PREFACE TO VOLUME 1

This 2025 Edition of the Standard California Codes incorporates all changes required by legislative enactments up to and including ch. 1017 of the second year of the 2023–2024 Regular Session.

This Edition gives the legislative history of each section. Amendments made in 2024 are highlighted by printing in boldface type all matter added to a section and indicating by a figure within brackets, such as [1], each point of deletion. The deleted matter is then shown by footnotes keyed to the corresponding figures. Where changes are extensive, the former section may be reprinted in full.

The following reproduction of Civil Code Section 2079.14, as amended by Stats. 2019 Chapter 310, clearly illustrates the "stressed amendment" feature:

> **§2079.14. Provision of disclosure form to buyer and seller; Acknowledgement of receipt.**
> (a) A [1] copy of the disclosure form specified in Section 2079.16 [2] **shall be provided in a real property transaction** as follows:
> [3] **(1)** The seller's agent, if any, shall provide the disclosure form to the seller [4] **before** entering into the listing agreement.
> [5] **(2)** The buyer's agent shall provide the disclosure form to the buyer as soon as practicable [6] **before** execution of the buyer's offer to purchase. If the offer to purchase is not prepared by the buyer's agent, the buyer's agent shall present the disclosure form to the buyer not later than the next business day after receiving the offer to purchase from the buyer.
> **(b) The agent providing the disclosure form specified in Section 2079.16 shall obtain a signed acknowledgment of receipt from the buyer or seller except as provided in Section 2079.15. Leg.H.** Added Stats. 1995 ch. 428 §3 (SB 467). Amended Stats. 2018 ch. 907 §39 (AB 1289), effective January 1, 2019; Stats. 2019 ch. 310 §10 (AB 892), effective January 1, 2020.
> **§2079.14. 2019 Deletes. [1]** seller's agent and buyer's agent shall provide the seller and buyer in a real property transaction with a **[2]** , and shall obtain a signed acknowledgment of receipt from that seller and buyer, except as provided in Section 2079.15 **[3]** (a) **[4]** prior to **[5]** (b) **[6]** prior to

To read Section 2079.14 as amended, you read the section as printed, omitting the bracketed figures "[1]" through "[6]":

> (a) A copy of the disclosure form specified in Section 2079.16 **shall be provided in a real property transaction** as follows:
> (1) The seller's agent, if any, shall provide the disclosure form to the seller before entering into the listing agreement.
> (2) The buyer's agent shall provide the disclosure form to the buyer as soon as practicable **before** execution of the buyer's offer to purchase. If the offer to purchase is not prepared by the buyer's agent, the buyer's agent shall present the disclosure form to the buyer not later than the next business day after receiving the offer to purchase from the buyer.
> **(b) The agent providing the disclosure form specified in Section 2079.16 shall obtain a signed acknowledgment of receipt from the buyer or seller except as provided in Section 2079.15.**

To reconstruct the section as it read before being amended, you read the section as printed, omitting the words in boldface type and inserting the words appearing in the footnote under Section 2079.14 and referred to by the bracketed figures [1] through [6] in the section:

> A seller's agent and buyer's agent shall provide the seller and buyer in a real property transaction with a copy of the disclosure form specified in Section 2079.16, and shall obtain a signed acknowledgment of receipt from that seller and buyer, except as provided in Section 2079.15, as follows:
> (a) The seller's agent, if any, shall provide the disclosure form to the seller prior to entering into the listing agreement.
> (b) The buyer's agent shall provide the disclosure form to the buyer as soon as practicable prior to execution of the buyer's offer to purchase. If the offer to purchase is not prepared by the buyer's agent, the buyer's agent shall present the disclosure form to the buyer not later than the next business day after receiving the offer to purchase from the buyer.

In presenting this Edition of the Standard California Codes, we wish to acknowledge with gratitude the many helpful suggestions received from users of our Codes, and to express the hope that this Edition will serve effectively the needs of bench and bar alike.

THE PUBLISHER

The STANDARD CIVIL CODE

of the

STATE OF CALIFORNIA

2025 EDITION

The Original Civil Code
Adopted March 21, 1872—Effective January 1, 1873
With All Subsequent Legislative Enactments

Table Showing 2024 Changes in the Civil Code

Effective January 1, 2025, unless otherwise noted at end of section.

Section	Effect	Chapter	Section	Effect	Chapter
51	Amended	779	1798.106	Amended	121
51.7	Amended	584	1798.120	Amended	940
52.66	Added	198	1798.121	Amended	940
55.32	Amended	227	1798.130	Amended	121
56.05	Amended	80	1798.135	Amended	121
56.101	Amended	853	1798.140	Amended	887
714.3	Amended	7	1798.150	Amendment	121
798.15	Amended	397	1798.155	Amended	121
798.28.5	Amended	79	1798.160	Amended	121
798.42	Amended	23	1798.185	Amended	121
798.44.1	Added	162	1798.199.25	Amended	121
798.56	Amended	395	1798.199.40	Amended	121
799.12	Added	162	1798.199.45	Amended	121
799.47	Added	351	1798.199.90	Amended	121
827	Amended	1015	1798.1980.95	Amended	121
835	Amended & Added	235	1798.202	Amended	783
1098.6	Amended	475	1798.203	Added	783
1102.6i	Added	443	1799.208	Added	986
1102.6j	Added	443	1799.209	Added	986
1102.156	Added	21	1799.302	Amended	194
1103.2	Amended	80	1812.117	Amended	853
1207	Amended	691	1916.1	Amended	601
1459.5	Amended	577	1939.23	Amended	970
1632	Amended	1015	1941.5	Repealed & Added	75
Title 4.1			1941.6	Amended	75
w/1670.50)	Added	516	1946	Amended	287
1670.50	Added	516	1946.1	Amended	1015
1708.89	Added	557	1946.2	Amended	8
Ch. 1.5 (comm.	Added	89	1946.9	Added	75
w/1748.50)			1947.1	Amended	420
1748.50	Added	89	1947.3	Amended	287
1749.8	Added	172	1950.5	Amended	287
1749.8.4	Amended & Added	172	1950.6	Amended	966
1749.8.9	Added	172	1950.9	Added	1015
1770	Amended	853	1954.06	Amended	519
1785.3	Amended	520	1954.07	Added	279
1785.11.11	Amended	846	1954.08	Amended	209
1785.12	Amended	846	1954.09	Amended	209
1785.13	Amended	520	1954.092	Amended	209
1785.20.6	Added	520	1954.093	Repealed	209
1785.26	Amended	80	1980.5	Repealed	91
1785.27	Added	520	2079.13	Amended	516
1786.18	Amended	520	2079.14	Amended	516
1788.1	Amended	522	2079.16	Amended	516
1788.2	Amended	522	Ch. 6		
1788.10	Amended	522	w/2213)	Added	742
1788.11	Amended	522	2213–2218	Added	742
1788.12	Amended	522	Art. 1		
1788.13	Amended	522	w/2213)	Added	742
1788.14	Amended	522	2213	Added	742
1788.14.5	Amended	522	Art. 2		
1788.15	Amended	522	w/2214)	Added	742
1788.16	Amended	522	2214	Added	742
1788.17	Amended	522	Art. 3		
1788.18	Amended	522	w/2215)	Added	742
1788.18	Amended	522	2215	Added	742
1788.20	Amended	522	Art. 4		
1788.21	Amended	522	w/2216)	Added	742
1788.22	Amended	522	2216	Added	742
1788.94	Added	853	Art. 5		
1788.106	Amended & Added	853	w/2217)	Added	742
1791	Amended	196	2217	Added	742
1793.2	Amended	196	Art. 6		
1798.99.31	Amendment	80	w/2218)	Added	742
1798.99.86	Amended	80	2218	Added	742

Section	Effect	Chapter	Section	Effect	Chapter
2923.5	Amended	311	3344.1	Amended	258
2923.7	Amended	601	3512	Amended	812
2923.55	Amended	311	3513	Amended	812
2924	Amended	142	3515	Amended	812
2924c	Amended	601	3517	Amended	812
2924f	Amended	311	3518	Amended	812
2924g	Amended	311	3519	Amended	812
2924h	Amended	601	3521	Amended	812
2924m	Amended	601	3526	Amended	812
2924p	Amended	580	3529	Amended	812
2924.15	Amended	601	3543	Amended	812
2924.18	Amended	601	4751	Amended	7
2924.21	Added	142	4775	Amended	288
2932.2	Added	311	5105	Amended	383
2951	Added	431	5110	Amended	383
2982.12	Amended	853	5115	Amended	401
3273.10	Amended	142	5120	Amended	383
Ch. 15.2			5125	Amended	383
w/3110)	Added	817	5200	Amended	383
3110–3111	Added	817	5260	Amended	383
3110	Added	817	5550	Amended	288
3111	Added	817	5551	Amended	100
3333.8	Amended	666	5610	Amended	288
3339	Amended	853			

CONTENTS

	Sections
TITLE OF THE ACT	1
PRELIMINARY PROVISIONS	2 – 21
DEFINITIONS AND SOURCES OF LAW	22 – 22.2
EFFECT OF THE 1872 CODES	23 – 23.6

DIVISION 1. PERSONS

Part 1.	Persons With Unsound Mind	38 – 41
Part 2.	Personal Rights	43 – 53.7
Part 2.5.	Blind and Other Physically Disabled Persons	54 – 55.32
Part 2.52.	Construction-Related Accessibility Standards Compliance	55.51 – 55.545
Part 2.53.	Attorney's Fees and Statutory Damages in Construction-Related Accessibility Standards Claims	55.55 – 55.57
Part 2.55.	Small Business Gender Discrimination In Services Compliance Act	55.61 – 55.63
Part 2.57.	Gender Neutral Retail Departments	55.7 – 55.8
Part 2.6.	Confidentiality of Medical Information	56 – 56.37
Part 2.7.	Medical Claims Data Error Correction	57
Part 2.9.	California Fair Dealership Law	80 – 86

DIVISION 2. PROPERTY

Part 1.	Property in General	654 – 749
Part 2.	Real or Immovable Property	755 – 945.5
Part 3.	Personal or Movable Property	946 – 998
Part 4.	Acquisition of Property	1000 – 1426a

DIVISION 3. OBLIGATIONS

Part 1.	Obligations in General	1427 – 1543
Part 2.	Contracts	1549 – 1701
Part 3.	Obligations Imposed by Law	1708 – 1725
Part 4.	Obligations Arising from Particular Transactions	1738 – 3273.69

DIVISION 4. GENERAL PROVISIONS

Part 1.	Relief	3274 – 3428
Part 2.	Special Relations of Debtor and Creditor	3429 – 3449
Part 3.	Nuisance	3479 – 3508.2
Part 4.	Maxims Of Jurisprudence	3509 – 3548
Part 5.	Common Interest Developments	4000 – 6150
Part 5.3.	Commercial and Industrial Common Interest Developments	6500 – 6876
Part 5.5.	Automatic Checkout System	7100 – 7106
Part 6.	Works of Improvement	8000 – 9566

CIVIL CODE

An act to Establish a Civil Code

TITLE OF THE ACT

§1. Title and Divisions of this Act

This Act shall be known as The Civil Code of the State of California, and is in Four Divisions, as follows:
1. The first relating to persons.
2. The second to property.
3. The third to obligations.
4. The fourth contains general provisions relating to the three preceding divisions. **Leg.H.** Enacted 1872.

PRELIMINARY PROVISIONS

When this Code takes effect. §2.
Not retroactive. §3.
Rules of construction. §4.
Provisions similar to existing laws, how construed. §5.
Actions, etc., not affected. §6.
Holidays. §7.
Optional bank holidays. §7.1.
[Section repealed 1905]. §8.
Business days. §9.
[Section repealed 1955]. §9.1.
Computation of time. §10.
Certain acts not to be done on holidays. §11.
Joint authority construed. §12.
Words and phrases, how construed. §13.
Significance of certain words. §14.
[Sections repealed 1874]. §§15, 16.
Notice by certified mail as compliance with requirement of notice by registered mail. §17.
Notice, actual and constructive. §18.
Constructive notice specified. §19.
Effect of repeal. §20.
This Act, how cited. §21.

§2. When this Code takes effect

This Code takes effect at twelve o'clock noon, on the first day of January, eighteen hundred and seventy-three. **Leg.H.** Enacted 1872.

§3. Not retroactive

No part of it is retroactive, unless expressly so declared. **Leg.H.** Enacted 1872.

§4. Rules of construction

The rule of the common law, that statutes in derogation thereof are to be strictly construed, has no application to this code. The code establishes the law of this state respecting the subjects to which it relates, and its provisions are to be liberally construed with a view to effect its objects and to promote justice. **Leg.H.** Enacted 1872.

§5. Provisions similar to existing laws, how construed

The provisions of this code, so far as they are substantially the same as existing statutes or the common law, must be construed as continuations thereof, and not as new enactments. **Leg.H.** Enacted 1872.

§6. Actions, etc., not affected

No action or proceeding commenced before this code takes effect, and no right accrued, is affected by its provisions. **Leg.H.** Enacted 1872.

§7. Holidays

Holidays within the meaning of this code are every Sunday and such other days as are specified or provided for as holidays in the Government Code of the State of California. **Leg.H.** Enacted 1872. Amended Stats 1880 ch 50 §1; Stats 1889 ch 44 §1; Stats 1893 ch 158 §1; Stats 1897 ch 18 §1; Stats 1907 ch 293 §1; Stats 1907 Ex Sess ch 5 §1; Stats 1909 ch 30 §1; Stats 1911 ch 320 §1; Stats 1925 ch 92 §1; Stats 1955 ch 165 §1.

§7.1. Optional bank holidays

Optional bank holidays within the meaning of Section 9 are:
(a) Any closing of a bank because of an extraordinary situation, as that term is defined in the Bank Extraordinary Situation Closing Act (Chapter 20 (commencing with Section 3600) of Division 1 of the Financial Code).
(b) Every Saturday.
(c) Every Sunday.
(d) January 1st.
(e) The third Monday in January, known as "Dr. Martin Luther King, Jr. Day."
(f) February 12, known as "Lincoln Day."
(g) The third Monday in February.
(h) The last Monday in May.
(i) July 4th.
(j) The first Monday in September.
(k) September 9th, known as "Admission Day."
(*l*) The second Monday in October, known as "Columbus Day."
(m) November 11th, known as "Veteran's Day."
(n) December 25th.
(o) Good Friday from 12 noon until closing.
(p) The Thursday in November appointed as "Thanksgiving Day."
(q) Any Monday following any Sunday on which January 1st, February 12th, July 4th, September 9th, November 11th, or December 25th falls.
(r) Any Friday preceding any Saturday on which July 4th, September 9th, or December 25th falls. **Leg.H.** Added Stats 1994 ch 668 §1 (SB 1405).

§8. [Section repealed 1905]

Leg.H. Enacted 1872. Repealed Stats 1905 ch 17 §1.

§9. Business days

All other days than those mentioned in Section 7 are business days for all purposes; provided, that as to any act appointed by law or contract, or in any other way, to be performed by, at, or through any bank organized under the laws of or doing business in this state, any optional bank holiday as defined in Section 7.1 is not a business day; and provided, that any act appointed by law or contract, or in any other way, to be performed on any day which is an optional bank holiday as defined in Section 7.1, by, at, or through any bank or branch or office thereof, whether acting in its own behalf or in any other capacity whatsoever, may be performed on that optional bank holiday if the bank or branch or office by, at, or through which the act is to be performed is open for the transaction of business on that optional bank holiday, or, at the option of the person obligated to perform the act, it may be performed on the next succeeding business day. **Leg.H.** Enacted 1872. Amended Stats 1905 ch 17 §2; Stats 1939 ch 414 §1; Stats 1955 ch 198 §1, ch 599 §1; Stats 1973 ch 285 §1; Stats 1979 ch 159 §1; Stats 1981 ch 67 §1, effective June 16, 1981; Stats 1982 ch 1203 §1, effective September 22, 1982; Stats 1985 ch 147 §1, effective July 8, 1985; Stats 1994 ch 668 §2 (SB 1405).

§9.1. [Section repealed 1955]

Leg.H. Added Stats 1953 ch 1213 §1. Repealed Stats 1955 ch 198 §3, ch 599 §3. The repealed section related to Saturday as a bank holiday.

§10. Computation of time

The time in which any act provided by law is to be done is computed by excluding the first day and including the last, unless the last day is a holiday, and then it is also excluded. **Leg.H.** Enacted 1872.

§11. Certain acts not to be done on holidays

Whenever any act of a secular nature, other than a work of necessity or mercy, is appointed by law or contract to be performed upon a particular day, which day falls upon a holiday, it may be performed upon the next business day, with the same effect as if it had been performed upon the day appointed. **Leg.H.** Enacted 1872.

§12. Joint authority construed

Words giving a joint authority to three or more public officers or other persons are construed as giving such authority to a majority of them, unless it is otherwise expressed in the act giving the authority. **Leg.H.** Enacted 1872.

§13. Words and phrases, how construed

Words and phrases are construed according to the context and the approved usage of the language; but technical words and phrases, and such others as may have acquired a peculiar and appropriate meaning in law, or are defined in the succeeding section, are to be construed according to such peculiar and appropriate meaning or definition. **Leg.H.** Enacted 1872.

§14. Significance of certain words

(a) Words used in this code in the present tense include the future as well as the present; words used in the masculine gender include the feminine and neuter; the singular number includes the plural, and the plural the singular; the word person includes a corporation as well as a natural person; county includes city and county; writing includes printing and typewriting; oath includes affirmation or declaration; and every mode of oral statement, under oath or affirmation, is embraced by the term "testify," and every written one in the term "depose"; signature or subscription includes mark, when the person cannot write, his name being written near it, by a person who writes his own name as a witness; provided, that when a signature is by mark it must in order that the same may be acknowledged or may serve as the signature to any sworn statement be witnessed by two persons who must subscribe their own names as witnesses thereto.

(b) The following words have in this code the signification attached to them in this section, unless otherwise apparent from the context:

(1) The word "property" includes property real and personal.

(2) The words "real property" are coextensive with lands, tenements, and hereditaments.

(3) The words "personal property" include money, goods, chattels, things in action, and evidences of debt.

(4) The word "month" means a calendar month, unless otherwise expressed.

(5) The word "will" includes codicil.

(6) The word "section" whenever hereinafter employed refers to a section of this code, unless some other code or statute is expressly mentioned.

(7) The word "spouse" includes a registered domestic partner, as required by Section 297.5 of the Family Code. **Leg.H.** Enacted 1872. Amended Code Amendments 1873–74 ch 612 §1; Stats 1903 ch 281 §1; Stats 2016 ch 50 §3 (SB 1005), effective January 1, 2017.

2016 Note: It is the intent of the Legislature that the changes made by this act have only technical and nonsubstantive effect. Hence, no change made by this act shall create any new right, duty, or other obligation that did not exist immediately preceding the effective date of this act, or result in the limitation or termination of any right, duty, or other obligation that existed immediately preceding the effective date of this act. Stats 2016 ch 50 (SB 1005) §125.

§§15, 16. [Sections repealed 1874]

Leg.H. Enacted 1872. Repealed Code Amdts 1873–74 ch 612 §2.

§17. Notice by certified mail as compliance with requirement of notice by registered mail

Wherever any notice or other communication is required by this code to be mailed by registered mail, the mailing of such notice or other communication by certified mail shall be deemed to be a sufficient compliance with the requirements of law. **Leg.H.** Added Stats 1959 ch 426 §1.

Prior Law: Former §17, relating to degrees of negligence, was enacted 1872 and repealed Code Amdts 1873–74 ch 612 §2.

§18. Notice, actual and constructive

Notice is:

1. Actual—which consists in express information of a fact; or,
2. Constructive—which is imputed by law. **Leg.H.** Enacted 1872.

§19. Constructive notice specified

Every person who has actual notice of circumstances sufficient to put a prudent person upon inquiry as to a particular fact has constructive notice of the fact itself in all cases in which, by prosecuting such inquiry, he or she might have learned that fact. **Leg.H.** Enacted 1872. Amended Code Amdts 1873–74 ch 612 §3; Stats 2017 ch 561 §15 (AB 1516), effective January 1, 2018.

§20. Effect of repeal

No statute, law, or rule is continued in force because it is consistent with the provisions of this code on the same subject; but in all cases provided for by this code, all statutes, laws, and rules heretofore in force in this state, whether consistent or not with the provisions of this code, unless expressly continued in force by it, are repealed or abrogated.

This repeal or abrogation does not revive any former law heretofore repealed, nor does it affect any right already existing or accrued, or any action or proceeding already taken, except as in this code provided. **Leg.H.** Enacted 1872.

§21. This Act, how cited

This Act, whenever cited, enumerated, referred to, or amended, may be designated simply as "The Civil Code," adding, when necessary, the number of the section. **Leg.H.** Enacted 1872.

DEFINITIONS AND SOURCES OF LAW

Law defined. §22.
Expression by Constitution and statutes. §22.1.
Common law as rule of decision. §22.2.
[Section repealed 1979]. §22.3.

§22. Law defined

Law is a solemn expression of the will of the supreme power of the State. **Leg.H.** Added Stats 1951 ch 655 §1.

§22.1. Expression by Constitution and statutes

The will of the supreme power is expressed:

(a) By the Constitution.

(b) By statutes. **Leg.H.** Added Stats 1951 ch 655 §1.

§22.2. Common law as rule of decision

The common law of England, so far as it is not repugnant to or inconsistent with the Constitution of the United States, or the Constitution or laws of this State, is the rule of decision in all the courts of this State. **Leg.H.** Added Stats 1951 ch 655 §1.

§22.3. [Section repealed 1979]

Leg.H. Added Stats 1961 ch 1404 §1, operative until September 20, 1963. Repealed Stats 1979 ch 373 §40.

EFFECT OF THE 1872 CODES

Construction of codes regarding date of passage. §23.
Conflict with laws passed at 1872 Session. §23.1.
Construction of codes with relation to each other. §23.2.
Conflicts between titles. §23.3.
Conflicts between chapters. §23.4.
Conflicts between articles. §23.5.
Conflicting sections of same chapter or article. §23.6.

§23. Construction of codes regarding date of passage

With relation to the laws passed at the 1872 Session of the Legislature, the Political Code, Civil Code, Code of Civil Procedure, and Penal Code, shall be construed as though each had been passed on the first day of the session. **Leg.H.** Added Stats 1951 ch 655 §2.

§23.1. Conflict with laws passed at 1872 Session

The provisions of any law passed at the 1872 Session of the Legislature which contravene or are inconsistent with the provisions of any of the four codes passed at the 1872 Session prevail. **Leg.H.** Added Stats 1951 ch 655 §2.

§23.2. Construction of codes with relation to each other

With relation to each other, the provisions of the four codes shall be construed as though all such codes had been passed at the same moment of time and were parts of the same statute. **Leg.H.** Added Stats 1951 ch 655 §2.

§23.3. Conflicts between titles

If the provisions of any title conflict with or contravene the provisions of another title, the provisions of each title shall prevail as to all matters and questions arising out of the subject matter of the title. **Leg.H.** Added Stats 1951 ch 655 §2.

§23.4. Conflicts between chapters

If the provisions of any chapter conflict with or contravene the provisions of another chapter of the same title, the provisions of each chapter shall prevail as to all matters and questions arising out of the subject matter of the chapter. **Leg.H.** Added Stats 1951 ch 655 §2.

§23.5. Conflicts between articles

If the provisions of any article conflict with or contravene the provisions of another article of the same chapter, the provisions of each article shall prevail as to all matters and questions arising out of the subject matter of the article. **Leg.H.** Added Stats 1951 ch 655 §2.

§23.6. Conflicting sections of same chapter or article

If conflicting provisions are found in different sections of the same chapter or article, the provisions of the sections last in numerical order shall prevail, unless such construction is inconsistent with the meaning of the chapter or article. **Leg.H.** Added Stats 1951 ch 655 §2.

DIVISION 1
PERSONS

Part 1. Persons With Unsound Mind.
Part 2. Personal Rights.
Part 2.5. Blind and Other Physically Disabled Persons.
Part 2.52. Construction-Related Accessibility Standards Compliance.
Part 2.53. Attorney's Fees and Statutory Damages in Construction-Related Accessibility Standards Claims.
Part 2.55. Small Business Gender Discrimination In Services Compliance Act.
Part 2.57. Gender Neutral Retail Departments.
Part 2.6. Confidentiality of Medical Information.
Part 2.7. Medical Claims Data Error Correction.
Part 2.9. California Fair Dealership Law.

PART 1
PERSONS WITH UNSOUND MIND

Contract by person without understanding; Liability for necessaries. §38.
Conveyance or contract by person of unsound mind before adjudged incapable. §39.
Person of unsound mind adjudged incapable. §40.
Civil liability of person of unsound mind. §41.

§25. [Section repealed 1993]

Leg.H. Enacted 1872. Amended Stats 1927 ch 661 §1; Stats 1931 ch 935 §1; Stats 1943 ch 154 §1; Stats 1953 ch 1128 §1; Stats 1955 ch 183 §1; Stats 1967 ch 1029 §1; Stats 1969 ch 1608 §1; Stats 1971 ch 1748 §23. Repealed Stats 1992 ch 163 §2, operative January 1, 1994, (amendment of §25.9 by Stats 1992 ch 252 §1 prevails to make repeal inoperative, see Stats 1992 ch 163 §160); Stats 1993 ch 219 §2. See Fam C §6500.

§25.1. [Section repealed 1993]

Leg.H. Added Stats 1973 ch 278 §1. Repealed Stats 1992 ch 163 §2, operative January 1, 1994 (amendment of §25.9 by Stats 1992 ch 252 §1 prevails to make repeal inoperative, see Stats 1992 ch 163 §160); Stats 1993 ch 219 §2. See Fam C §6502.

§25.5. [Section repealed 1993]

Leg.H. Added Stats 1959 ch 1280 §1. Amended Stats 1968 ch 1224 §1; Stats 1974 ch 1292 §1; Stats 1981 ch 23 §1. Repealed Stats 1992 ch 163 §2, operative January 1, 1994 (amendment of §25.9 by Stats 1992 ch 252 §1 prevails to make repeal inoperative, see Stats 1992 ch 163 §160); Stats 1993 ch 219 §2. The repealed section related to blood donation by minor.

§25.6. [Section repealed 1993]

Leg.H. Added Stats 1961 ch 1407 §1. Amended Stats 1969 ch 1608 §2, operative January 1, 1970. Repealed Stats 1992 ch 163 §2, operative January 1, 1994 (amendment of §25.9 by Stats 1992 ch 252 §1 prevails to make repeal inoperative, see Stats 1992 ch 163 §160); Stats 1993 ch 219 §2. See Fam C §§7002, 7050.

§25.7. [Section repealed 1993]

Leg.H. Added Stats 1961 ch 1407 §2. Repealed Stats 1992 ch 163 §2, operative January 1, 1994 (amendment of §25.9 by Stats 1992 ch 252 §1 prevails to make repeal inoperative, see Stats 1992 ch 163 §160); Stats 1993 ch 219 §2. See Fam C §§7002, 7050.

§25.8. [Section repealed 1993]

Leg.H. Added Stats 1965 ch 1524 §1. Amended Stats 1981 ch 714 §45. Repealed Stats 1992 ch 163 §2, operative January 1, 1994 (amendment of §25.9 by Stats 1992 ch 252 §1 prevails to make repeal inoperative, see Stats 1992 ch 163 §160); Stats 1993 ch 219 §2. See Fam C §§6901–6903, 6910.

§25.9. [Section repealed 1993]

Leg.H. Added Stats 1979 ch 832 §1. Amended Stats 1983 ch 928 §7. Repealed Stats 1992 ch 163 §2, operative January 1, 1994 (ch 252 prevails). Amended Stats 1992 ch 252 §1. Repealed Stats 1993 ch 219 §2. See Fam C §§6920, 6921, 6924.

§26. [Section repealed 1993]

Leg.H. Enacted 1872. Repealed Stats 1992 ch 163 §2, operative January 1, 1994 (amendment of §25.9 by Stats 1992 ch 252 §1 prevails to make repeal inoperative, see Stats 1992 ch 163 §160); Stats 1993 ch 219 §2. See Fam C §6500.

§27. [Section repealed 1993]

Leg.H. Enacted 1872. Repealed Stats 1992 ch 163 §2, operative January 1, 1994 (amendment of §25.9 by Stats 1992 ch 252 §1 prevails to make repeal inoperative, see Stats 1992 ch 163 §160); Stats 1993 ch 219 §2. See Fam C §6501.

§28. [Section repealed 1874]

Leg.H. Enacted 1872. Repealed Code Amdts 1873–74 ch 612 §4.

§29. [Section repealed 1993]

Leg.H. Enacted 1872. Amended Stats 1941 ch 337 §1. Repealed Stats 1992 ch 163 §2, operative January 1, 1994 (amendment of §25.9 by Stats 1992 ch 252 §1 prevails to make repeal inoperative, see Stats 1992 ch 163 §160); Stats 1993 ch 219 §2. The repealed section related to minor's change of status to adult upon marriage.

§§30, 31. [Sections repealed 1874]

Leg.H. Enacted 1872. Repealed Code Amdts 1873–74 ch 612 §4.

§32. [Section repealed 1981]

Leg.H. Enacted 1872. Repealed Stats 1979 ch 730 §3, operative January 1, 1981. The repealed section related to custody of minors and persons of unsound mind.

§33. [Section repealed 1993]

Leg.H. Enacted 1872. Amended Code Amdts 1873–74 ch 612 §5; Stats 1971 ch 1748 §24. Repealed Stats 1992 ch 163 §2, operative January 1, 1994 (amendment of §25.9 by Stats 1992 ch 252 §1 prevails to make repeal inoperative, see Stats 1992 ch 163 §160); Stats 1993 ch 219 §2. See Fam C §6701.

§34. [Section repealed 1993]

Leg.H. Enacted 1872. Amended Code Amdts 1873–74 ch 612 §6. Repealed Stats 1992 ch 163 §2, operative January 1, 1994 (amendment of §25.9 by Stats 1992 ch 252 §1 prevails to make repeal inoperative, see Stats 1992 ch 163 §160); Stats 1993 ch 219 §2. See Fam C §6700.

§34.5. [Section repealed 1993]

Leg.H. Added Stats 1953 ch 1654 §1. Amended Stats 1975 ch 820 §1; Stats 1987 ch 1237 §2. Repealed Stats 1992 ch 163 §2, operative January 1, 1994 (amendment of §25.9 by Stats 1992 ch 252 §1 prevails to make repeal inoperative, see Stats 1992 ch 163 §160); Stats 1993 ch 219 §2. See Fam C §§6920, 6921, 6925.

§34.6. [Section repealed 1993]

Leg.H. Added Stats 1968 ch 371 §1. Repealed Stats 1992 ch 163 §2, operative January 1, 1994 (amendment of §25.9 by Stats 1992 ch 252 §1 prevails to make repeal inoperative, see Stats 1992 ch 163 §160); Stats 1993 ch 219 §2. See Fam C §§6901, 6902, 6920–6922.

§34.7. [Section repealed 1993]

Leg.H. Added Stats 1968 ch 417 §1. Amended Stats 1980 ch 152 §1. Repealed Stats 1992 ch 163 §2, operative January 1, 1994 (amendment of §25.9 by Stats 1992 ch 252 §1 prevails to make repeal inoperative, see Stats 1992 ch 163 §160); Stats 1993 ch 219 §2. See Fam C §§6920, 6921, 6926.

§34.8. [Section repealed 1993]

Leg.H. Added Stats 1977 ch 354 §1. Repealed Stats 1992 ch 163 §2, operative January 1, 1994 (amendment of §25.9 by Stats 1992 ch 252 §1 prevails to make repeal inoperative, see Stats 1992 ch 163 §160); Stats 1993 ch 219 §2. See Fam C §§6920, 6921, 6927.

§34.9. [Section repealed 1993]

Leg.H. Added Stats 1977 ch 935 §1. Repealed Stats 1992 ch 163 §2, operative January 1, 1994 (amendment of §25.9 by Stats 1992 ch 252 §1 prevails to make repeal inoperative, see Stats 1992 ch 163 §160); Stats 1993 ch 219 §2. See Fam C §§6920, 6921, 6928.

§34.10. [Section repealed 1993]

Leg.H. Added Stats 1977 ch 979 §1. Repealed Stats 1992 ch 163 §2, operative January 1, 1994 (amendment of §25.9 by Stats 1992 ch 252 §1 prevails to make repeal inoperative, see Stats 1992 ch 163 §160); Stats 1993 ch 219 §2. See Fam C §§6920, 6921, 6929.

§35. [Section repealed 1993]

Leg.H. Enacted 1872. Amended Code Amdts 1873–74 ch 612 §7; Stats 1971 ch 1748 §25. Repealed Stats 1992 ch 163 §2, operative January 1, 1994 (amendment of §25.9 by Stats 1992 ch 252 §1 prevails to make repeal inoperative, see Stats 1992 ch 163 §160); Stats 1993 ch 219 §2. See Fam C §6710.

§35a. [Section repealed 1993]

Leg.H. Added Stats 1931 ch 1070 §12. Repealed Stats 1992 ch 163 §2, operative January 1, 1994 (amendment of §25.9 by Stats 1992 ch 252 §1 prevails to make repeal inoperative, see Stats 1992 ch 163 §160); Stats 1993 ch 219 §2. See Fam C §6713.

§36. [Section repealed 1993]

Leg.H. Enacted 1872. Amended Code Amdts 1873–74 ch 612 §8; Stats 1927 ch 876 §1; Stats 1931 ch 1070 §3; Stats 1941 ch 734 §1; Stats 1947 ch 526 §1; Stats 1963 ch 52 §1; Stats 1974 ch 771 §1; Stats 1980 ch 676 §37. Repealed Stats 1992 ch 163 §2, operative January 1, 1994 (amendment of §25.9 by Stats 1992 ch 252 §1 prevails to make repeal inoperative, see Stats 1992 ch 163 §160); Stats 1993 ch 219 §2. See Fam C §§6712, 6750, 6751.

§36.1. [Section repealed 1993]

Leg.H. Added Stats 1939 ch 637 §1. Repealed Stats 1992 ch 163 §2, operative January 1, 1994 (amendment of §25.9 by Stats 1992 ch 252 §1 prevails to make repeal inoperative, see Stats 1992 ch 163 §160); Stats 1993 ch 219 §2. See Fam C §6752.

§36.2. [Section repealed 1993]

Leg.H. Added Stats 1939 ch 637 §2. Repealed Stats 1992 ch 163 §2, operative January 1, 1994 (amendment of §25.9 by Stats 1992 ch 252 §1 prevails to make repeal inoperative, see Stats 1992 ch 163 §160); Stats 1993 ch 219 §2. See Fam C §6753.

§37. [Section repealed 1993]

Leg.H. Enacted 1872. Repealed Stats 1992 ch 163 §2, operative January 1, 1994 (amendment of §25.9 by Stats 1992 ch 252 §1 prevails to make repeal inoperative, see Stats 1992 ch 163 §160); Stats 1993 ch 219 §2. See Fam C §6711.

§38. Contract by person without understanding; Liability for necessaries

A person entirely without understanding has no power to make a contract of any kind, but the person is liable for the reasonable value of things furnished to the person necessary for the support of the person or the person's family. **Leg.H.** Added Stats 1992 ch 163 §3, operative January 1, 1994.

Prior Law: Former §38, similar to the present section, was enacted 1872, amended Code Amdts 1873–74 ch 612 §9, repealed Stats 1992 ch 163 §2, operative January 1, 1994 (amendment of §25.9 by Stats 1992 ch 252 §1 prevails to make repeal inoperative, see Stats 1992 ch 163 §160), and repealed Stats 1993 ch 219 §2.

§39. Conveyance or contract by person of unsound mind before adjudged incapable

(a) A conveyance or other contract of a person of unsound mind, but not entirely without understanding, made before the incapacity of the person has been judicially determined, is subject to rescission, as provided in Chapter 2 (commencing with Section 1688) of Title 5 of Part 2 of Division 3.

(b) A rebuttable presumption affecting the burden of proof that a person is of unsound mind shall exist for purposes of this section if the person is substantially unable to manage his or her own financial resources or resist fraud or undue influence. Substantial inability may not be proved solely by isolated incidents of negligence or improvidence. **Leg.H.** Added Stats 1992 ch 163 §3 (AB 2641), operative January 1, 1994. Amended Stats 1995 ch 842 §1 (SB 730).

Prior Law: Former §39, similar to the present section, was enacted 1872, amended Code Amdts 1873–74 ch 612 §10, repealed Stats 1992 ch 163 §2, operative January 1, 1994 (amendment of CC §25.9 by Stats 1992 ch 252 §1 prevails to make repeal inoperative, see Stats 1992 ch 163 §160), and repealed 1993 ch 219 §2.

1995 Notes: This act shall be known and may be cited as the Due Process in Competence Determinations Act. Stats 1995 ch 842 §12.

This act shall not apply to proceedings under the Welfare and Institutions Code. Stats 1995 ch 842 §13.

§40. Person of unsound mind adjudged incapable

(a) Subject to Section 1871 of the Probate Code, and subject to Part 1 (commencing with Section 5000) of Division 5 of the Welfare and Institutions Code, after his or her incapacity has been judicially determined a person of unsound mind can make no conveyance or other contract, nor delegate any power or waive any right, until his or her restoration to capacity.

(b) Subject to Sections 1873 to 1876, inclusive, of the Probate Code, the establishment of a conservatorship under Division 4 (commencing with Section 1400) of the Probate Code is a judicial determination of the incapacity of the conservatee for the purposes of this section. **Leg.H.** Added Stats 1992 ch 163 §3 (AB 2641), operative January 1, 1994.

Prior Law: Former CC §40, similar to the present section, was enacted 1872, amended Code Amdts 1877–78 ch 519 §1, Stats 1967 ch 638 §1, ch 1667 §30, Stats 1979 ch 730 §4, operative January 1, 1981, repealed Stats 1992 ch 163 §2, operative January 1, 1994 (amendment of §25.9 by Stats 1992 ch 252 §1 prevails to make repeal inoperative, see Stats 1992 ch 163 §160), and repealed Stats 1993 ch 219 §2.

§41. Civil liability of person of unsound mind

A person of unsound mind, of whatever degree, is civilly liable for a wrong done by the person, but is not liable in exemplary damages unless at the time of the act the person was capable of knowing that the act was wrongful. **Leg.H.** Added Stats 1992 ch 163 §3 (AB 2641), operative January 1, 1994.

Prior Law: Former §41, similar to the present section, was enacted 1872, repealed Stats 1992 ch 163 §2, operative January 1, 1994 (amendment of §25.9 by Stats 1992 ch 252 §1 prevails to make repeal inoperative, see Stats 1992 ch 163 §160), and repealed Stats 1993 ch 219 §2.

§42. [Section repealed 1993]

Leg.H. Enacted 1872. Repealed Stats 1992 ch 163 §2, operative January 1, 1994 (amendment of §25.9 by Stats 1992 ch 252 §1 prevails to make repeal inoperative, see Stats 1992 ch 163 §160); Stats 1993 ch 219 §2. See Fam C §6601.

PART 1.5
UNIFORM MINOR STUDENT CAPACITY TO BORROW ACT
[REPEALED]

§§42.1–42.5. [Sections repealed 1972]

Leg.H. Added Stats 1970 ch 747 §1. Repealed Stats 1972 ch 579 §9. The repealed sections related to citation of act; definitions of "person", "educational institution", and "educational loans", and contract for educational loan.

PART 2
PERSONAL RIGHTS

General personal rights. §43.
Child conceived but not yet born. §43.1.
Breastfeeding rights. §43.3.
No cause of action for damages from fraudulent promise to marry or to cohabit after marriage. §43.4.
Wrongs for which no cause of action arises. §43.5.
[Section renumbered 1986]. §43.5(a).
Civil arrest in a courthouse. §43.54.
No cause of action for arrest pursuant to warrant regular on its face. §43.55.
Alienation of affection of foster child. §43.56.
Wrongful life action. §43.6.
Immunity for members of mental health professional quality assurance committee, medical specialty society, professional society, or insurance underwriting committee. §43.7.
Immunity as to communication in aid of evaluation of practitioner of healing or veterinary arts. §43.8.
Immunity of health care provider from negligence on account of unsolicited referral arising from test by multiphasic screening unit. §43.9.
Immunity of members of professional society comprised of persons licensed under Real Estate Law. §43.91.
Psychotherapist's duty to protect of patient's violent behavior; Immunity from liability; Legislative intent. §43.92.
Patient's action against psychotherapist for sexual contact. §43.93.
Professional societies' immunity from liability for referrals. §43.95.
Notification of complainant against physician, surgeon or podiatrist of disciplinary agency; Immunity. §43.96.
Hospital's immunity for action taken pursuant to recommendation of medical staff or peer review committee. §43.97.
Immunity of consultant. §43.98.
Liability of person or entity under contract with residential building permit applicant for quality review of compliance with State Housing Law. §43.99.
Immunity from civil liability for motor vehicle property damage or trespass caused during rescue of animal. §43.100.
Liability of emergency responder for damage to unmanned aircraft or unmanned aircraft system. §43.101.
Liability of property damage rescuing a child. § 43.102.
Defamation. §44.
Libel defined. §45.
Libel on its face defined; Action for defamation not libelous on its face. §45a.
Slander defined. §46.
Privileged publication or broadcast. §47.
Communications about sexual assault, harassment, or discrimination incident privileged. § 47.1.
Action for defamation against individual filing false complaint against peace officer. §47.5.
Malice not inferred in specified privileged communication. §48.
Demand for publication or broadcast of correction. §48a.
Liability of owners, licensees and operators of radio stations and networks for broadcast of defamatory statements. §48.5.
Civil action for libel or slander arising from child abuse prosecution. §48.7.
Defamation liability for false threatening communications to school officials. §48.8.
Immunity for organization sponsoring or conducting anonymous witness program. §48.9.
Protection from abduction, seduction, and injury to servant. §49.
Defense of self or others; Protection from wrongful injury; Use of necessary force. §50.
Citation of section; Civil rights of persons in business establishments; Definitions. §51.
Actions requiring copy of petition and brief to be served on State Solicitor General. §51.1.
Age discrimination in housing sale or rental. §51.2.
Senior citizen housing. §51.3.
Legislative intent; Intergenerational housing development requirements; Creation of state policy supporting intergenerational housing; Definitions. § 51.3.5.
Legislative intent regarding senior housing. §51.4.
Discrimination by business establishment prohibited. §51.5.
Gender Tax Repeal Act of 1995. §51.6.
Freedom from violence; Preservation of legal right to pursue action for violations; Lawful labor dispute exception. §51.7.
Discrimination in granting of franchises prohibited. §51.8.
Sexual harassment. §51.9.
Discrimination by business establishment in housing based on age. §51.10.
Special living environments for senior citizens; Applicability to County of Riverside. §51.11.
Federal law. §51.12.
Discounts or benefits offered due to loss or reduction of employment. §51.13.
Charging different prices for substantially similar goods. § 51.14.
Establishment of pilot program [Repealed July 1, 2028]. § 51.17.
Actions for damages and other relief for denial of rights. §52.
Action for injunctive and other equitable relief to protect exercise or enjoyment of legal rights. §52.1.
"Court of competent jurisdiction". §52.2.
Action to obtain equitable and declaratory relief to eliminate pattern or practice by law enforcement officers depriving person of legal rights. §52.3.
Action for damages against party responsible for gender violence. §52.4.
Action for damages against party responsible for sexual orientation violence. §52.45.
Action by victim of human trafficking. §52.5.
Specified businesses to post notice related to slavery and human trafficking; Development of model notice; Manner of notice; Failure to comply. §52.6.
Civil action against hotel for sex trafficking activity. § 52.65.
Required notice by primary ticket seller. § 52.66.
Subcutaneous implanting of identification device; Penalties and remedies; Time for commencing action; Restitution. §52.7.
Civil actions for distribution of unauthorized obscene material; Definitions. § 52.8.
Prohibition against discriminating restrictions in real instruments. §53.
Privacy; Lodging; Common carriers. §53.5.
Political structure equal protection; Compelling government interest. §53.7.

§43. General personal rights

Besides the personal rights mentioned or recognized in the Government Code, every person has, subject to the qualifications and restrictions provided by law, the right of protection from bodily restraint or harm, from personal insult, from defamation, and from injury to his personal relations. **Leg.H.** Enacted 1872. Amended Stats 1953 ch 604 §1.

§43.1. Child conceived but not yet born

A child conceived, but not yet born, is deemed an existing person, so far as necessary for the child's interests in the event of the child's subsequent birth. **Leg.H.** Added Stats 1992 ch 163 §4 (AB 2641), operative January 1, 1994.

§43.3. Breastfeeding rights

Notwithstanding any other provision of law, a mother may breastfeed her child in any location, public or private, except the private home or residence of another, where the mother and the child are otherwise authorized to be present. **Leg.H.** Added Stats 1997 ch 59 §1 (AB 157).

§43.4. No cause of action for damages from fraudulent promise to marry or to cohabit after marriage

A fraudulent promise to marry or to cohabit after marriage does not give rise to a cause of action for damages. **Leg.H.** Added Stats 1959 ch 381 §1.

§43.5. Wrongs for which no cause of action arises

No cause of action arises for:
 (a) Alienation of affection.
 (b) Criminal conversation.
 (c) Seduction of a person over the age of legal consent.
 (d) Breach of promise of marriage. **Leg.H.** Added Stats 1939 ch 128 §2.

§43.5(a). [Section renumbered 1986]

Leg.H. Added Stats 1945 ch 1117 §1. Amended and renumbered to CC §43.55 by Stats 1986 ch 248 §15.

§43.54 Civil arrest in a courthouse

(a) A person shall not be subject to civil arrest in a courthouse while attending a court proceeding or having legal business in the courthouse.
(b) This section does not narrow, or in any way lessen, any existing common law privilege.
(c) This section does not apply to arrests made pursuant to a valid judicial warrant. **Leg.H.** Added Stats 2019 ch 787 §2 (AB 668), effective January 1, 2020.

§43.55. No cause of action for arrest pursuant to warrant regular on its face

(a) There shall be no liability on the part of, and no cause of action shall arise against, any peace officer who makes an arrest pursuant to a warrant of arrest regular upon its face if the peace officer in making the arrest acts without malice and in the reasonable belief that the person arrested is the one referred to in the warrant.

(b) As used in this section, a "warrant of arrest regular upon its face" includes both of the following:

(1) A paper arrest warrant that has been issued pursuant to a judicial order.

(2) A judicial order that is entered into an automated warrant system by law enforcement or court personnel authorized to make those entries at or near the time the judicial order is made. **Leg.H.** Added Stats 1945 ch 1117 §1, as §43.5(a). Amended and renumbered Stats 1986 ch 248 §15; Stats 2005 ch 706 §2 (AB 1742), effective January 1, 2006.

Prior Law: There was another section of this number which was added Stats 1986 ch 1330 §2, effective September 29, 1986, amended Stats 1988 ch 195 §1, effective June 16, 1988, and renumbered §43.56 by Stats 1990 ch 216 §5.

§43.56. Alienation of affection of foster child

No cause of action arises against a foster parent for alienation of affection of a foster child. **Leg.H.** Added Stats 1986 ch 1330 §2, effective September 29, 1986, as CC §43.55. Amended Stats 1988 ch 195 §1, effective June 16, 1988. Renumbered by Stats 1990 ch 216 §5.

§43.6. Wrongful life action

(a) No cause of action arises against a parent of a child based upon the claim that the child should not have been conceived or, if conceived, should not have been allowed to have been born alive.

(b) The failure or refusal of a parent to prevent the live birth of his or her child shall not be a defense in any action against a third party, nor shall the failure or refusal be considered in awarding damages in any such action.

(c) As used in this section "conceived" means the fertilization of a human ovum by a human sperm. **Leg.H.** Added Stats 1981 ch 331 §1.

§43.7. Immunity for members of mental health professional quality assurance committee, medical specialty society, professional society, or insurance underwriting committee

(a) There shall be no monetary liability on the part of, and no cause of action for damages shall arise against, any member of a duly appointed mental health professional quality assurance committee that is established in compliance with Section 14725 of the Welfare and Institutions Code, for any act or proceeding undertaken or performed within the scope of the functions of the committee which is formed to review and evaluate the adequacy, appropriateness, or effectiveness of the care and treatment planned for, or provided to, mental health patients in order to improve quality of care by mental health professionals if the committee member acts without malice, has made a reasonable effort to obtain the facts of the matter as to which he or she acts, and acts in reasonable belief that the action taken by him or her is warranted by the facts known to him or her after the reasonable effort to obtain facts.

(b) There shall be no monetary liability on the part of, and no cause of action for damages shall arise against, any professional society, any member of a duly appointed committee of a medical specialty society, or any member of a duly appointed committee of a state or local professional society, or duly appointed member of a committee of a professional staff of a licensed hospital (provided the professional staff operates pursuant to written bylaws that have been approved by the governing board of the hospital), for any act or proceeding undertaken or performed within the scope of the functions of the committee which is formed to maintain the professional standards of the society established by its bylaws, or any member of any peer review committee whose purpose is to review the quality of medical, dental, dietetic, chiropractic, optometric, acupuncture, psychotherapy, midwifery, or veterinary services rendered by physicians and surgeons, dentists, dental hygienists, podiatrists, registered dietitians, chiropractors, optometrists, acupuncturists, veterinarians, marriage and family therapists, professional clinical counselors, licensed midwives, or psychologists, which committee is composed chiefly of physicians and surgeons, dentists, dental hygienists, podiatrists, registered dietitians, chiropractors, optometrists, acupuncturists, veterinarians, marriage and family therapists, professional clinical counselors, licensed midwives or psychologists for any act or proceeding undertaken or performed in reviewing the quality of medical, dental, dietetic, chiropractic, optometric, acupuncture, psychotherapy, midwifery, or veterinary services rendered by physicians and surgeons, dentists, dental hygienists, podiatrists, registered dietitians, chiropractors, optometrists, acupuncturists, veterinarians, marriage and family therapists, professional clinical counselors, midwifery, or psychologists or any member of the governing board of a hospital in reviewing the quality of medical services rendered by members of the staff if the professional society, committee, or board member acts without malice, has made a reasonable effort to obtain the facts of the matter as to which he, she, or it acts, and acts in reasonable belief that the action taken by him, her, or it is warranted by the facts known to him, her, or it after the reasonable effort to obtain facts. "Professional society" includes legal, medical, psychological, dental, dental hygiene, dietetic, accounting, optometric, acupuncture, podiatric, pharmaceutic, chiropractic, physical therapist, veterinary, licensed marriage and family therapy, licensed clinical social work, licensed professional clinical counselor, and engineering organizations having as members at least 25 percent of the eligible persons or licentiates in the geographic area served by the particular society. However, if the society has fewer than 100 members, it shall have as members at least a majority of the eligible persons or licentiates in the geographic area served by the particular society.

"Medical specialty society" means an organization having as members at least 25 percent of the eligible physicians and surgeons within a given professionally recognized medical specialty in the geographic area served by the particular society.

(c) This section does not affect the official immunity of an officer or employee of a public corporation.

(d) There shall be no monetary liability on the part of, and no cause of action for damages shall arise against, any physician and surgeon, podiatrist, or chiropractor who is a member of an underwriting committee of an interindemnity or reciprocal or interinsurance exchange or mutual company for any act or proceeding undertaken or performed in evaluating physicians and surgeons, podiatrists, or chiropractors for the writing of professional liability insurance, or any act or proceeding undertaken or performed in evaluating physicians and surgeons for the writing of an interindemnity, reciprocal, or interinsurance contract as specified in Section 1280.7 of the Insurance Code, if the evaluating physician and surgeon, podiatrist, or chiropractor acts without malice, has made a reasonable effort to obtain the facts of the matter as to which he or she acts, and acts in reasonable belief that the action taken by him or her is warranted by the facts known to him or her after the reasonable effort to obtain the facts.

(e) This section shall not be construed to confer immunity from liability on any quality assurance committee established in compliance with Section 14725 of the Welfare and Institutions Code or hospital. In any case in which, but for the enactment of the preceding provisions of this section, a cause of action would arise against a quality assurance committee established in compliance with Section 14725 of the Welfare and Institutions Code or hospital, the cause of action shall exist as if the preceding provisions of this section had not been enacted. **Leg.H.** Added Stats 1961 ch 623 §1. Amended Stats 1963 ch 806 §1; Stats 1969 ch 264 §1; Stats 1973 ch 191 §1; Stats 1976 ch 532 §1; Stats 1977 ch 241 §1, ch 934 §1; Stats 1978 ch 268 §1, ch 503 §1; Stats 1980 ch 454 §1; Stats 1982 ch 234 §2, effective June 2, 1982, ch 705 §1; Stats 1983 ch 289 §1, ch 297 §1, ch 1081 §1.8; Stats 1984 ch 515 §1, ch 1012 §2; Stats 1986 ch 669 §1; Stats 1987 ch 1169 §2, operative January 1, 1990; Stats 1994 ch 815 §1 (SB 1279); Stats 2002 ch 1013 §72 (SB 2026); Stats 2010 ch 82 §1 (AB 1730), effective January 1, 2011; Stats 2011 ch 381 §14 (SB 146), effective January 1, 2012; Stats 2012 ch 34 §3 (SB 1009), effective June 27, 2012, operative July 1, 2012; Stats 2017 ch 775 §105 (SB 798), effective January 1, 2018.

2012 Note: This act is titled and may be cited as 2011 Realignment Legislation. Stats 2012 ch 34 (SB 1009) §1.

§43.8. Immunity as to communication in aid of evaluation of practitioner of healing or veterinary arts

(a) In addition to the privilege afforded by Section 47, there shall be no monetary liability on the part of, and no cause of action for damages shall arise against, any person on account of the communication of information in the possession of that person to any hospital, hospital medical staff, veterinary hospital staff, professional society, medical, dental, podiatric, psychology, marriage and family therapy, professional clinical counselor, midwifery, or veterinary school, professional licensing board or division, committee or panel of a licensing board, the Senior Assistant Attorney General of the Health Quality Enforcement Section appointed under Section 12529 of the Government Code, peer review committee, quality assurance committees established in compliance with Sections 4070 and 5624 of the Welfare and Institutions Code, or underwriting committee described in Section 43.7 when the communication is intended to aid in the evaluation of the qualifications, fitness, character, or insurability of a practitioner of the healing or veterinary arts.

(b) The immunities afforded by this section and by Section 43.7 shall not affect the availability of any absolute privilege that may be afforded by Section 47.

(c) Nothing in this section is intended in any way to affect the California Supreme Court's decision in Hassan v. Mercy American River Hospital (2003) 31 Cal.4th 709, holding that subdivision (a) provides a qualified privilege. **Leg.H.** Added Stats 1974 ch 1086 §1. Amended Stats 1975 2nd Ex Sess ch 1 §24.4; Stats 1976 ch 532 §2; Stats 1977 ch 934 §2; Stats 1982 ch 234 §3, effective June 2, 1982, ch 705 §2; Stats 1983 ch 1081 §2; Stats 1984 ch 515 §4; Stats 1983 ch 1081 §2, operative January 1, 1990; Stats 1990 ch 1597 §30 (SB 2375); Stats 2002 ch 664 §31 (AB 3034); Stats 2007 ch 36 §1 (SB 822), effective January 1, 2008; Stats 2008 ch 23 §1 (AB 164), effective January 1, 2009; Stats 2011 ch 381 §15 (SB 146), effective January 1, 2012; Stats 2017 ch 775 §106 (SB 798), effective January 1, 2018.

§43.9. Immunity of health care provider from negligence on account of unsolicited referral arising from test by multiphasic screening unit

(a) There shall be no liability on the part of, and no cause of action shall accrue against, any health care provider for professional negligence on account of the receipt by such provider of an unsolicited referral, arising from a test performed by a multiphasic screening unit, for any act or omission, including the failure to examine, treat, or refer for examination or treatment any person concerning whom an unsolicited referral has been received. The immunity from liability granted by this subdivision shall only apply where a health provider meets the obligations established in subdivision (c).

(b) Every multiphasic screening unit shall notify each person it tests that the person should contact the health provider to whom the test results are sent within 10 days and that the health provider may not be obligated to interpret the results or provide further care. The multiphasic screening unit shall include the words "PATIENT TEST RESULTS" on the envelope of any test results sent to a health care provider, and shall include the address of the person tested in the test result material sent to the health care provider.

Nothing contained in this section shall relieve any health care provider from liability, if any, when at the time of receipt of the unsolicited referral there exists a provider-patient relationship, or a contract for health care services, or following receipt of such unsolicited referral there is established or reestablished a provider-patient relationship.

(c) A health care provider who receives unsolicited test results from a multiphasic screening unit shall receive immunity from liability pursuant to subdivision (a) only if the provider who receives such test results and does not wish to evaluate them, or evaluates them and takes no further action, either notifies the multiphasic screening unit of that fact or returns the test results within 21 days. If the health care provider reviews the test results and determines that they indicate a substantial risk of serious illness or death the provider shall make a reasonable effort to notify the person tested of the presumptive finding within 14 days after the provider has received the test results.

(d) For the purposes of this section:

(1) "Health care provider" means any person licensed or certified pursuant to Division 2 (commencing with Section 500) of the Business and Professions Code, or licensed pursuant to the Osteopathic Initiative Act or the Chiropractic Initiative Act, or licensed pursuant to Chapter 2.5 (commencing with Section 1440) of Division 2 of the Health and Safety Code, and any clinic, health dispensary, or health facility licensed pursuant to Division 2 (commencing with Section 1200) of the Health and Safety Code. "Health care provider" also includes the legal representatives of a health care provider.

(2) "Professional negligence" means an action for personal injury or wrongful death proximately caused by a health care provider's negligent act or omission to act in the rendering of professional services, provided that such services are within the scope of services for which the health care provider is licensed and are not within any restriction imposed by the licensing agency or any licensed hospital.

(3) "Unsolicited referral" means any written report regarding the health, physical or mental condition of any person which was forwarded or delivered to a health care provider without prior request by such provider.

(4) A "multiphasic screening unit" means a facility which does not prescribe or treat patients but performs diagnostic testing only. **Leg.H.** Added Stats 1978 ch 1296 §1. Amended Stats 1980 ch 676 §38.

Note: Sections 43.55 and 43.56 appear following §43.5.

§43.91. Immunity of members of professional society comprised of persons licensed under Real Estate Law

(a) There shall be no monetary liability on the part of, and no cause of action shall arise against, any member of a duly appointed committee of a professional society which comprises a substantial percentage of the persons licensed pursuant to Part 1 (commencing with Section 10000) of Division 4 of the Business and Professions Code and situated in the geographic area served by the particular society, for any act or proceeding undertaken or performed within the scope of the functions of any such committee which is formed to maintain the professional standards of the society established by its bylaws, if such member acts without malice, has made a reasonable effort to obtain the facts of the matter as to which he acts, and acts in reasonable belief that the action taken by him is warranted by the facts known to him after such reasonable effort to obtain facts.

(b) There shall be no monetary liability on the part of, and no cause of action for damages shall arise against, any person on account of the communication of information in the possession of such person to any committee specified in subdivision (a) when such communication is intended to aid in the evaluation of the qualifications, fitness or character of a member or applicant for membership in any such professional society, and does not represent as true any matter not reasonably believed to be true.

(c) The immunities afforded by this section shall not affect the availability of any absolute privilege which may be afforded by Section 47.

(d) This section shall not be construed to confer immunity from liability on any professional society. In any case in which, but for the enactment of this section, a cause of action would arise against a professional society, such cause of action shall exist as if this section had not been enacted. **Leg.H.** Added Stats 1980 ch 492 §1.

§43.92. Psychotherapist's duty to protect of patient's violent behavior; Immunity from liability; Legislative intent

(a) There shall be no monetary liability on the part of, and no cause of action shall arise against, any person who is a psychotherapist as defined in Section 1010 of the Evidence Code in failing to protect from a patient's threatened violent behavior or failing to predict and protect from a patient's violent behavior except if the patient has communicated to the psychotherapist a serious threat of physical violence against a reasonably identifiable victim or victims.

(b) There shall be no monetary liability on the part of, and no cause of action shall arise against, a psychotherapist who, under the limited circumstances specified in subdivision (a), discharges his or her duty to protect by making reasonable efforts to communicate the threat to the victim or victims and to a law enforcement agency.

(c) It is the intent of the Legislature that the amendments made by the act adding this subdivision only change the name of the duty referenced in this section from a duty to warn and protect to a duty to protect. Nothing in this section shall be construed to be a substantive change, and any duty of a psychotherapist shall not be modified as a result of changing the wording in this section.

(d) It is the intent of the Legislature that a court interpret this section, as amended by the act adding this subdivision, in a manner consistent with the interpretation of this section as it read prior to January 1, 2013. **Leg.H.** Added Stats 1985 ch 737 §1. Amended Stats 2006 ch 136 §1 (AB 733), effective January 1, 2007; Stats 2012 ch 149 §1 (SB 1134), effective January 1, 2013.

§43.93. Patient's action against psychotherapist for sexual contact

(a) For the purposes of this section the following definitions are applicable:

(1) "Psychotherapy" means the professional treatment, assessment, or counseling of a mental or emotional illness, symptom, or condition.

(2) "Psychotherapist" means a physician and surgeon specializing in the practice of psychiatry, a psychologist, a psychological assistant, a marriage and family therapist, a registered marriage and family therapist intern or trainee, an educational psychologist, an associate clinical social worker, a licensed clinical social worker, a professional clinical counselor, or a registered clinical counselor intern or trainee.

(3) "Sexual contact" means the touching of an intimate part of another person. "Intimate part" and "touching" have the same meanings as defined in subdivisions (f) and (d), respectively, of Section 243.4 of the Penal Code. For the purposes of this section, sexual contact includes sexual intercourse, sodomy, and oral copulation.

(4) "Therapeutic relationship" exists during the time the patient or client is rendered professional service by the psychotherapist.

(5) "Therapeutic deception" means a representation by a psychotherapist that sexual contact with the psychotherapist is consistent with or part of the patient's or former patient's treatment.

(b) A cause of action against a psychotherapist for sexual contact exists for a patient or former patient for injury caused by sexual contact with the psychotherapist, if the sexual contact occurred under any of the following conditions:

(1) During the period the patient was receiving psychotherapy from the psychotherapist.

(2) Within two years following termination of therapy.

(3) By means of therapeutic deception.

(c) The patient or former patient may recover damages from a psychotherapist who is found liable for sexual contact. It is not a defense to the action that sexual contact with a patient occurred outside a therapy or treatment session or that it occurred off the premises regularly used by the psychotherapist for therapy or treatment sessions. No cause of action shall exist between spouses within a marriage.

(d) In an action for sexual contact, evidence of the plaintiff's sexual history is not subject to discovery and is not admissible as evidence except in either of the following situations:

(1) The plaintiff claims damage to sexual functioning.

(2) The defendant requests a hearing prior to conducting discovery and makes an offer of proof of the relevancy of the history, and the court finds that the history is relevant and the probative value of the history outweighs its prejudicial effect.

The court shall allow the discovery or introduction as evidence only of specific information or examples of the plaintiff's conduct that are determined by the court to be relevant. The court's order shall detail the information or conduct that is subject to discovery. **Leg.H.** Added Stats 1987 ch 1474 §1. Amended Stats 1992 ch 890 §5 (SB 1394); Stats 1993 ch 589 §19 (AB 2211); Stats 2002 ch 1013 §73 (SB 2026); Stats 2011 ch 381 §16 (SB 146), effective January 1, 2012.

§43.95. Professional societies' immunity from liability for referrals

(a) There shall be no monetary liability on the part of, and no cause of action for damages shall arise against, any professional society or any nonprofit corporation authorized by a professional society to operate a referral service, or their agents, employees, or members, for referring any member of the public to any professional member of the society or service, or for acts of negligence or conduct constituting unprofessional conduct committed by a professional to whom a member of the public was referred, so long as any of the foregoing persons or entities has acted without malice, and the referral was made at no cost added to the initial referral fee as part of a public service referral system organized under the auspices of the professional society. Further, there shall be no monetary liability on the part of, and no cause of action for damages shall arise against, any professional society for providing a telephone information library available for use by the general public without charge, nor against any nonprofit corporation authorized by a professional society for providing a telephone information library available for use by the general public without charge. "Professional society" includes legal, psychological, architectural, medical, dental, dietetic, accounting, optometric, podiatric, pharmaceutical, chiropractic, veterinary, licensed marriage and family therapy, licensed clinical social work, professional clinical counselor, and engineering organizations having as members at least 25 percent of the eligible persons or licentiates in the geographic area served by the particular society. However, if the society has less than 100 members, it shall have as members at least a majority of the eligible persons or licentiates in the geographic area served by the particular society. "Professional society" also includes organizations with referral services that have been authorized by the State Bar of California and operated in accordance with its Minimum Standards for a Lawyer Referral Service in California, and organizations that have been established to provide free assistance or representation to needy patients or clients.

(b) This section shall not apply whenever the professional society, while making a referral to a professional member of the society, fails to disclose the nature of any disciplinary action of which it has actual knowledge taken by a state licensing agency against that professional member. However, there shall be no duty to disclose a disciplinary action in either of the following cases:

(1) Where a disciplinary proceeding results in no disciplinary action being taken against the professional to whom a member of the public was referred.

(2) Where a period of three years has elapsed since the professional to whom a member of the public was referred has satisfied any terms, conditions, or sanctions imposed upon the professional as disciplinary action; except that if the professional is an attorney, there shall be no time limit on the duty to disclose. **Leg.H.** Added Stats 1987 ch 727 §4, operative July 1, 1993. Amended Stats 1988 ch 312 §2, operative July 1, 1993; Stats 2002 ch 1013 §74 (SB 2026); Stats 2011 ch 381 §17 (SB 146), effective January 1, 2012.

Prior Law: Former CC §43.95, similar to the present section, was added Stats 1978 ch 1297 §1, amended Stats 1980 ch 439 §1, ch 862 §2, Stats 1983 ch 289 §2, Stats 1986 ch 437 §1, ch 669 §3, ch 1274 §4.6, Stats 1987 ch 727 §3, Stats 1988 ch 312 §1, operative until July 1, 1993, and repealed, operative July 1, 1993, by its own terms.

§43.96. Notification of complainant against physician, surgeon or podiatrist of disciplinary agency; Immunity

(a) Any medical or podiatric society, health facility licensed or certified under Division 2 (commencing with Section 1200) of the Health and Safety Code, state agency as defined in Section 11000 of the Government Code, or local government agency that receives written complaints related to the professional competence or professional conduct of a physician and surgeon or doctor of podiatric medicine from the public shall inform the complainant that the Medical Board of California or the California Board of Podiatric Medicine, as the case may be, is the only authority in the state that may take disciplinary action against the license of the named licensee, and shall provide to the complainant the address and toll-free telephone number of the applicable state board.

(b) The immunity provided in Section 2318 of the Business and Professions Code and in Section 47 shall apply to complaints and information made or provided to a board pursuant to this section. **Leg.H.** Added Stats 1993 ch 1267 §48 (SB 916). Amended Stats 1994 ch 1206 §26 (SB 1775); Stats 1995 ch 708 §12 (SB 609).

§43.97. Hospital's immunity for action taken pursuant to recommendation of medical staff or peer review committee

There shall be no monetary liability on the part of, and no cause of action for damages, other than economic or pecuniary damages, shall arise against, a hospital for any action taken upon the recommendation of its medical staff, or against any other person or organization for any action taken, or restriction imposed, which is required to be reported pursuant to Section 805 of the Business and Professions Code, if that action or restriction is reported in accordance with Section 805 of the Business and Professions Code. This section shall not apply to an action knowingly and intentionally taken for the purpose of injuring a person affected by the action or infringing upon a person's rights. **Leg.H.** Added Stats 1981 ch 926 §1. Amended Stats 1986 ch 1274 §5; Stats 2006 ch 538 §36 (SB 1852), effective January 1, 2007.

§43.98. Immunity of consultant

(a) There shall be no monetary liability on the part of, and no cause of action shall arise against, any consultant on account of any communication by that consultant to the Director of the Department of Managed Health Care or any other officer, employee, agent, contractor, or consultant of the Department of Managed Health Care, when that communication is for the purpose of determining whether health care services have been or are being arranged or provided in accordance with the Knox–Keene Health Care Service Plan Act of 1975 (Chapter 2.2 (commencing with Section 1340) of Division 2 of the Health and Safety Code) and any regulation adopted thereunder and the consultant does all of the following:

(1) Acts without malice.

(2) Makes a reasonable effort to obtain the facts of the matter communicated.

(3) Acts with a reasonable belief that the communication is warranted by the facts actually known to the consultant after a reasonable effort to obtain the facts.

(4) Acts pursuant to a contract entered into on or after January 1, 1998, between the Commissioner of Corporations and a state licensing board or committee, including, but not limited to, the Medical Board of California, or pursuant to a contract entered into on or after January 1, 1998, with the Commissioner of Corporations pursuant to Section 1397.6 of the Health and Safety Code.

(5) Acts pursuant to a contract entered into on or after July 1, 2000, between the Director of the Department of Managed Health Care and a state licensing board or committee, including, but not limited to, the Medical Board of California, or pursuant to a contract entered into on or after July 1, 1999, with the Director of the Department of Managed Health Care pursuant to Section 1397.6 of the Health and Safety Code.

(b) The immunities afforded by this section shall not affect the availability of any other privilege or immunity which may be afforded under this part. Nothing in this section shall be construed to alter the laws regarding the confidentiality of medical records. **Leg.H.** Added Stats 1997 ch 139 §1 (AB 564). Amended Stats 1999 ch 525 §4 (AB 78); Stats 2000 ch 857 §3 (AB 2903).

§43.99. Liability of person or entity under contract with residential building permit applicant for quality review of compliance with State Housing Law

(a) There shall be no monetary liability on the part of, and no cause of action for damages shall arise against, any person or other legal entity that is under contract with an applicant for a residential building permit to provide independent quality review of the plans and specifications provided with the application in order to determine compliance with all applicable requirements imposed pursuant to the State Housing Law (Part 1.5 (commencing with Section 17910) of Division 13 of the Health and Safety Code), or any rules or regulations adopted pursuant to that law, or under contract with that applicant to provide independent quality review of the work of improvement to determine compliance with these plans and specifications, if the person or other legal entity meets the requirements of this section and one of the following applies:

(1) The person, or a person employed by any other legal entity, performing the work as described in this subdivision, has completed not less than five years of verifiable experience in the appropriate field and has obtained certification as a building inspector, combination inspector, or combination dwelling inspector from the International Conference of Building Officials (ICBO) and has successfully passed the technical written examination promulgated by ICBO for those certification categories.

(2) The person, or a person employed by any other legal entity, performing the work as described in this subdivision, has completed not less than five years of verifiable experience in the appropriate field and is a registered professional engineer, licensed general contractor, or a licensed architect rendering independent quality review of the work of improvement or plan examination services within the scope of his or her registration or licensure.

(3) The immunity provided under this section does not apply to any action initiated by the applicant who retained the qualified person.

(4) A "qualified person" for purposes of this section means a person holding a valid certification as one of those inspectors.

(b) Except for qualified persons, this section shall not relieve from, excuse, or lessen in any manner, the responsibility or liability of any person, company, contractor, builder, developer, architect, engineer, designer, or other individual or entity who develops, improves, owns, operates, or manages any residential building for any damages to persons or property caused by construction or design defects. The fact that an inspection by a qualified person has taken place may not be introduced as evidence in a construction defect action, including any reports or other items generated by the qualified person. This subdivision shall not apply in any action initiated by the applicant who retained the qualified person.

(c) Nothing in this section, as it relates to construction inspectors or plans examiners, shall be construed to alter the requirements for licensure, or the jurisdiction, authority, or scope of practice, of architects pursuant to Chapter 3 (commencing with Section 5500) of Division 3 of the Business and Professions Code, professional engineers pursuant to Chapter 7 (commencing with Section 6700) of Division 3 of the Business and Professions Code, or general contractors pursuant to Chapter 9 (commencing with Section 7000) of Division 3 of the Business and Professions Code.

(d) Nothing in this section shall be construed to alter the immunity of employees of the Department of Housing and Community Development under the Government Claims Act (Division 3.6 (commencing with Section 810) of Title 1 of the Government Code) when acting pursuant to Section 17965 of the Health and Safety Code.

(e) The qualifying person shall engage in no other construction, design, planning, supervision, or activities of any kind on the work of improvement, nor provide quality review services for any other party on the work of improvement.

(f) The qualifying person, or other legal entity, shall maintain professional errors and omissions insurance coverage in an amount not less than two million dollars ($2,000,000).

(g) The immunity provided by subdivision (a) does not inure to the benefit of the qualified person for damages caused to the applicant solely by the negligence or willful misconduct of the qualified person resulting from the provision of services under the contract with the applicant. **Leg.H.** Added Stats 2002 ch 722 §2 (SB 800). Amended Stats 2012 ch 759 §1 (AB 2690), effective January 1, 2013.

§43.100. Immunity from civil liability for motor vehicle property damage or trespass caused during rescue of animal

(a) There shall not be any civil liability on the part of, and no cause of action shall accrue against, a person for property damage or trespass to a motor vehicle, if the damage was caused while the person was rescuing an animal in accordance with subdivision (b) of Section 597.7 of the Penal Code.

(b) The immunity from civil liability for property damage to a motor vehicle that is established by subdivision (a) does not affect a person's civil liability or immunity from civil liability for rendering aid to an animal. **Leg.H.** Added Stats 2016 ch 554 §1 (AB 797), effective January 1, 2017.

§43.101. Liability of emergency responder for damage to unmanned aircraft or unmanned aircraft system

(a) An emergency responder shall not be liable for any damage to an unmanned aircraft or unmanned aircraft system, if that damage was caused while the emergency responder was providing, and the unmanned aircraft or unmanned aircraft system was interfering with, the operation, support, or enabling of the emergency services listed in Section 853 of the Government Code.

(b)(1) For purposes of this section, "emergency responder" means either of the following, if acting within the scope of authority implicitly or expressly provided by a local public entity or a public employee of a local public entity to provide emergency services:

(A) A paid or an unpaid volunteer.

(B) A private entity.

(2) All of the following terms shall have the same meaning as the terms as used in Chapter 4.5 (commencing with Section 853) of Part 2 of Division 3.6 of Title 1 of the Government Code:

(A) Local public entity.

(B) Public employee of a local public entity.

(C) Unmanned aircraft.

(D) Unmanned aircraft system. **Leg.H.** Added Stats 2016 ch 834 §1 (SB 807), effective January 1, 2017.

§ 43.102. Liability of property damage rescuing a child

There shall not be any civil liability on the part of, and no cause of action shall accrue against, a person for property damage or trespass to a motor vehicle, if the damage was caused while the person was rescuing a child in accordance with subdivision (a) or (b) of Section 1799.101 of the Health and Safety Code. For purposes of this section, "child" means a child who is six years of age or younger. **Leg.H.** Added Stats 2020 ch 352 §1 (AB 2717), effective January 1, 2021.

§44. Defamation

Defamation is effected by either of the following:

(a) Libel.

(b) Slander. **Leg.H.** Enacted 1872. Amended Stats 1980 ch 676 §39.

§45. Libel defined

Libel is a false and unprivileged publication by writing, printing, picture, effigy, or other fixed representation to the eye, which exposes any person to hatred, contempt, ridicule, or obloquy, or which causes him to be shunned or avoided, or which has a tendency to injure him in his occupation. **Leg.H.** Enacted 1872.

§45a. Libel on its face defined; Action for defamation not libelous on its face

A libel which is defamatory of the plaintiff without the necessity of explanatory matter, such as an inducement, innuendo or other extrinsic fact, is said to be a libel on its face. Defamatory language not libelous on its face is not actionable unless the plaintiff alleges and proves that he has suffered special damage as a proximate result thereof. Special damage is defined in Section 48a of this code. **Leg.H.** Added Stats 1945 ch 1489 §1.

§46. Slander defined

Slander is a false and unprivileged publication, orally uttered, and also communications by radio or any mechanical or other means which:

1. Charges any person with crime, or with having been indicted, convicted, or punished for crime;
2. Imputes in him the present existence of an infectious, contagious, or loathsome disease;
3. Tends directly to injure him in respect to his office, profession, trade or business, either by imputing to him general disqualification in those respects which the office or other occupation peculiarly requires, or by imputing something with reference to his office, profession, trade, or business that has a natural tendency to lessen its profits;
4. Imputes to him impotence or a want of chastity; or
5. Which, by natural consequence, causes actual damage. **Leg.H.** Enacted 1872. Amended Stats 1945 ch 1489 §2.

§47. Privileged publication or broadcast

A privileged publication or broadcast is one made:

(a) In the proper discharge of an official duty.

(b) In any (1) legislative proceeding, (2) judicial proceeding, (3) in any other official proceeding authorized by law, or (4) in the initiation or course of any other proceeding authorized by law and reviewable pursuant to Chapter 2 (commencing with Section 1084) of Title 1 of Part 3 of the Code of Civil Procedure, except as follows:

(1) An allegation or averment contained in any pleading or affidavit filed in an action for marital dissolution or legal separation made of or concerning a person by or against whom no affirmative relief is prayed in the action shall not be a privileged publication or broadcast as to the person making the allegation or averment within the meaning of this section unless the pleading is verified or affidavit sworn to, and is made without malice, by one having reasonable and probable cause for believing the truth of the allegation or averment and unless the allegation or averment is material and relevant to the issues in the action.

(2) This subdivision does not make privileged any communication made in furtherance of an act of intentional destruction or alteration of physical evidence undertaken for the purpose of depriving a party to litigation of the use of that evidence, whether or not the content of the communication is the subject of a subsequent publication or broadcast which is privileged pursuant to this section. As used in this paragraph, "physical evidence" means evidence specified in Section 250 of the Evidence Code or evidence that is property of any type specified in Chapter 14 (commencing with Section 2031.010) of Title 4 of Part 4 of the Code of Civil Procedure.

(3) This subdivision does not make privileged any communication made in a judicial proceeding knowingly concealing the existence of an insurance policy or policies.

(4) A recorded lis pendens is not a privileged publication unless it identifies an action previously filed with a court of competent jurisdiction which affects the title or right of possession of real property, as authorized or required by law.

(5) This subdivision does not make privileged any communication between a person and a law enforcement agency in which the person makes a false report that another person has committed, or is in the act of committing, a criminal act or is engaged in an activity requiring law enforcement intervention, knowing that the report is false, or with reckless disregard for the truth or falsity of the report.

(c) In a communication, without malice, to a person interested therein, (1) by one who is also interested, or (2) by one who stands in such a relation to the person interested as to afford a reasonable ground for supposing the motive for the communication to be innocent, or (3) who is requested by the person interested to give the information. This subdivision applies to and includes a communication concerning the job performance or qualifications of an applicant for employment, based upon credible evidence, made without malice, by a current or former employer of the applicant to, and upon request of, one whom the employer reasonably believes is a prospective employer of the applicant. This subdivision applies to and includes a complaint of sexual harassment by an employee, without malice, to an employer based upon credible evidence and communications between the employer and interested persons, without malice, regarding a complaint of sexual harassment. This subdivision authorizes a current or former employer, or the employer's agent, to answer, without malice, whether or not the employer would rehire a current or former employee and whether the decision to not rehire is based upon the employer's determination that the former employee engaged in sexual harassment. This subdivision does not apply to a communication concerning the speech or activities of an applicant for employment if the speech or activities are constitutionally protected, or otherwise protected by Section 527.3 of the Code of Civil Procedure or any other provision of law.

(d)(1) By a fair and true report in, or a communication to, a public journal, of (A) a judicial, (B) legislative, or (C) other public official proceeding, or (D) of anything said in the course thereof, or (E) of a verified charge or complaint made by any person to a public official, upon which complaint a warrant has been issued.

(2) Paragraph (1) does not make privileged any communication to a public journal that does any of the following:

(A) Violates Rule 3.6 of the State Bar Rules of Professional Conduct.

(B) Breaches a court order.

(C) Violates a requirement of confidentiality imposed by law.

(e) By a fair and true report of (1) the proceedings of a public meeting, if the meeting was lawfully convened for a lawful purpose and open to the public, or (2) the publication of the matter complained of was for the public benefit. **Leg.H.** Enacted 1872. Amended Code Amdts 1873–74 ch 612 §11; Stats 1895 ch 163 §1; Stats 1927 ch 866 §1; Stats 1945 ch 1489 §3; Stats 1979 ch 184 §1; Stats 1990 ch 1491 §1 (AB 3765); Stats 1991 ch 432 §1 (AB 529); Stats 1992 ch 615 §1 (SB 1804); Stats 1994 ch 364 §1 (AB 2778), ch 700 §2.5 (SB 1457); Stats 1996 ch 1055 §2 (SB 1540); Stats 2002 ch 1029 §1 (AB 2868), effective September 28, 2002; Stats 2004 ch 182 §4 (AB 3081), operative July 1, 2005; Stats 2018 ch 82 §1 (AB 2770), effective January 1, 2019; Stats 2020 ch 327 §2 (AB 1775), effective January 1, 2021; Stats 2023 ch 131 §9 (AB 1754), effective January 1, 2024.

1996 Note: In amending Section 47 of the Civil Code by this act, it is the intent of the Legislature to abrogate the decision in *Shahvar v. Superior Court* (1994), 25 Cal. App. 4th 653, to preserve the scarce resources of California's courts, to avoid using the courts for satellite litigation, and to increase public participation in the political, legislative, and judicial processes. It is not the intent of the Legislature to limit in any manner the application of subdivision (b) or (d) of Section 47 of the Civil Code. Specifically, it is not the intent of the Legislature to affect case law holding that certain prelitigation statements are privileged as described in, for example, *Lerette v. Dean Witter Organization, Inc.*, 60 Cal. App. 3d 573; *Martin v. Kearney*, 51 Cal. App. 3d 309; *Ascherman v. Natanson*, 23 Cal. App. 3d 861; and the Second Restatement of Torts, Section 586. Stats 1996 ch 1055 §1.

1994 Note: It is the intent of the Legislature in amending Section 47 of the Civil Code to overturn the decision in *California Dredging Company v. Insurance Company of North America*, 18 Cal. App. 4th 572. Stats 1994 ch 700 §1.

§ 47.1. Communications about sexual assault, harassment, or discrimination incident privileged

(a) A communication made by an individual, without malice, regarding an incident of sexual assault, harassment, or discrimination is privileged under Section 47.

(b) A prevailing defendant in any defamation action brought against that defendant for making a communication that is privileged under this section shall be entitled to their reasonable attorney's fees and costs for successfully defending themselves in the litigation, plus treble damages for any harm caused to them by the defamation action against them, in addition to punitive damages available under Section 3294 or any other relief otherwise permitted by law.

(c) This section shall only apply to an individual that has, or at any time had, a reasonable basis to file a complaint of sexual assault, harassment, or discrimination, whether the complaint is, or was, filed or not.

(d) For the purposes of this section, "communication" means factual information related to an incident of sexual assault, harassment, or discrimination experienced by the individual making the communication, including, but not limited to, any of the following:

(1) An act of sexual assault.

(2) An act of sexual harassment, as described in Section 51.9.

(3) An act of workplace harassment or discrimination, failure to prevent an act of workplace harassment or discrimination, aiding, abetting, inciting, compelling, or coercing an act of workplace harassment or discrimination, or an act of retaliation against a person for reporting or opposing workplace harassment or discrimination, as described in subdivision (a), (h), (i), (j), or (k) of Section 12940 of the Government Code.

(4) An act of harassment or discrimination, or an act of retaliation against a person for reporting harassment or discrimination, by the owner of a housing accommodation, as described in Section 12955 of the Government Code.

(5) An act of sexual harassment, as defined in Sections 212.5 and 66262.5 of the Education Code.

(6) An act of harassment or discrimination, or an act of retaliation against a person for reporting harassment or discrimination, based on any of the protected classes enumerated in Sections 220, 221.51, and 66270 of the Education Code.

(7) An act of cyber sexual bullying, as defined in Section 48900 of the Education Code. **Leg.H.** Added Stats 2023 ch 670 §1 (AB 933), effective January 1, 2024.

§47.5. Action for defamation against individual filing false complaint against peace officer

Notwithstanding Section 47, a peace officer may bring an action for defamation against an individual who has filed a complaint with that officer's employing agency alleging misconduct, criminal conduct, or incompetence, if that complaint is false, the complaint was made with knowledge that it was false and that it was made with spite, hatred, or ill will. Knowledge that the complaint was false may be proved by a showing that the complainant had no reasonable grounds to believe the statement was true and that the complainant exhibited a reckless disregard for ascertaining the truth. **Leg.H.** Added Stats 1982 ch 1588 §1.

§48. Malice not inferred in specified privileged communication

In the case provided for in subdivision (c) of Section 47, malice is not inferred from the communication. **Leg.H.** Enacted 1872. Amended Stats 1895 ch 163 §2; Stats 1945 ch 1489 §4; Stats 2003 ch 62 §11 (SB 600).

§48a. Demand for publication or broadcast of correction

(a) In any action for damages for the publication of a libel in a daily or weekly news publication, or of a slander by radio broadcast, plaintiff shall only recover special damages unless a correction is demanded and is not published or broadcast, as provided in this section. Plaintiff shall serve upon the publisher at the place of publication, or broadcaster at the place of broadcast, a written notice specifying the statements claimed to be libelous and demanding that those statements be corrected. The notice and demand must be served within 20 days after knowledge of the publication or broadcast of the statements claimed to be libelous.

(b) If a correction is demanded within 20 days and is not published or broadcast in substantially as conspicuous a manner in the same daily or weekly news publication, or on the same broadcasting station as were the statements claimed to be libelous, in a regular issue thereof published or broadcast within three weeks after service, plaintiff, if he or she pleads and proves notice, demand and failure to correct, and if his or her cause of action is maintained, may recover general, special, and exemplary damages. Exemplary damages shall not be recovered unless the plaintiff proves that defendant made the publication or broadcast with actual malice and then only in the discretion of the court or jury, and actual malice shall not be inferred or presumed from the publication or broadcast.

(c) A correction published or broadcast in substantially as conspicuous a manner in the daily or weekly news publication, or on the broadcasting station as the statements claimed in the complaint to be libelous, before receipt of a demand for correction, shall be of the same force and effect as though the correction had been published or broadcast within three weeks after a demand for correction.

(d) As used in this section, the following definitions shall apply:

(1) "General damages" means damages for loss of reputation, shame, mortification, and hurt feelings.

(2) "Special damages" means all damages that plaintiff alleges and proves that he or she has suffered in respect to his or her property, business, trade, profession, or occupation, including the amounts of money the plaintiff alleges and proves he or she has expended as a result of the alleged libel, and no other.

(3) "Exemplary damages" means damages that may in the discretion of the court or jury be recovered in addition to general and special damages for the sake of example and by way of punishing a defendant who has made the publication or broadcast with actual malice.

(4) "Actual malice" means that state of mind arising from hatred or ill will toward the plaintiff; provided, however, that a state of mind occasioned by a good faith belief on the part of the defendant in the truth of the libelous publication or broadcast at the time it is published or broadcast shall not constitute actual malice.

(5) "Daily or weekly news publication" means a publication, either in print or electronic form, that contains news on matters of public concern and that publishes at least once a week. **Leg.H.** Added Stats 1931 ch 1018 §1. Amended Stats 1945 ch 1489 §5; Stats 2015 ch 343 §2 (AB 998), effective January 1, 2016; Stats 2016 ch 86 §17 (SB 1171), effective January 1, 2017.

2015 Note: It is the intent of the Legislature to ensure that weekly and online publications are afforded the same protection under Section 48a of the Civil Code as is afforded to a daily newspaper to the extent that the weekly and online publications perform the same news-disseminating function as a daily newspaper. The Legislature finds and declares that the rulings in Burnett v. National Enquirer, Inc. (1983) 144 Cal.App.3d 991 and Condit v. National Enquirer, Inc. (2002) 248 F.Supp.2d 945 do not fully recognize that the policy of Section 48a of the Civil Code to protect enterprises engaged in the immediate dissemination of news on matters of public concern, insofar as time constraints do not reasonably permit such enterprises to check sources for accuracy and stories for inadvertent errors, should extend to online publications and weekly newspapers, which publish breaking news on deadlines indistinguishable from daily newspapers. It is not the intent of the Legislature that Section 48a of the Civil Code should apply to periodicals that publish at longer than weekly intervals, nor is it the intent of the Legislature that Section 48a of the Civil Code should apply to casual postings on a social networking Internet Web site, chat room, electronic bulletin board, discussion group, online forum, or other related Internet Web site. Stats 2015 ch 343 (AB 998) §1.

§48.5. Liability of owners, licensees and operators of radio stations and networks for broadcast of defamatory statements

(1) The owner, licensee or operator of a visual or sound radio broadcasting station or network of stations, and the agents or employees of any such owner, licensee or operator, shall not be liable for any damages for any defamatory statement or matter published or uttered in or as a part of a visual or sound radio broadcast by one other than such owner, licensee or operator, or agent or employee thereof, if it shall be alleged and proved by such owner, licensee or operator, or agent or employee thereof, that such owner, licensee or operator, or such agent or employee, has exercised due care to prevent the publication or utterance of such statement or matter in such broadcast.

(2) If any defamatory statement or matter is published or uttered in or as a part of a broadcast over the facilities of a network of visual or sound radio broadcasting stations, the owner, licensee or operator of any such station, or network of stations, and the agents or employees thereof, other than the owner, licensee or operator of the station, or network of stations, originating such broadcast, and the agents or employees thereof, shall in no event be liable for any damages for any such defamatory statement or matter.

(3) In no event, however, shall any owner, licensee or operator of such station or network of stations, or the agents or employees thereof, be liable for any damages for any defamatory statement or matter published or uttered, by one other than such owner, licensee or operator, or agent or employee thereof, in or as a part of a visual or sound radio broadcast by or on behalf of any candidate for public office, which broadcast cannot be censored by reason of the provisions of federal statute or regulation of the Federal Communications Commission.

(4) As used in this Part 2, the terms "radio," "radio broadcast," and "broadcast," are defined to include both visual and sound radio broadcasting.

(5) Nothing in this section contained shall deprive any such owner, licensee or operator, or the agent or employee thereof, of any rights under any other section of this Part 2. **Leg.H.** Added Stats 1949 ch 1258 §1.

§48.7. Civil action for libel or slander arising from child abuse prosecution

(a) No person charged by indictment, information, or other accusatory pleading of child abuse may bring a civil libel or slander action against the minor, the parent or guardian of the minor, or any witness, based upon any statements made by the minor, parent or guardian, or witness which are reasonably believed to be in furtherance of the prosecution of the criminal charges while the charges are pending before a trial court. The charges are not pending within the meaning of this section after dismissal, after pronouncement of judgment, or during an appeal from a judgment.

Any applicable statute of limitations shall be tolled during the period that such charges are pending before a trial court.

(b) Whenever any complaint for libel or slander is filed which is subject to the provisions of this section, no responsive pleading shall be required to be filed until 30 days after the end of the period set forth in subdivision (a).

(c) Every complaint for libel or slander based on a statement that the plaintiff committed an act of child abuse shall state that the complaint is not barred by subdivision (a). A failure to include that statement shall be grounds for a demurrer.

(d) Whenever a demurrer against a complaint for libel or slander is sustained on the basis that the complaint was filed in violation of this section, attorney's fees and costs shall be awarded to the prevailing party.

(e) Whenever a prosecutor is informed by a minor, parent, guardian, or witness that a complaint against one of those persons has been filed which may be subject to the provisions of this section, the prosecutor shall provide that person with a copy of this section.

(f) As used in this section, child abuse has the meaning set forth in Section 11165 of the Penal Code. **Leg.H.** Added Stats 1981 ch 253 §1.

§48.8. Defamation liability for false threatening communications to school officials

(a) A communication by any person to a school principal, or a communication by a student attending the school to the student's teacher or to a school counselor or school nurse and any report of that communication to the school principal, stating that a specific student or other specified person has made a threat to commit violence or potential violence on the school grounds involving the use of a firearm or other deadly or dangerous weapon, is a communication on a matter of public concern and is subject to liability in defamation only upon a showing by clear and convincing evidence that the communication or report was made with knowledge of its falsity or with reckless disregard for the truth or falsity of the communication. Where punitive damages are alleged, the provisions of Section 3294 shall also apply.

(b) As used in this section, "school" means a public or private school providing instruction in kindergarten or grades 1 to 12, inclusive. **Leg.H.** Added Stats 2001 ch 570 §1 (AB 1717).

§48.9. Immunity for organization sponsoring or conducting anonymous witness program

(a) An organization which sponsors or conducts an anonymous witness program, and its employees and agents, shall not be liable in a civil action for damages resulting from its receipt of information regarding possible criminal activity or from dissemination of that information to a law enforcement agency.

(b) The immunity provided by this section shall apply to any civil action for damages, including, but not limited to, a defamation action or an action for damages resulting from retaliation against a person who provided information.

(c) The immunity provided by this section shall not apply in any of the following instances:

(1) The information was disseminated with actual knowledge that it was false.

(2) The name of the provider of the information was disseminated without that person's authorization and the dissemination was not required by law.

(3) The name of the provider of information was obtained and the provider was not informed by the organization that the disclosure of his or her name may be required by law.

(d) As used in this section, an "anonymous witness program" means a program whereby information relating to alleged criminal activity is received from persons, whose names are not released without their authorization unless required by law, and disseminated to law enforcement agencies. **Leg.H.** Added Stats 1983 ch 495 §1.

§49. Protection from abduction, seduction, and injury to servant

The rights of personal relations forbid:

(a) The abduction or enticement of a child from a parent, or from a guardian entitled to its custody;

(b) The seduction of a person under the age of legal consent;

(c) Any injury to a servant which affects his ability to serve his master, other than seduction, abduction or criminal conversation. **Leg.H.** Enacted 1872. Amended Stats 1905 ch 70 §1; Stats 1939 ch 128 §1, ch 1103 §5.

§50. Defense of self or others; Protection from wrongful injury; Use of necessary force

Any necessary force may be used to protect from wrongful injury the person or property of oneself, or of a spouse, child, parent, or other relative, or member of one's family, or of a ward, servant, master, or guest. **Leg.H.** Enacted 1872. Amended Code Amdts 1873–74 ch 612 §12; Stats 2016 ch 50 §4 (SB 1005), effective January 1, 2017.

2016 Note: For legislative intent, see the 2016 Note following §14.

§51. Citation of section; Civil rights of persons in business establishments; Definitions

(a) This section shall be known, and may be cited, as the Unruh Civil Rights Act.

(b) All persons within the jurisdiction of this state are free and equal, and no matter what their sex, race, color, religion, ancestry, national origin, disability, medical condition, genetic information, marital status, sexual orientation, citizenship, primary language, or immigration status are entitled to the full and equal accommodations, advantages, facilities, privileges, or services in all business establishments of every kind whatsoever.

(c) This section shall not be construed to confer any right or privilege on a person that is conditioned or limited by law or that is applicable alike to persons of every sex, color, race, religion, ancestry, national origin, disability, medical condition, marital status, sexual orientation, citizenship, primary language, or immigration status, or to persons regardless of their genetic information.

(d) Nothing in this section shall be construed to require any construction, alteration, repair, structural or otherwise, or modification of any sort whatsoever, beyond that construction, alteration, repair, or modification that is otherwise required by other provisions of law, to any new or existing establishment, facility, building, improvement, or any other structure, nor shall anything in this section be construed to augment, restrict, or alter in any way the authority of the State Architect to require construction, alteration, repair, or modifications that the State Architect otherwise possesses pursuant to other laws.

(e) For purposes of this section:

(1) "Disability" means any mental or physical disability as defined in Sections 12926 and 12926.1 of the Government Code.

(2)(A) "Genetic information" means, with respect to any individual, information about any of the following:

(i) The individual's genetic tests.

(ii) The genetic tests of family members of the individual.

(iii) The manifestation of a disease or disorder in family members of the individual.

(B) "Genetic information" includes any request for, or receipt of, genetic services, or participation in clinical research that includes genetic services, by an individual or any family member of the individual.

(C) "Genetic information" does not include information about the sex or age of any individual.

(3) "Medical condition" has the same meaning as defined in subdivision (i) of Section 12926 of the Government Code.

(4) **"Race"** is inclusive of traits associated with race, including, but not limited to, hair texture and protective hairstyles. **"Protective hairstyles"** includes, but is not limited to, such hairstyles as braids, locs, and twists.

(5) "Religion" includes all aspects of religious belief, observance, and practice.

[1] **(6)** "Sex" includes, but is not limited to, pregnancy, childbirth, or medical conditions related to pregnancy or childbirth. "Sex" also includes, but is not limited to, a person's gender. "Gender" means sex, and includes a person's gender identity and gender expression. "Gender expression" means a person's gender-related appearance and behavior whether or not stereotypically associated with the person's assigned sex at birth.

[2] **(7)** "Sex, race, color, religion, ancestry, national origin, disability, medical condition, genetic information, marital status, sexual orientation, citizenship, primary language, or immigration status" includes [3] **any of the following:**

(A) Any combination of those characteristics.

(B) A perception that the person has any particular characteristic or characteristics within the listed categories or any combination of those characteristics.

(C) A perception that the person is associated with a person who has, or is perceived to have, any particular characteristic or characteristics, or any combination of characteristics, within the listed categories.

[4] **(8)** "Sexual orientation" has the same meaning as defined in subdivision (s) of Section 12926 of the Government Code.

(f) A violation of the right of any individual under the federal Americans with Disabilities Act of 1990 (Public Law 101-336) shall also constitute a violation of this section.

(g) Verification of immigration status and any discrimination based upon verified immigration status, where required by federal law, shall not constitute a violation of this section.

(h) Nothing in this section shall be construed to require the provision of services or documents in a language other than English, beyond that which is otherwise required by other provisions of federal, state, or local law, including Section 1632. **Leg.H.** Added Stats 1905 ch 413 §3. Amended Stats 1919 ch 210 §1; Stats 1923 ch 235 §1; Stats 1959 ch 1866 §1; Stats 1961 ch 1187 §1; Stats 1974 ch 1193 §1; Stats 1987 ch 159 §1; Stats 1992 ch 913 §3 (AB 1077); Stats 1998 ch 195 §1 (AB 2702); Stats 2000 ch 1049 §2 (AB 2222); Stats 2005 ch 420 §3 (AB 1400), effective January 1, 2006; Stats 2011 ch 261 §3 (SB 559), effective January 1, 2012, ch 719 §1.5 (AB 887), effective January 1, 2012; Stats 2015 ch 282 §1 (SB 600), effective January 1, 2016 (ch 282 prevails), ch 303 §25 (AB 731), effective January 1, 2016; Stats 2024 ch 619 §1 (AB 1815), effective January 1, 2025; Stats 2024 ch 779 §2.5 (SB 1137), effective January 1, 2025 (ch 779 prevails).

§51. 2024 Deletes. [1] (5) [2] (6) [3] a perception that the person has any particular characteristic or characteristics within the listed categories, or that the person is associated with a person who has, or is perceived to have, any particular characteristic or characteristics within the listed categories. [4] (7)

2015 Note: The amendment of Section 51 of the Civil Code by this act does not constitute a change in, but is declaratory of, existing law. It is not the intent of the Legislature in amending the Unruh Civil Rights Act to affect the protected status of any other classification, whether or not expressed in Section 51 of the Civil Code. Stats 2015 ch 282 (SB 600) §2.

2005 Notes: This act shall be known and may be cited as "The Civil Rights Act of 2005." Stats 2005 ch 420 (AB 1400) §1.

The Legislature affirms that the bases of discrimination prohibited by the Unruh Civil Rights Act include, but are not limited to, marital status and sexual orientation, as defined herein. By specifically enumerating these bases in the Unruh Civil Rights Act, the Legislature intends to clarify the existing law, rather than to change the law, as well as the principle that the bases enumerated in the act are illustrative rather than restrictive. Stats 2005 ch 420 (AB 1400) §2(c).

It is the intent of the Legislature that the amendments made to the Unruh Civil Rights Act by this act do not affect the California Supreme Court's rulings in *Marina Point, Ltd. v. Wolfson* (1982) 30 Cal.3d 721 and *O'Connor v. Village Green Owners Association* (1983) 33 Cal.3d 790. Stats 2005 ch 420 (AB 1400) §2(d).

§51.1. Actions requiring copy of petition and brief to be served on State Solicitor General

If a violation of Section 51, 51.5, 51.7, 51.9, or 52.1 is alleged or the application or construction of any of these sections is in issue in any proceeding in the Supreme Court of California, a state court of appeal, or the appellate division of a superior court, each party shall serve a copy of the party's brief or petition and brief, on the State Solicitor General at the Office of the Attorney General. No brief may be accepted for filing unless the proof of service shows service on the State Solicitor General. Any party failing to comply with this requirement shall be given a reasonable opportunity to cure the failure before the court imposes any sanction and, in that instance, the court shall allow the Attorney General reasonable additional time to file a brief in the matter. **Leg.H.** Added Stats 2002 ch 244 §1 (AB 2524).

§51.2. Age discrimination in housing sale or rental

(a) Section 51 shall be construed to prohibit a business establishment from discriminating in the sale or rental of housing based upon age. Where accommodations are designed to meet the physical and social needs of senior citizens, a business establishment may establish and preserve that housing for senior citizens, pursuant to Section 51.3, except housing as to which Section 51.3 is preempted by the prohibition in the federal Fair Housing Amendments Act of 1988 (Public Law 100-430) and implementing regulations against discrimination on the basis of familial status. For accommodations constructed before February 8, 1982, that meet all the criteria for senior citizen housing specified in Section 51.3, a business establishment may establish and preserve that housing development for senior citizens without the housing development being designed to meet physical and social needs of senior citizens.

(b) This section is intended to clarify the holdings in Marina Point, Ltd. v. Wolfson (1982) 30 Cal. 3d 721 and O'Connor v. Village Green Owners Association (1983) 33 Cal. 3d 790.

(c) This section shall not apply to the County of Riverside.

(d) A housing development for senior citizens constructed on or after January 1, 2001, shall be presumed to be designed to meet the physical and social needs of senior citizens if it includes all of the following elements:

(1) Entryways, walkways, and hallways in the common areas of the development, and doorways and paths of access to and within the housing units, shall be as wide as required by current laws applicable to new multifamily housing construction for provision of access to persons using a standard-width wheelchair.

(2) Walkways and hallways in the common areas of the development shall be equipped with standard height railings or grab bars to assist persons who have difficulty with walking.

(3) Walkways and hallways in the common areas shall have lighting conditions which are of sufficient brightness to assist persons who have difficulty seeing.

(4) Access to all common areas and housing units within the development shall be provided without use of stairs, either by means of an elevator or sloped walking ramps.

(5) The development shall be designed to encourage social contact by providing at least one common room and at least some common open space.

(6) Refuse collection shall be provided in a manner that requires a minimum of physical exertion by residents.

(7) The development shall comply with all other applicable requirements for access and design imposed by law, including, but not limited to, the Fair Housing Act (42 U.S.C. Sec. 3601 et seq.), the Americans with Disabilities Act (42 U.S.C. Sec. 12101 et seq.), and the regulations promulgated at Title 24 of the California Code of Regulations that relate to access for persons with disabilities or handicaps. Nothing in this section shall be construed to limit or reduce any right or obligation applicable under those laws.

(e) Selection preferences based on age, imposed in connection with a federally approved housing program, do not constitute age discrimination in housing. **Leg.H.** Added Stats 1984 ch 787 §1. Amended Stats 1989 ch 501 §1; Stats 1993 ch 830 §1 (SB 137), effective October 5, 1993; Stats 1996 ch 1147 §2 (SB 2097); Stats 1999 ch 324 §1 (SB 382); Stats 2000 ch 1004 §2 (SB 2011); Stats 2002 ch 726 §2 (AB 2787); Stats 2010 ch 524 §2 (SB 1252), effective January 1, 2011.

§51.3. Senior citizen housing

(a) The Legislature finds and declares that this section is essential to establish and preserve specially designed accessible housing for senior citizens. There are senior citizens who need special living environments and services, and find that there is an inadequate supply of this type of housing in the state.

(b) For the purposes of this section, the following definitions apply:

(1) "Qualifying resident" or "senior citizen" means a person 62 years of age or older, or 55 years of age or older in a senior citizen housing development.

(2) "Qualified permanent resident" means a person who meets both of the following requirements:

(A) Was residing with the qualifying resident or senior citizen prior to the death, hospitalization, or other prolonged absence of, or the dissolution of marriage with, the qualifying resident or senior citizen.

(B) Was 45 years of age or older, or was a spouse, cohabitant, or person providing primary physical or economic support to the qualifying resident or senior citizen.

(3) "Qualified permanent resident" also means a disabled person or person with a disabling illness or injury who is a child or grandchild of the senior citizen or a qualified permanent resident as defined in paragraph (2) who needs to live with the senior citizen or qualified permanent resident because of the disabling condition, illness, or injury. For purposes of this section, "disabled" means a person who has a disability as defined in subdivision (b) of Section 54. A "disabling injury or illness" means an illness or injury which results in a condition meeting the definition of disability set forth in subdivision (b) of Section 54.

(A) For any person who is a qualified permanent resident under this paragraph whose disabling condition ends, the owner, board of directors, or other governing body may require the formerly disabled resident to cease residing in the development upon receipt of six months' written notice; provided, however, that the owner, board of directors, or other governing body may allow the person to remain a resident for up to one year after the disabling condition ends.

(B) The owner, board of directors, or other governing body of the senior citizen housing development may take action to prohibit or terminate occupancy by a person who is a qualified permanent resident under this paragraph if the owner, board of directors, or other governing body finds, based on credible and objective evidence, that the person is likely to pose a significant threat to the health or safety of others that cannot be ameliorated by means of a reasonable accommodation; provided, however, that the action to prohibit or terminate the occupancy may be taken only after doing both of the following:

(i) Providing reasonable notice to and an opportunity to be heard for the disabled person whose occupancy is being challenged, and reasonable notice to the coresident parent or grandparent of that person.

(ii) Giving due consideration to the relevant, credible, and objective information provided in the hearing. The evidence shall be taken and held in a confidential manner, pursuant to a closed session, by the owner, board of directors, or other governing body in order to preserve the privacy of the affected persons.

The affected persons shall be entitled to have present at the hearing an attorney or any other person authorized by them to speak on their behalf or to assist them in the matter.

(4) "Senior citizen housing development" means a residential development developed, substantially rehabilitated, or substantially renovated for, senior citizens that has at least 35 dwelling units. Any senior citizen housing development which is required to obtain a public report under Section 11010 of the Business and Professions Code and which submits its application for a public report after July 1, 2001, shall be required to have been issued a public report as a senior citizen housing development under Section 11010.05 of the Business and Professions Code. No housing development constructed prior to January 1, 1985, shall fail to qualify as a senior citizen housing development because it was not originally developed or put to use for occupancy by senior citizens.

(5) "Dwelling unit" or "housing" means any residential accommodation other than a mobilehome.

(6) "Cohabitant" refers to persons who live together as spouses or persons who are domestic partners within the meaning of Section 297 of the Family Code.

(7) "Permitted health care resident" means a person hired to provide live-in, long-term, or terminal health care to a qualifying resident, or a family member of the qualifying resident providing that care. For the purposes of this section, the care provided by a permitted health care resident must be substantial in nature and must provide either assistance with necessary daily activities or medical treatment, or both.

A permitted health care resident shall be entitled to continue his or her occupancy, residency, or use of the dwelling unit as a permitted resident in the absence of the senior citizen from the dwelling unit only if both of the following are applicable:

(A) The senior citizen became absent from the dwelling unit due to hospitalization or other necessary medical treatment and expects to return to his or her residence within 90 days from the date the absence began.

(B) The absent senior citizen or an authorized person acting for the senior citizen submits a written request to the owner, board of directors, or governing board stating that the senior citizen desires that the permitted health care resident be allowed to remain in order to be present when the senior citizen returns to reside in the development.

Upon written request by the senior citizen or an authorized person acting for the senior citizen, the owner, board of directors, or governing board shall have the discretion to allow a permitted health care resident to remain for a time period longer than 90 days from the date that the senior citizen's absence began, if it appears that the senior citizen will return within a period of time not to exceed an additional 90 days.

(c) The covenants, conditions, and restrictions and other documents or written policy shall set forth the limitations on occupancy, residency, or use on the basis of age. Any such limitation shall not be more exclusive than to require that one person in residence in each dwelling unit may be required to be a senior citizen and that each other resident in the same dwelling unit may be required to be a qualified permanent resident, a permitted health care resident, or a person under 55 years of age whose occupancy is permitted under subdivision (h) of this section or under subdivision (b) of Section 51.4. That limitation may be less exclusive, but shall at least require that the persons commencing any occupancy of a dwelling unit include a senior citizen who intends to reside in the unit as his or her primary residence on a permanent basis. The application of the rules set forth in this subdivision regarding limitations on occupancy may result in less than all of the dwellings being actually occupied by a senior citizen.

(d) The covenants, conditions, and restrictions or other documents or written policy shall permit temporary residency, as a guest of a senior citizen or qualified permanent resident, by a person of less than 55 years of age for periods of time, not less than 60 days in any year, that are specified in the covenants, conditions, and restrictions or other documents or written policy.

(e) Upon the death or dissolution of marriage, or upon hospitalization, or other prolonged absence of the qualifying resident, any qualified permanent resident shall be entitled to continue his or her occupancy, residency, or use of the dwelling unit as a permitted resident. This subdivision shall not apply to a permitted health care resident.

(f) The condominium, stock cooperative, limited-equity housing cooperative, planned development, or multiple-family residential rental property shall have been developed for, and initially been put to use as, housing for senior citizens, or shall have been substantially rehabilitated or renovated for, and immediately afterward put to use as, housing for senior citizens, as provided in this section; provided, however, that no housing development constructed prior to January 1, 1985, shall fail to qualify as a senior citizen housing development because it was not originally developed for or originally put to use for occupancy by senior citizens.

(g) The covenants, conditions, and restrictions or other documents or written policies applicable to any condominium, stock cooperative, limited-equity housing cooperative, planned development, or multiple-family residential property that contained age restrictions on January 1, 1984, shall be enforceable only to the extent permitted by this section, notwithstanding lower age restrictions contained in those documents or policies.

(h) Any person who has the right to reside in, occupy, or use the housing or an unimproved lot subject to this section on January 1, 1985, shall not be deprived of the right to continue that residency, occupancy, or use as the result of the enactment of this section.

(i) The covenants, conditions, and restrictions or other documents or written policy of the senior citizen housing development shall permit the occupancy of a dwelling unit by a permitted health care resident during any period that the person is actually providing live-in, long-term, or hospice health care to a qualifying resident for compensation. For purposes of this subdivision, the term "for compensation" shall include provisions of lodging and food in exchange for care.

(j) Notwithstanding any other provision of this section, this section shall not apply to the County of Riverside. **Leg.H.** Added Stats 1984 ch 1333 §1. Amended Stats 1985 ch 1505 §2; Stats 1989 ch 190 §1; Stats 1994 ch 464 §1 (SB 1560); Stats 1995 ch 147 §1 (SB 332); Stats 1996 ch 1147 §3 (SB 2097); Stats 1999 ch 324 §2 (SB 382); Stats 2000 ch 1004 §3 (SB 2011); Stats 2016 ch 50 §5 (SB 1005), effective January 1, 2017.

2016 Note: For legislative intent, see the 2016 Note following §14.

§ 51.3.5. Legislative intent; Intergenerational housing development requirements; Creation of state policy supporting intergenerational housing; Definitions

(a) The Legislature finds and declares that this section is essential to establish and preserve specially designed, accessible, intergenerational housing for senior citizens. There are senior citizens who need special living environments and services and benefit from intergenerational housing environments, and find that there is an inadequate supply of this type of housing in the state.

(b) An intergenerational housing development may be established to provide intergenerational housing consisting of units for senior citizens, caregivers, or transition age youths if all of the following conditions are satisfied:

(1)(A) At least 80 percent of the occupied dwelling units are occupied by at least one senior citizen. This requirement shall commence when at least 25 percent of the units are occupied. A dwelling unit is occupied by at least one senior citizen if, on the date the exemption for housing designed for intergenerational housing is claimed, one of the following conditions is satisfied:

(i) At least one occupant of the dwelling unit is a senior citizen.

(ii) If the dwelling unit is temporarily vacant, at least one of the occupants immediately prior to the date on which the unit was temporarily vacated was a senior citizen.

(B) Up to 20 percent of the occupied dwelling units are occupied by at least one caregiver or transition age youth. A dwelling unit is occupied by at least one caregiver or transition age youth if, on the date the exemption for housing designed for intergenerational housing is claimed, one of the following conditions is satisfied:

(i) At least one occupant of the dwelling unit is a caregiver or transition age youth.

(ii) If the dwelling unit is temporarily vacant, at least one of the occupants immediately prior to the date on which the unit was temporarily vacant was a caregiver or transition age youth.

(2) The development is affordable to lower income households as defined in Section 50079.5 of the Health and Safety Code.

(3)(A) If a unit that is identified for occupancy by a caregiver or transition age youth ceases to house a caregiver or transition age youth, the owner, board of directors, or other governing body may require, at their discretion, the household in that unit to cease residing in the development upon receipt of a minimum of six months written notice, for the sole purpose of ensuring that the unit may be made available to a qualifying caregiver or transition age youth. This action shall not constitute a violation of Section 51 or of Article 2 (commencing with Section 12955) of Chapter 6 of Part 2.8 of Division 3 of Title 2 of the Government Code (California Fair Employment and Housing Act).

(B) The housing facility or community shall not evict or terminate the lease of a family with children in order to comply with the requirement that at least 80 percent of the occupied units be occupied by at least one senior citizen. This provision does not otherwise alter or affect applicable protections for tenants.

(C) The covenants, conditions, and restrictions and other documents or written policy for the development shall set forth the limitations on occupancy, residency, or use consistent with this section.

(4) Housing established pursuant to this section shall comply with all applicable fair housing laws, including, but not limited to, the California Fair Employment and Housing Act (Part 2.8 (commencing with Section 12900) of Division 3 of Title 2 of the Government Code) and the Fair Housing Act (42 U.S.C. Sec. 3601).

(5) Notwithstanding any other law, any occupied dwelling units within an intergenerational housing development established pursuant to this section that are occupied by caregivers or transition age youth as described in subparagraph (B) of paragraph (1) shall not count toward the housing type goal for seniors under the qualified allocation plan adopted by the California Tax Credit Allocation Committee in accordance with Section 50199.14 of the Health and Safety Code.

(c) This section specifically creates a state policy supporting intergenerational housing for senior citizens, caregivers, and transition age youth, as described in Section 42(g)(9) of the Internal Revenue Code, and, further, permits developers in receipt of local or state funds or tax credits designated for affordable rental housing to restrict occupancy to senior citizens, caregivers, and transition age youth, including permitting developers in receipt of tax credits designated for affordable rental housing to retain the right to prioritize and restrict occupancy, so long as that housing does not violate any other applicable laws.

(d) For the purposes of this section, the following terms have the following meanings:

(1) "Caregiver" means a person responsible for meeting the daily care needs of a senior citizen, or a person hired to provide live-in, long-term, or terminal health care to a qualifying resident, or a family member of the qualifying resident providing that care. For purposes of this section, the care provided shall be substantial in nature and shall include either assistance with necessary daily activities or medical treatment, or both.

(2) "Senior citizen" or "resident" means a person 55 years of age or older.

(3) "Transition age youth" means a person who is 18 to 24 years of age, inclusive, and who is either of the following:

(A) A current or former foster youth who has been adjudged a ward or dependent of the juvenile court pursuant to Section 300, 601, or 602 of the Welfare and Institutions Code.

(B) A homeless youth or former homeless youth, who has met the McKinney-Vento Homeless Assistance Act of 1987 definition of "homeless children and youths," as that term is defined in Section 11434a of Title 42 of the United States Code. **Leg.H.** Added Stats 2021 ch 364 §3 (SB 591), effective January 1, 2022.

§51.4. Legislative intent regarding senior housing

(a) The Legislature finds and declares that the requirements for senior housing under Sections 51.2 and 51.3 are more stringent than the requirements for that housing under the federal Fair Housing Amendments Act of 1988 (P.L. 100-430) in recognition of the acute shortage of housing for families with children in California. The Legislature further finds and declares that the special design requirements for senior housing under Sections 51.2 and 51.3 may pose a hardship to some housing developments that were constructed before the decision in Marina Point, Ltd. v. Wolfson (1982) 30 Cal.3d 721. The Legislature further finds and declares that the requirement for specially designed accommodations in senior housing under Sections 51.2 and 51.3 provides important benefits to senior citizens and also ensures that housing exempt from the prohibition of age discrimination is carefully tailored to meet the compelling societal interest in providing senior housing.

(b) Any person who resided in, occupied, or used, prior to January 1, 1990, a dwelling in a senior citizen housing development that relied on the exemption to the special design requirement provided by this section prior to January 1, 2001, shall not be deprived of the right to continue that residency, occupancy, or use as the result of the changes made to this section by the enactment of Chapter 1004 of the Statutes of 2000.

(c) This section shall not apply to the County of Riverside. **Leg.H.** Added Stats 1989 ch 501 §2. Amended Stats 1991 ch 59 §1 (AB 125), effective June 14, 1991; Stats 1996 ch 1147 §4 (SB 2097); Stats 2000 ch 1004 §4 (SB 2011); Stats 2006 ch 538 §37 (SB 1852), effective January 1, 2007.

§51.5. Discrimination by business establishment prohibited

(a) No business establishment of any kind whatsoever shall discriminate against, boycott or blacklist, or refuse to buy from, contract with, sell to, or trade with any person in this state on account of any characteristic listed or defined in subdivision (b) or (e) of Section 51, or of the person's partners, members, stockholders, directors, officers, managers, superintendents, agents, employees, business associates, suppliers, or customers, because the person is perceived to have one or more of those characteristics, or because the person is associated with a person who has, or is perceived to have, any of those characteristics.

(b) As used in this section, "person" includes any person, firm, association, organization, partnership, business trust, corporation, limited liability company, or company

(c) This section shall not be construed to require any construction, alteration, repair, structural or otherwise, or modification of any sort whatsoever, beyond that construction, alteration, repair, or modification that is otherwise required by other provisions of law, to any new or existing establishment, facility, building, improvement, or any other structure, nor shall this section be construed to augment, restrict, or alter in any way the authority of the State Architect to require construction, alteration, repair, or modifications that the State Architect otherwise possesses pursuant to other laws. **Leg.H.** Added Stats 1976 ch 366 §1. Amended Stats 1987 ch 159 §2; Stats 1992 ch 913 §3.2 (AB 1077); Stats

1994 ch 1010 §28 (SB 2053); Stats 1998 ch 195 §2 (AB 2702); Stats 1999 ch 591 §2 (AB 1670); Stats 2000 ch 1049 §3 (AB 2222); Stats 2005 ch 420 §4 (AB 1400), effective January 1, 2006.

2005 Notes: This act shall be known and may be cited as "The Civil Rights Act of 2005." Stats 2005 ch 420 (AB 1400) §1.

The Legislature affirms that the bases of discrimination prohibited by the Unruh Civil Rights Act include, but are not limited to, marital status and sexual orientation, as defined herein. By specifically enumerating these bases in the Unruh Civil Rights Act, the Legislature intends to clarify the existing law, rather than to change the law, as well as the principle that the bases enumerated in the act are illustrative rather than restrictive. Stats 2005 ch 420 (AB 1400) §2(c).

It is the intent of the Legislature that the amendments made to the Unruh Civil Rights Act by this act do not affect the California Supreme Court's rulings in *Marina Point, Ltd. v. Wolfson* (1982) 30 Cal.3d 721 and *O'Connor v. Village Green Owners Association* (1983) 33 Cal.3d 790. Stats 2005 ch 420 (AB 1400) §2(d).

1999 Note: The amendments made by Chapter 591 to Section 51.5 of the Civil Code do not constitute a change in, but are declaratory of existing law. Stats 1999 ch 591 §16.

§51.6. Gender Tax Repeal Act of 1995

(a) This section shall be known, and may be cited, as the Gender Tax Repeal Act of 1995.

(b) No business establishment of any kind whatsoever may discriminate, with respect to the price charged for services of similar or like kind, against a person because of the person's gender.

(c) Nothing in subdivision (b) prohibits price differences based specifically upon the amount of time, difficulty, or cost of providing the services.

(d) Except as provided in subdivision (f), the remedies for a violation of this section are the remedies provided in subdivision (a) of Section 52. However, an action under this section is independent of any other remedy or procedure that may be available to an aggrieved party.

(e) This act does not alter or affect the provisions of the Health and Safety Code, the Insurance Code, or other laws that govern health care service plan or insurer underwriting or rating practices.

(f)(1) The following business establishments shall clearly and conspicuously disclose to the customer in writing the pricing for each standard service provided:

(A) Tailors or businesses providing aftermarket clothing alterations.

(B) Barbers or hair salons.

(C) Dry cleaners and laundries providing services to individuals.

(2) The price list shall be posted in an area conspicuous to customers. Posted price lists shall be in no less than 14-point boldface type and clearly and completely display pricing for every standard service offered by the business under paragraph (1).

(3) The business establishment shall provide the customer with a complete written price list upon request.

(4) The business establishment shall display in a conspicuous place at least one clearly visible sign, printed in no less than 24-point boldface type, which reads: "CALIFORNIA LAW PROHIBITS ANY BUSINESS ESTABLISHMENT FROM DISCRIMINATING, WITH RESPECT TO THE PRICE CHARGED FOR SERVICES OF SIMILAR OR LIKE KIND, AGAINST A PERSON BECAUSE OF THE PERSON'S GENDER. A COMPLETE PRICE LIST IS AVAILABLE UPON REQUEST."

(5) A business establishment that fails to correct a violation of this subdivision within 30 days of receiving written notice of the violation is liable for a civil penalty of one thousand dollars ($1,000).

(6) For the purposes of this subdivision, "standard service" means the 15 most frequently requested services provided by the business.

(g)(1) Commencing January 1, 2021, a city, county, or city and county that issues business licenses shall provide a business, at the time the business is issued the license or when the license is renewed, written notice of these provisions in English, Spanish, Chinese, Tagalog, Vietnamese, and Korean. In order to comply with this paragraph, a city, county, or city and county may provide the business with the notice created by the Department of Consumer Affairs under subdivision (b) of Section 55.63.

(2) A city, county, or city and county that issues business licenses may increase the fee for that license in an amount not to exceed the reasonable costs of providing the written notice above.

(h) The Legislature finds and declares that this section addresses a matter of statewide concern rather than a municipal affair as that term is used in Section 5 of Article XI of the California Constitution. Therefore, this section applies to all cities, including charter cities. **Leg.H.** Added Stats 1995 ch 866 §1 (AB 1100). Amended Stats 2001 ch 312 §1 (AB 1088); Stats 2019 ch 293 §1 (AB 1607), effective January 1, 2020.

§51.7. Freedom from violence; Preservation of legal right to pursue action for violations; Lawful labor dispute exception

(a) This section shall be known, and may be cited, as the Ralph Civil Rights Act of 1976.

(b)(1) All persons within the jurisdiction of this state have the right to be free from any violence, or intimidation by threat of violence, committed against their persons or property because of political affiliation, or on account of any characteristic listed or defined in subdivision (b) or (e) of Section 51, or position in a labor dispute, or because another person perceives them to have one or more of those characteristics. The identification in this subdivision of particular bases of discrimination is illustrative rather than restrictive.

(2) For purposes of this subdivision, "intimidation by threat of violence" includes, but is not limited to, making or threatening to make a claim or report to a peace officer or law enforcement agency that falsely alleges that another person has engaged in unlawful activity or in an activity that requires law enforcement intervention, knowing that the claim or report is false, or with reckless disregard for the truth or falsity of the claim or report.

(3) For purposes of this subdivision, "intimidation by threat of violence" includes, but is not limited to, terrorizing the owner or occupant of private property with the distribution of materials on the private property, without authorization, with the purpose of terrorizing the owner or occupant of that private property.

(4) For purposes of this subdivision, "terrorize" means to cause a person of ordinary emotions and sensibilities to fear for personal safety.

(c)(1) A person shall not require another person to waive any legal right, penalty, remedy, forum, or procedure for a violation of this section, as a condition of entering into a contract for goods or services, including the right to file and pursue a civil action or complaint with, or otherwise notify, the Attorney General or any other public prosecutor, or law enforcement agency, the Civil Rights Department, or any court or other governmental entity.

(2) A person shall not refuse to enter into a contract with, or refuse to provide goods or services to, another person on the basis that the other person refuses to waive any legal right, penalty, remedy, forum, or procedure for a violation of this section, including the right to file and pursue a civil action or complaint with, or otherwise notify, the Attorney General or any other public prosecutor, or law enforcement agency, the Civil Rights Department, or any other governmental entity.

(3) Any waiver of any legal right, penalty, remedy, forum, or procedure for a violation of this section, including the right to file and pursue a civil action or complaint with, or otherwise notify, the Attorney General or any other public prosecutor, or law enforcement agency, the Civil Rights Department, or any other governmental entity shall be knowing and voluntary, in writing, and expressly not made as a condition of entering into a contract for goods or services or as a condition of providing or receiving goods and services.

(4) Any waiver of any legal right, penalty, remedy, forum, or procedure for a violation of this section that is required as a condition of entering into a contract for goods or services shall be deemed involuntary, unconscionable, against public policy, and unenforceable. This subdivision does not affect the enforceability or validity of any other provision of the contract.

(5) A person who seeks to enforce a waiver of any legal right, penalty, remedy, forum, or procedure for a violation of this section has the burden of proving that the waiver was knowing and voluntary and not made as a condition of the contract or of providing or receiving the goods or services.

(6) The exercise of a person's right to refuse to waive any legal right, penalty, remedy, forum, or procedure for a violation of this section, including a rejection of a contract requiring a waiver, does not affect any otherwise legal terms of a contract or an agreement.

(7) This subdivision does not apply to an agreement to waive any legal rights, penalties, remedies, forums, or procedures for a violation of this section after a legal claim has arisen.

(8) This subdivision applies to an agreement to waive any legal right, penalty, remedy, forum, or procedure for a violation of this section,

including an agreement to accept private arbitration, entered into, altered, modified, renewed, or extended on or after January 1, 2015.

(d) This section does not apply to statements concerning positions in a labor dispute that are made during otherwise lawful labor picketing.

(e)(1) Speech alone shall not support an action brought pursuant to this section, except upon a showing of all of the following:

(A) The speech itself threatens violence against a specific person or group of persons.

(B) The person or group of persons against whom the threat is directed reasonably fears that, because of the speech, violence will be committed against them or their property.

(C) The person threatening violence is acting in reckless disregard for the threatening nature of their speech.

(D) The person threatening violence has the apparent ability to carry out the threat.

(2) This subdivision shall not be construed to negate or otherwise abrogate the requirements set forth in subdivisions (b) to (d), inclusive, to bring an action pursuant to this section.

[1] (f) The Legislature finds and declares that this section was enacted as part of the Ralph Civil Rights Act of 1976, in Chapter 1293 of the Statutes of 1976.

[2] (g) This section does not negate or otherwise abrogate the provisions of Sections 1668, 1953, and 3513. **Leg.H.** Added Stats 1976 ch 1293 §2. Amended Stats 1984 ch 1437 §1; Stats 1985 ch 497 §1; Stats 1987 ch 1277 §2; Stats 1994 ch 407 §1 (SB 1595); Stats 2005 ch 420 §5 (AB 1400), effective January 1, 2006; Stats 2014 ch 910 §2 (AB 2617), effective January 1, 2015; Stats 2018 ch 776 §3 (AB 3250), effective January 1, 2019; Stats 2020 ch 327 §3 (AB 1775), effective January 1, 2021; Stats 2022 ch 48 §4 (SB 189), effective June 30, 2022; Stats 2024 ch 584 §1 (AB 3024), effective September 25, 2024.

§51.7. 2024 Deletes. [1] (e) [2] (f)

2014 Note: (a) The Legislature finds and declares that it is the policy of the State of California to ensure that all persons have the full benefit of the rights, penalties, remedies, forums, and procedures established by the Ralph Civil Rights Act and the Tom Bane Civil Rights Act, and that individuals shall not be deprived of those rights, penalties, remedies, forums, or procedures through the use of involuntary or coerced waivers.

(b) It is the purpose of this act to ensure that a contract to waive any of the rights, penalties, remedies, forums, or procedures under the Ralph Civil Rights Act or the Tom Bane Civil Rights Act, including any provision that has the effect of limiting the full application or enforcement of any right, remedy, forum, or procedure available under the Ralph Civil Rights Act or the Tom Bane Civil Rights Act, is a matter of voluntary consent, not coercion. Stats 2014 ch 910 (AB 2617) §1.

2005 Notes: This act shall be known and may be cited as "The Civil Rights Act of 2005." Stats 2005 ch 420 (AB 1400) §1.

The Legislature affirms that the bases of discrimination prohibited by the Unruh Civil Rights Act include, but are not limited to, marital status and sexual orientation, as defined herein. By specifically enumerating these bases in the Unruh Civil Rights Act, the Legislature intends to clarify the existing law, rather than to change the law, as well as the principle that the bases enumerated in the act are illustrative rather than restrictive. Stats 2005 ch 420 (AB 1400) §2(c).

It is the intent of the Legislature that the amendments made to the Unruh Civil Rights Act by this act do not affect the California Supreme Court's rulings in *Marina Point, Ltd. v. Wolfson* (1982) 30 Cal.3d 721 and *O'Connor v. Village Green Owners Association* (1983) 33 Cal.3d 790. Stats 2005 ch 420 (AB 1400) §2(d).

§51.8. Discrimination in granting of franchises prohibited

(a) No franchisor shall discriminate in the granting of franchises solely on account of any characteristic listed or defined in subdivision (b) or (e) of Section 51 of the franchisee and the composition of a neighborhood or geographic area reflecting any characteristic listed or defined in subdivision (b) or (e) of Section 51 in which the franchise is located. Nothing in this section shall be interpreted to prohibit a franchisor from granting a franchise to prospective franchisees as part of a program or programs to make franchises available to persons lacking the capital, training, business experience, or other qualifications ordinarily required of franchisees, or any other affirmative action program adopted by the franchisor.

(b) Nothing in this section shall be construed to require any construction, alteration, repair, structural or otherwise, or modification of any sort whatsoever, beyond that construction, alteration, repair, or modification that is otherwise required by other provisions of law, to any new or existing establishment, facility, building, improvement, or any other structure, nor shall anything in this section be construed to augment, restrict, or alter in any way the authority of the State Architect to require construction, alteration, repair, or modifications that the State Architect otherwise possesses pursuant to other laws. **Leg.H.** Added Stats 1980 ch 1303 §1. Amended Stats 1987 ch 159 §3; Stats 1992 ch 913 §3.4 (AB 1077); Stats 1998 ch 195 §3 (AB 2702); Stats 2005 ch 420 §6 (AB 1400), effective January 1, 2006.

2005 Notes: This act shall be known and may be cited as "The Civil Rights Act of 2005." Stats 2005 ch 420 (AB 1400) §1.

The Legislature affirms that the bases of discrimination prohibited by the Unruh Civil Rights Act include, but are not limited to, marital status and sexual orientation, as defined herein. By specifically enumerating these bases in the Unruh Civil Rights Act, the Legislature intends to clarify the existing law, rather than to change the law, as well as the principle that the bases enumerated in the act are illustrative rather than restrictive. Stats 2005 ch 420 (AB 1400) §2(c).

It is the intent of the Legislature that the amendments made to the Unruh Civil Rights Act by this act do not affect the California Supreme Court's rulings in *Marina Point, Ltd. v. Wolfson* (1982) 30 Cal.3d 721 and *O'Connor v. Village Green Owners Association* (1983) 33 Cal.3d 790. Stats 2005 ch 420 (AB 1400) §2(d).

§51.9. Sexual harassment

(a) A person is liable in a cause of action for sexual harassment under this section when the plaintiff proves all of the following elements:

(1) There is a business, service, or professional relationship between the plaintiff and defendant or the defendant holds himself or herself out as being able to help the plaintiff establish a business, service, or professional relationship with the defendant or a third party. Such a relationship may exist between a plaintiff and a person, including, but not limited to, any of the following persons:

(A) Physician, psychotherapist, or dentist. For purposes of this section, "psychotherapist" has the same meaning as set forth in paragraph (1) of subdivision (c) of Section 728 of the Business and Professions Code.

(B) Attorney, holder of a master's degree in social work, real estate agent, real estate appraiser, investor, accountant, banker, trust officer, financial planner loan officer, collection service, building contractor, or escrow loan officer.

(C) Executor, trustee, or administrator.

(D) Landlord or property manager.

(E) Teacher.

(F) Elected official.

(G) Lobbyist.

(H) Director or producer.

(I) A relationship that is substantially similar to any of the above.

(2) The defendant has made sexual advances, solicitations, sexual requests, demands for sexual compliance by the plaintiff, or engaged in other verbal, visual, or physical conduct of a sexual nature or of a hostile nature based on gender, that were unwelcome and pervasive or severe.

(3) The plaintiff has suffered or will suffer economic loss or disadvantage or personal injury, including, but not limited to, emotional distress or the violation of a statutory or constitutional right, as a result of the conduct described in paragraph (2).

(b) In an action pursuant to this section, damages shall be awarded as provided by subdivision (b) of Section 52.

(c) Nothing in this section shall be construed to limit application of any other remedies or rights provided under the law.

(d) The definition of sexual harassment and the standards for determining liability set forth in this section shall be limited to determining liability only with regard to a cause of action brought under this section. **Leg.H.** Added Stats 1994 ch 710 §2 (SB 612). Amended Stats 1996 ch 150 §1 (SB 195); Stats 1999 ch 964 §1 (AB 519); Stats 2018 ch 951 §1 (SB 224), effective January 1, 2019.

§51.10. Discrimination by business establishment in housing based on age

(a) Section 51 shall be construed to prohibit a business establishment from discriminating in the sale or rental of housing based upon age. A business establishment may establish and preserve housing for senior citizens, pursuant to Section 51.11, except housing as to which Section 51.11 is preempted by the prohibition in the federal Fair Housing Amendments Act of 1988 (Public Law 100-430) and implementing regulations against discrimination on the basis of familial status.

(b) This section is intended to clarify the holdings in Marina Point, Ltd. v. Wolfson (1982) 30 Cal.3d 721, and O'Connor v. Village Green Owners Association (1983) 33 Cal.3d 790.

(c) Selection preferences based on age, imposed in connection with a federally approved housing program, do not constitute age discrimination in housing.

(d) This section shall only apply to the County of Riverside. **Leg.H.** Added Stats 1996 ch 1147 §5 (SB 2097). Amended Stats 2004 ch 183 §23 (AB 3082); Stats 2010 ch 524 §3 (SB 1252), effective January 1, 2011.

2010 Note: It is the intent of the Legislature in enacting this act to clarify the characteristics that may not serve as a basis for discrimination in housing under the California Fair Employment and Housing Act (Part 2.8 (commencing with Section 12900) of Division 3 of Title 2 of the Government Code. The addition of "source of income" to Sections 12920, 12921, and 12955.8 of the Government Code is strictly intended to create consistency within the California Fair Employment and Housing Act, and does not create any substantive rights in addition to those already provided for under current law. Stats 2010 ch 524 (SB 1252) §1.

§51.11. Special living environments for senior citizens; Applicability to County of Riverside

(a) The Legislature finds and declares that this section is essential to establish and preserve housing for senior citizens. There are senior citizens who need special living environments, and find that there is an inadequate supply of this type of housing in the state.

(b) For the purposes of this section, the following definitions apply:

(1) "Qualifying resident" or "senior citizen" means a person 62 years of age or older, or 55 years of age or older in a senior citizen housing development.

(2) "Qualified permanent resident" means a person who meets both of the following requirements:

(A) Was residing with the qualifying resident or senior citizen prior to the death, hospitalization, or other prolonged absence of, or the dissolution of marriage with, the qualifying resident or senior citizen.

(B) Was 45 years of age or older, or was a spouse, cohabitant, or person providing primary physical or economic support to the qualifying resident or senior citizen.

(3) "Qualified permanent resident" also means a disabled person or person with a disabling illness or injury who is a child or grandchild of the senior citizen or a qualified permanent resident as defined in paragraph (2) who needs to live with the senior citizen or qualified permanent resident because of the disabling condition, illness, or injury. For purposes of this section, "disabled" means a person who has a disability as defined in subdivision (b) of Section 54. A "disabling injury or illness" means an illness or injury which results in a condition meeting the definition of disability set forth in subdivision (b) of Section 54.

(A) For any person who is a qualified permanent resident under paragraph (3) whose disabling condition ends, the owner, board of directors, or other governing body may require the formerly disabled resident to cease residing in the development upon receipt of six months' written notice; provided, however, that the owner, board of directors, or other governing body may allow the person to remain a resident for up to one year, after the disabling condition ends.

(B) The owner, board of directors, or other governing body of the senior citizen housing development may take action to prohibit or terminate occupancy by a person who is a qualified permanent resident under paragraph (3) if the owner, board of directors, or other governing body finds, based on credible and objective evidence, that the person is likely to pose a significant threat to the health or safety of others that cannot be ameliorated by means of a reasonable accommodation; provided, however, that action to prohibit or terminate the occupancy may be taken only after doing both of the following:

(i) Providing reasonable notice to and an opportunity to be heard for the disabled person whose occupancy is being challenged, and reasonable notice to the coresident parent or grandparent of that person.

(ii) Giving due consideration to the relevant, credible, and objective information provided in that hearing. The evidence shall be taken and held in a confidential manner, pursuant to a closed session, by the owner, board of directors, or other governing body in order to preserve the privacy of the affected persons.

The affected persons shall be entitled to have present at the hearing an attorney or any other person authorized by them to speak on their behalf or to assist them in the matter.

(4) "Senior citizen housing development" means a residential development developed with more than 20 units as a senior community by its developer and zoned as a senior community by a local governmental entity, or characterized as a senior community in its governing documents, as these are defined in Section 4150, or qualified as a senior community under the federal Fair Housing Amendments Act of 1988, as amended. Any senior citizen housing development which is required to obtain a public report under Section 11010 of the Business and Professions Code and which submits its application for a public report after July 1, 2001, shall be required to have been issued a public report as a senior citizen housing development under Section 11010.05 of the Business and Professions Code.

(5) "Dwelling unit" or "housing" means any residential accommodation other than a mobilehome.

(6) "Cohabitant" refers to persons who live together as spouses or persons who are domestic partners within the meaning of Section 297 of the Family Code.

(7) "Permitted health care resident" means a person hired to provide live-in, long-term, or terminal health care to a qualifying resident, or a family member of the qualifying resident providing that care. For the purposes of this section, the care provided by a permitted health care resident must be substantial in nature and must provide either assistance with necessary daily activities or medical treatment, or both.

A permitted health care resident shall be entitled to continue his or her occupancy, residency, or use of the dwelling unit as a permitted resident in the absence of the senior citizen from the dwelling unit only if both of the following are applicable:

(A) The senior citizen became absent from the dwelling unit due to hospitalization or other necessary medical treatment and expects to return to his or her residence within 90 days from the date the absence began.

(B) The absent senior citizen or an authorized person acting for the senior citizen submits a written request to the owner, board of directors, or governing board stating that the senior citizen desires that the permitted health care resident be allowed to remain in order to be present when the senior citizen returns to reside in the development.

Upon written request by the senior citizen or an authorized person acting for the senior citizen, the owner, board of directors, or governing board shall have the discretion to allow a permitted health care resident to remain for a time period longer than 90 days from the date that the senior citizen's absence began, if it appears that the senior citizen will return within a period of time not to exceed an additional 90 days.

(c) The covenants, conditions, and restrictions and other documents or written policy shall set forth the limitations on occupancy, residency, or use on the basis of age. Any limitation shall not be more exclusive than to require that one person in residence in each dwelling unit may be required to be a senior citizen and that each other resident in the same dwelling unit may be required to be a qualified permanent resident, a permitted health care resident, or a person under 55 years of age whose occupancy is permitted under subdivision (g) of this section or subdivision (b) of Section 51.12. That limitation may be less exclusive, but shall at least require that the persons commencing any occupancy of a dwelling unit include a senior citizen who intends to reside in the unit as his or her primary residence on a permanent basis. The application of the rules set forth in this subdivision regarding limitations on occupancy may result in less than all of the dwellings being actually occupied by a senior citizen.

(d) The covenants, conditions, and restrictions or other documents or written policy shall permit temporary residency, as a guest of a senior citizen or qualified permanent resident, by a person of less than 55 years of age for periods of time, not more than 60 days in any year, that are specified in the covenants, conditions, and restrictions or other documents or written policy.

(e) Upon the death or dissolution of marriage, or upon hospitalization, or other prolonged absence of the qualifying resident, any qualified permanent resident shall be entitled to continue his or her occupancy, residency, or use of the dwelling unit as a permitted resident. This subdivision shall not apply to a permitted health care resident.

(f) The covenants, conditions, and restrictions or other documents or written policies applicable to any condominium, stock cooperative, limited-equity housing cooperative, planned development, or multiple-family residential property that contained age restrictions on January 1, 1984, shall be enforceable only to the extent permitted by this section, notwithstanding lower age restrictions contained in those documents or policies.

(g) Any person who has the right to reside in, occupy, or use the housing or an unimproved lot subject to this section on or after January 1, 1985, shall not be deprived of the right to continue that residency, occupancy, or use as the result of the enactment of this section by Chapter 1147 of the Statutes of 1996.

(h) A housing development may qualify as a senior citizen housing development under this section even though, as of January 1, 1997, it does not meet the definition of a senior citizen housing development specified in subdivision (b), if the development complies with that definition for every unit that becomes occupied after January 1, 1997, and if the development was once within that definition, and then became noncompliant with the definition as the result of any one of the following:

(1) The development was ordered by a court or a local, state, or federal enforcement agency to allow persons other than qualifying residents, qualified permanent residents, or permitted health care residents to reside in the development.

(2) The development received a notice of a pending or proposed action in, or by, a court, or a local, state, or federal enforcement agency, which action could have resulted in the development being ordered by a court or a state or federal enforcement agency to allow persons other than qualifying residents, qualified permanent residents, or permitted health care residents to reside in the development.

(3) The development agreed to allow persons other than qualifying residents, qualified permanent residents, or permitted health care residents to reside in the development by entering into a stipulation, conciliation agreement, or settlement agreement with a local, state, or federal enforcement agency or with a private party who had filed, or indicated an intent to file, a complaint against the development with a local, state, or federal enforcement agency, or file an action in a court.

(4) The development allowed persons other than qualifying residents, qualified permanent residents, or permitted health care residents to reside in the development on the advice of counsel in order to prevent the possibility of an action being filed by a private party or by a local, state, or federal enforcement agency.

(i) The covenants, conditions, and restrictions or other documents or written policy of the senior citizen housing development shall permit the occupancy of a dwelling unit by a permitted health care resident during any period that the person is actually providing live-in, long-term, or hospice health care to a qualifying resident for compensation.

(j) This section shall only apply to the County of Riverside. **Leg.H.** Added Stats 1996 ch 1147 §6 (SB 2097). Amended Stats 1999 ch 324 §3 (SB 382); Stats 2000 ch 1004 §5 (SB 2011); Stats 2012 ch 181 §19 (AB 806), effective January 1, 2013, operative January 1, 2014; Stats 2016 ch 50 §6 (SB 1005), effective January 1, 2017.

2016 Note: For legislative intent, see the 2016 Note following §14.

§51.12. Federal law

(a) The Legislature finds and declares that the requirements for senior housing under Sections 51.10 and 51.11 are more stringent than the requirements for that housing under the federal Fair Housing Amendments Act of 1988 (Public Law 100-430).

(b) Any person who resided in, occupied, or used, prior to January 1, 1990, a dwelling in a senior citizen housing development which relied on the exemption to the special design requirement provided by Section 51.4 as that section read prior to January 1, 2001, shall not be deprived of the right to continue that residency, or occupancy, or use as the result of the changes made to this section by the enactment of Senate Bill 1382 or Senate Bill 2011 at the 1999–2000 Regular Session of the Legislature.

(c) This section shall only apply to the County of Riverside. **Leg.H.** Added Stats 1996 ch 1147 §7 (SB 2097). Amended Stats 2000 ch 1004 §6 (SB 2011).

§51.13. Discounts or benefits offered due to loss or reduction of employment

Any discount or other benefit offered to or conferred on a consumer or prospective consumer by a business because the consumer or prospective consumer has suffered the loss or reduction of employment or reduction of wages shall not be considered an arbitrary discrimination in violation of Section 51. **Leg.H.** Added Stats 2009 ch 641 §1 (SB 367), effective November 2, 2009.

§51.14. Charging different prices for substantially similar goods

(a) For the purposes of this section, the following terms apply:

(1) "Business" means any business acting within the State of California that sells goods to any individual or entity, including, but not limited to, retailers, suppliers, manufacturers, and distributors.

(2) "Goods" means any consumer products used, bought, or rendered primarily for personal, family, or household purposes.

(3)(A) "Substantially similar" means two goods that exhibit all of the following characteristics:

(i) No substantial differences in the materials used in production.

(ii) The intended use is similar.

(iii) The functional design and features are similar.

(iv) The brand is the same or both brands are owned by the same individual or entity.

(B) A difference in coloring among any of the goods shall not be construed as a substantial difference for the purposes of this paragraph.

(b) A person, firm, partnership, company, corporation, or business shall not charge a different price for any two goods that are substantially similar if those goods are priced differently based on the gender of the individuals for whom the goods are marketed and intended.

(c) This section does not prohibit price differences in goods or services based specifically upon any of the following:

(1) The amount of time it took to manufacture those goods.

(2) The difficulty in manufacturing those goods.

(3) The cost incurred in manufacturing those goods.

(4) The labor used in manufacturing those goods.

(5) The materials used in manufacturing those goods.

(6) Any other gender-neutral reason for charging a different price for those goods.

(d)(1) Notwithstanding any other law, whenever the Attorney General has cause to believe that a violation of this section has occurred, the Attorney General may, upon notice to the defendant of not less than five days, seek a court order to enjoin and restrain the continuance of those violations.

(2) If a court finds that the defendant has violated this section, an injunction may be issued by the court enjoining or restraining any violation, without requiring proof that any person has, in fact, been injured or damaged thereby. The court may make direct restitution, if applicable. In connection with the proposed application for an injunction, the Attorney General is authorized to take proof and make a determination of the relevant facts and to issue subpoenas in accordance with the civil practice law and rules.

(3) If a court finds that the defendant has violated this section, a court may impose a civil penalty not to exceed ten thousand dollars ($10,000) for the first violation, and a civil penalty not to exceed one thousand dollars ($1,000) for each subsequent violation. The total civil penalty imposed pursuant to this paragraph shall not exceed one hundred thousand dollars ($100,000).

(4) Notwithstanding paragraph (3), a court may impose additional civil penalties upon a defendant exceeding one hundred thousand dollars ($100,000) if the defendant subsequently violates this section with respect to the same goods for which the maximum civil penalty has been previously imposed under a separate civil action or for any good for which the Attorney General has not brought civil action pursuant to this section.

(e) For the purposes of this section, each instance of charging a different price for two goods that are substantially similar, as specified in subdivision (b), shall constitute a single violation.

(f) This section does not limit liability under the Unruh Civil Rights Act (Section 51). **Leg.H.** Added Stats 2022 ch 555 §1 (AB 1287), effective January 1, 2023.

§51.17. Establishment of pilot program [Repealed July 1, 2028]

(a) For purposes of this section, "department" refers to the Civil Rights Department.

(b)(1) On or before January 1, 2025, the department shall establish a pilot program that recognizes businesses for creating safe and welcoming environments free from discrimination and harassment of customers.

(2) To qualify for recognition under the pilot program, a business shall meet the criteria set out by the department, which may include, but not be limited to, the following:

(A) Demonstrating compliance with Section 51.

(B) Offering additional training to educate and inform employees or build skills.

(C) Informing the public of their rights to be free from discrimination and harassment and how to report violations.

(D) Outlining a code of conduct for the public that encourages respectful and civil behavior.

(E) Any other actions designed to prevent and respond to discrimination and harassment regardless of the identity of the perpetrator.

(3) The department shall provide a certificate to qualifying businesses that may be prominently displayed on site and publish on its internet website a database of businesses receiving that certificate.

(4) On or before January 1, 2028, the department shall evaluate whether that recognition is effective, including, at a minimum, whether it affects customer behavior, incentivizes compliance among businesses with Section 51, or reduces the incidence of discrimination and harassment at businesses.

(5) Recognition under the pilot program does not establish and is not relevant to any defense of claims brought under existing law.

(c) This section shall remain in effect only until July 1, 2028, and as of that date is repealed. **Leg.H.** Added Stats 2022 ch 315 §1 (AB 2448), effective January 1, 2023, repealed July 1, 2028.

§52. Actions for damages and other relief for denial of rights

(a) Whoever denies, aids or incites a denial, or makes any discrimination or distinction contrary to Section 51, 51.5, or 51.6, is liable for each and every offense for the actual damages, and any amount that may be determined by a jury, or a court sitting without a jury, up to a maximum of three times the amount of actual damage but in no case less than four thousand dollars ($4,000), and any attorney's fees that may be determined by the court in addition thereto, suffered by any person denied the rights provided in Section 51, 51.5, or 51.6.

(b) Whoever denies the right provided by Section 51.7 or 51.9, or aids, incites, or conspires in that denial, is liable for each and every offense for the actual damages suffered by any person denied that right and, in addition, the following:

(1) An amount to be determined by a jury, or a court sitting without a jury, for exemplary damages.

(2) A civil penalty of twenty-five thousand dollars ($25,000) to be awarded to the person denied the right provided by Section 51.7 in any action brought by the person denied the right, or by the Attorney General, a district attorney, or a city attorney. An action for that penalty brought pursuant to Section 51.7 shall be commenced within three years of the alleged practice.

(3) Attorney's fees as may be determined by the court.

(c) Whenever there is reasonable cause to believe that any person or group of persons is engaged in conduct of resistance to the full enjoyment of any of the rights described in this section, and that conduct is of that nature and is intended to deny the full exercise of those rights, the Attorney General, any district attorney or city attorney, or any person aggrieved by the conduct may bring a civil action in the appropriate court by filing with it a complaint. The complaint shall contain the following:

(1) The signature of the officer, or, in the officer's absence, the individual acting on behalf of the officer, or the signature of the person aggrieved.

(2) The facts pertaining to the conduct.

(3) A request for preventive relief, including an application for a permanent or temporary injunction, restraining order, or other order against the person or persons responsible for the conduct, as the complainant deems necessary to ensure the full enjoyment of the rights described in this section.

(d) Whenever an action has been commenced in any court seeking relief from the denial of equal protection of the laws under the Fourteenth Amendment to the Constitution of the United States on account of race, color, religion, sex, national origin, or disability, the Attorney General or any district attorney or city attorney for or in the name of the people of the State of California may intervene in the action upon timely application if the Attorney General or any district attorney or city attorney certifies that the case is of general public importance. In that action, the people of the State of California shall be entitled to the same relief as if it had instituted the action.

(e) Actions brought pursuant to this section are independent of any other actions, remedies, or procedures that may be available to an aggrieved party pursuant to any other law.

(f) Any person claiming to be aggrieved by an alleged unlawful practice in violation of Section 51 or 51.7 may also file a verified complaint with the Civil Rights Department pursuant to Section 12948 of the Government Code.

(g) This section does not require any construction, alteration, repair, structural or otherwise, or modification of any sort whatsoever, beyond that construction, alteration, repair, or modification that is otherwise required by other provisions of law, to any new or existing establishment, facility, building, improvement, or any other structure, nor does this section augment, restrict, or alter in any way the authority of the State Architect to require construction, alteration, repair, or modifications that the State Architect otherwise possesses pursuant to other laws.

(h) For the purposes of this section, "actual damages" means special and general damages. This subdivision is declaratory of existing law.

(i) Subdivisions (b) to (f), inclusive, shall not be waived by contract except as provided in Section 51.7. **Leg.H.** Added Stats 1905 ch 413 §2. Amended Stats 1919 ch 210 §2; Stats 1923 ch 235 §2; Stats 1959 ch 1866 §2; Stats 1974 ch 1193 §2; Stats 1976 ch 366 §2, ch 1293 §2.5; Stats 1978 ch 1212 §1; Stats 1981 ch 521 §1, effective September 16, 1981; Stats 1986 ch 244 §1; Stats 1987 ch 159 §4; Stats 1989 ch 459 §1; Stats 1991 ch 607 §2 (SB 98), ch 839 §2 (AB 1169); Stats 1992 ch 913 §3.6 (AB 1077); Stats 1994 ch 535 §1 (SB 1288); Stats 1998 ch 195 §4 (AB 2702); Stats 1999 ch 964 §2 (AB 519); Stats 2000 ch 98 §2 (AB 2719); Stats 2001 ch 261 §1 (AB 587); Stats 2005 ch 123 §1 (AB 378), effective January 1, 2006; Stats 2014 ch 910 §3 (AB 2617), effective January 1, 2015; Stats 2022 ch 48 §5 (SB 189), effective June 30, 2022.

2014 Note: For legislative findings and declarations, see 2014 Note following §51.7.

1991 Note: It is the intent of the Legislature to modify the prerequisite for injunctive relief under Section 52 of the Civil Code. By providing a civil remedy for the classes of persons specifically identified in Sections 51, 51.7, and 52 of the Civil Code, the Legislature does not intend to limit the availability of this remedy for any other form of discrimination which is prohibited by these sections. Stats 1991 ch 839 §3.

§52.1. Action for injunctive and other equitable relief to protect exercise or enjoyment of legal rights

(a) This section shall be known, and may be cited, as the Tom Bane Civil Rights Act.

(b) If a person or persons, whether or not acting under color of law, interferes by threat, intimidation, or coercion, or attempts to interfere by threat, intimidation, or coercion, with the exercise or enjoyment by any individual or individuals of rights secured by the Constitution or laws of the United States, or of the rights secured by the Constitution or laws of this state, the Attorney General, or any district attorney or city attorney may bring a civil action for injunctive and other appropriate equitable relief in the name of the people of the State of California, in order to protect the peaceable exercise or enjoyment of the right or rights secured. An action brought by the Attorney General, any district attorney, or any city attorney may also seek a civil penalty of twenty-five thousand dollars ($25,000). If this civil penalty is requested, it shall be assessed individually against each person who is determined to have violated this section and the penalty shall be awarded to each individual whose rights under this section are determined to have been violated.

(c) Any individual whose exercise or enjoyment of rights secured by the Constitution or laws of the United States, or of rights secured by the Constitution or laws of this state, has been interfered with, or attempted to be interfered with, as described in subdivision (b), may institute and prosecute in their own name and on their own behalf a civil action for damages, including, but not limited to, damages under Section 52, injunctive relief, and other appropriate equitable relief to protect the peaceable exercise or enjoyment of the right or rights secured, including appropriate equitable and declaratory relief to eliminate a pattern or practice of conduct as described in subdivision (b).

(d) An action brought pursuant to subdivision (b) or (c) may be filed either in the superior court for the county in which the conduct complained of occurred or in the superior court for the county in which a person whose conduct complained of resides or has their place of business. An action brought by the Attorney General pursuant to subdivision (b) also may be filed in the superior court for any county wherein the Attorney General has an office, and in that case, the jurisdiction of the court shall extend throughout the state.

(e) If a court issues a temporary restraining order or a preliminary or permanent injunction in an action brought pursuant to subdivision (b) or (c), ordering a defendant to refrain from conduct or activities, the order issued shall include the following statement: VIOLATION OF THIS

ORDER IS A CRIME PUNISHABLE UNDER SECTION 422.77 OF THE PENAL CODE.

(f) The court shall order the plaintiff or the attorney for the plaintiff to deliver, or the clerk of the court to mail, two copies of any order, extension, modification, or termination thereof granted pursuant to this section, by the close of the business day on which the order, extension, modification, or termination was granted, to each local law enforcement agency having jurisdiction over the residence of the plaintiff and any other locations where the court determines that acts of violence against the plaintiff are likely to occur. Those local law enforcement agencies shall be designated by the plaintiff or the attorney for the plaintiff. Each appropriate law enforcement agency receiving any order, extension, or modification of any order issued pursuant to this section shall serve forthwith one copy thereof upon the defendant. Each appropriate law enforcement agency shall provide to any law enforcement officer responding to the scene of reported violence, information as to the existence of, terms, and current status of, any order issued pursuant to this section.

(g) A court shall not have jurisdiction to issue an order or injunction under this section, if that order or injunction would be prohibited under Section 527.3 of the Code of Civil Procedure.

(h) An action brought pursuant to this section is independent of any other action, remedy, or procedure that may be available to an aggrieved individual under any other provision of law, including, but not limited to, an action, remedy, or procedure brought pursuant to Section 51.7.

(i) In addition to any damages, injunction, or other equitable relief awarded in an action brought pursuant to subdivision (c), the court may award the petitioner or plaintiff reasonable attorney's fees.

(j) A violation of an order described in subdivision (e) may be punished either by prosecution under Section 422.77 of the Penal Code, or by a proceeding for contempt brought pursuant to Title 5 (commencing with Section 1209) of Part 3 of the Code of Civil Procedure. However, in any proceeding pursuant to the Code of Civil Procedure, if it is determined that the person proceeded against is guilty of the contempt charged, in addition to any other relief, a fine may be imposed not exceeding one thousand dollars ($1,000), or the person may be ordered imprisoned in a county jail not exceeding six months, or the court may order both the imprisonment and fine.

(k) Speech alone is not sufficient to support an action brought pursuant to subdivision (b) or (c), except upon a showing that the speech itself threatens violence against a specific person or group of persons; and the person or group of persons against whom the threat is directed reasonably fears that, because of the speech, violence will be committed against them or their property and that the person threatening violence had the apparent ability to carry out the threat.

(*l*) No order issued in any proceeding brought pursuant to subdivision (b) or (c) shall restrict the content of any person's speech. An order restricting the time, place, or manner of any person's speech shall do so only to the extent reasonably necessary to protect the peaceable exercise or enjoyment of constitutional or statutory rights, consistent with the constitutional rights of the person sought to be enjoined.

(m) The rights, penalties, remedies, forums, and procedures of this section shall not be waived by contract except as provided in Section 51.7.

(n) The state immunity provisions provided in Sections 821.6, 844.6, and 845.6 of the Government Code shall not apply to any cause of action brought against any peace officer or custodial officer, as those terms are defined in Chapter 4.5 (commencing with Section 830) of Title 3 of Part 2 of the Penal Code, or directly against a public entity that employs a peace officer or custodial officer, under this section.

(o) Sections 825, 825.2, 825.4, and 825.6 of the Government Code, providing for indemnification of an employee or former employee of a public entity, shall apply to any cause of action brought under this section against an employee or former employee of a public entity. **Leg.H.** Added Stats 1987 ch 1277 §3. Amended Stats 1990 ch 392 §1 (AB 2683); Stats 1991 ch 607 §3 (SB 98); Stats 2000 ch 98 §3 (AB 2719); Stats 2001 ch 261 §2 (AB 587); Stats 2002 ch 784 §11 (SB 1316); Stats 2004 ch 700 §1 (SB 1234); Stats 2014 ch 296 §1 (AB 2634), effective January 1, 2015, ch 910 §4.5 (AB 2617), effective January 1, 2015; Stats 2018 ch 776 §4 (AB 3250), effective January 1, 2019; Stats 2021 ch 401 §1.5 (AB 1578), effective January 1, 2022; Stats 2021 ch 409 §3 (SB 2), effective January 1, 2022 (ch 409 prevails).

2014 Note: For legislative findings and declarations, see 2014 Note following §51.7.

2000 Note: (a) The Legislature hereby finds and declares all of the following:

(1) Section 52.1 of the Civil Code guarantees the exercise or enjoyment by any individual or individuals of rights secured by the Constitution or laws of the United States, or of the rights secured by the Constitution or laws of this state without regard to his or her membership in a protected class identified by its race, color, religion, or sex, among other things.

(2) The decision in *Boccato v. City of Hermosa Beach* (1994) 29 Cal.App.4th 1797 misconstrued Section 52.1 of the Civil Code to require that an individual who brings an action, or on whose behalf an action is brought, pursuant to that section, be a member of one of those specified protected classes.

(b) It is the intent of the Legislature in enacting this act to clarify that an action brought pursuant to Section 52.1 of the Civil Code does not require the individual whose rights are secured by the Constitution or laws of the United States, or of the rights secured by the Constitution or laws of California to be a member of a protected class identified by its race, color, religion, or sex, among other things. Stats 2000 ch 98 §1.

§52.2. "Court of competent jurisdiction"

An action pursuant to Section 52 or 54.3 may be brought in any court of competent jurisdiction. A "court of competent jurisdiction" shall include small claims court if the amount of the damages sought in the action does not exceed the jurisdictional limits stated in Sections 116.220 and 116.221 of the Code of Civil Procedure. **Leg.H.** Added Stats 1998 ch 195 §5 (AB 2702). Amended Stats 2006 ch 167 §1 (AB 2618), effective January 1, 2007.

§52.3. Action to obtain equitable and declaratory relief to eliminate pattern or practice by law enforcement officers depriving person of legal rights

(a) No governmental authority, or agent of a governmental authority, or person acting on behalf of a governmental authority, shall engage in a pattern or practice of conduct by law enforcement officers that deprives any person of rights, privileges, or immunities secured or protected by the Constitution or laws of the United States or by the Constitution or laws of California.

(b) The Attorney General may bring a civil action in the name of the people to obtain appropriate equitable and declaratory relief to eliminate the pattern or practice of conduct specified in subdivision (a), whenever the Attorney General has reasonable cause to believe that a violation of subdivision (a) has occurred. **Leg.H.** Added Stats 2000 ch 622 §1 (AB 2484).

§52.4. Action for damages against party responsible for gender violence

(a) Any person who has been subjected to gender violence may bring a civil action for damages against any responsible party. The plaintiff may seek actual damages, compensatory damages, punitive damages, injunctive relief, any combination of those, or any other appropriate relief. A prevailing plaintiff may also be awarded attorney's fees and costs.

(b) An action brought pursuant to this section shall be commenced within three years of the act, or if the victim was a minor when the act occurred, within eight years after the date the plaintiff attains the age of majority or within three years after the date the plaintiff discovers or reasonably should have discovered the psychological injury or illness occurring after the age of majority that was caused by the act, whichever date occurs later.

(c) For purposes of this section, "gender violence" is a form of sex discrimination and means either of the following:

(1) One or more acts that would constitute a criminal offense under state law that has as an element the use, attempted use, or threatened use of physical force against the person or property of another, committed at least in part based on the gender of the victim, whether or not those acts have resulted in criminal complaints, charges, prosecution, or conviction.

(2) A physical intrusion or physical invasion of a sexual nature under coercive conditions, whether or not those acts have resulted in criminal complaints, charges, prosecution, or conviction.

(d) For purposes of this section, "gender" has the meaning set forth in Section 51.

(e) Notwithstanding any other laws that may establish the liability of an employer for the acts of an employee, this section does not establish any civil liability of a person because of his or her status as an employer, unless the employer personally committed an act of gender violence. **Leg.H.** Added Stats 2002 ch 842 §2 (AB 1928). Amended Stats 2015 ch 202 §1 (AB 830), effective January 1, 2016.

§52.45. Action for damages against party responsible for sexual orientation violence

(a) Any person who has been subjected to sexual orientation violence may bring a civil action for damages against any responsible party. The plaintiff may seek actual damages, compensatory damages, punitive damages, injunctive relief, any combination of those, or any other appropriate relief. A prevailing plaintiff may also be awarded attorney's fees and costs.

(b) An action brought pursuant to this section shall be commenced within three years of the act, or if the victim was a minor when the act occurred, within eight years after the date the plaintiff attains the age of majority or within three years after the date the plaintiff discovers or reasonably should have discovered the psychological injury or illness occurring after the age of majority that was caused by the act, whichever date occurs later.

(c) For purposes of this section, "sexual orientation violence" means one or more acts that would constitute a criminal offense under state law that has as an element the use, attempted use, or threatened use of physical force against the person or property of another, committed at least in part based on the sexual orientation of the victim, whether or not those acts have resulted in criminal complaints, charges, prosecution, or conviction.

(d) Notwithstanding any other laws that may establish the liability of an employer for the acts of an employee, this section does not establish any civil liability of a person because of his or her status as an employer, unless the employer personally committed an act of sexual orientation violence. **Leg.H.** Added Stats 2015 ch 202 §2 (AB 830), effective January 1, 2016.

§52.5. Action by victim of human trafficking

(a) A victim of human trafficking, as defined in Section 236.1 of the Penal Code, may bring a civil action for actual damages, compensatory damages, punitive damages, injunctive relief, any combination of those, or any other appropriate relief. A prevailing plaintiff may also be awarded attorney's fees and costs.

(b) In addition to the remedies specified in this section, in an action under subdivision (a), both of the following apply:

(1) A plaintiff may be awarded up to three times the plaintiff's actual damages or ten thousand dollars ($10,000), whichever is greater. In addition, punitive damages may be awarded upon proof of the defendant's malice, oppression, fraud, or duress in committing the act of human trafficking.

(2)(A) A plaintiff may seek from the court a finding that specific debts attributed to the plaintiff were incurred as the result of trafficking and without the consent of the plaintiff.

(B) For purposes of this paragraph, the court may base its finding upon evidence that a debt attributed to the plaintiff was incurred as the result of any illegal act in which the plaintiff was the victim. A finding shall not affect the priority of any lien or other security interest.

(C) For purposes of this paragraph, a debt attributed to the plaintiff is incurred as the result of trafficking when the plaintiff is a victim of any illegal act associated with human trafficking and the debt or a portion of the debt meets all of the following criteria:

(i) It was incurred for personal, family, or household use.

(ii) It is in the name of the plaintiff.

(iii) It was incurred as a result of duress, intimidation, threat of force, force, fraud, or undue influence.

(c) An action brought pursuant to this section shall be commenced within seven years of the date on which the trafficking victim was freed from the trafficking situation or, if the victim was a minor when the act of human trafficking against the victim occurred, within 10 years after the date the plaintiff attains the age of majority.

(d) If a person entitled to sue is under a disability at the time the cause of action accrues so that it is impossible or impracticable for the person to bring an action, the time of the disability is not part of the time limited for the commencement of the action. Disability shall toll the running of the statute of limitations for this action.

(1) Disability includes being a minor, lacking legal capacity to make decisions, imprisonment, or other incapacity or incompetence.

(2) The statute of limitations shall not run against a plaintiff who is a minor or who lacks the legal competence to make decisions simply because a guardian ad litem has been appointed. A guardian ad litem's failure to bring a plaintiff's action within the applicable limitation period will not prejudice the plaintiff's right to bring an action after the plaintiff's disability ceases.

(3) A defendant is estopped from asserting a defense of the statute of limitations if the expiration of the statute is due to conduct by the defendant inducing the plaintiff to delay the filing of the action, or due to threats made by the defendant causing the plaintiff duress.

(4) The suspension of the statute of limitations due to disability, lack of knowledge, or estoppel applies to all other related claims arising out of the trafficking situation.

(5) The running of the statute of limitations is postponed during the pendency of criminal proceedings against the victim.

(e) The running of the statute of limitations may be suspended if a person entitled to sue could not have reasonably discovered the cause of action due to circumstances resulting from the trafficking situation, such as psychological trauma, cultural and linguistic isolation, and the inability to access services.

(f) A prevailing plaintiff may also be awarded reasonable attorney's fees and litigation costs including, but not limited to, expert witness fees and expenses as part of the costs.

(g) Restitution paid by the defendant to the victim shall be credited against a judgment, award, or settlement obtained pursuant to an action under this section. A judgment, award, or settlement obtained pursuant to an action under this section is subject to Section 13963 of the Government Code.

(h) A civil action filed under this section shall be stayed during the pendency of any criminal action arising out of the same occurrence in which the claimant is the victim. As used in this section, a "criminal action" includes investigation and prosecution, and is pending until a final adjudication in the trial court or dismissal. **Leg.H.** Added Stats 2005 ch 240 §2 (AB 22), effective January 1, 2006. Amended Stats 2014 ch 144 §1 (AB 1847), effective January 1, 2015; Stats 2015 ch 474 §1 (AB 15), effective January 1, 2016; Stats 2016 ch 86 §18 (SB 1171), effective January 1, 2017; Stats 2023 ch 632 §1 (SB 727), effective January 1, 2024.

2005 Note: Nothing in this act shall be construed as prohibiting or precluding prosecution under any other provision of law or to prevent punishment pursuant to any other provision of law that imposes a greater or more severe punishment than provided for in this act. Stats 2005 ch 240 (AB 22) §13.

§52.6. Specified businesses to post notice related to slavery and human trafficking; Development of model notice; Manner of notice; Failure to comply

(a) Each of the following businesses and other establishments shall, upon the availability of the model notice described in subdivision (d), post a notice that complies with the requirements of this section in a conspicuous place near the public entrance of the establishment or in another conspicuous location in clear view of the public and employees where similar notices are customarily posted:

(1) On-sale general public premises licensees under the Alcoholic Beverage Control Act (Division 9 (commencing with Section 23000) of the Business and Professions Code).

(2) Adult or sexually oriented businesses, as defined in subdivision (a) of Section 318.5 of the Penal Code.

(3) Primary airports, as defined in Section 47102(16) of Title 49 of the United States Code.

(4) Intercity passenger rail or light rail stations.

(5) Bus stations.

(6) Truck stops. For purposes of this section, "truck stop" means a privately owned and operated facility that provides food, fuel, shower or other sanitary facilities, and lawful overnight truck parking.

(7) Emergency rooms within general acute care hospitals.

(8) Urgent care centers.

(9) Facilities that provide pediatric care. For purposes of this section, "facilities that provide pediatric care" means a medical facility that provides pediatric services, as that term is defined in Section 16907.5 of the Welfare and Institutions Code.

(10) Farm labor contractors, as defined in subdivision (b) of Section 1682 of the Labor Code.

(11) Privately operated job recruitment centers.

(12) Roadside rest areas.

(13) Businesses or establishments that offer massage or bodywork services for compensation and are not described in paragraph (1) of subdivision (b) of Section 4612 of the Business and Professions Code.

(14) Hotels, motels, and bed and breakfast inns, as defined in subdivision (b) of Section 24045.12 of the Business and Professions Code, not including personal residences.

(15) Hair, nail, electrolysis, and skin care, and other related businesses or establishments subject to regulation under Chapter 10 (commencing with Section 7301) of Division 3 of the Business and Professions Code.

(b) The notice to be posted pursuant to subdivision (a) shall be at least 8½ inches by 11 inches in size, written in a 16-point font, and shall state the following:

If you or someone you know is being forced to engage in any activity and cannot leave—whether it is commercial sex, housework, farm work, construction, factory, retail, or restaurant work, or any other activity—text 233-733 (Be Free) or call the National Human Trafficking Hotline at 1-888-373-7888 or the California Coalition to Abolish Slavery and Trafficking (CAST) at 1-888-KEY-2-FRE(EDOM) or 1-888-539-2373 to access help and services.

Victims of slavery and human trafficking are protected under United States and California law.

The hotlines are:

- Available 24 hours a day, 7 days a week.
- Toll-free.
- Operated by nonprofit, nongovernmental organizations.
- Anonymous and confidential.
- Accessible in more than 160 languages.
- Able to provide help, referral to services, training, and general information.

(c) The notice to be posted pursuant to subdivision (a) shall be printed in English, Spanish, and in one other language that is the most widely spoken language in the county where the establishment is located and for which translation is mandated by the federal Voting Rights Act of 1965 (52 U.S.C. Sec. 10301 et seq.), as applicable. This section does not require a business or other establishment in a county where a language other than English or Spanish is the most widely spoken language to print the notice in more than one language in addition to English and Spanish.

(d)(1) On or before April 1, 2013, the Department of Justice shall develop a model notice that complies with the requirements of this section and make the model notice available for download on the department's internet website.

(2) On or before January 1, 2019, the Department of Justice shall revise and update the model notice to comply with the requirements of this section and make the updated model notice available for download on the department's internet website. A business or establishment required to post the model notice shall not be required to post the updated model notice until on and after January 1, 2019.

(e) On or before January 1, 2021, a business or other establishment that operates a facility described in paragraph (4) or (5) of subdivision (a) shall provide at least 20 minutes of training to its new and existing employees who may interact with, or come into contact with, a victim of human trafficking or who are likely to receive, in the course of their employment, a report from another employee about suspected human trafficking, in recognizing the signs of human trafficking and how to report those signs to the appropriate law enforcement agency.

(f) The employee training pursuant to subdivision (e) shall include, but not be limited to, all of the following:

(1) The definition of human trafficking, including sex trafficking and labor trafficking.

(2) Myths and misconceptions about human trafficking.

(3) Physical and mental signs to be aware of that may indicate that human trafficking is occurring.

(4) Guidance on how to identify individuals who are most at risk for human trafficking.

(5) Guidance on how to report human trafficking, including, but not limited to, national hotlines (1-888-373-7888 and text line 233733) and contact information for local law enforcement agencies that an employee may use to make a confidential report.

(6) Protocols for reporting human trafficking when on the job.

(g)(1) The human trafficking employee training pursuant to subdivision (e) may include, but shall not be limited to, information and material utilized in training Santa Clara County Valley Transportation Authority employees, private nonprofit organizations that represent the interests of human trafficking victims, and the Department of Justice.

(2) The failure to report human trafficking by an employee shall not, by itself, result in the liability of the business or other establishment that operates a facility described in paragraph (4) or (5) of subdivision (a) or of any other person or entity.

(h) A business or establishment that fails to comply with the requirements of this section is liable for a civil penalty of five hundred dollars ($500) for a first offense and one thousand dollars ($1,000) for each subsequent offense. A government entity identified in Section 17204 of the Business and Professions Code may bring an action to impose a civil penalty pursuant to this subdivision against a business or establishment if a local or state agency with authority to regulate that business or establishment has satisfied both of the following:

(1) Provided the business or establishment with reasonable notice of noncompliance, which informs the business or establishment that it is subject to a civil penalty if it does not correct the violation within 30 days from the date the notice is sent to the business or establishment.

(2) Verified that the violation was not corrected within the 30-day period described in paragraph (1).

(i) This section does not prevent a local governing body from adopting and enforcing a local ordinance, rule, or regulation to prevent slavery or human trafficking. If a local ordinance, rule, or regulation duplicates or supplements the requirements that this section imposes upon businesses and other establishments, this section does not supersede or preempt that local ordinance, rule, or regulation. **Leg.H.** Added Stats 2012 ch 515 §1 (SB 1193), effective January 1, 2013. Amended Stats 2017 ch 547 §1 (AB 260), effective January 1, 2018; Stats 2017 ch 565 §1.5 (SB 225), effective January 1, 2018 (ch 565 prevails); Stats 2018 ch 812 §1 (AB 2034), effective January 1, 2019; Stats 2019 ch 57 §1 (SB 630), effective January 1, 2020; Stats 2020 ch 370 §22 (SB 1371), effective January 1, 2021; Stats 2022 ch 106 §1 (AB 1661), effective January 1, 2023; Stats 2023 ch 104 §1 (AB 1740), effective January 1, 2024.

§ 52.65. Civil action against hotel for sex trafficking activity

(a) A hotel is in violation of this section, and subject to civil penalties, if either or both of the following conditions are met:

(1) Sex trafficking activity occurred in the hotel, a supervisory employee of the hotel either knew of the nature of the activity, or acted in reckless disregard of the activity constituting sex trafficking activity within the hotel, and the supervisory employee of the hotel failed to inform law enforcement, the National Human Trafficking Hotline, or another appropriate victim service organization within 24 hours.

(2) An employee of the hotel was acting within the scope of employment and knowingly benefited, financially or by receiving anything of value, by participating in a venture that the employee knew or acted in reckless disregard of the activity constituting sex trafficking within the hotel.

(b) If there is reasonable cause to believe there has been a violation pursuant to subdivision (a), a city, county, or city and county attorney may bring a civil action for injunctive and other equitable relief against a hotel for violation of this section. A city, county, or city and county attorney who brings a civil action under this section may also seek civil penalties in the amount of one thousand dollars ($1,000) for the first violation in a calendar year, three thousand dollars ($3,000) for the second violation within the same calendar year, and five thousand dollars ($5,000) for the third and any subsequent violation within the same calendar year.

(c) The court may exercise its discretion to increase the amount of the civil penalty, not to exceed ten thousand dollars ($10,000), for any fourth or subsequent violation, considering all of the following factors:

(1) The defendant's culpability.

(2) The relationship between the harm and the penalty.

(3) The penalties imposed for similar conduct in similar statutes.

(4) The defendant's ability to pay.

(d) The lack of reporting of a sex trafficking case that occurs in a hotel shall not, by itself, without meeting the conditions in either paragraph (1) or (2) of subdivision (a), result in the liability of an employer of that establishment to the sex trafficking victim or victims in the case in question or to any other party.

(e) No liability for civil penalties shall arise under this section against a hotel employee.

(f) Violation of this section, by itself, shall not result in criminal liability against the hotel.

(g) Nothing in this section affects criminal or civil liability that may arise pursuant to other provisions of law.

(h) For the purposes of this section, the following terms shall have the following definitions:

(1) "Hotel" means a motel, or any other operator or management company that offers and accepts payment for rooms, sleeping accommodations, or board and lodging and retains the right of access to, and control of, a dwelling unit that is required to provide training and education regarding human trafficking awareness pursuant to Section 12950.3 of the Government Code.

(2) "Sex trafficking" means human trafficking for the purposes of engaging in a commercial sex act as set forth in subdivision (c) of Section 236.1 of the Penal Code.

(3) "Supervisory employee" means any individual, regardless of the job description or title, who has each of the following capabilities and qualifications:

(A) Holds authority, in the interest of the employer, to hire, transfer, suspend, lay off, recall, promote, discharge, assign, reward, or discipline other employees, or responsibility to direct them, or to adjust their grievances, or effectively to recommend this action, if, in connection with the foregoing, the exercise of this authority is not of a merely routine or clerical nature, but requires the use of independent judgment.

(B) Holds responsibility for duties that are not substantially similar to those of their subordinates. Employees whose duties are substantially similar to those of their subordinates shall not be considered to be supervisory employees.

(i) An action brought pursuant to this section shall be commenced within five years of the date when the violation of subdivision (a) occurred, or, if the victim of that sex trafficking activity was a minor when the violation occurred, within five years of the date the victim attains the age of majority. **Leg.H.** Added Stats 2022 ch 760 §1 (AB 1788), effective January 1, 2023.

§ 52.66. Required notice by primary ticket seller

(a) For purposes of this section, both of the following definitions shall apply:

(1) "Entertainment facility" means a publicly or privately owned place of entertainment with a capacity of over 15,000 people, including, but not limited to, an arena, auditorium, concert hall, live performance venue, museum, racetrack, stadium, theater, or other place where entertainment events are presented for a price of admission. The facility does not have to be used exclusively for entertainment events. The term does not apply to an amusement park or fairground.

(2) "Primary ticket seller" means a primary contractor as defined in Section 22503.5 of the Business and Professions Code, ticket seller, or agent of the primary contractor or ticket seller that engages in the primary sale of tickets for an event.

(b) Upon the purchase of a mobile or electronic ticket for an event at an entertainment facility, the primary ticket seller shall include the following notice with the ticket purchase confirmation electronically to the buyer:

If you or someone you know is being forced to engage in commercial sex or labor trafficking, text 233-733 (Be Free) or call the National Human Trafficking Hotline at 1-888-373-7888 or the California Coalition to Abolish Slavery and Trafficking (CAST) at 1-888-key-2-fre(edom) or 1-888-539-2373 to access help and services.

It is a felony in California to knowingly engage in commercial trafficking and perpetrators of this offense shall be prosecuted under the law.

(c) The notice to be included pursuant to subdivision (b) shall be provided in English, Spanish, and in one other language that is the most widely spoken language in the county where the entertainment facility is located and for which translation is mandated by the federal Voting Rights Act of 1965 (52 U.S.C. Sec. 10301 et seq.), as applicable. **Leg.H.** Added Stats 2024 ch 198 §1 (AB 1966), effective January 1, 2025.

§52.7. Subcutaneous implanting of identification device; Penalties and remedies; Time for commencing action; Restitution

(a) Except as provided in subdivision (g), a person shall not require, coerce, or compel any other individual to undergo the subcutaneous implanting of an identification device.

(b)(1) Any person who violates subdivision (a) may be assessed an initial civil penalty of no more than ten thousand dollars ($10,000), and no more than one thousand dollars ($1,000) for each day the violation continues until the deficiency is corrected. That civil penalty may be assessed and recovered in a civil action brought in any court of competent jurisdiction. The court may also grant a prevailing plaintiff reasonable attorney's fees and litigation costs, including, but not limited to, expert witness fees and expenses as part of the costs.

(2) A person who is implanted with a subcutaneous identification device in violation of subdivision (a) may bring a civil action for actual damages, compensatory damages, punitive damages, injunctive relief, any combination of those, or any other appropriate relief.

(3) Additionally, punitive damages may also be awarded upon proof of the defendant's malice, oppression, fraud, or duress in requiring, coercing, or compelling the plaintiff to undergo the subcutaneous implanting of an identification device.

(c)(1) An action brought pursuant to this section shall be commenced within three years of the date upon which the identification device was implanted.

(2) If the victim was a dependent adult or minor when the implantation occurred, actions brought pursuant to this section shall be commenced within three years after the date the plaintiff, or his or her guardian or parent, discovered or reasonably should have discovered the implant, or within eight years after the plaintiff attains the age of majority, whichever date occurs later.

(3) The statute of limitations shall not run against a dependent adult or minor plaintiff simply because a guardian ad litem has been appointed. A guardian ad litem's failure to bring a plaintiff's action within the applicable limitation period will not prejudice the plaintiff's right to do so.

(4) A defendant is estopped to assert a defense of the statute of limitations when the expiration of the statute is due to conduct by the defendant inducing the plaintiff to delay the filing of the action, or due to threats made by the defendant causing duress upon the plaintiff.

(d) Any restitution paid by the defendant to the victim shall be credited against any judgment, award, or settlement obtained pursuant to this section. Any judgment, award, or settlement obtained pursuant to an action under this section shall be subject to the provisions of Section 13963 of the Government Code.

(e) The provisions of this section shall be liberally construed so as to protect privacy and bodily integrity.

(f) Actions brought pursuant to this section are independent of any other actions, remedies, or procedures that may be available to an aggrieved party pursuant to any other law.

(g) This section shall not in any way modify existing statutory or case law regarding the rights of parents or guardians, the rights of children or minors, or the rights of dependent adults.

(h) For purposes of this section:

(1) "Identification device" means any item, application, or product that is passively or actively capable of transmitting personal information, including, but not limited to, devices using radio frequency technology.

(2) "Person" means an individual, business association, partnership, limited partnership, corporation, limited liability company, trust, estate, cooperative association, or other entity.

(3) "Personal information" includes any of the following data elements to the extent they are used alone or in conjunction with any other information used to identify an individual:

(A) First or last name.

(B) Address.

(C) Telephone number.

(D) E-mail, Internet Protocol, or Web site address.

(E) Date of birth.

(F) Driver's license number or California identification card number.

(G) Any unique personal identifier number contained or encoded on a driver's license or identification card issued pursuant to Section 13000 of the Vehicle Code.

(H) Bank, credit card, or other financial institution account number.

(I) Any unique personal identifier contained or encoded on a health insurance, health benefit, or benefit card or record issued in conjunction with any government-supported aid program.

(J) Religion.

(K) Ethnicity or nationality.

(L) Photograph.

(M) Fingerprint or other biometric identifier.
(N) Social security number.
(O) Any unique personal identifier.

(4) "Require, coerce, or compel" includes physical violence, threat, intimidation, retaliation, the conditioning of any private or public benefit or care on consent to implantation, including employment, promotion, or other employment benefit, or by any means that causes a reasonable person of ordinary susceptibilities to acquiesce to implantation when he or she otherwise would not.

(5) "Subcutaneous" means existing, performed, or introduced under or on the skin. **Leg.H.** Added Stats 2007 ch 538 §1 (SB 362), effective January 1, 2008.

§ 52.8. Civil actions for distribution of unauthorized obscene material; Definitions

(a) In a civil action seeking damages or equitable relief against any person or entity that distributes, benefits from, promotes, or induces another person to distribute unauthorized obscene materials, including through electronic distribution, a prevailing plaintiff shall be awarded attorney's fees and costs.

(b) For purposes of this section:

(1) "Obscene material" means material, taken as a whole, that to the average person, applying contemporary statewide standards, appeals to the prurient interest, that, taken as a whole, depicts or describes sexual conduct in a patently offensive way, and that, taken as a whole, lacks serious literary, artistic, political, or scientific value.

(2) "Unauthorized" means either of the following:

(A) The obscene material was coerced, made, or obtained by trickery or subterfuge, or stolen, made, obtained, or distributed without the knowledge or without or beyond the express permission, freely given, of the person in the photograph, or the person whose identifiable likeness appears in the photograph.

(B) The obscene material is of a person who was less than 18 years of age at the time the obscene material was created. **Leg.H.** Added Stats 2022 ch 26 §1 (SB 1210), effective January 1, 2023.

§53. Prohibition against discriminating restrictions in real instruments

(a) Every provision in a written instrument relating to real property that purports to forbid or restrict the conveyance, encumbrance, leasing, or mortgaging of that real property to any person because of any characteristic listed or defined in subdivision (b) or (e) of Section 51 is void, and every restriction or prohibition as to the use or occupation of real property because of any characteristic listed or defined in subdivision (b) or (e) of Section 51 is void.

(b) Every restriction or prohibition, whether by way of covenant, condition upon use or occupation, or upon transfer of title to real property, which restriction or prohibition directly or indirectly limits the acquisition, use or occupation of that property because of any characteristic listed or defined in subdivision (b) or (e) of Section 51 is void.

(c) In any action to declare that a restriction or prohibition specified in subdivision (a) or (b) is void, the court shall take judicial notice of the recorded instrument or instruments containing the prohibitions or restrictions in the same manner that it takes judicial notice of the matters listed in Section 452 of the Evidence Code. **Leg.H.** Added Stats 1961 ch 1877 §1. Amended Stats 1965 ch 299 §6; Stats 1974 ch 1193 §3; Stats 1987 ch 159 §5; Stats 1992 ch 913 §3.8 (AB 1077); Stats 2005 ch 420 §7 (AB 1400), effective January 1, 2006.

Prior Law: Former §53, relating to admittance to places of amusement, etc., was added Stats 1905 ch 413 §3 and repealed Stats 1959 ch 1866 §3.

2005 Notes: This act shall be known and may be cited as "The Civil Rights Act of 2005." Stats 2005 ch 420 (AB 1400) §1.

The Legislature affirms that the bases of discrimination prohibited by the Unruh Civil Rights Act include, but are not limited to, marital status and sexual orientation, as defined herein. By specifically enumerating these bases in the Unruh Civil Rights Act, the Legislature intends to clarify the existing law, rather than to change the law, as well as the principle that the bases enumerated in the act are illustrative rather than restrictive. Stats 2005 ch 420 (AB 1400) §2(c).

It is the intent of the Legislature that the amendments made to the Unruh Civil Rights Act by this act do not affect the California Supreme Court's rulings in *Marina Point, Ltd. v. Wolfson* (1982) 30 Cal.3d 721 and *O'Connor v. Village Green Owners Association* (1983) 33 Cal.3d 790. Stats 2005 ch 420 (AB 1400) §2(d).

§53.5. Privacy; Lodging; Common carriers

(a) Notwithstanding any other law, except as specified in this section, an innkeeper, hotelkeeper, motelkeeper, lodginghouse keeper, or owner or operator of an inn, hotel, motel, lodginghouse, or other similar accommodations, or any employee or agent thereof, who offers or accepts payment for rooms, sleeping accommodations, or board and lodging, or other similar accommodation, shall not disclose, produce, provide, release, transfer, disseminate, or otherwise communicate, except to a California peace officer, all or any part of a guest record orally, in writing, or by electronic or any other means to a third party without a court-issued subpoena, warrant, or order.

(b) Notwithstanding any other law, except as specified in this section, an owner or operator of a private or charter bus transportation company, or any employee or agent thereof, shall not disclose, produce, provide, release, transfer, disseminate, or otherwise communicate, except to a California peace officer, all or any part of a passenger manifest record orally, in writing, or by electronic or any other means to a third party without a court-issued subpoena, warrant, or order.

(c) "Guest record" for purposes of this section includes any record that identifies an individual guest, boarder, occupant, lodger, customer, or invitee, including, but not limited to, their name, social security number or other unique identifying number, date of birth, location of birth, address, telephone number, driver's license number, other official form of identification, credit card number, or automobile license plate number.

(d) "Passenger manifest record" for purposes of this section includes any record that identifies an individual guest, passenger, customer, or invitee, including, but not limited to, their name, social security number or other unique identifying number, date of birth, location of birth, address, telephone number, driver's license number, other official form of identification, credit card number, or automobile license plate number.

(e) "Court issued subpoena, warrant, or order" for purposes of this section is limited to subpoenas, warrants, or orders issued by a judicial officer. An administrative subpoena, warrant, or order is not sufficient for purposes of this section.

(f) "Third-party service provider," for the purposes of this section, means an entity contracted to provide services outlined in the contract that has no independent right to use or share the data beyond the terms of the contract. Records shared with a third-party service provider shall be subject to limitations on further disclosure as described in subdivisions (a) and (b), except as otherwise permitted by this section.

(g) This section shall not be construed to prevent a government entity from requiring a private business to provide business records, including, but not limited to, guest and passenger manifest records, in a public health, civil rights, or consumer protection investigation, or in an investigation conducted pursuant to Section 308.5 of the Public Utilities Code.

(h) This section shall not be construed to prevent a government entity from requiring a private business to provide business records during an audit or inspection if those records omit the personal information described in subdivisions (c) and (d).

(i) This section shall not be construed to prevent a private business from providing business records containing a guest's or passenger's name, address, credit card number, or driver's license number to a third-party service provider, if required, for the sole purpose of effectuating financial payment, including, approving or processing negotiable instruments, electronic fund transfers, or similar methods of payment, from a guest or passenger to the private business for a good or service, or from providing business records to a third-party service provider that the private business contracts with for business-related services.

(j) This section shall not be construed to prevent a private business from providing, where required, business records to a government entity in order to comply with state and federal laws regarding financial oversight and privacy, including, but not limited to, the federal Gramm-Leach-Bliley Act (15 U.S.C. Sec. 6801). Records shared with a government entity or in compliance with the federal Gramm-Leach-Bliley Act shall be subject to the limitations on further disclosure as described in subdivisions (a) and (b), except as otherwise permitted by this section.

(k) This section shall not be construed to prevent a private business from disclosing records in a criminal investigation if a law enforcement officer in good faith believes that an emergency involving imminent danger of death or serious bodily injury to a person requires a warrantless search, to the extent permitted by law.

(*l*) This section shall not be construed to compel disclosure of a guest record or passenger manifest record by an innkeeper, motelkeeper, lodginghouse keeper, or owner or operator of an inn, hotel, motel, lodginghouse, or other similar accommodation, or an owner or operator of a private or charter bus transportation company, in the absence of a court-issued subpoena, warrant, or order. **Leg.H.** Added Stats 2018 ch 853 §2 (SB 1194), effective January 1, 2019. Amended Stats 2019 ch 2 §1 (AB 73), effective February 13, 2019; Stats 2020 ch 370 §23 (SB 1371), effective January 1, 2021.

§53.7. Political structure equal protection; Compelling government interest

(a) A statute, ordinance, or other state or local rule, regulation, or enactment shall not deny a minority group political structure equal protection of the law by altering, restructuring, or reordering the policy decisionmaking process in a manner that burdens the ability of members of the minority group to effect the enactment of future legislation, solely with respect to a matter that inures primarily to the benefit of, or is primarily of interest to, one or more minority groups.

(b)(1) A member of a minority group, as defined in paragraph (2), may bring a civil action challenging the validity of a statute, ordinance, or other state or local rule, regulation, or enactment, pursuant to subdivision (a).

(2) For purposes of this section, "minority group" means a group of persons who share in common any race, ethnicity, nationality, or sexual orientation.

(c) A statute, ordinance, or other state or local rule, regulation, or enactment shall be determined valid in an action brought pursuant to this section, only upon a showing by the government that the burden imposed by the statute, ordinance, or other state or local rule, regulation, or enactment satisfies both of the following criteria:

(1) The burden is necessary to serve a compelling government interest.

(2) The burden is no greater than necessary to serve the compelling government interest. **Leg.H.** Added Stats 2014 ch 912 §2 (AB 2646), effective January 1, 2015.

2014 Note: The Legislature finds and declares all of the following:

(a) The United States Supreme Court has interpreted the Equal Protection Clause of the Fourteenth Amendment of the United States Constitution as disfavoring and subjecting to "strict scrutiny" state and local laws that (1) target a suspect classification of persons, (2) restrict a fundamental right, or (3) alter the political policymaking process with respect to an issue of primary concern to a minority group or groups. This last doctrine is commonly referred to as "political structure equal protection."

(b) The doctrine of political structure equal protection was established primarily through two United States Supreme Court decisions, *Hunter v. Erickson* (1969) 393 U.S. 385, and *Washington v. Seattle School District No. 1* (1982) 458 U.S. 457. As a result, this doctrine has also been referred to as the "Hunter/Seattle" doctrine. In the recent case of *Schuette v. BAMN, et al.* (2014) 134 S. Ct. 1623, the United States Supreme Court has further interpreted the political structure equal protection doctrine, although the implications of this new interpretation are not yet clear.

(c) Because the Hunter/Seattle doctrine was established as a part of the Equal Protection Clause of the Fourteenth Amendment of the United States Constitution, there has not been the need or occasion for the California Supreme Court to determine whether the California Constitution, through its own guarantee of equal protection of the laws under Section 7 of Article I, also includes political structure equal protection.

(d) Because the California Constitution goes at least as far as the United States Constitution in protecting rights and liberties, and in some cases has been interpreted to go beyond the United States Constitution in providing such protections, the guarantee of political structure equal protection that has been part of the United States Constitution for nearly 50 years should appropriately be recognized in the California Constitution. Specifically, the Legislature believes that Section 7 of Article I of the California Constitution provides broader protection of individual liberties and rights than the Equal Protection Clause of the Fourteenth Amendment of the United States Constitution, and these broader protections should include the political structure equal protection doctrine, as interpreted prior to *Schuette v. BAMN*.

(e) Independent of the guarantees afforded by the California Constitution, the Legislature believes that the Hunter/Seattle doctrine provides a prudent and salutary rule for statutory protection against discriminatory statutes, ordinances, or other state or local rules, regulations, or enactments. Stats 2014 ch 912 (AB 2646) §1.

PART 2.5
BLIND AND OTHER PHYSICALLY DISABLED PERSONS

Right to use public ways and facilities. §54.
Rights concerning transportation, accommodations, and facilities. §54.1.
Right to be accompanied by guide dog, signal dog, or service dog. §54.2.
Peace officer or firefighter assigned to canine unit; Rights of and limitations with respect to dog. §54.25.
Requirements for prelitigation letter to, or complaint against, education entity; Violation; Report. §54.27.
Interference with admittance or enjoyment of public facilities. §54.3.
Pedestrian not using white cane or guide dog. §54.4.
White Cane Safety Day. §54.5.
"Visually impaired". §54.6.
Use of guide dogs in zoos. §54.7.
Assistive listening system or computer-aided transcription system for hearing impaired in court proceedings. §54.8.
Touch screen self-service devices to be accessible to visually impaired. §54.9.
Action to enjoin violation. §55.
Standing to bring action to enjoin violation. §55.1.
Actions requiring copy of petition and brief to be served on State Solicitor General. §55.2.
Construction-related accessibility claims; Demand for money or complaint made by attorney; Forms. §55.3.
Demand letter alleging construction-related accessibility claim; Demand for money; Violation. §55.31.
Requirements for attorney sending demand letter or serving complaint; Violation; Report. §55.32.

§54. Right to use public ways and facilities

(a) Individuals with disabilities or medical conditions have the same right as the general public to the full and free use of the streets, highways, sidewalks, walkways, public buildings, medical facilities, including hospitals, clinics, and physicians' offices, public facilities, and other public places.

(b) For purposes of this section:

(1) "Disability" means any mental or physical disability as defined in Section 12926 of the Government Code.

(2) "Medical condition" has the same meaning as defined in subdivision (h) of Section 12926 of the Government Code.

(c) A violation of the right of an individual under the Americans with Disabilities Act of 1990 (Public Law 101-336) also constitutes a violation of this section. **Leg.H.** Added Stats 1968 ch 461 §1. Amended Stats 1992 ch 913 §4 (AB 1077); Stats 1994 ch 1257 §1 (SB 1240); Stats 1996 ch 498 §1 (SB 1687); Stats 2000 ch 1049 §4 (AB 2222).

Prior Law: Former §54, relating to violation of right of admission to places of amusement, was added Stats 1905 ch 413 §4 and repealed Stats 1959 ch 1866 §3.

§54.1. Rights concerning transportation, accommodations, and facilities

(a)(1) Individuals with disabilities shall be entitled to full and equal access, as other members of the general public, to accommodations, advantages, facilities, medical facilities, including hospitals, clinics, and physicians' offices, and privileges of all common carriers, airplanes, motor vehicles, railroad trains, motorbuses, streetcars, boats, or any other public conveyances or modes of transportation (whether private, public, franchised, licensed, contracted, or otherwise provided), telephone facilities, adoption agencies, private schools, hotels, lodging places, places of public accommodation, amusement, or resort, and other places to which the general public is invited, subject only to the conditions and limitations established by law, or state or federal regulation, and applicable alike to all persons.

(2) As used in this section, "telephone facilities" means tariff items and other equipment and services that have been approved by the Public Utilities Commission to be used by individuals with disabilities in a manner feasible and compatible with the existing telephone network provided by the telephone companies.

(3) "Full and equal access," for purposes of this section in its application to transportation, means access that meets the standards of Titles II and III of the Americans with Disabilities Act of 1990 (Public Law 101-336) and federal regulations adopted pursuant thereto, except that, if the laws of this state prescribe higher standards, it shall mean access that meets those higher standards.

(b)(1) Individuals with disabilities shall be entitled to full and equal access, as other members of the general public, to all housing accommodations offered for rent, lease, or compensation in this state, subject to the conditions and limitations established by law, or state or federal regulation, and applicable alike to all persons.

(2) "Housing accommodations" means any real property, or portion of real property, that is used or occupied, or is intended, arranged, or designed to be used or occupied, as the home, residence, or sleeping place of one or more human beings, but shall not include any accommodations included within subdivision (a) or any single-family residence the occupants of which rent, lease, or furnish for compensation not more than one room in the residence.

(3)(A) A person renting, leasing, or otherwise providing real property for compensation shall not refuse to permit an individual with a disability, at that person's expense, to make reasonable modifications of the existing rented premises if the modifications are necessary to afford the person full enjoyment of the premises. However, any modifications under this paragraph may be conditioned on the disabled tenant entering into an agreement to restore the interior of the premises to the condition existing before the modifications. No additional security may be required on account of an election to make modifications to the rented premises under this paragraph, but the lessor and tenant may negotiate, as part of the agreement to restore the premises, a provision requiring the disabled tenant to pay an amount into an escrow account, not to exceed a reasonable estimate of the cost of restoring the premises.

(B) A person renting, leasing, or otherwise providing real property for compensation shall not refuse to make reasonable accommodations in rules, policies, practices, or services, when those accommodations may be necessary to afford individuals with a disability equal opportunity to use and enjoy the premises.

(4) This subdivision does not require a person renting, leasing, or providing for compensation real property to modify his or her property in any way or provide a higher degree of care for an individual with a disability than for an individual who is not disabled.

(5) Except as provided in paragraph (6), this part does not require a person renting, leasing, or providing for compensation real property, if that person refuses to accept tenants who have dogs, to accept as a tenant an individual with a disability who has a dog.

(6)(A) It shall be deemed a denial of equal access to housing accommodations within the meaning of this subdivision for a person, firm, or corporation to refuse to lease or rent housing accommodations to an individual who is blind or visually impaired on the basis that the individual uses the services of a guide dog, an individual who is deaf or hard of hearing on the basis that the individual uses the services of a signal dog, or to an individual with any other disability on the basis that the individual uses the services of a service dog, or to refuse to permit such an individual who is blind or visually impaired to keep a guide dog, an individual who is deaf or hard of hearing to keep a signal dog, or an individual with any other disability to keep a service dog on the premises.

(B) Except in the normal performance of duty as a mobility or signal aid, this paragraph does not prevent the owner of a housing accommodation from establishing terms in a lease or rental agreement that reasonably regulate the presence of guide dogs, signal dogs, or service dogs on the premises of a housing accommodation, nor does this paragraph relieve a tenant from any liability otherwise imposed by law for real and personal property damages caused by such a dog when proof of the damage exists.

(C)(i) As used in this subdivision, "guide dog" means a guide dog that was trained by a person licensed under Chapter 9.5 (commencing with Section 7200) of Division 3 of the Business and Professions Code or as defined in the regulations implementing Title III of the Americans with Disabilities Act of 1990 (Public Law 101-336).

(ii) As used in this subdivision, "signal dog" means a dog trained to alert an individual who is deaf or hard of hearing to intruders or sounds.

(iii) As used in this subdivision, "service dog" means a dog individually trained to the requirements of the individual with a disability, including, but not limited to, minimal protection work, rescue work, pulling a wheelchair, or fetching dropped items.

(7) It shall be deemed a denial of equal access to housing accommodations within the meaning of this subdivision for a person, firm, or corporation to refuse to lease or rent housing accommodations to an individual who is blind or visually impaired, an individual who is deaf or hard of hearing, or other individual with a disability on the basis that the individual with a disability is partially or wholly dependent upon the income of his or her spouse, if the spouse is a party to the lease or rental agreement. This subdivision does not prohibit a lessor or landlord from considering the aggregate financial status of an individual with a disability and his or her spouse.

(c) Visually impaired or blind persons and persons licensed to train guide dogs for individuals who are visually impaired or blind pursuant to Chapter 9.5 (commencing with Section 7200) of Division 3 of the Business and Professions Code or guide dogs as defined in the regulations implementing Title III of the Americans with Disabilities Act of 1990 (Public Law 101-336), and persons who are deaf or hard of hearing and persons authorized to train signal dogs for individuals who are deaf or hard of hearing, and other individuals with a disability and persons authorized to train service dogs for individuals with a disability, may take dogs, for the purpose of training them as guide dogs, signal dogs, or service dogs in any of the places specified in subdivisions (a) and (b). These persons shall ensure that the dog is on a leash and tagged as a guide dog, signal dog, or service dog by identification tag issued by the county clerk, animal control department, or other agency, as authorized by Chapter 3.5 (commencing with Section 30850) of Division 14 of the Food and Agricultural Code. In addition, the person shall be liable for any provable damage done to the premises or facilities by his or her dog.

(d) A violation of the right of an individual under the Americans with Disabilities Act of 1990 (Public Law 101-336) also constitutes a violation of this section, and this section does not limit the access of any person in violation of that act.

(e) This section does not preclude the requirement of the showing of a license plate or disabled placard when required by enforcement units enforcing disabled persons parking violations pursuant to Sections 22507.8 and 22511.8 of the Vehicle Code. **Leg.H.** Added Stats 1968 ch 461 §1. Amended Stats 1969 ch 832 §1; Stats 1972 ch 819 §1; Stats 1974 ch 108 §1; Stats 1976 ch 971 §1, ch 972 §1.5; Stats 1977 ch 700 §1; Stats 1978 ch 380 §12; Stats 1979 ch 293 §1; Stats 1980 ch 773 §1; Stats 1988 ch 1595 §2; Stats 1992 ch 913 §5 (AB 1077); Stats 1993 ch 1149 §4 (AB 1419), ch 1214 §1.5 (AB 551); Stats 1994 ch 1257 §2 (SB 1240); Stats 1996 ch 498 §1.5 (SB 1687); Stats 2016 ch 94 §1 (AB 1709), effective January 1, 2017.

§54.2. Right to be accompanied by guide dog, signal dog, or service dog

(a) Every individual with a disability has the right to be accompanied by a guide dog, signal dog, or service dog, especially trained for the purpose, in any of the places specified in Section 54.1 without being required to pay an extra charge or security deposit for the guide dog, signal dog, or service dog. However, the individual shall be liable for any damage done to the premises or facilities by his or her dog.

(b) Individuals who are blind or otherwise visually impaired and persons licensed to train guide dogs for individuals who are blind or visually impaired pursuant to Chapter 9.5 (commencing with Section 7200) of Division 3 of the Business and Professions Code or as defined in regulations implementing Title III of the Americans with Disabilities Act of 1990 (Public Law 101-336), and individuals who are deaf or hard of hearing and persons authorized to train signal dogs for individuals who are deaf or hard of hearing, and individuals with a disability and persons who are authorized to train service dogs for the individuals with a disability may take dogs, for the purpose of training them as guide dogs, signal dogs, or service dogs in any of the places specified in Section 54.1 without being required to pay an extra charge or security deposit for the guide dog, signal dog, or service dog. However, the person shall be liable for any damage done to the premises or facilities by his or her dog. These persons shall ensure the dog is on a leash and tagged as a guide dog, signal dog, or service dog by an identification tag issued by the county clerk, animal control department, or other agency, as authorized by Chapter 3.5 (commencing with Section 30850) of Title 14 of the Food and Agricultural Code.

(c) A violation of the right of an individual under the Americans with Disabilities Act of 1990 (Public Law 101-336) also constitutes a violation of this section, and this section does not limit the access of any person in violation of that act.

(d) As used in this section, the terms "guide dog," "signal dog," and "service dog" have the same meanings as defined in Section 54.1.

(e) This section does not preclude the requirement of the showing of a license plate or disabled placard when required by enforcement units enforcing disabled persons parking violations pursuant to Sections 22507.8 and 22511.8 of the Vehicle Code. **Leg.H.** Added Stats 1968 ch 461 §1. Amended Stats 1972 ch 819 §2; Stats 1979 ch 293 §2; Stats 1980 ch 773 §2; Stats 1988 ch 1595 §3; Stats 1992 ch 913 §6 (AB 1077); Stats 1994 ch 1257 §3 (SB 1240); Stats 1996 ch 498 §2 (SB 1687); Stats 2016 ch 94 §2 (AB 1709), effective January 1, 2017.

§54.25. Peace officer or firefighter assigned to canine unit; Rights of and limitations with respect to dog

(a)(1) A peace officer or firefighter assigned to a canine unit or the handler of a search and rescue dog assigned to duty away from his or her home jurisdiction because of a declared federal, state, or local emergency, or an official mutual aid request or training, and in the course and scope of his or her duties shall not be denied service based on the presence of the dog or discriminated against in hotels, lodging establishments, eating establishments, or public transportation by being required to pay an extra charge or security deposit for the dog. However, the peace officer's law enforcement agency, the firefighter's fire agency, or the handler of a search and rescue dog shall be liable for any damages to the premises or facilities caused by the dog.

(2) Any person, firm, association, or corporation, or the agent of any person, firm, association, or corporation that prevents a peace officer or a firefighter assigned to a canine unit and his or her dog or the handler of a search and rescue dog and his or her dog from exercising, or interferes in the exercise of, the rights specified in this section is subject to a civil fine not exceeding one thousand dollars ($1,000).

(b) For purposes of this section, the following definitions apply:

(1) "Declared emergency" is any emergency declared by the President of the United States, the Governor of a state, or local authorities.

(2) "Handler of a search and rescue dog" means a person in possession of a dog that is in training to become registered and approved as a search and rescue dog, or that is currently registered and approved for tasks, including, but not limited to, locating missing persons, discovering controlled substances, explosives, or cadavers, or locating victims in collapsed structures, and assisting with peace officer on-command searches for suspects and victims at crime scenes.

(3) "Peace officer's or firefighter's dog" means a dog owned by a public law enforcement agency or fire department and under the control of a peace officer or firefighter assigned to a canine unit that has been trained in matters, including, but not limited to, discovering controlled substances, explosives, cadavers, victims in collapsed structures, and peace officer on-command searches for suspects and victims at crime scenes.

(4) "Search and rescue dog" means a dog that is officially affiliated with, or sponsored by, a governmental agency and that has been trained and approved as a search and rescue dog, or that is currently registered and approved for search and rescue work with a search and rescue team affiliated with the California Emergency Management Agency. The term also includes a dog that is in training to become registered and approved for that work.

(c) Nothing in this section is intended to affect any civil remedies available for a violation of this section.

(d) This section is intended to provide accessibility without discrimination to a peace officer or firefighter with a peace officer's or firefighter's dog or a handler of a search and rescue dog with a search and rescue dog in hotels, lodging places, eating establishments, and public transportation.

(e) Nothing in this section is intended to prevent the removal of the search and rescue dog in the event the search and rescue dog creates an excessive disturbance to the quiet enjoyment of the property. In the event of an excessive disturbance, the peace officer, firefighter, or handler of the search and rescue dog shall be given a minimum of one warning notice of the excessive disturbance and an opportunity to correct the disturbance. The mere presence of the dog within the hotel, lodging establishment, food establishment, or public transportation shall not be considered an excessive disturbance. **Leg.H.** Added Stats 2008 ch 226 §1 (AB 2131), effective January 1, 2009. Amended Stats 2010 ch 92 §1 (AB 2243), effective January 1, 2011.

§54.27. Requirements for prelitigation letter to, or complaint against, education entity; Violation; Report

(a) An attorney who provides a prelitigation letter to an education entity shall do both of the following:

(1) Include the attorney's State Bar license number in the prelitigation letter.

(2) Within five business days of providing the prelitigation letter, send a copy of the prelitigation letter to the California Commission on Disability Access.

(b) An attorney who sends or serves a complaint against an education entity shall do both of the following:

(1) Send a copy of the complaint and submit information about the complaint in a standard format specified by the California Commission on Disability Access to the commission within five business days of sending or serving the complaint.

(2) Notify the California Commission on Disability Access within five business days of judgment, settlement, or dismissal of the claim or claims alleged in the complaint of the following information in a standard format specified by the commission:

(A) The date of the judgment, settlement, or dismissal.

(B) Whether or not the construction-related accessibility violations alleged in the complaint were remedied in whole or in part after the plaintiff filed a complaint.

(C) If the construction-related accessibility violations alleged in the complaint were not remedied in whole or in part after the plaintiff filed a complaint, whether or not another favorable result was achieved after the plaintiff filed the complaint.

(c) A violation of paragraph (2) of subdivision (a) or subdivision (b) shall constitute cause for the imposition of discipline of an attorney if a copy of the prelitigation letter, complaint, or notification of a case outcome is not sent to the California Commission on Disability Access within five business days. In the event the State Bar of California receives information indicating that an attorney has failed to send a copy of the prelitigation letter, complaint, or notification of a case outcome to the California Commission on Disability Access within five business days, the State Bar of California shall investigate to determine whether paragraph (2) of subdivision (a) or subdivision (b) has been violated.

(d) Notwithstanding subdivisions (a) and (b), an attorney is not required to send to the California Commission on Disability Access a copy of any subsequent prelitigation letter or amended complaint in the same dispute following the initial prelitigation letter or complaint, unless that subsequent prelitigation letter or amended complaint alleges a new construction-related accessibility claim.

(e) A prelitigation letter or notification of a case outcome sent to the California Commission on Disability Access shall be for the informational purposes of Section 8299.08 of the Government Code.

(f) The California Commission on Disability Access shall review and report on the prelitigation letters, complaints, and notifications of case outcomes it receives in the same manner as provided in Section 8299.08 of the Government Code.

(g) Paragraph (2) of subdivision (a) and subdivision (b) does not apply to a prelitigation letter or complaint sent or filed by an attorney employed or retained by a qualified legal services project or a qualified support center, as defined in Section 6213 of the Business and Professions Code, when acting within the scope of employment in asserting a construction-related accessibility claim. The Legislature finds and declares that qualified legal services projects and support centers are extensively regulated by the State Bar of California, and that there is no evidence of any abusive use of demand letters or complaints by these organizations. The Legislature further finds that, in light of the evidence of the extraordinarily small number of construction-related accessibility cases brought by regulated legal services programs, and given the resources of those programs, exempting regulated legal services programs from the requirements of this section to report to the California Commission on Disability Access will not affect the purpose of the reporting to, and tabulation by, the commission of all other construction-related accessibility claims.

(h) This section does not apply to a claim for money or damages against a public entity governed by Division 3.6 (commencing with Section 810) of Title 1 of the Government Code or make the requirements of this section applicable to such a claim.

(i) For purposes of this section, the following terms have the following meanings:

(1) "Complaint" means a civil complaint that is filed or is to be filed with a court and is sent to or served upon a defendant on the basis of one or more construction-related accessibility claims.

(2) "Construction-related accessibility claim" or "claim" means any claim of a violation of any construction-related accessibility standard, as defined in paragraph (6) of subdivision (a) of Section 55.52, with respect to a public building, public facility, or other public place of an education entity. "Construction-related accessibility claim" does not include a claim of interference with housing within the meaning of paragraph (2) of subdivision (b) of Section 54.1, or any claim of interference caused by something other than the construction-related accessibility condition of the property, including, but not limited to, the conduct of any person.

(3) "Education entity" means the Regents of the University of California, the Trustees of the California State University and the California State University, the office of the Chancellor of the California Community Colleges, a K–12 school district, or any local education agency.

(4) "Prelitigation letter" means a prelitigation written document that alleges the site is in violation of one or more construction-related accessibility standards, as defined in paragraph (6) of subdivision (a) of Section 55.52 and is provided to the education entity whether or not the attorney intends to file a complaint, or eventually files a complaint, in state or federal court. A prelitigation letter does not include a claim for money or damages against a local public entity governed by Division 3.6 (commencing with Section 810) of Title 1 of the Government Code.

Leg.H. Added Stats 2016 ch 892 §1 (SB 1406), effective January 1, 2017. Amended Stats 2017 ch 561 §16 (AB 1516), effective January 1, 2018.

§54.3. Interference with admittance or enjoyment of public facilities

(a) Any person or persons, firm or corporation who denies or interferes with admittance to or enjoyment of the public facilities as specified in Sections 54 and 54.1 or otherwise interferes with the rights of an individual with a disability under Sections 54, 54.1 and 54.2 is liable for each offense for the actual damages and any amount as may be determined by a jury, or the court sitting without a jury, up to a maximum of three times the amount of actual damages but in no case less than one thousand dollars ($1,000), and attorney's fees as may be determined by the court in addition thereto, suffered by any person denied any of the rights provided in Sections 54, 54.1, and 54.2. "Interfere," for purposes of this section, includes, but is not limited to, preventing or causing the prevention of a guide dog, signal dog, or service dog from carrying out its functions in assisting a disabled person.

(b) Any person who claims to be aggrieved by an alleged unlawful practice in violation of Section 54, 54.1, or 54.2 may also file a verified complaint with the Civil Rights Department pursuant to Section 12948 of the Government Code. The remedies in this section are nonexclusive and are in addition to any other remedy provided by law, including, but not limited to, any action for injunctive or other equitable relief available to the aggrieved party or brought in the name of the people of this state or of the United States.

(c) A person may not be held liable for damages pursuant to both this section and Section 52 for the same act or failure to act. **Leg.H.** Added Stats 1968 ch 461 §1. Amended Stats 1976 ch 971 §2, ch 972 §2.5; Stats 1977 ch 881 §1, effective September 17, 1977; Stats 1981 ch 395 §1; Stats 1992 ch 913 §7 (AB 1077); Stats 1994 ch 1257 §4 (SB 1240); Stats 1996 ch 498 §2.3 (SB 1687); Stats 2022 ch 48 §6 (SB 189), effective June 30, 2022.

§54.4. Pedestrian not using white cane or guide dog

A blind or otherwise visually impaired pedestrian shall have all of the rights and privileges conferred by law upon other persons in any of the places, accommodations, or conveyances specified in Sections 54 and 54.1, notwithstanding the fact that the person is not carrying a predominantly white cane (with or without a red tip), or using a guide dog. The failure of a blind or otherwise visually impaired person to carry such a cane or to use such a guide dog shall not constitute negligence per se. **Leg.H.** Added Stats 1968 ch 461 §1. Amended Stats 1994 ch 1257 §5 (SB 1240).

§54.5. White Cane Safety Day

Each year, the Governor shall publicly proclaim October 15 as White Cane Safety Day. He or she shall issue a proclamation in which:

(a) Comments shall be made upon the significance of this chapter.

(b) Citizens of the state are called upon to observe the provisions of this chapter and to take precautions necessary to the safety of disabled persons.

(c) Citizens of the state are reminded of the policies with respect to disabled persons declared in this chapter and he urges the citizens to cooperate in giving effect to them.

(d) Emphasis shall be made on the need of the citizenry to be aware of the presence of disabled persons in the community and to keep safe and functional for the disabled the streets, highways, sidewalks, walkways, public buildings, public facilities, other public places, places of public accommodation, amusement and resort, and other places to which the public is invited, and to offer assistance to disabled persons upon appropriate occasions.

(e) It is the policy of this state to encourage and enable disabled persons to participate fully in the social and economic life of the state and to engage in remunerative employment. **Leg.H.** Added Stats 1968 ch 461 §1. Amended Stats 1994 ch 1257 §6 (SB 1240).

§54.6. "Visually impaired"

As used in this part, "visually impaired" includes blindness and means having central visual acuity not to exceed 20/200 in the better eye, with corrected lenses, as measured by the Snellen test, or visual acuity greater than 20/200, but with a limitation in the field of vision such that the widest diameter of the visual field subtends an angle not greater than 20 degrees. **Leg.H.** Added Stats 1968 ch 461 §1. Amended Stats 1994 ch 1257 §7 (SB 1240); Stats 2006 ch 538 §38 (SB 1852), effective January 1, 2007.

§54.7. Use of guide dogs in zoos

(a) Notwithstanding any other provision of law, the provisions of this part shall not be construed to require zoos or wild animal parks to allow guide dogs, signal dogs, or service dogs to accompany individuals with a disability in areas of the zoo or park where zoo or park animals are not separated from members of the public by a physical barrier. As used in this section, "physical barrier" does not include an automobile or other conveyance.

(b) Any zoo or wild animal park that does not permit guide dogs, signal dogs, or service dogs to accompany individuals with a disability therein shall maintain, free of charge, adequate kennel facilities for the use of guide dogs, signal dogs, or service dogs belonging to these persons. These facilities shall be of a character commensurate with the anticipated daily attendance of individuals with a disability. The facilities shall be in an area not accessible to the general public, shall be equipped with water and utensils for the consumption thereof, and shall otherwise be safe, clean, and comfortable.

(c) Any zoo or wild animal park that does not permit guide dogs to accompany blind or visually impaired persons therein shall provide free transportation to blind or visually impaired persons on any mode of transportation provided for members of the public.

Each zoo or wild animal park that does not permit service dogs to accompany individuals with a disability shall provide free transportation to individuals with a disability on any mode of transportation provided for a member of the public in cases where the person uses a wheelchair and it is readily apparent that the person is unable to maintain complete or independent mobility without the aid of the service dog.

(d) Any zoo or wild animal park that does not permit guide dogs to accompany blind or otherwise visually impaired persons therein shall provide sighted escorts for blind or otherwise visually impaired persons if they are unaccompanied by a sighted person.

(e) As used in this section, "wild animal park" means any entity open to the public on a regular basis, licensed by the United States Department of Agriculture under the Animal Welfare Act as an exhibit, and operating for the primary purposes of conserving, propagating, and exhibiting wild and exotic animals, and any marine, mammal, or aquatic park open to the general public. **Leg.H.** Added Stats 1979 ch 525 §1. Amended Stats 1988 ch 1595 §4; Stats 1994 ch 1257 §8 (SB 1240).

§54.8. Assistive listening system or computer-aided transcription system for hearing impaired in court proceedings

(a) In any civil or criminal proceeding, including, but not limited to, traffic, small claims court, family court proceedings and services, and juvenile court proceedings, in any court-ordered or court-provided alternative dispute resolution, including mediation and arbitration, or in any administrative hearing of a public agency, where a party, witness, attorney, judicial employee, judge, juror, or other participant who is deaf or hard of hearing, the individual who is deaf or hard of hearing, upon his or her request, shall be provided with a functioning assistive listening system or a computer-aided transcription system. Any individual requiring this equipment shall give advance notice of his or her need to the appropriate court or agency at the time the hearing is set or not later than five days before the hearing.

(b) Assistive listening systems include, but are not limited to, special devices which transmit amplified speech by means of audio-induction loops, radio frequency systems (AM or FM), or infrared transmission. Personal receivers, headphones, and neck loops shall be available upon request by individuals who are deaf or hard of hearing.

(c) If a computer-aided transcription system is requested, sufficient display terminals shall be provided to allow the individual who is deaf or hard of hearing to read the real-time transcript of the proceeding without difficulty.

(d) A sign shall be posted in a prominent place indicating the availability of, and how to request, an assistive listening system and a computer-aided transcription system. Notice of the availability of the systems shall be posted with notice of trials.

(e) Each superior court shall have at least one portable assistive listening system for use in any court facility within the county. When not in use, the system shall be stored in a location determined by the court.

(f) The Judicial Council shall develop and approve official forms for notice of the availability of assistive listening systems and computer-aided transcription systems for individuals who are deaf or hard of hearing. The Judicial Council shall also develop and maintain a system to record utilization by the courts of these assistive listening systems and computer-aided transcription systems.

(g) If the individual who is deaf or hard of hearing is a juror, the jury deliberation room shall be equipped with an assistive listening system or a computer-aided transcription system upon the request of the juror.

(h) A court reporter may be present in the jury deliberating room during a jury deliberation if the services of a court reporter for the purpose of operating a computer-aided transcription system are required for a juror who is deaf or hard of hearing.

(i) In any of the proceedings referred to in subdivision (a), or in any administrative hearing of a public agency, in which the individual who is deaf or hard of hearing is a party, witness, attorney, judicial employee, judge, juror, or other participant, and has requested use of an assistive listening system or computer-aided transcription system, the proceedings shall not commence until the system is in place and functioning.

(j) As used in this section, individual who is deaf or hard of hearing means an individual with a hearing loss, who, with sufficient amplification or a computer-aided transcription system, is able to fully participate in the proceeding.

(k) In no case shall this section be construed to prescribe a lesser standard of accessibility or usability than that provided by Title II of the Americans with Disabilities Act of 1990 (Public Law 101-336) and federal regulations adopted pursuant to that act. **Leg.H.** Added Stats 1989 ch 1002 §1. Amended Stats 1992 ch 913 §8 (AB 1077); Stats 1993 ch 1214 §2 (AB 551); Stats 2001 ch 824 §1 (AB 1700); Stats 2018 ch 776 §5 (AB 3250), effective January 1, 2019.

§54.9. Touch screen self-service devices to be accessible to visually impaired

(a) On and after January 1, 2009, a manufacturer or distributor of touch-screen devices used for the purpose of self-service check-in at a hotel or at a facility providing passenger transportation services shall offer for availability touch-screen self-service check-in devices that contain the necessary technology.

(b) For purposes of this section, "necessary technology" means technology that enables a person with a visual impairment to do the following:

(1) Enter any personal information necessary to process a transaction in a manner that ensures the same degree of personal privacy afforded to those without visual impairments.

(2) Use the device independently and without the assistance of others in the same manner afforded to those without visual impairments.

(c) For purposes of this section, "hotel" means any hotel, motel, bed and breakfast inn, or other similar transient lodging establishment, but it does not include any residential hotel as defined in Section 50519 of the Health and Safety Code.

(d) This section shall not be construed to preclude or limit any other existing right or remedy as it pertains to self-service check-in devices and accessibility. **Leg.H.** Added Stats 2006 ch 546 §2 (AB 768), effective January 1, 2007.

§55. Action to enjoin violation

Any person who is aggrieved or potentially aggrieved by a violation of Section 54 or 54.1 of this code, Chapter 7 (commencing with Section 4450) of Division 5 of Title 1 of the Government Code, or Part 5.5 (commencing with Section 19955) of Division 13 of the Health and Safety Code may bring an action to enjoin the violation. The prevailing party in the action shall be entitled to recover reasonable attorney's fees. **Leg.H.** Added Stats 1974 ch 1443 §1.

Prior Law: Former §55, similar to present Fam C §300, was enacted 1872, amended Stats 1895 ch 129 §1, Stats 1945 ch 213 §1, and repealed Stats 1969 ch 1608 §3, operative January 1, 1970.

§55.1. Standing to bring action to enjoin violation

In addition to any remedies available under the federal Americans with Disabilities Act of 1990, Public Law 101-336 (42 U.S.C. Sec. 12102), or other provisions of law, the district attorney, the city attorney, the Department of Rehabilitation acting through the Attorney General, or the Attorney General may bring an action to enjoin any violation of Section 54 or 54.1. **Leg.H.** Added Stats 1976 ch 869 §1. Amended Stats 1994 ch 1257 §9 (SB 1240).

§55.2. Actions requiring copy of petition and brief to be served on State Solicitor General

If a violation of Section 54, 54.1, 54.2, or 54.3 is alleged or the application or construction of any of these sections is in issue in any proceeding in the Supreme Court of California, a state court of appeal, or the appellate division of a superior court, each party shall serve a copy of the party's brief or petition and brief, on the State Solicitor General at the Office of the Attorney General. No brief may be accepted for filing unless the proof of service shows service on the State Solicitor General. Any party failing to comply with this requirement shall be given a reasonable opportunity to cure the failure before the court imposes any sanction and, in that instance, the court shall allow the Attorney General reasonable additional time to file a brief in the matter. **Leg.H.** Added Stats 2002 ch 244 §2 (AB 2524).

§55.3. Construction-related accessibility claims; Demand for money or complaint made by attorney; Forms

(a) For purposes of this section, the following apply:

(1) "Complaint" means a civil complaint that is filed or is to be filed with a court and is sent to or served upon a defendant on the basis of one or more construction-related accessibility claims, as defined in this section.

(2) "Construction-related accessibility claim" means any claim of a violation of any construction-related accessibility standard, as defined by paragraph (6) of subdivision (a) of Section 55.52, with respect to a place of public accommodation. "Construction-related accessibility claim" does not include a claim of interference with housing within the meaning of paragraph (2) of subdivision (b) of Section 54.1, or any claim of interference caused by something other than the construction-related accessibility condition of the property, including, but not limited to, the conduct of any person.

(3) "Demand for money" means a prelitigation written document or oral statement that is provided or issued to a building owner or tenant, or the owner's or tenant's agent or employee, that does all of the following:

(A) Alleges that the site is in violation of one or more construction-related accessibility standards, as defined in paragraph (6) of subdivision (a) of Section 55.52, or alleges one or more construction-related accessibility claims, as defined in paragraph (2).

(B) Contains or makes a request or demand for money or an offer or agreement to accept money.

(C) Is provided or issued whether or not the attorney intends to file a complaint, or eventually files a complaint, in state or federal court.

(4) "Demand letter" means a prelitigation written document that is provided to a building owner or tenant, or the owner's or tenant's agent or employee, that alleges the site is in violation of one or more construction-related accessibility standards, as defined in paragraph (6) of subdivision (a) of Section 55.52, or alleges one or more construction-related accessibility claims, as defined in paragraph (2), and is provided whether or not the attorney intends to file a complaint, or eventually files a complaint, in state or federal court.

(b) An attorney shall provide the following items with each demand letter or complaint sent to or served upon a defendant or potential defendant alleging a construction-related accessibility claim:

(1) A written advisory on the form described in subparagraph (B), or, until that form is available, on a separate page or pages that are clearly distinguishable from the demand letter or complaint. The advisory shall not be required in subsequent communications following the initial demand letter or initial complaint unless a new construction-related accessibility claim is asserted in the subsequent demand letter or amended complaint.

(A) The advisory shall state as follows:

STATE LAW REQUIRES THAT YOU GET THIS IMPORTANT ADVISORY INFORMATION FOR BUILDING OWNERS AND TENANTS

This information is available in English, Spanish, Chinese, Vietnamese, and Korean through the Judicial Council of California. Persons with visual impairments can get assistance in viewing this form through the Judicial Council Internet Web site at www.courts.ca.gov.

California law requires that you receive this information because the demand letter or court complaint you received with this document claims that your building or property does not comply with one or more existing construction-related accessibility laws or regulations protecting the civil rights of persons with disabilities to access public places.

YOU HAVE IMPORTANT LEGAL OBLIGATIONS. Compliance with disability access laws is a serious and significant responsibility that applies to all California building owners and tenants with buildings open for business to the public. You may obtain information about your legal obligations and how to comply with disability access laws through the Division of the State Architect at www.dgs.ca.gov. Information is also available from the California Commission on Disability Access at www.ccda.ca.gov/guide.htm.

YOU HAVE IMPORTANT LEGAL RIGHTS. The allegations made in the accompanying demand letter or court complaint do not mean that you are required to pay any money unless and until a court finds you liable. Moreover, RECEIPT OF A DEMAND LETTER OR COURT COMPLAINT AND THIS ADVISORY DOES NOT NECESSARILY MEAN YOU WILL BE FOUND LIABLE FOR ANYTHING. You will have the right if you are later sued to fully present your explanation why you believe you have not in fact violated disability access laws or have corrected the violation or violations giving rise to the claim.

You have the right to seek assistance or advice about this demand letter or court complaint from any person of your choice. If you have insurance, you may also wish to contact your insurance provider. Your best interest may be served by seeking legal advice or representation from an attorney, but you may also represent yourself and file the necessary court papers to protect your interests if you are served with a court complaint. If you have hired an attorney to represent you, you should immediately notify your attorney.

If a court complaint has been served on you, you will get a separate advisory notice with the complaint advising you of special options and procedures available to you under certain conditions.

ADDITIONAL THINGS YOU SHOULD KNOW:

ATTORNEY MISCONDUCT. Except for limited circumstances, state law generally requires that a prelitigation demand letter from an attorney MAY NOT MAKE A REQUEST OR DEMAND FOR MONEY OR AN OFFER OR AGREEMENT TO ACCEPT MONEY. Moreover, a demand letter from an attorney MUST INCLUDE THE ATTORNEY'S STATE BAR LICENSE NUMBER.

If you believe the attorney who provided you with this notice and prelitigation demand letter is not complying with state law, you may send a copy of the demand letter you received from the attorney to the State Bar of California by facsimile transmission to 1-415-538-2171, or by mail to the State Bar of California, 180 Howard Street, San Francisco, CA, 94105, Attention: Professional Competence.

REDUCING YOUR DAMAGES. If you are a small business owner and correct all of the construction-related violations that are the basis of the complaint against you within 30 days of being served with the complaint, you may qualify for reduced damages. You may wish to consult an attorney to obtain legal advice. You may also wish to contact the California Commission on Disability Access for additional information about the rights and obligations of business owners.

COMMERCIAL TENANT. If you are a commercial tenant, you may not be responsible for ensuring that some or all portions of the premises you lease for your business, including common areas such as parking lots, are accessible to the public because those areas may be the responsibility of your landlord. You may want to refer to your lease agreement and consult with an attorney or contact your landlord, to determine if your landlord is responsible for maintaining and improving some or all of the areas you lease.

(B) On or before July 1, 2016, the Judicial Council shall update the advisory form that may be used by an attorney to comply with the requirements of subparagraph (A). The advisory form shall be in substantially the same format and include all of the text set forth in subparagraph (A). The advisory form shall be available in English, Spanish, Chinese, Vietnamese, and Korean, and shall include a statement that the advisory form is available in additional languages, and the Judicial Council Internet Web site address where the different versions of the advisory form are located. The advisory form shall include Internet Web site information for the Division of the State Architect and the California Commission on Disability Access.

(2) A verified answer form developed by the Judicial Council, which allows a defendant to respond to the complaint in the event a complaint is filed.

(A) The answer form shall be written in plain language and allow the defendant to state any relevant information affecting the defendant's liability or damages including, but not limited to, the following:

(i) Specific denials of the allegations in the complaint, including whether the plaintiff has demonstrated that he or she was denied full and equal access to the place of public accommodation on a particular occasion pursuant to Section 55.56.

(ii) Potential affirmative defenses available to the defendant, including:

(I) An assertion that the defendant's landlord is responsible for ensuring that some or all of the property leased by the defendant, including the areas at issue in the complaint, are accessible to the public. The defendant shall provide facts supporting that assertion, and the name and contact information of the defendant's landlord.

(II) Any other affirmative defense the defendant wishes to assert.

(iii) A request to meet in person at the subject premises, if the defendant qualifies for an early evaluation conference pursuant to Section 55.54.

(iv) Any other information that the defendant believes is relevant to his or her potential liability or damages, including that the defendant qualifies for reduced damages pursuant to paragraph (1) or (2) of subdivision (f) of Section 55.56, and, if so, any facts supporting that assertion.

(B) The answer form shall provide instructions to a defendant who wishes to file the form as an answer to the complaint. The form shall also notify the defendant that he or she may use the completed form as an informal response to a demand letter or for settlement discussion purposes.

(C) On or before July 1, 2016, the Judicial Council shall adopt the answer form that may be used by an attorney to comply with the requirements of this paragraph, and shall post the answer form on the Judicial Council Internet Web site.

(c) Subdivision (b) applies only to a demand letter or complaint made by an attorney. This section does not affect the right to file a civil complaint under any other law or regulation protecting the physical access rights of persons with disabilities. Additionally, this section does not require a party to provide or send a demand letter to another party before proceeding against that party with a civil complaint.

(d) This section does not apply to an action brought by the Attorney General or any district attorney, city attorney, or county counsel. **Leg.H.** Added Stats 2008 ch 549 §2 (SB 1608), effective January 1, 2009. Amended Stats 2011 ch 419 §2 (SB 384), effective January 1, 2012; Stats 2012 ch 162 §9 (SB 1171), effective January 1, 2013, ch 383 §3 (SB 1186), effective September 19, 2012 (ch 383 prevails); Stats 2015 ch 755 §1 (AB 1521), effective October 10, 2015.

2009 Note: The conditions of Stats 2008 ch 549 §12 were met as stated in a letter dated October 13, 2009. It is reproduced below:

October 13, 2009

Honorable Ellen Corbett, Chair
Senate Committee on Judiciary

Honorable Ronald M. George, Chair
Judicial Council of California

Honorable Mike Feuer, Chair
Assembly Committee on Judiciary

Mr. Howard Miller, President
State Bar of California

California Commission on Disability Access

Pursuant to Chapter 549, Statutes of 2008 (SB 1608, Corbett), specific activities associated with disability access shall only occur upon a declaration from the Director of Finance that the California Commission on Disability Access (Commission) has been funded and has commenced operations.

Chapter 549 appropriated $80,000 General Fund for the Commission which became available on May 1, 2009. The Commission members have been appointed and the first Commission meeting is scheduled to occur on October 19, 2009. As such, the conditions of Chapter 549 have been met.

Furthermore, as required by statute, this notice shall be posted on the Internet websites of the Department of Finance, the Division of the State Architect, and the Commission.

If you have any questions or need additional information regarding this matter, please contact Kristin Shelton, Principal Program Budget Analyst, at (916) 445-8913.

MICHAEL C. GENEST
Director
By:
/s/ Ana J. Matosantos
ANA J. MATOSANTOS
Chief Deputy Director
cc: Mr. David Thorman, Director, State Architect of California
Mr. Dave Walls, Director, Building Standards Commission
Ms. Mary Ann Dewitt, Budget Officer, Department of General Services
icc: CAPOFC, JERUE, MARTINEZ, SHELTON, WHITE

2008 Note: (a) Sections 2, 3, and 4 of Stats 2008 ch 549 (SB 1608) shall become operative only upon issuance of a notice by the Director of Finance declaring that the California Commission on Disability Access has been funded and has commenced operations.

(b) If the commission loses funding, or for any other reason ceases operations, both of the following shall apply:

(1) Sections 55.51 and 55.52, subdivision (c) of Section 55.53, and subdivision (a) of Section 55.54 of the Civil Code, as added by Section 3 of this act, shall become inoperative.

(2) The remaining provisions of Section 55.54 shall remain operative as follows:

(A) Subdivisions (j) and (k) shall have general application.

(B) The remaining subdivisions shall be available only to a defendant in a construction-related accessibility claim relating to a place of public accommodation for which a CASp inspection and report was obtained prior to the date of the commission ceasing operations.

(c) If the commission loses funding or ceases operations for any other reason on or before January 1, 2014, Sections 55.55 and 55.56 of the Civil Code, as added by Section 4 of this act shall become inoperative on the date the commission ceases operations, except as to a construction-related accessibility claim that was filed before the date the commission ceased operations.

(d) The commission shall issue a notice of its date of ceasing operation upon the occurrence of that event. The Director of Finance also shall issue a notice within 30 days of the commission losing its funding or ceasing operations.

(e) Any notice required under this section shall be sent to the chairs of the Committee on Judiciary of the Senate and the Assembly, the Judicial Council, and the State Bar of California, and posted on the respective Internet Web sites of the Department of Finance, the Division of the State Architect, and the Commission on Disability Access. Stats 2008 ch 549 (SB 1608) §12.

§55.31. Demand letter alleging construction-related accessibility claim; Demand for money; Violation

(a) Commencing January 1, 2013, a demand letter alleging a construction-related accessibility claim, as defined in subdivision (a) of Section 55.3, shall state facts sufficient to allow a reasonable person to identify the basis of the violation or violations supporting the claim, including all of the following:

(1) A plain language explanation of the specific access barrier or barriers the individual encountered, or by which the individual alleges he or she was deterred, with sufficient information about the location of the barrier to enable a reasonable person to identify the access barrier.

(2) The way in which the barrier encountered interfered with the individual's full and equal use or access, or in which it deterred the individual, on each particular occasion.

(3) The date or dates of each particular occasion on which the individual encountered the specific access barrier, or on which he or she was deterred.

(b) A demand letter may offer prelitigation settlement negotiations, but shall not include a request or demand for money or an offer or agreement to accept money.

(1) With respect to potential monetary damages for an alleged construction-related accessibility claim or claims, a demand letter shall not

state any specific potential monetary liability for any asserted claim or claims, and may only state: "The property owner or tenant, or both, may be civilly liable for actual and statutory damages for a violation of a construction-related accessibility requirement."

(2) Notwithstanding any other law, a demand letter meeting the requirements of this section shall be deemed to satisfy the requirements for prelitigation notice of a potential claim when prelitigation notice is required by statute or common law for an award of attorney's fees.

(3) This subdivision and subdivision (a) do not apply to a demand for money, which is governed by subdivision (c).

(c) An attorney, or a person acting at the direction of an attorney, shall not issue a demand for money as defined in subdivision (a) of Section 55.3. This subdivision does not apply to a demand letter as defined in subdivision (a) of Section 55.3.

(d)(1) A violation of subdivision (b) or (c) constitutes cause for the imposition of discipline of an attorney. Subdivisions (b) and (c) do not prohibit an attorney from presenting a settlement figure or specification of damages in response to a request from the building owner or tenant, or the owner's or tenant's authorized agent or employee, following a demand letter provided pursuant to Section 55.3.

(2) Any liability for a violation of subdivision (c) is as provided in paragraph (1) of this subdivision. A violation of subdivision (c) does not create a new cause of action.

(e) Subdivision (c) does not prohibit any prelitigation settlement discussion of liability for damages and attorney's fees that occurs after a written or oral agreement is reached between the parties for the repair or correction of the alleged violation or violations of a construction-related accessibility standard.

(f) Subdivision (c) shall not apply to a claim involving physical injury and resulting special damages, but a demand for money relating to that claim that is sent shall otherwise comply with the requirements of subdivision (a) and Section 55.32.

(g) Nothing in this section shall apply to a demand or statement of alleged damages made in a prelitigation claim presented to a governmental entity as required by state or federal law, including, but not limited to, claims made under Part 3 (commencing with Section 900) of Division 3.6 of the Government Code.

(h) If subdivision (c) is not operative or becomes inoperative for any reason, the requirements of subdivision (a) and Section 55.32 shall apply to any written demand for money. **Leg.H.** Added Stats 2012 ch 383 §4 (SB 1186), effective September 19, 2012.

2012 Note: The Legislature finds and declares that a very small number of plaintiffs' attorneys have been abusing the right of petition under Sections 52 and 54.3 of the Civil Code by issuing a demand for money to a California business owner that demands the owner pay a quick settlement of the attorney's alleged claim under those laws or else incur greater liability and legal costs if a lawsuit is filed. These demands for money allege one or more, but frequently multiple, claims for asserted violations of a construction-related accessibility standard and often demand a quick money settlement based on the alleged multiple claims without seeking and obtaining actual repair or correction of the alleged violations on the site. These "pay me now or pay me more" demands are used to scare businesses into paying quick settlements that only financially enrich the attorney and claimant and do not promote accessibility either for the claimant or the disability community as a whole. These practices, often involving a series of demand for money letters sent to numerous businesses, do not promote compliance with the accessibility requirements and erode public support for and confidence in our laws. Therefore, the Legislature finds and declares that it is necessary and appropriate to enact Sections 55.31 and 55.32 of the Civil Code, and Section 425.50 of the Code of Civil Procedure to protect the public's confidence and support of the right to petition under Sections 52 and 54.3 of the Civil Code. Stats 2012 ch 383 (SB 1186) §24.

§55.32. Requirements for attorney sending demand letter or serving complaint; Violation; Report

(a) An attorney who provides a demand letter, as defined in subdivision (a) of Section 55.3, shall do all of the following:

(1) Include the attorney's State Bar license number in the demand letter.

(2) Within five business days of providing the demand letter, send a copy of the demand letter, and submit information about the demand letter in a standard format specified by the California Commission on Disability Access on the commission's internet website pursuant to Section 14985.8 of the Government Code, to the commission.

(b) An attorney who sends or serves a complaint, as defined in subdivision (a) of Section 55.3, or a complaint alleging that an internet website is not accessible, shall do both of the following:

(1) Send a copy of the complaint and submit information about the complaint in a standard format specified by the California Commission on Disability Access on the commission's internet website pursuant to Section 14985.8 of the Government Code to the commission within five business days of sending or serving the complaint.

(2) Notify the California Commission on Disability Access within five business days of judgment, settlement, or dismissal of the claim or claims alleged in the complaint of the following information in a standard format specified by the commission on the commission's internet website pursuant to Section 14985.8 of the Government Code:

(A) The date of the judgment, settlement, or dismissal.

(B) Whether or not the construction-related accessibility violations or accessibility violations related to an internet website alleged in the complaint were remedied in whole or in part after the plaintiff filed a complaint or provided a demand letter, as defined by Section 55.3.

(C) If the construction-related accessibility violations or accessibility violations related to an internet website alleged in the complaint were not remedied in whole or in part after the plaintiff filed a complaint or provided a demand letter, as defined by Section 55.3, whether or not another favorable result was achieved after the plaintiff filed the complaint or provided the demand letter.

(D) Whether or not the defendant submitted an application for an early evaluation conference and stay pursuant to Section 55.54, whether the defendant requested a site inspection of an alleged construction-related accessibility violation, the date of any early evaluation conference, and the date of any site inspection of an alleged construction-related accessibility violation.

(c) A violation of paragraph (2) of subdivision (a) or subdivision (b) shall constitute cause for the imposition of discipline of an attorney if a copy of the demand letter, complaint, or notification of a case outcome is not sent to the California Commission on Disability Access in the standard format specified on the commission's internet website pursuant to Section 14985.8 of the Government Code within five business days. In the event the State Bar receives information indicating that an attorney has failed to send a copy of the demand letter, complaint, or notification of a case outcome to the California Commission on Disability Access in the standard format specified on the commission's internet website pursuant to Section 14985.8 of the Government Code within five business days, the State Bar shall investigate to determine whether paragraph (2) of subdivision (a) or subdivision (b) has been violated.

(d) Notwithstanding subdivisions (a) and (b), an attorney is not required to send to the California Commission on Disability Access a copy of any subsequent demand letter or amended complaint in the same dispute following the initial demand letter or complaint, unless that subsequent demand letter or amended complaint alleges a new construction-related accessibility claim.

(e) A demand letter or notification of a case outcome sent to the California Commission on Disability Access shall be for the informational purposes of Section 14985.8 of the Government Code. A demand letter received by the State Bar from the recipient of the demand letter shall be reviewed by the State Bar to determine whether subdivision (b) or (c) of Section 55.31 has been violated.

(f)(1) Notwithstanding Section 10231.5 of the Government Code, [1] and annually as part of the Annual Discipline Report, [2] the State Bar shall report to the Legislature and the Chairs of the Senate and Assembly Judiciary Committees, both of the following with respect to demand letters received by the State Bar:

(A) The number of investigations opened to date on a suspected violation of subdivision (b) or (c) of Section 55.31.

(B) Whether any disciplinary action resulted from the investigation, and the results of that disciplinary action.

(2) A report to be submitted pursuant to this subdivision shall be submitted in compliance with Section 9795 of the Government Code.

(g) The California Commission on Disability Access shall review and report on the demand letters, complaints, and notifications of case outcomes it receives as provided in Section 14985.8 of the Government Code.

(h) The expiration of any ground for discipline of an attorney shall not affect the imposition of discipline for any act prior to the expiration. An act or omission that constituted cause for imposition of discipline of an attorney when committed or omitted prior to January 1, 2019, shall continue to constitute cause for the imposition of discipline of that attorney on and after January 1, 2019.

(i) Paragraph (2) of subdivision (a) and subdivision (b) shall not apply to a demand letter or complaint sent or filed by an attorney employed or retained by a qualified legal services project or a qualified support center, as defined in Section 6213 of the Business and Professions Code, when acting within the scope of employment in asserting a construction-related accessibility claim. The Legislature finds and declares that qualified legal services projects and support centers are extensively regulated by the State Bar of California, and that there is no evidence of any abusive use of demand letters or complaints by these organizations. The Legislature further finds that, in light of the evidence of the extraordinarily small number of construction-related accessibility cases brought by regulated legal services programs, and given the resources of those programs, exempting regulated legal services programs from the requirements of this section to report to the California Commission on Disability Access will not affect the purpose of the reporting to, and tabulation by, the commission of all other construction-related accessibility claims. **Leg.H.** Added Stats 2012 ch 383 §6 (SB 1186), effective September 19, 2012, operative January 1, 2016. Amended Stats 2015 ch 755 §3 (AB 1521), effective October 10, 2015, operative January 1, 2019; Stats 2016 ch 872 §2 (AB 54), effective January 1, 2017, operative January 1, 2019; Stats 2018 ch 659 §147 (AB 3249), effective January 1, 2019, operative January 1, 2020; Stats 2020 ch 36 §11 (AB 3364), effective January 1, 2021; Stats 2022 ch 897 §1 (AB 2917), effective January 1, 2023; Stats 2024 ch 227 §27 (AB 3279), effective January 1, 2025.

§55.32. 2024 Deletes. [1] on or before April 30, 2019, **[2]** no later than April 30 thereafter,

2015 Note: The Legislature finds and declares that Section 3 of this act limits the public's right of access to public documents within the meaning of Section 3 of Article I of the California Constitution. Pursuant to that constitutional provision, the Legislature makes the following findings to demonstrate the interest and the need for protecting that interest:

(a) The interest protected by this limitation is the privacy rights of litigants.

(b) The need for protecting those interests is to preclude the chilling effect on litigation if public disclosure were required. Stats 2015 ch 755 (AB 1521) §9.

2012 Note: For legislative findings and declarations of Stats 2012 ch 383 (SB 1186), see the 2012 Note following §55.31.

Prior Law: Former CC §55.32, similar to the present section, was added Stats 2012 ch 383 §5 (SB 1186), effective September 19, 2012, operative January 1, 2013, repealed January 1, 2016, amended Stats 2015 ch 755 §2 (AB 1521), effective October 10, 2015, repealed January 1, 2019, Stats 2016 ch 872 §1 (AB 54), effective January 1, 2017, and repealed January 1, 2019, by its own terms.

PART 2.52
CONSTRUCTION-RELATED ACCESSIBILITY STANDARDS COMPLIANCE

Citation of part; Applicability [Operative term contingent]. §55.51.
Definitions [Operative term contingent]. §55.52.
Duties of certified access specialist; Conflict or difference between state and federal provision; Notice to property owner and tenant; Posting of disability access inspection certificate. §55.53.
Service of notice of stay and early evaluation conference; Application; Notice of substitution of counsel; Court order; Construction of part; Duties of Judicial Council. §55.54.
Mandatory evaluation conference; Scheduling; Purpose. §55.545.

§55.51. Citation of part; Applicability [Operative term contingent]

This part shall be known, and may be cited, as the Construction-Related Accessibility Standards Compliance Act. Notwithstanding any other provision of law, the provisions of this part shall apply to any construction-related accessibility claim, as defined in this part, including, but not limited to, any claim brought under Section 51, 54, 54.1, or 55. **Leg.H.** Added Stats 2008 ch 549 §3 (SB 1608), effective January 1, 2009.

2009 Note: See 2009 Note following §55.54 explaining when Part 2.52 (§55.51-55.54) became operative.

2008 Note: See Note following §55.54 explaining when Part 2.52 (§55.51-55.54) becomes operative and §12(b)(1) Note explaining when this section becomes inoperative.

§55.52. Definitions [Operative term contingent]

(a) For purposes of this part, the following definitions apply:

(1) "Construction-related accessibility claim" means any civil claim in a civil action with respect to a place of public accommodation, including, but not limited to, a claim brought under Section 51, 54, 54.1, or 55, based wholly or in part on an alleged violation of any construction-related accessibility standard, as defined in paragraph (6).

(2) "Application for stay and early evaluation conference" means an application to be filed with the court that meets the requirements of subdivision (c) of Section 55.54.

(3) "Certified access specialist" or "CASp" means any person who has been certified pursuant to Section 4459.5 of the Government Code.

(4) "Meets applicable standards" means the site was inspected by a CASp and determined to meet all applicable construction-related accessibility standards pursuant to paragraph (1) of subdivision (a) of Section 55.53. A site that is "CASp inspected" on or before the effective date of the amendments made to this section by Senate Bill 1186 of the 2011–12 Regular Session of the Legislature means that the site "meets applicable standards."

(5) "Inspected by a CASp" means the site was inspected by a CASp and is pending a determination by the CASp that the site meets applicable construction-related accessibility standards pursuant to paragraph (2) of subdivision (a) of Section 55.53. A site that is "CASp determination pending" on or before the effective date of the amendments made to this section by Senate Bill 1186 of the 2011–12 Regular Session of the Legislature means that the site was "inspected by a CASp."

(6) "Construction-related accessibility standard" means a provision, standard, or regulation under state or federal law requiring compliance with standards for making new construction and existing facilities accessible to persons with disabilities, including, but not limited to, any provision, standard, or regulation set forth in Section 51, 54, 54.1, or 55 of this code, Section 19955.5 of the Health and Safety Code, the California Building Standards Code (Title 24 of the California Code of Regulations), the federal Americans with Disabilities Act of 1990 (Public Law 101-336; 42 U.S.C. Sec. 12101 et seq.), and the federal Americans with Disabilities Act Accessibility Guidelines (Appendix A to Part 36, of Title 28, of the Code of Federal Regulations).

(7) "Place of public accommodation" has the same meaning as "public accommodation," as set forth in Section 12181(7) of Title 42 of the United States Code and the federal regulations adopted pursuant to that section.

(8) "Qualified defendant" means a defendant in an action that includes a construction-related accessibility claim that is asserted against a place of public accommodation that met the requirements of "meets applicable standards" or "inspected by a CASp" prior to the date the defendant was served with the summons and complaint in that action. To be a qualified defendant, the defendant is not required to have been the party who hired any CASp, so long as the basis of the alleged liability of the defendant is a construction-related accessibility claim. To determine whether a defendant is a qualified defendant, the court need not make a finding that the place of public accommodation complies with all applicable construction-related accessibility standards as a matter of law. The court need only determine that the place of public accommodation has a status of "meets applicable standards" or "inspected by a CASp."

(9) "Site" means a place of public accommodation.

(b) Unless otherwise indicated, terms used in this part relating to civil procedure have the same meanings that those terms have in the Code of Civil Procedure. **Leg.H.** Added Stats 2008 ch 549 §3 (SB 1608), effective January 1, 2009. Amended Stats 2012 ch 383 §7 (SB 1186), effective September 19, 2012.

2009 Note: See 2009 Note following §55.54 explaining when Part 2.52 (commencing with §55.51) became operative.

2008 Note: See Note following §55.54 explaining when Part 2.52 (commencing with §55.51) became operative and §12(b)(1) Note explaining when this section becomes inoperative.

§55.53. Duties of certified access specialist; Conflict or difference between state and federal provision; Notice to property owner and tenant; Posting of disability access inspection certificate

(a) For purposes of this part, a certified access specialist shall, upon completion of the inspection of a site, comply with the following:

(1) For a meets applicable standards site, if the CASp determines the site meets all applicable construction-related accessibility standards, the CASp shall provide a written inspection report to the requesting party that includes both of the following:

(A) An identification and description of the inspected structures and areas of the site.

(B) A signed and dated statement that includes both of the following:

(i) A statement that, in the opinion of the CASp, the inspected structures and areas of the site meet construction-related accessibility standards. The statement shall clearly indicate whether the determination of the CASp includes an assessment of readily achievable barrier removal.

(ii) If corrections were made as a result of the CASp inspection, an itemized list of all corrections and dates of completion.

(2) For an inspected by a CASp site, if the CASp determines that corrections are needed to the site in order for the site to meet all applicable construction-related accessibility standards, the CASp shall provide a signed and dated written inspection report to the requesting party that includes all of the following:

(A) An identification and description of the inspected structures and areas of the site.

(B) The date of the inspection.

(C) A statement that, in the opinion of the CASp, the inspected structures and areas of the site need correction to meet construction-related accessibility standards. This statement shall clearly indicate whether the determination of the CASp includes an assessment of readily achievable barrier removal.

(D) An identification and description of the structures or areas of the site that need correction and the correction needed.

(E) A schedule of completion for each of the corrections within a reasonable timeframe.

(3) The CASp shall provide, within 30 days of the date of the inspection of a business that qualifies for the provisions of subparagraph (A) of paragraph (3) of subdivision (g) of Section 55.56, a copy of a report prepared pursuant to that subparagraph to the business.

(4) The CASp shall file, within 10 days of inspecting a business pursuant to subparagraph (A) of paragraph (3) of subdivision (g) of Section 55.56, a notice with the State Architect for listing on the State Architect's Internet Web site, as provided by subdivision (d) of Section 4459.7 of the Government Code, indicating that the CASp has inspected

the business, the name and address of the business, the date of the filing, the date of the inspection of the business, the name and license number of the CASp, and a description of the structure or area inspected by the CASp.

(5) The CASp shall post the notice described in paragraph (4), in a form prescribed by the State Architect, in a conspicuous location within five feet of all public entrances to the building on the date of the inspection and instruct the business to keep it in place until the earlier of either of the following:

(A) One hundred twenty days after the date of the inspection.

(B) The date when all of the construction-related violations in the structure or area inspected by the CASp are corrected.

(b) For purposes of this section, in determining whether the site meets applicable construction-related accessibility standards when there is a conflict or difference between a state and federal provision, standard, or regulation, the state provision, standard, or regulation shall apply unless the federal provision, standard, or regulation is more protective of accessibility rights.

(c) Every CASp who conducts an inspection of a place of public accommodation shall, upon completing the inspection of the site, provide the building owner or tenant who requested the inspection with the following notice, which the State Architect shall make available as a form on the State Architect's Internet Web site:

NOTICE TO PRIVATE PROPERTY OWNER/TENANT:

YOU ARE ADVISED TO KEEP IN YOUR RECORDS ANY WRITTEN INSPECTION REPORT AND ANY OTHER DOCUMENTATION CONCERNING YOUR PROPERTY SITE THAT IS GIVEN TO YOU BY A CERTIFIED ACCESS SPECIALIST.

IF YOU BECOME A DEFENDANT IN A LAWSUIT THAT INCLUDES A CLAIM CONCERNING A SITE INSPECTED BY A CERTIFIED ACCESS SPECIALIST, YOU MAY BE ENTITLED TO A COURT STAY (AN ORDER TEMPORARILY STOPPING ANY LAWSUIT) OF THE CLAIM AND AN EARLY EVALUATION CONFERENCE.

IN ORDER TO REQUEST THE STAY AND EARLY EVALUATION CONFERENCE, YOU WILL NEED TO VERIFY THAT A CERTIFIED ACCESS SPECIALIST HAS INSPECTED THE SITE THAT IS THE SUBJECT OF THE CLAIM. YOU WILL ALSO BE REQUIRED TO PROVIDE THE COURT AND THE PLAINTIFF WITH THE COPY OF A WRITTEN INSPECTION REPORT BY THE CERTIFIED ACCESS SPECIALIST, AS SET FORTH IN CIVIL CODE SECTION 55.54. THE APPLICATION FORM AND INFORMATION ON HOW TO REQUEST A STAY AND EARLY EVALUATION CONFERENCE MAY BE OBTAINED AT www.courts.ca.gov/selfhelp-start.htm.

YOU ARE ENTITLED TO REQUEST, FROM A CERTIFIED ACCESS SPECIALIST WHO HAS CONDUCTED AN INSPECTION OF YOUR PROPERTY, A WRITTEN INSPECTION REPORT AND OTHER DOCUMENTATION AS SET FORTH IN CIVIL CODE SECTION 55.53. YOU ARE ALSO ENTITLED TO REQUEST THE ISSUANCE OF A DISABILITY ACCESS INSPECTION CERTIFICATE, WHICH YOU MAY POST ON YOUR PROPERTY.

(d)(1) Commencing July 1, 2010, a local agency shall employ or retain at least one building inspector who is a certified access specialist. The certified access specialist shall provide consultation to the local agency, permit applicants, and members of the public on compliance with state construction-related accessibility standards with respect to inspections of a place of public accommodation that relate to permitting, plan checks, or new construction, including, but not limited to, inspections relating to tenant improvements that may impact access. If a local agency employs or retains two or more certified access specialists to comply with this subdivision, at least one-half of the certified access specialists shall be building inspectors who are certified access specialists.

(2) Commencing January 1, 2014, a local agency shall employ or retain a sufficient number of building inspectors who are certified access specialists to conduct permitting and plan check services to review for compliance with state construction-related accessibility standards by a place of public accommodation with respect to new construction, including, but not limited to, projects relating to tenant improvements that may impact access. If a local agency employs or retains two or more certified access specialists to comply with this subdivision, at least one-half of the certified access specialists shall be building inspectors who are certified access specialists.

(3) If a permit applicant or member of the public requests consultation from a certified access specialist, the local agency may charge an amount limited to a reasonable hourly rate, an estimate of which shall be provided upon request in advance of the consultation. A local government may additionally charge or increase permitting, plan check, or inspection fees to the extent necessary to offset the costs of complying with this subdivision. Any revenues generated from an hourly or other charge or fee increase under this subdivision shall be used solely to offset the costs incurred to comply with this subdivision. A CASp inspection pursuant to subdivision (a) by a building inspector who is a certified access specialist shall be treated equally for legal and evidentiary purposes as an inspection conducted by a private CASp. Nothing in this subdivision shall preclude permit applicants or any other person with a legal interest in the property from retaining a private CASp at any time.

(e)(1) Every CASp who completes an inspection of a place of public accommodation shall, upon a determination that the site meets applicable standards pursuant to paragraph (1) of subdivision (a) or is inspected by a CASp pursuant to paragraph (2) of subdivision (a), provide the building owner or tenant requesting the inspection with a numbered disability access inspection certificate indicating that the site has undergone inspection by a certified access specialist. The disability access inspection certificate shall be dated and signed by the CASp inspector, and shall contain the inspector's name and license number. Upon issuance of a certificate, the CASp shall record the issuance of the numbered certificate, the name and address of the recipient, and the type of report issued pursuant to subdivision (a) in a record book the CASp shall maintain for that purpose.

(2) Beginning March 1, 2009, the State Architect shall make available for purchase by any local building department or CASp sequentially numbered disability access inspection certificates that are printed with a watermark or other feature to deter forgery and that comply with the information requirements specified in subdivision (a).

(3) The disability access inspection certificate may be posted on the premises of the place of public accommodation, unless, following the date of inspection, the inspected site has been modified or construction has commenced to modify the inspected site in a way that may impact compliance with construction-related accessibility standards.

(f) Nothing in this section or any other law is intended to require a property owner or tenant to hire a CASp. A property owner's or tenant's election not to hire a CASp shall not be admissible to prove that person's lack of intent to comply with the law. **Leg.H.** Added Stats 2008 ch 549 §3 (SB 1608), effective January 1, 2009. Amended Stats 2012 ch 383 §8 (SB 1186), effective September 19, 2012; Stats 2016 ch 13 §1 (SB 269), effective May 10, 2016.

2009 Note: See 2009 Note following §55.54 explaining when Part 2.52 (commencing with §55.51) became operative.

2008 Note: See Note following §55.54 explaining when Part 2.52 (commencing with §55.51) became operative and §12(b)(1) Note explaining when this section becomes inoperative.

§55.54. Service of notice of stay and early evaluation conference; Application; Notice of substitution of counsel; Court order; Construction of part; Duties of Judicial Council

(a)(1) An attorney who causes a summons and complaint to be served in an action that includes a construction-related accessibility claim, including, but not limited to, a claim brought under Section 51, 54, 54.1, or 55, shall, at the same time, cause to be served a copy of the application form specified in subdivision (c) and a copy of the following notice, including, until January 1, 2013, the bracketed text, to the defendant on separate papers that shall be served with the summons and complaint:

ADVISORY NOTICE TO DEFENDANT

YOU MAY BE ENTITLED TO ASK FOR A COURT STAY (AN ORDER TEMPORARILY STOPPING ANY LAWSUIT) AND EARLY EVALUATION CONFERENCE IN THIS LAWSUIT AND MAY BE ASSESSED REDUCED STATUTORY DAMAGES IF YOU MEET CERTAIN CONDITIONS.

If the construction-related accessibility claim pertains to a site that has a Certified Access Specialist (CASp) inspection report for that site, or to a site where new construction or improvement was approved after January 1, 2008, by the local building permit and inspection process, you may make an immediate request for a court stay and early evaluation conference in the construction-related accessibility claim by filing the attached application form with the court. You may be entitled to the court stay and early evaluation conference regarding the accessibility claim only if ALL of the statements in the application form applicable to you are true.

FURTHER, if you are a defendant described above (with a CASp inspection report or with new construction after January 1, 2008), and, to the best of your knowledge, there have been no modifications or alterations completed or commenced since the CASp report or building department approval of the new construction or improvement that impacted compliance with construction-related accessibility standards with respect to the plaintiff's claim, your liability for minimum statutory damages may be reduced to $1,000 for each offense, unless the violation was intentional, and if all construction-related accessibility violations giving rise to the claim are corrected within 60 days of being served with this complaint.

ALSO, if your business has been served with a complaint filed by a high-frequency litigant, as defined in subdivision (b) of Section 425.55 of the Code of Civil Procedure, asserting a construction-related accessibility claim, including, but not limited to, a claim brought under Section 51, 54, 54.1, or 55 of the Civil Code, you may also be entitled to a court stay and an early evaluation conference. If you choose to request a stay and early evaluation conference, you may also request to meet in person with the plaintiff and counsel for both parties, as well as experts if the parties so elect, at the subject premises no later than 30 days after issuance of the court order to jointly inspect the portions of the subject premises and review any conditions that are claimed to constitute a violation of a construction-related accessibility standard.

IN ADDITION, if your business is a small business that, over the previous three years, or the existence of the business if less than three years, employs 25 or fewer employees on average over that time period and meets specified gross receipts criteria, you may also be entitled to the court stay and early evaluation conference and your minimum statutory damages for each claim may be reduced to $2,000 for each offense, unless the violation was intentional, and if all the alleged construction-related accessibility violations are corrected within 30 days of being served with the complaint.

If you plan to correct the violations giving rise to the claim, you should take pictures and measurements or similar action to document the condition of the physical barrier asserted to be the basis for a violation before undertaking any corrective action in case a court needs to see the condition of a barrier before it was corrected.

The court will schedule the conference to be held within 70 days after you file the attached application form.

[If you are not a defendant with a CASp inspection report, until a form is adopted by the Judicial Council, you may use the attached form if you modify the form and supplement it with your declaration stating any one of the following:

(1) Until January 1, 2018, that the site's new construction or improvement on or after January 1, 2008, and before January 1, 2016, was approved pursuant to the local building permit and inspection process; that, to the best of your knowledge, there have been no modifications or alterations completed or commenced since the building department approval that impacted compliance with construction-related accessibility standards with respect to the plaintiff's claim; and that all violations giving rise to the claim have been corrected, or will be corrected within 60 days of the complaint being served.

(2) That the site's new construction or improvement passed inspection by a local building department inspector who is a certified access specialist; that, to the best of your knowledge, there have been no modifications or alterations completed or commenced since that inspection approval that impacted compliance with construction-related accessibility standards with respect to the plaintiff's claim; and that all violations giving rise to the claim have been corrected, or will be corrected within 60 days of the complaint being served.

(3) That your business is a small business with 25 or fewer employees and meets the gross receipts criteria set out in Section 55.56 of the Civil Code, and that all violations giving rise to the claim have been corrected, or will be corrected within 30 days of being served with the complaint.]

The court will also issue an immediate stay of the proceedings unless the plaintiff has obtained a temporary restraining order in the construction-related accessibility claim. You may obtain a copy of the application form, filing instructions, and additional information about the stay and early evaluation conference through the Judicial Council Internet Web site at www.courts.ca.gov/selfhelp-start.htm.

You may file the application after you are served with a summons and complaint, but no later than your first court pleading or appearance in this case, which is due within 30 days after you receive the summons and complaint. If you do not file the application, you will still need to file your reply to the lawsuit within 30 days after you receive the summons and complaint to contest it. You may obtain more information about how to represent yourself and how to file a reply without hiring an attorney at www.courts.ca.gov/selfhelp-start.htm.

You may file the application without the assistance of an attorney, but it may be in your best interest to immediately seek the assistance of an attorney experienced in disability access laws when you receive a summons and complaint. You may make an offer to settle the case, and it may be in your interest to put that offer in writing so that it may be considered under Section 55.55 of the Civil Code.

(2) An attorney who files a Notice of Substitution of Counsel to appear as counsel for a plaintiff who, acting in propria persona, had previously filed a complaint in an action that includes a construction-related accessibility claim, including, but not limited to, a claim brought under Section 51, 54, 54.1, or 55, shall, at the same time, cause to be served a copy of the application form specified in subdivision (c) and a copy of the notice specified in paragraph (1) upon the defendant on separate pages that shall be attached to the Notice of Substitution of Counsel.

(b)(1) Notwithstanding any other law, upon being served with a summons and complaint asserting a construction-related accessibility claim, including, but not limited to, a claim brought under Section 51, 54, 54.1, or 55, a qualified defendant, or other defendant as defined in paragraph (2), may file a request for a court stay and early evaluation conference in the proceedings of that claim prior to or simultaneous with that defendant's responsive pleading or other initial appearance in the action that includes the claim. If that defendant filed a timely request for stay and early evaluation conference before a responsive pleading was due, the period for filing a responsive pleading shall be tolled until the stay is lifted. Any responsive pleading filed simultaneously with a request for stay and early evaluation conference may be amended without prejudice, and the period for filing that amendment shall be tolled until the stay is lifted.

(2) This subdivision shall also apply to a defendant if any of the following apply:

(A) Until January 1, 2018, the site's new construction or improvement on or after January 1, 2008, and before January 1, 2016, was approved pursuant to the local building permit and inspection process, and the defendant declares with the application that, to the best of the defendant's knowledge, there have been no modifications or alterations completed or commenced since that approval that impacted compliance with construction-related accessibility standards with respect to the plaintiff's claim, and that all violations have been corrected, or will be corrected within 60 days of being served with the complaint.

(B) The site's new construction or improvement was approved by a local public building department inspector who is a certified access specialist, and the defendant declares with the application that, to the best of the defendant's knowledge, there have been no modifications or alterations completed or commenced since that approval that impacted compliance with construction-related accessibility standards with respect to the plaintiff's claim, and that all violations have been corrected, or will be corrected within 60 days of being served with the complaint.

(C) The defendant is a small business described in subdivision (f) of Section 55.56, and the defendant declares with the application that all violations have been corrected, or will be corrected within 30 days of being served with the complaint.

(D) The defendant is a business that has been served with a complaint filed by a high-frequency litigant, as defined in subdivision (b) of Section 425.55 of the Code of Civil Procedure, asserting a construction-related accessibility claim, including, but not limited to, a claim brought under Section 51, 54, 54.1, or 55.

(3) Notwithstanding any other law, if the plaintiff had acted in propria persona in filing a complaint that includes a construction-related accessibility claim, including, but not limited to, a claim brought under Section 51, 54, 54.1, or 55, a qualified defendant, or a defendant described by paragraph (2), who is served with a Notice of Substitution of Counsel

shall have 30 days to file an application for a stay and an early evaluation conference. The application may be filed prior to or after the defendant's filing of a responsive pleading or other initial appearance in the action that includes the claim, except that an application may not be filed in a claim in which an early evaluation conference or settlement conference has already been held on the claim.

(c)(1) An application for an early evaluation conference and stay by a qualified defendant shall include a signed declaration that states both of the following:

(A) The site identified in the complaint has been CASp-inspected or meets applicable standards, or is CASp determination pending or has been inspected by a CASp, and if the site is CASp-inspected or meets applicable standards, there have been no modifications completed or commenced since the date of inspection that may impact compliance with construction-related accessibility standards to the best of the defendant's knowledge.

(B) An inspection report pertaining to the site has been issued by a CASp. The inspection report shall be provided to the court and the plaintiff at least 15 days prior to the court date set for the early evaluation conference.

(2) An application for an early evaluation conference and stay by a defendant described by subparagraph (A) of paragraph (2) of subdivision (b), which may be filed until January 1, 2018, shall include a signed declaration that states all of the following:

(A) The site's new construction or improvement was approved pursuant to the local building permit and inspection process on or after January 1, 2008, and before January 1, 2016.

(B) To the best of the defendant's knowledge there have been no modifications or alterations completed or commenced since that approval that impacted compliance with construction-related accessibility standards with respect to the plaintiff's claim.

(C) All construction-related violations giving rise to the claim have been corrected, or will be corrected within 60 days of the complaint being served upon the defendant.

(3) An application for an early evaluation conference and stay by a defendant described in subparagraph (B) of paragraph (2) of subdivision (b) shall include a signed declaration that states all of the following:

(A) The site's new construction or improvement was approved by a local building department inspector who is a certified access specialist.

(B) To the best of the defendant's knowledge there have been no modifications or alterations completed or commenced since that approval that impacted compliance with construction-related accessibility standards with respect to the plaintiff's claim.

(C) All construction related violations giving rise to the claim have been corrected, or will be corrected within 60 days of the complaint being served upon the defendant.

(4) An application for an early evaluation conference and stay by a defendant described by subparagraph (C) of paragraph (2) of subdivision (b) shall include the materials listed in paragraphs (5) and (6) of this subdivision, and shall include a signed declaration that states both of the following:

(A) The defendant is a small business that employs 25 or fewer employees and meets the gross receipts eligibility criteria provided in paragraph (2) of subdivision (f) of Section 55.56.

(B) All construction-related violations giving rise to the claim have been corrected, or will be corrected within 30 days of the complaint being served upon the defendant.

(5) An application for an early evaluation conference and stay by a small business defendant under paragraph (4) shall include evidence showing correction of all violations within 30 days of the service of the complaint and served upon the plaintiff with the reply unless the application is filed prior to completion of the corrections. In that event, the evidence shall be provided to the court and served upon the plaintiff within 10 days of the court order as provided in paragraph (4) of subdivision (d). This paragraph shall not be construed to extend the permissible time under subdivision (f) of Section 55.56 to make the corrections.

(6) An application for an early evaluation conference and stay by a small business defendant under paragraph (4) shall also include both of the following, which shall be confidential documents filed only with the court and not served upon or available to the plaintiff:

(A) Proof of the defendant's number of employees, as shown by wage report forms filed with the Employment Development Department.

(B) Proof of the defendant's average gross receipts for the previous three years, or for the existence of the business if less than three years, as shown by a federal or state tax document.

(7) An application for an early evaluation conference and stay by a defendant described by subparagraph (D) of paragraph (2) of subdivision (b) shall include a signed declaration that the defendant was served with a complaint filed by a high-frequency litigant, as defined in subdivision (b) of Section 425.55 of the Code of Civil Procedure, asserting a construction-related accessibility claim, including, but not limited to, a claim brought under Section 51, 54, 54.1, or 55.

(8) The following provisional request and notice forms may be used and filed by a qualified defendant until forms are adopted by the Judicial Council for those purposes pursuant to subdivision (*l*):

CONSTRUCTION-RELATED ACCESSIBILITY STANDARDS COMPLIANCE — Sec. 55.54

ATTORNEY OR PARTY WITHOUT ATTORNEY (Name, State Bar number if attorney, and address):	FOR COURT USE ONLY
TELEPHONE NO.: FAX NO. (Optional): E-MAIL ADDRESS (Optional): ATTORNEY FOR (Name):	

SUPERIOR COURT OF CALIFORNIA, COUNTY OF _____
STREET ADDRESS:
MAILING ADDRESS:
CITY AND ZIP CODE:
BRANCH NAME:

PLAINTIFF:
DEFENDANT:

DEFENDANT'S APPLICATION FOR STAY AND EARLY EVALUATION CONFERENCE PURSUANT TO CIVIL CODE SECTION 55.54 (CONSTRUCTION-RELATED ACCESSIBILITY CLAIM)	CASE NUMBER:

(Information about this application and the filing instructions may be obtained at http://www.courtinfo.ca.gov/selfhelp/.)

1. Defendant (name) _____ requests a stay of proceedings and early evaluation conference pursuant to Civil Code Section 55.54.

2. The complaint in this case alleges a construction-related accessibility claim as defined under Civil Code Section 55.52(a)(1).

3. The claim concerns a site that (check the box if the statement is true):
   a. _____ Has been inspected by a Certified Access Specialist (CASp) and determined to be CASp inspected or CASp determination pending and, if CASp inspected, there have been no modifications completed or commenced since the date of inspection that may impact compliance with construction-related accessibility standards to the best of defendant's knowledge; and
   b. _____ An inspection report by a Certified Access Specialist (CASp) relating to the site has been issued.
   (Both (a) and (b) must be met for the court to order a Stay and Early Evaluation Conference.)

4. I am requesting the court to:
   a. Stay the proceedings relating to the construction-related accessibility claim.
   b. Schedule an early evaluation conference.
   c. Order Defendant to file a confidential copy of the Certified Access Specialist (CASp) report with the court and serve a copy of the report on the Plaintiff at least fifteen (15) days before the Early Evaluation Conference date.
   d. Order Plaintiff to file the statement required by Civil Code Section 55.54(d)(6)(A)–(D) with the court and serve a copy of the statement on the Defendant at least fifteen (15) days before the date of the Early Evaluation Conference.

I declare under penalty of perjury under the laws of the State of California that the foregoing is true and correct.

Date:

_____   _____
(TYPE OR PRINT NAME OF DECLARANT)   (SIGNATURE OF DECLARANT)

_____
(TITLE OF DECLARANT)

DEFENDANT'S APPLICATION FOR EARLY EVALUATION CONFERENCE AND STAY OF PROCEEDINGS
(Construction-related Accessibility Claim)   Provisional Form

Sec. 55.54   CIVIL CODE   42

ATTORNEY OR PARTY WITHOUT ATTORNEY (Name, State Bar number if attorney, and address):	FOR COURT USE ONLY
TELEPHONE NO.: FAX NO. (Optional): E-MAIL ADDRESS (Optional): ATTORNEY FOR (Name):	
SUPERIOR COURT OF CALIFORNIA, COUNTY OF _____ STREET ADDRESS: MAILING ADDRESS: CITY AND ZIP CODE: BRANCH NAME:	
PLAINTIFF: DEFENDANT:	
NOTICE OF STAY OR PROCEEDINGS AND EARLY EVALUATION CONFERENCE (CONSTRUCTION-RELATED ACCESSIBILITY CLAIM)	CASE NUMBER:

Stay of Proceedings

For a period of 90 days from the date of the filing of this court notice, unless otherwise ordered by the court, the parties are stayed from taking any further action relating to the construction-related accessibility claim or claims in this case.

This stay does not apply to any construction-related accessibility claim in which the plaintiff has obtained temporary injunctive relief which is still in place.

Notice of Early Evaluation Conference

1. This action includes a construction-related accessibility claim under Civil Code Section 55.52(a)(1) or other provision of law.

2. A defendant has requested an early evaluation conference and a stay of proceedings under Civil Code Section 55.54.

3. The early evaluation conference is scheduled as follows:

    a. Date: Time: Dept: Room:

    b. The conference will be held at _____ the court address shown above, or _____ at:

4. The plaintiff and defendant shall attend with any other person needed for settlement of the case unless, with court approval, a party's disability requires the party's participation by a telephone appearance or other alternate means or through the personal appearance of an authorized representative.

5. The defendant that requested the conference and stay of proceedings must file with the court and serve on all parties a copy of the CASp report for the site that is the subject of the construction-related accessibility claim at least fifteen (15) days before the date set for the early evaluation conference. The CASp report is confidential and only available as set forth below and in Civil Code Section 55.54(d)(4).

6. The CASp report shall be marked "CONFIDENTIAL" and may be disclosed only to counsel, the parties to the action, the parties' attorneys, those individuals employed or retained by the attorneys to assist in the litigation, and insurance representatives or others involved in the evaluation and settlement of the case.

7. The plaintiff shall file with the court and serve on all parties at least fifteen (15) days before the date set for the early evaluation conference a statement of, to the extent known, all of the following:
    a. An itemized list of specific issues on the subject premises that are the basis of the claimed construction-related accessibility violations in the plaintiff's complaint;
    b. The amount of damages claimed;
    c. The amount of attorney's fees and costs incurred to date, if any, that are being claimed; and
    d. Any demand for settlement of the case in its entirety.

8. A copy of this Notice and Order and the Defendant's Application shall be served on the plaintiff or plaintiff's attorney by hand delivering it or mailing it to the address listed on the complaint on the same date that the court issues this Notice and Order of Stay of Proceedings and Early Evaluation Conference.

Date: _____   Clerk, by _____, Deputy

More information about this Notice and Order and the defendant's application, and instructions to assist plaintiff and defendants in complying with this Notice and Order, may be obtained at http://www.courtinfo.ca.gov/selfhelp/.)

Requests for Accommodation

Assistive listening systems, computer-assisted real-time captioning, or sign language interpreter services are available if you ask at least 5 days before the date on which you are to appear. Contact the clerk's office or go to www.courtinfo.ca.gov/forms for Request for Accommodations by Persons with Disabilities and Order (form MC-410). (Civil Code Section 54.8)

Proof of Service
(Required from Defendant Filing Application for Stay and Early Evaluation Conference)

I served a copy of the defendant's Application For Stay and Early Evaluation Conference Pursuant To Civil Code Section 55.54 and the court Notice and Order of Stay of Proceedings and Early Evaluation Conference (check one):

_____ On the Plaintiff's attorney

_____ On the Plaintiff who is not represented by an attorney

By hand delivering it or mailing it to the address listed on the complaint on the day the court issued this Notice and Order of Stay of Proceedings and Early Evaluation Conference.

I declare under penalty of perjury of the laws of the State of California that the foregoing is true and correct.

Date: _____

_____   _____
Type or Print Name   Signature

_____
Address of named person

NOTICE OF STAY OF PROCEEDINGS AND EARLY EVALUATION CONFERENCE
(Construction-related Accessibility Claim)   Provisional Form

(9) The provisional forms and any replacement Judicial Council forms shall include the defendant's declaration of proof of service of the application, the notice of the court's order, and the court's order pursuant to subdivision (d).

(d) Upon the filing of an application for stay and early evaluation conference by a qualified defendant, or a defendant described by paragraph (2) of subdivision (b), the court shall immediately issue an order that does all of the following:

(1) Grants a 90-day stay of the proceedings with respect to the construction-related accessibility claim, unless the plaintiff has obtained temporary injunctive relief that is still in place for the construction-related accessibility claim.

(2) Schedules a mandatory early evaluation conference for a date as soon as possible from the date of the order, but in no event later than 70 days after issuance of the order, and in no event earlier than 50 days after the filing of the request.

(3) Directs the parties, and any other person whose authority is required to negotiate and enter into settlement, to appear in person at the time set for the conference. Appearance by counsel shall not satisfy the requirement that the parties or those with negotiation and settlement authority personally appear, provided, however, that the court may allow a party who is unable to attend in person due to his or her disability to participate in the hearing by telephone or other alternative means or through a representative authorized to settle the case.

(4)(A) Directs the qualified defendant to file with the court and serve on the plaintiff a copy of any relevant CASp inspection report at least 15 days before the date of the conference. The CASp inspection report is confidential and is available only as set forth in paragraph (5) of this subdivision and in paragraph (4) of subdivision (e).

(B) Directs a defendant described by subparagraph (A) or (B) of paragraph (2) of subdivision (b) who has filed a declaration stating that the violation or violations have been corrected, or will be corrected within 60 days of service of the complaint to file with the court and serve on the plaintiff evidence showing correction of the violation or violations within 10 calendar days after the completion of the corrections.

(C) Directs a defendant described by subparagraph (C) of paragraph (2) of subdivision (b) who has filed a declaration stating that the violation or violations have been corrected, or will be corrected within 30 days of service of the complaint to file with the court and serve on the plaintiff within 10 days after issuance of the court order evidence of correction of the violation or violations, if that evidence showing correction was not filed previously with the application and served on the plaintiff.

(5) Directs the parties that the CASp inspection report may be disclosed only to the court, the parties to the action, the parties' attorneys, those individuals employed or retained by the attorneys to assist in the litigation, and insurance representatives or others involved in the evaluation and settlement of the case.

(6) If the defendant so requests, directs the parties that no later than 30 days after issuance of the court order the parties and their counsel, accompanied by their experts if the parties so elect, shall meet in person at the subject premises. They shall jointly inspect the portions of the subject premises, and shall review any programmatic or policy issues, that are claimed to constitute a violation of a construction-related accessibility standard. The court may allow a plaintiff who is unable to meet in person at the subject premises to be excused from participating in a site visit or to participate by telephone or other alternative means for good cause. A plaintiff or plaintiff's counsel is not required, but may agree, to attend more than one in-person site meeting. A site inspection pursuant to this paragraph shall not affect the right of the parties to conduct otherwise appropriate discovery.

(7) Directs the plaintiff to file with the court and serve on the defendant at least 15 days before the date of the conference a statement that includes, to the extent reasonably known, for use solely for the purpose of the early evaluation conference, all of the following:

(A) An itemized list of specific conditions on the subject premises that are the basis of the claimed violations of construction-related accessibility standards in the plaintiff's complaint.

(B) The amount of damages claimed.

(C) The amount of attorney's fees and costs incurred to date, if any, that are being claimed.

(D) Any demand for settlement of the case in its entirety.

(e)(1) A party failing to comply with any court order may be subject to court sanction at the court's discretion.

(2)(A) The court shall lift the stay when the defendant has failed to file and serve the CASp inspection report prior to the early evaluation conference and has failed also to produce the report at the time of the early evaluation conference, unless the defendant shows good cause for that failure.

(B) The court shall lift the stay when a defendant described by paragraph (2) of subdivision (b) has failed to file and serve the evidence showing correction of the violation or violations as required by law.

(3) The court may lift the stay at the conclusion of the early evaluation conference upon a showing of good cause by the plaintiff. Good cause may include the defendant's failure to make reasonably timely progress toward completion of corrections noted by a CASp.

(4) The CASp inspection report filed and served pursuant to subdivision (d) shall remain confidential throughout the stay and shall continue to be confidential until the conclusion of the claim, whether by dismissal, settlement, or final judgment, unless there is a showing of good cause by any party. Good cause may include the defendant's failure to make reasonably timely progress toward completion of corrections noted by a CASp. The confidentiality of the inspection report shall terminate upon the conclusion of the claim, unless the owner of the report obtains a court order pursuant to the California Rules of Court to seal the record.

(f) All discussions at the early evaluation conference shall be subject to Section 1152 of the Evidence Code. It is the intent of the Legislature that the purpose of the evaluation conference shall include, but not be limited to, evaluation of all of the following, as applicable:

(1) Whether the defendant is entitled to the 90-day stay for some or all of the identified issues in the case, as a qualified defendant.

(2) The current condition of the site and the status of any plan of corrections, including whether the qualified defendant has corrected or is willing to correct the alleged violations, and the timeline for doing so.

(3) Whether subdivision (f) of Section 55.56 may be applicable to the case, and whether all violations giving rise to the claim have been corrected within the specified time periods.

(4) Whether the case, including any claim for damages or injunctive relief, can be settled in whole or in part.

(5) Whether the parties should share other information that may facilitate early evaluation and resolution of the dispute.

(g) Nothing in this section precludes any party from making an offer to compromise pursuant to Section 998 of the Code of Civil Procedure.

(h) For a claim involving a qualified defendant, as provided in paragraph (1) of subdivision (b), the court may schedule additional conferences and may extend the 90-day stay for good cause shown, but not to exceed one additional 90-day extension.

(i) Early evaluation conferences shall be conducted by a superior court judge or commissioner, or a court early evaluation conference officer. A commissioner shall not be qualified to conduct early evaluation conferences pursuant to this subdivision unless he or she has received training regarding disability access requirements imposed by the federal Americans with Disabilities Act of 1990 (Public Law 101-336; 42 U.S.C. Sec. 12101 et seq.), state laws that govern access to public facilities, and federal and state regulations adopted pursuant to those laws. For purposes of this subdivision, a "court early evaluation conference officer" means an attorney employed by the court who has received training regarding disability access requirements imposed by the federal Americans with Disabilities Act of 1990, state laws that govern access to public facilities, and federal and state regulations adopted pursuant to those laws. Attorneys serving in this capacity may also be utilized by the court for other purposes not related to these proceedings.

(j) Nothing in this part shall be deemed to make any inspection report, opinion, statement, or other finding or conclusion of a CASp binding on the court, or to abrogate in any manner the ultimate authority of the court to make all appropriate findings of fact and law. The CASp inspection report and any opinion, statement, finding, or conclusion therein shall be given the weight the trier of fact finds that it deserves.

(k) Nothing in this part shall be construed to invalidate or limit any California construction-related accessibility standard that provides greater or equal protection for the rights of individuals with disabilities than is afforded by the federal Americans with Disabilities Act (Public Law 101-336; 42 U.S.C. Sec. 12101 et seq.) and the federal regulations adopted pursuant to that act.

(*l*)(1) The Judicial Council shall, by January 1, 2013, prepare and post on its Internet Web site instructions and a form for use by a qualified defendant, or other defendant described by paragraph (2) of subdivision (b), to file an application for stay and early evaluation conference as provided in subdivisions (b) and (c), a form for the court's notice of stay and early evaluation conference, and any other forms appropriate to implement the provisions relating to early evaluation conferences. Until those forms are adopted, the Judicial Council shall post on its Internet Web site the provisional forms set forth in subdivision (c).

(2) Until the adoption of the forms as provided in paragraph (1), the provisional application form may be used by a defendant described by paragraph (2) of subdivision (b).

(3) In lieu of the provisions specified in number 3 of page 1 of the application form set forth in paragraph (7) of subdivision (c), the application shall include one of the following declarations of the defendant as to the basis for the application, as follows:

(A) That all of the following apply to a defendant described by subparagraph (A) of paragraph (2) of subdivision (b):

(i) The site's new construction or improvement was approved pursuant to the local building permit and inspection process on or after January 1, 2008, and before January 1, 2016.

(ii) To the best of the defendant's knowledge there have been no modifications or alterations completed or commenced since that approval that impacted compliance with construction-related accessibility standards with respect to the plaintiff's claim.

(iii) All the violations giving rise to the claim have been corrected, or will be corrected within 60 days of the complaint being served.

(B) That all of the following apply to a defendant described by subparagraph (B) of paragraph (2) of subdivision (b):

(i) The site's new construction or improvement was approved by a local public building department inspector who is a certified access specialist.

(ii) To the best of the defendant's knowledge there have been no modifications or alterations completed or commenced since that approval that impacted compliance with construction-related accessibility standards with respect to the plaintiff's claim.

(iii) All the violations giving rise to the claim have been corrected, or will be corrected within 60 days of the complaint being served.

(C) That both of the following apply to a defendant described by subparagraph (C) of paragraph (2) of subdivision (b):

(i) The defendant is a small business described in paragraph (2) of subdivision (f) of Section 55.56.

(ii) The violation or violations giving rise to the claim have been corrected, or will be corrected within 30 days of the complaint being served.

(4) In lieu of the provision specified in number 4(c) of page 1 of the application form set forth in paragraph (7) of subdivision (c), the application shall include a request that the court order the defendant to do either of the following:

(A) For a defendant who has filed a declaration stating that all violations have been corrected, or will be corrected within 60 days of service of the complaint, file with the court and serve on the plaintiff evidence showing correction of the violation or violations within 10 calendar days of the completion of the corrections.

(B) For a defendant who is a small business that has filed a declaration stating that all the violations have been corrected, or will be corrected within 30 days of the service of the complaint, file with the court and serve on the plaintiff evidence showing correction of the violation or violations within 10 calendar days after issuance of the court order, if that evidence showing correction was not filed previously with the application and served on the plaintiff.

(5) The Judicial Council shall also prepare and post on its Internet Web site instructions and cover pages to assist plaintiffs and defendants, respectively, to comply with their filing responsibilities under subdivision (d). The cover pages shall also provide for the party's declaration of proof of service of the pertinent document served under the court order.

(m) The stay provisions shall not apply to any construction-related accessibility claim in which the plaintiff has been granted temporary injunctive relief that remains in place.

(n) This section shall not apply to any action brought by the Attorney General, or by any district attorney, city attorney, or county counsel.

(o) The amendments to this section made by Senate Bill 1186 of the 2011–12 Regular Session of the Legislature shall apply only to claims filed on or after the operative date of that act. Nothing in this part is intended to affect any complaint filed before that date.

(p) Nothing in this part is intended to affect existing law regarding class action requirements. **Leg.H.** Added Stats 2008 ch 549 §3 (SB 1608), effective January 1, 2009. Amended Stats 2009 ch 569 §1 (SB 209), effective January 1, 2010; Stats 2012 ch 383 §9 (SB 1186), effective September 19, 2012; Stats 2015 ch 755 §4 (AB 1521), effective October 10, 2015.

2009 Note: The conditions of Stats 2008 ch 549 §12 were met as stated in a letter dated October 13, 2009. It is reproduced below:

October 13, 2009

Honorable Ellen Corbett, Chair
Senate Committee on Judiciary
Honorable Mike Feuer, Chair
Assembly Committee on Judiciary

Honorable Ronald M. George, Chair
Judicial Council of California
Mr. Howard Miller, President
State Bar of California

California Commission on Disability Access

Pursuant to Chapter 549, Statutes of 2008 (SB 1608, Corbett), specific activities associated with disability access shall only occur upon a declaration from the Director of Finance that the California Commission on Disability Access (Commission) has been funded and has commenced operations.

Chapter 549 appropriated $80,000 General Fund for the Commission which became available on May 1, 2009. The Commission members have been appointed and the first Commission meeting is scheduled to occur on October 19, 2009. As such, the conditions of Chapter 549 have been met.

Furthermore, as required by statute, this notice shall be posted on the Internet websites of the Department of Finance, the Division of the State Architect, and the Commission.

If you have any questions or need additional information regarding this matter, please contact Kristin Shelton, Principal Program Budget Analyst, at (916) 445-8913.

MICHAEL C. GENEST
Director
By:
/s/ Ana J. Matosantos
ANA J. MATOSANTOS
Chief Deputy Director
cc: Mr. David Thorman, Director, State Architect of California
Mr. Dave Walls, Director, Building Standards Commission
Ms. Mary Ann Dewitt, Budget Officer, Department of General Services
icc: CAPOFC, JERUE, MARTINEZ, SHELTON, WHITE

2008 Notes: *Legislative Intent and Declaration*

The Legislature finds and declares all of the following:

Subdivisions (a)–(d) not reproduced.

(e) (1) Section 55.54 of the Civil Code, as added by Section 3 of this act, requires a qualified defendant to file a copy of the relevant certified access specialist report with the court, which is to be maintained under seal and kept confidential during the litigation, except upon a showing of good cause. Similarly, a protective order is granted to the certified access specialist report that the qualified defendant is required to provide to the plaintiff.

(2) This act uniquely requires the submittal to the court of a document at a very early stage of the proceedings, whereas that document might not otherwise become a court record until the trial of the claim. Although court records are normally presumed to be public and open, statutorily mandated confidentiality is necessary for these reports because of the unique and special circumstances involved here. Specifically, there is an overriding interest in promoting greater compliance with construction-related accessibility standards by encouraging businesses to voluntarily obtain CASp reports and protecting those qualified defendants from unnecessary litigation. Thus, there is an overriding interest supporting the sealing of the CASp report that overcomes the normally paramount right of public access to the record, and there is a substantial probability that this interest will be prejudiced if the record is not sealed. In addition, the proposed sealing is narrowly tailored to the duration of the litigation, and there are no less restrictive means to achieve the overriding interest.

(3) This act also uniquely requires the defendant to provide the CASp report to the plaintiff at a very early stage of the proceedings. Normally, the exchange of potential evidence is handled through the discovery process, in which case a CASp report might not be furnished except pursuant to a protective order issued by the court or pursuant to a stipulation of the parties. In order to enhance the utility of the early evaluation conference and to avoid unnecessary court proceedings for a protective order, this act requires a qualified defendant to provide the plaintiff with the CASp report at a very early stage of the proceedings, but subject to a protective order for the duration of the proceedings, unless good cause is shown by any party for the court to lift the protective order. Stats 2008 ch 549 (SB 1608) §9(e).

Operative and Inoperative Conditions

(a) Sections 2, 3, and 4 of Stats 2008 ch 549 (SB 1608) shall become operative only upon issuance of a notice by the Director of Finance declaring that the

California Commission on Disability Access has been funded and has commenced operations.

(b) If the commission loses funding, or for any other reason ceases operations, both of the following shall apply:

(1) Sections 55.51 and 55.52, subdivision (c) of Section 55.53, and subdivision (a) of Section 55.54 of the Civil Code, as added by Section 3 of this act, shall become inoperative.

(2) The remaining provisions of Section 55.54 shall remain operative as follows:

(A) Subdivisions (j) and (k) shall have general application.

(B) The remaining subdivisions shall be available only to a defendant in a construction-related accessibility claim relating to a place of public accommodation for which a CASp inspection and report was obtained prior to the date of the commission ceasing operations.

(c) If the commission loses funding or ceases operations for any other reason on or before January 1, 2014, Sections 55.55 and 55.56 of the Civil Code, as added by Section 4 of this act shall become inoperative on the date the commission ceases operations, except as to a construction-related accessibility claim that was filed before the date the commission ceased operations.

(d) The commission shall issue a notice of its date of ceasing operation upon the occurrence of that event. The Director of Finance also shall issue a notice within 30 days of the commission losing its funding or ceasing operations.

(e) Any notice required under this section shall be sent to the chairs of the Committee on Judiciary of the Senate and the Assembly, the Judicial Council, and the State Bar of California, and posted on the respective Internet Web sites of the Department of Finance, the Division of the State Architect, and the Commission on Disability Access. Stats 2008 ch 549 (SB 1608) §12.

§55.545. Mandatory evaluation conference; Scheduling; Purpose

(a) A defendant who does not qualify for an early evaluation conference pursuant Section 55.54, or who forgoes the provisions of Section 55.54, may request a mandatory evaluation conference. A plaintiff may, if the defendant does not make the request with the filing of the responsive pleadings, request a mandatory evaluation conference by filing an application within 15 days of the defendant's filing of responsive pleadings.

(b) Upon being served with a summons and complaint asserting a construction-related accessibility claim, including, but not limited to, a claim brought under Section 51, 54, 54.1, or 55, a defendant may file an application for a mandatory evaluation conference in the proceedings of that claim simultaneous with the defendant's responsive pleading or other initial appearance in the action that includes the claim. Until the application form for the mandatory evaluation conference is developed by the Judicial Council and posted on its Internet Web site pursuant to subdivision (j), a defendant may request the calendaring of the mandatory evaluation conference in a separate application filed with the defendant's responsive pleadings.

(c) Upon the filing of a request or application for a mandatory evaluation conference by a defendant or plaintiff, the court shall schedule a mandatory evaluation conference for a date as soon as possible from the date of the request or application, but in no event later than 180 days after the date of request or application, or earlier than 120 days after the filing of the request or application. Upon mutual stipulation for an extension of the conference date, the mandatory evaluation conference may be extended for up to 30 days. The court's notice of conference shall also do all of the following:

(1) Direct the parties, and any other person whose authority is required to negotiate and enter into settlement, to appear in person at the time set for the conference. Appearance by counsel shall not satisfy the requirement that the parties, or those with negotiation and settlement authority, personally appear. However, the court may allow a party who is unable to attend in person due to his or her disability to participate in the hearing by telephone or other alternative means, or through a representative authorized to settle the case.

(2) Direct the plaintiff to file with the court and serve on the defendant, at least 30 days before the date of mandatory evaluation conference, a statement that includes, to the extent reasonably known, for use solely for the purpose of the mandatory evaluation conference, all of the following:

(A) An itemized list of specific conditions on the site that are the basis of the claimed violations of construction-related accessibility standards in the plaintiff's complaint.

(B) The amount of damages claimed.

(C) The amount of attorney's fees and costs incurred to date, if any, that are being claimed.

(D) Any demand for settlement of the case in its entirety.

(3) Direct the defendant to file with the court and serve on the plaintiff, at least 30 days before the date of the mandatory evaluation conference, a statement of the defendant detailing any remedial action or remedial correction plan undertaken, or to be undertaken, by the defendant to correct the alleged violations.

(d) A party failing to comply with any court order is subject to court sanction at the court's discretion.

(e) All discussions at the mandatory evaluation conference shall be subject to Section 1152 of the Evidence Code. It is the intent of the Legislature that the purpose of the evaluation conference shall include, but not be limited to, evaluation of all of the following:

(1) The current condition of the site and the status of any plan of correction, including whether the defendant has corrected, or is willing to correct, the alleged violations, and the timeline for doing so.

(2) Whether the case, including any claim for damages or injunctive relief, can be settled in whole or in part.

(3) Whether the parties should share other information that may facilitate evaluation and resolution of the dispute.

(f) Nothing in this section precludes any party from making an offer to compromise pursuant to Section 998 of the Code of Civil Procedure.

(g) The court may schedule additional conferences.

(h) Mandatory evaluation conferences shall be conducted by a superior court judge or commissioner, or by a court early evaluation conference officer as provided in subdivision (i) of Section 55.54.

(i) If an inspection report by a certified access specialist is offered by the defendant, the provisions of Section 55.54 relating to the use and confidentiality of that report shall apply.

(j)(1) The Judicial Council shall prepare and post on its Internet Web site instructions and a form for a party to use to file an application for a mandatory evaluation conference and a form for the court's notice of the mandatory evaluation conference. Until those forms are adopted, a party and the court may use an ad hoc form that complies with the requirements of this section.

(2) The Judicial Council shall also prepare and post on its Internet Web site instructions and cover pages to assist plaintiffs and defendants, respectively, to comply with their filing responsibilities under subdivision (c).

(k) The mandatory evaluation conference may, at the court's discretion, be scheduled or combined with the case management conference within the time period specified in subdivision (c).

(*l*) This section shall not apply to any action brought by the Attorney General, or by any district attorney, city attorney, or county counsel.

(m) This section shall apply only to claims filed on or after January 1, 2013. Nothing in this section is intended to affect any complaint filed before that date. **Leg.H.** Added Stats 2012 ch 383 §10 (SB 1186), effective September 19, 2012.

PART 2.53
ATTORNEY'S FEES AND STATUTORY DAMAGES IN CONSTRUCTION-RELATED ACCESSIBILITY STANDARDS CLAIMS

Attorney's fees and recoverable costs [Operative term contingent]. §55.55.
Statutory damages; Denial of full and equal access; Rebuttable presumption for certain technical violations; Assessment; Reduction of, or exemption from, liability [Operative term contingent]. §55.56.
Applicability of part. §55.57.

§55.55. Attorney's fees and recoverable costs [Operative term contingent]

Notwithstanding subdivision (f) of Section 55.54, in determining an award of reasonable attorney's fees and recoverable costs with respect to any construction-related accessibility claim, the court may consider, along with other relevant information, written settlement offers made and rejected by the parties. Nothing in this section affects or modifies the inadmissibility of evidence regarding offers of compromise pursuant to Section 1152 of the Evidence Code, including, but not limited to, inadmissibility to prove injury or damage. **Leg.H.** Added Stats 2008 ch 549 §4 (SB 1608), effective January 1, 2009.

2009 Note: See 2009 Note following §55.57 explaining when Part 2.53 (§55.55-55.57) became operative.

2008 Notes: *Legislative Intent and Declaration*
The Legislature finds and declares all of the following:
(a) Section 55.55 of the Civil Code, as added by Section 4 of this act, is intended to reflect the longstanding principle that when a party prevails in a civil rights case the amount of attorney's fees to be awarded is based upon equitable considerations and a variety of factors, including, but not limited to, any written settlement offers made and rejected and whether the prevailing party failed to obtain a more favorable judgment or award than the settlements offered. Stats 2008 ch 549 (SB 1608) §9(a).

Operative and Inoperative Conditions
See §12(a) Note following CC §55.57 explaining when Part 2.53 (§55.55-55.57) becomes operative and §12(c) Note explaining when this section becomes inoperative.

§55.56. Statutory damages; Denial of full and equal access; Rebuttable presumption for certain technical violations; Assessment; Reduction of, or exemption from, liability [Operative term contingent]

(a) Statutory damages under either subdivision (a) of Section 52 or subdivision (a) of Section 54.3 may be recovered in a construction-related accessibility claim against a place of public accommodation only if a violation or violations of one or more construction-related accessibility standards denied the plaintiff full and equal access to the place of public accommodation on a particular occasion.

(b) A plaintiff is denied full and equal access only if the plaintiff personally encountered the violation on a particular occasion, or the plaintiff was deterred from accessing a place of public accommodation on a particular occasion.

(c) A violation personally encountered by a plaintiff may be sufficient to cause a denial of full and equal access if the plaintiff experienced difficulty, discomfort, or embarrassment because of the violation.

(d) A plaintiff demonstrates that he or she was deterred from accessing a place of public accommodation on a particular occasion only if both of the following apply:
(1) The plaintiff had actual knowledge of a violation or violations that prevented or reasonably dissuaded the plaintiff from accessing a place of public accommodation that the plaintiff intended to use on a particular occasion.
(2) The violation or violations would have actually denied the plaintiff full and equal access if the plaintiff had accessed the place of public accommodation on that particular occasion.

(e)(1) The following technical violations are presumed to not cause a person difficulty, discomfort, or embarrassment for the purpose of an award of minimum statutory damages in a construction-related accessibility claim, as set forth in subdivision (c), where the defendant is a small business, as described by subparagraph (B) of paragraph (2) of subdivision (g), the defendant has corrected, within 15 days of the service of a summons and complaint asserting a construction-related accessibility claim or receipt of a written notice, whichever is earlier, all of the technical violations that are the basis of the claim, and the claim is based on one or more of the following violations:

(A) Interior signs, other than directional signs or signs that identify the location of accessible elements, facilities, or features, when not all such elements, facilities, or features are accessible.

(B) The lack of exterior signs, other than parking signs and directional signs, including signs that indicate the location of accessible pathways or entrance and exit doors when not all pathways, entrance and exit doors are accessible.

(C) The order in which parking signs are placed or the exact location or wording of parking signs, provided that the parking signs are clearly visible and indicate the location of accessible parking and van-accessible parking.

(D) The color of parking signs, provided that the color of the background contrasts with the color of the information on the sign.

(E) The color of parking lot striping, provided that it exists and provides sufficient contrast with the surface upon which it is applied to be reasonably visible.

(F) Faded, chipped, damaged, or deteriorated paint in otherwise fully compliant parking spaces and passenger access aisles in parking lots, provided that it indicates the required dimensions of a parking space or access aisle in a manner that is reasonably visible.

(G) The presence or condition of detectable warning surfaces on ramps, except where the ramp is part of a pedestrian path of travel that intersects with a vehicular lane or other hazardous area.

(2) The presumption set forth in paragraph (1) affects the plaintiff's burden of proof and is rebuttable by evidence showing, by a preponderance of the evidence, that the plaintiff did, in fact, experience difficulty, discomfort, or embarrassment on the particular occasion as a result of one or more of the technical violations listed in paragraph (1).

(3) This subdivision shall apply only to claims filed on or after the effective date of Senate Bill 269 of the 2015–16 Regular Session.

(f) Statutory damages may be assessed pursuant to subdivision (a) based on each particular occasion that the plaintiff was denied full and equal access, and not upon the number of violations of construction-related accessibility standards identified at the place of public accommodation where the denial of full and equal access occurred. If the place of public accommodation consists of distinct facilities that offer distinct services, statutory damages may be assessed based on each denial of full and equal access to the distinct facility, and not upon the number of violations of construction-related accessibility standards identified at the place of public accommodation where the denial of full and equal access occurred.

(g)(1) Notwithstanding any other law, a defendant's liability for statutory damages in a construction-related accessibility claim against a place of public accommodation is reduced to a minimum of one thousand dollars ($1,000) for each offense if the defendant demonstrates that it has corrected all construction-related violations that are the basis of a claim within 60 days of being served with the complaint, and the defendant demonstrates any of the following:

(A) The structure or area of the alleged violation was determined to be "CASp-inspected" or "meets applicable standards" and, to the best of the defendant's knowledge, there were no modifications or alterations that impacted compliance with construction-related accessibility standards with respect to the plaintiff's claim that were completed or commenced between the date of that determination and the particular occasion on which the plaintiff was allegedly denied full and equal access.

(B) The structure or area of the alleged violation was the subject of an inspection report indicating "CASp determination pending" or "Inspected by a CASp," and the defendant has either implemented reasonable measures to correct the alleged violation before the particular occasion on which the plaintiff was allegedly denied full and equal access, or the defendant was in the process of correcting the alleged violation within a reasonable time and manner before the particular occasion on which the plaintiff was allegedly denied full and equal access.

(C) For a claim alleging a construction-related accessibility violation filed before January 1, 2018, the structure or area of the alleged violation was a new construction or an improvement that was approved by, and passed inspection by, the local building department permit and inspection process on or after January 1, 2008, and before January 1, 2016, and, to the best of the defendant's knowledge, there were no modifications or alterations that impacted compliance with respect to the plaintiff's claim that were completed or commenced between the completion date of the new construction or improvement and the particular occasion on which the plaintiff was allegedly denied full and equal access.

(D) The structure or area of the alleged violation was new construction or an improvement that was approved by, and passed inspection by, a local building department official who is a certified access specialist, and, to the best of the defendant's knowledge, there were no modifications or alterations that affected compliance with respect to the plaintiff's claim that were completed or commenced between the completion date of the new construction or improvement and the particular occasion on which the plaintiff was allegedly denied full and equal access.

(2) Notwithstanding any other law, a defendant's liability for statutory damages in a construction-related accessibility claim against a place of public accommodation is reduced to a minimum of two thousand dollars ($2,000) for each offense if the defendant demonstrates both of the following:

(A) The defendant has corrected all construction-related violations that are the basis of a claim within 30 days of being served with the complaint.

(B) The defendant is a small business that has employed 25 or fewer employees on average over the past three years, or for the years it has been in existence if less than three years, as evidenced by wage report forms filed with the Economic Development Department, and has average annual gross receipts of less than three million five hundred thousand dollars ($3,500,000) over the previous three years, or for the years it has been in existence if less than three years, as evidenced by federal or state income tax returns. The average annual gross receipts dollar amount shall be adjusted biannually by the Department of General Services for changes in the California Consumer Price Index for All Urban Consumers, as compiled by the Department of Industrial Relations. The Department of General Services shall post that adjusted amount on its Internet Web site.

(3)(A) Notwithstanding any other law, a defendant shall not be liable for minimum statutory damages in a construction-related accessibility claim, with respect to a violation noted in a report by a certified access specialist (CASp), for a period of 120 days following the date of the inspection if the defendant demonstrates compliance with each of the following:

(i) The defendant is a business that, as of the date of inspection, has employed 50 or fewer employees on average over the past three years, or for the years it has been in existence if less than three years, as evidenced by wage report forms filed with the Employment Development Department.

(ii) The structure or area of the alleged violation was the subject of an inspection report indicating "CASp determination pending" or "Inspected by a CASp."

(iii) The inspection predates the filing of the claim by, or receipt of a demand letter from, the plaintiff regarding the alleged violation of a construction-related accessibility standard, and the defendant was not on notice of the alleged violation prior to the CASp inspection.

(iv) The defendant has corrected, within 120 days of the date of the inspection, all construction-related violations in the structure or area inspected by the CASp that are noted in the CASp report that are the basis of the claim.

(B) Notwithstanding any other law, a defendant who claims the benefit of the reduction of, or protection from liability for, minimum statutory damages under this subdivision shall disclose the date and findings of any CASp inspection to a plaintiff if relevant to a claim or defense in an action.

(4) A defendant may claim the protection from liability for minimum statutory damages under paragraph (3) only once for each structure or area inspected by a CASp, unless the inspected structure or area has undergone modifications or alterations that affect the compliance with construction-related accessibility standards of those structures or areas after the date of the last inspection, and the defendant obtains an additional CASp inspection within 30 days of final approval by the building department or certificate of occupancy, as appropriate, regarding the modification or alterations.

(5) If the defendant has failed to correct, within 120 days of the date of the inspection, all construction-related violations in the structure or area inspected by the CASp that are noted in the CASp report, the defendant shall not receive any protection from liability for minimum statutory damages pursuant to paragraph (3), unless a building permit is required for the repairs which cannot reasonably be completed by the defendant within 120 days and the defendant is in the process of correcting the violations noted in the CASp report, as evidenced by having, at least, an active building permit necessary for the repairs to correct the violation that was noted, but not corrected, in the CASp report and all of the repairs are completed within 180 days of the date of the inspection.

(6) This subdivision shall not be applicable to intentional violations.

(7) Nothing in this subdivision affects the awarding of actual damages, or affects the awarding of treble actual damages.

(8) This subdivision shall apply only to claims filed on or after the effective date of Chapter 383 of the Statutes of 2012, except for paragraphs (3), (4), and (5), which shall apply only to claims filed on or after the effective date of Senate Bill 269 of the 2015–16 Regular Session. Nothing in this subdivision is intended to affect a complaint filed before those dates, as applicable.

(h) This section does not alter the applicable law for the awarding of injunctive or other equitable relief for a violation or violations of one or more construction-related accessibility standards, nor alter any legal obligation of a party to mitigate damages.

(i) In assessing liability under subdivision (d), in an action alleging multiple claims for the same construction-related accessibility violation on different particular occasions, the court shall consider the reasonableness of the plaintiff's conduct in light of the plaintiff's obligation, if any, to mitigate damages.

(j) For purposes of this section, the "structure or area inspected" means one of the following: the interior of the premises, the exterior of the premises, or both the interior and exterior. **Leg.H.** Added Stats 2008 ch 549 §4 (SB 1608), effective January 1, 2009. Amended Stats 2012 ch 383 §11 (SB 1186), effective September 19, 2012; Stats 2013 ch 76 §9 (AB 383), effective January 1, 2014; Stats 2016 ch 13 §2 (SB 269), effective May 10, 2016.

2012 Note: The Legislature finds and declares all of the following:

(a) Subdivision (h) of Section 55.56 of the Civil Code, as added by Section 11 of this act, is intended to address the misuse of Sections 52 and 54.3 of the Civil Code by a small minority of disability rights lawyers and plaintiffs. These lawyers and plaintiffs have alleged in demand letters and complaints that they were deterred on repeated occasions by the same violation of a construction-related accessibility standard and thereby assert multiple claims for the same violation without a reasonable explanation for the repeated conduct in light of the obligation to mitigate damages. Their assertions of these "stacked" multiple claims for the same construction-related accessibility violation on different occasions are made to substantially increase the purported statutory liability of a defendant in order to intimidate and pressure the defendant into making a quick monetary settlement. The provisions of subdivision (h) of Section 55.56 of the Civil Code reiterate that where multiple claims for the same construction-related accessibility violation on separate particular occasions are alleged, a plaintiff's conduct must have a reasonable explanation for the asserted need for multiple visits to a site where a known barrier violation would deny full and equal access, in light of the obligation to mitigate damages.

(b) Correspondingly, if there is a reasonable explanation in light of the obligation to mitigate damages for the need to make multiple visits to a site where a known barrier violation would deny full and equal access, a multiple claim for repeated violations of the same construction-related accessibility standard may properly lie. In addition, there may be clear instances when the needs of a person with a disability and circumstances may make mitigation efforts impossible or futile in cases involving multiple instances of deterrence on separate particular occasions where the individual has a reasonable explanation for the need for multiple visits to the same site.

(c) Further, nothing in subdivision (h) of Section 55.56 of the Civil Code is intended to change existing law with respect to the fact that an alleged failure to mitigate damages is pled and proven as an affirmative defense. Stats 2012 ch 383 (SB 1186) §25.

2009 Note: See 2009 Note following §55.57 explaining when Part 2.53 (§55.55-55.57) became operative.

2008 Notes: *Legislative Intent and Declaration*

The Legislature finds and declares all of the following:

Subdivision (a) not reproduced.

(b) Section 55.56 of the Civil Code, as added by Section 4 of this act, concerns eligibility to recover statutory damages under the Unruh Civil Rights Act or the Disabled Persons Act. It provides that those damages may be recovered in a construction-related accessibility claim only when the plaintiff either personally encounters a violation on a particular occasion or is deterred from accessing a place of public accommodation on a particular occasion. With respect to deterrence, a plaintiff must, among other requirements, have had actual knowledge of the violation or violations in order to be deterred, based on the circumstances of the individual's experience. This statement is intended to reflect current case law.

(c) The term "full and equal access," as used in Section 55.56 of the Civil Code, as added by Section 4 of this act, is intended to encompass without change the existing obligations of both Section 51 of the Civil Code, including full and equal accommodations, advantages, facilities, privileges, and services, and Section 54.3 of the Civil Code, including full and equal access to accommodations, advantages, facilities, and privileges. "Full and equal access" is also intended to mean "equal access" as that term is used in case law, and therefore, is not an expansion of existing law.

(d) Subdivision (e) of Section 55.56 of the Civil Code, as added by Section 4 of this act, provides that not every violation of a construction-related accessibility standard constitutes a separate offense entitling a plaintiff to a separate award of statutory damages, even if the plaintiff personally encountered more than one violation. A restaurant, convenience store, or theater normally serves only one function—a place to eat, shop, or watch a movie—and multiple violations of one or more construction-related accessibility standards at such a place do not constitute separate denials of full and equal access. By contrast, other places of public accommodation offer more than one type of service, facility, or other function. For example, a hotel or resort may offer sleeping rooms, a restaurant, a golf course, and a spa. Likewise, a shopping center may consist of one large common area and many separate stores and restaurants. If the place of public accommodation consists of such distinct facilities offering distinct services, statutory damages may be assessed based on each denial of full and equal access to the distinct facility, but not upon the number of violations of construction-related accessibility standards identified at the place of public accommodation where the denial of full and equal access occurred. Stats 2008 ch 549 (SB 1608) §9(b)-(d).

Operative and Inoperative Conditions

See §12(a) Note following CC §55.57 explaining when Part 2.53 (§§55.55-55.57) becomes operative and §12(c) Note explaining when this section becomes inoperative.

§55.57. Applicability of part

(a) This part shall apply only to claims filed on or after January 1, 2009. Nothing in this part is intended to affect litigation filed before that date, and no inference shall be drawn from provisions contained in this part concerning the state of the law as it existed prior to January 1, 2009.

(b) Nothing in this part is intended to affect existing law regarding class action requirements. **Leg.H.** Added Stats 2008 ch 549 §4 (SB 1608), effective January 1, 2009.

2009 Note: The conditions of Stats 2008 ch 549 §12 were met as stated in a letter dated October 13, 2009. It is reproduced below:

October 13, 2009

Honorable Ellen Corbett, Chair
Senate Committee on Judiciary

Honorable Ronald M. George, Chair
Judicial Council of California

Honorable Mike Feuer, Chair
Assembly Committee on Judiciary

Mr. Howard Miller, President
State Bar of California

California Commission on Disability Access

Pursuant to Chapter 549, Statutes of 2008 (SB 1608, Corbett), specific activities associated with disability access shall only occur upon a declaration from the Director of Finance that the California Commission on Disability Access (Commission) has been funded and has commenced operations.

Chapter 549 appropriated $80,000 General Fund for the Commission which became available on May 1, 2009. The Commission members have been appointed and the first Commission meeting is scheduled to occur on October 19, 2009. As such, the conditions of Chapter 549 have been met.

Furthermore, as required by statute, this notice shall be posted on the Internet websites of the Department of Finance, the Division of the State Architect, and the Commission.

If you have any questions or need additional information regarding this matter, please contact Kristin Shelton, Principal Program Budget Analyst, at (916) 445-8913.

MICHAEL C. GENEST
Director
By:
/s/ Ana J. Matosantos
ANA J. MATOSANTOS
Chief Deputy Director
cc: Mr. David Thorman, Director, State Architect of California
Mr. Dave Walls, Director, Building Standards Commission
Ms. Mary Ann Dewitt, Budget Officer, Department of General Services
icc: CAPOFC, JERUE, MARTINEZ, SHELTON, WHITE

2008 Note: *Operative and Inoperative Conditions*

(a) Sections 2, 3, and 4 of Stats 2008 ch 549 (SB 1608) shall become operative only upon issuance of a notice by the Director of Finance declaring that the California Commission on Disability Access has been funded and has commenced operations.

(b) If the commission loses funding, or for any other reason ceases operations, both of the following shall apply:

(1) Sections 55.51 and 55.52, subdivision (c) of Section 55.53, and subdivision (a) of Section 55.54 of the Civil Code, as added by Section 3 of this act, shall become inoperative.

(2) The remaining provisions of Section 55.54 shall remain operative as follows:

(A) Subdivisions (j) and (k) shall have general application.

(B) The remaining subdivisions shall be available only to a defendant in a construction-related accessibility claim relating to a place of public accommodation for which a CASp inspection and report was obtained prior to the date of the commission ceasing operations.

(c) If the commission loses funding or ceases operations for any other reason on or before January 1, 2014, Sections 55.55 and 55.56 of the Civil Code, as added by Section 4 of this act shall become inoperative on the date the commission ceases operations, except as to a construction-related accessibility claim that was filed before the date the commission ceased operations.

(d) The commission shall issue a notice of its date of ceasing operation upon the occurrence of that event. The Director of Finance also shall issue a notice within 30 days of the commission losing its funding or ceasing operations.

(e) Any notice required under this section shall be sent to the chairs of the Committee on Judiciary of the Senate and the Assembly, the Judicial Council, and the State Bar of California, and posted on the respective Internet Web sites of the Department of Finance, the Division of the State Architect, and the Commission on Disability Access. Stats 2008 ch 549 (SB 1608) §12.

PART 2.55
SMALL BUSINESS GENDER DISCRIMINATION IN SERVICES COMPLIANCE ACT

Citation of part. §55.61.
Definitions; Required materials in demand letter or complaint alleging gender discrimination in pricing services; Adoption of written advisory notice by Judicial Council. §55.62.
Development and provision of pamphlet or other informational materials for specified businesses explaining rights and obligations under Gender Tax Repeal Act of 1995; Written notice. §55.63.

§55.61. Citation of part

This part shall be known, and may be cited, as the Small Business Gender Discrimination in Services Compliance Act. **Leg.H.** Added Stats 2017 ch 156 §1 (AB 1615), effective January 1, 2018.

§55.62. Definitions; Required materials in demand letter or complaint alleging gender discrimination in pricing services; Adoption of written advisory notice by Judicial Council

(a) For purposes of this part, the following definitions apply:

(1) "Gender discrimination in pricing services claim" means any civil claim in a civil action with respect to a business establishment, including, but not limited to, a claim brought under Section 51 or 51.6, based wholly or in part on an alleged price difference charged for services of similar or like kind, against a person because of the person's gender.

(2) "Demand letter" means a prelitigation written document that is provided to a business alleging a gender discrimination in pricing services claim and demanding money, whether or not the attorney intends to file a complaint, or eventually files a complaint, in state court.

(b) An attorney shall provide the following items with each demand letter or complaint sent to or served upon a defendant or potential defendant alleging gender discrimination in pricing services, including, but not limited to, claims brought pursuant to Section 51 or 51.6:

(1) A copy of the written advisory notice as specified in subdivision (c). Until the Judicial Council adopts this notice, the attorney shall provide a written statement that replicates the advisory notice described in subdivision (c).

(2) A copy of the pamphlet or other informational material specified in Section 55.63, after the pamphlet or material is developed by the Department of Consumer Affairs.

(c) On or before January 1, 2019, the Judicial Council shall adopt a written advisory notice that shall be used by a plaintiff's attorney to comply with the requirements of paragraph (1) of subdivision (b). The advisory notice shall be available in English, Spanish, Chinese, Vietnamese, and Korean, and shall include a statement that the advisory notice is available in additional languages, and the Judicial Council Internet Web site address where the different versions of the advisory notice are located. The advisory notice shall state the following:

ADVISORY NOTICE TO DEFENDANT
STATE LAW REQUIRES THAT YOU GET THIS IMPORTANT ADVISORY INFORMATION FOR BUSINESSES

This information is available in English, Spanish, Chinese, Vietnamese, and Korean through the Judicial Council of California. Persons with visual impairments can get assistance in viewing this form through the Judicial Council Internet Web site at www.courts.ca.gov.

California law requires that you receive this information because the demand letter or court complaint you received with this document claims that you have discriminated, with respect to the price charged for services of similar or like kind, against a person because of that person's gender.

YOU HAVE IMPORTANT LEGAL OBLIGATIONS. State law requires that businesses charge the same price for the same services, or services of the same or similar kind, regardless of the customer's gender. In addition, state law requires that certain business establishments clearly and conspicuously disclose to their customers in writing the pricing for each standard service provided. The posting requirement applies to the following businesses:

(1) Tailors or businesses providing aftermarket clothing alterations.
(2) Barbers or hair salons.
(3) Dry cleaners and laundries providing services to individuals.

YOU HAVE IMPORTANT LEGAL RIGHTS. The allegations made in the accompanying demand letter or court complaint do not mean that you are required to pay any money unless and until a court finds you liable. Moreover, RECEIPT OF A DEMAND LETTER OR COURT COMPLAINT AND THIS ADVISORY DOES NOT NECESSARILY MEAN YOU WILL BE FOUND LIABLE FOR ANYTHING.

You have the right to seek assistance or advice about this demand letter or complaint from any person of your choice. If you have insurance, you may also wish to contact your insurance provider. Your best interest may be served by seeking legal advice or representation from an attorney, but you may also represent yourself and file the necessary court papers to protect your interests if you are served with a court complaint. If you have hired an attorney to represent you, you should immediately notify your attorney.

ADDITIONAL THINGS YOU SHOULD KNOW

WHEN YOU CAN AND CANNOT CHARGE DIFFERENT PRICES: The Gender Tax Repeal Act of 1995 (California Civil Code Section 51.6) prohibits a business from charging a different price for the same service because of the gender of the person receiving the service. However, you may charge different prices based specifically upon the amount of time, difficulty, or cost of providing the services.

POSTING PRICES: The Gender Tax Repeal Act of 1995 also requires that certain businesses clearly disclose to the customer in writing the price of each standard service provided. This pricing disclosure is required for the following businesses: tailors or businesses providing aftermarket clothing alterations; barbers or hair salons; dry cleaners and laundries providing service to individuals. The price list must be posted in a place where customers will likely see it and it must be in no less than 14-point boldface font. A business must also provide a written copy of the prices to the customer if one is requested by the customer. Finally, a business must clearly and conspicuously display a sign, in no less than 24-point font, that reads:

"CALIFORNIA LAW PROHIBITS ANY BUSINESS ESTABLISHMENT FROM DISCRIMINATING, WITH RESPECT TO THE PRICE CHARGED FOR SERVICES OF SIMILAR OR LIKE KIND, AGAINST A PERSON BECAUSE OF THE PERSON'S GENDER. A COMPLETE PRICE LIST IS AVAILABLE UPON REQUEST."

RIGHT TO CORRECT A POSTING VIOLATION ONLY: If you receive a written notice claiming that you have failed to properly post any of the above information, you have 30 days to correct the violation. If you fail to correct the violation you will be liable for a civil penalty of $1,000. (Note that the 30-day period to correct applies only to posting violations, not to discriminatory pricing violations.)

(d) This section does not apply to an action brought by the Attorney General or any district attorney, city attorney, or county counsel. **Leg.H.** Added Stats 2017 ch 156 §1 (AB 1615), effective January 1, 2018.

§55.63. Development and provision of pamphlet or other informational materials for specified businesses explaining rights and obligations under Gender Tax Repeal Act of 1995; Written notice

(a)(1) On or before January 1, 2019, the Department of Consumer Affairs shall develop a pamphlet or other informational materials for use by the following business establishments: tailors and businesses providing aftermarket clothing alterations; barbers and hair salons; and dry cleaners and laundries providing services to individuals. The pamphlet shall explain the business' rights and obligations under Section 51.6 in clear and concise language. Specifically, the pamphlet shall explain that the business is prohibited from charging different prices for services of similar or like kind based on the customer's gender, unless the price difference is based upon the amount of time, difficulty, or cost of providing the services and that the business shall disclose a price list and sign in the manner prescribed in subdivision (f) of Section 51.6. The pamphlet shall explain that a business has 30 days to correct any violation of the posting requirements in subdivision (f) of Section 51.6 and that a business that fails to correct within 30 days of receiving notice of the violation is liable for a civil penalty of one thousand dollars ($1,000). The department may include any other information that would help the business comply with Section 51.6. The department shall subsequently revise the pamphlet, as necessary.

(2) The department shall provide the pamphlet or other informational materials required by paragraph (1) to an affected business establishment at the time that the business establishment applies for or renews a license, at the time of any inspection, or at both times. The department shall post a copy of the pamphlet or other informational materials on its internet website.

(3) Commencing October 1, 2020, the department shall provide the pamphlet and other informational materials required by paragraph (1) in English, Spanish, Chinese, Tagalog, Vietnamese, and Korean.

(b) By October 1, 2020, the department shall develop a written notice explaining the requirements and obligations specified in Section 51.6. The notice shall be available in English, Spanish, Chinese, Tagalog, Vietnamese, and Korean. The department shall post a copy of the notice in each language on its internet website in a format available for download. The department shall subsequently revise the notice, as necessary. **Leg.H.** Added Stats 2017 ch 156 §1 (AB 1615), effective January 1, 2018. Amended Stats 2019 ch 293 §2 (AB 1607), effective January 1, 2020.

PART 2.57
GENDER NEUTRAL RETAIL DEPARTMENTS

Legislative findings and declarations. § 55.7.
Gender neutral section or area for display of selection of childcare items and toys; Penalties. § 55.8.

§ 55.7. Legislative findings and declarations

The Legislature finds and declares both of the following:

(a) Unjustified differences in similar products that are traditionally marketed either for girls or for boys can be more easily identified by the consumer if similar items are displayed closer to one another in one, undivided area of the retail sales floor.

(b) Keeping similar items that are traditionally marketed either for girls or for boys separated makes it more difficult for the consumer to compare the products and incorrectly implies that their use by one gender is inappropriate. **Leg.H.** Added Stats 2021 ch 750 §1 (AB 1084), effective January 1, 2022.

§ 55.8. Gender neutral section or area for display of selection of childcare items and toys; Penalties

(a) A retail department store that offers childcare items or toys for sale shall maintain a gender neutral section or area, to be labeled at the discretion of the retailer, in which a reasonable selection of the items and toys for children that it sells shall be displayed, regardless of whether they have been traditionally marketed for either girls or for boys.

(b) This section shall apply only to retail department stores that are physically located in California that have a total of 500 or more employees across all California retail department store locations. This section shall not apply to retail department stores that are physically located outside California.

(c) Beginning on January 1, 2024, a retail department store that fails to comply with this section is liable for a civil penalty, not to exceed two hundred fifty dollars ($250) for a first violation or five hundred dollars ($500) for a subsequent violation, which may be assessed and recovered in a civil action brought in the name of the people of the State of California by the Attorney General, or a district attorney or city attorney, in any court of competent jurisdiction. If the Attorney General, district attorney, or city attorney prevails in an action under this subdivision, the court shall award to the Attorney General, district attorney, or city attorney reasonable attorney's fees and costs.

(d) For purposes of this section:

(1) "Childcare item" means any product designed or intended by the manufacturer to facilitate sleep, relaxation, or the feeding of children, or to help children with sucking or teething.

(2) "Children" means persons 12 years of age or less.

(3) "Toy" means a product designed or intended by the manufacturer to be used by children when they play. **Leg.H.** Added Stats 2021 ch 750 §1 (AB 1084), effective January 1, 2022.

PART 2.6
CONFIDENTIALITY OF MEDICAL INFORMATION

Chapter 1. Definitions.
Chapter 2. Disclosure of Medical Information by Providers.
Chapter 2.5. Disclosure of Genetic Test Results by Health Care Service Plan.
Chapter 2.6. Genetic Privacy.
Chapter 3. Use and Disclosure of Medical Information by Employers.
Chapter 4. Relationship of Chapters 2 and 3.
Chapter 4.1. Notifications.
Chapter 5. Use and Disclosure of Medical and Other Information by Third Party Administrators and Others.
Chapter 6. Relationship to Existing Law.
Chapter 7. Violations.

CHAPTER 1
DEFINITIONS

Short title. §56.
Definitions. §56.05.
Business organized to maintain medical information; Business offering software or hardware designed to maintain medical information; Cannabis licensee receiving identification cards or physician's recommendations; Mental health or reproductive or sexual health digital services. §56.06.
Access to records kept by corporation. §56.07.

§56. Short title

This part may be cited as the Confidentiality of Medical Information Act. **Leg.H.** Added Stats 1981 ch 782 §2.

Prior Law: Former §56, similar to the present section, was added Stats 1979 ch 773 §1 and repealed Stats 1981 ch 782 §1.5.

Former §56, similar to present Fam C §§301, 302, 304, was enacted 1872, amended Stats 1921 ch 233 §1, Stats 1929 ch 607 §1, Stats 1945 ch 1145 §1, Stats 1967 ch 601 §1, and repealed Stats 1969 ch 1608 §3, operative January 1, 1970.

§56.05. Definitions

For purposes of this part:

(a) "Authorization" means permission granted in accordance with Section 56.11 or 56.21 for the disclosure of medical information.

(b) "Authorized recipient" means a person who is authorized to receive medical information pursuant to Section 56.10 or 56.20.

(c) "Confidential communications request" means a request by a subscriber or enrollee that health care service plan communications containing medical information be communicated to them at a specific mail or email address or specific telephone number, as designated by the subscriber or enrollee.

(d) "Contractor" means a person or entity that is a medical group, independent practice association, pharmaceutical benefits manager, or a medical service organization and is not a health care service plan or provider of health care. "Contractor" does not include insurance institutions as defined in subdivision (k) of Section 791.02 of the Insurance Code or pharmaceutical benefits managers licensed pursuant to the Knox-Keene Health Care Service Plan Act of 1975 (Chapter 2.2 (commencing with Section 1340) of Division 2 of the Health and Safety Code).

(e) "Enrollee" has the same meaning as that term is defined in Section 1345 of the Health and Safety Code.

(f) "Expiration date or event" means a specified date or an occurrence relating to the individual to whom the medical information pertains or the purpose of the use or disclosure, after which the provider of health care, health care service plan, pharmaceutical company, or contractor is no longer authorized to disclose the medical information.

(g) "Health care service plan" means an entity regulated pursuant to the Knox-Keene Health Care Service Plan Act of 1975 (Chapter 2.2 (commencing with Section 1340) of Division 2 of the Health and Safety Code).

(h) "Licensed health care professional" means a person licensed or certified pursuant to Division 2 (commencing with Section 500) of the Business and Professions Code, the Osteopathic Initiative Act or the Chiropractic Initiative Act, or Division 2.5 (commencing with Section 1797) of the Health and Safety Code.

(i) "Marketing" means to make a communication about a product or service that encourages recipients of the communication to purchase or use the product or service.

"Marketing" does not include any of the following:

(1) Communications made orally or in writing for which the communicator does not receive direct or indirect remuneration, including, but not limited to, gifts, fees, payments, subsidies, or other economic benefits, from a third party for making the communication.

(2) Communications made to current enrollees solely for the purpose of describing a provider's participation in an existing health care provider network or health plan network of a Knox-Keene licensed health plan to which the enrollees already subscribe; communications made to current enrollees solely for the purpose of describing if, and the extent to which, a product or service, or payment for a product or service, is provided by a provider, contractor, or plan or included in a plan of benefits of a Knox-Keene licensed health plan to which the enrollees already subscribe; or communications made to plan enrollees describing the availability of more cost-effective pharmaceuticals.

(3) Communications that are tailored to the circumstances of a particular individual to educate or advise the individual about treatment options, and otherwise maintain the individual's adherence to a prescribed course of medical treatment, as provided in Section 1399.901 of the Health and Safety Code, for a chronic and seriously debilitating or life-threatening condition as defined in subdivisions (d) and (e) of Section 1367.21 of the Health and Safety Code, if the health care provider, contractor, or health plan receives direct or indirect remuneration, including, but not limited to, gifts, fees, payments, subsidies, or other economic benefits, from a third party for making the communication, if all of the following apply:

(A) The individual receiving the communication is notified in the communication in typeface no smaller than 14-point type of the fact that the provider, contractor, or health plan has been remunerated and the source of the remuneration.

(B) The individual is provided the opportunity to opt out of receiving future remunerated communications.

(C) The communication contains instructions in typeface no smaller than 14-point type describing how the individual can opt out of receiving further communications by calling a toll-free number of the health care provider, contractor, or health plan making the remunerated communications. Further communication shall not be made to an individual who has opted out after 30 calendar days from the date the individual makes the opt-out request.

(j) "Medical information" means any individually identifiable information, in electronic or physical form, in possession of or derived from a provider of health care, health care service plan, pharmaceutical company, or contractor regarding a patient's medical history, mental health application information, reproductive or sexual health application information, mental or physical condition, or treatment. "Individually identifiable" means that the medical information includes or contains any element of personal identifying information sufficient to allow identification of the individual, such as the patient's name, address, electronic mail address, telephone number, or social security number, or other information that, alone or in combination with other publicly available information, reveals the identity of the individual.

(k) "Mental health application information" means information related to a consumer's inferred or diagnosed mental health or substance use disorder, as defined in Section 1374.72 of the Health and Safety Code, collected by a mental health digital service.

(*l*) "Mental health digital service" means a mobile-based application or internet website that collects mental health application information from a consumer, markets itself as facilitating mental health services to a consumer, and uses the information to facilitate mental health services to a consumer.

(m) "Patient" means a natural person, whether or not still living, who received health care services from a provider of health care and to whom medical information pertains.

(n) "Pharmaceutical company" means a company or business, or an agent or representative thereof, that manufactures, sells, or distributes pharmaceuticals, medications, or prescription drugs. "Pharmaceutical company" does not include a pharmaceutical benefits manager, as included in subdivision (c), or a provider of health care.

(o) "Protected individual" means any adult covered by the subscriber's health care service plan or a minor who can consent to a health care service without the consent of a parent or legal guardian, pursuant to state or federal law. "Protected individual" does not include an individual that lacks the capacity to give informed consent for health care pursuant to Section 813 of the Probate Code.

(p) "Provider of health care" means a person licensed or certified pursuant to Division 2 (commencing with Section 500) of the Business and Professions Code; a person licensed pursuant to the Osteopathic Initiative Act or the Chiropractic Initiative Act; a person certified pursuant to Division 2.5 (commencing with Section 1797) of the Health and Safety Code; or a clinic, health dispensary, or health facility licensed pursuant to Division 2 (commencing with Section 1200) of the Health and Safety Code. "Provider of health care" does not include insurance institutions as defined in subdivision (k) of Section 791.02 of the Insurance Code.

(q) "Reproductive or sexual health application information" means information about a consumer's reproductive health, menstrual cycle, fertility, pregnancy, pregnancy outcome, plans to conceive, or type of sexual activity collected by a reproductive or sexual health digital service, including, but not limited to, information from which one can infer someone's pregnancy status, menstrual cycle, fertility, hormone levels, birth control use, sexual activity, or gender identity.

(r) "Reproductive or sexual health digital service" means a mobile-based application or internet website that collects reproductive or sexual health application information from a consumer, markets itself as facilitating reproductive or sexual health services to a consumer, and uses the information to facilitate reproductive or sexual health services to a consumer.

(s) "Sensitive services" means all health care services related to mental or behavioral health, sexual and reproductive health, sexually transmitted infections, substance use disorder, [1] **gender-affirming** care, and intimate partner violence, and includes services described in Sections 6924, 6925, 6926, 6927, 6928, 6929, and 6930 of the Family Code, and Sections 121020 and 124260 of the Health and Safety Code, obtained by a patient at or above the minimum age specified for consenting to the service specified in the section.

(t) "Subscriber" has the same meaning as that term is defined in Section 1345 of the Health and Safety Code. **Leg.H.** Added Stats 1981 ch 782 §2. Amended Stats 1984 ch 1391 §3; Stats 1999 ch 526 §1 (SB 19); Stats 2000 ch 1067 §1 (SB 2094); Stats 2002 ch 853 §1 (AB 2191); Stats 2003 ch 562 §1 (AB 715); Stats 2013 ch 444 §2 (SB 138), effective January 1, 2014; Stats 2021 ch 190 §1 (AB 1184), effective January 1, 2022; Stats 2022 ch 690 §1 (AB 2089), effective January 1, 2023; Stats 2023 ch 254 §1 (AB 254), effective January 1, 2024; Stats 2023 ch 374 §1.5 (AB 1697), effective January 1, 2024 (ch 374 prevails); Stats 2024 ch 80 §18 (SB 1525), effective January 1, 2025.

§56.05. 2024 Deletes. [1] gender affirming

Prior Law: Former §56.05, similar to the present section, was added Stats 1979 ch 773 §1 and repealed Stats 1981 ch 782 §1.5.

§56.06. Business organized to maintain medical information; Business offering software or hardware designed to maintain medical information; Cannabis licensee receiving identification cards or physician's recommendations; Mental health or reproductive or sexual health digital services

(a) Any business organized for the purpose of maintaining medical information in order to make the information available to an individual or to a provider of health care at the request of the individual or a provider of health care, for purposes of allowing the individual to manage the individual's information, or for the diagnosis and treatment of the individual, shall be deemed to be a provider of health care subject to the requirements of this part. However, this section shall not be construed to make a business specified in this subdivision a provider of health care for purposes of any law other than this part, including laws that specifically incorporate by reference the definitions of this part.

(b) Any business that offers software or hardware to consumers, including a mobile application or other related device that is designed to maintain medical information in order to make the information available to an individual or a provider of health care at the request of the individual or a provider of health care, for purposes of allowing the individual to manage the individual's information, or for the diagnosis, treatment, or management of a medical condition of the individual, shall be deemed to be a provider of health care subject to the requirements of this part. However, this section shall not be construed to make a business specified in this subdivision a provider of health care for purposes of any law other than this part, including laws that specifically incorporate by reference the definitions of this part.

(c) Any business that is licensed pursuant to Division 10 (commencing with Section 26000) of the Business and Professions Code that is authorized to receive or receives identification cards issued pursuant to Section 11362.71 of the Health and Safety Code or information contained in a physician's recommendation issued in accordance with Article 25 (commencing with Section 2525) of Chapter 5 of Division 2 of the Business and Professions Code shall be deemed to be a provider of health care subject to the requirements of this part. However, this section shall not be construed to make a business specified in this subdivision a provider of health care for purposes of any law other than this part, including laws that specifically incorporate by reference the definitions of this part.

(d) Any business that offers a mental health digital service to a consumer for the purpose of allowing the individual to manage the individual's information, or for the diagnosis, treatment, or management of a medical condition of the individual, shall be deemed to be a provider of health care subject to the requirements of this part. However, this section shall not be construed to make a business specified in this subdivision a provider of health care for purposes of any law other than this part, including laws that specifically incorporate by reference the definitions of this part.

(e) Any business that offers a reproductive or sexual health digital service to a consumer for the purpose of allowing the individual to manage the individual's information, or for the diagnosis, treatment, or management of a medical condition of the individual, shall be deemed to be a provider of health care subject to the requirements of this part. However, this section shall not be construed to make a business specified in this subdivision a provider of health care for purposes of any law other than this part, including, but not limited to, laws that specifically incorporate by reference the definitions of this part.

(f) Any business described in this section shall maintain the same standards of confidentiality required of a provider of health care with respect to medical information disclosed to the business.

(g) Any business described in this section is subject to the penalties for improper use and disclosure of medical information prescribed in this part. **Leg.H.** Added Stats 1993 ch 1004 §1 (AB 336). Amended Stats 2007 ch 699 §1 (AB 1298), effective January 1, 2008; Stats 2013 ch 296 §1 (AB 658), effective January 1, 2014; Stats 2014 ch 913 §2 (AB 2747), effective January 1, 2015; Stats 2017 ch 561 §17 (AB 1516), effective January 1, 2018; Stats 2018 ch 583 §3 (AB 2402), effective January 1, 2019; Stats 2022 ch 690 §2 (AB 2089), effective January 1, 2023; Stats 2023 ch 254 §2 (AB 254), effective January 1, 2024.

§56.07. Access to records kept by corporation

(a) Except as provided in subdivision (c), upon the patient's written request, any corporation described in Section 56.06, or any other entity that compiles or maintains medical information for any reason, shall provide the patient, at no charge, with a copy of any medical profile, summary, or information maintained by the corporation or entity with respect to the patient.

(b) A request by a patient pursuant to this section shall not be deemed to be an authorization by the patient for the release or disclosure of any information to any person or entity other than the patient.

(c) This section shall not apply to any patient records that are subject to inspection by the patient pursuant to Section 123110 of the Health and Safety Code and shall not be deemed to limit the right of a health care provider to charge a fee for the preparation of a summary of patient records as provided in Section 123130 of the Health and Safety Code. This section shall not apply to a health care service plan licensed pursuant to Chapter 2.2 (commencing with Section 1340) of Division 2 of the Health and Safety Code or a disability insurer licensed pursuant to the Insurance Code. This section shall not apply to medical information compiled or maintained by a fire and casualty insurer or its retained counsel in the regular course of investigating or litigating a claim under a policy of insurance that it has written. For the purposes of this section, a fire and casualty insurer is an insurer writing policies that may be sold by a fire and casualty licensee pursuant to Section 1625 of the Insurance Code. **Leg.H.** Added Stats 2000 ch 1066 §1 (SB 1903).

§56.1. [Section repealed 1969]

Leg.H. Added Stats 1967 ch 601 §2. Repealed Stats 1969 ch 1608 §3, See Fam C §303.

CHAPTER 2
DISCLOSURE OF MEDICAL INFORMATION BY PROVIDERS

Authorization for disclosure; When disclosure compelled; When disclosure allowed; Prohibitions. §56.10.

Disclosure to family member, partner, or friend; Disclosure for notification purposes; Disaster relief efforts. §56.1007.

Preservation of confidentiality of records; Patient's right to access or receive copy of electronic medical records. §56.101.

Patients not required to sign release form as condition of receiving pharmaceuticals; Exceptions. §56.102.

Disclosure of minor's medical information or minor's mental health condition for purpose of coordinating health care services and medical treatment. §56.103.

Release of information on outpatient psychotherapy treatment. §56.104.

Authorization to accompany settlement demand by patient; Notice of request for information. §56.105.

Disclosure or release of information on minor removed from physical custody of parent or guardian; Restrictions; Applicability. §56.106.

Confidentiality of medical information. § 56.107.

Release of medical information related to abortion; Restrictions. § 56.108.

Release of medical information related to child receiving gender-affirming health care or gender-affirming mental health care. § 56.109.

Protection of identifying information relating to lawful abortion. § 56.110.

Form and contents of authorization. §56.11.

Furnishing copy of authorization. §56.12.

Disclosure by recipient. §56.13.

Communication of limits of authorization. §56.14.

Cancellation and modification of authorization. §56.15.

Information that may be released without authorization. §56.16.

§56.10. Authorization for disclosure; When disclosure compelled; When disclosure allowed; Prohibitions

(a) A provider of health care, health care service plan, or contractor shall not disclose medical information regarding a patient of the provider of health care or an enrollee or subscriber of a health care service plan without first obtaining an authorization, except as provided in subdivision (b) or (c).

(b) A provider of health care, a health care service plan, or a contractor shall disclose medical information if the disclosure is compelled by any of the following:

(1) A court order.

(2) A board, commission, or administrative agency for purposes of adjudication pursuant to its lawful authority.

(3) A party to a proceeding before a court or administrative agency pursuant to a subpoena, subpoena duces tecum, notice to appear served pursuant to Section 1987 of the Code of Civil Procedure, or any provision authorizing discovery in a proceeding before a court or administrative agency.

(4) A board, commission, or administrative agency pursuant to an investigative subpoena issued under Article 2 (commencing with Section 11180) of Chapter 2 of Part 1 of Division 3 of Title 2 of the Government Code.

(5) An arbitrator or arbitration panel, when arbitration is lawfully requested by either party, pursuant to a subpoena duces tecum issued under Section 1282.6 of the Code of Civil Procedure, or another provision authorizing discovery in a proceeding before an arbitrator or arbitration panel.

(6) A search warrant lawfully issued to a governmental law enforcement agency.

(7) The patient or the patient's representative pursuant to Chapter 1 (commencing with Section 123100) of Part 1 of Division 106 of the Health and Safety Code.

(8) A medical examiner, forensic pathologist, or coroner, when requested in the course of an investigation by a medical examiner, forensic pathologist, or coroner's office for the purpose of identifying the decedent or locating next of kin, or when investigating deaths that may involve public health concerns, organ or tissue donation, child abuse, elder abuse, suicides, poisonings, accidents, sudden infant deaths, suspicious deaths, unknown deaths, or criminal deaths, or upon notification of, or investigation of, imminent deaths that may involve organ or tissue donation pursuant to Section 7151.15 of the Health and Safety Code, or when otherwise authorized by the decedent's representative. Medical information requested by a medical examiner, forensic pathologist, or coroner under this paragraph shall be limited to information regarding the patient who is the decedent and who is the subject of the investigation or who is the prospective donor and shall be disclosed to a medical examiner, forensic pathologist, or coroner without delay upon request. A medical examiner, forensic pathologist, or coroner shall not disclose the information contained in the medical record obtained pursuant to this paragraph to a third party without a court order or authorization pursuant to paragraph (4) of subdivision (c) of Section 56.11.

(9) When otherwise specifically required by law.

(c) A provider of health care or a health care service plan may disclose medical information as follows:

(1) The information may be disclosed to providers of health care, health care service plans, contractors, or other health care professionals or facilities for purposes of diagnosis or treatment of the patient. This includes, in an emergency situation, the communication of patient information by radio transmission or other means between emergency medical personnel at the scene of an emergency, or in an emergency medical transport vehicle, and emergency medical personnel at a health facility licensed pursuant to Chapter 2 (commencing with Section 1250) of Division 2 of the Health and Safety Code.

(2) The information may be disclosed to an insurer, employer, health care service plan, hospital service plan, employee benefit plan, governmental authority, contractor, or other person or entity responsible for paying for health care services rendered to the patient, to the extent necessary to allow responsibility for payment to be determined and payment to be made. If (A) the patient is, by reason of a comatose or other disabling medical condition, unable to consent to the disclosure of medical information and (B) no other arrangements have been made to pay for the health care services being rendered to the patient, the information may be disclosed to a governmental authority to the extent necessary to determine the patient's eligibility for, and to obtain, payment under a governmental program for health care services provided to the patient. The information may also be disclosed to another provider of health care or health care service plan as necessary to assist the other provider or health care service plan in obtaining payment for health care services rendered by that provider of health care or health care service plan to the patient.

(3) The information may be disclosed to a person or entity that provides billing, claims management, medical data processing, or other administrative services for providers of health care or health care service plans or for any of the persons or entities specified in paragraph (2). However, that disclosed information shall not be further disclosed by the recipient in a way that would violate this part.

(4) The information may be disclosed to organized committees and agents of professional societies or of medical staffs of licensed hospitals, licensed health care service plans, professional standards review organizations, independent medical review organizations and their selected reviewers, utilization and quality control peer review organizations as established by Congress in Public Law 97-248 in 1982, contractors, or persons or organizations insuring, responsible for, or defending professional liability that a provider may incur, if the committees, agents, health care service plans, organizations, reviewers, contractors, or persons are engaged in reviewing the competence or qualifications of health care professionals or in reviewing health care services with respect to medical necessity, level of care, quality of care, or justification of charges.

(5) The information in the possession of a provider of health care or a health care service plan may be reviewed by a private or public body responsible for licensing or accrediting the provider of health care or a health care service plan. However, no patient-identifying medical information may be removed from the premises except as expressly permitted or required elsewhere by law, nor shall that information be further disclosed by the recipient in a way that would violate this part.

(6) The information may be disclosed to a medical examiner, forensic pathologist, or county coroner in the course of an investigation by a medical examiner, forensic pathologist, or coroner's office when requested for all purposes not included in paragraph (8) of subdivision (b). A medical examiner, forensic pathologist, or coroner shall not disclose the

information contained in the medical record obtained pursuant to this paragraph to a third party without a court order or authorization pursuant to paragraph (4) of subdivision (c) of Section 56.11.

(7) The information may be disclosed to public agencies, clinical investigators, including investigators conducting epidemiologic studies, health care research organizations, and accredited public or private nonprofit educational or health care institutions for bona fide research purposes. However, no information so disclosed shall be further disclosed by the recipient in a way that would disclose the identity of a patient or violate this part.

(8) A provider of health care or health care service plan that has created medical information as a result of employment-related health care services to an employee conducted at the specific prior written request and expense of the employer may disclose to the employee's employer that part of the information that:

(A) Is relevant in a lawsuit, arbitration, grievance, or other claim or challenge to which the employer and the employee are parties and in which the patient has placed in issue the patient's medical history, mental or physical condition, or treatment, provided that information may only be used or disclosed in connection with that proceeding.

(B) Describes functional limitations of the patient that may entitle the patient to leave from work for medical reasons or limit the patient's fitness to perform the patient's present employment, provided that no statement of medical cause is included in the information disclosed.

(9) Unless the provider of health care or a health care service plan is notified in writing of an agreement by the sponsor, insurer, or administrator to the contrary, the information may be disclosed to a sponsor, insurer, or administrator of a group or individual insured or uninsured plan or policy that the patient seeks coverage by or benefits from, if the information was created by the provider of health care or health care service plan as the result of services conducted at the specific prior written request and expense of the sponsor, insurer, or administrator for the purpose of evaluating the application for coverage or benefits.

(10) The information may be disclosed to a health care service plan by providers of health care that contract with the health care service plan and may be transferred between providers of health care that contract with the health care service plan, for the purpose of administering the health care service plan. Medical information shall not otherwise be disclosed by a health care service plan except in accordance with this part.

(11) This part does not prevent the disclosure by a provider of health care or a health care service plan to an insurance institution, agent, or support organization, subject to Article 6.6 (commencing with Section 791) of Chapter 1 of Part 2 of Division 1 of the Insurance Code, of medical information if the insurance institution, agent, or support organization has complied with all of the requirements for obtaining the information pursuant to Article 6.6 (commencing with Section 791) of Chapter 1 of Part 2 of Division 1 of the Insurance Code.

(12) The information relevant to the patient's condition, care, and treatment provided may be disclosed to a probate court investigator in the course of an investigation required or authorized in a conservatorship proceeding under the Guardianship-Conservatorship Law as defined in Section 1400 of the Probate Code, or to a probate court investigator, probation officer, or domestic relations investigator engaged in determining the need for an initial guardianship or continuation of an existing guardianship.

(13) The information may be disclosed to an organ procurement organization or a tissue bank processing the tissue of a decedent for transplantation into the body of another person, but only with respect to the donating decedent, for the purpose of aiding the transplant. For the purpose of this paragraph, "tissue bank" and "tissue" have the same meanings as defined in Section 1635 of the Health and Safety Code.

(14) The information may be disclosed when the disclosure is otherwise specifically authorized by law, including, but not limited to, the voluntary reporting, either directly or indirectly, to the federal Food and Drug Administration of adverse events related to drug products or medical device problems, or to disclosures made pursuant to subdivisions (b) and (c) of Section 11167 of the Penal Code by a person making a report pursuant to Sections 11165.9 and 11166 of the Penal Code, provided that those disclosures concern a report made by that person.

(15) Basic information, including the patient's name, city of residence, age, sex, and general condition, may be disclosed to a state-recognized or federally recognized disaster relief organization for the purpose of responding to disaster welfare inquiries.

(16) The information may be disclosed to a third party for purposes of encoding, encrypting, or otherwise anonymizing data. However, no information so disclosed shall be further disclosed by the recipient in a way that would violate this part, including the unauthorized manipulation of coded or encrypted medical information that reveals individually identifiable medical information.

(17) For purposes of disease management programs and services as defined in Section 1399.901 of the Health and Safety Code, information may be disclosed as follows: (A) to an entity contracting with a health care service plan or the health care service plan's contractors to monitor or administer care of enrollees for a covered benefit, if the disease management services and care are authorized by a treating physician, or (B) to a disease management organization, as defined in Section 1399.900 of the Health and Safety Code, that complies fully with the physician authorization requirements of Section 1399.902 of the Health and Safety Code, if the health care service plan or its contractor provides or has provided a description of the disease management services to a treating physician or to the health care service plan's or contractor's network of physicians. This paragraph does not require physician authorization for the care or treatment of the adherents of a well-recognized church or religious denomination who depend solely upon prayer or spiritual means for healing in the practice of the religion of that church or denomination.

(18) The information may be disclosed, as permitted by state and federal law or regulation, to a local health department for the purpose of preventing or controlling disease, injury, or disability, including, but not limited to, the reporting of disease, injury, vital events, including, but not limited to, birth or death, and the conduct of public health surveillance, public health investigations, and public health interventions, as authorized or required by state or federal law or regulation.

(19) The information may be disclosed, consistent with applicable law and standards of ethical conduct, by a psychotherapist, as defined in Section 1010 of the Evidence Code, if the psychotherapist, in good faith, believes the disclosure is necessary to prevent or lessen a serious and imminent threat to the health or safety of a reasonably foreseeable victim or victims, and the disclosure is made to a person or persons reasonably able to prevent or lessen the threat, including the target of the threat.

(20) The information may be disclosed as described in Section 56.103.

(21)(A) The information may be disclosed to an employee welfare benefit plan, as defined under Section 3(1) of the Employee Retirement Income Security Act of 1974 (29 U.S.C. Sec. 1002(1)), which is formed under Section 302(c)(5) of the Taft-Hartley Act (29 U.S.C. Sec. 186(c)(5)), to the extent that the employee welfare benefit plan provides medical care, and may also be disclosed to an entity contracting with the employee welfare benefit plan for billing, claims management, medical data processing, or other administrative services related to the provision of medical care to persons enrolled in the employee welfare benefit plan for health care coverage, if all of the following conditions are met:

(i) The disclosure is for the purpose of determining eligibility, coordinating benefits, or allowing the employee welfare benefit plan or the contracting entity to advocate on the behalf of a patient or enrollee with a provider, a health care service plan, or a state or federal regulatory agency.

(ii) The request for the information is accompanied by a written authorization for the release of the information submitted in a manner consistent with subdivision (a) and Section 56.11.

(iii) The disclosure is authorized by and made in a manner consistent with the federal Health Insurance Portability and Accountability Act of 1996 (Public Law 104-191).

(iv) Any information disclosed is not further used or disclosed by the recipient in any way that would directly or indirectly violate this part or the restrictions imposed by Part 164 of Title 45 of the Code of Federal Regulations, including the manipulation of the information in any way that might reveal individually identifiable medical information.

(B) For purposes of this paragraph, Section 1374.8 of the Health and Safety Code shall not apply.

(22) Information may be disclosed pursuant to subdivision (a) of Section 15633.5 of the Welfare and Institutions Code by a person required to make a report pursuant to Section 15630 of the Welfare and Institutions Code, provided that the disclosure under subdivision (a) of Section 15633.5 concerns a report made by that person. Covered entities, as they

are defined in Section 160.103 of Title 45 of the Code of Federal Regulations, shall comply with the requirements of the federal Health Insurance Portability and Accountability Act of 1996 (HIPAA) privacy rule pursuant to subsection (c) of Section 164.512 of Title 45 of the Code of Federal Regulations if the disclosure is not for the purpose of public health surveillance, investigation, intervention, or reporting an injury or death.

(23) The information may be disclosed to a school-linked services coordinator pursuant to a written authorization between the health provider and the patient or client that complies with the federal Health Insurance Portability and Accountability Act of 1996.

(24) Mental health records, as defined in subdivision (c) of Section 5073 of the Penal Code, may be disclosed by a county correctional facility, county medical facility, state correctional facility, or state hospital, as required by Section 5073 of the Penal Code.

(d) Except to the extent expressly authorized by a patient, enrollee, or subscriber, or as provided by subdivisions (b) and (c), a provider of health care, health care service plan, contractor, or corporation and its subsidiaries and affiliates shall not intentionally share, sell, use for marketing, or otherwise use medical information for a purpose not necessary to provide health care services to the patient.

(e) Except to the extent expressly authorized by a patient or enrollee or subscriber or as provided by subdivisions (b) and (c), a contractor or corporation and its subsidiaries and affiliates shall not further disclose medical information regarding a patient of the provider of health care or an enrollee or subscriber of a health care service plan or insurer or self-insured employer received under this section to a person or entity that is not engaged in providing direct health care services to the patient or the patient's provider of health care or health care service plan or insurer or self-insured employer.

(f) For purposes of this section, the following definitions apply:

(1) "Medical examiner, forensic pathologist, or coroner" means a coroner or deputy coroner, as described in subdivision (c) of Section 830.35 of the Penal Code, or a licensed physician who currently performs official autopsies on behalf of a county coroner's office or a medical examiner's office, whether as a government employee or under contract to that office.

(2) "School-linked services coordinator" means an individual located on a school campus or under contract by a county behavioral health provider agency for the treatment and health care operations and referrals of students and their families that holds any of the following:

(A) A services credential with a specialization in pupil personnel services, as described in Section 44266 of the Education Code.

(B) A services credential with a specialization in health authorizing service as a school nurse, as described in Section 44877 of the Education Code.

(C) A license to engage in the practice of marriage and family therapy issued pursuant to Chapter 13 (commencing with Section 4980) of Division 2 of the Business and Professions Code.

(D) A license to engage in the practice of educational psychology issued pursuant to Chapter 13.5 (commencing with Section 4989.10) of Division 2 of the Business and Professions Code.

(E) A license to engage in the practice of professional clinical counseling issued pursuant to Chapter 16 (commencing with Section 4999.10) of Division 2 of the Business and Professions Code. **Leg.H.** Added Stats 2000 ch 1068 §1.16 (AB 1836), operative January 1, 2003. Amended Stats 2002 ch 123 §1 (AB 1958); Stats 2003 ch 562 §2 (AB 715); Stats 2006 ch 874 §2 (SB 1430), effective January 1, 2007; Stats 2007 ch 506 §1 (AB 1178) (ch 553 prevails), effective January 1, 2008; Stats 2007 ch 552 §2 (AB 1687) (ch 553 prevails), effective January 1, 2008; Stats 2007 ch 553 §1.9 (AB 1727), effective January 1, 2008; Stats 2008 ch 179 §27 (SB 1498), effective January 1, 2009; Stats 2009 ch 493 §1 (AB 952), effective January 1, 2010; Stats 2010 ch 540 §1 (AB 2028), effective January 1, 2011; Stats 2013 ch 341 §1 (AB 1297), effective January 1, 2014; Stats 2016 ch 690 §1 (AB 2119), effective January 1, 2017; Stats 2022 ch 968 §1 (AB 2526), effective January 1, 2023; Stats 2022 ch 993 §1.5 (SB 1184), effective January 1, 2023 (ch 993 prevails).

Prior Law: Former §56.10, similar to the present section, was added Stats 1981 ch 782 §2, amended Stats 1983 ch 1246 §1, Stats 1984 ch 442 §1, ch 967 §2, Stats 1986 ch 633 §1, Stats 1990 ch 911 §1, Stats 1991 ch 591 §1; Stats 1992 ch 427 §9, ch 572 §1 (ch 572 prevails), Stats 1993 ch 659 §1, Stats 1994 ch 700 §3, Stats 1999 ch 526 §2, Stats 2000 ch 1065 §1, ch 1066 §2, ch 1067 §2.3, ch 1068 §1.8, operative until January 1, 2003.

Former §56.10, similar to present CC §§56.11, 56.21, was added Stats 1979 ch 773 §1, amended Stats 1981 ch 143 §1, and repealed Stats 1981 ch 782 §1.5.

2016 Note: The Legislature finds and declares that this act imposes a limitation on the public's right of access to the meetings of public bodies or the writings of public officials and agencies within the meaning of Section 3 of Article I of the California Constitution. Pursuant to that constitutional provision, the Legislature makes the following findings to demonstrate the interest protected by this limitation and the need for protecting that interest:

The privacy rights of the decedent would be impaired if the records released to a medical examiner, forensic pathologist, or coroner regarding the decedent were released to the public. Stats 2016 ch 690 (AB 2119) §4.

2006 Note: This act shall be known, and may be cited as the Local Pandemic and Emergency Health Preparedness Act of 2006. Stats 2006 ch 874 (SB 1430) §1.

Former Sections: Former CC §56.10, similar to the present section, was added Stats 1981 ch 782 §2 and repealed operative January 1, 2003, by its own provisions. Stats 2000 ch 1068 §1.8.

Former CC §56.10, similar to present CC §§56.11, 56.21, was added Stats 1979 ch 773 §1 and repealed Stats 1981 ch 782 §1.5.

§56.1007. Disclosure to family member, partner, or friend; Disclosure for notification purposes; Disaster relief efforts

(a) A provider of health care, health care service plan, or contractor may, in accordance with subdivision (c) or (d), disclose to a family member, other relative, domestic partner, or a close personal friend of the patient, or any other person identified by the patient, the medical information directly relevant to that person's involvement with the patient's care or payment related to the patient's health care.

(b) A provider of health care, health care service plan, or contractor may use or disclose medical information to notify, or assist in the notification of, including identifying or locating, a family member, a personal representative of the patient, a domestic partner, or another person responsible for the care of the patient of the patient's location, general condition, or death. Any use or disclosure of medical information for those notification purposes shall be in accordance with the provisions of subdivision (c), (d), or (e), as applicable.

(c)(1) Except as provided in paragraph (2), if the patient is present for, or otherwise available prior to, a use or disclosure permitted by subdivision (a) or (b) and has the capacity to make health care decisions, the provider of health care, health care service plan, or contractor may use or disclose the medical information if it does any of the following:

(A) Obtains the patient's agreement.

(B) Provides the patient with the opportunity to object to the disclosure, and the patient does not express an objection.

(C) Reasonably infers from the circumstances, based on the exercise of professional judgment, that the patient does not object to the disclosure.

(2) A provider of health care who is a psychotherapist, as defined in Section 1010 of the Evidence Code, may use or disclose medical information pursuant to this subdivision only if the psychotherapist complies with subparagraph (A) or (B) of paragraph (1).

(d) If the patient is not present, or the opportunity to agree or object to the use or disclosure cannot practicably be provided because of the patient's incapacity or an emergency circumstance, the provider of health care, health care service plan, or contractor may, in the exercise of professional judgment, determine whether the disclosure is in the best interests of the patient and, if so, disclose only the medical information that is directly relevant to the person's involvement with the patient's health care. A provider of health care, health care service plan, or contractor may use professional judgment and its experience with common practice to make reasonable inferences of the patient's best interest in allowing a person to act on behalf of the patient to pick up filled prescriptions, medical supplies, X-rays, or other similar forms of medical information.

(e) A provider of health care, health care service plan, or contractor may use or disclose medical information to a public or private entity authorized by law or by its charter to assist in disaster relief efforts, for the purpose of coordinating with those entities the uses or disclosures permitted by subdivision (b). The requirements in subdivisions (c) and (d) apply to those uses and disclosures to the extent that the provider of health care, health care service plan, or contractor, in the exercise of professional judgment, determines that the requirements do not interfere with the ability to respond to the emergency circumstances.

(f) Nothing in this section shall be construed to interfere with or limit the access authority of Protection and Advocacy, Inc., the Office of Patients' Rights, or any county patients' rights advocates to access medical information pursuant to any state or federal law. **Leg.H.** Added Stats 2006 ch 833 §1 (AB 3013), effective January 1, 2007.

§56.101. Preservation of confidentiality of records; Patient's right to access or receive copy of electronic medical records

(a) Every provider of health care, health care service plan, pharmaceutical company, or contractor who creates, maintains, preserves, stores, abandons, destroys, or disposes of medical information shall do so in a manner that preserves the confidentiality of the information contained therein. Any provider of health care, health care service plan, pharmaceutical company, or contractor who negligently creates, maintains, preserves, stores, abandons, destroys, or disposes of medical information shall be subject to the remedies and penalties provided under subdivisions (b) and (c) of Section 56.36.

(b)(1) An electronic health record system or electronic medical record system shall do all of the following:

(A) Protect and preserve the integrity of electronic medical information.

(B) Automatically record and preserve any change or deletion of any electronically stored medical information. The record of any change or deletion shall include the identity of the person who accessed and changed the medical information, the date and time the medical information was accessed, and the change that was made to the medical information.

(2) A patient's right to access or receive a copy of the patient's electronic medical records upon request shall be consistent with applicable state and federal laws governing patient access to, and the use and disclosures of, medical information.

(c)(1) A business, as described in Section 56.06, that electronically stores or maintains medical information on the provision of sensitive services, including, but not limited to, on an electronic health record system or electronic medical record system, on behalf of a provider of health care, health care service plan, pharmaceutical company, contractor, or employer, shall develop capabilities, policies, and procedures, on or before July 1, 2024, to enable all of the following:

(A) Limit user access privileges to information systems that contain medical information related to gender affirming care, abortion and abortion-related services, and contraception only to those persons who are authorized to access specified medical information.

(B) Prevent the disclosure, access, transfer, transmission, or processing of medical information related to gender affirming care, abortion and abortion-related services, and contraception to persons and entities outside of this state in accordance to this part.

(C) Segregate medical information related to gender affirming care, abortion and abortion-related services, and contraception from the rest of the patient's record.

(D) Provide the ability to automatically disable access to segregated medical information related to gender affirming care, abortion and abortion-related services, and contraception by individuals and entities in another state.

(2) Any fees charged to providers of health care, health care service plans, pharmaceutical company, contractors, employers, or patients to comply with this subdivision shall be consistent with Section 171.302 of Title 45 of the Code of Federal Regulations.

(3) For the purposes of this subdivision, "gender affirming care" means gender affirming health care and gender affirming mental health care as defined in subdivision (b) of Section 16010.2 of the Welfare and Institutions Code.

(4) This subdivision does not apply to a **contractor, health care service plan, or** provider of health care [1] **as those terms are** defined in Section 56.05.

(d) This section shall apply to an "electronic medical record" or "electronic health record" that meets the definition of "electronic health record," as that term is defined in Section 17921(5) of Title 42 of the United States Code. **Leg.H.** Added Stats 1999 ch 526 §3 (SB 19). Amended Stats 2000 ch 1067 §4 (SB 2094); Stats 2002 ch 853 §2 (AB 2191); Stats 2011 ch 714 §1 (SB 850), effective January 1, 2012; Stats 2023 ch 255 §1 (AB 352), effective January 1, 2024; Stats 2024 ch 853 §9 (AB 3281), effective January 1, 2025.

§56.101. 2024 Deletes. [1] , as

§56.102. Patients not required to sign release form as condition of receiving pharmaceuticals; Exceptions

(a) A pharmaceutical company may not require a patient, as a condition of receiving pharmaceuticals, medications, or prescription drugs, to sign an authorization, release, consent, or waiver that would permit the disclosure of medical information that otherwise may not be disclosed under Section 56.10 or any other provision of law, unless the disclosure is for one of the following purposes:

(1) Enrollment of the patient in a patient assistance program or prescription drug discount program.

(2) Enrollment of the patient in a clinical research project.

(3) Prioritization of distribution to the patient of a prescription medicine in limited supply in the United States.

(4) Response to an inquiry from the patient communicated in writing, by telephone, or by electronic mail.

(b) Except as provided in subdivision (a) or Section 56.10, a pharmaceutical company may not disclose medical information provided to it without first obtaining a valid authorization from the patient. **Leg.H.** Added Stats 2002 ch 853 §3 (AB 2191).

§56.103. Disclosure of minor's medical information or minor's mental health condition for purpose of coordinating health care services and medical treatment

(a) A provider of health care may disclose medical information to a county social worker, a probation officer, a foster care public health nurse acting pursuant to Section 16501.3 of the Welfare and Institutions Code, or any other person who is legally authorized to have custody or care of a minor for the purpose of coordinating health care services and medical treatment provided to the minor, including, but not limited to, the sharing of information related to screenings, assessments, and laboratory tests necessary to monitor the administration of psychotropic medications.

(b) For purposes of this section, health care services and medical treatment includes one or more providers of health care providing, coordinating, or managing health care and related services, including, but not limited to, a provider of health care coordinating health care with a third party, consultation between providers of health care and medical treatment relating to a minor, or a provider of health care referring a minor for health care services to another provider of health care.

(c) For purposes of this section, a county social worker, a probation officer, foster care public health nurse, or any other person who is legally authorized to have custody or care of a minor shall be considered a third party who may receive any of the following:

(1) Medical information described in Sections 56.05 and 56.10.

(2) Protected health information described in Section 160.103 of Title 45 of the Code of Federal Regulations.

(d) Medical information disclosed to a county social worker, probation officer, foster care public health nurse, or any other person who is legally authorized to have custody or care of a minor shall not be further disclosed by the recipient unless the disclosure is for the purpose of coordinating health care services and medical treatment of the minor and the disclosure is authorized by law. Medical information disclosed pursuant to this section may not be admitted into evidence in any criminal or delinquency proceeding against the minor. Nothing in this subdivision shall prohibit identical evidence from being admissible in a criminal proceeding if that evidence is derived solely from lawful means other than this section and is permitted by law.

(e)(1) Notwithstanding Section 56.104, if a provider of health care determines that the disclosure of medical information concerning the diagnosis and treatment of a mental health condition of a minor is reasonably necessary for the purpose of assisting in coordinating the treatment and care of the minor, that information may be disclosed to a county social worker, probation officer, foster care public health nurse, or any other person who is legally authorized to have custody or care of the minor. The information shall not be further disclosed by the recipient unless the disclosure is for the purpose of coordinating mental health services and treatment of the minor and the disclosure is authorized by law.

(2) As used in this subdivision, "medical information" does not include psychotherapy notes as defined in Section 164.501 of Title 45 of the Code of Federal Regulations.

(f) The disclosure of information pursuant to this section is not intended to limit the disclosure of information when that disclosure is otherwise required by law.

(g) For purposes of this section, "minor" means a minor taken into temporary custody or as to whom a petition has been filed with the court, or who has been adjudged to be a dependent child or ward of the juvenile court pursuant to Section 300 or 601 of the Welfare and Institutions Code.

(h)(1) Except as described in paragraph (1) of subdivision (e), nothing in this section shall be construed to limit or otherwise affect existing privacy protections provided for in state or federal law.

(2) Nothing in this section shall be construed to expand the authority of a social worker, probation officer, foster care public health nurse, or custodial caregiver beyond the authority provided under existing law to a parent or a patient representative regarding access to medical information. **Leg.H.** Added Stats 2007 ch 552 §3 (AB 1687), effective January 1, 2008. Amended Stats 2008 ch 699 §1 (SB 1241), ch 700 §1 (AB 2352) (ch 700 prevails), effective January 1, 2009; Stats 2015 ch 535 §1 (SB 319), effective January 1, 2016.

§56.104. Release of information on outpatient psychotherapy treatment

(a) Notwithstanding subdivision (c) of Section 56.10, except as provided in subdivision (e), no provider of health care, health care service plan, or contractor may release medical information to persons or entities who have requested that information and who are authorized by law to receive that information pursuant to subdivision (c) of Section 56.10, if the requested information specifically relates to the patient's participation in outpatient treatment with a psychotherapist, unless the person or entity requesting that information submits to the patient pursuant to subdivision (b) and to the provider of health care, health care service plan, or contractor a written request, signed by the person requesting the information or an authorized agent of the entity requesting the information, that includes all of the following:

(1) The specific information relating to a patient's participation in outpatient treatment with a psychotherapist being requested and its specific intended use or uses.

(2) The length of time during which the information will be kept before being destroyed or disposed of. A person or entity may extend that timeframe, provided that the person or entity notifies the provider, plan, or contractor of the extension. Any notification of an extension shall include the specific reason for the extension, the intended use or uses of the information during the extended time, and the expected date of the destruction of the information.

(3) A statement that the information will not be used for any purpose other than its intended use.

(4) A statement that the person or entity requesting the information will destroy the information and all copies in the person's or entity's possession or control, will cause it to be destroyed, or will return the information and all copies of it before or immediately after the length of time specified in paragraph (2) has expired.

(b) The person or entity requesting the information shall submit a copy of the written request required by this section to the patient within 30 days of receipt of the information requested, unless the patient has signed a written waiver in the form of a letter signed and submitted by the patient to the provider of health care or health care service plan waiving notification.

(c) For purposes of this section, "psychotherapist" means a person who is both a "psychotherapist" as defined in Section 1010 of the Evidence Code and a "provider of health care" as defined in Section 56.05.

(d) This section does not apply to the disclosure or use of medical information by a law enforcement agency or a regulatory agency when required for an investigation of unlawful activity or for licensing, certification, or regulatory purposes, unless the disclosure is otherwise prohibited by law.

(e) This section shall not apply to any of the following:

(1) Information authorized to be disclosed pursuant to paragraph (1) of subdivision (c) of Section 56.10.

(2) Information requested from a psychotherapist by law enforcement or by the target of the threat subsequent to a disclosure by that psychotherapist authorized by paragraph (19) of subdivision (c) of Section 56.10, in which the additional information is clearly necessary to prevent the serious and imminent threat disclosed under that paragraph.

(3) Information disclosed by a psychotherapist pursuant to paragraphs (14) and (22) of subdivision (c) of Section 56.10 and requested by an agency investigating the abuse reported pursuant to those paragraphs.

(f) Nothing in this section shall be construed to grant any additional authority to a provider of health care, health care service plan, or contractor to disclose information to a person or entity without the patient's consent. **Leg.H.** Added Stats 1999 ch 527 §3 (AB 416). Amended Stats 2004 ch 463 §1 (SB 598); Stats 2009 ch 464 §1 (AB 681), effective January 1, 2010; Stats 2010 ch 540 §2 (AB 2028), effective January 1, 2011; Stats 2013 ch 444 §3 (SB 138), effective January 1, 2014.

§56.105. Authorization to accompany settlement demand by patient; Notice of request for information

Whenever, prior to the service of a complaint upon a defendant in any action arising out of the professional negligence of a person holding a valid physician's and surgeon's certificate issued pursuant to Chapter 5 (commencing with Section 2000) of Division 2 of the Business and Professions Code, a person holding a valid license as a marriage and family therapist issued pursuant to Chapter 13 (commencing with Section 4980) of Division 2 of the Business and Professions Code, a person holding a valid license as a clinical social worker issued pursuant to Chapter 14 (commencing with Section 4991) of Division 2 of the Business and Professions Code, or a person holding a valid license as a professional clinical counselor issued pursuant to Chapter 16 (commencing with Section 4999.10) of Division 2 of the Business and Professions Code, a demand for settlement or offer to compromise is made on a patient's behalf, the demand or offer shall be accompanied by an authorization to disclose medical information to persons or organizations insuring, responsible for, or defending professional liability that the certificate holder may incur. The authorization shall be in accordance with Section 56.11 and shall authorize disclosure of that information that is necessary to investigate issues of liability and extent of potential damages in evaluating the merits of the demand for settlement or offer to compromise.

Notice of any request for medical information made pursuant to an authorization as provided by this section shall be given to the patient or the patient's legal representative. The notice shall describe the inclusive subject matter and dates of the materials requested and shall also authorize the patient or the patient's legal representative to receive, upon request, copies of the information at his or her expense.

Nothing in this section shall be construed to waive or limit any applicable privileges set forth in the Evidence Code except for the disclosure of medical information subject to the patient's authorization. Nothing in this section shall be construed as authorizing a representative of any person from whom settlement has been demanded to communicate in violation of the physician-patient privilege with a treating physician, or to communicate in violation of the psychotherapist-patient privilege with a treating licensed marriage and family therapist, licensed clinical social worker, or licensed professional clinical counselor, except for the medical information request.

The requirements of this section are independent of the requirements of Section 364 of the Code of Civil Procedure. **Leg.H.** Added Stats 1985 ch 484 §1. Amended Stats 2013 ch 58 §1 (SB 282), effective January 1, 2014; Stats 2018 ch 389 §8 (AB 2296), effective January 1, 2019.

§56.106. Disclosure or release of information on minor removed from physical custody of parent or guardian; Restrictions; Applicability

(a) Notwithstanding Section 3025 of the Family Code, paragraph (2) of subdivision (c) of Section 56.11, or any other provision of law, a psychotherapist who knows that a minor has been removed from the custody of his or her parent or guardian pursuant to Article 6 (commencing with Section 300) to Article 10 (commencing with Section 360), inclusive, of Chapter 2 of Part 1 of Division 2 of the Welfare and Institutions Code shall not release the mental health records of the minor patient and shall not disclose mental health information about that minor patient based upon an authorization to release those records signed by the minor's parent or guardian. This restriction shall not apply if the juvenile court has issued an order authorizing the parent or guardian to sign an authorization for the release of the mental health records or the information about the minor patient after finding that such an order would not be detrimental to the minor patient.

(b) For purposes of this section, the following definitions apply:

(1) "Mental health records" means mental health records as defined by subdivision (b) of Section 123105 of the Health and Safety Code.

(2) "Psychotherapist" means a provider of health care as defined in Section 1010 of the Evidence Code.

(c) When the juvenile court has issued an order authorizing the parent or guardian to sign an authorization for the release of the mental health records or information about that minor patient under the circumstances described in subdivision (a), the parent or guardian seeking the release of the minor's records or information about the minor shall present a copy of the court order to the psychotherapist before any records or information may be released pursuant to the signed authorization.

(d) Nothing in this section shall be construed to prevent or limit a psychotherapist's authority under subdivision (a) of Section 123115 of the Health and Safety Code to deny a parent's or guardian's written request to inspect or obtain copies of the minor patient's mental health records, notwithstanding the fact that the juvenile court has issued an order authorizing the parent or guardian to sign an authorization for the release of the mental health records or information about that minor patient. Liability for a psychotherapist's decision not to release the mental health records of the minor patient or not to disclose information about the minor patient pursuant to the authority of subdivision (a) of Section 123115 of the Health and Safety Code shall be governed by that section.

(e) Nothing in this section shall be construed to impose upon a psychotherapist a duty to inquire or investigate whether a child has been removed from the physical custody of his or her parent or guardian pursuant to Article 6 (commencing with Section 300) to Article 10 (commencing with Section 360), inclusive, of Chapter 2 of Part 1 of Division 2 of the Welfare and Institutions Code when a parent or guardian presents the minor's psychotherapist with an authorization to release information or the mental health records regarding the minor patient. **Leg.H.** Added Stats 2012 ch 657 §1 (SB 1407), effective January 1, 2013.

§ 56.107. Confidentiality of medical information

Notwithstanding any other law, and to the extent permitted by federal law, a health care service plan shall take the following steps to protect the confidentiality of a subscriber's or enrollee's medical information:

(a)(1) A health care service plan shall not require a protected individual to obtain the policyholder, primary subscriber, or other enrollee's authorization to receive sensitive services or to submit a claim for sensitive services if the protected individual has the right to consent to care.

(2) A health care service plan shall recognize the right of a protected individual to exclusively exercise rights granted under this section regarding medical information related to sensitive services that the protected individual has received.

(3) A health care service plan shall direct all communications regarding a protected individual's receipt of sensitive services directly to the protected individual receiving care as follows:

(A) If the protected individual has designated an alternative mailing address, email address, or telephone number pursuant to subdivision (b), the health care service plan shall send or make all communications related to the protected individual's receipt of sensitive services to the alternative mailing address, email address, or telephone number designated.

(B) If the protected individual has not designated an alternative mailing address, email address, or telephone number pursuant to subdivision (b), the health care service plan shall send or make all communications related to the protected individual's receipt of sensitive services in the name of the protected individual at the address or telephone number on file.

(C) Communications subject to this paragraph shall include the following written, verbal, or electronic communications related to the receipt of sensitive services:

(i) Bills and attempts to collect payment.

(ii) A notice of adverse benefits determinations.

(iii) An explanation of benefits notice.

(iv) A health care service plan's request for additional information regarding a claim.

(v) A notice of a contested claim.

(vi) The name and address of a provider, description of services provided, and other information related to a visit.

(vii) Any written, oral, or electronic communication from a health care service plan that contains protected health information.

(4) A health care service plan shall not disclose medical information related to sensitive health care services provided to a protected individual to the policyholder, primary subscriber, or any plan enrollees other than the protected individual receiving care, absent an express written authorization of the protected individual receiving care.

(b)(1) A health care service plan shall permit subscribers and enrollees to request, and shall accommodate requests for, confidential communication in the form and format requested by the individual, if it is readily producible in the requested form and format, or at alternative locations.

(2) A health care service plan may require the subscriber or enrollee to make a request for a confidential communication described in paragraph (1), in writing or by electronic transmission.

(3) The confidential communication request shall be valid until the subscriber or enrollee submits a revocation of the request or a new confidential communication request is submitted.

(4) The confidential communication request shall apply to all communications that disclose medical information or provider name and address related to receipt of medical services by the individual requesting the confidential communication.

(5) For the purposes of this section, a confidential communications request shall be implemented by the health care service plan within 7 calendar days of receipt of an electronic transmission or telephonic request or within 14 calendar days of receipt by first-class mail. The health care service plan shall acknowledge receipt of the confidential communications request and advise the subscriber or enrollee of the status of implementation of the request if a subscriber or enrollee contacts the health care service plan.

(c)(1) A health care service plan shall notify subscribers and enrollees that they may request a confidential communication pursuant to subdivision (b) and how to make the request.

(2) The information required to be provided pursuant to this subdivision shall be provided to subscribers and enrollees with individual or group coverage upon initial enrollment and annually thereafter upon renewal. The information shall also be provided in the following manner:

(A) In a conspicuously visible location in the evidence of coverage.

(B) On the health care service plan's internet website, accessible through a hyperlink on the internet website's home page and in a manner that allows subscribers, enrollees, prospective subscribers, prospective enrollees, and members of the public to easily locate the information.

(d) Notwithstanding subdivision (b), the provider of health care may make arrangements with the subscriber or enrollee for the payment of benefit cost sharing and communicate that arrangement with the health care service plan.

(e) A health care service plan shall not condition enrollment or coverage on the waiver of rights provided in this section.

(f) This section shall become operative on July 1, 2022. **Leg.H.** Added Stats 2021 ch 190 §3 (AB 1184), effective January 1, 2022, operative July 1, 2022.

Prior Law: Former CC §56.107, relating to confidentiality of medical information, was added Stats 2013 ch 444 §4 (SB 138), effective January 1, 2014, amended Stats 2021 ch190 §2 (AB 1184), effective January 1, 2022, and repealed July 1, 2022, by its own terms.

§56.108. Release of medical information related to abortion; Restrictions

(a) Notwithstanding subdivisions (b) and (c) of Section 56.10 or subdivision (c) of Section 56.20, a provider of health care, health care service plan, contractor, or employer shall not release medical information related to an individual seeking or obtaining an abortion in response to a subpoena or request if that subpoena or request is based on either another state's laws that interfere with a person's rights under the Reproductive Privacy Act (Article 2.5 (commencing with Section 123460) of Chapter 2 of Part 2 of Division 106 of the Health and Safety Code) or a foreign penal civil action, as defined in Section 2029.200 of the Code of Civil Procedure.

(b) A provider of health care, health care service plan, contractor, or employer shall not release medical information that would identify an individual or that is related to an individual seeking or obtaining an abortion to law enforcement for either of the following purposes, unless that release is pursuant to a subpoena not otherwise prohibited by subdivision (a):

(1) Enforcement of another state's law that would interfere with a person's rights under the Reproductive Privacy Act (Article 2.5 (commencing with Section 123460) of Chapter 2 of Part 2 of Division 106 of the Health and Safety Code).

(2) Enforcement of a foreign penal civil action, as defined in Section 2029.200 of the Code of Civil Procedure.

(c) Notwithstanding subdivisions (b) and (c) of Section 56.10 or subdivision (c) of Section 56.20, a provider of health care, health care service plan, contractor, or employer shall not cooperate with any inquiry or investigation by, or provide medical information to, any individual, agency, or department from another state or, to the extent permitted by federal law, to a federal law enforcement agency that would identify an individual and that is related to an individual seeking or obtaining an abortion or abortion-related services that are lawful under the laws of this state, unless the request for medical information is authorized under Section 56.110.

(d) This section does not prohibit compliance with the investigation of activity that is punishable as a crime under the laws of this state. **Leg.H.** Added Stats 2022 ch 628 §2 (AB 2091), effective September 27, 2022. Amended Stats 2023 ch 255 §2 (AB 352), effective January 1, 2024.

§ 56.109. Release of medical information related to child receiving gender-affirming health care or gender-affirming mental health care

(a) Notwithstanding subdivision (b) of Section 56.10, a provider of health care, health care service plan, or contractor shall not release medical information related to a person or entity allowing a child to receive gender-affirming health care or gender-affirming mental health care in response to any civil action, including a foreign subpoena, based on another state's law that authorizes a person to bring a civil action against a person or entity that allows a child to receive gender-affirming health care or gender-affirming mental health care.

(b) Notwithstanding subdivision (c) of Section 56.10, a provider of health care, health care service plan, or contractor shall not release medical information to persons or entities who have requested that information and who are authorized by law to receive that information pursuant to subdivision (c) of Section 56.10, if the information is related to a person or entity allowing a child to receive gender-affirming health care or gender-affirming mental health care, and the information is being requested pursuant to another state's law that authorizes a person to bring a civil action against a person or entity who allows a child to receive gender-affirming health care or gender-affirming mental health care.

(c) For the purposes of this section, "person" means an individual or governmental subdivision, agency, or instrumentality.

(d) For the purpose of this section, "gender-affirming health care" and "gender-affirming mental health care" shall have the same meaning as provided in Section 16010.2 of the Welfare and Institutions Code. **Leg.H.** Added Stats 2022 ch 810 §1 (SB 107), effective January 1, 2023.

§ 56.110. Protection of identifying information relating to lawful abortion

(a) Notwithstanding subdivision (c) of Section 56.10, a provider of health care, health care service plan, pharmaceutical company, contractor, or employer shall not knowingly disclose, transmit, transfer, share, or grant access to medical information in an electronic health records system or through a health information exchange that would identify an individual and that is related to an individual seeking, obtaining, providing, supporting, or aiding in the performance of an abortion that is lawful under the laws of this state to any individual or entity from another state, unless the disclosure, transmittal, transfer, sharing, or granting of access is authorized under any of the following conditions:

(1) In accordance with a valid, written authorization pursuant to Section 56.11 that clearly states that medical information on abortion or abortion-related services may be disclosed, and only to the extent and for the purposes expressly stated in the authorization.

(2) In accordance with paragraphs (2) and (3) of subdivision (c) of Section 56.10, to the extent necessary to allow responsibility for payment to be determined and payment to be made or to the extent that it is not further disclosed by the recipient in a way that would violate this part.

(3) In accordance with paragraphs (4) and (5) of subdivision (c) of Section 56.10 for the purpose of accreditation, in reviewing the competence or qualifications of health care professionals, or in reviewing health care services with respect to medical necessity, level of care, quality of care, or justification of charges.

(4) In accordance with paragraph (7) of subdivision (c) of Section 56.10, for the purpose of bona fide research. Institutional Review Boards shall consider the potential harm to the patient and the patient's privacy when the research uses data that contains information related to abortion or abortion-related services and the research is performed out of state.

(b) Notwithstanding subdivision (a), the content of the health records containing medical information described in subdivision (a) shall be disclosed to any of the following:

(1) A patient, or their personal representative, consistent with the Patient Access to Health Records Act (Chapter 1 (commencing with Section 123100) of Part 1 of Division 106 of the Health and Safety Code).

(2) In response to an order of a California or federal court, but only to the extent clearly stated in the order and consistent with Section 1543 of the Penal Code, if applicable, and only if all information about the patient's identity and records are protected from public scrutiny through mechanisms, including, but not limited to, a sealed proceeding or court record.

(3) When expressly required by federal law that preempts California law, but only to the extent expressly required.

(c) Nothing in this section shall prohibit a provider of health care, health care service plan, pharmaceutical company, contractor, or employer from cooperating or complying with the investigation of activity that is punishable as a crime under the laws of California, and that took place in California.

(d) A provider of health care, as defined in Section 56.05, shall not be subject to liability for damages or to civil or enforcement actions, including disciplinary actions, fines, or penalties, for failure to meet the requirements of this section before January 31, 2026, if the provider of health care is working diligently and in good faith to come into compliance with this section. **Leg.H.** Added Stats 2023 ch 255 §3 (AB 352), effective January 1, 2024.

§56.11. Form and contents of authorization

(a) Any person or entity that wishes to obtain medical information pursuant to subdivision (a) of Section 56.10, other than a person or entity authorized to receive medical information pursuant to subdivision (b) or (c) of Section 56.10, except as provided in paragraph (21) of subdivision (c) of Section 56.10, shall obtain a valid authorization for the release of this information.

(b) An authorization for the release of medical information by a provider of health care, health care service plan, pharmaceutical company, or contractor shall be valid if it meets the following conditions:

(1) Is handwritten or is in a typeface no smaller than 14-point type.

(2) Is clearly separate from any other language present on the same page and is executed by a signature that serves no other purpose than to execute the authorization.

(3) Is signed, including with an electronic or handwritten signature, and dated by one of the following:

(A) The patient. A patient who is a minor may only sign an authorization for the release of medical information obtained by a provider of health care, health care service plan, pharmaceutical company, or contractor in the course of furnishing services to which the minor could lawfully have consented under Part 4 (commencing with Section 6900) of Division 11 of the Family Code.

(B) The legal representative of the patient, if the patient is a minor or lacks the capacity to make the decision to authorize the release of medical information. However, authorization may not be given under this subdivision for the disclosure of medical information obtained by the provider of health care, health care service plan, pharmaceutical company, or contractor in the course of furnishing services to which a minor patient could lawfully have consented under Part 4 (commencing with Section 6900) of Division 11 of the Family Code.

(C) The spouse of the patient or the person financially responsible for the patient, where the medical information is being sought for the sole purpose of processing an application for health insurance or for enrollment in a nonprofit hospital plan, a health care service plan, or an employee benefit plan, and where the patient is to be an enrolled spouse or dependent under the policy or plan.

(D) The beneficiary, as defined in Section 24 of the Probate Code, or personal representative, as defined in Section 58 of the Probate Code, of a deceased patient.

(4) States the specific uses and limitations on the types of medical information to be disclosed.

(5) States the name or functions of the provider of health care, health care service plan, pharmaceutical company, or contractor that may disclose the medical information.

(6) States the name or functions of the persons or entities authorized to receive the medical information.

(7) States the specific uses and limitations on the use of the medical information by the persons or entities authorized to receive the medical information.

(8) States an expiration date or event. The expiration date or event shall limit the duration of the authorization to one year or less, unless the person signing the authorization requests a specific date beyond a year or unless the authorization is related to an approved clinical trial, as defined in Section 1370.6 of the Health and Safety Code, or medical research study, in which case the authorization may extend beyond one year if the expiration date or event extends no longer than the completion of the relevant clinical trial or research study.

(9) Advises the person signing the authorization of the right to receive a copy of the authorization.

(c) If a provider of health care, health care service plan, pharmaceutical company, contractor, or any other entity seeks an authorization from an individual for a use or disclosure of protected health information, the provider of health care, health care service plan, pharmaceutical company, contractor, or other entity shall provide the individual with a copy of the signed authorization, and instructions on how to access additional copies or a digital version of the signed authorization. **Leg.H.** Added Stats 1981 ch 782 §2. Amended Stats 1999 ch 526 §4 (SB 19); Stats 2000 ch 1066 §3 (SB 1903); Stats 2002 ch 853 §4 (AB 2191); Stats 2003 ch 562 §3 (AB 715); Stats 2009 ch 493 §2 (AB 952), effective January 1, 2010; Stats 2023 ch 374 §2 (AB 1697), effective January 1, 2024.

§56.12. Furnishing copy of authorization

Upon demand by the patient or the person who signed an authorization, a provider of health care, health care service plan, pharmaceutical company, or contractor possessing the authorization shall furnish a true copy thereof. **Leg.H.** Added Stats 1981 ch 782 §2. Amended Stats 1999 ch 526 §5 (SB 19); Stats 2002 ch 853 §5 (AB 2191).

§56.13. Disclosure by recipient

A recipient of medical information pursuant to an authorization as provided by this chapter or pursuant to the provisions of subdivision (c) of Section 56.10 may not further disclose that medical information except in accordance with a new authorization that meets the requirements of Section 56.11, or as specifically required or permitted by other provisions of this chapter or by law. **Leg.H.** Added Stats 1981 ch 782 §2.

§56.14. Communication of limits of authorization

A provider of health care, health care service plan, or contractor that discloses medical information pursuant to the authorizations required by this chapter shall communicate to the person or entity to which it discloses the medical information any limitations in the authorization regarding the use of the medical information. No provider of health care, health care service plan, or contractor that has attempted in good faith to comply with this provision shall be liable for any unauthorized use of the medical information by the person or entity to which the provider, plan, or contractor disclosed the medical information. **Leg.H.** Added Stats 1981 ch 782 §2. Amended Stats 1999 ch 526 §6 (SB 19).

§56.15. Cancellation and modification of authorization

Nothing in this part shall be construed to prevent a person who could sign the authorization pursuant to subdivision (c) of Section 56.11 from cancelling or modifying an authorization. However, the cancellation or modification shall be effective only after the provider of health care actually receives written notice of the cancellation or modification. **Leg.H.** Added Stats 1981 ch 782 §2.

Prior Law: Former §56.15, similar to present CC §56.10, was added Stats 1979 ch 773 §1 and repealed Stats 1981 ch 782 §1.5.

§56.16. Information that may be released without authorization

For disclosures not addressed by Section 56.1007, unless there is a specific written request by the patient to the contrary, nothing in this part shall be construed to prevent a general acute care hospital, as defined in subdivision (a) of Section 1250 of the Health and Safety Code, upon an inquiry concerning a specific patient, from releasing at its discretion any of the following information: the patient's name, address, age, and sex; a general description of the reason for treatment (whether an injury, a burn, poisoning, or some unrelated condition); the general nature of the injury, burn, poisoning, or other condition; the general condition of the patient; and any information that is not medical information as defined in Section 56.05. **Leg.H.** Added Stats 1981 ch 782 §2. Amended Stats 2006 ch 833 §2 (AB 3013), effective January 1, 2007; Stats 2013 ch 76 §10 (AB 383), effective January 1, 2014, ch 444 §5 (AB 138), effective January 1, 2014 (ch 444 prevails).

Prior Law: Former §56.16, relating to collection of individually identifiable medical information, was added Stats 1979 ch 773 §1 and repealed Stats 1981 ch 782 §1.5.

CHAPTER 2.5
DISCLOSURE OF GENETIC TEST RESULTS BY HEALTH CARE SERVICE PLAN

Disclosure of genetic test results. §56.17.

§56.17. Disclosure of genetic test results

(a) This section shall apply to the disclosure of genetic test results by a health care service plan that are contained in an applicant's or enrollee's medical records.

(b) Any person who negligently discloses results of a test for a genetic characteristic to any third party in a manner that identifies or provides identifying characteristics of the person to whom the test results apply, except pursuant to a written authorization as described in subdivision (g), shall be assessed a civil penalty in an amount not to exceed one thousand dollars ($1,000) plus court costs, as determined by the court, which penalty and costs shall be paid to the subject of the test.

(c) Any person who willfully discloses the results of a test for a genetic characteristic to any third party in a manner that identifies or provides identifying characteristics of the person to whom the test results apply, except pursuant to a written authorization as described in subdivision (g), shall be assessed a civil penalty in an amount not less than one thousand dollars ($1,000) and no more than five thousand dollars ($5,000) plus court costs, as determined by the court, which penalty and costs shall be paid to the subject of the test.

(d) Any person who willfully or negligently discloses the results of a test for a genetic characteristic to a third party in a manner that identifies or provides identifying characteristics of the person to whom the test results apply, except pursuant to a written authorization as described in subdivision (g), that results in economic, bodily, or emotional harm to the subject of the test, is guilty of a misdemeanor punishable by a fine not to exceed ten thousand dollars ($10,000).

(e) In addition to the penalties listed in subdivisions (b) and (c), any person who commits any act described in subdivision (b) or (c) shall be liable to the subject for all actual damages, including damages for economic, bodily, or emotional harm which is proximately caused by the act.

(f) Each disclosure made in violation of this section is a separate and actionable offense.

(g) The applicant's "written authorization," as used in this section, shall satisfy the following requirements:

(1) Is written in plain language and is in a typeface no smaller than 14-point type.

(2) Is dated and signed, including with an electronic or handwritten signature, by the individual or a person authorized to act on behalf of the individual.

(3) Specifies the types of persons authorized to disclose information about the individual.

(4) Specifies the nature of the information authorized to be disclosed.

(5) States the name or functions of the persons or entities authorized to receive the information.

(6) Specifies the purposes for which the information is collected.

(7) Specifies the length of time the authorization shall remain valid or states an expiration date or event. The expiration date or event shall limit the duration of the authorization to one year or less, unless the person signing the authorization requests a specific date beyond a year or unless the authorization is related to an approved clinical trial, as defined in Section 1370.6 of the Health and Safety Code, or medical research study, in which case the authorization may extend beyond one year if the expiration date or event extends no longer than the completion of the relevant clinical trial or research study.

(8) Advises the person signing the authorization of the right to receive a copy of the authorization. Written authorization is required for each separate disclosure of the test results.

(h) If a provider of health care, health care service plan, pharmaceutical company, contractor, or any other entity seeks an authorization from an individual for a use or disclosure of protected health information, the provider of health care, health care service plan, pharmaceutical company, contractor, or other entity shall provide the individual with a copy of the signed authorization and instructions on how to access additional copies or a digital version of the signed authorization.

(i) This section shall not apply to disclosures required by the State Department of Health Care Services necessary to monitor compliance with Chapter 1 (commencing with Section 124975) of Part 5 of Division 106 of the Health and Safety Code, nor to disclosures required by the Department of Managed Health Care necessary to administer and enforce compliance with Section 1374.7 of the Health and Safety Code.

(j) For purposes of this section, "genetic characteristic" has the same meaning as that set forth in subdivision (d) of Section 1374.7 of the Health and Safety Code. **Leg.H.** Added Stats 1995 ch 695 §1 (SB 1020). Amended Stats 1996 ch 532 §1 (SB 1740) (ch 532 prevails), ch 1023 §25 (SB 1497), effective September 29, 1996; Stats 1999 ch 311 §1 (SB 1185), ch 525 §5 (AB 78); Stats 2000 ch 857 §4 (AB 2903) (ch 941 prevails), ch 941 §1 (SB 1364); Stats 2003 ch 562 §4 (AB 715); Stats 2023 ch 374 §3 (AB 1697), effective January 1, 2024.

Prior Law: Former §56.17, relating to responsibility for securing a release from applicant, was added Stats 1979 ch 773 §1 and repealed Stats 1981 ch 782 §1.5.

§56.18. [Section repealed 1981]

Leg.H. Added Stats 1979 ch 773 §1. Repealed Stats 1981 ch 782 §1.5. The repealed section related to release of patient information, see now CC §56.16.

§56.19. [Section repealed 1981]

Leg.H. Added Stats 1979 ch 773 §1. Repealed Stats 1981 ch 782 §1.5. The repealed section related to effect on existing law, see now CC §56.28.

CHAPTER 2.6
GENETIC PRIVACY

Genetic Information Privacy Act; Definitions. § 56.18.
Requirements for direct-to-consumer genetic testing company to safeguard privacy, confidentiality, security, and integrity of consumer's genetic data; Consent; Discrimination; Disclosure. § 56.181.
Violations; Penalties; Procedure. § 56.182.
Relationship of chapter to other laws; Applicability of chapter. § 56.184.
Severability. § 56.186.

§ 56.18. Genetic Information Privacy Act; Definitions

(a) This chapter shall be known, and may be cited, as the Genetic Information Privacy Act.

(b) For purposes of this chapter, the following definitions apply:

(1) "Affirmative authorization" means an action that demonstrates an intentional decision by the consumer.

(2) "Biological sample" means any material part of the human, discharge therefrom, or derivative thereof, such as tissue, blood, urine, or saliva, known to contain deoxyribonucleic acid (DNA).

(3) "Consumer" means a natural person who is a California resident.

(4) "Dark pattern" means a user interface designed or manipulated with the substantial effect of subverting or impairing user autonomy, decisionmaking, or choice.

(5) "Direct-to-consumer genetic testing company" means an entity that does any of the following:

(A) Sells, markets, interprets, or otherwise offers consumer-initiated genetic testing products or services directly to consumers.

(B) Analyzes genetic data obtained from a consumer, except to the extent that the analysis is performed by a person licensed in the healing arts for diagnosis or treatment of a medical condition.

(C) Collects, uses, maintains, or discloses genetic data collected or derived from a direct-to-consumer genetic testing product or service, or is directly provided by a consumer.

(6) "Express consent" means a consumer's affirmative authorization to grant permission in response to a clear, meaningful, and prominent notice regarding the collection, use, maintenance, or disclosure of genetic data for a specific purpose. The nature of the data collection, use, maintenance, or disclosure shall be conveyed in clear and prominent terms in such a manner that an ordinary consumer would notice and understand it. Express consent cannot be inferred from inaction. Agreement obtained through use of dark patterns does not constitute consent.

(7)(A) "Genetic data" means any data, regardless of its format, that results from the analysis of a biological sample from a consumer, or from another element enabling equivalent information to be obtained, and concerns genetic material. Genetic material includes, but is not limited to, deoxyribonucleic acids (DNA), ribonucleic acids (RNA), genes, chromosomes, alleles, genomes, alterations or modifications to DNA or RNA, single nucleotide polymorphisms (SNPs), uninterpreted data that results from the analysis of the biological sample, and any information extrapolated, derived, or inferred therefrom.

(B) "Genetic data" does not include deidentified data. For purposes of this subparagraph, "deidentified data" means data that cannot be used to infer information about, or otherwise be linked to, a particular individual, provided that the business that possesses the information does all of the following:

(i) Takes reasonable measures to ensure that the information cannot be associated with a consumer or household.

(ii) Publicly commits to maintain and use the information only in deidentified form and not to attempt to reidentify the information, except that the business may attempt to reidentify the information solely for the purpose of determining whether its deidentification processes satisfy the requirements of this subparagraph, provided that the business does not use or disclose any information reidentified in this process and destroys the reidentified information upon completion of that assessment.

(iii) Contractually obligates any recipients of the information to take reasonable measures to ensure that the information cannot be associated with a consumer or household and to commit to maintaining and using the information only in deidentified form and not to reidentify the information.

(C) "Genetic data" does not include data or a biological sample to the extent that data or a biological sample is collected, used, maintained, and disclosed exclusively for scientific research conducted by an investigator with an institution that holds an assurance with the United States Department of Health and Human Services pursuant to Part 46 (commencing with Section 46.101) of Title 45 of the Code of Federal Regulations, in compliance with all applicable federal and state laws and regulations for the protection of human subjects in research, including, but not limited to, the Common Rule pursuant to Part 46 (commencing with Section 46.101) of Title 45 of the Code of Federal Regulations, United States Food and Drug Administration regulations pursuant to Parts 50 and 56 of Title 21 of the Code of Federal Regulations, the federal Family Educational Rights and Privacy Act (20 U.S.C. Sec. 1232g), and the Protection of Human Subjects in Medical Experimentation Act, Chapter 1.3 (commencing with Section 24170) of Division 20 of the Health and Safety Code.

(8) "Genetic testing" means any laboratory test of a biological sample from a consumer for the purpose of determining information concerning genetic material contained within the biological sample, or any information extrapolated, derived, or inferred therefrom.

(9) "Person" means an individual, partnership, corporation, association, business, business trust, or legal representative of an organization.

(10) "Service provider" means a sole proprietorship, partnership, limited liability company, corporation, association, or other legal entity that is organized or operated for the profit or financial benefit of its shareholders or other owners, that is involved in the collection, transportation, and analysis of the consumer's biological sample or extracted genetic material on behalf of the direct-to-consumer genetic testing company, or on behalf of any other company that collects, uses, maintains, or discloses genetic data collected or derived from a direct-to-consumer genetic testing product or service, or is directly provided by a consumer, or the delivery of the results of the analysis of the biological sample or genetic material. The contract between the company and the service provider shall prohibit the service provider from retaining, using, or disclosing the biological sample, extracted genetic material, genetic data, or any information regarding the identity of the consumer, including whether that consumer has solicited or received genetic testing, as applicable, for any purpose other than for the specific purpose of performing the services specified in the contract for the business, including both of the following:

(A) A provision prohibiting the service provider from retaining, using, or disclosing the biological sample, extracted genetic material, genetic data, or any information regarding the identity of the consumer, including whether that consumer has solicited or received genetic testing, as applicable, for a commercial purpose other than providing the services specified in the contract with the business.

(B) A provision prohibiting the service provider from associating or combining the biological sample, extracted genetic material, genetic data, or any information regarding the identity of the consumer, including whether that consumer has solicited or received genetic testing, as applicable, with information the service provider has received from or on behalf of another person or persons, or has collected from its own interaction with consumers or as required by law. **Leg.H.** Added Stats 2021 ch 596 §2 (SB 41), effective January 1, 2022.

§ 56.181. Requirements for direct-to-consumer genetic testing company to safeguard privacy, confidentiality, security, and integrity of consumer's genetic data; Consent; Discrimination; Disclosure

(a) To safeguard the privacy, confidentiality, security, and integrity of a consumer's genetic data, a direct-to-consumer genetic testing company shall do both of the following:

(1) Provide clear and complete information regarding the company's policies and procedures for the collection, use, maintenance, and disclosure, as applicable, of genetic data by making available to a consumer all of the following:

(A) A summary of its privacy practices, written in plain language, that includes information about the company's collection, use, maintenance, and disclosure, as applicable, of genetic data.

(B) A prominent and easily accessible privacy notice that includes, at a minimum, complete information about the company's data collection, consent, use, access, disclosure, maintenance, transfer, security, and retention and deletion practices, and information that clearly describes how to file a complaint alleging a violation of this chapter, pursuant to subdivision (c) of Section 56.182.

(C) A notice that the consumer's deidentified genetic or phenotypic information may be shared with or disclosed to third parties for research purposes in accordance with Part 46 (commencing with Section 46.101) of Title 45 of the Code of Federal Regulations.

(2) Obtain a consumer's express consent for collection, use, and disclosure of the consumer's genetic data, including, at a minimum, separate and express consent for each of the following:

(A) The use of the genetic data collected through the genetic testing product or service offered to the consumer, including who has access to genetic data, and how genetic data may be shared, and the specific purposes for which it will be collected, used, and disclosed.

(B) The storage of a consumer's biological sample after the initial testing requested by the consumer has been fulfilled.

(C) Each use of genetic data or the biological sample beyond the primary purpose of the genetic testing or service and inherent contextual uses.

(D) Each transfer or disclosure of the consumer's genetic data or biological sample to a third party other than to a service provider, including the name of the third party to which the consumer's genetic data or biological sample will be transferred or disclosed.

(E)(i) The marketing or facilitation of marketing to a consumer based on the consumer's genetic data or the marketing or facilitation of marketing by a third party based upon the consumer having ordered, purchased, received, or used a genetic testing product or service.

(ii) This subparagraph does not require a direct-to-consumer genetic testing company to obtain a consumer's express consent to market to the consumer on the company's own website or mobile application based upon the consumer having ordered, purchased, received, or used a genetic testing product or service from that company if the content of the advertisement does not depend upon any information specific to that consumer, except for the product or service that the consumer ordered, purchased, received, or used, and the placement of the advertisement is not intended to result in disparate exposure to advertising content on the basis of any characteristic specified in Section 51. Nothing in this subparagraph alters, limits, or negates the requirements of any other antidiscrimination law or targeted advertising law.

(iii) Any advertisement of a third-party product or service presented to a consumer pursuant to either clause (i) or (ii) shall be prominently labeled as advertising content and be accompanied by the name of any third party that has contributed to the placement of the advertising. If applicable, the advertisement also shall clearly indicate that the advertised product or service, and any associated claims, have not been vetted or endorsed by the direct-to-consumer genetic testing company.

(F) For the purpose of this paragraph, "third party" does not include a public or private nonprofit postsecondary educational institution to the extent that the consumer's genetic data or biological sample is disclosed to a public or private nonprofit postsecondary educational institution for the purpose of scientific research or educational activities as described in paragraph (4) of subdivision (b) of Section 56.184.

(b) A company that is subject to the requirements described in paragraph (2) of subdivision (a) shall provide effective mechanisms, without any unnecessary steps, for a consumer to revoke their consent after it is given, at least one of which utilizes the primary medium through which the company communicates with consumers.

(c) If a consumer revokes the consent that they provided pursuant to paragraph (2) of subdivision (a), the company shall honor the consumer's consent revocation as soon as practicable, but not later than 30 days after the individual revokes consent, in accordance with both of the following:

(1) Revocation of consent under this section shall comply with Part 46 of Title 45 of the Code of Federal Regulations.

(2) The company shall destroy a consumer's biological sample within 30 days of receipt of revocation of consent to store the sample.

(d) The direct-to-consumer genetic testing company shall do both of the following:

(1) Implement and maintain reasonable security procedures and practices to protect a consumer's genetic data against unauthorized access, destruction, use, modification, or disclosure.

(2) Develop procedures and practices to enable a consumer to easily do any of the following:

(A) Access the consumer's genetic data.

(B) Delete the consumer's account and genetic data, except for genetic data that is required to be retained by the company to comply with applicable legal and regulatory requirements.

(C) Have the consumer's biological sample destroyed.

(e) A person or public entity shall not discriminate against a consumer because the consumer exercised any of the consumer's rights under this chapter by doing any of the following, including, but not limited to:

(1) Denying goods, services, or benefits to the customer.

(2) Charging different prices or rates for goods or services, including through the use of discounts or other incentives or imposing penalties.

(3) Providing a different level or quality of goods, services, or benefits to the consumer.

(4) Suggesting that the consumer will receive a different price or rate for goods, services, or benefits, or a different level or quality of goods, services, or benefits.

(5) Considering the consumer's exercise of rights under this chapter as a basis for suspicion of criminal wrongdoing or unlawful conduct.

(f)(1) Notwithstanding any other provision in this section, and except as provided in paragraph (2), a direct-to-consumer genetic testing company shall not disclose a consumer's genetic data to any entity that is responsible for administering or making decisions regarding health insurance, life insurance, long-term care insurance, disability insurance, or employment or to any entity that provides advice to an entity that is responsible for performing those functions.

(2) A direct-to-consumer genetic testing company may disclose a consumer's genetic data or biological sample to an entity described in paragraph (1) if all of the following are true:

(A) The entity is not primarily engaged in administering health insurance, life insurance, long-term care insurance, disability insurance, or employment.

(B) The consumer's genetic data or biological sample is not disclosed to the entity in that entity's capacity as a party that is responsible for administering, advising, or making decisions regarding health insurance, life insurance, long-term care insurance, disability insurance, or employment.

(C) Any agent or division of the entity that is involved in administering, advising, or making decisions regarding health insurance, life insurance, long-term care insurance, disability insurance, or employment is prohibited from accessing the consumer's genetic data or biological sample. **Leg.H.** Added Stats 2021 ch 596 §2 (SB 41), effective January 1, 2022.

§ 56.182. Violations; Penalties; Procedure

(a) Any person who negligently violates this chapter shall be assessed a civil penalty in an amount not to exceed one thousand dollars ($1,000) plus court costs, as determined by the court.

(b) Any person who willfully violates this chapter shall be assessed a civil penalty in an amount not less than one thousand dollars ($1,000) and not more than ten thousand dollars ($10,000) plus court costs, as determined by the court.

(c) Actions for relief pursuant to this chapter shall be prosecuted exclusively in a court of competent jurisdiction by the Attorney General or a district attorney or by a county counsel authorized by agreement with the district attorney in actions involving violation of a county ordinance, or by a city attorney of a city having a population in excess of 750,000, or by a city attorney in a city and county or, with the consent of the district attorney, by a city prosecutor in a city having a full-time city prosecutor in the name of the people of the State of California upon their own complaint or upon the complaint of a board, officer, person, corporation, or association, or upon a complaint by a person who has suffered injury in fact and has lost money or property as a result of the violation of this chapter.

(d) Court costs recovered pursuant to this section shall be paid to the party or parties that prosecuted the violation. Penalties recovered pursuant to this section shall be paid to the individual to whom the genetic data at issue pertains.

(e) Any provision of a contract or agreement between a consumer and a person governed by this chapter that has, or would have, the effect of delaying or limiting access to a legal remedy for a violation of this chapter shall not apply to the exercise of rights or enforcement pursuant to this chapter.

(f) Each violation of this chapter is a separate and actionable violation. **Leg.H.** Added Stats 2021 ch 596 §2 (SB 41), effective January 1, 2022.

§ 56.184. Relationship of chapter to other laws; Applicability of chapter

(a) The provisions of this chapter shall not reduce a direct-to-consumer genetic testing company's duties, obligations, requirements, or standards under any applicable state and federal laws for the protection of privacy and security.

(b) In the event of a conflict between the provisions of this chapter and any other law, the provisions of the law that afford the greatest protection for the right of privacy for consumers shall control.

(c) This chapter shall not apply to any of the following:

(1) Medical information governed by the Confidentiality of Medical Information Act, Part 2.6 (commencing with Section 56), or to protected health information that is collected, maintained, used, or disclosed by a covered entity or business associate governed by the privacy, security, and breach notification rules issued by the United States Department of Health and Human Services, Parts 160 and 164 of Title 45 of the Code of Federal Regulations established pursuant to the federal Health Insurance Portability and Accountability Act of 1996 (Public Law 104-191) and the federal Health Information Technology for Economic and Clinical Health Act (Public Law 111-5).

(2) A provider of health care governed by the Confidentiality of Medical Information Act (Part 2.6 (commencing with Section 56)) or a covered entity governed by the privacy, security, and breach notification rules issued by the United States Department of Health and Human Services, Parts 160 and 164 of Title 45 of the Code of Federal Regulations, established pursuant to the Health Insurance Portability and Accountability Act of 1996 (Public Law 104-191) and the federal Health Information Technology for Economic and Clinical Health Act, Title XIII of the federal American Recovery and Reinvestment Act of 2009 (Public Law 111-5), to the extent that the provider or covered entity maintains, uses, and discloses genetic information in the same manner as medical information or protected health information, as described in paragraph (1).

(3) A business associate of a covered entity governed by the privacy, security, and data breach notification rules issued by the United States Department of Health and Human Services, Parts 160 and 164 of Title 45 of the Code of Federal Regulations, established pursuant to the federal Health Insurance Portability and Accountability Act of 1996 (Public Law 104-191) and the federal Health Information Technology for Economic and Clinical Health Act, Title XIII of the federal American Recovery and Reinvestment Act of 2009 (Public Law 111-5), to the extent that the business associate maintains, uses, and discloses genetic information in the same manner as medical information or protected health information, as described in paragraph (1).

(4) Scientific research or educational activities conducted by a public or private nonprofit postsecondary educational institution that holds an assurance with the United States Department of Health and Human Services pursuant to Part 46 of Title 45 of the Code of Federal Regulations, to the extent that the scientific research and educational activities conducted by that institution comply with all applicable federal and state laws and regulations for the protection of human subjects in research, including, but not limited to, the Common Rule pursuant to Part 46 (commencing with Section 46.101) of Title 45 of the Code of Federal Regulations, United States Food and Drug Administration regulations pursuant to Parts 50 and 56 of Title 21 of the Code of Federal Regulations, the federal Family Educational Rights and Privacy Act (20 U.S.C. Sec. 1232g), and the Protection of Human Subjects in Medical Experimentation Act, Chapter 1.3 (commencing with Section 24170) of Division 20 of the Health and Safety Code.

(5) The California Newborn Screening Program authorized by Chapter 1 (commencing with Section 124975) of Part 5 of Division 106 of the Health and Safety Code.

(6) Tests conducted exclusively to diagnose whether an individual has a specific disease, to the extent that all persons involved in the conduct of the test maintain, use, and disclose genetic information in the same manner as medical information or protected health information, as described in paragraph (1).

(7) Genetic data used or maintained by an employer, or disclosed by an employee to an employer, to the extent that the use, maintenance, or disclosure of that data is necessary to comply with a local, state, or federal workplace health and safety ordinance, law, or regulation.

(d) Nothing in this chapter shall be construed to affect access to information made available to the public by the consumer. **Leg.H.** Added Stats 2021 ch 596 §2 (SB 41), effective January 1, 2022.

§ 56.186. Severability

The provisions of this chapter are severable. If any provision of this chapter or its application is held invalid, that invalidity shall not affect other provisions or applications that can be given effect without the invalid provision or application. **Leg.H.** Added Stats 2021 ch 596 §2 (SB 41), effective January 1, 2022.

CHAPTER 3
USE AND DISCLOSURE OF MEDICAL INFORMATION BY EMPLOYERS

Confidentiality; Necessity of authorization. §56.20.
Form and contents of authorization. §56.21.
Furnishing copy of authorization. §56.22.
Communication of limits of authorization. §56.23.
Cancellation and modification of authorization. §56.24.
Disclosure by recipient. §56.245.

§56.20. Confidentiality; Necessity of authorization

(a) Each employer who receives medical information shall establish appropriate procedures to ensure the confidentiality and protection from unauthorized use and disclosure of that information. These procedures may include, but are not limited to, instruction regarding confidentiality of employees and agents handling files containing medical information, and security systems restricting access to files containing medical information.

(b) No employee shall be discriminated against in terms or conditions of employment due to that employee's refusal to sign an authorization under this part. However, nothing in this section shall prohibit an employer from taking such action as is necessary in the absence of medical information due to an employee's refusal to sign an authorization under this part.

(c) No employer shall use, disclose, or knowingly permit its employees or agents to use or disclose medical information which the employer possesses pertaining to its employees without the patient having first signed an authorization under Section 56.11 or Section 56.21 permitting such use or disclosure, except as follows:

(1) The information may be disclosed if the disclosure is compelled by judicial or administrative process or by any other specific provision of law.

(2) That part of the information which is relevant in a lawsuit, arbitration, grievance, or other claim or challenge to which the employer and employee are parties and in which the patient has placed in issue his

or her medical history, mental or physical condition, or treatment may be used or disclosed in connection with that proceeding.

(3) The information may be used only for the purpose of administering and maintaining employee benefit plans, including health care plans and plans providing short-term and long-term disability income, workers' compensation and for determining eligibility for paid and unpaid leave from work for medical reasons.

(4) The information may be disclosed to a provider of health care or other health care professional or facility to aid the diagnosis or treatment of the patient, where the patient or other person specified in subdivision (c) of Section 56.21 is unable to authorize the disclosure.

(d) If an employer agrees in writing with one or more of its employees or maintains a written policy which provides that particular types of medical information shall not be used or disclosed by the employer in particular ways, the employer shall obtain an authorization for such uses or disclosures even if an authorization would not otherwise be required by subdivision (c). **Leg.H.** Added Stats 1981 ch 782 §2.

Prior Law: Former §56.20, similar to present CC §56.29, was added Stats 1979 ch 773 §1 and repealed Stats 1981 ch 782 §1.5.

§56.21. Form and contents of authorization

An authorization for an employer to disclose medical information shall be valid if the authorization complies with all of the following:

(a) Is handwritten or is in a typeface no smaller than 14-point type.

(b) Is clearly separate from any other language present on the same page and is executed by a signature that serves no purpose other than to execute the authorization.

(c) Is signed, including with an electronic or handwritten signature, and dated by one of the following:

(1) The patient, except that a patient who is a minor may only sign an authorization for the disclosure of medical information obtained by a provider of health care in the course of furnishing services to which the minor could lawfully have consented under Part 4 (commencing with Section 6900) of Division 11 of the Family Code.

(2) The legal representative of the patient, if the patient is a minor or lacks the capacity to make the decision to authorize the release of medical information. However, authorization may not be given under this subdivision for the disclosure of medical information that pertains to a competent minor and that was created by a provider of health care in the course of furnishing services to which a minor patient could lawfully have consented under Part 4 (commencing with Section 6900) of Division 11 of the Family Code.

(3) The beneficiary, as defined in Section 24 of the Probate Code, or personal representative, as defined in Section 58 of the Probate Code, of a deceased patient.

(d) States the limitations, if any, on the types of medical information to be disclosed.

(e) States the name or functions of the employer or person authorized to disclose the medical information.

(f) States the names or functions of the persons or entities authorized to receive the medical information.

(g) States the limitations, if any, on the use of the medical information by the persons or entities authorized to receive the medical information.

(h) States an expiration date or event. The expiration date or event shall limit the duration of the authorization to one year or less, unless the person signing the authorization requests a specific date beyond a year or unless the authorization is related to an approved clinical trial, as defined in Section 1370.6 of the Health and Safety Code, or medical research study, in which case the authorization may extend beyond one year if the expiration date or event extends no longer than the completion of the relevant clinical trial or research study.

(i) Advises the person who signed the authorization of the right to receive a copy of the authorization.

(j) If an employer or any other entity seeks an authorization from an individual for a use or disclosure of protected health information, the employer or other entity shall provide the individual with a copy of the signed authorization and instructions on how to access additional copies or a digital version of the signed authorization. **Leg.H.** Added Stats 1981 ch 782 §2. Amended Stats 2003 ch 562 §5 (AB 715); Stats 2006 ch 538 §39 (SB 1852), effective January 1, 2007; Stats 2023 ch 374 §4 (AB 1697), effective January 1, 2024.

Prior Law: Former §56.21, similar to present CC §56.29, was added Stats 1979 ch 773 §1 and repealed Stats 1981 ch 782 §1.5.

§56.22. Furnishing copy of authorization

Upon demand by the patient or the person who signed an authorization, an employer possessing the authorization shall furnish a true copy thereof. **Leg.H.** Added Stats 1981 ch 782 §2.

Prior Law: Former §56.22, similar to present CC §56.29, was added Stats 1979 ch 773 §1, amended Stats 1981 ch 714 §46, and repealed Stats 1981 ch 782 §1.5.

§56.23. Communication of limits of authorization

An employer that discloses medical information pursuant to an authorization required by this chapter shall communicate to the person or entity to which it discloses the medical information any limitations in the authorization regarding the use of the medical information. No employer that has attempted in good faith to comply with this provision shall be liable for any unauthorized use of the medical information by the person or entity to which the employer disclosed the medical information. **Leg.H.** Added Stats 1981 ch 782 §2.

§56.24. Cancellation and modification of authorization

Nothing in this part shall be construed to prevent a person who could sign the authorization pursuant to subdivision (c) of Section 56.21 from cancelling or modifying an authorization. However, the cancellation or modification shall be effective only after the employer actually receives written notice of the cancellation or modification. **Leg.H.** Added Stats 1981 ch 782 §2.

Prior Law: Former §56.24, similar to present CC §56.20, was added Stats 1979 ch 773 §1 and repealed Stats 1981 ch 782 §1.5.

§56.245. Disclosure by recipient

A recipient of medical information pursuant to an authorization as provided by this chapter may not further disclose such medical information unless in accordance with a new authorization that meets the requirements of Section 56.21, or as specifically required or permitted by other provisions of this chapter or by law. **Leg.H.** Added Stats 1981 ch 782 §2.

CHAPTER 4
RELATIONSHIP OF CHAPTERS 2 AND 3

Employer-providers. §56.25.

§56.25. Employer-providers

(a) An employer that is a provider of health care shall not be deemed to have violated Section 56.20 by disclosing, in accordance with Chapter 2 (commencing with Section 56.10), medical information possessed in connection with providing health care services to the provider's patients.

(b) An employer shall not be deemed to have violated Section 56.20 because a provider of health care that is an employee or agent of the employer uses or discloses, in accordance with Chapter 2 (commencing with Section 56.10), medical information possessed by the provider in connection with providing health care services to the provider's patients.

(c) A provider of health care that is an employer shall not be deemed to have violated Section 56.10 by disclosing, in accordance with Chapter 3 (commencing with Section 56.20), medical information possessed in connection with employing the provider's employees. Information maintained by a provider of health care in connection with employing the provider's employees shall not be deemed to be medical information for purposes of Chapter 3 (commencing with Section 56.20), unless it would be deemed medical information if received or maintained by an employer that is not a provider of health care. **Leg.H.** Added Stats 1981 ch 782 §2.

Prior Law: Former §56.25, similar to present CC §56.30, was added Stats 1979 ch 773 §1, amended Stats 1980 ch 1025 §1, and repealed Stats 1981 ch 782 §1.5.

CHAPTER 4.1
NOTIFICATIONS

Mental health digital service business to provide information on reported data breaches. § 56.251.

§ 56.251. Mental health digital service business to provide information on reported data breaches

When partnering with a provider of health care to provide a mental health digital service, any business that offers a mental health digital service shall provide to the provider of health care information regarding how to find data breaches reported pursuant to Section 1798.82 on the internet website of the Attorney General. **Leg.H.** Added Stats 2022 ch 690 §3 (AB 2089), effective January 1, 2023.

CHAPTER 5
USE AND DISCLOSURE OF MEDICAL AND OTHER INFORMATION BY THIRD PARTY ADMINISTRATORS AND OTHERS

Necessity for authorization; Form and contents. §56.26.
Confidentiality of health, medical, or genetic information. §56.265.

§56.26. Necessity for authorization; Form and contents

(a) No person or entity engaged in the business of furnishing administrative services to programs that provide payment for health care services shall knowingly use, disclose, or permit its employees or agents to use or disclose medical information possessed in connection with performing administrative functions for a program, except as reasonably necessary in connection with the administration or maintenance of the program, or as required by law, or with an authorization.

(b) An authorization required by this section shall be in the same form as described in Section 56.21, except that "third party administrator" shall be substituted for "employer" wherever it appears in Section 56.21.

(c) This section shall not apply to any person or entity that is subject to the Insurance Information Privacy Act or to Chapter 2 (commencing with Section 56.10) or Chapter 3 (commencing with Section 56.20). **Leg.H.** Added Stats 1981 ch 782 §2. Amended Stats 2004 ch 183 §24 (AB 3082).

Prior Law: Former §56.26, similar to present CC §56.30, was added Stats 1980 ch 384 §1 and repealed Stats 1981 ch 782 §1.5.

§56.265. Confidentiality of health, medical, or genetic information

A person or entity that underwrites or sells annuity contracts or contracts insuring, guaranteeing, or indemnifying against loss, harm, damage, illness, disability, or death, and any affiliate of that person or entity, shall not disclose individually identifiable information concerning the health of, or the medical or genetic history of, a customer, to any affiliated or nonaffiliated depository institution, or to any other affiliated or nonaffiliated third party for use with regard to the granting of credit. **Leg.H.** Added Stats 2000 ch 278 §2 (AB 2797).

CHAPTER 6
RELATIONSHIP TO EXISTING LAW

Employer-insurers. §56.27.
Patient's right of access. §56.28.
Disclosure of personal and confidential information. §56.29.
Disclosures not subject to part. §56.30.
Disclosure of human immunodeficiency virus. §56.31.

§56.27. Employer-insurers

An employer that is an insurance institution, insurance agent, or insurance support organization subject to the Insurance Information and Privacy Protection Act, Article 6.6 (commencing with Section 791) of Part 2 of Division 1 of the Insurance Code, shall not be deemed to have violated Section 56.20 by disclosing medical information gathered in connection with an insurance transaction in accordance with that act. **Leg.H.** Added Stats 1981 ch 782 §2.

§56.28. Patient's right of access

Nothing in this part shall be deemed to affect existing laws relating to a patient's right of access to his or her own medical information, or relating to disclosures made pursuant to Section 1158 of the Evidence Code, or relating to privileges established under the Evidence Code. **Leg.H.** Added Stats 1981 ch 782 §2.

§56.29. Disclosure of personal and confidential information

(a) Nothing in Chapter 1 (commencing with Section 1798) of Title 1.8 of Part 4 of Division 3 shall be construed to permit the acquisition or disclosure of medical information regarding a patient without an authorization, where the authorization is required by this part.

(b) The disclosure of medical information regarding a patient which is subject to subdivision (b) of Section 1798.24 shall be made only with an authorization which complies with the provisions of this part. Such disclosure may be made only within the time limits specified in subdivision (b) of Section 1798.24.

(c) Where the acquisition or disclosure of medical information regarding a patient is prohibited or limited by any provision of Chapter 1 (commencing with Section 1798) of Title 1.8 of Part 4 of Division 3, the prohibition or limit shall be applicable in addition to the requirements of this part. **Leg.H.** Added Stats 1981 ch 782 §2.

Prior Law: Former §56.29, relating to disclosure of medical information by health care provider, was added Stats 1981 ch 106 §1, effective June 29, 1981, and repealed Stats 1981 ch 782 §1.5.

§56.30. Disclosures not subject to part

The disclosure and use of the following medical information shall not be subject to the limitations of this part:

(a) (Mental health and developmental disabilities) Information and records obtained in the course of providing services under Division 4 (commencing with Section 4000), Division 4.1 (commencing with Section 4400), Division 4.5 (commencing with Section 4500), Division 5 (commencing with Section 5000), Division 6 (commencing with Section 6000), or Division 7 (commencing with Section 7100) of the Welfare and Institutions Code.

(b) (Public social services) Information and records that are subject to Sections 10850, 14124.1, and 14124.2 of the Welfare and Institutions Code.

(c) (State health services, communicable diseases, developmental disabilities) Information and records maintained pursuant to former Chapter 2 (commencing with Section 200) of Part 1 of Division 1 of the Health and Safety Code and pursuant to the Communicable Disease Prevention and Control Act (subdivision (a) of Section 27 of the Health and Safety Code).

(d) (Licensing and statistics) Information and records maintained pursuant to Division 2 (commencing with Section 1200) and Part 1 (commencing with Section 102100) of Division 102 of the Health and Safety Code; pursuant to Chapter 3 (commencing with Section 1200) of Division 2 of the Business and Professions Code; and pursuant to Section 8608, 8817, or 8909 of the Family Code.

(e) (Medical survey, workers' safety) Information and records acquired and maintained or disclosed pursuant to Sections 1380 and 1382 of the Health and Safety Code and pursuant to Division 5 (commencing with Section 6300) of the Labor Code.

(f) (Industrial accidents) Information and records acquired, maintained, or disclosed pursuant to Division 1 (commencing with Section 50), Division 4 (commencing with Section 3200), Division 4.5 (commencing with Section 6100), and Division 4.7 (commencing with Section 6200) of the Labor Code.

(g) (Law enforcement) Information and records maintained by a health facility which are sought by a law enforcement agency under Chapter 3.5 (commencing with Section 1543) of Title 12 of Part 2 of the Penal Code.

(h) (Investigations of employment accident or illness) Information and records sought as part of an investigation of an on-the-job accident or illness pursuant to Division 5 (commencing with Section 6300) of the Labor Code or pursuant to Section 105200 of the Health and Safety Code.

(i) (Alcohol or drug abuse) Information and records subject to the federal alcohol and drug abuse regulations (Part 2 (commencing with Section 2.1) of Subchapter A of Chapter 1 of Title 42 of the Code of Federal Regulations) or to Section 11845.5 of the Health and Safety Code dealing with alcohol and drug abuse.

(j) (Patient discharge data) Nothing in this part shall be construed to limit, expand, or otherwise affect the authority of the California Health Facilities Commission to collect patient discharge information from health facilities.

(k) Medical information and records disclosed to, and their use by, the Insurance Commissioner, the Director of the Department of Managed Health Care, the Division of Industrial Accidents, the Workers' Compensation Appeals Board, the Department of Insurance, or the Department of Managed Health Care.

(*l*) Medical information and records related to services provided on and after January 1, 2006, disclosed to, and their use by, the Managed Risk Medical Insurance Board to the same extent that those records are required to be provided to the board related to services provided on and after July 1, 2009, to comply with Section 403 of the federal Children's Health Insurance Program Reauthorization Act of 2009 (Public Law 111-3), applying subdivision (c) of Section 1932 of the federal Social Security Act. **Leg.H.** Added Stats 1981 ch 782 §2. Amended Stats 1990 ch 1363 §1 (AB 3532), operative July 1, 1991; Stats 1992 ch 163 §5 (AB 2641), operative January 1, 1994; Stats 1993 ch 1004 §2 (AB 336); Stats 1996 ch 1023 §26 (SB 1497), effective September 29, 1996; Stats 1999 ch 526 §7 (SB 19); Stats 2000 ch 1067 §3 (SB 2094); Stats 2010 ch 717 §1

(SB 853), effective October 19, 2010; Stats 2014 ch 71 §14 (SB 1304), effective January 1, 2015.

Prior Law: Former §56.30, similar to present CC §56.35, was added Stats 1979 ch 773 §1 and repealed Stats 1981 ch 782 §1.5.

§56.31. Disclosure of human immunodeficiency virus

Notwithstanding any other provision of law, nothing in subdivision (f) of Section 56.30 shall permit the disclosure or use of medical information regarding whether a patient is infected with or exposed to the human immunodeficiency virus without the prior authorization from the patient unless the patient is an injured worker claiming to be infected with or exposed to the human immunodeficiency virus through an exposure incident arising out of and in the course of employment. **Leg.H.** Added Stats 1999 ch 766 §1 (AB 435).

Prior Law: Former §56.31, similar to present CC §56.36, was added Stats 1979 ch 773 §1, amended Stats 1980 ch 676 §40, and repealed Stats 1981 ch 782 §1.5.

1999 Note: The addition of Section 56.31 to the Civil Code by Chapter 766 is not intended either to abrogate the holdings in *Allison v. Workers' Comp. Appeals Bd.* (1999) 72 Cal.App.4th 654, or to prohibit a redaction decision by a workers' compensation judge from being appealed to the Workers' Compensation Appeals Board. Stats 1999 ch 766 §3.

§56.32. [Section repealed 1981]

Leg.H. Added Stats 1979 ch 773 §1. Repealed Stats 1981 ch 782 §1.5. See CC §56.37.

CHAPTER 7
VIOLATIONS

Damages. §56.35.
Violation as misdemeanor; Damages; Administrative fines and civil penalties; Affirmative defense. §56.36.
Waiver of provisions. §56.37.

§56.35. Damages

In addition to any other remedies available at law, a patient whose medical information has been used or disclosed in violation of Section 56.10, 56.104, 56.107, or 56.20 or subdivision (a) of Section 56.26 and who has sustained economic loss or personal injury therefrom may recover compensatory damages, punitive damages not to exceed three thousand dollars ($3,000), attorney's fees not to exceed one thousand dollars ($1,000), and the costs of litigation. **Leg.H.** Added Stats 1981 ch 782 §2. Amended Stats 1999 ch 527 §4 (AB 416); Stats 2021 ch 190 §4 (AB 1184), effective January 1, 2022.

§56.36. Violation as misdemeanor; Damages; Administrative fines and civil penalties; Affirmative defense

(a) A violation of the provisions of this part that results in economic loss or personal injury to a patient is punishable as a misdemeanor.

(b) In addition to any other remedies available at law, an individual may bring an action against a person or entity who has negligently released confidential information or records concerning him or her in violation of this part, for either or both of the following:

(1) Except as provided in subdivision (e), nominal damages of one thousand dollars ($1,000). In order to recover under this paragraph, it is not necessary that the plaintiff suffered or was threatened with actual damages.

(2) The amount of actual damages, if any, sustained by the patient.

(c)(1) In addition, a person or entity that negligently discloses medical information in violation of the provisions of this part shall also be liable, irrespective of the amount of damages suffered by the patient as a result of that violation, for an administrative fine or civil penalty not to exceed two thousand five hundred dollars ($2,500) per violation.

(2)(A) A person or entity, other than a licensed health care professional, who knowingly and willfully obtains, discloses, or uses medical information in violation of this part shall be liable for an administrative fine or civil penalty not to exceed twenty-five thousand dollars ($25,000) per violation.

(B) A licensed health care professional who knowingly and willfully obtains, discloses, or uses medical information in violation of this part shall be liable on a first violation for an administrative fine or civil penalty not to exceed two thousand five hundred dollars ($2,500) per violation, on a second violation for an administrative fine or civil penalty not to exceed ten thousand dollars ($10,000) per violation, or on a third and subsequent violation for an administrative fine or civil penalty not to exceed twenty-five thousand dollars ($25,000) per violation. This subdivision shall not be construed to limit the liability of a health care service plan, a contractor, or a provider of health care that is not a licensed health care professional for a violation of this part.

(3)(A) A person or entity, other than a licensed health care professional, who knowingly or willfully obtains or uses medical information in violation of this part for the purpose of financial gain shall be liable for an administrative fine or civil penalty not to exceed two hundred fifty thousand dollars ($250,000) per violation and shall also be subject to disgorgement of any proceeds or other consideration obtained as a result of the violation.

(B) A licensed health care professional who knowingly and willfully obtains, discloses, or uses medical information in violation of this part for financial gain shall be liable on a first violation for an administrative fine or civil penalty not to exceed five thousand dollars ($5,000) per violation, on a second violation for an administrative fine or civil penalty not to exceed twenty-five thousand dollars ($25,000) per violation, or on a third and subsequent violation for an administrative fine or civil penalty not to exceed two hundred fifty thousand dollars ($250,000) per violation and shall also be subject to disgorgement of any proceeds or other consideration obtained as a result of the violation. This subdivision shall not be construed to limit the liability of a health care service plan, a contractor, or a provider of health care that is not a licensed health care professional for any violation of this part.

(4) This subdivision shall not be construed as authorizing an administrative fine or civil penalty under both paragraphs (2) and (3) for the same violation.

(5) A person or entity who is not permitted to receive medical information pursuant to this part and who knowingly and willfully obtains, discloses, or uses medical information without written authorization from the patient shall be liable for a civil penalty not to exceed two hundred fifty thousand dollars ($250,000) per violation.

(d) In assessing the amount of an administrative fine or civil penalty pursuant to subdivision (c), the State Department of Public Health, licensing agency, or certifying board or court shall consider any of the relevant circumstances presented by any of the parties to the case including, but not limited to, the following:

(1) Whether the defendant has made a reasonable, good faith attempt to comply with this part.

(2) The nature and seriousness of the misconduct.

(3) The harm to the patient, enrollee, or subscriber.

(4) The number of violations.

(5) The persistence of the misconduct.

(6) The length of time over which the misconduct occurred.

(7) The willfulness of the defendant's misconduct.

(8) The defendant's assets, liabilities, and net worth.

(e)(1) In an action brought by an individual pursuant to subdivision (b) on or after January 1, 2013, in which the defendant establishes the affirmative defense in paragraph (2), the court shall award any actual damages and reasonable attorney's fees and costs, but shall not award nominal damages for a violation of this part.

(2) The defendant is entitled to an affirmative defense if all of the following are established, subject to the equitable considerations in paragraph (3):

(A) The defendant is a covered entity or business associate, as defined in Section 160.103 of Title 45 of the Code of Federal Regulations, in effect as of January 1, 2012.

(B) The defendant has complied with any obligations to notify all persons entitled to receive notice regarding the release of the information or records.

(C) The release of confidential information or records was solely to another covered entity or business associate.

(D) The release of confidential information or records was not an incident of medical identity theft. For purposes of this subparagraph, "medical identity theft" means the use of an individual's personal information, as defined in Section 1798.80, without the individual's knowledge or consent, to obtain medical goods or services, or to submit false claims for medical services.

(E) The defendant took appropriate preventive actions to protect the confidential information or records against release consistent with the defendant's obligations under this part or other applicable state law and the Health Insurance Portability and Accountability Act of 1996 (Public

Law 104-191) (HIPAA) and all HIPAA Administrative Simplification Regulations in effect on January 1, 2012, contained in Parts 160, 162, and 164 of Title 45 of the Code of Federal Regulations, and Part 2 of Title 42 of the Code of Federal Regulations, including, but not limited to, all of the following:

(i) Developing and implementing security policies and procedures.

(ii) Designating a security official who is responsible for developing and implementing its security policies and procedures, including educating and training the workforce.

(iii) Encrypting the information or records, and protecting against the release or use of the encryption key and passwords, or transmitting the information or records in a manner designed to provide equal or greater protections against improper disclosures.

(F) The defendant took reasonable and appropriate corrective action after the release of the confidential information or records, and the covered entity or business associate that received the confidential information or records destroyed or returned the confidential information or records in the most expedient time possible and without unreasonable delay, consistent with any measures necessary to determine the scope of the breach and restore the reasonable integrity of the data system. A court may consider this subparagraph to be established if the defendant shows in detail that the covered entity or business associate could not destroy or return the confidential information or records because of the technology utilized.

(G) The covered entity or business associate that received the confidential information or records, or any of its agents, independent contractors, or employees, regardless of the scope of the employee's employment, did not retain, use, or release the information or records.

(H) After the release of the confidential information or records, the defendant took reasonable and appropriate action to prevent a future similar release of confidential information or records.

(I) The defendant has not previously established an affirmative defense pursuant to this subdivision, or the court determines, in its discretion, that application of the affirmative defense is compelling and consistent with the purposes of this section to promote reasonable conduct in light of all the facts.

(3)(A) In determining whether the affirmative defense may be established pursuant to paragraph (2), the court shall consider the equity of the situation, including, but not limited to, (i) whether the defendant has previously violated this part, regardless of whether an action has previously been brought, and (ii) the nature of the prior violation.

(B) To the extent the court allows discovery to determine whether there has been any other violation of this part that the court will consider in balancing the equities, the defendant shall not provide any medical information, as defined in Section 56.05. The court, in its discretion, may enter a protective order prohibiting the further use of any personal information, as defined in Section 1798.80, about the individual whose medical information may have been disclosed in a prior violation.

(4) In an action under this subdivision in which the defendant establishes the affirmative defense pursuant to paragraph (2), a plaintiff shall be entitled to recover reasonable attorney's fees and costs without regard to an award of actual or nominal damages or the imposition of administrative fines or civil penalties.

(5) In an action brought by an individual pursuant to subdivision (b) on or after January 1, 2013, in which the defendant establishes the affirmative defense pursuant to paragraph (2), a defendant shall not be liable for more than one judgment on the merits under this subdivision for releases of confidential information or records arising out of the same event, transaction, or occurrence.

(f)(1) The civil penalty pursuant to subdivision (c) shall be assessed and recovered in a civil action brought in the name of the people of the State of California in any court of competent jurisdiction by any of the following:

(A) The Attorney General.

(B) A district attorney.

(C) A county counsel authorized by agreement with the district attorney in actions involving violation of a county ordinance.

(D) A city attorney of a city.

(E) A city attorney of a city and county having a population in excess of 750,000, with the consent of the district attorney.

(F) A city prosecutor in a city having a full-time city prosecutor or, with the consent of the district attorney, by a city attorney in a city and county.

(G) The State Public Health Officer, or his or her designee, may recommend that a person described in subparagraphs (A) to (F), inclusive, bring a civil action under this section.

(2) If the action is brought by the Attorney General, one-half of the penalty collected shall be paid to the treasurer of the county in which the judgment was entered, and one-half to the General Fund. If the action is brought by a district attorney or county counsel, the penalty collected shall be paid to the treasurer of the county in which the judgment was entered. Except as provided in paragraph (3), if the action is brought by a city attorney or city prosecutor, one-half of the penalty collected shall be paid to the treasurer of the city in which the judgment was entered and one-half to the treasurer of the county in which the judgment was entered.

(3) If the action is brought by a city attorney of a city and county, the entire amount of the penalty collected shall be paid to the treasurer of the city and county in which the judgment was entered.

(4) This section shall not be construed as authorizing both an administrative fine and civil penalty for the same violation.

(5) Imposition of a fine or penalty provided for in this section shall not preclude imposition of other sanctions or remedies authorized by law.

(6) Administrative fines or penalties issued pursuant to Section 1280.15 of the Health and Safety Code shall offset any other administrative fine or civil penalty imposed under this section for the same violation.

(g) For purposes of this section, "knowing" and "willful" shall have the same meanings as in Section 7 of the Penal Code.

(h) A person who discloses protected medical information in accordance with the provisions of this part is not subject to the penalty provisions of this part. **Leg.H.** Added Stats 1981 ch 782 §2. Amended Stats 1999 ch 526 §8 (SB 19); Stats 2008 ch 602 §1 (AB 211), effective January 1, 2009; Stats 2012 ch 437 §1 (AB 439), effective January 1, 2013; Stats 2014 ch 31 §1 (SB 857), effective June 20, 2014; Stats 2015 ch 303 §26 (AB 731), effective January 1, 2016.

2008 Note: Subsection (e)(6), as added by Stats 2008 ch 602, became operative due to enactment of Stats 2008 ch 605 (SB 541).

§56.37. Waiver of provisions

(a) No provider of health care, health care service plan, or contractor may require a patient, as a condition of receiving health care services, to sign an authorization, release, consent, or waiver that would permit the disclosure of medical information that otherwise may not be disclosed under Section 56.10 or any other provision of law. However, a health care service plan or disability insurer may require relevant enrollee or subscriber medical information as a condition of the medical underwriting process, provided that Sections 1374.7 and 1389.1 of the Health and Safety Code are strictly observed.

(b) Any waiver by a patient of the provisions of this part, except as authorized by Section 56.11 or 56.21 or subdivision (b) of Section 56.26, shall be deemed contrary to public policy and shall be unenforceable. **Leg.H.** Added Stats 1981 ch 782 §2. Amended Stats 1999 ch 526 §9 (SB 19).

§58. [Section repealed 1905]

Leg.H. Enacted 1872. Repealed Stats 1905 ch 414 §1. The repealed section related to marriage.

§59. [Section repealed 1969]

Leg.H. Enacted 1872. Repealed Stats 1969 ch 1608 §3. See Fam C §2200.

PART 2.7
MEDICAL CLAIMS DATA ERROR CORRECTION

Requests for error correction. §57.

§57. Requests for error correction

(a) A qualified entity, as defined in Section 1395kk(e)(2) of Title 42 of the United States Code, that receives claims data from a health care service plan or health insurer shall comply with the requirements governing provider and supplier requests for error correction established under Section 401.717 of Title 42 of the Code of Federal Regulations for all claims data received, including data from sources other than Medicare.

(b) For purposes of this section, the following definitions apply:

(1) "Provider" means a hospital, a skilled nursing facility, a comprehensive outpatient rehabilitation facility, a home health agency, a hospice, a clinic, or a rehabilitation agency.

(2) "Supplier" means a physician and surgeon or other health care practitioner, or an entity that furnishes health care services other than a provider. **Leg.H.** Added Stats 2012 ch 869 §1 (SB 1196), effective January 1, 2013.

Prior Law: Former CC §57 was enacted 1872, amended Stats 1895 ch 129 §2, and repealed Stats 1969 ch 1068 §3. See Fam C §305.

PART 2.9
CALIFORNIA FAIR DEALERSHIP LAW

Citation. §80.
Definitions. §81.
Purposes. §82.
New dealerships. §83.
Existing dealerships. §84.
Transfer of dealerships. §85.
Litigation costs. §86.

§80. Citation

This part may be cited as the California Fair Dealership Law. **Leg.H.** Added Stats 1980 ch 914 §1.

Prior Law: Former §80, relating to marriage, was added Code Amendments 1875–76 ch 217 §1, amended Stats 1880 ch 41 §3, and repealed Stats 1969 ch 1608 §3, operative January 1, 1970.

§81. Definitions

As used in this part:

(a) "Person" means a natural person, partnership, joint venture, corporation, limited liability company, or other entity.

(b) "Dealership" means a contract or agreement, either express or implied, whether oral or written, between two or more persons, by which a person is granted the right to sell or distribute goods or services, or to use a trade name, trademark, service mark, logotype, or advertising or other commercial symbol, in which there is a community of interest in the business of offering, selling, or distributing goods or services at wholesale, or at retail, by lease, agreement, or otherwise.

(c) "Grantor" means a person who sells, leases, or otherwise transfers a dealership.

(d) "Community of interest" means a continuing financial interest between the grantor and grantee in either the operation of the dealership or the marketing of goods or services.

(e) "Dealer" means a person who is a grantee of a dealership situated in this state.

(f) "Grant" means a sale, lease, or transfer of any kind. **Leg.H.** Added Stats 1980 ch 914 §1. Amended Stats 1994 ch 1010 §29 (SB 2053).

§82. Purposes

This part shall be liberally construed and applied to promote its underlying purposes and policies, which are as follows:

(a) The prohibition of discrimination based upon any characteristic listed or defined in subdivision (b) or (e) of Section 51 in the granting, sale, transfer, bequest, termination, and nonrenewal of dealerships.

(b) The requirements of this part shall not be varied by contract or agreement and any portion of a contract or agreement purporting to do so is void and unenforceable. **Leg.H.** Added Stats 1980 ch 914 §1. Amended Stats 2007 ch 568 §10 (AB 14), effective January 1, 2008.

Prior Law: Former §82, similar to present Fam C §2210, was enacted 1872, amended Code Amendments 1873–74 ch 612 §20, Stats 1957 ch 1299 §2, and repealed Stats 1969 ch 1608 §3, operative January 1, 1970.

2007 Notes: The Legislature finds and declares as follows:

(a) Even prior to passage of the Unruh Civil Rights Act, California law afforded broad protection against arbitrary discrimination by business establishments. The Unruh Civil Rights Act was enacted to provide broader, more effective protection against arbitrary discrimination. California's interest in preventing that discrimination is longstanding and compelling.

(b) In keeping with that history and the legislative history of the Unruh Civil Rights Act, California courts have interpreted the categories enumerated in the act to be illustrative rather than restrictive. It is the intent of the Legislature that these enumerated bases shall continue to be construed as illustrative rather than restrictive, and, consistent with the Unruh Civil Rights Act, that the civil rights provisions of this act that reference Section 51 of the Civil Code also be interpreted to be illustrative rather than restrictive. Stats 2007 ch 568 (AB 14) §1.

This act shall be known and may be cited as the Civil Rights Act of 2007. Stats 2007 ch 568 (AB 14) §1.5.

§83. New dealerships

On or after January 1, 1981, no grantor, directly or indirectly, shall refuse to grant a dealership to any person because of any characteristic listed or defined in subdivision (b) or (e) of Section 51. **Leg.H.** Added Stats 1980 ch 914 §1. Amended Stats 2007 ch 568 §11 (AB 14), effective January 1, 2008.

Prior Law: Former §83, similar to present Fam C §2211, was enacted 1872, amended Code Amendments 1873–74 ch 612 §21, and repealed Stats 1969 ch 1608 §3, operative January 1, 1970.

2007 Notes: The Legislature finds and declares as follows:

(a) Even prior to passage of the Unruh Civil Rights Act, California law afforded broad protection against arbitrary discrimination by business establishments. The Unruh Civil Rights Act was enacted to provide broader, more effective protection against arbitrary discrimination. California's interest in preventing that discrimination is longstanding and compelling.

(b) In keeping with that history and the legislative history of the Unruh Civil Rights Act, California courts have interpreted the categories enumerated in the act to be illustrative rather than restrictive. It is the intent of the Legislature that these enumerated bases shall continue to be construed as illustrative rather than restrictive, and, consistent with the Unruh Civil Rights Act, that the civil rights provisions of this act that reference Section 51 of the Civil Code also be interpreted to be illustrative rather than restrictive. Stats 2007 ch 568 (AB 14) §1.

This act shall be known and may be cited as the Civil Rights Act of 2007. Stats 2007 ch 568 (AB 14) §1.5.

§84. Existing dealerships

On or after January 1, 1981, no grantor, directly or indirectly, may terminate, cancel, or refuse to renew a dealership agreement with a dealer because of any characteristic listed or defined in subdivision (b) or (e) of Section 51. **Leg.H.** Added Stats 1980 ch 914 §1. Amended Stats 2007 ch 568 §12 (AB 14), effective January 1, 2008.

Prior Law: Former §84, similar to Fam C §§7600 et seq., was enacted 1872, amended Stats 1905 ch 414 §5, Stats 1929 ch 415 §1, Stats 1951 ch 230 §1, and repealed Stats 1969 ch 1608 §3, operative January 1, 1970.

2007 Notes: The Legislature finds and declares as follows:

(a) Even prior to passage of the Unruh Civil Rights Act, California law afforded broad protection against arbitrary discrimination by business establishments. The Unruh Civil Rights Act was enacted to provide broader, more effective protection against arbitrary discrimination. California's interest in preventing that discrimination is longstanding and compelling.

(b) In keeping with that history and the legislative history of the Unruh Civil Rights Act, California courts have interpreted the categories enumerated in the act to be illustrative rather than restrictive. It is the intent of the Legislature that these enumerated bases shall continue to be construed as illustrative rather than restrictive, and, consistent with the Unruh Civil Rights Act, that the civil rights provisions of this act that reference Section 51 of the Civil Code also be interpreted to be illustrative rather than restrictive. Stats 2007 ch 568 (AB 14) §1.

This act shall be known and may be cited as the Civil Rights Act of 2007. Stats 2007 ch 568 (AB 14) §1.5.

§85. Transfer of dealerships

On or after January 1, 1981, no grantor or dealer, directly or indirectly, shall refuse to make or to consent to an assignment, sale, transfer, or bequest of a dealership to any person, or to the intestate succession to the dealership by any person, because of any characteristic listed or defined in subdivision (b) or (e) of Section 51. This section shall not be construed to create any right in a dealer to assign, sell, transfer, or bequeath a dealership where the right did not exist prior to January 1, 1981. **Leg.H.** Added Stats 1980 ch 914 §1. Amended Stats 2007 ch 568 §13 (AB 14), effective January 1, 2008.

Prior Law: Former §85, similar to Fam C §§7600 et seq., was added Stats 1933 ch 355 §1, amended Stats 1969 ch 1615 §1, and repealed Stats 1969 ch 1608 §3, operative January 1, 1970, Stats 1970 ch 269 §1.

Original §85, similar to Fam C §§7600 et seq., was repealed Stats 1929 ch 415.

2007 Notes: The Legislature finds and declares as follows:

(a) Even prior to passage of the Unruh Civil Rights Act, California law afforded broad protection against arbitrary discrimination by business establishments. The Unruh Civil Rights Act was enacted to provide broader, more effective protection against arbitrary discrimination. California's interest in preventing that discrimination is longstanding and compelling.

(b) In keeping with that history and the legislative history of the Unruh Civil Rights Act, California courts have interpreted the categories enumerated in the act to be illustrative rather than restrictive. It is the intent of the Legislature that these enumerated bases shall continue to be construed as illustrative rather than restrictive, and, consistent with the Unruh Civil Rights Act, that the civil rights provisions of this act that reference Section 51 of the Civil Code also be interpreted to be illustrative rather than restrictive. Stats 2007 ch 568 (AB 14) §1.

This act shall be known and may be cited as the Civil Rights Act of 2007. Stats 2007 ch 568 (AB 14) §1.5.

§86. Litigation costs

The prevailing party in any action based on a violation of the provisions of this part shall be entitled to recover reasonable attorney's fees and taxable court costs. **Leg.H.** Added Stats 1980 ch 914 §1.

Prior Law: Former §86, similar to present Fam C §2212, was enacted 1872 and repealed Stats 1969 ch 1608 §3, operative January 1, 1970.

§87. [Section repealed 1970]

Leg.H. Added Stats 1947 ch 951 §1. Repealed Stats 1969 ch 1608 §3, operative January 1, 1970. See Fam C §2255.

§88. [Section repealed 1970]

Leg.H. Added Stats 1951 ch 233 §1. Repealed Stats 1969 ch 1608 §3, operative January 1, 1970. The repealed section related to restoration of maiden name in action to null or void marriage.

§89. [Section repealed 1965]

Leg.H. Added Stats 1961 ch 1722 §3. Repealed Stats 1965 ch 1893 §1.5. The repealed section related to payment of fee for annulment of marriage.

§§90–92. [Sections repealed 1970]

Leg.H. Enacted 1872. Amended Code Amdts 1873–74 ch 612 §22; Amended Code Amdts 1873–74 ch 612 §23; Amended Code Amdts 1873–74 ch 612 §24, Stats 1941 ch 951 §1. Repealed Stats 1969 ch 1608 §3, operative January 1, 1970. See Fam C §§310, 2300, 2310.

§§93–108. [Sections repealed 1970]

Leg.H. Enacted 1872. Repealed Stats 1969 ch 1608 §3, operative January 1, 1970. The repealed sections related to dissolution of marriage.

§§111–127. [Sections repealed 1970]

Leg.H. Enacted 1872. Repealed Stats 1969 ch 1608 §3, operative January 1, 1970. The repealed sections related to reasons for denying divorce.

§128. [Section repealed 1970]

Leg.H. Enacted 1872. Amended Stats 1891 ch 55 §1, Stats 1911 ch 376 §1, Stats 1965 ch 232 §1. Repealed Stats 1969 ch 1608 §3, operative January 1, 1970. See Fam C §§2320, 2321.

§128.1. [Section repealed 1970]

Leg.H. Added Stats 1965 ch 232 §2. Repealed Stats 1969 ch 1608 §3, operative January 1, 1970. See Fam C §§2320, 2321.

§§129, 130. [Sections repealed 1970]

Leg.H. Enacted 1872. Amended Stats 1925 ch 287 §1. Repealed Stats 1969 ch 1608 §3, operative January 1, 1970. See Fam C §2322.

§131. [Section repealed 1970]

Leg.H. Added Stats 1903 ch 67 §1. Amended Stats 1909 ch 621 §1, Stats 1915 ch 115 §1, Stats 1945 ch 175 §1, ch 721 §1, Stats 1947 ch 1029 §1. Repealed Stats 1969 ch 1608 §3, operative January 1, 1970. See Fam C §2338.

§131.5. [Section repealed 1970]

Leg.H. Added Stats 1939 ch 332 §1. Amended Stats 1951 ch 229 §1. Repealed Stats 1969 ch 1608 §3, operative January 1, 1970. See Fam C §2346.

§132. [Section repealed 1970]

Leg.H. Added Stats 1903 ch 67 §1. Amended Stats 1965 ch 1108 §1, Stats 1969 ch 489 §1. Repealed Stats 1969 ch 1608 §3, operative January 1, 1970. See Fam C §§2339–2344.

§133. [Section repealed 1970]

Leg.H. Added Stats 1935 ch 407 §1. Amended Stats 1941 ch 995 §1, Stats 1951 ch 229 §2, Stats 1967 ch 1137 §2. Repealed Stats 1969 ch 1608 §3, operative January 1, 1970. See Fam C §2346.

§134. [Section repealed 1965]

Leg.H. Added Stats 1961 ch 1722 §4. Repealed Stats 1965 ch 1893 §2. The repealed section related to payment of fee for annulment of marriage.

§§136, 137. [Sections repealed 1970]

Leg.H. Enacted 1872. Amended Code Amdts 1877–78 ch 298 §1, Code Amdts 1880 ch 41 §4, Stats 1905 ch 216 §1, Stats 1907 ch 63 §1, Stats 1917 ch 36 §1, Stats 1927 ch 249 §1, Stats 1941 ch 1038 §1. Repealed Stats 1969 ch 1608 §3, operative January 1, 1970. See Fam C §§63, 270–275, 780, 2030, 2550–2553, 2600–2627, 3600–3604.

§§137.1–137.3. [Sections repealed 1970]

Leg.H. Added Stats 1951 ch 1700 §§3, 4. Repealed Stats 1969 ch 1608 §3, operative January 1, 1970. See Fam C §§270, 273, 2030, 2031, 3557, 3600–3604.

§137.5. [Section repealed 1970]

Leg.H. Added Stats 1937 ch 183 §1. Repealed Stats 1969 ch 1608 §3, operative January 1, 1970. See Fam C §§272, 275.

§137.6. [Section repealed 1970]

Leg.H. Added Stats 1967 ch 1205 §1. Repealed Stats 1969 ch 1608 §3, operative January 1, 1970. The repealed section related to order of payment to creditor in divorce, annulment, or separate maintenance action.

§138. [Section repealed 1970]

Leg.H. Enacted 1872. Amended Stats 1905 ch 49 §1; Stats 1931 ch 930 §1; Stats 1951 ch 1700 §6. Repealed Stats 1969 ch 1608 §3, operative January 1, 1970. See Fam C §§3020 et seq.

§138.5. [Section repealed 1967]

Leg.H. Added Stats 1965 ch 1963 §1. Repealed Stats 1967 ch 291 §1. The repealed section related to visitation rights of grandparents upon death of child.

§139. [Section repealed 1970]

Leg.H. Enacted 1872. Amended Stats 1933 ch 412 §1; Stats 1951 ch 1700 §7; Stats 1957 ch 1837 §1; Stats 1959 ch 1399 §1; Stats 1961 ch 2098 §1; Stats 1963 ch 861 §1; Stats 1967 ch 133 §2, ch 844 §1, ch 1308 §1. Repealed Stats 1969 ch 1608 §3, operative January 1, 1970. See Fam C §§92, 270, 3028, 3585 et seq.

§139.1. [Section repealed 1970]

Leg.H. Added Stats 1967 ch 133 §3. Repealed Stats 1969 ch 1608 §3, operative January 1, 1970. See Fam C §3592.

§139.5. [Section repealed 1970]

Leg.H. Added Stats 1963 ch 883 §1. Repealed Stats 1969 ch 1608 §3, operative January 1, 1970. The repealed section related to support payment to probation officer.

§139.7. [Section repealed 1970]

Leg.H. Added Stats 1965 ch 1109 §1. Repealed Stats 1969 ch 1608 §3, operative January 1, 1970. The repealed section related to termination of support order.

§139.8. [Section repealed 1970]

Leg.H. Added Stats 1968 ch 633 §1. Repealed Stats 1969 ch 1608 §3, operative January 1, 1970. The repealed section related to termination of contingent support order.

§140. [Section repealed 1970]

Leg.H. Enacted 1872. Amended Stats 1927 ch 249 §2; Stats 1951 ch 1700 §8. Repealed Stats 1969 ch 1608 §3, operative January 1, 1970. See Fam C §§63, 780, 2500 et seq.

§§140.5, 140.7. [Sections repealed 1970]

Leg.H. Added Stats 1961 ch 636 §§2, 3. Repealed Stats 1969 ch 1608 §3, operative January 1, 1970. See Fam C §§125, 2502, 3515.

§§141–146. [Sections repealed 1970]

Leg.H. Enacted 1872. Amended Code Amdts 1873–74 ch 612 §33, Stats 1941 ch 951 §3, Stats 1949 ch 1589 §1, Stats 1951 ch 1700 §10, Stats 1961 ch 636 §4, Stats 1968 ch 457 §1. Repealed Stats 1969 ch 1608 §3, operative January 1, 1970. See Fam C §§63, 780, 2500 et seq., 4321 et seq., 4008.

§147. [Section repealed 1970]

Leg.H. Added Stats 1963 ch 605 §1. Repealed Stats 1969 ch 1608 §3, operative January 1, 1970. The repealed section related to notice required for modification of final decree.

Prior Law: Former §147 was enacted 1872 and repealed Stats 1951 ch 1700 §11.

§148. [Section repealed 1970]

Leg.H. Enacted 1872. Amended Code Amdts 1873–74 ch 612 §35; Stats 1961 ch 636 §5. Repealed Stats 1969 ch 1608 §3, operative January 1, 1970. See Fam C §2555.

§149. [Section repealed 1970]

Leg.H. Added Stats 1939 ch 484 §1. Repealed Stats 1969 ch 1608 §3, operative January 1, 1970, Stats 1970 ch 269 §2, ch 962 §1. The repealed section related to jurisdiction over community property.

§§150–150.4. [Sections repealed 1970]

Leg.H. Added Stats 1949 ch 1292 §1. Repealed Stats 1969 ch 1608 §3, operative January 1, 1970. See Fam C §§3, 2090–2093.

§§155–161. [Sections repealed 1970]

Leg.H. Enacted 1872. Amended Stats 1957 ch 2145 §1. Repealed Stats 1969 ch 1608 §3, operative January 1, 1970. See Fam C §§720–754, 6321, 6340.

§161a. [Section repealed 1970]

Leg.H. Added Stats 1927 ch 205 §1. Repealed Stats 1969 ch 1608 §3, operative January 1, 1970. See Fam C §751.

§161b. [Section repealed 1970]

Leg.H. Added Stats 1949 ch 522 §1. Amended Stats 1951 ch 1542 §1. Repealed Stats 1969 ch 1608 §3, operative January 1, 1970. See Fam C §755.

§§162, 163. [Sections repealed 1970]

Leg.H. Enacted 1872. Repealed Stats 1969 ch 1608 §3, operative January 1, 1970. See Fam C §§700, 751, 760, 803.

§163.5. [Section repealed 1970]

Leg.H. Added Stats 1957 ch 2334 §1. Amended Stats 1968 ch 457 §2. Repealed Stats 1969 ch 1608 §3, operative January 1, 1970. See Fam C §781.

§164. [Section repealed 1970]

Leg.H. Enacted Stats 1872. Amended Stats 1889 ch 219 §1; Stats 1893 ch 62 §1; Stats 1897 ch 72 §1; Stats 1917 ch 581 §1; Stats 1923 ch 360 §1; Stats 1927 ch 487 §1; Stats 1935 ch 707 §1; Stats 1941 ch 455 §1; Stats 1961 ch 636 §1; Stats 1965 ch 1710 §1. Repealed Stats 1969 ch 1608 §3, operative January 1, 1970. See Fam C §§700, 760, 803.

§164.5. [Section repealed 1970]

Leg.H. Added Stats 1965 ch 299 §7. Repealed Stats 1969 ch 1608 §3, operative January 1, 1970. See Fam C §802.

§§164.6, 164.7. [Sections repealed 1970]

Leg.H. Added Stats 1968 ch 457 §§3, 4. Repealed Stats 1969 ch 1608 §3, operative January 1, 1970. See Fam C §§782, 783.

§164.8. [Section repealed 1970]

Leg.H. Added Stats 1969 ch 647 §1. Repealed Stats 1969 ch 1608 §3, operative January 1, 1970. The repealed section related to transfer of community property to trust.

§§165–169. [Sections repealed 1970]

Leg.H. Enacted 1872. Repealed Stats 1969 ch 1608 §3, operative January 1, 1970. See Fam C §§771, 900, 910.

§169.1. [Section repealed 1970]

Leg.H. Added Stats 1951 ch 1700 §12. Repealed Stats 1969 ch 1608 §3, operative January 1, 1970. See Fam C §772.

§169.2. [Section repealed 1970]

Leg.H. Added Stats 1959 ch 1459 §1. Repealed Stats 1969 ch 1608 §3, operative January 1, 1970. The repealed section related to husbands and wives.

§169.3. [Section repealed 1970]

Leg.H. Added Stats 1968 ch 457 §5. Repealed Stats 1969 ch 1608 §3, operative January 1, 1970. See Fam C §781.

§170. [Section repealed 1970]

Leg.H. Enacted Stats 1872. Amended Stats 1935 ch 810 §1. Repealed Stats 1969 ch 1608 §3, operative January 1, 1970. See Fam C §§910, 911.

§171. [Section repealed 1970]

Leg.H. Enacted Stats 1872. Amended Stats 1905 ch 217 §1; Stats 1915 ch 544 §1. Repealed Stats 1969 ch 1608 §3, operative January 1, 1970. See Fam C §916.

§171a. [Section repealed 1970]

Leg.H. Added Stats 1913 ch 131 §1. Amended Stats 1968 ch 457 §6. Repealed Stats 1969 ch 1608 §3, operative January 1, 1970. See Fam C §1000.

§171b. [Section repealed 1970]

Leg.H. Added Stats 1937 ch 508 §1. Repealed Stats 1969 ch 1608 §3, operative January 1, 1970. The repealed section related to liability of wife's separate property.

§171c. [Section repealed 1970]

Leg.H. Added Stats 1951 ch 1102 §1. Amended Stats 1957 ch 2334 §2; Stats 1968 ch 458 §2. Repealed Stats 1969 ch 1608 §3, operative January 1, 1970. See Fam C §1100.

§172. [Section repealed 1970]

Leg.H. Enacted Stats 1872. Amended Stats 1891 ch 220 §1; Stats 1901 ch 190 §1; Stats 1917 ch 583 §1; Stats 1959 ch 125 §21; Stats 1969 ch 647 §2, ch 1609 §34. Repealed Stats 1969 ch 1608 §3, operative January 1, 1970. See Fam C §1100.

§172a. [Section repealed 1970]

Leg.H. Added Stats 1917 ch 583 §2. Amended Stats 1925 ch 37 §1; Stats 1927 ch 488 §1; Stats 1959 ch 125 §22; Stats 1969 ch 647 §3, ch 1609 §4. Repealed Stats 1969 ch 1608 §3, operative January 1, 1970. See Fam C §1102.

§172b. [Section repealed 1959]

Leg.H. Added Stats 1959 ch 125 §23. Repealed Stats 1969 ch 1608 §3, operative January 1, 1970. See Fam C §1103. The repealed section related to incompetent spouse.

Prior Law: Former §172b was added Stats 1919 ch 615 §1 and repealed Stats 1941 ch 1220 §3.

§§172c, 172d. [Sections repealed 1970]

Leg.H. Added Stats 1919 ch 615 §§2, 3. Repealed Stats 1941 ch 1220 §3. The repealed section related to notice of application for permit and validity of sale.

§§173–181. [Sections repealed 1970]

Leg.H. Enacted Stats 1872. Amended Code Amdts 1873–74 ch 612 §41, Stats 1961 ch 636 §10. Repealed Stats 1969 ch 1608 §3, operative January 1, 1970. See Fam C §§1500, 1502, 1611, 4301.

§182. [Section repealed 1970]

Leg.H. Added Stats 1957 ch 2121 §1. Amended Stats 1969 ch 120 §1, ch 1609 §5. Repealed Stats 1969 ch 1608 §3, operative January 1, 1970. See Fam C §295.

§193. [Section repealed 1967]

Leg.H. Enacted 1872. Repealed Stats 1965 ch 299 §8, operative January 1, 1967.

§194. [Section repealed 1967]

Leg.H. Enacted 1872. Amended Code Amdts 1873–74 ch 612 §42. Repealed Stats 1965 ch 299 §9, operative January 1, 1967.

§195. [Section repealed 1975]

Leg.H. Added Stats 1969 ch 1608 §4, operative January 1, 1970. Amended Stats 1970 ch 269 §3. Repealed Stats 1975 ch 1244 §1. See CC §7004.

Prior Law: Former §195, similar to Ev C §661, was enacted 1872, amended Stats 1955 ch 948 §2, and repealed Stats 1965 ch 299 §10, operative January 1, 1967.

PART 3
PERSONAL RELATIONS [REPEALED]

§196. **[Section repealed 1994]**

Leg.H. Added Stats 1990 ch 1493 §2 (AB 3974), operative January 1, 1993. Repealed Stats 1992 ch 162 §2 (AB 2650), operative January 1, 1994. See Fam C §3900.

Prior Law: Former §196, similar to present Fam C §3900, was added Stats 1980 ch 1341 §2, amended Stats 1988 ch 1577 §2, Stats 1990 ch 1493 §1, and repealed, operative January 1, 1993, by its own terms.

Former §196, similar to present Fam C §3900, was enacted 1872, amended Stats 1975 ch 1244 §2, and repealed Stats 1980 ch 1341 §1.

§196a. **[Section repealed 1994]**

Leg.H. Added Stats 1913 ch 132 §1. Amended Stats 1939 ch 424 §1; Stats 1965 ch 422 §1; Stats 1969 ch 1608 §1, effective January 1, 1970; Stats 1975 ch 1244 §2.5. Repealed Stats 1992 ch 162 §2 (AB 2650), operative January 1, 1994. See Fam C §§3900, 4000.

§196b. **[Section repealed 1969]**

Leg.H. Added Stats 1968 ch 235 §1. Repealed Stats 1969 ch 1615 §1.5.

§196.5. **[Section repealed 1993]**

Leg.H. Added Stats 1985 ch 379 §1, effective July 30, 1985. Repealed Stats 1992 ch 162 §2 (AB 2650), operative January 1, 1994 (ch 718 prevails). Amended Stats 1992 ch 718 §1 (AB 568). Repealed Stats 1993 ch 219 §5 (AB 1500). See Fam C §§3901, 4000.

§197. **[Section repealed 1994]**

Leg.H. Enacted 1872. Amended Code Amendments 1873–74 ch 612 §43; Stats 1913 ch 50 §1; Stats 1975 ch 1244 §3. Repealed Stats 1992 ch 162 §2 (AB 2650), operative January 1, 1994. See Fam C §§3010, 7500.

§197.5. **[Section repealed 1994]**

Leg.H. Added Stats 1967 ch 276 §1. Amended Stats 1970 ch 1188 §1; Stats 1973 ch 200 §1, ch 823 §1. Repealed Stats 1992 ch 162 §2 (AB 2650), operative January 1, 1994. See Fam C §3102.

§198. **[Section repealed 1976]**

Leg.H. Enacted 1872. Repealed Stats 1976 ch 1399 §1. The repealed section related to right to custody of children by husband and wife living separate.

§199. **[Section repealed 1984]**

Leg.H. Added Stats 1973 ch 987 §1, operative January 1, 1975. Amended Stats 1979 ch 1030 §1. Repealed Stats 1984 ch 1671 §1. The repealed section related to support obligation of father for natural child.

Prior Law: Former §199, similar to present Fam C §3120, was enacted 1872 and repealed Stats 1969 ch 1608 §6, operative January 1, 1970.

§200. **[Section repealed 1975]**

Leg.H. Enacted 1872. Repealed Stats 1975 ch 1244 §4. The repealed section related to entitlement of mother of illegitimate minor.

§201. **[Section repealed 1994]**

Leg.H. Enacted 1872. Repealed Stats 1992 ch 162 §2 (AB 2650), operative January 1, 1994. See Fam C §3902.

§202. **[Section repealed 1994]**

Leg.H. Enacted 1872. Repealed Stats 1992 ch 162 §2 (AB 2650), operative January 1, 1994. See Fam C §7502.

§203. **[Section repealed 1994]**

Leg.H. Enacted 1872. Repealed Stats 1992 ch 162 §2 (AB 2650), operative January 1, 1994. See Fam C §7507.

§204. **[Section repealed 1994]**

Leg.H. Enacted 1872. Repealed Stats 1992 ch 162 §2 (AB 2650), operative January 1, 1994. See Fam C §7505.

§205. **[Section repealed 1994]**

Leg.H. Enacted 1872. Amended Stats 1957 ch 1557 §1. Repealed Stats 1992 ch 162 §2 (AB 2650), operative January 1, 1994. See Fam C §3952.

§206. **[Section repealed 1994]**

Leg.H. Enacted 1872. Amended Stats 1971 ch 578 §3, effective August 13, 1971, operative October 1, 1971. Repealed Stats 1992 ch 162 §2 (AB 2650), operative January 1, 1994. See Fam C §§3910, 4400, 4401.

§206.5. **[Section repealed 1994]**

Leg.H. Added Stats 1955 ch 613 §1. Amended Stats 1957 ch 1557 §2; Stats 1959 ch 1186 §1; Stats 1961 ch 1872 §1; Stats 1979 ch 730 §5, operative January 1, 1981. Repealed Stats 1992 ch 162 §2 (AB 2650), operative January 1, 1994. See Fam C §§4410–4412, 4414.

§206.6. **[Section repealed 1994]**

Leg.H. Added Stats 1961 ch 2177 §1. Repealed Stats 1992 ch 162 §2 (AB 2650), operative January 1, 1994. See Fam C §4413.

§206.7. **[Section repealed 1994]**

Leg.H. Added Stats 1955 ch 613 §2. Amended Stats 1957 ch 1557 §3; Stats 1959 ch 1186 §2; Stats 1961 ch 1872 §2, ch 1995 §7, operative January 1, 1962, ch 1996 §4, operative January 1, 1962; Stats 1969 ch 59 §1; Stats 1974 ch 485 §1. Repealed Stats 1992 ch 162 §2 (AB 2650), operative January 1, 1994. The repealed section related to proceedings by adult for release from obligation to support parent, where parent is applicant for or recipient of aid.

§207. **[Section repealed 1994]**

Leg.H. Enacted 1872. Repealed Stats 1992 ch 162 §2 (AB 2650), operative January 1, 1994. See Fam C §3950.

§208. **[Section repealed 1994]**

Leg.H. Enacted 1872. Amended Stats 1982 ch 1276 §1, effective September 22, 1982. Repealed Stats 1992 ch 162 §2 (AB 2650), operative January 1, 1994. See Fam C §3951.

§208.5. **[Section repealed 1994]**

Leg.H. Added Stats 1975 ch 924 §1, effective September 20, 1975. Repealed Stats 1992 ch 162 §2 (AB 2650), operative January 1, 1994. See Fam C §3930.

§209. **[Section repealed 1979]**

Leg.H. Enacted 1872. Amended Stats 1976 ch 130 §1. Repealed Stats 1979 ch 1170 §1.3. The repealed section related to the husband's duty to support wife's children by former marriage.

§210. **[Section repealed 1994]**

Leg.H. Enacted 1872. Repealed Stats 1992 ch 162 §2 (AB 2650), operative January 1, 1994. See Fam C §7506.

§211. **[Section repealed 1994]**

Leg.H. Enacted 1872. Repealed Stats 1992 ch 162 §2 (AB 2650), operative January 1, 1994. See Fam C §7504.

§212. **[Section repealed 1994]**

Leg.H. Enacted 1872. Amended Code Amdts 1873–74 ch 612 §44. Repealed Stats 1992 ch 162 §2 (AB 2650), operative January 1, 1994. See Fam C §7503.

§213. **[Section repealed 1994]**

Leg.H. Enacted 1872. Repealed Stats 1992 ch 162 §2 (AB 2650), operative January 1, 1994. See Fam C §7501.

§214. **[Section repealed 1970]**

Leg.H. Enacted 1872. Repealed Stats 1969 ch 1608 §7, effective January 1, 1970.

§215. **[Section repealed 1975]**

Leg.H. Added Code Amdts 1873–74 ch 612 §45. Repealed Stats 1975 ch 1244 §5. The repealed section related to when child becomes legitimate.

§216. **[Section repealed 1975]**

Leg.H. Added Stats 1969 ch 1615 §2. Repealed Stats 1975 ch 1244 §6. The repealed section related to legitimacy of child born by artificial insemination.

§220.10. [Section repealed 1994]

Leg.H. Added Stats 1990 ch 1363 §3 (AB 3532), operative July 1, 1991. Repealed Stats 1992 ch 162 §2 (AB 2650), operative January 1, 1994. The repealed section related to legislative findings and declarations.

§220.15. [Section repealed 1993]

Leg.H. Added Stats 1992 ch 1353 §1.5 (SB 1148), operative January 1, 1994. Repealed Stats 1993 ch 219 §6 (AB 1500). The repealed section related to the purpose of adoption.

§220.20. [Section repealed 1993]

Leg.H. Added Stats 1990 ch 1363 §3 (AB 3532), operative July 1, 1991. Repealed Stats 1992 ch 162 §2 (AB 2650), operative January 1, 1994 (ch 1353 prevails). Amended Stats 1992 ch 472 §1 (AB 2887) ch 1353 §2 (SB 1148), operative January 1, 1994. Repealed Stats 1993 ch 219 §7 (AB 1500). See Fam C §§8500 et seq.

§221. [Section repealed 1991]

Leg.H. Enacted 1872. Amended Stats 1951 ch 880 §1; Stats 1953 ch 1220 §1. Repealed Stats 1990 ch 1363 §2 (AB 3532), operative July 1, 1991. See Fam C §8500.

§221.05. [Section repealed 1993]

Leg.H. Added Stats 1992 ch 1353 §3 (SB 1148), operative January 1, 1994. Repealed Stats 1993 ch 219 §8 (AB 1500). See Fam C §8621.

§221.07. [Section repealed 1993]

Leg.H. Added Stats 1992 ch 1353 §4 (SB 1148), operative January 1, 1994. Repealed Stats 1993 ch 219 §9 (AB 1500). See Fam C §8622.

§221.5. [Section repealed 1991]

Leg.H. Added Stats 1987 ch 1022 §1. Amended Stats 1988 ch 557 §1; Stats 1989 ch 1142 §2. Repealed Stats 1990 ch 1363 §2 (AB 3532), operative July 1, 1991. See Fam C §8500.

§221.10. [Section repealed 1994]

Leg.H. Added Stats 1990 ch 1363 §3 (AB 3532), operative July 1, 1991. Repealed Stats 1992 ch 162 §2 (AB 2650), operative January 1, 1994. See Fam C §8600.

§221.12. [Section repealed 1994]

Leg.H. Added Stats 1990 ch 1363 §3 (AB 3532), operative July 1, 1991. Repealed Stats 1992 ch 162 §2 (AB 2650), operative January 1, 1994. See Fam C §8601.

§221.13. [Section repealed 1994]

Leg.H. Added Stats 1990 ch 1363 §3 (AB 3532), operative July 1, 1991. Repealed Stats 1992 ch 162 §2 (AB 2650), operative January 1, 1994. See Fam C §8602.

§221.14. [Section repealed 1994]

Leg.H. Added Stats 1990 ch 1363 §3 (AB 3532), operative July 1, 1991. Repealed Stats 1992 ch 162 §2 (AB 2650), operative January 1, 1994. See Fam C §8603.

§221.20. [Section repealed 1994]

Leg.H. Added Stats 1990 ch 1363 §3 (AB 3532), operative July 1, 1991. Repealed Stats 1992 ch 162 §2 (AB 2650), operative January 1, 1994. See Fam C §§8604–8606.

§221.30. [Section repealed 1994]

Leg.H. Added Stats 1990 ch 1363 §3 (AB 3532), operative July 1, 1991. Amended Stats 1991 ch 372 §1 (SB 735), effective September 8, 1991. Repealed Stats 1992 ch 162 §2 (AB 2650), operative January 1, 1994. See Fam C §8607.

§221.40. [Section repealed 1994]

Leg.H. Added Stats 1990 ch 1363 §3 (AB 3532), operative July 1, 1991. Repealed Stats 1992 ch 162 §2 (AB 2650), operative January 1, 1994. See Fam C §8609.

§221.50. [Section repealed 1994]

Leg.H. Added Stats 1990 ch 1363 §3 (AB 3532), operative July 1, 1991. Repealed Stats 1992 ch 162 §2 (AB 2650), operative January 1, 1994. See Fam C §8610.

§221.60. [Section repealed 1994]

Leg.H. Added Stats 1990 ch 1363 §3 (AB 3532), operative July 1, 1991. Repealed Stats 1992 ch 162 §2 (AB 2650), operative January 1, 1994. See Fam C §8611.

§221.62. [Section repealed 1994]

Leg.H. Added Stats 1990 ch 1363 §3 (AB 3532), operative July 1, 1991. Repealed Stats 1992 ch 162 §2 (AB 2650), operative January 1, 1994. See Fam C §§8718, 8823, 8913, 9007.

§221.63. [Section repealed 1994]

Leg.H. Added Stats 1990 ch 1363 §3 (AB 3532), operative July 1, 1991. Repealed Stats 1992 ch 162 §2 (AB 2650), operative January 1, 1994. See Fam C §§8612, 8616.

§221.65. [Section repealed 1994]

Leg.H. Added Stats 1990 ch 1363 §3 (AB 3532), operative July 1, 1991. Repealed Stats 1992 ch 162 §2 (AB 2650), operative January 1, 1994. See Fam C §8613.

§221.70. [Section repealed 1994]

Leg.H. Added Stats 1990 ch 1363 §3 (AB 3532), operative July 1, 1991. Repealed Stats 1992 ch 162 §2 (AB 2650), operative January 1, 1994. See Fam C §8614.

§221.72. [Section repealed 1994]

Leg.H. Added Stats 1990 ch 1363 §3 (AB 3532), operative July 1, 1991. Repealed Stats 1992 ch 162 §2 (AB 2650), operative January 1, 1994. See Fam C §8615.

§221.74. [Section repealed 1994]

Leg.H. Added Stats 1990 ch 1363 §3 (AB 3532), operative July 1, 1991. Repealed Stats 1992 ch 162 §2 (AB 2650), operative January 1, 1994. See Fam C §§8616, 8618.

§221.76. [Section repealed 1994]

Leg.H. Added Stats 1990 ch 1363 §3 (AB 3532), operative July 1, 1991. Repealed Stats 1992 ch 162 §2 (AB 2650), operative January 1, 1994. See Fam C §8617.

§221.80. [Section repealed 1994]

Leg.H. Added Stats 1990 ch 1363 §3 (AB 3532), operative July 1, 1991. Repealed Stats 1992 ch 162 §2 (AB 2650), operative January 1, 1994. Fam C §8619.

§222. [Section repealed 1991]

Leg.H. Enacted 1872. Amended Code Amendments 1873–74 ch 612 §46; Stats 1968 ch 568 §1; Stats 1976 ch 497 §1. Repealed Stats 1990 ch 1363 §2 (AB 3532), operative July 1, 1991. See Fam C §8601.

§222.10. [Section repealed 1993]

Leg.H. Added Stats 1990 ch 1363 §3 (AB 3532), operative July 1, 1991. Repealed Stats 1992 ch 162 §2 (AB 2650), operative January 1, 1994. See Fam C §8700 (ch 667 prevails). Amended Stats 1992 ch 667 §1 (AB 3456). Repealed Stats 1993 ch 219 §10 (AB 1500). See Fam C §8700.

§222.13. [Section repealed 1994]

Leg.H. Added Stats 1990 ch 1363 §3 (AB 3532), operative July 1, 1991. Repealed Stats 1992 ch 162 §2 (AB 2650), operative January 1, 1994. See Fam C §8701.

§222.15. [Section repealed 1994]

Leg.H. Added Stats 1990 ch 1363 §3 (AB 3532), operative July 1, 1991. Repealed Stats 1992 ch 162 §2 (AB 2650), operative January 1, 1994. See Fam C §8702.

§222.18. [Section repealed 1994]

Leg.H. Added Stats 1990 ch 1363 §3 (AB 3532), operative July 1, 1991. Repealed Stats 1992 ch 162 §2 (AB 2650), operative January 1, 1994. See Fam C §8703.

§222.20. [Section repealed 1994]

Leg.H. Added Stats 1990 ch 1363 §3 (AB 3532), operative July 1, 1991. Repealed Stats 1992 ch 162 §2 (AB 2650), operative January 1, 1994. See Fam C §8704.

§222.22. [Section repealed 1994]
Leg.H. Added Stats 1990 ch 1363 §3 (AB 3532), operative July 1, 1991. Repealed Stats 1992 ch 162 §2 (AB 2650), operative January 1, 1994. See Fam C §8705.

§222.26. [Section repealed 1994]
Leg.H. Added Stats 1990 ch 1363 §3 (AB 3532), operative July 1, 1991. Repealed Stats 1992 ch 162 §2 (AB 2650), operative January 1, 1994. See Fam C §§8608, 8706.

§222.30. [Section repealed 1994]
Leg.H. Added Stats 1990 ch 1363 §3 (AB 3532), operative July 1, 1991. Repealed Stats 1992 ch 162 §2 (AB 2650), operative January 1, 1994. See Fam C §8707.

§222.35. [Section repealed 1994]
Leg.H. Added Stats 1990 ch 1581 §1 (AB 548), operative July 1, 1991. Repealed Stats 1992 ch 162 §2 (AB 2650), operative January 1, 1994. See Fam C §8708.

§222.36. [Section repealed 1994]
Leg.H. Added Stats 1990 ch 1581 §2 (AB 548), operative July 1, 1991. Repealed Stats 1992 ch 162 §2 (AB 2650), operative January 1, 1994. See Fam C §8709.

§222.37. [Section repealed 1994]
Leg.H. Added Stats 1990 ch 1581 §3 (AB 548), operative July 1, 1991. Repealed Stats 1992 ch 162 §2 (AB 2650), operative January 1, 1994. See Fam C §8710.

§222.38. [Section repealed 1994]
Leg.H. Added Stats 1990 ch 1581 §4 (AB 548), operative July 1, 1991. Repealed Stats 1992 ch 162 §2 (AB 2650), operative January 1, 1994. See Fam C §8711.

§222.40. [Section repealed 1994]
Leg.H. Added Stats 1990 ch 1363 §3 (AB 3532), operative July 1, 1991. Repealed Stats 1992 ch 162 §2 (AB 2650), operative January 1, 1994. See Fam C §8712.

§222.50. [Section repealed 1994]
Leg.H. Added Stats 1990 ch 1363 §3 (AB 3532), operative July 1, 1991. Repealed Stats 1992 ch 162 §2 (AB 2650), operative January 1, 1994. See Fam C §8713.

§222.70. [Section repealed 1994]
Leg.H. Added Stats 1990 ch 1363 §3 (AB 3532), operative July 1, 1991. Repealed Stats 1992 ch 162 §2 (AB 2650), operative January 1, 1994. See Fam C §8714.

§222.71. [Section repealed 1993]
Leg.H. Added Stats 1992 ch 455 §1 (SB 1564). Repealed Stats 1993 ch 219 §11 (AB 1500). See Fam C §8714(a).

§222.72. [Section repealed 1994]
Leg.H. Added Stats 1990 ch 1363 §3 (AB 3532), operative July 1, 1991. Repealed Stats 1992 ch 162 §2 (AB 2650), operative January 1, 1994. See Fam C §8716.

§222.75. [Section repealed 1994]
Leg.H. Added Stats 1990 ch 1363 §3 (AB 3532), operative July 1, 1991. Repealed Stats 1992 ch 162 §2 (AB 2650), operative January 1, 1994. See Fam C §8715.

§222.77. [Section repealed 1994]
Leg.H. Added Stats 1990 ch 1363 §3 (AB 3532), operative July 1, 1991. Repealed Stats 1992 ch 162 §2 (AB 2650), operative January 1, 1994. See Fam C §8717.

§222.78. [Section repealed 1994]
Leg.H. Added Stats 1990 ch 1363 §3 (AB 3532), operative July 1, 1991. Repealed Stats 1992 ch 162 §2 (AB 2650), operative January 1, 1994. See Fam C §8718.

§222.80. [Section repealed 1994]
Leg.H. Added Stats 1990 ch 1363 §3 (AB 3532), operative July 1, 1991. Repealed Stats 1992 ch 162 §2 (AB 2650), operative January 1, 1994. See Fam C §8719.

§222.90. [Section repealed 1994]
Leg.H. Added Stats 1990 ch 1363 §3 (AB 3532), operative July 1, 1991. Repealed Stats 1992 ch 162 §2 (AB 2650), operative January 1, 1994. See Fam C §8720.

§223. [Section repealed 1991]
Leg.H. Enacted 1872. Amended Code Amendments 1873–74 ch 612 §47. Repealed Stats 1990 ch 1363 §2 (AB 3532), operative July 1, 1991. See Fam C §8603.

§224. [Section repealed 1991]
Leg.H. Enacted 1872. Amended Stats 1891 ch 37 §1; Stats 1893 ch 96 §1; Stats 1895 ch 36 §1; Stats 1903 ch 102 §1; Stats 1907 ch 268 §1; Stats 1911 ch 450 §1; Stats 1913 ch 92 §1; Stats 1917 ch 558 §1; Stats 1921 ch 229 §1; Stats 1927 ch 691 §1; Stats 1931 ch 1130 §1; Stats 1933 ch 541 §1; Stats 1937 ch 179 §1, ch 366 §1; Stats 1939 ch 463 §1; Stats 1943 ch 283 §1; Stats 1945 ch 1317 §1; Stats 1949 ch 960 §1; Stats 1951 ch 638 §1; Stats 1955 ch 758 §1; Stats 1963 ch 374 §1; Stats 1965 ch 1173 §1; Stats 1969 ch 1611 §2, operative July 1, 1970; Stats 1974 ch 246 §1; Stats 1975 ch 1244 §7; Stats 1981 ch 714 §47. Repealed Stats 1990 ch 1363 §2 (AB 3532), operative July 1, 1991. See Fam C §§8604–8606.

§224a. [Section repealed 1991]
Leg.H. Added Stats 1979 ch 809 §1. Amended Stats 1981 ch 714 §48. Repealed Stats 1990 ch 1363 §2 (AB 3532), operative July 1, 1991. See Fam C §8619.

§224b. [Section repealed 1991]
Leg.H. Added Stats 1986 ch 445 §1. Amended Stats 1988 ch 412 §1. Repealed Stats 1990 ch 1363 §2 (AB 3532), operative July 1, 1991. See Fam C §8707.

§224m. [Section repealed 1991]
Leg.H. Added Stats 1927 ch 691 §2. Amended Stats 1931 ch 1130 §2; Stats 1947 ch 530 §1; Stats 1953 ch 1391 §1; Stats 1971 ch 1593 §47.1, operative July 1, 1973; Stats 1977 ch 1252 §51, operative July 1, 1978; Stats 1980 ch 1229 §1. Repealed Stats 1990 ch 1363 §2 (AB 3532), operative July 1, 1991. See Fam C §8700.

§224n. [Section repealed 1991]
Leg.H. Added Stats 1953 ch 1122 §1. Amended Stats 1955 ch 949 §1; Stats 1957 ch 1237 §1; Stats 1970 ch 1091 §1; Stats 1976 ch 404 §1; Stats 1982 ch 977 §1, effective September 13, 1982, operative October 1, 1982; Stats 1987 ch 360 §1; Stats 1989 ch 994 §1; Stats 1990 ch 130 §1 (SB 2188) (ch 1363 prevails). Repealed Stats 1990 ch 1363 §2 (AB 3532), operative July 1, 1991. See Fam C §§8614, 8704.

§224o. [Section repealed 1991]
Leg.H. Added Stats 1982 ch 773 §1. Repealed Stats 1990 ch 1363 §2 (AB 3532), operative July 1, 1991. See Fam C §§8701, 8813.

§224p. [Section repealed 1991]
Leg.H. Added Stats 1945 ch 1317 §2. Amended Stats 1951 ch 638 §2; Stats 1971 ch 1593 §47.2, operative July 1, 1973; Stats 1977 ch 1252 §52, operative July 1, 1978; Stats 1987 ch 940 §1. Repealed Stats 1990 ch 1363 §2 (AB 3532), operative July 1, 1991. See Fam C §8609.

§224q. [Section repealed 1991]
Leg.H. Added Stats 1945 ch 1317 §2.5. Amended Stats 1971 ch 1593 §47.3, operative July 1, 1973; Stats 1977 ch 1252 §53, operative July 1, 1978; Stats 1987 ch 940 §2. Repealed Stats 1990 ch 1363 §2 (AB 3532), operative July 1, 1991. See Fam C §8500.

§224r. [Section repealed 1991]
Leg.H. Added Stats 1963 ch 1893 §1. Repealed Stats 1990 ch 1363 §2 (AB 3532), operative July 1, 1991. See Fam C §8610.

§224s. [Section repealed 1991]

Leg.H. Added Stats 1974 ch 1087 §1. Amended Stats 1978 ch 429 §21, effective July 17, 1978, operative July 1, 1978; Stats 1980 ch 1229 §2; Stats 1983 ch 1162 §3; Stats 1984 ch 1116 §1, effective September 13, 1984. Repealed Stats 1990 ch 1363 §2 (AB 3532), operative July 1, 1991. See Fam C §§8608, 8706, 8817, 8909.

§224t. [Section repealed 1991]

Leg.H. Added Stats 1983 ch 1162 §4, operative January 1, 1986. Amended Stats 1984 ch 288 §1. Repealed Stats 1990 ch 1363 §2 (AB 3532), operative July 1, 1991. See Fam C §9202.

§224u. [Section repealed 1991]

Leg.H. Added Stats 1983 ch 1162 §5, operative January 1, 1986. Amended Stats 1984 ch 288 §2. Repealed Stats 1990 ch 1363 §2 (AB 3532), operative July 1, 1991. See Fam C §§8703, 8819.

§224v. [Section repealed 1991]

Leg.H. Added Stats 1983 ch 1162 §6, operative January 1, 1986. Amended Stats 1984 ch 288 §3. Repealed Stats 1990 ch 1363 §2 (AB 3532), operative July 1, 1991. See Fam C §§8702, 8818, 9004.

§224.1. [Section repealed 1991]

Leg.H. Added Stats 1977 ch 376 §1. Amended Stats 1983 ch 842 §2, operative January 1, 1985. Repealed Stats 1990 ch 1363 §2 (AB 3532), operative July 1, 1991. See Fam C §8705.

§224.10. [Section repealed 1994]

Leg.H. Added Stats 1990 ch 1363 §3 (AB 3532), operative July 1, 1991. Repealed Stats 1992 ch 162 §2 (AB 2650), operative January 1, 1994. See Fam C §§270, 8800.

§224.20. [Section repealed 1994]

Leg.H. Added Stats 1990 ch 1363 §3 (AB 3532), operative July 1, 1991. Repealed Stats 1992 ch 162 §2 (AB 2650), operative January 1, 1994. See Fam C §8801.

§224.21. [Section repealed 1993]

Leg.H. Added Stats 1992 ch 1353 §5 (SB 1148), operative January 1, 1994. Repealed Stats 1993 ch 219 §12 (AB 1500). See Fam C §8801.3.

§224.24. [Section repealed 1993]

Leg.H. Added Stats 1992 ch 1353 §6 (SB 1148), operative January 1, 1994. Repealed Stats 1993 ch 219 §13 (AB 1500). See Fam C §8801.5.

§224.26. [Section repealed 1993]

Leg.H. Added Stats 1992 ch 1353 §7 (SB 1148), operative January 1, 1994. Repealed Stats 1993 ch 219 §14 (AB 1500). See Fam C §8801.7.

§224.30. [Section repealed 1993]

Leg.H. Added Stats 1990 ch 1363 §3 (AB 3532), operative July 1, 1991. Repealed Stats 1992 ch 162 §2 (AB 2650), operative January 1, 1994 (ch 1353 prevails). Amended Stats 1992 ch 1353 §8 (SB 1148), operative January 1, 1994. Repealed Stats 1993 ch 219 §15 (AB 1500). See Fam C §8802.

§224.33. [Section repealed 1994]

Leg.H. Added Stats 1990 ch 1363 §3 (AB 3532), operative July 1, 1991. Repealed Stats 1992 ch 162 §2 (AB 2650), operative January 1, 1994. See Fam C §8803.

§224.36. [Section repealed 1993]

Leg.H. Added Stats 1990 ch 1363 §3 (AB 3532), operative July 1, 1991. Amended Stats 1991 ch 697 §1 (AB 1202), effective October 7, 1991. Repealed Stats 1992 ch 162 §2 (AB 2650) (ch 1353 prevails). Amended Stats 1992 ch 1353 §9 (SB 1148), operative January 1, 1994. Repealed Stats 1993 ch 219 §16 (AB 1500). See Fam C §8804.

§224.37. [Section repealed 1994]

Leg.H. Added Stats 1990 ch 1363 §3 (AB 3532), operative July 1, 1991. Repealed Stats 1992 ch 162 §2 (AB 2650), operative January 1, 1994. See Fam C §8805.

§224.40. [Section repealed 1994]

Leg.H. Added Stats 1990 ch 1363 §3 (AB 3532), operative July 1, 1991. Repealed Stats 1992 ch 162 §2 (AB 2650), operative January 1, 1994. See Fam C §8806.

§224.42. [Section repealed 1994]

Leg.H. Added Stats 1990 ch 1363 §3 (AB 3532), operative July 1, 1991. Repealed Stats 1992 ch 162 §2 (AB 2650), operative January 1, 1994. See Fam C §8807.

§224.44. [Section repealed 1993]

Leg.H. Added Stats 1990 ch 1363 §3 (AB 3532), operative July 1, 1991. Repealed Stats 1992 ch 162 §2 (AB 2650), operative January 1, 1994. See Fam C §8808.

§224.45. [Section repealed 1993]

Leg.H. Added Stats 1991 ch 697 §2 (AB 1202), effective October 7, 1991, operative July 1, 1991. Repealed operative January 1, 1993, by its own provisions. The repealed section related to request to sign consent in presence of court.

§224.47. [Section repealed 1993]

Leg.H. Added Stats 1990 ch 1363 §3 (AB 3532), operative July 1, 1991. Repealed operative January 1, 1993, by its own provisions. See Fam C §8810.

§224.49. [Section repealed 1994]

Leg.H. Added Stats 1990 ch 1363 §3 (AB 3532), operative July 1, 1991. Repealed Stats 1992 ch 162 §2 (AB 2650), operative January 1, 1994. See Fam C §8811.

§224.50. [Section repealed 1994]

Leg.H. Added Stats 1990 ch 1363 §3 (AB 3532), operative July 1, 1991, operative until January 1, 1994. Amended Stats 1991 ch 697 §3 (AB 1202), effective October 7, 1991, operative until January 1, 1994. Repealed Stats 1992 ch 162 §2 (AB 2650), operative January 1, 1994. Amended Stats 1992 ch 427 §10 (AB 3355) (ch 162 prevails). The repealed section related to conditions for early interview of persons from whom consent is required, advice to birth parent, disclosure of relationship between attorney and agency, and the Independent Adoption Preplacement Program.

§224.61. [Section repealed 1994]

Leg.H. Added Stats 1990 ch 1363 §3 (AB 3532), operative July 1, 1991. Repealed Stats 1992 ch 162 §2 (AB 2650), operative January 1, 1994. See Fam C §8813.

§224.62. [Section repealed 1993]

Leg.H. Added Stats 1990 ch 1363 §3 (AB 3532), operative July 1, 1991. Repealed Stats 1992 ch 162 §2 (AB 2650), operative January 1, 1994. See Fam C §8814.

§224.63. [Section repealed 1993]

Leg.H. Added Stats 1992 ch 1353 §12 (SB 1148), operative January 1, 1994. Repealed Stats 1993 ch 219 §19 (AB 1500). See Fam C §8814.5.

§224.64. [Section repealed 1994]

Leg.H. Added Stats 1990 ch 1363 §3 (AB 3532), operative July 1, 1991. Repealed Stats 1992 ch 162 §2 (AB 2650), operative January 1, 1994. See Fam C §8815.

§224.66. [Section repealed 1994]

Leg.H. Added Stats 1990 ch 1363 §3 (AB 3532), operative July 1, 1991. Repealed Stats 1992 ch 162 §2 (AB 2650), operative January 1, 1994. See Fam C §8816.

§224.70. [Section repealed 1994]

Leg.H. Added Stats 1990 ch 1363 §3 (AB 3532), operative July 1, 1991. Repealed Stats 1992 ch 162 §§2 (AB 2650), operative January 1, 1994. See Fam C §§8608, 8817.

§224.73. [Section repealed 1994]

Leg.H. Added Stats 1990 ch 1363 §3 (AB 3532), operative July 1, 1991. Amended Stats 1991 ch 697 §4 (AB 1202), effective October 7, 1991. Repealed Stats 1992 ch 162 §2 (AB 2650), operative January 1, 1994. See Fam C §8818.

§224.76. [Section repealed 1994]

Leg.H. Added Stats 1990 ch 1363 §3 (AB 3532), operative July 1, 1991. Repealed Stats 1992 ch 162 §2 (AB 2650), operative January 1, 1994. See Fam C §8819.

§224.80. [Section repealed 1994]

Leg.H. Added Stats 1990 ch 1363 §3 (AB 3532), operative July 1, 1991. Repealed Stats 1992 ch 162 §2 (AB 2650), operative January 1, 1994. See Fam C §8820.

§224.91. [Section repealed 1994]

Leg.H. Added Stats 1990 ch 1363 §3 (AB 3532), operative July 1, 1991. Repealed Stats 1992 ch 162 §2 (AB 2650), operative January 1, 1994. See Fam C §8821.

§224.93. [Section repealed 1994]

Leg.H. Added Stats 1990 ch 1363 §3 (AB 3532), operative July 1, 1991. Repealed Stats 1992 ch 162 §2 (AB 2650), operative January 1, 1994. See Fam C §8822.

§224.95. [Section repealed 1994]

Leg.H. Added Stats 1990 ch 1363 §3 (AB 3532), operative July 1, 1991. Repealed Stats 1992 ch 162 §2 (AB 2650), operative January 1, 1994. See Fam C §8823.

§225. [Section repealed 1991]

Leg.H. Enacted 1872. Repealed Stats 1990 ch 1363 §2 (AB 3532), operative July 1, 1991. See Fam C §8602.

§225m. [Section repealed 1991]

Leg.H. Added Stats 1977 ch 718 §1. Amended Stats 1988 ch 1001 §1. Repealed Stats 1990 ch 1363 §2 (AB 3532), operative July 1, 1991. See Fam C §§270, 8800.

Prior Law: Former §225m, similar to present W & I C §16100, was added Stats 1947 ch 532 §1 and repealed Stats 1953 ch 1342 §1, operative July 1, 1954.

§225p. [Section repealed 1991]

Leg.H. Added Stats 1947 ch 1126 §1. Amended Stats 1953 ch 1341 §1, operative July 1, 1954; Stats 1957 ch 1321 §5; Stats 1965 ch 1824 §1; Stats 1968 ch 879 §1; Stats 1970 ch 838 §1; Stats 1971 ch 1593 §47.4, operative July 1, 1973; Stats 1977 ch 1252 §54, operative July 1, 1978; Stats 1985 ch 269 §1; Stats 1989 ch 85 §1, effective July 5, 1989, operative September 1, 1989. Repealed Stats 1990 ch 1363 §2 (AB 3532), operative July 1, 1991. See Fam C §8716.

§225q. [Section repealed 1991]

Leg.H. Added Stats 1989 ch 85 §2, effective July 5, 1989, operative September 1, 1989, operative until January 1, 1993. Repealed Stats 1990 ch 1363 §2 (AB 3532), operative July 1, 1991. See Fam C §§8810, 9002.

Prior Law: Former §225q, similar to present W & I C §§16101, 16105, was added Stats 1951 ch 1112 §1 and repealed Stats 1953 ch 1342 §1, operative July 1, 1954.

§226. [Section repealed 1991]

Leg.H. Enacted 1872. Amended Code Amendments 1875–76 ch 57 §1; Code Amendments 1880 ch 41 §5; Stats 1905 ch 415 §1; Stats 1907 ch 266 §1; Stats 1927 ch 691 §3; Stats 1931 ch 1130 §3; Stats 1935 ch 563 §1; Stats 1939 ch 463 §2; Stats 1943 ch 283 §2, ch 901 §1; Stats 1945 ch 1316 §1, ch 1317 §3; Stats 1947 ch 529 §1; Stats 1951 ch 637 §1; Stats 1953 ch 1220 §2; Stats 1955 ch 725 §1; Stats 1961 ch 1074 §1; Stats 1963 ch 676 §1, ch 1806 §1; Stats 1965 ch 174 §1; Stats 1968 ch 694 §1; Stats 1971 ch 1593 §47.5, operative July 1, 1973; Stats 1977 ch 1252 §55, operative July 1, 1978; Stats 1982 ch 977 §2, effective September 13, 1982, operative October 1, 1982; Stats 1983 ch 477 §1; Stats 1984 ch 1116 §1.5, effective September 13, 1984; Stats 1988 ch 1382 §1. Repealed Stats 1990 ch 1363 §2 (AB 3532), operative July 1, 1991. See Fam C §§8714, 8802.

§226a. [Section repealed 1991]

Leg.H. Added Stats 1949 ch 731 §1. Amended Stats 1951 ch 638 §3; Stats 1965 ch 816 §1; Stats 1971 ch 1593 §47.6, operative July 1, 1974; Stats 1977 ch 1252 §56, operative July 1, 1978; Stats 1988 ch 1382 §2. Repealed Stats 1990 ch 1363 §2 (AB 3532), operative July 1, 1991. See Fam C §§8815, 9005.

§226b. [Section repealed 1991]

Leg.H. Added Stats 1949 ch 731 §2. Amended Stats 1951 ch 638 §4; Stats 1961 ch 1074 §2; Stats 1971 ch 1593 §47.7, operative July 1, 1973; Stats 1977 ch 1252 §57, operative July 1, 1978; Stats 1984 ch 1116 §2, effective September 13, 1984. Repealed Stats 1990 ch 1363 §2 (AB 3532), operative July 1, 1991. See Fam C §§8719, 8804, 8916, 9006.

§226c. [Section repealed 1991]

Leg.H. Added Stats 1953 ch 1343 §1, operative July 1, 1954. Amended Stats 1961 ch 1074 §3; Stats 1971 ch 1593 §47.8, operative July 1, 1973; Stats 1977 ch 1252 §58, operative July 1, 1978; Stats 1984 ch 1116 §3, effective September 13, 1984. Repealed Stats 1990 ch 1363 §2 (AB 3532), operative July 1, 1991. See Fam C §§8805, 8917, 8918.

§226m. [Section repealed 1991]

Leg.H. Added Stats 1947 ch 534 §1. Amended Stats 1971 ch 762 §1. Repealed Stats 1990 ch 1363 §2 (AB 3532), operative July 1, 1991. See Fam C §8611.

§226.1. [Section repealed 1991]

Leg.H. Added Stats 1963 ch 1806 §3. Amended Stats 1971 ch 1593 §47.9, operative July 1, 1973; Stats 1977 ch 1252 §59, operative July 1, 1978. Repealed Stats 1990 ch 1363 §2 (AB 3532), operative July 1, 1991. See Fam C §§8805, 8814, 9003.

§226.2. [Section repealed 1991]

Leg.H. Added Stats 1963 ch 1806 §4. Amended Stats 1971 ch 1593 §47.10, operative July 1, 1973; Stats 1977 ch 1252 §60, operative July 1, 1978. Repealed Stats 1990 ch 1363 §2 (AB 3532), operative July 1, 1991. See Fam C §200.

§226.3. [Section repealed 1991]

Leg.H. Added Stats 1963 ch 1806 §5. Amended Stats 1971 ch 1593 §47.11, operative July 1, 1973; Stats 1977 ch 1252 §61, operative July 1, 1978; Stats 1984 ch 1116 §4, effective September 13, 1984. Repealed Stats 1990 ch 1363 §2 (AB 3532), operative July 1, 1991. See Fam C §8816.

§226.4. [Section repealed 1991]

Leg.H. Added Stats 1963 ch 1806 §6. Amended Stats 1971 ch 1593 §47.12, operative July 1, 1973; Stats 1977 ch 1252 §62, operative July 1, 1978; Stats 1980 ch 676 §41; Stats 1984 ch 1116 §5, effective September 13, 1984. Repealed Stats 1990 ch 1363 §2 (AB 3532), operative July 1, 1991. See Fam C §8820.

§226.5. [Section repealed 1991]

Leg.H. Added Stats 1963 ch 1806 §7. Amended Stats 1971 ch 1593 §47.13, operative July 1, 1973; Stats 1977 ch 1252 §63, operative July 1, 1978; Stats 1983 ch 309 §1; Stats 1989 ch 85 §3, effective July 5, 1989, operative September 1, 1989, ch 1142 §3; Stats 1990 ch 864 §1.5 (AB4145), operative until July 1, 1991. Repealed Stats 1990 ch 1363 §2 (AB 3532), operative July 1, 1991. See Fam C §8808.

§226.6. [Section repealed 1991]

Leg.H. Added Stats 1963 ch 1806 §8. Amended Stats 1971 ch 1593 §47.14, operative July 1, 1973; Stats 1977 ch 1252 §65, operative July 1, 1978; Stats 1984 ch 1116 §6, effective September 13, 1984; Stats 1986 ch 767 §1. Repealed Stats 1990 ch 1363 §2 (AB 3532), operative July 1, 1991. See Fam C §§8715, 8914.

§226.7. [Section repealed 1991]

Leg.H. Added Stats 1963 ch 1806 §9. Amended Stats 1971 ch 1593 §47.15, operative July 1, 1973; Stats 1977 ch 1252 §66, operative July 1, 1978; Stats 1984 ch 1116 §7, effective September 13, 1984. Repealed Stats 1990 ch 1363 §2 (AB 3532), operative July 1, 1991. See Fam C §§8717, 8821, 8915.

§226.8. [Section repealed 1991]

Leg.H. Added Stats 1963 ch 1806 §10. Amended Stats 1971 ch 1593 §47.16, operative July 1, 1973; Stats 1977 ch 1252 §67, operative July 1, 1978; Stats 1984 ch 1116 §8, effective September 13, 1984. Repealed Stats 1990 ch 1363 §2 (AB 3532), operative July 1, 1991. See Fam C §§8720, 8822.

§226.9. [Section repealed 1991]

Leg.H. Added Stats 1963 ch 1806 §11. Amended Stats 1971 ch 1593 §47.17, operative July 1, 1973; Stats 1973 ch 237 §1; Stats 1977 ch 1252 §68, operative July 1, 1978; Stats 1983 ch 477 §2. Repealed Stats 1990 ch 1363 §2 (AB 3532), operative July 1, 1991. See Fam C §§9000 et seq.

§226.10. [Section repealed 1994]

Leg.H. Added Stats 1990 ch 1363 §3 (AB 3532), operative July 1, 1991. Repealed Stats 1992 ch 162 §2 (AB 2650), operative January 1, 1994. See Fam C §8900.

Prior Law: Former §226.10, similar to present Fam C §§8713, 8803, 8910, was added Stats 1969 ch 1251 §1, amended Stats 1971 ch 1593 §47.18, operative July 1, 1973, Stats 1977 ch 1252 §69, operative July 1, 1978, and repealed Stats 1990 ch 1363 §2, operative July 1, 1991.

§226.11. [Section repealed 1994]

Leg.H. Added Stats 1990 ch 1363 §3 (AB 3532), operative July 1, 1991. Repealed Stats 1992 ch 162 §2 (AB 2650), operative January 1, 1994. See Fam C §8901.

Prior Law: Former §226.11, relating to forms releasing child from health facilities required to delineate types of available adoptions, was added Stats 1974 ch 196 §1, amended Stats 1977 ch 1252 §70, operative July 1, 1978, and repealed Stats 1990 ch 1363 §2, operative July 1, 1991.

§226.12. [Section repealed 1991]

Leg.H. Added Stats 1983 ch 842 §3, operative January 1, 1985. Amended Stats 1984 ch 892 §1. Repealed Stats 1990 ch 1363 §2 (AB 3532), operative July 1, 1991. See Fam C §§9003, 9004.

§226.20. [Section repealed 1994]

Leg.H. Added Stats 1990 ch 1363 §3 (AB 3532), operative July 1, 1991. Repealed Stats 1992 ch 162 §2 (AB 2650), operative January 1, 1994. See Fam C §8902.

§226.21. [Section repealed 1994]

Leg.H. Added Stats 1990 ch 1363 §3 (AB 3532), operative July 1, 1991. Repealed Stats 1992 ch 162 §2 (AB 2650), operative January 1, 1994. See Fam C §8903.

§226.23. [Section repealed 1993]

Leg.H. Added Stats 1990 ch 1363 §3 (AB 3532), operative July 1, 1991. Repealed Stats 1992 ch 162 §2 (AB 2650), operative January 1, 1994. See Family Code §8904 (ch 435 prevails). Amended Stats 1992 ch 435 §1 (AB 2840). Repealed Stats 1993 ch 219 §21 (AB 1500). See Fam C §8904.

§226.25. [Section repealed 1994]

Leg.H. Added Stats 1990 ch 1363 §3 (AB 3532), operative July 1, 1991. Repealed Stats 1992 ch 162 §2 (AB 2650), operative January 1, 1994. See Fam C §8905.

§226.27. [Section repealed 1994]

Leg.H. Added Stats 1990 ch 1363 §3 (AB 3532), operative July 1, 1991. Repealed Stats 1992 ch 162 §2 (AB 2650), operative January 1, 1994. See Fam C §8906.

§226.28. [Section repealed 1994]

Leg.H. Added Stats 1990 ch 1363 §3 (AB 3532), operative July 1, 1991. Repealed Stats 1992 ch 162 §2 (AB 2650), operative January 1, 1994. See Fam C §8907.

§226.30. [Section repealed 1994]

Leg.H. Added Stats 1990 ch 1363 §3 (AB 3532), operative July 1, 1991. Repealed Stats 1992 ch 162 §2 (AB 2650), operative January 1, 1994. See Fam C §8908.

§226.35. [Section repealed 1994]

Leg.H. Added Stats 1990 ch 1363 §3 (AB 3532), operative July 1, 1991. Repealed Stats 1992 ch 162 §2 (AB 2650), operative January 1, 1994. See Fam C §§8608, 8909.

§226.40. [Section repealed 1994]

Leg.H. Added Stats 1990 ch 1363 §3 (AB 3532), operative July 1, 1991. Repealed Stats 1992 ch 162 §2 (AB 2650), operative January 1, 1994. See Fam C §8910.

§226.50. [Section repealed 1994]

Leg.H. Added Stats 1990 ch 1363 §3 (AB 3532), operative July 1, 1991. Repealed Stats 1992 ch 162 §2 (AB 2650), operative January 1, 1994. See Fam C §8911.

§226.51. [Section repealed 1991]

Leg.H. Added Stats 1989 ch 1142 §4. Repealed Stats 1990 ch 1363 §2 (AB 3532), operative July 1, 1991. See Fam C §8911.

§226.52. [Section repealed 1994]

Leg.H. Added Stats 1990 ch 1363 §3 (AB 3532), operative July 1, 1991. Repealed Stats 1992 ch 162 §2 (AB 2650), operative January 1, 1994. See Fam C §8912.

§226.55. [Section repealed 1994]

Leg.H. Added Stats 1990 ch 1363 §3 (AB 3532), operative July 1, 1991. Repealed Stats 1992 ch 162 §2 (AB 2650), operative January 1, 1994. See Fam C §8913.

Prior Law: Former §226.55, similar to present Fam C §§8712, 8811, 8908, was added Stats 1973 ch 596 §1, amended Stats 1977 ch 1252 §64, operative July 1, 1978, Stats 1986 ch 1345 §1, and repealed Stats 1990 ch 1363 §2, operative July 1, 1991.

§226.57. [Section repealed 1994]

Leg.H. Added Stats 1990 ch 1363 §3 (AB 3532), operative July 1, 1991. Repealed Stats 1992 ch 162 §2 (AB 2650), operative January 1, 1994. See Fam C §8914.

§226.59. [Section repealed 1994]

Leg.H. Added Stats 1990 ch 1363 §3 (AB 3532), operative July 1, 1991. Repealed Stats 1992 ch 162 §2 (AB 2650), operative January 1, 1994. See Fam C §8915.

§226.60. [Section repealed 1994]

Leg.H. Added Stats 1990 ch 1363 §3 (AB 3532), operative July 1, 1991. Repealed Stats 1992 ch 162 §2 (AB 2650), operative January 1, 1994. See Fam C §8916.

§226.64. [Section repealed 1994]

Leg.H. Added Stats 1990 ch 1363 §3 (AB 3532), operative July 1, 1991. Repealed Stats 1992 ch 162 §2 (AB 2650), operative January 1, 1994. See Fam C §8917.

§226.66. [Section repealed 1994]

Leg.H. Added Stats 1990 ch 1363 §3 (AB 3532), operative July 1, 1991. Repealed Stats 1992 ch 162 §2 (AB 2650), operative January 1, 1994. See Fam C §8918.

§226.69. [Section repealed 1993]

Leg.H. Added Stats 1992 ch 435 §2 (AB 2840). Repealed Stats 1993 ch 219 §22 (AB 1500). See Fam C §8919.

§227. [Section repealed 1991]

Leg.H. Enacted 1872. Amended Stats 1905 ch 415 §2; Stats 1927 ch 691 §3; Stats 1931 ch 1130 §4; Stats 1943 ch 208 §1; Stats 1945 ch 1316 §2; Stats 1961 ch 605 §1; Stats 1965 ch 193 §1; Stats 1968 ch 551 §1, ch 1106 §2; Stats 1970 ch 655 §1; Stats 1971 ch 1593 §47.19, operative July 1, 1973; Stats 1977 ch 1252 §71, operative July 1, 1978; Stats 1983 ch 1162 §7, operative January 1, 1986; Stats 1984 ch 288 §4. Repealed Stats 1990 ch 1363 §2 (AB 3532), operative July 1, 1991. See Fam C §§8612–8614, 8616, 8718, 8823, 8913, 9007.

§227a. [Section repealed 1991]

Leg.H. Added Stats 1933 ch 541 §2. Amended Stats 1943 ch 283 §3; Stats 1945 ch 1317 §4; Stats 1963 ch 1806 §2; Stats 1972 ch 1132 §1; Stats 1985 ch 588 §1. Repealed Stats 1990 ch 1363 §2 (AB 3532), operative July 1, 1991. See Fam C §§8807, 9001.

§227aa. [Section repealed 1979]

Leg.H. Added Stats 1943 ch 208 §2. Amended Stats 1945 ch 1317 §5, operative until noon, December 31, 1946. Repealed Stats 1979 ch 373 §41. The repealed section related to adoption by stepparent.

§227aaa. [Section repealed 1991]

Leg.H. Added Stats 1945 ch 1317 §6. Amended Stats 1971 ch 1593 §47.20, operative July 1, 1973; Stats 1977 ch 1252 §72, operative July 1, 1978. Repealed Stats 1990 ch 1363 §2 (AB 3532), operative July 1, 1991. See Fam C §9201.

§227b. [Section repealed 1991]

Leg.H. Added Stats 1972 ch 380 §1.5, operative July 1, 1973. Amended Stats 1977 ch 1252 §73, operative July 1, 1978; Stats 1978 ch 429 §22, effective July 17, 1978, operative July 1, 1978. Repealed Stats 1990 ch 1363 §2 (AB 3532), operative July 1, 1991. See Fam C §9100.

Prior Law: Former §227b, similar to the repealed section, was added Stats 1937 ch 366 §2, amended Stats 1947 ch 531 §1, and repealed, effective July 1, 1973, by its own terms.

§227c. [Section repealed 1991]

Leg.H. Added Stats 1939 ch 1102 §1. Amended Stats 1972 ch 380 §2. Repealed Stats 1990 ch 1363 §2 (AB 3532), operative July 1, 1991. See Fam C §9101.

§227d. [Section repealed 1991]

Leg.H. Added Stats 1951 ch 638 §5. Repealed Stats 1990 ch 1363 §2 (AB 3532), operative July 1, 1991. See Fam C §9102.

§227p. [Section repealed 1991]

Leg.H. Added Stats 1951 ch 880 §2. Amended Stats 1953 ch 1220 §3; Stats 1971 ch 1593 §47.22, operative July 1, 1973; Stats 1977 ch 1252 §74, operative July 1, 1978; Stats 1981 ch 734 §1; Stats 1985 ch 356 §1. Repealed Stats 1990 ch 1363 §2 (AB 3532), operative July 1, 1991. See Fam C §§9300 et seq.

§227.5. [Section repealed 1991]

Leg.H. Added Stats 1983 ch 477 §3. Repealed Stats 1990 ch 1363 §2 (AB 3532), operative July 1, 1991. See Fam C §9002.

§227.10. [Section repealed 1994]

Leg.H. Added Stats 1990 ch 1363 §3 (AB 3532), operative July 1, 1991. Repealed Stats 1992 ch 162 §2 (AB 2650), operative January 1, 1994. See Fam C §9000.

§227.20. [Section repealed 1993]

Leg.H. Added Stats 1990 ch 1363 §3 (AB 3532), operative July 1, 1991. Repealed Stats 1992 ch 162 §2 (AB 2650) (ch 472 prevails). Amended Stats 1992 ch 472 §2 (AB 2887). Repealed Stats 1993 ch 219 §23 (AB 1500). See Fam C §9001.

§227.30. [Section repealed 1993]

Leg.H. Added Stats 1990 ch 1363 §3 (AB 3532), operative July 1, 1991. Amended Stats 1991 ch 120 §1 (AB 1804). Repealed Stats 1992 ch 162 §2 (AB 2650) (ch 472 prevails). Amended Stats 1992 ch 472 §3 (AB 2887). Repealed Stats 1993 ch 219 §24 (AB 1500). See Fam C §9002.

§227.40. [Section repealed 1993]

Leg.H. Added Stats 1990 ch 1363 §3 (AB 3532), operative July 1, 1991. Repealed Stats 1992 ch 162 §2 (AB 2650) (ch 472 prevails). Amended Stats 1992 ch 472 §4 (AB 2887). Repealed Stats 1993 ch 219 §25 (AB 1500). See Fam C §9003.

§227.44. [Section repealed 1994]

Leg.H. Added Stats 1990 ch 1363 §3 (AB 3532), operative July 1, 1991. Repealed Stats 1992 ch 162 §2 (AB 2650), operative January 1, 1994. See Fam C §9004.

§227.46. [Section repealed 1993]

Leg.H. Added Stats 1990 ch 1363 §3 (AB 3532), operative July 1, 1991. Repealed Stats 1992 ch 162 §2 (AB 2650) (ch 472 prevails). Amended Stats 1992 ch 472 §5 (AB 2887). Repealed Stats 1993 ch 219 §26 (AB 1500). See Fam C §9005.

§227.50. [Section repealed 1993]

Leg.H. Added Stats 1990 ch 1363 §3 (AB 3532), operative July 1, 1991. Repealed Stats 1992 ch 162 §2 (AB 2650) (ch 472 prevails). Amended Stats 1992 ch 472 §6 (AB 2887). Repealed Stats 1993 ch 219 §27 (AB 1500). See Fam C §9006.

§227.60. [Section repealed 1994]

Leg.H. Added Stats 1990 ch 1363 §3 (AB 3532), operative July 1, 1991. Repealed Stats 1992 ch 162 §2 (AB 2650), operative January 1, 1994. See Fam C §9007.

§228. [Section repealed 1991]

Leg.H. Enacted 1872. Amended Code Amendments 1873–74 ch 612 §48. Repealed Stats 1990 ch 1363 §2 (AB 3532), operative July 1, 1991. See Fam C §§8616, 8618, 9304, 9305.

§228.10. [Section repealed 1994]

Leg.H. Added Stats 1990 ch 1363 §3 (AB 3532), operative July 1, 1991. Repealed Stats 1992 ch 162 §2 (AB 2650), operative January 1, 1994. See Fam C §9100.

§228.13. [Section repealed 1994]

Leg.H. Added Stats 1990 ch 1363 §3 (AB 3532), operative July 1, 1991. Repealed Stats 1992 ch 162 §2 (AB 2650), operative January 1, 1994. See Fam C §9101.

§228.15. [Section repealed 1994]

Leg.H. Added Stats 1990 ch 1363 §3 (AB 3532), operative July 1, 1991. Repealed Stats 1992 ch 162 §2 (AB 2650), operative January 1, 1994. See Fam C §9102.

§229. [Section repealed 1991]

Leg.H. Enacted 1872. Repealed Stats 1990 ch 1363 §2 (AB 3532), operative July 1, 1991. See Fam C §9306.

§229.10. [Section repealed 1994]

Leg.H. Added Stats 1990 ch 1363 §3 (AB 3532), operative July 1, 1991. Repealed Stats 1992 ch 162 §2 (AB 2650), operative January 1, 1994. See Fam C §9200.

§229.20. [Section repealed 1994]

Leg.H. Added Stats 1990 ch 1363 §3 (AB 3532), operative July 1, 1991. Repealed Stats 1992 ch 162 §2 (AB 2650), operative January 1, 1994. See Fam C §9201.

§229.30. [Section repealed 1994]

Leg.H. Added Stats 1990 ch 1363 §3 (AB 3532), operative July 1, 1991. Repealed Stats 1992 ch 162 §2 (AB 2650), operative January 1, 1994. See Fam C §9202.

§229.40. [Section repealed 1994]

Leg.H. Added Stats 1990 ch 1363 §3 (AB 3532), operative July 1, 1991. Repealed Stats 1992 ch 162 §2 (AB 2650), operative January 1, 1994. See Fam C §9203.

§229.50. [Section repealed 1994]

Leg.H. Added Stats 1990 ch 1363 §3 (AB 3532), operative July 1, 1991. Amended Stats 1991 ch 135 §1 (AB 1896). Repealed Stats 1992 ch 162 §2 (AB 2650), operative January 1, 1994. See Fam C §9204.

§229.60. [Section repealed 1994]

Leg.H. Added Stats 1990 ch 1363 §3 (AB 3532), operative July 1, 1991. Amended Stats 1991 ch 697 §5 (AB 1202), effective October 7, 1991. Repealed Stats 1992 ch 162 §2 (AB 2650), operative January 1, 1994. See Fam C §9205.

§229.70. [Section repealed 1994]

Leg.H. Added Stats 1990 ch 1363 §3 (AB 3532), operative July 1, 1991. Repealed Stats 1992 ch 162 §2 (AB 2650), operative January 1, 1994. See Fam C §9206.

§230. [Section repealed 1975]

Leg.H. Enacted 1872. Repealed Stats 1975 ch 1244 §8. The repealed section related to the adoption of illegitimate child.

§230.5. [Section repealed 1991]

Leg.H. Added Stats 1969 ch 485 §1. Repealed Stats 1990 ch 1363 §2 (AB 3532), operative July 1, 1991. See Fam C §8615.

§230.6. [Section repealed 1991]

Leg.H. Added Stats 1982 ch 990 §1. Repealed Stats 1990 ch 1363 §2 (AB 3532), operative July 1, 1991. See Fam C §9204.

§230.7. [Section repealed 1991]

Leg.H. Added Stats 1984 ch 1049 §1. Amended Stats 1985 ch 1493 §1. Repealed Stats 1990 ch 1363 §2 (AB 3532), operative July 1, 1991. See Fam C §9206.

§230.8. [Section repealed 1991]

Leg.H. Added Stats 1985 ch 559 §1. Repealed Stats 1990 ch 1363 §2 (AB 3532), operative July 1, 1991. See Fam C §9205.

§230.10. [Section repealed 1994]

Leg.H. Added Stats 1990 ch 1363 §4 (AB 3532), operative July 1, 1991. Repealed Stats 1992 ch 162 §2 (AB 2650), operative January 1, 1994. See Fam C §9300.

§230.12. [Section repealed 1994]

Leg.H. Added Stats 1990 ch 1363 §4 (AB 3532), operative July 1, 1991. Repealed Stats 1992 ch 162 §2 (AB 2650), operative January 1, 1994. See Fam C §9303.

§230.14. [Section repealed 1994]

Leg.H. Added Stats 1990 ch 1363 §4 (AB 3532), operative July 1, 1991. Repealed Stats 1992 ch 162 §2 (AB 2650), operative January 1, 1994. See Fam C §§9304, 9305.

§230.16. [Section repealed 1994]

Leg.H. Added Stats 1990 ch 1363 §4 (AB 3532), operative July 1, 1991. Repealed Stats 1992 ch 162 §2 (AB 2650), operative January 1, 1994. See Fam C §9306.

§230.20. [Section repealed 1994]

Leg.H. Added Stats 1990 ch 1363 §4 (AB 3532), operative July 1, 1991. Repealed Stats 1992 ch 162 §2 (AB 2650), operative January 1, 1994. See Fam C §§9301, 9302, 9307, 9320–9328, 9340.

§231. [Section repealed 1975]

Leg.H. Added Stats 1921 ch 136 §1. Amended Stats 1963 ch 1413 §1. Repealed Stats 1975 ch 1244 §9. The repealed section related to action to determine parental relation.

§232. [Section repealed 1994]

Leg.H. Added Stats 1961 ch 1616 §4. Amended Stats 1963 ch 938 §1; Stats 1965 ch 1065 §1; Stats 1967 ch 1052 §1; Stats 1970 ch 240 §1, ch 735 §1; Stats 1971 ch 438 §14, ch 1210 §1; Stats 1972 ch 579 §10; Stats 1973 ch 686 §1; Stats 1976 ch 653 §1, ch 940 §2; Stats 1977 ch 1252 §75, operative July 1, 1978; Stats 1978 ch 391 §1, ch 429 §23, effective July 17, 1978, operative July 1, 1978, ch 1269 §2; Stats 1979 ch 245 §1; Stats 1982 ch 978 §1, effective September 13, 1982, operative July 1, 1982; Stats 1983 ch 309 §2; Stats 1984 ch 1246 §1, ch 1608 §1, effective September 30, 1984, ch 1608 §9.5, effective September 30, 1984, operative January 1, 1985; Stats 1985 ch 528 §1; Stats 1986 ch 1122 §1; Stats 1987 ch 1485 §1; Stats 1988 ch 701 §1, effective August 29, 1988; Stats 1990 ch 1363 §5 (AB 3532), operative July 1, 1991; Stats 1991 ch 372 §2 (SB 735), effective September 8, 1991. Repealed Stats 1992 ch 162 §2 (AB 2650), operative January 1, 1994. See Fam C §§7802, 7807, 7808, 7820–7829, 7890, 7892.

§232.1. [Section repealed 1984]

Leg.H. Added Stats 1977 ch 21 §1, effective April 6, 1977. Amended Stats 1978 ch 429 §24, effective July 17, 1978, operative July 1, 1978; Stats 1981 ch 104 §1, effective June 29, 1981. Repealed operative July 1, 1984, by the provisions of Stats 1976 ch 977 §30, as amended Stats 1981 ch 104 §18. The repealed section related to action to declare child free from parental control in demonstration county.

§232.3. [Section repealed 1994]

Leg.H. Added Stats 1978 ch 124 §2. Amended Stats 1981 ch 714 §49; Stats 1982 ch 990 §2. Repealed Stats 1992 ch 162 §2 (AB 2650), operative January 1, 1994. See Fam C §§7870, 7871.

§232.5. [Section repealed 1994]

Leg.H. Added Stats 1965 ch 1064 §1. Amended Stats 1983 ch 309 §3. Repealed Stats 1992 ch 162 §2 (AB 2650), operative January 1, 1994. See Fam C §§7801, 7890.

§232.6. [Section repealed 1994]

Leg.H. Added Stats 1980 ch 1229 §3. Repealed Stats 1992 ch 162 §2 (AB 2650), operative January 1, 1994. See Fam C §§7800, 7803.

§232.9. [Section repealed 1994]

Leg.H. Added Stats 1970 ch 583 §2. Amended Stats 1971 ch 1077 §1; Stats 1977 ch 21 §1.3, effective April 6, 1977; Stats 1978 ch 429 §25, effective July 17, 1978, operative July 1, 1978; Stats 1982 ch 978 §2, effective September 13, 1982, operative July 1, 1982. Repealed Stats 1992 ch 162 §2 (AB 2650), operative January 1, 1994. See Fam C §7840.

§233. [Section repealed 1993]

Leg.H. Added Stats 1961 ch 1616 §4. Amended Stats 1967 ch 877 §1; Stats 1973 ch 205 §1; Stats 1981 ch 810 §1. Repealed Stats 1992 ch 162 §2 (AB 2650) (ch 472 prevails). Amended Stats 1992 ch 472 §7 (AB 2887). Repealed Stats 1993 ch 219 §28 (AB 1500). See Fam C §§7806, 7841, 7845, 7850–7852.

§233.5. [Section repealed 1994]

Leg.H. Added Stats 1965 ch 1530 §1. Amended Stats 1973 ch 205 §2; Stats 1980 ch 503 §1. Repealed Stats 1992 ch 162 §2 (AB 2650), operative January 1, 1994. See Fam C §7805.

§233.6. [Section repealed 1994]

Leg.H. Added Stats 1965 ch 1530 §1.5. Amended Stats 1978 ch 429 §26, effective July 17, 1978, operative July 1, 1978. Repealed Stats 1992 ch 162 §2 (AB 2650), operative January 1, 1994. See Fam C §7805.

§234. [Section repealed 1994]

Leg.H. Added Stats 1961 ch 1616 §4. Amended Stats 1963 ch 493 §1; Stats 1974 ch 246 §2; Stats 1981 ch 810 §2. Repealed Stats 1992 ch 162 §2 (AB 2650), operative January 1, 1994. See Fam C §§7880, 7891.

§235. [Section repealed 1994]

Leg.H. Added Stats 1961 ch 1616 §4. Amended Stats 1969 ch 1611 §3; Stats 1970 ch 1091 §2; Stats 1972 ch 575 §1; Stats 1976 ch 1376 §1; Stats 1990 ch 1363 §6 (AB 3532), operative July 1, 1991. Repealed Stats 1992 ch 162 §2 (AB 2650), operative January 1, 1994. See Fam C §§7881, 7882.

§235.5. [Section repealed 1994]

Leg.H. Added Stats 1965 ch 1530 §2. Repealed Stats 1992 ch 162 §2 (AB 2650), operative January 1, 1994. See Fam C §7884.

§236. [Section repealed 1994]

Leg.H. Added Stats 1961 ch 1616 §4. Repealed Stats 1992 ch 162 §2 (AB 2650), operative January 1, 1994. See Fam C §7883.

Prior Law: Former §236, relating to general and special guardians, was enacted 1872 and repealed Stats 1931 ch 281 (Prob C §1700).

§237. [Section repealed 1994]

Leg.H. Added Stats 1961 ch 1616 §4. Repealed Stats 1992 ch 162 §2 (AB 2650), operative January 1, 1994. See Fam C §7804.

Prior Law: Former §237, relating to general and special guardians, was enacted 1872 and repealed Stats 1931 ch 281 (Prob C §1700).

§237.5. [Section repealed 1994]

Leg.H. Added Stats 1981 ch 810 §3. Repealed Stats 1992 ch 162 §2 (AB 2650), operative January 1, 1994. See Fam C §§7860–7864.

Prior Law: Former §237.5, similar to the repealed section, was added Stats 1965 ch 1530 §3, amended Stats 1969 ch 489 §1, Stats 1974 ch 246 §3, and repealed Stats 1981 ch 810 §4.

§237.7. [Section repealed 1994]

Leg.H. Added Stats 1984 ch 605 §1. Amended Stats 1986 ch 823 §1. Repealed Stats 1992 ch 162 §2 (AB 2650), operative January 1, 1994. See Fam C §7895.

§238. [Section repealed 1994]

Leg.H. Added Stats 1961 ch 1616 §4. Repealed Stats 1992 ch 162 §2 (AB 2650), operative January 1, 1994. See Fam C §7894.

Prior Law: Former §238, relating to general and special guardians, was enacted 1872 and repealed Stats 1931 ch 281 (Prob C §1700).

§239. [Section repealed 1994]

Leg.H. Added Stats 1981 ch 810 §6. Repealed Stats 1992 ch 162 §2 (AB 2650), operative January 1, 1994. See Fam C §7893.

Prior Law: Former §239, similar to the Fam C §7893, was added Stats 1967 ch 1099 §1 and repealed Stats 1981 ch 810 §5.

Former §239, relating to general and special guardians, was enacted 1872 and repealed Stats 1931 ch 281 (Prob C §1700).

§240. [Section repealed 1931]

Leg.H. Enacted 1872. Repealed Stats 1931 ch 281 (Prob C §1700). The repealed section related to general and special guardians.

§241. [Section repealed 1994]

Leg.H. Added Stats 1955 ch 835 §1. Amended Stats 1971 ch 1748 §25.5; Stats 1980 ch 676 §42. Repealed Stats 1992 ch 162 §2 (AB 2650), operative January 1, 1994. See Fam C §§3550, 3910.

Prior Law: Former §241, similar to Prob C §§1500–1502, was enacted 1872, amended Code Amdts 1873–74 ch 612 §49, Stats 1925 ch 431 §1, and repealed Stats 1931 ch 281 (Prob C §1700).

§242. [Section repealed 1994]

Leg.H. Added Stats 1955 ch 835 §1. Amended Stats 1972 ch 1167 §1; Stats 1976 ch 130 §2; Stats 1983 ch 1304 §2, operative July 1, 1984; Stats 1984 ch 1605 §1, operative July 1, 1985. Repealed Stats 1992 ch 162 §2 (AB 2650), operative January 1, 1994. See Fam C §§3900, 3910, 4300, 4400.

Prior Law: Former §242, relating to guardianship of person and/or estate of incompetent person, was added Stats 1917 ch 511 §1 and repealed Stats 1931 ch 281.

Former §242, providing that no person to be guardian of estate without appointment, was enacted 1872 and repealed Stats 1905 ch 562 §1.

§243. [Section repealed 1976]

Leg.H. Added Stats 1955 ch 835 §1. Repealed Stats 1976 ch 130 §3. See Fam C §§4300, 4400.

§244. [Section repealed 1994]

Leg.H. Added Stats 1955 ch 835 §1. Repealed Stats 1992 ch 162 §2 (AB 2650), operative January 1, 1994. See Fam C §3550.

Prior Law: Former §244, relating to appointment of guardian by court, was enacted 1872, amended Code Amdts 1880 ch 41 §7, and repealed Stats 1905 ch 562 §3.

§245. [Section repealed 1994]

Leg.H. Added Stats 1955 ch 835 §1. Repealed Stats 1992 ch 162 §2 (AB 2650), operative January 1, 1994. See Fam C §200.

Prior Law: Former §245, relating to jurisdiction of court in appointment of guardian, was enacted 1872 and repealed Stats 1905 ch 562 §4.

§246. [Section repealed 1992]

Leg.H. Added Stats 1955 ch 835 §1. Amended Stats 1976 ch 130 §4; Stats 1983 ch 1304 §3, operative July 1, 1984. Repealed Stats 1992 ch 46 §1 (SB 370), effective May 11, 1992, operative July 1, 1992, ch 162 §2 (AB 2650), operative January 1, 1994 (ch 46 prevails). See Fam C §§4320, 4404.

Prior Law: Former §246, similar to Prob C §1514, was enacted 1872, amended Code Amdts 1873–74 ch 612 §51, Stats 1905 ch 562 §5, and repealed Stats 1931 ch 281 (Prob C §1700).

§247. [Section repealed 1994]

Leg.H. Added Stats 1955 ch 835 §1. Repealed Stats 1992 ch 162 §2 (AB 2650), operative January 1, 1994. See Fam C §§3651, 4405.

Prior Law: Former §247, relating to powers of guardian appointed by court, was enacted 1872 and repealed Stats 1905 ch 562 §6.

§248. [Section repealed 1994]

Leg.H. Added Stats 1955 ch 835 §1. Amended Stats 1971 ch 578 §3.3, effective August 13, 1971. Repealed Stats 1992 ch 162 §2 (AB 2650), operative January 1, 1994. See Fam C §§4000, 4002, 4303, 4403.

Prior Law: Former §248, relating to duties of guardian of person, was enacted 1872 and repealed Stats 1905 ch 562 §7.

§249. [Section repealed 1994]

Leg.H. Added Stats 1955 ch 835 §1. Repealed Stats 1992 ch 162 §2 (AB 2650), operative January 1, 1994. See Fam C §3554.

Prior Law: Former §249, relating to duties of guardian of estate was enacted 1872, amended Code Amdts 1873–74 ch 612 §52, Code Amdts 1880 ch 41 §8, and repealed Stats 1905 ch 562 §8.

§250. [Section repealed 1994]

Leg.H. Added Stats 1955 ch 835 §1. Repealed Stats 1992 ch 162 §2 (AB 2650), operative January 1, 1994. See Fam C §3551.

Prior Law: Former §250, similar to Prob C §§2101, 2102, 2104, was enacted 1872 and repealed Stats 1931 ch 281 (Prob C §1700).

§251. [Section repealed 1994]

Leg.H. Added Stats 1955 ch 835 §1. Repealed Stats 1992 ch 162 §2 (AB 2650), operative January 1, 1994. See Fam C §4402.

Prior Law: Former §251, similar to Prob C §§2101, 2102, 2104, was enacted 1872 and repealed Stats 1931 ch 281 (Prob C §1700).

§252. [Section repealed 1994]

Leg.H. Added Stats 1955 ch 835 §1. Repealed Stats 1992 ch 162 §2 (AB 2650), operative January 1, 1994. The repealed section related to effect of partial invalidity.

Prior Law: Former §252, similar to Prob C §2105, was enacted 1872 and repealed Stats 1931 ch 281 (Prob C §1700).

§253. [Section repealed 1994]

Leg.H. Added Stats 1955 ch 835 §1. Repealed Stats 1992 ch 162 §2 (AB 2650), operative January 1, 1994. The repealed section related to interpretation and construction.

Prior Law: Former §253, similar to Prob C §§1601, 2650–2654, was enacted 1872, amended Code Amdts 1880 ch 41 §9, and repealed Stats 1931 ch 281 (Prob C §1700).

§254. [Section repealed 1994]

Leg.H. Added Stats 1955 ch 835 §1. Repealed Stats 1992 ch 162 §2 (AB 2650), operative January 1, 1994. The repealed section related to citation of act.

Prior Law: Former §254, relating to guardian appointed by parent, was enacted 1872 and repealed Stats 1931 ch 281 (Prob C §1700).

§255. [Section repealed 1931]

Leg.H. Enacted 1872. Amended Code Amdts 1873–74 ch 612 §53. Repealed Stats 1931 ch 281.

§§256, 257. [Sections repealed 1931]

Leg.H. Enacted 1872. Repealed Stats 1931 ch 281. See Prob C §2627.

§258. [Section repealed 1905]

Leg.H. Enacted 1872. Repealed Stats 1905 ch 562 §9.

§264. [Section repealed 1994]

Leg.H. Added Stats 1974 ch 956 §1. Repealed Stats 1992 ch 162 §2 (AB 2650), operative January 1, 1994. See Fam C §7900.

Prior Law: Former §264, relating to master and apprentice, was repealed Stats 1937 ch 90.

§265. [Section repealed 1994]

Leg.H. Added Stats 1974 ch 956 §1. Repealed Stats 1992 ch 162 §2 (AB 2650), operative January 1, 1994. See Fam C §7901.

Prior Law: Former §265, relating to apprenticeship, was repealed Stats 1937 ch 90.

§266. [Section repealed 1994]

Leg.H. Added Stats 1974 ch 956 §1. Repealed Stats 1992 ch 162 §2 (AB 2650), operative January 1, 1994. See Fam C §7902.

Prior Law: Former §266, relating to the definition of apprentice and apprenticeship agreements, was repealed Stats 1937 ch 90.

§267. [Section repealed 1994]

Leg.H. Added Stats 1974 ch 956 §1. Amended Stats 1978 ch 429 §27, effective July 17, 1978, operative July 1, 1978. Repealed Stats 1992 ch 162 §2 (AB 2650), operative January 1, 1994. See Fam C §7903.

Prior Law: Former §267, relating to the Administrator of Apprenticeship and appointment of assistants, was repealed Stats 1937 ch 90.

§268. [Section repealed 1994]

Leg.H. Added Stats 1974 ch 956 §1. Amended Stats 1978 ch 429 §28, effective July 17, 1978, operative July 1, 1978. Repealed Stats 1992 ch 162 §2 (AB 2650), operative January 1, 1994. See Fam C §7904.

Prior Law: Former §268, relating to requirements of apprenticeship agreements, was repealed Stats 1937 ch 90.

§269. [Section repealed 1994]

Leg.H. Added Stats 1974 ch 956 §1. Repealed Stats 1992 ch 162 §2 (AB 2650), operative January 1, 1994. See Fam C §7905.

Prior Law: Former §269, relating to investigation, determination and appeal of violations of apprenticeship agreement, was repealed Stats 1937 ch 90.

§270. [Section repealed 1994]

Leg.H. Added Stats 1974 ch 956 §1. Repealed Stats 1992 ch 162 §2 (AB 2650), operative January 1, 1994. See Fam C §7906.

Prior Law: Former §270, relating to conclusiveness of Apprenticeship Council's decision, was repealed Stats 1937 ch 90.

§271. [Section repealed 1994]

Leg.H. Added Stats 1974 ch 956 §1. Repealed Stats 1992 ch 162 §2 (AB 2650), operative January 1, 1994. See Fam C §7907.

Prior Law: Former §271, relating to judicial review of questions of law, was repealed Stats 1937 ch 90.

§272. [Section repealed 1994]

Leg.H. Added Stats 1974 ch 956 §1. Repealed Stats 1992 ch 162 §2 (AB 2650), operative January 1, 1994. See Fam C §7908.

Prior Law: Former §272, relating to actions to enforce apprenticeship agreements, was repealed Stats 1937 ch 90.

§273. [Section repealed 1994]

Leg.H. Added Stats 1974 ch 956 §1. Repealed Stats 1992 ch 162 §2 (AB 2650), operative January 1, 1994. See Fam C §7909.

Prior Law: Former §273, relating to apprenticeship agreements for higher standards, was repealed Stats 1937 ch 90.

§274. [Section repealed 1994]

Leg.H. Added Stats 1974 ch 956 §1. Amended Stats 1990 ch 1363 §7 (AB 3532), operative July 1, 1991. Repealed Stats 1992 ch 162 §2 (AB 2650), operative January 1, 1994. See Fam C §7910.

Prior Law: Former §274, relating to severability, was repealed Stats 1937 ch 90.

§275. [Section repealed 1994]

Leg.H. Added Stats 1990 ch 1581 §6 (AB 548). Repealed Stats 1992 ch 162 §2 (AB 2650), operative January 1, 1994. See Fam C §7950.

Prior Law: Former §275, similar to Fam C §7950, was added Stats 1982 ch 1051 §1 and repealed Stats 1990 ch 1581 §5.

Former §275, similar to present Lab C §3090, was enacted Stats 1905 ch 417 §1 and repealed Stats 1937 ch 90 (Lab C §8100).

Former §275 was enacted 1872, amended Code Amdts 1880 ch 41, Stats 1901 ch 157 and repealed Stats 1905 ch 417 §1.

§275.1. [Section repealed 1994]

Leg.H. Added Stats 1990 ch 1581 §6 (AB 548). Repealed Stats 1992 ch 162 §2 (AB 2650), operative January 1, 1994. See Fam C §7951.

§275.2. [Section repealed 1994]

Leg.H. Added Stats 1990 ch 1581 §6 (AB 548). Repealed Stats 1992 ch 162 §2 (AB 2650), operative January 1, 1994. See Fam C §7952.

§275.3. [Section repealed 1994]

Leg.H. Added Stats 1990 ch 1581 §6 (AB 548). Repealed Stats 1992 ch 162 §2 (AB 2650), operative January 1, 1994. See Fam C §7951.

§275.4. [Section repealed 1994]

Leg.H. Added Stats 1990 ch 1581 §6 (AB 548). Repealed Stats 1992 ch 162 §2 (AB 2650), operative January 1, 1994. See Fam C §7952.

§276. [Section repealed 1991]

Leg.H. Added Stats 1990 ch 1581 §7 (AB 548), operative until July 1, 1991. Repealed Stats 1990 ch 1581 §8 (AB 548), operative July 1, 1991. See Fam C §8708.

Prior Law: Former §276, similar to Fam C §8708, was added Stats 1982 ch 1051 §1 and repealed Stats 1990 ch 1581 §5 (AB 548).

Former §276, similar to present Lab C §3089, was enacted Stats 1905 ch 417 §1 and repealed Stats 1937 ch 90 (Lab C §8100).

Former §276 was enacted 1872, amended Code Amdts 1880 ch 41, Stats 1901 ch 157 and repealed Stats 1905 ch 417 §1.

§276.1. [Section repealed 1991]

Leg.H. Added Stats 1990 ch 1581 §7 (AB 548), operative until July 1, 1991. Repealed Stats 1990 ch 1581 §8 (AB 548), operative July 1, 1991. See Fam C §8804.

§276.2. [Section repealed 1991]

Leg.H. Added Stats 1990 ch 1581 §7 (AB 548), operative until July 1, 1991. Repealed Stats 1990 ch 1581 §8 (AB 548), operative July 1, 1991. See Fam C §8710.

§276.3. [Section repealed 1991]

Leg.H. Added Stats 1990 ch 1581 §7 (AB 548), operative until July 1, 1991. Repealed Stats 1990 ch 1581 §8 (AB 548), operative July 1, 1991. See Fam C §8711.

§277. [Section repealed 1990]

Leg.H. Added Stats 1984 ch 317 §1. Repealed Stats 1990 ch 1581 §5 (AB 548). See Fam C §7952.

Prior Law: Former §277, similar to present Corp C §100, was added Stats 1931 ch 862 §1 and repealed Stats 1947 ch 1038 (Corp 100001).

PART 4
CORPORATIONS [REPEALED]

§§278–280.   [Sections repealed 1947]

Leg.H. Enacted Stats 1931 ch 862 §2. Repealed Stats 1947 ch 1038. See Corp C §§100, 102, 154–188.

§281.   [Section repealed 1947]

Leg.H. Added Stats 1933 ch 533. Repealed Stats 1947 ch 1038.

§283.   [Section repealed 1931]

Leg.H. Added Stats 1929 ch 711. Repealed Stats 1931 ch 862 §1. See Corp C §102.

§284.   [Section repealed 1931]

Leg.H. Added Code Amdts 1873–74 ch 612. Repealed Stats 1931 ch 862 §1. See Corp C §§154–188, 200.

§§285–288.   [Sections repealed 1947]

Leg.H. Enacted Stats 1931 ch 862 §2. Repealed Stats 1947 ch 1038 (Corp C §100001). See Corp C §200.

Prior Law: Former §§285–288, were enacted 1872 and superseded Stats 1931 ch 862 §1.

§289.   [Section repealed 1931]

Leg.H. Enacted 1872. Repealed Stats 1931 ch 862.

§290.   [Section repealed 1947]

Leg.H. Enacted Stats 1931 ch 862 §2. Repealed Stats 1947 ch 1038 (Corp C §100001). See Corp C §§202–204.

Prior Law: Former §290, similar to present Corp C §§202–204, 300, 303 was enacted 1872 and superseded Stats 1931 ch 862 §1.

§290a.   [Section repealed 1951]

Leg.H. Enacted Stats 1931 ch 862 §2. Repealed Stats 1951 ch 364 (Fin C §50000).

Prior Law: Former §290a, similar to the repealed section, was enacted 1872 and superseded Stats 1931 ch 862 §1.

§290b.   [Section repealed 1947]

Leg.H. Enacted Stats 1931 ch 862 §2. Repealed Stats 1947 ch 1038 (Corp C §100001). See Corp C §§202–204, 406–409.

Prior Law: Former §290b, was enacted 1872 and superseded Stats 1931 ch 862 §1.

§290c.   [Section repealed 1929]

Leg.H. Enacted 1872. Repealed Stats 1929 ch 711.

§290d.   [Section repealed 1931]

Leg.H. Enacted 1872. Repealed Stats 1931 ch 862.

§§290e–290½.   [Sections repealed 1929]

Leg.H. Enacted 1872. Repealed Stats 1929 ch 711.

§§291–293.   [Sections repealed 1947]

Leg.H. Enacted Stats 1931 ch 862 §2. Repealed Stats 1947 ch 1038 (Corp C §100001). See Corp C §§110, 200, 201.

Prior Law: Former §§292, 293, similar to present Corp C §§110, 200, were enacted 1872 and superseded Stats 1931 ch 862 §1.

§§294–299.   [Sections repealed 1947]

Leg.H. Enacted Stats 1931 ch 862 §2. Repealed Stats 1947 ch 1038 (Corp C §100001). See Corp C §§201, 400–409.

Prior Law: Former §§296, 296a, 297, 298, 299, similar to present Corp C §§110, 154–158, 200, 201, 209, were enacted 1872 and superseded Stats 1931 ch 862 §1.

§300.   [Section repealed 1933]

Leg.H. Enacted 1872. Repealed Stats 1933 ch 79.

Prior Law: Former §300, similar to the repealed section, was enacted 1872 and superseded Stats 1931 ch 862 §1.

§§300a, 300b.   [Sections repealed 1947]

Leg.H. Enacted Stats 1931 ch 862 §2. Repealed Stats 1947 ch 1038 (Corp C §100001). See Corp C §409.

§§301, 302.   [Sections repealed 1947]

Leg.H. Enacted Stats 1931 ch 862 §2. Repealed Stats 1947 ch 1038 (Corp C §100001). See Corp C §§211, 213.

Prior Law: Former §§301, 302, similar to present Corp C §§211, 600, were enacted 1872 and superseded Stats 1931 ch 862 §1.

§302a.   [Section repealed 1931]

Leg.H. Enacted 1872. Repealed Stats 1931 ch 862.

§303.   [Section repealed 1947]

Leg.H. Enacted Stats 1931 ch 862 §2. Repealed Stats 1947 ch 1038 (Corp C §100001). See Corp C §§204, 212.

Prior Law: Former §303 was enacted 1872 and superseded Stats 1931 ch 862 §1.

§§305–311.   [Sections repealed 1947]

Leg.H. Enacted Stats 1931 ch 862 §2. Repealed Stats 1947 ch 1038 (Corp C §100001). See Corp C §§192, 300 et seq.

Prior Law: Former §§305–311 were enacted 1872 and superseded Stats 1931 ch 862 §1.

§§312–321a.   [Sections repealed 1947]

Leg.H. Enacted Stats 1931 ch 862 §2. Repealed Stats 1947 ch 1038 (Corp C §100001). See Corp C §§204, 400, 600–603, 700 et seq.

Prior Law: Former §§312–321 were enacted 1872 and superseded Stats 1931 ch 862 §1.

§§322–325a.   [Sections repealed 1947]

Leg.H. Enacted Stats 1931 ch 862 §2. Repealed Stats 1947 ch 1038 (Corp C §100001). See Corp C §§410–415.

Prior Law: Former §§322–325 were enacted 1872 and superseded Stats 1931 ch 862 §1.

§§326, 326a.   [Sections repealed 1947]

Leg.H. Enacted Stats 1931 ch 862 §2. Repealed Stats 1947 ch 1038 (Corp C §100001). See Corp C §§416–419.

Prior Law: Former §§326, 326a, similar to present UCC §8402, were enacted 1872 and superseded Stats 1931 ch 862 §1.

§326b.   [Section repealed 1947]

Leg.H. Added Stats 1933 ch 533 §28. Repealed Stats 1947 ch 1038 (Corp C §100001). See Corp C §§422.

§§327–330.23.   [Sections repealed 1947]

Leg.H. Enacted Stats 1931 ch 862 §2. Repealed Stats 1947 ch 1038 (Corp C §100001). See Corp C §§419, 420; UCC §§8206, 8302 et seq., 8401 et seq.

§330.24.   [Section repealed 1997]

Leg.H. Added Stats 1931 ch 862 §2. Amended Stats 1933 ch 533 §36, Stats 1935 ch 305 §1, Stats 1951 ch 790 §1, effective June 1, 1951, Stats 1955 ch 1587 §1, Stats 1957 ch 217 §1. Repealed Stats 1997 ch 598 §1 (SB 633). See Corp C §14300.

§330.25.   [Section repealed 1997]

Leg.H. Added Stats 1941 ch 629 §2. Repealed Stats 1997 ch 598 §1 (SB 633). See Corp C §14301.

§330.26.   [Section repealed 1997]

Leg.H. Added Stats 1953 ch 71 §1. Repealed Stats 1997 ch 598 §1 (SB 633). See Corp C §14302.

§331.   [Section repealed 1997]

Leg.H. Added Stats 1931 ch 862 §2. Amended Stats 1933 ch 533 §37, ch 928 §1; Stats 1976 ch 641 §1, operative January 1, 1977; Stats 1981 ch 587 §1. Repealed Stats 1997 ch 598 §1 (SB 633). See Corp C §14303.

Prior Law: Former §331, similar to Corp C §423(a), was enacted 1872, amended Code Amdts 1873–74 ch 612 §72, Stats 1929 ch 711 §17, and repealed Stats 1931 ch 862 §1.

§331a. [Section repealed 1931]
Leg.H. Enacted Stats 1872. Repealed Stats 1931 ch 862 §1.

§§332–340. [Sections repealed 1947]
Leg.H. Enacted Stats 1931 ch 862 §2. Repealed Stats 1947 ch 1038 (Corp C §100001). See Corp C §423.

§§341–343. [Sections repealed 1947]
Leg.H. Enacted Stats 1931 ch 862 §2. Repealed Stats 1947 ch 1038 (Corp C §100001). See Corp C §§207, 500 et seq., 1001.

§343a. [Section repealed 1933]
Leg.H. Enacted Stats 1931 ch 862 §2. Repealed Stats 1933 ch 533. The repealed section related to sale of assets and distribution of shares.

§§343b–345. [Sections repealed 1947]
Leg.H. Enacted Stats 1931 ch 862 §2. Repealed Stats 1947 ch 1038 (Corp C §100001). See Corp C §§208, 1000, 1002.

§§346–348c. [Sections repealed 1947]
Leg.H. Enacted Stats 1931 ch 862 §2. Repealed Stats 1947 ch 1038 (Corp C §100001). See Corp C §§409, 500 et seq.

§349. [Section repealed 1929]
Leg.H. Enacted 1872. Repealed Stats 1929 ch 711.

§§352–359. [Sections repealed 1947]
Leg.H. Enacted Stats 1931 ch 862 §2. Repealed Stats 1947 ch 1038 (Corp C §100001). See Corp C §§114, 1500, 1501, 1600, 1602, 1603.

§360. [Section repealed 1929]
Leg.H. Enacted 1872. Repealed Stats 1929 ch 711.

§§361–362c. [Sections repealed 1947]
Leg.H. Enacted Stats 1931 ch 862 §2. Repealed Stats 1947 on 1038 (Corp C §100001). See Corp C §§100, 190, 212, 900 et seq. 1100 et seq.

§§363–375. [Sections repealed 1947]
Leg.H. Enacted Stats 1931 ch 862 §2. Repealed Stats 1947 ch 1038 (Corp C §100001). See Corp C §§209, 309, 314–317, 506, 1502–1504, 1507, 2200–2202, 1300–1312.

§§382, 383. [Sections repealed 1931]
Leg.H. Enacted 1872. Repealed Stats 1931 ch 862.

§384. [Section repealed 1907]
Leg.H. Enacted 1872. Repealed Stats 1907 ch 304.

§§388–393. [Sections repealed 1931]
Leg.H. Enacted 1872. Repealed Stats 1931 ch 862 §1.

§§399–401a. [Sections repealed 1947]
Leg.H. Enacted Stats 1931 ch 862 §2. Repealed Stats 1947 on 1038 (Corp C §100001). The repealed sections related to winding up and distribution of corporation.

§401b. [Section repealed 1933]
Leg.H. Enacted Stats 1931 ch 862 §2. Repealed Stats 1933 ch 533. The repealed section related to winding up and distribution of corporation.

§§401c–404c. [Sections repealed 1947]
Leg.H. Enacted Stats 1931 ch 862 §2. Repealed Stats 1947 ch 1038 (Corp C §100001). The repealed sections related to winding up and distribution of corporation.

§§405–413. [Sections repealed 1947]
Leg.H. Enacted Stats 1931 ch 862 §2. Repealed Stats 1947 ch 1038 (Corp C §100001). The repealed sections related to winding up and distribution of corporation.

§§414–418. [Sections repealed 1935]
Leg.H. Enacted 1872. Repealed Stats 1935 ch 145 (Ins C §13001). See Ins C §§386, 1140, 1152, 1194.86, 1194.87, 1194.88.

§§419, 420. [Sections repealed 1907]
Leg.H. Enacted 1872. Repealed Stats 1907 ch 119.

§§421–426. [Sections repealed 1935]
Leg.H. Enacted 1872. Repealed Stats 1935 ch 145 (Ins C §13001). See Ins C §§1100 et seq., 1170 et seq., 1190 et seq., 1220, 1221, 1240, 1250–1253.

§427. [Section repealed 1905]
Leg.H. Enacted 1872. Repealed Stats 1905 ch 39.

§§428–430. [Sections repealed 1935]
Leg.H. Enacted 1872. Repealed Stats 1935 ch 145 (Ins C §13001). See Ins C §928.

§431. [Section repealed 1905]
Leg.H. Enacted 1872. Repealed Stats 1905 ch 39.

§432. [Section repealed 1913]
Leg.H. Enacted 1872. Repealed Stats 1913 ch 270.

§§437–443. [Sections repealed 1935]
Leg.H. Enacted 1872. Repealed Stats 1935 ch 145 (Ins C §13001). See Ins C §739.10.

§444. [Section repealed 1907]
Leg.H. Enacted 1872. Repealed Stats 1907 ch 486.

§§445, 446. [Sections repealed 1935]
Leg.H. Enacted 1872. Repealed Stats 1935 ch 145 (Ins C §13001).

§§447–449. [Sections repealed 1907]
Leg.H. Enacted 1872. Repealed Stats 1907 ch 119.

§450. [Section repealed 1935]
Leg.H. Enacted 1872. Repealed Stats 1935 ch 145 (Ins C §13001). See Ins C §§10150–10154.

§451. [Section repealed 1907]
Leg.H. Enacted 1872. Repealed Stats 1907 ch 119.

§452. [Section repealed 1935]
Leg.H. Added Stats 1905 ch 442 §1. Repealed Stats 1935 ch 145 (Ins C §13001). See Ins C §10530.

§§452a–453c. [Sections repealed 1935]
Leg.H. Enacted 1872. Repealed Stats 1935 ch 145 (Ins C §13001). See Ins C §§10020 et seq.

§§453d–453h. [Sections repealed 1935]
Leg.H. Added Stats 1905 ch 353 §1. Repealed Stats 1935 ch 145 (Ins C §13001). The repealed section related to different types of insurance on assessment plan.

§453i. [Section repealed 1941]
Leg.H. Added Stats 1905 ch 353 §1. Repealed Stats 1941 ch 311. The repealed section related to different types of insurance on assessment plan.

§§453j–453r. [Sections repealed 1935]
Leg.H. Added Stats 1905 ch 353 §1. Repealed Stats 1935 ch 145 (Ins C §13001). The repealed section related to mortgage insurance companies.

§§453s–453z. [Sections repealed 1935]
Leg.H. Added Stats 1913 ch 270 §1. Repealed Stats 1935 ch 145 (Ins C §13001). See Ins C §§12340 et seq.

§§453aa–453gg½. [Sections repealed 1933]
Leg.H. Added Stats 1913 ch 268 §1. Repealed Stats 1933 ch 97 (Ins C §13001). The repealed section related to mortgage insurance companies.

§453hh. [Section repealed 1935]
Leg.H. Added Stats 1913 ch 268 §1. Repealed Stats 1935 ch 145 (Ins C §13001). The repealed section related to mortgage insurance companies.

§§453.1–453.13. [Sections repealed 1935]

Leg.H. Added Stats 1933 ch 97 §2. Repealed Stats 1935 ch 145 (Ins C §13001). See Ins C §§12420 et seq.

§453.14. [Section repealed 1941]

Leg.H. Added Stats 1933 ch 97 §2. Repealed Stats 1941 ch 311. The repealed section related to mortgage insurance companies.

§§454–470. [Sections repealed 1951]

Leg.H. Enacted 1872. Repealed Stats 1951 ch 764 Pub Util C §25003. See Pub Util C §§7526 et seq.

§471. [Section repealed 1878]

Leg.H. Enacted 1872. Repealed Code Amdts 1877–78 ch 621.

§472. [Section repealed 1951]

Leg.H. Enacted 1872. Repealed Stats 1951 ch 764 (Pub Util C §25003). See Pub Util C §7536.

§473. [Section repealed 1929]

Leg.H. Enacted 1872. Repealed Stats 1929 ch 711.

§§473a–494. [Sections repealed 1951]

Leg.H. Enacted 1872. Repealed Stats 1951 ch 764 (Pub Util C §25003). See Pub Util C §§7526 et seq., 7551 et seq.

§§497–511. [Sections repealed 1951]

Leg.H. Enacted 1872. Repealed Stats 1951 ch 764 (Pub Util C §25003). See Pub Util C §§7801 et seq.

§512. [Section repealed 1947]

Leg.H. Enacted 1872. Amended Code Amdts 1873–74 ch 612 §91. Repealed Stats 1947 ch 176 §2 (Sts & H C §50009). The repealed section related to certain special statutes relating to roads, bridges and highways.

§513. [Section repealed 1947]

Leg.H. Enacted 1872. Amended Stats 1901 ch 157 §146; Stats 1905 ch 426 §1. Repealed Stats 1947 ch 176 §2 (Sts & H C §50009). The repealed section related to certain special statutes relating to roads, bridges and highways.

§514. [Section repealed 1947]

Leg.H. Enacted 1872. Amended Code Amdts 1873–74 ch 524 §1, ch 612 §92; Stats 1901 ch 157 §147; Stats 1905 ch 426 §2. Repealed Stats 1947 ch 176 §2 (Sts & H C §50009). The repealed section related to certain special statutes relating to roads, bridges and highways.

§515. [Section repealed 1947]

Leg.H. Enacted 1872. Repealed Stats 1947 ch 176 §2 (Sts & H C §50009). The repealed section related to certain special statutes relating to roads, bridges and highways.

§516. [Section repealed 1947]

Leg.H. Enacted 1872. Amended Stats 1901 ch 10 §1. Repealed Stats 1947 ch 176 §2 (Sts & H C §50009). The repealed section related to certain special statutes relating to roads, bridges and highways.

§§517, 518. [Sections repealed 1947]

Leg.H. Enacted 1872. Amended Stats 1901 ch 157 §§148, 149; Stats 1905 ch 426 §§3, 4. Repealed Stats 1947 ch 176 §2 (Sts & H C §50009). The repealed section related to certain special statutes relating to roads, bridges and highways.

§§519, 520. [Sections repealed 1947]

Leg.H. Enacted 1872. Repealed Stats 1947 ch 176 §2 (Sts & H C §50009). The repealed section related to certain special statutes relating to roads, bridges and highways.

§521. [Section repealed 1947]

Leg.H. Enacted 1872. Amended Code Amdts 1873–74 ch 612 §93. Repealed Stats 1947 ch 176 §2 (Sts & H C §50009). The repealed section related to certain special statutes relating to roads, bridges and highways.

§522. [Section repealed 1947]

Leg.H. Enacted 1872. Amended Stats 1901 ch 157 §150; Stats 1905 ch 426 §5; Stats 1929 ch 169 §1. Repealed Stats 1947 ch 176 §2 (Sts & H C §50009). The repealed section related to certain special statutes relating to roads, bridges and highways.

§523. [Section repealed 1947]

Leg.H. Enacted 1872. Repealed Stats 1947 ch 176 §2 (Sts & H C §50009). The repealed section related to certain special statutes relating to roads, bridges and highways.

§524. [Section repealed 1947]

Leg.H. Added Stats 1901 ch 157 §151. Stats 1905 ch 427 §1. Repealed Stats 1947 ch 176 §2 (Sts & H C §50009) ch 424 §2. The repealed section related to certain special statutes relating to roads, bridges and highways.

§528. [Section repealed 1997]

Leg.H. Enacted 1872. Amended Stats 1905 ch 428 §1. Repealed Stats 1997 ch 598 §1 (SB 633). See Corp C §14350.

§529. [Section repealed 1997]

Leg.H. Enacted 1872. Amended Stats 1905 ch 428 §2; Stats 1925 ch 451 §1; Stats 1927 ch 694 §1. Repealed Stats 1997 ch 598 §1 (SB 633). See Corp C §14351.

§530. [Section repealed 1997]

Leg.H. Enacted 1872. Amended Stats 1905 ch 428 §3. Repealed Stats 1997 ch 598 §1 (SB 633). See Corp C §14352.

§531. [Section repealed 1997]

Leg.H. Enacted 1872. Repealed Stats 1997 ch 598 §1 (SB 633). See Corp C §14353.

§536. [Section repealed 1997]

Leg.H. Added Stats 1986 ch 756 §1. Repealed Stats 1997 ch 598 §1 (SB 633). See Corp C §14400.

Prior Law: Former §536, similar to present Pub Util C §7901, was enacted Stats 1905 ch 385 §1 and repealed Stats 1951 ch 764 (Pub Util C §25003).

Original §536 was enacted 1872 and repealed Stats 1905 ch 385 §1.

§§537–540. [Sections repealed 1951]

Leg.H. Enacted Stats 1905 ch 385 §1. Repealed Stats 1951 ch 764 (Pub Util C §25003). See Pub Util C §§7951–7953.

Prior Law: Former §§537–540 were enacted 1872 and repealed Stats 1905 ch 385 §1.

§541. [Section repealed 1874]

Leg.H. Enacted 1872. Repealed Code Amdts 1873–74 ch 612.

§548. [Section repealed 1997]

Leg.H. Enacted 1872. Repealed Stats 1997 ch 598 §1 (SB 633). See Corp C §14450.

§549. [Section repealed 1997]

Leg.H. Enacted 1872. Amended Code Amdts 1873–74 ch 612 §95; Stats 1905 ch 429 §1; Stats 1979 ch 862 §1. Repealed Stats 1997 ch 598 §1 (SB 633). See Corp C §14451.

§550. [Section repealed 1905]

Leg.H. Enacted 1872. Repealed Stats 1905 ch 429 §2.

§551. [Section repealed 1943]

Leg.H. Enacted 1872. Amended Stats 1905 ch 429 §3; Stats 1927 ch 358 §1. Repealed Stats 1943 ch 368 (Wat C §150001). See Wat C §§7032, 7034.

§552. [Section repealed 1997]

Leg.H. Added Code Amdts 1875–76 ch 499 §1. Repealed Stats 1997 ch 598 §1 (SB 633). See Corp C §14452.

§§557–566. [Sections repealed 1951]

Leg.H. Enacted 1872. Repealed Stats 1951 ch 41 §1, ch 364 (Fin C §50000).

§571. [Section repealed 1951]

Leg.H. Enacted 1872. Amended Stats 1901 ch 135 §1. Repealed Stats 1951 ch 364 (Fin C §50000).

§§572, 573. [Sections repealed 1951]

Leg.H. Enacted 1872. Repealed Stats 1951 ch 364 (Fin C §50000).

§574. [Section repealed 1951]

Leg.H. Enacted 1872. Amended Code Amdts 1873–74 ch 318 §1; Stats 1901 ch 220 §1. Repealed Stats 1951 ch 364 (Fin C §50000).

§§575–579. [Sections repealed 1951]

Leg.H. Enacted 1872. Repealed Stats 1951 ch 364 (Fin C §50000).

§580. [Section repealed 1907]

Leg.H. Added Stats 1903 ch 78 §1. Amended Stats 1905 ch 394 §1. Repealed Stats 1907 ch 320 §8. The repealed section related to amount of capital stock required for banks.

§§581–583a. [Sections repealed 1951]

Leg.H. Added Stats 1903 ch 256 §§1–4. Repealed Stats 1951 ch 364 (Fin C §50000).

§583b. [Section repealed 1951]

Leg.H. Added Stats 1905 ch 430 §1. Repealed Stats 1951 ch 364 (Fin C §50000).

§584. [Section repealed 1876]

Leg.H. Enacted 1872. Repealed Code Amdts 1875–76 ch 608 §2.

§585. [Section repealed 1905]

Leg.H. Enacted 1872. Repealed Stats 1905 ch 432 §1.

§586. [Section repealed 1939]

Leg.H. Enacted 1872. Repealed and re-enacted Stats 1905 ch 432 §1. Repealed Stats 1939 ch 93 (Pub Res C §10002). See Pub Res C §3983.

§587. [Section repealed 1933]

Leg.H. Enacted 1872. Repealed and re-enacted Stats 1905 ch 432 §1. Repealed Stats 1933 ch 533 §96. The repealed section related to consolidation of corporations.

§§587a, 588. [Sections repealed 1929]

Leg.H. Added Stats 1905 ch 432 §1. Repealed Stats 1929 ch 711 §44.

§589. [Section repealed 1939]

Leg.H. Added Stats 1905 ch 432 §1. Repealed Stats 1939 ch 93 (Pub Res C §10002). See Pub Res C §3984.

§590. [Section repealed 1929]

Leg.H. Added Stats 1905 ch 432 §1. Repealed Stats 1929 ch 711 §44.

§§591–592e. [Sections repealed 1947]

Leg.H. Added Stats 1905 ch 433 §1. Repealed Stats 1947 ch 1038 (Corp C §100001).

§§593–604. [Sections repealed 1947]

Leg.H. Enacted 1872. Revised Stats 1931 ch 871 §1. Repealed Stats 1947 ch 1038 (Corp C §100001). See Corp C §§5000 et seq.

§604a. [Section repealed 1929]

Leg.H. Enacted 1872. Repealed Stats 1929 ch 711.

§§605–606. [Sections repealed 1947]

Leg.H. Enacted 1872. Revised Stats 1931 ch 871 §1. Repealed Stats 1947 ch 1038 (Corp C §100001). See Corp C §§5000 et seq.

§607. [Section repealed 1947]

Leg.H. Added Stats 1905 ch 434 §1. Amended Stats 1943 ch 1023 §1. Repealed Stats 1947 ch 1038 (Corp C §100001). See Corp C §§10400 et seq.

§§607a–607c. [Sections repealed 1947]

Leg.H. Added Stats 1905 ch 434 §1. Repealed Stats 1947 ch 1038 (Corp C §100001). See Corp C §§10403–10405.

§607d. [Section repealed 1997]

Leg.H. Added Stats 1905 ch 434 §1. Repealed Stats 1997 ch 598 §1 (SB 633). See Corp C §14500.

§607e. [Section repealed 1997]

Leg.H. Added Stats 1905 ch 434 §1. Amended Stats 1909 ch 343 §1; Stats 1911 ch 295 §1; Stats 1913 ch 325 §1. Repealed Stats 1997 ch 598 §1 (SB 633). See Corp C §14501.

§607f. [Section repealed 1997]

Leg.H. Added Stats 1905 ch 434 §1. Amended Stats 1909 ch 38 §1; Stats 1913 ch 279 §1; Stats 1943 ch 1023 §2; Stats 1959 ch 2166 §1; Stats 1971 ch 1094 §1; Stats 1972 ch 1377 §7; Stats 1979 ch 139 §1; Stats 1985 ch 998 §1; Stats 1994 ch 84 §1 (SB 477); Stats 1995 ch 806 §1 (AB 1571); Stats 1996 ch 872 §22 (AB 3472). Repealed Stats 1997 ch 598 §1 (SB 633). See Corp C §14502.

§607g. [Section repealed 1997]

Leg.H. Added Stats 1973 ch 1155 §1. Repealed Stats 1997 ch 598 §1 (SB 633). See Corp C §14503.

Prior Law: Former §607g, relating to arresting children, was added Stats 1905 ch 434 §1 and repealed Stats 1937 ch 369 (W & I C §20000).

§§608, 609. [Sections repealed 1931]

Leg.H. Enacted 1872. Repealed Stats 1931 ch 1148 §32.

§610. [Section repealed 1997]

Leg.H. Added Stats 1923 ch 103 §1 as §653aa. Amended and renumbered Stats 1980 ch 676 §47. Repealed Stats 1997 ch 598 §1 (SB 633). See Corp C §14550.

Prior Law: Former §610, relating to cemetery corporations, was enacted 1872 and repealed Stats 1931 ch 1148 §32.

§611. [Section repealed 1997]

Leg.H. Added Stats 1923 ch 103 §1 as §653ee. Renumbered Stats 1980 ch 676 §48. Repealed Stats 1997 ch 598 §1 (SB 633). See Corp C §14551.

Prior Law: Former §611, relating to cemetery corporations, was enacted 1872, amended Code Amdts 1880 ch 103 §1, and repealed Stats 1931 ch 1148 §32.

§612. [Section repealed 1931]

Leg.H. Enacted 1872. Amended Stats 1901 ch 267 §1. Repealed Stats 1931 ch 1148 §32. The repealed section related to cemetery associations holding title to property.

§613. [Section repealed 1931]

Leg.H. Enacted 1872. Amended Stats 1885 ch 2 §1. Repealed Stats 1931 ch 1148 §32.

§614. [Section repealed 1931]

Leg.H. Enacted 1872. Repealed Stats 1931 ch 1148 §32.

§615. [Section repealed 1931]

Leg.H. Added Stats 1889 ch 64 §1. Repealed Stats 1931 ch 1148 §32.

§616. [Section repealed 1931]

Leg.H. Added Stats 1895 ch 157 §1. Amended Stats 1901 ch 267 §2; Stats 1927 ch 144 §1. Repealed Stats 1931 ch 1148 §32.

§617. [Section repealed 1931]

Leg.H. Added Stats 1921 ch 316 §1. Amended Stats 1927 ch 144 §2. Repealed Stats 1931 ch 1148 §32.

§§620–622. [Sections repealed 1974]

Leg.H. Enacted 1872. Repealed Stats 1974 ch 370 §6.

§628. [Section repealed 1905]

Leg.H. Enacted 1872. Repealed Stats 1905 ch 435 §1.

§629. [Section repealed 1915]

Leg.H. Enacted 1905 ch 435 §1. Amended Stats 1911 ch 434 §1. Repealed Stats 1915 ch 91 §86.

Prior Law: Former §629 was enacted 1872, amended Stats 1901 ch 157 §191, and repealed Stats 1905 ch 435 §1.

§630. [Section repealed 1915]

Leg.H. Enacted Stats 1905 ch 435 §1. Repealed Stats 1915 ch 91 §86.

Prior Law: Former §629 was enacted 1872, amended Stats 1901 ch 157 §192, and repealed Stats 1905 ch 435 §1.

§630a. [Section repealed 1915]

Leg.H. Added Stats 1905 ch 435 §1. Repealed Stats 1915 ch 91 §86.

§§631, 632. [Sections repealed 1915]

Leg.H. Enacted Stats 1905 ch 435 §1. Repealed Stats 1915 ch 91 §86.

Prior Law: Former §§631, 632 were enacted 1872, amended Stats 1901 ch 157 §§193, 194, and repealed Stats 1905 ch 435 §1.

§§633–648. [Sections repealed 1931]

Leg.H. Enacted Stats 1907 ch 502 §1. Repealed Stats 1931 ch 269. See Fin C §§5000 et seq.

Prior Law: Former §§633–648 were enacted 1872, amended Stats 1891 ch 174, and repealed Stats 1907 ch 502 §1.

§§648a, 648b. [Sections repealed 1907]
Leg.H. Enacted 1872. Repealed Stats 1907 ch 502 §1.

§648½. [Section repealed 1905]
Leg.H. Enacted 1872. Repealed Stats 1905 ch 565.

§§649–651e. [Sections repealed 1943]
Leg.H. Added Stats 1885 ch 143 §1, Stats 1927 ch 152 §1, Stats 1940 1st Ex Sess ch 22 §1. Repealed Stats 1943 ch 71 (Ed C §40001). The repealed section related to colleges and seminaries of learning.

§§652–653. [Sections repealed 1943]
Leg.H. Added Stats 1893 ch 6 §1. Stats 1935 ch 452 §§1–5. Repealed Stats 1943 ch 71 (Ed C §40001). See Ed C §§94400 et seq.

§653a. [Section repealed 1931]
Leg.H. Added Stats 1905 ch 436 §1. Repealed Stats 1931 ch 867 §1.

§§653b, 653c. [Sections repealed 1931]
Leg.H. Added Stats 1905 ch 437 §1. Repealed Stats 1931 ch 867 §1.

§653d. [Section repealed 1931]
Leg.H. Added Stats 1905 ch 437 §1. Amended Stats 1921 ch 170 §1; Stats 1929 ch 711 §39. Repealed Stats 1931 ch 867 §1.

§§653e–653h. [Sections repealed 1931]
Leg.H. Added Stats 1905 ch 437 §1. Repealed Stats 1931 ch 867 §1.

§653ha. [Section repealed 1931]
Leg.H. Added Stats 1915 ch 523 §1. Repealed Stats 1931 ch 867 §1.

§653i. [Section repealed 1931]
Leg.H. Added Stats 1905 ch 437 §1. Amended Stats 1921 ch 170 §2. Repealed Stats 1931 ch 867 §1.

§§653j–653l. [Sections repealed 1931]
Leg.H. Added Stats 1905 ch 437 §1. Repealed Stats 1931 ch 867 §1.

§§653m, 653n. [Sections repealed 1931]
Leg.H. Added Stats 1909 ch 26 §1. Amended Stats 1921 ch 341 §1. Repealed Stats 1931 ch 868 §1.

§653o. [Section repealed 1931]
Leg.H. Added Stats 1909 ch 26 §1. Amended Stats 1921 ch 170 §3, ch 341 §1; Stats 1929 ch 711 §40. Repealed Stats 1931 ch 868 §1.

§653p. [Section repealed 1931]
Leg.H. Added Stats 1909 ch 26 §1. Amended Stats 1921 ch 341 §1; Stats 1927 ch 339 §40. Repealed Stats 1931 ch 868 §1.

§§653q–653s. [Sections repealed 1931]
Leg.H. Added Stats 1909 ch 26 §1. Amended Stats 1921 ch 341 §1. Repealed Stats 1931 ch 868 §1.

§653sa. [Section repealed 1931]
Leg.H. Added Stats 1921 ch 341 §1. Repealed Stats 1931 ch 868 §1.

§653sb. [Section repealed 1931]
Leg.H. Added Stats 1921 ch 341 §1. Amended Stats 1923 ch 107 §1. Repealed Stats 1931 ch 868 §1.

§653sc. [Section repealed 1931]
Leg.H. Added Stats 1921 ch 341 §1. Repealed Stats 1931 ch 868 §1.

§§653t, 653u. [Sections repealed 1931]
Leg.H. Added Stats 1909 ch 524 §1. Amended Stats 1921 ch 342 §1. Repealed Stats 1931 ch 869 §1.

§653v. [Section repealed 1931]
Leg.H. Added Stats 1909 ch 524 §1. Amended Stats 1921 ch 170 §4, 342 §1; Stats 1929 ch 711 §41. Repealed Stats 1931 ch 869 §1.

§653w. [Section repealed 1931]
Leg.H. Added Stats 1909 ch 624 §1. Amended Stats 1921 ch 342 §1; Stats 1927 ch 338 §1. Repealed Stats 1931 ch 869 §1.

§§653x–653zb. [Sections repealed 1931]
Leg.H. Added Stats 1909 ch 524 §1. Amended Stats 1921 ch 342 §1. Repealed Stats 1931 ch 869 §1.

§§653zc, 653zd. [Sections repealed 1931]
Leg.H. Added Stats 1921 ch 342 §1. Repealed Stats 1931 ch 869 §1.

§653aa. [Section renumbered 1980]
Leg.H. Added Stats 1923 ch 103 §1. Amended and renumbered §610 Stats 1980 ch 676 §47.

§§653bb, 653cc. [Sections repealed 1933]
Leg.H. Added Stats 1923 ch 103 §1. Amended Stats 1931 ch 870 §§1, 2. Repealed Stats 1933 ch 25 (Ag C §1301). See Fd & Ag C §§54001–54004, 54033, 54061.

§653dd. [Section repealed 1945]
Leg.H. Added Stats 1923 ch 103 §1. Amended Stats 1939 ch 801 §1. Repealed Stats 1945 ch 1379 §13.

§653ee. [Section renumbered 1980]
Leg.H. Added Stats 1923 ch 103 §1. Amended and renumbered §611 Stats 1980 ch 676 §48.

§653ff. [Section repealed 1933]
Leg.H. Added Stats 1923 ch 103 §1. Amended Stats 1927 ch 340 §1. Repealed Stats 1933 ch 25 (Ag C §1301). See Fd & Ag C §§54171–54179.

§653gg. [Section repealed 1933]
Leg.H. Added Stats 1923 ch 103 §1. Repealed Stats 1933 ch 25 (Ag C §1301). See Fd & Ag C §§54231–54233.

§653hh. [Section repealed 1933]
Leg.H. Added Stats 1923 ch 103 §1. Amended Stats 1929 ch 711 §42; Stats 1931 ch 870 §3. Repealed Stats 1933 ch 25. See Fd & Ag C §54081.

§§653hh(1), 653hh(2). [Sections repealed 1945]
Leg.H. Added Stats 1931 ch 870 §11, 12. Repealed Stats 1945 1379 §13. See Fd & Ag C §§54082, 54202.

§653ii. [Section repealed 1933]
Leg.H. Added Stats 1923 ch 103 §1. Amended Stats 1931 ch 870 §4. Repealed Stats 1933 ch 25 (Ag C §1301). See Fd & Ag C §54083.

§§653jj, 653kk. [Sections repealed 1933]
Leg.H. Added Stats 1923 ch 103 §1. Amended Stats 1927 ch 340 §§2, 3; Stats 1931 ch 870 §3. Repealed Stats 1933 ch 25 (Ag C §1301). See Fd & Ag C §§54111–54122, 54141–54148.

§653ll. [Section repealed 1933]
Leg.H. Added Stats 1923 ch 103 §1. Repealed Stats 1933 ch 25 (Ag C §1301). See Fd & Ag C §54149.

§653mm. [Section repealed 1933]
Leg.H. Added Stats 1923 ch 103 §1. Amended Stats 1931 ch 870 §7. Repealed Stats 1933 ch 25 (Ag C §1301). See Fd & Ag C §54149.

§§653nn–653pp. [Sections repealed 1933]
Leg.H. Added Stats 1923 ch 103 §1. Repealed Stats 1933 ch 25 (Ag C §1301). See Fd & Ag C §§54150, 54261, 54262, 54264–54266.

§653qq. [Section repealed 1933]
Leg.H. Added Stats 1923 ch 103 §1. Amended Stats 1931 ch 870 §8. Repealed Stats 1933 ch 25 (Ag C §1301). See Fd & Ag C §54203.

§§653rr, 653ss. [Sections repealed 1933]
Leg.H. Added Stats 1923 ch 103 §1. Repealed Stats 1933 ch 25 (Ag C §1301). See Fd & Ag C §§54034–54036.

§653tt. [Section repealed 1933]
Leg.H. Added Stats 1923 ch 103 §1. Amended Stats 1931 ch 870 §9. Repealed Stats 1933 ch 25 (Ag C §1301). See Fd & Ag C §54180.

§653uu. [Section repealed 1933]
Leg.H. Added Stats 1923 ch 103 §1. Repealed Stats 1933 ch 25 (Ag C §1301). See Fd & Ag C §54181.

§653vv. [Section repealed 1933]

Leg.H. Added Stats 1923 ch 103 §1. Amended Stats 1931 ch 870 §10. Repealed Stats 1933 ch 25 (Ag C §1301). See Fd & Ag C §54037.

§§653ww, 653xx. [Sections repealed 1933]

Leg.H. Added Stats 1923 ch 103 §1. Repealed Stats 1933 ch 25 (Ag C §1301). See Fd & Ag C §§54038–54040.

§653yy. [Section repealed 1933]

Leg.H. Added Stats 1931 ch 870 §13. Repealed Stats 1933 ch 25 (Ag C §1301). See Fd & Ag C §54201.

§§653ab–653ag. [Sections repealed 1943]

Leg.H. Added Stats 1927 ch 722 §1. Repealed Stats 1943 ch 71 (Ed C §40001). The repealed section related to incorporation of libraries.

§§653.1–653.3. [Sections repealed 1947]

Leg.H. Added Stats 1939 ch 2359 §1. Repealed Stats 1947 ch 1038 (Corp C §10000.1). See Corp C §§12201 et seq.

§653.4. [Section repealed 1947].

Leg.H. Added Stats 1939 ch 2359 §1. Repealed Stats 1947 ch 1091 §2.

§§653.5–653.16. [Sections repealed 1947]

Leg.H. Added Stats 1939 ch 2359 §1. Repealed Stats 1947 ch 1038 (Corp C §10000.1). See Corp C §§12201 et seq.

DIVISION 2
PROPERTY

Part 1. Property in General.
Part 2. Real or Immovable Property.
Part 3. Personal or Movable Property.
Part 4. Acquisition of Property.

PART 1
PROPERTY IN GENERAL

Title 1. Nature of Property.
Title 2. Ownership.
Title 3. General Definitions.

TITLE 1
NATURE OF PROPERTY

"Property defined". §654.
In what property may exist. §655.
Wild animals. §656.
Real and personal. §657.
Definition of real property; Severance by agreement. §658.
Land. §659.
Definition of fixtures; Severance by agreement. §660.
Appurtenances. §662.
Personal property. §663.

§654. "Property defined"
The ownership of a thing is the right of one or more persons to possess and use it to the exclusion of others. In this code, the thing of which there may be ownership is called property. **Leg.H.** Enacted 1872.

§655. In what property may exist
There may be ownership of all inanimate things which are capable of appropriation or of manual delivery; of all domestic animals; of all obligations; of such products of labor or skill as the composition of an author, the goodwill of a business, trademarks and signs, and of rights created or granted by statute. **Leg.H.** Enacted 1872.

§656. Wild animals
Animals wild by nature are the subjects of ownership, while living, only when on the land of the person claiming them, or when tamed, or taken and held in possession, or disabled and immediately pursued. **Leg.H.** Enacted 1872.

§657. Real and personal
Property is either:
1. Real or immovable; or,
2. Personal or movable. **Leg.H.** Enacted 1872.

§658. Definition of real property; Severance by agreement
Real or immovable property consists of:
1. Land;
2. That which is affixed to land;
3. That which is incidental or appurtenant to land;
4. That which is immovable by law; except that for the purposes of sale, emblements, industrial growing crops and things attached to or forming part of the land, which are agreed to be severed before sale or under the contract of sale, shall be treated as goods and be governed by the provisions of the title of this code regulating the sales of goods. **Leg.H.** Enacted 1872. Amended Stats 1931 ch 1070 §4.

§659. Land
Land is the material of the earth, whatever may be the ingredients of which it is composed, whether soil, rock, or other substance, and includes free or occupied space for an indefinite distance upwards as well as downwards, subject to limitations upon the use of airspace imposed, and rights in the use of airspace granted, by law. **Leg.H.** Enacted 1872. Amended Stats 1963 ch 860 §5.

§660. Definition of fixtures; Severance by agreement
A thing is deemed to be affixed to land when it is attached to it by roots, as in the case of trees, vines, or shrubs; or imbedded in it, as in the case of walls; or permanently resting upon it, as in the case of buildings; or permanently attached to what is thus permanent, as by means of cement, plaster, nails, bolts, or screws; except that for the purposes of sale, emblements, industrial growing crops and things attached to or forming part of the land, which are agreed to be severed before sale or under the contract of sale, shall be treated as goods and be governed by the provisions of the title of this code regulating the sales of goods. **Leg.H.** Enacted 1872. Amended Stats 1931 ch 1070 §5.

§661. [Section repealed 1939]
Leg.H. Enacted 1872. Repealed Stats 1939 ch 93 p 1215. See Pub Res C §3980.

§662. Appurtenances
A thing is deemed to be incidental or appurtenant to land when it is by right used with the land for its benefit, as in the case of a way, or watercourse, or of a passage for light, air, or heat from or across the land of another. **Leg.H.** Enacted 1872.

§663. Personal property
Every kind of property that is not real is personal. **Leg.H.** Enacted 1872.

TITLE 2
OWNERSHIP

Chapter 1. Owners.
Chapter 2. Modifications of Ownership.
Chapter 2.6. Legal Estates Principal and Income Law.
Chapter 3. Rights of Owners.
Chapter 4. Termination of Ownership.

CHAPTER 1
OWNERS

Owner. §669.
Property of the State. §670.
Who may own property. §671.

§669. Owner
All property has an owner, whether that owner is the state, and the property public, or the owner an individual, and the property private. The state may also hold property as a private proprietor. **Leg.H.** Enacted 1872.

§670. Property of the State
The State is the owner of all land below tide water, and below ordinary high-water mark, bordering upon tide water within the State; of all land below the water of a navigable lake or stream; of all property lawfully appropriated by it to its own use; of all property dedicated to the State; and of all property of which there is no other owner. **Leg.H.** Enacted 1872. Amended Code Amendments 1873–74 ch 612 §99.

§671. Who may own property
Any person, regardless of their citizenship status, may take, hold, and dispose of property, real or personal, within this state. **Leg.H.** Enacted 1872. Amended Code Amendments 1873–74 ch 612 §100; Stats 2021 ch 296 §12 (AB 1096), effective January 1, 2022.

§672. [Section repealed 1933]
Leg.H. Enacted 1872. Repealed Stats 1933 ch 969 §25. See Prob C §12203.

CHAPTER 2
MODIFICATIONS OF OWNERSHIP

Article 1. Interests in Property.
Article 2. Conditions of Ownership.
Article 3. Duration of Leases.

Article 4. Accumulations.

ARTICLE 1
Interests in Property

Ownership, absolute or qualified. §678.
When absolute. §679.
When qualified. §680.
Several ownership. §681.
Estates in property; Ownership by several persons. §682.
Community property; Express declaration in transfer document. §682.1.
Joint tenancy. §683.
Joint tenancy or other ownership of contents of safe-deposit boxes; When not established. §683.1.
Severance of joint tenancy. §683.2.
Partnership interest. §684.
Interest in common. §685.
What interests are in common. §686.
Community property. §687.
Interests as to time. §688.
Present interest. §689.
Future interest. §690.
Perpetual interest. §691.
Limited interest. §692.
Two or more future interests. §696.
Certain future interests not to be void. §697.
Posthumous children. §698.
Qualities of expectant estates. §699.
Mere possibility; Effect. §700.
Interests in real property. §701.
Names and classifications of interests in real property. §702.
What future interests are recognized. §703.

§678. Ownership, absolute or qualified
The ownership of property is either:
1. Absolute; or,
2. Qualified. **Leg.H.** Enacted 1872.

§679. When absolute
The ownership of property is absolute when a single person has the absolute dominion over it, and may use it or dispose of it according to his pleasure, subject only to general laws. **Leg.H.** Enacted 1872.

§680. When qualified
The ownership of property is qualified:
1. When it is shared with one or more persons;
2. When the time of enjoyment is deferred or limited;
3. When the use is restricted. **Leg.H.** Enacted 1872.

§681. Several ownership
The ownership of property by a single person is designated as a sole or several ownership. **Leg.H.** Enacted 1872.

§682. Estates in property; Ownership by several persons
The ownership of property by several persons is either:
(a) Of joint interest.
(b) Of partnership interests.
(c) Of interests in common.
(d) Of community interest of spouses. **Leg.H.** Enacted 1872. Amended Stats 2016 ch 50 §7 (SB 1005), effective January 1, 2017.

2016 Note: For legislative intent, see the 2016 Note following §14.

§682.1. Community property; Express declaration in transfer document
(a)(1) Community property of spouses, when expressly declared in the transfer document to be community property with right of survivorship, and which may be accepted in writing on the face of the document by a statement signed or initialed by the grantees, shall, upon the death of one of the spouses, pass to the survivor, without administration, pursuant to the terms of the instrument, subject to the same procedures, as property held in joint tenancy. Prior to the death of either spouse, the right of survivorship may be terminated pursuant to the same procedures by which a joint tenancy may be severed.

(2) Part 1 (commencing with Section 5000) of Division 5 of the Probate Code and Chapter 2 (commencing with Section 13540), Chapter 3 (commencing with Section 13550), and Chapter 3.5 (commencing with Section 13560) of Part 2 of Division 8 of the Probate Code apply to this property.

(3) For the purposes of Chapter 3 (commencing with Section 13550) of Part 2 of Division 8 of the Probate Code, this property shall be treated as if it had passed without administration under Part 2 (commencing with Section 13500) of Division 8 of the Probate Code.

(b) This section does not apply to a joint account in a financial institution to which Part 2 (commencing with Section 5100) of Division 5 of the Probate Code applies.

(c) This section shall become operative on July 1, 2001, and shall apply to instruments created on or after that date. **Leg.H.** Added Stats 2000 ch 645 §1 (AB 2913), operative July 1, 2001. Amended Stats 2016 ch 50 §8 (SB 1005), effective January 1, 2017, operative July 1, 2001; Stats 2022 ch 29 §1 (AB 1716), effective January 1, 2023.

2016 Note: For legislative intent, see the 2016 Note following §14.

§683. Joint tenancy
(a) A joint interest is one owned by two or more persons in equal shares, by a title created by a single will or transfer, when expressly declared in the will or transfer to be a joint tenancy, or by transfer from a sole owner to himself or herself and others, or from tenants in common or joint tenants to themselves or some of them, or to themselves or any of them and others, or from spouses, when holding title as community property or otherwise to themselves or to themselves and others or to one of them and to another or others, when expressly declared in the transfer to be a joint tenancy, or when granted or devised to executors or trustees as joint tenants. A joint tenancy in personal property may be created by a written transfer, instrument, or agreement.

(b) Provisions of this section do not apply to a joint account in a financial institution if Part 2 (commencing with Section 5100) of Division 5 of the Probate Code applies to such account. **Leg.H.** Enacted 1872. Amended Stats 1929 ch 93 §1; Stats 1931 ch 1051 §1; Stats 1935 ch 234 §1; Stats 1955 ch 178 §1; Stats 1983 ch 92 §1, operative July 1, 1984; Stats 1989 ch 397 §1, operative July 1, 1990; Stats 1990 ch 79 §1 (AB 759), operative July 1, 1991; Stats 2016 ch 50 §9 (SB 1005), effective January 1, 2017.

2016 Note: It is the intent of the Legislature that the changes made by this act have only technical and nonsubstantive effect. Hence, no change made by this act shall create any new right, duty, or other obligation that did not exist immediately preceding the effective date of this act, or result in the limitation or termination of any right, duty, or other obligation that existed immediately preceding the effective date of this act. Stats 2016 ch 50 (SB 1005) §125.

§683.1. Joint tenancy or other ownership of contents of safe-deposit boxes; When not established
No contract or other arrangement made after the effective date of this section between any person, firm, or corporation engaged in the business of renting safe-deposit boxes and the renter or renters of a safe-deposit box, shall create a joint tenancy in or otherwise establish ownership in any of the contents of such safe-deposit box. Any such contract or other arrangement purporting so to do shall be to such extent void and of no effect. **Leg.H.** Added Stats 1949 ch 1597 §1.

§683.2. Severance of joint tenancy
(a) Subject to the limitations and requirements of this section, in addition to any other means by which a joint tenancy may be severed, a joint tenant may sever a joint tenancy in real property as to the joint tenant's interest without the joinder or consent of the other joint tenants by any of the following means:

(1) Execution and delivery of a deed that conveys legal title to the joint tenant's interest to a third person, whether or not pursuant to an agreement that requires the third person to reconvey legal title to the joint tenant.

(2) Execution of a written instrument that evidences the intent to sever the joint tenancy, including a deed that names the joint tenant as transferee, or of a written declaration that, as to the interest of the joint tenant, the joint tenancy is severed.

(b) Nothing in this section authorizes severance of a joint tenancy contrary to a written agreement of the joint tenants, but a severance contrary to a written agreement does not defeat the rights of a purchaser or encumbrancer for value in good faith and without knowledge of the written agreement.

(c) Severance of a joint tenancy of record by deed, written declaration, or other written instrument pursuant to subdivision (a) is not effective to terminate the right of survivorship of the other joint tenants as to the severing joint tenant's interest unless one of the following requirements is satisfied:

(1) Before the death of the severing joint tenant, the deed, written declaration, or other written instrument effecting the severance is recorded in the county where the real property is located.

(2) The deed, written declaration, or other written instrument effecting the severance is executed and acknowledged before a notary public by the severing joint tenant not earlier than three days before the death of that joint tenant and is recorded in the county where the real property is located not later than seven days after the death of the severing joint tenant.

(d) Nothing in subdivision (c) limits the manner or effect of:

(1) A written instrument executed by all the joint tenants that severs the joint tenancy.

(2) A severance made by or pursuant to a written agreement of all the joint tenants.

(3) A deed from a joint tenant to another joint tenant.

(e) Subdivisions (a) and (b) apply to all joint tenancies in real property, whether the joint tenancy was created before, on, or after January 1, 1985, except that in the case of the death of a joint tenant before January 1, 1985, the validity of a severance under subdivisions (a) and (b) is determined by the law in effect at the time of death. Subdivisions (c) and (d) do not apply to or affect a severance made before January 1, 1986, of a joint tenancy. **Leg.H.** Added Stats 1984 ch 519 §1. Amended Stats 1985 ch 157 §1.

§684. Partnership interest

A partnership interest is one owned by several persons, in partnership, for partnership purposes. **Leg.H.** Enacted 1872.

§685. Interest in common

An interest in common is one owned by several persons, not in joint ownership or partnership. **Leg.H.** Enacted 1872.

§686. What interests are in common

Every interest created in favor of several persons in their own right is an interest in common, unless acquired by them in partnership, for partnership purposes, or unless declared in its creation to be a joint interest, as provided in Section 683, or unless acquired as community property. **Leg.H.** Enacted 1872.

§687. Community property

Community property is property that is community property under Part 2 (commencing with Section 760) of Division 4 of the Family Code. **Leg.H.** Enacted 1872. Amended Stats 1992 ch 163 §6 (AB 2641), operative January 1, 1994.

§688. Interests as to time

In respect to the time of enjoyment, an interest in property is either:
1. Present or future; and,
2. Perpetual or limited. **Leg.H.** Enacted 1872.

§689. Present interest

A present interest entitles the owner to the immediate possession of the property. **Leg.H.** Enacted 1872.

§690. Future interest

A future interest entitles the owner to the possession of the property only at a future period. **Leg.H.** Enacted 1872.

§691. Perpetual interest

A perpetual interest has a duration equal to that of the property. **Leg.H.** Enacted 1872.

§692. Limited interest

A limited interest has a duration less than that of the property. **Leg.H.** Enacted 1872.

§§693–695. [Sections repealed 1963]

Leg.H. Enacted 1872. Repealed Stats 1963 ch 1455 §§1–3. The repealed sections related to vested and contingent future interests.

§696. Two or more future interests

Two or more future interests may be created to take effect in the alternative, so that if the first in order fails to vest, the next in succession shall be substituted for it, and take effect accordingly. **Leg.H.** Enacted 1872.

§697. Certain future interests not to be void

A future interest is not void merely because of the improbability of the contingency on which it is limited to take effect. **Leg.H.** Enacted 1872.

§698. Posthumous children

When a future interest is limited to successors, heirs, issue, or children, posthumous children are entitled to take in the same manner as if living at the death of their parent. **Leg.H.** Enacted 1872.

§699. Qualities of expectant estates

Future interests pass by succession, will, and transfer, in the same manner as present interests. **Leg.H.** Enacted 1872.

§700. Mere possibility; Effect

A mere possibility, such as the expectancy of an heir apparent, is not to be deemed an interest of any kind. **Leg.H.** Enacted 1872.

§701. Interests in real property

In respect to real or immovable property, the interests mentioned in this chapter are denominated estates, and are specially named and classified in part two of this division. **Leg.H.** Enacted 1872.

§702. Names and classifications of interests in real property

The names and classification of interests in real property have only such application to interests in personal property as is in this division of the code expressly provided. **Leg.H.** Enacted 1872.

§703. What future interests are recognized

No future interest in property is recognized by the law, except such as is defined in this division of the code. **Leg.H.** Enacted 1872.

§704. [Section repealed 1991]

Leg.H. Added Stats 1943 ch 51 §1, effective February 10, 1943. Repealed Stats 1991 ch 1055 §1. The repealed section related to entitlement to savings bonds upon death of co-owner.

ARTICLE 2
Conditions of Ownership

Fixing time of enjoyment. §707.
Conditions. §708.
Certain conditions precedent void. §709.
Conditions restraining marriage void. §710.
Conditions restraining alienation void. §711.
Loans by public entity; Denial of assumption by subsequent ineligible purchaser or transferee and acceleration of payment upon sale or transfer; Assumption with increase in interest. §711.5.
Restrictions on placing for sale sign on property as void; Retrospective operation of statute. §712.
Right to display sign advertising property for sale, lease, or exchange. §713.
Unenforceability of restrictions on use of solar energy system; Standards for solar energy systems; Approval process; Penalty for willful violation; Attorneys' fees; Compliance by public entity seeking grant or loan funds. §714.
Permitted restrictions by common interest development associations. §714.1.
Unenforceability of accessory dwelling unit prohibitions. §714.3.
Application of governing documents to structure intended for occupancy constructed in offsite facility or factory and subsequently moved or transported in sections or modules. §714.5.
Recorded covenants limiting use of public or private land unenforceable against affordable housing development owner with approved and recorded restrictive covenant affordable housing modification document; Limitations and exceptions. §714.6.
Sale of units constructed pursuant to a local inclusionary zoning ordinance; Penalty for violations; Requirements for a nonprofit housing corporation. §714.7.

§707. Fixing time of enjoyment

The time when the enjoyment of property is to begin or end may be determined by computation, or be made to depend on events. In the latter case, the enjoyment is said to be upon condition. **Leg.H.** Enacted 1872.

§708. Conditions

Conditions are precedent or subsequent. The former fix the beginning, the latter the ending, of the right. **Leg.H.** Enacted 1872.

§709. Certain conditions precedent void

If a condition precedent requires the performance of an act wrong of itself, the instrument containing it is so far void, and the right cannot exist. If it requires the performance of an act not wrong of itself, but otherwise unlawful, the instrument takes effect and the condition is void. **Leg.H.** Enacted 1872.

§710. Conditions restraining marriage void

Conditions imposing restraints upon marriage, except upon the marriage of a minor, are void; but this does not affect limitations where the intent was not to forbid marriage, but only to give the use until marriage. **Leg.H.** Enacted 1872. Amended Code Amdts 1873–74 ch 612 §101.

§711. Conditions restraining alienation void

Conditions restraining alienation, when repugnant to the interest created, are void. **Leg.H.** Enacted 1872.

§711.5. Loans by public entity; Denial of assumption by subsequent ineligible purchaser or transferee and acceleration of payment upon sale or transfer; Assumption with increase in interest

(a) Notwithstanding the provisions of Sections 711 and 1916.5, a state or local public entity directly or indirectly providing housing purchase or rehabilitation loans shall have the authority to deny assumptions, or require the denial of assumptions, by a subsequent ineligible purchaser or transferee of the prior borrower of the obligation of any such loan made for the purpose of rehabilitating or providing affordable housing. If such a subsequent purchaser or transferee does not meet such an entity's eligibility requirements, that entity may accelerate or may require the acceleration of the principal balance of the loan to be all due and payable upon the sale or transfer of the property.

(b) As a condition of authorizing assumption of a loan pursuant to this section, the entity may recast the repayment schedule for the remainder of the term of the loan by increasing the interest to the current market rate at the time of assumption, or to such lower rate of interest as is the maximum allowed by an entity that provided any insurance or other assistance which results in an assumption being permitted. Any additional increment of interest produced by increasing the rate of interest upon a loan pursuant to this subdivision shall be transmitted or forwarded to the entity for deposit in the specified fund from which the loan was made, or, if no such fund exists, or the public entity has directed otherwise, then to the general fund of such entity.

(c) The state or local public entity providing assistance as specified in this section may implement appropriate measures to assure compliance with this section. **Leg.H.** Added Stats 1979 ch 971 §1, effective September 22, 1979.

§712. Restrictions on placing for sale sign on property as void; Retrospective operation of statute

(a) Every provision contained in or otherwise affecting a grant of a fee interest in, or purchase money security instrument upon, real property in this state heretofore or hereafter made, which purports to prohibit or restrict the right of the property owner or his or her agent to display or have displayed on the real property, or on real property owned by others with their consent, or both, signs which are reasonably located, in plain view of the public, are of reasonable dimensions and design, and do not adversely affect public safety, including traffic safety, and which advertise the property for sale, lease, or exchange, or advertise directions to the property, by the property owner or his or her agent is void as an unreasonable restraint upon the power of alienation.

(b) This section shall operate retrospectively, as well as prospectively, to the full extent that it may constitutionally operate retrospectively.

(c) A sign that conforms to the ordinance adopted in conformity with Section 713 shall be deemed to be of reasonable dimension and design pursuant to this section. **Leg.H.** Added Stats 1965 ch 1591 §1. Amended Stats 1975 ch 147 §1; Stats 1983 ch 51 §1; Stats 1990 ch 1282 §1 (AB 2949); Stats 1992 ch 773 §2 (SB 1474); Stats 1993 ch 589 §20 (AB 2211).

§713. Right to display sign advertising property for sale, lease, or exchange

(a) Notwithstanding any provision of any ordinance, an owner of real property or his or her agent may display or have displayed on the owner's real property, and on real property owned by others with their consent, signs which are reasonably located, in plain view of the public, are of reasonable dimensions and design, and do not adversely affect public safety, including traffic safety, as determined by the city, county, or city and county, advertising the following:

(1) That the property is for sale, lease, or exchange by the owner or his or her agent.

(2) Directions to the property.

(3) The owner's or agent's name.

(4) The owner's or agent's address and telephone number.

(b) Nothing in this section limits any authority which a person or local governmental entity may have to limit or regulate the display or placement of a sign on a private or public right-of-way. **Leg.H.** Added Stats 1975 ch 147 §2. Amended Stats 1983 ch 51 §2; Stats 1990 ch 1282 §2 (AB 2949); Stats 1992 ch 773 §3 (SB 1474).

§714. Unenforceability of restrictions on use of solar energy system; Standards for solar energy systems; Approval process; Penalty for willful violation; Attorneys' fees; Compliance by public entity seeking grant or loan funds

(a) Any covenant, restriction, or condition contained in any deed, contract, security instrument, or other instrument affecting the transfer or sale of, or any interest in, real property, and any provision of a governing document, as defined in Section 4150 or 6552, that effectively prohibits or restricts the installation or use of a solar energy system is void and unenforceable.

(b) This section does not apply to provisions that impose reasonable restrictions on solar energy systems. However, it is the policy of the state to promote and encourage the use of solar energy systems and to remove obstacles thereto. Accordingly, reasonable restrictions on a solar energy system are those restrictions that do not significantly increase the cost of the system or significantly decrease its efficiency or specified performance, or that allow for an alternative system of comparable cost, efficiency, and energy conservation benefits.

(c)(1) A solar energy system shall meet applicable health and safety standards and requirements imposed by state and local permitting authorities, consistent with Section 65850.5 of the Government Code.

(2) Solar energy systems used for heating water in single family residences and solar collectors used for heating water in commercial or swimming pool applications shall be certified by an accredited listing agency as defined in the Plumbing and Mechanical Codes.

(3) A solar energy system for producing electricity shall also meet all applicable safety and performance standards established by the California Electrical Code, the Institute of Electrical and Electronics Engineers, and accredited testing laboratories such as Underwriters Laboratories and, where applicable, rules of the Public Utilities Commission regarding safety and reliability.

(d) For the purposes of this section:

(1)(A) For solar domestic water heating systems or solar swimming pool heating systems that comply with state and federal law, "significantly" means an amount exceeding 10 percent of the cost of the system, but in no case more than one thousand dollars ($1,000), or decreasing the efficiency of the solar energy system by an amount exceeding 10 percent, as originally specified and proposed.

(B) For photovoltaic systems that comply with state and federal law, "significantly" means an amount not to exceed one thousand dollars ($1,000) over the system cost as originally specified and proposed, or a decrease in system efficiency of an amount exceeding 10 percent as originally specified and proposed.

(2) "Solar energy system" has the same meaning as defined in paragraphs (1) and (2) of subdivision (a) of Section 801.5.

(e)(1) Whenever approval is required for the installation or use of a solar energy system, the application for approval shall be processed and approved by the appropriate approving entity in the same manner as an application for approval of an architectural modification to the property, and shall not be willfully avoided or delayed.

(2) For an approving entity that is an association, as defined in Section 4080 or 6528, and that is not a public entity, both of the following shall apply:

(A) The approval or denial of an application shall be in writing.

(B) If an application is not denied in writing within 45 days from the date of receipt of the application, the application shall be deemed approved, unless that delay is the result of a reasonable request for additional information.

(f) Any entity, other than a public entity, that willfully violates this section shall be liable to the applicant or other party for actual damages occasioned thereby, and shall pay a civil penalty to the applicant or other party in an amount not to exceed one thousand dollars ($1,000).

(g) In any action to enforce compliance with this section, the prevailing party shall be awarded reasonable attorney's fees.

(h)(1) A public entity that fails to comply with this section may not receive funds from a state-sponsored grant or loan program for solar energy. A public entity shall certify its compliance with the requirements of this section when applying for funds from a state-sponsored grant or loan program.

(2) A local public entity may not exempt residents in its jurisdiction from the requirements of this section. **Leg.H.** Added Stats 1978 ch 1154 §3. Amended Stats 1990 ch 1517 §2 (AB 3689), operative July 1, 1991; Stats 1992 ch 1222 §1 (AB 3554); Stats 1994 ch 382 §1 (SB 1553); Stats 1995 ch 91 §16 (SB 975); Stats 2002 ch 570 §1 (SB 1534); Stats 2003 ch 290 §1 (AB 1407); Stats 2004 ch 789 §2 (AB 2473); Stats 2008 ch 40 §1 (AB 1892), ch 539 §2 (AB 2180), effective January 1, 2009; Stats 2012 ch 181 §20 (AB 806), effective January 1, 2013, operative January 1, 2014; Stats 2013 ch 605 §8 (SB 752), effective January 1, 2014; Stats 2014 ch 521 §2 (AB 2188), effective January 1, 2015.

§714.1. Permitted restrictions by common interest development associations

(a) Notwithstanding Section 714, an association may impose reasonable provisions that:

(1) Restrict the installation of solar energy systems in common areas to those systems approved by the association.

(2) Require the owner of a separate interest to obtain the approval of the association for the installation of a solar energy system in a separate interest owned by another.

(3) Provide for the maintenance, repair, or replacement of roofs or other building components.

(4) Require installers of solar energy systems to indemnify or reimburse the association or its members for loss or damage caused by the installation, maintenance, or use of the solar energy system.

(b) An association shall not:

(1) Establish a general policy prohibiting the installation or use of a rooftop solar energy system for household purposes on the roof of the building in which the owner resides, or a garage or carport adjacent to the building that has been assigned to the owner for exclusive use.

(2) Require approval by a vote of members owning separate interests in the common interest development, including that specified by Section 4600, for installation of a solar energy system for household purposes on the roof of the building in which the owner resides, or a garage or carport adjacent to the building that has been assigned to the owner for exclusive use.

An action by an association that contravenes paragraph (1) or (2) shall be void and unenforceable.

(c) For purposes of this section:

(1) "Association" has the same meaning as defined in Section 4080 or 6528.

(2) "Common area" has the same meaning as defined in Section 4095 or 6532.

(3) "Separate interest" has the same meaning as defined in Section 4185 or 6564. **Leg.H.** Added Stats 1992 ch 1222 §2 (AB 3554). Amended Stats 2012 ch 181 §21 (AB 806), effective January 1, 2013, operative January 1, 2014; Stats 2013 ch 605 §9 (SB 752), effective January 1, 2014; Stats 2017 ch 818 §1 (AB 634), effective January 1, 2018.

§ 714.3. Unenforceability of accessory dwelling unit prohibitions

(a) Any covenant, restriction, or condition contained in any deed, contract, security instrument, or other instrument affecting the transfer or sale of any interest in real property that either effectively prohibits or unreasonably restricts the construction or use of an accessory dwelling unit or junior accessory dwelling unit on a lot zoned for single-family residential use that meets the requirements of [1] **Article 2 (commencing with Section 66314) of Chapter 13 or Article 3 (commencing with Section 66333) of Chapter 13 of Division of Title 7** of the Government Code is void and unenforceable.

(b) This section does not apply to provisions that impose reasonable restrictions on accessory dwelling units or junior accessory dwelling units. For purposes of this subdivision, "reasonable restrictions" means restrictions that do not unreasonably increase the cost to construct, effectively prohibit the construction of, or extinguish the ability to otherwise construct, an accessory dwelling unit or junior accessory dwelling unit consistent with the provisions of [2] **Article 2 (commencing with Section 66314) or Article 3 (commencing with Section 66333) of Chapter 13 of Division 1 of Title 7** of the Government Code. **Leg.H.** Added Stats 2021 ch 360 §1 (AB 1584), effective January 1, 2022. Amended Stats 2024 ch 7 §1 (SB 477), effective March 25, 2024.

§ 714.3. 2024 Deletes. [1] Section 65852.2 or 65852.22 [2] Section 65852.2 or 65852.22

§714.5. Application of governing documents to structure intended for occupancy constructed in offsite facility or factory and subsequently moved or transported in sections or modules

The covenants, conditions, and restrictions or other management documents shall not prohibit the sale, lease, rent, or use of real property on the basis that the structure intended for occupancy on the real property is constructed in an offsite facility or factory, and subsequently moved or transported in sections or modules to the real property. Nothing herein shall preclude the governing instruments from being uniformly applied to all structures subject to the covenants, conditions, and restrictions or other management documents.

This section shall apply to covenants, conditions, and restrictions or other management documents adopted on and after the effective date of this section. **Leg.H.** Added Stats 1987 ch 1339 §1.

§ 714.6. Recorded covenants limiting use of public or private land unenforceable against affordable housing development owner with approved and recorded restrictive covenant affordable housing modification document; Limitations and exceptions

(a) Recorded covenants, conditions, restrictions, or private limits on the use of private or publicly owned land contained in any deed, contract, security instrument, or other instrument affecting the transfer or sale of any interest in real property that restrict the number, size, or location of the residences that may be built on the property, or that restrict the number of persons or families who may reside on the property, shall not be enforceable against the owner of an affordable housing development, if an approved restrictive covenant affordable housing modification document has been recorded in the public record as provided for in this section, except as explicitly provided in this section.

(b)(1) The owner of an affordable housing development shall be entitled to establish that an existing restrictive covenant is unenforceable under subdivision (a) by submitting a restrictive covenant modification document pursuant to Section 12956.2 of the Government Code that modifies or removes any existing restrictive covenant language that restricts the number, size, or location of the residences that may be built on the property, or that restricts the number of persons or families that may reside on the property, to the extent necessary to allow the affordable housing development to proceed under the existing declaration of restrictive covenants.

(2)(A) The owner shall submit to the county recorder a copy of the original restrictive covenant, a copy of any notice the owner believes is required pursuant to paragraph (3) of subdivision (g), and any documents the owner believes necessary to establish that the property qualifies as an affordable housing development under this section prior to, or simultaneously with, the submission of the request for recordation of the restrictive covenant modification document.

(B) Before recording the restrictive covenant modification document, pursuant to subdivision (b) of Section 12956.2 of the Government Code, the county recorder shall, within five business days of receipt, submit the documentation provided to the county recorder by the owner pursuant to subparagraph (A) and the modification document to the county counsel for review. The county counsel shall determine whether the original restrictive covenant document restricts the property in a manner prohibited by subdivision (a), whether the owner has submitted documents sufficient to establish that the property qualifies as an affordable housing development under this section, whether any notice required under this section has been provided, whether any exemption provided in subdivision (g) or (h) applies, and whether the restriction may no longer be enforced against the owner of the affordable housing development and that the owner may record a modification document pursuant to this section.

(C) Pursuant to Section 12956.2 of the Government Code, the county counsel shall return the documents and inform the county recorder of the county counsel's determination within 15 days of submission to the county counsel. If the county counsel is unable to make a determination, the county counsel shall specify the documentation that is needed in order to make the determination. If the county counsel has authorized the county recorder to record the modification document, that authorization shall be noted on the face of the modification or on a cover sheet affixed thereto, and the county recorder shall notify the owner or submitting party of the county counsel's determination without delay so that the notice described in subparagraph (D) may be given.

(D) Upon being notified that the county counsel has authorized the county recorder to record the modification document, the owner may mail, by certified mail to anyone who the owner knows has an interest in the property or in the restrictive covenant, a copy of the modification document, together with a copy of this section and a written explanation that the modification has been applied for and approved for recordation by the county counsel pursuant to this section. That notice shall be deemed given if the notice is actually received by the intended recipient or if the notice is mailed by certified mail both to an address for notice indicated in the restrictive covenant, if any, and to the intended recipient's address as shown in the last equalized assessment roll, if that address reasonably can be ascertained from the assessment roll. The owner may also publish notice pursuant to Section 6061 of the Government Code identifying that a modification document pursuant to this section has been submitted to the county recorder and approved for recordation by the county counsel, and that the modification document is available for public inspection in the office of the county recorder. The notice shall also identify the property by assessor's parcel number and mailing address. If no mailing address has been assigned for the property, then the property shall be identified instead by its nearest intersection. If the owner elects to publish notice in this manner, then notice shall be deemed given to anyone whose interest does not appear of record or for whom an address for notice does not appear of record and cannot reasonably be ascertained from the assessment roll. Notice as described in this subparagraph is optional, and failure to provide it shall not, in any manner, invalidate a restrictive covenant modification document recorded pursuant to this section.

(E) The county recorder shall not record the modification document if the county counsel finds that the original restrictive covenant document does not contain a restriction prohibited by this section or if the county counsel finds that the property does not qualify as an affordable housing development. If the owner of the property is not yet its record title owner, but is instead a beneficial owner with a right pursuant to a purchase and sale or similar agreement to purchase the property, then the owner shall not record the modification document until the owner closes escrow on the property and becomes its record title owner.

(F) A modification document shall be indexed in the same manner as the original restrictive covenant document being modified. It shall contain a recording reference to the original restrictive covenant document, in the form of a book and page or instrument number, and date of the recording. The effective date of the terms and conditions of the modification document shall be the same as the effective date of the original restrictive covenant document, subject to any intervening amendments or modifications, except to the extent modified by the recorded modification document.

(3) If the holder of an ownership interest of record in property causes to be recorded a modification document pursuant to this section that modifies or removes a restrictive covenant that is not authorized by this section, the county shall not incur liability for recording the document. The liability that may result from the unauthorized recordation shall be the sole responsibility of the holder of the ownership interest of record who caused the unauthorized recordation.

(4) A restrictive covenant that was originally invalidated by this section shall become and remain enforceable while the property subject to the restrictive covenant modification is utilized in any manner that violates the terms of the affordability restrictions required by this section.

(5) If the property is utilized in any manner that violates the terms of the affordability restrictions required by this section, the city or county may, after notice and an opportunity to be heard, record a notice of that violation. If the owner complies with the applicable affordability restrictions, the owner may apply to the agency of the city or county that recorded the notice of violation for a release of the notice of violation, and if approved by the city or county, a release of the notice of violation may be recorded.

(6) The county recorder may charge a standard recording fee to an owner who submits a modification document for recordation pursuant to this section.

(c)(1) Subject to paragraph (2), this section shall only apply to restrictive covenants that restrict the number, size, or location of the residences that may be built on a property or that restrict the number of persons or families who may reside on a property. This section does not apply to any other covenant, including, but not limited to, covenants that:

(A) Relate to purely aesthetic objective design standards, as long as the objective design standards are not applied in a manner that renders the affordable housing development infeasible.

(B) Provide for fees or assessments for the maintenance of common areas.

(C) Provide for limits on the amount of rent that may be charged to tenants.

(2) Paragraph (1) shall not apply to restrictive covenants, fees, and assessments that have not been consistently enforced or assessed prior to the construction of the affordable housing development.

(d)(1) Any suit filed by a party that is deemed to have been given notice as described in subparagraph (D) of paragraph (2) of subdivision (b), which challenges the validity of a restrictive covenant modification document pursuant to this section, shall be filed within 35 days of that notice.

(2) In any suit filed to enforce the rights provided in this section or defend against a suit filed against them, a prevailing owner of an affordable housing development, and any successors or assigns, or a holder of a conservation easement, shall be entitled to recover, as part of any judgment, litigation costs and reasonable attorney's fees, provided that any judgment entered shall be limited to those costs incurred after the modification document was recorded as provided by subdivision (b).

(3) This subdivision shall not prevent the court from awarding any prevailing party litigation costs and reasonable attorney's fees otherwise authorized by applicable law, including, but not limited to, subdivision (d) of Section 815.7 of the Civil Code.

(e) This section shall not be interpreted to modify, weaken, or invalidate existing laws protecting affordable and fair housing and prohibiting unlawful discrimination in the provision of housing, including, but not limited to, prohibitions on discrimination in, or resulting from, the enforcement of restrictive covenants.

(f)(1) Provided that the restrictions are otherwise compliant with all applicable laws, this section does not invalidate local building codes or other rules regulating either of the following:

(A) The number of persons who may reside in a dwelling.

(B) The size of a dwelling.

(2) This section shall not be interpreted to authorize any development that is not otherwise consistent with the local general plan, zoning ordinances, and any applicable specific plan that apply to the affordable housing development, including any requirements regarding the number of residential units, the size of residential units, and any other zoning restriction relevant to the affordable housing development.

(3) This section does not prevent an affordable housing development from receiving any bonus or incentive pursuant to any statute listed in Section 65582.1 of the Government Code or any related local ordinance.

(g)(1) Subject to paragraph (2), this section does not apply to:

(A) Any conservation easement, as defined in Section 815.1, that is recorded as required by Section 815.5, and held by any of the entities or organizations set forth in Section 815.3.

(B) Any interest in land comparable to a conservation easement that is held by any political subdivision and recorded in the office of the county recorder of the county where the land is situated.

(2) The exclusion from this section of conservation easements held by tax-exempt nonprofit organizations, as provided in subparagraph (A) of paragraph (1), applies only if the conservation easement satisfies one or more of the following:

(A) It was recorded in the office of the county recorder where the property is located before January 1, 2022.

(B) It is, as of the date of recordation of the conservation easement, held by a land trust or other entity that is accredited by the Land Trust Accreditation Commission, or any successor organization, or is a member of the California Council of Land Trusts, or any successor organization, and notice of that ownership is provided in the text of the recorded conservation easement document, or if that notice is not provided in the text of the recorded conservation easement document, the land trust or other entity provides documentation of that accreditation or membership within 30 days of receipt of either of the following:

(i) A written request for that documentation.

(ii) Any written notice of the intended modification of the conservation easement provided pursuant to paragraph (3).

(C) It was funded in whole or in part by a local, state, federal, or tribal government or was required by a local, state, federal, or tribal government as mitigation for, or as a condition of approval of, a project, and notice of that funding or mitigation requirement is provided in the text of the recorded conservation easement document.

(D) It is held by a land trust or other entity whose purpose is to conserve or protect indigenous cultural resources, and that purpose of the land trust or other entity is provided in the text of the recorded conservation easement document.

(E) It, as of the date of recordation of the conservation easement, burdens property that is located entirely outside the boundaries of any urbanized area or urban cluster, as designated by the United States Census Bureau.

(3)(A) At least 60 days before submission of a modification document modifying a conservation easement to a county recorder pursuant to subdivision (b), the owner of an affordable housing development shall provide written notice of the intended modification of any conservation easement to the parties to that conservation easement and any third-party beneficiaries or other entities that are entitled to receive notice of changes to or termination of the conservation easement with the notice being sent to the notice address of those parties as specified in the recorded conservation easement. The notice shall include a return mailing address of the owner of the affordable housing development, the approximate number, size, and location of intended structures to be built on the property for the purposes of affordable housing, and a copy of the intended modification document, and shall specify that it is being provided pursuant to this section.

(B) The county recorder shall not record any restrictive covenant modification document unless the county recorder has received confirmation from the county counsel that any notice required pursuant to subparagraph (A) was provided in accordance with subparagraph (A).

(h) This section shall not apply to any settlement, conservation agreement, or conservation easement, notice of which has been recorded, for which either of the following apply:

(1) It was entered into before January 1, 2022, and limits the density of or precludes development in order to mitigate for the environmental impacts of a proposed project or to resolve a dispute about the level of permitted development on the property.

(2) It was entered into after January 1, 2022, and limits the density of or precludes development where the settlement is approved by a court of competent jurisdiction and the court finds that the density limitation is for the express purpose of protecting the natural resource or open-space value of the property.

(i) The provisions of this section shall not apply to any recorded deed restriction, public access easement, or other similar covenant that was required by a state agency for the purpose of compliance with a state or federal law, provided that the recorded deed restriction, public access easement, or similar covenant contains notice within the recorded document, inclusive of its recorded exhibits, that it was recorded to satisfy a state agency requirement.

(j) For purposes of this section:

(1) "Affordable housing development" means a development located on the property that is the subject of the recorded restrictive covenant and that meets one of the following requirements:

(A) The property is subject to a recorded affordability restriction requiring 100 percent of the units, exclusive of a manager's unit or units, be made available at affordable rent to, and be occupied by, lower income households for 55 years for rental housing, unless a local ordinance or the terms of a federal, state, or local grant, tax credit, or other project financing requires, as a condition of the development of residential units, that the development include a certain percentage of units that are affordable to, and occupied by, low-income, lower income, very low income, or extremely low income households for a term that exceeds 55 years for rental housing units.

(B)(i) The property is owned or controlled by an entity or individual that has submitted a permit application to the relevant jurisdiction to develop a project that complies with subparagraph (A).

(ii) For purposes of this subparagraph:

(I) "Controlled" includes, without limitation, the right to acquire the property under an option agreement, purchase and sale agreement, or similar agreement.

(II) "Permit application" includes, without limitation, a building permit application, an application pursuant to Chapter 4.5 (commencing with Section 65920) of Division 1 of Title 7 of the Government Code, including a preliminary application pursuant to Section 65941.1 of the Government Code, an application for a zoning or general plan amendment, an application for a specific plan or amendment to a specific plan, a notice of intent or an application for development pursuant to Section 65913.4 of the Government Code, or an application for development pursuant to Section 65912.110 of the Government Code.

(2) "Affordable rent" shall have the same meaning as defined in Section 50053 of the Health and Safety Code.

(3) "Lower income households" shall have the same meaning as defined in Section 50079.5 of the Health and Safety Code.

(4) "Modification document" means a restrictive covenant modification document described in paragraph (1) of subdivision (b).

(5) "Owner" means any record title owner of the property, any beneficial owner of the property, or an entity or individual controlling the property for purposes of subparagraph (B) of paragraph (1).

(6) "Restrictive covenant" means any recorded covenant, condition, restriction, or limit on the use of private or publicly owned land contained in any deed, contract, security instrument, or other instrument affecting the transfer or sale of any interest that restricts the number, size, or location of the residences that may be built on the property or that restricts the number of persons or families who may reside on the property, as described in subdivision (a). **Leg.H.** Added Stats 2021 ch 349 §2 (AB 721), effective January 1, 2022. Amended Stats 2022 ch 28 §20 (SB 1380), effective January 1, 2023; Stats 2023 ch 750 §1 (AB 911), effective January 1, 2024.

§ 714.7. Sale of units constructed pursuant to a local inclusionary zoning ordinance; Penalty for violations; Requirements for a nonprofit housing corporation

(a) Notwithstanding any other provision of law, a developer shall not sell a unit constructed pursuant to a local inclusionary zoning ordinance that is intended for owner-occupancy by persons or families of extremely low, very low, low, or moderate income to a purchaser that is not a person or family of extremely low, very low, low, or moderate income, except that if such a unit has not been purchased by an income-qualifying person or family within 180 days of the issuance of the certificate of occupancy a developer may sell the unit to a qualified nonprofit housing corporation that will ensure owner occupancy pursuant to the income limitation recorded on the deed or other instrument defining the terms of conveyance eligibility.

(b) Every unit sold in a manner inconsistent with subdivision (a) shall constitute a violation of this section.

(c) A person who violates this section is subject to a civil penalty of not more than fifteen thousand dollars ($15,000) for each violation, which shall be assessed and recovered in a civil action brought in the name of the people of the State of California by the county counsel or city attorney for the jurisdiction in which the violation occurred in a court of competent jurisdiction. This subdivision shall be the exclusive enforcement mechanism used against violators of this section.

(d) For purposes of this section, a qualified nonprofit housing corporation means a nonprofit corporation that meets all of the following requirements:

(1) The nonprofit corporation has a determination letter from the Internal Revenue Service affirming its tax-exempt status pursuant to Section 501(c)(3) of the Internal Revenue Code and is not a private foundation as that term is defined in Section 509 of the Internal Revenue Code.

(2) The nonprofit corporation is based in California.

(3) All of the board members of the nonprofit corporation have their primary residence in California.

(4) The primary activity of the nonprofit corporation is the development and preservation of affordable home ownership housing in California. **Leg.H.** Added Stats 2023 ch 738 §1 (AB 323), effective January 1, 2024.

ARTICLE 3
Duration of Leases

Commencement period. §715.
Period of lease of land for agricultural purposes. §717.

Leases of town and city lots; Maximum term; Mineral lands; Tidelands and submerged lands. §718.
Period of lease of land for purpose of producing minerals, oil, or gas. §718f.
Conditions for longer lease of property owned by city. §719.

§715. Commencement period

A lease to commence at a time certain or upon the happening of a future event becomes invalid if its term does not actually commence in possession within 30 years after its execution. **Leg.H.** Added Stats 1991 ch 156 §3 (AB 1577).

Prior Law: Former §715, relating to perpetuities, was added Stats 1970 ch 789 §1, operative November 3, 1970, and repealed Stats 1991 ch 156 §2.

Former §715, relating to restraints upon alienation, was enacted 1872, amended Stats 1917 ch 539 §1, and repealed Stats 1951 ch 1463 §7.

§715.1. [Section repealed 1959]

Leg.H. Added Stats 1951 ch 1463 §1. Repealed Stats 1959 ch 470 §1. The repealed section related to suspension of power of alienation.

§715.2. [Section repealed 1991]

Leg.H. Added Stats 1951 ch 1463 §2. Repealed Stats 1991 ch 156 §4. See Prob C §§21201, 21205–21208, 21230.

§715.3. [Section repealed 1991]

Leg.H. Added Stats 1951 ch 1463 §3. Amended Stats 1959 ch 470 §2, ch 726 §1; Stats 1961 ch 71 §1. Repealed Stats 1991 ch 156 §5. See Prob C §21225.

§715.4. [Section repealed 1991]

Leg.H. Added Stats 1959 ch 1240 §1. Repealed Stats 1991 ch 156 §6. See Prob C §21225.

§715.5. [Section repealed 1991]

Leg.H. Added Stats 1963 ch 1455 §4. Repealed Stats 1991 ch 156 §7. See Prob C §21220.

§715.6. [Section repealed 1991]

Leg.H. Added Stats 1963 ch 1455 §5. Repealed Stats 1991 ch 156 §8. See Prob C §§21205–21207.

§715.7. [Section repealed 1991]

Leg.H. Added Stats 1963 ch 1455 §6. Repealed Stats 1991 ch 156 §9. See Prob C §21231.

§715.8. [Section repealed 1970]

Leg.H. Added Stats 1963 ch 1455 §7. Repealed Stats 1970 ch 45 §1.

§716. [Section repealed 1991]

Leg.H. Enacted 1872. Amended Stats 1951 ch 1463 §4; Stats 1959 ch 470 §3. Repealed Stats 1991 ch 156 §10. See Prob C §21211.

§716.5. [Section repealed 1991]

Leg.H. Added Stats 1986 ch 820 §1, operative July 1, 1987. Repealed Stats 1991 ch 156 §11. See Prob C §§15000 et seq., 15413, 15414.

§717. Period of lease of land for agricultural purposes

No lease or grant of land for agricultural or horticultural purposes for a longer period than 51 years, in which shall be reserved any rent or service of any kind, shall be valid. **Leg.H.** Enacted 1872. Amended Stats 1895 ch 82 §1; Stats 1909 ch 662 §1; Stats 1915 ch 176 §1; Stats 1963 ch 1906 §1.

§718. Leases of town and city lots; Maximum term; Mineral lands; Tidelands and submerged lands

No lease or grant of any town or city lot, which reserves any rent or service of any kind, and which provides for a leasing or granting period in excess of 99 years, shall be valid. The property owned by, or that held by, or under the management and control of, any municipality, or any department or board thereof, may be leased for a period not to exceed 55 years. The property of any municipality not acquired for park purposes may, for the purpose of producing, or effecting the production of minerals, oil, gas or other hydrocarbon substances, be leased for a period not to exceed 35 years. Any tidelands or submerged lands, granted to any city by the State of California, may be leased for a period not to exceed 66 years unless the grant from the state of the use thereof provides specifically the term for which said lands may be leased. Tidelands and submerged lands owned or controlled by any city, together with the wharves, docks, piers and other structures or improvements thereon, and so much of the uplands abutting thereon as, in the judgment of the city council, or other governing body, of said city, may be necessary for the proper development and use of its waterfront and harbor facilities, may be leased for a period not to exceed 66 years. Said tidelands, submerged lands and uplands may be so leased only for industrial uses, the improvement and development of any harbor, or harbors, of said city, the construction and maintenance of wharves, docks, piers or bulkhead piers, or any other public use or purpose consistent with the requirements of commerce or navigation at, or in, any such harbor or harbors. **Leg.H.** Enacted 1872. Amended Stats 1903 ch 210 §1; Stats 1911 ch 708 §1; Stats 1915 ch 176 §2; Stats 1917 ch 572 §1; Stats 1927 ch 689 §1; Stats 1929 ch 170 §1; Stats 1935 ch 695 §1; Stats 1941 ch 492 §1; Stats 1961 ch 2010 §1; Stats 1967 ch 228 §1.

§718a. [Section repealed 1949]

Leg.H. Added Stats 1947 ch 1161 §1. Repealed Stats 1949 ch 79 §2 (Gov C §500041). See Gov C §37388.

§718c. [Section repealed 1979]

Leg.H. Added Stats 1931 ch 999 §1. Amended Stats 1935 ch 167 §1; Stats 1937 ch 834 §1. Repealed Stats 1949 ch 79 §2 (Gov C §500041). Amended Stats 1949 ch 536 §10. Repealed Stats 1979 ch 373 §43. See Gov C §§37389–37392.

§§718d, 718e. [Sections repealed 1949]

Leg.H. Added Stats 1931 ch 999 §§2, 3. Repealed Stats 1949 ch 79 §2 (Gov C §500041). See Gov C §§37387, 37393.

§718f. Period of lease of land for purpose of producing minerals, oil, or gas

A lease of land for the purpose of effecting the production of minerals, oil, gas, or other hydrocarbon substances from other lands may be made for a period certain or determinable by any future event prescribed by the parties but no such lease shall be enforceable after 99 years from the commencement of the term thereof. **Leg.H.** Added Stats 1953 ch 1344 §1.

§719. Conditions for longer lease of property owned by city

Notwithstanding the 55-year limitation imposed by Section 718, property owned by, or held by, or under the management and control of, any city, or any department or board thereof, may be leased for a period which exceeds 55 years but does not exceed 99 years, if all of the following conditions are met:

(a) The lease shall be subject to periodic review by the city and shall take into consideration the then current market conditions. The local legislative body may, prior to final execution of the lease, establish the lease provisions which will periodically be reviewed, and determine when those provisions are to be reviewed.

(b) Any lease entered into by any city pursuant to this section shall be authorized by an ordinance adopted by the legislative body. The ordinance shall be subject to referendum in the manner prescribed by law for ordinances of cities.

(c) Prior to adopting an ordinance authorizing a lease, the legislative body shall hold a public hearing. Notice of the time and place of the hearing shall be published pursuant to Section 6066 of the Government Code, in one or more newspapers of general circulation within the city and shall be mailed to any person requesting special notice, to any present tenant of the public property, and to all owners of land adjoining the property.

(d) Any lease shall be awarded to the bidder which, in the determination of the legislative body, offers the greatest economic return to the city, after competitive bidding conducted in the manner determined by the legislative body. Notice inviting bids shall be published pursuant to Section 6066 in one or more newspapers of general circulation within the city.

(e) The provisions of subdivisions (b), (c), and (d) of this section do not apply to any charter city, which may utilize a procedure as specified by charter or adopted by ordinance in accordance with its charter.

(f) This section shall not apply to leases of property acquired for park purposes; to leases for the purpose of producing mineral, oil, gas, or other hydrocarbon substances; nor to leases of tidelands or submerged lands or improvements thereon. **Leg.H.** Added Stats 1983 ch 720 §1.

ARTICLE 4
Accumulations

Dispositions of income. §722.
Accumulations, when void. §723.

Rights; Limitations. §724.
Other directions, when void in part. §725.
Application of income to support of beneficiaries. §726.

§722. Dispositions of income

Dispositions of the income of property to accrue and to be received at any time subsequent to the execution of the instrument creating such disposition are governed by the rules relating to future interests. **Leg.H.** Enacted 1872. Amended Stats 1991 ch 156 §12 (AB 1577).

§723. Accumulations, when void

All directions for the accumulation of the income of property, except such as are allowed by this Title, are void. **Leg.H.** Enacted 1872.

§724. Rights; Limitations

(a) An accumulation of the income of property may be directed by any will, trust or transfer in writing sufficient to pass the property or create the trust out of which the fund is to arise, for the benefit of one or more persons, objects or purposes, but may not extend beyond the time permitted for the vesting of future interests.

(b) Notwithstanding subdivision (a), the income arising from real or personal property held in a trust forming part of a profit-sharing plan of an employer for the exclusive benefit of its employees or their beneficiaries or forming part of a retirement plan formed primarily for the purpose of providing benefits for employees on or after retirement may be permitted to accumulate until the fund is sufficient, in the opinion of the trustee or trustees, to accomplish the purposes of the trust. **Leg.H.** Enacted 1872. Amended Stats 1929 ch 143 §1; Stats 1959 ch 470 §4; Stats 1991 ch 156 §13 (AB 1577).

§725. Other directions, when void in part

If the direction for an accumulation of the income of property is for a longer term than is limited in the last section, the direction only, whether separable or not from the other provisions of the instrument, is void as respects the time beyond the limit prescribed in said last section, and no other part of such instrument is affected by the void portion of such direction. **Leg.H.** Enacted 1872. Amended Stats 1929 ch 143 §2.

§726. Application of income to support of beneficiaries

When one or more persons for whose benefit an accumulation of income has been directed is or are destitute of other sufficient means of support or education, the proper court, upon application, may direct a suitable sum to be applied thereto out of the fund directed to be accumulated for the benefit of such person or persons. **Leg.H.** Enacted 1872. Amended Stats 1929 ch 143 §3.

CHAPTER 2.5
PRINCIPAL AND INCOME LAW [REPEALED]

§730. [Section repealed 1987]

Leg.H. Added Stats 1967 ch 1508 §2, operative July 1, 1968. Repealed Stats 1986 ch 820 §2, operative July 1, 1987. See Prob C §§16320 et seq.

Prior Law: Former §730, similar to present Prob C §16320, was added Stats 1953 ch 137 §1 and repealed Stats 1967 ch 1508 §1, operative July 1, 1968.

§730a. [Section repealed 1987]

Leg.H. Added Stats 1967 ch 1508 §2, operative July 1, 1968. Repealed Stats 1986 ch 820 §2, operative July 1, 1987. The repealed section related to Personal Income Tax Law and Bank and Corporations Tax Law.

§730.01. [Section repealed 1987]

Leg.H. Added Stats 1967 ch 1508 §2, operative July 1, 1968. Repealed Stats 1986 ch 820 §2, operative July 1, 1984. See Prob C §§16301, 16321, 16325.

Prior Law: Former §730.01, relating to Personal Income Tax Law and Bank and Corporations Tax Law, was added Stats 1953 ch 37 §1 and repealed Stats 1967 ch 1508 §1, operative July 1, 1968.

§730.02. [Section repealed 1987]

Leg.H. Added Stats 1967 ch 1508 §2, operative July 1, 1968. Repealed Stats 1986 ch 820 §2, operative July 1, 1987. See Prob C §§16040, 16335.

Prior Law: Former §730.02, similar to present Prob C §15001, was added Stats 1953 ch 37 §1 and repealed Stats 1967 ch 1508 §1, operative July 1, 1968.

§730.03. [Section repealed 1987]

Leg.H. Added Stats 1967 ch 1508 §2, operative July 1, 1968. Repealed Stats 1986 ch 820 §2, operative July 1, 1987. See Prob C §§16371–16373.

Prior Law: Former §730.03, similar to present Prob C §§84, 16321, 16325, 16371–16373, was added Stats 1953 ch 37 §1 and repealed Stats 1967 ch 1508 §1, operative July 1, 1968.

§730.04. [Section repealed 1987]

Leg.H. Added Stats 1967 ch 1508 §2, operative July 1, 1968. Amended Stats 1968 ch 448 §1, effective July 1, 1968, operative July 1, 1968. Repealed Stats 1986 ch 820 §2, operative July 1, 1987. See Prob C §16341.

Prior Law: Former §730.04, relating to application of the chapter, was added Stats 1953 ch 37 §1 and repealed Stats 1967 ch 1508 §1, operative July 1, 1968.

§730.05. [Section repealed 1987]

Leg.H. Added Stats 1967 ch 1508 §2, operative July 1, 1968. Amended Stats 1968 ch 448 §2, effective July 1, 1968, operative July 1, 1968; Stats 1983 ch 842 §4, operative January 1, 1985. Repealed Stats 1986 ch 820 §2, operative July 1, 1987. See Prob C §16340.

Prior Law: Former §730.05, similar to present Prob C §§16371–16373, was added Stats 1953 ch 37 §1 and repealed Stats 1967 ch 1508 §1, operative July 1, 1968.

§730.06. [Section repealed 1987]

Leg.H. Added Stats 1967 ch 1508 §2, operative July 1, 1968. Repealed Stats 1986 ch 820 §2, operative July 1, 1987. See Prob C §16350.

Prior Law: Former §730.06, similar to present Prob C §§16340 et seq., was added Stats 1953 ch 37 §1 and repealed Stats 1968 ch 1508 §1, operative July 1, 1968.

§730.07. [Section repealed 1987]

Leg.H. Added Stats 1967 ch 1508 §2, operative July 1, 1968. Repealed Stats 1986 ch 820 §2, operative July 1, 1987. See Prob C §16357.

Prior Law: Former §730.07, similar to present Prob C §16350, was added Stats 1953 ch 37 §1, amended Stats 1967 ch 726 §1, and repealed Stats 1967 ch 1508 §1, operative July 1, 1968.

§730.08. [Section repealed 1987]

Leg.H. Added Stats 1967 ch 1508 §2, operative July 1, 1968. Amended Stats 1968 ch 448 §3, effective July 1, 1968, operative July 1, 1968. Repealed Stats 1986 ch 820 §2, operative July 1, 1987. See Prob C §§16350, 16352.

Prior Law: Former §730.08, similar to present Prob C §16357, was added Stats 1953 ch 37 §1 and repealed Stats 1967 ch 1508 §1, operative July 1, 1968.

§730.09. [Section repealed 1987]

Leg.H. Added Stats 1967 ch 1508 §2, operative July 1, 1968. Repealed Stats 1986 ch 820 §2, operative July 1, 1987. See Prob C §§16081, 16363, 16364.

Prior Law: Former §730.09, similar to present Prob C §§16350, 16352, was added Stats 1953 ch 37 §1 and repealed Stats 1967 ch 1508 §1, operative July 1, 1968.

§730.10. [Section repealed 1987]

Leg.H. Added Stats 1967 ch 1508 §2, operative July 1, 1968. Repealed Stats 1986 ch 820 §2, operative July 1, 1987. See Prob C §§16081, 16361, 16362, 16364.

Prior Law: Former §730.10, similar to present Prob C §§16350, 16352, was added Stats 1953 ch 37 §1 and repealed Stats 1967 ch 1508 §1, operative July 1, 1968.

§730.11. [Section repealed 1987]

Leg.H. Added Stats 1967 ch 1508 §2, operative July 1, 1968. Repealed Stats 1986 ch 820 §2, operative July 1, 1987. See Prob C §§16081, 16361, 16362, 16364.

Prior Law: Former §730.11, similar to present Prob C §§16081, 16350, 16352, 16361, 16362, 16364, was added Stats 1953 ch 37 §1 and repealed Stats 1967 ch 1508 §1, operative July 1, 1968.

§730.12. [Section repealed 1987]

Leg.H. Added Stats 1967 ch 1508 §2, operative July 1, 1968. Repealed Stats 1986 ch 820 §2, operative July 1, 1987. The repealed section related to underproductive property.

Prior Law: Former §730.12, similar to present Prob C §§16081, 16371–16373, was added Stats 1953 ch 37 §1 and repealed Stats 1967 ch 1508 §1, operative July 1, 1968.

§730.13. [Section repealed 1987]

Leg.H. Added Stats 1967 ch 1508 §2, operative July 1, 1968. Amended Stats 1968 ch 448 §4, effective July 1, 1968, operative July 1, 1968. Repealed Stats 1986 ch 820 §2, operative July 1, 1987. See Prob C §§16081, 16371–16373.

Prior Law: Former §730.13, relating to underproductive property, was added Stats 1953 ch 37 §1 and repealed Stats 1967 ch 1508 §1, operative July 1, 1968.

§730.14. [Section repealed 1987]

Leg.H. Added Stats 1967 ch 1508 §2, operative July 1, 1968. Repealed Stats 1986 ch 820 §2, operative July 1, 1987. See Prob C §§15001, 16372.

Prior Law: Former §730.14, relating to underproductive property, was added Stats 1953 ch 37 §1 and repealed Stats 1967 ch 1508 §1, operative July 1, 1968.

§730.15. [Section repealed 1987]

Leg.H. Added Stats 1967 ch 1508 §2, operative July 1, 1968. Repealed Stats 1986 ch 820 §2, operative July 1, 1987. See Prob C §15001.

Prior Law: Former §730.15, similar to present Prob C §§16081, 16371–16373, was added Stats 1953 ch 37 §1 and repealed Stats 1967 ch 1508 §1, operative July 1, 1968.

§730.16. [Section repealed 1987]

Leg.H. Added Stats 1967 ch 1508 §2, operative July 1, 1968. Repealed Stats 1986 ch 820 §2, operative July 1, 1987. The repealed section related to operative date of chapter.

Prior Law: Former §730.16, similar to present Prob C §§15001, 16372, was added Stats 1967 ch 776 §1 and repealed Stats 1967 ch 1508 §1, operative July 1, 1968.

§730.17. [Section repealed 1987]

Leg.H. Added Stats 1967 ch 1508 §2, operative July 1, 1968. Repealed Stats 1986 ch 820 §2, operative July 1, 1987. See Prob C §11.

CHAPTER 2.6
LEGAL ESTATES PRINCIPAL AND INCOME LAW

Citation of chapter. §731.
Chapter not to affect Personal Income Tax Law and Bank and Corporation Tax Law. §731.01.
Applicability of chapter. §731.02.
"Principal"; "Income"; "Tenant"; "Remainderman". §731.03.
Principal established without interposition of trust; Ascertainment of income and principal and apportionment of receipts and expenses; Direction of manner of ascertainment. §731.04.
Receipts deemed to be income; Receipts, deemed to be principal; Disposition of income after payment of expenses; Liability of principal for ultimate distribution. §731.05.
Cessation of tenant's right to income; Effect on payments. §731.06.
Corporate dividends, stock subscription rights, liquidated corporate assets; When deemed principal or income; Date of accrual of dividends; Distributions by investment company or trust; Reliance of tenant on statement as to source of dividends. §731.07.
Principal consisting of bonds or other obligations for payment of money; When deemed principal or income. §731.08.
Authorized use of principal in continuance of business; Net profits as income; Business consisting or not consisting of buying and selling property; Ascertainment of net profits in income; Increase in value deemed principal; Burden for losses. §731.09.
Principal consisting of animals employed in business; Determination of whether principal or income. §731.10.
Principal consisting of property in land from which timber may be taken; Determination of proceeds as income or principal; Application of section to tenant developing resources for own benefit. §731.11.
Principal consisting of property subject to depletion; When rents deemed income to tenant; When deemed part income and remainder principal. §731.12.
Principal consisting of realty or personalty failing to produce certain average net income; Tenant under duty to change form of investment; Extent tenant to share in net proceeds; Provisions governing determination and disposition; Apportionment to successive tenants. §731.13.
Principal consisting of obligation for payment secured by mortgage, etc.; When property treated as single substituted asset; Apportionment of proceeds of sale; Credit of gain or profit as income or principal; Apportionment between successive tenants; What constitutes cost price of property. §731.14.
Ordinary expenses to be paid out of income; Exception; Source for payment of attorneys' fees and taxes levied upon profit or gain deemed income. §731.15.

§731. Citation of chapter

This chapter may be cited as the Legal Estates Principal and Income Law. **Leg.H.** Added Stats 1968 ch 193 §1, effective May 28, 1968, operative July 1, 1968.

§731.01. Chapter not to affect Personal Income Tax Law and Bank and Corporation Tax Law

Nothing in this chapter shall affect the provisions of the Personal Income Tax Law and the Bank and Corporation Tax Law. **Leg.H.** Added Stats 1968 ch 193 §1, effective May 28, 1968, operative July 1, 1968.

§731.02. Applicability of chapter

This chapter shall apply to all transactions by which a principal was established without the interposition of a trust on or after September 13, 1941, or is hereafter so established. Transactions by which a principal is held in trust are governed by Chapter 3 (commencing with Section 16300) of Part 4 of Division 9 of the Probate Code. **Leg.H.** Added Stats 1968 ch 193 §1, effective May 28, 1968, operative July 1, 1968. Amended Stats 1986 ch 820 §3, operative July 1, 1987.

§731.03. "Principal"; "Income"; "Tenant"; "Remainderman"

(a) "Principal" as used in this chapter means any realty or personalty which has been so set aside or limited by the owner thereof or a person thereto legally empowered that it and any substitutions for it are eventually to be conveyed, delivered, or paid to a person, while the return therefrom or use thereof or any part of such return or use is in the meantime to be taken or received by or held for accumulation for the same or another person;

(b) "Income" as used in this chapter means the return derived from principal;

(c) "Tenant" as used in this chapter means the person to whom income is presently or currently payable, or for whom it is accumulated or who is entitled to the beneficial use of the principal presently and for a time prior to its distribution;

(d) "Remainderman" as used in this chapter means the person ultimately entitled to the principal, whether named or designated by the terms of the transaction by which the principal was established or determined by operation of law. **Leg.H.** Added Stats 1968 ch 193 §1, effective May 28, 1968, operative July 1, 1968.

§731.04. Principal established without interposition of trust; Ascertainment of income and principal and apportionment of receipts and expenses; Direction of manner of ascertainment

This chapter shall govern the ascertainment of income and principal and the apportionment of receipts and expenses between tenants and remaindermen in all cases where a principal has been established without the interposition of a trust, except that in the establishment of the principal, provision may be made touching all matters covered by this chapter, and the person establishing the principal may himself direct the manner of ascertainment of income and principal and the apportionment of receipts and expenses or grant discretion to the tenant or other person to do so, and such provision and direction, where not otherwise contrary to law shall control notwithstanding this chapter. The exercise by the tenant or other designated person, of such discretionary power if in good faith and according to his best judgment, shall be conclusive, irrespective of whether it may be in accordance with the determination which the court having jurisdiction would have made. **Leg.H.** Added Stats 1968 ch 193 §1, effective May 28, 1968, operative July 1, 1968.

§731.05. Receipts deemed to be income; Receipts, deemed to be principal; Disposition of income after payment of expenses; Liability of principal for ultimate distribution

(a) All receipts of money or other property paid or delivered as rent of realty or hire of personalty, or interest on money loaned, or interest on or the rental or use value of property wrongfully withheld or tortiously damaged or otherwise in return for the use of principal, shall be deemed income unless otherwise expressly provided in this chapter. Dividends on corporate shares, payable in stock or otherwise, shall be deemed income except as provided in Section 731.07.

(b) All receipts of money or other property paid or delivered as the consideration for the sale or other transfer, not a leasing or letting, of property forming a part of principal, or as a repayment of loans, or in liquidation of the assets of a corporation, or as the proceeds of property taken on eminent domain proceedings where separate awards to tenant and remainderman are not made, or as proceeds of insurance upon property forming a part of the principal except where such insurance has been issued for the benefit of either tenant or remainderman alone, or otherwise as a refund or replacement or change in form of principal, shall be deemed principal unless otherwise expressly provided in this chapter. Any profit or loss resulting upon any change in form of principal shall inure to or fall upon principal, except in the case of property referred to and defined by Section 731.14, in which case the provisions of Section 731.14 shall govern.

(c) All income, after payment of expenses properly chargeable to it, shall be paid and delivered to the tenant or retained by him if already in his possession or held for accumulation where legally so directed by the terms of the transaction by which the principal was established; while the principal shall be held for ultimate distribution as determined by the terms of the transaction by which it was established or by law, except in the case of property referred to and defined by Section 731.14, in which case the provisions of Section 731.14 shall govern. **Leg.H.** Added Stats 1968 ch 193 §1, effective May 28, 1968, operative July 1, 1968.

§731.06. Cessation of tenant's right to income; Effect on payments

Whenever a tenant's right to income shall cease by death, or in any other manner, all payments theretofore actually paid to the tenant shall belong to the tenant or to his personal representative; all income actually received after such termination shall be paid to the person next entitled to income by the terms of the transaction by which the principal was established. **Leg.H.** Added Stats 1968 ch 193 §1, effective May 28, 1968, operative July 1, 1968.

§731.07. Corporate dividends, stock subscription rights, liquidated corporate assets; When deemed principal or income; Date of accrual of dividends; Distributions by investment company or trust; Reliance of tenant on statement as to source of dividends

(a) All dividends on shares of a corporation forming a part of the principal which are payable

(1) In shares of the declaring corporation of the same kind and rank as the shares on which such dividend is paid; and

(2) In shares of the declaring corporation of a different kind or rank to the extent that they represent a capitalization of surplus not derived from earnings, shall be deemed principal.

Subject to the provisions of this section, all dividends, other than those awarded to principal under (1) and (2) above, including ordinary and extraordinary dividends and dividends payable in shares or other securities or obligations of corporations other than the declaring corporation, shall be deemed income.

Where the tenant shall have the option of receiving a dividend either in cash or in the shares of the declaring corporation, it shall be considered as a cash dividend and deemed income, irrespective of the choice made by the tenant except as provided in subdivision (f) of this section.

(b) All rights to subscribe to the shares or other securities or obligations of a corporation accruing on account of the ownership of shares or other securities in such corporation, and the proceeds of any sale of such rights, shall be deemed principal. All rights to subscribe to the shares or other securities or obligations of a corporation accruing on account of the ownership of shares or other securities in another corporation, and the proceeds of any sale of such rights shall be deemed income.

(c) Where the assets of a corporation are liquidated, amounts paid upon corporate shares as cash dividends declared before such liquidation occurred or as arrears of preferred or guaranteed dividends shall be deemed income; all other amounts paid upon corporate shares on disbursement of the corporate assets to the stockholders shall be deemed principal. All disbursements of corporate assets to the stockholders, whenever made, which are designated by the corporation as a return of capital or division of corporate property shall be deemed principal.

(d) Where a corporation succeeds another by merger, consolidation, or reorganization or otherwise acquires its assets, and the corporate shares of the succeeding corporation are issued to the shareholders of the original corporation in like proportion to, or in substitution for, their shares of the original corporation, the two corporations shall be considered a single corporation in applying the provisions of this section. But, two corporations shall not be considered a single corporation under this section merely because one owns corporate shares of or otherwise controls or directs the other.

(e) In applying this section the date when a dividend accrues to the person who is entitled to it shall be held to be the date specified by the corporation as the one on which the stockholders entitled thereto are determined, or in default thereof the date of declaration of the dividend.

(f) Distributions made from ordinary income by a regulated investment company or by a trust qualifying and electing to be taxed under federal law as a real estate investment trust are income. All other distributions made by the company or trust, including distributions from capital gains, depreciation, or depletion, whether in the form of cash or an option to take new stock or cash or an option to purchase additional shares, are principal.

(g) The tenant may rely upon the statement of the paying corporation as to whether dividends are paid from profits or earnings or are a return of capital or division of corporate property, and as to any other fact, relevant under any provision of this chapter, concerning the source or character of dividends or disbursements of corporate assets. **Leg.H.** Added Stats 1968 ch 193 §1, effective May 28, 1968, operative July 1, 1968.

§731.08. Principal consisting of bonds or other obligations for payment of money; When deemed principal or income

Where any part of the principal consists of bonds or other obligations for the payment of money, they shall be deemed principal at their inventory value as fixed by the appraiser or appraisers regularly appointed by the court, or, in default thereof, at their market value at the time the principal was established, or at their cost where purchased later, regardless of their par or maturity value; and upon their respective maturities or upon their sale or other disposition any loss or gain realized thereon shall fall upon or inure to the principal, except in the case of property referred to and defined by Section 731.14, in which case the provisions of Section 731.14 shall govern. Where any part of the principal consists of a bond or other obligation for the payment of money, bearing no stated interest but redeemable at maturity or a future time at an amount in excess of the amount in consideration of which it was issued, such accretion, as when realized, shall inure to income. **Leg.H.** Added Stats 1968 ch 193 §1, effective May 28, 1968, operative July 1, 1968.

§731.09. Authorized use of principal in continuance of business; Net profits as income; Business consisting or not consisting of buying and selling property; Ascertainment of net profits in income; Increase in value deemed principal; Burden for losses

(a) Whenever a tenant is authorized by the terms of the transaction by which the principal was established or by law, to use any part of the principal in the continuance of a business which the original owner of the property comprising the principal had been carrying on, the net profits of such business attributable to such principal shall be deemed income.

(b) Where such business consists of buying and selling property, the net profits for any period shall be ascertained by deducting from the gross returns during, and the inventory value of the property at the end of, such period, the expenses during, and the inventory value of the property at the beginning of, such period.

(c) Where such business does not consist of buying and selling property, the net income shall be computed in accordance with the customary practice of such business, but not in such way as to decrease the principal.

(d) Any increase in the value of the principal used in such business shall be deemed principal, and all losses in any one calendar year, after the income from such business for that year has been exhausted, shall fall upon principal. **Leg.H.** Added Stats 1968 ch 193 §1, effective May 28, 1968, operative July 1, 1968.

§731.10. Principal consisting of animals employed in business; Determination of whether principal or income

Where any part of the principal consists of animals employed in business, the provisions of Section 731.09 shall apply; and in other cases where the animals are held as a part of the principal partly or wholly because of the offspring or increase which they are expected to produce, all offspring or increase shall be deemed principal to the extent necessary to maintain the original number of such animals and the remainder shall be deemed income; and in all other cases such offspring or increase shall be deemed income. **Leg.H.** Added Stats 1968 ch 193 §1, effective May 28, 1968, operative July 1, 1968.

§731.11. Principal consisting of property in land from which timber may be taken; Determination of proceeds as income or principal; Application of section to tenant developing resources for own benefit

(a) Where any part of the principal consists of property in lands from which may be taken timber, minerals, oils, gas, or other natural resources, and the tenant in possession is not under a duty to change the form of the investment of the principal, or (the duty to change the form of the investment being absent) is authorized by law or by the terms of the transaction by which the principal was established, to lease or otherwise develop such natural resources, and no provision is made for the disposition of the net proceeds thereof after the payment of expenses and carrying charges on such property, such proceeds shall be deemed income, whether received as rent or bonus on a lease or as a consideration, by way of royalties or otherwise for the permanent severance of such natural resources from the lands. A duty to change the form of the investment shall be negatived, and authority to develop such natural resources shall be deemed to exist (not excluding other cases where appropriate intent is manifested) where: (1) the resources or the right to exploit them is specifically devised or granted, or (2) where development or exploitation of the resources had begun prior to the transaction by which the principal was established, or (3) where by the terms of that transaction a general authority to lease or otherwise develop is conferred, or (4) where the lands are directed to be retained. The fact that such property received upon creation of the principal does not fall within the category of investments which the tenant or a trustee would be authorized to make under the law or the terms of the particular instrument by which the principal is established, nor the conferring of a mere authority, as distinguished from a direction, to sell such property, shall not be deemed to evidence an intent that the form of the investment shall be changed.

(b) Where any part of the principal consists of property in lands containing such natural resources, and the conditions under which the proceeds thereof become income shall not exist, then in the absence of the expression of contrary intent in the terms of the transaction by which the principal was established, all such proceeds from such resources, not in excess of 5 percent per annum of the inventory value of such resources as fixed by the appraiser or appraisers regularly appointed by the court, or in default thereof their fair market value at the time the principal was established, or their cost if acquired later, shall be deemed income and the remainder principal.

(c) Nothing in this section shall be construed to abrogate or extend any right which may otherwise have accrued by law to a tenant to develop or work such natural resources for his own benefit. **Leg.H.** Added Stats 1968 ch 193 §1, effective May 28, 1968, operative July 1, 1968.

§731.12. Principal consisting of property subject to depletion; When rents deemed income to tenant; When deemed part income and remainder principal

Where any part of the principal consists of property subject to depletion, such as leaseholds, patents, copyrights, and royalty rights, and the tenant in possession is not under a duty to change the form of the investment of the principal, the full amount of rents, royalties, or income from the property shall be income to the tenant; but where the tenant is under a duty to change the form of the investment, either at once or as soon as a reasonable price, not representing an undue sacrifice of value, may be obtained, then the rents, royalties or income from such property not in excess of 5 percent per annum of its inventory value as fixed by the appraiser or appraisers regularly appointed by the court, or in default thereof its market value at the time the principal was established or at its cost where purchased later, shall be deemed income and the remainder principal. **Leg.H.** Added Stats 1968 ch 193 §1, effective May 28, 1968, operative July 1, 1968.

§731.13. Principal consisting of realty or personalty failing to produce certain average net income; Tenant under duty to change form of investment; Extent tenant to share in net proceeds; Provisions governing determination and disposition; Apportionment to successive tenants

(a) Where any part of a principal in the possession of a tenant consists of realty or personalty which for more than a year and until disposed of as hereinafter stated has not produced an average net income of at least 1 percent per annum of its inventory value as fixed by the appraiser or appraisers regularly appointed by the court, or in default thereof its market value at the time the principal was established or of its cost where purchased or otherwise acquired later, and the tenant is under a duty to change the form of the investment as soon as a reasonable price, not representing an undue sacrifice of value, may be obtained and such change is delayed, but is made before the principal is finally distributed, then the tenant shall be entitled to share in the net proceeds received from the property as delayed income to the extent hereinafter stated.

(b) Such income shall be the difference between the net proceeds received from the property and the amount which, had it been placed at simple interest at the rate of 5 percent per annum for the period during which the change was delayed, would have produced the net proceeds at the time of change, but in no event shall such income be more than the amount by which the net proceeds exceed the inventory value of the property as fixed by the appraiser or appraisers regularly appointed by the court, or in default thereof its market value at the time the principal was established or its cost where purchased later. The net proceeds shall consist of the gross proceeds received from the property less any expenses incurred in disposing of it and less all carrying charges which have been paid out of principal during the period while it has been unproductive.

(c) The change shall be taken to have been delayed from the time when the duty to make it first arose, which shall be presumed in the absence of evidence to the contrary, to be one year after the tenant first received the property if then unproductive, otherwise one year after it became unproductive.

(d) If the tenant has received any income from the property or has had any beneficial use thereof during the period while the change has been delayed, his share of the delayed income shall be reduced by the amount of such income received or the value of the use had.

(e) As between successive tenants, or a tenant and a remainderman, delayed income shall be apportioned in the same manner as provided for income by Section 731.06. **Leg.H.** Added Stats 1968 ch 193 §1, effective May 28, 1968, operative July 1, 1968.

§731.14. Principal consisting of obligation for payment secured by mortgage, etc.; When property treated as single substituted asset; Apportionment of proceeds of sale; Credit of gain or profit as income or principal; Apportionment between successive tenants; What constitutes cost price of property

(a) Where any part of the principal in possession of the tenant consists of an obligation for the payment of money secured by a mortgage or other hypothecation of real or personal property, and by reason of the enforcement of such obligation or by agreement in lieu of enforcement the tenant acquires any property, real or personal, of whatsoever kind, including a money judgment, such property shall be treated as a single substituted asset, and thereafter all income therefrom, expenses incident thereto and proceeds received upon sale, satisfaction, or transfer thereof, not a leasing or letting, excepting gain or profit on such sale, satisfaction or transfer, shall be apportioned in the same manner as provided by this chapter for property of like character acquired by purchase or held as a part of the estate at the time the principal was established.

Gain or profit realized on sale, satisfaction, or transfer, not a leasing or a letting, of property referred to in this section shall be credited to the income in an amount up to, but not exceeding, the accrued unpaid interest on the original obligation secured by such property as of the date of its acquisition by enforcement of the obligation or agreement in lieu thereof, and the balance shall be credited to principal. Such credit to income on account of accrued interest shall be in addition to any and all other credits due income by the terms of any other section of this chapter. Should any portion of such credit to income on account of accrued interest be in a form other than cash, then, and in that event, the full amount of such credit to income shall be paid first out of any sums received from the conversion of such asset into cash whether by payment, sale, or transfer before any sums so received shall be paid to principal.

As between successive tenants or a tenant and a remainderman, all sums paid hereunder on account of accrued interest shall be apportioned in the same manner as provided for income by Section 731.06.

The cost price of the property shall be the unpaid balance of the principal sum of the debt secured by such property, plus all sums whenever paid on any of the following items:

(1) All costs, charges, and expenses incident to the acquisition of such property;

(2) All taxes, bonds, and assessments, or any of them, which were payable at the date of the acquisition of such property by the tenant, excepting, however, interest accruing thereon from the date of the acquisition of such property by the tenant; and all such sums shall be a charge against the principal.

(b) Upon the sale, surrender, or other disposition of a bond, debenture, note, or other evidence of an indebtedness, voluntarily created, or of a certificate of deposit evidencing the deposit of any such instrument with a protective or reorganization committee, or of stock or other security received through participation in the enforcement of such obligation or the foreclosure of the security therefor, upon which bond or other obligation there is overdue unpaid interest which accrued after the establishment of the principal, the proceeds realized upon such sale, surrender, or other disposition, after repayment (1) of expenses incurred in connection therewith and (2) of any sums paid to protect or preserve such security, shall be divided pro rata between income and principal, computing interest at the rate specified in such obligation. The amount allocable to income shall in no case exceed the interest accrued and unpaid on the original obligation up to the time of such sale or other disposition or, where another security has been received in lieu of the original obligation, the income which would have accrued on the latter up to such time, less income received from the original or the substituted security. The terms sale, surrender, or other disposition, as above used, shall include compromise, settlement, accord and satisfaction, and similar arrangements. **Leg.H.** Added Stats 1968 ch 193 §1, effective May 28, 1968, operative July 1, 1968.

§731.15. Ordinary expenses to be paid out of income; Exception; Source for payment of attorneys' fees and taxes levied upon profit or gain deemed income

(a) All ordinary expenses incurred in connection with the principal or with its administration and management, including regularly recurring taxes assessed against any portion of the principal, water rates, premiums on insurance taken upon the estates of both tenant and remainderman, interest on mortgages on the principal, ordinary repairs, compensation of assistants and court costs on regular accountings, except attorneys' fees, shall be paid out of income. But such expenses where incurred in disposing of, or as carrying charges on, unproductive property as defined in Section 731.13, shall be paid out of principal, subject to the provisions of subdivision (b) of Section 731.13. Attorneys' fees for ordinary or current services shall be paid one-half out of income; one-half out of principal or in such other proportion as the court may direct.

(b) Attorneys' fees and other costs incurred in maintaining or defending any action to protect the property or assure the title thereof, unless due to the fault or cause of the tenant, costs of, or assessments for, improvements to property forming part of the principal, brokers' commissions, title charges, and other costs incurred in connection with purchasing, selling, or leasing property, or investing or reinvesting principal, and all other expenses, except as specified in subdivision (a) of this section, shall be paid out of principal. Any tax levied by any authority, federal, state, or foreign, upon profit or gain defined under the terms of subdivision (b) of Section 731.05 shall be paid out of principal, notwithstanding such tax may be denominated a tax upon income by the taxing authority. **Leg.H.** Added Stats 1968 ch 193 §1, effective May 28, 1968, operative July 1, 1968.

CHAPTER 3
RIGHTS OF OWNERS

Increase of property. §732.
In certain cases who entitled to income of property. §733.

§732. Increase of property

The owner of a thing owns also all its products and accessions. **Leg.H.** Enacted 1872.

§733. In certain cases who entitled to income of property

When, in consequence of a valid limitation of a future interest, there is a suspension of the power of alienation or of the ownership during the continuation of which the income is undisposed of, and no valid direction for its accumulation is given, such income belongs to the persons presumptively entitled to the next eventual interest. **Leg.H.** Enacted 1872.

§734. [Section repealed 1949]

Leg.H. Added Stats 1935 ch 476 §1. Repealed Stats 1949 ch 79 §2 (Gov C §500041). See Gov C §37359.

CHAPTER 4
TERMINATION OF OWNERSHIP

Future interests, when defeated. §739.
Same. §740.
Future interests, when not defeated. §741.
Same. §742.

§739. Future interests, when defeated

A future interest, depending on the contingency of the death of any person without successors, heirs, issue, or children, is defeated by the birth of a posthumous child of such person, capable of taking by succession. **Leg.H.** Enacted 1872.

§740. Same

A future interest may be defeated in any manner or by any act or means which the party creating such interest provided for or authorized in the creation thereof; nor is a future interest, thus liable to be defeated, to be on that ground adjudged void in its creation. **Leg.H.** Enacted 1872.

§741. Future interests, when not defeated

No future interest can be defeated or barred by any alienation or other act of the owner of the intermediate or precedent interest, nor by any destruction of such precedent interest by forfeiture, surrender, merger, or otherwise, except as provided by the next section, or where a forfeiture is imposed by statute as a penalty for the violation thereof. **Leg.H.** Enacted 1872.

§742. Same

No future interest, valid in its creation, is defeated by the determination of the precedent interest before the happening of the contingency on which the future interest is limited to take effect; but should such contingency afterwards happen, the future interest takes effect in the same manner and to the same extent as if the precedent interest had continued to the same period. **Leg.H.** Enacted 1872.

TITLE 3
GENERAL DEFINITIONS

Income. §748.
Time of creation. §749.

§748. Income

The income of property, as the term is used in this part of the code, includes the rents and profits of real property, the interest of money, dividends upon stock, and other produce of personal property. **Leg.H.** Enacted 1872.

§749. Time of creation

The delivery of the grant, where a limitation, condition, or future interest is created by grant, and the death of the testator, where it is created by will, is to be deemed the time of the creation of the limitation, condition, or interest, within the meaning of this part of the code. **Leg.H.** Enacted 1872.

PART 2
REAL OR IMMOVABLE PROPERTY

Title 1. General Provisions.
Title 2. Estates in Real Property.
Title 3. Rights and Obligations of Owners.
Title 5. Marketable Record Title.
Title 6. Rent Skimming.
Title 7. Requirements for Actions for Construction Defects.

TITLE 1
GENERAL PROVISIONS

Real property, how governed. §755.

§755. Real property, how governed
Real property within this State is governed by the laws of this State, except where the title is in the United States. **Leg.H.** Enacted 1872. Amended Code Amdts 1873–74 ch 612 §102.

TITLE 2
ESTATES IN REAL PROPERTY

Chapter 1. Estates in General.
Chapter 2. Termination of Estates.
Chapter 2.5. Mobilehome Residency Law.
Chapter 2.6. Recreational Vehicle Park Occupancy Law.
Chapter 2.7. Floating Home Residency Law.
Chapter 3. Servitudes.
Chapter 4. Conservation Easements.
Chapter 4.5. Greenway Easements.
Chapter 5. Housing Cooperatives and Housing Cooperative Trusts.

CHAPTER 1
ESTATES IN GENERAL

Enumeration of estates. §761.
What estate a fee simple. §762.
Conditional fees and estates tail abolished. §763.
Certain remainders valid. §764.
Freeholds; Chattels real; Chattel interests. §765.
Estates for life of a third person, when a freehold, etc. §766.
Future estates, what. §767.
Reversions. §768.
Remainders. §769.
Remainders, future and contingent estates, how created. §773.
Remainder upon a contingency. §778.
Heirs of tenant for life, when to take as purchasers. §779.
Construction of certain remainders. §780.
Effect of power of appointment. §781.
Provision in deed of real property. §782.
Revision of instrument to omit provision for restriction as to race or color or any other prohibited basis. §782.5.
"Condominium". §783.
Separate and correlative interests as interests in real property. §783.1.
"Restriction". §784.

§761. Enumeration of estates
Estates in real property, in respect to the duration of their enjoyment, are either:
1. Estates of inheritance or perpetual estates;
2. Estates for life;
3. Estates for years; or
4. Estates at will. **Leg.H.** Enacted 1872.

§762. What estate a fee simple
Every estate of inheritance is a fee, and every such estate, when not defeasible or conditional, is a fee simple or an absolute fee. **Leg.H.** Enacted 1872. Amended Code Amdts 1873–74 ch 612 §103.

§763. Conditional fees and estates tail abolished
Estates tail are abolished, and every estate which would be at common law adjudged to be a fee tail is a fee simple; and if no valid remainder is limited thereon, is a fee simple absolute. **Leg.H.** Enacted 1872.

§764. Certain remainders valid
Where a remainder in fee is limited upon any estate, which would by the common law be adjudged a fee tail, such remainder is valid as a contingent limitation upon a fee, and vests in possession on the death of the first taker, without issue living at the time of his death. **Leg.H.** Enacted 1872.

§765. Freeholds; Chattels real; Chattel interests
Estates of inheritance and for life are called estates of freehold; estates for years are chattels real; and estates at will are chattel interests, but are not subject to enforcement of a money judgment. **Leg.H.** Enacted 1872. Amended Stats 1982 ch 497 §2, operative July 1, 1983.

§766. Estates for life of a third person, when a freehold, etc.
An estate during the life of a third person, whether limited to heirs or otherwise, is a freehold. **Leg.H.** Enacted 1872. Amended Code Amdts 1873–74 ch 612 §104.

§767. Future estates, what
A future estate may be limited by the act of the party to commence in possession at a future day, either without the intervention of a precedent estate, or on the termination, by lapse of time or otherwise, of a precedent estate created at the same time. **Leg.H.** Enacted 1872.

§768. Reversions
A reversion is the residue of an estate left by operation of law in the grantor or his successors, or in the successors of a testator, commencing in possession on the determination of a particular estate granted or devised. **Leg.H.** Enacted 1872.

§769. Remainders
When a future estate, other than a reversion, is dependent on a precedent estate, it may be called a remainder, and may be created and transferred by that name. **Leg.H.** Enacted 1872.

§770. [Section repealed 1959]
Leg.H. Enacted 1872. Amended Code Amdts 1873–74 ch 612 §105. Repealed Stats 1959 ch 470 §5.

§771. [Section repealed 1987]
Leg.H. Added Stats 1959 ch 470 §6. Repealed Stats 1986 ch 820 §4, operative July 1, 1987. See CC §716.5.

Prior Law: Former §771, relating to suspension by trust, was enacted 1872, amended Stats 1951 ch 1463 §5, and repealed Stats 1959 ch 470 §5.

§772. [Section repealed 1951]
Leg.H. Enacted 1872. Repealed Stats 1951 ch 1463 §7. See CC §715.2.

§773. Remainders, future and contingent estates, how created
Subject to the rules of this title, and of Part 1 of this division, a freehold estate, as well as a chattel real, may be created to commence at a future day; an estate for life may be created in a term of years, and a remainder limited thereon; a remainder of a freehold or chattel real, either contingent or vested, may be created, expectant on the determination of a term of years; and a fee may be limited on a fee, upon a contingency, which, if it should occur, must happen within the period prescribed by the statutory rule against perpetuities in Article 2 (commencing with Section 21205) of Chapter 1 of Part 2 of Division 11 of the Probate Code. **Leg.H.** Enacted 1872. Amended Stats 1951 ch 1463 §6; Stats 1991 ch 156 §14 (AB 1577).

§§774, 775. [Sections repealed 1959]
Leg.H. Enacted 1872. Amended Code Amdts 1873–74 ch 612 §§106, 107. Repealed Stats 1959 ch 470 §7.

§776. [Section repealed 1951]
Leg.H. Enacted 1872. Repealed Stats 1951 ch 1463 §7.

§777. [Section repealed 1959]
Leg.H. Enacted 1872. Repealed Stats 1959 ch 470 §7.

§778. Remainder upon a contingency
A remainder may be limited on a contingency which, in case it should happen, will operate to abridge or determine the precedent estate; and

every such remainder is to be deemed a conditional limitation. **Leg.H.** Enacted 1872.

§779. Heirs of tenant for life, when to take as purchasers

When a remainder is limited to the heirs, or heirs of the body, of a person to whom a life estate in the same property is given, the persons who, on the termination of the life estate, are the successors or heirs of the body of the owner for life, are entitled to take by virtue of the remainder so limited to them, and not as mere successors of the owner for life. **Leg.H.** Enacted 1872.

§780. Construction of certain remainders

When a remainder on an estate for life or for years is not limited on a contingency defeating or avoiding such precedent estate, it is to be deemed intended to take effect only on the death of the first taker, or the expiration, by lapse of time, of such term of years. **Leg.H.** Enacted 1872.

§781. Effect of power of appointment

A general or special power of appointment does not prevent the vesting of a future estate limited to take effect in case such power is not executed. **Leg.H.** Enacted 1872.

§782. Provision in deed of real property

(a) Any provision in any deed of real property in California, whether executed before or after the effective date of this section, that purports to restrict the right of any persons to sell, lease, rent, use, or occupy the property to persons having any characteristic listed in subdivision (a) or (d) of Section 12955 of the Government Code, as those bases are defined in Sections 12926, 12926.1, subdivision (m) and paragraph (1) of subdivision (p) of Section 12955 and Section 12955.2 of the Government Code, by providing for payment of a penalty, forfeiture, reverter, or otherwise, is void.

(b) Notwithstanding subdivision (a), with respect to familial status, subdivision (a) shall not be construed to apply to housing for older persons, as defined in Section 12955.9 of the Government Code. With respect to familial status, nothing in subdivision (a) shall be construed to affect Sections 51.2, 51.3, 51.4, 51.10, 51.11, and 799.5 of this code, relating to housing for senior citizens. Subdivision (d) of Section 51, Section 4760, and Section 6714 of this code, and subdivisions (n), (o), and (p) of Section 12955 of the Government Code shall apply to subdivision (a). **Leg.H.** Added Stats 1961 ch 1078 §1. Amended Stats 1965 ch 283 §2; Stats 2006 ch 578 §4 (AB 2800), effective January 1, 2007; Stats 2012 ch 181 §22 (AB 806), effective January 1, 2013, operative January 1, 2014; Stats 2013 ch 605 §10 (SB 752), effective January 1, 2014.

2006 Note: This act shall be known, and may be cited, as the Civil Rights Housing Act of 2006. Stats 2006 ch 578 (AB 2800) §1.

§782.5. Revision of instrument to omit provision for restriction as to race or color or any other prohibited basis

(a) Any deed or other written instrument that relates to title to real property, or any written covenant, condition, or restriction annexed or made a part of, by reference or otherwise, any deed or instrument that relates to title to real property, which contains any provision that purports to forbid, restrict, or condition the right of any person or persons to sell, buy, lease, rent, use, or occupy the property on account of any basis listed in subdivision (a) or (d) of Section 12955 of the Government Code, as those bases are defined in Sections 12926, 12926.1, subdivision (m) and paragraph (1) of subdivision (p) of Section 12955, and Section 12955.2 of the Government Code, with respect to any person or persons, shall be deemed to be revised to omit that provision.

(b) Notwithstanding subdivision (a), with respect to familial status, subdivision (a) shall not be construed to apply to housing for older persons, as defined in Section 12955.9 of the Government Code. With respect to familial status, nothing in subdivision (a) shall be construed to affect Sections 51.2, 51.3, 51.4, 51.10, 51.11, and 799.5 of this code, relating to housing for senior citizens. Subdivision (d) of Section 51, Section 4760, and Section 6714 of this code, and subdivisions (n), (o), and (p) of Section 12955 of the Government Code shall apply to subdivision (a).

(c) This section shall not be construed to limit or expand the powers of a court to reform a deed or other written instrument. **Leg.H.** Added Stats 1987 ch 500 §1. Amended Stats 2006 ch 578 §5 (AB 2800), effective January 1, 2007; Stats 2012 ch 181 §23 (AB 806), effective January 1, 2013, operative January 1, 2014; Stats 2013 ch 605 §11 (SB 752), effective January 1, 2014.

2006 Note: This act shall be known, and may be cited, as the Civil Rights Housing Act of 2006. Stats 2006 ch 578 (AB 2800) §1.

§783. "Condominium"

A condominium is an estate in real property described in Section 4125 or 6542. A condominium may, with respect to the duration of its enjoyment, be either (1) an estate of inheritance or perpetual estate, (2) an estate for life, (3) an estate for years, such as a leasehold or a subleasehold, or (4) any combination of the foregoing. **Leg.H.** Added Stats 1985 ch 874 §9. Amended Stats 2012 ch 181 §24 (AB 806), effective January 1, 2013, operative January 1, 2014; Stats 2013 ch 605 §12 (SB 752), effective January 1, 2014.

Prior Law: Former §783, similar to the present section, was added Stats 1963 ch 860 §1, amended Stats 1969 ch 275 §1, Stats 1984 ch 291 §1, and repealed Stats 1985 ch 874 §8.

§783.1. Separate and correlative interests as interests in real property

In a stock cooperative, as defined in Section 4190 or 6566, both the separate interest, as defined in paragraph (4) of subdivision (a) of Section 4185 or in paragraph (3) of subdivision (a) of Section 6564, and the correlative interest in the stock cooperative corporation, however designated, are interests in real property. **Leg.H.** Added Stats 1985 ch 874 §10. Amended Stats 2012 ch 181 §25 (AB 806), effective January 1, 2013, operative January 1, 2014; Stats 2013 ch 605 §13 (SB 752), effective January 1, 2014.

§784. "Restriction"

"Restriction," when used in a statute that incorporates this section by reference, means a limitation on, or provision affecting, the use of real property in a deed, declaration, or other instrument, whether in the form of a covenant, equitable servitude, condition subsequent, negative easement, or other form of restriction. **Leg.H.** Added Stats 1998 ch 14 §1 (AB 707).

CHAPTER 2
TERMINATION OF ESTATES

Termination of estates. §789.
Prohibition of interruption or termination of utility service, restriction of access of tenant to property. §789.3.
[Section renumbered 1978]. §789.16.
Effect of notice. §790.
Re-entry, when and how to be made. §791.
Summary proceedings in certain cases provided for. §792.
Notice not necessary before action. §793.

§789. Termination of estates

A tenancy or other estate at will, however created, may be terminated by the landlord's giving notice in writing to the tenant, in the manner prescribed by Section 1162 of the Code of Civil Procedure, to remove from the premises within a period of not less than 30 days, to be specified in the notice. **Leg.H.** Enacted 1872. Amended Stats 1911 ch 44 §1; Stats 2002 ch 664 §32 (AB 3034).

§789.3. Prohibition of interruption or termination of utility service, restriction of access of tenant to property

(a) A landlord shall not with intent to terminate the occupancy under any lease or other tenancy or estate at will, however created, of property used by a tenant as his residence willfully cause, directly or indirectly, the interruption or termination of any utility service furnished the tenant, including, but not limited to, water, heat, light, electricity, gas, telephone, elevator, or refrigeration, whether or not the utility service is under the control of the landlord.

(b) In addition, a landlord shall not, with intent to terminate the occupancy under any lease or other tenancy or estate at will, however created, of property used by a tenant as his or her residence, willfully:

(1) Prevent the tenant from gaining reasonable access to the property by changing the locks or using a bootlock or by any other similar method or device;

(2) Remove outside doors or windows; or

(3) Remove from the premises the tenant's personal property, the furnishings, or any other items without the prior written consent of the tenant, except when done pursuant to the procedure set forth in Chapter 5 (commencing with Section 1980) of Title 5 of Part 4 of Division 3.

Nothing in this subdivision shall be construed to prevent the lawful eviction of a tenant by appropriate legal authorities, nor shall anything in this subdivision apply to occupancies defined by subdivision (b) of Section 1940.

(c) Any landlord who violates this section shall be liable to the tenant in a civil action for all of the following:

(1) Actual damages of the tenant.

(2) An amount not to exceed one hundred dollars ($100) for each day or part thereof the landlord remains in violation of this section. In determining the amount of such award, the court shall consider proof of such matters as justice may require; however, in no event shall less than two hundred fifty dollars ($250) be awarded for each separate cause of action. Subsequent or repeated violations, which are not committed contemporaneously with the initial violation, shall be treated as separate causes of action and shall be subject to a separate award of damages.

(d) In any action under subdivision (c) the court shall award reasonable attorney's fees to the prevailing party. In any such action the tenant may seek appropriate injunctive relief to prevent continuing or further violation of the provisions of this section during the pendency of the action. The remedy provided by this section is not exclusive and shall not preclude the tenant from pursuing any other remedy which the tenant may have under any other provision of law. **Leg.H.** Added Stats 1971 ch 1275 §1. Amended Stats 1979 ch 333 §1.

§789.4. [Section repealed 1978]

Leg.H. Added Stats 1975 ch 146 §1. Repealed Stats 1978 ch 1031 §2. The repealed section related to finding of necessity for protection from eviction from mobilehome parks.

§ 789.4. Additional damages for tenants in COVID-19 financial distress [Repealed]

Leg.H. Added Stats 2020 ch 37 §3 (AB 3088), effective August 31, 2020, repealed February 1, 2021. Amended Stats 2021 ch 2 §1 (SB 91), effective January 29, 2021, repealed July 1, 2021 (repealer amended); Stats 2021 ch 5 §1 (AB 81), effective February 23, 2021, repealed July 1, 2021; Stats 2021 ch 27 §1 (AB 832), effective June 28, 2021, repealed October 1, 2021 (repealer amended).

Prior Law: Former CC §789.4, relating to finding of necessity for protection from eviction from mobilehome park, was added Stats 1975 ch 146 §1 and repealed Stats 1978 ch 1031 §2.

§789.5. [Section repealed 1978]

Leg.H. Added Stats 1969 ch 1500 §1. Amended Stats 1971 ch 649 §1; Stats 1973 ch 351 §1; Stats 1975 ch 1092 §1. Repealed Stats 1978 ch 1031 §3. See CC §§798, 798.19, 798.25, 798.50, 798.55–798.57, 798.60.

§789.5c. [Section repealed 1978]

Leg.H. Added Stats 1977 ch 817 §1. Repealed Stats 1978 ch 1031 §4. See CC §798.15.

§789.6. [Section repealed 1978]

Leg.H. Added Stats 1971 ch 1143 §1. Repealed Stats 1978 ch 1031 §5. See CC §798.58.

§789.7. [Section repealed 1978]

Leg.H. Added Stats 1971 ch 1143 §2. Amended Stats 1975 ch 613 §1, ch 1092 §2. Repealed Stats 1978 ch 1031 §6. See CC §§798.15, 798.31, 798.33–798.36.

§789.7a. [Section repealed 1978]

Leg.H. Added Stats 1975 ch 1092 §2.5. Repealed Stats 1978 ch 1031 §7. See CC §798.34.

§789.7b. [Section repealed 1978]

Leg.H. Added Stats 1975 ch 1092 §3. Amended Stats 1976 ch 923 §2, effective September 14, 1976. Repealed Stats 1978 ch 1031 §8. See CC §798.38.

§789.7c. [Section repealed 1978]

Leg.H. Added Stats 1975 ch 1092 §3.5. Repealed Stats 1978 ch 1031 §9. See CC §798.20.

§789.8. [Section repealed 1978]

Leg.H. Added Stats 1972 ch 1001 §1. Amended Stats 1975 ch 1092 §4. Repealed Stats 1978 ch 1031 §10. See CC §§798.32, 798.37, 798.72.

§789.9. [Section repealed 1978]

Leg.H. Added Stats 1972 ch 1001 §2. Amended Stats 1975 ch 146 §2; Stats 1976 ch 438 §1; Stats 1977 ch 736 §1. Repealed Stats 1978 ch 1031 §11. See CC §§798.30, 798.59.

§789.10. [Section repealed 1978]

Leg.H. Added Stats 1973 ch 785 §1. Amended Stats 1975 ch 146 §3; Stats 1976 ch 438 §2. Repealed Stats 1978 ch 1031 §12. See CC §§798.70, 798.73, 798.74, 798.76, 798.77, 799.1, 799.3–799.5.

§789.11. [Section repealed 1978]

Leg.H. Added Stats 1973 ch 785 §2. Repealed Stats 1978 ch 1031 §13. See CC §§798.71, 799.2, 799.6.

§789.12. [Section repealed 1978]

Leg.H. Added Stats 1975 ch 1092 §5. Repealed Stats 1978 ch 1031 §14. See CC §798.85.

§789.13. [Section repealed 1978]

Leg.H. Added Stats 1975 ch 1092 §6. Repealed Stats 1978 ch 1031 §15. See CC §798.86.

§789.14. [Section repealed 1978]

Leg.H. Added Stats 1977 ch 54 §1. Repealed Stats 1978 ch 1031 §16. See CC §798.18.

§789.15. [Section repealed 1978]

Leg.H. Added Stats 1977 ch 677 §1. Repealed Stats 1978 ch 1031 §17. See CC §798.75.

§789.16. [Section renumbered 1978]

Leg.H. Added Stats 1978 ch 396 §1. Renumbered CC §798.26 by Stats 1978 ch 1033 §10.5.

§790. Effect of notice

After such notice has been served, and the period specified by such notice has expired, but not before, the landlord may re-enter, or proceed according to law to recover possession. **Leg.H.** Enacted 1872.

§791. Re-entry, when and how to be made

Whenever the right of re-entry is given to a grantor or a lessor in any grant or lease or otherwise, such re-entry may be made at any time after the right has accrued, upon three days' notice, as provided in sections 1161 and 1162, Code of Civil Procedure; provided, however, that the said three days' notice shall not be required in cases where the hiring of real property is for a term not specified by the parties and where such hiring was terminated under and in accordance with the provisions of section 1946 of the Civil Code. **Leg.H.** Enacted 1872. Amended Stats 1931 ch 1033 §1.

§792. Summary proceedings in certain cases provided for

Summary proceedings for obtaining possession of real property forcibly entered, or forcibly and unlawfully detained, are provided for in Sections 1159 to 1175, both inclusive, of the Code of Civil Procedure. **Leg.H.** Enacted 1872.

§793. Notice not necessary before action

An action for the possession of real property leased or granted, with a right of re-entry, may be maintained at any time, after the right to re-enter has accrued, without the notice prescribed in section seven hundred and ninety-one. **Leg.H.** Enacted 1872. Amended Stats 1905 ch 438 §1.

§794. [Section repealed 1984]

Leg.H. Added Stats 1953 ch 945 §1. Repealed Stats 1984 ch 240 §1. See CC §883.140.

CHAPTER 2.5
MOBILEHOME RESIDENCY LAW

Article 1. General.
Article 2. Rental Agreement.
Article 3. Rules and Regulations.
Article 3.5. Fees and Charges.
Article 4. Utilities.
Article 4.5. Rent Control.
Article 5. Homeowner Communications and Meetings.
Article 5.5. Homeowners Meetings with Management.
Article 6. Termination of Tenancy.

Article 7. Transfer of Mobilehome or Mobilehome Park.
Article 8. Actions, Proceedings, and Penalties.
Article 9. Subdivisions, Cooperatives, and Condominiums.

ARTICLE 1
General

Citation of chapter. §798.
Definitions. §798.1.
"Management". §798.2.
"Mobilehome". §798.3.
"Mobilehome park". §798.4.
[Section renumbered 1980]. §798.5.
"Park". §798.6.
New construction; "New mobilehome park construction". §798.7.
"Rental agreement". §798.8.
"Homeowner". §798.9.
"Change of use". §798.10.
"Resident". §798.11.
"Tenancy". §798.12.
Application of chapter. §798.13.
Delivery of required notices. §798.14.

§798. Citation of chapter
This chapter shall be known and may be cited as the "Mobilehome Residency Law." **Leg.H.** Added Stats 1978 ch 1035 §4. Amended Stats 1992 ch 958 §1 (SB 1655), effective September 26, 1992.

§798.1. Definitions
Unless the provisions or context otherwise requires, the following definitions shall govern the construction of this chapter. **Leg.H.** Added Stats 1978 ch 1031 §1.

§798.2. "Management"
"Management" means the owner of a mobilehome park or an agent or representative authorized to act on his behalf in connection with matters relating to a tenancy in the park. **Leg.H.** Added Stats 1978 ch 1031 §1.

§798.3. "Mobilehome"
(a) "Mobilehome" is a structure designed for human habitation and for being moved on a street or highway under permit pursuant to Section 35790 of the Vehicle Code. Mobilehome includes a manufactured home, as defined in Section 18007 of the Health and Safety Code, and a mobilehome, as defined in Section 18008 of the Health and Safety Code, but, except as provided in subdivision (b), does not include a recreational vehicle, as defined in Section 799.29 of this code and Section 18010 of the Health and Safety Code or a commercial coach as defined in Section 18001.8 of the Health and Safety Code.

(b) "Mobilehome," for purposes of this chapter, other than Section 798.73, also includes trailers and other recreational vehicles of all types defined in Section 18010 of the Health and Safety Code, other than motor homes, truck campers, and camping trailers, which are used for human habitation if the occupancy criteria of either paragraph (1) or (2), as follows, are met:

(1) The trailer or other recreational vehicle occupies a mobilehome site in the park, on November 15, 1992, under a rental agreement with a term of one month or longer, and the trailer or other recreational vehicle occupied a mobilehome site in the park prior to January 1, 1991.

(2) The trailer or other recreational vehicle occupies a mobilehome site in the park for nine or more continuous months commencing on or after November 15, 1992.

"Mobilehome" does not include a trailer or other recreational vehicle located in a recreational vehicle park subject to Chapter 2.6 (commencing with Section 799.20). **Leg.H.** Added Stats 1978 ch 1033 §2. Amended Stats 1980 ch 502 §1; Stats 1982 ch 419 §1; Stats 1983 ch 1124 §1, operative July 1, 1984; Stats 1992 ch 958 §2 (SB 1655), effective September 26, 1992; Stats 1993 ch 666 §1 (AB 503); Stats 2005 ch 595 §1 (SB 253), effective January 1, 2006.

§798.4. "Mobilehome park"
"Mobilehome park" is an area of land where two or more mobilehome sites are rented, or held out for rent, to accommodate mobilehomes used for human habitation. **Leg.H.** Added Stats 1978 ch 1031 §1.

§798.5. [Section renumbered 1980]
Leg.H. Added Stats 1978 ch 1031 §1. Renumbered CC §798.6 by Stats 1980 ch 502 §5.

§798.6. "Park"
"Park" is a manufactured housing community as defined in Section 18210.7 of the Health and Safety Code, or a mobilehome park. **Leg.H.** Added Stats 1978 ch 1031 §1 as §798.5. Renumbered CC §798.8 by Stats 1980 ch 502 §5. Amended Stats 1993 ch 858 §1 (AB 2177); Stats 2007 ch 596 §1 (AB 382), effective January 1, 2008.

Prior Law: Former §798.6, was added Stats 1978 ch 1031 §1, and renumbered CC §798.8 by Stats 1980 ch 502 §6.

§798.7. New construction; "New mobilehome park construction"
(a) "New construction" means any newly constructed spaces initially held out for rent after January 1, 1990. A mobilehome park space shall be considered "initially held out for rent" on the date of issuance of a permit or certificate of occupancy for that space by the enforcement agency in accordance with Section 18551 or 18613 of the Health and Safety Code.

(b) "New mobilehome park construction" means all spaces contained in a newly constructed mobilehome park for which a permit to operate is first issued by the enforcement agency on or after January 1, 2023. **Leg.H.** Added Stats 1989 ch 412 §1. Amended Stats 2022 ch 666 §1 (SB 940), effective January 1, 2023.

Prior Law: Former §798.7, was added Stats 1978 ch 1031 §1, and renumbered CC §798.10 by Stats 1980 ch 502 §7.

§798.8. "Rental agreement"
"Rental agreement" is an agreement between the management and the homeowner establishing the terms and conditions of a park tenancy. A lease is a rental agreement. **Leg.H.** Added Stats 1978 ch 1031 §1 as CC §798.6. Renumbered CC §798.12 by Stats 1980 ch 502 §6. Amended Stats 1982 ch 1397 §1.

Prior Law: Former §798.8, was added Stats 1978 ch 1031 §1, amended Stats 1978 ch 1033 §3, and renumbered CC §798.12 by Stats 1980 ch 502 §8.

§798.9. "Homeowner"
"Homeowner" is a person who has a tenancy in a mobilehome park under a rental agreement. **Leg.H.** Added Stats 1978 ch 1031 §1. Amended Stats 1982 ch 1397 §2.

§798.10. "Change of use"
"Change of use" means a use of the park for a purpose other than the rental, or the holding out for rent, of two or more mobilehome sites to accommodate mobilehomes used for human habitation, and does not mean the adoption, amendment, or repeal of a park rule or regulation. A change of use may affect an entire park or any portion thereof. "Change of use" includes, but is not limited to, a change of the park or any portion thereof to a condominium, stock cooperative, planned unit development, or any form of ownership wherein spaces within the park are to be sold. **Leg.H.** Added Stats 1979 ch 945 §1. Amended Stats 1980 ch 137 §1.

Prior Law: There was another section of this number which was added by Stats 1978 ch 1031 §1 as CC §798.7, renumbered §798.10 by Stats 1980 ch 502 §7, and renumbered CC §798.11 by Stats 1981 ch 714 §50.

§798.11. "Resident"
"Resident" is a homeowner or other person who lawfully occupies a mobilehome. **Leg.H.** Added Stats 1978 ch 1031 §1 as CC §798.7. Renumbered CC §798.10 by Stats 1980 ch 502 §7. Amended Stats 1981 ch 714 §50; Stats 1982 ch 1397 §3.

§798.12. "Tenancy"
"Tenancy" is the right of a homeowner to the use of a site within a mobilehome park on which to locate, maintain, and occupy a mobilehome, site improvements, and accessory structures for human habitation, including the use of the services and facilities of the park. **Leg.H.** Added Stats 1978 ch 1031 §1 as §798.8. Amended Stats 1978 ch 1033 §3. Renumbered by Stats 1980 ch 502 §8. Amended Stats 1982 ch 1397 §4.

§798.13. Application of chapter
(a) This chapter does not apply to any area owned, operated, or maintained by the state for the purpose of providing employee housing or space for a mobilehome owned or occupied by an employee of the state.

(b) Notwithstanding subdivision (a), a state employer shall provide the occupant of a privately owned mobilehome that is situated in an employee housing area owned, operated, or maintained by the state, and that is occupied by a state employee by agreement with his or her state employer and subject to the terms and conditions of that state employment, with a minimum of 60-days' notice prior to terminating the tenancy for any reason. **Leg.H.** Added Stats 2000 ch 471 §1 (AB 2008).

§798.14. Delivery of required notices

(a) Unless otherwise provided, all notices required by this chapter shall be either delivered personally to the homeowner or deposited in the United States mail, postage prepaid, addressed to the homeowner at his or her site within the mobilehome park.

(b) All notices required by this chapter to be delivered prior to February 1 of each year may be combined in one notice that contains all the information required by the sections under which the notices are given. **Leg.H.** Added Stats 1988 ch 301 §1. Amended Stats 2012 ch 478 §1 (AB 2150), effective January 1, 2013.

ARTICLE 2
Rental Agreement

Required provisions; Incorporation by reference of chapter. §798.15.
Rules and regulations included in agreement; Copy to homeowner. §798.16.
Term; Charges and fees. §798.18.
Waiver of homeowner rights void. §798.19.
Rental agreement not to grant management right of first refusal to purchase mobilehome; Separate agreement not precluded. §798.19.5.
Discrimination prohibited. §798.20.
Exemption. §798.21.
Rental of space for recreational vehicles. §798.22.
Application of park rules and regulations to management. §798.23.
Circumstances where homeowner may rent or sublet primary residence; Approval of prospective renter or sublessee; Limitations on amount of rent charged. §798.23.5.

§798.15. Required provisions; Incorporation by reference of chapter

The rental agreement shall be in writing and shall contain, in addition to the provisions otherwise required by law to be included, all of the following:

(a) The term of the tenancy and the rent therefor.

(b) The rules and regulations of the park.

(c) A copy of the text of this chapter shall be provided as an exhibit and shall be incorporated into the rental agreement by reference. Management shall do one of the following prior to February 1 of each year, if a significant change was made in this chapter by legislation enacted in the prior year:

(1) Provide all homeowners with a copy of this chapter.

(2) Provide written notice to all homeowners that there has been a change to this chapter and that they may obtain one copy of this chapter from management at no charge. Management shall provide a copy within a reasonable time, not to exceed seven days, upon request.

(d) A provision specifying that (1) it is the responsibility of the management to provide and maintain physical improvements in the common facilities in good working order and condition and (2) with respect to a sudden or unforeseeable breakdown or deterioration of these improvements, the management shall have a reasonable period of time to repair the sudden or unforeseeable breakdown or deterioration and bring the improvements into good working order and condition after management knows or should have known of the breakdown or deterioration. For purposes of this subdivision, a reasonable period of time to repair a sudden or unforeseeable breakdown or deterioration shall be as soon as possible in situations affecting a health or safety condition, and shall not exceed 30 days in any other case except where exigent circumstances justify a delay.

(e) A description of the physical improvements to be provided the homeowner during [1] **the homeowner's** tenancy.

(f) A provision listing those services which will be provided at the time the rental agreement is executed and will continue to be offered for the term of tenancy and the fees, if any, to be charged for those services.

(g) A provision stating that management may charge a reasonable fee for services relating to the maintenance of the land and premises upon which a mobilehome is situated in the event the homeowner fails to maintain the land or premises in accordance with the rules and regulations of the park after written notification to the homeowner and the failure of the homeowner to comply within 14 days. The written notice shall state the specific condition to be corrected and an estimate of the charges to be imposed by management if the services are performed by management or its agent.

(h) All other provisions governing the tenancy.

(i) A copy of the following notice. Management shall also, prior to February 1 of each year, provide a copy of the following notice to all homeowners:

IMPORTANT NOTICE TO ALL MANUFACTURED HOME/MOBILEHOME OWNERS: CALIFORNIA LAW REQUIRES THAT YOU BE MADE AWARE OF THE FOLLOWING:The Mobilehome Residency Law (MRL), found in Section 798 et seq. of the Civil Code, establishes the rights and responsibilities of homeowners and park management. The MRL is deemed a part of the terms of any park rental agreement or lease. This notice is intended to provide you with a general awareness of selected parts of the MRL and other important laws. It does not serve as a legal explanation or interpretation. For authoritative information, you must read and understand the laws. These laws change from time to time. In any year in which the law has changed, you may obtain one copy of the full text of the law from management at no charge. This notice is required by Civil Code Section 798.15(i) and the information provided may not be current.Homeowners and park management have certain rights and responsibilities under the MRL. These include, but are not limited to:1.Management must give a homeowner written notice of any increase in [2] the rent at least 90 days before the date of the increase. (Civil Code Section 798.30)2.No rental or sales agreement may contain a provision by which a purchaser or a homeowner waives any of [3] their rights under the MRL. (Civil Code Sections 798.19, 798.77)3.Management may not terminate or refuse to renew a homeowner's tenancy except for one or more of the authorized reasons set forth in the MRL. (Civil Code Sections 798.55, 798.56) Homeowners must pay rent, utility charges, and reasonable incidental service charges in a timely manner. Failure to comply could be grounds for eviction from the park. (Civil Code Section 798.56)4.Homeowners, residents, and their guests must comply with the rental agreement or lease, including the reasonable rules and regulations of the park and all applicable local ordinances and state laws and regulations relating to mobilehomes. Failure to comply could be grounds for eviction from the park. (Civil Code Section 798.56)5.Homeowners have a right to peacefully assemble and freely communicate with respect to mobilehome living and for social or educational purposes. Homeowners have a right to meet in the park, at reasonable hours and in a reasonable manner, for any lawful purpose. Homeowners may not be charged a cleaning deposit in order to use the park clubhouse for meetings of resident organizations or for other lawful purposes, such as to hear from political candidates, so long as a homeowner of the park is hosting the meeting and all park residents are allowed to attend. Homeowners may not be required to obtain liability insurance in order to use common facilities unless alcohol is served. (Civil Code Sections 798.50, 798.51)6.If a home complies with certain standards, the homeowner is entitled to sell it in place in the park. If you sell your home, you are required to provide a manufactured home and mobilehome transfer disclosure statement to the buyer prior to sale. (Civil Code Section 1102.6d) When a home is sold, the owner is required to transfer the title to the buyer. The sale of the home is not complete until you receive the title from the seller. It is the responsibility of the buyer to also file paperwork with the Department of Housing and Community Development to register the home in [4] the buyer's name. (Civil Code Sections 798.70–798.74)7.Management has the right to enter the space upon which a mobilehome is situated for maintenance of utilities, trees, and driveways; for inspection and maintenance of the space in accordance with the rules and regulations of the park when the homeowner or resident fails to maintain the space; and for protection and maintenance of the mobilehome park at any reasonable time, but not in a manner or at a time that would interfere with the resident's quiet enjoyment of [5] the resident's home. (Civil Code Section 798.26)8.A homeowner may not make any improvements or alterations to [6] the homeowner's space or home without following the rules and regulations of the park and all applicable local ordinances and state laws and regulations, which may include obtaining a permit to construct, and, if required by park rules or the rental agreement, without prior written approval of management. Failure to comply could be grounds for eviction from the park. (Civil Code Section 798.56)9.In California, mobilehome owners must pay annual property tax to the county tax collector or an annual fee in lieu of taxes to the Department of Housing and Community Development (HCD). If you are unsure which to pay, contact HCD. Failure to pay taxes or in lieu fees can have serious consequences, including losing your home at a tax sale.10.For more information on registration, titling, and taxes, contact:

the Department of Housing and Community Development at www.hcd.ca.gov (800) 952-8356; your County Tax Collector; or call your local county government.11.The Mobilehome Residency Law Protection Program (MRLPP), found in Section 18800 et seq. of the Health and Safety Code, protects and safeguards mobilehome homeowners and residents by affording them an additional avenue to enforce violations of the MRL. The Department of Housing and Community Development (HCD) administers the program by providing assistance in taking complaints and helping to resolve and coordinate the resolution of those complaints from homeowners and residents relating to the MRL. The HCD contracts with nonprofit legal service providers and refers complaints of alleged MRL violations to these legal service providers. The HCD may not arbitrate, mediate, negotiate, or provide legal advice in connection with mobilehome park rent disputes, lease or rental agreements, or disputes arising from lease or rental agreements, but may provide information on these issues to the complaining party, management, or other responsible party. The MRLPP is funded by an annual registration fee of $10.00 for each permitted mobilehome lot, collected from management, which management may pass on and collect from the homeowner at the time of rent payment. The annual MRLPP registration fee must appear as a separate line item on the rent bill and be accompanied by a clear written description of the purposes of the charge, along with contact information for the HCD. For questions regarding the fee or the MRLPP, contact: the HCD at MHAssistance@hcd.ca.gov or by calling (800) 952-8356. **Leg.H.** Added Stats 1978 ch 1031 §1. Amended Stats 1978 ch 1033 §4; Stats 1980 ch 137 §2; Stats 1981 ch 667 §1; Stats 1982 ch 1397 §5; Stats 1983 ch 519 §1; Stats 1987 ch 126 §1; Stats 1993 ch 666 §2 (AB 503); Stats 2010 ch 90 §1 (AB 2120), effective January 1, 2011; Stats 2012 ch 478 §2 (AB 2150), effective January 1, 2013; Stats 2016, ch 396, §1 (AB 587), effective January 1, 2017; Stats 2024 ch 397 §1 (AB 2399), effective January 1, 2025.

§798.15. 2024 Deletes. [1] his or her [2] his or her [3] his or her [4] his or her [5] his or her [6] his or her

§798.16. Rules and regulations included in agreement; Copy to homeowner

(a) The rental agreement may include other provisions permitted by law, but need not include specific language contained in state or local laws not a part of this chapter.

(b) Management shall return an executed copy of the rental agreement to the homeowner within 15 business days after management has received the rental agreement signed by the homeowner. **Leg.H.** Added Stats 1978 ch 1031 §1. Amended Stats 1978 ch 1033 §5; Stats 1981 ch 667 §2; Stats 2004 ch 302 §1 (AB 2351).

§798.17. Exemption of certain mobilehomes from rent control; Notice to homeowner; Time for homeowner to respond; Exceptions [Repealed]

Leg.H. Added Stats 1985 ch 1084 §1. Amended Stats 1986 ch 1416 §1; Stats 1990 ch 1013 §1 (SB 2010) ch 1046 §2 (SB 2009); Stats 1991 ch 24 §1 (SB 132), effective May 6, 1991, operative May 10, 1991, ch 170 §1 (SB 360); Stats 1992 ch 289 §1 (SB 1454) ch 427 §11 (AB 3355) (ch 289 prevails); Stats 1993 ch 9 §1 (SB 6), effective April 28, 1993; Stats 2012 ch 477 §1 (AB 1938), effective January 1, 2013; Stats 2020 ch 35 §2 (AB 2782), effective January 1, 2021, repealed January 1, 2025; Stats 2020 ch 35 §2 (AB 2782), effective January 1, 2021, repealed January 1, 2025.

Prior Law: Former §798.17, similar to present CC §798.27, was added Stats 1980 ch 879 §1, and repealed Stats 1981 ch 667 §3.

Former §798.17, relating to termination of the rental agreement, was added Stats 1978 ch 1031 §1, and repealed Stats 1978 ch 1033 §6.

§798.18. Term; Charges and fees

(a) A homeowner shall be offered a rental agreement for (1) a term of 12 months, or (2) a lesser period as the homeowner may request, or (3) a longer period as mutually agreed upon by both the homeowner and management.

(b) No rental agreement shall contain any terms or conditions with respect to charges for rent, utilities, or incidental reasonable service charges that would be different during the first 12 months of the rental agreement from the corresponding terms or conditions that would be offered to the homeowners on a month-to-month basis.

(c) No rental agreement for a term of 12 months or less shall include any provision which authorizes automatic extension or renewal of, or automatically extends or renews, the rental agreement beyond the initial term for a term longer than 12 months at the sole option of either the management or the homeowner. **Leg.H.** Added Stats 1978 ch 1031 §1. Amended Stats 1978 ch 1032 §2, ch 1033 §7.5; Stats 1980 ch 206 §1; Stats 1981 ch 667 §4; Stats 1982 ch 1397 §6; Stats 1992 ch 289 §2 (SB 1454).

§798.19. Waiver of homeowner rights void

No rental agreement for a mobilehome shall contain a provision by which the homeowner waives his or her rights under the provisions of Articles 1 to 8, inclusive, of this chapter. Any such waiver shall be deemed contrary to public policy and void. **Leg.H.** Added Stats 1978 ch 1031 §1. Amended Stats 1978 ch 1033 §8; Stats 1982 ch 1397 §7.

§798.19.5. Rental agreement not to grant management right of first refusal to purchase mobilehome; Separate agreement not precluded

A rental agreement entered into or renewed on and after January 1, 2006, shall not include a clause, rule, regulation, or any other provision that grants to management the right of first refusal to purchase a homeowner's mobilehome that is in the park and offered for sale to a third party pursuant to Article 7 (commencing with Section 798.70). This section does not preclude a separate agreement for separate consideration granting the park owner or management a right of first refusal to purchase the homeowner's mobilehome that is in the park and offered for sale. **Leg.H.** Added Stats 2005 ch 35 §1 (SB 237), effective January 1, 2006.

§798.20. Discrimination prohibited

(a) Membership in any private club or organization that is a condition for tenancy in a park shall not be denied on any basis listed in subdivision (a) or (d) of Section 12955 of the Government Code, as those bases are defined in Sections 12926, 12926.1, subdivision (m) and paragraph (1) of subdivision (p) of Section 12955, and Section 12955.2 of the Government Code.

(b) Notwithstanding subdivision (a), with respect to familial status, subdivision (a) shall not be construed to apply to housing for older persons, as defined in Section 12955.9 of the Government Code. With respect to familial status, nothing in subdivision (a) shall be construed to affect Sections 51.2, 51.3, 51.4, 51.10, 51.11, and 799.5, relating to housing for senior citizens. Subdivision (d) of Section 51 and Section 4760 of this code and subdivisions (n), (o), and (p) of Section 12955 of the Government Code shall apply to subdivision (a). **Leg.H.** Added Stats 1978 ch 1031 §1. Amended Stats 2006 ch 578 §6 (AB 2800), effective January 1, 2007; Stats 2012 ch 181 §26 (AB 806), effective January 1, 2013, operative January 1, 2014.

2006 Note: This act shall be known, and may be cited, as the Civil Rights Housing Act of 2006. Stats 2006 ch 578 (AB 2800) §1.

§798.21. Exemption

(a) Notwithstanding Section 798.17, if a mobilehome space within a mobilehome park is not the principal residence of the homeowner and the homeowner has not rented the mobilehome to another party, it shall be exempt from any ordinance, rule, regulation, or initiative measure adopted by any city, county, or city and county, which establishes a maximum amount that the landlord may charge a tenant for rent.

(b) Nothing in this section is intended to require any homeowner to disclose information concerning his or her personal finances. Nothing in this section shall be construed to authorize management to gain access to any records which would otherwise be confidential or privileged.

(c) For purposes of this section, a mobilehome shall be deemed to be the principal residence of the homeowner, unless a review of state or county records demonstrates that the homeowner is receiving a homeowner's exemption for another property or mobilehome in this state, or unless a review of public records reasonably demonstrates that the principal residence of the homeowner is out of state.

(d) Before modifying the rent or other terms of tenancy as a result of a review of records, as described in subdivision (c), the management shall notify the homeowner, in writing, of the proposed changes and provide the homeowner with a copy of the documents upon which management relied.

(e) The homeowner shall have 90 days from the date the notice described in subdivision (d) is mailed to review and respond to the notice. Management may not modify the rent or other terms of tenancy prior to the expiration of the 90-day period or prior to responding, in writing, to information provided by the homeowner. Management may not modify the rent or other terms of tenancy if the homeowner provides documentation reasonably establishing that the information provided by management is incorrect or that the homeowner is not the same person identified in the documents. However, nothing in this subdivision shall be construed to authorize the homeowner to change the homeowner's exemption status of the other property or mobilehome owned by the homeowner.

(f) This section does not apply under any of the following conditions:

(1) The homeowner is unable to rent or lease the mobilehome because the owner or management of the mobilehome park in which the mobilehome is located does not permit, or the rental agreement limits or prohibits, the assignment of the mobilehome or the subletting of the park space.

(2) The mobilehome is being actively held available for sale by the homeowner, or pursuant to a listing agreement with a real estate broker licensed pursuant to Chapter 3 (commencing with Section 10130) of Part 1 of Division 4 of the Business and Professions Code, or a mobilehome dealer, as defined in Section 18002.6 of the Health and Safety Code. A homeowner, real estate broker, or mobilehome dealer attempting to sell a mobilehome shall actively market and advertise the mobilehome for sale in good faith to bona fide purchasers for value in order to remain exempt pursuant to this subdivision.

(3) The legal owner has taken possession or ownership, or both, of the mobilehome from a registered owner through either a surrender of ownership interest by the registered owner or a foreclosure proceeding. **Leg.H.** Added Stats 1996 ch 392 §1 (SB 1181). Amended Stats 2003 ch 132 §1 (AB 1173).

§798.22. Rental of space for recreational vehicles

(a) In any new mobilehome park that is developed after January 1, 1982, mobilehome spaces shall not be rented for the accommodation of recreational vehicles as defined by Section 799.29 unless the mobilehome park has a specifically designated area within the park for recreational vehicles, which is separate and apart from the area designated for mobilehomes. Recreational vehicles may be located only in the specifically designated area.

(b) Any new mobilehome park that is developed after January 1, 1982, is not subject to the provisions of this section until 75 percent of the spaces have been rented for the first time. **Leg.H.** Added Stats 1982 ch 1146 §1. Amended Stats 1993 ch 666 §3 (AB 503).

§798.23. Application of park rules and regulations to management

(a) Management shall be subject to, and comply with, all park rules and regulations to the same extent as residents and their guests.

(b) Subdivision (a) of this section does not apply to either of the following:

(1) Any rule or regulation that governs the age of any resident or guest.

(2) Acts of management that are undertaken to fulfill management's maintenance, management, and business operation responsibilities.

(c)(1) Notwithstanding subdivision (b) and subject to paragraph (2), management shall be subject to, and comply with, all rules and regulations that prohibit a homeowner from renting or subleasing the homeowner's mobilehome or mobilehome space.

(2)(A) If a rule or regulation has been enacted that prohibits either renting or subleasing by a homeowner, management shall not directly rent a mobilehome except as follows:

(i) Management may directly rent up to two mobilehomes within the park for the purpose of housing onsite employees.

(ii) For every 200 mobilehomes in a park, the management may directly rent one more mobilehome within the park, in addition to the mobilehomes authorized for direct rental pursuant to clause (i), for the purpose of housing onsite employees.

(B) For purposes of this paragraph, "the purpose of housing onsite employees" includes directly renting a mobilehome to a person who is not an onsite employee to avoid a vacancy during times when the mobilehome is authorized for direct rental pursuant to subparagraph (A) and not needed for housing onsite employees.

(d) Notwithstanding subdivision (c), management may continue to directly rent a mobilehome to a tenant if both of the following apply:

(1) The tenancy was initially established by a rental agreement executed before January 1, 2022.

(2) A tenant listed on the rental agreement described in paragraph (1) continues to occupy the mobilehome.

(e)(1) A park shall be exempt from the provisions of subdivision (c) if either of the following apply:

(A) The park is owned and operated by an organization that qualifies as an exempt organization under Section 501(c)(3) of the United States Internal Revenue Code of 1986, and the property has been granted an exemption from property taxation pursuant to Section 214 of the Revenue and Taxation Code.

(B) The park is owned by a government agency or an entity controlled by a government agency, and has an affordability covenant in place.

(2) The exemption contained in paragraph (1) applies only to those mobilehomes or mobilehome sites within a park that are restricted for use as affordable housing pursuant to either a written regulatory agreement or the policy or practice of the exempt organization or government agency. **Leg.H.** Added Stats 1993 ch 520 §1 (AB 217). Amended Stats 1994 ch 340 §1; Stats 2002 ch 672 §1 (SB 1410); Stats 2021 ch 706 §1 (AB 861), effective January 1, 2022.

§798.23.5. Circumstances where homeowner may rent or sublet primary residence; Approval of prospective renter or sublessee; Limitations on amount of rent charged

(a)(1) Management shall permit a homeowner to rent his or her home that serves as the homeowner's primary residence or sublet his or her space, under the circumstances described in paragraph (2) and subject to the requirements of this section.

(2) A homeowner shall be permitted to rent or sublet pursuant to paragraph (1) if a medical emergency or medical treatment requires the homeowner to be absent from his or her home and this is confirmed in writing by an attending physician.

(b) The following provisions shall apply to a rental or sublease pursuant to this section:

(1) The minimum term of the rental or sublease shall be six months, unless the management approves a shorter term, but no greater than 12 months, unless management approves a longer term.

(2) The management may require approval of a prospective renter or sublessee, subject to the process and restrictions provided by subdivision (a) of Section 798.74 for prospective purchasers of mobilehomes. A prospective sublessee shall comply with any rule or regulation limiting residency based on age requirements, pursuant to Section 798.76. The management may charge a prospective sublessee a credit screening fee for the actual cost of any personal reference check or consumer credit report that is provided by a consumer credit reporting agency, as defined in Section 1785.3, if the management or his or her agent requires that personal reference check or consumer credit report.

(3) The renter or sublessee shall comply with all rules and regulations of the park. The failure of a renter or sublessee to comply with the rules and regulations of the park may result in the termination of the homeowner's tenancy in the mobilehome park, in accordance with Section 798.56. A homeowner's tenancy may not be terminated under this paragraph if the homeowner completes an action for unlawful detainer or executes a judgment for possession, pursuant to Chapter 4 (commencing with Section 1159) of Title 3 of Part 3 of the Code of Civil Procedure within 60 days of the homeowner receiving notice of termination of tenancy.

(4) The homeowner shall remain liable for the mobilehome park rent and other park charges.

(5) The management may require the homeowner to reside in the mobilehome park for a term of one year before management permits the renting or subletting of a mobilehome or mobilehome space.

(6) Notwithstanding subdivision (a) of Section 798.39, if a security deposit has been refunded to the homeowner pursuant to subdivision (b) or (c) of Section 798.39, the management may require the homeowner to resubmit a security deposit in an amount or value not to exceed two months' rent in addition to the first month's rent. Management may retain this security deposit for the duration of the term of the rental or sublease.

(7) The homeowner shall keep his or her current address and telephone number on file with the management during the term of rental or sublease. If applicable, the homeowner may provide the name, address, and telephone number of his or her legal representative.

(c) A homeowner may not charge a renter or sublessee more than an amount necessary to cover the cost of space rent, utilities, and scheduled loan payments on the mobilehome, if any. **Leg.H.** Added Stats 2002 ch 672 §2 (SB 1410). Amended Stats 2011 ch 296 §32 (AB 1023), effective January 1, 2012.

ARTICLE 3
Rules and Regulations

Common area facilities. §798.24.
Amendment procedures. §798.25.
Void and unenforceable rule or regulation. §798.25.5.
Protection of mobilehome occupant's quiet enjoyment; Right of entry. §798.26.
Notice by management. §798.27.
Required disclosures. §798.28.
Removal of vehicle. §798.28.5.
[Section renumbered 2004]. §798.285.
Posting of Mobilehome Assistance Center sign. §798.29.
[Section renumbered 2010]. §798.29.5.
Accommodations for the disabled authorized. §798.29.6.

§798.24. Common area facilities

Each common area facility shall be open or available to residents at all reasonable hours and the hours of the common area facility shall be posted at the facility. **Leg.H.** Added Stats 1983 ch 503 §1. Amended Stats 1994 ch 380 §1 (SB 1508); Stats 2001 ch 83 §1 (AB 1202).

§798.25. Amendment procedures

(a) Except as provided in subdivision (d), when the management proposes an amendment to the park's rules and regulations, the management shall meet and consult with the homeowners in the park, their representatives, or both, after written notice has been given to all the homeowners in the park 10 days or more before the meeting. The notice shall set forth the proposed amendment to the park's rules and regulations and shall state the date, time, and location of the meeting.

(b) Except as provided in subdivision (d) following the meeting and consultation with the homeowners, the noticed amendment to the park's rules and regulations may be implemented, as to any homeowner, with the consent of that homeowner, or without the homeowner's consent upon written notice of not less than six months, except for regulations applicable to recreational facilities, which may be amended without homeowner consent upon written notice of not less than 60 days.

(c) Written notice to a homeowner whose tenancy commences within the required period of notice of a proposed amendment to the park's rules and regulations under subdivision (b) or (d) shall constitute compliance with this section where the written notice is given before the inception of the tenancy.

(d) When the management proposes an amendment to the park's rules and regulations mandated by a change in the law, including, but not limited to, a change in a statute, ordinance, or governmental regulation, the management may implement the amendment to the park's rules and regulations, as to any homeowner, with the consent of that homeowner or without the homeowner's consent upon written notice of not less than 60 days. For purposes of this subdivision, the management shall specify in the notice the citation to the statute, ordinance, or regulation, including the section number, that necessitates the proposed amendment to the park's rules and regulations.

(e) Any amendment to the park's rules and regulations that creates a new fee payable by the homeowner and that has not been expressly agreed upon by the homeowner and management in the written rental agreement or lease, shall be void and unenforceable. **Leg.H.** Added Stats 1978 ch 1033 §10. Amended Stats 1982 ch 1397 §8; Stats 1983 ch 519 §2; Stats 1993 ch 102 §1 (AB 285); Stats 1999 ch 323 §1 (SB 351); Stats 2004 ch 622 §1 (SB 1176); Stats 2005 ch 22 §11 (SB 1108), effective January 1, 2006.

1999 Note: The Legislature finds and declares that this act is intended to prohibit park owners from amending park rules and regulations to impose new fees on park residents. The act is not intended to limit the provisions of Article 4 (commencing with Section 798.30) of Chapter 2.5 of Title 2 of Part 2 of Division 2 of the Civil Code with respect to the imposition of fees. Stats 1999 ch 323 §2.

§798.25.5. Void and unenforceable rule or regulation

Any rule or regulation of a mobilehome park that (a) is unilaterally adopted by the management, (b) is implemented without the consent of the homeowners, and (c) by its terms purports to deny homeowners their right to a trial by jury or which would mandate binding arbitration of any dispute between the management and homeowners shall be void and unenforceable. **Leg.H.** Added Stats 1993 ch 889 §1 (AB 1012).

§798.26. Protection of mobilehome occupant's quiet enjoyment; Right of entry

(a) Except as provided in subdivision (b), the ownership or management of a park shall have no right of entry to a mobilehome or enclosed accessory structure without the prior written consent of the resident. The consent may be revoked in writing by the resident at any time. The ownership or management shall have a right of entry upon the land upon which a mobilehome is situated for maintenance of utilities, trees, and driveways, for maintenance of the premises in accordance with the rules and regulations of the park when the homeowner or resident fails to so maintain the premises, and protection of the mobilehome park at any reasonable time, but not in a manner or at a time that would interfere with the resident's quiet enjoyment.

(b) The ownership or management of a park may enter a mobilehome or enclosed accessory structure without the prior written consent of the resident in case of an emergency or when the resident has abandoned the mobilehome or accessory structure. **Leg.H.** Added Stats 1978 ch 396 §1 as CC §789.16. Renumbered by Stats 1978 ch 1033 §10.5. Amended Stats 1981 ch 667 §5; Stats 1982 ch 1397 §9; Stats 1983 ch 519 §3; Stats 2000 ch 423 §1 (AB 862); Stats 2004 ch 302 §2 (AB 2351); Stats 2008 ch 115 §1 (SB 1234), effective January 1, 2009.

§798.27. Notice by management

(a) The management shall give written notice to all homeowners and prospective homeowners concerning the following matters: (1) the nature of the zoning or use permit under which the mobilehome park operates. If the mobilehome park is operating pursuant to a permit subject to a renewal or expiration date, the relevant information and dates shall be included in the notice. (2) The duration of any lease of the mobilehome park, or any portion thereof, in which the management is a lessee.

(b) If a change occurs concerning the zoning or use permit under which the park operates or a lease in which the management is a lessee, all homeowners shall be given written notice within 30 days of that change. Notification regarding the change of use of the park, or any portion thereof, shall be governed by subdivision (g) of Section 798.56. A prospective homeowner shall be notified prior to the inception of the tenancy. **Leg.H.** Added Stats 1980 ch 864 §1. Amended Stats 1981 ch 667 §6; Stats 1982 ch 1397 §10; Stats 1991 ch 190 §1 (AB 600).

§798.28. Required disclosures

The management of a mobilehome park shall disclose, in writing, within 10 business days, the name, business address, and business telephone number of the mobilehome park owner upon the receipt of a written request of a homeowner. **Leg.H.** Added Stats 1981 ch 505 §1. Amended Stats 1982 ch 1397 §11; Stats 1991 ch 62 §1 (AB 577); Stats 2017 ch 31 §1 (AB 294), effective January 1, 2018.

§798.28.5. Removal of vehicle

(a) Except as otherwise provided in this section, the management may cause the removal, pursuant to Section 22658 of the Vehicle Code, of a vehicle other than a mobilehome that is parked in the park when there is displayed a sign at each entrance to the park as provided in paragraph (1) of subdivision (a) of Section 22658 of the Vehicle Code.

(b)(1) Management may not cause the removal of a vehicle from a homeowner's or resident's driveway or a homeowner's or resident's designated parking space except if management has first posted on the windshield of the vehicle a notice stating management's intent to remove the vehicle in seven days and stating the specific park rule that the vehicle has violated that justifies its removal. After the expiration of seven days following the posting of the notice, management may remove a vehicle that remains in violation of a rule for which notice has been posted upon the vehicle. If a vehicle rule violation is corrected within seven days after the rule violation notice is posted on the vehicle, the vehicle may not be removed. If a vehicle upon which a rule violation notice has been posted is removed from the park by a homeowner or resident and subsequently is returned to the park still in violation of the rule stated in the notice, management is not required to post any additional notice on the vehicle, and the vehicle may be removed after the expiration of the seven-day period following the original notice posting.

(2) If a vehicle poses a significant danger to the health or safety of a park resident or guest, or if a homeowner or resident requests to have a vehicle removed from [1] **their** driveway or designated parking space, the requirements of paragraph (1) do not apply, and management may remove the vehicle pursuant to Section 22658 of the Vehicle Code.

(c)(1) Management shall not cause the removal from a homeowner's or resident's driveway, a homeowner's or resident's designated parking space, or a space provided by management for parking vehicles, any vehicle used or required by the homeowner for work or employment or which advertises any trade or services on the vehicle.

(2) If any part of the vehicle extends into the park roadway or otherwise poses a significant danger to the health or safety of a park

resident or guest, or if a homeowner or resident requests to have the vehicle removed from their driveway or designated parking space, paragraph (1) shall not apply, and management may remove the vehicle pursuant to Section 22658 of the Vehicle Code. **Leg.H.** Added Stats 1993 ch 32 §1 (SB 209) as CC §798.285. Amended and Renumbered Civ C §798.28.5 by Stats 2004 ch 302 §3 (AB 2351); Stats 2024 ch 79 §1 (SB 1408), effective January 1, 2025.

§798.28.5. 2024 Deletes. [1] his or her

§798.285. [Section renumbered 2004]

Leg.H. Added Stats 1993 ch 32 §1. Amended and renumbered to CC §798.28.5 by Stats 2004 ch 302 §3 (AB 2351).

§798.29. Posting of Mobilehome Assistance Center sign

The management shall post a Mobilehome Assistance Center sign provided by the Department of Housing and Community Development, as required by Section 18253.5 of the Health and Safety Code. **Leg.H.** Added Stats 1988 ch 333 §1. Amended Stats 1996 ch 402 §1 (SB 1594); Stats 2018 ch 957 §1 (SB 1078), effective January 1, 2019.

§798.29.5. [Section renumbered 2010]

Leg.H. Added Stats 1992 ch 317 §1 (SB 1389). Renumbered CC §798.42 by Stats 2009 ch 558 §1 (SB 111), effective January 1, 2010.

2009 Note: Nothing in this act shall be construed to affect the application of any other statute, regulation, or any existing contract, lease, rental agreement, or related document. Stats 2009 ch 558 (SB 111) §8.

§798.29.6. Accommodations for the disabled authorized

The management shall not prohibit a homeowner or resident from installing accommodations for the disabled on the home or the site, lot, or space on which the mobilehome is located, including, but not limited to, ramps or handrails on the outside of the home, as long as the installation of those facilities complies with code, as determined by an enforcement agency, and those facilities are installed pursuant to a permit, if required for the installation, issued by the enforcement agency. The management may require that the accommodations installed pursuant to this section be removed by the current homeowner at the time the mobilehome is removed from the park or pursuant to a written agreement between the current homeowner and the management prior to the completion of the resale of the mobilehome in place in the park. This section is not exclusive and shall not be construed to condition, affect, or supersede any other provision of law or regulation relating to accessibility or accommodations for the disabled. **Leg.H.** Added Stats 2008 ch 170 §1 (SB 1107), effective January 1, 2009.

ARTICLE 3.5
Fees and Charges

Notice of increase. §798.30.
Restrictions on gross rental rate for a tenancy in a qualified mobilehome park [Repealed January 1, 2030]. § 798.30.5.
Rent, utilities, and services rendered. §798.31.
Fees for services actually rendered not listed in rental agreement. §798.32.
Facilities or services for pets. §798.33.
Guests; Provision of live-in health or supportive care; No tenancy rights or duty to guest; Violations. §798.34.
Number of members in family. §798.35.
Enforcement of rules and regulations. §798.36.
Entry, installation, hookup, landscaping and maintenance. §798.37.
Responsibility for trees. §798.37.5.
Acquisition of lien or security interest in mobilehome by park management. §798.38.
Security deposits. §798.39.

§798.30. Notice of increase

The management shall give a homeowner written notice of any increase in his or her rent at least 90 days before the date of the increase. **Leg.H.** Added Stats 1978 ch 1031 §1. Amended Stats 1982 ch 1397 §12; Stats 1993 ch 448 §1 (AB 870).

§ 798.30.5. Restrictions on gross rental rate for a tenancy in a qualified mobilehome park [Repealed January 1, 2030]

(a)(1) Subject to subdivision (b), management shall not, over the course of any 12-month period, increase the gross rental rate for a tenancy in a qualified mobilehome park more than 3 percent plus the percentage change in the cost of living, or 5 percent, whichever is lower, of the lowest gross rental rate charged for a tenancy at any time during the 12 months prior to the effective date of the increase.

(2) If the same homeowner maintains a tenancy over any 12-month period, the gross rental rate for the tenancy shall not be increased in more than two increments over that 12-month period, subject to the other restrictions of this subdivision governing gross rental rate increase.

(b) For a new tenancy in which no homeowner from the prior tenancy remains in lawful possession of the mobilehome space, management may establish the initial rental rate not subject to subdivision (a), unless the applicable local agency or jurisdiction has adopted an ordinance, rule, regulation, or initiative measure that limits the allowable rental rate for a new tenancy, in which case that ordinance, rule, regulation, or initiative measure shall apply. Subdivision (a) shall be applicable to subsequent increases after that initial rental rate has been established, except as otherwise provided in this section.

(c) A homeowner with a tenancy subject to this section shall not enter into a sublease that results in a total rent for the premises that exceeds the allowable rental rate authorized by subdivision (c) of Section 798.23.5. Nothing in this subdivision authorizes a homeowner to sublet or assign the homeowner's interest where otherwise prohibited.

(d) Management shall provide notice of any increase in the rental rate, pursuant to subdivision (a), to each homeowner in accordance with Section 798.30.

(e) This section shall not apply to a tenancy for any of the following:

(1) A mobilehome space restricted by deed, regulatory restriction contained in an agreement with a government agency, or other recorded document as affordable housing for persons and families of very low, low, or moderate income, as defined in Section 50093 of the Health and Safety Code, or subject to an agreement that provides housing subsidies for affordable housing for persons and families of very low, low, or moderate income, as defined in Section 50093 of the Health and Safety Code or comparable federal statutes.

(2) A mobilehome space constructed and maintained in connection with any higher education institution within the state for use and occupancy by students in attendance at the institution.

(3) A mobilehome space subject to any ordinance, rule, regulation, or initiative measure that restricts annual increases in the rental rate to an amount less than that provided in subdivision (a).

(4) A mobilehome space within a resident-owned mobilehome park, as defined in Section 799.

(f)(1)(A) This section shall apply to all rent increases occurring on or after February 18, 2021.

(B) This section shall become operative January 1, 2022.

(2) In the event that management has increased the rent by more than the amount permissible under subdivision (a) between February 18, 2021, and January 1, 2022, both of the following shall apply:

(A) The applicable rent on January 1, 2022, shall be the rent as of February 18, 2021, plus the maximum permissible increase under subdivision (a).

(B) Management shall not be liable to a homeowner for any corresponding rent overpayment.

(3) Management subject to subdivision (a) who increased the rental rate for a tenancy on or after February 18, 2021, but prior to January 1, 2022, by an amount less than the rental rate increase permitted by subdivision (a) shall be allowed to increase the rental rate twice, as provided in paragraph (2) of subdivision (a), within 12 months of February 18, 2021, but in no event shall that rental rate increase exceed the maximum rental rate increase permitted by subdivision (a).

(g) Any waiver of the rights under this section shall be void as contrary to public policy.

(h) For the purposes of this section:

(1) "Consumer Price Index for All Urban Consumers for All Items" means the following:

(A) The Consumer Price Index for All Urban Consumers for All Items (CPI-U) for the metropolitan area in which the property is located, as published by the United States Bureau of Labor Statistics, which are as follows:

(i) The CPI-U for the Los Angeles-Long Beach-Anaheim metropolitan area covering the Counties of Los Angeles and Orange.

(ii) The CPI-U for the Riverside-San Bernardo-Ontario metropolitan area covering the Counties of Riverside and San Bernardino.

(iii) The CPI-U for the San Diego-Carlsbad metropolitan area covering the County of San Diego.

(iv) The CPI-U for the San Francisco-Oakland-Hayward metropolitan area covering the Counties of Alameda, Contra Costa, Marin, San Francisco, and San Mateo.

(v) Any successor metropolitan area index to any of the indexes listed in clauses (i) to (iv), inclusive.

(B) If the United States Bureau of Labor Statistics does not publish a CPI-U for the metropolitan area in which the property is located, the California Consumer Price Index for All Urban Consumers for All Items as published by the Department of Industrial Relations.

(C) On or after January 1, 2022, if the United States Bureau of Labor Statistics publishes a CPI-U index for one or more metropolitan areas not listed in subparagraph (A), that CPI-U index shall apply in those areas with respect to rent increases that take effect on or after August 1 of the calendar year in which the 12-month change in that CPI-U, as described in subparagraph (B) of paragraph (3), is first published.

(2) "Management" means the management, as defined in Section 798.2, of a qualified mobilehome park.

(3)(A) "Percentage change in the cost of living" means the percentage change in the applicable Consumer Price Index for All Urban Consumers for All Items, as described in paragraph (1) and computed pursuant to subparagraph (B) of this paragraph.

(B)(i) For rent increases that take effect before August 1 of any calendar year, the following shall apply:

(I) The percentage change shall be the percentage change in the amount published for April of the immediately preceding calendar year and April of the year before that.

(II) If there is not an amount published in April for the applicable geographic area, the percentage change shall be the percentage change in the amount published for March of the immediately preceding calendar year and March of the year before that.

(ii) For rent increases that take effect on or after August 1 of any calendar year, the following shall apply:

(I) The percentage change shall be the percentage change in the amount published for April of that calendar year and April of the immediately preceding calendar year.

(II) If there is not an amount published in April for the applicable geographic area, the percentage change shall be the percentage change in the amount published for March of that calendar year and March of the immediately preceding calendar year.

(iii) The percentage change shall be rounded to the nearest one-tenth of 1 percent.

(4) "Qualified mobilehome park" means a mobilehome park, as defined in Section 798.4, that is located within and governed by the jurisdictions of two or more incorporated cities.

(i)(1) Nothing in this section affects the authority of a local government to adopt or maintain an ordinance, rule, regulation, or initiative measure that establishes a maximum amount that may be charged for rent. However, if a local ordinance, rule, regulation, or initiative measure allows for a rental rate increase greater than that provided in subdivision (a), this section shall apply.

(2) Nothing in this section alters the application of Sections 798.17, 798.45, or 798.49 to any ordinance, rule, regulation, or initiative measure that establishes a maximum amount that may be charged for rent.

(3) This section is not intended to express any policy regarding the appropriate, allowable rental rate increase limitations when a local government or jurisdiction adopts an ordinance, rule, regulation, or initiative measure regulating rent increases.

(j) This section shall remain in effect only until January 1, 2030, and as of that date is repealed. **Leg.H.** Added Stats 2021 ch 125 §2 (AB 978), effective January 1, 2022, operative January 1, 2022, repealed January 1, 2030.

§798.31. Rent, utilities, and services rendered

A homeowner shall not be charged a fee for other than rent, utilities, and incidental reasonable charges for services actually rendered.

A homeowner shall not be charged a fee for obtaining a lease on a mobilehome lot for (1) a term of 12 months, or (2) a lesser period as the homeowner may request. A fee may be charged for a lease of more than one year if the fee is mutually agreed upon by both the homeowner and management. **Leg.H.** Added Stats 1978 ch 1031 §1. Amended Stats 1982 ch 1397 §13; Stats 1984 ch 624 §1.

§798.32. Fees for services actually rendered not listed in rental agreement

(a) A homeowner shall not be charged a fee for services actually rendered which are not listed in the rental agreement unless he or she has been given written notice thereof by the management, at least 60 days before imposition of the charge.

(b) Those fees and charges specified in subdivision (a) shall be separately stated on any monthly or other periodic billing to the homeowner. If the fee or charge has a limited duration or is amortized for a specified period, the expiration date shall be stated on the initial notice and each subsequent billing to the homeowner while the fee or charge is billed to the homeowner. **Leg.H.** Added Stats 1978 ch 1031 §1. Amended Stats 1982 ch 1397 §14; Stats 1992 ch 338 §1 (SB 1365).

§798.33. Facilities or services for pets

(a) No lease agreement entered into, modified, or renewed on or after January 1, 2001, shall prohibit a homeowner from keeping at least one pet within the park, subject to reasonable rules and regulations of the park. This section may not be construed to affect any other rights provided by law to a homeowner to keep a pet within the park.

(b) A homeowner shall not be charged a fee for keeping a pet in the park unless the management actually provides special facilities or services for pets. If special pet facilities are maintained by the management, the fee charged shall reasonably relate to the cost of maintenance of the facilities or services and the number of pets kept in the park.

(c) For purposes of this section, "pet" means any domesticated bird, cat, dog, aquatic animal kept within an aquarium, or other animal as agreed to between the management and the homeowner. **Leg.H.** Added Stats 1978 ch 1031 §1. Amended Stats 1978 ch 1033 §11; Stats 1982 ch 1397 §15; Stats 1989 ch 42 §1; Stats 2000 ch 551 §1 (AB 860).

§798.34. Guests; Provision of live-in health or supportive care; No tenancy rights or duty to guest; Violations

(a) A homeowner shall not be charged a fee for a guest who does not stay with the homeowner for more than a total of 20 consecutive days or a total of 30 days in a calendar year. A person who is a guest, as described in this subdivision, shall not be required to register with the management.

(b) A homeowner who is living alone in the mobilehome and who wishes to share occupancy of their mobilehome with one other person, to be designated as the homeowner's companion, may do so, and management shall not impose a fee for that person. For purposes of this subdivision, a homeowner may only designate one person at a time as a companion and shall not designate more than three companions in total during any calendar year, unless otherwise authorized by management. Management may refuse to allow a homeowner to share their mobilehome with a companion under this subdivision if park residency is subject to age restrictions and the proposed companion is unable or unwilling to provide documentation that the proposed companion meets those age restrictions.

(c) A homeowner may share their mobilehome with any person over 18 years of age if that person is providing live-in health care, live-in supportive care, or supervision to the homeowner. Management shall not charge a fee for the live-in caregiver but may require written confirmation from a licensed health care professional of the homeowner's need for the care or supervision, if the need is not readily apparent or already known to management.

(d) A senior homeowner who resides in a mobilehome park that has implemented rules or regulations limiting residency based on age requirements for housing for older persons, pursuant to Section 798.76, may share their mobilehome with any person over 18 years of age if this person is a parent, sibling, child, or grandchild of the senior homeowner and requires live-in health care, live-in supportive care, or supervision. Management shall not charge a fee for this parent, sibling, child, or grandchild, but may require written confirmation from a licensed health care professional of the need for the care or supervision, if the need is not readily apparent or already known to management. As used in this section, "senior homeowner" means a homeowner who is 55 years of age or older.

(e) A guest, companion, live-in caregiver, or family member under the care of a senior homeowner, as they are described in this section, shall have no rights of tenancy in the park, and any agreement between the homeowner and the guest, companion, live-in caregiver, or family member under the care of a senior homeowner shall not change the terms and conditions of the rental agreement between management and the homeowner.

(f) A violation of the mobilehome park rules and regulations by a guest, companion, live-in caregiver, or family member under the care of a senior homeowner, as they are described in this section, shall be deemed a violation of the rules and regulations by the homeowner and subject to subdivision (d) of Section 798.56.

(g) Nothing in this section shall be interpreted to create a duty on the part of management to manage, supervise, or provide care for a homeowner's guest, companion, live-in caregiver, or family member under the care of a senior homeowner, during that person's stay in the mobilehome park. **Leg.H.** Added Stats 1978 ch 1031 §1. Amended Stats 1981 ch 240 §1; Stats 1982 ch 1397 §16; Stats 1983 ch 128 §1; Stats 1990 ch 881 §1 (SB 2547); Stats 1992 ch 337 §1 (SB 1314); Stats 1996 ch 157 §1 (SB 1624); Stats 2008 ch 170 §2 (SB 1107), effective January 1, 2009; Stats 2017 ch 767 §1 (SB 147), effective January 1, 2018; Stats 2019 ch 504 §1 (SB 274), effective January 1, 2020.

§798.35. Number of members in family

A homeowner shall not be charged a fee based on the number of members in his or her immediate family. As used in this section, the "immediate family" shall be limited to the homeowner, his or her spouse, their parents, their children, and their grandchildren under 18 years of age. **Leg.H.** Added Stats 1978 ch 1031 §1. Amended Stats 1980 ch 845 §1; Stats 1982 ch 1397 §17; Stats 1995 ch 24 §1 (AB 283).

§798.36. Enforcement of rules and regulations

(a) A homeowner shall not be charged a fee for the enforcement of any of the rules and regulations of the park, except a reasonable fee may be charged by management for the maintenance or cleanup, as described in subdivision (b), of the land and premises upon which the mobilehome is situated in the event the homeowner fails to do so in accordance with the rules and regulations of the park after written notification to the homeowner and the failure of the homeowner to comply within 14 days. The written notice shall state the specific condition to be corrected and an estimate of the charges to be imposed by management if the services are performed by management or its agent.

(b)(1) If management determines, in good faith, that the removal of a homeowner's or resident's personal property from the land and premises upon which the mobilehome is situated is necessary to bring the premises into compliance with the reasonable rules and regulations of the park or the provisions of the Mobilehome Parks Act (Part 2.1 (commencing with Section 18200) of Division 13 of the Health and Safety Code) or Title 25 of the California Code of Regulations, management may remove the property to a reasonably secure storage facility. Management shall provide written notice of at least 14 days of its intent to remove the personal property, including a description of the property to be removed. The notice shall include the rule, regulation, or code justifying the removal and shall provide an estimate of the charges to be imposed by management. The property to be removed shall not include the mobilehome or its appurtenances or accessory structures.

(2) The homeowner or resident shall be responsible for reimbursing to management the actual, reasonable costs, if any, of removing and storing the property. These costs incurred by management in correcting the rules violation associated with the removal and storage of the property, are deemed reasonable incidental service charges and may be collected pursuant to subdivision (e) of Section 798.56 if a notice of nonpayment of the removal and storage fees, as described in paragraph (3), is personally served on the homeowner.

(3) Within seven days from the date the property is removed to a storage area, management shall provide the homeowner or resident a written notice that includes an inventory of the property removed, the location where the property may be claimed, and notice that the cost of removal and storage shall be paid by the resident or homeowner. If, within 60 days, the homeowner or resident does not claim the property, the property shall be deemed to be abandoned, and management may dispose of the property in any manner. The homeowner's or resident's liability for storage charges shall not exceed 60 days. If the homeowner or resident claims the property, but has not reimbursed management for storage costs, management may bill those costs in a monthly statement which shall constitute notice of nonpayment, and the costs shall become the obligation of the homeowner or resident. If a resident or homeowner communicates in writing his or her intent to abandon the property before 60 days has expired, management may dispose of the property immediately and no further storage charges shall accrue.

(4) If management elects to dispose of the property by way of sale or auction, and the funds received from the sale or auction exceed the amount owed to management, management shall refund the difference to the homeowner or resident within 15 days from the date of management's receipt of the funds from the sale or auction. The refund shall be delivered to the homeowner or resident by first-class mail postage prepaid to his or her address in the park, or by personal delivery, and shall include an accounting specifying the costs of removal and storage of the property incurred by management in correcting the rules violation and the amount of proceeds realized from any sale or auction. If a sale or auction of the property yields less than the costs incurred by management, the homeowner or resident shall be responsible for the difference, and this amount shall be deemed a reasonable incidental service charge and may be collected pursuant to subdivision (e) of Section 798.56 if a notice of nonpayment of the removal and storage fees, as described in paragraph (3), is personally served on the homeowner. If management elects to proceed under this section, it may not also terminate the tenancy pursuant to subdivision (d) of Section 798.56 based upon the specific violations relied upon to proceed under this section. In any proceeding under this section, management shall bear the burden of proof that enforcement was undertaken in a nondiscriminatory, nonselective fashion. **Leg.H.** Added Stats 1978 ch 1031 §1. Amended Stats 1982 ch 1397 §18; Stats 1983 ch 519 §4; Stats 2005 ch 24 §1 (SB 125), effective January 1, 2006.

§798.37. Entry, installation, hookup, landscaping and maintenance

A homeowner may not be charged a fee for the entry, installation, hookup, or landscaping as a condition of tenancy except for an actual fee or cost imposed by a local governmental ordinance or requirement directly related to the occupancy of the specific site upon which the mobilehome is located and not incurred as a portion of the development of the mobilehome park as a whole. However, reasonable landscaping and maintenance requirements may be included in the park rules and regulations. The management may not require a homeowner or prospective homeowner to purchase, rent, or lease goods or services for landscaping, remodeling, or maintenance from any person, company, or corporation. **Leg.H.** Added Stats 1978 ch 1031 §1. Amended Stats 1980 ch 845 §2; Stats 1982 ch 1397 §19; Stats 1983 ch 519 §5; Stats 2004 ch 302 §4 (AB 2351).

§798.37.5. Responsibility for trees

(a) With respect to trees on rental spaces in a mobilehome park, park management shall be solely responsible for the trimming, pruning, or removal of any tree, and the costs thereof, upon written notice by a homeowner or a determination by park management that the tree poses a specific hazard or health and safety violation. In the case of a dispute over that assertion, the park management or a homeowner may request an inspection by the Department of Housing and Community Development or a local agency responsible for the enforcement of the Mobilehome Parks Act (Part 2.1 (commencing with Section 18200) of Division 13 of the Health and Safety Code) in order to determine whether a violation of that act exists.

(b) With respect to trees in the common areas of a mobilehome park, park management shall be solely responsible for the trimming, pruning, or removal of any tree, and the costs thereof.

(c) Park management shall be solely responsible for the maintenance, repair, replacement, paving, sealing, and the expenses related to the maintenance of all driveways installed by park management including, but not limited to, repair of root damage to driveways and foundation systems and removal. Homeowners shall be responsible for the maintenance, repair, replacement, paving, sealing, and the expenses related to the maintenance of a homeowner installed driveway. A homeowner may be charged for the cost of any damage to the driveway caused by an act of the homeowner or a breach of the homeowner's responsibilities under the rules and regulations so long as those rules and regulations are not inconsistent with the provisions of this section.

(d) No homeowner may plant a tree within the mobilehome park without first obtaining written permission from the management.

(e) This section shall not apply to alter the terms of any rental agreement in effect prior to January 1, 2001, between the park management and the homeowner regarding the responsibility for the maintenance of trees and driveways within the mobilehome park, except that upon any renewal or extension, the rental agreement shall be subject to this section.

This section is not intended to abrogate the content of any existing rental agreement or other written agreements regarding trees or driveways that are in effect prior to January 1, 2001.

(f) This section shall only apply to rental agreements entered into, renewed, or extended on or after January 1, 2001.

(g) Any mobilehome park rule or regulation shall be in compliance with this section. **Leg.H.** Added Stats 2000 ch 423 §2 (AB 862). Amended Stats 2014 ch 298 §1 (AB 2753), effective January 1, 2015.

§798.38. Acquisition of lien or security interest in mobilehome by park management

The management shall not acquire a lien or security interest, other than an interest arising by reason of process issued to enforce a judgment of any court, in a mobilehome located in the park unless it is mutually agreed upon by both the homeowner and management. Any billing and payment upon the obligation shall be kept separate from current rent. **Leg.H.** Added Stats 1986 ch 390 §1, as CC §798.40. Renumbered Stats 2009 ch 558 §5 (SB 111), effective January 1, 2010.

Prior Law: Former CC §798.38 was added Stats 1978 ch 1031 §1, amended Stats 1981 ch 714 §51, Stats 1982 ch 1397 §20, Stats 2004 ch 728 §1, and renumbered CC §798.40 by Stats 2009 ch 558 §3 (SB 111), effective January 1, 2010.

2009 Note: Nothing in this act shall be construed to affect the application of any other statute, regulation, or any existing contract, lease, rental agreement, or related document. Stats 2009 ch 558 (SB 111) §8.

§798.39. Security deposits

(a) The management may only demand a security deposit on or before initial occupancy and the security deposit may not be in an amount or value in excess of an amount equal to two months' rent that is charged at the inception of the occupancy, in addition to any rent for the first month. In no event shall additional security deposits be demanded of a homeowner following the initial occupancy.

(b) As to all security deposits collected on or after January 1, 1989, after the homeowner has promptly paid to the management, within five days of the date the amount is due, all of the rent, utilities, and reasonable service charges for any 12-consecutive-month period subsequent to the collection of the security deposit by the management, or upon resale of the mobilehome, whichever occurs earlier, the management shall, upon the receipt of a written request from the homeowner, refund to the homeowner the amount of the security deposit within 30 days following the end of the 12-consecutive-month period of the prompt payment or the date of the resale of the mobilehome.

(c) As to all security deposits collected prior to January 1, 1989, upon the extension or renewal of the rental agreement or lease between the homeowner and the management, and upon the receipt of a written request from the homeowner, if the homeowner has promptly paid to the management, within five days of the date the amount is due, all of the rent, utilities, and reasonable service charges for the 12-consecutive-month period preceding the receipt of the written request, the management shall refund to the homeowner the amount of the security deposit within 60 days.

(d) As to all security deposits collected prior to January 1, 1989, and not disbursed pursuant to subdivision (c), in the event that the mobilehome park is sold or transferred to any other party or entity, the selling park owner shall deposit in escrow an amount equal to all security deposits that the park owner holds. The seller's escrow instructions shall direct that, upon close of escrow, the security deposits therein that were held by the selling park owner (including the period in escrow) for 12 months or more, shall be disbursed to the persons who paid the deposits to the selling park owner and promptly paid, within five days of the date the amount is due, all rent, utilities, and reasonable service charges for the 12-month period preceding the close of escrow.

(e) Any and all security deposits in escrow that were held by the selling park owner that are not required to be disbursed pursuant to subdivision (b), (c), or (d) shall be disbursed to the successors in interest to the selling or transferring park owner, who shall have the same obligations of the park's management and ownership specified in this section with respect to security deposits. The disbursal may be made in escrow by a debit against the selling park owner and a credit to the successors in interest to the selling park owner.

(f) The management shall not be required to place any security deposit collected in an interest-bearing account or to provide a homeowner with any interest on the security deposit collected.

(g) Nothing in this section shall affect the validity of title to real property transferred in violation of this section. **Leg.H.** Added Stats 1988 ch 59 §1. Amended Stats 1994 ch 119 §1 (SB 1386); Stats 2001 ch 151 §1 (AB 210).

ARTICLE 4
Utilities

Fee or rent increase reflecting penalty assessed for violation of specified laws pertaining to mobilehome parks. §798.39.5.

Charges per billing period; Posting of specific current residential utility rate schedule or internet website address of specific current residential utility rate schedule; Third-party billing agent information. § 798.40.

Utility service fees. §798.41.

Advance notice of nonemergency interruption in utility service. §798.42.

Disclosure by management of measurement of service for common area facilities by meter on homeowner's site. §798.43.

Duties of management for California Alternate Rates for Energy (CARE) program. §798.43.1.

Cost of liquefied petroleum gas sold by park management to mobilehome owners or park tenants. §798.44.

Restriction on solar energy system for mobilehome void. § 798.44.1.

§798.39.5. Fee or rent increase reflecting penalty assessed for violation of specified laws pertaining to mobilehome parks

(a)(1) The management shall not charge or impose upon a homeowner any fee or increase in rent which reflects the cost to the management of any fine, forfeiture, penalty, money damages, or fee assessed or awarded by a court of law or an enforcement agency against the management for a violation of this chapter or Part 2.1 (commencing with Section 18200) of Division 13 of the Health and Safety Code, including any attorney's fees and costs incurred by the management in connection therewith.

(2) This section shall not apply to violations for which the registered owner of the mobilehome is initially responsible pursuant to subdivision (b) of Section 18420 of the Health and Safety Code.

(b) A court shall consider the remoteness in time of the assessment or award against the management of any fine, forfeiture, penalty, money damages, or fee in determining whether the homeowner has met the burden of proof that the fee or increase in rent is in violation of this section.

(c) Any provision in a rental agreement entered into, renewed, or modified on or after January 1, 1995, that permits a fee or increase in rent that reflects the cost to the management of any money damages awarded against the management for a violation of this chapter shall be void. **Leg.H.** Added Stats 1990 ch 1374 §1 (SB 2446), as CC §798.42. Renumbered Stats 2009 ch 558 §6 (SB 111), effective January 1, 2010. Amended Stats 2012 ch 477 §2 (AB 1938), effective January 1, 2013.

2009 Note: Nothing in this act shall be construed to affect the application of any other statute, regulation, or any existing contract, lease, rental agreement, or related document. Stats 2009 ch 558 (SB 111) §8.

§ 798.40. Charges per billing period; Posting of specific current residential utility rate schedule or internet website address of specific current residential utility rate schedule; Third-party billing agent information

(a) Where management provides both master-meter and submeter service of utilities to a homeowner, for each billing period the cost of the charges for the period shall be separately stated along with the opening and closing readings for the homeowner's meter. Management shall post, in a conspicuous place, the specific current residential utility rate schedule as published by the serving utility or the internet website address of the specific current residential utility rate schedule. If management elects to post the internet website address where the schedule may be accessed, management shall do both of the following:

(1) Provide a copy of the specific current residential utility rate schedule, upon request, at no cost.

(2) State in the posting that a homeowner may request a copy of the rate schedule from management.

(b) If a third-party billing agent or company prepares utility billing for the park, management shall disclose on each resident's billing, the name, address, and telephone number of the billing agent or company.

(c) Whenever management elects to separately bill water service to a homeowner as a utility service pursuant to Section 798.41, and to provide submetered water service to homeowners as a master-meter customer of the water purveyor, as a part of the regular bill for water service, management shall only bill a homeowner for the following water service:

(1) A charge for volumetric usage, which may be calculated in any of the following ways:

(A) The amount shall be calculated by first determining the proportion of the homeowner's usage, as shown by the submeter, to the total usage as shown by the water purveyor's billing. The dollar amount billed to the homeowner for usage shall be in that same proportion to the dollar amount for usage shown by the water purveyor's billing.

(B) If the water purveyor charges for volumetric usage based on a tiered rate schedule, management may calculate the charge for a homeowner's volumetric usage as described in subparagraph (A) or management may instead divide each tier's volume evenly among the number of mobilehome spaces, and the rate applicable to each block shall be applied to the consumption recorded for each mobilehome space.

(C) If the water purveyor charges the property rates on a per-mobilehome-space basis, the homeowners may be charged at those exact per-mobilehome-space rates.

(D) In no event shall the charge for volumetric usage under this paragraph include in its calculation water used by or for any common area facility in the park, or water used by any other person or entity, other than the homeowner being billed.

(2) Any recurring fixed charge, however that charge may be designated, for water service billed to the property by the water purveyors that, at management's discretion, shall be calculated by either of the following:

(A) The homeowner's proportion of the total fixed charges charged to management for the park's water use. The homeowner's proportion shall be based on the percentage of the homeowner's volumetric water use in relation to the total volumetric water use of the entire park, as shown on management's water bill during that period.

(B) Dividing the total fixed charges charged to the park equally among the total number of spaces at the park.

(3) A billing, administrative, or other fee representing the combined total of management's and the billing agent's costs, which shall be the lesser of an amount not to exceed four dollars and seventy-five cents ($4.75), as adjusted pursuant to this paragraph, or 25 percent of the amount billed pursuant to paragraph (1). Beginning January 1, 2022, the maximum fee authorized by this paragraph may be adjusted each calendar year by management, no higher than a commensurate increase in the Consumer Price Index based on a California fiscal year average for the previous fiscal year, for all urban consumers, as determined by the Department of Finance.

(d) For the purposes of this section, the following definitions apply:

(1) "Billing agent" means a person or entity that contracts to provide submetering services to management, including billing.

(2) "Submeter" means a device that measures water consumption of an individual mobilehome space within a park, and that is owned and operated by management.

(3) "Water service" includes any charges, whether presented for payment on local water purveyor bills, tax bills, or bills from other entities, related to water treatment, distribution, or usage, including, but not limited to, water, sewer, stormwater, and flood control.

(4) "Water purveyor" means a water purveyor as defined in Section 512 of the Water Code.

(e) Nothing in this section shall be construed to prevent management from recovering its costs to install, maintain, or improve its internal water delivery system, as may otherwise be allowed in any rental agreement or local regulation.

(f) The provisions of subdivision (c) shall apply to all management that elects to separately bill water service to a homeowner as a utility service pursuant to Section 798.41, and to provide submetered water service to homeowners as a master-meter customer of the water purveyor, as a part of the regular bill for water service, including where the water purveyor or the mobilehome park is subject to the jurisdiction, control, or regulation of the Public Utilities Commission. **Leg.H.** Added Stats 1978 ch 1031 §1, as CC §798.38. Amended Stats 1981 ch 714 §51; Stats 1982 ch 1397 §20; Stats 2004 ch 728 §1 (SB 1163). Renumbered Stats 2009 ch 558 §3 (SB 111), effective January 1, 2010; Stats 2013 ch 201 §1 (SB 196), effective January 1, 2014. Amended Stats 2021 ch 625 §1 (AB 1061), effective January 1, 2022; Stats 2023 ch 807 §1 (AB 604), effective January 1, 2024.

Prior Law: Former CC §798.40 was added Stats 1986 ch 390 §1. Renumbered CC §798.38 by Stats 2009 ch 558 §5 (SB 111), effective January 1, 2010.

2009 Note: Nothing in this act shall be construed to affect the application of any other statute, regulation, or any existing contract, lease, rental agreement, or related document. Stats 2009 ch 558 (SB 111) §8.

§798.41. Utility service fees

(a) Where a rental agreement, including a rental agreement specified in Section 798.17, does not specifically provide otherwise, the park management may elect to bill a homeowner separately for utility service fees and charges assessed by the utility for services provided to or for spaces in the park. Any separately billed utility fee and charges shall not be deemed to be included in the rent charged for those spaces under the rental agreement, and shall not be deemed to be rent or a rent increase for purposes of any ordinance, rule, regulation, or initiative measure adopted or enforced by any local governmental entity which establishes a maximum amount that a landlord may charge a tenant for rent, provided that at the time of the initial separate billing of any utility fees and charges the rent chargeable under the rental agreement or the base rent chargeable under the terms of a local rent control provision is simultaneously reduced by an amount equal to the fees and charges separately billed. The amount of this reduction shall be equal to the average amount charged to the park management for that utility service for that space during the 12 months immediately preceding notice of the commencement of the separate billing for that utility service.

Utility services to which this section applies are natural gas or liquid propane gas, electricity, water, cable television, garbage or refuse service, and sewer service.

(b) This section does not apply to rental agreements entered into prior to January 1, 1991, until extended or renewed on or after that date.

(c) Nothing in this section shall require rental agreements to provide for separate billing to homeowners of fees and charges specified in subdivision (a).

(d) Those fees and charges specified in subdivision (a) shall be separately stated on any monthly or other periodic billing to the homeowner. If the fee or charge has a limited duration or is amortized for a specified period, the expiration date shall be stated on the initial notice and each subsequent billing to the homeowner while the fee or charge is billed to the homeowner. **Leg.H.** Added Stats 1990 ch 1013 §2 (SB 2010). Amended Stats 1992 ch 160 §1 (SB 1658) ch 338 §2 (SB 1365).

Prior Law: There was another section of this number which was added Stats 1990 ch 380 §1, and amended and renumbered CC §798.43 by Stats 1991 ch 1091 §15.

§798.42. Advance notice of nonemergency interruption in utility service

(a) The management shall provide [1] all affected homeowners and residents [2] at least 72 hours' written advance notice of an interruption in utility service of more than two hours for the maintenance, repair, or replacement of facilities of utility systems over which the management has control within the park, provided that the interruption is not due to an emergency. The management shall be liable only for actual damages sustained by a homeowner or resident for violation of this section.

(b)(1) Upon voluntary, written consent of a homeowner or resident, the management may provide notice under this section by electronic communication in a form of electronic communication to which the homeowner or resident consents.

(2) For each homeowner or resident not provided notice by electronic communication, the management shall post written notice on the mobilehome of the affected homeowner or resident.

(c) For purposes of this section, the following definitions apply:

(1) "Electronic communication" means email, text, or automated telephone call.

(2) [3] "Emergency" means the interruption of utility service resulting from an accident or act of nature, or cessation of service caused by other than the management's regular or planned maintenance, repair, or replacement of utility facilities.

(3) "Voluntary, written consent" means written consent obtained separately from, and not contained in, any lease or rental agreement. Voluntary consent may be revoked by the homeowner or resident in writing at any time. Leg.H. Added Stats 1992 ch 317 §1 (SB 1389), as CC §798.29.5. Renumbered Stats 2009 ch 558 §1 (SB 111), effective

January 1, 2010. Amended Stats 2024 ch 23 §1 (AB 661), effective January 1, 2025.

§798.42. 2024 Deletes. [1], by posting notice on the mobilehomes of **[2]** , **[3]** "Emergency," for purposes of this section,

Prior Law: Former CC §798.42, was added Stats 1990 ch 1374 §1, amended Stats 1994 ch 1254 §1, and renumbered CC §798.39.5 by Stats 2009 ch 558 §6 (SB 111), effective January 1, 2010.

2009 Note: Nothing in this act shall be construed to affect the application of any other statute, regulation, or any existing contract, lease, rental agreement, or related document. Stats 2009 ch 558 (SB 111) §8.

§798.43. Disclosure by management of measurement of service for common area facilities by meter on homeowner's site

(a) Except as provided in subdivision (b), whenever a homeowner is responsible for payment of gas, water, or electric utility service, management shall disclose to the homeowner any condition by which a gas, water, or electric meter on the homeowner's site measures gas, water, or electric service for common area facilities or equipment, including lighting, provided that management has knowledge of the condition.

Management shall disclose this information prior to the inception of the tenancy or upon discovery and shall complete either of the following:

(1) Enter into a mutual written agreement with the homeowner for compensation by management for the cost of the portion of the service measured by the homeowner's meter for the common area facilities or equipment to the extent that this cost accrues on or after January 1, 1991.

(2) Discontinue using the meter on the homeowner's site for the utility service to the common area facilities and equipment.

(b) On and after January 1, 1994, if the electric meter on the homeowner's site measures electricity for lighting mandated by Section 18602 of the Health and Safety Code and this lighting provides lighting for the homeowner's site, management shall be required to comply with subdivision (a). **Leg.H.** Added Stats 1990 ch 380 §1 as CC §798.41 (AB 3259). Amended and renumbered by Stats 1991 ch 1091 §15 (AB 1487). Amended Stats 1993 ch 147 §1 (AB 1140).

§798.43.1. Duties of management for California Alternate Rates for Energy (CARE) program

(a) The management of a master-meter park shall give written notice to homeowners and residents on or before February 1 of each year in their utility billing statements about assistance to low-income persons for utility costs available under the California Alternate Rates for Energy (CARE) program, established pursuant to Section 739.1 of the Public Utilities Code. The notice shall include CARE information available to master-meter customers from their serving utility, to include, at a minimum: (1) the fact that CARE offers a discount on monthly gas or electric bills for qualifying low-income residents; and (2) the telephone number of the serving utility which provides CARE information and applications. The park shall also post the notice in a conspicuous place in the clubhouse, or if there is no clubhouse, in a conspicuous public place in the park.

(b) The management of a master-meter park may accept and help process CARE program applications from homeowners and residents in the park, fill in the necessary account or other park information required by the serving utility to process the applications, and send the applications to the serving utility. The management shall not deny a homeowner or resident who chooses to submit a CARE application to the utility himself or herself any park information, including a utility account number, the serving utility requires to process a homeowner or resident CARE program application.

(c) The management of a master-meter park shall pass through the full amount of the CARE program discount in monthly utility billings to homeowners and residents who have qualified for the CARE rate schedule, as defined in the serving utility's applicable rate schedule. The management shall notice the discount on the billing statement of any homeowner or resident who has qualified for the CARE rate schedule as either the itemized amount of the discount or a notation on the statement that the homeowner or resident is receiving the CARE discount on the electric bill, the gas bill, or both the electric and gas bills.

(d) "Master-meter park" as used in this section means "master-meter customer" as used in Section 739.5 of the Public Utilities Code. **Leg.H.** Added Stats 2001 ch 437 §1 (SB 920).

§798.44. Cost of liquefied petroleum gas sold by park management to mobilehome owners or park tenants

(a) The management of a park that does not permit mobilehome owners or park residents to purchase liquefied petroleum gas for use in the mobilehome park from someone other than the mobilehome park management shall not sell liquefied petroleum gas to mobilehome owners and residents within the park at a cost which exceeds 110 percent of the actual price paid by the management of the park for liquefied petroleum gas.

(b) The management of a park shall post in a visible location the actual price paid by management for liquefied petroleum gas sold pursuant to subdivision (a).

(c) This section shall apply only to mobilehome parks regulated under the Mobilehome Residency Law. This section shall not apply to recreational vehicle parks, as defined in Section 18215 of the Health and Safety Code, which exclusively serve recreational vehicles, as defined in Section 18010 of the Health and Safety Code.

(d) Nothing in this section is intended to abrogate any rights a mobilehome park owner may have under Section 798.31 of the Civil Code.

(e) In addition to a mobilehome park described in subdivision (a), the requirements of subdivisions (a) and (b) shall apply to a mobilehome park where requirements of federal, state, or local law or regulation, including, but not limited to, requirements for setbacks between mobilehomes, prohibit homeowners or residents from installing their own liquefied petroleum gas supply tanks, notwithstanding that the management of the mobilehome park permits mobilehome owners and park residents to buy their own liquefied petroleum gas. **Leg.H.** Added Stats 1999 ch 326 §2 (SB 476). Amended Stats 2000 ch 232 §1 (SB 1612); Stats 2009 ch 558 §7 (SB 111), effective January 1, 2010.

2009 Note: Nothing in this act shall be construed to affect the application of any other statute, regulation, or any existing contract, lease, rental agreement, or related document. Stats 2009 ch 558 (SB 111) §8.

§798.44.1. Restriction on solar energy system for mobilehome void

(a) Any covenant, restriction, or condition contained in any rental agreement or other instrument affecting the tenancy of a homeowner or resident in a mobilehome park that effectively prohibits or restricts the installation or use of a solar energy system on the mobilehome or the site, lot, or space on which the mobilehome is located is void and unenforceable.

(b) Management shall not prohibit or restrict a homeowner or resident from installing or using a solar energy system on a mobilehome or the site, lot, or space on which the mobilehome is located. Management shall not do any of the following:

(1) Charge any fee to a homeowner or resident in connection with the installation or use of a solar energy system.

(2) Require a homeowner or resident to use a specific solar installation contractor or solar energy system or product.

(3) Claim or receive any rebate, credit, or commission in connection with a homeowner's or resident's installation or use of a solar energy system.

(c) This section does not apply to imposition of reasonable restrictions on solar energy systems. However, it is the policy of the state to promote and encourage the use of solar energy systems and to remove obstacles thereto. Accordingly, reasonable restrictions on a solar energy system are those restrictions that do not significantly increase the cost of the system or significantly decrease its efficiency or specified performance, or that allow for an alternative system of comparable cost, efficiency, and energy conservation benefits.

(d)(1) For purposes of this section, "solar energy system" has the same meaning as defined in paragraphs (1) and (2) of subdivision (a) of Section 801.5.

(2) A solar energy system shall meet applicable health and safety standards and requirements imposed by state and local permitting authorities, consistent with Section 65850.5 of the Government Code.

(3) Solar energy systems and solar collectors used for heating water shall be certified by an accredited listing agency as defined in the California Plumbing and Mechanical Codes.

(4) A solar energy system for producing electricity shall also meet all applicable safety and performance standards established by the California Electrical Code, the Institute of Electrical and Electronics Engineers, and

accredited testing laboratories such as Underwriters Laboratories and, if applicable, rules of the Public Utilities Commission regarding safety and reliability.

(e) This section shall not apply to a master-meter park. "Master-meter park" as used in this section means "master-meter customer" as used in Section 739.5 of the Public Utilities Code. **Leg.H.** Added Stats 2024 ch 162 §1 (SB 1190), effective January 1, 2025.

ARTICLE 4.5
Rent Control

Exemption for new construction and new mobilehome park construction. §798.45.
Separate fees, assessments or other charges. §798.49.

§798.45. Exemption for new construction and new mobilehome park construction

(a) Notwithstanding Section 798.17, "new construction," as defined in subdivision (a) of Section 798.7, shall be exempt from any ordinance, rule, regulation, or initiative measure adopted by any city, county, or city and county, that establishes a maximum amount that a landlord may charge a tenant for rent, for a period of 15 years from the date upon which the space is initially held out for rent, as defined in subdivision (a) of Section 798.7.

(b) Notwithstanding Section 798.17, "new mobilehome park construction," as defined in subdivision (b) of Section 798.7, shall be exempt from any ordinance, rule, regulation, or initiative measure adopted by any city, county, or city and county, that establishes a maximum amount that a landlord may charge a tenant for rent for a period of 15 years from the date upon which 50 percent of the spaces in the new mobilehome park are initially held out for rent measured from the date of issuance of a permit or certificate of occupancy for that space by the enforcement agency in accordance with Section 18551 or 18613 of the Health and Safety Code. **Leg.H.** Added Stats 1989 ch 412 §2. Amended Stats 2022 ch 666 §2 (SB 940), effective January 1, 2023.

§798.49. Separate fees, assessments or other charges

(a) Except as provided in subdivision (d), the local agency of any city, including a charter city, county, or city and county, which administers an ordinance, rule, regulation, or initiative measure that establishes a maximum amount that management may charge a tenant for rent shall permit the management to separately charge a homeowner for any of the following:

(1) The amount of any fee, assessment or other charge first imposed by a city, including a charter city, a county, a city and county, the state, or the federal government on or after January 1, 1995, upon the space rented by the homeowner.

(2) The amount of any increase on or after January 1, 1995, in an existing fee, assessment or other charge imposed by any governmental entity upon the space rented by the homeowner.

(3) The amount of any fee, assessment or other charge upon the space first imposed or increased on or after January 1, 1993, pursuant to any state or locally mandated program relating to housing contained in the Health and Safety Code.

(b) If management has charged the homeowner for a fee, assessment, or other charge specified in subdivision (a) that was increased or first imposed on or after January 1, 1993, and the fee, assessment, or other charge is decreased or eliminated thereafter, the charge to the homeowner shall be decreased or eliminated accordingly.

(c) The amount of the fee, assessment or other charges authorized by subdivision (a) shall be separately stated on any billing to the homeowner. Any change in the amount of the fee, assessment, or other charges that are separately billed pursuant to subdivision (a) shall be considered when determining any rental adjustment under the local ordinance.

(d) This section shall not apply to any of the following:

(1) Those fees, assessments, or charges imposed pursuant to the Mobilehome Parks Act (Part 2.1 (commencing with Section 18200) of Division 13 of the Health and Safety Code), unless specifically authorized by Section 18502 of the Health and Safety Code.

(2) Those costs that are imposed on management by a court pursuant to Section 798.39.5.

(3) Any fee or other exaction imposed upon management for the specific purpose of defraying the cost of administration of any ordinance, rule, regulation, or initiative measure that establishes a maximum amount that management may charge a tenant for rent.

(4) Any tax imposed upon the property by a city, including a charter city, county, or city and county.

(e) Those fees and charges specified in subdivision (a) shall be separately stated on any monthly or other periodic billing to the homeowner. If the fee or charge has a limited duration or is amortized for a specified period, the expiration date shall be stated on the initial notice and each subsequent billing to the homeowner while the fee or charge is billed to the homeowner. **Leg.H.** Added Stats 1992 ch 338 §3 (SB 1365). Amended Stats 1994 ch 340 §2 (SB 1510); Stats 2012 ch 770 §1 (AB 2697), effective January 1, 2013.

ARTICLE 5
Homeowner Communications and Meetings

Legislative intent. §798.50.
Right of homeowners to meet in park; Use of community or recreation halls; Speakers; Political canvassing; Campaign signs. §798.51.
Injunctions. §798.52.

§798.50. Legislative intent

It is the intent of the Legislature in enacting this article to ensure that homeowners and residents of mobilehome parks have the right to peacefully assemble and freely communicate with one another and with others with respect to mobilehome living or for social or educational purposes. **Leg.H.** Added Stats 1989 ch 198 §2.

Prior Law: Former §798.50, relating to use of community or recreation halls, was added Stats 1978 ch 1031 §1, amended Stats 1982 ch 1397 §22; Stats 1983 ch 503 §2, ch 519 §17, Stats 1987 ch 33 §13, and repealed Stats 1989 ch 198 §1.

§798.51. Right of homeowners to meet in park; Use of community or recreation halls; Speakers; Political canvassing; Campaign signs

(a) No provision contained in any mobilehome park rental agreement, rule, or regulation shall deny or prohibit the right of any homeowner or resident in the park to do any of the following:

(1) Peacefully assemble or meet in the park, at reasonable hours and in a reasonable manner, for any lawful purpose. Meetings may be held in the park community or recreation hall or clubhouse when the facility is not otherwise in use, and, with the consent of the homeowner, in any mobilehome within the park.

(2) Invite public officials, candidates for public office, or representatives of mobilehome owner organizations to meet with homeowners and residents and speak upon matters of public interest, in accordance with Section 798.50.

(3) Canvass and petition homeowners and residents for noncommercial purposes relating to mobilehome living, election to public office, or the initiative, referendum, or recall processes, at reasonable hours and in a reasonable manner, including the distribution or circulation of information.

(b) A homeowner or resident may not be charged a cleaning deposit in order to use the park recreation hall or clubhouse for meetings of resident organizations for any of the purposes stated in Section 798.50 and this section, whether or not guests or visitors from outside the park are invited to attend the meeting, if a homeowner or resident of the park is hosting the meeting and all homeowners or residents of the park are allowed to attend.

(c) A homeowner or resident may not be required to obtain liability insurance in order to use common area facilities for the purposes specified in this section and Section 798.50. However, if alcoholic beverages are to be served at any meeting or private function, a liability insurance binder may be required by the park ownership or management. The ownership or management of a mobilehome park may prohibit the consumption of alcoholic beverages in the park common area facilities if the terms of the rental agreement or the rules and regulations of the park prohibit it.

(d) A homeowner, organization, or group of homeowners using a recreation hall or clubhouse pursuant to this section shall be required to adhere to any limitations or restrictions regarding vehicle parking or maximum occupancy for the clubhouse or recreation hall.

(e) A homeowner or resident may not be prohibited from displaying a political campaign sign relating to a candidate for election to public office or to the initiative, referendum, or recall process in the window or on the side of a manufactured home or mobilehome, or within the site on which the home is located or installed. The size of the face of a political sign may not exceed six square feet, and the sign may not be displayed in excess of a period of time from 90 days prior to an election to 15 days following the election, unless a local ordinance within the jurisdiction where the mobilehome park is located imposes a more restrictive period of time for the display of such a sign. **Leg.H.** Added Stats 1989 ch 198 §2. Amended Stats 2001 ch 83 §2 (AB 1202); Stats 2003 ch 249 §1 (SB 116).

Prior Law: Former §798.51, relating to meetings between homeowners and management, was added Stats 1981 ch 667 §7, amended Stats 1982 ch 1397 §23, Stats 1984 ch 299 §1, Stats 1986 ch 1416 §2, and repealed Stats 1989 ch 198 §1.

§798.52. Injunctions

Any homeowner or resident who is prevented by management from exercising the rights provided for in Section 798.51 may bring an action in a court of law to enjoin enforcement of any rule, regulation, or other policy which unreasonably deprives a homeowner or resident of those rights. **Leg.H.** Added Stats 1989 ch 198 §2.

ARTICLE 5.5
Homeowners Meetings with Management

Meetings between homeowners and management. §798.53.

§798.53. Meetings between homeowners and management

(a)(1) The management shall meet and consult with the homeowners, upon written request, within 30 days of the request, either individually, collectively, or with representatives of a group of homeowners who have signed a request to be so represented on the following matters:

(A) Resident concerns regarding interpretation, or enforcement or lack thereof, of existing park rules that are not subject to Section 798.25.

(B) Standards for maintenance of trees, driveways, or physical improvements in the park.

(C) Addition, alteration, or deletion of service, equipment, or physical improvements in the park.

(D) Rental agreements offered to existing residents pursuant to Section 798.17 or 798.18.

(E) Resident concerns regarding utility billing or utility charges.

(F) Common area facility hours and availability.

(2) The meeting may be conducted either in person or virtually using telephone, audio-video, or other audio-only conferencing.

(A) Management shall offer in-person and telephone options. If management allows audio-video conferencing options, management shall provide a list of audio-video conferencing options upon request of the homeowner or homeowners.

(B) Management shall comply with the method of meeting requested by the homeowner or homeowners requesting the meeting provided the method was offered by management pursuant to subparagraph (A).

(b) A collective meeting with a group of homeowners shall be conducted only after notice thereof has been given to all the requesting homeowners 10 days or more before the meeting.

(c) If an individual homeowner or group of homeowners consents to be represented at a meeting, management shall meet with either the designated representative on their behalf, or with both the homeowners and the designated representative, as the homeowners may choose in the written request. If requested by an individual homeowner or group of homeowners, a designated representative may participate in a meeting in person, by telephone, or virtually if management allows audio-video conferencing options pursuant to paragraph (2) of subdivision (a).

(d) Management shall permit the attendance of language interpreters at any meeting pursuant to this section. Interpreters may or may not be the homeowner's designated representative. **Leg.H.** Added Stats 1989 ch 198 §3. Amended Stats 1994 ch 340 §3 (SB 1510); Stats 2022 ch 648 §1 (AB 2031), effective January 1, 2023.

ARTICLE 6
Termination of Tenancy

Legislative findings; Notice of termination by management; Sale of mobile home by owner authorized. §798.55.
Reasons for termination of tenancy; Written notice; Cure of default [Repealed February 1, 2025]. §798.56
Reasons for termination of tenancy; Written notice; Cure of default [Operative February 1, 2025]. § 798.56.
Notice by owner or junior lienholder following notice of termination of tenancy; Retention of mobilehome in park pending sale to third party; Filing of notice of disposal of mobilehome; Information required for completion of disposal process. §798.56a.
Reason to be included in notice. §798.57.
Making site available for purchaser of mobilehome. §798.58.
Notice to management by homeowner. §798.59.
Proceeding for obtaining possession. §798.60.
Abandoned mobilehomes; Notice; Petition for declaration of abandonment; Hearing; Sale; Disposal. §798.61.
Renewed tenancy after destruction and rebuilding. §798.62.

§798.55. Legislative findings; Notice of termination by management; Sale of mobile home by owner authorized

(a) The Legislature finds and declares that, because of the high cost of moving mobilehomes, the potential for damage resulting therefrom, the requirements relating to the installation of mobilehomes, and the cost of landscaping or lot preparation, it is necessary that the owners of mobilehomes occupied within mobilehome parks be provided with the unique protection from actual or constructive eviction afforded by the provisions of this chapter.

(b)(1) The management may not terminate or refuse to renew a tenancy, except for a reason specified in this article and upon the giving of written notice to the homeowner, in the manner prescribed by Section 1162 of the Code of Civil Procedure, to sell or remove, at the homeowner's election, the mobilehome from the park within a period of not less than 60 days, which period shall be specified in the notice. A copy of this notice shall be sent to the legal owner, as defined in Section 18005.8 of the Health and Safety Code, each junior lienholder, as defined in Section 18005.3 of the Health and Safety Code, and the registered owner of the mobilehome, if other than the homeowner, by United States mail within 10 days after notice to the homeowner. The copy may be sent by regular mail or by certified or registered mail with return receipt requested, at the option of the management.

(2) The homeowner shall pay past due rent and utilities upon the sale of a mobilehome pursuant to paragraph (1).

(c) If the homeowner has not paid the rent due within three days after notice to the homeowner, and if the first notice was not sent by certified or registered mail with return receipt requested, a copy of the notice shall again be sent to the legal owner, each junior lienholder, and the registered owner, if other than the homeowner, by certified or registered mail with return receipt requested within 10 days after notice to the homeowner. Copies of the notice shall be addressed to the legal owner, each junior lienholder, and the registered owner at their addresses, as set forth in the registration card specified in Section 18091.5 of the Health and Safety Code.

(d) If management obtains a court judgment against a homeowner or resident, the cost incurred by management in obtaining a title search for the purpose of complying with the notice requirements of this section shall be recoverable as a cost of suit.

(e) The resident of a mobilehome that remains in the mobilehome park after service of the notice to sell or remove the mobilehome shall continue to be subject to this chapter and the rules and regulations of the park, including rules regarding maintenance of the space.

(f) No lawful act by the management to enforce this chapter or the rules and regulations of the park may be deemed or construed to waive or otherwise affect the notice to remove the mobilehome. **Leg.H.** Added Stats 1978 ch 1031 §1. Amended Stats 1978 ch 1033 §13; Stats 1979 ch 493 §1; Stats 1980 ch 1149 §4; Stats 1982 ch 1397 §24; Stats 1983 ch 519 §7, ch 1124 §2, operative July 1, 1984; Stats 1992 ch 835 §1 (AB 2715); Stats 1993 ch 666 §4 (AB 503); Stats 1998 ch 542 §1 (SB 2095); Stats 2003 ch 561 §1 (AB 682); Stats 2005 ch 24 §2 (SB 125), effective January 1, 2006.

2003 Note: This act is not intended to affect park management's existing rights and remedies to recover unpaid rent, utility charges, or reasonable incidental charges, and may not be construed to provide for an exclusive remedy. Stats 2003 ch 561 (AB 682) §4.

§798.56. Reasons for termination of tenancy; Written notice; Cure of default [Repealed February 1, 2025]

A tenancy shall be terminated by the management only for one or more of the following reasons:

(a) Failure of the homeowner or resident to comply with a local ordinance or state law or regulation relating to mobilehomes within a reasonable time after the homeowner receives a notice of noncompliance from the appropriate governmental agency.

(b) Conduct by the homeowner or resident, upon the park premises, that constitutes a substantial annoyance to other homeowners or residents.

(c)(1) Conviction of the homeowner or resident for prostitution, for a violation of subdivision (d) of Section 243, paragraph (2) of subdivision (a), or subdivision (b), of Section 245, Section 288, or Section 451, of the

Penal Code, or a felony controlled substance offense, if the act resulting in the conviction was committed anywhere on the premises of the mobilehome park, including, but not limited to, within the homeowner's mobilehome.

(2) However, the tenancy may not be terminated for the reason specified in this subdivision if the person convicted of the offense has permanently vacated, and does not subsequently reoccupy, the mobilehome.

(d) Failure of the homeowner or resident to comply with a reasonable rule or regulation of the park that is part of the rental agreement or any amendment thereto.

No act or omission of the homeowner or resident shall constitute a failure to comply with a reasonable rule or regulation unless and until the management has given the homeowner written notice of the alleged rule or regulation violation and the homeowner or resident has failed to adhere to the rule or regulation within seven days. However, if a homeowner has been given a written notice of an alleged violation of the same rule or regulation on three or more occasions within a 12-month period after the homeowner or resident has violated that rule or regulation, no written notice shall be required for a subsequent violation of the same rule or regulation.

Nothing in this subdivision shall relieve the management from its obligation to demonstrate that a rule or regulation has in fact been violated.

(e)(1) Except as provided for in the COVID-19 Tenant Relief Act of 2020 (Chapter 5 (commencing with Section 1179.01) of Title 3 of Part 3 of the Code of Civil Procedure), nonpayment of rent, utility charges, or reasonable incidental service charges; provided that the amount due has been unpaid for a period of at least five days from its due date, and provided that the homeowner shall be given a three-day written notice subsequent to that five-day period to pay the amount due or to vacate the tenancy. For purposes of this subdivision, the five-day period does not include the date the payment is due. The three-day written notice shall be given to the homeowner in the manner prescribed by Section 1162 of the Code of Civil Procedure. A copy of this notice shall be sent to the persons or entities specified in subdivision (b) of Section 798.55 within 10 days after notice is delivered to the homeowner. If the homeowner cures the default, the notice need not be sent. The notice may be given at the same time as the 60 days' notice required for termination of the tenancy. A three-day notice given pursuant to this subdivision shall contain the following provisions printed in at least 12-point boldface type at the top of the notice, with the appropriate number written in the blank: "Warning: This notice is the (insert number) three-day notice for nonpayment of rent, utility charges, or other reasonable incidental services that has been served upon you in the last 12 months. Pursuant to Civil Code Section 798.56 (e) (5), if you have been given a three-day notice to either pay rent, utility charges, or other reasonable incidental services or to vacate your tenancy on three or more occasions within a 12-month period, management is not required to give you a further three-day period to pay rent or vacate the tenancy before your tenancy can be terminated."

(2) Payment by the homeowner prior to the expiration of the three-day notice period shall cure a default under this subdivision. If the homeowner does not pay prior to the expiration of the three-day notice period, the homeowner shall remain liable for all payments due up until the time the tenancy is vacated.

(3) Payment by the legal owner, as defined in Section 18005.8 of the Health and Safety Code, any junior lienholder, as defined in Section 18005.3 of the Health and Safety Code, or the registered owner, as defined in Section 18009.5 of the Health and Safety Code, if other than the homeowner, on behalf of the homeowner prior to the expiration of 30 calendar days following the mailing of the notice to the legal owner, each junior lienholder, and the registered owner provided in subdivision (b) of Section 798.55, shall cure a default under this subdivision with respect to that payment.

(4) Cure of a default of rent, utility charges, or reasonable incidental service charges by the legal owner, any junior lienholder, or the registered owner, if other than the homeowner, as provided by this subdivision, may not be exercised more than twice during a 12-month period.

(5) If a homeowner has been given a three-day notice to pay the amount due or to vacate the tenancy on three or more occasions within the preceding 12-month period and each notice includes the provisions specified in paragraph (1), no written three-day notice shall be required in the case of a subsequent nonpayment of rent, utility charges, or reasonable incidental service charges.

In that event, the management shall give written notice to the homeowner in the manner prescribed by Section 1162 of the Code of Civil Procedure to remove the mobilehome from the park within a period of not less than 60 days, which period shall be specified in the notice. A copy of this notice shall be sent to the legal owner, each junior lienholder, and the registered owner of the mobilehome, if other than the homeowner, as specified in [1] **subdivision** (b) of Section 798.55, by certified or registered mail, return receipt requested, within 10 days after notice is sent to the homeowner.

(6) When a copy of the 60 days' notice described in paragraph (5) is sent to the legal owner, each junior lienholder, and the registered owner of the mobilehome, if other than the homeowner, the default may be cured by any of them on behalf of the homeowner prior to the expiration of 30 calendar days following the mailing of the notice, if all of the following conditions exist:

(A) A copy of a three-day notice sent pursuant to subdivision (b) of Section 798.55 to a homeowner for the nonpayment of rent, utility charges, or reasonable incidental service charges was not sent to the legal owner, junior lienholder, or registered owner, of the mobilehome, if other than the homeowner, during the preceding 12-month period.

(B) The legal owner, junior lienholder, or registered owner of the mobilehome, if other than the homeowner, has not previously cured a default of the homeowner during the preceding 12-month period.

(C) The legal owner, junior lienholder, or registered owner, if other than the homeowner, is not a financial institution or mobilehome dealer.

If the default is cured by the legal owner, junior lienholder, or registered owner within the 30-day period, the notice to remove the mobilehome from the park described in paragraph (5) shall be rescinded.

(f) Condemnation of the park.

(g) Change of use of the park or any portion thereof, provided:

(1) The management gives the homeowners at least 60 days' written notice that the management will be appearing before a local governmental board, commission, or body to request permits for a change of use of the mobilehome park.

(2)(A) After all required permits requesting a change of use have been approved by the local governmental board, commission, or body, the management shall give the homeowners six months' or more written notice of termination of tenancy.

(B) If the change of use requires no local governmental permits, then notice shall be given 12 months or more prior to the management's determination that a change of use will occur. The management in the notice shall disclose and describe in detail the nature of the change of use.

(3) The management gives each proposed homeowner written notice thereof prior to the inception of the proposed homeowner's tenancy that the management is requesting a change of use before local governmental bodies or that a change of use request has been granted.

(4) The notice requirements for termination of tenancy set forth in this section and Section 798.57 shall be followed if the proposed change actually occurs.

(5) A notice of a proposed change of use given prior to January 1, 1980, that conforms to the requirements in effect at that time shall be valid. The requirements for a notice of a proposed change of use imposed by this subdivision shall be governed by the law in effect at the time the notice was given.

(h) The report required pursuant to subdivisions (b) and (i) of Section 65863.7 of the Government Code shall be given to the homeowners or residents at the same time that notice is required pursuant to subdivision (g) of this section.

(i) A tenancy shall not be terminated pursuant to subdivision (e) or (g), and a notice of termination based thereon shall not be issued pursuant to Section 798.55 unless the park has a valid permit to operate issued by the enforcement agency pursuant to Chapter 4 (commencing with Section 18500) of Part 2.1 of Division 13 of the Health and Safety Code.

[2] **(j)** For purposes of this section, "financial institution" means a state or national bank, state or federal savings and loan association or credit union, or similar organization, and mobilehome dealer as defined in Section 18002.6 of the Health and Safety Code or any other organization that, as part of its usual course of business, originates, owns, or provides loan servicing for loans secured by a mobilehome.

[3] **(k)** This section remain in effect until February 1, 2025, and as of that date is repealed. **Leg.H.** Added Stats 1978 ch 1031 §1. Amended Stats 1978 ch 1033 §14; Stats 1979 ch 945 §2, ch 1185 §1.5; Stats 1980 ch 1149 §5; Stats 1981 ch 714 §52 (ch 458 prevails) ch 458 §1; Stats 1982 ch 777 §1, ch 1397 §25.5; Stats 1983 ch 519 §8, ch 1124 §3, operative July 1, 1984; Stats 1987 ch 55 §1, ch 883 §2; Stats 1988 ch 171 §1, ch 301 §2.5; Stats 1990 ch 42 §1 (AB 1209) ch 1357 §1.5 (AB 4156); Stats 1998 ch 427 §1 (AB 1888); Stats 2003 ch 85 §1 (AB 805) ch 388 §1.5 (AB 767); Stats 2020 ch 35 §3 (AB 2782), effective January 1, 2021; Stats 2020 ch 37 §4 (AB 3088), effective August 31, 2020, repealed February 1, 2025 (ch 37 prevails); Stats 2021 ch 360 §2 (AB 1584), effective January 1, 2022, repealed February 1, 2025; Stats 2024 ch 395 §1 (AB 2373), effective January 1, 2025, repealed February 1, 2025.

§798.56. 2024 Deletes. [1] paragraph [2] (i) [3] (j)

§ 798.56. Reasons for termination of tenancy; Written notice; Cure of default [Operative February 1, 2025]

A tenancy shall be terminated by the management only for one or more of the following reasons:

(a) Failure of the homeowner or resident to comply with a local ordinance or state law or regulation relating to mobilehomes within a reasonable time after the homeowner receives a notice of noncompliance from the appropriate governmental agency.

(b) Conduct by the homeowner or resident, upon the park premises, that constitutes a substantial annoyance to other homeowners or residents.

(c)(1) Conviction of the homeowner or resident for prostitution, for a violation of subdivision (d) of Section 243, paragraph (2) of subdivision (a), or subdivision (b), of Section 245, Section 288, or Section 451, of the Penal Code, or a felony controlled substance offense, if the act resulting in the conviction was committed anywhere on the premises of the mobilehome park, including, but not limited to, within the homeowner's mobilehome.

(2) However, the tenancy may not be terminated for the reason specified in this subdivision if the person convicted of the offense has permanently vacated, and does not subsequently reoccupy, the mobilehome.

(d) Failure of the homeowner or resident to comply with a reasonable rule or regulation of the park that is part of the rental agreement or any amendment thereto.

No act or omission of the homeowner or resident shall constitute a failure to comply with a reasonable rule or regulation unless and until the management has given the homeowner written notice of the alleged rule or regulation violation and the homeowner or resident has failed to adhere to the rule or regulation within seven days. However, if a homeowner has been given a written notice of an alleged violation of the same rule or regulation on three or more occasions within a 12-month period after the homeowner or resident has violated that rule or regulation, no written notice shall be required for a subsequent violation of the same rule or regulation.

Nothing in this subdivision shall relieve the management from its obligation to demonstrate that a rule or regulation has in fact been violated.

(e)(1) Nonpayment of rent, utility charges, or reasonable incidental service charges; provided that the amount due has been unpaid for a period of at least five days from its due date, and provided that the homeowner shall be given a three-day written notice subsequent to that five-day period to pay the amount due or to vacate the tenancy. For purposes of this subdivision, the five-day period does not include the date the payment is due. The three-day written notice shall be given to the homeowner in the manner prescribed by Section 1162 of the Code of Civil Procedure. A copy of this notice shall be sent to the persons or entities specified in subdivision (b) of Section 798.55 within 10 days after notice is delivered to the homeowner. If the homeowner cures the default, the notice need not be sent. The notice may be given at the same time as the 60 days' notice required for termination of the tenancy. A three-day notice given pursuant to this subdivision shall contain the following provisions printed in at least 12-point boldface type at the top of the notice, with the appropriate number written in the blank:

"Warning: This notice is the (insert number) three-day notice for nonpayment of rent, utility charges, or other reasonable incidental services that has been served upon you in the last 12 months. Pursuant to Civil Code Section 798.56 (e) (5), if you have been given a three-day notice to either pay rent, utility charges, or other reasonable incidental services or to vacate your tenancy on three or more occasions within a 12-month period, management is not required to give you a further three-day period to pay rent or vacate the tenancy before your tenancy can be terminated."

(2) Payment by the homeowner prior to the expiration of the three-day notice period shall cure a default under this subdivision. If the homeowner does not pay prior to the expiration of the three-day notice period, the homeowner shall remain liable for all payments due up until the time the tenancy is vacated.

(3) Payment by the legal owner, as defined in Section 18005.8 of the Health and Safety Code, any junior lienholder, as defined in Section 18005.3 of the Health and Safety Code, or the registered owner, as defined in Section 18009.5 of the Health and Safety Code, if other than the homeowner, on behalf of the homeowner prior to the expiration of 30 calendar days following the mailing of the notice to the legal owner, each junior lienholder, and the registered owner provided in subdivision (b) of Section 798.55, shall cure a default under this subdivision with respect to that payment.

(4) Cure of a default of rent, utility charges, or reasonable incidental service charges by the legal owner, any junior lienholder, or the registered owner, if other than the homeowner, as provided by this subdivision, may not be exercised more than twice during a 12-month period.

(5) If a homeowner has been given a three-day notice to pay the amount due or to vacate the tenancy on three or more occasions within the preceding 12-month period and each notice includes the provisions specified in paragraph (1), no written three-day notice shall be required in the case of a subsequent nonpayment of rent, utility charges, or reasonable incidental service charges.

In that event, the management shall give written notice to the homeowner in the manner prescribed by Section 1162 of the Code of Civil Procedure to remove the mobilehome from the park within a period of not less than 60 days, which period shall be specified in the notice. A copy of this notice shall be sent to the legal owner, each junior lienholder, and the registered owner of the mobilehome, if other than the homeowner, as specified in [1] **subdivision** (b) of Section 798.55, by certified or registered mail, return receipt requested, within 10 days after notice is sent to the homeowner.

(6) When a copy of the 60 days' notice described in paragraph (5) is sent to the legal owner, each junior lienholder, and the registered owner of the mobilehome, if other than the homeowner, the default may be cured by any of them on behalf of the homeowner prior to the expiration of 30 calendar days following the mailing of the notice, if all of the following conditions exist:

(A) A copy of a three-day notice sent pursuant to subdivision (b) of Section 798.55 to a homeowner for the nonpayment of rent, utility charges, or reasonable incidental service charges was not sent to the legal owner, junior lienholder, or registered owner, of the mobilehome, if other than the homeowner, during the preceding 12-month period.

(B) The legal owner, junior lienholder, or registered owner of the mobilehome, if other than the homeowner, has not previously cured a default of the homeowner during the preceding 12-month period.

(C) The legal owner, junior lienholder, or registered owner, if other than the homeowner, is not a financial institution or mobilehome dealer.

If the default is cured by the legal owner, junior lienholder, or registered owner within the 30-day period, the notice to remove the mobilehome from the park described in paragraph (5) shall be rescinded.

(f) Condemnation of the park.

(g) Change of use of the park or any portion thereof, provided:

(1) The management gives the homeowners at least 60 days' written notice that the management will be appearing before a local governmental board, commission, or body to request permits for a change of use of the mobilehome park.

(2)(A) After all required permits requesting a change of use have been approved by the local governmental board, commission, or body, the management shall give the homeowners six months' or more written notice of termination of tenancy.

(B) If the change of use requires no local governmental permits, then notice shall be given 12 months or more prior to the management's determination that a change of use will occur. The management in the notice shall disclose and describe in detail the nature of the change of use.

(3) The management gives each proposed homeowner written notice thereof prior to the inception of the proposed homeowner's tenancy that

the management is requesting a change of use before local governmental bodies or that a change of use request has been granted.

(4) The notice requirements for termination of tenancy set forth in Sections 798.56 and 798.57 shall be followed if the proposed change actually occurs.

(5) A notice of a proposed change of use given prior to January 1, 1980, that conforms to the requirements in effect at that time shall be valid. The requirements for a notice of a proposed change of use imposed by this subdivision shall be governed by the law in effect at the time the notice was given.

(h) The report required pursuant to subdivisions (b) and (i) of Section 65863.7 of the Government Code shall be given to the homeowners or residents at the same time that notice is required pursuant to subdivision (g) of this section.

(i) A tenancy shall not be terminated pursuant to subdivision (e) or (g), and a notice of termination based thereon shall not be issued pursuant to Section 798.55 unless the park has a valid permit to operate issued by the enforcement agency pursuant to Chapter 4 (commencing with Section 18500) of Part 2.1 of Division 13 of the Health and Safety Code.

[2] **(j)** For purposes of this section, "financial institution" means a state or national bank, state or federal savings and loan association or credit union, or similar organization, and mobilehome dealer as defined in Section 18002.6 of the Health and Safety Code or any other organization that, as part of its usual course of business, originates, owns, or provides loan servicing for loans secured by a mobilehome.

[3] **(k)** This section shall become operative on February 1, 2025. **Leg.H.** Added Stats 2020 ch 37 §5 (AB 3088), effective August 31, 2020, operative February 1, 2025. Amended Stats 2021 ch 360 §3 (AB 1584), effective January 1, 2022, operative February 1, 2025; Stats 2024 ch 395 §2 (AB 2373), effective January 1, 2025, operative February 1, 2025.

§ 798.56. 2024 Deletes. [1] paragraph [2] (i) [3] (j)

§798.56a. Notice by owner or junior lienholder following notice of termination of tenancy; Retention of mobilehome in park pending sale to third party; Filing of notice of disposal of mobilehome; Information required for completion of disposal process

(a) Within 60 days after receipt of, or no later than 65 days after the mailing of, the notice of termination of tenancy pursuant to any reason provided in Section 798.56, the legal owner, if any, and each junior lienholder, if any, shall notify the management in writing of at least one of the following:

(1) Its offer to sell the obligation secured by the mobilehome to the management for the amount specified in its written offer. In that event, the management shall have 15 days following receipt of the offer to accept or reject the offer in writing. If the offer is rejected, the person or entity that made the offer shall have 10 days in which to exercise one of the other options contained in this section and shall notify management in writing of its choice.

(2) Its intention to foreclose on its security interest in the mobilehome.

(3) Its request that the management pursue the termination of tenancy against the homeowner and its offer to reimburse management for the reasonable attorney's fees and court costs incurred by the management in that action. If this request and offer are made, the legal owner, if any, or junior lienholder, if any, shall reimburse the management the amount of reasonable attorney's fees and court costs, as agreed upon by the management and the legal owner or junior lienholder, incurred by the management in an action to terminate the homeowner's tenancy, on or before the earlier of (A) the 60th calendar day following receipt of written notice from the management of the aggregate amount of those reasonable attorney's fees and costs or (B) the date the mobilehome is resold.

(b) A legal owner, if any, or junior lienholder, if any, may sell the mobilehome within the park to a third party and keep the mobilehome on the site within the mobilehome park until it is resold only if all of the following requirements are met:

(1) The legal owner, if any, or junior lienholder, if any, notifies management in writing of the intention to exercise either option described in paragraph (2) or (3) of subdivision (a) within 60 days following receipt of, or no later than 65 days after the mailing of, the notice of termination of tenancy and satisfies all of the responsibilities and liabilities of the homeowner owing to the management for the 90 days preceding the mailing of the notice of termination of tenancy and then continues to satisfy these responsibilities and liabilities as they accrue from the date of the mailing of that notice until the date the mobilehome is resold.

(2) Within 60 days following receipt of, or no later than 65 days after the mailing of, the notice of termination of tenancy, the legal owner or junior lienholder commences all repairs and necessary corrective actions so that the mobilehome complies with park rules and regulations in existence at the time the notice of termination of tenancy was given as well as the health and safety standards specified in Sections 18550, 18552, and 18605 of the Health and Safety Code, and completes these repairs and corrective actions within 90 calendar days of that notice, or before the date that the mobilehome is sold, whichever is earlier.

(3) The legal owner, if any, or junior lienholder, if any, complies with the requirements of Article 7 (commencing with Section 798.70) as it relates to the transfer of the mobilehome to a third party.

(c) For purposes of subdivision (b), the "homeowner's responsibilities and liabilities" means all rents, utilities, reasonable maintenance charges of the mobilehome and its premises, and reasonable maintenance of the mobilehome and its premises pursuant to existing park rules and regulations.

(d) If the homeowner files for bankruptcy, the periods set forth in this section are tolled until the mobilehome is released from bankruptcy.

(e)(1) Notwithstanding any other provision of law, including, but not limited to, Section 18099.5 of the Health and Safety Code, if neither the legal owner nor a junior lienholder notifies the management of its decision pursuant to subdivision (a) within the period allowed, or performs as agreed within 30 days, or if a registered owner of a mobilehome, that is not encumbered by a lien held by a legal owner or a junior lienholder, fails to comply with a notice of termination and is either legally evicted or vacates the premises, the management may either remove the mobilehome from the premises and place it in storage or store it on its site. In this case, notwithstanding any other provision of law, the management shall have a warehouse lien in accordance with Section 7209 of the Commercial Code against the mobilehome for the costs of dismantling and moving, if appropriate, as well as storage, that shall be superior to all other liens, except the lien provided for in Section 18116.1 of the Health and Safety Code, and may enforce the lien pursuant to Section 7210 of the Commercial Code either after the date of judgment in an unlawful detainer action or after the date the mobilehome is physically vacated by the resident, whichever occurs earlier. Upon completion of any sale to enforce the warehouse lien in accordance with Section 7210 of the Commercial Code, the management shall provide the purchaser at the sale with evidence of the sale, as shall be specified by the Department of Housing and Community Development, that shall, upon proper request by the purchaser of the mobilehome, register title to the mobilehome to this purchaser, whether or not there existed a legal owner or junior lienholder on this title to the mobilehome.

(2)(A) Notwithstanding any other law, if the management of a mobilehome park acquires a mobilehome after enforcing the warehouse lien and files a notice of disposal pursuant to subparagraph (B) with the Department of Housing and Community Development to designate the mobilehome for disposal, management or any other person enforcing this warehouse lien shall not be required to pay past or current vehicle license fees required by Section 18115 of the Health and Safety Code or obtain a tax clearance certificate, as set forth in Section 5832 of the Revenue and Taxation Code, provided that management notifies the county tax collector in the county in which the mobilehome is located of management's intent to apply to have the mobilehome designated for disposal after a warehouse lien sale. The written notice shall be sent to the county tax collector no less than 30 days after the date of the sale to enforce the lien against the mobilehome by first class mail, postage prepaid.

(B)(i) In order to dispose of a mobilehome after a warehouse lien sale, the management shall file a notice of disposal with the Department of Housing and Community Development in the form and manner as prescribed by the department, no less than 30 days after the date of sale to enforce the lien against the mobilehome.

(ii) After filing a notice of disposal pursuant to clause (i), the management may dispose of the mobilehome after obtaining the information required by applicable laws.

(C)(i) Within 30 days of the date of the disposal of the mobilehome, the management shall submit to the Department of Housing and Community

Development all of the following information required for completing the disposal process:

(I) Photographs identifying and demonstrating that the mobilehome was uninhabitable by the removal or destruction of all appliances and fixtures such as ovens, stoves, bathroom fixtures, and heating or cooling appliances prior to its being moved.

(II) A statement of facts as to the condition of the mobilehome when moved, the date it was moved, and the anticipated site of further dismantling or disposal.

(III) The name, address, and license number of the person or entity removing the mobilehome from the mobilehome park.

(ii) The information required pursuant to clause (i) shall be submitted under penalty of perjury.

(D) For purposes of this paragraph, "dispose" or "disposal" shall mean the removal and destruction of an abandoned mobilehome from a mobilehome park, thus making it unusable for any purpose and not subject to, or eligible for, use in the future as a mobilehome.

(f) All written notices required by this section, except the notice in paragraph (2) of subdivision (e), shall be sent to the other party by certified or registered mail with return receipt requested.

(g) Satisfaction, pursuant to this section, of the homeowner's accrued or accruing responsibilities and liabilities shall not cure the default of the homeowner. **Leg.H.** Added Stats 1990 ch 1357 §2 (AB 4156). Amended Stats 1992 ch 88 §1 (AB 2548) ch 835 §2 (AB 2715); Stats 1996 ch 95 §1 (AB 2781); Stats 1998 ch 542 §2 (SB 2095); Stats 2010 ch 610 §1.6 (AB 2762), effective January 1, 2011; Stats 2015 ch 376 §1 (AB 999), effective January 1, 2016; Stats 2016 §2 (SB 944), effective January 1, 2017.

§798.57. Reason to be included in notice

The management shall set forth in a notice of termination, the reason relied upon for the termination with specific facts to permit determination of the date, place, witnesses, and circumstances concerning that reason. Neither reference to the section number or a subdivision thereof, nor a recital of the language of this article will constitute compliance with this section. **Leg.H.** Added Stats 1978 ch 1031 §1.

§798.58. Making site available for purchaser of mobilehome

Tenancy may only be terminated for reasons contained in Section 798.56, and a tenancy may not be terminated for the purpose of making a homeowner's site available for a person who purchased or proposes to purchase, or rents or proposes to rent, a mobilehome from the owner of the park or the owner's agent. **Leg.H.** Added Stats 1978 ch 1031 §1. Amended Stats 1982 ch 1397 §26; Stats 2002 ch 672 §3 (SB 1410).

§798.59. Notice to management by homeowner

A homeowner shall give written notice to the management of not less than 60 days before vacating his or her tenancy. **Leg.H.** Added Stats 1978 ch 1031 §1. Amended Stats 1982 ch 1397 §27.

§798.60. Proceeding for obtaining possession

The provisions of this article shall not affect any rights or proceedings set forth in Chapter 4 (commencing with Section 1159) of Title 3 of Part 3 of the Code of Civil Procedure except as otherwise provided herein. **Leg.H.** Added Stats 1978 ch 1031 §1. Amended Stats 1978 ch 1033 §15.

§798.61. Abandoned mobilehomes; Notice; Petition for declaration of abandonment; Hearing; Sale; Disposal

(a)(1) As used in this section, "abandoned mobilehome" means a mobilehome about which all of the following are true:

(A) It is located in a mobilehome park on a site for which no rent has been paid to the management for the preceding 60 days.

(B) It is unoccupied.

(C) A reasonable person would believe it to be abandoned.

(D) It is not permanently affixed to the land.

(2) As used in this section:

(A) "Mobilehome" shall include a trailer coach, as defined in Section 635 of the Vehicle Code, or a recreational vehicle, as defined in Section 18010 of the Health and Safety Code, if the trailer coach or recreational vehicle also satisfies the requirements of paragraph (1), including being located on any site within a mobilehome park, even if the site is in a separate designated section pursuant to Section 18215 of the Health and Safety Code.

(B) "Abandoned mobilehome" shall include a mobilehome that is uninhabitable because of its total or partial destruction that cannot be rehabilitated, if the mobilehome also satisfies the requirements of paragraph (1).

(C) "Dispose" or "disposal" shall mean the removal and destruction of an abandoned mobilehome from a mobilehome park, thus making it unusable for any purpose and not subject to, or eligible for, use in the future as a mobilehome.

(b) After determining a mobilehome in a mobilehome park to be an abandoned mobilehome, the management shall post a notice of belief of abandonment on the mobilehome for not less than 30 days, and shall deposit copies of the notice in the United States mail, postage prepaid, addressed to the homeowner at the last known address and to any known registered owner, if different from the homeowner, and to any known holder of a security interest in the abandoned mobilehome. This notice shall be mailed by registered or certified mail with a return receipt requested.

(c)(1) Thirty or more days following posting pursuant to subdivision (b), the management may file a petition in the superior court in the county in which the mobilehome park is located, for a judicial declaration of abandonment of the mobilehome. A proceeding under this subdivision is a limited civil case. Copies of the petition shall be served upon the homeowner, any known registered owner, and any known person having a lien or security interest of record in the mobilehome by posting a copy on the mobilehome and mailing copies to those persons at their last known addresses by registered or certified mail with a return receipt requested in the United States mail, postage prepaid.

(2) To dispose of an abandoned mobilehome pursuant to subdivision (f), the management shall also do all of the following:

(A) Declare in the petition that the management will dispose of the abandoned mobilehome, and therefore will not seek a tax clearance certificate as set forth in Section 5832 of the Revenue and Taxation Code.

(B) Declare in the petition whether the management intends to sell the contents of the abandoned mobilehome before its disposal.

(C) Notify the county tax collector in the county in which the mobilehome park is located of the declaration that management will dispose of the abandoned mobilehome by sending a copy of the petition by first class mail.

(D) Declare in the petition that management intends to file a notice of disposal with the Department of Housing and Community Development and complete the disposal process consistent with the requirements of subdivision (f).

(d)(1) Hearing on the petition shall be given precedence over other matters on the court's calendar.

(2) If, at the hearing, the petitioner shows by a preponderance of the evidence that the criteria for an abandoned mobilehome has been satisfied and no party establishes an interest therein at the hearing and tenders all past due rent and other charges, the court shall enter a judgment of abandonment, determine the amount of charges to which the petitioner is entitled, and award attorney's fees and costs to the petitioner. For purposes of this subdivision, an interest in the mobilehome shall be established by evidence of a right to possession of the mobilehome or a security or ownership interest in the mobilehome.

(3) A default may be entered by the court clerk upon request of the petitioner, and a default judgment shall be thereupon entered, if no responsive pleading is filed within 15 days after service of the petition by mail.

(e) To sell an abandoned mobilehome, the management shall do all of the following:

(1)(A) Within 10 days following a judgment of abandonment, the management shall enter the abandoned mobilehome and complete an inventory of the contents and submit the inventory to the court.

(B) During this period the management shall post and mail a notice of intent to sell the abandoned mobilehome and its contents under this section, and announcing the date of sale, in the same manner as provided for the notice of determination of abandonment under subdivision (b). The management shall also provide notice to the county tax collector in the county in which the mobilehome park is located.

(C) At any time prior to the sale of an abandoned mobilehome or its contents under this section, any person having a right to possession of the abandoned mobilehome may recover and remove it from the premises upon payment to the management of all rent or other charges due, including reasonable costs of storage and other costs awarded by the court. Upon receipt of this payment and removal of the abandoned mobilehome from the premises pursuant to this paragraph, the management shall immediately file an acknowledgment of satisfaction of judgment pursuant to Section 724.030 of the Code of Civil Procedure.

(2) Following the judgment of abandonment, but not less than 10 days following the notice of sale specified in paragraph (1), the management may conduct a public sale of the abandoned mobilehome, its contents, or both. The management may bid at the sale and shall have the right to offset its bids to the extent of the total amount due it under this section. The proceeds of the sale shall be retained by the management, but any unclaimed amount thus retained over and above the amount to which the management is entitled under this section shall be deemed abandoned property and shall be paid into the treasury of the county in which the sale took place within 30 days of the date of the sale. The former homeowner or any other owner may claim any or all of that unclaimed amount within one year from the date of payment to the county by making application to the county treasurer or other official designated by the county. If the county pays any or all of that unclaimed amount to a claimant, neither the county nor any officer or employee of the county is liable to any other claimant as to the amount paid.

(3) Within 30 days of the date of the sale, the management shall submit to the court an accounting of the moneys received from the sale and the disposition of the money and the items contained in the inventory submitted to the court pursuant to paragraph (1).

(4) The management shall provide the purchaser at the sale of an abandoned mobilehome with a copy of the judgment of abandonment and evidence of the sale, as shall be specified by the Department of Housing and Community Development, which shall register title in the abandoned mobilehome to the purchaser upon presentation thereof within 20 days of purchase. The sale shall pass title to the purchaser free of any prior interest, including any security interest or lien, except the lien provided for in Section 18116.1 of the Health and Safety Code, in the abandoned mobilehome.

(f) To dispose of an abandoned mobilehome, the management shall do all of the following:

(1)(A) Within 10 days following a judgment of abandonment, the management shall enter the abandoned mobilehome and complete an inventory of the contents and submit the inventory to the court.

(B) Within 10 days following a judgment of abandonment, the management shall post and mail a notice of intent to dispose of the abandoned mobilehome and its contents under this section, and announcing the date of disposal, in the same manner as provided for the notice of determination of abandonment under subdivision (b). The management shall also provide notice to the county tax collector in the county in which the mobilehome park is located.

(C)(i) Within 30 days following a judgment of abandonment, the management shall file a notice of disposal with the Department of Housing and Community Development in the form and manner as prescribed by the department.

(ii) Notwithstanding any other law, when filing a notice of disposal pursuant to clause (i), the management shall not be required to pay past or current vehicle license fees required by Section 18115 of the Health and Safety Code or obtain a tax clearance certificated as set forth in Section 5832 of the Revenue and Taxation Code, provided that the management notifies the county tax collector in the county in which the mobilehome is located of the management's intent to apply to have the mobilehome designated for disposal pursuant to this subdivision. The written notice shall be sent to the county tax collector no less than 10 days after the date of the abandonment judgment by first class mail, postage prepaid.

(D) At any time prior to the disposal of an abandoned mobilehome or its contents under this section, any person having a right to possession of the abandoned mobilehome may recover and remove it from the premises upon payment to the management of all rent or other charges due, including reasonable costs of storage and other costs awarded by the court. Upon receipt of this payment and removal of the abandoned mobilehome from the premises pursuant to this subparagraph, the management shall immediately file an acknowledgment of satisfaction of judgment pursuant to Section 724.030 of the Code of Civil Procedure and a cancellation of the notice of disposal with the Department of Housing and Community Development.

(2) Following the judgment of abandonment and approval of the notice of disposal by the Department of Housing and Community Development, but not less than 10 days following the notice of disposal specified in paragraph (1), the management may dispose of the abandoned mobilehome after obtaining the information required in subparagraph (A) of paragraph (3).

(3)(A) Within 30 days of the date of the disposal of an abandoned mobilehome and its contents, the management shall do both of the following:

(i) Submit to the court and the county tax collector in the county in which the mobilehome park is located a statement that the abandoned mobilehome and its contents were disposed with supporting documentation.

(ii)(I) Submit to the Department of Housing and Community Development all of the following information required for completing the disposal process:

(ia) Photographs identifying and demonstrating that the mobilehome was uninhabitable by the removal or destruction of all appliances and fixtures such as ovens, stoves, bathroom fixtures, and heating or cooling appliances prior to its being moved.

(ib) A statement of facts as to the condition of the mobilehome when moved, the date it was moved, and the anticipated site of further dismantling or disposal.

(ic) The name, address, and license number of the person or entity removing the mobilehome from the mobilehome park.

(II) The information required pursuant to subclause (I) shall be submitted under penalty of perjury.

(B) Within 30 days of the date of the disposal of an abandoned mobilehome or the date of the sale of its contents, whichever date is later, the management shall submit to the court and the county tax collector in the county in which the mobilehome park is located an accounting of the moneys received from the sale and the disposition of the money and the items contained in the inventory submitted to the court pursuant to paragraph (1) and a statement that the abandoned mobilehome was disposed with supporting documentation.

(g) Notwithstanding any other law, the management shall not be required to obtain a tax clearance certificate, as set forth in Section 5832 of the Revenue and Taxation Code, to dispose of an abandoned mobilehome and its contents pursuant to subdivision (f). However, any sale pursuant to this section shall be subject to the registration requirements of Section 18100.5 of the Health and Safety Code and the tax clearance certificate requirements of Section 18092.7 of the Health and Safety Code.

(h) Notwithstanding any other law, forms and procedures made available for the implementation of Chapter 376 of the Statutes of 2015 shall not be subject to Chapter 4.5 (commencing with Section 11400) of Part 1 of Division 3 of Title 2 of the Government Code. **Leg.H.** Added Stats 1986 ch 1153 §1. Amended Stats 1988 ch 301 §3; Stats 1991 ch 564 §1 (AB 743); Stats 1995 ch 446 §1 (SB 69); Stats 1998 ch 931 §12 (SB 2139), effective September 28, 1998; Stats 2003 ch 449 §2 (AB 1712); Stats 2015 ch 376 §2 (AB 999), effective January 1, 2016; Stats 2016 ch 714 §3 (SB 944), effective January 1, 2017.

Prior Law: Former §798.61, relating to application of requirements for notice of termination, was added Stats 1978 ch 1031 §1 and repealed Stats 1978 ch 1033 §6.

§798.62. Renewed tenancy after destruction and rebuilding

(a) If a mobilehome park is destroyed as a result of a wildfire or other natural disaster, and management elects to rebuild the park at the same location, management shall offer a renewed tenancy in the rebuilt mobilehome park to all previous homeowners in accordance with the following:

(1) The offer of renewed tenancy shall be on substantially the same terms as the previous homeowner's rental agreement that was in existence at the time of the wildfire or other natural disaster. However, management may adjust terms in the previous rental agreement to reflect costs and expenses to rebuild the park that were incurred from the time of the disaster until management received a final certificate of occupancy for all spaces in the park. These costs and expenses may include, but are not limited to, costs associated with demolition, reconstruction, and environmental remediation, as well as taxes and interest expenses.

(2) Management shall provide the previous homeowner, upon request, a statement listing the costs and expenses incurred in rebuilding the park and how the costs and expenses relate to the adjustment of terms in the rental agreement.

(3) The offer shall include an application to accept the renewed tenancy, the terms of the renewed tenancy, the deposit required to secure the renewed tenancy, and a clear statement of when the offer expires.

(4) Management shall send each previous homeowner the offer by certified mail, at least 240 days before the park is reopened, to the last postal address for the previous homeowner known to management, which may be the previous homeowner's former address within the park. If management has an email address or telephone number for the previous homeowner, management shall additionally attempt to notify the homeowner of the offer by those means.

(5) A previous homeowner may accept the offer by submitting, within 60 days from the date the homeowner receives the offer, the application and required deposit to secure the renewed tenancy to management and sign a rental agreement. If the previous homeowner fails to accept the offer within this time period, then the previous homeowner's right to a renewed tenancy under this section is deemed forfeited.

(6) Management shall process applications for renewed tenancy on a first-come-first-served basis.

(7) The previous homeowner shall not transfer the right to a renewed tenancy.

(b) For purposes of this section, "previous homeowner" means a homeowner with a valid tenancy in a mobilehome park at the time of a wildfire or other natural disaster. **Leg.H.** Added Stats 2019 ch 504 §2 (SB 274), effective January 1, 2020.

ARTICLE 7
Transfer of Mobilehome or Mobilehome Park

Advertisement for sale, exchange, or rent. §798.70.
Showing or listing for sale; Use of specific broker or dealer not required. §798.71.
Charging of fee for performance of services by management. §798.72.
Removal from park during term of rental agreement. §798.73.
Mobilehome that will remain in park. §798.73.5.
Management approval of purchaser; Notices and information. §798.74.
Transfer disclosure requirements. §798.74.4.
"Information for Prospective Homeowners" document to be given upon request for residency application. §798.74.5.
Attachment of rental agreement or statement. §798.75.
Mobilehome park rental agreement disclosure form. §798.75.5.
Compliance with regulation limiting residency based on age requirements to older persons. §798.76.
Waiver of provisions void. §798.77.
Ownership gained through death. §798.78.
Right of resale by legal owner or junior lienholder; Homeowner's responsibilities. §798.79.
Notice to resident organization that mobilehome park is for sale. §798.80.
Listing or sale within park; Management as agent as condition of residency. §798.81.
Disclosure by management that mobilehome may be subject to school facilities fee. §798.82.
Repairs or improvements to mobilehome park space. §798.83.

§798.70. Advertisement for sale, exchange, or rent

(a) A homeowner, an heir, joint tenant, or personal representative of the estate who gains ownership of a mobilehome in the mobilehome park through the death of the owner of the mobilehome who was a homeowner at the time of his or her death, or the agent of any such person, may advertise the sale or exchange of his or her mobilehome, or, if not prohibited by the terms of an agreement with the management, may advertise the rental of his or her mobilehome, by displaying one sign in the window of the mobilehome, or by one sign posted on the side of the mobilehome facing the street, or by one sign in front of the mobilehome facing the street, stating that the mobilehome is for sale or exchange or, if not prohibited, for rent by the owner of the mobilehome or his or her agent. Any such person also may display one sign conforming to these requirements indicating that the mobilehome is on display for an "open house," if allowed by the park. The park may allow open houses and may establish reasonable rules or regulations governing how an open house may be conducted, including rules regarding the number of houses allowed to be open at one time, hours, and parking. The sign shall state the name, address, and telephone number of the owner of the mobilehome or his or her agent and the sign face shall not exceed 24 inches in width and 36 inches in height. Signs posted in front of a mobilehome pursuant to this section may be of an H-frame, A-frame, L-frame, or generally accepted yard-arm type design with the sign face perpendicular to, but not extending into, the street. Management may require the use of a step-in L-frame sign. Homeowners may attach to the sign or their mobilehome tubes or holders for leaflets that provide information on the mobilehome for sale, exchange, or rent.

(b) This section shall become operative on July 1, 2016. **Leg.H.** Added Stats 2015 ch 288 §2 (SB 419), effective January 1, 2016, operative July 1, 2016.

Prior Law: Former CC §798.70 was enacted in 1978 and repealed operative July 1, 2016, by its own provisions. Stats 2015 ch 288 (SB 419) §1.

§798.71. Showing or listing for sale; Use of specific broker or dealer not required

(a)(1) The management may not show or list for sale a manufactured home or mobilehome without first obtaining the owner's written authorization. The authorization shall specify the terms and conditions regarding the showing or listing.

(2) Management may require that a homeowner advise management in writing that his or her manufactured home or mobilehome is for sale. If management requires that a homeowner advise management in writing that his or her manufactured home or mobilehome is for sale, failure to comply with this requirement does not invalidate a transfer.

(b) The management shall prohibit neither the listing nor the sale of a manufactured home or mobilehome within the park by the homeowner, an heir, joint tenant, or personal representative of the estate who gains ownership of a manufactured home or mobilehome in the mobilehome park through the death of the owner of the manufactured home or mobilehome who was a homeowner at the time of his or her death, or the agent of any such person other than the management. For purposes of this section, "listing" includes advertising the address of the home to the general public.

(c) The management shall not require the selling homeowner, or an heir, joint tenant, or personal representative of the estate who gains ownership of a manufactured home or mobilehome in the mobilehome park through the death of the owner of the manufactured home or mobilehome who was a homeowner at the time of his or her death, to authorize the management or any other specified broker, dealer, or person to act as the agent in the sale of a manufactured home or mobilehome as a condition of resale of the home in the park or of management's approval of the buyer or prospective homeowner for residency in the park.

(d) The management shall not require a homeowner, who is replacing a mobilehome or manufactured home on a space in the park, in which he or she resides, to use a specific broker, dealer, or other person as an agent in the purchase of or installation of the replacement home.

(e) Nothing in this section shall be construed as affecting the provisions of the Health and Safety Code governing the licensing of manufactured home or mobilehome salespersons or dealers.

(f) This section shall become operative on July 1, 2016. **Leg.H.** Added Stats 2015 ch 288 §4 (SB 419), effective January 1, 2016, operative July 1, 2016.

Prior Law: Former CC §798.71 was enacted in 1978 and repealed operative July 1, 2016, by its own provisions. Stats 2015 ch 288 (SB 419) §3.

§798.72. Charging of fee for performance of services by management

(a) The management shall not charge a homeowner, an heir, joint tenant, or personal representative of the estate who gains ownership of a mobilehome in the mobilehome park through the death of the owner of the mobilehome who was a homeowner at the time of his or her death, or the agent of any such person a transfer or selling fee as a condition of a sale of his mobilehome within a park unless the management performs a service in the sale. The management shall not perform any such service in connection with the sale unless so requested, in writing, by the homeowner, an heir, joint tenant, or personal representative of the estate who gains ownership of a mobilehome in the mobilehome park through the death of the owner of the mobilehome who was a homeowner at the time of his or her death, or the agent of any such person.

(b) The management shall not charge a prospective homeowner or his or her agent, upon purchase of a mobilehome, a fee as a condition of approval for residency in a park unless the management performs a specific service in the sale. The management shall not impose a fee, other than for a credit check in accordance with subdivision (b) of Section 798.74, for an interview of a prospective homeowner. **Leg.H.** Added Stats 1978 ch 1031 §1. Amended Stats 1982 ch 1397 §29; Stats 1988 ch 498 §2; Stats 1989 ch 745 §3.

§798.73. Removal from park during term of rental agreement

The management shall not require the removal of a mobilehome from the park in the event of the sale of the mobilehome to a third party during the term of the homeowner's rental agreement or in the 60 days following the initial notice required by paragraph (1) of subdivision (b) of Section 798.55. However, in the event of a sale to a third party, in order to upgrade the quality of the park, the management may require that a mobilehome be removed from the park where:

(a) It is not a "mobilehome" within the meaning of Section 798.3.

(b) It is more than 20 years old, or more than 25 years old if manufactured after September 15, 1971, and is 20 feet wide or more, and the mobilehome does not comply with the health and safety standards provided in Sections 18550, 18552, and 18605 of the Health and Safety Code and the regulations established thereunder, as determined following an inspection by the appropriate enforcement agency, as defined in Section 18207 of the Health and Safety Code.

(c) The mobilehome is more than 17 years old, or more than 25 years old if manufactured after September 15, 1971, and is less than 20 feet wide, and the mobilehome does not comply with the construction and safety standards under Sections 18550, 18552, and 18605 of the Health and Safety Code and the regulations established thereunder, as determined following an inspection by the appropriate enforcement agency, as defined in Section 18207 of the Health and Safety Code.

(d) It is in a significantly rundown condition or in disrepair, as determined by the general condition of the mobilehome and its acceptability to the health and safety of the occupants and to the public, exclusive of its age. The management shall use reasonable discretion in determining the general condition of the mobilehome and its accessory structures. The management shall bear the burden of demonstrating that the mobilehome is in a significantly rundown condition or in disrepair. The management of the park may not require repairs or improvements to the park space or property owned by the management, except for damage caused by the actions or negligence of the homeowner or an agent of the homeowner.

(e) The management shall not require a mobilehome to be removed from the park, pursuant to this section, unless the management has provided to the homeowner notice particularly specifying the condition that permits the removal of the mobilehome. **Leg.H.** Added Stats 1978 ch 1034 §2. Amended Stats 1982 ch 1392 §1, ch 1397 §30.5; Stats 1991 ch 576 §1 (AB 932); Stats 1994 ch 729 §1 (AB 3203); Stats 1997 ch 367 §1 (AB 672); Stats 1991 ch 576 §1 (AB 932); Stats 1994 ch 729 §1 (AB 3203); Stats 1997 ch 367 §1 (AB 672); Stats 2003 ch 561 §2 (AB 682); Stats 2007 ch 549 §1 (AB 446), effective January 1, 2008; Stats 2008 ch 179 §28 (SB 1498), effective January 1, 2009.

2003 Note: This act is not intended to provide the purchaser of a mobilehome a right to a tenancy in a mobilehome park when the selling tenant has had his or her tenancy terminated pursuant to subdivision (f) or (g) of Section 798.56 of the Civil Code. Stats 2003 ch 561 (AB 682) §3.

§798.73.5. Mobilehome that will remain in park

(a) In the case of a sale or transfer of a mobilehome that will remain in the park, the management may only require repairs or improvements to the mobilehome, its appurtenances, or an accessory structure that meet all of the following conditions:

(1) Except as provided by Section 798.83, the repair or improvement is to the mobilehome, its appurtenances, or an accessory structure that is not owned and installed by the management.

(2) The repair or improvement is based upon or is required by a local ordinance or state statute or regulation relating to mobilehomes, or a rule or regulation of the mobilehome park that implements or enforces a local ordinance or a state statute or regulation relating to mobilehomes.

(3) The repair or improvement relates to the exterior of the mobilehome, its appurtenances, or an accessory structure that is not owned and installed by the management.

(b) The management, in the case of sale or transfer of a mobilehome that will remain in the park, shall provide a homeowner with a written summary of repairs or improvements that management requires to the mobilehome, its appurtenances, or an accessory structure that is not owned and installed by the management no later than 10 business days following the receipt of a request for this information, as part of the notice required by Section 798.59. This summary shall include specific references to park rules and regulations, local ordinances, and state statutes and regulations relating to mobilehomes upon which the request for repair or improvement is based.

(c) The provisions of this section enacted at the 1999–2000 Regular Session of the Legislature are declarative of existing law as they pertain to allowing park management to enforce park rules and regulations; these provisions specifically limit repairs and improvements that can be required of a homeowner by park management at the time of sale or transfer to the same repairs and improvements that can be required during any other time of a residency. **Leg.H.** Added Stats 2000 ch 554 §1 (AB 2239).

§798.74. Management approval of purchaser; Notices and information

(a) The management may require the right of prior approval of a prospective purchaser of a mobilehome that will remain in the park.

(b)(1) A selling homeowner or their agent shall give notice of a sale of a mobilehome that will remain in the park to management before the close of the sale.

(2) Management shall, within 15 days, provide the seller and the prospective purchaser both of the following, in writing, upon receiving the notice required in paragraph (1):

(A) The standards that management customarily utilizes to approve a tenancy application, including the minimum reported credit score from a consumer credit reporting agency that management requires for approval.

(B) A list of all documentation that management will require to determine if the prospective purchaser will qualify for tenancy in the park.

(c) Management shall not withhold approval from a prospective purchase of a mobilehome unless any of the following apply:

(1) Management reasonably determines that, based upon the purchaser's prior tenancies, they will not comply with the rules and regulations of the park.

(2) The purchaser does not have the financial ability to pay the rent, estimated utilities, and other charges of the park.

(3) The purchaser has committed fraud, deceit, or concealment of material facts during the application process.

(d) In determining whether the prospective purchaser has the financial ability to pay the rent and charges of the park pursuant to paragraph (2) of subdivision (c), the management may require the prospective purchaser to document the amount and source of their gross monthly income or means of financial support. However, management shall not require the prospective purchaser to submit any of the following:

(1) Documentation beyond that disclosed pursuant to subparagraph (B) of paragraph (2) of subdivision (b).

(2) Copies of any personal income tax returns.

(e)(1) Within 15 business days of receiving all of the information requested from the prospective purchaser, management shall notify the seller and the prospective purchaser, in writing, of either acceptance or rejection of the application. During this 15-day period, the prospective purchaser shall comply with management's request, if any, for a personal interview.

(2)(A) If management rejects the application, management shall state the reason for the rejection in accordance with subdivision (c). If the rejection is based upon an alleged lack of financial ability to pay the rent, estimated utilities, and other charges of the park, as described in paragraph (2) of subdivision (c), the prospective purchaser may elect to provide additional financial or asset information to management to demonstrate their financial ability to pay the rent, estimated utilities, and other charges of the park. For purposes of this paragraph, "additional financial information" includes, but is not limited to, the following:

(i) Savings accounts.

(ii) Certificates of deposit.

(iii) Stock portfolios.

(iv) Trust interests of which the purchaser is a beneficiary.

(v) Real property.

(vi) Similar financial assets that can be liquidated or sold.

(B) If the prospective purchaser elects to provide additional financial and asset information specified in subparagraph (A), management shall consider the information together with the prospective purchaser's gross monthly income to determine whether the purchaser has the financial ability to pay the rent, estimated utilities, and other charges of the park.

(C) If a prospective purchaser provides additional financial and asset information, management may also consider any liabilities of the prospective purchaser when making a final determination of the prospective purchaser's ability to pay the rent, estimated utilities, and other charges of the park under this subdivision.

(f) If the management collects a fee or charge from a prospective purchaser of a mobilehome in order to obtain a financial report or credit rating, the full amount of the fee or charge shall be credited toward payment of the first month's rent for that mobilehome purchaser. If, for whatever reason, the prospective purchaser is rejected by the management, the management shall refund to the prospective purchaser the full amount of that fee or charge within 30 days from the date of rejection. If the prospective purchaser is approved by the management, but, for whatever reason, the prospective purchaser elects not to purchase the mobilehome, the management may retain the fee, or a portion thereof, to defray its administrative costs under this section.

(g) Management may be held liable by the selling homeowner for any and all damages proximately caused by management's failure to comply with this section.

(h) For purposes of this section:

(1) "Charges" means all charges authorized and imposed by management under Section 798.31.

(2) "Consumer credit reporting agency" has the same meaning as defined in subdivision (d) of Section 1785.3.

(3) "Credit score" has the same meaning as defined in subdivision (b) of Section 1785.15.1. **Leg.H.** Added Stats 2015 ch 288 §6 (SB 419), effective January 1, 2016, operative July 1, 2016. Amended Stats 2019 ch 504 §3 (SB 274), effective January 1, 2020.

Prior Law: Former CC §798.74 was enacted in 1978 and repealed operative July 1, 2016, by its own provisions. Stats 2015 ch 288 (SB 419) §5.

Former Sections: Former CC §798.74 was enacted in 1978 and repealed operative July 1, 2016, by its own provisions. Stats 2015 ch 288 (SB 419) §5.

§798.74.4. Transfer disclosure requirements

The transfer or sale of a manufactured home or mobilehome in a mobilehome park is subject to the transfer disclosure requirements and provisions set forth in Article 1.5 (commencing with Section 1102) of Chapter 2 of Title 4 of Part 4 of the Civil Code. The requirements include, but are not limited to, the use of the Manufactured Home and Mobilehome Transfer Disclosure Statement set forth in Section 1102.6d of the Civil Code. **Leg.H.** Added Stats 2003 ch 249 §2 (SB 116).

§798.74.5. "Information for Prospective Homeowners" document to be given upon request for residency application

(a) Within two business days of receiving a request from a prospective homeowner for an application for residency for a specific space within a mobilehome park, if the management has been advised that the mobilehome occupying that space is for sale, the management shall give the prospective homeowner a separate document in at least 12-point type entitled "INFORMATION FOR PROSPECTIVE HOMEOWNERS," which includes the following statements:

"As a prospective homeowner you are being provided with certain information you should know prior to applying for tenancy in a mobilehome park. This is not meant to be a complete list of information.

Owning a home in a mobilehome park incorporates the dual role of "homeowner" (the owner of the home) and park resident or tenant (also called a "homeowner" in the Mobilehome Residency Law). As a homeowner under the Mobilehome Residency Law, you will be responsible for paying the amount necessary to rent the space for your home, in addition to other fees and charges described below. You must also follow certain rules and regulations to reside in the park.

If you are approved for tenancy, and your tenancy commences within the next 30 days, your beginning monthly rent will be $_____ (must be completed by the management) for space number _____ (must be completed by the management). Additional information regarding future rent or fee increases may also be provided.

In addition to the monthly rent, you will be obligated to pay to the park the following additional fees and charges listed below. Other fees or charges may apply depending upon your specific requests. Metered utility charges are based on use.

_____

(Management shall describe the fee or charge and a good faith estimate of each fee or charge.)

Some spaces are governed by an ordinance, rule, regulation, or initiative measure that limits or restricts rents in mobilehome parks. These laws are commonly known as "rent control." Prospective purchasers who do not occupy the mobilehome as their principal residence may be subject to rent levels which are not governed by these laws. (Civil Code Section 798.21) Long-term leases specify rent increases during the term of the lease. By signing a rental agreement or lease for a term of more than one year, you may be removing your rental space from a local rent control ordinance during the term, or any extension, of the lease if a local rent control ordinance is in effect for the area in which the space is located.

A fully executed lease or rental agreement, or a statement signed by the park's management and by you stating that you and the management have agreed to the terms and conditions of a rental agreement, is required to complete the sale or escrow process of the home. You have no rights to tenancy without a properly executed lease or agreement or that statement. (Civil Code Section 798.75)

If the management collects a fee or charge from you in order to obtain a financial report or credit rating, the full amount of the fee or charge will be either credited toward your first month's rent or, if you are rejected for any reason, refunded to you. However, if you are approved by management, but, for whatever reason, you elect not to purchase the mobilehome, the management may retain the fee to defray its administrative costs. (Civil Code Section 798.74)

We encourage you to request from management a copy of the lease or rental agreement, the park's rules and regulations, and a copy of the Mobilehome Residency Law. Upon request, park management will provide you a copy of each document. We urge you to read these documents before making the decision that you want to become a mobilehome park resident.

Dated: _____

Signature of Park Manager: _____

Acknowledge Receipt by Prospective Homeowner: _____"

(b) Management shall provide a prospective homeowner, upon his or her request, with a copy of the rules and regulations of the park and with a copy of this chapter. **Leg.H.** Added Stats 2003 ch 767 §2 (AB 1287), operative October 1, 2004. Amended Stats 2012 ch 337 §1 (AB 317), effective January 1, 2013.

§798.75. Attachment of rental agreement or statement

(a) An escrow, sale, or transfer agreement involving a mobilehome located in a park at the time of the sale, where the mobilehome is to remain in the park, shall contain a copy of either a fully executed rental agreement or a statement signed by the park's management and the prospective homeowner that the parties have agreed to the terms and conditions of a rental agreement.

(b) In the event the purchaser fails to execute the rental agreement, the purchaser shall not have any rights of tenancy.

(c) In the event that an occupant of a mobilehome has no rights of tenancy and is not otherwise entitled to occupy the mobilehome pursuant to this chapter, the occupant is considered an unlawful occupant if, after a demand is made for the surrender of the mobilehome park site, for a period of five days, the occupant refuses to surrender the site to the mobilehome park management. In the event the unlawful occupant fails to comply with the demand, the unlawful occupant shall be subject to the proceedings set forth in Chapter 4 (commencing with Section 1159) of Title 3 of Part 3 of the Code of Civil Procedure.

(d) The occupant of the mobilehome shall not be considered an unlawful occupant and shall not be subject to the provisions of subdivision (c) if all of the following conditions are present:

(1) The occupant is the registered owner of the mobilehome.

(2) The management has determined that the occupant has the financial ability to pay the rent and charges of the park; will comply with the rules and regulations of the park, based on the occupant's prior tenancies; and will comply with this article.

(3) The management failed or refused to offer the occupant a rental agreement. **Leg.H.** Added Stats 1978 ch 1031 §1. Amended Stats 1981 ch 667 §8; Stats 1983 ch 519 §9; Stats 1987 ch 323 §1; Stats 1989 ch 119 §1; Stats 1990 ch 645 §2, (SB 2340).

§798.75.5. Mobilehome park rental agreement disclosure form

(a) The management shall provide a prospective homeowner with a completed written disclosure form concerning the park described in subdivision (b) at least three days prior to execution of a rental agreement or statement signed by the park management and the prospective homeowner that the parties have agreed to the terms and conditions of the rental agreement. The management shall update the information on the disclosure form annually, or, in the event of a material change in the condition of the mobilehome park, at the time of the material change in that condition.

(b) The written disclosure form shall read as follows:

Mobilehome Park Rental Agreement Disclosure Form

THIS DISCLOSURE STATEMENT CONCERNS THE MOBILEHOME PARK KNOWN AS _____ LOCATED AT _____
park name

_____
park address

IN THE CITY OF _____ COUNTY OF _____
STATE OF CALIFORNIA.

THIS STATEMENT IS A DISCLOSURE OF THE CONDITION OF THE PARK AND PARK COMMON AREAS AS OF _____
date

IN COMPLIANCE WITH SECTION 798.75.5 OF THE CIVIL CODE.

IT IS NOT A WARRANTY OF ANY KIND BY THE MOBILEHOME PARK OWNER OR PARK MANAGEMENT AND IS NOT A SUBSTITUTE FOR ANY INSPECTION BY THE PROSPECTIVE HOMEOWNER/LESSEE OF THE SPACE TO BE RENTED OR LEASED OR OF THE PARK, INCLUDING ALL COMMON AREAS REFERENCED IN THIS STATEMENT. THIS STATEMENT DOES NOT CREATE ANY NEW DUTY OR NEW LIABILITY ON THE PART OF THE MOBILEHOME PARK OWNER OR MOBILEHOME PARK MANAGEMENT OR AFFECT ANY DUTIES THAT MAY HAVE EXISTED PRIOR TO THE ENACTMENT OF SECTION 798.75.5 OF THE CIVIL CODE, OTHER THAN THE DUTY TO DISCLOSE THE INFORMATION REQUIRED BY THE STATEMENT.

Are you (the mobilehome park owner/mobilehome park manager) aware of any of the following:

A. Park or common area facilities	B. Does the park contain this facility?		C. Is the facility in operation?		D. Does the facility have any known substantial defects?		E. Are there any uncorrected park citations or notices of abatement relating to the facilities issued by a public agency?		F. Is there any substantial, uncorrected damage to the facility from fire, flood, earthquake, or landslides?		G. Are there any pending lawsuits by or against the park affecting the facilities or alleging defects in the facilities?		H. Is there any encroachment, easement, nonconforming use, or violation of setback requirements regarding this park common area facility?	
	Yes	No	Yes	No	Yes	No	Yes	No	Yes	No	Yes	No	Yes	No
Clubhouse														
Walkways														
Streets, roads, and access														
Electric utility system														
Water utility system														
Gas utility system														
Common area lighting system														
Septic or sewer system														
Playground														
RV storage														
Parking areas														
Swimming pool														
Spa pool														
Laundry														
Other common area facilities*														

*If there are other important park or common area facilities, please specify (attach additional sheets if necessary): _____

If any item in C is checked "no", or any item in D, E, F, G, or H is checked "yes", please explain (attach additional sheets if necessary): _____

The mobilehome park owner/park manager states that the information herein has been delivered to the prospective homeowner/lessee a minimum of three days prior to execution of a rental agreement and is true and correct to the best of the park owner/park manager's knowledge as of the date signed by the park owner/manager.

Park Owner/Manager: _____ By: _____
                         print name   signature

Date: _____

I/WE ACKNOWLEDGE RECEIPT OF A COMPLETED COPY OF THE PARK OWNER/MANAGER STATEMENT.

Prospective Homeowner
Lessee _____ Park Owner/Manager _____
                                              Title

Date: _____
Prospective Homeowner
Lessee _____ Park Owner/Manager _____
                                              Title

Date: _____

Leg.H. Added Stats 1999 ch 517 §1 (SB 534).

§798.76. Compliance with regulation limiting residency based on age requirements to older persons

The management may require that a prospective purchaser comply with any rule or regulation limiting residency based on age requirements for housing for older persons, provided that the rule or regulation complies with the federal Fair Housing Act, as amended by Public Law 104-76, and implementing regulations. **Leg.H.** Added Stats 1978 ch 1031 §1. Amended Stats 1992 ch 182 §1.5 (SB 1234) ch 666 §1 (AB 3453); Stats 1993 ch 1277 §1 (AB 2244); Stats 1996 ch 61 §1 (SB 1585), effective June 10, 1996.

§798.77. Waiver of provisions void

No rental or sale agreement shall contain a provision by which the purchaser or homeowner waives his or her rights under this chapter. Any such waiver shall be deemed contrary to public policy and shall be void and unenforceable. **Leg.H.** Added Stats 1978 ch 1031 §1. Amended Stats 1978 ch 1033 §19; Stats 1982 ch 1397 §32; Stats 1983 ch 519 §10.

§798.78. Ownership gained through death

(a) An heir, joint tenant, or personal representative of the estate who gains ownership of a mobilehome in the mobilehome park through the death of the owner of the mobilehome who was a homeowner at the time of his or her death shall have the right to sell the mobilehome to a third party in accordance with the provisions of this article, but only if all the homeowner's responsibilities and liabilities to the management regarding rent, utilities, and reasonable maintenance of the mobilehome and its premises which have arisen since the death of the homeowner have been satisfied as they have accrued pursuant to the rental agreement in effect at the time of the death of the homeowner up until the date the mobilehome is resold.

(b) In the event that the heir, joint tenant, or personal representative of the estate does not satisfy the requirements of subdivision (a) with respect to the satisfaction of the homeowner's responsibilities and liabilities to the management which accrue pursuant to the rental agreement in effect at the time of the death of the homeowner, the management shall have the right to require the removal of the mobilehome from the park.

(c) Prior to the sale of a mobilehome by an heir, joint tenant, or personal representative of the estate, that individual may replace the existing mobilehome with another mobilehome, either new or used, or repair the existing mobilehome so that the mobilehome to be sold complies with health and safety standards provided in Sections 18550, 18552, and 18605 of the Health and Safety Code, and the regulations established thereunder. In the event the mobilehome is to be replaced, the replacement mobilehome shall also meet current standards of the park as contained in the park's most recent written requirements issued to prospective homeowners.

(d) In the event the heir, joint tenant, or personal representative of the estate desires to establish a tenancy in the park, that individual shall comply with those provisions of this article which identify the requirements for a prospective purchaser of a mobilehome that remains in the park. **Leg.H.** Added Stats 1979 ch 198 §1. Amended Stats 1982 ch 477 §1, ch 1397 §32.5; Stats 1989 ch 745 §4.

§798.79. Right of resale by legal owner or junior lienholder; Homeowner's responsibilities

(a) Any legal owner or junior lienholder who forecloses on his or her security interest in a mobilehome located in a mobilehome park shall have the right to sell the mobilehome within the park to a third party in accordance with this article, but only if all of the homeowner's responsibilities and liabilities to the management regarding rent, utilities, and reasonable maintenance of a mobilehome and its premises are satisfied by the foreclosing creditor as they accrue through the date the mobilehome is resold.

(b) In the event the legal owner or junior lienholder has received from the management a copy of the notice of termination of tenancy for nonpayment of rent or other charges, the foreclosing creditor's right to sell the mobilehome within the park to a third party shall also be governed by Section 798.56a. **Leg.H.** Added Stats 1979 ch 1185 ch 1185 §2. Amended Stats 1982 ch 1397 §33.5; Stats 1983 ch 1124 §4, operative July 1, 1984; Stats 1990 ch 1357 §3 (AB 4156); Stats 1991 ch 190 §2 (AB 600).

§798.80. Notice to resident organization that mobilehome park is for sale

(a) Not less than 30 days nor more than one year prior to an owner of a mobilehome park entering into a written listing agreement with a licensed real estate broker, as defined in Article 1 (commencing with Section 10130) of Chapter 3 of Part 1 of Division 4 of the Business and Professions Code, for the sale of the park, or offering to sell the park to any party, the owner shall provide written notice of his or her intention to sell the mobilehome park by first-class mail or by personal delivery to the president, secretary, and treasurer of any resident organization formed by homeowners in the mobilehome park as a nonprofit corporation, pursuant to Section 23701v of the Revenue and Taxation Code, stock cooperative corporation, or other entity for purposes of converting the mobilehome park to condominium or stock cooperative ownership interests and for purchasing the mobilehome park from the management of the mobilehome park. An offer to sell a park shall not be construed as an offer under this subdivision unless it is initiated by the park owner or agent.

(b) An owner of a mobilehome park shall not be required to comply with subdivision (a) unless the following conditions are met:

(1) The resident organization has first furnished the park owner or park manager a written notice of the name and address of the president, secretary, and treasurer of the resident organization to whom the notice of sale shall be given.

(2) The resident organization has first notified the park owner or manager in writing that the park residents are interested in purchasing the park. The initial notice by the resident organization shall be made prior to a written listing or offer to sell the park by the park owner, and the resident organization shall give subsequent notice once each year thereafter that the park residents are interested in purchasing the park.

(3) The resident organization has furnished the park owner or park manager a written notice, within five days, of any change in the name or address of the officers of the resident organization to whom the notice of sale shall be given.

(c) Nothing in this section affects the validity of title to real property transferred in violation of this section, although a violation shall subject the seller to civil action pursuant to Article 8 (commencing with Section 798.84) by homeowner residents of the park or the resident organization.

(d) Nothing in this section affects the ability of a licensed real estate broker, as defined in Article 1 (commencing with Section 10130) of Chapter 3 of Part 1 of Division 4 of the Business and Professions Code, to collect a commission pursuant to an executed contract between the broker and the mobilehome park owner.

(e) Subdivision (a) does not apply to any of the following:

(1) Any sale or other transfer by a park owner who is a natural person to any relation specified in Section 6401 or 6402 of the Probate Code.

(2) Any transfer by gift, devise, or operation of law.

(3) Any transfer by a corporation to an affiliate. As used in this paragraph, "affiliate" means any shareholder of the transferring corporation, any corporation or entity owned or controlled, directly or indirectly, by the transferring corporation, or any other corporation or entity controlled, directly or indirectly, by any shareholder of the transferring corporation.

(4) Any transfer by a partnership to any of its partners.

(5) Any conveyance resulting from the judicial or nonjudicial foreclosure of a mortgage or deed of trust encumbering a mobilehome park or any deed given in lieu of such a foreclosure.

(6) Any sale or transfer between or among joint tenants or tenants in common owning a mobilehome park.

(7) The purchase of a mobilehome park by a governmental entity under its powers of eminent domain. **Leg.H.** Added Stats 1986 ch 648 §2. Amended Stats 1990 ch 421 §1 (AB 2944), operative until January 1, 1995; Stats 1994 ch 219 §1 (SB 1280).

§798.81. Listing or sale within park; Management as agent as condition of residency

The management (1) shall not prohibit the listing or sale of a used mobilehome within the park by the homeowner, an heir, joint tenant, or personal representative of the estate who gains ownership of a mobilehome in the mobilehome park through the death of the owner of the mobilehome who was a homeowner at the time of his or her death, or the agent of any such person other than the management, (2) nor require the selling homeowner to authorize the management to act as the agent in the sale of a mobilehome as a condition of approval of the buyer or prospective homeowner for residency in the park. **Leg.H.** Added Stats 1988 ch 1033 §1. Amended Stats 1989 ch 745 §5.

§798.82. Disclosure by management that mobilehome may be subject to school facilities fee

The management, at the time of an application for residency, shall disclose in writing to any person who proposes to purchase or install a manufactured home or mobilehome on a space, on which the construction of the pad or foundation system commenced after September 1, 1986, and no other manufactured home or mobilehome was previously located, installed, or occupied, that the manufactured home or mobilehome may be subject to a school facilities fee under Sections 53080 and 53080.4 of, and Chapter 4.9 (commencing with Section 65995) of Division 1 of Title 7 of, the Government Code. **Leg.H.** Added Stats 1994 ch 983 §1 (SB 1461).

§798.83. Repairs or improvements to mobilehome park space

In the case of a sale or transfer of a mobilehome that will remain in the park, the management of the park shall not require repairs or improvements to the park space or property owned by the management, except for damage caused by the actions or negligence of the homeowner or an agent of the homeowner. **Leg.H.** Added Stats 1997 ch 367 §2 (AB 672).

ARTICLE 8
Actions, Proceedings, and Penalties

Notice of intention to commence action based on failure to maintain physical improvements in common facilities or reduction in service. §798.84.
Allowance of attorney fees and costs. §798.85.
Award for willful violation in addition to damages; Punitive damages or statutory penalty. §798.86.
Failure of management to maintain facilities as public nuisance; Violations as public nuisance; Remedy; Civil action. §798.87.
Injunction for violations. §798.88.

§798.84. Notice of intention to commence action based on failure to maintain physical improvements in common facilities or reduction in service

(a) No action based upon the management's alleged failure to maintain the physical improvements in the common facilities in good working order or condition or alleged reduction of service may be commenced by a homeowner unless the management has been given at least 30 days' prior notice of the intention to commence the action.

(b) The notice shall be in writing, signed by the homeowner or homeowners making the allegations, and shall notify the management of the basis of the claim, the specific allegations, and the remedies requested. A notice by one homeowner shall be deemed to be sufficient notice of the specific allegation to the management of the park by all of the homeowners in the park.

(c) The notice may be served in the manner prescribed in Chapter 5 (commencing with Section 1010) of Title 14 of Part 2 of the Code of Civil Procedure.

(d) For purposes of this section, management shall be deemed to be notified of an alleged failure to maintain the physical improvements in the common facilities in good working order or condition or of an alleged reduction of services upon substantial compliance by the homeowner or homeowners with the provisions of subdivisions (b) and (c), or when management has been notified of the alleged failure to maintain or the alleged reduction of services by a state or local agency.

(e) If the notice is served within 30 days of the expiration of the applicable statute of limitations, the time for the commencement of the action shall be extended 30 days from the service of the notice.

(f) This section does not apply to actions for personal injury or wrongful death. **Leg.H.** Added Stats 1988 ch 1592 §1.

§798.85. Allowance of attorney fees and costs

In any action arising out of the provisions of this chapter the prevailing party shall be entitled to reasonable attorney's fees and costs. A party shall be deemed a prevailing party for the purposes of this section if the judgment is rendered in his or her favor or where the litigation is dismissed in his or her favor prior to or during the trial, unless the parties otherwise agree in the settlement or compromise. **Leg.H.** Added Stats 1978 ch 1031 §1. Amended Stats 1978 ch 1033 §21; Stats 1983 ch 519 §11.

§798.86. Award for willful violation in addition to damages; Punitive damages or statutory penalty

(a) If a homeowner or former homeowner of a park is the prevailing party in a civil action, including a small claims court action, against the management to enforce his or her rights under this chapter, the homeowner, in addition to damages afforded by law, may, in the discretion of the court, be awarded an amount not to exceed two thousand dollars ($2,000) for each willful violation of this chapter by the management.

(b) A homeowner or former homeowner of a park who is the prevailing party in a civil action against management to enforce his or her rights under this chapter may be awarded either punitive damages pursuant to Section 3294 of the Civil Code or the statutory penalty provided by subdivision (a). **Leg.H.** Added Stats 1978 ch 1031 §1. Amended Stats 1978 ch 1033 §22; Stats 1982 ch 1397 §34; Stats 1983 ch 519 §12; Stats 1997 ch 141 §1 (AB 591); Stats 2003 ch 98 §1 (AB 693).

§798.87. Failure of management to maintain facilities as public nuisance; Violations as public nuisance; Remedy; Civil action

(a) The substantial failure of the management to provide and maintain physical improvements in the common facilities in good working order and condition shall be deemed a public nuisance. Notwithstanding Section 3491, this nuisance may only be remedied by a civil action or abatement.

(b) The substantial violation of a mobilehome park rule shall be deemed a public nuisance. Notwithstanding Section 3491, this nuisance may only be remedied by a civil action or abatement.

(c) A civil action pursuant to this section may be brought by a park resident, the park management, or in the name of the people of the State of California, by any of the following:

(1) The district attorney or the county counsel of the jurisdiction in which the park, or the greater portion of the park, is located.

(2) The city attorney or city prosecutor if the park is located within the jurisdiction of the city.

(3) The Attorney General. **Leg.H.** Added Stats 1982 ch 1392 §2. Amended Stats 1983 ch 187 §1; Stats 1990 ch 1374 §2 (SB 2446); Stats 2002 ch 141 §1 (AB 2382).

§798.88. Injunction for violations

(a) In addition to any right under Article 6 (commencing with Section 798.55) to terminate the tenancy of a homeowner, any person in violation of a reasonable rule or regulation of a mobilehome park may be enjoined from the violation as provided in this section.

(b) A petition for an order enjoining a continuing or recurring violation of any reasonable rule or regulation of a mobilehome park may be filed by the management thereof within the limited jurisdiction of the superior court of the county in which the mobilehome park is located. At the time of filing the petition, the petitioner may obtain a temporary restraining order in accordance with subdivision (a) of Section 527 of the Code of Civil Procedure. A temporary order restraining the violation may be granted, with notice, upon the petitioner's affidavit showing to the satisfaction of the court reasonable proof of a continuing or recurring violation of a rule or regulation of the mobilehome park by the named homeowner or resident and that great or irreparable harm would result to the management or other homeowners or residents of the park from continuance or recurrence of the violation.

(c) A temporary restraining order granted pursuant to this subdivision shall be personally served upon the respondent homeowner or resident with the petition for injunction and notice of hearing thereon. The restraining order shall remain in effect for a period not to exceed 15 days, except as modified or sooner terminated by the court.

(d) Within 15 days of filing the petition for an injunction, a hearing shall be held thereon. If the court, by clear and convincing evidence, finds the existence of a continuing or recurring violation of a reasonable rule or regulation of the mobilehome park, the court shall issue an injunction prohibiting the violation. The duration of the injunction shall not exceed three years.

(e) However, not more than three months prior to the expiration of an injunction issued pursuant to this section, the management of the mobilehome park may petition under this section for a new injunction where there has been recurring or continuous violation of the injunction or there is a threat of future violation of the mobilehome park's rules upon termination of the injunction.

(f) Nothing shall preclude a party to an action under this section from appearing through legal counsel or in propria persona.

(g) The remedy provided by this section is nonexclusive and nothing in this section shall be construed to preclude or limit any rights the management of a mobilehome park may have to terminate a tenancy. **Leg.H.** Added Stats 1991 ch 270 §1 (SB 459). Amended Stats 2012 ch 99 §1 (AB 2272), effective January 1, 2013, repealed January 1, 2016; Stats 2015 ch 176 §1 (SB 244), effective January 1, 2016.

Prior Law: Former CC §798.88, similar to the present section, was added Stats 2012 ch 99 §2, effective January 1, 2013, operative January 1, 2016, and repealed Stats 2015 ch 176 §2, effective January 1, 2016.

Former CC §798.88 was enacted in 2012 and repealed Stats 2015 ch 176 (SB 244) §2.

ARTICLE 9
Subdivisions, Cooperatives, and Condominiums

Definitions. §799.
Application of article; Ownership and operation by nonprofit mutual benefit corporation. §799.1.
Advertisement for sale or exchange of mobilehome. §799.1.5.
Showing or listing for sale. §799.2.
Right of entry by ownership or management. §799.2.5.
Removal of mobilehome in event of sale. §799.3.
Approval of purchaser. §799.4.
Limitation of residency based on age requirements for older persons. §799.5.
Waiver of provisions void. §799.6.
Advance notice of nonemergency interruption in utility service. §799.7.
Disclosure by management that mobilehome may be subject to school facilities fee. §799.8.
Sharing of homeowner's mobilehome with adult caregiver; Sharing of mobilehome in older persons' complex with relative requiring care or supervision. §799.9.
Display of political campaign sign. §799.10.
Accommodations for the disabled authorized. §799.11.
Prohibition on solar energy system voided. §799.12.

§799. Definitions

As used in this article:

(a) "Ownership or management" means the ownership or management of a subdivision, cooperative, or condominium for mobilehomes, or of a resident-owned mobilehome park.

(b) "Resident" means a person who maintains a residence in a subdivision, cooperative, or condominium for mobilehomes, or a resident-owned mobilehome park.

(c) "Resident-owned mobilehome park" means any entity other than a subdivision, cooperative, or condominium for mobilehomes, through which the residents have an ownership interest in the mobilehome park. **Leg.H.** Added Stats 1978 ch 1031 §1. Amended Stats 1979 ch 198 §2; Stats 1996 ch 61 §2 (SB 1585), effective June 10, 1996; Stats 1997 ch 72 §1 (SB 484).

§799.1. Application of article; Ownership and operation by nonprofit mutual benefit corporation

(a) Except as provided in subdivision (b), this article shall govern the rights of a resident who has an ownership interest in the subdivision, cooperative, or condominium for mobilehomes, or a resident-owned mobilehome park in which his or her mobilehome is located or installed. In a subdivision, cooperative, or condominium for mobilehomes, or a resident-owned mobilehome park, Article 1 (commencing with Section 798) to Article 8 (commencing with Section 798.84), inclusive, shall apply only to a resident who does not have an ownership interest in the subdivision, cooperative, or condominium for mobilehomes, or the resident-owned mobilehome park, in which his or her mobilehome is located or installed.

(b) Notwithstanding subdivision (a), in a mobilehome park owned and operated by a nonprofit mutual benefit corporation, established pursuant to Section 11010.8 of the Business and Professions Code, whose members consist of park residents where there is no recorded subdivision declaration or condominium plan, Article 1 (commencing with Section 798) to Article 8 (commencing with Section 798.84), inclusive, shall govern the rights of members who are residents that rent their space from the corporation. **Leg.H.** Added Stats 1995 ch 103 §2 (SB 110). Amended Stats 1996 ch 61 §3 (SB 1585), effective June 10, 1996; Stats 1997 ch 72 §2 (SB 484); Stats 2010 ch 175 §1 (SB 1047), effective January 1, 2011; Stats 2011 ch 296 §33 (AB 1023), effective January 1, 2012; Stats 2012 ch 492 §1 (SB 1421), effective September 23, 2012.

Prior Law: Former CC §799.1 was added Stats 1978 ch 1031 §1, amended Stats 1978 ch 1033 §23, Stats 1979 ch 198 §3, Stats 1983 ch 519 §13, and renumbered CC §799.1.5 by Stats 1995 ch 103 §1.

§799.1.5. Advertisement for sale or exchange of mobilehome

A homeowner or resident, or an heir, joint tenant, or personal representative of the estate who gains ownership of a mobilehome through the death of the resident of the mobilehome who was a resident at the time of his or her death, or the agent of any of those persons, may advertise the sale or exchange of his or her mobilehome or, if not prohibited by the terms of an agreement with the management or ownership, may advertise the rental of his or her mobilehome by displaying a sign in the window of the mobilehome, or by a sign posted on the side of the mobilehome facing the street, or by a sign in front of the mobilehome facing the street, stating that the mobilehome is for sale or exchange or, if not prohibited, for rent by the owner of the mobilehome or his or her agent. Any such person also may display a sign conforming to these requirements indicating that the mobilehome is on display for an "open house," unless the park rules prohibit the display of an open house sign. The sign shall state the name, address, and telephone number of the owner of the mobilehome or his or her agent. The sign face may not exceed 24 inches in width and 36 inches in height. Signs posted in front of a mobilehome pursuant to this section may be of an H-frame or A-frame design with the sign face perpendicular to, but not extending into, the street. A homeowner or resident, or an heir, joint tenant, or personal representative of the estate who gains ownership of a mobilehome through the death of the resident of the mobilehome who was a resident at the time of his or her death, or the agent of any of those persons, may attach to the sign or their mobilehome tubes or holders for leaflets that provide information on the mobilehome for sale, exchange, or rent. **Leg.H.** Added Stats 1978 ch 1031 §1 as CC §799.1. Amended Stats 1978 ch 1033 §23; Stats 1979 ch 198 §3; Stats 1983 ch 519 §13. Renumbered by Stats 1995 ch 103 §1 (SB 110). Amended Stats 2004 ch 302 §5 (AB 2351); Stats 2005 ch 22 §12 (SB 1108), effective January 1, 2006.

§799.2. Showing or listing for sale

The ownership or management shall not show or list for sale a mobilehome owned by a resident without first obtaining the resident's written authorization. The authorization shall specify the terms and conditions regarding the showing or listing.

Nothing contained in this section shall be construed to affect the provisions of the Health and Safety Code governing the licensing of mobilehome salesmen. **Leg.H.** Added Stats 1978 ch 1031 §1. Amended Stats 1979 ch 198 §4; Stats 1983 ch 519 §14.

§799.2.5. Right of entry by ownership or management

(a) Except as provided in subdivision (b), the ownership or management shall have no right of entry to a mobilehome without the prior written consent of the resident. The consent may be revoked in writing by the resident at any time. The ownership or management shall have a right of entry upon the land upon which a mobilehome is situated for maintenance of utilities, trees, and driveways, for maintenance of the premises in accordance with the rules and regulations of the subdivision, cooperative, or condominium for mobilehomes, or resident-owned mobilehome park when the homeowner or resident fails to so maintain the premises, and protection of the subdivision, cooperative, or condominium for mobilehomes, or resident-owned mobilehome park at any reasonable time, but not in a manner or at a time that would interfere with the resident's quiet enjoyment.

(b) The ownership or management may enter a mobilehome without the prior written consent of the resident in case of an emergency or when the resident has abandoned the mobilehome. **Leg.H.** Added Stats 2004 ch 302 §6 (AB 2351). Amended Stats 2006 ch 538 §40 (SB 1852), effective January 1, 2007.

§799.3. Removal of mobilehome in event of sale

The ownership or management shall not require the removal of a mobilehome from a subdivision, cooperative, or condominium for mobilehomes, or resident-owned mobilehome park in the event of its sale to a third party. **Leg.H.** Added Stats 1978 ch 1031 §1. Amended Stats 1978 ch 1033 §24; Stats 1979 ch 198 §5; Stats 1996 ch 61 §4 (SB 1585), effective June 10, 1996; Stats 1997 ch 72 §3 (SB 484); Stats 1996 ch 61 §4 (SB 1585), effective June 10, 1996; Stats 1997 ch 72 §3 (SB 484).

§799.4. Approval of purchaser

The ownership or management may require the right to prior approval of the purchaser of a mobilehome that will remain in the subdivision, cooperative, or condominium for mobilehomes, or resident-owned mobilehome park and that the selling resident, or his or her agent give notice of the sale to the ownership or management before the close of the sale. Approval cannot be withheld if the purchaser has the financial ability to pay the fees and charges of the subdivision, cooperative, or condominium for mobilehomes, or resident-owned mobilehome park unless the ownership or management reasonably determines that, based on the purchaser's prior residences, he or she will not comply with the rules and regulations of the subdivision, cooperative, or condominium for mobilehomes, or resident-owned mobilehome park. **Leg.H.** Added Stats 1978 ch 1031 §1. Amended Stats 1979 ch 198 §6; Stats 1983 ch 519 §15; Stats 1996 ch 61 §5 (SB 1585), effective June 10, 1996; Stats 1997 ch 72 §4 (SB 484); Stats 1996 ch 61 §5 (SB 1585), effective June 10, 1996; Stats 1997 ch 72 §4 (SB 484).

§799.5. Limitation of residency based on age requirements for older persons

The ownership or management may require that a purchaser of a mobilehome that will remain in the subdivision, cooperative, or condominium for mobilehomes, or resident-owned mobilehome park comply with any rule or regulation limiting residency based on age requirements for housing for older persons, provided that the rule or regulation complies with the provisions of the federal Fair Housing Act, as amended by Public Law 104-76, and implementing regulations. **Leg.H.** Added Stats 1978 ch 1031 §1. Amended Stats 1993 ch 1277 §2 (AB 2244); Stats 1996 ch 61 §6 (SB 1585), effective June 10, 1996; Stats 1997 ch 72 §5 (SB 484).

§799.6. Waiver of provisions void

No agreement shall contain any provision by which the purchaser waives his or her rights under the provisions of this article. Any such waiver shall be deemed contrary to public policy and void and unenforceable. **Leg.H.** Added Stats 1978 ch 1031 §1 as CC §799.8. Amended and renumbered by Stats 1978 ch 1033 §27. Amended Stats 1983 ch 519 §16.

§799.7. Advance notice of nonemergency interruption in utility service

The ownership or management shall provide, by posting notice on the mobilehomes of all affected homeowners and residents, at least 72 hours' written advance notice of an interruption in utility service of more than two hours for the maintenance, repair, or replacement of facilities of utility systems over which the management has control within the subdivision, cooperative, or condominium for mobilehomes, or resident-owned mobilehome park, if the interruption is not due to an emergency. The ownership or management shall be liable only for actual damages sustained by a homeowner or resident for violation of this section.

"Emergency," for purposes of this section, means the interruption of utility service resulting from an accident or act of nature, or cessation of service caused by other than the management's regular or planned maintenance, repair, or replacement of utility facilities. **Leg.H.** Added Stats 1992 ch 317 §2 (SB 1389). Amended Stats 1996 ch 61 §7 (SB 1585), effective June 10, 1996; Stats 1997 ch 72 §6 (SB 484).

§799.8. Disclosure by management that mobilehome may be subject to school facilities fee

The management, at the time of an application for residency, shall disclose in writing to any person who proposes to purchase or install a manufactured home or mobilehome on a space or lot, on which the construction of the pad or foundation system commenced after September 1, 1986, and no other manufactured home or mobilehome was previously located, installed, or occupied, that the manufactured home or mobilehome may be subject to a school facilities fee under Sections 53080 and 53080.4 of, and Chapter 4.9 (commencing with Section 65995) of Division 1 of Title 7 of, the Government Code. **Leg.H.** Added Stats 1994 ch 983 §2 (SB 1461).

Prior Law: There was another section of this number, which was added Stats 1978 ch 1031 §1. Amended and renumbered CC §799.6 by Stats 1978 ch 1033 §27.

§799.9. Sharing of homeowner's mobilehome with adult caregiver; Sharing of mobilehome in older persons' complex with relative requiring care or supervision

(a) A homeowner may share his or her mobilehome with any person 18 years of age or older if that person is providing live-in health care, live-in supportive care, or supervision to the homeowner. Management shall not charge a fee for the live-in caregiver, but may require written confirmation from a licensed health care professional of the need for the care or supervision, if the need is not readily apparent or already known to management. That person shall have no rights of tenancy in, and shall comply with the rules and regulations of, the subdivision, cooperative, or condominium for mobilehomes, or resident-owned mobilehome park.

(b) A senior homeowner who resides in a subdivision, cooperative, or condominium for mobilehomes, or a resident-owned mobilehome park, that has implemented rules or regulations limiting residency based on age requirements for housing for older persons, pursuant to Section 799.5, may share his or her mobilehome with any person 18 years of age or older if this person is a parent, sibling, child, or grandchild of the senior homeowner and requires live-in health care, live-in supportive care, or supervision. Management shall not charge a fee for this parent, sibling, child, or grandchild, but may require written confirmation from a licensed health care professional of the need for the care or supervision, if the need is not readily apparent or already known to management. Unless otherwise agreed upon, the management shall not be required to manage, supervise, or provide for this person's care during his or her stay in the subdivision, cooperative, or condominium for mobilehomes, or resident-owned mobilehome park. That person shall have no rights of tenancy in, and shall comply with the rules and regulations of, the subdivision, cooperative, or condominium for mobilehomes, or resident-owned mobilehome park. As used in this subdivision, "senior homeowner" means a homeowner or resident who is 55 years of age or older. **Leg.H.** Added Stats 1997 ch 72 §7 (SB 484). Amended Stats 2008 ch 170 §3 (SB 1107), effective January 1, 2009; Stats 2017 ch 767 §2 (SB 147), effective January 1, 2018.

§799.10. Display of political campaign sign

A resident may not be prohibited from displaying a political campaign sign relating to a candidate for election to public office or to the initiative, referendum, or recall process in the window or on the side of a manufactured home or mobilehome, or within the site on which the home is located or installed. The size of the face of a political sign may not exceed six square feet, and the sign may not be displayed in excess of a period of time from 90 days prior to an election to 15 days following the election, unless a local ordinance within the jurisdiction where the manufactured home or mobilehome subject to this article is located imposes a more restrictive period of time for the display of such a sign. In the event of a conflict between the provisions of this section and the provisions of Part 5 (commencing with Section 4000) of Division 4, relating to the size and display of political campaign signs, the provisions of this section shall prevail. **Leg.H.** Added Stats 2003 ch 249 §3 (SB 116). Amended Stats 2012 ch 181 §27 (AB 806), effective January 1, 2013, operative January 1, 2014.

2003 Note: It is the intent of the Legislature that enactment of this bill not affect any other form of political expression by a homeowner or resident of a mobilehome park where that expression is not associated with an election or political campaign. Stats 2003 ch 249 (SB 116) §4.

§799.11. Accommodations for the disabled authorized

The ownership or management shall not prohibit a homeowner or resident from installing accommodations for the disabled on the home or the site, lot, or space on which the mobilehome is located, including, but not limited to, ramps or handrails on the outside of the home, as long as the installation of those facilities complies with code, as determined by an enforcement agency, and those facilities are installed pursuant to a permit, if required for the installation, issued by the enforcement agency. The management may require that the accommodations installed pursuant to this section be removed by the current homeowner at the time the mobilehome is removed from the park or pursuant to a written agreement between the current homeowner and the management prior to the completion of the resale of the mobilehome in place in the park. This section is not exclusive and shall not be construed to condition, affect, or supersede any other provision of law or regulation relating to accessibility or accommodation for the disabled. **Leg.H.** Added Stats 2008 ch 170 §4 (SB 1107), effective January 1, 2009.

§799.12. Prohibition on solar energy system voided

(a) Any covenant, restriction, or condition contained in any rental agreement or other instrument affecting the tenancy of a homeowner or resident in a subdivision, cooperative, or condominium for mobilehomes, or resident-owned mobilehome park that effectively prohibits or restricts the installation or use of a solar energy system on the mobilehome or the site, lot, or space on which the mobilehome is located is void and unenforceable.

(b) Ownership or management shall not prohibit or restrict a homeowner or resident from installing or using a solar energy system on a mobilehome or the site, lot, or space on which the mobilehome is located. Ownership or management shall not do any of the following:

(1) Charge any fee to a homeowner or resident in connection with the installation or use of a solar energy system.

(2) Require a homeowner or resident to use a specific solar installation contractor or solar energy system or product.

(3) Claim or receive any rebate, credit, or commission in connection with a homeowner's or resident's installation or use of a solar energy system.

(c) This section does not apply to imposition of reasonable restrictions on solar energy systems. However, it is the policy of the state to promote and encourage the use of solar energy systems and to remove obstacles thereto. Accordingly, reasonable restrictions on a solar energy system are those restrictions that do not significantly increase the cost of the system or significantly decrease its efficiency or specified performance, or that allow for an alternative system of comparable cost, efficiency, and energy conservation benefits.

(d)(1) For purposes of this section, "solar energy system" has the same meaning as defined in paragraphs (1) and (2) of subdivision (a) of Section 801.5.

(2) A solar energy system shall meet applicable health and safety standards and requirements imposed by state and local permitting authorities, consistent with Section 65850.5 of the Government Code.

(3) Solar energy systems and solar collectors used for heating water shall be certified by an accredited listing agency as defined in the California Plumbing and Mechanical Codes.

(4) A solar energy system for producing electricity shall also meet all applicable safety and performance standards established by the California Electrical Code, the Institute of Electrical and Electronics Engineers, and accredited testing laboratories such as Underwriters Laboratories and, if applicable, rules of the Public Utilities Commission regarding safety and reliability.

(e) This section shall not apply to a master-meter park. "Master-meter park" as used in this section means "master-meter customer" as used in Section 739.5 of the Public Utilities Code.

(f) Any entity that willfully violates this section shall be liable to the homeowner, resident, or other party for actual damages occasioned thereby, and shall pay a civil penalty to the homeowner, resident, or other party in an amount not to exceed two thousand dollars ($2,000).

(g) In any action to enforce compliance with this section, the prevailing party shall be awarded reasonable attorney's fees. **Leg.H.** Added Stats 2024 ch 162 §2 (SB 1190), effective January 1, 2025.

CHAPTER 2.6
RECREATIONAL VEHICLE PARK OCCUPANCY LAW

Article 1. Definitions.
Article 2. General Provisions.
Article 3. Defaulting Occupants.
Article 4. Defaulting Tenants.
Article 5. Defaulting Residents.
Article 6. Liens for Recreational Vehicles and Abandoned Possessions.
Article 7. Actions and Proceedings.

ARTICLE 1
Definitions

Citation of chapter. §799.20.
Governing definitions. §799.21.
"Defaulting occupant". §799.22.
"Defaulting resident". §799.23.
"Defaulting tenant". §799.24.
"Guest". §799.25.
"Management". §799.26.
"Occupancy"; "Occupy". §799.27.
"Occupant". §799.28.
"Recreational vehicle". §799.29.
"Recreational vehicle park"; "Park". §799.30.
"Resident". §799.31.
"Tenant". §799.32.

§799.20. Citation of chapter

This chapter shall be known and may be cited as the Recreational Vehicle Park Occupancy Law. **Leg.H.** Added Stats 1992 ch 310 §2 (AB 3074).

Prior Law: Former §799.20, similar to the present section, was added Stats 1979 ch 1185 §3 and repealed Stats 1992 ch 310 §1.

§799.21. Governing definitions

Unless the provisions or context otherwise require, the following definitions shall govern the construction of this chapter. **Leg.H.** Added Stats 1992 ch 310 §2 (AB 3074).

Prior Law: Former §799.21, similar to the present section, was added Stats 1979 ch 1185 §3 and repealed Stats 1992 ch 310 §1.

§799.22. "Defaulting occupant"

"Defaulting occupant" means an occupant who fails to pay for his or her occupancy in a park or who fails to comply with reasonable written rules and regulations of the park given to the occupant upon registration. **Leg.H.** Added Stats 1992 ch 310 §2 (AB 3074).

Prior Law: Former §799.22, similar to the present section, was added Stats 1979 ch 1185 §3 as §799.24, amended and renumbered by Stats 1980 ch 502 §11, and repealed Stats 1992 ch 310 §1.

Former §799.22 was added Stats 1979 ch 1185 §3 and amended and renumbered §799.24 by Stats 1980 ch 502 §9.

§799.23. "Defaulting resident"

"Defaulting resident" means a resident who fails to pay for his or her occupancy in a park, fails to comply with reasonable written rules and regulations of the park given to the resident upon registration or during the term of his or her occupancy in the park, or who violates any of the provisions contained in Article 5 (commencing with Section 799.70). **Leg.H.** Added Stats 1992 ch 310 §2 (AB 3074).

Prior Law: Former §799.23, similar to present CC §799.28, was added Stats 1980 ch 502 §15 and repealed Stats 1992 ch 310 §1.

Former §799.23 was added Stats 1979 ch 1185 §3 and renumbered §799.25 by Stats 1980 ch 502 §10.

§799.24. "Defaulting tenant"

"Defaulting tenant" means a tenant who fails to pay for his or her occupancy in a park or fails to comply with reasonable written rules and regulations of the park given to the person upon registration or during the term of his or her occupancy in the park. **Leg.H.** Added Stats 1992 ch 310 §2 (AB 3074).

Prior Law: Former §799.24, similar to present CC §799.29, was added Stats 1990 ch 1160 §2 and repealed Stats 1992 ch 310 §1.

Former §799.24, similar to present CC §799.29, was added Stats 1979 ch 1185 §3 as §799.22, amended and renumbered by Stats 1980 ch 502 §9, amended Stats 1984 ch 1527 §1, Stats 1986 ch 1078 §1, effective September 24, 1986, and repealed Stats 1990 ch 1160 §1.

§799.25. "Guest"

"Guest" means a person who is lawfully occupying a recreational vehicle located in a park but who is not an occupant, tenant, or resident. An occupant, tenant, or resident shall be responsible for the actions of his or her guests. **Leg.H.** Added Stats 1992 ch 310 §2 (AB 3074).

Prior Law: Former §799.25, similar to present CC §799.30, was added Stats 1990 ch 1160 §4 and repealed Stats 1992 ch 310 §1.

Former §799.25, similar to present CC §799.30, was added Stats 1979 ch 1185 §3 as §799.23, renumbered by Stats 1980 ch 502 §10, and repealed Stats 1990 ch 1160 §3.

§799.26. "Management"

"Management" means the owner of a recreational vehicle park or an agent or representative authorized to act on his or her behalf in connection with matters relating to the park. **Leg.H.** Added Stats 1992 ch 310 §2 (AB 3074).

Prior Law: Former §799.26, similar to present CC §799.32, was added Stats 1980 ch 502 §16 and repealed Stats 1992 ch 310 §1.

Former §799.26 was added Stats 1979 ch 1185 §13 and renumbered CC §799.28 by Stats 1980 ch 502 §16.

§799.27. "Occupancy"; "Occupy"

"Occupancy" and "occupy" refer to the use of a recreational vehicle park lot by an occupant, tenant, or resident. **Leg.H.** Added Stats 1992 ch 310 §2 (AB 3074).

Prior Law: Former §799.27, similar to present CC §799.40, was added Stats 1979 ch 1185 §3 as §799.25, amended and renumbered by Stats 1980 ch 502 §12, and repealed Stats 1992 ch 310 §1.

§799.28. "Occupant"

"Occupant" means the owner or operator of a recreational vehicle who has occupied a lot in a park for 30 days or less. **Leg.H.** Added Stats 1992 ch 310 §2 (AB 3074).

Prior Law: Former §799.28, similar to present CC §799.41, was added Stats 1979 ch 1185 §3 as §799.26, renumbered by Stats 1980 ch 502 §13, and repealed Stats 1992 ch 310 §1.

§799.29. "Recreational vehicle"

"Recreational vehicle" has the same meaning as defined in Section 18010 of the Health and Safety Code. **Leg.H.** Added Stats 1992 ch 310 §2 (AB 3074).

Prior Law: Former §799.29, similar to present CC §799.42, was added Stats 1980 ch 502 §17 and repealed Stats 1992 ch 310 §1).

§799.30. "Recreational vehicle park"; "Park"

"Recreational vehicle park" or "park" has the same meaning as defined in Section 18862.39 of the Health and Safety Code. **Leg.H.** Added Stats 1992 ch 310 §2 (AB 3074). Amended Stats 2004 ch 530 §1 (AB 1964).

Prior Law: Former §799.30, similar to present CC §799.43, was added Stats 1979 ch 1185 §3, amended Stats 1980 ch 502 §2, Stats 1990 ch 317 §2, and repealed Stats 1992 ch 310 §1.

§799.31. "Resident"

"Resident" means a tenant who has occupied a lot in a park for nine months or more. **Leg.H.** Added Stats 1992 ch 310 §2 (AB 3074).

Prior Law: Former §799.31, similar to present CC §799.44, was added Stats 1979 ch 1185 §3 and repealed Stats 1992 ch 310 §1.

§799.32. "Tenant"

"Tenant" means the owner or operator of a recreational vehicle who has occupied a lot in a park for more than 30 consecutive days. **Leg.H.** Added Stats 1992 ch 310 §2 (AB 3074).

§799.35. [Section repealed 1992]

Leg.H. Added Stats 1979 ch 1185 §3. Repealed Stats 1992 ch 310 §1 (AB 3074). See CC §799.55.

§799.36. [Section repealed 1992]

Leg.H. Added Stats 1979 ch 1185 §3. Repealed Stats 1992 ch 310 §1 (AB 3074). See CC §799.56.

§799.37. [Section repealed 1992]

Leg.H. Added Stats 1979 ch 1185 §3. Repealed Stats 1992 ch 310 §1 (AB 3074). See CC §799.57.

§799.38. [Section repealed 1992]

Leg.H. Added Stats 1979 ch 1185 §3. Repealed Stats 1992 ch 310 §1 (AB 3074). See CC §799.58.

§799.39. [Section repealed 1992]

Leg.H. Added Stats 1979 ch 1185 §3. Amended Stats 1980 ch 502 §3; Stats 1990 ch 317 §3 (AB 3177). Repealed Stats 1992 ch 310 §1 (AB 3074). See CC §799.59.

ARTICLE 2
General Provisions

Cumulative nature of rights. §799.40.
Application to mobilehomes. §799.41.
Waiver of rights. §799.42.
Registration agreement requirements. §799.43.
Copy to be given to occupant at registration. §799.44.
Offer of rental agreement. §799.45.
Sign indicating reasons for removal of recreational vehicle from premises. §799.46.
Reregistration requirement to prevent the occupant, tenant, or resident from gaining or maintaining status as a resident. § 799.47.

§799.40. Cumulative nature of rights

The rights created by this chapter shall be cumulative and in addition to any other legal rights the management of a park may have against a defaulting occupant, tenant, or resident, or that an occupant, tenant, or resident may have against the management of a park. **Leg.H.** Added Stats 1992 ch 310 §2 (AB 3074).

Prior Law: Former §799.40, relating to removal of recreational vehicles whose occupants had been continuous residents for nine months following January 1, 1979, was added Stats 1979 ch 1185 §3 and repealed Stats 1980 ch 502 §20.

§799.41. Application to mobilehomes

Nothing in this chapter shall apply to a mobilehome as defined in Section 18008 of the Health and Safety Code or to a manufactured home as defined in Section 18007 of the Health and Safety Code. **Leg.H.** Added Stats 1992 ch 310 §2 (AB 3074).

§799.42. Waiver of rights

No occupant registration agreement or tenant rental agreement shall contain a provision by which the occupant or tenant waives his or her rights under the provisions of this chapter, and any waiver of these rights shall be deemed contrary to public policy and void. **Leg.H.** Added Stats 1992 ch 310 §2 (AB 3074).

§799.43. Registration agreement requirements

The registration agreement between a park and an occupant thereof shall be in writing and shall contain, in addition to the provisions otherwise required by law to be included, the term of the occupancy and the rent therefor, the fees, if any, to be charged for services which will be provided by the park, and a statement of the grounds for which a defaulting occupant's recreational vehicle may be removed as specified in Section 799.22 without a judicial hearing after the service of a 72-hour notice pursuant to this chapter and the telephone number of the local traffic law enforcement agency. **Leg.H.** Added Stats 1992 ch 310 §2 (AB 3074).

§799.44. Copy to be given to occupant at registration

At the time of registration, an occupant shall be given a copy of the rules and regulations of the park. **Leg.H.** Added Stats 1992 ch 310 §2 (AB 3074).

§799.45. Offer of rental agreement

The management may offer a rental agreement to an occupant of the park who intends to remain in the park for a period in excess of 30 consecutive days. **Leg.H.** Added Stats 1992 ch 310 §2 (AB 3074).

Prior Law: Former §799.45, similar to present CC §799.65, was added Stats 1980 ch 502 §18 and repealed Stats 1992 ch 310 §1.

§799.46. Sign indicating reasons for removal of recreational vehicle from premises

At the entry to a recreational vehicle park, or within the separate designated section for recreational vehicles within a mobilehome park, there shall be displayed in plain view on the property a sign indicating that the recreational vehicle may be removed from the premises for the reasons specified in Sections 799.22 and 1866 and containing the telephone number of the local traffic law enforcement agency. Nothing in this section shall prevent management from additionally displaying the sign in other locations within the park. **Leg.H.** Added Stats 1992 ch 310 §2 (AB 3074). Amended Stats 2004 ch 530 §2 (AB 1964).

Prior Law: Former §799.46, relating to notice by tenant of intent to vacate, was added Stats 1980 ch 502 §18 and repealed Stats 1992 ch 310 §1.

§799.47. [Section repealed 1992]

Leg.H. Added Stats 1980 ch 502 §18. Repealed Stats 1992 ch 310 §1 (AB 3074). See CC §799.75.

§799.47. Reregistration requirement to prevent the occupant, tenant, or resident from gaining or maintaining status as a resident

(a) A person shall not require an occupant, tenant, or resident in a qualified recreational vehicle park to reregister if the purpose of the reregistration requirement is to prevent the occupant, tenant, or resident from gaining or maintaining status as a resident.

(b) A person who violates subdivision (a) shall be liable for a civil penalty of five hundred dollars ($500).

(c) In an action brought pursuant to this section, if it is established by a preponderance of the evidence that an occupant, tenant, or resident was required to reregister, there shall be a rebuttable presumption that the purpose of that requirement was to prevent the occupant, tenant, or resident from gaining or maintaining status as a resident.

(d) In an action brought pursuant to this section, the court shall award reasonable attorney's fees and costs to the prevailing party.

(e) For the purposes of this section:

(1) "Qualified recreational vehicle park" means a recreational vehicle park, as defined in Section 799.30, that is located within the City of Imperial Beach.

(2) Notwithstanding Section 799.31 "resident" means a tenant who has occupied a lot in a park for at least 9 months in a 12-month period. **Leg.H.** Added Stats 2024 ch 353 §1 (AB 1472), effective January 1, 2025.

§799.48. [Section repealed 1990]

Leg.H. Added Stats 1980 ch 502 §18. Repealed Stats 1990 ch 317 §4 (AB 3177). The repealed section related to termination of tenancy.

§799.49. [Section repealed 1992]

Leg.H. Added Stats 1990 ch 1160 §5 (AB 3601). Repealed Stats 1992 ch 310 §1 (AB 3074). See CC §799.46.

§799.50. [Section repealed 1992]

Leg.H. Added Stats 1980 ch 502 §19. Repealed Stats 1992 ch 310 §1 (AB 3074). See CC §799.78.

§799.51. [Section repealed 1992]

Leg.H. Added Stats 1980 ch 502 §19. Repealed Stats 1992 ch 310 §1 (AB 3074). See CC §799.79.

ARTICLE 3
Defaulting Occupants

Notice prerequisite to removal of defaulting occupant's vehicle. §799.55.
Service of notice; Curing default. §799.56.
Contents of notice. §799.57.
Removal of vehicle; Duration of notice. §799.58.
Care required for removal. §799.59.

§799.55. Notice prerequisite to removal of defaulting occupant's vehicle

Except as provided in subdivision (b) of Section 1866, as a prerequisite to the right of management to have a defaulting occupant's recreational vehicle removed from the lot which is the subject of the registration agreement between the park and the occupant pursuant to Section 799.57, the management shall serve a 72-hour written notice as prescribed in Section 799.56. A defaulting occupant may correct his or her payment deficiency within the 72-hour period during normal business hours. **Leg.H.** Added Stats 1992 ch 310 §2 (AB 3074). Amended Stats 2004 ch 530 §3 (AB 1964).

§799.56. Service of notice; Curing default

(a) The 72-hour written notice shall be served by delivering a copy to the defaulting occupant personally or to a person of suitable age and discretion who is occupying the recreational vehicle located on the lot. In the latter event, a copy of the notice shall also be affixed in a conspicuous place on the recreational vehicle and shall be sent through the mail addressed to the occupant at the place where the property is located and, if available, any other address which the occupant has provided to management in the registration agreement. Delivery of the 72-hour notice to a defaulting occupant who is incapable of removing the occupant's recreational vehicle from the park because of a physical incapacity shall not be sufficient to satisfy the requirements of this section.

(b) In the event that the defaulting occupant is incapable of removing the occupant's recreational vehicle from the park because of a physical incapacity or because the recreational vehicle is not motorized and cannot be moved by the occupant's vehicle, the default shall be cured within 72 hours, but the date to quit shall be no less than seven days after service of the notice.

(c) The management shall also serve a copy of the notice to the city police if the park is located in a city, or, if the park is located in an unincorporated area, to the county sheriff. **Leg.H.** Added Stats 1992 ch 310 §2 (AB 3074).

§799.57. Contents of notice

The written 72-hour notice shall state that if the defaulting occupant does not remove the recreational vehicle from the premises of the park within 72 hours after receipt of the notice, the management has authority pursuant to Section 799.58 to have the recreational vehicle removed from the lot to the nearest secured storage facility. **Leg.H.** Added Stats 1992 ch 310 §2 (AB 3074).

§799.58. Removal of vehicle; Duration of notice

Subsequent to serving a copy of the notice specified in this article to the city police or county sheriff, whichever is appropriate, and after the expiration of 72 hours following service of the notice on the defaulting occupant, the police or sheriff, shall remove or cause to be removed any person in the recreational vehicle. The management may then remove or cause the removal of a defaulting occupant's recreational vehicle parked on the premises of the park to the nearest secured storage facility. The notice shall be void seven days after the date of service of the notice. **Leg.H.** Added Stats 1992 ch 310 §2 (AB 3074).

§799.59. Care required for removal

When the management removes or causes the removal of a defaulting occupant's recreational vehicle, the management and the individual or entity that removes the recreational vehicle shall exercise reasonable and ordinary care in removing the recreational vehicle to the storage area. **Leg.H.** Added Stats 1992 ch 310 §2 (AB 3074).

ARTICLE 4
Defaulting Tenants

Termination for nonpayment of charges; Notice; Curing default. §799.65.
Termination or refusal to renew for other reasons. §799.66.
Eviction requirements. §799.67.

§799.65. Termination for nonpayment of charges; Notice; Curing default

The management may terminate the tenancy of a defaulting tenant for nonpayment of rent, utilities, or reasonable incidental service charges, provided the amount due shall have been unpaid for a period of five days from its due date, and provided the tenant has been given a three-day written notice subsequent to that five-day period to pay the total amount due or to vacate the park. For purposes of this section, the five-day period does not include the date the payment is due. The three-day notice shall be given to the tenant in the manner prescribed by Section 1162 of the Code of Civil Procedure. Any payment of the total charges due, prior to the expiration of the three-day period, shall cure any default of the tenant. In the event the tenant does not pay prior to the expiration of the three-day notice period, the tenant shall remain liable for all payments due up until the time the tenancy is vacated. **Leg.H.** Added Stats 1992 ch 310 §2 (AB 3074).

§799.66. Termination or refusal to renew for other reasons

The management may terminate or refuse to renew the right of occupancy of a tenant for other than nonpayment of rent or other charges upon the giving of a written notice to the tenant in the manner prescribed by Section 1162 of the Code of Civil Procedure to remove the recreational vehicle from the park. The notice need not state the cause for termination but shall provide not less than 30 days' notice of termination of the tenancy. **Leg.H.** Added Stats 1992 ch 310 §2 (AB 3074). Amended Stats 1994 ch 167 §1 (SB 1349).

§799.67. Eviction requirements

Evictions pursuant to this article shall be subject to the requirements set forth in Chapter 4 (commencing with Section 1159) of Title 3 of Part 3 of the Code of Civil Procedure, except as otherwise provided in this article. **Leg.H.** Added Stats 1992 ch 310 §2 (AB 3074).

ARTICLE 5
Defaulting Residents

Notice of termination or refusal to renew right of occupancy. §799.70.
Eviction requirements. §799.71.

§799.70. Notice of termination or refusal to renew right of occupancy

The management may terminate or refuse to renew the right of occupancy of a defaulting resident upon the giving of a written notice to the defaulting resident in the manner prescribed by Section 1162 of the Code of Civil Procedure to remove the recreational vehicle from the park. This notice shall provide not less than 60 days' notice of termination of the right of occupancy and shall specify one of the following reasons for the termination of the right of occupancy:

(a) Nonpayment of rent, utilities, or reasonable incidental service charges; provided, that the amount due has been unpaid for a period of five days from its due date, and provided that the resident shall be given a three-day written notice subsequent to that five-day period to pay the total amount due or to vacate the park. For purposes of this subdivision, the five-day period does not include the date the payment is due. The three-day notice shall be given to the resident in the manner prescribed by Section 1162 of the Code of Civil Procedure. The three-day notice may be given at the same time as the 60-day notice required for termination of the right of occupancy; provided, however, that any payment of the total charges due, prior to the expiration of the three-day period, shall cure any default of the resident. In the event the resident does not pay prior to the expiration of the three-day notice period, the resident shall remain liable for all payments due up until the time the tenancy is vacated.

(b) Failure of the resident to comply with a local ordinance or state law or regulation relating to the recreational vehicle park or recreational vehicles within a reasonable time after the resident or the management receives a notice of noncompliance from the appropriate governmental agency and the resident has been provided with a copy of that notice.

(c) Conduct by the resident or guest, upon the park premises, which constitutes a substantial annoyance to other occupants, tenants, or residents.

(d) Conviction of the resident of prostitution, or a felony controlled substance offense, if the act resulting in the conviction was committed anywhere on the premises of the park, including, but not limited to, within the resident's recreational vehicle.

However, the right of occupancy may not be terminated for the reason specified in this subdivision if the person convicted of the offense has permanently vacated, and does not subsequently reoccupy, the recreational vehicle.

(e) Failure of the resident or a guest to comply with a rule or regulation of the park which is part of the rental agreement or any amendment thereto.

No act or omission of the resident or guest shall constitute a failure to comply with a rule or regulation unless the resident has been notified in writing of the violation and has failed to correct the violation within seven days of the issuance of the written notification.

(f) Condemnation of the park.

(g) Change of use of the park or any portion thereof. **Leg.H.** Added Stats 1992 ch 310 §2 (AB 3074).

§799.71. Eviction requirements

Evictions pursuant to this article shall be subject to the requirements set forth in Chapter 4 (commencing with Section 1159) of Title 3 of Part 3 of the Code of Civil Procedure, except as otherwise provided in this article. **Leg.H.** Added Stats 1992 ch 310 §2 (AB 3074).

ARTICLE 6
Liens for Recreational Vehicles and Abandoned Possessions

Nature of lien; Disposition of abandoned possessions. §799.75.

§799.75. Nature of lien; Disposition of abandoned possessions

The management shall have a lien upon the recreational vehicle and the contents therein for the proper charges due from a defaulting occupant, tenant, or resident. Such a lien shall be identical to that authorized by Section 1861, and shall be enforced as provided by Sections 1861 to 1861.28, inclusive. Disposition of any possessions abandoned by an occupant, tenant, or resident at a park shall be performed pursuant to Chapter 5 (commencing with Section 1980) of Title 5 of Part 4 of Division 3. **Leg.H.** Added Stats 1992 ch 310 §2 (AB 3074).

ARTICLE 7
Actions and Proceedings

Attorney fees and costs. §799.78.
Damages for willful violation. §799.79.

§799.78. Attorney fees and costs

In any action arising out of the provisions of this chapter, the prevailing party shall be entitled to reasonable attorney's fees and costs. A party shall be deemed a prevailing party for the purposes of this section if the judgment is rendered in his or her favor or where the litigation is dismissed in his or her favor prior to or during the trial, unless the parties otherwise agree in the settlement or compromise. **Leg.H.** Added Stats 1992 ch 310 §2 (AB 3074).

§799.79. Damages for willful violation

In the event that an occupant, tenant, or resident or a former occupant, tenant, or resident is the prevailing party in a civil action against the management to enforce his or her rights under this chapter, the occupant, tenant, or resident, in addition to damages afforded by law, may, in the discretion of the court, be awarded an amount not to exceed five hundred dollars ($500) for each willful violation of any provision of this chapter by the management. **Leg.H.** Added Stats 1992 ch 310 §2 (AB 3074).

CHAPTER 2.7
FLOATING HOME RESIDENCY LAW

Article 1. General Provisions.
Article 2. Rental Agreement.
Article 3. Rules and Regulations.
Article 4. Fees and Charges.
Article 5. Homeowner Meetings.
Article 6. Termination of Tenancy.
Article 7. Transfer of a Floating Home.
Article 8. Transfer of a Floating Home Marina.
Article 9. Actions, Proceedings, and Penalties.
Article 10. Cooperatives and Condominiums.

ARTICLE 1
General Provisions

Citation of chapter. §800.
Definitions to govern construction of chapter. §800.1.
"Management". §800.2.
"Floating home". §800.3.
"Floating home marina". §800.4.
"Rental agreement". §800.5.
"Homeowner". §800.6.
"Change of use". §800.7.
"Resident". §800.8.
"Tenancy". §800.9.

§800. Citation of chapter

This chapter shall be known and may be cited as the Floating Home Residency Law. **Leg.H.** Added Stats 1990 ch 1505 §1 (AB 3139).

Prior Law: Former §800, relating to citation and application of Recreational Vehicle and Trailer Law chapter, was added Stats 1979 ch 371 §1 and repealed Stats 1980 ch 502 §21.

§800.1. Definitions to govern construction of chapter

Unless the provisions or context otherwise requires, the following definitions shall govern the construction of this chapter. **Leg.H.** Added Stats 1990 ch 1505 §1 (AB 3139).

Prior Law: Former §800.1, relating to termination of tenancy, was added Stats 1979 ch 371 §1 and repealed Stats 1980 ch 502 §21.

§800.2. "Management"

"Management" means the owner of a floating home marina or an agent or representative authorized to act on his or her behalf in connection with matters relating to a tenancy in the floating home marina. **Leg.H.** Added Stats 1990 ch 1505 §1 (AB 3139).

Prior Law: Former §800.2, relating to termination or refusal to renew right of occupancy, was added Stats 1979 ch 371 §1 and repealed Stats 1980 ch 502 §21.

§800.3. "Floating home"

"Floating home" has the same meaning as defined in subdivision (d) of Section 18075.55 of the Health and Safety Code. **Leg.H.** Added Stats 1990 ch 1505 §1 (AB 3139).

Prior Law: Former §800.3, relating to reason for termination to be included in notice, was added Stats 1979 ch 371 §1 and repealed Stats 1980 ch 502 §21.

§800.4. "Floating home marina"

"Floating home marina" means an area where five or more floating home berths are rented, or held out for rent, to accommodate floating homes, but does not include a marina or harbor that satisfies all of the following:

(a) The marina or harbor is managed by a nonprofit organization, the property, assets, and profits of which may not inure to any individual or group of individuals, but only to another nonprofit organization.

(b) The rules and regulations of the marina or harbor are set by majority vote of the berthholders thereof.

(c) The marina or harbor contains berths for fewer than 25 floating homes. **Leg.H.** Added Stats 1990 ch 1505 §1 (AB 3139). Amended Stats 1991 ch 942 §1 (AB 628); Stats 2022 ch 633 §1 (AB 252), effective January 1, 2023.

§800.5. "Rental agreement"

"Rental agreement" means an agreement between the management and the homeowner establishing the terms and conditions of a tenancy. A lease is a rental agreement. **Leg.H.** Added Stats 1990 ch 1505 §1 (AB 3139).

§800.6. "Homeowner"

"Homeowner" means a person who owns or resides in a floating home which is in a floating home marina pursuant to a rental agreement with management. **Leg.H.** Added Stats 1990 ch 1505 §1 (AB 3139).

§800.7. "Change of use"

"Change of use" means a use of the floating home marina for a purpose other than the rental, or the holding out for rent, of five or more floating home berths and does not mean the adoption, amendment, or repeal of a floating home marina rule or regulation. A change of use may affect an entire floating home marina or any portion thereof. "Change of use" includes, but is not limited to, a change of the floating home marina or any portion thereof to a condominium, stock cooperative, or any form of ownership wherein spaces within the floating home marina are to be sold. **Leg.H.** Added Stats 1990 ch 1505 §1 (AB 3139).

§800.8. "Resident"

"Resident" means a homeowner or other person who lawfully occupies a floating home. **Leg.H.** Added Stats 1990 ch 1505 §1 (AB 3139).

§800.9. "Tenancy"

"Tenancy" means the right of a homeowner to the use of a berth within a floating home marina on which to locate, maintain, and occupy a floating home, and accessory structures or vessels, including the use of the services and facilities of the floating home marina. **Leg.H.** Added Stats 1990 ch 1505 §1 (AB 3139).

ARTICLE 2
Rental Agreement

Availability of notices. §800.20.
Contents of rental agreement. §800.21.
Scope of provisions in rental agreement. §800.22.
Term. §800.23.
Waiver of rights. §800.24.
Nondiscrimination in private club membership. §800.25.
Availability of copy of Floating Home Residency Law; Notice. §800.26.

§800.20. Availability of notices

Unless otherwise provided, the management shall make available to floating homeowners, upon request, copies of all notices required by this article and Article 3 (commencing with Section 800.30). **Leg.H.** Added Stats 1990 ch 1505 §1 (AB 3139).

§800.21. Contents of rental agreement

The rental agreement shall be in writing and shall contain, in addition to the provisions otherwise required by law to be included, all of the following:

(a) The term of the tenancy and the rent therefor.

(b) The rules and regulations of the floating home marina.

(c) A reference to this chapter and a statement that a copy of it is available from the marina upon request.

(d) A provision specifying that it is the responsibility of the management to provide and maintain physical improvements in the common facilities in good working order and condition.

(e) A description of the physical improvements to be provided the homeowner during his or her tenancy.

(f) A provision listing those services which will be provided at the time the rental agreement is executed and will continue to be offered for the term of tenancy and the fees, if any, to be charged for those services.

(g) All other provisions governing the tenancy. **Leg.H.** Added Stats 1990 ch 1505 §1 (AB 3139).

§800.22. Scope of provisions in rental agreement

The rental agreement may include other provisions permitted by law, but need not include specific language contained in state or local laws not a part of this chapter. **Leg.H.** Added Stats 1990 ch 1505 §1 (AB 3139).

§800.23. Term

(a) A homeowner shall be offered a rental agreement for (1) a term of 12 months, (2) a lesser period as mutually agreed upon by both the homeowner and the management, (3) a longer period as mutually agreed upon by both the homeowner and the management, or (4) a longer period as necessary to secure financing from a conventional lending institution.

(b) Rental agreements for a prescribed term shall not contain any terms or conditions with respect to charges for rent, utilities, or incidental reasonable service charges that would be different during the first 12 months of the agreement from the corresponding terms or conditions that would be offered to the homeowner or homeowners on a month-to-month basis. **Leg.H.** Added Stats 1990 ch 1505 §1 (AB 3139).

§800.24. Waiver of rights

No rental agreement for a floating home berth shall contain a provision by which the homeowner waives his or her rights under any of the provisions of this chapter. Any waiver of these rights shall be deemed contrary to public policy and void. **Leg.H.** Added Stats 1990 ch 1505 §1 (AB 3139).

§800.25. Nondiscrimination in private club membership

(a) Membership in any private club or organization that is a condition for tenancy in a floating home marina shall not be denied on any basis listed in subdivision (a) or (d) of Section 12955 of the Government Code, as those bases are defined in Sections 12926, 12926.1, subdivision (m) and paragraph (1) of subdivision (p) of Section 12955, and Section 12955.2 of the Government Code.

(b) Notwithstanding subdivision (a), with respect to familial status, subdivision (a) shall not be construed to apply to housing for older persons, as defined in Section 12955.9 of the Government Code. With respect to familial status, nothing in subdivision (a) shall be construed to affect Sections 51.2, 51.3, 51.4, 51.10, 51.11, and 799.5, relating to housing for senior citizens. Subdivision (d) of Section 51 and Section 4760 of this code and subdivisions (n), (o), and (p) of Section 12955 of the Government Code shall apply to subdivision (a). **Leg.H.** Added Stats 1990 ch 1505 §1 (AB 3139). Amended Stats 2006 ch 578 §7 (AB 2800), effective January 1, 2007; Stats 2012 ch 181 §28 (AB 806), effective January 1, 2013, operative January 1, 2014.

2006 Note: This act shall be known, and may be cited, as the Civil Rights Housing Act of 2006. Stats 2006 ch 578 (AB 2800) §1.

§800.26. Availability of copy of Floating Home Residency Law; Notice

On or before March 12, 1991, the management shall notify all floating homeowners, in writing, that a copy of the Floating Home Residency Law is available to them, upon request, from the management. **Leg.H.** Added Stats 1990 ch 1505 §1 (AB 3139).

ARTICLE 3
Rules and Regulations

Common areas. §800.30.
Amendments. §800.31.
Right of entry for management. §800.32.
Written notice for change of use. §800.33.
Disclosure of owner's name and address. §800.34.
Entry into floating home marina by management. §800.35.
Notice of belief of abandonment. §800.36.
Abandonment of floating home owned by floating home marina. §800.37.

§800.30. Common areas

Each common area facility shall be open or available to residents at all reasonable hours, and the hours of the common area facility shall be posted at the facility. **Leg.H.** Added Stats 1990 ch 1505 §1 (AB 3139).

§800.31. Amendments

A rule or regulation of the floating home marina may be amended at any time with the consent of a homeowner, or without his or her consent upon written notice to him or her of not less than six months. Written notice to a new homeowner, whose tenancy commences within the required period of notice, of a proposed amendment shall constitute compliance with this section where the written notice is given to him or her before the inception of his or her tenancy. **Leg.H.** Added Stats 1990 ch 1505 §1 (AB 3139).

§800.32. Right of entry for management

(a) Except as provided in subdivision (b), and notwithstanding any other provision of law to the contrary, the ownership or management of a floating home marina, cooperative, or condominium for floating homes shall have no right of entry to a floating home without the prior written consent of the resident. This consent may be revoked in writing by the resident at any time. The ownership or management shall have a right of entry into the berth in which a floating home is situated for correction of what management determines to be a hazardous condition at any time, or for maintenance of utilities, docks, and common areas at any reasonable time, but not in a manner or at a time which would interfere with the resident's quiet enjoyment.

(b) The ownership or management of a floating home marina, cooperative, or condominium may enter a floating home without the prior written consent of the resident in case of an emergency or when the resident has abandoned the floating home. **Leg.H.** Added Stats 1990 ch 1505 §1 (AB 3139).

§800.33. Written notice for change of use

(a) The management shall give written notice to all homeowners and prospective homeowners concerning the following matters: (1) the nature of the zoning or use permit under which the floating home marina operates, (2) if the floating home marina is operating pursuant to a permit subject to a renewal or expiration date, the relevant information and dates shall be included in the notice, and (3) the duration of any lease of the floating home marina, or any portion thereof, in which the management is a lessee.

(b) If a change occurs concerning the zoning or use permit under which the floating home marina operates, a change occurs to the lease under which the management is a lessee and that change could affect the homeowner, including the termination of the lease, litigation occurs regarding termination of the lease, or expiration of a use permit occurs, all homeowners shall be given written notice at least 30 days prior to the effective date of the change. Notification regarding the change of use of the floating home marina, or any portion thereof, shall be governed by subdivision (f) of Section 800.71. A prospective homeowner shall be notified prior to the inception of the tenancy. **Leg.H.** Added Stats 1990 ch 1505 §1 (AB 3139).

§800.34. Disclosure of owner's name and address

The management of a floating home marina shall disclose, in writing, the name and address of the floating home marina owner upon the request of a homeowner. **Leg.H.** Added Stats 1990 ch 1505 §1 (AB 3139).

§800.35. Entry into floating home marina by management

(a) The management of a floating home marina may enter a floating home, which is owned by the marina, only upon the prior written consent of the renter, except:

(1) In case of an emergency.

(2) Upon reasonable notice and during regular business hours, to make necessary or agreed repairs.

(3) When the homeowner has abandoned the premises.

(4) Pursuant to court order.

(b) The management of a floating home marina may enter a floating home, not owned by the marina, only upon prior written consent, except:

(1) In case of an emergency.

(2) When the homeowner has abandoned the premises.

(3) Pursuant to a court order. **Leg.H.** Added Stats 1991 ch 942 §2 (AB 628).

§800.36. Notice of belief of abandonment

(a) A floating home not owned by a floating home marina shall be deemed abandoned by the homeowner, and the lease shall terminate, if the floating home marina gives written notice of its belief of abandonment as provided in this section and the homeowner fails to give the marina written notice, prior to the date of termination specified in the marina's notice, stating that he or she does not intend to abandon the floating home and stating an address at which the homeowner may be served by certified mail in any action for unlawful detainer of the marina.

(b) The marina may give a notice of belief of abandonment to the homeowner pursuant to this section only where the rent on the marina has been due and unpaid for at least 45 consecutive days and the marina management reasonably believes that the homeowner has abandoned the floating home. The date of termination of the lease shall be specified in the marina's notice and shall be not less than 15 days after the notice is served personally or, if mailed, not less than 18 days after the notice is deposited in the mail.

(c) The marina's notice of belief of abandonment shall be personally delivered to the homeowner or sent by first-class mail, postage prepaid, to the homeowner at his or her last known address and, if there is reason to believe that the notice sent to that address will not be received by the homeowner, also to such other address, if any, known to the marina where the homeowner may reasonably be expected to receive the notice.

(d) The notice of belief of abandonment shall be in substantially the following form:

Notice of Belief of Abandonment

To: _____

_____
(Name of homeowner)

_____
(Address of homeowner)

This notice is given pursuant to Section 800.36 of the Civil Code concerning the floating home marina leased by you at _____ (state location of the property by address or other sufficient description). The rent on this marina has been due and unpaid for 45 consecutive days and the marina believes that you have abandoned the floating home.

The floating home will be deemed abandoned within the meaning of Section 1951.2 of the Civil Code and your lease will terminate on ____ (here insert a date not less than 15 days after this notice is served personally or, if mailed, not less than 18 days after this notice is deposited in the mail) unless before that date the undersigned receives at the address indicated below a written notice from you stating both of the following:

(1) Your intent not to abandon the floating home.

(2) An address at which you may be served by certified mail in any action for unlawful detainer of the floating home marina.

You are required to pay the rent due and unpaid on this marina as required by the lease, and your failure to do so can lead to a court proceeding against you.

Dated: ____

_____
(Signature of marina manager/owner)

_____
(Type or print name of marina manager/owner)

_____
(Address to which the homeowner is to send notice)

(e) The floating home shall not be deemed to be abandoned pursuant to this section if the homeowner proves any of the following:

(1) At the time the notice of belief of abandonment was given, the rent was not due and unpaid for 45 consecutive days.

(2) At the time the notice of belief of abandonment was given, it was not reasonable for the marina to believe that the homeowner had abandoned the floating home. The fact that the marina management knew that the homeowner left personal property on the floating home does not, of itself, justify a finding that the marina management did not reasonably believe that the homeowner had abandoned the floating home.

(3) Prior to the date specified in the marina's notice, the homeowner gave written notice to the lessor stating his or her intent not to abandon the floating home and stating an address at which he or she may be served by certified mail in any action for unlawful detainer of the marina.

(4) During the period commencing 45 days before the time the notice of belief of abandonment was given and ending on the date the lease would have terminated pursuant to the notice, the homeowner paid to the marina all or a portion of the rent due and unpaid.

(f) Nothing in this section precludes the marina or the homeowner from otherwise proving that the floating home has been abandoned by the homeowner within the meaning of Section 1951.2.

(g) Nothing in this section precludes the marina from serving a notice requiring the homeowner to pay rent or quit as provided in Section 800.71 at any time permitted by that section, or affects the time and manner of giving any other notice required or permitted by law. The giving of the notice provided by this section does not satisfy the requirements of Sections 1161 and 1162 of the Code of Civil Procedure. **Leg.H.** Added Stats 1991 ch 942 §3 (AB 628).

§800.37. Abandonment of floating home owned by floating home marina

A floating home which is owned by a floating home marina shall be deemed abandoned according to the procedures and requirements of Section 1951.3. **Leg.H.** Added Stats 1991 ch 942 §4 (AB 628).

ARTICLE 4
Fees and Charges

Rent increases. §800.40.
Rental caps; Notice; Application [Repealed January 1, 2030]. § 800.40.5.
Fees for rental agreements. §800.41.
Fees not listed in rental agreement. §800.42.
Pet fees. §800.43.
Guest fees. §800.44.
Fees based on the number of members in immediate family. §800.45.

Fees for rule enforcement. §800.46.
Landscaping, installation, and hookup fees. §800.47.
Utilities. §800.48.
Security deposits; Interest. §800.49.
Liens and security interests. §800.50.

§800.40. Rent increases

The management shall give a homeowner written notice of any increase in his or her rent at least 30 days before the date of the increase, and the reason for the increase, including the basis for any calculation used in determining the amount of the increase. **Leg.H.** Added Stats 1990 ch 1505 §1 (AB 3139). Amended Stats 1991 ch 942 §5 (AB 628).

§ 800.40.5. Rental caps; Notice; Application [Repealed January 1, 2030]

(a)(1) Subject to subdivision (b), management shall not, over the course of any 12-month period, increase the gross rental rate for a tenancy for a floating home berth in a floating home marina more than 3 percent plus the percentage change in the cost of living, or 5 percent, whichever is lower, of the lowest gross rental rate charged for a tenancy at any time during the 12 months prior to the effective date of the increase.

(2) If the same homeowner maintains a tenancy over any 12-month period, the gross rental rate for the tenancy shall not be increased in more than two increments over that 12-month period, subject to the other restrictions of this subdivision governing gross rental rate increases.

(b)(1) For a new tenancy in which no homeowner from the prior tenancy remains in lawful possession of the floating home berth, management may establish the initial rental rate not subject to subdivision (a). However, if the applicable local agency or jurisdiction has adopted an ordinance, rule, regulation, or initiative measure that limits the allowable rental rate for a new tenancy, that ordinance, rule, regulation, or initiative measure shall apply. Subdivision (a) shall be applicable to subsequent increases after the initial rental rate has been established, except as otherwise provided in this section.

(2) Notwithstanding paragraph (1), management shall not impose an increase in rent on a homeowner that purchases a floating home if the purchase qualifies as an in-place transfer, and the initial rental rate shall be set at the rental rate of the previous tenancy. Subdivision (a) shall be applicable to subsequent increases after the initial rental rate has been established.

(c) Management shall provide notice of any increase in the rental rate, pursuant to subdivision (a), to each homeowner in accordance with Section 800.40.

(d) Subdivision (a) shall not apply to a tenancy for any of the following:

(1) A floating home berth restricted by deed, regulatory restriction contained in an agreement with a government agency, or other recorded document as affordable housing for persons and families of very low, low, or moderate income, as defined in Section 50093 of the Health and Safety Code, or subject to an agreement that provides housing subsidies for affordable housing for persons and families of very low, low, or moderate income, as defined in Section 50093 of the Health and Safety Code or comparable federal statutes.

(2) A floating home berth subject to any ordinance, rule, regulation, or initiative measure that restricts annual increases in the rental rate to an amount less than that provided in subdivision (a).

(e)(1)(A) This section shall apply to all rent increases occurring on or after January 1, 2022.

(B) This section shall become operative January 1, 2023.

(2) In the event that management has increased the rent by more than the amount permissible under subdivision (a) between January 1, 2022, and January 1, 2023, both of the following shall apply:

(A) The applicable rent on January 1, 2023, shall be the rent as of January 1, 2022, plus the maximum permissible increase under subdivision (a).

(B) Management shall not be liable to a homeowner for any corresponding rent overpayment.

(f) Any waiver of the rights under this section shall be void as contrary to public policy.

(g) For the purposes of this section:

(1) "Consumer Price Index for All Urban Consumers for All Items" means the CPI-U for the San Francisco-Oakland-Hayward metropolitan area, or any successor metropolitan area index.

(2)(A) "Percentage change in the cost of living" means the percentage change in the applicable CPI-U, as described in paragraph (1) and computed pursuant to subparagraph (B) of this paragraph.

(B)(i) For rent increases that take effect before August 1 of any calendar year, the following shall apply:

(I) The percentage change shall be the percentage change in the amount published for April of the immediately preceding calendar year and April of the year before that.

(II) If there is not an amount published in April for the applicable geographic area, the percentage change shall be the percentage change in the amount published for March of the immediately preceding calendar year and March of the year before that.

(ii) For rent increases that take effect on or after August 1 of any calendar year, the following shall apply:

(I) The percentage change shall be the percentage change in the amount published for April of that calendar year and April of the immediately preceding calendar year.

(II) If there is not an amount published in April for the applicable geographic area, the percentage change shall be the percentage change in the amount published for March of that calendar year and March of the immediately preceding calendar year.

(iii) The percentage change shall be rounded to the nearest one-tenth of 1 percent.

(3) "In place transfer" means the sale of a floating home where the floating home is transferred by a homeowner to a subsequent homeowner and remains docked at the same berth.

(h)(1) Nothing in this section affects the authority of a local government to adopt or maintain an ordinance, rule, regulation, or initiative measure that establishes a maximum amount that may be charged for rent or the rental rate for a new tenancy, including any ordinance, rule, regulation, or initiative measure adopted before the effective date of this section. However, if a local ordinance, rule, regulation, or initiative measure allows for the rental rate for a new tenancy or a rental rate increase greater than that provided in subdivision (a), this section shall apply.

(2) This section is not intended to express any policy regarding the appropriate, allowable rental rate increase limitations imposed by ordinance, rule, regulation, or initiative measure regulating rent increases adopted before or after the effective date of this section.

(i) This section shall only apply to floating home marinas in the Counties of Alameda, Contra Costa, and Marin.

(j) This section shall remain in effect only until January 1, 2030, and as of that date is repealed. **Leg.H.** Added Stats 2022 ch 633 §2 (AB 252), effective January 1, 2023, repealed January 1, 2030.

§800.41. Fees for rental agreements

A homeowner shall not be charged a fee for other than rent, utilities, and incidental reasonable charges for services actually rendered.

A homeowner shall not be charged a fee for obtaining a rental agreement on a floating home berth for (1) a term of 12 months, or (2) a lesser period as mutually agreed upon by both the homeowner and the management. A fee may be charged for a rental agreement of more than one year if the fee is mutually agreed upon by both the homeowner and management. **Leg.H.** Added Stats 1990 ch 1505 §1 (AB 3139).

§800.42. Fees not listed in rental agreement

A homeowner shall not be charged a fee for services actually rendered which are not listed in the rental agreement unless he or she has been given written notice thereof by the management, at least 60 days before imposition of the charge. **Leg.H.** Added Stats 1990 ch 1505 §1 (AB 3139).

§800.43. Pet fees

A homeowner shall not be charged a fee for keeping a pet in the floating home marina unless the management actually provides special facilities or services for pets. If special pet facilities are maintained by the management, the fee charged shall reasonably relate to the cost of maintenance of the facilities or services and the number of pets kept in the floating home marina. **Leg.H.** Added Stats 1990 ch 1505 §1 (AB 3139).

§800.44. Guest fees

(a) A homeowner shall not be charged a fee for a guest who does not stay with him or her for more than a total of 20 consecutive days or a total of 30 days in a calendar year. Such a guest shall not be required to register with the management.

(b) A homeowner who is living alone and who wishes to share his or her floating home with one person may do so, and a fee shall not be imposed by management for that person. The person shall be considered a guest of the homeowner and any agreement between the homeowner and the person shall not change the terms and conditions of the rental agreement between management and the homeowner. The guest shall comply with the provisions of the rules and regulations of the floating home marina. **Leg.H.** Added Stats 1990 ch 1505 §1 (AB 3139).

§800.45. Fees based on the number of members in immediate family

A homeowner shall not be charged a fee based on the number of members in his or her immediate family. As used in this section, the "immediate family" includes the homeowner and his or her spouse, their parents, and their children. **Leg.H.** Added Stats 1990 ch 1505 §1 (AB 3139).

§800.46. Fees for rule enforcement

A homeowner shall not be charged a fee for the enforcement of any of the rules and regulations of the floating home marina. **Leg.H.** Added Stats 1990 ch 1505 §1 (AB 3139).

§800.47. Landscaping, installation, and hookup fees

Unless the homeowner specifically requests the service in writing from the management, a homeowner shall not be charged a fee for the entry, installation, hookup, or landscaping as a condition of tenancy except for an actual fee or cost imposed by a local governmental ordinance or requirement directly related to the occupancy of the specific berth where the floating home is located and not incurred as a portion of the development of the floating home marina as a whole. However, reasonable landscaping and maintenance requirements may be included in the floating home marina rules and regulations. The management shall not require a homeowner or prospective homeowner to purchase, rent, or lease goods or services for landscaping from any person, company, or corporation. **Leg.H.** Added Stats 1990 ch 1505 §1 (AB 3139).

§800.48. Utilities

Where the management provides both master meter and submeter service of utilities to a homeowner, for each billing period the cost of the charges for the period shall be separately stated along with the opening and closing readings for his or her meter. The management shall post in a conspicuous place, the prevailing residential utilities rate schedule as published by the serving utility. **Leg.H.** Added Stats 1990 ch 1505 §1 (AB 3139).

§800.49. Security deposits; Interest

(a) The management may only demand a security deposit on or before initial occupancy and the security deposit may not be in an amount or value in excess of an amount equal to two months' rent that is charged at the inception of the tenancy, in addition to any rent for the first month. In no event shall additional security deposits be demanded of a homeowner following initial occupancy.

(b) After the homeowner has promptly paid to the management within five days of the date the amount is due, all of the rent, utilities, and reasonable service charges for any 12-consecutive-month period subsequent to the collection of the security deposit by the management, or upon resale of the floating home, whichever occurs earlier, the management shall, upon the receipt of a written request from the homeowner, refund to the homeowner the amount of the security deposit within 30 days following the end of the 12-consecutive-month period of prompt payment or the date of the resale of the floating home.

(c) In the event that the interest in the floating home marina is transferred to any other party or entity, the successor in interest shall have the same obligations of management contained in this section with respect to the security deposit.

(d) The management shall not be required to place any security deposit collected in an interest-bearing account or to provide a homeowner with any interest on the security deposit collected.

(e) This section applies to all security deposits collected on or after January 1, 1991. **Leg.H.** Added Stats 1990 ch 1505 §1 (AB 3139). Amended Stats 1991 ch 942 §6 (AB 628).

§800.50. Liens and security interests

The management shall not acquire a lien or security interest, other than an interest arising by reason of process issued to enforce a judgment of any court, in a floating home located in the floating home marina unless it is mutually agreed upon by both the homeowner and management. Any billing and payment upon the obligation shall be kept separate from current rent. **Leg.H.** Added Stats 1990 ch 1505 §1 (AB 3139).

ARTICLE 5
Homeowner Meetings

Meeting place. §800.60.
Meetings with management and homeowners; Matters. §800.61.

§800.60. Meeting place

The management shall permit meetings by homeowners or residents of a floating home in the marina, or any or all of them, relating to floating home living or social or educational purposes, including forums for or speeches of public officials or candidates for public office, to be held in any community facility if the meeting is held at reasonable hours and when the facility is not otherwise in use. The management's private office is not to be considered a community facility unless so designated by the management. **Leg.H.** Added Stats 1990 ch 1505 §1 (AB 3139).

§800.61. Meetings with management and homeowners; Matters

The management shall meet and consult with the homeowners, upon written request, within 30 days of the request, either individually, collectively, or with representatives of a group of homeowners who have signed a request to be so represented on the following matters:

(a) Amendments to floating home marina rules and regulations.

(b) Standards for maintenance or physical improvements in the floating home marina.

(c) Addition, alteration, or deletion of services, equipment or physical improvements.

(d) Rental agreements offered pursuant to Article 2 (commencing with Section 800.20).

Any collective meeting shall be conducted only after notice thereof has been given to all the requesting homeowners 10 days or more before the meeting. **Leg.H.** Added Stats 1990 ch 1505 §1 (AB 3139).

ARTICLE 6
Termination of Tenancy

Legislative findings and declarations. §800.70.
Reasons for terminating tenancy. §800.71.
Notice of termination. §800.72.
Impermissible reason for termination. §800.73.
Homeowner's written notice before vacating. §800.74.
Effect of provisions on rights set forth in Code of Civil Procedure. §800.75.

§800.70. Legislative findings and declarations

(a) The Legislature finds and declares that, because of the high cost of moving floating homes, the potential for damage resulting therefrom, the requirements relating to the installation of floating homes, and current government policy limiting the availability of floating home berths, it is necessary that the owners of floating homes within floating home marinas be provided with the unique protection from actual or constructive eviction afforded by the provisions of this chapter.

(b) The management shall not terminate or refuse to renew a tenancy, except for a reason specified in this article and upon the giving of written notice to the homeowner in the manner prescribed by Section 1162 of the Code of Civil Procedure, to remove the floating home from the floating home marina within a period of not less than 60 days, which period shall be specified in the notice. A copy of this notice shall be sent to the legal owner, as defined in Section 18005.8 of the Health and Safety Code, each junior lienholder, as defined in Section 18005.3 of the Health and Safety Code, and the registered owner of the floating home, if other than the homeowner, by United States mail within 10 days after notice to the homeowner, addressed to the legal owner, each junior lienholder, and the registered owner at their addresses, as set forth in the registration card specified in Section 18091.5 of the Health and Safety Code. **Leg.H.** Added Stats 1990 ch 1505 §1 (AB 3139).

§800.71. Reasons for terminating tenancy

A tenancy shall be terminated by the management only for one or more of the following reasons:

(a) Failure of the homeowner or resident to comply with a local ordinance or state law or regulation relating to floating homes within a reasonable time after the homeowner receives a notice of noncompliance from the appropriate governmental agency.

(b) Conduct by the homeowner or resident, upon the floating home marina premises, which constitutes a substantial annoyance to other homeowners or residents.

(c) Failure of the homeowner or resident to comply with a reasonable rule or regulation of the floating home marina as set forth in the rental agreement or any amendment thereto. The management may not impose unreasonable restrictions on the right of the homeowner to sublet his or her floating home.

No act or omission of the homeowner or resident shall constitute a failure to comply with a reasonable rule or regulation unless and until the management has given the homeowner written notice of the alleged rule or regulation violation and the homeowner or resident has failed to adhere to the rule or regulation within seven days. However, if a homeowner has been given a written notice of an alleged violation of the same rule or regulation on three or more occasions within a 12-month period after the homeowner or resident has violated that rule or regulation, no written notice shall be required for a subsequent violation of the same rule or regulation.

Nothing in this subdivision shall relieve the management from its obligation to demonstrate that a rule or regulation has in fact been violated.

(d)(1) Nonpayment of rent, utility charges, or reasonable incidental service charges; if the amount due has been unpaid for a period of at least five days from its due date, and provided, that the homeowner shall be given a three-day written notice subsequent to that five-day period to pay the amount due or to vacate the tenancy. The three-day written notice shall be given to the homeowner in the manner prescribed by Section 1162 of the Code of Civil Procedure. The notice may be given at the same time as the 60 days' notice required for termination of the tenancy.

Payment by the homeowner prior to the expiration of the three-day notice period shall cure a default under this subdivision.

(2) However, if a homeowner has been given a three-day notice to pay the amount due or to vacate the tenancy on three or more occasions within the preceding 12-month period, no written three-day notice shall be required for a subsequent nonpayment of rent, utility charges, or reasonable incidental service charges.

(3) Payment by the legal owner, any junior lienholder, or the registered owner, if other than the homeowner, on behalf of the homeowner prior to the expiration of 30 calendar days following the mailing of the notice to the legal owner, each junior lienholder, and the registered owner provided in subdivision (b) of Section 800.70, shall cure a default under this subdivision with respect to that payment.

(4) The homeowner shall remain liable for all payments due up until the time the tenancy is vacated.

(5) Cure of a default of rent, utility charges, or reasonable incidental service charges by the legal owner, any junior lienholder, or the registered owner, if other than the homeowner, as provided by this subdivision, may not be exercised more than twice during a 12-month period.

(e) Condemnation of the floating home marina.

(f) Change of use of the floating home marina or any portion thereof, provided:

(1) The management gives the homeowners at least 60 days' written notice that the management will be appearing before a local governmental board commission, or body to request permits for a change of use of the floating home marina.

(2) After all required permits requesting a change of use have been approved by the local governmental board, commission, or body, the management shall give the homeowners six months' or more written notice of termination of tenancy.

If the change of use requires no local governmental permits, then notice shall be given 12 months or more prior to the management's determination that a change of use will occur. The management in the notice shall disclose and describe in detail the nature of the change of use.

(3) The management gives each proposed homeowner written notice thereof prior to the inception of his or her tenancy that the management is requesting a change of use before local governmental bodies or that a change of use request has been granted.

(4) The notice requirements for termination of tenancy set forth in this section and Section 800.72 shall be followed if the proposed change actually occurs.

(5) The requirements for a notice of a proposed change of use imposed by this subdivision shall be governed by the law in effect at the time the notice was given. **Leg.H.** Added Stats 1990 ch 1505 §1 (AB 3139).

§800.72. Notice of termination

The management shall set forth in a notice of termination the reason relied upon for the termination with specific facts to permit determination of the date, place, witnesses, and circumstances concerning that reason. Neither reference to the section number or a subdivision thereof nor a recital of the language of this article constitutes compliance with this section. **Leg.H.** Added Stats 1990 ch 1505 §1 (AB 3139).

§800.73. Impermissible reason for termination

No tenancy shall be terminated for the purpose of making a homeowner's berth available for a person who purchases a floating home from the owner of the floating home marina or his or her agent. **Leg.H.** Added Stats 1990 ch 1505 §1 (AB 3139).

§800.74. Homeowner's written notice before vacating

A homeowner shall give written notice to the management of not less than 60 days before vacating his or her tenancy. **Leg.H.** Added Stats 1990 ch 1505 §1 (AB 3139).

§800.75. Effect of provisions on rights set forth in Code of Civil Procedure

The provisions of this article shall not affect any rights or proceedings set forth in Chapter 4 (commencing with Section 1159) of Title 3 of Part 3 of the Code of Civil Procedure except as otherwise provided in those sections. **Leg.H.** Added Stats 1990 ch 1505 §1 (AB 3139).

ARTICLE 7
Transfer of a Floating Home

Advertising sale or exchange of home. §800.80.
Written authorization necessary for management to show or list home for sale. §800.82.
Transfers or selling fees. §800.83.
Sale of home to third party; Removal from marina. §800.84.
Right of prior approval of purchaser. §800.85.
Purchaser's execution of rental agreement; Unlawful occupancy. §800.86.
Waiver of rights provision. §800.87.
Rights of heir or joint tenant to sell. §800.88.
Rights of junior lienholder to sell. §800.89.
Sale of used floating home by homeowner. §800.90.
Notice for action based on management's failure to maintain common facilities. §800.91.

§800.80. Advertising sale or exchange of home

A homeowner or his or her agent may advertise the sale or exchange of his or her floating home, or, if not prohibited by the terms of an agreement with the management, may advertise the rental of his or her floating home, by displaying a sign in the window of the floating home, or by a sign posted on the side of the floating home facing the dock or water or both, stating that the floating home is for sale or exchange or, if not prohibited, for rent by the owner of the floating home or his or her agent. The sign shall state the name, address, and telephone number of the owner of the floating home or his or her agent and may be at least 24 inches in width and 18 inches in height. **Leg.H.** Added Stats 1990 ch 1505 §1 (AB 3139).

§800.82. Written authorization necessary for management to show or list home for sale

(a) The management shall not show or list for sale a floating home without first obtaining the owner's written authorization. The authorization shall specify the terms and conditions regarding the showing or listing.

(b) The management shall prohibit neither the listing nor the sale of a floating home within the floating home marina by the homeowner, or an agent of the homeowner to authorize the management to act as the agent in the sale of a floating home as a condition of management's approval of buyer or prospective homeowner for residency in the floating home marina. **Leg.H.** Added Stats 1990 ch 1505 §1 (AB 3139).

§800.83. Transfers or selling fees

(a) The management shall not charge a homeowner, or his or her agent a transfer or selling fee as a condition of a sale of his or her floating home within a floating home marina unless the management performs a service in the sale. The management shall not perform any such service in connection with the sale unless so requested in writing, by the homeowner or his or her agent.

(b) The management shall not charge a prospective homeowner or his or her agent, upon purchase of a floating home, a fee as a condition of approval for residency in a floating home marina unless the management performs a specific service in the sale. The management shall not impose a fee, other than for a credit check in accordance with subdivision (b) of Section 800.85, for an interview of a prospective homeowner. **Leg.H.** Added Stats 1990 ch 1505 §1 (AB 3139).

§800.84. Sale of home to third party; Removal from marina

The management shall not require the removal of a floating home from the floating home marina in the event of its sale to a third party during the term of the homeowner's rental agreement. **Leg.H.** Added Stats 1990 ch 1505 §1 (AB 3139).

§800.85. Right of prior approval of purchaser

(a) The management may require the right of prior approval of a purchaser of a floating home that will remain in the floating home marina and that the selling homeowner or his or her agent give notice of the sale to the management before the close of the sale. Approval cannot be withheld if the purchaser has the financial ability to pay the rent and charges of the floating home marina unless the management reasonably determines that, based on the purchaser's prior tenancies, he or she will not comply with the rules and regulations of the floating home marina. In determining whether the purchaser has the financial ability to pay the rent and charges of the floating home marina, the management shall not require the purchaser to submit copies of any personal income tax returns in order to obtain approval for residency in the floating home marina. However, management may require the purchaser to document the amount and source of his or her gross monthly income or means of financial support. If the ownership or management rejects a purchaser as a prospective homeowner, the ownership or management shall inform the selling homeowner in writing of its reasons for the rejection. If the approval of a purchaser is withheld for any reason other than those stated in this article, the management or owner may be held liable for all damages proximately resulting therefrom.

(b) If the management collects a fee or charge from a prospective purchaser of a floating home in order to obtain a financial report or credit rating, the full amount of the fee or charge shall be credited toward payment of the first month's rent for that floating home purchaser. If, for whatever reason, the prospective purchaser is rejected by the management, the management shall refund to the prospective purchaser the full amount of that fee or charge within 30 days from the date of rejection. If the prospective purchaser is approved by the management, but, for whatever reason, the prospective purchaser elects not to purchase the floating home, the management may retain the fee, or a portion thereof, to defray its administrative costs under this section. **Leg.H.** Added Stats 1990 ch 1505 §1 (AB 3139).

§800.86. Purchaser's execution of rental agreement; Unlawful occupancy

(a) An escrow, sale, or transfer agreement involving a floating home located in the floating home marina at the time of sale, where the floating home is to remain in the floating home marina, shall contain a provision signed by the purchaser stating that by his or her signature he or she has agreed to the terms of a rental agreement. A copy of a fully executed rental agreement signed by both the purchaser and floating home marina management will satisfy the requirements of this section.

(b) In the event the purchaser fails to execute the rental agreement, the purchaser shall not have any rights of tenancy.

(c) In the event that an occupant of a floating home has no rights of tenancy and is not otherwise entitled to occupy the floating home pursuant to this chapter, the occupant shall be considered an unlawful occupant if, after a demand is made for the surrender of the floating home marina berth, for a period of five days, the occupant has refused to surrender the berth to the floating home marina management. In the event the unlawful occupant fails to comply with the demand, the unlawful occupant shall be subject to the proceedings set forth in Chapter 4 (commencing with Section 1159) of Title 3 of Part 3 of the Code of Civil Procedure.

(d) The occupant of the floating home shall not be considered an unlawful occupant and shall not be subject to the provisions of subdivision (c) if all of the following conditions exist:

(1) The occupant is the registered owner of the floating home.

(2) The management has determined that the occupant has the financial ability to pay the rent and charges of the floating home marina, will comply with the rules and regulations of the floating home marina, based on the occupant's prior tenancies, and will comply with this article.

(3) The management failed or refused to offer the occupant a rental agreement. **Leg.H.** Added Stats 1990 ch 1505 §1 (AB 3139).

§800.87. Waiver of rights provision

No rental or sale agreement shall contain a provision by which the purchaser or homeowner waives his or her rights under this article. Any waiver thereof shall be deemed contrary to public policy and shall be void and unenforceable. **Leg.H.** Added Stats 1990 ch 1505 §1 (AB 3139).

§800.88. Rights of heir or joint tenant to sell

An heir or joint tenant who gains ownership of a floating home in the floating home marina through the death of the owner of the floating home who is a homeowner shall have the right to sell the floating home to a third party in accordance with this article, but only if all the homeowner's responsibilities and liabilities to the management regarding rent, utilities, and reasonable maintenance of the floating home and its premises which have arisen after the transfer of ownership to the heir or joint tenant have been satisfied up until the date the floating home is resold. **Leg.H.** Added Stats 1990 ch 1505 §1 (AB 3139). Amended Stats 1991 ch 942 §7 (AB 628).

§800.89. Rights of junior lienholder to sell

Any legal owner or junior lienholder who forecloses on his or her security interest in a floating home located in a floating home marina shall have the right to sell the floating home within the floating home marina to a third party in accordance with the provisions of this article, but only if all the homeowner's responsibilities and liabilities to the management regarding rent, utilities, and reasonable maintenance of a floating home and it's premises are satisfied by the foreclosing creditor through the date the floating home is resold. **Leg.H.** Added Stats 1990 ch 1505 §1 (AB 3139).

1990 Note: It appears that the Legislature inadvertently substituted the word "it's" for "its."

§800.90. Sale of used floating home by homeowner

The management (1) shall not prohibit the listing or sale of a used floating home within the floating home marina by the homeowner, or an agent of the homeowner other than the management, (2) nor require the selling homeowner to authorize the management to act as the agent in the sale of a floating home as a condition of approval of the buyer or prospective homeowner for residency in the floating home marina. **Leg.H.** Added Stats 1990 ch 1505 §1 (AB 3139).

§800.91. Notice for action based on management's failure to maintain common facilities

(a) No action based upon the management's alleged failure to maintain the physical improvements in the common facilities in good working order or condition or alleged reduction of service may be commenced by a homeowner unless the management has been given at least 30 days' prior notice of the intention to commence the action.

(b) The notice shall be in writing, signed by the homeowner or homeowners making the allegations, and shall notify the management of the basis of the claim, the specific allegations, and the remedies requested. A notice by one homeowner shall be deemed to be sufficient notice of the specific allegation to the management of the floating home marina by all of the homeowners in the floating home marina.

(c) The notice may be served in the manner prescribed in Chapter 5 (commencing with Section 1010) of Title 14 of Part 2 of the Code of Civil Procedure.

(d) For purposes of this section, management shall be deemed to be notified of an alleged failure to maintain the physical improvements in the common facilities in good working order or condition or of an alleged reduction of services upon substantial compliance by the homeowner or homeowners with the provisions of subdivisions (b) and (c), or when management has been notified of the alleged failure to maintain or the alleged reduction of services by a state or local agency.

(e) If the notice is served within 30 days of the expiration of the applicable statute of limitations, the time for the commencement of the action shall be extended 30 days from the service of the notice.

(f) This section does not apply to actions for personal injury or wrongful death. **Leg.H.** Added Stats 1990 ch 1505 §1 (AB 3139).

ARTICLE 8
Transfer of a Floating Home Marina

Written notice prior to entering into listing agreement. §800.100.

§800.100. Written notice prior to entering into listing agreement

(a) When the owner of a floating home marina enters into a written listing agreement with a licensed real estate broker, as defined in Article 1 (commencing with Section 10130) of Chapter 2 of Part 1 of Division 4 of the Business and Professions Code, for the sale of the marina or offers to sell the marina to any party, the owner shall provide written notice by first-class mail or by personal delivery to the president, secretary, and treasurer of the resident organization, not less than 30 days but no more than one year prior to entering into any written listing agreement for the sale of the marina, or making any offer to sell the marina to any party. An offer to sell a marina shall not be construed as an offer under this subdivision unless it is initiated by the marina owner or his or her agent.

(b) An owner of a floating home marina is not required to comply with subdivision (a) unless the following conditions are met:

(1) The resident organization has first furnished the marina owner or marina manager a written notice of the name and address of the president, secretary, and treasurer of the resident organization to whom the notice of sale shall be given.

(2) The resident organization has first notified the marina owner or manager in writing that the marina residents are interested in purchasing the marina. The initial notice by the resident organization shall be made prior to a written listing or offer to sell the marina by the marina owner, and the resident organization shall give subsequent notice once each year thereafter that the marina residents are interested in purchasing the marina.

(3) The resident organization has furnished the marina owner or marina manager a written notice, within five days, of any change in the name or address of the officers of the resident organization to whom the notice of sale shall be given.

(c) Nothing in this section affects the validity of title to real property transferred in violation of this section, although a violation shall subject the seller to civil action pursuant to Article 9 (commencing with Section 800.200) by homeowner residents of the marina or by the resident organization.

(d) Nothing in this section affects the ability of a licensed real estate broker to collect a commission pursuant to an executed contract between the broker and the floating home marina owner.

(e) This section does not apply to any of the following:

(1) Any sale or other transfer by a marina owner who is a natural person to any relation specified in Section 6401 or 6402 of the Probate Code.

(2) Any transfer by gift, devise, or operation of law.

(3) Any transfer by a corporation to an affiliate. As used in this paragraph, "affiliate" means any shareholder of the transferring corporation, any corporation or entity owned or controlled, directly or indirectly, by the transferring corporation, or any other corporation or entity controlled, directly or indirectly, by any shareholder of the transferring corporation.

(4) Any transfer by a partnership to any of its partners.

(5) Any conveyance resulting from the judicial or nonjudicial foreclosure of a mortgage or deed of trust encumbering a floating home marina or any deed given in lieu of such a foreclosure.

(6) Any sale or transfer between or among joint tenants or tenants in common owning a floating home marina.

(7) The purchase of a floating home marina by a governmental entity under its powers of eminent domain. **Leg.H.** Added Stats 1990 ch 1505 §1 (AB 3139). Amended Stats 1991 ch 942 §8 (AB 628); Stats 2004 ch 183 §25 (AB 3082).

ARTICLE 9
Actions, Proceedings, and Penalties

Attorney's fees. §800.200.
Public nuisance. §800.201.

§800.200. Attorney's fees

In any action arising out of the provisions of this chapter the prevailing party shall be entitled to reasonable attorney's fees and costs. A party shall be deemed a prevailing party for the purposes of this section if the judgment is rendered in his or her favor or where the litigation is dismissed in his or her favor prior to or during the trial, unless the parties otherwise agree in the settlement or compromise.

In the event a homeowner or former homeowner of a floating home marina is the prevailing party in a civil action against the management to enforce his or her rights under the provisions of this chapter, the homeowner, in addition to damages afforded by law, may, in the discretion of the court, be awarded an amount not to exceed five hundred dollars ($500) for each willful violation of those provisions by the management. **Leg.H.** Added Stats 1990 ch 1505 §1 (AB 3139).

§800.201. Public nuisance

(a) The substantial failure of the management to provide and maintain physical improvements in the common facilities in good working order and condition shall be deemed a public nuisance. Notwithstanding the provisions of Section 3491, such a nuisance only may be remedied by a civil action or abatement.

(b) The substantial violation of a floating home marina rule shall be deemed a public nuisance. Notwithstanding the provisions of Section 3491, such a nuisance only may be remedied by a civil action or abatement. **Leg.H.** Added Stats 1990 ch 1505 §1 (AB 3139).

ARTICLE 10
Cooperatives and Condominiums

"Ownership or management"; "Resident". §800.300.
Advertising sale or rental of home. §800.301.
Resident's authorization necessary for management to show or list home. §800.302.
Sale to third party; Removal of home. §800.303.
Management's right to prior approval of purchaser. §800.304.
Purchaser's waiver of rights. §800.305.
Applicability of chapter. §800.306.

§800.300. "Ownership or management"; "Resident"

As used in this article:

(a) "Ownership or management" means the ownership or management of a cooperative or condominium for floating homes.

(b) "Resident" means a person who maintains a residence in a cooperative or condominium for floating homes. **Leg.H.** Added Stats 1990 ch 1505 §1 (AB 3139).

§800.301. Advertising sale or rental of home

A resident may advertise the sale or exchange of his or her floating home or, if not prohibited by the terms of an agreement with the management or ownership, may advertise the rental of his or her floating home by displaying a sign in the window of his or her floating home stating that the floating home is for sale or exchange or, if not prohibited, for rent by the owner of the floating home or his or her agent. The sign shall state the name, address, and telephone number of the owner of the floating home or his or her agent, and shall be 24 inches in width and 18 inches in length. **Leg.H.** Added Stats 1990 ch 1505 §1 (AB 3139). Amended Stats 1991 ch 942 §9 (AB 628).

§800.302. Resident's authorization necessary for management to show or list home

The ownership or management shall not show or list for sale a floating home owned by a resident without first obtaining the resident's written authorization. The authorization shall specify the terms and conditions regarding the showing or listing. **Leg.H.** Added Stats 1990 ch 1505 §1 (AB 3139). Amended Stats 1991 ch 942 §10 (AB 628).

§800.303. Sale to third party; Removal of home

The ownership or management shall not require the removal of a floating home from a cooperative or condominium in the event of its sale to a third party. **Leg.H.** Added Stats 1990 ch 1505 §1 (AB 3139).

§800.304. Management's right to prior approval of purchaser

The ownership or management may require the right to prior approval of the purchaser of a floating home that will remain in the cooperative or condominium for floating homes and that the selling resident or his or her agent give notice of the sale to the ownership or management before the close of the sale. Approval cannot be withheld if the purchaser has the financial ability to pay the fees and charges of the cooperative or condominium unless the ownership or management reasonably determines that, based on the purchaser's prior residences, he or she will not comply with the rules and regulations of the cooperative or condominium. **Leg.H.** Added Stats 1990 ch 1505 §1 (AB 3139).

§800.305. Purchaser's waiver of rights

No agreement shall contain any provision by which the purchaser waives his or her rights under this article. Any waiver thereof shall be deemed contrary to public policy and void and unenforceable. **Leg.H.** Added Stats 1990 ch 1505 §1 (AB 3139).

§800.306. Applicability of chapter

This chapter applies only to the relationship between the management and the homeowners and residents of floating home marinas. Nothing in this chapter affects residential use of tide and submerged lands, including the public trust doctrine or any legislative grant of tide and submerged lands to a public entity, or the administration of these lands by the State Lands Commission or a legislative grantee. In addition, this chapter does not supplant, lessen, modify, or otherwise affect past or future regulation of floating homes or floating home marinas by the San Francisco Bay Conservation and Development Commission pursuant to the McAteer–Petris Act. **Leg.H.** Added Stats 1990 ch 1505 §1 (AB 3139).

CHAPTER 3
SERVITUDES

Servitudes attached to land. §801.
Solar easement. §801.5.
Scope of right-of-way granted to railroad transporting passengers. §801.7.
Servitudes not attached to land. §802.
Designation of estates. §803.
By whom grantable. §804.
By whom held. §805.
Extent of servitudes. §806.
Apportioning easements. §807.
Rights of owner of future estate. §808.
Actions by owner and occupant of dominant tenement. §809.
Actions by owner of servient tenement. §810.
How extinguished. §811.
Recordation of notice of consent to use land; Effect; Revocation; Mailing notice; Restrictions in notice. §813.

§801. Servitudes attached to land

The following land burdens, or servitudes upon land, may be attached to other land as incidents or appurtenances, and are then called easements:

1. The right of pasture;
2. The right of fishing;
3. The right of taking game;
4. The right-of-way;
5. The right of taking water, wood, minerals, and other things;
6. The right of transacting business upon land;
7. The right of conducting lawful sports upon land;
8. The right of receiving air, light, or heat from or over, or discharging the same upon or over land;
9. The right of receiving water from or discharging the same upon land;
10. The right of flooding land;
11. The right of having water flow without diminution or disturbance of any kind;
12. The right of using a wall as a party wall;
13. The right of receiving more than natural support from adjacent land or things affixed thereto;
14. The right of having the whole of a division fence maintained by a coterminous owner;
15. The right of having public conveyances stopped, or of stopping the same on land;
16. The right of a seat in church;
17. The right of burial;
18. The right of receiving sunlight upon or over land as specified in Section 801.5. **Leg.H.** Enacted 1872. Amended Stats 1978 ch 1154 §4.

§801.5. Solar easement

(a) The right of receiving sunlight as specified in subdivision 18 of Section 801 shall be referred to as a solar easement. "Solar easement" means the right of receiving sunlight across real property of another for any solar energy system.

As used in this section, "solar energy system" means either of the following that is designed to serve one utility retail customer on the same property, more than one utility retail customer on the same property, one utility retail customer on the same, adjacent, or contiguous properties, or more than one utility retail customer on the same, adjacent or contiguous properties, and is not designed for procurement of electricity by an electric utility:

(1) Any solar collector or other solar energy device whose primary purpose is to provide for the collection, storage, and distribution of solar energy for space heating, space cooling, electric generation, or water heating.

(2) A structural design feature, including the following:

(A) Solar racking, solar mounting, and elevated solar support structures, including, but not limited to, solar carports, solar shade structures, solar awnings, solar canopies, and solar patio covers, regardless of whether the feature is on the ground or on a building. Elevated solar support structures include the aboveground superstructure and associated foundation elements that support the solar collectors or other solar energy devices described in paragraph (1).

(B) Any design feature whose primary purpose is to provide for the collection, storage, and distribution of solar energy for electricity generation, space heating or cooling, or for water heating.

(C) Any photovoltaic device or technology that is integrated into a building, including, but not limited to, photovoltaic windows, siding, and roofing shingles or tiles.

(b) Any instrument creating a solar easement shall include, at a minimum, all of the following:

(1) A description of the dimensions of the easement expressed in measurable terms, such as vertical or horizontal angles measured in degrees, or the hours of the day on specified dates during which direct sunlight to a specified surface of a solar collector, device, or structural design feature may not be obstructed, or a combination of these descriptions.

(2) The restrictions placed upon vegetation, structures, and other objects that would impair or obstruct the passage of sunlight through the easement.

(3) The terms or conditions, if any, under which the easement may be revised or terminated.

(c) As used in this section, "electric utility" means an electrical corporation as defined in Section 218 of the Public Utilities Code or a local publicly owned electric utility as defined in Section 224.3 of the Public Utilities Code. **Leg.H.** Added Stats 1978 ch 1154 §5. Amended Stats 2000 ch 537 §2 (SB 1345); Stats 2017 ch 849 §1 (AB 1414), effective January 1, 2018; Stats 2021 ch 235 §2 (AB 1124), effective January 1, 2022.

§801.7. Scope of right-of-way granted to railroad transporting passengers

(a) When a right-of-way is granted pursuant to Section 801 or 802 to a railroad corporation whose primary business is the transportation of passengers, the grant shall include, but not be limited to, a right-of-way for the location, construction, and maintenance of the railroad corporation's necessary works and for every necessary adjunct thereto.

(b) A "railroad corporation" shall have the same definition as provided in Section 230 of the Public Utilities Code. **Leg.H.** Added Stats 1982 ch 1553 §1.

§802. Servitudes not attached to land

The following land burdens, or servitudes upon land, may be granted and held, though not attached to land:

One—The right to pasture, and of fishing and taking game.
Two—The right of a seat in church.
Three—The right of burial.
Four—The right of taking rents and tolls.
Five—The right of way.
Six—The right of taking water, wood, minerals, or other things. **Leg.H.** Enacted 1872. Amended by Code Amdts 1873–74 ch 612 §108.

§803. Designation of estates

The land to which an easement is attached is called the dominant tenement; the land upon which a burden or servitude is laid is called the servient tenement. **Leg.H.** Enacted 1872.

§804. By whom grantable

A servitude can be created only by one who has a vested estate in the servient tenement. **Leg.H.** Enacted 1872.

§805. By whom held

A servitude thereon cannot be held by the owner of the servient tenement. **Leg.H.** Enacted 1872.

§806. Extent of servitudes

The extent of a servitude is determined by the terms of the grant, or the nature of the enjoyment by which it was acquired. **Leg.H.** Enacted 1872.

§807. Apportioning easements

In case of partition of the dominant tenement the burden must be apportioned according to the division of the dominant tenement, but not in such a way as to increase the burden upon the servient tenement. **Leg.H.** Enacted 1872.

§808. Rights of owner of future estate

The owner of a future estate in a dominant tenement may use easements attached thereto for the purpose of viewing waste, demanding rent, or removing an obstruction to the enjoyment of such easements, although such tenement is occupied by a tenant. **Leg.H.** Enacted 1872.

§809. Actions by owner and occupant of dominant tenement

The owner of any estate in a dominant tenement, or the occupant of such tenement, may maintain an action for the enforcement of an easement attached thereto. **Leg.H.** Enacted 1872.

§810. Actions by owner of servient tenement

The owner in fee of a servient tenement may maintain an action for the possession of the land, against any one unlawfully possessed thereof, though a servitude exists thereon in favor of the public. **Leg.H.** Enacted 1872.

§811. How extinguished

A servitude is extinguished:

1. By the vesting of the right to the servitude and the right to the servient tenement in the same person;
2. By the destruction of the servient tenement;
3. By the performance of any act upon either tenement, by the owner of the servitude, or with his assent, which is incompatible with its nature or exercise; or,
4. When the servitude was acquired by enjoyment, by disuse thereof by the owner of the servitude for the period prescribed for acquiring title by enjoyment. **Leg.H.** Enacted 1872.

§812. [Section repealed 1980]

Leg.H. Added Stats 1949 ch 996 §1. Repealed Stats 1980 ch 1050 §1. See Sts & H C §8353.

§812.5. [Section repealed 1980]

Leg.H. Added Stats 1974 ch 1340 §1. Repealed Stats 1980 ch 1050 §2. See Sts & H C §§8345–8350.

§813. Recordation of notice of consent to use land; Effect; Revocation; Mailing notice; Restrictions in notice

The holder of record title to land may record in the office of the recorder of any county in which any part of the land is situated, a description of said land and a notice reading substantially as follows: "The right of the public or any person to make any use whatsoever of the above described land or any portion thereof (other than any use expressly allowed by a written or recorded map, agreement, deed or dedication) is by permission, and subject to control, of owner: Section 813, Civil Code."

The recorded notice is conclusive evidence that subsequent use of the land during the time such notice is in effect by the public or any user for any purpose (other than any use expressly allowed by a written or recorded map, agreement, deed or dedication) is permissive and with consent in any judicial proceeding involving the issue as to whether all or any portion of such land has been dedicated to public use or whether any user has a prescriptive right in such land or any portion thereof. The notice may be revoked by the holder of record title by recording a notice of revocation in the office of the recorder wherein the notice is recorded. After recording a notice pursuant to this section, and prior to any revocation thereof, the owner shall not prevent any public use appropriate thereto by physical obstruction, notice or otherwise.

In the event of use by other than the general public, any such notices, to be effective, shall also be served by registered mail on the user.

The recording of a notice pursuant to this section shall not be deemed to affect rights vested at the time of recording.

The permission for public use of real property provided for in such a recorded notice may be conditioned upon reasonable restrictions on the time, place, and manner of such public use, and no use in violation of such restrictions shall be considered public use for purposes of a finding of implied dedication. **Leg.H.** Added Stats 1963 ch 735 §1. Amended Stats 1971 ch 941 §1.

CHAPTER 4
CONSERVATION EASEMENTS

Legislative finding. §815.
"Conservation easement". §815.1.
Legal effect. §815.2.
Who may acquire and hold. §815.3.
Limitation on interest conveyed. §815.4.
Recording of conveyances. §815.5.
Enforceability; Remedies. §815.7.
Right of political subdivisions to hold similar interests. §815.9.
Conservation easement as enforceable restriction for assessment purposes. §815.10.
Liberal construction. §816.

§815. Legislative finding

The Legislature finds and declares that the preservation of land in its natural, scenic, agricultural, historical, forested, or open-space condition is among the most important environmental assets of California. The Legislature further finds and declares it to be the public policy and in the public interest of this state to encourage the voluntary conveyance of conservation easements to qualified nonprofit organizations. **Leg.H.** Added Stats 1979 ch 179 §1.

§815.1. "Conservation easement"

For the purposes of this chapter, "conservation easement" means any limitation in a deed, will, or other instrument in the form of an easement, restriction, covenant, or condition, which is or has been executed by or on behalf of the owner of the land subject to such easement and is binding upon successive owners of such land, and the purpose of which is to retain land predominantly in its natural, scenic, historical, agricultural, forested, or open-space condition. **Leg.H.** Added Stats 1979 ch 179 §1.

§815.2. Legal effect

(a) A conservation easement is an interest in real property voluntarily created and freely transferable in whole or in part for the purposes stated in Section 815.1 by any lawful method for the transfer of interests in real property in this state.

(b) A conservation easement shall be perpetual in duration.

(c) A conservation easement shall not be deemed personal in nature and shall constitute an interest in real property notwithstanding the fact that it may be negative in character.

(d) The particular characteristics of a conservation easement shall be those granted or specified in the instrument creating or transferring the easement. **Leg.H.** Added Stats 1979 ch 179 §1.

§815.3. Who may acquire and hold

Only the following entities or organizations may acquire and hold conservation easements:

(a) A tax-exempt nonprofit organization qualified under Section 501(c)(3) of the Internal Revenue Code and qualified to do business in this state which has as its primary purpose the preservation, protection, or enhancement of land in its natural, scenic, historical, agricultural, forested, or open-space condition or use.

(b) The state or any city, county, city and county, district, or other state or local governmental entity, if otherwise authorized to acquire and hold title to real property and if the conservation easement is voluntarily conveyed. No local governmental entity may condition the issuance of an entitlement for use on the applicant's granting of a conservation easement pursuant to this chapter.

(c) A federally recognized California Native American tribe or a nonfederally recognized California Native American tribe that is on the contact list maintained by the Native American Heritage Commission to protect a California Native American prehistoric, archaeological, cultural, spiritual, or ceremonial place, if the conservation easement is voluntarily conveyed. **Leg.H.** Added Stats 1979 ch 179 §1. Amended Stats 1981 ch 170 §1; Stats 2004 ch 905 §2 (SB 18).

§815.4. Limitation on interest conveyed

All interests not transferred and conveyed by the instrument creating the easement shall remain in the grantor of the easement, including the right to engage in all uses of the land not affected by the easement nor prohibited by the easement or by law. **Leg.H.** Added Stats 1979 ch 179 §1.

§815.5. Recording of conveyances

Instruments creating, assigning, or otherwise transferring conservation easements shall be recorded in the office of the county recorder of the county where the land is situated, in whole or in part, and such instruments shall be subject in all respects to the recording laws. **Leg.H.** Added Stats 1979 ch 179 §1.

§815.7. Enforceability; Remedies

(a) No conservation easement shall be unenforceable by reason of lack of privity of contract or lack of benefit to particular land or because not expressed in the instrument creating it as running with the land.

(b) Actual or threatened injury to or impairment of a conservation easement or actual or threatened violation of its terms may be prohibited or restrained, or the interest intended for protection by such easement may be enforced, by injunctive relief granted by any court of competent jurisdiction in a proceeding initiated by the grantor or by the owner of the easement.

(c) In addition to the remedy of injunctive relief, the holder of a conservation easement shall be entitled to recover money damages for any injury to such easement or to the interest being protected thereby or for the violation of the terms of such easement. In assessing such damages there may be taken into account, in addition to the cost of restoration and other usual rules of the law of damages, the loss of scenic, aesthetic, or environmental value to the real property subject to the easement.

(d) The court may award to the prevailing party in any action authorized by this section the costs of litigation, including reasonable attorney's fees. **Leg.H.** Added Stats 1979 ch 179 §1.

§815.9. Right of political subdivisions to hold similar interests

Nothing in this chapter shall be construed to impair or conflict with the operation of any law or statute conferring upon any political subdivision the right or power to hold interests in land comparable to conservation easements, including, but not limited to, Chapter 12 (commencing with Section 6950) of Division 7 of Title 1 of, Chapter 6.5 (commencing with Section 51050) chapter 6.6 (commencing with Section 51070) and Chapter 7 (commencing with Section 51200) of Part 1 of Division 1 of Title 5 of, and Article 10.5 (commencing with Section 65560) of Chapter 3 of Title 7 of, the Government Code, and Article 1.5 (commencing with Section 421) of Chapter 3 of Part 2 of Division 1 of the Revenue and Taxation Code. **Leg.H.** Added Stats 1979 ch 179 §1.

§815.10. Conservation easement as enforceable restriction for assessment purposes

A conservation easement granted pursuant to this chapter constitutes an enforceable restriction, for purposes of Section 402.1 of the Revenue and Taxation Code. **Leg.H.** Added Stats 1984 ch 777 §1.

§815.11. Landowner maintenance and improvement of forest health [Repealed]

Leg.H. Added Stats 2018 ch 626 §2 (SB 901), effective January 1, 2019. Repealed Stats 2022 ch 131 §1 (AB 2966), effective January 1, 2023.

§816. Liberal construction

The provisions of this chapter shall be liberally construed in order to effectuate the policy and purpose of Section 815. **Leg.H.** Added Stats 1979 ch 179 §1.

CHAPTER 4.5
GREENWAY EASEMENTS

Findings and declarations. §816.50.
Definitions. §816.52.
Interest in real property. §816.54.
Entities which may acquire greenway easement. §816.56.
Interests not transferred in instrument. §816.58.
Recording of instruments. §816.60.
Enforceability. §816.62.
Conflicts. §816.64.
Enforceability for purposes of Section 402.1 of Revenue and Tax Code. §816.66.

§816.50. Findings and declarations

The Legislature finds and declares the following with regard to the development of greenways along urban waterways:

(a) The restoration and preservation of land in its natural, scenic, forested, recreational, or open-space condition is among the most important environmental assets in California.

(b) Greenways have the potential to improve the quality of life in, and connectivity between, communities, and provide important recreational, open-space, wildlife, flood management, greenhouse gas reduction, and urban waterfront revitalization opportunities.

(c) It is the policy of the Legislature and in the best interest in the state to encourage the voluntary conveyance of greenway easements to qualified nonprofit organizations. **Leg.H.** Added Stats 2015 ch 639 §3 (AB 1251), effective January 1, 2016.

2015 Notes: The Legislature finds and declares the following with regard to the development of a greenway along the Los Angeles River and its tributaries:

(a) The area along the Los Angeles River and its tributaries is particularly suited for the development of a greenway.

(b) A Los Angeles River greenway that focuses on public-private partnerships aimed at establishing a continuous pedestrian bikeway along the Los Angeles River and its tributaries would foster job creation, economic development, and community revitalization. Stats 2015 ch 639 (AB 1251) §1.

This act shall be known, and may be cited, as the Greenway Development and Sustainment Act. Stats 2015 ch 639 (AB 1251) §2.

§816.52. Definitions

For purposes of this chapter, the following definitions apply:

(a)(1) "Adjacent" means within 400 yards from the property boundary of an existing urban waterway.

(2) This subdivision does not create a new authority to place or extend an easement on private property that is not part of a voluntary agreement.

(b) "Greenway" means a pedestrian and bicycle, nonmotorized vehicle transportation, and recreational travel corridor that meets the following requirements:

(1) Includes landscaping that improves rivers and streams, provides flood protection benefits, and incorporates the significance and value of natural, historical, and cultural resources, as documented in the local agency's applicable planning document, including, but not limited to, a master plan, a general plan, or a specific plan.

(2) Is separated and protected from shared roadways, is adjacent to an urban waterway, and incorporates both ease of access to nearby communities and an array of amenities within an urbanized area and services for the users of the corridor and nearby communities.

(3) Is located on public lands or private lands, or a combination of public and private lands, where public access to those lands for greenway purposes has been legally authorized by, or legally obtained from, the fee owner of the land and, if applicable, the operator of any facility or improvement located on the land, through leases, easements, or other agreements entered into by the fee owner and the operator of any affected facility or improvement on the land.

(4) Reflects design standards regarding appropriate widths, clearances, setbacks from obstructions, and centerlines protecting directional travel, and other considerations, as appropriate, that are applicable for each affected local agency, as documented in the local agency's applicable planning document, including, but not limited to, a master plan, general plan, or specific plan, and that are consistent with plans and facilities for controlling the floodwater of rivers and their tributaries, as applicable.

(5) May incorporate appropriate lighting, public amenities within an urbanized area, art, and other features that are consistent with a local agency's planning document, including, but not limited to, a general plan, master plan, or specific plan.

(c) "Greenway easement" means any limitation in a deed, will, or other instrument in the form of an easement, restriction, covenant, or condition that is or has been executed by or on behalf of the owner of the land subject to the easement and is binding upon successive owners of that land, for either of the following purposes:

(1) Developing greenways adjacent to urban waterways consistent with restoration efforts undertaken at those waterways at the time of the creation of the easement, if any.

(2) Preserving greenways adjacent to urban waterways.

(d) "Local agency" means a city, county, or city and county.

(e) "Urbanized area" has the same meaning as set forth in Section 21071 of the Public Resources Code.

(f) "Urban waterway" means a creek, stream, or river that crosses (1) developed residential, commercial, or industrial property or (2) open space where the land use is designated as residential, commercial, or industrial, as referenced in a local agency's planning document, including, but not limited to, a general plan, master plan, or specific general plan. **Leg.H.** Added Stats 2015 ch 639 §3 (AB 1251), effective January 1, 2016. Amended Stats 2016 ch 471 §1 (AB 2651), effective September 22, 2016.

2015 Note: For legislative findings and declarations and citation of act, see the 2015 Notes following §816.50.

§816.54. Interest in real property

(a) A greenway easement is an interest in real property voluntarily created and freely transferable in whole or in part for the purposes stated in subdivision (c) of Section 816.52 by any lawful method for the transfer of interests in real property in this state.

(b) A greenway easement shall be perpetual in duration.

(c) Notwithstanding the fact that it may be negative in character, a greenway easement is not personal in nature and shall constitute an interest in real property.

(d) The particular characteristics of a greenway easement shall be those granted or specified in the instrument creating or transferring the easement. **Leg.H.** Added Stats 2015 ch 639 §3 (AB 1251), effective January 1, 2016.

2015 Note: For legislative findings and declarations and citation of act, see the 2015 Notes following §816.50.

§816.56. Entities which may acquire greenway easement

Only the following entities or organizations may acquire and hold a greenway easement:

(a) A tax-exempt nonprofit organization qualified under Section 501(c)(3) of the Internal Revenue Code and qualified to do business in this state that has as its primary purpose the preservation, protection, or enhancement of land in its natural, scenic, historical, agricultural, forested, or open-space condition or use, or the preservation or development of a greenway.

(b) The state or any city, county, city and county, district, or other state or local governmental entity, if otherwise authorized to acquire and hold title to real property and if the greenway easement is voluntarily conveyed. A local governmental entity shall not condition the issuance of an entitlement for use on the applicant's granting of a greenway easement pursuant to this chapter.

(c) A federally recognized California Native American tribe or a nonfederally recognized California Native American tribe that is on the contact list maintained by the Native American Heritage Commission to protect a California Native American prehistoric, archaeological, cultural, spiritual, or ceremonial place, if the greenway easement is voluntarily conveyed. **Leg.H.** Added Stats 2015 ch 639 §3 (AB 1251), effective January 1, 2016.

2015 Note: For legislative findings and declarations and citation of act, see the 2015 Notes following §816.50.

§816.58. Interests not transferred in instrument

All interests not transferred and conveyed by the instrument creating the greenway easement shall remain in the grantor of the greenway easement, including the right to engage in all uses of the land not affected by the greenway easement nor prohibited by the greenway easement or by law. **Leg.H.** Added Stats 2015 ch 639 §3 (AB 1251), effective January 1, 2016.

2015 Note: For legislative findings and declarations and citation of act, see the 2015 Notes following §816.50.

§816.60. Recording of instruments

Instruments creating, assigning, or otherwise transferring greenway easements shall be recorded in the office of the county recorder of the county where the land is situated, in whole or in part, and those instruments shall be subject in all respects to the recording laws. **Leg.H.** Added Stats 2015 ch 639 §3 (AB 1251), effective January 1, 2016.

2015 Note: For legislative findings and declarations and citation of act, see the 2015 Notes following §816.50.

§816.62. Enforceability

(a) No greenway easement shall be unenforceable by reason of lack of privity of contract or lack of benefit to particular land or because not expressed in the instrument creating it as running with the land.

(b) Actual or threatened injury to or impairment of a greenway easement or actual or threatened violation of its terms may be prohibited or restrained, or the interest intended for protection by that easement may be enforced, by injunctive relief granted by any court of competent jurisdiction in a proceeding initiated by the grantor or by the owner of the greenway easement.

(c) In addition to the remedy of injunctive relief, the holder of a greenway easement shall be entitled to recover money damages for any injury to the greenway easement or to the interest being protected thereby or for the violation of the terms of the greenway easement. In assessing the damages, there may be taken into account, in addition to the cost of restoration and other usual rules of the law of damages, the loss of scenic, aesthetic, or environmental value to the real property subject to the greenway easement.

(d) The court may award to the prevailing party in any action authorized by this section the costs of litigation, including reasonable attorney's fees. **Leg.H.** Added Stats 2015 ch 639 §3 (AB 1251), effective January 1, 2016.

2015 Note: For legislative findings and declarations and citation of act, see the 2015 Notes following §816.50.

§816.64. Conflicts

Nothing in this chapter shall be construed to impair or conflict with the operation of any law or statute conferring upon any political subdivision the right or power to hold interests in land comparable to greenway easements, including, but not limited to, Chapter 12 (commencing with Section 6950) of Division 7 of Title 1 of, Chapter 6.5 (commencing with Section 51050), Chapter 6.6 (commencing with Section 51070) and Chapter 7 (commencing with Section 51200) of Part 1 of Division 1 of Title 5 of, and Article 10.5 (commencing with Section 65560) of Chapter 3 of Title 7 of, the Government Code, and Article 1.5 (commencing with Section 421) of Chapter 3 of Part 2 of Division 1 of the Revenue and Taxation Code. **Leg.H.** Added Stats 2015 ch 639 §3 (AB 1251), effective January 1, 2016.

2015 Note: For legislative findings and declarations and citation of act, see the 2015 Notes following §816.50.

§816.66. Enforceability for purposes of Section 402.1 of Revenue and Tax Code

A greenway easement granted pursuant to this chapter constitutes an enforceable restriction, for purposes of Section 402.1 of the Revenue and Taxation Code. **Leg.H.** Added Stats 2015 ch 639 §3 (AB 1251), effective January 1, 2016.

2015 Note: For legislative findings and declarations and citation of act, see the 2015 Notes following §816.50.

CHAPTER 5
HOUSING COOPERATIVES AND HOUSING COOPERATIVE TRUSTS

"Limited-equity housing cooperative"; "Workforce housing cooperative trust". §817.

"Workforce housing cooperative trust". §817.1.

Procedure for dissolution of limited-equity housing cooperative or workforce housing cooperative trust that receives or has received public subsidy. §817.2.

Standing of entity named as sponsor organization of workforce housing cooperative trust. §817.3.

Breach of corporate or fiduciary duties or failure to comply; Attorney fees and costs; Use of funds. §817.4.

§817. "Limited-equity housing cooperative"; "Workforce housing cooperative trust"

"Limited-equity housing cooperative" or a "workforce housing cooperative trust" means a corporation organized on a cooperative basis that, in addition to complying with Section 817.1 as may be applicable, meets all of the following requirements:

(a) The corporation is any of the following:

(1) Organized as a nonprofit public benefit corporation pursuant to Part 2 (commencing with Section 5110) of Division 2 of Title 1 of the Corporations Code.

(2) Holds title to real property as the beneficiary of a trust providing for distribution for public or charitable purposes upon termination of the trust.

(3) Holds title to real property subject to conditions that will result in reversion to a public or charitable entity upon dissolution of the corporation.

(4) Holds a leasehold interest, of at least 20 years' duration, conditioned on the corporation's continued qualification under this section, and provides for reversion to a public entity or charitable corporation.

(b)(1) The articles of incorporation or bylaws require the purchase and sale of the stock or membership interest of resident owners who cease to be permanent residents, at no more than a transfer value determined as provided in the articles or bylaws, and that shall not exceed the aggregate of the following:

(A) The consideration paid for the membership or shares by the first occupant of the unit involved, as shown on the books of the corporation.

(B) The value, as determined by the board of directors of the corporation, of any improvements installed at the expense of the member or a prior member with the prior approval of the board of directors.

(C) Accumulated simple interest, an inflation allowance at a rate that may be based on a cost-of-living index, an income index, or market-interest index, or compound interest if specified in the articles of incorporation or bylaws. For newly formed corporations, accumulated simple interest shall apply. Any increment pursuant to this paragraph shall not exceed a 10-percent annual increase on the consideration paid for the membership or share by the first occupant of the unit involved.

(2)(A) Except as provided in subparagraph (B), for purposes of a return of transfer value, both of the following are prohibited:

(i) A board of directors returning transfer value, either full or partial, to a member while he or she still remains a member.

(ii) An existing member accepting the return of his or her transfer value, either full or partial.

(B) A board of directors may return to an existing member and the existing member may accept return of his or her transfer value in the event that the member moves within the cooperative from a category of unit initially valued at a higher price to a different category of unit valued at a lower price.

(c) The articles of incorporation or bylaws require the board of directors to sell the stock or membership interest purchased as provided in subdivision (b) to new member-occupants or resident shareholders at a price that does not exceed the "transfer value" paid for the unit.

(d) The "corporate equity," that is defined as the excess of the current fair market value of the corporation's real property over the sum of the current transfer values of all shares or membership interests, reduced by the principal balance of outstanding encumbrances upon the corporate real property as a whole, shall be applied as follows:

(1) So long as any such encumbrance remains outstanding, the corporate equity shall not be used for distribution to members, but only for the following purposes, and only to the extent authorized by the board, subject to the provisions and limitations of the articles of incorporation and bylaws:

(A) For the benefit of the corporation or the improvement of the real property.

(B) For expansion of the corporation by acquisition of additional real property.

(C) For public benefit or charitable purposes.

(2) Upon sale of the property, dissolution of the corporation, or occurrence of a condition requiring termination of the trust or reversion of title to the real property, the corporate equity is required by the articles, bylaws, or trust or title conditions to be paid out, or title to the property transferred, subject to outstanding encumbrances and liens, for the transfer value of membership interests or shares, for use for a public or charitable purpose.

(e) Amendment of the bylaws and articles of incorporation requires the affirmative vote of at least two-thirds of the resident-owner members or shareholders. **Leg.H.** Added Stats 2009 ch 520 §2 (AB 1246), effective January 1, 2010.

§817.1. "Workforce housing cooperative trust"

(a) A "workforce housing cooperative trust" is an entity organized pursuant to this section that complies with Section 817 and with all of the following:

(1) Allows the governing board to be composed of two classes of board members. One class is elected by the residents, and one class is appointed by sponsor organizations, including employer and employee organizations, chambers of commerce, government entities, unions, religious organizations, nonprofit organizations, cooperative organizations, and other forms of organizations. Resident members shall elect a majority of the board members. However, sponsor organizations may appoint up to one less than a majority of the board members. The numerical composition and class of the sponsor and resident board members shall be set in the articles of incorporation and in the bylaws.

(2) Requires the charter board of a workforce housing cooperative trust to be composed of only sponsor board members, to remain in place for one year after the first resident occupancy. One year after the first resident occupancy, the resident members shall elect a single board member. Three years after the first resident occupancy, resident members shall elect a majority of the board members.

(3) Prohibits the removal of the appointees of sponsor organizations, except for cause.

(4) Allows for the issuance of separate classes of shares to sponsor organizations or support organizations. These shares shall be denominated as "workforce housing shares" and shall receive a rate of return of no more than 10 percent simple interest pursuant to subparagraph (C) of paragraph (1) of subdivision (b) of Section 817.

(5) Requires, in order to amend the bylaws or articles of incorporation of a workforce housing cooperative trust, the affirmative vote of at least a majority of the resident-owner members or shareholders and a majority of each class of board members. The rights of the sponsor board members or the sponsors shall not be changed without the affirmative vote of two-thirds of the sponsor board members.

(b) A workforce housing cooperative trust shall be entitled to operate at multiple locations in order to sponsor limited-equity housing cooperatives. A workforce housing cooperative trust may either own or lease land for the purpose of developing limited-equity housing cooperatives.

(c) A workforce housing cooperative trust may be created when at least 51 percent of the occupied units in a multifamily property that is in foreclosure support efforts to buy the building or property. **Leg.H.** Added Stats 2009 ch 520 §2 (AB 1246), effective January 1, 2010.

§817.2. Procedure for dissolution of limited-equity housing cooperative or workforce housing cooperative trust that receives or has received public subsidy

The procedure for the dissolution of a limited-equity housing cooperative or workforce housing cooperative trust that receives or has received a public subsidy shall be as follows:

(a) The city, or the county for any unincorporated area, in which the limited-equity housing cooperative or workforce housing cooperative trust is located, shall hold a public hearing. The cooperative or trust shall pay for all costs associated with the public hearing.

(b) The city or county shall provide notice to all interested parties. The notice shall be given at least 120 days prior to the date of the hearing. The city or county shall obtain a list of all other limited-equity housing cooperatives and cooperative development organizations in the state from the California Center for Cooperative Development, if the list exists, and provide notice to all of the entities on the list in an effort to create a merger with an existing limited-equity housing cooperative or workforce housing cooperative trust. The notice shall be mailed first class, postage prepaid, in the United States mail.

(c) If the dissolving limited-equity housing cooperative or workforce housing cooperative trust merges with an existing cooperative or trust, to the extent possible, the merger shall be with the geographically closest cooperative or trust.

(d) If the dissolving limited-equity housing cooperative or workforce housing cooperative trust does not merge with an existing cooperative or trust, both of the following shall occur:

(1) Upon completion of the public hearing required pursuant to subdivision (a), the city or county shall adopt a resolution approving of the dissolution and make a finding that the dissolution plan meets the requirements of state and federal law, meets the donative intent standards of the United States Internal Revenue Service, and is free of private inurement, which includes, but is not limited to, a prohibition on any member receiving any payment in excess of the transfer value to which he or she is entitled pursuant to subdivision (b) of Section 817.

(2) The city or county shall forward all of the information and written testimony from the hearing to the Office of the Attorney General for the Attorney General to consider as part of his or her ruling on the dissolution. **Leg.H.** Added Stats 2009 ch 520 §2 (AB 1246), effective January 1, 2010.

§817.3. Standing of entity named as sponsor organization of workforce housing cooperative trust

Each entity named as a sponsor organization of a workforce housing cooperative trust formed pursuant to Section 817 shall have the legal standing of a member unless it revokes, in writing, its sponsorship. **Leg.H.** Added Stats 2009 ch 520 §2 (AB 1246), effective January 1, 2010.

§817.4. Breach of corporate or fiduciary duties or failure to comply; Attorney fees and costs; Use of funds

(a) In any action instituted on or after January 1, 2010, against a board of directors and its members based upon a breach of corporate or fiduciary duties or a failure to comply with the requirements of this chapter, a prevailing plaintiff may recover reasonable attorney's fees and costs.

(b) If an organization formed under this chapter uses public funds, it shall not use any corporate funds to avoid compliance with this chapter or to pursue dissolution if the intent or outcome is for some or all of the members to receive any payment in excess of the transfer value to which he or she is entitled pursuant to subdivision (b) of Section 817. **Leg.H.** Added Stats 2009 ch 520 §2 (AB 1246), effective January 1, 2010.

TITLE 3
RIGHTS AND OBLIGATIONS OF OWNERS

Chapter 1. Rights of Owners.
Chapter 2. Obligations of Owners.
Chapter 3. Environmental Responsibility Acceptance Act.

CHAPTER 1
RIGHTS OF OWNERS

Article 1. Incidents of Ownership.
Article 2. Boundaries.

ARTICLE 1
Incidents of Ownership

Rights of tenant for life. §818.
Rights of tenant for years, etc. §819.
Same. §820.
Rights of grantees of rents and reversion. §821.
Remedies of lessor against assignee of lessee. §822.
Rights of lessees and their assignees, etc. §823.
Remedy on leases for life. §824.
Rent dependent on life. §825.
Remedy of reversioners, etc. §826.
Changes in terms of lease; Notice. §827.

§818. Rights of tenant for life

The owner of a life estate may use the land in the same manner as the owner of a fee simple, except that he must do no act to the injury of the inheritance. **Leg.H.** Enacted Stats 1872.

§819. Rights of tenant for years, etc

A tenant for years or at will, unless he is a wrong-doer by holding over, may occupy the buildings, take the annual products of the soil, work mines and quarries open at the commencement of his tenancy. **Leg.H.** Enacted Stats 1872.

§820. Same

A tenant for years or at will has no other rights to the property than such as are given to him by the agreement or instrument by which his tenancy is acquired, or by the last section. **Leg.H.** Enacted Stats 1872.

§821. Rights of grantees of rents and reversion

A person to whom any real property is transferred or devised, upon which rent has been reserved, or to whom any such rent is transferred, is entitled to the same remedies for recovery of rent, for non-performance of any of the terms of the lease, or for any waste or cause of forfeiture, as his grantor or devisor might have had. **Leg.H.** Enacted Stats 1872.

§822. Remedies of lessor against assignee of lessee

Whatever remedies the lessor of any real property has against his immediate lessee for the breach of any agreement in the lease, or for recovery of the possession, he has against the assignees of the lessee, for any cause of action accruing while they are such assignees, except where the assignment is made by way of security for a loan, and is not accompanied by possession of the premises. **Leg.H.** Enacted Stats 1872. Amended Code Amdts 1873–74 ch 612 §109; Stats 1905 ch 439 §1.

§823. Rights of lessees and their assignees, etc

Whatever remedies the lessee of any real property may have against his immediate lessor, for the breach of any agreement in the lease, he may have against the assigns of the lessor, and the assigns of the lessee may have against the lessor and his assigns, except upon covenants against incumbrances or relating to the title or possession of the premises. **Leg.H.** Enacted Stats 1872.

§824. Remedy on leases for life

Rent due upon a lease for life may be recovered in the same manner as upon a lease for years. **Leg.H.** Enacted Stats 1872.

§825. Rent dependent on life

Rent dependent on the life of a person may be recovered after as well as before his death. **Leg.H.** Enacted Stats 1872.

§826. Remedy of reversioners, etc

A person having an estate in fee, in remainder or reversion, may maintain an action for any injury done to the inheritance, notwithstanding an intervening estate for life or years, and although, after its commission, his estate is transferred, and he has no interest in the property at the commencement of the action. **Leg.H.** Enacted Stats 1872.

§827. Changes in terms of lease; Notice

(a)(1) Except as provided in subdivision (b), in all leases of lands or tenements, or of any interest therein, from week to week, month to month, or other period less than a month, the landlord may, upon giving notice in writing to the tenant, in the manner prescribed by Section 1162 of the Code of Civil Procedure, change the terms of the lease to take effect, as to tenancies for less than one month, upon the expiration of a period at least as long as the term of the hiring itself, and, as to tenancies from month to month, to take effect at the expiration of not less than 30 days, but if that change takes effect within a rental term, the rent accruing from the first day of the term to the date of that change shall be computed at the rental rate obtained immediately prior to that change; provided, however, that it shall be competent for the parties to provide by an agreement in writing that a notice changing the terms thereof may be given at any time not less than seven days before the expiration of a term, to be effective upon the expiration of the term.

(2) The notice, when served upon the tenant, shall in and of itself operate and be effectual to create and establish, as a part of the lease, the terms, rents, and conditions specified in the notice, if the tenant shall continue to hold the premises after the notice takes effect.

(b)(1) In all leases of a residential dwelling, **commercial real property by a qualified commercial tenant,** or of any interest therein, from week to week, month to month, or other period less than a month, the landlord may increase the rent provided in the lease or rental agreement, upon giving written notice to the tenant, as follows, by either of the following procedures:

(A) By delivering a copy to the tenant personally.

(B) By serving a copy by mail under the procedures prescribed in Section 1013 of the Code of Civil Procedure.

(2) If the proposed rent increase for that tenant is 10 percent or less of the rental amount charged to that tenant at any time during the 12 months before the effective date of the increase, either in and of itself or when combined with any other rent increases for the 12 months before the effective date of the increase, the notice shall be delivered at least 30 days before the effective date of the increase, and subject to Section 1013 of the Code of Civil Procedure if served by mail.

(3)(A) If the proposed rent increase for that tenant is greater than 10 percent of the rental amount charged to that tenant at any time during the 12 months before the effective date of the increase, either in and of itself or when combined with any other rent increases for the 12 months before the effective date of the increase, the notice shall be delivered at least 90 days before the effective date of the increase, and subject to Section 1013 of the Code of Civil Procedure if served by mail.

(B) If the proposed rent increase for that tenant is caused by a change in a tenant's income or family composition as determined by a recertification required by statute or regulation, the notice shall be delivered at least 30 days before the effective date of the increase as described in paragraph (2), and subparagraph (A) of this paragraph shall not apply.

(4) A landlord of a commercial real property shall include in the notice information on the provisions of this subdivision.

(5) In all leases for commercial real property by a qualified commercial tenant, a rent increase shall not be effective until the notice period required by this subdivision has expired.

(6) Notwithstanding any other provision of law, a violation of this subdivision by a landlord of a commercial real property does not entitle a qualified commercial tenant to civil penalties.

(7) For the purposes of this subdivision, the following definitions apply:

(A) "Commercial real property" means all real property in this state, except dwelling units subject to Chapter 2 (commencing with Section 1940) of Title 5 of Part 4 of Division 3, mobilehomes as defined in Section 798.3, and recreational vehicles as defined in Section 799.29.

(B) "Microenterprise" has the same meaning as that term is defined in subdivision (a) of Section 18000 of the Business and Professions Code.

(C) "Nonprofit organization" means any private, nonprofit organization that qualifies under Section 501(c)(3) of the United States Internal Revenue Code of 1986.

(D) "Qualified commercial tenant" means a tenant of commercial real property that meets both of the following requirements:

(i) The tenant is a microenterprise, a restaurant with fewer than 10 employees, or a nonprofit organization with fewer than 20 employees.

(ii)(I) Subject to subclause (II), the tenant has provided the landlord, within the previous 12 months, a written notice that the tenant is a qualified commercial tenant and a self-attestation regarding the number of employees, at such time the protections under this subdivision come into place.

(II) Unless the tenancy is from week to week, month to month, or other period less than a month, the tenant provided the notice and self-attestation described in subclause (I) before or upon execution of the lease, and annually thereafter, at such time the protections under this subdivision come into place.

(c) If a state or federal statute, state or federal regulation, recorded regulatory agreement, or contract provides for a longer period of notice regarding a rent increase than that provided in subdivision (a) or (b), the personal service or mailing of the notice shall be in accordance with the longer period. **Leg.H.** Added Code Amdts 1873–74 ch 612 §110. Amended Stats 1907 ch 39 §1; Stats 1929 ch 138 §1; Stats 1937 ch 356 §1; Stats 1939 ch 1013 §1; Stats 1947 ch 676 §1; Stats 2000 ch 680 §2 (SB 1745), operative until January 1, 2006; Stats 2001 ch 593 §1 (AB 1160), effective October 9, 2001; Stats 2002 ch 664 §33 (AB 3034); Stats 2004 ch 568 §1 (SB 1145); Stats 2019 ch 595 §2 (AB 1110), effective January 1, 2020; Stats 2024 ch 1015 §1 (SB 1103), effective January 1, 2025.

Prior Law: Former §827, similar to present Civ §827, was added Stats 2000 ch 680 §3, amended Stats 2002 ch 664 §34, operative January 1, 2006, and repealed Stats 2004 ch 568 §2.

2019 Note: It is the intent of the Legislature to respond to tight rental market conditions by providing tenants with additional notice when served with rent increases of more than 10 percent. The longer notice period prescribed in this act provide tenants with additional time to respond to rent increases. The longer notice period is not intended to constitute rent control, nor is it intended as a statement of public policy regarding acceptable or unacceptable levels of rent increases. Stats 2019 ch 595 §1.

2000 Note: It is the intent of the Legislature to respond to tight rental market conditions by providing tenants with longer notice when served with a rent increase of more than 10 percent in a 12-month period and providing owners with an easier method of service for notices of rent increases. The longer notice prescribed in this act provides tenants with additional time to respond to rent increases by, for example, augmenting their income with an additional job, finding a roommate, or relocating. The longer notice is not intended to constitute rent control, nor is it a statement of public policy regarding acceptable or unacceptable levels of rent increases. Stats 2000 ch 680 §1.

Former Sections: Former CC §827, similar to the present section, was added Stats 2000 ch 680 §3 and repealed Stats 2004 ch 568 §2 (SB 1145).

ARTICLE 2
Boundaries

Rights of owner. §829.
Boundaries by water. §830.
Boundaries by ways. §831.
Lateral and subjacent support. §832.
Trees whose trunks are wholly on land of one. §833.
Line trees. §834.
"Electrified security fence"; Installation and operation requirements [Repealed January 1, 2028]. §835.
Electrified security fences; Requirements; Local regulation for that one [Operative January 1, 2028]. § 835.

§829. Rights of owner

The owner of land in fee has the right to the surface and to everything permanently situated beneath or above it. **Leg.H.** Enacted Stats 1872.

§830. Boundaries by water

Except where the grant under which the land is held indicates a different intent, the owner of the upland, when it borders on tide-water, takes to ordinary high-water mark; when it borders upon a navigable lake or stream, where there is no tide, the owner takes to the edge of the lake or stream, at low-water mark; when it borders upon any other water, the owner takes to the middle of the lake or stream. **Leg.H.** Enacted Stats 1872. Amended Code Amdts 1873–74 ch 612 §111.

§831. Boundaries by ways

An owner of land bounded by a road or street is presumed to own to the center of the way, but the contrary may be shown. **Leg.H.** Enacted Stats 1872.

§832. Lateral and subjacent support

Each coterminous owner is entitled to the lateral and subjacent support which his land receives from the adjoining land, subject to the right of the owner of the adjoining land to make proper and usual excavations on the same for purposes of construction or improvement, under the following conditions:

1. Any owner of land or his lessee intending to make or to permit an excavation shall give reasonable notice to the owner or owners of adjoining lands and of buildings or other structures, stating the depth to which such excavation is intended to be made, and when the excavating will begin.

2. In making any excavation, ordinary care and skill shall be used, and reasonable precautions taken to sustain the adjoining land as such, without regard to any building or other structure which may be thereon, and there shall be no liability for damage done to any such building or other structure by reason of the excavation, except as otherwise provided or allowed by law.

3. If at any time it appears that the excavation is to be of a greater depth than are the walls or foundations of any adjoining building or other structure, and is to be so close as to endanger the building or other structure in any way, then the owner of the building or other structure must be allowed at least 30 days, if he so desires, in which to take measures to protect the same from any damage, or in which to extend the foundations thereof, and he must be given for the same purposes reasonable license to enter on the land on which the excavation is to be or is being made.

4. If the excavation is intended to be or is deeper than the standard depth of foundations, which depth is defined to be a depth of nine feet below the adjacent curb level, at the point where the joint property line intersects the curb and if on the land of the coterminous owner there is any building or other structure the wall or foundation of which goes to standard depth or deeper then the owner of the land on which the excavation is being made shall, if given the necessary license to enter on the adjoining land, protect the said adjoining land and any such building or other structure thereon without cost to the owner thereof, from any damage by reason of the excavation, and shall be liable to the owner of such property for any such damage, excepting only for minor settlement cracks in buildings or other structures. **Leg.H.** Enacted Stats 1872. Amended Code Amdts 1873–74 ch 612 §112; Stats 1931 ch 776 §1; Stats 1968 ch 835 §1.

§833. Trees whose trunks are wholly on land of one

Trees whose trunks stand wholly upon the land of one owner belong exclusively to him, although their roots grow into the land of another. **Leg.H.** Enacted Stats 1872.

§834. Line trees

Trees whose trunks stand partly on the land of two or more coterminous owners, belong to them in common. **Leg.H.** Enacted Stats 1872.

§835. "Electrified security fence"; Installation and operation requirements [Repealed January 1, 2028]

(a) As used in this chapter, "electrified security fence" means any fence, other than an electrified fence as defined in Section 17151 of the Food and Agricultural Code, that meets the following requirements:

(1) The **electrified security** fence is powered by an electrical energizer, **driven by solar-charged batteries of no more than 12 volts of direct current,** with both of the following output characteristics:

(A) The impulse repetition rate does not exceed 1 hertz (hz).

(B) The impulse duration does not exceed 10 milliseconds, or **10/1000** of a second.

(2) The **electrified security** fence is used to protect and secure **manufacturing** or industrial property, or property zoned under another designation, but legally authorized to be used for a commercial

purpose that stores, parks, services, sells, or rents vehicles, vessels, equipment, materials, freight, or utility infrastructure within an outdoor lot or yard, provided that the secured area does not include any existing residential or hospitality uses.

(b) An owner of real property may install and operate an electrified security fence on their property, subject to all of the following:

(1) The property is not located in a residential zone **and falls within the description of property described in paragraph (2) of subdivision (a).**

(2) The **electrified security** fence meets the [4] standards and specifications of the International Electrotechnical Commission for electric **security** fence energizers in "International Standard IEC 60335, [5] **Part 2-76:2018.**"

(3) The **electrified security** fence is identified by prominently placed warning signs that are legible from both sides of the fence. At a minimum, the warning signs shall meet all of the following criteria:

(A) The warning signs are placed at each gate and access point, and at intervals along the **electrified security** fence not exceeding 30 feet.

(B) The warning signs are adjacent to any other signs relating to chemical, radiological, or biological hazards.

(C) The warning signs are marked with a written warning or a commonly recognized symbol for shock, a written warning or a commonly recognized symbol to warn people with pacemakers, and a written warning or commonly recognized symbol about the danger of touching the **electrified security** fence in wet conditions.

(4) The height of the **electrified security** fence does not exceed 10 feet or 2 feet higher than an existing [6] **nonelectrified perimeter fence or wall**, whichever is greater. The electrified security fence shall be located behind a **nonelectrified** perimeter fence **or wall** that is not less than [7] **five** feet in height.

(5) **The electrified security fence includes a device that enables first responders to deactivate the electrified security fence in response to an emergency, if utilized by a city, county, or city and county.**

(c) The electrified security fence may interface with a monitored alarm device in a manner that enables the alarm system to transmit a signal intended to summon the business, a monitoring service, or both the business and a monitoring service, in response to an intrusion or burglary.

(d)(1) An owner of real property **not specified in paragraph (2) of subdivision (a)** shall not install or operate an electrified security fence where a local ordinance prohibits the installation or operation of an electrified security fence. A local ordinance **may prohibit the installation and operation of an electrified security fence that does not comply with subdivisions (a) to (c), inclusive. A local ordinance** that prohibits or regulates only the installation or operation of an electrified fence as defined in Section 17151 of the Food and Agricultural Code [8] **shall not be construed to** apply to an electrified security fence.

(2) [9] **For property specified under paragraph (2) of subdivision (a) and in compliance with subdivisions (a) to (c), inclusive, a city, county, or city and county ordinance, regulation, or code shall not prohibit** the installation and operation of an electrified security fence, [10] **nor require a permit or approval that is in addition to an alarm system permit issued by the city, county, or city and county. A city, county, or city and county may require an administrative permit confirming the fence meets** the requirements of [11] **this section if it is on a property abutting a property in residential use, or within 300 feet of a public park, childcare facility, recreation center, community center, or school facility.**

(e) Nothing in this section shall be construed to alter the authority of a jurisdiction to adopt and enforce an ordinance relating to nonelectrified perimeter fences or walls as legally authorized, if applicable.

(f) This section shall remain in effect only until **January 1, 2028, and as of that date is repealed. Leg.H.** Added Stats 2015 ch 273 §1 (SB 582), effective January 1, 2016. Amended Stats 2021 ch 148 §1 (AB 358), effective January 1, 2022; Stats 2024 ch 235 §1 (AB 2371), effective September 14, 2024, repealed January 1, 2028.

§835. 2024 Deletes. [1] 10/10000 [2] commercial, manufacturing, [3] , manufacturing, or industrial purpose [4] 2006 international [5] Part 2-76 [6] perimeter fence [7] 5 [8] does not [9] If a local ordinance allows [10] the installation and operation of the fence shall meet [11] that ordinance and the requirements of subdivision (b)

§835. Electrified security fences; Requirements; Local regulation for that one [Operative January 1, 2028]

(a) As used in this chapter, "electrified security fence" means any fence, other than an electrified fence as defined in Section 17151 of the Food and Agricultural Code, that meets the following requirements:

(1) The fence is powered by an electrical energizer with both of the following output characteristics:

(A) The impulse repetition rate does not exceed 1 hertz (hz).

(B) The impulse duration does not exceed 10 milliseconds, or 10/1000 of a second.

(2) The fence is used to protect and secure commercial, manufacturing, or industrial property, or property zoned under another designation, but legally authorized to be used for a commercial, manufacturing, or industrial purpose.

(b) An owner of real property may install and operate an electrified security fence on their property, subject to all of the following:

(1) The property is not located in a residential zone.

(2) The fence meets the 2006 international standards and specifications of the International Electrotechnical Commission for electric fence energizers in "International Standard IEC 60335, Part 2-76."

(3) The fence is identified by prominently placed warning signs that are legible from both sides of the fence. At a minimum, the warning signs shall meet all of the following criteria:

(A) The warning signs are placed at each gate and access point, and at intervals along the fence not exceeding 30 feet.

(B) The warning signs are adjacent to any other signs relating to chemical, radiological, or biological hazards.

(C) The warning signs are marked with a written warning or a commonly recognized symbol for shock, a written warning or a commonly recognized symbol to warn people with pacemakers, and a written warning or commonly recognized symbol about the danger of touching the fence in wet conditions.

(4) The height of the fence does not exceed 10 feet or 2 feet higher than an existing perimeter fence, whichever is greater. The electrified security fence shall be located behind a perimeter fence that is not less than 5 feet in height.

(c) The electrified security fence may interface with a monitored alarm device in a manner that enables the alarm system to transmit a signal intended to summon the business, a monitoring service, or both the business and a monitoring service, in response to an intrusion or burglary.

(d)(1) An owner of real property shall not install or operate an electrified security fence where a local ordinance prohibits the installation or operation of an electrified security fence. A local ordinance that prohibits or regulates only the installation or operation of an electrified fence as defined in Section 17151 of the Food and Agricultural Code does not apply to an electrified security fence.

(2) If a local ordinance allows the installation and operation of an electrified security fence, the installation and operation of the fence shall meet the requirements of that ordinance and the requirements of subdivision (b).

(e) This section shall become operative on January 1, 2028. **Leg.H.** Added Stats 2024 ch 235 §2 (AB 2371), effective September 14, 2024, operative January 1, 2028.

CHAPTER 2
OBLIGATIONS OF OWNERS

Duties of tenant for life. §840.

Boundaries and monuments; Presumption of equal benefit from and responsibility for fences; Required notice to adjoining landowner of costs for fence; Factors overcoming presumption; Definitions. §841.

Fence exceeding specified height as nuisance. §841.4.

Ouster of cotenant out of possession by cotenant in possession. §843.

Maintenance of right of way; Sharing of costs by co-owners. §845.

Duty of care or warning to persons entering property for recreation; Effect of permission to enter. §846.

Attorney fees claim by property owner or public entity allowing public access to land. §846.1.

Persons invited on land to glean agricultural products for charitable purpose. §846.2.

Access to property to perform surveys; Monuments within freeway right-of-ways. §846.5.

Limitation on liability for injuries to persons committing certain felonies. §847.

Owner of mineral rights; Notice prior to first entry. §848.

§840. Duties of tenant for life

The owner of a life estate must keep the buildings and fences in repair from ordinary waste, and must pay the taxes and other annual charges, and a just proportion of extraordinary assessments benefiting the whole inheritance. **Leg.H.** Enacted Stats 1872.

§841. Boundaries and monuments; Presumption of equal benefit from and responsibility for fences; Required notice to adjoining landowner of costs for fence; Factors overcoming presumption; Definitions

(a) Adjoining landowners shall share equally in the responsibility for maintaining the boundaries and monuments between them.

(b)(1) Adjoining landowners are presumed to share an equal benefit from any fence dividing their properties and, unless otherwise agreed to by the parties in a written agreement, shall be presumed to be equally responsible for the reasonable costs of construction, maintenance, or necessary replacement of the fence.

(2) Where a landowner intends to incur costs for a fence described in paragraph (1), the landowner shall give 30 days' prior written notice to each affected adjoining landowner. The notice shall include notification of the presumption of equal responsibility for the reasonable costs of construction, maintenance, or necessary replacement of the fence. The notice shall include a description of the nature of the problem facing the shared fence, the proposed solution for addressing the problem, the estimated construction or maintenance costs involved to address the problem, the proposed cost sharing approach, and the proposed timeline for getting the problem addressed.

(3) The presumption in paragraph (1) may be overcome by a preponderance of the evidence demonstrating that imposing equal responsibility for the reasonable costs of construction, maintenance, or necessary replacement of the fence would be unjust. In determining whether equal responsibility for the reasonable costs would be unjust, the court shall consider all of the following:

(A) Whether the financial burden to one landowner is substantially disproportionate to the benefit conferred upon that landowner by the fence in question.

(B) Whether the cost of the fence would exceed the difference in the value of the real property before and after its installation.

(C) Whether the financial burden to one landowner would impose an undue financial hardship given that party's financial circumstances as demonstrated by reasonable proof.

(D) The reasonableness of a particular construction or maintenance project, including all of the following:

(i) The extent to which the costs of the project appear to be unnecessary or excessive.

(ii) The extent to which the costs of the project appear to be the result of the landowner's personal aesthetic, architectural, or other preferences.

(E) Any other equitable factors appropriate under the circumstances.

(4) Where a party rebuts the presumption in paragraph (1) by a preponderance of the evidence, the court shall, in its discretion, consistent with the party's circumstances, order either a contribution of less than an equal share for the costs of construction, maintenance, or necessary replacement of the fence, or order no contribution.

(c) For the purposes of this section, the following terms have the following meanings:

(1) "Landowner" means a private person or entity that lawfully holds any possessory interest in real property, and does not include a city, county, city and county, district, public corporation, or other political subdivision, public body, or public agency.

(2) "Adjoining" means contiguous to or in contact with. **Leg.H.** Added Stats 2013 ch 86 §3 (AB 1404), effective January 1, 2014.

Prior Law: Former CC §841, relating to boundaries, monuments, and fences, was enacted Stats 1872 and repealed January 1, 2014, by Stats 2013 ch 86 §2 (AB 1404).

2013 Note: This act shall be known, and may be cited, as the Good Neighbor Fence Act of 2013. Stats 2013 ch 86 (AB 1404) §1.

Former Sections: Former CC §841, relating to boundaries, monuments, and fences, was enacted Stats 1872 and repealed operative January 1, 2014, by Stats 2013 ch 86 §2 (AB 1404).

§841.4. Fence exceeding specified height as nuisance

Any fence or other structure in the nature of a fence unnecessarily exceeding 10 feet in height maliciously erected or maintained for the purpose of annoying the owner or occupant of adjoining property is a private nuisance. Any owner or occupant of adjoining property injured either in his comfort or the enjoyment of his estate by such nuisance may enforce the remedies against its continuance prescribed in Title 3, Part 3, Division 4 of this code. **Leg.H.** Added Stats 1953 ch 37 §2.

§842. [Section repealed 1943]

Leg.H. Added Stats 1905 ch 440 §1. Amended Stats 1941 ch 499 §1. Repealed Stats 1943 ch 368 (Wat C §150001). See Wat C §7001.

§843. Ouster of cotenant out of possession by cotenant in possession

(a) If real property is owned concurrently by two or more persons, a tenant out of possession may establish an ouster from possession by a tenant in possession in the manner provided in this section. This section does not apply to the extent the tenant out of possession is not entitled to possession or an alternative remedy is provided under the terms of an agreement between the cotenants or the instrument creating the cotenancy or another written instrument that indicates the possessory rights or remedies of the cotenants. This section supplements and does not limit any other means by which an ouster may be established.

(b) A tenant out of possession may serve on a tenant in possession a written demand for concurrent possession of the property. The written demand shall make specific reference to this section and to the time within which concurrent possession must be offered under this section. Service of the written demand shall be made in the same manner as service of summons in a civil action. An ouster is established 60 days after service is complete if, within that time, the tenant in possession does not offer and provide unconditional concurrent possession of the property to the tenant out of possession.

(c) A claim for damages for an ouster established pursuant to this section may be asserted by an independent action or in an action for possession or partition of the property or another appropriate action or proceeding, subject to any applicable statute of limitation.

(d) Nothing in this section precludes the cotenants, at any time before or after a demand is served, from seeking partition of the property or from making an agreement as to the right of possession among the cotenants, the payment of reasonable rental value in lieu of possession, or any other terms that may be appropriate. **Leg.H.** Added Stats 1984 ch 241 §1.

Prior Law: Former §843, similar to present Wat C §§7002, 7003, was added Stats 1905 ch 440 §2 and repealed Stats 1943 ch 368 (Wat C §150001.)

1984 Note: This act applies to property acquired before, on, or after the operative date of the act. Stats 1984 ch 241 §2.

§844. [Section repealed 1943]

Leg.H. Added Stats 1935 ch 315 §1. Amended Stats 1941 ch 499 §2. Repealed Stats 1943 ch 368 (Wat C §150001). See Wat C §§7005–7010.

§845. Maintenance of right of way; Sharing of costs by co-owners

(a) The owner of any easement in the nature of a private right-of-way, or of any land to which any such easement is attached, shall maintain it in repair.

(b) If the easement is owned by more than one person, or is attached to parcels of land under different ownership, the cost of maintaining it in repair shall be shared by each owner of the easement or the owners of the parcels of land, as the case may be, pursuant to the terms of any agreement entered into by the parties for that purpose. In the absence of an agreement, the cost shall be shared proportionately to the use made of the easement by each owner.

(c) If any owner refuses to perform, or fails after demand in writing to pay the owner's proportion of the cost, an action to recover that owner's share of the cost, or for specific performance or contribution, may be brought by the other owners, either jointly or severally. The action may be brought before, during, or after performance of the maintenance work, as follows:

(1) The action may be brought in small claims court if the amount claimed to be due as the owner's proportion of the cost does not exceed the jurisdictional limit of the small claims court. A small claims judgment shall not affect apportionment of any future costs that are not requested in the small claims action.

(2) Except as provided in paragraph (1), the action shall be filed in superior court and, notwithstanding Section 1141.13 of the Code of Civil

Procedure, the action shall be subject to judicial arbitration pursuant to Chapter 2.5 of Title 3 of Part 3 (commencing with Section 1141.10) of the Code of Civil Procedure. A superior court judgment shall not affect apportionment of any future costs that are not requested in the action, unless otherwise provided in the judgment.

(3) In the absence of an agreement addressing the maintenance of the easement, any action for specific performance or contribution shall be brought in a court in the county in which the easement is located.

(4) Nothing in this section precludes the use of any available alternative dispute resolution program to resolve actions regarding the maintenance of easements in the small claims court or the superior court.

(d) In the event that snow removal is not required under subdivision (a), or under any independent contractual or statutory duty, an agreement entered into pursuant to subdivision (b) to maintain the easement in repair shall be construed to include snow removal within the maintenance obligations of the agreement if all of the following exist:

(1) Snow removal is not expressly precluded by the terms of the agreement.

(2) Snow removal is necessary to provide access to the properties served by the easement.

(3) Snow removal is approved in advance by the property owners or their elected representatives in the same manner as provided by the agreement for repairs to the easement.

(e) This section does not apply to rights-of-way held or used by railroad common carriers subject to the jurisdiction of the Public Utilities Commission. **Leg.H.** Added Stats 1939 ch 755 §1. Amended Stats 1985 ch 985 §1; Stats 1993 ch 196 §1 (SB 370); Stats 2012 ch 244 §1 (AB 1927), effective January 1, 2013.

§846. Duty of care or warning to persons entering property for recreation; Effect of permission to enter

(a) An owner of any estate or any other interest in real property, whether possessory or nonpossessory, owes no duty of care to keep the premises safe for entry or use by others for any recreational purpose or to give any warning of hazardous conditions, uses of, structures, or activities on those premises to persons entering for a recreational purpose, except as provided in this section.

(b) A "recreational purpose," as used in this section, includes activities such as fishing, hunting, camping, water sports, hiking, spelunking, sport parachuting, riding, including animal riding, snowmobiling, and all other types of vehicular riding, rock collecting, sightseeing, picnicking, nature study, nature contacting, recreational gardening, gleaning, hang gliding, private noncommercial aviation activities, winter sports, and viewing or enjoying historical, archaeological, scenic, natural, or scientific sites.

(c) An owner of any estate or any other interest in real property, whether possessory or nonpossessory, who gives permission to another for entry or use for the above purpose upon the premises does not thereby do any of the following:

(1) Extend any assurance that the premises are safe for that purpose.

(2) Constitute the person to whom permission has been granted the legal status of an invitee or licensee to whom a duty of care is owed.

(3) Assume responsibility for or incur liability for any injury to person or property caused by any act of the person to whom permission has been granted except as provided in this section.

(d) This section does not limit the liability which otherwise exists for any of the following:

(1) Willful or malicious failure to guard or warn against a dangerous condition, use, structure or activity.

(2) Injury suffered in any case where permission to enter for the above purpose was granted for a consideration other than the consideration, if any, paid to said landowner by the state, or where consideration has been received from others for the same purpose.

(3) Any persons who are expressly invited rather than merely permitted to come upon the premises by the landowner.

(e) This section does not create a duty of care or ground of liability for injury to person or property. **Leg.H.** Added Stats 1963 ch 1759 §1. Amended Stats 1970 ch 807 §1; Stats 1971 ch 1028 §1; Stats 1972 ch 1200 §1; Stats 1976 ch 1303 §1; Stats 1978 ch 86 §1; Stats 1979 ch 150 §1; Stats 1980 ch 408 §1; Stats 1988 ch 129 §1; Stats 2014 ch 52 §1 (SB 1072), effective January 1, 2015; Stats 2018 ch 92 §33 (SB 1289), effective January 1, 2019.

§846.1. Attorney fees claim by property owner or public entity allowing public access to land

(a) Except as provided in subdivision (c), an owner of any estate or interest in real property, whether possessory or nonpossessory, who gives permission to the public for entry on or use of the real property pursuant to an agreement with a public or nonprofit agency for purposes of recreational trail use, and is a defendant in a civil action brought by, or on behalf of, a person who is allegedly injured or allegedly suffers damages on the real property, may present a claim to the Department of General Services for reasonable attorney's fees incurred in this civil action if any of the following occurs:

(1) The court has dismissed the civil action upon a demurrer or motion for summary judgment made by the owner or upon its own motion for lack of prosecution.

(2) The action was dismissed by the plaintiff without any payment from the owner.

(3) The owner prevails in the civil action.

(b) Except as provided in subdivision (c), a public entity, as defined in Section 831.5 of the Government Code, that gives permission to the public for entry on or use of real property for a recreational purpose, as defined in Section 846, and is a defendant in a civil action brought by, or on behalf of, a person who is allegedly injured or allegedly suffers damages on the real property, may present a claim to the Department of General Services for reasonable attorney's fees incurred in this civil action if any of the following occurs:

(1) The court has dismissed the civil action upon a demurrer or motion for summary judgment made by this public entity or upon its own motion for lack of prosecution.

(2) The action was dismissed by the plaintiff without any payment from the public entity.

(3) The public entity prevails in the civil action.

(c) An owner of any estate or interest in real property, whether possessory or nonpossessory, or a public entity, as defined in Section 831.5 of the Government Code, that gives permission to the public for entry on, or use of, the real property for a recreational purpose, as defined in Section 846, pursuant to an agreement with a public or nonprofit agency, and is a defendant in a civil action brought by, or on behalf of, a person who seeks to restrict, prevent, or delay public use of that property, may present a claim to the Department of General Services for reasonable attorney's fees incurred in the civil action if any of the following occurs:

(1) The court has dismissed the civil action upon a demurrer or motion for summary judgment made by the owner or public entity or upon its own motion for lack of prosecution.

(2) The action was dismissed by the plaintiff without any payment from the owner or public entity.

(3) The owner or public entity prevails in the civil action.

(d) The Department of General Services shall allow the claim if the requirements of this section are met. The claim shall be paid from an appropriation to be made for that purpose. Reasonable attorney's fees, for purposes of this section, may not exceed an hourly rate greater than the rate charged by the Attorney General at the time the award is made, and may not exceed an aggregate amount of twenty-five thousand dollars ($25,000). This subdivision shall not apply if a public entity has provided for the defense of this civil action pursuant to Section 995 of the Government Code. This subdivision shall also not apply if an owner or public entity has been provided a legal defense by the state pursuant to any contract or other legal obligation.

(e) The total of claims allowed by the Department of General Services pursuant to this section shall not exceed two hundred thousand dollars ($200,000) per fiscal year. **Leg.H.** Added Stats 1996 ch 932 §1 (AB 2291). Amended Stats 1999 ch 775 §1 (SB 243); Stats 2006 ch 538 §41 (SB 1852), effective January 1, 2007; Stats 2016 ch 31 §8 (SB 836), effective June 27, 2016.

§846.2. Persons invited on land to glean agricultural products for charitable purpose

No cause of action shall arise against the owner, tenant, or lessee of land or premises for injuries to any person who has been expressly invited on that land or premises to glean agricultural or farm products for charitable purposes, unless that person's injuries were caused by the gross negligence or willful and wanton misconduct of the owner, tenant, or lessee. The immunity provided by this section does not apply if the owner, tenant, or lessee received any consideration for permitting the gleaning activity. **Leg.H.** Added Stats 1988 ch 1062 §1.

§846.5. Access to property to perform surveys; Monuments within freeway right-of-ways

(a) The right of entry upon or to real property to investigate and utilize boundary evidence, and to perform surveys, is a right of persons legally authorized to practice land surveying and it shall be the responsibility of the owner or tenant who owns or controls property to provide reasonable access without undue delay. The right of entry is not contingent upon the provision of prior notice to the owner or tenant. However, the owner or tenant shall be notified of the proposed time of entry where practicable.

(b) The requirements of subdivision (a) do not apply to monuments within access-controlled portions of freeways.

(c) When required for a property survey, monuments within a freeway right-of-way shall be referenced to usable points outside the access control line by the agency having jurisdiction over the freeway when requested in writing by the registered civil engineer or licensed land surveyor who is to perform the property survey. The work shall be done within a reasonable time period by the agency in direct cooperation with the engineer or surveyor and at no charge to him. **Leg.H.** Added Stats 1973 ch 435 §1. Amended Stats 1982 ch 427 §1.

§846.6. [Section repealed 1985]

Leg.H. Added Stats 1984 ch 650 §1. Repealed Stats 1985 ch 874 §11. See CC §1357.

§847. Limitation on liability for injuries to persons committing certain felonies

(a) An owner, including, but not limited to, a public entity, as defined in Section 811.2 of the Government Code, of any estate or any other interest in real property, whether possessory or nonpossessory, shall not be liable to any person for any injury or death that occurs upon that property during the course of or after the commission of any of the felonies set forth in subdivision (b) by the injured or deceased person.

(b) The felonies to which the provisions of this section apply are the following: (1) Murder or voluntary manslaughter; (2) mayhem; (3) rape; (4) sodomy by force, violence, duress, menace, or threat of great bodily harm; (5) oral copulation by force, violence, duress, menace, or threat of great bodily harm; (6) lewd acts on a child under the age of 14 years; (7) any felony punishable by death or imprisonment in the state prison for life; (8) any other felony in which the defendant inflicts great bodily injury on any person, other than an accomplice, or any felony in which the defendant uses a firearm; (9) attempted murder; (10) assault with intent to commit rape or robbery; (11) assault with a deadly weapon or instrument on a peace officer; (12) assault by a life prisoner on a noninmate; (13) assault with a deadly weapon by an inmate; (14) arson; (15) exploding a destructive device or any explosive with intent to injure; (16) exploding a destructive device or any explosive causing great bodily injury; (17) exploding a destructive device or any explosive with intent to murder; (18) burglary; (19) robbery; (20) kidnapping; (21) taking of a hostage by an inmate of a state prison; (22) any felony in which the defendant personally used a dangerous or deadly weapon; (23) selling, furnishing, administering, or providing heroin, cocaine, or phencyclidine (PCP) to a minor; (24) grand theft as defined in Sections 487 and 487a of the Penal Code; and (25) any attempt to commit a crime listed in this subdivision other than an assault.

(c) The limitation on liability conferred by this section arises at the moment the injured or deceased person commences the felony or attempted felony and extends to the moment the injured or deceased person is no longer upon the property.

(d) The limitation on liability conferred by this section applies only when the injured or deceased person's conduct in furtherance of the commission of a felony specified in subdivision (b) proximately or legally causes the injury or death.

(e) The limitation on liability conferred by this section arises only upon the charge of a felony listed in subdivision (b) and the subsequent conviction of that felony or a lesser included felony or misdemeanor arising from a charge of a felony listed in subdivision (b). During the pendency of any such criminal action, a civil action alleging this liability shall be abated and the statute of limitations on the civil cause of action shall be tolled.

(f) This section does not limit the liability of an owner or an owner's agent which otherwise exists for willful, wanton, or criminal conduct, or for willful or malicious failure to guard or warn against a dangerous condition, use, structure, or activity.

(g) The limitation on liability provided by this section shall be in addition to any other available defense. **Leg.H.** Added Stats 1985 ch 1541 §1.

Prior Law: Former §847 was enacted Stats 1872 and repealed Stats 1929 ch 146 §2.

§848. Owner of mineral rights; Notice prior to first entry

(a) Except as provided in subdivision (c), the owner of mineral rights, as defined by Section 883.110, in real property shall give a written notice prior to the first entry to the owner of the real property who is listed as the assessee on the current local assessment roll or to the owner's representative, or to the lessee of the real property if different from the mineral rights owner, and to any public utility that has a recorded interest in the real property if there is to be excavation of the utility interest, under the following circumstances:

(1) If the mineral rights owner or its agent intends to enter real property for the purpose of undertaking non-surface-disrupting activities such as surveying, water and mineral testing, and removal of debris and equipment not involving use of an articulated vehicle on the real property, the owner or agent shall provide a minimum of five days' notice. Reasonable attempts shall be made to deliver the notice by acknowledged personal delivery, but if that cannot occur, the notice shall be delivered by registered letter and be received a minimum of five days prior to the entrance on the property. The notice shall specify all of the following:

(A) Date of entry.

(B) Estimated length of time the property will be occupied.

(C) General nature of the work.

(2) If the mineral rights owner or its agent intends to enter real property for the purpose of excavation or other surface-disrupting activities such as drilling new wells, constructing structures, bringing articulated vehicles or excavation equipment on the real property, or reclamation of the real property after the surface has been disturbed, the owner or agent shall provide a minimum of 30 days' notice. The notice shall specify both of the following:

(A) The extent and location of the prospecting, mining, or extraction operation.

(B) The approximate time or times of entry and exit upon the real property.

(3) If a mineral rights owner's entry to the real property ceases for a period of one year or more, any further entry by the mineral rights owner for the purpose of surface-disturbing activities pursuant to paragraph (2) shall require written notice pursuant to this subdivision.

(b)(1) If a mineral rights owner has been authorized by the Geologic Energy Management Division to drill a relief well or to take other immediate actions in response to an emergency situation, or if the division or its agent is drilling a relief well or taking other immediate actions in response to an emergency situation, the notice provisions under paragraph (2) of subdivision (a) shall be waived.

(2) For purposes of this subdivision, an "emergency" means immediate action is necessary to protect life, health, property, or natural resources.

(c) The notice specified in subdivision (a) shall not be required if the owner of the real property or assessee has a current, already negotiated surface use, access use, or similar agreement with the mineral rights owner, lessee, agent, or operator.

(d) If the mineral rights owner has not complied with the notice requirement specified in subdivision (a), the owner of the real property listed on the current assessment roll or any public utility which has a recorded interest in the real property may request a court to enjoin the prospecting, mining, or extracting operation until the mineral rights owner has complied. The absence of a known owner on the assessment roll or any public utility which has a recorded interest in the real property relieves the mineral rights owner of the obligation to give the written notice to the owner or public utility.

(e) For purposes of this section, an "acknowledged personal delivery" means that the written notice is personally delivered to the owner, the owner's representative, or lessee, and the owner, the owner's representative, or lessee acknowledges, in writing, receipt of the notice. **Leg.H.** Added Stats 1988 ch 535 §1. Amended Stats 2012 ch 542 §1 (AB 1966), effective January 1, 2013; Stats 2019 ch 771 §1 (AB 1057), effective January 1, 2020.

Prior Law: Former §848 was enacted Stats 1872 and repealed Code Amdts 1873–74 ch 612 §113.

§849. [Section repealed 1873–74]

Leg.H. Enacted Stats 1872. Repealed Code Amdts 1873–74 ch 612 §113.

CHAPTER 3
ENVIRONMENTAL RESPONSIBILITY ACCEPTANCE ACT

Definitions [Operative January 1, 2024]. §850.
Responsibilities and notices [Operative January 1, 2024]. §851.
Commitment statement procedure. §852.
Construction of chapter; Cause of action [Operative January 1, 2024]. §853.
Form of commitment statement. §854.
Notification requirements effective date. §855.

§850. Definitions [Operative January 1, 2024]

The definitions set forth in Section 25260 of the Health and Safety Code govern the construction of this chapter. In addition, the following definitions apply for purposes of this chapter only:

(a) "Actual awareness" means actual knowledge of a fact pertaining to an obligation under this chapter, including actual knowledge of a release exceeding the notification threshold. Only actual awareness possessed by those employees or representatives of an owner of a site who are responsible for monitoring, responding to or otherwise addressing the release shall be attributable to the owner. Only actual awareness possessed by those employees or representatives of a potentially responsible party who are responsible for monitoring, responding to, or otherwise addressing, the release shall be attributable to the potentially responsible party.

(b) "Commitment statement" means a written statement executed by the notice recipient which recites expressly the language specified in Section 854.

(c) "Mediation" means an informal process in which the disputing parties select a neutral third party to assist them in reaching a negotiated settlement in which the neutral third party has no power to impose a solution on the parties, but rather has the power only to assist the parties in shaping solutions to meet their interests and objectives.

(d) "Negative response" means a written response by the recipient of a notice of potential liability indicating that the recipient will not undertake any response action, or a deemed negative response pursuant to subdivision (c) of Section 851 in the event of the recipient's failure to respond.

(e) "Neutral third party" means an experienced professional, such as an attorney, engineer, environmentalist, hydrologist, or retired judge, who has served as a mediator.

(f) "Notice of potential liability" means a notice, sent by the owner of the site, stating that a release that exceeds the notification threshold has occurred at the site and that the owner believes that the recipient of the notice is a responsible party with respect to the release. The notice of potential liability shall describe the location of the site and the nature of the release.

(g) "Notice recipient" means any one of the following:

(1) A person who receives a notice of potential liability pursuant to subdivision (a) of Section 851.

(2) A person who provides a release report pursuant to subdivision (b) of Section 851.

(3) A person who offers a commitment statement to the owner of a site pursuant to subdivision (c) of Section 851.

(h) "Notification threshold" means any release of such a magnitude that:

(1) The release is the subject of a response action which has been ordered by, or is being performed by, an oversight agency; or

(2) The release is impeding the ability of the owner of the site to sell, lease, or otherwise use the site.

(i) "Operation and maintenance" means any activity as defined in Section 78080 of the Health and Safety Code.

(j) "Oversight agency" means any agency, as defined in subdivision (c) of Section 25260 of the Health and Safety Code, that has jurisdiction over a response action performed in connection with a release that is the subject of a notice of potential liability. Subject to any other limitation imposed by law, an oversight agency retains full discretion as to when it exercises jurisdiction over a site.

(k) "Reasonable steps," as used in subdivision (a) of Section 851, means the least expensive means available to ascertain the potentially responsible parties. If the owner cannot otherwise identify any apparent, potentially responsible parties, then "reasonable steps" includes:

(1) Conducting a title search; and

(2) Reviewing all environmental reports in the owner's possession of which the owner has actual awareness pertaining to the site.

(*l*) "Release" means the release, as defined in Section 78105 of the Health and Safety Code, of a hazardous material or hazardous materials.

(m) "Release report" means a notice sent by a responsible party to the owner of the site stating that a release has occurred on the site which is likely to exceed the notification threshold. The release report shall describe the location of the site and the nature of the release.

(n) "Remedial action" means any action as defined in Section 78125 of the Health and Safety Code.

(o) "Removal action" means any action as defined in Section 78135 of the Health and Safety Code.

(p) "Response action" means any removal actions, including, but not limited to, site investigations and remedial actions, including, but not limited to, operation and maintenance measures.

(q) "Responsible party" means any person who is liable under state or local law for taking action in response to a release.

(r) "Site" means any parcel of commercial, industrial, or agricultural real property where a hazardous materials release has occurred.

(s) "Written action" means any official action by any oversight agency where the oversight agency has expressly exercised its cleanup authority in writing, pursuant to the oversight agency's procedures, directing a response action at the site. **Leg.H.** Added Stats 1997 ch 873 §1 (SB 1081). Amended Stats 2022 ch 258 §2 (AB 2327), effective January 1, 2023, operative January 1, 2024.

Prior Law: Former CC §850, relating to uses and trusts, was enacted Stats 1872 and repealed Stats 1873-74 ch 612 §113.

§851. Responsibilities and notices [Operative January 1, 2024]

(a) An owner of a site who has actual awareness of a release exceeding the notification threshold shall take all reasonable steps as defined in subdivision (j) of Section 850 to expeditiously identify the potentially responsible parties. The owner shall, as soon as reasonably possible after obtaining actual awareness of the potentially responsible parties, send a notice of potential liability to the identified potentially responsible parties and the agency, as defined in subdivision (c) of Section 25260 of the Health and Safety Code, that the owner believes to be the appropriate oversight agency. For any release exceeding the notification threshold of which the owner has actual awareness that occurred prior to, but within three years of, the effective date of this section, the notice shall be given on or before December 31, 1998.

(b) A potentially responsible party who has actual awareness of a release which is likely to exceed the notification threshold shall as soon as reasonably possible after obtaining actual awareness of the release provide the owner of the site where the release occurred with a release report. For any release exceeding the notification threshold of which the potentially responsible party has actual awareness that occurred prior to, but within three years of, the effective date of this section, the release report shall be given on or before December 31, 1998. A potentially responsible party may issue, at the potentially responsible party's option, a commitment statement to the owner of the site within 120 days of the potentially responsible party's issuance of a release report. The fact that a release report is issued shall not constitute an admission of liability and may not be admitted as evidence against a potentially responsible party in any litigation.

(c) When a notice of potential liability is issued, a notice recipient shall respond to the owner, in writing, and by certified mail, return receipt requested, within 120 days from the date that the notice of potential liability was mailed. The notice recipient's response shall be either a commitment statement or a negative response. The notice recipient's failure to submit the written response within the 120-day period, or failure to strictly comply with the form of the written response, as provided in Section 854, shall be deemed a negative response. The owner may agree in writing to extend the period during which the notice recipient may respond to the notice of potential liability. An extension of up to 120 days shall be provided if the notice recipient commits to do a site investigation, the results of which shall be provided to the owner and the oversight agency.

(d)(1) The common law duty to mitigate damages shall apply to any failure of the owner of a site to give a timely notice of potential liability when the owner is required to give this notice pursuant to this chapter. Where an owner fails to mitigate damages by not giving a timely notice of potential liability, the owner's damage claim shall be reduced in accordance with common law principles by the amount that the potentially responsible party proves would have likely been mitigated had a timely notice of potential liability been given.

(2) Common law principles shall apply to the failure of the potentially responsible party to issue a timely release report. Where a potentially responsible party fails to give a timely release report, the potentially responsible party, in accordance with common law principles, shall be responsible to the owner of the site, for damages that the owner proves are likely caused by the failure to provide a release report.

(3) Any party who argues the applicability of this subdivision carries the burden of proof in that regard.

(4) Nothing in this section is intended to create a new cause of action or defense beyond that which already exists under common law.

(5) Subdivisions (a) and (b), and paragraphs (1) and (2) of this subdivision, shall not apply when the party to whom a notice of potential liability or release report is owed already possesses actual awareness of the information required to be transmitted in the notice of potential liability or release report.

(e)(1) Except as provided in paragraph (2), the requirements of this chapter shall not apply to a site listed pursuant to Article 5 (commencing with Section 78760) of Chapter 4 of Part 2 of Division 45 of for response action pursuant to Part 2 (commencing with Section 7800) of Division 45 of the Health and Safety Code or to a site where an oversight agency has issued an order or entered into an enforceable agreement pursuant to any authority, including, but not limited to, an order or enforceable agreement entered into by a local agency, the Department of Toxic Substance Control, the State Water Resources Control Board, or a regional water quality control board pursuant to Chapter 6.5 (commencing with Section 25100), Chapter 6.7 (commencing with Section 25280), Chapter 6.75 (commencing with Section 25299.10), Chapter 6.86 (commencing with Section 25396), or Chapter 6.11 (commencing with Section 25404) of Division 20 of, or Part 2 (commencing with Section 78000) of Division 45 of, the Health and Safety Code, or pursuant to Division 7 (commencing with Section 13000) of the Water Code.

(2) The requirements of this chapter shall apply if either of the following applies:

(A) The order or enforceable agreement is issued or entered into after the owner accepts a commitment statement.

(B) The Department of Toxic Substance Control, State Water Resources Control Board, or regional water quality control board that issued the order or entered into an enforceable agreement consents in writing to the applicability of this chapter to the site.

(f) It is the intent of the Legislature for this chapter to resolve disputes between, and affect the rights of, private parties only. Nothing in this chapter shall affect the authority of the Department of Toxic Substance Control, the State Water Resources Control Board, a regional water quality control board, or any other oversight agency.

(g) Notwithstanding any other provision of this chapter, any time prior to accepting a commitment statement, the owner may provide the notice to the notice recipient that the provisions of subdivision (c), paragraph (2) of subdivision (e), and Sections 852 and 854, shall not apply to the site, in which case the provisions of subdivision (c), paragraph (2) of subdivision (e), and Sections 852 and 854 shall not apply to the site and the owner and notice recipient shall be entitled to pursue all other legal remedies and defenses authorized by law. **Leg.H.** Added Stats 1997 ch 873 §1 (SB 1081). Amended Stats 2022 ch 258 §3 (AB 2327), effective January 1, 2023, operative January 1, 2024.

Prior Law Former CC §851, relating to uses and trusts, was enacted Stats 1872 and repealed Stats 1873-74 ch 612 §113.

§852. Commitment statement procedure

(a) Within 45 days after issuance of the commitment statement, the owner may transmit to the notice recipient by certified mail, return receipt requested, an executed copy of the commitment statement, indicating its acceptance. If the owner does not execute the commitment statement, the commitment statement shall be deemed to have been rejected upon expiration of the 45-day period. A notice recipient has no obligation with respect to the provisions of a rejected commitment statement.

(b)(1) Except as otherwise provided in this chapter, or unless the owner or the notice recipient has elected not to proceed with the mediation, if the owner rejects the commitment statement, the owner and notice recipient shall participate in a mediation process prior to the commencement of any litigation which pertains to a release covered by the commitment statement. The mediation process shall be supervised by a neutral third party mutually agreed upon by the owner and the notice recipient in order to mediate a mutually agreeable settlement between the owner and notice recipient of all issues related to the release.

(2) Either the notice recipient or the owner may elect not to proceed further with the mediation process at any time prior to completion of those proceedings.

(3) To the extent a mutually agreeable settlement is reached which allocates the liability and assigns the rights and obligations of the owner and notice recipient in a manner different from or inconsistent with this chapter, the settlement shall supersede the terms of this chapter pursuant to subdivision (f) of Section 853. If a settlement of all issues cannot be reached within 90 days after the owner's rejection of the commitment statement, the neutral third party shall declare the mediation process unsuccessful and terminate the process. The owner and notice recipient may mutually agree to extend the mediation process but shall communicate any such extension in writing to the neutral third party. If the party issuing the commitment statement fails, for any reason, to participate in the mediation within 90 days of the rejection of the commitment statement, the owner may proceed with litigation.

(4) After the termination of an unsuccessful mediation process, the parties shall be free to litigate or otherwise resolve their respective claims. The parties may mutually agree to the terms of the commitment statement at any time after the termination of an unsuccessful mediation process, in which case this chapter shall govern the rights and obligations of the parties.

(5) Any applicable statute of limitations shall be tolled for 90 days following issuance of a notice of potential liability, a release report, or a commitment statement.

(6) Any applicable statute of limitations shall be tolled from the time the owner rejects a commitment statement until the termination of the mediation process. If mediation is not commenced within 90 days after the owner's rejection of the commitment statement, the tolling of the statute of limitations shall terminate unless otherwise agreed to by the parties.

(7) Unless the owner and notice recipient agree otherwise, the fees and costs of the neutral third party shall be borne equally by the notice recipient and the owner.

(c) Upon taking effect, the commitment statement shall have all of the following results:

(1) The commitment statement shall constitute a binding promise that the notice recipient will undertake any response action as required by an oversight agency through a written action, directed to the owner or notice recipient, in connection with the release that is the subject of the notice of potential liability or release report. The commitment statement shall not create any obligations with respect to releases occurring after the commitment statement is signed, or with respect to any other release that is not the subject of the notice of potential liability.

(2) The commitment statement shall constitute a binding promise that the owner shall provide reasonable site access to the notice recipient to take any action that is reasonably necessary or appropriate to conduct a response action. This grant of access shall not affect the rights of the owner if the notice recipient's activities onsite result in physical damage to the site which the notice recipient fails to repair within a reasonable period after completion of all onsite activities. Unless otherwise ordered by the oversight agency, the notice recipient shall take all reasonable steps to avoid interfering with the owner's use of the site.

(3) Except for civil actions seeking damages for personal injury or wrongful death, once a commitment statement has been accepted, the court shall stay any action brought by the owner of the site against the notice recipient that issued the commitment statement, including, but not limited to, actions in trespass, nuisance, negligence, and strict liability, which arise from or relate to a release for which a commitment statement has been issued. The stay shall be effective for a period of not more than two years from the date of acceptance of the commitment statement, but only so long as the site response action is proceeding to the satisfaction of an oversight agency. The stay shall not apply to any civil action that is based on fraud, failure to disclose, or misrepresentation related to any transaction between the owner of the site and the notice recipient, to any civil action for breach of the commitment statement, or to any civil action which is unrelated to the release. The owner and notice recipient may elect to extend the period of the stay by written agreement.

(4) In an action by an owner who has accepted a commitment statement against the notice recipient who issued the commitment statement, and which arises from or relates to a release for which a commitment statement has been issued, only the following damages shall be recoverable to the extent otherwise authorized by law:

(A) Damages for personal injuries or wrongful death caused by the release.

(B) Damages for breach of a commitment statement.

(C) Damages from the failure of a prospective purchaser to perform under a sales contract because of the release, where such failure to perform occurs prior to the issuance of the commitment statement.

(D) Damages for the lost use of the property prior to the issuance of a commitment statement caused by the release.

(E) Recovery of costs of investigating and responding to the release where such costs are incurred prior to the issuance of the commitment statement.

(F) Remedies for any breach of a preexisting contract entered into prior to the acceptance of a commitment statement.

(G) Damages for lost rents and any other damages recoverable under law associated with lost use of the site caused by any notice recipient during site response action activities.

(5) An owner may obtain rescission of a commitment statement if a notice recipient repudiates its obligations under the commitment statement, in which case Sections 852 and 854 shall no longer apply to the site.

(6) The notice recipient and owner shall copy each other with respect to all correspondence and proposed workplans to and from the oversight agency that relate to the site.

(d) Nothing in this chapter shall affect the authority of an oversight agency under the law to bring an administrative, criminal, or civil action against either a notice recipient or the owner, nor does it compel any action on the part of the oversight agency.

(e) At any time after the commitment statement is accepted, either the owner or the notice recipient may file an action against the other for material breach of rights and obligations associated with the commitment statement. Subject to the stay provided for in paragraph (3) of subdivision (c), the parties may litigate these claims in the same action as any other claims they may have in connection with the release that is the subject of the commitment statement.

(f) Whenever a notice recipient issues a commitment statement, the following notice shall be provided in 14 point boldface type if printed or in boldface capital letters if typed:

"THIS FORM WAS DEVELOPED AS PART OF A PROCESS ENACTED BY THE CALIFORNIA LEGISLATURE TO PROVIDE OWNERS OF PROPERTY AND POTENTIALLY RESPONSIBLE PARTIES AN ALTERNATIVE TO LITIGATING DISPUTES OVER CONTAMINATION. IT IS YOUR OPTION AS TO WHETHER YOU SIGN THIS FORM OR OTHERWISE PARTICIPATE IN THIS PROCESS. IF YOU CHOOSE NOT TO PARTICIPATE IN THE PROCESS, YOU SHOULD NOTIFY THE PARTY WHO SENT YOU THIS FORM. THIS FORM INVOLVES A TRADEOFF WHEREBY EACH PARTY ACQUIRES AND RELINQUISHES CERTAIN RIGHTS. UNDER THIS FORM, THE PROPERTY OWNER GETS THE ASSURANCE THAT THE POTENTIALLY RESPONSIBLE PARTY IS OBLIGATED TO PERFORM INVESTIGATORY AND CLEANUP ACTIONS IN THE EVENT THAT GOVERNMENT AUTHORITIES ELECT TO REQUIRE THESE ACTIONS. ON THE OTHER HAND, THE PROPERTY OWNER FOREGOES CERTAIN CLAIMS ASSOCIATED WITH RESIDUAL CONTAMINATION THAT GOVERNMENTAL AUTHORITIES ALLOW TO REMAIN IN PLACE ON THE PROPERTY. IF YOU ELECT NOT TO SIGN THIS FORM, THE PROCESS DEVELOPED BY THE LEGISLATURE CONTEMPLATES THAT YOU WILL ATTEMPT TO MEDIATE ANY DISPUTES REGARDING THE CONTAMINATION. HOWEVER, MEDIATION IS NEITHER MANDATORY NOR BINDING. IF YOU HAVE QUESTIONS ABOUT THE PROCESS, YOU MAY WISH TO CONSULT AN ATTORNEY."

(g) Any applicable statute of limitations shall be tolled for two and one-half years from the date of acceptance of the commitment statement. If at the end of two years from the date of acceptance of the commitment statement an oversight agency has not issued a written action directed to the owner or notice recipient, the owner has 60 days in which he or she may terminate the commitment statement; and, in this event, it shall have no further force or effect. In the event the owner terminates the commitment statement, subdivision (c) shall no longer apply to the site and shall no longer govern the rights and obligations of the owner or notice recipient. **Leg.H.** Added Stats 1997 ch 873 §1 (SB 1081).

Prior Law: Former §852, similar to present Prob C §15206, was enacted Stats 1872 and repealed Stats 1986 ch 820 §5, operative July 1, 1987.

§853. Construction of chapter; Cause of action [Operative January 1, 2024]

(a) Neither the failure to issue a commitment statement nor its issuance shall be construed as an admission that the recipient of the notice of potential liability is liable under any federal, state, or local law, including common law, for the release that the party agrees to investigate or respond. Neither the failure to issue a commitment statement nor the contents of the commitment statement shall be admissible evidence in any proceeding, as defined in Section 901 of the Evidence Code, except that the contents of the commitment statement shall be admissible evidence in an action to enforce the commitment statement to the extent that the contents would be admissible under other applicable law.

(b) Nothing in this chapter shall subject a notice recipient to any damages, fines, or penalties for a failure to make a written response, either positive or negative, to a notice of potential liability.

(c) Nothing in this chapter shall subject the owner of a site to any damages, fines, or penalties for a failure to send a notice of potential liability pursuant to Section 851. Failure by the owner of a site to send a notice of potential liability of a release in a timely fashion shall not be deemed to create any liability for the owner under a theory of negligence per se.

(d) Nothing in this chapter imposes an affirmative duty on the owner of a site, or any potentially responsible party, to discover, or determine the nature or extent of, a hazardous materials release at the site. This chapter does not affect an affirmative duty described in this subdivision to the extent that duty is imposed by any other law.

(e) Subject to the defenses specified in Sections 101(35) and 107(b) of the federal Comprehensive Environmental Response, Compensation, and Liability Act of 1980, as amended (42 U.S.C. Secs. 9601(35) and 9607(b)), a cause of action is hereby established whereby a notice recipient may recover from any responsible party any reasonable response costs for conducting a response action as may be approved or overseen by an oversight agency or as incurred pursuant to a commitment statement. Liability among responsible parties shall be allocated based upon the equitable factors specified in former subdivision (c) of former Section 25356.3 of the Health and Safety Code, as it existed prior to its repeal by Chapter 39 of the Statutes of 2012. No third-party beneficiary rights are created by a commitment statement, except as provided in subdivision (b) of Section 854. This cause of action applies to costs incurred prior to enactment of this subdivision. However, no recovery may be obtained under this subdivision for costs incurred more than three years prior to the filing of litigation to recover those costs. The cause of action established pursuant to this subdivision shall not apply against a current or former owner of a site unless that owner operated a business that caused a release being addressed by a response action at the site and the costs incurred by the notice recipient were in response to a release caused by the owner.

(f) Nothing in this chapter shall affect or limit the rights of an owner under preexisting contract. Nothing in this chapter shall affect or limit the right of a notice recipient and owner to agree to an allocation of liability or to an assignment of rights and obligations that is different from or inconsistent with this chapter. Agreements allocating liability or assigning rights and obligations shall supersede the terms of this chapter.

(g) Nothing in this chapter shall make a notice recipient a responsible party, beyond the obligations the notice recipient undertakes pursuant to this chapter.

(h) Nothing in this chapter shall apply to causes of action for wrongful death or personal injury. However, the pleading of a cause of action for wrongful death or personal injury shall not affect the applicability of this chapter to other causes of action in the same civil action. **Leg.H.** Added Stats 1997 ch 873 §1 (SB 1081). Amended Stats 2022 ch 258 §4 (AB 2327), effective January 1, 2023, operative January 1, 2024.

Prior Law Former CC §853, concerning resulting trusts, was enacted Stats 1872, amended Code Amdts 1873–74 ch 612 §114, and repealed Stats 1986 ch 820 §5, operative July 1, 1987.

§854. Form of commitment statement

A commitment statement shall be executed in substantially the following form:

COUNTY OF _____
STATE OF CALIFORNIA
} NOTICE OF ASSUMPTION OF GOVERNMENT IMPOSED SITE INVESTIGATION AND/OR REMEDIAL ACTION ORDERS ("COMMITMENT STATEMENT")

(a) The undersigned notice recipient is aware of, or has received a notice of potential liability pursuant to, Section 851 of the Civil Code ("notice of potential liability") in connection with a release of hazardous materials at a parcel of property ("site") having the following legal description: (Insert description here)

(b) The undersigned notice recipient and the undersigned owner of the site and the owner's successors, heirs, and assigns agree, upon the proper and timely execution and delivery of this commitment statement, to abide by the requirements of Chapter 3 (commencing with Section 850) of Title 3 of Part 2 of Division 2 in connection with the release that is the subject of the notice of potential liability.

(c) The undersigned notice recipient hereby commits to undertake any response action as required by an oversight agency through a written action, directed to the owner or notice recipient, in connection with the release that is the subject of the notice of potential liability or release report. This commitment runs with the land and binds, in addition to the current owner of the site, all of the owner's successors in interest, including current and future lenders having a security interest in the site.

(d) The owner of the site and the owner's successors, heirs, and assigns agree, upon the proper and timely execution and delivery of this commitment statement, to all of the following:

(1) The undersigned notice recipient or the party's designee shall be allowed such access to the site as may be required to perform its obligations under this commitment statement, provided that the undersigned notice recipient shall be liable for any physical damage it causes in conducting a response action, which the notice recipient fails to repair within a reasonable period after completion of all onsite activities.

(2) The parties, their successors, heirs, and assigns shall provide each other with copies of any communication or correspondence with an oversight agency in connection with the release of hazardous materials at the site.

(3) Provided that the undersigned notice recipient performs all of its obligations under this commitment statement, and except as otherwise provided in subdivisions (c) and (e) of Section 852 of the Civil Code, no claim for damages, accruing after the acceptance of the commitment statement, shall be brought against the undersigned notice recipient by the owner of the site or by the owner's successors, heirs, and assigns.

(e) The contents of this commitment statement shall be inadmissible evidence in any proceeding, as defined in Section 901 of the Evidence Code, except in an action to enforce this commitment statement to the extent that such contents would be admissible under other applicable law. This commitment statement may be enforced fully by the owner of the site and all parties identified in paragraph (b). There are no third-party beneficiary rights created by this commitment statement.

(f) The owner of the site shall provide a copy of this commitment statement to any prospective purchaser or lessee of the site until this commitment statement is terminated or until all response actions have been completed in accordance with the commitment statement.

(g) If the owner transfers the site, the owner shall notify the undersigned parties to this commitment statement, by mail, within 14 business days of the property transfer.

(h) As provided by law, this commitment statement shall become effective if the owner executes this commitment statement within 45 days from the date of issuance, in which case its terms shall go into effect upon receipt of that acceptance by the issuer of this commitment statement. If the owner rejects this commitment statement, the rejection shall be subject to the mediation provisions of subdivision (b) of Section 852.

(i) If at the end of two years from the date of acceptance of this commitment statement, an oversight agency has not issued a written action directed to the owner or notice recipient, the owner has 60 days in which he or she may terminate the commitment statement; and, in this event, it shall have no further force or effect.

_____   _____
Notice recipient   Date

(Notice recipient's name, address, and telephone number)
(Notarial affidavit)

_____   _____
Owner   Date

(Owner's name, address, and telephone number)
(Notarial affidavit)

Leg.H. Added Stats 1997 ch 873 §1 (SB 1081).

§855. Notification requirements effective date
The notification requirements of Section 851 shall not become effective until 180 days after the effective date of this chapter. **Leg.H.** Added Stats 1997 ch 873 §1 (SB 1081).

TITLE 4
USES AND TRUSTS [REPEALED]

§856. [Section repealed 1987]
Leg.H. Enacted Stats 1872. Repealed Stats 1986 ch 820 §5, operative July 1, 1987.

§857. [Section repealed 1929]
Leg.H. Enacted Stats 1872. Amended Code Amdts 1873–74 ch 612 §116, Stats 1913 ch 252 §1 p 438. Repealed Stats 1929 ch 146 §2. The repealed section related to purpose of express trusts.

§858. [Section repealed 1987]
Leg.H. Added Code Amdts 1873–74 ch 612 §117. Repealed Stats 1986 ch 820 §5, operative July 1, 1987. See CC §2932.5.

Prior Law: Former §858, relating to certain devises in trust deemed powers, was enacted Stats 1872 and repealed by Code Amdts 1873–74 ch 612 §117 p 222.

§859. [Section repealed 1987]
Leg.H. Enacted Stats 1872. Amended Stats 1935 ch 408 §1; Stats 1982 ch 497 §3, operative July 1, 1983. Repealed Stats 1986 ch 820 §5, operative July 1, 1987. See Prob C §15307.

§860. [Section repealed 1987]
Leg.H. Added Code Amdts 1873–74 ch 612 §118. Amended Stats 1969 ch 113 §1. Repealed Stats 1986 ch 820 §5, operative July 1, 1987. See Prob C §§15620–15622.

Prior Law: Former §860, providing that certain express trusts should be valid as powers trust, was enacted Stats 1872 and repealed by Code Amdts 1873–74 ch 612 §118 p 222.

§§861, 862. [Sections repealed 1873–74]
Leg.H. Enacted Stats 1872. Repealed Code Amdts 1873–74 ch 612 §119.

§863. [Section repealed 1987]
Leg.H. Enacted Stats 1872. Repealed Stats 1986 ch 820 §5, operative July 1, 1987. See Prob C §§15200, 16000–16081, 16420, 17200.

§§864–866. [Sections repealed 1987]
Leg.H. Enacted Stats 1872. Repealed Stats 1986 ch 820 §5, operative July 1, 1987. See Prob C §§15000 et seq., 15410.

§867. [Section repealed 1987]
Leg.H. Enacted Stats 1872. Amended Code Amdts 1873–74 ch 612 §120. Repealed Stats 1986 ch 820 §5, operative July 1, 1987. See Prob C §15300.

§868. [Section repealed 1873–74]
Leg.H. Enacted Stats 1872. Repealed Code Amdts 1873–74 ch 612 §121.

§869. [Section repealed 1987]
Leg.H. Enacted Stats 1872. Amended Code Amdts 1873–74 ch 612 §122. Repealed Stats 1986 ch 820 §5, operative July 1, 1987. See Prob C §18103.

§869a. [Section repealed 1987]
Leg.H. Added Stats 1923 ch 134 §1. Amended Stats 1943 ch 312 §1. Repealed Stats 1986 ch 820 §5, operative July 1, 1987. See Prob C §18104.

§870. [Section repealed 1987]

Leg.H. Enacted Stats 1872. Repealed Stats 1986 ch 820 §5, operative July 1, 1987. See Prob C §§16200 et seq. 16420, and 18100.

§871. [Section repealed 1987]

Leg.H. Enacted Stats 1872. Repealed Stats 1986 ch 820 §5, operative July 1, 1987. See Prob C §§15407, 15409.

§§878–880. [Sections repealed 1874]

Leg.H. Enacted Stats 1872. Repealed Code Amdts 1873–74 ch 612 §123.

TITLE 5
MARKETABLE RECORD TITLE

Chapter 1. General Provisions.
Chapter 2. Ancient Mortgages and Deeds of Trust.
Chapter 3. Mineral Rights.
Chapter 4. Unexercised Options.
Chapter 5. Powers of Termination.
Chapter 6. Unperformed Contracts for Sale of Real Property.
Chapter 7. Abandoned Easements.

CHAPTER 1
GENERAL PROVISIONS

Article 1. Construction.
Article 2. Application of Title.
Article 3. Preservation of Interests.

ARTICLE 1
Construction

Legislative policy and purpose. §880.020.
Construction of title. §880.030.

§880.020. Legislative policy and purpose

(a) The Legislature declares as public policy that:

(1) Real property is a basic resource of the people of the state and should be made freely alienable and marketable to the extent practicable in order to enable and encourage full use and development of the real property, including both surface and subsurface interests.

(2) Interests in real property and defects in titles created at remote times, whether or not of record, often constitute unreasonable restraints on alienation and marketability of real property because the interests are no longer valid or have been abandoned or have otherwise become obsolete.

(3) Such interests and defects produce litigation to clear and quiet titles, cause delays in real property title transactions, and hinder marketability of real property.

(4) Real property title transactions should be possible with economy and expediency. The status and security of recorded real property titles should be determinable to the extent practicable from an examination of recent records only.

(b) It is the purpose of the Legislature in enacting this title to simplify and facilitate real property title transactions in furtherance of public policy by enabling persons to rely on record title to the extent provided in this title, with respect to the property interests specified in this title, subject only to the limitations expressly provided in this title and notwithstanding any provision or implication to the contrary in any other statute or in the common law. This title shall be liberally construed to effect the legislative purpose. **Leg.H.** Added Stats 1982 ch 1268 §1. Amended Stats 2011 ch 46 §1 (SB 284), effective January 1, 2012.

§880.030. Construction of title

Nothing in this title shall be construed to:

(a) Limit application of the principles of waiver and estoppel, laches, and other equitable principles.

(b) Affect the operation of any statute governing the effect of recording or failure to record, except as specifically provided in this title. **Leg.H.** Added Stats 1982 ch 1268 §1.

ARTICLE 2
Application of Title

Interests not subject to expiration of record. §880.240.
Time limitations. §880.250.
Effect of commencement of action. §880.260.

§880.240. Interests not subject to expiration of record

The following interests are not subject to expiration or expiration of record pursuant to this title:

(a) The interest of a person in possession (including use or occupancy) of real property and the interest of a person under whom a person in possession claims, to the extent the possession would have been revealed by reasonable inspection or inquiry.

(b) An interest of the United States or pursuant to federal law in real property that is not subjected by federal law to the recording requirements of the state and that has not terminated under federal law.

(c) An interest of the state or a local public entity in real property.

(d) A conservation easement pursuant to Chapter 4 (commencing with Section 815) of Title 2. **Leg.H.** Added Stats 1982 ch 1268 §1.

§880.250. Time limitations

(a) The times prescribed in this title for expiration or expiration of record of an interest in real property or for enforcement, for bringing an action, or for doing any other required act are absolute and apply notwithstanding any disability or lack of knowledge of any person or any provisions for tolling a statute of limitation and notwithstanding any longer time applicable pursuant to any statute of limitation.

(b) Nothing in this title extends the period for enforcement, for bringing an action, or for doing any other required act, or revives an interest in real property that expires and is unenforceable, pursuant to any applicable statute of limitation. **Leg.H.** Added Stats 1982 ch 1268 §1.

§880.260. Effect of commencement of action

An interest in real property, as specified in this title, does not expire or expire of record and is not unenforceable pursuant to this title at the time prescribed in this title if within the time an action is commenced to enforce, establish, clear title to, or otherwise affect the interest and a notice of the pendency of the action is recorded as provided by law. For the purpose of this section, action includes special proceeding and arbitration proceeding. **Leg.H.** Added Stats 1982 ch 1268 §1.

ARTICLE 3
Preservation of Interests

Requirement of notice; Effect of recordation of notice. §880.310.
Persons who may record notice. §880.320.
Verification and content of notice. §880.330.
Form of notice. §880.340.
Recording procedure. §880.350.
Slander of title. §880.360.
Retroactivity of limitation statutes. §880.370.

§880.310. Requirement of notice; Effect of recordation of notice

(a) If the time within which an interest in real property expires pursuant to this title depends upon recordation of a notice of intent to preserve the interest, a person may preserve the person's interest from expiration by recording a notice of intent to preserve the interest before the interest expires pursuant to this title. Recordation of a notice of intent to preserve an interest in real property after the interest has expired pursuant to this title does not preserve the interest.

(b) Recordation of a notice of intent to preserve an interest in real property does not preclude a court from determining that an interest has been abandoned or is otherwise unenforceable pursuant to other law, whether before or after the notice of intent to preserve the interest is recorded, and does not validate or make enforceable a claim or interest that is otherwise invalid or unenforceable. Recordation of a notice of intent to preserve an interest in real property creates a presumption affecting the burden of proof that the person who claims the interest has not abandoned and does not intend to abandon the interest. **Leg.H.** Added Stats 1982 ch 1268 §1.

§880.320. Persons who may record notice

A notice of intent to preserve an interest in real property may be recorded by any of the following persons:

(a) A person who claims the interest.

(b) Another person acting on behalf of a claimant if the person is authorized to act on behalf of the claimant or if the claimant is one of a class whose identity cannot be established or is uncertain at the time of recording the notice of intent to preserve the interest. **Leg.H.** Added Stats 1982 ch 1268 §1.

§880.330. Verification and content of notice

Subject to all statutory requirements for recorded documents:

(a) A notice of intent to preserve an interest in real property shall be in writing and signed and verified by or on behalf of the claimant. If the notice is made on behalf of a claimant, the notice shall include a statement of the authority of the person making the notice.

(b) The notice shall contain all of the following information:

(1) The name and mailing address of the claimant. If the notice is made by or on behalf of more than one claimant the notice shall contain the name and mailing address of each claimant.

(2) A statement of the character of interest claimed. The statement shall include a reference by record location to the recorded document that creates or evidences the interest in the claimant.

(3) A legal description of the real property in which the interest is claimed. The description may be the same as that contained in the recorded document that creates or evidences the interest in the claimant. **Leg.H.** Added Stats 1982 ch 1268 §1.

§880.340. Form of notice

Subject to all statutory requirements for recorded documents, a notice of intent to preserve an interest in real property shall be in substantially the following form:

RECORDING INFORMATION

Recording requested by:	FOR USE OF COUNTY RECORDER
After recording return to:	Indexing instructions. This notice must be indexed as follows: Grantor and grantee index—each claimant is a grantor.

NOTICE OF INTENT TO PRESERVE INTEREST

This notice is intended to preserve an interest in real property from extinguishment pursuant to Title 5 (commencing with Section 880.020) of Part 2 of Division 2 of the Civil Code (Marketable Record Title).

Claimant	Name: Mailing address: (must be given for each claimant)
Interest	Character (e.g., power of termination): Record location of document creating or evidencing interest in claimant:
Real Property	Legal description (may be same as in recorded document creating or evidencing interest in claimant):

I assert under penalty of perjury that this notice is not recorded for the purpose of slandering title to real property and I am informed and believe that the information contained in this notice is true. If this notice is made on behalf of a claimant, I assert under penalty of perjury that I am authorized to act on behalf of the claimant.

Signed: _____ Date: _____
(claimant)

_____
(person acting on behalf of claimant)
Certificate of acknowledgment required.

Leg.H. Added Stats 1982 ch 1268 §1. Amended Stats 2012 ch 94 §1 (AB 1642), effective January 1, 2013.

§880.350. Recording procedure

(a) A notice of intent to preserve an interest in real property shall be recorded in the county in which the real property is situated.

(b) The county recorder shall index a notice of intent to preserve an interest in real property in the index of grantors and grantees. The index entry shall be for the grantor, and for the purpose of this index, the claimant under the notice shall be deemed to be the grantor. If a notice of intent to preserve is recorded by or on behalf of more than one claimant, each claimant shall be deemed to be a grantor and a separate index entry shall be made for each claimant. **Leg.H.** Added Stats 1982 ch 1268 §1.

§880.360. Slander of title

A person shall not record a notice of intent to preserve an interest in real property for the purpose of slandering title to the real property. If the court in an action or proceeding to establish or quiet title determines that a person recorded a notice of intent to preserve an interest for the purpose of slandering title, the court shall award against the person the cost of the action or proceeding, including a reasonable attorney's fee, and the damages caused by the recording. **Leg.H.** Added Stats 1982 ch 1268 §1.

§880.370. Retroactivity of limitation statutes

If the period prescribed by statute during which a notice of intent to preserve an interest in real property must be recorded expires before, on, or within five years after the operative date of the statute, the period is extended until five years after the operative date of the statute. **Leg.H.** Added Stats 1982 ch 1268 §1.

§§881, 882. [Sections repealed 1874]

Leg.H. Enacted Stats 1872. Repealed Code Amdts 1873–74 ch 612 §123.

CHAPTER 2
ANCIENT MORTGAGES AND DEEDS OF TRUST

Expiration of security interests. §882.020.
Effect of expiration of security interest. §882.030.
Application of chapter. §882.040.

§882.020. Expiration of security interests

(a) Unless the lien of a mortgage, deed of trust, or other instrument that creates a security interest of record in real property to secure a debt or other obligation has earlier expired pursuant to Section 2911, the lien expires at, and is not enforceable by action for foreclosure commenced, power of sale exercised, or any other means asserted after, the later of the following times:

(1) If the final maturity date or the last date fixed for payment of the debt or performance of the obligation is ascertainable from the recorded evidence of indebtedness, 10 years after that date.

(2) If the final maturity date or the last date fixed for payment of the debt or performance of the obligation is not ascertainable from the recorded evidence of indebtedness, or if there is no final maturity date or last date fixed for payment of the debt or performance of the obligation, 60 years after the date the instrument that created the security interest was recorded.

(3) If a notice of intent to preserve the security interest is recorded within the time prescribed in paragraph (1) or (2), 10 years after the date the notice is recorded.

(b) For the purpose of this section, a power of sale is deemed to be exercised upon recordation of the deed executed pursuant to the power of sale.

(c) The times prescribed in this section may be extended in the same manner and to the same extent as a waiver made pursuant to Section 360.5 of the Code of Civil Procedure, except that an instrument is effective to extend the prescribed times only if it is recorded before expiration of the prescribed times. **Leg.H.** Added Stats 1982 ch 1268 §1. Amended Stats 2006 ch 575 §1 (AB 2624), effective January 1, 2007.

§882.030. Effect of expiration of security interest

Expiration of the lien of a mortgage, deed of trust, or other security interest pursuant to this chapter or any other statute renders the lien unenforceable by any means commenced or asserted thereafter and is equivalent for all purposes to a certificate of satisfaction, reconveyance, release, or other discharge of the security interest, and execution and recording of a certificate of satisfaction, reconveyance, release, or other discharge is not necessary to terminate or evidence the termination of the security interest. Nothing in this section precludes execution and recording at any time of a certificate of satisfaction, reconveyance, release, or other discharge. **Leg.H.** Added Stats 1982 ch 1268 §1.

§882.040. Application of chapter

(a) Subject to Section 880.370 (grace period for recording notice) and except as otherwise provided in this section, this chapter applies on the operative date to all mortgages, deeds of trust, and other instruments that create a security interest in real property to secure a debt or other obligation, whether executed or recorded before, on, or after the operative date.

(b) This chapter shall not cause the lien of a mortgage, deed of trust, or other security interest in real property to expire or become unenforceable before the passage of five years after the operative date of this chapter. **Leg.H.** Added Stats 1982 ch 1268 §1.

§883. [Section repealed 1874]

Leg.H. Enacted Stats 1982. Repealed Code Amdts 1873–74 ch 612 §123.

CHAPTER 3
MINERAL RIGHTS

Article 1. General Provisions.
Article 2. Termination of Dormant Mineral Right.

ARTICLE 1
General Provisions

"Mineral right". §883.110.
Application of chapter. §883.120.
Effect on common law. §883.130.
Expiration or abandonment of lease; Quitclaim deed; Instrument or notice of surrender or termination; Damages for failure to comply. §883.140.

§883.110. "Mineral right"

As used in this chapter, "mineral right" means an interest in minerals, regardless of character, whether fugacious or nonfugacious, organic or inorganic, that is created by grant or reservation, regardless of form, whether a fee or lesser interest, mineral, royalty, or leasehold, absolute or fractional, corporeal or incorporeal, and includes express or implied appurtenant surface rights. **Leg.H.** Added Stats 1984 ch 240 §2.

§883.120. Application of chapter

(a) This chapter does not apply to a mineral right reserved to the United States (whether in a patent, pursuant to federal law, or otherwise) or to an oil or gas lease, mining claim, or other mineral right of a person entitled pursuant thereto, to the extent provided in Section 880.240.

(b) This chapter does not apply to a mineral right of the state or a local public entity, or of any other person, to the extent provided in Section 880.240. **Leg.H.** Added Stats 1984 ch 240 §2.

§883.130. Effect on common law

Nothing in this chapter limits or affects the common law governing abandonment of a mineral right or any other procedure provided by statute for clearing an abandoned mineral right from title to real property. **Leg.H.** Added Stats 1984 ch 240 §2.

§883.140. Expiration or abandonment of lease; Quitclaim deed; Instrument or notice of surrender or termination; Damages for failure to comply

(a) As used in this section:

(1) "Lessee" includes an assignee or other successor in interest of the lessee.

(2) "Lessor" includes a successor in interest or heir or grantee of the lessor.

(b) If the term of a mineral right lease has expired or a mineral right lease has been abandoned by the lessee, the lessee shall, within 30 days after demand therefor by the lessor, execute, acknowledge, and deliver, or cause to be recorded, a deed quitclaiming all interest in and to the mineral rights covered by the lease. If the expiration or abandonment covers less than the entire interest of the lessee, the lessee shall execute, acknowledge, and deliver an appropriate instrument or notice of surrender or termination that covers the interest that has expired or been abandoned.

(c) If the lessee fails to comply with the requirements of this section, the lessee is liable for all damages sustained by the lessor as a result of the failure, including, but not limited to, court costs and reasonable attorney's fees in an action to clear title to the lessor's interest. The lessee shall also forfeit to the lessor the sum of one hundred fifty dollars ($150).

(d) Nothing in this section makes a quitclaim deed or other instrument or notice of surrender or termination, or a demand therefor, a condition precedent to an action to clear title to the lessor's interest. **Leg.H.** Added Stats 1984 ch 240 §2.

ARTICLE 2
Termination of Dormant Mineral Right

Authorization to bring action. §883.210.
Conditions for dormancy of mineral right. §883.220.
Notice of intent to preserve mineral right; Recordation. §883.230.
Venue. §883.240.
Recordation of late notice of intent as condition of dismissal; Payment of litigation expenses. §883.250.
Terminated mineral rights deemed unenforceable and expired. §883.260.
Application of article. §883.270.

§883.210. Authorization to bring action

The owner of real property subject to a mineral right may bring an action to terminate the mineral right pursuant to this article if the mineral right is dormant. **Leg.H.** Added Stats 1984 ch 240 §2.

§883.220. Conditions for dormancy of mineral right

For the purpose of this article, a mineral right is dormant if all of the following conditions are satisfied for a period of 20 years immediately preceding commencement of the action to terminate the mineral right:

(a) There is no production of the minerals and no exploration, drilling, mining, development, or other operations that affect the minerals, whether on or below the surface of the real property or on other property, whether or not unitized or pooled with the real property.

(b) No separate property tax assessment is made of the mineral right or, if made, no taxes are paid on the assessment.

(c) No instrument creating, reserving, transferring, or otherwise evidencing the mineral right is recorded. **Leg.H.** Added Stats 1984 ch 240 §2.

§883.230. Notice of intent to preserve mineral right; Recordation

(a) An owner of a mineral right may at any time record a notice of intent to preserve the mineral right.

(b) In lieu of the statement of the character of the interest claimed and the record location of the documents creating or evidencing the mineral rights claimed as otherwise required by paragraph (2) of subdivision (b) of Section 880.330 and in lieu of the legal description of the real property in which the interest is claimed as otherwise required by paragraph (3) of subdivision (b) of Section 880.330 and notwithstanding the provisions of Section 880.340 or any other provision in this title, a notice of intent to preserve a mineral right may refer generally and without specificity to any or all mineral rights claimed by claimant in any real property situated in the county.

(c) A mineral right is not dormant for the purpose of this article if:

(1) A notice of intent to preserve the mineral right is recorded within 20 years immediately preceding commencement of the action to terminate the mineral right.

(2) A notice of intent to preserve the mineral right is recorded pursuant to Section 883.250 after commencement of the action to terminate the mineral right. **Leg.H.** Added Stats 1984 ch 240 §2.

§883.240. Venue

(a) An action to terminate a mineral right pursuant to this article shall be brought in the superior court of the county in which the real property subject to the mineral right is located.

(b) The action shall be brought in the same manner and shall be subject to the same procedure as an action to quiet title pursuant to Chapter 4 (commencing with Section 760.010) of Title 10 of Part 2 of the Code of Civil Procedure, to the extent applicable. **Leg.H.** Added Stats 1984 ch 240 §2.

§883.250. Recordation of late notice of intent as condition of dismissal; Payment of litigation expenses

In an action to terminate a mineral right pursuant to this article, the court shall permit the owner of the mineral right to record a late notice of intent to preserve the mineral right as a condition of dismissal of the action, upon payment into court for the benefit of the owner of the real property the litigation expenses attributable to the mineral right or portion thereof as to which the notice is recorded. As used in this section, the term "litigation expenses" means recoverable costs and expenses reasonably and necessarily incurred in preparation for the action, including a reasonable attorney's fee. **Leg.H.** Added Stats 1984 ch 240 §2.

§883.260. Terminated mineral rights deemed unenforceable and expired

A mineral right terminated pursuant to this article is unenforceable and is deemed to have expired. A court order terminating a mineral right pursuant to this article is equivalent for all purposes to a conveyance of the mineral right to the owner of the real property. **Leg.H.** Added Stats 1984 ch 240 §2.

§883.270. Application of article

Subject to Section 880.370 (grace period for recording notice), this article applies to all mineral rights, whether executed or recorded before, on, or after January 1, 1985. **Leg.H.** Added Stats 1984 ch 240 §2.

§884. [Section repealed 1874]

Leg.H. Enacted Stats 1872. Repealed Code Amdts 1873–74 ch 612 §123.

CHAPTER 4
UNEXERCISED OPTIONS

Expiration. §884.010.
Effect of expiration. §884.020.
Application of chapter. §884.030.

§884.010. Expiration

If a recorded instrument creates or gives constructive notice of an option to purchase real property, the option expires of record if no conveyance, contract, or other instrument that gives notice of exercise or extends the option is recorded within the following times:

(a) If the expiration date of the option is ascertainable from the recorded instrument, six months after that expiration date.

(b) If the expiration date of the option is not ascertainable from the recorded instrument or the recorded instrument indicates that the option provides no expiration date, six months after the date the instrument that creates or gives constructive notice of the option is recorded.

(c) This section shall become operative on January 1, 2013. **Leg.H.** Added Stats 2011 ch 46 §3 (SB 284), effective January 1, 2012, operative January 1, 2013.

Prior Law: Former CC §884.010, similar to the present section, was added Stats 1982 ch 1268 §1; amended Stats 2011 ch 46 §2 (SB 284), effective January 1, 2012, repealed January 1, 2013.**Former Sections:** Former CC §884.010, similar to the present section, was added Stats 1982 ch 1268 §1 and repealed operative January 1, 2013, by its own provisions. Stats 2011 ch 46 (SB 284) §2.

§884.020. Effect of expiration

Upon the expiration of record of an option to purchase real property, the recorded instrument that creates or gives constructive notice of the option ceases to be notice to any person or to put any person on inquiry with respect to the exercise or existence of the option or of any contract, conveyance, or other writing that may have been executed pursuant to the option. **Leg.H.** Added Stats 1982 ch 1268 §1.

§884.030. Application of chapter

(a) Except as otherwise provided in this section, this chapter applies on the operative date to all recorded instruments that create or give constructive notice of options to purchase real property, whether executed or recorded before, on, or after the operative date.

(b) This chapter shall not cause an option that expires according to its terms within one year before, on, or within one year after the operative date of this chapter to expire of record until one year after the operative date.

(c) This chapter shall not cause an option that provides no expiration date and that is recorded before the operative date of this chapter to expire of record until five years after the operative date of this chapter.

(d) Nothing in this chapter affects a recorded instrument that has ceased to be notice to any person or put any person on inquiry with respect to the exercise or existence of an option pursuant to former Section 1213.5 before the operative date of this chapter. **Leg.H.** Added Stats 1982 ch 1268 §1.

§885. [Section repealed 1874]

Leg.H. Enacted Stats 1872. Repealed Code Amdts 1873–74 ch 612 §123.

CHAPTER 5
POWERS OF TERMINATION

Definitions. §885.010.
Application of chapter. §885.015.
Abolition and redefinition of former terms. §885.020.
Expiration of power of termination. §885.030.
Expiration of power of termination by obsolescence. §885.040.
Exercise of power of termination. §885.050.
Effect of expiration of power of termination; Exception. §885.060.
Application of chapter. §885.070.

§885.010. Definitions

(a) As used in this chapter:

(1) "Power of termination" means the power to terminate a fee simple estate in real property to enforce a restriction in the form of a condition subsequent to which the fee simple estate is subject, whether the power is characterized in the instrument that creates or evidences it as a power of termination, right of entry or reentry, right of possession or repossession, reserved power of revocation, or otherwise, and includes a possibility of reverter that is deemed to be and is enforceable as a power of termination pursuant to Section 885.020.

(2) "Power of termination" includes the power created in a transferee to terminate a fee simple estate in real property to enforce a restriction on the use of the real property in the form of a limitation or condition subsequent to which the fee simple estate is subject, whether the power is characterized in the instrument that creates or evidences it as an executory interest, executory limitation, or otherwise, and includes the interest known at common law as an executory interest preceded by a fee simple determinable.

(b) A power of termination is an interest in the real property.

(c) For the purpose of applying this chapter to other statutes relating to powers of termination, the terms "right of reentry," "right of repossession for breach of condition subsequent," and comparable terms used in the other statutes mean power of termination" as defined in this section. **Leg.H.** Added Stats 1982 ch 1268 §1. Amended Stats 1991 ch 156 §15 (AB 1577).

§885.015. Application of chapter

This chapter does not apply to any of the following:

(a) A power of termination conditioned upon the continued production or removal of oil or gas or other minerals.

(b) A power of termination as to separately owned improvements or fixtures conditioned upon the continued leasehold or possessory interest in the underlying land. **Leg.H.** Added Stats 1982 ch 1268 §1. Amended Stats 1991 ch 156 §16 (AB 1577).

§885.020. Abolition and redefinition of former terms

Fees simple determinable and possibilities of reverter are abolished. Every estate that would be at common law a fee simple determinable is deemed to be a fee simple subject to a restriction in the form of a condition subsequent. Every interest that would be at common law a possibility of reverter is deemed to be and is enforceable as a power of termination. **Leg.H.** Added Stats 1982 ch 1268 §1.

§885.030. Expiration of power of termination

(a) A power of termination of record expires at the later of the following times:

(1) Thirty years after the date the instrument reserving, transferring, or otherwise evidencing the power of termination is recorded.

(2) Thirty years after the date a notice of intent to preserve the power of termination is recorded, if the notice is recorded within the time prescribed in paragraph (1).

(3) Thirty years after the date an instrument reserving, transferring, or otherwise evidencing the power of termination or a notice of intent to preserve the power of termination is recorded, if the instrument or notice is recorded within 30 years after the date such an instrument or notice was last recorded.

(b) This section applies notwithstanding any provision to the contrary in the instrument reserving, transferring, or otherwise evidencing the power of termination or in another recorded document unless the instrument or other recorded document provides an earlier expiration date. **Leg.H.** Added Stats 1982 ch 1268 §1.

§885.040. Expiration of power of termination by obsolescence

(a) If a power of termination becomes obsolete, the power expires.

(b) As used in this section, a power of termination is obsolete if any of the following circumstances applies:

(1) The restriction to which the fee simple estate is subject is of no actual and substantial benefit to the holder of the power.

(2) Enforcement of the power would not effectuate the purpose of the restriction to which the fee simple estate is subject.

(3) It would be otherwise inequitable to enforce the power because of changed conditions or circumstances.

(c) No power of termination shall expire under this section during the life of the grantor if it arises from a grant by a natural person without consideration to a public entity or to a society, corporation, institution, or association exempt by the laws of this state from taxation. **Leg.H.** Added Stats 1982 ch 1268 §1.

§885.050. Exercise of power of termination

A power of termination shall be exercised only by notice or by civil action and, if the power of termination is of record, the exercise shall be of record. The notice shall be given, and any civil action shall be commenced, within five years after breach of the restriction to which the fee simple estate is subject, or such longer period as may be agreed to by the parties by a waiver or extension recorded before expiration of that period. **Leg.H.** Added Stats 1982 ch 1268 §1.

§885.060. Effect of expiration of power of termination; Exception

(a) Expiration of a power of termination pursuant to this chapter makes the power unenforceable and is equivalent for all purposes to a termination of the power of record and a quitclaim of the power to the owner of the fee simple estate, and execution and recording of a termination and quitclaim is not necessary to terminate or evidence the termination of the power.

(b) Expiration of a power of termination pursuant to this chapter terminates the restriction to which the fee simple estate is subject and makes the restriction unenforceable by any other means, including, but not limited to, injunction and damages.

(c) However, subdivision (b) does not apply to a restriction for which a power of termination has expired under this chapter if the restriction is also an equitable servitude alternatively enforceable by injunction. Such an equitable servitude shall remain enforceable by injunction and any other available remedies, but shall not be enforceable by a power of termination. This subdivision does not constitute a change in, but is declaratory of, the existing law. However, nothing in this subdivision shall be construed to make enforceable any restriction prohibited or made unenforceable by other provisions of law, including Section 53. **Leg.H.** Added Stats 1982 ch 1268 §1. Amended Stats 1990 ch 1114 §1 (AB 3220).

§885.070. Application of chapter

(a) Subject to Section 880.370 (grace period for recording notice) and except as otherwise provided in this section, this chapter applies on the operative date to all powers of termination, whether executed or recorded before, on, or after the operative date.

(b) If breach of the restriction to which the fee simple estate is subject occurred before the operative date of this chapter and the power of termination is not exercised before the operative date of this chapter, the power of termination shall be exercised, or in the case of a power of termination of record, exercised of record, within the earlier of the following times:

(1) The time that would be applicable pursuant to the law in effect immediately prior to the operative date of this chapter.

(2) Five years after the operative date of this chapter.

(c) As used in this section, "operative date" means the operative date of this chapter as enacted or, with respect to any amendment of a section of this chapter, the operative date of the amendment. **Leg.H.** Added Stats 1982 ch 1268 §1. Amended Stats 1991 ch 156 §17 (AB 1577).

§886. [Section repealed 1874]

Leg.H. Enacted Stats 1872. Repealed Code Amdts 1873–74 ch 612 §123.

CHAPTER 6
UNPERFORMED CONTRACTS FOR SALE OF REAL PROPERTY

Definitions. §886.010.
Liability of defaulting purchaser. §886.020.
Expiration. §886.030.
Effect of expiration. §886.040.
Application of chapter. §886.050.

§886.010. Definitions

As used in this chapter:

(a) "Contract for sale of real property" means an agreement wherein one party agrees to convey title to real property to another party upon the satisfaction of specified conditions set forth in the contract and which requires conveyance of title within one year from the date of formation of the contract, whether designated in the agreement a "contract for sale of real property," "land sale contract," "deposit receipt," "agreement for sale," "agreement to convey," or otherwise.

(b) "Recorded contract for sale of real property" includes the entire terms of a contract for sale of real property that is recorded in its entirety or is evidenced by a recorded memorandum or short form of the contract. **Leg.H.** Added Stats 1982 ch 1268 §1.

§886.020. Liability of defaulting purchaser

If the party to whom title to real property is to be conveyed pursuant to a recorded contract for the sale of real property fails to satisfy the specified conditions set forth in the contract and does not seek performance of the contract or restitution of amounts paid under the contract, the party shall, upon demand therefor made after the operative date of this chapter, execute a release of the contract, duly acknowledged for record, to the party who agreed to convey title. Willful violation of this section by the party to whom title is to be conveyed without good cause makes the party liable for the damages the party who agreed to convey title sustains by reason of the violation, including but not limited to court costs and reasonable attorney's fees in an action to clear title to the real property. Nothing in this section makes a release or a demand therefor a condition precedent to an action to clear title to the real property. **Leg.H.** Added Stats 1982 ch 1268 §1.

§886.030. Expiration

(a) Except as otherwise provided in this section, a recorded contract for sale of real property expires of record at the later of the following times:

(1) Five years after the date for conveyance of title provided in the contract or, if no date for conveyance of title is provided in the contract, five years after the last date provided in the contract for satisfaction of the specified conditions set forth in the contract.

(2) If there is a recorded extension of the contract within the time prescribed in paragraph (1), five years after the date for conveyance of title provided in the extension or, if no date for conveyance of title is provided in the extension, five years after the last date provided in the extension for satisfaction of the specified conditions set forth in the contract.

(b) The time prescribed in this section may be waived or extended only by an instrument that is recorded before expiration of the prescribed times. **Leg.H.** Added Stats 1982 ch 1268 §1.

§886.040. Effect of expiration

Upon the expiration of record of a recorded contract for sale of real property pursuant to this chapter, the contract has no effect, and does not constitute an encumbrance or cloud, on the title to the real property as against a person other than a party to the contract. **Leg.H.** Added Stats 1982 ch 1268 §1.

§886.050. Application of chapter

(a) Except as otherwise provided in this section, this chapter applies on the operative date to all recorded contracts for sale of real property, whether recorded before, on, or after the operative date.

(b) This chapter shall not cause a recorded contract for sale of real property to expire of record before the passage of two years after the operative date of this chapter. **Leg.H.** Added Stats 1982 ch 1268 §1.

§887. [Section repealed 1874]

Leg.H. Enacted Stats 1872. Repealed Code Amdts 1873–74 ch 612 §123.

CHAPTER 7
ABANDONED EASEMENTS

"Easement". §887.010.
Exceptions. §887.020.
Effect of common law and statutory procedures. §887.030.
Actions to establish abandonment. §887.040.
Conditions for abandonment. §887.050.
Notice of intent to preserve easement. §887.060.
Late notice of intent; Litigation expenses. §887.070.
Effect of abandoned easement. §887.080.
Application of chapter. §887.090.

§887.010. "Easement"

As used in this chapter, "easement" means a burden or servitude upon land, whether or not attached to other land as an incident or appurtenance, that allows the holder of the burden or servitude to do acts upon the land. **Leg.H.** Added Stats 1985 ch 157 §2.

§887.020. Exceptions

This chapter does not apply to an easement that is part of a unified or reciprocal system for the mutual benefit of multiple parties. **Leg.H.** Added Stats 1985 ch 157 §2.

§887.030. Effect of common law and statutory procedures

This chapter supplements and does not limit or otherwise affect the common law governing abandonment of an easement or any other procedure provided by statute or otherwise for clearing an abandoned easement from title to real property. **Leg.H.** Added Stats 1985 ch 157 §2.

§887.040.   Actions to establish abandonment

(a) The owner of real property subject to an easement may bring an action to establish the abandonment of the easement and to clear record title of the easement.

(b) The action shall be brought in the superior court of the county in which the real property subject to the easement is located.

(c) The action shall be brought in the same manner and shall be subject to the same procedure as an action to quiet title pursuant to Chapter 4 (commencing with Section 760.010) of Title 10 of Part 2 of the Code of Civil Procedure, to the extent applicable. **Leg.H.** Added Stats 1985 ch 157 §2.

§887.050.   Conditions for abandonment

(a) For purposes of this chapter, an easement is abandoned if all of the following conditions are satisfied for a period of 20 years immediately preceding commencement of the action to establish abandonment of the easement:

(1) The easement is not used at any time.

(2) No separate property tax assessment is made of the easement or, if made, no taxes are paid on the assessment.

(3) No instrument creating, reserving, transferring, or otherwise evidencing the easement is recorded.

(b) This section applies notwithstanding any provision to the contrary in the instrument creating, reserving, transferring, or otherwise evidencing the easement or in another recorded document, unless the instrument or other document provides an earlier expiration date. **Leg.H.** Added Stats 1985 ch 157 §2.

§887.060.   Notice of intent to preserve easement

(a) The owner of an easement may at any time record a notice of intent to preserve the easement.

(b) In lieu of the statement of the character of the interest claimed and the record location of the documents creating or evidencing the easement claimed, as otherwise required by paragraph (2) of subdivision (b) of Section 880.330, and in lieu of the legal description of the real property in which the interest is claimed, as otherwise required by paragraph (3) of subdivision (b) of Section 880.330, and notwithstanding the provisions of Section 880.340, or any other provision in this title, a notice of intent to preserve an easement may refer generally and without specificity to any or all easements claimed by the claimant in any real property situated in the county.

(c) An easement is not abandoned for purposes of this chapter if either of the following occurs:

(1) A notice of intent to preserve the easement is recorded within 20 years immediately preceding commencement of the action to establish the abandonment of the easement.

(2) A notice of intent to preserve the easement is recorded pursuant to Section 887.070 after commencement of the action to establish the abandonment of the easement and before judgment is entered in the action. **Leg.H.** Added Stats 1985 ch 157 §2.

§887.070.   Late notice of intent; Litigation expenses

In an action to establish the abandonment of an easement pursuant to this chapter, the court shall permit the owner of the easement to record a late notice of intent to preserve the easement as a condition of dismissal of the action, upon payment into court for the benefit of the owner of the real property the litigation expenses attributable to the easement or portion thereof as to which the notice is recorded. As used in this section, the term "litigation expenses" means recoverable costs and expenses reasonably and necessarily incurred in preparation for the action, including a reasonable attorney's fee. **Leg.H.** Added Stats 1985 ch 157 §2.

§887.080.   Effect of abandoned easement

An abandoned easement is unenforceable and is deemed to have expired. A court order establishing abandonment of an easement pursuant to this chapter is equivalent for all purposes to a conveyance of the easement to the owner of the real property. **Leg.H.** Added Stats 1985 ch 157 §2.

§887.090.   Application of chapter

Subject to Sections 880.370 (grace period for recording notice) and 887.020, this chapter applies to all easements, whether executed or recorded before, on, or after January 1, 1986. **Leg.H.** Added Stats 1985 ch 157 §2.

§§888, 889.   [Sections repealed 1874]

Leg.H. Enacted Stats 1872. Repealed Code Amdts 1873–74 ch 612 §123.

TITLE 6
RENT SKIMMING

Definitions. §890.
Civil cause of action; Treble damages. §891.
Criminal prosecution. §892.
Affirmative defenses. §893.
Savings provision. §894.

§890.   Definitions

(a)(1) "Rent skimming" means using revenue received from the rental of a parcel of residential real property at any time during the first year period after acquiring that property without first applying the revenue or an equivalent amount to the payments due on all mortgages and deeds of trust encumbering that property.

(2) For purposes of this section, "rent skimming" also means receiving revenue from the rental of a parcel of residential real property where the person receiving that revenue, without the consent of the owner or owner's agent, asserted possession or ownership of the residential property, whether under a false claim of title, by trespass, or any other unauthorized means, rented the property to another, and collected rents from the other person for the rental of the property. This paragraph does not apply to any tenant, subtenant, lessee, sublessee, or assignee, nor to any other hirer having a lawful occupancy interest in the residential dwelling.

(b) "Multiple acts of rent skimming" means knowingly and willfully rent skimming with respect to each of five or more parcels of residential real property acquired within any two-year period.

(c) "Person" means any natural person, any form of business organization, its officers and directors, and any natural person who authorizes rent skimming or who, being in a position of control, fails to prevent another from rent skimming. **Leg.H.** Added Stats 1986 ch 838 §1. Amended Stats 1998 ch 193 §1 (AB 583).

Prior Law: Former §890, relating to powers, was enacted Stats 1872 and repealed Code Amdts 1873–74 ch 612 §123.

§891.   Civil cause of action; Treble damages

(a) A seller of an interest in residential real property who received a promissory note or other evidence of indebtedness for all or a portion of its purchase price secured by a lien on the property may bring an action against any person who has engaged in rent skimming with respect to that property. A seller who prevails in the action shall recover all actual damages and reasonable attorney's fees and costs. The court may award any appropriate equitable relief. The court shall award exemplary damages of not less than three times the actual damages if the defendant has engaged in multiple acts of rent skimming and may award exemplary damages in other cases.

(b) A seller of an interest in residential real property who reacquires the interest from a person who has engaged in rent skimming with respect to that property, or a law enforcement agency, may request the court for an order declaring that the reacquired interest is not encumbered by any lien that is or has the effect of a judgment lien against the person who engaged in rent skimming if the lien is not related to any improvement of the property and does not represent security for loan proceeds made by a bona fide lien holder without knowledge of facts constituting a violation of this title. The motion or application shall be made with at least 30 days' advance written notice to all persons who may be affected by the order, including lienholders, and shall be granted unless the interests of justice would not be served by such an order.

(c) A mortgagee or beneficiary under a deed of trust encumbering residential real property may bring an action against a person who has engaged in rent skimming with respect to that property as one of multiple acts of rent skimming, whether or not the person has become contractually bound by an obligation secured by the mortgage or deed of trust. The mortgagee or beneficiary who prevails in the action shall recover actual damages to the extent of the amount of the rent collected on the encumbered property and attorney's fees and costs. The court also may order any appropriate equitable relief and may award exemplary damages.

(d) A tenant of residential real property may bring an action against a person who has engaged in rent skimming with respect to that property for the recovery of actual damages, including any security, as defined in Section 1950.5, and moving expenses if the property is sold at a foreclosure sale and the tenant was required to move. A prevailing plaintiff in such an action shall be awarded reasonable attorney's fees and costs. The court also may award exemplary damages; it shall award exemplary damages of at least three times the amount of actual damages if the payments due under any deed of trust or mortgage were two or more months delinquent at the time the tenant rented the premises or if the defendant has engaged in multiple acts of rent skimming.

(e) The rights and remedies provided in this section are in addition to any other rights and remedies provided by law.

(f) Rent skimming is unlawful, and any waiver of the provisions of this section are void and unenforceable as contrary to public policy.

(g) Sections 580a, 580b, 580d, and 726 of the Code of Civil Procedure do not apply to any action brought under this title. **Leg.H.** Added Stats 1986 ch 838 §1.

Prior Law: Former §891, relating to powers, was enacted Stats 1872 and repealed Code Amdts 1873–74 ch 612 §123.

§892. Criminal prosecution

(a) Any person who engages in multiple acts of rent skimming is subject to criminal prosecution. Each act of rent skimming comprising the multiple acts of rent skimming shall be separately alleged. A person found guilty of five acts shall be punished by imprisonment pursuant to subdivision (h) of Section 1170 of the Penal Code or by imprisonment in a county jail for not more than one year, by a fine of not more than ten thousand dollars ($10,000), or by both that fine and imprisonment. A person found guilty of additional acts shall be separately punished for each additional act by imprisonment pursuant to subdivision (h) of Section 1170 of the Penal Code or by imprisonment in a county jail for not more than one year, by a fine of not more than ten thousand dollars ($10,000), or by both that fine and imprisonment.

(b) If a defendant has been once previously convicted of a violation of subdivision (a), any subsequent knowing and willful act of rent skimming shall be punishable by imprisonment pursuant to subdivision (h) of Section 1170 of the Penal Code or by imprisonment in a county jail for not more than one year, or by a fine of not more than ten thousand dollars ($10,000), or by both that fine and imprisonment.

(c) A prosecution for a violation of this section shall be commenced within three years after the date of the acquisition of the last parcel of property that was the subject of the conduct for which the defendant is prosecuted.

(d) The penalties under this section are in addition to any other remedies or penalties provided by law for the conduct proscribed by this section. **Leg.H.** Added Stats 1986 ch 838 §1. Amended Stats 2011 ch 15 §31 (AB 109), effective April 4, 2011, operative October 1, 2011.

Prior Law: Former §892, relating to powers, was enacted Stats 1872 and repealed Code Amdts 1873–74 ch 612 §123.

2011 Notes: This act is titled and may be cited as the 2011 Realignment Legislation addressing public safety. Stats 2011 ch 15 (AB 109) §1.

This act will become operative no earlier than October 1, 2011, and only upon creation of a community corrections grant program to assist in implementing this act and upon an appropriation to fund the grant program. Stats 2011 ch 15 (AB 109) §636; Stats 2011 ch 39 (AB 117) §68.

The Community Corrections Grant Program referred to in Stats 2011 ch 15 (AB 109) §636, as amended by Stats 2011 ch 39 (AB 117) §68, was created by Stats 2011 ch 40 (AB 118) §3, operative October 1, 2011.

§893. Affirmative defenses

(a) It is an affirmative defense for a natural person who is a defendant in a civil action brought under Section 891, or a criminal action brought under Section 892, if all of the following occurred:

(1) The defendant used the rental revenue due but not paid to holders of mortgages or deeds of trust to make payments to any of the following:

(A) Health care providers, as defined in paragraph (2) of subdivision (c) of Section 6146 of the Business and Professions Code, for the unforeseen and necessary medical treatment of the defendant or his or her spouse, parents, or children.

(B) Licensed contractors or material suppliers to correct the violation of any statute, ordinance, or regulation relating to the habitability of the premises.

(2) The defendant made the payments within 30 days of receiving the rental revenue.

(3) The defendant had no other source of funds from which to make the payments.

(b) The defendant has the burden of producing evidence of each element of the defense specified in subdivision (a) in a criminal action under Section 892 and the burden of proof of each element of the defense in a civil action under Section 891. **Leg.H.** Added Stats 1986 ch 838 §1.

Prior Law: Former §893, relating to powers, was enacted Stats 1872 and repealed Code Amdts 1873–74 ch 612 §123.

§894. Savings provision

If any provision of this title or the application thereof to any person or circumstances is held to be unconstitutional, the remainder of the title and the application of its provisions to other persons and circumstances shall not be affected thereby. **Leg.H.** Added Stats 1986 ch 838 §1.

Prior Law: Former §894, relating to powers, was enacted Stats 1872 and repealed Code Amdts 1873–74 ch 612 §123.

TITLE 7
REQUIREMENTS FOR ACTIONS FOR CONSTRUCTION DEFECTS

Chapter 1. Definitions.
Chapter 2. Actionable Defects.
Chapter 3. Obligations.
Chapter 4. Prelitigation Procedure.
Chapter 5. Procedure.

CHAPTER 1
DEFINITIONS

Definitions. §895.

§895. Definitions

(a) "Structure" means any residential dwelling, other building, or improvement located upon a lot or within a common area.

(b) "Designed moisture barrier" means an installed moisture barrier specified in the plans and specifications, contract documents, or manufacturer's recommendations.

(c) "Actual moisture barrier" means any component or material, actually installed, that serves to any degree as a barrier against moisture, whether or not intended as a barrier against moisture.

(d) "Unintended water" means water that passes beyond, around, or through a component or the material that is designed to prevent that passage.

(e) "Close of escrow" means the date of the close of escrow between the builder and the original homeowner. With respect to claims by an association, as defined in Section 4080, "close of escrow" means the date of substantial completion, as defined in Section 337.15 of the Code of Civil Procedure, or the date the builder relinquishes control over the association's ability to decide whether to initiate a claim under this title, whichever is later.

(f) "Claimant" or "homeowner" includes the individual owners of single-family homes, individual unit owners of attached dwellings and, in the case of a common interest development, any association as defined in Section 4080. **Leg.H.** Added Stats 2002 ch 722 §3 (SB 800). Amended Stats 2012 ch 181 §29 (AB 806), effective January 1, 2013, operative January 1, 2014.

Prior Law: Former §895, relating to repeal of title, was enacted Stats 1986 and repealed Stats 1991 ch 1007 §2 (SB 892), ch 1155 §1 (AB 2146).

Former §895, similar to present §2932.5, was enacted Stats 1872 and repealed Code Amdts 1873–74 ch 612 §123.

CHAPTER 2
ACTIONABLE DEFECTS

Standards for residential construction. §896.
Intent of standards. §897.

§896. Standards for residential construction

In any action seeking recovery of damages arising out of, or related to deficiencies in, the residential construction, design, specifications, surveying, planning, supervision, testing, or observation of construction, a builder, and to the extent set forth in Chapter 4 (commencing with Section 910), a general contractor, subcontractor, material supplier, individual product manufacturer, or design professional, shall, except as specifically set forth in this title, be liable for, and the claimant's claims or causes of action shall be limited to violation of, the following standards, except as specifically set forth in this title. This title applies to original construction intended to be sold as an individual dwelling unit. As to condominium conversions, this title does not apply to or does not supersede any other statutory or common law.

(a) With respect to water issues:

(1) A door shall not allow unintended water to pass beyond, around, or through the door or its designed or actual moisture barriers, if any.

(2) Windows, patio doors, deck doors, and their systems shall not allow water to pass beyond, around, or through the window, patio door, or deck door or its designed or actual moisture barriers, including, without limitation, internal barriers within the systems themselves. For purposes of this paragraph, "systems" include, without limitation, windows, window assemblies, framing, substrate, flashings, and trim, if any.

(3) Windows, patio doors, deck doors, and their systems shall not allow excessive condensation to enter the structure and cause damage to another component. For purposes of this paragraph, "systems" include, without limitation, windows, window assemblies, framing, substrate, flashings, and trim, if any.

(4) Roofs, roofing systems, chimney caps, and ventilation components shall not allow water to enter the structure or to pass beyond, around, or through the designed or actual moisture barriers, including, without limitation, internal barriers located within the systems themselves. For purposes of this paragraph, "systems" include, without limitation, framing, substrate, and sheathing, if any.

(5) Decks, deck systems, balconies, balcony systems, exterior stairs, and stair systems shall not allow water to pass into the adjacent structure. For purposes of this paragraph, "systems" include, without limitation, framing, substrate, flashing, and sheathing, if any.

(6) Decks, deck systems, balconies, balcony systems, exterior stairs, and stair systems shall not allow unintended water to pass within the systems themselves and cause damage to the systems. For purposes of this paragraph, "systems" include, without limitation, framing, substrate, flashing, and sheathing, if any.

(7) Foundation systems and slabs shall not allow water or vapor to enter into the structure so as to cause damage to another building component.

(8) Foundation systems and slabs shall not allow water or vapor to enter into the structure so as to limit the installation of the type of flooring materials typically used for the particular application.

(9) Hardscape, including paths and patios, irrigation systems, landscaping systems, and drainage systems, that are installed as part of the original construction, shall not be installed in such a way as to cause water or soil erosion to enter into or come in contact with the structure so as to cause damage to another building component.

(10) Stucco, exterior siding, exterior walls, including, without limitation, exterior framing, and other exterior wall finishes and fixtures and the systems of those components and fixtures, including, but not limited to, pot shelves, horizontal surfaces, columns, and plant-ons, shall be installed in such a way so as not to allow unintended water to pass into the structure or to pass beyond, around, or through the designed or actual moisture barriers of the system, including any internal barriers located within the system itself. For purposes of this paragraph, "systems" include, without limitation, framing, substrate, flashings, trim, wall assemblies, and internal wall cavities, if any.

(11) Stucco, exterior siding, and exterior walls shall not allow excessive condensation to enter the structure and cause damage to another component. For purposes of this paragraph, "systems" include, without limitation, framing, substrate, flashings, trim, wall assemblies, and internal wall cavities, if any.

(12) Retaining and site walls and their associated drainage systems shall not allow unintended water to pass beyond, around, or through its designed or actual moisture barriers including, without limitation, any internal barriers, so as to cause damage. This standard does not apply to those portions of any wall or drainage system that are designed to have water flow beyond, around, or through them.

(13) Retaining walls and site walls, and their associated drainage systems, shall only allow water to flow beyond, around, or through the areas designated by design.

(14) The lines and components of the plumbing system, sewer system, and utility systems shall not leak.

(15) Plumbing lines, sewer lines, and utility lines shall not corrode so as to impede the useful life of the systems.

(16) Sewer systems shall be installed in such a way as to allow the designated amount of sewage to flow through the system.

(17) Showers, baths, and related waterproofing systems shall not leak water into the interior of walls, flooring systems, or the interior of other components.

(18) The waterproofing system behind or under ceramic tile and tile countertops shall not allow water into the interior of walls, flooring systems, or other components so as to cause damage. Ceramic tile systems shall be designed and installed so as to deflect intended water to the waterproofing system.

(b) With respect to structural issues:

(1) Foundations, load bearing components, and slabs, shall not contain significant cracks or significant vertical displacement.

(2) Foundations, load bearing components, and slabs shall not cause the structure, in whole or in part, to be structurally unsafe.

(3) Foundations, load bearing components, and slabs, and underlying soils shall be constructed so as to materially comply with the design criteria set by applicable government building codes, regulations, and ordinances for chemical deterioration or corrosion resistance in effect at the time of original construction.

(4) A structure shall be constructed so as to materially comply with the design criteria for earthquake and wind load resistance, as set forth in the applicable government building codes, regulations, and ordinances in effect at the time of original construction.

(c) With respect to soil issues:

(1) Soils and engineered retaining walls shall not cause, in whole or in part, damage to the structure built upon the soil or engineered retaining wall.

(2) Soils and engineered retaining walls shall not cause, in whole or in part, the structure to be structurally unsafe.

(3) Soils shall not cause, in whole or in part, the land upon which no structure is built to become unusable for the purpose represented at the time of original sale by the builder or for the purpose for which that land is commonly used.

(d) With respect to fire protection issues:

(1) A structure shall be constructed so as to materially comply with the design criteria of the applicable government building codes, regulations, and ordinances for fire protection of the occupants in effect at the time of the original construction.

(2) Fireplaces, chimneys, chimney structures, and chimney termination caps shall be constructed and installed in such a way so as not to cause an unreasonable risk of fire outside the fireplace enclosure or chimney.

(3) Electrical and mechanical systems shall be constructed and installed in such a way so as not to cause an unreasonable risk of fire.

(e) With respect to plumbing and sewer issues:

Plumbing and sewer systems shall be installed to operate properly and shall not materially impair the use of the structure by its inhabitants. However, no action may be brought for a violation of this subdivision more than four years after close of escrow.

(f) With respect to electrical system issues:

Electrical systems shall operate properly and shall not materially impair the use of the structure by its inhabitants. However, no action shall be brought pursuant to this subdivision more than four years from close of escrow.

(g) With respect to issues regarding other areas of construction:

(1) Exterior pathways, driveways, hardscape, sidewalls, sidewalks, and patios installed by the original builder shall not contain cracks that display significant vertical displacement or that are excessive. However, no action shall be brought upon a violation of this paragraph more than four years from close of escrow.

(2) Stucco, exterior siding, and other exterior wall finishes and fixtures, including, but not limited to, pot shelves, horizontal surfaces, columns, and plant-ons, shall not contain significant cracks or separations.

(3)(A) To the extent not otherwise covered by these standards, manufactured products, including, but not limited to, windows, doors, roofs, plumbing products and fixtures, fireplaces, electrical fixtures, HVAC units, countertops, cabinets, paint, and appliances shall be installed so as not to interfere with the products' useful life, if any.

(B) For purposes of this paragraph, "useful life" means a representation of how long a product is warranted or represented, through its limited warranty or any written representations, to last by its manufacturer, including recommended or required maintenance. If there is no representation by a manufacturer, a builder shall install manufactured products so as not to interfere with the product's utility.

(C) For purposes of this paragraph, "manufactured product" means a product that is completely manufactured offsite.

(D) If no useful life representation is made, or if the representation is less than one year, the period shall be no less than one year. If a manufactured product is damaged as a result of a violation of these standards, damage to the product is a recoverable element of damages. This subparagraph does not limit recovery if there has been damage to another building component caused by a manufactured product during the manufactured product's useful life.

(E) This title does not apply in any action seeking recovery solely for a defect in a manufactured product located within or adjacent to a structure.

(4) Heating shall be installed so as to be capable of maintaining a room temperature of 70 degrees Fahrenheit at a point three feet above the floor in any living space if the heating was installed pursuant to a building permit application submitted prior to January 1, 2008, or capable of maintaining a room temperature of 68 degrees Fahrenheit at a point three feet above the floor and two feet from exterior walls in all habitable rooms at the design temperature if the heating was installed pursuant to a building permit application submitted on or before January 1, 2008.

(5) Living space air-conditioning, if any, shall be provided in a manner consistent with the size and efficiency design criteria specified in Title 24 of the California Code of Regulations or its successor.

(6) Attached structures shall be constructed to comply with interunit noise transmission standards set by the applicable government building codes, ordinances, or regulations in effect at the time of the original construction. If there is no applicable code, ordinance, or regulation, this paragraph does not apply. However, no action shall be brought pursuant to this paragraph more than one year from the original occupancy of the adjacent unit.

(7) Irrigation systems and drainage shall operate properly so as not to damage landscaping or other external improvements. However, no action shall be brought pursuant to this paragraph more than one year from close of escrow.

(8) Untreated wood posts shall not be installed in contact with soil so as to cause unreasonable decay to the wood based upon the finish grade at the time of original construction. However, no action shall be brought pursuant to this paragraph more than two years from close of escrow.

(9) Untreated steel fences and adjacent components shall be installed so as to prevent unreasonable corrosion. However, no action shall be brought pursuant to this paragraph more than four years from close of escrow.

(10) Paint and stains shall be applied in such a manner so as not to cause deterioration of the building surfaces for the length of time specified by the paint or stain manufacturers' representations, if any. However, no action shall be brought pursuant to this paragraph more than five years from close of escrow.

(11) Roofing materials shall be installed so as to avoid materials falling from the roof.

(12) The landscaping systems shall be installed in such a manner so as to survive for not less than one year. However, no action shall be brought pursuant to this paragraph more than two years from close of escrow.

(13) Ceramic tile and tile backing shall be installed in such a manner that the tile does not detach.

(14) Dryer ducts shall be installed and terminated pursuant to manufacturer installation requirements. However, no action shall be brought pursuant to this paragraph more than two years from close of escrow.

(15) Structures shall be constructed in such a manner so as not to impair the occupants' safety because they contain public health hazards as determined by a duly authorized public health official, health agency, or governmental entity having jurisdiction. This paragraph does not limit recovery for any damages caused by a violation of any other paragraph of this section on the grounds that the damages do not constitute a health hazard. **Leg.H.** Added Stats 2002 ch 722 §3 (SB 800). Amended Stats 2003 ch 762 §1 (AB 903); Stats 2006 ch 567 §2 (AB 2303), effective January 1, 2007; Stats 2012 ch 770 §2 (AB 2697), effective January 1, 2013.

Prior Law: Former §896, was enacted Stats 1872 and repealed Code Amdts 1873–74 ch 612 §123.

§897. Intent of standards

The standards set forth in this chapter are intended to address every function or component of a structure. To the extent that a function or component of a structure is not addressed by these standards, it shall be actionable if it causes damage. **Leg.H.** Added Stats 2002 ch 722 §3 (SB 800).

Prior Law: Former §897, was enacted Stats 1872 and repealed Code Amdts 1873–74 ch 612 §123.

§898. [Section repealed 1874]

Leg.H. Enacted Stats 1872. Repealed Code Amdts 1873–74 ch 612 §123.

§899. [Section repealed 1874]

Leg.H. Enacted Stats 1872. Repealed Code Amdts 1873–74 ch 612 §123.

CHAPTER 3
OBLIGATIONS

Warranty covering fit and finish items. §900.
Enhanced protection agreement. §901.
Effect of enhanced protection agreement. §902.
Written copy of enhanced protection agreement. §903.
Enforcement of construction standards in lieu of particular enhanced protection agreement provision. §904.
Responsive pleading in action to enforce construction standards of this chapter in lieu of enhanced protection agreement. §905.
Effect of election of enhanced protection agreement on provisions of prelitigation procedures. §906.
Obligation of homeowner to follow reasonable maintenance obligations. §907.

§900. Warranty covering fit and finish items

As to fit and finish items, a builder shall provide a homebuyer with a minimum one-year express written limited warranty covering the fit and finish of the following building components. Except as otherwise provided by the standards specified in Chapter 2 (commencing with Section 896), this warranty shall cover the fit and finish of cabinets, mirrors, flooring, interior and exterior walls, countertops, paint finishes, and trim, but shall not apply to damage to those components caused by defects in other components governed by the other provisions of this title. Any fit and finish matters covered by this warranty are not subject to the provisions of this title. If a builder fails to provide the express warranty required by this section, the warranty for these items shall be for a period of one year. **Leg.H.** Added Stats 2002 ch 722 §3 (SB 800).

Prior Law: Former §900 was enacted Stats 1872 and repealed Code Amdts 1873–74 ch 612 §123.

§901. Enhanced protection agreement

A builder may, but is not required to, offer greater protection or protection for longer time periods in its express contract with the homeowner than that set forth in Chapter 2 (commencing with Section 896). A builder may not limit the application of Chapter 2 (commencing with Section 896) or lower its protection through the express contract with the homeowner. This type of express contract constitutes an "enhanced protection agreement." **Leg.H.** Added Stats 2002 ch 722 §3 (SB 800).

Prior Law: Former §901 was enacted Stats 1872 and repealed Code Amdts 1873–74 ch 612 §123.

§902. Effect of enhanced protection agreement

If a builder offers an enhanced protection agreement, the builder may choose to be subject to its own express contractual provisions in place of the provisions set forth in Chapter 2 (commencing with Section 896). If an enhanced protection agreement is in place, Chapter 2 (commencing with Section 896) no longer applies other than to set forth minimum provisions by which to judge the enforceability of the particular provisions of the enhanced protection agreement. **Leg.H.** Added Stats 2002 ch 722 §3 (SB 800).

Prior Law: Former §902 was enacted Stats 1872 and repealed Code Amdts 1873–74 ch 612 §123.

§903. Written copy of enhanced protection agreement

If a builder offers an enhanced protection agreement in place of the provisions set forth in Chapter 2 (commencing with Section 896), the election to do so shall be made in writing with the homeowner no later than the close of escrow. The builder shall provide the homeowner with a complete copy of Chapter 2 (commencing with Section 896) and advise the homeowner that the builder has elected not to be subject to its provisions. If any provision of an enhanced protection agreement is later found to be unenforceable as not meeting the minimum standards of Chapter 2 (commencing with Section 896), a builder may use this chapter in lieu of those provisions found to be unenforceable. **Leg.H.** Added Stats 2002 ch 722 §3 (SB 800).

Prior Law: Former §903 was enacted Stats 1872 and repealed Code Amdts 1873–74 ch 612 §123.

§904. Enforcement of construction standards in lieu of particular enhanced protection agreement provision

If a builder has elected to use an enhanced protection agreement, and a homeowner disputes that the particular provision or time periods of the enhanced protection agreement are not greater than, or equal to, the provisions of Chapter 2 (commencing with Section 896) as they apply to the particular deficiency alleged by the homeowner, the homeowner may seek to enforce the application of the standards set forth in this chapter as to those claimed deficiencies. If a homeowner seeks to enforce a particular standard in lieu of a provision of the enhanced protection agreement, the homeowner shall give the builder written notice of that intent at the time the homeowner files a notice of claim pursuant to Chapter 4 (commencing with Section 910). **Leg.H.** Added Stats 2002 ch 722 §3 (SB 800).

Prior Law: Former §904 was enacted Stats 1872 and repealed Code Amdts 1873–74 ch 612 §123.

§905. Responsive pleading in action to enforce construction standards of this chapter in lieu of enhanced protection agreement

If a homeowner seeks to enforce Chapter 2 (commencing with Section 896), in lieu of the enhanced protection agreement in a subsequent litigation or other legal action, the builder shall have the right to have the matter bifurcated, and to have an immediately binding determination of his or her responsive pleading within 60 days after the filing of that pleading, but in no event after the commencement of discovery, as to the application of either Chapter 2 (commencing with Section 896) or the enhanced protection agreement as to the deficiencies claimed by the homeowner. If the builder fails to seek that determination in the timeframe specified, the builder waives the right to do so and the standards set forth in this title shall apply. As to any nonoriginal homeowner, that homeowner shall be deemed in privity for purposes of an enhanced protection agreement only to the extent that the builder has recorded the enhanced protection agreement on title or provided actual notice to the nonoriginal homeowner of the enhanced protection agreement. If the enhanced protection agreement is not recorded on title or no actual notice has been provided, the standards set forth in this title apply to any nonoriginal homeowners' claims. **Leg.H.** Added Stats 2002 ch 722 §3 (SB 800).

Prior Law: Former §905 was enacted Stats 1872 and repealed Code Amdts 1873–74 ch 612 §123.

§906. Effect of election of enhanced protection agreement on provisions of prelitigation procedures

A builder's election to use an enhanced protection agreement addresses only the issues set forth in Chapter 2 (commencing with Section 896) and does not constitute an election to use or not use the provisions of Chapter 4 (commencing with Section 910). The decision to use or not use Chapter 4 (commencing with Section 910) is governed by the provisions of that chapter. **Leg.H.** Added Stats 2002 ch 722 §3 (SB 800).

Prior Law: Former §906 was enacted Stats 1872 and repealed Code Amdts 1873–74 ch 612 §123.

§907. Obligation of homeowner to follow reasonable maintenance obligations

A homeowner is obligated to follow all reasonable maintenance obligations and schedules communicated in writing to the homeowner by the builder and product manufacturers, as well as commonly accepted maintenance practices. A failure by a homeowner to follow these obligations, schedules, and practices may subject the homeowner to the affirmative defenses contained in Section 944. **Leg.H.** Added Stats 2002 ch 722 §3 (SB 800).

Prior Law: Former §907 was enacted Stats 1872 and repealed Code Amdts 1873–74 ch 612 §123.

§908. [Section repealed 1874]

Leg.H. Enacted Stats 1872. Repealed Code Amdts 1873–74 ch 612 §123.

§909. [Section repealed 1874]

Leg.H. Enacted Stats 1872. Repealed Code Amdts 1873–74 ch 612 §123.

CHAPTER 4
PRELITIGATION PROCEDURE

Procedures required prior to filing action for violation of construction standards. §910.
"Builder" defined. §911.
Builder's duties. §912.
Acknowledgment of receipt of notice. §913.
Nonadversarial procedure established. §914.
Actions resulting in nonapplication of chapter. §915.
Inspection of claimed unmet standards by builder. §916.
Offer to repair. §917.
Authorization to proceed with repair. §918.
Offer to mediate dispute. §919.
Actions resulting in filing of an action by homeowner; Applicable standards. §920.
Procedure when resolution involves repair by builder. §921.
Observation and electronic recording, video recording, or photographing of repair allowed. §922.
Availability to homeowner of correspondence, photographs and other material pertaining to repairs. §923.
Offer to repair some, but not all, of claimed unmet standards. §924.
Failure to timely complete repairs. §925.
Release or waiver in exchange for repair work prohibited. §926.
Statute of limitations. §927.
Mediation procedure. §928.
Cash offer in lieu of repair. §929.
Strict construction of requirements; Failure of claimant to conform. §930.
Claim combined with other causes of action. §931.
Subsequent discovered claims of unmet standards. §932.
Evidence of repair work. §933.
Evidence of parties' conduct. §934.
Similar requirements of Civil Code Section 6000. §935.
Applicability of title to other entities involved in construction process. §936.
Claims and damages not covered by this title. §937.
Date of sale for applicability of title. §938.

§910. Procedures required prior to filing action for violation of construction standards

Prior to filing an action against any party alleged to have contributed to a violation of the standards set forth in Chapter 2 (commencing with Section 896), the claimant shall initiate the following prelitigation procedures:

(a) The claimant or his or her legal representative shall provide written notice via certified mail, overnight mail, or personal delivery to the builder, in the manner prescribed in this section, of the claimant's claim that the construction of his or her residence violates any of the standards set forth in Chapter 2 (commencing with Section 896). That notice shall provide the claimant's name, address, and preferred method of contact, and shall state that the claimant alleges a violation pursuant to this part against the builder, and shall describe the claim in reasonable detail sufficient to determine the nature and location, to the extent known, of the claimed violation. In the case of a group of homeowners or an association, the notice may identify the claimants solely by address or other description sufficient to apprise the builder of the locations of the subject residences. That document shall have the same force and effect as a notice of commencement of a legal proceeding.

(b) The notice requirements of this section do not preclude a homeowner from seeking redress through any applicable normal customer service procedure as set forth in any contractual, warranty, or other builder-generated document; and, if a homeowner seeks to do so, that request shall not satisfy the notice requirements of this section. **Leg.H.** Added Stats 2002 ch 722 §3 (SB 800).

Prior Law: Former §910 was enacted Stats 1872 and repealed Code Amdts 1873–74 ch 612 §123.

§911. "Builder" defined

(a) For purposes of this title, except as provided in subdivision (b), "builder" means any entity or individual, including, but not limited to a builder, developer, general contractor, contractor, or original seller, who, at the time of sale, was also in the business of selling residential units to the public for the property that is the subject of the homeowner's claim or was in the business of building, developing, or constructing residential units for public purchase for the property that is the subject of the homeowner's claim.

(b) For the purposes of this title, "builder" does not include any entity or individual whose involvement with a residential unit that is the subject of the homeowner's claim is limited to his or her capacity as general contractor or contractor and who is not a partner, member of, subsidiary of, or otherwise similarly affiliated with the builder. For purposes of this title, these nonaffiliated general contractors and nonaffiliated contractors shall be treated the same as subcontractors, material suppliers, individual product manufacturers, and design professionals. **Leg.H.** Added Stats 2002 ch 722 §3 (SB 800). Amended Stats 2003 ch 762 §2 (AB 903).

Prior Law: Former §911 was enacted Stats 1872 and repealed Code Amdts 1873–74 ch 612 §123.

§912. Builder's duties

A builder shall do all of the following:

(a) Within 30 days of a written request by a homeowner or his or her legal representative, the builder shall provide copies of all relevant plans, specifications, mass or rough grading plans, final soils reports, Bureau of Real Estate public reports, and available engineering calculations, that pertain to a homeowner's residence specifically or as part of a larger development tract. The request shall be honored if it states that it is made relative to structural, fire safety, or soils provisions of this title. However, a builder is not obligated to provide a copying service, and reasonable copying costs shall be borne by the requesting party. A builder may require that the documents be copied onsite by the requesting party, except that the homeowner may, at his or her option, use his or her own copying service, which may include an offsite copy facility that is bonded and insured. If a builder can show that the builder maintained the documents, but that they later became unavailable due to loss or destruction that was not the fault of the builder, the builder may be excused from the requirements of this subdivision, in which case the builder shall act with reasonable diligence to assist the homeowner in obtaining those documents from any applicable government authority or from the source that generated the document. However, in that case, the time limits specified by this section do not apply.

(b) At the expense of the homeowner, who may opt to use an offsite copy facility that is bonded and insured, the builder shall provide to the homeowner or his or her legal representative copies of all maintenance and preventative maintenance recommendations that pertain to his or her residence within 30 days of service of a written request for those documents. Those documents shall also be provided to the homeowner in conjunction with the initial sale of the residence.

(c) At the expense of the homeowner, who may opt to use an offsite copy facility that is bonded and insured, a builder shall provide to the homeowner or his or her legal representative copies of all manufactured products maintenance, preventive maintenance, and limited warranty information within 30 days of a written request for those documents. These documents shall also be provided to the homeowner in conjunction with the initial sale of the residence.

(d) At the expense of the homeowner, who may opt to use an offsite copy facility that is bonded and insured, a builder shall provide to the homeowner or his or her legal representative copies of all of the builder's limited contractual warranties in accordance with this part in effect at the time of the original sale of the residence within 30 days of a written request for those documents. Those documents shall also be provided to the homeowner in conjunction with the initial sale of the residence.

(e) A builder shall maintain the name and address of an agent for notice pursuant to this chapter with the Secretary of State or, alternatively, elect to use a third party for that notice if the builder has notified the homeowner in writing of the third party's name and address, to whom claims and requests for information under this section may be mailed. The name and address of the agent for notice or third party shall be included with the original sales documentation and shall be initialed and acknowledged by the purchaser and the builder's sales representative.

This subdivision applies to instances in which a builder contracts with a third party to accept claims and act on the builder's behalf. A builder shall give actual notice to the homeowner that the builder has made such an election, and shall include the name and address of the third party.

(f) A builder shall record on title a notice of the existence of these procedures and a notice that these procedures impact the legal rights of the homeowner. This information shall also be included with the original sales documentation and shall be initialed and acknowledged by the purchaser and the builder's sales representative.

(g) A builder shall provide, with the original sales documentation, a written copy of this title, which shall be initialed and acknowledged by the purchaser and the builder's sales representative.

(h) As to any documents provided in conjunction with the original sale, the builder shall instruct the original purchaser to provide those documents to any subsequent purchaser.

(i) Any builder who fails to comply with any of these requirements within the time specified is not entitled to the protection of this chapter, and the homeowner is released from the requirements of this chapter and may proceed with the filing of an action, in which case the remaining chapters of this part shall continue to apply to the action. **Leg.H.** Added Stats 2002 ch 722 §3 (SB 800). Amended Stats 2003 ch 762 §3 (AB 903); Stats 2013 ch 352 §50 (AB 1317), effective September 26, 2013, operative July 1, 2013.

Prior Law: Former §912 was enacted Stats 1872 and repealed Code Amdts 1873–74 ch 612 §123.

§913. Acknowledgment of receipt of notice

A builder or his or her representative shall acknowledge, in writing, receipt of the notice of the claim within 14 days after receipt of the notice of the claim. If the notice of the claim is served by the claimant's legal representative, or if the builder receives a written representation letter from a homeowner's attorney, the builder shall include the attorney in all subsequent substantive communications, including, without limitation, all written communications occurring pursuant to this chapter, and all substantive and procedural communications, including all written communications, following the commencement of any subsequent complaint or other legal action, except that if the builder has retained or involved legal counsel to assist the builder in this process, all communications by the builder's counsel shall only be with the claimant's legal representative, if any. **Leg.H.** Added Stats 2002 ch 722 §3 (SB 800).

Prior Law: Former §913 was enacted Stats 1872 and repealed Code Amdts 1873–74 ch 612 §123.

§914. Nonadversarial procedure established

(a) This chapter establishes a nonadversarial procedure, including the remedies available under this chapter which, if the procedure does not resolve the dispute between the parties, may result in a subsequent action to enforce the other chapters of this title. A builder may attempt to commence nonadversarial contractual provisions other than the nonadversarial procedures and remedies set forth in this chapter, but may not, in addition to its own nonadversarial contractual provisions, require adherence to the nonadversarial procedures and remedies set forth in this chapter, regardless of whether the builder's own alternative nonadversarial contractual provisions are successful in resolving the dispute or ultimately deemed enforceable.

At the time the sales agreement is executed, the builder shall notify the homeowner whether the builder intends to engage in the nonadversarial procedure of this section or attempt to enforce alternative nonadversarial contractual provisions. If the builder elects to use alternative nonadversarial contractual provisions in lieu of this chapter, the election is binding, regardless of whether the builder's alternative nonadversarial contractual provisions are successful in resolving the ultimate dispute or are ultimately deemed enforceable.

(b) Nothing in this title is intended to affect existing statutory or decisional law pertaining to the applicability, viability, or enforceability of alternative dispute resolution methods, alternative remedies, or contractual arbitration, judicial reference, or similar procedures requiring a binding resolution to enforce the other chapters of this title or any other disputes between homeowners and builders. Nothing in this title is intended to affect the applicability, viability, or enforceability, if any, of contractual arbitration or judicial reference after a nonadversarial procedure or provision has been completed. **Leg.H.** Added Stats 2002 ch 722 §3 (SB 800).

Prior Law: Former §914 was enacted Stats 1872 and repealed Code Amdts 1873–74 ch 612 §123.

§915. Actions resulting in nonapplication of chapter

If a builder fails to acknowledge receipt of the notice of a claim within the time specified, elects not to go through the process set forth in this chapter, or fails to request an inspection within the time specified, or at the conclusion or cessation of an alternative nonadversarial proceeding, this chapter does not apply and the homeowner is released from the requirements of this chapter and may proceed with the filing of an action. However, the standards set forth in the other chapters of this title shall continue to apply to the action. **Leg.H.** Added Stats 2002 ch 722 §3 (SB 800).

Prior Law: Former §915 was enacted Stats 1872 and repealed Code Amdts 1873–74 ch 612 §123.

§916. Inspection of claimed unmet standards by builder

(a) If a builder elects to inspect the claimed unmet standards, the builder shall complete the initial inspection and testing within 14 days after acknowledgment of receipt of the notice of the claim, at a mutually convenient date and time. If the homeowner has retained legal representation, the inspection shall be scheduled with the legal representative's office at a mutually convenient date and time, unless the legal representative is unavailable during the relevant time periods. All costs of builder inspection and testing, including any damage caused by the builder inspection, shall be borne by the builder. The builder shall also provide written proof that the builder has liability insurance to cover any damages or injuries occurring during inspection and testing. The builder shall restore the property to its pretesting condition within 48 hours of the testing. The builder shall, upon request, allow the inspections to be observed and electronically recorded, video recorded, or photographed by the claimant or his or her legal representative.

(b) Nothing that occurs during a builder's or claimant's inspection or testing may be used or introduced as evidence to support a spoliation defense by any potential party in any subsequent litigation.

(c) If a builder deems a second inspection or testing reasonably necessary, and specifies the reasons therefor in writing within three days following the initial inspection, the builder may conduct a second inspection or testing. A second inspection or testing shall be completed within 40 days of the initial inspection or testing. All requirements concerning the initial inspection or testing shall also apply to the second inspection or testing.

(d) If the builder fails to inspect or test the property within the time specified, the claimant is released from the requirements of this section and may proceed with the filing of an action. However, the standards set forth in the other chapters of this title shall continue to apply to the action.

(e) If a builder intends to hold a subcontractor, design professional, individual product manufacturer, or material supplier, including an insurance carrier, warranty company, or service company, responsible for its contribution to the unmet standard, the builder shall provide notice to that person or entity sufficiently in advance to allow them to attend the initial, or if requested, second inspection of any alleged unmet standard and to participate in the repair process. The claimant and his or her legal representative, if any, shall be advised in a reasonable time prior to the inspection as to the identity of all persons or entities invited to attend. This subdivision does not apply to the builder's insurance company. Except with respect to any claims involving a repair actually conducted under this chapter, nothing in this subdivision shall be construed to relieve a subcontractor, design professional, individual product manufacturer, or material supplier of any liability under an action brought by a claimant. **Leg.H.** Added Stats 2002 ch 722 §3 (SB 800). Amended Stats 2003 ch 762 §4 (AB 903); Stats 2009 ch 88 §12 (AB 176), effective January 1, 2010.

Prior Law: Former §916 was enacted Stats 1872 and repealed Code Amdts 1873–74 ch 612 §123.

§917. Offer to repair

Within 30 days of the initial or, if requested, second inspection or testing, the builder may offer in writing to repair the violation. The offer to repair shall also compensate the homeowner for all applicable damages recoverable under Section 944, within the timeframe for the repair set forth in this chapter. Any such offer shall be accompanied by a detailed, specific, step-by-step statement identifying the particular violation that is being repaired, explaining the nature, scope, and location of the repair, and setting a reasonable completion date for the repair. The offer shall also include the names, addresses, telephone numbers, and license numbers of the contractors whom the builder intends to have perform the repair. Those contractors shall be fully insured for, and shall be responsible for, all damages or injuries that they may cause to occur during the repair, and evidence of that insurance shall be provided to the homeowner upon request. Upon written request by the homeowner or his or her legal representative, and within the timeframes set forth in this chapter, the builder shall also provide any available technical documentation, including, without limitation, plans and specifications, pertaining to the claimed violation within the particular home or development tract. The offer shall also advise the homeowner in writing of his or her right to request up to three additional contractors from which to select to do the repair pursuant to this chapter. **Leg.H.** Added Stats 2002 ch 722 §3 (SB 800).

Prior Law: Former §917 was enacted Stats 1872 and repealed Code Amdts 1873–74 ch 612 §123.

§918. Authorization to proceed with repair

Upon receipt of the offer to repair, the homeowner shall have 30 days to authorize the builder to proceed with the repair. The homeowner may alternatively request, at the homeowner's sole option and discretion, that the builder provide the names, addresses, telephone numbers, and license numbers for up to three alternative contractors who are not owned or financially controlled by the builder and who regularly conduct business in the county where the structure is located. If the homeowner so elects, the builder is entitled to an additional noninvasive inspection, to occur at a mutually convenient date and time within 20 days of the election, so as to permit the other proposed contractors to review the proposed site of the repair. Within 35 days after the request of the homeowner for alternative contractors, the builder shall present the homeowner with a choice of contractors. Within 20 days after that presentation, the homeowner shall authorize the builder or one of the alternative contractors to perform the repair. **Leg.H.** Added Stats 2002 ch 722 §3 (SB 800).

Prior Law: Former §918 was enacted Stats 1872 and repealed Code Amdts 1873–74 ch 612 §123.

§919. Offer to mediate dispute

The offer to repair shall also be accompanied by an offer to mediate the dispute if the homeowner so chooses. The mediation shall be limited to a four-hour mediation, except as otherwise mutually agreed before a nonaffiliated mediator selected and paid for by the builder. At the homeowner's sole option, the homeowner may agree to split the cost of the mediator, and if he or she does so, the mediator shall be selected jointly. The mediator shall have sufficient availability such that the mediation occurs within 15 days after the request to mediate is received and occurs at a mutually convenient location within the county where the action is pending. If a builder has made an offer to repair a violation, and the mediation has failed to resolve the dispute, the homeowner shall allow the repair to be performed either by the builder, its contractor, or the selected contractor. **Leg.H.** Added Stats 2002 ch 722 §3 (SB 800).

Prior Law: Former §919 was enacted Stats 1872 and repealed Code Amdts 1873–74 ch 612 §123.

§920. Actions resulting in filing of an action by homeowner; Applicable standards

If the builder fails to make an offer to repair or otherwise strictly comply with this chapter within the times specified, the claimant is released from the requirements of this chapter and may proceed with the filing of an action. If the contractor performing the repair does not complete the repair in the time or manner specified, the claimant may file an action. If this occurs, the standards set forth in the other chapters of this part shall continue to apply to the action. **Leg.H.** Added Stats 2002 ch 722 §3 (SB 800).

Prior Law: Former §920 was enacted Stats 1872 and repealed Code Amdts 1873–74 ch 612 §123.

§921. Procedure when resolution involves repair by builder

(a) In the event that a resolution under this chapter involves a repair by the builder, the builder shall make an appointment with the claimant, make all appropriate arrangements to effectuate a repair of the claimed unmet standards, and compensate the homeowner for all damages resulting therefrom free of charge to the claimant. The repair shall be scheduled through the claimant's legal representative, if any, unless he or she is unavailable during the relevant time periods. The repair shall be commenced on a mutually convenient date within 14 days of acceptance or, if an alternative contractor is selected by the homeowner, within 14 days of the selection, or, if a mediation occurs, within seven days of the mediation, or within five days after a permit is obtained if one is required.

The builder shall act with reasonable diligence in obtaining any such permit.

(b) The builder shall ensure that work done on the repairs is done with the utmost diligence, and that the repairs are completed as soon as reasonably possible, subject to the nature of the repair or some unforeseen event not caused by the builder or the contractor performing the repair. Every effort shall be made to complete the repair within 120 days. **Leg.H.** Added Stats 2002 ch 722 §3 (SB 800).

Prior Law: Former §921 was enacted Stats 1872 and repealed Code Amdts 1873–74 ch 612 §123.

§922. Observation and electronic recording, video recording, or photographing of repair allowed

The builder shall, upon request, allow the repair to be observed and electronically recorded, video recorded, or photographed by the claimant or his or her legal representative. Nothing that occurs during the repair process may be used or introduced as evidence to support a spoliation defense by any potential party in any subsequent litigation. **Leg.H.** Added Stats 2002 ch 722 §3 (SB 800). Amended Stats 2009 ch 88 §13 (AB 176), effective January 1, 2010.

Prior Law: Former §922 was enacted Stats 1872 and repealed Code Amdts 1873–74 ch 612 §123.

§923. Availability to homeowner of correspondence, photographs and other material pertaining to repairs

The builder shall provide the homeowner or his or her legal representative, upon request, with copies of all correspondence, photographs, and other materials pertaining or relating in any manner to the repairs. **Leg.H.** Added Stats 2002 ch 722 §3 (SB 800).

Prior Law: Former §923 was enacted Stats 1872 and repealed Code Amdts 1873–74 ch 612 §123.

§924. Offer to repair some, but not all, of claimed unmet standards

If the builder elects to repair some, but not all of, the claimed unmet standards, the builder shall, at the same time it makes its offer, set forth with particularity in writing the reasons, and the support for those reasons, for not repairing all claimed unmet standards. **Leg.H.** Added Stats 2002 ch 722 §3 (SB 800).

Prior Law: Former §924 was enacted Stats 1872 and repealed Code Amdts 1873–74 ch 612 §123.

§925. Failure to timely complete repairs

If the builder fails to complete the repair within the time specified in the repair plan, the claimant is released from the requirements of this chapter and may proceed with the filing of an action. If this occurs, the standards set forth in the other chapters of this title shall continue to apply to the action. **Leg.H.** Added Stats 2002 ch 722 §3 (SB 800).

Prior Law: Former §925 was enacted Stats 1872 and repealed Code Amdts 1873–74 ch 612 §123.

§926. Release or waiver in exchange for repair work prohibited

The builder may not obtain a release or waiver of any kind in exchange for the repair work mandated by this chapter. At the conclusion of the repair, the claimant may proceed with filing an action for violation of the applicable standard or for a claim of inadequate repair, or both, including all applicable damages available under Section 944. **Leg.H.** Added Stats 2002 ch 722 §3 (SB 800).

Prior Law: Former §926 was enacted Stats 1872 and repealed Code Amdts 1873–74 ch 612 §123.

§927. Statute of limitations

If the applicable statute of limitations has otherwise run during this process, the time period for filing a complaint or other legal remedies for violation of any provision of this title, or for a claim of inadequate repair, is extended from the time of the original claim by the claimant to 100 days after the repair is completed, whether or not the particular violation is the one being repaired. If the builder fails to acknowledge the claim within the time specified, elects not to go through this statutory process, or fails to request an inspection within the time specified, the time period for filing a complaint or other legal remedies for violation of any provision of this title is extended from the time of the original claim by the claimant to 45 days after the time for responding to the notice of claim has expired. If the builder elects to attempt to enforce its own nonadversarial procedure in lieu of the procedure set forth in this chapter, the time period for filing a complaint or other legal remedies for violation of any provision of this part is extended from the time of the original claim by the claimant to 100 days after either the completion of the builder's alternative nonadversarial procedure, or 100 days after the builder's alternative nonadversarial procedure is deemed unenforceable, whichever is later. **Leg.H.** Added Stats 2002 ch 722 §3 (SB 800).

Prior Law: Former §927 was enacted Stats 1872 and repealed Code Amdts 1873–74 ch 612 §123.

§928. Mediation procedure

If the builder has invoked this chapter and completed a repair, prior to filing an action, if there has been no previous mediation between the parties, the homeowner or his or her legal representative shall request mediation in writing. The mediation shall be limited to four hours, except as otherwise mutually agreed before a nonaffiliated mediator selected and paid for by the builder. At the homeowner's sole option, the homeowner may agree to split the cost of the mediator and if he or she does so, the mediator shall be selected jointly. The mediator shall have sufficient availability such that the mediation will occur within 15 days after the request for mediation is received and shall occur at a mutually convenient location within the county where the action is pending. In the event that a mediation is used at this point, any applicable statutes of limitations shall be tolled from the date of the request to mediate until the next court day after the mediation is completed, or the 100-day period, whichever is later. **Leg.H.** Added Stats 2002 ch 722 §3 (SB 800).

Prior Law: Former §928 was enacted Stats 1872 and repealed Code Amdts 1873–74 ch 612 §123.

§929. Cash offer in lieu of repair

(a) Nothing in this chapter prohibits the builder from making only a cash offer and no repair. In this situation, the homeowner is free to accept the offer, or he or she may reject the offer and proceed with the filing of an action. If the latter occurs, the standards of the other chapters of this title shall continue to apply to the action.

(b) The builder may obtain a reasonable release in exchange for the cash payment. The builder may negotiate the terms and conditions of any reasonable release in terms of scope and consideration in conjunction with a cash payment under this chapter. **Leg.H.** Added Stats 2002 ch 722 §3 (SB 800).

Prior Law: Former §929 was enacted Stats 1872 and repealed Code Amdts 1873–74 ch 612 §123.

§930. Strict construction of requirements; Failure of claimant to conform

(a) The time periods and all other requirements in this chapter are to be strictly construed, and, unless extended by the mutual agreement of the parties in accordance with this chapter, shall govern the rights and obligations under this title. If a builder fails to act in accordance with this section within the timeframes mandated, unless extended by the mutual agreement of the parties as evidenced by a postclaim written confirmation by the affected homeowner demonstrating that he or she has knowingly and voluntarily extended the statutory timeframe, the claimant may proceed with filing an action. If this occurs, the standards of the other chapters of this title shall continue to apply to the action.

(b) If the claimant does not conform with the requirements of this chapter, the builder may bring a motion to stay any subsequent court action or other proceeding until the requirements of this chapter have been satisfied. The court, in its discretion, may award the prevailing party on such a motion, his or her attorney's fees and costs in bringing or opposing the motion. **Leg.H.** Added Stats 2002 ch 722 §3 (SB 800).

Prior Law: Former §930 was enacted Stats 1872 and repealed Code Amdts 1873–74 ch 612 §123.

§931. Claim combined with other causes of action

If a claim combines causes of action or damages not covered by this part, including, without limitation, personal injuries, class actions, other statutory remedies, or fraud-based claims, the claimed unmet standards shall be administered according to this part, although evidence of the property in its unrepaired condition may be introduced to support the respective elements of any such cause of action. As to any fraud-based claim, if the fact that the property has been repaired under this chapter is deemed admissible, the trier of fact shall be informed that the repair was not voluntarily accepted by the homeowner. As to any class action claims that address solely the incorporation of a defective component into a residence, the named and unnamed class members need not comply with this chapter. **Leg.H.** Added Stats 2002 ch 722 §3 (SB 800).

Prior Law: Former §931 was enacted Stats 1872 and repealed Code Amdts 1873–74 ch 612 §123.

§932. Subsequent discovered claims of unmet standards

Subsequently discovered claims of unmet standards shall be administered separately under this chapter, unless otherwise agreed to by the parties. However, in the case of a detached single family residence, in the same home, if the subsequently discovered claim is for a violation of the same standard as that which has already been initiated by the same claimant and the subject of a currently pending action, the claimant need not reinitiate the process as to the same standard. In the case of an attached project, if the subsequently discovered claim is for a violation of the same standard for a connected component system in the same building as has already been initiated by the same claimant, and the subject of a currently pending action, the claimant need not reinitiate this process as to that standard. **Leg.H.** Added Stats 2002 ch 722 §3 (SB 800).

Prior Law: Former §932 was enacted Stats 1872 and repealed Code Amdts 1873–74 ch 612 §123.

§933. Evidence of repair work

If any enforcement of these standards is commenced, the fact that a repair effort was made may be introduced to the trier of fact. However, the claimant may use the condition of the property prior to the repair as the basis for contending that the repair work was inappropriate, inadequate, or incomplete, or that the violation still exists. The claimant need not show that the repair work resulted in further damage nor that damage has continued to occur as a result of the violation. **Leg.H.** Added Stats 2002 ch 722 §3 (SB 800).

Prior Law: Former §933 was enacted Stats 1872 and repealed Code Amdts 1873–74 ch 612 §123.

§934. Evidence of parties' conduct

Evidence of both parties' conduct during this process may be introduced during a subsequent enforcement action, if any, with the exception of any mediation. Any repair efforts undertaken by the builder, shall not be considered settlement communications or offers of settlement and are not inadmissible in evidence on such a basis. **Leg.H.** Added Stats 2002 ch 722 §3 (SB 800).

Prior Law: Former §934 was enacted Stats 1872 and repealed Code Amdts 1873–74 ch 612 §123.

§935. Similar requirements of Civil Code Section 6000

To the extent that provisions of this chapter are enforced and those provisions are substantially similar to provisions in Section 6000, but an action is subsequently commenced under Section 6000, the parties are excused from performing the substantially similar requirements under Section 6000. **Leg.H.** Added Stats 2002 ch 722 §3 (SB 800). Amended Stats 2012 ch 181 §30 (AB 806), effective January 1, 2013, operative January 1, 2014.

Prior Law: Former §935 was enacted Stats 1872 and repealed Code Amdts 1873–74 ch 612 §123.

§936. Applicability of title to other entities involved in construction process

Each and every provision of the other chapters of this title apply to general contractors, subcontractors, material suppliers, individual product manufacturers, and design professionals to the extent that the general contractors, subcontractors, material suppliers, individual product manufacturers, and design professionals caused, in whole or in part, a violation of a particular standard as the result of a negligent act or omission or a breach of contract. In addition to the affirmative defenses set forth in Section 945.5, a general contractor, subcontractor, material supplier, design professional, individual product manufacturer, or other entity may also offer common law and contractual defenses as applicable to any claimed violation of a standard. All actions by a claimant or builder to enforce an express contract, or any provision thereof, against a general contractor, subcontractor, material supplier, individual product manufacturer, or design professional is preserved. Nothing in this title modifies the law pertaining to joint and several liability for builders, general contractors, subcontractors, material suppliers, individual product manufacturer, and design professionals that contribute to any specific violation of this title. However, the negligence standard in this section does not apply to any general contractor, subcontractor, material supplier, individual product manufacturer, or design professional with respect to claims for which strict liability would apply. **Leg.H.** Added Stats 2002 ch 722 §3 (SB 800). Amended Stats 2003 ch 762 §5 (AB 903).

Prior Law: Former §936 was enacted Stats 1872 and repealed Code Amdts 1873–74 ch 612 §123.

§937. Claims and damages not covered by this title

Nothing in this title shall be interpreted to eliminate or abrogate the requirement to comply with Section 411.35 of the Code of Civil Procedure or to affect the liability of design professionals, including architects and architectural firms, for claims and damages not covered by this title. **Leg.H.** Added Stats 2002 ch 722 §3 (SB 800).

Prior Law: Former §937 was enacted Stats 1872 and repealed Code Amdts 1873–74 ch 612 §123.

§938. Date of sale for applicability of title

This title applies only to new residential units where the purchase agreement with the buyer was signed by the seller on or after January 1, 2003. **Leg.H.** Added Stats 2002 ch 722 §3 (SB 800). Amended Stats 2003 ch 762 §6 (AB 903).

Prior Law: Former §938 was enacted Stats 1872 and repealed Code Amdts 1873–74 ch 612 §123.

§939. [Section repealed 1874]

Leg.H. Enacted Stats 1872. Repealed Code Amdts 1873–74 ch 612 §123.

§940. [Section repealed 1874]

Leg.H. Enacted Stats 1872. Repealed Code Amdts 1873–74 ch 612 §123.

CHAPTER 5
PROCEDURE

Time limit for bringing action. §941.
Showing required for claim. §942.
Other causes of action; Claims involving detached single-family home. §943.
Damages. §944.
Original purchasers and successors-in-interest. §945.
Affirmative defenses. §945.5.

§941. Time limit for bringing action

(a) Except as specifically set forth in this title, no action may be brought to recover under this title more than 10 years after substantial completion of the improvement but not later than the date of recordation of a valid notice of completion.

(b) As used in this section, "action" includes an action for indemnity brought against a person arising out of that person's performance or furnishing of services or materials referred to in this title, except that a cross-complaint for indemnity may be filed pursuant to subdivision (b) of Section 428.10 of the Code of Civil Procedure in an action which has been brought within the time period set forth in subdivision (a).

(c) The limitation prescribed by this section may not be asserted by way of defense by any person in actual possession or the control, as owner, tenant or otherwise, of such an improvement, at the time any deficiency in the improvement constitutes the proximate cause for which it is proposed to make a claim or bring an action.

(d) Sections 337.15 and 337.1 of the Code of Civil Procedure do not apply to actions under this title.

(e) Existing statutory and decisional law regarding tolling of the statute of limitations shall apply to the time periods for filing an action or making a claim under this title, except that repairs made pursuant to Chapter 4 (commencing with Section 910), with the exception of the tolling provision contained in Section 927, do not extend the period for filing an action, or restart the time limitations contained in subdivision (a) or (b) of Section 7091 of the Business and Professions Code. If a builder arranges for a contractor to perform a repair pursuant to Chapter 4 (commencing with Section 910), as to the builder the time period for calculating the statute of limitation in subdivision (a) or (b) of Section 7091 of the Business and Professions Code shall pertain to the substantial completion of the original construction and not to the date of repairs under this title. The time limitations established by this title do not apply to any action by a claimant for a contract or express contractual provision. Causes of action and damages to which this chapter does not apply are not limited by this section. **Leg.H.** Added Stats 2002 ch 722 §3 (SB 800). Amended Stats 2003 ch 62 §12 (SB 600), ch 762 §7 (AB 903) (ch 762 prevails).

§942. Showing required for claim

In order to make a claim for violation of the standards set forth in Chapter 2 (commencing with Section 896), a homeowner need only demonstrate, in accordance with the applicable evidentiary standard, that the home does not meet the applicable standard, subject to the affirmative defenses set forth in Section 945.5. No further showing of causation or damages is required to meet the burden of proof regarding a violation of a standard set forth in Chapter 2 (commencing with Section 896), provided that the violation arises out of, pertains to, or is related to, the original construction. **Leg.H.** Added Stats 2003 ch 762 §9 (AB 903).

Prior Law: Former §942 was added Stats 2002 ch 722 §3 and renumbered CC §943 by Stats 2003 ch 762 §8.

§943. Other causes of action; Claims involving detached single-family home

(a) Except as provided in this title, no other cause of action for a claim covered by this title or for damages recoverable under Section 944 is allowed. In addition to the rights under this title, this title does not apply to any action by a claimant to enforce a contract or express contractual provision, or any action for fraud, personal injury, or violation of a statute. Damages awarded for the items set forth in Section 944 in such other cause of action shall be reduced by the amounts recovered pursuant to Section 944 for violation of the standards set forth in this title.

(b) As to any claims involving a detached single-family home, the homeowner's right to the reasonable value of repairing any nonconformity is limited to the repair costs, or the diminution in current value of the home caused by the nonconformity, whichever is less, subject to the personal use exception as developed under common law. **Leg.H.** Added Stats 2002 ch 722 §3 (SB 800), as CC §942. Renumbered by Stats 2003 ch 762 §8 (AB 903).

§944. Damages

If a claim for damages is made under this title, the homeowner is only entitled to damages for the reasonable value of repairing any violation of the standards set forth in this title, the reasonable cost of repairing any damages caused by the repair efforts, the reasonable cost of repairing and rectifying any damages resulting from the failure of the home to meet the standards, the reasonable cost of removing and replacing any improper repair by the builder, reasonable relocation and storage expenses, lost business income if the home was used as a principal place of a business licensed to be operated from the home, reasonable investigative costs for each established violation, and all other costs or fees recoverable by contract or statute. **Leg.H.** Added Stats 2002 ch 722 §3 (SB 800).

§945. Original purchasers and successors-in-interest

The provisions, standards, rights, and obligations set forth in this title are binding upon all original purchasers and their successors-in-interest. For purposes of this title, associations and others having the rights set forth in Sections 5980 and 5985 shall be considered to be original purchasers and shall have standing to enforce the provisions, standards, rights, and obligations set forth in this title. **Leg.H.** Added Stats 2002 ch 722 §3 (SB 800). Amended Stats 2005 ch 37 §1 (SB 853), effective January 1, 2006; Stats 2012 ch 181 §31 (AB 806), effective January 1, 2013, operative January 1, 2014; Stats 2018 ch 92 §34 (SB 1289), effective January 1, 2019.

§945.5. Affirmative defenses

A builder, general contractor, subcontractor, material supplier, individual product manufacturer, or design professional, under the principles of comparative fault pertaining to affirmative defenses, may be excused, in whole or in part, from any obligation, damage, loss, or liability if the builder, general contractor, subcontractor, material supplier, individual product manufacturer, or design professional, can demonstrate any of the following affirmative defenses in response to a claimed violation:

(a) To the extent it is caused by an unforeseen act of nature which caused the structure not to meet the standard. For purposes of this section an "unforeseen act of nature" means a weather condition, earthquake, or manmade event such as war, terrorism, or vandalism, in excess of the design criteria expressed by the applicable building codes, regulations, and ordinances in effect at the time of original construction.

(b) To the extent it is caused by a homeowner's unreasonable failure to minimize or prevent those damages in a timely manner, including the failure of the homeowner to allow reasonable and timely access for inspections and repairs under this title. This includes the failure to give timely notice to the builder after discovery of a violation, but does not include damages due to the untimely or inadequate response of a builder to the homeowner's claim.

(c) To the extent it is caused by the homeowner or his or her agent, employee, general contractor, subcontractor, independent contractor, or consultant by virtue of their failure to follow the builder's or manufacturer's recommendations, or commonly accepted homeowner maintenance obligations. In order to rely upon this defense as it relates to a builder's recommended maintenance schedule, the builder shall show that the homeowner had written notice of these schedules and recommendations and that the recommendations and schedules were reasonable at the time they were issued.

(d) To the extent it is caused by the homeowner or his or her agent's or an independent third party's alterations, ordinary wear and tear, misuse, abuse, or neglect, or by the structure's use for something other than its intended purpose.

(e) To the extent that the time period for filing actions bars the claimed violation.

(f) As to a particular violation for which the builder has obtained a valid release.

(g) To the extent that the builder's repair was successful in correcting the particular violation of the applicable standard.

(h) As to any causes of action to which this statute does not apply, all applicable affirmative defenses are preserved. **Leg.H.** Added Stats 2002 ch 722 §3 (SB 800). Amended Stats 2003 ch 762 §10 (AB 903).

TITLE 8
RECONSTRUCTION OF HOMES LOST IN CEDAR FIRE, OCTOBER 2003 [REPEALED]

§945.6. [Section repealed 2008]

Leg.H. Added Stats 2005 ch 40 §2 (AB 662), effective July 11, 2005, repealed January 1, 2008. Repealed operative January 1, 2008, by its own provisions. The repealed section related to voluntary incorporation of Title 7 rights and remedies in reconstruction contracts and definition of contractor.

PART 3
PERSONAL OR MOVABLE PROPERTY

Title 1. Personal Property in General.
Title 2. Particular Kinds of Personal Property.

TITLE 1
PERSONAL PROPERTY IN GENERAL

By what law governed. §946.

§946. By what law governed

If there is no law to the contrary, in the place where personal property is situated, it is deemed to follow the person of its owner, and is governed by the law of his domicile. **Leg.H.** Enacted Stats 1872. Repealed Code Amdts 1873–74 ch 612 §123. Reenacted Code Amdts 1875–76 ch 167 §1.

§947. [Section repealed 1874]

Leg.H. Enacted Stats 1872. Repealed Code Amdts 1873–74 ch 612 §124.

TITLE 2
PARTICULAR KINDS OF PERSONAL PROPERTY

Chapter 1. Things in Action.
Chapter 2. Shipping.
Chapter 3. Products of the Mind.
Chapter 4. Other Kinds of Personal Property.

CHAPTER 1
THINGS IN ACTION

Article 1. Transfer of Things in Action.

ARTICLE 1
Transfer of Things in Action

Thing in action. §953.
Transfer of thing in action. §954.
Perfecting transfer of right as against third persons. §954.5.
Perfection of transfer of nonnegotiable instrument. §955.
Perfection of transfer of payment intangible, account, or chattel paper. §955.1.

§953. Thing in action

A thing in action is a right to recover money or other personal property by a judicial proceeding. **Leg.H.** Enacted Stats 1872. Amended Code Amdts 1873–74 ch 612 §125.

§954. Transfer of thing in action

A thing in action, arising out of the violation of a right of property, or out of an obligation, may be transferred by the owner. **Leg.H.** Enacted Stats 1872. Amended Stats 1990 ch 79 §2 (AB 759), operative July 1, 1991.

§954.5. Perfecting transfer of right as against third persons

(a) Subject to subdivisions (b) and (c), a transfer of a right represented by a judgment excluded from coverage of Division 9 of the Commercial Code by paragraph (9) of subdivision (d) of Section 9109 of the Commercial Code shall be deemed perfected as against third persons upon there being executed and delivered to the transferee an assignment thereof in writing.

(b) As between bona fide assignees of the same right for value without notice, the assignee who first becomes an assignee of record, by filing an acknowledgment of assignment of judgment with the court as provided in Section 673 of the Code of Civil Procedure or otherwise becoming an assignee of record, has priority.

(c) The filing of an acknowledgment of assignment of the judgment with the court under Section 673 of the Code of Civil Procedure is not, of itself, notice to the judgment debtor so as to invalidate any payments made by the judgment debtor that would otherwise be applied to the satisfaction of the judgment. **Leg.H.** Added Stats 1982 ch 497 §4, operative July 1, 1983. Amended Stats 1999 ch 991 §1.8 (SB 45), operative July 1, 2001.

§955. Perfection of transfer of nonnegotiable instrument

A transfer other than one intended to create a security interest (paragraph (1) or (3) of subdivision (a) of Section 9109 of the Commercial Code) of a nonnegotiable instrument which is otherwise negotiable within Division 3 of the Commercial Code but which is not payable to order or to bearer and a sale of accounts, chattel paper, payment intangibles, or promissory notes as part of a sale of the business out of which they arose (paragraph (4) of subdivision (d) of Section 9109 of the Commercial Code) shall be deemed perfected against third persons when such property rights have been endorsed or assigned in writing and in the case of such instruments or chattel paper delivered to the transferee, whether or not notice of such transfer or sale has been given to the obligor; but such endorsement, assignment, or delivery is not, of itself, notice to the obligor so as to invalidate any payments made by the obligor to the transferor. **Leg.H.** Added Stats 1941 ch 1025 §1. Amended Stats 1953 ch 1242 §2; Stats 1963 ch 819 §3, effective January 1, 1965; Stats 1982 ch 497 §5, operative July 1, 1983; Stats 1999 ch 991 §2 (SB 45), operative July 1, 2001.

Prior Law: Former §955, incorporated in Lab C §300, was added by Stats 1913 ch 287 §1 p 537 and repealed by Stats 1937 ch 90 (Lab C §8100) p 328.

§955.1. Perfection of transfer of payment intangible, account, or chattel paper

(a) Except as provided in Sections 954.5 and 955 and subject to subdivisions (b) and (c), a transfer other than one intended to create a security interest pursuant to paragraph (1) or (3) of subdivision (a) of Section 9109 of the Commercial Code, of any payment intangible, as defined in Section 9102 of the Commercial Code, and any transfer of accounts, chattel paper, payment intangibles, or promissory notes excluded from the coverage of Division 9 of the Commercial Code by paragraph (4) of subdivision (d) of Section 9109 of the Commercial Code shall be deemed perfected as against third persons upon there being executed and delivered to the transferee an assignment thereof in writing.

(b) As between bona fide assignees of the same right for value without notice, the assignee first giving notice of the right to the obligor in writing has priority.

(c) The assignment is not, of itself, notice to the obligor so as to invalidate any payments made by the obligor to the transferor.

(d) This section does not apply to transfers or assignments of water supply property, as defined in Section 849 of the Public Utilities Code.

(e) This section does not apply to transfers or assignments of recovery property, as defined in Section 848 of the Public Utilities Code. **Leg.H.** Added Stats 1953 ch 1242 §3. Amended Stats 1955 ch 741 §1; Stats 1963 ch 819 §4; Stats 1982 ch 497 §6, operative July 1, 1983; Stats 1996 ch 854 §2 (AB 1890), effective September 24, 1996; Stats 1999 ch 991 §3 (SB 45), operative July 1, 2001; Stats 2004 ch 46 §2 (SB 772), effective June 7, 2004; Stats 2014 ch 482 §2 (SB 936), effective January 1, 2015.

2014 Note: The Legislature finds and declares all of the following:

(a) Under existing law, the Public Utilities Commission has regulatory authority over public utilities, including water utilities. Existing law authorizes the commission to fix just and reasonable rates and charges.

(b) To address the unique needs for integrated water management on the Monterey Peninsula, the Legislature adopted special legislation creating the Monterey Peninsula Water Management District (Monterey Peninsula Water Management District Law, as added by Section 118 of Chapter 527 of the Statutes of 1977, as amended).

(c) California American Water (CAW) is the water utility that provides water to most of the residents and businesses within the Monterey Peninsula.

(d) CAW provides water to its customers from the surface water in the Carmel River and its tributaries, water in the Carmel Valley Alluvial Aquifer that underlies the Carmel River, and water in the Seaside Groundwater Basin that includes the Northern and Southern Coastal Subunits and the Northern and Southern Inland Subareas.

(e) CAW's lawful right to obtain water supplies from the Carmel Valley Alluvial Aquifer was determined by the State Water Resources Control Board (SWRCB) in SWRCB Order No. WR 95-10, dated July 6, 1995. The SWRCB found that CAW does not possess the legal right to divert from the Carmel River system the amount of water historically, and presently, being diverted, and required CAW to diligently pursue a substitute water supply. SWRCB Order No. WR 95-10 limited CAW production from the Carmel River system to 10,308 acre-feet annually (Water Year 2012), and ordered CAW to terminate its unpermitted diversions from the Carmel River, and in the interim, to maximize its production from the Seaside Groundwater Basin.

(f) Subsequently, the SWRCB issued a cease and desist order (CDO) against CAW in October 2009 as Order No. WR 2009-0060. The CDO prescribed a series of significant cutbacks to CAW's production from the Carmel River system from January 2010 to December 2016, inclusive. Pursuant to the CDO, CAW's customers are subject to a moratorium on water permits for new construction and remodels, and may be subject to water rationing, fines, or both if CAW production limits are exceeded.

(g) CAW's ability to produce water from the Seaside Groundwater Basin has also been limited by the adjudication of the Monterey County Superior Court. CAW's right to groundwater from Coastal Subareas and the Laguna Seca Subarea of the Seaside Groundwater Basin, without causing adverse effects such as seawater intrusion, declining water levels, or land subsidence, characterized as a "safe yield," was determined in *California American Water v. City of Seaside* (2010) (183 Cal.App.4th 471). The 2006 final judgment imposes a series of pumping reductions designed to limit production of natural basin water to its safe yield, initially set at 3,000 acre-feet per year. CAW's share of the safe yield is reduced proportionately at each stage.

(h) The need for infrastructure to expand CAW sources of water has been heightened by the lack of legal water supplies resulting from the CDO, SWRCB Order No. WR 95-10, the listing of the California red-legged frog and the steelhead trout as threatened species under the federal Endangered Species Act of 1973 (16 U.S.C. Sec. 1531 et seq.) and the limitations on water from the Seaside Groundwater Basin adjudication.

(i) These circumstances create a special and unique need to augment potable water supplies on the Monterey Peninsula. Potential infrastructure projects necessary to develop new sources of supply to resolve the critical water supply shortage within CAW's Monterey County District include desalination, aquifer storage and recovery projects, and the production and use of recycled water.

(j) It may benefit the customers of CAW to finance the capital costs associated with the construction and installation of water infrastructure, plants, and facilities necessary to resolve the critical water supply shortage through an alternative financing mechanism.

(k) Alternative financing mechanisms exist that can result in lower costs to customers of CAW as compared to traditional utility financing mechanisms. To use alternative financing mechanisms, the Public Utilities Commission must be empowered to issue financing orders to allow the issuance of bonds secured by water supply property.

(*l*) CAW customers may take advantage of additional costs savings if a public agency assists in the financing of water project capital costs on a tax-exempt basis. It is necessary for California to provide express authority for a public agency to issue bonds or other evidences of indebtedness on this basis.

(m) In confirming the Public Utilities Commission's authority to approve water supply property, including a dedicated customer surcharge to support the issuance of water rate relief bonds, the Legislature is not ratifying or endorsing any particular outcome for proceeding A.12-04-019, but rather is authorizing a means by which the commission may reduce the cost impact on Monterey Peninsula customers if a water supply project is approved by the commission in proceeding A.12-04-019. Stats 2014 ch 482 (SB 936) §1.

ARTICLE 2
Survival of Tort Actions [Repealed]

§956.   [Section repealed 1961]

Leg.H. Added Stats 1949 ch 1380 §2. Repealed Stats 1961 ch 657 §1. The repealed section related to tort action surviving death of wrongdoer or injured person.

CHAPTER 2
SHIPPING

§§960–966.   [Sections repealed 1937]

Leg.H. Enacted Stats 1872. Repealed Stats 1937 ch 368 (H & N C §10001). See H & N C §§21, 400–405.

§§970–973.   [Sections repealed 1937]

Leg.H. Enacted Stats 1872. Repealed Stats 1937 ch 368 (H & N C §10001). See H & N C §§280–285, 290–292.

CHAPTER 3
PRODUCTS OF THE MIND

Works of authorship; Sound recordings; Inventions and designs. §980.
Joint ownership. §981.
Transfer of ownership. §982.
Effect of publication. §983.
Subsequent and original production. §984.
Private writings. §985.
Sale of fine art. §986.
Protection of fine art against alteration or destruction; Actions; Removal of work from property. §987.
Residual rights. §988.
Preservation of integrity of cultural and artistic creations; Right of organization to commence action; Removal of art from property. §989.

§980.   Works of authorship; Sound recordings; Inventions and designs

(a)(1) The author of any original work of authorship that is not fixed in any tangible medium of expression has an exclusive ownership in the representation or expression thereof as against all persons except one who orginally and independently creates the same or similar work. A work shall be considered not fixed when it is not embodied in a tangible medium of expression or when its embodiment in a tangible medium of expression is not sufficiently permanent or stable to permit it to be perceived, reproduced, or otherwise communicated for a period of more than transitory duration, either directly or with the aid of a machine or device.

(2) The author of an original work of authorship consisting of a sound recording initially fixed prior to February 15, 1972, has an exclusive ownership therein until February 15, 2047, as against all persons except one who independently makes or duplicates another sound recording that does not directly or indirectly recapture the actual sounds fixed in such prior sound recording, but consists entirely of an independent fixation of other sounds, even though such sounds imitate or simulate the sounds contained in the prior sound recording.

(b) The inventor or proprietor of any invention or design, with or without delineation, or other graphical representation, has an exclusive ownership therein, and in the representation or expression thereof, which continues so long as the invention or design and the representations or expressions thereof made by him remain in his possession. **Leg.H.** Enacted Stats 1872. Amended Stats 1947 ch 1107 §1; Stats 1949 ch 921 §1; Stats 1982 ch 574 §2.

§981.   Joint ownership

(a) Unless otherwise agreed, an original work of authorship not fixed in any tangible medium of expression and in the creation of which several persons are jointly concerned, is owned by them in equal proportion.

(b) Unless otherwise agreed, an invention or design in the production of which several persons are jointly concerned is owned by them as follows:

(1) If the invention or design is single, in equal proportions.

(2) If it is not single, in proportion to the contribution of each. **Leg.H.** Enacted Stats 1872. Amended Stats 1947 ch 1107 §2; Stats 1949 ch 921 §2; Stats 1982 ch 574 §3.

§982.   Transfer of ownership

(a) The owner of any rights in any original works of authorship not fixed in any tangible medium of expression may transfer the ownership therein.

(b) The owner of any invention or design, or of any representation or expression thereof, may transfer his or her proprietary interest in it.

(c) Notwithstanding any other provision in this section, whenever a work of fine art is transferred, whether by sale or on commission or otherwise, by or on behalf of the artist who created it, or that artist's heir, legatee, or personal representative, the right of reproduction thereof is reserved to such artist or such heir, legatee, or personal representative until it passes into the public domain by act or operation of law, unless that right is expressly transferred by a document in writing in which reference is made to the specific right of reproduction, signed by the owner of the rights conveyed or that person's duly authorized agent. If the transfer is pursuant to an employment relationship, the right of reproduction is transferred to the employer, unless it is expressly reserved in writing. If the transfer is pursuant to a legacy or inheritance, the right of reproduction is transferred to the legatee or heir, unless it is expressly reserved by will or codicil. Nothing contained herein, however, shall be construed to prohibit the fair use of such work of fine art.

(d) As used in subdivision (c):

(1) "Fine art" means any work of visual art, including but not limited to, a drawing, painting, sculpture, mosaic, or photograph, a work of calligraphy, work of graphic art (including an etching, lithograph, offset print, silk screen, or a work of graphic art of like nature), crafts (including crafts in clay, textile, fiber, wood, metal, plastic, and like materials), or mixed media (including a collage, assemblage, or any combination of the foregoing art media).

(2) "Artist" means the creator of a work of fine art.

(3) "Right of reproduction", at the present state of commerce and technology shall be interpreted as including, but shall not be limited to, the following: reproduction of works of fine art as prints suitable for framing; facsimile casts of sculpture; reproductions used for greeting cards; reproductions in general books and magazines not devoted primarily to art, and in newspapers in other than art or news sections, when such reproductions in books, magazines, and newspapers are used for purposes similar to those of material for which the publishers customarily pay; art films; television, except from stations operated for educational purposes, or on programs for educational purposes from all stations; and reproductions used in any form of advertising, including magazines, calendars, newspapers, posters, billboards, films or television.

(e) The amendments to this section made at the 1975-76 Regular Session shall only apply to transfers made on or after January 1, 1976. **Leg.H.** Enacted Stats 1872. Amended Stats 1947 ch 1107 §3; Stats 1949 ch 921 §3; Stats 1975 ch 952 §1; Stats 1982 ch 574 §4.

§983. Effect of publication

If the owner of any invention or design intentionally makes it public, a copy or reproduction may be made public by any person, without responsiblily to the owner, so far as the law of this state is concerned. **Leg.H.** Enacted Stats 1872. Amended Stats 1947 ch 1107 §4; Stats 1949 ch 921 §4; Stats 1982 ch 574 §5.

§984. Subsequent and original production

If the owner of an invention or design does not make it public, any other person subsequently and originally producing the same thing has the same right therein as the prior inventor, which is exclusive to the same extent against all persons except the prior inventor, or those claiming under him. **Leg.H.** Added Stats 1949 ch 921 §5.

Prior Law: Former §984, relating to subsequent inventor, author, etc., was enacted Stats 1872 and repealed by Stats 1947 ch 1107 §5 p 2546.

§985. Private writings

Letters and other private communications in writing belong to the person to whom they are addressed and delivered; but they cannot be published against the will of the writer, except by authority of law. **Leg.H.** Enacted Stats 1872.

§986. Sale of fine art

(a) Whenever a work of fine art is sold and the seller resides in California or the sale takes place in California, the seller or the seller's agent shall pay to the artist of such work of fine art or to such artist's agent 5 percent of the amount of such sale. The right of the artist to receive an amount equal to 5 percent of the amount of such sale may be waived only by a contract in writing providing for an amount in excess of 5 percent of the amount of such sale. An artist may assign the right to collect the royalty payment provided by this section to another individual or entity. However, the assignment shall not have the effect of creating a waiver prohibited by this subdivision.

(1) When a work of fine art is sold at an auction or by a gallery, dealer, broker, museum, or other person acting as the agent for the seller the agent shall withhold 5 percent of the amount of the sale, locate the artist and pay the artist.

(2) If the seller or agent is unable to locate and pay the artist within 90 days, an amount equal to 5 percent of the amount of the sale shall be tranferred to the Arts Council.

(3) If a seller or the seller's agent fails to pay an artist the amount equal to 5 percent of the sale of a work of fine art by the artist or fails to transfer such amount to the Arts Council, the artist may bring an action for damages within three years after the date of sale or one year after the discovery of the sale, whichever is longer. The prevailing party in any action brought under this paragraph shall be entitled to reasonable attorney fees, in an amount as determined by the court.

(4) Moneys received by the council pursuant to this section shall be deposited in an account in the Special Deposit Fund in the State Treasury.

(5) The Arts Council shall attempt to locate any artist for whom money is received pursuant to this section. If the council is unable to locate the artist and the artist does not file a written claim for the money received by the council within seven years of the date of sale of the work of fine art, the right of the artist terminates and such money shall be transferred to the council for use in acquiring fine art pursuant to the Art in Public Buildings program set forth in Chapter 2.1 (commencing with Section 15813) of Part 10b of Division 3 of Title 2, of the Government Code.

(6) Any amounts of money held by any seller or agent for the payment of artists pursuant to this section shall be exempt from enforcement of a money judgment by the creditors of the seller or agent.

(7) Upon the death of an artist, the rights and duties created under this section shall inure to his or her heirs, legatees, or personal representative, until the 20th anniversary of the death of the artist. The provisions of this paragraph shall be applicable only with respect to an artist who dies after January 1, 1983.

(b) Subdivision (a) shall not apply to any of the following:

(1) To the initial sale of a work of fine art where legal title to such work at the time of such initial sale is vested in the artist thereof.

(2) To the resale of a work of fine art for a gross sales price of less than one thousand dollars ($1,000).

(3) Except as provided in paragraph (7) of subdivision (a), to a resale after the death of such artist.

(4) To the resale of the work of fine art for a gross sales price less than the purchase price paid by the seller.

(5) To a transfer of a work of fine art which is exchanged for one or more works of fine art or for a combination of cash, other property, and one or more works of fine art where the fair market value of the property exchanged is less than one thousand dollars ($1,000).

(6) To the resale of a work of fine art by an art dealer to a purchaser within 10 years of the initial sale of the work of fine art by the artist to an art dealer, provided all intervening resales are between art dealers.

(7) To a sale of a work of stained glass artistry where the work has been permanently attached to real property and is sold as part of the sale of the real property to which it is attached.

(c) For purposes of this section, the following terms have the following meanings:

(1) "Artist" means the person who creates a work of fine art and who, at the time of resale, is a citizen of the United States, or a resident of the state who has resided in the state for a minimum of two years.

(2) "Fine art" means an original painting, sculpture, or drawing, or an original work of art in glass.

(3) "Art dealer" means a person who is actively and principally engaged in or conducting the business of selling works of fine art for which business such person validly holds a sales tax permit.

(d) This section shall become operative on January 1, 1977, and shall apply to works of fine art created before and after its operative date.

(e) If any provision of this section or the application thereof to any person or circumstance is held invalid for any reason, such invalidity shall not affect any other provisions or applications of this section which can be effected, without the invalid provision or application, and to this end the provisions of this section are severable.

(f) The amendments to this section enacted during the 1981-82 Regular Session of the Legislature shall apply to transfers of works of fine art, when created before or after January 1, 1983, that occur on or after that date. **Leg.H.** Added Stats 1976 ch 1228 §1. Amended Stats 1982 ch 497 §7, ch 1601 §1, ch 1609 §1.5.

§987. Protection of fine art against alteration or destruction; Actions; Removal of work from property

(a) The Legislature hereby finds and declares that the physical alteration or destruction of fine art, which is an expression of the artist's personality, is detrimental to the artist's reputation, and artists therefore have an interest in protecting their works of fine art against any alteration or destruction; and that there is also a public interest in preserving the integrity of cultural and artistic creations.

(b) As used in this section:

(1) "Artist" means the individual or individuals who create a work of fine art.

(2) "Fine art" means an original painting, sculpture, or drawing, or an original work of art in glass, of recognized quality, but shall not include work prepared under contract for commercial use by its purchaser.

(3) "Person" means an individual, partnership, corporation, limited liability company, association or other group, however organized.

(4) "Frame" means to prepare, or cause to be prepared, a work of fine art for display in a manner customarily considered to be appropriate for a work of fine art in the particular medium.

(5) "Restore" means to return, or cause to be returned, a deteriorated or damaged work of fine art as nearly as is feasible to its original state or condition, in accordance with prevailing standards.

(6) "Conserve" means to preserve, or cause to be preserved, a work of fine art by retarding or preventing deterioration or damage through appropriate treatment in accordance with prevailing standards in order to maintain the structural integrity to the fullest extent possible in an unchanging state.

(7) "Commercial use" means fine art created under a work-for-hire arrangement for use in advertising, magazines, newspapers, or other print and electronic media.

(c)(1) No person, except an artist who owns and possesses a work of fine art which the artist has created, shall intentionally commit, or authorize the intentional commission of, any physical defacement, mutilation, alteration, or destruction of a work of fine art.

(2) In addition to the prohibitions contained in paragraph (1), no person who frames, conserves, or restores a work of fine art shall commit, or authorize the commission of, any physical defacement, mutilation, alteration, or destruction of a work of fine art by any act constituting gross negligence. For purposes of this section, the term "gross negligence" shall mean the exercise of so slight a degree of care as to justify the belief that there was an indifference to the particular work of fine art.

(d) The artist shall retain at all times the right to claim authorship, or, for a just and valid reason, to disclaim authorship of his or her work of fine art.

(e) To effectuate the rights created by this section, the artist may commence an action to recover or obtain any of the following:

(1) Injunctive relief.

(2) Actual damages.

(3) Punitive damages. In the event that punitive damages are awarded, the court shall, in its discretion, select an organization or organizations engaged in charitable or educational activities involving the fine arts in California to receive any punitive damages.

(4) Reasonable attorneys' and expert witness fees.

(5) Any other relief which the court deems proper.

(f) In determining whether a work of fine art is of recognized quality, the trier of fact shall rely on the opinions of artists, art dealers, collectors of fine art, curators of art museums, and other persons involved with the creation or marketing of fine art.

(g) The rights and duties created under this section:

(1) Shall, with respect to the artist, or if any artist is deceased, his or her heir, beneficiary, devisee, or personal representative, exist until the 50th anniversary of the death of the artist.

(2) Shall exist in addition to any other rights and duties which may now or in the future be applicable.

(3) Except as provided in paragraph (1) of subdivision (h), may not be waived except by an instrument in writing expressly so providing which is signed by the artist.

(h)(1) If a work of fine art cannot be removed from a building without substantial physical defacement, mutilation, alteration, or destruction of the work, the rights and duties created under this section, unless expressly reserved by an instrument in writing signed by the owner of the building, containing a legal description of the property and properly recorded, shall be deemed waived. The instrument, if properly recorded, shall be binding on subsequent owners of the building.

(2) If the owner of a building wishes to remove a work of fine art which is a part of the building but which can be removed from the building without substantial harm to the fine art, and in the course of or after removal, the owner intends to cause or allow the fine art to suffer physical defacement, mutilation, alteration, or destruction, the rights and duties created under this section shall apply unless the owner has diligently attempted without success to notify the artist, or, if the artist is deceased, his or her heir, beneficiary, devisee, or personal representative, in writing of his or her intended action affecting the work of fine art, or unless he or she did provide notice and that person failed within 90 days either to remove the work or to pay for its removal. If the work is removed at the expense of the artist, his or her heir, beneficiary, devisee, or personal representative, title to the fine art shall pass to that person.

(3) If a work of fine art can be removed from a building scheduled for demolition without substantial physical defacement, mutilation, alteration, or destruction of the work, and the owner of the building has notified the owner of the work of fine art of the scheduled demolition or the owner of the building is the owner of the work of fine art, and the owner of the work of fine art elects not to remove the work of fine art, the rights and duties created under this section shall apply, unless the owner of the building has diligently attempted without success to notify the artist, or, if the artist is deceased, his or her heir, beneficiary, devisee, or personal representative, in writing of the intended action affecting the work of fine art, or unless he or she did provide notice and that person failed within 90 days either to remove the work or to pay for its removal. If the work is removed at the expense of the artist, his or her heir, beneficiary, devisee, or personal representative, title to the fine art shall pass to that person.

(4) Nothing in this subdivision shall affect the rights of authorship created in subdivision (d) of this section.

(i) No action may be maintained to enforce any liability under this section unless brought within three years of the act complained of or one year after discovery of the act, whichever is longer.

(j) This section shall become operative on January 1, 1980, and shall apply to claims based on proscribed acts occurring on or after that date to works of fine art whenever created.

(k) If any provision of this section or the application thereof to any person or circumstance is held invalid for any reason, the invalidity shall not affect any other provisions or applications of this section which can be effected without the invalid provision or application, and to this end the provisions of this section are severable. **Leg.H.** Added Stats 1979 ch 409 §1. Amended Stats 1982 ch 1517 §1, ch 1609 §2.5; Stats 1989 ch 482 §1; Stats 1994 ch 1010 §30 (SB 2053).

1979 Note: This act shall be known and may be cited as "The California Art Preservation Act." Stats 1979 ch 409 §2.

§988. Residual rights

(a) For the purpose of this section:

(1) The term "artist" means the creator of a work of art.

(2) The term "work of art" means any work of visual or graphic art of any media including, but not limited to, a painting, print, drawing, sculpture, craft, photograph, or film.

(b) Whenever an exclusive or nonexclusive conveyance of any right to reproduce, prepare derivative works based on, distribute copies of, publicly perform, or publicly display a work of art is made by or on behalf of the artist who created it or the owner at the time of the conveyance, ownership of the physical work of art shall remain with and be reserved to the artist or owner, as the case may be, unless such right of ownership is expressly transferred by an instrument, note, memorandum, or other writing, signed by the artist, the owner, or their duly authorized agent.

(c) Whenever an exclusive or nonexclusive conveyance of any right to reproduce, prepare derivative works based on, distribute copies of, publicly perform, or publicly display a work of art is made by or on behalf of the artist who created it or the owner at the time of the conveyance, any ambiguity with respect to the nature or extent of the rights conveyed shall be resolved in favor of the reservation of rights by the artist or owner, unless in any given case the federal copyright law provides to the contrary. **Leg.H.** Added Stats 1982 ch 1319 §1.

§989. Preservation of integrity of cultural and artistic creations; Right of organization to commence action; Removal of art from property

(a) The Legislature hereby finds and declares that there is a public interest in preserving the integrity of cultural and artistic creations.

(b) As used in this section:

(1) "Fine art" means an original painting, sculpture, or drawing, or an original work of art in glass, of recognized quality, and of substantial public interest.

(2) "Organization" means a public or private not-for-profit entity or association, in existence at least three years at the time an action is filed pursuant to this section, a major purpose of which is to stage, display, or otherwise present works of art to the public or to promote the interests of the arts or artists.

(3) "Cost of removal" includes reasonable costs, if any, for the repair of damage to the real property caused by the removal of the work of fine art.

(c) An organization acting in the public interest may commence an action for injunctive relief to preserve or restore the integrity of a work of fine art from acts prohibited by subdivision (c) of Section 987.

(d) In determining whether a work of fine art is of recognized quality and of substantial public interest the trier of fact shall rely on the opinions of those described in subdivision (f) of Section 987.

(e)(1) If a work of fine art cannot be removed from real property without substantial physical defacement, mutilation, alteration, or destruction of such work, no action to preserve the integrity of the work of fine art may be brought under this section. However, if an organization offers some evidence giving rise to a reasonable likelihood that a work of art can be removed from the real property without substantial physical defacement, mutilation, alteration, or destruction of the work, and is prepared to pay the cost of removal of the work, it may bring a legal action for a determination of this issue. In that action the organization shall be entitled to injunctive relief to preserve the integrity of the work of fine art, but shall also have the burden of proof. The action shall commence within 30 days after filing. No action may be brought under this paragraph if the organization's interest in preserving the work of art is in conflict with an instrument described in paragraph (1) of subdivision (h) of Section 987.

(2) If the owner of the real property wishes to remove a work of fine art which is part of the real property, but which can be removed from the real property without substantial harm to such fine art, and in the course of or after removal, the owner intends to cause or allow the fine art to suffer physical defacement, mutilation, alteration, or destruction the owner shall do the following:

(A) If the artist or artist's heir, legatee, or personal representative fails to take action to remove the work of fine art after the notice provided by paragraph (2) of subdivision (h) of Section 987, the owner shall provide 30 days' notice of his or her intended action affecting the work of art. The written notice shall be a display advertisement in a newspaper of general circulation in the area where the fine art is located. The notice required by this paragraph may run concurrently with the notice required by subdivision (h) of Section 987.

(i) If within the 30-day period an organization agrees to remove the work of fine art and pay the cost of removal of the work, the payment and removal shall occur within 90 days of the first day of the 30-day notice.

(ii) If the work is removed at the expense of an organization, title to the fine art shall pass to that organization.

(B) If an organization does not agree to remove the work of fine art within the 30-day period or fails to remove and pay the cost of removal of the work of fine art within the 90-day period the owner may take the intended action affecting the work of fine art.

(f) To effectuate the rights created by this section, the court may do the following:

(1) Award reasonable attorney's and expert witness fees to the prevailing party, in an amount as determined by the court.

(2) Require the organization to post a bond in a reasonable amount as determined by the court.

(g) No action may be maintained under this section unless brought within three years of the act complained of or one year after discovery of such act, whichever is longer.

(h) This section shall become operative on January 1, 1983, and shall apply to claims based on acts occurring on or after that date to works of fine art, whenever created.

(i) If any provision of this section or the application thereof to any person or circumstances is held invalid, such invalidity shall not affect other provisions or applications of this section which can be given effect without the invalid provision or application, and to this end the provisions of this section are severable. **Leg.H.** Added Stats 1982 ch 1517 §4, operative January 1, 1983.

CHAPTER 4
OTHER KINDS OF PERSONAL PROPERTY

[Section renumbered 1999]. §990.
Title deeds. §994.
Furbearing wild animals in captivity. §996.
Porcelain painting; Stained glass artistry. §997.
Sale of electronic data processing equipment or telecommunications goods and services. §998.

§990. [Section renumbered 1999]
Leg.H. Added Stats 1984 ch 1704 §1. Amended Stats 1988 ch 113 §2, effective May 25, 1988, operative July 1, 1988. Renumbered to be CC §3344.1 by Stats 1999 ch 998 §1 (SB 209), ch 1000 §9.5 (SB 284).

§991. [Section repealed 1941]
Leg.H. Enacted Stats 1872. Amended Code Amdts 1873–74 ch 612 §127; Stats 1931 ch 103 §1. Repealed Stats 1941 ch 58 §3 (B & P C §30024). See B & P C §§14207, 14220.

§992. [Section repealed 1941]
Leg.H. Enacted Stats 1872. Repealed Stats 1941 ch 57 §2 (B & P C §30023). See B & P C §§14100, 14101.

§993. [Section repealed 1941]
Leg.H. Enacted Stats 1872. Amended Stats 1905 ch 442 §1. Repealed Stats 1941 ch 57 §2 (B & P C §30023). See B & P C §§14102, 14103.

§994. Title deeds
Instruments essential to the title of real property, and which are not kept in a public office as a record, pursuant to law, belong to the person in whom, for the time being, such title may be vested, and pass with the title. **Leg.H.** Enacted Stats 1872.

§995. [Section repealed 1943]
Leg.H. Added Stats 1907 ch 455 §1. Repealed Stats 1943 ch 129 §1 (B & P C §30022.1). The repealed section related to "tare" on baled hops.

§996. Furbearing wild animals in captivity
Whenever fur bearing animals, which are by their nature known as wild animals, have been brought into, or born in, restraint or captivity upon any farm or ranch for the purpose of cultivating or pelting their furs, such animals, together with their offspring or increase, shall be the subjects of ownership, lien, and all kinds of absolute and other property rights, the same as purely domestic animals, in whatever situation, location, or condition such fur bearing animals may thereafter come or be, and regardless of their remaining in or escaping from such restraint or captivity. Such fur bearing animals shall receive the same protection of law, and in the same way and to the same extent shall be the subject of trespass or larceny as other personal property and shall be considered and classified as domestic animals for the purpose of and within the meaning of any statute or law relating generally to domestic animals, other than dogs and cats or other pets, or relating to farming, to animal husbandry, or to the encouragement of agriculture, unless any such statute or law is impossible of application to such fur bearing animals. **Leg.H.** Added Stats 1941 ch 404 §1.

§997. Porcelain painting; Stained glass artistry
In this state, for any purpose, porcelain painting and stained glass artistry shall be considered a fine art and not a craft. **Leg.H.** Added Stats 1979 ch 202 §1. Amended Stats 1982 ch 1609 §3.

§998. Sale of electronic data processing equipment or telecommunications goods and services
Any private vendor of electronic data processing equipment or telecommunications goods and services may sell or lease equipment, goods, or services to a private school for the same price and on similar terms as the vendor sells or leases the equipment, goods, or services to a public school or school district. **Leg.H.** Added Stats 1988 ch 858 sec 1.

PART 4
ACQUISITION OF PROPERTY

Title 1. Modes in Which Property May Be Acquired.
Title 2. Occupancy.
Title 3. Accession.
Title 4. Transfer.
Title 8. Water Rights.

TITLE 1
MODES IN WHICH PROPERTY MAY BE ACQUIRED

Property, how acquired. §1000.
Easement to provide utility service. §1001.
Exercise of eminent domain by owner; Acquisition of right to enter; Conditions. §1002.

§1000. Property, how acquired

Property is acquired by:
1. Occupancy;
2. Accession;
3. Transfer;
4. Will; or,
5. Succession. **Leg.H.** Enacted Stats 1872.

§1001. Easement to provide utility service

(a) As used in this section, "utility service" means water, gas, electric, drainage, sewer, or telephone service.

(b) Any owner of real property may acquire by eminent domain an appurtenant easement to provide utility service to the owner's property.

(c) In lieu of the requirements of Section 1240.030 of the Code of Civil Procedure, the power of eminent domain may be exercised to acquire an appurtenant easement under this section only if all of the following are established:

(1) There is a great necessity for the taking.

(2) The location of the easement affords the most reasonable service to the property to which it is appurtenant, consistent with the least damage to the burdened property.

(3) The hardship to the owner of the appurtenant property, if the taking is not permitted, clearly outweighs any hardship to the owner of the burdened property. **Leg.H.** Added Stats 1976 ch 994 §1.

Prior Law: Former §1001, relating to acquisition of property exercise of eminent domain, was enacted Stats 1872 and repealed Stats 1975 ch 1240 §1, operative July 1, 1976, under the terms of Stats 1976 ch 22, as amended Stats 1976 ch 393.

§1002. Exercise of eminent domain by owner; Acquisition of right to enter; Conditions

(a) Subject to the provisions of Article 3 (commencing with Section 1245.310) of Chapter 4 of Title 7 of Part 3 of the Code of Civil Procedure, the power of eminent domain may be exercised by an owner of real property to acquire a temporary right to enter upon adjacent or nearby property to repair or reconstruct land or improvements, if all of the following conditions are established or met:

(1) There is a necessity to do the repair or reconstruction work and there is a great necessity to enter upon the adjacent or nearby property to do the repair or reconstruction work because (A) the repair or reconstruction work cannot be done safely without entry, or the cost of performing the repair or reconstruction work without entry would be substantially higher; and (B) the property without repair or reconstruction adversely affects the surrounding community.

(2) The right to enter upon the adjacent or nearby land will be exercised in a manner which provides the least damage to the property and the least inconvenience or annoyance to the occupants or owners thereof consistent with satisfactory completion of the repair or reconstruction work.

(3) The hardship to the person seeking to exercise the power of eminent domain, if that power is not exercised, clearly outweighs any hardship to the owner or occupant of the adjacent or nearby property.

(b) No entry shall be made upon the property to be condemned until an eminent domain proceeding has been commenced and then only after a court order permitting entry is issued or after judgment is entered for the plaintiff.

A deposit of security, in the form of cash or a bond, shall be made to the court in an amount the court determines is necessary to permit the owner of the adjacent or nearby property to restore the property to the condition it was in prior to the entry, if the person exercising the power of eminent domain does not do so within a reasonable period of time as determined by the court.

(c) The court may order the person acquiring the temporary right to enter the land of another, pursuant to this section, to pay the owner of the land subject to that temporary right a reasonable amount of rent for the use of the land.

(d) "Adjacent" or "nearby" for purposes of this section shall mean land contiguous with the property needing repair or reconstruction, or land through which the party granted temporary access must pass to reach adjacent land.

(e) The provisions of this section shall not apply to the temporary entry upon lands used primarily for the commercial production of agricultural commodities and forest products. **Leg.H.** Added Stats 1982 ch 1239 §1.

TITLE 2
OCCUPANCY

Title conferred by occupancy. §1006.
Title by prescription. §1007.
Posting of signs to preclude easement by prescription. §1008.
Public use of private lands; Dedication prerequisite to vested right; Offer to governmental entity; Vested right from governmental expenditure; Coastal property affected; Owners precluding evidence of implied dedication. §1009.

§1006. Title conferred by occupancy

Occupancy for any period confers a title sufficient against all except the state and those who have title by prescription, accession, transfer, will, or succession; but the title conferred by occupancy is not a sufficient interest in real property to enable the occupant or the occupant's privies to commence or maintain an action to quiet title, unless the occupancy has ripened into title by prescription. **Leg.H.** Enacted Stats 1872. Amended Stats 1915 ch 554 §1; Stats 1980 ch 44 §1.

§1007. Title by prescription

Occupancy for the period prescribed by the Code of Civil Procedure as sufficient to bar any action for the recovery of the property confers a title thereto, denominated a title by prescription, which is sufficient against all, but no possession by any person, firm or corporation no matter how long continued of any land, water, water right, easement, or other property whatsoever dedicated to a public use by a public utility, or dedicated to or owned by the state or any public entity, shall ever ripen into any title, interest or right against the owner thereof. **Leg.H.** Enacted Stats 1872. Amended Stats 1935 ch 519 §1; Stats 1968 ch 1112 §1.

§1008. Posting of signs to preclude easement by prescription

No use by any person or persons, no matter how long continued, of any land, shall ever ripen into an easement by prescription, if the owner of such property posts at each entrance to the property or at intervals of not more than 200 feet along the boundary a sign reading substantially as follows: "Right to pass by permission, and subject to control, of owner: Section 1008, Civil Code." **Leg.H.** Added Stats 1965 ch 926 §1.

§1009. Public use of private lands; Dedication prerequisite to vested right; Offer to governmental entity; Vested right from governmental expenditure; Coastal property affected; Owners precluding evidence of implied dedication

(a) The Legislature finds that:

(1) It is in the best interests of the state to encourage owners of private real property to continue to make their lands available for public recreational use to supplement opportunities available on tax-supported publicly owned facilities.

(2) Owners of private real property are confronted with the threat of loss of rights in their property if they allow or continue to allow members

of the public to use, enjoy or pass over their property for recreational purposes.

(3) The stability and marketability of record titles is clouded by such public use, thereby compelling the owner to exclude the public from his property.

(b) Regardless of whether or not a private owner of real property has recorded a notice of consent to use of any particular property pursuant to Section 813 of the Civil Code or has posted signs on such property pursuant to Section 1008 of the Civil Code, except as otherwise provided in subdivision (d), no use of such property by the public after the effective date of this section shall ever ripen to confer upon the public or any governmental body or unit a vested right to continue to make such use permanently, in the absence of an express written irrevocable offer of dedication of such property to such use, made by the owner thereof in the manner prescribed in subdivision (c) of this section, which has been accepted by the county, city, or other public body to which the offer of dedication was made, in the manner set forth in subdivision (c).

(c) In addition to any procedure authorized by law and not prohibited by this section, an irrevocable offer of dedication may be made in the manner prescribed in Section 7050 of the Government Code to any county, city, or other public body, and may be accepted or terminated, in the manner prescribed in that section, by the county board of supervisors in the case of an offer of dedication to a county, by the city council in the case of an offer of dedication to a city, or by the governing board of any other public body in the case of an offer of dedication to such body.

(d) Where a governmental entity is using private lands by an expenditure of public funds on visible improvements on or across such lands or on the cleaning or maintenance related to the public use of such lands in such a manner so that the owner knows or should know that the public is making such use of his land, such use, including any public use reasonably related to the purposes of such improvement, in the absence of either express permission by the owner to continue such use or the taking by the owner of reasonable steps to enjoin, remove or prohibit such use, shall after five years ripen to confer upon the governmental entity a vested right to continue such use.

(e) Subdivision (b) shall not apply to any coastal property which lies within 1,000 yards inland of the mean high tide line of the Pacific Ocean, and harbors, estuaries, bays and inlets thereof, but not including any property lying inland of the Carquinez Straits bridge, or between the mean high tide line and the nearest public road or highway, whichever distance is less.

(f) No use, subsequent to the effective date of this section, by the public of property described in subdivision (e) shall constitute evidence or be admissible as evidence that the public or any governmental body or unit has any right in such property by implied dedication if the owner does any of the following actions:

(1) Posts signs, as provided in Section 1008, and renews the same, if they are removed, at least once a year, or publishes annually, pursuant to Section 6066 of the Government Code, in a newspaper of general circulation in the county or counties in which the land is located, a statement describing the property and reading substantially as follows: "Right to pass by permission and subject to control of owner: Section 1008, Civil Code."

(2) Records a notice as provided in Section 813.

(3) Enters into a written agreement with any federal, state, or local agency providing for the public use of such land.

After taking any of the actions set forth in paragraph (1), (2), or (3), and during the time such action is effective, the owner shall not prevent any public use which is appropriate under the permission granted pursuant to such paragraphs by physical obstruction, notice, or otherwise.

(g) The permission for public use of real property referred to in subdivision (f) may be conditioned upon reasonable restrictions on the time, place, and manner of such public use, and no use in violation of such restrictions shall be considered public use for purposes of a finding of implied dedication. **Leg.H.** Added Stats 1971 ch 941 §2.

TITLE 3
ACCESSION

Chapter 1. Accession to Real Property.
Chapter 2. Accession to Personal Property.

CHAPTER 1
ACCESSION TO REAL PROPERTY

Fixtures. §1013.
Improvements affixed to land. §1013.5.
Alluvion. §1014.
Sudden removal of bank. §1015.
Islands, in navigable streams. §1016.
In unnavigable streams. §1017.
Islands formed by division of stream. §1018.
Removal of fixtures by tenant. §1019.

§1013. Fixtures

When a person affixes his property to the land of another, without an agreement permitting him to remove it, the thing affixed, except as otherwise provided in this chapter, belongs to the owner of the land, unless he chooses to require the former to remove it or the former elects to exercise the right of removal provided for in Section 1013.5 of this chapter. **Leg.H.** Enacted Stats 1872. Amended Code Amdts 1873–74 ch 612 §128; Stats 1953 ch 1175 §1.

§1013.5. Improvements affixed to land

(a) When any person, acting in good faith and erroneously believing because of a mistake either of law or fact that he has a right to do so, affixes improvements to the land of another, such person, or his successor in interest, shall have the right to remove such improvements upon payment, as their interests shall appear, to the owner of the land, and any other person having any interest therein who acquired such interest for value after the commencement of the work of improvement and in reliance thereon, of all their damages proximately resulting from the affixing and removal of such improvements.

(b) In any action brought to enforce such right the owner of the land and encumbrancers of record shall be named as defendants, a notice of pendency of action shall be recorded before trial, and the owner of the land shall recover his costs of suit and a reasonable attorney's fee to be fixed by the court.

(c) If it appears to the court that the total amount of damages cannot readily be ascertained prior to the removal of the improvements, or that it is otherwise in the interests of justice, the court may order an interlocutory judgment authorizing the removal of the improvements upon condition precedent that the plaintiff pay into court the estimated total damages, as found by the court or as stipulated.

(d) If the court finds that the holder of any lien upon the property acquired his lien in good faith and for value after the commencement of the work of improvement and in reliance thereon, or that as a result of the making or affixing of the improvements there is any lien against the property under Article XX, Section 15, of the Constitution of this State, judgment authorizing removal, final or interlocutory, shall not be given unless the holder of each such lien shall have consented to the removal of the improvements. Such consent shall be in writing and shall be filed with the court.

(e) The right created by this section is a right to remove improvements from land which may be exercised at the option of one who, acting in good faith and erroneously believing because of a mistake either of law or fact that he has a right to do so, affixes such improvements to the land of another. This section shall not be construed to affect or qualify the law as it existed prior to the 1953 amendment of this section with regard to the circumstances under which a court of equity will refuse to compel removal of an encroachment. **Leg.H.** Added Stats 1953 ch 1175 §2. Amended Stats 1955 ch 73 §1.

§1014. Alluvion

Where, from natural causes, land forms by imperceptible degrees upon the bank of a river or stream, navigable or not navigable, either by accumulation of material or by the recession of the stream, such land belongs to the owner of the bank, subject to any existing right of way over the bank. **Leg.H.** Enacted Stats 1872.

§1015. Sudden removal of bank

If a river or stream, navigable or not navigable, carries away, by sudden violence, a considerable and distinguishable part of a bank, and bears it to the opposite bank, or to another part of the same bank, the owner of the part carried away may reclaim it within a year after the owner of the land to which it has been united takes possession thereof. **Leg.H.** Enacted Stats 1872.

§1016. Islands, in navigable streams
Islands and accumulations of land, formed in the beds of streams which are navigable, belong to the State, if there is no title or prescription to the contrary. **Leg.H.** Enacted Stats 1872.

§1017. In unnavigable streams
An island, or an accumulation of land, formed in a stream which is not navigable, belongs to the owner of the shore on that side where the island or accumulation is formed; or, if not formed on one side only, to the owners of the shore on the two sides, divided by an imaginary line drawn through the middle of the river. **Leg.H.** Enacted Stats 1872.

§1018. Islands formed by division of stream
If a stream, navigable or not navigable, in forming itself a new arm, divides itself and surrounds land belonging to the owner of the shore, and thereby forms an island, the island belongs to such owner. **Leg.H.** Enacted Stats 1872.

§1019. Removal of fixtures by tenant
A tenant may remove from the demised premises, any time during the continuance of his term, anything affixed thereto for purposes of trade, manufacture, ornament, or domestic use, if the removal can be effected without injury to the premises, unless the thing has, by the manner in which it is affixed, become an integral part of the premises. **Leg.H.** Added Code Amdts 1873–74 ch 612 §129.

Prior Law: Former §1019, relating to abandoned bed of stream, was enacted Stats 1872 and repealed Code Amdts 1873–74 ch 612 §129 p 224.

CHAPTER 2
ACCESSION TO PERSONAL PROPERTY

Accession by uniting several things. §1025.
Principal part, what. §1026.
Same. §1027.
Uniting materials and workmanship. §1028.
Inseparable materials. §1029.
Materials of several owners. §1030.
Willful trespassers. §1031.
Owner may elect between the thing and its value. §1032.
Wrongdoer liable in damages. §1033.

§1025. Accession by uniting several things
When things belonging to different owners have been united so as to form a single thing, and cannot be separated without injury, the whole belongs to the owner of the thing which forms the principal part; who must, however, reimburse the value of the residue to the other owner, or surrender the whole to him. **Leg.H.** Enacted Stats 1872.

§1026. Principal part, what
That part is to be deemed the principal to which the other has been united only for the use, ornament, or completion of the former, unless the latter is the more valuable, and has been united without the knowledge of its owner, who may, in the latter case, require it to be separated and returned to him, although some injury should result to the thing to which it has been united. **Leg.H.** Enacted Stats 1872.

§1027. Same
If neither part can be considered the principal, within the rule prescribed by the last section, the more valuable, or, if the values are nearly equal, the more considerable in bulk, is to be deemed the principal part. **Leg.H.** Enacted Stats 1872.

§1028. Uniting materials and workmanship
If one makes a thing from materials belonging to another, the latter may claim the thing on reimbursing the value of the workmanship, unless the value of the workmanship exceeds the value of the materials, in which case the thing belongs to the maker, on reimbursing the value of the materials. **Leg.H.** Enacted Stats 1872.

§1029. Inseparable materials
Where one has made use of materials which in part belong to him and in part to another, in order to form a thing of a new description, without having destroyed any of the materials, but in such a way that they cannot be separated without inconvenience, the thing formed is common to both proprietors; in proportion, as respects the one, of the materials belonging to him, and as respects the other, of the materials belonging to him and the price of his workmanship. **Leg.H.** Enacted Stats 1872.

§1030. Materials of several owners
When a thing has been formed by the admixture of several materials of different owners, and neither can be considered the principal substance, an owner without whose consent the admixture was made may require a separation, if the materials can be separated without inconvenience. If they cannot be thus separated, the owners acquire the thing in common, in proportion to the quantity, quality, and value of their materials; but if the materials of one were far superior to those of the others, both in quantity and value, he may claim the thing on reimbursing to the others the value of their materials. **Leg.H.** Enacted Stats 1872.

§1031. Willful trespassers
The foregoing sections of this Article are not applicable to cases in which one willfully uses the materials of another without his consent; but, in such cases, the product belongs to the owner of the material, if its identity can be traced. **Leg.H.** Enacted Stats 1872.

§1032. Owner may elect between the thing and its value
In all cases where one whose material has been used without his knowledge, in order to form a product of a different description, can claim an interest in such product, he has an option to demand either restitution of his material in kind, in the same quantity, weight, measure, and quality, or the value thereof; or where he is entitled to the product, the value thereof in place of the product. **Leg.H.** Enacted Stats 1872.

§1033. Wrongdoer liable in damages
One who wrongfully employs materials belonging to another is liable to him in damages, as well as under the foregoing provisions of this Chapter. **Leg.H.** Enacted Stats 1872.

TITLE 4
TRANSFER

Chapter 1. Transfers in General.
Chapter 2. Transfer of Real Property.
Chapter 3. Transfer of Personal Property.
Chapter 4. Recording Transfers.
Chapter 5. Unlawful Transfers.

CHAPTER 1
TRANSFERS IN GENERAL

Article 1. Definition of Transfer.
Article 2. What May Be Transferred.
Article 3. Mode of Transfer.
Article 4. Interpretation of Grants.
Article 5. Effect of Transfer.
Article 6. Agency Listings for the Transfer of Certain Property.
Article 7. Unlawful Influence of Appraisers.

ARTICLE 1
Definition of Transfer

"Transfer" defined. §1039.
Voluntary transfer. §1040.

§1039. "Transfer" defined
Transfer is an act of the parties, or of the law, by which the title to property is conveyed from one living person to another. **Leg.H.** Enacted Stats 1872.

§1040. Voluntary transfer
A voluntary transfer is an executed contract, subject to all rules of law concerning contracts in general; except that a consideration is not necessary to its validity. **Leg.H.** Enacted Stats 1872.

ARTICLE 2
What May Be Transferred

What may be transferred. §1044.
Possibility. §1045.
Right of re-entry can be transferred. §1046.
Owner ousted of possession may transfer. §1047.

§1044. What may be transferred
Property of any kind may be transferred, except as otherwise provided by this article. **Leg.H.** Enacted Stats 1872.

§1045. Possibility
A mere possibility, not coupled with an interest, cannot be transferred. **Leg.H.** Enacted Stats 1872.

§1046. Right of re-entry can be transferred
A right of re-entry, or of repossession for breach of condition subsequent, can be transferred. **Leg.H.** Enacted Stats 1872.

§1047. Owner ousted of possession may transfer
Any person claiming title to real property in the adverse possession of another may transfer it with the same effect as if in actual possession. **Leg.H.** Enacted Stats 1872.

ARTICLE 3
Mode of Transfer

Oral transfer. §1052.
Transfer in writing; "Grant". §1053.
Delivery necessary. §1054.
Delivery date. §1055.
Delivery to grantee is necessarily absolute. §1056.
Delivery in escrow. §1057.
Return of escrow funds. §1057.3.
Referral fee prohibited; Contingent fee. §1057.5.
Notice to be provided to buyer or parties exchanging property when title insurance will not be issued. §1057.6.
Required statement for all written escrow instructions. §1057.7.
Surrendering or canceling grant does not reconvey. §1058.
Notice of nonacceptance of recorded deed; Notice of rescission of trustee's deed. §1058.5.
Constructive delivery. §1059.

§1052. Oral transfer
A transfer may be made without writing, in every case in which a writing is not expressly required by statute. **Leg.H.** Enacted Stats 1872.

§1053. Transfer in writing; "Grant"
A transfer in writing is called a grant, or conveyance, or bill of sale. The term "grant," in this and the next two articles, includes all these instruments, unless it is specially applied to real property. **Leg.H.** Enacted Stats 1872. Amended Code Amdts 1873–74 ch 612 §130.

§1054. Delivery necessary
A grant takes effect, so as to vest the interest intended to be transferred, only upon its delivery by the grantor. **Leg.H.** Enacted Stats 1872.

§1055. Delivery date
A grant duly executed is presumed to have been delivered at its date. **Leg.H.** Enacted Stats 1872.

§1056. Delivery to grantee is necessarily absolute
A grant cannot be delivered to the grantee conditionally. Delivery to him, or to his agent as such, is necessarily absolute, and the instrument takes effect thereupon, discharged of any condition on which the delivery was made. **Leg.H.** Enacted Stats 1872.

§1057. Delivery in escrow
A grant may be deposited by the grantor with a third person, to be delivered on performance of a condition, and, on delivery by the depositary, it will take effect. While in the possession of the third person, and subject to condition, it is called an escrow. **Leg.H.** Enacted Stats 1872.

§1057.3. Return of escrow funds
(a) It shall be the obligation of a buyer and seller who enter into a contract to purchase and sell real property to ensure that all funds deposited into an escrow account are returned to the person who deposited the funds or who is otherwise entitled to the funds under the contract, if the purchase of the property is not completed by the date set forth in the contract for the close of escrow or any duly executed extension thereof.

(b) Any buyer or seller who fails to execute any document required by the escrow holder to release funds on deposit in an escrow account as provided in subdivision (a) within 30 days following a written demand for the return of funds deposited in escrow by the other party shall be liable to the person making the deposit for all of the following:

(1) The amount of the funds deposited in escrow not held in good faith to resolve a good faith dispute.

(2) Damages of treble the amount of the funds deposited in escrow not held to resolve a good faith dispute, but liability under this paragraph shall not be less than one hundred dollars ($100) or more than one thousand dollars ($1,000).

(3) Reasonable attorney's fees incurred in any action to enforce this section.

(c) Notwithstanding subdivision (b), there shall be no cause of action under this section, and no party to a contract to purchase and sell real property shall be liable, for failure to return funds deposited in an escrow account by a buyer or seller, if the funds are withheld in order to resolve a good faith dispute between a buyer and seller. A party who is denied the return of the funds deposited in escrow is entitled to damages under this section only upon proving that there was no good faith dispute as to the right to the funds on deposit.

(d) Upon the filing of a cause of action pursuant to this section, the escrow holder shall deposit the sum in dispute, less any cancellation fee and charges incurred, with the court in which the action is filed and be discharged of further responsibility for the funds.

(e) Neither any document required by the escrow holder to release funds deposited in an escrow account nor the acceptance of funds released from escrow, by any principal to the escrow transaction, shall be deemed a cancellation or termination of the underlying contract to purchase and sell real property, unless the cancellation is specifically stated therein. If the escrow instructions constitute the only contract between the buyer and seller, no document required by the escrow holder to release funds deposited in an escrow account shall abrogate a cause of action for breach of a contractual obligation to purchase or sell real property unless the cancellation is specifically stated therein.

(f) For purposes of this section:

(1) "Close of escrow" means the date, specified event, or performance of prescribed condition upon which the escrow agent is to deliver the subject of the escrow to the person specified in the buyer's instructions to the escrow agent.

(2) "Good faith dispute" means a dispute in which the trier of fact finds that the party refusing to return the deposited funds had a reasonable belief of his or her legal entitlement to withhold the deposited funds. The existence of a "good faith dispute" shall be determined by the trier of fact.

(3) "Property" means real property containing one to four residential units at least one of which at the time the escrow is created is to be occupied by the buyer. The buyer's statement as to his or her intention to occupy one of the units is conclusive for the purposes of this section.

(g) Nothing in this section restricts the ability of an escrow holder to file an interpleader action in the event of a dispute as to the proper distribution of funds deposited in an escrow account. **Leg.H.** Added Stats 1990 ch 13 §1 (AB 546).

§1057.5. Referral fee prohibited; Contingent fee
Except for the normal compensation of his own employees, no person acting as an escrow agent whether required to be licensed as such or not, shall pay over to any other person any commission, fee, or other consideration as compensation for referring, soliciting, handling, or servicing escrow customers or accounts.

No escrow agent shall enter into any arrangement, either of his own making or of a subsidiary nature, or through any other person having a dual capacity, or through any person having a direct or indirect interest in the escrow, or other device, permitting any fee, commission, or compensation which is contingent upon the performance of any act, condition, or instruction set forth in an escrow, to be drawn or paid, either in whole or in part, or in kind or its equivalent, prior to the actual closing and completion of the escrow.

The provisions of this section shall not be deemed to supersede, negate, or modify any of the provisions of Section 12404 of the Insurance Code. **Leg.H.** Added Stats 1967 ch 678 §1.

§1057.6. Notice to be provided to buyer or parties exchanging property when title insurance will not be issued
In an escrow transaction for the purchase or simultaneous exchange of real property, where a policy of title insurance will not be issued to the buyer or to the parties to the exchange, the following notice shall be provided in a separate document to the buyer or parties exchanging real property, which shall be signed and acknowledged by them:

"IMPORTANT: IN A PURCHASE OR EXCHANGE OF REAL PROPERTY, IT MAY BE ADVISABLE TO OBTAIN TITLE INSURANCE IN CONNECTION WITH THE CLOSE OF ESCROW SINCE THERE MAY BE PRIOR RECORDED LIENS AND ENCUMBRANCES WHICH AFFECT YOUR INTEREST IN THE PROPERTY BEING ACQUIRED. A NEW POLICY OF TITLE INSURANCE SHOULD BE OBTAINED IN ORDER TO ENSURE YOUR INTEREST

IN THE PROPERTY THAT YOU ARE ACQUIRING." **Leg.H.** Added Stats 1992 ch 194 §1 (SB 1738).

§1057.7. Required statement for all written escrow instructions

All written escrow instructions executed by a buyer or seller, whether prepared by a person subject to Division 6 (commencing with Section 17000) of the Financial Code, or by a person exempt from that division under Section 17006 of the Financial Code, shall contain a statement in not less than 10-point type which shall include the license name and the name of the department issuing the license or authority under which the person is operating. This section shall not apply to supplemental escrow instructions or modifications to escrow instructions.

This section shall become operative on July 1, 1993. **Leg.H.** Added Stats 1992 ch 861 §2 AB 2583, operative July 1, 1993.

§1058. Surrendering or canceling grant does not reconvey

Redelivering a grant of real property to the grantor, or canceling it, does not operate to retransfer the title. **Leg.H.** Enacted Stats 1872.

§1058.5. Notice of nonacceptance of recorded deed; Notice of rescission of trustee's deed

(a) A notice of nonacceptance of a recorded deed executed by a holder of a security interest, which notice identifies the security interest, contains a legal description of the property, properly identifies the parties to the deed, the date of recordation of the deed, the county in which the project is located, and the county assessor's parcel number of the real property referenced in the deed, may be recorded in the office of the county recorder where the real property is located.

(b) Where a trustee's deed is invalidated by a pending bankruptcy or otherwise, recordation of a notice of rescission of the trustee's deed, which notice properly identifies the deed of trust, the identification numbers used by the recorder or the books and pages at which the trustee's deed and deed of trust are recorded, the names of all trustors and beneficiaries, the location of the property subject to the deed of trust, and the reason for rescission, shall restore the condition of record title to the real property described in the trustee's deed and the existence and priority of all lienholders to the status quo prior to the recordation of the trustee's deed upon sale. Only the trustee or beneficiary who caused the trustee's deed to be recorded, or his or her successor in interest, may record a notice of rescission. **Leg.H.** Added Stats 1993 ch 724 §1 (AB 1196). Amended Stats 1997 ch 74 §1 (SB 665).

§1059. Constructive delivery

Though a grant be not actually delivered into the possession of the grantee, it is yet to be deemed constructively delivered in the following cases:

1. Where the instrument is, by the agreement of the parties at the time of execution, understood to be delivered, and under such circumstances that the grantee is entitled to immediate delivery; or,

2. Where it is delivered to a stranger for the benefit of the grantee, and his assent is shown, or may be presumed. **Leg.H.** Enacted Stats 1872.

§1060. [Section repealed 1969]

Leg.H. Added Stats 1945 ch 318 §1, effective May 12, 1945. Repealed Stats 1969 ch 155 §2, operative July 1, 1970. The repealed section related to release of power.

Prior Law: Former §1060, providing that gratuitous grants take effect immediately, was enacted Stats 1872 and repealed by Code Amdts 1873-1874 ch 612 §131 p 225.

ARTICLE 4
Interpretation of Grants

Grants, how interpreted. §1066.
Limitations, how controlled. §1067.
Recitals, when resorted to. §1068.
Interpretation against grantor. §1069.
Irreconcilable provisions. §1070.
Words of inheritance unnecessary. §1072.

§1066. Grants, how interpreted

Grants are to be interpreted in like manner with contracts in general, except so far as is otherwise provided in this article. **Leg.H.** Enacted Stats 1872.

§1067. Limitations, how controlled

A clear and distinct limitation in a grant is not controlled by other words less clear and distinct. **Leg.H.** Enacted Stats 1872.

§1068. Recitals, when resorted to

If the operative words of a grant are doubtful, recourse may be had to its recitals to assist the construction. **Leg.H.** Enacted Stats 1872.

§1069. Interpretation against grantor

A grant is to be interpreted in favor of the grantee, except that a reservation in any grant, and every grant by a public officer or body, as such, to a private party, is to be interpreted in favor of the grantor. **Leg.H.** Enacted Stats 1872.

§1070. Irreconcilable provisions

If several parts of a grant are absolutely irreconcilable, the former part prevails. **Leg.H.** Enacted Stats 1872.

§1071. [Section repealed 2002]

Leg.H. Enacted Stats 1872. Repealed Stats 2002 ch 138 §1 (AB 1784). The repealed section related to the meaning of "heirs" and "issue" in certain remainders.

§1072. Words of inheritance unnecessary

Words of inheritance or succession are not requisite to transfer a fee in real property. **Leg.H.** Enacted Stats 1872.

§1073. [Section repealed 2002]

Leg.H. Added Stats 1959 ch 122 §1. Repealed Stats 2002 ch 138 §2 (AB 1784). The repealed section related to the granting of a legal or equitable interest to a grantor's own heirs or next of kin.

ARTICLE 5
Effect of Transfer

Incidents. §1084.
Grant may inure to benefit of stranger. §1085.

§1083. [Section repealed 1931]

Leg.H. Enacted Stats 1872. Repealed Stats 1931 ch 1070 §2. The repealed section related to vesting of transfers.

§1084. Incidents

The transfer of a thing transfers also all its incidents, unless expressly excepted; but the transfer of an incident to a thing does not transfer the thing itself. **Leg.H.** Enacted Stats 1872.

§1085. Grant may inure to benefit of stranger

A present interest, and the benefit of a condition or covenant respecting property, may be taken by any natural person under a grant, although not named a party thereto. **Leg.H.** Enacted Stats 1872.

ARTICLE 6
Agency Listings for the Transfer of Certain Property

Definitions. §1086.
Multiple listing services. §1087.
Authorization for listing; Responsibility for truth of statements in listing. §1088.
Applicability of Section 1102.1(d) to article. §1089.
Application of article. §1089.5.

§1086. Definitions

(a) For purposes of this article, the definitions contained in Chapter 1 (commencing with Section 10000) of Part 1 of Division 4 of the Business and Professions Code apply.

(b) An "agent" is one authorized by law to act in that capacity for that type of property and is licensed as a real estate broker under Chapter 3 (commencing with Section 10130) of Part 1 of Division 4 of the Business and Professions Code, or is a licensee, as defined in Section 18006 of the Health and Safety Code **Leg.H.** Added Stats 1982 ch 547 §1. Amended Stats 1988 ch 113 §3, effective May 25, 1988, operative July 1, 1988; Stats 1993 ch 331 §3 (SB 914); Stats 2018 ch 907 §1 (AB 1289), effective January 1, 2019.

§1087. Multiple listing services

A multiple listing service (MLS) is a facility of cooperation of agents and appraisers, operating through an intermediary that does not itself act as an agent or appraiser, through which agents establish express or implied contracts for compensation between agents that are MLS participants in accordance with its MLS rules with respect to listed properties in a listing agreement, or that may be used by agents and appraisers, pursuant to the rules of the service, to prepare market evaluations and appraisals of real property. **Leg.H.** Added Stats 1982 ch 547 §1. Amended Stats 1993 ch

331 §4 (SB 914); Stats 2018 ch 907 §2 (AB 1289), effective January 1, 2019.

§1088. Authorization for listing; Responsibility for truth of statements in listing

(a) A listing may not be placed in a multiple listing service unless authorized or directed by the seller in the listing.

(b) If an agent or appraiser places a listing or other information in the multiple listing service, that agent or appraiser shall be responsible for the truth of all representations and statements made by the agent or appraiser of which that agent or appraiser had knowledge or reasonably should have had knowledge to anyone injured by their falseness or inaccuracy.

(c) A multiple listing service shall retain and make accessible on its computer system, if any, all listing and other information placed in the multiple listing service by an agent or appraiser for no less than three years from the date the listing was placed in the multiple listing service.

(d) This section shall not alter the obligations of a licensed real estate broker to retain documents as specified in subdivision (a) of Section 10148 of the Business and Professions Code. **Leg.H.** Added Stats 1982 ch 547 §1. Amended Stats 1993 ch 331 §5 (SB 914); Stats 2018 ch 907 §3 (AB 1289), effective January 1, 2019; Stats 2019 ch 310 §1 (AB 892), effective January 1, 2020.

§1089. Applicability of Section 1102.1(d) to article

The provisions of subdivision (d) of Section 1102.1 shall apply to this article. **Leg.H.** Added Stats 2018 ch 907 §5 (AB 1289), effective January 1, 2019.

Prior Law Former CC §1089, relating to agreements for payment of compensation to listing agent, was added Stats 1982 ch 547 §1 and repealed Stats 2018 ch 907 §4 (AB 1289), effective January 1, 2019.

Former Sections: Former CC §1089, relating to agreements for payment of compensation to listing agent, was added Stats 1982 ch 547 §1 and repealed Stats 2018 ch 907 §4 (AB 1289).

§1089.5. Application of article

Subject to the limitations, conditions, and requirements of Chapter 18 (commencing with Section 10000) of Part 5 of Division 7 of the Probate Code, this article applies to property defined in Section 1086 that is covered by a contract described in Section 10150 of the Probate Code. **Leg.H.** Added Stats 1988 ch 113 sec 4, effective May 25, 1988, operative July 1, 1988.

§1090. Listing agent not precluded from being selling agent [Repealed]

Leg.H. Added Stats 1982 ch 547 §1. Repealed Stats 2018 ch 907 §6 (AB 1289), effective January 1, 2019.

ARTICLE 7
Unlawful Influence of Appraisers

Improper attempt to influence the development, reporting, result, or review of a real estate valuation; Prohibited acts; Construction. §1090.5.

§1090.5. Improper attempt to influence the development, reporting, result, or review of a real estate valuation; Prohibited acts; Construction

(a) No person with an interest in a real estate transaction involving a valuation shall improperly influence or attempt to improperly influence the development, reporting, result, or review of that valuation, through coercion, extortion, bribery, intimidation, compensation, or instruction. For purposes of this section, a valuation is defined as an estimate of the value of real property in written or electronic form, other than one produced solely by an automated valuation model or system. Prohibited acts include, but are not limited to, the following:

(1) Seeking to influence a person who prepares a valuation to report a minimum or maximum value for the property being valued. Such influence may include, but is not limited to:

(A) Requesting that a person provide a preliminary estimate or opinion of value prior to entering into a contract with that person for valuation services.

(B) Conditioning whether to hire a person based on an expectation of the value conclusion likely to be returned by that person.

(C) Conditioning the amount of a person's compensation on the value conclusion returned by that person.

(D) Providing to a person an anticipated, estimated, encouraged, or desired valuation prior to their completion of a valuation.

(2) Withholding or threatening to withhold timely payment to a person or entity that prepares a valuation, or provides valuation management functions, because that person or entity does not return a value at or above a certain amount.

(3) Implying to a person who prepares a valuation that current or future retention of that person depends on the amount at which the person estimates the value of real property.

(4) Excluding a person who prepares a valuation from consideration for future engagement because the person reports a value that does not meet or exceed a predetermined threshold.

(5) Conditioning the compensation paid to a person who prepares a valuation on consummation of the real estate transaction for which the valuation is prepared.

(6) Requesting the payment of compensation to achieve higher priority in the assignment of valuation business.

(b) Subdivision (a) does not prohibit a person with an interest in a real estate transaction from doing any of the following:

(1) Asking a person who performs a valuation to do any of the following:

(A) Consider additional, appropriate property information, including information about comparable properties.

(B) Provide further detail, substantiation, or explanation for the person's value conclusion.

(C) Correct errors in a valuation report.

(2) Obtaining multiple valuations, for purposes of selecting the most reliable valuation.

(3) Withholding compensation due to breach of contract or substandard performance of services.

(4) Providing a copy of the sales contract in connection with a purchase transaction.

(c) If a person who violates this section is licensed or registered under any state licensing or registration law and the violation occurs within the course and scope of the person's duties as a licensee or registrant, the violation shall be deemed a violation of that law.

(d) Nothing in this section shall be construed to authorize communications that are otherwise prohibited under existing law. **Leg.H.** Added Stats 2007 ch 291 §2 (SB 223), effective October 5, 2007. Amended Stats 2009 ch 173 §21 (SB 237), effective January 1, 2010; Stats 2011 ch 716 §5 (SB 6), effective January 1, 2012.

CHAPTER 2
TRANSFER OF REAL PROPERTY

Article 1. Mode of Transfer.
Article 1.4. Installation of Water Use Efficiency Improvements.
Article 1.5. Disclosures Upon Transfer of Residential Property.
Article 1.7. Disclosure of Natural and Environmental Hazards, Right-to-Farm, and Other Disclosures Upon Transfer of Residential Property.
Article 1.8. Buyer's Choice Act.
Article 2. Effect of Transfer.

ARTICLE 1
Mode of Transfer

Requisites for transfer of certain estates. §1091.
Form of grant. §1092.
Consolidation of separate real property descriptions into subsequent single instrument. §1093.
Attorney in fact, how must execute for principal. §1095.
Change in name of titleholder; Effect of failure to comply with statute. §1096.
Maximum fee on transfer in exercising option to purchase single family residence. §1097.
Transfer fee defined. §1098.
Recording transfer fees prior to, and subsequent to, January 1, 2008; Recorder's responsibilities. §1098.5.
Prohibition against creation of transfer fee on or after January 1, 2019; Excepted transfer fee covenants. §1098.6.
Structural pest control inspection report prior to transfer of title or execution of sales contract. §1099.

§1091. Requisites for transfer of certain estates

An estate in real property, other than an estate at will or for a term not exceeding one year, can be transferred only by operation of law, or by an instrument in writing, subscribed by the party disposing of the same, or by his agent thereunto authorized by writing. **Leg.H.** Enacted Stats 1872.

§1092. Form of grant

A grant of an estate in real property may be made in substance as follows:

"I, A B, grant to C D all that real property situated in (insert name of county) County, State of California, bounded (or described) as follows: (here insert property description, or if the land sought to be conveyed has a descriptive name, it may be described by the name, as for instance, 'The Norris Ranch.')

Witness my hand this (insert day) day of (insert month), 20_____.
            A B"

Leg.H. Enacted Stats 1872. Amended Stats 1999 ch 608 §4 (AB 1342).

§1093. Consolidation of separate real property descriptions into subsequent single instrument

Absent the express written statement of the grantor contained therein, the consolidation of separate and distinct legal descriptions of real property contained in one or more deeds, mortgages, patents, deeds of trust, contracts of sale, or other instruments of conveyance or security documents, into a subsequent single deed, mortgage, patent, deed of trust, contract of sale, or other instrument of conveyance or security document (whether by means of an individual listing of the legal descriptions in a subsequent single instrument of conveyance or security document, or by means of a consolidated legal description comprised of more than one previously separate and distinct legal description), does not operate in any manner to alter or affect the separate and distinct nature of the real property so described in the subsequent single instrument of conveyance or security document containing either the listing of or the consolidated legal description of the parcels so conveyed or secured thereby.

This section does not constitute a change in, but is declaratory of, the existing law. **Leg.H.** Added Stats 1985 ch 911 §1.

Prior Law: Former §1093, relating to acknowledgment of grant by married woman, was enacted Stats 1872, amended by Stats 1895 ch 53 §1, and repealed by Stats 1976 ch 1171 §2.

§1094. [Section repealed 1976]

Leg.H. Enacted Stats 1872. Amended Stats 1895 ch 35 §1. Repealed Stats 1976 ch 1171 §3.

§1095. Attorney in fact, how must execute for principal

When an attorney in fact executes an instrument transferring an estate in real property, he must subscribe the name of his principal to it, and his own name as attorney in fact. **Leg.H.** Enacted Stats 1872.

§1096. Change in name of titleholder; Effect of failure to comply with statute

Any person in whom the title of real estate is vested, who shall afterwards, from any cause, have his or her name changed, must, in any conveyance of said real estate so held, set forth the name in which he or she derived title to said real estate. Any conveyance, though recorded as provided by law, which does not comply with the foregoing provision shall not impart constructive notice of the contents thereof to subsequent purchasers and encumbrancers, but such conveyance is valid as between the parties thereto and those who have notice thereof. **Leg.H.** Added Stats 1905 ch 443 §1. Amended Stats 1947 ch 1314 §1.

§1097. Maximum fee on transfer in exercising option to purchase single family residence

No vendor or lessor of a single family residential property shall contract for or exact any fee in excess of ten dollars ($10) for the act of signing and delivering a document in connection with the transfer, cancellation or reconveyance of any title or instrument at the time the buyer or lessee exercises an option to buy, or completes performance of the contract for the sale of, the property.

The provisions of this section shall apply prospectively only. **Leg.H.** Added Stats 1965 ch 352 §1.

§1098. Transfer fee defined

(a) A "transfer fee" is any fee payment requirement imposed within a covenant, restriction, or condition contained in any deed, contract, security instrument, or other document affecting the transfer or sale of, or any interest in, real property that requires a fee be paid as a result of transfer of the real property. A transfer fee does not include any of the following:

(1) Fees or taxes imposed by a governmental entity.

(2) Fees pursuant to mechanics' liens.

(3) Fees pursuant to court-ordered transfers, payments, or judgments.

(4) Fees pursuant to property agreements in connection with a legal separation or dissolution of marriage.

(5) Fees, charges, or payments in connection with the administration of estates or trusts pursuant to Division 7 (commencing with Section 7000), Division 8 (commencing with Section 13000), or Division 9 (commencing with Section 15000) of the Probate Code.

(6) Fees, charges, or payments imposed by lenders or purchasers of loans, as these entities are described in subdivision (c) of Section 10232 of the Business and Professions Code.

(7) Assessments, charges, penalties, or fees authorized by the Davis-Stirling Common Interest Development Act (Part 5 (commencing with Section 4000) of Division 4) or by the Commercial and Industrial Common Interest Development Act (Part 5.3 (commencing with Section 6500) of Division 4).

(8) Fees, charges, or payments for failing to comply with, or for transferring the real property prior to satisfying, an obligation to construct residential improvements on the real property.

(9)(A) Any fee reflected in a document recorded against the property on or before December 31, 2007, that is separate from any covenants, conditions, and restrictions, and that substantially complies with subdivision (a) of Section 1098.5 by providing a prospective transferee notice of the following:

(i) Payment of a transfer fee is required.

(ii) The amount or method of calculation of the fee.

(iii) The date or circumstances under which the transfer fee payment requirement expires, if any.

(iv) The entity to which the fee will be paid.

(v) The general purposes for which the fee will be used.

(B) A fee reflected in a document recorded against the property on or before December 31, 2007, that is not separate from any covenants, conditions, and restrictions, or that incorporates by reference from another document, is a "transfer fee" for purposes of Section 1098.5. A transfer fee recorded against the property on or before December 31, 2007, that complies with subparagraph (A) and incorporates by reference from another document is unenforceable unless recorded against the property on or before December 31, 2016, in a single document that complies with subdivision (b) and with Section 1098.5.

(b) The information in paragraph (9) of subdivision (a) shall be set forth in a single document and shall not be incorporated by reference from any other document. **Leg.H.** Added Stats 2007 ch 689 §1 (AB 980), effective January 1, 2008. Amended Stats 2012 ch 181 §32 (AB 806), effective January 1, 2013, operative January 1, 2014; Stats 2013 ch 605 §14 (SB 752), effective January 1, 2014; Stats 2015 ch 634 §1 (AB 807), effective January 1, 2016.

2015 Note: The Legislature finds and declares that the addition of subdivision (b) to Section 1098 of, and the amendments to Sections 1098.5 and 1102.6e of, the Civil Code made by this act are clarifying and declaratory of existing law. Stats 2015 ch 634 (AB 807) §4.

§1098.5. Recording transfer fees prior to, and subsequent to, January 1, 2008; Recorder's responsibilities

(a) For transfer fees, as defined in Section 1098, imposed prior to January 1, 2008, the receiver of the fee, as a condition of payment of the fee on or after January 1, 2009, shall record, on or before December 31, 2008, against the real property in the office of the county recorder for the county in which the real property is located a separate document that meets all of the following requirements:

(1) The title of the document shall be "Payment of Transfer Fee Required" in at least 14-point boldface type.

(2) The document shall include all of the following information:

(A) The names of all current owners of the real property subject to the transfer fee, and the legal description and assessor's parcel number for the affected real property.

(B) The amount, if the fee is a flat amount, or the percentage of the sales price constituting the cost of the fee.

(C) If the real property is residential property, actual dollar-cost examples of the fee for a home priced at two hundred fifty thousand dollars ($250,000), five hundred thousand dollars ($500,000), and seven hundred fifty thousand dollars ($750,000).

(D) The date or circumstances under which the transfer fee payment requirement expires, if any.

(E) The purpose for which the funds from the fee will be used.

(F) The entity to which funds from the fee will be paid and specific contact information regarding where the funds are to be sent.

(G) The signature of the authorized representative of the entity to which funds from the fee will be paid.

(b) When a transfer fee, as defined in Section 1098, is imposed upon real property on or after January 1, 2008, the person or entity imposing the transfer fee, as a condition of payment of the fee, shall record in the office of the county recorder for the county in which the real property is located, concurrently with the instrument creating the transfer fee requirement, a separate document that meets all of the following requirements:

(1) The title of the document shall be "Payment of Transfer Fee Required" in at least 14-point boldface type.

(2) The document shall include all of the following information:

(A) The names of all current owners of the real property subject to the transfer fee, and the legal description and assessor's parcel number for the affected real property.

(B) The amount, if the fee is a flat amount, the percentage of the sales price constituting the cost of the fee, or the method for calculating the amount.

(C) If the real property is residential property and the amount of the fee is based on the price of the real property, actual dollar-cost examples of the fee for a home priced at two hundred fifty thousand dollars ($250,000), five hundred thousand dollars ($500,000), and seven hundred fifty thousand dollars ($750,000).

(D) The date or circumstances under which the transfer fee payment requirement expires, if any.

(E) The purpose for which the funds from the fee will be used.

(F) The entity to which funds from the fee will be paid and specific contact information regarding where the funds are to be sent.

(G) The signature of the authorized representative of the entity to which funds from the fee will be paid.

(H) For private transfer fees created on or after February 8, 2011, unless the exception in Section 1228.3 of Title 12 of the Code of Federal Regulations applies, the following notice in at least 14-point boldface type:

The Federal Housing Finance Agency and the Federal Housing Administration are prohibited from dealing in mortgages on properties encumbered by private transfer fee covenants that do not provide a "direct benefit" to the real property encumbered by the covenant. As a result, if you purchase such a property, you or individuals you want to sell the property to may have difficulty obtaining financing.

(c) The recorder shall only be responsible for examining that the document required by subdivision (a) or (b) contains the information required by subparagraphs (A), (F), and (G) of paragraph (2) of subdivision (a) or (b). The recorder shall index the document under the names of the persons and entities identified in subparagraphs (A) and (F) of paragraph (2) of subdivision (a) or (b). The recorder shall not examine any other information contained in the document required by subdivision (a) or (b). **Leg.H.** Added Stats 2007 ch 689 §2 (AB 980), effective January 1, 2008. Amended Stats 2015 ch 634 §2 (AB 807), effective January 1, 2016; Stats 2017 ch 148 §1 (AB 1139), effective January 1, 2018.

2015 Note: The Legislature finds and declares that the addition of subdivision (b) to Section 1098 of, and the amendments to Sections 1098.5 and 1102.6e of, the Civil Code made by this act are clarifying and declaratory of existing law. Stats 2015 ch 634 (AB 807) §4.

§1098.6. Prohibition against creation of transfer fee on or after January 1, 2019; Excepted transfer fee covenants

(a)(1) On or after January 1, 2019, a transfer fee shall not be created.

(2) This subdivision does not apply to excepted transfer fee covenants as defined by Section 1228.1 of Title 12 of the Code of Federal Regulations. Excepted transfer fee covenants are not required to comply with subparagraph (H) of paragraph (2) of subdivision (b) of Section 1098.5.

(3) This subdivision does not apply to a private transfer fee covenant if all of the following requirements are met:

(A) The covenant is created pursuant to an agreement entered into before June 1, 2009.

(B) The covenant is applicable to land that is identified in the agreement.

(C) The agreement was in settlement of litigation or approved by a government agency or body.

(D) The agreement was recorded in each county in which the land identified in the agreement is located.

(E) The agreement specifies the development area in which the covenant shall apply to any covered parcel to be created within that development area.

(F) The covenant complies with the requirements of Section 1098.5, except that the requirement of subparagraph (H) of paragraph (2) of subdivision (b) of Section 1098.5 does not apply.

(b) Any transfer fee created in violation of subdivision (a) is void as against public policy.

(c) For purposes of this section, "transfer fee" has the same meaning as that term is defined in Section 1098. **Leg.H.** Added Stats 2018 ch 306 §1 (AB 3041), effective January 1, 2019. Amended Stats 2024 ch 475 §1 (SB 1399), effective January 1, 2025.

§1099. Structural pest control inspection report prior to transfer of title or execution of sales contract

(a) As soon as practical before transfer of title of any real property or the execution of a real property sales contract as defined in Section 2985, the transferor, fee owner, or his or her agent, shall deliver to the transferee a copy of a structural pest control inspection report prepared pursuant to Section 8516 of the Business and Professions Code upon which any certification in accordance with Section 8519 of the Business and Professions Code may be made, provided that certification or preparation of a report is a condition of the contract effecting that transfer, or is a requirement imposed as a condition of financing such transfer.

(b) If a notice of work completed as contemplated by Section 8518 of the Business and Professions Code, indicating action by a structural pest control licensee in response to an inspection report delivered or to be delivered under provisions of subdivision (a), or a certification pursuant to Section 8519 of the Business and Professions Code, has been received by a transferor or his or her agent before transfer of title or execution of a real property sales contract as defined in Section 2985, it shall be furnished to the transferee as soon as practical before transfer of title or the execution of such real property sales contract.

(c) Delivery to a transferee as used in this section means delivery in person or by mail to the transferee himself or herself or any person authorized to act for him or her in the transaction or to such additional transferees who have requested such delivery from the transferor or his or her agent in writing. For the purposes of this section, delivery to either spouse shall be deemed delivery to a transferee, unless the contract affecting the transfer states otherwise.

(d) No transfer of title of real property shall be invalidated solely because of the failure of any person to comply with the provisions of this section unless such failure is an act or omission which would be a valid ground for rescission of such transfer in the absence of this section. **Leg.H.** Added Stats 1974 ch 649 §2, operative July 1, 1975. Amended Stats 2016 ch 50 §10 (SB 1005), effective January 1, 2017.

2016 Note: For legislative intent, see the 2016 Note following §14.

ARTICLE 1.4
Installation of Water Use Efficiency Improvements

Legislative findings and declarations. §1101.1.
Applicability of article. §1101.2.
Definitions. §1101.3.
Single-family residential real property; Compliance. §1101.4.
Water-conserving plumbing fixtures; Replacement of noncompliant plumbing fixtures. §1101.5.
Requirements of article postponed with respect to building for which demolition permit has been issued. §1101.6.
Applicability of article. §1101.7.
Enactment of local ordinances; Establishment of policies. §1101.8.
City, county, or city and county exempted from requirements of article; Conditions. §1101.9.

§1101.1. Legislative findings and declarations

The Legislature finds and declares all of the following:

(a) Adequate water supply reliability for all uses is essential to the future economic and environmental health of California.

(b) Environmentally sound strategies to meet future water supply and wastewater treatment needs are key to protecting and restoring aquatic resources in California.

(c) There is a pressing need to address water supply reliability issues raised by growing urban areas.

(d) Economic analysis by urban water agencies has identified urban water conservation as a cost-effective approach to addressing water supply needs.

(e) There are many water conservation practices that produce significant energy and other resource savings that should be encouraged as a matter of state policy.

(f) Since the 1991 signing of the "Memorandum of Understanding Regarding Urban Water Conservation in California," many urban water and wastewater treatment agencies have gained valuable experience that can be applied to produce significant statewide savings of water, energy, and associated infrastructure costs. This experience indicates a need to regularly revise and update water conservation methodologies and practices.

(g) To address these concerns, it is the intent of the Legislature to require that residential and commercial real property built and available for use or occupancy on or before January 1, 1994, be equipped with water-conserving plumbing fixtures.

(h) It is further the intent of the Legislature that retail water suppliers are encouraged to provide incentives, financing mechanisms, and funding to assist property owners with these retrofit obligations. **Leg.H.** Added Stats 2009 ch 587 §1 (SB 407), effective January 1, 2010.

§1101.2. Applicability of article

Except as provided in Section 1101.7, this article shall apply to residential and commercial real property built and available for use on or before January 1, 1994. **Leg.H.** Added Stats 2009 ch 587 §1 (SB 407), effective January 1, 2010.

§1101.3. Definitions

For the purposes of this article:

(a) "Commercial real property" means any real property that is improved with, or consisting of, a building that is intended for commercial use, including hotels and motels, that is not a single-family residential real property or a multifamily residential real property.

(b) "Multifamily residential real property" means any real property that is improved with, or consisting of, a building containing more than one unit that is intended for human habitation, or any mixed residential-commercial buildings or portions thereof that are intended for human habitation. Multifamily residential real property includes residential hotels but does not include hotels and motels that are not residential hotels.

(c) "Noncompliant plumbing fixture" means any of the following:

(1) Any toilet manufactured to use more than 1.6 gallons of water per flush.

(2) Any urinal manufactured to use more than one gallon of water per flush.

(3) Any showerhead manufactured to have a flow capacity of more than 2.5 gallons of water per minute.

(4) Any interior faucet that emits more than 2.2 gallons of water per minute.

(d) "Single-family residential real property" means any real property that is improved with, or consisting of, a building containing not more than one unit that is intended for human habitation.

(e) "Water-conserving plumbing fixture" means any fixture that is in compliance with current building standards applicable to a newly constructed real property of the same type.

(f) "Sale or transfer" means the sale or transfer of an entire real property estate or the fee interest in that real property estate and does not include the sale or transfer of a partial interest, including a leasehold. **Leg.H.** Added Stats 2009 ch 587 §1 (SB 407), effective January 1, 2010.

§1101.4. Single-family residential real property; Compliance

(a) For all building alterations or improvements to single-family residential real property, as a condition for issuance of a certificate of final completion and occupancy or final permit approval by the local building department, the permit applicant shall replace all noncompliant plumbing fixtures with water-conserving plumbing fixtures.

(b) On or before January 1, 2017, noncompliant plumbing fixtures in any single-family residential real property shall be replaced by the property owner with water-conserving plumbing fixtures.

(c) A seller or transferor of single-family residential real property shall disclose in writing to the prospective purchaser or transferee the requirements of subdivision (b) and whether the real property includes any noncompliant plumbing fixtures. **Leg.H.** Added Stats 2009 ch 587 §1 (SB 407), effective January 1, 2010. Amended Stats 2019 ch 310 §2 (AB 892), effective January 1, 2020.

§1101.5. Water-conserving plumbing fixtures; Replacement of noncompliant plumbing fixtures

(a) On or before January 1, 2019, all noncompliant plumbing fixtures in any multifamily residential real property and in any commercial real property shall be replaced with water-conserving plumbing fixtures.

(b) An owner or the owner's agent may enter the owner's property for the purpose of installing, repairing, testing, and maintaining water-conserving plumbing fixtures required by this section, consistent with notice requirements of Section 1954.

(c) On and after January 1, 2019, the water-conserving plumbing fixtures required by this section shall be operating at the manufacturer's rated water consumption at the time that the tenant takes possession. A tenant shall be responsible for notifying the owner or owner's agent if the tenant becomes aware that a water-conserving plumbing fixture within his or her unit is not operating at the manufacturer's rated water consumption. The owner or owner's agent shall correct an inoperability in a water-conserving plumbing fixture upon notice by the tenant or if detected by the owner or the owner's agent.

(d)(1) On and after January 1, 2014, all noncompliant plumbing fixtures in any multifamily residential real property and any commercial real property shall be replaced with water-conserving plumbing fixtures in the following circumstances:

(A) For building additions in which the sum of concurrent building permits by the same permit applicant would increase the floor area of the space in a building by more than 10 percent, the building permit applicant shall replace all noncompliant plumbing fixtures in the building.

(B) For building alterations or improvements in which the total construction cost estimated in the building permit is greater than one hundred fifty thousand dollars ($150,000), the building permit applicant shall replace all noncompliant plumbing fixtures that service the specific area of the improvement.

(C) Notwithstanding subparagraph (A) or (B), for any alterations or improvements to a room in a building that require a building permit and that room contains any noncompliant plumbing fixtures, the building permit applicant shall replace all noncompliant plumbing fixtures in that room.

(2) Replacement of all noncompliant plumbing fixtures with water-conserving plumbing fixtures, as described in paragraph (1), shall be a condition for issuance of a certificate of final completion and occupancy or final permit approval by the local building department.

(e) On and after January 1, 2019, a seller or transferor of multifamily residential real property or of commercial real property shall disclose to the prospective purchaser or transferee, in writing, the requirements of subdivision (a) and whether the property includes any noncompliant plumbing fixtures. This disclosure may be included in other transactional documents. **Leg.H.** Added Stats 2009 ch 587 §1 (SB 407), effective January 1, 2010. Amended Stats 2013 ch 183 §1 (SB 745), effective January 1, 2014.

§1101.6. Requirements of article postponed with respect to building for which demolition permit has been issued

The duty of an owner or building permit applicant to comply with the requirements of this article shall be postponed for one year from the date of issuance of a demolition permit for the building. If the building is demolished within the one-year postponement, the requirements of this article shall not apply. If the building is not demolished after the expiration of one year, the provisions of this article shall apply, subject to appeal to the local building department, even though the demolition permit is still in effect or a new demolition permit has been issued. **Leg.H.** Added Stats 2009 ch 587 §1 (SB 407), effective January 1, 2010.

§1101.7. Applicability of article

This article shall not apply to any of the following:

(a) Registered historical sites.

(b) Real property for which a licensed plumber certifies that, due to the age or configuration of the property or its plumbing, installation of water-conserving plumbing fixtures is not technically feasible.

(c) A building for which water service is permanently disconnected. **Leg.H.** Added Stats 2009 ch 587 §1 (SB 407), effective January 1, 2010.

§1101.8. Enactment of local ordinances; Establishment of policies

A city, county, or city and county, or a retail water supplier may do either of the following:

(a) Enact local ordinances or establish policies that promote compliance with this article.

(b) Enact local ordinances or establish policies that will result in a greater amount of water savings than those provided for in this article. **Leg.H.** Added Stats 2009 ch 587 §1 (SB 407), effective January 1, 2010.

§1101.9. City, county, or city and county exempted from requirements of article; Conditions

Any city, county, or city and county that has adopted an ordinance requiring retrofit of noncompliant plumbing fixtures prior to July 1, 2009, shall be exempt from the requirements of this article so long as the ordinance remains in effect. **Leg.H.** Added Stats 2009 ch 587 §1 (SB 407), effective January 1, 2010.

ARTICLE 1.5
Disclosures Upon Transfer of Residential Property

Transactions to which article applies; Waiver void as against public policy. §1102.
Legislative intent regarding use of disclosure statement. §1102.1.
Transactions to which article does not apply. §1102.2.
Delivery of disclosure statement by seller of single-family real property. §1102.3.
Delivery of disclosure statement by transferor of manufactured home or mobilehome; Effect of delivery of specified disclosure after execution of purchase offer. §1102.3a.
Liability for errors or omissions. §1102.4.
Information rendered inaccurate due to subsequent events; Use of approximations; Article applicability to contract or agreement. §1102.5.
Form of disclosure statement. §1102.6.
Additional disclosures; Disclosure form; Proximity to airport. §1102.6a.
Disclosure notice requirements; Substantially equivalent and modified notices. §1102.6b.
Disclosure notice of supplemental property tax bills. §1102.6c.
Manufactured home and mobilehome transfer disclosure statement. §1102.6d.
Additional disclosure statement for property transferred on or after January 1, 2008. §1102.6e.
Disclosure notice by seller to buyer of real property in high or very high fire hazard severity zone; Statement contents. §1102.6f.
Required sales contract notice provision regarding unbiased appraisal and complaint process; Loan refinance and mortgage disclosure statement. § 1102.6g.
Additional disclosures. § 1102.6h.
Disclosure; Limited electrical capacity. § 1102.6i.
Gas-powered appliances. § 1102.6j.
Disclosures to be made in good faith; "Good faith". §1102.7.
Effect of article on other required disclosures. §1102.8.
Amendment of disclosure statement. §1102.9.
Means of delivering statement. §1102.10.
Escrow agents. §1102.11.
Broker's duties. §1102.12.
Failure to comply with article; Liability for damages. §1102.13.
Disclosure of former ordnance locations within neighborhood area. §1102.15.
Disclosures relating to water-conserving plumbing fixtures. §1102.155.
Required disclosure of domestic water storage tank assistance. § 1102.156.
Disclosure relating to window security bars. §1102.16.
Notice that property is adjacent to, zoned to allow, or affected by nuisance created by industrial use. §1102.17.
Applicability of Section 1102.1(d) to article. §1102.18.
Documentation to buyer of compliance with Public Resources Code Section 4291 or local ordinances for property in high or very high fire hazard severity zone. §1102.19.

§1102. Transactions to which article applies; Waiver void as against public policy

(a) Except as provided in Section 1102.2, this article applies to any transfer by sale, exchange, real property sales contract as defined in Section 2985, lease with an option to purchase, any other option to purchase, or ground lease coupled with improvements of any single-family residential property.

(b) For purposes of this article, the definitions contained in Chapter 1 (commencing with Section 10000) of Part 1 of Division 4 of the Business and Professions Code shall apply.

(c) Any waiver of the requirements of this article is void as against public policy. **Leg.H.** Added Stats 1985 ch 1574 §2, operative January 1, 1987. Amended Stats 1986 ch 460 §1; Stats 1994 ch 817 §1 (SB 1377); Stats 1995 ch 335 §1 (AB 530); Stats 1996 ch 677 §1 (SB 1704); Stats 1997 ch 71 §1 (SB 384), effective July 14, 1997; Stats 1998 ch 693 §1 (SB 1988); Stats 1999 ch 517 §2 (SB 534); Stats 2018 ch 907 §7 (AB 1289), effective January 1, 2019; Stats 2019 ch 310 §3 (AB 892), effective January 1, 2020.

§1102.1. Legislative intent regarding use of disclosure statement

(a) In enacting Chapter 817 of the Statutes of 1994, it was the intent of the Legislature to clarify and facilitate the use of the real estate disclosure statement, as specified in Section 1102.6. The Legislature intended the statement to be used by transferors making disclosures required under this article and by agents making disclosures required by Section 2079 on the agent's portion of the real estate disclosure statement, in transfers subject to this article. In transfers not subject to this article, agents may make required disclosures in a separate writing. The Legislature did not intend to affect the existing obligations of the parties to a real estate contract, or their agents, to disclose any fact materially affecting the value and desirability of the property, including, but not limited to, the physical conditions of the property and previously received reports of physical inspections noted on the disclosure form set forth in Section 1102.6 or 1102.6a, and that nothing in this article shall be construed to change the duty of a real estate broker or salesperson pursuant to Section 2079.

It is also the intent of the Legislature that the delivery of a real estate transfer disclosure statement may not be waived in an "as is" sale, as held in Loughrin v. Superior Court (1993) 15 Cal. App. 4th 1188.

(b) In enacting Chapter 677 of the Statutes of 1996, it was the intent of the Legislature to clarify and facilitate the use of the manufactured home and mobilehome transfer disclosure statement applicable to the resale of a manufactured home or mobilehome pursuant to subdivision (b) of Section 1102. The Legislature intended the statements to be used by transferors making disclosures required under this article and by agents making disclosures required by Section 2079 on the agent's portion of the disclosure statement and as required by Section 18046 of the Health and Safety Code on the dealer's portion of the manufactured home and mobilehome transfer disclosure statement, in transfers subject to this article. In transfers not subject to this article, agents may make required disclosures in a separate writing. The Legislature did not intend to affect the existing obligations of the parties to a real estate contract, or their agents, to disclose any fact materially affecting the value and desirability of the property, including, but not limited to, the physical conditions of the property and previously received reports of physical inspections noted on the disclosure form set forth in Section 1102.6 or 1102.6a or to affect the existing obligations of the parties to a manufactured home or mobilehome purchase contract, and nothing in this article shall be construed to change the duty of a real estate broker or salesperson pursuant to Section 2079 or the duty of a manufactured home or mobilehome dealer or salesperson pursuant to Section 18046 of the Health and Safety Code.

It is also the intent of the Legislature that the delivery of a mobilehome transfer disclosure statement may not be waived in an "as is" sale.

(c) It is the intent of the Legislature that manufactured home and mobilehome dealers and salespersons and real estate brokers and salespersons use the form provided pursuant to Section 1102.6d. It is also the intent of the Legislature for sellers of manufactured homes or mobilehomes who are neither manufactured home dealers or salespersons nor real estate brokers or salespersons to use the Manufactured Home/Mobilehome Transfer Disclosure Statement contained in Section 1102.6d.

(d) Nothing in Assembly Bill 1289 of the 2017–18 Regular Session or Assembly Bill 2884 of the 2017–18 Regular Session shall be construed to affect any of the following:

(1) A real estate broker's duties under existing statutory or common law as an agent of a person who retains that broker to perform acts for which a license is required under this division.

(2) Any fiduciary duties owed by a real estate broker to a person who retains that broker to perform acts for which a license is required under this division.

(3) Any duty of disclosure or any other duties or obligations of a real estate broker, which arise under this division or other existing, applicable California law, including common law.

(4) Any duties or obligations of a salesperson or a broker associate, which arise under this division or existing, applicable California law, including common law, and duties and obligations to the salesperson's or broker associate's responsible broker.

(5) A responsible broker's duty of supervision and oversight for the acts of retained salespersons or broker associates, which arise under this division or other existing, applicable California law, including common law.

For purposes of this subdivision, references to "existing statutory law" and "existing, applicable California law" refer to the law as it read immediately prior to enactment of Assembly Bill 1289 of the 2017–18 Regular Session and Assembly Bill 2884 of the 2017–18 Regular Session. **Leg.H.** Added Stats 1995 ch 335 §2 (AB 530). Amended Stats 1996 ch 240 §1 (AB 2383); Stats 1999 ch 517 §3 (SB 534); Stats 2018 ch 907 §8 (AB 1289), effective January 1, 2019.

Prior Law: Former §1102.1 was added Stats 1985 ch 1574 §2, operative January 1, 1987, amended Stats 1986 ch 460 §2, Stats 1992 ch 163 §7, operative January 1, 1994, and renumbered to be CC §1102.2 by Stats 1995 ch 335 §3.

§1102.2. Transactions to which article does not apply

This article does not apply to the following:

(a) Sales or transfers that are required to be preceded by the furnishing to a prospective buyer of a copy of a public report pursuant to Section 11018.1 of the Business and Professions Code and transfers that can be made without a public report pursuant to Section 11010.4 of the Business and Professions Code.

(b) Sales or transfers pursuant to court order, including, but not limited to, sales ordered by a probate court in the administration of an estate, sales pursuant to a writ of execution, sales by any foreclosure sale, transfers by a trustee in bankruptcy, sales by eminent domain, and sales resulting from a decree for specific performance.

(c) Sales or transfers to a mortgagee by a mortgagor or successor in interest who is in default, sales to a beneficiary of a deed of trust by a trustor or successor in interest who is in default, any foreclosure sale after default, any foreclosure sale after default in an obligation secured by a mortgage, a sale under a power of sale or any foreclosure sale under a decree of foreclosure after default in an obligation secured by a deed of trust or secured by any other instrument containing a power of sale, sales by a mortgagee or a beneficiary under a deed of trust who has acquired the real property at a sale conducted pursuant to a power of sale under a mortgage or deed of trust or a sale pursuant to a decree of foreclosure or has acquired the real property by a deed in lieu of foreclosure, sales to the legal owner or lienholder of a manufactured home or mobilehome by a registered owner or successor in interest who is in default, or sales by reason of any foreclosure of a security interest in a manufactured home or mobilehome.

(d) Sales or transfers by a fiduciary in the course of the administration of a trust, guardianship, conservatorship, or decedent's estate. This exemption shall not apply to a sale if the trustee is a natural person who is a trustee of a revocable trust and is a former owner of the property or was an occupant in possession of the property within the preceding year.

(e) Sales or transfers from one coowner to one or more other coowners.

(f) Sales or transfers made to a spouse, or to a person or persons in the line of consanguinity of one or more of the transferors.

(g) Sales or transfers between spouses resulting from a judgment of dissolution of marriage or of legal separation or from a property settlement agreement incidental to that judgment.

(h) Sales or transfers by the Controller in the course of administering Chapter 7 (commencing with Section 1500) of Title 10 of Part 3 of the Code of Civil Procedure.

(i) Sales or transfers under Chapter 7 (commencing with Section 3691) or Chapter 8 (commencing with Section 3771) of Part 6 of Division 1 of the Revenue and Taxation Code.

(j) Sales or transfers or exchanges to or from any governmental entity.

(k) Sales or transfers of any portion of a property not constituting single-family residential property.

(l) The sale, creation, or transfer of any lease of any duration with the exception of a lease with an option to purchase or a ground lease coupled with improvements.

(m) Notwithstanding the definition of sale in Section 10018.10 of the Business and Professions Code and Section 2079.13, the terms "sale" and "transfer," as they are used in this section, shall have their commonly understood meanings. The changes made to this section by Assembly Bill 1289 of the 2017–18 Legislative Session shall not be interpreted to change the application of the law as it read prior to January 1, 2019. **Leg.H.** Added Stats 1985 ch 1574 §2, operative January 1, 1987, as §1102.1. Amended Stats 1986 ch 460 §2; Stats 1992 ch 163 §7 (AB 2641), operative January 1, 1994. Renumbered by Stats 1995 ch 335 §3 (AB 530). Amended Stats 1999 ch 119 §1 (AB 594), ch 517 §4.5 (SB 534); Stats 2000 ch 135 §11 (AB 2539); Stats 2018 ch 907 §9 (AB 1289), effective January 1, 2019; Stats 2019 ch 310 §4 (AB 892), effective January 1, 2020; Stats 2019 ch 497 §20 (AB 991), effective January 1, 2020 (ch 310 prevails; ch 497 not effective); Stats 2020 ch 370 §24 (SB 1371), effective January 1, 2021.

Prior Law: Former §1102.2 was added Stats 1985 ch 1574 §2, operative January 1, 1987, amended Stats 1986 ch 460 §3, and renumbered to be CC §1102.3 by Stats 1995 ch 335 §4.

§1102.3. Delivery of disclosure statement by seller of single-family real property

The seller of any single-family real property subject to this article shall deliver to the prospective buyer the completed written statement required by this article, as follows:

(a) In the case of a sale, as soon as practicable before transfer of title.

(b) In the case of sale by a real property sales contract, as defined in Section 2985, or by a lease together with an option to purchase, or a ground lease coupled with improvements, as soon as practicable before execution of the contract. For the purpose of this subdivision, "execution" means the making or acceptance of an offer.

(c) With respect to any sale subject to subdivision (a) or (b), the seller shall indicate compliance with this article on the real property sales contract, the lease, or any addendum attached thereto or on a separate document.

If any disclosure, or any material amendment of any disclosure, required to be made by this article, is delivered after the execution of an offer to purchase, the prospective buyer shall have three days after delivery in person, five days after delivery by deposit in the mail, or five days after delivery of an electronic record in transactions where the parties have agreed to conduct the transaction by electronic means, pursuant to provisions of the Uniform Electronic Transactions Act (Title 2.5 (commencing with Section 1633.1) of Part 2 of Division 3), to terminate the offer by delivery of a written notice of termination to the seller or the seller's agent. The period of time the prospective buyer has in which to terminate the offer commences when Sections I and II, and, if the seller is represented by an agent in the transaction, then also Section III, in the form described in Section 1102.6, are completed and delivered to the buyer or buyer's agent. A real estate agent may complete their own portion of the required disclosure by providing all of the information on the agent's inspection disclosure set forth in Section 1102.6. **Leg.H.** Added Stats 1985 ch 1574 §2, operative January 1, 1987, as §1102.2. Amended Stats 1986 ch 460 §3. Renumbered by Stats 1995 ch 335 §4 (AB 530). Amended Stats 2018 ch 907 §10 (AB 1289), effective January 1, 2019; Stats 2019 ch 310 §5 (AB 892), effective January 1, 2020; Stats 2019 ch 497 §21 (AB 991), effective January 1, 2020 (ch 310 prevails; ch 497 not effective).

§1102.3a. Delivery of disclosure statement by transferor of manufactured home or mobilehome; Effect of delivery of specified disclosure after execution of purchase offer

(a) The transferor of any manufactured home or mobilehome subject to this article shall deliver to the prospective transferee the written statement required by this article, as follows:

(1) In the case of a sale, or a lease with an option to purchase, of a manufactured home or mobilehome, involving an agent, as defined in Section 18046 of the Health and Safety Code, as soon as practicable, but no later than the close of escrow for the purchase of the manufactured home or mobilehome.

(2) In the case of a sale, or lease with an option to purchase, of a manufactured home or mobilehome, not involving an agent, as defined in Section 18046 of the Health and Safety Code, at the time of execution of any document by the prospective transferee with the transferor for the purchase of the manufactured home or mobilehome.

(b) With respect to any transfer subject to this section, the transferor shall indicate compliance with this article either on the transfer disclosure statement, any addendum thereto, or on a separate document.

(c) If any disclosure, or any material amendment of any disclosure, required to be made pursuant to subdivision (b) of Section 1102, is delivered after the execution of an offer to purchase, the transferee shall have three days after delivery in person or five days after delivery by deposit in the mail, to terminate his or her offer by delivery of a written notice of termination to the transferor. **Leg.H.** Added Stats 1999 ch 517 §5 (SB 534).

§1102.4. Liability for errors or omissions

(a) Neither the seller nor any seller's agent or buyer's agent shall be liable for any error, inaccuracy, or omission of any information delivered pursuant to this article if the error, inaccuracy, or omission was not within the personal knowledge of the seller or that listing or buyer's agent, was based on information timely provided by public agencies or by other persons providing information as specified in subdivision (c) that is required to be disclosed pursuant to this article, and ordinary care was exercised in obtaining and transmitting it.

(b) The delivery of any information required to be disclosed by this article to a prospective buyer by a public agency or other person providing information required to be disclosed pursuant to this article shall be deemed to comply with the requirements of this article and shall relieve the seller or any listing or buyer's agent of any further duty under this article with respect to that item of information.

(c) The delivery of a report or opinion prepared by a licensed engineer, land surveyor, geologist, structural pest control operator, contractor, a C-39 roofing contractor conducting a roof inspection pursuant to subdivision (d) of Section 7197 of the Business and Professions Code, or other expert, dealing with matters within the scope of the professional's license or expertise, shall be sufficient compliance for application of the exemption provided by subdivision (a) if the information is provided to the prospective buyer pursuant to a request therefor, whether written or oral. In responding to such a request, an expert may indicate, in writing, an understanding that the information provided will be used in fulfilling the requirements of Section 1102.6 and, if so, shall indicate the required disclosures, or parts thereof, to which the information being furnished is applicable. Where such a statement is furnished, the expert shall not be responsible for any items of information or parts thereof, other than those expressly set forth in the statement. **Leg.H.** Added Stats 1985 ch 1574 §2, operative January 1, 1987. Amended Stats 1986 ch 460 §4; Stats 2017 ch 508 §2 (AB 1357), effective January 1, 2018; Stats 2018 ch 907 §11 (AB 1289), effective January 1, 2019.

§1102.5. Information rendered inaccurate due to subsequent events; Use of approximations; Article applicability to contract or agreement

(a) If information disclosed in accordance with this article is subsequently rendered inaccurate as a result of any act, occurrence, or agreement subsequent to the delivery of the required disclosures, any inaccuracy resulting therefrom does not constitute a violation of this article. If at the time the disclosures are required to be made, an item of information required to be disclosed is unknown or not available to the seller, and the seller or the seller's agent has made a reasonable effort to ascertain it, the seller may use an approximation of the information, provided the approximation is clearly identified as such, is reasonable, is based on the best information reasonably available to the seller or the seller's agent, and is not used for the purpose of circumventing or evading this article.

(b) The requirements of this article in effect on the date that all of the parties enter into a contract or agreement subject to this article are the requirements that shall apply to that contract or agreement. An amendment to this article that becomes effective after that date does not alter the requirements under this article that shall apply to that contract or agreement, unless the applicable statute provides otherwise. **Leg.H.** Added Stats 1985 ch 1574 §2, operative January 1, 1987. Amended Stats 2018 ch 907 §12 (AB 1289), effective January 1, 2019; Stats 2022 ch 420 §9 (AB 2960), effective January 1, 2023.

§1102.6. Form of disclosure statement

(a) The disclosures required by this article pertaining to the property proposed to be transferred are set forth in, and shall be made on a copy of, the following disclosure form:

Sec. 1102.6   CIVIL CODE

REAL ESTATE TRANSFER DISCLOSURE STATEMENT

THIS DISCLOSURE STATEMENT CONCERNS THE REAL PROPERTY SITUATED IN THE CITY OF _____, COUNTY OF _____, STATE OF CALIFORNIA, DESCRIBED AS _____
_____. THIS STATEMENT IS A DISCLOSURE OF THE CONDITION OF THE ABOVE DESCRIBED PROPERTY IN COMPLIANCE WITH SECTION 1102 OF THE CIVIL CODE AS OF _____, 20___. IT IS NOT A WARRANTY OF ANY KIND BY THE SELLER(S) OR ANY AGENT(S) REPRESENTING ANY PRINCIPAL(S) IN THIS TRANSACTION, AND IS NOT A SUBSTITUTE FOR ANY INSPECTIONS OR WARRANTIES THE PRINCIPAL(S) MAY WISH TO OBTAIN.

I
COORDINATION WITH OTHER DISCLOSURE FORMS

This Real Estate Transfer Disclosure Statement is made pursuant to Section 1102 of the Civil Code. Other statutes require disclosures, depending upon the details of the particular real estate transaction (for example: special study zone and purchase-money liens on residential property).

Substituted Disclosures: The following disclosures and other disclosures required by law, including the Natural Hazard Disclosure Report/Statement that may include airport annoyances, earthquake, fire, flood, or special assessment information, have or will be made in connection with this real estate transfer, and are intended to satisfy the disclosure obligations on this form, where the subject matter is the same:

☐ Inspection reports completed pursuant to the contract of sale or receipt for deposit.

☐ Additional inspection reports or disclosures:
_____
_____
_____

☐ *No substituted disclosures for this transfer.*

II
SELLER'S INFORMATION

The Seller discloses the following information with the knowledge that even though this is not a warranty, prospective Buyers may rely on this information in deciding whether and on what terms to purchase the subject property. Seller hereby authorizes any agent(s) representing any principal(s) in this transaction to provide a copy of this statement to any person or entity in connection with any actual or anticipated sale of the property.

THE FOLLOWING ARE REPRESENTATIONS MADE BY THE SELLER(S) AND ARE NOT THE REPRESENTATIONS OF THE AGENT(S), IF ANY. THIS INFORMATION IS A DISCLOSURE AND IS NOT INTENDED TO BE PART OF ANY CONTRACT BETWEEN THE BUYER AND SELLER:

Seller __is __is not occupying the property.
A. The subject property has the items checked below (read across):*

__Range	__Oven	__Microwave
__Dishwasher	__Trash Compactor	__Garbage Disposal
__Washer/Dryer Hookups		__Rain Gutters
__Burglar Alarms	__Carbon Monoxide	__Fire Alarm
__TV Antenna	Device(s)	__Intercom
__Central Heating	__Satellite Dish	__Evaporator Cooler(s)
__Wall/Window Air Cndtng.	__Central Air Cndtng.	__Public Sewer System
__Septic Tank	__Sprinklers	__Water Softener
__Patio/Decking	__Sump Pump	__Gazebo
__Sauna	__Built-in Barbecue	
__Hot Tub __Locking		__Spa __Locking
Safety Cover	__Pool __Child	Safety Cover
__Security Gate(s)	Resistant Barrier	__Number Remote
	__Automatic Garage	Controls
Garage: __Attached	Door Opener(s)	__Carport
Pool/Spa Heater: __Gas	__Not Attached	__Electric
Water Heater: __Gas	__Solar	__Private Utility or
		Other_____
	__Well	__Water-conserving
Water Supply: __City	__Bottled	plumbing fixtures
Gas Supply: __Utility	__Window Security	
__Window Screens	Bars __Quick-Release	
	Mechanism on	
	Bedroom Windows	

Exhaust Fan(s) in _____ 220 Volt Wiring in _____ Fireplace(s) in _____
Gas Starter _____ Roof(s): Type: _____ Age: _____ (approx.)
Other: _____
Are there, to the best of your (Seller's) knowledge, any of the above that are not in operating condition? __Yes __No. If yes, then describe.
(Attach additional sheets if necessary): _____
_____
_____

B. Are you (Seller) aware of any significant defects/malfunctions in any of the following?
__Yes __No. If yes, check appropriate space(s) below.
__Interior Walls __Ceilings __Floors __Exterior Walls __Insulation __Roof(s)
__Windows __Doors __Foundation __Slab(s) __Driveways __Sidewalks
__Walls/Fences __Electrical Systems __Plumbing/Sewers/Septics __Other
Structural Components (Describe: _____
_____)
If any of the above is checked, explain. (Attach additional sheets if necessary): _____
_____
_____

* Installation of a listed appliance, device, or amenity is not a precondition of sale or transfer of the dwelling. The carbon monoxide device, garage door opener, or child-resistant pool barrier may not be in compliance with the safety standards relating to, respectively, carbon monoxide device standards of Chapter 8 (commencing with Section 13260) of Part 2 of Division 12 of, automatic reversing device standards of Chapter 12.5 (commencing with Section 19890) of Part 3 of Division 13 of, or the pool safety standards of Article 2.5 (commencing with Section 115920) of Chapter 5 of Part 10 of Division 104 of, the Health and Safety Code. Window security bars may not have quick-release mechanisms in compliance with the 1995 edition of the California Building Standards Code. Section 1101.4 of the Civil Code requires all single-family residences built on or before January 1, 1994, to be equipped with water-conserving plumbing fixtures after January 1, 2017. Additionally, on and after January 1, 2014, a single-family residence built on or before January 1, 1994, that is altered or improved is required to be equipped with water-conserving plumbing fixtures as a condition of final approval. Fixtures in this dwelling may not comply with Section 1101.4 of the Civil Code.

C. Are you (Seller) aware of any of the following:
1. Substances, materials, or products which may be an environmental hazard such as, but not limited to, asbestos, formaldehyde, radon gas, lead-based paint, mold, fuel or chemical storage tanks, and contaminated soil or water on the subject property .... __Yes __No
2. Features of the property shared in common with adjoining landowners, such as walls, fences, and driveways, whose use or responsibility for maintenance may have an effect on the subject property .... __Yes __No
3. Any encroachments, easements or similar matters that may affect your interest in the subject property .... __Yes __No
4. Room additions, structural modifications, or other alterations or repairs made without necessary permits.. __Yes __No
5. Room additions, structural modifications, or other alterations or repairs not in compliance with building codes... __Yes __No
6. Fill (compacted or otherwise) on the property or any portion thereof .... __Yes __No
7. Any settling from any cause, or slippage, sliding, or other soil problems .... __Yes __No
8. Flooding, drainage or grading problems .... __Yes __No
9. Major damage to the property or any of the structures from fire, earthquake, floods, or landslides .... __Yes __No
10. Any zoning violations, nonconforming uses, violations of "setback" requirements .... __Yes __No
11. Neighborhood noise problems or other nuisances .... __Yes __No
12. CC&Rs or other deed restrictions or obligations .... __Yes __No
13. Homeowners' Association which has any authority over the subject property .... __Yes __No
14. Any "common area" (facilities such as pools, tennis courts, walkways, or other areas co-owned in undivided interest with others)... __Yes __No
15. Any notices of abatement or citations against the property.. __Yes __No
16. Any lawsuits by or against the Seller threatening to or affecting this real property, claims for damages by the Seller pursuant to Section 910 or 914 of the Civil Code threatening to or affecting this real property, claims for breach of warranty pursuant to Section 900 of the Civil Code threatening to or affecting this real property, or claims for breach of an enhanced protection agreement pursuant to Section 903 of the Civil Code threatening to or affecting this real property, including any lawsuits or claims for damages pursuant to Section 910 or 914 of the Civil Code alleging a defect or deficiency in this real property or "common areas" (facilities such as pools, tennis courts, walkways, or other areas co-owned in undivided interest with others).................. __Yes __No

If the answer to any of these is yes, explain. (Attach additional sheets if necessary.): _____
_____
_____

D. 1. The Seller certifies that the property, as of the close of escrow, will be in compliance with Section 13113.8 of the Health and Safety Code by having operable smoke detectors(s) which are approved, listed, and installed in accordance with the State Fire Marshal's regulations and applicable local standards.

2. The Seller certifies that the property, as of the close of escrow, will be in compliance with Section 19211 of the Health and Safety Code by having the water heater tank(s) braced, anchored, or strapped in place in accordance with applicable law.

Seller certifies that the information herein is true and correct to the best of the Seller's knowledge as of the date signed by the Seller.

Seller _____ Date _____

Seller _____ Date _____

III

AGENT'S INSPECTION DISCLOSURE

(To be completed only if the Seller is represented by an agent in this transaction.)

THE UNDERSIGNED, BASED ON THE ABOVE INQUIRY OF THE SELLER(S) AS TO THE CONDITION OF THE PROPERTY AND BASED ON A REASONABLY COMPETENT AND DILIGENT VISUAL INSPECTION OF THE ACCESSIBLE AREAS OF THE PROPERTY IN CONJUNCTION WITH THAT INQUIRY, STATES THE FOLLOWING:

☐ Agent notes no items for disclosure.

☐ Agent notes the following items:
_____
_____
_____

Agent (Broker
Representing Seller) _____ By _____ Date _____
(Please Print)   (Associate Licensee
                                  or Broker Signature)

IV
AGENT'S INSPECTION DISCLOSURE

(To be completed only if the agent who has obtained the offer is other than the agent above.)

THE UNDERSIGNED, BASED ON A REASONABLY COMPETENT AND DILIGENT VISUAL INSPECTION OF THE ACCESSIBLE AREAS OF THE PROPERTY, STATES THE FOLLOWING:

☐ Agent notes no items for disclosure.

☐ Agent notes the following items:
_____
_____
_____
_____

Agent (Broker
Obtaining the Offer) _____ By _____ Date _____
                  (Please Print)   (Associate Licensee
                                     or Broker Signature)

V

BUYER(S) AND SELLER(S) MAY WISH TO OBTAIN PROFESSIONAL ADVICE AND/OR INSPECTIONS OF THE PROPERTY AND TO PROVIDE FOR APPROPRIATE PROVISIONS IN A CONTRACT BETWEEN BUYER(S) AND SELLER(S) WITH RESPECT TO ANY ADVICE/INSPECTIONS/DEFECTS.

I/WE ACKNOWLEDGE RECEIPT OF A COPY OF THIS STATEMENT.

Seller _____ Date _____ Buyer _____ Date _____
Seller _____ Date _____ Buyer _____ Date _____

Agent (Broker
Representing Seller) _____ By _____ Date _____
                  (Please Print)   (Associate Licensee
                                     or Broker Signature)

Agent (Broker
Obtaining the Offer) _____ By _____ Date _____
                  (Please Print)   (Associate Licensee
                                     or Broker Signature)

SECTION 1102.3 OF THE CIVIL CODE PROVIDES A BUYER WITH THE RIGHT TO RESCIND A PURCHASE CONTRACT FOR AT LEAST THREE DAYS AFTER THE DELIVERY OF THIS DISCLOSURE IF DELIVERY OCCURS AFTER THE SIGNING OF AN OFFER TO PURCHASE. IF YOU WISH TO RESCIND THE CONTRACT, YOU MUST ACT WITHIN THE PRESCRIBED PERIOD.

A REAL ESTATE BROKER IS QUALIFIED TO ADVISE ON REAL ESTATE.
IF YOU DESIRE LEGAL ADVICE, CONSULT YOUR ATTORNEY.

(b) The amendments to this section by the act adding this subdivision shall become operative on July 1, 2014. **Leg.H.** Added Stats 1985 ch 1574 §2, operative January 1, 1987. Amended Stats 1986 ch 460 §5; Stats 1989 ch 171 §1; Stats 1990 ch 1336 §2 (AB 3600), operative July 1, 1991; Stats 1994 ch 817 §2 (SB 1377); Stats 1996 ch 240 §2 (AB 2383), ch 925 §1 (AB 3305), operative until July 1, 1997; Stats 1996 ch 926 §1.5 (AB 3026), operative July 1, 1997; Stats 2001 ch 584 §1 (SB 732); Stats 2002 ch 496 §3 (AB 2776), operative January 1, 2004, ch 664 §35 (AB 3034) (ch 496 prevails); Stats 2003 ch 62 §13 (SB 600); Stats 2010 ch 19 §1 (SB 183), effective January 1, 2011; Stats 2011 ch 61 §1 (SB 837), effective January 1, 2012; Stats 2013 ch 431 §1 (SB 652), effective September 30, 2013, operative July 1, 2014; Stats 2014 ch 71 §15 (SB 1304), effective January 1, 2015; Stats 2019 ch 310 §6 (AB 892), effective January 1, 2020; Stats 2020 ch 370 §25 (SB 1371), effective January 1, 2021.

§1102.6a. Additional disclosures; Disclosure form; Proximity to airport

(a) On and after July 1, 1990, any city or county may elect to require disclosures on the form set forth in subdivision (b) in addition to those disclosures required by Section 1102.6. However, this section does not affect or limit the authority of a city or county to require disclosures on a different disclosure form in connection with transactions subject to this article pursuant to an ordinance adopted prior to July 1, 1990. An ordinance like this adopted prior to July 1, 1990, may be amended thereafter to revise the disclosure requirements of the ordinance, in the discretion of the city council or county board of supervisors.

(b) Disclosures required pursuant to this section pertaining to the property proposed to be sold, shall be set forth in, and shall be made on a copy of, the following disclosure form:

LOCAL OPTION
REAL ESTATE TRANSFER DISCLOSURE STATEMENT
THIS DISCLOSURE STATEMENT CONCERNS THE REAL PROPERTY SITUATED IN THE CITY OF _____, COUNTY OF _____, STATE OF CALIFORNIA, DESCRIBED AS _____. THIS STATEMENT IS A DISCLOSURE OF THE CONDITION OF THE ABOVE-DESCRIBED PROPERTY IN COMPLIANCE WITH ORDINANCE NO. ____ OF THE _____ CITY OR COUNTY CODE AS OF _____, 20 ____. IT IS NOT A WARRANTY OF ANY KIND BY THE SELLER(S) OR ANY REAL ESTATE LICENSEE(S) REPRESENTING ANY PRINCIPAL(S) IN THIS TRANSACTION, AND IS NOT A SUBSTITUTE FOR ANY INSPECTIONS OR WARRANTIES THE PRINCIPAL(S) MAY WISH TO OBTAIN.

I
SELLER'S INFORMATION

The Seller discloses the following information with the knowledge that even though this is not a warranty, prospective Buyers may rely on this information in deciding whether and on what terms to purchase the subject property. Seller hereby authorizes any real estate licensee(s) representing any principal(s) in this transaction to provide a copy of this statement to any person or entity in connection with any actual or anticipated sale of the property.
THE FOLLOWING ARE REPRESENTATIONS MADE BY THE SELLER(S) AS REQUIRED BY THE CITY OR COUNTY OF _____, AND ARE NOT THE REPRESENTATIONS OF THE REAL ESTATE LICENSEE(S), IF ANY. THIS INFORMATION IS A DISCLOSURE AND IS NOT INTENDED TO BE PART OF ANY CONTRACT BETWEEN THE BUYER AND SELLER.

1. _____
   _____
   _____

2. _____
   _____
   _____

(Example: Adjacent land is zoned for timber production which may be subject to harvest.)
Seller certifies that the information herein is true and correct to the best of the Seller's knowledge as of the date signed by the Seller.
Seller _____ Date _____
Seller _____ Date _____

II
BUYER(S) MAY WISH TO OBTAIN PROFESSIONAL ADVICE AND/OR INSPECTIONS OF THE PROPERTY AND TO PROVIDE FOR APPROPRIATE PROVISIONS IN A CONTRACT BETWEEN BUYER AND SELLER(S) WITH RESPECT TO ANY ADVICE/INSPECTIONS/DEFECTS.
I/WE ACKNOWLEDGE RECEIPT OF A COPY OF THIS STATEMENT.

Buyer _____ Date _____
Buyer _____ Date _____

A REAL ESTATE BROKER IS QUALIFIED TO ADVISE ON REAL ESTATE. IF YOU DESIRE LEGAL ADVICE, CONSULT YOUR ATTORNEY.

(c) This section does not preclude the use of addenda to the form specified in subdivision (b) to facilitate the required disclosures. This section does not preclude a city or county from using the disclosure form specified in subdivision (b) for a purpose other than that specified in this section.

(d)(1) On and after January 1, 2005, if a city or county adopts a different or additional disclosure form pursuant to this section regarding the proximity or effects of an airport, the statement in that form shall contain, at a minimum, the information in the statement "Notice of Airport in Vicinity" found in Section 11010 of the Business and Professions Code, or Section 1103.4 or 4255.

(2) On and after January 1, 2006, if a city or county does not adopt a different or additional disclosure form pursuant to this section, then the provision of an "airport influence area" disclosure pursuant to Section 11010 of the Business and Professions Code, or Section 1103.4 or 4255, or if there is not a current airport influence map, a written disclosure of an airport within two statute miles, shall be deemed to satisfy any city or county requirements for the disclosure of airports in connection with sales of real property. **Leg.H.** Added Stats 1989 ch 171 §2. Amended Stats 2004 ch 66 §1 (AB 920); Stats 2012 ch 181 §33 (AB 806), effective January 1, 2013, operative January 1, 2014; Stats 2018 ch 907 §13 (AB 1289), effective January 1, 2019.

§1102.6b. Disclosure notice requirements; Substantially equivalent and modified notices

(a) This section applies to all sales of real property for which all of the following apply:

(1) The sale is subject to this article.

(2) The property being sold is subject to a continuing lien securing the levy of special taxes pursuant to the Mello-Roos Community Facilities Act (Chapter 2.5 (commencing with Section 53311) of Part 1 of Division 2 of Title 5 of the Government Code), to a fixed lien assessment collected in installments to secure bonds issued pursuant to the Improvement Bond Act of 1915 (Division 10 (commencing with Section 8500) of the Streets and Highways Code), or to a contractual assessment program authorized pursuant to Chapter 29 (commencing with Section 5898.10) of Part 3 of Division 7 of the Streets and Highway Code.

(3) A notice is not required pursuant to Section 53341.5 of the Government Code.

(b) In addition to any other disclosure required pursuant to this article, the seller of any real property subject to this section shall make a good faith effort to obtain a disclosure notice concerning the special tax as provided for in Section 53340.2 of the Government Code, or a disclosure notice concerning an assessment installment as provided in Section 53754 of the Government Code, from each local agency that levies a special tax pursuant to the Mello-Roos Community Facilities Act, or that collects assessment installments to secure bonds issued pursuant to the Improvement Bond Act of 1915 (Division 10 (commencing with Section 8500) of the Streets and Highways Code), or a disclosure notice concerning the contractual assessment as provided in Section 5898.24 of the Streets and Highways Code, on the property being sold, and shall deliver that notice or those notices to the prospective buyer, as long as the notices are made available by the local agency.

(c)(1) The seller of real property subject to this section may satisfy the disclosure notice requirements in regard to the bonds issued pursuant to the Improvement Bond Act of 1915 (Division 10 (commencing with Section 8500) of the Streets and Highways Code) by delivering a disclosure notice that is substantially equivalent and obtained from another source until December 31, 2004.

(2) The seller of real property subject to this section may satisfy the disclosure notice requirements in regard to the assessments collected under the contractual assessment program authorized pursuant to Chapter 29 (commencing with Section 5898.10) of Part 3 of Division 7 of the Streets and Highway Code by delivering a disclosure notice that is substantially equivalent and obtained from another source.

(3) For the purposes of this section, a substantially equivalent disclosure notice includes, but is not limited to, a copy of the most recent year's property tax bill or an itemization of current assessment amounts applicable to the property.

(d)(1) Notwithstanding subdivision (c), the seller of real property subject to this section may satisfy the disclosure notice requirements of this section by delivering a disclosure notice obtained from a nongovernmental source that satisfies the requirements of paragraph (2).

(2) A notice provided by a private entity other than a designated office, department, or bureau of the levying entity may be modified as needed to clearly and accurately describe a special tax pursuant to the Mello-Roos Community Facilities Act levied against the property or to clearly and accurately consolidate information about two or more districts that levy or are authorized to levy a special tax pursuant to the Mello-Roos Community Facilities Act against the property, and shall include the name of the Mello-Roos entity levying taxes against the property, the annual tax due for the Mello-Roos entity for the current tax year, the maximum tax that may be levied against the property in any year, the percentage by which the maximum tax for the Mello-Roos entity may increase per year, and the date until the tax may be levied against the property for the Mello-Roos entity and a contact telephone number, if available, for further information about the Mello-Roos entity. A notice provided by a private entity other than a designated office, department, or bureau of the levying entity may be modified as needed to clearly and accurately describe special assessments and bonds pursuant to the Improvement Bond Act of 1915 levied against the property, or to clearly and accurately consolidate information about two or more districts that levy or are authorized to levy special assessments and bonds pursuant to the Improvement Bond Act of 1915 against the property, and shall include the name of the special assessments and bonds issued pursuant to the Improvement Bond Act of 1915, the current annual tax on the property for the special assessments and bonds issued pursuant to the Improvement Bond Act of 1915 and a contact telephone number, if available, for further information about the special assessments and bonds issued pursuant to the Improvement Bond Act of 1915.

(3) This section does not change the ability to make disclosures pursuant to Section 1102.4 of the Civil Code.

(e) If a disclosure received pursuant to subdivision (b), (c), or (d) has been delivered to the buyer, a seller or his or her agent is not required to provide additional information concerning, and information in the disclosure shall be deemed to satisfy the responsibility of the seller or his or her agent to inform the buyer regarding the special tax or assessment installments and the district. Notwithstanding subdivision (b), (c), or (d), nothing in this section imposes a duty to discover a special tax or assessment installments or the existence of any levying district not actually known to the agents. **Leg.H.** Added Stats 1992 ch 772 §1.3 (SB 1464), operative July 1, 1993. Amended Stats 2001 ch 673 §1 (SB 1122), ch 771; Stats 2002 ch 770 §1 (SB 1879), effective September 21, 2002, ch 771 §1 (AB 337); Stats 2003 ch 62 §14 (SB 600); Stats 2009 ch 444 §1 (AB 474), effective January 1, 2010; Stats 2018 ch 907 §14 (AB 1289), effective January 1, 2019.

2002 Note: This act is intended to ensure that prospective purchasers of real property have the relevant information that they need to make an informed decision, and to clarify that substantial compliance by property owners continues to be legally sufficient in lieu of formal disclosures by public entities. Stats 2002 ch 771 (AB 337) §2.

§1102.6c. Disclosure notice of supplemental property tax bills

(a) In addition to any other disclosure required pursuant to this article, it shall be the sole responsibility of the seller of any real property subject to this article, or his or her agent, to deliver to the prospective buyer a disclosure notice that includes both of the following:

(1) A notice, in at least 12-point type or a contrasting color, as follows:

"California property tax law requires the Assessor to revalue real property at the time the ownership of the property changes. Because of this law, you may receive one or two supplemental tax bills, depending on when your loan closes.

The supplemental tax bills are not mailed to your lender. If you have arranged for your property tax payments to be paid through an impound account, the supplemental tax bills will not be paid by your lender. It is your responsibility to pay these supplemental bills directly to the tax collector. If you have any question concerning this matter, please call your local tax collector's office."

(2) A title, in at least 14-point type or a contrasting color, that reads as follows: "Notice of Your 'Supplemental' Property Tax Bill."

(b) The disclosure notice requirements of this section may be satisfied by delivering a disclosure notice pursuant to Section 1102.6b that satisfies the requirements of subdivision (a). **Leg.H.** Added Stats 2005 ch 392 §2 (AB 459), effective January 1, 2006. Amended Stats 2018 ch 907 §15 (AB 1289), effective January 1, 2019.

Prior Law: Former CC §1102.6c, similar to the present section was added Stats 1998 ch 65 §2, effective June 9, 1998, operative June 1, 1998, amended Stats 1999 ch 83 §19 and repealed Stats 1999 ch 876 §1 (ch 876 prevails). See CC §1103.2.

There was another section of this number, similar to the present section, which was added Stats 1st Ex Sess 1997–98 ch 7 §1, effective December 1, 1998, operative June 1, 1998. It was then repealed Stats 1998 ch 65 §1, effective June 9, 1998, operative December 1, 1998. The source of the effective date of the addition and the operative date of the repeal was the effective date of legislation enacted during the First Extraordinary Session of 1997–98; by virtue of Const Art IV §8 (c)(1), that was 91 days after adjournment of the session on September 1, 1998. The operative date of the addition was set by Stats 1st Ex Sess 1997–98 ch 7 §14, as amended Stats 1998 ch 2 §1.

Former CC §1102.6c, similar to the present section, was added Stats 1998 ch 65 §2, effective June 9, 1998, operative June 1, 1998, and repealed Stats 1999 ch 876 §1. See CC §1103.2.

1998 Note: It is the intent of the Legislature that the provisions of Stats 1998 ch 65 shall supersede the provisions of Chapter 7 of the Statutes of 1997, First Extraordinary Session, in their entirety and, to that intent, the provisions of that chapter shall not become operative. Stats 1998 ch 65 §20.

Former Sections: Former CC §1102.6c, similar to the present section, was added Stats 1997–98 1st Ex Sess ch 7 §1, effective December 1, 1998, operative June 1, 1998, and repealed Stats 1998 ch 65 §1.

§1102.6d. Manufactured home and mobilehome transfer disclosure statement

Except for manufactured homes and mobilehomes located in a common interest development governed by Part 5 (commencing with Section 4000) of Division 4, the disclosures applicable to the resale of a manufactured home or mobilehome pursuant to subdivision (b) of Section 1102 are set forth in, and shall be made on a copy of, the following disclosure form:

MANUFACTURED HOME AND MOBILEHOME:
TRANSFER DISCLOSURE STATEMENT

THIS DISCLOSURE STATEMENT CONCERNS THE MANUFACTURED HOME OR MOBILEHOME (HEREAFTER REFERRED TO AS "HOME") LOCATED AT _____ IN THE CITY OF _____, COUNTY OF _____, STATE OF CALIFORNIA, DESCRIBED AS

YEAR   MAKE SERIAL #(s)   HCD DECAL # or Equivalent
THIS STATEMENT IS A DISCLOSURE OF THE CONDITION OF THE ABOVE-DESCRIBED HOME IN COMPLIANCE WITH SUBDIVISION (b) OF SECTION 1102 OF THE CIVIL CODE AND SECTIONS 18025 AND 18046 OF THE HEALTH AND SAFETY CODE AS OF

_____
DATE
IT IS NOT A WARRANTY OF ANY KIND BY THE LAWFUL OWNER OF THE MANUFACTURED HOME OR MOBILEHOME WHO OFFERS THE HOME FOR SALE (HEREAFTER THE SELLER), OR ANY AGENT(S) REPRESENTING ANY PRINCIPAL(S) IN THIS TRANSACTION, AND IS NOT A SUBSTITUTE FOR ANY INSPECTIONS OR WARRANTIES THE PRINCIPAL(S) MAY WISH TO OBTAIN. AN "AGENT" MEANS ANY DEALER OR SALESPERSON LICENSED PURSUANT TO PART 2 (COMMENCING WITH SECTION 18000) OF

THE HEALTH AND SAFETY CODE, OR A REAL ESTATE BROKER OR SALESPERSON LICENSED PURSUANT TO DIVISION 4 (COMMENCING WITH SECTION 10000) OF DIVISION 13 OF THE BUSINESS AND PROFESSIONS CODE.

I
COORDINATION WITH OTHER DISCLOSURE & INFORMATION

This Manufactured Home and Mobilehome Transfer Disclosure Statement is made pursuant to Article 1.5 (commencing with Section 1102) of Chapter 2 of Title 4 of Part 4 of Division 2 of the Civil Code. Other statutes require disclosures, or other information may be important to the prospective buyer, depending upon the details of the particular transaction (including, but not limited to, the condition of the park in which the manufactured home or mobilehome will be located; disclosures required or information provided by the Mobilehome Residency Law, Section 798 of the Civil Code et seq.; the mobilehome park rental agreement or lease; the mobilehome park rules and regulations; and park and lot inspection reports, if any, completed by the state or a local enforcement agency). Substituted Disclosures: The following disclosures have or will be made in connection with this transfer, and are intended to satisfy the disclosure obligations of this form, where the subject matter is the same:

☐ Home inspection reports completed pursuant to the contract of sale or receipt for deposit.

☐ Additional inspection reports or disclosures: _____
_____

II
SELLER'S INFORMATION

The Seller discloses the following information with the knowledge that even though this is not a warranty, prospective buyers may rely on this information in deciding whether, and on what terms, to purchase the subject Home. Seller hereby authorizes any agent(s), as defined in Section 18046 of the Health and Safety Code, representing any principal(s) in this transaction to provide a copy of this statement to any person or entity in connection with any actual or anticipated sale of the Home.

THE FOLLOWING ARE REPRESENTATIONS MADE BY THE SELLER(S) AND ARE NOT THE REPRESENTATIONS OF THE AGENT(S), IF ANY, AS DEFINED IN SECTION 18046 OF THE HEALTH AND SAFETY CODE. THIS INFORMATION IS A DISCLOSURE AND IS NOT INTENDED TO BE PART OF ANY CONTRACT BETWEEN THE BUYER AND THE SELLER.

Seller ____ is ____ is not occupying the Home.

A. The subject Home includes the items checked below which are being sold with the Home (read across): *

____ Range   ____ Oven   ____ Microwave
____ Dishwasher   ____ Trash Compactor   ____ Garbage Disposal
____ Burglar Alarm   ____ Carbon Monoxide   ____ Fire Alarm
                           Device(s)
____ TV Antenna   ____ Satellite Dish   ____ Intercom
____ Central Heating ____ Central Air   ____ Wall/Window Air Cndtng.
                           Cndtng.
____ Evaporative Cool-____ Sump Pump   ____ Water Softener
er(s)
____ Porch Decking   ____ Porch Awning   ____ Gazebo
____ Private Sauna   ____ Private Spa   ____ Spa Locking Safety Cvr
____ Private Hot Tub ____ Hot Tub Locking   ____ Gas/Spa Heater
                           Cvr
____ Solar/Spa Heater ____ Gas Water Heater   ____ Solar Water Heater
____ Electric Water   ____ Bottled Propane
Heater
____ Carport Awning
                      ____ Attached Garage   ____ Detached Garage
____ Automatic Garage ____ # Remote Controls ____ Window Screens
Door Opener(s)
____ Window Secure   ____ Bedroom Window
Bars   Quick   Release
                           Mechanism
____ Earthquake Resis-____ Washer/Dryer   ____ Rain Gutters
tant Bracing System   Hookups

Exhaust Fan(s) in _____ 220 Volt Wiring in _____
Fireplace(s) in _____ Gas Starter(s) _____
Roof(s) and type(s) _____ Roof age (Approximate) _____
Other _____

* Installation of a listed appliance, device, or amenity is not a precondition of sale or transfer of the home. The carbon monoxide device, garage door opener, or child-resistant pool barrier may not be in compliance with the safety standards relating to, respectively, carbon monoxide device standards of Chapter 8 (commencing with Section 13260) of Part 2 of Division 12 of, automatic reversing device standards of Chapter 12.5 (commencing with Section 19890) of Part 3 of Division 13 of, or the pool safety standards of Article 2.5 (commencing with Section 115920) of Chapter 5 of Part 10 of Division 104 of, the Health and Safety Code. Window security bars may not have quick-release mechanisms in compliance with the 1995 edition of the California Building Standards Code. Are there, to the best of your (Seller's) knowledge, any of the above that are not in operating condition? ____ Yes ____ No. If yes, then describe. (Attach additional sheets if necessary): _____
_____
_____

B. Are you (the Seller) aware of any significant defects/malfunctions in any of the following in connection with the Home?
____ Yes ____ No   If yes, check appropriate space(s) below:
____ Interior Walls, ____ Ceilings, ____ Floors, ____ Exterior Walls,
____ Insulation, ____ Roof(s), ____ Windows, ____ Doors,
____ Home Electrical Systems, ____ Plumbing, ____ Porch or Deck,
____ Porch Steps & Railings, ____ Other Steps & Railings,
____ Porch Awning, ____ Carport Awning, ____ Other Awnings,
____ Skirting, ____ Home Foundation or Support System,
____ Other Structural Components (Describe: _____
_____
_____)

If any of the above is checked, explain. (Attach additional sheets if necessary): _____
_____

C. Are you (the Seller) aware of any of the following:

1. Substances, materials, or products which may be an environmental hazard, such as, but not limited to, asbestos, formaldehyde, radon gas, lead-based paint, or chemical storage tanks on the subject home interior or exterior .... ____ Yes ____ No
2. Room additions, structural modifications, or other alterations or repairs made without necessary permits .... ____ Yes ____ No
3. Room additions, structural modifications, or other alterations or repairs not in compliance with applicable codes .... ____ Yes ____ No
4. Any settling from slippage, sliding or problems with leveling of the home or the foundation or support system .... ____ Yes ____ No
5. Drainage or grading problems with the home, space or lot .... ____ Yes ____ No
6. Damage to the home or accessory structures being sold with the home from fire, flood, earthquake, or landslides .... ____ Yes ____ No
7. Any notices of abatement or citations against the home or accessory structures being sold with the home .... ____ Yes ____ No
8. Any lawsuits by or against the seller threatening to or affecting the home or the accessory structures being sold with the home, including any lawsuits alleging any defect or deficiency in the home or accessories sold with the home .... ____ Yes ____ No
9. Neighborhood noise problems or other nuisances .... ____ Yes ____ No
10. Any encroachment, easement, nonconforming use or violation of setback requirements with the home, accessory structures being sold with the home, or space .... ____ Yes ____ No

If the answer to any of these is yes, explain. (Attach additional sheets if necessary.): _____
_____

D. 1. The Seller certifies that the home, as of the close of escrow, will be in compliance with Section 13113.8 of the Health and Safety Code by having operable smoke detectors(s) which are approved, listed, and installed in accordance with the State Fire Marshal's regulations and applicable local standards.

2. The Seller certifies that the home, as of the close of escrow, will be in compliance with Section 19211 of the Health and Safety Code by having the water heater tank(s) braced, anchored, or strapped in place in accordance with applicable law.

Seller certifies that the information herein is true and correct to the best of the Seller's knowledge as of the date signed by the Seller.

Seller _____ Date _____
Seller _____ Date _____

III
AGENT'S INSPECTION DISCLOSURE

(To be completed only if the Seller is represented by an Agent in this transaction)

THE UNDERSIGNED, BASED ON THE ABOVE INQUIRY OF THE SELLER(S) AS TO THE CONDITION OF THE HOME AND BASED ON A REASONABLY COMPETENT AND DILIGENT VISUAL INSPECTION OF THE ACCESSIBLE AREAS OF THE HOME IN CONJUNCTION WITH THAT INQUIRY, STATES THE FOLLOWING:

☐ Agent notes no items for disclosure.
☐ Agent notes the following items:

_____
_____
_____

Agent
Representing
Seller _____ By _____ Date _____
(Please Print)   (Signature)

IV
AGENT'S INSPECTION DISCLOSURE

(To be completed only if the Agent who has obtained the offer is other than the Agent above.)

THE UNDERSIGNED, BASED ON A REASONABLY COMPETENT AND DILIGENT VISUAL INSPECTION OF THE ACCESSIBLE AREAS OF THE HOME, STATES THE FOLLOWING:

☐ Agent notes no items for disclosure.
☐ Agent notes the following items:

_____
_____
_____

Agent
Representing
Buyer _____ By _____ Date _____
(Please Print)   (Signature)

V

BUYER(S) AND SELLER(S) MAY WISH TO OBTAIN PROFESSIONAL ADVICE AND/OR INSPECTIONS OF THE HOME AND TO PROVIDE FOR APPROPRIATE PROVISIONS IN A CONTRACT BETWEEN THE BUYER(S) AND SELLER(S) WITH RESPECT TO ANY ADVICE/INSPECTIONS/DEFECTS.

I/WE ACKNOWLEDGE RECEIPT OF A COPY OF THIS STATEMENT.

Seller _____ Date _____ Buyer _____ Date _____
Seller _____ Date _____ Buyer _____ Date _____
Agent
Representing
Seller _____ By _____ Date _____
(Please Print)   (Signature)
Agent
Representing
Buyer _____ By _____ Date _____
(Please Print)   (Signature)

VI

SECTION 1102.3a OF THE CIVIL CODE PROVIDES A PROSPECTIVE BUYER WITH THE RIGHT TO RESCIND THE PURCHASE OF THE MANUFACTURED HOME OR MOBILEHOME FOR AT LEAST THREE DAYS AFTER DELIVERY OF THIS DISCLOSURE, IF DELIVERY OCCURS AFTER THE SIGNING OF AN OFFER TO PURCHASE. IF YOU WISH TO RESCIND THE CONTRACT, YOU MUST ACT WITHIN THE PRESCRIBED PERIOD.

A MANUFACTURED HOME OR MOBILEHOME DEALER OR A REAL ESTATE BROKER IS QUALIFIED TO PROVIDE ADVICE ON THE SALE OF A MANUFACTURED HOME OR MOBILEHOME. IF YOU DESIRE LEGAL ADVICE, CONSULT YOUR ATTORNEY.

Leg.H. Added Stats 1999 ch 517 §6 (SB 534). Amended Stats 2010 ch 19 §2 (SB 183), effective January 1, 2011; Stats 2012 ch 181 §34 (AB 806), effective January 1, 2013, operative January 1, 2014.

§1102.6e. Additional disclosure statement for property transferred on or after January 1, 2008

If a property being transferred on or after January 1, 2008, is subject to a transfer fee, as defined in Section 1098, the transferor shall provide, at the same time as the transfer disclosure statement required pursuant to Section 1102.6 is provided if the document required by subdivision (b) of Section 1098.5 has not already been provided, an additional disclosure statement containing all of the following:

(a) Notice that payment of a transfer fee is required as a result of transfer of the property.

(b) The amount of the fee required for the asking price of the real property, if the amount of the fee is based on the price of the real property, and a description of how the fee is calculated.

(c) Notice that the final amount of the fee may be different if the fee is based upon a percentage of the final sale price.

(d) The entity to which funds from the fee will be paid.

(e) The purposes for which funds from the fee will be used.

(f) The date or circumstances under which the obligation to pay the transfer fee expires, if any. **Leg.H.** Added Stats 2007 ch 689 §3 (AB 980), effective January 1, 2008. Amended Stats 2015 ch 634 §3 (AB 807), effective January 1, 2016.

2015 Note: The Legislature finds and declares that the addition of subdivision (b) to Section 1098 of, and the amendments to Sections 1098.5 and 1102.6e of, the Civil Code made by this act are clarifying and declaratory of existing law. Stats 2015 ch 634 (AB 807) §4.

§1102.6f. Disclosure notice by seller to buyer of real property in high or very high fire hazard severity zone; Statement contents

(a) On or after January 1, 2021, in addition to any other disclosure required pursuant to this article, the seller of any real property subject to this article that is located in a high or very high fire hazard severity zone, as identified by the Director of Forestry and Fire Protection pursuant to Section 51178 of the Government Code or Article 9 (commencing with Section 4201) of Chapter 1 of Part 2 of Division 4 of the Public Resources Code, shall provide a disclosure notice to the buyer, if the home was constructed before January 1, 2010, that includes the following information:

(1) A statement as follows: "This home is located in a high or very high fire hazard severity zone and this home was built before the implementation of the Wildfire Urban Interface building codes which help to fire harden a home. To better protect your home from wildfire, you might need to consider improvements. Information on fire hardening, including current building standards and information on minimum annual vegetation management standards to protect homes from wildfires, can be obtained on the internet website http://www.readyforwildfire.org."

(2) On or after July 1, 2025, a list of low-cost retrofits developed and listed pursuant to Section 51189 of the Government Code. The notice shall disclose which listed retrofits, if any, have been completed during the time that the seller has owned the property.

(3) A list of the following features that may make the home vulnerable to wildfire and flying embers. The notice shall disclose which of the listed features, if any, that exist on the home of which the seller is aware:

(A) Eave, soffit, and roof ventilation where the vents have openings in excess of one-eighth of an inch or are not flame and ember resistant.

(B) Roof coverings made of untreated wood shingles or shakes.

(C) Combustible landscaping or other materials within five feet of the home and under the footprint of any attached deck.

(D) Single pane or nontempered glass windows.

(E) Loose or missing bird stopping or roof flashing.

(F) Rain gutters without metal or noncombustible gutter covers.

(b) If, pursuant to Section 51182 of the Government Code, a seller has obtained a final inspection report described in that section, the seller shall provide to the buyer a copy of that report or information on where a copy of the report may be obtained.

(c) This section shall not be construed as a requirement, instruction, or consideration for present or future building code formulation, including, but not limited to, the Wildland Urban Interface building standards (Chapter 7A (commencing with Section 701A.1) of Part 2 of Title 24 of the California Code of Regulations). **Leg.H.** Added Stats 2019 ch 391 §2 (AB 38), effective January 1, 2020. Amended Stats 2020 ch 370 §26 (SB 1371), effective January 1, 2021.

§ 1102.6g. Required sales contract notice provision regarding unbiased appraisal and complaint process; Loan refinance and mortgage disclosure statement

(a) After July 1, 2022, every contract for the sale of real property shall contain, in no less than 8-point type, the following notice:

"Any appraisal of the property is required to be unbiased, objective, and not influenced by improper or illegal considerations, including, but not limited to, any of the following: race, color, religion (including religious dress, grooming practices, or both), gender (including, but not limited to, pregnancy, childbirth, breastfeeding, and related conditions, and gender identity and gender expression), sexual orientation, marital status, medical condition, military or veteran status, national origin (including language use and possession of a driver's license issued to persons unable to provide their presence in the United States is authorized under federal law), source of income, ancestry, disability (mental and physical, including, but not limited to, HIV/AIDS status, cancer diagnosis, and genetic characteristics), genetic information, or age. If a buyer or seller believes that the appraisal has been influenced by any of the above factors, the seller or buyer can report this information to the lender or mortgage broker that retained the appraiser and may also file a complaint with the Bureau of Real Estate Appraisers at https://www2.brea.ca.gov/complaint/ or call (916) 552-9000 for further information on how to file a complaint."

(b) The notice described in subdivision (a) shall also be delivered by a licensed person refinancing a first lien purchase money loan secured by residential real property containing no more than four dwelling units, either prior to, or with, the loan estimate as required by the federal Truth in Lending Act, as amended (15 U.S.C. Sec. 1601 et seq.), or the mortgage loan disclosure statement as required pursuant to Section 10240 of the Business and Professions Code. The notice described in subdivision (a) may be included as part of the disclosure required under Section 1002.14(a)(2) of the federal Equal Credit Opportunity Act (Regulation B) (12 C.F.R. Sec. 1002 et seq.).

(c) For purposes of this section, a "licensed person" means a depository institution chartered under federal or state law, a person covered by the licensing requirements of Division 9 (commencing with Section 22000) or Division 20 (commencing with Section 50000) of the Financial Code, or a person licensed pursuant to Part 1 (commencing with Section 10000) of Division 4 of the Business and Professions Code. **Leg.H.** Added Stats 2021 ch 352 §6 (AB 948), effective January 1, 2022.

Prior Law: Stats 2021 ch 352 provides:

SECTION 1. This act shall be known, and may be cited, as the Fair Appraisal Act.

§ 1102.6h. Additional disclosures

(a) A seller of a single-family residential property who accepts an offer for the sale of the single-family residential property within 18 months from the date that title for the single-family residential property was transferred to the seller shall disclose, in addition to any other disclosure required pursuant to this article, to the buyer both of the following:

(1) Any room additions, structural modifications, other alterations, or repairs made to the property since title to the property was transferred to the seller that were performed by a contractor with whom the seller entered into a contract.

(2) The name of each contractor with whom the seller entered into a contract with for the room additions, structural modifications, other alterations, or repairs disclosed in paragraph (1) and any contact information for the contractor provided by the contractor to the seller. The obligation to provide the name of the contractor shall only apply to contracts where the aggregate contract price for labor, material, and all other items for the project or undertaking is in excess of the dollar amount specified in Section 7027.2 of the Business and Professions Code.

(b) The seller's obligation to disclose the room additions, structural modifications, other alterations, or repairs made to the property performed by a contractor may also be satisfied by providing a list of room additions, structural modifications, other alterations, or repairs performed by, and provided by, the contractor with whom the seller contracted for the room additions, structural modifications, other alterations, or repairs.

(c)(1) If the seller obtained a permit for any room additions, structural modifications, other alterations, or repairs provided to the buyer pursuant to subdivision (a), the seller shall provide a copy of the permit to the buyer.

(2) If the seller contracted with a third party for any room additions, structural modifications, or repairs, and the seller was not provided with a copy of any permits obtained, the seller may satisfy the obligation in paragraph (1) by informing the buyer that any information on permits may be obtained from the third party and providing the contact information for the third party provided by the third party to the seller.

(d) This section shall apply to the sale of a single-family residential property where the seller accepts an offer from a buyer to purchase the property on or after July 1, 2024. **Leg.H.** Added Stats 2023 ch 95 §1 (AB 968), effective January 1, 2024.

§1102.6i. Disclosure; Limited electrical capacity

(a) Except as provided in subdivision (b), on or after January 1, 2026, in addition to any other disclosure required pursuant to this article, the seller of any real property subject to this article, or the seller's agent, shall deliver to the prospective buyer a disclosure statement that provides as follows: "In a purchase of real property, it may be advisable to obtain an inspection by a qualified professional of the electrical system(s) of any buildings, including, but not limited to, the main service panel, the subpanel(s), and wiring. Substandard, recalled, or faulty wiring may cause a fire risk and may make it difficult to obtain property insurance. Limited electrical capacity may make it difficult to support future electrical additions to the building(s), such as solar generation, electric space heating, electric water heating, or electric vehicle charging equipment."

(b) This section does not apply to the sale of a building within three years of the issuance of the certificate of occupancy for the building. **Leg.H.** Added Stats 2024 ch 443 §1 (SB 382), effective January 1, 2025.

§1102.6j. Gas-powered appliances

On or after January 1, 2026, the seller of a single-family residential property subject to this article shall disclose, in writing, the existence of any state or local requirements or restrictions relating to the future replacement of existing gas-powered appliances that are being transferred with the property to the extent they or their agent are aware of those requirements or restrictions. For purposes of this section, "gas-powered appliance" includes, but is not limited to, appliances fueled by natural gas or liquid propane. **Leg.H.** Added Stats 2024 ch 443 §2 (SB 382), effective January 1, 2025.

§1102.7. Disclosures to be made in good faith; "Good faith"

Each disclosure required by this article and each act which may be performed in making the disclosure, shall be made in good faith. For purposes of this article, "good faith" means honesty in fact in the conduct of the transaction. **Leg.H.** Added Stats 1985 ch 1574 §2, operative January 1, 1987.

§1102.8. Effect of article on other required disclosures

The specification of items for disclosure in this article does not limit or abridge any obligation for disclosure created by any other provision of law or which may exist in order to avoid fraud, misrepresentation, or deceit in the transfer transaction. **Leg.H.** Added Stats 1985 ch 1574 §2, operative January 1, 1987.

§1102.9. Amendment of disclosure statement

Any disclosure made pursuant to this article may be amended in writing by the seller or his or her agent, but the amendment shall be subject to Section 1102.3 or 1102.3a. **Leg.H.** Added Stats 1985 ch 1574 §2, operative January 1, 1987. Amended Stats 1996 ch 240 §3 (AB 2383); Stats 1999 ch 517 §7 (SB 534); Stats 2018 ch 907 §16 (AB 1289), effective January 1, 2019.

§1102.10. Means of delivering statement

Delivery of disclosures required by this article shall be by personal delivery to the tranferee or by mail to the prospective transferee. For the purposes of this article, delivery to the spouse of a transferee shall be deemed delivery to the transferee, unless provided otherwise by contract. **Leg.H.** Added Stats 1985 ch 1574 §2, operative January 1, 1987.

1985 Note: It appears that the Legislature inadvertently substituted "tranferee" for the word "transferee."

§1102.11. Escrow agents

Any person or entity, other than a real estate licensee licensed pursuant to Part 1 (commencing with Section 10000) of Division 4 of the Business and Professions Code, acting in the capacity of an escrow agent for the transfer of real property subject to this article shall not be deemed the agent of the transferor or transferee for purposes of the disclosure requirements of this article, unless the person or entity is empowered to so act by an express written agreement to that effect. The extent of such an agency shall be governed by the written agreement. **Leg.H.** Added Stats 1985 ch 1574 §2, operative January 1, 1987.

§1102.12. Broker's duties

(a) If more than one licensed real estate broker is acting as an agent in a transaction subject to this article, the broker who has obtained the offer made by the transferee shall, except as otherwise provided in this article, deliver the disclosure required by this article to the transferee, unless the transferor has given other written instructions for delivery.

(b) If a licensed real estate broker responsible for delivering the disclosures under this section cannot obtain the disclosure document required and does not have written assurance from the transferee that the disclosure has been received, the broker shall advise the transferee in writing of his or her rights to the disclosure. A licensed real estate broker responsible for delivering disclosures under this section shall maintain a record of the action taken to effect compliance in accordance with Section 10148 of the Business and Professions Code. **Leg.H.** Added Stats 1985 ch 1574 §2, operative January 1, 1987. Amended Stats 1986 ch 460 §6.

§1102.13. Failure to comply with article; Liability for damages

No transfer subject to this article shall be invalidated solely because of the failure of any person to comply with any provision of this article. However, any person who willfully or negligently violates or fails to perform any duty prescribed by any provision of this article shall be liable in the amount of actual damages suffered by a transferee. **Leg.H.** Added Stats 1985 ch 1574 §2, operative January 1, 1987.

§1102.14. "Listing agent"; "Selling agent" [Repealed]

Leg.H. Added Stats 1986 ch 460 §7. Repealed Stats 2018 ch 907 §17 (AB 1289), effective January 1, 2019.

§1102.15. Disclosure of former ordnance locations within neighborhood area

The seller of residential real property subject to this article who has actual knowledge of any former federal or state ordnance locations within the neighborhood area shall give written notice of that knowledge as soon as practicable before transfer of title.

For purposes of this section, "former federal or state ordnance locations" means an area identified by an agency or instrumentality of the federal or state government as an area once used for military training purposes which may contain potentially explosive munitions. "Neighborhood area" means within one mile of the residential real property.

The disclosure required by this section does not limit or abridge any obligation for disclosure created by any other law or that may exist in order to avoid fraud, misrepresentation, or deceit in the transfer transaction. **Leg.H.** Added Stats 1989 ch 294 §1.

§1102.155. Disclosures relating to water-conserving plumbing fixtures

(a)(1) The seller of single-family residential real property subject to this article shall disclose, in writing, that Section 1101.4 requires that California single-family residences be equipped with water-conserving plumbing fixtures on or after January 1, 2017, and shall disclose whether the property includes any noncompliant plumbing fixtures as defined in subdivision (c) of Section 1101.3.

(2) The seller shall affirm that this representation is that of the seller and not a representation of any agent, and that this disclosure is not intended to be part of any contract between the buyer and the seller. The seller shall further affirm that this disclosure is not a warranty of any kind by the seller or any agent representing any principal in the transaction and is not a substitute for any inspections or warranties that any principal may wish to obtain.

(b) This section shall become operative on January 1, 2017. **Leg.H.** Added Stats 2009 ch 587 §2 (SB 407), effective January 1, 2010, operative January 1, 2017. Amended Stats 2018 ch 907 §18 (AB 1289), effective January 1, 2019.

§ 1102.156. Required disclosure of domestic water storage tank assistance

On or after January 1, 2025, in addition to any other disclosure required pursuant to this article, a seller of any real property who received domestic water storage tank assistance pursuant to Section 13194 of the Water Code, or is aware the real property received such assistance and the real property currently still has the domestic water storage tank, shall deliver to the prospective buyer a disclosure statement that includes all of the following information in substantially the following form:

(a) This property has a domestic water storage tank provided by a county, community water system, local public agency, or nonprofit organization, pursuant to Section 13194 of the Water Code.

(b) The domestic water storage tank was made available to households that had a private water well that had gone dry, or had been destroyed due to drought, wildfire, other natural disasters, or was otherwise nonfunctioning.

(c) The domestic water storage tank provided pursuant to Section 13194 of the Water Code might not convey with the real property.

(d) Due to the water well issues that led to this property obtaining assistance pursuant to Section 13194 of the Water Code, the buyer is advised to have an inspection of the water well and to have a professional evaluate the availability of water to the property to ensure it suits the purposes for which the buyer is purchasing the property. **Leg.H.** Added Stats 2024 ch 21 §1 (SB 1366), effective January 1, 2025.

§1102.16. Disclosure relating to window security bars

The disclosure of the existence of any window security bars and any safety release mechanism on those window security bars shall be made pursuant to Section 1102.6 or 1102.6a of the Civil Code. **Leg.H.** Added Stats 1996 ch 926 §2 (AB 3026), operative July 1, 1997. Amended Stats 2004 ch 183 §26 (AB 3082).

§1102.17. Notice that property is adjacent to, zoned to allow, or affected by nuisance created by industrial use

The seller of residential real property subject to this article who has actual knowledge that the property is adjacent to, or zoned to allow, an industrial use described in Section 731a of the Code of Civil Procedure, or affected by a nuisance created by such a use, shall give written notice of that knowledge as soon as practicable before transfer of title. **Leg.H.** Added Stats 1999 ch 876 §2 (AB 248). Amended Stats 2004 ch 66 §2 (AB 920).

Prior Law: Former §1102.17, relating to disclosure that property is located in a special flood hazard area, was added Stats 1st Ex Sess 1997–98 ch 7 §2, effective December 1, 1998, operative June 1, 1998, and repealed Stats 1998 ch 65 §3, effective June 9, 1998, operative December 1, 1998.

1998 Note: It is the intent of the Legislature that the provisions of Stats 1998 ch 65 shall supersede the provisions of Chapter 7 of the Statutes of 1997, First Extraordinary Session, in their entirety and, to that intent, the provisions of that chapter shall not become operative. Stats 1998 ch 65 §20.

Former Sections: Former CC §1102.17, relating to disclosure that property is located in a special flood hazard area, was added Stats 1997–98 1st Ex Sess ch 7 §2, effective December 1, 1998, operative June 1, 1998, and repealed Stats 1998 ch 65 §3.

§1102.18. Applicability of Section 1102.1(d) to article

The provisions of subdivision (d) of Section 1102.1 shall apply to this article. **Leg.H.** Added Stats 2018 ch 907 §19 (AB 1289), effective January 1, 2019.

Prior Law: Former CC §1102.18, relating to notice of illegal controlled substance releases on residential real property prior to sale of property, was added Stats 2001 ch 466 §1 (SB 189), amended Stats 2003 ch 422 §1 (AB 24), and repealed January 1, 2006, by its own terms.

Former CC §1102.18 was enacted in 2001 and repealed operative January 1, 2006, by its own provisions. Stats 2003 ch 422 §1 (AB 24).

§1102.19. Documentation to buyer of compliance with Public Resources Code Section 4291 or local ordinances for property in high or very high fire hazard severity zone

(a) On and after July 1, 2021, a seller of a real property subject to this article that is located in a high or very high fire hazard severity zone, as identified by the Director of Forestry and Fire Protection pursuant to Section 51178 of the Government Code or Article 9 (commencing with Section 4201) of Chapter 1 of Part 2 of Division 4 of the Public Resources Code, shall provide to the buyer documentation stating that the property is in compliance with Section 4291 of the Public Resources Code or local vegetation management ordinances, as follows:

(1) In a local jurisdiction that has enacted an ordinance requiring an owner of real property to obtain documentation that the property is in compliance with Section 4291 of the Public Resources Code or a local vegetation management ordinance, the seller shall provide the buyer with a copy of the documentation that complies with the requirements of that local ordinance and information on the local agency from which a copy of that documentation may be obtained.

(2) In a local jurisdiction that has not enacted an ordinance for an owner of real property to obtain documentation that a property is in compliance with Section 4291 of the Public Resources Code or a local vegetation management ordinance, and if a state or local agency, or other government entity, or other qualified nonprofit entity, provides an inspection with documentation for the jurisdiction in which the property is located, the seller shall provide the buyer with the documentation obtained in the six-month period preceding the date the seller enters into a transaction to sell that real property and provide information on the local agency from which a copy of that documentation may be obtained.

(b) On and after July 1, 2021, if the seller of a real property described in subdivision (a) has not obtained documentation of compliance in accordance with paragraph (1) or (2) of subdivision (a), the seller and the buyer shall enter into a written agreement pursuant to which the buyer agrees to obtain documentation of compliance with Section 4291 of the Public Resources Code or a local vegetation management ordinance as follows:

(1) In a local jurisdiction that has enacted an ordinance requiring an owner or buyer to obtain documentation of compliance with Section 4291 of the Public Resources Code or a local vegetation management ordinance, the buyer shall comply with that ordinance.

(2) In a local jurisdiction that has not enacted an ordinance requiring an owner or buyer to obtain documentation of compliance, and if a state or local agency, or other government entity, or other qualified nonprofit entity, provides an inspection with documentation for the jurisdiction in which the property is located, the buyer shall obtain documentation of compliance within one year of the date of the close of escrow.

(c) Nothing in this section, including the existence of an agreement between a buyer and seller pursuant to subdivision (b), shall limit the ability of a state or local agency to enforce defensible space requirements pursuant to Section 51182 of the Government Code, Section 4291 of the Public Resources Code, or other applicable statutes, regulations, and local ordinances. **Leg.H.** Added Stats 2019 ch 391 §3 (AB 38), effective January 1, 2020. Amended Stats 2020 ch 36 §12 (AB 3364), effective January 1, 2021.

ARTICLE 1.7
Disclosure of Natural and Environmental Hazards, Right-to-Farm, and Other Disclosures Upon Transfer of Residential Property

Application of statutory provisions. §1103.
Exempt transfers. §1103.1.
Natural hazard disclosure statement. §1103.2.
Delivery of written statement. §1103.3.
Liability and compliance; Expert's report; Notice of airport in vicinity; Notice of San Francisco Bay Conservation and Development Commission Jurisdiction; Notice of right to farm; Notice of mining operations. §1103.4.
Relief from further duties. §1103.5.
Good faith requirement. §1103.7.
Obligations under other laws. §1103.8.
Amendment of disclosure. §1103.9.
Means of delivery of disclosures. §1103.10.
Persons deemed agents. §1103.11.
Delivery and receipt of disclosures. §1103.12.
Effect of failure to comply. §1103.13.
Applicability of Section 1102.1(d) to article. §1103.15.

§1103. Application of statutory provisions

(a) For purpose of this article, the definitions in Chapter 1 (commencing with Section 10000) of Part 1 of Division 4 of the Business and Professions Code shall apply.

(b) Except as provided in Section 1103.1, this article applies to a sale, exchange, real property sales contract, as defined in Section 2985, lease with an option to purchase, any other option to purchase, or ground lease coupled with improvements, of any single-family residential real property.

(c) This article shall apply to the transactions described in subdivision (b) only if the seller or his or her agent is required by one or more of the following to disclose the property's location within a hazard zone:

(1) A seller's agent for a seller of real property that is located within a special flood hazard area (any type Zone "A" or "V") designated by the Federal Emergency Management Agency, or the seller if the seller is acting without a seller's agent, shall disclose to any prospective buyer the fact that the property is located within a special flood hazard area if either:

(A) The seller, or the seller's agent, has actual knowledge that the property is within a special flood hazard area.

(B) The local jurisdiction has compiled a list, by parcel, of properties that are within the special flood hazard area and a notice has been posted at the offices of the county recorder, county assessor, and county planning agency that identifies the location of the parcel list.

(2) A seller's agent for a seller of real property that is located within an area of potential flooding designated pursuant to Section 6161 of the Water Code, or the seller if the seller is acting without a seller's agent, shall disclose to any prospective buyer the fact that the property is located within an area of potential flooding if either:

(A) The seller, or the seller's agent, has actual knowledge that the property is within an inundation area.

(B) The local jurisdiction has compiled a list, by parcel, of properties that are within the inundation area and a notice has been posted at the offices of the county recorder, county assessor, and county planning agency that identifies the location of the parcel list.

(3) A seller of real property that is located within a very high fire hazard severity zone, designated pursuant to Section 51178 of the Government Code, or the seller's agent, shall disclose to any prospective buyer the fact that the property is located within a very high fire hazard severity zone and is subject to the requirements of Section 51182 of the Government Code if either:

(A) The seller or the seller's agent, has actual knowledge that the property is within a very high fire hazard severity zone.

(B) A map that includes the property has been provided to the local agency pursuant to Section 51178 of the Government Code and a notice has been posted at the offices of the county recorder, county assessor, and county planning agency that identifies the location of the map and any information regarding changes to the map received by the local agency.

(4) A seller's agent for a seller of real property that is located within an earthquake fault zone, designated pursuant to Section 2622 of the Public Resources Code, or the seller, if the seller is acting without an agent, shall disclose to any prospective buyer the fact that the property is located within a delineated earthquake fault zone if either:

(A) The seller, or the seller's agent, has actual knowledge that the property is within a delineated earthquake fault zone.

(B) A map that includes the property has been provided to the city or county pursuant to Section 2622 of the Public Resources Code and a notice has been posted at the offices of the county recorder, county assessor, and county planning agency that identifies the location of the map and any information regarding changes to the map received by the county.

(5) A seller's agent for a seller of real property that is located within a seismic hazard zone, designated pursuant to Section 2696 of the Public Resources Code, or the seller if the seller is acting without an agent, shall disclose to any prospective buyer the fact that the property is located within a seismic hazard zone if either:

(A) The seller, or the seller's agent, has actual knowledge that the property is within a seismic hazard zone.

(B) A map that includes the property has been provided to the city or county pursuant to Section 2696 of the Public Resources Code and a notice has been posted at the offices of the county recorder, county assessor, and county planning agency that identifies the location of the map and any information regarding changes to the map received by the county.

(6) A seller of real property that is located within a state responsibility area determined by the board, pursuant to Section 4125 of the Public Resources Code, or the seller's agent, shall disclose to any prospective buyer the fact that the property is located within a wildland area that may

contain substantial forest fire risks and hazards and is subject to the requirements of Section 4291 of the Public Resources Code if either:

(A) The seller, or the seller's agent, has actual knowledge that the property is within a wildland fire zone.

(B) A map that includes the property has been provided to the city or county pursuant to Section 4125 of the Public Resources Code and a notice has been posted at the offices of the county recorder, county assessor, and county planning agency that identifies the location of the map and any information regarding changes to the map received by the county.

(d) Any waiver of the requirements of this article is void as against public policy. **Leg.H.** Added Stats 1999 ch 876 §3 (AB 248). Amended Stats 2000 ch 135 §12 (AB 2539); Stats 2003 1st Ex Sess 2003–2004 ch 8 §1 (SBX1-25), effective May 5, 2003; Stats 2003 ch 741 §2 (SB 1049) (ch 741 prevails); Stats 2004 ch 183 §27 (AB 3082); Stats 2017 ch 26 §1 (SB 92), effective June 27, 2017; Stats 2018 ch 907 §20 (AB 1289), effective January 1, 2019.

§1103.1. Exempt transfers

(a) This article does not apply to the following sales:

(1) Sales or transfers pursuant to court order, including, but not limited to, sales ordered by a probate court in administration of an estate, sales pursuant to a writ of execution, sales by any foreclosure sale, sales by a trustee in bankruptcy, sales by eminent domain, and sales resulting from a decree for specific performance.

(2) Sales or transfers to a mortgagee by a mortgagor or successor in interest who is in default, sales to a beneficiary of a deed of trust by a trustor or successor in interest who is in default, transfers by any foreclosure sale after default, any foreclosure sale after default in an obligation secured by a mortgage, sale under a power of sale or any foreclosure sale under a decree of foreclosure after default in an obligation secured by a deed of trust or secured by any other instrument containing a power of sale, or sales by a mortgagee or a beneficiary under a deed of trust who has acquired the real property at a sale conducted pursuant to a power of sale under a mortgage or deed of trust or a sale pursuant to a decree of foreclosure or has acquired the real property by a deed in lieu of foreclosure.

(3) Sales or transfers by a fiduciary in the course of the administration of a trust, guardianship, conservatorship, or decedent's estate. This exemption shall not apply to a sale if the trustee is a natural person who is a trustee of a revocable trust and the seller is a former owner of the property or an occupant in possession of the property within the preceding year.

(4) Sales or transfers from one coowner to one or more other coowners.

(5) Sales or transfers made to a spouse, or to a person or persons in the line of consanguinity of one or more of the sellers.

(6) Sales or transfers between spouses resulting from a judgment of dissolution of marriage or of legal separation of the parties or from a property settlement agreement incidental to that judgment.

(7) Sales or transfers by the Controller in the course of administering Chapter 7 (commencing with Section 1500) of Title 10 of Part 3 of the Code of Civil Procedure.

(8) Sales or transfers under Chapter 7 (commencing with Section 3691) or Chapter 8 (commencing with Section 3771) of Part 6 of Division 1 of the Revenue and Taxation Code.

(9) Sales, transfers, or exchanges to or from any governmental entity.

(10) The sale, creation, or transfer of any lease of any duration except a lease with an option to purchase or a ground lease coupled with improvements.

(b) Sales and transfers not subject to this article may be subject to other disclosure requirements, including those under Sections 8589.3, 8589.4, and 51183.5 of the Government Code and Sections 2621.9, 2694, and 4136 of the Public Resources Code. In sales not subject to this article, agents may make required disclosures in a separate writing.

(c) Notwithstanding the definition of sale in Section 10018.5 of the Business and Professions Code and Section 2079.13, the terms "sale" and "transfer," as they are used in this section, shall have their commonly understood meanings. The changes made to this section by Assembly Bill 1289 of the 2017-18 Legislative Session shall not be interpreted to change the application of the law as it read prior to January 1, 2019. **Leg.H.** Added Stats 1999 ch 876 §3 (AB 248). Amended Stats 2018 ch 907 §21 (AB 1289), effective January 1, 2019; Stats 2019 ch 310 §7 (AB 892), effective January 1, 2020; Stats 2019 ch 497 §22 (AB 991), effective January 1, 2020 (ch 310 prevails; ch 497 not effective); Stats 2020 ch 370 §27 (SB 1371), effective January 1, 2021.

§1103.2. Natural hazard disclosure statement

(a) The disclosures required by this article are set forth in, and shall be made on a copy of, the following Natural Hazard Disclosure Statement:

NATURAL HAZARD DISCLOSURE STATEMENT

This statement applies to the following property: _____

The seller and the seller's agent(s) or a third-party consultant disclose the following information with the knowledge that even though this is not a warranty, prospective buyers may rely on this information in deciding whether and on what terms to purchase the subject property. Seller hereby authorizes any agent(s) representing any principal(s) in this action to provide a copy of this statement to any person or entity in connection with any actual or anticipated sale of the property.

The following are representations made by the seller and the seller's agent(s) based on their knowledge and maps drawn by the state and federal governments. This information is a disclosure and is not intended to be part of any contract between the seller and buyer.

THIS REAL PROPERTY LIES WITHIN THE FOLLOWING HAZARDOUS AREA(S):

A SPECIAL FLOOD HAZARD AREA (Any type Zone "A" or "V") designated by the Federal Emergency Management Agency.

Yes ____ No ____ Do not know and information not available from local jurisdiction ____

AN AREA OF POTENTIAL FLOODING shown on a dam failure inundation map pursuant to Section 8589.5 of the Government Code.

Yes ____ No ____ Do not know and information not available from local jurisdiction ____

A HIGH or VERY HIGH FIRE HAZARD SEVERITY ZONE (FHSZ) as identified by the Director of Forestry and Fire Protection pursuant to Section 51178 of the Government Code or Article 9 (commencing with Section 4201) of Chapter 1 of Part 2 of Division 4 of the Public Resources Code. The owner of this property is subject to the maintenance requirements of Section 51182 of the Government Code.

Yes ____ No ____

High FHSZ in a state responsibility area ____
Very High FHSZ in a state responsibility area ____
Very High FHSZ in a local responsibility area ____

A WILDLAND AREA THAT MAY CONTAIN SUBSTANTIAL FOREST FIRE RISKS AND HAZARDS pursuant to Section 4125 of the Public Resources Code. The owner of this property is subject to the maintenance requirements of Section 4291 of the Public Resources Code. Additionally, it is not the state's responsibility to provide fire protection services to any building or structure located within the wildlands unless the Department of Forestry and Fire Protection has entered into a cooperative agreement with a local agency for those purposes pursuant to Section 4142 of the Public Resources Code.

Yes ____ No ____

AN EARTHQUAKE FAULT ZONE pursuant to Section 2622 of the Public Resources Code.

Yes ____ No ____

A SEISMIC HAZARD ZONE pursuant to Section 2696 of the Public Resources Code.

Yes (Landslide Zone) ____ Yes (Liquefaction Zone) ____

No ____ Map not yet released by state ____

THESE HAZARDS MAY LIMIT YOUR ABILITY TO DEVELOP THE REAL PROPERTY, TO OBTAIN INSURANCE, OR TO RECEIVE ASSISTANCE AFTER A DISASTER.

THE MAPS ON WHICH THESE DISCLOSURES ARE BASED ESTIMATE WHERE NATURAL HAZARDS EXIST. THEY ARE NOT DEFINITIVE INDICATORS OF WHETHER OR NOT A PROPERTY

WILL BE AFFECTED BY A NATURAL DISASTER. SELLER(S) AND BUYER(S) MAY WISH TO OBTAIN PROFESSIONAL ADVICE REGARDING THOSE HAZARDS AND OTHER HAZARDS THAT MAY AFFECT THE PROPERTY.

Signature of Seller(s) _____ Date _____
Signature of Seller(s) _____ Date _____

Seller's Agent(s) _____
Seller's Agent(s) _____ Date _____

Check only one of the following:

☐ Seller(s) and their agent(s) represent that the information herein is true and correct to the best of their knowledge as of the date signed by the transferor(s) and agent(s).

☐ Seller(s) and their agent(s) acknowledge that they have exercised good faith in the selection of a third-party report provider as required in Section 1103.7 of the Civil Code, and that the representations made in this Natural Hazard Disclosure Statement are based upon information provided by the independent third-party disclosure provider as a substituted disclosure pursuant to Section 1103.4 of the Civil Code. Neither seller(s) nor their agent(s) (1) has independently verified the information contained in this statement and report or (2) is personally aware of any errors or inaccuracies in the information contained on the statement. This statement was prepared by the provider below:

Third-Party
Disclosure Provider(s) _____ Date _____

Buyer represents that Buyer has read and understands this document. Pursuant to Section 1103.8 of the Civil Code, the representations made in this Natural Hazard Disclosure Statement do not constitute all of the seller's or agent's disclosure obligations in this transaction.

Signature of Buyer(s) _____ Date _____
Signature of Buyer(s) _____ Date _____

(b) If an earthquake fault zone, seismic hazard zone, high or very high fire hazard severity zone, or wildland fire area map or accompanying information is not of sufficient accuracy or scale that a reasonable person can determine if the subject real property is included in a natural hazard area, the seller or seller's agent shall mark "Yes" on the Natural Hazard Disclosure Statement. The seller's agent may mark "No" on the Natural Hazard Disclosure Statement if the seller attaches a report prepared pursuant to subdivision (c) of Section 1103.4 that verifies the property is not in the hazard zone. This subdivision is not intended to limit or abridge any existing duty of the seller or the seller's agent to exercise reasonable care in making a determination under this subdivision.

(c) If the Federal Emergency Management Agency has issued a Letter of Map Revision confirming that a property is no longer within a special flood hazard area, then the seller or seller's agent may mark "No" on the Natural Hazard Disclosure Statement, even if the map has not yet been updated. The seller or seller's agent shall attach a copy of the Letter of Map Revision to the disclosure statement.

(d) If the Federal Emergency Management Agency has issued a Letter of Map Revision confirming that a property is within a special flood hazard area and the location of the letter has been posted pursuant to subdivision (g) of Section 8589.3 of the Government Code, then the seller or seller's agent shall mark "Yes" on the Natural Hazard Disclosure Statement, even if the map has not yet been updated. The seller or seller's agent shall attach a copy of the Letter of Map Revision to the disclosure statement.

(e) The disclosure required pursuant to this article may be provided by the seller and the seller's agent in the Local Option Real Estate **Transfer** Disclosure Statement described in Section 1102.6a, provided that the Local Option Real Estate **Transfer** Disclosure Statement includes substantially the same information and substantially the same warnings that are required by this section.

(f)(1) The legal effect of a consultant's report delivered to satisfy the exemption provided by Section 1103.4 is not changed when it is accompanied by a Natural Hazard Disclosure Statement.

(2) A consultant's report shall always be accompanied by a completed and signed Natural Hazard Disclosure Statement.

(3) In a disclosure statement required by this section, an agent and third-party provider may cause the agent and third-party provider's name to be preprinted in lieu of an original signature in the portions of the form reserved for signatures. The use of a preprinted name shall not change the legal effect of the acknowledgment.

(g) The disclosure required by this article is only a disclosure between the seller, the seller's agent, and the prospective buyer, and shall not be used by any other party, including, but not limited to, insurance companies, lenders, or governmental agencies, for any purpose.

(h) In any transaction in which a seller has accepted, prior to June 1, 1998, an offer to purchase, the seller, or the seller's agent shall be deemed to have complied with the requirement of subdivision (a) if the seller or agent delivers to the prospective buyer a statement that includes substantially the same information and warning as the Natural Hazard Disclosure Statement. **Leg.H.** Added Stats 1999 ch 876 §3 (AB 248). Amended Stats 2003 1st Ex Sess 2003–2004 ch 8 §2 (SBX1-25), effective May 5, 2003; Stats 2003 ch 741 §3 (SB 1049); Stats 2004 ch 66 §3 (AB 920); Stats 2018 ch 907 §22 (AB 1289), effective January 1, 2019; Stats 2019 ch 497 §23 (AB 991), effective January 1, 2020; Stats 2023 ch 99 §1 (AB 1280), effective January 1, 2024; Stats 2024 ch 80 §19 (SB 1525), effective January 1, 2025.

§1103.3. Delivery of written statement

(a) The seller of any real property subject to this article shall deliver to the prospective buyer the written statement required by this article, as follows:

(1) In the case of a sale, as soon as practicable before transfer of title.

(2) In the case of a sale by a real property sales contract, as defined in Section 2985, or by a lease together with an option to purchase, or a ground lease coupled with improvements, as soon as practicable before the prospective buyer's execution of the contract. For the purpose of this subdivision, "execution" means the making or acceptance of an offer.

(b) The seller shall indicate compliance with this article either on the real property sales contract, the lease, any addendum attached thereto, or on a separate document.

(c) If any disclosure, or any material amendment of any disclosure, required to be made pursuant to this article is delivered after the execution of an offer to purchase, the prospective buyer shall have three days after delivery in person, five days after delivery by deposit in the mail, or five days after delivery of an electronic record in transactions where the parties have agreed to conduct the transaction by electronic means, pursuant to provisions of the Uniform Electronic Transactions Act (Title 2.5 (commencing with Section 1633.1) of Part 2 of Division 3), to terminate his or her offer by delivery of a written notice of termination to the seller or the seller's agent. **Leg.H.** Added Stats 1999 ch 876 §3 (AB 248). Amended Stats 2018 ch 907 §23 (AB 1289), effective January 1, 2019.

§1103.4. Liability and compliance; Expert's report; Notice of airport in vicinity; Notice of San Francisco Bay Conservation and Development Commission Jurisdiction; Notice of right to farm; Notice of mining operations

(a) Neither the seller nor any seller's agent or buyer's agent shall be liable for any error, inaccuracy, or omission of any information delivered pursuant to this article if the error, inaccuracy, or omission was not within the personal knowledge of the seller or the seller's agent or buyer's agent and was based on information timely provided by public agencies or by other persons providing information as specified in subdivision (c) that is required to be disclosed pursuant to this article, and ordinary care was exercised in obtaining and transmitting the information.

(b) The delivery of any information required to be disclosed by this article to a prospective buyer by a public agency or other person providing information required to be disclosed pursuant to this article shall be deemed to comply with the requirements of this article and shall relieve the seller, seller's agent, and buyer's agent of any further duty under this article with respect to that item of information.

(c) The delivery of a report or opinion prepared by a licensed engineer, land surveyor, geologist, or expert in natural hazard discovery dealing with matters within the scope of the professional's license or expertise shall be sufficient compliance for application of the exemption provided by subdivision (a) if the information is provided to the prospective buyer pursuant to a request therefor, whether written or oral. In responding to that request, an expert may indicate, in writing, an understanding that the information provided will be used in fulfilling the requirements of Section 1103.2 and, if so, shall indicate the required disclosures, or parts thereof, to which the information being furnished is applicable. Where such a statement is furnished, the expert shall not be responsible for any items of information or parts thereof, other than those expressly set forth in the statement.

(1) In responding to the request, the expert shall determine whether the property is within an airport influence area as defined in subdivision (b) of Section 11010 of the Business and Professions Code. If the property is within an airport influence area, the report shall contain the following statement:

NOTICE OF AIRPORT IN VICINITY

This property is presently located in the vicinity of an airport, within what is known as an airport influence area. For that reason, the property may be subject to some of the annoyances or inconveniences associated with proximity to airport operations (for example: noise, vibration, or odors). Individual sensitivities to those annoyances can vary from person to person. You may wish to consider what airport annoyances, if any, are associated with the property before you complete your purchase and determine whether they are acceptable to you.

(2) In responding to the request, the expert shall determine whether the property is within the jurisdiction of the San Francisco Bay Conservation and Development Commission, as defined in Section 66620 of the Government Code. If the property is within the commission's jurisdiction, the report shall contain the following notice:

NOTICE OF SAN FRANCISCO BAY CONSERVATION AND DEVELOPMENT COMMISSION JURISDICTION

This property is located within the jurisdiction of the San Francisco Bay Conservation and Development Commission. Use and development of property within the commission's jurisdiction may be subject to special regulations, restrictions, and permit requirements. You may wish to investigate and determine whether they are acceptable to you and your intended use of the property before you complete your transaction.

(3) In responding to the request, the expert shall determine whether the property is presently located within one mile of a parcel of real property designated as "Prime Farmland," "Farmland of Statewide Importance," "Unique Farmland," "Farmland of Local Importance," or "Grazing Land" on the most current "Important Farmland Map" issued by the California Department of Conservation, Division of Land Resource Protection, utilizing solely the county-level GIS map data, if any, available on the Farmland Mapping and Monitoring Program Web site. If the residential property is within one mile of a designated farmland area, the report shall contain the following notice:

NOTICE OF RIGHT TO FARM

This property is located within one mile of a farm or ranch land designated on the current county-level GIS "Important Farmland Map," issued by the California Department of Conservation, Division of Land Resource Protection. Accordingly, the property may be subject to inconveniences or discomforts resulting from agricultural operations that are a normal and necessary aspect of living in a community with a strong rural character and a healthy agricultural sector. Customary agricultural practices in farm operations may include, but are not limited to, noise, odors, dust, light, insects, the operation of pumps and machinery, the storage and disposal of manure, bee pollination, and the ground or aerial application of fertilizers, pesticides, and herbicides. These agricultural practices may occur at any time during the 24-hour day. Individual sensitivities to those practices can vary from person to person. You may wish to consider the impacts of such agricultural practices before you complete your purchase. Please be advised that you may be barred from obtaining legal remedies against agricultural practices conducted in a manner consistent with proper and accepted customs and standards pursuant to Section 3482.5 of the Civil Code or any pertinent local ordinance.

(4) In responding to the request, the expert shall determine, utilizing map coordinate data made available by the Office of Mine Reclamation, whether the property is presently located within one mile of a mine operation for which map coordinate data has been reported to the director pursuant to Section 2207 of the Public Resources Code. If the expert determines, from the available map coordinate data, that the residential property is located within one mile of a mine operation, the report shall contain the following notice:

NOTICE OF MINING OPERATIONS:

This property is located within one mile of a mine operation for which the mine owner or operator has reported mine location data to the Department of Conservation pursuant to Section 2207 of the Public Resources Code. Accordingly, the property may be subject to inconveniences resulting from mining operations. You may wish to consider the impacts of these practices before you complete your transaction. **Leg.H.** Added Stats 1999 ch 876 §3 (AB 248). Amended Stats 2002 ch 496 §4 (AB 2776), operative January 1, 2004; Stats 2004 ch 618 §2 (SB 1568); Stats 2008 ch 686 §3 (AB 2881), effective January 1, 2009; Stats 2011 ch 253 §1 (SB 110), effective January 1, 2012; Stats 2018 ch 907 §24 (AB 1289), effective January 1, 2019.

§1103.5. Relief from further duties

(a) After a seller and his or her agent comply with Section 1103.2, they shall be relieved of further duty under this article with respect to those items of information. The seller and the seller's agent shall not be required to provide notice to the prospective buyer if the information provided subsequently becomes inaccurate as a result of any governmental action, map revision, changed information, or other act or occurrence, unless the seller or agent has actual knowledge that the information has become inaccurate.

(b) If information disclosed in accordance with this article is subsequently rendered inaccurate as a result of any governmental action, map revision, changed information, or other act or occurrence subsequent to the delivery of the required disclosures, the inaccuracy resulting therefrom does not constitute a violation of this article. **Leg.H.** Added Stats 1999 ch 876 §3 (AB 248). Amended Stats 2018 ch 907 §25 (AB 1289), effective January 1, 2019.

§1103.7. Good faith requirement

Each disclosure required by this article and each act that may be performed in making the disclosure shall be made in good faith. For purposes of this article, "good faith" means honesty in fact in the conduct of the transaction. **Leg.H.** Added Stats 1999 ch 876 §3 (AB 248).

§1103.8. Obligations under other laws

(a) The specification of items for disclosure in this article does not limit or abridge any obligation for disclosure created by any other provision of law or that may exist in order to avoid fraud, misrepresentation, or deceit in the sale transaction. The Legislature does not intend to affect the existing obligations of the parties to a real estate contract, or their agents, to disclose any fact materially affecting the value and desirability of the property, including, but not limited to, the physical condition of the property and previously received reports of physical inspection noted on the disclosure form provided pursuant to Section 1102.6 or 1102.6a.

(b) Nothing in this article shall be construed to change the duty of a real estate broker or salesperson pursuant to Section 2079. **Leg.H.** Added Stats 1999 ch 876 §3 (AB 248). Amended Stats 2018 ch 907 §26 (AB 1289), effective January 1, 2019.

§1103.9. Amendment of disclosure

Any disclosure made pursuant to this article may be amended in writing by the seller or the seller's agent, but the amendment shall be subject to Section 1103.3. **Leg.H.** Added Stats 1999 ch 876 §3 (AB 248). Amended Stats 2018 ch 907 §27 (AB 1289), effective January 1, 2019.

§1103.10. Means of delivery of disclosures

Delivery of disclosures required by this article shall be by personal delivery to the transferee or by mail to the prospective transferee. For the purposes of this article, delivery to the spouse of a transferee shall be deemed delivery to the transferee, unless provided otherwise by contract. **Leg.H.** Added Stats 1999 ch 876 §3 (AB 248).

§1103.11. Persons deemed agents

Any person or entity, other than a real estate licensee licensed pursuant to Part 1 (commencing with Section 10000) of Division 4 of the Business and Professions Code, acting in the capacity of an escrow agent for the transfer of real property subject to this article shall not be deemed the agent of the transferor or transferee for purposes of the disclosure requirements of this article, unless the person or entity is empowered to so act by an express written agreement to that effect. The extent of that agency shall be governed by the written agreement. **Leg.H.** Added Stats 1999 ch 876 §3 (AB 248).

§1103.12. Delivery and receipt of disclosures

(a) If more than one licensed real estate broker is acting as an agent in a transaction subject to this article, the broker who has obtained the offer made by the transferee shall, except as otherwise provided in this article, deliver the disclosure required by this article to the transferee, unless the transferor has given other written instructions for delivery.

(b) If a licensed real estate broker responsible for delivering the disclosures under this section cannot obtain the disclosure document required and does not have written assurance from the transferee that the disclosure has been received, the broker shall advise the transferee in writing of his or her rights to the disclosure. A licensed real estate broker responsible for delivering disclosures under this section shall maintain a record of the action taken to effect compliance in accordance with Section 10148 of the Business and Professions Code. **Leg.H.** Added Stats 1999 ch 876 §3 (AB 248).

§1103.13. Effect of failure to comply

No transfer subject to this article shall be invalidated solely because of the failure of any person to comply with any provision of this article. However, any person who willfully or negligently violates or fails to perform any duty prescribed by any provision of this article shall be liable in the amount of actual damages suffered by a transferee. **Leg.H.** Added Stats 1999 ch 876 §3 (AB 248).

§1103.14. Definitions [Repealed]

Leg.H. Added Stats 1999 ch 876 §3 (AB 248). Repealed Stats 2018 ch 907 §28 (AB 1289), effective January 1, 2019.

§1103.15. Applicability of Section 1102.1(d) to article

The provisions of subdivision (d) of Section 1102.1 shall apply to this article. **Leg.H.** Added Stats 2018 ch 907 §29 (AB 1289), effective January 1, 2019.

ARTICLE 1.8
Buyer's Choice Act

Citation of article. §1103.20.
Findings and declaration. §1103.21.
Option to choose title insurer or escrow agent; Violation of section. §1103.22.

§1103.20. Citation of article

This article shall be known, and may be cited, as the Buyer's Choice Act. **Leg.H.** Added Stats 2009 ch 264 §1 (AB 957), effective October 11, 2009. Amended Stats 2014 ch 198 §1 (SB 1051), effective January 1, 2015.

§1103.21. Findings and declaration

(a) The Legislature finds and declares:

(1) Sales of foreclosed properties have become a dominant portion of homes on the resale real estate market.

(2) The recent troubled real estate market has resulted in a concentration of the majority of homes available for resale within the hands of foreclosing lenders and has dramatically changed the market dynamics affecting ordinary home buyers.

(3) Preserving the fair negotiability of contract terms is an important policy goal to be preserved in real estate transactions.

(4) The potential for unfairness occasioned by the resale of large numbers of foreclosed homes on the market requires that protections against abuses be made effective immediately.

(5) The federal Real Estate Settlement Procedures Act (RESPA) creates general rules for fair negotiation of settlement services, prohibits kickbacks and specifically prohibits a seller in a federally related transaction from requiring a buyer to purchase title insurance from a particular insurer.

(6) California law does not specifically prohibit a seller from imposing, as a condition of sale of a foreclosed home, the purchase of title insurance or escrow services from a particular insurer or provider.

(7) Therefore it is necessary to add this act to California law to provide to a home buyer protection that follows the RESPA model and applies to, and prevents, the conditioning of a sale of a foreclosed home on the buyer's purchase of title insurance from a particular insurer or title company and/or the buyer's purchase of escrow services from a particular provider.

(b) It is the intent of the Legislature that, for the purpose of this act, the sale of a residential real property is deemed to include the receipt of an offer to purchase that residential real property. **Leg.H.** Added Stats 2009 ch 264 §1 (AB 957), effective October 11, 2009. Amended Stats 2014 ch 198 §1 (SB 1051), effective January 1, 2015.

§1103.22. Option to choose title insurer or escrow agent; Violation of section

(a) A seller of residential real property improved by four or fewer dwelling units shall not require directly or indirectly, as a condition of selling the property, that title insurance covering the property or escrow service provided in connection with the sale of the property be purchased by the buyer from a particular title insurer or escrow agent. This section does not prohibit a buyer from agreeing to accept the services of a title insurer or an escrow agent recommended by the seller if written notice of the right to make an independent selection of those services is first provided by the seller to the buyer.

(b) For purposes of this section:

(1) Escrow service" means service provided by a person licensed pursuant to Division 6 (commencing with Section 17000) of the Financial Code, or exempt from licensing pursuant to Section 17006 of the Financial Code.

(2) "Seller" means a mortgagee or beneficiary under a deed of trust who acquired title to residential real property improved by four or fewer dwelling units at a foreclosure sale, including a trustee, agent, officer, or other employee of any such mortgagee or beneficiary.

(3) "Title insurance" means insurance offered by an insurer admitted in this state to transact title insurance pursuant to Chapter 1 (commencing with Section 12340) of Part 6 of the Insurance Code.

(c) A seller who violates this section shall be liable to a buyer in an amount equal to three times all charges made for the title insurance or escrow service. In addition, any person who violates this section shall be deemed to have violated his or her license law and shall be subject to discipline by his or her licensing entity.

(d) A transaction subject to this section shall not be invalidated solely because of the failure of any person to comply with any provision of this act. **Leg.H.** Added Stats 2009 ch 264 §1 (AB 957), effective October 11, 2009. Amended Stats 2014 ch 198 §1 (SB 1051), effective January 1, 2015.

§1103.23. [Section repealed 2015]

Leg.H. Added Stats 2009 ch 264 §1 (AB 957), effective October 11, 2009. Repealed Stats 2014 ch 198 §1 (SB 1051), effective January 1, 2015. The repealed section related to repeal of the article.

ARTICLE 2
Effect of Transfer

What easements pass with property. §1104.
When fee simple title is presumed to pass. §1105.
Subsequently acquired title passes by operation of law. §1106.
Grant, how far conclusive on purchasers. §1107.
Conveyances by owner for life or for years. §1108.
Grant made on condition subsequent. §1109.
Grant to take effect upon condition precedent. §1110.
Grant of rents, reversions, and remainders. §1111.
Transfer of land bounded by highway. §1112.
Implied covenants. §1113.
"Incumbrances". §1114.
Lineal and collateral warranties abolished. §1115.
Sale or lease of subdivision lot subject to blanket encumbrance; Required notice to buyer or lessee. §1133.
Disclosures required in condominium transfer. §1134.

§1104. What easements pass with property

A transfer of real property passes all easements attached thereto, and creates in favor thereof an easement to use other real property of the person whose estate is transferred in the same manner and to the same extent as such property was obviously and permanently used by the person whose estate is transferred, for the benefit thereof, at the time when the transfer was agreed upon or completed. **Leg.H.** Enacted Stats 1872.

§1105. When fee simple title is presumed to pass

A fee simple title is presumed to be intended to pass by a grant of real property, unless it appears from the grant that a lesser estate was intended. **Leg.H.** Enacted Stats 1872.

§1106. Subsequently acquired title passes by operation of law

Where a person purports by proper instrument to grant real property in fee simple, and subsequently acquires any title, or claim of title thereto, the same passes by operation of law to the grantee, or his successors. **Leg.H.** Enacted Stats 1872.

§1107. Grant, how far conclusive on purchasers

Every grant of an estate in real property is conclusive against the grantor, also against every one subsequently claiming under him, except a purchaser or incumbrancer who in good faith and for a valuable consideration acquires a title or lien by an instrument that is first duly recorded. **Leg.H.** Enacted Stats 1872.

§1108. Conveyances by owner for life or for years

A grant made by the owner of an estate for life or years, purporting to transfer a greater estate than he could lawfully transfer, does not work a forfeiture of his estate, but passes to the grantee all the estate which the grantor could lawfully transfer. **Leg.H.** Enacted Stats 1872.

§1109. Grant made on condition subsequent

Where a grant is made upon condition subsequent, and is subsequently defeated by the non-performance of the condition, the person otherwise entitled to hold under the grant must reconvey the property to the grantor or his successors, by grant, duly acknowledged for record. **Leg.H.** Enacted Stats 1872.

§1110. Grant to take effect upon condition precedent

An instrument purporting to be a grant of real property, to take effect upon condition precedent, passes the estate upon the performance of the condition. **Leg.H.** Enacted Stats 1872. Amended Code Amdts 1873–74 ch 612 §132.

§1111. Grant of rents, reversions, and remainders

Grants of rents or of reversions or of remainders are good and effectual without attornments of the tenants; but no tenant who, before notice of the grant, shall have paid rent to the grantor, must suffer any damage thereby. **Leg.H.** Enacted Stats 1872.

§1112. Transfer of land bounded by highway

A transfer of land, bounded by a highway, passes the title of the person whose estate is transferred to the soil of the highway in front to the center thereof, unless a different intent appears from the grant. **Leg.H.** Enacted Stats 1872. Amended Code Amdts 1873–74 ch 612 §133.

§1113. Implied covenants

From the use of the word "grant" in any conveyance by which an estate of inheritance or fee simple is to be passed, the following covenants, and none other, on the part of the grantor for himself and his heirs to the grantee, his heirs, and assigns, are implied, unless restrained by express terms contained in such conveyance:

1. That previous to the time of the execution of such conveyance, the grantor has not conveyed the same estate, or any right, title, or interest therein, to any person other than the grantee;

2. That such estate is at the time of the execution of such conveyance free from incumbrances done, made, or suffered by the grantor, or any person claiming under him.

Such covenants may be sued upon in the same manner as if they had been expressly inserted in the conveyance. **Leg.H.** Enacted Stats 1872.

§1114. "Incumbrances"

The term "incumbrances" includes taxes, assessments, and all liens upon real property. **Leg.H.** Enacted Stats 1872. Amended Code Amdts 1873–74 ch 612 §134.

§1115. Lineal and collateral warranties abolished

Lineal and collateral warranties, with all their incidents, are abolished; but the heirs and devisees of every person who has made any covenant or agreement in reference to the title of, in, or to any real property, are answerable upon such covenant or agreement to the extent of the land descended or devised to them, in the cases and in the manner prescribed by law. **Leg.H.** Enacted Stats 1872.

§1133. Sale or lease of subdivision lot subject to blanket encumbrance; Required notice to buyer or lessee

(a) If a lot, parcel, or unit of a subdivision is subject to a blanket encumbrance, as defined in Section 11013 of the Business and Professions Code, but is exempt from a requirement of compliance with Section 11013.2 of the Business and Professions Code, the subdivider, his or her agent, or representative, shall not sell, or lease for a term exceeding five years, the lot, parcel, or unit, nor cause it to be sold, or leased for a term exceeding five years, until the prospective purchaser or lessee of the lot, parcel, or unit has been furnished with and has signed a true copy of the following notice:

BUYER/LESSEE IS AWARE OF THE FACT THAT THE LOT, PARCEL, OR UNIT WHICH HE OR SHE IS PROPOSING TO PURCHASE OR LEASE IS SUBJECT TO A DEED OF TRUST, MORTGAGE, OR OTHER LIEN KNOWN AS A "BLANKET ENCUMBRANCE".

IF BUYER/LESSEE PURCHASES OR LEASES THIS LOT, PARCEL, OR UNIT, HE OR SHE COULD LOSE THAT INTEREST THROUGH FORECLOSURE OF THE BLANKET ENCUMBRANCE OR OTHER LEGAL PROCESS EVEN THOUGH BUYER/LESSEE IS NOT DELINQUENT IN HIS OR HER PAYMENTS OR OTHER OBLIGATIONS UNDER THE MORTGAGE, DEED OF TRUST, OR LEASE.

_____
Date

_____
Signature of Buyer or Lessee

(b) "Subdivision," as used in subdivision (a), means improved or unimproved land that is divided or proposed to be divided for the purpose of sale, lease, or financing, whether immediate or future, into two or more lots, parcels, or units and includes a condominium project, as defined in Section 4125 or 6542, a community apartment project, as defined in Section 4105, a stock cooperative, as defined in Section 4190 or 6566, and a limited equity housing cooperative, as defined in Section 4190.

(c) The failure of the buyer or lessee to sign the notice shall not invalidate any grant, conveyance, lease, or encumbrance.

(d) Any person or entity who willfully violates the provisions of this section shall be liable to the purchaser of a lot or unit which is subject to the provisions of this section for actual damages, and, in addition thereto, shall be guilty of a public offense punishable by a fine in an amount not to exceed five hundred dollars ($500). In an action to enforce the liability or fine, the prevailing party shall be awarded reasonable attorney's fees. **Leg.H.** Added Stats 1982 ch 148 §3, effective April 5, 1982. Amended Stats 1985 ch 874 §12; Stats 2012 ch 181 §35 (AB 806), effective January 1, 2013, operative January 1, 2014; Stats 2013 ch 605 §15 (SB 752), effective January 1, 2014.

§1134. Disclosures required in condominium transfer

(a) As soon as practicable before transfer of title for the first sale of a unit in a residential condominium, community apartment project, or stock cooperative which was converted from an existing dwelling to a condominium project, community apartment project, or stock cooperative, the owner or subdivider, or agent of the owner or subdivider, shall deliver to a prospective buyer a written statement listing all substantial defects or malfunctions in the major systems in the unit and common areas of the premises, or a written statement disclaiming knowledge of any such substantial defects or malfunctions. The disclaimer may be delivered only after the owner or subdivider has inspected the unit and the common areas and has not discovered a substantial defect or malfunction which a reasonable inspection would have disclosed.

(b) If any disclosure required to be made by this section is delivered after the execution of an agreement to purchase, the buyer shall have three days after delivery in person or five days after delivery by deposit in the mail, to terminate his or her agreement by delivery of written notice of that termination to the owner, subdivider, or agent. Any disclosure delivered after the execution of an agreement to purchase shall contain a statement describing the buyer's right, method and time to rescind as prescribed by this subdivision.

(c) For the purposes of this section:

(1) "Major systems" includes, but is not limited to, the roof, walls, floors, heating, air conditioning, plumbing, electrical systems or components of a similar or comparable nature, and recreational facilities.

(2) Delivery to a prospective buyer of the written statement required by this section shall be deemed effected when delivered personally or by mail to the prospective buyer or to an agent thereof, or to a spouse unless the agreement provides to the contrary. Delivery shall also be made to additional prospective buyers who have made a request therefor in writing.

(3) "Prospective buyer" includes any person who makes an offer to purchase a unit in the condominium, community apartment project, or stock cooperative.

(d) Any person who willfully fails to carry out the requirements of this section shall be liable in the amount of actual damages suffered by the buyer.

(e) Nothing in this section shall preclude the injured party from pursuing any remedy available under any other provision of law.

(f) No transfer of title to a unit subject to the provisions of this chapter shall be invalid solely because of the failure of any person to comply with the requirements of this section.

(g) The written statement required by this section shall not abridge or limit any other obligation of disclosure created by any other provision of law or which is or may be required to avoid fraud, deceit, or misrepresentation in the transaction. **Leg.H.** Added Stats 1981 ch 811 §1, operative July 1, 1982.

§1134.5. [Section repealed 1986]

Leg.H. Added Stats 1984 ch 1183 §1, operative July 1, 1985. Amended Stats 1985 ch 982 §1. Repealed Stats 1986 ch 460 §8. See CC §§1102 et seq.

CHAPTER 3
TRANSFER OF PERSONAL PROPERTY

Article 1. Mode of Transfer.
Article 3. Gifts.

ARTICLE 1
Mode of Transfer

Transfer of interest in ship. §1135.
Ownership of dies, molds, and forms. §1140.

§1135. Transfer of interest in ship

An interest in a ship can be transferred only by operation of law, or by written instrument, subscribed by the person making the transfer, or by his agent. **Leg.H.** Enacted Stats 1872. Amended Stats 1931 ch 1070 §6.

§1136. [Section repealed 1931]

Leg.H. Enacted Stats 1872. Repealed Stats 1931 ch 1070 §2.

§1140. Ownership of dies, molds, and forms

(a) For purposes of this section:

(1) The term "customer" means any individual or entity who causes or caused a molder to fabricate, cast, or otherwise make a die, mold, or form.

(2) The term "molder" means any individual or entity, including, but not limited to, a tool or die maker, who fabricates, casts, or otherwise makes a die, mold, or form.

(3) For purposes of this section, the term "within three years following the last prior use" shall be construed to include any period following the last prior use of a die, mold, or form regardless of whether or not that period precedes the effective date of this section.

(b) In the absence of any agreement to the contrary, the customer shall have all rights and title to any die, mold, or form in the possession of the molder.

(c) If a customer does not claim possession from a molder of a die, mold, or form within three years following the last prior use thereof, all rights and title to any die, mold, or form may be transferred by operation of law to the molder for the purpose of destroying or otherwise disposing of such die, mold, or form, consistent with this section.

(d) If a molder chooses to have all rights and title to any die, mold, or form transferred to the molder by operation of law, the molder shall send written notice by registered mail to the chief executive officer of the customer or, if the customer is not a business entity, to the customer himself or herself at the customer's last known address indicating that the molder intends to terminate the customer's rights and title by having all such rights and title transferred to the molder by operation of law pursuant to this section.

(e) If a customer does not respond in person or by mail to claim possession of the particular die, mold, or form within 120 days following the date the notice was sent, or does not make other contractual arrangements with the molder for storage thereof, all rights and title of the customer shall transfer by operation of law to the molder. Thereafter, the molder may destroy or otherwise dispose of the particular mold, tool, or die as the molder's own property without any risk of liability to the customer, except that this section shall not be construed in any manner to affect any right of the customer, under federal patent or copyright law or any state or federal law pertaining to unfair competition. **Leg.H.** Added Stats 1979 ch 180 §1. Amended Stats 1981 ch 290 §1.

Prior Law: Former §1140, relating to operation as transfer, was enacted Stats 1872 and repealed by Stats 1931 ch 1070 §2.

ARTICLE 2
What Operates as a Transfer [Repealed]

§§1141, 1142. [Sections repealed 1931]

Leg.H. Enacted Stats 1872. Repealed Stats 1931 ch 1070 §2.

ARTICLE 3
Gifts

Gifts defined. §1146.
Gift, how made. §1147.
Gift not revocable. §1148.

§1146. Gifts defined

A gift is a transfer of personal property, made voluntarily, and without consideration. **Leg.H.** Enacted Stats 1872.

§1147. Gift, how made

A verbal gift is not valid, unless the means of obtaining possession and control of the thing are given, nor, if it is capable of delivery, unless there is an actual or symbolical delivery of the thing to the donee. **Leg.H.** Enacted Stats 1872.

§1148. Gift not revocable

A gift, other than a gift in view of impending death, cannot be revoked by the giver. **Leg.H.** Enacted Stats 1872. Amended Stats 1991 ch 1055 §2 (SB 271).

§1149. [Section repealed 1991]

Leg.H. Enacted Stats 1872. Repealed Stats 1991 ch 1055 §3 (SB 271). See Prob C §5702.

§1150. [Section repealed 1991]

Leg.H. Enacted Stats 1872. Repealed Stats 1991 ch 1055 §4 (SB 271). See Prob C §5703.

§1151. [Section repealed 1991]

Leg.H. Enacted Stats 1872. Amended Code Amdts 1873–74 ch 612 §135. Repealed Stats 1991 ch 1055 §5 (SB 271). See Prob C §5704.

§1152. [Section repealed 1991]

Leg.H. Enacted Stats 1872. Repealed Stats 1991 ch 1055 §6 (SB 271). See Prob C §5704.

§1153. [Section repealed 1991]

Leg.H. Enacted Stats 1872. Repealed Stats 1991 ch 1055 §7 (SB 271). See Prob C §5705.

ARTICLE 4
California Uniform Gifts to Minors Act [Repealed]

§1154. [Section repealed 1984]

Leg.H. Added Stats 1959 ch 709 §2. Repealed Stats 1984 ch 243 §1. The repealed section related to application of California Uniform Gifts to Minors Act.

§1155. [Section repealed 1984]

Leg.H. Added Stats 1959 ch 709 §2. Amended Stats 1961 ch 613 §1; Stats 1963 ch 2110 §1; Stats 1970 ch 584 §1; Stats 1972 ch 579 §11; Stats 1979 ch 730 §6, operative January 1, 1981; Stats 1982 ch 355 §1, ch 591 §1.5. Repealed Stats 1984 ch 243 §1. See Prob C §3901.

§1156. [Section repealed 1984]

Leg.H. Added Stats 1959 ch 709 §2. Amended Stats 1961 ch 613 §2; Stats 1970 ch 584 §2; Stats 1982 ch 591 §2. Repealed Stats 1984 ch 243 §1. See Prob C §§3904, 3909–3911.

§1157. [Section repealed 1984]

Leg.H. Added Stats 1959 ch 709 §2. Amended Stats 1963 ch 2110 §3. Repealed Stats 1984 ch 243 §1. See Prob C §3911.

§1158. [Section repealed 1984]

Leg.H. Added Stats 1959 ch 709 §2. Amended Stats 1963 ch 2110 §4; Stats 1970 ch 584 §3; Stats 1972 ch 579 §12; Stats 1982 ch 591 §3. Repealed Stats 1984 ch 243 §1. See Prob C §§3912–3914, 3920.5.

Prior Law: Former §1158, relating to liability of custodian, was added by Stats 1955 ch 1958 §1 p 3590 and repealed by Stats 1959 ch 709 §1 p 2684.

Original §1158, similar to Gov C §§27280, 27281, was enacted in 1872, amended by Stats 1921 ch 143 §1 p 143, Stats 1933 ch 127 §1 p 580, and repealed by Stats 1947 ch 424 §2 (Gov C §500036) p 1307.

§1158.5. [Section repealed 1984]

Leg.H. Added Stats 1965 ch 1616 §1. Repealed Stats 1984 ch 243 §1. The repealed section related to expenditures of custodian.

§1159. [Section repealed 1984]

Leg.H. Added Stats 1959 ch 709 §2. Repealed Stats 1984 ch 243 §1. See Prob C §3915.

Prior Law: Former §1159, relating to resignation of custodian, was added by Stats 1955 ch 1958 §1 p 3590 and repealed by Stats 1959 ch 709 §1 p 2684.

Original §1159, similar to Gov C §§27282–27284, was enacted in 1872, amended by Stats 1897 ch 94 §1 p 97, and repealed by Stats 1947 ch 424 §2 (Gov C §500036) p 1307.

§1160. [Section repealed 1984]

Leg.H. Added Stats 1959 ch 709 §2. Amended Stats 1963 ch 2110 §5; Stats 1970 ch 584 §4; Stats 1980 ch 676 §49. Repealed Stats 1984 ch 243 §1. See Prob C §3916.

Prior Law: Former §1160, relating to death of custodian, was added by Stats 1955 ch 1958 §1 p 3590 and repealed by Stats 1959 ch 709 §1 p 2684.

Original §1160, similar to Gov C §§27285, 27286, was enacted in 1872, amended by Code Amdts 1877–78 ch 615 §1 p 85, Stats 1945 ch 834 §1 p 1532, and repealed by Stats 1947 ch 424 §2 (Gov C §500036) p 1307.

§1161. [Section repealed 1984]

Leg.H. Added Stats 1959 ch 709 §2. Amended Stats 1963 ch 478 §1; Stats 1969 ch 1074 §1. Repealed Stats 1984 ch 243 §1. See Prob C §3918.

Prior Law: Former §1161, relating to custodian's failure to render an accounting, was added Stats 1955 ch 1958 §1 and repealed Stats 1959 ch 709 §1.

Original §1161, similar to Gov C §§27287–27289, was enacted in 1872, amended Code Amdts 1873–74 ch 612 §136, Stats 1901 ch 157 §239, Stats 1905 ch 444 §1, Stats 1941 ch 1018 §1, Stats 1945 ch 292 §1, and repealed Stats 1947 ch 424 §2 (Gov C §500036), ch 435 §3, ch 1497 §4.

§1162. [Section repealed 1984]

Leg.H. Added Stats 1959 ch 709 §2. Repealed Stats 1984 ch 243 §1.1 See Prob C §3919.

Prior Law: Former §1162, relating to definition of "security", was added by Stats 1955 ch 1958 §1 p 3590 and repealed by Stats 1959 ch 709 §1 p 2684.

Original §1162, similar to Gov C §27290, was enacted in 1872 and repealed by Stats 1947 ch 424 §2 (Gov C §500036) p 1307.

§1162.5. [Section repealed 1984]

Leg.H. Added Stats 1972 ch 440 §1. Repealed Stats 1984 ch 243 §1. See Prob C §3921.

§1163. [Section repealed 1984]

Leg.H. Added Stats 1959 ch 709 §2. Repealed Stats 1984 ch 243 §1. See Prob C §3925.

Prior Law: Former §1163, similar to present Prob C §3925, was added by Stats 1955 ch 1958 §1 p 3591 and repealed by Stats 1959 ch 709 §1 p 2684.

Original §1163, similar to Gov C §27291, was enacted in 1872, repealed by Code Amdts 1873–74 ch 612 §137 p 226, added by Stats 1905 ch 138 §1 p 139, and repealed by Stats 1947 ch 424 §2 (Gov C §500036) p 1307.

§1164. [Section repealed 1984]

Leg.H. Added Stats 1959 ch 709 §2. Repealed Stats 1984 ch 243 §1. The repealed section related to citation of article as California Gifts of Securities to Minors Act.

Prior Law: Former §1164, similar to present §1164, was added by Stats 1955 ch 1958 §1 p 3591 and repealed by Stats 1959 ch 709 §1 p 2684.

Original §1164, similar to Gov C §27292, was enacted in 1872 and repealed by Stats 1947 ch 424 §2 (Gov C §500036) p 1307.

§1165. [Section repealed 1984]

Leg.H. Added Stats 1959 ch 709 §2. Repealed Stats 1984 ch 243 §1. The repealed section related to severability of individual sections of article.

Prior Law: Original §1165, similar to Gov C §27294, was added by Code Amdts 1873–74 ch 744 §1 p 274 and repealed by Stats 1947 ch 424 §2 (Gov C §500036) p 1307.

CHAPTER 4
RECORDING TRANSFERS

Article 2. Mode of Recording.
Article 3. Proof and Acknowledgment of Instruments.
Article 4. Effect of Recording, or the Want Thereof.

ARTICLE 1
What May Be Recorded [Repealed]
ARTICLE 2
Mode of Recording

In what office. §1169.
Instrument deemed recorded. §1170.
Books of record. §1171.
Duties of recorder. §1172.
Transfer of vessels. §1173.

§1169. In what office

Instruments entitled to be recorded must be recorded by the County Recorder of the county in which the real property affected thereby is situated. **Leg.H.** Enacted Stats 1872.

§1170. Instrument deemed recorded

An instrument is deemed to be recorded when, being duly acknowledged or proved and certified, it is deposited in the Recorder's office, with the proper officer, for record. **Leg.H.** Enacted Stats 1872. Amended Code Amdts 1873–74 ch 612 §138.

§1171. Books of record

Grants, absolute in terms, are to be recorded in one set of books, and mortgages in another. **Leg.H.** Enacted Stats 1872.

§1172. Duties of recorder

The duties of county recorders, in respect to recording instruments, are prescribed by the Government Code. **Leg.H.** Enacted Stats 1872. Amended Stats 1959 ch 593 §1.

§1173. Transfer of vessels

The mode of recording transfers of ships registered under the laws of the United States is regulated by acts of Congress. **Leg.H.** Enacted Stats 1872.

ARTICLE 3
Proof and Acknowledgment of Instruments

Court and legislative personnel. §1180.
Notary public; City or county officer. §1181.
Online notarization [Repeal date contingent]. § 1181.1.
Online notarization [Operative date contingent]. § 1181.1.
Officers outside state. §1182.
Officers outside United States. §1183.
Notarial acts for military personnel. §1183.5.
Deputies of officers. §1184.
Satisfactory evidence as prerequisite to acknowledgment; What is satisfactory evidence; Presumption and burden of proof; Effect of perjury conviction. §1185.
Officer must endorse certificate. §1188.
Notice and form for certificate of acknowledgment taken within state; Acknowledgment taken in another place or to be filed in another state. §1189.
Certificate of acknowledgment by corporation. §1190.
Officers must affix their signatures. §1193.
Proof of execution; Notice and form for certificate for proof of execution taken within state. §1195.
Proof that witness is subscribing witness; Documentation and oath. §1196.
Witness must prove, what. §1197.
Handwriting may be proved, when. §1198.
Requirements for proof by handwriting. §1199.
Certificate of proof. §1200.
Officers authorized to do certain things. §1201.
Action to correct certificate. §1202.
Action for judgment proving instrument. §1203.
Effect of judgment in such action. §1204.
Conveyances heretofore made to be governed by then existing laws. §1205.
Recording, and as evidence, to be governed by then existing laws. §1206.
Notice to subsequent purchasers and encumbrancers; Certified copies as evidence. §1207.

§1180. Court and legislative personnel

The proof or acknowledgment of an instrument may be made at any place within this state before a justice, retired justice, or Clerk/Executive Officer of the Supreme Court, a justice, retired justice, or clerk of any court of appeal or judge or retired judge of a superior court, or the Secretary of the Senate or Chief Clerk of the Assembly. **Leg.H.** Enacted Stats 1872. Amended Code Amdts 1880 ch 39 §1; Stats 1953 ch 457 §1; Stats 1967 ch 17 §3; Stats 1986 ch 1417 §1; Stats 1999 ch 20 §1 (SB 301); Stats 2017 ch 36 §3 (AB 452), effective January 1, 2018.

§1181. Notary public; City or county officer

The proof or acknowledgment of an instrument may be made before a notary public at any place within this state, or within the county or city and county in this state in which the officer specified below was elected or appointed, before either:

(a) A clerk of a superior court.
(b) A county clerk.
(c) A court commissioner.
(d) A retired judge of a municipal or justice court.
(e) A district attorney.
(f) A clerk of a board of supervisors.
(g) A city clerk.
(h) A county counsel.
(i) A city attorney.
(j) Secretary of the Senate.
(k) Chief Clerk of the Assembly. **Leg.H.** Enacted Stats 1872. Amended Code Amdts 1880 ch 39 §2; Stats 1891 ch 150 §1; Stats 1905 ch 445 §1; Stats 1911 ch 247 §1; Stats 1941 ch 1096 §1; Stats 1945 ch 240 §2; Stats 1951 ch 1676 §3, operative January 1, 1952; Stats 1953 ch 457 §2; Stats 1959 ch 1162 §1; Stats 1961 ch 49 §1; Stats 1963 ch 200 §1; Stats 1968 ch 576 §1; Stats 1971 ch 27 §1; Stats 1981 ch 390 §1; Stats 1986 ch 1417 §2; Stats 1992 ch 876 §3 (AB 3296); Stats 1998 ch 931 §13 (SB 2139), effective September 28, 1998; Stats 1999 ch 20 §2 (SB 301); Stats 2002 ch 784 §12 (SB 1316).

§ 1181.1. Online notarization [Repeal date contingent]

(a) Section 1181 shall not be construed to authorize any person, other than a notary public authorized by the Secretary of State to perform online notarizations pursuant to Article 2 (commencing with Section 8231) of Chapter 3 of Division 1 of Title 2 of the Government Code, to take a proof or acknowledgment of an instrument by means of appearances using audio-video communication, as that term is defined in subdivision (a) of Section 8231.1 of the Government Code.

(b) A California notary public shall not provide online notarization for any principal, and an online notarization platform shall not be authorized for use by a California notary public, until the earlier of the following:

(1) Certification by the Secretary of State on its internet website that the Secretary of State's technology project necessary to implement statutes related to online notarization is complete.

(2) January 1, 2030, unless the Secretary of State informs the Legislature and the Governor in writing on or before January 1, 2029, that the technology project necessary to implement statutes related to online notarization will not be completed by January 1, 2030, including a detailed status of the technology project.

(c) This section shall remain in effect until the attainment of paragraph (1) or (2) of subdivision (b), and as of that date is repealed. **Leg.H.** Added Stats 2023 ch 291 §1 (SB 696), effective January 1, 2024, repeal date contingent.

§ 1181.1. Online notarization [Operative date contingent]

(a) Section 1181 shall not be construed to authorize any person, other than a notary public authorized by the Secretary of State to perform online notarizations pursuant to Article 2 (commencing with Section 8231) of Chapter 3 of Division 1 of Title 2 of the Government Code, to take a proof or acknowledgment of an instrument by means of appearances using audio-video communication, as that term is defined in subdivision (a) of Section 8231.1 of the Government Code.

(b) This section shall become operative upon the earlier of the following:

(1) Certification by the Secretary of State on its internet website that the Secretary of State's technology project necessary to implement statutes related to online notarization is complete.

(2) January 1, 2030, unless the Secretary of State informs the Legislature and the Governor in writing on or before January 1, 2029, that the technology project necessary to implement statutes related to online notarization will not be completed by January 1, 2030, including a detailed status of the technology project. **Leg.H.** Added Stats 2023 ch 291 §2 (SB 696), effective January 1, 2024, operative date contingent.

§1182. Officers outside state

The proof or acknowledgment of an instrument may be taken without this state, but within the United States, and within the jurisdiction of the officer, by any of the following:

(a) A justice, judge, or clerk of any court of record of the United States.
(b) A justice, judge, or clerk of any court of record of any state.
(c) A commissioner appointed by the Governor or Secretary of State for that purpose.
(d) A notary public.
(e) Any other officer of the state where the acknowledgment is made authorized by its laws to take such proof or acknowledgment. **Leg.H.** Enacted Stats 1872. Amended Stats 1971 ch 1611 §1; Stats 2023 ch 291 §3 (SB 696), effective January 1, 2024.

§1183. Officers outside United States

(a) The proof or acknowledgment of an instrument may be taken without the United States, by any of the following:

(1) A minister, commissioner, or chargè d'affaires of the United States, resident and accredited in the country where the proof or acknowledgment is made.

(2) A consul, vice consul, or consular agent of the United States, resident in the country where the proof or acknowledgment is made.

(3) A judge of a court of record of the country where the proof or acknowledgment is made.

(4) Commissioners appointed by the Governor or Secretary of State for that purpose.

(5) A notary public.

(b) If the proof or acknowledgment is taken by a notary public, the signature of the notary public shall be proved or acknowledged (1) before a judge of a court of record of the country where the proof or acknowledgment is taken, or (2) by any American diplomatic officer, consul general, consul, vice consul, or consular agent, or (3) by an apostille (certification) affixed to the instrument pursuant to the terms of The Hague Convention Abolishing the Requirement of Legalization for Foreign Public Documents. **Leg.H.** Enacted Stats 1872. Amended Code Amdts 1873–74 ch 612 §139; Stats 1939 ch 249 §1; Stats 1943 ch 28 §1, effective February 9, 1943; Stats 1963 ch 144 §1; Stats 1971 ch 1611 §2; Stats 1982 ch 520 §13; Stats 1984 ch 1017 §1; Stats 2023 ch 291 §4 (SB 696), effective January 1, 2024.

§1183.5. Notarial acts for military personnel

Any officer on active duty or performing inactive-duty training in the armed forces having the general powers of a notary public pursuant to Section 936 or 1044a of Title 10 of the United States Code (Public Law 90-632 and 101-510) and any successor statutes may perform all notarial acts for any person serving in the armed forces of the United States, wherever he or she may be, or for any spouse of a person serving in the armed forces, wherever he or she may be, or for any person eligible for legal assistance under laws and regulations of the United States, wherever he or she may be, for any person serving with, employed by, or accompanying such armed forces outside the United States and outside the Canal Zone, Puerto Rico, Guam and the Virgin Islands, and any person subject to the Uniform Code of Military Justice outside of the United States.

Any instrument acknowledged by any such officer or any oath or affirmation made before such officer shall not be rendered invalid by the failure to state therein the place of execution or acknowledgment. No seal or authentication of the officer's certificate of acknowledgment or of any jurat signed by him or her shall be required but the officer taking the acknowledgment shall endorse thereon or attach thereto a certificate substantially in a form authorized by the laws of this state or in the following form:

On this the ____ day of ____, 19 ____, before me ____, the undersigned officer, personally appeared ____ known to me (or satisfactorily proven) to be (a) serving in the armed forces of the United States, (b) a spouse of a person serving in the armed forces of the United States, or (c) a person serving with, employed by, or accompanying the armed forces of the United States outside the United States and outside the Canal Zone, Puerto Rico, Guam, and the Virgin Islands, and to be the person whose name is subscribed to the within instrument and acknowledged that he or she executed the same. And the undersigned does further certify that he or she is at the date of this certificate a commissioned officer of the armed forces of the United States having the general powers of a notary public under the provisions of Section 936 or 1044a of Title 10 of the United States Code (Public Law 90-632 and 101-510).

_____

_____
Signature of officer, rank, branch of

service and capacity in which signed.

To any affidavit subscribed and sworn to before such officer there shall be attached a jurat substantially in the following form:

Subscribed and sworn to before me on this ___ day of ____, 19___.

_____
Signature of officer, rank, branch of service and capacity in which signed.

The recitals contained in any such certificate or jurat shall be prima facie evidence of the truth thereof, and any certificate of acknowledgment, oath or affirmation purporting to have been made by any commissioned officer of the Army, Air Force, Navy, Marine Corps or Coast Guard shall, notwithstanding the omission of any specific recitals therein, constitute presumptive evidence of the existence of the facts necessary to authorize such acknowledgment, oath or affirmation to be taken by the certifying officer pursuant to this section. **Leg.H.** Added Stats 1943 ch 28 §2, effective February 1, 1943. Amended Stats 1943 ch 365 §1; effective May 12, 1943; Stats 1945 ch 106 §1; Stats 1947 ch 10 §1, effective February 4, 1947; Stats 1949 ch 1186 §2; Stats 1951 ch 386 §1; Stats 1953 ch 603 §1; Stats 1957 ch 898 §1; Stats 1974 ch 91 §1; Stats 1992 ch 77 §1 (SB 208); Stats 1994 ch 587 §1 (AB 3600).

§1184. Deputies of officers

When any of the officers mentioned in Sections 1180, 1181, 1182, and 1183 are authorized by law to appoint a deputy, the acknowledgment or proof may be taken by such deputy, in the name of his principal. **Leg.H.** Enacted Stats 1872. Amended Stats 1953 ch 457 §3.

§1185. Satisfactory evidence as prerequisite to acknowledgment; What is satisfactory evidence; Presumption and burden of proof; Effect of perjury conviction

(a) The acknowledgment of an instrument shall not be taken unless the officer taking it has satisfactory evidence that the person making the acknowledgment is the individual who is described in and who executed the instrument.

(b) For purposes of this section, "satisfactory evidence" means the absence of information, evidence, or other circumstances that would lead a reasonable person to believe that the person making the acknowledgment is not the individual he or she claims to be and any one of the following:

(1)(A) The oath or affirmation of a credible witness personally known to the officer, whose identity is proven to the officer upon presentation of a document satisfying the requirements of paragraph (3) or (4), that the person making the acknowledgment is personally known to the witness and that each of the following are true:

(i) The person making the acknowledgment is the person named in the document.

(ii) The person making the acknowledgment is personally known to the witness.

(iii) That it is the reasonable belief of the witness that the circumstances of the person making the acknowledgment are such that it would be very difficult or impossible for that person to obtain another form of identification.

(iv) The person making the acknowledgment does not possess any of the identification documents named in paragraphs (3) and (4).

(v) The witness does not have a financial interest in the document being acknowledged and is not named in the document.

(B) A notary public who violates this section by failing to obtain the satisfactory evidence required by subparagraph (A) shall be subject to a civil penalty not exceeding ten thousand dollars ($10,000). An action to impose this civil penalty may be brought by the Secretary of State in an administrative proceeding or a public prosecutor in superior court, and shall be enforced as a civil judgment. A public prosecutor shall inform the secretary of any civil penalty imposed under this subparagraph.

(2) The oath or affirmation under penalty of perjury of two credible witnesses, whose identities are proven to the officer upon the presentation of a document satisfying the requirements of paragraph (3) or (4), that each statement in paragraph (1) is true.

(3) Reasonable reliance on the presentation to the officer of any one of the following, if the document or other form of identification is current or has been issued within five years:

(A) An identification card or driver's license issued by the Department of Motor Vehicles.

(B) A passport issued by the Department of State of the United States.

(C) An inmate identification card issued by the Department of Corrections and Rehabilitation, if the inmate is in custody in prison.

(D) Any form of inmate identification issued by a sheriff's department, if the inmate is in custody in a local detention facility.

(4) Reasonable reliance on the presentation of any one of the following, provided that a document specified in subparagraphs (A) to (F), inclusive, shall either be current or have been issued within five years and shall contain a photograph and description of the person named on it, shall be signed by the person, and shall bear a serial or other identifying number:

(A) A valid consular identification document issued by a consulate from the applicant's country of citizenship, or a valid passport from the applicant's country of citizenship.

(B) A driver's license issued by a state other than California or by a Canadian or Mexican public agency authorized to issue driver's licenses.

(C) An identification card issued by a state other than California.

(D) An identification card issued by any branch of the Armed Forces of the United States.

(E) An employee identification card issued by an agency or office of the State of California, or by an agency or office of a city, county, or city and county in this state.

(F) An identification card issued by a federally recognized tribal government.

(c) An officer who has taken an acknowledgment pursuant to this section shall be presumed to have operated in accordance with the provisions of law.

(d) A party who files an action for damages based on the failure of the officer to establish the proper identity of the person making the acknowledgment shall have the burden of proof in establishing the negligence or misconduct of the officer.

(e) A person convicted of perjury under this section shall forfeit any financial interest in the document. **Leg.H.** Enacted Stats 1872. Amended Stats 1905 ch 445 §2; Stats 1982 ch 197 §1, effective May 12, 1982; Stats 1987 ch 307 §1; Stats 1988 ch 842 §1; Stats 1993 ch 1044 §1 (AB 1090); Stats 2007 ch 399 §1 (AB 886), effective January 1, 2008; Stats 2008 ch 67 §1 (AB 2452) (ch 67 prevails), ch 179 §29 (SB 1498), effective January 1, 2009; Stats 2010 ch 328 §28 (SB 1330), effective January 1, 2011; Stats 2013 ch 159 §2 (AB 625), effective January 1, 2014; Stats 2015 ch 42 §1 (AB 1036), effective January 1, 2016; Stats 2016 ch 491 §1 (SB 997), effective January 1, 2017; Stats 2016 ch 762 §1.5 (AB 2566), effective January 1, 2017.

2013 Note: The Legislature finds and declares the following:

(a) The state and its counties have a financial and public safety interest in ensuring the children of people convicted of felonies and sentenced to state prison time have access to appropriate schooling and medical treatment. Eighty percent of imprisoned women are mothers and the vast majority were the primary care provider of minor children at the time of their arrest and imprisonment. These minor children's access to school and medical treatment may be unnecessarily interrupted should their incarcerated parent lack timely and affordable access to a notary necessary for them to complete paperwork to establish temporary guardianship for their children.

(b) The state and its counties have a financial and public safety interest in ensuring people convicted of felonies and sentenced to state prison time are able to successfully reenter their communities upon completion of their sentences and live a crime-free life. Evidence-based research demonstrates a clear connection between decreased recidivism rates and strength of familial bonds during periods of incarceration. These bonds are weakened when minor children are unnecessarily prevented from visiting incarcerated parents due merely to the incarcerated parents' lack of timely and affordable access to a notary public required to complete required visitation forms.

(c) The state has taken significant measures to ensure due process and accuracy in determining the identity of people convicted of felonies and held in control of the Department of Corrections and Rehabilitation, and in tracking these individuals' appropriate identity through issuance and monitoring of state inmate identification cards. Stats 2013 ch 159 (AB 625) §1.

§1186. [Section repealed 1891]

Leg.H. Enacted Stats 1872. Repealed Stats 1891 ch 125 §1. The repealed section related to conveyance by unmarried woman.

§1187. [Section repealed 1976]

Leg.H. Enacted Stats 1872. Amended Stats 1891 ch 125 §2. Repealed Stats 1976 ch 1171 §4. The repealed section related to conveyance by married woman.

§1188. Officer must endorse certificate

An officer taking the acknowledgment of an instrument shall endorse thereon or attach thereto a certificate pursuant to Section 1189. **Leg.H.** Enacted Stats 1872. Amended Code Amdts 1873–74 ch 612 §140; Stats 1990 ch 1070 §1 (SB 2251); Stats 2013 ch 78 §1 (AB 464), effective January 1, 2014.

§1189. Notice and form for certificate of acknowledgment taken within state; Acknowledgment taken in another place or to be filed in another state

(a)(1) Any certificate of acknowledgment taken within this state shall include a notice at the top of the certificate of acknowledgment in an enclosed box stating: "A notary public or other officer completing this certificate verifies only the identity of the individual who signed the document to which this certificate is attached, and not the truthfulness, accuracy, or validity of that document." This notice shall be legible.

(2) The physical format of the boxed notice at the top of the certificate of acknowledgment required pursuant to paragraph (3) is an example, for purposes of illustration and not limitation, of the physical format of a boxed notice fulfilling the requirements of paragraph (1).

(3) A certificate of acknowledgment taken within this state shall be in the following form:

> A notary public or other officer completing this certificate verifies only the identity of the individual who signed the document to which this certificate is attached, and not the truthfulness, accuracy, or validity of that document.

State of California
County of _____ }

On ____ before me, (here insert name and title of the officer), personally appeared _____, who proved to me on the basis of satisfactory evidence to be the person(s) whose name(s) is/are subscribed to the within instrument and acknowledged to me that he/she/they executed the same in his/her/their authorized capacity(ies), and that by his/her/their signature(s) on the instrument the person(s), or the entity upon behalf of which the person(s) acted, executed the instrument.

I certify under PENALTY OF PERJURY under the laws of the State of California that the foregoing paragraph is true and correct.

WITNESS my hand and official seal.

Signature _____ (Seal)

(4) A notary public who willfully states as true any material fact that he or she knows to be false shall be subject to a civil penalty not exceeding ten thousand dollars ($10,000). An action to impose a civil penalty under this subdivision may be brought by the Secretary of State in an administrative proceeding or any public prosecutor in superior court, and shall be enforced as a civil judgment. A public prosecutor shall inform the secretary of any civil penalty imposed under this section.

(b) Any certificate of acknowledgment taken in another place shall be sufficient in this state if it is taken in accordance with the laws of the place where the acknowledgment is made.

(c) On documents to be filed in another state or jurisdiction of the United States, a California notary public may complete any acknowledgment form as may be required in that other state or jurisdiction on a document, provided the form does not require the notary to determine or certify that the signer holds a particular representative capacity or to make other determinations and certifications not allowed by California law.

(d) An acknowledgment provided prior to January 1, 1993, and conforming to applicable provisions of former Sections 1189, 1190, 1190a, 1190.1, 1191, and 1192, as repealed by Chapter 335 of the Statutes of 1990, shall have the same force and effect as if those sections had not been repealed. **Leg.H.** Added Stats 1990 ch 335 §2 (AB 2581). Amended Stats 1990 ch 1070 §2 (SB 2251); Stats 1991 ch 157 §1 (AB 1750); Stats 1996 ch 97 §1 (AB 3304); Stats 2005 ch 295 §1 (AB 361), effective January 1, 2006; Stats 2007 ch 399 §2 (AB 886), effective January 1, 2008; Stats 2014 ch 197 §1 (SB 1050), effective January 1, 2015.

Prior Law: Former §1189, similar to the present section, was enacted Stats 1872, amended Stats 1891 ch 125 §3, Stats 1897 ch 46 §1, Stats 1980 ch 188 §1, Stats 1982 ch 197 §2, effective May 12, 1982, and repealed Stats 1990 ch 335 §1.

§1190. Certificate of acknowledgment by corporation

The certificate of acknowledgment of an instrument executed on behalf of an incorporated or unincorporated entity by a duly authorized person in the form specified in Section 1189 shall be prima facie evidence that the instrument is the duly authorized act of the entity named in the instrument and shall be conclusive evidence thereof in favor of any good faith purchaser, lessee, or encumbrancer. "Duly authorized person," with respect to a domestic or foreign corporation, includes the president, vice president, secretary, and assistant secretary of the corporation. **Leg.H.** Added Stats 1990 ch 1070 §3 (SB 2251).

Prior Law: Former §1190, similar to present §1189, was enacted Stats 1872, amended Stats 1905 ch 445 §3; Stats 1982 ch 197 §3, effective May 12, 1982 and repealed Stats 1990 ch 335 §3 (AB 2581).

§1190.1. [Section repealed 1990]

Leg.H. Added Stats 1951 ch 482 §1. Repealed Stats 1990 ch 335 §4 (AB 2581). See CC §1189.

§1190a. [Section repealed 1990]

Leg.H. Added Stats 1931 ch 766 §1. Amended Stats 1982 ch 197 §4, effective May 12, 1982. Repealed Stats 1990 ch 335 §5 (AB 2581). See CC §1189.

§1191. [Section repealed 1990]

Leg.H. Added Stats 1963 ch 880 §1, operative January 1, 1964. Amended Stats 1982 ch 197 §5, effective May 12, 1982. Repealed Stats 1990 ch 335 §6 (AB 2581). See CC §1189.

Prior Law: Former §1191, giving the form of the certificate of acknowledgment by married women, was enacted Stats 1872 and repealed by Stats 1891 ch 125 §4 p 137.

§1192. [Section repealed 1990]

Leg.H. Enacted Stats 1872. Amended Stats 1982 ch 197 §6, effective May 12, 1982. Repealed Stats 1990 ch 335 §7 (AB 2581). See CC §1189.

§1193. Officers must affix their signatures

Officers taking and certifying acknowledgments, or proof of instruments for record, must authenticate their certificates by affixing thereto their signatures, followed by the names of their offices; also, their seals of office, if by the laws of the state or county where the acknowledgment or proof is taken, or by authority of which they are acting, they are required to have official seals. **Leg.H.** Enacted Stats 1872.

§1194. [Section repealed 1939]

Leg.H. Enacted Stats 1872. Repealed Stats 1939 ch 824 §1.

§1195. Proof of execution; Notice and form for certificate for proof of execution taken within state

(a) Proof of the execution of an instrument, when not acknowledged, may be made by any of the following:

(1) By the party executing it, or either of them.

(2) By a subscribing witness.

(3) By other witnesses, in cases mentioned in Section 1198.

(b)(1) Proof of the execution of a power of attorney, grant deed, mortgage, deed of trust, quitclaim deed, security agreement, or any instrument affecting real property is not permitted pursuant to Section 27287 of the Government Code, though proof of the execution of a trustee's deed or deed of reconveyance is permitted.

(2) Proof of the execution for any instrument requiring a notary public to obtain a thumbprint from the party signing the document in the notary public's journal is not permitted.

(c) Any certificate for proof of execution taken within this state shall include a notice at the top of the certificate for proof of execution in an enclosed box stating: "A notary public or other officer completing this certificate verifies only the identity of the individual who signed the document to which this certificate is attached, and not the truthfulness, accuracy, or validity of that document." This notice shall be legible.

(d) The physical format of the boxed notice at the top of the certificate for proof of execution required pursuant to subdivision (e) is an example, for purposes of illustration and not limitation, of the physical format of a boxed notice fulfilling the requirements of subdivision (c).

(e) A certificate for proof of execution taken within this state shall be in the following form:

> A notary public or other officer completing this certificate verifies only the identity of the individual who signed the document to which this certificate is attached, and not the truthfulness, accuracy, or validity of that document.

State of California } ss.
County of _____

On ____ (date), before me, _____ (name and title of officer), personally appeared _____ (name of subscribing witness), proved to me to be the person whose name is subscribed to the within instrument, as a witness thereto, on the oath of _____ (name of credible witness), a credible witness who is known to me and provided a satisfactory identifying document. _____ (name of subscribing witness), being by me duly sworn, said that he/she was present and saw/heard _____ (name[s] of principal[s]), the same person(s) described in and whose name(s) is/are subscribed to the within or attached instrument in his/her/their authorized capacity(ies) as (a) party(ies) thereto, execute or acknowledge executing the same, and that said affiant subscribed his/her name to the within or attached instrument as a witness at the request of _____ (name[s] of principal[s]).

WITNESS my hand and official seal.

Signature _____ (Seal)

Leg.H. Enacted Stats 1872. Amended Stats 1997 ch 319 §1 (SB 618); Stats 2011 ch 269 §3 (AB 75) (ch 269 prevails), effective January 1, 2012, ch 296 §34 (AB 1023), effective January 1, 2012; Stats 2012 ch 202 §1 (AB 2326), effective January 1, 2013; Stats 2013 ch 76 §11 (AB 383), effective January 1, 2014, ch 78 §2 (AB 464), effective January 1, 2014 (ch 78 prevails); Stats 2014 ch 197 §2 (SB 1050), effective January 1, 2015.

§1196. Proof that witness is subscribing witness; Documentation and oath

A witness shall be proved to be a subscribing witness by the oath of a credible witness who provides the officer with any document satisfying the requirements of paragraph (3) or (4) of subdivision (b) of Section 1185. Leg.H. Enacted Stats 1872. Amended Stats 1982 ch 197 §7, effective May 12, 1982; Stats 2008 ch 67 §2 (AB 2452), effective January 1, 2009.

§1197. Witness must prove, what

The subscribing witness must prove that the person whose name is subscribed to the instrument as a party is the person described in it, and that such person executed it, and that the witness subscribed his name thereto as a witness. Leg.H. Enacted Stats 1872.

§1198. Handwriting may be proved, when

The execution of an instrument may be established by proof of the handwriting of the party and of a subscribing witness, if there is one, in the following cases:

1. When the parties and all the subscribing witnesses are dead; or,
2. When the parties and all the subscribing witnesses are nonresidents of the state; or,
3. When the place of their residence is unknown to the party desiring the proof, and cannot be ascertained by the exercise of due diligence; or,
4. When the subscribing witness conceals himself, or cannot be found by the officer by the exercise of due diligence in attempting to serve the subpoena or attachment; or,
5. In case of the continued failure or refusal of the witness to testify, for the space of one hour, after his appearance. Leg.H. Enacted Stats 1872.

§1199. Requirements for proof by handwriting

The evidence taken under the preceding section must satisfactorily prove to the officer the following facts:

One. The existence of one or more of the conditions mentioned therein; and,

Two. That the witness testifying knew the person whose name purports to be subscribed to the instrument as a party, and is well acquainted with his signature, and that it is genuine; and,

Three. That the witness testifying personally knew the person who subscribed the instrument as a witness, and is well acquainted with his signature, and that it is genuine; and,

Four. The place of residence of the witness. Leg.H. Enacted Stats 1872. Amended Code Amdts 1873–74 ch 612 §141.

§1200. Certificate of proof

An officer taking proof of the execution of any instrument must, in his certificate indorsed thereon or attached thereto, set forth all the matters required by law to be done or known by him, or proved before him on the proceeding, together with the names of all the witnesses examined before him, their places of residence respectively, and the substance of their testimony. Leg.H. Enacted Stats 1872.

§1201. Officers authorized to do certain things

Officers authorized to take the proof of instruments are authorized in such proceedings:

1. To administer oaths or affirmations, as prescribed in section two thousand and ninety-three, Code of Civil Procedure;
2. To employ and swear interpreters;
3. To issue subpoenas, as prescribed in section nineteen hundred and eighty-six, Code of Civil Procedure;
4. To punish for contempt, as prescribed in sections nineteen hundred and ninety-one, nineteen hundred and ninety-three, nineteen hundred and ninety-four, Code of Civil Procedure.

The civil damages and forfeiture to the party aggrieved are prescribed in section nineteen hundred and ninety-two, Code of Civil Procedure. Leg.H. Enacted Stats 1872.

§1202. Action to correct certificate

When the acknowledgment or proof of the execution of an instrument is properly made, but defectively certified, any party interested may have an action in the superior court to obtain a judgment correcting the certificate. Leg.H. Enacted Stats 1872. Amended Stats 1905 ch 445 §4.

§1203. Action for judgment proving instrument

Any person interested under an instrument entitled to be proved for record, may institute an action in the superior court against the proper parties to obtain a judgment proving such instrument. Leg.H. Enacted Stats 1872. Amended Stats 1905 ch 445 §5.

§1204. Effect of judgment in such action

A certified copy of the judgment in a proceeding instituted under either of the two preceding sections, showing the proof of the instrument, and attached thereto, entitles such instrument to record, with like effect as if acknowledged. Leg.H. Enacted Stats 1872.

§1205. Conveyances heretofore made to be governed by then existing laws

The legality of the execution, acknowledgment, proof, form, or record of any conveyance or other instrument made before this code goes into effect, executed, acknowledged, proved, or recorded is not affected by anything contained in this chapter, but depends for its validity and legality upon the laws in force when the act was performed. Leg.H. Enacted Stats 1872.

§1206. Recording, and as evidence, to be governed by then existing laws

All conveyances of real property made before this code goes into effect, and acknowledged or proved according to the laws in force at the time of such making and acknowledgment or proof, have the same force as evidence, and may be recorded in the same manner and with the like effect, as conveyances executed and acknowledged in pursuance of this chapter. Leg.H. Enacted Stats 1872.

§1207. Notice to subsequent purchasers and encumbrancers; Certified copies as evidence

Any instrument affecting the title to real property, [1] **90 days** after the same has been copied into the proper book of record, kept in the office of any county recorder, imparts notice of its contents to subsequent purchasers and encumbrancers, notwithstanding any defect, omission, or informality in the execution of the instrument, or in the certificate of acknowledgment thereof, or the absence of any such certificate; but nothing herein affects the rights of purchasers or encumbrancers previous to the taking effect of this act. Duly certified copies of the record of any such instrument may be read in evidence with like effect as copies of an instrument duly acknowledged and recorded; provided, when such copying in the proper book of record occurred within five years prior to the trial of the action, it is first shown that the original instrument was genuine. **Leg.H.** Added Code Amdts 1873–74 ch 612 §142. Amended Stats 1897 ch 74 §1; Stats 1903 ch 97 §1; Stats 1909 ch 54 §1; Stats 1913 ch 71 §1; Stats 1915 ch 626 §1; Stats 1919 ch 163 §1; Stats 1921 ch 97 §1; Stats 1927 ch 489 §1; Stats 2024 ch 691 §1 (AB 2004), effective January 1, 2025.

§1207. 2024 Deletes. [1] one year

ARTICLE 4
Effect of Recording, or the Want Thereof

Recorded conveyance as constructive notice to subsequent purchasers and mortgagees; Certified copies. §1213.
Unrecorded conveyance void as to subsequent purchaser or mortgagee. §1214.
Conveyance defined. §1215.
Revocation of powers of attorney. §1216.
Unrecorded instrument valid between the parties. §1217.
Recordation of certified copy in another county. §1218.
Oil and gas leases; Fictitious leases; Recordation. §1219.
Contracts and instruments creating interest in standing timber or trees; Unrecorded contracts and instruments before effective date of 1959 amendment. §1220.

§1213. Recorded conveyance as constructive notice to subsequent purchasers and mortgagees; Certified copies

Every conveyance of real property or an estate for years therein acknowledged or proved and certified and recorded as prescribed by law from the time it is filed with the recorder for record is constructive notice of the contents thereof to subsequent purchasers and mortgagees; and a certified copy of such a recorded conveyance may be recorded in any other county and when so recorded the record thereof shall have the same force and effect as though it was of the original conveyance and where the original conveyance has been recorded in any county wherein the property therein mentioned is not situated a certified copy of the recorded conveyance may be recorded in the county where such property is situated with the same force and effect as if the original conveyance had been recorded in that county. **Leg.H.** Enacted Stats 1872. Amended Stats 1897 ch 68 §1; Stats 1909 ch 179 §1; Stats 1989 ch 698 §1.

§1213.5. [Section repealed 1982]

Leg.H. Added Stats 1965 ch 1948 §1, operative January 1, 1967. Repealed Stats 1982 ch 1268 §2. See CC §§884.010–884.030.

§1214. Unrecorded conveyance void as to subsequent purchaser or mortgagee

Every conveyance of real property or an estate for years therein, other than a lease for a term not exceeding one year, is void as against any subsequent purchaser or mortgagee of the same property, or any part thereof, in good faith and for a valuable consideration, whose conveyance is first duly recorded, and as against any judgment affecting the title, unless the conveyance shall have been duly recorded prior to the record of notice of action. **Leg.H.** Enacted Stats 1872. Amended Stats 1895 ch 48 §1; Stats 1989 ch 698 sec 2.

§1215. Conveyance defined

The term "conveyance," as used in sections twelve hundred and thirteen and twelve hundred and fourteen, embraces every instrument in writing by which any estate or interest in real property is created, aliened, mortgaged, or encumbered, or by which the title to any real property may be affected, except wills. **Leg.H.** Enacted Stats 1872.

§1216. Revocation of powers of attorney

No power contained in an instrument to convey or execute instruments affecting real property which has been recorded is revoked by any act of the party by whom it was executed, unless the instrument containing such revocation is also acknowledged or proved, certified and recorded, in the same office in which the instrument containing the power was recorded. **Leg.H.** Enacted Stats 1872. Amended Stats 1970 ch 323 §1.

§1217. Unrecorded instrument valid between the parties

An unrecorded instrument is valid as between the parties thereto and those who have notice thereof. **Leg.H.** Enacted Stats 1872.

§1218. Recordation of certified copy in another county

A certified copy of an instrument affecting the title to real property, once recorded, or a certified copy of the record of such instrument may be recorded in any other county, and, when so recorded, the record thereof has the same force and effect as though it was of the original instrument. **Leg.H.** Added Stats 1905 ch 446 §1. Amended Stats 1913 ch 191 §1.

§1219. Oil and gas leases; Fictitious leases; Recordation

Oil and gas leases may be acknowledged or proved, certified and recorded in like manner and with like effect, as grants of real property. However, an oil and gas lease may be recorded and constructive notice of the same and the contents of that lease given in the following manner:

Any person may record in the office of county recorder of any county fictitious oil and gas leases. Those fictitious oil and gas leases need not be acknowledged, or proved, or certified, to be recorded or entitled to record. Oil and gas leases shall have noted upon the face thereof that they are fictitious. The county recorder shall index and record fictitious oil and gas leases in the same manner as other oil and gas leases are recorded, and shall note on all indices and records of the same that they are fictitious. Thereafter, any of the provisions of any recorded fictitious oil and gas lease may be included for any and all purposes in any oil and gas lease by reference therein to those provisions, without setting the same forth in full, if the fictitious oil and gas lease is of record in the county in which the oil and gas lease adopting or including by reference any of the provisions of the lease is recorded. The reference shall contain a statement, as to each county in which the oil and gas lease containing such a reference is recorded, of the date the fictitious oil and gas lease was recorded, the county recorder's office in which it is recorded, and the book or volume and the first page of the records or the recorder's instrument number in the recorder's office in which the fictitious oil and gas lease was recorded, and a statement by paragraph numbers or any other method that will definitely identify the same, of the specific provisions of any fictitious oil and gas lease that are being adopted and included therein. The recording of any oil and gas lease which has included any provisions by reference shall operate as constructive notice of the whole including the terms, as a part of the written contents of any oil and gas lease, of any provisions so included by reference as though the same were written in full therein. The parties bound or to be bound by provisions so adopted and included by reference shall be bound thereby in the same manner and with like effect for all purposes as though the provisions had been and were set forth in full in the oil and gas lease. **Leg.H.** Added Stats 1955 ch 1541 §1. Amended Stats 2009 ch 54 §4 (SB 544), effective January 1, 2010.

§1220. Contracts and instruments creating interest in standing timber or trees; Unrecorded contracts and instruments before effective date of 1959 amendment

Contracts for the purchase or sale of standing timber or trees, for severance or otherwise, and all instruments in writing by which any estate or interest in, or right to cut, standing timber or trees is created, aliened, mortgaged or encumbered or by which the title to any standing timber or trees may be affected, may be acknowledged or proved, certified and recorded in like manner and with like effect, as grants of real property, and all statutory provisions relating to the recordation or nonrecordation of conveyances of real property and to the effect thereof shall apply to such contracts and instruments with like effect.

Any such contracts for purchase and sale or instruments in writing affecting the title to standing timber or trees, executed and delivered before the effective date of the amendment of this section at the 1959 Regular Session of the Legislature but unrecorded before such date, shall become subject to all statutory provisions relating to the recordation or nonrecordation of conveyances of real property and to the effect thereof one year from said effective date. **Leg.H.** Added Stats 1957 ch 1937 §1. Amended Stats 1959 ch 1795 §1.

CHAPTER 5
UNLAWFUL TRANSFERS

Certain instruments void against purchasers, etc. §1227.
Not void against purchaser having notice, unless fraud is mutual. §1228.

Power to revoke, when deemed executed. §1229.
Same. §1230.
Other provisions. §1231.

§1227. Certain instruments void against purchasers, etc

Every instrument, other than a will, affecting an estate in real property, including every charge upon real property, or upon its rents or profits, made with intent to defraud prior or subsequent purchasers thereof, or incumbrancers thereon, is void as against every purchaser or incumbrancer, for value, of the same property, or the rents or profits thereof. **Leg.H.** Enacted Stats 1872.

§1228. Not void against purchaser having notice, unless fraud is mutual

No instrument is to be avoided under the last section, in favor of a subsequent purchaser or incumbrancer having notice thereof at the time his purchase was made, or his lien acquired, unless the person in whose favor the instrument was made was privy to the fraud intended. **Leg.H.** Enacted Stats 1872.

§1229. Power to revoke, when deemed executed

Where a power to revoke or modify an instrument affecting the title to, or the enjoyment of, an estate in real property, is reserved to the grantor, or given to any other person, a subsequent grant of, or charge upon, the estate, by the person having the power of revocation, in favor of a purchaser or incumbrancer for value, operates as a revocation of the original instrument, to the extent of the power, in favor of such purchaser or incumbrancer. **Leg.H.** Enacted Stats 1872.

§1230. Same

Where a person having a power of revocation, within the provisions of the last section, is not entitled to execute it until after the time at which he makes such a grant or charge as is described in that section, the power is deemed to be executed as soon as he is entitled to execute it. **Leg.H.** Enacted Stats 1872.

§1231. Other provisions

Other provisions concerning unlawful transfers are contained in part two, division fourth, of this code, concerning the special relations of debtor and creditor. **Leg.H.** Enacted Stats 1872.

2012 Note: See the Disposition Table, on pp. v-vii, that shows the old provision to corresponding new provision repealed and added by Stats 2012 ch 180 (AB 805), operative January 1, 2014, recodifying the Davis-Stirling Common Interest Development Act (provisions of Title 6 (commencing with Section 1350) of Part 4 of Division 2 to new Part 5 (commencing with Section 4000) of Division 4).

TITLE 5
HOMESTEADS [REPEALED]

§1237. [Section repealed 1983]

Leg.H. Enacted Stats 1872. Amended Code Amdts 1873–74 ch 612 §143; Stats 1945 ch 789 §1; Stats 1970 ch 687 §1; Stats 1973 ch 281 §1. Repealed Stats 1982 ch 497 §8, operative July 1, 1983. The repealed section related to permissible homesteads.

§1237.5. [Section repealed 1983]

Leg.H. Added Stats 1961 ch 636 §11. Amended Stats 1970 ch 312 §1. Repealed Stats 1982 ch 497 §8, operative July 1, 1983. The repealed section related to definition of "quasi-community property" and "separate property.".

§§1237a, 1237b. [Sections repealed 1955]

Leg.H. Added Stats 1901 ch 157. Repealed Stats 1955 ch 33 §1. See note to §4 for history of Stats 1901 ch 157 p 332 which added sections of these numbers.

§1238. [Section repealed 1983]

Leg.H. Enacted Stats 1872. Amended Code Amdts 1873–74 ch 612 §144; Stats 1929 ch 184 §1; Stats 1935 ch 444 §1; Stats 1937 ch 570 §1; Stats 1961 ch 636 §12; Stats 1970 ch 687 §2; Stats 1976 ch 463 §1. Repealed Stats 1982 ch 497 §8, operative July 1, 1983. The repealed section related to types of property from which homestead could be selected.

§1239. [Section repealed 1976]

Leg.H. Enacted Stats 1872. Amended Code Amdts 1873–74 ch 612 §145. Repealed Stats 1976 ch 463 §2. The repealed section related to homestead from separate property of wife.

§1240. [Section repealed 1983]

Leg.H. Enacted Stats 1872. Repealed Stats 1982 ch 497 §8, operative July 1, 1983. See CCP §704.720.

§1241. [Section repealed 1983]

Leg.H. Enacted Stats 1872. Amended Code Amdts 1873–74 ch 612 §146; Code Amdts 1880 ch 4 §17; Stats 1887 ch 71 §1; Stats 1951 ch 1109 §1; Stats 1957 ch 1317 §1; Stats 1959 ch 1805 §2. Repealed Stats 1982 ch 497 §8, operative July 1, 1983. See CCP §704.950.

§1242. [Section repealed 1983]

Leg.H. Enacted Stats 1872. Amended Stats 1951 ch 438 §1; Stats 1957 ch 1619 §1; Stats 1959 ch 125 §24, ch 1805 §3; Stats 1979 ch 730 §7, operative January 1, 1981. Repealed Stats 1982 ch 497 §8, operative July 1, 1983. See CCP §704.940.

§1243. [Section repealed 1983]

Leg.H. Enacted Stats 1872. Amended Stats 1949 ch 772 §1; Stats 1951 ch 438 §2; Stats 1959 ch 125 §25, ch 1805 §4, ch 1960 §1; Stats 1979 ch 730 §8, operative January 1, 1981. Repealed Stats 1982 ch 497 §8, operative July 1, 1983. See CCP §§704.980, 704.990.

§1243.5. [Section repealed 1983]

Leg.H. Added Stats 1979 ch 730 §9, operative January 1, 1981. Repealed Stats 1982 ch 497 §8, operative July 1, 1983. The repealed section related to conveyance of homestead by spouse having conservator or lacking legal capacity.

§1244. [Section repealed 1983]

Leg.H. Enacted Stats 1872. Amended Stats 1967 ch 79 §4. Repealed Stats 1982 ch 497 §8, operative July 1, 1983. See CCP §704.980.

§1245. [Section repealed 1983]

Leg.H. Added Stats 1979 ch 185 §2. Repealed Stats 1982 ch 497 §8, operative July 1, 1983. The repealed section related to application to enforce judgment upon homestead; contents of application; determination of value.

Prior Law: Former §1245, relating to proceedings on execution against homesteads, was enacted Stats 1872, amended Code Amdts 1880 ch 41 §18, Stats 1911 ch 436 §1, and repealed Stats 1979 ch 185 §1.

§1246. [Section repealed 1983]

Leg.H. Added Stats 1979 ch 185 §4. Repealed Stats 1982 ch 497 §8, operative July 1, 1983. See CCP §§704.770, 704.780.

Prior Law: Former §1246, relating to form and contents of application, was enacted Stats 1872, amended Stats 1911 ch 436 §2, Stats 1945 ch 789 §2, and repealed Stats 1979 ch 185 §3.

§1247. [Section repealed 1983]

Leg.H. Added 1979 ch 185 §6. Repealed Stats 1982 ch 497 §8, operative July 1, 1983. The repealed section related to burden of proof; appointment of appraiser.

Prior Law: Former §1247, relating to filing of petition, was enacted Stats 1872, amended Code Amdts 1880 ch 41 §19, and repealed Stats 1979 ch 185 §5.

§1248. [Section repealed 1983]

Leg.H. Added Stats 1979 ch 185 §8. Repealed Stats 1982 ch 497 §8, operative July 1, 1983. The repealed section related to division of land.

Prior Law: Former §1248, relating to service of petition and notice of hearing, was enacted Stats 1872, amended Stats 1911 ch 436 §3, and repealed Stats 1979 ch 185 §7.

§1249. [Section repealed 1983]

Leg.H. Added Stats 1979 ch 185 §10. Repealed Stats 1982 ch 497 §8, operative July 1, 1983. The repealed section related to sale of land.

Prior Law: Former §1249, relating to appointment of appraisers, was enacted Stats 1872 and repealed Stats 1979 ch 185 §9.

§1250. [Section repealed 1983]

Leg.H. Added Stats 1979 ch 185 §12. Repealed Stats 1982 ch 497 §8, operative July 1, 1983. The repealed section related to writ of execution.

Prior Law: Former §1250, relating to oath of appraisers, was enacted Stats 1872 and repealed Stats 1979 ch 185 §11.

§1251. [Section repealed 1983]

Leg.H. Added Stats 1979 ch 185 §14. Repealed Stats 1982 ch 497 §8, operative July 1, 1983. The repealed section related to notice of issuance of writ.

Prior Law: Former §1251, relating to duties of appraisers, was enacted Stats 1872, amended Stats 1945 ch 789 §3, and repealed Stats 1979 ch 185 §13.

§1252. [Section repealed 1983]

Leg.H. Added Stats 1979 ch 185 §16. Repealed Stats 1982 ch 497 §8, operative July 1, 1983. The repealed section related to recall of writ.

Prior Law: Former §1252, relating to appraisers' report, was enacted Stats 1872, amended Stats 1945 ch 789 §4, and repealed Stats 1979 ch 185 §15.

§1253. [Section repealed 1983]

Leg.H. Added Stats 1979 ch 185 §18. Repealed Stats 1982 ch 497 §8, operative July 1, 1983. The repealed section related to subsequent application for writ.

Prior Law: Former §1253, relating to proceedings where land can be divided without material injury, was enacted Stats 1872, amended Stats 1945 ch 789 §5, and repealed Stats 1979 ch 185 §17.

§1254. [Section repealed 1983]

Leg.H. Added Stats 1979 ch 185 §20. Repealed Stats 1982 ch 497 §8, operative July 1, 1983. The repealed section related to conduct of sale; minimum bid.

Prior Law: Former §1254, relating to sale where property cannot be divided, was enacted Stats 1872, amended Stats 1945 ch 789 §6, and repealed Stats 1979 ch 185 §19.

§1255. [Section repealed 1983]

Leg.H. Added Stats 1979 ch 185 §22. Repealed Stats 1982 ch 497 §8, operative July 1, 1983. See CCP §704.850.

Prior Law: Former §1255, relating to necessity of bid exceeding exemption and lien, was enacted Stats 1872, amended Stats 1945 ch 789 §7, and repealed Stats 1979 ch 185 §21.

§1256. [Section repealed 1983]

Leg.H. Added Stats 1979 ch 185 §24. Repealed Stats 1982 ch 497 §8, operative July 1, 1983. See CCP §704.960.

Prior Law: Former §1256, relating to application of proceeds of sale, was enacted Stats 1872, amended Stats 1945 ch 789 §8, and repealed Stats 1979 ch 185 §23.

§1257. [Section repealed 1983]

Leg.H. Added Stats 1979 ch 185 §26. Repealed Stats 1982 ch 497 §8, operative July 1, 1983. The repealed section related to service of documents.

Prior Law: Former §1257, relating to protection of money equal to homestead exemption, was enacted Stats 1872, amended Code Amdts 1873–74 ch 612 §153, Stats 1976 ch 463 §3, and repealed Stats 1979 ch 185 §25.

§1258. [Section repealed 1983]

Leg.H. Added Stats 1979 ch 185 §28. Repealed Stats 1982 ch 497 §8, operative July 1, 1983. The repealed section related to transmittal of copies of judgments to levying officer; notice of extensions of time.

Prior Law: Former §1258, relating to compensation of appraisers, was enacted Stats 1872, amended Stats 1949 ch 946 §1, Stats 1968 ch 450 §1, and repealed Stats 1979 ch 185 §27.

§1259. [Section repealed 1983]

Leg.H. Added Stats 1979 ch 185 §30. Repealed Stats 1982 ch 497 §8, operative July 1, 1983. See CCP §704.840.

Prior Law: Former §1259, relating to costs, was enacted Stats 1872 and repealed Stats 1979 ch 185 §29.

§1259.1. [Section repealed 1983]

Leg.H. Added Stats 1979 ch 185 §31. Repealed Stats 1982 ch 497 §8, operative July 1, 1983. The repealed section related to appeals.

§1259.2. [Section repealed 1983]

Leg.H. Added Stats 1979 ch 185 §32. Repealed Stats 1982 ch 497 §8, operative July 1, 1983. The repealed section related to exemption of dwelling house from execution of judgment in civil action.

§1260. [Section repealed 1983]

Leg.H. Enacted Stats 1872. Amended Stats 1945 ch 789 §7; Stats 1947 ch 1077 §1, effective July 2, 1947; Stats 1949 ch 357 §1; Stats 1953 ch 943 §1; Stats 1963 ch 1288 §1; Stats 1969 ch 1099 §1; Stats 1970 ch 319 §1; Stats 1976 ch 132 §1; Stats 1978 ch 993 §1; Stats 1979 ch 118 §1; Stats 1980 ch 15 §1. Repealed Stats 1982 ch 497 §8, operative July 1, 1983. See CCP §§704.710, 704.910.

§1261. [Section repealed 1983]

Leg.H. Enacted Stats 1872. Amended Code Amdts 1873–74 ch 612 §155; Stats 1893 ch 107 §1; Stats 1921 ch 786 §1; Stats 1976 ch 463 §4. Repealed Stats 1982 ch 497 §8, operative July 1, 1983. The repealed section related to the definition of "head of family".

§1261.1. [Section repealed 1983]

Leg.H. Added Stats 1969 ch 1099 §2. Repealed Stats 1982 ch 497 §8, operative July 1, 1983. The repealed section related to claim of homestead on property previously homesteaded as not constituting abandonment of prior homestead.

§1262. [Section repealed 1983]

Leg.H. Enacted Stats 1872. Amended Code Amdts 1873–74 ch 612 §156; Stats 1976 ch 463 §5. Repealed Stats 1982 ch 497 §8, operative July 1, 1983. See CCP §704.930.

§1263. [Section repealed 1983]

Leg.H. Enacted Stats 1872. Amended Code Amdts 1873–74 ch 612 §157; Stats 1905 ch 447 §1; Stats 1927 ch 490 §1; Stats 1943 ch 63 §1; Stats 1945 ch 789 §10; Stats 1953 ch 330 §1; Stats 1969 ch 564 §1; Stats 1970 ch 80 §1; Stats 1976 ch 463 §6. Repealed Stats 1982 ch 497 §8, operative July 1, 1983. See CCP §704.930.

§1264. [Section repealed 1983]

Leg.H. Enacted Stats 1872. Repealed Stats 1982 ch 497 §8, operative July 1, 1983. See CCP §704.920.

§1265. [Section repealed 1983]

Leg.H. Enacted Stats 1872. Amended Code Amdts 1873–74 ch 612 §158; Code Amdts 1880 ch 41 §20; Stats 1909 ch 637 §1; Stats 1911 ch 45 §1; Stats 1951 ch 438 §3; Stats 1959 ch 1805 §5; Stats 1961 ch 636 §13; Stats 1980 ch 119 §1. Repealed Stats 1982 ch 497 §8, operative July 1, 1983. The repealed section related to when property becomes homestead, disposition in case of death, exemption of property or proceeds from liability for debts, and exceptions.

§1265a. [Section repealed 1983]

Leg.H. Added Stats 1939 ch 515 §1. Repealed Stats 1982 ch 497 §8, operative July 1, 1983. The repealed section related to retroactive effect of new declaration on property purchased with proceeds of former homestead.

§1266. [Section repealed 1983]

Leg.H. Enacted Stats 1872. Repealed Stats 1982 ch 497 §8, operative July 1, 1983. See CCP §704.920.

§1267. [Section repealed 1983]

Leg.H. Enacted Stats 1872. Amended Stats 1927 ch 491 §1; Stats 1969 ch 564 §2, ch 1099 §3. Repealed 1982 ch 497 §8, operative July 1, 1983. See CCP §704.920.

§1268. [Section repealed 1983]

Leg.H. Enacted Stats 1872. Repealed Stats 1982 ch 497 §8, operative July 1, 1983. See CCP §704.920.

§1269. [Section repealed 1983]

Leg.H. Enacted Stats 1872. Repealed Stats 1982 ch 497 §8, operative July 1, 1983. See CCP §704.920.

§1269a. [Section repealed 1941]

Leg.H. Added Stats 1905 ch 560 §1. Amended Stats 1923 ch 71 §1; Stats 1931 ch 79 §1; Stats 1937 ch 73 §1. Repealed Stats 1941 ch 1220 §3. See Prob C §§3071, 3100–3102.

§1269b. [Section repealed 1941]

Leg.H. Added Stats 1905 ch 560 §1. Repealed Stats 1941 ch 1220 §3. See Prob C §§3131, 3140.

§1269c. [Section repealed 1941]

Leg.H. Added Stats 1905 ch 560 §1. Amended Stats 1931 ch 79 §2; Stats 1937 ch 73 §2. Repealed Stats 1941 ch 1220 §3. See Prob C §§3144, 3150.

§1270. [Section repealed 1931]

Leg.H. Enacted Stats 1872. Repealed Stats 1931 ch 281 (Prob C §1700). See Prob C §§6100, 6101.

§1271. [Section repealed 1873–74]

Leg.H. Enacted Stats 1872. Repealed Code Amdts 1873–74 ch 612.

§§1272–1274. [Sections repealed 1931]

Leg.H. Enacted Stats 1872. Repealed Stats 1931 ch 281 (Prob C §1700). See Prob C §§6100, 6101.

§1275. [Section repealed 1931]

Leg.H. Enacted Stats 1872. Amended Code Amdts 1873–74 ch 43 §1; Stats 1901 ch 157 §268; Stats 1903 ch 223 §1; Stats 1905 ch 448 §1; Stats 1923 ch 53 §1. Repealed Stats 1931 ch 281 (Prob C §1700). See Prob C §6102.

§1276. [Section repealed 1931]

Leg.H. Enacted Stats 1872. Amended Stats 1901 ch 157 §269 (amendment repealed Stats 1955 ch 28 §1); Stats 1905 ch 448 §2. Repealed Stats 1931 ch 281 (Prob C §1700). See Prob C §6110.

§§1277–1282. [Sections repealed 1931]

Leg.H. Enacted Stats 1872. Repealed Stats 1931 ch 281 (Prob C §1700). See Prob C §§6105, 6110–6112, 8220, 8221, 21700.

§1283. [Section repealed 1931]

Leg.H. Enacted Stats 1872. Amended Code Amdts 1873–74 ch 612 §163. Repealed Stats 1931 ch 281 (Prob C §1700). See Prob C §6112.

§1284. [Section repealed 1873–74]

Leg.H. Enacted Stats 1872. Repealed Code Amdts 1873–74 ch 612.

§1285. [Section repealed 1931]

Leg.H. Enacted Stats 1872. Amended Code Amdts 1873–74 ch 612 §165; Stats 1901 ch 157 §270 (amendment repealed Stats 1955 ch 28 §1); Stats 1905 ch 448 §3. Repealed Stats 1931 ch 281 (Prob C §1700). See Prob C §6113.

§1286. [Section repealed 1873–74]

Leg.H. Enacted Stats 1872. Repealed Code Amdts 1873–74 ch 612.

§§1287–1293. [Sections repealed 1931]

Leg.H. Enacted Stats 1872. Repealed Stats 1931 ch 281 (Prob C §1700). See Prob C §§6120, 6130, 21105.

§1294. [Section repealed 1873–74]

Leg.H. Enacted Stats 1872. Repealed Code Amdts 1873–74 ch 612.

§§1295–1299. [Sections repealed 1931]

Leg.H. Enacted Stats 1872. Repealed 1931 ch 281 (Prob C §1700). See Prob C §§6120, 6121, 6123, 21610–21612, 21620–21623.

§1300. [Section repealed 1983]

Leg.H. Added Stats 1959 ch 1805 §1. Amended Stats 1972 ch 1210 §2. Repealed Stats 1982 ch 497 §8, operative July 1, 1983. The repealed section related to execution, acknowledgment, and declaration of separate homestead after entry of decree of separate maintenance or interlocutory decree of divorce.

Prior Law: Former §1300, similar to Prob C §§21610–21612, was enacted Stats 1872, amended Stats 1901 ch 157 §271, Stats 1905 ch 448 §4, Stats 1919 ch 595 §1, and repealed Stats 1931 ch 281 (Prob C §1700) p 687.

§1300a. [Section repealed 1931]

Leg.H. Added Stats 1919 ch 595 §2. Repealed Stats 1931 ch 281 (Prob C §1700). See Prob C §§21620–21623.

§1301. [Section repealed 1983]

Leg.H. Added Stats 1959 ch 1805 §1. Amended Stats 1969 ch 564 §3; Stats 1971 ch 1210 §3. Repealed Stats 1982 ch 497 §8, operative July 1, 1983. The repealed section related to contents of declaration of married person separated or divorced.

Prior Law: Former §1301, relating to the rights of a beneficiary of a specific gift when the transferor enters into an agreement for sale or transfer of the specifically given property, was enacted Stats 1872 and repealed Stats 1931 ch 281 (Prob C §1700) p 687.

§1302. [Section repealed 1983]

Leg.H. Added Stats 1959 ch 1805 §1. Repealed Stats 1982 ch 497 §8, operative July 1, 1983. The repealed section related to definition of "head of family".

Prior Law: Former §1302, relating to the rights of a beneficiary of a specific gift when the transferor alters his or her interest in the property, was enacted Stats 1872 and repealed Stats 1931 ch 281 (Prob C §1700) p 687.

§1303. [Section repealed 1983]

Leg.H. Added Stats 1959 ch 1805 §1. Repealed Stats 1982 ch 497 §8, operative July 1, 1983. The repealed section related to when land became homestead.

Prior Law: Former §1303, relating to the rights of a beneficiary of a specific gift when the transferor alters his or her interest in the property, was enacted Stats 1872 and repealed Stats 1931 ch 281 (Prob C §1700) p 687.

§1304. [Section repealed 1983]

Leg.H. Added Stats 1959 ch 1805 §1. Amended Stats 1971 ch 1210 §4. Repealed Stats 1982 ch 497 §8, operative July 1, 1983. The repealed section related to transformation of married person's separate homestead on reconciliation of parties.

Prior Law: Former §1304, was enacted Stats 1872 and repealed Stats 1931 ch 281 (Prob C §1700) p 687.

§1305. [Section repealed 1931]

Leg.H. Enacted Stats 1872. Repealed Stats 1931 ch 281 (Prob C §1700).

§§1306, 1307. [Sections repealed 1931]

Leg.H. Enacted Stats 1872. Amended Stats 1901 ch 157 §§272, 273; Stats 1905 ch 448 §§5, 6. Repealed Stats 1931 ch 281 (Prob C §1700). See Prob C §§21620–21623.

§§1308, 1309. [Sections repealed 1931]

Leg.H. Enacted Stats 1872. Repealed Stats 1931 ch 281 (Prob C §1700). See Prob C §§21620–21623.

§1310. [Section repealed 1931]

Leg.H. Enacted Stats 1872. Amended Stats 1905 ch 155 §1; Stats 1921 ch 116 §1. Repealed Stats 1931 ch 281 (Prob C §1700). See Prob C §§21109, 21110.

§1311. [Section repealed 1931]

Leg.H. Enacted Stats 1872. Repealed Stats 1931 ch 281 (Prob C §1700). See Prob C §6142.

§1312. [Section repealed 1931]

Leg.H. Enacted Stats 1872. Amended Code Amdts 1873–74 ch 612 §169. Repealed Stats 1931 ch 281 (Prob C §1700). See Prob C §21105.

§1313. [Section repealed 1931]

Leg.H. Enacted Stats 1872. Repealed Stats 1931 ch 281 (Prob C §1700).

§§1317–1326. [Sections repealed 1931]

Leg.H. Enacted Stats 1872. Repealed Stats 1931 ch 281 (Prob C §1700). See Prob C §§6120, 21102, 21103, 21120–21122.

§1327. [Section repealed 1931]

Leg.H. Enacted Stats 1872. Amended Stats 1901 ch 157 §275 (amendment repealed Stats 1955 ch 28 §1); Stats 1905 ch 448 §8. Repealed Stats 1931 ch 281 (Prob C §1700). See Prob C §21122.

§§1328–1331. [Sections repealed 1931]

Leg.H. Enacted Stats 1872. Repealed Stats 1931 ch 281 (Prob C §1700). See Prob C §§21105, 21122.

§§1332, 1333. [Sections repealed 1931]

Leg.H. Enacted Stats 1872. Amended Code Amdts 1873–74 ch 612 §§170, 171. Repealed Stats 1931 ch 281 Prob C §1700. See Prob C §21105.

§§1334–1342. [Sections repealed 1931]

Leg.H. Enacted Stats 1872. Repealed Stats 1931 ch 281 (Prob C §1700). See Prob C §§21107, 21113–21116.

§1343. [Section repealed 1931]

Leg.H. Enacted Stats 1872. Amended Code Amdts 1873–74 ch 612 §182. Repealed 1931 (Prob C §1700). See Prob C §§21109, 21110.

§§1344–1349. [Sections repealed 1931]

Leg.H. Enacted Stats 1872. Repealed Stats 1931 ch 281 (Prob C §1700).

TITLE 6
COMMON INTEREST DEVELOPMENTS [REPEALED]

CHAPTER 1
GENERAL PROVISIONS [REPEALED]

ARTICLE 1
Preliminary Provisions [Repealed]

§1350. [Section repealed 2014]

Leg.H. Added Stats 1985 ch 874 §14. Repealed Stats 2012 ch 180 §1 (AB 805), effective January 1, 2013, operative January 1, 2014. The repealed section related to short title provisions.

Prior Law: Former CC §1350, similar to present CC §1351, was added Stats 1963 ch 860 §3, amended Stats 1984 ch 291 §2, and repealed Stats 1985 ch 874 §13.

Former CC §1350, similar to present Prob C §21106, was enacted Stats 1872 and repealed Stats 1931 ch 281 (Prob C §1700).

See CC §4000.

§1350.5. [Section repealed 2014]

Leg.H. Added Stats 2003 ch 557 §3 (AB 512). Repealed Stats 2012 ch 180 §1 (AB 805), effective January 1, 2013, operative January 1, 2014. The repealed section related to effect of headings on title.

See CC §4005.

§1350.7. [Section repealed 2014]

Leg.H. Added Stats 2003 ch 557 §4 (AB 512). Amended Stats 2009 ch 484 §1 (AB 899), effective January 1, 2010. Repealed Stats 2012 ch 180 §1 (AB 805), effective January 1, 2013, operative January 1, 2014. The repealed section related to delivery of a document listed in Section 1363.005 or to the extent the section was made applicable by another provision of this title.

Omitted, but see CC §§4040, 4045, 4050.

ARTICLE 2
Definitions [Repealed]

§1351. [Section repealed 2014]

Leg.H. Added Stats 1985 ch 874 §14. Amended Stats 1987 ch 357 §1; Stats 1989 ch 1150 §2; Stats 1991 ch 263 §3 (AB 1840); Stats 2000 ch 26 §1 (SB 453), effective May 24, 2000; Stats 2002 ch 1111 §1 (AB 2289); Stats 2009 ch 520 §3 (AB 1246), effective January 1, 2010. Repealed Stats 2012 ch 180 §1 (AB 805), effective January 1, 2013, operative January 1, 2014. The repealed section related to definitions of title.

Prior Law: Former CC §1351, similar to present CC §§1352, 1353, and 1355, was added Stats 1963 ch 860 §3, amended Stats 1984 ch 291 §3, and repealed Stats 1985 ch 874 §13.

Former CC §1351, similar to present Prob C §§6174, 6409, was enacted Stats 1872 and repealed Stats 1931 ch 281 (Prob C §1700).

See CC §§4075, 4080, 4095, 4100, 4105, 4285, 4290, 4295, 4125, 4130, 4135, 4145, 4150, 4175, 4185, 4190.

CHAPTER 2
GOVERNING DOCUMENTS [REPEALED]

ARTICLE 1
Creation [Repealed]

§1352. [Section repealed 2014]

Leg.H. Added Stats 1985 ch 874 §14. Amended Stats 1986 ch 9 §1, effective February 25, 1986. Repealed Stats 2012 ch 180 §1 (AB 805), effective January 1, 2013, operative January 1, 2014. The repealed section related to applicability of title.

Prior Law: Former CC §1352, similar to present CC §1358, was added Stats 1963 ch 860 §3 and repealed Stats 1985 ch 874 §13.

See CC §4200.

§1352.5. [Section repealed 2014]

Leg.H. Added Stats 1999 ch 589 §1 (SB 1148). Repealed Stats 2012 ch 180 §1 (AB 805), effective January 1, 2013, operative January 1, 2014. The repealed section related to restrictive covenant that discriminates on basis of race, color, religion or other prohibited basis.

See CC §4225.

§1353. [Section repealed 2014]

Leg.H. Added Stats 1985 ch 874 §14. Amended Stats 1986 ch 9 §2, effective February 25, 1986; Stats 2002 ch 496 §5 (AB 2776), operative January 1, 2004; Stats 2004 ch 618 §3 (SB 1568). Repealed Stats 2012 ch 180 §1 (AB 805), effective January 1, 2013, operative January 1, 2014. The repealed section related to contents of declaration.

Prior Law: Former §1353, similar to present CC §§1361, 1362, was added Stats 1963 ch 860 §3 and repealed Stats 1985 ch 874 §13.

See CC §§4250, 4255.

§1353.5. [Section repealed 2014]

Leg.H. Added Stats 2002 ch 178 §2 (SB 2032). Repealed Stats 2012 ch 180 §1 (AB 805), effective January 1, 2013, operative January 1, 2014. The repealed section related to displaying flag of the United States.

See CC §4705.

§1353.6. [Section repealed 2014]

Leg.H. Added Stats 2003 ch 774 §2 (AB 1525). Repealed Stats 2012 ch 180 §1 (AB 805), effective January 1, 2013, operative January 1, 2014. The repealed section related to display of noncommercial signs, posters, flags or banners.

See CC §4710.

§1353.7. [Section repealed 2014]

Leg.H. Added Stats 2004 ch 318 §1 (AB 224). Repealed Stats 2012 ch 180 §1 (AB 805), effective January 1, 2013, operative January 1, 2014. The repealed section related to requirements for fire retardant roof covering.

See CC §4720.

§1353.8. [Section repealed 2014]

Leg.H. Added Stats 2009 ch 503 §3 (AB 1061), effective January 1, 2010. Repealed Stats 2012 ch 180 §1 (AB 805), effective January 1, 2013, operative January 1, 2014. The repealed section related to prohibition on use of low water-using plants or water-efficient landscape void.

Prior Law: Former CC §1353.8, relating to conditions having the effect of prohibiting the use of low water-using plants as a group, was added Stats 2006 ch 559 §1 and repealed Stats 2009 ch 503 §2.

See CC §4735.

§1353.9. [Section repealed 2014]

Leg.H. Added Stats 2011 ch 121 §1 (SB 209), effective January 1, 2012. Amended Stats 2012 ch 6 §1 (SB 880), effective February 29, 2012. Repealed Stats 2012 ch 180 §1 (AB 805), effective January 1, 2013, operative January 1, 2014. The repealed section related to Prohibition or restriction on installation or use of electric vehicle charging station; Standards and requirements; Application for approval; Placement in common areas; Violations and penalties; Attorney's fees.

ARTICLE 2
Enforcement [Repealed]

§1354. [Section repealed 2014]

Leg.H. Added Stats 1985 ch 874 §14. Amended Stats 1990 ch 1517 §3 (AB 3689), operative July 1, 1991; Stats 1993 ch 303 §1 (AB 55); Stats 1996 ch 1101 §1 (AB 1317); Stats 2004 ch 754 §1 (AB 1836). Repealed Stats 2012 ch 180 §1 (AB 805), effective January 1, 2013, operative January 1, 2014. The repealed section related to enforceability of covenants and restrictions as equitable servitudes; governing document other than declaration.

Prior Law: Former CC §1354, similar to present CC §1359, was added Stats 1963 ch 860 §3, amended Stats 1976 ch 73 §1, and repealed Stats 1985 ch 874 §13.

See CC §5975.

ARTICLE 3
Amendment [Repealed]

§1355. [Section repealed 2014]

Leg.H. Added Stats 1985 ch 874 §14. Amended Stats 1988 ch 1409 §1; Stats 1993 ch 21 §1 (AB 199). Repealed Stats 2012 ch 180 §1 (AB 805), effective January 1, 2013, operative January 1, 2014. The repealed section related to amendment of declaration.

Prior Law: Former §1355, similar to present CC §1354, was added Stats 1963 ch 860 §3, amended Stats 1976 ch 73 §2, and repealed Stats 1985 ch 874 §13.

See CC §§4270, 4260, 5115.

§1355.5. [Section repealed 2014]

Leg.H. Added Stats 1992 ch 124 §1 (AB 1384). Repealed Stats 2012 ch 180 §1 (AB 805), effective January 1, 2013, operative January 1, 2014. The repealed section related to amendment of governing documents to delete provisions intended to facilitate developer in completing construction or marketing.

See CC §4230.

§1356. [Section repealed 2014]

Leg.H. Added Stats 1985 ch 1003 §1. Repealed Stats 2012 ch 180 §1 (AB 805), effective January 1, 2013, operative January 1, 2014. The repealed section related to amendment of declaration; petition; hearing; grounds for granting or denying petition.

Prior Law: Former §1356, similar to present CC §§1366, 1367, was added Stats 1963 ch 860 §3 and repealed Stats 1985 ch 874 §13.

See CC §4275.

§1357. [Section repealed 2014]

Leg.H. Added Stats 1985 ch 874 §14. Repealed Stats 2012 ch 180 §1 (AB 805), effective January 1, 2013, operative January 1, 2014. The repealed section related to extension of term of declaration.

Prior Law: Former CC §1357, similar to present CC §1369, was added Stats 1960 ch 860 §3 and repealed Stats 1985 ch 874 §13.

Former CC §1357, similar to present Prob C §§21117, 21132, 21134, 21402, 21403, was enacted Stats 1872 and repealed Stats 1931 ch 281 (Prob C §1700).

See CC §4265.

ARTICLE 4
Operating Rules [Repealed]

§1357.100. [Section repealed 2014]

Leg.H. Added Stats 2003 ch 557 §10 (AB 512). Repealed Stats 2012 ch 180 §1 (AB 805), effective January 1, 2013, operative January 1, 2014. The repealed section related to definitions.

See CC §4340.

§1357.110. [Section repealed 2014]

Leg.H. Added Stats 2003 ch 557 §10 (AB 512). Repealed Stats 2012 ch 180 §1 (AB 805), effective January 1, 2013, operative January 1, 2014. The repealed section related to requirements for valid rule.

See CC §4350.

§1357.120. [Section repealed 2014]

Leg.H. Added Stats 2003 ch 557 §10 (AB 512). Amended Stats 2004 ch 346 §1 (AB 2376), ch 754 §2.5 (AB 1836); Stats 2005 ch 450 §1 (SB 61), effective January 1, 2006, operative July 1, 2006. Repealed Stats 2012 ch 180 §1 (AB 805), effective January 1, 2013, operative January 1, 2014. The repealed section related to application of Sections 1357.130, 1357.140.

See CC §4355.

§1357.130. [Section repealed 2014]

Leg.H. Added Stats 2003 ch 557 §10 (AB 512). Repealed Stats 2012 ch 180 §1 (AB 805), effective January 1, 2013, operative January 1, 2014. The repealed section related to notice of proposed rule change.

See CC §4360.

§1357.140. [Section repealed 2014]

Leg.H. Added Stats 2003 ch 557 §10 (AB 512). Repealed Stats 2012 ch 180 §1 (AB 805), effective January 1, 2013, operative January 1, 2014. The repealed section related to calling special meeting to reverse rule change.

See CC §4365.

§1357.150. [Section repealed 2014]

Leg.H. Added Stats 2003 ch 557 §10 (AB 512). Repealed Stats 2012 ch 180 §1 (AB 805), effective January 1, 2013, operative January 1, 2014. The repealed section related to application and effect of article; commencement of rule change.

See CC §4370.

CHAPTER 3
OWNERSHIP RIGHTS AND INTERESTS [REPEALED]

§1358. [Section repealed 2014]

Leg.H. Added Stats 1985 ch 874 §14. Repealed Stats 2012 ch 180 §1 (AB 805), effective January 1, 2013, operative January 1, 2014. The repealed section related to transfer or conveyance of separate interest.

Prior Law: Former CC §1358, similar to the present section, was added Stats 1963 ch 860 §3 and repealed Stats 1985 ch 874 §13.

Former CC §1358, similar to present Prob C §§7000, 7001, was enacted Stats 1872, amended Code Amdts 1873–74 ch 612 §173, and repealed Stats 1931 ch 281 (Prob C §1700).

See CC §§4625, 4630, 4635, 4640, 4645, 4650.

§1359. [Section repealed 2014]

Leg.H. Added Stats 1985 ch 874 §14. Repealed Stats 2012 ch 180 §1 (AB 805), effective January 1, 2013, operative January 1, 2014. The repealed section related to condominium projects; partition actions.

Prior Law: Former CC §1359, similar to present CC §1370, was added Stats 1963 ch 860 §3 and repealed Stats 1985 ch 874 §13.

Former CC §1359, similar to present Prob C §§21400–21403, was enacted Stats 1872, amended Code Amdts 1873–74 ch 612 §174, and repealed Stats 1931 ch 281 (Prob C §1700).

See CC §4610.

§1360. [Section repealed 2014]

Leg.H. Added Stats 1985 ch 874 §14. Repealed Stats 2012 ch 180 §1 (AB 805), effective January 1, 2013, operative January 1, 2014. The repealed section related to right of owner of separate interest to make improvements or modifications.

Prior Law: Former CC §1360, similar to present CC §1368, was added Stats 1976 ch 395 §1, amended Stats 1982 ch 805 §1, Stats 1983 ch 1288 §1, effective September 30, 1983, and repealed Stats 1985 ch 874 §13.

Former CC §1360, similar to present Prob C §§21401, 21402, was enacted Stats 1872, amended Code Amdts 1873–74 ch 612 §175, Stats 1901 ch 157 §278, and repealed Stats 1931 ch 281 (Prob C §1700).

See CC §4760.

§1360.2. [Section repealed 2014]

Leg.H. Added Stats 2011 ch 62 §2 (SB 150), effective January 1, 2012. Repealed Stats 2012 ch 180 §1 (AB 805), effective January 1, 2013, operative January 1, 2014. The repealed section related to rental or leasing separate interests; requirements.

§1360.5. [Section repealed 2014]

Leg.H. Added Stats 2000 ch 551 §2 (AB 860), operative January 1, 2001. Amended Stats 2001 ch 176 §2 (SB 210). Repealed Stats 2012 ch 180 §1 (AB 805), effective January 1, 2013, operative January 1, 2014. The repealed section related to responsibility for pets.

See CC §4715.

§1361. [Section repealed 2014]

Leg.H. Added Stats 1985 ch 874 §14. Repealed Stats 2012 ch 180 §1 (AB 805), effective January 1, 2013, operative January 1, 2014. The repealed section related to ingress, egress, and support.

Prior Law: Former CC §1361, similar to present CC §1360, was added Stats 1983 ch 163 §1 and repealed Stats 1985 ch 874 §13.

Former CC §1361, similar to present Prob C §§21400, 21402, 21403, was enacted Stats 1872 and repealed Stats 1931 ch 281 (Prob C §1700).

See CC §4505.

§1361.5. [Section repealed 2014]

Leg.H. Added Stats 2002 ch 1111 §2 (AB 2289). Repealed Stats 2012 ch 180 §1 (AB 805), effective January 1, 2013, operative January 1, 2014. The repealed section related to denial of physical access to separate interest prohibited.

See CC §4510.

§1362. [Section repealed 2014]

Leg.H. Added Stats 1985 ch 874 §14. Repealed Stats 2012 ch 180 §1 (AB 805), effective January 1, 2013, operative January 1, 2014. The repealed section related to ownership of common areas as tenants in common.

Prior Law: Former CC §1362, similar to present Prob C §§12400, 12402, 12403, was enacted Stats 1872 and repealed Stats 1931 ch 281 (Prob C §1700).

See CC §4500.

CHAPTER 4
GOVERNANCE [REPEALED]

ARTICLE 1
Association [Repealed]

§1363. [Section repealed 2014]

Leg.H. Added Stats 1985 ch 874 §14. Amended Stats 1988 ch 123 §1; Stats 1989 ch 571 §1; Stats 1991 ch 621 §1 (AB 839); Stats 1992 ch 178 §1 (SB 1496), ch 1250 §1 (AB 790), effective September 29, 1992, ch 1332 §1.5 (SB 1750); Stats 1993 ch 151 §1 (AB 1704), effective July 16, 1993; Stats 1995 ch 661 §1 (AB 46); Stats 2000 ch 257 §1 (AB 1823), ch 636 §5 (AB 2284); Stats 2003 ch 557 §14 (AB 512); Stats 2005 ch 37 §2 (SB 853), effective January 1, 2006; Stats 2011 ch 257 §1 (SB 563), effective January 1, 2012. Repealed Stats 2012 ch 180 §1 (AB 805), effective January 1, 2013, operative January 1, 2014. The repealed section related to community association.

Prior Law: Former CC §1363, similar to present Prob C §§7000, 7001, was enacted Stats 1872, amended Code Amdts 1880 ch 41 §21, and repealed Stats 1931 ch 281 (Prob C §1700).

See CC §§4800, 4805, 4820, 5000, 5240, 5850, 5855, 5865.

§1363.001. [Section repealed 2014]

Leg.H. Added Stats 2005 ch 452 §1 (SB 137), effective January 1, 2006. Repealed Stats 2012 ch 180 §1 (AB 805), effective January 1, 2013, operative January 1, 2014. The repealed section related to on-line education course.

See CC §5400.

§1363.005. [Section repealed 2014]

Leg.H. Added Stats 2009 ch 484 §2 (AB 899), effective January 1, 2010. Repealed Stats 2012 ch 180 §1 (AB 805), effective January 1, 2013, operative January 1, 2014. The repealed section related to distribution of disclosure documents index.

ARTICLE 2
Elections and Meetings [Repealed]

§1363.03. [Section repealed 2014]

Leg.H. Added Stats 2005 ch 450 §4 (SB 61), operative July 1, 2006. Amended Stats 2006 ch 310 §1 (SB 1560), effective September 18, 2006; Stats 2009 ch 547 §1 (AB 1572), effective January 1, 2010; Stats 2010 ch 328 §29 (SB 1330), effective January 1, 2011. Repealed Stats 2012 ch 180 §1 (AB 805), effective January 1, 2013, operative January 1, 2014. The repealed section related to adoption of rules; election; inspectors of election; procedures.

See CC §§5100, 5105, 5110, 5115, 5120, 5125, 5130.

§1363.04. [Section repealed 2014]

Leg.H. Added Stats 2005 ch 450 §4 (SB 61), operative July 1, 2006. Amended Stats 2006 ch 538 §42 (SB 1852), effective January 1, 2007. Repealed Stats 2012 ch 180 §1 (AB 805), effective January 1, 2013, operative January 1, 2014. The repealed section related to use of funds for campaign purposes.

See CC §5135.

§1363.05. [Section repealed 2014]

Leg.H. Added Stats 1995 ch 661 §2 (AB 46). Amended Stats 1996 ch 1101 §2 (AB 1317); Stats 2002 ch 195 §1 (AB 2417), ch 1111 §3 (AB 2289); Stats 2007 ch 250 §1 (SB 528), effective January 1, 2008; Stats 2011 ch 257 §2 (SB 563), effective January 1, 2012. Repealed Stats 2012 ch 180 §1 (AB 805), effective January 1, 2013, operative January 1, 2014. Amended Stats 2012 ch 770 §3 (AB 2697), effective January 1, 2013. Repealed Stats 2013 ch 183 §2 (SB 745), effective January 1, 2014. The repealed section related to the Common Interest Development Open Meeting Act.

See CC §4090, 4155, 4900, 4910, 4920, 4923, 4925, 4930, 4935, 4950, 5000.

§1363.07. [Section repealed 2014]

Leg.H. Added Stats 2005 ch 458 §1 (AB 1098), effective January 1, 2006. Amended Stats 2006 ch 538 §43 (SB 1852), effective January 1, 2007; Stats 2012 ch 6 §2 (SB 880), effective February 29, 2012. Repealed Stats 2012 ch 180 §1 (AB 805), effective January 1, 2013, operative January 1, 2014. The repealed section related to grant of exclusive use of part of common area; when vote required.

See CC §§4202, 4600.

§1363.09. [Section repealed 2014]

Leg.H. Added Stats 2005 ch 450 §5 (SB 61), effective January 1, 2006, operative July 1, 2006. Repealed Stats 2012 ch 180 §1 (AB 805), effective January 1, 2013, operative January 1, 2014. The repealed section related to civil action for violation of article.

See CC §§4605, 4955, 5145.

ARTICLE 3
Managing Agents [Repealed]

§1363.1. [Section repealed 2014]

Leg.H. Added Stats 1997 ch 632 §1 (AB 76). Repealed Stats 2012 ch 180 §1 (AB 805), effective January 1, 2013, operative January 1, 2014. The repealed section related to statement by prospective managing agent; contents.

Prior Law: Former CC §1363.1, relating to statement of information about managing agent, was added Stats 1989 ch 709 §1, and repealed, operative January 1, 1997, by its own terms.

See CC §§4158, 5375, 5385.

§1363.2. [Section repealed 2014]

Leg.H. Added Stats 1990 ch 1483 §1 (SB 2181). Amended Stats 1993 ch 589 §21 (AB 2211). Repealed Stats 2012 ch 180 §1 (AB 805), effective January 1, 2013, operative January 1, 2014. The repealed section related to management of funds received by managing agent.

See CC §§4158, 5380, 5385.

ARTICLE 4
Public Information [Repealed]

§1363.5. [Section repealed 2014]

Leg.H. Added Stats 1994 ch 204 §1 (AB 2551). Amended Stats 2002 ch 1116 §6 (AB 555); Stats 2003 ch 147 §5 (AB 1423), effective August 1, 2003; Stats 2011 ch 204 §1 (AB 657), effective January 1, 2012. Repealed Stats 2012 ch 180 §1 (AB 805), effective January 1, 2013, operative January 1, 2014. The repealed section related to statement in articles of incorporation; statement in biennial statement filed by incorporated association; requirements.

See CC §4280.

§1363.6. [Section repealed 2014]

Leg.H. Added Stats 2002 ch 1117 §2 (AB 643). Amended Stats 2003 ch 557 §18 (AB 512); Stats 2011 ch 204 §2 (AB 657), effective January 1, 2012. Repealed Stats 2012 ch 180 §1 (AB 805), effective January 1, 2013, operative January 1, 2014. The repealed section related to information to be submitted by association to secretary of state.

Prior Law: There was another section of this number, added Stats 1997, ch 181 §1 (AB 1025), renumbered CC §1366.2 by Stats 2002 ch 1117 §1.

See CC §5405.

ARTICLE 5
Dispute Resolution Procedure [Repealed]

§1363.810. [Section repealed 2014]

Leg.H. Added Stats 2004 ch 754 §3 (AB 1836). Repealed Stats 2012 ch 180 §1 (AB 805), effective January 1, 2013, operative January 1, 2014. The repealed section related to the application of article.

See CC §5900.

§1363.820. [Section repealed 2014]

Leg.H. Added Stats 2004 ch 754 §3 (AB 1836). Repealed Stats 2012 ch 180 §1 (AB 805), effective January 1, 2013, operative January 1, 2014. The repealed section related to development of fair, reasonable and expeditious procedure.

See CC §5905.

§1363.830. [Section repealed 2014]

Leg.H. Added Stats 2004 ch 754 §3 (AB 1836). Repealed Stats 2012 ch 180 §1 (AB 805), effective January 1, 2013, operative January 1, 2014. The repealed section related to requirements for procedure.

See CC §5910.

§1363.840. [Section repealed 2014]

Leg.H. Added Stats 2004 ch 754 §3 (AB 1836). Repealed Stats 2012 ch 180 §1 (AB 805), effective January 1, 2013, operative January 1, 2014. The repealed section related to procedure provided for association not otherwise providing one of their own.

See CC §5915.

§1363.850. [Section repealed 2014]

Leg.H. Added Stats 2004 ch 754 §3 (AB 1836). Repealed Stats 2012 ch 180 §1 (AB 805), effective January 1, 2013, operative January 1, 2014. The repealed section related to notice to include description of process.

See CC §5920.

CHAPTER 5
OPERATIONS [REPEALED]
ARTICLE 1
Common Areas [Repealed]

§1364. [Section repealed 2014]

Leg.H. Added Stats 1985 ch 874 §14. Amended Stats 1987 ch 357 §2, ch 1151 §1. Repealed Stats 2012 ch 180 §1 (AB 805), effective January 1, 2013, operative January 1, 2014. The repealed section related to responsibility for maintaining common areas and separate interests; access to telephone wiring.

See CC §§4775, 4780, 4785, 4790.

ARTICLE 2
Fiscal Matters [Repealed]

§1365. [Section repealed 2014]

Leg.H. Added Stats 1985 ch 874 §14. Amended Stats 1988 ch 1388 §1, ch 1409 §2; Stats 1990 ch 716 §1 (AB 2438); Stats 1991 ch 412 §1 (AB 623); Stats 1995 ch 199 §1 (SB 300); Stats 1996 ch 396 §1 (SB 1525); Stats 1997 ch 17 §14 (SB 947); Stats 1999 ch 898 §1 (AB 1048); Stats 2000 ch 1055 §8 (AB 2889), effective September 30, 2000; Stats 2002 ch 1116 §7 (AB 555); Stats 2004 ch 766 §1 (AB 2718); Stats 2005 ch 348 §1 (AB 1754), effective January 1, 2006; Stats 2006 ch 188 §1 (AB 2100), effective January 1, 2007. Repealed Stats 2012 ch 180 §1 (AB 805), effective January 1, 2013, operative January 1, 2014. The repealed section related to preparation and distribution of financial documents.

Prior Law: Former CC §1365 was enacted Stats 1872 and repealed Stats 1931 ch 281 (Prob C §1700).

See CC §§5300, 5305, 5310, 5320, 5565, 5810.

§1365.1. [Section repealed 2014]

Leg.H. Added Stats 2002 ch 1111 §4 (AB 2289). Amended Stats 2004 ch 697 §15 (AB 2252); Stats 2005 ch 452 §2 (SB 137), effective January 1, 2006; Stats 2008 ch 502 §1 (AB 2846), effective January 1, 2009. Repealed Stats 2012 ch 180 §1 (AB 805), effective January 1, 2013, operative January 1, 2014. The repealed section related to distribution of written notice by association prior to beginning of fiscal year; contents.

See CC §§4040, 5730.

§1365.2. [Section repealed 2014]

Leg.H. Added Stats 2005 ch 458 §3 (AB 1098), effective January 1, 2006, operative July 1, 2006. Amended Stats 2006 ch 310 §2 (SB 1560), effective September 18, 2006; Stats 2010 ch 322 §1 (SB 1128), effective January 1, 2011; Stats 2011 ch 257 §3 (SB 563), effective January 1, 2012. Repealed Stats 2012 ch 180 §1 (AB 805), effective January 1, 2013, operative January 1, 2014. The repealed section related to association records and enhanced association records; definitions; availability for inspection and copying; redaction of information; use; action for violation; effect on corporations code sections 8330, 8333; applicability.

See CC §§5210, 5200, 5205, 5215, 5220, 5225, 5230, 5235, 5240.

§1365.2.5. [Section repealed 2014]

Leg.H. Added Stats 2004 ch 766 §2 (AB 2718). Amended Stats 2005 ch 22 §13 (SB 1108), effective January 1, 2006; Stats 2006 ch 188 §2 (AB 2100), effective January 1, 2007; Stats 2009 ch 484 §3 (AB 899), effective January 1, 2010. Repealed Stats 2012 ch 180 §1 (AB 805), effective January 1, 2013, operative January 1, 2014. The repealed section related to assessment and reserve funding disclosure summary form.

See CC §§5300, 5570.

§1365.3. [Section repealed 2014]

Leg.H. Added Stats 2004 ch 766 §3 (AB 2718). Repealed Stats 2012 ch 180 §1 (AB 805), effective January 1, 2013, operative January 1, 2014. The repealed section related to community organizations to report administrative costs and payees of those costs.

See CC §5580.

§1365.5. [Section repealed 2014]

Leg.H. Added Stats 1986 ch 294 §1. Amended Stats 1991 ch 355 §1 (AB 871); Stats 1992 ch 866 §1 (AB 2693); Stats 1994 ch 885 §1 (AB 2770); Stats 1995 ch 13 §1 (AB 463); Stats 1996 ch 80 §1 (AB 3015); Stats 1999 ch 898 §2 (AB 1048); Stats 2004 ch 766 §4 (AB 2718); Stats 2006 ch 188 §3 (AB 2100), effective January 1, 2007. Repealed Stats 2012 ch 180 §1 (AB 805), effective January 1, 2013, operative January 1, 2014. The repealed section related to fiscal duties of board of directors; signatures required for withdrawal of money; use of reserve accounts; visual inspection.

See CC §§4177, 4178, 5500, 5510, 5515, 5520, 5550, 5560.

§1365.6. [Section repealed 2014]

Leg.H. Added Stats 2006 ch 188 §4 (AB 2100), effective January 1, 2007. Repealed Stats 2012 ch 180 §1 (AB 805), effective January 1, 2013, operative January 1, 2014. The repealed section related to application of Corp C §310.

See CC §5350.

ARTICLE 3
Insurance [Repealed]

§1365.7. [Section repealed 2014]

Leg.H. Added Stats 1988 ch 1188 §1. Amended Stats 1992 ch 866 §2 (AB 2693); Stats 1996 ch 185 §1 (SB 1711). Repealed Stats 2012 ch 180 §1 (AB 805), effective January 1, 2013, operative January 1, 2014. The repealed section related to personal liability of volunteer officer or director for injury.

See CC §5800.

§1365.9. [Section repealed 2014]

Leg.H. Added Stats 1994 ch 833 §1 (SB 2072). Amended Stats 1995 ch 199 §2 (SB 300). Repealed Stats 2012 ch 180 §1 (AB 805), effective January 1, 2013, operative January 1, 2014. The repealed section related to liability for common areas; action against association; insurance requirements.

See CC §5805.

ARTICLE 4
Assessments [Repealed]

§1366. [Section repealed 2014]

Leg.H. Added Stats 1985 ch 874 §14. Amended Stats 1987 ch 596 §1; Stats 1990 ch 1517 §4 (AB 3689), operative July 1, 1991; Stats 1991 ch 355 §2 (AB 871), ch 412 §2 (AB 623); Stats 1992 ch 1250 §2 (AB 790), effective September 29, 1992; Stats 2000 ch 125 §1 (AB 1859); Stats 2002 ch 1111 §5 (AB 2289). Repealed Stats 2012 ch 180 §1 (AB 805), effective

January 1, 2013, operative January 1, 2014. The repealed section related to regular and special assessment; increases; emergency situations; delinquent assessments; exemption for associations.

Prior Law: Former CC §1366, similar to present Prob C §§16340, 16341, 16345–16347, was enacted Stats 1872 and repealed Stats 1931 ch 281 (Prob C §1700).

See CC §§5600, 5605, 5610, 5615, 5620, 5650.

§1366.1. [Section repealed 2014]

Leg.H. Added Stats 1986 ch 548 §1. Amended Stats 1992 ch 1332 §2 (SB 1750). Repealed Stats 2012 ch 180 §1 (AB 805), effective January 1, 2013, operative January 1, 2014. The repealed section related to excessive assessments.

See CC §5600.

§1366.2. [Section repealed 2014]

Leg.H. Added Stats 1997 ch 181 §1 as CC §1363.6. Amended and renumbered by Stats 2002 ch 1117 §1. Repealed Stats 2012 ch 180 §1 (AB 805), effective January 1, 2013, operative January 1, 2014. The repealed section related to recording statement of relevant information.

See CC §4210.

§1366.3. [Section repealed 2006]

Leg.H. Added Stats 1996 ch 1101 §3 (AB 1317). Amended Stats 2002 ch 1111 §6 (AB 2289). Repealed Stats 2005 ch 452 §3 (SB 137), effective January 1, 2006. The repealed section related to alternative dispute resolution.

§1366.4. [Section repealed 2014]

Leg.H. Added Stats 2009 ch 431 §1 (AB 313), effective January 1, 2010. Repealed Stats 2012 ch 180 §1 (AB 805), effective January 1, 2013, operative January 1, 2014. The repealed section related to levy of assessments on separate interests.

See CC §5625.

§1367. [Section repealed 2014]

Leg.H. Added Stats 1985 ch 874 §14. Amended Stats 1986 ch 9 §3, effective February 25, 1986; Stats 1996 ch 1101 §4 (AB 1317); Stats 2002 ch 1111 §7 (AB 2289). Repealed Stats 2012 ch 180 §1 (AB 805), effective January 1, 2013, operative January 1, 2014. The repealed section related to lien for delinquent assessments.

Prior Law: Former CC §1367, similar to present Prob C §§6409, 21135, was enacted Stats 1872, amended Code Amdts 1873–74 ch 612 §176, and repealed Stats 1931 ch 281 (Prob C §1700).

Omitted, but see CC §5740.

§1367.1. [Section repealed 2014]

Leg.H. Added Stats 2002 ch 1111 §8 (AB 2289). Amended Stats 2004 ch 697 §16 (AB 2252); Stats 2005 ch 452 §4 (SB 137), effective January 1, 2006; Stats 2006 ch 575 §2 (AB 2624), effective January 1, 2007. Repealed Stats 2012 ch 180 §1 (AB 805), effective January 1, 2013, operative January 1, 2014. The repealed section related to assessment as debt; written notice of lien; application of payments; dispute resolution; payment plan; monetary penalty; assignability of rights; costs.

See CC §§4040, 5650, 5655, 5660, 5665, 5670, 5673, 5675, 5680, 5685, 5690, 5700, 5705, 5710, 5725, 5735, 5740.

§1367.4. [Section repealed 2014]

Leg.H. Added Stats 2005 ch 452 §5 (SB 137), effective January 1, 2006. Amended Stats 2006 ch 575 §3 (AB 2624), effective January 1, 2007. Repealed Stats 2012 ch 180 §1 (AB 805), effective January 1, 2013, operative January 1, 2014. The repealed section related to collection of debts for assessments arising on and after January 1, 2006; when judicial or nonjudicial foreclosure may be used.

See CC §§5705, 5715, 5720.

§1367.5. [Section repealed 2014]

Leg.H. Added Stats 2005 ch 452 §6 (SB 137), effective January 1, 2006. Repealed Stats 2012 ch 180 §1 (AB 805), effective January 1, 2013, operative January 1, 2014. The repealed section related to reversal and release of lien recorded in error; costs.

See CC §5685.

§1367.6. [Section repealed 2014]

Leg.H. Added Stats 2008 ch 502 §2 (AB 2846), effective January 1, 2009. Repealed Stats 2012 ch 180 §1 (AB 805), effective January 1, 2013, operative January 1, 2014. The repealed section related to dispute of charge or sum levied by association; dispute resolution; collection of delinquent assessments.

See CC §5658.

CHAPTER 6
TRANSFER OF OWNERSHIP INTERESTS [REPEALED]

§1368. [Section repealed 2014]

Leg.H. Added Stats 1985 ch 1596 §4. Amended Stats 1987 ch 596 §2; Stats 1991 ch 412 §3 (AB 623); Stats 1995 ch 199 §3 (SB 300); Stats 1997 ch 632 §2 (AB 76); Stats 2000 ch 257 §2 (AB 1823); Stats 2002 ch 1111 §9 (AB 2289), ch 1117 §3.5 (AB 643); Stats 2003 ch 393 §1 (AB 1086), ch 557 §25.5 (AB 512); Stats 2004 ch 766 §5 (AB 2718); Stats 2010 ch 322 §2 (SB 1128), effective January 1, 2011; Stats 2011 ch 62 §3 (SB 150), effective January 1, 2012; Stats 2012 ch. 162 §10 (SB 1171), effective January 1, 2013. Repealed Stats 2012 ch 180 §1 (AB 805), effective January 1, 2013, operative January 1, 2014. Amended Stats 2012 ch 475 §1 (AB 1838), effective January 1, 2013, ch 770 §4.5 (AB 2697), effective January 1, 2013. Repealed Stats 2013 ch 183 §3 (SB 745), effective January 1, 2014. The repealed section related to documents to be provided to a prospective purchaser and civil penalties for willful violations of section.

See CC §§4110, 4525, 4530, 4535, 4540, 4545, 4575, 4580.

§1368.1. [Section repealed 2014]

Leg.H. Added Stats 2002 ch 817 §1 (AB 2546). Repealed Stats 2012 ch 180 §1 (AB 805), effective January 1, 2013, operative January 1, 2014. The repealed section related to unreasonable restrictions on marketability of property void.

See CC §4730.

§1368.2. [Section repealed 2013]

Leg.H. Added Stats 2011 ch 206 §2 (AB 771), effective January 1, 2012. Repealed Stats 2012 ch 180 §1 (AB 805), effective January 1, 2013, operative January 1, 2014. Amended Stats 2012 ch 475 §2 (AB 1838), effective January 1, 2013. Repealed Stats 2013 ch 183 §4 (SB 745), effective January 1, 2014. The repealed section related to the form for billing disclosures required by former CC §1368.

See CC §4528.

CHAPTER 7
CIVIL ACTIONS AND LIENS [REPEALED]
ARTICLE 1
Miscellaneous Provisions [Repealed]

§1368.3. [Section repealed 2014]

Leg.H. Added Stats 2004 ch 754 §4 (AB 1836). Repealed Stats 2012 ch 180 §1 (AB 805), effective January 1, 2013, operative January 1, 2014. The repealed section related to standing of association in specified matters.

See CC §5980.

§1368.4. [Section repealed 2014]

Leg.H. Added Stats 2004 ch 754 §4 (AB 1836). Repealed Stats 2012 ch 180 §1 (AB 805), effective January 1, 2013, operative January 1, 2014. The repealed section related to recovery of damages.

Prior Law: Former CC §1368.4, relating to notice of civil actions, was added Stats 1995 ch 13 §2, and amended and renumbered Civ C §1368.5 by Stats 2004 ch 754 §5.

See CC §5985.

§1368.5. [Section repealed 2014]

Leg.H. Added Stats 1995 ch 13 §2 (AB 463), as CC §1368.4. Amended and renumbered by Stats 2004 ch 754 §5 (AB 1836). Repealed Stats 2012 ch 180 §1 (AB 805), effective January 1, 2013, operative January 1, 2014. The repealed section related to notice of civil action.

See CC §6150.

§1369. [Section repealed 2014]

Leg.H. Added Stats 1985 ch 874 §14. Repealed Stats 2012 ch 180 §1 (AB 805), effective January 1, 2013, operative January 1, 2014. The repealed section related to lien for labor or materials furnished to condominium owner; emergency repairs; labor and materials for common areas.

Prior Law: Former CC §1369, similar to present Prob C §§12001, 12003–12005, 16340, 16341, 16345–13647, was enacted Stats 1872 and repealed Stats 1931 ch 281 (Prob C §1700).

See CC §4615.

ARTICLE 2
Alternative Dispute Resolution [Repealed]

§1369.510. [Section repealed 2014]

Leg.H. Added Stats 2004 ch 754 §6 (AB 1836). Repealed Stats 2012 ch 180 §1 (AB 805), effective January 1, 2013, operative January 1, 2014. The repealed section related to definitions.

See CC §5925.

§1369.520. [Section repealed 2014]

Leg.H. Added Stats 2004 ch 754 §6 (AB 1836). Amended Stats 2006 ch 167 §2 (AB 2618), effective January 1, 2007. Repealed Stats 2012 ch 180 §1 (AB 805), effective January 1, 2013, operative January 1, 2014. The repealed section related to filing of specified enforcement actions to be preceded by alternate dispute resolution attempt.

See CC §5930.

§1369.530. [Section repealed 2014]

Leg.H. Added Stats 2004 ch 754 §6 (AB 1836). Repealed Stats 2012 ch 180 §1 (AB 805), effective January 1, 2013, operative January 1, 2014. The repealed section related to service of request for resolution; contents of request.

See CC §5935.

§1369.540. [Section repealed 2014]

Leg.H. Added Stats 2004 ch 754 §6 (AB 1836). Repealed Stats 2012 ch 180 §1 (AB 805), effective January 1, 2013, operative January 1, 2014. The repealed section related to time limit for resolution upon acceptance; application of evidence code; costs.

See CC §5940.

§1369.550. [Section repealed 2014]

Leg.H. Added Stats 2004 ch 754 §6 (AB 1836). Repealed Stats 2012 ch 180 §1 (AB 805), effective January 1, 2013, operative January 1, 2014. The repealed section related to tolling of time limitation.

See CC §5945.

§1369.560. [Section repealed 2014]

Leg.H. Added Stats 2004 ch 754 §6 (AB 1836). Repealed Stats 2012 ch 180 §1 (AB 805), effective January 1, 2013, operative January 1, 2014. The repealed section related to filing of certificate required at commencement of enforcement action.

See CC §5950.

§1369.570. [Section repealed 2014]

Leg.H. Added Stats 2004 ch 754 §6 (AB 1836). Repealed Stats 2012 ch 180 §1 (AB 805), effective January 1, 2013, operative January 1, 2014. The repealed section related to referring to alternative dispute resolution subsequent to commencement of enforcement action.

See CC §5955.

§1369.580. [Section repealed 2014]

Leg.H. Added Stats 2004 ch 754 §6 (AB 1836). Repealed Stats 2012 ch 180 §1 (AB 805), effective January 1, 2013, operative January 1, 2014. The repealed section related to determination of fees and costs.

See CC §5960.

§1369.590. [Section repealed 2014]

Leg.H. Added Stats 2004 ch 754 §6 (AB 1836). Repealed Stats 2012 ch 180 §1 (AB 805), effective January 1, 2013, operative January 1, 2014. The repealed section related to annual summary to be provided.

See CC §5965.

CHAPTER 8
CONSTRUCTION OF INSTRUMENTS AND ZONING [REPEALED]

§1370. [Section repealed 2014]

Leg.H. Added Stats 1985 ch 874 §14. Repealed Stats 2012 ch 180 §1 (AB 805), effective January 1, 2013, operative January 1, 2014. The repealed section related to liberal construction of governing documents; severability of provisions.

Prior Law: Former CC §1370, similar to present CC §1372, was added Stats 1963 ch 860 §3 and repealed Stats 1985 ch 874 §13.

Former CC §1370, similar to present Prob C §12000, was enacted Stats 1872 and repealed Stats 1931 ch 281 (Prob C §1700).

See CC §4215.

§1371. [Section repealed 2014]

Leg.H. Added Stats 1985 ch 874 §14. Repealed Stats 2012 ch 180 §1 (AB 805), effective January 1, 2013, operative January 1, 2014. The repealed section related to presumption regarding unit boundaries.

Prior Law: Former CC §1371, similar to present Prob C §8421, was enacted Stats 1872 and repealed Stats 1931 ch 281 (Prob C §1700).

See CC §4220.

§1372. [Section repealed 2014]

Leg.H. Added Stats 1985 ch 874 §14. Repealed Stats 2012 ch 180 §1 (AB 805), effective January 1, 2013, operative January 1, 2014. The repealed section related to construction of local zoning ordinances.

Prior Law: Former CC §1372 was enacted Stats 1872 and repealed Stats 1931 ch 281 (Prob C §1700).

See CC §4020.

§1373. [Section repealed 2014]

Leg.H. Added Stats 1988 ch 123 §2. Amended Stats 2003 ch 557 §30 (AB 512); Stats 2004 ch 346 §2 (AB 2376); Stats 2011 ch 62 §4 (SB 150), effective January 1, 2012. Repealed Stats 2012 ch 180 §1 (AB 805), effective January 1, 2013, operative January 1, 2014. The repealed section related to industrial or commercial developments.

Prior Law: Former CC §1373, similar to present Prob C §8400, was enacted Stats 1872 and repealed Stats 1931 ch 281 (Prob C §1700).

See CC §4202.

§1374. [Section repealed 2014]

Leg.H. Added Stats 1994 ch 245 §1 (AB 67). Amended Stats 2005 ch 37 §3 (SB 853), effective January 1, 2006. Repealed Stats 2012 ch 180 §1 (AB 805), effective January 1, 2013, operative January 1, 2014. The repealed section related to inapplicability to development without specified common area.

Prior Law: Former CC §1374, was enacted Stats 1872 and repealed Stats 1931 ch 281 (Prob C §1700).

See CC §4201.

CHAPTER 9
CONSTRUCTION DEFECT LITIGATION [REPEALED]

§1375. [Section repealed 2014]

Leg.H. Added Stats 1995 ch 864 §1 (SB 1029). Amended Stats 1997 ch 17 §15 (SB 947), ch 632 §4 (AB 76) (ch 632 prevails); Stats 2001 ch 824 §1.5 (AB 1700), operative July 1, 2002, inoperative July 1, 2010, repealed January 1, 2011; Stats 2002 ch 664 §36 (AB 3034), operative July 1, 2002, inoperative July 1, 2010, repealed January 1, 2011; Stats 2009 ch 7 §1 (AB 927), effective January 1, 2010, inoperative July 1, 2017, repealed January 1, 2018. Repealed Stats 2012 ch 180 §1 (AB 805), effective January 1, 2013, operative January 1, 2014. The repealed section related to claim against builder for defects in design or construction.

Prior Law: Former CC §1375, was enacted Stats 1872 and repealed Stats 1931 ch 281 (Prob C §1700).

See CC §6000.

§1375.05. [Section repealed 2011]

Leg.H. Added Stats 2001 ch 824 §1.7 (AB 1700), operative July 1, 2002, inoperative July 1, 2010, repealed January 1, 2011. Amended Stats 2002 ch 664 §37 (AB 3034), inoperative July 1, 2010, repealed January 1, 2011. Repealed operative January 1, 2011, by its own provisions. The repealed section related to claim against builder for defects in design or construction and trial procedure.

§1375.1. [Section repealed 2014]

Leg.H. Added Stats 1997 ch 632 §3 (AB 76). Repealed Stats 2012 ch 180 §1 (AB 805), effective January 1, 2013, operative January 1, 2014. The repealed section related to disclosure to association members of settlement agreement regarding defects.

See CC §6100.

CHAPTER 10
IMPROVEMENTS [REPEALED]

§1376. [Section repealed 2014]

Leg.H. Added Stats 1995 ch 978 §1 (AB 104). Repealed Stats 2012 ch 180 §1 (AB 805), effective January 1, 2013, operative January 1, 2014. The repealed section related to restrictions on installation or use of video or television antenna.

> **Prior Law:** Former CC §1376, similar to Prob C §§21102, 21103, was enacted Stats 1872, amended Code Amdts 1873–74 ch 612 §177, Stats 1901 ch 157 §280, Stats 1905 ch 448 §10, and repealed Stats 1931 ch 281 (Prob C §1700).

See CC §4725.

§1377. [Section repealed 1931]

Leg.H. Enacted Stats 1872. Repealed Stats 1931 ch 281 (Prob C §1700). See Prob C §§7000, 7001.

§1378. [Section repealed 2014]

Leg.H. Added Stats 2004 ch 346 §3.5 (AB 2376). Amended Stats 2005 ch 37 §4 (SB 853), effective January 1, 2006. Repealed Stats 2012 ch 180 §1 (AB 805), effective January 1, 2013, operative January 1, 2014. The repealed section related to requirements for reviewing proposed physical changes to owner's separate interests or to common area; notice to members.

See CC §4765.

TITLE 7
POWERS OF APPOINTMENT
[REPEALED]

§1380.1. [Section repealed 1992]

Leg.H. Added Stats 1969 ch 155 §1, operative July 1, 1970. Repealed Stats 1992 ch 30 §1 (AB 1722). See Prob C §600.

§1380.2. [Section repealed 1992]

Leg.H. Added Stats 1969 ch 155 §1, operative July 1, 1970. Repealed Stats 1992 ch 30 §1 (AB 1722). See Prob C §601.

§1381.1. [Section repealed 1992]

Leg.H. Added Stats 1969 ch 155 §1, operative July 1, 1970. Repealed Stats 1992 ch 30 §1 (AB 1722). See Prob C §610.

§1381.2. [Section repealed 1992]

Leg.H. Added Stats 1969 ch 155 §1, operative July 1, 1970. Repealed Stats 1992 ch 30 §1 (AB 1722). See Prob C §611.

§1381.3. [Section repealed 1992]

Leg.H. Added Stats 1969 ch 155 §1, operative July 1, 1970. Repealed Stats 1992 ch 30 §1 (AB 1722). See Prob C §612.

§1381.4. [Section repealed 1992]

Leg.H. Added Stats 1969 ch 155 §1, operative July 1, 1970. Repealed Stats 1992 ch 30 §1 (AB 1722). See Prob C §613.

§1382.1. [Section repealed 1992]

Leg.H. Added Stats 1969 ch 155 §1, operative July 1, 1970. Repealed Stats 1992 ch 30 §1 (AB 1722). See Prob C §620.

§1383. [Section repealed 1931]

Leg.H. Enacted Stats 1872. Repealed Stats 1931 ch 281 (Prob C §1700). See Prob C §6400.

§1384. [Section repealed 1931]

Leg.H. Enacted Stats 1872. Amended Code Amdts 1873–74 ch 612 §178, Repealed Stats 1931 ch 281 (Prob C §1700). See Prob C §§7000, 7001.

§1384.1. [Section repealed 1992]

Leg.H. Added Stats 1969 ch 155 §1, operative July 1, 1970. Amended Stats 1972 ch 579 §13; Stats 1978 ch 266 §1. Repealed Stats 1992 ch 30 §1 (AB 1722). See Prob C §625.

§1385. [Section repealed 1873–74]

Leg.H. Enacted Stats 1872. Repealed Code Amdts 1873–74 ch 612 §179.

§1385.1. [Section repealed 1992]

Leg.H. Added Stats 1969 ch 155 §1, operative July 1, 1970. Repealed Stats 1992 ch 30 §1 (AB 1722). See Prob C §630.

§1385.2. [Section repealed 1992]

Leg.H. Added Stats 1969 ch 155 §1, operative July 1, 1970. Repealed Stats 1992 ch 30 §1 (AB 1722). See Prob C §632.

§1385.3. [Section repealed 1992]

Leg.H. Added Stats 1969 ch 155 §1, operative July 1, 1970. Repealed Stats 1992 ch 30 §1 (AB 1722). See Prob C §633.

§1385.4. [Section repealed 1992]

Leg.H. Added Stats 1969 ch 155 §1, operative July 1, 1970. Repealed Stats 1992 ch 30 §1 (AB 1722). See Prob C §634.

§1385.5. [Section repealed 1992]

Leg.H. Added Stats 1969 ch 155 §1, operative July 1, 1970. Repealed Stats 1992 ch 30 §1 (AB 1722). See Prob C §635.

§1386. [Section repealed 1931]

Leg.H. Enacted Stats 1872. Amended Code Amdts 1873–74 ch 612 §180; Code Amdts 1880 ch 115 §1; Stats 1901 ch 157 §281; Stats 1905 ch 449 §1; Stats 1907 ch 297 §1. Repealed Stats 1931 ch 281 (Prob C §1700). See Prob C §§101, 102, 140–147, 240, 6400–6402, 6402.5, 6404, 6806.

§1386.1. [Section repealed 1992]

Leg.H. Added Stats 1969 ch 155 §1, operative July 1, 1970. Repealed Stats 1992 ch 30 §1 (AB 1722). See Prob C §640.

§1386.2. [Section repealed 1992]

Leg.H. Added Stats 1981 ch 63 §2, operative July 1, 1982. Repealed Stats 1992 ch 30 §1 (AB 1722). See Prob C §641.

> **Prior Law:** Former §1386.2, similar to present Prob C §641, was added Stats 1969 ch 155 §1, operative July 1, 1970, and repealed Stats 1981 ch 63 §1, operative July 1, 1982.

§1386.3. [Section repealed 1992]

Leg.H. Added Stats 1969 ch 155 §1, operative July 1, 1970. Repealed Stats 1992 ch 30 §1 (AB 1722). See Prob C §642.

§1387. [Section repealed 1931]

Leg.H. Enacted Stats 1872. Amended Stats 1901 ch 157 §282. Repealed Stats 1931 ch 281 (Prob C §1700). See Prob C §6450.

§1387.1. [Section repealed 1992]

Leg.H. Added Stats 1969 ch 155 §1, operative July 1, 1970. Repealed Stats 1992 ch 30 §1 (AB 1722). See Prob C §650.

§1387.2. [Section repealed 1992]

Leg.H. Added Stats 1969 ch 155 §1, operative July 1, 1970. Repealed Stats 1992 ch 30 §1 (AB 1722). See Prob C §651.

§1387.3. [Section repealed 1992]

Leg.H. Added Stats 1969 ch 155 §1, operative July 1, 1970. Repealed Stats 1992 ch 30 §1 (AB 1722). See Prob C §652.

§1388. [Section repealed 1931]

Leg.H. Enacted Stats 1872. Amended Stats 1901 ch 157 §283; Stats 1905 ch 449 §2; Stats 1921 ch 186 §1. Repealed Stats 1931 ch 281 (Prob C §1700).

§1388.1. [Section repealed 1992]

Leg.H. Added Stats 1969 ch 155 §1, operative July 1, 1970. Amended Stats 1978 ch 266 §2. Repealed Stats 1992 ch 30 §1 (AB 1722). See Prob C §660.

§1388.2. [Section repealed 1992]

Leg.H. Added Stats 1969 ch 155 §1, operative July 1, 1970. Amended Stats 1969 ch 468 §1; Stats 1981 ch 63 §3, operative July 1, 1982. Repealed Stats 1992 ch 30 §1 (AB 1722). See Prob C §661.

§1388.3. [Section repealed 1992]

Leg.H. Added Stats 1981 ch 63 §4, operative July 1, 1982. Repealed Stats 1992 ch 30 §1 (AB 1722). See Prob C §662.

§1389. [Section repealed 1931]

Leg.H. Enacted Stats 1872. Repealed Stats 1931 ch 281 (Prob C §1700). See Prob C §§6402, 6402.5.

§1389.1. [Section repealed 1992]

Leg.H. Added Stats 1969 ch 155 §1, operative July 1, 1970. Repealed Stats 1992 ch 30 §1 (AB 1722). See Prob C §670.

§1389.2. [Section repealed 1992]

Leg.H. Added Stats 1969 ch 155 §1, operative July 1, 1970. Repealed Stats 1992 ch 30 §1 (AB 1722). See Prob C §671.

§1389.3. [Section repealed 1992]

Leg.H. Added Stats 1969 ch 155 §1, operative July 1, 1970. Amended Stats 1981 ch 63 §5, operative July 1, 1982. Repealed Stats 1992 ch 30 §1 (AB 1722). See Prob C §672.

§1389.4. [Section repealed 1992]

Leg.H. Added Stats 1969 ch 155 §1, operative July 1, 1970. Amended Stats 1981 ch 63 §6, operative July 1, 1982; Stats 1983 ch 842 §5, operative January 1, 1985; Stats 1985 ch 982 §2. Repealed Stats 1992 ch 30 §1 (AB 1722). See Prob C §673.

§1389.5. [Section repealed 1992]

Leg.H. Added Stats 1981 ch 63 §7, operative July 1, 1982. Repealed Stats 1992 ch 30 §1 (AB 1722). See Prob C §674.

§1390. [Section repealed 1931]

Leg.H. Enacted Stats 1872. Repealed Stats 1931 ch 281 (Prob C §1700).

§1390.1. [Section repealed 1992]

Leg.H. Added Stats 1969 ch 155 §1, operative July 1, 1970. Amended Stats 1981 ch 63 §8, operative July 1, 1982. Repealed Stats 1992 ch 30 §1 (AB 1722). See Prob C §680.

§1390.2. [Section repealed 1992]

Leg.H. Added Stats 1969 ch 155 §1, operative July 1, 1970. Repealed Stats 1992 ch 30 §1 (AB 1722). See Prob C §681.

§1390.3. [Section repealed 1992]

Leg.H. Added Stats 1969 ch 155 §1, operative July 1, 1970. Repealed Stats 1992 ch 30 §1 (AB 1722). See Prob C §682.

§1390.4. [Section repealed 1992]

Leg.H. Added Stats 1969 ch 155 §1, operative July 1, 1970. Repealed Stats 1992 ch 30 §1 (AB 1722). See Prob C §683.

§1390.5. [Section repealed 1992]

Leg.H. Added Stats 1981 ch 63 §9, operative July 1, 1982. Repealed Stats 1992 ch 30 §1 (AB 1722). See Prob C §684.

§1391. [Section repealed 1992]

Leg.H. Added Stats 1991 ch 156 §18 (AB 1577). Repealed Stats 1992 ch 30 §1 (AB 1722). See Prob C §690.

Prior Law: Former §1391 was enacted Stats 1872 and repealed Stats 1931 ch 281.

§1391.1. [Section repealed 1991]

Leg.H. Added Stats 1969 ch 155 §1, operative July 1, 1970. Repealed Stats 1991 ch 156 §19 (AB 1577). See Prob C §§21210, 21211.

§1391.2. [Section repealed 1991]

Leg.H. Added Stats 1969 ch 155 §1, operative July 1, 1970. Repealed Stats 1991 ch 156 §19 (AB 1577). See Prob C §21206.

§1392. [Section repealed 1931]

Leg.H. Enacted Stats 1872. Repealed Stats 1931 ch 281 (Prob C §1700).

§1392.1. [Section repealed 1992]

Leg.H. Added Stats 1969 ch 155 §1, operative July 1, 1970. Amended Stats 1986 ch 820 §6, operative July 1, 1987. Repealed Stats 1992 ch 30 §1 (AB 1722). See Prob C §695.

§§1393–1400. [Sections repealed 1931]

Leg.H. Enacted Stats 1872. Repealed Stats 1931 ch 281 (Prob C §1700). See Prob C §§6406, 6409, 21135.

§1401. [Section repealed 1931]

Leg.H. Enacted Stats 1872. Amended Code Amdts 1873–74 ch 612 §181; Stats 1919 ch 611 §1; Stats 1923 ch 18 §1. Repealed Stats 1931 ch 281 (Prob C §1700). See Prob C §§100, 6101, 6401.

§1402. [Section repealed 1931]

Leg.H. Enacted Stats 1872. Amended Stats 1919 ch 611 §2; Stats 1923 ch 18 §2. Repealed Stats 1931 ch 281 (Prob C §1700). See Prob C §§13501, 13540, 13541, 13550–13554.

§§1403, 1404. [Sections repealed 1931]

Leg.H. Enacted Stats 1872. Repealed Stats 1931 ch 281 (Prob C §1700). See Prob C §§240, 6407.

§1405. [Section repealed 1931]

Leg.H. Enacted Stats 1872. Amended Stats 1901 ch 157 §286 (amendment repealed Stats 1955 ch 28 §1); Stats 1905 ch 449 §5; Stats 1917 ch 170 §1. Repealed Stats 1931 ch 281 (Prob C §1700). See Prob C §§6404, 6806.

§1406. [Section repealed 1931]

Leg.H. Enacted Stats 1872. Amended Stats 1901 ch 157 §287 (amendment repealed Stats 1955 ch 28 §1); Stats 1905 ch 449 §6. Repealed Stats 1931 ch 281 (Prob C §1700). See Prob C §§6404, 6806.

§§1407, 1408. [Sections repealed 1931]

Leg.H. Enacted Stats 1872. Repealed Stats 1931 ch 281 (Prob C §1700). See Prob C §§6404, 6806.

§1409. [Section repealed 1931]

Leg.H. Added Stats 1905 ch 449 §7. Repealed Stats 1931 ch 281 (Prob C §1700). See Prob C §§250–257.

TITLE 8
WATER RIGHTS

First in time, first in right. §1414.
Notice of appropriation. §1415.
Work to be done in appropriation of waters. §1416.
Completion defined. §1417.
Doctrine of relation applied. §1418.
Forfeiture. §1419.
Rights of present claimant. §1420.
Recorder to keep book in which to record notices. §1421.
Time within which to commence excavation on public reservation. §1422.

§1410. [Section repealed 1943]

Leg.H. Enacted Stats 1872. Amended Stats 1911 ch 407 §1. Repealed Stats 1943 ch 368 (Wat C §150001). See Wat C §102.

§1410a. [Section repealed 2015]

Leg.H. Added Stats 1913 ch 88 §1. Repealed Stats 2014 ch 274 §1 (AB 2759), effective January 1, 2015. The repealed section related to use of waters flowing out of the State.

§1410b. [Section repealed 1943]

Leg.H. Added Stats 1915 ch 700 §1. Repealed Stats 1943 ch 368 (Wat C §150001). See Wat C §§7040–7045.

§§1411–1413. [Sections repealed 1943]

Leg.H. Enacted Stats 1872. Repealed Stats 1943 ch 368 (Wat C §150001). See Wat C §§1240, 1706, 7075.

§1414. First in time, first in right

As between appropriators, the one first in time is the first in right.
Leg.H. Enacted Stats 1872.

§1415. Notice of appropriation

A person desiring to appropriate water must post a notice, in writing, in a conspicuous place at the point of intended diversion, stating therein:

1. That he claims the water there flowing to the extent of (giving the number) inches, measured under a four-inch pressure;
2. The purposes for which he claims it, and the place of intended use;
3. The means by which he intends to divert it, and the size of the flume, ditch, pipe, or aqueduct in which he intends to divert it.

A copy of the notice must, within ten days after it is posted, be recorded in the office of the recorder of the county in which it is posted. After filing such copy for record, the place of intended diversion or the place of intended use or the means by which it is intended to divert the water, may be changed by the person posting said notice or his assigns, if others are not injured by such change. This provision applies to notices already filed as well as to notices hereafter filed. **Leg.H.** Enacted Stats 1872. Amended Stats 1903 ch 262 §1.

§1416. Work to be done in appropriation of waters

Within sixty days after the notice is posted, the claimant must commence the excavation or construction of the works in which he intends to divert the water, or the survey, road or trail building, necessarily incident thereto, and must prosecute the work diligently and uninterruptedly to completion, unless temporarily interrupted by snows or rain; provided, that if the erection of a dam has been recommended by the California debris commission at or near the place where it is intended to divert the water, the claimant shall have sixty days after the completion of such dam in which to commence the excavation or construction of the works in which he intends to divert the water; provided, that whenever any city and county, or any incorporated city or town within this state makes, or has made, or acquires, or has acquired any appropriation of any of the waters of this state in accordance with the provisions of section 1415 of this code, it shall not be necessary for such city and county, city or town to commence the work for development of more of the water so claimed than is actually necessary for the immediate needs of such city and county, city or town, and it shall be held to be a sufficient compliance with the requirements of this chapter, to the full amount of water stated in the notice posted and recorded, for such city and county, city or town to within sixty days make the necessary surveys, or within six months to authorize the issuance of municipal bonds, for the construction of the necessary works designed to supply such city and county, city or town with the water required for immediate use. Any appropriation heretofore made by any such city and county, city or town in connection with which surveys were at any time made, or an issue of bonds authorized for the construction of any portion of the works necessary for a diversion of any part of the water appropriated, is hereby confirmed to the full amount of water stated in the original notice or notices. **Leg.H.** Enacted Stats 1872. Amended Stats 1895 ch 74 §1; Stats 1903 ch 272 §1; Stats 1907 ch 429 §1; Stats 1911 ch 730 §1.

§1417. Completion defined

By "completion" is meant conducting the waters to the place of intended use. **Leg.H.** Enacted Stats 1872.

§1418. Doctrine of relation applied

By a compliance with the above rules the claimant's right to the use of the water relates back to the time the notice was posted. **Leg.H.** Enacted Stats 1872.

§1419. Forfeiture

A failure to comply with such rules deprives the claimants of the right to the use of the water as against a subsequent claimant who complies therewith. **Leg.H.** Enacted Stats 1872.

§1420. Rights of present claimant

Persons who have heretofore claimed the right to water, and who have not constructed works in which to divert it, and who have not diverted nor applied it to some useful purpose, must, after this title takes effect, and within twenty days thereafter, proceed as in this title provided, or their right ceases. **Leg.H.** Enacted Stats 1872.

§1421. Recorder to keep book in which to record notices

The recorder of each county must keep a book, in which he must record the notices provided for in this title. **Leg.H.** Enacted Stats 1872.

§1422. Time within which to commence excavation on public reservation

If the place of intended diversion or any part of the route of intended conveyance of water so claimed, be within, and a part of, any national park, forest reservation, or other public reservation, and be so shown in the notice of appropriation of said water, then the claimant shall have sixty days, after the grant of authority to occupy and use such park or reservation for such intended purpose, within which to commence the excavation or construction of said works; provided that within sixty days after the posting of said notice of appropriation, as provided in section fourteen hundred and fifteen of the Civil Code, the claimant shall in good faith commence (and thereafter diligently and continuously, except when temporarily interrupted by snow or rain, prosecute to completion) such surveys and other work as under the regulations governing such park or reservations, may be required as preliminary to, or for use with, an application for such authority; and provided also that the claimant shall in good faith on completion of said survey and preliminary work, apply to the officer, board, or body, having charge of such park or reservation, for such authority, and shall thereafter, prosecute said application with reasonable diligence. **Leg.H.** Added Stats 1903 ch 272 §2.

Prior Law: Former §1422, relating to the rights of riparian proprietors as affected by this title, was enacted Stats 1872 and repealed Stats 1887 ch 99 §1.

TITLE 9
HYDRAULIC MINING [REPEALED]

§§1424, 1425. [Sections repealed 1939]

Leg.H. Added Stats 1893 ch 223 §1. Repealed Stats 1939 ch 93 (Pub Res C §10002). See Pub Res C §§3981, 3982.

TITLE 10
MINING CLAIMS, TUNNEL RIGHTS AND MILL SITES [REPEALED]

§1426. [Section repealed 1939]

Leg.H. Added Stats 1909 ch 205 §1. Repealed Stats 1939 ch 93 (Pub Res C §10002). See Pub Res C §3900.

§1426a. [Section repealed 1939]

Leg.H. Added Stats 1909 ch 205 §1. Amended Stats 1935 ch 839 §1. Repealed Stats 1939 ch 93 (Pub Res C §10002). See Pub Res C §3901.

§§1426b–1426d. [Sections repealed 1939]

Leg.H. Added Stats 1909 ch 205 §1. Repealed Stats 1939 ch 93 (Pub Res C §10002). See Pub Res C §§3902, 3911.

§§1426da–1426dc. [Sections repealed 1939]

Leg.H. Added Stats 1935 ch 839 §§2–4. Repealed Stats 1939 ch 93 (Pub Res C §10002). See Pub Res C §3903.

§§1426e–1426r. [Sections repealed 1939]

Leg.H. Added Stats 1909 ch 205 §1. Repealed Stats 1939 ch 93 (Pub Res C §10002). See Pub Res C §§3906–3913, 3917–3920, 3921–3923.

§1426ra. [Section repealed 1939]

Leg.H. Added Stats 1935 ch 839 §5. Repealed Stats 1939 ch 93 (Pub Res C §10002). See Pub Res C §§3905.

§1426s. [Section repealed 1939]

Leg.H. Added Stats 1909 ch 205 §1. Repealed Stats 1939 ch 93 (Pub Res C §10002).

DIVISION 3
OBLIGATIONS

Part 1. Obligations in General.
Part 2. Contracts.
Part 3. Obligations Imposed by Law.
Part 4. Obligations Arising from Particular Transactions.

PART 1
OBLIGATIONS IN GENERAL

Title 1. Definition of Obligations.
Title 2. Interpretation of Obligations.
Title 3. Transfer of Obligations.
Title 4. Extinction of Obligations.

TITLE 1
DEFINITION OF OBLIGATIONS

Obligation, what. §1427.
How created and enforced. §1428.

§1427. Obligation, what

An obligation is a legal duty, by which a person is bound to do or not to do a certain thing. **Leg.H.** Enacted Stats 1872.

§1428. How created and enforced

An obligation arises either from:

One. The contract of the parties; or,

Two. The operation of law. An obligation arising from operation of law may be enforced in the manner provided by law, or by civil action or proceeding. **Leg.H.** Enacted Stats 1872. Amended Code Amdts 1873–74 ch 612 §181½.

TITLE 2
INTERPRETATION OF OBLIGATIONS

Chapter 1. General Rules of Interpretation.
Chapter 2. Joint or Several Obligations.
Chapter 3. Conditional Obligations.
Chapter 4. Alternative Obligations.

CHAPTER 1
GENERAL RULES OF INTERPRETATION

General rules. §1429.

§1429. General rules

The rules which govern the interpretation of contracts are prescribed by Part II of this Division. Other obligations are interpreted by the same rules by which statutes of a similar nature are interpreted. **Leg.H.** Enacted Stats 1872.

CHAPTER 2
JOINT OR SEVERAL OBLIGATIONS

Obligations, joint or several, etc. §1430.
Joint Liability. §1431.
Findings and Declaration of Purpose. §1431.1.
Several liability for non-economic damages. §1431.2.
Immunity. §1431.3.
Amendment or Repeal of Measure. §1431.4.
Severability. §1431.5.
Contribution between joint parties. §1432.

§1430. Obligations, joint or several, etc.

An obligation imposed upon several persons, or a right created in favor of several persons, may be:
1. Joint;
2. Several; or,
3. Joint and several. **Leg.H.** Enacted Stats 1872.

§1431. Joint Liability

An obligation imposed upon several persons, or a right created in favor of several persons, is presumed to be joint, and not several, except as provided in Section 1431.2, and except in the special cases mentioned in the title on the interpretation of contracts. This presumption, in the case of a right, can be overcome only by express words to the contrary. **Leg.H.** Enacted Stats 1872. Amended by initiative measure (Prop. 51), adopted June 3, 1986.

§1431.1. Findings and Declaration of Purpose

The People of the State of California find and declare as follows:

(a) The legal doctrine of joint and several liability, also known as "the deep pocket rule", has resulted in a system of inequity and injustice that has threatened financial bankruptcy of local governments, other public agencies, private individuals and businesses and has resulted in higher prices for goods and services to the public and in higher taxes to the taxpayers.

(b) Some governmental and private defendants are perceived to have substantial financial resources or insurance coverage and have thus been included in lawsuits even though there was little or no basis for finding them at fault. Under joint and several liability, if they are found to share even a fraction of the fault, they often are held financially liable for all the damage. The People—taxpayers and consumers alike—ultimately pay for these lawsuits in the form of higher taxes, higher prices and higher insurance premiums.

(c) Local governments have been forced to curtail some essential police, fire and other protections because of the soaring costs of lawsuits and insurance premiums.

Therefore, the People of the State of California declare that to remedy these inequities, defendants in tort actions shall be held financially liable in closer proportion to their degree of fault. To treat them differently is unfair and inequitable.

The People of the State of California further declare that reforms in the liability laws in tort actions are necessary and proper to avoid catastrophic economic consequences for state and local governmental bodies as well as private individuals and businesses. **Leg.H.** Added by initiative measure (Prop. 51), adopted June 3, 1986.

§1431.2. Several liability for non-economic damages

(a) In any action for personal injury, property damage, or wrongful death, based upon principles of comparative fault, the liability of each defendant for non-economic damages shall be several only and shall not be joint. Each defendant shall be liable only for the amount of non-economic damages allocated to that defendant in direct proportion to that defendant's percentage of fault, and a separate judgment shall be rendered against that defendant for that amount.

(b)(1) For purposes of this section, the term "economic damages" means objectively verifiable monetary losses including medical expenses, loss of earnings, burial costs, loss of use of property, costs of repair or replacement, costs of obtaining substitute domestic services, loss of employment and loss of business or employment opportunities.

(2) For the purposes of this section, the term "non-economic damages" means subjective, non-monetary losses including, but not limited to, pain, suffering, inconvenience, mental suffering, emotional distress, loss of society and companionship, loss of consortium, injury to reputation and humiliation. **Leg.H.** Added by initiative measure (Prop. 51), adopted June 3, 1986.

§1431.3. Immunity

Nothing contained in this measure is intended, in any way, to alter the law of immunity. **Leg.H.** Added by initiative measure (Prop. 51), adopted June 3, 1986.

§1431.4. Amendment or Repeal of Measure

This measure may be amended or repealed by either of the procedures set forth in this section. If any portion of subsection (a) is declared invalid, then subsection (b) shall be the exclusive means of amending or repealing this measure.

(a) This measure may be amended to further its purposes by statute, passed in each house by rollcall vote entered in the journal, two-thirds of the membership concurring and signed by the Governor, if at least 20 days prior to passage in each house the bill in its final form has been delivered to the Secretary of State for distribution to the news media.

(b) This measure may be amended or repealed by a statute that becomes effective only when approved by the electors. **Leg.H.** Added by initiative measure (Prop. 51), adopted June 3, 1986.

§1431.5. Severability

If any provision of this measure, or the application of any such provision to any person or circumstances, shall be held invalid, the remainder of this measure to the extent it can be given effect, or the application of such provision to persons or circumstances other than those as to which it is held invalid, shall not be affected thereby, and to this end the provisions of this measure are severable. **Leg.H.** Added by initiative measure (Prop. 51), adopted June 3, 1986.

§1432. Contribution between joint parties

Except as provided in Section 877 of the Code of Civil Procedure, a party to a joint, or joint and several obligation, who satisfies more than his share of the claim against all, may require a proportionate contribution from all the parties joined with him. **Leg.H.** Enacted Stats 1872. Amended Stats 1987 ch 677 §1.

CHAPTER 3
CONDITIONAL OBLIGATIONS

Obligation, when conditional. §1434.
Conditions, kinds of. §1435.
Conditions precedent. §1436.
Conditions concurrent. §1437.
Condition subsequent. §1438.
Performance, etc., of conditions, when essential. §1439.
When performance, etc., excused. §1440.
Impossible or unlawful conditions void. §1441.
Conditions involving forfeiture, how construed. §1442.

§1434. Obligation, when conditional

An obligation is conditional, when the rights or duties of any party thereto depend upon the occurrence of an uncertain event. **Leg.H.** Enacted Stats 1872.

§1435. Conditions, kinds of

Conditions may be precedent, concurrent, or subsequent. **Leg.H.** Enacted Stats 1872.

§1436. Conditions precedent

A condition precedent is one which is to be performed before some right dependent thereon accrues, or some act dependent thereon is performed. **Leg.H.** Enacted Stats 1872.

§1437. Conditions concurrent

Conditions concurrent are those which are mutually dependent, and are to be performed at the same time. **Leg.H.** Enacted Stats 1872.

§1438. Condition subsequent

A condition subsequent is one referring to a future event, upon the happening of which the obligation becomes no longer binding upon the other party, if he chooses to avail himself of the condition. **Leg.H.** Enacted Stats 1872.

§1439. Performance, etc., of conditions, when essential

Before any party to an obligation can require another party to perform any act under it, he must fulfill all conditions precedent thereto imposed upon himself; and must be able and offer to fulfill all conditions concurrent so imposed upon him on the like fulfillment by the other party, except as provided by the next section. **Leg.H.** Enacted Stats 1872.

§1440. When performance, etc., excused

If a party to an obligation gives notice to another, before the latter is in default, that he will not perform the same upon his part, and does not retract such notice before the time at which performance upon his part is due, such other party is entitled to enforce the obligation without previously performing or offering to perform any conditions upon his part in favor of the former party. **Leg.H.** Enacted Stats 1872.

§1441. Impossible or unlawful conditions void

A condition in a contract, the fulfillment of which is impossible or unlawful, within the meaning of the article on the object of contracts, or which is repugnant to the nature of the interest created by the contract, is void. **Leg.H.** Enacted Stats 1872.

§1442. Conditions involving forfeiture, how construed

A condition involving a forfeiture must be strictly interpreted against the party for whose benefit it is created. **Leg.H.** Enacted Stats 1872.

CHAPTER 4
ALTERNATIVE OBLIGATIONS

Who has the right of selection. §1448.
Right of selection, how lost. §1449.
Alternatives indivisible. §1450.
Nullity of one or more alternative obligations. §1451.

§1448. Who has the right of selection

If an obligation requires the performance of one of two acts, in the alternative, the party required to perform has the right of selection, unless it is otherwise provided by the terms of the obligation. **Leg.H.** Enacted Stats 1872.

§1449. Right of selection, how lost

If the party having the right of selection between alternative acts does not give notice of his selection to the other party within the time, if any, fixed by the obligation for that purpose, or, if none is so fixed, before the time at which the obligation ought to be performed, the right of selection passes to the other party. **Leg.H.** Enacted Stats 1872.

§1450. Alternatives indivisible

The party having the right of selection between alternative acts must select one of them in its entirety, and cannot select part of one and part of another without the consent of the other party. **Leg.H.** Enacted Stats 1872.

§1451. Nullity of one or more alternative obligations

If one of the alternative acts required by an obligation is such as the law will not enforce, or becomes unlawful, or impossible of performance, the obligation is to be interpreted as though the other stood alone. **Leg.H.** Enacted Stats 1872.

TITLE 3
TRANSFER OF OBLIGATIONS

Burden of obligation not transferable. §1457.
Rights arising out of obligation transferable. §1458.
Non-negotiable instruments may be transferred. §1459.
Preservation of consumers' contract claims and defenses; Attorney's fees, costs, and expenses. §1459.5.
Covenants that run with land. §1460.
Restrictions on covenants that run with land. §1461.
Covenants contained in grant of estate in real property run with land. §1462.
Covenants included in Section 1462. §1463.
Persons bound by covenants. §1465.
Persons not bound by covenants. §1466.
Apportionment of covenants. §1467.
Covenants running with land; Apportionment of burden. §1468.
Covenant by lessor of real property. §1469.
Same; When description of contiguous parcel to be included. §1470.
Covenant to do or refrain from doing act for benefit of covenantee to run with land. §1471.

§1457. Burden of obligation not transferable

The burden of an obligation may be transferred with the consent of the party entitled to its benefit, but not otherwise, except as provided by Section 1466. **Leg.H.** Enacted Stats 1872.

§1458. Rights arising out of obligation transferable

A right arising out of an obligation is the property of the person to whom it is due, and may be transferred as such. **Leg.H.** Enacted Stats 1872.

§1459. Non-negotiable instruments may be transferred

A non-negotiable written contract for the payment of money or personal property may be transferred by indorsement, in like manner with negotiable instruments. Such indorsement shall transfer all the rights of the assignor under the instrument to the assignee, subject to all equities and defenses existing in favor of the maker at the time of the indorsement. **Leg.H.** Enacted Stats 1872.

§1459.5. Preservation of consumers' contract claims and defenses; Attorney's fees, costs, and expenses

(a) A plaintiff who prevails on a cause of action against a defendant named pursuant to Part 433 of Title 16 of the Code of Federal Regulations or any successor thereto, or pursuant to the contractual language required by that part or any successor thereto, may claim attorney's fees, costs, and expenses from that defendant to the fullest extent permissible if the plaintiff had prevailed on that cause of action against the seller.

(b) Any waiver of subdivision (a) is contrary to public policy and is void and unenforceable. **Leg.H.** Added Stats 2019 ch 116 §1 (AB 1821), effective January 1, 2020. Amended Stats 2020 ch 370 §28 (SB 1371), effective January 1, 2021; Stats 2024 ch 853 §10 (AB 3281), effective January 1, 2025.

§1460. Covenants that run with land

Certain covenants, contained in grants of estates in real property, are appurtenant to such estates, and pass with them, so as to bind the assigns of the covenantor and to vest in the assigns of the covenantee, in the same manner as if they had personally entered into them. Such covenants are said to run with the land. **Leg.H.** Enacted Stats 1872.

§1461. Restrictions on covenants that run with land

The only covenants which run with the land are those specified in this Title, and those which are incidental thereto. **Leg.H.** Enacted Stats 1872.

§1462. Covenants contained in grant of estate in real property run with land

Every covenant contained in a grant of an estate in real property, which is made for the direct benefit of the property, or some part of it then in existence, runs with the land. **Leg.H.** Enacted Stats 1872.

§1463. Covenants included in Section 1462

The last section includes covenants "of warranty," "for quiet enjoyment," or for further assurance on the part of a grantor, and covenants for the payment of rent, or of taxes or assessments upon the land, on the part of the grantee. **Leg.H.** Enacted Stats 1872.

§1464. [Section repealed 1998]

Leg.H. Enacted Stats 1872. Repealed Stats 1998 ch 14 §2 (AB 707). The repealed section related to covenants that run with land when assigns are named.

§1465. Persons bound by covenants

A covenant running with the land binds those only who acquire the whole estate of the covenantor in some part of the property. **Leg.H.** Enacted Stats 1872.

§1466. Persons not bound by covenants

No one, merely by reason of having acquired an estate subject to a covenant running with the land, is liable for a breach of the covenant before he acquired the estate, or after he has parted with it or ceased to enjoy its benefits. **Leg.H.** Enacted Stats 1872.

§1467. Apportionment of covenants

Where several persons, holding by several titles, are subject to the burden or entitled to the benefit of a covenant running with the land, it must be apportioned among them according to the value of the property subject to it held by them respectively, if such value can be ascertained, and if not, then according to their respective interests in point of quantity. **Leg.H.** Enacted Stats 1872.

§1468. Covenants running with land; Apportionment of burden

Each covenant, made by an owner of land with the owner of other land or made by a grantor of land with the grantee of land conveyed, or made by the grantee of land conveyed with the grantor thereof, to do or refrain from doing some act on his own land, which doing or refraining is expressed to be for the benefit of the land of the covenantee, runs with both the land owned by or granted to the covenantor and the land owned by or granted to the covenantee and shall, except as provided by Section 1466, or as specifically provided in the instrument creating such covenant, and notwithstanding the provisions of Section 1465, benefit or be binding upon each successive owner, during his ownership, of any portion of such land affected thereby and upon each person having any interest therein derived through any owner thereof where all of the following requirements are met:

(a) The land of the covenantor which is to be affected by such covenants, and the land of covenantee to be benefited, are particularly described in the instrument containing such covenants;

(b) Such successive owners of the land are in such instrument expressed to be bound thereby for the benefit of the land owned by, granted by, or granted to the covenantee;

(c) Each such act relates to the use, repair, maintenance or improvement of, or payment of taxes and assessments on, such land or some part thereof, or if the land owned by or granted to each consists of undivided interests in the same parcel or parcels, the suspension of the right of partition or sale in lieu of partition for a period which is reasonable in relation to the purpose of the covenant;

(d) The instrument containing such covenants is recorded in the office of the recorder of each county in which such land or some part thereof is situated.

Where several persons are subject to the burden of any such covenant, it shall be apportioned among them pursuant to Section 1467, except that where only a portion of such land is so affected thereby, such apportionment shall be only among the several owners of such portion. This section shall apply to the mortagee, trustee or beneficiary of a mortgage or deed of trust upon such land or any part thereof while but only while he, in such capacity, is in possession thereof. **Leg.H.** Added Stats 1905 ch 450 §1. Amended Stats 1968 ch 680 §1; Stats 1969 ch 245 §1; Stats 1973 ch 474 §1, effective September 11, 1973.

§1469. Covenant by lessor of real property

Each covenant made by the lessor in a lease of real property to do any act or acts on other real property which is owned by the lessor and is contiguous (except for intervening public streets, alleys or sidewalks) to the real property demised to the lessee shall, except as provided by Section 1466, be binding upon each successive owner, during his ownership, of any portion of such contiguous real property affected thereby where all of the following requirements are met:

(a) Such contiguous real property is particularly described in the lease;

(b) Such successive owners are in the lease expressed to be bound thereby for the benefit of the demised real property;

(c) Each such act relates to the use, repair, maintenance or improvement of, or payment of taxes and assessments on, such contiguous real property or some part thereof;

(d) The lease is recorded in the same manner as grants of real property, in the office of the recorder of each county in which such contiguous real property or some part thereof is situate. Such lease shall include the description of any such contiguous land described in any unrecorded instrument, the contents of which unrecorded instrument are incorporated by reference in such recorded lease.

Where several persons are subject to the burden of any such covenant, it shall be apportioned among them pursuant to Section 1467, except that where only a portion of such contiguous real property is so affected thereby, such apportionment shall be only among the several owners of such portion. This section shall apply to the mortgagee, trustee or beneficiary of a mortgage or deed of trust upon such contiguous real property or any part thereof while but only while he, in such capacity, is in possession thereof. **Leg.H.** Added Stats 1953 ch 652 §1. Amended Stats 1965 ch 1502 §1.

§1470. Same; When description of contiguous parcel to be included

Each covenant made by the lessor in a lease of real property not to use or permit to be used contrary to the terms of such lease any other real property which is owned by the lessor and is contiguous (except for intervening public streets, alleys or sidewalks) to the real property demised to the lessee shall, except as provided by Section 1466, be binding upon each successive owner, during his ownership, of any portion of such contiguous real property affected thereby and upon each person having any interest therein derived through any owner thereof where all of the following requirements are met:

(a) Such contiguous real property is particularly described in the lease:

(b) Such successive owners and persons having any such interest are in the lease expressed to be bound thereby for the benefit of the demised real property;

(c) The lease is recorded in the same manner as grants of real property, in the office of the recorder of each county in which such contiguous real property or some part thereof is situate. Such lease shall include therein the description of any such contiguous land described in any unrecorded instrument, the contents of which unrecorded instrument are incorporated by reference in such recorded lease.

Where several persons are subject to the burden of any such covenant, it shall be apportioned among them pursuant to Section 1467, except that where only a portion of such contiguous real property is so affected

Compensation after delay in performance. §1492.
Offer to be made in good faith. §1493.
Conditional offer. §1494.
Ability and willingness essential. §1495.
Production of thing to be delivered not necessary. §1496.
Thing offered to be kept separate. §1497.
Performance of condition precedent. §1498.
Written receipts. §1499.
Extinction of pecuniary obligation. §1500.
Objections to mode of offer. §1501.
Title to thing offered. §1502.
Custody of thing offered. §1503.
Effect of offer on accessories of obligation. §1504.
Creditor's retention of thing which he refuses to accept. §1505.

§1485. Obligation extinguished by offer of performance
An obligation is extinguished by an offer of performance, made in conformity to the rules herein prescribed, and with intent to extinguish the obligation. **Leg.H.** Enacted Stats 1872.

§1486. Offer of partial performance
An offer of partial performance is of no effect. **Leg.H.** Enacted Stats 1872.

§1487. By whom to be made
An offer of performance must be made by the debtor, or by some person on his behalf and with his assent. **Leg.H.** Enacted Stats 1872.

§1488. To whom to be made
An offer of performance must be made to the creditor, or to any one of two or more joint creditors, or to a person authorized by one or more of them to receive or collect what is due under the obligation, if such creditor or authorized person is present at the place where the offer may be made; and if not, wherever the creditor may be found. **Leg.H.** Enacted Stats 1872. Amended by Code Amdts 1873–74 ch 612 §183.

§1489. Where offer may be made
In the absence of an express provision to the contrary, an offer of performance may be made, at the option of the debtor:
1. At any place appointed by the creditor; or,
2. Wherever the person to whom the offer ought to be made can be found; or,
3. If such person cannot, with reasonable diligence, be found within this state, and within a reasonable distance from his residence or place of business, or if he evades the debtor, then at his residence or place of business, if the same can, with reasonable diligence, be found within the state; or,
4. If this cannot be done, then at any place within this state. **Leg.H.** Enacted Stats 1872.

§1490. When offer must be made
Where an obligation fixes a time for its performance, an offer of performance must be made at that time, within reasonable hours, and not before nor afterwards. **Leg.H.** Enacted Stats 1872.

§1491. Same
Where an obligation does not fix the time for its performance, an offer of performance may be made at any time before the debtor, upon a reasonable demand, has refused to perform. **Leg.H.** Enacted Stats 1872.

§1492. Compensation after delay in performance
Where delay in performance is capable of exact and entire compensation, and time has not been expressly declared to be of the essence of the obligation, an offer of performance, accompanied with an offer of such compensation, may be made at any time after it is due, but without prejudice to any rights acquired by the creditor, or by any other person, in the meantime. **Leg.H.** Enacted Stats 1872.

§1493. Offer to be made in good faith
An offer of performance must be made in good faith, and in such manner as is most likely, under the circumstances, to benefit the creditor. **Leg.H.** Enacted Stats 1872.

§1494. Conditional offer
An offer of performance must be free from any conditions which the creditor is not bound, on his part, to perform. **Leg.H.** Enacted Stats 1872.

§1495. Ability and willingness essential
An offer of performance is of no effect if the person making it is not able and willing to perform according to the offer. **Leg.H.** Enacted Stats 1872.

§1496. Production of thing to be delivered not necessary
The thing to be delivered, if any, need not in any case be actually produced, upon an offer of performance, unless the offer is accepted. **Leg.H.** Enacted Stats 1872.

§1497. Thing offered to be kept separate
A thing, when offered by way of performance, must not be mixed with other things from which it cannot be separated immediately and without difficulty. **Leg.H.** Enacted Stats 1872.

§1498. Performance of condition precedent
When a debtor is entitled to the performance of a condition precedent to, or concurrent with, performance on his part, he may make his offer to depend upon the due performance of such condition. **Leg.H.** Enacted Stats 1872.

§1499. Written receipts
A debtor has a right to require from his creditor a written receipt for any property delivered in performance of his obligation. **Leg.H.** Enacted Stats 1872.

§1500. Extinction of pecuniary obligation
An obligation for the payment of money is extinguished by a due offer of payment, if the amount is immediately deposited in the name of the creditor, with some bank or savings and loan association within this state, of good repute, and notice thereof is given to the creditor. **Leg.H.** Enacted Stats 1872. Amended Stats 1981 ch 632 §1, effective September 23, 1981.

§1501. Objections to mode of offer
All objections to the mode of an offer of performance, which the creditor has an opportunity to state at the time to the person making the offer, and which could be then obviated by him, are waived by the creditor, if not then stated. **Leg.H.** Enacted Stats 1872.

§1502. Title to thing offered
The title to a thing duly offered in performance of an obligation passes to the creditor, if the debtor at the time signifies his intention to that effect. **Leg.H.** Enacted Stats 1872.

§1503. Custody of thing offered
The person offering a thing, other than money, by way of performance, must, if he means to treat it as belonging to the creditor, retain it as a depositary for hire, until the creditor accepts it, or until he has given reasonable notice to the creditor that he will retain it no longer, and, if with reasonable diligence he can find a suitable depositary therefor, until he has deposited it with such person. **Leg.H.** Enacted Stats 1872.

§1504. Effect of offer on accessories of obligation
An offer of payment or other performance, duly made, though the title to the thing offered be not transferred to the creditor, stops the running of interest on the obligation, and has the same effect upon all its incidents as a performance thereof. **Leg.H.** Enacted Stats 1872.

§1505. Creditor's retention of thing which he refuses to accept
If anything is given to a creditor by way of performance, which he refuses to accept as such, he is not bound to return it without demand; but if he retains it, he is a gratuitous depositary thereof. **Leg.H.** Enacted Stats 1872.

CHAPTER 3
PREVENTION OF PERFORMANCE OR OFFER

What excuses performance, etc. §1511.
Effect of prevention of performance. §1512.
Same; Debtor entitled to ratable proportion of consideration, when. §1514.
Effect of refusal to accept performance before offer. §1515.

§1511. What excuses performance, etc.
The want of performance of an obligation, or of an offer of performance, in whole or in part, or any delay therein, is excused by the following causes, to the extent to which they operate:
1. When such performance or offer is prevented or delayed by the act of the creditor, or by the operation of law, even though there may have been a stipulation that this shall not be an excuse; however, the parties may expressly require in a contract that the party relying on the provisions of this paragraph give written notice to the other party or parties, within a reasonable time after the occurrence of the event excusing performance, of an intention to claim an extension of time or of an intention to bring suit

thereby, such apportionment shall be only among the several owners of, and persons having any such interest in, such portion. This section shall apply to the mortgagee, trustee or beneficiary of a mortgage or deed of trust upon such contiguous real property or any part thereof while and only while he, in such capacity, is in possession thereof. **Leg.H.** Added by Stats 1953 ch 652 §2. Amended Stats 1963 ch 2054 §1.

§1471. Covenant to do or refrain from doing act for benefit of covenantee to run with land

(a) Notwithstanding Section 1468 or any other provision of law, a covenant made by an owner of land or by the grantee of land to do or refrain from doing some act on his or her own land, which doing or refraining is expressed to be for the benefit of the covenantee, regardless of whether or not it is for the benefit of land owned by the covenantee, shall run with the land owned by or granted to the covenantor if all the following requirements are met:

(1) The land of the covenantor that is to be affected by the covenant is particularly described in the instrument containing the covenant.

(2) The successive owners of the land are expressed to be bound thereby for the benefit of the covenantee in the instrument containing the covenant.

(3) Each act that the owner or grantee will do or refrain from doing relates to the use of land and each act is reasonably necessary to protect present or future human health or safety or the environment as a result of the presence on the land of hazardous materials, as defined in Section 25260 of the Health and Safety Code.

(4) The instrument containing the covenant is recorded in the office of the recorder of each county in which the land or some portion thereof is situated and the instrument includes in its title the words: "Environmental Restriction."

(b) Except as provided by Section 1466 or as specifically provided in the instrument creating a covenant made pursuant to this section, the covenant shall be binding upon each successive owner, during his or her ownership, of any portion of the land affected thereby and upon each person having any interest therein derived through any owner thereof.

(c) If several persons are subject to the burden of a covenant recorded pursuant to this section, it shall be apportioned among them pursuant to Section 1467, except if only a portion of the land is so affected thereby, the apportionment shall be only among the several owners of that portion.

(d) This section shall apply to the mortgagee, trustee, or beneficiary of a mortgage or deed of trust upon the land or any part thereof while, but only while, he or she, in that capacity, is in possession thereof.

(e)(1) If an instrument containing a covenant is recorded pursuant to paragraph (4) of subdivision (a) as an "Environmental Restriction," in accordance with this section, the office of the recorder of the county may send a certified copy of the instrument to the California Environmental Protection Agency, for posting on its Web site, for informational purposes only, pursuant to Section 57012 of the Health and Safety Code, unless the instrument indicates that it is required by a board or department specified in paragraphs (1) to (3), inclusive, of subdivision (d) of Section 57012 of the Health and Safety Code.

(2) Notwithstanding any provision of law, the office of the recorder of the county and any of its employees shall not be subject to any liability under any state law or in any action for damages if the office of the recorder does not send a certified copy of the instrument pursuant to paragraph (1).

(f) The office of the recorder of the county may assess a reasonable fee, as determined by resolution of its governing body, to cover the costs of taking the action authorized by subdivision (e). **Leg.H.** Added Stats 1995 ch 188 §1 (AB 1120). Amended Stats 2002 ch 592 §1 (AB 2436).

TITLE 4
EXTINCTION OF OBLIGATIONS

Chapter 1. Performance.
Chapter 2. Offer of Performance.
Chapter 3. Prevention of Performance or Offer.
Chapter 4. Accord and Satisfaction.
Chapter 5. Novation.
Chapter 6. Release.

CHAPTER 1
PERFORMANCE

Obligation extinguished by performance. §1473.
Performance by one of several joint debtors. §1474.
Performance to one of joint creditors. §1475.
Effect of directions by creditors. §1476.
Partial performance. §1477.
Payment, defined. §1478.
Application of general performance. §1479.

§1473. Obligation extinguished by performance

Full performance of an obligation, by the party whose duty it is to perform it, or by any other person on his behalf, and with his assent, if accepted by the creditor, extinguishes it. **Leg.H.** Enacted Stats 1872.

§1474. Performance by one of several joint debtors

Performance of an obligation, by one of several persons who are jointly liable under it, extinguishes the liability of all. **Leg.H.** Enacted Stats 1872.

§1475. Performance to one of joint creditors

An obligation in favor of several persons is extinguished by performance rendered to any of them, except in the case of a deposit made by owners in common, or in joint ownership, which is regulated by the title on deposit. **Leg.H.** Enacted Stats 1872.

§1476. Effect of directions by creditors

If a creditor, or any one of two or more joint creditors, at any time directs the debtor to perform his obligation in a particular manner, the obligation is extinguished by performance in that manner, even though the creditor does not receive the benefit of such performance. **Leg.H.** Enacted Stats 1872.

§1477. Partial performance

A partial performance of an indivisible obligation extinguishes a corresponding portion thereof, if the benefit of such performance is voluntarily retained by the creditor, but not otherwise. If such partial performance is of such nature that the creditor cannot avoid retaining it without injuring his own property, his retention thereof is not presumed to be voluntary. **Leg.H.** Enacted Stats 1872.

§1478. Payment, defined

Performance of an obligation for the delivery of money only, is called payment. **Leg.H.** Enacted Stats 1872.

§1479. Application of general performance

Where a debtor under several obligations to another, does an act, by way of performance, in whole or in part, which is equally applicable to two or more of such obligations, such performance must be applied as follows:

One—If, at the time of performance, the intention or desire of the debtor that such performance should be applied to the extinction of any particular obligation, be manifested to the creditor, it must be so applied.

Two—If no such application be then made, the creditor, within a reasonable time after such performance, may apply it toward the extinction of any obligation, performance of which was due to him from the debtor at the time of such performance; except that if similar obligations were due to him both individually and as a trustee, he must, unless otherwise directed by the debtor, apply the performance to the extinction of all such obligations in equal proportion; and an application once made by the creditor cannot be rescinded without the consent of [the] debtor.

Three—If neither party makes such application within the time prescribed herein, the performance must be applied to the extinction of obligations in the following order; and, if there be more than one obligation of a particular class, to the extinction of all in that class, ratably:

1. Of interest due at the time of the performance.
2. Of principal due at that time.
3. Of the obligation earliest in date of maturity.
4. Of an obligation not secured by a lien or collateral undertaking.
5. Of an obligation secured by a lien or collateral undertaking. **Leg.H.** Enacted Stats 1872. Amended by Code Amdts 1873–74 ch 612 §182.

CHAPTER 2
OFFER OF PERFORMANCE

Obligation extinguished by offer of performance. §1485.
Offer of partial performance. §1486.
By whom to be made. §1487.
To whom to be made. §1488.
Where offer may be made. §1489.
When offer must be made. §1490.
Same. §1491.

or of any other similar or related intent, provided the requirement of such notice is reasonable and just;

2. When it is prevented or delayed by an irresistible, superhuman cause, or by the act of public enemies of this state or of the United States, unless the parties have expressly agreed to the contrary; or,

3. When the debtor is induced not to make it, by any act of the creditor intended or naturally tending to have that effect, done at or before the time at which such performance or offer may be made, and not rescinded before that time. **Leg.H.** Enacted Stats 1872. Amended Stats 1965 ch 1730 §1.

§1512. Effect of prevention of performance

If the performance of an obligation be prevented by the creditor, the debtor is entitled to all the benefits which he would have obtained if it had been performed by both parties. **Leg.H.** Enacted Stats 1872. Amended by Code Amdts 1873–74 ch 612 §184.

§1513. [Section repealed 1873–74]

Leg.H. Enacted Stats 1872. Repealed by Code Amdts 1873–74 ch 612 §185.

§1514. Same; Debtor entitled to ratable proportion of consideration, when

If performance of an obligation is prevented by any cause excusing performance, other than the act of the creditor, the debtor is entitled to a ratable proportion of the consideration to which he would have been entitled upon full performance, according to the benefits which the creditor receives from the actual performance. **Leg.H.** Enacted Stats 1872.

§1515. Effect of refusal to accept performance before offer

A refusal by a creditor to accept performance, made before an offer thereof, is equivalent to an offer and refusal, unless before performance is actually due, he gives notice to the debtor of his willingness to accept it. **Leg.H.** Enacted Stats 1872.

CHAPTER 4
ACCORD AND SATISFACTION

Accord defined. §1521.
Effect of accord. §1522.
Satisfaction defined. §1523.
Part performance of obligation. §1524.
Payment of undisputed part of money due under contract; Conditional payment. §1525.
Acceptance of check or draft as accord and satisfaction. §1526.

§1521. Accord defined

An accord is an agreement to accept, in extinction of an obligation, something different from or less than that to which the person agreeing to accept is entitled. **Leg.H.** Enacted Stats 1872. Amended by Code Amdts 1873–74 ch 612 §186.

§1522. Effect of accord

Though the parties to an accord are bound to execute it, yet it does not extinguish the obligation until it is fully executed. **Leg.H.** Enacted Stats 1872.

§1523. Satisfaction defined

Acceptance, by the creditor, of the consideration of an accord extinguishes the obligation, and is called satisfaction. **Leg.H.** Enacted Stats 1872.

§1524. Part performance of obligation

Part performance of an obligation, either before or after a breach thereof, where expressly accepted by the creditor in writing, in satisfaction, or rendered in pursuance of an agreement in writing for that purpose, though without any new consideration, extinguishes the obligation. **Leg.H.** Enacted Stats 1872. Amended by Code Amdts 1873–74 ch 612 §187.

§1525. Payment of undisputed part of money due under contract; Conditional payment

It is the public policy of this State, in the best interests of the taxpayer and of the litigant, to encourage fair dealing and to promote justice by reducing litigated matters to the lowest level of jurisdiction.

In case of a dispute over total money due on a contract and it is conceded by the parties that part of the money is due, the debtor may pay, without condition, the amount conceded to be due, leaving to the other party all remedies to which he might otherwise be entitled as to any balance claimed.

If any conditions are attached to the payment, this section shall not be deemed to have limited the remedies available to the other party under other provisions of law on the original amount claimed. **Leg.H.** Added Stats 1963 ch 1495 §1.

§1526. Acceptance of check or draft as accord and satisfaction

(a) Where a claim is disputed or unliquidated and a check or draft is tendered by the debtor in settlement thereof in full discharge of the claim, and the words "payment in full" or other words of similar meaning are notated on the check or draft, the acceptance of the check or draft does not constitute an accord and satisfaction if the creditor protests against accepting the tender in full payment by striking out or otherwise deleting that notation or if the acceptance of the check or draft was inadvertent or without knowledge of the notation.

(b) Notwithstanding subdivision (a), the acceptance of a check or draft constitutes an accord and satisfaction if a check or draft is tendered pursuant to a composition or extension agreement between a debtor and its creditors, and pursuant to that composition or extension agreement, all creditors of the same class are accorded similar treatment, and the creditor receives the check or draft with knowledge of the restriction.

A creditor shall be conclusively presumed to have knowledge of the restriction if a creditor either:

(1) Has, previous to the receipt of the check or draft, executed a written consent to the composition or extension agreement.

(2) Has been given, not less than 15 days nor more than 90 days prior to receipt of the check or draft, notice, in writing, that a check or draft will be tendered with a restrictive endorsement and that acceptance and cashing of the check or draft will constitute an accord and satisfaction.

(c) Notwithstanding subdivision (a), the acceptance of a check or draft by a creditor constitutes an accord and satisfaction when the check or draft is issued pursuant to or in conjunction with a release of a claim.

(d) For the purposes of paragraph (2) of subdivision (b), mailing the notice by first-class mail, postage prepaid, addressed to the address shown for the creditor on the debtor's books or such other address as the creditor may designate in writing constitutes notice. **Leg.H.** Added Stats 1987 ch 1268 §1.

CHAPTER 5
NOVATION

Novation defined. §1530.
Modes of novation. §1531.
Novation a contract. §1532.
Rescission of novation. §1533.

§1530. Novation defined

Novation is the substitution of a new obligation for an existing one. **Leg.H.** Enacted Stats 1872.

§1531. Modes of novation

Novation is made:

1. By the substitution of a new obligation between the same parties, with intent to extinguish the old obligation;

2. By the substitution of a new debtor in place of the old one, with intent to release the latter; or,

3. By the substitution of a new creditor in place of the old one, with intent to transfer the rights of the latter to the former. **Leg.H.** Enacted Stats 1872.

§1532. Novation a contract

Novation is made by contract, and is subject to all the rules concerning contracts in general. **Leg.H.** Enacted Stats 1872.

§1533. Rescission of novation

When the obligation of a third person, or an order upon such person is accepted in satisfaction, the creditor may rescind such acceptance if the debtor prevents such person from complying with the order, or from fulfilling the obligation; or if, at the time the obligation or order is received, such person is insolvent, and this fact is unknown to the creditor, or if, before the creditor can with reasonable diligence present the order to the person upon whom it is given, he becomes insolvent. **Leg.H.** Enacted Stats 1872. Amended by Code Amdts 1873–74 ch 612 §188.

CHAPTER 6
RELEASE

Obligation extinguished by release. §1541.
Certain claims not affected by general release. §1542.
Release of state from claims. §1542.1.
Release of one of several joint debtors. §1543.

§1541. Obligation extinguished by release

An obligation is extinguished by a release therefrom given to the debtor or the released party by the creditor or releasing party, upon a new consideration, or in writing, with or without new consideration. **Leg.H.** Enacted Stats 1872. Amended Stats 2018 ch 157 §1 (SB 1431), effective January 1, 2019.

2018 Note: The amendments to Sections 1541 and 1542 of the Civil Code made by this act are declaratory of existing law. Stats 2018 ch 157 §3 (SB 1431).

§1542. Certain claims not affected by general release

A general release does not extend to claims that the creditor or releasing party does not know or suspect to exist in his or her favor at the time of executing the release and that, if known by him or her, would have materially affected his or her settlement with the debtor or released party. **Leg.H.** Enacted Stats 1872. Amended by Code Amdts 1873–74 ch 612 §189; Stats 2004 ch 183 §28 (AB 3082); Stats 2018 ch 157 §2 (SB 1431), effective January 1, 2019.

2018 Note: The amendments to Sections 1541 and 1542 of the Civil Code made by this act are declaratory of existing law. Stats 2018 ch 157 §3 (SB 1431).

§1542.1. Release of state from claims

Notwithstanding Section 1542, a provider of health care, as defined in Section 56.05, or its officers, employees, agents, or subcontractors, shall release the state and its officers, employees, and agents, from any claim arising from the defense of the provider of health care by the Attorney General, or other legal counsel provided by the state pursuant to Section 12511.5 of the Government Code. **Leg.H.** Added Stats 1995 ch 749 §2 (AB 1177), effective October 10, 1995.

§1543. Release of one of several joint debtors

A release of one of two or more joint debtors does not extinguish the obligations of any of the others, unless they are mere guarantors; nor does it affect their right to contribution from him or her, except as provided in Section 877 of the Code of Civil Procedure. **Leg.H.** Enacted Stats 1872. Amended Stats 1987 ch 677 §1.5.

PART 2
CONTRACTS

Title 1. Nature of a Contract.
Title 2. Manner of Creating Contracts.
Title 2.5. Electronic Transactions.
Title 3. Interpretation of Contracts.
Title 4. Unlawful Contracts.
Title 4.1. Buyer-broker representation agreement requirements and limitations.
Title 4.5. Liquidated Damages.
Title 5. Extinction of Contracts.

TITLE 1
NATURE OF A CONTRACT

Chapter 1. Definition.
Chapter 2. Parties.
Chapter 3. Consent.
Chapter 4. Object of a Contract.
Chapter 5. Consideration.

CHAPTER 1
DEFINITION

Contract defined. §1549.
Essential elements of contract. §1550.
Lawful commercial cannabis activity. §1550.5.

§1549. Contract defined
A contract is an agreement to do or not to do a certain thing. **Leg.H.** Enacted Stats 1872.

§1550. Essential elements of contract
It is essential to the existence of a contract that there should be:
1. Parties capable of contracting;
2. Their consent;
3. A lawful object; and,
4. A sufficient cause or consideration. **Leg.H.** Enacted Stats 1872.

§1550.5. Lawful commercial cannabis activity
(a) The Legislature finds and declares all of the following:
(1) The Compassionate Use Act of 1996, an initiative measure enacted by the approval of Proposition 215 at the November 5, 1996, statewide general election, authorized the use of marijuana for medical purposes in this state.
(2) The Legislature passed the Medical Cannabis Regulation and Safety Act, formerly Chapter 3.5 (commencing with Section 19300) of Division 8 of the Business and Professions Code, to regulate and license medical cannabis in the state.
(3) The Control, Regulate and Tax Adult Use of Marijuana Act (AUMA), an initiative measure enacted by the approval of Proposition 64 at the November 8, 2016, statewide general election, authorized the consumption of nonmedical marijuana by persons over 21 years of age and provided for the licensure and regulation of certain commercial nonmedical marijuana activities in this state.
(4) The Legislature passed the Medicinal and Adult-Use Cannabis Regulation and Safety Act (Division 10 (commencing with Section 26000) of the Business and Professions Code) to consolidate the licensure and regulation of certain commercial activities with respect to medicinal cannabis and nonmedical marijuana, now known as adult-use cannabis.
(b) Notwithstanding any law, including, but not limited to, Sections 1550, 1667, and 1668 and federal law, commercial activity relating to medicinal cannabis or adult-use cannabis conducted in compliance with California law and any applicable local standards, requirements, and regulations shall be deemed to be all of the following:
(1) A lawful object of a contract.
(2) Not contrary to, an express provision of law, any policy of express law, or good morals.
(3) Not against public policy. **Leg.H.** Added Stats 2017 ch 530 §1 (AB 1159), effective January 1, 2018. Amended Stats 2018 ch 92 §35 (SB 1289), effective January 1, 2019.

CHAPTER 2
PARTIES

Who may contract. §1556.
Capacity of minors and persons of unsound mind to contract. §1557.
Identification of parties necessary. §1558.
When contract for benefit of third person may be enforced. §1559.

§1556. Who may contract
All persons are capable of contracting, except minors, persons of unsound mind, and persons deprived of civil rights. **Leg.H.** Enacted Stats 1872.

§1557. Capacity of minors and persons of unsound mind to contract
(a) The capacity of a minor to contract is governed by Division 11 (commencing with Section 6500) of the Family Code.
(b) The capacity of a person of unsound mind to contract is governed by Part 1 (commencing with Section 38) of Division 1. **Leg.H.** Added Stats 1992 ch 163 §9 (AB 2641), operative January 1, 1994.

Prior Law: Former §1557, similar to the present section, was enacted Stats 1872 and repealed Stats 1992 ch 163 §8, operative January 1, 1994.

§1558. Identification of parties necessary
It is essential to the validity of a contract, not only that the parties should exist, but that it should be possible to identify them. **Leg.H.** Enacted Stats 1872.

§1559. When contract for benefit of third person may be enforced
A contract, made expressly for the benefit of a third person, may be enforced by him at any time before the parties thereto rescind it. **Leg.H.** Enacted Stats 1872.

CHAPTER 3
CONSENT

Essentials of consent. §1565.
Consent, when voidable. §1566.
Apparent consent, when not free. §1567.
When deemed to have been obtained by fraud, etc. §1568.
Consent by parent or legal guardian. §1568.5.
Duress defined. §1569.
Menace defined. §1570.
Fraud, actual or constructive. §1571.
Actual fraud defined. §1572.
Constructive fraud. §1573.
Actual fraud a question of fact. §1574.
Undue influence defined. §1575.
Mistake defined. §1576.
Mistake of fact. §1577.
Mistake of law. §1578.
Mistake of foreign laws. §1579.
Mutuality of consent. §1580.
Communication of consent. §1581.
Mode of communication of acceptance of proposal. §1582.
When communication deemed complete. §1583.
Acceptance by performance of conditions. §1584.
Voluntary and unsolicited sending of goods or services; Receipt as unconditional gift. §1584.5.
Organization selling to its members at retail; Subsequent sending of unordered goods as unconditional gift. §1584.6.
Acceptance must be absolute. §1585.
Revocation of proposal. §1586.
Revocation, how made. §1587.
Ratification of contract, void for want of consent. §1588.
Assumption of obligation by acceptance of benefits. §1589.
Recovery of gift made in contemplation of marriage. §1590.

§1565. Essentials of consent
The consent of the parties to a contract must be:
1. Free;
2. Mutual; and,
3. Communicated by each to the other. **Leg.H.** Enacted Stats 1872.

§1566. Consent, when voidable
A consent which is not free is nevertheless not absolutely void, but may be rescinded by the parties, in the manner prescribed by the chapter on rescission. **Leg.H.** Enacted Stats 1872.

§1567. Apparent consent, when not free

An apparent consent is not real or free when obtained through:
1. Duress;
2. Menace;
3. Fraud;
4. Undue influence; or
5. Mistake. **Leg.H.** Enacted Stats 1872.

§1568. When deemed to have been obtained by fraud, etc.

Consent is deemed to have been obtained through one of the causes mentioned in the last section only when it would not have been given had such cause not existed. **Leg.H.** Enacted Stats 1872.

§ 1568.5. Consent by parent or legal guardian

A representation by a minor that the minor's parent or legal guardian has consented shall not be considered to be consent for purposes of this chapter. **Leg.H.** Added Stats 2021 ch 28 §1 (AB 891), effective January 1, 2022.

§1569. Duress defined

Duress consists in any of the following:

(a) Unlawful confinement of the person of the party, or of the spouse of such party, or of an ancestor, descendant, or adopted child of such party or spouse.

(b) Unlawful detention of the property of any such person.

(c) Confinement of such person, lawful in form, but fraudulently obtained, or fraudulently made unjustly harassing or oppressive. **Leg.H.** Enacted Stats 1872. Amended Stats 2016 ch 50 §11 (SB 1005), effective January 1, 2017.

2016 Note: For legislative intent, see the 2016 Note following §14.

§1570. Menace defined

Menace consists in a threat:
1. Of such duress as is specified in subdivisions one and three of the last section;
2. Of unlawful and violent injury to the person or property of any such person as is specified in the last section; or,
3. Of injury to the character of any such person. **Leg.H.** Enacted Stats 1872.

§1571. Fraud, actual or constructive

Fraud is either actual or constructive. **Leg.H.** Enacted Stats 1872.

§1572. Actual fraud defined

Actual fraud, within the meaning of this chapter, consists in any of the following acts, committed by a party to the contract, or with his connivance, with intent to deceive another party thereto, or to induce him to enter into the contract:
1. The suggestion, as a fact, of that which is not true, by one who does not believe it to be true;
2. The positive assertion, in a manner not warranted by the information of the person making it, of that which is not true, though he believes it to be true;
3. The suppression of that which is true, by one having knowledge or belief of the fact;
4. A promise made without any intention of performing it; or,
5. Any other act fitted to deceive. **Leg.H.** Enacted Stats 1872.

§1573. Constructive fraud

Constructive fraud consists:
1. In any breach of duty which, without an actually fraudulent intent, gains an advantage to the person in fault, or anyone claiming under him, by misleading another to his prejudice, or to the prejudice of anyone claiming under him; or,
2. In any such act or omission as the law specially declares to be fraudulent, without respect to actual fraud. **Leg.H.** Enacted Stats 1872.

§1574. Actual fraud a question of fact

Actual fraud is always a question of fact. **Leg.H.** Enacted Stats 1872.

§1575. Undue influence defined

Undue influence consists:
1. In the use, by one in whom a confidence is reposed by another, or who holds a real or apparent authority over him, of such confidence or authority for the purpose of obtaining an unfair advantage over him;
2. In taking an unfair advantage of another's weakness of mind; or,
3. In taking a grossly oppressive and unfair advantage of another's necessities or distress. **Leg.H.** Enacted Stats 1872.

§1576. Mistake defined

Mistake may be either of fact or law. **Leg.H.** Enacted Stats 1872.

§1577. Mistake of fact

Mistake of fact is a mistake, not caused by the neglect of a legal duty on the part of the person making the mistake, and consisting in:
1. An unconscious ignorance or forgetfulness of a fact past or present, material to the contract; or,
2. Belief in the present existence of a thing material to the contract, which does not exist, or in the past existence of such a thing, which has not existed. **Leg.H.** Enacted Stats 1872.

§1578. Mistake of law

Mistake of law constitutes a mistake, within the meaning of this article, only when it arises from:
1. A misapprehension of the law by all parties, all supposing that they knew and understood it, and all making substantially the same mistake as to the law; or,
2. A misapprehension of the law by one party, of which the others are aware at the time of contracting, but which they do not rectify. **Leg.H.** Enacted Stats 1872.

§1579. Mistake of foreign laws

Mistake of foreign laws is a mistake of fact. **Leg.H.** Enacted Stats 1872.

§1580. Mutuality of consent

Consent is not mutual, unless the parties all agree upon the same thing in the same sense. But in certain cases defined by the chapter on interpretation, they are to be deemed so to agree without regard to the fact. **Leg.H.** Enacted Stats 1872.

§1581. Communication of consent

Consent can be communicated with effect, only by some act or omission of the party contracting, by which he intends to communicate it, or which necessarily tends to such communication. **Leg.H.** Enacted Stats 1872.

§1582. Mode of communication of acceptance of proposal

If a proposal prescribes any conditions concerning the communication of its acceptance, the proposer is not bound unless they are conformed to; but in other cases any reasonable and usual mode may be adopted. **Leg.H.** Enacted Stats 1872.

§1583. When communication deemed complete

Consent is deemed to be fully communicated between the parties as soon as the party accepting a proposal has put his acceptance in the course of transmission to the proposer, in conformity to the last section. **Leg.H.** Enacted Stats 1872.

§1584. Acceptance by performance of conditions

Performance of the conditions of a proposal, or the acceptance of the consideration offered with a proposal, is an acceptance of the proposal. **Leg.H.** Enacted Stats 1872.

§1584.5. Voluntary and unsolicited sending of goods or services; Receipt as unconditional gift

No person, firm, partnership, association, or corporation, or agent or employee thereof, shall, in any manner, or by any means, offer for sale goods, wares, merchandise, or services, where the offer includes the voluntary and unsolicited sending or providing of goods, wares, merchandise, or services not actually ordered or requested by the recipient, either orally or in writing. The receipt of any goods, wares, merchandise, or services shall for all purposes be deemed an unconditional gift to the recipient who may use or dispose of the goods, wares, merchandise, or services in any manner he or she sees fit without any obligation on his or her part to the sender or provider.

If, after any receipt deemed to be an unconditional gift under this section, the sender or provider continues to send bill statements or requests for payment with respect to the gift, an action may be brought by the recipient to enjoin the conduct, in which action there may also be awarded reasonable attorney's fees and costs to the prevailing party.

For the purposes of this section and limited to merchandise or services offered for sale through the mails, the "voluntary and unsolicited sending or providing of goods, wares, merchandise, or services not actually ordered or requested by the recipient, either orally or in writing," includes any merchandise or services selected by the company and offered to the consumer which will be mailed to him or her for sale or on approval or provided to him or her unless he or she exercises an option to reject the offer of sale or receipt on approval. Merchandise or services selected by the seller and offered for sale on a periodic basis must be affirmatively ordered by a statement or card signed by the consumer as to each periodic offer of merchandise or services. This paragraph shall not apply to any of the following:

(a) Contractual plans or arrangements complying with this subdivision under which the seller periodically provides the consumer with a form or announcement card which the consumer may use to instruct the seller not to ship the offered merchandise. Any instructions not to ship merchandise included on the form or card shall be printed in type as large as all other instructions and terms stated on the form or card. The form or card shall specify a date by which it shall be mailed by the consumer (the "mailing date") or received by the seller (the "return date") to prevent shipment of the offered merchandise. The seller shall mail the form or card either at least 25 days prior to the return date or at least 20 days prior to the mailing date, or provide a mailing date of at least 10 days after receipt by the consumer, except that whichever system the seller chooses for mailing the form or card, the system must be calculated to afford the consumer at least 10 days in which to mail his or her form or card. The form or card shall be preaddressed to the seller so that it may serve as a postal reply card or, alternatively, the form or card shall be accompanied by a return envelope addressed to seller. Upon the membership contract or application form or on the same page and immediately adjacent to the contract or form, and in clear and conspicuous language, there shall be disclosed the material terms of the plan or arrangement including all of the following:

(1) That aspect of the plan under which the subscriber must notify the seller, in the manner provided for by the seller, if he or she does not wish to purchase or receive the selection.

(2) Any obligation assumed by the subscriber to purchase a minimum quantity of merchandise.

(3) The right of a contract-complete subscriber to cancel his or her membership at any time.

(4) Whether billing charges will include an amount for postage and handling.

(b) Other contractual plans or arrangements not covered under subdivision (a), such as continuity plans, subscription arrangements, standing order arrangements, supplements and series arrangements under which the seller periodically ships merchandise to a consumer who has consented in advance to receive the merchandise on a periodic basis. **Leg.H.** Added Stats 1969 ch 265 §1, ch 400 §1. Amended Stats 1971 ch 1623 §1, operative July 1, 1972; Stats 1973 ch 916 §1, operative January 1, 1975; Stats 1985 ch 80 §1.

Prior Law: Former §1584.5, similar to present §1584.5, was added Stats 1969 ch 265 §1 and repealed by Stats 1971 ch 1623 §2, operative July 1, 1972.

§1584.6. Organization selling to its members at retail; Subsequent sending of unordered goods as unconditional gift

If a person is a member of an organization which makes retail sales of any goods, wares, or merchandise to its members, and the person notifies the organization of his termination of membership by certified mail, return receipt requested, any unordered goods, wares, or merchandise which are sent to the person after 30 days following execution of the return receipt for the certified letter by the organization, shall for all purposes be deemed unconditional gifts to the person, who may use or dispose of the goods, wares, or merchandise in any manner he sees fit without any obligation on his part to the organization.

If the termination of a person's membership in such organization breaches any agreement with the organization, nothing in this section shall relieve the person from liability for damages to which he might be otherwise subjected to pursuant to law, but he shall not be subject to any damages with respect to any goods, wares, or merchandise which are deemed unconditional gifts to him under this section.

If after any receipt deemed to be an unconditional gift under this section, the sender continues to send bill statements or requests for payment with respect thereto, an action may be brought by the recipient to enjoin such conduct, in which action there may also be awarded reasonable attorneys' fees and costs to the prevailing party. **Leg.H.** Added Stats 1969 ch 400 §2.

§1585. Acceptance must be absolute

An acceptance must be absolute and unqualified, or must include in itself an acceptance of that character which the proposer can separate from the rest, and which will conclude the person accepting. A qualified acceptance is a new proposal. **Leg.H.** Enacted Stats 1872.

§1586. Revocation of proposal

A proposal may be revoked at any time before its acceptance is communicated to the proposer, but not afterwards. **Leg.H.** Enacted Stats 1872.

§1587. Revocation, how made

A proposal is revoked by any of the following:

(a) By the communication of notice of revocation by the proposer to the other party, in the manner prescribed by Sections 1581 and 1583, before his or her acceptance has been communicated to the former.

(b) By the lapse of the time prescribed in the proposal for its acceptance or, if no time is prescribed, the lapse of a reasonable time without communication of the acceptance.

(c) By the failure of the acceptor to fulfill a condition precedent to acceptance.

(d) By the death or legal incapacity to make decisions of the proposer. **Leg.H.** Enacted Stats 1872. Amended Stats 2014 ch 144 §2 (AB 1847), effective January 1, 2015.

§1588. Ratification of contract, void for want of consent

A contract which is voidable solely for want of due consent, may be ratified by a subsequent consent. **Leg.H.** Enacted Stats 1872.

§1589. Assumption of obligation by acceptance of benefits

A voluntary acceptance of the benefit of a transaction is equivalent to a consent to all the obligations arising from it, so far as the facts are known, or ought to be known, to the person accepting. **Leg.H.** Enacted Stats 1872.

§1590. Recovery of gift made in contemplation of marriage

Where either party to a contemplated marriage in this State makes a gift of money or property to the other on the basis or assumption that the marriage will take place, in the event that the donee refuses to enter into the marriage as contemplated or that it is given up by mutual consent, the donor may recover such gift or such part of its value as may, under all of the circumstances of the case, be found by a court or jury to be just. **Leg.H.** Added by Stats 1939 ch 128 §3 p 1245.

CHAPTER 4
OBJECT OF A CONTRACT

Object defined. §1595.
Requisites of object. §1596.
Impossibility defined. §1597.
When contract wholly void. §1598.
When contract partially void. §1599.

§1595. Object defined

The object of a contract is the thing which it is agreed, on the part of the party receiving the consideration, to do or not to do. **Leg.H.** Enacted Stats 1872.

§1596. Requisites of object

The object of a contract must be lawful when the contract is made, and possible and ascertainable by the time the contract is to be performed. **Leg.H.** Enacted Stats 1872.

§1597. Impossibility defined

Everything is deemed possible except that which is impossible in the nature of things. **Leg.H.** Enacted Stats 1872.

§1598. When contract wholly void

Where a contract has but a single object, and such object is unlawful, whether in whole or in part, or wholly impossible of performance, or so vaguely expressed as to be wholly unascertainable, the entire contract is void. **Leg.H.** Enacted Stats 1872.

§1599. When contract partially void

Where a contract has several distinct objects, of which one at least is lawful, and one at least is unlawful, in whole or in part, the contract is void as to the latter and valid as to the rest. **Leg.H.** Enacted Stats 1872.

CHAPTER 5
CONSIDERATION

Good consideration defined. §1605.
How far legal or moral obligation is a good consideration. §1606.

Consideration lawful. §1607.
Effect of its illegality. §1608.
Consideration executed or executory. §1609.
Executory consideration. §1610.
How ascertained. §1611.
Consideration Impossible to Execute on Its Face. §1612.
Consideration impossible to execute in fact. §1613.
Written instrument presumptive evidence of consideration. §1614.
Burden of proof to invalidate sufficient consideration. §1615.

§1605. Good consideration defined

Any benefit conferred, or agreed to be conferred, upon the promisor, by any other person, to which the promisor is not lawfully entitled, or any prejudice suffered, or agreed to be suffered, by such person, other than such as he is at the time of consent lawfully bound to suffer, as an inducement to the promisor, is a good consideration for a promise. **Leg.H.** Enacted Stats 1872.

§1606. How far legal or moral obligation is a good consideration

An existing legal obligation resting upon the promisor, or a moral obligation originating in some benefit conferred upon the promisor, or prejudice suffered by the promisee, is also a good consideration for a promise, to an extent corresponding with the extent of the obligation, but no further or otherwise. **Leg.H.** Enacted Stats 1872.

§1607. Consideration lawful

The consideration of a contract must be lawful within the meaning of section sixteen hundred and sixty-seven. **Leg.H.** Enacted Stats 1872.

§1608. Effect of its illegality

If any part of a single consideration for one or more objects, or of several considerations for a single object, is unlawful, the entire contract is void. **Leg.H.** Enacted Stats 1872.

§1609. Consideration executed or executory

A consideration may be executed or executory, in whole or in part. In so far as it is executory, it is subject to the provisions of chapter four of this title. **Leg.H.** Enacted Stats 1872.

§1610. Executory consideration

When a consideration is executory, it is not indispensable that the contract should specify its amount or the means of ascertaining it. It may be left to the decision of a third person, or regulated by any specified standard. **Leg.H.** Enacted Stats 1872.

§1611. How ascertained

When a contract does not determine the amount of the consideration, nor the method by which it is to be ascertained, or when it leaves the amount thereof to the discretion of an interested party, the consideration must be so much money as the object of the contract is reasonably worth. **Leg.H.** Enacted Stats 1872.

§1612. Consideration Impossible to Execute on Its Face

Where a contract provides an exclusive method by which its consideration is to be ascertained, which method is on its face impossible of execution, the entire contract is void; but this section shall not apply to the cases provided for in sections 1729 and 1730 of this code. **Leg.H.** Enacted Stats 1872. Amended Stats 1931 ch 1070 §7.

§1613. Consideration impossible to execute in fact

Where a contract provides an exclusive method by which its consideration is to be ascertained, which method appears possible on its face, but in fact is, or becomes, impossible of execution, such provision only is void; but this section shall not apply to the cases provided for in sections 1729 and 1730 of this code. **Leg.H.** Enacted Stats 1872. Amended Stats 1931 ch 1070 §8.

§1614. Written instrument presumptive evidence of consideration

A written instrument is presumptive evidence of a consideration. **Leg.H.** Enacted Stats 1872.

§1615. Burden of proof to invalidate sufficient consideration

The burden of showing a want of consideration sufficient to support an instrument lies with the party seeking to invalidate or avoid it. **Leg.H.** Enacted Stats 1872.

TITLE 2
MANNER OF CREATING CONTRACTS

Contracts, express or implied. §1619.
Express contract, what. §1620.
Implied contract, what. §1621.
What contracts may be oral. §1622.
Contract not in writing through fraud, may be enforced against fraudulent party. §1623.
Statute of frauds; Qualified financial contracts; Personal property leases; Electronic message. §1624.
Contract, requirements; Exceptions. §1624.5.
Effect of written contract. §1625.
Contract in writing, takes effect when. §1626.
Provisions of chapter on transfers of real property. §1627.
Corporate seal, how affixed. §1628.
Provisions abolishing seals made applicable. §1629.
Bailment contract for parking or storage of vehicle. §1630.
Bailee's liability for theft of motor vehicle. §1630.5.
Sale of mining machinery; Bill of sale; Record of transaction. §1631.
Trade or business negotiating primarily in Spanish, Chinese, Tagalog, Vietnamese, or Korean. §1632.
Delivery of form summarizing residential mortgage loan terms or modified terms in applicable foreign language; Penalties; Development of forms [Operative date contingent]. §1632.5.
Validity of contract with broker-dealer resulting from customer's electronically transmitted application. §1633.

§1619. Contracts, express or implied

A contract is either express or implied. **Leg.H.** Enacted 1872.

§1620. Express contract, what

An express contract is one, the terms of which are stated in words. **Leg.H.** Enacted 1872.

§1621. Implied contract, what

An implied contract is one, the existence and terms of which are manifested by conduct. **Leg.H.** Enacted 1872.

§1622. What contracts may be oral

All contracts may be oral, except such as are especially required by statute to be in writing. **Leg.H.** Enacted 1872.

§1623. Contract not in writing through fraud, may be enforced against fraudulent party

Where a contract, which is required by law to be in writing, is prevented from being put into writing by the fraud of a party thereto, any other party who is by such fraud led to believe that it is in writing, and acts upon such belief to his prejudice, may enforce it against the fraudulent party. **Leg.H.** Enacted 1872.

§1624. Statute of frauds; Qualified financial contracts; Personal property leases; Electronic message

(a) The following contracts are invalid, unless they, or some note or memorandum thereof, are in writing and subscribed by the party to be charged or by the party's agent:

(1) An agreement that by its terms is not to be performed within a year from the making thereof.

(2) A special promise to answer for the debt, default, or miscarriage of another, except in the cases provided for in Section 2794.

(3) An agreement for the leasing for a longer period than one year, or for the sale of real property, or of an interest therein; such an agreement, if made by an agent of the party sought to be charged, is invalid, unless the authority of the agent is in writing, subscribed by the party sought to be charged.

(4) An agreement authorizing or employing an agent, broker, or any other person to purchase or sell real estate, or to lease real estate for a longer period than one year, or to procure, introduce, or find a purchaser or seller of real estate or a lessee or lessor of real estate where the lease is for a longer period than one year, for compensation or a commission.

(5) An agreement that by its terms is not to be performed during the lifetime of the promisor.

(6) An agreement by a purchaser of real property to pay an indebtedness secured by a mortgage or deed of trust upon the property purchased, unless assumption of the indebtedness by the purchaser is specifically provided for in the conveyance of the property.

(7) A contract, promise, undertaking, or commitment to loan money or to grant or extend credit, in an amount greater than one hundred thousand

dollars ($100,000), not primarily for personal, family, or household purposes, made by a person engaged in the business of lending or arranging for the lending of money or extending credit. For purposes of this section, a contract, promise, undertaking, or commitment to loan money secured solely by residential property consisting of one to four dwelling units shall be deemed to be for personal, family, or household purposes.

(b) Notwithstanding paragraph (1) of subdivision (a):

(1) An agreement or contract that is valid in other respects and is otherwise enforceable is not invalid for lack of a note, memorandum, or other writing and is enforceable by way of action or defense, provided that the agreement or contract is a qualified financial contract as defined in paragraph (2) and one of the following apply:

(A) There is, as provided in paragraph (3), sufficient evidence to indicate that a contract has been made.

(B) The parties thereto by means of a prior or subsequent written contract, have agreed to be bound by the terms of the qualified financial contract from the time they reached agreement (by telephone, by exchange of electronic messages, or otherwise) on those terms.

(2) For purposes of this subdivision, a "qualified financial contract" means an agreement as to which each party thereto is other than a natural person and that is any of the following:

(A) For the purchase and sale of foreign exchange, foreign currency, bullion, coin, or precious metals on a forward, spot, next-day value or other basis.

(B) A contract (other than a contract for the purchase of a commodity for future delivery on, or subject to the rules of, a contract market or board of trade) for the purchase, sale, or transfer of any commodity or any similar good, article, service, right, or interest that is presently or in the future becomes the subject of a dealing in the forward contract trade, or any product or byproduct thereof, with a maturity date more than two days after the date the contract is entered into.

(C) For the purchase and sale of currency, or interbank deposits denominated in United States dollars.

(D) For a currency option, currency swap, or cross-currency rate swap.

(E) For a commodity swap or a commodity option (other than an option contract traded on, or subject to the rules of, a contract market or board of trade).

(F) For a rate swap, basis swap, forward rate transaction, or an interest rate option.

(G) For a security-index swap or option, or a security or securities price swap or option.

(H) An agreement that involves any other similar transaction relating to a price or index (including, without limitation, any transaction or agreement involving any combination of the foregoing, any cap, floor, collar, or similar transaction with respect to a rate, commodity price, commodity index, security or securities price, security index, other price index, or loan price).

(I) An option with respect to any of the foregoing.

(3) There is sufficient evidence that a contract has been made in any of the following circumstances:

(A) There is evidence of an electronic communication (including, without limitation, the recording of a telephone call or the tangible written text produced by computer retrieval), admissible in evidence under the laws of this state, sufficient to indicate that in the communication a contract was made between the parties.

(B) A confirmation in writing sufficient to indicate that a contract has been made between the parties and sufficient against the sender is received by the party against whom enforcement is sought no later than the fifth business day after the contract is made (or any other period of time that the parties may agree in writing) and the sender does not receive, on or before the third business day after receipt (or the other period of time that the parties may agree in writing), written objection to a material term of the confirmation. For purposes of this subparagraph, a confirmation or an objection thereto is received at the time there has been an actual receipt by an individual responsible for the transaction or, if earlier, at the time there has been constructive receipt, which is the time actual receipt by that individual would have occurred if the receiving party, as an organization, had exercised reasonable diligence. For the purposes of this subparagraph, a "business day" is a day on which both parties are open and transacting business of the kind involved in that qualified financial contract that is the subject of confirmation.

(C) The party against whom enforcement is sought admits in its pleading, testimony, or otherwise in court that a contract was made.

(D) There is a note, memorandum, or other writing sufficient to indicate that a contract has been made, signed by the party against whom enforcement is sought or by its authorized agent or broker.

For purposes of this paragraph, evidence of an electronic communication indicating the making in that communication of a contract, or a confirmation, admission, note, memorandum, or writing is not insufficient because it omits or incorrectly states one or more material terms agreed upon, as long as the evidence provides a reasonable basis for concluding that a contract was made.

(4) For purposes of this subdivision, the tangible written text produced by telex, telefacsimile, computer retrieval, or other process by which electronic signals are transmitted by telephone or otherwise shall constitute a writing, and any symbol executed or adopted by a party with the present intention to authenticate a writing shall constitute a signing. The confirmation and notice of objection referred to in subparagraph (B) of paragraph (3) may be communicated by means of telex, telefacsimile, computer, or other similar process by which electronic signals are transmitted by telephone or otherwise, provided that a party claiming to have communicated in that manner shall, unless the parties have otherwise agreed in writing, have the burden of establishing actual or constructive receipt by the other party as set forth in subparagraph (B) of paragraph (3).

(c) This section does not apply to leases subject to Division 10 (commencing with Section 10101) of the Commercial Code.

(d) An electronic message of an ephemeral nature that is not designed to be retained or to create a permanent record, including, but not limited to, a text message or instant message format communication, is insufficient under this title to constitute a contract to convey real property, in the absence of a written confirmation that conforms to the requirements of subparagraph (B) of paragraph (3) of subdivision (b). **Leg.H.** Enacted 1872. Amended by Code Amdts 1873–74; Code Amdts 1877–78 ch 165; Stats 1905 ch 451 §1; Stats 1931 ch 1070 §9; Stats 1937 ch 316 §2; Stats 1963 ch 814 §1; Stats 1967 ch 52 §1; Stats 1983 ch 842 §6, operative January 1, 1985; Stats 1985 ch 1315 §1; Stats 1988 ch 1096 §1, ch 1368 §1.5, operative January 1, 1990; Stats 1998 ch 78 §1 (SB 1865); Stats 2014 ch 107 §2 (AB 2136), effective January 1, 2015.

1988 Notes: It is the intent of the Legislature that subdivision (a)(7) of Civil Code Section 1624 shall only apply prospectively to any claim or cause of action arising on or after January 1, 1989, and not otherwise affect any statutory or common law rights in a civil action.

It is also the intent of the Legislature that judicially and legislatively recognized defenses and exceptions to the application of subdivisions (a)(1) to (a)(6), inclusive, of Section 1624 also apply to subdivision (g) of Section 1624. Stats 1988 ch 1096 §3.

§1624.5. Contract, requirements; Exceptions

(a) Except in the cases described in subdivision (b), a contract for the sale of personal property is not enforceable by way of action or defense beyond five thousand dollars ($5,000) in amount or value of remedy unless there is some record, as defined in subdivision (m) of Section 1633.2, but solely to the extent permitted by applicable law, that indicates that a contract for sale has been made between the parties at a defined or stated price, reasonably identifies the subject matter, and is signed, including by way of electronic signature, as defined in subdivision (h) of Section 1633.2, but solely to the extent permitted by applicable law, by the party against whom enforcement is sought or by his or her authorized agent.

(b) Subdivision (a) does not apply to contracts governed by the Commercial Code, including contracts for the sale of goods (Section 2201 of the Commercial Code), contracts for the sale of securities (Section 8113 of the Commercial Code), and security agreements (Sections 9201 and 9203 of the Commercial Code).

(c) Subdivision (a) does not apply to a qualified financial contract as that term is defined in paragraph (2) of subdivision (b) of Section 1624 if either of the following exists:

(1) There is, as provided in paragraph (3) of subdivision (b) of Section 1624, sufficient evidence to indicate that a contract has been made.

(2) The parties thereto, by means of a prior or subsequent written contract, have agreed to be bound by the terms of the qualified financial contract from the time they reach agreement (by telephone, by exchange of electronic messages, or otherwise) on those terms. **Leg.H.** Added Stats 2006 ch 254 §1 (SB 1481), effective January 1, 2007.

§1624a. [Section repealed 1965]
Leg.H. Added Stats 1931 ch 1070 §13. Repealed Stats 1963 ch 819 §5, effective January 1, 1965. See UCC §2201.

§1625. Effect of written contract
The execution of a contract in writing, whether the law requires it to be written or not, supersedes all the negotiations or stipulations concerning its matter which preceded or accompanied the execution of the instrument. **Leg.H.** Enacted 1872. Amended Stats 1905 ch 451 §2.

§1626. Contract in writing, takes effect when
A contract in writing takes effect upon its delivery to the party in whose favor it is made, or to his agent. **Leg.H.** Enacted 1872.

§1627. Provisions of chapter on transfers of real property
The provisions of the chapter on transfers in general, concerning the delivery of grants, absolute and conditional, apply to all written contracts. **Leg.H.** Enacted 1872.

§1628. Corporate seal, how affixed
A corporate seal or official seal may be affixed to an instrument by a mere impression upon the paper or other material on which such instrument is written. **Leg.H.** Enacted 1872.

§1629. Provisions abolishing seals made applicable
All distinctions between sealed and unsealed instruments are abolished. **Leg.H.** Enacted 1872.

§1630. Bailment contract for parking or storage of vehicle
Except as provided in Section 1630.5, a printed contract of bailment providing for the parking or storage of a motor vehicle shall not be binding, either in whole or in part, on the vehicle owner or on the person who leaves the vehicle with another, unless the contract conforms to the following:

(a) "This contract limits our liability—read it" is printed at the top in capital letters of 10-point type or larger.

(b) All the provisions of the contract are printed legibly in eight-point type or larger.

(c) Acceptance of benefits under a contract included within the provisions of this section shall not be construed a waiver of this section, and it shall be unlawful to issue such a contract on condition that provisions of this section are waived.

A copy of the contract printed in large type, in an area at least 17 by 22 inches, shall be posted in a conspicuous place at each entrance of the parking lot.

Nothing in this section shall be construed to prohibit the enactment of city ordinances on this subject that are not less restrictive, and such enactments are expressly authorized. **Leg.H.** Added Stats 1957 ch 1472 §1. Amended Stats 1970 ch 1277 §1.

§1630.5. Bailee's liability for theft of motor vehicle
The provisions of any contract of bailment for the parking or storage of a motor vehicle shall not exempt the bailee from liability, either in whole or in part, for the theft of any motor vehicle, when such motor vehicle is parked or stored with such bailee, and the keys are required by such bailee to be left in the parked or stored vehicle. **Leg.H.** Added Stats 1970 ch 1277 §2.

§1631. Sale of mining machinery; Bill of sale; Record of transaction
Every person in this State who sells machinery used or to be used for mining purposes shall, at the time of sale, give to the buyer a bill of sale for the machinery. The seller shall keep a written record of the sale, giving the date thereof, describing the machinery, and showing the name and address of the buyer, and the buyer, if in this State, shall keep a record of his purchase, giving the name and address of the seller, describing the machinery, and showing the date of the purchase. **Leg.H.** Added Stats 1959 ch 222 §1.

§1632. Trade or business negotiating primarily in Spanish, Chinese, Tagalog, Vietnamese, or Korean
(a) The Legislature hereby finds and declares all of the following:

(1) This section was enacted in 1976 to increase consumer information and protections for the state's sizeable and growing Spanish-speaking population.

(2) Since 1976, the state's population has become increasingly diverse and the number of Californians who speak languages other than English as their primary language at home has increased dramatically.

(3) According to data from the American Community Survey, which has replaced the decennial census for detailed socioeconomic information about United States residents, approximately 15.2 million Californians speak a language other than English at home, based on data from combined years 2009 through 2011. This compares to approximately 19.6 million people who speak only English at home. Among the Californians who speak a language other than English at home, approximately 8.4 million speak English very well, and another 3 million speak English well. The remaining 3.8 million Californians surveyed do not speak English well or do not speak English at all. Among this group, the five languages other than English that are most widely spoken at home are Spanish, Chinese, Tagalog, Vietnamese, and Korean. These five languages are spoken at home by approximately 3.5 million of the 3.8 million Californians with limited or no English proficiency, who speak a language other than English at home.

(b) [1] A person engaged in a trade or business who negotiates primarily in Spanish, Chinese, Tagalog, Vietnamese, or Korean, orally or in writing, in the course of entering into any of the following, shall deliver to the other party to the contract or agreement, and any other person who will be signing the contract or agreement, and before the execution thereof, a translation of the contract or agreement in the language in which the contract or agreement was negotiated, that includes a translation of every term and condition in that contract or agreement:

(1) A contract or agreement subject to the provisions of Title 2 (commencing with Section 1801) of, and Chapter 2b (commencing with Section 2981) and Chapter 2d (commencing with Section 2985.7) of Title 14 of, Part 4 of Division 3.

(2) A loan or extension of credit secured other than by real property, or unsecured, for use primarily for personal, family, or household purposes.

(3) A lease, sublease, rental contract or agreement, or other term of tenancy contract or agreement, for a period of longer than one month, covering a dwelling, an apartment, or mobilehome, or other dwelling unit normally occupied as a residence.

(4) Notwithstanding paragraph (2), a loan or extension of credit for use primarily for personal, family, or household purposes in which the loan or extension of credit is subject to the provisions of Article 7 (commencing with Section 10240) of Chapter 3 of Part 1 of Division 4 of the Business and Professions Code, or Division 7 (commencing with Section 18000), or Division 9 (commencing with Section 22000) of the Financial Code.

(5) Notwithstanding paragraph (2), a reverse mortgage as described in Chapter 8 (commencing with Section 1923) of Title 4 of Part 4 of Division 3.

(6) A contract or agreement, containing a statement of fees or charges, entered into for the purpose of obtaining legal services, when the person who is engaged in business is currently licensed to practice law pursuant to Chapter 4 (commencing with Section 6000) of Division 3 of the Business and Professions Code.

(7) A foreclosure consulting contract subject to Article 1.5 (commencing with Section 2945) of Chapter 2 of Title 14 of Part 4 of Division 3.

(8) A lease, sublease, rental contract or agreement, or other term of tenancy contract or agreement covering a nonresidential-zoned commercial space entered into between a landlord and a qualified commercial tenant, on or after January 1, 2025.

(c) Notwithstanding subdivision (b), for a loan subject to this part and to Article 7 (commencing with Section 10240) of Chapter 3 of Part 1 of Division 4 of the Business and Professions Code, the delivery of a translation of the statement to the borrower required by Section 10240 of the Business and Professions Code in any of the languages specified in subdivision (b) in which the contract or agreement was negotiated, is in compliance with subdivision (b).

(d) At the time and place where a lease, sublease, or rental contract or agreement described in subdivision (b) is executed, notice in any of the languages specified in subdivision (b) in which the contract or agreement was negotiated shall be provided to the lessee or tenant.

(e) Provision by a supervised financial organization of a translation of the disclosures required by Regulation M or Regulation Z, and, if applicable, Division 7 (commencing with Section 18000) or Division 9 (commencing with Section 22000) of the Financial Code in any of the languages specified in subdivision (b) in which the contract or agreement was negotiated, [2] **before** the execution of the contract or agreement, shall also be deemed in compliance with the requirements of subdivision (b) with regard to the original contract or agreement.

(1) "Regulation M" and "Regulation Z" mean any rule, regulation, or interpretation promulgated by the Board of Governors of the Federal Reserve System and any interpretation or approval issued by an official or employee duly authorized by the board to issue interpretations or approvals dealing with, respectively, consumer leasing or consumer lending, pursuant to the Federal Truth in Lending Act, as amended (15 U.S.C. Sec. 1601 et seq.).

(2) As used in this section, "supervised financial organization" means a bank, savings association as defined in Section 5102 of the Financial Code, credit union, or holding company, affiliate, or subsidiary thereof, or [3] **a** person subject to Article 7 (commencing with Section 10240) of Chapter 3 of Part 1 of Division 4 of the Business and Professions Code, or Division 7 (commencing with Section 18000) or Division 9 (commencing with Section 22000) of the Financial Code.

(f) At the time and place where a contract or agreement described in paragraph (1) or (2) of subdivision (b) is executed, a notice in any of the languages specified in subdivision (b) in which the contract or agreement was negotiated shall be conspicuously displayed to the effect that the person described in subdivision (b) is required to provide a contract or agreement in the language in which the contract or agreement was negotiated, or a translation of the disclosures required by law in the language in which the contract or agreement was negotiated, as the case may be. If a person described in subdivision (b) does business at more than one location or branch, the requirements of this section shall apply only with respect to the location or branch at which the language in which the contract or agreement was negotiated is used.

(g)**(1)** The term "contract" or "agreement," as used in this section, means the document creating the rights and obligations of the parties and includes any subsequent document making substantial changes in the rights and obligations of the parties. The term "contract" or "agreement" does not include any subsequent documents authorized or contemplated by the original document such as periodic statements, sales slips or invoices representing purchases made pursuant to a credit card agreement, a retail installment contract or account or other revolving sales or loan account, memoranda of purchases in an add-on sale, or refinancing of a purchase as provided by, or pursuant to, the original document.

(2) The term "contract" or "agreement" does not include a home improvement contract as defined in Sections 7151.2 and 7159 of the Business and Professions Code, nor does it include plans, specifications, description of work to be done and materials to be used, or collateral security taken or to be taken for the retail buyer's obligation contained in a contract for the installation of goods by a contractor licensed pursuant to Chapter 9 (commencing with Section 7000) of Division 3 of the Business and Professions Code, if the home improvement contract or installation contract is otherwise a part of a contract described in subdivision (b).

(3) Matters ordinarily incorporated by reference in contracts or agreements as described in paragraph (3) of subdivision (b), including, but not limited to, rules and regulations governing a tenancy and inventories of furnishings to be provided by the person described in subdivision (b), are not included in the term "contract" or "agreement."

(h)(1) This section does not apply to [4] **a** person engaged in a trade or business who negotiates primarily in a language other than English, as described by subdivision (b), if the party with whom that person is negotiating is a buyer of goods or services, or receives a loan or extension of credit, or enters an agreement obligating that party as a tenant, lessee, or sublessee, or similarly obligates the party by contract or lease, and the party negotiates the terms of the contract, lease, or other obligation through the party's own interpreter.

(2) As used in this subdivision, "the party's own interpreter" means a person who is not a minor and who is able to speak fluently and read with full understanding both the English language and any of the languages specified in subdivision (b) in which the contract, lease, or other obligation was negotiated, and who is not employed by, or whose service is not made available through, the person engaged in the trade or business.

(3) This subdivision does not apply to a contract or agreement described in paragraph (8) of subdivision (b).

(i) Notwithstanding subdivision (b), a translation may retain the following elements of the executed English-language contract or agreement without translation: names and titles of individuals and other persons, addresses, brand names, trade names, trademarks, registered service marks, full or abbreviated designations of the make and model of goods or services, alphanumeric codes, numerals, dollar amounts expressed in numerals, dates, and individual words or expressions having no generally accepted non-English translation. It is permissible, but not required, that this translation be signed.

(j) The terms of the contract or agreement that is executed in the English language shall determine the rights and obligations of the parties. However, the translation of the contract or the disclosures required by subdivision (e) in any of the languages specified in subdivision (b) in which the contract or agreement was negotiated shall be admissible in evidence only to show that no contract was entered into because of a substantial difference in the material terms and conditions of the contract and the translation.

(k)(1) Upon a failure to comply with the provisions of this section, the person aggrieved may rescind the contract or agreement in the manner provided by this chapter. If the contract for a consumer credit sale or consumer lease that has been sold and assigned to a financial institution is rescinded pursuant to this subdivision, the consumer shall make restitution to and have restitution made by the person with whom the consumer made the contract and shall give notice of rescission to the assignee. Notwithstanding that the contract was assigned without recourse, the assignment shall be deemed rescinded, and the assignor shall promptly repurchase the contract from the assignee.

(2) Notwithstanding paragraph (1), only a qualified commercial tenant may rescind a contract described in paragraph (8) of subdivision (b) pursuant to this subdivision.

(*l*) Any waiver of a provision of this section is contrary to public policy and is void and unenforceable.

(m) For the purposes of this section, the following definitions apply:

(1) "Commercial real property" means all real property in this state, except dwelling units subject to Chapter 2 (commencing with Section 1940) of Title 5 of Part 4, mobilehomes, as defined in Section 798.3, and recreational vehicles, as defined in Section 799.29.

(2) "Microenterprise" has the same meaning as that term is defined in subdivision (a) of Section 18000 of the Business and Professions Code.

(3) "Nonprofit organization" means any private, nonprofit organization that qualifies under Section 501(c)(3) of the United States Internal Revenue Code of 1986.

(4) "Qualified commercial tenant" means a tenant of commercial real property that meets both of the following requirements:

(A) The tenant is a microenterprise, a restaurant with fewer than 10 employees, or a nonprofit organization with fewer than 20 employees.

(B)(i) Subject to clause (ii), the tenant has provided the landlord, within the prior 12 months, a written notice that the tenant is a qualified commercial tenant and a self-attestation regarding the number of employees, at such time the protections under this section come into place.

(ii) Unless the tenancy is from week to week, month to month, or other period less than a month, the tenant provided the notice and self-attestation described in clause (i) before or upon execution of the lease, and annually thereafter, at such time the protections under this section come into place. Leg.H. Added Stats 1974 ch 1446 §1. Amended Stats 1975 ch 892 §1; Stats 1976 ch 312 §1, effective July 2, 1976; Stats 1981 ch 724 §3; Stats 1988 ch 1531 §1; Stats 2001 ch 306 §35 (AB 446); Stats 2002 ch 664 §38 (AB 3034); Stats 2003 ch 330 §1 (AB 309), operative July 1, 2004, ch 589 §1 (SB 146), operative until July 1, 2004, ch 589 §1.5 (SB 146), operative July 1, 2004. (As amended Stats 2003 ch 589, compared to the section as it read prior to 2003. This section was also amended by an earlier chapter, ch 330. See Gov C §9605; Stats 2006 ch 202 §1 (SB 1609), effective January 1, 2007; Stats 2008 ch 278 §1 (AB 180), effective January 1, 2009, operative July 1, 2009; Stats 2014 ch 117 §1 (SB 245), effective January 1, 2015; Stats 2020 ch 161 §1 (AB 3254), effective January 1, 2021; Stats 2024 ch 853 §11 (AB 3281), effective January 1, 2025; Stats 2024 §2.5 (SB 1103), effective January 1, 2025 (ch 1015 prevails).

§1632. 2024 Deletes. [1] Any [2] prior to [3] any [4] any

§1632.5. Delivery of form summarizing residential mortgage loan terms or modified terms in applicable foreign language; Penalties; Development of forms [Operative date contingent]

(a)(1) A supervised financial organization that negotiates primarily in

Spanish, Chinese, Tagalog, Vietnamese, or Korean, whether orally or in writing, in the course of entering into a contract or agreement for a loan or extension of credit secured by residential real property, shall deliver to the other party to that contract or agreement prior to the execution of the contract or agreement the applicable form or forms described in subdivision (i) for that language.

(2) A supervised financial organization that negotiates the modification of any of the terms of a loan or extension of credit secured by residential real property primarily in Spanish, Chinese, Tagalog, Vietnamese, or Korean, and that offers a borrower a final loan modification in writing, shall deliver to that borrower, at the time the final loan modification offer is made, one of the forms described in paragraph (4) of subdivision (i) summarizing the modified terms of the loan in the same language as the negotiation.

(b) For purposes of this section:

(1) "Contract" or "agreement" has the same meaning as defined in subdivision (g) of Section 1632.

(2) "Supervised financial organization" means a bank, savings association, as defined in Section 5102 of the Financial Code, credit union, or holding company, affiliate, or subsidiary thereof, or any person subject to Division 7 (commencing with Section 18000), Division 9 (commencing with Section 22000), or Division 20 (commencing with Section 50000) of the Financial Code.

(c)(1) With respect to a contract or agreement for a loan or extension of credit secured by residential real property as described in subdivision (a), a supervised financial organization that complies with this section shall be deemed in compliance with Section 1632.

(2) Except with respect to a loan or extension of credit described in paragraph (2) of subdivision (a), a supervised financial organization that complies with Section 1632, with respect to a contract or agreement for a loan or extension of credit secured by residential real property as described in subdivision (a), shall be deemed in compliance with this section.

(d)(1) Except as provided in paragraphs (2) and (3), the supervised financial organization shall provide the Good Faith Estimate disclosure form described in paragraph (1) of subdivision (i) to the borrower no later than three business days after receipt of the written application, and if any of the loan terms summarized materially change after provision of the translated form but prior to consummation of the loan, the supervised financial organization shall provide an updated version of the translated form prior to consummation of the loan.

(2) For a transaction subject to subsection (e) of Section 1026.19 of Title 12 of the Code of Federal Regulations, the supervised financial organization shall provide the Loan Estimate form described in paragraph (2) of subdivision (i) translated in the applicable language no later than three business days after receipt of the written application. If any of the summarized loan terms materially change after provision of the Loan Estimate form but prior to consummation of the loan, the supervised financial organization shall provide an updated version of the translated form prior to consummation of the loan.

(3) For a transaction subject to subsection (f) of Section 1026.19 of Title 12 of the Code of Federal Regulations, the supervised financial organization shall provide the Closing Disclosure form described in paragraph (3) of subdivision (i) translated in the applicable language at least three business days prior to consummation of the loan.

(e)(1) This section does not apply to a supervised financial organization that negotiates primarily in a language other than English, as described by subdivision (a), if the party with whom the supervised financial organization is negotiating, negotiates the terms of the contract through the party's own interpreter.

(2) For purposes of this subdivision, "the party's own interpreter" means a person, not a minor, who is able to speak fluently and read with full understanding both the English language and one of the languages specified in subdivision (a) that is the language in which the contract was negotiated, who is not employed by, and whose services are not made available through, the person engaged in the trade or business.

(f) Notwithstanding subdivision (a), a translated form may retain any of the following elements of the executed English language contract or agreement without translation:

(1) Names and titles of individuals and other persons.

(2) Addresses, brand names, trade names, trademarks, or registered service marks.

(3) Full or abbreviated designations of the make and model of goods or services.

(4) Alphanumeric codes.

(5) Individual words or expressions having no generally accepted non-English translation.

(g) The terms of the contract or agreement that is executed in the English language shall determine the rights and obligations of the parties. However, the translation of the forms described in subdivision (i) and required by subdivision (a) shall be admissible in evidence only to show that no contract or agreement was entered into because of a substantial difference in the material terms and conditions of the contract or agreement and the prior translated forms provided to the borrower.

(h)(1) A licensing agency may, by order, after appropriate notice and opportunity for hearing, levy administrative penalties against a supervised financial organization that violates any provision of this section, and the supervised financial organization may be liable for administrative penalties, up to the amounts of two thousand five hundred dollars ($2,500) for the first violation, five thousand dollars ($5,000) for the second violation, and ten thousand dollars ($10,000) for each subsequent violation. Except for licensing agencies exempt from the provisions of the Administrative Procedure Act, any hearing shall be held in accordance with the Administrative Procedure Act (Chapter 5 (commencing with Section 11500) of Part 1 of Division 3 of Title 2 of the Government Code), and the licensing agency shall have all the powers granted under that act.

(2) A licensing agency may exercise any and all authority and powers available to it under any other provisions of law to administer and enforce this section, including, but not limited to, investigating and examining the licensed person's books and records, and charging and collecting the reasonable costs for these activities. The licensing agency shall not charge a licensed person twice for the same service. Any civil, criminal, and administrative authority and remedies available to the licensing agency pursuant to its licensing law may be sought and employed in any combination deemed advisable by the licensing agency to enforce the provisions of this section.

(3) Any supervised financial organization that violates this section shall be deemed to have violated its licensing law.

(4) This section shall not be construed to impair or impede the Attorney General from bringing an action to enforce this division.

(i) The Department of Financial Protection and Innovation shall make available each of the following forms based on existing forms in each of the languages set forth in subdivision (a) for use by a supervised financial organization to summarize the terms of a mortgage loan pursuant to subdivision (a). In making available the forms, the Department of Financial Protection and Innovation may use as guidance the following existing forms:

(1) The Good Faith Estimate disclosure form from the United States Department of Housing and Urban Development.

(2) The Loan Estimate form from the Consumer Financial Protection Bureau.

(3) The Closing Disclosure form from the Consumer Financial Protection Bureau.

(4) The Agreement for Modification, Re-Amortization, or Extension of a Mortgage (Form 181), the Loan Modification Agreement (Providing for Fixed Interest Rate) (Form 3179), and the Loan Modification Agreement (Providing for Adjustable Interest Rate) (Form 3161) from the Federal National Mortgage Association.

(j) This section does not apply to federally chartered banks, credit unions, savings banks, or thrifts.

(k) Except as otherwise provided in subdivision (h), this section shall not be construed to create or enhance any claim, right of action, or civil liability that did not previously exist under state law, or limit any claim, right of action, or civil liability that otherwise exists under state law.

(*l*) An action against a supervised financial organization for a violation of this section may only be brought by a licensing agency or by the Attorney General. **Leg.H.** Added Stats 2009 ch 274 §1 (AB 1160), effective January 1, 2010, operative September 26, 2010. Amended Stats 2015 ch 190 §2 (AB 1517), effective January 1, 2016; Stats 2018 ch 356 §1 (SB 1201), effective January 1, 2019, operative date contingent; Stats 2019 ch 497 §24 (AB 991), effective January 1, 2020, operative date contingent; Stats 2022 ch 452 §18 (SB 1498), effective January 1, 2023; Stats 2018 ch 356 §1 (SB 1201), effective January 1, 2019, operative date contingent.

2018 Note: The amendments made by Section 1 of this act to Section 1632.5 of the Civil Code shall become operative 90 days following the issuance of forms by the Department of Business Oversight pursuant to subdivision (i) of that section, but in no instance before January 1, 2019. Stats 2018 ch 356 §3 (SB 1201).

2009 Note: This act is not intended to affect the obligations of a real estate broker, as defined in Section 10131 of the Business and Professions Code, subject to Section 1632, or the remedies under Section 1632 applicable to real estate brokers who violate that section. Further, it is the intent of the Legislature that a supervised financial organization that is subject to both Section 1632 and this section, and who seeks to comply with this section, shall be subject to the remedies set forth in this section and not Section 1632. Stats 2009 ch 274 (AB 1160) §2.

§1633. Validity of contract with broker-dealer resulting from customer's electronically transmitted application

(a) Notwithstanding any other provision of law, an application by a prospective customer to enter into a brokerage agreement with a broker–dealer, which application is transmitted electronically and is accompanied by the prospective customer's electronic signature or digital signature as described in subdivisions (d), (e), (f), and (g), shall be deemed, upon acceptance by the broker-dealer, to be a fully executed, valid, enforceable, and irrevocable written contract, unless grounds exist which would render any other contract invalid, unenforceable, or revocable.

(b) Nothing in this section abrogates or limits any existing law that would otherwise apply to contracts governed by this section, or any theory of liability or any remedy otherwise available at law.

(c) "Broker-dealer," for purposes of this section, means any broker-dealer licensed pursuant to Part 3 (commencing with Section 25200) of Division 1 of Title 4 of the Corporations Code or exempted from licensing pursuant thereto.

(d) "Electronic" means relating to technology having electrical, digital, magnetic, wireless, optical, electromagnetic, or similar capabilities.

(e) "Electronic record" means a record created, generated, sent, communicated, received, or stored electronically.

(f) "Electronic signature" means an electronic sound, symbol, or process attached to or logically associated with an electronic record and executed or adopted by a person with the intent to sign the electronic record.

(g) "Digital signature," for the purposes of this section, means an electronic identifier, created by a computer, that is intended by the party using it to have the same force and effect as the use of a manual signature. The use of a digital signature shall have the same force or effect as a manual signature if it embodies all of the following attributes:

(1) It is unique to the person using it.

(2) It is capable of verification.

(3) It is under the sole control of the person using it.

(4) It is linked to data in a manner that if the data is changed, the digital signature is invalidated.

(h) The use of an electronic signature or digital signature shall have the same force or effect as a manual signature.

(i) The application that is transmitted electronically pursuant to subdivision (a) shall comply with all applicable federal and state securities laws and regulations relating to disclosures to prospective customers. Unless those laws and regulations currently require disclosures to be displayed or printed in bold, to be of specific type or print size, and to be placed prominently at specified locations within the application, the disclosures shall be displayed prominently and printed in capital letters, in bold type and displayed or printed immediately above the signature line. Disclosures shall be written in plain English. The full text of the disclosures shall be contained in the application as required by this subdivision.

(j) Whenever a disclosure to a prospective customer is required under federal or state law or regulation to be confirmed as having been made, the application that is transmitted electronically pursuant to subdivision (a) shall provide a means by which the prospective customer shall confirm that he or she has read the disclosure. **Leg.H.** Added Stats 1999 ch 213 §1 (SB 1124), effective July 28, 1999.

TITLE 2.5
ELECTRONIC TRANSACTIONS

Citation of title. §1633.1.
Definitions. §1633.2.
Transactions governed by title; Exceptions. §1633.3.
Date following which transactions are governed by title. §1633.4.
Application of title. §1633.5.
Construction of title. §1633.6.
Influence of electronic form on effect or enforceability of record or signature. §1633.7.
Satisfaction of writing requirement by sending of electronic record; Effect of requirement that record be sent or formatted in a certain way. §1633.8.
Attributing electronic signature or record to a person. §1633.9.
Effect of change or error in electronic record. §1633.10.
Notarization of electronic signature. §1633.11.
Retention of record. §1633.12.
Evidence of record or signature. §1633.13.
Formation and terms of contract in automated transaction. §1633.14.
Time that electronic record is sent; Place of sending and receiving; Effect of electronic acknowledgment. §1633.15.
Requirements for notice of right to cancel. §1633.16.
Prohibition of use of electronic signature by state agency that is not party to transaction. §1633.17.

§1633.1. Citation of title

This title may be cited as the Uniform Electronic Transactions Act. **Leg.H.** Added Stats 1999 ch 428 §1 (SB 820).

§1633.2. Definitions

In this title the following terms have the following definitions:

(a) "Agreement" means the bargain of the parties in fact, as found in their language or inferred from other circumstances and from rules, regulations, and procedures given the effect of agreements under laws otherwise applicable to a particular transaction.

(b) "Automated transaction" means a transaction conducted or performed, in whole or in part, by electronic means or electronic records, in which the acts or records of one or both parties are not reviewed by an individual in the ordinary course in forming a contract, performing under an existing contract, or fulfilling an obligation required by the transaction.

(c) "Computer program" means a set of statements or instructions to be used directly or indirectly in an information processing system in order to bring about a certain result.

(d) "Contract" means the total legal obligation resulting from the parties' agreement as affected by this title and other applicable law.

(e) "Electronic" means relating to technology having electrical, digital, magnetic, wireless, optical, electromagnetic, or similar capabilities.

(f) "Electronic agent" means a computer program or an electronic or other automated means used independently to initiate an action or respond to electronic records or performances in whole or in part, without review by an individual.

(g) "Electronic record" means a record created, generated, sent, communicated, received, or stored by electronic means.

(h) "Electronic signature" means an electronic sound, symbol, or process attached to or logically associated with an electronic record and executed or adopted by a person with the intent to sign the electronic record. For purposes of this title, a "digital signature" as defined in subdivision (d) of Section 16.5 of the Government Code is a type of electronic signature.

(i) "Governmental agency" means an executive, legislative, or judicial agency, department, board, commission, authority, institution, or instrumentality of the federal government or of a state or of a county, municipality, or other political subdivision of a state.

(j) "Information" means data, text, images, sounds, codes, computer programs, software, databases, or the like.

(k) "Information processing system" means an electronic system for creating, generating, sending, receiving, storing, displaying, or processing information.

(*l*) "Person" means an individual, corporation, business trust, estate, trust, partnership, limited liability company, association, joint venture, governmental agency, public corporation, or any other legal or commercial entity.

(m) "Record" means information that is inscribed on a tangible medium or that is stored in an electronic or other medium and is retrievable in perceivable form.

(n) "Security procedure" means a procedure employed for the purpose of verifying that an electronic signature, record, or performance is that of a specific person or for detecting changes or errors in the information in an electronic record. The term includes a procedure that requires the use of algorithms or other codes, identifying words or numbers, encryption, or callback or other acknowledgment procedures.

(o) "Transaction" means an action or set of actions occurring between two or more persons relating to the conduct of business, commercial, or governmental affairs. **Leg.H.** Added Stats 1999 ch 428 §1 (SB 820). Amended Stats 2016 ch 144 §2 (AB 2296), effective January 1, 2017.

§1633.3. Transactions governed by title; Exceptions

(a) Except as otherwise provided in subdivisions (b) and (c), this title applies to electronic records and electronic signatures relating to a transaction.

(b) This title does not apply to transactions subject to any of the following laws:

(1) A law governing the creation and execution of wills, codicils, or testamentary trusts.

(2) Division 1 (commencing with Section 1101) of the Uniform Commercial Code, except Sections 1206 and 1306.

(3) Divisions 3 (commencing with Section 3101), 4 (commencing with Section 4101), 5 (commencing with Section 5101), 8 (commencing with Section 8101), 9 (commencing with Section 9101), and 11 (commencing with Section 11101) of the Uniform Commercial Code.

(4) A law that requires that specifically identifiable text or disclosures in a record or a portion of a record be separately signed, including initialed, from the record. However, this paragraph does not apply to Section 1677 or 1678 of this code or Section 1298 of the Code of Civil Procedure.

(c) This title does not apply to any specific transaction described in Section 17511.5 of the Business and Professions Code, Section 798.14, 1133, or 1134 of, Section 1689.6, 1689.7, or 1689.13 of, Chapter 2.5 (commencing with Section 1695) of Title 5 of Part 2 of Division 3 of, Section 1720, 1785.15, 1789.14, 1789.16, or 1793.23 of, Chapter 1 (commencing with Section 1801) of Title 2 of Part 4 of Division 3 of, Section 1861.24, 1862.5, 1917.712, 1917.713, 1950.6, 1983, 2924b, 2924c, 2924f, 2924i, 2924j, 2924.3, or 2937 of, Article 1.5 (commencing with Section 2945) of Chapter 2 of Title 14 of Part 4 of Division 3 of, Section 2954.5 or 2963 of, Chapter 2b (commencing with Section 2981) or 2d (commencing with Section 2985.7) of Title 14 of Part 4 of Division 3 of, Section 3071.5 of, Part 5 (commencing with Section 4000) of Division 4 of, or Part 5.3 (commencing with Section 6500) of Division 4 of, this code; subdivision (b) of Section 18608 or Section 22328 of the Financial Code, Section 1358.15, 1365, 1368.01, 1368.1, 1371, or 18035.5 of the Health and Safety Code, Section 786 as it applies to individual and group disability policies, 10199.44, 10199.46, 10235.16, 10235.40, 11624.09, or 11624.1 of the Insurance Code, Section 779.1, 10010.1, or 16482 of the Public Utilities Code, or Section 9975 or 11738 of the Vehicle Code. An electronic record may not be substituted for any notice that is required to be sent pursuant to Section 1162 of the Code of Civil Procedure. This subdivision does not prohibit the recordation of any document with a county recorder by electronic means.

(d) This title applies to an electronic record or electronic signature otherwise excluded from the application of this title under subdivision (b) when used for a transaction subject to a law other than those specified in subdivision (b).

(e) A transaction subject to this title is also subject to other applicable substantive law.

(f) The exclusion of a transaction from the application of this title under subdivision (b) or (c) shall be construed only to exclude the transaction from the application of this title, but shall not be construed to prohibit the transaction from being conducted by electronic means if the transaction may be conducted by electronic means under any other applicable law.

(g) Notwithstanding subdivisions (b) and (c), this title shall apply to electronic records and electronic signatures relating to transactions conducted by a person licensed, certified, or registered pursuant to the Alarm Company Act (Chapter 11.6 (commencing with Section 7590) of Division 3 of the Business and Professions Code) for purposes of activities authorized by Section 7599.54 of the Business and Professions Code. **Leg.H.** Added Stats 2013 ch 369 §3 (SB 251), effective January 1, 2014, operative January 1, 2019. Amended Stats 2014 ch 913 §4 (AB 2747), effective January 1, 2015, operative January 1, 2019; Stats 2015 ch 439 §4 (AB 1097), effective January 1, 2016, operative January 1, 2019, repealed January 1, 2021, Stats 2015 ch 638 §2.5 (AB 2747), effective January 1, 2016, operative January 1, 2019, repealed January 1, 2021; Stats 2016 ch 617 §2 (AB 2591), effective January 1, 2017, repealed January 1, 2021; Stats 2019 ch 235 §1 (AB 1065), effective January 1, 2020; Stats 2022 ch 39 §1 (SB 1179), effective January 1, 2023; Stats 2023 ch 374 §5 (AB 1697), effective January 1, 2024.

Prior Law: Former CC §1633.3, similar to the present section, was added Stats 1999 ch 428 §1 (SB 820), amended Stats 2009 ch 433 §1 (AB 328), effective January 1, 2010, Stats 2012 ch 181 §36 (AB 806), effective January 1, 2013, operative January 1, 2014, Stats 2013 ch 369 §1 (SB 251), effective January 1, 2014, ch 605 §16.5 (SB 752), effective January 1, 2014, repealed January 1, 2019, Stats 2014 ch 913 §3 (AB 2747), effective January 1, 2015, repealed January 1, 2019, Stats 2015 ch 439 §3 (AB 1097), effective January 1, 2016, repealed January 1, 2019, Stats 2015 ch 638 §1.5 (AB 1131), effective January 1, 2016, repealed January 1, 2019, and repealed Stats 2016 ch 617 §1 (AB 2591), effective January 1, 2017.

Former CC §1633.3, similar to the present section, was added Stats 1999 ch 428 §1 (SB 820) and repealed Stats 2016 ch 617 §1 (AB 2591), effective January 1, 2017.

Former Civ C §1633.3, similar to the present section, was added Stats 2015 ch 638 §3.5 (AB 1131), effective January 1, 2016, operative January 1, 2021, amended Stats 2016 ch 617 §3 (AB 2591), effective January 1, 2017, operative January 1, 2021, and repealed Stats 2019 ch 235 §2 (AB 1065), effective January 1, 2020.

§1633.4. Date following which transactions are governed by title

This title applies to any electronic record or electronic signature created, generated, sent, communicated, received, or stored on or after January 1, 2000. **Leg.H.** Added Stats 1999 ch 428 §1 (SB 820).

§1633.5. Application of title

(a) This title does not require a record or signature to be created, generated, sent, communicated, received, stored, or otherwise processed or used by electronic means or in electronic form.

(b) This title applies only to a transaction between parties each of which has agreed to conduct the transaction by electronic means. Whether the parties agree to conduct a transaction by electronic means is determined from the context and surrounding circumstances, including the parties' conduct. Except for a separate and optional agreement the primary purpose of which is to authorize a transaction to be conducted by electronic means, an agreement to conduct a transaction by electronic means may not be contained in a standard form contract that is not an electronic record. An agreement in such a standard form contract may not be conditioned upon an agreement to conduct transactions by electronic means. An agreement to conduct a transaction by electronic means may not be inferred solely from the fact that a party has used electronic means to pay an account or register a purchase or warranty. This subdivision may not be varied by agreement.

(c) A party that agrees to conduct a transaction by electronic means may refuse to conduct other transactions by electronic means. If a seller sells goods or services by both electronic and nonelectronic means and a buyer purchases the goods or services by conducting the transaction by electronic means, the buyer may refuse to conduct further transactions regarding the goods or services by electronic means. This subdivision may not be varied by agreement.

(d) Except as otherwise provided in this title, the effect of any of its provisions may be varied by agreement. The presence in certain provisions of this title of the words "unless otherwise agreed," or words of similar import, does not imply that the effect of other provisions may not be varied by agreement. **Leg.H.** Added Stats 1999 ch 428 §1 (SB 820).

§1633.6. Construction of title

This title shall be construed and applied according to all of the following:

(1) To facilitate electronic transactions consistent with other applicable law.

(2) To be consistent with reasonable practices concerning electronic transactions and with the continued expansion of those practices.

(3) To effectuate its general purpose to make uniform the law with respect to the subject of this title among states enacting it. **Leg.H.** Added Stats 1999 ch 428 §1 (SB 820).

§1633.7. Influence of electronic form on effect or enforceability of record or signature

(a) A record or signature may not be denied legal effect or enforceability solely because it is in electronic form.

(b) A contract may not be denied legal effect or enforceability solely because an electronic record was used in its formation.

(c) If a law requires a record to be in writing, an electronic record satisfies the law.

(d) If a law requires a signature, an electronic signature satisfies the law. **Leg.H.** Added Stats 1999 ch 428 §1 (SB 820).

§1633.8. Satisfaction of writing requirement by sending of electronic record; Effect of requirement that record be sent or formatted in a certain way

(a) If parties have agreed to conduct a transaction by electronic means and a law requires a person to provide, send, or deliver information in writing to another person, that requirement is satisfied if the information is provided, sent, or delivered, as the case may be, in an electronic record capable of retention by the recipient at the time of receipt. An electronic record is not capable of retention by the recipient if the sender or its information processing system inhibits the ability of the recipient to print or store the electronic record.

(b) If a law other than this title requires a record to be posted or displayed in a certain manner, to be sent, communicated, or transmitted by a specified method, or to contain information that is formatted in a certain manner, all of the following rules apply:

(1) The record shall be posted or displayed in the manner specified in the other law.

(2) Except as otherwise provided in paragraph (2) of subdivision (d), the record shall be sent, communicated, or transmitted by the method specified in the other law.

(3) The record shall contain the information formatted in the manner specified in the other law.

(c) If a sender inhibits the ability of a recipient to store or print an electronic record, the electronic record is not enforceable against the recipient.

(d) The requirements of this section may not be varied by agreement, except as follows:

(1) To the extent a law other than this title requires information to be provided, sent, or delivered in writing but permits that requirement to be varied by agreement, the requirement under subdivision (a) that the information be in the form of an electronic record capable of retention may also be varied by agreement.

(2) A requirement under a law other than this title to send, communicate, or transmit a record by first-class mail may be varied by agreement to the extent permitted by the other law. **Leg.H.** Added Stats 1999 ch 428 §1 (SB 820).

§1633.9. Attributing electronic signature or record to a person

(a) An electronic record or electronic signature is attributable to a person if it was the act of the person. The act of the person may be shown in any manner, including a showing of the efficacy of any security procedure applied to determine the person to which the electronic record or electronic signature was attributable.

(b) The effect of an electronic record or electronic signature attributed to a person under subdivision (a) is determined from the context and surrounding circumstances at the time of its creation, execution, or adoption, including the parties' agreement, if any, and otherwise as provided by law. **Leg.H.** Added Stats 1999 ch 428 §1 (SB 820).

§1633.10. Effect of change or error in electronic record

If a change or error in an electronic record occurs in a transmission between parties to a transaction, the following rules apply:

(1) If the parties have agreed to use a security procedure to detect changes or errors and one party has conformed to the procedure, but the other party has not, and the nonconforming party would have detected the change or error had that party also conformed, the conforming party may avoid the effect of the changed or erroneous electronic record.

(2) In an automated transaction involving an individual, the individual may avoid the effect of an electronic record that resulted from an error made by the individual in dealing with the electronic agent of another person if the electronic agent did not provide an opportunity for the prevention or correction of the error and, at the time the individual learns of the error, all of the following conditions are met:

(i) The individual promptly notifies the other person of the error and that the individual did not intend to be bound by the electronic record received by the other person.

(ii) The individual takes reasonable steps, including steps that conform to the other person's reasonable instructions, to return to the other person or, if instructed by the other person, to destroy the consideration received, if any, as a result of the erroneous electronic record.

(iii) The individual has not used or received any benefit or value from the consideration, if any, received from the other person.

(3) If neither paragraph (1) nor (2) applies, the change or error has the effect provided by other law, including the law of mistake, and the parties' contract, if any.

(4) Paragraphs (2) and (3) may not be varied by agreement. **Leg.H.** Added Stats 1999 ch 428 §1 (SB 820).

§1633.11. Notarization of electronic signature

(a) If a law requires that a signature be notarized, the requirement is satisfied with respect to an electronic signature if an electronic record includes, in addition to the electronic signature to be notarized, the electronic signature of a notary public together with all other information required to be included in a notarization by other applicable law.

(b) In a transaction, if a law requires that a statement be signed under penalty of perjury, the requirement is satisfied with respect to an electronic signature, if an electronic record includes, in addition to the electronic signature, all of the information as to which the declaration pertains together with a declaration under penalty of perjury by the person who submits the electronic signature that the information is true and correct. **Leg.H.** Added Stats 1999 ch 428 §1 (SB 820).

§1633.12. Retention of record

(a) If a law requires that a record be retained, the requirement is satisfied by retaining an electronic record of the information in the record, if the electronic record reflects accurately the information set forth in the record at the time it was first generated in its final form as an electronic record or otherwise, and the electronic record remains accessible for later reference.

(b) A requirement to retain a record in accordance with subdivision (a) does not apply to any information the sole purpose of which is to enable the record to be sent, communicated, or received.

(c) A person may satisfy subdivision (a) by using the services of another person if the requirements of subdivision (a) are satisfied.

(d) If a law requires a record to be retained in its original form, or provides consequences if the record is not retained in its original form, that law is satisfied by an electronic record retained in accordance with subdivision (a).

(e) If a law requires retention of a check, that requirement is satisfied by retention of an electronic record of the information on the front and back of the check in accordance with subdivision (a).

(f) A record retained as an electronic record in accordance with subdivision (a) satisfies a law requiring a person to retain a record for evidentiary, audit, or like purposes, unless a law enacted after the effective date of this title specifically prohibits the use of an electronic record for a specified purpose.

(g) This section does not preclude a governmental agency from specifying additional requirements for the retention of a record subject to the agency's jurisdiction. **Leg.H.** Added Stats 1999 ch 428 §1 (SB 820).

§1633.13. Evidence of record or signature

In a proceeding, evidence of a record or signature may not be excluded solely because it is in electronic form. **Leg.H.** Added Stats 1999 ch 428 §1 (SB 820).

§1633.14. Formation and terms of contract in automated transaction

(a) In an automated transaction, the following rules apply:

(1) A contract may be formed by the interaction of electronic agents of the parties, even if no individual was aware of or reviewed the electronic agents' actions or the resulting terms and agreements.

(2) A contract may be formed by the interaction of an electronic agent and an individual, acting on the individual's own behalf or for another person, including by an interaction in which the individual performs actions that the individual is free to refuse to perform and which the individual knows or has reason to know will cause the electronic agent to complete the transaction or performance.

(b) The terms of the contract are determined by the substantive law applicable to it. **Leg.H.** Added Stats 1999 ch 428 §1 (SB 820).

§1633.15. Time that electronic record is sent; Place of sending and receiving; Effect of electronic acknowledgment

(a) Unless the sender and the recipient agree to a different method of sending that is reasonable under the circumstances, an electronic record is sent when the information is addressed properly or otherwise directed properly to the recipient and either (1) enters an information processing system outside the control of the sender or of a person that sent the electronic record on behalf of the sender, or (2) enters a region of an information processing system that is under the control of the recipient.

(b) Unless the sender and the recipient agree to a different method of receiving that is reasonable under the circumstances, an electronic record is received when the electronic record enters an information processing system that the recipient has designated or uses for the purpose of receiving electronic records or information of the type sent, in a form capable of being processed by that system, and from which the recipient is able to retrieve the electronic record.

(c) Subdivision (b) applies even if the place the information processing system is located is different from the place the electronic record is deemed to be received under subdivision (d).

(d) Unless otherwise expressly provided in the electronic record or agreed between the sender and the recipient, an electronic record is deemed to be sent from the sender's place of business and to be received at the recipient's place of business or, if the recipient is an individual acting on his or her own behalf, at the recipient's place of residence. For purposes of this subdivision, the following rules apply:

(1) If the sender or recipient has more than one place of business, the place of business of that person is the place having the closest relationship to the underlying transaction.

(2) If the sender or the recipient does not have a place of business, the place of business is the sender's or recipient's residence, as the case may be.

(e) An electronic record is received under subdivision (b) even if no individual is aware of its receipt.

(f) Receipt of an electronic acknowledgment from an information processing system described in subdivision (b) establishes that a record was received but, by itself, does not establish that the content sent corresponds to the content received.

(g) If a person is aware that an electronic record purportedly sent under subdivision (a), or purportedly received under subdivision (b), was not actually sent or received, the legal effect of the sending or receipt is determined by other applicable law. Except to the extent permitted by the other law, this subdivision may not be varied by agreement. **Leg.H.** Added Stats 1999 ch 428 §1 (SB 820).

§1633.16. Requirements for notice of right to cancel

If a law other than this title requires that a notice of the right to cancel be provided or sent, an electronic record may not substitute for a writing under that other law unless, in addition to satisfying the requirements of that other law and this title, the notice of cancellation may be returned by electronic means. This section may not be varied by agreement. **Leg.H.** Added Stats 1999 ch 428 §1 (SB 820).

§1633.17. Prohibition of use of electronic signature by state agency that is not party to transaction

No state agency, board, or commission may require, prohibit, or regulate the use of an electronic signature in a transaction in which the agency, board, or commission is not a party unless a law other than this title expressly authorizes the requirement, prohibition, or regulation. **Leg.H.** Added Stats 1999 ch 428 §1 (SB 820).

TITLE 3
INTERPRETATION OF CONTRACTS

Uniformity of interpretation. §1635.
Contracts, how to be interpreted. §1636.
Intention of parties, how ascertained. §1637.
Intention to be ascertained from language. §1638.
Interpretation of written contracts. §1639.
Writing, when disregarded. §1640.
Effect to be given to every part of contract. §1641.
Several contracts, when taken together. §1642.
Interpretation in favor of contract. §1643.
Words to be understood in usual sense. §1644.
Technical words. §1645.
Law of place. §1646.
Exception to law of place for specified contracts. §1646.5.
Contracts explained by circumstances. §1647.
Contract restricted to its evident object. §1648.
Interpretation in sense in which promisor believed promisee to rely. §1649.
Particular clauses subordinate to general intent. §1650.
Contract, partly written and partly printed. §1651.
Repugnancies, how reconciled. §1652.
Inconsistent words rejected. §1653.
Language interpreted against party who caused uncertainty. §1654.
Reasonable stipulations, when implied. §1655.
Necessary incidents implied. §1656.
Sales tax reimbursement included in retail sale price; Rebuttable presumption. §1656.1.
Addition of estimated personal property tax reimbursement on rental of qualified heavy equipment; Rebuttable presumptions. §1656.5.
Time of performance of contract. §1657.
Reasonable time required in contract of adhesion. § 1657.1.
When joint and several. §1659.
Same. §1660.
Executed and executory contracts, what. §1661.
Uniform Vendor and Purchaser Risk Act. §1662.
Definitions; Effect of euro on certain contracts, securities, or instruments. §1663.

§1635. Uniformity of interpretation

All contracts, whether public or private, are to be interpreted by the same rules, except as otherwise provided by this code. **Leg.H.** Enacted 1872.

§1636. Contracts, how to be interpreted

A contract must be so interpreted as to give effect to the mutual intention of the parties as it existed at the time of contracting, so far as the same is ascertainable and lawful. **Leg.H.** Enacted 1872.

§1637. Intention of parties, how ascertained

For the purpose of ascertaining the intention of the parties to a contract, if otherwise doubtful, the rules given in this chapter are to be applied. **Leg.H.** Enacted 1872.

§1638. Intention to be ascertained from language

The language of a contract is to govern its interpretation, if the language is clear and explicit, and does not involve an absurdity. **Leg.H.** Enacted 1872.

§1639. Interpretation of written contracts

When a contract is reduced to writing, the intention of the parties is to be ascertained from the writing alone, if possible; subject, however, to the other provisions of this title. **Leg.H.** Enacted 1872.

§1640. Writing, when disregarded

When, through fraud, mistake, or accident, a written contract fails to express the real intention of the parties, such intention is to be regarded, and the erroneous parts of the writing disregarded. **Leg.H.** Enacted 1872.

§1641. Effect to be given to every part of contract

The whole of a contract is to be taken together, so as to give effect to every part, if reasonably practicable, each clause helping to interpret the other. **Leg.H.** Enacted 1872.

§1642. Several contracts, when taken together

Several contracts relating to the same matters, between the same parties, and made as parts of substantially one transaction, are to be taken together. **Leg.H.** Enacted 1872.

§1643. Interpretation in favor of contract

A contract must receive such an interpretation as will make it lawful, operative, definite, reasonable, and capable of being carried into effect, if it can be done without violating the intention of the parties. **Leg.H.** Enacted 1872.

§1644. Words to be understood in usual sense

The words of a contract are to be understood in their ordinary and popular sense, rather than according to their strict legal meaning; unless used by the parties in a technical sense, or unless a special meaning is given to them by usage, in which case the latter must be followed. **Leg.H.** Enacted 1872.

§1645. Technical words

Technical words are to be interpreted as usually understood by persons in the profession or business to which they relate, unless clearly used in a different sense. **Leg.H.** Enacted 1872.

§1646. Law of place

A contract is to be interpreted according to the law and usage of the place where it is to be performed; or, if it does not indicate a place of performance, according to the law and usage of the place where it is made. **Leg.H.** Enacted 1872.

§1646.5. Exception to law of place for specified contracts

Notwithstanding Section 1646, the parties to any contract, agreement, or undertaking, contingent or otherwise, relating to a transaction involving in the aggregate not less than two hundred fifty thousand dollars ($250,000), including a transaction otherwise covered by subdivision (a) of Section 1301 of the Commercial Code, may agree that the law of this state shall govern their rights and duties in whole or in part, whether or not the contract, agreement, or undertaking or transaction bears a reasonable relation to this state. This section does not apply to any contract, agreement, or undertaking (a) for labor or personal services, (b) relating to any transaction primarily for personal, family, or household purposes, or (c) to the extent provided to the contrary in subdivision (c) of Section 1301 of the Commercial Code.

This section applies to contracts, agreements, and undertakings entered into before, on, or after its effective date; it shall be fully retroactive. Contracts, agreements, and undertakings selecting California law entered into before the effective date of this section shall be valid, enforceable, and effective as if this section had been in effect on the date they were entered into; and actions and proceedings commencing in a court of this state before the effective date of this section may be maintained as if this section were in effect on the date they were commenced. **Leg.H.** Added Stats 1992 ch 615 §2 (SB 1804). Amended Stats 2006 ch 254 §1.5 (SB 1481), effective January 1, 2007.

Prior Law: Former §1646.5, relating to agreement regarding applicable law, was added Stats 1986 ch 968 §1, effective September 22, 1986, and repealed, operative January 1, 1992, by its own terms.

§1647. Contracts explained by circumstances
A contract may be explained by reference to the circumstances under which it was made, and the matter to which it relates. **Leg.H.** Enacted 1872.

§1648. Contract restricted to its evident object
However broad may be the terms of a contract, it extends only to those things concerning which it appears that the parties intended to contract. **Leg.H.** Enacted 1872.

§1649. Interpretation in sense in which promisor believed promisee to rely
If the terms of a promise are in any respect ambiguous or uncertain, it must be interpreted in the sense in which the promisor believed, at the time of making it, that the promisee understood it. **Leg.H.** Enacted 1872.

§1650. Particular clauses subordinate to general intent
Particular clauses of a contract are subordinate to its general intent. **Leg.H.** Enacted 1872.

§1651. Contract, partly written and partly printed
Where a contract is partly written and partly printed, or where part of it is written or printed under the special directions of the parties, and with a special view to their intention, and the remainder is copied from a form originally prepared without special reference to the particular parties and the particular contract in question, the written parts control the printed parts, and the parts which are purely original control those which are copied from a form. And if the two are absolutely repugnant, the latter must be so far disregarded. **Leg.H.** Enacted 1872.

§1652. Repugnancies, how reconciled
Repugnancy in a contract must be reconciled, if possible, by such an interpretation as will give some effect to the repugnant clauses, subordinate to the general intent and purpose of the whole contract. **Leg.H.** Enacted 1872.

§1653. Inconsistent words rejected
Words in a contract which are wholly inconsistent with its nature, or with the main intention of the parties, are to be rejected. **Leg.H.** Enacted 1872.

§1654. Language interpreted against party who caused uncertainty
In cases of uncertainty not removed by the preceding rules, the language of a contract should be interpreted most strongly against the party who caused the uncertainty to exist. **Leg.H.** Enacted 1872. Amended Stats 1982 ch 1120 §1.

§1655. Reasonable stipulations, when implied
Stipulations which are necessary to make a contract reasonable, or conformable to usage, are implied, in respect to matters concerning which the contract manifests no contrary intention. **Leg.H.** Enacted 1872.

§1656. Necessary incidents implied
All things that in law or usage are considered as incidental to a contract, or as necessary to carry it into effect, are implied therefrom, unless some of them are expressly mentioned therein, when all other things of the same class are deemed to be excluded. **Leg.H.** Enacted 1872.

§1656.1. Sales tax reimbursement included in retail sale price; Rebuttable presumption
(a) Whether a retailer may add sales tax reimbursement to the sales price of the tangible personal property sold at retail to a purchaser depends solely upon the terms of the agreement of sale. It shall be presumed that the parties agreed to the addition of sales tax reimbursement to the sales price of tangible personal property sold at retail to a purchaser if:

(1) The agreement of sale expressly provides for such addition of sales tax reimbursement;

(2) Sales tax reimbursement is shown on the sales check or other proof of sale; or

(3) The retailer posts in his or her premises in a location visible to purchasers, or includes on a price tag or in an advertisement or other printed material directed to purchasers, a notice to the effect that reimbursement for sales tax will be added to the sales price of all items or certain items, whichever is applicable.

(b) It shall be presumed that the property, the gross receipts from the sale of which is subject to the sales tax, is sold at a price which includes tax reimbursement if the retailer posts in his or her premises, or includes on a price tag or in an advertisement (whichever is applicable) one of the following notices:

(1) "All prices of taxable items include sales tax reimbursement computed to the nearest mill."

(2) "The price of this item includes sales tax reimbursement computed to the nearest mill."

(c)(1) The State Board of Equalization shall prepare and make available for inspection and duplication or reproduction a sales tax reimbursement schedule which shall be identical with the following tables up to the amounts specified therein:

4¾ percent

Price	Tax
.01–.10	.00
.11–.31	.01
.32–.52	.02
.53–.73	.03
.74–.94	.04
.95–1.15	.05

5 percent

Price	Tax
.01–.09	.00
.10–.29	.01
.30–.49	.02
.50–.69	.03
.70–.89	.04
.90–1.09	.05

5¼ percent

Price	Tax
.01–.09	.00
.10–.28	.01
.29–.47	.02
.48–.66	.03
.67–.85	.04
.86–1.04	.05

5½ percent

Price	Tax
.01–.09	.00
.10–.27	.01
.28–.45	.02
.46–.63	.03
.64–.81	.04
.82–.99	.05
1.00–1.18	.06

5¾ percent

Price	Tax
.01–.08	.00
.09–.26	.01
.27–.43	.02
.44–.60	.03
.61–.78	.04
.79–.95	.05
.96–1.13	.06

6 percent

Price	Tax
.01–.08	.00
.09–.24	.01
.25–.41	.02
.42–.58	.03
.59–.74	.04
.75–.91	.05
.92–1.08	.06

6¼ percent

Price	Tax
.01–.07	.00
.08–.23	.01
.24–.39	.02
.40–.55	.03
.56–.71	.04
.72–.87	.05
.88–1.03	.06

6½ percent

Price	Tax
.01–.07	.00
.08–.23	.01
.24–.38	.02
.39–.53	.03
.54–.69	.04
.70–.84	.05
.85–.99	.06
1.00–1.15	.07

6¾ percent

Price	Tax
.01–.07	.00
.08–.22	.01
.23–.37	.02
.38–.51	.03
.52–.66	.04
.67–.81	.05
.82–.96	.06
.97–1.11	.07

7 percent

Price	Tax
.01–.07	.00
.08–.21	.01
.22–.35	.02
.36–.49	.03
.50–.64	.04
.65–.78	.05
.79–.92	.06
.93–1.07	.07

7¼ percent

Price	Tax
.01–.06	.00
.07–.20	.01
.21–.34	.02
.35–.48	.03
.49–.62	.04
.63–.75	.05
.76–.89	.06
.90–1.03	.07

7½ percent

Price	Tax
.01–.06	.00
.07–.19	.01
.20–.33	.02
.34–.46	.03
.47–.59	.04
.60–.73	.05
.74–.86	.06
.87–.99	.07
1.00–1.13	.08

(2) Reimbursement on sales prices in excess of those shown in the schedules may be computed by applying the applicable tax rate to the sales price, rounded off to the nearest cent by eliminating any fraction less than one-half cent and increasing any fraction of one-half cent or over to the next higher cent.

(3) If sales tax reimbursement is added to the sales price of tangible personal property sold at retail, the retailer shall use a schedule provided by the board, or a schedule approved by the board.

(d) The presumptions created by this section are rebuttable presumptions. **Leg.H.** Added Stats 1978 ch 1211 §1. Amended Stats 1985 ch 20 §1, effective March 29, 1985, operative April 1, 1985; Stats 1990 ch 1528 §1 (SB 2196).

§1656.2. [Section repealed 1990]

Leg.H. Added Stats 1983–84 1st Ex Sess ch 10 §2, effective February 17, 1983. Repealed Stats 1990 ch 1528 §2 (SB 2196). The repealed section related to preparation of sales tax reimbursement schedule.

§1656.5. Addition of estimated personal property tax reimbursement on rental of qualified heavy equipment; Rebuttable presumptions

(a) Whether a qualified heavy equipment renter may add estimated personal property tax reimbursement to the rental price of heavy equipment property to a lessee depends solely upon the terms of the rental agreement. It shall be presumed that the parties agreed to the addition of estimated personal property tax reimbursement to the rental price of heavy equipment property to a lessee if all of the following conditions occur:

(1) The rental agreement expressly provides for the addition of estimated personal property tax reimbursement.

(2) Estimated personal property tax reimbursement is separately stated and charged on the rental agreement.

(3) The estimated personal property tax reimbursement amount shall not exceed 0.75 percent of the rental price of the heavy equipment property.

(b) The presumptions created by this section are rebuttable presumptions.

(c) For purposes of this section:

(1) "Qualified heavy equipment renter" shall have the same meaning as provided in Section 31202 of the Revenue and Taxation Code.

(2) "Rental price" means the total amount of the charge for renting the heavy equipment property, excluding any separately stated charges that are not rental charges, including, but not limited to, separately stated charges for delivery and pickup fees, damage waivers, environmental mitigation fees, sales tax reimbursement, or use taxes. **Leg.H.** Added Stats 2017 ch 505 §1 (AB 1130), effective January 1, 2018.

§1657. Time of performance of contract

If no time is specified for the performance of an act required to be performed, a reasonable time is allowed. If the act is in its nature capable of being done instantly—as, for example, if it consists in the payment of money only—it must be performed immediately upon the thing to be done being exactly ascertained. **Leg.H.** Enacted 1872.

§ 1657.1. Reasonable time required in contract of adhesion

Any time specified in a contract of adhesion for the performance of an act required to be performed shall be reasonable. **Leg.H.** Added Stats 2021 ch 222 §1 (SB 762), effective January 1, 2022.

§1658. [Section repealed 1873–74]

Leg.H. Enacted 1872. Repealed by Code Amdts 1873–74 ch 612 §191.

§1659. When joint and several

Where all the parties who unite in a promise receive some benefit from the consideration, whether past or present, their promise is presumed to be joint and several. **Leg.H.** Enacted 1872.

§1660. Same

A promise, made in the singular number, but executed by several persons, is presumed to be joint and several. **Leg.H.** Enacted 1872.

§1661. Executed and executory contracts, what

An executed contract is one, the object of which is fully performed. All others are executory. **Leg.H.** Enacted 1872.

§1662. Uniform Vendor and Purchaser Risk Act

Any contract hereafter made in this State for the purchase and sale of real property shall be interpreted as including an agreement that the parties shall have the following rights and duties, unless the contract expressly provides otherwise:

(a) If, when neither the legal title nor the possession of the subject matter of the contract has been transferred, all or a material part thereof is destroyed without fault of the purchaser or is taken by eminent domain, the vendor cannot enforce the contract, and the purchaser is entitled to recover any portion of the price that he has paid;

(b) If, when either the legal title or the possession of the subject matter of the contract has been transferred, all or any part thereof is destroyed without fault of the vendor or is taken by eminent domain, the purchaser is not thereby relieved from a duty to pay the price, nor is he entitled to recover any portion thereof that he has paid.

This section shall be so interpreted and construed as to effectuate its general purpose to make uniform the law of those states which enact it.

This section may be cited as the Uniform Vendor and Purchaser Risk Act. **Leg.H.** Added Stats 1947 ch 497 §1.

§1663. Definitions; Effect of euro on certain contracts, securities, or instruments

(a) As used in this section, the following terms shall have the following meanings:

(1) "Euro" means the currency of participating member states of the European Union that adopt a single currency in accordance with the Treaty on European Union signed February 7, 1992, as amended from time to time.

(2) "Introduction of the euro" includes, but is not limited to, the implementation from time to time of economic and monetary union in member states of the European Union in accordance with the Treaty on European Union signed February 7, 1992, as amended from time to time.

(3) "ECU" or "European Currency Unit" means the currency basket that is from time to time used as the unit of account of the European community, as defined in European Council Regulation No. 3320/94.

(b) If a subject or medium of payment of a contract, security, or instrument is the ECU or a currency that has been substituted or replaced by the euro, the euro shall be a commercially reasonable substitute and substantial equivalent that may be either tendered or used in determining the value of the ECU or currency, in each case at the conversion rate specified in, and otherwise calculated in accordance with, the regulations adopted by the Council of the European Union.

(c) The introduction of the euro, the tendering of euros in connection with any obligation in compliance with subdivision (b), the determining of the value of any obligation in compliance with subdivision (b), or the calculating or determining of the subject or medium of payment of a contract, security, or instrument with reference to an interest rate or other basis that has been substituted or replaced due to the introduction of the euro and that is a commercially reasonable substitute and substantial equivalent, shall neither have the effect of discharging or excusing performance under any contract, security, or instrument, nor give a party the right unilaterally to alter or terminate any contract, security, or instrument.

(d) This section shall be subject to any agreements between parties with specific reference to, or agreement regarding, the introduction of the euro.

(e) Notwithstanding the Commercial Code or any other law of this state, this section shall apply to all contracts, securities, and instruments, including contracts with respect to commercial transactions, and shall not be deemed to be displaced by any other law of this state.

(f) In the event of other currency changes, the provisions of this section with respect to the euro shall not be interpreted as creating any negative inference or negative presumption regarding the validity or enforceability of contracts, securities, or instruments denominated in whole or part in those other currencies. **Leg.H.** Added Stats 1998 ch 62 §1 (AB 185), effective June 5, 1998.

TITLE 4
UNLAWFUL CONTRACTS

What is unlawful. §1667.
Certain contracts unlawful. §1668.
Restraint of marriage. §1669.
Contract to pay minor who is allegedly victim of unlawful sex act. §1669.5.
Contract for payment of money for person to be called as witness in criminal prosecution. §1669.7.
Arbitration of construction contracts with public agency. §1670.
Unconscionable contract. §1670.5.
Failure to comply with federal Telemarketing Sales Rule. §1670.6.
Deduction from wages for cost of transporting person to United States void. §1670.7.
Prohibition against provision waiving consumer's right to make statement regarding seller or lessor, or concerning goods or services, in specified consumer contract. §1670.8.
Provision limiting consumer's ability to file complaint against licensing board. §1670.8.5.
Contracts for detention of noncitizens for purposes of civil immigration custody; New contracts prohibited; Renewal or modification of existing contracts prohibited; Requirements for conveyance of land or permit for building used for detention. §1670.9.
Prohibition against transactions making transfer of ownership of dog or cat contingent on payments or by way of lease over time. §1670.10.
Contracts; Waiver of right to testify regarding criminal conduct or sexual harassment; Void. §1670.11.
Exclusive listing agreements. § 1670.12.

§1667. What is unlawful

That is not lawful which is:

1. Contrary to an express provision of law;

2. Contrary to the policy of express law, though not expressly prohibited; or,

3. Otherwise contrary to good morals. **Leg.H.** Enacted 1872.

§1668. Certain contracts unlawful

All contracts which have for their object, directly or indirectly, to exempt anyone from responsibility for his own fraud, or willful injury to the person or property of another, or violation of law, whether willful or negligent, are against the policy of the law. **Leg.H.** Enacted 1872.

§1669. Restraint of marriage

Every contract in restraint of the marriage of any person, other than a minor, is void. **Leg.H.** Added Stats 1977 ch 198 §1, operative July 1, 1978.

Prior Law: Former §1669 was enacted 1872 and repealed Code Amdts 1873–74 ch 612 §191.

§1669.5. Contract to pay minor who is allegedly victim of unlawful sex act

(a) Any contract for the payment of money or other consideration to a minor who has been alleged to be the victim of an unlawful sex act, or to his or her legal representative, by the alleged perpetrator of that unlawful sex act, or his or her legal representative, entered into on or after the time of the alleged unlawful sex act, and providing for any payments to be made more than one year after the date of the execution of the contract, is void as contrary to public policy. A district attorney may bring an action or intervene in any action to enjoin enforcement of any contract which is in violation of this section.

(b) This section does not apply after the date of the final judgment in a criminal case against the alleged perpetrator for the unlawful sex act described in subdivision (a).

(c) This section does not apply to a contract for the payment of money or other consideration made from a nonrevocable trust established for the benefit of the minor if the alleged perpetrator has no direct or indirect access to, or control over, the trust.

(d) This section does not apply to an alleged perpetrator of an unlawful sex act against a minor to the extent he or she agrees to pay, or is required by court order to pay, child support for that minor upon a dissolution or legal separation.

(e) For purposes of this section, "unlawful sex act," means a felony sex offense committed against a minor.

(f) Notwithstanding subdivision (a), any contract declared void as contrary to public policy under this section may still be enforced by a district attorney against the payor, and the proceeds thereof shall be deposited in the State Children's Trust Fund pursuant to Section 18969 of the Welfare and Institutions Code. **Leg.H.** Added Stats 1994 1st Ex Sess 1993–1994 ch 54 §1 (SBX1-35).

§1669.7. Contract for payment of money for person to be called as witness in criminal prosecution

A contract for the payment of money or other consideration in violation of Section 132.5 of the Penal Code is void as contrary to public policy. The Attorney General or the district attorney of the county in which a violation of Section 132.5 of the Penal Code occurs may bring a civil action, or intervene in any civil action, to enjoin the enforcement of a contract that violates that section. **Leg.H.** Added Stats 1994 ch 869 §1 (SB 1999).

§1670. Arbitration of construction contracts with public agency

Any dispute arising from a construction contract with a public agency, which contract contains a provision that one party to the contract or one party's agent or employee shall decide any disputes arising under that contract, shall be resolved by submitting the dispute to independent arbitration, if mutually agreeable, otherwise by litigation in a court of competent jurisdiction. **Leg.H.** Added Stats 1978 ch 1374 §1.

Prior Law: Former §1670, similar to present CC §1671, was enacted 1872 and repealed Stats 1977 ch 198 §2, operative July 1, 1978.

§1670.5. Unconscionable contract

(a) If the court as a matter of law finds the contract or any clause of the contract to have been unconscionable at the time it was made the court may refuse to enforce the contract, or it may enforce the remainder of the contract without the unconscionable clause, or it may so limit the application of any unconscionable clause as to avoid any unconscionable result.

(b) When it is claimed or appears to the court that the contract or any clause thereof may be unconscionable the parties shall be afforded a reasonable opportunity to present evidence as to its commercial setting, purpose, and effect to aid the court in making the determination. **Leg.H.** Added Stats 1979 ch 819 §3, effective September 19, 1979.

§1670.6. Failure to comply with federal Telemarketing Sales Rule

A contract with a consumer located in California for the purchase of a good or service that is made in connection with a telephone solicitation made in or from outside of California and is primarily for personal, family, or household use, is unlawful if, with respect to that telephone solicitation, the telemarketer is in violation of Section 310.4(a)(6)(i) of, or has not complied with Section 310.5(a)(5) of, the Federal Trade Commission's Telemarketing Sales Rule (16 C.F.R. Part 310), as published in the Federal Register, Volume 68, Number 19, on January 29, 2003. This section shall apply only to those entities subject to, and does not apply to any transaction exempted under Section 310.6 of, the Telemarketing Sales Rule (16 C.F.R. Part 310), as published in the Federal Register, Volume 68, Number 19, on January 29, 2003. **Leg.H.** Added Stats 2003 ch 77 §1 (AB 88).

§1670.7. Deduction from wages for cost of transporting person to United States void

Any provision of a contract that purports to allow a deduction from a person's wages for the cost of emigrating and transporting that person to the United States is void as against public policy. **Leg.H.** Added Stats 2008 ch 258 §1 (AB 1278), effective January 1, 2009. Amended Stats 2009 ch 35 §2 (SB 174), effective January 1, 2010.

§1670.8. Prohibition against provision waiving consumer's right to make statement regarding seller or lessor, or concerning goods or services, in specified consumer contract

(a)(1) A contract or proposed contract for the sale or lease of consumer goods or services may not include a provision waiving the consumer's right to make any statement regarding the seller or lessor or its employees or agents, or concerning the goods or services.

(2) It shall be unlawful to threaten or to seek to enforce a provision made unlawful under this section, or to otherwise penalize a consumer for making any statement protected under this section.

(b) Any waiver of the provisions of this section is contrary to public policy, and is void and unenforceable.

(c) Any person who violates this section shall be subject to a civil penalty not to exceed two thousand five hundred dollars ($2,500) for the first violation, and five thousand dollars ($5,000) for the second and for each subsequent violation, to be assessed and collected in a civil action brought by the consumer, by the Attorney General, or by the district attorney or city attorney of the county or city in which the violation occurred. When collected, the civil penalty shall be payable, as appropriate, to the consumer or to the general fund of whichever governmental entity brought the action to assess the civil penalty.

(d) In addition, for a willful, intentional, or reckless violation of this section, a consumer or public prosecutor may recover a civil penalty not to exceed ten thousand dollars ($10,000).

(e) The penalty provided by this section is not an exclusive remedy, and does not affect any other relief or remedy provided by law. This section shall not be construed to prohibit or limit a person or business that hosts online consumer reviews or comments from removing a statement that is otherwise lawful to remove. **Leg.H.** Added Stats 2014 ch 308 §1 (AB 2365), effective January 1, 2015.

§ 1670.8.5. Provision limiting consumer's ability to file complaint against licensing board

(a) A contract or proposed contract for the provision of a consumer service by a licensee regulated by a licensing board shall not include a provision limiting the consumer's ability to file a complaint with that board or to participate in the board's investigation into the licensee.

(b) Any waiver of the provisions of this section is contrary to public policy, and is void and unenforceable.

(c) For purposes of this section, the following terms apply:

(1) "Consumer service" means any service that is obtained for use primarily for personal, family, or household purposes.

(2) "Licensing board" means any entity described in Section 101 of the Business and Professions Code, the State Bar of California, the Department of Real Estate, or any other state agency that issues a license, certificate, or registration authorizing a person to engage in a business or profession.

(d) Violation of this section by a licensee shall constitute unprofessional conduct subject to discipline by the licensee's licensing board. **Leg.H.** Added Stats 2020 ch 312 §98 (SB 1474), effective January 1, 2021.

§1670.9. Contracts for detention of noncitizens for purposes of civil immigration custody; New contracts prohibited; Renewal or modification of existing contracts prohibited; Requirements for conveyance of land or permit for building used for detention

(a) A city, county, city and county, or local law enforcement agency that does not, as of January 1, 2018, have a contract with the federal government or any federal agency or a private corporation to house or detain noncitizens for purposes of civil immigration custody, shall not, on and after January 1, 2018, enter into a contract with the federal government or any federal agency or a private corporation, to house or detain in a locked detention facility noncitizens for purposes of civil immigration custody.

(b) A city, county, city and county, or local law enforcement agency that, as of January 1, 2018, has an existing contract with the federal government or any federal agency or a private corporation to detain noncitizens for purposes of civil immigration custody, shall not, on and after January 1, 2018, renew or modify that contract in a manner that would expand the maximum number of contract beds that may be utilized to house or detain in a locked detention facility noncitizens for purposes of civil immigration custody.

(c) Any facility that detains a noncitizen pursuant to a contract with a city, county, city and county, or a local law enforcement agency is subject to the California Public Records Act (Division 10 (commencing with Section 7920.000) of Title 1 of the Government Code).

(d) A city, county, city and county, or public agency shall not, on and after January 1, 2018, approve or sign a deed, instrument, or other document related to a conveyance of land or issue a permit for the building or reuse of existing buildings by any private corporation, contractor, or vendor to house or detain noncitizens for purposes of civil immigration proceedings unless the city, county, city and county, or public agency has done both of the following:

(1) Provided notice to the public of the proposed conveyance or permitting action at least 180 days before execution of the conveyance or permit.

(2) Solicited and heard public comments on the proposed conveyance or permit action in at least two separate meetings open to the public. **Leg.H.** Added Stats 2017 ch 494 §2 (SB 29), effective January 1, 2018. Amended Stats 2021 ch 615 §42 (AB 474), effective January 1, 2022.

§1670.10. Prohibition against transactions making transfer of ownership of dog or cat contingent on payments or by way of lease over time

(a)(1) Except as provided in paragraph (2), a contract entered into on or after January 1, 2018, to transfer ownership of a dog or cat in which ownership is contingent upon the making of payments over a period of time subsequent to the transfer of possession of the dog or cat is void as against public policy.

(2) Paragraph (1) shall not apply to payments to repay an unsecured loan for the purchase of the dog or cat.

(b) A contract entered into on or after January 1, 2018, for the lease of a dog or cat that provides for or offers the option of transferring ownership of the dog or cat at the end of the lease term is void as against public policy.

(c) In addition to any other remedies provided by law, the consumer taking possession of a dog or cat transferred under a contract described in paragraph (1) of subdivision (a) or in subdivision (b) shall be deemed the owner of the dog or cat and shall also be entitled to the return of all amounts the consumer paid under the contract. **Leg.H.** Added Stats 2017 ch 761 §1 (AB 1491), effective January 1, 2018.

§1670.11. Contracts; Waiver of right to testify regarding criminal conduct or sexual harassment; Void

Notwithstanding any other law, a provision in a contract or settlement agreement entered into on or after January 1, 2019, that waives a party's right to testify in an administrative, legislative, or judicial proceeding concerning alleged criminal conduct or alleged sexual harassment on the part of the other party to the contract or settlement agreement, or on the part of the agents or employees of the other party, when the party has been required or requested to attend the proceeding pursuant to a court order, subpoena, or written request from an administrative agency or the Legislature, is void and unenforceable. **Leg.H.** Added Stats 2018 ch 949 §1 (AB 3109), effective January 1, 2019. Amended Stats 2019 ch 497 §25 (AB 991), effective January 1, 2020.

§ 1670.12. Exclusive listing agreements

(a) For purposes of this section, the following definitions apply:

(1) "Exclusive listing agreement" means any contract or agreement providing an exclusive right to list or sell residential real property, including:

(A) An exclusive agreement as described in Section 10018.15 or 10018.16 of the Business and Professions Code.

(B) A contract or agreement to enter into any such agreement or arrangement.

(2) "Single-family residential property" means one of the following:

(A) Real property improved with one to four dwelling units.

(B) A unit in a residential stock cooperative, condominium, or planned unit development.

(C) A mobilehome or manufactured home when offered for sale or sold through a real estate licensee pursuant to Section 10131.6 of the Business and Professions Code.

(D) A qualified ownership interest in real property subject to an agreement providing the owner the right to occupy one to four dwelling units on that property.

(b)(1) It is unlawful for an exclusive listing agreement regarding single-family residential property to last longer than 24 months from the date the agreement was made. This paragraph shall not apply to exclusive listing agreements entered into between a real estate broker and a corporation, limited liability company, or partnership.

(2) No exclusive listing agreement shall renew automatically, and any renewal of an exclusive listing agreement shall be in writing and be dated and signed by all parties to the agreement. It is unlawful for a renewal of an exclusive listing agreement subject to paragraph (1) to last longer than 12 months from the date the renewal was made.

(c) It is unlawful to present for recording or filing, or otherwise attempt to record or file, with a county recorder an exclusive listing agreement of any duration or any memoranda or notice of such an agreement.

(d) It is unlawful to enforce or attempt to enforce an exclusive listing agreement that is made, or that is presented for recording or filing with a county recorder, in violation of this section.

(e)(1) An exclusive listing agreement that is made, or that is presented for recording or filing with a county recorder, in violation of this section is void and unenforceable. A homeowner who entered into any such agreement may retain any consideration received thereunder.

(2) A violation of this section constitutes a violation under Section 1770.

(3) Any person licensed pursuant to Division 4 (commencing with Section 10000) of the Business and Professions Code who violates any provision of this section shall be deemed to have violated that person's licensing law. **Leg.H.** Added Stats 2023 ch 577 §2 (AB 1345), effective January 1, 2024.

TITLE 4.1
BUYER-BROKER REPRESENTATION AGREEMENT REQUIREMENTS AND LIMITATIONS

Buyer-broker representation agreement requirements and limitations. § 1670.50.

§ 1670.50. Buyer-broker representation agreement requirements and limitations

(a) A buyer-broker representation agreement shall be executed between a buyer's agent and a buyer as soon as practicable, but no later than the execution of the buyer's offer to purchase real property.

(b) The buyer-broker representation agreement shall include, but not be limited to, terms related to all of the following:

(1) Compensation of the real estate broker.

(2) Services to be rendered.

(3) When compensation is due.

(4) Contract termination.

(c) Prior to execution of a buyer-broker representation agreement between the buyer and the buyers's agent, the buyer's agent shall provide the disclosure form required by Section 2079.14 to the buyer.

(d)(1) A buyer-broker representation agreement shall not last longer than three months from the date the agreement was made. This paragraph shall not apply to a buyer-broker representation agreement entered into between a real estate broker and a corporation, limited liability company, or partnership.

(2) A buyer-broker representation agreement shall not renew automatically, and a renewal of a buyer-broker representation agreement shall be in writing and be dated and signed by all parties to the agreement. A renewal of a buyer-broker representation agreement subject to paragraph (1) shall not last longer than three months from the date the renewal was made.

(3) A buyer-broker representation agreement that is made in violation of this subdivision is void and unenforceable.

(e) A person licensed pursuant to Division 4 (commencing with Section 10000) of the Business and Professions Code who violates this section shall be deemed to have violated that person's licensing law.

(f) For the purposes of this section, "buyer-broker representation agreement" means the same as it is defined in subdivision (p) of Section 2079.13. **Leg.H.** Added Stats 2024 ch 516 §2 (AB 2992), effective January 1, 2025.

TITLE 4.5
LIQUIDATED DAMAGES

Chapter 1. General Provisions.
Chapter 2. Default on Real Property Purchase Contract.

CHAPTER 1
GENERAL PROVISIONS

Liquidated damages provision for breach of contract. §1671.

§1671. Liquidated damages provision for breach of contract

(a) This section does not apply in any case where another statute expressly applicable to the contract prescribes the rules or standard for determining the validity of a provision in the contract liquidating the damages for the breach of the contract.

(b) Except as provided in subdivision (c), a provision in a contract liquidating the damages for the breach of the contract is valid unless the party seeking to invalidate the provision establishes that the provision was unreasonable under the circumstances existing at the time the contract was made.

(c) The validity of a liquidated damages provision shall be determined under subdivision (d) and not under subdivision (b) where the liquidated damages are sought to be recovered from either:

(1) A party to a contract for the retail purchase, or rental, by such party of personal property or services, primarily for the party's personal, family, or household purposes; or

(2) A party to a lease of real property for use as a dwelling by the party or those dependent upon the party for support.

(d) In the cases described in subdivision (c), a provision in a contract liquidating damages for the breach of the contract is void except that the parties to such a contract may agree therein upon an amount which shall be presumed to be the amount of damage sustained by a breach thereof, when, from the nature of the case, it would be impracticable or extremely difficult to fix the actual damage. **Leg.H.** Enacted 1872. Amended Stats 1977 ch 198 §5, operative July 1, 1978.

§1672. [Section repealed 1873–74]

Leg.H. Enacted 1872. Repealed Code Amdts 1873–74 ch 612 §191.

§§1673, 1674. [Sections repealed 1941]

Leg.H. Enacted 1872. Repealed Stats 1941 ch 526 §2 (B & P C §30028). See B & P C §§16600, 16601.

CHAPTER 2
DEFAULT ON REAL PROPERTY PURCHASE CONTRACT

Purchase and sale of residential property; Liquidated damages; Provisions relating to initial sale of newly constructed attached condominium units. §1675.
Validity of liquidated damages provision. §1676.
Requirements for validity of liquidated damages provision. §1677.
More than one payment constituting liquidated damages. §1678.
Application of chapter. §1679.
Right to specific performance. §1680.
Sales contracts excluded. §1681.

§1675. Purchase and sale of residential property; Liquidated damages; Provisions relating to initial sale of newly constructed attached condominium units

(a) As used in this section, "residential property" means real property primarily consisting of a dwelling that meets both of the following requirements:

(1) The dwelling contains not more than four residential units.

(2) At the time the contract to purchase and sell the property is made, the buyer intends to occupy the dwelling or one of its units as his or her residence.

(b) A provision in a contract to purchase and sell residential property that provides that all or any part of a payment made by the buyer shall constitute liquidated damages to the seller upon the buyer's failure to complete the purchase of the property is valid to the extent that payment in the form of cash or check, including a postdated check, is actually made if the provision satisfies the requirements of Sections 1677 and 1678 and either subdivision (c) or (d) of this section.

(c) If the amount actually paid pursuant to the liquidated damages provision does not exceed 3 percent of the purchase price, the provision is valid to the extent that payment is actually made unless the buyer establishes that the amount is unreasonable as liquidated damages.

(d) If the amount actually paid pursuant to the liquidated damages provision exceeds 3 percent of the purchase price, the provision is invalid unless the party seeking to uphold the provision establishes that the amount actually paid is reasonable as liquidated damages.

(e) For the purposes of subdivisions (c) and (d), the reasonableness of an amount actually paid as liquidated damages shall be determined by taking into account both of the following:

(1) The circumstances existing at the time the contract was made.

(2) The price and other terms and circumstances of any subsequent sale or contract to sell and purchase the same property if the sale or contract is made within six months of the buyer's default.

(f)(1) Notwithstanding either subdivision (c) or (d), for the initial sale of newly constructed attached condominium units, as defined pursuant to Section 783, that involves the sale of an attached residential condominium unit located within a structure of 10 or more residential condominium units and the amount actually paid to the seller pursuant to the liquidated damages provision exceeds 3 percent of the purchase price of the residential unit in the transaction both of the following shall occur in the event of a buyer's default:

(A) The seller shall perform an accounting of its costs and revenues related to and fairly allocable to the construction and sale of the residential unit within 60 calendar days after the final close of escrow of the sale of the unit within the structure.

(B) The accounting shall include any and all costs and revenues related to the construction and sale of the residential property and any delay caused by the buyer's default. The seller shall make reasonable efforts to mitigate any damages arising from the default. The seller shall refund to the buyer any amounts previously retained as liquidated damages in excess of the greater of either 3 percent of the originally agreed-upon purchase price of the residential property or the amount of the seller's losses resulting from the buyer's default, as calculated by the accounting.

(2) The refund shall be sent to the buyer's last known address within 90 days after the final close of escrow of the sale or lease of all the residential condominium units within the structure.

(3) If the amount retained by the seller after the accounting does not exceed 3 percent of the purchase price, the amount is valid unless the buyer establishes that the amount is unreasonable as liquidated damages pursuant to subdivision (e).

(4) Subdivision (d) shall not apply to any dispute regarding the reasonableness of any amount retained as liquidated damages pursuant to this subdivision.

(5) Notwithstanding the time periods regarding the performance of the accounting set forth in paragraph (1), if a new qualified buyer has entered into a contract to purchase the residential property in question, the seller shall perform the accounting within 60 calendar days after a new qualified buyer has entered into a contract to purchase.

(6) As used in this subdivision, "structure" means either of the following:

(A) Improvements constructed on a common foundation.

(B) Improvements constructed by the same owner that must be constructed concurrently due to the design characteristics of the improvements or physical characteristics of the property on which the improvements are located.

(7) As used in this subdivision, "new qualified buyer" means a buyer who either:

(A) Has been issued a loan commitment, which satisfies the purchase agreement loan contingency requirement, by an institutional lender to obtain a loan for an amount equal to the purchase price less any downpayment possessed by the buyer.

(B) Has contracted to pay a purchase price that is greater than or equal to the purchase price to be paid by the original buyer.

(g) This section shall become operative on July 1, 2014. **Leg.H.** Added Stats 2008 ch 665 §2 (AB 2020), effective January 1, 2009, operative July 1, 2014.

Prior Law: Former CC §1675, similar to present section, added Stats 1977 ch 198 §7, operative July 1, 1978, amended Stats 2003 ch 434 §3, Stats 2008 ch 665 §1, effective January 1, 2009, inoperative July 1, 2014, repealed January 1, 2015, Stats 2009 ch 140 §25, effective January 1, 2010, inoperative July 1, 2014, repealed January 1, 2015, Stats 2013 ch 352 §51, effective September 26, 2013, operative July 1, 2013, inoperative July 1, 2014, and repealed January 1, 2015, by its own terms.

Former §1675, similar to present B & P C §16602, was enacted 1872 and repealed Stats 1941 ch 526 §2 (B & P C §30028).

Former CC §1675, similar to present section, was added Stats 1977 ch 198 §7, operative July 1, 1978, and became inoperative July 1, 2014, and repealed operative January 1, 2015, by its own provisions. Stats 2013 ch 352 (AB 1317) §51, effective September 26, 2013.

Former CC §1675, similar to present B & P C §16602, was enacted 1872 and repealed Stats 1941 ch 526 §2 (B & P C §30028).

§1676. Validity of liquidated damages provision

Except as provided in Section 1675, a provision in a contract to purchase and sell real property liquidating the damages to the seller if the buyer fails to complete the purchase of the property is valid if it satisfies the requirements of Section 1677 and the requirements of subdivision (b) of Section 1671. **Leg.H.** Added Stats 1977 ch 198 §7, operative July 1, 1978.

Prior Law: Former §1676, similar to present CC §1669, was enacted 1872 and repealed Stats 1977 ch 198 §6, operative July 1, 1978.

§1677. Requirements for validity of liquidated damages provision

A provision in a contract to purchase and sell real property liquidating the damages to the seller if the buyer fails to complete the purchase of the property is invalid unless:

(a) The provision is separately signed or initialed by each party to the contract; and

(b) If the provision is included in a printed contract, it is set out either in at least 10-point bold type or in contrasting red print in at least eight-point bold type. **Leg.H.** Added Stats 1977 ch 198 §7, operative July 1, 1978.

§1678. More than one payment constituting liquidated damages

If more than one payment made by the buyer is to constitute liquidated damages under Section 1675, the amount of any payment after the first payment is valid as liquidated damages only if (1) the total of all such payments satisfies the requirements of Section 1675 and (2) a separate liquidated damages provision satisfying the requirements of Section 1677 is separately signed or initialed by each party to the contract for each such subsequent payment. **Leg.H.** Added Stats 1977 ch 198 §7, operative July 1, 1978.

§1679. Application of chapter

This chapter applies only to a provision for liquidated damages to the seller if the buyer fails to complete the purchase of real property. The validity of any other provision for liquidated damages in a contract to purchase and sell real property shall be determined under Section 1671. **Leg.H.** Added Stats 1977 ch 198 §7, operative July 1, 1978.

§1680. Right to specific performance

Nothing in this chapter affects any right a party to a contract for the purchase and sale of real property may have to obtain specific performance. **Leg.H.** Added States 1977 ch 198 §7, operative July 1, 1978.

§1681. Sales contracts excluded

This chapter does not apply to real property sales contracts as defined in Section 2985. **Leg.H.** Added Stats 1977 ch 198 §7, operative July 1, 1978.

TITLE 5
EXTINCTION OF CONTRACTS

Chapter 1. Contracts, How Extinguished.
Chapter 2. Rescission.
Chapter 2.1. Dating Service Contracts.
Chapter 2.2. Weight Loss Contracts.
Chapter 2.5. Home Equity Sales Contracts.
Chapter 3. Modification and Cancellation.

CHAPTER 1
CONTRACTS, HOW EXTINGUISHED

Contract, how extinguished. §1682.

§1682. Contract, how extinguished

A contract may be extinguished in like manner with any other obligation, and also in the manner prescribed by this title. **Leg.H.** Enacted 1872.

CHAPTER 2
RESCISSION

Rescission extinguishes contract. §1688.
When party to a contract may rescind. §1689.
Rescission in endless chain scheme. §1689.2.
Rescission for dental services contract. §1689.3.
Definitions. §1689.5.
Right to cancel home solicitation contract or offer. §1689.6.
Form of home solicitation contract or offer; Notice of cancellation. §1689.7.
Home solicitation contract or offer for home improvements which provides for lien on real property. §1689.8.
Absence of buyer's right to cancel home solicitation contract or offer if goods affixed to sold or encumbered real property. §1689.9.
Tender of payments to buyer upon cancellation of home solicitation contract or offer. §1689.10.
Tender of goods by buyer upon cancellation of home solicitation contract or offer. §1689.11.
Waiver or confession of judgment invalid. §1689.12.
Applicability to emergency repairs or services. §1689.13.
Home solicitation contract or offer for repair signed following disaster; Void as specified. §1689.14.
Commencement of work; Right of cancellation. §1689.15.
Right to cancel seminar sales solicitation contract or offer. §1689.20.
Form of seminar sales solicitation contract or offer; Notice of cancellation. §1689.21.
Tender of payments to buyer upon cancellation of seminar sales solicitation contract or offer. §1689.22.
Tender goods by buyer upon cancellation of seminar sales solicitation contract or offer of goods received after cancellation. §1689.23.
Definitions; "Seminar sales solicitation contract or offer". §1689.24.
When stipulations against right to rescind do not defeat it. §1690.
Rescission, how effected. §1691.
Relief based upon rescission; Claim for damages. §1692.
Delay in giving notice of rescission; Delay in restoration. §1693.

§1688. Rescission extinguishes contract

A contract is extinguished by its rescission. **Leg.H.** Enacted 1872.

§1689. When party to a contract may rescind

(a) A contract may be rescinded if all the parties thereto consent.

(b) A party to a contract may rescind the contract in the following cases:

(1) If the consent of the party rescinding, or of any party jointly contracting with him, was given by mistake, or obtained through duress, menace, fraud, or undue influence, exercised by or with the connivance of the party as to whom he rescinds, or of any other party to the contract jointly interested with such party.

(2) If the consideration for the obligation of the rescinding party fails, in whole or in part, through the fault of the party as to whom he rescinds.

(3) If the consideration for the obligation of the rescinding party becomes entirely void from any cause.

(4) If the consideration for the obligation of the rescinding party, before it is rendered to him, fails in a material respect from any cause.

(5) If the contract is unlawful for causes which do not appear in its terms or conditions, and the parties are not equally at fault.

(6) If the public interest will be prejudiced by permitting the contract to stand.

(7) Under the circumstances provided for in Sections 39, 1533, 1566, 1785, 1789, 1930 and 2314 of this code, Section 2470 of the Corporations Code, Sections 331, 338, 359, 447, 1904 and 2030 of the Insurance Code or any other statute providing for rescission. **Leg.H.** Enacted 1872. Amended Stats 1931 ch 1070 §10; Stats 1961 ch 589 §1.

§1689.2. Rescission in endless chain scheme

A participant in an endless chain scheme, as defined in Section 327 of the Penal Code, may rescind the contract upon which the scheme is based, and may recover all consideration paid pursuant to the scheme, less any amounts paid or consideration provided to the participant pursuant to the scheme. In addition, the court may, upon motion, award reasonable attorney's fees to a prevailing plaintiff. **Leg.H.** Added Stats 1989 ch 436 §1.

§1689.3. Rescission for dental services contract

Any patient who contracts directly with a dental office or plan for services may rescind the contract or plan until midnight of the third business day after the day on which the patient signs the contract or plan. If services have been provided to the patient, the dental office shall be entitled to compensation for those services. **Leg.H.** Added Stats 1991 ch 596 §2 (AB 1283).

§1689.5. Definitions

As used in Sections 1689.6 to 1689.11, inclusive, and in Section 1689.14, all of the following definitions apply:

(a) "Home solicitation contract or offer" means any contract, whether single or multiple, or any offer which is subject to approval, for the sale, lease, or rental of goods or services or both, made at other than appropriate trade premises in an amount of twenty-five dollars ($25) or more, including any interest or service charges. "Home solicitation contract" does not include any contract under which the buyer has the right to rescind pursuant to Title 1, Chapter 2, Section 125 of the Federal Consumer Credit Protection Act (P.L. 90-321) and the regulations promulgated pursuant thereto.

(b) "Appropriate trade premises," means premises where either the owner or seller normally carries on a business, or where goods are normally offered or exposed for sale in the course of a business carried on at those premises.

(c) "Goods" means tangible chattels bought for use primarily for personal, family, or household purposes, including certificates or coupons exchangeable for these goods, and including goods that, at the time of the sale or subsequently, are to be so affixed to real property as to become a part of the real property whether or not severable therefrom, but does not include any vehicle required to be registered under the Vehicle Code, nor any goods sold with this vehicle if sold under a contract governed by Section 2982, and does not include any mobilehome, as defined in Section 18008 of the Health and Safety Code, nor any goods sold with this mobilehome if either are sold under a contract subject to Section 18036.5 of the Health and Safety Code.

(d) "Services" means work, labor and services, including, but not limited to, services furnished in connection with the repair, restoration, alteration, or improvement of residential premises, or services furnished in connection with the sale or repair of goods as defined in Section 1802.1, and courses of instruction, regardless of the purpose for which they are taken, but does not include the services of attorneys, real estate brokers and salesmen, securities dealers or investment counselors, physicians, optometrists, or dentists, nor financial services offered by banks, savings institutions, credit unions, industrial loan companies, personal property brokers, consumer finance lenders, or commercial finance lenders, organized pursuant to state or federal law, that are not connected with the sale of goods or services, as defined herein, nor the sale of insurance that is not connected with the sale of goods or services as defined herein, nor services in connection with the sale or installation of mobilehomes or of goods sold with a mobilehome if either are sold or installed under a contract subject to Section 18036.5 of the Health and Safety Code, nor services for which the tariffs, rates, charges, costs, or expenses, including in each instance the time sale price, is required by law to be filed with and approved by the federal government or any official, department, division, commission, or agency of the United States or of the state.

(e) "Business day" means any calendar day except Sunday, or the following business holidays: New Year's Day, Washington's Birthday, Memorial Day, Independence Day, Labor Day, Columbus Day, Veterans' Day, Thanksgiving Day, and Christmas Day.

(f) "Senior citizen" means an individual who is 65 years of age or older. **Leg.H.** Added Stats 2005 ch 48 §23 (SB 1113), effective July 18, 2005, operative January 1, 2006. Amended Stats 2020 ch 158 §4 (AB 2471), effective January 1, 2021.

Prior Law: Former CC §1689.5, similar to the present section, was added Stats 1971 ch 375 §1, amended Stats 1972 ch 1415 §2; Stats 1973 ch 554 §1; Stats 1981 ch 975 §1.5; Stats 1985 ch 660 §1; Stats 1986 ch 1229 §2; Stats 1988 ch 1104 §1 Stats 1st Ex Sess 1993-1994 ch 51 §1; Stats 2004 ch 566 §15 (SB 30), operative July 1, 2005; Stats 2005 ch 48 §22, effective July 18, 2005, repealed January 1, 2006.

Former CC §1689.5, similar to the present section, was added Stats 1971 ch 375 §1 and repealed operative January 1, 2006, by its own provisions. Stats 2005 ch 48 (SB 1113) §22, effective July 18, 2005.

§1689.6. Right to cancel home solicitation contract or offer

(a)(1) Except for a contract written pursuant to Section 7151.2 or 7159.10 of the Business and Professions Code, in addition to any other right to revoke an offer, the buyer has the right to cancel a home solicitation contract or offer until midnight of the third business day, or until midnight of the fifth business day if the buyer is a senior citizen, after the day on which the buyer signs an agreement or offer to purchase which complies with Section 1689.7.

(2) In addition to any other right to revoke an offer, the buyer has the right to cancel a home solicitation contract written pursuant to Section 7151.2 of the Business and Professions Code until midnight of the third business day, or until midnight of the fifth business day if the buyer is a senior citizen, after the buyer receives a signed and dated copy of the contract or offer to purchase that complies with Section 1689.7 of this code.

(3)(A) In addition to any other right to revoke an offer, the buyer has the right to cancel a home solicitation contract or offer to purchase written pursuant to Section 7159.10 of the Business and Professions Code, until the buyer receives a signed and dated copy of a service and repair contract that complies with the contract requirements specified in Section 7159.10 of the Business and Professions Code and the work commences.

(B) For any contract written pursuant to Section 7159.10 of the Business and Professions Code, or otherwise presented to the buyer as a service and repair contract, unless all of the conforming requirements listed under subdivision (a) of that section are met, the requirements set forth under Section 7159 of the Business and Professions Code shall be applicable, regardless of the aggregate contract price, including the right to cancel as set forth under this section.

(4) The five-day right to cancel added by the act that amended paragraphs (1) and (2) shall apply to contracts entered into, or offers to purchase conveyed, on or after January 1, 2021.

(b) In addition to any other right to revoke an offer, any buyer has the right to cancel a home solicitation contract or offer for the purchase of a personal emergency response unit until midnight of the seventh business day after the day on which the buyer signs an agreement or offer to purchase which complies with Section 1689.7. This subdivision shall not apply to a personal emergency response unit installed with, and as part of, a home security alarm system subject to the Alarm Company Act (Chapter 11.6 (commencing with Section 7590) of Division 3 of the Business and Professions Code) which has two or more stationary protective devices used to enunciate an intrusion or fire and is installed by an alarm company operator operating under a current license issued pursuant to the Alarm Company Act, which shall instead be subject to subdivision (a).

(c) In addition to any other right to revoke an offer, a buyer has the right to cancel a home solicitation contract or offer for the repair or restoration of residential premises damaged by a disaster that was not void pursuant to Section 1689.14, until midnight of the seventh business day after the buyer signs and dates the contract unless the provisions of Section 1689.15 are applicable.

(d) Cancellation occurs when the buyer gives written notice of cancellation to the seller at the address specified in the agreement or offer.

(e) Notice of cancellation, if given by mail, is effective when deposited in the mail properly addressed with postage prepaid.

(f) Notice of cancellation given by the buyer need not take the particular form as provided with the contract or offer to purchase and, however expressed, is effective if it indicates the intention of the buyer not to be bound by the home solicitation contract or offer.

(g) "Personal emergency response unit," for purposes of this section, means an in-home radio transmitter device or two-way radio device generally, but not exclusively, worn on a neckchain, wrist strap, or clipped to clothing, and connected to a telephone line through which a monitoring station is alerted of an emergency and emergency assistance is summoned. **Leg.H.** Added Stats 2005 ch 48 §25 (SB 1113), effective July 18, 2005, operative January 1, 2006. Amended Stats 2005 ch 385 §11 (AB 316); Stats 2020 ch 158 §5 (AB 2471), effective January 1, 2021.

Prior Law: Former CC §1689.6, similar to present section, was added Stats 1971 ch 375 §2, amended Stats 1973 ch 554 §2; Stats 1991 ch 394 §1; Stats 1992 ch 145 §1; Stats 1st Ex Sess 1993–1994 ch 51 §2; Stats 2004 ch 566 §16, operative July 1, 2005; Stats 2005 ch 48 §24, effective July 18, 2005, repealed January 1, 2006.

Former CC §1689.6, similar to the present section, was added Stats 1971 ch 375 §2 and repealed operative January 1, 2006, by its own provisions. Stats 2005 ch 48 (SB 1113) §24, effective July 18, 2005.

§1689.7. Form of home solicitation contract or offer; Notice of cancellation

(a)(1) Except for contracts written pursuant to Sections 7151.2 and 7159.10 of the Business and Professions Code, in a home solicitation contract or offer, the buyer's agreement or offer to purchase shall be written in the same language, e.g., Spanish, as principally used in the oral sales presentation, shall be dated, shall be signed by the buyer, and except as provided in paragraph (2), shall contain in immediate proximity to the space reserved for the buyer's signature, a conspicuous statement in a size equal to at least 10-point boldface type, as follows:

(A) For a buyer who is a senior citizen: "You, the buyer, may cancel this transaction at any time prior to midnight of the fifth business day after the date of this transaction. See the attached notice of cancellation form for an explanation of this right."

(B) For all other buyers: "You, the buyer, may cancel this transaction at any time prior to midnight of the third business day after the date of this transaction. See the attached notice of cancellation form for an explanation of this right."

(2) The statement required pursuant to this subdivision for a home solicitation contract or offer for the purchase of a personal emergency response unit, as defined in Section 1689.6, that is not installed with and as part of a home security alarm system subject to the Alarm Company Act (Chapter 11.6 (commencing with Section 7590) of Division 3 of the Business and Professions Code) that has two or more stationary protective devices used to enunciate an intrusion or fire and is installed by an alarm company operator operating under a current license issued pursuant to the Alarm Company Act, is as follows: "You, the buyer, may cancel this transaction at any time prior to midnight of the seventh business day after the date of this transaction. See the attached notice of cancellation form for an explanation of this right."

(3) Except for contracts written pursuant to Sections 7151.2 and 7159.10 of the Business and Professions Code, the statement required pursuant to this subdivision for the repair or restoration of residential premises damaged by a disaster pursuant to subdivision (c) of Section 1689.6 is as follows: "You, the buyer, may cancel this transaction at any time prior to midnight of the seventh business day after the date of this transaction. See the attached notice of cancellation form for an explanation of this right."

(4)(A) A home solicitation contract written pursuant to Section 7151.2 of the Business and Professions Code shall be written in the same language, e.g., Spanish, as principally used in the oral sales presentation. The contract, or an attachment to the contract that is subject to Section 7159 of the Business and Professions Code shall include in immediate proximity to the space reserved for the buyer's signature, the following statement in a size equal to at least 12-point boldface type, which shall be dated and signed by the buyer:

Three-Day Right to Cancel

You, the buyer, have the right to cancel this contract within three business days. You may cancel by e-mailing, mailing, faxing, or delivering a written notice to the contractor at the contractor's place of business by midnight of the third business day after you received a signed and dated copy of the contract that includes this notice. Include your name, your address, and the date you received the signed copy of the contract and this notice.

If you cancel, the contractor must return to you anything you paid within 10 days of receiving the notice of cancellation. For your part, you must make available to the contractor at your residence, in substantially as good condition as you received it, any goods delivered to you under this contract or sale. Or, you may, if you wish, comply with the contractor's instructions on how to return the goods at the contractor's expense and risk. If you do make the goods available to the contractor and the contractor does not pick them up within 20 days of the date of your notice of cancellation, you may keep them without any further obligation. If you fail to make the goods available to the contractor, or if you agree to return the goods to the contractor and fail to do so, then you remain liable for performance of all obligations under the contract.

(B) References to "three" and "third" in the statement set forth in subparagraph (A) shall be changed to "five" and "fifth," respectively, for a buyer who is a senior citizen.

(b) The agreement or offer to purchase shall contain on the first page, in a type size no smaller than that generally used in the body of the document, the following: (1) the name and address of the seller to which the notice is to be mailed, and (2) the date the buyer signed the agreement or offer to purchase.

(c)(1) Except for contracts written pursuant to Sections 7151.2 and 7159.10 of the Business and Professions Code, or except as provided in subdivision (d), the agreement or offer to purchase shall be accompanied by a completed form in duplicate, captioned "Notice of Cancellation" which shall be attached to the agreement or offer to purchase and be easily detachable, and which shall contain in type of at least 10-point the following statement written in the same language, e.g., Spanish, as used in the contract:

"Notice of Cancellation"
/enter date of transaction/
_____
(Date)

You may cancel this transaction, without any penalty or obligation, within three business days from the above date.

If you cancel, any property traded in, any payments made by you under the contract or sale, and any negotiable instrument executed by you will be returned within 10 days following receipt by the seller of your cancellation notice, and any security interest arising out of the transaction will be canceled.

If you cancel, you must make available to the seller at your residence, in substantially as good condition as when received, any goods delivered to you under this contract or sale, or you may, if you wish, comply with the instructions of the seller regarding the return shipment of the goods at the seller's expense and risk.

If you do make the goods available to the seller and the seller does not pick them up within 20 days of the date of your notice of cancellation, you may retain or dispose of the goods without any further obligation. If you fail to make the goods available to the seller, or if you agree to return the goods to the seller and fail to do so, then you remain liable for performance of all obligations under the contract.

_____

To cancel this transaction, mail or deliver a signed and dated copy of this cancellation notice, or any other written notice, or send a telegram
to _____ , at _____
/name of seller/ /address of seller's place of business/
not later than midnight of _____
(Date)
I hereby cancel this transaction. _____
(Date)
_____
(Buyer's signature)

(2) The reference to "three" in the statement set forth in paragraph (1) shall be changed to "five" for a buyer who is a senior citizen.

(d) Any agreement or offer to purchase a personal emergency response unit, as defined in Section 1689.6, which is not installed with and as part of a home security alarm system subject to the Alarm Company Act which has two or more stationary protective devices used to enunciate an intrusion or fire and is installed by an alarm company operator operating under a current license issued pursuant to the Alarm Company Act, shall be subject to the requirements of subdivision (c), and shall be accompanied by the "Notice of Cancellation" required by subdivision (c), except that the first paragraph of that notice shall be deleted and replaced with the following paragraph:

You may cancel this transaction, without any penalty or obligation, within seven business days from the above date.

(e) A home solicitation contract written pursuant to Section 7151.2 of the Business and Professions Code for the repair or restoration of residential premises damaged by a disaster that is subject to subdivision (c) of Section 1689.6, shall be written in the same language, e.g., Spanish, as principally used in the oral sales presentation. The contract, or an attachment to the contract that is subject to Section 7159 of the Business and Professions Code shall include, in immediate proximity to the space reserved for the buyer's signature, the following statement in a size equal to at least 12-point boldface type, which shall be signed and dated by the buyer:

Seven-Day Right to Cancel

You, the buyer, have the right to cancel this contract within seven business days. You may cancel by e-mailing, mailing, faxing, or delivering a written notice to the contractor at the contractor's place of business by midnight of the seventh business day after you received a signed and dated copy of the contract that includes this notice. Include your name, your address, and the date you received the signed copy of the contract and this notice.

If you cancel, the contractor must return to you anything you paid within 10 days of receiving the notice of cancellation. For your part, you must make available to the contractor at your residence, in substantially as good condition as you received it, any goods delivered to you under this contract or sale. Or, you may, if you wish, comply with the contractor's instructions on how to return the goods at the contractor's expense and risk. If you do make the goods available to the contractor and the contractor does not pick them up within 20 days of the date of your notice of cancellation, you may keep them without any further obligation. If you fail to make the goods available to the contractor, or if you agree to return the goods to the contractor and fail to do so, then you remain liable for performance of all obligations under the contract.

(f) The seller shall provide the buyer with a copy of the contract or offer to purchase and the attached notice of cancellation, and shall inform the buyer orally of the buyer's right to cancel and the requirement that cancellation be in writing, at the time the home solicitation contract or offer is executed.

(g) Until the seller has complied with this section the buyer may cancel the home solicitation contract or offer.

(h) "Contract or sale" as used in subdivision (c) means "home solicitation contract or offer" as defined by Section 1689.5.

(i) The five-day right to cancel added by the act that added subparagraph (A) to paragraph (1) and subparagraph (B) to paragraph (4) of subdivision (a), and paragraph (2) to subdivision (c) applies to contracts, or offers to purchase conveyed, entered into, on or after January 1, 2021. **Leg.H.** Added Stats 2005 ch 48 §27 (SB 1113), effective July 18, 2005, operative January 1, 2006. Amended Stats 2005 ch 385 §12 (AB 316), effective January 1, 2006; Stats 2020 ch 158 §6 (AB 2471), effective January 1, 2021; Stats 2021 ch 124 §4 (AB 938), effective January 1, 2022.

Prior Law: Former CC §1689.7, similar to the present section, was added Stats 1971 ch 375 §3, amended Stats 1973 ch 544 §3; Stats 1974 ch 175 §1, effective April 17, 1974; Stats 1991 ch 394 §2; Stats 1992 ch 145 §2; Stats 1993 ch 589 §22; Stats 1st Ex Sess 1993–1994 ch 51 §3, effective November 30, 1994; Stats 2004 ch 566 §17, operative July 1, 2005; Stats 2005 ch 48 §26, effective July 18, 2005, repealed January 1, 2006.

Former CC §1689.7, similar to the present section, was added Stats 1971 ch 375 §3 and repealed operative January 1, 2006, by its own provisions. Stats 2005 ch 48 (SB 1113) §26, effective July 18, 2005.

§1689.8. Home solicitation contract or offer for home improvements which provides for lien on real property

(a) Every home solicitation contract or offer for home improvement goods or services which provides for a lien on real property is subject to the provisions of Chapter 1 (commencing with Section 1801) of Title 2 of Part 4 of Division 3.

(b) For purposes of this section, "home improvement goods or services" means goods and services, as defined in Section 1689.5, which are bought in connection with the improvement of real property. Such home improvement goods and services include, but are not limited to, burglar alarms, carpeting, texture coating, fencing, air conditioning or heating equipment, and termite extermination. Home improvement goods include goods which, at the time of sale or subsequently, are to be so affixed to real property as to become a part of real property whether or not severable therefrom. **Leg.H.** Added Stats 1979 ch 1012 §6.

Prior Law: Former §1689.8, relating to form and contents of statement of buyer's right, was added Stats 1971 ch 375 §4 and repealed Stats 1973 ch 554 §4.

§1689.9. Absence of buyer's right to cancel home solicitation contract or offer if goods affixed to sold or encumbered real property

Where the goods sold under any home solicitation contract are so affixed to real property as to become a part thereof, whether or not severable therefrom, the buyer shall not have the right to cancel as provided in Section 1689.6 or Section 1689.7 if, subsequent to his signing such contract, he has sold or encumbered such real property to a bona fide purchaser or encumbrancer who was not a party to such sale of goods or to any loan agreement in connection therewith. **Leg.H.** Added Stats 1971 ch 375 §5.

§1689.10. Tender of payments to buyer upon cancellation of home solicitation contract or offer

(a) Except as provided in Sections 1689.6 to 1689.11, inclusive, within 10 days after a home solicitation contract or offer has been canceled, the seller must tender to the buyer any payments made by the buyer and any note or other evidence of indebtedness.

(b) If the downpayment includes goods traded in, the goods must be tendered in substantially as good condition as when received.

(c) Until the seller has complied with the obligations imposed by Sections 1689.7 to 1689.11, inclusive, the buyer may retain possession of goods delivered to him by the seller and has a lien on the goods for any recovery to which he is entitled. **Leg.H.** Added Stats 1971 ch 375 §6. Amended Stats 1973 ch 554 §5.

§1689.11. Tender of goods by buyer upon cancellation of home solicitation contract or offer

(a) Except as provided in subdivision (c) of Section 1689.10, within 20 days after a home solicitation contract or offer has been canceled, the buyer, upon demand, must tender to the seller any goods delivered by the seller pursuant to the sale or offer, but he is not obligated to tender at any place other than his own address. If the seller fails to demand possession of goods within 20 days after cancellation, the goods become the property of the buyer without obligation to pay for them.

(b) The buyer has a duty to take reasonable care of the goods in his possession both prior to cancellation and during the 20-day period following. During the 20-day period after cancellation, except for the buyer's duty of care, the goods are at the seller's risk.

(c) If the seller has performed any services pursuant to a home solicitation contract or offer prior to its cancellation, the seller is entitled to no compensation. If the seller's services result in the alteration of property of the buyer, the seller shall restore the property to substantially as good condition as it was at the time the services were rendered. **Leg.H.** Added Stats 1971 ch 375 §7. Amended Stats 1973 ch 554 §6.

§1689.12. Waiver or confession of judgment invalid

Any waiver or confession of judgment of the provisions of Sections 1689.5 to 1689.11, inclusive, shall be deemed contrary to public policy and shall be void and unenforceable. **Leg.H.** Added Stats 1971 ch 375 §8. Amended Stats 1973 ch 554 §7.

§1689.13. Applicability to emergency repairs or services

Sections 1689.5, 1689.6, 1689.7, 1689.10, 1689.12, and 1689.14 do not apply to a contract that meets all of the following requirements:

(a) The contract is initiated by the buyer or the buyer's agent or insurance representative.

(b) The contract is executed in connection with making of emergency or immediately necessary repairs that are necessary for the immediate protection of persons or real or personal property.

(c)(1) The buyer gives the seller a separate statement that is dated and signed that describes the situation that requires immediate remedy, and expressly acknowledges and waives the right to cancel the sale within three, five, or seven business days, whichever applies.

(2) The waiver of the five-day right to cancel added by the act that amended paragraph (1) shall apply to contracts entered into, or offers to purchase conveyed, on or after January 1, 2021. **Leg.H.** Added Stats 2005 ch 48 §29 (SB 1113), effective July 18, 2005, operative January 1, 2006. Amended Stats 2020 ch 158 §7 (AB 2471), effective January 1, 2021.

Prior Law: Former CC §1689.13, similar to the present section, was added Stats 1971 ch 375 §9, amended Stats 1973 ch 554 §8, Stats 1st Ex Sess 1993–1994 ch 51 §4 (AB 57X) and repealed Stats 2004 ch 566 §18.

Former CC §1689.13, similar to the present section, was added Stats 2004 ch 566 §19, operative July 1, 2005, amended Stats 2005 ch 48 §28, effective July 18, 2005, and repealed January 1, 2006.

Former CC §1689.13, similar to the present section, was added Stats 2004 ch 566 §19, operative July 1, 2005, and repealed operative January 1, 2006, by its own provisions. Stats 2005 ch 48 (SB 1113) §28, effective July 18, 2005.

Former CC §1689.13, similar to the present section, was added Stats 1971 ch 375 §9, and repealed Stats 2004 ch 566 §18.

§1689.14. Home solicitation contract or offer for repair signed following disaster; Void as specified

(a) Any home solicitation contract or offer for the repair or restoration of residential premises signed by the buyer on or after the date on which a disaster causes damage to the residential premises, but not later than midnight of the seventh business day after this date, shall be void, unless the buyer or his or her agent or insurance representative solicited the contract or offer at the appropriate trade premises of the seller. Any contract covered by this subdivision shall not be void if solicited by the buyer or his or her agent or insurance representative regardless of where the contract is made. For purposes of this section, buyer solicitation includes a telephone call from the buyer to the appropriate trade premises of the seller whether or not the call is in response to a prior home solicitation.

(b) As used in this section and Section 1689.6, "disaster" means an earthquake, flood, fire, hurricane, riot, storm, tidal wave, or other similar sudden or catastrophic occurrence for which a state of emergency has been declared by the President of the United States or the Governor or for which a local emergency has been declared by the executive officer or governing body of any city, county, or city and county. **Leg.H.** Added Stats 1994 1st Ex Sess 1993–1994 ch 51 §5 (ABX1-57). Amended Stats 1995 ch 123 §1 (AB 1610), effective July 18, 1995.

§1689.15. Commencement of work; Right of cancellation

Notwithstanding any other provision of law, a contractor who is duly licensed pursuant to Chapter 9 (commencing with Section 7000) of Division 3 of the Business and Professions Code may commence work on a service and repair project as soon as the buyer receives a signed and dated copy of a service and repair contract that meets all of the contract requirements specified in Section 7159.10 of the Business and Professions Code. The buyer retains any right of cancellation applicable to home solicitations under Sections 1689.5 to 1689.14, inclusive, until such time as the buyer receives a signed and dated copy of a service and repair contract that meets all of the contract requirements specified in Section 7159.10 of the Business and Professions Code and the licensee in fact commences that project, at which time any cancellation rights provided in Sections 1689.5 to 1689.14, inclusive, are extinguished by operation of law. **Leg.H.** Added Stats 2004 ch 566 §20 (SB 30), operative July 1, 2005. Amended Stats 2005 ch 48 §30 (SB 1113), effective July 18, 2005, operative January 1, 2006, ch 385 §13 (AB 316).

§1689.20. Right to cancel seminar sales solicitation contract or offer

(a)(1) In addition to any other right to revoke an offer, the buyer has the right to cancel a seminar sales solicitation contract or offer until midnight of the third business day, or until midnight of the fifth business day if the buyer is a senior citizen, after the day on which the buyer signs an agreement or offer to purchase which complies with Section 1689.21.

(2) The five-day right to cancel added by the act that amended paragraph (1) shall apply to contracts entered into, or offers to purchase conveyed, on or after January 1, 2021.

(b) Cancellation occurs when the buyer gives written notice of cancellation to the seller at the address specified in the agreement or offer.

(c) Notice of cancellation, if given by mail, is effective when deposited in the mail properly addressed with postage prepaid.

(d) Notice of cancellation given by the buyer need not take the particular form as provided with the contract or offer to purchase and, however expressed, is effective if it indicates the intention of the buyer not to be bound by the seminar sales solicitation contract or offer. **Leg.H.** Added Stats 1989 ch 724 §1. Amended Stats 2020 ch 158 §8 (AB 2471), effective January 1, 2021.

1989 Note: This act is declaratory of existing law with respect to contracts made at seminars held at locations other than appropriate trade premises, as defined in subdivision (b) of Section 1689.5 of the Civil Code. Stats 1989 ch 724 §6.

§1689.21. Form of seminar sales solicitation contract or offer; Notice of cancellation

(a) In a seminar sales solicitation contract or offer, the buyer's agreement or offer to purchase shall be written in the same language, e.g., Spanish, as principally used in the oral sales presentation, shall be dated, signed by the buyer, and shall contain in immediate proximity to the space reserved for the buyer's signature, a conspicuous statement in a size equal to at least 10-point bold type, as follows:

(1) For a buyer who is a senior citizen: "You, the buyer, may cancel this transaction at any time prior to midnight of the fifth business day after the date of this transaction. See the attached notice of cancellation form for an explanation of this right."

(2) For all other buyers: "You, the buyer, may cancel this transaction at any time prior to midnight of the third business day after the date of this transaction. See the attached notice of cancellation form for an explanation of this right."

(b) The agreement or offer to purchase shall contain on the first page, in a type size no smaller than that generally used in the body of the document, each of the following:

(1) The name and address of the seller to which the notice is to be mailed.

(2) The date the buyer signed the agreement or offer to purchase.

(c)(1) The agreement or offer to purchase shall be accompanied by a completed form in duplicate, captioned "Notice of Cancellation," which shall be attached to the agreement or offer to purchase and be easily detachable, and which shall contain in type of at least 10-point, the following statement written in the same language, e.g., Spanish, as used in the contract:

"Notice of Cancellation"

/enter date of transaction/

_____

(Date)

You may cancel this transaction, without any penalty or obligation, within three business days from the above date.

If you cancel, any property traded in, any payments made by you under the contract or sale, and any negotiable instrument executed by you will be returned within 10 days following receipt by the seller of your cancellation notice, and any security interest arising out of the transaction will be canceled.

If you cancel, you must make available to the seller at your residence, in substantially as good condition as when received, any goods delivered to you under this contract or sale, or you may, if you wish, comply with the instructions of the seller regarding the return shipment of the goods at the seller's expense and risk. If you do make the goods available to the seller and the seller does not pick them up within 20 days of the date of your notice of cancellation, you may retain or dispose of the goods without any further obligation. If you fail to make the goods available to the seller, or if you agree to return the goods to the seller and fail to do so, then you remain liable for performance of all obligations under the contract.

To cancel this transaction, mail or deliver a signed and dated copy of this cancellation notice, or any other written notice, or send a telegram to _____, at _____

/name of seller/   /address of seller's place of business/

not later than midnight of _____

(Date)

I hereby cancel this transaction. _____

(Date)

_____

(Buyer's signature)

(2) The reference to "three" in the statement set forth in paragraph (1) shall be changed to "five" for a buyer who is a senior citizen.

(d) The seller shall provide the buyer with a copy of the contract or offer to purchase and the attached notice of cancellation, and shall inform the buyer orally of the buyer's right to cancel at the time the seminar sales solicitation contract or offer is executed.

(e) Until the seller has complied with this section, the buyer may cancel the seminar sales solicitation contract or offer.

(f) "Contract or sale" as used in subdivision (c), means "seminar sales solicitation contract or offer" as defined by Section 1689.24.

(g) The five-day right to cancel added by the act that added paragraph (1) to subdivision (a) and added paragraph (2) to subdivision (c) shall apply to contracts entered into or offers to purchase conveyed on or after January 1, 2021. **Leg.H.** Added Stats 1989 ch 724 §2. Amended Stats 2020 ch 158 §9 (AB 2471), effective January 1, 2021.

1989 Note: See the note to CC §1689.20.

§1689.22. Tender of payments to buyer upon cancellation of seminar sales solicitation contract or offer

(a) Except as provided in Sections 1689.20 and 1689.21, within 10 days after a seminar sales solicitation contract or offer has been cancelled, the seller must tender to the buyer any payments made by the buyer and any note or other evidence of indebtedness.

(b) If the downpayment includes goods traded in, the goods must be tendered in substantially as good condition as when received.

(c) Until the seller has complied with the obligations imposed by Sections 1689.20 and 1689.21, the buyer may retain possession of goods delivered to him or her by the seller and has a lien on the goods for any recovery to which he or she is entitled. **Leg.H.** Added Stats 1989 ch 724 §3.

1989 Note: See the note to CC §1689.20.

§1689.23. Tender goods by buyer upon cancellation of seminar sales solicitation contract or offer of goods received after cancellation

(a) Except as provided in subdivision (c) of Section 1689.22, within 20 days after a seminar sales solicitation contract or offer has been canceled, the buyer, upon demand, must tender to the seller any goods delivered by the seller pursuant to the sale or offer, but he or she is not obligated to tender at any place other than his or her own address. If the seller fails to demand possession of goods within 20 days after cancellation, the goods become the property of the buyer without obligation to pay for them.

(b) The buyer has a duty to take reasonable care of the goods in his or her possession, both prior to cancellation and during the 20-day period following. During the 20-day period after cancellation, except for the buyer's duty of care, the goods are at the seller's risk.

(c) If the seller has performed any services pursuant to a seminar sales solicitation contract or offer prior to its cancellation, the seller is entitled to no compensation. If the seller's services result in the alteration of property of the buyer, the seller shall restore the property to substantially as good condition as it was at the time the services were rendered. **Leg.H.** Added Stats 1989 ch 724 §4.

1989 Note: See the note to CC §1689.20.

§1689.24. Definitions; "Seminar sales solicitation contract or offer"

As used in Sections 1689.20 to 1689.23, inclusive:

(a) "Seminar sales solicitation contract or offer" means any contract, whether single or multiple, or any offer which is subject to approval, for the sale, lease, or rental of goods or services or both, made using selling techniques in a seminar setting in an amount of twenty-five dollars ($25) or more, including any interest or service charges. "Seminar sales solicitation contract" does not include any contract under which the buyer has the right to rescind pursuant to Title 1, Chapter 2, Section 125 of the Federal Consumer Credit Protection Act (Public Law 90-321) and the regulations promulgated pursuant thereto or any contract which contains a written and dated statement signed by the prospective buyer stating that the negotiation between the parties was initiated by the prospective buyer.

(b) "Seminar setting" means premises other than the residence of the buyer.

(c) "Goods" means tangible chattels bought for use primarily for personal, family, or household purposes, including certificates or coupons exchangeable for these goods, and including goods which, at the time of the sale or subsequently, are to be so affixed to real property as to become a part of the real property whether or not severable therefrom, but does not include any vehicle required to be registered under the Vehicle Code, nor any goods sold with a vehicle if sold under a contract governed by Section 2982, and does not include any mobilehome, as defined in Section 18008 of the Health and Safety Code, nor any goods sold with a mobilehome if either are sold under a contract subject to Section 18036.5 of the Health and Safety Code.

(d) "Services" means work, labor and services, including, but not limited to, services furnished in connection with the repair, alteration, or improvement of residential premises, or services furnished in connection with the sale or repair of goods as defined in Section 1802.1, and courses of instruction, regardless of the purpose for which they are taken, but does not include the services of attorneys, real estate brokers and salesmen, securities dealers or investment counselors, physicians, optometrists, or dentists, nor financial services offered by banks, savings institutions, credit unions, industrial loan companies, personal property brokers, consumer finance lenders, or commercial finance lenders, organized pursuant to state or federal law, which are not connected with the sale of goods or services, as defined herein, nor the sale of insurance which is not connected with the sale of goods or services as defined herein, nor services in connection with the sale or installation of mobilehomes or of goods sold with a mobilehome if either are sold or installed under a contract subject to Section 18036.5 of the Health and Safety Code, nor services for which the tariffs, rates, charges, costs, or expenses, including in each instance the time sale price, is required by law to be filed with and approved by the federal government or any official, department, division, commission, or agency of the United States or of the State of California.

(e) "Business day" means any calendar day except Sunday, or the following business holidays: New Year's Day, Washington's Birthday, Memorial Day, Independence Day, Labor Day, Columbus Day, Veterans' Day, Thanksgiving Day, and Christmas Day.

(f) "Senior citizen" means an individual who is 65 years of age or older. **Leg.H.** Added Stats 1989 ch 724 §5. Amended Stats 2020 ch 158 §10 (AB 2471), effective January 1, 2021.

1989 Note: See the note to CC §1689.20.

§1690. When stipulations against right to rescind do not defeat it

A stipulation that errors of description shall not avoid a contract, or shall be the subject of compensation, or both, does not take away the right of rescission for fraud, nor for mistake, where such mistake is in a matter essential to the inducement of the contract, and is not capable of exact and entire compensation. **Leg.H.** Enacted 1872.

§1691. Rescission, how effected

Subject to Section 1693, to effect a rescission a party to the contract must, promptly upon discovering the facts which entitle him to rescind if he is free from duress, menace, undue influence or disability and is aware of his right to rescind:

(a) Give notice of rescission to the party as to whom he rescinds; and

(b) Restore to the other party everything of value which he has received from him under the contract or offer to restore the same upon condition that the other party do likewise, unless the latter is unable or positively refuses to do so.

When notice of rescission has not otherwise been given or an offer to restore the benefits received under the contract has not otherwise been made, the service of a pleading in an action or proceeding that seeks relief based on rescission shall be deemed to be such notice or offer or both. **Leg.H.** Enacted 1872. Amended Stats 1961 ch 589 §2.

§1692. Relief based upon rescission; Claim for damages

When a contract has been rescinded in whole or in part, any party to the contract may seek relief based upon such rescission by (a) bringing an action to recover any money or thing owing to him by any other party to the contract as a consequence of such rescission or for any other relief to which he may be entitled under the circumstances or (b) asserting such rescission by way of defense or cross-complaint.

If in an action or proceeding a party seeks relief based upon rescission and the court determines that the contract has not been rescinded, the court may grant any party to the action any other relief to which he may be entitled under the circumstances.

A claim for damages is not inconsistent with a claim for relief based upon rescission. The aggrieved party shall be awarded complete relief, including restitution of benefits, if any, conferred by him as a result of the transaction and any consequential damages to which he is entitled; but such relief shall not include duplicate or inconsistent items of recovery.

If in an action or proceeding a party seeks relief based upon rescission, the court may require the party to whom such relief is granted to make any compensation to the other which justice may require and may otherwise in its judgment adjust the equities between the parties. **Leg.H.** Added Stats 1961 ch 589 §3. Amended Stats 1971 ch 244 §1.

§1693. Delay in giving notice of rescission; Delay in restoration

When relief based upon rescission is claimed in an action or proceeding, such relief shall not be denied because of delay in giving notice of rescission unless such delay has been substantially prejudicial to the other party.

A party who has received benefits by reason of a contract that is subject to rescission and who in an action or proceeding seeks relief based upon rescission shall not be denied relief because of a delay in restoring or in tendering restoration of such benefits before judgment unless such delay has been substantially prejudicial to the other party; but the court may make a tender of restoration a condition of its judgment. **Leg.H.** Added Stats 1961 ch 589 §4.

CHAPTER 2.1
DATING SERVICE CONTRACTS

"Dating service contract"; "Online dating service". §1694.
Right to cancel dating service contract; Notice of cancellation. §1694.1.
Dating service requirements; Notice to buyer of right to cancel. §1694.2.

Dating service contract provision on death, disability, or relocation of buyer; Online dating services safety provisions. §1694.3.

Validity and enforceability of dating service contract; Action for damages; Refunds. §1694.4.

§1694. "Dating service contract"; "Online dating service"

(a) As used in this chapter, a dating service contract is any contract with any organization that offers dating, matrimonial, or social referral services by any of the following means:

(1) An exchange of names, telephone numbers, addresses, and statistics.

(2) A photograph or video selection process.

(3) Personal introductions provided by the organization at its place of business.

(4) A social environment provided by the organization intended primarily as an alternative to other singles' bars or club-type environments.

(b) As used in this chapter, an "online dating service" means any person or organization engaged in the business of offering dating, matrimonial, or social referral services online, where the services are offered primarily online, such as by means of an Internet Web site or a mobile application. **Leg.H.** Added Stats 1989 ch 138 §1. Amended Stats 2017 ch 578 §1 (AB 314), effective January 1, 2018.

§1694.1. Right to cancel dating service contract; Notice of cancellation

(a) In addition to any other right to revoke an offer, the buyer has the right to cancel a dating service contract or offer, until midnight of the third business day after the day on which the buyer signs an agreement or offer to purchase those services.

(b)(1) Cancellation occurs when the buyer gives written notice of cancellation by mail, telegram, or delivery to the seller at the address specified in the agreement or offer.

(2) In the case of a dating service contract with an online dating service, cancellation occurs when the buyer gives written notice of cancellation by email to an email address provided by the seller. Additional electronic means of cancellation may be provided by the agreement or offer.

(c) Notice of cancellation, if given by mail, is effective when deposited in the mail properly addressed with postage prepaid.

(d) Notice of cancellation given by the buyer need not take the particular form as provided in the contract or offer to purchase and, however expressed, is effective if it indicates the intention of the buyer not to be bound by the dating service contract.

(e) All moneys paid pursuant to any contract for dating services shall be refunded within 10 days of receipt of the notice of cancellation.

(f) The buyer may notify the dating service of his or her intent to cancel the contract within the three-day period specified in this section and stop the processing of a credit card voucher or check by telephone notification to the dating service. However, this does not negate the obligation of the buyer to cancel the contract by mail, email or other electronic means, telegram, or delivery as required pursuant to this section. **Leg.H.** Added Stats 1989 ch 138 §1. Amended Stats 1993 ch 359 §1 (AB 1323); Stats 2017 ch 578 §2 (AB 314), effective January 1, 2018.

§1694.2. Dating service requirements; Notice to buyer of right to cancel

(a) A dating service contract shall be in writing, which, in the case of an online dating service contract, may be an electronic writing made available for viewing online. A copy of the contract shall be provided to the buyer at the time he or she signs the contract, except that an online dating service shall not be required to provide a copy of the contract where (1) the contract is available through a direct link that is provided in a clear and conspicuous manner on the Internet Web site page where the buyer provides consent to the agreement and, (2) upon request by the buyer, the online dating service provides a PDF format or retainable digital copy of the contract.

(b)(1) Every dating service contract shall contain on its face, and in close proximity to the space reserved for the signature of the buyer, a conspicuous statement in a size equal to at least 10-point boldface type, as follows:

"You, the buyer, may cancel this agreement, without any penalty or obligation, at any time prior to midnight of the original contract seller's third business day following the date of this contract, excluding Sundays and holidays. To cancel this agreement, mail or deliver a signed and dated notice, or send a telegram which states that you, the buyer, are canceling this agreement, or words of similar effect. This notice shall be sent to:

_____
(Name of the business that sold you the contract)

_____
(Address of the business that sold you the contract)."

(2) Paragraph (1) shall not otherwise apply to an online dating service if the online dating service contract includes the statement in paragraph (1) in a clear and conspicuous manner in a stand-alone first paragraph of the contract.

(c)(1) The dating service contract shall contain on the first page, in a type size no smaller than that generally used in the body of the document, the name and address of the dating service operator to which the notice of cancellation is to be mailed, and the date the buyer signed the contract.

(2) In the case of an online dating service contract, if the name of the dating service operator and the email address that can be used for cancellation appears in the first paragraph of the contract, in a type size no smaller than that generally used in the body of the document, the other requirements of paragraph (1) shall not apply.

(d)(1) No dating service contract shall require payments or financing by the buyer over a period in excess of two years from the date the contract is entered into, nor shall the term of any such contract be measured by the life of the buyer. However, the services to be rendered to the buyer under the contract may extend over a period beginning within six months and ending within three years of the date the contract is entered into.

(2) In the case of an online dating service contract, if the initial term is one year or less, and subsequent terms are one year or less, paragraph (1) shall not apply.

(e) If a dating service contract is not in compliance with this chapter, the buyer may, at any time, cancel the contract. **Leg.H.** Added Stats 1989 ch 138 §1. Amended Stats 1993 ch 359 §2 (AB 1323); Stats 2017 ch 578 §3 (AB 314), effective January 1, 2018.

§1694.3. Dating service contract provision on death, disability, or relocation of buyer; Online dating services safety provisions

(a) Every dating service contract shall contain language providing that:

(1) If by reason of death or disability the buyer is unable to receive all services for which the buyer has contracted, the buyer and the buyer's estate may elect to be relieved of the obligation to make payments for services other than those received before death or the onset of disability, except as provided in paragraph (4).

(2) If the buyer has prepaid any amount for services, so much of the amount prepaid that is allocable to services that the buyer has not received shall be promptly refunded to the buyer or his or her representative.

(3) "Disability" means a condition which precludes the buyer from physically using the services specified in the contract during the term of disability and the condition is verified in writing by a physician designated and remunerated by the buyer. The written verification of the physician shall be presented to the seller.

(4) If the physician determines that the duration of the disability will be less than six months, the seller may extend the term of the contract for a period of six months at no additional charge to the buyer in lieu of cancellation.

(b)(1) If the buyer relocates his or her primary residence further than 50 miles from the dating service office and is unable to transfer the contract to a comparable facility, the buyer may elect to be relieved of the obligation to make payment for services other than those received prior to that relocation, and if the buyer has prepaid any amount for dating services, so much of the amount prepaid that is allocable to services that the buyer has not received shall be promptly refunded to the buyer. A buyer who elects to be relieved of further obligation pursuant to this subdivision may be charged a predetermined fee not to exceed one hundred dollars ($100) or, if more than half the life of the contract has expired, a predetermined fee not to exceed fifty dollars ($50).

(2) Paragraph (1) shall not apply to online dating services that are generally available to users on a regional, national, or global basis.

(c) In addition to any other requirements, online dating services shall also maintain both of the following features:

(1) A reference or link to dating safety awareness information that includes, at a minimum, a list or descriptions of safety measures reasonably aimed at increasing awareness of safer dating practices.

(2) A means to report issues or concerns relating to the behavior of other users of the online dating service arising out of their use of the service. **Leg.H.** Added Stats 1989 ch 138 §1. Amended Stats 2017 ch 578 §4 (AB 314), effective January 1, 2018.

§1694.4. Validity and enforceability of dating service contract; Action for damages; Refunds

(a) Any contract for dating services which does not comply with this chapter is void and unenforceable.

(b) Any contract for dating services entered into under willful and fraudulent or misleading information or advertisements of the seller is void and unenforceable.

(c) Any buyer injured by a violation of this chapter may bring an action for the recovery of damages in a court of competent jurisdiction. Judgment may be entered for three times the amount at which the actual damages are assessed. Reasonable attorney fees may be awarded to the prevailing party.

(d) Notwithstanding the provisions of any contract to the contrary, whenever the contract price is payable in installments and the buyer is relieved from making further payments or entitled to a refund under this chapter, the buyer shall be entitled to receive a refund or refund credit of that portion of the cash price as is allocable to the services not actually received by the buyer. The refund of any finance charge shall be computed according to the "sum of the balance method," also known as the "Rule of 78."

(e) Any waiver by the buyer of this chapter is void and unenforceable. **Leg.H.** Added Stats 1989 ch 138 §1.

CHAPTER 2.2
WEIGHT LOSS CONTRACTS

"Weight loss contract". §1694.5.
Right to cancel weight loss contract; Notice to seller of cancellation. §1694.6.
Weight loss contract requirements; Notice to buyer of right to cancel. §1694.7.
Weight loss contract provision on death, disability, or relocation of buyer. §1694.8.
Validity and enforceability of weight loss contract; Action for damages; Refunds. §1694.9.

§1694.5. "Weight loss contract"

(a) As used in this chapter, a weight loss contract is a contract with any weight loss program or center that offers any of the following:

(1) Instruction, counseling, supervision, or assistance in weight reduction, body shaping, diet, and eating habits, by persons who are not licensed health care professionals.

(2) Use of facilities of a weight loss center for any of the purposes specified in paragraph (1).

(3) Membership in any group, club, association, or organization formed for any of the purposes specified in paragraph (1).

(4) Prepackaged, or premeasured "diet foods" provided by the weight loss program or center.

(b) This chapter does not apply to any contract for health studio services as defined in Section 1812.81. **Leg.H.** Added Stats 1989 ch 138 §2.

§1694.6. Right to cancel weight loss contract; Notice to seller of cancellation

(a) In addition to any other right to revoke an offer, the buyer has the right to cancel a weight loss contract or offer until midnight of the third business day after the day on which the buyer signs an agreement or offer to purchase those services.

(b) Cancellation occurs when the buyer gives written notice of cancellation by mail, telegram, or delivery to the seller at the address specified in the agreement or offer.

(c) Notice of cancellation, if given by mail, is effective when deposited in the mail properly addressed with postage prepaid.

(d) Notice of cancellation given by the buyer need not take the particular form as provided in the contract or offer to purchase and, however expressed, is effective if it indicates the intention of the buyer not to be bound by the weight loss contract.

(e) All moneys paid pursuant to any weight loss contract shall be refunded within 10 days of receipt of the notice of cancellation.

(f) The buyer may notify the weight loss program of his or her intent to cancel the contract within the three-day period specified in this section and stop the processing of a credit card voucher or check by telephone notification to the weight loss program. However, this does not negate the obligation of the buyer to cancel the contract by mail, telegram, or delivery as required pursuant to this section. **Leg.H.** Added Stats 1989 ch 138 §2. Amended Stats 1993 ch 359 §3 (AB 1323).

§1694.7. Weight loss contract requirements; Notice to buyer of right to cancel

(a) A weight loss contract shall be in writing. A copy of the contract shall be provided to the buyer at the time he or she signs the contract.

(b) Every weight loss contract shall contain on its face, and in close proximity to the space reserved for the signature of the buyer, a conspicuous statement in a size equal to at least 10-point boldface type, as follows:

"You, the buyer, may cancel this agreement, without any penalty or obligation, at any time prior to midnight of the original contract seller's third business day following the date of this contract, excluding Sundays and holidays. To cancel this agreement, mail or deliver a signed and dated notice, or send a telegram which states that you, the buyer, are canceling this agreement, or words of similar effect. This notice shall be sent to:

_____
(Name of the business that sold you the contract)

_____
(Address of the business that sold you the contract)."

(c) The weight loss contract shall contain on the first page, in a type size no smaller than that generally used in the body of the document, the name and address of the weight loss program operator to which the notice of cancellation is to be mailed; and the date the buyer signed the contract.

(d) No weight loss contract shall require payments or financing by the buyer over a period in excess of two years from the date the contract is entered into, nor shall the term of any such contract be measured by the life of the buyer. The services to be rendered to the buyer under the contract shall not extend for more than three years after the date the contract is entered into.

(e) If a weight loss contract is not in compliance with this chapter, the buyer may, at any time, cancel the contract. **Leg.H.** Added Stats 1989 ch 138 §2. Amended Stats 1993 ch 359 §4 (AB 1323).

§1694.8. Weight loss contract provision on death, disability, or relocation of buyer

Every weight loss contract shall contain language providing that:

(a) If by reason of death or disability the buyer is unable to receive all services for which the buyer has contracted, the buyer and the buyer's estate may elect to be relieved of the obligation to make payments for services other than those received before death or the onset of disability, except as provided in paragraph (3).

(1) If the buyer has prepaid any amount for services, so much of the amount prepaid that is allocable to services that the buyer has not received shall be promptly refunded to the buyer or his or her representative.

(2) "Disability" means a condition which precludes the buyer from physically using the services specified in the contract during the term of disability and the condition is verified in writing by a physician designated and remunerated by the buyer. The written verification of the physician shall be presented to the seller.

(3) If the physician determines that the duration of the disability will be less than six months, the seller may extend the term of the contract for a period of six months at no additional charge to the buyer in lieu of cancellation.

(b) If the buyer relocates his or her primary residence further than 50 miles from the weight loss center and is unable to transfer the contract to a comparable facility, the buyer may elect to be relieved of the obligation to make payment for services other than those received prior to that relocation, and if the buyer has prepaid any amount for weight loss services, so much of the amount prepaid that is allocable to services that the buyer has not received shall be promptly refunded to the buyer. A buyer who elects to be relieved of further obligation pursuant to this subdivision may be charged a predetermined fee not to exceed one hundred dollars ($100) or, if more than half the life of the contract has expired, a predetermined fee not to exceed fifty dollars ($50). **Leg.H.** Added Stats 1989 ch 138 §2.

§1694.9. Validity and enforceability of weight loss contract; Action for damages; Refunds

(a) Any contract for weight loss services which does not comply with this chapter is void and unenforceable.

(b) Any contract for weight loss services entered into under willful and fraudulent or misleading information or advertisements of the seller is void and unenforceable.

(c) Any buyer injured by a violation of this chapter may bring an action for the recovery of damages in a court of competent jurisdiction. Judgment may be entered for three times the amount at which the actual damages are assessed if the violation is willful. Reasonable attorney fees may be awarded to the prevailing party.

(d) Notwithstanding the provisions of any contract to the contrary, whenever the contract price is payable in installments and the buyer is relieved from making further payments or entitled to a refund under this chapter, the buyer shall be entitled to receive a refund or refund credit of that portion of the cash price as is allocable to the services not actually received by the buyer. The refund of any finance charge shall be computed according to the "sum of the balance method," also known as the "Rule of 78."

(e) Any waiver by the buyer of this chapter is void and unenforceable.
Leg.H. Added Stats 1989 ch 138 §2.

CHAPTER 2.5
HOME EQUITY SALES CONTRACTS

Legislative findings and declarations; Intent and purposes of chapter. §1695.
Definitions. §1695.1.
Form of home equity sales contract. §1695.2.
Terms of home equity sales contract. §1695.3.
Right to cancellation of home equity sales contract. §1695.4.
Notice of cancellation; Right to cancel pending compliance. §1695.5.
Provision of contract by equity purchaser; Prohibited acts pending end of cancellation period; Misrepresentation by equity purchaser; Encumbrance when there is option to repurchase. §1695.6.
Seller's right to bring action; Exemplary damages; Civil penalty; Time limitation. §1695.7.
Violations by equity purchaser; Punishment. §1695.8.
Provisions of chapter not exclusive. §1695.9.
Waiver of provisions of chapter. §1695.10.
Effect of unconstitutional provision. §1695.11.
Presumption of loan transaction. §1695.12.
Unconscionability; Transactions involving real property. §1695.13.
Rescission of transactions involving residential real property in foreclosure. §1695.14.
Liability of equity purchaser for damages resulting from statements of representative. §1695.15.
Contract provisions attempting to limit liability. §1695.16.
Statements required of representatives. §1695.17.

§1695. Legislative findings and declarations; Intent and purposes of chapter

(a) The Legislature finds and declares that homeowners whose residences are in foreclosure have been subjected to fraud, deception, and unfair dealing by home equity purchasers. The recent rapid escalation of home values, particularly in the urban areas, has resulted in a significant increase in home equities which are usually the greatest financial asset held by the homeowners of this state. During the time period between the commencement of foreclosure proceedings and the scheduled foreclosure sale date, homeowners in financial distress, especially the poor, elderly, and financially unsophisticated, are vulnerable to the importunities of equity purchasers who induce homeowners to sell their homes for a small fraction of their fair market values through the use of schemes which often involve oral and written misrepresentations, deceit, intimidation, and other unreasonable commercial practices.

(b) The Legislature declares that it is the express policy of the state to preserve and guard the precious asset of home equity, and the social as well as the economic value of homeownership.

(c) The Legislature further finds that equity purchasers have a significant impact upon the economy and well-being of this state and its local communities, and therefore the provisions of this chapter are necessary to promote the public welfare.

(d) The intent and purposes of this chapter are the following:

(1) To provide each homeowner with information necessary to make an informed and intelligent decision regarding the sale of his or her home to an equity purchaser; to require that the sales agreement be expressed in writing; to safeguard the public against deceit and financial hardship; to insure, foster, and encourage fair dealing in the sale and purchase of homes in foreclosure; to prohibit representations that tend to mislead; to prohibit or restrict unfair contract terms; to afford homeowners a reasonable and meaningful opportunity to rescind sales to equity purchasers; and to preserve and protect home equities for the homeowners of this state.

(2) This chapter shall be liberally construed to effectuate this intent and to achieve these purposes. Leg.H. Added Stats 1979 ch 1029 §1.

§1695.1. Definitions

The following definitions apply to this chapter:

(a) "Equity purchaser" means any person who acquires title to any residence in foreclosure, except a person who acquires such title as follows:

(1) For the purpose of using such property as a personal residence.

(2) By a deed in lieu of foreclosure of any voluntary lien or encumbrance of record.

(3) By a deed from a trustee acting under the power of sale contained in a deed of trust or mortgage at a foreclosure sale conducted pursuant to Article 1 (commencing with Section 2920) of Chapter 2 of Title 14 of Part 4 of Division 3.

(4) At any sale of property authorized by statute.

(5) By order or judgment of any court.

(6) From a spouse, blood relative, or blood relative of a spouse.

(b) "Residence in foreclosure" and "residential real property in foreclosure" means residential real property consisting of one- to four-family dwelling units, one of which the owner occupies as his or her principal place of residence, and against which there is an outstanding notice of default, recorded pursuant to Article 1 (commencing with Section 2920) of Chapter 2 of Title 14 of Part 4 of Division 3.

(c) "Equity seller" means any seller of a residence in foreclosure.

(d) "Business day" means any calendar day except Sunday, or the following business holidays: New Year's Day, Washington's Birthday, Memorial Day, Independence Day, Labor Day, Columbus Day, Veterans' Day, Thanksgiving Day, and Christmas Day.

(e) "Contract" means any offer or any contract, agreement, or arrangement, or any term thereof, between an equity purchaser and equity seller incident to the sale of a residence in foreclosure.

(f) "Property owner" means the record title owner of the residential real property in foreclosure at the time the notice of default was recorded.
Leg.H. Added Stats 1979 ch 1029 §1. Amended Stats 1980 ch 423 §4, effective July 11, 1980.

§1695.2. Form of home equity sales contract

Every contract shall be written in letters of a size equal to 10-point bold type, in the same language principally used by the equity purchaser and equity seller to negotiate the sale of the residence in foreclosure and shall be fully completed and signed and dated by the equity seller and equity purchaser prior to the execution of any instrument of conveyance of the residence in foreclosure. Leg.H. Added Stats 1979 ch 1029 §1.

§1695.3. Terms of home equity sales contract

Every contract shall contain the entire agreement of the parties and shall include the following terms:

(a) The name, business address, and the telephone number of the equity purchaser.

(b) The address of the residence in foreclosure.

(c) The total consideration to be given by the equity purchaser in connection with or incident to the sale.

(d) A complete description of the terms of payment or other consideration including, but not limited to, any services of any nature which the equity purchaser represents he will perform for the equity seller before or after the sale.

(e) The time at which possession is to be transferred to the equity purchaser.

(f) The terms of any rental agreement.

(g) A notice of cancellation as provided in subdivision (b) of Section 1695.5.

(h) The following notice in at least 14-point boldface type, if the contract is printed or in capital letters if the contract is typed, and completed with the name of the equity purchaser, immediately above the statement required by Section 1695.5(a):

"NOTICE REQUIRED BY CALIFORNIA LAW

Until your right to cancel this contract has ended, _____ (Name) or anyone working for _____ (Name) CANNOT ask you to sign or have you sign any deed or any other document."

The contract required by this section shall survive delivery of any instrument of conveyance of the residence in foreclosure, and shall have no effect on persons other than the parties to the contract. **Leg.H.** Added Stats 1979 ch 1029 §1. Amended Stats 1980 ch 423 §5, effective July 11, 1980.

§1695.4. Right to cancellation of home equity sales contract

(a) In addition to any other right of rescission, the equity seller has the right to cancel any contract with an equity purchaser until midnight of the fifth business day following the day on which the equity seller signs a contract that complies with this chapter or until 8 a.m. on the day scheduled for the sale of the property pursuant to a power of sale conferred in a deed of trust, whichever occurs first.

(b) Cancellation occurs when the equity seller personally delivers written notice of cancellation to the address specified in the contract or sends a telegram indicating cancellation to that address.

(c) A notice of cancellation given by the equity seller need not take the particular form as provided with the contract and, however expressed, is effective if it indicates the intention of the equity seller not to be bound by the contract. **Leg.H.** Added Stats 1979 ch 1029 §1. Amended Stats 1997 ch 50 §1 (AB 669).

§1695.5. Notice of cancellation; Right to cancel pending compliance

(a) The contract shall contain in immediate proximity to the space reserved for the equity seller's signature a conspicuous statement in a size equal to at least 12-point bold type, if the contract is printed or in capital letters if the contract is typed, as follows:

"You may cancel this contract for the sale of your house without any penalty or obligation at any time before

_____
(Date and time of day)
See the attached notice of cancellation form for an explanation of this right."

The equity purchaser shall accurately enter the date and time of day on which the rescission right ends.

(b) The contract shall be accompanied by a completed form in duplicate, captioned "notice of cancellation" in a size equal to 12-point bold type, if the contract is printed or in capital letters if the contract is typed, followed by a space in which the equity purchaser shall enter the date on which the equity seller executes any contract. This form shall be attached to the contract, shall be easily detachable, and shall contain in type of at least 10-point, if the contract is printed or in capital letters if the contract is typed, the following statement written in the same language as used in the contract:

"NOTICE OF CANCELLATION

_____
(Enter date contract signed)
You may cancel this contract for the sale of your house, without and penalty or obligation, at any time before

_____
(Enter date and time of day)
To cancel this transaction, personally deliver a signed and dated copy of this cancellation notice, or send a telegram
to _____
(Name of purchaser)
at _____
(Street address of purchaser's place of business)
NOT LATER THAN _____
(Enter date and time of day)
I hereby cancel this transaction. _____
(Date)
_____"
(Seller's signature)

(c) The equity purchaser shall provide the equity seller with a copy of the contract and the attached notice of cancellation.

(d) Until the equity purchaser has complied with this section, the equity seller may cancel the contract. **Leg.H.** Added Stats 1979 ch 1029 §1. Amended Stats 1980 ch 423 §6, effective July 11, 1980; Stats 1997 ch 50 §2 (AB 669).

§1695.6. Provision of contract by equity purchaser; Prohibited acts pending end of cancellation period; Misrepresentation by equity purchaser; Encumbrance when there is option to repurchase

(a) The contract as required by Sections 1695.2, 1695.3, and 1695.5, shall be provided and completed in conformity with those sections by the equity purchaser.

(b) Until the time within which the equity seller may cancel the transaction has fully elapsed, the equity purchaser shall not do any of the following:

(1) Accept from any equity seller an execution of, or induce any equity seller to execute, any instrument of conveyance of any interest in the residence in foreclosure.

(2) Record with the county recorder any document, including, but not limited to, any instrument of conveyance, signed by the equity seller.

(3) Transfer or encumber or purport to transfer or encumber any interest in the residence in foreclosure to any third party, provided no grant of any interest or encumbrance shall be defeated or affected as against a bona fide purchaser or encumbrancer for value and without notice of a violation of this chapter, and knowledge on the part of any such person or entity that the property was "residential real property in foreclosure" shall not constitute notice of a violation of this chapter. This section shall not be deemed to abrogate any duty of inquiry which exists as to rights or interests of persons in possession of the residential real property in foreclosure.

(4) Pay the equity seller any consideration.

(c) Within 10 days following receipt of a notice of cancellation given in accordance with Sections 1695.4 and 1695.5, the equity purchaser shall return without condition any original contract and any other documents signed by the equity seller.

(d) An equity purchaser shall make no untrue or misleading statements regarding the value of the residence in foreclosure, the amount of proceeds the equity seller will receive after a foreclosure sale, any contract term, the equity seller's rights or obligations incident to or arising out of the sale transaction, the nature of any document which the equity purchaser induces the equity seller to sign, or any other untrue or misleading statement concerning the sale of the residence in foreclosure to the equity purchaser.

(e) Whenever any equity purchaser purports to hold title as a result of any transaction in which the equity seller grants the residence in foreclosure by any instrument which purports to be an absolute conveyance and reserves or is given by the equity purchaser an option to repurchase such residence, the equity purchaser shall not cause any encumbrance or encumbrances to be placed on such property or grant any interest in such property to any other person without the written consent of the equity seller. Nothing in this subdivision shall preclude the application of paragraph (3) of subdivision (b). **Leg.H.** Added Stats 1979 ch 1029 §1. Amended Stats 1980 ch 423 §7, effective July 11, 1980; Stats 1997 ch 50 §3 (AB 669).

1997 Note: It is the intent of the Legislature in enacting Stats 1997 ch 50 to abrogate the holding in *Boquilon v. Beckwith* (1996) 49 Cal. App. 4th 1697, 1713-1716, as it related to the relationship between paragraph (3) of subdivision (b) of Section 1695.6 of the Civil Code and subdivision (e) of that section. Stats 1997 ch 50 §6.

§1695.7. Seller's right to bring action; Exemplary damages; Civil penalty; Time limitation

An equity seller may bring an action for the recovery of damages or other equitable relief against an equity purchaser for a violation of any subdivision of Section 1695.6 or Section 1695.13. The equity seller shall recover actual damages plus reasonable attorneys' fees and costs. In addition, the court may award exemplary damages or equitable relief, or both, if the court deems such award proper, but in any event shall award exemplary damages in an amount not less than three times the equity seller's actual damages for any violation of paragraph (3) of subdivision (b) of Section 1695.6 or Section 1695.13; or the court may award a civil penalty of up to two thousand five hundred dollars ($2,500), but it may not award both exemplary damages and a civil penalty. Any action brought pursuant to this section shall be commenced within four years after the date of the alleged violation. **Leg.H.** Added Stats 1979 ch 1029 §1.

Amended Stats 1980 ch 423 §8, effective July 11, 1980; Stats 2003 ch 74 §1 (SB 455).

§1695.8. Violations by equity purchaser; Punishment

Any equity purchaser who violates any subdivision of Section 1695.6 or who engages in any practice which would operate as a fraud or deceit upon an equity seller shall, upon conviction, be punished by a fine of not more than twenty-five thousand dollars ($25,000), by imprisonment in the county jail for not more than one year, or pursuant to subdivision (h) of Section 1170 of the Penal Code, or by both that fine and imprisonment for each violation. **Leg.H.** Added Stats 1979 ch 1029 §1. Amended Stats 1985 ch 270 §1; Stats 2003 ch 74 §2 (SB 455); Stats 2011 ch 15 §32 (AB 109), effective April 4, 2011, operative October 1, 2011.

2011 Notes: This act is titled and may be cited as the 2011 Realignment Legislation addressing public safety. Stats 2011 ch 15 (AB 109) §1.

This act will become operative no earlier than October 1, 2011, and only upon creation of a community corrections grant program to assist in implementing this act and upon an appropriation to fund the grant program. Stats 2011 ch 15 (AB 109) §636; Stats 2011 ch 39 (AB 117) §68.

The Community Corrections Grant Program referred to in Stats 2011 ch 15 (AB 109) §636, as amended by Stats 2011 ch 39 (AB 117) §68, was created by Stats 2011 ch 40 (AB 118) §3, operative October 1, 2011.

§1695.9. Provisions of chapter not exclusive

The provisions of this chapter are not exclusive and are in addition to any other requirements, rights, remedies, and penalties provided by law. **Leg.H.** Added Stats 1979 ch 1029 §1.

§1695.10. Waiver of provisions of chapter

Any waiver of the provisions of this chapter shall be void and unenforceable as contrary to the public policy. **Leg.H.** Added Stats 1979 ch 1029 §1.

§1695.11. Effect of unconstitutional provision

If any provision of this chapter, or if any application thereof to any person or circumstance is held unconstitutional, the remainder of this chapter and the application of its provisions to other persons and circumstances shall not be affected thereby. **Leg.H.** Added Stats 1979 ch 1029 §1.

§1695.12. Presumption of loan transaction

In any transaction in which an equity seller purports to grant a residence in foreclosure to an equity purchaser by any instrument which appears to be an absolute conveyance and reserves to himself or herself or is given by the equity purchaser an option to repurchase, such transaction shall create a presumption affecting the burden of proof, which may be overcome by clear and convincing evidence to the contrary that the transaction is a loan transaction, and the purported absolute conveyance is a mortgage; however, such presumption shall not apply to a bona fide purchaser or encumbrancer for value without notice of a violation of this chapter, and knowledge on the part of any such person or entity that the property was "residential real property in foreclosure" shall not constitute notice of a violation of this chapter. This section shall not be deemed to abrogate any duty of inquiry which exists as to rights or interests of persons in possession of the residential real property in foreclosure. **Leg.H.** Added Stats 1979 ch 1029 §1. Amended Stats 1980 ch 423 §9, effective July 11, 1980.

§1695.13. Unconscionability; Transactions involving real property

It is unlawful for any person to initiate, enter into, negotiate, or consummate any transaction involving residential real property in foreclosure, as defined in Section 1695.1, if such person, by the terms of such transaction, takes unconscionable advantage of the property owner in foreclosure. **Leg.H.** Added Stats 1980 ch 423 §10, effective July 11, 1980.

§1695.14. Rescission of transactions involving residential real property in foreclosure

(a) In any transaction involving residential real property in foreclosure, as defined in Section 1695.1, which is in violation of Section 1695.13 is voidable and the transaction may be rescinded by the property owner within two years of the date of the recordation of the conveyance of the residential real property in foreclosure.

(b) Such rescission shall be effected by giving written notice as provided in Section 1691 to the equity purchaser and his successor in interest, if the successor is not a bona fide purchaser or encumbrancer for value as set forth in subdivision (c), and by recording such notice with the county recorder of the county in which the property is located, within two years of the date of the recordation of the conveyance to the equity purchaser. The notice of rescission shall contain the names of the property owner and the name of the equity purchaser in addition to any successor in interest holding record title to the real property and shall particularly describe such real property. The equity purchaser and his successor in interest if the successor is not a bona fide purchaser or encumbrancer for value as set forth in subdivision (c), shall have 20 days after the delivery of the notice in which to reconvey title to the property free and clear of encumbrances created subsequent to the rescinded transaction. Upon failure to reconvey title within such time, the rescinding party may bring an action to enforce the rescission and for cancellation of the deed.

(c) The provisions of this section shall not affect the interest of a bona fide purchaser or encumbrancer for value if such purchase or encumbrance occurred prior to the recordation of the notice of rescission pursuant to subdivision (b). Knowledge that the property was residential real property in foreclosure shall not impair the status of such persons or entities as bona fide purchasers or encumbrancers for value. This subdivision shall not be deemed to abrogate any duty of inquiry which exists as to rights or interests of persons in possession of the residential real property in foreclosure.

(d) In any action brought to enforce a rescission pursuant to this section, the prevailing party shall be entitled to costs and reasonable attorneys fees.

(e) The remedies provided by this section shall be in addition to any other remedies provided by law. **Leg.H.** Added Stats 1980 ch 423 §11, effective July 11, 1980.

§1695.15. Liability of equity purchaser for damages resulting from statements of representative

(a) An equity purchaser is liable for all damages resulting from any statement made or act committed by the equity purchaser's representative in any manner connected with the equity purchaser's acquisition of a residence in foreclosure, receipt of any consideration or property from or on behalf of the equity seller, or the performance of any act prohibited by this chapter.

(b) "Representative" for the purposes of this section means a person who in any manner solicits, induces, or causes any property owner to transfer title or solicits any member of the property owner's family or household to induce or cause any property owner to transfer title to the residence in foreclosure to the equity purchaser. **Leg.H.** Added Stats 1990 ch 1537 §1 (SB 2641).

§1695.16. Contract provisions attempting to limit liability

(a) Any provision of a contract which attempts or purports to limit the liability of the equity purchaser under Section 1695.15 shall be void and shall at the option of the equity seller render the equity purchase contract void. The equity purchaser shall be liable to the equity seller for all damages proximately caused by that provision. Any provision in a contract which attempts or purports to require arbitration of any dispute arising under this chapter shall be void at the option of the equity seller only upon grounds as exist for the revocation of any contract.

(b) This section shall apply to any contract entered into on or after January 1, 1991. **Leg.H.** Added Stats 1990 ch 1537 §2 (SB 2641).

§1695.17. Statements required of representatives

(a) Any representative, as defined in subdivision (b) of Section 1695.15, deemed to be the agent or employee, or both the agent and the employee of the equity purchaser shall be required to provide both of the following:

(1) Written proof to the equity seller that the representative has a valid current California Real Estate Sales License and that the representative is bonded by an admitted surety insurer in an amount equal to twice the fair market value of the real property which is the subject of the contract.

(2) A statement in writing, under penalty of perjury, that the representative has a valid current California Real Estate Sales License, is bonded by an admitted surety insurer in an amount equal to at least twice the value of the real property which is the subject of the contract and has complied with paragraph (1). The written statement required by this paragraph shall be provided to all parties to the contract prior to the transfer of any interest in the real property which is the subject of the contract.

(b) The failure to comply with subdivision (a) shall at the option of the equity seller render the equity purchase contract void and the equity purchaser shall be liable to the equity seller for all damages proximately caused by the failure to comply. **Leg.H.** Added Stats 1990 ch 1537 §3 (SB 2641).

CHAPTER 3
MODIFICATION AND CANCELLATION

Modification of verbal contract. §1697.
Modification of written contract. §1698.
Extinction by cancellation, etc. §1699.
Extinction by unauthorized alteration. §1700.
Alteration of duplicate, not to prejudice. §1701.

§1697. Modification of verbal contract

A contract not in writing may be modified in any respect by consent of the parties, in writing, without a new consideration, and is extinguished thereby to the extent of the modification. **Leg.H.** Enacted 1872. Amended Code Amdts 1873–74 ch 612 §192; Stats 1976 ch 109 §2.

§1698. Modification of written contract

(a) A contract in writing may be modified by a contract in writing.

(b) A contract in writing may be modified by an oral agreement to the extent that the oral agreement is executed by the parties.

(c) Unless the contract otherwise expressly provides, a contract in writing may be modified by an oral agreement supported by new consideration. The statute of frauds (Section 1624) is required to be satisfied if the contract as modified is within its provisions.

(d) Nothing in this section precludes in an appropriate case the application of rules of law concerning estoppel, oral novation and substitution of a new agreement, rescission of a written contract by an oral agreement, waiver of a provision of a written contract, or oral independent collateral contracts. **Leg.H.** Added Stats 1976 ch 109 §4.

Prior Law: Former §1698, similar to the present section, was enacted 1872, amended Code Amdts 1873–74 ch 612 §193, and repealed Stats 1976 ch 109 §3.

§1699. Extinction by cancellation, etc

The destruction or cancellation of a written contract, or of the signature of the parties liable thereon, with intent to extinguish the obligation thereof, extinguishes it as to all the parties consenting to the act. **Leg.H.** Enacted 1872.

§1700. Extinction by unauthorized alteration

The intentional destruction, cancellation or material alteration of a written contract, by a party entitled to any benefit under it, or with his consent, extinguishes all the executory obligations of the contract in his favor, against parties who do not consent to the act. **Leg.H.** Enacted 1872.

§1701. Alteration of duplicate, not to prejudice

Where a contract is executed in duplicate, an alteration or destruction of one copy, while the other exists, is not within the provisions of the last section. **Leg.H.** Enacted 1872.

PART 3
OBLIGATIONS IMPOSED BY LAW

Abstinence from injury. §1708.
Liability of person who commits sexual battery; "Intimate part"; "Offensive contact". §1708.5.
Limitation on consent as a defense under Section 1708.5; "Position of authority"; "Undue influence". §1708.5.5.
Cause of action for misuse of sperm, ova, or embryos. § 1708.5.6.
Tort of domestic violence; Damages. §1708.6.
Stalking. §1708.7.
Invasion of privacy to capture physical impression; Liability for damages; Civil fines. §1708.8.
Private cause of action for distribution of material exposing private body parts or sexual acts of another without permission; Affirmative defenses. §1708.85.
Cause of action for creating or disclosing sexually explicit depiction of individual; Exceptions; Damages. §1708.86.
Cause of action for knowingly sending electronic message depicting obscene material. § 1708.88.
Definitions. § 1708.89.
Unlawful acts toward minors. §1708.9.
Fraudulent deceit. §1709.
What constitutes deceit. §1710.
Removal or alteration of serial number on equipment. §1710.1.
Disclosure of death or HIV-positive status of prior occupant in real property transfers; Preemption by state. §1710.2.
Deceit upon the public, etc. §1711.
Restoration of thing wrongfully acquired. §1712.
When demand necessary. §1713.
Responsibility for willful acts or negligence; Proximate cause of injuries resulting from furnishing alcohol to intoxicated person; Liability of social host; Provision of alcoholic beverages to persons under 21 years of age. §1714.
Recovery of damages by domestic partner for negligent infliction of emotional distress. §1714.01.
Civil liability of parents for minor's acts of willful misconduct resulting in death, personal injury, or property damage. §1714.1.
Civil liability of persons rendering emergency care. §1714.2.
Liability for damages. §1714.21.
Prescribing, dispensing, or administering opioid antagonist; Report. §1714.22.
No liability for administration of epinephrine auto-injector to person experiencing anaphylaxis; Applicability. §1714.23.
Limitation on liability for injury or harm from maintenance of secure drug take-back bin. §1714.24.
Limitation on liability for damage or injury from donated food. §1714.25.
Limitation on liability for damage or injury from provision of vision screenings and donated or recycled eyeglasses by nonprofit charitable organization; Applicability; Definitions. §1714.26.
Limitation of liability to person rendering emergency aid by use of trauma kit. § 1714.29.
Civil liability of parents for injuries from discharge of firearm by minor under 18; Maximum liability. §1714.3.
Liability for knowingly assisting child support obligor to escape, evade, or avoid payment; Application to financial institutions. §1714.4.
Liability for knowingly assisting child support obligor to escape, evade, or avoid payment; Examples of actions taken knowingly. §1714.41.
Disclosure of efforts to eradicate slavery and human trafficking; Posting disclosures on Internet Web site; Remedies for violation. §1714.43.
Manufacturer or seller's liability in product liability action; Tobacco products; Actions by public entities to recover benefits for tobacco related illnesses. §1714.45.
Liability of owner of premises designated as emergency shelter; Liability of disaster service workers. §1714.5.
Liability of provider of telecommunications service involved in providing 9-1-1 service; Applicability; Construction. §1714.55.
Violation of statute or ordinance where act or omission required by military order, or order under California Emergency Services Act. §1714.6.
Right to damages for injuries sustained while unauthorizedly boarding, traveling, etc., on locomotive or railroad car. §1714.7.
Liability of health care provider for negligence or malpractice; Natural course of disease. §1714.8.
Liability for injury to peace officer, firefighter, or emergency medical personnel; Legislative intent regarding common law exception to firefighter's rule. §1714.9.
Cause of action against attorney based on civil conspiracy with client. §1714.10.
Limitation on liability for damage or injury from donated fire protection apparatus or equipment. §1714.11.
Other obligations. §1715.
Statement or invoice for goods not ordered or services not performed; Requirements for warning; Damages; Civil penalty. §1716.
Contract provision for attorney fees and costs. §1717.
Contract action based on book account; Attorney's fees and costs. §1717.5.
Farm machinery repair shop work; Invoice; Written estimate furnished on request; Violation as misdemeanor. §1718.
Passage of checks on insufficient funds; Liability for specified amounts including treble damages. §1719.
Inquiries of obligor about credit account; Obligee's failure to respond. §1720.
Vandalism at construction site; Damages; Attorney's fees. §1721.
Time period for delivery of contract goods, or for service or repair by retailer; Cable television companies; Utilities; Waiver of rights. §1722.
Display by retail store of policy regarding refunds and exchanges. §1723.
Unlawful to sell illegally obtained or accessed data or access to such data; Unlawful for unauthorized person to purchase or use data from source known or reasonably should have been known to be illegally obtained or accessed. § 1724.
Prohibition against requiring credit card as condition of acceptance of negotiable instrument. §1725.

§1708. Abstinence from injury

Every person is bound, without contract, to abstain from injuring the person or property of another, or infringing upon any of his or her rights. **Leg.H.** Enacted Stats 1872. Amended Stats 2002 ch 664 §38.5 (AB 3034).

§1708.5. Liability of person who commits sexual battery; "Intimate part"; "Offensive contact"

(a) A person commits a sexual battery who does any of the following:

(1) Acts with the intent to cause a harmful or offensive contact with an intimate part of another, and a sexually offensive contact with that person directly or indirectly results.

(2) Acts with the intent to cause a harmful or offensive contact with another by use of the person's intimate part, and a sexually offensive contact with that person directly or indirectly results.

(3) Acts to cause an imminent apprehension of the conduct described in paragraph (1) or (2), and a sexually offensive contact with that person directly or indirectly results.

(4) Causes contact between a sexual organ, from which a condom has been removed, and the intimate part of another who did not verbally consent to the condom being removed.

(5) Causes contact between an intimate part of the person and a sexual organ of another from which the person removed a condom without verbal consent.

(b) A person who commits a sexual battery upon another is liable to that person for damages, including, but not limited to, general damages, special damages, and punitive damages.

(c) The court in an action pursuant to this section may award equitable relief, including, but not limited to, an injunction, costs, and any other relief the court deems proper.

(d) For the purposes of this section:

(1) "Intimate part" means the sexual organ, anus, groin, or buttocks of any person, or the breast of a female.

(2) "Offensive contact" means contact that offends a reasonable sense of personal dignity.

(e) The rights and remedies provided in this section are in addition to any other rights and remedies provided by law. **Leg.H.** Added Stats 1990 ch 1531 §1 (SB 2336). Amended Stats 2021 ch 613 §1 (AB 453), effective January 1, 2022.

§1708.5.5. Limitation on consent as a defense under Section 1708.5; "Position of authority"; "Undue influence"

(a) Notwithstanding Section 3515, consent shall not be a defense in any civil action under Section 1708.5 if the person who commits the sexual battery is an adult who is in a position of authority over the minor.

(b) For purposes of this section, an adult is in a "position of authority" if he or she, by reason of that position, is able to exercise undue influence over a minor. A "position of authority" includes, but is not limited to, a natural parent, stepparent, foster parent, relative, partner of any such parent or relative, caretaker, youth leader, recreational director, athletic manager, coach, teacher, counselor, therapist, religious leader, doctor, employee of one of those aforementioned persons, or coworker.

(c) For purposes of this section, "undue influence" has the same meaning as in Section 15610.70 of the Welfare and Institutions Code. **Leg.H.** Added Stats 2015 ch 128 §1 (SB 14), effective January 1, 2016.

§ 1708.5.6. Cause of action for misuse of sperm, ova, or embryos

(a) A private cause of action for damages lies against a person who misuses sperm, ova, or embryos in violation of Section 367g of the Penal Code.

(b) A prevailing plaintiff who suffers harm as a result of a violation of Section 367g of the Penal Code may be awarded actual damages or statutory damages of not less than fifty thousand dollars ($50,000), whichever is greater. **Leg.H.** Added Stats 2021 ch 170 §1 (AB 556), effective January 1, 2022.

§1708.6. Tort of domestic violence; Damages

(a) A person is liable for the tort of domestic violence if the plaintiff proves both of the following elements:

(1) The infliction of injury upon the plaintiff resulting from abuse, as defined in subdivision (a) of Section 13700 of the Penal Code.

(2) The abuse was committed by the defendant, a person having a relationship with the plaintiff as defined in subdivision (b) of Section 13700 of the Penal Code.

(b) A person who commits an act of domestic violence upon another is liable to that person for damages, including, but not limited to, general damages, special damages, and punitive damages pursuant to Section 3294.

(c) The court, in an action pursuant to this section, may grant to a prevailing plaintiff equitable relief, an injunction, costs, and any other relief that the court deems proper, including reasonable attorney's fees.

(d) The rights and remedies provided in this section are in addition to any other rights and remedies provided by law.

(e) The time for commencement of an action under this section is governed by Section 340.15 of the Code of Civil Procedure. **Leg.H.** Added Stats 2002 ch 193 §2 (AB 1933).

§1708.7. Stalking

(a) A person is liable for the tort of stalking when the plaintiff proves all of the following elements of the tort:

(1) The defendant engaged in a pattern of conduct the intent of which was to follow, alarm, place under surveillance, or harass the plaintiff. In order to establish this element, the plaintiff shall be required to support his or her allegations with independent corroborating evidence.

(2) As a result of that pattern of conduct, either of the following occurred:

(A) The plaintiff reasonably feared for his or her safety, or the safety of an immediate family member. For purposes of this subparagraph, "immediate family" means a spouse, parent, child, any person related by consanguinity or affinity within the second degree, or any person who regularly resides, or, within the six months preceding any portion of the pattern of conduct, regularly resided, in the plaintiff's household.

(B) The plaintiff suffered substantial emotional distress, and the pattern of conduct would cause a reasonable person to suffer substantial emotional distress.

(3) One of the following:

(A) The defendant, as a part of the pattern of conduct specified in paragraph (1), made a credible threat with either (i) the intent to place the plaintiff in reasonable fear for his or her safety, or the safety of an immediate family member, or (ii) reckless disregard for the safety of the plaintiff or that of an immediate family member. In addition, the plaintiff must have, on at least one occasion, clearly and definitively demanded that the defendant cease and abate his or her pattern of conduct and the defendant persisted in his or her pattern of conduct unless exigent circumstances make the plaintiff's communication of the demand impractical or unsafe.

(B) The defendant violated a restraining order, including, but not limited to, any order issued pursuant to Section 527.6 of the Code of Civil Procedure, prohibiting any act described in subdivision (a).

(b) For the purposes of this section:

(1) "Pattern of conduct" means conduct composed of a series of acts over a period of time, however short, evidencing a continuity of purpose. Constitutionally protected activity is not included within the meaning of "pattern of conduct."

(2) "Credible threat" means a verbal or written threat, including that communicated by means of an electronic communication device, or a threat implied by a pattern of conduct, including, but not limited to, acts in which a defendant directly, indirectly, or through third parties, by any action, method, device, or means, follows, harasses, monitors, surveils, threatens, or interferes with or damages the plaintiff's property, or a combination of verbal, written, or electronically communicated statements and conduct, made with the intent and apparent ability to carry out the threat so as to cause the person who is the target of the threat to reasonably fear for his or her safety or the safety of his or her immediate family.

(3) "Electronic communication device" includes, but is not limited to, telephones, cellular telephones, computers, video recorders, fax machines, or pagers. "Electronic communication" has the same meaning as the term defined in Subsection 12 of Section 2510 of Title 18 of the United States Code.

(4) "Follows" means to move in relative proximity to a person as that person moves from place to place or to remain in relative proximity to a person who is stationary or whose movements are confined to a small area but does not include following the plaintiff within the residence of the defendant. For purposes of the liability created by subdivision (a), "follows" does not include any lawful activity of private investigators licensed pursuant to Article 3 (commencing with Section 7520) of Chapter 11.3 of Division 3 of the Business and Professions Code, or of law enforcement personnel or employees of agencies, either public or private, who, in the course and scope of their employment, encourage or attempt to engage in any conduct or activity to obtain evidence of suspected illegal activity or other misconduct, suspected violation of any administrative rule or regulation, suspected fraudulent conduct, or any suspected activity involving a violation of law or business practice or conduct of a public official that adversely affects public welfare, health, or safety. For purposes of the liability created by subdivision (a), "follows" also does not include any newsgathering conduct connected to a newsworthy event.

(5) "Harass" means a knowing and willful course of conduct directed at a specific person which seriously alarms, annoys, torments, or terrorizes the person, and which serves no legitimate purpose. The course of conduct must be such as would cause a reasonable person to suffer substantial emotional distress, and must actually cause substantial emotional distress to the person.

(6) "Place under surveillance" means remaining present outside of the plaintiff's school, place of employment, vehicle, residence, other than the residence of the defendant, or other place occupied by the plaintiff. For purposes of the liability created by subdivision (a), "place under surveillance" does not include any lawful activity of private investigators licensed pursuant to Article 3 (commencing with Section 7520) of Chapter 11.3 of Division 3 of the Business and Professions Code, or of law enforcement personnel or employees of agencies, either public or private, who, in the course and scope of their employment, encourage or attempt to engage in any conduct or activity to obtain evidence of suspected illegal activity or other misconduct, suspected violation of any administrative rule or regulation, suspected fraudulent conduct, or any suspected activity involving a violation of law or business practice or conduct of a public official that adversely affects public welfare, health, or safety. For purposes of the liability created by subdivision (a), "place under surveillance" also does not include any newsgathering conduct connected to a newsworthy event.

(7) "Substantial emotional distress" shall not be construed to have the same meaning as the "severe emotional distress" requirement for intentional infliction of emotional distress. "Substantial emotional distress" does not require a showing of physical manifestations of emotional distress; rather, it requires the evaluation of the totality of the circumstances to determine whether the defendant reasonably caused the plaintiff substantial fear, anxiety, or emotional torment.

(c) A person who commits the tort of stalking upon another is liable to that person for damages, including, but not limited to, general damages, special damages, and punitive damages pursuant to Section 3294.

(d) In an action pursuant to this section, the court may grant equitable relief, including, but not limited to, an injunction.

(e) The rights and remedies provided in this section are cumulative and in addition to any other rights and remedies provided by law.

(f) This section shall not be construed to impair any constitutionally protected activity, including, but not limited to, speech, protest, and assembly.

(g) This act is an exercise of the police power of the state for the protection of the health, safety, and welfare of the people of the State of California, and shall be liberally construed to effectuate those purposes.
Leg.H. Added Stats 1993 ch 582 §1 (AB 1548). Amended Stats 1994 ch 509 §1 (AB 2676); Stats 1998 ch 825 §2 (SB 1796); Stats 2014 ch 853 §1 (AB 1356), effective January 1, 2015.

§1708.8. Invasion of privacy to capture physical impression; Liability for damages; Civil fines

(a) A person is liable for physical invasion of privacy when the person knowingly enters onto the land or into the airspace above the land of another person without permission or otherwise commits a trespass in order to capture any type of visual image, sound recording, or other physical impression of the plaintiff engaging in a private, personal, or familial activity and the invasion occurs in a manner that is offensive to a reasonable person.

(b) A person is liable for constructive invasion of privacy when the person attempts to capture, in a manner that is offensive to a reasonable person, any type of visual image, sound recording, or other physical impression of the plaintiff engaging in a private, personal, or familial activity, through the use of any device, regardless of whether there is a physical trespass, if this image, sound recording, or other physical impression could not have been achieved without a trespass unless the device was used.

(c) An assault or false imprisonment committed with the intent to capture any type of visual image, sound recording, or other physical impression of the plaintiff is subject to subdivisions (d), (e), and (h).

(d) A person who commits any act described in subdivision (a), (b), or (c) is liable for up to three times the amount of any general and special damages that are proximately caused by the violation of this section. This person may also be liable for punitive damages, subject to proof according to Section 3294. If the plaintiff proves that the invasion of privacy was committed for a commercial purpose, the person shall also be subject to disgorgement to the plaintiff of any proceeds or other consideration obtained as a result of the violation of this section. A person who comes within the description of this subdivision is also subject to a civil fine of not less than five thousand dollars ($5,000) and not more than fifty thousand dollars ($50,000).

(e) A person who directs, solicits, actually induces, or actually causes another person, regardless of whether there is an employer-employee relationship, to violate any provision of subdivision (a), (b), or (c) is liable for any general, special, and consequential damages resulting from each said violation. In addition, the person that directs, solicits, actually induces, or actually causes another person, regardless of whether there is an employer-employee relationship, to violate this section shall be liable for punitive damages to the extent that an employer would be subject to punitive damages pursuant to subdivision (b) of Section 3294. A person who comes within the description of this subdivision is also subject to a civil fine of not less than five thousand dollars ($5,000) and not more than fifty thousand dollars ($50,000).

(f)(1) The transmission, publication, broadcast, sale, offer for sale, or other use of any visual image, sound recording, or other physical impression that was taken or captured in violation of subdivision (a), (b), or (c) shall not constitute a violation of this section unless the person, in the first transaction following the taking or capture of the visual image, sound recording, or other physical impression, publicly transmitted, published, broadcast, sold, or offered for sale the visual image, sound recording, or other physical impression with actual knowledge that it was taken or captured in violation of subdivision (a), (b), or (c), and provided compensation, consideration, or remuneration, monetary or otherwise, for the rights to the unlawfully obtained visual image, sound recording, or other physical impression.

(2) For the purposes of paragraph (1), "actual knowledge" means actual awareness, understanding, and recognition, obtained prior to the time at which the person purchased or acquired the visual image, sound recording, or other physical impression, that the visual image, sound recording, or other physical impression was taken or captured in violation of subdivision (a), (b), or (c). The plaintiff shall establish actual knowledge by clear and convincing evidence.

(3) Any person that publicly transmits, publishes, broadcasts, sells, or offers for sale, in any form, medium, format, or work, a visual image, sound recording, or other physical impression that was previously publicly transmitted, published, broadcast, sold, or offered for sale by another person, is exempt from liability under this section.

(4) If a person's first public transmission, publication, broadcast, or sale or offer for sale of a visual image, sound recording, or other physical impression that was taken or captured in violation of subdivision (a), (b), or (c) does not constitute a violation of this section, that person's subsequent public transmission, publication, broadcast, sale, or offer for sale, in any form, medium, format, or work, of the visual image, sound recording, or other physical impression, does not constitute a violation of this section.

(5) This section applies only to a visual image, sound recording, or other physical impression that is captured or taken in California in violation of subdivision (a), (b), or (c) after January 1, 2010, and shall not apply to any visual image, sound recording, or other physical impression taken or captured outside of California.

(6) Nothing in this subdivision shall be construed to impair or limit a special motion to strike pursuant to Section 425.16, 425.17, or 425.18 of the Code of Civil Procedure.

(7) This section shall not be construed to limit all other rights or remedies of the plaintiff in law or equity, including, but not limited to, the publication of private facts.

(g) This section shall not be construed to impair or limit any otherwise lawful activities of law enforcement personnel or employees of governmental agencies or other entities, either public or private, who, in the course and scope of their employment, and supported by an articulable suspicion, attempt to capture any type of visual image, sound recording, or other physical impression of a person during an investigation, surveillance, or monitoring of any conduct to obtain evidence of suspected illegal activity or other misconduct, the suspected violation of any administrative rule or regulation, a suspected fraudulent conduct, or any activity involving a violation of law or business practices or conduct of public officials adversely affecting the public welfare, health, or safety.

(h) In any action pursuant to this section, the court may grant equitable relief, including, but not limited to, an injunction and restraining order against further violations of subdivision (a), (b), or (c).

(i) The rights and remedies provided in this section are cumulative and in addition to any other rights and remedies provided by law.

(j) It is not a defense to a violation of this section that no image, recording, or physical impression was captured or sold.

(k) For the purposes of this section, "for a commercial purpose" means any act done with the expectation of a sale, financial gain, or other consideration. A visual image, sound recording, or other physical impression shall not be found to have been, or intended to have been, captured for a commercial purpose unless it is intended to be, or was in fact, sold, published, or transmitted.

(*l*)(1) For the purposes of this section, "private, personal, and familial activity" includes, but is not limited to:

(A) Intimate details of the plaintiff's personal life under circumstances in which the plaintiff has a reasonable expectation of privacy.

(B) Interaction with the plaintiff's family or significant others under circumstances in which the plaintiff has a reasonable expectation of privacy.

(C) If and only after the person has been convicted of violating Section 626.8 of the Penal Code, any activity that occurs when minors are present at any location set forth in subdivision (a) of Section 626.8 of the Penal Code.

(D) Any activity that occurs on a residential property under circumstances in which the plaintiff has a reasonable expectation of privacy.

(E) Other aspects of the plaintiff's private affairs or concerns under circumstances in which the plaintiff has a reasonable expectation of privacy.

(2) "Private, personal, and familial activity" does not include illegal or otherwise criminal activity as delineated in subdivision (g). However, "private, personal, and familial activity" shall include the activities of victims of crime in circumstances under which subdivision (a), (b), or (c) would apply.

(m)(1) A proceeding to recover the civil fines specified in subdivision (d) or (e) may be brought in any court of competent jurisdiction by a county counsel or city attorney.

(2) Fines collected pursuant to this subdivision shall be allocated, as follows:

(A) One-half shall be allocated to the prosecuting agency.

(B) One-half shall be deposited in the Arts and Entertainment Fund, which is hereby created in the State Treasury.

(3) Funds in the Arts and Entertainment Fund created pursuant to paragraph (2) may be expended by the California Arts Council, upon appropriation by the Legislature, to issue grants pursuant to the Dixon-Zenovich-Maddy California Arts Act of 1975 (Chapter 9 (commencing with Section 8750) of Division 1 of Title 2 of the Government Code).

(4) The rights and remedies provided in this subdivision are cumulative and in addition to any other rights and remedies provided by law.

(n) The provisions of this section are severable. If any provision of this section or its application is held invalid, that invalidity shall not affect other provisions or applications that can be given effect without the invalid provision or application. **Leg.H.** Added Stats 1998 ch 1000 §1 (SB 262). Amended Stats 2005 ch 424 §1 (AB 381), effective January 1, 2006; Stats 2009 ch 449 §2 (AB 524), effective January 1, 2010; Stats 2010 ch 685 §1 (AB 2479), effective January 1, 2011; Stats 2014 ch 852 §1 (AB 1256), effective January 1, 2015; Stats 2014 ch 858 §1.5 (AB 2306), effective January 1, 2015; Stats 2015 ch 521 §1 (AB 856), effective January 1, 2016.

§1708.85. Private cause of action for distribution of material exposing private body parts or sexual acts of another without permission; Affirmative defenses

(a) A private cause of action lies against a person who intentionally distributes by any means a photograph, film, videotape, recording, or any other reproduction of another, without the other's consent, if (1) the person knew, or reasonably should have known, that the other person had a reasonable expectation that the material would remain private, (2) the distributed material exposes an intimate body part of the other person, or shows the other person engaging in an act of intercourse, oral copulation, sodomy, or other act of sexual penetration, and (3) the other person suffers general or special damages as described in Section 48a.

(b) As used in this section, "intimate body part" means any portion of the genitals, and, in the case of a female, also includes any portion of the breast below the top of the areola, that is uncovered or visible through less than fully opaque clothing.

(c) There shall be no liability on the part of the person distributing material under subdivision (a) under any of the following circumstances:

(1) The distributed material was created under an agreement by the person appearing in the material for its public use and distribution or otherwise intended by that person for public use and distribution.

(2) The person possessing or viewing the distributed material has permission from the person appearing in the material to publish by any means or post the material on an internet website.

(3) The person appearing in the material waived any reasonable expectation of privacy in the distributed material by making it accessible to the general public.

(4) The distributed material constitutes a matter of public concern.

(5) The distributed material was photographed, filmed, videotaped, recorded, or otherwise reproduced in a public place and under circumstances in which the person depicted had no reasonable expectation of privacy.

(6) The distributed material was previously distributed by another person, unless the plaintiff served on the defendant, by certified mail, a notice to cease distribution of the material, and the defendant failed to cease distribution within 20 days of receiving the notice.

(d) In addition to any other relief available at law, the court may order equitable relief against the person violating subdivision (a), including a temporary restraining order, or a preliminary injunction or a permanent injunction ordering the defendant to cease distribution of material. The court may grant injunctive relief maintaining the confidentiality of a plaintiff using a pseudonym as provided in subdivision (f).

(e) The court may also grant, after holding a properly noticed hearing, reasonable attorney's fees and costs to the prevailing plaintiff.

(f)(1) A plaintiff in a civil proceeding pursuant to subdivision (a), may proceed using a pseudonym, either John Doe, Jane Doe, or Doe, for the true name of the plaintiff and may exclude or redact from all pleadings and documents filed in the action other identifying characteristics of the plaintiff. A plaintiff who proceeds using a pseudonym and excluding or redacting identifying characteristics as provided in this section shall file with the court and serve upon the defendant a confidential information form for this purpose that includes the plaintiff's name and other identifying characteristics excluded or redacted. The court shall keep the plaintiff's name and excluded or redacted characteristics confidential.

(2) In cases where a plaintiff proceeds using a pseudonym under this section, the following provisions shall apply:

(A) All other parties and their agents and attorneys shall use this pseudonym in all pleadings, discovery documents, and other documents filed or served in the action, and at hearings, trial, and other court proceedings that are open to the public.

(B)(i) Any party filing a pleading, discovery document, or other document in the action shall exclude or redact any identifying characteristics of the plaintiff from the pleading, discovery document, or other document, except for a confidential information form filed pursuant to this subdivision.

(ii) A party excluding or redacting identifying characteristics as provided in this section shall file with the court and serve upon all other parties a confidential information form that includes the plaintiff's name and other identifying characteristics excluded or redacted. The court shall keep the plaintiff's name and excluded or redacted characteristics confidential.

(C) All court decisions, orders, petitions, discovery documents, and other documents shall be worded so as to protect the name or other identifying characteristics of the plaintiff from public revelation.

(3) The following definitions apply to this subdivision:

(A) "Identifying characteristics" means name or any part thereof, address or any part thereof, city or unincorporated area of residence, age, marital status, relationship to defendant, and race or ethnic background, telephone number, email address, social media profiles, online identifiers, contact information, or any other information, including images of the plaintiff, from which the plaintiff's identity can be discerned.

(B) "Online identifiers" means any personally identifying information or signifiers that would tie an individual to a particular electronic service, device, or Internet application, website, or platform account, including, but not limited to, access names, access codes, account names, aliases, avatars, credentials, gamer tags, display names, handles, login names, member names, online identities, pseudonyms, screen names, user accounts, user identifications, usernames, Uniform Resource Locators (URLs), domain names, Internet Protocol (IP) addresses, and media access control (MAC) addresses.

(4) The responsibility for excluding or redacting the name or identifying characteristics of the plaintiff from all documents filed with the court rests solely with the parties and their attorneys. Nothing in this section requires the court to review pleadings or other papers for compliance with this provision.

(5) Upon request of the plaintiff, the clerk shall allow access to the court file in an action filed under this section only as follows:

(A) To a party to the action, including a party's attorney.

(B) To a person by order of the court on a showing of good cause for access.

(C) To any person 60 days after judgment is entered unless the court grants a plaintiff's motion to seal records pursuant to Chapter 3 of Division 4 of Title 2 of the California Rules of Court.

(g) In an action pursuant to this section, the plaintiff shall state in the caption of the complaint "ACTION BASED ON CIVIL CODE SECTION 1708.85."

(h) Nothing in this section shall be construed to alter or negate any rights, obligations, or immunities of an interactive service provider under Section 230 of Title 47 of the United States Code. Nothing in this section shall be construed to limit or preclude a plaintiff from securing or recovering any other available remedy.

(i) The provisions of this section are severable. If any provision of this section or its application is held invalid, that invalidity shall not affect other provisions or applications that can be given effect without the invalid provision or application.

(j) The Judicial Council shall, on or before January 1, 2019, adopt or revise as appropriate rules and forms in order to implement subdivision (f). **Leg.H.** Added Stats 2014 ch 859 §1 (AB 2643), effective January 1, 2015, operative July 1, 2015. Amended Stats 2017 ch 233 §1 (SB 157), effective January 1, 2018; Stats 2021 ch 518 §1 (AB 514), effective January 1, 2022.

2017 Note: The Legislature finds and declares that Section 1 of this act, which amends Section 1708.85 of the Civil Code, and Section 2 of this act, which amends Section 6276.12 of the Government Code, impose a limitation on the public's right of access to the meetings of public bodies or the writings of public officials and agencies within the meaning of Section 3 of Article I of the California Constitution. Pursuant to that constitutional provision, the Legislature makes the following findings to demonstrate the interest protected by this limitation and the need for protecting that interest:

In order to protect the identity of victims whose privacy was violated by the unconsented distribution of material that exposes his or her intimate body part or shows him or her engaging in specified sexual acts. Stats 2017 ch 233 (SB 157) §3.

2014 Note: The Judicial Council shall, by July 1, 2015, develop the confidential information form specified in subdivision (f) of Section 1708.85 of the Civil Code. Stats 2014 ch 859 (AB 2643) §1.

§1708.86. Cause of action for creating or disclosing sexually explicit depiction of individual; Exceptions; Damages

(a) For purposes of this section:

(1) "Altered depiction" means a performance that was actually performed by the depicted individual but was subsequently altered to be in violation of this section.

(2) "Authorized Representative" means an attorney, talent agent, or personal manager authorized to represent a depicted individual if the depicted individual is represented.

(3)(A) "Consent" means an agreement written in plain language signed knowingly and voluntarily by the depicted individual that includes a general description of the sexually explicit material and the audiovisual work in which it will be incorporated.

(B) A depicted individual may rescind consent by delivering written notice within three business days from the date consent was given to the person in whose favor consent was made, unless one of the following requirements is satisfied:

(i) The depicted individual is given at least 72 hours to review the terms of the agreement before signing it.

(ii) The depicted individual's authorized representative provides written approval of the signed agreement.

(4) "Depicted individual" means an individual who appears, as a result of digitization, to be giving a performance they did not actually perform or to be performing in an altered depiction.

(5) "Despicable conduct" means conduct that is so vile, base, or contemptible that it would be looked down on and despised by a reasonable person.

(6) "Digitization" means to realistically depict any of the following:

(A) The nude body parts of another human being as the nude body parts of the depicted individual.

(B) Computer-generated nude body parts as the nude body parts of the depicted individual.

(C) The depicted individual engaging in sexual conduct in which the depicted individual did not engage.

(7) "Disclose" means to publish, make available, or distribute to the public.

(8) "Individual" means a natural person.

(9) "Malice" means that the defendant acted with intent to cause harm to the plaintiff or despicable conduct that was done with a willful and knowing disregard of the rights of the plaintiff. A person acts with knowing disregard within the meaning of this paragraph when they are aware of the probable harmful consequences of their conduct and deliberately fail to avoid those consequences.

(10) "Nude" means visible genitals, pubic area, anus, or a female's postpubescent nipple or areola.

(11) "Person" means a human being or legal entity.

(12) "Plaintiff" includes cross-plaintiff.

(13) "Sexual conduct" means any of the following:

(A) Masturbation.

(B) Sexual intercourse, including genital, oral, or anal, whether between persons regardless of sex or gender or between humans and animals.

(C) Sexual penetration of the vagina or rectum by, or with, an object.

(D) The transfer of semen by means of sexual conduct from the penis directly onto the depicted individual as a result of ejaculation.

(E) Sadomasochistic abuse involving the depicted individual.

(14) "Sexually explicit material" means any portion of an audiovisual work that shows the depicted individual performing in the nude or appearing to engage in, or being subjected to, sexual conduct.

(b) A depicted individual has a cause of action against a person who does either of the following:

(1) Creates and intentionally discloses sexually explicit material and the person knows or reasonably should have known the depicted individual in that material did not consent to its creation or disclosure.

(2) Intentionally discloses sexually explicit material that the person did not create and the person knows the depicted individual in that material did not consent to the creation of the sexually explicit material.

(c)(1) A person is not liable under this section in either of the following circumstances:

(A) The person discloses the sexually explicit material in the course of any of the following:

(i) Reporting unlawful activity.

(ii) Exercising the person's law enforcement duties.

(iii) Hearings, trials, or other legal proceedings.

(B) The material is any of the following:

(i) A matter of legitimate public concern.

(ii) A work of political or newsworthy value or similar work.

(iii) Commentary, criticism, or disclosure that is otherwise protected by the California Constitution or the United States Constitution.

(2) For purposes of this subdivision, sexually explicit material is not of newsworthy value solely because the depicted individual is a public figure.

(d) It shall not be a defense to an action under this section that there is a disclaimer included in the sexually explicit material that communicates that the inclusion of the depicted individual in the sexually explicit material was unauthorized or that the depicted individual did not participate in the creation or development of the material.

(e)(1) A prevailing plaintiff who suffers harm as a result of the violation of subdivision (b) may recover any of the following:

(A) An amount equal to the monetary gain made by the defendant from the creation, development, or disclosure of the sexually explicit material.

(B) One of the following:

(i) Economic and noneconomic damages proximately caused by the disclosure of the sexually explicit material, including damages for emotional distress.

(ii) Upon request of the plaintiff at any time before the final judgment is rendered, the plaintiff may instead recover an award of statutory damages for all unauthorized acts involved in the action, with respect to any one work, as follows:

(I) A sum of not less than one thousand five hundred dollars ($1,500) but not more than thirty thousand dollars ($30,000).

(II) If the unlawful act was committed with malice, the award of statutory damages may be increased to a maximum of one hundred fifty thousand dollars ($150,000).

(C) Punitive damages.

(D) Reasonable attorney's fees and costs.

(E) Any other available relief, including injunctive relief.

(2) The remedies provided by this section are cumulative and shall not be construed as restricting a remedy that is available under any other law.

(f) An action under this section shall be commenced no later than three years from the date the unauthorized creation, development, or disclosure was discovered or should have been discovered with the exercise of reasonable diligence.

(g) The provisions of this section are severable. If any provision of this section or its application is held invalid, that invalidity shall not affect other provisions. **Leg.H.** Added Stats 2019 ch 491 §1 (AB 602), effective January 1, 2020.

§ 1708.88. Cause of action for knowingly sending electronic message depicting obscene material

(a) A private cause of action lies against a person 18 years of age or older who knowingly sends an image, that the person knows or reasonably should know is unsolicited, by electronic means, depicting obscene material.

(b) For purposes of this section, the following terms have the following meanings:

(1) An "image" includes, but is not limited to, a moving visual image.

(2) "Obscene material" means material, including, but not limited to, images depicting a person engaging in an act of sexual intercourse, sodomy, oral copulation, sexual penetration, or masturbation, or depicting the exposed genitals or anus of any person, taken as a whole, that to the average person, applying contemporary statewide standards, appeals to the prurient interest, that, taken as a whole, depicts or describes sexual

conduct in a patently offensive way, and that, taken as a whole, lacks serious literary, artistic, political, or scientific value.

(3) An image is "unsolicited" if the recipient has not consented to or has expressly forbidden the receipt of the image.

(c)(1) A prevailing plaintiff who suffers harm as a result of receiving an image in violation of subdivision (a) may recover economic and noneconomic damages proximately caused by the receipt of the image, including damages for emotional distress.

(2) A prevailing plaintiff who suffers harm as a result of receiving an image, the receipt of which had been expressly forbidden by the plaintiff, in violation of subdivision (a), may recover the following:

(A) Economic and noneconomic damages proximately caused by the receipt of the image, including damages for emotional distress.

(B) Upon request of the plaintiff at any time before the final judgment is rendered, the plaintiff may, in lieu of those damages specified in subparagraph (A), recover an award of statutory damages of a sum of not less than one thousand five hundred dollars ($1,500) but not more than thirty thousand dollars ($30,000).

(C) Punitive damages.

(3) A prevailing plaintiff described in paragraph (1) or (2) may recover the following:

(A) Reasonable attorney's fees and costs.

(B) Any other available relief, including injunctive relief.

(4) The remedies provided by this section are cumulative and shall not be construed as restricting a remedy that is available under any other law.

(d) This section does not apply to any of the following:

(1) An internet service provider, mobile data provider, or operator of an online or mobile application, to the extent that the entity is transmitting, routing, or providing connections for electronic communications initiated by or at the direction of another person.

(2) Any service that transmits images or audiovisual works, including, without limitation, an on-demand, subscription, or advertising-supported service.

(3) A health care provider transmitting an image for a legitimate medical purpose.

(4) An individual who has not expressly opted-out of receiving sexually explicit images on the service in which the image is transmitted, where such an option is available. **Leg.H.** Added Stats 2022 ch 504 §1 (SB 53), effective January 1, 2023.

§ 1708.89. Definitions

(a) For purposes of this section, the following terms apply:

(1) "Doxes" means an act when a person, with intent to place another person in reasonable fear for their safety, or the safety of the other person's immediate family, by means of an electronic communication device, and without consent of the other person, and for the purpose of imminently causing that other person unwanted physical contact, injury, or harassment, by a third party, electronically distributes, publishes, emails, hyperlinks, or makes available for downloading, personal identifying information, including, but not limited to, a digital image of another person, or an electronic message of a harassing nature about another person, which would be likely to incite or produce that unlawful action.

(2) "Electronic communication" has the same meaning as the term is defined in paragraph (12) of Section 2510 of Title 18 of the United States Code.

(3) "Electronic communication device" includes, but is not limited to, telephones, cell phones, computers, internet web pages or websites, internet phones, hybrid cellular/wireless devices, personal digital assistants, video recorders, fax machines, or pagers.

(4) "Harassment" means a knowing and willful course of conduct directed at a specific person that a reasonable person would consider as seriously alarming, seriously annoying, seriously tormenting, or seriously terrorizing the person and that serves no legitimate purpose.

(5) "Identifying characteristics" means name or any part thereof, address or any part thereof, city or unincorporated area of residence, age, marital status, relationship to defendant, and race or ethnic background, telephone number, email address, social media profiles, online identifiers, contact information, or any other information, including images of the plaintiff, from which the plaintiff's identity can be discerned.

(6) "Of a harassing nature" means of a nature that a reasonable person would consider as seriously alarming, seriously annoying, seriously tormenting, or seriously terrorizing of the person and that serves no legitimate purpose.

(7) "Online identifiers" means any personally identifying information or signifiers that would tie an individual to a particular electronic service, device, or internet application, website, or platform account, including, but not limited to, access names, access codes, account names, aliases, avatars, credentials, gamer tags, display names, handles, login names, member names, online identities, pseudonyms, screen names, user accounts, user identifications, usernames, Uniform Resource Locators (URLs), domain names, Internet Protocol (IP) addresses, and media access control (MAC) addresses.

(b) A private cause of action lies against a person who doxes another person.

(c) A prevailing plaintiff who suffers harm as a result of being doxed in violation of subdivision (b) may recover any of the following:

(1) Economic and noneconomic damages proximately caused by being doxed, including, but not limited to, damages for physical harm, emotional distress, or property damage.

(2) Statutory damages of a sum of not less than one thousand five hundred dollars ($1,500) but not more than thirty thousand dollars ($30,000).

(3) Punitive damages.

(4) Upon the court holding a properly noticed hearing, reasonable attorney's fees and costs to the prevailing plaintiff.

(d) In addition to any other relief available at law, the court may order equitable relief against the person violating subdivision (b), including a temporary restraining order, or a preliminary injunction or a permanent injunction ordering the defendant to cease doxing activities. The court may grant injunctive relief maintaining the confidentiality of a plaintiff using a pseudonym as provided in subdivision (e).

(e)(1) A plaintiff in a civil proceeding pursuant to subdivision (b) may proceed using a pseudonym, either John Doe, Jane Doe, or Doe, for the true name of the plaintiff and may exclude or redact from all pleadings and documents filed in the action other identifying characteristics of the plaintiff. A plaintiff who proceeds using a pseudonym and excluding or redacting identifying characteristics as provided in this section shall file with the court and serve upon the defendant a confidential information form for this purpose that includes the plaintiff's name and other identifying characteristics excluded or redacted. The court shall keep the plaintiff's name and excluded or redacted characteristics confidential.

(2) In cases where a plaintiff proceeds using a pseudonym under this section, the following applies:

(A) All other parties and their agents and attorneys shall use this pseudonym in all pleadings, discovery documents, and other documents filed or served in the action, and at hearings, trial, and other court proceedings that are open to the public.

(B)(i) Any party filing a pleading, discovery document, or other document in the action shall exclude or redact any identifying characteristics of the plaintiff from the pleading, discovery document, or other document, except for a confidential information form filed pursuant to this subdivision.

(ii) A party excluding or redacting identifying characteristics as provided in this section shall file with the court and serve upon all other parties a confidential information form that includes the plaintiff's name and other identifying characteristics excluded or redacted. The court shall keep the plaintiff's name and excluded or redacted characteristics confidential.

(C) All court decisions, orders, petitions, discovery documents, and other documents shall be worded so as to protect the name or other identifying characteristics of the plaintiff from public revelation.

(3) The responsibility for excluding or redacting the name or identifying characteristics of the plaintiff from all documents filed with the court shall be the responsibility of the parties and their attorneys. This section does not require the court to review pleadings or other papers for compliance with this subdivision.

(4) Upon request of the plaintiff, the court shall limit access to the court records in an action filed under this section to the following individuals:

(A) A party to the action, including a party's attorney.

(B) A person by order of the court on a showing of good cause for access.

(C) A person 60 days after judgment is entered unless the court grants a plaintiff's motion to seal records pursuant to Chapter 3 of Division 4 of Title 2 of the California Rules of Court.

(f) In an action pursuant to this section, the plaintiff shall state in the caption of the complaint "ACTION BASED ON CIVIL CODE SECTION 1708.89."

(g) This section does not alter or negate any rights, obligations, or immunities of an interactive service provider under Section 230 of Title 47 of the United States Code. This section does not limit or preclude a plaintiff from securing or recovering any other available remedy.

(h) On or before January 1, 2026, the Judicial Council shall adopt or revise as appropriate rules and forms to implement subdivision (e).

(i) This section shall not apply against a person who solely does either of the following:

(1) Provide a person's personal identifying information or sensitive personal information in connection with the reporting of criminal activity to an employee of a law enforcement agency or with any lawfully authorized investigative, protective, or intelligence activity of any law enforcement agency or of an intelligence agency of the United States and the person making the report reasonably believes it is true.

(2) Disseminate the personally identifiable information for the purpose of, or in connection with, the reporting of conduct reasonably believed to be unlawful.

(j) The provisions of this section are severable. If any provision of this section or its application is held invalid, that invalidity shall not affect other provisions or applications that can be given effect without the invalid provision or application. **Leg.H.** Added Stats 2024 ch 557 §2 (AB 1979), effective January 1, 2025.

§1708.9. Unlawful acts toward minors

(a) It is unlawful for any person, except a parent or guardian acting toward his or her minor child, to commit any of the following acts:

(1) By force, threat of force, or physical obstruction that is a crime of violence, to intentionally injure, intimidate, interfere with, or attempt to injure, intimidate, or interfere with, any person attempting to enter or exit a facility.

(2) By nonviolent physical obstruction, to intentionally injure, intimidate, interfere with, or attempt to injure, intimidate, or interfere with, any person attempting to enter or exit a facility.

(b) For purposes of this section:

(1) "Facility" means any public or private school grounds, as described in subdivision (a) of Section 626.8 of the Penal Code, or any health facility, as described in Section 1250 of the Health and Safety Code.

(2) To "interfere" means to restrict a person's freedom of movement.

(3) To "intimidate" means to place a person in reasonable apprehension of bodily harm to himself, herself, or another person.

(4) "Nonviolent" means conduct that would not constitute a crime of violence.

(5) "Physical obstruction" means rendering ingress to or egress from a facility impassable to another person, or rendering passage to or from a facility unreasonably difficult or hazardous to another person.

(c) A person aggrieved by a violation of subdivision (a) may bring a civil action to enjoin the violation, for compensatory and punitive damages, for injunctive relief, and for the cost of suit and reasonable attorney's and expert witness' fees. With respect to compensatory damages, the plaintiff may elect, at any time prior to the rendering of a final judgment, to recover, in lieu of actual damages, an award of statutory damages in the amount of five thousand dollars ($5,000) per violation of paragraph (1) of subdivision (a), and one thousand dollars ($1,000) per violation of paragraph (2) of subdivision (a).

(d) The Attorney General, a district attorney, or a city attorney may bring a civil action to enjoin a violation of subdivision (a), for compensatory damages to persons or entities aggrieved by the violation, and for the imposition of a civil penalty against each respondent. The civil penalty for a violation of paragraph (1) of subdivision (a) shall not exceed fifteen thousand dollars ($15,000), or twenty-five thousand dollars ($25,000) for a second or subsequent violation. The civil penalty for a violation of paragraph (2) of subdivision (a) shall not exceed five thousand dollars ($5,000), or twenty-five thousand dollars ($25,000) for a second or subsequent violation.

(e) This section shall not be construed to impair the right to engage in any constitutionally protected activity, including, but not limited to, speech, protest, or assembly.

(f) The adoption of the act that added this section is an exercise of the police power of the state for purposes of protecting the health, safety, and welfare of the people of California, and this section shall be liberally construed to effectuate that purpose.

(g) This section shall not be construed to restrict, inhibit, prevent, or bring a chilling effect upon any actions by a person that are reasonable under the circumstances to protect, secure, provide safety to, or prevent illness in any child or adult in a facility. **Leg.H.** Added Stats 2014 ch 852 §2 (AB 1256), effective January 1, 2015.

§1709. Fraudulent deceit

One who willfully deceives another with intent to induce him to alter his position to his injury or risk, is liable for any damage which he thereby suffers. **Leg.H.** Enacted Stats 1872.

§1710. What constitutes deceit

A deceit, within the meaning of the last section, is either:

1. The suggestion, as a fact, of that which is not true, by one who does not believe it to be true;

2. The assertion, as a fact, of that which is not true, by one who has no reasonable ground for believing it to be true;

3. The suppression of a fact, by one who is bound to disclose it, or who gives information of other facts which are likely to mislead for want of communication of that fact; or,

4. A promise, made without any intention of performing it. **Leg.H.** Enacted Stats 1872.

§1710.1. Removal or alteration of serial number on equipment

Any person who, with intent to defraud, sells or disposes of a radio, piano, phonograph, sewing machine, washing machine, typewriter, adding machine, comptometer, bicycle, firearm, safe, vacuum cleaner, dictaphone, watch, watch movement, watchcase, or any other mechanical or electrical device, appliance, contrivance, material, piece of apparatus or equipment, from which the manufacturer's nameplate, serial number or any other distinguishing number or identification mark has been removed, defaced, covered, altered or destroyed, is civilly liable to the manufacturer in the sum of five hundred dollars ($500) per transaction and civilly liable to the purchaser for treble the actual damages sustained by the purchaser.

This section does not apply to those cases or instances where any of the changes or alterations enumerated in this section have been customarily made or done as an established practice in the ordinary and regular conduct of business by the original manufacturer or his duly appointed direct representative or under specific authorization from the original manufacturer. **Leg.H.** Added Stats 1971 ch 1713 §1.

§1710.2. Disclosure of death or HIV-positive status of prior occupant in real property transfers; Preemption by state

(a)(1) Subject to subdivision (d), an owner of real property or his or her agent, or any agent of a transferee of real property, is not required to disclose either of the following to the transferee, as these are not material facts that require disclosure:

(A) The occurrence of an occupant's death upon the real property or the manner of death where the death has occurred more than three years prior to the date the transferee offers to purchase, lease, or rent the real property.

(B) That an occupant of that property was living with human immunodeficiency virus (HIV) or died from AIDS-related complications.

(2) As used in this section:

(A) "Agent" includes any person licensed pursuant to Part 1 (commencing with Section 10000) of Division 4 of the Business and Professions Code.

(B) "Transferee" includes a purchaser, lessee, or renter of real property.

(3) No cause of action shall arise against an owner or his or her agent or any agent of a transferee for not disclosing facts pursuant to paragraph (1).

(b) It is the intent of the Legislature to occupy the field of regulation of disclosure related to either of the following:

(1) Deaths occurring upon real property.

(2) The HIV-positive status of a prior occupant in situations affecting the transfer of real property or any estate or interest in real property.

(c) This section shall not be construed to alter the law relating to disclosure pertaining to any other physical or mental condition or disease, and this section shall not relieve any owner or agent of any obligation to disclose the physical condition of the premises.

(d) This section shall not be construed to immunize an owner or his or her agent from making an intentional misrepresentation in response to a direct inquiry from a transferee or a prospective transferee of real property, concerning deaths on the real property. **Leg.H.** Added Stats 1986 ch 498 §2. Amended Stats 1987 ch 494 §1; Stats 2016 ch 548 §1 (AB 73), effective September 24, 2016.

§1711. Deceit upon the public, etc

One who practices a deceit with intent to defraud the public, or a particular class of persons, is deemed to have intended to defraud every individual in that class, who is actually misled by the deceit. **Leg.H.** Enacted Stats 1872.

§1712. Restoration of thing wrongfully acquired

One who obtains a thing without the consent of its owner, or by a consent afterwards rescinded, or by an unlawful exaction which the owner could not at the time prudently refuse, must restore it to the person from whom it was thus obtained, unless he has acquired a title thereto superior to that of such other person, or unless the transaction was corrupt and unlawful on both sides. **Leg.H.** Enacted Stats 1872.

§1713. When demand necessary

The restoration required by the last section must be made without demand, except where a thing is obtained by mutual mistake, in which case the party obtaining the thing is not bound to return it until he has notice of the mistake. **Leg.H.** Enacted Stats 1872.

§1714. Responsibility for willful acts or negligence; Proximate cause of injuries resulting from furnishing alcohol to intoxicated person; Liability of social host; Provision of alcoholic beverages to persons under 21 years of age

(a) Everyone is responsible, not only for the result of his or her willful acts, but also for an injury occasioned to another by his or her want of ordinary care or skill in the management of his or her property or person, except so far as the latter has, willfully or by want of ordinary care, brought the injury upon himself or herself. The design, distribution, or marketing of firearms and ammunition is not exempt from the duty to use ordinary care and skill that is required by this section. The extent of liability in these cases is defined by the Title on Compensatory Relief.

(b) It is the intent of the Legislature to abrogate the holdings in cases such as Vesely v. Sager (1971) 5 Cal.3d 153, Bernhard v. Harrah's Club (1976) 16 Cal.3d 313, and Coulter v. Superior Court (1978) 21 Cal.3d 144 and to reinstate the prior judicial interpretation of this section as it relates to proximate cause for injuries incurred as a result of furnishing alcoholic beverages to an intoxicated person, namely that the furnishing of alcoholic beverages is not the proximate cause of injuries resulting from intoxication, but rather the consumption of alcoholic beverages is the proximate cause of injuries inflicted upon another by an intoxicated person.

(c) Except as provided in subdivision (d), no social host who furnishes alcoholic beverages to any person may be held legally accountable for damages suffered by that person, or for injury to the person or property of, or death of, any third person, resulting from the consumption of those beverages.

(d)(1) Nothing in subdivision (c) shall preclude a claim against a parent, guardian, or another adult who knowingly furnishes alcoholic beverages at his or her residence to a person whom he or she knows, or should have known, to be under 21 years of age, in which case, notwithstanding subdivision (b), the furnishing of the alcoholic beverage may be found to be the proximate cause of resulting injuries or death.

(2) A claim under this subdivision may be brought by, or on behalf of, the person under 21 years of age or by a person who was harmed by the person under 21 years of age. **Leg.H.** Enacted Stats 1872. Amended Stats 1978 ch 929 §2; Stats 2002 ch 913 §1 (SB 682); Stats 2003 ch 62 §15 (SB 600); Stats 2010 ch 154 §1 (AB 2486), effective January 1, 2011; Stats 2011 ch 410 §1 (AB 1407), effective January 1, 2012.

§1714¼. [Section repealed 1935]

Leg.H. Added Stats 1929 ch 261 §1. Repealed Stats 1935 ch 27 (Veh C §802). See Veh C §§17150–17157.

§1714½. [Section repealed 1935]

Leg.H. Added Stats 1929 ch 260 §1. Amended Stats 1931 ch 122 §1. Repealed Stats 1935 ch 27 (Veh C §802). See Veh C §§17000–17002.

§1714.01. Recovery of damages by domestic partner for negligent infliction of emotional distress

(a) Domestic partners shall be entitled to recover damages for negligent infliction of emotional distress to the same extent that spouses are entitled to do so under California law.

(b) For the purpose of this section, "domestic partners" has the meaning provided in Section 297 of the Family Code. **Leg.H.** Added Stats 2001 ch 893 §1 (AB 25).

§1714.1. Civil liability of parents for minor's acts of willful misconduct resulting in death, personal injury, or property damage

(a) Any act of willful misconduct of a minor that results in injury or death to another person or in any injury to the property of another shall be imputed to the parent or guardian having custody and control of the minor for all purposes of civil damages, and the parent or guardian having custody and control shall be jointly and severally liable with the minor for any damages resulting from the willful misconduct.

Subject to the provisions of subdivision (c), the joint and several liability of the parent or guardian having custody and control of a minor under this subdivision shall not exceed twenty-five thousand dollars ($25,000) for each tort of the minor, and in the case of injury to a person, imputed liability shall be further limited to medical, dental and hospital expenses incurred by the injured person, not to exceed twenty-five thousand dollars ($25,000). The liability imposed by this section is in addition to any liability now imposed by law.

(b) Any act of willful misconduct of a minor that results in the defacement of property of another with paint or a similar substance shall be imputed to the parent or guardian having custody and control of the minor for all purposes of civil damages, including court costs, and attorney's fees, to the prevailing party, and the parent or guardian having custody and control shall be jointly and severally liable with the minor for any damages resulting from the willful misconduct, not to exceed twenty-five thousand dollars ($25,000), except as provided in subdivision (c), for each tort of the minor.

(c) The amounts listed in subdivisions (a) and (b) shall be adjusted every two years by the Judicial Council to reflect any increases in the cost of living in California, as indicated by the annual average of the California Consumer Price Index. The Judicial Council shall round this adjusted amount up or down to the nearest hundred dollars. On or before July 1 of each odd-numbered year, the Judicial Council shall compute and publish the amounts listed in subdivisions (a) and (b), as adjusted according to this subdivision.

(d) The maximum liability imposed by this section is the maximum liability authorized under this section at the time that the act of willful misconduct by a minor was committed.

(e) Nothing in this section shall impose liability on an insurer for a loss caused by the willful act of the insured for purposes of Section 533 of the Insurance Code. An insurer shall not be liable for the conduct imputed to a parent or guardian by this section for any amount in excess of ten thousand dollars ($10,000). **Leg.H.** Added Stats 1955 ch 820 §1. Amended Stats 1965 ch 407 §1; Stats 1970 ch 640 §1; Stats 1972 ch 442 §1; Stats 1974 ch 340 §1; Stats 1979 ch 127 §1; Stats 1983 ch 981 §1; Stats 1994 ch 568 §1 (AB 308), ch 909 §1 (SB 1779); Stats 2007 ch 738 §2 (AB 1248), effective January 1, 2008.

§1714.2. Civil liability of persons rendering emergency care

(a) In order to encourage citizens to participate in emergency medical services training programs and to render emergency medical services to fellow citizens, no person who has completed a basic cardiopulmonary resuscitation course which complies with the standards adopted by the American Heart Association or the American Red Cross for cardiopulmonary resuscitation and emergency cardiac care, and who, in good faith, renders emergency cardiopulmonary resuscitation at the scene of an emergency, shall be liable for any civil damages as a result of any acts or omissions by such person rendering the emergency care.

(b) This section shall not be construed to grant immunity from civil damages to any person whose conduct in rendering such emergency care constitutes gross negligence.

(c) In order to encourage local agencies and other organizations to train citizens in cardiopulmonary resuscitation techniques, no local agency, entity of state or local government, or other public or private organization which sponsors, authorizes, supports, finances, or supervises the training of citizens in cardiopulmonary resuscitation shall be liable for any civil damages alleged to result from such training programs.

(d) In order to encourage qualified individuals to instruct citizens in cardiopulmonary resuscitation, no person who is certified to instruct in cardiopulmonary resuscitation by either the American Heart Association or the American Red Cross shall be liable for any civil damages alleged to result from the acts or omissions of an individual who received instruction on cardiopulmonary resuscitation by that certified instructor.

(e) This section shall not be construed to grant immunity from civil damages to any person who renders such emergency care to an individual with the expectation of receiving compensation from the individual for providing the emergency care. **Leg.H.** Added Stats 1977 ch 595 §1.

§1714.21. Liability for damages

(a) For purposes of this section, the following definitions shall apply:

(1) "AED" or "defibrillator" means an automated external defibrillator.

(2) "CPR" means cardiopulmonary resuscitation.

(b) Any person who, in good faith and not for compensation, renders emergency care or treatment by the use of an AED at the scene of an emergency is not liable for any civil damages resulting from any acts or omissions in rendering the emergency care.

(c) A person or entity who provides CPR and AED training to a person who renders emergency care pursuant to subdivision (b) is not liable for any civil damages resulting from any acts or omissions of the person rendering the emergency care.

(d)(1) A person or entity that acquires an AED for emergency use pursuant to this section is not liable for any civil damages resulting from any acts or omissions in the rendering of the emergency care by use of an AED if that person or entity has complied with subdivision (b) of Section 1797.196 of the Health and Safety Code.

(2) A physician and surgeon or other health care professional that is involved in the selection, placement, or installation of an AED pursuant to Section 1797.196 of the Health and Safety Code is not liable for civil damages resulting from acts or omissions in the rendering of emergency care by use of that AED.

(e) The protections specified in this section do not apply in the case of personal injury or wrongful death that results from the gross negligence or willful or wanton misconduct of the person who renders emergency care or treatment by the use of an AED.

(f) This section does not relieve a manufacturer, designer, developer, distributor, installer, or supplier of an AED or defibrillator of any liability under any applicable statute or rule of law. **Leg.H.** Added Stats 1999 ch 163 §2 (SB 911). Amended Stats 2002 ch 718 §1 (AB 2041); Stats 2015 ch 264 §1 (SB 658), effective January 1, 2016.

§1714.22. Prescribing, dispensing, or administering opioid antagonist; Report

(a) For purposes of this section, the following definitions apply:

(1) "Opioid antagonist" means naloxone hydrochloride or any other opioid antagonist that is approved by the United States Food and Drug Administration for the treatment of an opioid overdose.

(2) "Opioid overdose prevention and treatment training program" means any program operated by a local health jurisdiction or that is registered by a local health jurisdiction to train individuals to prevent, recognize, and respond to an opiate overdose, and that provides, at a minimum, training in all of the following:

(A) The causes of an opiate overdose.

(B) Mouth to mouth resuscitation.

(C) How to contact appropriate emergency medical services.

(D) How to administer an opioid antagonist.

(b) A licensed health care provider who is authorized by law to prescribe an opioid antagonist may, if acting with reasonable care, prescribe and subsequently dispense or distribute an opioid antagonist to a person at risk of an opioid-related overdose or to a family member, friend, or other person in a position to assist a person at risk of an opioid-related overdose.

(c)(1) A licensed health care provider who is authorized by law to prescribe an opioid antagonist may issue standing orders for the distribution of an opioid antagonist to a person at risk of an opioid-related overdose or to a family member, friend, or other person in a position to assist a person at risk of an opioid-related overdose.

(2) A licensed health care provider who is authorized by law to prescribe an opioid antagonist may issue standing orders for the administration of an opioid antagonist to a person at risk of an opioid-related overdose by a family member, friend, or other person in a position to assist a person experiencing or reasonably suspected of experiencing an opioid overdose.

(d)(1) A person who is prescribed or possesses an opioid antagonist pursuant to a standing order shall receive the training provided by an opioid overdose prevention and treatment training program.

(2) A person who is prescribed an opioid antagonist directly from a licensed prescriber shall not be required to receive training from an opioid prevention and treatment training program.

(e) A licensed health care provider who acts with reasonable care shall not be subject to professional review, be liable in a civil action, or be subject to criminal prosecution for issuing a prescription or order pursuant to subdivision (b) or (c).

(f) Notwithstanding any other law, a person who possesses or distributes an opioid antagonist pursuant to a prescription or standing order shall not be subject to professional review, be liable in a civil action, or be subject to criminal prosecution for this possession or distribution. Notwithstanding any other law, a person not otherwise licensed to administer an opioid antagonist, but trained as required under paragraph (1) of subdivision (d), who acts with reasonable care in administering an opioid antagonist, in good faith and not for compensation, to a person who is experiencing or is suspected of experiencing an overdose shall not be subject to professional review, be liable in a civil action, or be subject to criminal prosecution for this administration. **Leg.H.** Added Stats 2007 ch 477 §2 (SB 767), effective January 1, 2008, repealed January 1, 2011. Amended Stats 2010 ch 545 §1 (AB 2145), effective January 1, 2011, repealed January 1, 2016; Stats 2013 ch 707 §1 (AB 635), effective January 1, 2014; Stats 2021 ch 554 §1 (SB 823), effective January 1, 2022.

§1714.23. No liability for administration of epinephrine auto-injector to person experiencing anaphylaxis; Applicability

(a) For purposes of this section, the following definitions shall apply:

(1) "Anaphylaxis" means a potentially life-threatening hypersensitivity or allergic reaction to a substance.

(A) Symptoms of anaphylaxis may include shortness of breath, wheezing, difficulty breathing, difficulty talking or swallowing, hives, itching, swelling, shock, or asthma.

(B) Causes of anaphylaxis may include, but are not limited to, insect stings or bites, foods, drugs, and other allergens, as well as idiopathic or exercise-induced anaphylaxis.

(2) "Epinephrine auto-injector" means a disposable delivery device designed for the automatic injection of a premeasured dose of epinephrine into the human body to prevent or treat a life-threatening allergic reaction.

(b)(1) Any person described in subdivision (b) of Section 1797.197a of the Health and Safety Code who administers an epinephrine auto-injector, in good faith and not for compensation, to another person who appears to be experiencing anaphylaxis at the scene of an emergency situation is not liable for any civil damages resulting from his or her acts or omissions in administering the epinephrine auto-injector, if that person has complied with the requirements and standards of Section 1797.197a of the Health and Safety Code.

(2)(A) An authorized entity shall not be liable for any civil damages resulting from any act or omission other than an act or omission constituting gross negligence or willful or wanton misconduct connected to the administration of an epinephrine auto-injector by any one of its employees, volunteers, or agents who is a lay rescuer, as defined by paragraph (4) of subdivision (a) of Section 1797.197a of the Health and Safety Code, if the entity has complied with all applicable requirements of Section 1797.197a of the Health and Safety Code.

(B) The failure of an authorized entity to possess or administer an epinephrine auto-injector shall not result in civil liability.

(3) This subdivision does not affect any other immunity or defense that is available under law.

(c) The protection specified in paragraph (1) of subdivision (b) shall not apply in a case of personal injury or wrongful death that results from the gross negligence or willful or wanton misconduct of the person who renders emergency care treatment by the use of an epinephrine auto-injector.

(d) Nothing in this section relieves a manufacturer, designer, developer, distributor, or supplier of an epinephrine auto-injector of liability under any other applicable law.

(e) An authorizing physician and surgeon is not subject to professional review, liable in a civil action, or subject to criminal prosecution for the issuance of a prescription or order in accordance with Section 1797.197a of the Health and Safety Code unless the physician and surgeon's issuance of the prescription or order constitutes gross negligence or willful or malicious conduct. **Leg.H.** Added Stats 2013 ch 725 §2 (SB 669), effective January 1, 2014. Amended Stats 2016 ch 374 §2 (AB 1386), effective January 1, 2017.

§1714.24. Limitation on liability for injury or harm from maintenance of secure drug take-back bin

(a) For purposes of this section, the following definitions shall apply:

(1) "Collector" includes only those entities authorized by and registered with the federal Drug Enforcement Administration to receive a controlled substance for the purpose of destruction, if the entity is in good standing with any applicable licensing authority.

(2) "Compensation" means reimbursement or funds received from a customer to compensate for the cost incurred in obtaining, installing, or maintaining a secure drug take-back bin. "Compensation" does not include reimbursement or funds received from any other person or entity, other than a customer, to compensate for the costs incurred in obtaining, installing, or maintaining a secure drug take-back bin.

(3) "Home-generated pharmaceutical waste" means a pharmaceutical that is no longer wanted or needed by the consumer and includes any delivery system, such as pills, liquids, and inhalers.

(4) "Maintains" includes owning, leasing, operating, or otherwise hosting a secure drug take-back bin on the collector's premises.

(5) "Pharmaceutical" means a prescription or over-the-counter human or veterinary drug, including, but not limited to, a drug as defined in Section 109925 of the Health and Safety Code and Section 321(g)(1) of Title 21 of the United States Code. "Pharmaceutical" includes controlled substances included in Schedule II, III, IV, or V of the California Uniform Controlled Substances Act (Division 10 (commencing with Section 11000) of the Health and Safety Code), but does not include a controlled substance included in Schedule I.

(6) "Secure drug take-back bin" means a collection receptacle as described in Section 1317.75 of Title 21 of the Code of Federal Regulations.

(b) Any collector that maintains a secure drug take-back bin shall not be liable in a civil action, or be subject to criminal prosecution, for any injury or harm that results from the collector maintaining a secure drug take-back bin on its premises provided that the collector, not for compensation, acts in good faith to take all of the following steps to ensure the health and safety of consumers and employees and the proper disposal in the waste stream of the home-generated pharmaceutical waste contained in a secure drug take-back bin, unless the injury or harm results from the collector's gross negligence or willful and wanton misconduct:

(1) Complies with all applicable state and federal laws and regulations relating to the collection of home-generated pharmaceutical waste for disposal in secure drug take-back bins, including, but not limited to, the federal Secure and Responsible Drug Disposal Act of 2010 (Public Law 111-273).

(2) Notifies local law enforcement and any local environmental health department as to the existence and location of any secure drug take-back bin on the collector's premises and the status of the collector's registration as a collector with the federal Drug Enforcement Administration.

(3) Ensures that the secure drug take-back bin is placed in a location that is regularly monitored by employees of the registered collector.

(4) Ensures that conspicuous signage is posted on the secure drug take-back bin that clearly notifies customers as to what controlled and noncontrolled substances are and are not acceptable for deposit into the bin, as well as the hours during which collection is allowed.

(5) Ensures that public access to the secure drug take-back bin is limited to hours in which employees of the registered collector are present and able to monitor the operation of the secure drug take-back bin.

(6) Regularly inspects the area surrounding the secure drug take-back bin for potential tampering or diversion. Record logs of those inspections shall be maintained and retained for two years, reflecting the date and time of the inspection, and the initials of the employee inspecting the area. The logs shall be maintained in writing or electronically and may be combined with logs required by state or federal regulations. The logs may be used to demonstrate regular inspection of the area. Other records or reports mandated by federal or state regulations shall also be retained for a minimum of two years unless regulations mandate a longer period.

(7) Notifies local law enforcement authorities of any suspected or known tampering, theft, or significant loss of controlled substances, within one business day of discovery. If the collector maintains daily business hours, this notification shall be made within one calendar day.

(8) Notify local law enforcement as to any decision to discontinue its voluntary collection of controlled substances and provide documentation of its written notification to the federal Drug Enforcement Administration's Registration Unit as otherwise required under federal laws and regulations.

(c) Nothing in this section shall be construed to require entities that may qualify as a collector to acquire, maintain, or make available to the public a secure drug take-back bin on its premises. **Leg.H.** Added Stats 2016 ch 238 §2 (SB 1229), effective January 1, 2017.

2016 Note: (a) The Legislature finds and declares the following:

(1) On October 12, 2010, the federal Secure and Responsible Drug Disposal Act of 2010 (Public Law 111-273; hereafter referred to as the Disposal Act) was enacted. Before the Disposal Act, individuals who wanted to dispose of unused, unwanted, or expired pharmaceutical controlled substances had limited disposal options. The federal Controlled Substances Act (21 U.S.C. Sec. 801 et seq.; hereafter referred to as the CSA) only permitted individuals to destroy those substances themselves (e.g., by flushing or discarding), surrender them to law enforcement, or seek assistance from the federal Drug Enforcement Administration (DEA). These restrictions resulted in the accumulation of pharmaceutical controlled substances in household medicine cabinets that were available for abuse, misuse, diversion, and accidental ingestion. The Disposal Act amended the CSA to authorize specified individuals, referred to as "ultimate users," to deliver their pharmaceutical controlled substances to another person for the purpose of disposal in accordance with regulations promulgated by the United States Attorney General.

(2) On September 9, 2014, the DEA issued its final rule governing the secure disposal of controlled substances by registrants and ultimate users. Those regulations implement the Disposal Act by expanding the options available to collect controlled substances from ultimate users for the purpose of disposal, including take-back events, mail-back programs, and collection receptacle locations. Those regulations, among other things, allow authorized manufacturers, distributors, reverse distributors, narcotic treatment programs, hospitals/clinics with an onsite pharmacy, and retail pharmacies to voluntarily administer mail-back programs and maintain collection receptacles.

(b) It is the intent of the Legislature, with the enactment of this act, to do both of the following:

(1) Encourage the good faith participation of federally authorized entities to maintain secure drug take-back bins on their premises for the convenience and public health and safety of prescription drug consumers and the proper disposal in the waste stream of the pharmaceutical waste contained in the bins.

(2) Limit the civil and criminal liability of participating entities that meet certain minimum standards and take reasonable care to ensure the health and safety of consumers and employees when maintaining secure drug take-back bins on their premises.

(c) The terms and conditions provided by subdivision (b) of Section 1714.24 of the Civil Code, as added by this act, shall be construed in a manner consistent with the requirements imposed by the DEA's final rule governing the secure disposal of controlled substances (79 Fed. Reg. 53519-70 (September 9, 2014)) and any regulations promulgated by the state. Stats 2016 ch 238 (SB 1229) §1.

§1714.25. Limitation on liability for damage or injury from donated food

(a) Except for injury resulting from gross negligence or intentional misconduct in the preparation or handling of donated food, no person, gleaner, or food facility that donates food that is fit for human consumption at the time it was donated to a nonprofit charitable organization or food bank shall be liable for any damage or injury resulting from the consumption of the donated food. Food facilities may donate food directly to end recipients for consumption.

The immunity from civil liability provided by this subdivision applies regardless of compliance with any laws, regulations, or ordinances regulating the packaging or labeling of food, and regardless of compliance with any laws, regulations, or ordinances regulating the storage or handling of the food by the donee after the donation of the food. The donation of perishable food that is fit for human consumption but that has exceeded the labeled shelf life date recommended by the manufacturer is protected under the California Good Samaritan Food Donation Act if the person that distributes the food to the end recipient makes a good faith evaluation that the food to be donated is wholesome.

(b) A nonprofit charitable organization or a food bank that, in good faith, receives and distributes food without charge that is fit for human consumption at the time it was distributed is not liable for an injury or death due to the food unless the injury or death is a direct result of the gross negligence or intentional misconduct of the organization.

(c) Nothing in this chapter shall be construed to limit the ability of a person, gleaner, or food facility to donate food.

(d) For the purposes of this section:

(1) "Food bank" has the same meaning as defined in Section 113783 of the Health and Safety Code.

(2) Food facility has the same meaning as defined in Section 113789 of the Health and Safety Code.

(3) "Gleaner" means a person who harvests for free distribution to the needy, or for donation to a nonprofit organization for ultimate distribution to the needy, an agricultural crop that has been donated by the owner.

(4) "Nonprofit charitable organization" has the same meaning as defined in Section 113841 of the Health and Safety Code.

(5) "Person" means an individual, school, local educational agency as defined in Section 421 of the Education Code, corporation, partnership, limited liability company, organization, association, or governmental entity, including a retail grocer, wholesaler, hotel, motel, manufacturer, restaurant, caterer, farmer, and nonprofit food distributor or hospital. In the case of a corporation, partnership, organization, association, or governmental entity, the term includes an officer, director, partner, manager or managing member, deacon, trustee, council member, or other elected or appointed individual responsible for the governance of the entity. **Leg.H.** Added Stats 1988 ch 735 §1. Amended Stats 1996 ch 1023 §27 (SB 1497), effective September 29, 1996; Stats 2017 ch 619 §3 (AB 1219), effective January 1, 2018.

2017 Note: This act shall be known, and may be cited, as the California Good Samaritan Food Donation Act. Stats 2017 ch 619 (AB 1219) §1.

§1714.26. Limitation on liability for damage or injury from provision of vision screenings and donated or recycled eyeglasses by nonprofit charitable organization; Applicability; Definitions

(a) Except for damage or injury resulting from gross negligence or a willful act, there is no liability for any damage or injury on the part of a nonprofit charitable organization that provides vision screenings and, if applicable, provides donated or recycled eyeglasses, or a participating licensed optometrist, ophthalmologist, or trained volunteer who works with such a nonprofit charitable organization in the performance of vision screenings, if all of the following conditions are met:

(1) The vision screening is provided to address ocular health concerns and, if applicable, to provide a temporary solution in the form of donated or recycled eyeglasses until the patient can get a full examination and eyeglasses.

(2) The vision screening is not intended to replace a full ocular health examination provided by a licensed optometrist or ophthalmologist.

(3) The patient signs a waiver acknowledging that the services provided are a temporary solution until the patient can get a full examination by a licensed optometrist or ophthalmologist.

(4) Each vision screening is supervised by an attending licensed optometrist or ophthalmologist.

(5) The eyeglass prescription determinations and ocular health recommendations are provided by an attending licensed optometrist or ophthalmologist.

(6) A written prescription is not provided to the patient.

(7) The eyeglasses provided to the patients are a close or approximate match, within tolerances allowed by the attending licensed optometrist or ophthalmologist, to the prescription determined during the vision screening.

(8) The vision screening and eyeglasses are provided without a charge.

(9) The optometrist, ophthalmologist, or volunteer is authorized by the nonprofit organization to provide the vision screening and eyeglasses on behalf of the nonprofit organization and is acting within the scope of his or her authorized responsibilities and the guidelines of the nonprofit charitable organization when providing the vision screening or eyeglasses.

(10) The nonprofit charitable organization provides procedural, risk management, and quality control training, as applicable, to the participating optometrist, ophthalmologist, or volunteer who provides the vision screening or eyeglasses.

(b) The limitation of liability provided in subdivision (a) is not applicable if an action is brought by an officer of a state or local government pursuant to state or local law.

(c) The limitation of liability provided in subdivision (a) is not applicable if the conduct of the nonprofit charitable organization, optometrist, ophthalmologist, or volunteer includes any of the following types of misconduct:

(1) A crime of violence.

(2) A hate crime.

(3) An act involving a sexual offense.

(4) An act involving misconduct in violation of federal or state civil rights laws.

(5) An act performed while the defendant was under the influence of drugs or alcohol.

(d) For the purposes of this section:

(1) "Nonprofit charitable organization" means an organization exempt from federal income tax as an organization described in Section 501(c)(3) of the Internal Revenue Code.

(2) "Vision screening" means a test or examination of an individual using a portion of the usual examination procedures in a comprehensive eye examination and refraction, that are selected or directed by an attending licensed optometrist or ophthalmologist, and are within the guidelines of the nonprofit charitable organization. **Leg.H.** Added Stats 2013 ch 68 §1 (SB 724), effective January 1, 2014.

§ 1714.29. Limitation of liability to person rendering emergency aid by use of trauma kit

(a) For purposes of this section, "trauma kit" means a first aid response kit that contains at least all of the following:

(1) One tourniquet endorsed by the Committee on Tactical Combat Casualty Care.

(2) One bleeding control bandage.

(3) One pair of nonlatex protective gloves and a marker.

(4) One pair of scissors.

(5) Instructional documents developed by the Stop the Bleed national awareness campaign of the United States Department of Homeland Security or the American College of Surgeons Committee on Trauma, the American Red Cross, the Committee for Tactical Emergency Casualty Care, or any other partner of the United States Department of Defense.

(b) Medical materials and equipment similar to those described in paragraphs (1) to (4), inclusive, of subdivision (a) and any additional items that are approved by the medical director of the local emergency medical services agency may be included as supplements in addition to the items described in paragraphs (1) to (4), inclusive, of subdivision (a) if they adequately treat a traumatic injury and can be stored in a readily available kit.

(c) Subdivision (b) of Section 1799.102 of the Health and Safety Code, the "Good Samaritan Law," applies to any lay rescuer or person who, in good faith and not for compensation, renders emergency care or treatment by the use of a trauma kit at the scene of an emergency.

(d) A person who renders emergency care or treatment by the use of a trauma kit at the scene of an emergency and who receives compensation as a result of their employment by a property managing entity, a tenant of a building, or any other private or public employer, but is not compensated to provide emergency medical care, is not providing emergency medical care "for compensation" for purposes of Section 1799.102 of the Health and Safety Code.

(e) Section 1799.100 of the Health and Safety Code applies to a person or entity that voluntarily, and without expectation and receipt of compensation, does either of the following:

(1) Provides training in the use of a trauma kit to provide emergency medical treatment to victims of trauma, including, but not limited to, training in the use of the trauma kit in emergency first care response to an active shooter.

(2) Certifies persons, other than physicians and surgeons, registered nurses, and licensed vocational nurses, who are trained in the use of a trauma kit to provide emergency medical treatment to victims of trauma.

(f) This section does not require a property manager or person employed by a property managing entity to respond to an emergency with the use of trauma kits. **Leg.H.** Added Stats 2022 ch 586 §2 (AB 2260), effective January 1, 2023.

§1714.3. Civil liability of parents for injuries from discharge of firearm by minor under 18; Maximum liability

Civil liability for any injury to the person or property of another proximately caused by the discharge of a firearm by a minor under the age of 18 years shall be imputed to a parent or guardian having custody and control of the minor for all purposes of civil damages, and such parent or guardian shall be jointly and severally liable with such minor for any damages resulting from such act, if such parent or guardian either permitted the minor to have the firearm or left the firearm in a place accessible to the minor.

The liability imposed by this section is in addition to any liability otherwise imposed by law. However, no person, or group of persons collectively, shall incur liability under this section in any amount exceeding thirty thousand dollars ($30,000) for injury to or death of one person as a result of any one occurrence or, subject to the limit as to one person, exceeding sixty thousand dollars ($60,000) for injury to or death of all persons as a result of any one such occurrence. **Leg.H.** Added Stats 1970 ch 843 §1. Amended Stats 1977 ch 87 §1; Stats 1986 ch 1099 §1.

§1714.4. Liability for knowingly assisting child support obligor to escape, evade, or avoid payment; Application to financial institutions

(a) Any person or business entity that knowingly assists a child support obligor who has an unpaid child support obligation to escape, evade, or avoid paying court-ordered or court-approved child support shall be liable for three times the value of the assistance provided, such as the fair market value of the obligor's assets transferred or hidden. The maximum liability imposed by this section shall not exceed the entire child support obligation due. Any funds or assets collected pursuant to this section shall be paid to the child support obligee, and shall not reduce the amount of the unpaid child support obligation. Upon the satisfaction of the unpaid child support obligation, this section shall not apply.

(b) For purposes of this section, actions taken to knowingly assist a child support obligor to escape, evade, or avoid paying court-ordered or court-approved child support include, with actual knowledge of the child support obligation, helping to hide or transfer assets of the child support obligor.

(c) This section shall not apply to a financial institution unless the financial institution has actual knowledge of the child support obligation and, with that knowledge, knowingly assists the obligor to escape, evade, or avoid paying the child support obligation. However, a financial institution with knowledge of an asset transfer has no duty to inquire into the rightfulness of the transaction, nor shall it be deemed to have knowingly assisted an obligor to escape, evade, or avoid paying the child support obligation if that assistance is provided by an employee or agent of the financial institution acting outside the terms and conditions of employment or agency without the actual knowledge of the financial institution. **Leg.H.** Added Stats 2006 ch 820 §2 (AB 2440), effective January 1, 2007.

Prior Law: Former CC §1714.4, relating to exemption of firearm or ammunition design from products liability in certain cases, was added Stats 1983 ch 1299 §1 and repealed Stats 2002 ch 906 §2, ch 913 §2.

Former CC §1714.4, relating to exemption of firearm or ammunition design from products liability in certain cases, was added Stats 1983 ch 1299 §1 and repealed Stats 2002 ch 906 §2, ch 913 §2.

§1714.41. Liability for knowingly assisting child support obligor to escape, evade, or avoid payment; Examples of actions taken knowingly

(a) Any person or business entity that knowingly assists a child support obligor who has an unpaid child support obligation to escape, evade, or avoid paying court-ordered or court-approved child support shall be liable for three times the value of the assistance provided, such as the fair market value of the assets transferred or hidden, or the amount of the wages or other compensation paid to the child support obligor but not reported. The maximum liability imposed by this section shall not exceed the entire child support obligation due. Any funds or assets collected pursuant to this section shall be paid to the child support obligee, and shall not reduce the amount of the unpaid child support obligation. Upon the satisfaction of the unpaid child support obligation, this section shall not apply.

(b) For purposes of this section, actions taken to knowingly assist a child support obligor to escape, evade, or avoid paying court-ordered or court-approved child support include, but are not limited to, any of the following actions taken when the individual or entity knew or should have known of the child support obligation:

(1) Hiring or employing the child support obligor as an employee in a trade or business and failing to timely file a report of new employees with the California New Employee Registry maintained by the Employment Development Department.

(2) Engaging the child support obligor as a service provider and failing to timely file a report with the Employment Development Department as required by Section 1088.8 of the Unemployment Insurance Code.

(3) When engaged in a trade or business, paying wages or other forms of compensation for services rendered by a child support obligor that are not reported to the Employment Development Department as required, including, but not limited to, payment in cash or via barter or trade. **Leg.H.** Added Stats 2006 ch 820 §3 (AB 2440), effective January 1, 2007.

§1714.43. Disclosure of efforts to eradicate slavery and human trafficking; Posting disclosures on Internet Web site; Remedies for violation

(a)(1) Every retail seller and manufacturer doing business in this state and having annual worldwide gross receipts that exceed one hundred million dollars ($100,000,000) shall disclose, as set forth in subdivision (c), its efforts to eradicate slavery and human trafficking from its direct supply chain for tangible goods offered for sale.

(2) For the purposes of this section, the following definitions shall apply:

(A) "Doing business in this state" shall have the same meaning as set forth in Section 23101 of the Revenue and Taxation Code.

(B) "Gross receipts" shall have the same meaning as set forth in Section 25120 of the Revenue and Taxation Code.

(C) "Manufacturer" means a business entity with manufacturing as its principal business activity code, as reported on the entity's tax return filed under Part 10.2 (commencing with Section 18401) of Division 2 of the Revenue and Taxation Code.

(D) "Retail seller" means a business entity with retail trade as its principal business activity code, as reported on the entity's tax return filed under Part 10.2 (commencing with Section 18401) of Division 2 of the Revenue and Taxation Code.

(b) The disclosure described in subdivision (a) shall be posted on the retail seller's or manufacturer's Internet Web site with a conspicuous and easily understood link to the required information placed on the business' homepage. In the event the retail seller or manufacturer does not have an Internet Web site, consumers shall be provided the written disclosure within 30 days of receiving a written request for the disclosure from a consumer.

(c) The disclosure described in subdivision (a) shall, at a minimum, disclose to what extent, if any, that the retail seller or manufacturer does each of the following:

(1) Engages in verification of product supply chains to evaluate and address risks of human trafficking and slavery. The disclosure shall specify if the verification was not conducted by a third party.

(2) Conducts audits of suppliers to evaluate supplier compliance with company standards for trafficking and slavery in supply chains. The disclosure shall specify if the verification was not an independent, unannounced audit.

(3) Requires direct suppliers to certify that materials incorporated into the product comply with the laws regarding slavery and human trafficking of the country or countries in which they are doing business.

(4) Maintains internal accountability standards and procedures for employees or contractors failing to meet company standards regarding slavery and trafficking.

(5) Provides company employees and management, who have direct responsibility for supply chain management, training on human trafficking and slavery, particularly with respect to mitigating risks within the supply chains of products.

(d) The exclusive remedy for a violation of this section shall be an action brought by the Attorney General for injunctive relief. Nothing in this section shall limit remedies available for a violation of any other state or federal law.

(e) The provisions of this section shall take effect on January 1, 2012. **Leg.H.** Added Stats 2010 ch 556 §3 (SB 657), effective January 1, 2011, operative January 1, 2012.

2010 Note: This act shall be known, and may be cited, as the California Transparency in Supply Chains Act of 2010. Stats 2010 ch 556 (SB 657) §1.

§1714.45. Manufacturer or seller's liability in product liability action; Tobacco products; Actions by public entities to recover benefits for tobacco related illnesses

(a) In a product liability action, a manufacturer or seller shall not be liable if both of the following apply:

(1) The product is inherently unsafe and the product is known to be unsafe by the ordinary consumer who consumes the product with the ordinary knowledge common to the community.

(2) The product is a common consumer product intended for personal consumption, such as sugar, castor oil, alcohol, and butter, as identified in comment i to Section 402A of the Restatement (Second) of Torts.

(b) This section does not exempt the manufacture or sale of tobacco products by tobacco manufacturers and their successors in interest from product liability actions, but does exempt the sale or distribution of tobacco products by any other person, including, but not limited to, retailers or distributors.

(c) For purposes of this section, the term "product liability action" means any action for injury or death caused by a product, except that the term does not include an action based on a manufacturing defect or breach of an express warranty.

(d) This section is intended to be declarative of and does not alter or amend existing California law, including Cronin v. J.B.E. Olson Corp. (1972), 8 Cal. 3d 121, and shall apply to all product liability actions pending on, or commenced after, January 1, 1988.

(e) This section does not apply to, and never applied to, an action brought by a public entity to recover the value of benefits provided to individuals injured by a tobacco-related illness caused by the tortious conduct of a tobacco company or its successor in interest, including, but not limited to, an action brought pursuant to Section 14124.71 of the Welfare and Institutions Code. In the action brought by a public entity, the fact that the injured individual's claim against the defendant may be barred by a prior version of this section shall not be a defense. This subdivision does not constitute a change in, but is declaratory of, existing law relating to tobacco products.

(f) It is the intention of the Legislature in enacting the amendments to subdivisions (a) and (b) of this section adopted at the 1997–98 Regular Session to declare that there exists no statutory bar to tobacco-related personal injury, wrongful death, or other tort claims against tobacco manufacturers and their successors in interest by California smokers or others who have suffered or incurred injuries, damages, or costs arising from the promotion, marketing, sale, or consumption of tobacco products. It is also the intention of the Legislature to clarify that those claims that were or are brought shall be determined on their merits, without the imposition of any claim of statutory bar or categorical defense.

(g) This section shall not be construed to grant immunity to a tobacco industry research organization. **Leg.H.** Added Stats 1987 ch 1498 §3. Amended Stats 1997 ch 25 §1 (AB 1603), effective June 12, 1997, ch 570 §1 (SB 67); Stats 1998 ch 485 §38 (AB 2803).

1997 Note: The Legislature hereby finds and declares that to the extent that the common law rules as to product liability actions with respect to tobacco were superseded by the version of Section 1714.45 of the Civil Code added by Chapter 1498 of the Statutes of 1987, this act restores those common law rules with respect to the manufacture or sale of tobacco products by tobacco manufacturers and their successors in interest. Stats 1997 ch 570 §2.

§1714.5. Liability of owner of premises designated as emergency shelter; Liability of disaster service workers

(a) There shall be no liability on the part of one, including the State of California, county, city and county, city or any other political subdivision of the State of California, who owns or maintains any building or premises which have been designated as a shelter from destructive operations or attacks by enemies of the United States by any disaster council or any public office, body, or officer of this state or of the United States, or which have been designated or are used as mass care centers, first aid stations, temporary hospital annexes, or as other necessary facilities for mitigating the effects of a natural, manmade, or war-caused emergency, for any injuries arising out of the use thereof for such purposes sustained by any person while in or upon said building or premises as a result of the condition of said building or premises or as a result of any act or omission, or in any way arising from the designation of such premises as a shelter, or the designation or use thereof as a mass care center, first aid station, temporary hospital annex, or other necessary facility for emergency purposes, except a willful act, of such owner or occupant or his or her servants, agents or employees when such person has entered or gone upon or into said building or premises for the purpose of seeking refuge, treatment, care, or assistance therein during destructive operations or attacks by enemies of the United States or during tests ordered by lawful authority or during a natural or manmade emergency.

(b) Notwithstanding any other provision of law, no disaster service worker who is performing disaster services during a state of war emergency, a state of emergency, or a local emergency, as such emergencies are defined in Section 8558 of the Government Code, shall be liable for civil damages on account of personal injury to or death of any person or damage to property resulting from any act or omission while performing disaster services anywhere within any jurisdiction covered by such emergency, except one that is willful.

(c) For purposes of this subdivision, a disaster service worker shall be performing disaster services when acting within the scope of the disaster service worker's responsibilities under the authority of the governmental emergency organization.

(d) For purposes of this subdivision, "governmental emergency organization" shall mean the emergency organization of any state, city, city and county, county, district, or other local governmental agency or public agency, which is authorized pursuant to the California Emergency Services Act (Chapter 7 (commencing with Section 8550) of Division 1 of Title 2 of the Government Code).

(e) Nothing in this section shall be construed to alter any existing legal duties or obligations. The amendments to this section made by the act amending this section shall apply exclusively to any legal action filed on or after the effective date of the act. **Leg.H.** Added Stats 1943 ch 463 §1, effective May 15, 1943. Amended Stats 1951 ch 247 §1, effective May 4, 1951; Stats 1955 ch 1777 §1; Stats 1971 ch 38 §1; Stats 1974 ch 1158 §1; Stats 2009 ch 27 §1 (SB 39), effective August 6, 2009.

2009 Note: Because the state has long encouraged Californians to assist others facing danger in an emergency, and the ability to do so without fear of potential suit has been thrown into question by the recent California Supreme Court decision of *Van Horn v. Watson*, (2008) 45 Cal.4th 322, decided on December 18, 2008, this legislation clarifying the intent of the Legislature needs to go into effect immediately so as to avoid any confusion in this important area of the law. Stats 2009 ch 27 (SB 39) §2.

§1714.55. Liability of provider of telecommunications service involved in providing 9-1-1 service; Applicability; Construction

(a) A retail or wholesale service provider of telecommunications service, or other service, involved in providing 9-1-1 service in accordance with the Warren-911-Emergency Assistance Act (Article 6 (commencing with Section 53100) of Chapter 1 of Part 1 of Division 2 of Title 5 of the Government Code), shall not be liable for any civil claim, damage, or loss caused by an act or omission in the design, development, installation, maintenance, or provision of 9-1-1 service, unless the act or omission that proximately caused the claim, damage, or loss constituted gross negligence, wanton or willful misconduct, or intentional misconduct.

(b) For purposes of this section:

(1) "Public safety agency" means a public safety agency as defined in accordance with the Warren-911-Emergency Assistance Act (Article 6 (commencing with Section 53100) of Chapter 1 of Part 1 of Division 2 of Title 5 of the Government Code).

(2) "9-1-1 service" means a telecommunications service, or other wireline or wireless service, that provides to the user of the public telephone system the ability to reach a public safety agency by utilizing the digits 9-1-1 or otherwise facilitates the provision of emergency services pursuant to the Warren-911-Emergency Assistance Act (Article 6 (commencing with Section 53100) of Chapter 1 of Part 1 of Division 2 of Title 5 of the Government Code). "9-1-1 service" includes a 9-1-1 service that utilizes in whole or in part an Internet Protocol.

(c) This section shall not apply to services provided under tariff.

(d) This section shall not be construed to modify the liability of a manufacturer, distributor, or other person arising from a claim, damage, or loss, related to the operation or performance of an end-user device that is not related to the provision of 9-1-1 service. **Leg.H.** Added Stats 2011 ch 297 §1 (AB 1074), effective September 21, 2011.

2011 Note: The Legislature finds and declares that the general public increasingly relies on wireless telephones for their primary means of communication, and that more 9-1-1 calls are now placed on wireless telephones than on traditional landline telephones. People expect to be able to call for help using the technology that they use for their everyday communications. Next Generation 9-1-1 (NG 9-1-1), which utilizes Internet Protocol-based communication technology, will improve a 9-1-1 operator's ability to locate a wireless caller who cannot speak or give their location, and make possible future applications that will allow emergency responders to receive text messages, real-time images of the site of an emergency before they arrive on the scene, telemetric data from crash sensors in automobiles even when the injured occupants cannot call 9-1-1, and a wealth of other data that can save lives, including their own. NG 9-1-1 involves service providers beyond the traditional landline telephone companies that have provided 9-1-1 service for decades. The Federal Communications Commission has an open proceeding to adopt the rapid adoption of NG 9-1-1 by the states. It is the intent of the Legislature that state law should be amended to encourage qualified service providers beyond traditional landline telephone companies to develop NG 9-1-1 services, and that California should lead the nation in the deployment of NG 9-1-1. Stats 2011 ch 297 (AB 1074) §2.

§1714.6. Violation of statute or ordinance where act or omission required by military order, or order under California Emergency Services Act

The violation of any statute or ordinance shall not establish negligence as a matter of law where the act or omission involved was required in order to comply with an order or proclamation of any military commander who is authorized to issue such orders or proclamations; nor when the act or omission involved is required in order to comply with any regulation, directive, or order of the Governor promulgated under the California Emergency Services Act. No person shall be prosecuted for a violation of any statute or ordinance when violation of such statute or ordinance is required in order to comply with an order or proclamation of any military commander who is authorized to issue such orders or proclamations; nor shall any person be prosecuted for a violation of any statute or ordinance when violation of such statute or ordinance is required in order to comply with any regulation, directive, or order of the Governor promulgated under the California Emergency Services Act. The provisions of this section shall apply to such acts or omissions whether occurring prior to or after the effective date of this section. **Leg.H.** Added Stats 1943 ch 895 §1, effective May 29, 1943, as §1714.5. Amended and renumbered by Stats 1951 ch 514 §1. Amended Stats 1971 ch 438 §15.

§1714.7. Right to damages for injuries sustained while unauthorizedly boarding, traveling, etc., on locomotive or railroad car

No person who is injured while getting on, or attempting to get on, a moving locomotive or railroad car, without authority from the owner or operator of the railroad, or who, having gotten on a locomotive or railroad car while in motion without such authority, is injured while so riding or getting off, shall recover any damages from the owner or operator thereof for such injuries unless proximately caused by an intentional act of such owner or operator with knowledge that serious injury is the probable result of such act, or with a wanton and reckless disregard of the probable result of such act. **Leg.H.** Added by Stats 1971 ch 1554 §1.

§1714.8. Liability of health care provider for negligence or malpractice; Natural course of disease

(a) No health care provider shall be liable for professional negligence or malpractice for any occurrence or result solely on the basis that the occurrence or result was caused by the natural course of a disease or condition, or was the natural or expected result of reasonable treatment rendered for the disease or condition. This section shall not be construed so as to limit liability for the failure to inform of the risks of treatment or failure to accept treatment, or for negligent diagnosis or treatment or the negligence failure to diagnose or treat.

(b) As used in this section, "health care provider" means any person licensed or certified pursuant to Division 2 (commencing with Section 500) of the Business and Professions Code, or licensed pursuant to the Osteopathic Initiative Act or the Chiropractic Initiative Act, or certified pursuant to Chapter 2.5 (commencing with Section 1440) of Division 2 of the Health and Safety Code, and any clinic, health dispensary, or health facility licensed pursuant to Division 2 (commencing with Section 1200) of the Health and Safety Code. **Leg.H.** Added Stats 1978 ch 1358 §1.

§1714.9. Liability for injury to peace officer, firefighter, or emergency medical personnel; Legislative intent regarding common law exception to firefighter's rule

(a) Notwithstanding statutory or decisional law to the contrary, any person is responsible not only for the results of that person's willful acts causing injury to a peace officer, firefighter, or any emergency medical personnel employed by a public entity, but also for any injury occasioned to that person by the want of ordinary care or skill in the management of the person's property or person, in any of the following situations:

(1) Where the conduct causing the injury occurs after the person knows or should have known of the presence of the peace officer, firefighter, or emergency medical personnel.

(2) Where the conduct causing injury violates a statute, ordinance, or regulation, and the conduct causing injury was itself not the event that precipitated either the response or presence of the peace officer, firefighter, or emergency medical personnel.

(3) Where the conduct causing the injury was intended to injure the peace officer, firefighter, or emergency medical personnel.

(4) Where the conduct causing the injury is arson as defined in Section 451 of the Penal Code.

(b) This section does not preclude the reduction of an award of damages because of the comparative fault of the peace officer, firefighter, or emergency medical personnel in causing the injury.

(c) The employer of a firefighter, peace officer or emergency medical personnel may be subrogated to the rights granted by this section to the extent of the worker's compensation benefits, and other liabilities of the employer, including all salary, wage, pension, or other emolument paid to the employee or the employee's dependents.

(d) The liability imposed by this section shall not apply to an employer of a peace officer, firefighter, or emergency medical personnel.

(e) This section is not intended to change or modify the common law independent cause exception to the firefighter's rule as set forth in Donohue v. San Francisco Housing Authority (1993) 16 Cal.App.4th 658. **Leg.H.** Added Stats 1982 ch 258 §1. Amended Stats 1983 ch 136 §1; Stats 2001 ch 140 §2 (SB 448).

§1714.10. Cause of action against attorney based on civil conspiracy with client

(a) No cause of action against an attorney for a civil conspiracy with his or her client arising from any attempt to contest or compromise a claim or dispute, and which is based upon the attorney's representation of the client, shall be included in a complaint or other pleading unless the court enters an order allowing the pleading that includes the claim for civil conspiracy to be filed after the court determines that the party seeking to file the pleading has established that there is a reasonable probability that the party will prevail in the action. The court may allow the filing of a pleading claiming liability based upon such a civil conspiracy following the filing of a verified petition therefor accompanied by the proposed pleading and supporting affidavits stating the facts upon which the liability is based. The court shall order service of the petition upon the party against whom the action is proposed to be filed and permit that party to submit opposing affidavits prior to making its determination. The filing of the petition, proposed pleading, and accompanying affidavits shall toll the running of any applicable statute of limitations until the final determination of the matter, which ruling, if favorable to the petitioning party, shall permit the proposed pleading to be filed.

(b) Failure to obtain a court order where required by subdivision (a) shall be a defense to any action for civil conspiracy filed in violation thereof. The defense shall be raised by the attorney charged with civil conspiracy upon that attorney's first appearance by demurrer, motion to strike, or such other motion or application as may be appropriate. Failure to timely raise the defense shall constitute a waiver thereof.

(c) This section shall not apply to a cause of action against an attorney for a civil conspiracy with his or her client, where (1) the attorney has an independent legal duty to the plaintiff, or (2) the attorney's acts go beyond the performance of a professional duty to serve the client and involve a conspiracy to violate a legal duty in furtherance of the attorney's financial gain.

(d) This section establishes a special proceeding of a civil nature. Any order made under subdivision (a), (b), or (c) which determines the rights of a petitioner or an attorney against whom a pleading has been or is proposed to be filed, shall be appealable as a final judgment in a civil action.

(e) Subdivision (d) does not constitute a change in, but is declaratory of, the existing law. **Leg.H.** Added Stats 1988 ch 1052 §1. Amended Stats 1991 ch 916 §1 (SB 820); Stats 1992 ch 427 §12 (AB 3355); Stats 1993 ch 645 §1 (SB 764); Stats 2000 ch 472 §2 (AB 2069).

1988 Note: It is the intent of the Legislature in enacting this measure to modify the decision of the Court of Appeal in *Wolfrich Corp. v. United Services Automobile Assn.*, (149 Cal. App. 3d 1206 (1st Dist. 1983)). Stats 1988 ch 1052 §2.

§1714.11. Limitation on liability for damage or injury from donated fire protection apparatus or equipment

(a) Except for damage or injury proximately caused by a grossly negligent act or omission or willful or wanton misconduct of the donor, no public employee or public entity, including, but not limited to, a fire department, a fire protection district, or the Department of Forestry and Fire Protection, that donates fire protection apparatus or equipment to a volunteer fire department, volunteer fire protection district, or volunteer fire company is liable for any damage or injury that results from the use of that apparatus or equipment by the recipient fire department, fire protection district, or fire company.

(b)(1) The immunity provided by this section only shall apply if the donor of the fire protection apparatus or equipment discloses in writing to the recipient fire department, fire protection district, or fire company any known damage to, or deficiencies in, the apparatus and equipment.

(2) A volunteer fire department, volunteer fire protection district, or volunteer fire company that receives donated fire protection apparatus or equipment shall inspect and repair the apparatus and equipment prior to use for public safety purposes. **Leg.H.** Added Stats 2002 ch 388 §1 (AB 1821).

§1715. Other obligations

Other obligations are prescribed by divisions one and two of this code. **Leg.H.** Enacted Stats 1872.

§1716. Statement or invoice for goods not ordered or services not performed; Requirements for warning; Damages; Civil penalty

(a) It is unlawful for a person to solicit payment of money by another by means of a written statement or invoice, or any writing that reasonably could be considered a bill, invoice, or statement of account due, but is in fact a solicitation for an order, unless the solicitation conforms to subdivisions (b) to (f), inclusive.

(b) A solicitation described in subdivision (a) shall bear on its face either the disclaimer prescribed by subparagraph (A) of paragraph (2) of subsection (d) of Section 3001 of Title 39 of the United States Code or the following notice:

"THIS IS NOT A BILL. THIS IS A SOLICITATION. YOU ARE UNDER NO OBLIGATION TO PAY THE AMOUNT STATED ABOVE UNLESS YOU ACCEPT THIS OFFER."

The statutory disclaimer or the alternative notice shall be displayed in conspicuous boldface capital letters of a color prominently contrasting with the background against which they appear, including all other print on the face of the solicitation and shall be at least as large, bold, and conspicuous as any other print on the face of the solicitation but no smaller than 30-point type.

(c) The notice or disclaimer required by this section shall be displayed conspicuously apart from other print on the page and immediately below each portion of the solicitation that reasonably could be construed to specify a monetary amount due and payable by the recipient. The notice or disclaimer shall not be preceded, followed, or surrounded by words, symbols, or other matter that reduces its conspicuousness or that introduces, modifies, qualifies, or explains the required text, such as "legal notice required by law."

(d) The notice or disclaimer may not, by folding or any other device, be rendered unintelligible or less prominent than any other information on the face of the solicitation.

(e) If a solicitation consists of more than one page or if any page is designed to be separated into portions, such as by tearing along a perforated line, the notice or disclaimer shall be displayed in its entirety on the face of each page or portion of a page that reasonably might be considered a bill, invoice, or statement of account due as required by subdivisions (b) and (c).

(f) For the purposes of this section, "color" includes black and "color prominently contrasting" excludes any color, or any intensity of an otherwise included color, that does not permit legible reproduction by ordinary office photocopying equipment used under normal operating conditions, and that is not at least as vivid as any other color on the face of the solicitation.

(g) Any person damaged by noncompliance with this section, in addition to other remedies, is entitled to damages in an amount equal to three times the sum solicited.

(h) Any person who violates this section shall be liable for a civil penalty not to exceed ten thousand dollars ($10,000) for each violation, which shall be assessed and recovered in a civil action brought in the name of the people of the State of California by the Attorney General or by any district attorney, county counsel, or city attorney in any court of competent jurisdiction. If the action is brought by the Attorney General, one-half of the penalty collected shall be paid to the treasurer of the county in which the judgment was entered and one-half to the State Treasurer. If brought by a district attorney or county counsel, the entire amount of the penalty collected shall be paid to the treasurer of the county in which the judgment was entered. If brought by a city attorney or city prosecutor, one-half of the penalty shall be paid to the treasurer of the county and one-half to the city.

(i) A violation of this section is a misdemeanor punishable by imprisonment in a county jail not exceeding six months, by a fine not exceeding two thousand five hundred dollars ($2,500), or by both that fine and imprisonment. **Leg.H.** Added Stats 1967 ch 346 §1. Amended Stats 1978 ch 492 §1; Stats 1996 ch 397 §1 (SB 1530).

§1717. Contract provision for attorney fees and costs

(a) In any action on a contract, where the contract specifically provides that attorney's fees and costs, which are incurred to enforce that contract, shall be awarded either to one of the parties or to the prevailing party, then the party who is determined to be the party prevailing on the contract, whether he or she is the party specified in the contract or not, shall be entitled to reasonable attorney's fees in addition to other costs.

Where a contract provides for attorney's fees, as set forth above, that provision shall be construed as applying to the entire contract, unless each party was represented by counsel in the negotiation and execution of the contract, and the fact of that representation is specified in the contract.

Reasonable attorney's fees shall be fixed by the court, and shall be an element of the costs of suit.

Attorney's fees provided for by this section shall not be subject to waiver by the parties to any contract which is entered into after the effective date of this section. Any provision in any such contract which provides for a waiver of attorney's fees is void.

(b)(1) The court, upon notice and motion by a party, shall determine who is the party prevailing on the contract for purposes of this section, whether or not the suit proceeds to final judgment. Except as provided in paragraph (2), the party prevailing on the contract shall be the party who recovered a greater relief in the action on the contract. The court may also determine that there is no party prevailing on the contract for purposes of this section.

(2) Where an action has been voluntarily dismissed or dismissed pursuant to a settlement of the case, there shall be no prevailing party for purposes of this section.

Where the defendant alleges in his or her answer that he or she tendered to the plaintiff the full amount to which he or she was entitled, and thereupon deposits in court for the plaintiff, the amount so tendered, and the allegation is found to be true, then the defendant is deemed to be a party prevailing on the contract within the meaning of this section.

Where a deposit has been made pursuant to this section, the court shall, on the application of any party to the action, order the deposit to be invested in an insured, interest-bearing account. Interest on the amount shall be allocated to the parties in the same proportion as the original funds are allocated.

(c) In an action which seeks relief in addition to that based on a contract, if the party prevailing on the contract has damages awarded against it on causes of action not on the contract, the amounts awarded to the party prevailing on the contract under this section shall be deducted from any damages awarded in favor of the party who did not prevail on the contract. If the amount awarded under this section exceeds the amount of damages awarded the party not prevailing on the contract, the net amount shall be awarded the party prevailing on the contract and judgment may be entered in favor of the party prevailing on the contract for that net amount. **Leg.H.** Added Stats 1968 ch 266 §1. Amended Stats 1981 ch 888 §1; Stats 1983 ch 1073 §1; Stats 1986 ch 377 §1, ch 785 §1; Stats 1987 ch 1080 §1.

§1717.5. Contract action based on book account; Attorney's fees and costs

(a) Except as otherwise provided by law or where waived by the parties to an agreement, in any action on a contract based on a book account, as defined in Section 337a of the Code of Civil Procedure, entered into on or after January 1, 1987, which does not provide for attorney's fees and costs, as provided in Section 1717, the party who is determined to be the party prevailing on the contract shall be entitled to reasonable attorney's fees, as provided below, in addition to other costs. The prevailing party on the contract shall be the party who recovered a greater relief in the action on the contract. The court may determine that there is no party prevailing on the contract for purposes of this section.

Reasonable attorney's fees awarded pursuant to this section for the prevailing party bringing the action on the book account shall be fixed by the court in an amount that shall not exceed the lesser of: (1) nine hundred sixty dollars ($960) for book accounts based upon an obligation owing by a natural person for goods, moneys, or services which were primarily for personal, family, or household purposes; and one thousand two hundred dollars ($1,200) for all other book accounts to which this section applies; or (2) 25 percent of the principal obligation owing under the contract.

For the party against whom the obligation on the book account was asserted in the action subject to this section, if that party is found to have no obligation owing on a book account, the court shall award that prevailing party reasonable attorney's fees not to exceed nine hundred sixty dollars ($960) for book accounts based upon an obligation owing by a natural person for goods, moneys, or services which were primarily for personal, family, or household purposes, and one thousand two hundred dollars ($1,200) for all other book accounts to which this section applies. These attorney's fees shall be an element of the costs of the suit.

If there is a written agreement between the parties signed by the person to be charged, the fees provided by this section may not be imposed unless that agreement contains a statement that the prevailing party in any action between the parties is entitled to the fees provided by this section.

(b) The attorney's fees allowed pursuant to this section shall be the lesser of either the maximum amount allowed by this section, the amount provided by any default attorney's fee schedule adopted by the court applicable to the suit, or an amount as otherwise provided by the court. Any claim for attorney's fees pursuant to this section in excess of the amounts set forth in the default attorney's fee schedule shall be reasonable attorney's fees, as proved by the party, as actual and necessary for the claim that is subject to this section.

(c) This section does not apply to any action in which an insurance company is a party nor shall an insurance company, surety, or guarantor be liable under this section, in the absence of a specific contractual provision, for the attorney's fees and costs awarded a prevailing party against its insured.

This section does not apply to any action in which a bank, a savings association, a federal association, a state or federal credit union, or a subsidiary, affiliate, or holding company of any of those entities, or an authorized industrial loan company, a licensed consumer finance lender, or a licensed commercial finance lender, is a party. **Leg.H.** Added Stats 1986 ch 884 §1. Amended Stats 1987 ch 764 §4; Stats 1991 ch 406 §1 (SB 182); Stats 1992 ch 530 §2 (AB 2516); Stats 2004 ch 328 §1 (AB 2347); Stats 2015 ch 80 §1 (SB 363), effective January 1, 2016.

§1718. Farm machinery repair shop work; Invoice; Written estimate furnished on request; Violation as misdemeanor

(a) As used in this section:

(1) "Farm machinery" means all tools and equipment used in relation to the operation of a farm.

(2) "Farm machinery repair shop" means a business which, for compensation, engages in the operation, on or off its premises, of repairing farm machinery.

(3) "Per-job basis" means each act of maintenance or repair which is performed on farm machinery.

(b) All work done by a farm machinery repair shop, including all warranty work, shall be recorded on an invoice, which shall describe all service work done and parts supplied. If more than one act of maintenance or repair is performed by a farm machinery repair shop, the invoice shall be written in such a way that the labor cost per hour and total labor cost, as well as the specific parts used and their cost, shall be recorded on a per-job basis.

However, where work is done on an agreed total-cost-per-job basis, or the work includes an agreed total cost for component unit replacement, the invoice shall describe the work done on such basis and the total cost for such work.

(c) Each farm machinery repair shop shall give each customer, upon request, a written estimated price for labor and parts necessary, on a per–job basis. It shall not charge for work done or parts supplied in excess of the estimated price without the consent of the customer, which shall be obtained at some time after it is determined that the estimated price is insufficient and before the work not included in the estimate is done, or the parts not included in the estimate are supplied. Nothing in this section shall be construed to require a farm machinery repair shop to give a written estimated price if the shop does not agree to perform the requested repair.

(d) Any violation of this section is a misdemeanor. **Leg.H.** Added Stats 1972 ch 302 §1. Amended Stats 1973 ch 235 §1.

Prior Law: Former §1718, similar to present §§1747.02, 1747.10, was added Stats 1969 ch 904 §1 and repealed Stats 1971 ch 1019 §1.

§1719. Passage of checks on insufficient funds; Liability for specified amounts including treble damages

(a)(1) Notwithstanding any penal sanctions that may apply, any person who passes a check on insufficient funds shall be liable to the payee for the amount of the check and a service charge payable to the payee for an amount not to exceed twenty-five dollars ($25) for the first check passed on insufficient funds and an amount not to exceed thirty-five dollars ($35) for each subsequent check to that payee passed on insufficient funds.

(2) Notwithstanding any penal sanctions that may apply, any person who passes a check on insufficient funds shall be liable to the payee for damages equal to treble the amount of the check if a written demand for payment is mailed by certified mail to the person who had passed a check on insufficient funds and the written demand informs this person of (A) the provisions of this section, (B) the amount of the check, and (C) the amount of the service charge payable to the payee. The person who had passed a check on insufficient funds shall have 30 days from the date the written demand was mailed to pay the amount of the check, the amount of the service charge payable to the payee, and the costs to mail the written demand for payment. If this person fails to pay in full the amount of the check, the service charge payable to the payee, and the costs to mail the written demand within this period, this person shall then be liable instead for the amount of the check, minus any partial payments made toward the amount of the check or the service charge within 30 days of the written demand, and damages equal to treble that amount, which shall not be less than one hundred dollars ($100) nor more than one thousand five hundred dollars ($1,500). When a person becomes liable for treble damages for a check that is the subject of a written demand, that person shall no longer be liable for any service charge for that check and any costs to mail the written demand.

(3) Notwithstanding paragraphs (1) and (2), a person shall not be liable for the service charge, costs to mail the written demand, or treble damages if he or she stops payment in order to resolve a good faith dispute with the payee. The payee is entitled to the service charge, costs to mail the written demand, or treble damages only upon proving by clear and convincing evidence that there was no good faith dispute, as defined in subdivision (b).

(4) Notwithstanding paragraph (1), a person shall not be liable under that paragraph for the service charge if, at any time, he or she presents the payee with written confirmation by his or her financial institution that the check was returned to the payee by the financial institution due to an error on the part of the financial institution.

(5) Notwithstanding paragraph (1), a person shall not be liable under that paragraph for the service charge if the person presents the payee with written confirmation that his or her account had insufficient funds as a result of a delay in the regularly scheduled transfer of, or the posting of, a direct deposit of a social security or government benefit assistance payment.

(6) As used in this subdivision, to "pass a check on insufficient funds" means to make, utter, draw, or deliver any check, draft, or order for the payment of money upon any bank, depository, person, firm, or corporation that refuses to honor the check, draft, or order for any of the following reasons:

(A) Lack of funds or credit in the account to pay the check.

(B) The person who wrote the check does not have an account with the drawee.

(C) The person who wrote the check instructed the drawee to stop payment on the check.

(b) For purposes of this section, in the case of a stop payment, the existence of a "good faith dispute" shall be determined by the trier of fact. A "good faith dispute" is one in which the court finds that the drawer had a reasonable belief of his or her legal entitlement to withhold payment. Grounds for the entitlement include, but are not limited to, the following: services were not rendered, goods were not delivered, goods or services purchased are faulty, not as promised, or otherwise unsatisfactory, or there was an overcharge.

(c) In the case of a stop payment, the notice to the drawer required by this section shall be in substantially the following form:

NOTICE

To: _____
  (name of drawer)
_____
  (name of payee) is the payee of a check you wrote
for $ _____
  (amount)

The check was not paid because you stopped payment, and the payee demands payment. You may have a good faith dispute as to whether you owe the full amount. If you do not have a good faith dispute with the payee and fail to pay the payee the full amount of the check in cash, a service charge of an amount not to exceed twenty-five dollars ($25) for the first check passed on insufficient funds and an amount not to exceed thirty-five dollars ($35) for each subsequent check passed on insufficient funds, and the costs to mail this notice within 30 days after this notice was mailed, you could be sued and held responsible to pay at least both of the following:

(1) The amount of the check.

(2) Damages of at least one hundred dollars ($100) or, if higher, three times the amount of the check up to one thousand five hundred dollars ($1,500).

If the court determines that you do have a good faith dispute with the payee, you will not have to pay the service charge, treble damages, or mailing cost. If you stopped payment because you have a good faith dispute with the payee, you should try to work out your dispute with the payee. You can contact the payee at:

_____
  (name of payee)
_____
  (street address)
_____
  (telephone number)

You may wish to contact a lawyer to discuss your legal rights and responsibilities.

_____
  (name of sender of notice)

(d) In the case of a stop payment, a court may not award damages or costs under this section unless the court receives into evidence a copy of the written demand that, in that case, shall have been sent to the drawer and a signed certified mail receipt showing delivery, or attempted delivery if refused, of the written demand to the drawer's last known address.

(e) A cause of action under this section may be brought in small claims court by the original payee, if it does not exceed the jurisdiction of that court, or in any other appropriate court. The payee shall, in order to recover damages because the drawer instructed the drawee to stop payment, show to the satisfaction of the trier of fact that there was a reasonable effort on the part of the payee to reconcile and resolve the dispute prior to pursuing the dispute through the courts.

(f) A cause of action under this section may be brought by a holder of the check or an assignee of the payee. A proceeding under this section is a limited civil case. However, if the assignee is acting on behalf of the payee, for a flat fee or a percentage fee, the assignee may not charge the payee a greater flat fee or percentage fee for that portion of the amount collected that represents treble damages than is charged the payee for collecting the face amount of the check, draft, or order. This subdivision shall not apply to an action brought in small claims court.

(g) Notwithstanding subdivision (a), if the payee is the court, the written demand for payment described in subdivision (a) may be mailed to the drawer by the court clerk. Notwithstanding subdivision (d), in the case of a stop payment where the demand is mailed by the court clerk, a court may not award damages or costs pursuant to subdivision (d), unless the court receives into evidence a copy of the written demand, and a certificate of mailing by the court clerk in the form provided for in subdivision (4) of Section 1013a of the Code of Civil Procedure for service in civil actions. For purposes of this subdivision, in courts where a single court clerk serves more than one court, the clerk shall be deemed the court clerk of each court.

(h) The requirements of this section in regard to remedies are mandatory upon a court.

(i) The assignee of the payee or a holder of the check may demand, recover, or enforce the service charge, damages, and costs specified in this section to the same extent as the original payee.

(j)(1) A drawer is liable for damages and costs only if all of the requirements of this section have been satisfied.

(2) The drawer shall in no event be liable more than once under this section on each check for a service charge, damages, or costs.

(k) Nothing in this section is intended to condition, curtail, or otherwise prejudice the rights, claims, remedies, and defenses under Division 3 (commencing with Section 3101) of the Commercial Code of a drawer, payee, assignee, or holder, including a holder in due course as defined in Section 3302 of the Commercial Code, in connection with the enforcement of this section. **Leg.H.** Added Stats 1983 ch 522 §1. Amended Stats 1985 ch 196 §1; Stats 1986 ch 225 §1, ch 708 §1; Stats 1987 ch 4 §1, effective March 17, 1987; Stats 1990 ch 599 §1 (SB 2130); Stats 1994 ch 926 §1 (AB 2533); Stats 1995 ch 134 §1 (AB 522); Stats 1996 ch 1000 §1 (AB 2643); Stats 1998 ch 931 §14 (SB 2139), effective September 28, 1998.

§1720. Inquiries of obligor about credit account; Obligee's failure to respond

(a) If an obligee fails to give a timely response to an inquiry of an obligor concerning any debit or credit applicable to an obligation, he shall not be entitled to interest, financing charges, service charges, or any other similar charges thereon, from the date of mailing of the inquiry to the date of mailing of the response.

(b) For the purpose of subdivision (a):

(1) An "inquiry" is a writing which is posted by certified mail to the address of the obligee to which payments are normally tendered, unless another address is specifically indicated on the statement for such purpose, then to such address.

(2) A "response" is a writing which is responsive to an inquiry and mailed to the last known address of the obligor.

(3) A response is "timely" if it is mailed within 60 days from the date on which the inquiry was mailed.

(c) This section shall only apply to an obligation created pursuant to a retail installment account as defined by Section 1802.7. **Leg.H.** Added Stats 1970 ch 191 §1. Amended Stats 1971 ch 1019 §3.

§1721. Vandalism at construction site; Damages; Attorney's fees

In an action for the intentional and malicious destruction of real or personal property at a site where substantial improvements to real property are under construction, upon judgment in favor of the plaintiff, the court may, in its discretion, award the plaintiff an amount not to exceed three times the amount of actual damages, and may award reasonable attorney's fees. **Leg.H.** Added Stats 1983 ch 474 §1.

Prior Law: Former §1721, similar to present UCC §§2106, 2204–2206, was added Stats 1931 ch 1070 §1 and repealed Stats 1963 ch 819 §2, effective January 1, 1965.

Former §1721, defining sale (based on Field's Draft NY CC §855), was enacted 1872 and repealed Stats 1931 ch 1070 §1.

§1722. Time period for delivery of contract goods, or for service or repair by retailer; Cable television companies; Utilities; Waiver of rights

(a)(1) Whenever a contract is entered into between a consumer and a retailer with 25 or more employees relating to the sale of merchandise which is to be delivered by the retailer or the retailer's agent to the consumer at a later date, and the parties have agreed that the presence of the consumer is required at the time of delivery, the retailer and the consumer shall agree, either at the time of the sale or at a later date prior to the delivery date, on a four-hour time period within which any delivery shall be made. Whenever a contract is entered into between a consumer and a retailer with 25 or more employees for service or repair of merchandise, whether or not the merchandise was sold by the retailer to the consumer, and the parties have agreed that the presence of the consumer is required at the time of service or repair, upon receipt of a request for service or repair under the contract, the retailer and the consumer shall agree, prior to the date of service or repair, on a four-hour period within which the service or repair shall be commenced. Once a delivery, service, or repair time is established, the retailer or the retailer's agent shall deliver the merchandise to the consumer, or commence service or repair of the merchandise, within that four-hour period.

(2) If the merchandise is not delivered, or service or repair are not commenced, within the specified four-hour period, except for delays caused by unforeseen or unavoidable occurrences beyond the control of the retailer, the consumer may bring an action in small claims court against the retailer for lost wages, expenses actually incurred, or other actual damages not exceeding a total of six hundred dollars ($600).

(3) No action shall be considered valid if the consumer was not present at the time, within the specified period, when the retailer or the retailer's agent attempted to make the delivery, service, or repairs or made a diligent attempt to notify the consumer by telephone or in person of its inability to do so because of unforeseen or unavoidable occurrences beyond its control. If notification is by telephone, the retailer or the retailer's agent shall leave a telephone number for a return telephone call by the consumer to the retailer or its agent, to enable the consumer to arrange a new two-hour period for delivery, service, or repair with the retailer or the retailer's agent.

(4) In any small claims action, logs and other business records maintained by the retailer or the retailer's agent in the ordinary course of business shall be prima facie evidence of the time period specified for the delivery, service, or repairs and of the time when the merchandise was delivered, or of a diligent attempt by the retailer or the retailer's agent to notify the consumer of delay caused by unforeseen or unavoidable occurrences.

(5) It shall be a defense to the action if a diligent attempt was made to notify the consumer of the delay caused by unforeseen or unavoidable occurrences beyond the control of the retailer or the retailer's agent, or the retailer or the retailer's agent was unable to notify the consumer of the delay because of the consumer's absence or unavailability during the four-hour period, and, in either instance, the retailer or the retailer's agent makes the delivery, service, or repairs within two hours of a newly agreed upon time or, if the consumer unreasonably declines to arrange a new time for the delivery, service, or repairs.

(b)(1) Cable television companies shall inform their subscribers of their right to service connection or repair within a four-hour period, if the presence of the subscriber is required, by offering the four-hour period at the time the subscriber calls for service connection or repair. Whenever a subscriber contracts with a cable television company for a service connection or repair which is to take place at a later date, and the parties have agreed that the presence of the subscriber is required, the cable company and the subscriber shall agree, prior to the date of service connection or repair, on the time for the commencement of the four-hour period for the service connection or repair.

(2) If the service connection or repair is not commenced within the specified four-hour period, except for delays caused by unforeseen or unavoidable occurrences beyond the control of the company, the subscriber may bring an action in small claims court against the company for lost wages, expenses actually incurred or other actual damages not exceeding a total of six hundred dollars ($600).

(3) No action shall be considered valid if the subscriber was not present at the time, within the specified period, that the company attempted to make the service connection or repair or made a diligent attempt to notify the subscriber by telephone or in person of its inability to do so because of unforeseen or unavoidable occurrences beyond its control. If notification is by telephone, the cable television company or its agent shall leave a telephone number for a return telephone call by the subscriber to the company or its agent, to enable the consumer to arrange a new two-hour period for service connection or repair.

(4) In any small claims action, logs and other business records maintained by the company or its agents in the ordinary course of business shall be prima facie evidence of the time period specified for the commencement of the service connection or repair and the time that the company or its agents attempted to make the service connection or repair, or of a diligent attempt by the company to notify the subscriber in person or by telephone of a delay caused by unforeseen or unavoidable occurrences.

(5) It shall be a defense to the action if a diligent attempt was made to notify the subscriber of a delay caused by unforeseen or unavoidable occurrences beyond the control of the company or its agents, or the company or its agents were unable to notify the subscriber because of the subscriber's absence or unavailability during the four-hour period, and, in either instance, the cable television company commenced service or repairs within a newly agreed upon two-hour period.

(6) No action shall be considered valid against a cable television company pursuant to this section when the franchise or any local ordinance provides the subscriber with a remedy for a delay in commencement of a service connection or repair and the subscriber has elected to pursue that remedy. If a subscriber elects to pursue his or her remedies against a cable television company under this section, the franchising or state or local licensing authority shall be barred from imposing any fine, penalty, or other sanction against the company, arising out of the same incident.

(c)(1) Utilities shall inform their subscribers of their right to service connection or repair within a four-hour period, if the presence of the subscriber is required, by offering the four-hour period at the time the subscriber calls for service connection or repair. Whenever a subscriber contracts with the utility for a service connection or repair, and the parties have agreed that the presence of the subscriber is required, and the subscriber has requested a four-hour appointment, the utility and the subscriber shall agree, prior to the date of service connection or repair, on the time for the commencement of the four-hour period for the service connection or repair.

(2) If the service connection or repair is not commenced within the four-hour period provided under paragraph (1) or another period otherwise agreed to by the utility and the subscriber, except for delays caused by unforeseen or unavoidable circumstances beyond the control of the utility, the subscriber may bring an action in small claims court against the utility for lost wages, expenses actually incurred, or other actual damages not exceeding a total of six hundred dollars ($600).

(3) No action shall be considered valid if the subscriber was not present at the time, within the specified period, that the utility attempted to make the service connection or repair or made a diligent attempt to notify the subscriber by telephone or in person of its inability to do so because of unforeseen or unavoidable occurrences beyond its control. If notification is by telephone, the utility or its agent shall leave a telephone number for a return telephone call by the subscriber to the utility or its agent, to enable the consumer to arrange a new two-hour period for service connection or repair.

(4) In any small claims action, logs and other business records maintained by the utility or its agents in the ordinary course of business shall be prima facie evidence of the time period specified for the commencement of the service connection or repair and of the time that the utility attempted to make the service connection or repair, or of a diligent attempt by a utility to notify the subscriber in person or by telephone of a delay caused by unforeseen or unavoidable occurrences.

(5) It shall be a defense to the action if a diligent attempt was made by the utility to notify the subscriber of a delay caused by unforeseen or unavoidable occurrences beyond the control of the utility, and the utility commenced service within a newly agreed upon two-hour period.

(d) Any provision of a delivery, service, or repair contract in which the consumer or subscriber agrees to modify or waive any of the rights afforded by this section is void as contrary to public policy. **Leg.H.** Added Stats 1989 ch 1075 §1. Amended Stats 1990 ch 193 §1 (SB 1968); Stats 1991 ch 394 §3 (AB 585); Stats 1992 ch 427 §13 (AB 3355), ch 693 §1 (SB 1387) (ch 693 prevails); Stats 1993 ch 28 §1 (SB 47); Stats 2002 ch 279 §1 (SB 500).

Prior Law: Former §1722, similar to present UCC §1103, was added Stats 1931 ch 1070 §1 and repealed Stats 1963 ch 819 §2, effective January 1, 1965.

Former §1722, relating to the subject of sale (based on Field's Draft NY CC §856), was enacted 1872 and repealed Stats 1931 ch 1070 §1.

§1723. Display by retail store of policy regarding refunds and exchanges

(a) Every retail seller which sells goods to the public in this state that has a policy as to any of those goods of not giving full cash or credit refunds, or of not allowing equal exchanges, or any combination thereof, for at least seven days following purchase of the goods if they are returned and proof of their purchase is presented, shall conspicuously display that policy either on signs posted at each cash register and sales counter, at each public entrance, on tags attached to each item sold under that policy, or on the retail seller's order forms, if any. This display shall state the store's policy, including, but not limited to, whether cash refund, store credit, or exchanges will be given for the full amount of the purchase price; the applicable time period; the types of merchandise which are covered by the policy; and any other conditions which govern the refund, credit, or exchange of merchandise.

(b) This section does not apply to food, plants, flowers, perishable goods, goods marked "as is," "no returns accepted," "all sales final," or with similar language, goods used or damaged after purchase, customized goods received as ordered, goods not returned with their original package, and goods which cannot be resold due to health considerations.

(c)(1) Any retail store which violates this section shall be liable to the buyer for the amount of the purchase if the buyer returns, or attempts to return, the purchased goods on or before the 30th day after their purchase.

(2) Violations of this section shall be subject to the remedies provided in the Consumers Legal Remedies Act (Title 1.5 (commencing with Section 1750) of Part 4).

(3) The duties, rights, and remedies provided in this section are in addition to any other duties, rights, and remedies provided by state law. **Leg.H.** Added Stats 1990 ch 422 §2 (AB 3047).

Prior Law: Former §1723, similar to present UCC §§2204–2206, was added Stats 1931 ch 1070 §1 and repealed Stats 1963 ch 819 §2, effective January 1, 1965.

§1724. Unlawful to sell illegally obtained or accessed data or access to such data; Unlawful for unauthorized person to purchase or use data from source known or reasonably should have been known to be illegally obtained or accessed

(a) As used in this section:

(1) "Authorized person" means a person who has come to possess or access the data lawfully and who continues to maintain the legal authority to possess, access, or use that data, under state or federal law, as applicable.

(2) "Data" has the same meaning as defined in Section 502 of the Penal Code.

(b) It is unlawful for a person to sell data, or sell access to data, that the person has obtained or accessed pursuant to the commission of a crime.

(c) It is unlawful for a person, who is not an authorized person, to purchase or use data from a source that the person knows or reasonably should know has obtained or accessed that data through the commission of a crime.

(d) This section shall not be construed to limit the constitutional rights of the public, the rights of whistleblowers, and the press regarding matters of public concern, including, but not limited to, those described in Bartnicki v. Vopper, (2001) 532 U.S. 514.

(e) This section does not limit providing or obtaining data in an otherwise lawful manner for the purpose of protecting a computer system or data stored in a computer system or protecting an individual from risk of identity theft or fraud.

(f) The court in an action pursuant to this section may award equitable relief, including, but not limited to, an injunction, costs, and any other relief the court deems proper.

(g) Liability under this section shall not limit or preclude liability under any other law.

(h) A violation of this section shall not constitute a crime. **Leg.H.** Added Stats 2021 ch 594 §1 (AB 1391), effective January 1, 2022.

Prior Law Former Civ C §1724 was added Stats 1931 ch 1070 §1 ad repealed Stats 1963 ch 819 §2, effective January 1, 1965. See former UCC §1206.

§1725. Prohibition against requiring credit card as condition of acceptance of negotiable instrument

(a) Unless permitted under subdivision (c), no person accepting a negotiable instrument as payment in full or in part for goods or services sold or leased at retail shall do any of the following:

(1) Require the person paying with a negotiable instrument to provide a credit card as a condition of acceptance of the negotiable instrument, or record the number of the credit card.

(2) Require, as a condition of acceptance of the negotiable instrument, or cause the person paying with a negotiable instrument to sign a statement agreeing to allow his or her credit card to be charged to cover the negotiable instrument if returned as no good.

(3) Record a credit card number in connection with any part of the transaction described in this subdivision.

(4) Contact a credit card issuer to determine if the amount of any credit available to the person paying with a negotiable instrument will cover the amount of the negotiable instrument.

(b) For the purposes of this section, the following terms have the following meanings:

(1) "Check guarantee card" means a card issued by a financial institution, evidencing an agreement under which the financial institution will not dishonor a check drawn upon itself, under the terms and conditions of the agreement.

(2) "Credit card" has the meaning specified in Section 1747.02, and does not include a check guarantee card or a card that is both a credit card and a check guarantee card.

(3) "Negotiable instrument" has the meaning specified in Section 3104 of the Commercial Code.

(4) "Retail" means a transaction involving the sale or lease of goods or services or both, between an individual, corporation, or other entity regularly engaged in business and a consumer, for use by the consumer and not for resale.

(c) This section does not prohibit any person from doing any of the following:

(1) Requiring the production of reasonable forms of positive identification, other than a credit card, which may include a driver's license or a California state identification card, or where one of these is not available, another form of photo identification, as a condition of acceptance of a negotiable instrument.

(2) Requesting, but not requiring, a purchaser to voluntarily display a credit card as an indicia of creditworthiness or financial responsibility, or as an additional identification, provided the only information concerning the credit card which is recorded is the type of credit card displayed, the issuer of the card, and the expiration date of the card. All retailers that request the display of a credit card pursuant to this paragraph shall inform the customer, by either of the following methods, that displaying the credit card is not a requirement for check writing:

(A) By posting the following notice in a conspicuous location in the unobstructed view of the public within the premises where the check is being written, clearly and legibly: "Check writing ID: credit card may be requested but not required for purchases."

(B) By training and requiring the sales clerks or retail employees requesting the credit card to inform all check writing customers that they are not required to display a credit card to write a check.

(3) Requesting production of, or recording, a credit card number as a condition for cashing a negotiable instrument that is being used solely to receive cash back from the person.

(4) Requesting, receiving, or recording a credit card number in lieu of requiring a deposit to secure payment in event of default, loss, damage, or other occurrence.

(5) Requiring, verifying, and recording the purchaser's name, address, and telephone number.

(6) Requesting or recording a credit card number on a negotiable instrument used to make a payment on that credit card account.

(d) This section does not require acceptance of a negotiable instrument whether or not a credit card is presented.

(e) Any person who violates this section is subject to a civil penalty not to exceed two hundred fifty dollars ($250) for a first violation, and to a civil penalty not to exceed one thousand dollars ($1,000) for a second or subsequent violation, to be assessed and collected in a civil action brought by the person paying with a negotiable instrument, by the Attorney General, or by the district attorney or city attorney of the county or city in which the violation occurred. However, no civil penalty shall be assessed for a violation of this section if the defendant shows by a preponderance of the evidence that the violation was not intentional and resulted from a bona fide error made notwithstanding the defendant's maintenance of procedures reasonably adopted to avoid such an error. When collected, the civil penalty shall be payable, as appropriate, to the person paying with a negotiable instrument who brought the action or to the general fund of whichever governmental entity brought the action to assess the civil penalty.

(f) The Attorney General, or any district attorney or city attorney within his or her respective jurisdiction, may bring an action in the superior court in the name of the people of the State of California to enjoin violation of subdivision (a) and, upon notice to the defendant of not less than five days, to temporarily restrain and enjoin the violation. If it appears to the satisfaction of the court that the defendant has, in fact, violated subdivision (a), the court may issue an injunction restraining further violations, without requiring proof that any person has been damaged by the violation. In these proceedings, if the court finds that the defendant has violated subdivision (a), the court may direct the defendant to pay any or all costs incurred by the Attorney General, district attorney, or city attorney in seeking or obtaining injunctive relief pursuant to this subdivision.

(g) Actions for collection of civil penalties under subdivision (e) and for injunctive relief under subdivision (f) may be consolidated. **Leg.H.** Added Stats 1990 ch 637 §1 (AB 2880). Amended Stats 1991 ch 1089 §1 (AB 1477), effective October 14, 1991; Stats 1995 ch 458 §1 (AB 1316).

Prior Law: Former §1725, similar to present §1366, was added Stats 1982 ch 1237 §1 and repealed Stats 1985 ch 874 §15.

Former §1725, relating to contracts for swimming pool construction, was added Stats 1969 ch 583 §1 and repealed Stats 1979 ch 747 §3.

PART 4
OBLIGATIONS ARISING FROM PARTICULAR TRANSACTIONS

Title 1. Consignment of Fine Art.
Title 1A. Independent Wholesale Sales Representatives.
Title 1.1. Sale and Manufacture of Political Items.
Title 1.1A. Autographed Memorabilia.
Title 1.2. Sale of Fine Prints.
Title 1.2A. Violent Video Games.
Title 1.3. Credit Cards.
Title 1.3A. Credit Card Disclosure.
Title 1.3B. Charge Card Disclosures.
Title 1.3C. Debit Cards.
Title 1.3.5. Consumer Refunds.
Title 1.4. Layaway Practices.
Title 1.4A. Gift Certificates.
Title 1.4B. Supermarket Club Cards.
Title 1.4C. Clarity of Marketplace Terms and Conditions and Dispute Resolution Minimum Fairness.
Title 1.4D. Online Marketplaces.
Title 1.5. Consumers Legal Remedies Act.
Title 1.5A. Vehicle History Reports.
Title 1.6. Consumer Credit Reporting Agencies Act.
Title 1.61. Commercial Credit Reports.
Title 1.6A. Investigative Consumer Reporting Agencies.
Title 1.6B. Consumer Credit Denial.
Title 1.6C. Fair Debt Collection Practices.
Title 1.6C.5. Fair Debt Buying Practices.
Title 1.6C.7. Educational Debt Collection Practices.
Title 1.6C.10. Student Loans: Borrower Rights.
Title 1.6C.15. Private Student Loan Collections Reform Act.
Title 1.6C.17. Fair Debt Settlement Practices.
Title 1.6D. Electronic Commerce.
Title 1.6E. Credit Services.
Title 1.6F. Check Cashers.
Title 1.7. Consumer Warranties.
Title 1.8. Personal Data.
Title 1.80. Identification Documents.
Title 1.807. Domestic Violence, Sexual Assault, and Stalking: Personal Information.
Title 1.81. Customer Records.
Title 1.81.1. Confidentiality of Social Security Numbers.
Title 1.81.15. Reader Privacy Act.
Title 1.81.2. Confidentiality of Driver's License Information.
Title 1.81.23. Collection of License Plate Information.
Title 1.81.25. Consumer Privacy Protection.
Title 1.81.26. Security of Connected Devices.
Title 1.81.27. Commercial Use of Booking Photographs.
Title 1.81.3. Identity Theft.
Title 1.81.35. Coerced Debt.
Title 1.81.4. Privacy of Customer Electrical or Natural Gas Usage Data.
Title 1.81.45. Parent accountability and child protection.
Title 1.81.46. Online Violence Prevention Act.
Title 1.81.47. The California Age-Appropriate Design Code Act.
Title 1.81.48. Data Broker Registration.
Title 1.81.49. Family Planning Center Location Data.
Title 1.81.5. California Consumer Privacy Act of 2018.
Title 1.81.6. Identity Theft in Business Entity Filings.
Title 1.81.7. Reproductive and Gender-Affirming Health Care Services.
Title 1.82. Business Records.
Title 1.83. Precomputed Interest.
Title 1.84. Precomputed Finance Charge Contract.
Title 1.85. Consumer Credit Contracts.
Title 1.86. Consumer Contract Awareness Act of 1990.
Title 1.90. Commercial Financing Transactions with Small Businesses.
Title 2. Credit Sales.
Title 2.4. Contracts For Dance Studio Lessons And Other Services.
Title 2.5. Contracts For Health Studio Services.
Title 2.55. Contracts for the Lease or Rental of Athletic Facilities.
Title 2.6. Contracts for Discount Buying Services.
Title 2.7. Contracts for Seller Assisted Marketing Plans.
Title 2.8. Membership Camping Contracts.
Title 2.9. Creditor Remedies: Disability Insurance.
Title 2.91. Employment Agency, Employment Counseling, and Job Listing Services Act.
Title 2.95. Auctioneer and Auction Companies.
Title 2.96. California Rental-Purchase Act.
Title 2.97. Consumer Collection Notice.
Title 3. Deposit.
Title 3.5. Utility Services.
Title 4. Loan.
Title 5. Hiring.
Title 6. Service.
Title 7. Carriage.
Title 8. Involuntary Trusts.
Title 9. Agency.
Title 10. Recording Artist Contracts.
Title 10.1. Shared Mobility Devices.
Title 11. Pharmaceutical Services.
Title 12. Indemnity.
Title 13. Suretyship.
Title 13.5. Obligation To Defend Action.
Title 13.7. Obligation To Settle Insurance Claims Fairly [Inoperative].
Title 14. Lien.
Title 15. Internet Neutrality.
Title 15.2. Artificial Intelligence Training Data Transparency.
Title 15.5. Digital Equity Bill of Rights.
Title 16. General Provisions.
Title 17. Year 2000 Information Disclosures.
Title 18. Providers of Health and Safety Labor or Services.
Title 19. COVID-19 Small Landlord and Homeowner Relief Act.
Title 20. Firearm Industry Responsibility Act.
Title 21. Firearm Manufacturing.
Title 22. Child Sexual Abuse Material Hosted on a Social Media Platform.

TITLE 1
CONSIGNMENT OF FINE ART

Chapter 1. Definitions.
Chapter 2. General Provisions.

CHAPTER 1
DEFINITIONS

Definitions. §1738.

§§1726–1729. [Sections repealed 1979]

Leg.H. Added Stats 1969 ch 583 §1. Repealed Stats 1979 ch 747 §3. The repealed section related to contracts for swimming pool construction.

Prior Law: Former §1726, similar to present UCC §1201, was added Stats 1931 ch 1070 §1 and repealed Stats 1963 ch 819 §2, effective January 1, 1965.

Former §1726, relating to sales, was enacted 1872 and repealed Stats 1931 ch 1070 §1.

Former §§1727, 1728, similar to present UCC §2613, was added Stats 1931 ch 1070 §1 and repealed Stats 1963 ch 819 §2, effective January 1, 1965.

Former §1729, similar to present UCC §2305, was added Stats 1931 ch 1070 §1 and repealed Stats 1963 ch 819 §2, effective January 1, 1965.

§1730. [Section repealed 1985]

Leg.H. Added Stats 1983 ch 1288 §2, effective September 30, 1983. Repealed Stats 1985 ch 874 §16. See CC §1365.

Prior Law: Former §1730, relating to contracts for swimming pool construction, was added Stats 1969 ch 583 §1 and repealed Stats 1979 ch 747 §3.

Former §1730, similar to present UCC §2305, was added Stats 1931 ch 1070 §1 and repealed Stats 1963 ch 819 §2, effective January 1, 1965.

§1730.5. [Section repealed 1979]

Leg.H. Added Stats 1974 ch 1228 §1. Repealed 1979 ch 747 §3. The repealed section related to payments on swimming pool construction contracts.

§1731. [Section repealed 1979]

Leg.H. Added Stats 1969 ch 583 §1. Repealed Stats 1979 ch 747 §3. The repealed section related to contracts for swimming pool construction.

Prior Law: Former §1731, relating to contracts for swimming pool construction, was added Stats 1969 ch 583 §1 and repealed Stats 1979 ch 747 §3.

Former §1731, similar to present UCC §§2106, 2301, 2503, 2507, 2601, was added Stats 1931 ch 1070 §1 and repealed Stats 1963 ch 819 §2, effective January 1, 1965.

Former §1731, relating to sales was enacted 1872, amended Code Amdts 1873–74 ch 612 §194, and repealed Stats 1931 ch 1070 §1.

§1732. [Section repealed 1979]

Leg.H. Added Stats 1969 ch 583 §1. Repealed Stats 1979 ch 747 §3. See B & P C §7168.

Prior Law: Former §1732, similar to present UCC §2313, was added Stats 1931 ch 1070 §1 and repealed Stats 1963 ch 819 §2, effective January 1, 1965.

Former §1732, relating to sales was enacted 1872, amended Code Amdts 1873–74 ch 612 §195, and repealed Stats 1931 ch 1070 §1.

§1733. [Section repealed 1979]

Leg.H. Added Stats 1969 ch 583 §1. Repealed Stats 1979 ch 747 §3. See B & P C §7166.

Prior Law: Former §1733, similar to present UCC §2312, was added Stats 1931 ch 1070 §1 and repealed Stats 1963 ch 819 §2, effective January 1, 1965.

Former §1733, relating to sales was enacted 1872 and repealed Stats 1931 ch 1070 §1.

§1734. [Section repealed 1979]

Leg.H. Added Stats 1969 ch 583 §1. Repealed Stats 1979 ch 747 §3. The repealed section related to exclusivity and application of provisions of the title.

Prior Law: Former §1734, similar to present UCC §§2313, 2317 was added Stats 1931 ch 1070 §1 and repealed Stats 1963 ch 819 §2, effective January 1, 1965.

Former §1734, relating to sales was enacted 1872 and repealed Stats 1931 ch 1070 §1.

§1735. [Section repealed 1979]

Leg.H. Added Stats 1969 ch 583 §1. Repealed Stats 1979 ch 747 §3. See B & P C §7167.

Prior Law: Former §1735, similar to present UCC §2312, was added Stats 1931 ch 1070 §1 and repealed Stats 1963 ch 819 §2, effective January 1, 1965.

Former §1735, relating to sales was enacted 1872 and repealed Stats 1931 ch 1070 §1.

§1736. [Section repealed 1979]

Leg.H. Added Stats 1969 ch 583 §1. Repealed Stats 1979 ch 747 §3. The repealed section related to contracts for swimming pool construction.

Prior Law: Former §1736, similar to present UCC §§2313, 2317 was added Stats 1931 ch 1070 §1 and repealed Stats 1963 ch 819 §2, effective January 1, 1965.

Former §1736, relating to sales was enacted 1872 and repealed Stats 1931 ch 1070 §1.

§1737. [Section repealed 1963]

Leg.H. Added Stats 1931 ch 1070 §1. Repealed Stats 1963 ch 819 §2 p 1997, effective January 1, 1965. See UCC §§2401, 2501, 2502.

§1738. Definitions

As used in this title:

(a) "Artist" means the person who creates a work of fine art or, if that person is deceased, that person's heir, legatee, or personal representative.

(b) "Fine art" means a painting, sculpture, drawing, work of graphic art (including an etching, lithograph, offset print, silk screen, or a work of graphic art of like nature), a work of calligraphy, or a work in mixed media (including a collage, assemblage, or any combination of the foregoing art media).

(c) "Art dealer" means a person engaged in the business of selling works of fine art, other than a person exclusively engaged in the business of selling goods at public auction.

(d) "Person" means an individual, partnership, corporation, limited liability company, association or other group, however organized.

(e) "Consignment" means that no title to, estate in, or right to possession of, fine art, superior to that of the consignor shall vest in the consignee, notwithstanding the consignee's power or authority to transfer and convey to a third person all of the right, title and interest of the consignor in and to such fine art. **Leg.H.** Added Stats 1975 ch 953 §1. Amended Stats 1994 ch 1010 §31 (SB 2053).

Prior Law: Former §1738, similar to UCC §§1205, 2401, 2502, was added Stats 1931 ch 1070 §1, and repealed Stats 1963 ch 819 §2, effective January 1, 1965.

CHAPTER 2
GENERAL PROVISIONS

Delivery constituting consignment. §1738.5.
Results of consignment. §1738.6.
Consigned art to be trust property. §1738.7.
Contrary agreements void. §1738.8.
Application; Relation to Commercial Code. §1738.9.

§1738.5. Delivery constituting consignment

Notwithstanding any custom, practice or usage of the trade to the contrary, whenever an artist delivers or causes to be delivered a work of fine art of the artist's own creation to an art dealer in this state for the purpose of exhibition or sale, or both, on a commission, fee or other basis of compensation, the delivery to and acceptance of such work of fine art by the art dealer shall constitute a consignment, unless the delivery to the art dealer is pursuant to an outright sale for which the artist receives or has received full compensation for the work of fine art upon delivery. **Leg.H.** Added Stats 1975 ch 953 §1.

§1738.6. Results of consignment

A consignment of a work of fine art shall result in all of the following:

(a) The art dealer, after delivery of the work of fine art, shall constitute an agent of the artist for the purpose of sale or exhibition of the consigned work of fine art within the State of California.

(b) The work of fine art shall constitute property held in trust by the consignee for the benefit of the consignor, and shall not be subject to claim by a creditor of the consignee.

(c) The consignee shall be responsible for the loss of, or damage to, the work of fine art.

(d) The proceeds from the sale of the work of fine art shall constitute funds held in trust by the consignee for the benefit of the consignor. Such proceeds shall first be applied to pay any balance due to the consignor, unless the consignor expressly agrees otherwise in writing. **Leg.H.** Added Stats 1975 ch 953 §1.

§1738.7. Consigned art to be trust property

A work of fine art received as a consignment shall remain trust property, notwithstanding the subsequent purchase thereof by the consignee directly or indirectly for the consignee's own account until the price is paid in full to the consignor. If such work is thereafter resold to a bona fide purchaser before the consignor has been paid in full, the proceeds of the resale received by the consignee shall constitute funds held in trust for the benefit of the consignor to the extent necessary to pay any balance still due to the consignor and such trusteeship shall continue until the fiduciary obligation of the consignee with respect to such transaction is discharged in full. **Leg.H.** Added Stats 1975 ch 953 §1.

§1738.8. Contrary agreements void

Any provision of a contract or agreement whereby the consignor waives any provision of this title is void. **Leg.H.** Added Stats 1975 ch 953 §1.

§1738.9. Application; Relation to Commercial Code

This title shall not apply to a written contract executed prior to the effective date of this title, unless either the parties agree by mutual written consent that this title shall apply or such contract is extended or renewed after the effective date of this title.

The provisions of this title shall prevail over any conflicting or inconsistent provisions of the Commercial Code affecting the subject matter of this title. **Leg.H.** Added Stats 1975 ch 953 §1.

TITLE 1A
INDEPENDENT WHOLESALE SALES REPRESENTATIVES

Legislative findings and declarations. §1738.10.
Citation of chapter. §1738.11.
Definitions. §1738.12.
Requirement of written contract; Contents. §1738.13.
Doing business in state. §1738.14.
Civil action for damages. §1738.15.
Attorney fees and costs. §1738.16.
Application of chapter. §1738.17.

§1738.10. Legislative findings and declarations

The Legislature finds and declares that independent wholesale sales representatives are a key ingredient to the California economy. The Legislature further finds and declares the wholesale sales representatives spend many hours developing their territory in order to properly market their products, and therefore should be provided unique protection from unjust termination of the territorial market areas. Therefore, it is the intent of the Legislature, in enacting this act to provide security and clarify the contractual relations between manufacturers and their nonemployee sales representatives. **Leg.H.** Added Stats 1990 ch 964 §1 (AB 3456).

§1738.11. Citation of chapter
This chapter shall be known and cited as the Independent Wholesale Sales Representatives Contractual Relations Act of 1990. **Leg.H.** Added Stats 1990 ch 964 §1 (AB 3456).

§1738.12. Definitions
For purposes of this chapter the following terms have the following meaning:

(a) "Manufacturer" means any organization engaged in the business of producing, assembling, mining, weaving, importing or by any other method of fabrication, a product tangible or intangible, intended for resale to, or use by the consumers of this state.

(b) "Jobber" means any business organization engaged in the business of purchasing products intended for resale and invoicing to purchasers for resale to, or use by, the consumers of this state.

(c) "Distributor" means any business organization engaged in offering for sale products which are shipped from its inventory, or from goods in transit to its inventory, to purchasers and intended for resale to, or use by the consumers of this state.

(d) "Chargeback" means any deduction taken against the commissions earned by the sales representative which are not required by state or federal law.

(e) "Wholesale sales representative" means any person who contracts with a manufacturer, jobber, or distributor for the purpose of soliciting wholesale orders, is compensated, in whole or part, by commission, but shall not include one who places orders or purchases exclusively for his own account for resale and shall not include one who sells or takes orders for the direct sale of products to the ultimate consumer. **Leg.H.** Added Stats 1990 ch 964 §1 (AB 3456).

§1738.13. Requirement of written contract; Contents
(a) Whenever a manufacturer, jobber, or distributor is engaged in business within this state and uses the services of a wholesale sales representative, who is not an employee of the manufacturer, jobber, or distributor, to solicit wholesale orders at least partially within this state, and the contemplated method of payment involves commissions, the manufacturer, jobber, or distributor shall enter into a written contract with the sales representative.

(b) The written contract shall include all of the following:
(1) The rate and method by which the commission is computed.
(2) The time when commissions will be paid.
(3) The territory assigned to the sales representative.
(4) All exceptions to the assigned territory and customers therein.
(5) What chargebacks will be made against the commissions, if any.

(c) The sales representative and the manufacturer, jobber, or distributor shall each be provided with a signed copy of the written contract and the sales representative shall sign a receipt acknowledging receipt of the signed contract.

(d) The sales representative shall be provided with the following written information and documentation with payment of the commission:
(1) An accounting of the orders for which payment is made, including the customer's name and invoice number.
(2) The rate of commission on each order.
(3) Information relating to any chargebacks included in the accounting.

(e) No contract shall contain any provision which waives any rights established pursuant to this chapter. Any such waiver is deemed contrary to public policy and void. **Leg.H.** Added Stats 1990 ch 964 §1 (AB 3456).

§1738.14. Doing business in state
A manufacturer, jobber, or distributor who is not a resident of this state, and who enters into a contract regulated by this chapter is deemed to be doing business in this state for purposes of personal jurisdiction. **Leg.H.** Added Stats 1990 ch 964 §1 (AB 3456).

§1738.15. Civil action for damages
A manufacturer, jobber, or distributor who willfully fails to enter into a written contract as required by this chapter or willfully fails to pay commissions as provided in the written contract shall be liable to the sales representative in a civil action for treble the damages proved at trial. **Leg.H.** Added Stats 1990 ch 964 §1 (AB 3456).

§1738.16. Attorney fees and costs
In a civil action brought by the sales representative pursuant to this chapter, the prevailing party shall be entitled to reasonable attorney's fees and costs in addition to any other recovery. **Leg.H.** Added Stats 1990 ch 964 §1 (AB 3456).

§1738.17. Application of chapter
This chapter shall not apply to any person licensed pursuant to Division 9 (commencing with Section 23000) of the Business and Professions Code. **Leg.H.** Added Stats 1990 ch 964 §1 (AB 3456).

TITLE 1.1
SALE AND MANUFACTURE OF POLITICAL ITEMS

Prohibition as to items not original in fact. §1739.
"Political item". §1739.1.
"Original political item". §1739.2.
Items labeled "copy" or "reproduction" excepted. §1739.3.
Action to enforce liability for violation. §1739.4.

§1739. Prohibition as to items not original in fact
No person shall sell, advertise for sale, or offer for sale any political item which is purported to be an original political item but which is not in fact an original political item. **Leg.H.** Added Stats 1977 ch 69 §1.

Prior Law: Former §1739, similar to UCC §§2326, 2327, 2401, 2501–2503, was added Stats 1931 ch 1070 §1 and repealed Stats 1963 ch 819 §2, effective January 1, 1965.

Former §1739, relating to contract for sale of personal property, was enacted 1872, amended Code Amdts 1873–74 ch 612 §196, and repealed Stats 1931 ch 1070 §1.

§1739.1. "Political item"
For purposes of this title, a "political item" is any button, ribbon, poster, sticker, literature, or advertising concerning any candidate or ballot proposition in any electoral campaign. **Leg.H.** Added Stats 1977 ch 69 §1.

§1739.2. "Original political item"
For purposes of this title, an "original political item" is any political item produced during any electoral campaign for use in support of or in opposition to any candidate or ballot proposition before the voters in that campaign. **Leg.H.** Added Stats 1977 ch 69 §1.

§1739.3. Items labeled "copy" or "reproduction" excepted
No political item which is labeled "copy" or "reproduction" at the time of sale, advertising for sale, or offering for sale shall violate Section 1739. **Leg.H.** Added Stats 1977 ch 69 §1.

§1739.4. Action to enforce liability for violation
(a) A person who offers or sells any political item in violation of this title shall be liable to the person purchasing such political item from him, who may sue to recover the consideration paid for the political item, with interest at the legal rate thereon, upon the tender of the political item.

(b) In any case in which a person knowingly offers or sells a political item in violation of this title, the person purchasing such political item may recover from the person who offers or sells such political item an amount equal to three times the amount required under subdivision (a).

(c) No action shall be maintained to enforce any liability under this section unless brought within one year after discovery of the violation upon which it is based and in no event more than three years after the political item was sold. **Leg.H.** Added Stats 1977 ch 69 §1.

TITLE 1.1A
AUTOGRAPHED MEMORABILIA

Requirements for sale or offer for sale. §1739.7.

§1739.7. Requirements for sale or offer for sale
(a) As used in this section:
(1) "Autographed collectible" means an item bearing the signature of a particular person that is sold or offered for sale for fifty dollars ($50) or more, excluding sales tax and shipping fees, when the dealer offers the signed item at a higher price than the dealer would charge for a comparable item without the signature.

(2) For purposes of this section, an autographed collectible shall be limited to the following items:

(A) Sports items, including, but not limited to, a photograph, ticket, plaque, sports program, trading card, item of sports equipment or clothing, or other sports memorabilia.

(B) Entertainment media items related to music, television, and films, including, but not limited to, a picture, photo, record, compact disc, digital video disc, ticket, program, playbill, clothing, hat, poster, toy, plaque, trading card, musical instrument, or other entertainment memorabilia.

(3) For purposes of this section, and notwithstanding paragraph (2), an autographed collectible does not include the following items:

(A) Works of fine art, as defined by paragraph (1) of subdivision (d) of Section 982 that are originals or numbered multiples, and signed by the artist or maker.

(B) Furniture and decorative objects, including works of pottery, jewelry, and design that are signed by the artist or maker.

(C) Signed books, manuscripts, and correspondence, as well as ephemera not related to sports or entertainment media.

(D) Signed numismatic items or bullion.

(4) "Consumer" means any natural person who purchases an autographed collectible from a dealer for personal, family, or household purposes. "Consumer" also includes a prospective purchaser meeting these criteria.

(5)(A) "Dealer" means a person who is in the business of selling or offering for sale autographed collectibles exclusively or nonexclusively, and sells three or more autographed collectibles in a period of 12 months. "Dealer" includes an auctioneer or auction company that sells autographed collectibles at a public auction. "Dealer" includes a person engaged in a mail-order, telephone-order, online, or television business for the sale of autographed collectibles.

(B) "Dealer" does not include any of the following:

(i) A pawnbroker licensed pursuant to Chapter 3 (commencing with Section 21300) of Division 8 of the Financial Code, if the autographed collectible was acquired through a foreclosure on a collateral loan, provided that the pawnbroker does not hold himself or herself out as having knowledge or skill peculiar to autographed collectibles.

(ii) The person who autographed the collectible.

(6) "Limited edition" means any autographed collectible that meets all of the following requirements:

(A) A company has produced a specific quantity of an autographed collectible and placed it on the open market.

(B) The producer of the autographed collectible has posted a notice, at its primary place of business, that it will provide any consumer, upon request, with a copy of a notice that states the exact number of an autographed collectible produced in that series of limited editions.

(C) The producer makes available, upon request of a consumer, evidence that the electronic encoding, films, molds, or plates used to create the autographed collectible have been destroyed after the specified number of autographed collectibles have been produced.

(D) The sequence number of the autographed collectible and the number of the total quantity produced in the limited edition are printed on the autographed collectible.

(7) "Person" means any natural person, partnership, corporation, limited liability company, company, trust, association, or other entity, however organized.

(8) "Representation" means any oral or written representation, including, but not limited to, a representation in an advertisement, brochure, catalog, flyer, invoice, sign, radio or television broadcast, online communication, Internet Web page, email, or other commercial or promotional material.

(9) "Auctioneer" means an auctioneer as defined in subdivision (d) of Section 1812.601, or a representative or agent of an auctioneer.

(10) "Auction company" means an auction company as defined in subdivision (c) of Section 1812.601, or a representative or agent of an auction company.

(b) A dealer who, in selling or offering to sell to a consumer an autographed collectible, makes a representation to a consumer that the signature on the autographed collectible is the authentic signature of a particular person in that person's own hand, shall furnish an express warranty to the consumer at the time of sale. The dealer shall retain a copy of the express warranty for not less than seven years. The express warranty, which may be included in the bill of sale or invoice, shall meet all of the following criteria:

(1) Is written in at least 10-point type.

(2) Is signed by the dealer or his or her authorized agent, and contains the dealer's true legal name, business street address, and the last four digits of the dealer's seller's permit account number from the California Department of Tax and Fee Administration, if applicable.

(3) Specifies the date of sale and the purchase price.

(4) Describes the autographed collectible and specifies the name of the person who autographed it.

(5) Expressly warrants the autographed collectible as authentic, and that the warranty is conclusively presumed to be part of the bargain. The warranty shall not be negated or limited by reason of the lack of words such as "warranty" or "guarantee" or because the dealer does not have a specific intent or authorization to make the warranty or because any statement relevant to the autographed collectible is or purports to be, or is capable of being, merely the dealer's opinion.

(6) If the autographed collectible is offered as one of a limited edition, specifies (A) how the autographed collectible and edition are numbered and (B) the size of the edition and the size of any prior or anticipated future edition, if known by the dealer. If the size of the edition and the size of any prior or anticipated future edition is not known, the warranty shall contain an explicit statement to that effect.

(7) Indicates whether the dealer is surety bonded or is otherwise insured to protect the consumer against errors and omissions of the dealer and, if bonded or insured, provides proof thereof.

(8) Indicates if the autographed collectible was autographed in the presence of the dealer, and any proof thereof. Specify the date and location of, and the name of a witness to, the autograph signing, if known, and applicable.

(9) Identifies all information upon which the dealer relied when making the representation that the autographed collectible is authentic.

(10) Indicates an identifying serial number that corresponds to an identifying number printed on the autographed collectible item, if any.

(11) Indicates whether the item was obtained or purchased from a third party.

(c) The dealer shall retain, after January 1, 2018, a record of the name and address of the third party, as described in paragraph (11) of subdivision (b). This third-party information may be discoverable during a civil dispute. However, nothing in this subdivision prohibits a party from objecting to a discovery request on the grounds of a right to privacy. This third-party information shall be kept on file for seven years.

(d)(1) In addition to any other right or remedy provided under existing law, including, but not limited to, any rights and remedies provided under contract law, a consumer shall have the right to cancel the contract for the purchase of an autographed collectible represented by a dealer as authentic until midnight of the third day after the day on which the consumer purchased the autographed collectible. Notice of the cancellation may be provided in person or in a written or electronic form, and is deemed effective once communicated or sent. The autographed collectible shall be returned to the dealer within 30 days of the sale in the same condition in which it was sold, the cost of which shall be borne by the consumer. The price paid by the consumer shall be refunded within 10 days of receipt of the returned autographed collectible. Nothing in this section prevents the parties from agreeing to cancel a contract after midnight of the third day after the day on which the consumer purchases the autographed collectible.

(2) This subdivision does not apply to the following:

(A) Autographed collectibles sold by an auctioneer or auction company at auction.

(B) Autographed collectibles purchased by barter or trade of other items.

(C) Autographed collectibles sold at a trade show.

(D) Autographed collectibles sold by one dealer to another dealer.

(e)(1) No dealer shall display or offer for sale an autographed collectible unless, at the location where the autographed collectible is offered for sale and in close proximity to the autographed collectible merchandise, there is a conspicuous sign that reads as follows:

"SALE OF AUTOGRAPHED COLLECTIBLES: AS REQUIRED BY LAW, A DEALER WHO SELLS TO A CONSUMER ANY COLLECTIBLE DESCRIBED AS BEING AUTOGRAPHED MUST PROVIDE A WRITTEN EXPRESS WARRANTY AT THE TIME OF SALE AND A THREE-DAY RIGHT OF RETURN. THIS DEALER MAY BE SURETY BONDED OR OTHERWISE INSURED TO ENSURE THE AUTHENTICITY OF ANY AUTOGRAPHED COLLECTIBLE SOLD BY THIS DEALER."

(2) This subdivision does not apply to an autographed collectible sold by an auctioneer or auction company at auction or an autographed collectible sold at a trade show.

(f) No dealer selling at a trade show, nor an auctioneer or auction company shall display or offer for sale an autographed collectible unless, at the location where the autographed collectible is offered for sale and in close proximity to the autographed collectible merchandise, there is a conspicuous sign that reads as follows:

"SALE OF AUTOGRAPHED COLLECTIBLES: AS REQUIRED BY LAW, A DEALER WHO SELLS TO A CONSUMER ANY COLLECTIBLE DESCRIBED AS BEING AUTOGRAPHED MUST PROVIDE A WRITTEN EXPRESS WARRANTY AT THE TIME OF SALE. THIS DEALER MAY BE SURETY BONDED OR OTHERWISE INSURED TO ENSURE THE AUTHENTICITY OF ANY AUTOGRAPHED COLLECTIBLE SOLD BY THIS DEALER."

(g) Any dealer engaged in a mail-order, telephone-order, or online business for the sale of autographed collectibles:

(1) Shall include the disclosure specified in subdivision (e), in type of conspicuous size, in any written advertisement relating to an autographed collectible.

(2) Shall include in each television or online advertisement relating to an autographed collectible the following written onscreen message, which shall be prominently displayed, easily readable, and clearly visible for no less than five seconds, and which shall be repeated for five seconds once during each four-minute segment of the advertisement following the initial four minutes:

A written express warranty is provided with each autographed collectible, as required by law. This dealer may be surety bonded or otherwise insured to ensure the authenticity of any autographed collectible sold by this dealer.

(3) Shall include as part of the oral message of each radio advertisement for an autographed collectible the disclosure specified in subdivision (e).

(h) In a civil action brought by a consumer against a dealer, the following shall apply:

(1) A dealer who fails to provide an express warranty, or provides an express warranty that does not comply with all of the requirements of subdivision (b), shall be subject to a civil penalty of up to one thousand dollars ($1,000), payable to the consumer.

(2) A dealer who provides a false express warranty that injures the consumer shall be subject to a civil penalty of up to one thousand dollars ($1,000) payable to the consumer.

(3) A dealer who provides a false express warranty and whose act or omission amounts to gross negligence that injures the consumer, shall be subject to a civil penalty of three thousand dollars ($3,000), or an amount equal to three times actual damages, whichever is greater, payable to the consumer.

(4) A dealer who knowingly provides a false express warranty, or knowingly fails to provide an express warranty required by this section, and whose act or omission results in an injury to a consumer shall be subject to a civil penalty of five thousand dollars ($5,000), or an amount equal to(five) times actual damages, whichever is greater, payable to the consumer.

(5) A consumer may recover court costs, reasonable attorney's fees, interest, and expert witness fees, if applicable, pursuant to an action described in paragraphs (2) to (4), inclusive.

(6) The remedies specified in this section are in addition to, and not in lieu of, any other remedy that may be provided by law. The court, in its discretion, may award punitive damages based on the egregiousness of the dealer's conduct.

(i) A dealer may be surety bonded or otherwise insured for purposes of indemnification against errors and omissions arising from the authentication, sale, or resale of autographed collectibles.

(j) It is the intent of the Legislature that neither the amendment to this section by Assembly Bill 1570 of the 2015–2016 Regular Session, adding an exclusion of a provider or operator of an online marketplace to the definition of a dealer, nor the amendment to this section by Assembly Bill 228 of the 2017–2018 Regular Session, removing that exclusion from the definition of a dealer, be construed to affect the decision of the Court of Appeal in Gentry v. eBay, Inc. (2002) 99 Cal.App.4th 816. **Leg.H.** Added Stats 1992 ch 656 §1 (AB 3113). Amended Stats 1994 ch 1010 §32 (SB 2053); Stats 1995 ch 360 §3 (AB 434); Stats 1998 ch 494 §1 (SB 2024); Stats 1999 ch 83 §20 (SB 966); Stats 2016 ch 258 §2 (AB 1570), effective January 1, 2017; Stats 2017 ch 696 §1 (AB 228), effective October 12, 2017.

TITLE 1.2
SALE OF FINE PRINTS

Chapter 1. General Provisions.
Chapter 2. Full Disclosure in the Sale of Fine Prints.
Chapter 3. Remedies and Penalties.

CHAPTER 1
GENERAL PROVISIONS

Definitions. §1740.
Prints subject to chapter. §1741.

§1740. Definitions

As used in this title:

(a) "Fine art multiple" or "multiple" for the purposes of this title means any fine print, photograph (positive or negative), sculpture cast, collage, or similar art object produced in more than one copy. Pages or sheets taken from books and magazines and offered for sale or sold as art objects shall be included, but books and magazines shall be excluded.

(b) "Fine print" or "print" means a multiple produced by, but not limited to, engraving, etching, woodcutting, lithography, and serigraphy, and means multiples produced or developed from photographic negatives, or any combination thereof.

(c) "Master" is used in lieu of and has the same meaning as a printing plate, stone, block, screen, photographic negative, or mold or other process as to a sculpture, which contains an image used to produce fine art objects in multiples.

(d) "Artist" means the person who created the image which is contained in, or constitutes, the master or conceived of, and approved the image which is contained in, or constitutes, the master.

(e) Whether a multiple is "signed" or "unsigned" as these terms are used in this title relating to prints and photographs, depends upon whether or not the multiple was autographed by the artist's own hand, and not by mechanical means, after the multiple was produced, irrespective of whether it was signed or unsigned in the plate.

(f) "Impression" means each individual fine art multiple made by printing, stamping, casting, or any other process.

(g) "Art dealer" means a person who is in the business of dealing, exclusively or nonexclusively, in the fine art multiples to which this title is applicable, or a person who by his or her occupation holds himself or herself out as having knowledge or skill peculiar to these works, or to whom that knowledge or skill may be attributed by his or her employment of an agent or other intermediary who by his or her occupation holds himself or herself out as having that knowledge or skill. The term "art dealer" includes an auctioneer who sells these works at public auction, but excludes persons, not otherwise defined or treated as art dealers herein, who are consignors or principals of auctioneers.

(h) "Limited edition" means fine art multiples produced from a master, all of which are the same image and bear numbers or other markings to denote the limited production thereof to a stated maximum number of multiples, or are otherwise held out as limited to a maximum number of multiples.

(i) "Proofs" means multiples which are the same as, and which are produced from the same master as, the multiples in a limited edition, but which, whether so designated or not, are set aside from and are in addition to the limited edition to which they relate.

(j) "Certificate of authenticity" means a written or printed description of the multiple which is to be sold, exchanged, or consigned by an art dealer. Every certificate shall contain the following statement:

"This is to certify that all information and the statements contained herein are true and correct."

(k) "Person" means an individual, partnership, corporation, limited liability company, association, or other entity, however organized. **Leg.H.** Added Stats 1970 ch 1223 §1, operative July 1, 1971. Amended Stats 1982 ch 1320 §1; Stats 1988 ch 819 §1; Stats 1994 ch 1010 §33 (SB 2053).

Prior Law: Former §1740, similar to UCC §§2401, 2403, 2503, 2505, 7502, was added Stats 1931 ch 1070 §1, and repealed Stats 1963 ch 819 §2, effective January 1, 1965.

Former §1740, relating to an agreement to manufacture, was enacted 1872, and repealed Stats 1931 ch 1070 §1.

§1741. Prints subject to chapter

This title shall apply to any fine art multiple when offered for sale or sold at wholesale or retail for one hundred dollars ($100) or more, exclusive of any frame. **Leg.H.** Added Stats 1970 ch 1223 §1, operative July 1, 1971. Amended Stats 1982 ch 1320 §2.

Prior Law: Former §1741, similar to UCC §2328, was added Stats 1931 ch 1070 §1 and repealed Stats 1963 ch 819 §2, effective January 1, 1965.

Former §1741, relating to contract for sale of real property, was enacted 1872, amended Code Amdts 1873–74 ch 612 §197, and repealed Stats 1931 ch 1070 §1.

CHAPTER 2
FULL DISCLOSURE IN THE SALE OF FINE PRINTS

Information required. §1742.
Exemption of charitable organizations. §1742.6.
Detail required. §1744.
Disclosures as warranties. §1744.7.
Liability of artist or dealer. §1744.9.

§1742. Information required

(a) An art dealer shall not sell or consign a multiple into or from this state unless a certificate of authenticity is furnished to the purchaser or consignee, at his or her request, or in any event prior to a sale or consignment, which sets forth as to each multiple, the descriptive information required by Section 1744 for any period. If a prospective purchaser so requests, the certificate shall be transmitted to him or her prior to the payment or placing of an order for a multiple. If payment is made by a purchaser prior to delivery of such a multiple, this certificate shall be supplied at the time of or prior to delivery. With respect to auctions, this information may be furnished in catalogues or other written materials which are made readily available for consultation and purchase prior to sale, provided that a bill of sale, receipt, or invoice describing the transaction is then provided which makes reference to the catalogue and lot number in which this information is supplied. Information supplied pursuant to this subdivision shall be clearly, specifically and distinctly addressed to each of the items listed in Section 1744 unless the required data is not applicable. This section is applicable to transactions by and between art dealers and others considered to be art dealers for the purposes of this title.

(b) An art dealer shall not cause a catalogue, prospectus, flyer, or other written material or advertisement to be distributed in, into, or from this state which solicits a direct sale, by inviting transmittal of payment for a specific multiple, unless it clearly sets forth, in close physical proximity to the place in such material where the multiple is described, the descriptive information required by Section 1744 for any time period. In lieu of this required information, the written material or advertising may set forth the material contained in the following quoted passage, or the passage itself, if the art dealer then supplies the required information prior to or with delivery of the multiple. The nonobservance of the terms within the following passage shall constitute a violation of this title:

"California law provides for disclosure in writing of information concerning certain fine prints, photographs, and sculptures prior to effecting a sale of them. This law requires disclosure of such matters as the identity of the artist, the artist's signature, the medium, whether the multiple is a reproduction, the time when the multiple was produced, use of the plate which produced the multiple, and the number of multiples in a "limited edition." If a prospective purchaser so requests, the information shall be transmitted to him or her prior to payment, or the placing of an order for a multiple. If payment is made by a purchaser prior to delivery of the multiple, this information will be supplied at the time of or prior to delivery, in which case the purchaser is entitled to a refund if, for reasons related to matter contained in such information, he or she returns the multiple in the condition in which received, within 30 days of receiving it. In addition, if after payment and delivery, it is ascertained that the information provided is incorrect, the purchaser may be entitled to certain remedies, including refund upon return of the multiple in the condition in which received."

This requirement is not applicable to general written material or advertising which does not constitute an offer to effect a specific sale.

(c) In each place of business in the state where an art dealer is regularly engaged in sales of multiples, the art dealer shall post in a conspicuous place, a sign which, in a legible format, contains the information included in the following passage:

"California law provides for the disclosure in writing of certain information concerning prints, photographs, and sculpture casts. This information is available to you, and you may request to receive it prior to purchase."

(d) If an art dealer offering multiples by means of a catalogue, prospectus, flyer or other written material or advertisement distributed in, into or from this state disclaims knowledge as to any relevant detail referred to in Section 1744, he or she shall so state specifically and categorically with regard to each such detail to the end that the purchaser shall be enabled to judge the degree of uniqueness or scarcity of each multiple contained in the edition so offered. Describing the edition as an edition of "reproductions" eliminates the need to furnish further informational details unless the edition was allegedly published in a signed, numbered, or limited edition, or any combination thereof, in which case all of the informational details are required to be furnished.

(e) Whenever an artist sells or consigns a multiple of his or her own creation or conception, the artist shall disclose the information required by Section 1744, but an artist shall not otherwise be regarded as an art dealer. **Leg.H.** Added Stats 1970 ch 1223 §1, operative July 1, 1971. Amended Stats 1982 ch 1320 §3; Stats 1988 ch 819 §2.

Prior Law: Former §1742, similar to UCC §2509, was added Stats 1931 ch 1070 §1 and repealed Stats 1963 ch 819 §2, effective January 1, 1965.

§1742.6. Exemption of charitable organizations

Any charitable organization which conducts a sale or auction of fine art multiples shall be exempt from the disclosure requirements of this title if it posts in a conspicuous place, at the site of the sale or auction, a disclaimer of any knowledge of the information specified in Section 1744, and includes such a disclaimer in a catalogue, if any, distributed by the organization with respect to the sale or auction of fine art multiples. If a charitable organization uses or employs an art dealer to conduct a sale or auction of fine art multiples, the art dealer shall be subject to all disclosure requirements otherwise required of an art dealer under this title. **Leg.H.** Added Stats 1982 ch 1320 §4.

§1743. [Section repealed 1982]

Leg.H. Added Stats 1970 ch 1223 §1, operative July 1, 1971. Repealed Stats 1982 ch 1320 §4.2. See CC §1742.

Prior Law: Former §1743, similar to UCC §2403, was added Stats 1931 ch 1070 §1 and repealed Stats 1963 ch 819 §2, effective January 1, 1965.

§1744. Detail required

(a) Except as provided in subdivisions (c), (d), (e), and otherwise in this title, a certificate of authenticity containing the following informational details shall be required to be supplied in all transactions covered by subdivisions (a), (b), and (e) of Section 1742:

(1) The name of the artist.

(2) If the artist's name appears on the multiple, a statement whether the multiple was signed by the artist.

If the multiple was not signed by the artist, a statement of the source of the artist's name on the multiple, such as whether the artist placed his signature on the multiple or on the master, whether his name was stamped or estate stamped on the multiple or on the master, or was from some other source or in some other manner placed on the multiple or on the master.

(3) A description of the medium or process, and where pertinent to photographic processes, the material used in producing the multiple, such as whether the multiple was produced through the etching, engraving, lithographic, serigraphic, or a particular method or material used in photographic developing processes. If an established term, in accordance with the usage of the trade, cannot be employed accurately to describe the medium or process, a brief, clear description shall be made.

(4) If the multiple or the image on or in the master constitutes, as to prints and photographs, a photomechanical or photographic type of reproduction, or as to sculptures a surmoulage or other form of reproduction of sculpture cases, of an image produced in a different medium, for a purpose other than the creation of the multiple being described, a statement of this information and the respective mediums.

(5) If paragraph (4) is applicable, and the multiple is not signed, a statement whether the artist authorized or approved in writing the multiple or the edition of which the multiple being described is one.

(6) If the purported artist was deceased at the time the master was made which produced the multiple, this shall be stated.

(7) If the multiple is a "posthumous" multiple, that is, if the master was created during the life of the artist but the multiple was produced after the artist's death, this shall be stated.

(8) If the multiple was made from a master which produced a prior limited edition, or from a master which constitutes or was made from a reproduction or surmoulage of a prior multiple or the master which produced the prior limited edition, this shall be stated as shall the total number of multiples, including proofs, of all other editions produced from that master.

(9) As to multiples produced after 1949, the year, or approximate year, the multiple was produced shall be stated. As to multiples produced prior to 1950, state the year, approximate year or period when the master was made which produced the multiple and when the particular multiple being described was produced. The requirements of this subdivision shall be satisfied when the year stated is approximately accurate.

(10) Whether the edition is being offered as a limited edition, and if so: (i) the authorized maximum number of signed or numbered impressions, or both, in the edition; (ii) the authorized maximum number of unsigned or unnumbered impressions, or both, in the edition; (iii) the authorized maximum number of artist's, publisher's or other proofs, if any, outside of the regular edition; and (iv) the total size of the edition.

(11) Whether or not the master has been destroyed, effaced, altered, defaced, or canceled after the current edition.

(b) If the multiple is part of a limited edition, and was printed after January 1, 1983, the statement of the size of the limited edition, as stated pursuant to paragraph (10) of subdivision (a) of Section 1744 shall also constitute an express warranty that no additional multiples of the same image, including proofs, have been produced in this or in any other limited edition.

(c) If the multiple was produced in the period from 1950 to the effective date of this section, the information required to be supplied need not include the information required by paragraphs (5) and (8) of subdivision (a).

(d) If the multiple was produced in the period from 1900 to 1949, the information required to be supplied need only consist of the information required by paragraphs (1), (2), (3), and (9) of subdivision (a).

(e) If the multiple was produced before the year 1900, the information to be supplied need only consist of the information required by paragraphs (1), (3), and (9) of subdivision (a). **Leg.H.** Added Stats 1982 ch 1320 §5. Amended Stats 1988 ch 819 §3.

Prior Law: Former §1744, similar to the present section, was added Stats 1970 ch 1223 §1, operative July 1, 1971, and repealed Stats 1982 ch 1320 §4.5.

Former §1744, similar to UCC §2403, was added Stats 1931 ch 1070 §1 and repealed Stats 1963 ch 819 §2, effective January 1, 1965.

§1744.7. Disclosures as warranties

Whenever an art dealer furnishes the name of the artist pursuant to Section 1744 for any time period after 1949, and otherwise furnishes information required by any of the subdivisions of Section 1744 for any time period, as to transactions including offers, sales, or consignments made to other than art dealers, and to other art dealers, such information shall be a part of the basis of the bargain and shall create express warranties as to the information provided. Such warranties shall not be negated or limited because the art dealer in the written instrument did not use formal words such as "warrant" or "guarantee" or because the art dealer did not have a specific intention or authorization to make a warranty or because any required statement is, or purports to be, or is capable of being merely the seller's opinion. The existence of a basis in fact for information warranted by virtue of this subdivision shall not be a defense in an action to enforce such warranty. However, with respect to photographs and sculptures produced prior to 1950, and other multiples produced prior to 1900, as to information required by paragraphs (3), (4), (5), and (6) of subdivision (a) of Section 1744, the art dealer shall be deemed to have satisfied this section if a reasonable basis in fact existed for the information provided. When information is not supplied as to any subdivision or paragraph of Section 1744 because not applicable, this shall constitute the express warranty that the paragraph is not applicable.

Whenever an art dealer disclaims knowledge as to a particular item about which information is required, such disclaimer shall be ineffective unless clearly, specifically, and categorically stated as to the particular item and contained in the physical context of other language setting forth the required information as to a specific multiple. **Leg.H.** Added Stats 1982 ch 1320 §6.

§1744.9. Liability of artist or dealer

(a) An artist or art dealer who consigns a multiple to an art dealer for the purpose of effecting a sale of the multiple, shall have no liability to a purchaser under this article if the consignor, as to the consignee, has complied with the provisions of this title.

(b) When an art dealer has agreed to sell a multiple on behalf of a consignor, who is not an art dealer, or an artist has not consigned a multiple to an art dealer but the art dealer has agreed to act as the agent for an artist for the purpose of supplying the information required by this title, the art dealer shall incur the liabilities of other art dealers prescribed by this title, as to a purchaser. **Leg.H.** Added Stats 1982 ch 1320 §7.

CHAPTER 3
REMEDIES AND PENALTIES

Liability; Damages; Limitation of actions; Disclaimers. §1745.
Injunctions; Civil penalties. §1745.5.

§1745. Liability; Damages; Limitation of actions; Disclaimers

(a) An art dealer, including a dealer consignee, who offers or sells a multiple in, into or from this state without providing the certificate of authenticity required in Sections 1742 and 1744 of this title for any time period, or who provides information which is mistaken, erroneous or untrue, except for harmless errors, such as typographical errors, shall be liable to the purchaser of the multiple. The art dealer's liability shall consist of the consideration paid by the purchaser for the multiple, with interest at the legal rate thereon, upon the return of the multiple in the condition in which received by the purchaser.

(b) In any case in which an art dealer, including a dealer consignee, willfully offers or sells a multiple in violation of this title, the person purchasing such multiple may recover from the art dealer, including a dealer consignee, who offers or sells such multiple an amount equal to three times the amount required under subdivision (a).

(c) No action shall be maintained to enforce any liability under this section unless brought within one year after discovery of the violation upon which it is based and in no event more than three years after the multiple was sold.

(d) In any action to enforce any provision of this title, the court may allow the prevailing purchaser the costs of the action together with reasonable attorneys' and expert witnesses' fees. In the event, however, the court determines that an action to enforce was brought in bad faith, it may allow such expenses to the seller as it deems appropriate.

(e) These remedies shall not bar or be deemed inconsistent with a claim for damages or with the exercise of additional remedies otherwise available to the purchaser.

(f) In any proceeding in which an art dealer relies upon a disclaimer of knowledge as to any relevant information set forth in Section 1744 for any time period, such disclaimer shall be effective unless the claimant is able to establish that the art dealer failed to make reasonable inquiries, according to the custom and usage of the trade, to ascertain the relevant information or that such relevant information would have been ascertained as a result of such reasonable inquiries. **Leg.H.** Added Stats 1970 ch 1223 §1, operative July 1, 1971. Amended Stats 1982 ch 1320 §8; Stats 1988 ch 819 §4.

Prior Law: Former §1745, similar to UCC §§2403, 7502, was added Stats 1931 ch 1070 §1 and repealed Stats 1963 ch 819 §2, effective January 1, 1965.

§1745.5. Injunctions; Civil penalties

(a) Any person performing or proposing to perform an act in violation of this title within this state may be enjoined in any court of competent jurisdiction.

(b) Actions for injunction pursuant to this title may be prosecuted by the following persons:

(1) The Attorney General.
(2) Any district attorney.
(3) Any city attorney.
(4) With the consent of the district attorney, a city prosecutor in any city or city and county having a full-time city prosecutor in the name of the people of the State of California upon their own complaint, or upon the complaint of any board, officer, person, corporation, or association.

(5) Any person acting in his or her own interests, or in the interests of the members of a corporation or association, or in the interests of the general public.

(c) Any person who violates any provision of this title may also be liable for a civil penalty not to exceed one thousand dollars ($1,000) for each violation, which may be assessed and recovered in a civil action brought in the name of the people of the State of California by the Attorney General or by any district attorney or any city attorney, and, with the consent of the district attorney, by a city prosecutor in any city or city and county having a full-time city prosecutor in any court of competent jurisdiction.

If the action is brought by the Attorney General, one-half of the penalty collected shall be paid to the treasurer of the county in which the judgment was entered, and one-half to the General Fund. If brought by a district attorney, the penalty collected shall be paid to the treasurer of the county in which the judgment was entered. If brought by a city attorney or city prosecutor, one-half of the penalty collected shall be paid to the treasurer of the city in which the judgment was entered, and one-half to the treasurer of the county in which the judgment was entered.

(d) Any person who violates any provision of this title may also be liable for a civil penalty surcharge not to exceed one thousand dollars ($1,000) for each violation which shall be assessed and recovered in the manner provided in subdivision (c). Any penalty surcharge collected shall be applied to the costs of enforcing this title by the prosecuting officer. **Leg.H.** Added Stats 1982 ch 1320 §9. Amended Stats 1988 ch 819 §5.

TITLE 1.2A
VIOLENT VIDEO GAMES

Definitions. §1746.
Sale or rental of violent video game to minor prohibited. §1746.1.
Labeling of violent video games. §1746.2.
Penalty for violation of title. §1746.3.
Reporting violations; Prosecution. §1746.4.
Severability of title. §1746.5.

§1746. Definitions

For purposes of this title, the following definitions shall apply:

(a) "Minor" means any natural person who is under 18 years of age.

(b) "Person" means any natural person, partnership, firm, association, corporation, limited liability company, or other legal entity.

(c) enjoining enforcement of the Act was granted.

(d)(1) "Violent video game" means a video game in which the range of options available to a player includes killing, maiming, dismembering, or sexually assaulting an image of a human being, if those acts are depicted in the game in a manner that does either of the following:

(A) Comes within all of the following descriptions:

(i) A reasonable person, considering the game as a whole, would find appeals to a deviant or morbid interest of minors.

(ii) It is patently offensive to prevailing standards in the community as to what is suitable for minors.

(iii) It causes the game, as a whole, to lack serious literary, artistic, political, or scientific value for minors.

(B) Enables the player to virtually inflict serious injury upon images of human beings or characters with substantially human characteristics in a manner which is especially heinous, cruel, or depraved in that it involves torture or serious physical abuse to the victim.

(2) For purposes of this subdivision, the following definitions apply:

(A) "Cruel" means that the player intends to virtually inflict a high degree of pain by torture or serious physical abuse of the victim in addition to killing the victim.

(B) "Depraved" means that the player relishes the virtual killing or shows indifference to the suffering of the victim, as evidenced by torture or serious physical abuse of the victim.

(C) "Heinous" means shockingly atrocious. For the killing depicted in a video game to be heinous, it must involve additional acts of torture or serious physical abuse of the victim as set apart from other killings.

(D) "Serious physical abuse" means a significant or considerable amount of injury or damage to the victim's body which involves a substantial risk of death, unconsciousness, extreme physical pain, substantial disfigurement, or substantial impairment of the function of a bodily member, organ, or mental faculty. Serious physical abuse, unlike torture, does not require that the victim be conscious of the abuse at the time it is inflicted. However, the player must specifically intend the abuse apart from the killing.

(E) "Torture" includes mental as well as physical abuse of the victim. In either case, the virtual victim must be conscious of the abuse at the time it is inflicted; and the player must specifically intend to virtually inflict severe mental or physical pain or suffering upon the victim, apart from killing the victim.

(3) Pertinent factors in determining whether a killing depicted in a video game is especially heinous, cruel, or depraved include infliction of gratuitous violence upon the victim beyond that necessary to commit the killing, needless mutilation of the victim's body, and helplessness of the victim. **Leg.H.** Added Stats 2005 ch 638 §2 (AB 1179), effective January 1, 2006.

Prior Law: Former CC §1746, relating to rights of seller's creditors against sold goods, was added Stats 1931 ch 1070 §1 and repealed Stats 1963 ch 819 §2, effective January 1, 1965.

§1746.1. Sale or rental of violent video game to minor prohibited

(a) A person may not sell or rent a video game that has been labeled as a violent video game to a minor.

(b) Proof that a defendant, or his or her employee or agent, demanded, was shown, and reasonably relied upon evidence that a purchaser or renter of a violent video game was not a minor or that the manufacturer failed to label a violent video game as required pursuant to Section 1746.2 shall be an affirmative defense to any action brought pursuant to this title. That evidence may include, but is not limited to, a driver's license or an identification card issued to the purchaser or renter by a state or by the Armed Forces of the United States.

(c) This section shall not apply if the violent video game is sold or rented to a minor by the minor's parent, grandparent, aunt, uncle, or legal guardian. **Leg.H.** Added Stats 2005 ch 638 §2 (AB 1179), effective January 1, 2006.

§1746.2. Labeling of violent video games

Each violent video game that is imported into or distributed in California for retail sale shall be labeled with a solid white "18" outlined in black. The "18" shall have dimensions of no less than 2 inches by 2 inches. The "18" shall be displayed on the front face of the video game package. **Leg.H.** Added Stats 2005 ch 638 §2 (AB 1179), effective January 1, 2006.

§1746.3. Penalty for violation of title

Any person who violates any provision of this title shall be liable in an amount of up to one thousand dollars ($1,000), or a lesser amount as determined by the court. However, this liability shall not apply to any person who violates those provisions if he or she is employed solely in the capacity of a salesclerk or other, similar position and he or she does not have an ownership interest in the business in which the violation occurred and is not employed as a manager in that business. **Leg.H.** Added Stats 2005 ch 638 §2 (AB 1179), effective January 1, 2006.

§1746.4. Reporting violations; Prosecution

A suspected violation of this title may be reported to a city attorney, county counsel, or district attorney by a parent, legal guardian, or other adult acting on behalf of a minor to whom a violent video game has been sold or rented. A violation of this title may be prosecuted by any city attorney, county counsel, or district attorney. **Leg.H.** Added Stats 2005 ch 638 §2 (AB 1179), effective January 1, 2006.

§1746.5. Severability of title

The provisions of this title are severable. If any provision of this title or its application is held to be invalid, that invalidity shall not affect other provisions or applications that can be given effect without the invalid provision or application. **Leg.H.** Added Stats 2005 ch 638 §2 (AB 1179), effective January 1, 2006.

TITLE 1.3
CREDIT CARDS

Citation. §1747.
Construction of title in conformance with federal law. §1747.01.
Definitions. §1747.02.
Electronic fund transfers; Use of card keys. §1747.03.
Waiver of provisions of title void. §1747.04.
Limitations on issuance of card. §1747.05.

Verification of change of offeree's address. §1747.06.
Requiring identification information as condition of acceptance. §1747.08.
Printing of account number on receipt. §1747.09.
[Section renumbered 2004]. §1747.8.
[Section renumbered 2004]. §1747.9.
Liability for unauthorized use of card. §1747.10.
Agreements between issuers and organizations as to liability for unauthorized card use. §1747.20.
Rights on failure of issuer to respond to inquiry. §1747.40.
Correction of billing errors by issuer. §1747.50.
Correction of billing errors by retailer. §1747.60.
Exclusivity of liability. §1747.65.
Prohibited acts; Remedies. §1747.70.
Discrimination in refusing to issue card. §1747.80.
Name on card issued to married woman. §1747.81.
Cancellation of card. §1747.85.
Issuer as subject to cardholder's claims and defenses. §1747.90.
Identification and disclosure regarding security of credit instrument. §1747.94.
Validity of contracts prohibiting cash discounts. §1748.
Credit card surcharges; Cash discounts. §1748.1.
Annual statement. §1748.5.
Payment of charges without furnishing of goods or services. §1748.7.
Required disclosures. §1748.9.
Access to personal identifying information used by unauthorized person for unlawful purpose. §1748.95.

§1747. Citation

This title may be cited as the "Song-Beverly Credit Card Act of 1971."
Leg.H. Added Stats 1971 ch 1019 §4.

Prior Law: Former §1747, similar to UCC §7104, was added Stats 1931 ch 1070 §1 and repealed Stats 1963 ch 819 §2, effective January 1, 1965.

§1747.01. Construction of title in conformance with federal law

It is the intent of the Legislature that the provisions of this title as to which there are similar provisions in the federal Truth in Lending Act, as amended (15 U.S.C. 1601, et seq.), essentially conform, and be interpreted by anyone construing the provisions of this title to so conform, to the Truth in Lending Act and any rule, regulation, or interpretation promulgated thereunder by the Board of Governors of the Federal Reserve System, and any interpretation issued by an official or employee of the Federal Reserve System duly authorized to issue such interpretation.
Leg.H. Added Stats 1982 ch 545 §1.

§1747.02. Definitions

As used in this title:

(a) "Credit card" means any card, plate, coupon book, or other single credit device existing for the purpose of being used from time to time upon presentation to obtain money, property, labor, or services on credit. "Credit card" does not mean any of the following:

(1) Any single credit device used to obtain telephone property, labor, or services in any transaction under public utility tariffs.

(2) Any device that may be used to obtain credit pursuant to an electronic fund transfer, but only if the credit is obtained under an agreement between a consumer and a financial institution to extend credit when the consumer's asset account is overdrawn or to maintain a specified minimum balance in the consumer's asset account.

(3) Any key or card key used at an automated dispensing outlet to obtain or purchase petroleum products, as defined in subdivision (c) of Section 13401 of the Business and Professions Code, that will be used primarily for business rather than personal or family purposes.

(b) "Accepted credit card" means any credit card that the cardholder has requested or applied for and received or has signed, or has used, or has authorized another person to use, for the purpose of obtaining money, property, labor, or services on credit. Any credit card issued in renewal of, or in substitution for, an accepted credit card becomes an accepted credit card when received by the cardholder, whether the credit card is issued by the same or a successor card issuer.

(c) "Card issuer" means any person who issues a credit card or the agent of that person for that purpose with respect to the credit card.

(d) "Cardholder" means a natural person to whom a credit card is issued for consumer credit purposes, or a natural person who has agreed with the card issuer to pay consumer credit obligations arising from the issuance of a credit card to another natural person. For purposes of Sections 1747.05, 1747.10, and 1747.20, the term includes any person to whom a credit card is issued for any purpose, including business, commercial, or agricultural use, or a person who has agreed with the card issuer to pay obligations arising from the issuance of that credit card to another person.

(e) "Retailer" means every person other than a card issuer who furnishes money, goods, services, or anything else of value upon presentation of a credit card by a cardholder. "Retailer" shall not mean the state, a county, city, city and county, or any other public agency.

(f) "Unauthorized use" means the use of a credit card by a person, other than the cardholder, (1) who does not have actual, implied, or apparent authority for that use and (2) from which the cardholder receives no benefit. "Unauthorized use" does not include the use of a credit card by a person who has been given authority by the cardholder to use the credit card. Any attempted termination by the cardholder of the person's authority is ineffective as against the card issuer until the cardholder complies with the procedures required by the card issuer to terminate that authority. Notwithstanding the above, following the card issuer's receipt of oral or written notice from a cardholder indicating that it wishes to terminate the authority of a previously authorized user of a credit card, the card issuer shall follow its usual procedures for precluding any further use of a credit card by an unauthorized person.

(g) An "inquiry" is a writing that is posted by mail to the address of the card issuer to which payments are normally tendered, unless another address is specifically indicated on the statement for that purpose, then to that other address, and that is received by the card issuer no later than 60 days after the card issuer transmitted the first periodic statement that reflects the alleged billing error, and that does all of the following:

(1) Sets forth sufficient information to enable the card issuer to identify the cardholder and the account.

(2) Sufficiently identifies the billing error.

(3) Sets forth information providing the basis for the cardholder's belief that the billing error exists.

(h) A "response" is a writing that is responsive to an inquiry and mailed to the cardholder's address last known to the card issuer.

(i) A "timely response" is a response that is mailed within two complete billing cycles, but in no event later than 90 days, after the card issuer receives an inquiry.

(j) A "billing error" means an error by omission or commission in (1) posting any debit or credit, or (2) in computation or similar error of an accounting nature contained in a statement given to the cardholder by the card issuer. A "billing error" does not mean any dispute with respect to value, quality, or quantity of goods, services, or other benefit obtained through use of a credit card.

(k) "Adequate notice" means a printed notice to a cardholder that sets forth the pertinent facts clearly and conspicuously so that a person against whom it is to operate could reasonably be expected to have noticed it and understood its meaning.

(*l*) "Secured credit card" means any credit card issued under an agreement or other instrument that pledges, hypothecates, or places a lien on real property or money or other personal property to secure the cardholder's obligations to the card issuer.

(m) "Student credit card" means any credit card that is provided to a student at a public or private college or university and is provided to that student solely based on his or her enrollment in a public or private university, or is provided to a student who would not otherwise qualify for that credit card on the basis of his or her income. A "student credit card" does not include a credit card issued to a student who has a cocardholder or cosigner who would otherwise qualify for a credit card other than a student credit card.

(n) "Retail motor fuel dispenser" means a device that dispenses fuel that is used to power internal combustion engines, including motor vehicle engines, that processes the sale of fuel through a remote electronic payment system, and that is in a location where an employee or other agent of the seller is not present.

(o) "Retail motor fuel payment island automated cashier" means a remote electronic payment processing station that processes the retail sale of fuel that is used to power internal combustion engines, including motor vehicle engines, that is in a location where an employee or other agent of the seller is not present, and that is located in close proximity to a retail motor fuel dispenser. **Leg.H.** Added Stats 1971 ch 1019 §4. Amended Stats 1979 ch 574 §1, effective September 12, 1979; Stats 1982 ch 545 §2, ch 646 §1.5; Stats 1991 ch 608 §1 (AB 998); Stats 1992 ch 523 §1 (SB

1683); Stats 2001 ch 294 §1 (AB 521); Stats 2011 ch 690 §1 (AB 1219), effective October 9, 2011.

§1747.03. Electronic fund transfers; Use of card keys

(a) Any rights or responsibilities created by this title that are based on the use of a credit card shall have no effect with respect to:

(1) Those transactions that constitute an electronic fund transfer as defined by Regulation E of the Federal Reserve Board (12 CFR, Part 205).

(2) Those transactions involving the use of any key or a card key used at an automated dispensing outlet to obtain or purchase petroleum products, as defined in subdivision (c) of Section 13401 of the Business and Professions Code, which will be used primarily for business rather than personal or family purposes.

(b) Notwithstanding subdivision (a), a person, company, or corporation that has been issued a key or card key described in paragraph (2) of subdivision (a) shall not be liable for losses due to the loss or theft of the key or card key incurred after receipt by the issuer of the key or card key of written or oral notification of the loss or theft. **Leg.H.** Added Stats 1979 ch 574 §2, effective September 12, 1979. Amended Stats 1982 ch 646 §2.

§1747.04. Waiver of provisions of title void

Any waiver of the provisions of this title is contrary to public policy, and is void and unenforceable. **Leg.H.** Added Stats 2002 ch 815 §2 (AB 2331).

§1747.05. Limitations on issuance of card

(a) No credit card shall be issued except:

(1) In response to an oral or written request or application therefore.

(2) As a renewal of, or in substitution for, an accepted credit card whether that card is issued by the same or a successor card issuer.

(b) A credit card issued in substitution for an accepted credit card may be issued only if the card issuer provides an activation process whereby the cardholder is required to contact the card issuer to activate the credit card prior to the first use of the credit card in a credit transaction.

(c) This section does not prohibit the completion of an overdraft protection advance or recurring-charge transaction that a cardholder has previously authorized on an accepted credit card. **Leg.H.** Added Stats 1971 ch 1019 §4. Amended Stats 1982 ch 545 §3; Stats 2002 ch 862 §1 (SB 1617).

§1747.06. Verification of change of offeree's address

(a) A credit card issuer that mails an offer or solicitation to receive a credit card and, in response, receives a completed application for a credit card that lists an address that is different from the address on the offer or solicitation shall verify the change of address by contacting the person to whom the solicitation or offer was mailed.

(b) Notwithstanding any other provision of law, a person to whom an offer or solicitation to receive a credit card is made shall not be liable for the unauthorized use of a credit card issued in response to that offer or solicitation if the credit card issuer does not verify the change of address pursuant to subdivision (a) prior to the issuance of the credit card, unless the credit card issuer proves that this person actually incurred the charge on the credit card.

(c) When a credit card issuer receives a written or oral request for a change of the cardholder's billing address and then receives a written or oral request for an additional credit card within 10 days after the requested address change, the credit card issuer shall not mail the requested additional credit card to the new address or, alternatively, activate the requested additional credit card, unless the credit card issuer has verified the change of address.

(d) This section shall become operative on July 1, 2000. **Leg.H.** Added Stats 1999 ch 423 §1 (SB 930), operative July 1, 2000.

§1747.08. Requiring identification information as condition of acceptance

(a) Except as provided in subdivision (c), no person, firm, partnership, association, or corporation that accepts credit cards for the transaction of business shall do any of the following:

(1) Request, or require as a condition to accepting the credit card as payment in full or in part for goods or services, the cardholder to write any personal identification information upon the credit card transaction form or otherwise.

(2) Request, or require as a condition to accepting the credit card as payment in full or in part for goods or services, the cardholder to provide personal identification information, which the person, firm, partnership, association, or corporation accepting the credit card writes, causes to be written, or otherwise records upon the credit card transaction form or otherwise.

(3) Utilize, in any credit card transaction, a credit card form which contains preprinted spaces specifically designated for filling in any personal identification information of the cardholder.

(b) For purposes of this section "personal identification information," means information concerning the cardholder, other than information set forth on the credit card, and including, but not limited to, the cardholder's address and telephone number.

(c) Subdivision (a) does not apply in the following instances:

(1) If the credit card is being used as a deposit to secure payment in the event of default, loss, damage, or other similar occurrence.

(2) Cash advance transactions.

(3) If any of the following applies:

(A) The person, firm, partnership, association, or corporation accepting the credit card is contractually obligated to provide personal identification information in order to complete the credit card transaction.

(B) The person, firm, partnership, association, or corporation accepting the credit card in a sales transaction at a retail motor fuel dispenser or retail motor fuel payment island automated cashier uses the Zip Code information solely for prevention of fraud, theft, or identity theft.

(C) The person, firm, partnership, association, or corporation accepting the credit card is obligated to collect and record the personal identification information by federal or state law or regulation.

(4) If personal identification information is required for a special purpose incidental but related to the individual credit card transaction, including, but not limited to, information relating to shipping, delivery, servicing, or installation of the purchased merchandise, or for special orders.

(d) This section does not prohibit any person, firm, partnership, association, or corporation from requiring the cardholder, as a condition to accepting the credit card as payment in full or in part for goods or services, to provide reasonable forms of positive identification, which may include a driver's license or a California state identification card, or where one of these is not available, another form of photo identification, provided that none of the information contained thereon is written or recorded on the credit card transaction form or otherwise. If the cardholder pays for the transaction with a credit card number and does not make the credit card available upon request to verify the number, the cardholder's driver's license number or identification card number may be recorded on the credit card transaction form or otherwise.

(e) Any person who violates this section shall be subject to a civil penalty not to exceed two hundred fifty dollars ($250) for the first violation and one thousand dollars ($1,000) for each subsequent violation, to be assessed and collected in a civil action brought by the person paying with a credit card, by the Attorney General, or by the district attorney or city attorney of the county or city in which the violation occurred. However, no civil penalty shall be assessed for a violation of this section if the defendant shows by a preponderance of the evidence that the violation was not intentional and resulted from a bona fide error made notwithstanding the defendant's maintenance of procedures reasonably adopted to avoid that error. When collected, the civil penalty shall be payable, as appropriate, to the person paying with a credit card who brought the action, or to the general fund of whichever governmental entity brought the action to assess the civil penalty.

(f) The Attorney General, or any district attorney or city attorney within his or her respective jurisdiction, may bring an action in the superior court in the name of the people of the State of California to enjoin violation of subdivision (a) and, upon notice to the defendant of not less than five days, to temporarily restrain and enjoin the violation. If it appears to the satisfaction of the court that the defendant has, in fact, violated subdivision (a), the court may issue an injunction restraining further violations, without requiring proof that any person has been damaged by the violation. In these proceedings, if the court finds that the defendant has violated subdivision (a), the court may direct the defendant to pay any or all costs incurred by the Attorney General, district attorney, or city attorney in seeking or obtaining injunctive relief pursuant to this subdivision.

(g) Actions for collection of civil penalties under subdivision (e) and for injunctive relief under subdivision (f) may be consolidated.

(h) The changes made to this section by Chapter 458 of the Statutes of 1995 apply only to credit card transactions entered into on and after January 1, 1996. Nothing in those changes shall be construed to affect any civil action which was filed before January 1, 1996. **Leg.H.** Added Stats 1990 ch 999 §1, as CC §1747.8. Amended Stats 1991 ch 1089 §2 (AB 1477), effective October 14, 1991; Stats 1995 ch 458 §2 (AB 1316). Amended and renumbered by Stats 2004 ch 183 §29 (AB 3082). Amended Stats 2005 ch 22 §14 (SB 1108), effective January 1, 2006; Stats 2011 ch 690 §2 (AB 1219), effective October 9, 2011.

§1747.09. Printing of account number on receipt

(a) Except as provided in this section, no person, firm, partnership, association, corporation, or limited liability company that accepts credit or debit cards for the transaction of business shall print more than the last five digits of the credit or debit card account number or the expiration date upon any of the following:

(1) Any receipt provided to the cardholder.

(2) Any receipt retained by the person, firm, partnership, association, corporation, or limited liability company, which is printed at the time of the purchase, exchange, refund, or return, and is signed by the cardholder.

(3) Any receipt retained by the person, firm, partnership, association, corporation, or limited liability company, which is printed at the time of the purchase, exchange, refund, or return, but is not signed by the cardholder, because the cardholder used a personal identification number to complete the transaction.

(b) This section shall apply only to receipts that include a credit or debit card account number that are electronically printed and shall not apply to transactions in which the sole means of recording the person's credit or debit card account number is by handwriting or by an imprint or copy of the credit or debit card.

(c) This section shall not apply to documents, other than the receipts described in paragraphs (1) to (3), inclusive, of subdivision (a), used for internal administrative purposes.

(d) Paragraphs (2) and (3) of subdivision (a) shall become operative on January 1, 2009. **Leg.H.** Added Stats 1999 ch 423 §2 (SB 930), operative January 1, 2001, as CC §1747.9. Amended and renumbered by Stats 2004 ch 183 §30 (AB 3082); Stats 2005 ch 445 §1 (SB 802), effective January 1, 2006; Stats 2006 ch 682 §1 (SB 1699), effective January 1, 2007.

§1747.8 [Section renumbered 2004]

Leg.H. Amended and renumbered to CC §1747.08 by Stats 2004 ch 183 §29.

§1747.9 [Section renumbered 2004]

Leg.H. Amended and renumbered to CC §1747.09 by Stats 2004 ch 183 §30.

§1747.10. Liability for unauthorized use of card

A cardholder shall be liable for the unauthorized use of a credit card only if all of the following conditions are met:

(a) The card is an accepted credit card.

(b) The liability is not in excess of fifty dollars ($50).

(c) The card issuer gives adequate notice to the cardholder of the potential liability.

(d) The card issuer has provided the cardholder with a description of a means by which the card issuer may be notified of loss or theft of the card.

(e) The unauthorized use occurs before the card issuer has been notified that an unauthorized use of the credit card has occurred or may occur as the result of loss, theft, or otherwise.

(f) The card issuer has provided a method whereby the user of such card can be identified as the person authorized to use it. **Leg.H.** Added Stats 1982 ch 545 §5.

Prior Law: Former §1747.10, similar to the present section, was added Stats 1971 ch 1019 §4 and repealed Stats 1982 ch 545 §4.

§1747.20. Agreements between issuers and organizations as to liability for unauthorized card use

If 10 or more credit cards are issued by one card issuer for use by the employees of an organization, Section 1747.10 does not prohibit the card issuer and the organization from agreeing to liability for unauthorized use without regard to Section 1747.10. However, liability for unauthorized use may be imposed on an employee of the organization, by either the card issuer or the organization, only in accordance with Section 1747.10. **Leg.H.** Added Stats 1982 ch 545 §7.

Prior Law: Former §1747.20, similar to present §1747.10, was added Stats 1971 ch 1019 §4 and repealed Stats 1982 ch 545 §6.

§1747.30. [Section repealed 1982]

Leg.H. Added Stats 1971 ch 1019 §4. Repealed Stats 1982 ch 545 §8. The repealed section related to statement of fees, charges and penalties.

§1747.40. Rights on failure of issuer to respond to inquiry

If a card issuer fails to give a timely response to an inquiry of a cardholder concerning any debit or credit applicable to an obligation incurred through the use of a credit card, he shall not be entitled to interest, finance charges, service charges, or any other charges thereon, from the date of mailing of the inquiry to the date of mailing of the response. **Leg.H.** Added Stats 1971 ch 1019 §4.

§1747.50. Correction of billing errors by issuer

(a) Every card issuer shall correct any billing error made by the card issuer within two complete billing cycles, but in no event later than 90 days, after receiving an inquiry.

(b) Any card issuer who fails to correct a billing error made by the card issuer within the period prescribed by subdivision (a) shall not be entitled to the amount by which the outstanding balance of the cardholder's account is greater than the correct balance, nor any interest, finance charges, service charges, or other charges on the obligation giving rise to the billing error.

(c) Any cardholder who is injured by a willful violation of this section may bring an action for the recovery of damages. Judgment may be entered for three times the amount at which actual damages are assessed. The cardholder shall be entitled to recover reasonable attorney's fees and costs incurred in the action. **Leg.H.** Added Stats 1971 ch 1019 §4. Amended Stats 1982 ch 545 §9.

§1747.60. Correction of billing errors by retailer

(a) Every retailer shall correct any billing error made by the retailer within 60 days from the date on which an inquiry concerning a billing error was mailed.

(b) Any retailer who fails to correct a billing error made by the retailer within the period prescribed by subdivision (a) shall be liable to the cardholder in the amount by which the outstanding balance of the cardholder's account is greater than the correct balance, and any interest, finance charges, service charges, or other charges on the obligation giving rise to the billing error.

(c) Any cardholder who is injured by a willful violation of this section may bring an action for the recovery of damages. Judgment may be entered for three times the amount at which actual damages are assessed. The cardholder shall be entitled to recover reasonable attorney's fees and costs incurred in the action.

(d) As used in this section, an "inquiry" is a writing which is posted by mail to the address of the retailer, unless another address is specifically indicated by the retailer for the purpose of mailing inquiries with respect to billing errors, then to such address. **Leg.H.** Added Stats 1971 ch 1019 §4.

§1747.65. Exclusivity of liability

(a) A card issuer shall not be liable for a billing error made by the retailer.

(b) A retailer shall not be liable for a billing error made by a card issuer. **Leg.H.** Added Stats 1971 ch 1019 §4.

§1747.70. Prohibited acts; Remedies

(a) No card issuer shall knowingly give any untrue credit information to any other person concerning a cardholder.

(b) No card issuer, after receiving an inquiry from a cardholder regarding a billing error and prior to satisfying the requirements of Section 1747.50, shall communicate unfavorable credit information concerning the cardholder to any person solely because of the cardholder's failure to pay the amount by which the outstanding balance of the cardholder's account is greater than the correct balance.

(c) No card issuer shall cancel or refuse to renew a credit card for the reason that the cardholder has obtained relief under Section 1747.50.

(d) Any cardholder who is injured by a willful violation of this section may bring an action for the recovery of damages. Judgment may be entered for three times the amount at which actual damages are assessed.

The cardholder shall be entitled to recover reasonable attorney's fees and costs incurred in the action. **Leg.H.** Added Stats 1971 ch 1019 §4.

§1747.80. Discrimination in refusing to issue card

(a) No card issuer shall refuse to issue a credit card to any person solely because of any characteristic listed or defined in subdivision (b) or (e) of Section 51.

(b) Any card issuer who willfully violates this section is liable for each and every offense for the actual damages, and two hundred fifty dollars ($250) in addition thereto, suffered by any person denied a credit card solely for the reasons set forth in subdivision (a). In addition, that person may petition the court to order the card issuer to issue him or her a credit card upon the terms, conditions, and standards as the card issuer normally utilizes in granting credit to other individuals. **Leg.H.** Added Stats 1971 ch 1019 §4. Amended Stats 2007 ch 568 §14 (AB 14), effective January 1, 2008.

2007 Notes: The Legislature finds and declares as follows:

(a) Even prior to passage of the Unruh Civil Rights Act, California law afforded broad protection against arbitrary discrimination by business establishments. The Unruh Civil Rights Act was enacted to provide broader, more effective protection against arbitrary discrimination. California's interest in preventing that discrimination is longstanding and compelling.

(b) In keeping with that history and the legislative history of the Unruh Civil Rights Act, California courts have interpreted the categories enumerated in the act to be illustrative rather than restrictive. It is the intent of the Legislature that these enumerated bases shall continue to be construed as illustrative rather than restrictive, and, consistent with the Unruh Civil Rights Act, that the civil rights provisions of this act that reference Section 51 of the Civil Code also be interpreted to be illustrative rather than restrictive. Stats 2007 ch 568 (AB 14) §1.

This act shall be known and may be cited as the Civil Rights Act of 2007. Stats 2007 ch 568 (AB14) §1.5.

§1747.81. Name on card issued to married woman

(a) If a card issuer has determined in the normal course of business that it will issue a card to a married woman, the card shall be issued bearing either the maiden name or married name of the woman, as the woman may direct.

(b) Card issuers may require that a married woman requesting a card in her maiden name open a new account in that name. **Leg.H.** Added Stats 1974 ch 1252 §1.

§1747.85. Cancellation of card

Unless requested by the cardholder, no card issuer shall cancel a credit card without having first given the cardholder 30 days' written notice of its intention to do so unless the cardholder is or has been within the last 90 days in default of payment or otherwise in violation of any provision of the agreement between the card issuer and the cardholder governing the cardholder's use of the credit card or unless the card issuer has evidence or reasonable belief that the cardholder is unable or unwilling to repay obligations incurred under the agreement or that an unauthorized use of the card may be made.

Nothing provided herein shall be construed to prohibit a card issuer from placing the account of a cardholder on inactive status if the cardholder has not used the card for a period in excess of 18 months or from requiring that cardholder, upon subsequent reuse of a card, to provide to the card issuer such updated information as will enable the card issuer to verify the current creditworthiness of the cardholder. **Leg.H.** Added Stats 1976 ch 34 §1. Amended Stats 1983 ch 1247 §1.

§1747.90. Issuer as subject to cardholder's claims and defenses

(a)(1) Subject to the limitation contained in subdivision (b), a card issuer who has issued a credit card to a cardholder pursuant to an open-end consumer credit plan shall be subject to all claims and defenses, other than tort claims, arising out of any transaction in which the credit card is used as a method of payment or extension of credit if the following conditions are met:

(A) The cardholder has made a good faith attempt to obtain satisfactory resolution of a disagreement or problem relative to the transaction from the person honoring the credit card.

(B) The amount of the initial transaction exceeds fifty dollars ($50).

(C) The place where the initial transaction occurred was in California, or, if not within California, then within 100 miles from the cardholder's current designated address in California.

(2) The limitations set forth in subparagraphs (B) and (C) of paragraph (1) with respect to a cardholder's right to assert claims and defenses against a card issuer shall not be applicable to any transaction in which the person honoring the credit card satisfies any of the following requirements:

(A) Is the same person as the card issuer.

(B) Is controlled by the card issuer.

(C) Is under direct or indirect common control with the card issuer.

(D) Is a franchised dealer in the card issuer's products or services.

(E) Has obtained the order for such transaction through a mail solicitation made by or participated in by the card issuer in which the cardholder is solicited to enter into such transaction by using the credit card issued by the card issuer.

(b) The amount of claims or defenses asserted by the cardholder may not exceed the amount of credit outstanding with respect to such transaction at the time the cardholder first notifies the card issuer or the person honoring the credit card of such claim or defense. For the purpose of determining the amount of credit outstanding, payments and credits to the cardholder's account are deemed to have been applied, in the order indicated, to the payment of the following:

(1) Late charges in the order of their entry to the account.

(2) Finance charges in order of their entry to the account.

(3) Debits to the account other than those set forth above, in the order in which each debit entry to the account was made.

(c) This section does not apply to the use of a check guarantee card or a debit card in connection with an overdraft credit plan, or to a check guarantee card used in connection with cash advance checks. **Leg.H.** Added Stats 1982 ch 545 §11.

Prior Law: Former §1747.90, similar to the present section, was added Stats 1971 ch 1019 §4 and repealed Stats 1982 ch 545 §10.

§1747.94. Identification and disclosure regarding security of credit instrument

(a) In addition to any other disclosures required by law, a card issuer of a secured credit card shall, in every advertisement or solicitation to prospective cardholders, expressly identify the credit instrument offered as a "secured credit card" and prominently disclose that credit extended under the secured credit card is secured, and shall describe the security by item or type.

(b) Any deed of trust executed in connection with a secured credit card shall contain a statement that it is security for a secured credit card obligation. However, failure to include the statement shall not invalidate the deed of trust.

(c) This section does not apply to either of the following:

(1) Any credit card which is issued under an agreement or other instrument creating a purchase money security interest in property purchased with the credit card, but which does not pledge, hypothecate, or place a lien on other property of the cardholder or any co-obligor.

(2) Loans or extensions of credit subject to the Federal Home Equity Loan Consumer Protection Act of 1988 (P. L. 100-709).

(d) Any violation of this section shall constitute unfair competition within the meaning of Section 17200 of the Business and Professions Code. **Leg.H.** Added Stats 1991 ch 608 §2 (AB 998).

§1748. Validity of contracts prohibiting cash discounts

Any provision in a contract between a card issuer and a retailer which has the effect of prohibiting the retailer from offering price discounts or from charging a different and lower price to customers who pay for goods or services by cash instead of by credit card is contrary to public policy and void. **Leg.H.** Added Stats 1974 ch 1520 §1.

Prior Law: Former §1748, similar to UCC §7501, was added Stats 1931 ch 1070 §1 and repealed Stats 1963 ch 819 §2, effective January 1, 1965.

Former §1748, relating to settler acting as depositary, was enacted 1872 and repealed Stats 1931 ch 1070 §1.

§1748.1. Credit card surcharges; Cash discounts

(a) No retailer in any sales, service, or lease transaction with a consumer may impose a surcharge on a cardholder who elects to use a credit card in lieu of payment by cash, check, or similar means. A retailer may, however, offer discounts for the purpose of inducing payment by cash, check, or other means not involving the use of a credit card, provided that the discount is offered to all prospective buyers.

(b) Any retailer who willfully violates this section by imposing a surcharge on a cardholder who elects to use a credit card and who fails to pay that amount to the cardholder within 30 days of a written demand by the cardholder to the retailer by certified mail, shall be liable to the cardholder for three times the amount at which actual damages are assessed. The cardholder shall also be entitled to recover reasonable attorney's fees and costs incurred in the action.

A cause of action under this section may be brought in small claims court, if it does not exceed the jurisdiction of that court, or in any other appropriate court.

(c) A consumer shall not be deemed to have elected to use a credit card in lieu of another means of payment for purposes of this section in a transaction with a retailer if only credit cards are accepted by that retailer in payment for an order made by a consumer over a telephone, and only cash is accepted at a public store or other facility of the same retailer.

(d) Charges for third-party credit card guarantee services, when added to the price charged by the retailer if cash were to be paid, shall be deemed surcharges for purposes of this section even if they are payable directly to the third party or are charged separately.

(e) It is the intent of the Legislature to promote the effective operation of the free market and protect consumers from deceptive price increases for goods and services by prohibiting credit card surcharges and encouraging the availability of discounts by those retailers who wish to offer a lower price for goods and services purchased by some form of payment other than credit card.

(f) This section does not apply to charges for payment by credit card or debit card that are made by an electrical, gas, or water corporation and approved by the Public Utilities Commission pursuant to Section 755 of the Public Utilities Code. **Leg.H.** Added Stats 1985 ch 913 §1. Amended Stats 1990 ch 309 §1 (SB 1763); Stats 2005 ch 426 §1 (AB 746), effective January 1, 2006.

§1748.5. Annual statement

(a) A cardholder may request, not more frequently than once a year, that the card issuer inform the cardholder of the total amount of finance charges assessed on the account during the preceding calendar year and the card issuer shall provide that information to the cardholder within 30 days of receiving the request, without charge.

If the cardholder's request for the information is made in writing, the card issuer shall provide the information in writing. However, if the card issuer is required to furnish the cardholder with a periodic billing or periodic statement of account or furnishes the billing or statement of account, the requested statement of finance charges may be furnished along with the periodic billing or periodic statement of account.

(b) This section shall not apply to card issuers or cardholders who issue or use credit cards in connection with a retail installment account, as defined by Section 1802.7. **Leg.H.** Added Stats 1996 ch 180 §2 (SB 1871).

Prior Law: Former §1748.5, similar to the present section, was added Stats 1976 ch 747 §1, operative January 1, 1978, and repealed Stats 1996 ch 180 §1.

§1748.7. Payment of charges without furnishing of goods or services

(a) No person shall process, deposit, negotiate, or obtain payment of a credit card charge through a retailer's account with a financial institution or through a retailer's agreement with a financial institution, card issuer, or organization of financial institutions or card issuers if that retailer did not furnish or agree to furnish the goods or services which are the subject of the charge.

(b) No retailer shall permit any person to process, deposit, negotiate, or obtain payment of a credit card charge through the retailer's account with a financial institution or the retailer's agreement with a financial institution, card issuer, or organization of financial institutions or card issuers if that retailer did not furnish or agree to furnish the goods or services which are the subject of the charge.

(c) Subdivisions (a) and (b) do not apply to any of the following:

(1) A person who furnishes goods or services on the business premises of a general merchandise retailer and who processes, deposits, negotiates, or obtains payment of a credit card charge through that general merchandise retailer's account or agreement.

(2) A general merchandise retailer who permits a person described in paragraph (1) to process, deposit, negotiate, or obtain payment of a credit card charge through that general merchandise retailer's account or agreement.

(3) A franchisee who furnishes the cardholder with goods or services that are provided in whole or in part by the franchisor and who processes, deposits, negotiates, or obtains payment of a credit card charge through that franchisor's account or agreement.

(4) A franchisor who permits a franchisee described in paragraph (3) to process, deposit, negotiate, or obtain payment of a credit card charge through that franchisor's account or agreement.

(5) The credit card issuer or a financial institution or a parent, subsidiary, or affiliate of the card issuer or a financial institution.

(6) A person who processes, deposits, negotiates, or obtains payment of less than five hundred dollars ($500) of credit card charges in any one year period through a retailer's account or agreement. The person shall have the burden of producing evidence that the person transacted less than five hundred dollars ($500) in credit card charges during any one year period.

(d) Any person injured by a violation of this section may bring an action for the recovery of damages, equitable relief, and reasonable attorney's fees and costs.

(e) Any person who violates this section shall be guilty of a misdemeanor. Each occurrence in which a person processes, deposits, negotiates, or otherwise seeks to obtain payment of a credit card charge in violation of subdivision (a) constitutes a separate offense.

(f) The penalties and remedies provided in this section are in addition to any other remedies or penalties provided by law.

(g) The exemptions from this title specified in Section 1747.03 do not apply to this section.

(h) As used in this section:

(1) "General merchandise retailer" means any person or entity, regardless of the form of organization, that has continuously offered for sale or lease more than 100 different types of goods or services to the public in this state throughout a period which includes the immediately preceding five years.

(2) "Franchisor" has the same meaning as defined in Section 31007 of the Corporations Code.

(3) "Franchisee" has the same meaning as defined in Section 31006 of the Corporations Code. **Leg.H.** Added Stats 1989 ch 855 §1.

§1748.9. Required disclosures

(a) A credit card issuer that extends credit to a cardholder through the use of a preprinted check or draft shall disclose on the front of an attachment that is affixed by perforation or other means to the preprinted check or draft, in clear and conspicuous language, all of the following information:

(1) That "use of the attached check or draft will constitute a charge against your credit account."

(2) The annual percentage rate and the calculation of finance charges, as required by Section 226.16 of Regulation Z of the Code of Federal Regulations, associated with the use of the attached check or draft.

(3) Whether the finance charges are triggered immediately upon the use of the check or draft. **Leg.H.** Added Stats 1999 ch 171 §1 (SB 545), operative July 1, 2000.

§1748.95. Access to personal identifying information used by unauthorized person for unlawful purpose

(a)(1) Upon the request of a person who has obtained a police report pursuant to Section 530.6 of the Penal Code, a credit card issuer shall provide to the person, or to a law enforcement officer specified by the person, copies of all application forms or application information containing the person's name, address, or other identifying information pertaining to the application filed with the credit card issuer by an unauthorized person in violation of Section 530.5 of the Penal Code.

(2) Before providing copies pursuant to paragraph (1), the credit card issuer shall inform the requesting person of the categories of identifying information that the unauthorized person used to complete the application and shall require the requesting person to provide identifying information in those categories and a copy of the police report.

(3) The credit card issuer shall provide copies of all forms and information required by this section, without charge, within 10 business days of receipt of the person's request and submission of the required copy of the police report and identifying information.

(b)(1) Before a credit card issuer provides copies to a law enforcement officer pursuant to paragraph (1) of subdivision (a), the credit card issuer may require the requesting person to provide them with a signed and dated statement by which the person does all of the following:

(A) Authorizes disclosure for a stated period.

(B) Specifies the name of the agency or department to which the disclosure is authorized.

(C) Identifies the type of records that the person authorizes to be disclosed.

(2) The credit card issuer shall include in the statement to be signed by the requesting person a notice that the person has the right at any time to revoke the authorization.

(c) As used in this section, "law enforcement officer" means a peace officer as defined by Section 830.1 of the Penal Code. **Leg.H.** Added Stats 2001 ch 493 §1 (SB 125).

TITLE 1.3A
CREDIT CARD DISCLOSURE

Citation of act. §1748.10.
Disclosure requirements. §1748.11.
Disclosure of information. §1748.12.
Statement to include time at various payment rates to pay off balance on open-end account; Toll-free telephone number; Establishment of illustration table; Definitions; Non-applicability of section. §1748.13.
Waiver of provisions of title void. §1748.14.

§1748.10. Citation of act

This act shall be known and may be cited as the "Areias Credit Card Full Disclosure Act of 1986." **Leg.H.** Added Stats 1986 ch 1397 §2. Amended Stats 2000 ch 375 §2 (AB 1331), ch 977 §1 (AB 2869); Stats 2001 ch 159 §32 (SB 662).

§1748.11. Disclosure requirements

(a) Any application form or preapproved written solicitation for an open-end credit card account to be used for personal, family, or household purposes that is mailed on or after October 1, 1987, to a consumer residing in this state by or on behalf of a creditor, whether or not the creditor is located in this state, other than an application form or solicitation included in a magazine, newspaper, or other publication distributed by someone other than the creditor, shall contain or be accompanied by either of the following disclosures:

(1) A disclosure of each of the following, if applicable:

(A) Any periodic rate or rates that may be applied to the account, expressed as an annual percentage rate or rates. If the account is subject to a variable rate, the creditor may instead either disclose the rate as of a specific date and indicate that the rate may vary, or identify the index and any amount or percentage added to, or subtracted from, that index and used to determine the rate. For purposes of this section, that amount or percentage shall be referred to as the "spread."

(B) Any membership or participation fee that may be imposed for availability of a credit card account, expressed as an annualized amount.

(C) Any per transaction fee that may be imposed on purchases, expressed as an amount or as a percentage of the transaction, as applicable.

(D) If the creditor provides a period during which the consumer may repay the full balance reflected on a billing statement that is attributable to purchases of goods or services from the creditor or from merchants participating in the credit card plan, without the imposition of additional finance charges, the creditor shall either disclose the number of days of that period, calculated from the closing date of the prior billing cycle to the date designated in the billing statement sent to the consumer as the date by which that payment must be received to avoid additional finance charges, or describe the manner in which the period is calculated. For purposes of this section, the period shall be referred to as the "free period" or "free-ride period." If the creditor does not provide this period for purchases, the disclosure shall so indicate.

(2) A disclosure that satisfies the initial disclosure statement requirements of Regulation Z.

(b) A creditor need not present the disclosures required by paragraph (1) of subdivision (a) in chart form or use any specific terminology, except as expressly provided in this section. The following chart shall not be construed in any way as a standard by which to determine whether a creditor who elects not to use such a chart has provided the required disclosures in a manner that satisfies paragraph (1) of subdivision (a). However, disclosures shall be conclusively presumed to satisfy the requirements of paragraph (1) of subdivision (a) if a chart with captions substantially as follows is completed with the applicable terms offered by the creditor, or if the creditor presents the applicable terms in tabular, list, or narrative format using terminology substantially similar to the captions included in the following chart:

THE FOLLOWING INFORMATION IS PROVIDED PURSUANT TO THE AREIAS CREDIT CARD FULL DISCLOSURE ACT OF 1986:

INTEREST RATES, FEES, AND FREE-RIDE PERIOD FOR PURCHASES UNDER THIS CREDIT CARD ACCOUNT

ANNUAL PERCENTAGE RATE (1)	VARIABLE RATE INDEX AND SPREAD (2)	ANNUALIZED MEMBERSHIP OR PARTICIPATION FEE	TRANSACTION FEE	FREE-RIDE PERIOD (3)

(1) For fixed interest rates. If variable rate, creditor may elect to disclose a rate as of a specified date and indicate that the rate may vary.

(2) For variable interest rates. If fixed rate, creditor may eliminate the column, leave the column blank, or indicate "No" or "None" or "Does not apply."

(3) For example, "30 days" or "Yes, if full payment is received by next billing date" or "Yes, if full new balance is paid by due date."

(c) For purposes of this section, "Regulation Z" has the meaning attributed to it under Section 1802.18, and all of the terms used in this section have the same meaning as attributed to them in federal Regulation Z (12 C.F.R. 226.1 et seq.). For the purposes of this section, "open-end credit card account" does not include an account accessed by a device described in paragraph (2) of subdivision (a) of Section 1747.02.

(d) Nothing in this section shall be deemed or construed to prohibit a creditor from disclosing additional terms, conditions, or information, whether or not relating to the disclosures required under this section, in conjunction with the disclosures required by this section.

(e) If a creditor is required under federal law to make any disclosure of the terms applicable to a credit card account in connection with application forms or solicitations, the creditor shall be deemed to have complied with the requirements of paragraph (1) of subdivision (a) with respect to those application forms or solicitations if the creditor complies with the federal disclosure requirement. For example, in lieu of complying with the requirements of paragraph (1) of subdivision (a), a creditor has the option of disclosing the specific terms required to be disclosed in an advertisement under Regulation Z, if the application forms or solicitations constitute advertisements in which specific terms must be disclosed under Regulation Z.

(f) If for any reason the requirements of this section do not apply equally to creditors located in this state and creditors not located in this state, then the requirements applicable to creditors located in this state shall automatically be reduced to the extent necessary to establish equal requirements for both categories of creditors, until it is otherwise determined by a court of law in a proceeding to which the creditor located in this state is a party.

(g) All application forms for an open-end credit card account distributed in this state on or after October 1, 1987, other than by mail, shall contain a statement in substantially the following form:

"If you wish to receive disclosure of the terms of this credit card, pursuant to the Areias Credit Card Full Disclosure Act of 1986, check here and return to the address on this application."

A box shall be printed in or next to this statement for placement of such a checkmark.

However, this subdivision does not apply if the application contains the disclosures provided for in this title.

(h) This title does not apply to any application form or written advertisement or an open-end credit card account where the credit to be extended will be secured by a lien on real or personal property or both real and personal property.

(i) This title does not apply to any person who is subject to Article 10.5 (commencing with Section 1810.20) of Chapter 1 of Title 2. **Leg.H.**

Added Stats 1986 ch 1397 §2. Amended Stats 2000 ch 375 §3 (AB 1331); Stats 2001 ch 159 §33 (SB 662).

§1748.12. Disclosure of information

(a) For purposes of this section:

(1) "Cardholder" means any consumer to whom a credit card is issued, provided that, when more than one credit card has been issued for the same account, all persons holding those credit cards may be treated as a single cardholder.

(2) "Credit card" means any card, plate, coupon book, or other single credit device existing for the purpose of being used from time to time upon presentation to obtain money, property, labor, or services on credit. "Credit card" does not mean any of the following:

(A) Any single credit device used to obtain telephone property, labor, or services in any transaction under public utility tariffs.

(B) Any device that may be used to obtain credit pursuant to an electronic fund transfer but only if the credit is obtained under an agreement between a consumer and a financial institution to extend credit when the consumer's asset account is overdrawn or to maintain a specified minimum balance in the consumer's asset account.

(C) Any key or card key used at an automated dispensing outlet to obtain or purchase petroleum products, as defined in subdivision (c) of Section 13401 of the Business and Professions Code, which will be used primarily for business rather than personal or family purposes.

(3) "Marketing information" means the categorization of cardholders compiled by a credit card issuer, based on a cardholder's shopping patterns, spending history, or behavioral characteristics derived from account activity which is provided to a marketer of goods or services or a subsidiary or affiliate organization of the company that collects the information for consideration. "Marketing information" does not include aggregate data that does not identify a cardholder based on the cardholder's shopping patterns, spending history, or behavioral characteristics derived from account activity or any communications to any person in connection with any transfer, processing, billing, collection, chargeback, fraud prevention, credit card recovery, or acquisition of or for credit card accounts.

(b) If the credit card issuer discloses marketing information concerning a cardholder to any person, the credit card issuer shall provide a written notice to the cardholder that clearly and conspicuously describes the cardholder's right to prohibit the disclosure of marketing information concerning the cardholder which discloses the cardholder's identity. The notice shall be in 10-point type and shall advise the cardholder of his or her ability to respond either by completing a preprinted form or a toll-free telephone number that the cardholder may call to exercise this right.

(c) The requirements of subdivision (b) shall be satisfied by furnishing the notice to the cardholder:

(1) At least 60 days prior to the initial disclosure of marketing information concerning the cardholder by the credit card issuer.

(2) For all new credit cards issued on or after April 1, 2002, on the form containing the new credit card when the credit card is delivered to the cardholder.

(3) At least once per calendar year, to every cardholder entitled to receive an annual statement of billings rights pursuant to 12 C.F.R. 226.9 (Regulation Z). The notice required by this paragraph may be included on or with any periodic statement or with the delivery of the renewal card.

(d)(1) The cardholder's election to prohibit disclosure of marketing information shall be effective only with respect to marketing information that is disclosed to any party beginning 30 days after the credit card issuer has received, at the designated address on the form containing the new credit card or on the preprinted form, or by telephone, the cardholder's election to prohibit disclosure. This does not apply to the disclosure of marketing information prior to the cardholder's notification to the credit card issuer of the cardholder's election.

(2) An election to prohibit disclosure of marketing information shall terminate upon receipt by the credit card issuer of notice from the cardholder that the cardholder's election to prohibit disclosure is no longer effective.

(e) The requirements of this section do not apply to any of the following communications of marketing information by a credit card issuer:

(1) Communications to any party to, or merchant specified in, the credit card agreement, or to any person whose name appears on the credit card or on whose behalf the credit card is issued.

(2) Communications to consumer credit reporting agencies, as defined in subdivision (d) of Section 1785.3.

(3) To the extent that the Fair Credit Reporting Act preempts the requirements of this section as to communication by a credit card issuer to a corporate subsidiary or affiliate, the credit card issuer may communicate information about a cardholder to a corporate subsidiary or affiliate to the extent and in the manner permitted under that act.

(4) Communications to a third party when the third party is responsible for conveying information from the card issuer to any of its cardholders.

(f) If the laws of the United States require disclosure to cardholders regarding the use of personal information, compliance with the federal requirements shall be deemed to be compliance with this section.

(g) This section shall become operative on April 1, 2002. **Leg.H.** Added Stats 2000 ch 977 §3 (AB 2869), operative April 1, 2002.

Prior Law: Former §1748.12, similar to present section, was added Stats 1993 ch 622 §1, operative July 1, 1994, amended Stats 1994 ch 188 §1, effective July 9, 1994, operative July 1, 1994, Stats 2000 ch 977 §2, inoperative April 1, 2002, and repealed, January 1, 2003, by its own terms.

Former CC §1748.12, similar to the present section, was added Stats 1993 ch 622 §1, operative July 1, 1994, and became inoperative April 1, 2002, and repealed operative January 1, 2003, by its own provisions. Stats 2000 ch 977 §2.

§1748.13. Statement to include time at various payment rates to pay off balance on open-end account; Toll-free telephone number; Establishment of illustration table; Definitions; Non-applicability of section

(a) A credit card issuer shall, with each billing statement provided to a cardholder in this state, provide the following on the front of the first page of the billing statement in type no smaller than that required for any other required disclosure, but in no case in less than 8-point capitalized type:

(1) A written statement in the following form: "Minimum Payment Warning: Making only the minimum payment will increase the interest you pay and the time it takes to repay your balance."

(2) Either of the following:

(A) A written statement in the form of and containing the information described in clause (i) or (ii), as applicable, as follows:

(i) A written three-line statement, as follows:

"A one thousand dollar ($1,000) balance will take 17 years and three months to pay off at a total cost of two thousand five hundred ninety dollars and thirty-five cents ($2,590.35). A two thousand five hundred dollar ($2,500) balance will take 30 years and three months to pay off at a total cost of seven thousand seven hundred thirty-three dollars and forty-nine cents ($7,733.49). A five thousand dollar ($5,000) balance will take 40 years and two months to pay off at a total cost of sixteen thousand three hundred five dollars and thirty-four cents ($16,305.34). This information is based on an annual percentage rate of 17 percent and a minimum payment of 2 percent or ten dollars ($10), whichever is greater."

In the alternative, a credit card issuer may provide this information for the three specified amounts at the annual percentage rate and required minimum payment which are applicable to the cardholder's account. The statement provided shall be immediately preceded by the statement required by paragraph (1).

(ii) Instead of the information required by clause (i), retail credit card issuers shall provide a written three-line statement to read, as follows:

"A two hundred fifty dollar ($250) balance will take two years and eight months to pay off a total cost of three hundred twenty-five dollars and twenty-four cents ($325.24). A five hundred dollar ($500) balance will take four years and five months to pay off at a total cost of seven hundred nine dollars and ninety cents ($709.90). A seven hundred fifty dollar ($750) balance will take five years and five months to pay off at a total cost of one thousand ninety-four dollars and forty-nine cents ($1,094.49). This information is based on an annual percentage rate of 21 percent and a minimum payment of 5 percent or ten dollars ($10), whichever is greater."

In the alternative, a retail credit card issuer may provide this information for the three specified amounts at the annual percentage rate and required minimum payment which are applicable to the cardholder's account. The statement provided shall be immediately preceded by the statement required by paragraph (1). A retail credit card issuer is not required to provide this statement if the cardholder has a balance of less than five hundred dollars ($500).

(B) A written statement providing individualized information indicating an estimate of the number of years and months and the approximate total cost to pay off the entire balance due on an open-end credit card account if the cardholder were to pay only the minimum amount due on the open-ended account based upon the terms of the credit agreement. For purposes of this subparagraph only, if the account is subject to a variable rate, the creditor may make disclosures based on the rate for the entire balance as of the date of the disclosure and indicate that the rate may vary. In addition, the cardholder shall be provided with referrals or, in the alternative, with the "800" telephone number of the National Foundation for Credit Counseling through which the cardholder can be referred, to credit counseling services in, or closest to, the cardholder's county of residence. The credit counseling service shall be in good standing with the National Foundation for Credit Counseling or accredited by the Council on Accreditation for Children and Family Services. The creditor is required to provide, or continue to provide, the information required by this paragraph only if the cardholder has not paid more than the minimum payment for six consecutive months, after July 1, 2002.

(3)(A) A written statement in the following form: "For an estimate of the time it would take to repay your balance, making only minimum payments, and the total amount of those payments, call this toll-free telephone number: (Insert toll-free telephone number)." This statement shall be provided immediately following the statement required by subparagraph (A) of paragraph (2). A credit card issuer is not required to provide this statement if the disclosure required by subparagraph (B) of paragraph (2) has been provided.

(B) The toll-free telephone number shall be available between the hours of 8 a.m. and 9 p.m., Pacific standard time, seven days a week, and shall provide consumers with the opportunity to speak with a person, rather than a recording, from whom the information described in subparagraph (A) may be obtained.

(C) The Department of Financial Protection and Innovation shall establish a detailed table illustrating the approximate number of months that it would take and the approximate total cost to repay an outstanding balance if the consumer pays only the required minimum monthly payments and if no other additional charges or fees are incurred on the account, such as additional extension of credit, voluntary credit insurance, late fees, or dishonored check fees by assuming all of the following:

(i) A significant number of different annual percentage rates.

(ii) A significant number of different account balances, with the difference between sequential examples of balances being no greater than one hundred dollars ($100).

(iii) A significant number of different minimum payment amounts.

(iv) That only minimum monthly payments are made and no additional charges or fees are incurred on the account, such as additional extensions of credit, voluntary credit insurance, late fees, or dishonored check fees.

(D) A creditor that receives a request for information described in subparagraph (A) from a cardholder through the toll-free telephone number disclosed under subparagraph (A), or who is required to provide the information required by subparagraph (B) of paragraph (2), may satisfy its obligation to disclose an estimate of the time it would take and the approximate total cost to repay the cardholder's balance by disclosing only the information set forth in the table described in subparagraph (C). Including the full chart along with a billing statement does not satisfy the obligation under this section.

(b) For purposes of this section:

(1) "Credit card" has the same meaning as in paragraph (2) of subdivision (a) of Section 1748.12.

(2) "Open-end credit card account" means an account in which consumer credit is granted by a creditor under a plan in which the creditor reasonably contemplates repeated transactions, the creditor may impose a finance charge from time to time on an unpaid balance, and the amount of credit that may be extended to the consumer during the term of the plan is generally made available to the extent that any outstanding balance is repaid and up to any limit set by the creditor.

(3) "Retail credit card" means a credit card is issued by or on behalf of a retailer, or a private label credit card that is limited to customers of a specific retailer.

(c)(1) This section shall not apply in any billing cycle in which the account agreement requires a minimum payment of at least 10 percent of the outstanding balance.

(2) This section shall not apply in any billing cycle in which finance charges are not imposed. **Leg.H.** Added Stats 2001 ch 711 §1 (AB 865), operative July 1, 2002. Amended Stats 2002 ch 664 §39 (AB 3034); Stats 2015 ch 190 §3 (AB 1517), effective January 1, 2016; Stats 2022 ch 452 §19 (SB 1498), effective January 1, 2023.

2001 Notes: Except for the provisions of subparagraph (C) of paragraph (3) of subdivision (a) of Section 1748.13 which shall become operative of January 1, 2002, this act shall become operative on July 1, 2002. Stats 2001 ch 711 §3.

If the federal Bankruptcy Reform Act of 2001, as proposed by H.R. No. 333 of the 107th Congress, is enacted and includes the provisions of Section 1301 (Enhanced Disclosures Under an Open End Credit Plan) as it read on July 17, 2001, credit card issuers and retail credit card issuers shall be exempt from the following provisions of Section 1748.13 of the Civil Code: (a) The provisions of paragraph (1) of subdivision (a). (b) (1) The provisions of clause (i) f subparagraph (A) of paragraph (2) of subdivision (a) as it relates to that portion of the statement describing the payments made on a balance of one thousand dollars ($1,000). However, the portion of the statement describing the payments made on balances of two thousand five hundred dollars ($2,500) and five thousand dollars ($5,000) shall be inserted immediately after the statement required by Section 1301 (Enhanced Disclosures Under an Open End Credit Plan) of the federal act. (2) For retail credit card issuers, the provisions of clause (ii) of subparagraph (A) of paragraph (2) of subdivision (a) as it related to that portion of the statement describing the payments made on balances of five hundred dollars ($500) and seven hundred fifty dollars ($750) shall be inserted immediately after the statement required by Section 1301 (Enhanced Disclosures Under an Open End Credit Plan) of the federal act. (c) The provisions of §2.

§1748.14. Waiver of provisions of title void

Any waiver of the provisions of this title is contrary to public policy, and is void and unenforceable. **Leg.H.** Added Stats 2002 ch 815 §3 (AB 2331).

TITLE 1.3B
CHARGE CARD DISCLOSURES

Citation of title. §1748.20.
Definitions. §1748.21.
Mailed solicitations; Disclosure requirements. §1748.22.
Waiver of provisions of title void. §1748.23.

§1748.20. Citation of title

This title may be cited as the "Areias-Robbins Charge Card Full Disclosure Act of 1986." **Leg.H.** Added Stats 1986 ch 1397 §3.

§1748.21. Definitions

For the purposes of this title:

(a) "Charge card" means any card, plate, or other credit device pursuant to which the charge card issuer extends credit to the charge cardholder, primarily for personal, family, or household purposes where (1) the credit extended does not subject the charge cardholder to a finance charge and (2) the charge cardholder cannot automatically access credit that is repayable in installments.

(b) "Charge cardholder" means the person to whom a charge card is issued.

(c) "Charge card issuer" means any person that issues a charge card or that person's agent with respect to the card. **Leg.H.** Added Stats 1986 ch 1397 §3.

§1748.22. Mailed solicitations; Disclosure requirements

(a) On and after October 1, 1987, issuers of charge cards shall clearly and conspicuously disclose in any charge card application form or preapproved written solicitation for a charge card mailed to a consumer who resides in this state to apply for a charge card, whether or not the charge card issuer is located in this state, other than an application form or solicitation included in a magazine, newspaper, or other publication distributed by someone other than the charge card issuer, the following information:

(1) Any fee or charge assessed for or which may be assessed for the issuance or renewal of the charge card, expressed as an annualized amount. The fee or charge required to be disclosed pursuant to this paragraph shall be denominated as an "annual fee."

(2) The charge card does not permit the charge cardholder to defer payment of charges incurred by the use of the charge card upon receipt of a periodic statement of charges from the charge card issuer.

(3) Any fee that may be assessed for an extension of credit to a charge cardholder where the extension of credit is made by the charge card issuer, and is not a credit sale and where the charge cardholder receives the extension of credit in the form of cash or where the charge cardholder obtains the extension of credit through the use of a preprinted check, draft, or similar credit device provided by the charge card issuer to obtain an

extension of credit. This fee shall be denominated as a "cash advance fee" in the disclosure required by this paragraph.

(b) A charge card issuer shall be conclusively presumed to have complied with the disclosure requirements of subdivision (a) if the table set out in subdivision (b) of Section 1748.11 is completed with the applicable terms offered by the charge card issuer in a clear and conspicuous manner and the completed table in subdivision (b) of Section 1748.11 is then provided to the person invited to apply for the charge card as a part of or in material which accompanies the charge card application or written advertisement which invites a person to apply for a charge card.

The charge card issuer shall include as part of table set out in subdivision (b) of Section 1748.11 the following sentences in the boxes or in a footnote outside of the boxes that relate to the interest rate disclosure: "This is a charge card which does not permit the charge cardholder to pay for purchases made using this charge card in installments. All charges made by a person to whom the charge card is issued are due and payable upon the receipt of a periodic statement of charges by the charge cardholder."

The inclusion or exclusion of an expiration date with table set out in subdivision (b) of Section 1748.11 or the use of footnotes in the boxes of the table to set out the information required to be disclosed by this section outside of the boxes of the table set out in subdivision (b) of Section 1748.11 shall not affect the conclusive presumption of compliance pursuant to this subdivision. If a charge card issuer does not offer or require one of the selected attributes of credit cards in the table set out in subdivision (b) of Section 1748.11 the charge card issuer shall employ the phrase in the appropriate box or in the appropriate footnote "Not offered" or "Not required" or a substantially similar phrase without losing the conclusive presumption of compliance with the requirements of subdivision (a). If one of the selected attributes of charge cards required to be disclosed pursuant to subdivision (a) is not applicable to the charge card issuer, the charge card issuer may employ in the appropriate box or in the appropriate footnote outside of the box in the table set out in subdivision (b) of Section 1748.11 the phrase "Not applicable" or a substantially similar phrase without losing the conclusive presumption of compliance with the requirements of subdivision (a).

(c) Nothing in this section shall be deemed or construed to prohibit a charge card issuer from disclosing additional terms, conditions, or information, whether or not relating to the disclosures required under this section by subdivision (a) or in connection with the disclosure provided in subdivision (b), in conjunction with the disclosures required by this section.

(d) If the charge card issuer offers to the charge cardholder any program or service under which the charge cardholder may elect to access open-end credit, the charge card issuer shall provide to the charge cardholder, before the charge cardholder has the right to access that credit, the initial disclosure statement required by Regulation Z, as defined in subdivision (c) of Section 1748.10.

(e) All charge card application forms distributed in this state on or after October 1, 1987, other than by mail, shall contain a statement in substantially the following form:

"If you wish to receive disclosure of the terms of this credit card, pursuant to the Areias Charge Card Full Disclosure Act of 1986, check here and return to the address on this application."

A box shall be printed in or next to this statement for placing such a checkmark.

However, this subdivision does not apply if the application contains the disclosures provided for in this title. **Leg.H.** Added Stats 1986 ch 1397 §3. Amended Stats 2000 ch 375 §4 (AB 1331).

§1748.23. Waiver of provisions of title void

Any waiver of the provisions of this title is contrary to public policy, and is void and unenforceable. **Leg.H.** Added Stats 2002 ch 815 §4 (AB 2331).

TITLE 1.3C
DEBIT CARDS

Definitions. §1748.30.
Cardholder's liability for unauthorized use of debit card; Effect of failure to make timely report of unauthorized use appearing on statement. §1748.31.
Waiver of provisions of title void. §1748.32.

§1748.30. Definitions

For purposes of this title, the following definitions shall apply:

(a) "Accepted debit card" means any debit card which the debit cardholder has requested and received or has signed, or has used, or has authorized another person to use, for the purpose of obtaining money, property, labor, or services. Any debit card issued in renewal of, or in substitution for, an accepted debit card becomes an accepted debit card when received by the debit cardholder, whether the debit card is issued by the same or by a successor card issuer.

(b) "Account" means a demand deposit (checking), savings, or other consumer asset account, other than an occasional or incidental credit balance in a credit plan, established primarily for personal, family, or household purposes.

(c) "Adequate notice" has the same meaning as found in subdivision (k) of Section 1747.02.

(d) "Debit card" means an accepted debit card or other means of access to a debit cardholder's account that may be used to initiate electronic funds transfers and may be used without unique identifying information such as a personal identification number to initiate access to the debit cardholder's account.

(e) "Debit card issuer" means any person who issues a debit card or the agent of that person for that purpose.

(f) "Debit cardholder" means a natural person to whom a debit card is issued.

(g) "Unauthorized use" means the use of a debit card by a person, other than the debit cardholder, to initiate an electronic fund transfer from the debit cardholder's account without actual authority to initiate the transfer and from which the debit cardholder receives no benefit. The term does not include an electronic fund transfer initiated in any of the following manners:

(1) By a person who was furnished the debit card to the debit cardholder's account by the debit cardholder, unless the debit cardholder has notified the debit card issuer that transfers by that person are no longer authorized.

(2) With fraudulent intent by the debit cardholder or any person acting in concert with the debit cardholder.

(3) By the debit card issuer or its employee. **Leg.H.** Added Stats 1999 ch 244 §1 (SB 313).

§1748.31. Cardholder's liability for unauthorized use of debit card; Effect of failure to make timely report of unauthorized use appearing on statement

(a) A debit cardholder shall be liable for an unauthorized use of a debit card only if all of the following conditions are met:

(1) The card is an accepted debit card.

(2) Except as provided in subdivision (b), the liability is not in excess of fifty dollars ($50).

(3) The debit card issuer has given adequate notice to the debit cardholder of the potential liability.

(4) The debit card issuer has provided the debit cardholder with a description of the means by which the debit card issuer may be notified of loss or theft of the card.

(5) The unauthorized use occurs before the debit card issuer has been notified by the debit cardholder that an unauthorized use of the debit card has occurred or may occur as a result of loss, theft, or otherwise.

(6) The debit card issuer has provided a means to identify the debit cardholder to whom the debit card was issued.

(b) Notwithstanding subdivision (a), if the debit cardholder fails to report an unauthorized use that appears on a periodic statement within 60 days of the debit card issuer's transmittal of the statement, and if the issuer establishes that an unauthorized use would not have occurred had the debit cardholder notified the issuer within the 60-day period, the debit cardholder shall be liable for the amount of each unauthorized transfer that occurs after the close of the 60 days and before notice to the issuer. If the debit cardholder's delay in notifying the debit card issuer was due to extenuating circumstances beyond the debit cardholder's reasonable control, the time specified above shall be extended by a reasonable period. For the purposes of this subdivision, examples of extenuating circumstances include, but are not limited to, extended travel, the death or serious illness of the debit cardholder or a member of the debit cardholder's family, hospitalization, permanent mental impairment, or serious physical impairment, unless the circumstance did not reasonably contribute to the cardholder's delay in notifying the debit card issuer within the 60-day period.

(c) A debit cardholder shall have no liability for erroneous or fraudulent transfers initiated by a debit card issuer, its agent, or employee. **Leg.H.** Added Stats 1999 ch 244 §1 (SB 313).

§1748.32. Waiver of provisions of title void

Any waiver of the provisions of this title is contrary to public policy, and is void and unenforceable. **Leg.H.** Added Stats 2002 ch 815 §5 (AB 2331).

TITLE 1.3.5
CONSUMER REFUNDS

Chapter 1. Prepaid Debit Cards.
Chapter 1.5. Consumer Refund Conditioned on Nondisclosure Agreement.
Chapter 2. Hotel and Private Residence Rental Reservation Refunds.

CHAPTER 1
PREPAID DEBIT CARDS

Definitions. §1748.40.
Refund via prepaid debit card. §1748.41.

§1748.40. Definitions

For purposes of this chapter:

(a) "Accepted debit card" means any debit card which the debit cardholder has requested and received or has signed, or has used, or has authorized another person to use, for the purpose of obtaining money, property, labor, or services. Any debit card issued in renewal of, or in substitution for, an accepted debit card becomes an accepted debit card when received by the debit cardholder, whether the debit card is issued by the same or by a successor card issuer.

(b) "Business" means a proprietorship, partnership, corporation, or other form of commercial enterprise. "Business" does not include a restaurant.

(c) "Cardholder" means a natural person to whom a prepaid debit card is issued.

(d) "Debit card" means an accepted debit card or other means of access to a debit cardholder's account that may be used to initiate electronic funds transfers and may be used without unique identifying information such as a personal identification number to initiate access to the debit cardholder's account.

(e) "Prepaid debit card" means a debit card that meets either of the following:

(1) A card, code, or other means of access to funds of a recipient that is usable at multiple, unaffiliated merchants for goods or services, or usable at automated teller machines.

(2) The same as those terms or related terms are defined in the regulations adopted under the Electronic Fund Transfer Act regarding general use reloadable cards.

(f) "Refund" means a return of a sum of money to a customer who has overpaid for services or property or is otherwise owed money by the business. **Leg.H.** Added Stats 2019 ch 130 §1 (AB 1428), effective January 1, 2020. Amended Stats 2023 ch 718 §2 (SB 644), effective January 1, 2024.

§1748.41. Refund via prepaid debit card

If a business offers a refund to a customer via a prepaid debit card for a purchase initiated by the customer in California, the business shall provide the customer with at least one other method of receiving the refund other than a prepaid debit card. **Leg.H.** Added Stats 2019 ch 130 §1 (AB 1428), effective January 1, 2020.

CHAPTER 1.5
CONSUMER REFUND CONDITIONED ON NONDISCLOSURE AGREEMENT

Refund conditioned on nondisclosure agreements void. § 1748.50.

§ 1748.50. Refund conditioned on nondisclosure agreements void

Any provision in a contract or agreement that prohibits a consumer from publishing or making statements about the business as a condition of receiving a partial or complete refund or any other consideration or thing of value is contrary to public policy and shall be void and unenforceable. **Leg.H.** Added Stats 2024 ch 89 §1 (AB 1900), effective January 1, 2025.

CHAPTER 2
HOTEL AND PRIVATE RESIDENCE RENTAL RESERVATION REFUNDS

Definitions. § 1748.80.
Reservation cancellation without penalty. § 1748.81.
Refunds for cancellations. § 1748.82.
Actions for violations; Penalties. § 1748.83.
Applicability of chapter. § 1748.84.

§ 1748.80. Definitions

For purposes of this chapter:

(a) "Hosting platform" has the same meaning as defined in Section 22590 of the Business and Professions Code.

(b)(1) "Hotel" means a hotel, motel, bed and breakfast inn, or other similar transient lodging establishment located in this state.

(2) "Hotel" does not include a residential hotel, as defined in Section 50519 of the Health and Safety Code.

(c) "Third-party booking service" means a person that facilitates the booking of a hotel room or short-term rental in this state.

(d) "Short-term rental" means a residential dwelling, or any portion of a residential dwelling, that is rented to a person or persons for 30 or fewer consecutive days and that is located in this state. **Leg.H.** Added Stats 2023 ch 718 §3 (SB 644), effective January 1, 2024.

§ 1748.81. Reservation cancellation without penalty

A hosting platform, hotel, third-party booking service, or short-term rental shall allow a reservation for a hotel accommodation or a short-term rental located in California to be canceled without penalty for at least 24 hours after the reservation is confirmed if the reservation is made 72 hours or more before the time of check-in. **Leg.H.** Added Stats 2023 ch 718 §3 (SB 644), effective January 1, 2024.

§ 1748.82. Refunds for cancellations

(a) If a consumer cancels a reservation pursuant to Section 1748.81, the hosting platform, hotel, third-party booking service, or short-term rental shall issue a refund to a consumer of all amounts paid to the hosting platform, hotel, third-party booking service, or short-term rental to the original form of payment within 30 days of the cancellation of the reservation.

(b) The refund required by this section shall include a refund of all fees charged to the consumer for optional services. **Leg.H.** Added Stats 2023 ch 718 §3 (SB 644), effective January 1, 2024.

§ 1748.83. Actions for violations; Penalties

(a) An action for a violation of this chapter may be brought only by any of the following:

(1) The Attorney General.

(2) A district attorney.

(3) A city attorney of a city having a population in excess of 750,000.

(4) A county counsel of any county within which a city has a population in excess of 750,000.

(5) With the consent of the district attorney, a city prosecutor in a city that has a full-time city prosecutor.

(b) In an action alleging a violation of this chapter, the court shall assess a civil penalty of not more than ten thousand dollars ($10,000) for each violation. In determining the amount of the civil penalty, the court shall consider any of the relevant circumstances presented by any of the parties to the case, including, but not limited to, all of the following:

(1) The nature and seriousness of the misconduct.

(2) The number of violations.

(3) The persistence of the misconduct.

(4) The length of time over which the misconduct occurred.

(5) The willfulness of the misconduct.

(6) The defendant's assets, liabilities, and net worth.

(c) Each day that a defendant remains in violation of this chapter shall constitute a single violation.

(d) The duties and obligations imposed by this chapter are cumulative with any other duties or obligations imposed under other law and shall not be construed to relieve any party from any duties or obligations imposed under other law. **Leg.H.** Added Stats 2023 ch 718 §3 (SB 644), effective January 1, 2024.

§ 1748.84. Applicability of chapter

This chapter does not apply to a reservation that meets any of the following criteria:

(a) The reservation was made for a negotiated rate that was not advertised, or otherwise made available, for booking by the general public.

(b) The reservation is for a hotel accommodation or short-term rental reservation that was confirmed before July 1, 2024.

(c) The reservation is one in which the specific hotel or short-term rental is not disclosed to the consumer until after the booking is confirmed. **Leg.H.** Added Stats 2023 ch 718 §3 (SB 644), effective January 1, 2024.

TITLE 1.4
LAYAWAY PRACTICES

Disclosure requirements. §1749.
Definitions. §1749.1.
Waiver contrary to public policy. §1749.2.
Remedies cumulative. §1749.3.
Construction of title. §1749.4.

§1749. Disclosure requirements

Any retail seller which permits consumers to lay away consumer goods shall provide to any consumer entering into a layaway agreement with the seller a written statement of the terms and conditions of the agreement, including the following information:

(1) The amount of the deposit received.

(2) The length of time the goods will be held on layaway which may be expressed as a period of time or as a date when final payment for the goods is due.

(3) A specific description of the goods.

(4) The total purchase price of the goods including a separate listing of any handling or processing charges.

(5) Any other terms and conditions of the layaway agreement.

(6) That the seller will refund any layaway deposit and subsequent payments, if any, when, before the end of the stated layaway period, the goods have for any reason become no longer available in the same condition as at the time of the sale to the consumer. **Leg.H.** Added Stats 1975 ch 825 §1.

Prior Law: Former §1749, similar to UCC §7501, was added Stats 1931 ch 1070 §1 and repealed Stats 1963 ch 819 §2, effective January 1, 1965.

Former §1749, relating to when seller may resell, was enacted 1872 and repealed Stats 1931 ch 1070 §1.

§1749.1. Definitions

For purposes of this title, the following terms have the following meanings:

(a) "Consumer good" means any article which is used or bought for use primarily for personal, family, or household purposes.

(b) "Retail seller" means an individual, firm, partnership, corporation, joint stock company, association, organization, or other legal entity which engages in the business of selling consumer goods to retail buyers.

(c) "Layaway" means an agreement by a retail seller with a consumer to retain specified consumer goods for sale to the consumer at a specified price, in earnest of which sale the consumer has deposited with the retail seller an agreed upon sum of money, and any other terms and conditions not contrary to law which are mutually agreed upon. **Leg.H.** Added Stats 1975 ch 825 §1.

§1749.2. Waiver contrary to public policy

Any waiver by the buyer of consumer goods of the provisions of this title, except as expressly provided in this title, shall be deemed contrary to public policy and shall be unenforceable and void. **Leg.H.** Added Stats 1975 ch 825 §1.

§1749.3. Remedies cumulative

The remedies provided by this title are cumulative and shall not be construed as restricting any remedy that is otherwise available. **Leg.H.** Added Stats 1975 ch 825 §1.

§1749.4. Construction of title

Nothing in this title shall be construed to limit or reduce any legal obligations imposed under Title 2 (commencing with Section 1801) of Part 4 of Division 3 or under any other applicable law. **Leg.H.** Added Stats 1975 ch 825 §1.

TITLE 1.4A
GIFT CERTIFICATES

"Gift Certificate" defined. §1749.45.
Proscription on expiration dates and service fees in gift certificates; Exceptions. §1749.5.
Waiver of provisions of title void. §1749.51.
Gift certificate is trust property of beneficiary and must be honored by issuer in bankruptcy. §1749.6.

§1749.45. "Gift Certificate" defined

(a) As used in this title, "gift certificate" includes gift cards, but does not include any gift card usable with multiple sellers of goods or services, provided the expiration date, if any, is printed on the card. This exemption does not apply to a gift card usable only with affiliated sellers of goods or services.

(b) Nothing in this title prohibits those fees or practices expressly permitted by Section 17538.9 of the Business and Professions Code with respect to a prepaid calling card, as defined in that section, that is issued solely to provide an access number and authorization code for prepaid calling services. **Leg.H.** Added Stats 2003 ch 116 §1 (AB 1092).

§1749.5. Proscription on expiration dates and service fees in gift certificates; Exceptions

(a) It is unlawful for any person or entity to sell a gift certificate to a purchaser that contains any of the following:

(1) An expiration date.

(2) A service fee, including, but not limited to, a service fee for dormancy, except as provided in subdivision (e).

(b)(1) Any gift certificate sold after January 1, 1997, is redeemable in cash for its cash value, or subject to replacement with a new gift certificate at no cost to the purchaser or holder.

(2) Notwithstanding paragraph (1), any gift certificate with a cash value of less than ten dollars ($10) is redeemable in cash for its cash value.

(c) A gift certificate sold without an expiration date is valid until redeemed or replaced.

(d) This section does not apply to any of the following gift certificates issued on or after January 1, 1998, provided the expiration date appears in capital letters in at least 10-point font on the front of the gift certificate:

(1) Gift certificates that are distributed by the issuer to a consumer pursuant to an awards, loyalty, or promotional program without any money or other thing of value being given in exchange for the gift certificate by the consumer.

(2) Gift certificates that are donated or sold below face value at a volume discount to employers or to nonprofit and charitable organizations for fundraising purposes if the expiration date on those gift certificates is not more than 30 days after the date of sale.

(3) Gift certificates that are issued for perishable food products.

(e) Paragraph (2) of subdivision (a) does not apply to a dormancy fee on a gift card that meets all of the following criteria:

(1) The remaining value of the gift card is five dollars ($5) or less each time the fee is assessed.

(2) The fee does not exceed one dollar ($1) per month.

(3) There has been no activity on the gift card for 24 consecutive months, including, but not limited to, purchases, the adding of value, or balance inquiries.

(4) The holder may reload or add value to the gift card.

(5) A statement is printed on the gift card in at least 10-point font stating the amount of the fee, how often the fee will occur, that the fee is triggered by inactivity of the gift card, and at what point the fee will be charged. The statement may appear on the front or back of the gift card, but shall appear in a location where it is visible to any purchaser prior to the purchase thereof.

(f) An issuer of gift certificates may accept funds from one or more contributors toward the purchase of a gift certificate intended to be a gift for a recipient, provided that each contributor is provided with a full refund of the amount that he or she paid toward the purchase of the gift certificate upon the occurrence of all of the following:

(1) The funds are contributed for the purpose of being redeemed by the recipient by purchasing a gift certificate.

(2) The time in which the recipient may redeem the funds by purchasing a gift certificate is clearly disclosed in writing to the contributors and the recipient.

(3) The recipient does not redeem the funds within the time described in paragraph (2).

(g) The changes made to this section by the act adding this subdivision shall apply only to gift certificates issued on or after January 1, 2004.

(h) For purposes of this section, "cash" includes, but is not limited to, currency or check. If accepted by both parties, an electronic funds transfer or an application of the balance to a subscriber's wireless telecommunications account is permissible. **Leg.H.** Added Stats 1996 ch 933 §1 (AB 2466). Amended Stats 1997 ch 472 §1 (AB 1054); Stats 2003 ch 116 §2 (AB 1092); Stats 2004 ch 319 §1 (AB 656); Stats 2007 ch 640 §1 (SB 250), effective January 1, 2008.

2003 Note: The enactment of this act creates no inference with respect to the validity or invalidity of any service fee imposed prior to the effective date of this act. Stats 2003 ch 116 (AB 1092) §4.

§1749.51. Waiver of provisions of title void

Any waiver of the provisions of this title is contrary to public policy, and is void and unenforceable. **Leg.H.** Added Stats 2002 ch 815 §6 (AB 2331).

§1749.6. Gift certificate is trust property of beneficiary and must be honored by issuer in bankruptcy

(a) A gift certificate constitutes value held in trust by the issuer of the gift certificate on behalf of the beneficiary of the gift certificate. The value represented by the gift certificate belongs to the beneficiary, or to the legal representative of the beneficiary to the extent provided by law, and not to the issuer.

(b) An issuer of a gift certificate who is in bankruptcy shall continue to honor a gift certificate issued prior to the date of the bankruptcy filing on the grounds that the value of the gift certificate constitutes trust property of the beneficiary.

(c)(1) This section does not alter the terms of a gift certificate. The terms of a gift certificate may not make its redemption or other use invalid in the event of a bankruptcy.

(2) This section does not require, unless otherwise required by law, the issuer of a gift certificate to:

(A) Redeem a gift certificate for cash.

(B) Replace a gift certificate that has been lost or stolen.

(C) Maintain a separate account for the funds used to purchase the gift certificate.

(d)(1) This section does not create an interest in favor of the beneficiary of the gift certificate in any specific property of the issuer.

(2) This section does not create a fiduciary or quasi-fiduciary relationship between the beneficiary of the gift certificates and the issuer, unless otherwise provided by law.

(3) The issuer of a gift certificate has no obligation to pay interest on the value of the gift certificate held in trust under this section, unless otherwise provided by law. **Leg.H.** Added Stats 2002 ch 997 §1 (AB 2473).

TITLE 1.4B
SUPERMARKET CLUB CARDS

Citation of title. §1749.60.
Definition. §1749.61.
Violation as unfair competition. §1749.63.
Proscription on requiring driver's license or social security number for club card application. §1749.64.
Restrictions on dissemination of personal identification information about cardholders. §1749.65.
Waiver of provisions of title void. §1749.66.

§1749.60. Citation of title

This title shall be known and may be cited as the "Supermarket Club Card Disclosure Act of 1999." **Leg.H.** Added Stats 1999 ch 586 §1 (SB 926), operative July 1, 2000.

§1749.61. Definition

For purposes of this title:

(a) "Cardholder" means any consumer to whom a supermarket club card is issued, provided that in cases where more than one supermarket club card has been issued for the same account, all persons holding those supermarket club cards may be treated as a single cardholder.

(b) "Supermarket" means any retailer that sells food items.

(c) "Supermarket club card" means any card, plate, coupon book, or other single device existing for the purpose of being used from time to time upon presentation for price discounts on retail products offered by the club card issuer. "Supermarket club card" does not include any credit card that is subject to Section 1748.12.

(d) "Club card issuer" means a supermarket that provides supermarket club cards to consumers, and includes a supermarket's contract information services provider.

(e) "Marketing information" means the categorization of cardholders compiled by a club card issuer, based on a cardholder's shopping patterns, spending history, or behavioral characteristics derived from account activity which is provided to any person or entity for consideration. "Marketing information" does not include aggregate data which does not identify a cardholder based on the cardholder's shopping patterns, spending history, or behavioral characteristics derived from account activity. **Leg.H.** Added Stats 1999 ch 586 §1 (SB 926), operative July 1, 2000.

§1749.63. Violation as unfair competition

A violation of this title constitutes "unfair competition" as defined in Section 17200 of the Business and Professions Code and is punishable as prescribed in Chapter 5 (commencing with Section 17200) of Part 2 of Division 7 of the Business and Professions Code. **Leg.H.** Added Stats 1999 ch 586 §1 (SB 926), operative July 1, 2000.

§1749.64. Proscription on requiring driver's license or social security number for club card application

Notwithstanding any other provision of law, no club card issuer shall request in a supermarket club card application, or require as a condition of obtaining a supermarket club card, that an applicant provide a driver's license number or a social security account number. This section shall not be construed to prohibit a club card issuer from requesting a driver's license number or a social security account number for a supermarket club card that can also be used as identification for check cashing purposes or to debit the checking or savings account of the cardholder. However, no club card issuer shall, as a condition of obtaining a supermarket club card, require a cardholder to obtain a supermarket club card that can also be used as identification for check cashing purposes or to debit the checking or savings account of the cardholder. **Leg.H.** Added Stats 1999 ch 586 §1 (SB 926), operative July 1, 2000.

§1749.65. Restrictions on dissemination of personal identification information about cardholders

(a) Notwithstanding any other provision of law, no club card issuer may sell or share a cardholder's name, address, telephone number, or other personal identification information.

(b) Nothing in this section is intended to prevent a club card issuer from providing names and addresses of cardholders to a third party for purposes of mailing supermarket club card information to cardholders on behalf of the club card issuer. However, that third party shall not use the information for any other purpose.

(c) Notwithstanding subdivision (a), this section does not prohibit a club card issuer from sharing marketing information that includes cardholder names and addresses if the club card issuer complies with all of the following:

(1) The club card issuer charges an annual fee for its supermarket club card.

(2) The club card issuer requires cardholders to renew supermarket club cards annually and to pay an annual renewal fee.

(3) The club card issuer allows only cardholders, and not members of the public, to make purchases in the supermarket.

(4) The club card issuer provides a privacy statement to the cardholder in the supermarket club card application and in the club card issuer's annual renewal material notifying cardholders that outside companies will be receiving marketing information including names and addresses of cardholders, and the cardholder has agreed to allow the club card issuer to share this information.

(5) Prior to selling or transferring names and addresses of cardholders to an outside company, the club card issuer has obtained a written confidentiality agreement from the outside company that the outside company will not sell or share the information with any other entity. **Leg.H.** Added Stats 1999 ch 586 §1 (SB 926), operative July 1, 2000.

§1749.66. Waiver of provisions of title void

Any waiver of the provisions of this title is contrary to public policy, and is void and unenforceable. **Leg.H.** Added Stats 2002 ch 815 §7 (AB 2331).

(c) "Online marketplace" means a consumer-directed, electronically accessed platform that includes features that allow for, facilitate, or enable a third-party seller to engage in the sale, purchase, payment, storage, shipment, or delivery of a consumer product in this state.

(d) "Third-party seller" means a person or entity, independent of an online marketplace, who sells, offers to sell, or contracts with an online marketplace to sell a consumer product in the state by utilizing an online marketplace.

(e) "Verify" means to confirm that information provided to an online marketplace pursuant to this title is accurate. Methods of confirmation include the use of one or more methods that enable the online marketplace to reliably determine that the information and documents are valid, correspond to the seller or an individual acting on the seller's behalf, are not misappropriated, and are not falsified.

(f) This section shall become operative on July 1, 2025. **Leg.H.** Added Stats 2024 ch 172 §3 (SB 1144), operative July 1, 2025.

§ 1749.8.1. High-volume third-party seller information requirements

(a) An online marketplace shall require each high-volume third-party seller on the online marketplace to provide, not later than 10 days after qualifying as a high-volume third-party seller, all of the following information to the online marketplace:

(1)(A) A bank account number, or, if the high-volume third-party seller does not have a bank account, the name of the payee for payments issued by the online marketplace to the seller.

(B) The high-volume third-party seller shall provide the information required by this paragraph to one of the following as specified by the online marketplace:

(i) The online marketplace.

(ii) A payment processor or other third party designated by the online marketplace that is required, pursuant to a contract with the online marketplace, to maintain the information in a confidential manner and disclose the information only in response to a court order or to the online marketplace upon its request.

(2) If the high-volume third-party seller is an individual, the individual's name.

(3) If the high-volume third-party seller is not an individual, one of the following:

(A) A copy of a valid government-issued identification for an individual who has the legal authority to act on behalf of the high-volume third-party seller that includes the individual's name.

(B) A copy of a valid government record or tax document dated within the past 24 months that includes the business name and physical address of the high-volume third-party seller.

(4) A business tax identification number, or, if the high-volume third-party seller does not have a business tax identification number, a taxpayer identification number.

(5) A valid email address and telephone number for the high-volume third-party seller.

(b) An online marketplace shall verify the information provided pursuant to subdivision (a) within 10 days and shall verify within 10 days any changes to the information that is provided to the marketplace by a high-volume third-party seller. If a high-volume third-party seller provides a copy of a valid government-issued tax document, information contained within the tax document shall be presumed to be verified as of the date of issuance of the record or document.

(c)(1) The online marketplace shall, on at least an annual basis, notify each high-volume third-party seller operating on the online marketplace of the requirement to inform the online marketplace of any changes to the information provided by the seller pursuant to subdivision (a) within 10 days of receiving the notification and shall instruct each high-volume third-party seller, as part of the notification, to electronically certify that the information is accurate and that either that the seller's information is unchanged or that the seller is providing updated information.

(2) If a high-volume third-party seller does not provide the information or certification required under this section, the online marketplace shall, after providing the seller with written or electronic notice and opportunity to provide the information or certification not later than 10 days after the issuance of the notice, suspend any future sales activity of the seller until the seller provides the information or certification. **Leg.H.** Added Stats 2022 ch 857 §1 (SB 301), effective January 1, 2023, operative July 1, 2023. Amended Stats 2023 ch 131 §11 (AB 1754), effective January 1, 2024.

§ 1749.8.2. Additional information and disclosure requirements for high-volume third-party seller with at least twenty thousand dollars ($20,000) of gross annual revenues; Criteria for suspension

(a) An online marketplace shall require a high-volume third-party seller with at least twenty thousand dollars ($20,000) of gross annual revenues from transactions with buyers in California through the online marketplace in either of the two prior calendar years to provide, in addition to the information required by 1749.8.1, the following information to the online marketplace and to disclose the information about the high-volume third-party seller to consumers in a clear and conspicuous manner in the order confirmation message, or other communication made to a consumer after a purchase is finalized, and in the consumer's account transaction history:

(1)(A) Except as provided in subparagraph (B), the high-volume third-party seller shall provide all of the following identifying information:

(i) The full name of the high-volume third-party seller, which may include the seller's name or company name, or the name by which the seller or company operates on the online marketplace.

(ii) The high-volume third-party seller's physical address.

(iii) Contact information for the high-volume third-party seller, including a current working telephone number, email address, or any other means of direct electronic messaging, to allow users of the online marketplace to have direct and unhindered communication with the seller.

(B) A high-volume third-party seller may request that the online marketplace accept the following partial disclosures of information in lieu of the disclosures required pursuant to subparagraph (A):

(i) If the high-volume third-party seller certifies to the online marketplace that they do not have a physical address other than a residential physical address, or a combined business and residential physical address, the online marketplace may disclose only the country and state, if applicable, in which the seller resides and inform consumers that inquiries should be submitted to the seller by telephone, email, or electronic means provided by the online marketplace.

(ii) If the high-volume third-party seller certifies to the online marketplace that they do not have a telephone number other than a personal telephone number, the online marketplace shall inform consumers that no telephone number is available for the seller, and inquiries should be submitted to the seller's email address or electronic means provided by the online marketplace.

(2)(A) Whether or not another party is responsible for supplying the product to the consumer upon purchase.

(B) If requested by an authenticated purchaser, the contact information described in paragraph (1) for the party who is responsible for supplying the product to the consumer upon purchase.

(b) An online marketplace shall disclose to consumers, in a clear and conspicuous manner on the product listing of a high-volume third-party seller, a reporting mechanism that allows for electronic and telephonic reporting of suspicious activity by the high-volume third-party seller to the online marketplace.

(c)(1)(A) An online marketplace shall suspend future sales activity of a high-volume third-party seller that meets any of the following criteria:

(i) The high-volume third-party seller is not in compliance with the requirements of this section.

(ii) The high-volume third-party seller made a false representation to the online marketplace about the applicability of subparagraph (B) of paragraph (1) of subdivision (a).

(iii) The high-volume third-party seller made a false representation to consumers.

(B) An online marketplace may suspend future sales activity of a high-volume third-party seller that has not answered consumer inquiries within a reasonable timeframe.

(2)(A) An online marketplace shall provide notice of an impending suspension pursuant to clause (i) of subparagraph (A) of paragraph (1) and shall not suspend the high-volume third-party seller if the seller becomes in compliance with this section within 10 days of the date on which the notice was issued.

TITLE 1.4C
CLARITY OF MARKETPLACE TERMS AND CONDITIONS AND DISPUTE RESOLUTION MINIMUM FAIRNESS

Terms and conditions for commercial relationships with marketplace sellers; Payment to influence search results; Suspension or termination of marketplace seller; Definitions. §1749.7.

§1749.7. Terms and conditions for commercial relationships with marketplace sellers; Payment to influence search results; Suspension or termination of marketplace seller; Definitions

(a) Every marketplace shall ensure that their terms and conditions regarding commercial relationships with marketplace sellers meet all of the following requirements:

(1) Are drafted in plain and intelligible language.

(2) Are easily available online for marketplace sellers at all stages of their commercial relationship with the marketplace, including, but not limited to, during the stage prior to the formation of a contract.

(3) Set out the grounds for decisions to retain, or refuse to disburse, funds in its possession belonging to a marketplace seller pending investigation or resolution of a dispute between the marketplace and the marketplace seller and the grounds for suspending or terminating a marketplace seller from participating in the marketplace.

(b) If a marketplace permits a marketplace seller to pay the marketplace to influence search results through ranking or preferential placement within the marketplace of tangible personal property or services sold by marketplace sellers through the marketplace, the marketplace, in its terms and conditions or policies, shall describe those possibilities and the effects of such payment on the ranking or preferential placement, and either (1) the price of that ranking or preferential placement or (2) how a marketplace seller may obtain written price information for such ranking or preferential placement.

(c) If a marketplace decides to suspend or terminate a marketplace seller based upon an alleged violation of law or a term, condition, or policy of the marketplace, the marketplace shall provide the marketplace seller, without undue delay, with a written statement of reasons for that decision. The written statement of reasons shall, at a minimum, do all of the following:

(1) Without disclosing information that would result in the disclosure of any proprietary, confidential, or trade secret information, or disclosing information that would hinder any investigation or prevention of deceptive, fraudulent, or illegal activity, describe the facts and circumstances that led to the decision unless the marketplace reasonably believes that giving a written statement of reasons could negatively impact the safety or property of another user or the marketplace itself.

(2) Identify the term, condition, or policy that serves as the basis for the suspension or termination.

(3) Explain whether or not the decision may be appealed, and, if so, the procedure for such an appeal.

(d) For purposes of this section, the following definitions shall apply:

(1) "Marketplace" means a physical or electronic place, including, but not limited to, a store, booth, internet website, catalog, television or radio broadcast, or a dedicated sales software application, that sells or offers for retail sale services or tangible personal property for delivery in this state and has an agreement with a marketplace seller to make retail sales of services or tangible personal property through that marketplace, regardless of whether the tangible personal property or the marketplace has a physical presence in the state.

(2) "Marketplace seller" means a person residing in the state who has an agreement with a marketplace and makes retail sales of services or tangible personal property through a marketplace owned, operated, or controlled by that marketplace.

(3) "Ranking" means the relative prominence given to the tangible personal property or services offered to consumers through a marketplace, as organized or communicated to those consumers by the marketplace, irrespective of the technological means used for that organization or communication. **Leg.H.** Added Stats 2019 ch 635 §1 (AB 1790), effective January 1, 2020.

TITLE 1.4D
ONLINE MARKETPLACES

Definitions [Inoperative July 1, 2025; Repealed January 1, 2026]. § 1749.8.
Definitions [Operative July 1, 2025]. § 1749.8.
High-volume third-party seller information requirements. § 1749.8.1.
Additional information and disclosure requirements for high-volume third-party seller with at least twenty thousand dollars ($20,000) of gross annual revenues; Criteria for suspension. § 1749.8.2.
Information retention and security; Redaction. § 1749.8.3.
Penalties and other relief [Inoperative July 1, 2025; Repealed January 1, 2026]. § 1749.8.4.
Penalties [Operative July 1, 2025]. § 1749.8.4.
Applicability of title; Operative date of title. § 1749.8.5.
Duties of online marketplaces to alert [Operative July 1, 2025]. § 1749.8.9.

§ 1749.8. Definitions [Inoperative July 1, 2025; Repealed January 1, 2026]

For purposes of this title:

(a) "Consumer product" means tangible personal property that is distributed in commerce and normally used for personal, family, or household purposes, including property intended to be attached to or installed in real property regardless of whether it is actually attached or installed.

(b)(1) "High-volume third-party seller" means a third-party seller who, in any continuous 12-month period during the previous 24 months, has entered into 200 or more discrete transactions through an online marketplace for the sale of new or unused consumer products to buyers located in California resulting in the accumulation of an aggregate total of five thousand dollars ($5,000) or more in gross revenues.

(2) The number of discrete transactions referenced in paragraph (1) includes only those transactions through the online marketplace for which payment is processed by the online marketplace directly or through its payment processor.

(c) "Online marketplace" means a consumer-directed, electronically accessed platform for which all of the following are true:

(1) The platform includes features that allow for, facilitate, or enable third-party sellers to engage in the sale, purchase, payment, storage, shipping, or delivery of a consumer product in this state.

(2) The features described in paragraph (1) are used by third-party sellers.

(3) The platform has a contractual relationship with consumers governing their use of the platform to purchase consumer products.

(d) "Third-party seller" means a person or entity, independent of an online marketplace, who sells, offers to sell, or contracts with an online marketplace to sell a consumer product in the state by or through an online marketplace.

(e) "Verify" means to confirm that information provided to an online marketplace pursuant to this title is accurate. Methods of confirmation include the use of one or more methods that enable the online marketplace to reliably determine that the information and documents are valid, correspond to the seller or an individual acting on the seller's behalf, are not misappropriated, and are not falsified.

(f) This section shall become inoperative on July 1, 2025, and shall be repealed on January 1, 2026. **Leg.H.** Added Stats 2022 ch 857 §1 (SB 301), effective January 1, 2023, operative July 1, 2023. Amended Stats 2023 ch 131 §10 (AB 1754), effective January 1, 2024; Stats 2024 ch 172 §2 (SB 1144), effective January 1, 2025, inoperative July 1, 2025, repealed January 1, 2026.

§1749.8. Definitions [Operative July 1, 2025]

For purposes of this title:

(a) "Consumer product" means tangible personal property that is distributed in commerce and normally used for personal, family, or household purposes, including property intended to be attached to or installed in real property regardless of whether it is actually attached or installed.

(b) "High-volume third-party seller" means a third-party seller on an online marketplace who, in any continuous 12-month period during the previous 24 months, has entered into 200 or more discrete transactions utilizing the online marketplace for the sale of new or unused consumer products to buyers located in California resulting in the accumulation of an aggregate total of five thousand dollars ($5,000) or more in gross revenues.

(B) If the high-volume third-party seller provides the information required by subdivision (a) more than 10 days after the date of the notice, the online marketplace shall restore the ability of the seller to have transactions facilitated by or through the online marketplace within 10 days of receiving all of the information. **Leg.H.** Added Stats 2022 ch 857 §1 (SB 301), effective January 1, 2023, operative July 1, 2023.

§ 1749.8.3. Information retention and security; Redaction

(a)(1) An online marketplace shall keep the information provided to comply with the requirements of this title for no less than two years.

(2) Information provided solely to comply with the requirements of this title shall not be used for any other purpose unless required by law.

(3) An online marketplace shall implement and maintain reasonable security procedures and practices, including administrative, physical, and technical safeguards, appropriate to the nature of the information and the purposes for which the information will be used, to protect the information provided to comply with the requirements of this title from unauthorized use, disclosure, access, destruction, and modification.

(b) A high-volume third-party seller may redact from a document provided solely to comply with a requirement of this title any information that is not necessary for either of the following:

(1) To comply with a requirement of this title.

(2) To verify the authenticity of the document as a copy of a valid government-issued identification, government record, or tax document, as applicable. **Leg.H.** Added Stats 2022 ch 857 §1 (SB 301), effective January 1, 2023, operative July 1, 2023.

§ 1749.8.4. Penalties and other relief [Inoperative July 1, 2025; Repealed January 1, 2026]

(a) A person or entity who violates any provision of this title shall be liable for a civil penalty not to exceed ten thousand dollars ($10,000) for each violation, which may be assessed and recovered only in a civil action brought in the name of the people of the State of California by the Attorney General.

(b) In addition to the civil penalty provided by subdivision (a), the Attorney General who prevails in an action to enforce this title shall be entitled to the following relief:

(1) Reasonable attorney's fees and costs, including expert witness fees and other litigation expenses.

(2) Preventive relief, including a permanent or temporary injunction, restraining order, or other order against any person responsible for the conduct.

(c) **This section shall become inoperative on July 1, 2025, and shall be repealed on January 1, 2026. Leg.H.** Added Stats 2022 ch 857 §1 (SB 301), effective January 1, 2023, operative July 1, 2023. Amended Stats 2024 ch 172 §4 (SB 1144), effective January 1, 2025, inoperative July 1, 2025, repealed January 1, 2026.

§1749.8.4. Penalties [Operative July 1, 2025]

(a) A person or entity who violates any provision of this title shall be liable for a civil penalty not to exceed ten thousand dollars ($10,000) for each violation, which may be assessed and recovered only in a civil action brought in the name of the people of the State of California by the Attorney General, a district attorney in any county, a city attorney in any city or city and county, or a county counsel in any county.

(b) In addition to the civil penalty provided by subdivision (a), the Attorney General, a district attorney, a city attorney in any city or city and county, or county counsel who prevails in an action to enforce this title shall be entitled to the following relief:

(1) Reasonable attorney's fees and costs, including expert witness fees and other litigation expenses.

(2) Preventive relief, including a permanent or temporary injunction, restraining order, or other order against any person responsible for the conduct.

(c) This section shall become operative on July 1, 2025. **Leg.H.** Added Stats 2024 ch 172 §5 (SB 1144), effective January 1, 2025, operative July 1, 2025.

§ 1749.8.5. Applicability of title; Operative date of title

(a) This title does not apply to or affect the liability of an entity, including an entity that meets the definition of a high-volume third-party seller under this title, for damages caused by a consumer product that is sold online.

(b) This title shall become operative July 1, 2023. **Leg.H.** Added Stats 2022 ch 857 §1 (SB 301), effective January 1, 2023, operative July 1, 2023.

§1749.8.9. Duties of online marketplaces to alert [Operative July 1, 2025]

(a) An online marketplace shall alert local, regional, or state law enforcement agencies in California if it knows or should know that a third-party seller is selling or attempting to sell stolen goods to a California resident, unless the online marketplace has received a notice from the law enforcement agency that the same third-party seller is suspected of selling or attempting to sell the same stolen goods on the online marketplace to a California resident.

(b)(1) An online marketplace shall do all of the following:

(A) Establish and maintain a policy prohibiting the sale of stolen goods on the online marketplace, which shall include consequences for knowingly selling stolen goods on the online marketplace, including, but not limited to, suspension or termination of the seller's account.

(B) Provide a mechanism on the online marketplace that allows any individual to notify the online marketplace that a seller is or may be selling stolen goods.

(C) Provide a mechanism on the online marketplace that allows the online marketplace and law enforcement to communicate in a timely and confidential manner, including by means of a link to a dedicated web page, online portal, or point of contact and ensure timely replies to law enforcement requests, including warrants, subpoenas, and other legal processes.

(D) Maintain internal written policies, systems, and staff to monitor listings in order to affirmatively prevent and detect organized retail crime.

(2) The policy and mechanism required by this subdivision shall be publicly posted and readily accessible to users.

(c) This section shall become operative on July 1, 2025. **Leg.H.** Added Stats 2024 ch 172 §6 (SB 1144), effective January 1, 2025, operative July 1, 2025.

TITLE 1.5
CONSUMERS LEGAL REMEDIES ACT

Chapter 1. General Provisions.
Chapter 2. Construction and Definitions.
Chapter 3. Deceptive Practices.
Chapter 4. Remedies and Procedures.

CHAPTER 1
GENERAL PROVISIONS

Title. §1750.
Waiver prohibited. §1751.
Remedies nonexclusive. §1752.
Severability. §1753.
Transactions excluded. §1754.
Applicability to advertising media. §1755.
Applicability to pending legal actions. §1756.
[Section renumbered 1973]. §1757.

§1750. Title

This title may be cited as the Consumers Legal Remedies Act. **Leg.H.** Added Stats 1970 ch 1550 §1.

Prior Law: Former §1750, similar to present §1785.2, was added Stats 1970 ch 1348 §1 and renumbered §1785.1 by Stats 1973 ch 167 §2.

Former §1750, relating to negotiable documents marked "not negotiable," was added Stats 1931 ch 1070 §1 and repealed Stats 1963 ch 819 §2, effective January 1, 1965.

§1751. Waiver prohibited

Any waiver by a consumer of the provisions of this title is contrary to public policy and shall be unenforceable and void. **Leg.H.** Added Stats 1970 ch 1550 §1 p 3157.

Prior Law: Former §1751, similar to present §1785.3, was added Stats 1970 ch 1348 §1 and renumbered §1785.2 by Stats 1973 ch 167 §3.

Former §1751, similar to present UCC §7501, was added Stats 1931 ch 1070 §1 and repealed Stats 1963 ch 819 §2, effective January 1, 1965.

§1752. Remedies nonexclusive

The provisions of this title are not exclusive. The remedies provided herein for violation of any section of this title or for conduct proscribed by any section of this title shall be in addition to any other procedures or remedies for any violation or conduct provided for in any other law.

Nothing in this title shall limit any other statutory or any common law rights of the Attorney General or any other person to bring class actions. Class actions by consumers brought under the specific provisions of Chapter 3 (commencing with Section 1770) of this title shall be governed exclusively by the provisions of Chapter 4 (commencing with Section 1780); however, this shall not be construed so as to deprive a consumer of any statutory or common law right to bring a class action without resort to this title. If any act or practice proscribed under this title also constitutes a cause of action in common law or a violation of another statute, the consumer may assert such common law or statutory cause of action under the procedures and with the remedies provided for in such law. **Leg.H.** Added Stats 1970 ch 1550 §1. Amended Stats 1975 ch 615 §1.

Prior Law: Former §1752, similar to present §1785.10, was added Stats 1970 ch 1348 §1 and renumbered §1785.3 by Stats 1973 ch 167 §4.

Former §1752, similar to present UCC §7501, was added Stats 1931 ch 1070 §1 and repealed Stats 1963 ch 819 §2, effective January 1, 1965.

§1753. Severability

If any provision of this title or the application thereof to any person or circumstance is held to be unconstitutional, the remainder of the title and the application of such provision to other persons or circumstances shall not be affected thereby. **Leg.H.** Added Stats 1970 ch 1550 §1.

Prior Law: Former §1753, similar to present §1785.15, was added Stats 1970 ch 1348 §1 and renumbered §1785.4 by Stats 1973 ch 167 §5.

Former §1753, similar to present UCC §7503, was added by Stats 1931 ch 1070 §1 and repealed Stats 1963 ch 819 §2, effective January 1, 1965.

Former §1753, relating to delivery on demand, was enacted 1872 and repealed Stats 1931 ch 1070 §1.

§1754. Transactions excluded

The provisions of this title shall not apply to any transaction which provides for the construction, sale, or construction and sale of an entire residence or all or part of a structure designed for commercial or industrial occupancy, with or without a parcel of real property or an interest therein, or for the sale of a lot or parcel of real property, including any site preparation incidental to such sale. **Leg.H.** Added Stats 1970 ch 1550 §1.

Prior Law: Former §1754, similar to present §1785.20, was added Stats 1970 ch 1348 §1, amended Stats 1972 ch 1422 §1, and renumbered §1785.5 by Stats 1973 ch 167 §6.

Former §1754, similar to present UCC §7504, was added Stats 1931 ch 1070 §1 and repealed Stats 1963 ch 819 §2, effective January 1, 1965.

Former §1754, relating to delivery of personal property, was enacted 1872 and repealed Stats 1931 ch 1070 §1.

§1755. Applicability to advertising media

Nothing in this title shall apply to the owners or employees of any advertising medium, including, but not limited to, newspapers, magazines, broadcast stations, billboards and transit ads, by whom any advertisement in violation of this title is published or disseminated, unless it is established that such owners or employees had knowledge of the deceptive methods, acts or practices declared to be unlawful by Section 1770. **Leg.H.** Added Stats 1970 ch 1550 §1.

Prior Law: Former §1755, similar to present §1785.16, was added Stats 1970 ch 1348 §1 and renumbered §1785.6 by Stats 1973 ch 167 §7.

Former §1755, similar to present UCC §7506, was added Stats 1931 ch 1070 §1 and repealed Stats 1963 ch 819 §2, effective January 1, 1965.

Former §1755, relating to the expense of transportation, was enacted 1872 and repealed Stats 1931 ch 1070 §1.

§1756. Applicability to pending legal actions

The substantive and procedural provisions of this title shall only apply to actions filed on or after January 1, 1971. **Leg.H.** Added Stats 1970 ch 1550 §1.

Prior Law: Former §1756, relating to grounds for civil or criminal proceedings, was added Stats 1970 ch 1348 §1 and renumbered §1785.7 by Stats 1973 ch 167 §8.

Former §1756, similar to present UCC §7507, was added Stats 1931 ch 1070 §1 and repealed Stats 1963 ch 819 §2, effective January 1, 1965.

Former §1756, relating to notice of election as to delivery, was enacted 1872 and repealed Stats 1931 ch 1070 §1.

§1757. [Section renumbered 1973]

Leg.H. Added Stats 1970 ch 1348 §1. Renumbered §1785.8 by Stats 1973 ch 167 §9. See CC §1785.35.

§§1758, 1759. [Sections repealed 1965]

Leg.H. Added Stats 1931 ch 1070 §1. Repealed Stats 1963 ch 819 §2, effective January 1, 1965. See UCC §§7501, 7502.

Prior Law: Former §1758, relating to delivery within reasonable hours, was enacted 1872 and repealed Stats 1931 ch 1070 §1.

CHAPTER 2
CONSTRUCTION AND DEFINITIONS

Construction. §1760.
Definitions. §1761.

§1760. Construction

This title shall be liberally construed and applied to promote its underlying purposes, which are to protect consumers against unfair and deceptive business practices and to provide efficient and economical procedures to secure such protection. **Leg.H.** Added Stats 1970 ch 1550 §1.

Prior Law: Former CC §1760, relating to creditors' remedies to reach negotiable documents, was added Stats 1931 ch 1070 §1 and repealed Stats 1963 ch 819 §2, effective January 1, 1965.

§1761. Definitions

As used in this title:

(a) "Goods" means tangible chattels bought or leased for use primarily for personal, family, or household purposes, including certificates or coupons exchangeable for these goods, and including goods that, at the time of the sale or subsequently, are to be so affixed to real property as to become a part of real property, whether or not they are severable from the real property.

(b) "Services" means work, labor, and services for other than a commercial or business use, including services furnished in connection with the sale or repair of goods.

(c) "Person" means an individual, partnership, corporation, limited liability company, association, or other group, however organized.

(d) "Consumer" means an individual who seeks or acquires, by purchase or lease, any goods or services for personal, family, or household purposes.

(e) "Transaction" means an agreement between a consumer and another person, whether or not the agreement is a contract enforceable by action, and includes the making of, and the performance pursuant to, that agreement.

(f) "Senior citizen" means a person who is 65 years of age or older.

(g) "Disabled person" means a person who has a physical or mental impairment that substantially limits one or more major life activities.

(1) As used in this subdivision, "physical or mental impairment" means any of the following:

(A) A physiological disorder or condition, cosmetic disfigurement, or anatomical loss substantially affecting one or more of the following body systems: neurological; musculoskeletal; special sense organs; respiratory, including speech organs; cardiovascular; reproductive; digestive; genito-urinary; hemic and lymphatic; skin; or endocrine.

(B) A mental or psychological disorder, including intellectual disability, organic brain syndrome, emotional or mental illness, and specific learning disabilities. "Physical or mental impairment" includes, but is not limited to, diseases and conditions that include orthopedic, visual, speech, and hearing impairment, cerebral palsy, epilepsy, muscular dystrophy, multiple sclerosis, cancer, heart disease, diabetes, intellectual disability, and emotional illness.

(2) "Major life activities" means functions that include caring for one's self, performing manual tasks, walking, seeing, hearing, speaking, breathing, learning, and working.

(h) "Home solicitation" means a transaction made at the consumer's primary residence, except those transactions initiated by the consumer. A consumer response to an advertisement is not a home solicitation. **Leg.H.** Added Stats 1970 ch 1550 §1. Amended Stats 1988 ch 823 §2; Stats 1994 ch 1010 §34 (SB 2053); Stats 1995 ch 255 §1 (SB 320); Stats 2006 ch 538 §44 (SB 1852), effective January 1, 2007; Stats 2012 ch 448 §4 (AB 2370), effective January 1, 2013, ch 457 §4 (SB 1381), effective January 1, 2013.

1995 Note: The provisions of this act shall be applicable to contracts entered into on or after January 1, 1996. Stats 1995 ch 255 §3.

Prior Law: Former §1761, similar to present UCC §§2301, 2507, 2607, was added Stats 1931 ch 1070 §1, and repealed Stats 1963 ch 819 §2, effective January 1, 1965.

§§1762–1769. [Sections repealed 1965]

Leg.H. Added Stats 1931 ch 1070 §1. Repealed Stats 1963 ch 819 §2, effective January 1, 1965. See UCC §§2106, 2307–2310, 2503, 2504, 2507, 2511–2513, 2601, 2606, 2607, 2612.

Prior Law: Former §§1763–1769, relating to warranties, were enacted 1872 and repealed Stats 1931 ch 1070 §1.

CHAPTER 3
DECEPTIVE PRACTICES

Unlawful acts and practices. § 1770.

§ 1770. Unlawful acts and practices

(a) The unfair methods of competition and unfair or deceptive acts or practices listed in this subdivision undertaken by any person in a transaction intended to result or that results in the sale or lease of goods or services to any consumer are unlawful:

(1) Passing off goods or services as those of another.

(2) Misrepresenting the source, sponsorship, approval, or certification of goods or services.

(3) Misrepresenting the affiliation, connection, or association with, or certification by, another.

(4) Using deceptive representations or designations of geographic origin in connection with goods or services.

(5) Representing that goods or services have sponsorship, approval, characteristics, ingredients, uses, benefits, or quantities that they do not have or that a person has a sponsorship, approval, status, affiliation, or connection that the person does not have.

(6) Representing that goods are original or new if they have deteriorated unreasonably or are altered, reconditioned, reclaimed, used, or secondhand.

(7) Representing that goods or services are of a particular standard, quality, or grade, or that goods are of a particular style or model, if they are of another.

(8) Disparaging the goods, services, or business of another by false or misleading representation of fact.

(9) Advertising goods or services with intent not to sell them as advertised.

(10) Advertising goods or services with intent not to supply reasonably expectable demand, unless the advertisement discloses a limitation of quantity.

(11) Advertising furniture without clearly indicating that it is unassembled if that is the case.

(12) Advertising the price of unassembled furniture without clearly indicating the assembled price of that furniture if the same furniture is available assembled from the seller.

(13) Making false or misleading statements of fact concerning reasons for, existence of, or amounts of, price reductions.

(14) Representing that a transaction confers or involves rights, remedies, or obligations that it does not have or involve, or that are prohibited by law.

(15) Representing that a part, replacement, or repair service is needed when it is not.

(16) Representing that the subject of a transaction has been supplied in accordance with a previous representation when it has not.

(17) Representing that the consumer will receive a rebate, discount, or other economic benefit, if the earning of the benefit is contingent on an event to occur subsequent to the consummation of the transaction.

(18) Misrepresenting the authority of a salesperson, representative, or agent to negotiate the final terms of a transaction with a consumer.

(19) Inserting an unconscionable provision in the contract.

(20) Advertising that a product is being offered at a specific price plus a specific percentage of that price unless (A) the total price is set forth in the advertisement, which may include, but is not limited to, shelf tags, displays, and media advertising, in a size larger than any other price in that advertisement, and (B) the specific price plus a specific percentage of that price represents a markup from the seller's costs or from the wholesale price of the product. This subdivision shall not apply to in-store advertising by businesses that are open only to members or cooperative organizations organized pursuant to Division 3 (commencing with Section 12000) of Title 1 of the Corporations Code if more than 50 percent of purchases are made at the specific price set forth in the advertisement.

(21) Selling or leasing goods in violation of Chapter 4 (commencing with Section 1797.8) of Title 1.7.

(22)(A) Disseminating an unsolicited prerecorded message by telephone without an unrecorded, natural voice first informing the person answering the telephone of the name of the caller or the organization being represented, and either the address or the telephone number of the caller, and without obtaining the consent of that person to listen to the prerecorded message.

(B) This subdivision does not apply to a message disseminated to a business associate, customer, or other person having an established relationship with the person or organization making the call, to a call for the purpose of collecting an existing obligation, or to any call generated at the request of the recipient.

(23)(A) The home solicitation, as defined in subdivision (h) of Section 1761, of a consumer who is a senior citizen where a loan or assessment is made encumbering the primary residence of that consumer for purposes of paying for home improvements and where the transaction is part of a pattern or practice in violation any of the following:

(i) Subsection (h) or (i) of Section 1639 of Title 15 of the United States Code.

(ii) Paragraph (1), (2), or (4) of subdivision (a) of Section 226.34 of Title 12 of the Code of Federal Regulations.

(iii) Section 22684, 22685, 22686, or 22687 of the Financial Code.

(iv) Section 5898.16, 5898.17, 5913, 5922, 5923, 5924, 5925, 5926, or 5940 of the Streets and Highways Code.

(B) A third party shall not be liable under this subdivision unless (i) there was an agency relationship between the party who engaged in home solicitation and the third party, or (ii) the third party had actual knowledge of, or participated in, the unfair or deceptive transaction. A third party who is a holder in due course under a home solicitation transaction shall not be liable under this subdivision.

(24)(A) Charging or receiving an unreasonable fee to prepare, aid, or advise any prospective applicant, applicant, or recipient in the procurement, maintenance, or securing of public social services.

(B) For purposes of this paragraph:

(i) "Public social services" means those activities and functions of state and local government administered or supervised by the State Department of Health Care Services, the State Department of Public Health, or the State Department of Social Services, and involved in providing aid or services, or both, including health care services, and medical assistance, to those persons who, because of their economic circumstances or social condition, are in need of that aid or those services and may benefit from them.

(ii) "Public social services" also includes activities and functions administered or supervised by the United States Department of Veterans Affairs or the California Department of Veterans Affairs involved in providing aid or services, or both, to veterans, including pension benefits.

(iii) "Unreasonable fee" means a fee that is exorbitant and disproportionate to the services performed. Factors to be considered, if appropriate, in determining the reasonableness of a fee, are based on the circumstances existing at the time of the service and shall include, but not be limited to, all of the following:

(I) The time and effort required.

(II) The novelty and difficulty of the services.

(III) The skill required to perform the services.

(IV) The nature and length of the professional relationship.

(V) The experience, reputation, and ability of the person providing the services.

(C) This paragraph shall not apply to attorneys licensed to practice law in California, who are subject to the California Rules of Professional Conduct and to the mandatory fee arbitration provisions of Article 13 (commencing with Section 6200) of Chapter 4 of Division 3 of the Business and Professions Code, when the fees charged or received are for providing representation in administrative agency appeal proceedings or court proceedings for purposes of procuring, maintaining, or securing public social services on behalf of a person or group of persons.

(25)(A) Advertising or promoting any event, presentation, seminar, workshop, or other public gathering regarding veterans' benefits or entitlements that does not include the following statement in the same type size and font as the term "veteran" or any variation of that term:

(i) "I am not authorized to file an initial application for Veterans' Aid and Attendance benefits on your behalf, or to represent you before the

Board of Veterans' Appeals within the United States Department of Veterans Affairs in any proceeding on any matter, including an application for those benefits. It would be illegal for me to accept a fee for preparing that application on your behalf." The requirements of this clause do not apply to a person licensed to act as an agent or attorney in proceedings before the Agency of Original Jurisdiction and the Board of Veterans' Appeals within the United States Department of Veterans Affairs when that person is offering those services at the advertised event.

(ii) The statement in clause (i) shall also be disseminated, both orally and in writing, at the beginning of any event, presentation, seminar, workshop, or public gathering regarding veterans' benefits or entitlements.

(B) Advertising or promoting any event, presentation, seminar, workshop, or other public gathering regarding veterans' benefits or entitlements that is not sponsored by, or affiliated with, the United States Department of Veterans Affairs, the California Department of Veterans Affairs, or any other congressionally chartered or recognized organization of honorably discharged members of the Armed Forces of the United States, or any of their auxiliaries that does not include the following statement, in the same type size and font as the term "veteran" or the variation of that term:

"This event is not sponsored by, or affiliated with, the United States Department of Veterans Affairs, the California Department of Veterans Affairs, or any other congressionally chartered or recognized organization of honorably discharged members of the Armed Forces of the United States, or any of their auxiliaries. None of the insurance products promoted at this sales event are endorsed by those organizations, all of which offer free advice to veterans about how to qualify and apply for benefits."

(i) The statement in this subparagraph shall be disseminated, both orally and in writing, at the beginning of any event, presentation, seminar, workshop, or public gathering regarding veterans' benefits or entitlements.

(ii) The requirements of this subparagraph shall not apply in a case where the United States Department of Veterans Affairs, the California Department of Veterans Affairs, or other congressionally chartered or recognized organization of honorably discharged members of the Armed Forces of the United States, or any of their auxiliaries have granted written permission to the advertiser or promoter for the use of its name, symbol, or insignia to advertise or promote the event, presentation, seminar, workshop, or other public gathering.

(26) Advertising, offering for sale, or selling a financial product that is illegal under state or federal law, including any cash payment for the assignment to a third party of the consumer's right to receive future pension or veteran's benefits.

(27) Representing that a product is made in California by using a Made in California label created pursuant to Section 12098.10 of the Government Code, unless the product complies with Section 12098.10 of the Government Code.

(28)(A) Failing to include either of the following in a solicitation by a covered person, or an entity acting on behalf of a covered person, to a consumer for a consumer financial product or service:

(i) The name of the covered person, and, if applicable, the entity acting on behalf of the covered person, and relevant contact information, including a mailing address and telephone number.

(ii)(I) The following disclosure statement in at least 18-point bold type and in the language in which [1] **a solicitation described by this paragraph** is drafted: "This is an advertisement. You are not required to make any payment or take any other action in response to this offer."

(II)(ia) The disclosure statement described in subclause (I) shall appear in at least 16-point bold type on the front of an envelope that contains a solicitation described by this paragraph.

(ib) This subclause applies only to solicitations made by physical mail.

(B) For purposes of this paragraph:

(i) "Consumer financial product or service" has the same meaning as defined in Section 90005 of the Financial Code.

(ii)(I) "Covered person" has the same meaning as defined in Section 90005 of the Financial Code.

(II) "Covered person" does not mean an entity exempt from Division 24 (commencing with Section 90000) of the Financial Code pursuant to Section 90002 of the Financial Code.

(iii) "Solicitation" means an advertisement or marketing communication through writing or graphics that is directed to, or likely to give the impression of being directed to, an individually identified person, residence, or business location. "Solicitation" does not include any of the following:

(I) Communication through a mass advertisement, including in a catalog, on a radio or television broadcast, or on a publicly accessible internet website, if that communication is not directed to, or is not likely to give the impression of being directed to, an individually identified person, residence, or business location.

(II) Communication via a telephone, mail, or electronic communication that was initiated by a consumer.

(III) A written credit or insurance solicitation that is subject to the disclosure requirements of subsection (d) of Section 1681m of Title 15 of the United States Code.

(29)(A) Advertising, displaying, or offering a price for a good or service that does not include all mandatory fees or charges other than either of the following:

(i) Taxes or fees imposed by a government on the transaction.

(ii) Postage or carriage charges that will be reasonably and actually incurred to ship the physical good to the consumer.

(B) Compliance by a person providing broadband internet access service on its own or as part of a bundle, as defined in Section 8.1(b) of Title 47 of the Code of Federal Regulations, with the broadband consumer label requirements adopted by the Federal Communications Commission in FCC 22-86 on November 14, 2022, codified in Section 8.1(a) of Title 47 of the Code of Federal Regulations, shall be deemed compliance with this paragraph.

(C)(i) For purposes of this subparagraph, "financial entity" means an entity that is exempt from Division 24 (commencing with Section 90000) of the Financial Code pursuant to Section 90002 of the Financial Code.

(ii) A financial entity that is required to provide disclosures in compliance with any of the following federal or state acts or regulations with respect to a financial transaction is exempt from this paragraph for purposes of that financial transaction:

(I) The federal Truth in Savings Act, as amended (12 U.S.C. Sec. 4301 et seq.).

(II) The federal Electronic Fund Transfer Act, as amended (15 U.S.C. Sec. 1693 et seq.).

(III) Section 19 of the Federal Reserve Act, as amended (12 U.S.C. Sec. 461 et seq.).

(IV) The federal Truth in Lending Act, as amended (15 U.S.C. Sec. 1601 et seq.).

(V) The federal Real Estate Settlement Procedures Act, as amended (12 U.S.C. Sec. 2601 et seq.).

(VI) The federal Home Ownership and Equity Protection Act (15 U.S.C. Sec. 1639).

(VII) Any regulation adopted pursuant to any of the federal acts in subclauses (I) to (VI), inclusive.

(VIII) The California Financing Law (Division 9 (commencing with Section 22000) of the Financial Code).

(IX) The California Residential Mortgage Lending Act (Division 20 (commencing with Section 50000) of the Financial Code).

(X) The Real Estate Law (Part 1 (commencing with Section 10000) of Division 4 of the Business and Professions Code).

(XI) Any regulation adopted pursuant to any of the state acts in subclauses (VIII) to (X), inclusive.

(D)(i) Subject to clause (ii), this paragraph does not apply to a mandatory fee or charge for individual food or beverage items sold directly to a customer by a restaurant, bar, food concession, grocery store, or grocery delivery service, or by means of a menu or contract for banquet or catering services that fully discloses the terms of service.

(ii) A mandatory fee or charge under clause (i) shall be clearly and conspicuously displayed, with an explanation of its purpose, on any advertisement, menu, or other display that contains the price of the food or beverage item.

(iii) "Grocery delivery service" means a company owned by, or under contract with, a grocery store or distributor that delivers food, primarily fresh produce, meat, poultry, fish, deli products, dairy products, perishable beverages, baked foods, and prepared foods, from the grocery store or distributor to a consumer.

(iv) The exemption in this subparagraph does not apply to a "third-party food delivery platform," as defined in Section 113930.5 of the Health and Safety Code, or any other food delivery platform.

(b)(1) It is an unfair or deceptive act or practice for a mortgage broker or lender, directly or indirectly, to use a home improvement contractor to negotiate the terms of any loan that is secured, whether in whole or in part, by the residence of the borrower and that is used to finance a home improvement contract or any portion of a home improvement contract. For purposes of this subdivision, "mortgage broker or lender" includes a finance lender licensed pursuant to the California Financing Law (Division 9 (commencing with Section 22000) of the Financial Code), a residential mortgage lender licensed pursuant to the California Residential Mortgage Lending Act (Division 20 (commencing with Section 50000) of the Financial Code), or a real estate broker licensed under the Real Estate Law (Division 4 (commencing with Section 10000) of the Business and Professions Code).

(2) This section shall not be construed to either authorize or prohibit a home improvement contractor from referring a consumer to a mortgage broker or lender by this subdivision. However, a home improvement contractor may refer a consumer to a mortgage lender or broker if that referral does not violate Section 7157 of the Business and Professions Code or any other law. A mortgage lender or broker may purchase an executed home improvement contract if that purchase does not violate Section 7157 of the Business and Professions Code or any other law. Nothing in this paragraph shall have any effect on the application of Chapter 1 (commencing with Section 1801) of Title 2 to a home improvement transaction or the financing of a home improvement transaction.

(c) As of July 1, 2025, any disclosure, advertisement, or notice that is required to be "clearly" or "clearly and conspicuously" made must have text that is "clear and conspicuous," as defined in subdivision (u) of Section 1791.

(d) This section shall become operative on July 1, 2024. **Leg.H.** Added Stats 2023 ch 400 §3 (SB 478), effective January 1, 2024, operative July 1, 2024. Stats 2024 ch 20 §1 (SB 1096), effective January 1, 2025; Stats 2024 ch 43 §1 (SB 1524), effective June 29, 2024, operative July 1, 2024; Stats 2024 ch 853 §12 (AB 3281), effective January 1, 2025 (ch 853 prevails).

§ 1770. 2024 Deletes. [1] the solicitation

Prior Law: Former CC §1770, similar to the present section, was added Stats 1970 ch 1550 §1, and amended Stats 1975 ch 379 §1, Stats 1979 ch 819 §4, Stats 1984 ch 1171 §1, Stats 1986 ch 1497 §1, Stats 1990 ch 1641 §1 (AB 4084), Stats 1995 ch 255 §2 (SB 320), Stats 1996 ch 684 §1 (SB 2045), Stats 2008 ch 479 §1 (SB 1136), Stats 2009 ch 140 §26 (AB 1164), Stats 2011 ch 79 §1 (SB 180), Stats 2012 ch 653 §1 (SB 1170), Stats 2013 ch 541 §1 (SB 12), Stats 2015 ch 246 §1 (SB 386), Stats 2016 ch 86 §19 (SB 1171), Stats 2019 ch 143 §14 (SB 251), Stats 2021 ch 589 §1 (AB 790), Stats 2022 ch 324 §1 (AB 1904), Stats 2023 ch 400 §2 (SB 478), and repealed July 1, 2024 by its own terms.

§§1771–1779.   [Sections repealed 1965]

Leg.H. Added Stats 1931 ch 1070 §1. Repealed Stats 1963 ch 819 §2, effective January 1, 1965. See UCC §§2503, 2609, 2702, 2705.

Prior Law: Former §§1771–1778, relating to merchandise inaccessible to examination of buyer, trademarks, and warranties, were enacted 1872, amended Code Amdts 1873–74 ch 612 §198, and repealed Stats 1931 ch 1070 §1.

CHAPTER 4
REMEDIES AND PROCEDURES

Action for damages and other relief; Additional remedy for senior citizens and disabled persons; Treble damages for charging unreasonable fee to assist applicant or recipient in securing public social services; Venue; Court costs and attorney's fees. §1780.
Class actions. §1781.
Prerequisites to commencement of action. §1782.
Limitation of actions. §1783.
Defenses. §1784.

§1780.   Action for damages and other relief; Additional remedy for senior citizens and disabled persons; Treble damages for charging unreasonable fee to assist applicant or recipient in securing public social services; Venue; Court costs and attorney's fees

(a) Any consumer who suffers any damage as a result of the use or employment by any person of a method, act, or practice declared to be unlawful by Section 1770 may bring an action against that person to recover or obtain any of the following:

(1) Actual damages, but in no case shall the total award of damages in a class action be less than one thousand dollars ($1,000).

(2) An order enjoining the methods, acts, or practices.

(3) Restitution of property.

(4) Punitive damages.

(5) Any other relief that the court deems proper.

(b)(1) Any consumer who is a senior citizen or a disabled person, as defined in subdivisions (f) and (g) of Section 1761, as part of an action under subdivision (a), may seek and be awarded, in addition to the remedies specified therein, up to five thousand dollars ($5,000) where the trier of fact does all of the following:

(A) Finds that the consumer has suffered substantial physical, emotional, or economic damage resulting from the defendant's conduct.

(B) Makes an affirmative finding in regard to one or more of the factors set forth in subdivision (b) of Section 3345.

(C) Finds that an additional award is appropriate.

(2) Judgment in a class action by senior citizens or disabled persons under Section 1781 may award each class member that additional award if the trier of fact has made the foregoing findings.

(c) Whenever it is proven by a preponderance of the evidence that a defendant has engaged in conduct in violation of paragraph (24) of subdivision (a) of Section 1770, in addition to all other remedies otherwise provided in this section, the court shall award treble actual damages to the plaintiff. This subdivision shall not apply to attorneys licensed to practice law in California, who are subject to the California Rules of Professional Conduct and to the mandatory fee arbitration provisions of Article 13 (commencing with Section 6200) of Chapter 4 of Division 3 of the Business and Professions Code, when the fees charged or received are for providing representation in administrative agency appeal proceedings or court proceedings for purposes of procuring, maintaining, or securing public social services on behalf of a person or group of persons.

(d) An action under subdivision (a) or (b) may be commenced in the county in which the person against whom it is brought resides, has his or her principal place of business, or is doing business, or in the county where the transaction or any substantial portion thereof occurred.

In any action subject to this section, concurrently with the filing of the complaint, the plaintiff shall file an affidavit stating facts showing that the action has been commenced in a county described in this section as a proper place for the trial of the action. If a plaintiff fails to file the affidavit required by this section, the court shall, upon its own motion or upon motion of any party, dismiss the action without prejudice.

(e) The court shall award court costs and attorney's fees to a prevailing plaintiff in litigation filed pursuant to this section. Reasonable attorney's fees may be awarded to a prevailing defendant upon a finding by the court that the plaintiff's prosecution of the action was not in good faith. **Leg.H.** Added Stats 1970 ch 1550 §1. Amended Stats 1988 ch 823 §3, ch 1343 §2; Stats 1998 ch 931 §15 (SB 2139), effective September 28, 1998; Stats 2003 ch 449 §3 (AB 1712); Stats 2008 ch 479 §2 (SB 1136), effective January 1, 2009; Stats 2009 ch 140 §27 (AB 1164), effective January 1, 2010.

Prior Law: Former §1780, similar to present UCC §2706, was added Stats 1931 ch 1070 §1 and repealed Stats 1963 ch 819 §2, effective January 1, 1965.

§1781.   Class actions

(a) Any consumer entitled to bring an action under Section 1780 may, if the unlawful method, act, or practice has caused damage to other consumers similarly situated, bring an action on behalf of himself and such other consumers to recover damages or obtain other relief as provided for in Section 1780.

(b) The court shall permit the suit to be maintained on behalf of all members of the represented class if all of the following conditions exist:

(1) It is impracticable to bring all members of the class before the court.

(2) The questions of law or fact common to the class are substantially similar and predominate over the questions affecting the individual members.

(3) The claims or defenses of the representative plaintiffs are typical of the claims or defenses of the class.

(4) The representative plaintiffs will fairly and adequately protect the interests of the class.

(c) If notice of the time and place of the hearing is served upon the other parties at least 10 days prior thereto, the court shall hold a hearing, upon motion of any party to the action which is supported by affidavit of any person or persons having knowledge of the facts, to determine if any of the following apply to the action:

(1) A class action pursuant to subdivision (b) is proper.

(2) Published notice pursuant to subdivision (d) is necessary to adjudicate the claims of the class.

(3) The action is without merit or there is no defense to the action.

A motion based upon Section 437c of the Code of Civil Procedure shall not be granted in any action commenced as a class action pursuant to subdivision (a).

(d) If the action is permitted as a class action, the court may direct either party to notify each member of the class of the action. The party required to serve notice may, with the consent of the court, if personal notification is unreasonably expensive or it appears that all members of the class cannot be notified personally, give notice as prescribed herein by publication in accordance with Section 6064 of the Government Code in a newspaper of general circulation in the county in which the transaction occurred.

(e) The notice required by subdivision (d) shall include the following:

(1) The court will exclude the member notified from the class if he so requests by a specified date.

(2) The judgment, whether favorable or not, will include all members who do not request exclusion.

(3) Any member who does not request exclusion, may, if he desires, enter an appearance through counsel.

(f) A class action shall not be dismissed, settled, or compromised without the approval of the court, and notice of the proposed dismissal, settlement, or compromise shall be given in such manner as the court directs to each member who was given notice pursuant to subdivision (d) and did not request exclusion.

(g) The judgment in a class action shall describe those to whom the notice was directed and who have not requested exclusion and those the court finds to be members of the class. The best possible notice of the judgment shall be given in such manner as the court directs to each member who was personally served with notice pursuant to subdivision (d) and did not request exclusion. **Leg.H.** Added Stats 1970 ch 1550 §1.

Prior Law: Former §1781, relating to when and how the seller may rescind the sale, was added Stats 1931 ch 1070 §1 and repealed Stats 1963 ch 819 §2, effective January 1, 1965.

§1782. Prerequisites to commencement of action

(a) Thirty days or more prior to the commencement of an action for damages pursuant to this title, the consumer shall do the following:

(1) Notify the person alleged to have employed or committed methods, acts, or practices declared unlawful by Section 1770 of the particular alleged violations of Section 1770.

(2) Demand that the person correct, repair, replace, or otherwise rectify the goods or services alleged to be in violation of Section 1770.

The notice shall be in writing and shall be sent by certified or registered mail, return receipt requested, to the place where the transaction occurred or to the person's principal place of business within California.

(b) Except as provided in subdivision (c), no action for damages may be maintained under Section 1780 if an appropriate correction, repair, replacement, or other remedy is given, or agreed to be given within a reasonable time, to the consumer within 30 days after receipt of the notice.

(c) No action for damages may be maintained under Section 1781 upon a showing by a person alleged to have employed or committed methods, acts, or practices declared unlawful by Section 1770 that all of the following exist:

(1) All consumers similarly situated have been identified, or a reasonable effort to identify such other consumers has been made.

(2) All consumers so identified have been notified that upon their request the person shall make the appropriate correction, repair, replacement, or other remedy of the goods and services.

(3) The correction, repair, replacement, or other remedy requested by the consumers has been, or, in a reasonable time, shall be, given.

(4) The person has ceased from engaging, or if immediate cessation is impossible or unreasonably expensive under the circumstances, the person will, within a reasonable time, cease to engage, in the methods, act, or practices.

(d) An action for injunctive relief brought under the specific provisions of Section 1770 may be commenced without compliance with subdivision (a). Not less than 30 days after the commencement of an action for injunctive relief, and after compliance with subdivision (a), the consumer may amend his or her complaint without leave of court to include a request for damages. The appropriate provisions of subdivision (b) or (c) shall be applicable if the complaint for injunctive relief is amended to request damages.

(e) Attempts to comply with this section by a person receiving a demand shall be construed to be an offer to compromise and shall be inadmissible as evidence pursuant to Section 1152 of the Evidence Code. Furthermore, these attempts to comply with a demand shall not be considered an admission of engaging in an act or practice declared unlawful by Section 1770. Evidence of compliance or attempts to comply with this section may be introduced by a defendant for the purpose of establishing good faith or to show compliance with this section. **Leg.H.** Added Stats 1970 ch 1550 §1. Amended Stats 1999 ch 1000 §10 (SB 284).

Prior Law: Former §1782, similar to present UCC §7502, was added Stats 1931 ch 1070 §1 and repealed Stats 1963 ch 819 §2, effective January 1, 1965.

§1783. Limitation of actions

Any action brought under the specific provisions of Section 1770 shall be commenced not more than three years from the date of the commission of such method, act, or practice. **Leg.H.** Added Stats 1970 ch 1550 §1.

Prior Law: Former §1783, similar to present UCC §§2609, 2610, 2704, 2709, was added Stats 1931 ch 1070 §1 and repealed Stats 1963 ch 819 §2, effective January 1, 1965.

§1784. Defenses

No award of damages may be given in any action based on a method, act, or practice declared to be unlawful by Section 1770 if the person alleged to have employed or committed such method, act, or practice (a) proves that such violation was not intentional and resulted from a bona fide error notwithstanding the use of reasonable procedures adopted to avoid any such error and (b) makes an appropriate correction, repair or replacement or other remedy of the goods and services according to the provisions of subdivisions (b) and (c) of Section 1782. **Leg.H.** Added Stats 1970 ch 1550 §1.

Prior Law: Former §1784, similar to present UCC §§2704, 2708, 2710, was added Stats 1931 ch 1070 §1 and repealed Stats 1963 ch 819 §2, effective January 1, 1965.

§1785. [Section repealed 1965]

Leg.H. Added Stats 1931 ch 1070 §1. Repealed Stats 1963 ch 819 §2, effective January 1, 1965. See UCC §2610.

Prior Law: Former §1785, relating to right to inspect goods, was enacted 1872 and repealed Stats 1931 ch 1070 §1.

TITLE 1.5A
VEHICLE HISTORY REPORTS

Required contents of report; Duties of report providers. § 1784.1.

§ 1784.1. Required contents of report; Duties of report providers

(a) For purposes of this section, the following definitions apply:

(1) "Affiliate" means any person or persons controlling, controlled by, or under common control with, other persons.

(2) "Dealer" has the same meaning as in Section 285 of the Vehicle Code.

(3) "Vehicle" has the same meaning as in Section 670 of the Vehicle Code.

(4) "Vehicle history database" means a database from which a person may obtain vehicle history information specific to a vehicle identification number (VIN).

(5) "Vehicle history report provider" means an entity that generates vehicle history reports from a vehicle history database that are provided directly to consumers for the purpose of selling or purchasing a vehicle. "Vehicle history report provider" does not include a dealer that obtains a vehicle history report from a third party that is not an affiliate of the dealer and who then communicates the vehicle history report without altering the vehicle history information therein.

(6) "Vehicle history information" includes, but is not limited to, any of the following related to a vehicle:

(A) Accident or damage information.
(B) The number of previous owners.
(C) Information regarding service or maintenance history.
(D) Odometer reading.

(7) "Vehicle history report" means any written or electronic communication of vehicle history information made by a vehicle history report provider that is made available to consumers.

(b)(1) Every vehicle history report shall clearly and conspicuously disclose the vehicle history report provider's contact information by which an owner can submit an inquiry regarding the vehicle history information contained in a vehicle history report, including a request for a vehicle history report provider to research and address any potential discrepancies found within the vehicle history report.

(2) A vehicle history report provider shall confirm receipt of a California resident's inquiry under paragraph (1) promptly, within three days of receipt. The confirmation shall include a means to obtain regular updates until the request is completed.

(3) A vehicle history report provider shall use reasonable efforts to complete the inquiry within 14 days from the date it was received. If there is a delay in completing the inquiry that is beyond the reasonable control of the vehicle history report provider, the 14-day requirement is waived and the vehicle history report provider shall promptly notify the consumer of the delay no later than the 15th day from the date the inquiry was received and shall provide the requester weekly updates thereafter until the inquiry is completed.

(c) Any attempted waiver of the provisions of this section is contrary to public policy, and is void and unenforceable.

(d) This section does not relieve any party of its responsibilities under Section 11713.26 of the Vehicle Code. To the extent that a provision of this section conflicts with Section 11713.26 of the Vehicle Code, Section 11713.26 of the Vehicle Code shall control. **Leg.H.** Added Stats 2022 ch 863 §1 (AB 1871), effective January 1, 2023.

TITLE 1.6
CONSUMER CREDIT REPORTING AGENCIES ACT

Chapter 1. General Provisions.
Chapter 2. Obligations of Consumer Credit Reporting Agencies.
Chapter 3. Requirements on Users of Consumer Credit Reports.
Chapter 3.5. Obligations of Furnishers of Credit Information.
Chapter 3.6. Escrow Agent Rating Service [Repealed effective January 1, 2027].
Chapter 4. Remedies.

CHAPTER 1
GENERAL PROVISIONS

Legislative findings and declarations. §1785.1.
Citation of Act. §1785.2.
Definitions. §1785.3.
Persons to whom title not applicable. §1785.4.
Application to persons dealing in information on checking account experiences. §1785.5.
Application of provisions regarding notices and disclosures. §1785.6.

§1785.1. Legislative findings and declarations

The Legislature finds and declares as follows:

(a) An elaborate mechanism has been developed for investigating and evaluating the credit worthiness, credit standing, credit capacity, and general reputation of consumers.

(b) Consumer credit reporting agencies have assumed a vital role in assembling and evaluating consumer credit and other information on consumers.

(c) There is a need to insure that consumer credit reporting agencies exercise their grave responsibilities with fairness, impartiality, and a respect for the consumer's right to privacy.

(d) It is the purpose of this title to require that consumer credit reporting agencies adopt reasonable procedures for meeting the needs of commerce for consumer credit, personnel, insurance, hiring of a dwelling unit, and other information in a manner which is fair and equitable to the consumer, with regard to the confidentiality, accuracy, relevancy, and proper utilization of such information in accordance with the requirements of this title.

(e) The Legislature hereby intends to regulate consumer credit reporting agencies pursuant to this title in a manner which will best protect the interests of the people of the State of California.

(f) The extension of credit is a privilege and not a right. Nothing in this title shall preclude a creditor from denying credit to any applicant providing such denial is based on factors not inconsistent with present law.

(g) Any clauses in contracts which prohibit any action required by this title are not in the public interest and shall be considered unenforceable. This shall not invalidate the other terms of such a contract. **Leg.H.** Added Stats 1975 ch 1271 §1. Amended Stats 1976 ch 666 §1; Stats 1982 ch 1127 §1.

Prior Law: Former §1785.1, similar to present §1785.2, was added Stats 1970 ch 1348 §1 as §1750, renumbered by Stats 1973 ch 167 §2, and repealed Stats 1975 ch 1271 §2.

§1785.2. Citation of Act

This act may be referred to as the Consumer Credit Reporting Agencies Act. **Leg.H.** Added Stats 1975 ch 1271 §1.

Prior Law: Former §1785.2, similar to present §1785.3, was added Stats 1970 ch 1348 §1as §1751, renumbered by Stats 1973 ch 167 §3, and repealed Stats 1975 ch 1271 §2.

§1785.3. Definitions

The following terms as used in this title have the meaning expressed in this section:

(a) "Adverse action" means a denial or revocation of credit, a change in the terms of an existing credit arrangement which is adverse to the interests of the consumer, or a refusal to grant credit in substantially the amount or on substantially the terms requested. "Adverse action" includes all of the following:

(1) Any denial of, increase in any charge for, or reduction in the amount of, insurance for personal, family, or household purposes made in connection with the underwriting of insurance.

(2) Any denial of employment or any other decision made for employment purposes which adversely affects any current or prospective employee.

(3) Any action taken, or determination made, with respect to a consumer (A) for an application for an extension of credit, or an application for the hiring of a dwelling unit, and (B) that is adverse to the interests of the consumer.

"Adverse action" does not include (A) a refusal to extend additional credit to a consumer under an existing credit arrangement if (i) the applicant is delinquent or otherwise in default under that credit arrangement or (ii) the additional credit would exceed a credit limit previously established for the consumer or (B) a refusal or failure to authorize an account transaction at a point of sale.

(b) "Consumer" means a natural individual.

(c) "Consumer credit report" means any written, oral, or other communication of any information by a consumer credit reporting agency bearing on a consumer's credit worthiness, credit standing, or credit capacity, which is used or is expected to be used, or collected in whole or in part, for the purpose of serving as a factor in establishing the consumer's eligibility for: (1) credit to be used primarily for personal, family, or household purposes, or (2) employment purposes, or (3) hiring of a dwelling unit, as defined in subdivision (c) of Section 1940, or (4) other purposes authorized in Section 1785.11.

The term does not include (1) any report containing information solely as to transactions or experiences between the consumer and the person making the report, (2) any communication of that information or information from a credit application by a consumer that is internal within the organization that is the person making the report or that is made to an entity owned by, or affiliated by corporate control with, that person; provided that the consumer is informed by means of a clear and conspicuous written disclosure that information contained in the credit application may be provided to these persons; however, where a credit application is taken by telephone, disclosure shall initially be given orally at the time the application is taken, and a clear and conspicuous written disclosure shall be made to the consumer in the first written communication to that consumer after the application is taken, (3) any authorization or approval of a specific extension of credit directly or indirectly by the issuer of a credit card or similar device, (4) any report by a person conveying a decision whether to make a specific extension of credit directly or indirectly to a consumer in response to a request by a third party, if the third party advises the consumer of the name and address of the person to whom the request was made and the person makes the disclosures to the consumer required under Section 1785.20, (5) any report containing information solely on a consumer's character, general reputation, personal characteristics, or mode of living which is obtained through personal interviews with neighbors, friends, or associates of the consumer reported on, or others with whom [1] the consumer is acquainted or who may have knowledge concerning those items of information, (6) any communication about a consumer in connection with a credit transaction which is not initiated by the consumer, between persons who are affiliated (as defined in Section 150 of the Corporations Code) by common ownership or common corporate control (as defined by Section 160 of the Corporations Code), if either of those persons has complied with paragraph (2) of subdivision (b) of Section 1785.20.1 with respect to a prequalifying report from which the information communicated is taken and provided the consumer has consented to the provision and use of the prequalifying report in writing, or (7) any consumer credit report furnished for use in connection with a transaction which consists of an extension of credit to be used solely for a commercial purpose.

(d) "Consumer credit reporting agency" means any person who, for monetary fees, dues, or on a cooperative nonprofit basis, regularly engages in whole or in part in the business of assembling or evaluating consumer credit information or other information on consumers for the purpose of furnishing consumer credit reports to third parties, but does not include any governmental agency whose records are maintained primarily for traffic safety, law enforcement, or licensing purposes.

(e) "Credit transaction that is not initiated by the consumer" does not include the use of a consumer credit report by an assignee for collection or by a person with which the consumer has an account for purposes of (1) reviewing the account or (2) collecting the account. For purposes of this subdivision, "reviewing the account" includes activities related to account maintenance and monitoring, credit line increases, and account upgrades and enhancements.

(f) "Employment purposes," when used in connection with a consumer credit report, means a report used for the purpose of evaluating a consumer for employment, promotion, reassignment, or retention as an employee.

(g) "File," when used in connection with information on any consumer, means all of the information on that consumer recorded and retained by a consumer credit reporting agency, regardless of how the information is stored.

(h) "Firm offer of credit" means any offer of credit to a consumer that will be honored if, based on information in a consumer credit report on the consumer and other information bearing on the creditworthiness of the consumer, the consumer is determined to meet the criteria used to select the consumer for the offer and the consumer is able to provide any real property collateral specified in the offer. For purposes of this subdivision, the phrase "other information bearing on the creditworthiness of the consumer" means information that the person making the offer is permitted to consider pursuant to any rule, regulation, or formal written policy statement relating to the federal Fair Credit Reporting Act, as amended (15 U.S.C. Sec. 1681 et seq.), promulgated by the Federal Trade Commission or any federal bank regulatory agency.

(i) "Item of information" means any of one or more informative entries in a credit report which causes a creditor to deny credit to an applicant or increase the cost of credit to an applicant or deny an applicant a checking account with a bank or other financial institution.

(j)(1) **"Medical debt" means a debt owed by a consumer to a person whose primary business is providing medical services, products, or devices, or to the person's agent or assignee, for the provision of medical services, products, or devices. Medical debt includes, but is not limited to, medical bills that are not past due or that have been paid.**

(2) **For the purposes of this subdivision, "medical service, product, or device" does not include cosmetic surgery, as defined in Section 1367.63 of the Health and Safety Code, and includes, but is not limited to, all of the following:**

(A) **Any service, drug, medication, product, or device sold, offered, or provided to a patient by either of the following:**

(i) **A person or facility licensed under Division 2 (commencing with Section 1200) of the Health and Safety Code, except for Chapters 3.35 (commencing with Section 1596.60) to 3.65 (commencing with Section 1597.70), inclusive, of that division.**

(ii) **A person licensed under Division 2 (commencing with Section 500) of the Business and Professions Code, except for Chapter 11 (commencing with Section 4800) of that division.**

(B) **Initial or subsequent reconstructive surgeries, as defined in Section 1367.63 of the Health and Safety Code, and followup care deemed necessary by the attending physician and surgeon.**

(C) **Initial or subsequent prosthetic devices, as defined in Section 1367.635 of the Health and Safety Code, and followup care deemed necessary by the attending physician and surgeon.**

(D) **A mastectomy, as defined in Section 1367.635 of the Health and Safety Code.**

[2] (k) "Person" means any individual, partnership, corporation, trust, estate, cooperative, association, government or governmental subdivision or agency, or other entity.

[3] (*l*) "Prequalifying report" means a report containing the limited information permitted under paragraph (2) of subdivision (b) of Section 1785.11.

[4] (m) "State or local child support enforcement agency" means the Department of Child Support Services or local child support agency acting pursuant to Division 17 (commencing with Section 17000) of the Family Code to establish, enforce or modify child support obligations, and any state or local agency or official that succeeds to these responsibilities under a successor statute. **Leg.H.** Added Stats 1975 ch 1271 §1. Amended Stats 1976 ch 666 §2; Stats 1982 ch 1127 §2; Stats 1990 ch 1144 §1 (SB 2751); Stats 1992 ch 1194 §1 (AB 1629), operative July 1, 1993; Stats 1993 ch 285 §1 (AB 1340), effective July 30, 1993; Stats 1994 ch 225 §1 (SB 1483) (ch 225 prevails), ch 1010 §35 (SB 2053); Stats 2000 ch 808 §3 (AB 1358), effective September 28, 2000; Stats 2024 ch 520 §1 (SB 1061), effective January 1, 2025.

§1785.3. 2024 Deletes. [1] he [2] (j) [3] (k) [4] (l)

Prior Law: Former §1785.3, similar to present §1785.10, was added Stats 1970 ch 1348 §1 as §1752, renumbered by Stats 1973 ch 167 §4, and repealed Stats 1975 ch 1271 §2.

§1785.4. Persons to whom title not applicable

Nothing in this title shall apply to any person licensed pursuant to the provisions of Chapter 11 (commencing with Section 7500) of Division 3 of the Business and Professions Code, or to any employee of such person, unless such person is employed directly by a consumer credit reporting agency. **Leg.H.** Added Stats 1975 ch 1271 §1.

Prior Law: Former §1785.4, similar to present §1785.15, was added Stats 1970 ch 1348 §1 as §1753, renumbered by Stats 1973 ch 167 §5, and repealed Stats 1975 ch 1271 §2.

§1785.5. Application to persons dealing in information on checking account experiences

Any person who, for monetary fees, dues, or on a cooperative nonprofit basis, regularly engages in whole or in part in the practice of assembling, evaluating, or disseminating information on the checking account experiences of consumer customers of banks or other financial institutions is, with the exception of compliance with the requirements of Section 1785.10, subdivisions (c), (d), and (e), only with regard to the provision of the address and telephone number, subject to the same laws which govern consumer credit reporting agencies. **Leg.H.** Added Stats 1990 ch 1144 §2 (SB2751). Amended Stats 2001 ch 236 §1 (AB 488), operative January 1, 2003.

Prior Law: Former §1785.5, similar to present §1785.20, was added Stats 1970 ch 1348 §1 as §1754, amended Stats 1972 ch 1422 §1, renumbered by Stats 1973 ch 167 §6, and repealed Stats 1975 ch 1271 §2.

§1785.6. Application of provisions regarding notices and disclosures

The notices and disclosures to consumers provided for in this title shall be required to be made only to those consumers who have a mailing address in California. **Leg.H.** Added Stats 1993 ch 285 §2 (AB 1340), effective July 30, 1993.

Prior Law: Former §1785.6, similar to present §1785.16, was added Stats 1970 ch 1348 §1 as §1755, renumbered by Stats 1973 ch 167 §7, and repealed by Stats 1975 ch 1271 §2.

§1785.7 [Section repealed 1975]

Leg.H. Added Stats 1970 ch 1348 §1 as §1756. Amended Stats 1972 ch 1422 §1. Renumbered Stats 1973 ch 167 §8. Repealed Stats 1975 ch 1271 §2. The repealed section related to grounds for suit.

§1785.8 [Section repealed 1975]

Leg.H. Added Stats 1970 ch 1348 §1 as §1757. Amended Stats 1972 ch 1422 §1. Renumbered Stats 1973 ch 167 §9. Repealed Stats 1975 ch 1271 §2. See now CC §1785.35.

CHAPTER 2
OBLIGATIONS OF CONSUMER CREDIT REPORTING AGENCIES

Inspection rights; Disclosures. §1785.10.
Agency may not discourage consumer access to reports. §1785.10.1.
Issuance of reports not initiated by consumer. §1785.11.
Placement of security alert in credit report; Notice to persons requesting consumer credit information; Toll-free telephone number; Duration of alert; Penalty for noncompliance. §1785.11.1.
Security freeze on credit report at request of consumer; Written confirmation; Time requirements; Procedures; Removal or temporary lifting of freeze; Fee. §1785.11.2.
Credit reporting agency duties if security freeze in place. §1785.11.3.
Exemptions from requirements of security alert or security freeze; Honoring other agency security freeze. §1785.11.4.
Entities not required to place security alert or security freeze in credit report. §1785.11.6.
Removal of consumer name from solicitation list; Notification to credit reporting agency. §1785.11.8.
Protected consumer security freezes; Definitions. §1785.11.9.
Protected consumer security freezes; Applicability. §1785.11.10.
Protected consumer security freezes; Placement; Removal. §1785.11.11.
Information furnished government agencies. §1785.12.
Contents of reports. §1785.13.
Lien or encumbrance accompanied by strike order. §1785.135.
Maintenance of reporting procedures. §1785.14.
Time and manner of supplying information and making disclosures; Information which consumer has right to receive; Summary of consumer's rights. §1785.15.
"Credit score" information. §1785.15.1.
Credit scoring assessment or model; Fee. §1785.15.2.
Statement of rights of victims of identity theft. §1785.15.3.
Disputed information; Liability for disclosure of credit score. §1785.16.
Deletion of credit report inquiries initiated as a result of identity theft. §1785.16.1.
Prohibition against selling consumer debt when debt is blocked; Victim of identity theft. §1785.16.2.
Exception to blocking provisions for certain agencies that act only as reseller of credit information. §1785.16.3.
Charges for information. §1785.17.
Information based on public record. §1785.18.
Action for civil penalty. §1785.19.
Use of files for marketing purposes. §1785.19.5.

§1785.10. Inspection rights; Disclosures

(a) Every consumer credit reporting agency shall, upon request and proper identification of any consumer, allow the consumer to visually inspect all files maintained regarding that consumer at the time of the request.

(b) Every consumer reporting agency, upon contact by a consumer by telephone, mail, or in person regarding information which may be contained in the agency files regarding that consumer, shall promptly advise the consumer of his or her rights under Sections 1785.11.8, 1785.19, and 1785.19.5, and of the obligation of the agency to provide disclosure of the files in person, by mail, or by telephone pursuant to Section 1785.15, including the obligation of the agency to provide a decoded written version of the file or a written copy of the file with an explanation of any code, including any credit score used, and the key factors, as defined in Section 1785.15.1, if the consumer so requests that copy. The disclosure shall be provided in the manner selected by the consumer, chosen from among any reasonable means available to the consumer credit reporting agency.

The agency shall determine the applicability of subdivision (1) of Section 1785.17 and, where applicable, the agency shall inform the consumer of the rights under that section.

(c) All information on a consumer in the files of a consumer credit reporting agency at the time of a request for inspection under subdivision (a), shall be available for inspection, including the names, addresses and, if provided by the sources of information, the telephone numbers identified for customer service for the sources of information.

(d)(1) The consumer credit reporting agency shall also disclose the recipients of any consumer credit report on the consumer which the consumer credit reporting agency has furnished:

(A) For employment purposes within the two-year period preceding the request.

(B) For any other purpose within the 12-month period preceding the request.

(2) Disclosure of recipients of consumer credit reports for purposes of this subdivision shall include the name of the recipient or, if applicable, the fictitious business name under which the recipient does business disclosed in full. The identification shall also include the address and, if provided by the recipient, the telephone number identified for customer service for the recipient.

(e) The consumer credit reporting agency shall also disclose a record of all inquiries received by the agency in the 12-month period preceding the request that identified the consumer in connection with a credit transaction which is not initiated by the consumer. This record of inquiries shall include the name, address and, if provided by the recipient, the telephone number identified for customer service for each recipient making an inquiry.

(f) Any consumer credit reporting agency when it is subject to the provisions of Section 1785.22 is exempted from the requirements of subdivisions (c), (d), and (e), only with regard to the provision of the address and telephone number.

(g) Any consumer credit reporting agency, that provides a consumer credit report to another consumer credit reporting agency that procures the consumer credit report for the purpose of resale and is subject to Section 1785.22, is exempted from the requirements of subdivisions (d) and (e), only with regard to the provision of the address and telephone number regarding each prospective user to which the consumer credit report was sold.

(h) This section shall become operative on January 1, 2003. **Leg.H.** Added Stats 2002 ch 9 §2 (AB 1531), effective February 19, 2002, operative January 1, 2003.

Prior Law: Former §1785.10, similar to present section, was added Stats 1975 ch 1271 §1, amended Stats 1980 ch 1113 §1, Stats 1990 ch 842 §1, Stats 1992 ch 1194 §2, operative July 1, 1993, amended Stats 1993 ch 285 §3, effective July 30, 1993, amended Stats 2000 ch 978 §1, operative July 1, 2001, Stats 2001 ch 354 §1, Stats 2002 ch 9 §1, effective February 19, 2002, and repealed, operative January 1, 2003, by its own terms.

Former CC §1785.10, similar to the present section, was added Stats 1975 ch 1271 §1 and repealed operative January 1, 2003, by its own provisions. Stats 2002 ch 9 (AB 1531) §1, effective February 19, 2002.

§1785.10.1. Agency may not discourage consumer access to reports

(a) It is unlawful for a consumer credit reporting agency to prohibit in any manner, including, but not limited to, in the terms of a contract enforceable in the state, or to dissuade or attempt to dissuade, a user of a consumer credit report furnished by the credit reporting agency from providing a copy of the consumer's credit report to the consumer, upon the consumer's request, if the user has taken adverse action against the consumer based in whole or in part upon information in the report.

(b) The Attorney General, any district attorney or city attorney, or a city prosecutor in any city or city and county having a full-time city prosecutor, may bring a civil action in any court of competent jurisdiction against any credit reporting agency violating this section for a civil penalty not to exceed five thousand dollars ($5,000) which may be assessed and recovered in a civil action brought in the name of the people of the State of California. **Leg.H.** Added Stats 2013 ch 433 §1 (AB 1220), effective January 1, 2014.

§1785.11. Issuance of reports not initiated by consumer

(a) A consumer credit reporting agency shall furnish a consumer credit report only under the following circumstances:

(1) In response to the order of a court having jurisdiction to issue an order.

(2) In accordance with the written instructions of the consumer to whom it relates.

(3) To a person whom it has reason to believe:

(A) Intends to use the information in connection with a credit transaction, or entering or enforcing an order of a court of competent jurisdiction for support, involving the consumer as to whom the information is to be furnished and involving the extension of credit to, or review or collection of an account of, the consumer; or

(B) Intends to use the information for employment purposes; or

(C) Intends to use the information in connection with the underwriting of insurance involving the consumer, or for insurance claims settlements; or

(D) Intends to use the information in connection with a determination of the consumer's eligibility for a license or other benefit granted by a governmental instrumentality required by law to consider the applicant's financial responsibility or status; or

(E) Intends to use the information in connection with the hiring of a dwelling unit, as defined in subdivision (c) of Section 1940; or

(F) Otherwise has a legitimate business need for the information in connection with a business transaction involving the consumer.

(b) A consumer credit reporting agency may furnish information for purposes of a credit transaction specified in subparagraph (A) of paragraph (3) of subdivision (a), where it is a credit transaction that is not initiated by the consumer, only under the circumstances specified in paragraph (1) or (2), as follows:

(1) The consumer authorizes the consumer credit reporting agency to furnish the consumer credit report to the person.

(2) The proposed transaction involves a firm offer of credit to the consumer, the consumer credit reporting agency has complied with subdivision (d), and the consumer has not elected pursuant to paragraph (1) of subdivision (d) to have the consumer's name excluded from lists of names provided by the consumer credit reporting agency for purposes of reporting in connection with the potential issuance of firm offers of credit. A consumer credit reporting agency may provide only the following information pursuant to this paragraph:

(A) The name and address of the consumer.

(B) Information pertaining to a consumer that is not identified or identifiable with a particular consumer.

(c) Except as provided in paragraph (3) of subdivision (a) of Section 1785.15, a consumer credit reporting agency shall not furnish to any person a record of inquiries solely resulting from credit transactions that are not initiated by the consumer.

(d)(1) A consumer may elect to have his or her name and address excluded from any list provided by a consumer credit reporting agency pursuant to paragraph (2) of subdivision (b) by notifying the consumer credit reporting agency, by telephone or in writing, through the notification system maintained by the consumer credit reporting agency pursuant to subdivision (e), that the consumer does not consent to any use of consumer credit reports relating to the consumer in connection with any transaction that is not initiated by the consumer.

(2) An election of a consumer under paragraph (1) shall be effective with respect to a consumer credit reporting agency, and any affiliate of the consumer credit reporting agency, on the date on which the consumer notifies the consumer credit reporting agency.

(3) An election of a consumer under paragraph (1) shall terminate and be of no force or effect following notice from the consumer to the consumer credit reporting agency, through the system established pursuant to subdivision (e), that the election is no longer effective.

(e) Each consumer credit reporting agency that furnishes a prequalifying report pursuant to subdivision (b) in connection with a credit transaction not initiated by the consumer shall establish and maintain a notification system, including a toll-free telephone number, that permits any consumer, with appropriate identification and for which the consumer credit reporting agency has a file, to notify the consumer credit reporting agency of the consumer's election to have the consumer's name removed from any list of names and addresses provided by the consumer credit reporting agency, and by any affiliated consumer credit reporting agency, pursuant to paragraph (2) of subdivision (b). Compliance with the requirements of this subdivision by a consumer credit reporting agency shall constitute compliance with those requirements by any affiliate of that consumer credit reporting agency.

(f) Each consumer credit reporting agency that compiles and maintains files on consumers on a nationwide basis shall establish and maintain a notification system under paragraph (1) of subdivision (e) jointly with its affiliated consumer credit reporting agencies. **Leg.H.** Added Stats 1975 ch 1271 §1. Amended Stats 1982 ch 1127 §3; Stats 1992 ch 1194 §3 (AB 1629), operative July 1, 1993; Stats 1993 ch 285 §4 (AB 1340), effective July 30, 1993; Stats 1994 ch 146 §11 (AB 3601); Stats 2000 ch 1012 §1 (SB 2166); Stats 2002 ch 664 §40 (AB 3034).

2000 Note: The Legislature inadvertently made an incorrect reference to paragraph (1) of subdivision (e) in subsection (f). The paragraph (1) and (2) designations were deleted from subsection (e).

§1785.11.1. Placement of security alert in credit report; Notice to persons requesting consumer credit information; Toll-free telephone number; Duration of alert; Penalty for noncompliance

(a) A consumer may elect to place a security alert in his or her credit report by making a request in writing or by telephone to a consumer credit reporting agency. "Security alert" means a notice placed in a consumer's credit report, at the request of the consumer, that notifies a recipient of the credit report that the consumer's identity may have been used without the consumer's consent to fraudulently obtain goods or services in the consumer's name.

(b) A consumer credit reporting agency shall notify each person requesting consumer credit information with respect to a consumer of the existence of a security alert in the credit report of that consumer, regardless of whether a full credit report, credit score, or summary report is requested.

(c) Each consumer credit reporting agency shall maintain a toll-free telephone number to accept security alert requests from consumers 24 hours a day, seven days a week.

(d) The toll-free telephone number shall be included in any written disclosure by a consumer credit reporting agency to any consumer pursuant to Section 1785.15 and shall be printed in a clear and conspicuous manner.

(e) A consumer credit reporting agency shall place a security alert on a consumer's credit report no later than five business days after receiving a request from the consumer.

(f) The security alert shall remain in place for at least 90 days, and a consumer shall have the right to request a renewal of the security alert.

(g) Any person who uses a consumer credit report in connection with the approval of credit based on an application for an extension of credit, or with the purchase, lease, or rental of goods or non-credit-related services and who receives notification of a security alert pursuant to subdivision (a) may not lend money, extend credit, or complete the purchase, lease, or rental of goods or non-credit-related services without taking reasonable steps to verify the consumer's identity, in order to ensure that the application for an extension of credit or for the purchase, lease, or rental of goods or non-credit-related services is not the result of identity theft. If the consumer has placed a statement with the security alert in his or her file requesting that identity be verified by calling a specified telephone number, any person who receives that statement with the security alert in a consumer's file pursuant to subdivision (a) shall take reasonable steps to verify the identity of the consumer by contacting the consumer using the specified telephone number prior to lending money, extending credit, or completing the purchase, lease, or rental of goods or non-credit-related services. If a person uses a consumer credit report to facilitate the extension of credit or for another permissible purpose on behalf of a subsidiary, affiliate, agent, assignee, or prospective assignee, that person may verify a consumer's identity under this section in lieu of the subsidiary, affiliate, agent, assignee, or prospective assignee.

(h) For purposes of this section, "extension of credit" does not include an increase in the dollar limit of an existing open-end credit plan, as defined in Regulation Z issued by the Board of Governors of the Federal Reserve System (12 C.F.R. 226.2), or any change to, or review of, an existing credit account.

(i) If reasonable steps are taken to verify the identity of the consumer pursuant to subdivision (b) of Section 1785.20.3, those steps constitute compliance with the requirements of this section, except that if a consumer has placed a statement including a telephone number with the security alert in his or her file, his or her identity shall be verified by contacting the consumer using that telephone number as specified pursuant to subdivision (g).

(j) A consumer credit reporting agency shall notify each consumer who has requested that a security alert be placed on his or her consumer credit report of the expiration date of the alert.

(k) Notwithstanding Section 1785.19, any consumer credit reporting agency that recklessly, willfully, or intentionally fails to place a security alert pursuant to this section shall be liable for a penalty in an amount of up to two thousand five hundred dollars ($2,500) and reasonable attorneys' fees. **Leg.H.** Added Stats 2001 ch 720 §1, operative July 1, 2002. Amended Stats 2003 ch 533 §2; Stats 2003 ch 533 §2.5 (SB 602), ch 907 §1.5 (SB 25), operative July 1, 2004.

§1785.11.2. Security freeze on credit report at request of consumer; Written confirmation; Time requirements; Procedures; Removal or temporary lifting of freeze; Fee

(a) A consumer may elect to place a security freeze on his or her credit report by making a request in writing by mail to a consumer credit reporting agency. "Security freeze" means a notice placed in a consumer's credit report, at the request of the consumer, and subject to certain exceptions, that prohibits the consumer credit reporting agency from releasing the consumer's credit report or any information from it without the express authorization of the consumer. If a security freeze is in place, information from a consumer's credit report may not be released to a third party without prior express authorization from the consumer. This subdivision does not prevent a consumer credit reporting agency from advising a third party that a security freeze is in effect with respect to the consumer's credit report.

(b) A consumer credit reporting agency shall place a security freeze on a consumer's credit report no later than three business days after receiving a written request from the consumer.

(c) The consumer credit reporting agency shall send a written confirmation of the security freeze to the consumer within 10 business days and shall provide the consumer with a unique personal identification number or password to be used by the consumer when providing authorization for the release of his or her credit for a specific party or period of time.

(d) If the consumer wishes to allow his or her credit report to be accessed for a specific party or period of time while a freeze is in place, he or she shall contact the consumer credit reporting agency, request that the freeze be temporarily lifted, and provide the following:

(1) Proper identification, as defined in subdivision (c) of Section 1785.15.

(2) The unique personal identification number or password provided by the credit reporting agency pursuant to subdivision (c).

(3) The proper information regarding the third party who is to receive the credit report or the time period for which the report shall be available to users of the credit report.

(e) A consumer credit reporting agency that receives a request from a consumer to temporarily lift a freeze on a credit report pursuant to subdivision (d) shall comply with the request no later than three business days after receiving the request.

(f) A consumer credit reporting agency may develop procedures involving the use of telephone, fax, the Internet, or other electronic media to receive and process a request from a consumer to temporarily lift a freeze on a credit report pursuant to subdivision (d) in an expedited manner.

(g) A consumer credit reporting agency shall remove or temporarily lift a freeze placed on a consumer's credit report only in the following cases:

(1) Upon consumer request, pursuant to subdivision (d) or (j).

(2) If the consumer's credit report was frozen due to a material misrepresentation of fact by the consumer. If a consumer credit reporting agency intends to remove a freeze upon a consumer's credit report pursuant to this paragraph, the consumer credit reporting agency shall notify the consumer in writing prior to removing the freeze on the consumer's credit report.

(h) A third party who requests access to a consumer credit report in connection with an application for credit or any other use may treat the application as incomplete if a security freeze is in effect and the consumer does not allow his or her credit report to be accessed for that specific party or period of time.

(i) If a consumer requests a security freeze, the consumer credit reporting agency shall disclose the process of placing and temporarily lifting a freeze and the process for allowing access to information from the consumer's credit report for a specific party or period of time while the freeze is in place.

(j) A security freeze shall remain in place until the consumer requests that the security freeze be removed. A consumer credit reporting agency shall remove a security freeze within three business days of receiving a request for removal from the consumer if the consumer provides both of the following:

(1) Proper identification, as defined in subdivision (c) of Section 1785.15.

(2) The unique personal identification number or password provided by the credit reporting agency pursuant to subdivision (c).

(k) A consumer credit reporting agency shall require proper identification, as defined in subdivision (c) of Section 1785.15, of the person making a request to place or remove a security freeze.

(l) The provisions of this section do not apply to the use of a consumer credit report by any of the following:

(1)(A)(i) A person or entity with which the consumer has or had, prior to any assignment, an account or contract, including a demand deposit account, or to which the consumer issued a negotiable instrument, for the purpose of reviewing the account or collecting the financial obligation owing for the account, contract, or negotiable instrument.

(ii) A subsidiary, affiliate, or agent of a person or entity described in clause (i), an assignee of a financial obligation owing by the consumer to such a person or entity, or a prospective assignee of a financial obligation owing by the consumer to such a person or entity in conjunction with the proposed purchase of the financial obligation, for the purpose of reviewing the account or collecting the financial obligation owing for the account, contract, or negotiable instrument.

(B) For purposes of this paragraph, "reviewing the account" includes activities related to account maintenance, monitoring, credit line increases, and account upgrades and enhancements.

(2) A subsidiary, affiliate, agent, assignee, or prospective assignee of a person to whom access has been granted under subdivision (d) for purposes of facilitating the extension of credit or other permissible use.

(3) Any state or local agency, law enforcement agency, trial court, or private collection agency acting pursuant to a court order, warrant, or subpoena.

(4) A child support agency acting pursuant to Chapter 2 (commencing with Section 17400) of Division 17 of the Family Code or Title IV-D of the Social Security Act (42 U.S.C. et seq.).

(5) The State Department of Health Care Services or its agents or assigns acting to investigate Medi-Cal fraud.

(6) The Franchise Tax Board or its agents or assigns acting to investigate or collect delinquent taxes or unpaid court orders or to fulfill any of its other statutory responsibilities.

(7) The use of credit information for the purposes of prescreening as provided for by the federal Fair Credit Reporting Act.

(8) Any person or entity administering a credit file monitoring subscription service to which the consumer has subscribed.

(9) Any person or entity for the purpose of providing a consumer with a copy of his or her credit report upon the consumer's request.

(m)(1) Except as provided in paragraph (2), this title does not prevent a consumer credit reporting agency from charging a fee of no more than ten dollars ($10) to a consumer for the placement of each freeze, the removal of the freeze, the temporary lift of the freeze for a period of time, or the temporary lift of the freeze for a specific party, regarding access to a consumer credit report, except that a consumer credit reporting agency may not charge a fee to a victim of identity theft who has submitted a valid police report or valid Department of Motor Vehicles investigative report that alleges a violation of Section 530.5 of the Penal Code.

(2) With respect to a consumer who is 65 years of age or older and who has provided identification confirming his or her age, a consumer credit reporting agency shall not charge a fee for the placement of an initial security freeze, but may charge a fee not to exceed five dollars ($5) for the removal of the freeze, the temporary lift of the freeze for a period of time, the temporary lift of the freeze for a specific party, or replacing the freeze.

(n) Regardless of the existence of a security freeze, a consumer reporting agency may disclose public record information lawfully obtained by, or for, the consumer reporting agency from an open public record to the extent otherwise permitted by law. This subdivision does not prohibit a consumer reporting agency from electing to apply a valid security freeze to the entire contents of a credit report. **Leg.H.** Added Stats 2001 ch 720 §2 (SB 168), operative January 1, 2003. Amended Stats 2002 ch 664 §41 (AB 3034), ch 786 §1 (SB 1730); Stats 2003 ch 533 §3 (SB 602); Stats 2007 ch 699 §2 (AB 1298), effective January 1, 2008; Stats 2008 ch 151 §1 (AB 372), effective January 1, 2009; Stats 2012 ch 645 §1 (AB 2374), effective January 1, 2013.

§1785.11.3. Credit reporting agency duties if security freeze in place

(a) If a security freeze is in place, a consumer credit reporting agency shall not change any of the following official information in a consumer credit report without sending a written confirmation of the change to the consumer within 30 days of the change being posted to the consumer's file: name, date of birth, social security number, and address. Written confirmation is not required for technical modifications of a consumer's official information, including name and street abbreviations, complete spellings, or transposition of numbers or letters. In the case of an address change, the written confirmation shall be sent to both the new address and to the former address.

(b) If a consumer has placed a security alert, a consumer credit reporting agency shall provide the consumer, upon request, with a free copy of his or her credit report at the time the 90-day security alert period expires. **Leg.H.** Added Stats 2001 ch 720 §3 (SB 168), operative January 1, 2003.

§1785.11.4. Exemptions from requirements of security alert or security freeze; Honoring other agency security freeze

The provisions of Sections 1785.11.1, 1785.11.2, and 1785.11.3 do not apply to a consumer credit reporting agency that acts only as a reseller of credit information pursuant to Section 1785.22 by assembling and merging information contained in the data base of another consumer credit reporting agency or multiple consumer credit reporting agencies, and does not maintain a permanent data base of credit information from which new consumer credit reports are produced. However, a consumer credit reporting agency acting pursuant to Section 1785.22 shall honor any security freeze placed on a consumer credit report by another consumer credit reporting agency. **Leg.H.** Added Stats 2001 ch 720 §4 (SB 168).

§1785.11.6. Entities not required to place security alert or security freeze in credit report

The following entities are not required to place in a credit report either a security alert, pursuant to Section 1785.11.1, or a security freeze, pursuant to Section 1785.11.2:

(a) A check services or fraud prevention services company, which issues reports on incidents of fraud or authorizations for the purpose of approving or processing negotiable instruments, electronic funds transfers, or similar methods of payments.

(b) A deposit account information service company, which issues reports regarding account closures due to fraud, substantial overdrafts, ATM abuse, or similar negative information regarding a consumer, to inquiring banks or other financial institutions for use only in reviewing a consumer request for a deposit account at the inquiring bank or financial institution. **Leg.H.** Added Stats 2001 ch 720 §5 (SB 168). Amended Stats 2002 ch 786 §2 (SB 1730); Stats 2003 ch 907 §2 (SB 25).

§1785.11.8. Removal of consumer name from solicitation list; Notification to credit reporting agency

A consumer may elect that his or her name shall be removed from any list that a consumer credit reporting agency furnishes for credit card solicitations, by notifying the consumer credit reporting agency, by telephone or in writing, pursuant to the notification system maintained by the consumer credit reporting agency pursuant to subdivision (d) of Section 1785.11. The election shall be effective for a minimum of two years, unless otherwise specified by the consumer. **Leg.H.** Added Stats 2001 ch 354 §2 (AB 655).

§1785.11.9. Protected consumer security freezes; Definitions

For purposes of Sections 1785.11.10 and 1785.11.11, the following terms shall have the following meanings:

(a) "Protected consumer" means an individual who is any of the following:

(1) Under 16 years of age at the time a request for the placement of a security freeze is made.

(2) An incapacitated person or a protected person for whom a guardian or conservator has been appointed.

(3) Under the jurisdiction of a county welfare department or county probation department, has been placed in a foster care setting, and is under 16 years of age at the time a request for placement of a security freeze is made.

(b) "Record" means a compilation of information that:

(1) Identifies a protected consumer.

(2) Was created by a consumer credit reporting agency solely for the purpose of complying with this section.

(3) Is not otherwise authorized to be created or used to consider the protected consumer's creditworthiness, credit standing, credit capacity, character, general reputation, personal characteristics, or mode of living.

(c)(1) "Representative" means a person who provides to a consumer credit reporting agency sufficient proof of authority to act on behalf of a protected consumer.

(2) For a protected consumer who has been placed in a foster care setting, "representative" means either of the following:

(A) A county welfare department or its agent or designee.

(B) A county probation department or its agent or designee.

(3) For a protected consumer who has been placed in a foster care setting, "representative" does not mean a foster parent.

(d) "Security freeze" means:

(1) If a consumer credit reporting agency does not have a file pertaining to a protected consumer, a restriction that:

(A) Is placed on the protected consumer's record in accordance with this section.

(B) Prohibits the consumer credit reporting agency from releasing the protected consumer's record except as authorized in this section.

(2) If a consumer credit reporting agency has a file pertaining to a protected consumer, a restriction that:

(A) Is placed on the protected consumer's consumer credit report in accordance with this section.

(B) Prohibits the consumer credit reporting agency from releasing the protected consumer's consumer credit report or any information derived from the protected consumer's consumer credit report except as authorized in this section.

(e) "Sufficient proof of authority" means documentation that shows that a representative has authority to act on behalf of a protected consumer in a financial matter. This documentation includes, but is not limited to:

(1) A court order or relevant enabling document issued by a court.

(2) A legally sufficient and valid power of attorney, or a durable power of attorney.

(3) A written, notarized statement signed by a representative that expressly describes the authority of the representative to act on behalf of a protected consumer, including a temporary conservator or temporary guardian.

(4) A written communication from a county welfare department or its agent or designee or a county probation department or its agent or designee certifying that the protected consumer is a foster youth under its jurisdiction.

(f) "Sufficient proof of identification" means information or documentation that identifies a protected consumer or a representative of a protected consumer. This information or documentation includes, but is not limited to:

(1) A social security number or a copy of a social security card issued by the Social Security Administration.

(2) A certified copy or official copy of a birth certificate issued by the entity authorized to issue the birth certificate.

(3) A copy of a driver's license, an identification issued by the Department of Motor Vehicles, or any other government-issued identification.

(4) A copy of a bill for telephone, sewer, septic tank, water, electric, oil, or natural gas services that shows a name and a home address.

(5) A written communication from a county welfare department or its agent or designee or a county probation department or its agent or designee certifying that the protected consumer is a foster youth under its jurisdiction. **Leg.H.** Added Stats 2016 ch 494 §1 (AB 1580), effective January 1, 2017.

§1785.11.10. Protected consumer security freezes; Applicability

Sections 1785.11.9 to 1785.11.11, inclusive, do not apply to the use of a protected consumer's consumer credit report or record by any of the following:

(a) A person or entity listed in paragraph (1) or (2) of subdivision (*l*) of Section 1785.11.2, or Section 1785.11.4 or 1785.11.6.

(b) A person administering a credit file monitoring subscription service to which the representative of the protected consumer has subscribed on behalf of the protected consumer.

(c) A person who provides the protected consumer or the protected consumer's representative with a copy of the protected consumer's consumer credit report at the request of the protected consumer or at the request of the protected consumer's representative.

(d) Any state or local agency, law enforcement agency, trial court, or private collection agency acting pursuant to a court order, warrant, or subpoena.

(e) A child support agency acting pursuant to Chapter 2 (commencing with Section 17400) of Division 17 of the Family Code and Title IV-D of the Social Security Act (42 U.S.C. Sec. 651 et seq.).

(f) The State Department of Health Care Services or its agents or assigns acting to investigate Medi-Cal fraud.

(g) The Franchise Tax Board or its agents or assigns acting to investigate or collect delinquent taxes or unpaid court orders or to fulfill any of its other statutory responsibilities. **Leg.H.** Added Stats 2016 ch 494 §2 (AB 1580), effective January 1, 2017.

§1785.11.11. Protected consumer security freezes; Placement; Removal

(a)(1) A consumer credit reporting agency shall place a security freeze for a protected consumer if both of the following occur:

[1] **(A)** The consumer credit reporting agency receives a request from the protected consumer's representative for the placement of the security freeze pursuant to this section.

[2] **(B)** The protected consumer's representative does all of the following:

[3] **(i)** Submits the request to the consumer credit reporting agency at the address or other point of contact and in the manner specified by the consumer credit reporting agency.

[4] **(ii)** Provides to the consumer credit reporting agency sufficient proof of identification of the protected consumer and the representative.

[5] **(iii) Provides to the consumer credit reporting agency sufficient proof of authority to act on behalf of the protected consumer.**

[6] **(iv) Pays to the consumer credit reporting agency a fee as authorized by subdivision (i).**

(2)(A) **If the request for the placement or removal of a security freeze is for a protected consumer who has been placed in a foster care setting, the credit reporting agency shall deem the requirements of clauses (ii) and (iii) of subparagraph (B) of paragraph (1) to have been met if the request is from a county welfare department or a county probation department appearing on the most recent list provided or available to a consumer credit reporting agency by the State Department of Social Services and the requesting entity provides sufficient proof of identification under 15 U.S.C. Sec. 1681c-1(j)(1)(G). A county welfare department or county probation department shall not have the authority to request a security freeze for a protected consumer placed in foster care that continues beyond the protected consumer's 18th birthday. A consumer credit reporting agency may use whatever lawful mechanism is available to it, including mechanisms for thawing or unfreezing reports by dates certain, to ensure the freeze does not extend beyond a protected consumer's 18th birthday.**

(B) Notwithstanding any other law, the State Department of Social Services may, at the request of a consumer credit reporting agency, provide or, in the State Department of Social Service's discretion, otherwise make available to consumer reporting agencies in any other manner, a list of county welfare departments or county probation departments whose employees may be representatives of protected consumers who have been placed in a foster care setting.

(b) If a consumer credit reporting agency does not have a file pertaining to a protected consumer when the consumer credit reporting agency receives a request pursuant to paragraph (1) of subdivision (a), the consumer credit reporting agency shall create a record for the protected consumer.

(c) If a protected consumer's representative requests a security freeze, the consumer credit reporting agency shall disclose the process for placing and removing a security freeze.

(d) Within 30 days after receiving a request that meets the requirements of subdivision (a), a consumer credit reporting agency shall place a security freeze for the protected consumer. The consumer credit reporting agency shall send written confirmation of the security freeze to the address on file within 10 days of the placement of the security freeze.

(e) Unless a security freeze for a protected consumer is removed pursuant to subdivision (h) or (j), a consumer credit reporting agency shall not release the protected consumer's consumer credit report, any information derived from the protected consumer's consumer credit report, or any record created for the protected consumer.

(f) A security freeze for a protected consumer placed pursuant to this section shall remain in effect until either of the following occurs:

(1) The protected consumer or the protected consumer's representative requests that the consumer credit reporting agency remove the security freeze in accordance with subdivision (h).

(2) The security freeze is removed in accordance with subdivision (j).

(g) To remove a security freeze, a protected consumer or a protected consumer's representative shall do all of the following:

(1) Submit a request for removal of the security freeze to the consumer credit reporting agency at the address or other point of contact and in the manner specified by the consumer credit reporting agency.

(2) Provide to the consumer credit reporting agency:

(A) If the request is made by the protected consumer:

(i) Proof that the sufficient proof of authority for the protected consumer's representative to act on behalf of the protected consumer is no longer valid, [7] **they have** been emancipated, or [8] **they are** 16 years of age or older.

(ii) Sufficient proof of identification of the protected consumer.

(B) If the request is made by the representative of a protected consumer:

(i) Sufficient proof of identification of the protected consumer and the representative.

(ii) Sufficient proof of authority to act on behalf of the protected consumer.

(3) Pay to the consumer credit reporting agency a fee as authorized by subdivision (i).

(h) Within 30 days after receiving a request that meets the requirements of subdivision (g), a consumer credit reporting agency shall remove a security freeze for a protected consumer.

(i)(1) Except as provided in paragraph (2), a consumer credit reporting agency may not charge a fee for any service performed pursuant to this section.

(2) A consumer credit reporting agency is authorized to charge a reasonable fee, not exceeding ten dollars ($10), for each placement or removal of a security freeze for a protected consumer.

(3) Notwithstanding paragraph (2), a consumer credit reporting agency shall not charge any fee pursuant to this section under any of the following circumstances:

(A) The protected consumer's representative has received a report of alleged identity theft against the protected consumer under Section 530.5 of the Penal Code and has provided copy of the report to the consumer credit reporting agency.

(B) The request for the placement or removal of a security freeze is for a protected consumer who is under 16 years of age at the time of the request and the consumer credit reporting agency has a report pertaining to the protected consumer.

(C) The request for the placement or removal of a security freeze is for a protected consumer who has been placed in a foster care setting.

(j)(1) A consumer credit reporting agency is authorized to remove a security freeze for a protected consumer or to delete a record of a protected consumer if the security freeze was placed or the record was created based upon a material misrepresentation of fact by the protected consumer or the protected consumer's representative.

(2) With respect to a security freeze placed for a protected consumer under paragraph (2) of subdivision (a), the freeze may be removed prior to the protected consumer's 18th birthday at the request of the representative of the protected consumer, or by the protected consumer if the protected consumer is 16 years of age or older at the time they make the request, under any of the following circumstances:

(A) Upon the protected consumer's removal from foster care.

(B) Upon the protected consumer's request, if the protected consumer is 16 years of age or older.

(C) Upon a determination by the representative of the protected consumer that removal of the security freeze is in the best interest of the protected consumer.

(3) A representative of the protected consumer may also remove the freeze pursuant to paragraph (2) at a time when the representative inquires with each of the three major credit reporting agencies

pursuant to paragraph (1) of subdivision (a) of Section 10618.6 the Welfare and Institutions Code.

(k) A consumer credit reporting agency may develop procedures involving the use of telephone, mail, fax, the [9] **internet**, or other electronic media to receive and process a request for a protected consumer's security freeze to be placed or removed. **Leg.H.** Added Stats 2016 ch 494 §3 (AB 1580), effective January 1, 2017. Amended Stats 2024 ch 846 §1 (AB 2935), effective January 1, 2025.

§1785.11.11. 2024 Deletes. [1] (1) [2] (2) [3] (A) [4] (B) [5] (C) [6] (D) [7] he or she has [8] he or she is [9] Internet

§1785.12. Information furnished government agencies

(a) Notwithstanding the provisions of Section 1785.11, a consumer credit reporting agency may furnish to a governmental agency a consumer's name, address, former address, places of employment, or former places of employment.

(b) If a request received pursuant to subdivision (a) of Section 10618.6 of the Welfare and Institutions Code indicates that the protected consumer who has been placed in a foster care setting has a consumer credit history, any information that appears on the protected consumer's credit report shall be promptly blocked and not reported, in the same manner set forth in subdivision (k) of Section 1785.16 as if the agency had received a police report pursuant to Section 530.5 of the Penal Code. The credit reporting agency shall also comply with subdivisions (k) and (l) of Section 1785.16, regarding the protected consumer who has been placed in a foster care setting. **Leg.H.** Added Stats 1975 ch 1271 §1. Amended Stats 2024 ch 846 §2 (AB 2935), effective January 1, 2025.

§1785.13. Contents of reports

(a) No consumer credit reporting agency shall make any consumer credit report containing any of the following items of information:

(1) Bankruptcies that, from the date of the order for relief, antedate the report by more than 10 years.

(2) Suits and judgments that, from the date of entry or renewal, antedate the report by more than seven years or until the governing statute of limitations has expired, whichever is the longer period.

(3) Unlawful detainer actions, unless the lessor was the prevailing party. For purposes of this paragraph, the lessor shall be deemed to be the prevailing party only if (A) final judgment was awarded to the lessor (i) upon entry of the tenant's default, (ii) upon the granting of the lessor's motion for summary judgment, or (iii) following trial, or (B) the action was resolved by a written settlement agreement between the parties that states that the unlawful detainer action may be reported. In any other instance in which the action is resolved by settlement agreement, the lessor shall not be deemed to be the prevailing party for purposes of this paragraph.

(4) Paid tax liens that, from the date of payment, antedate the report by more than seven years.

(5) Accounts placed for collection or charged to profit and loss that antedate the report by more than seven years.

(6) Records of arrest, indictment, information, misdemeanor complaint, or conviction of a crime that, from the date of disposition, release, or parole, antedate the report by more than seven years. These items of information shall no longer be reported if at any time it is learned that in the case of a conviction a full pardon has been granted, or in the case of an arrest, indictment, information, or misdemeanor complaint a conviction did not result.

(7) **Medical debt.**

[1] (8) Any other adverse information that antedates the report by more than seven years.

(b) The seven-year period specified in paragraphs (5) and [2] (8) of subdivision (a) shall commence to run, with respect to any account that is placed for collection (internally or by referral to a third party, whichever is earlier), charged to profit and loss, or subjected to any similar action, upon the expiration of the 180-day period beginning on the date of the commencement of the delinquency that immediately preceded the collection activity, charge to profit and loss, or similar action. Where more than one of these actions is taken with respect to a particular account, the seven-year period specified in paragraphs (5) and [3] (8) shall commence concurrently for all these actions on the date of the first of these actions.

(c) Any consumer credit reporting agency that furnishes a consumer credit report containing information regarding any case involving a consumer arising under the bankruptcy provisions of Title 11 of the United States Code shall include an identification of the chapter of Title 11 of the United States Code under which the case arose if that can be ascertained from what was provided to the consumer credit reporting agency by the source of the information.

(d) A consumer credit report shall not include any adverse information concerning a consumer antedating the report by more than 10 years or that otherwise is prohibited from being included in a consumer credit report.

(e) If a consumer credit reporting agency is notified by a furnisher of credit information that an open-end credit account of the consumer has been closed by the consumer, any consumer credit report thereafter issued by the consumer credit reporting agency with respect to that consumer, and that includes information respecting that account, shall indicate the fact that the consumer has closed the account. For purposes of this subdivision, "open-end credit account" does not include any demand deposit account, such as a checking account, money market account, or share draft account.

(f) Consumer credit reporting agencies shall not include medical information in their files on consumers or furnish medical information for employment, insurance, or credit purposes in a consumer credit report without the consent of the consumer.

(g) A consumer credit reporting agency shall include in any consumer credit report information, if any, on the failure of the consumer to pay overdue child or spousal support, where the information either was provided to the consumer credit reporting agency pursuant to Section 4752 or has been provided to the consumer credit reporting agency and verified by another federal, state, or local governmental agency. **Leg.H.** Added Stats 1975 ch 1271 §1. Amended Stats 1982 ch 1127 §4; Stats 1988 ch 900 §1; Stats 1991 ch 965 §1 (AB 1796), ch 1145 §1.1 (AB 2032); Stats 1992 ch 1194 §4 (AB 1629), operative July 1, 1993; Stats 1993 ch 285 §5 (AB 1340), effective July 30, 1993; Stats 1994 ch 146 §12 (AB 3601); Stats 2000 ch 1012 §2 (SB 2166); Stats 2009 ch 500 §10 (AB 1059), effective January 1, 2010; Stats 2024 ch 520 §2 (SB 1061), effective January 1, 2025.

§1785.13. 2024 Deletes. [1] (7) [2] (7) [3] (7)

§1785.135. Lien or encumbrance accompanied by strike order

No consumer credit reporting agency shall make any consumer credit report with respect to a document which acts as a lien or other encumbrance, including, but not limited to, a notice of lis pendens, but which has together with it a court order striking or releasing the lien or other encumbrance pursuant to Section 765.030 of the Code of Civil Procedure. **Leg.H.** Added Stats 1998 ch 779 §1 (SB 1759).

§1785.14. Maintenance of reporting procedures

(a) Every consumer credit reporting agency shall maintain reasonable procedures designed to avoid violations of Section 1785.13 and to limit furnishing of consumer credit reports to the purposes listed under Section 1785.11. These procedures shall require that prospective users of the information identify themselves, certify the purposes for which the information is sought and certify that the information will be used for no other purposes. From the effective date of this act the consumer credit reporting agency shall keep a record of the purposes as stated by the user. Every consumer credit reporting agency shall make a reasonable effort to verify the identity of a new prospective user and the uses certified by the prospective user prior to furnishing the user a consumer report. No consumer credit reporting agency may furnish a consumer credit report to any person unless the consumer credit reporting agency has reasonable grounds for believing that the consumer credit report will be used by the person for the purposes listed in Section 1785.11. A consumer credit reporting agency does not have reasonable grounds for believing that a consumer credit report will be used by the person for the purposes listed in Section 1785.11 unless all of the following requirements are met:

(1) If the prospective user is a retail seller, as defined in Section 1802.3, and intends to issue credit to a consumer who appears in person on the basis of an application for credit submitted in person, the consumer credit reporting agency shall, with a reasonable degree of certainty, match at least three categories of identifying information within the file maintained by the consumer credit reporting agency on the consumer with the information provided to the consumer credit reporting agency by the retail seller. The categories of identifying information may include, but are not limited to, first and last name, month and date of birth, driver's license

number, place of employment, current residence address, previous residence address, or social security number. The categories of information shall not include mother's maiden name.

(2) If the prospective user is a retail seller, as defined in Section 1802.3, and intends to issue credit to a consumer who appears in person on the basis of an application for credit submitted in person, the retail seller certifies, in writing, to the consumer credit reporting agency that it instructs its employees and agents to inspect a photo identification of the consumer at the time the application was submitted in person. This paragraph does not apply to an application for credit submitted by mail.

(3) If the prospective user intends to extend credit by mail pursuant to a solicitation by mail, the extension of credit shall be mailed to the same address as on the solicitation unless the prospective user verifies any address change by, among other methods, contacting the person to whom the extension of credit will be mailed.

(b) Whenever a consumer credit reporting agency prepares a consumer credit report, it shall follow reasonable procedures to assure maximum possible accuracy of the information concerning the individual about whom the report relates. These reasonable procedures shall include, but not be limited to, permanent retention by the consumer credit reporting agency in the consumer's file, or a separately individualized file, of that portion of the data in the file that is used by the consumer credit reporting agency to identify the individual consumer pursuant to paragraph (1) of subdivision (a). This permanently retained data shall be available for use in either a reinvestigation pursuant to subdivision (a) of Section 1785.16, an investigation where the consumer has filed a police report pursuant to subdivision (k) of Section 1785.16, or a restoration of a file involving the consumer. If the permanently retained identifying information is retained in a consumer's file, it shall be clearly identified in the file in order for an individual who reviews the file to easily distinguish between the permanently stored identifying information and any other identifying information that may be a part of the file. This retention requirement shall not apply to data that is reported in error, that is obsolete, or that is found to be inaccurate through the results of a reinvestigation initiated by a consumer pursuant to subdivision (a) of Section 1785.16.

(c) No consumer credit reporting agency may prohibit any user of any consumer credit report furnished by the consumer credit reporting agency from disclosing the contents of the consumer credit report to the consumer who is the subject of the report if adverse action may be taken by the user based in whole or in part on the consumer credit report. The act of disclosure to the consumer by the user of the contents of a consumer credit report shall not be a basis for liability of the consumer credit reporting agency or the user under Section 1785.31.

(d) A consumer credit reporting agency shall provide a written notice to any person who regularly and in the ordinary course of business supplies information to the consumer credit reporting agency concerning any consumer or to whom a consumer credit report is provided by the consumer credit reporting agency. The notice shall specify the person's obligations under this title. Copies of the appropriate code sections shall satisfy the requirement of this subdivision. **Leg.H.** Added Stats 1975 ch 1271 §1. Amended Stats 1992 ch 1194 §5 (AB 1629), operative July 1, 1993; Stats 1993 ch 285 §6 (AB 1340), effective July 30, 1993; Stats 1997 ch 768 §1 (AB 156), operative July 1, 1998.

§1785.15. Time and manner of supplying information and making disclosures; Information which consumer has right to receive; Summary of consumer's rights

(a) A consumer credit reporting agency shall supply files and information required under Section 1785.10 during normal business hours and on reasonable notice. In addition to the disclosure provided by this chapter and any disclosures received by the consumer, the consumer has the right to request and receive all of the following:

(1) Either a decoded written version of the file or a written copy of the file, including all information in the file at the time of the request, with an explanation of any code used.

(2) A credit score for the consumer, the key factors, and the related information, as defined in and required by Section 1785.15.1.

(3) A record of all inquiries, by recipient, that result in the provision of information concerning the consumer in connection with a credit transaction not initiated by the consumer and that were received by the consumer credit reporting agency in the 12-month period immediately preceding the request for disclosure under this section.

(4) The recipients, including end users specified in Section 1785.22, of any consumer credit report on the consumer which the consumer credit reporting agency has furnished:

(A) For employment purposes within the two-year period preceding the request.

(B) For any other purpose within the 12-month period preceding the request.

Identification for purposes of this paragraph shall include the name of the recipient or, if applicable, the fictitious business name under which the recipient does business disclosed in full. If requested by the consumer, the identification shall also include the address of the recipient.

(b) Files maintained on a consumer shall be disclosed promptly as follows:

(1) In person, at the location where the consumer credit reporting agency maintains the trained personnel required by subdivision (d), if he or she appears in person and furnishes proper identification.

(2) By mail, if the consumer makes a written request with proper identification for a copy of the file or a decoded written version of that file to be sent to the consumer at a specified address. A disclosure pursuant to this paragraph shall be deposited in the United States mail, postage prepaid, within five business days after the consumer's written request for the disclosure is received by the consumer credit reporting agency. Consumer credit reporting agencies complying with requests for mailings under this section shall not be liable for disclosures to third parties caused by mishandling of mail after the mailings leave the consumer credit reporting agencies.

(3) A summary of all information contained in files on a consumer and required to be provided by Section 1785.10 shall be provided by telephone, if the consumer has made a written request, with proper identification for telephone disclosure.

(4) Information in a consumer's file required to be provided in writing under this section may also be disclosed in another form if authorized by the consumer and if available from the consumer credit reporting agency. For this purpose, a consumer may request disclosure in person pursuant to Section 1785.10, by telephone upon disclosure of proper identification by the consumer, by electronic means if available from the consumer credit reporting agency, or by any other reasonable means that is available from the consumer credit reporting agency.

(c) "Proper identification," as used in subdivision (b) means that information generally deemed sufficient to identify a person. Only if the consumer is unable to reasonably identify himself or herself with the information described above may a consumer credit reporting agency require additional information concerning the consumer's employment and personal or family history in order to verify his or her identity.

(d) The consumer credit reporting agency shall provide trained personnel to explain to the consumer any information furnished him or her pursuant to Section 1785.10.

(e) The consumer shall be permitted to be accompanied by one other person of his or her choosing, who shall furnish reasonable identification. A consumer credit reporting agency may require the consumer to furnish a written statement granting permission to the consumer credit reporting agency to discuss the consumer's file in that person's presence.

(f) Any written disclosure by a consumer credit reporting agency to any consumer pursuant to this section shall include a written summary of all rights the consumer has under this title and, in the case of a consumer credit reporting agency that compiles and maintains consumer credit reports on a nationwide basis, a toll-free telephone number that the consumer can use to communicate with the consumer credit reporting agency. The written summary of rights required under this subdivision is sufficient if in substantially the following form:

"You have a right to obtain a copy of your credit file from a consumer credit reporting agency. You may be charged a reasonable fee not exceeding eight dollars ($8). There is no fee, however, if you have been turned down for credit, employment, insurance, or a rental dwelling because of information in your credit report within the preceding 60 days. The consumer credit reporting agency must provide someone to help you interpret the information in your credit file.

You have a right to dispute inaccurate information by contacting the consumer credit reporting agency directly. However, neither you nor any credit repair company or credit service organization has the right to have accurate, current, and verifiable information removed from your credit report. Under the Federal Fair Credit Reporting Act, the consumer credit reporting agency must remove accurate, negative information from your report only if it is over seven years old. Bankruptcy information can be reported for 10 years.

If you have notified a consumer credit reporting agency in writing that you dispute the accuracy of information in your file, the consumer credit reporting agency must then, within 30 business days, reinvestigate and modify or remove inaccurate information. The consumer credit reporting agency may not charge a fee for this service. Any pertinent information and copies of all documents you have concerning an error should be given to the consumer credit reporting agency.

If reinvestigation does not resolve the dispute to your satisfaction, you may send a brief statement to the consumer credit reporting agency to keep in your file, explaining why you think the record is inaccurate. The consumer credit reporting agency must include your statement about disputed information in a report it issues about you.

You have a right to receive a record of all inquiries relating to a credit transaction initiated in 12 months preceding your request. This record shall include the recipients of any consumer credit report.

You may request in writing that the information contained in your file not be provided to a third party for marketing purposes.

You have a right to place a "security alert" in your credit report, which will warn anyone who receives information in your credit report that your identity may have been used without your consent. Recipients of your credit report are required to take reasonable steps, including contacting you at the telephone number you may provide with your security alert, to verify your identity prior to lending money, extending credit, or completing the purchase, lease, or rental of goods or services. The security alert may prevent credit, loans, and services from being approved in your name without your consent. However, you should be aware that taking advantage of this right may delay or interfere with the timely approval of any subsequent request or application you make regarding a new loan, credit, mortgage, or cellular phone or other new account, including an extension of credit at point of sale. If you place a security alert on your credit report, you have a right to obtain a free copy of your credit report at the time the 90-day security alert period expires. A security alert may be requested by calling the following toll-free telephone number: (Insert applicable toll-free telephone number). California consumers also have the right to obtain a "security freeze."

You have a right to place a "security freeze" on your credit report, which will prohibit a consumer credit reporting agency from releasing any information in your credit report without your express authorization. A security freeze must be requested in writing by mail. The security freeze is designed to prevent credit, loans, and services from being approved in your name without your consent. However, you should be aware that using a security freeze to take control over who gets access to the personal and financial information in your credit report may delay, interfere with, or prohibit the timely approval of any subsequent request or application you make regarding a new loan, credit, mortgage, or cellular phone or other new account, including an extension of credit at point of sale. When you place a security freeze on your credit report, you will be provided a personal identification number or password to use if you choose to remove the freeze on your credit report or authorize the release of your credit report for a specific party or period of time after the freeze is in place. To provide that authorization you must contact the consumer credit reporting agency and provide all of the following:

(1) The personal identification number or password.
(2) Proper identification to verify your identity.
(3) The proper information regarding the third party who is to receive the credit report or the period of time for which the report shall be available to users of the credit report.

A consumer credit reporting agency must authorize the release of your credit report no later than three business days after receiving the above information.

A security freeze does not apply when you have an existing account and a copy of your report is requested by your existing creditor or its agents or affiliates for certain types of account review, collection, fraud control, or similar activities.

If you are actively seeking credit, you should understand that the procedures involved in lifting a security freeze may slow your application for credit. You should plan ahead and lift a freeze, either completely if you are shopping around, or specifically for a certain creditor, before applying for new credit.

A consumer credit reporting agency may not charge a fee to a consumer for placing or removing a security freeze if the consumer is a victim of identity theft and submits a copy of a valid police report or valid Department of Motor Vehicles investigative report. A person 65 years of age or older with proper identification shall not be charged a fee for placing an initial security freeze, but may be charged a fee of no more than five dollars ($5) for lifting, removing, or replacing a security freeze. All other consumers may be charged a fee of no more than ten dollars ($10) for each of these steps.

You have a right to bring civil action against anyone, including a consumer credit reporting agency, who improperly obtains access to a file, knowingly or willfully misuses file data, or fails to correct inaccurate file data.

If you are a victim of identity theft and provide to a consumer credit reporting agency a copy of a valid police report or a valid investigative report made by a Department of Motor Vehicles investigator with peace officer status describing your circumstances, the following shall apply:

(1) You have a right to have any information you list on the report as allegedly fraudulent promptly blocked so that the information cannot be reported. The information will be unblocked only if (A) the information you provide is a material misrepresentation of the facts, (B) you agree that the information is blocked in error, or (C) you knowingly obtained possession of goods, services, or moneys as a result of the blocked transactions. If blocked information is unblocked, you will be promptly notified.

(2) You have a right to receive, free of charge and upon request, one copy of your credit report each month for up to 12 consecutive months."

Leg.H. Added Stats 1975 ch 1271 §1. Amended Stats 1976 ch 666 §3; Stats 1980 ch 1113 §2; Stats 1992 ch 1194 §6 (AB 1629), operative July 1, 1993; Stats 2000 ch 978 §2 (SB 1607), operative July 1, 2001; Stats 2001 ch 720 §6 (SB 168); Stats 2002 ch 860 §1 (SB 1239); Stats 2003 ch 907 §3 (SB 25); Stats 2008 ch 151 §2 (AB 372), effective January 1, 2009; Stats 2012 ch 645 §2 (AB 2374), effective January 1, 2013.

§1785.15.1. "Credit score" information

(a) Upon the consumer's request for a credit score, a consumer credit reporting agency shall supply to a consumer a notice which shall include the information described in paragraphs (1) to (5), inclusive, and a statement indicating that the information and credit scoring model may be different than the credit score that may be used by the lender. However, if the consumer requests the credit file and not the credit score, then the consumer shall receive the credit file and a statement that he or she may request and obtain a credit score.

(1) The consumer's current credit score or the consumer's most recent credit score that was previously calculated by the credit reporting agency for a purpose related to the extension of credit.

(2) The range of possible credit scores under the model used.

(3) All the key factors that adversely affected the consumer's credit score in the model used, the total number of which shall not exceed four.

(4) The date the credit score was created.

(5) The name of the person or entity that provided the credit score or credit file upon which the credit score was created.

(b) For purposes of this act, "credit score" means a numerical value or a categorization derived from a statistical tool or modeling system used by a person who makes or arranges a loan to predict the likelihood of certain credit behaviors, including default. The numerical value or the categorization derived from this analysis may also be referred to as a "risk predictor" or "risk score." "Credit score" does not include any mortgage score or rating of an automated underwriting system that considers one or more factors in addition to credit information, including, but not limited to, the loan to value ratio, the amount of down payment, or a consumer's financial assets. "Credit score" does not include other elements of the underwriting process or underwriting decision.

(c) For the purposes of this section, "key factors" means all relevant elements or reasons adversely affecting the credit score for the particular individual listed in the order of their importance based on their effect on the credit score.

(d) The information required by this section shall be provided in the same timeframe and manner as the information described in Section 1785.15.

(e) This section shall not be construed to compel a consumer reporting agency to develop or disclose a score if the agency does not (1) distribute scores that are used in connection with residential real property loans, or

(2) develop scores that assist credit providers in understanding a consumer's general credit behavior and predicting his or her future credit behavior.

(f) This section shall not be construed to require a consumer credit reporting agency that distributes credit scores developed by another person or entity to provide a further explanation of them, or to process a dispute arising pursuant to subdivision (a) of Section 1785.16, except that the consumer credit reporting agency shall provide the consumer with the name and address and website for contacting the person or entity who developed the score or developed the methodology of the score. This subdivision does not apply to a consumer credit reporting agency that develops or modifies scores that are developed by another person or entity.

(g) This section shall not be construed to require a consumer reporting agency to maintain credit scores in its files. **Leg.H.** Added Stats 2000 ch 978 §3 (SB 1607), operative July 1, 2001.

§1785.15.2. Credit scoring assessment or model; Fee

(a) In complying with Section 1785.15.1, a consumer credit reporting agency shall supply the consumer with a credit score that is derived from a credit scoring model that is widely distributed to users by that consumer credit reporting agency in connection with residential real property loans or with a credit score that assists the consumer in understanding the credit scoring assessment of his or her credit behavior and predictions about his or her future credit behavior, and a statement indicating that the information and credit scoring model may be different than that used by the lender.

(b) A consumer credit reporting agency may charge a reasonable fee for providing the information required under Section 1785.15.1. **Leg.H.** Added Stats 2000 ch 978 §4 (SB 1607), operative July 1, 2001.

§1785.15.3. Statement of rights of victims of identity theft

(a) In addition to any other rights the consumer may have under this title, every consumer credit reporting agency, after being contacted by telephone, mail, or in person by any consumer who has reason to believe he or she may be a victim of identity theft, shall promptly provide to that consumer a statement, written in a clear and conspicuous manner, describing the statutory rights of victims of identity theft under this title.

(b) Every consumer credit reporting agency shall, upon the receipt from a victim of identity theft of a police report prepared pursuant to Section 530.6 of the Penal Code, or a valid investigative report made by a Department of Motor Vehicles investigator with peace officer status regarding the public offenses described in Section 530.5 of the Penal Code, provide the victim, free of charge and upon request, with up to 12 copies of his or her file during a consecutive 12-month period, not to exceed one copy per month, following the date of the police report. Notwithstanding any other provision of this title, the maximum number of free reports a victim of identity theft is entitled to obtain under this title is 12 per year, as provided by this subdivision.

(c) Subdivision (a) does not apply to a consumer reporting agency that acts only as a reseller of credit information by assembling and merging information contained in the database of another consumer reporting agency or agencies and that does not maintain a permanent database of credit information from which new credit reports are produced.

(d) The provisions of this section shall become effective July 1, 2003. **Leg.H.** Added Stats 2002 ch 860 §2 (SB 1239), effective July 1, 2003.

§1785.16. Disputed information; Liability for disclosure of credit score

(a) If the completeness or accuracy of any item of information contained in his or her file is disputed by a consumer, and the dispute is conveyed directly to the consumer credit reporting agency by the consumer or user on behalf of the consumer, the consumer credit reporting agency shall within a reasonable period of time and without charge, reinvestigate and record the current status of the disputed information before the end of the 30-business-day period beginning on the date the agency receives notice of the dispute from the consumer or user, unless the consumer credit reporting agency has reasonable grounds to believe and determines that the dispute by the consumer is frivolous or irrelevant, including by reason of a failure of the consumer to provide sufficient information, as requested by the consumer credit reporting agency, to investigate the dispute. Unless the consumer credit reporting agency determines that the dispute is frivolous or irrelevant, before the end of the five-business-day period beginning on the date the consumer credit reporting agency receives notice of dispute under this section, the agency shall notify any person who provided information in dispute at the address and in the manner specified by the person. A consumer credit reporting agency may require that disputes by consumers be in writing.

(b) In conducting that reinvestigation the consumer credit reporting agency shall review and consider all relevant information submitted by the consumer with respect to the disputed item of information. If the consumer credit reporting agency determines that the dispute is frivolous or irrelevant, it shall notify the consumer by mail or, if authorized by the consumer for that purpose, by any other means available to the consumer credit reporting agency, within five business days after that determination is made that it is terminating its reinvestigation of the item of information. In this notification, the consumer credit reporting agency shall state the specific reasons why it has determined that the consumer's dispute is frivolous or irrelevant. If the disputed item of information is found to be inaccurate, missing, or can no longer be verified by the evidence submitted, the consumer credit reporting agency shall promptly add, correct, or delete that information from the consumer's file.

(c) No information may be reinserted in a consumer's file after having been deleted pursuant to this section unless the person who furnished the information certifies that the information is accurate. If any information deleted from a consumer's file is reinserted in the file, the consumer credit reporting agency shall promptly notify the consumer of the reinsertion in writing or, if authorized by the consumer for that purpose, by any other means available to the consumer credit reporting agency. As part of, or in addition to, this notice the consumer credit reporting agency shall, within five business days of reinserting the information, provide the consumer in writing (1) a statement that the disputed information has been reinserted, (2) a notice that the agency will provide to the consumer, within 15 days following a request, the name, address, and telephone number of any furnisher of information contacted or which contacted the consumer credit reporting agency in connection with the reinsertion, (3) the toll-free telephone number of the consumer credit reporting agency that the consumer can use to obtain this name, address, and telephone number, and (4) a notice that the consumer has the right to a reinvestigation of the information reinserted by the consumer credit reporting agency and to add a statement to his or her file disputing the accuracy or completeness of the information.

(d) A consumer credit reporting agency shall provide written notice to the consumer of the results of any reinvestigation under this subdivision, within five days of completion of the reinvestigation. The notice shall include (1) a statement that the reinvestigation is completed, (2) a consumer credit report that is based on the consumer's file as that file is revised as a result of the reinvestigation, (3) a description or indication of any changes made in the consumer credit report as a result of those revisions to the consumer's file and a description of any changes made or sought by the consumer that were not made and an explanation why they were not made, (4) a notice that, if requested by the consumer, a description of the procedure used to determine the accuracy and completeness of the information shall be provided to the consumer by the consumer credit reporting agency, including the name, business address, and telephone number of any furnisher of information contacted in connection with that information, (5) a notice that the consumer has the right to add a statement to the consumer's file disputing the accuracy or completeness of the information, (6) a notice that the consumer has the right to request that the consumer credit reporting agency furnish notifications under subdivision (h), (7) a notice that the dispute will remain on file with the agency as long as the credit information is used, and (8) a statement about the details of the dispute will be furnished to any recipient as long as the credit information is retained in the agency's data base. A consumer credit reporting agency shall provide the notice pursuant to this subdivision respecting the procedure used to determine the accuracy and completeness of information, not later than 15 days after receiving a request from the consumer.

(e) The presence of information in the consumer's file that contradicts the contention of the consumer shall not, in and of itself, constitute reasonable grounds for believing the dispute is frivolous or irrelevant.

(f) If the consumer credit reporting agency determines that the dispute is frivolous or irrelevant, or if the reinvestigation does not resolve the dispute, or if the information is reinserted into the consumer's file pursuant to subdivision (c), the consumer may file a brief statement setting forth the nature of the dispute. The consumer credit reporting agency may limit these statements to not more than 100 words if it provides the consumer with assistance in writing a clear summary of the dispute.

(g) Whenever a statement of dispute is filed, the consumer credit reporting agency shall, in any subsequent consumer credit report containing the information in question, clearly note that the information is disputed by the consumer and shall include in the report either the consumer's statement or a clear and accurate summary thereof.

(h) Following the deletion of information from a consumer's file pursuant to this section, or following the filing of a statement of dispute pursuant to subdivision (f), the consumer credit reporting agency, at the request of the consumer, shall furnish notification that the item of information has been deleted or that the item of information is disputed. In the case of disputed information, the notification shall include the statement or summary of the dispute filed pursuant to subdivision (f). This notification shall be furnished to any person designated by the consumer who has, within two years prior to the deletion or the filing of the dispute, received a consumer credit report concerning the consumer for employment purposes, or who has, within 12 months of the deletion or the filing of the dispute, received a consumer credit report concerning the consumer for any other purpose, if these consumer credit reports contained the deleted or disputed information. The consumer credit reporting agency shall clearly and conspicuously disclose to the consumer his or her rights to make a request for this notification. The disclosure shall be made at or prior to the time the information is deleted pursuant to this section or the consumer's statement regarding the disputed information is received pursuant to subdivision (f).

(i) A consumer credit reporting agency shall maintain reasonable procedures to prevent the reappearance in a consumer's file and in consumer credit reports of information that has been deleted pursuant to this section and not reinserted pursuant to subdivision (c).

(j) If the consumer's dispute is resolved by deletion of the disputed information within three business days, beginning with the day the consumer credit reporting agency receives notice of the dispute in accordance with subdivision (a), and provided that verification thereof is provided to the consumer in writing within five business days following the deletion, then the consumer credit reporting agency shall be exempt from requirements for further action under subdivisions (d), (f), and (g).

(k) If a consumer submits to a credit reporting agency a copy of a valid police report, or a valid investigative report made by a Department of Motor Vehicles investigator with peace officer status, filed pursuant to Section 530.5 of the Penal Code, the consumer credit reporting agency shall promptly and permanently block reporting any information that the consumer alleges appears on his or her credit report as a result of a violation of Section 530.5 of the Penal Code so that the information cannot be reported. The consumer credit reporting agency shall promptly notify the furnisher of the information that the information has been so blocked. Furnishers of information and consumer credit reporting agencies shall ensure that information is unblocked only upon a preponderance of the evidence establishing the facts required under paragraph (1), (2), or (3). The permanently blocked information shall be unblocked only if: (1) the information was blocked due to a material misrepresentation of fact by the consumer or fraud, or (2) the consumer agrees that the blocked information, or portions of the blocked information, were blocked in error, or (3) the consumer knowingly obtained possession of goods, services, or moneys as a result of the blocked transaction or transactions or the consumer should have known that he or she obtained possession of goods, services, or moneys as a result of the blocked transaction or transactions. If blocked information is unblocked pursuant to this subdivision, the consumer shall be promptly notified in the same manner as consumers are notified of the reinsertion of information pursuant to subdivision (c). The prior presence of the blocked information in the consumer credit reporting agency's file on the consumer is not evidence of whether the consumer knew or should have known that he or she obtained possession of any goods, services, or moneys. For the purposes of this subdivision, fraud may be demonstrated by circumstantial evidence. In unblocking information pursuant to this subdivision, furnishers and consumer credit reporting agencies shall be subject to their respective requirements pursuant to this title regarding the completeness and accuracy of information.

(*l*) In unblocking information as described in subdivision (k), a consumer reporting agency shall comply with all requirements of this section and 15 U.S.C. Sec. 1681i relating to reinvestigating disputed information. In addition, a consumer reporting agency shall accept the consumer's version of the disputed information and correct or delete the disputed item when the consumer submits to the consumer reporting agency documentation obtained from the source of the item in dispute or from public records confirming that the report was inaccurate or incomplete, unless the consumer reporting agency, in the exercise of good faith and reasonable judgment, has substantial reason based on specific, verifiable facts to doubt the authenticity of the documentation submitted and notifies the consumer in writing of that decision, explaining its reasons for unblocking the information and setting forth the specific, verifiable facts on which the decision was based.

(m) Any provision in a contract that prohibits the disclosure of a credit score by a person who makes or arranges loans or a consumer credit reporting agency is void. A lender shall not have liability under any contractual provision for disclosure of a credit score. **Leg.H.** Added Stats 1975 ch 1271 §1. Amended Stats 1976 ch 666 §4; Stats 1980 ch 1113 §3; Stats 1990 ch 1315 §1 (SB 2750); Stats 1992 ch 1194 §7 (AB 1629), operative July 1, 1993; Stats 1993 ch 285 §7 (AB 1340), effective July 30, 1993; Stats 1997 ch 768 §2 (AB 156), operative July 1, 1998; Stats 2000 ch 978 §5 (SB 1607), operative July 1, 2001; Stats 2001 ch 354 §3 (AB 655).

§1785.16.1. Deletion of credit report inquiries initiated as a result of identity theft

A consumer credit reporting agency shall delete from a consumer credit report inquiries for credit reports based upon credit requests that the consumer credit reporting agency verifies were initiated as the result of identity theft, as defined in Section 1798.92. **Leg.H.** Added Stats 2001 ch 354 §4 (AB 655).

§1785.16.2. Prohibition against selling consumer debt when debt is blocked; Victim of identity theft

(a) No creditor may sell a consumer debt to a debt collector, as defined in 15 U.S.C. Sec. 1692a, if the consumer is a victim of identity theft, as defined in Section 1798.2, and with respect to that debt, the creditor has received notice pursuant to subdivision (k) of Section 1785.16 or paragraph (2) of subdivision (g) of Section 1788.18.

(b) Subdivision (a) does not apply to a creditor's sale of a debt to a subsidiary or affiliate of the creditor, if, with respect to that debt, the subsidiary or affiliate does not take any action to collect the debt.

(c) For the purposes of this section, the requirement in 15 U.S.C. Sec. 1692a, that a person must use an instrumentality of interstate commerce or the mails in the collection of any debt to be considered a debt collector, does not apply. **Leg.H.** Added Stats 2001 ch 354 §4.5 (AB 655). Amended Stats 2002 ch 1030 §1 (AB 1068), effective September 28, 2002; Stats 2016 ch 376 §2 (AB 1723), effective January 1, 2017.

2016 Note: This act shall be known, and may be cited, as the Identity Theft Resolution Act. Stats 2016 ch 376 (AB 1723) §1.

§1785.16.3. Exception to blocking provisions for certain agencies that act only as reseller of credit information

The provisions of subdivisions (k) and (*l*) of Section 1785.16 do not apply to a consumer reporting agency that acts only as a reseller of credit information by assembling and merging information contained in the database of another consumer reporting agency or agencies, and that does not maintain a permanent database of credit information from which new credit reports are produced. **Leg.H.** Added Stats 2002 ch 1029 §2 (AB 2868), effective September 28, 2002.

§1785.17. Charges for information

(a) Except as otherwise provided, a consumer credit reporting agency may impose a reasonable charge upon a consumer, as follows:

(1) For making a disclosure pursuant to Section 1785.10 or 1785.15, the consumer credit reporting agency may charge a fee not exceeding eight dollars ($8).

(2) For furnishing a notification, statement, or summary, to any person pursuant to subdivision (h) of Section 1785.16, the consumer credit reporting agency may charge a fee not exceeding the charge that it would impose on each designated recipient for a consumer credit report, and the amount of the charge shall be indicated to the consumer before furnishing the notification, statement, or summary.

(b) A consumer credit reporting agency shall make all disclosures pursuant to Sections 1785.10 and 1785.15 and furnish all consumer reports pursuant to Section 1785.16 without charge, if requested by the consumer within 60 days after receipt by the consumer of a notification of adverse action pursuant to Section 1785.20 or of a notification from a debt collection agency affiliated with the consumer credit reporting agency stating that the consumer's credit rating may be or has been adversely affected.

(c) A consumer credit reporting agency shall not impose any charge for (1) providing notice to a consumer required under Section 1785.16 or (2) notifying a person pursuant to subdivision (h) of Section 1785.16 of the deletion of any information which is found to be inaccurate or which can no longer be verified, if the consumer designates that person to the consumer credit reporting agency before the end of the 30-day period beginning on that date of notice under subdivision (d) of Section 1785.16. **Leg.H.** Added Stats 1975 ch 1271 §1. Amended Stats 1976 ch 666 §5; Stats 1980 ch 1113 §4; Stats 1992 ch 651 §1, ch 1194 §8 (AB 1629), operative July 1, 1993.

§1785.18. Information based on public record

(a) Each consumer credit reporting agency which compiles and reports items of information concerning consumers which are matters of public record, shall specify in any report containing public record information the source from which that information was obtained, including the particular court, if there be such, and the date that the information was initially reported or publicized.

(b) A consumer credit reporting agency which furnishes a consumer credit report for employment purposes, and which for that purpose compiles and reports items of information on consumers which are matters of public record and are likely to have an adverse effect upon a consumer's ability to obtain employment shall, in addition, maintain strict procedures designed to ensure that whenever public record information which is likely to have an adverse effect on a consumer's ability to obtain employment is reported it is complete and up to date. For purposes of this paragraph, items of public record relating to arrests, indictments, convictions, suits, tax liens, and outstanding judgments shall be considered up to date if the current public record status of the item at the time of the report is reported.

(c) No consumer credit reporting agency which furnishes a consumer credit report for employment purposes shall report information on the age, marital status, race, color, or creed of any consumer. **Leg.H.** Added Stats 1975 ch 1271 §1. Amended Stats 1991 ch 971 §1 (AB 1102).

§1785.19. Action for civil penalty

(a) In addition to any other remedy provided by law, a consumer may bring an action for a civil penalty, not to exceed two thousand five hundred dollars ($2,500), against any of the following:

(1) A person who knowingly and willfully obtains access to a file other than as provided in Section 1785.11.

(2) Any person who knowingly and willfully obtains data from a file other than as provided in Section 1785.11.

(3) A person who uses the data received from a file in a manner contrary to an agreement with the consumer credit reporting agency.

Such an action may also be brought by the person or entity responsible for the file accessed. This remedy is in addition to any other remedy which may exist.

(b) If a plaintiff prevails in an action under subdivision (a) he or she shall be awarded the civil penalty, costs, and reasonable attorney fees. **Leg.H.** Added Stats 1990 ch 842 §2 (AB 2908).

§1785.19.5. Use of files for marketing purposes

Every consumer credit reporting agency, upon written request and the furnishing of sufficient identification to identify the consumer and the subject file, shall create reasonable procedures to prevent a consumer credit report or information from a consumer's file from being provided to any third party for marketing purposes or for any offer of credit not requested by the consumer. This section does not apply to the use of information by a credit grantor for purposes related to an existing credit relationship. **Leg.H.** Added Stats 1990 ch 842 §3 (AB 2908).

CHAPTER 3
REQUIREMENTS ON USERS OF CONSUMER CREDIT REPORTS

Notice following adverse action. §1785.20.
Transactions not initiated by consumer. §1785.20.1.
"Credit score" information. §1785.20.2.
Verification of consumer address; Reasonable steps before extending credit to determine identity theft; Violation; Recoverable damages. §1785.20.3.
Prohibition on negative use of COVID-19 rental debt in evaluating housing application. §1785.20.4.
Reports for employment purposes. §1785.20.5.
Prohibition on use of medical debt as negative factor in credit decisions. §1785.20.6.
Request for investigation. §1785.21.
Reselling credit reports. §1785.22.

§1785.20. Notice following adverse action

(a) If any person takes any adverse action with respect to any consumer, and the adverse action is based, in whole or in part, on any information contained in a consumer credit report, that person shall do all of the following:

(1) Provide written notice of the adverse action to the consumer.

(2) Provide the consumer with the name, address, and telephone number of the consumer credit reporting agency which furnished the report to the person.

(3) Provide a statement that the credit grantor's decision to take adverse action was based in whole or in part upon information contained in a consumer credit report.

(4) Provide the consumer with a written notice of the following rights of the consumer:

(A) The right of the consumer to obtain within 60 days a free copy of the consumer's consumer credit report from the consumer credit reporting agency identified pursuant to paragraph (2) and from any other consumer credit reporting agency which compiles and maintains files on consumers on a nationwide basis.

(B) The right of the consumer under Section 1785.16 to dispute the accuracy or completeness of any information in a consumer credit report furnished by the consumer credit reporting agency.

(b) Whenever credit or insurance for personal, family, or household purposes involving a consumer is denied or the charge for such credit is increased either wholly or in part because of information obtained from a person other than a consumer credit reporting agency bearing upon consumer's credit worthiness or credit standing, the user of that information shall, within a reasonable period of time, and upon the consumer's written request for the reasons for that adverse action received within 60 days after learning of the adverse action, disclose the nature and substance of the information to the consumer. The user of the information shall clearly and accurately disclose to the consumer his or her right to make such a written request at the time the adverse action is communicated to the consumer.

(c) No person shall be held liable for any violation of this section if he or she shows by a preponderance of the evidence that at the time of the alleged violation he or she maintained reasonable procedures to assure compliance with this section.

(d) Nothing in this chapter shall excuse compliance with the requirements of Section 1787.2. **Leg.H.** Added Stats 1975 ch 1271 §1. Amended Stats 1980 ch 1113 §5; Stats 1982 ch 1127 §5; Stats 1992 ch 1194 §9 (AB 1629), operative July 1, 1993.

§1785.20.1. Transactions not initiated by consumer

(a) Except as provided in subdivision (b), any person who uses a consumer credit report in connection with any credit transaction not initiated by the consumer and which consists of a firm offer of credit shall provide with any solicitation made to the consumer a clear and conspicuous statement as to all of the following:

(1) Information contained in the consumer's prequalifying report was used in connection with the transaction.

(2) The consumer received the offer of credit, because the consumer satisfied the criteria for creditworthiness under which the consumer was selected for the offer.

(3) Where applicable, the credit may not be extended if, after the consumer responds to the offer, the consumer does not meet the criteria used to select the consumer for the offer.

(4) The consumer has a right to prohibit use of information contained in the consumer's file with any consumer credit reporting agency in connection with any credit transaction that is not initiated by the consumer. The consumer may exercise this right by notifying the notification system or joint notification system established under subdivision (d) or (e) of Section 1785.11.

(b) Subdivision (a) does not apply to any person using a prequalifying report if all of the following conditions are met:

(1) The person using the prequalifying report is affiliated by common ownership or common corporate control with the person who procured the report.

(2) The person who procures the prequalifying report from the consumer credit reporting agency clearly and conspicuously discloses to the consumer to whom the report relates, before the prequalifying report is provided to the person who uses the report, that the prequalifying report might be provided to, and used by, persons affiliated in the manner specified in paragraph (1) with the person that procured the report.

(3) The consumer consents in writing to this provision and use of the prequalifying report.

(c) No person shall be denied credit on the basis of the consumer's refusal to provide consent pursuant to paragraph (3) of subdivision (b), unless that consent is necessary for the extension of credit, related to that transaction, by an affiliate. **Leg.H.** Added Stats 1992 ch 1194 §9.5 (AB 1629), operative July 1, 1993.

§1785.20.2. "Credit score" information

Any person who makes or arranges loans and who uses a consumer credit score as defined in Section 1785.15.1 in connection with an application initiated or sought by a consumer for a closed end loan or establishment of an open end loan for a consumer purpose that is secured by one to four units of residential real property shall provide the following to the consumer as soon as reasonably practicable:

(a) A copy of the information identified in subdivision (a) of Section 1785.15.1 that was obtained from a credit reporting agency or was developed and used by the user of the information. In addition to the information provided to it by a third party that provided the credit score or scores, a lender is only required to provide the notice contained in subdivision (d).

(b) If a person who is subject to this section uses an automated underwriting system to underwrite a loan, that person may satisfy the obligation to provide a credit score by disclosing a credit score and associated key factors supplied by a consumer credit reporting agency. However, if a numerical credit score is generated by an automated underwriting system used by an enterprise, and that score is disclosed to the person, it shall be disclosed to the consumer consistent with subdivision (c). For purposes of this subdivision, the term "enterprise" shall have the meaning provided in paragraph (6) of Section 4502 of Title 12 of the United States Code.

(c) A person subject to the provisions of this section who uses a credit score other than a credit score provided by a consumer reporting agency may satisfy the obligation to provide a credit score by disclosing a credit score and associated key factors supplied by a consumer credit reporting agency.

(d) A copy of the following notice, which shall include the name, address, and telephone number of each credit bureau providing a credit score that was used:

NOTICE TO THE HOME LOAN APPLICANT

In connection with your application for a home loan, the lender must disclose to you the score that a credit bureau distributed to users and the lender used in connection with your home loan, and the key factors affecting your credit scores.

The credit score is a computer generated summary calculated at the time of the request and based on information a credit bureau or lender has on file. The scores are based on data about your credit history and payment patterns. Credit scores are important because they are used to assist the lender in determining whether you will obtain a loan. They may also be used to determine what interest rate you may be offered on the mortgage. Credit scores can change over time, depending on your conduct, how your credit history and payment patterns change, and how credit scoring technologies change.

Because the score is based on information in your credit history, it is very important that you review the credit-related information that is being furnished to make sure it is accurate. Credit records may vary from one company to another.

If you have questions about your credit score or the credit information that is furnished to you, contact the credit bureau at the address and telephone number provided with this notice, or contact the lender, if the lender developed or generated the credit score. The credit bureau plays no part in the decision to take any action on the loan application and is unable to provide you with specific reasons for the decision on a loan application.

If you have questions concerning the terms of the loan, contact the lender.

(e) This section shall not require any person to do the following:

(1) Explain the information provided pursuant to Section 1785.15.1.

(2) Disclose any information other than a credit score or key factor, as defined in Section 1785.15.1.

(3) Disclose any credit score or related information obtained by the user after a loan has closed.

(4) Provide more than one disclosure per loan transaction.

(5) Provide the disclosure required by this section when another person has made the disclosure to the consumer for that loan transaction.

(f) Any person's obligation pursuant to this section shall be limited solely to providing a copy of the information that was received from the consumer credit reporting agency. No person has liability under this section for the content of that information or for the omission of any information within the report provided by the consumer credit reporting agency.

(g) As used in this section, the term "person" does not include an "enterprise" as defined in paragraph (6) of Section 4502 of Title 12 of the United States Code. **Leg.H.** Added Stats 2000 ch 978 §6 (SB 1607), operative July 1, 2001.

§1785.20.3. Verification of consumer address; Reasonable steps before extending credit to determine identity theft; Violation; Recoverable damages

(a) Any person who uses a consumer credit report in connection with the approval of credit based on an application for an extension of credit, and who discovers that the consumer's first and last name, address, or social security number, on the credit application does not match, within a reasonable degree of certainty, the consumer's first and last name, address or addresses, or social security number listed, if any, on the consumer credit report, shall take reasonable steps to verify the accuracy of the consumer's first and last name, address, or social security number provided on the application to confirm that the extension of credit is not the result of identity theft, as defined in Section 1798.92.

(b) Any person who uses a consumer credit report in connection with the approval of credit based on an application for an extension of credit, and who has received notification pursuant to subdivision (k) of Section 1785.16 that the applicant has been a victim of identity theft, as defined in Section 1798.92, may not lend money or extend credit without taking reasonable steps to verify the consumer's identity and confirm that the application for an extension of credit is not the result of identity theft.

(c) Any consumer who suffers damages as a result of a violation of this section by any person may bring an action in a court of appropriate jurisdiction against that person to recover actual damages, court costs, attorney's fees, and punitive damages of not more than thirty thousand dollars ($30,000) for each violation, as the court deems proper.

(d) As used in this section, "identity theft" has the meaning given in subdivision (b) of Section 1798.92.

(e) For the purposes of this section, "extension of credit" does not include an increase in an existing open-end credit plan, as defined in Regulation Z of the Federal Reserve System (12 C.F.R. 226.2), or any change to or review of an existing credit account.

(f) If a consumer provides initial written notice to a creditor that he or she is a victim of identity theft, as defined in subdivision (d) of Section 1798.92, the creditor shall provide written notice to the consumer of his or her rights under subdivision (k) of Section 1785.16.

(g) The provisions of subdivisions (k) and (l) of Section 1785.16 do not apply to a consumer credit reporting agency that acts only as a reseller of credit information by assembling and merging information contained in the database of another consumer credit reporting agency or the databases of multiple consumer credit reporting agencies, and does not maintain a permanent database of credit information from which new credit reports are produced.

(h) This section does not apply if one of the addresses at issue is a United States Army or Air Force post office address or a United States Fleet post office address. **Leg.H.** Added Stats 2001 ch 354 §5 (AB 655). Amended Stats 2002 ch 1030 §2 (AB 1068), effective September 28, 2002; Stats 2003 ch 41 §1 (AB 1610).

2002 Note: Subsection (f) of Section 1785.20.3 of the Civil Code, as added by 2002 ch 1030, shall become operative 90 days after the effective date of chapter 1030 (December 27, 2002). Stats 2002 ch 1030 (AB 1068) §10.

§ 1785.20.4. Prohibition on negative use of COVID-19 rental debt in evaluating housing application

A housing provider, tenant screening company, or other entity that evaluates tenants on behalf of a housing provider shall not use an alleged COVID-19 rental debt, as defined in Section 1179.02 of the Code of Civil Procedure, as a negative factor for the purpose of evaluating a prospective housing application or as the basis for refusing to rent a dwelling unit to an otherwise qualified prospective tenant. **Leg.H.** Added Stats 2021 ch 2 §2 (SB 91), effective January 29, 2021. Amended Stats 2021 ch 5 §3 (AB 81), effective February 23, 2021.

Prior Law This section, as added Stats 2021 ch 2 §2 (SB 91), effective January 29, 2021, until February 23, 2021, read:

A housing provider, tenant screening company, or other entity that evaluates tenants on behalf of a housing provider shall not use an alleged COVID-19 rental debt, as that term is defined in Section 1179.02, as a negative factor for the purpose of evaluating a prospective housing application or as the basis for refusing to rent a dwelling unit to an otherwise qualified prospective tenant.

§1785.20.5. Reports for employment purposes

(a) Prior to requesting a consumer credit report for employment purposes, the user of the report shall provide written notice to the person involved. The notice shall inform the person that a report will be used, and shall identify the specific basis under subdivision (a) of Section 1024.5 of the Labor Code for use of the report. The notice shall also inform the person of the source of the report, and shall contain a box that the person may check off to receive a copy of the credit report. If the consumer indicates that he or she wishes to receive a copy of the report, the user shall request that a copy be provided to the person when the user requests its copy from the credit reporting agency. The report to the user and to the subject person shall be provided contemporaneously and at no charge to the subject person.

(b) Whenever employment involving a consumer is denied either wholly or partly because of information contained in a consumer credit report from a consumer credit reporting agency, the user of the consumer credit report shall so advise the consumer against whom the adverse action has been taken and supply the name and address or addresses of the consumer credit reporting agency making the report. No person shall be held liable for any violation of this section if he or she shows by a preponderance of the evidence that, at the time of the alleged violation, he or she maintained reasonable procedures to assure compliance with this section. **Leg.H.** Added Stats 1976 ch 666 §7.5. Amended Stats 1991 ch 971 §2 (AB 1102); Stats 2011 ch 724 §1 (AB 22), effective January 1, 2012.

§ 1785.20.6. Prohibition on use of medical debt as negative factor in credit decisions

A person who uses a consumer credit report in connection with a credit transaction shall not use a medical debt listed on the report as a negative factor when making a credit decision. **Leg.H.** Added Stats 2024 ch 520 §3 (SB 1061), effective January 1, 2025.

§1785.21. Request for investigation

(a) A user in its discretion may notify the consumer that upon request the user may contact the consumer reporting agency and request that the consumer reporting agency investigate the current status of an item or items of information contained in the consumer report if the consumer disputes the completeness or accuracy of an item or items of information as provided to the user.

(b) The consumer credit reporting agency may require identification from the user to insure the validity of the request and, in that regard, may require that the request be put in writing with proper identification.

(c) In the event that any such request is made and identification given in the form or manner demanded by the consumer credit reporting agency, such agency shall review the file of the consumer and report the current status of the disputed information to the user and the consumer by the most expeditious means possible.

(d) No user who furnishes information pursuant to this section shall be liable to any person for furnishing such information. **Leg.H.** Added Stats 1976 ch 666 §8.

§1785.22. Reselling credit reports

(a) A person may not procure a consumer credit report for the purpose of reselling the report or any information therein unless the person discloses to the consumer credit reporting agency which issues the report the identity of the ultimate end user and each permissible purpose for which the report is furnished to the end user of the consumer credit report or information therein.

(b) A person that procures a consumer credit report for the purpose of reselling the report or any information therein shall do all of the following:

(1) Establish and comply with reasonable procedures designed to ensure that the consumer credit report or information is resold by the person only for a purpose for which the report may be furnished under this title. These procedures shall include all of the following:

(A) Identification of each prospective user of the resold consumer credit report or information.

(B) Certification of each purpose for which the consumer credit report or information will be used.

(C) Certification that the consumer credit report or information will be used for no other purpose.

(2) Before reselling the consumer credit report or information, the person shall make reasonable efforts to verify the identities and certifications made under paragraph (1). **Leg.H.** Added Stats 1992 ch 1194 §10 (AB 1629), operative July 1, 1993.

CHAPTER 3.5
OBLIGATIONS OF FURNISHERS OF CREDIT INFORMATION

Incomplete, inaccurate or disputed information; Closed or delinquent accounts information. §1785.25.
Negative credit information from creditors. §1785.26.
Prohibition on furnishing medical debt information to consumer credit reporting agencies. § 1785.27.

§1785.25. Incomplete, inaccurate or disputed information; Closed or delinquent accounts information

(a) A person shall not furnish information on a specific transaction or experience to any consumer credit reporting agency if the person knows or should know the information is incomplete or inaccurate.

(b) A person who (1) in the ordinary course of business regularly and on a routine basis furnishes information to one or more consumer credit reporting agencies about the person's own transactions or experiences with one or more consumers and (2) determines that information on a specific transaction or experience so provided to a consumer credit reporting agency is not complete or accurate, shall promptly notify the consumer credit reporting agency of that determination and provide to the consumer credit reporting agency any corrections to that information, or any additional information, that is necessary to make the information provided by the person to the consumer credit reporting agency complete and accurate.

(c) So long as the completeness or accuracy of any information on a specific transaction or experience furnished by any person to a consumer credit reporting agency is subject to a continuing dispute between the affected consumer and that person, the person may not furnish the information to any consumer credit reporting agency without also including a notice that the information is disputed by the consumer.

(d) A person who regularly furnishes information to a consumer credit reporting agency regarding a consumer who has an open-end credit account with that person, and which is closed by the consumer, shall notify the consumer credit reporting agency of the closure of that account by the consumer, in the information regularly furnished for the period in which the account is closed.

(e) A person who places a delinquent account for collection (internally or by referral to a third party), charges the delinquent account to profit or loss, or takes similar action, and subsequently furnishes information to a credit reporting agency regarding that action, shall include within the information furnished the approximate commencement date of the delinquency which gave rise to that action, unless that date was previously reported to the credit reporting agency. Nothing in this provision shall require that a delinquency must be reported to a credit reporting agency.

(f) Upon receiving notice of a dispute noticed pursuant to subdivision (a) of Section 1785.16 with regard to the completeness or accuracy of any information provided to a consumer credit reporting agency, the person that provided the information shall (1) complete an investigation with respect to the disputed information and report to the consumer credit reporting agency the results of that investigation before the end of the

30-business-day period beginning on the date the consumer credit reporting agency receives the notice of dispute from the consumer in accordance with subdivision (a) of Section 1785.16 and (2) review relevant information submitted to it.

(g) A person who furnishes information to a consumer credit reporting agency is liable for failure to comply with this section, unless the furnisher establishes by a preponderance of the evidence that, at the time of the failure to comply with this section, the furnisher maintained reasonable procedures to comply with those provisions. **Leg.H.** Added Stats 1992 ch 1194 §11 (AB 1629), operative July 1, 1993. Amended Stats 1993 ch 285 §8 (AB 1340), effective July 30, 1993.

§1785.26. Negative credit information from creditors

(a) As used in this section:

(1) "Creditor" includes an agent or assignee of a creditor, including an agent engaged in administering or collecting the creditor's accounts.

(2) "Negative credit information" means information concerning the credit history of a consumer that, because of the consumer's past delinquencies, late or irregular payment history, insolvency, or any form of default, would reasonably be expected to affect adversely the consumer's ability to obtain or maintain credit. "Negative credit information" does not include information or credit histories arising from a nonconsumer transaction or any other credit transaction outside the scope of this title, nor does it include inquiries about a consumer's credit record.

(b) A creditor may submit negative credit information concerning a consumer to a consumer credit reporting agency, only if the creditor notifies the consumer affected. After providing this notice, a creditor may submit additional information to a credit reporting agency respecting the same transaction or extension of credit that gave rise to the original negative credit information without providing additional notice.

(c) The notice shall be in writing and shall be delivered in person or mailed first class, postage prepaid, to the party's last known address, prior to or within 30 days after the transmission of the negative credit information.

(1) The notice may be part of any notice of default, billing statement, or other correspondence, and may be included as preprinted or standard form language in any of these from the creditor to the consumer.

(2) The notice is sufficient if it is in substantially the following form: "As required by law, you are hereby notified that a negative credit report reflecting on your credit record may be submitted to a credit reporting agency if you fail to fulfill the terms of your credit obligations."

(3) The notice may, in the creditor's discretion, be more specific than the form given in paragraph (2). The notice may include, but shall not be limited to, particular information regarding an account or information respecting the approximate date on which the creditor submitted or intends to submit a negative credit report.

(4) The giving of notice by a creditor as provided in this subdivision does not create any requirement for the creditor to actually submit negative credit information to a consumer credit reporting agency. However, this section shall not be construed to authorize the use of notice as provided in this subdivision in violation of the federal Fair Debt Collection Practices Act (15 U.S.C., Sec. [1] **1692** et seq.).

(d) A creditor is liable for failure to provide notice pursuant to this section, unless the creditor establishes, by a preponderance of the evidence, that at the time of that failure to give notice the creditor maintained reasonable procedures to comply with this section. **Leg.H.** Added Stats 1992 ch 1194 §11 (AB 1629), operative July 1, 1993. Amended Stats 2024 ch 80 §20 (SB 1525), effective January 1, 2025.

§1785.26. 2024 Deletes. [1] 1592

§ 1785.27. Prohibition on furnishing medical debt information to consumer credit reporting agencies

(a) A person shall not furnish information regarding a medical debt to a consumer credit reporting agency.

(b) A medical debt is void and unenforceable if a person knowingly violates this section by furnishing information regarding the medical debt to a consumer credit reporting agency.

(c)(1) On or after July 1, 2025, it is unlawful to enter into a contract creating a medical debt that does not include the following term:

"A holder of this medical debt contract is prohibited by Section 1785.27 of the Civil Code from furnishing any information related to this debt to a consumer credit reporting agency. In addition to any other penalties allowed by law, if a person knowingly violates that section by furnishing information regarding this debt to a consumer credit reporting agency, the debt shall be void and unenforceable."

(2) A contract entered into on or after July 1, 2025, that does not include the term described in paragraph (1) is void and unenforceable.

(d) A violation of this section by a person holding a license or permit issued by the state shall be deemed to be a violation of the law governing that license or permit. **Leg.H.** Added Stats 2024 ch 520 §4 (SB 1061), effective January 1, 2025.

CHAPTER 3.6
ESCROW AGENT RATING SERVICE
[REPEALED EFFECTIVE JANUARY 1, 2027]

Compliance by escrow agent rating service with specified sections applicable to consumer credit reporting agency; Policies and procedures to safeguard personally identifiable information; Action by escrow agent for damages [Repealed January 1, 2027]. §1785.28.

Repeal of chapter [Repealed January 1, 2027]. §1785.28.6.

§1785.28. Compliance by escrow agent rating service with specified sections applicable to consumer credit reporting agency; Policies and procedures to safeguard personally identifiable information; Action by escrow agent for damages [Repealed January 1, 2027]

(a) For the purposes of this section, the following definitions shall apply:

(1) Escrow means any transaction in which one person, for the purpose of effecting the sale, transfer, encumbering, or leasing of real or personal property to another person, delivers any written instrument, money, evidence of title to real or personal property, or other thing of value to a third person to be held by that third person until the happening of a specified event or the performance of a prescribed condition, when it is then to be delivered by that third person to a grantee, grantor, promisee, promisor, obligee, obligor, bailee, bailor, or any agent or employee of any of the latter.

(2) An escrow agent is any of the following:

(A) A natural person who performs escrow services for an entity licensed pursuant to the Escrow Law contained in Division 6 (commencing with Section 17000) of the Financial Code.

(B) A natural person performing escrow services for a title insurer admitted pursuant to Article 3 (commencing with Section 699) of Chapter 1 of Part 2 of Division 1 of the Insurance Code or an underwritten title company licensed pursuant to Article 3.7 (commencing with Section 12389) of Chapter 1 of Part 6 of Division 2 of the Insurance Code.

(C) A natural person performing escrow services for a controlled escrow company, as defined in Section 12340.6 of the Insurance Code.

(D) A natural person licensed pursuant to Division 4 (commencing with Section 10000) of the Business and Professions Code, who performs escrow services, in accordance with Section 17006 of the Financial Code.

(3) An escrow agent rating service is a person or entity that prepares a report, for compensation or in expectation of compensation, for use by a creditor in evaluating the capacity of an escrow agent to perform escrow services in connection with an extension of credit. An escrow agent rating service does not include either of the following:

(A) A creditor or an employee of a creditor evaluating an escrow agent in connection with an extension of credit by that creditor.

(B) An entity described in paragraph (2) for which a natural person performs escrow services as an employee or an independent contractor.

(4) An escrow agent rating service shall be considered a reseller of credit information within the meaning of Section 1785.22 if it assembles and merges information contained in the database or databases maintained by a consumer credit reporting agency.

(5) "Consumer" also means escrow agent.

(b) An escrow agent rating service shall comply with and be subject to the following sections of this title applicable to a consumer credit reporting agency:

(1) Subdivision (a) of Section 1785.10.

(2) Subdivision (b) of Section 1785.10, limited to the obligation to advise a consumer of his or her right to a decoded written version of a file.

(3) Subdivision (d) of Section 1785.10.

(4) Paragraph (2) of subdivision (a) of Section 1785.11.

(5) Section 1785.13.

(6) Section 1785.14.

(7) Paragraph (1) of subdivision (a) of Section 1785.15, limited to the right to request and receive a decoded written version of the file.

(8) Section 1785.16.

(9) Section 1785.18.

(c) An escrow agent rating service that acts as a reseller of credit information as described in paragraph (4) of subdivision (a) shall comply with and be subject to Section 1785.22.

(d) An escrow agent rating service shall establish policies and procedures reasonably intended to safeguard from theft or misuse any personally identifiable information it obtains from an escrow agent.

(e) An escrow agent who suffers damages as a result of the failure of an escrow agent rating service to comply with subdivision (b), (c), or (d) may bring an action in a court of competent jurisdiction pursuant to Section 1785.31 of the Civil Code.

(f) If an escrow agent rating service is also a consumer credit reporting agency as defined in subdivision (d) of Section 1785.3, nothing in this section shall be construed to suggest that an escrow agent reporting service that is also a consumer credit reporting agency is not otherwise required to comply with other provisions of this title applicable to consumer credit reporting agencies.

(g) Nothing in this section shall be construed to authorize a person, who was not otherwise legally authorized to perform escrow services prior to the effective date of this section, to legally perform escrow services.

(h) Nothing in this section is intended to alter the provisions of Section 17420 of the Financial Code, including the legal authority of an escrow agent to compensate an escrow agent rating service for a report prepared pursuant to paragraph (3) of subdivision (a). **Leg.H.** Added Stats 2013 ch 380 §1 (AB 1169), effective January 1, 2014, repealed January 1, 2017. Amended Stats 2016 ch 135 §1 (AB 2416), effective January 1, 2017, repealed January 1, 2022 (repealer amended); Stats 2021 ch 105 §1 (SB 360), effective January 1, 2022, repealed January 1, 2027 (repealer amended).

2013 Note: See §1785.28.6 for repealer.

§1785.28.6. Repeal of chapter [Repealed January 1, 2027]

This chapter shall remain in effect only until January 1, 2027, and as of that date is repealed. **Leg.H.** Added Stats 2013 ch 380 §1 (AB 1169), effective January 1, 2014, repealed January 1, 2017. Amended Stats 2016 ch 135 §1 (AB 2416), effective January 1, 2017, repealed January 1, 2022; Stats 2021 ch 105 §1 (SB 360), effective January 1, 2022, repealed January 1, 2027.

CHAPTER 4
REMEDIES

Reinvestigation; Correction. §1785.30.
Damages. §1785.31.
Actions barred. §1785.32.
Limitation of actions. §1785.33.
Effect of federal action. §1785.34.
Application to disclosures relating to land records. §1785.35.
Waiver of provisions of title void. §1785.36.

§1785.30. Reinvestigation; Correction

Upon notification of the results of a consumer credit reporting agency's reinvestigation pursuant to Section 1785.16, a consumer may make a written demand on any person furnishing information to the consumer credit reporting agency to correct any information that the consumer believes to be inaccurate. The person upon whom the written demand is made shall acknowledge the demand within 30 days. The consumer may require the consumer credit reporting agency to indicate on any subsequent reports issued during the dispute that the item or items of information are in dispute. If upon investigation the information is found to be inaccurate or incorrect, the consumer may require the consumer credit reporting agency to delete or correct the item or items of information within a reasonable time. If within 90 days the consumer credit reporting agency does not receive any information from the person requested to furnish the same or any communication relative to this information from this person, the consumer credit reporting agency shall delete the information from the report. **Leg.H.** Added Stats 1976 ch 666 §10. Amended Stats 1997 ch 768 §3 (AB 156), operative July 1, 1998; Stats 2004 ch 183 §31 (AB 3082).

Prior Law: Former §1785.30, similar to present CC §1785.31, was added Stats 1975 ch 1271 §1 and repealed Stats 1976 ch 666 §9.

§1785.31. Damages

(a) Any consumer who suffers damages as a result of a violation of this title by any person may bring an action in a court of appropriate jurisdiction against that person to recover the following:

(1) In the case of a negligent violation, actual damages, including court costs, loss of wages, attorney's fees and, when applicable, pain and suffering.

(2) In the case of a willful violation:

(A) Actual damages as set forth in paragraph (1) above:

(B) Punitive damages of not less than one hundred dollars ($100) nor more than five thousand dollars ($5,000) for each violation as the court deems proper;

(C) Any other relief that the court deems proper.

(3) In the case of liability of a natural person for obtaining a consumer credit report under false pretenses or knowingly without a permissible purpose, an award of actual damages pursuant to paragraph (1) or subparagraph (A) of paragraph (2) shall be in an amount of not less than two thousand five hundred dollars ($2,500).

(b) Injunctive relief shall be available to any consumer aggrieved by a violation or a threatened violation of this title whether or not the consumer seeks any other remedy under this section.

(c) Notwithstanding any other provision of this section, any person who willfully violates any requirement imposed under this title may be liable for punitive damages in the case of a class action, in an amount that the court may allow. In determining the amount of award in any class action, the court shall consider among relevant factors the amount of any actual damages awarded, the frequency of the violations, the resources of the violator and the number of persons adversely affected.

(d) Except as provided in subdivision (e), the prevailing plaintiffs in any action commenced under this section shall be entitled to recover court costs and reasonable attorney's fees.

(e) If a plaintiff brings an action pursuant to this section against a debt collector, as defined in subdivision (c) of Section 1788.2, and the basis for the action is related to the collection of a debt, whether issues relating to the debt collection are raised in the same or another proceeding, the debt collector shall be entitled to recover reasonable attorney's fees upon a finding by the court that the action was not brought in good faith.

(f) If a plaintiff only seeks and obtains injunctive relief to compel compliance with this title, court costs and attorney's fees shall be awarded pursuant to Section 1021.5 of the Code of Civil Procedure.

(g) Nothing in this section is intended to affect remedies available under Section 128.5 of the Code of Civil Procedure. **Leg.H.** Added Stats 1976 ch 666 §12. Amended Stats 1992 ch 1194 §12 (AB 1629), operative July 1, 1993; Stats 1997 ch 768 §4 (AB 156), operative July 1, 1998; Stats 1999 ch 836 §1 (AB 758).

Prior Law: Former §1785.31 was added Stats 1975 ch 1271 §1, and amended and renumbered to be CC §1785.32 by Stats 1976 ch 666 §11.

§1785.32. Actions barred

Except as provided in Section 1785.31, no consumer may bring any action or proceeding in the nature of defamation, invasion of privacy or negligence with respect to the reporting of information against any consumer reporting agency, any user of information, or any person who furnishes information to a consumer reporting agency, based on information disclosed pursuant to Sections 1785.10, 1785.15 or 1785.20 of this title, except as to false information furnished with malice or willful intent to injure such consumer. **Leg.H.** Added Stats 1975 ch 1271 §1 as §1785.31. Amended and renumbered by Stats 1976 ch 666 §11.

Prior Law: Former §1785.32 was added Stats 1975 ch 1271 §1 and amended and renumbered §1785.33 by Stats 1976 ch 666 §13.

§1785.33. Limitation of actions

An action to enforce any liability created under this chapter may be brought in any appropriate court of competent jurisdiction within two years from the date the plaintiff knew of, or should have known of, the violation of this title, but not more than seven years from the earliest date on which liability could have arisen, except that where a defendant has materially and willfully misrepresented any information required under this chapter to be disclosed to a consumer and the information so misrepresented is material to the establishment of the defendant's liability to the consumer under this chapter, the action may be brought at any time within two years after the discovery by the consumer of the misrepresentation. **Leg.H.** Added Stats 1975 ch 1271 §1, as CC §1785.32.

Renumbered by Stats 1976 ch 666 §13. Amended Stats 1997 ch 768 §5 (AB 156), operative July 1, 1998.

Prior Law: Former §1785.33 was added Stats 1975 ch 1271 §1, and amended and renumbered to be CC §1785.34 by Stats 1976 ch 666 §14.

§1785.34. Effect of federal action

(a) Any consumer credit reporting agency or user of information against whom an action brought pursuant to Section 1681n or 1681o of Title 15 of the United States Code is pending shall not be subject to suit for the same act or omission under Section 1785.31.

(b) The entry of a final judgment against a consumer credit reporting agency or user of information in an action brought pursuant to the provisions of Section 1681n or 1681o of Title 15 of the United States Code shall be a bar to the maintenance of any action based on the same act or omission which might be brought under this chapter. **Leg.H.** Added Stats 1975 ch 1271 §1 as §1785.33. Amended and renumbered by Stats 1976 ch 666 §14.

Prior Law: Former §1785.34 was added Stats 1975 ch 1271 §1 and amended and renumbered §1785.35 by Stats 1976 ch 666 §15.

§1785.35. Application to disclosures relating to land records

This title does not apply to any consumer credit report that by its terms is limited to disclosures from public records relating to land and land titles and does not apply to any person whose records and files are maintained for the primary purpose of reporting those portions of the public records that impart constructive notice under the law of matters relating to land and land titles. **Leg.H.** Added Stats 1975 ch 1271 §1 as §1785.34. Amended and renumbered by Stats 1976 ch 666 §15. Amended Stats 1999 ch 836 §2 (AB 758).

§1785.36. Waiver of provisions of title void

Any waiver of the provisions of this title is contrary to public policy, and is void and unenforceable. **Leg.H.** Added Stats 2002 ch 815 §8 (AB 2331).

TITLE 1.61
COMMERCIAL CREDIT REPORTS

Application of Consumer Credit Reporting Agencies Act. §1785.41.
Definitions. §1785.42.
Issuance of reports. §1785.43.
Waiver of provisions of title void. §1785.44.

§1785.41. Application of Consumer Credit Reporting Agencies Act

Consumer credit reporting is subject to the regulations of the Consumer Credit Reporting Agencies Act. Commercial credit reports, which differ significantly, are not subject to that act. The circumstances, business practices, and reports themselves differ sufficiently to make it impractical to include commercial credit reports under the Consumer Credit Reporting Agencies Act. **Leg.H.** Added Stats 1992 ch 101 §1 (SB 652).

§1785.42. Definitions

(a) "Commercial credit report" means any report provided to a commercial enterprise for a legitimate business purpose, relating to the financial status or payment habits of a commercial enterprise which is the subject of the report. It does not include a report subject to Title 1.6 (commencing with Section 1785.1), Title 1.6A (commencing with Section 1786), or a report prepared for commercial insurance underwriting, claims, or auditing purposes.

The term does not include (1) any report containing information related to transactions or experiences between the subject and the person making the report; (2) any authorization or approval of a specific extension of credit directly or indirectly by the issuer of a credit card or similar device; or (3) any report in which a person who has been requested by a third party to make a specific extension of credit directly or indirectly to the subject conveys its decision with respect to that request.

(b) "Commercial credit reporting agency" means any person who, for monetary fees, dues, or on a cooperative nonprofit basis, provides commercial credit reports to third parties.

(c) "Subject" means the commercial enterprise about which a commercial credit report has been compiled. **Leg.H.** Added Stats 1992 ch 101 §1 (SB 652). Amended Stats 1993 ch 285 §9 (AB 1340), effective July 30, 1993.

§1785.43. Issuance of reports

(a) Commercial credit reporting agencies may protect the identity of sources of information to be used in commercial credit reports.

(b) Upon the request of a representative of the subject of a report, the commercial credit reporting agency shall provide one printed copy of the subject's commercial credit report in a format routinely made available to third parties, at a cost no greater than the cost usually charged to third parties.

(c) In the event that the subject of a commercial credit report believes the report contains an inaccurate statement of fact, a representative of the subject of the report may, within 30 days of receipt of the report pursuant to subdivision (b), file with the commercial credit reporting agency a written summary statement of not more than 50 words identifying the particular statement of fact that is disputed, and indicating the nature of the disagreement with the statement in the report. Within 30 days of receipt of a subject's summary statement of disagreement, the commercial credit reporting agency shall either delete the disputed item of information from the report, or include in the report an indication that the subject's summary statement of disagreement will be provided upon request. **Leg.H.** Added Stats 1992 ch 101 §1 (SB 652).

§1785.44. Waiver of provisions of title void

Any waiver of the provisions of this title is contrary to public policy, and is void and unenforceable. **Leg.H.** Added Stats 2002 ch 815 §9 (AB 2331).

TITLE 1.6A
INVESTIGATIVE CONSUMER REPORTING AGENCIES

Article 1. General Provisions.
Article 2. Obligations of Investigative Consumer Reporting Agencies.
Article 4. Remedies.

ARTICLE 1
General Provisions

Legislative findings and declarations. §1786.
Title. §1786.1.
Definitions. §1786.2.

§1786. Legislative findings and declarations

The Legislature finds and declares as follows:

(a) Investigative consumer reporting agencies have assumed a vital role in collecting, assembling, evaluating, compiling, reporting, transmitting, transferring, or communicating information on consumers for employment and insurance purposes, and for purposes relating to the hiring of dwelling units, subpoenas and court orders, licensure, and other lawful purposes.

(b) There is a need to insure that investigative consumer reporting agencies exercise their grave responsibilities with fairness, impartiality, and a respect for the consumer's right to privacy.

(c) The crime of identity theft in this new computer era has exploded to become the fastest growing white collar crime in America.

(d) The unique nature of this crime means it can often go undetected for years without the victim being aware his identity has been misused.

(e) Because notice of identity theft is critical before the victim can take steps to stop and prosecute this crime, consumers are best protected if they are automatically given copies of any investigative consumer reports made on them.

(f) It is the purpose of this title to require that investigative consumer reporting agencies adopt reasonable procedures for meeting the needs of commerce for employment, insurance information, and information relating to the hiring of dwelling units in a manner which is fair and equitable to the consumer, with regard to the confidentiality, accuracy, relevancy, and proper utilization of the information in accordance with the requirements of this title.

(g) The Legislature hereby intends to regulate investigative consumer reporting agencies pursuant to this title in a manner which will best protect the interests of the people of the State of California. **Leg.H.** Added Stats 1975 ch 1272 §1. Amended Stats 1982 ch 1127 §6; Stats 2001 ch 354 §6 (AB 655).

Prior Law: Former §1786, similar to UCC §1201, was added Stats 1931 ch 1070 §1 and repealed Stats 1963 ch 819 §2, effective January 1, 1965.

Former §1786, relating to breach of warranty, was enacted 1872 and repealed Stats 1931 ch 1070 §1.

§1786.1. Title

This title may be referred to as the Investigative Consumer Reporting Agencies Act. **Leg.H.** Added Stats 1975 ch 1272 §1.

§1786.2. Definitions

The following terms as used in this title have the meaning expressed in this section:

(a) The term "person" means any individual, partnership, corporation, limited liability company, trust, estate, cooperative, association, government or governmental subdivision or agency, or other entity. The term "person" as used in this title shall not be construed to require duplicative reporting by any individual, corporation, trust, estate, cooperative, association, government, or governmental subdivision or agency, or other entity involved in the same transaction.

(b) The term "consumer" means a natural individual who has made application to a person for employment purposes, for insurance for personal, family, or household purposes, or the hiring of a dwelling unit, as defined in subdivision (c) of Section 1940.

(c) The term "investigative consumer report" means a consumer report in which information on a consumer's character, general reputation, personal characteristics, or mode of living is obtained through any means. The term does not include a consumer report or other compilation of information that is limited to specific factual information relating to a consumer's credit record or manner of obtaining credit obtained directly from a creditor of the consumer or from a consumer reporting agency when that information was obtained directly from a potential or existing creditor of the consumer or from the consumer. Notwithstanding the foregoing, for transactions between investigative consumer reporting agencies and insurance institutions, agents, or insurance-support organizations subject to Article 6.6 (commencing with Section 791) of Chapter 1 of Part 2 of Division 1 of the Insurance Code, the term "investigative consumer report" shall have the meaning set forth in Section 791.02 of the Insurance Code.

(d) The term "investigative consumer reporting agency" means any person who, for monetary fees or dues, engages in whole or in part in the practice of collecting, assembling, evaluating, compiling, reporting, transmitting, transferring, or communicating information concerning consumers for the purposes of furnishing investigative consumer reports to third parties, but does not include any governmental agency whose records are maintained primarily for traffic safety, law enforcement, or licensing purposes, or any licensed insurance agent, insurance broker, or solicitor, insurer, or life insurance agent.

(e) The term "file," when used in connection with information on any consumer, means all of the information on that consumer recorded and retained by an investigative consumer reporting agency regardless of how the information is stored.

(f) The term "employment purposes," when used in connection with an investigative consumer report, means a report used for the purpose of evaluating a consumer for employment, promotion, reassignment, or retention as an employee.

(g) The term "medical information" means information on a person's medical history or condition obtained directly or indirectly from a licensed physician, medical practitioner, hospital, clinic, or other medical or medically related facility. **Leg.H.** Added Stats 1975 ch 1272 §1. Amended Stats 1976 ch 1150 §1; Stats 1982 ch 1127 §7; Stats 1994 ch 1010 §36 (SB 2053); Stats 1998 ch 988 §1 (SB 1454); Stats 2001 ch 354 §7 (AB 655); Stats 2013 ch 444 §6 (SB 138), effective January 1, 2014.

ARTICLE 2
Obligations of Investigative Consumer Reporting Agencies

Inspection rights; Disclosure. §1786.10.
Availability to consumer of report provided to third party. §1786.11.
Circumstances permitting report to be furnished. §1786.12.
Information furnished government agencies. §1786.14.
Conditions precedent to preparation of report. §1786.16.
Contents of report. §1786.18.
Maintenance of reporting procedures; Purposes for which information is sought; Retention of reports; Information to be posted on Internet Web site; Contents of privacy statement; Liability. §1786.20.
Time and manner of supplying information. §1786.22.
Disputed information. §1786.24.
Charges for information. §1786.26.
Information based on public record. §1786.28.
Notice requirements; Providing report. §1786.29.
Information contained in subsequent reports. §1786.30.
Circumstances requiring user of investigative consumer report to notify consumer. §1786.40.

§1786.10. Inspection rights; Disclosure

(a) Every investigative consumer reporting agency shall, upon request and proper identification of any consumer, allow the consumer to visually inspect all files maintained regarding the consumer at the time of the request.

(b)(1) All items of information shall be available for inspection, except that the sources of information, other than public records and records from databases available for sale, acquired solely for use in preparing an investigative consumer report and actually used for no other purpose need not be disclosed. However, if an action is brought under this title, those sources shall be available to the consumer under appropriate discovery procedures in the court in which the action is brought.

(2) This title shall not be interpreted to mean that investigative consumer reporting agencies are required to divulge to consumers the sources of investigative consumer reports, except in appropriate discovery procedures as outlined in this title.

(c) The investigative consumer reporting agency shall also identify the recipients of any investigative consumer report on the consumer that the investigative consumer reporting agency has furnished for either of the following purposes:

(1) For employment or insurance purposes within the three-year period preceding the request.

(2) For any other purpose within the three-year period preceding the request.

(d) The identification of a recipient under subdivision (c) shall include the name of the recipient or, if applicable, the trade name (written in full) under which the recipient conducts business and, upon request of the consumer, the address and telephone number of the recipient.

(e) The investigative consumer reporting agency shall also disclose the dates, original payees, and amounts of any checks or charges upon which is based any adverse characterization of the consumer, included in the file at the time of the disclosure. **Leg.H.** Added Stats 1975 ch 1272 §1. Amended Stats 1998 ch 988 §2 (SB 1454); Stats 2001 ch 354 §8 (AB 655); Stats 2006 ch 538 §45 (SB 1852), effective January 1, 2007.

§1786.11. Availability to consumer of report provided to third party

Every investigative consumer reporting agency that provides an investigative consumer report to a person other than the consumer shall make a copy of that report available, upon request and proper identification, to the consumer for at least two years after the date that the report is provided to the other person. **Leg.H.** Added Stats 1998 ch 988 §3 (SB 1454). Amended Stats 2001 ch 354 §9 (AB 655); Stats 2002 ch 1029 §3 (AB 2868), effective September 28, 2002.

§1786.12. Circumstances permitting report to be furnished

An investigative consumer reporting agency shall only furnish an investigative consumer report under the following circumstances:

(a) In response to the order of a court having jurisdiction to issue the order.

(b) In compliance with a lawful subpoena issued by a court of competent jurisdiction.

(c) In accordance with the written instructions of the consumer to whom it relates.

(d) To a person that it has reason to believe:

(1) Intends to use the information for employment purposes; or

(2) Intends to use the information serving as a factor in determining a consumer's eligibility for insurance or the rate for any insurance; or

(3) Intends to use the information in connection with a determination of the consumer's eligibility for a license or other benefit granted by a governmental instrumentality required by law to consider the applicant's financial responsibility or status; or

(4) Intends to use the information in connection with an order of a court of competent jurisdiction to provide support where the imposition or enforcement of the order involves the consumer; or

(5) Intends to use the information in connection with the hiring of a dwelling unit, as defined in subdivision (c) of Section 1940.

(e) An investigative consumer reporting agency shall not prepare or furnish an investigative consumer report to a person described in subdivision (d) unless the agency has received the certification under paragraph (4) of subdivision (a) of Section 1786.16 from the person requesting the report.

(f) An investigative consumer reporting agency shall not furnish an investigative consumer report to a person described in subdivision (d) if that report contains medical information about a consumer, unless the consumer consents to the furnishing of the report. **Leg.H.** Added Stats 1975 ch 1272 §1. Amended Stats 1976 ch 1150 §2; Stats 1982 ch 1127 §8; Stats 1998 ch 988 §4 (SB 1454).

§1786.14. Information furnished government agencies

Notwithstanding the provisions of Section 1786.12 an investigative consumer reporting agency may furnish to a governmental agency a consumer's name, address, former address, places of employment, or former places of employment. **Leg.H.** Added Stats 1975 ch 1272 §1.

§1786.16. Conditions precedent to preparation of report

(a) Any person described in subdivision (d) of Section 1786.12 shall not procure or cause to be prepared an investigative consumer report unless the following applicable conditions are met:

(1) If an investigative consumer report is sought in connection with the underwriting of insurance, it shall be clearly and accurately disclosed in writing at the time the application form, medical form, binder, or similar document is signed by the consumer that an investigative consumer report regarding the consumer's character, general reputation, personal characteristics, and mode of living may be made. If no signed application form, medical form, binder, or similar document is involved in the underwriting transaction, the disclosure shall be made to the consumer in writing and mailed or otherwise delivered to the consumer not later than three days after the report was first requested. The disclosure shall include the name and address of any investigative consumer reporting agency conducting an investigation, plus the nature and scope of the investigation requested, and a summary of the provisions of Section 1786.22.

(2) If, at any time, an investigative consumer report is sought for employment purposes other than suspicion of wrongdoing or misconduct by the subject of the investigation, the person seeking the investigative consumer report may procure the report, or cause the report to be made, only if all of the following apply:

(A) The person procuring or causing the report to be made has a permissible purpose, as defined in Section 1786.12.

(B) The person procuring or causing the report to be made provides a clear and conspicuous disclosure in writing to the consumer at any time before the report is procured or caused to be made in a document that consists solely of the disclosure, that:

(i) An investigative consumer report may be obtained.

(ii) The permissible purpose of the report is identified.

(iii) The disclosure may include information on the consumer's character, general reputation, personal characteristics, and mode of living.

(iv) Identifies the name, address, and telephone number of the investigative consumer reporting agency conducting the investigation.

(v) Notifies the consumer in writing of the nature and scope of the investigation requested, including a summary of the provisions of Section 1786.22.

(vi) Notifies the consumer of the Internet Web site address of the investigative consumer reporting agency identified in clause (iv), or, if the agency has no Internet Web site address, the telephone number of the agency, where the consumer may find information about the investigative reporting agency's privacy practices, including whether the consumer's personal information will be sent outside the United States or its territories and information that complies with subdivision (d) of Section 1786.20. This clause shall become operative on January 1, 2012.

(C) The consumer has authorized in writing the procurement of the report.

(3) If an investigative consumer report is sought in connection with the hiring of a dwelling unit, as defined in subdivision (c) of Section 1940, the person procuring or causing the request to be made shall, not later than three days after the date on which the report was first requested, notify the consumer in writing that an investigative consumer report will be made regarding the consumer's character, general reputation, personal characteristics, and mode of living. The notification shall also include the name and address of the investigative consumer reporting agency that will prepare the report and a summary of the provisions of Section 1786.22.

(4) The person procuring or causing the request to be made shall certify to the investigative consumer reporting agency that the person has made the applicable disclosures to the consumer required by this subdivision and that the person will comply with subdivision (b).

(5) The person procuring the report or causing it to be prepared agrees to provide a copy of the report to the subject of the investigation, as provided in subdivision (b).

(b) Any person described in subdivision (d) of Section 1786.12 who requests an investigative consumer report, in accordance with subdivision (a) regarding that consumer, shall do the following:

(1) Provide the consumer a means by which the consumer may indicate on a written form, by means of a box to check, that the consumer wishes to receive a copy of any report that is prepared. If the consumer wishes to receive a copy of the report, the recipient of the report shall send a copy of the report to the consumer within three business days of the date that the report is provided to the recipient, who may contract with any other entity to send a copy to the consumer. The notice to request the report may be contained on either the disclosure form, as required by subdivision (a), or a separate consent form. The copy of the report shall contain the name, address, and telephone number of the person who issued the report and how to contact them.

(2) Comply with Section 1786.40, if the taking of adverse action is a consideration.

(c) Subdivisions (a) and (b) do not apply to an investigative consumer report procured or caused to be prepared by an employer, if the report is sought for employment purposes due to suspicion held by an employer of wrongdoing or misconduct by the subject of the investigation.

(d) Those persons described in subdivision (d) of Section 1786.12 constitute the sole and exclusive class of persons who may cause an investigative consumer report to be prepared. **Leg.H.** Added Stats 1975 ch 1272 §1. Amended Stats 1976 ch 1150 §3; Stats 1982 ch 1127 §9; Stats 1998 ch 988 §5 (SB 1454); Stats 2001 ch 354 §10 (AB 655); Stats 2002 ch 1030 §3 (AB 1068), effective September 28, 2002; Stats 2010 ch 481 §1 (SB 909), effective January 1, 2011.

§1786.18. Contents of report

(a) Except as authorized under subdivision (b), an investigative consumer reporting agency may not make or furnish any investigative consumer report containing any of the following items of information:

(1) Bankruptcies that, from the date of the order for relief, antedate the report by more than 10 years.

(2) Suits that, from the date of filing, and satisfied judgments that, from the date of entry, antedate the report by more than seven years.

(3) Unsatisfied judgments that, from the date of entry, antedate the report by more than seven years.

(4) Unlawful detainer actions where the defendant was the prevailing party or where the action is resolved by settlement agreement.

(5) Paid tax liens that, from the date of payment, antedate the report by more than seven years.

(6) Accounts placed for collection or charged to profit and loss that antedate the report by more than seven years.

(7) Records of arrest, indictment, information, misdemeanor complaint, or conviction of a crime that, from the date of disposition, release, or parole, antedate the report by more than seven years. These items of information shall no longer be reported if at any time it is learned that, in the case of a conviction, a full pardon has been granted or, in the case of an arrest, indictment, information, or misdemeanor complaint, a conviction did not result; except that records of arrest, indictment, information, or misdemeanor complaints may be reported pending pronouncement of judgment on the particular subject matter of those records.

(8) Any other adverse information that antedates the report by more than seven years.

(9) Medical debt, as defined in Section 1785.3.

(b) The provisions of subdivision (a) are not applicable in either of the following circumstances:

(1) If the investigative consumer report is to be used in the underwriting of life insurance involving, or that may reasonably be expected to involve, an amount of two hundred fifty thousand dollars ($250,000) or more.

(2) If the investigative consumer report is to be used by an employer who is explicitly required by a governmental regulatory agency to check for records that are prohibited by subdivision (a) when the employer is reviewing a consumer's qualification for employment.

(c) Except as otherwise provided in Section 1786.28, an investigative consumer reporting agency shall not furnish an investigative consumer report that includes information that is a matter of public record and that relates to an arrest, indictment, conviction, civil judicial action, tax lien, or outstanding judgment, unless the agency has verified the accuracy of the information during the 30-day period ending on the date on which the report is furnished.

(d) An investigative consumer reporting agency shall not prepare or furnish an investigative consumer report on a consumer that contains information that is adverse to the interest of the consumer and that is obtained through a personal interview with a neighbor, friend, or associate of the consumer or with another person with whom the consumer is acquainted or who has knowledge of the item of information, unless either (1) the investigative consumer reporting agency has followed reasonable procedures to obtain confirmation of the information, from an additional source that has independent and direct knowledge of the information, or (2) the person interviewed is the best possible source of the information. **Leg.H.** Added Stats 1975 ch 1272 §1. Amended Stats 1982 ch 1127 §10; Stats 1991 ch 965 §2 (AB 1796); Stats 1998 ch 988 §6 (SB 1454); Stats 2001 ch 354 §11 (AB 655); Stats 2002 ch 1029 §4 (AB 2868), effective September 28, 2002; Stats 2009 ch 500 §11 (AB 1059), effective January 1, 2010; Stats 2024 ch 520 §5 (SB 1061), effective January 1, 2025.

§1786.20. Maintenance of reporting procedures; Purposes for which information is sought; Retention of reports; Information to be posted on Internet Web site; Contents of privacy statement; Liability

(a) An investigative consumer reporting agency shall maintain reasonable procedures designed to avoid violations of Section 1786.18 and to limit furnishing of investigative consumer reports for the purposes listed under Section 1786.12. These procedures shall require that prospective users of the information identify themselves, certify the purposes for which the information is sought and that the information will be used for no other purposes, and make the certifications described in paragraph (4) of subdivision (a) of Section 1786.16. From the effective date of this title, the investigative consumer reporting agency shall keep a record of the purposes for which information is sought, as stated by the user. The investigative consumer reporting agency may assume that the purpose for which a user seeks information remains the same as that which a user has previously stated. The investigative consumer reporting agency shall inform the user that the user is obligated to notify the agency of any change in the purpose for which information will be used. An investigative consumer reporting agency shall make a reasonable effort to verify the identity of a new prospective user and the uses certified by the prospective user prior to furnishing the user any investigative consumer reports. An investigative consumer reporting agency may not furnish an investigative consumer report to a person unless it has a written agreement that the investigative consumer reports will be used by that person only for purposes listed in Section 1786.12.

(b) Whenever an investigative consumer reporting agency prepares an investigative consumer report, it shall follow reasonable procedures to assure maximum possible accuracy of the information concerning the individual about whom the report relates. An investigative consumer reporting agency shall retain the investigative consumer report for two years after the report is provided.

(c) An investigative consumer reporting agency may not make an inquiry for the purpose of preparing an investigative consumer report on a consumer for employment purposes if the making of the inquiry by an employer or prospective employer of the consumer would violate applicable federal or state equal employment opportunity law or regulation.

(d)(1) An investigative consumer reporting agency doing business in this state shall conspicuously post, as defined in subdivision (b) of Section 22577 of the Business and Professions Code, on its primary Internet Web site information describing its privacy practices with respect to its preparation and processing of investigative consumer reports. If the investigative consumer reporting agency does not have an Internet Web site, it shall, upon request, mail a written copy of the privacy statement to consumers. The privacy statement shall conspicuously include, but not be limited to, both of the following:

(A) A statement entitled "Personal Information Disclosure: United States or Overseas," that indicates whether the personal information will be transferred to third parties outside the United States or its territories.

(B) A separate section that includes the name, mailing address, e-mail address, and telephone number of the investigative consumer reporting agency representatives who can assist a consumer with additional information regarding the investigative consumer reporting agency's privacy practices or policies in the event of a compromise of his or her information.

(2) For purposes of this subdivision, "third party" shall include, but not be limited to, a contractor, foreign affiliate, wholly owned entity, or an employee of the investigative consumer reporting agency.

(e) An investigative consumer reporting agency shall be liable to a consumer who is the subject of a report if the consumer is harmed by any unauthorized access of the consumer's personally identifiable information, act, or omission that occurs outside the United States or its territories as a result of the investigative consumer reporting agency negligently preparing or processing an investigative consumer report, or portion thereof, outside of the United States or its territories. Liability shall be in an amount equal to the sum of (1) any actual damages sustained by the consumer as a result of the unauthorized access, and (2) in the case of any successful action to enforce any liability under this section, the costs of the action together with reasonable attorney's fees, as determined by the court. **Leg.H.** Added Stats 1975 ch 1272 §1. Amended Stats 1998 ch 988 §7 (SB 1454); Stats 2001 ch 354 §12 (AB 655); Stats 2002 ch 1029 §5 (AB 2868), effective September 28, 2002; Stats 2003 ch 146 §1 (AB 1399); Stats 2010 ch 481 §2 (SB 909), effective January 1, 2011.

§1786.22. Time and manner of supplying information

(a) An investigative consumer reporting agency shall supply files and information required under Section 1786.10 during normal business hours and on reasonable notice.

(b) Files maintained on a consumer shall be made available for the consumer's visual inspection, as follows:

(1) In person, if he appears in person and furnishes proper identification. A copy of his file shall also be available to the consumer for a fee not to exceed the actual costs of duplication services provided.

(2) By certified mail, if he makes a written request, with proper identification, for copies to be sent to a specified addressee. Investigative consumer reporting agencies complying with requests for certified mailings under this section shall not be liable for disclosures to third parties caused by mishandling of mail after such mailings leave the investigative consumer reporting agencies.

(3) A summary of all information contained in files on a consumer and required to be provided by Section 1786.10 shall be provided by telephone, if the consumer has made a written request, with proper identification for telephone disclosure, and the toll charge, if any, for the telephone call is prepaid by or charged directly to the consumer.

(c) The term "proper identification" as used in subdivision (b) shall mean that information generally deemed sufficient to identify a person. Such information includes documents such as a valid driver's license, social security account number, military identification card, and credit cards. Only if the consumer is unable to reasonably identify himself with the information described above, may an investigative consumer reporting agency require additional information concerning the consumer's employment and personal or family history in order to verify his identity.

(d) The investigative consumer reporting agency shall provide trained personnel to explain to the consumer any information furnished him pursuant to Section 1786.10.

(e) The investigative consumer reporting agency shall provide a written explanation of any coded information contained in files maintained on a consumer. This written explanation shall be distributed whenever a file is provided to a consumer for visual inspection as required under Section 1786.22.

(f) The consumer shall be permitted to be accompanied by one other person of his choosing, who shall furnish reasonable identification. An investigative consumer reporting agency may require the consumer to furnish a written statement granting permission to the consumer reporting agency to discuss the consumer's file in such person's presence. **Leg.H.** Added Stats 1975 ch 1272 §1. Amended Stats 1976 ch 666 §16.

§1786.24. Disputed information

(a) If the completeness or accuracy of any item of information contained in his or her file is disputed by a consumer, and the dispute is conveyed directly to the investigative consumer reporting agency by the consumer, the investigative consumer reporting agency shall, without charge, reinvestigate and record the current status of the disputed information or delete the item from the file in accordance with subdivision (c), before the end of the 30-day period beginning on the date on which the agency receives the notice of the dispute from the consumer.

(b) The agency shall notify any person who provided information in dispute at the address and in the manner specified by that person. The notice shall include all relevant information regarding the dispute that the investigative consumer reporting agency has received from the consumer. The agency shall also promptly provide to the person who provided the information in dispute all relevant information regarding the dispute that is received by the agency from the consumer during the reinvestigation.

(c) In conducting a reinvestigation, the investigative consumer reporting agency shall review and consider all relevant information submitted by the consumer with respect to the disputed item of information.

(d) Notwithstanding subdivision (a), an investigative consumer reporting agency may terminate a reinvestigation of information disputed by a consumer if the investigative consumer reporting agency reasonably determines that the dispute is frivolous or irrelevant, including by reason of a failure by a consumer to provide sufficient information to investigate the disputed information. Upon making a determination that a dispute is frivolous or irrelevant, the investigative consumer reporting agency shall notify the consumer, by mail or, if authorized by the consumer for that purpose, by any other means available to the agency. In this notification, the investigative consumer reporting agency shall state the specific reasons why it has determined that the consumer's dispute is frivolous or irrelevant and provide a description of any information required to investigate the disputed information, that may consist of a standardized form describing the general nature of the required information.

(e) If a reinvestigation is made and, after reinvestigation, the disputed item of information is found to be inaccurate, incomplete, or cannot be verified by the evidence submitted, the investigative consumer reporting agency shall promptly delete that information from the consumer's file or modify the information, as appropriate, based on the results of the reinvestigation, and shall notify the consumer that the information has been deleted or modified. The consumer reporting agency shall also notify any and all sources from which the disputed information was obtained and inform them in writing of the reasons and results of the reinvestigation, and send a copy of this notification to the consumer. In accordance with subdivision (b) of Section 1786.10, the copy of the notification sent to the consumer need not reveal the identity of the source of information, unless otherwise required by law.

(f) No information may be reinserted in the file of a consumer after having been deleted pursuant to this section, unless the person who furnished the information verifies that the information is complete and accurate. If any information deleted from the file of a consumer is reinserted in the file, the investigative consumer reporting agency shall promptly notify the consumer of the reinsertion in writing or, if authorized by the consumer for that purpose, by any other means available to the agency. As part of, or in addition to, this notice, the investigative consumer reporting agency shall provide to the consumer in writing (1) a statement that the disputed information has been reinserted, (2) the name, address, and telephone number of any furnisher of information contacted or that contacted the investigative consumer reporting agency in connection with the reinsertion, and the telephone number of the furnisher, if reasonably available, and (3) a notice that the consumer has the right to a reinvestigation of the information reinserted by the investigative consumer reporting agency and to add a statement to his or her file disputing the accuracy or completeness of the information.

(g) An investigative consumer reporting agency shall provide notice to the consumer of the results of any reinvestigation under this section by mail or, if authorized by the consumer for that purpose, by other means available to the agency. The notice shall include (1) a statement that the reinvestigation is completed, (2) an investigative consumer report that is based on the consumer's file as that file is revised as a result of the reinvestigation, (3) a description or indication of any changes made in the investigative consumer report as a result of those revisions to the consumer's file, (4) a notice that, if requested by the consumer, a description of the procedure used to determine the accuracy and completeness of the information shall be provided to the consumer by the investigative consumer reporting agency, including the name, business address, and telephone number of any furnisher of information contacted in connection with that information, (5) a notice that the consumer has the right to add a statement to the consumer's file disputing the accuracy or completeness of the information, and (6) a notice that the consumer has the right to request that the investigative consumer reporting agency furnish notifications under subdivision (k).

(h) The presence of information in the consumer's file that contradicts the contention of the consumer shall not, in and of itself, constitute reasonable grounds for believing the dispute is frivolous or irrelevant.

(i) If the investigative consumer reporting agency determines that the dispute is frivolous or irrelevant, or if the reinvestigation does not resolve the dispute, or if the information is reinserted into the file of a consumer pursuant to subdivision (f), the consumer may file a brief statement setting forth the nature of the dispute. The investigative consumer reporting agency may limit these statements to not more than 500 words if it provides the consumer with assistance in writing a clear summary of the dispute.

(j) If a statement of dispute is filed, the investigative consumer reporting agency shall, in any subsequent investigative consumer report containing the information in question, clearly note that the information is disputed by the consumer and shall include in the report either the statement of the consumer or a clear and accurate summary thereof.

(k) Following the deletion of information from the file of a consumer pursuant to this section, or following the filing of a dispute pursuant to subdivision (i), the investigative consumer reporting agency shall, at the request of the consumer, furnish notification that the item of information has been deleted or that the item of information is disputed. In the case of disputed information, the notification shall include the statement or summary of the dispute filed pursuant to subdivision (i). This notification shall be furnished to any person who has, within two years prior to the deletion or the filing of the dispute, received an investigative consumer report concerning the consumer for employment purposes, or who has, within one year of the deletion or the filing of the dispute, received an investigative consumer report concerning the consumer for any other purpose, if these investigative consumer reports contained the deleted or disputed information, unless the consumer specifically requests in writing that this notification not be given to all persons or to any specified persons. The investigative consumer reporting agency shall clearly and conspicuously disclose to the consumer his or her rights to make a request that this notification not be made.

(*l*) An investigative consumer reporting agency shall maintain reasonable procedures designed to prevent the reappearance in the file of a consumer and in investigative consumer reports information that has been deleted pursuant to this section and not reinserted pursuant to subdivision (f).

(m) If the dispute of a consumer is resolved by deletion of the disputed information within three business days, beginning with the day the investigative consumer reporting agency receives notice of the dispute in accordance with subdivision (a), the investigative consumer reporting agency is exempt from requirements for further action under subdivisions (g), (i), and (j), if the agency: (1) provides prompt notice of the deletion to the consumer by telephone, (2) provides written confirmation of the deletion and a copy of an investigative consumer report of the consumer that is based on the file of a consumer after the deletion, and (3) includes, in the telephone notice or in a written notice that accompanies the confirmation and report, a statement of the consumer's right to request under subdivision (k) that the agency not furnish notifications under that subdivision.

(n) Any investigative consumer reporting agency that compiles and maintains files on consumers on a nationwide basis, as defined in the federal Fair Credit Reporting Act, as amended (15 U.S.C. Sec. 1681 et seq.), shall implement an automated system through which furnishers of information to that agency may report the results of a reinvestigation that finds incomplete or inaccurate information in the file of a consumer to other investigative consumer reporting agencies.

(o) All actions to be taken by an investigative consumer reporting agency under this section are governed by the applicable time periods specified in Section 611 of the federal Fair Credit Reporting Act, as amended (15 U.S.C. Sec. 1681i). **Leg.H.** Added Stats 1975 ch 1272 §1.

Amended Stats 1998 ch 988 §8 (SB 1454); Stats 2001 ch 354 §13 (AB 655); Stats 2002 ch 1029 §6 (AB 2868), ch 1030 §4 (AB 1068); Stats 2004 ch 183 §32 (AB 3082).

§1786.26. Charges for information

(a) Except as otherwise provided in subdivision (c), an investigative consumer reporting agency may charge a consumer a fee not exceeding eight dollars ($8) for making disclosures to the consumer pursuant to Sections 1786.10, 1786.11, and 1786.22. Any charges shall be indicated to the consumer prior to disclosure.

(b) An investigative consumer reporting agency shall not impose any charge for providing notice to a consumer required under Section 1786.24, furnishing an investigative consumer report pursuant to Section 1786.24, or notifying a person pursuant to subdivision (k) of Section 1786.24 of the deletion of information that is found to be inaccurate or that cannot be verified.

(c) Upon the request of the consumer, an investigative consumer reporting agency shall make all disclosures pursuant to Section 1786.10 and 1786.22 once during any 12-month period without charge to that consumer if the consumer certifies in writing that he or she (1) is unemployed and intends to apply for employment in the 60-day period beginning on the date the certification is made, (2) is a recipient of public welfare assistance, or (3) has reason to believe that the file on the consumer at the investigative consumer reporting agency contains inaccurate information due to fraud.

(d) An investigative consumer reporting agency shall not impose any charge on a consumer for providing any notification or making any disclosure required by this title, except as authorized by this section. **Leg.H.** Added Stats 1975 ch 1272 §1. Amended Stats 1976 ch 666 §17; Stats 1977 ch 579 §31; Stats 1998 ch 988 §9 (SB 1454); Stats 2001 ch 354 §14 (AB 655).

§1786.28. Information based on public record

(a) Each investigative consumer reporting agency that collects, assembles, evaluates, compiles, reports, transmits, transfers, or communicates items of information concerning consumers which are matters of public record shall specify in any report containing public record information the source from which this information was obtained, including the particular court, if applicable, and the date that this information was initially reported or publicized.

(b) A consumer reporting agency which furnishes a consumer report for employment purposes and which for that purpose compiles, collects, assembles, evaluates, reports, transmits, transfers, or communicates items of information on consumers which are matters of public record and are likely to have an adverse effect upon a consumer's ability to obtain employment shall in addition maintain strict procedures designed to insure that whenever public record information which is likely to have an adverse effect on a consumer's ability to obtain employment is reported it is complete and up to date. For purposes of this paragraph, items of public record relating to arrests, indictments, convictions, suits, tax liens, and outstanding judgments shall be considered up to date if the current public record status of the item at the time of the report is reported. **Leg.H.** Added Stats 1975 ch 1272 §1. Amended Stats 2001 ch 354 §15 (AB 655).

§1786.29. Notice requirements; Providing report

An investigative consumer reporting agency shall provide the following notices on the first page of an investigative consumer report:

(a) A notice in at least 12-point boldface type setting forth that the report does not guarantee the accuracy or truthfulness of the information as to the subject of the investigation, but only that it is accurately copied from public records, and information generated as a result of identity theft, including evidence of criminal activity, may be inaccurately associated with the consumer who is the subject of the report.

(b) An investigative consumer reporting agency shall provide a consumer seeking to obtain a copy of a report or making a request to review a file, a written notice in simple, plain English and Spanish setting forth the terms and conditions of his or her right to receive all disclosures, as provided in Section 1786.26. **Leg.H.** Added Stats 2001 ch 354 §16 (AB 655). Amended Stats 2002 ch 1030 §5 (AB 1068), effective September 28, 2002.

§1786.30. Information contained in subsequent reports

Whenever an investigative consumer reporting agency prepares an investigative consumer report, no adverse information in the report (other than information that is a matter of public record, the status of which has been updated pursuant to Section 1786.28) may be included in a subsequent investigative consumer report unless that adverse information has been verified in the process of making the subsequent investigative consumer report, or the adverse information was received within the three-month period preceding the date the subsequent report is furnished. **Leg.H.** Added Stats 1975 ch 1272 §1. Amended Stats 1998 ch 988 §10 (SB 1454).

§1786.40. Circumstances requiring user of investigative consumer report to notify consumer

(a) Whenever insurance for personal, family, or household purposes, employment, or the hiring of a dwelling unit involving a consumer is denied, or the charge for that insurance or the hiring of a dwelling unit is increased, under circumstances in which a report regarding the consumer was obtained from an investigative consumer reporting agency, the user of the investigative consumer report shall so advise the consumer against whom the adverse action has been taken and supply the name and address of the investigative consumer reporting agency making the report.

(b) Whenever insurance for personal, family, or household purposes involving a consumer is denied or the charge for that insurance is increased, either wholly or in part because of information bearing upon the consumer's general reputation, personal characteristics, or mode of living, that was obtained from a person other than an investigative consumer reporting agency, the consumer, or another person related to the consumer and acting on the consumer's behalf, the user of the information shall, within a reasonable period of time, and upon the consumer's written request for the reasons for the adverse action received within 60 days after learning of the adverse action, disclose the nature and substance of the information to the consumer. The user of the information shall clearly and accurately disclose to the consumer his or her right to make this written request at the time the adverse action is communicated to the consumer. **Leg.H.** Added Stats 2002 ch 1030 §6 (AB 1068).

Prior Law: Former 1786.40, relating to notice and disclosures following adverse action, was added Stats 1975 ch 1272 §1, amended Stats 1976 ch 1150 §4; Stats 1982 ch 1127 §11; Stats 1998 ch 988 §11 and repealed Stats 2001 ch 354 §17.

Former CC §1786.40, relating to notice and disclosures following adverse action, was added Stats 1975 ch 1272 §1 and repealed Stats 2001 ch 354 §17.

ARTICLE 3
Requirements on Users of Investigative Consumer Reports [Repealed]

ARTICLE 4
Remedies

Liability; Actual damages; Costs and fees; Punitive damages. §1786.50.
Actions. §1786.52.
Disclosure requirement when investigative consumer reporting agency not used. §1786.53.
Application to disclosures relating to land records. §1786.54.
Construction of chapter with other statutory law. §1786.55.
Severability of provisions. §1786.56.
Waiver of provisions of title void. §1786.57.
Printing individual's social security number on certain documents mailed to individual. §1786.60.

§1786.50. Liability; Actual damages; Costs and fees; Punitive damages

(a) An investigative consumer reporting agency or user of information that fails to comply with any requirement under this title with respect to an investigative consumer report is liable to the consumer who is the subject of the report in an amount equal to the sum of all the following:

(1) Any actual damages sustained by the consumer as a result of the failure or, except in the case of class actions, ten thousand dollars ($10,000), whichever sum is greater.

(2) In the case of any successful action to enforce any liability under this chapter, the costs of the action together with reasonable attorney's fees as determined by the court.

(b) If the court determines that the violation was grossly negligent or willful, the court may, in addition, assess, and the consumer may recover, punitive damages.

(c) Notwithstanding subdivision (a), an investigative consumer reporting agency or user of information that fails to comply with any requirement under this title with respect to an investigative consumer report shall not be liable to a consumer who is the subject of the report where the failure to comply results in a more favorable investigative consumer report than if there had not been a failure to comply. **Leg.H.** Added Stats 1975 ch 1272 §1. Amended Stats 1998 ch 988 §12 (SB 1454); Stats 2001 ch 354 §18 (AB 655); Stats 2002 ch 1029 §7 (AB 2868), effective September 28, 2002; Stats 2003 ch 146 §2 (AB 1399).

§1786.52. Actions

Nothing in this chapter shall in any way affect the right of any consumer to maintain an action against an investigative consumer reporting agency, a user of an investigative consumer report, or an informant for invasion of privacy or defamation.

An action to enforce any liability created under this title may be brought in any appropriate court of competent jurisdiction within two years from the date of discovery.

(a) Any investigative consumer reporting agency or user of information against whom an action brought pursuant to Section 1681n or 1681o of Title 15 of the United States Code is pending shall not be subject to suit for the same act or omission under Section 1786.50.

(b) The entry of a final judgment against the investigative consumer reporting agency or user of information in an action brought pursuant to the provisions of Section 1681n or 1681o of Title 15 of the United States Code shall be a bar to the maintenance of any action based on the same act or omission which might be brought under this title. **Leg.H.** Added Stats 1975 ch 1272 §1. Amended Stats 2001 ch 354 §19 (AB 655).

§1786.53. Disclosure requirement when investigative consumer reporting agency not used

(a) Any person who collects, assembles, evaluates, compiles, reports, transmits, transfers, or communicates information on a consumer's character, general reputation, personnel characteristics, or mode of living, for employment purposes, which are matters of public record, and does not use the services of an investigative consumer reporting agency, shall provide that information to the consumer pursuant to subdivision (b). For purposes of this section:

(1) "Adverse action," as relating to employment, means a denial of employment or any decision made for an employment purpose that adversely affects any current or prospective employee.

(2) The term "person" does not include an agency subject to the Information Practices Act of 1977 (Chapter 1 (commencing with Section 1798) of Title 1.8).

(3) "Public records" means records documenting an arrest, indictment, conviction, civil judicial action, tax lien, or outstanding judgment.

(b)(1) Any person described in subdivision (a), or any person who receives information pursuant to subdivision (a), shall provide a copy of the related public record to the consumer within seven days after receipt of the information, regardless of whether the information is received in a written or oral form.

(2) Any person shall provide on any job application form, or any other written form, a box that, if checked by the consumer, permits the consumer to waive his or her right to receive a copy of any public record obtained pursuant to this section.

(3) If any person obtains a public record pursuant to this section for the purpose of conducting an investigation for suspicion of wrongdoing or misconduct by the subject of the investigation, the person may withhold the information until the completion of the investigation. Upon completion, the person shall provide a copy of the public record pursuant to paragraph (1), unless the consumer waived his or her rights pursuant to paragraph (2).

(4) If any person takes any adverse action as a result of receiving information pursuant to subdivision (a), the person shall provide to the consumer a copy of the public record, regardless of whether the consumer waived his or her rights pursuant to paragraph (2).

(c) Nothing in subdivision (a) or (b) requires any person to provide the same information to any consumer on more than one occasion. **Leg.H.** Added Stats 2001 ch 354 §20 (AB 655). Amended Stats 2002 ch 1030 §7 (AB 1068), effective September 28, 2002.

§1786.54. Application to disclosures relating to land records

This title does not apply to any investigative consumer report which by its terms is limited to disclosures from public records relating to land and land titles or which is a report issued preliminary to the issuance of a policy of title insurance, and it does not apply to any person whose records are maintained for the primary purpose of reporting those portions of public records which impart constructive notice under the law of matters relating to land and land titles and which may be issued as the basis for the issuance of a policy of title insurance. **Leg.H.** Added Stats 1975 ch 1272 §1.

§1786.55. Construction of chapter with other statutory law

Nothing in this chapter is intended to modify Section 1198.5 of the Labor Code or existing law concerning information obtained by an employer or employment agency without the use of the services of an investigative consumer reporting agency for employment reference checks, background investigations, credential verifications, or employee investigations, except as provided in Section 1786.53. Nothing in this chapter is intended to change or supersede existing law related to privileged attorney-client communications or attorney work product, or require the production or disclosure of that information. **Leg.H.** Added Stats 2002 ch 1030 §8 (AB 1068), effective September 28, 2002.

§1786.56. Severability of provisions

If any provision of this act or the application thereof to any person or circumstances is held invalid, such invalidity shall not affect other provisions or applications of the act which can be given effect without the invalid provision or application, and to this end the provisions of this act are severable. **Leg.H.** Added Stats 1975 ch 1272 §1.

§1786.57. Waiver of provisions of title void

Any waiver of the provisions of this title is contrary to public policy, and is void and unenforceable. **Leg.H.** Added Stats 2002 ch 815 §10 (AB 2331).

§1786.60. Printing individual's social security number on certain documents mailed to individual

Notwithstanding subdivision (a) of Section 1798.85, prior to July 1, 2004, any financial institution may print the social security number of an individual on any account statement or similar document mailed to that individual, if the social security number is provided in connection with a transaction governed by the rules of the National Automated Clearing House Association, or a transaction initiated by a federal governmental entity through an automated clearing house network. **Leg.H.** Added Stats 2002 ch 1030 §9 (AB 1068), effective September 28, 2002. Amended Stats 2003 ch 907 §4 (SB 25).

§1787. [Section repealed 1965]

Leg.H. Added Stats 1931 ch 1070 §1. Repealed Stats 1963 ch 819 §2, effective January 1, 1965. See UCC §2713.

TITLE 1.6B
CONSUMER CREDIT DENIAL

Article 1. General Provisions.
Article 2. Remedies.

ARTICLE 1
General Provisions

Citation. §1787.1.
Statement of reasons for denial of credit. §1787.2.

§1787.1. Citation

This title may be cited as "The Holden Credit Denial Disclosure Act of 1976." **Leg.H.** Added Stats 1976 ch 1072 §1, operative March 31, 1977.

§1787.2. Statement of reasons for denial of credit

(a) Within 30 days, or at a later reasonable time as specified in federal law or regulations, after receipt of a completed written application for credit, a creditor shall notify the applicant of its action on the application.

(b) Each applicant denied credit shall be entitled to a statement of reasons for such action from the creditor. A creditor satisfies this obligation by:

(1) Providing statements of reasons in writing as a matter of course to applicants denied credit; or

(2) Giving written notification of credit denial which discloses:

(i) The applicant's right to a statement of reasons within 30 days after receipt by the creditor of a request made within 60 days after such notification; and

(ii) The identity and address of the person or office from which the statement of reasons may be obtained.

(3) The statement of reasons may be given orally if the written notification advises the applicant of the right to have the statement of reasons confirmed in writing on written request.

(c) A statement of reasons meets the requirements of this section only if it contains the specific reasons for the credit denial.

(d) Where a creditor has been requested by a third party to make a specific extension of credit directly or indirectly to an applicant, the notification and statement of reasons required by this section may be made directly by such creditor, or indirectly through the third party, provided in either case that the identity of the creditor is disclosed.

(e) For purposes of this section:

(1) The term "applicant" means a natural person who applies for credit primarily for personal, family or household purposes.

(2) The term "credit denial" means a denial or revocation of credit, a change in the terms of an existing credit arrangement, or a refusal to grant credit in substantially the amount or on substantially the terms requested. Such term does not include a refusal to extend additional credit under an existing credit arrangement where the applicant is delinquent or otherwise in default, or where such additional credit would exceed a previously established credit limit without a specific written application or written request for an increase in the credit limit.

(3) The term "creditor" refers only to creditors who regularly extend, or arrange for the extension of, credit whether in connection with loans, sales of property or services, or otherwise.

(f) Nothing in this section shall be construed to limit any authority, derived from other provisions of law, of any state department or agency. **Leg.H.** Added Stats 1976 ch 1072 §1, operative March 31, 1977.

ARTICLE 2
Remedies

Damages; Exemption; Limitation. §1787.3.
Waiver of provisions of title void. §1787.4.

§1787.3. Damages; Exemption; Limitation

(a) Any creditor who fails to comply with any requirement of Section 1787.2 shall be liable for any actual damages sustained by an applicant as a result of such failure.

(b) Any creditor, other than a government or governmental subdivision or agency, who fails to comply with any requirement imposed under this title shall be liable to the aggrieved applicant for punitive damages in an amount not greater than ten thousand dollars ($10,000), in addition to any actual damages provided in subdivision (a), except that in the case of a class action the total recovery under this subdivision shall not exceed the lesser of five hundred thousand dollars ($500,000) or 1 percent of the net worth of the creditor. In determining the amount of such damages in any action, the court shall consider, among other relevant factors, the amount of any actual damages awarded, the frequency and persistence of failures of compliance by the creditor, the resources of the creditor, the number of persons adversely affected, and the extent to which the creditor's failure of compliance was intentional.

(c) In the case of any action brought by an aggrieved applicant under subdivision (a) or (b), the costs of the action, together with a reasonable attorney's fee as determined by the court, shall be added to any damages awarded by the court.

(d) No provision of this title imposing liability shall apply to any act done or omitted in good faith in conformity with any official rule, regulation, or interpretation thereby by the Board of Governors of the Federal Reserve System or in conformity with any interpretation or approval by an official or employee of the Federal Reserve System duly authorized by the board to issue such interpretations or approvals under such procedures as the board may prescribe therefor, notwithstanding that after such act or omission has occurred, such rule, regulation, interpretation, or approval is amended, rescinded, or determined by judicial or other authority to be invalid for any reason.

(e) Actions alleging a failure to comply with any requirement of Section 1787.2 shall be brought within two years from the date of the occurrence of the violation. **Leg.H.** Added Stats 1976 ch 1072 §1, operative March 31, 1977.

§1787.4. Waiver of provisions of title void

Any waiver of the provisions of this title is contrary to public policy, and is void and unenforceable. **Leg.H.** Added Stats 2002 ch 815 §11 (AB 2331).

TITLE 1.6C
FAIR DEBT COLLECTION PRACTICES

Article 1. General Provisions.
Article 2. Debt Collector Responsibilities.
Article 3. Debtor Responsibilities.
Article 4. Enforcement.

ARTICLE 1
General Provisions

Short title. §1788.
Legislative findings; Purpose. §1788.1.
Definitions and rules of construction. §1788.2.
Information furnished by credit union to employer. §1788.3.

§1788. Short title

This title may be cited as the Rosenthal Fair Debt Collection Practices Act. **Leg.H.** Added Stats 1977 ch 907 §1. Amended Stats 1999 ch 319 §1 (AB 969); Stats 2000 ch 375 §5 (AB 1331).

Prior Law: Former §1788, similar to UCC §2716, was added Stats 1931 ch 1070 §1 and repealed Stats 1963 ch 819 §2, effective January 1, 1965.

§1788.1. Legislative findings; Purpose

(a) The Legislature makes the following findings:

(1) The banking and credit system and grantors of credit to consumers are dependent upon the collection of just and owing debts. Unfair or deceptive collection practices undermine the public confidence, which is essential to the continued functioning of the banking and credit system and sound extensions of credit to consumers **and small businesses**.

(2) There is need to ensure that debt collectors and debtors exercise their responsibilities to one another with fairness, honesty and due regard for the rights of the other.

(b) It is the purpose of this title to prohibit debt collectors from engaging in unfair or deceptive acts or practices in the collection of consumer debts and **small business debts and** to require debtors to act fairly in entering into and honoring [1] **those** debts, as specified in this title.

(c) Nothing in this title is intended to create or impose an additional licensing requirement under Division 25 (commencing with Section 100000) of the Financial Code on a debt collector with respect to the collection of covered commercial debt or covered commercial credit.

(d) The provisions of this title related to covered commercial credit or covered commercial debt apply to covered commercial credit or covered commercial debt entered into, renewed, sold, or assigned on or after July 1, 2025. Leg.H. Added Stats 1977 ch 907 §1. Amended Stats 2024 ch 522 §1 (SB 1286), effective January 1, 2025.

§1788.1. 2024 Deletes. [1] such

§1788.2. Definitions and rules of construction

(a) Definitions and rules of construction set forth in this section are applicable for the purpose of this title.

(b) The term "debt collection" means any act or practice in connection with the collection of [1] **covered** debts.

(c) The term "debt collector" means any person who, in the ordinary course of business, regularly, on behalf of that person or others, engages in debt collection. The term includes any person who composes and sells, or offers to compose and sell, forms, letters, and other collection media used or intended to be used for debt collection.

(d) The term "debt" means money, property, or their equivalent that is due or owing or alleged to be due or owing from a natural person to another person.

(e) The term "consumer credit transaction" means a transaction between a natural person and another person in which property, services, or money is acquired on credit by that natural person from the other person primarily for personal, family, or household purposes.

(f) The terms "consumer debt" and "consumer credit" mean money, property, or their equivalent, due or owing or alleged to be due or owing from a natural person by reason of a consumer credit transaction. The term "consumer debt" includes a mortgage debt.

(g) The term "person" means a natural person, partnership, corporation, limited liability company, trust, estate, cooperative, association, or other similar entity.

(h)(1) Except as provided in Section 1788.18, the term "debtor" means a natural person from whom a debt collector seeks to collect a [2] **covered** debt that is due and owing or alleged to be due and owing from [3] **that** person.

(2) In relation to a covered commercial debt or covered commercial credit, a "debtor" shall mean a natural person who guarantees an obligation related to a covered commercial credit transaction.

(i) The term "creditor" means a person who extends [4] **covered** credit to a debtor.

(j) The term "consumer credit report" means any written, oral, or other communication of any information by a consumer reporting agency bearing on a consumer's creditworthiness, credit standing, credit capacity, character, general reputation, personal characteristics, or mode of living that is used or expected to be used or collected in whole or in part for the purpose of serving as a factor in establishing the consumer's eligibility for (1) credit or insurance to be used primarily for personal, family, or household purposes, or (2) employment purposes, or (3) other purposes authorized under any applicable federal or state law or regulation. The term does not include (a) any report containing information solely as to transactions or experiences between the consumer and the person making the report; (b) any authorization or approval of a specific extension of credit directly or indirectly by the issuer of a credit card or similar device; or (c) any report in which a person who has been requested by a third party to make a specific extension of credit directly or indirectly to a consumer conveys that person's decision with respect to that request, if the third party advises the consumer of the name and address of the person to whom the request was made, and the person makes the disclosures to the consumer required under any applicable federal or state law or regulation.

(k) The term "consumer reporting agency" means any person that, for monetary fees, dues, or on a cooperative nonprofit basis, regularly engages, in whole or in part, in the practice of assembling or evaluating consumer credit information or other information on consumers for the purpose of furnishing consumer credit reports to third parties and uses any means or facility for the purpose of preparing or furnishing consumer credit reports.

(*l*) **The term "covered debt" means a consumer debt or a covered commercial debt.**

(m) **The term "covered credit" means consumer credit or covered commercial credit.**

(n) **The terms "covered commercial debt" and "covered commercial credit" mean money due or owing or alleged to be due or owing from a natural person to a lender, a commercial financing provider, as defined in Section 22800 of the Financial Code, or a debt buyer, as defined in Section 1788.50, by reason of one or more covered commercial credit transactions, provided the total amount of all covered commercial credit transactions and all other noncovered commercial credit transactions due and owing by the debtor or other person obligated under the transactions to the same lender, commercial financing provider, or debt buyer is no more than five hundred thousand dollars ($500,000).**

(1) For credit owed to a lender or commercial financing provider, the total value of credit per transaction is determined as of when the transaction is first entered into and is the maximum amount that the creditor is contractually required to provide or make available to the debtor over the life of the transaction or is the maximum amount that is enumerated in an open-end credit agreement.

(2) The value of credit for each transaction for a debt buyer is the amount owing or alleged to be owing to the debt buyer when the debt buyer acquires the rights of the lender or commercial financing provider in the commercial credit.

(o) **The term "covered commercial credit transaction" means a transaction between a person and another person in which a total value of no more than five hundred thousand dollars ($500,000), is acquired on credit by that person from the other person for use primarily for other than personal, family, or household purposes.** **Leg.H.** Added Stats 1977 ch 907 §1. Amended Stats 1994 ch 1010 §37 (SB 2053); Stats 2006 ch 521 §1 (AB 2043) (ch 521 prevails), ch 583 §46 (SB 1852), effective January 1, 2007; Stats 2019 ch 545 §2 (SB 187), effective January 1, 2020; Stats 2024 ch 522 §2 (SB 1286), effective January 1, 2025.

§1788.2. 2024 **Deletes.** [1] consumer [2] consumer [3] such [4] consumer

2019 Note: The amendments of subdivision (f) of Section 1788.2 of the Civil Code made by this act do not constitute a change in, but are declaratory of, existing law. Stats 2019 ch 545 §1 (SB 187).

§1788.3. Information furnished by credit union to employer

Nothing contained in this title shall be construed to prohibit a credit union chartered under Division 5 (commencing with Section 14000) of the Financial Code or under the Federal Credit Union Act (Chapter 14 (commencing with Section 1751) of Title 12 of the United States Code) from providing information to an employer when the employer is ordinarily and necessarily entitled to receive such information because he is an employee, officer, committee member, or agent of such credit union. **Leg.H.** Added Stats 1977 ch 907 §1.

ARTICLE 2
Debt Collector Responsibilities

Threats. §1788.10.
Profane language; Telephone practices. §1788.11.
Communication of information regarding debt. §1788.12.
Representations. §1788.13.
Collection of fee or discharged debt; Communication with debtor represented by attorney. §1788.14.
Required statement by debt collector to debtor upon debtor's request; Prerequisites to debt collector's statement; Required contents of statement. § 1788.14.5.
Improper use of judicial proceedings. §1788.15.
Simulation of legal process. §1788.16.
Compliance with federal law. §1788.17.
Identity theft; Debt collector to stop collection activities when certain information provided; Written statement; Penalty for false information; Recommencement of collection upon good faith determination; Notification to credit reporting agencies and creditors of specified information; Definition. §1788.18.
Complaint; Redaction of confidential information; Judgments. § 1788.185.

§1788.10. Threats

No debt collector shall collect or attempt to collect a [1] **covered** debt by means of the following conduct:

(a) The use, or threat of use, of physical force or violence or any criminal means to cause harm to the person, or the reputation, or the property of any person [2].

(b) The threat that the failure to pay a [3] **covered** debt will result in an accusation that the debtor has committed a crime where [4] **the** accusation, if made, would be false [5].

(c) The communication of, or threat to communicate to any person the fact that a debtor has engaged in conduct, other than the failure to pay a [6] **covered** debt, which the debt collector knows or has reason to believe will defame the debtor [7].

(d) The threat to the debtor to sell or assign to another person the obligation of the debtor to pay a [8] **covered** debt, with an accompanying false representation that the result of [9] **the** sale or assignment would be that the debtor would lose any defense to the [10] **covered debt.**

(e) The threat to any person that nonpayment of the [11] **covered** debt may result in the arrest of the debtor or the seizure, garnishment, attachment, or sale of any property or the garnishment or attachment of wages of the debtor, unless [12] **the** action is in fact contemplated by the debt collector and permitted by the law [13].

(f) The threat to take any action against the debtor, which is prohibited by this title. **Leg.H.** Added Stats 1977 ch 907 §1. Amended Stats 2024 ch 522 §3 (SB 1286), effective January 1, 2025.

§1788.10. 2024 **Deletes.** [1] consumer [2] ; [3] consumer [4] such [5] ; [6] consumer [7] ; [8] consumer [9] such [10] consumer debt; [11] consumer [12] such [13] ; or

§1788.11. Profane language; Telephone practices

No debt collector shall collect or attempt to collect a [1] **covered** debt by means of the following practices:

(a) Using obscene or profane language.

(b) Placing a telephone call without disclosing the caller's identity, provided that an employee of a licensed collection agency may identify oneself by using their registered alias name if they correctly identify the agency that they represent. A debt collector shall provide its California debt collector license number, **if applicable,** upon the consumer's request.

(c) Causing expense to any person for long distance telephone calls, telegram fees, or charges for other similar communications, by misrepresenting to the person the purpose of the telephone call, telegram or similar communication.

(d) Causing a telephone to ring repeatedly or continuously to annoy the person called.

(e) Communicating, by telephone or in person, with the debtor with such frequency as to be unreasonable, and to constitute harassment of the debtor under the circumstances.

(f) Sending written or digital communication to the person that does not display the California license number of the collector, **if applicable,** in at least 12-point type. **Leg.H.** Added Stats 1977 ch 907 §1. Amended Stats 2020 ch 163 §1 (SB 908), effective January 1, 2021; Stats 2024 ch 522 §4 (SB 1286), effective January 1, 2025.

§1788.11. 2024 Deletes. [1] consumer

§1788.12. Communication of information regarding debt

No debt collector shall collect or attempt to collect a **covered debt or** consumer debt**, as specified,** by means of the following practices:

(a) Communicating with the debtor's employer regarding the debtor's consumer debt unless such a communication is necessary to the collection of the **consumer** debt, or unless the debtor or [1] **their** attorney has consented in writing to [2] **that** communication. A communication is necessary to the collection of the **consumer** debt only if it is made for the purposes of verifying the debtor's employment, locating the debtor, or effecting garnishment, after judgment, of the debtor's wages, or in the case of a medical debt for the purpose of discovering the existence of medical insurance. Any such communication, other than a communication in the case of a medical debt by a health care provider or its agent for the purpose of discovering the existence of medical insurance, shall be in writing unless [3] **that** written communication receives no response within 15 days and shall be made only as many times as is necessary to the collection of the **consumer** debt. Communications to a debtor's employer regarding a **consumer** debt shall not contain language that would be improper if the communication were made to the debtor. One communication solely for the purpose of verifying the debtor's employment may be oral without prior written contact.

(b) Communicating information regarding a consumer debt to any member of the debtor's family, other than the debtor's spouse or the parents or guardians of the debtor who is either a minor or who resides in the same household with [4] **that** parent or guardian, prior to obtaining a judgment against the debtor, except where the purpose of the communication is to locate the debtor, or where the debtor or [5] **their** attorney has consented in writing to [6] **that communication.**

(c) Communicating to any person any list of debtors [7] **that** discloses the nature or existence of a [8] **covered** debt, commonly known as deadbeat lists [9]**, or advertising any [10] covered** debt for sale, by naming the debtor [11].

(d) Communicating with the debtor by means of a written communication that displays or conveys any information about the [12] **covered** debt or the debtor other than the name, address**,** and telephone number of the debtor and the debt collector and [13] **that** is intended both to be seen by any other person and also to embarrass the debtor.

(e) Notwithstanding the foregoing provisions of this section, the disclosure, publication, or communication by a debt collector of information relating to a [14] **covered** debt or the debtor to a consumer reporting agency or to any other person reasonably believed to have a legitimate business need for [15] **that** information shall not be deemed to violate this title. **Leg.H.** Added Stats 1977 ch 907 §1. Amended Stats 1978 ch 390 §1, effective July 11, 1978; Stats 2024 ch 522 §5 (SB 1286), effective January 1, 2025.

§1788.12. 2024 Deletes. [1] his [2] such [3] such [4] such [5] his [6] such communication; [7] which [8] consumer [9] [10] consumer [11] ; or [12] consumer [13] which [14] consumer [15] such

§1788.13. Representations

No debt collector shall collect or attempt to collect a [1] **covered** debt by means of the following practices:

(a) Any communication with the debtor other than in the name either of the debt collector or the person on whose behalf the debt collector is acting [2].

(b) Any false representation that any person is an attorney or counselor at law [3].

(c) Any communication with a debtor in the name of an attorney or counselor at law or upon stationery or like written instruments bearing the name of the attorney or counselor at law, unless [4] **that** communication is by an attorney or counselor at law or shall have been approved or authorized by [5] **that** attorney or counselor at law [6].

(d) The representation that any debt collector is vouched for, bonded by, affiliated with, or is an instrumentality, agent or official of any federal, state or local government or any agency of federal, state or local government, unless the collector is actually employed by the particular governmental agency in question and is acting on behalf of [7] **that** agency in the debt collection matter [8].

(e) The false representation that the [9] **covered** debt may be increased by the addition of attorney's fees, investigation fees, service fees, finance charges, or other charges if, in fact, [10] **those** fees or charges may not legally be added to the existing obligation [11].

(f) The false representation that information concerning a debtor's failure or alleged failure to pay a [12] **covered** debt has been or is about to be referred to a consumer reporting agency [13].

(g) The false representation that a debt collector is a consumer reporting agency [14].

(h) The false representation that collection letters, notices or other printed forms are being sent by or on behalf of a claim, credit, audit**,** or legal department [15].

(i) The false representation of the true nature of the business or services being rendered by the debt collector [16].

(j) The false representation that a legal proceeding has been, is about to be, or will be instituted unless payment of a [17] **covered** debt is made [18].

(k) The false representation that a [19] **covered** debt has been, is about to be, or will be sold, assigned, or referred to a debt collector for collection [20].

(*l*) Any communication by a [21] collection agency to a debtor demanding money unless the claim is actually assigned to the collection agency. **Leg.H.** Added Stats 1977 ch 907 §1. Amended Stats 1980 ch 1126 §7; Stats 2024 ch 522 §6 (SB 1286), effective January 1, 2025.

§1788.13. 2024 Deletes. [1] consumer [2] ; [3] ; [4] such [5] such [6] ; [7] such [8] ; [9] consumer [10] such [11] ; [12] consumer [13] ; [14] ; [15] ; [16] ; [17] consumer [18] ; [19] consumer [20] ; or [21] licensed

§1788.14. Collection of fee or discharged debt; Communication with debtor represented by attorney

No debt collector shall collect or attempt to collect a [1] **covered** debt by means of the following practices:

(a) Obtaining an affirmation from a debtor of a [2] **covered** debt that has been discharged in bankruptcy, without clearly and conspicuously disclosing to the debtor, in writing, at the time the affirmation is sought, the fact that the debtor is not legally obligated to make an affirmation.

(b) Collecting or attempting to collect from the debtor the whole or any part of the debt collector's fee or charge for services rendered, or other expense incurred by the debt collector in the collection of the [3] **covered** debt, except as permitted by law.

(c) Initiating communications, other than statements of account, with the debtor with regard to the [4] **covered** debt, when the debt collector has been previously notified in writing by the debtor's attorney that the debtor is represented by the attorney with respect to the [5] **covered** debt and the notice includes the attorney's name and address and a request by the attorney that all communications regarding the [6] **covered** debt be addressed to the attorney, unless the attorney fails to answer correspondence, return telephone calls, or discuss the obligation in question. This subdivision shall not apply if prior approval has been obtained from the debtor's attorney, or if the communication is a response in the ordinary course of business to a debtor's inquiry.

(d) Sending a written communication to a debtor in an attempt to collect a time-barred debt without providing the debtor with one of the following written notices:

(1) If the debt is not past the date for obsolescence set forth in Section 605(a) of the federal Fair Credit Reporting Act (15 U.S.C. Sec. 1681c), the following notice shall be included in the first written communication provided to the debtor after the debt has become time-barred:

"The law limits how long you can be sued on a debt. Because of the age of your debt, we will not sue you for it. If you do not pay the debt, [insert name of debt collector] may [continue to] report it to the credit reporting agencies as unpaid for as long as the law permits this reporting."

(2) If the debt is past the date for obsolescence set forth in Section 605(a) of the federal Fair Credit Reporting Act (15 U.S.C. Sec. 1681c), the following notice shall be included in the first written communication provided to the debtor after the date for obsolescence:

"The law limits how long you can be sued on a debt. Because of the age of your debt, we will not sue you for it, and we will not report it to any credit reporting agency."

(e) Collecting consumer debt that originated with a hospital licensed pursuant to subdivision (a) of Section 1250 of the Health and Safety Code without including in the first written communication to the debtor a copy of the notice required pursuant to subdivision (e) of Section 127425 of the Health and Safety Code and a statement that the debt collector will wait at least 180 days from the date the debtor was initially billed for the hospital services that are the basis of the debt before [7] filing a lawsuit against the debtor.

(f) For purposes of this section, "first written communication" means the first communication sent to the debtor in writing or by facsimile, email, or other similar means. **Leg.H.** Added Stats 1977 ch 907 §1. Amended Stats 2009 ch 500 §12 (AB 1059), effective January 1, 2010; Stats 2018 ch 247 §1 (AB 1526), effective January 1, 2019; Stats 2021 ch 473 §1 (AB 1020), effective January 1, 2022; Stats 2024 ch 520 §6 (SB 1061), effective January 1, 2025; Stats 2024 ch 522 §7.5 (SB 1286), effective January 1, 2025 (ch 522 prevails).

§1788.14. 2024 Deletes. [1] consumer [2] consumer [3] consumer [4] consumer [5] consumer [6] consumer [7] reporting adverse information to a credit reporting agency or

§ 1788.14.5. Required statement by debt collector to debtor upon debtor's request; Prerequisites to debt collector's statement; Required contents of statement

(a) A debt collector to which delinquent debt has been assigned shall provide to the debtor, upon the debtor's written request, a statement that includes all of the following information pursuant to subdivision (c):

(1) That the debt collector has authority to assert the rights of the creditor to collect the debt.

(2)(A) The debt balance and an explanation of the amount, nature, and reason for all interest and fees, if any, imposed by the creditor or any subsequent entities to which the debt was assigned.

(B) The explanation required by subparagraph (A) shall identify separately the balance, the total of any interest, and the total of any fees.

(3) The date the debt became delinquent or the date of the last payment.

(4) The name and an address of the creditor and the creditor's account number associated with the debt. The creditor's name and address shall be in sufficient form so as to reasonably identify the creditor.

(5) The name and last known address of the debtor as they appeared in the creditor's records before the assignment of the debt to the debt collector.

(6) The names and addresses of all persons or entities other than the debt collector to which the debt was assigned. The names and addresses shall be in sufficient form so as to reasonably identify each assignee.

(7) The California license number of the debt collector, **if applicable**.

(b) A debt collector to which delinquent debt has been assigned shall not make a written statement to a debtor in an attempt to collect a delinquent debt unless the debt collector has access to a copy of a contract or other document evidencing the debtor's agreement to the debt, except in the following circumstances:

(1) If the claim is based on debt for which no signed contract or agreement exists, the debt collector shall have access to a copy of a document provided to the debtor while the account was active, demonstrating that the debt was incurred by the debtor.

(2) For a revolving credit account, the most recent monthly statement recording a purchase transaction, last payment, or balance transfer shall be deemed sufficient to satisfy the requirements of this subparagraph.

(c)(1) A debt collector to which delinquent debt has been assigned shall provide the information or documents identified in subdivisions (a) and (b) to the debtor without charge within 30 calendar days of receipt of a debtor's written request for information regarding the debt or proof of the debt.

(2) If the debt collector cannot provide the information or documents within 30 calendar days, the debt collector shall cease all collection of the debt until the debt collector provides the debtor the information or documents described in subdivisions (a) and (b).

(d)(1) A debt collector shall provide a debtor with whom it has contact an active postal address to which a debtor may send a request for the information described in this section.

(2) A debt collector may also provide an active email address to which these requests can be sent and through which information and documents can be delivered if the parties agree.

(e)(1) A debt collector to which delinquent debt has been assigned shall include in its first written communication with the debtor in no smaller than 12-point type, a separate prominent notice that contains the following statement:

"You may request records showing the following: (1) that [insert name of debt collector] has the right to seek collection of the debt; (2) the debt balance, including an explanation of any interest charges and additional fees; (3) the date the debt became delinquent or the date of the last payment; (4) the name of the creditor and the account number associated with the debt; (5) the name and last known address of the debtor as it appeared in the creditor's records prior to assignment of the debt; and (6) the names of all persons or entities other than the debt collector to which the debt has been assigned, if applicable. You may also request from us a copy of the contract or other document evidencing your agreement to the debt.

A request for these records may be addressed to: [insert debt collector's active mailing address and email address, if applicable]."

(2) If a language other than English is principally used by the debt collector in the initial oral contact with the debtor, the notice required by this subdivision shall be provided to the debtor in that language within five business days.

(f)(1) A debt buyer that complies with the requirements of Section 1788.52 shall be deemed to be in compliance with this section.

(2) For purposes of this subdivision, "debt buyer" shall have the same meaning as in Section 1788.50.

(g) For the purposes of this section, the term "delinquent debt" means a [1] **covered** debt, other than a mortgage debt, that is past due at least 90 days and has not been charged off.

(h) This section shall apply to all delinquent **consumer** debt sold or assigned on or after July 1, 2022.

(i) This section shall [2] **apply to all delinquent covered commercial debt sold or assigned on or after** July 1, [3] **2025**. **Leg.H.** Added Stats 2021 ch 455 §1 (SB 531), effective January 1, 2022, operative July 1, 2022. Amended Stats 2024 ch 522 §8 (SB 1286), effective January 1, 2025.

§ 1788.14.5. 2024 Deletes. [1] consumer [2] become operative on [3] 2022

§1788.15. Improper use of judicial proceedings

(a) No debt collector shall collect or attempt to collect a [1] **covered** debt by means of judicial proceedings when the debt collector knows that service of process, where essential to jurisdiction over the debtor or [2] **their** property, has not been legally effected.

(b) No debt collector shall collect or attempt to collect a [3] **covered** debt, other than one reduced to judgment, by means of judicial proceedings in a county other than the county in which the debtor has incurred the [4] **covered** debt or the county in which the debtor resides at the time [5] **those** proceedings are instituted, or resided at the time the debt was incurred.

(c) **Notwithstanding subdivision (b), when the obligation of the debtor arises from a guaranty by the debtor of a covered commercial debt, a debt collector may collect or attempt to collect covered commercial debt by means of a judicial proceeding in the county in which the nonnatural person for whose purpose the commercial debt was incurred is located.**

(d) **This section shall apply to all delinquent covered commercial debt sold or assigned on or after July 1, 2025. Leg.H.** Added Stats 1977 ch 907 §1. Amended Stats 2024 ch 522 §9 (SB 1286), effective January 1, 2025.

§1788.15. 2024 Deletes. [1] consumer [2] his [3] consumer [4] consumer [5] such

§1788.16. Simulation of legal process

It is unlawful, with respect to attempted collection of a [1] **covered** debt, for a debt collector, creditor, or an attorney [2] to send a communication [3] **that** simulates legal or judicial process or [4] **that** gives the appearance of being authorized, issued, or approved by a governmental agency or attorney when it is not. Any violation of the provisions of this section is a misdemeanor punishable by imprisonment in the county jail not exceeding six months, or by a fine not exceeding two thousand five hundred dollars ($2,500) or by both. **Leg.H.** Added Stats 1980 ch 1126 §8. Amended Stats 2024 ch 522 §10 (SB 1286), effective January 1, 2025.

§1788.16. 2024 Deletes. [1] consumer [2] , [3] which [4] which

§1788.17. Compliance with federal law

Notwithstanding any other provision of this title, every debt collector collecting or attempting to collect a consumer debt shall comply with the provisions of Sections 1692b to 1692j, inclusive, of, and shall be subject to the remedies in Section 1692k of, Title 15 of the United States Code. However, subsection (11) of Section 1692e and Section 1692g shall not apply to any person specified in paragraphs (A) and (B) of subsection (6) of Section 1692a of Title 15 of the United States Code or that person's principal. The references to federal codes in this section refer to those codes as they read January 1, 2001. **Leg.H.** Added Stats 1999 ch 319 §2 (AB 969). Amended Stats 2000 ch 688 §1 (AB 1669); Stats 2024 ch 522 §11 (SB 1286), effective January 1, 2025.

§1788.18. Identity theft; Debt collector to stop collection activities when certain information provided; Written statement; Penalty for false information; Recommencement of collection upon good faith determination; Notification to credit reporting agencies and creditors of specified information; Definition

(a) Upon receipt from a debtor of all of the following, a debt collector shall cease collection activities until completion of the review provided in subdivision (d):

(1) A copy of a Federal Trade Commission (FTC) identity theft report, completed and signed by the debtor. The debtor may choose, instead, to send a copy of a police report filed by the debtor alleging that the debtor is the victim of an identity theft crime, including, but not limited to, a violation of Section 530.5 of the Penal Code, for the specific debt being collected by the debt collector; however, the debt collector shall not also require a police report if the debtor submits an FTC identity theft report.

(2) The debtor's written statement that the debtor claims to be the victim of identity theft with respect to the specific debt being collected by the debt collector.

(b) The written statement described in paragraph (2) of subdivision (a) shall consist of [1] **either** of the following:

(1) A written statement that contains the content of the Identity Theft Victim's Fraudulent Account Information Request offered to the public by the California Office of Privacy Protection.

(2) A written statement that certifies that the representations are true, correct, and contain no material omissions of fact to the best knowledge and belief of the person submitting the certification. A person submitting the certification who declares as true any material matter pursuant to this subdivision that they know to be false is guilty of a misdemeanor. The statement shall contain or be accompanied by the following, to the extent that an item listed below is relevant to the debtor's allegation of identity theft with respect to the debt in question:

(A) A statement that the debtor is a victim of identity theft.

(B) A copy of the debtor's driver's license or identification card, as issued by the state.

(C) Any other identification document that supports the statement of identity theft.

(D) Specific facts supporting the claim of identity theft, if available.

(E) Any explanation showing that the debtor did not incur the debt.

(F) Any available correspondence disputing the debt after transaction information has been provided to the debtor.

(G) Documentation of the residence of the debtor at the time of the alleged debt. This may include copies of bills and statements, such as utility bills, tax statements, or other statements from businesses sent to the debtor, showing that the debtor lived at another residence at the time the debt was incurred.

(H) A telephone number for contacting the debtor concerning any additional information or questions, or direction that further communications to the debtor be in writing only, with the mailing address specified in the statement.

(I) To the extent the debtor has information concerning who may have incurred the debt, the identification of any person whom the debtor believes is responsible.

(J) An express statement that the debtor did not authorize the use of the debtor's name or personal information for incurring the debt.

(K) The certification required pursuant to this paragraph shall be sufficient if it is in substantially the following form:

I certify the representations made are true, correct, and contain no material omissions of fact. [2]

I certify the representations made are true, correct, and contain no material omissions of fact.

_____
(Date and Place)
_____
(Signature)

(c) If a debtor notifies a debt collector orally that they are a victim of identity theft, the debt collector shall notify the debtor, orally or in writing, that the debtor's claim must be in writing. If a debtor notifies a debt collector in writing that they are a victim of identity theft, but omits information required pursuant to subdivision (a) or, if applicable, the certification required pursuant to paragraph (2) of subdivision (b), if the debt collector does not cease collection activities, the debt collector shall provide written notice to the debtor of the additional information that is required, or the certification required pursuant to paragraph (2) of subdivision (b), as applicable, or send the debtor a copy of the Federal Trade Commission's identity theft form.

(d) Within 10 business days of receiving the complete statement and information described in subdivision (a), the debt collector shall, if it furnished adverse information about the debtor to a consumer credit reporting agency, notify the consumer credit reporting agency that the account is disputed, and initiate a review considering all of the information provided by the debtor and other information available to the debt collector in its file or from the creditor. The debt collector shall send notice of its determination to the debtor no later than 10 business days after concluding the review. The debt collector may recommence debt collection activities only upon making a good faith determination that the information does not establish that the debtor is not responsible for the specific debt in question. The debt collector's determination shall be made in a manner consistent with the provisions of subsection (1) of Section 1692f of Title 15 of the United States Code, as incorporated by Section 1788.17 of this code. The debt collector shall notify the debtor in writing of that determination and the basis for that determination before proceeding with any further collection activities. The debt collector's determination shall be based on all of the information provided by the debtor and other information available to the debt collector in its file or from the creditor.

(e) No inference or presumption that the debt is valid or invalid, or that the debtor is liable or not liable for the debt, shall arise if the debt collector decides after the review described in subdivision (d) to cease or recommence the debt collection activities. The exercise or nonexercise of rights under this section is not a waiver of any other right or defense of the debtor or debt collector.

(f) The statement and supporting documents that comply with subdivision (a) may also satisfy, to the extent those documents meet the requirements of, the notice requirement of paragraph (5) of subdivision (c) of Section 1798.93.

(g) A debt collector who ceases collection activities under this section and does not recommence those collection activities shall do [4] **both** of the following:

(1) If the debt collector has furnished adverse information to a consumer credit reporting agency, notify the agency to delete that information no later than 10 business days after making its determination.

(2) Notify the creditor no later than 10 business days after making its determination that debt collection activities have been terminated based upon the debtor's claim of identity theft.

(h) A debt collector who has possession of documents that the debtor is entitled to request from a creditor pursuant to Section 530.8 of the Penal Code is authorized to provide those documents to the debtor.

(i) Notwithstanding subdivision (h) of Section 1788.2, for the purposes of this section, "debtor" means a natural person, firm, association, organization, partnership, business trust, company, corporation, or limited liability company from which a debt collector seeks to collect a debt that is due and owing or alleged to be due and owing from the person or entity. The remedies provided by this title shall apply equally to violations of this section. **Leg.H.** Added Stats 2003 ch 287 §1 (AB 1294). Amended Stats 2006 ch 521 §2 (AB 2043), effective January 1, 2007; Stats 2007 ch 130 §34 (AB 299), effective January 1, 2008; Stats 2016 ch 376 §3 (AB 1723), effective January 1, 2017; Stats 2020 ch 36 §13 (AB 3364), effective January 1, 2021; Stats 2021 ch 265 §1 (AB 430), effective January 1, 2022; Stats 2023 ch 100 §1 (AB 1312), effective January 1, 2024; Stats 2023 ch 131 §12 (AB 1754), effective January 1, 2024 (ch 100 prevails); Stats 2024 ch 522 §12 (SB 1286), effective January 1, 2025.

§1788.18. 2024 Deletes. [1] any [2] (Date and Place) [3] (Date and Place) (Signature) [5] (Signature) [4] all

2016 Note: This act shall be known, and may be cited, as the Identity Theft Resolution Act. Stats 2016 ch 376 (AB 1723) §1.

§ 1788.185. Complaint; Redaction of confidential information; Judgments

(a) The complaint in an action brought by a debt collector for debt that originated with a general acute care hospital licensed pursuant to subdivision (a) of Section 1250 of the Health and Safety Code shall allege all of the following:

(1) That the plaintiff is a debt collector.

(2) That the underlying debt originated with a general acute care hospital.

(3) The information contained in paragraph (6) of subdivision (e) of Section 127425 of the Health and Safety Code and a statement identifying the language in which that information was sent to the debtor.

(4) The balance of the debt upon assignment to the debt collector and an explanation of the amount, nature, and reason for any interest and fees that are added to the debt balance by the debt collector after the assignment of the debt. This paragraph shall not be deemed to require a specific itemization, but the explanation shall identify separately the charge-off balance of the debt upon assignment to the debt collector, the total of any interest, and the total of any fees added to the debt balance by the debt collector after the assignment of the debt.

(5) The date of default or the date of the last payment, and the date the debt was assigned.

(6) The name and address of the hospital at the time of assignment.

(7) The hospital's account number associated with the debt.

(b) Copies of the application for financial assistance that was provided to the debtor by the hospital and the notice that was provided to the debtor by the hospital about applying for financial assistance shall be attached to the complaint. If the notice was provided as part of the hospital bill that cannot be separated, the bill shall be redacted to remove confidential information or a sample hospital bill with the substance of the notice regarding financial assistance in the format in use at the time the patient was billed may be provided.

(c) This title does not require the disclosure in public records of personal, financial, or medical information, the confidentiality of which is protected by state or federal law. The plaintiff shall redact protected information filed with the complaint.

(d) A default or other judgment shall not be entered against a debtor for debt pursuant to this section unless business records, authenticated through a sworn declaration, are submitted by the debt collector to the court to establish the facts required to be alleged pursuant to subdivision (a).

(e) If a debt collector plaintiff seeks a default judgment and has not complied with this title, the court shall not enter a default judgment for the plaintiff and may, in its discretion, dismiss the action.

(f) Except as provided in this title, this section does not modify or otherwise amend the procedures established in Section 585 of the Code of Civil Procedure. **Leg.H.** Added Stats 2021 ch 473 §2 (AB 1020), effective January 1, 2022.

ARTICLE 3
Debtor Responsibilities

Representations regarding ability to pay. §1788.20.
Change of name, address, or employment. §1788.21.
Unauthorized use of account. §1788.22.

§1788.20. Representations regarding ability to pay

In connection with any request or application for [1] **covered** credit, no person shall:

(a) Request or apply for [2] **that** credit at a time when [3] **that** person knows there is no reasonable probability of [4] **that** person's being able, or [5] **that** person then lacks the intention, to pay the obligation created thereby in accordance with the terms and conditions of the credit extension [6].

(b) Knowingly submit false or inaccurate information or willfully conceal adverse information bearing upon [7] **that** person's credit worthiness, credit standing, or credit capacity. **Leg.H.** Added Stats 1977 ch 907 §1. Amended Stats 2024 ch 522 §13 (SB 1286), effective January 1, 2025.

§1788.20. 2024 Deletes. [1] consumer [2] such [3] such [4] such [5] such [6] ; or [7] such

§1788.21. Change of name, address, or employment

(a) In connection with any [1] **covered** credit existing or requested to be extended to a person, [2] **that** person shall within a reasonable time notify the creditor or prospective creditor of any change in [3] **that** person's name, address, or employment.

(b) Each responsibility set forth in subdivision (a) shall apply only if and after the creditor clearly and conspicuously in writing discloses [4] **that** responsibility to [5] **that** person. **Leg.H.** Added Stats 1977 ch 907 §1. Amended Stats 2024 ch 522 §14 (SB 1286), effective January 1, 2025.

§1788.21. 2024 Deletes. [1] consumer [2] such [3] such [4] such [5] such

§1788.22. Unauthorized use of account

(a) In connection with any [1] **covered** credit extended to a person under an account:

(1) No such person shall attempt to consummate any [2] **covered** credit transaction thereunder knowing that credit privileges under the account have been terminated or suspended.

(2) Each such person shall notify the creditor by telephone, telegraph, letter, or any other reasonable means that an unauthorized use of the account has occurred or may occur as the result of loss or theft of a credit card, or other instrument identifying the account, within a reasonable time after [3] **that** person's discovery thereof, and shall reasonably assist the creditor in determining the facts and circumstances relating to any unauthorized use of the account.

(b) Each responsibility set forth in subdivision (a) shall apply only if and after the creditor clearly and conspicuously in writing discloses [4] **that** responsibility to [5] **that** person. **Leg.H.** Added Stats 1977 ch 907 §1. Amended Stats 2024 ch 522 §15 (SB 1286), effective January 1, 2025.

§1788.22. 2024 Deletes. [1] consumer [2] consumer [3] such [4] such [5] such

ARTICLE 4
Enforcement

Remedies; Jurisdiction; Defenses. §1788.30.
Separability of provisions. §1788.31.
Remedies cumulative; Administrative regulations saved. §1788.32.
Waiver of provisions of title void. §1788.33.

§1788.30. Remedies; Jurisdiction; Defenses

(a) Any debt collector who violates this title with respect to any debtor shall be liable to that debtor only in an individual action, and his liability therein to that debtor shall be in an amount equal to the sum of any actual damages sustained by the debtor as a result of the violation.

(b) Any debt collector who willfully and knowingly violates this title with respect to any debtor shall, in addition to actual damages sustained by the debtor as a result of the violation, also be liable to the debtor only in an individual action, and his additional liability therein to that debtor shall be for a penalty in such amount as the court may allow, which shall not be less than one hundred dollars ($100) nor greater than one thousand dollars ($1,000).

(c) In the case of any action to enforce any liability under this title, the prevailing party shall be entitled to costs of the action. Reasonable attorney's fees, which shall be based on time necessarily expended to enforce the liability, shall be awarded to a prevailing debtor; reasonable attorney's fees may be awarded to a prevailing creditor upon a finding by the court that the debtor's prosecution or defense of the action was not in good faith.

(d) A debt collector shall have no civil liability under this title if, within 15 days either after discovering a violation which is able to be cured, or after the receipt of a written notice of such violation, the debt collector notifies the debtor of the violation, and makes whatever adjustments or corrections are necessary to cure the violation with respect to the debtor.

(e) A debt collector shall have no civil liability to which such debt collector might otherwise be subject for a violation of this title, if the debt collector shows by a preponderance of evidence that the violation was not intentional and resulted notwithstanding the maintenance of procedures reasonably adapted to avoid any such violation.

(f) Any action under this section may be brought in any appropriate court of competent jurisdiction in an individual capacity only, within one year from the date of the occurrence of the violation.

(g) Any intentional violation of the provisions of this title by the debtor may be raised as a defense by the debt collector, if such violation is pertinent or relevant to any claim or action brought against the debt collector by or on behalf of the debtor. **Leg.H.** Added Stats 1977 ch 907 §1.

§1788.31. Separability of provisions

If any provision of this title, or the application thereof to any person or circumstances, is held invalid, the remaining provisions of this title, or the application of such provisions to other persons or circumstances, shall not be affected thereby. **Leg.H.** Added Stats 1977 ch 907 §1.

§1788.32. Remedies cumulative; Administrative regulations saved

The remedies provided herein are intended to be cumulative and are in addition to any other procedures, rights, or remedies under any other provision of law. The enactment of this title shall not supersede existing administrative regulations of the Director of Consumer Affairs except to the extent that those regulations are inconsistent with the provisions of this title. **Leg.H.** Added Stats 1977 ch 907 §1.

§1788.33. Waiver of provisions of title void

Any waiver of the provisions of this title is contrary to public policy, and is void and unenforceable. **Leg.H.** Added Stats 2002 ch 815 §12 (AB 2331).

TITLE 1.6C.5
FAIR DEBT BUYING PRACTICES

Definitions; Applicability of title. §1788.50.
Prohibition against making written statement in attempt to collect consumer debt unless requirements satisfied; Provision of information or documents to debtor; Required notice to debtor; Language other than English; Conflict with federal law. §1788.52.
Settlement agreements; Receipt or monthly statement of payment on debt; Final statement of payment in full or as full and final compromise of debt; Prohibition against sale of interest in or information related to resolved debt. §1788.54.
Prohibition against bringing suit to collect consumer debt if statute of limitations expired. §1788.56.
Complaint in action on consumer debt; No requirement to disclose protected personal, financial, or medical information. §1788.58.
Requirements for default judgment against debtor. §1788.60.
Notice of motion and motion to set aside default or default judgment and for leave to defend action. §1788.61.
Amount of liability for violation; Costs and fees; Factors affecting amount of liability; Violation not intentional and result of error; Limitation on action; Preclusion of recovery. §1788.62.
Waiver of provisions of title void. §1788.64.
Prohibition on the sale or assignment of COVID-19 rental debt of persons qualified for certain rental assistance. § 1788.66.

§1788.50. Definitions; Applicability of title

(a) As used in this title:

(1) "Debt buyer" means a person or entity that is regularly engaged in the business of purchasing charged-off consumer debt for collection purposes, whether it collects the debt itself, hires a third party for collection, or hires an attorney-at-law for collection litigation. "Debt buyer" does not mean a person or entity that acquires a charged-off consumer debt incidental to the purchase of a portfolio predominantly consisting of consumer debt that has not been charged off.

(2) "Charged-off consumer debt" means a consumer debt that has been removed from a creditor's books as an asset and treated as a loss or expense.

(b) The acquisition by a check services company of the right to collect on a paper or electronic check instrument, including an Automated Clearing House item, that has been returned unpaid to a merchant does not constitute a purchase of delinquent consumer debt under this title.

(c) Terms defined in Title 1.6C (commencing with Section 1788) shall apply to this title.

(d) This title shall apply to debt buyers with respect to all consumer debt sold or resold on or after January 1, 2014. **Leg.H.** Added Stats 2013 ch 64 §2 (SB 233), effective January 1, 2014.

§1788.52. Prohibition against making written statement in attempt to collect consumer debt unless requirements satisfied; Provision of information or documents to debtor; Required notice to debtor; Language other than English; Conflict with federal law

(a) A debt buyer shall not make any written statement to a debtor in an attempt to collect a consumer debt unless the debt buyer possesses the following information:

(1) That the debt buyer is the sole owner of the debt at issue or has authority to assert the rights of all owners of the debt.

(2) The debt balance at charge off and an explanation of the amount, nature, and reason for all post-charge-off interest and fees, if any, imposed by the charge-off creditor or any subsequent purchasers of the debt. This paragraph shall not be deemed to require a specific itemization, but the explanation shall identify separately the charge-off balance, the total of any post-charge-off interest, and the total of any post-charge-off fees.

(3) The date of default or the date of the last payment.

(4) The name and an address of the charge-off creditor at the time of charge off, and the charge-off creditor's account number associated with the debt. The charge-off creditor's name and address shall be in sufficient form so as to reasonably identify the charge-off creditor.

(5) The name and last known address of the debtor as they appeared in the charge-off creditor's records prior to the sale of the debt. If the debt was sold prior to January 1, 2014, the name and last known address of the debtor as they appeared in the debt owner's records on December 31, 2013, shall be sufficient.

(6) The names and addresses of all persons or entities that purchased the debt after charge off, including the debt buyer making the written statement. The names and addresses shall be in sufficient form so as to reasonably identify each such purchaser.

(7) The California license number of the debt buyer.

(b) A debt buyer shall not make any written statement to a debtor in an attempt to collect a consumer debt unless the debt buyer has access to a copy of a contract or other document evidencing the debtor's agreement to the debt. If the claim is based on debt for which no signed contract or agreement exists, the debt buyer shall have access to a copy of a document provided to the debtor while the account was active, demonstrating that the debt was incurred by the debtor. For a revolving credit account, the most recent monthly statement recording a purchase transaction, last payment, or balance transfer shall be deemed sufficient to satisfy this requirement.

(c) A debt buyer shall provide the information or documents identified in subdivisions (a) and (b) to the debtor without charge within 15 calendar days of receipt of a debtor's written request for information regarding the debt or proof of the debt. If the debt buyer cannot provide the information or documents within 15 calendar days, the debt buyer shall cease all collection of the debt until the debt buyer provides the debtor the information or documents described in subdivisions (a) and (b). Except as provided otherwise in this title, the request by the debtor shall be consistent with the validation requirements contained in Section 1692g of Title 15 of the United States Code. A debt buyer shall provide all debtors with whom it has contact an active postal address to which these requests can be sent. A debt buyer may also provide an active email address to which these requests can be sent and through which information and documents can be delivered, if the parties agree.

(d)(1) A debt buyer shall include with its first written communication with the debtor in no smaller than 12-point type, a separate prominent notice that provides:

"You may request records showing the following: (1) that [insert name of debt buyer] has the right to seek collection of the debt; (2) the debt balance, including an explanation of any interest charges and additional fees; (3) the date of default or the date of the last payment; (4) the name of the charge-off creditor and the account number associated with the debt; (5) the name and last known address of the debtor as it appeared in the charge-off creditor's or debt buyer's records prior to the sale of the debt, as appropriate; and (6) the names of all persons or entities that have purchased the debt. You may also request from us a copy of the contract or other document evidencing your agreement to the debt.

"A request for these records may be addressed to: [insert debt buyer's active mailing address and email address, if applicable]."

(2) When collecting on a time-barred debt where the debt is not past the date for obsolescence provided for in Section 605(a) of the federal Fair Credit Reporting Act (15 U.S.C. Sec. 1681c):

"The law limits how long you can be sued on a debt. Because of the age of your debt, we will not sue you for it. If you do not pay the debt, [insert name of debt buyer] may [continue to] report it to the credit reporting agencies as unpaid for as long as the law permits this reporting."

(3) When collecting on a time-barred debt where the debt is past the date for obsolescence provided for in Section 605(a) of the federal Fair Credit Reporting Act (15 U.S.C. Sec. 1681c):

"The law limits how long you can be sued on a debt. Because of the age of your debt, we will not sue you for it, and we will not report it to any credit reporting agency."

(e) If a language other than English is principally used by the debt buyer in the initial oral contact with the debtor, the notice required by subdivision (d) shall be provided to the debtor in that language within five working days.

(f) A debt buyer shall not collect, or make any attempt to collect consumer debt that originated with a hospital licensed pursuant to subdivision (a) of Section 1250 of the Health and Safety Code without including in the first written communication to the debtor a copy of the notice required pursuant to subdivision (e) of Section 127425 of the Health and Safety Code.

(g) In the event of a conflict between the requirements of subdivision (d) and federal law, so that it is impracticable to comply with both, the requirements of federal law shall prevail. **Leg.H.** Added Stats 2013 ch 64 §2 (SB 233), effective January 1, 2014. Amended Stats 2020 ch 163 §2 (SB 908), effective January 1, 2021; Stats 2021 ch 473 §3 (AB 1020), effective January 1, 2022.

§1788.54. Settlement agreements; Receipt or monthly statement of payment on debt; Final statement of payment in full or as full and final compromise of debt; Prohibition against sale of interest in or information related to resolved debt

(a) All settlement agreements between a debt buyer and a debtor shall be documented in open court or otherwise reduced to writing. The debt buyer shall ensure that a copy of the written agreement is provided to the debtor.

(b) A debt buyer that receives payment on a debt shall provide, within 30 calendar days, a receipt or monthly statement, to the debtor. The receipt or statement shall clearly and conspicuously show the amount and date paid, the name of the entity paid, the current account number, the name of the charge-off creditor, the account number issued by the charge-off creditor, and the remaining balance owing, if any. The receipt or statement may be provided electronically if the parties agree.

(c) A debt buyer that accepts a payment as payment in full, or as a full and final compromise of the debt, shall provide, within 30 calendar days, a final statement that complies with subdivision (b). A debt buyer shall not sell an interest in a resolved debt, or any personal or financial information related to the resolved debt. **Leg.H.** Added Stats 2013 ch 64 §2 (SB 233), effective January 1, 2014.

§1788.56. Prohibition against bringing suit to collect consumer debt if statute of limitations expired

A debt buyer shall not bring suit or initiate an arbitration or other legal proceeding to collect a consumer debt if the applicable statute of limitations on the debt buyer's claim has expired. **Leg.H.** Added Stats 2013 ch 64 §2 (SB 233), effective January 1, 2014.

§1788.58. Complaint in action on consumer debt; No requirement to disclose protected personal, financial, or medical information

In an action brought by a debt buyer on a consumer debt:

(a) The complaint shall allege all of the following:

(1) That the plaintiff is a debt buyer.

(2) The nature of the underlying debt and the consumer transaction or transactions from which it is derived, in a short and plain statement.

(3) That the debt buyer is the sole owner of the debt at issue, or has authority to assert the rights of all owners of the debt.

(4) The debt balance at charge off and an explanation of the amount, nature, and reason for all post-charge-off interest and fees, if any, imposed by the charge-off creditor or any subsequent purchasers of the debt. This paragraph shall not be deemed to require a specific itemization, but the explanation shall identify separately the charge-off balance, the total of any post-charge-off interest, and the total of any post-charge-off fees.

(5) The date of default or the date of the last payment.

(6) The name and an address of the charge-off creditor at the time of charge off and the charge-off creditor's account number associated with the debt. The charge-off creditor's name and address shall be in sufficient form so as to reasonably identify the charge-off creditor.

(7) The name and last known address of the debtor as they appeared in the charge-off creditor's records prior to the sale of the debt. If the debt was sold prior to January 1, 2014, the debtor's name and last known address as they appeared in the debt owner's records on December 31, 2013, shall be sufficient.

(8) The names and addresses of all persons or entities that purchased the debt after charge off, including the plaintiff debt buyer. The names and addresses shall be in sufficient form so as to reasonably identify each such purchaser.

(9) That the debt buyer has complied with Section 1788.52.

(b) A copy of the contract or other document described in subdivision (b) of Section 1788.52 shall be attached to the complaint.

(c) The complaint in an action brought by a debt buyer for debt that originated with a general acute care hospital licensed pursuant to subdivision (a) of Section 1250 of the Health and Safety Code shall also contain both of the following:

(1) The information contained in paragraph (6) of subdivision (e) of Section 127425 of the Health and Safety Code and a statement identifying the language in which that information was sent to the debtor.

(2) Copies of the application for financial assistance that was provided to the debtor by the hospital and the notice that was provided to the debtor by the hospital about applying for financial assistance, attached to the complaint. If the notice was provided as part of the hospital bill that cannot be separated, the bill shall be redacted to remove confidential information, or a sample hospital bill with the substance of the notice regarding financial assistance in the format in use at the time the patient was billed may be provided.

(d) The requirements of this title shall not be deemed to require the disclosure in public records of personal, financial, or medical information, the confidentiality of which is protected by any state or federal law. **Leg.H.** Added Stats 2013 ch 64 §2 (SB 233), effective January 1, 2014. Amended Stats 2014 ch 71 §16 (SB 1304), effective January 1, 2015; Stats 2021 ch 473 §4 (AB 1020), effective January 1, 2022.

§1788.60. Requirements for default judgment against debtor

(a) In an action initiated by a debt buyer, no default or other judgment may be entered against a debtor unless business records, authenticated through a sworn declaration, are submitted by the debt buyer to the court to establish the facts required to be alleged by paragraphs (3) to (8), inclusive, of subdivision (a) of Section 1788.58.

(b) No default or other judgment may be entered against a debtor unless a copy of the contract or other document described in subdivision (b) of Section 1788.52, authenticated through a sworn declaration, has been submitted by the debt buyer to the court.

(c) In any action on a consumer debt, if a debt buyer plaintiff seeks a default judgment and has not complied with the requirements of this title, the court shall not enter a default judgment for the plaintiff and may, in its discretion, dismiss the action.

(d) Except as provided in this title, this section is not intended to modify or otherwise amend the procedures established in Section 585 of the Code of Civil Procedure. **Leg.H.** Added Stats 2013 ch 64 §2 (SB 233), effective January 1, 2014.

§1788.61. Notice of motion and motion to set aside default or default judgment and for leave to defend action

(a)(1) Notwithstanding Section 473.5 of the Code of Civil Procedure, if service of a summons has not resulted in actual notice to a person in time to defend an action brought by a debt buyer and a default or default judgment has been entered against the person in the action, the person may serve and file a notice of motion and motion to set aside the default or default judgment and for leave to defend the action.

(2) Except as provided in paragraph (3), the notice of motion shall be served and filed within a reasonable time, but in no event exceeding the earlier of:

(A) Six years after entry of the default or default judgment against the person.

(B) One hundred eighty days of the first actual notice of the action.

(3)(A) Notwithstanding paragraph (2), in the case of identity theft or mistaken identity, the notice of motion shall be served and filed within a reasonable time, but in no event exceeding 180 days of the first actual notice of the action.

(B)(i) In the case of identity theft, the person alleging that they are a victim of identity theft shall provide the court with either a copy of a Federal Trade Commission identity theft report or a copy of a police report filed by the person alleging that they are the victim of an identity theft crime, including, but not limited to, a violation of Section 530.5 of the Penal Code, for the specific debt associated with the judgment.

(ii) In the case of mistaken identity, the moving party shall provide relevant information or documentation to support the claim that they are not the party named in the judgment or is not the person who incurred or owes the debt.

(b) A notice of motion to set aside a default or default judgment and for leave to defend the action shall designate as the time for making the motion a date prescribed by Section 1005 of the Code of Civil Procedure, and it shall be accompanied by an affidavit stating under oath that the person's lack of actual notice in time to defend the action was not caused by their avoidance of service or inexcusable neglect. The person shall serve and file with the notice a copy of the answer, motion, or other pleading proposed to be filed in the action. Either party may introduce, and the court may consider, evidence in support of its motion or opposition, including evidence relating to the process server who appears on the proof of service of the summons and complaint.

(c) Upon a finding by the court that the motion was made within the period permitted by subdivision (a) and that the person's lack of actual notice in time to defend the action was not caused by their avoidance of service or inexcusable neglect, the court may set aside the default or default judgment on whatever terms as may be just and allow the party to defend the action. If the validity of the judgment is not challenged, the court may select an appropriate remedy other than setting aside the default or default judgment.

(d) This section shall apply to a default or default judgment entered on or after January 1, 2010, except in the case of identity theft or mistaken identity, in which case this section shall apply regardless of the date of the default or default judgment.

(e) This section shall not limit the equitable authority of the court or other available remedies under law. **Leg.H.** Added Stats 2015 ch 804 §1 (SB 641), effective January 1, 2016. Amended Stats 2021 ch 265 §2 (AB 430), effective January 1, 2022.

§1788.62. Amount of liability for violation; Costs and fees; Factors affecting amount of liability; Violation not intentional and result of error; Limitation on action; Preclusion of recovery

(a) In the case of an action brought by an individual or individuals, a debt buyer that violates any provision of this title with respect to any person shall be liable to that person in an amount equal to the sum of the following:

(1) Any actual damages sustained by that person as a result of the violation, including, but not limited to, the amount of any judgment obtained by the debt buyer as a result of a time-barred suit to collect a debt from that person.

(2) Statutory damages in an amount as the court may allow, which shall not be less than one hundred dollars ($100) nor greater than one thousand dollars ($1,000).

(b) In the case of a class action, a debt buyer that violates any provision of this title shall be liable for any statutory damages for each named plaintiff as provided in paragraph (2) of subdivision (a). If the court finds that the debt buyer engaged in a pattern and practice of violating any provision of this title, the court may award additional damages to the class in an amount not to exceed the lesser of five hundred thousand dollars ($500,000) or 1 percent of the net worth of the debt buyer.

(c)(1) In the case of any successful action to enforce liability under this section, the court shall award costs of the action, together with reasonable attorney's fees as determined by the court.

(2) Reasonable attorney's fees may be awarded to a prevailing debt buyer upon a finding by the court that the plaintiff's prosecution of the action was not in good faith.

(d) In determining the amount of liability under subdivision (b), the court shall consider, among other relevant factors, the frequency and persistence of noncompliance by the debt buyer, the nature of the noncompliance, the resources of the debt buyer, and the number of persons adversely affected.

(e) A debt buyer shall have no civil liability under this section if the debt buyer shows by a preponderance of evidence that the violation was not intentional and resulted from a bona fide error, and occurred notwithstanding the maintenance of procedures reasonably adopted to avoid any error.

(f) An action to enforce any liability created by this title shall be brought within one year from the date of the last violation.

(g) Recovery in an action brought under the Rosenthal Fair Debt Collection Practices Act (Title 1.6C (commencing with Section 1788)) or the federal Fair Debt Collection Practices Act (15 U.S.C. Sec. 1692 et seq.) shall preclude recovery for the same acts in an action brought under this title. **Leg.H.** Added Stats 2013 ch 64 §2 (SB 233), effective January 1, 2014.

§1788.64. Waiver of provisions of title void

Any waiver of the provisions of this title is contrary to public policy, and is void and unenforceable. **Leg.H.** Added Stats 2013 ch 64 §2 (SB 233), effective January 1, 2014.

§ 1788.65. Sale or assignment of COVID-19 rental debt; Limitations [Repealed]

Leg.H. Added Stats 2021 ch 2 §3 (SB 91), effective January 29, 2021, repealed July 1, 2021. Amended Stats 2021 ch 5 §4 (AB 81), effective February 23, 2021, repealed July 1, 2021; Stats 2021 ch 27 §2 (AB 832), effective June 28, 2021, repealed October 1, 2021.

§ 1788.66. Prohibition on the sale or assignment of COVID-19 rental debt of persons qualified for certain rental assistance

Notwithstanding any other law, a person shall not sell or assign any unpaid COVID-19 rental debt, as defined in Section 1179.02 of the Code of Civil Procedure, for the time period between March 1, 2020, and September 30, 2021, of any person who would have qualified for rental assistance funding provided by the Secretary of the Treasury pursuant to Section 501 of Subtitle A of Title V of Division N of the federal Consolidated Appropriations Act, 2021 (Public Law 116-260) or Section 3201 of Subtitle B of Title III of the federal American Rescue Plan Act of 2021 (Public Law 117-2), if the person's household income is at or below 80 percent of the area median income for the 2020 or 2021 calendar year. **Leg.H.** Added Stats 2021 ch 2 §4 (SB 91), effective January 29, 2021. Amended Stats 2021 ch 5 §5 (AB 81), effective February 23, 2021; Stats 2021 ch 27 §3 (AB 832), effective June 28, 2021.

TITLE 1.6C.7
EDUCATIONAL DEBT COLLECTION PRACTICES

Citation of title. §1788.90.
Legislative findings and declarations. §1788.91.
Definitions. §1788.92.
Prohibited debt collection practices by school. §1788.93.
Waiver of provisions void and unenforceable. § 1788.94.

§1788.90. Citation of title

This title shall be known, and may be cited, as the Educational Debt Collection Practices Act. **Leg.H.** Added Stats 2019 ch 518 §1 (AB 1313), effective January 1, 2020.

§1788.91. Legislative findings and declarations

The Legislature finds and declares all of the following:

(a) Schools and colleges have threatened to withhold transcripts from students as a debt collection tactic. The practice can cause severe hardship by preventing students from pursuing educational and career opportunities, and it is therefore unfair and contrary to public policy. Moreover, the practice is counterproductive as it may further delay the payment of the debt by creating obstacles to student employment.

(b) It is the purpose of this title to prohibit schools from interfering with student educational and career opportunity by the withholding of transcripts. **Leg.H.** Added Stats 2019 ch 518 §1 (AB 1313), effective January 1, 2020.

§1788.92. Definitions

For purposes of this title, the following terms shall have the following meanings:

(a) "School" means any public or private postsecondary school, or any public or private entity, responsible for providing transcripts to current or former students of a school.

(b) "Debt" means any money, obligation, claim, or sum, due or owing, or alleged to be due or owing, from a student, but does not include the fee, if any, charged to all students for the actual costs of providing the transcripts. **Leg.H.** Added Stats 2019 ch 518 §1 (AB 1313), effective January 1, 2020.

§1788.93. Prohibited debt collection practices by school

Notwithstanding any provision of law, a school shall not do any of the following:

(a) Refuse to provide a transcript for a current or former student on the grounds that the student owes a debt.

(b) Condition the provision of a transcript on the payment of a debt, other than a fee charged to provide the transcript.

(c) Charge a higher fee for obtaining a transcript, or provide less favorable treatment of a transcript request because a student owes a debt.

(d) Use transcript issuance as a tool for debt collection. **Leg.H.** Added Stats 2019 ch 518 §1 (AB 1313), effective January 1, 2020.

§1788.94. Waiver of provisions void and unenforceable

Any waiver of a provision of this title is contrary to public policy and is void and unenforceable. **Leg.H.** Added Stats 2024 ch 853 §13 (AB 3281), effective January 1, 2025.

TITLE 1.6C.10
STUDENT LOANS: BORROWER RIGHTS

Chapter 1. Student Borrower Bill Of Rights.
Chapter 2. Setting Clear "Rules of the Road" for the Student Loan Industry.
Chapter 3. Enforcement of the Student Borrower Bill of Rights.
Chapter 4. Establishment of The California Student Loan Ombudsman.
Chapter 5. Shining a Spotlight on Student Loan Industry Practices.

CHAPTER 1
STUDENT BORROWER BILL OF RIGHTS

Definitions. § 1788.100.
Prohibition against engaging in abusive acts or practices. § 1788.101.

§ 1788.100. Definitions

For purposes of this title, the following definitions apply:

(a) "Borrower" means either of the following:

(1) A person who has received or agreed to pay a student loan.

(2) A person who shares responsibility for repaying a student loan with a person described in paragraph (1).

(b) "Borrower with disabilities" means a borrower who a student loan servicer knows, or reasonably should know, is a person who has a disability, as defined in Section 54.

(c) "Borrower working in public service" means a borrower who a student loan servicer knows, or reasonably should know, is employed in a public service job, as defined in the Higher Education Act (20 U.S.C. Sec. 1087e(m)) and its implementing regulations.

(d) "Commissioner" means the Commissioner of Financial Protection and Innovation.

(e) "Department" means the Department of Financial Protection and Innovation.

(f) "Engage in the business" means, without limitation, servicing student loans.

(g) "In this state" means any activity of a person relating to servicing student loans that originates from this state and is directed to persons outside this state, that originates from outside this state and is directed to persons inside this state, or that originates inside this state and is directed to persons inside this state.

(h) "Licensee" means a person licensed pursuant to the Student Loan Servicing Act (Division 12.5 (commencing with Section 28100) of the Financial Code).

(i) "Military borrower" means any of the following:

(1) A borrower who is one of the following:

(A) A servicemember as defined in the Servicemember Civil Relief Act (50 U.S.C. Sec. 3911).

(B) Self-identifies as a service member when interacting with a student loan servicer.

(C) Is a service member as defined in Section 400 of the Military and Veterans Code.

(2) A borrower who is a veteran of a branch of the Armed Forces as defined in Section 101 of Title 38 of the United States Code.

(3) An authorized representative of a borrower described in paragraph (1) or (2).

(j) "Older borrower" means a borrower who a student loan servicer knows, or reasonably should know, is a senior citizen, as defined in Section 51.3.

(k) "Overpayment" means a payment on a student loan account in excess of the monthly amount due from a borrower on a student loan, also commonly referred to as a prepayment.

(*l*) "Partial payment" means a payment on a student loan account in an amount less than the current amount due from a borrower on the student loan account, also commonly referred to as an underpayment.

(m) "Person" means an individual, a corporation, a partnership, a limited liability company, an association, a trust, an unincorporated organization, a government, or a political subdivision of a government, and any other entity.

(n) "Qualified request" means any inbound telephone call, the subject of which cannot be resolved in a single phone call, made by a borrower to a student loan servicer in which either the borrower requests specific information from the student loan servicer or reports what the borrower believes to be an error regarding the borrower's account.

(o) "Qualified written request" means a written correspondence made by a borrower, other than notice on a payment medium supplied by a student loan servicer, that is transmitted by mail, facsimile, or electronically through an email address or internet website designated by the student loan servicer to receive communications from a borrower that does all of the following:

(1) Enables the student loan servicer to identify the name and account of the borrower.

(2) Includes a statement of the reasons for the belief by the borrower, to the extent applicable, that the account is in error or that provides sufficient detail to the servicer regarding information sought by the borrower, such as requesting a complete payment history for the loan or the borrower's account, a copy of the borrower's student loan promissory note, or the contact information for the creditor to whom the borrower's student loan is owed.

(p) "Servicing" means any of the following activities related to a student loan of a borrower:

(1) Performing both of the following:

(A) Receiving any scheduled periodic payments from a borrower or any notification that a borrower made a scheduled periodic payment.

(B) Applying payments to the borrower's account pursuant to the terms of the student loan or the contract governing the servicing.

(2) During a period when no payment is required on a student loan, performing both of the following:

(A) Maintaining account records for the student loan.

(B) Communicating with the borrower regarding the student loan on behalf of the owner of the student loan promissory note.

(3) Interacting with a borrower related to that borrower's student loan, with the goal of helping the borrower avoid default on their student loan or facilitating the activities described in paragraph (1) or (2).

(q)(1) "Student loan" means any loan made solely for use to finance a postsecondary education and costs of attendance at a postsecondary institution, including, but not limited to, tuition, fees, books and supplies, room and board, transportation, and miscellaneous personal expenses. A "student loan" includes a loan made to refinance a student loan.

(2)(A) A "student loan" shall not include an extension of credit under an open-end consumer credit plan, a reverse mortgage transaction, a residential mortgage transaction, or any other loan that is secured by real property or a dwelling.

(B) A "student loan" shall not include an extension of credit made by a postsecondary educational institution to a borrower if one of the following applies:

(i) The term of the extension of credit is no longer than the borrower's education program.

(ii) The remaining, unpaid principal balance of the extension of credit is less than one thousand five hundred dollars ($1,500) at the time of the borrower's graduation or completion of the program.

(iii) The borrower fails to graduate or successfully complete their education program and has a balance due at the time of their disenrollment from the postsecondary institution.

(r) "Student loan account" means student loans owed by a borrower grouped together for billing purposes by a student loan servicer.

(s) "Student loan servicer" means any person engaged in the business of servicing student loans in this state. A "student loan servicer" does not include any of the following:

(1) A debt collector, as defined in subdivision (c) of Section 1788.2, whose student loan debt collection business, and business operations, involve collecting, or attempting to collect, on defaulted student loans, that is, federal student loans for which no payment has been received for 270 days or more, or private student loans, in default, according to the terms of the loan documents. Debt collectors who also service nondefaulted student loans as part of their business and business operations are "student loan servicers."

(2) In connection with its responsibilities as a guaranty agency engaged in default aversion, a state or nonprofit private institution or organization having an agreement with the United States Secretary of Education under the Higher Education Act of 1965 (20 U.S.C. Sec. 1078(b)).

(3) A federally chartered credit union. **Leg.H.** Added Stats 2020 ch 154 §2 (AB 376), effective January 1, 2021. Amended Stats 2022 ch 452 §20 (SB 1498), effective January 1, 2023.

§ 1788.101. Prohibition against engaging in abusive acts or practices

(a)(1) A person shall not engage in abusive acts or practices when servicing a student loan in this state.

(2) An act or practice is abusive in connection with the servicing of a student loan, if the act or practice does either of the following:

(A) Materially interferes with the ability of a borrower to understand a term or condition of a student loan.

(B) Takes unreasonable advantage of any of the following:

(i) A lack of understanding on the part of a borrower of the material risks, costs, or conditions of the student loan.

(ii) The inability of a borrower to protect the interests of the borrower when selecting or using either of the following:

(I) A student loan.

(II) A feature, term, or condition of a student loan.

(iii) The reasonable reliance by the borrower on a person engaged in servicing a student loan to act in the interests of the borrower.

(3) Abusive acts and practices include, but are not limited to, those described in paragraph (2).

(b) A student loan servicer shall not do any of the following:

(1) Directly or indirectly employ a scheme, device, or artifice to defraud or mislead a borrower.

(2) Engage in an unfair or deceptive practice toward a borrower or misrepresent or omit material information in connection with the servicing of a student loan, including, but not limited to, misrepresenting the amount, nature, or terms of a fee or payment due or claimed to be due on a student loan, the terms and conditions of the student loan agreement, or the borrower's obligations under the student loan.

(3) Misapply payments made by a borrower to the outstanding balance of a student loan.

(4)(A) If the student loan servicer is required to or voluntarily reports to a consumer reporting agency, fail to accurately report each borrower's payment performance to at least one consumer reporting agency that compiles and maintains files on consumers on a nationwide basis, upon acceptance as a data furnisher by that consumer reporting agency.

(B) For purposes of this paragraph, "consumer reporting agency that compiles and maintains files on consumers on a nationwide basis" has the same meaning as defined in the federal Fair Credit Reporting Act (15 U.S.C. Sec. 1681a(p)).

(5) Refuse to communicate with an authorized representative of the borrower who provides a written authorization signed by the borrower, provided the student loan servicer may adopt reasonable procedures for verifying that the representative is in fact authorized to act on behalf of the borrower and for protecting the borrower from fraud or abusive practices.

(6) Negligently or intentionally make a false statement or knowingly and willfully make an omission of a material fact in connection with information or reports filed with the department or another governmental agency.

(7) Engage in an unfair or deceptive practice toward a military borrower or misrepresent or omit material information in connection with the servicing of a student loan owed by a military borrower. For purposes of this paragraph, "misrepresent or omit material information" includes, but is not limited to:

(A) Misrepresenting or omitting the availability of a program or protection specific to military borrowers or applicable to military borrowers.

(B) A misrepresentation or omission in violation of paragraph (2) of this subdivision.

(8) Engage in an unfair or deceptive practice toward any borrower working in public service or misrepresent or omit material information in connection with the servicing of a student loan owed by a borrower working in public service. For purposes of this paragraph, "misrepresent or omit material information" includes, but is not limited to:

(A) Misrepresenting or omitting the availability of a program or protection specific to borrowers working in public service or applicable to those borrowers.

(B) A misrepresentation or omission in violation of paragraph (2).

(9) Engage in an unfair or deceptive practice toward an older borrower or older cosigner or misrepresent or omit material information in connection with the servicing of a student loan owed or cosigned by an older borrower. For purposes of this paragraph, "misrepresent or omit material information" includes, but is not limited to:

(A) Misrepresenting or omitting the availability of a program or protection specific to older borrowers or older cosigners or applicable to those borrowers or cosigners.

(B) Misrepresenting or omitting the older borrower's or older cosigner's obligations under the student loan.

(C) A misrepresentation or omission in violation of paragraph (2).

(10) Engage in an unfair or deceptive practice toward a borrower with a disability or misrepresent or omit material information in connection with the servicing of a student loan owed by a borrower with a disability. For purposes of this paragraph, "misrepresent or omit material information" includes, but is not limited to:

(A) Misrepresenting or omitting the availability of a program or protection specific to borrowers with disabilities or applicable to those borrowers.

(B) A misrepresentation or omission in violation of paragraph (2) of this subdivision. **Leg.H.** Added Stats 2020 ch 154 §2 (AB 376), effective January 1, 2021.

CHAPTER 2
SETTING CLEAR "RULES OF THE ROAD" FOR THE STUDENT LOAN INDUSTRY

Requirements on student loan servicers. § 1788.102.

§ 1788.102. Requirements on student loan servicers

Except to the extent that this section is inconsistent with any provision of federal law or regulation, and then only to the extent of the inconsistency, a student loan servicer shall do all of the following:

(a) Post and process student loan payments in a timely manner pursuant to the servicer's established payment processing policies that shall be disclosed to and readily accessible by borrowers and credit student loan payments in a timely manner in accordance with the following:

(1) A payment received on or before 11:59 p.m. on the date on which that payment is due, in the amount, manner, and location indicated by the person engaged in student loan servicing, shall be credited as effective on the date on which the payment was received by the person engaged in student loan servicing in this state. A person engaged in student loan servicing in this state shall treat a payment received from the borrower on the borrower's due date as an "on-time" payment.

(2) If a payment is made by check, credit the payment on the date the check was received by the student loan servicer regardless of the date of processing. A borrower's online account shall reflect payments made within three business days of the date of payment unless payment is made by check and contains no information identifying to which account or loan the payment should be credited. In the event the student loan servicer receives a paper check with no information identifying to which account or loan the payment should be credited, the student loan servicer shall determine, within 10 business days, to which account and loan the payment should be credited. When the servicer determines to which account and loan the payment should be credited, the servicer shall credit

the payment as of the date the payment was received by the servicer and update the borrower's online account within one business day.

(b) If a person engaged in servicing a student loan makes a material change in the mailing address, office, or procedures for handling borrower payments, and that change causes a material delay in the crediting of a borrower payment made during the 60-day period following the date on which that change took effect, the person engaged in servicing the student loan shall not impose on the borrower any negative consequences related to that material change, including negative credit reporting, lost eligibility for a borrower benefit, late fees, interest capitalization, or other financial injury.

(c)(1) Inquire of a borrower how to apply an overpayment to a student loan. A borrower's direction on how to apply an overpayment to a student loan shall be effective with respect to future overpayments during the term of a student loan until the borrower provides a different direction.

(2)(A) In the absence of a direction provided by a borrower pursuant to paragraph (1), allocate an overpayment on a student loan account in a manner that is in the best financial interest of a student loan borrower.

(B) As used in this paragraph, "best financial interest of a student loan borrower" means reducing the total cost of the student loan, including principal balance, interest, and fees.

(3) A student loan servicer shall be considered to meet the requirements of paragraph (2) if the servicer allocates the overpayment to the loan with the highest interest rate on the borrower's student loan account, unless the borrower specifies otherwise.

(d)(1) Except as provided in federal law or required by a student loan agreement, comply with a direction provided by a borrower as to how to allocate a partial payment to a student loan.

(2) In the absence of a direction provided by a borrower pursuant to paragraph (1) of this subdivision, allocate a partial payment in a manner that minimizes late fees and negative credit reporting.

(3) A student loan servicer shall be considered to have satisfied paragraph (2) if, when there are multiple loans on a borrower's student loan account at an equal stage of delinquency, the student loan servicer allocates partial payments to satisfy as many loans as possible on a borrower's student loan account.

(e)(1) If a student loan servicer imposes a fee on a borrower for a past due student loan payment, that fee shall be reasonable and proportional to the total costs incurred as a result of the late payment by a borrower, and shall not exceed 6 percent of any amount past due.

(2) A student loan servicer shall not impose a minimum late fee. For purposes of this paragraph, "minimum late fee" includes any fee that is not assessed as a percentage of any amount past due.

(f) Diligently oversee its service providers. For purposes of this subdivision, "diligently oversee its service providers" includes maintaining policies and procedures to oversee compliance by third-party service providers engaged in any aspect of student loan servicing. Student loan servicers have joint and several liability for the conduct of their service providers for any act or practice that violates this title.

(g)(1) Timely process its paperwork, consistent with existing federal requirements, including, but not limited to, ensuring that customer service personnel have received both of the following:

(A) Appropriate training about the handling of paperwork.

(B) Access to necessary information about forms and applications that are in process, have been approved, or have been denied.

(2) The requirements of this subdivision include ensuring that customer service personnel have access to applications for income-driven repayment plans and other forms required to access benefits and protections for federal student loans, as described in Section 1070 and following of Title 20 of the United States Code.

(h) Except as required by a student loan agreement, all records about a borrower's account shall be maintained for the period of time during which a person performs student loan servicing for a borrower's account and for a minimum of three years after the loan serviced has been paid in full, assigned to collection, or the servicing rights have been transferred.

(i) Treat a qualified request as if it were a qualified written request and comply with subdivision (t) with respect to that qualified request.

(j) Maintain policies and procedures permitting a borrower who is dissatisfied with the outcome of an initial qualified request to escalate the borrower's concern to a supervisor.

(k)(1) Protect borrowers from any negative consequences that are directly related to the issue identified in a borrower's qualified request or qualified written request until that request has been resolved. For purposes of this subdivision, "negative consequences" include, but are not limited to, negative credit reporting, lost eligibility for a borrower benefit, late fees, interest capitalization, or other financial injury.

(2) Notwithstanding paragraph (1), after receipt of a qualified request or qualified written request related to a dispute on a borrower's payment on a student loan, a student loan servicer shall not, for 60 days, furnish information to a consumer reporting agency regarding a payment that is the subject of the qualified request or the qualified written request.

(l) Protect borrowers from any negative consequences stemming from a sale, assignment, transfer, system conversion, or payment made by the borrower to the original student loan servicer consistent with the original student loan servicer's policy. For purposes of this subdivision, "negative consequences" include, but are not limited to, any of the following:

(1) Negative credit reporting.

(2) The imposition of late fees not required by the promissory note.

(3) Loss of or denial of eligibility for any benefit or protection established under federal law or included in a loan contract.

(m) If the sale, assignment, or other transfer of the servicing of a student loan results in a change in the identity of the party to whom the borrower is required to send payments or direct any communications concerning the student loan, the student loan servicer shall notify the borrower in writing at least 15 days before the borrower is required to send a payment on the student loan of all of the following:

(1) The identity of the new student loan servicer and the number of the license, issued by the commissioner, of the new student loan servicer.

(2) The name and address of the new student loan servicer to whom subsequent payments or communications are required to be sent.

(3) The telephone numbers and internet websites of the new student loan servicer.

(4) The effective date of the sale, assignment, or transfer.

(5) The date on which the current student loan servicer will stop accepting payments on the borrower's student loan.

(6) The date on which the new student loan servicer will begin accepting payments on the borrower's student loan.

(n) Ensure all necessary information regarding a borrower, a borrower's account, and a borrower's student loan accompanies a loan when it transfers to a new student loan servicer within 45 calendar days of the effective date of the sale, assignment, or transfer. For purposes of this subdivision, "necessary information" shall include, at minimum, all of the following:

(1) A schedule of all transactions credited or debited to the student loan account.

(2) A copy of the promissory note for the student loan.

(3) Any notes created by the student loan servicer's personnel reflecting communications with the borrower about the student loan account.

(4) A report of the data fields relating to the borrower's student loan account created by the student loan servicer's electronic systems in connection with servicing practices.

(5) Copies or electronic records of any information or documents provided by the borrower to the student loan servicer.

(6) Usable data fields with information necessary to assess qualification for forgiveness, including public service loan forgiveness, if applicable.

(7) Any information necessary to compile a payment history.

(o) Provide specialized training for any customer service personnel that advises military borrowers about student loan repayment benefits and protections.

(p) Provide specialized training for any customer service personnel that advises borrowers working in public service about student loan repayment benefits and protections.

(q) Provide specialized training for any customer service personnel that advises older borrowers about risks specifically applicable to older borrowers to ensure that, once identified, older borrowers are informed about student loan repayment benefits and protections, including disability discharge programs for private and federal loans, if applicable, and, to the extent an older borrower serves as cosigner, about cosigner release provisions in private student loan contracts.

(r) Provide specialized training for any customer service personnel that advises borrowers with disabilities about student loan repayment benefits and protections, including disability discharge programs for private and federal loans. Under no circumstances shall a person engage in any unfair or deceptive practice toward any borrower with a disability or misrepresent or omit any material information in connection with the servicing of a student loan owed by a borrower with a disability. For purposes of this subdivision, "misrepresent or omit any material information" includes, but is not limited to, misrepresenting or omitting any of the following:

(1) The availability of any program or protection specific to borrowers with disabilities or applicable to those borrowers.

(2) The amount, nature, or terms of any fee or payment due or claimed to be due on a student loan.

(3) The terms and conditions of the student loan agreement.

(4) The borrower's obligations under the student loan.

(s) Respond within 10 business days to communications from the Student Loan Ombudsman, established pursuant to Chapter 4 (commencing with Section 1788.104), or within a shorter, reasonable time as the Student Loan Ombudsman may request in that person's communication.

(t)(1) Respond to a qualified written request by acknowledging receipt of the request within 10 business days and within 30 business days, provide information relating to the request and, if applicable, either the action the student loan servicer will take to correct the account or an explanation for the position that the borrower's account is correct.

(2) The 30-day period described in paragraph (1) may be extended for not more than 15 days if, before the end of the 30-day period, the student loan servicer notifies the borrower of the extension and the reason for the delay in responding. **Leg.H.** Added Stats 2020 ch 154 §2 (AB 376), effective January 1, 2021. Amended Stats 2021 ch 124 §5 (AB 938), effective January 1, 2022.

CHAPTER 3
ENFORCEMENT OF THE STUDENT BORROWER BILL OF RIGHTS

Compliance; Actions against student a loan servicer. § 1788.103.

§ 1788.103. Compliance; Actions against student a loan servicer

(a) A student loan servicer shall do both of the following:

(1) Comply with this title.

(2) Comply with all applicable federal laws relating to student loan servicing, as from time to time amended, and the regulations promulgated thereunder.

(b) Any consumer who suffers damage as a result of the failure of a student loan servicer to comply with paragraph (1) or (2) of subdivision (a) may, subject to the requirements of subdivisions (d) to (g), inclusive, bring an action on that consumer's behalf and on behalf of a similarly situated class of consumers against that student loan servicer to recover or obtain any of the following:

(1) Actual damages, but in no case, shall the total award of damages be less than five hundred dollars ($500) per plaintiff, per violation.

(2) An order enjoining the methods, acts, or practices.

(3) Restitution of property.

(4) Punitive damages.

(5) Attorney's fees.

(6) Any other relief that the court deems proper.

(c) In addition to any other remedies provided by this subdivision or otherwise provided by law, whenever it is proven by a preponderance of the evidence that a student loan servicer has engaged in conduct that substantially interferes with a borrower's right to an alternative payment arrangement; loan forgiveness, cancellation, or discharge; or any other financial benefit as established under the terms of a borrower's promissory note or under the Higher Education Act of 1965 (20 U.S.C. Sec. 1070a et seq.), as from time to time amended, and the regulations promulgated thereunder, the court shall award treble actual damages to the plaintiff, but in no case shall the award of damages be less than one thousand five hundred dollars ($1,500) per plaintiff, per violation.

(d)(1) At least 45 days before bringing an action for damages or injunctive relief pursuant to this chapter, a consumer shall do all of the following:

(A) Provide written notice to the person alleged to have violated subdivision (a) regarding the nature of the alleged violations.

(B) Demand that the person correct and remedy the method, acts, or practices to which the notice required by subparagraph (A) refers.

(2) The notice required by this subdivision shall be sent by certified or registered mail, return receipt requested, to the person's address on file with the Department of Financial Protection and Innovation or to the person's principal place of business within California.

(e) An action for damages or injunctive relief brought by a consumer only on that consumer's behalf may not be maintained under subdivision (b) upon a showing by a person that an appropriate correction and remedy is given, or agreed to be given within a reasonable time, to the consumer within 30 days after receipt of the notice.

(f) An action for damages brought by a consumer on both the consumer's behalf and on behalf of a similarly situated class of consumers may not be maintained under subdivision (b) upon a showing by a person alleged to have employed or committed methods, acts, or practices declared unlawful that all of the following are true:

(1) All consumers similarly situated have been identified, or a reasonable effort to identify those other consumers has been made.

(2) All consumers so identified have been notified that, upon their request, the person shall make the appropriate correction and remedy.

(3) The correction and remedy requested by the consumers has been, or, in a reasonable time, will be, given.

(4) The person has ceased from engaging, or if immediate cessation is impossible or unreasonably expensive under the circumstances, the person will, within a reasonable time, cease to engage, in the methods, act, or practices.

(g) Attempts to comply with a demand described in paragraph (2) of subdivision (d) by a person receiving that demand shall be construed to be an offer to compromise and shall be inadmissible as evidence pursuant to Section 1152 of the Evidence Code. Furthermore, these attempts to comply with a demand shall not be considered an admission of engaging in an act or practice declared unlawful by subdivision (a). Evidence of compliance or attempts to comply with this section may be introduced by a defendant for the purpose of establishing good faith or to show compliance with subdivision (a).

(h) An award of damages shall not be given in an action based on a method, act, or practice in violation of subdivision (a) if the person alleged to have employed or committed that method, act, or practice does both of the following:

(1) Proves by a preponderance of the evidence that the violation was not intentional and resulted from a bona fide error notwithstanding the use of reasonable procedures adopted to avoid that error.

(2) Makes an appropriate correction, repair, replacement, or other remedy according to the provisions of subdivisions (d) and (e) as required by law.

(i) The commissioner shall administer and enforce the provisions of this title and may promulgate rules and regulations and issue orders consistent with that authority.

(1) The commissioner shall have the authority to carry over any regulations issued pursuant to the Student Loan Servicing Act in order to implement equivalent provisions of this act.

(2) Any rules issued pursuant to the Student Loan Servicing Act in effect at the time of enactment of this act shall remain in effect until the commissioner repeals or reissues those regulations. **Leg.H.** Added Stats 2020 ch 154 §2 (AB 376), effective January 1, 2021. Amended Stats 2022 ch 452 §21 (SB 1498), effective January 1, 2023.

CHAPTER 4
ESTABLISHMENT OF THE CALIFORNIA STUDENT LOAN OMBUDSMAN

Designation of a Student Loan Ombudsman; Complaints from student loan borrowers; Duties. § 1788.104.

§ 1788.104. Designation of a Student Loan Ombudsman; Complaints from student loan borrowers; Duties

(a) Not later than 180 days following the operative date of this chapter, the commissioner shall designate a Student Loan Ombudsman to work within the department. The Student Loan Ombudsman shall hire additional staff as necessary to implement this section.

(b) The Student Loan Ombudsman shall receive and review complaints from student loan borrowers.

(c) Any complaint regarding a student loan servicer licensed or subject to licensing under the Student Loan Servicing Act (Division 12.5 (commencing with Section 28100) of the Financial Code) shall be referred to the appropriate unit within the department. This unit may investigate complaints referred by the Student Loan Ombudsman, and from the public, who may also submit complaints directly to the department.

(d) Complaints regarding student loans not subject to the Student Loan Servicing Act (Division 12.5 (commencing with Section 28100) of the Financial Code) shall be referred to the Department of Justice. The Department of Justice may investigate complaints regarding student loans referred by the Student Loan Ombudsman, and from the public, who may also submit complaints directly to the Department of Justice.

(e) Complaints regarding any private postsecondary educational institution licensed by the Bureau for Private Postsecondary Education shall be referred to the Bureau for Private Postsecondary Education's Office of Student Assistance and Relief.

(f) The Student Loan Ombudsman shall confer with the Department of Justice and the Office of Student Assistance and Relief regarding the student loan complaints, the proper referral processes for those complaints, and the reporting requirements of the Student Loan Ombudsman under this title.

(g) The Student Loan Ombudsman has all of the following duties:

(1) Compiling and analyzing data on the number of student loan borrower complaints received by the Department of Financial Protection and Innovation and referred to the Department of Justice.

(2) Providing information to the public, agencies, legislators, and others regarding the problems and concerns of student loan borrowers and making recommendations for resolving those problems and concerns.

(3) Analyzing and monitoring the development and implementation of federal and state laws, rules, regulations, and policies relating to student loan borrowers.

(4) Disseminating information concerning the availability of the Department of Financial Protection and Innovation, the Department of Justice, and the Bureau of Private Postsecondary Education to accept complaints from individual student loan borrowers and potential student loan borrowers.

(5) Requesting and compiling information provided by any student loan servicer if reasonably determined by the Student Loan Ombudsman to be necessary to effectuate the duties described in this subdivision, except if that student loan servicer is a national bank, as defined in Section 25b of Title 12 of the United States Code, and only to the extent that the requirements of this paragraph are preempted with respect to national banks pursuant to Section 25b and following of Title 12 of the United States Code.

(6) Not later than 18 months after the operative date of this chapter, and not less frequently than once per year thereafter, the Student Loan Ombudsman shall submit a report to the appropriate committees of the Legislature having jurisdiction over higher education and financial institutions. The Student Loan Ombudsman shall report on all of the following:

(A) The implementation of this section.

(B) The types of complaints received regarding student loan borrowing, student loan repayment and servicing, and how these complaints are resolved.

(C) Other data and analysis on outstanding student loan issues faced by borrowers.

(h) Notwithstanding subdivision (l) of Section 1788.100, for purposes of this chapter, "student loan servicer" includes a state or nonprofit private institution or organization having an agreement with the United States Secretary of Education under the Higher Education Act of 1965 (20 U.S.C. Sec. 1078(b)) in connection with its responsibilities as a guaranty agency engaged in default aversion.

(i) The operation of this chapter is contingent upon the enactment of an appropriation in the annual Budget Act for its purposes.

(j) This chapter shall become operative on July 1, 2021. **Leg.H.** Added Stats 2020 ch 154 §2 (AB 376), effective January 1, 2021, operative July 1, 2021. Amended Stats 2022 ch 452 §22 (SB 1498), effective January 1, 2023.

CHAPTER 5
SHINING A SPOTLIGHT ON STUDENT LOAN INDUSTRY PRACTICES

Monitoring of risks to consumers. §1788.105.
Waiver of provisions void and unenforceable. § 1788.106.

1788.105. Monitoring of risks to consumers

(a) The commissioner may monitor for risks to consumers in the provision of student loan servicing in this state, including developments in the market for those services, by compiling and analyzing data and other information based on any of the following considerations:

(1) The likely risks and costs to consumers associated with using or repaying a student loan or with the servicing of a student loan.

(2) The understanding by consumers of the risks of a student loan or the servicing of a student loan.

(3) The legal protections applicable to the offering or provision of a student loan or the servicing of a student loan, including the extent to which the law is likely to adequately protect consumers.

(4) The rates of growth in the offering or provision of a student loan or the servicing of that loan.

(5) The extent, if any, to which the risks of a student loan or the servicing of a student loan disproportionately affect traditionally underserved consumers.

(6) The type, number, and other pertinent characteristics of student loan servicers in this state.

(b) In conducting any monitoring or assessment authorized by this section, the commissioner may gather information regarding the organization, business conduct, markets, and activities of student loan servicers in this state, except if that student loan servicer is a national bank, as defined in Section 25b of Title 12 of the United States Code, and only to the extent that the requirements of this paragraph are preempted with respect to national banks pursuant to Section 25b and following of Title 12 of the United States Code. The commissioner may enter into contracts to perform the duties required in this section, as necessary.

(c) In order to gather information described in subdivision (b), the commissioner may do both of the following:

(1) Gather and compile information from a variety of sources, including consumer complaints, voluntary surveys and voluntary interviews of consumers, surveys and interviews with student loan servicers and service providers, and review of available databases.

(2) Require persons engaged in student loan servicing and licensed or subject to the licensing requirements of the Student Loan Servicing Act (Division 12.5 (commencing with Section 28100) of the Financial Code) to file, under oath or otherwise, in the form and within a reasonable period of time as the commissioner may prescribe, annual or special reports, or answers in writing to specific questions, as necessary for the commissioner to fulfill the monitoring, assessment, and reporting responsibilities required in this title.

(d)(1) In addition to any other market monitoring activities deemed necessary by the commissioner, pursuant to subdivision (a), the department may gather and compile information from student loan servicers to assemble data that assesses the total size of the student loan market in this state, the servicing of loans owed by borrowers at risk of default, the servicing of private student loans owed by borrowers experiencing financial distress, and the servicing of federal student loans for borrowers who seek to repay their loans under an Income Driven Repayment Plan as described in Section 1070 et seq. of Title 20 of the United States Code.

(2) The commissioner may, on a quarterly basis, develop and publicize metrics based on data collected pursuant to this subdivision, and those metrics may identify each student loan servicer and publish relevant metrics related to performance of student loan servicing by each person. In executing the function described in this subdivision, the commissioner may meet and confer with the Student Loan Ombudsman established pursuant to Chapter 4.

(e) Notwithstanding subdivision (l) of Section 1788.100, for purposes of this chapter, "student loan servicer" includes a state or nonprofit private institution or organization having an agreement with the United States Secretary of Education under the Higher Education Act of 1965 (20 U.S.C. Sec. 1078(b)) in connection with its responsibilities as a guaranty agency engaged in default aversion.

(f) This chapter shall become operative on July 1, 2021.

(g) The operation of this chapter is contingent upon the enactment of an appropriation in the annual Budget Act for its purposes. **Leg.H.** Added Stats 2020 ch 154 §2 (AB 376), effective January 1, 2021, operative July 1, 2021. Amended Stats 2021 ch 124 §6 (AB 938), effective January 1, 2022.

§1788.106. Waiver of provisions void and unenforceable

Any waiver of a provision of this title is contrary to public policy and is void and unenforceable. **Leg.H.** Added Stats 2024 ch 853 §14 (AB 3281), effective January 1, 2025.

TITLE 1.6C.15
PRIVATE STUDENT LOAN COLLECTIONS REFORM ACT

Citation of title. § 1788.200.
Definitions. § 1788.201.
Information required before private education lender or loan collector may make a written statement to debtor. § 1788.202.
Settlement agreements; Acceptance as payment in full. § 1788.203.
Effect of statute of limitations. § 1788.204.
Complaint; Confidential information. § 1788.205.
Judgment against debtor, including default judgment. § 1788.206.
Failure to provide actual notice. § 1788.207.
Action against creditor, private education lender, or private education loan collector for violation; Damages or other relief; Class action; Costs and fees; Time limitations. § 1788.208.
Waiver prohibited. § 1788.209.
Severability of provisions. § 1788.210.
Operative date of title. § 1788.211.

§ 1788.200. Citation of title

This title shall be known and may be cited as the Private Student Loan Collections Reform Act. **Leg.H.** Added Stats 2021 ch 559 §1 (AB 424), effective January 1, 2022, operative July 1, 2022.

§ 1788.201. Definitions

For purposes of this title, the following definitions apply:

(a) "Borrower" or "student loan borrower" means a person who has received or agreed to pay a private education loan.

(b) "Consumer report" and "consumer reporting agency" shall each have the same meaning that these terms have under the federal Fair Credit Reporting Act (15 U.S.C. Sec. 1681 et seq.).

(c)(1) "Cosigner" means any individual who is liable for the obligation of another without compensation, regardless of how the individual is designated in the contract or instrument with respect to that obligation, including an obligation under a private education loan extended to consolidate a borrower's preexisting private education loans, and shall include any person whose signature is requested as a condition to grant credit or to forbear on collection.

(2) "Cosigner" does not include a spouse of an individual described in paragraph (1), the signature of whom is needed to perfect the security interest in a loan.

(d) "Creditor" means any of the following:

(1) The original creditor, where ownership of a private education loan has not been sold, assigned, or transferred.

(2) The person or entity that owned the private education loan at the time the private education loan defaulted, even if that person or entity did not originate the private education loan, and where such a private education loan has not subsequently been sold, transferred, or assigned.

(3) A person or entity that purchased a defaulted private education loan, whether it collects the private education loan itself or hires a third party for collection, or hires an attorney for collection litigation.

(e) "Debtor" means a borrower, cosigner, or other person that owes or is alleged to owe an unpaid amount on a private education loan.

(f)(1) "Exempt entity" means an entity that meets both of the following requirements:

(A) It is a depository institution as defined in Section 1420 of the Financial Code.

(B) It, together with its affiliates, will be, in the aggregate, a plaintiff in 35 or fewer private student loan collection actions in the current calendar year. Private education loans assigned to a third party for the purposes of collection shall count towards the numerical limit set forth in this subparagraph.

(2) For purposes of this subdivision, an entity is an "affiliate" of another specified entity if it directly, or indirectly through one or more intermediaries, controls, is controlled by, or is under common control with, the other specified entity.

(g) "Original creditor" means the private education lender identified in a promissory note, loan agreement, or loan contract entered into with a student loan borrower or cosigner.

(h) "Private education lender" means either of the following:

(1) Any person or entity engaged in the business of securing, making, or extending private education loans.

(2) Any holder of a private education loan.

(i) "Private education loan" means an extension of credit that meets all of the following conditions:

(1) Is not made, insured, or guaranteed under Title IV of the Higher Education Act of 1965 (20 U.S.C. Sec. 1070 et seq.).

(2) Is extended to a consumer expressly, in whole or in part, for postsecondary educational expenses, regardless of whether the loan is provided by the educational institution that the student attends.

(3) Does not include open-end credit or any loan that is secured by real property or a dwelling.

(4) Does not include an extension of credit in which the covered educational institution is the original creditor if either:

(A) The term of the extension of credit is 90 days or less.

(B) An interest rate will not be applied to the credit balance and the term of the extension of credit is one year or less, even if the credit is payable in more than four installments.

(j) "Private education loan collection action" means any suit, arbitration, or other legal proceeding in which a claim is asserted to collect a private education loan.

(k) "Private education loan collector" means a person, other than a private education lender, collecting or attempting to collect on a defaulted private education loan. **Leg.H.** Added Stats 2021 ch 559 §1 (AB 424), effective January 1, 2022, operative July 1, 2022.

§ 1788.202. Information required before private education lender or loan collector may make a written statement to debtor

(a) A private education lender or a private education loan collector shall not make any written statement to a debtor in an attempt to collect a private education loan unless the private education lender or private education loan collector possesses the following information:

(1) The name of the owner of the private education loan.

(2) The creditor's name at the time of default, if applicable.

(3) The creditor's account number used to identify the private education loan at the time of default, if the original creditor used an account number to identify the private education loan at the time of default.

(4) The amount due at default.

(5) An itemization of interest, if any, that has accrued on the private education loan.

(6) An itemization of fees, if any, claimed to be owed on the private education loan and whether those fees were imposed by the original creditor or any subsequent owners of the private education loan.

(7) The date that the private education loan was incurred.

(8) The date of the first partial payment or the first day that a payment was missed, whichever is earlier, that precipitated default.

(9) The date and amount of the last payment, if applicable.

(10) Any payments, settlement, or financial remuneration of any kind paid to the creditor by a guarantor, surety, or other party not obligated on the loan as compensation under a separate contract that provides coverage for financial losses incurred as a result of default, if applicable.

(11) The names of all persons or entities that owned the private education loan after the time of default, if applicable, and the date of each sale or transfer.

(12) A copy of the self-certification form and any other "needs analysis" conducted by the original creditor prior to origination of the loan.

(13) Documentation establishing that the creditor is the owner of the specific individual private education loan at issue. If the private education loan was assigned more than once, the creditor shall possess each assignment or other writing evidencing the transfer of ownership of the specific individual private education loan to establish an unbroken chain of ownership, beginning with the original creditor to the first subsequent creditor and each additional creditor. Each assignment or other writing evidencing transfer of ownership or the right to collect shall contain the original creditor's account number (redacted for security purposes to show only the last four digits) of the private education loan purchased or otherwise assigned, the date of purchase and assignment, and shall clearly show the borrower's correct name associated with the original account number. The assignment or other writing attached shall be that by which the creditor or other assignee acquired the private education loan, not a document prepared for litigation.

(14) A copy of all pages of the contract, application, or other documents evidencing the debtor's liability for the private education loan, stating all terms and conditions applicable to the private education loan.

(15) A list of all collection attempts made in the last 12 months, including date and time of all calls and written communications.

(16) A statement as to whether the creditor is willing to renegotiate the terms of the private student loan.

(17) Copies of all written settlement communications made in the last 12 months, or, in the alternative, a statement that the creditor has not attempted to settle or otherwise renegotiate the debt prior to suit.

(18) A statement as to whether the private education loan is eligible for an income-based repayment plan.

(b)(1) In addition to any other information required under applicable federal or state law, a private education lender or private education loan collector shall provide the information set forth in subdivision (a) in the first written collection communication with a debtor after the first of either of the following:

(A) Default and acceleration.

(B) A period of 12 consecutive months of default.

(2) A private education lender or private education loan collector shall provide the information set forth in subdivision (a) to the debtor upon the debtor's request if both of the following are true:

(A) An event described in subparagraph (A) or (B) of paragraph (1) has occurred.

(B) The debtor has not requested or received the information set forth in subdivision (a) within the previous 12 months. **Leg.H.** Added Stats 2021 ch 559 §1 (AB 424), effective January 1, 2022, operative July 1, 2022.

§ 1788.203. Settlement agreements; Acceptance as payment in full

(a) All settlement agreements between a private education lender or private education loan collector and a debtor shall be documented in open court or otherwise reduced to writing. The private education lender or private education loan collector shall ensure that a copy of the written agreement is provided to the debtor.

(b) A private education lender or private education loan collector that accepts a payment as payment in full, or as a full and final compromise of a private education loan, shall provide, within 30 calendar days, a final statement that shall clearly and conspicuously show the amount and date paid, the name of the entity paid, the current account number, the name of the private education lender or private education loan collector, the account number issued by the private education lender or private education loan collector, the name of the owner of the private education loan, and that a zero balance is owing. The statement may be provided electronically if the parties agree. **Leg.H.** Added Stats 2021 ch 559 §1 (AB 424), effective January 1, 2022, operative July 1, 2022.

§ 1788.204. Effect of statute of limitations

A private education lender or private education loan collector shall not bring suit or initiate an arbitration or other legal proceeding to collect a private education loan if the applicable statute of limitations for the private education lender's or private education loan collector's claim has expired. **Leg.H.** Added Stats 2021 ch 559 §1 (AB 424), effective January 1, 2022, operative July 1, 2022.

§ 1788.205. Complaint; Confidential information

In an action brought by a private education lender or private education loan collector to collect a private education loan:

(a) The complaint shall allege all of the following:

(1) The information required by paragraphs (1) to (11), inclusive, of subdivision (a) of Section 1788.202.

(2) That the applicable statute of limitations has not expired.

(3) That the plaintiff has complied with Section 1788.202.

(b) Copies of the documents required by paragraphs (12) to (14), inclusive, of subdivision (a) of Section 1788.202 shall be attached to the complaint.

(c) The requirements of this title shall not be deemed to require the disclosure in public records of personal, financial, or medical information, the confidentiality of which is protected by any state or federal law.

(d) This section does not apply to a plaintiff that attaches to the complaint a declaration or affidavit pursuant to Section 2015.5 of the Code of Civil Procedure that is signed by a natural person and states all of the following:

(1) That the plaintiff is an exempt entity.

(2) The category in subdivision (a) of Section 1420 of the Financial Code under which the plaintiff falls.

(3) The name and title of the signer.

(4) That the signer has been authorized by the entity to make the affidavit or declaration. **Leg.H.** Added Stats 2021 ch 559 §1 (AB 424), effective January 1, 2022, operative July 1, 2022.

§ 1788.206. Judgment against debtor, including default judgment

(a) In an action initiated by a private education lender or private education loan collector, no default or other judgment may be entered against a defendant unless documents are submitted by the plaintiff to the court to establish the facts required to be alleged by paragraphs (1) and (2) of subdivision (a) of Section 1788.205. The documents shall be properly authenticated and each shall be in a form that would be admissible as a business record under Section 1271 of the Evidence Code.

(b) In an action initiated by a private education lender or private education loan collector, no default or other judgment may be entered against a defendant unless copies of the documents described in subdivision (b) of Section 1788.205 have been submitted by the plaintiff to the court. These documents shall be properly authenticated and each shall be in a form that would be admissible as a business record under Section 1271 of the Evidence Code.

(c) In any action on a private education loan, if a plaintiff seeks a default judgment and has not complied with the requirements of this title, the court shall not enter a default judgment for the plaintiff and may, in its discretion, dismiss the action.

(d) Except as provided in this title, this section is not intended to modify or otherwise amend the procedures established in Section 585 of the Code of Civil Procedure.

(e) This section does not apply to a plaintiff that attaches to the complaint a declaration or affidavit pursuant to Section 2015.5 of the Code of Civil Procedure that is signed by a natural person and states all of the following:

(1) That the plaintiff is an exempt entity.

(2) The category in subdivision (a) of Section 1420 of the Financial Code under which the plaintiff falls.

(3) The name and title of the signer.

(4) That the signer has been authorized by the entity to make the affidavit or declaration. **Leg.H.** Added Stats 2021 ch 559 §1 (AB 424), effective January 1, 2022, operative July 1, 2022.

§ 1788.207. Failure to provide actual notice

Notwithstanding Section 473.5 of the Code of Civil Procedure, if service of a summons has not resulted in actual notice to a person in time to defend an action brought by a private education lender or a private education loan collector and a default or default judgment has been entered against the person in the action, the person may serve and file a notice of motion and motion to set aside the default or default judgment and for leave to defend the action utilizing the procedures set forth in Section 1788.61. **Leg.H.** Added Stats 2021 ch 559 §1 (AB 424), effective January 1, 2022, operative July 1, 2022.

§ 1788.208. Action against creditor, private education lender, or private education loan collector for violation; Damages or other relief; Class action; Costs and fees; Time limitations

(a) A person may bring a cause of action against a creditor, private education lender, or private education loan collector for a violation of any provision of this title in order to recover or obtain any of the following:

(1) Damages in an amount equal to the sum of the following:

(A) Any actual damages sustained by that person as a result of the violation.

(B) Statutory damages in an amount as the court may allow, which shall not be less than five hundred dollars ($500) per violation.

(2) Damages pursuant to Section 3294.

(3) An order vacating any default judgment entered against that person.

(4) Restitution of all moneys taken from or paid by that person after a default judgment was entered in favor of the private education lender or private education loan collector.

(5) An order directing the private education lender or private education loan collector to do one or more of the following:

(A) Request that a consumer reporting agency correct a consumer report that it issues.

(B) Request that a consumer reporting agency remove derogatory information furnished to it after default.

(C) Furnish correct information to a consumer reporting agency.

(6) Any other relief that the court deems proper.

(b) In the case of a class action, a defendant that violates any provision of this title shall be liable for any statutory damages for each named plaintiff as provided in subparagraph (B) of paragraph (1) of subdivision (a). If the court finds that the defendant engaged in a pattern and practice of violating any provision of this title, the court may award additional damages to the class in an amount not to exceed the lesser of five hundred thousand dollars ($500,000) or 1 percent of the net worth of the defendant.

(c)(1) In the case of any successful cause of action under this section, the court shall award costs of the action, together with reasonable attorney's fees as determined by the court.

(2) Reasonable attorney's fees may be awarded to a prevailing defendant upon a finding by the court that the plaintiff's prosecution of the cause of action was not in good faith.

(d) A private education lender or private education loan collector shall have no civil liability for damages under this section if the private education lender or private education loan collector shows by a preponderance of evidence that the violation was not intentional and resulted from a bona fide error, and occurred notwithstanding the maintenance of procedures reasonably adopted to avoid any error.

(e) A cause of action to enforce any liability created by this title shall be brought within one year from the date of the discovery by the plaintiff of the last violation, or, in the event a default judgment is entered against the debtor, one year from the date the borrower first receives a writ, notice, or order under Division 1 (commencing with Section 680.010) or Division 2 (commencing with Section 695.010) of Title 9 of Part 2 of the Code of Civil Procedure, whichever is later. **Leg.H.** Added Stats 2021 ch 559 §1 (AB 424), effective January 1, 2022, operative July 1, 2022.

§ 1788.209. Waiver prohibited

Any waiver of the provisions of this title is contrary to public policy, and is void and unenforceable. **Leg.H.** Added Stats 2021 ch 559 §1 (AB 424), effective January 1, 2022, operative July 1, 2022.

§ 1788.210. Severability of provisions

The provisions of this title are severable. If any provision of this title or its application is held invalid, that invalidity shall not affect other provisions or applications that can be given effect without the invalid provision or application. **Leg.H.** Added Stats 2021 ch 559 §1 (AB 424), effective January 1, 2022, operative July 1, 2022.

§ 1788.211. Operative date of title

This title shall become operative on July 1, 2022. **Leg.H.** Added Stats 2021 ch 559 §1 (AB 424), effective January 1, 2022, operative July 1, 2022.

TITLE 1.6C.17
FAIR DEBT SETTLEMENT PRACTICES

Chapter 1. General Provisions.
Chapter 2. Application of the Fair Debt Settlement Practices Act.
Chapter 3. Enforcement of the Fair Debt Settlement Practices Act.

CHAPTER 1
GENERAL PROVISIONS

Citation of title. § 1788.300.
Definitions. § 1788.301.
Debt settlement provider and payment processor duties and responsibilities; False, unfair, abusive, deceptive, or misleading acts or practices; Contract termination by consumer. § 1788.302.

§ 1788.300. Citation of title

This title may be cited as the Fair Debt Settlement Practices Act. **Leg.H.** Added Stats 2021 ch 454 §1 (AB 1405), effective January 1, 2022.

§ 1788.301. Definitions

For purposes of this title:

(a) "Debt settlement provider" means a person who, for compensation and on behalf of a consumer, provides debt settlement services.

(b) "Debt settlement services" means any of the following:

(1) Providing advice, or offering to act or acting as an intermediary, including, but not limited to, offering debt negotiation, debt reduction, or debt relief services between a consumer and one or more of the consumer's creditors, if the primary purpose of that advice or action is to obtain a settlement for less than the full amount of the debt.

(2) Advising, encouraging, or counseling a consumer to accumulate funds in an account for future payment of a reduced amount of debt to one or more of the consumer's creditors.

(c) "Settlement account" means a depository account established and used for the purpose of holding funds of a consumer to be distributed to a creditor in the event of a settlement of a consumer's debt with the creditor.

(d) "Consumer" means a person who is allegedly legally responsible for a debt.

(e) "Person" means a natural person or entity, whether a corporation, partnership, association, trust, limited liability company, cooperative, or other organization.

(f) "Creditor" means the person who originated the debt or is assigned, or has purchased for collection, a debt for which a consumer is allegedly legally responsible.

(g) "Debt" means money, whether in principal, interest, fees, or other charges, which is due or owing or alleged to be due or owing from a natural person to another person and incurred primarily for personal, family, or household purposes.

(h) "Payment processor" means a person who provides payment processing services.

(i) "Payment processing services" means accepting, maintaining, holding, or distributing funds, or facilitating the acceptance, maintenance, holding, or distribution of funds, on behalf of a consumer for the purpose of facilitating debt settlement services. **Leg.H.** Added Stats 2021 ch 454 §1 (AB 1405), effective January 1, 2022.

§ 1788.302. Debt settlement provider and payment processor duties and responsibilities; False, unfair, abusive, deceptive, or misleading acts or practices; Contract termination by consumer

(a) A debt settlement provider shall not engage in false, deceptive, or misleading acts or practices when providing debt settlement services. Without limiting the general application of the foregoing, an act or practice is false, deceptive, or misleading, in connection with providing debt settlement services, if the act or practice consists of any of the following:

(1) Making or permitting another entity to publicly make on behalf of the debt settlement provider, a statement or representation that is false, deceptive, or misleading.

(2) Posting directly, or indirectly causing to be posted, an online review or ranking on an internet website if the debt settlement provider, or its agent, provided anything of value in exchange for favorable treatment in that review or ranking.

(3) Omitting any material information.

(b) A debt settlement provider shall provide to the consumer the following disclosures along with an unsigned copy of the written contract proposed to be entered into between the debt settlement provider and the consumer no less than three calendar days prior to the execution of that contract by the consumer. A fully executed copy of the contract shall be delivered to the consumer by the debt settlement provider immediately after the debt settlement provider receives the contract.

(1) The contract shall be preceded by a disclosure that contains all of the following information in conspicuous boldface type that is larger than the typeface provided in the contract typeface:

(A) There is no guarantee that any particular debt or all of the consumer's enrolled debts will be reduced, eliminated, or otherwise settled.

(B) The deposits made pursuant to the contract will not be distributed to the creditor until a settlement is obtained. This may take months to achieve.

(C) If the consumer stops paying any creditor, any of the following may occur:

(i) The creditors may still try to collect.

(ii) The creditors may sue.

(iii) If a creditor obtains a judgment against the consumer, the creditor may garnish the consumer's wages or levy the consumer's bank account or accounts, or both garnish the consumer's wages and levy the consumer's bank account or accounts.

(iv) The consumer's credit score or credit rating may be negatively impacted.

(D) Failing to pay debts on time may adversely affect the consumer's credit rating or credit scores.

(E) Specific results cannot be predicted or guaranteed, and the debt settlement provider cannot require a creditor to negotiate or settle a debt.

(F) A consumer may cancel the debt settlement contract at any time without any penalty.

(G) Debt settlement services may not be suitable for all individuals.

(H) Bankruptcy may provide an alternative to debt settlement.

(I) Canceled debt may be counted as income under federal tax law, and the consumer may have to pay income taxes on the amount of forgiven or reduced debt.

(J) Many sources of income may be protected from debt collection. Common sources of protected income include disability insurance benefits, life insurance benefits, military benefits, pension plans, retirement benefits, public assistance, social security benefits, supplemental security income (SSI), unemployment benefits, veterans benefits, workers compensation, and student aid. See form EJ-155 from the Judicial Council for a complete list.

(K) The number of months estimated to enter into settlement agreements that completely resolve all enrolled debts.

(L) All conditions that the consumer must satisfy before the debt settlement provider will make a settlement offer to a creditor.

(M) Whether the debt settlement provider pays or receives referral fees.

(2) Each contract between a consumer and debt settlement provider:

(A) Shall list each debt to be serviced, including, for each debt, the name of the creditor and the total amount of the debt. The total amount of the debt may be based on either a billing statement for the debt or information in the consumer's consumer report, as that term is defined under the federal Fair Credit Reporting Act (15 U.S.C. Sec. 1681 et seq.). The billing statement or consumer report must have been issued within 30 calendar days of the date of the contract.

(B) Shall provide the estimated period of time it will take the consumer to accumulate in a settlement account the amount of money estimated to be required to settle all debts.

(C) Shall provide the amount of time necessary to achieve the represented results.

(D) Shall provide, in terms easily understood by the least sophisticated consumer, the method that the debt settlement provider will use to calculate the charges and fees for debt settlement services.

(E) Shall provide the name and mailing address of the debt settlement provider and of the consumer.

(F) Shall provide a telephone number at which the consumer may speak, during normal business hours, with a live representative of the debt settlement provider during normal business hours who is able to access information about the consumer's account.

(G) Shall be provided to the consumer in English and in the language in which it was negotiated or in which the debt settlement services were offered, if that language is one of the languages set forth in Section 1632.

(H) Shall not require a compulsory agreement with any other party. A debt settlement provider may require that the consumer obtain a dedicated settlement account and provide a list of preferred vendors, however a payment processor who receives compensation from the consumer for payment processing services must supply its own contract to the consumer for engagement.

(I) Shall not be entered into by a consumer who is not already allegedly legally responsible for all the debt that will be enrolled in the debt settlement services. In the event multiple consumers engage in a single contract for debt settlement services, if any consumer is not proficient in English and speaks a language set forth in Section 1632, a translated copy of the disclosures and contract shall be provided to the consumer in that language and in a manner that complies with this subdivision.

(3) A debt settlement provider shall not communicate with any of a consumer's creditors until five calendar days after full execution of a contract for debt settlement services.

(c) A debt settlement provider and a payment processor shall not engage in unfair, abusive, or deceptive acts or practices when providing debt settlement services or payment processing services. Without limiting the general application of the foregoing, in connection with providing debt settlement services and payment processing services, an act or practice is unfair, abusive, or deceptive if the act or practice consists of any of the following:

(1) For a debt settlement provider and payment processor, offering to lend money or extend credit to the consumer, or purchase an enrolled debt.

(2) For a debt settlement provider requesting or receiving payment of any fee or consideration for debt settlement services, unless and until all of the following occur:

(A) The debt settlement provider has renegotiated, settled, reduced, or otherwise altered the terms of at least one debt pursuant to a settlement agreement approved and executed by the consumer.

(B) The consumer has made at least one payment pursuant to that settlement agreement between the consumer and the creditor.

(C) To the extent that debts enrolled in a debt settlement service are negotiated, settled, or modified individually, the fee or consideration must either:

(i) Bear the same proportional relationship to the total fee for renegotiating, settling, reducing, or altering the terms of the entire debt balance as the individual debt amount bears to the entire debt amount. The individual debt amount and the entire debt amount are those owed at the time the debt was enrolled in the service.

(ii) Represent a percentage of the amount saved as a result of the renegotiation, settlement, reduction, or alteration. The percentage charged cannot change from one individual debt to another. The amount saved is the difference between the amount owed at the time the debt was enrolled in the service and the amount agreed pursuant to the settlement agreement between the consumer and the creditor to satisfy the debt.

(3) Beginning July 1, 2022, for a payment processor, facilitating the distribution of payment of any fee or consideration for debt settlement services before the requirements set forth in paragraph (2) have been met.

(4) For a payment processor, failing to distribute a statement of accounting to a consumer at least once a month while the consumer is engaged with the payment processor, as well as on or before the fifth business day after a consumer requests a statement of accounting.

(A) When an accounting is available to the consumer online, the payment processor must make prominent and ongoing the ability for a consumer to opt in to a paper accounting to be mailed to the consumer under the terms of this section.

(B) The statement of accounting must contain the following information to the extent applicable:

(i) A list of deposits made into, and withdrawals from, the consumer's settlement account during the previous month.

(ii) The fees that the debt settlement provider has billed and collected in connection with each of the debts settled during the previous month.

(iii) The fees that the payment processor has billed and collected in connection with payment processing services during the previous month.

(iv) The amount of money that the consumer holds in the consumer's settlement account.

(C) Within five business days of a consumer's request, a payment processor shall provide a consolidated statement of accounting containing all of the following:

(i) A list of deposits made into, and withdrawals from, the consumer's settlement account starting from the outset of the contract.

(ii) A list of fees that the debt settlement provider has billed and collected in connection with each of the debts settled starting from the outset of the contract.

(iii) A list of fees that the payment processor has billed and collected in connection with payment processing services starting from the outset of the contract.

(iv) The amount of money that the consumer holds in the consumer's settlement account.

(5) For a debt settlement provider, failing to distribute a statement of accounting to a consumer at least once a month while the contract for debt settlement services is in effect, as well as on or before the fifth business day after a consumer requests a statement of accounting.

(A) When an accounting is available to the consumer online, the debt settlement provider must make prominent and ongoing the ability for a consumer to opt in to a paper accounting to be mailed to the consumer under the terms of this section.

(B) The statement of accounting must contain the following information to the extent applicable:

(i) The amounts, dates, and creditors associated with each settlement obtained by the debt settlement provider on behalf of the consumer.

(ii) The fees that the debt settlement provider has billed and collected in connection with each of the debts settled.

(iii) With respect to any debt settled by the debt settlement provider on behalf of the consumer, all of the following information:

(I) The total amount of money that the consumer paid or will pay to the creditor to settle the debt.

(II) The amount of the debt at the time the debt settlement provider and the consumer entered into the contract.

(III) The amount of the debt at the time the creditor agreed to settle the debt.

(IV) The amount of compensation that the debt settlement provider received, or may receive, to settle the debt.

(d)(1) A consumer may terminate a contract for debt settlement services at any time without a fee or penalty of any sort by notifying the debt settlement provider in writing, electronically, or orally.

(2) The notice described in paragraph (1) shall be deemed effective immediately upon being sent if made electronically, including via text message or orally. When the notice is sent via certified mail, notice shall be deemed effective upon receipt. When written notice is sent via noncertified mail, notice shall be deemed effective seven calendar days from the date of mailing.

(3) Upon effective notice of request for cancellation of the contract, the debt settlement provider shall do all of the following:

(A) Immediately cancel the contract.

(B) Immediately notify the payment processor that the consumer has canceled the debt settlement services and transmit to the payment processor the consumer's instruction to close the settlement account and deliver the balance in the settlement account to the consumer.

(C) Provide, within three business days, a detailed accounting of any amounts received or expected to be received by the debt settlement provider from the consumer's settlement account after the debt settlement provider received effective notice of request for cancellation. The detailed accounting shall include an explanation of how the amounts were calculated in accordance with the requirements of paragraph (2) of subdivision (c).

(D) Provide within three business days copies of all documents, notices, or other communications it has received from any creditor on behalf of the consumer.

(4) The items in subparagraphs (C) and (D) of paragraph (3) shall be sent by United States mail or by electronic means reasonably calculated to reach the consumer.

(5) Upon receipt of notice of cancellation of the contract from the consumer or debt settlement provider, the payment processor shall stop accumulating service fees, close the settlement account, and deliver to the consumer the balance in the settlement account within seven days. The payment processor shall provide, within 10 business days, a detailed accounting of the amount refunded and any amounts sent to the debt settlement provider after or upon the payment processor receiving notice of the cancellation of the contract.

(e) A debt settlement provider shall immediately forward the following notices to the consumer, either by United States mail or by electronic means reasonably calculated to reach the consumer:

(1) Any notice of a lawsuit on an enrolled debt from any person other than the consumer.

(2) Any settlement agreement that a debt settlement provider has negotiated on the consumer's behalf. **Leg.H.** Added Stats 2021 ch 454 §1 (AB 1405), effective January 1, 2022.

CHAPTER 2
APPLICATION OF THE FAIR DEBT SETTLEMENT PRACTICES ACT

Applicability of title. § 1788.303.
Exemptions. § 1788.304.

§ 1788.303. Applicability of title

This title applies to persons providing payment processing services, debt settlement services, and persons purporting to engage in debt settlement services. **Leg.H.** Added Stats 2021 ch 454 §1 (AB 1405), effective January 1, 2022.

§ 1788.304. Exemptions

This title does not apply to any of the following:

(a) Any person, or the person's authorized agent, doing business under license and authority of the Commissioner of Financial Protection and Innovation under Divisions 1.1 (commencing with Section 1000), 2 (commencing with Section 5000), and 5 (commencing with Section 14000) of the Financial Code or under any law of this state or of the United States relating to banks or credit unions.

(b) Any nonprofit business organization that is certified as tax-exempt by the Internal Revenue Service and that does not receive compensation from the consumer for providing debt settlement services.

(c) Attorneys and law firms that meet all of the following criteria:

(1) The attorney or law firm does not charge for services regulated by this title.

(2) The fees and disbursements are not charges or costs shared, directly or indirectly, with a debt settlement provider.

(3) Any of the following is true:

(A) The attorney or law firm is retained by a consumer for the purpose of legal representation in consumer debt litigation.

(B) The attorney or law firm provides debt settlement services pursuant to representation by retainer for a debt collection matter that does not involve consumer debt.

(C) The attorney or law firm is retained by the consumer primarily for purposes other than the settlement of consumer debt.

(d) A merchant-owned credit or creditors association, or a member-owned, member-controlled, or member-directed association whose principal function is that of servicing the community as a reporting agency. **Leg.H.** Added Stats 2021 ch 454 §1 (AB 1405), effective January 1, 2022.

CHAPTER 3
ENFORCEMENT OF THE FAIR DEBT SETTLEMENT PRACTICES ACT

Compliance; Cause of action; Costs and fees; Civil liability; Time limitations. § 1788.305.
Waiver void and unenforceable. § 1788.306.
Severability and effect of invalid provisions. § 1788.307.

§ 1788.305. Compliance; Cause of action; Costs and fees; Civil liability; Time limitations

(a) A debt settlement provider and a payment processor shall comply with this title.

(b) A consumer may bring a cause of action against a debt settlement provider and a payment processor for violation of any provision of this title in order to recover or obtain any of the following:

(1) Damages in an amount equal to the sum of the following:

(A) Statutory damages in an amount to be determined by the court of no less than one thousand dollars ($1,000) and no more than five thousand dollars ($5,000) per violation of this title.

(B) Any actual damages sustained by the consumer as a result of the violation.

(2) Injunctive relief.

(3) Any other relief that the court deems proper.

(c)(1) In the case of any successful cause of action under this section, the court shall award costs of the action, together with reasonable attorney's fees as determined by the court.

(2) Reasonable attorney's fees may be awarded to a prevailing debt settlement provider and a prevailing payment processor upon a finding by the court that the consumer's prosecution of the cause of action was not in good faith.

(d) A debt settlement provider or a prevailing payment processor shall have no civil liability for damages under this section if the debt settlement provider or a prevailing payment processor shows by a preponderance of evidence that the violation was not intentional and resulted from a bona fide error, and occurred notwithstanding the maintenance of procedures reasonably adopted to avoid any error.

(e) A cause of action brought under this section shall be brought within four years of the latter of the following dates:

(1) The last payment by or on behalf of the consumer.

(2) The date on which the consumer discovered or reasonably should have discovered the facts giving rise to the consumer's claim. **Leg.H.** Added Stats 2021 ch 454 §1 (AB 1405), effective January 1, 2022.

§ 1788.306. Waiver void and unenforceable

Any waiver of the provisions of this title is contrary to public policy, and is void and unenforceable. **Leg.H.** Added Stats 2021 ch 454 §1 (AB 1405), effective January 1, 2022.

§ 1788.307. Severability and effect of invalid provisions

The provisions of this title are severable. If any provision of this title or its application is held invalid, that invalidity shall not affect other provisions or applications that can be given effect without the invalid provision or application. **Leg.H.** Added Stats 2021 ch 454 §1 (AB 1405), effective January 1, 2022.

TITLE 1.6D
ELECTRONIC COMMERCE

Article 1. General Provisions.

ARTICLE 1
General Provisions

Legislative findings and declarations. §1789.
Citation. §1789.1.
Definitions. §1789.2.
Disclosures required of service providers. §1789.3.
Penalties. §1789.5.
Construction with respect to operational liability. §1789.6.
Applicability of title. §1789.7.
Covered transactions. §1789.8.
Waiver of provisions of title void. §1789.9.

§1789. Legislative findings and declarations

The Legislature hereby finds and declares that it is in the public interest that consumers have comprehensive knowledge of services available through electronic commerce and to that end hereby enacts the Electronic Commerce Act of 1984. **Leg.H.** Added Stats 1984 ch 638 §1.

Prior Law: Former §1789, similar to present UCC §§2106, 2507, 2601, 2607, 2608, 2711, 2714, 2715, 2717.

§1789.1. Citation

This title may be cited as "The Electronic Commerce Act of 1984." **Leg.H.** Added Stats 1984 ch 638 §1.

§1789.2. Definitions

For the purposes of this title, the following terms have the meanings expressed in this section:

(a) "Electronic commercial service" or "service" means an electronic shopping system to conduct the purchase of goods and services via a telecommunications network, but does not mean conventional voice-only telephone service, one-way television or radio broadcasting, an electronic fund transfer system, or a service provided through an electronic terminal located at a place of business where the sale of goods or services sold through that service otherwise occurs.

(b) "Consumer" means a natural person who purchases goods or services using an electronic commercial service.

(c) "Provider of service" means a person who contracts with consumers to provide an electronic commercial service.

(d) "Goods or services" means tangible items or physical services provided to the consumer, or tickets or vouchers for such tangible items or physical services, but does not mean computerized data delivered to the consumer via a computer terminal or in printed form. **Leg.H.** Added Stats 1984 ch 638 §1. Amended Stats 1987 ch 49 §1, effective June 17, 1987.

§1789.3. Disclosures required of service providers

The provider of an electronic commercial service shall provide to consumers with which it contracts to provide the service, at the time it contracts to provide the service and annually, on or before June 30 of each year thereafter, all of the following information:

(a) The name, address, and telephone number of the provider of service.

(b) Any charges to the consumer imposed by the provider for the use of the service.

(c) The procedures a consumer may follow in order to resolve a complaint regarding the service or to receive further information regarding use of the service, including the telephone number and address of the Complaint Assistance Unit of the Division of Consumer Services of the Department of Consumer Affairs. **Leg.H.** Added Stats 1984 ch 638 §1. Amended Stats 1986 ch 508 §1.

§1789.5. Penalties

(a) Any provider who knowingly and willfully violates any provision of this title is liable for a civil penalty not to exceed five thousand dollars ($5,000) which may be assessed and recovered in a civil action brought in the name of the people of the State of California by the Attorney General, by any district attorney or city attorney, or by a city prosecutor in any city or city and county having a full-time city prosecutor, in any court of competent jurisdiction.

(b) If the action is brought by the Attorney General, one-half of the penalty collected shall be paid to the treasurer of the county in which the judgment was entered, and one-half to the General Fund. If the action is brought by a district attorney, the penalty collected shall be paid to the treasurer of the county in which the judgment was entered. If the action is brought by a city attorney or city prosecutor, one-half of the penalty shall be paid to the treasurer of the city in which the judgment was entered, and one-half to the treasurer of the county in which the judgment was entered. **Leg.H.** Added Stats 1984 ch 638 §1.

§1789.6. Construction with respect to operational liability

Nothing in this title shall be construed to limit the liability of a provider of service to a consumer for errors or omissions arising from the operation of an electronic commercial service. **Leg.H.** Added Stats 1984 ch 638 §1.

§1789.7. Applicability of title

(a) This title does not apply where it is inconsistent with, or infringes upon, federal law or regulation.

(b) This title does not apply to the rights and obligations of a cardholder and a card issuer with respect to the use of a credit card arising from the purchase of goods or services conducted through an electronic commercial service. For the purpose of this subdivision, "cardholder," "card issuer," and "credit card" have the same meaning as those terms are given in the federal Fair Credit Billing Act (15 U.S.C. Sec. 1601 et seq.) and regulations adopted thereunder, or, if applicable, the Song-Beverly Credit Card Act of 1971 (Title 1.3 (commencing with Section 1747)).

(c) This title does not apply to the rights and obligations of a consumer and a financial institution with respect to any electronic fund transfer arising from purchase of goods or services conducted through an electronic commercial service. For the purposes of this subdivision, "consumer," "financial institution," and "electronic fund transfer" have the same meaning as those terms are given in the Electronic Fund Transfer Act (15 U.S.C. Sec. 1601 et seq.) and regulations adopted thereunder. **Leg.H.** Added Stats 1984 ch 638 §1.

§1789.8. Covered transactions

This title applies to transactions entered into on or after July 1, 1985. **Leg.H.** Added Stats 1984 ch 638 §1.

§1789.9. Waiver of provisions of title void

Any waiver of the provisions of this title is contrary to public policy, and is void and unenforceable. **Leg.H.** Added Stats 2002 ch 815 §13 (AB 2331).

TITLE 1.6E
CREDIT SERVICES

Citation. §1789.10.
Legislative findings and declarations. §1789.11.
Definitions. §1789.12.
Prohibited acts. §1789.13.
Communication with credit services organization concerning account; Exceptions. § 1789.134.
Protection of personal information by credit services organization. § 1789.135.
Required statement of information. §1789.14.
Contents of information statement. §1789.15.
Contracts. §1789.16.
Breach of contract. §1789.17.
Surety bond. §1789.18.
Defenses. §1789.19.
Injunctions; Criminal proceedings. §1789.20.
Civil actions. §1789.21.
Applicability of other provisions. §1789.22.
Severability of provisions. §1789.23.
Claims against deposits made in lieu of bond. §1789.24.
Registration of organization; Change in required information. §1789.25.
Filing of bonds. §1789.26.

§1789.10. Citation

This title shall be known and may be cited as the "Credit Services Act of 1984." **Leg.H.** Added Stats 1984 ch 1177 §1.

§1789.11. Legislative findings and declarations

The Legislature finds and declares that:

(a) The ability to obtain and use credit has become of great importance to consumers, who have a vital interest in establishing and maintaining their creditworthiness and credit standing. As a result, consumers who have experienced credit problems may seek assistance from credit services organizations which offer to obtain credit or improve the credit standing of those consumers.

Certain advertising and business practices of some credit services organizations have worked a financial hardship upon the people of this state, often those who are of limited economic means and inexperienced in credit matters. Credit services organizations have significant impact upon the economy and well-being of this state and its people.

(b) The purposes of this title are to provide prospective consumers of services of credit services organizations with the information necessary to make an intelligent decision regarding the purchase of those services and to protect the public from unfair or deceptive advertising and business practices.

(c) This title shall be construed liberally to achieve these purposes. **Leg.H.** Added Stats 1984 ch 1177 §1. Amended Stats 2022 ch 965 §1 (AB 2424), effective January 1, 2023.

§1789.12. Definitions

As used in this title:

(a) "Communication" means the conveyance of any information regarding a debt, credit record, credit history, or credit rating, directly or indirectly, to any person by any means or through any medium.

(b) "Consumer" means any natural person who is solicited to purchase or who purchases the services of a credit services organization.

(c) "Consumer credit reporting agency" has the same meaning as in Section 1785.3.

(d) "Credit services organization" means a person who, with respect to the extension of credit by others, sells, provides, or performs, or represents that the person can or will sell, provide, or perform, any of the following services, in return for the payment of money or other valuable consideration:

(1) Improving a consumer's credit record, history, or rating.

(2) Obtaining a loan or other extension of credit for a consumer.

(3) Providing advice or assistance to a consumer with regard to either paragraph (1) or (2).

(e) "Credit services organization" does not include any of the following:

(1) Any person holding a license to make loans or extensions of credit pursuant to the laws of this state or the United States who is subject to regulation and supervision with respect to the making of those loans or extensions of credit by an official or agency of this state or the United States and whose business is the making of those loans or extensions of credit.

(2) Any bank, as defined in Section 103 of the Financial Code, or any savings institution, as specified in subdivision (a) or (b) of Section 5102 of the Financial Code, whose deposits or accounts are eligible for insurance by the Federal Deposit Insurance Corporation.

(3) Any person licensed as a prorater by the Department of Financial Protection and Innovation when the person is acting within the course and scope of that license.

(4) Any person licensed as a real estate broker performing an act for which a real estate license is required under the Real Estate Law (Part 1 (commencing with Section 10000) of Division 4 of the Business and Professions Code) and who is acting within the course and scope of that license.

(5) Any attorney licensed to practice law in this state, where the attorney renders services within the course and scope of the practice of law, unless the attorney is an employee of, or otherwise directly affiliated with, a credit services organization. This includes attorneys that regularly engage in litigation in furtherance of assisting consumers with credit issues.

(6) Any broker-dealer registered with the Securities and Exchange Commission or the Commodity Futures Trading Commission where the broker-dealer is acting within the course and scope of the regulation.

(7) Any nonprofit organization described in Section 501(c)(3) of the Internal Revenue Code that, according to a final ruling or determination by the Internal Revenue Service, is both of the following:

(A) Exempt from taxation under Section 501(a) of the Internal Revenue Code.

(B) Not a private foundation as defined in Section 509 of the Internal Revenue Code.

An advance ruling or determination of tax-exempt or foundation status by the Internal Revenue Service does not meet the requirements of this paragraph.

(f) "Data furnisher" has the same meaning as the term "furnisher" is defined in Section 660.2 of Title 16 of the Code of Federal Regulations.

(g) "Extension of credit" means the right to defer payment of debt or to incur debt and defer its payment, offered or granted primarily for personal, family, or household purposes.

(h) "Person" includes an individual, corporation, partnership, joint venture, or any business entity. **Leg.H.** Added Stats 1984 ch 1177 §1. Amended Stats 1992 ch 651 §2 (AB 2999); Stats 1994 ch 792 §1 (AB 1922), ch 1010 §38 (SB 2053) (ch 792 prevails); Stats 1996 ch 648 §1 (AB 2279); Stats 2015 ch 190 §4 (AB 1517), effective January 1, 2016; Stats 2022 ch 452 §23 (SB 1498), effective January 1, 2023; Stats 2022 ch 965 §2 (AB 2424), effective January 1, 2023 (ch 965 prevails).

§1789.13. Prohibited acts

A credit services organization and its salespersons, agents, representatives, and independent contractors who sell or attempt to sell the services of a credit services organization shall not do any of the following:

(a) Charge or receive any money or other valuable consideration prior to full and complete performance of the services the credit services organization has agreed to perform for or on behalf of the consumer.

(b) Fail to perform the agreed services within 180 days following the date the consumer signs the contract for those services.

(c) Fail to provide a monthly statement to the consumer detailing the services performed.

(d) Charge or receive any money or other valuable consideration for referral of the consumer to a retail seller or other credit grantor who will or may extend credit to the consumer, if either of the following apply:

(1) The credit that is or will be extended to the consumer (A) is upon substantially the same terms as those available to the general public or (B) is upon substantially the same terms that would have been extended to the consumer without the assistance of the credit services organization.

(2) The money or consideration is paid by the credit grantor or is derived from the consumer's payments to the credit grantor for costs, fees, finance charges, or principal.

(e) Make, or counsel or advise a consumer to make, a statement that is untrue or misleading and that is known, or that by the exercise of reasonable care should be known, to be untrue or misleading, to a consumer credit reporting agency or to a person who has extended credit to a consumer, to a data furnisher, or to any person with whom a consumer is applying for an extension of credit, such as statements concerning a consumer's identification, home address, creditworthiness, credit standing, or credit capacity.

(f) Remove, or assist or advise the consumer to remove, adverse information from the consumer's credit record that is accurate or not obsolete.

(g) Create, or assist or advise the consumer to create, a new credit record by using a different name, address, social security number, or employee identification number.

(h) Make or use untrue or misleading representations in the offer or sale of the services of a credit services organization, including either of the following:

(1) Guaranteeing or otherwise stating that the credit services organization is able to delete an adverse credit history, unless the representation clearly discloses, in a manner equally as conspicuous as the guarantee, that this can be done only if the credit history is inaccurate or obsolete and is not claimed to be accurate by the creditor who submitted the information.

(2) Guaranteeing or otherwise stating that the credit services organization is able to obtain an extension of credit, regardless of the consumer's previous credit problems or credit history, unless the representation clearly discloses, in a manner equally as conspicuous as the guarantee, the eligibility requirements for obtaining an extension of credit.

(i) Engage, directly or indirectly, in an act, practice, or course of business that operates or would operate as a fraud or deception upon a person in connection with the offer or sale of the services of a credit services organization.

(j) Advertise or cause to be advertised, in any manner, the services of the credit services organization, without being registered with the Department of Justice.

(k) Fail to maintain an agent for service of process in this state.

(*l*) Transfer or assign its certificate of registration.

(m) Call or submit any communication to a consumer credit reporting agency, creditor, debt collector, or debt buyer without the prior written authorization of the consumer. A relevant authorization in the agreement or contract between a consumer and a credit services organization is sufficient for the purpose of this subdivision.

(n) Submit a consumer's dispute to a consumer credit reporting agency, creditor, debt collector, or debt buyer more than 180 days after the account subject to the dispute has been removed from the consumer's credit report.

(o) Use the online electronic portal, electronic mail system, or telephone system of a consumer credit reporting agency, creditor, debt collector, or debt buyer to submit a dispute of a consumer or to request disclosure without the prior written authorization of the consumer. A relevant authorization in the agreement or contract between a consumer and a credit services organization is sufficient for the purpose of this subdivision.

(p) Directly or indirectly extend credit to a consumer.

(q) Refer a consumer to a credit grantor that is related to the credit services organization by a common ownership, management, or control, including a common owner, director, or officer.

(r) Refer a consumer to a credit grantor for which the credit services organization provides, or arranges for a third party to provide, services related to the extension of credit such as underwriting, billing, payment processing, or debt collection.

(s) Provide a credit grantor with an assurance that a portion of an extension of credit to a consumer referred by the credit services organization will be repaid, including providing a guaranty, letter of credit, or agreement to acquire a part of the credit grantor's financial interest in the extension of credit.

(t) Use a scheme, device, or contrivance to evade the prohibitions contained in this section.

(u) Fail to make a written communication sent on behalf of a consumer to any credit reporting agency, data furnisher, or legal counsel for either of the foregoing available to the consumer.

(v) Fail to provide along with its first written communication to a credit reporting agency or data furnisher any sufficient information to investigate an account.

(w) The seeking to obtain, or the obtaining of, a consumer's credit report and the performance of other services necessary to determine the needs of a consumer for the reinvestigation of any accounts shall not constitute services of a credit services organization for which a contract is required pursuant to subdivision (a) of Section 1789.16, if that activity is undertaken with the consumer's prior written, electronic, or recorded oral consent. **Leg.H.** Added Stats 1984 ch 1177 §1. Amended Stats 1992 ch 651 §3 (AB 2999); Stats 1994 ch 792 §2 (AB 1922); Stats 2007 ch 91 §1 (SB 500), effective January 1, 2008; Stats 2008 ch 179 §30 (SB 1498), effective January 1, 2009; Stats 2022 ch 965 §3 (AB 2424), effective January 1, 2023.

§ 1789.134. Communication with credit services organization concerning account; Exceptions

(a) A consumer credit reporting agency, creditor, debt collector, or debt buyer that knows that a consumer is represented by a credit services organization, and that also has knowledge of, or can readily ascertain the credit services organization's name and address shall communicate with the credit services organization unless either of the following circumstances apply:

(1) The credit services organization fails to respond within 30 days to a communication from a consumer credit reporting agency, creditor, debt collector, or debt buyer.

(2) The consumer expressly directs the consumer credit reporting agency, creditor, debt collector, or debt buyer not to communicate with the credit services organization.

(b) Notwithstanding subdivision (a), a consumer credit reporting agency, creditor, or debt collector shall not be required to communicate with a credit services organization concerning an account that is subject to a dispute if any of the following apply:

(1) The account subject to the dispute has been paid, settled, or otherwise resolved and has been reported as paid, settled, or otherwise resolved on the consumer's credit report.

(2) The account subject to the dispute has been removed from the consumer's credit report.

(3) The debt collector has provided to the credit services organization or to the consumer the verification information or documentation described in Section 1692g(b) of Title 15 of the United States Code regarding the account subject to dispute.

(4) The debt buyer has provided to the credit services organization or to the consumer the information or documentation described in subdivisions (a) and (b) of Section 1788.52 regarding the account subject to the dispute.

(5) The consumer credit reporting agency, creditor, or debt collector reasonably determines that the dispute is frivolous or irrelevant pursuant to Section 1681i(a)(3) or Section 1681s-2(a)(1)(F) of Title 15 of the United States Code. **Leg.H.** Added Stats 2022 ch 965 §4 (AB 2424), effective January 1, 2023.

§ 1789.135. Protection of personal information by credit services organization

To protect against fraud and identity theft, when a credit services organization sends a written communication by facsimile, electronic mail, United States mail, overnight courier, or other means that contains personal information of a consumer, the credit services organization shall redact the personal information to include only the last four digits of the social security number, taxpayer identification number, or state identification number, the last four digits of the financial account number, credit card number, or debit card number, or the month and year of the consumer's date of birth, unless the inclusion of the full number or date is otherwise required by law, or is legally permissible and required to achieve the desired objective. Redacting information pursuant to this subdivision shall not be considered a violation of subdivision (w) of Section 1789.13. **Leg.H.** Added Stats 2022 ch 965 §5 (AB 2424), effective January 1, 2023.

§1789.14. Required statement of information

Before the execution of a contract or agreement between the consumer and a credit services organization, the credit services organization shall provide the consumer a statement in writing containing all the information required by Section 1789.15. The credit services organization shall maintain on file for a period of four years following the completion or termination of the credit services organization agreement with the consumer an exact copy of the statement. **Leg.H.** Added Stats 1984 ch 1177 §1. Amended Stats 1992 ch 651 §4 (AB 2999); Stats 2022 ch 965 §6 (AB 2424), effective January 1, 2023.

§1789.15. Contents of information statement

The information statement shall include all of the following:

(a) A complete and detailed description of the services to be performed by the credit services organization for or on behalf of the consumer and the total amount the consumer will have to pay, or become obligated to pay, for the services.

(b) The consumer's right to proceed against the bond under the circumstances and in the manner set forth in Section 1789.18.

(c) The name and address of the surety company which issued the bond.

(d) A complete and accurate statement of the availability of nonprofit credit counseling services.

(e) The following notice: If you have a complaint about the services provided by this credit services organization or the fees charged by this credit services organization, you may submit that complaint to the Attorney General's office, California Department of Justice, Attn: ____, P.O. Box 944255, Sacramento, CA 94244-2550.

The information statement shall be printed in at least 10-point boldface type and shall include the following statement:

CONSUMER CREDIT FILE RIGHTS UNDER STATE AND FEDERAL LAW.

You have a right to obtain a free copy of your credit report from a credit reporting agency. You may obtain this free copy of your credit report one time per year by visiting www.AnnualCreditReport.com. You will be able to view your credit report, dispute alleged inaccuracies, and obtain additional information at no fee. If requested, the consumer credit reporting agency must provide someone to help you interpret the information in your credit file.

You have a right to dispute inaccurate information by contacting the consumer credit reporting agency directly. However, neither you nor any credit repair company or credit services organization has the right to have accurate, current, and verifiable information removed from your credit report. Under the Federal Fair Credit Reporting Act, the consumer credit reporting agency must remove accurate, negative information from your report only if it is over seven years old. Bankruptcy information can be reported for 10 years.

If you have notified a credit reporting agency in writing that you dispute the accuracy of information in your credit file, the consumer credit reporting agency must then reinvestigate and modify or remove inaccurate information. The consumer credit reporting agency may not charge a fee for this service. Any pertinent information and copies of all documents you have concerning an error should be given to the consumer credit reporting agency.

If the reinvestigation does not resolve the dispute to your satisfaction, you may send a brief statement to the consumer credit reporting agency to keep in your file, explaining why you think the record is inaccurate. The consumer credit reporting agency must include your statement about disputed information in any report it issues about you.

You have a right to cancel the contract with the credit services organization for any reason before midnight on the fifth working day after you signed it. If for any reason you cancel the contract during this time, you do not owe any money.

You have a right to sue a credit services organization if it misleads you. **Leg.H.** Added Stats 1984 ch 1177 §1. Amended Stats 1992 ch 651 §5 (AB 2999); Stats 2022 ch 965 §7 (AB 2424), effective January 1, 2023.

§1789.16. Contracts

(a) A credit services organization shall not provide any service to a consumer except pursuant to a written contract that complies with this section. Every contract between the consumer and a credit services organization for the purchase of the services of the credit services organization shall identify the physical address, electronic mail address, and facsimile number if applicable, of the credit services organization, shall be in writing, shall be dated, shall be signed by the consumer, and shall include all of the following:

(1) A conspicuous statement in size equal to at least 10-point boldface type, in immediate proximity to the space reserved for the signature of the buyer, as follows:

"You, the consumer, may cancel this contract at any time before midnight on the fifth working day after you sign it. See the attached notice of cancellation form for an explanation of this right."

(2) The terms and conditions of payment, including the total of all payments to be made by the consumer, whether to the credit services organization or to some other person.

(3) A full and detailed description of the services to be performed by the credit services organization for the consumer, including a list of the information appearing on the consumer's credit report that the credit services organization will seek a reasonable reinvestigation of, as described in Title 15 of Section 1681i of the United States Code, all guarantees and all promises of full or partial refunds, and the estimated length of time for performing the services, not to exceed 180 days, or a shorter period consistent with the purposes of this title as may be prescribed by the Department of Justice.

(4) The credit services organization's principal business address and the name and address of its agent, other than the Secretary of State, in the State of California, authorized to receive service of process.

(b) The contract shall be accompanied by a completed form in duplicate, captioned "Notice of Cancellation," which shall be attached to the contract and easily detachable, and which shall contain in type of at least 10-point the following statement written in the same language as used in the contract:

"Notice of Cancellation"

You may cancel this contract, without any penalty or obligation, before midnight on the fifth working day after you sign it.

If you cancel, any payment made by you under this contract must be returned within 15 days following receipt by the seller of your cancellation notice.

To cancel this contract, mail or deliver a signed and dated copy of this cancellation notice, or any other written notice, to _____ (name of seller) at

_____ (address of seller)
_____ (place of business)
not later than midnight _____ (date)
"I hereby cancel this transaction."
_____ (date) _____ (purchaser's signature)

A copy of the fully completed contract and all other documents the credit services organization requires the buyer to sign shall be given to the consumer at the time they are signed. **Leg.H.** Added Stats 1984 ch 1177 §1. Amended Stats 1992 ch 651 §6 (AB 2999); Stats 1993 ch 285 §10 (AB 1340), effective July 30, 1993; Stats 1994 ch 792 §3 (AB 1922); Stats 2022 ch 965 §8 (AB 2424), effective January 1, 2023.

§1789.17. Breach of contract

The seller's breach of a contract under this title or of any obligation arising therefrom shall constitute a violation of this title. **Leg.H.** Added Stats 1984 ch 1177 §1.

§1789.18. Surety bond

No credit services organization shall conduct business in this state unless the credit services organization has first obtained a surety bond in the principal amount of one hundred thousand dollars ($100,000) issued by an admitted surety and the bond complies with all of the following:

(a) The bond shall be in favor of the State of California for the benefit of any person who is damaged by any violation of this title. The bond shall also be in favor of any individual damaged by those practices.

(b) Any person claiming against the bond for a violation of this title may maintain an action at law against the credit services organization and against the surety. The surety shall be liable only for actual damages and not the punitive damages permitted under Section 1789.21. The aggregate liability of the surety to all persons damaged by a credit services organization's violation of this title shall in no event exceed the amount of the bond.

(c) The bond shall be maintained for two years following the date on which the credit services organization ceases to conduct business in this state.

A copy of the bond shall be filed with the Secretary of State. **Leg.H.** Added Stats 1984 ch 1177 §1. Amended Stats 1992 ch 651 §7 (AB 2999).

§1789.19. Defenses

(a) Any waiver by a consumer of the provisions of this title shall be deemed contrary to public policy and shall be void and unenforceable. Any attempt by a credit services organization to have a consumer waive rights given by this title shall constitute a violation of this title.

(b) In any proceeding involving this title, the burden of proving an exemption or an exception from a definition is upon the person claiming it. **Leg.H.** Added Stats 1984 ch 1177 §1. Amended Stats 2022 ch 965 §9 (AB 2424), effective January 1, 2023.

§1789.20. Injunctions; Criminal proceedings

(a) Any person who violates any provision of this title is guilty of a misdemeanor. Any superior court of this state shall have jurisdiction in equity to restrain and enjoin the violation of any provision of this title.

The duty to institute actions for violation of this title, including equity proceedings to restrain and enjoin such a violation, is hereby vested in the Attorney General, district attorneys, and city attorneys. The Attorney General, any district attorney, or any city attorney may prosecute misdemeanor actions or institute equity proceedings, or both.

This section shall not be deemed to prohibit the enforcement by any person of any right provided by this or any other law.

(b) The misdemeanor provision of this section does not apply to a seller's breach of a contract subject to this title. **Leg.H.** Added Stats 1984 ch 1177 §1.

§1789.21. Civil actions

(a) Any consumer injured by a violation of this title or by the credit services organization's breach of a contract subject to this title may bring any action for recovery of damages, or for injunctive relief, or both. Judgment shall be entered for actual damages, but in no case less than the amount paid by the consumer to the credit services organization, plus reasonable attorney's fees and costs. An award, if the trial court deems it proper, may be entered for punitive damages.

(b) Any person, including, but not limited to, a consumer credit reporting agency, as defined in subdivision (d) of Section 1785.3, and any consumer of, or user of, a consumer credit report under the Consumer Credit Reporting Agencies Act (Title 1.6 (commencing with Section 1785.1)), and any furnisher of credit information under the Consumer Credit Reporting Agencies Act, may bring an action for the recovery of damages or for injunctive relief, or both, for a violation of this title. Any person bringing such an action who prevails in the action shall be entitled to reasonable attorney's fees and costs. **Leg.H.** Added Stats 1984 ch 1177

§1. Amended Stats 1992 ch 651 §8 (AB 2999); Stats 1994 ch 792 §4 (AB 1922); Stats 2004 ch 183 §33 (AB 3082); Stats 2022 ch 965 §10 (AB 2424), effective January 1, 2023.

§1789.22. Applicability of other provisions

The provisions of this title are not exclusive and do not relieve the parties or the contracts subject thereto from compliance with any other applicable provision of law.

The remedies provided in this title for violation of any section of this title shall be in addition to any other procedures or remedies for any violation or conduct provided for in any other law. **Leg.H.** Added Stats 1984 ch 1177 §1.

§1789.23. Severability of provisions

If any provision of this title or if any application thereof to any person or circumstance is held invalid, the remainder of the title and the application of the provision to other persons and circumstances shall not be affected thereby. **Leg.H.** Added Stats 1984 ch 1177 §1.

§1789.24. Claims against deposits made in lieu of bond

(a) When a deposit has been made in lieu of a bond pursuant to Section 995.710 of the Code of Civil Procedure, the person asserting a claim against the deposit shall, in lieu of proceeding under Section 996.430 of the Code of Civil Procedure, establish the claim by furnishing evidence to the Secretary of State of a money judgment entered by a court, together with evidence that the claimant is a person described in subdivision (b) of Section 1789.18.

(b) When a person has established the claim with the Secretary of State, the Secretary of State shall review and approve the claim and enter the date of approval thereon. The claim shall be designated an "approved claim."

(c) When the first claim against a particular deposit has been approved, it shall not be paid until the expiration of a period of 240 days after the date of its approval by the Secretary of State. Subsequent claims that are approved by the Secretary of State within the same 240-day period shall similarly not be paid until the expiration of the 240-day period. Upon the expiration of the 240-day period, the Secretary of State shall pay all approved claims from that 240-day period in full unless the deposit is insufficient, in which case each approved claim shall be paid a pro rata share of the deposit.

(d) When the Secretary of State approves the first claim against a particular deposit after the expiration of a 240-day period, the date of approval of that claim shall begin a new 240-day period to which subdivision (c) shall apply with respect to any amount remaining in the deposit.

(e) After a deposit is exhausted, no further claims shall be paid by the Secretary of State. Claimants who have had their claims paid in full or in part pursuant to subdivision (c) or (d) shall not be required to return funds received from the deposit for the benefit of other claimants.

(f) When a deposit has been made in lieu of a bond, as specified in subdivision (a), the amount of the deposit shall not be subject to attachment, garnishment, or execution with respect to an action or judgment against the credit services organization, other than as to an amount as no longer needed or required for the purpose of this title which would otherwise be returned to the credit services organization by the Secretary of State.

(g) The Secretary of State shall retain a cash deposit for two years from the date the Secretary of State receives written notification from the assignor of the deposit that the assignor has ceased to engage in the business of a credit services organization or has filed a bond pursuant to Section 1789.18, provided that there are no outstanding claims against the deposit. The written notice shall include all of the following: (1) name, address, and telephone number of the assignor; (2) name, address, and telephone number of the bank at which the deposit is located; (3) account number of the deposit; and (4) a statement whether the assignor is ceasing to engage in the business of a credit services organization or has filed a bond with the Secretary of State. The Secretary of State shall forward an acknowledgment of receipt of the written notice to the assignor at the address indicated therein, specifying the date of receipt of the written notice and anticipated date of release of the deposit.

(h) This section shall apply to all deposits retained by the Secretary of State.

(i) A judge of a superior court may order the return of the deposit prior to the expiration of two years upon evidence satisfactory to the judge that there are no outstanding claims against the deposit or order the Secretary of State to retain the deposit for a sufficient period beyond the two years specified in subdivision (g) to resolve outstanding claims against the deposit account. **Leg.H.** Added Stats 1985 ch 275 §1. Amended Stats 1996 ch 633 §4 (SB 1978); Stats 1998 ch 829 §6 (SB 1652); Stats 2002 ch 784 §13 (SB 1316).

§1789.25. Registration of organization; Change in required information

(a) Every credit services organization shall file a registration application with, and receive a certificate of registration from, the Department of Justice before conducting business in this state. The Department of Justice shall not issue a certificate of registration until the bond required by Section 1789.18 has been filed with the Office of the Secretary of State and the department establishes that the organization seeking a certificate satisfies the requirements of subdivision (f). The application shall be accompanied by a registration fee of one hundred dollars ($100). The registration application shall contain all of the following information:

(1) The name and address where business is actually conducted of the credit services organization.

(2) The names, addresses, and driver's license numbers of any and all persons who directly or indirectly own or control 10 percent or more of the outstanding shares of stock in the credit services organization.

(3) Either of the following:

(A) A full and complete disclosure of any litigation commenced against the credit services organization or any resolved or unresolved complaint that relates to the operation of the credit services organization and that is filed with the Attorney General, or any other governmental authority of this state, any other state, or the federal government. With respect to each resolved complaint identified by the disclosure, the disclosure shall include a brief description of the resolution.

(B) An acknowledged declaration, under penalty of perjury, stating that no litigation has been commenced and no unresolved complaint relating to the operation of the organization has been filed with the Attorney General, or any other governmental authority of this state, any other state, or the federal government.

(4) Other information that the Department of Justice requires, either at the time of application or thereafter.

(b) The Department of Justice may conduct an investigation to verify the accuracy of the registration application. If the application involves investigation outside this state, the applicant credit services organization may be required by the Department of Justice to advance sufficient funds to pay the actual expenses of the investigation. Any nonresident applying for registration under this section shall designate and maintain a resident of this state as the applicant's agent for the purpose of receipt of service of process.

(c) Each credit services organization shall notify the Department of Justice in writing within 30 days after the date of a change in the information required by subdivision (a), except that 30 days' advance notice and approval by the Department of Justice shall be required before changing the corporate name or address, or persons owning more than 10 percent of the shares of stock in the organization. Each credit services organization registering under this section may use no more than one fictitious or trade name and shall maintain a copy of the registration application in its files. The organization shall allow a buyer to inspect the registration application upon request.

(d) A certificate of registration issued pursuant to this section shall expire one year after it was issued, but may be renewed by filing a renewal application accompanied by a fee in an amount to be determined annually by the Department of Justice as is reasonable and necessary to satisfy its costs in complying with its duties under this title to regulate credit services organizations. The Department of Justice may, periodically, increase the fee, but the amount of the fee shall not exceed that which is reasonable and necessary to satisfy its costs in complying with its duties under this title to regulate credit services organizations.

(e) The credit services organization shall attach to the registration statement a copy of the contract or contracts which the credit services organization intends to execute with its customers and a copy of the required bond.

(f) The Department of Justice shall not issue a certificate of registration under this title to any person who has engaged in, or proposes to engage in, any activity that is in violation of Section 1789.13, any law prohibiting the use of untrue or misleading statements, or any law related to the extension of credit to persons for personal, family, or household purposes.

(g) The Department of Justice shall maintain on a publicly available internet website a list of the credit services organizations that are registered in this state. **Leg.H.** Added Stats 1992 ch 651 §9 (AB 2999). Amended Stats 2007 ch 91 §2 (SB 500), effective January 1, 2008; Stats 2022 ch 965 §11 (AB 2424), effective January 1, 2023.

§1789.26. Filing of bonds

(a) The Secretary of State shall enforce the provisions of this title that govern the filing and maintenance of bonds and deposits in lieu of bonds.

(b) The Secretary of State shall charge and collect a filing fee not to exceed the cost of filing the bond or the deposit in lieu of a bond pursuant to Section 995.710 of the Code of Civil Procedure. **Leg.H.** Added Stats 1996 ch 633 §5 (SB 1978).

TITLE 1.6F
CHECK CASHERS

Disclosures. §1789.30.
Definitions. §1789.31.
Violations. §1789.32.
Fees; Penalties for violations; Willful violation as misdemeanor; Civil actions; Damages. §1789.35.
Permits; Regulations; Violations. §1789.37.
Waiver of provisions of title void. §1789.38.

§1789.30. Disclosures

(a)(1) Every check casher, as applicable to the services provided, shall post a complete, detailed, and unambiguous schedule of all fees for (A) cashing checks, drafts, money orders, or other commercial paper serving the same purpose, (B) the sale or issuance of money orders, and (C) the initial issuance of any identification card. Each check casher shall also post a list of valid identification which is acceptable in lieu of identification provided by the check casher. The information required by this section shall be clear, legible, and in letters not less than one-half inch in height. The information shall be posted in a conspicuous location in the unobstructed view of the public within the check casher's premises.

(2) A check casher may be required to file a return required by Section 18631.7 of the Revenue and Taxation Code.

(b)(1) Except as provided in paragraph (2), this section shall become operative December 31, 2004.

(2)(A) Except as provided in subparagraph (B), paragraph (2) of subdivision (a) shall apply to checks cashed on or after January 1, 2006.

(B) The amendments to this section made by the act adding this subparagraph shall become operative on January 1, 2008. **Leg.H.** Added Stats 2004 ch 17 §2 (AB 971), effective February 23, 2004, operative December 31, 2004. Amended Stats 2005 ch 74 §24 (AB 139), effective July 19, 2005; Stats 2007 ch 341 §1 (AB 1747), effective January 1, 2008.

Prior Law: Former §1789.30, similar to the present section, was added Stats 1990 ch 1391 §1, amended Stats 1996 ch 682 §1, Stats 2004 ch 17 §1, effective February 23, 2004, inoperative December 31, 2004, repealed January 1, 2005, by its own terms.

2004 Note: Notwithstanding the December 31, 2004 operative and inoperative dates specified in this act, the provisions of this act may become operative and inoperative on an earlier date established by an executive order issued by the Governor if that date is not less than 30 days after the issuance of the executive order. Stats 2004 ch 17 (AB 971) §20.

Former Sections: Former CC §1789.30, similar to the present section, was added Stats 1990 ch 1391 §1 and became inoperative December 31, 2004, and repealed operative January 1, 2005, by its own provisions. Stats 2004 ch 17 (AB 971) §1, effective February 23, 2004.

§1789.31. Definitions

(a) As used in this title, a "check casher" means a person or entity that for compensation engages, in whole or in part, in the business of cashing checks, warrants, drafts, money orders, or other commercial paper serving the same purpose. "Check casher" does not include a state or federally chartered bank, savings association, credit union, or industrial loan company. "Check casher" also does not include a retail seller engaged primarily in the business of selling consumer goods, including consumables, to retail buyers that cashes checks or issues money orders for a fee not exceeding two dollars ($2) as a service to its customers that is incidental to its main purpose or business.

(b) This section shall become operative December 31, 2004. **Leg.H.** Added Stats 2002 ch 777 §3 (SB 898); Stats 2004 ch 17 §4 (AB 971), effective February 23, 2004, operative December 31, 2004.

Prior Law: Former §1789.31, similar to the present section, was added Stats 1990 ch 1391 §1, amended Stats 1991 ch 228 §1, Stats 1996 ch 682 §2, Stats 2002 ch 777 §2, Stats 2004 ch 17 §3, effective February 23, 2004, inoperative December 31, 2004, repealed January 1, 2005, by its own terms.

2004 Note: Notwithstanding the December 31, 2004 operative and inoperative dates specified in this act, the provisions of this act may become operative and inoperative on an earlier date established by an executive order issued by the Governor if that date is not less than 30 days after the issuance of the executive order. Stats 2004 ch 17 (AB 971) §20.

Former Sections: Former CC §1789.31, similar to the present section, was added Stats 1990 ch 1391 §1 and became inoperative December 31, 2004, and repealed operative January 1, 2005, by its own provisions. Stats 2004 ch 17 (AB 971) §3, effective February 23, 2004.

§1789.32. Violations

Failure to post information as required by this title, or the imposition of fees or identification requirements contrary to the information posted, shall constitute an unfair business practice within the meaning of Section 17200 of the Business and Professions Code. **Leg.H.** Added Stats 1990 ch 1391 §1 (AB 3096).

§1789.33. [Section repealed 2005]

Leg.H. Added Stats 1996 ch 682 §2.5 (SB 1959). Amended Stats 2002 ch 777 §4 (SB 898). Repealed Stats 2004 ch 17 §5 (AB 971), effective February 23, 2004, inoperative December 31, 2004, repealed January 1, 2005, by its own provisions. The repealed section related to deferred deposit agreement.

2004 Note: Notwithstanding the December 31, 2004 operative and inoperative dates specified in this act, the provisions of this act may become operative and inoperative on an earlier date established by an executive order issued by the Governor if that date is not less than 30 days after the issuance of the executive order. Stats 2004 ch 17 (AB 971) §20.

§1789.35. Fees; Penalties for violations; Willful violation as misdemeanor; Civil actions; Damages

(a) A check casher shall not charge a fee for cashing a payroll check or government check in excess of 3 percent if identification is provided by the customer, or 3.5 percent without the provision of identification, of the face amount of the check, or three dollars ($3), whichever is greater. Identification, for purposes of this section, is limited to a California driver's license, a California identification card, or a valid United States military identification card.

(b) A check casher may charge a fee of no more than ten dollars ($10) to set up an initial account and issue an optional identification card for providing check cashing services. A replacement optional identification card may be issued at a cost not to exceed five dollars ($5).

(c) A check casher shall provide a receipt to the customer for each transaction.

(d) A check casher may charge a fee for cashing a personal check, as posted pursuant to Section 1789.30, for immediate deposit in an amount not to exceed 12 percent of the face value of the check.

(e) Any person who violates any provision of this section shall be liable for a civil penalty not to exceed two thousand dollars ($2,000) for each violation, which shall be assessed and recovered in a civil action brought in the name of the people of the State of California by the Attorney General in any court of competent jurisdiction. Any action brought pursuant to this subdivision shall be commenced within four years of the date on which the act or transaction upon which the action is based occurred.

(f) A willful violation of this section is a misdemeanor.

(g) Any person who is injured by any violation of this section may bring an action for the recovery of damages, an equity proceeding to restrain and enjoin those violations, or both. The amount awarded may be up to three times the damages actually incurred, but in no event less than the amount paid by the aggrieved consumer to a person subject to this section. If the plaintiff prevails, the plaintiff shall be awarded reasonable attorney's fees and costs. If a court determines by clear and convincing evidence that a breach or violation was willful, the court, in its discretion, may award punitive damages in addition to the amounts set forth above.

(h) This section shall become operative December 31, 2004. **Leg.H.** Added Stats 2002 ch 777 §6 (SB 898). Amended Stats 2004 ch 17 §7 (AB 971), effective February 23, 2004, operative December 31, 2004, ch 28 §2 (SB 31), effective April 1, 2004, operative December 31, 2004.

Prior Law: Former §1789.35, similar to the present section, was added Stats 1992 ch 1043 §2, amended Stats 1996 ch 682 §3, Stats 2002 ch 777 §5, Stats 2004 ch 17 §6, effective February 23, 2004, inoperative December 31, 2004, repealed January 1, 2005, ch 28 §1, effective April 1, 2004, inoperative December 31, 2004, repealed January 1, 2005, by its own terms.

2004 Note: Notwithstanding the December 31, 2004, operative and inoperative dates specified in the sections amended by Sections 1 and 2 of this act, the provisions of those sections may become operative and inoperative on an earlier date established by an executive order issued by the Governor if that date is not less than 30 days after the issuance of the executive order. Stats 2004 ch 28 (SB 31) §3.

Former Sections: Former CC §1789.35, similar to the present section, was added Stats 1992 ch 1043 §2 and became inoperative December 31, 2004, and repealed operative January 1, 2005, by its own provisions. Stats 2004 ch 28 (SB 31) §1, effective April 1, 2004.

§1789.37. Permits; Regulations; Violations

(a) Every owner of a check casher's business shall obtain a permit from the Department of Justice to conduct a check casher's business.

(b) All applications for a permit to conduct a check casher's business shall be filed with the department in writing, signed by the applicant, if an individual, or by a member or officer authorized to sign, if the applicant is a corporation or other entity, and shall state the name of the business, the type of business engaged in, and the business address. Each applicant shall be fingerprinted.

(c) Each applicant for a permit to conduct a check casher's business shall pay a fee not to exceed the cost of processing the application, fingerprinting the applicant, and checking or obtaining the criminal record of the applicant, at the time of filing the application.

(d) Each applicant shall annually, beginning one year from the date of issuance of a check casher's permit, file an application for renewal of the permit with the department, along with payment of a renewal fee not to exceed the cost of processing the application for renewal and checking or obtaining the criminal record of the applicant.

(e) The department shall deny an application for a permit to conduct a check casher's business, or for renewal of a permit, if the applicant has a felony conviction involving dishonesty, fraud, or deceit, if the crime is substantially related to the qualifications, functions, or duties of a person engaged in the business of check cashing.

(f) The department shall adopt regulations to implement this section and shall determine the amount of the application fees required by this section. The department shall prescribe forms for the applications and permit required by this section, which shall be uniform throughout the state.

(g) In any action brought by a city attorney or district attorney to enforce a violation of this section, an owner of a check casher's business who engages in the business of check cashing without holding a current and valid permit issued by the department pursuant to this section is subject to a civil penalty, as follows:

(1) For the first offense, not more than one thousand dollars ($1,000).

(2) For the second offense, not more than five thousand dollars ($5,000).

(h) Any person who has twice been found in violation of subdivision (g) and who, within 10 years of the date of the first offense, engages in the business of check cashing without holding a current and valid permit issued by the department pursuant to this section is guilty of a misdemeanor punishable by imprisonment in a county jail not exceeding six months, or by a fine not exceeding five thousand dollars ($5,000), or by both that fine and imprisonment.

(i) All civil penalties, forfeited bail, or fines received by any court pursuant to this section shall, as soon as practicable after the receipt thereof, be deposited with the county treasurer of the county in which the court is situated. Fines and forfeitures deposited shall be disbursed pursuant to the Penal Code. Civil penalties deposited shall be paid at least once a month as follows:

(1) Fifty percent to the Treasurer by warrant of the county auditor drawn upon the requisition of the clerk or judge of the court, to be deposited in the State Treasury on order of the Controller.

(2) Fifty percent to the city treasurer of the city, if the offense occurred in a city, otherwise to the treasurer of the county in which the prosecution is conducted. Any money deposited in the State Treasury under this section that is determined by the Controller to have been erroneously deposited shall be refunded out of any money in the State Treasury that is available by law for that purpose.

(j) This section shall become operative December 31, 2004. **Leg.H.** Added Stats 2004 ch 17 §9 (AB 971), effective February 23, 2004, operative December 31, 2004. Amended Stats 2006 ch 538 §47 (SB 1852), effective January 1, 2007; Stats 2016 ch 31 §9 (SB 836), effective June 27, 2016.

Prior Law: Former §1789.37, similar to the present section, was added Stats 1992 ch 1043 §3, amended Stats 1993 ch 327 §1, Stats 1996 ch 682 §4, Stats 1997 ch 369 §1, Stats 2004 ch 17 §8, effective February 23, 2004, inoperative December 31, 2004, repealed January 1, 2005, by its own terms.

2004 Note: Notwithstanding the December 31, 2004 operative and inoperative dates specified in this act, the provisions of this act may become operative and inoperative on an earlier date established by an executive order issued by the Governor if that date is not less than 30 days after the issuance of the executive order. Stats 2004 ch 17 (AB 971) §20.

Former Sections: Former CC §1789.37, similar to the present section, was added Stats 1992 ch 1043 §3 and became inoperative December 31, 2004, and repealed operative January 1, 2005, by its own provisions. Stats 2004 ch 17 (AB 971) §8, effective February 23, 2004.

§1789.38. Waiver of provisions of title void

Any waiver of the provisions of this title is contrary to public policy, and is void and unenforceable. **Leg.H.** Added Stats 2002 ch 815 §14 (AB 2331).

§1789.39. [Section repealed 2005]

Leg.H. Added Stats 2004 ch 17 §10 (AB 971), effective February 23, 2004, inoperative December 31, 2004, repealed January 1, 2005, by its own provisions. The repealed section related to extension of certain permits.

2004 Note: Notwithstanding the December 31, 2004 operative and inoperative dates specified in this act, the provisions of this act may become operative and inoperative on an earlier date established by an executive order issued by the Governor if that date is not less than 30 days after the issuance of the executive order. Stats 2004 ch 17 (AB 971) §20.

TITLE 1.7
CONSUMER WARRANTIES

Chapter 1. Consumer Warranty Protection.
Chapter 1.5. Motor Vehicle Warranty Adjustment Programs.
Chapter 2. Standards for Warranty Work.
Chapter 3. Mobilehome Warranties.
Chapter 4. Grey Market Goods.
Chapter 5. Home Roof Warranties.

CHAPTER 1
CONSUMER WARRANTY PROTECTION

Article 1. General Provisions.
Article 2. Definitions.
Article 3. Sale Warranties.

ARTICLE 1
General Provisions

Title. §1790.
Enforceability of waiver. §1790.1.
Severability. §1790.2.
Construction in case of conflict with Commercial Code. §1790.3.
Cumulative remedies. §1790.4.

§1790. Title

This chapter may be cited as the "Song-Beverly Consumer Warranty Act." **Leg.H.** Added Stats 1970 ch 1333 §1.

Prior Law: Former §1790, similar to UCC §§2710, 2715, was added Stats 1931 ch 1070 §1 and repealed Stats 1963 ch 819 §2, effective January 1, 1965.

§1790.1. Enforceability of waiver

Any waiver by the buyer of consumer goods of the provisions of this chapter, except as expressly provided in this chapter, shall be deemed contrary to public policy and shall be unenforceable and void. **Leg.H.** Added Stats 1970 ch 1333 §1.

§1790.2. Severability

If any provision of this chapter or the application thereof to any person or circumstance is held unconstitutional, such invalidity shall not affect other provisions or applications of this chapter which can be given effect without the invalid provision or application, and to this end the provisions of this chapter are severable. **Leg.H.** Added Stats 1970 ch 1333 §1.

§1790.3. Construction in case of conflict with Commercial Code

The provisions of this chapter shall not affect the rights and obligations of parties determined by reference to the Commercial Code except that, where the provisions of the Commercial Code conflict with the rights guaranteed to buyers of consumer goods under the provisions of this chapter, the provisions of this chapter shall prevail. **Leg.H.** Added Stats 1970 ch 1333 §1.

§1790.4. Cumulative remedies

The remedies provided by this chapter are cumulative and shall not be construed as restricting any remedy that is otherwise available, and, in particular, shall not be construed to supplant the provisions of the Unfair Practices Act. **Leg.H.** Added Stats 1971 ch 1523 §1, operative January 1, 1972. Amended Stats 1976 ch 416 §1.

ARTICLE 2
Definitions

Definitions. §1791.
"Implied warranty of merchantability"; "Implied warranty of fitness". §1791.1.
"Express warranty". §1791.2.
"As is"; "With all faults". §1791.3.

§1791. Definitions

As used in this chapter:

(a) "Consumer goods" means any new product or part thereof that is used, bought, or leased for use primarily for personal, family, or household purposes, except for clothing and consumables. "Consumer goods" shall include new and used assistive devices sold at retail.

(b) "Buyer" or "retail buyer" means any individual who buys consumer goods from a person engaged in the business of manufacturing, distributing, or selling consumer goods at retail. As used in this subdivision, "person" means any individual, partnership, corporation, limited liability company, association, or other legal entity that engages in any of these businesses.

(c) "Clothing" means any wearing apparel, worn for any purpose, including under and outer garments, shoes, and accessories composed primarily of woven material, natural or synthetic yarn, fiber, or leather or similar fabric.

(d) "Consumables" means any product that is intended for consumption by individuals, or use by individuals for purposes of personal care or in the performance of services ordinarily rendered within the household, and that usually is consumed or expended in the course of consumption or use.

(e) "Distributor" means any individual, partnership, corporation, association, or other legal relationship that stands between the manufacturer and the retail seller in purchases, consignments, or contracts for sale of consumer goods.

(f) "Independent repair or service facility" or "independent service dealer" means any individual, partnership, corporation, association, or other legal entity, not an employee or subsidiary of a manufacturer or distributor, that engages in the business of servicing and repairing consumer goods.

(g) "Lease" means any contract for the lease or bailment for the use of consumer goods by an individual, for a term exceeding four months, primarily for personal, family, or household purposes, whether or not it is agreed that the lessee bears the risk of the consumer goods' depreciation.

(h) "Lessee" means an individual who leases consumer goods under a lease.

(i) "Lessor" means a person who regularly leases consumer goods under a lease.

(j) "Manufacturer" means any individual, partnership, corporation, association, or other legal relationship that manufactures, assembles, or produces consumer goods.

(k) "Place of business" means, for the purposes of any retail seller that sells consumer goods by catalog or mail order, the distribution point for consumer goods.

(*l*) "Retail seller," "seller," or "retailer" means any individual, partnership, corporation, association, or other legal relationship that engages in the business of selling or leasing consumer goods to retail buyers.

(m) "Return to the retail seller" means, for the purposes of any retail seller that sells consumer goods by catalog or mail order, the retail seller's place of business, as defined in subdivision (k).

(n) "Sale" means either of the following:

(1) The passing of title from the seller to the buyer for a price.

(2) A consignment for sale.

(o) "Service contract" means a contract in writing to perform, over a fixed period of time or for a specified duration, services relating to the maintenance or repair of a consumer product, except that this term does not include a policy of automobile insurance, as defined in Section 116 of the Insurance Code.

(p) "Assistive device" means any instrument, apparatus, or contrivance, including any component or part thereof or accessory thereto, that is used or intended to be used, to assist an individual with a disability in the mitigation or treatment of an injury or disease or to assist or affect or replace the structure or any function of the body of an individual with a disability, except that this term does not include prescriptive lenses and other ophthalmic goods unless they are sold or dispensed to a blind person, as defined in Section 19153 of the Welfare and Institutions Code and unless they are intended to assist the limited vision of the person so disabled.

(q) "Catalog or similar sale" means a sale in which neither the seller nor any employee or agent of the seller nor any person related to the seller nor any person with a financial interest in the sale participates in the diagnosis of the buyer's condition or in the selection or fitting of the device.

(r) "Home appliance" means any refrigerator, freezer, range, microwave oven, washer, dryer, dishwasher, garbage disposal, trash compactor, or room air-conditioner normally used or sold for personal, family, or household purposes.

(s) "Home electronic product" means any television, radio, antenna rotator, audio or video recorder or playback equipment, video camera, video game, video monitor, computer equipment, telephone, telecommunications equipment, electronic alarm system, electronic appliance control system, or other kind of electronic product, if it is normally used or sold for personal, family, or household purposes. The term includes any electronic accessory that is normally used or sold with a home electronic product for one of those purposes. The term excludes any single product with a wholesale price to the retail seller of less than fifty dollars ($50).

(t) "Member of the Armed Forces" means a person on full-time active duty in the Army, Navy, Marine Corps, Air Force, National Guard, Space Force, or Coast Guard. Full-time active duty shall also include active military service at a military service school designated by law or the Adjutant General of the Military Department concerned.

(u) "Clear and conspicuous" and "clearly and conspicuously" means a larger type than the surrounding text, or in a contrasting type, font, or color to the surrounding text of the same size, or set off from the surrounding text of the same size by symbols or other marks, in a manner that clearly calls attention to the language. For an audio disclosure, "clear and conspicuous" and "clearly and conspicuously" means in a volume and cadence sufficient to be readily audible and understandable.

(v) **"Motor home" has the same meaning as defined in Section 1793.22.**

(w) **"Mobilehome" means a vehicle as defined in Section 18008 of the Health and Safety Code.**

(x) **"Travel trailer" means a vehicular unit without motive power that is designed to be towed or carried by a motor vehicle. "Travel trailer" does not include a mobilehome. Leg.H.** Added Stats 1993 ch 1265 §12.5 (SB 798), operative January 1, 1998. Amended Stats 1994 ch 1010 §39.5 (SB 2053), operative January 1, 1998; Stats 1995 ch 461 §2 (AB 40), operative January 1, 1998; Stats 1997 ch 401 §63 (SB 780), operative January 1, 2003; Stats 2002 ch 405 §62 (AB 2973); Stats 2007 ch 151 §1 (SB 234), effective January 1, 2008; Stats 2021 ch 452 §1 (AB 1221), effective January 1, 2022; Stats 2022 ch 379 §2 (AB 1715), effective January 1, 2023; Stats 2024 ch 196 §1 (AB 1849), effective January 1, 2025.

Prior Law: Former §1791, similar to present section, was added Stats 1970 ch 1333 §1, amended 1971 ch 1523 §2, operative January 1, 1972; Stats 1976 ch 416 §1.5, Stats 1977 ch 598 §1, Stats 1978 ch 991 §1, Stats 1979 ch 1023 §1, Stats 1982 ch 619 §1, Stats 1984 ch 1169 §1, Stats 1985 ch 1047 §1, Stats 1988 ch 581 §1, Stats 1993 ch 1265 §12, operative until January 1, 1998, amended Stats 1994 ch 1010 §39, operative until January 1, 1998; Stats 1995 ch 461 §1, operative until January 1, 1998, Stats 1997 ch 401 §62, operative until January 1, 2003; Stats 1998 ch 196 §2, operative until January 1, 2003; Stats 2002 ch 405 §63, operative until January 1, 2008 and repealed, January 1, 2008, by its own terms.

Former §1791, similar to present section, was added Stats 1970 ch 1333 §1, amended 1971 ch 1523 §2, operative January 1, 1972; Stats 1976 ch 416 §1.5, Stats 1977 ch 598 §1, Stats 1978 ch 991 §1, Stats 1979 ch 1023 §1, Stats 1982 ch 619 §1, Stats 1984 ch 1169 §1, Stats 1985 ch 1047 §1, Stats 1988 ch 581 §1, Stats 1993 ch 1265 §12, operative until January 1, 1998, amended Stats 1994 ch 1010 §39, operative until January 1, 1998; Stats 1995 ch 461 §1, operative until January 1, 1998, Stats 1997 ch 401 §62, operative until January 1, 2003, Stats 1998 ch 196 §2, operative until January 1, 2003.

Former §1791, similar to UCC §§1201, 1205, 2104, was added Stats 1931 ch 1070 §1, and repealed Stats 1963 ch 819 §2, effective January 1, 1965.

Former CC §1791, similar to present section, was added Stats 1970 ch 1333 §1 and repealed operative January 1, 2008, by its own provisions. Stats 2002 ch 405 (AB 2973) §63.

Former CC §1791, similar to UCC §§1201, 1205, 2104, was added Stats 1931 ch 1070 §1 and repealed Stats 1963 ch 819 §2, effective January 1, 1965.

§1791.1. "Implied warranty of merchantability"; "Implied warranty of fitness"

As used in this chapter:

(a) "Implied warranty of merchantability" or "implied warranty that goods are merchantable" means that the consumer goods meet each of the following:

(1) Pass without objection in the trade under the contract description.

(2) Are fit for the ordinary purposes for which such goods are used.

(3) Are adequately contained, packaged, and labeled.

(4) Conform to the promises or affirmations of fact made on the container or label.

(b) "Implied warranty of fitness" means (1) that when the retailer, distributor, or manufacturer has reason to know any particular purpose for which the consumer goods are required, and further, that the buyer is relying on the skill and judgment of the seller to select and furnish suitable goods, then there is an implied warranty that the goods shall be fit for such purpose and (2) that when there is a sale of an assistive device sold at retail in this state, then there is an implied warranty by the retailer that the device is specifically fit for the particular needs of the buyer.

(c) The duration of the implied warranty of merchantability and where present the implied warranty of fitness shall be coextensive in duration with an express warranty which accompanies the consumer goods, provided the duration of the express warranty is reasonable; but in no event shall such implied warranty have a duration of less than 60 days nor more than one year following the sale of new consumer goods to a retail buyer. Where no duration for an express warranty is stated with respect to consumer goods, or parts thereof, the duration of the implied warranty shall be the maximum period prescribed above.

(d) Any buyer of consumer goods injured by a breach of the implied warranty of merchantability and where applicable by a breach of the implied warranty of fitness has the remedies provided in Chapter 6 (commencing with Section 2601) and Chapter 7 (commencing with Section 2701) of Division 2 of the Commercial Code, and, in any action brought under such provisions, Section 1794 of this chapter shall apply. **Leg.H.** Added Stats 1970 ch 1333 §1. Amended Stats 1971 ch 1523 §3, operative January 1, 1972; Stats 1978 ch 991 §2; Stats 1979 ch 1023 §1.5.

§1791.2. "Express warranty"

(a) "Express warranty" means:

(1) A written statement arising out of a sale to the consumer of a consumer good pursuant to which the manufacturer, distributor, or retailer undertakes to preserve or maintain the utility or performance of the consumer good or provide compensation if there is a failure in utility or performance; or

(2) In the event of any sample or model, that the whole of the goods conforms to such sample or model.

(b) It is not necessary to the creation of an express warranty that formal words such as "warrant" or "guarantee" be used, but if such words are used then an express warranty is created. An affirmation merely of the value of the goods or a statement purporting to be merely an opinion or commendation of the goods does not create a warranty.

(c) Statements or representations such as expressions of general policy concerning customer satisfaction which are not subject to any limitation do not create an express warranty. **Leg.H.** Added Stats 1970 ch 1333 §1. Amended Stats 1978 ch 991 §2.5.

§1791.3. "As is"; "With all faults"

As used in this chapter, a sale "as is" or "with all faults" means that the manufacturer, distributor, and retailer disclaim all implied warranties that would otherwise attach to the sale of consumer goods under the provisions of this chapter. **Leg.H.** Added Stats 1970 ch 1333 §1.

ARTICLE 3
Sale Warranties

Implied warranty of merchantability. §1792.
Manufacturer's implied warranty of fitness for particular purpose. §1792.1.
Retailer's or distributor's implied warranty of fitness for particular purpose. §1792.2.
Waiver of implied warranties. §1792.3.
Disclaimer of implied warranty. §1792.4.
"As is" sales. §1792.5.
Express warranties. §1793.
Express warranties prior to delivery of consumer good prohibited. § 1793.01.
Assistive devices; Hearing aids. §1793.02.
Motorized wheelchairs. §1793.025.
Manufacturers of consumer electronics or appliances making express warranties; Availability of service literature and parts. §1793.03.
Vehicle manufacturers altering new vehicles into housecars. §1793.05.
Form of express warranties; Requirements on distribution of warranty or product registration car or form, or electronic online warranty or product registration forms. §1793.1.
Duties of manufacturer making express warranty. §1793.2.
Reasonable number of attempts to conform vehicle to warranties; Dispute resolution process; Transfer of vehicle. §1793.22.
Disclosures required of seller of returned vehicle; "Lemon Law Buyback". §1793.23.
Warranty buyback notice. §1793.24.
Sales tax reimbursement to vehicle manufacturer after restitution under express warranty. §1793.25.
Restrictions on confidentiality clause, gag clause, or other similar clause associated with reacquisition of motor vehicle. §1793.26.
Failure to provide service facility in conjunction with express warranty. §1793.3.
Replacement of or reimbursement for clothing or consumables under express warranty. §1793.35.
Time to exercise option for service of item under express warranty. §1793.4.
Liability of manufacturer making express warranties for failure to maintain service facilities. §1793.5.
Manufacturer's liability to independent serviceman performing services or incurring obligations on express warranties. §1793.6.
Buyer's damages, penalties and fees. §1794.
Seller's and serviceman's damages. §1794.1.
Effect of unauthorized or unreasonable use of goods. §1794.3.
Service contract in lieu of warranty. §1794.4.
Vehicle, home appliance, or home electronic product service contract; Requirements; Applicability; Conflicts with insurance provisions. §1794.41.
Service contract; Duty of retailer; Applicability. §1794.45.
Alternative suggestions for repair of item under express warranty. §1794.5.
Liability of nonmanufacturer making express warranty. §1795.
Application of chapter to components of air conditioning system. §1795.1.
Rules applicable to leases of consumer goods. §1795.4.
Obligations of distributors or sellers of used goods. §1795.5.
Obligations of buy-here-pay-here dealer; Written warranty required. §1795.51.
Tolling the warranty period. §1795.6.
Effect of tolling on manufacturer's liability. §1795.7.
Application of chapter. §1795.8.

§1792. Implied warranty of merchantability

Unless disclaimed in the manner prescribed by this chapter, every sale of consumer goods that are sold at retail in this state shall be accompanied by the manufacturer's and the retail seller's implied warranty that the goods are merchantable. The retail seller shall have a right of indemnity against the manufacturer in the amount of any liability under this section. **Leg.H.** Added Stats 1970 ch 1333 §1. Amended Stats 1971 ch 1523 §4, operative January 1, 1972; Stats 1978 ch 991 §3.

Prior Law: Former CC §1792, similar to UCC §1106, was added Stats 1931 ch 1060 §1 and repealed Stats 1963 ch 819 §2, effective January 1, 1965.

Former CC §1792, relating to sale by auction, was enacted 1872 and repealed Stats 1931 ch 1070 §1.

§1792.1. Manufacturer's implied warranty of fitness for particular purpose

Every sale of consumer goods that are sold at retail in this state by a manufacturer who has reason to know at the time of the retail sale that the goods are required for a particular purpose and that the buyer is relying on the manufacturer's skill or judgment to select or furnish suitable goods shall be accompanied by such manufacturer's implied warranty of fitness. **Leg.H.** Added Stats 1970 ch 1333 §1. Amended Stats 1971 ch 1523 §5, operative January 1, 1972; Stats 1978 ch 991 §4.

§1792.2. Retailer's or distributor's implied warranty of fitness for particular purpose

(a) Every sale of consumer goods that are sold at retail in this state by a retailer or distributor who has reason to know at the time of the retail sale that the goods are required for a particular purpose, and that the buyer is relying on the retailer's or distributor's skill or judgment to select or furnish suitable goods shall be accompanied by such retailer's or distributor's implied warranty that the goods are fit for that purpose.

(b) Every sale of an assistive device sold at retail in this state shall be accompanied by the retail seller's implied warranty that the device is specifically fit for the particular needs of the buyer. **Leg.H.** Added Stats 1970 ch 1333 §1. Amended Stats 1971 ch 1523 §6, operative January 1, 1972; Stats 1978 ch 991 §5; Stats 1979 ch 1023 §2.

§1792.3. Waiver of implied warranties

No implied warranty of merchantability and, where applicable, no implied warranty of fitness shall be waived, except in the case of a sale of consumer goods on an "as is" or "with all faults" basis where the provisions of this chapter affecting "as is" or "with all faults" sales are strictly complied with. **Leg.H.** Added Stats 1970 ch 1333 §1.

§1792.4. Disclaimer of implied warranty

(a) No sale of goods, governed by the provisions of this chapter, on an "as is" or "with all faults" basis, shall be effective to disclaim the implied warranty of merchantability or, where applicable, the implied warranty of fitness, unless a conspicuous writing is attached to the goods which clearly informs the buyer, prior to the sale, in simple and concise language of each of the following:

(1) The goods are being sold on an "as is" or "with all faults" basis.

(2) The entire risk as to the quality and performance of the goods is with the buyer.

(3) Should the goods prove defective following their purchase, the buyer and not the manufacturer, distributor, or retailer assumes the entire cost of all necessary servicing or repair.

(b) In the event of sale of consumer goods by means of a mail order catalog, the catalog offering such goods shall contain the required writing as to each item so offered in lieu of the requirement of notification prior to the sale. **Leg.H.** Added Stats 1970 ch 1333 §1. Amended Stats 1971 ch 1523 §6.5, operative January 1, 1972.

§1792.5. "As is" sales

Every sale of goods that are governed by the provisions of this chapter, on an "as is" or "with all faults" basis, made in compliance with the provisions of this chapter, shall constitute a waiver by the buyer of the implied warranty of merchantability and, where applicable, of the implied warranty of fitness. **Leg.H.** Added Stats 1970 ch 1333 §1. Amended Stats 1971 ch 1523 §6.5, operative January 1, 1972.

§1793. Express warranties

Except as provided in Sections 1793.01 and 1793.02, nothing in this chapter shall affect the right of the manufacturer, distributor, or retailer to make express warranties with respect to consumer goods. However, a manufacturer, distributor, or retailer, in transacting a sale in which express warranties are given, may not limit, modify, or disclaim the implied warranties guaranteed by this chapter to the sale of consumer goods. **Leg.H.** Added Stats 1970 ch 1333 §1. Amended Stats 1971 ch 1523 §7, operative January 1, 1972; Stats 1978 ch 991 §6; Stats 1979 ch 1023 §3; Stats 2022 ch 464 §1 (AB 2912), effective January 1, 2023.

Prior Law: Former §1793, similar to UCC §1103, was added Stats 1931 ch 1070 §1 and repealed Stats 1963 ch 819 §2, effective January 1, 1965.

Former §1793, relating to when sale by auction is complete, was enacted 1872 and repealed Stats 1931 ch 1070 §1.

§ 1793.01. Express warranties prior to delivery of consumer good prohibited

A manufacturer, distributor, or retail seller shall not make an express warranty with respect to a consumer good that commences earlier than the date of delivery of the good. This section does not limit an express warranty made before July 1, 2023. **Leg.H.** Added Stats 2022 ch 464 §2 (AB 2912), effective January 1, 2023.

§1793.02. Assistive devices; Hearing aids

(a)(1) Except as provided in paragraph (2), all new and used assistive devices sold at retail in this state shall be accompanied by the retail seller's written warranty which shall contain the following language: "This assistive device is warranted to be specifically fit for the particular needs of you, the buyer. If the device is not specifically fit for your particular needs, it may be returned to the seller within 30 days of the date of actual receipt by you or completion of fitting by the seller, whichever occurs later. If you return the device, the seller will either adjust or replace the device or promptly refund the total amount paid. This warranty does not affect the protections and remedies you have under other laws." In lieu of the words "30 days" the retail seller may specify any longer period.

(2)(A) All new and used hearing aids sold in this state shall be accompanied by the retail seller's written warranty and shall contain the following language: "This hearing aid is warranted to be specifically fit for the particular needs of you, the buyer. If the hearing aid is not initially fit for your particular needs, it may be returned to the seller within 45 days of the initial date of delivery to you. If you return the hearing aid, the seller will either adjust or replace the hearing aid or promptly refund the total amount paid. This warranty does not affect the protections and remedies you have under other laws."

(B) In lieu of the words "45 days" the retail seller may specify any longer period.

(C) On the initial date of delivery, the retail seller shall revise the written warranty to include the initial date of delivery to the buyer of the hearing aid and expiration date of the warranty.

(b) The language prescribed in subdivision (a) shall appear on the first page of the warranty in at least 10-point bold type. The warranty shall be delivered to the buyer at the time of the sale of the device.

(c) If the buyer returns the device within the period specified in the written warranty, the seller shall, without charge and within a reasonable time, adjust the device or, if appropriate, replace it with a device that is specifically fit for the particular needs of the buyer. If the seller does not adjust or replace the device so that it is specifically fit for the particular needs of the buyer, the seller shall promptly refund to the buyer the total amount paid, the transaction shall be deemed rescinded, and the seller shall promptly return to the buyer all payments and any assistive device or other consideration exchanged as part of the transaction and shall promptly cancel or cause to be canceled all contracts, instruments, and security agreements executed by the buyer in connection with the sale. When a sale is rescinded under this section, no charge, penalty, or other fee may be imposed in connection with the purchase, fitting, financing, or return of the device.

(d) With respect to the retail sale of an assistive device to an individual, organization, or agency known by the seller to be purchasing for the ultimate user of the device, this section and subdivision (b) of Section 1792.2 shall be construed to require that the device be specifically fit for the particular needs of the ultimate user.

(e) This section and subdivision (b) of Section 1792.2 shall not apply to any of the following sales of assistive devices:

(1) A catalog or similar sale, as defined in subdivision (q) of Section 1791, except a sale of a hearing aid.

(2) A sale which involves a retail sale price of less than fifteen dollars ($15).

(3) A surgical implant performed by a physician and surgeon, or a restoration or dental prosthesis provided by a dentist.

(f) The rights and remedies of the buyer under this section and subdivision (b) of Section 1792.2 are not subject to waiver under Section 1792.3. The rights and remedies of the buyer under this section and subdivision (b) of Section 1792.2 are cumulative, and shall not be construed to affect the obligations of the retail seller or any other party or to supplant the rights or remedies of the buyer under any other section of this chapter or under any other law or instrument.

(g) Section 1795.5 shall not apply to a sale of used assistive devices, and for the purposes of the Song-Beverly Consumer Warranty Act the buyer of a used assistive device shall have the same rights and remedies as the buyer of a new assistive device.

(h) The language in subdivision (a) shall not constitute an express warranty for purposes of Sections 1793.2 and 1793.3. **Leg.H.** Added Stats 1979 ch 1023 §4. Amended Stats 1982 ch 619 §2; Stats 1991 ch 228 §2 (AB 1889); Stats 2014 ch 226 §1 (SB 1326), effective January 1, 2015.

§1793.025. Motorized wheelchairs

(a) All new and used wheelchairs, including, but not limited to, wheelchairs that are motorized or have been otherwise customized to suit the needs of the user, shall be accompanied by the manufacturer's or lessor's written express warranty that the wheelchair is free of defects. The duration of the warranty shall be for a period of at least one year from the date of the first delivery of a new wheelchair to the consumer, or at least 60 days from the date of the first delivery of a used, refurbished, or reconditioned wheelchair to the consumer. If the written express warranty is not furnished to the consumer, the wheelchair nonetheless shall be deemed to be covered by the express warranty. This section shall not apply to wheelchairs manufactured specifically for athletic, competitive, or off-road use.

(b) The provisions of this chapter for express warranties govern the express warranty described in subdivision (a), whether or not those provisions only apply to the sale, and not the lease, of goods.

(c) A reasonable number of attempts have been made to conform a wheelchair to the express warranty if, within the warranty period or within one year of inception of the warranty, whichever occurs first, (1) the same nonconformity has been subject to repair four or more times by the manufacturer, lessor, or an agent thereof, and continues to exist, or (2) the wheelchair is out of service by reason of repair of nonconformities by the manufacturer, lessor, or an agent thereof, for a cumulative total of more than 30 calendar days since inception of the warranty.

(d) No wheelchair that has been returned to the manufacturer, lessor, or an agent thereof, by the consumer for failure to repair a nonconformity after a reasonable number of attempts, either in this state or in another state pursuant to a similar statute of that state, may be sold or leased again in this state unless the reasons for the return are fully disclosed to the prospective buyer or lessee.

(e) If the wheelchair is out of service for a period of at least 24 hours for the repair of a nonconformity by the manufacturer, lessor, or agent thereof, a temporary replacement wheelchair shall be made available to the consumer, if requested. The provider of the temporary replacement wheelchair may not charge the consumer more than the cost to the provider to make the wheelchair available to the consumer. Nothing in this subdivision is intended to prevent a consumer and a provider from negotiating an agreement in which the provider assumes the cost of providing a temporary replacement wheelchair to the consumer. **Leg.H.** Added Stats 1993 ch 374 §1 (AB 1945). Amended Stats 1995 ch 461 §3 (AB 40).

§1793.03. Manufacturers of consumer electronics or appliances making express warranties; Availability of service literature and parts

(a) Every manufacturer making an express warranty with respect to an electronic or appliance product described in subdivision (h), (i), (j), or (k) of Section 9801 of the Business and Professions Code, with a wholesale price to the retailer of not less than fifty dollars ($50) and not more than ninety-nine dollars and ninety-nine cents ($99.99), shall make available to service and repair facilities sufficient service literature and functional parts to effect the repair of a product for at least three years after the date a product model or type was manufactured, regardless of whether the three-year period exceeds the warranty period for the product.

(b) Every manufacturer making an express warranty with respect to an electronic or appliance product described in subdivision (h), (i), (j), or (k) of Section 9801 of the Business and Professions Code, with a wholesale price to the retailer of one hundred dollars ($100) or more, shall make available to service and repair facilities sufficient service literature and functional parts to effect the repair of a product for at least seven years after the date a product model or type was manufactured, regardless of whether the seven-year period exceeds the warranty period for the product **Leg.H.** Added Stats 1986 ch 547 §1.

§1793.05. Vehicle manufacturers altering new vehicles into housecars

Vehicle manufacturers who alter new vehicles into housecars shall, in addition to any new product warranty, assume any warranty responsibility of the original vehicle manufacturer for any and all components of the finished product which are, by virtue of any act of the alterer, no longer covered by the warranty issued by the original vehicle manufacturer. **Leg.H.** Added Stats 1977 ch 873 §1, operative July 1, 1978.

§1793.1. Form of express warranties; Requirements on distribution of warranty or product registration car or form, or electronic online warranty or product registration forms

(a)(1) Every manufacturer, distributor, or retailer making express warranties with respect to consumer goods shall fully set forth those warranties in simple and readily understood language, which shall clearly identify the party making the express warranties, and which shall conform to the federal standards for disclosure of warranty terms and conditions set forth in the federal Magnuson-Moss Warranty-Federal Trade Commission Improvement Act (15 U.S.C. Sec. 2301 et seq.), and in the regulations of the Federal Trade Commission adopted pursuant to the provisions of that act. If the manufacturer, distributor, or retailer provides a warranty or product registration card or form, or an electronic online warranty or product registration form, to be completed and returned by the consumer, the card or form shall contain statements, each displayed in a clear and conspicuous manner, that do all of the following:

(A) Informs the consumer that the card or form is for product registration.

(B) Informs the consumer that failure to complete and return the card or form does not diminish his or her warranty rights.

(2) Every work order or repair invoice for warranty repairs or service shall clearly and conspicuously incorporate in 10-point boldface type the following statement either on the face of the work order or repair invoice, or on the reverse side, or on an attachment to the work order or repair invoice: "A buyer of this product in California has the right to have this product serviced or repaired during the warranty period. The warranty period will be extended for the number of whole days that the product has been out of the buyer's hands for warranty repairs. If a defect exists within the warranty period, the warranty will not expire until the defect has been fixed. The warranty period will also be extended if the warranty repairs have not been performed due to delays caused by circumstances beyond the control of the buyer, or if the warranty repairs did not remedy the defect and the buyer notifies the manufacturer or seller of the failure of the repairs within 60 days after they were completed. If, after a reasonable number of attempts, the defect has not been fixed, the buyer may return this product for a replacement or a refund subject, in either case, to deduction of a reasonable charge for usage. This time extension does not affect the protections or remedies the buyer has under other laws."

If the required notice is placed on the reverse side of the work order or repair invoice, the face of the work order or repair invoice shall include the following notice in 10-point boldface type: "Notice to Consumer: Please read important information on back."

A copy of the work order or repair invoice and any attachment shall be presented to the buyer at the time that warranty service or repairs are made.

(b) No warranty or product registration card or form, or an electronic online warranty or product registration form, may be labeled as a warranty registration or a warranty confirmation.

(c) The requirements imposed by this section on the distribution of any warranty or product registration card or form, or an electronic online warranty or product registration form, shall become effective on January 1, 2004.

(d) This section does not apply to any warranty or product registration card or form that was printed prior to January 1, 2004, and was shipped or included with a product that was placed in the stream of commerce prior to January 1, 2004.

(e) Every manufacturer, distributor, or retailer making express warranties and who elects to maintain service and repair facilities within this state pursuant to this chapter shall perform one or more of the following:

(1) At the time of sale, provide the buyer with the name and address of each service and repair facility within this state.

(2) At the time of the sale, provide the buyer with the name and address and telephone number of a service and repair facility central directory within this state, or the toll-free telephone number of a service and repair facility central directory outside this state. It shall be the duty of the central directory to provide, upon inquiry, the name and address of the authorized service and repair facility nearest the buyer.

(3) Maintain at the premises of retail sellers of the warrantor's consumer goods a current listing of the warrantor's authorized service and repair facilities, or retail sellers to whom the consumer goods are to be returned for service and repair, whichever is applicable, within this state. It shall be the duty of every retail seller provided with that listing to provide, on inquiry, the name, address, and telephone number of the nearest authorized service and repair facility, or the retail seller to whom the consumer goods are to be returned for service and repair, whichever is applicable. **Leg.H.** Added Stats 1970 ch 1333 §1. Amended Stats 1971 ch 1523 §8, operative January 1, 1972; Stats 1972 ch 1293 §1; Stats 1980 ch 394 §1; Stats 1981 ch 150 §1, effective July 8, 1981; Stats 1982 ch 381 §1; Stats 2002 ch 306 §1 (SB 1765).

§1793.2. Duties of manufacturer making express warranty

(a) Every manufacturer of consumer goods sold in this state and for which the manufacturer has made an express warranty shall:

(1)(A) Maintain in this state sufficient service and repair facilities reasonably close to all areas where its consumer goods are sold to carry out the terms of those warranties or designate and authorize in this state as service and repair facilities independent repair or service facilities reasonably close to all areas where its consumer goods are sold to carry out the terms of the warranties.

(B) As a means of complying with this paragraph, a manufacturer may enter into warranty service contracts with independent service and repair facilities. The warranty service contracts may provide for a fixed schedule of rates to be charged for warranty service or warranty repair work. However, the rates fixed by those contracts shall be in conformity with the requirements of subdivision (c) of Section 1793.3. The rates established pursuant to subdivision (c) of Section 1793.3, between the manufacturer and the independent service and repair facility, do not preclude a good faith discount that is reasonably related to reduced credit and general overhead cost factors arising from the manufacturer's payment of warranty charges direct to the independent service and repair facility. The warranty service contracts authorized by this paragraph may not be executed to cover a period of time in excess of one year, and may be renewed only by a separate, new contract or letter of agreement between the manufacturer and the independent service and repair facility.

(2) In the event of a failure to comply with paragraph (1) [1], be subject to Section 1793.5.

(3) Make available to authorized service and repair facilities sufficient service literature and replacement parts to effect repairs during the express warranty period.

(b) Where those service and repair facilities are maintained in this state and service or repair of the goods is necessary because they do not conform with the applicable express warranties, service and repair shall be commenced within a reasonable time by the manufacturer or its representative in this state. Unless the buyer agrees in writing to the contrary, the goods shall be serviced or repaired so as to conform to the applicable warranties within 30 days. Delay caused by conditions beyond the control of the manufacturer or its representatives shall serve to extend this 30-day requirement. Where delay arises, conforming goods shall be tendered as soon as possible following termination of the condition giving rise to the delay.

(c) The buyer shall deliver nonconforming goods to the manufacturer's service and repair facility within this state, unless, due to reasons of size and weight, or method of attachment, or method of installation, or nature of the nonconformity, delivery cannot reasonably be accomplished. If the buyer cannot return the nonconforming goods for any of these reasons, [2] **the buyer** shall notify the manufacturer or its nearest service and repair facility within the state. Written notice of nonconformity to the manufacturer or its service and repair facility shall constitute return of the goods for purposes of this section. Upon receipt of that notice of nonconformity, the manufacturer shall, at its option, service or repair the goods at the buyer's residence, or pick up the goods for service and repair, or arrange for transporting the goods to its service and repair facility. All reasonable costs of transporting the goods when a buyer cannot return them for any of the above reasons shall be at the manufacturer's expense. The reasonable costs of transporting nonconforming goods after delivery to the service and repair facility until return of the goods to the buyer shall be at the manufacturer's expense.

(d)(1) Except as provided in paragraph (2), if the manufacturer or its representative in this state does not service or repair the goods to conform to the applicable express warranties after a reasonable number of attempts, the manufacturer shall either replace the goods or reimburse the buyer in an amount equal to the purchase price paid by the buyer, less that amount directly attributable to use by the buyer prior to the discovery of the nonconformity. **However, if the manufacturer or its representative in this state does not service or repair a travel trailer or a portion of a motor home designed, used, or maintained for human habitation, to conform to the applicable express warranties after a reasonable number of attempts, the buyer shall be free to elect reimbursement in lieu of replacement, and in no event shall the buyer be required by the manufacturer to accept a replacement travel trailer or motor home.**

(2) If the manufacturer or its representative in this state is unable to service or repair a new motor vehicle, as that term is defined in paragraph (2) of subdivision (e) of Section 1793.22, to conform to the applicable express warranties after a reasonable number of attempts, the manufacturer shall either promptly replace the new motor vehicle in accordance with subparagraph (A) or promptly make restitution to the buyer in accordance with subparagraph (B). However, the buyer shall be free to elect restitution in lieu of replacement, and in no event shall the buyer be required by the manufacturer to accept a replacement vehicle.

(A) In the case of replacement, the manufacturer shall replace the buyer's vehicle with a new motor vehicle substantially identical to the vehicle replaced. The replacement vehicle shall be accompanied by all express and implied warranties that normally accompany new motor vehicles of that specific kind. The manufacturer also shall pay for, or to, the buyer the amount of any sales or use tax, license fees, registration fees, and other official fees which the buyer is obligated to pay in connection with the replacement, plus any incidental damages to which the buyer is entitled under Section 1794, including, but not limited to, reasonable repair, towing, and rental car costs actually incurred by the buyer.

(B) In the case of restitution, the manufacturer shall make restitution in an amount equal to the actual price paid or payable by the buyer, including any charges for transportation and manufacturer-installed options, but excluding nonmanufacturer items installed by a dealer or the buyer, and including any collateral charges such as sales or use tax, license fees, registration fees, and other official fees, plus any incidental damages to which the buyer is entitled under Section 1794, including, but not limited to, reasonable repair, towing, and rental car costs actually incurred by the buyer.

(C) When the manufacturer replaces the new motor vehicle pursuant to subparagraph (A), the buyer shall only be liable to pay the manufacturer an amount directly attributable to use by the buyer of the replaced vehicle prior to the time the buyer first delivered the vehicle to the manufacturer or distributor, or its authorized service and repair facility for correction of the problem that gave rise to the nonconformity. When restitution is made pursuant to subparagraph (B), the amount to be paid by the manufacturer to the buyer may be reduced by the manufacturer by that amount directly attributable to use by the buyer prior to the time the buyer first delivered the vehicle to the manufacturer or distributor, or its authorized service and repair facility for correction of the problem that gave rise to the nonconformity. The amount directly attributable to use by the buyer shall be determined by multiplying the actual price of the new motor vehicle paid or payable by the buyer, including any charges for transportation and manufacturer-installed options, by a fraction having as its denominator 120,000 and having as its numerator the number of miles traveled by the new motor vehicle prior to the time the buyer first delivered the vehicle to the manufacturer or distributor, or its authorized service and repair facility for correction of the problem that gave rise to the nonconformity. Nothing in this paragraph shall in any way limit the rights or remedies available to the buyer under any other law.

(D) Pursuant to Section 1795.4, a buyer of a new motor vehicle shall also include a lessee of a new motor vehicle.

(e)(1) If the goods cannot practicably be serviced or repaired by the manufacturer or its representative to conform to the applicable express warranties because of the method of installation or because the goods have become so affixed to real property as to become a part thereof, the manufacturer shall either replace and install the goods or reimburse the buyer in an amount equal to the purchase price paid by the buyer, including installation costs, less that amount directly attributable to use by the buyer prior to the discovery of the nonconformity.

(2) With respect to claims arising out of deficiencies in the construction of a new residential dwelling, paragraph (1) shall not apply to either of the following:

(A) A product that is not a manufactured product, as defined in subdivision (g) of Section 896.

(B) A claim against a person or entity that is not the manufacturer that originally made the express warranty for that manufactured product.

Leg.H. Added Stats 1970 ch 1333 §1. Amended Stats 1971 ch 1523 §9, operative January 1, 1972; Stats 1976 ch 416 §2; Stats 1978 ch 991 §7; Stats 1982 ch 388 §1; Stats 1986 ch 547 §2; Stats 1987 ch 1280 §2; Stats 1988 ch 697 §1; Stats 1989 ch 193 §2; Stats 1991 ch 689 §10 (AB 211); Stats 1992 ch 1232 §6 (SB 1762); Stats 2004 ch 331 §1 (AB 2723); Stats 2011 ch 727 §1 (AB 242), effective January 1, 2012; Stats 2024 ch 196 §2 (AB 1849), effective January 1, 2025.

§1793.2. 2024 Deletes. [1] of this subdivision [2] he or she

2011 Note: Sections 1 and 2 of this act are declaratory of existing law. Stats 2011 ch 727 (AB 242) §21.

§1793.22. Reasonable number of attempts to conform vehicle to warranties; Dispute resolution process; Transfer of vehicle

(a) This section shall be known and may be cited as the Tanner Consumer Protection Act.

(b) It shall be presumed that a reasonable number of attempts have been made to conform a new motor vehicle to the applicable express warranties if, within 18 months from delivery to the buyer or 18,000 miles on the odometer of the vehicle, whichever occurs first, one or more of the following occurs:

(1) The same nonconformity results in a condition that is likely to cause death or serious bodily injury if the vehicle is driven and the nonconformity has been subject to repair two or more times by the manufacturer or its agents, and the buyer or lessee has at least once directly notified the manufacturer of the need for the repair of the nonconformity.

(2) The same nonconformity has been subject to repair four or more times by the manufacturer or its agents and the buyer has at least once directly notified the manufacturer of the need for the repair of the nonconformity.

(3) The vehicle is out of service by reason of repair of nonconformities by the manufacturer or its agents for a cumulative total of more than 30 calendar days since delivery of the vehicle to the buyer. The 30-day limit shall be extended only if repairs cannot be performed due to conditions beyond the control of the manufacturer or its agents. The buyer shall be required to directly notify the manufacturer pursuant to paragraphs (1) and (2) only if the manufacturer has clearly and conspicuously disclosed to the buyer, with the warranty or the owner's manual, the provisions of this section and that of subdivision (d) of Section 1793.2, including the requirement that the buyer must notify the manufacturer directly pursuant to paragraphs (1) and (2). The notification, if required, shall be sent to the address, if any, specified clearly and conspicuously by the manufacturer in the warranty or owner's manual. This presumption shall be a rebuttable presumption affecting the burden of proof, and it may be asserted by the buyer in any civil action, including an action in small claims court, or other formal or informal proceeding.

(c) If a qualified third-party dispute resolution process exists, and the buyer receives timely notification in writing of the availability of that qualified third-party dispute resolution process with a description of its operation and effect, the presumption in subdivision (b) may not be asserted by the buyer until after the buyer has initially resorted to the qualified third-party dispute resolution process as required in subdivision (d). Notification of the availability of the qualified third-party dispute resolution process is not timely if the buyer suffers any prejudice resulting from any delay in giving the notification. If a qualified third-party dispute resolution process does not exist, or if the buyer is dissatisfied with that third-party decision, or if the manufacturer or its agent neglects to promptly fulfill the terms of the qualified third-party dispute resolution process decision after the decision is accepted by the buyer, the buyer may assert the presumption provided in subdivision (b) in an action to enforce the buyer's rights under subdivision (d) of Section 1793.2. The findings and decision of a qualified third-party dispute resolution process shall be admissible in evidence in the action without further foundation. Any period of limitation of actions under any federal or California laws with respect to any person shall be extended for a period equal to the number of days between the date a complaint is filed with a third-party dispute resolution process and the date of its decision or the date before which the manufacturer or its agent is required by the decision to fulfill its terms if the decision is accepted by the buyer, whichever occurs later.

(d) A qualified third-party dispute resolution process shall be one that does all of the following:

(1) Complies with the minimum requirements of the Federal Trade Commission for informal dispute settlement procedures as set forth in Part 703 of Title 16 of the Code of Federal Regulations, as those regulations read on January 1, 1987.

(2) Renders decisions which are binding on the manufacturer if the buyer elects to accept the decision.

(3) Prescribes a reasonable time, not to exceed 30 days after the decision is accepted by the buyer, within which the manufacturer or its agent must fulfill the terms of its decisions.

(4) Provides arbitrators who are assigned to decide disputes with copies of, and instruction in, the provisions of the Federal Trade Commission's regulations in Part 703 of Title 16 of the Code of Federal Regulations as those regulations read on January 1, 1987, Division 2 (commencing with Section 2101) of the Commercial Code, and this chapter.

(5) Requires the manufacturer, when the process orders, under the terms of this chapter, either that the nonconforming motor vehicle be replaced if the buyer consents to this remedy or that restitution be made to the buyer, to replace the motor vehicle or make restitution in accordance with paragraph (2) of subdivision (d) of Section 1793.2.

(6) Provides, at the request of the arbitrator or a majority of the arbitration panel, for an inspection and written report on the condition of a nonconforming motor vehicle, at no cost to the buyer, by an automobile expert who is independent of the manufacturer.

(7) Takes into account, in rendering decisions, all legal and equitable factors, including, but not limited to, the written warranty, the rights and remedies conferred in regulations of the Federal Trade Commission contained in Part 703 of Title 16 of the Code of Federal Regulations as those regulations read on January 1, 1987, Division 2 (commencing with Section 2101) of the Commercial Code, this chapter, and any other equitable considerations appropriate in the circumstances. Nothing in this chapter requires that, to be certified as a qualified third-party dispute resolution process pursuant to this section, decisions of the process must consider or provide remedies in the form of awards of punitive damages or multiple damages, under subdivision (c) of Section 1794, or of attorneys' fees under subdivision (d) of Section 1794, or of consequential damages other than as provided in subdivisions (a) and (b) of Section 1794, including, but not limited to, reasonable repair, towing, and rental car costs actually incurred by the buyer.

(8) Requires that no arbitrator deciding a dispute may be a party to the dispute and that no other person, including an employee, agent, or dealer for the manufacturer, may be allowed to participate substantively in the merits of any dispute with the arbitrator unless the buyer is allowed to participate also. Nothing in this subdivision prohibits any member of an arbitration board from deciding a dispute.

(9) Obtains and maintains certification by the Department of Consumer Affairs pursuant to Chapter 9 (commencing with Section 472) of Division 1 of the Business and Professions Code.

(e) For the purposes of subdivision (d) of Section 1793.2 and this section, the following terms have the following meanings:

(1) "Nonconformity" means a nonconformity which substantially impairs the use, value, or safety of the new motor vehicle to the buyer or lessee.

(2) "New motor vehicle" means a new motor vehicle that is bought or used primarily for personal, family, or household purposes. "New motor vehicle" also means a new motor vehicle with a gross vehicle weight under 10,000 pounds that is bought or used primarily for business purposes by a person, including a partnership, limited liability company, corporation, association, or any other legal entity, to which not more than five motor vehicles are registered in this state. "New motor vehicle" includes the chassis, chassis cab, and that portion of a motor home devoted to its propulsion, but does not include any portion designed, used, or maintained primarily for human habitation, a dealer-owned vehicle and a "demonstrator" or other motor vehicle sold with a manufacturer's new car warranty but does not include a motorcycle or a motor vehicle which is not registered under the Vehicle Code because it is to be operated or used exclusively off the highways. A demonstrator is a vehicle assigned by a dealer for the purpose of demonstrating qualities and characteristics common to vehicles of the same or similar model and type.

(3) "Motor home" means a vehicular unit built on, or permanently attached to, a self-propelled motor vehicle chassis, chassis cab, or van, which becomes an integral part of the completed vehicle, designed for human habitation for recreational or emergency occupancy.

(f)(1) Except as provided in paragraph (2), no person shall sell, either at wholesale or retail, lease, or transfer a motor vehicle transferred by a buyer or lessee to a manufacturer pursuant to paragraph (2) of subdivision (d) of Section 1793.2 or a similar statute of any other state, unless the nature of the nonconformity experienced by the original buyer or lessee is clearly and conspicuously disclosed to the prospective buyer, lessee, or transferee, the nonconformity is corrected, and the manufacturer warrants to the new buyer, lessee, or transferee in writing for a period of one year that the motor vehicle is free of that nonconformity.

(2) Except for the requirement that the nature of the nonconformity be disclosed to the transferee, paragraph (1) does not apply to the transfer of a motor vehicle to an educational institution if the purpose of the transfer is to make the motor vehicle available for use in automotive repair courses. **Leg.H.** Added Stats 1992 ch 1232 §7 (SB 1762). Amended Stats 1998 ch 352 §1 (AB 1848); Stats 1999 ch 83 §21 (SB 966), ch 448 §1 (AB 1290) (ch 448 prevails); Stats 2000 ch 679 §1 (SB 1718).

§1793.23. Disclosures required of seller of returned vehicle; "Lemon Law Buyback"

(a) The Legislature finds and declares all of the following:

(1) That the expansion of state warranty laws covering new and used cars has given important and valuable protection to consumers.

(2) That, in states without this valuable warranty protection, used and irrepairable motor vehicles are being resold in the marketplace without notice to the subsequent purchaser.

(3) That other states have addressed this problem by requiring notices on the title of these vehicles or other notice procedures to warn consumers that the motor vehicles were repurchased by a dealer or manufacturer because the vehicle could not be repaired in a reasonable length of time or a reasonable number of repair attempts or the dealer or manufacturer was not willing to repair the vehicle.

(4) That these notices serve the interests of consumers who have a right to information relevant to their buying decisions.

(5) That the disappearance of these notices upon the transfer of title from another state to this state encourages the transport of "lemons" to this state for sale to the drivers of this state.

(b) This section and Section 1793.24 shall be known, and may be cited as, the Automotive Consumer Notification Act.

(c) Any manufacturer who reacquires or assists a dealer or lienholder to reacquire a motor vehicle registered in this state, any other state, or a federally administered district shall, prior to any sale, lease, or transfer of the vehicle in this state, or prior to exporting the vehicle to another state for sale, lease, or transfer if the vehicle was registered in this state and reacquired pursuant to paragraph (2) of subdivision (d) of Section 1793.2, cause the vehicle to be retitled in the name of the manufacturer, request the Department of Motor Vehicles to inscribe the ownership certificate with the notation "Lemon Law Buyback," and affix a decal to the vehicle in accordance with Section 11713.12 of the Vehicle Code if the manufacturer knew or should have known that the vehicle is required by law to be replaced, accepted for restitution due to the failure of the manufacturer to conform the vehicle to applicable warranties pursuant to paragraph (2) of subdivision (d) of Section 1793.2, or accepted for restitution by the manufacturer due to the failure of the manufacturer to conform the vehicle to warranties required by any other applicable law of the state, any other state, or federal law.

(d) Any manufacturer who reacquires or assists a dealer or lienholder to reacquire a motor vehicle in response to a request by the buyer or lessee that the vehicle be either replaced or accepted for restitution because the vehicle did not conform to express warranties shall, prior to the sale, lease, or other transfer of the vehicle, execute and deliver to the subsequent transferee a notice and obtain the transferee's written acknowledgment of a notice, as prescribed by Section 1793.24.

(e) Any person, including any dealer, who acquires a motor vehicle for resale and knows or should have known that the vehicle was reacquired by the vehicle's manufacturer in response to a request by the last retail owner or lessee of the vehicle that it be replaced or accepted for restitution because the vehicle did not conform to express warranties shall, prior to the sale, lease, or other transfer, execute and deliver to the subsequent transferee a notice and obtain the transferee's written acknowledgment of a notice, as prescribed by Section 1793.24.

(f) Any person, including any manufacturer or dealer, who sells, leases, or transfers ownership of a motor vehicle when the vehicle's ownership certificate is inscribed with the notation "Lemon Law Buyback" shall, prior to the sale, lease, or ownership transfer of the vehicle, provide the transferee with a disclosure statement signed by the transferee that states:

"THIS VEHICLE WAS REPURCHASED BY ITS MANUFACTURER DUE TO A DEFECT IN THE VEHICLE PURSUANT TO CONSUMER WARRANTY LAWS. THE TITLE TO THIS VEHICLE HAS BEEN PERMANENTLY BRANDED WITH THE NOTATION 'LEMON LAW BUYBACK'."

(g) The disclosure requirements in subdivisions (d), (e), and (f) are cumulative with all other consumer notice requirements and do not relieve any person, including any dealer or manufacturer, from complying with any other applicable law, including any requirement of subdivision (f) of Section 1793.22.

(h) For purposes of this section, "dealer" means any person engaged in the business of selling, offering for sale, or negotiating the retail sale of, a used motor vehicle or selling motor vehicles as a broker or agent for another, including the officers, agents, and employees of the person and any combination or association of dealers. **Leg.H.** Added Stats 1995 ch 503 §1 (AB 1381). Amended Stats 1998 ch 932 §7 (AB 1094).

1995 Note: This act shall apply only to vehicles reacquired by a manufacturer on or after January 1, 1996, and shall not affect any proceeding relating to vehicles reacquired prior to January 1, 1996. Stats 1995 ch 503 §7.

§1793.24. Warranty buyback notice

(a) The notice required in subdivisions (d) and (e) of Section 1793.23 shall be prepared by the manufacturer of the reacquired vehicle and shall disclose all of the following:

(1) Year, make, model, and vehicle identification number of the vehicle.

(2) Whether the title to the vehicle has been inscribed with the notation "Lemon Law Buyback."

(3) The nature of each nonconformity reported by the original buyer or lessee of the vehicle.

(4) Repairs, if any, made to the vehicle in an attempt to correct each nonconformity reported by the original buyer or lessee.

(b) The notice shall be on a form 8½ × 11 inches in size and printed in no smaller than 10-point black type on a white background.

The form shall only contain the following information prior to it being filled out by the manufacturer:

WARRANTY BUYBACK NOTICE

(Check One)

☐ This vehicle was repurchased by the vehicle's manufacturer after the last retail owner or lessee requested its repurchase due to the problem(s) listed below.

☐ THIS VEHICLE WAS REPURCHASED BY ITS MANUFACTURER DUE TO A DEFECT IN THE VEHICLE PURSUANT TO CONSUMER WARRANTY LAWS. THE TITLE TO THIS VEHICLE HAS BEEN PERMANENTLY BRANDED WITH THE NOTATION "LEMON LAW BUYBACK." Under California law, the manufacturer must warrant to you, for a one year period, that the vehicle is free of the problem(s) listed below.

V.I.N.	Year	Make	Model
Problem(s) Reported by Original Owner		Repairs Made, if any, to Correct Reported Problem(s)	

Signature of Manufacturer _____ Date _____

Signature of Dealer(s) _____ Date _____

Signature of Retail Buyer or Lessee _____ Date _____

(c) The manufacturer shall provide an executed copy of the notice to the manufacturer's transferee. Each transferee, including a dealer, to whom the motor vehicle is transferred prior to its sale to a retail buyer or lessee shall be provided an executed copy of the notice by the previous transferor. **Leg.H.** Added Stats 1995 ch 503 §2 (AB 1381).

1995 Note: This act shall apply only to vehicles reacquired by a manufacturer on or after January 1, 1996, and shall not affect any proceeding relating to vehicles reacquired prior to January 1, 1996. Stats 1995 ch 503 §7.

§1793.25. Sales tax reimbursement to vehicle manufacturer after restitution under express warranty

(a) Notwithstanding Part 1 (commencing with Section 6001) of Division 2 of the Revenue and Taxation Code, the State Board of Equalization shall reimburse the manufacturer of a new motor vehicle for an amount equal to the sales tax or use tax which the manufacturer pays to or for the buyer or lessee when providing a replacement vehicle pursuant to subparagraph (A) of paragraph (2) of subdivision (d) of Section 1793.2 or includes in making restitution to the buyer or lessee pursuant to subparagraph (B) of paragraph (2) of subdivision (d) of Section 1793.2, when the manufacturer provides satisfactory proof that it has complied with subdivision (c) of Section 1793.23, and satisfactory proof is provided for one of the following:

(1) The retailer of the motor vehicle for which the manufacturer is making restitution has reported and paid the sales tax on the gross receipts from the sale of that motor vehicle.

(2) The buyer of the motor vehicle has paid the use tax on the sales price for the storage, use, or other consumption of that motor vehicle in this state.

(3) The lessee of the motor vehicle has paid the use tax on the rentals payable from the lease of that motor vehicle.

(b) The State Board of Equalization may adopt rules and regulations to carry out, facilitate compliance with, or prevent circumvention or evasion of, this section.

(c) This section shall not change the application of the sales and use tax to the gross receipts, the rentals payable, and the sales price from the sale, lease, and the storage, use, or other consumption, in this state of tangible personal property pursuant to Part 1 (commencing with Section 6001) of Division 2 of the Revenue and Taxation Code.

(d) The manufacturer's claim for reimbursement and the State Board of Equalization's approval or denial of the claim shall be subject to the provisions of Article 1 (commencing with Section 6901) of Chapter 7 of Part 1 of Division 2 of the Revenue and Taxation Code, except Sections 6907 and 6908, insofar as those provisions are not inconsistent with this section.

(e) For purposes of this section, the amount of use tax that the State Board of Equalization is required to reimburse the manufacturer shall be limited to the amount of use tax the manufacturer is required to pay to or for the lessee pursuant to Section 1793.2. **Leg.H.** Added Stats 1987 ch 1280 §3. Amended Stats 1995 ch 503 §3 (AB 1381); Stats 2011 ch 727 §2 (AB 242), effective January 1, 2012.

2011 Note: Sections 1 and 2 of this act are declaratory of existing law. Stats 2011 ch 727 (AB 242) §21.

1995 Note: This act shall apply only to vehicles reacquired by a manufacturer on or after January 1, 1996, and shall not affect any proceeding relating to vehicles reacquired prior to January 1, 1996. Stats 1995 ch 503 §7.

§1793.26. Restrictions on confidentiality clause, gag clause, or other similar clause associated with reacquisition of motor vehicle

(a) Any automobile manufacturer, importer, distributor, dealer, or lienholder who reacquires, or who assists in reacquiring, a motor vehicle, whether by judgment, decree, arbitration award, settlement agreement, or voluntary agreement, is prohibited from doing either of the following:

(1) Requiring, as a condition of the reacquisition of the motor vehicle, that a buyer or lessee who is a resident of this state agree not to disclose the problems with the vehicle experienced by the buyer or lessee or the nonfinancial terms of the reacquisition.

(2) Including, in any release or other agreement, whether prepared by the manufacturer, importer, distributor, dealer, or lienholder, for signature by the buyer or lessee, a confidentiality clause, gag clause, or similar clause prohibiting the buyer or lessee from disclosing information to anyone about the problems with the vehicle, or the nonfinancial terms of the reacquisition of the vehicle by the manufacturer, importer, distributor, dealer, or lienholder.

(b) Any confidentiality clause, gag clause, or similar clause in such a release or other agreement in violation of this section shall be null and void as against the public policy of this state.

(c) Nothing in this section is intended to prevent any confidentiality clause, gag clause, or similar clause regarding the financial terms of the reacquisition of the vehicle. **Leg.H.** Added Stats 1998 ch 1063 §1 (AB 2410). Amended Stats 2000 ch 258 §1 (AB 2517).

§1793.3. Failure to provide service facility in conjunction with express warranty

If the manufacturer of consumer goods sold in this state for which the manufacturer has made an express warranty does not provide service and repair facilities within this state pursuant to subdivision (a) of Section 1793.2, or does not make available to authorized service and repair facilities service literature and replacement parts sufficient to effect repair during the express warranty period, the buyer of such manufacturer's nonconforming goods may follow the course of action prescribed in either subdivision (a), (b), or (c), below, as follows:

(a) Return the nonconforming consumer goods to the retail seller thereof. The retail seller shall do one of the following:

(1) Service or repair the nonconforming goods to conform to the applicable warranty.

(2) Direct the buyer to a reasonably close independent repair or service facility willing to accept service or repair under this section.

(3) Replace the nonconforming goods with goods that are identical or reasonably equivalent to the warranted goods.

(4) Refund to the buyer the original purchase price less that amount directly attributable to use by the buyer prior to the discovery of the nonconformity.

(b) Return the nonconforming consumer goods to any retail seller of like goods of the same manufacturer within this state who may do one of the following:

(1) Service or repair the nonconforming goods to conform to the applicable warranty.

(2) Direct the buyer to a reasonably close independent repair or service facility willing to accept service or repair under this section.

(3) Replace the nonconforming goods with goods that are identical or reasonably equivalent to the warranted goods.

(4) Refund to the buyer the original purchase price less that amount directly attributable to use by the buyer prior to the discovery of the nonconformity.

(c) Secure the services of an independent repair or service facility for the service or repair of the nonconforming consumer goods, when service or repair of the goods can be economically accomplished. In that event the manufacturer shall be liable to the buyer, or to the independent repair or service facility upon an assignment of the buyer's rights, for the actual and reasonable cost of service and repair, including any cost for parts and any reasonable cost of transporting the goods or parts, plus a reasonable profit. It shall be a rebuttable presumption affecting the burden of producing evidence that the reasonable cost of service or repair is an amount equal to that which is charged by the independent service dealer for like services or repairs rendered to service or repair customers who are not entitled to warranty protection. Any waiver of the liability of a manufacturer shall be void and unenforceable.

The course of action prescribed in this subdivision shall be available to the buyer only after the buyer has followed the course of action prescribed in either subdivision (a) or (b) and such course of action has not furnished the buyer with appropriate relief. In no event, shall the provisions of this subdivision be available to the buyer with regard to consumer goods with a wholesale price to the retailer of less than fifty dollars ($50). In no event shall the buyer be responsible or liable for service or repair costs charged by the independent repair or service facility which accepts service or repair of nonconforming consumer goods under this section. Such independent repair or service facility shall only be authorized to hold the manufacturer liable for such costs.

(d) A retail seller to which any nonconforming consumer good is returned pursuant to subdivision (a) or (b) shall have the option of providing service or repair itself or directing the buyer to a reasonably close independent repair or service facility willing to accept service or repair under this section. In the event the retail seller directs the buyer to an independent repair or service facility, the manufacturer shall be liable for the reasonable cost of repair services in the manner provided in subdivision (c).

(e) In the event a buyer is unable to return nonconforming goods to the retailer due to reasons of size and weight, or method of attachment, or method of installation, or nature of the nonconformity, the buyer shall give notice of the nonconformity to the retailer. Upon receipt of such notice of nonconformity the retailer shall, at its option, service or repair the goods at the buyer's residence, or pick up the goods for service or repair, or arrange for transporting the goods to its place of business. The reasonable costs of transporting the goods shall be at the retailer's expense. The retailer shall be entitled to recover all such reasonable costs of transportation from the manufacturer pursuant to Section 1793.5. The reasonable costs of transporting nonconforming goods after delivery to the retailer until return of the goods to the buyer, when incurred by a retailer, shall be recoverable from the manufacturer pursuant to Section 1793.5. Written notice of nonconformity to the retailer shall constitute return of the goods for the purposes of subdivisions (a) and (b).

(f) The manufacturer of consumer goods with a wholesale price to the retailer of fifty dollars ($50) or more for which the manufacturer has made express warranties shall provide written notice to the buyer of the courses of action available to him under subdivision (a), (b), or (c). **Leg.H.** Added Stats 1970 ch 1333 §1. Amended Stats 1971 ch 1523 §10, operative January 1, 1972; Stats 1976 ch 416 §3; Stats 1978 ch 991 §8; Stats 1986 ch 547 §3.

§1793.35. Replacement of or reimbursement for clothing or consumables under express warranty

(a) Where the retail sale of clothing or consumables is accompanied by an express warranty and such items do not conform with the terms of the express warranty, the buyer thereof may return the goods within 30 days of purchase or the period specified in the warranty, whichever is greater. The manufacturer may, in the express warranty, direct the purchaser to return nonconforming goods to a retail seller of like goods of the same manufacturer for replacement.

(b) When clothing or consumables are returned to a retail seller for the reason that they do not conform to an express warranty, the retailer shall replace the nonconforming goods where the manufacturer has directed replacement in the express warranty. In the event the manufacturer has not directed replacement in the express warranty, the retailer may replace the nonconforming goods or reimburse the buyer in an amount equal to the purchase price paid by the buyer for the goods, at the option of the retailer. Costs of reimbursement or replacement are recoverable by a retailer from the manufacturer in the manner provided in Section 1793.5.

(c) Where the retail sale of draperies is not accompanied by an express warranty and the sale of such draperies is accompanied by a conspicuous writing disclaiming the retailer's implied warranty of merchantability on the fabric, the retailer's implied warranty of merchantability shall not apply to the fabric. **Leg.H.** Added Stats 1971 ch 1523 §10.5, operative January 1, 1972. Amended Stats 1978 ch 991 §8.5.

§1793.4. Time to exercise option for service of item under express warranty

Where an option is exercised in favor of service and repair under Section 1793.3, such service and repair must be commenced within a reasonable time, and, unless the buyer agrees in writing to the contrary, goods conforming to the applicable express warranties shall be tendered within 30 days. Delay caused by conditions beyond the control of the retail seller or his representative shall serve to extend this 30-day requirement. Where such a delay arises, conforming goods shall be tendered as soon as possible following termination of the condition giving rise to the delay. **Leg.H.** Added Stats 1970 ch 1333 §1. Amended Stats 1971 ch 1523 §11, operative January 1, 1972; Stats 1978 ch 991 §9.

§1793.5. Liability of manufacturer making express warranties for failure to maintain service facilities

Every manufacturer making express warranties who does not provide service and repair facilities within this state pursuant to subdivision (a) of Section 1793.2 shall be liable as prescribed in this section to every retail seller of such manufacturer's goods who incurs obligations in giving effect to the express warranties that accompany such manufacturer's consumer goods. The amount of such liability shall be determined as follows:

(a) In the event of replacement, in an amount equal to the actual cost to the retail seller of the replaced goods, and cost of transporting the goods, if such costs are incurred plus a reasonable handling charge.

(b) In the event of service and repair, in an amount equal to that which would be received by the retail seller for like service rendered to retail consumers who are not entitled to warranty protection, including actual and reasonable costs of the service and repair and the cost of transporting the goods, if such costs are incurred, plus a reasonable profit.

(c) In the event of reimbursement under subdivision (a) of Section 1793.3, in an amount equal to that reimbursed to the buyer, plus a reasonable handling charge. **Leg.H.** Added Stats 1970 ch 1333 §1. Amended Stats 1971 ch 1523 §12, operative January 1, 1972.

§1793.6. Manufacturer's liability to independent serviceman performing services or incurring obligations on express warranties

Except as otherwise provided in the terms of a warranty service contract, as specified in subdivision (a) of Section 1793.2, entered into between a manufacturer and an independent service and repair facility, every manufacturer making express warranties whose consumer goods are sold in this state shall be liable as prescribed in this section to every independent serviceman who performs services or incurs obligations in giving effect to the express warranties that accompany such manufacturer's consumer goods whether the independent serviceman is acting as an authorized service and repair facility designated by the manufacturer pursuant to paragraph (1) of subdivision (a) of Section 1793.2 or is acting as an independent serviceman pursuant to subdivisions (c) and (d) of Section 1793.3. The amount of such liability shall be an amount equal to the actual and reasonable costs of the service and repair, including any cost for parts and any reasonable cost of transporting the goods or parts, plus a reasonable profit. It shall be a rebuttable presumption affecting the burden of producing evidence that the reasonable cost of service or repair is an amount equal to that which is charged by the independent serviceman for like services or repairs rendered to service or repair customers who are not entitled to warranty protection. Any waiver of the liability of a manufacturer shall be void and unenforceable. **Leg.H.** Added Stats 1976 ch 416 §4.

§1794. Buyer's damages, penalties and fees

(a) Any buyer of consumer goods who is damaged by a failure to comply with any obligation under this chapter or under an implied or express warranty or service contract may bring an action for the recovery of damages and other legal and equitable relief.

(b) The measure of the buyer's damages in an action under this section shall include the rights of replacement or reimbursement as set forth in subdivision (d) of Section 1793.2, and the following:

(1) Where the buyer has rightfully rejected or justifiably revoked acceptance of the goods or has exercised any right to cancel the sale, Sections 2711, 2712, and 2713 of the Commercial Code shall apply.

(2) Where the buyer has accepted the goods, Sections 2714 and 2715 of the Commercial Code shall apply, and the measure of damages shall include the cost of repairs necessary to make the goods conform.

(c) If the buyer establishes that the failure to comply was willful, the judgment may include, in addition to the amounts recovered under subdivision (a), a civil penalty which shall not exceed two times the amount of actual damages. This subdivision shall not apply in any class action under Section 382 of the Code of Civil Procedure or under Section 1781, or with respect to a claim based solely on a breach of an implied warranty.

(d) If the buyer prevails in an action under this section, the buyer shall be allowed by the court to recover as part of the judgment a sum equal to the aggregate amount of costs and expenses, including attorney's fees based on actual time expended, determined by the court to have been reasonably incurred by the buyer in connection with the commencement and prosecution of such action.

(e)(1) Except as otherwise provided in this subdivision, if the buyer establishes a violation of paragraph (2) of subdivision (d) of Section 1793.2, the buyer shall recover damages and reasonable attorney's fees and costs, and may recover a civil penalty of up to two times the amount of damages.

(2) If the manufacturer maintains a qualified third-party dispute resolution process which substantially complies with Section 1793.22, the manufacturer shall not be liable for any civil penalty pursuant to this subdivision.

(3) After the occurrence of the events giving rise to the presumption established in subdivision (b) of Section 1793.22, the buyer may serve upon the manufacturer a written notice requesting that the manufacturer comply with paragraph (2) of subdivision (d) of Section 1793.2. If the buyer fails to serve the notice, the manufacturer shall not be liable for a civil penalty pursuant to this subdivision.

(4) If the buyer serves the notice described in paragraph (3) and the manufacturer complies with paragraph (2) of subdivision (d) of Section 1793.2 within 30 days of the service of that notice, the manufacturer shall not be liable for a civil penalty pursuant to this subdivision.

(5) If the buyer recovers a civil penalty under subdivision (c), the buyer may not also recover a civil penalty under this subdivision for the same violation. **Leg.H.** Added Stats 1982 ch 385 §2. Amended Stats 1987 ch 1280 §4; Stats 1992 ch 1232 §9 (SB 1762).

Prior Law: Former §1794, similar to the present section, was added 1970 ch 1333 §1, amended Stats 1971 ch 1523 §13, operative January 1, 1972, Stats 1978 ch 991 §10, and repealed Stats 1982 ch 385 §1.

Former §1794, similar to UCC §1102, was added Stats 1931 ch 1070 §1 and repealed Stats 1963 ch 819 §2, effective January 1, 1965.

Former §1794, relating to withdrawal of bid, was enacted 1872 and repealed Stats 1931 ch 1070 §1.

§1794.1. Seller's and serviceman's damages

(a) Any retail seller of consumer goods injured by the willful or repeated violation of the provisions of this chapter may bring an action for the recovery of damages. Judgment may be entered for three times the amount at which the actual damages are assessed plus reasonable attorney fees.

(b) Any independent serviceman of consumer goods injured by the willful or repeated violation of the provisions of this chapter may bring an action for the recovery of damages. Judgment may be entered for three times the amount at which the actual damages are assessed plus reasonable attorney fees. Leg.H. Added Stats 1970 ch 1333 §1. Amended Stats 1976 ch 416 §5.

§1794.2. [Section repealed 1982]

Leg.H. Added Stats 1979 ch 1023 §6. Repealed Stats 1982 ch 385 §3. The repealed section related to the inapplicability of the treble damages provision of former CC §1794.

Prior Law: Former §1794.2, similar to the repealed section, was added Stats 1970 ch 1333 §3, operative March 1, 1971, amended Stats 1971 ch 1523 §14, operative January 1, 1972, and repealed Stats 1979 ch 1023 §5.

Former §1794.2, similar to the repealed section, was added Stats 1970 ch 1333 §1 and repealed Stats 1970 ch 1333 §3, operative March 1, 1971.

§1794.3. Effect of unauthorized or unreasonable use of goods

The provisions of this chapter shall not apply to any defect or nonconformity in consumer goods caused by the unauthorized or unreasonable use of the goods following sale. Leg.H. Added Stats 1970 ch 1333 §1. Amended Stats 1971 ch 1523 §15, operative January 1, 1972.

§1794.4. Service contract in lieu of warranty

(a) Nothing in this chapter shall be construed to prevent the sale of a service contract to the buyer in addition to or in lieu of an express warranty if that contract fully and conspicuously discloses in simple and readily understood language the terms, conditions, and exclusions of that contract, provided that nothing in this section shall apply to a home protection contract issued by a home protection company that is subject to Part 7 (commencing with Section 12740) of Division 2 of the Insurance Code.

(b) Except as otherwise expressly provided in the service contract, every service contract shall obligate the service contractor to provide to the buyer of the product all of the services and functional parts that may be necessary to maintain proper operation of the entire product under normal operation and service for the duration of the service contract and without additional charge.

(c) The service contract shall contain all of the following items of information:

(1) If the service contract covers a single product, a clear description and identification of the covered product. If the service contract covers a class of products, a description of the class of products covered by the service contract that is sufficiently clear so the buyer is able to discern the products covered.

(2) The point in time or event when the term of the service contract commences, and its duration measured by elapsed time or an objective measure of use.

(3)(A) A service contract may be offered on a month-to-month or other periodic basis and continue until canceled by the buyer or the service contractor in accordance with Section 1794.41 and, for electronic and appliance repair dealers, Section 9855.6 of the Business and Professions Code. If the service contract continues until canceled by the buyer or service contractor, the service contract shall do all of the following:

(i) Disclose to the buyer in a clear and conspicuous manner that the service contract shall continue until canceled by the buyer or service contractor and require the buyer's affirmative consent to this provision.

(ii) Disclose to the buyer all alternatives that the seller offering the service contract offers, including any fixed-term service contracts or other service contract basis that does not continue until it is canceled.

(iii) Provide, at a minimum, a toll-free number, email address, postal address, and, if one exists, internet website the buyer can use to cancel the service contract. Cancellation shall not require the use of more than one of these methods to be completed and shall be effective immediately upon receipt of the request for cancellation.

(iv) If the service contract was entered into online, allow the buyer the option to cancel the service contract exclusively online, without engaging in any unnecessary steps that obstruct or delay the buyer's ability to cancel the continuation of the service contract.

(v)(I) Provide for a refund to the buyer of any unearned amounts in accordance with Section 1794.41 and, for electronic and appliance repair dealers, Section 9855.6 of the Business and Professions Code.

(II) The amount of any refund, as well as any cancellation or administrative fees, under this paragraph shall be calculated based on the period, whether month to month or otherwise, for which payment is made and the amount of the payment for the period.

(III) A written notice of cancellation other than notice required by clauses (iii) and (iv) shall not be required to obtain a refund.

(B) This paragraph does not apply to vehicle service contracts.

(4) If the enforceability of the service contract is limited to the original buyer or is limited to persons other than every consumer owner of the covered product during the term of the service contract, a description of the limits on transfer or assignment of the service contract.

(5) A statement of the general obligation of the service contractor in the same language set forth in subdivision (b), with equally clear and conspicuous statements of the following:

(A) Any services, parts, characteristics, components, properties, defects, malfunctions, causes, conditions, repairs, or remedies that are excluded from the scope of the service contract.

(B) Any other limits on the application of the language in subdivision (b) such as a limit on the total number of service calls.

(C) Any additional services that the service contractor will provide.

(D) Whether the obligation of the service contractor includes preventive maintenance and, if so, the nature and frequency of the preventive maintenance that the service contractor will provide.

(E) Whether the buyer has an obligation to provide preventive maintenance or perform any other obligations and, if so, the nature and frequency of the preventive maintenance and of any other obligations, and the consequences of any noncompliance.

(6) A step-by-step explanation of the procedure that the buyer should follow in order to obtain performance of any obligation under the service contract including the following:

(A) The full legal and business name of the service contractor.

(B) The mailing address of the service contractor.

(C) The persons or class of persons that are authorized to perform service.

(D) The name or title and address of any agent, employee, or department of the service contractor that is responsible for the performance of any obligations.

(E) The method of giving notice to the service contractor of the need for service.

(F) Whether in-home service is provided or, if not, whether the costs of transporting the product for service or repairs will be paid by the service contractor.

(G) If the product must be transported to the service contractor, either the place where the product may be delivered for service or repairs or a toll-free telephone number that the buyer may call to obtain that information.

(H) All other steps that the buyer must take to obtain service.

(I) All fees, charges, and other costs that the buyer must pay to obtain service.

(7) An explanation of the steps that the service contractor will take to carry out its obligations under the service contract.

(8) A description of any right to cancel the contract if the buyer returns the product or the product is sold, lost, stolen, or destroyed, or, if there is no right to cancel or the right to cancel is limited, a statement of the fact.

(9) Information respecting the availability of any informal dispute settlement process.

(d) A service contractor may cancel a service contract offered on a month-to-month or other periodic basis only if any of the following occurs:

(1) The buyer fails to make timely payment.

(2) The buyer is otherwise in material breach of the service contract.

(3) The buyer has committed fraud in connection with the service contract.

(4)(A) The service contractor or its affiliate is the obligor under the service contract, and the service contractor or its affiliate is discontinuing this category of service contract no later than 30 days after the effective date of the cancellation.

(B) A cancellation or administrative fee shall not be charged to the buyer for a cancellation pursuant to this paragraph.

(5)(A) Neither the seller offering the service contract nor any of its affiliates is the obligor under the service contract, and the seller is discontinuing its offering of the service contract no later than 30 days after the effective date of the cancellation in favor of a service contract with a different obligor.

(B) A cancellation or administrative fee shall not be charged to the buyer for a cancellation pursuant to this paragraph.

(e) As used in this section:

(1) "Affiliate" means an entity that directly, or indirectly through one or more intermediaries, controls, is controlled by, or is under common control with another specified entity.

(2)(A) "Affirmative consent" means any freely given, specific, informed, and unambiguous indication of the consumer's wishes by which the consumer, or the consumer's legal guardian, a person who has power of attorney, or a person acting as a conservator for the consumer, including by a statement or by a clear affirmative action, signifies agreement to the continuous until canceled nature of the service contract.

(B) "Affirmative consent" does not mean any of the following:

(i) Acceptance of a general or broad terms of use, or similar document, that contains descriptions of the coverages under the service contract along with other, unrelated information.

(ii) Hovering over, muting, pausing, or closing a given piece of content.

(iii) Agreement obtained through the use of dark patterns.

(f) Subdivisions (b) and (c) are applicable to service contracts on new or used home appliances and home electronic products entered into on or after July 1, 1989. They are applicable to service contracts on all other new or used products entered into on and after July 1, 1991.

(g) The amendments to this section made by the act adding this subdivision are applicable only to a service contract entered into on or after January 1, 2022. **Leg.H.** Added Stats 1993 ch 1265 §13.5 (SB 798), operative January 1, 1998. Amended Stats 1997 ch 401 §65 (SB 780), operative January 1, 2003; Stats 2002 ch 405 §64 (AB 2973), operative January 1, 2008; Stats 2021 ch 452 §2 (AB 1221), effective January 1, 2022.

Prior Law: Former CC §1794.4, similar to the present section was added Stats 1970 ch 1333 §1, amended Stats 1971 ch 1523 §16, operative January 1, 1972; Stats 1985 ch 1047 §2; Stats 1988 ch 581 §2; Stats 1990 ch 127 §1; Stats 1993 ch 1265 §13, operative until January 1, 1998; Stats 1997 ch 401 §64 (SB 780), operative until January 1, 2003; Stats 2002 ch 405 §65 (AB 2973), operative until January 1, 2008 and repealed, January 1, 2008, by its own terms.

Former CC §1794.4, similar to present section, which was added Stats 1970 ch 1333 §1, amended Stats 1971 ch 1523 §16, operative January 1, 1972, Stats 1985 ch 1047 §2, Stats 1988 ch 581 §2, Stats 1990 ch 127 §1, Stats 1993 ch 1265 §13, operative until January 1, 1998, amended Stats 1997 ch 401 §64, and repealed, January 1, 2003, by its own terms.

Former CC §1794.4, similar to the present section was added Stats 1970 ch 1333 §1 and repealed operative January 1, 2008, by its own provisions. Stats 2002 ch 405 (AB 2973) §65.

§1794.41. Vehicle, home appliance, or home electronic product service contract; Requirements; Applicability; Conflicts with insurance provisions

(a) No service contract covering any motor vehicle, home appliance, or home electronic product purchased for use in this state may be offered for sale or sold unless all of the following elements exist:

(1) The contract shall contain the disclosures specified in Section 1794.4 and shall disclose in the manner described in that section the buyer's cancellation and refund rights provided by this section.

(2) The contract shall be available for inspection by the buyer prior to purchase and either the contract, or a brochure which specifically describes the terms, conditions, and exclusions of the contract, and the provisions of this section relating to contract delivery, cancellation, and refund, shall be delivered to the buyer at or before the time of purchase of the contract. Within 60 days after the date of purchase, the contract itself shall be delivered to the buyer. If a service contract for a home appliance or a home electronic product is sold by means of a telephone solicitation, the seller may elect to satisfy the requirements of this paragraph by mailing or delivering the contract to the buyer not later than 30 days after the date of the sale of the contract.

(3) The contract is applicable only to items, costs, and time periods not covered by the express warranty. However, a service contract may run concurrently with or overlap an express warranty if (A) the contract covers items or costs not covered by the express warranty or (B) the contract provides relief to the purchaser not available under the express warranty, such as automatic replacement of a product where the express warranty only provides for repair.

(4) The contract shall be cancelable by the purchaser under the following conditions:

(A) Unless the contract provides for a longer period, within the first 60 days after receipt of the contract, or with respect to a contract covering a used motor vehicle without manufacturer warranties, a home appliance, or a home electronic product, within the first 30 days after receipt of the contract, the full amount paid shall be refunded by the seller to the purchaser if the purchaser provides a written notice of cancellation to the person specified in the contract, and if no claims have been made against the contract. If a claim has been made against the contract either within the first 60 days after receipt of the contract, or with respect to a used motor vehicle without manufacturer warranties, home appliance, or home electronic product, within the first 30 days after receipt of the contract, a pro rata refund, based on either elapsed time or an objective measure of use, such as mileage or the retail value of any service performed, at the seller's option as indicated in the contract, or for a vehicle service contract at the obligor's option as determined at the time of cancellation, shall be made by the seller to the purchaser if the purchaser provides a written notice of cancellation to the person specified in the contract.

(B) Unless the contract provides for a longer period for obtaining a full refund, after the first 60 days after receipt of the contract, or with respect to a contract covering a used motor vehicle without manufacturer warranties, a home appliance, or a home electronic product, after the first 30 days after the receipt of the contract, a pro rata refund, based on either elapsed time or an objective measure of use, such as mileage or the retail value of any service performed, at the seller's option as indicated in the contract, or for a vehicle service contract at the obligor's option as determined at the time of cancellation, shall be made by the seller to the purchaser if the purchaser provides a written notice of cancellation to the person specified in the contract. In addition, the seller may assess a cancellation or administrative fee, not to exceed 10 percent of the price of the service contract or twenty-five dollars ($25), whichever is less.

(C) If the purchase of the service contract was financed, the seller may make the refund payable to the purchaser, the assignee, or lender of record, or both.

(b) Nothing in this section shall apply to a home protection plan that is issued by a home protection company which is subject to Part 7 (commencing with Section 12740) of Division 2 of the Insurance Code.

(c) If any provision of this section conflicts with any provision of Part 8 (commencing with Section 12800) of Division 2 of the Insurance Code, the provision of the Insurance Code shall apply instead of this section. **Leg.H.** Added Stats 1985 ch 1047 §3. Amended Stats 1988 ch 581 §3; Stats 1990 ch 1183 §1 (AB 2226); Stats 2003 ch 439 §1 (AB 984), operative July 1, 2004; Stats 2010 ch 543 §7 (AB 2111), effective January 1, 2011.

§1794.45. Service contract; Duty of retailer; Applicability

(a) A retailer that sells a service contract pursuant to Section 1794.4 shall do either of the following during the period that the service contract is in effect:

(1) Maintain contract information that includes a description of the terms and conditions of the service contract, and provide that information to the purchaser of the service contract or other beneficiary upon request.

(2) Upon request from the purchaser of the service contract or other beneficiary, obtain a copy of the service contract, and provide that copy to the requester within 10 business days after receiving the request.

(b) This section shall not apply to a vehicle service contract, as defined in subdivision (c) of Section 12800 of the Insurance Code. **Leg.H.** Added Stats 2009 ch 74 §1 (AB 63), effective January 1, 2010.

§1794.5. Alternative suggestions for repair of item under express warranty

The provisions of this chapter shall not preclude a manufacturer making express warranties from suggesting methods of effecting service and repair, in accordance with the terms and conditions of the express warranties, other than those required by this chapter. **Leg.H.** Added Stats 1970 ch 1333 §1.

§1795. Liability of nonmanufacturer making express warranty

If express warranties are made by persons other than the manufacturer of the goods, the obligation of the person making such warranties shall be the same as that imposed on the manufacturer under this chapter. **Leg.H.** Added Stats 1970 ch 1333 §.

Prior Law: Former §1795, similar to UCC §2102, was added Stats 1931 ch 1070 §1 and repealed Stats 1963 ch 819 §2, effective January 1, 1965.

Former §1795, relating to sale by auction under written conditions, was enacted 1872 and repealed Stats 1931 ch 1070 §1.

§1795.1. Application of chapter to components of air conditioning system

This chapter shall apply to any equipment or mechanical, electrical, or thermal component of a system designed to heat, cool, or otherwise condition air, but, with that exception, shall not apply to the system as a whole where such a system becomes a fixed part of a structure. **Leg.H.** Added Stats 1971 ch 1523 §16.5, operative January 1, 1972. Amended Stats 1978 ch 991 §11; Stats 1983 ch 728 §1.

§1795.4. Rules applicable to leases of consumer goods

For the purposes of this chapter only, the following rules apply to leases of both new and used consumer goods:

(a) If express warranties are regularly furnished to purchasers of substantially the same kind of goods, (1) those warranties will be deemed to apply to the leased goods and (2) the lessor and lessee shall each be deemed to be the first purchaser of the goods for the purpose of any warranty provision limiting warranty benefits to the original purchaser.

(b) The lessee of goods has the same rights under this chapter against the manufacturer and any person making express warranties that the lessee would have had under this chapter if the goods had been purchased by the lessee, and the manufacturer and any person making express warranties have the same duties and obligations under this chapter with respect to the goods that such manufacturer and other person would have had under this chapter if the goods had been sold to the lessee.

(c) If a lessor leases goods to a lessee from the lessor's inventory, the lessee has the same rights under this chapter against the lessor that the lessee would have had if the goods had been purchased by the lessee, and the lessor has the same duties and obligations under this chapter with respect to the goods that the lessor would have had under this chapter if the goods had been sold to the lessee. For purposes of this section, "inventory" shall include both goods in the lessor's possession prior to negotiation of the lease and goods ordered from another party in order to lease those goods to the lessee where the lessor is a dealer in goods of that type.

(d) If a lessor leases goods to a lessee which the lessor acquires other than from the lessor's inventory, the lessee has the same rights under this chapter against the seller of the goods to the lessor that the lessee would have had under this chapter if the goods had been purchased by the lessee from the seller, and the seller of the goods to the lessor has the same duties and obligations under this chapter with respect to the goods that the seller would have had under this chapter if the goods had been purchased by the lessee from the seller.

(e) A lessor who re-leases goods to a new lessee and does not retake possession of the goods prior to consummation of the re-lease may, notwithstanding the provisions of Section 1793, disclaim as to that lessee any and all warranties created by this chapter by conspicuously disclosing in the lease that these warranties are disclaimed.

(f) A lessor who has obligations to the lessee with relation to warranties in connection with a lease of goods and the seller of goods to a lessor have the same rights and remedies against the manufacturer and any person making express warranties that a seller of the goods would have had if the seller had sold the goods to the lessee. **Leg.H.** Added Stats 1984 ch 1169 §2.

§1795.5. Obligations of distributors or sellers of used goods

Notwithstanding the provisions of subdivision (a) of Section 1791 defining consumer goods to mean "new" goods, the obligation of a distributor or retail seller of used consumer goods in a sale in which an express warranty is given shall be the same as that imposed on manufacturers under this chapter except:

(a) It shall be the obligation of the distributor or retail seller making express warranties with respect to used consumer goods (and not the original manufacturer, distributor, or retail seller making express warranties with respect to such goods when new) to maintain sufficient service and repair facilities within this state to carry out the terms of such express warranties.

(b) The provisions of Section 1793.5 shall not apply to the sale of used consumer goods sold in this state.

(c) The duration of the implied warranty of merchantability and where present the implied warranty of fitness with respect to used consumer goods sold in this state, where the sale is accompanied by an express warranty, shall be coextensive in duration with an express warranty which accompanies the consumer goods, provided the duration of the express warranty is reasonable, but in no event shall such implied warranties have a duration of less than 30 days nor more than three months following the sale of used consumer goods to a retail buyer. Where no duration for an express warranty is stated with respect to such goods, or parts thereof, the duration of the implied warranties shall be the maximum period prescribed above.

(d) The obligation of the distributor or retail seller who makes express warranties with respect to used goods that are sold in this state, shall extend to the sale of all such used goods, regardless of when such goods may have been manufactured. **Leg.H.** Added Stats 1971 ch 1523 §17, operative January 1, 1972. Amended Stats 1974 ch 169 §1; Stats 1978 ch 991 §12; Stats 1983 ch 728 §2.

§1795.51. Obligations of buy-here-pay-here dealer; Written warranty required

(a) No buy-here-pay-here dealer, as that term is defined in Section 241 of the Vehicle Code, shall sell or lease a used vehicle, as defined in Section 665 of the Vehicle Code, at retail price without giving the buyer or lessee a written warranty that shall have a minimum duration of at least 30 days from the date of delivery or when the odometer has registered 1,000 miles from what is shown on the contract, whichever occurs first.

(b) The written warranty shall provide that if the buyer or lessee notifies the buy-here-pay-here dealer that the vehicle does not conform to the written warranty, the buy-here-pay-here dealer shall either repair the vehicle to conform to the written warranty, reimburse the buyer or lessee for the reasonable cost of repairs, or cancel the sale or lease contract and provide the buyer or lessee with a full refund, less a reasonable amount for any damage sustained by the vehicle after the sale or lease, excepting damage caused by any nonconformity with the written warranty.

(c) The written warranty shall provide that the buy-here-pay-here dealer shall pay 100 percent of the cost of labor and parts for any repairs pursuant to the warranty, and may not charge the buyer or lessee for the cost of repairs or for inspecting the vehicle, tearing down the engine or transmission or other part, or for any deductible. Any person performing repairs pursuant to this subdivision shall comply with the requirements of an automotive repair dealer pursuant to Chapter 20.3 (commencing with Section 9880) of Division 3 of the Business and Professions Code.

(d) The buy-here-pay-here dealer or its agent may elect to refund the buyer or lessee a full refund, less a reasonable amount for any damage sustained by the vehicle after the sale or lease, excepting damage caused by any nonconformity with the written warranty, rather than performing a repair. In the event that the buy-here-pay-here dealer cancels the sale or lease, all of the following shall apply:

(1) The buy-here-pay-here dealer shall give written notice to the buyer or lessee of the election to cancel the sale or lease by personal delivery or first-class mail.

(2) The buyer or lessee shall return the vehicle in substantially the same condition as when it was delivered by the buy-here-pay-here dealer, reasonable wear and tear and any nonconformity with the written warranty excepted.

(3) The buy-here-pay-here dealer shall provide the buyer or lessee with a receipt stating all of the following:

(A) The date the vehicle was returned to the buy-here-pay-here dealer.

(B) The vehicle identification number.

(C) The make, year, and model of the vehicle.

(D) The odometer reading at the time that the vehicle was returned to the buy-here-pay-here dealer.

(E) A statement that the buy-here-pay-here dealer has canceled the sale or lease.

(F) The amount of the buyer's or lessee's refund.

(4) The buy-here-pay-here dealer shall not treat the return of the vehicle pursuant to the contract cancellation provisions of this subdivision as a repossession.

(5) The buyer or lessee shall execute the documents necessary to transfer any interest in the vehicle to the buy-here-pay-here dealer or to remove the buyer or lessee from any registration or title documents.

(6) The buy-here-pay-here dealer shall refund to the buyer or lessee, no later than the day after the day on which the buyer or lessee returns the vehicle and the notice of election to cancel is given to the buyer or lessee, all amounts paid under the sale or lease agreement, less a reasonable amount for property damage sustained by the vehicle after the sale or lease, excepting damage caused by any nonconformity with the warranty.

(e) The written warranty shall cover at least the following components:

(1) Engine, including all internally lubricated parts.

(2) Transmission and transaxle.

(3) Front and rear wheel drive components.

(4) Engine cooling system.

(5) Alternator, generator, starter, and ignition system, not including the battery.

(6) Braking system.

(7) Front and rear suspension systems.

(8) Steering system and components.

(9) Seatbelts.

(10) Inflatable restraint systems installed on the vehicle as originally manufactured.

(11) Catalytic converter and other emissions components necessary for the vehicle to pass a California emissions test.

(12) Heater.

(13) Seals and gaskets on components described in this subdivision.

(14) Electrical, electronic, and computer components, to the extent that those components substantially affect the functionality of other components described in this subdivision.

(f) Any Used Car Buyer's Guide displayed on a vehicle offered for sale or lease by a buy-here-pay-here dealer shall list each of the above systems and components and shall specify that the buy-here-pay-here dealer will pay 100 percent of the cost of parts and labor for repairs covered by the warranty.

(g) The buy-here-pay-here dealer shall make the repair or provide a refund notwithstanding the fact that the warranty period has expired if the buyer or lessee notified the buy-here-pay-here dealer of the failure of a covered system or part within the warranty period.

(h) This section shall not apply to any defect or nonconformity caused by the unauthorized or unreasonable use of the vehicle following the sale, or to any property damage not to the vehicle arising out of the failure of a covered part.

(i) In any proceeding in which the exclusion of coverage permitted by subdivision (h) or the deduction allowed by paragraph (6) of subdivision (d) is an issue, the buy-here-pay-here dealer shall have the burden of proof.

(j) A buy-here-pay-here dealer shall not sell or lease any vehicle unless the vehicle meets all of the equipment requirements of Division 12 (commencing with Section 24000) of the Vehicle Code.

(k) Any agreement between a buy-here-pay-here dealer and a buyer or lessee that disclaims, limits, or waives the rights set forth in this section shall be void as contrary to public policy.

(*l*) If a buy-here-pay-here dealer fails to give a buyer a written warranty pursuant to this section, the buy-here-pay-here dealer shall be deemed to have provided the warranty as a matter of law. **Leg.H.** Added Stats 2012 ch 740 §2 (AB 1447), effective January 1, 2013.

§1795.6. **Tolling the warranty period**

(a)(1) Except as provided in paragraph (2) warranty period relating to an implied or express warranty accompanying a sale or consignment for sale of consumer goods selling for fifty dollars ($50) or more shall automatically be tolled for the period from the date upon which the buyer either (1) delivers nonconforming goods to the manufacturer or seller for warranty repairs or service or (2), pursuant to subdivision (c) of Section 1793.2 or Section 1793.22, notifies the manufacturer or seller of the nonconformity of the goods up to, and including, the date upon which (1) the repaired or serviced goods are delivered to the buyer, (2) the buyer is notified the goods are repaired or serviced and are available for the buyer's possession or (3) the buyer is notified that repairs or service is completed, if repairs or service is made at the buyer's residence.

(2) With respect to hearing aids, the warranty period shall resume on the date upon which (1) the repaired or serviced hearing aid is delivered to the buyer or (2) five days after the buyer is notified the hearing aid is repaired or serviced and is available for the buyer's possession, whichever is earlier.

(b) Notwithstanding the date or conditions set for the expiration of the warranty period, such warranty period shall not be deemed expired if either or both of the following situations occur: (1) after the buyer has satisfied the requirements of subdivision (a), the warranty repairs or service has not been performed due to delays caused by circumstances beyond the control of the buyer or (2) the warranty repairs or service performed upon the nonconforming goods did not remedy the nonconformity for which such repairs or service was performed and the buyer notified the manufacturer or seller of this failure within 60 days after the repairs or service was completed. When the warranty repairs or service has been performed so as to remedy the nonconformity, the warranty period shall expire in accordance with its terms, including any extension to the warranty period for warranty repairs or service.

(c) For purposes of this section only, "manufacturer" includes the manufacturer's service or repair facility.

(d)(1) Except as provided in paragraph (2), every manufacturer or seller of consumer goods selling for fifty dollars ($50) or more shall provide a receipt to the buyer showing the date of purchase. Every manufacturer or seller performing warranty repairs or service on the goods shall provide to the buyer a work order or receipt with the date of return and either the date the buyer was notified that the goods were repaired or serviced or, where applicable, the date the goods were shipped or delivered to the buyer.

(2) With respect to hearing aids, the seller, after receiving the hearing aid for warranty repairs or service, shall also provide at the time of delivery to the buyer a work order or receipt with the following: (1) the date the warranty period resumes and (2) the revised expiration date of the warranty, as adjusted to reflect the suspension of the warranty period provided under this section. **Leg.H.** Added Stats 1974 ch 844 §1, operative July 1, 1975. Amended Stats 1980 ch 394 §2; Stats 1983 ch 728 §3; Stats 1992 ch 1232 §10 (SB 1762); Stats 2014 ch 226 §2 (SB 1326), effective January 1, 2015.

2014 Note: It appears the Legislature inadvertently deleted "every" in subdivision (a)(1). It is the Publisher's belief that the text should read: "Except as provided in paragraph (2), every warranty period..."

§1795.7. **Effect of tolling on manufacturer's liability**

Whenever a warranty, express or implied, is tolled pursuant to Section 1795.6 as a result of repairs or service performed by any retail seller, the warranty shall be extended with regard to the liability of the manufacturer to a retail seller pursuant to law. In such event, the manufacturer shall be liable in accordance with the provisions of Section 1793.5 for the period that an express warranty has been extended by virtue of Section 1795.6 to every retail seller who incurs obligations in giving effect to such express warranty. The manufacturer shall also be liable to every retail seller for the period that an implied warranty has been extended by virtue of Section 1795.6, in the same manner as he would be liable under Section 1793.5 for an express warranty. If a manufacturer provides for warranty repairs and service through its own service and repair facilities and through independent repair facilities in the state, its exclusive liability pursuant to this section shall be to such facilities. **Leg.H.** Added Stats 1974 ch 844 §2, operative July 1, 1975.

§1795.8. **Application of chapter**

Notwithstanding any other provision of law, this chapter shall apply to a purchase in the United States of a motor vehicle, as defined in paragraph (2) of subdivision (e) of Section 1793.22, with a manufacturer's express warranty by a member of the Armed Forces regardless of in which state his or her motor vehicle is purchased or registered, if both of the following apply:

(a) The member of the Armed Forces purchases a motor vehicle, as defined in paragraph (2) of subdivision (e) of Section 1793.22, with a manufacturer's express warranty from a manufacturer who sells motor vehicles in this state or from an agent or representative of that manufacturer.

(b) The member of the Armed Forces was stationed in or a resident of this state at the time he or she purchased the motor vehicle or at the time he or she filed an action pursuant to this chapter. **Leg.H.** Added Stats 2007 ch 151 §2 (SB 234), effective January 1, 2008.

Prior Law: Former CC §1795.8, similar to CC §1793.23, was added Stats 1989 ch 862 §1, amended Stats 1992 ch 1232 §11 and repealed Stats 1995 ch 503 §4.

Former CC §1795.8, similar to CC §1793.23, was added Stats 1989 ch 862 §1 and repealed Stats 1995 ch 503 §4.

CHAPTER 1.5
MOTOR VEHICLE WARRANTY ADJUSTMENT PROGRAMS

Definitions. §1795.90.
Duties of dealers. §1795.91.
Duties of manufacturers. §1795.92.
Remedies as cumulative. §1795.93.

§1795.90. Definitions

For purposes of this chapter:

(a) "Consumer" means the purchaser, other than for purposes of resale, of a motor vehicle, a lessee of a motor vehicle, any person to whom the motor vehicle is transferred during the duration of an express warranty applicable to that motor vehicle, and any person entitled by the terms of the warranty to enforce the obligations of the warranty.

(b) "Manufacturer" means any person, firm, or corporation, whether resident or nonresident, that manufactures or assembles motor vehicles for sale or distribution in this state. In the case of motor vehicles not manufactured in the United States, the term "manufacturer" shall also include any person, firm, or corporation that is engaged in the business of importing motor vehicles.

(c) "Dealer" means any person, firm, or corporation selling or agreeing to sell in this state one or more new motor vehicles under a retail agreement with a manufacturer, manufacturer branch, distributor, distributor branch, or agent of any of them.

(d) "Adjustment program" means any program or policy that expands or extends the consumer's warranty beyond its stated limit or under which a manufacturer offers to pay for all or any part of the cost of repairing, or to reimburse consumers for all or any part of the cost of repairing, any condition that may substantially affect vehicle durability, reliability, or performance, other than service provided under a safety or emission-related recall campaign. "Adjustment program" does not include ad hoc adjustments made by a manufacturer on a case-by-case basis.

(e) "Motor vehicle" means a motor vehicle, excluding motorcycles, motor homes, and off-road vehicles, which is registered in this state.

(f) "Lessee" means any person who leases a motor vehicle pursuant to a written lease which provides that the lessee is responsible for repairs to the motor vehicle.

(g) "Service bulletin" means any notice issued by a manufacturer and filed with the National Highway Traffic Safety Administration relating to vehicle durability, reliability, or performance. **Leg.H.** Added Stats 1993 ch 814 §1 (SB 486).

§1795.91. Duties of dealers

Dealers shall have the following duties:

(a) A dealer shall provide notice to prospective purchasers and lessees that provides information on how to get copies of service bulletins. This notice shall not be construed as an admission by the dealer or manufacturer of the existence or nonexistence of a vehicle defect.

The notice shall be deemed sufficient if posted in the showroom or other area conspicuous to motor vehicle purchasers and written in the following form:

FEDERAL LAW REQUIRES MANUFACTURERS TO FURNISH THE NATIONAL HIGHWAY TRAFFIC SAFETY ADMINISTRATION (NHTSA) WITH BULLETINS DESCRIBING ANY DEFECTS IN THEIR VEHICLES. THESE BULLETINS ARE NOT RECALLS.

YOU MAY OBTAIN COPIES OF THESE TECHNICAL SERVICE BULLETINS FROM THE NHTSA, THE MANUFACTURER (ASK YOUR DEALER FOR THE TOLL-FREE NUMBER), OR CERTAIN CONSUMER PUBLICATIONS, WHICH PUBLISH THESE BULLETINS. SOME COMPANIES WILL SEND THEM TO YOU, FOR A FEE.

(b) A dealer shall disclose to a consumer seeking repairs for a particular condition at its repair shop, the principal terms and conditions of the manufacturer's adjustment program covering the condition if the dealer has received a service bulletin concerning the adjustment program. **Leg.H.** Added Stats 1993 ch 814 §1 (SB 486). Amended Stats 2019 ch 490 §1 (AB 596), effective January 1, 2020.

§1795.92. Duties of manufacturers

Manufacturers shall have the following duties:

(a) A manufacturer shall, within 90 days of the adoption of an adjustment program, subject to priority for safety or emission-related recalls, notify by first-class mail all owners or lessees of motor vehicles eligible under the program of the condition giving rise to and the principal terms and conditions of the program.

(b) Copies of all notices mailed in accordance with subdivision (a) shall be sent to the New Motor Vehicle Board within the Department of Motor Vehicles and made available for public inquiries.

(c) A manufacturer shall, within 30 days of the adoption of any new adjustment program, notify its dealers, in writing, of all the terms and conditions thereof.

(d) A manufacturer who establishes an adjustment program shall implement procedures to assure reimbursement of each consumer eligible under an adjustment program who incurs expenses for repair of a condition subject to the program prior to acquiring knowledge of the program. The reimbursement shall be consistent with the terms and conditions of the particular program. The manufacturer shall notify the consumer within 21 business days of receiving a claim for reimbursement whether the claim will be allowed or denied. If the claim is denied, the specific reasons for the denial shall be stated in writing.

(e) Any consumer who, prior to acquiring knowledge of an adjustment program, incurs expenses for repair of a condition subject to the adjustment program may file a claim for reimbursement under subdivision (d). The claim shall be made in writing to the manufacturer within two years of the date of the consumer's payment for repair of the condition. **Leg.H.** Added Stats 1993 ch 814 §1 (SB 486).

§1795.93. Remedies as cumulative

Nothing in this chapter shall be construed to exclude, modify, or otherwise limit any other remedy provided by law to a consumer or lessee. **Leg.H.** Added Stats 1993 ch 814 §1 (SB 486).

CHAPTER 2
STANDARDS FOR WARRANTY WORK

Duty to install new or used goods. §1796.
Duty to service or repair new or used goods. §1796.5.

§1796. Duty to install new or used goods

Any individual, partnership, corporation, association, or other legal relationship which engages in the business of installing new or used consumer goods, has a duty to the buyer to install them in a good and workmanlike manner. **Leg.H.** Added Stats 1978 ch 991 §13.

Prior Law: Former §1796, similar to UCC §§1201, 2103, 2107, 2702, 7102, 7104, was added Stats 1931 ch 1070 §1 and repealed Stats 1963 ch 819 §2, effective January 1, 1965.

Former §1796, relating to rights of buyer upon sale without reserve, was enacted 1872 and repealed Stats 1931 ch 1070 §1.

§1796.5. Duty to service or repair new or used goods

Any individual, partnership, corporation, association, or other legal relationship which engages in the business of providing service or repair to new or used consumer goods has a duty to the purchaser to perform those services in a good and workmanlike manner. **Leg.H.** Added Stats 1978 ch 991 §13.

CHAPTER 3
MOBILEHOME WARRANTIES

Mobilehomes covered by warranty. §1797.
Definitions. §1797.1.
Application of warranty to manufacturer, contractor, and dealer. §1797.2.
Required written warranty; Contents. §1797.3.
Additional rights and privileges; Prohibited waiver. §1797.4.
Display of copy of warranty. §1797.5.
Records required to be kept. §1797.6.
Deadline for correcting defects. §1797.7.

§1797. Mobilehomes covered by warranty

All new mobilehomes and manufactured homes sold to a buyer shall be covered by the warranty set forth in this chapter. **Leg.H.** Added Stats 1971 ch 1492 §1. Amended Stats 1982 ch 730 §1.

Prior Law: Former §1797, relating to inapplicability of act to sales or contracts to sell made prior to act, was added Stats 1931 ch 1070 §1 and repealed Stats 1963 ch 819 §2, effective January 1, 1965.

Former §1797, relating to employment by a seller of a person to bid at sale, was enacted 1872 and repealed Stats 1931 ch 1070 §1.

§1797.1. Definitions

As used in this chapter:

(a) "Contractor" means any person who is a general building contractor within the meaning of Section 7057 of the Business and Professions Code.

(b) "Dealer" means any person who is a dealer within the meaning of Section 18002.6 of the Health and Safety Code.

(c) "Mobilehome" and "manufactured home" have the meanings, respectively, defined in Sections 18007 and 18008 of the Health and Safety Code.

(d) "Substantial defects in materials and workmanship" means defects objectively manifested by broken, ripped, cracked, stained, or missing parts or components, or workmanship resulting in improper function of materials, components, appliances, or systems as installed or manufactured by the contractor, dealer, or manufacturer. **Leg.H.** Added Stats 1971 ch 1492 §1. Amended Stats 1982 ch 730 §2; Stats 1985 ch 763 §1; Stats 1988 ch 793 §1; Stats 1993 ch 458 §1 (AB 247).

§1797.2. Application of warranty to manufacturer, contractor, and dealer

(a) The warranty provided for in this chapter shall apply to the manufacturer of the mobilehome or the manufactured home as well as to the contractor or dealer who sells the mobilehome or the manufactured home to the buyer. The warranty shall cover the electrical, plumbing, heating, cooling, fire safety, and structural systems, and all appliances of the mobilehome or manufactured home as installed or manufactured by the contractor, dealer, or manufacturer.

(b) Where a manufacturer sells a mobilehome or manufactured home directly to a city, city and county, or other public agency pursuant to the exception established in Section 18015.7, the manufacturer shall be responsible for providing the warranty required by this chapter. **Leg.H.** Added Stats 1971 ch 1492 §1. Amended Stats 1982 ch 730 §3; Stats 1985 ch 763 §2; Stats 1993 ch 458 §2 (AB 247); Stats 1995 ch 185 §1 (AB 431).

§1797.3. Required written warranty; Contents

The mobilehome/manufactured home warranty from the contractor, manufacturer, or dealer to the buyer shall be set forth in a separate written document that reprints all of the provisions of this chapter and shall be delivered to the buyer by the contractor or dealer at the time the contract of sale is signed, and shall contain, but is not limited to, the following terms:

(a) That the mobilehome or manufactured home is free from any substantial defects in materials or workmanship.

(b) That the contractor, manufacturer, or dealer or any or all of them shall take appropriate corrective action at the site of the mobilehome or manufactured home in instances of substantial defects in materials or workmanship which become evident within one year from the date of delivery of the mobilehome or manufactured home to the buyer, provided the buyer or his or her transferee gives written notice of those defects to the contractor, manufacturer, or dealer at their business address not later than one year and 10 days after date of delivery.

(c) That the manufacturer and the contractor or dealer shall be jointly and severally liable to the buyer for the fulfillment of the terms of warranty, and that the buyer may notify either one or both of the need for appropriate corrective action in instances of substantial defects in materials or workmanship.

(d) That the address and the phone number of where to mail or deliver written notices of defects shall be set forth in the document.

(e) That the one-year warranty period applies to the plumbing, heating, electrical, cooling, fire safety, and structural systems and all appliances of the mobilehome or manufactured home.

(f) That, while the manufacturers of any or all appliances may also issue their own warranties, the primary responsibility for appropriate corrective action under the warranty rests with the contractor or dealer and the manufacturer, and the buyer should report all complaints to the contractor or dealer and the manufacturer initially.

(g) That, if corrective action taken by the manufacturer or the contractor or dealer fails to eliminate a substantial defect, then the material, system, appliance, or component shall be replaced in kind. As used in this subdivision, "replaced in kind" means (1) replacement with the identical material, system, appliance, or component, and, if not available (2) replacement with a comparable or better material, system, appliance, or component. **Leg.H.** Added Stats 1971 ch 1492 §1. Amended Stats 1973 ch 807 §1; Stats 1982 ch 730 §4; Stats 1985 ch 763 §3; Stats 1990 ch 765 §1 (AB 4079); Stats 1993 ch 458 §3 (AB 247).

§1797.4. Additional rights and privileges; Prohibited waiver

The warranty under this chapter shall be in addition to, and not in derogation of, all other rights and privileges which the buyer may have under any other law or instrument. The contractor, manufacturer, or dealer shall not require the buyer to waive his or her rights under this chapter, and any waiver of these rights shall be deemed contrary to public policy and shall be unenforceable and void. **Leg.H.** Added Stats 1971 ch 1492 §1. Amended Stats 1993 ch 458 §4 (AB 247).

§1797.5. Display of copy of warranty

Every contractor or dealer shall display a copy of all of the warranty provisions required by this chapter. The copy of the warranty provisions required by this chapter shall be posted in each area where purchase orders and conditional sales contracts are written. **Leg.H.** Added Stats 1974 ch 1286 §1, operative July 1, 1975. Amended Stats 1990 ch 765 §2 (AB 4079); Stats 1993 ch 458 §5 (AB 247).

§1797.6. Records required to be kept

Manufacturers, contractors, and dealers shall keep records of all actions taken pursuant to this chapter, including all correspondence to or from the buyer for a period of three years from the date of delivery. **Leg.H.** Added Stats 1985 ch 763 §4. Amended Stats 1993 ch 458 §6 (AB 247).

§1797.7. Deadline for correcting defects

The contractor, dealer, or manufacturer shall complete warranty service to correct all substantial defects within 90 days of receiving the buyer's written notice specified in subdivision (b) of Section 1797.3, unless there are circumstances which are beyond the control of the contractor, dealer, or manufacturer. **Leg.H.** Added Stats 1988 ch 793 §2. Amended Stats 1993 ch 458 §7 (AB 247).

CHAPTER 4
GREY MARKET GOODS

Definitions. §1797.8.
Disclosures required. §1797.81.
Advertisements. §1797.82.
Language in disclosures. §1797.83.
Application of other laws and regulations. §1797.84.
Liability for violation of chapter. §1797.85.
Violation as unfair competition and deceptive practice. §1797.86.

§1797.8. Definitions

(a) As used in this chapter, the term "grey market goods" means consumer goods bearing a trademark and normally accompanied by an express written warranty valid in the United States of America which are imported into the United States through channels other than the manufacturer's authorized United States distributor and which are not accompanied by the manufacturer's express written warranty valid in the United States.

(b) As used in this chapter, the term "sale" includes a lease of more than four months. **Leg.H.** Added Stats 1986 ch 1497 §2.

§1797.81. Disclosures required

(a) Every retail seller who offers grey market goods for sale shall post a conspicuous sign at the product's point of display and affix to the product or its package a conspicuous ticket, label, or tag disclosing any or all of the following, whichever is applicable:

(1) The item is not covered by a manufacturer's express written warranty valid in the United States (however, any implied warranty provided by law still exists).

(2) The item is not compatible with United States electrical currents.

(3) The item is not compatible with United States broadcast frequencies.

(4) Replacement parts are not available through the manufacturer's United States distributors.

(5) Compatible accessories are not available through the manufacturer's United States distributors.

(6) The item is not accompanied by instructions in English.

(7) The item is not eligible for a manufacturer's rebate.

(8) Any other incompatibility or nonconformity with relevant domestic standards known to the seller.

(b) The disclosure described in paragraph (1) of subdivision (a) shall not be required to be made by a retail seller with respect to grey market goods that are accompanied by an express written warranty provided by the retail seller, provided that each of the following conditions is satisfied:

(1) The protections and other benefits that are provided to the buyer by the express written warranty provided by the retail seller are equal to or better than the protections and other benefits that are provided to buyers in the United States of America by the manufacturer's express written warranty that normally accompanies the goods.

(2) The express written warranty conforms to the requirements of the Song-Beverly Consumer Warranty Act, (Chapter 1 (commencing with Section 1790)), including, but not limited to, the warranty disclosure standards specified in Section 1793.1, and the standards applicable to service and repair facilities specified in Section 1793.2.

(3) The retail seller has posted a conspicuous sign at the product's point of sale or display, or has affixed to the product or its package a conspicuous ticket, label, or tag that informs prospective buyers that copies of all of the warranties applicable to the products offered for sale by the retail seller are available to prospective buyers for inspection upon request.

(4) The retail seller has complied with the provisions on presale availability of written warranties set forth in the regulations of the Federal Trade Commission adopted pursuant to the federal Magnuson-Moss Warranty-Federal Trade Commission Improvement Act (see 15 U.S.C.A. Sec. 2302(b)(1)(A) and 16 C.F.R. 702.1 et seq.).

(c) Nothing in subdivision (b) shall affect the obligations of a retail seller to make the disclosures, if any, required by any other paragraph of subdivision (a). **Leg.H.** Added Stats 1986 ch 1497 §2.

§1797.82. Advertisements

Every retail dealer who offers for sale grey market goods shall be required to disclose in any advertisement of those goods the disclosures required by Section 1797.81. The disclosure shall be made in a type of conspicuous size. **Leg.H.** Added Stats 1986 ch 1497 §2.

§1797.83. Language in disclosures

In making the disclosures prescribed by this chapter, the retail seller may use reasonably equivalent language if necessary or appropriate to achieve a clearer, or more accurate, disclosure. **Leg.H.** Added Stats 1986 ch 1497 §2.

§1797.84. Application of other laws and regulations

Nothing in this chapter shall be construed to authorize any sale of goods which is specifically prohibited by a federal or state statute or regulation or a local ordinance or regulation, or to relieve the seller of any responsibility for bringing the goods into compliance with any applicable federal or state statute or regulation or local ordinance or regulation. **Leg.H.** Added Stats 1986 ch 1497 §2.

§1797.85. Liability for violation of chapter

Any retail seller who violates this chapter shall be liable to the buyer who returns the product for a refund, or credit on credit purchases, if the product purchased has not been used in a manner inconsistent with any printed instructions provided by the seller. **Leg.H.** Added Stats 1986 ch 1497 §2.

§1797.86. Violation as unfair competition and deceptive practice

Any violation of this chapter constitutes unfair competition under Section 17200 of the Business and Professions Code, grounds for rescission under Section 1689 of this code, and an unfair method of competition or deceptive practice under Section 1770 of this code. **Leg.H.** Added Stats 1986 ch 1497 §2.

CHAPTER 5
HOME ROOF WARRANTIES

Application of chapter. §1797.90.
Necessity for written contract. §1797.91.
Beneficiaries of warranty. §1797.92.
Lifetime warranties. §1797.93.
Transferability. §1797.94.
Multiple-state warranties. §1797.95.
Timing of warranty disclosures. §1797.96.

§1797.90. Application of chapter

This chapter shall apply to all contracts and warranties for roofing materials used on a residential structure, including, but not limited to, a manufactured home or mobilehome, and to all contracts and warranties for the installation, repair, or replacement of all or any portion of the roof of a residential structure, including, but not limited to, a manufactured home or mobilehome. **Leg.H.** Added Stats 1993 ch 835 §1 (SB 409).

§1797.91. Necessity for written contract

Any contract for roofing materials, or for the installation, repair, or replacement of all or any portion of the roof of a residential structure, including, but not limited to, a manufactured home or mobilehome, shall be in writing if the contract includes any warranty of the materials or workmanship that extends for any period of time beyond completion of the work. **Leg.H.** Added Stats 1993 ch 835 §1 (SB 409).

§1797.92. Beneficiaries of warranty

For any contract subject to this chapter that is entered into on or after January 1, 1994, the warranty obligations shall inure to the benefit of, and shall be directly enforceable by, all subsequent purchasers and transferees of the residential structure, without limitation, unless the contract contains a clear and conspicuous provision limiting transferability of the warranty. **Leg.H.** Added Stats 1993 ch 835 §1 (SB 409).

§1797.93. Lifetime warranties

If any warranty subject to this chapter, uses the term "lifetime," "life," or a similar representation to describe the duration of the warranty, then the warranty shall disclose with such clarity and prominence as will be noticed and understood by prospective purchasers, the life to which the representation refers. **Leg.H.** Added Stats 1993 ch 835 §1 (SB 409).

§1797.94. Transferability

Any warranty subject to this chapter, shall inure to the benefit of, and shall be directly enforceable by, all subsequent purchasers and transferees of the residential structure, without limitation, unless the warranty contains a provision limiting transferability of the warranty. A provision limiting transferability shall be set forth at the top of the first page of the warranty in 14-point boldface type, and shall be enclosed in a rectangular box in at least 4-point type.

(b) Any disclosure required by Section 1797.93 shall also be set forth at the top of the first page of the warranty in 14-point boldface type, and shall be enclosed in a rectangular box in at least 4-point type. This disclosure may be included in a disclosure required under subdivision (a). **Leg.H.** Added Stats 1993 ch 835 §1 (SB 409).

1993 Note: The Legislature inadvertently omitted a subsection (a) designation from §1797.94.

§1797.95. Multiple-state warranties

A warrantor who provides roof warranties in multiple states may standardize the warranty to meet warranty requirements of other states. However, those standardized warranties shall meet requirements which are no less than those imposed by this chapter. **Leg.H.** Added Stats 1993 ch 835 §1 (SB 409).

§1797.96. Timing of warranty disclosures

Where a warranty subject to this chapter is provided for the benefit of the purchaser of a newly constructed residential structure, the seller shall provide the warranty disclosures required by this chapter to the purchaser prior to the close of escrow. No transfer shall be invalidated for failure to comply with this section. **Leg.H.** Added Stats 1993 ch 835 §1 (SB 409).

TITLE 1.8
PERSONAL DATA

Chapter 1. Information Practices Act of 1977.

CHAPTER 1
INFORMATION PRACTICES ACT OF 1977

Article 1. General Provisions and Legislative Findings.
Article 2. Definitions.
Article 4. Notification Requirements.
Article 5. Agency Requirements.

Article 6. Conditions of Disclosure.
Article 7. Accounting of Disclosures.
Article 8. Access to Records and Administrative Remedies.
Article 9. Civil Remedies.
Article 10. Penalties.
Article 11. Miscellaneous Provisions.
Article 12. Construction With Other Laws.

ARTICLE 1
General Provisions and Legislative Findings

Title. §1798.
Legislative declaration and findings. §1798.1.

§1798. Title

This chapter shall be known and may be cited as the Information Practices Act of 1977. **Leg.H.** Added Stats 1977 ch 709 §1, operative July 1, 1978.

Prior Law: Former §1798 was added Stats 1931 ch 1070 §1 and repealed Stats 1963 ch 819 §2, effective January 1, 1965.

Former §1798, relating to auctioneer's memorandum of sale, was enacted 1872, amended Code Amdts 1873–74 ch 612 §199, and repealed Stats 1931 ch 1070 §1.

§1798.1. Legislative declaration and findings

The Legislature declares that the right to privacy is a personal and fundamental right protected by Section 1 of Article I of the Constitution of California and by the United States Constitution and that all individuals have a right of privacy in information pertaining to them. The Legislature further makes the following findings:

(a) The right to privacy is being threatened by the indiscriminate collection, maintenance, and dissemination of personal information and the lack of effective laws and legal remedies.

(b) The increasing use of computers and other sophisticated information technology has greatly magnified the potential risk to individual privacy that can occur from the maintenance of personal information.

(c) In order to protect the privacy of individuals, it is necessary that the maintenance and dissemination of personal information be subject to strict limits. **Leg.H.** Added Stats 1977 ch 709 §1, operative July 1, 1978.

§1798.2. [Section repealed 1985]

Leg.H. Added Stats 1977 ch 709 §1, operative July 1, 1978. Repealed Stats 1985 ch 595 §1. The repealed section related to application of chapter.

ARTICLE 2
Definitions

Definitions. §1798.3.

§1798.3. Definitions

As used in this chapter:

(a) The term "personal information" means any information that is maintained by an agency that identifies or describes an individual, including, but not limited to, the individual's name, social security number, physical description, home address, home telephone number, education, financial matters, and medical or employment history. It includes statements made by, or attributed to, the individual.

(b) The term "agency" means every state office, officer, department, division, bureau, board, commission, or other state agency, except that the term agency shall not include:

(1) The California Legislature.

(2) Any agency established under Article VI of the California Constitution.

(3) The State Compensation Insurance Fund, except as to any records that contain personal information about the employees of the State Compensation Insurance Fund.

(4) A local agency, as defined in Section 7920.510 of the Government Code.

(c) The term "disclose" means to disclose, release, transfer, disseminate, or otherwise communicate all or any part of any record orally, in writing, or by electronic or any other means to any person or entity.

(d) The term "individual" means a natural person.

(e) The term "maintain" includes maintain, acquire, use, or disclose.

(f) The term "person" means any natural person, corporation, partnership, limited liability company, firm, or association.

(g) The term "record" means any file or grouping of information about an individual that is maintained by an agency by reference to an identifying particular such as the individual's name, photograph, finger or voice print, or a number or symbol assigned to the individual.

(h) The term "system of records" means one or more records, which pertain to one or more individuals, which is maintained by any agency, from which information is retrieved by the name of an individual or by some identifying number, symbol, or other identifying particular assigned to the individual.

(i) The term "governmental entity," except as used in Section 1798.26, means any branch of the federal government or of the local government.

(j) The term "commercial purpose" means any purpose that has financial gain as a major objective. It does not include the gathering or dissemination of newsworthy facts by a publisher or broadcaster.

(k) The term "regulatory agency" means the Department of Financial Protection and Innovation, the Department of Insurance, the Bureau of Real Estate, and agencies of the United States or of any other state responsible for regulating financial institutions. **Leg.H.** Added Stats 1977 ch 709 §1, operative July 1, 1978. Amended Stats 1978 ch 874 §1, effective September 19, 1978; Stats 1979 ch 143 §1, effective June 22, 1979; Stats 1980 ch 174 §1; Stats 1982 ch 604 §1; Stats 1985 ch 595 §2; Stats 1987 ch 1453 §1; Stats 1994 ch 1010 §40 (SB 2053); Stats 1996 ch 1064 §4 (AB 3351), operative July 1, 1997; Stats 2005 ch 677 §1 (SB 512), effective October 7, 2005; Stats 2013 ch 352 §52 (AB 1317), effective September 26, 2013, operative July 1, 2013; Stats 2021 ch 615 §43 (AB 474), effective January 1, 2022; Stats 2022 ch 452 §25 (SB 1498), effective January 1, 2023; Stats 2022 ch 452 §24 (SB 1498), effective January 1, 2023.

ARTICLE 3
Office of Information Practices [Repealed]

§1798.4. [Section repealed 1993]

Leg.H. Added Stats 1977 ch 709 §1, operative July 1, 1978. Repealed Stats 1991 1st Ex Sess 1991-1992 ch 21 §33.1 (ABX1-66), effective March 1, 1993. The repealed section related to establishment of Office of Information Practices.

§1798.5. [Section repealed 1993]

Leg.H. Added Stats 1977 ch 709 §1, operative July 1, 1978. Repealed Stats 1991 1st Ex Sess 1991-1992 ch 21 §33.1 (ABX1-66), effective March 1, 1993. The repealed section related to assistance to individuals in identifying records.

§1798.6. [Section repealed 1993]

Leg.H. Added Stats 1977 ch 709 §1, operative July 1, 1978. Repealed Stats 1991 1st Ex Sess 1991-1992 ch 21 §33.1 (ABX1-66), effective March 1, 1993. The repealed section related to investigation of complaints and report of violations.

§1798.7. [Section repealed 1993]

Leg.H. Added Stats 1977 ch 709 §1, operative July 1, 1978. Amended Stats 1978 ch 874 §2, effective September 19, 1978. Repealed Stats 1991 1st Ex Sess 1991-1992 ch 21 §33.1 (ABX1-66), effective March 1, 1993. The repealed section related to development of guidelines.

§1798.8. [Section repealed 1993]

Leg.H. Added Stats 1977 ch 709 §1, operative July 1, 1978. Repealed Stats 1991 1st Ex Sess 1991-1992 ch 21 §33.1 (ABX1-66), effective March 1, 1993. The repealed section related to mediation of disputes and statement of findings and recommendations.

ARTICLE 4
Notification Requirements

§1798.9. [Section repealed 1993]

Leg.H. Added Stats 1977 ch 709 §1, operative July 1, 1978. Amended Stats 1982 ch 604 §1.5; Stats 1985 ch 595 §3; Stats 1987 ch 1113 §2, effective September 25, 1987, operative January 1, 1989; Stats 1990 ch 478 §1 (SB 2466). Repealed Stats 1991 1st Ex Sess 1991-1992 ch 21 §33.2 (ABX1-66), effective March 1, 1993. The repealed section related to agencies required to file notice.

§1798.10. [Section repealed 1993]

Leg.H. Added Stats 1977 ch 709 §1, operative July 1, 1978. Amended Stats 1978 ch 874 §3, effective September 19, 1978; Stats 1982 ch 604 §2; Stats 1985 ch 595 §4; Stats 1987 ch 1113 §3, effective September 25,

1987; Stats 1990 ch 478 §2 (SB 2466). Repealed Stats 1991 1st Ex Sess 1991-1992 ch 21 §33.3 (ABX1-66), effective March 1, 1993. The repealed section related to specification of notice.

§1798.11. [Section repealed 1993]
Leg.H. Added Stats 1987 ch 1113 §4, effective September 25, 1987. Amended Stats 1990 ch 478 §3 (SB 2466). Repealed Stats 1991 1st Ex Sess 1991-1992 ch 21 §33.4 (ABX1-66), effective March 1, 1993. The repealed section related to report to Legislature.

ARTICLE 5
Agency Requirements

Records limited to relevant and necessary information. §1798.14.
Information sources. §1798.15.
Maintenance of sources of personal information collected by agency; Accessibility of sources. §1798.16.
Contents of form used to collect information. §1798.17.
Maintenance of information. §1798.18.
Record requirements applied to contractor. §1798.19.
Establishment of rules of conduct and penalties for noncompliance. §1798.20.
Safeguards to ensure compliance. §1798.21.
Designation of employee responsible for ensuring compliance. §1798.22.
Review of information by Department of Justice. §1798.23.

§1798.14. Records limited to relevant and necessary information
Each agency shall maintain in its records only personal information which is relevant and necessary to accomplish a purpose of the agency required or authorized by the California Constitution or statute or mandated by the federal government. **Leg.H.** Added Stats 1977 ch 709 §1, operative July 1, 1978. Amended Stats 1985 ch 595 §5.

§1798.15. Information sources
Each agency shall collect personal information to the greatest extent practicable directly from the individual who is the subject of the information rather than from another source. **Leg.H.** Added Stats 1977 ch 709 §1, operative July 1, 1978. Amended Stats 1985 ch 595 §6.

§1798.16. Maintenance of sources of personal information collected by agency; Accessibility of sources
(a) Whenever an agency collects personal information, the agency shall maintain the source or sources of the information, unless the source is the data subject or he or she has received a copy of the source document, including, but not limited to, the name of any source who is an individual acting in his or her own private or individual capacity. If the source is an agency, governmental entity or other organization, such as a corporation or association, this requirement can be met by maintaining the name of the agency, governmental entity, or organization, as long as the smallest reasonably identifiable unit of that agency, governmental entity, or organization is named.

(b) On or after July 1, 2001, unless otherwise authorized by the Department of Information Technology pursuant to Executive Order D-3-99, whenever an agency electronically collects personal information, as defined by Section 11015.5 of the Government Code, the agency shall retain the source or sources or any intermediate form of the information, if either are created or possessed by the agency, unless the source is the data subject that has requested that the information be discarded or the data subject has received a copy of the source document.

(c) The agency shall maintain the source or sources of the information in a readily accessible form so as to be able to provide it to the data subject when they inspect any record pursuant to Section 1798.34. This section shall not apply if the source or sources are exempt from disclosure under the provisions of this chapter. **Leg.H.** Added Stats 1977 ch 709 §1, operative July 1, 1978. Amended Stats 1998 ch 429 §1 (SB 1386); Stats 1999 ch 784 §7 (AB 724), effective October 10, 1999.

§1798.17. Contents of form used to collect information
Each agency shall provide on or with any form used to collect personal information from individuals the notice specified in this section. When contact with the individual is of a regularly recurring nature, an initial notice followed by a periodic notice of not more than one-year intervals shall satisfy this requirement. This requirement is also satisfied by notification to individuals of the availability of the notice in annual tax-related pamphlets or booklets provided for them. The notice shall include all of the following:

(a) The name of the agency and the division within the agency that is requesting the information.

(b) The title, business address, and telephone number of the agency official who is responsible for the system of records and who shall, upon request, inform an individual regarding the location of his or her records and the categories of any persons who use the information in those records.

(c) The authority, whether granted by statute, regulation, or executive order which authorizes the maintenance of the information.

(d) With respect to each item of information, whether submission of such information is mandatory or voluntary.

(e) The consequences, if any, of not providing all or any part of the requested information.

(f) The principal purpose or purposes within the agency for which the information is to be used.

(g) Any known or foreseeable disclosures which may be made of the information pursuant to subdivision (e) or (f) of Section 1798.24.

(h) The individual's right of access to records containing personal information which are maintained by the agency.

This section does not apply to any enforcement document issued by an employee of a law enforcement agency in the performance of his or her duties wherein the violator is provided an exact copy of the document, or to accident reports whereby the parties of interest may obtain a copy of the report pursuant to Section 20012 of the Vehicle Code.

The notice required by this section does not apply to agency requirements for an individual to provide his or her name, identifying number, photograph, address, or similar identifying information, if this information is used only for the purpose of identification and communication with the individual by the agency, except that requirements for an individual's social security number shall conform with the provisions of the Federal Privacy Act of 1974 (Public Law 93-579). **Leg.H.** Added Stats 1977 ch 709 §1, operative July 1, 1978. Amended Stats 1978 ch 874 §3.5, effective September 19, 1978; Stats 1982 ch 604 §2.5; Stats 1985 ch 595 §7.

§1798.18. Maintenance of information
Each agency shall maintain all records, to the maximum extent possible, with accuracy, relevance, timeliness, and completeness.

Such standard need not be met except when such records are used to make any determination about the individual. When an agency transfers a record outside of state government, it shall correct, update, withhold, or delete any portion of the record that it knows or has reason to believe is inaccurate or untimely. **Leg.H.** Added Stats 1977 ch 709 §1, operative July 1, 1978.

§1798.19. Record requirements applied to contractor
Each agency when it provides by contract for the operation or maintenance of records containing personal information to accomplish an agency function, shall cause, consistent with its authority, the requirements of this chapter to be applied to those records. For purposes of Article 10 (commencing with Section 1798.55), any contractor and any employee of the contractor, if the contract is agreed to on or after July 1, 1978, shall be considered to be an employee of an agency. Local government functions mandated by the state are not deemed agency functions within the meaning of this section. **Leg.H.** Added Stats 1977 ch 709 §1, operative July 1, 1978. Amended Stats 1978 ch 874 §4, effective September 19, 1978; Stats 1985 ch 595 §8.

§1798.20. Establishment of rules of conduct and penalties for noncompliance
Each agency shall establish rules of conduct for persons involved in the design, development, operation, disclosure, or maintenance of records containing personal information and instruct each such person with respect to such rules and the requirements of this chapter, including any other rules and procedures adopted pursuant to this chapter and the remedies and penalties for noncompliance. **Leg.H.** Added Stats 1977 ch 709 §1, operative July 1, 1978. Amended Stats 1985 ch 595 §9.

§1798.21. Safeguards to ensure compliance
Each agency shall establish appropriate and reasonable administrative, technical, and physical safeguards to ensure compliance with the provisions of this chapter, to ensure the security and confidentiality of records, and to protect against anticipated threats or hazards to their security or integrity which could result in any injury. **Leg.H.** Added Stats 1977 ch 709 §1, operative July 1, 1978.

§1798.22. Designation of employee responsible for ensuring compliance

Each agency shall designate an agency employee to be responsible for ensuring that the agency complies with all of the provisions of this chapter. **Leg.H.** Added Stats 1977 ch 709 §1, operative July 1, 1978.

§1798.23. Review of information by Department of Justice

The Department of Justice shall review all personal information in its possession every five years commencing July 1, 1978, to determine whether it should continue to be exempt from access pursuant to Section 1798.40. **Leg.H.** Added Stats 1977 ch 709 §1, operative July 1, 1978. Amended Stats 1985 ch 595 §10.

ARTICLE 6
Conditions of Disclosure

Specification of restrictions. §1798.24.
Exception for screening of prospective concessionaire. §1798.24a.
Disclosure of information to agencies designated to protect rights of developmentally disabled. §1798.24b.

§1798.24. Specification of restrictions

An agency shall not disclose any personal information in a manner that would link the information disclosed to the individual to whom it pertains unless the information is disclosed, as follows:

(a) To the individual to whom the information pertains.

(b) With the prior written voluntary consent of the individual to whom the information pertains, but only if that consent has been obtained not more than 30 days before the disclosure, or in the time limit agreed to by the individual in the written consent.

(c) To the duly appointed guardian or conservator of the individual or a person representing the individual if it can be proven with reasonable certainty through the possession of agency forms, documents, or correspondence that this person is the authorized representative of the individual to whom the information pertains.

(d) To those officers, employees, attorneys, agents, or volunteers of the agency that have custody of the information if the disclosure is relevant and necessary in the ordinary course of the performance of their official duties and is related to the purpose for which the information was acquired.

(e) To a person, or to another agency if the transfer is necessary for the transferee agency to perform its constitutional or statutory duties, and the use is compatible with a purpose for which the information was collected and the use or transfer is in accordance with Section 1798.25. With respect to information transferred from a law enforcement or regulatory agency, or information transferred to another law enforcement or regulatory agency, a use is compatible if the use of the information requested is needed in an investigation of unlawful activity under the jurisdiction of the requesting agency or for licensing, certification, or regulatory purposes by that agency.

(f) To a governmental entity if required by state or federal law.

(g) Pursuant to the California Public Records Act (Division 10 (commencing with Section 7920.000) of Title 1 of the Government Code).

(h) To a person who has provided the agency with advance, adequate written assurance that the information will be used solely for statistical research or reporting purposes, but only if the information to be disclosed is in a form that will not identify any individual.

(i) Pursuant to a determination by the agency that maintains information that compelling circumstances exist that affect the health or safety of an individual, if upon the disclosure notification is transmitted to the individual to whom the information pertains at the individual's last known address. Disclosure shall not be made if it is in conflict with other state or federal laws.

(j) To the State Archives as a record that has sufficient historical or other value to warrant its continued preservation by the California state government, or for evaluation by the Director of General Services or the director's designee to determine whether the record has further administrative, legal, or fiscal value.

(k) To any person pursuant to a subpoena, court order, or other compulsory legal process if, before the disclosure, the agency reasonably attempts to notify the individual to whom the record pertains, and if the notification is not prohibited by law.

(*l*) To any person pursuant to a search warrant.

(m) Pursuant to Article 3 (commencing with Section 1800) of Chapter 1 of Division 2 of the Vehicle Code.

(n) For the sole purpose of verifying and paying government health care service claims made pursuant to Division 9 (commencing with Section 10000) of the Welfare and Institutions Code.

(o) To a law enforcement or regulatory agency when required for an investigation of unlawful activity or for licensing, certification, or regulatory purposes, unless the disclosure is otherwise prohibited by law.

(p) To another person or governmental organization to the extent necessary to obtain information from the person or governmental organization for an investigation by the agency of a failure to comply with a specific state law that the agency is responsible for enforcing.

(q) To an adopted person and disclosure is limited to general background information pertaining to the adopted person's biological parents, if the information does not include or reveal the identity of the biological parents.

(r) To a child or a grandchild of an adopted person and disclosure is limited to medically necessary information pertaining to the adopted person's biological parents. However, the information, or the process for obtaining the information, shall not include or reveal the identity of the biological parents. The State Department of Social Services shall adopt regulations governing the release of information pursuant to this subdivision. The regulations shall require licensed adoption agencies to provide the same services provided by the department as established by this subdivision.

(s) To a committee of the Legislature or to a Member of the Legislature, or the member's staff if authorized in writing by the member, if the member has permission to obtain the information from the individual to whom it pertains or if the member provides reasonable assurance that the member is acting on behalf of the individual.

(t)(1) To the University of California, a nonprofit educational institution, an established nonprofit research institution performing health or social services research, the Cradle-to-Career Data System, for purposes consistent with the creation and execution of the Cradle-to-Career Data System Act pursuant to Article 2 (commencing with Section 10860) of Chapter 8.5 of Part 7 of Division 1 of Title 1 of the Education Code, or, in the case of education-related data, another nonprofit entity, conducting scientific research, if the request for information is approved by the Committee for the Protection of Human Subjects (CPHS) for the California Health and Human Services Agency (CHHSA) or an institutional review board, as authorized in paragraphs (5) and (6). The approval shall include a review and determination that all the following criteria have been satisfied:

(A) The researcher has provided a plan sufficient to protect personal information from improper use and disclosures, including sufficient administrative, physical, and technical safeguards to protect personal information from reasonable anticipated threats to the security or confidentiality of the information.

(B) The researcher has provided a sufficient plan to destroy or return all personal information as soon as it is no longer needed for the research project, unless the researcher has demonstrated an ongoing need for the personal information for the research project and has provided a long-term plan sufficient to protect the confidentiality of that information.

(C) The researcher has provided sufficient written assurances that the personal information will not be reused or disclosed to any other person or entity, or used in any manner, not approved in the research protocol, except as required by law or for authorized oversight of the research project.

(2) The CPHS shall enter into a written agreement with the Office of Cradle-to-Career Data, as defined in Section 10862 of the Education Code, to assist the managing entity of that office in its role as the institutional review board for the Cradle-to-Career Data System.

(3) The CPHS or institutional review board shall, at a minimum, accomplish all of the following as part of its review and approval of the research project for the purpose of protecting personal information held in agency databases:

(A) Determine whether the requested personal information is needed to conduct the research.

(B) Permit access to personal information only if it is needed for the research project.

(C) Permit access only to the minimum necessary personal information needed for the research project.

(D) Require the assignment of unique subject codes that are not derived from personal information in lieu of social security numbers if the research can still be conducted without social security numbers.

(E) If feasible, and if cost, time, and technical expertise permit, require the agency to conduct a portion of the data processing for the researcher to minimize the release of personal information.

(4) Reasonable costs to the agency associated with the agency's process of protecting personal information under the conditions of CPHS approval may be billed to the researcher, including, but not limited to, the agency's costs for conducting a portion of the data processing for the researcher, removing personal information, encrypting or otherwise securing personal information, or assigning subject codes.

(5) The CPHS may enter into written agreements to enable other institutional review boards to provide the data security approvals required by this subdivision, if the data security requirements set forth in this subdivision are satisfied.

(6) Pursuant to paragraph (5), the CPHS shall enter into a written agreement with the institutional review board established pursuant to former Section 49079.6 of the Education Code. The agreement shall authorize, commencing July 1, 2010, or the date upon which the written agreement is executed, whichever is later, that board to provide the data security approvals required by this subdivision, if the data security requirements set forth in this subdivision and the act specified in subdivision (a) of Section 49079.5 of the Education Code are satisfied.

(u) To an insurer if authorized by Chapter 5 (commencing with Section 10900) of Division 4 of the Vehicle Code.

(v) Pursuant to Section 450, 452, 8009, or 18396 of the Financial Code.

(w) For the sole purpose of participation in interstate data sharing of prescription drug monitoring program information pursuant to the California Uniform Controlled Substances Act (Division 10 (commencing with Section 11000) of the Health and Safety Code), if disclosure is limited to prescription drug monitoring program information.

This article does not require the disclosure of personal information to the individual to whom the information pertains if that information may otherwise be withheld as set forth in Section 1798.40. **Leg.H.** Added Stats 1977 ch 709 §1, operative July 1, 1978. Amended Stats 1978 ch 874 §5, effective September 19, 1978; Stats 1979 ch 143 §2, effective June 22, 1979; Stats 1982 ch 604 §3, ch 957 §1; Stats 1984 ch 2 §1, ch 724 §1; Stats 1985 ch 595 §11; Stats 1987 ch 1453 §2; Stats 1991 1st Ex Sess 1991-1992 ch 21 §33.5 (ABX1-66), effective March 1, 1993; Stats 1995 ch 480 §1.1 (AB 1482), effective October 2, 1995, operative October 2, 1995; Stats 2005 ch 241 §2 (SB 13), effective January 1, 2006; Stats 2006 ch 567 §2.5 (AB 2303), effective January 1, 2007; Stats 2008 ch 501 §1 (AB 2749), effective January 1, 2009; Stats 2010 5th Ex Sess 2009–2010 ch 1 §1 (SBX5-2), effective April 13, 2010; Stats 2010 ch 725 §1 (AB 1612), effective October 19, 2010; Stats 2014 ch 64 §2 (AB 2742), effective January 1, 2015; Stats 2018 ch 478 §1 (AB 1751), effective January 1, 2019; Stats 2022 ch 28 §21 (SB 1380), effective January 1, 2023.

§1798.24a. Exception for screening of prospective concessionaire

Notwithstanding Section 1798.24, information may be disclosed to any city, county, city and county, or district, or any officer or official thereof, if a written request is made to a local law enforcement agency and the information is needed to assist in the screening of a prospective concessionaire, and any affiliate or associate thereof, as these terms are defined in subdivision (k) of Section 432.7 of the Labor Code for purposes of consenting to, or approving of, the prospective concessionaire's application for, or acquisition of, any beneficial interest in a concession, lease, or other property interest. However, any summary criminal history information that may be disclosed pursuant to this section shall be limited to information pertaining to criminal convictions. **Leg.H.** Added Stats 1992 ch 1026 §2 (SB 1769).

§1798.24b. Disclosure of information to agencies designated to protect rights of developmentally disabled

(a) Notwithstanding Section 1798.24, except subdivision (v) thereof, information shall be disclosed to the protection and advocacy agency designated by the Governor in this state pursuant to federal law to protect and advocate for the rights of people with disabilities, as described in Division 4.7 (commencing with Section 4900) of the Welfare and Institutions Code.

(b) Information that shall be disclosed pursuant to this section includes all of the following information:

(1) Name.
(2) Address.
(3) Telephone number.
(4) Any other information necessary to identify that person whose consent is necessary for either of the following purposes:

(A) To enable the protection and advocacy agency to exercise its authority and investigate incidents of abuse or neglect of people with disabilities.

(B) To obtain access to records pursuant to Section 4903 of the Welfare and Institutions Code. **Leg.H.** Added Stats 1991 ch 534 §2 (SB 1088). Amended Stats 2003 ch 878 §2 (SB 577).

ARTICLE 7
Accounting of Disclosures

General requirement. §1798.25.
Sale of motor vehicle registration or driver's license information. §1798.26.
Retention requirement. §1798.27.
Information of disclosure and correction of error. §1798.28.
Disclosure of breach of security by agency that owns or maintains computerized data. §1798.29.

§1798.25. General requirement

(a) Each agency shall keep an accurate accounting of the date, nature, and purpose of each disclosure of a record made pursuant to subdivision (i), (k), (l), (o), or (p) of Section 1798.24. This accounting shall also be required for disclosures made pursuant to subdivision (e) or (f) of Section 1798.24 unless notice of the type of disclosure has been provided pursuant to Sections 1798.9 and 1798.10. The accounting shall also include the name, title, and business address of the person or agency to whom the disclosure was made. For the purpose of an accounting of a disclosure made under subdivision (o) of Section 1798.24, it shall be sufficient for a law enforcement or regulatory agency to record the date of disclosure, the law enforcement or regulatory agency requesting the disclosure, and whether the purpose of the disclosure is for an investigation of unlawful activity under the jurisdiction of the requesting agency, or for licensing, certification, or regulatory purposes by that agency.

(b) Routine disclosures of information pertaining to crimes, offenders, and suspected offenders to law enforcement or regulatory agencies of federal, state, and local government shall be deemed to be disclosures pursuant to subdivision (e) of Section 1798.24 for the purpose of meeting this requirement. **Leg.H.** Added Stats 1977 ch 709 §1, operative July 1, 1978. Amended Stats 1978 ch 874 §6, effective September 19, 1978; Stats 1985 ch 595 §12; Stats 1987 ch 1453 §3; Stats 2018 ch 92 §36 (SB 1289), effective January 1, 2019.

§1798.26. Sale of motor vehicle registration or driver's license information

With respect to the sale of information concerning the registration of any vehicle or the sale of information from the files of drivers' licenses, the Department of Motor Vehicles shall, by regulation, establish administrative procedures under which any person making a request for information shall be required to identify himself or herself and state the reason for making the request. These procedures shall provide for the verification of the name and address of the person making a request for the information and the department may require the person to produce the information as it determines is necessary in order to ensure that the name and address of the person are his or her true name and address. These procedures may provide for a 10-day delay in the release of the requested information. These procedures shall also provide for notification to the person to whom the information primarily relates, as to what information was provided and to whom it was provided. The department shall, by regulation, establish a reasonable period of time for which a record of all the foregoing shall be maintained.

The procedures required by this subdivision do not apply to any governmental entity, any person who has applied for and has been issued a requester code by the department, or any court of competent jurisdiction. **Leg.H.** Added Stats 1977 ch 709 §1, operative July 1, 1978. Amended Stats 1987 ch 961 §1, effective September 22, 1987; Stats 1989 ch 1213 §2.

§1798.27. Retention requirement

Each agency shall retain the accounting made pursuant to Section 1798.25 for at least three years after the disclosure for which the accounting is made, or until the record is destroyed, whichever is shorter.

Nothing in this section shall be construed to require retention of the original documents for a three-year period, providing that the agency can otherwise comply with the requirements of this section. **Leg.H.** Added Stats 1977 ch 709 §1, operative July 1, 1978.

§1798.28. Information of disclosure and correction of error

Each agency, after July 1, 1978, shall inform any person or agency to whom a record containing personal information has been disclosed during the preceding three years of any correction of an error or notation of dispute made pursuant to Sections 1798.35 and 1798.36 if (1) an accounting of the disclosure is required by Section 1798.25 or 1798.26, and the accounting has not been destroyed pursuant to Section 1798.27, or (2) the information provides the name of the person or agency to whom the disclosure was made, or (3) the person who is the subject of the disclosed record provides the name of the person or agency to whom the information was disclosed. **Leg.H.** Added Stats 1977 ch 709 §1, operative July 1, 1978. Amended Stats 1985 ch 595 §13.

§1798.29. Disclosure of breach of security by agency that owns or maintains computerized data

(a) Any agency that owns or licenses computerized data that includes personal information shall disclose any breach of the security of the system following discovery or notification of the breach in the security of the data to any resident of California (1) whose unencrypted personal information was, or is reasonably believed to have been, acquired by an unauthorized person, or, (2) whose encrypted personal information was, or is reasonably believed to have been, acquired by an unauthorized person and the encryption key or security credential was, or is reasonably believed to have been, acquired by an unauthorized person and the agency that owns or licenses the encrypted information has a reasonable belief that the encryption key or security credential could render that personal information readable or usable. The disclosure shall be made in the most expedient time possible and without unreasonable delay, consistent with the legitimate needs of law enforcement, as provided in subdivision (c), or any measures necessary to determine the scope of the breach and restore the reasonable integrity of the data system.

(b) Any agency that maintains computerized data that includes personal information that the agency does not own shall notify the owner or licensee of the information of any breach of the security of the data immediately following discovery, if the personal information was, or is reasonably believed to have been, acquired by an unauthorized person.

(c) The notification required by this section may be delayed if a law enforcement agency determines that the notification will impede a criminal investigation. The notification required by this section shall be made after the law enforcement agency determines that it will not compromise the investigation.

(d) Any agency that is required to issue a security breach notification pursuant to this section shall meet all of the following requirements:

(1) The security breach notification shall be written in plain language, shall be titled "Notice of Data Breach," and shall present the information described in paragraph (2) under the following headings: "What Happened," "What Information Was Involved," "What We Are Doing," "What You Can Do," and "For More Information." Additional information may be provided as a supplement to the notice.

(A) The format of the notice shall be designed to call attention to the nature and significance of the information it contains.

(B) The title and headings in the notice shall be clearly and conspicuously displayed.

(C) The text of the notice and any other notice provided pursuant to this section shall be no smaller than 10-point type.

(D) For a written notice described in paragraph (1) of subdivision (i), use of the model security breach notification form prescribed below or use of the headings described in this paragraph with the information described in paragraph (2), written in plain language, shall be deemed to be in compliance with this subdivision.

[name of institution / logo]	date: [insert date]
Notice of data breach	
What Happened?	
What Information Was Involved?	
What We Are Doing.	
What You Can Do.	
Other Important Information. [insert other important information]	
For More Information.	Call [telephone number] or go to [internet website]

(E) For an electronic notice described in paragraph (2) of subdivision (i), use of the headings described in this paragraph with the information described in paragraph (2), written in plain language, shall be deemed to be in compliance with this subdivision.

(2) The security breach notification described in paragraph (1) shall include, at a minimum, the following information:

(A) The name and contact information of the reporting agency subject to this section.

(B) A list of the types of personal information that were or are reasonably believed to have been the subject of a breach.

(C) If the information is possible to determine at the time the notice is provided, then any of the following: (i) the date of the breach, (ii) the estimated date of the breach, or (iii) the date range within which the breach occurred. The notification shall also include the date of the notice.

(D) Whether the notification was delayed as a result of a law enforcement investigation, if that information is possible to determine at the time the notice is provided.

(E) A general description of the breach incident, if that information is possible to determine at the time the notice is provided.

(F) The toll-free telephone numbers and addresses of the major credit reporting agencies, if the breach exposed a social security number or a driver's license or California identification card number.

(3) At the discretion of the agency, the security breach notification may also include any of the following:

(A) Information about what the agency has done to protect individuals whose information has been breached.

(B) Advice on steps that people whose information has been breached may take to protect themselves.

(e) Any agency that is required to issue a security breach notification pursuant to this section to more than 500 California residents as a result of a single breach of the security system shall electronically submit a single sample copy of that security breach notification, excluding any personally identifiable information, to the Attorney General. A single sample copy of a security breach notification shall not be deemed to be within Article 1 (commencing with Section 7923.600) of Chapter 1 of Part 5 of Division 10 of Title 1 of the Government Code.

(f) For purposes of this section, "breach of the security of the system" means unauthorized acquisition of computerized data that compromises the security, confidentiality, or integrity of personal information maintained by the agency. Good faith acquisition of personal information by an employee or agent of the agency for the purposes of the agency is not a breach of the security of the system, provided that the personal information is not used or subject to further unauthorized disclosure.

(g) For purposes of this section, "personal information" means either of the following:

(1) An individual's first name or first initial and last name in combination with any one or more of the following data elements, when either the name or the data elements are not encrypted:

(A) Social security number.

(B) Driver's license number, California identification card number, tax identification number, passport number, military identification number, or other unique identification number issued on a government document commonly used to verify the identity of a specific individual.

(C) Account number or credit or debit card number, in combination with any required security code, access code, or password that would permit access to an individual's financial account.

(D) Medical information.
(E) Health insurance information.
(F) Unique biometric data generated from measurements or technical analysis of human body characteristics, such as a fingerprint, retina, or iris image, used to authenticate a specific individual. Unique biometric data does not include a physical or digital photograph, unless used or stored for facial recognition purposes.
(G) Information or data collected through the use or operation of an automated license plate recognition system, as defined in Section 1798.90.5.
(H) Genetic data.
(2) A username or email address, in combination with a password or security question and answer that would permit access to an online account.
(h)(1) For purposes of this section, "personal information" does not include publicly available information that is lawfully made available to the general public from federal, state, or local government records.
(2) For purposes of this section, "medical information" means any information regarding an individual's medical history, mental or physical condition, or medical treatment or diagnosis by a health care professional.
(3) For purposes of this section, "health insurance information" means an individual's health insurance policy number or subscriber identification number, any unique identifier used by a health insurer to identify the individual, or any information in an individual's application and claims history, including any appeals records.
(4) For purposes of this section, "encrypted" means rendered unusable, unreadable, or indecipherable to an unauthorized person through a security technology or methodology generally accepted in the field of information security.
(5) For purposes of this section, "genetic data" means any data, regardless of its format, that results from the analysis of a biological sample of an individual, or from another source enabling equivalent information to be obtained, and concerns genetic material. Genetic material includes, but is not limited to, deoxyribonucleic acids (DNA), ribonucleic acids (RNA), genes, chromosomes, alleles, genomes, alterations or modifications to DNA or RNA, single nucleotide polymorphisms (SNPs), uninterpreted data that results from analysis of the biological sample or other source, and any information extrapolated, derived, or inferred therefrom.
(i) For purposes of this section, "notice" may be provided by one of the following methods:
(1) Written notice.
(2) Electronic notice, if the notice provided is consistent with the provisions regarding electronic records and signatures set forth in Section 7001 of Title 15 of the United States Code.
(3) Substitute notice, if the agency demonstrates that the cost of providing notice would exceed two hundred fifty thousand dollars ($250,000), or that the affected class of subject persons to be notified exceeds 500,000, or the agency does not have sufficient contact information. Substitute notice shall consist of all of the following:
(A) Email notice when the agency has an email address for the subject persons.
(B) Conspicuous posting, for a minimum of 30 days, of the notice on the agency's internet website, if the agency maintains one. For purposes of this subparagraph, conspicuous posting on the agency's internet website means providing a link to the notice on the home page or first significant page after entering the internet website that is in larger type than the surrounding text, or in contrasting type, font, or color to the surrounding text of the same size, or set off from the surrounding text of the same size by symbols or other marks that call attention to the link.
(C) Notification to major statewide media and the Office of Information Security within the Department of Technology.
(4) In the case of a breach of the security of the system involving personal information defined in paragraph (2) of subdivision (g) for an online account, and no other personal information defined in paragraph (1) of subdivision (g), the agency may comply with this section by providing the security breach notification in electronic or other form that directs the person whose personal information has been breached to promptly change the person's password and security question or answer, as applicable, or to take other steps appropriate to protect the online account with the agency and all other online accounts for which the person uses the same username or email address and password or security question or answer.

(5) In the case of a breach of the security of the system involving personal information defined in paragraph (2) of subdivision (g) for login credentials of an email account furnished by the agency, the agency shall not comply with this section by providing the security breach notification to that email address, but may, instead, comply with this section by providing notice by another method described in this subdivision or by clear and conspicuous notice delivered to the resident online when the resident is connected to the online account from an Internet Protocol address or online location from which the agency knows the resident customarily accesses the account.
(j) Notwithstanding subdivision (i), an agency that maintains its own notification procedures as part of an information security policy for the treatment of personal information and is otherwise consistent with the timing requirements of this part shall be deemed to be in compliance with the notification requirements of this section if it notifies subject persons in accordance with its policies in the event of a breach of security of the system.
(k) Notwithstanding the exception specified in paragraph (4) of subdivision (b) of Section 1798.3, for purposes of this section, "agency" includes a local agency, as defined in Section 7920.510 of the Government Code.
(*l*) For purposes of this section, "encryption key" and "security credential" mean the confidential key or process designed to render the data usable, readable, and decipherable.
(m) Notwithstanding any other law, the State Bar of California shall comply with this section. This subdivision shall not be construed to apply other provisions of this chapter to the State Bar. **Leg.H.** Added Stats 2002 ch 1054 §2 (AB 700), operative July 1, 2003. Amended Stats 2007 ch 699 §4 (AB 1298), effective January 1, 2008; Stats 2011 ch 197 §1 (SB 24), effective January 1, 2012; Stats 2013 ch 395 §1 (AB 1149) effective January 1, 2014, ch 396 §1.5 (SB 46), effective January 1, 2014; Stats 2015 ch 522 §1 (AB 964), effective January 1, 2016, ch 532 §1 (SB 34), effective January 1, 2016, ch 543 §1.3 (SB 570), effective January 1, 2016; Stats 2016 ch 86 §20 (SB 1171), effective January 1, 2017, Stats 2016 ch 337 §1 (AB 2828), effective January 1, 2017 (ch 337 prevails); Stats 2019 ch 750 §1 (AB 1130), effective January 1, 2020; Stats 2021 ch 527 §1 (AB 825), effective January 1, 2022; Stats 2021 ch 615 §45 (AB 474), effective January 1, 2022 (ch 527 prevails); Stats 2022 ch 28 §22 (SB 1380), effective January 1, 2023; Stats 2022 ch 419 §14 (AB 2958), effective September 18, 2022 (ch 419 prevails).

2002 Note: This act deals with subject matter that is of statewide concern, and it is the intent of the Legislature that this act supersede and preempt all rules, regulations, codes, statutes, or ordinances or all cities, counties, cities and counties, municipalities, and other local agencies regarding the matters expressly set forth in this act. Stats 2002 ch 1054 (AB 700) §6.

Former Sections: Former CC §1798.29, similar to the present section, was added Stats 2002 ch 915 §2 and repealed Stats 2007 ch 699 §3 (AB 1298).

ARTICLE 8
Access to Records and Administrative Remedies

Regulations to implement rights of individuals. §1798.30.
Right to inquire and be notified. §1798.32.
Fees established. §1798.33.
Permission to inspect information. §1798.34.
Permission to request amendment of record. §1798.35.
Review of refusal to amend record. §1798.36.
Disclosure required to note portion of record in dispute. §1798.37.
Protection of information source. §1798.38.
Property records. §1798.39.
Disclosure of personal information to individual to whom information pertains. §1798.40.
Procedure for disclosure of information exempt from access. §1798.41.
Deletion from disclosure of personal information to individual. §1798.42.
Disclosure of exempt information to individual. §1798.43.
Applicability of article. §1798.44.

§1798.30. Regulations to implement rights of individuals
Each agency shall either adopt regulations or publish guidelines specifying procedures to be followed in order fully to implement each of the rights of individuals set forth in this article. **Leg.H.** Added Stats 1977 ch 709 §1, operative July 1, 1978. Amended Stats 1978 ch 874 §7, effective September 19, 1978.

§1798.31. [Section repealed 1985]
Leg.H. Added Stats 1977 ch 709 §1, operative July 1, 1978. Repealed Stats 1985 ch 595 §14. The repealed section related to application of chapter.

§1798.32. Right to inquire and be notified

Each individual shall have the right to inquire and be notified as to whether the agency maintains a record about himself or herself. Agencies shall take reasonable steps to assist individuals in making their requests sufficiently specific.

Any notice sent to an individual which in any way indicates that the agency maintains any record concerning that individual shall include the title and business address of the agency official responsible for maintaining the records, the procedures to be followed to gain access to the records, and the procedures to be followed for an individual to contest the contents of these records unless the individual has received this notice from the agency during the past year.

In implementing the right conferred by this section, an agency may specify in its rules or regulations reasonable times, places, and requirements for identifying an individual who requests access to a record, and for disclosing the contents of a record. **Leg.H.** Added Stats 1977 ch 709 §1, operative July 1, 1978. Amended Stats 1978 ch 874 §8, effective September 19, 1978; Stats 1991 1st Ex Sess 1991-1992 ch 21 §33.6 (ABX1-66), effective March 1, 1993.

§1798.33. Fees established

Each agency may establish fees to be charged, if any, to an individual for making copies of a record. Such fees shall exclude the cost of any search for and review of the record, and shall not exceed ten cents ($0.10) per page, unless the agency fee for copying is established by statute. **Leg.H.** Added Stats 1977 ch 709 §1, operative July 1, 1978. Amended Stats 1978 ch 874 §9, effective September 19, 1978.

§1798.34. Permission to inspect information

(a) Except as otherwise provided in this chapter, each agency shall permit any individual upon request and proper identification to inspect all the personal information in any record containing personal information and maintained by reference to an identifying particular assigned to the individual within 30 days of the agency's receipt of the request for active records, and within 60 days of the agency's receipt of the request for records that are geographically dispersed or which are inactive and in central storage. Failure to respond within these time limits shall be deemed denial. In addition, the individual shall be permitted to inspect any personal information about himself or herself where it is maintained by reference to an identifying particular other than that of the individual, if the agency knows or should know that the information exists. The individual also shall be permitted to inspect the accounting made pursuant to Article 7 (commencing with Section 1798.25).

(b) The agency shall permit the individual, and, upon the individual's request, another person of the individual's own choosing to inspect all the personal information in the record and have an exact copy made of all or any portion thereof within 15 days of the inspection. It may require the individual to furnish a written statement authorizing disclosure of the individual's record to another person of the individual's choosing.

(c) The agency shall present the information in the record in a form reasonably comprehensible to the general public.

(d) Whenever an agency is unable to access a record by reference to name only, or when access by name only would impose an unreasonable administrative burden, it may require the individual to submit such other identifying information as will facilitate access to the record.

(e) When an individual is entitled under this chapter to gain access to the information in a record containing personal information, the information or a true copy thereof shall be made available to the individual at a location near the residence of the individual or by mail, whenever reasonable. **Leg.H.** Added Stats 1977 ch 709 §1, operative July 1, 1978. Amended Stats 1982 ch 604 §4; Stats 1985 ch 595 §15.

§1798.35. Permission to request amendment of record

Each agency shall permit an individual to request in writing an amendment of a record and, shall within 30 days of the date of receipt of such request:

(a) Make each correction in accordance with the individual's request of any portion of a record which the individual believes is not accurate, relevant, timely, or complete and inform the individual of the corrections made in accordance with their request; or

(b) Inform the individual of its refusal to amend the record in accordance with such individuals' request, the reason for the refusal, the procedures established by the agency for the individual to request a review by the head of the agency or an official specifically designated by the head of the agency of the refusal to amend, and the name, title, and business address of the reviewing official. **Leg.H.** Added Stats 1977 ch 709 §1, operative July 1, 1978.

§1798.36. Review of refusal to amend record

Each agency shall permit any individual who disagrees with the refusal of the agency to amend a record to request a review of such refusal by the head of the agency or an official specifically designated by the head of such agency, and, not later than 30 days from the date on which the individual requests such review, complete such review and make a final determination unless, for good cause shown, the head of the agency extends such review period by 30 days. If, after such review, the reviewing official refuses to amend the record in accordance with the request, the agency shall permit the individual to file with the agency a statement of reasonable length setting forth the reasons for the individual's disagreement. **Leg.H.** Added Stats 1977 ch 709 §1, operative July 1, 1978.

§1798.37. Disclosure required to note portion of record in dispute

The agency, with respect to any disclosure containing information about which the individual has filed a statement of disagreement, shall clearly note any portion of the record which is disputed and make available copies of such individual's statement and copies of a concise statement of the reasons of the agency for not making the amendment to any person or agency to whom the disputed record has been or is disclosed. **Leg.H.** Added Stats 1977 ch 709 §1, operative July 1, 1978.

§1798.38. Protection of information source

If information, including letters of recommendation, compiled for the purpose of determining suitability, eligibility, or qualifications for employment, advancement, renewal of appointment or promotion, status as adoptive parents, or for the receipt of state contracts, or for licensing purposes, was received with the promise or, prior to July 1, 1978, with the understanding that the identity of the source of the information would be held in confidence and the source is not in a supervisory position with respect to the individual to whom the record pertains, the agency shall fully inform the individual of all personal information about that individual without identification of the source. This may be done by providing a copy of the text of the material with only such deletions as are necessary to protect the identity of the source or by providing a comprehensive summary of the substance of the material. Whichever method is used, the agency shall insure that full disclosure is made to the subject of any personal information that could reasonably in any way reflect or convey anything detrimental, disparaging, or threatening to an individual's reputation, rights, benefits, privileges, or qualifications, or be used by an agency to make a determination that would affect an individual's rights, benefits, privileges, or qualifications. In institutions of higher education, "supervisory positions" shall not be deemed to include chairpersons of academic departments. **Leg.H.** Added Stats 1977 ch 709 §1, operative July 1, 1978. Amended Stats 1985 ch 595 §16.

§1798.39. Property records

Sections 1798.35, 1798.36, and 1798.37 shall not apply to any record evidencing property rights. **Leg.H.** Added Stats 1977 ch 709 §1, operative July 1, 1978.

§1798.40. Disclosure of personal information to individual to whom information pertains

This chapter shall not be construed to require an agency to disclose personal information to the individual to whom the information pertains, if the information meets any of the following criteria:

(a) Is compiled for the purpose of identifying individual criminal offenders and alleged offenders and consists only of identifying data and notations of arrests, the nature and disposition of criminal charges, sentencing, confinement, release, and parole and probation status.

(b) Is compiled for the purpose of a criminal investigation of suspected criminal activities, including reports of informants and investigators, and associated with an identifiable individual.

(c) Is contained in any record which could identify an individual and which is compiled at any stage of the process of enforcement of the criminal laws, from the arrest or indictment stage through release from supervision and including the process of extradition or the exercise of executive clemency.

(d) Is maintained for the purpose of an investigation of an individual's fitness for licensure or public employment, or of a grievance or complaint, or a suspected civil offense, so long as the information is withheld only so as not to compromise the investigation, or a related investigation. The identities of individuals who provided information for the investigation may be withheld pursuant to Section 1798.38.

(e) Would compromise the objectivity or fairness of a competitive examination for appointment or promotion in public service, or to determine fitness for licensure, or to determine scholastic aptitude.

(f) Pertains to the physical or psychological condition of the individual, if the agency determines that disclosure would be detrimental to the individual. The information shall, upon the individual's written authorization, be disclosed to a licensed medical practitioner or psychologist designated by the individual.

(g) Relates to the settlement of claims for work related illnesses or injuries and is maintained exclusively by the State Compensation Insurance Fund.

(h) Is required by statute to be withheld from the individual to whom it pertains.

This section shall not be construed to deny an individual access to information relating to him or her if access is allowed by another statute or decisional law of this state. **Leg.H.** Added Stats 1985 ch 595 §18.

Prior Law: Former §1798.40 was added Stats 1977 ch 709 §1, operative July 1, 1978, amended Stats 1982 ch 604 §5, and amended and renumbered §1798.41 by Stats 1985 ch 595 §17.

§1798.41. Procedure for disclosure of information exempt from access

(a) Except as provided in subdivision (c), if the agency determines that information requested pursuant to Section 1798.34 is exempt from access, it shall inform the individual in writing of the agency's finding that disclosure is not required by law.

(b) Except as provided in subdivision (c), each agency shall conduct a review of its determination that particular information is exempt from access pursuant to Section 1798.40, within 30 days from the receipt of a request by an individual directly affected by the determination, and inform the individual in writing of the findings of the review. The review shall be conducted by the head of the agency or an official specifically designated by the head of the agency.

(c) If the agency believes that compliance with subdivision (a) would seriously interfere with attempts to apprehend persons who are wanted for committing a crime or attempts to prevent the commission of a crime or would endanger the life of an informant or other person submitting information contained in the record, it may petition the presiding judge of the superior court of the county in which the record is maintained to issue an ex parte order authorizing the agency to respond to the individual that no record is maintained. All proceedings before the court shall be in camera. If the presiding judge finds that there are reasonable grounds to believe that compliance with subdivision (a) will seriously interfere with attempts to apprehend persons who are wanted for committing a crime or attempts to prevent the commission of a crime or will endanger the life of an informant or other person submitting information contained in the record, the judge shall issue an order authorizing the agency to respond to the individual that no record is maintained by the agency. The order shall not be issued for longer than 30 days but can be renewed at 30-day intervals. If a request pursuant to this section is received after the expiration of the order, the agency must either respond pursuant to subdivision (a) or seek a new order pursuant to this subdivision. **Leg.H.** Added Stats 1977 ch 709 §1, operative July 1, 1978, as §1798.40. Amended Stats 1982 ch 604 §5. Amended and renumbered by Stats 1985 ch 595 §17.

Prior Law: Former §1798.41 was added Stats 1977 ch 709 §1, operative July 1, 1978, amended Stats 1982 ch 604 §6, and amended and renumbered §1798.42 by Stats 1985 ch 595 §19.

§1798.42. Deletion from disclosure of personal information to individual

In disclosing information contained in a record to an individual, an agency shall not disclose any personal information relating to another individual which may be contained in the record. To comply with this section, an agency shall, in disclosing information, delete from disclosure such information as may be necessary. This section shall not be construed to authorize withholding the identities of sources except as provided in Sections 1798.38 and 1798.40. **Leg.H.** Added Stats 1977 ch 709 §1, operative July 1, 1978, as §1798.41. Amended Stats 1982 ch 604 §6. Amended and renumbered by Stats 1985 ch 595 §19.

Prior Law: Former §1798.42 was added Stats 1977 ch 709 §1, operative July 1, 1978, amended Stats 1982 ch 604 §7, and amended and renumbered §1798.43 by Stats 1985 ch 595 §20.

§1798.43. Disclosure of exempt information to individual

In disclosing information contained in a record to an individual, an agency need not disclose any information pertaining to that individual which is exempt under Section 1798.40. To comply with this section, an agency may, in disclosing personal information contained in a record, delete from the disclosure any exempt information. **Leg.H.** Added Stats 1977 ch 709 §1, operative July 1, 1978, as §1798.42. Amended Stats 1982 ch 604 §7. Amended and renumbered by Stats 1985 ch 595 §20.

Prior Law: There was another section of this number which was added Stats 1978 ch 874 §10, effective September 19, 1978, and amended and renumbered §1798.44 by Stats 1985 ch 595 §21.

§1798.44. Applicability of article

This article applies to the rights of an individual to whom personal information pertains and not to the authority or right of any other person, agency, other state governmental entity, or governmental entity to obtain this information. **Leg.H.** Added Stats 1978 ch 874 §10, effective September 19, 1978, as §1798.43. Amended and renumbered by Stats 1985 ch 595 §21.

ARTICLE 9
Civil Remedies

Actions. §1798.45.
Production and examination of records. §1798.46.
Injunction. §1798.47.
Damages and costs. §1798.48.
Jurisdiction. §1798.49.
Actions limited to factual assertion. §1798.50.
Limitation of actions. §1798.51.
Liability for disclosure of information. §1798.53.

§1798.45. Actions

An individual may bring a civil action against an agency whenever such agency does any of the following:

(a) Refuses to comply with an individual's lawful request to inspect pursuant to subdivision (a) of Section 1798.34.

(b) Fails to maintain any record concerning any individual with such accuracy, relevancy, timeliness, and completeness as is necessary to assure fairness in any determination relating to the qualifications, character, rights, opportunities of, or benefits to the individual that may be made on the basis of such record, if, as a proximate result of such failure, a determination is made which is adverse to the individual.

(c) Fails to comply with any other provision of this chapter, or any rule promulgated thereunder, in such a way as to have an adverse effect on an individual. **Leg.H.** Added Stats 1977 ch 709 §1, operative July 1, 1978.

§1798.46. Production and examination of records

In any suit brought under the provisions of subdivision (a) of Section 1798.45:

(a) The court may enjoin the agency from withholding the records and order the production to the complainant of any agency records improperly withheld from the complainant. In such a suit the court shall determine the matter de novo, and may examine the contents of any agency records in camera to determine whether the records or any portion thereof may be withheld as being exempt from the individual's right of access and the burden is on the agency to sustain its action.

(b) The court shall assess against the agency reasonable attorney's fees and other litigation costs reasonably incurred in any suit under this section in which the complainant has prevailed. A party may be considered to have prevailed even though he or she does not prevail on all issues or against all parties. **Leg.H.** Added Stats 1977 ch 709 §1, operative July 1, 1978. Amended Stats 1985 ch 595 §22.

§1798.47. Injunction

Any agency that fails to comply with any provision of this chapter may be enjoined by any court of competent jurisdiction. The court may make any order or judgment as may be necessary to prevent the use or employment by an agency of any practices which violate this chapter.

Actions for injunction under this section may be prosecuted by the Attorney General, or any district attorney in this state, in the name of the people of the State of California whether upon his or her own complaint, or of a member of the general public, or by any individual acting in his or her own behalf. **Leg.H.** Added Stats 1977 ch 709 §1, operative July 1, 1978. Amended Stats 1991 1st Ex Sess 1991-1992 ch 21 §33.7 (ABX1-66), effective March 1, 1993.

§1798.48. Damages and costs

In any suit brought under the provisions of subdivision (b) or (c) of Section 1798.45, the agency shall be liable to the individual in an amount equal to the sum of:

(a) Actual damages sustained by the individual, including damages for mental suffering.

(b) The costs of the action together with reasonable attorney's fees as determined by the court. **Leg.H.** Added Stats 1977 ch 709 §1, operative July 1, 1978.

§1798.49. Jurisdiction

An action to enforce any liability created under Sections 1798.45 to 1798.48, inclusive, may be brought in any court of competent jurisdiction in the county in which the complainant resides, or has his principal place of business, or in which the defendant's records are situated, within two years from the date on which the cause of action arises, except that where a defendant has materially and willfully misrepresented any information required under this section to be disclosed to an individual who is the subject of the information and the information so misrepresented is material to the establishment of the defendant's liability to that individual under this section, the action may be brought at any time within two years after discovery by the complainant of the misrepresentation. Nothing in Sections 1798.45 to 1798.48, inclusive, shall be construed to authorize any civil action by reason of any injury sustained as the result of any information practice covered by this chapter prior to July 1, 1978.

The rights and remedies set forth in this chapter shall be deemed to be nonexclusive and are in addition to all those rights and remedies which are otherwise available under any other provision of law. **Leg.H.** Added Stats 1977 ch 709 §1, operative July 1, 1978.

§1798.50. Actions limited to factual assertion

A civil action shall not lie under this article based upon an allegation that an opinion which is subjective in nature, as distinguished from a factual assertion, about an individual's qualifications, in connection with a personnel action concerning such an individual, was not accurate, relevant, timely, or complete. **Leg.H.** Added Stats 1977 ch 709 §1, operative July 1, 1978.

§1798.51. Limitation of actions

Where a remedy other than those provided in Articles 8 and 9 is provided by law but is not available because of lapse of time an individual may obtain a correction to a record under this chapter but such correction shall not operate to revise or restore a right or remedy not provided by this chapter that has been barred because of lapse of time. **Leg.H.** Added Stats 1977 ch 709 §1, operative July 1, 1978.

§1798.53. Liability for disclosure of information

Any person, other than an employee of the state or of a local government agency acting solely in his or her official capacity, who intentionally discloses information, not otherwise public, which they know or should reasonably know was obtained from personal information maintained by a state agency or from "records" within a "system of records" (as these terms are defined in the Federal Privacy Act of 1974 (P. L. 93-579; 5 U.S.C. 552a)) maintained by a federal government agency, shall be subject to a civil action, for invasion of privacy, by the individual to whom the information pertains.

In any successful action brought under this section, the complainant, in addition to any special or general damages awarded, shall be awarded a minimum of two thousand five hundred dollars ($2,500) in exemplary damages as well as attorney's fees and other litigation costs reasonably incurred in the suit.

The right, remedy, and cause of action set forth in this section shall be nonexclusive and is in addition to all other rights, remedies, and causes of action for invasion of privacy, inherent in Section 1 of Article I of the California Constitution. **Leg.H.** Added Stats 1977 ch 709 §1, operative July 1, 1978. Amended Stats 1985 ch 595 §23.

ARTICLE 10
Penalties

Violation by officer or employee of agency. §1798.55.
Requesting or obtaining record under false pretenses. §1798.56.
Wrongful disclosure resulting in economic loss or personal injury. §1798.57.

§1798.55. Violation by officer or employee of agency

The intentional violation of any provision of this chapter or of any rules or regulations adopted thereunder, by an officer or employee of any agency shall constitute a cause for discipline, including termination of employment. **Leg.H.** Added Stats 1977 ch 709 §1, operative July 1, 1978.

§1798.56. Requesting or obtaining record under false pretenses

Any person who willfully requests or obtains any record containing personal information from an agency under false pretenses shall be guilty of a misdemeanor and fined not more than five thousand dollars ($5,000), or imprisoned not more than one year, or both. **Leg.H.** Added Stats 1977 ch 709 §1, operative July 1, 1978. Amended Stats 1985 ch 595 §24.

§1798.57. Wrongful disclosure resulting in economic loss or personal injury

Except for disclosures which are otherwise required or permitted by law, the intentional disclosure of medical, psychiatric, or psychological information in violation of the disclosure provisions of this chapter is punishable as a misdemeanor if the wrongful disclosure results in economic loss or personal injury to the individual to whom the information pertains. **Leg.H.** Added Stats 1986 ch 94 §1, effective May 13, 1986.

ARTICLE 11
Miscellaneous Provisions

Distribution of name and address for commercial purpose. §1798.60.
Release of names and addresses of persons licensed to engage in professional occupations. §1798.61.
Removal of name from mailing list upon request. §1798.62.
Liberal construction. §1798.63.
Records accepted for storage, processing, and servicing by General Services; Records transferred to State Archives. §1798.64.
Extension of time limits. §1798.66.
Disclosure of real property lien or encumbrance records. §1798.67.
Disclosure of information when requested by district attorney. §1798.68.
Release of names and addresses by State Board of Equalization. §1798.69.

§1798.60. Distribution of name and address for commercial purpose

An individual's name and address may not be distributed for commercial purposes, sold, or rented by an agency unless such action is specifically authorized by law. **Leg.H.** Added Stats 1977 ch 709 §1, operative July 1, 1978.

§1798.61. Release of names and addresses of persons licensed to engage in professional occupations

(a) Nothing in this chapter shall prohibit the release of only names and addresses of persons possessing licenses to engage in professional occupations.

(b) Nothing in this chapter shall prohibit the release of only names and addresses of persons applying for licenses to engage in professional occupations for the sole purpose of providing those persons with informational materials relating to available professional educational materials or courses. **Leg.H.** Added Stats 1977 ch 709 §1, operative July 1, 1978. Amended Stats 1978 ch 874 §11, effective September 19, 1978; Stats 1979 ch 143 §3, effective June 22, 1979; Stats 1982 ch 1001 §1; Stats 2000 ch 962 §1 (AB 1965).

§1798.62. Removal of name from mailing list upon request

Upon written request of any individual, any agency which maintains a mailing list shall remove the individuals' name and address from such list, except that such agency need not remove the individuals' name if such name is exclusively used by the agency to directly contact the individual. **Leg.H.** Added Stats 1977 ch 709 §1, operative July 1, 1978.

§1798.63. Liberal construction

The provisions of this chapter shall be liberally construed so as to protect the rights of privacy arising under this chapter or under the Federal or State Constitution. **Leg.H.** Added Stats 1977 ch 709 §1, operative July 1, 1978.

§1798.64. Records accepted for storage, processing, and servicing by General Services; Records transferred to State Archives

(a) Each agency record which is accepted by the Director of General Services for storage, processing, and servicing in accordance with provisions of the State Administrative Manual for the purposes of this chapter shall be considered to be maintained by the agency which deposited the record and shall continue to be subject to the provisions of this chapter. The Director of General Services shall not disclose the record except to the agency which maintains the record, or pursuant to rules established by such agency which are not inconsistent with the provisions of this chapter.

(b) Each agency record pertaining to an identifiable individual which was or is transferred to the State Archives as a record which has sufficient historical or other value to warrant its continued preservation by the California state government, prior to or after July 1, 1978, shall, for the purposes of this chapter, be considered to be maintained by the archives. **Leg.H.** Added Stats 1977 ch 709 §1, operative July 1, 1978.

§1798.65. [Section repealed 1985]

Leg.H. Added Stats 1977 ch 709 §1 operative July 1, 1978. Repealed Stats 1985 ch 595 §25. The repealed section related to report to Legislature.

§1798.66. Extension of time limits

The time limits specified in Article 8 (commencing with Section 1798.30) may be extended to 60 days by the Franchise Tax Board if the following conditions exist:

(a) The request is made during the period January 1 through June 30; and

(b) The records requested are stored on magnetic tape. **Leg.H.** Added Stats 1977 ch 709 §1, operative July 1, 1978.

§1798.67. Disclosure of real property lien or encumbrance records

Where an agency has recorded a document creating a lien or encumbrance on real property in favor of the state, nothing herein shall prohibit any such agency from disclosing information relating to the identity of the person against whom such lien or encumbrance has been recorded for the purpose of distinguishing such person from another person bearing the same or a similar name. **Leg.H.** Added Stats 1977 ch 709 §1, operative July 1, 1978.

§1798.68. Disclosure of information when requested by district attorney

(a) Information which is permitted to be disclosed under the provisions of subdivision (e), (f), or (o), of Section 1798.24 shall be provided when requested by a district attorney.

A district attorney may petition a court of competent jurisdiction to require disclosure of information when an agency fails or refuses to provide the requested information within 10 working days of a request. The court may require the agency to permit inspection unless the public interest or good cause in withholding such records clearly outweighs the public interest in disclosure.

(b) Disclosure of information to a district attorney under the provisions of this chapter shall effect no change in the status of the records under any other provision of law. **Leg.H.** Added Stats 1979 ch 601 §1.

§1798.69. Release of names and addresses by State Board of Equalization

(a) Except as provided in subdivision (b), the State Board of Equalization may not release the names and addresses of individuals who are registered with, or are holding licenses or permits issued by, the State Board of Equalization except to the extent necessary to verify resale certificates or to administer the tax and fee provisions of the Revenue and Taxation Code.

(b) Nothing in this section shall prohibit the release by the State Board of Equalization to, or limit the use by, any federal or state agency, or local government, of any data collected by the board that is otherwise authorized by law. **Leg.H.** Added Stats 2000 ch 962 §2 (AB 1965).

ARTICLE 12
Construction With Other Laws

State laws authorizing withholding of records. §1798.70.
Rights of litigants. §1798.71.
Limited disclosure. §1798.72.
Right of privacy under California Constitution. §1798.73.
Student records. §1798.74.
Superseding effect of chapter. §1798.75.
Law enforcement records; Discovery. §1798.76.
Removal or alteration of records to avoid compliance with chapter; Civil actions. §1798.77.
Construction of chapter. §1798.78.

§1798.70. State laws authorizing withholding of records

This chapter shall be construed to supersede any other provision of state law, including Article 2 (commencing with Section 7924.100) of Chapter 2 of Part 5 of Division 10 of Title 1 of the Government Code, or any exemption in Section 7922.000 of the Government Code or in any provision listed in Section 7920.505 of the Government Code, which authorizes any agency to withhold from an individual any record containing personal information that is otherwise accessible under the provisions of this chapter. **Leg.H.** Added Stats 1977 ch 709 §1, operative July 1, 1978. Amended Stats 1978 ch 874 §12, effective September 19, 1978; Stats 2021 ch 615 §46 (AB 474), effective January 1, 2022.

§1798.71. Rights of litigants

This chapter shall not be deemed to abridge or limit the rights of litigants, including parties to administrative proceedings, under the laws, or case law, of discovery of this state. **Leg.H.** Added Stats 1977 ch 709 §1, operative July 1, 1978.

§1798.72. Limited disclosure

Nothing in this chapter shall be construed to authorize the disclosure of any record containing personal information, other than to the subject of such records, in violation of any other law. **Leg.H.** Added Stats 1977 ch 709 §1, operative July 1, 1978.

§1798.73. Right of privacy under California Constitution

Nothing in this chapter shall be construed to deny or limit any right of privacy arising under Section 1 of Article I of the California Constitution. **Leg.H.** Added Stats 1977 ch 709 §1, operative July 1, 1978.

§1798.74. Student records

The provisions of Chapter 13 (commencing with Section 67110) of Part 40 of the Education Code shall, with regard to student records, prevail over the provisions of this chapter. **Leg.H.** Added Stats 1977 ch 709 §1, operative July 1, 1978.

§1798.75. Superseding effect of chapter

This chapter shall not be deemed to supersede Division 10 (commencing with Section 7920.000) of Title 1 of the Government Code, except as to the provisions of Sections 1798.60, 1798.69, and 1798.70. **Leg.H.** Added Stats 1977 ch 709 §1, operative July 1, 1978. Amended Stats 1979 ch 143 §4, effective June 22, 1979; Stats 2000 ch 962 §3 (AB 1965); Stats 2021 ch 615 §47 (AB 474), effective January 1, 2022.

§1798.76. Law enforcement records; Discovery

Nothing in this chapter shall be construed to revoke, modify, or alter in any manner any statutory provision or any judicial decision which (a) authorizes an individual to gain access to any law enforcement record, or (b) authorizes discovery in criminal or civil litigation. **Leg.H.** Added Stats 1977 ch 709 §1, operative July 1, 1978.

§1798.77. Removal or alteration of records to avoid compliance with chapter; Civil actions

Each agency shall ensure that no record containing personal information shall be modified, transferred, or destroyed to avoid compliance with any of the provisions of this chapter. In the event that an agency fails to comply with the provisions of this section, an individual may bring a civil action and seek the appropriate remedies and damages in accordance with the provisions of Article 9 (commencing with Section 1798.45).

An agency shall not remove or destroy personal information about an individual who has requested access to the information before allowing the individual access to the record containing the information. **Leg.H.** Added Stats 1985 ch 595 §26.

§1798.78. Construction of chapter

This chapter shall not be deemed to supersede the provisions of Chapter 1299 of the Statutes of 1976. **Leg.H.** Added Stats 1985 ch 595 §27.

TITLE 1.80
IDENTIFICATION DOCUMENTS

Reading or attempting to remotely read a person's identification document using

radio frequency identification; Disclosure of operational system keys; Applicability; Penalties. §1798.79.
Definitions. §1798.795.

§1798.79. Reading or attempting to remotely read a person's identification document using radio frequency identification; Disclosure of operational system keys; Applicability; Penalties

(a) Except as provided in this section, a person or entity that intentionally remotely reads or attempts to remotely read a person's identification document using radio frequency identification (RFID), for the purpose of reading that person's identification document without that person's knowledge and prior consent, shall be punished by imprisonment in a county jail for up to one year, a fine of not more than one thousand five hundred dollars ($1,500), or both that fine and imprisonment.

(b) A person or entity that knowingly discloses, or causes to be disclosed, the operational system keys used in a contactless identification document system shall be punished by imprisonment in a county jail for up to one year, a fine of not more than one thousand five hundred dollars ($1,500), or both that fine and imprisonment.

(c) Subdivision (a) shall not apply to:

(1) The reading of a person's identification document for triage or medical care during a disaster and immediate hospitalization or immediate outpatient care directly related to a disaster, as defined by the local emergency medical services agency organized under Section 1797.200 of the Health and Safety Code.

(2) The reading of a person's identification document by a health care professional for reasons relating to the health or safety of that person or an identification document issued to a patient by emergency services.

(3) The reading of an identification document of a person who is incarcerated in the state prison or a county jail, detained in a juvenile facility operated by the Division of Juvenile Facilities in the Department of Corrections and Rehabilitation, or housed in a mental health facility, pursuant to a court order after having been charged with a crime, or to a person pursuant to a court-ordered electronic monitoring.

(4) Law enforcement or government personnel who need to read a lost identification document when the owner is unavailable for notice, knowledge, or consent, or those parties specifically authorized by law enforcement or government personnel for the limited purpose of reading a lost identification document when the owner is unavailable for notice, knowledge, or consent.

(5) Law enforcement personnel who need to read a person's identification document after an accident in which the person is unavailable for notice, knowledge, or consent.

(6) Law enforcement personnel who need to read a person's identification document pursuant to a search warrant.

(d) Subdivision (a) shall not apply to a person or entity that unintentionally remotely reads a person's identification document using RFID in the course of operating a contactless identification document system unless it knows it unintentionally read the document and thereafter intentionally does any of the following acts:

(1) Discloses what it read to a third party whose purpose is to read a person's identification document, or any information derived therefrom, without that person's knowledge and consent.

(2) Stores what it read for the purpose of reading a person's identification document, or any information derived therefrom, without that person's knowledge and prior consent.

(3) Uses what it read for the purpose of reading a person's identification document, or any information derived therefrom, without that person's knowledge and prior consent.

(e) Subdivisions (a) and (b) shall not apply to the reading, storage, use, or disclosure to a third party of a person's identification document, or information derived therefrom, in the course of an act of good faith security research, experimentation, or scientific inquiry, including, but not limited to, activities useful in identifying and analyzing security flaws and vulnerabilities.

(f) Nothing in this section shall affect the existing rights of law enforcement to access data stored electronically on driver's licenses.

(g) The penalties set forth in subdivisions (a) and (b) are independent of, and do not supersede, any other penalties provided by state law, and in the case of any conflict, the greater penalties shall apply. **Leg.H.** Added Stats 2008 ch 746 §2 (SB 31), effective January 1, 2009. Amended Stats 2009 ch 54 §5 (SB 544), effective January 1, 2010.

§1798.795. Definitions

For purposes of this title, the following definitions shall apply:

(a) "Contactless identification document system" means a group of identification documents issued and operated under a single authority that use RFID to transmit data remotely to readers intended to read that data. In a contactless identification document system, every reader must be able to read every identification document in the system.

(b) "Data" means any information stored or transmitted on an identification document in machine-readable form.

(c) "Identification document" means any document containing data that is issued to an individual and which that individual, and only that individual, uses alone or in conjunction with any other information for the primary purpose of establishing his or her identity. Identification documents specifically include, but are not limited to, the following:

(1) Driver's licenses or identification cards issued pursuant to Section 13000 of the Vehicle Code.

(2) Identification cards for employees or contractors.

(3) Identification cards issued by educational institutions.

(4) Health insurance or benefit cards.

(5) Benefit cards issued in conjunction with any government-supported aid program.

(6) Licenses, certificates, registration, or other means to engage in a business or profession regulated by the Business and Professions Code.

(7) Library cards issued by any public library.

(d) "Key" means a string of bits of information used as part of a cryptographic algorithm used in encryption.

(e) "Radio frequency identification" or "RFID" means the use of electromagnetic radiating waves or reactive field coupling in the radio frequency portion of the spectrum to communicate to or from an identification document through a variety of modulation and encoding schemes.

(f) "Reader" means a scanning device that is capable of using RFID to communicate with an identification document and read the data transmitted by that identification document.

(g) "Remotely" means that no physical contact between the identification document and a reader is necessary in order to transmit data using RFID. **Leg.H.** Added Stats 2008 ch 746 §2 (SB 31), effective January 1, 2009.

TITLE 1.807
DOMESTIC VIOLENCE, SEXUAL ASSAULT, AND STALKING: PERSONAL INFORMATION

Definitions. §1798.79.8.
Award of grants; Limitations. §1798.79.9.
Remedies. §1798.79.95.

§1798.79.8. Definitions

For purposes of this title:

(a) "Person or entity" means any individual, corporation, partnership, joint venture, or any business entity, or any state or local agency.

(b) "Personally identifying information" means:

(1) First and last name or last name only.

(2) Home or other physical address, including, but not limited to, a street name or ZIP Code, other than an address obtained pursuant to the California Safe At Home program or a business mailing address for the victim service provider.

(3) Electronic mail address or other online contact information, such as an instant messaging user identifier or a screen name that reveals an individual's electronic mail address.

(4) Telephone number, other than a business telephone number for the victim service provider.

(5) Social security number.

(6) Date of birth, with the exception of the year of birth.

(7) Internet protocol address or host name that identifies an individual.

(8) Any other information, including, but not limited to, the first and last names of children and relatives, racial or ethnic background, or religious affiliation, that, in combination with any other nonpersonally identifying information, would serve to identify any individual.

(c) "Victim service provider" means a nongovernmental organization or entity that provides shelter, programs, or services at low cost, no cost, or on a sliding scale to victims of domestic violence, dating violence, sexual assault, or stalking, or their children, either directly or through other contractual arrangements, including rape crisis centers, domestic violence shelters, domestic violence transitional housing programs, and other programs with the primary mission to provide services to victims of domestic violence, dating violence, sexual assault, or stalking, or their children, whether or not that program exists in an agency that provides additional services. **Leg.H.** Added Stats 2006 ch 54 §1 (SB 1491), effective January 1, 2007.

§1798.79.9. Award of grants; Limitations

(a) In the course of awarding grants, including, but not limited to, requests for proposals, contracts, or billing procedures, implementing programs, or providing financial support or assistance for the purpose of providing shelter, programs, or services at low cost, no cost, or on a sliding scale to victims of domestic violence, dating violence, sexual assault, or stalking, or their children, to any victim service provider, it is unlawful for any person or entity to request or require that victim service provider to provide personally identifying information regarding any of the persons to whom it is providing services, it has provided services, or it has considered or is considering providing services.

(b) In the course of awarding grants, including, but not limited to, requests for proposals, contracts, or billing procedures, implementing programs, or providing financial support or assistance for the purpose of providing shelter, programs, or services at low cost, no cost, or on a sliding scale to victims of domestic violence, dating violence, sexual assault, or stalking, or their children, to any victim service provider, it is unlawful for any person or entity to request or require that victim service provider to use any computer software, computer program, computer protocol, or other computer system that requires the disclosure of personally identifying information regarding any of the persons to whom it is providing services, it has provided services, or it has considered or is considering providing services.

(c) Nothing in this section is intended to prevent the collection of information for statistical purposes that are necessary for the proper administration of the grant, program, or financial assistance, provided that collection does not require the disclosure of information that would serve to identify any specific individual. **Leg.H.** Added Stats 2006 ch 54 §1 (SB 1491), effective January 1, 2007.

§1798.79.95. Remedies

Injunctive relief shall be available to any victim service provider aggrieved by a violation of this title. The prevailing plaintiff in any action commenced under this section shall be entitled to recover court costs and reasonable attorney's fees if the victim service provider has provided notice of this section and the asserted violation of this section to the defendant and the defendant has failed to cease the violation within five business days of receiving that notice. **Leg.H.** Added Stats 2006 ch 54 §1 (SB 1491), effective January 1, 2007.

TITLE 1.81
CUSTOMER RECORDS

Definitions. §1798.80.
Disposal of records. §1798.81.
Intent of Legislature; Reasonable security procedures; Contract required for similar protection upon disclosure; Definitions; Exceptions to applicability. §1798.81.5.
Personal information protection measures for consumer credit reporting agencies; Software updates. §1798.81.6.
Disclosure of breach in security by business maintaining computerized data that includes personal information. §1798.82.
Disclosure to customer on request of personal information provided to third parties for direct marketing purposes; Format; Privacy policy. §1798.83.
Customer records; Age information; Commercial online entertainment of employment service providers. §1798.83.5.
Violations and remedies; Safe harbor. §1798.84.

§1798.80. Definitions

The following definitions apply to this title:

(a) "Business" means a sole proprietorship, partnership, corporation, association, or other group, however organized and whether or not organized to operate at a profit, including a financial institution organized, chartered, or holding a license or authorization certificate under the law of this state, any other state, the United States, or of any other country, or the parent or the subsidiary of a financial institution. The term includes an entity that disposes of records.

(b) "Records" means any material, regardless of the physical form, on which information is recorded or preserved by any means, including in written or spoken words, graphically depicted, printed, or electromagnetically transmitted. "Records" does not include publicly available directories containing information an individual has voluntarily consented to have publicly disseminated or listed, such as name, address, or telephone number.

(c) "Customer" means an individual who provides personal information to a business for the purpose of purchasing or leasing a product or obtaining a service from the business.

(d) "Individual" means a natural person.

(e) "Personal information" means any information that identifies, relates to, describes, or is capable of being associated with, a particular individual, including, but not limited to, his or her name, signature, social security number, physical characteristics or description, address, telephone number, passport number, driver's license or state identification card number, insurance policy number, education, employment, employment history, bank account number, credit card number, debit card number, or any other financial information, medical information, or health insurance information. "Personal information" does not include publicly available information that is lawfully made available to the general public from federal, state, or local government records. **Leg.H.** Added Stats 2000 ch 1039 §1 (AB 2246). Amended Stats 2009 ch 134 §1 (AB 1094), effective January 1, 2010.

§1798.81. Disposal of records

A business shall take all reasonable steps to dispose, or arrange for the disposal, of customer records within its custody or control containing personal information when the records are no longer to be retained by the business by (a) shredding, (b) erasing, or (c) otherwise modifying the personal information in those records to make it unreadable or undecipherable through any means. **Leg.H.** Added Stats 2000 ch 1039 §1 (AB 2246). Amended Stats 2009 ch 134 §2 (AB 1094), effective January 1, 2010.

§1798.81.5. Intent of Legislature; Reasonable security procedures; Contract required for similar protection upon disclosure; Definitions; Exceptions to applicability

(a)(1) It is the intent of the Legislature to ensure that personal information about California residents is protected. To that end, the purpose of this section is to encourage businesses that own, license, or maintain personal information about Californians to provide reasonable security for that information.

(2) For the purpose of this section, the terms "own" and "license" include personal information that a business retains as part of the business' internal customer account or for the purpose of using that information in transactions with the person to whom the information relates. The term "maintain" includes personal information that a business maintains but does not own or license.

(b) A business that owns, licenses, or maintains personal information about a California resident shall implement and maintain reasonable security procedures and practices appropriate to the nature of the information, to protect the personal information from unauthorized access, destruction, use, modification, or disclosure.

(c) A business that discloses personal information about a California resident pursuant to a contract with a nonaffiliated third party that is not subject to subdivision (b) shall require by contract that the third party implement and maintain reasonable security procedures and practices appropriate to the nature of the information, to protect the personal information from unauthorized access, destruction, use, modification, or disclosure.

(d) For purposes of this section, the following terms have the following meanings:

(1) "Personal information" means either of the following:

(A) An individual's first name or first initial and the individual's last name in combination with any one or more of the following data elements, when either the name or the data elements are not encrypted or redacted:

(i) Social security number.

(ii) Driver's license number, California identification card number, tax identification number, passport number, military identification number, or other unique identification number issued on a government document commonly used to verify the identity of a specific individual.

(iii) Account number or credit or debit card number, in combination with any required security code, access code, or password that would permit access to an individual's financial account.

(iv) Medical information.

(v) Health insurance information.

(vi) Unique biometric data generated from measurements or technical analysis of human body characteristics, such as a fingerprint, retina, or iris image, used to authenticate a specific individual. Unique biometric data does not include a physical or digital photograph, unless used or stored for facial recognition purposes.

(vii) Genetic data.

(B) A username or email address in combination with a password or security question and answer that would permit access to an online account.

(2) "Medical information" means any individually identifiable information, in electronic or physical form, regarding the individual's medical history or medical treatment or diagnosis by a health care professional.

(3) "Health insurance information" means an individual's insurance policy number or subscriber identification number, any unique identifier used by a health insurer to identify the individual, or any information in an individual's application and claims history, including any appeals records.

(4) "Personal information" does not include publicly available information that is lawfully made available to the general public from federal, state, or local government records.

(5) "Genetic data" means any data, regardless of its format, that results from the analysis of a biological sample of an individual, or from another source enabling equivalent information to be obtained, and concerns genetic material. Genetic material includes, but is not limited to, deoxyribonucleic acids (DNA), ribonucleic acids (RNA), genes, chromosomes, alleles, genomes, alterations or modifications to DNA or RNA, single nucleotide polymorphisms (SNPs), uninterpreted data that results from analysis of the biological sample or other source, and any information extrapolated, derived, or inferred therefrom.

(e) The provisions of this section do not apply to any of the following:

(1) A provider of health care, health care service plan, or contractor regulated by the Confidentiality of Medical Information Act (Part 2.6 (commencing with Section 56) of Division 1).

(2) A financial institution as defined in Section 4052 of the Financial Code and subject to the California Financial Information Privacy Act (Division 1.4 (commencing with Section 4050) of the Financial Code).

(3) A covered entity governed by the medical privacy and security rules issued by the federal Department of Health and Human Services, Parts 160 and 164 of Title 45 of the Code of Federal Regulations, established pursuant to the Health Insurance Portability and Availability Act of 1996 (HIPAA).

(4) An entity that obtains information under an agreement pursuant to Article 3 (commencing with Section 1800) of Chapter 1 of Division 2 of the Vehicle Code and is subject to the confidentiality requirements of the Vehicle Code.

(5) A business that is regulated by state or federal law providing greater protection to personal information than that provided by this section in regard to the subjects addressed by this section. Compliance with that state or federal law shall be deemed compliance with this section with regard to those subjects. This paragraph does not relieve a business from a duty to comply with any other requirements of other state and federal law regarding the protection and privacy of personal information. **Leg.H.** Added Stats 2004 ch 877 §1 (AB 1950). Amended Stats 2005 ch 22 §15 (SB 1108), effective January 1, 2006; Stats 2014 ch 855 §1 (AB 1710), effective January 1, 2015; Stats 2015 ch 96 §1 (AB 1541), effective January 1, 2016; Stats 2019 ch 750 §2 (AB 1130), effective January 1, 2020; Stats 2021 ch 527 §2 (AB 825), effective January 1, 2022.

§1798.81.6. Personal information protection measures for consumer credit reporting agencies; Software updates

(a) A consumer credit reporting agency, as defined in 15 U.S.C. Sec. 1681a(p), that owns, licenses, or maintains personal information about a California resident, or a third party that maintains personal information about a California resident on behalf of a consumer credit reporting agency, that knows, or reasonably should know, that a computer system it owns, operates, or maintains, and for which it controls the security protocols, is subject to a security vulnerability that poses a significant risk, as defined in subdivision (c), to the security of computerized data that contains personal information, as defined in subdivision (h) of Section 1798.82, shall do all of the following:

(1) If a consumer credit reporting agency knows or reasonably should know that a software update is available to address the vulnerability as described in subdivision (a), the agency shall begin the necessary testing, planning, and assessment of its systems for implementation of that software update in the most expedient time possible and without unreasonable delay, in keeping with industry best practices, but in any case no later than three business days after becoming aware, or after the point at which it reasonably should have become aware, of the vulnerability and the available software update. The software update shall be completed in the most expedient time possible and without unreasonable delay, in keeping with industry best practices, but in any case no later than 90 days after becoming aware, or after the point at which it reasonably should have become aware, of the vulnerability and the available software update.

(2) Until the software update described in paragraph (1) is complete, the consumer credit reporting agency shall, in keeping with industry best practices, employ reasonable compensating controls to reduce the risk of a breach caused by computer system vulnerability as described in subdivision (a).

(b) Notwithstanding whether a software update is available, the consumer credit reporting agency, in keeping with industry best practices, shall do all of the following:

(1) Identify, prioritize, and address the highest risk security vulnerabilities most quickly in order to reduce the likelihood that the vulnerabilities that pose the greatest security risk will be exploited.

(2) Test and evaluate the impact of compensating controls and software updates and how they affect the vulnerability of the system to threats to the security of computerized data.

(3) Require, by contract, that the third party implement and maintain appropriate security measures for personal information. Contracting with a third party to maintain personal information about California residents shall not relieve the consumer credit agency of the requirements of this section.

(c) As used in this section, "significant risk" means a vulnerability score, calculated using a standard measurement system that is accepted as a best practice for the industry, to determine that the risk could reasonably result in a breach of the security of the system, as defined in subdivision (g) of Section 1798.82, of personal information, as defined in subdivision (h) of Section 1798.82.

(d) As used in this section, "compensating controls" means controls that the agency reasonably believes will prevent the computer system vulnerability as described in subdivision (a) from being exploited while the software update is being tested, assessed, and a plan for implementation is being developed, and have been adequately tested and confirmed to sufficiently offset the risk of breach caused by computer system vulnerability as described in subdivision (a).

(e) Nothing in this section shall reduce the responsibilities and obligations of a consumer credit reporting agency or third party under this title, including, but not limited to, Section 1798.81.5.

(f) The Attorney General has exclusive authority to enforce this section. **Leg.H.** Added Stats 2018 ch 532 §1 (AB 1859), effective January 1, 2019.

§1798.82. Disclosure of breach in security by business maintaining computerized data that includes personal information

(a) A person or business that conducts business in California, and that owns or licenses computerized data that includes personal information, shall disclose a breach of the security of the system following discovery or notification of the breach in the security of the data to a resident of California (1) whose unencrypted personal information was, or is reasonably believed to have been, acquired by an unauthorized person, or, (2) whose encrypted personal information was, or is reasonably believed to have been, acquired by an unauthorized person and the encryption key or security credential was, or is reasonably believed to have been, acquired by an unauthorized person and the person or business that owns or licenses the encrypted information has a reasonable belief that the encryption key or security credential could render that personal information readable or usable. The disclosure shall be made in the most expedient time possible and without unreasonable delay, consistent with the legitimate needs of law enforcement, as provided in subdivision (c), or any measures necessary to determine the scope of the breach and restore the reasonable integrity of the data system.

(b) A person or business that maintains computerized data that includes personal information that the person or business does not own shall notify the owner or licensee of the information of the breach of the security of the data immediately following discovery, if the personal information was, or is reasonably believed to have been, acquired by an unauthorized person.

(c) The notification required by this section may be delayed if a law enforcement agency determines that the notification will impede a criminal investigation. The notification required by this section shall be made promptly after the law enforcement agency determines that it will not compromise the investigation.

(d) A person or business that is required to issue a security breach notification pursuant to this section shall meet all of the following requirements:

(1) The security breach notification shall be written in plain language, shall be titled "Notice of Data Breach," and shall present the information described in paragraph (2) under the following headings: "What Happened," "What Information Was Involved," "What We Are Doing," "What You Can Do," and "For More Information." Additional information may be provided as a supplement to the notice.

(A) The format of the notice shall be designed to call attention to the nature and significance of the information it contains.

(B) The title and headings in the notice shall be clearly and conspicuously displayed.

(C) The text of the notice and any other notice provided pursuant to this section shall be no smaller than 10-point type.

(D) For a written notice described in paragraph (1) of subdivision (j), use of the model security breach notification form prescribed below or use of the headings described in this paragraph with the information described in paragraph (2), written in plain language, shall be deemed to be in compliance with this subdivision.

[name of institution / logo] date: [insert date]	
Notice of data breach	
What Happened?	
What Information Was Involved?	
What We Are Doing.	
What You Can Do.	
Other Important Information. [insert other important information]	
For More Information.	Call [telephone number] or go to [Internet Web site]

(E) For an electronic notice described in paragraph (2) of subdivision (j), use of the headings described in this paragraph with the information described in paragraph (2), written in plain language, shall be deemed to be in compliance with this subdivision.

(2) The security breach notification described in paragraph (1) shall include, at a minimum, the following information:

(A) The name and contact information of the reporting person or business subject to this section.

(B) A list of the types of personal information that were or are reasonably believed to have been the subject of a breach.

(C) If the information is possible to determine at the time the notice is provided, then any of the following: (i) the date of the breach, (ii) the estimated date of the breach, or (iii) the date range within which the breach occurred. The notification shall also include the date of the notice.

(D) Whether notification was delayed as a result of a law enforcement investigation, if that information is possible to determine at the time the notice is provided.

(E) A general description of the breach incident, if that information is possible to determine at the time the notice is provided.

(F) The toll-free telephone numbers and addresses of the major credit reporting agencies if the breach exposed a social security number or a driver's license or California identification card number.

(G) If the person or business providing the notification was the source of the breach, an offer to provide appropriate identity theft prevention and mitigation services, if any, shall be provided at no cost to the affected person for not less than 12 months along with all information necessary to take advantage of the offer to any person whose information was or may have been breached if the breach exposed or may have exposed personal information defined in subparagraphs (A) and (B) of paragraph (1) of subdivision (h).

(3) At the discretion of the person or business, the security breach notification may also include any of the following:

(A) Information about what the person or business has done to protect individuals whose information has been breached.

(B) Advice on steps that people whose information has been breached may take to protect themselves.

(C) In breaches involving biometric data, instructions on how to notify other entities that used the same type of biometric data as an authenticator to no longer rely on data for authentication purposes.

(e) A covered entity under the federal Health Insurance Portability and Accountability Act of 1996 (42 U.S.C. Sec. 1320d et seq.) will be deemed to have complied with the notice requirements in subdivision (d) if it has complied completely with Section 13402(f) of the federal Health Information Technology for Economic and Clinical Health Act (Public Law 111-5). However, nothing in this subdivision shall be construed to exempt a covered entity from any other provision of this section.

(f) A person or business that is required to issue a security breach notification pursuant to this section to more than 500 California residents as a result of a single breach of the security system shall electronically submit a single sample copy of that security breach notification, excluding any personally identifiable information, to the Attorney General. A single sample copy of a security breach notification shall not be deemed to be within Article 1 (commencing with Section 7923.600) of Chapter 1 of Part 5 of Division 10 of Title 1 of the Government Code.

(g) For purposes of this section, "breach of the security of the system" means unauthorized acquisition of computerized data that compromises the security, confidentiality, or integrity of personal information maintained by the person or business. Good faith acquisition of personal information by an employee or agent of the person or business for the purposes of the person or business is not a breach of the security of the system, provided that the personal information is not used or subject to further unauthorized disclosure.

(h) For purposes of this section, "personal information" means either of the following:

(1) An individual's first name or first initial and last name in combination with any one or more of the following data elements, when either the name or the data elements are not encrypted:

(A) Social security number.

(B) Driver's license number, California identification card number, tax identification number, passport number, military identification number, or other unique identification number issued on a government document commonly used to verify the identity of a specific individual.

(C) Account number or credit or debit card number, in combination with any required security code, access code, or password that would permit access to an individual's financial account.

(D) Medical information.

(E) Health insurance information.

(F) Unique biometric data generated from measurements or technical analysis of human body characteristics, such as a fingerprint, retina, or iris image, used to authenticate a specific individual. Unique biometric data does not include a physical or digital photograph, unless used or stored for facial recognition purposes.

(G) Information or data collected through the use or operation of an automated license plate recognition system, as defined in Section 1798.90.5.

(H) Genetic data.

(2) A username or email address, in combination with a password or security question and answer that would permit access to an online account.

(i)(1) For purposes of this section, "personal information" does not include publicly available information that is lawfully made available to the general public from federal, state, or local government records.

(2) For purposes of this section, "medical information" means any information regarding an individual's medical history, mental or physical condition, or medical treatment or diagnosis by a health care professional.

(3) For purposes of this section, "health insurance information" means an individual's health insurance policy number or subscriber identification number, any unique identifier used by a health insurer to identify the individual, or any information in an individual's application and claims history, including any appeals records.

(4) For purposes of this section, "encrypted" means rendered unusable, unreadable, or indecipherable to an unauthorized person through a security technology or methodology generally accepted in the field of information security.

(5) "Genetic data" means any data, regardless of its format, that results from the analysis of a biological sample of an individual, or from another source enabling equivalent information to be obtained, and concerns genetic material. Genetic material includes, but is not limited to, deoxyribonucleic acids (DNA), ribonucleic acids (RNA), genes, chromosomes, alleles, genomes, alterations or modifications to DNA or RNA, single nucleotide polymorphisms (SNPs), uninterpreted data that results from analysis of the biological sample or other source, and any information extrapolated, derived, or inferred therefrom.

(j) For purposes of this section, "notice" may be provided by one of the following methods:

(1) Written notice.

(2) Electronic notice, if the notice provided is consistent with the provisions regarding electronic records and signatures set forth in Section 7001 of Title 15 of the United States Code.

(3) Substitute notice, if the person or business demonstrates that the cost of providing notice would exceed two hundred fifty thousand dollars ($250,000), or that the affected class of subject persons to be notified exceeds 500,000, or the person or business does not have sufficient contact information. Substitute notice shall consist of all of the following:

(A) Email notice when the person or business has an email address for the subject persons.

(B) Conspicuous posting, for a minimum of 30 days, of the notice on the internet website page of the person or business, if the person or business maintains one. For purposes of this subparagraph, conspicuous posting on the person's or business's internet website means providing a link to the notice on the home page or first significant page after entering the internet website that is in larger type than the surrounding text, or in contrasting type, font, or color to the surrounding text of the same size, or set off from the surrounding text of the same size by symbols or other marks that call attention to the link.

(C) Notification to major statewide media.

(4) In the case of a breach of the security of the system involving personal information defined in paragraph (2) of subdivision (h) for an online account, and no other personal information defined in paragraph (1) of subdivision (h), the person or business may comply with this section by providing the security breach notification in electronic or other form that directs the person whose personal information has been breached promptly to change the person's password and security question or answer, as applicable, or to take other steps appropriate to protect the online account with the person or business and all other online accounts for which the person whose personal information has been breached uses the same username or email address and password or security question or answer.

(5) In the case of a breach of the security of the system involving personal information defined in paragraph (2) of subdivision (h) for login credentials of an email account furnished by the person or business, the person or business shall not comply with this section by providing the security breach notification to that email address, but may, instead, comply with this section by providing notice by another method described in this subdivision or by clear and conspicuous notice delivered to the resident online when the resident is connected to the online account from an Internet Protocol address or online location from which the person or business knows the resident customarily accesses the account.

(k) For purposes of this section, "encryption key" and "security credential" mean the confidential key or process designed to render data usable, readable, and decipherable.

(*l*) Notwithstanding subdivision (j), a person or business that maintains its own notification procedures as part of an information security policy for the treatment of personal information and is otherwise consistent with the timing requirements of this part, shall be deemed to be in compliance with the notification requirements of this section if the person or business notifies subject persons in accordance with its policies in the event of a breach of security of the system. **Leg.H.** Added Stats 2002 ch 915 §4 (SB 1386), ch 1054, §4 (AB 700). Amended Stats 2007 ch 699 §6 (AB 1298), effective January 1, 2008; Stats 2011 ch 197 §2 (SB 24), effective January 1, 2012; Stats 2013 ch 396 §2 (SB 46), effective January 1, 2014; Stats 2014 ch 855 §2 (AB 1710), effective January 1, 2015; Stats 2015 ch 522 §2 (AB 964), effective January 1, 2016, ch 532 §2 (SB 34), effective January 1, 2016, ch 543 §2,3 (SB 570), effective January 1, 2016; Stats 2016 ch 86 §21 (SB 1171), effective January 1, 2017; Stats 2016 ch 337 §2 (AB 2828), effective January 1, 2017 (ch 337 prevails); Stats 2019 ch 750 §3 (AB 1130), effective January 1, 2020; Stats 2020 ch 370 §29 (SB 1371), effective January 1, 2021; Stats 2021 ch 615 §48 (AB 474), effective January 1, 2022 (ch 527 prevails); Stats 2021 ch 527 §3 (AB 825), effective January 1, 2022; Stats 2022 ch 28 §23 (SB 1380), effective January 1, 2023.

2002 Note: This act deals with a subject matter that is of statewide concern, and it is the intent of the Legislature that this act supersede and preempt all rules, regulations, codes, statutes, or ordinances or all cities, counties, cities and counties, municipalities, and other local agencies regarding the matters expressly set forth in this act. Stats 2002 ch 1054 (AB 700) §6.

Former Sections: Former CC §1798.82 was renumbered to CC §1798.84 by Stats 2002 chs 915 (SB 1386) §3, 1054 (AB 700) §3, operative July 1, 2003.

Former CC §1798.82 was added Stats 2002 ch 915 §4 and repealed Stats 2007 ch 699 (AB 1298) §5.

§1798.83. Disclosure to customer on request of personal information provided to third parties for direct marketing purposes; Format; Privacy policy

(a) Except as otherwise provided in subdivision (d), if a business has an established business relationship with a customer and has within the immediately preceding calendar year disclosed personal information that corresponds to any of the categories of personal information set forth in paragraph (6) of subdivision (e) to third parties, and if the business knows or reasonably should know that the third parties used the personal information for the third parties' direct marketing purposes, that business shall, after the receipt of a written or electronic mail request, or, if the business chooses to receive requests by toll-free telephone or facsimile numbers, a telephone or facsimile request from the customer, provide all of the following information to the customer free of charge:

(1) In writing or by electronic mail, a list of the categories set forth in paragraph (6) of subdivision (e) that correspond to the personal information disclosed by the business to third parties for the third parties' direct marketing purposes during the immediately preceding calendar year.

(2) In writing or by electronic mail, the names and addresses of all of the third parties that received personal information from the business for the third parties' direct marketing purposes during the preceding calendar year and, if the nature of the third parties' business cannot reasonably be determined from the third parties' name, examples of the products or services marketed, if known to the business, sufficient to give the customer a reasonable indication of the nature of the third parties' business.

(b)(1) A business required to comply with this section shall designate a mailing address, electronic mail address, or, if the business chooses to receive requests by telephone or facsimile, a toll-free telephone or facsimile number, to which customers may deliver requests pursuant to subdivision (a). A business required to comply with this section shall, at its election, do at least one of the following:

(A) Notify all agents and managers who directly supervise employees who regularly have contact with customers of the designated addresses or numbers or the means to obtain those addresses or numbers and instruct those employees that customers who inquire about the business's privacy practices or the business's compliance with this section shall be informed of the designated addresses or numbers or the means to obtain the addresses or numbers.

(B) Add to the home page of its Web site a link either to a page titled "Your Privacy Rights" or add the words "Your Privacy Rights" to the home page's link to the business's privacy policy. If the business elects to add the words "Your Privacy Rights" to the link to the business's privacy policy, the words "Your Privacy Rights" shall be in the same style and size as the link to the business's privacy policy. If the business does not display a link to its privacy policy on the home page of its Web site, or does not have a privacy policy, the words "Your Privacy Rights" shall be written in larger type than the surrounding text, or in contrasting type, font, or color to the surrounding text of the same size, or set off from the surrounding text of the same size by symbols or other marks that call attention to the language. The first page of the link shall describe a customer's rights pursuant to this section and shall provide the designated mailing address, e-mail address, as required, or toll-free telephone number or facsimile number, as appropriate. If the business elects to add the words "Your California Privacy Rights" to the home page's link to the business's privacy policy in a manner that complies with this subdivision, and the first page of the link describes a customer's rights pursuant to this section, and provides the designated mailing address, electronic mailing address, as required, or toll-free telephone or facsimile number, as appropriate, the business need not respond to requests that are not received at one of the designated addresses or numbers.

(C) Make the designated addresses or numbers, or means to obtain the designated addresses or numbers, readily available upon request of a customer at every place of business in California where the business or its agents regularly have contact with customers.

The response to a request pursuant to this section received at one of the designated addresses or numbers shall be provided within 30 days. Requests received by the business at other than one of the designated addresses or numbers shall be provided within a reasonable period, in light of the circumstances related to how the request was received, but not to exceed 150 days from the date received.

(2) A business that is required to comply with this section and Section 6803 of Title 15 of the United States Code may comply with this section by providing the customer the disclosure required by Section 6803 of Title 15 of the United States Code, but only if the disclosure also complies with this section.

(3) A business that is required to comply with this section is not obligated to provide information associated with specific individuals and may provide the information required by this section in standardized format.

(c)(1) A business that is required to comply with this section is not obligated to do so in response to a request from a customer more than once during the course of any calendar year. A business with fewer than 20 full-time or part-time employees is exempt from the requirements of this section.

(2) If a business that is required to comply with this section adopts and discloses to the public, in its privacy policy, a policy of not disclosing personal information of customers to third parties for the third parties' direct marketing purposes unless the customer first affirmatively agrees to that disclosure, or of not disclosing the personal information of customers to third parties for the third parties' direct marketing purposes if the customer has exercised an option that prevents that information from being disclosed to third parties for those purposes, as long as the business maintains and discloses the policies, the business may comply with subdivision (a) by notifying the customer of his or her right to prevent disclosure of personal information, and providing the customer with a cost-free means to exercise that right.

(d) The following are among the disclosures not deemed to be disclosures of personal information by a business for a third party's direct marketing purposes for purposes of this section:

(1) Disclosures between a business and a third party pursuant to contracts or arrangements pertaining to any of the following:

(A) The processing, storage, management, or organization of personal information, or the performance of services on behalf of the business during which personal information is disclosed, if the third party that processes, stores, manages, or organizes the personal information does not use the information for a third party's direct marketing purposes and does not disclose the information to additional third parties for their direct marketing purposes.

(B) Marketing products or services to customers with whom the business has an established business relationship where, as a part of the marketing, the business does not disclose personal information to third parties for the third parties' direct marketing purposes.

(C) Maintaining or servicing accounts, including credit accounts and disclosures pertaining to the denial of applications for credit or the status of applications for credit and processing bills or insurance claims for payment.

(D) Public record information relating to the right, title, or interest in real property or information relating to property characteristics, as defined in Section 408.3 of the Revenue and Taxation Code, obtained from a governmental agency or entity or from a multiple listing service, as defined in Section 1087, and not provided directly by the customer to a business in the course of an established business relationship.

(E) Jointly offering a product or service pursuant to a written agreement with the third party that receives the personal information, provided that all of the following requirements are met:

(i) The product or service offered is a product or service of, and is provided by, at least one of the businesses that is a party to the written agreement.

(ii) The product or service is jointly offered, endorsed, or sponsored by, and clearly and conspicuously identifies for the customer, the businesses that disclose and receive the disclosed personal information.

(iii) The written agreement provides that the third party that receives the personal information is required to maintain the confidentiality of the information and is prohibited from disclosing or using the information other than to carry out the joint offering or servicing of a product or service that is the subject of the written agreement.

(2) Disclosures to or from a consumer reporting agency of a customer's payment history or other information pertaining to transactions or experiences between the business and a customer if that information is to be reported in, or used to generate, a consumer report as defined in subdivision (d) of Section 1681a of Title 15 of the United States Code, and use of that information is limited by the federal Fair Credit Reporting Act (15 U.S.C. Sec. 1681 et seq.).

(3) Disclosures of personal information by a business to a third party financial institution solely for the purpose of the business obtaining payment for a transaction in which the customer paid the business for goods or services with a check, credit card, charge card, or debit card, if the customer seeks the information required by subdivision (a) from the business obtaining payment, whether or not the business obtaining payment knows or reasonably should know that the third party financial institution has used the personal information for its direct marketing purposes.

(4) Disclosures of personal information between a licensed agent and its principal, if the personal information disclosed is necessary to complete, effectuate, administer, or enforce transactions between the principal and the agent, whether or not the licensed agent or principal also uses the personal information for direct marketing purposes, if that personal information is used by each of them solely to market products and services directly to customers with whom both have established business relationships as a result of the principal and agent relationship.

(5) Disclosures of personal information between a financial institution and a business that has a private label credit card, affinity card, retail installment contract, or cobranded card program with the financial institution, if the personal information disclosed is necessary for the financial institution to maintain or service accounts on behalf of the business with which it has a private label credit card, affinity card, retail installment contract, or cobranded card program, or to complete, effectuate, administer, or enforce customer transactions or transactions between the institution and the business, whether or not the institution or the business also uses the personal information for direct marketing purposes, if that personal information is used solely to market products and services directly to customers with whom both the business and the financial institution have established business relationships as a result of the private label credit card, affinity card, retail installment contract, or cobranded card program.

(e) For purposes of this section, the following terms have the following meanings:

(1) "Customer" means an individual who is a resident of California who provides personal information to a business during the creation of, or throughout the duration of, an established business relationship if the business relationship is primarily for personal, family, or household purposes.

(2) "Direct marketing purposes" means the use of personal information to solicit or induce a purchase, rental, lease, or exchange of products, goods, property, or services directly to individuals by means of the mail, telephone, or electronic mail for their personal, family, or household purposes. The sale, rental, exchange, or lease of personal information for consideration to businesses is a direct marketing purpose of the business that sells, rents, exchanges, or obtains consideration for the personal information. "Direct marketing purposes" does not include the use of personal information (A) by bona fide tax exempt charitable or religious organizations to solicit charitable contributions, (B) to raise funds from and communicate with individuals regarding politics and government, (C) by a third party when the third party receives personal information solely as a consequence of having obtained for consideration permanent ownership of accounts that might contain personal information, or (D) by a third party when the third party receives personal information solely as a consequence of a single transaction where, as a part of the transaction, personal information had to be disclosed in order to effectuate the transaction.

(3) "Disclose" means to disclose, release, transfer, disseminate, or otherwise communicate orally, in writing, or by electronic or any other means to any third party.

(4) "Employees who regularly have contact with customers" means employees whose contact with customers is not incidental to their primary employment duties, and whose duties do not predominantly involve ensuring the safety or health of the business's customers. It includes, but is not limited to, employees whose primary employment duties are as cashier, clerk, customer service, sales, or promotion. It does not, by way of example, include employees whose primary employment duties consist of food or beverage preparation or service, maintenance and repair of the business's facilities or equipment, direct involvement in the operation of a motor vehicle, aircraft, watercraft, amusement ride, heavy machinery or similar equipment, security, or participation in a theatrical, literary, musical, artistic, or athletic performance or contest.

(5) "Established business relationship" means a relationship formed by a voluntary, two-way communication between a business and a customer, with or without an exchange of consideration, for the purpose of purchasing, renting, or leasing real or personal property, or any interest therein, or obtaining a product or service from the business, if the relationship is ongoing and has not been expressly terminated by the business or the customer, or if the relationship is not ongoing, but is solely established by the purchase, rental, or lease of real or personal property from a business, or the purchase of a product or service, and no more than 18 months have elapsed from the date of the purchase, rental, or lease.

(6)(A) The categories of personal information required to be disclosed pursuant to paragraph (1) of subdivision (a) are all of the following:
(i) Name and address.
(ii) Electronic mail address.
(iii) Age or date of birth.
(iv) Names of children.
(v) Electronic mail or other addresses of children.
(vi) Number of children.
(vii) The age or gender of children.
(viii) Height.
(ix) Weight.
(x) Race.
(xi) Religion.
(xii) Occupation.
(xiii) Telephone number.
(xiv) Education.
(xv) Political party affiliation.
(xvi) Medical condition.
(xvii) Drugs, therapies, or medical products or equipment used.
(xviii) The kind of product the customer purchased, leased, or rented.
(xix) Real property purchased, leased, or rented.
(xx) The kind of service provided.
(xxi) Social security number.
(xxii) Bank account number.
(xxiii) Credit card number.
(xxiv) Debit card number.
(xxv) Bank or investment account, debit card, or credit card balance.
(xxvi) Payment history.
(xxvii) Information pertaining to the customer's creditworthiness, assets, income, or liabilities.

(B) If a list, description, or grouping of customer names or addresses is derived using any of these categories, and is disclosed to a third party for direct marketing purposes in a manner that permits the third party to identify, determine, or extrapolate any other personal information from which the list was derived, and that personal information when it was disclosed identified, described, or was associated with an individual, the categories set forth in this subdivision that correspond to the personal information used to derive the list, description, or grouping shall be considered personal information for purposes of this section.

(7) "Personal information" as used in this section means any information that when it was disclosed identified, described, or was able to be associated with an individual and includes all of the following:
(A) An individual's name and address.
(B) Electronic mail address.
(C) Age or date of birth.
(D) Names of children.
(E) Electronic mail or other addresses of children.
(F) Number of children.
(G) The age or gender of children.
(H) Height.
(I) Weight.
(J) Race.
(K) Religion.
(L) Occupation.
(M) Telephone number.
(N) Education.
(O) Political party affiliation.
(P) Medical condition.
(Q) Drugs, therapies, or medical products or equipment used.
(R) The kind of product the customer purchased, leased, or rented.
(S) Real property purchased, leased, or rented.
(T) The kind of service provided.
(U) Social security number.
(V) Bank account number.
(W) Credit card number.
(X) Debit card number.
(Y) Bank or investment account, debit card, or credit card balance.
(Z) Payment history.
(AA) Information pertaining to creditworthiness, assets, income, or liabilities.

(8) "Third party" or "third parties" means one or more of the following:
(A) A business that is a separate legal entity from the business that has an established business relationship with a customer.
(B) A business that has access to a database that is shared among businesses, if the business is authorized to use the database for direct marketing purposes, unless the use of the database is exempt from being considered a disclosure for direct marketing purposes pursuant to subdivision (d).
(C) A business not affiliated by a common ownership or common corporate control with the business required to comply with subdivision (a).

(f)(1) Disclosures of personal information for direct marketing purposes between affiliated third parties that share the same brand name are exempt from the requirements of paragraph (1) of subdivision (a) unless the personal information disclosed corresponds to one of the following categories, in which case the customer shall be informed of those categories listed in this subdivision that correspond to the categories of personal information disclosed for direct marketing purposes and the third party recipients of personal information disclosed for direct marketing purposes pursuant to paragraph (2) of subdivision (a):
(A) Number of children.
(B) The age or gender of children.
(C) Electronic mail or other addresses of children.
(D) Height.
(E) Weight.

(F) Race.
(G) Religion.
(H) Telephone number.
(I) Medical condition.
(J) Drugs, therapies, or medical products or equipment used.
(K) Social security number.
(L) Bank account number.
(M) Credit card number.
(N) Debit card number.
(O) Bank or investment account, debit card, or credit card balance.

(2) If a list, description, or grouping of customer names or addresses is derived using any of these categories, and is disclosed to a third party or third parties sharing the same brand name for direct marketing purposes in a manner that permits the third party to identify, determine, or extrapolate the personal information from which the list was derived, and that personal information when it was disclosed identified, described, or was associated with an individual, any other personal information that corresponds to the categories set forth in this subdivision used to derive the list, description, or grouping shall be considered personal information for purposes of this section.

(3) If a business discloses personal information for direct marketing purposes to affiliated third parties that share the same brand name, the business that discloses personal information for direct marketing purposes between affiliated third parties that share the same brand name may comply with the requirements of paragraph (2) of subdivision (a) by providing the overall number of affiliated companies that share the same brand name.

(g) The provisions of this section are severable. If any provision of this section or its application is held invalid, that invalidity shall not affect other provisions or applications that can be given effect without the invalid provision or application.

(h) This section does not apply to a financial institution that is subject to the California Financial Information Privacy Act (Division 1.2 (commencing with Section 4050) of the Financial Code) if the financial institution is in compliance with Sections 4052, 4052.5, 4053, 4053.5, and 4054.6 of the Financial Code, as those sections read when they were chaptered on August 28, 2003, and as subsequently amended by the Legislature or by initiative.

(i) This section shall become operative on January 1, 2005. **Leg.H.** Added Stats 2003 ch 505 §3 (SB 27), operative January 1, 2005. Amended Stats 2004 ch 183 §34 (AB 3082); Stats 2005 ch 22 §16 (SB 1108), effective January 1, 2006.

Prior Law: Former section 1798.83, related to the waiver of provisions of the title being void, was added Stats 2002 ch 815 §15 and repealed Stats 2003 ch 505 §2.

Former CC §1798.83, related to the waiver of provisions of the title being void, was added Stats 2002 ch 815 §15 and repealed Stats 2003 ch 505 §2 (SB 27).

§1798.83.5. Customer records; Age information; Commercial online entertainment of employment service providers

(a) The purpose of this section is to ensure that information obtained on an Internet Web site regarding an individual's age will not be used in furtherance of employment or age discrimination.

(b) A commercial online entertainment employment service provider that enters into a contractual agreement to provide employment services to an individual for a subscription payment shall not, upon request by the subscriber, do either of the following:

(1) Publish or make public the subscriber's date of birth or age information in an online profile of the subscriber.

(2) Share the subscriber's date of birth or age information with any Internet Web sites for the purpose of publication.

(c) A commercial online entertainment employment service provider subject to subdivision (b) shall, within five days, remove from public view in an online profile of the subscriber the subscriber's date of birth and age information on any companion Internet Web sites under its control upon specific request by the subscriber naming the Internet Web sites. A commercial online entertainment employment service provider that permits members of the public to upload or modify Internet content on its own Internet Web site or any Internet Web site under its control without prior review by that provider shall not be deemed in violation of this section unless first requested by the subscriber to remove age information.

(d) For purposes of this section, the following definitions apply:

(1) "Commercial online entertainment employment service provider" means a person or business that owns, licenses, or otherwise possesses computerized information, including, but not limited to, age and date of birth information, about individuals employed in the entertainment industry, including television, films, and video games, and that makes the information available to the public or potential employers.

(2) "Payment" means a fee in exchange for advertisements, or any other form of compensation or benefit.

(3) "Provide employment services" means post resumes, photographs, or other information about a subscriber when one of the purposes is to provide individually identifiable information about the subscriber to a prospective employer.

(4) "Subscriber" means a natural person who enters into a contractual agreement with a commercial online entertainment employment service provider to receive employment services in return for a subscription payment. **Leg.H.** Added Stats 2016 ch 555 §1 (AB 1687), effective January 1, 2017.

§1798.84. Violations and remedies; Safe harbor

(a) Any waiver of a provision of this title is contrary to public policy and is void and unenforceable.

(b) Any customer injured by a violation of this title may institute a civil action to recover damages.

(c) In addition, for a willful, intentional, or reckless violation of Section 1798.83, a customer may recover a civil penalty not to exceed three thousand dollars ($3,000) per violation; otherwise, the customer may recover a civil penalty of up to five hundred dollars ($500) per violation for a violation of Section 1798.83.

(d) Unless the violation is willful, intentional, or reckless, a business that is alleged to have not provided all the information required by subdivision (a) of Section 1798.83, to have provided inaccurate information, failed to provide any of the information required by subdivision (a) of Section 1798.83, or failed to provide information in the time period required by subdivision (b) of Section 1798.83, may assert as a complete defense in any action in law or equity that it thereafter provided regarding the information that was alleged to be untimely, all the information, or accurate information, to all customers who were provided incomplete or inaccurate information, respectively, within 90 days of the date the business knew that it had failed to provide the information, timely information, all the information, or the accurate information, respectively.

(e) Any business that violates, proposes to violate, or has violated this title may be enjoined.

(f)(1) A cause of action shall not lie against a business for disposing of abandoned records containing personal information by shredding, erasing, or otherwise modifying the personal information in the records to make it unreadable or undecipherable through any means.

(2) The Legislature finds and declares that when records containing personal information are abandoned by a business, they often end up in the possession of a storage company or commercial landlord. It is the intent of the Legislature in paragraph (1) to create a safe harbor for such a record custodian who properly disposes of the records in accordance with paragraph (1).

(g) A prevailing plaintiff in any action commenced under Section 1798.83 shall also be entitled to recover his or her reasonable attorney's fees and costs.

(h) The rights and remedies available under this section are cumulative to each other and to any other rights and remedies available under law. **Leg.H.** Added Stats 2000 ch 1039 §1, as CC §1798.82. Renumbered by Stats 2002 ch 915 §3, ch 1054 §3. Amended Stats 2003 ch 505 §4 (SB 27); Stats 2009 ch 134 §3 (AB 1094), effective January 1, 2010.

TITLE 1.81.1
CONFIDENTIALITY OF SOCIAL SECURITY NUMBERS

Prohibition against certain uses of social security numbers; Exceptions; Applicability of section. §1798.85.
Waiver of provisions of title void. §1798.86.
Filing prohibited when untruncated social security number displayed; Compliance. §1798.89.

§1798.85. Prohibition against certain uses of social security numbers; Exceptions; Applicability of section

(a) Except as provided in this section, a person or entity may not do any of the following:

(1) Publicly post or publicly display in any manner an individual's social security number. "Publicly post" or "publicly display" means to intentionally communicate or otherwise make available to the general public.

(2) Print an individual's social security number on any card required for the individual to access products or services provided by the person or entity.

(3) Require an individual to transmit the individual's social security number over the internet, unless the connection is secure or the social security number is encrypted.

(4) Require an individual to use the individual's social security number to access an internet website, unless a password or unique personal identification number or other authentication device is also required to access the internet website.

(5) Print an individual's social security number on any materials that are mailed to the individual, unless state or federal law requires the social security number to be on the document to be mailed. Notwithstanding this paragraph, social security numbers may be included in applications and forms sent by mail, including documents sent as part of an application or enrollment process, or to establish, amend, or terminate an account, contract, or policy, or to confirm the accuracy of the social security number. A social security number that is permitted to be mailed under this section may not be printed, in whole or in part, on a postcard or other mailer not requiring an envelope, or visible on the envelope or without the envelope having been opened.

(6) Sell, advertise for sale, or offer to sell an individual's social security number. For purposes of this paragraph, the following apply:

(A) "Sell" shall not include the release of an individual's social security number if the release of the social security number is incidental to a larger transaction and is necessary to identify the individual in order to accomplish a legitimate business purpose. Release of an individual's social security number for marketing purposes is not permitted.

(B) "Sell" shall not include the release of an individual's social security number for a purpose specifically authorized or specifically allowed by federal or state law.

(b) This section does not prevent the collection, use, or release of a social security number as required by state or federal law or the use of a social security number for internal verification or administrative purposes.

(c) This section does not prevent an adult state correctional facility, an adult city jail, or an adult county jail from releasing an inmate's social security number, with the inmate's consent and upon request by the county veterans service officer or the United States Department of Veterans Affairs, for the purposes of determining the inmate's status as a military veteran and the inmate's eligibility for federal, state, or local veterans' benefits or services.

(d) This section does not apply to documents that are recorded or required to be open to the public pursuant to Chapter 14 (commencing with Section 7150) or Chapter 14.5 (commencing with Section 7220) of Division 7 of Title 1 of, Division 10 (commencing with Section 7920.000) of Title 1 of, Article 9 (commencing with Section 11120) of Chapter 1 of Part 1 of Division 3 of Title 2 of, or Chapter 9 (commencing with Section 54950) of Part 1 of Division 2 of Title 5 of, the Government Code. This section does not apply to records that are required by statute, case law, or California Rules of Court, to be made available to the public by entities provided for in Article VI of the California Constitution.

(e)(1) In the case of a health care service plan, a provider of health care, an insurer or a pharmacy benefits manager, a contractor as defined in Section 56.05, or the provision by any person or entity of administrative or other services relative to health care or insurance products or services, including third-party administration or administrative services only, this section shall become operative in the following manner:

(A) On or before January 1, 2003, the entities listed in paragraph (1) shall comply with paragraphs (1), (3), (4), and (5) of subdivision (a) as these requirements pertain to individual policyholders or individual contractholders.

(B) On or before January 1, 2004, the entities listed in paragraph (1) shall comply with paragraphs (1) to (5), inclusive, of subdivision (a) as these requirements pertain to new individual policyholders or new individual contractholders and new groups, including new groups administered or issued on or after January 1, 2004.

(C) On or before July 1, 2004, the entities listed in paragraph (1) shall comply with paragraphs (1) to (5), inclusive, of subdivision (a) for all individual policyholders and individual contractholders, for all groups, and for all enrollees of the Healthy Families and Medi-Cal programs, except that for individual policyholders, individual contractholders and groups in existence prior to January 1, 2004, the entities listed in paragraph (1) shall comply upon the renewal date of the policy, contract, or group on or after July 1, 2004, but no later than July 1, 2005.

(2) A health care service plan, a provider of health care, an insurer or a pharmacy benefits manager, a contractor, or another person or entity as described in paragraph (1) shall make reasonable efforts to cooperate, through systems testing and other means, to ensure that the requirements of this article are implemented on or before the dates specified in this section.

(3) Notwithstanding paragraph (2), the Director of the Department of Managed Health Care, pursuant to the authority granted under Section 1346 of the Health and Safety Code, or the Insurance Commissioner, pursuant to the authority granted under Section 12921 of the Insurance Code, and upon a determination of good cause, may grant extensions not to exceed six months for compliance by health care service plans and insurers with the requirements of this section when requested by the health care service plan or insurer. Any extension granted shall apply to the health care service plan or insurer's affected providers, pharmacy benefits manager, and contractors.

(f) If a federal law takes effect requiring the United States Department of Health and Human Services to establish a national unique patient health identifier program, a provider of health care, a health care service plan, a licensed health care professional, or a contractor, as those terms are defined in Section 56.05, that complies with the federal law shall be deemed in compliance with this section.

(g) A person or entity may not encode or embed a social security number in or on a card or document, including, but not limited to, using a barcode, chip, magnetic strip, or other technology, in place of removing the social security number, as required by this section.

(h) This section shall become operative, with respect to the University of California, in the following manner:

(1) On or before January 1, 2004, the University of California shall comply with paragraphs (1), (2), and (3) of subdivision (a).

(2) On or before January 1, 2005, the University of California shall comply with paragraphs (4) and (5) of subdivision (a).

(i) This section shall become operative with respect to the Franchise Tax Board on January 1, 2007.

(j) This section shall become operative with respect to the California community college districts on January 1, 2007.

(k) This section shall become operative with respect to the California State University system on July 1, 2005.

(*l*) This section shall become operative, with respect to the California Student Aid Commission and its auxiliary organization, in the following manner:

(1) On or before January 1, 2004, the commission and its auxiliary organization shall comply with paragraphs (1), (2), and (3) of subdivision (a).

(2) On or before January 1, 2005, the commission and its auxiliary organization shall comply with paragraphs (4) and (5) of subdivision (a).
Leg.H. Added Stats 2001 ch 720 §7 (SB 168). Amended Stats 2002 ch 664 §42 (AB 3034), ch 786 §3 (SB 1730); Stats 2003 ch 532 §1 (AB 763), ch 907 §5.5 (SB 25); Stats 2004 ch 183 §35; (AB 3082), ch 282 §1 (AB 3016), operative July 1, 2006 (ch 282 prevails); Stats 2013 ch 103 §1 (AB 555), effective January 1, 2014; Stats 2014 ch 855 §3 (AB 1710), effective January 1, 2015; Stats 2021 ch 615 §49 (AB 474), effective January 1, 2022.

§1798.86. Waiver of provisions of title void
Any waiver of the provisions of this title is contrary to public policy, and is void and unenforceable. **Leg.H.** Added Stats 2002 ch 815 §16 (AB 2331).

§1798.89. Filing prohibited when untruncated social security number displayed; Compliance
(a) Unless otherwise required to do so by state or federal law, no person, entity, or governmental agency shall present for recording or filing with a county recorder a document that is required by any provision of law to be open to the public if that record displays more than the last four digits of a social security number. Unless otherwise authorized by state or

federal law, a document containing more than the last four digits of a social security number is not entitled for recording.

(b) A recorder shall be deemed to be in compliance with the requirements of this section if he or she uses due diligence to truncate social security numbers in documents recorded, as provided in Article 3.5 (commencing with Section 27300) of Chapter 6 of Part 3 of Division 2 of Title 3 of the Government Code.

(c) This section shall not apply to documents created prior to January 1, 2010. **Leg.H.** Added Stats 2009 ch 552 §2 (SB 40), effective January 1, 2010.

Prior Law: Former §1798.89, similar to the present section, was added Stats 2007 ch 627 §1, effective January 1, 2008 and repealed Stats 2009 ch 552 §1, effective January 1, 2010.

Former CC §1798.89, similar to the present section, was added Stats 2007 ch 627 §1 and repealed Stats 2009 ch 552 §1.

TITLE 1.81.15
READER PRIVACY ACT

Citation; Definitions; Personal information of users confidential; Exceptions; Court safeguards; Violations and penalties; Defenses; Reports. §1798.90.
Applicability to search warrants under federal law. §1798.90.05.

§1798.90. Citation; Definitions; Personal information of users confidential; Exceptions; Court safeguards; Violations and penalties; Defenses; Reports

(a) This title shall be known and may be cited as the Reader Privacy Act.

(b) For purposes of this section:

(1) "Book" means paginated or similarly organized content in printed, audio, electronic, or other format, including fiction, nonfiction, academic, or other works of the type normally published in a volume or finite number of volumes, excluding serial publications such as a magazine or newspaper.

(2) "Book service" means a service that, as its primary purpose, provides the rental, purchase, borrowing, browsing, or viewing of books. "Book service" does not include a store that sells a variety of consumer products when the book service sales do not exceed 2 percent of the store's total annual gross sales of consumer products sold in the United States.

(3) "Government entity" means any state or local agency, including, but not limited to, a law enforcement entity or any other investigative entity, agency, department, division, bureau, board, or commission, or any individual acting or purporting to act for or on behalf of a state or local agency.

(4) "Law enforcement entity" means a district attorney, a district attorney's office, a municipal police department, a sheriff's department, a county probation department, a county social services agency, the Department of Justice, the Department of Corrections and Rehabilitation, the Department of Corrections and Rehabilitation Division of Juvenile Facilities, the Department of the California Highway Patrol, the police department of a campus of a community college, the University of California, or the California State University, or any other department or agency of the state authorized to investigate or prosecute the commission of a crime.

(5) "Personal information" means all of the following:

(A) Any information that identifies, relates to, describes, or is associated with a particular user, including, but not limited to, the information specifically listed in Section 1798.80.

(B) A unique identifier or Internet Protocol address, when that identifier or address is used to identify, relate to, describe, or be associated with a particular user or book, in whole or in partial form.

(C) Any information that relates to, or is capable of being associated with, a particular user's access to or use of a book service or a book, in whole or in partial form.

(6) "Provider" means any commercial entity offering a book service to the public.

(7) "User" means any person or entity that uses a book service.

(c) A provider shall not knowingly disclose to any government entity, or be compelled to disclose to any person, private entity, or government entity, any personal information of a user, except under any of the following circumstances:

(1) A provider shall disclose personal information of a user to a law enforcement entity only pursuant to a court order issued by a duly authorized court with jurisdiction over an offense that is under investigation and only if all of the following conditions are met:

(A) The court issuing the order finds that probable cause exists to believe the personal information requested is relevant evidence to the investigation of an offense and any of the grounds in Section 1524 of the Penal Code is satisfied.

(B) The court issuing the order finds that the law enforcement entity seeking disclosure has a compelling interest in obtaining the personal information sought.

(C) The court issuing the order finds that the personal information sought cannot be obtained by the law enforcement entity seeking disclosure through less intrusive means.

(D) Prior to issuance of the court order, the law enforcement entity seeking disclosure provides, in a timely manner, the provider with reasonable notice of the proceeding to allow the provider the opportunity to appear and contest issuance of the order.

(E) The law enforcement entity seeking disclosure has informed the provider that it has given notice of the court order to the user contemporaneously with the execution of the order, unless there is a judicial determination of a strong showing of necessity to delay that notification for a reasonable period of time, not to exceed 90 days.

(2)(A) A provider shall disclose personal information of a user to any of the following only if all of the conditions listed in subparagraph (B) are satisfied:

(i) A government entity, other than a law enforcement entity, pursuant to a court order issued by a court having jurisdiction over an offense under investigation by that government entity.

(ii) A government entity, other than a law enforcement entity, or a person or private entity pursuant to a court order in a pending action brought by the government entity or by the person or private entity.

(B) A provider shall disclose personal information of a user pursuant to subparagraph (A) only if all of the following conditions are satisfied:

(i) The court issuing the order finds that the person or entity seeking disclosure has a compelling interest in obtaining the personal information sought.

(ii) The court issuing the order finds that the personal information sought cannot be obtained by the person or entity seeking disclosure through less intrusive means.

(iii) Prior to issuance of the court order, the person or entity seeking disclosure provides, in a timely manner, the provider with reasonable notice of the proceeding to allow the provider the opportunity to appear and contest the issuance of the court order.

(iv) The provider refrains from disclosing any personal information pursuant to the court order until it provides, in a timely manner, notice to the user about the issuance of the order and the ability to appear and quash the order, and the user has been given a minimum of 35 days prior to disclosure of the information within which to appear and quash the order.

(3) A provider shall disclose the personal information of a user to any person, private entity, or government entity if the user has given his or her informed, affirmative consent to the specific disclosure for a particular purpose.

(4) A provider may disclose personal information of a user to a government entity, if the government entity asserts, and the provider in good faith believes, that there is an imminent danger of death or serious physical injury requiring the immediate disclosure of the requested personal information and there is insufficient time to obtain a court order. The government entity seeking the disclosure shall provide the provider with a written statement setting forth the facts giving rise to the emergency upon request or no later than 48 hours after seeking disclosure.

(5) A provider may disclose personal information of a user to a government entity if the provider in good faith believes that the personal information is evidence directly related and relevant to a crime against the provider or that user.

(d)(1) Any court issuing a court order requiring the disclosure of personal information of a user shall impose appropriate safeguards against the unauthorized disclosure of personal information by the provider and by the person, private entity, or government entity seeking disclosure pursuant to the order.

(2) The court may, in its discretion, quash or modify a court order requiring the disclosure of the user's personal information upon a motion made by the user, provider, person, or entity seeking disclosure.

(e) A provider, upon the request of a law enforcement entity, shall take all necessary steps to preserve records and other evidence in its possession of a user's personal information related to the use of a book or part of a book, pending the issuance of a court order or a warrant pursuant to this section or Section 1798.90.05. The provider shall retain the records and evidence for a period of 90 days from the date of the request by the law enforcement entity, which shall be extended for an additional 90-day period upon a renewed request by the law enforcement entity.

(f) Except in an action for a violation of this section, no evidence obtained in violation of this section shall be admissible in any civil or administrative proceeding.

(g)(1) Violations of this section shall be subject to the following penalties:

(A) Any provider that knowingly provides personal information about a user to a government entity in violation of this section shall be subject to a civil penalty not to exceed five hundred dollars ($500) for each violation, which shall be paid to the user in a civil action brought by the user.

(B) Any provider that knowingly provides personal information about a user to a government entity in violation of this section shall, in addition to the penalty prescribed by subparagraph (A), be subject to a civil penalty not to exceed five hundred dollars ($500) for each violation, which may be assessed and recovered in a civil action brought by the Attorney General, by any district attorney or city attorney, or by a city prosecutor in any city having a full-time city prosecutor, in any court of competent jurisdiction.

(2) If an action is brought by the Attorney General, one-half of the penalty collected shall be paid to the treasurer of the county in which the judgment was entered, and one-half to the General Fund. If the action is brought by a district attorney, the penalty collected shall be paid to the treasurer of the county in which the judgment was entered. If the action is brought by a city attorney or city prosecutor, one-half of the penalty shall be paid to the treasurer of the city in which the judgment was entered, and one-half to the treasurer of the county in which the judgment was entered.

(3) The penalties provided by this section are not the exclusive remedy and do not affect any other relief or remedy provided by law.

(4) A civil action brought pursuant to this section shall be commenced within two years after the date upon which the claimant first discovered the violation.

(h) An objectively reasonable reliance by the provider on a warrant or court order for the disclosure of personal information of a user, or on any of the enumerated exceptions to the confidentiality of a user's personal information set forth in this section, is a complete defense to any civil action for the violation of this section.

(i)(1) Unless disclosure of information pertaining to a particular request or set of requests is specifically prohibited by law, a provider shall prepare a report including all of the following information, to the extent it can be reasonably determined:

(A) The number of federal and state warrants, federal and state grand jury subpoenas, federal and state civil and administrative subpoenas, federal and state civil and criminal court orders, and requests for information made with the informed consent of the user as described in paragraph (3) of subdivision (c), seeking disclosure of any personal information of a user related to the access or use of a book service or book, received by the provider from January 1 to December 31, inclusive, of the previous year.

(B) The number of disclosures made by the provider pursuant to paragraphs (4) and (5) of subdivision (c) from January 1 to December 31, inclusive, of the previous year.

(C) For each category of demand or disclosure, the provider shall include all of the following information:

(i) The number of times notice of a court order in a criminal, civil, or administrative action has been provided by the provider and the date the notice was provided.

(ii) The number of times personal information has been disclosed by the provider.

(iii) The number of times no personal information has been disclosed by the provider.

(iv) The number of times the provider contests the demand.

(v) The number of times the user contests the demand.

(vi) The number of users whose personal information was disclosed by the provider.

(vii) The type of personal information that was disclosed and the number of times that type of personal information was disclosed.

(2) Notwithstanding paragraph (1), a provider is not required to prepare a report pursuant to this subdivision unless it has disclosed personal information related to the access or use of a book service or book of more than 30 total users consisting of users located in this state or users whose location is unknown or of both types of users.

(3) The reporting requirements of this subdivision shall not apply to information disclosed to a government entity that is made by a provider serving a postsecondary educational institution when the provider is required to disclose the information in order to be reimbursed for the sale or rental of a book that was purchased or rented by a student using book vouchers or other financial aid subsidies for books.

(j) Reports prepared pursuant to subdivision (i) shall be made publicly available in an online, searchable format on or before March 1 of each year. If the provider does not have an Internet Web site, the provider shall post the reports prominently on its premises or send the reports to the Office of Privacy Protection on or before March 1 of each year.

(k) On or before March 1 of each year, a provider subject to Section 22575 of the Business and Professions Code shall complete one of the following actions:

(1) Create a prominent hyperlink to its latest report prepared pursuant to subdivision (i) in the disclosure section of its privacy policy applicable to its book service.

(2) Post the report prepared pursuant to subdivision (i) in the section of its Internet Web site explaining the way in which user information and privacy issues related to its book service are addressed.

(3) State on its Internet Web site in one of the areas described in paragraphs (1) and (2) that no report prepared pursuant to subdivision (i) is available because the provider is exempt from the reporting requirement pursuant to paragraph (2) of subdivision (i).

(*l*) Nothing in this section shall otherwise affect the rights of any person under the California Constitution or any other law or be construed as conflicting with the federal Privacy Protection Act of 1980 (42 U.S.C. 2000aa et seq.). **Leg.H.** Added Stats 2011 ch 424 §1 (SB 602), effective January 1, 2012.

§1798.90.05. Applicability to search warrants under federal law

Section 1798.90 does not make it unlawful for a law enforcement entity subject to Section 2000aa of Title 42 of the United States Code to obtain a search warrant for the personal information of a user pursuant to otherwise applicable law in connection with the investigation or prosecution of a criminal offense when probable cause exists to believe that the person possessing the personal information has committed, or is committing, a criminal offense involving the production, possession, receipt, mailing, sale, distribution, shipment, or transportation of child pornography, the sexual exploitation of children, or the sale or purchase of children prohibited by Sections 2251, 2251A, 2252, and 2252A of Title 18 of the United States Code. Nothing in Section 1798.90 shall prevent a provider from complying with a proper search warrant issued by a duly authorized court in connection with the investigation or prosecution of any of those offenses. **Leg.H.** Added Stats 2011 ch 424 §1 (SB 602), effective January 1, 2012.

TITLE 1.81.2
CONFIDENTIALITY OF DRIVER'S LICENSE INFORMATION

Scan or swipe of driver's license or identification card in electronic device by business; Authorized uses; Punishment for violation; Organ donation and anatomical gifts. §1798.90.1.

§1798.90.1. Scan or swipe of driver's license or identification card in electronic device by business; Authorized uses; Punishment for violation; Organ donation and anatomical gifts

(a)(1) A business may scan or swipe a driver's license or identification card issued by the Department of Motor Vehicles in any electronic device for the following purposes:

(A) To verify age or the authenticity of the driver's license or identification card.

(B) To comply with a legal requirement to record, retain, or transmit that information.

(C) To transmit information to a check service company for the purpose of approving negotiable instruments, electronic funds transfers, or similar methods of payments, provided that only the name and identification number from the license or the card may be used or retained by the check service company.

(D) To collect or disclose personal information that is required for reporting, investigating, or preventing fraud, abuse, or material misrepresentation.

(2)(A) An organ procurement organization may scan or swipe a driver's license or identification card issued by the Department of Motor Vehicles in any electronic device to transmit information to the Donate Life California Organ and Tissue Donor Registry established pursuant to Section 7150.90 of the Health and Safety Code for the purposes of allowing an individual to identify himself or herself as a registered organ donor. Information gathered or transmitted pursuant to this paragraph shall comply with the Department of Motor Vehicles Information Security Agreement.

(B) Prior to scanning or swiping a driver's license or identification card issued by the Department of Motor Vehicles, an organ procurement organization shall provide clear and conspicuous notice to the applicant and shall follow the procedure prescribed in this subparagraph:

(i) Once the applicant's information is populated on the electronic form, the applicant shall verify that the information is accurate and shall click "submit" after reading a clear and conspicuous consent message, which shall not be combined with or contained within another message, acknowledging that the applicant's information will be used for the sole purpose of being added to the registry.

(ii) The applicant shall provide his or her signature to complete registration.

(iii) The organization or registry system shall provide a written confirmation to the applicant confirming that he or she is signed up as an organ and tissue donor.

(3) A business or organ procurement organization shall not retain or use any of the information obtained by that electronic means for any purpose other than as provided herein.

(b) As used in this section:

(1) "Business" means a proprietorship, partnership, corporation, or any other form of commercial enterprise.

(2) "Organ procurement organization" means a person designated by the Secretary of the federal Department of Health and Human Services as an organ procurement organization.

(c) A violation of this section constitutes a misdemeanor punishable by imprisonment in a county jail for no more than one year, or by a fine of no more than ten thousand dollars ($10,000), or by both. **Leg.H.** Added Stats 2003 ch 533 §4 (SB 602). Amended Stats 2014 ch 569 §1 (AB 2399), effective January 1, 2015; Stats 2018 ch 548 §1 (AB 2769), effective January 1, 2019.

TITLE 1.81.23
COLLECTION OF LICENSE PLATE INFORMATION

Definitions. §1798.90.5.
Duties of ALPR operator. §1798.90.51.
Duties of ALPR operator when accessing or providing access to ALPR information. §1798.90.52.
Duties of ALPR end-user. §1798.90.53.
Remedies. §1798.90.54.
Opportunity for public comment; Sale, sharing, or transfer of ALPR information. §1798.90.55.

§1798.90.5. Definitions

The following definitions shall apply for purposes of this title:

(a) "Automated license plate recognition end-user" or "ALPR end-user" means a person that accesses or uses an ALPR system, but does not include any of the following:

(1) A transportation agency when subject to Section 31490 of the Streets and Highways Code.

(2) A person that is subject to Sections 6801 to 6809, inclusive, of Title 15 of the United States Code and state or federal statutes or regulations implementing those sections, if the person is subject to compliance oversight by a state or federal regulatory agency with respect to those sections.

(3) A person, other than a law enforcement agency, to whom information may be disclosed as a permissible use pursuant to Section 2721 of Title 18 of the United States Code.

(b) "Automated license plate recognition information," or "ALPR information" means information or data collected through the use of an ALPR system.

(c) "Automated license plate recognition operator" or "ALPR operator" means a person that operates an ALPR system, but does not include a transportation agency when subject to Section 31490 of the Streets and Highways Code.

(d) "Automated license plate recognition system" or "ALPR system" means a searchable computerized database resulting from the operation of one or more mobile or fixed cameras combined with computer algorithms to read and convert images of registration plates and the characters they contain into computer-readable data.

(e) "Person" means any natural person, public agency, partnership, firm, association, corporation, limited liability company, or other legal entity.

(f) "Public agency" means the state, any city, county, or city and county, or any agency or political subdivision of the state or a city, county, or city and county, including, but not limited to, a law enforcement agency. **Leg.H.** Added Stats 2015 ch 532 §3 (SB 34), effective January 1, 2016.

§1798.90.51. Duties of ALPR operator

An ALPR operator shall do all of the following:

(a) Maintain reasonable security procedures and practices, including operational, administrative, technical, and physical safeguards, to protect ALPR information from unauthorized access, destruction, use, modification, or disclosure.

(b)(1) Implement a usage and privacy policy in order to ensure that the collection, use, maintenance, sharing, and dissemination of ALPR information is consistent with respect for individuals' privacy and civil liberties. The usage and privacy policy shall be available to the public in writing, and, if the ALPR operator has an Internet Web site, the usage and privacy policy shall be posted conspicuously on that Internet Web site.

(2) The usage and privacy policy shall, at a minimum, include all of the following:

(A) The authorized purposes for using the ALPR system and collecting ALPR information.

(B) A description of the job title or other designation of the employees and independent contractors who are authorized to use or access the ALPR system, or to collect ALPR information. The policy shall identify the training requirements necessary for those authorized employees and independent contractors.

(C) A description of how the ALPR system will be monitored to ensure the security of the information and compliance with applicable privacy laws.

(D) The purposes of, process for, and restrictions on, the sale, sharing, or transfer of ALPR information to other persons.

(E) The title of the official custodian, or owner, of the ALPR system responsible for implementing this section.

(F) A description of the reasonable measures that will be used to ensure the accuracy of ALPR information and correct data errors.

(G) The length of time ALPR information will be retained, and the process the ALPR operator will utilize to determine if and when to destroy retained ALPR information. **Leg.H.** Added Stats 2015 ch 532 §3 (SB 34), effective January 1, 2016.

§1798.90.52. Duties of ALPR operator when accessing or providing access to ALPR information

If an ALPR operator accesses or provides access to ALPR information, the ALPR operator shall do both of the following:

(a) Maintain a record of that access. At a minimum, the record shall include all of the following:

(1) The date and time the information is accessed.

(2) The license plate number or other data elements used to query the ALPR system.

(3) The username of the person who accesses the information, and, as applicable, the organization or entity with whom the person is affiliated.

(4) The purpose for accessing the information.

(b) Require that ALPR information only be used for the authorized purposes described in the usage and privacy policy required by subdivision (b) of Section 1798.90.51. **Leg.H.** Added Stats 2015 ch 532 §3 (SB 34), effective January 1, 2016.

§1798.90.53. Duties of ALPR end-user

An ALPR end-user shall do all of the following:

(a) Maintain reasonable security procedures and practices, including operational, administrative, technical, and physical safeguards, to protect ALPR information from unauthorized access, destruction, use, modification, or disclosure.

(b)(1) Implement a usage and privacy policy in order to ensure that the access, use, sharing, and dissemination of ALPR information is consistent with respect for individuals' privacy and civil liberties. The usage and privacy policy shall be available to the public in writing, and, if the ALPR end-user has an Internet Web site, the usage and privacy policy shall be posted conspicuously on that Internet Web site.

(2) The usage and privacy policy shall, at a minimum, include all of the following:

(A) The authorized purposes for accessing and using ALPR information.

(B) A description of the job title or other designation of the employees and independent contractors who are authorized to access and use ALPR information. The policy shall identify the training requirements necessary for those authorized employees and independent contractors.

(C) A description of how the ALPR system will be monitored to ensure the security of the information accessed or used, and compliance with all applicable privacy laws and a process for periodic system audits.

(D) The purposes of, process for, and restrictions on, the sale, sharing, or transfer of ALPR information to other persons.

(E) The title of the official custodian, or owner, of the ALPR information responsible for implementing this section.

(F) A description of the reasonable measures that will be used to ensure the accuracy of ALPR information and correct data errors.

(G) The length of time ALPR information will be retained, and the process the ALPR end-user will utilize to determine if and when to destroy retained ALPR information. **Leg.H.** Added Stats 2015 ch 532 §3 (SB 34), effective January 1, 2016.

§1798.90.54. Remedies

(a) In addition to any other sanctions, penalties, or remedies provided by law, an individual who has been harmed by a violation of this title, including, but not limited to, unauthorized access or use of ALPR information or a breach of security of an ALPR system, may bring a civil action in any court of competent jurisdiction against a person who knowingly caused the harm.

(b) The court may award a combination of any one or more of the following:

(1) Actual damages, but not less than liquidated damages in the amount of two thousand five hundred dollars ($2,500).

(2) Punitive damages upon proof of willful or reckless disregard of the law.

(3) Reasonable attorney's fees and other litigation costs reasonably incurred.

(4) Other preliminary and equitable relief as the court determines to be appropriate. **Leg.H.** Added Stats 2015 ch 532 §3 (SB 34), effective January 1, 2016.

§1798.90.55. Opportunity for public comment; Sale, sharing, or transfer of ALPR information

Notwithstanding any other law or regulation:

(a) A public agency that operates or intends to operate an ALPR system shall provide an opportunity for public comment at a regularly scheduled public meeting of the governing body of the public agency before implementing the program.

(b) A public agency shall not sell, share, or transfer ALPR information, except to another public agency, and only as otherwise permitted by law. For purposes of this section, the provision of data hosting or towing services shall not be considered the sale, sharing, or transferring of ALPR information. **Leg.H.** Added Stats 2015 ch 532 §3 (SB 34), effective January 1, 2016.

TITLE 1.81.25
CONSUMER PRIVACY PROTECTION

Requirements for business to request medical information to use, share or otherwise disclose for direct marketing purposes. §1798.91.

§1798.91. Requirements for business to request medical information to use, share or otherwise disclose for direct marketing purposes

(a) For purposes of this title, the following definitions shall apply:

(1) "Direct marketing purposes" means the use of personal information for marketing or advertising products, goods, or services directly to individuals. "Direct marketing purposes" does not include the use of personal information (A) by bona fide tax exempt charitable or religious organizations to solicit charitable contributions or (B) to raise funds from and communicate with individuals regarding politics and government.

(2) "Medical information" means any individually identifiable information, in electronic or physical form, regarding the individual's medical history, or medical treatment or diagnosis by a health care professional. "Individually identifiable" means that the medical information includes or contains any element of personal identifying information sufficient to allow identification of the individual, such as the individual's name, address, electronic mail address, telephone number, or social security number, or other information that, alone or in combination with other publicly available information, reveals the individual's identity. For purposes of this section, "medical information" does not mean a subscription to, purchase of, or request for a periodical, book, pamphlet, video, audio, or other multimedia product or nonprofit association information.

(3) "Clear and conspicuous" means in larger type than the surrounding text, or in contrasting type, font, or color to the surrounding text of the same size, or set off from the surrounding text of the same size by symbols or other marks that call attention to the language.

(4) For purposes of this section, the collection of medical information online constitutes "in writing." For purposes of this section, "written consent" includes consent obtained online.

(b) A business may not orally request medical information directly from an individual regardless of whether the information pertains to the individual or not, and use, share, or otherwise disclose that information for direct marketing purposes, without doing both of the following prior to obtaining that information:

(1) Orally disclosing to the individual in the same conversation during which the business seeks to obtain the information, that it is obtaining the information to market or advertise products, goods, or services to the individual.

(2) Obtaining the consent of either the individual to whom the information pertains or a person legally authorized to consent for the individual, to permit his or her medical information to be used or shared to market or advertise products, goods, or services to the individual, and making and maintaining for two years after the date of the conversation, an audio recording of the entire conversation.

(c) A business may not request in writing medical information directly from an individual regardless of whether the information pertains to the individual or not, and use, share, or otherwise disclose that information for direct marketing purposes, without doing both of the following prior to obtaining that information:

(1) Disclosing in a clear and conspicuous manner that it is obtaining the information to market or advertise products, goods, or services to the individual.

(2) Obtaining the written consent of either the individual to whom the information pertains or a person legally authorized to consent for the individual, to permit his or her medical information to be used or shared to market or advertise products, goods, or services to the individual.

(d) This section does not apply to a provider of health care, health care service plan, or contractor, as defined in Section 56.05.

(e) This section shall not apply to an insurance institution, agent, or support organization, as defined in Section 791.02 of the Insurance Code, when engaged in an insurance transaction, as defined in Section 791.02 of the Insurance Code, pursuant to all the requirements of Article 6.6 (commencing with Section 791) of Chapter 1 of Part 2 of Division 1 of the Insurance Code, and the regulations promulgated thereunder.

(f) This section does not apply to a telephone corporation, as defined in Section 234 of the Public Utilities Code, when that corporation is engaged in providing telephone services and products pursuant to Sections 2881, 2881.1, and 2881.2 of the Public Utilities Code, if the corporation does not share or disclose medical information obtained as a consequence of complying with those sections of the Public Utilities Code, to third parties for direct marketing purposes. **Leg.H.** Added Stats 2004 ch 861 §1 (SB 1633). Amended Stats 2013 ch 444 §7 (SB 138), effective January 1, 2014.

TITLE 1.81.26
SECURITY OF CONNECTED DEVICES

Security features of connected devices. §1798.91.04.
Definitions. §1798.91.05.
Duties of third party software or applications. §1798.91.06.

§1798.91.04. Security features of connected devices

(a) A manufacturer of a connected device shall equip the device with a reasonable security feature or features that are all of the following:

(1) Appropriate to the nature and function of the device.

(2) Appropriate to the information it may collect, contain, or transmit.

(3) Designed to protect the device and any information contained therein from unauthorized access, destruction, use, modification, or disclosure.

(b) Subject to all of the requirements of subdivision (a), if a connected device is equipped with a means for authentication outside a local area network, it shall be deemed a reasonable security feature under subdivision (a) if either of the following requirements are met:

(1) The preprogrammed password is unique to each device manufactured.

(2) The device contains a security feature that requires a user to generate a new means of authentication before access is granted to the device for the first time.

(c) A manufacturer of a connected device may elect to satisfy the requirements of subdivision (a) by ensuring the connected device does all of the following:

(1) Meets or exceeds the baseline product criteria of a NIST conforming labeling scheme.

(2) Satisfies a conformity assessment as described by a NIST conforming labeling scheme that includes a third-party test, inspection, or certification.

(3) Bears the binary label as described by a NIST conforming labeling scheme. **Leg.H.** Added Stats 2018 ch 860 §1 (AB 1906), effective January 1, 2019, operative January 1, 2020. Amended Stats 2022 ch 785 §2 (AB 2392), effective January 1, 2023.

2018 Note: For operative date of title, see CC §1798.91.06.

§1798.91.05. Definitions

For the purposes of this title, the following terms have the following meanings:

(a) "Authentication" means a method of verifying the authority of a user, process, or device to access resources in an information system.

(b) "Connected device" means any device, or other physical object that is capable of connecting to the internet, directly or indirectly, and that is assigned an internet protocol address or Bluetooth address.

(c) "Manufacturer" means the person who manufactures, or contracts with another person to manufacture on the person's behalf, connected devices that are sold or offered for sale in California. For the purposes of this subdivision, a contract with another person to manufacture on the person's behalf does not include a contract only to purchase a connected device, or only to purchase and brand a connected device.

(d) "NIST conforming labeling scheme" means a labeling scheme conforming to the Cybersecurity White Paper titled "Recommended Criteria for Cybersecurity Labeling for Consumer Internet of Things (IoT) Products" published by the National Institute of Standards and Technology (NIST) on February 4, 2022, including any revisions or successor publications.

(e) "Security feature" means a feature of a device designed to provide security for that device.

(f) "Unauthorized access, destruction, use, modification, or disclosure" means access, destruction, use, modification, or disclosure that is not authorized by the consumer. **Leg.H.** Added Stats 2018 ch 860 §1 (AB 1906), effective January 1, 2019, operative January 1, 2020. Amended Stats 2022 ch 785 §3 (AB 2392), effective January 1, 2023.

2018 Note: For operative date of title, see CC §1798.91.06.

§1798.91.06. Duties of third party software or applications

(a) This title shall not be construed to impose any duty upon the manufacturer of a connected device related to unaffiliated third-party software or applications that a user chooses to add to a connected device.

(b) This title shall not be construed to impose any duty upon a provider of an electronic store, gateway, marketplace, or other means of purchasing or downloading software or applications, to review or enforce compliance with this title.

(c) This title shall not be construed to impose any duty upon the manufacturer of a connected device to prevent a user from having full control over a connected device, including the ability to modify the software or firmware running on the device at the user's discretion.

(d) This title shall not apply to any connected device the functionality of which is subject to security requirements under federal law, regulations, or guidance promulgated by a federal agency pursuant to its regulatory enforcement authority.

(e) This title shall not be construed to provide a basis for a private right of action. The Attorney General, a city attorney, a county counsel, or a district attorney shall have the exclusive authority to enforce this title.

(f) The duties and obligations imposed by this title are cumulative with any other duties or obligations imposed under other law, and shall not be construed to relieve any party from any duties or obligations imposed under other law.

(g) This title shall not be construed to limit the authority of a law enforcement agency to obtain connected device information from a manufacturer as authorized by law or pursuant to an order of a court of competent jurisdiction.

(h) A covered entity, provider of health care, business associate, health care service plan, contractor, employer, or any other person subject to the federal Health Insurance Portability and Accountability Act of 1996 (HIPAA) (Public Law 104-191) or the Confidentiality of Medical Information Act (Part 2.6 (commencing with Section 56) of Division 1) shall not be subject to this title with respect to any activity regulated by those acts.

(i) This title shall become operative on January 1, 2020. **Leg.H.** Stats 2018 ch 860 §1 (AB 1906), effective January 1, 2019, operative January 1, 2020.

TITLE 1.81.27
COMMERCIAL USE OF BOOKING PHOTOGRAPHS

Prohibition against soliciting or accepting fee to remove or refrain from publishing booking photograph; Civil action for violation. §1798.91.1.

§1798.91.1. Prohibition against soliciting or accepting fee to remove or refrain from publishing booking photograph; Civil action for violation

(a) For the purposes of this section, the following definitions shall apply:

(1) "Booking photograph" means a photograph of a subject individual taken pursuant to an arrest or other involvement in the criminal justice system.

(2) "Subject individual" means an individual who was arrested.

(3) "Person" means a natural person, partnership, joint venture, corporation, limited liability company, or other entity.

(4) "Public entity" means the state, county, city, special district, or other political subdivision therein.

(b) It shall be unlawful practice for any person engaged in publishing or otherwise disseminating a booking photograph through a print or electronic medium to solicit, require, or accept the payment of a fee or other consideration from a subject individual to remove, correct, modify, or to refrain from publishing or otherwise disseminating that booking photograph.

(c) Notwithstanding subdivision (b), a public entity may require and accept a reasonable administrative fee to correct a booking photograph.

(d) Each payment solicited or accepted in violation of these provisions constitutes a separate violation.

(e) In addition to any other sanctions, penalties, or remedies provided by law, a subject individual may bring a civil action in any court of competent jurisdiction against any person in violation of this section for damages in an amount equal to the greater of one thousand dollars ($1,000) per violation or the actual damages suffered by him or her as a result, along with costs, reasonable attorney's fees, and any other legal or equitable relief.

(f) The jurisdiction of a civil action brought pursuant to subdivision (e) shall also include the county in which the subject individual resides at the time of the violation of this section. **Leg.H.** Added Stats 2014 ch 194 §1 (SB 1027), effective January 1, 2015.

TITLE 1.81.3
IDENTITY THEFT

Definitions. §1798.92.
Action requirements; Results of favorable judgment; Notice requirements. §1798.93.
Joinder of claimants as defendants. §1798.94.
Continuing jurisdiction. §1798.95.
Time limitations of actions. §1798.96.
Nonapplicability of title. §1798.97.

§1798.92. Definitions

For the purposes of this title:

(a) "Claimant" means a person who has or purports to have a claim for money or an interest in property in connection with a transaction procured through identity theft.

(b) "Identity theft" means the unauthorized use of another person's personal identifying information to obtain credit, goods, services, money, or property.

(c) "Personal identifying information" means a person's name, address, telephone number, driver's license number, social security number, place of employment, employee identification number, mother's maiden name, demand deposit account number, savings account number, or credit card number.

(d) "Victim of identity theft" means a person who had their personal identifying information used without authorization by another to obtain credit, goods, services, money, or property, and did not use or possess the credit, goods, services, money, or property obtained by the identity theft, and has submitted a Federal Trade Commission identity theft report. In the alternative, the person may have filed a police report in this regard pursuant to Section 530.5 of the Penal Code. **Leg.H.** Added Stats 2001 ch 354 §21 (AB 655). Amended Stats 2021 ch 265 §3 (AB 430), effective January 1, 2022.

§1798.93. Action requirements; Results of favorable judgment; Notice requirements

(a) A person may bring an action against a claimant to establish that the person is a victim of identity theft in connection with the claimant's claim against that person. If the claimant has brought an action to recover on its claim against the person, the person may file a cross-complaint to establish that the person is a victim of identity theft in connection with the claimant's claim.

(b) A person shall establish that they are a victim of identity theft by a preponderance of the evidence.

(c) A person who proves that they are a victim of identity theft, as defined in Section 530.5 of the Penal Code, as to a particular claim, shall be entitled to a judgment providing all of the following, as appropriate:

(1) A declaration that they are not obligated to the claimant on that claim.

(2) A declaration that any security interest or other interest the claimant had purportedly obtained in the victim's property in connection with that claim is void and unenforceable.

(3) An injunction restraining the claimant from collecting or attempting to collect from the victim on that claim, from enforcing or attempting to enforce any security interest or other interest in the victim's property in connection with that claim, or from enforcing or executing on any judgment against the victim on that claim.

(4) If the victim has filed a cross-complaint against the claimant, the dismissal of any cause of action in the complaint filed by the claimant based on a claim which arose as a result of the identity theft.

(5) Actual damages, attorney's fees, and costs, and any equitable relief that the court deems appropriate. In order to recover actual damages or attorney's fees in an action or cross-complaint filed by a person alleging that they are a victim of identity theft, the person shall show that they provided written notice to the claimant that a situation of identity theft might exist, including, upon written request of the claimant, a valid, signed Federal Trade Commission (FTC) identity theft report completed at least 30 days before filing the action, or within their cross-complaint pursuant to this section. In the alternative, the person may provide a valid copy of a police report or of a Department of Motor Vehicles (DMV) investigative report, filed pursuant to Section 530.5 of the Penal Code, at least 30 days before filing the action or within their cross-complaint pursuant to this section. For the purposes of this paragraph, if the person submits an FTC identity theft report, the claimant shall not also require a DMV or police report.

(6) A civil penalty, in addition to any other damages, of up to thirty thousand dollars ($30,000) if the victim establishes by clear and convincing evidence all of the following:

(A) That at least 30 days prior to filing an action or within the cross-complaint pursuant to this section, they provided written notice to the claimant at the address designated by the claimant for complaints related to credit reporting issues that a situation of identity theft might exist and explaining the basis for that belief.

(B) That the claimant failed to diligently investigate the victim's notification of a possible identity theft.

(C) That the claimant continued to pursue its claim against the victim after the claimant was presented with facts that were later held to entitle the victim to a judgment pursuant to this section. **Leg.H.** Added Stats 2001 ch 354 §21 (AB 655). Amended Stats 2021 ch 265 §4 (AB 430), effective January 1, 2022.

§1798.94. Joinder of claimants as defendants

An action or cross-complaint brought under this title that joins other claimants as defendants in the same action or cross-complaint shall be deemed to comply with Section 379 of the Code of Civil Procedure. **Leg.H.** Added Stats 2001 ch 354 §21 (AB 655).

§1798.95. Continuing jurisdiction

A court shall have continuing jurisdiction over an action or cross-complaint filed pursuant to this title in order to provide for the joinder of related causes of action based on the theft of the same person's identity and the joinder of further defendants based upon the theft of the same person's identity, regardless of whether a final judgment has been entered as to any defendant. The court's continuing jurisdiction shall terminate 10 years after filing of the original action unless the court, prior to that date, finds good cause to extend jurisdiction over the matter. **Leg.H.** Added Stats 2001 ch 354 §21 (AB 655).

§1798.96. Time limitations of actions

Any action brought pursuant to this title or any joinder of a defendant pursuant to Section 1798.82 may be brought within four years of the date the person who alleges that he or she is a victim of identity theft knew or, in the exercise of reasonable diligence, should have known of the existence of facts which would give rise to the bringing of the action or joinder of the defendant. **Leg.H.** Added Stats 2001 ch 354 §21 (AB 655).

§1798.97. Nonapplicability of title

(a) This title does not apply to a transaction subject to Section 1747.10.

(b) Nothing is this title shall be construed to affect a claimant's rights and remedies against a person who perpetrates identity theft or against any person who used or possessed the credit, goods, services, or property obtained by identity theft.

(c) This title is cumulative to the rights and remedies provided under other laws. **Leg.H.** Added Stats 2001 ch 354 §21 (AB 655).

TITLE 1.81.35
COERCED DEBT

Definitions. § 1798.97.1.
Causing another person to incur coerced debt; Civil liability; Collection activities. § 1798.97.2.
Action to establish debt as coerced. § 1798.97.3.
Applicability and effect of title. § 1798.97.4.
Applicability of title to debts incurred on or after July 1, 2023. § 1798.97.5.
Severability of title provisions. § 1798.97.6.

§ 1798.97.1. Definitions

For purposes of this title, the following definitions apply:

(a) "Adequate documentation" means documentation that identifies a particular debt, or portion thereof, as coerced debt, describes the circumstances under which the coerced debt was incurred, and takes the form of any of the following:

(1) A police report.

(2) A Federal Trade Commission identity theft report identifying a particular debt, or portion thereof, as coerced, but not as identity theft.

(3) A court order issued pursuant to Section 6340 of the Family Code relating to domestic violence, Section 213.5 of the Welfare and Institutions Code relating to a dependent or ward of the juvenile court, or Section 15657.03 of the Welfare and Institutions Code relating to elder or dependent adult abuse.

(4)(A) A sworn written certification from a qualified third-party professional based on information they received while acting in a professional capacity.

(B) The documentation described by subparagraph (A) shall be signed by a qualified third-party professional and display the letterhead, address, and telephone number of the office, institution, center, or organization, as appropriate, that engages or employs, whether financially compensated or not, the qualified third-party professional, or, if the qualified third-party professional is self-employed, the documentation shall display the letterhead, address, and telephone number of the qualified third-party professional.

(b) "Claim" means a right to payment, whether or not that right is reduced to judgment, liquidated, unliquidated, fixed, contingent, matured, unmatured, disputed, undisputed, legal, or equitable.

(c)(1) "Claimant" means a person or an entity who has or purports to have a claim against a debtor arising from coerced debt, or that person's or entity's successor or assignee. "Claimant" includes, but is not limited to, a debt collector or a debt buyer.

(2) Notwithstanding paragraph (1), "claimant" shall not include a person who caused the claim described in paragraph (1) to arise through duress, intimidation, threat of force, force, fraud, or undue influence perpetrated against the debtor.

(d) "Coerced debt" means a particular debt, or portion thereof, for personal, family, or household use in the name of a debtor who is a victim of domestic violence, or a victim of elder or dependent adult abuse, or a person who is a foster youth, incurred as a result of duress, intimidation, threat of force, force, fraud, or undue influence.

(1) For purposes of this subdivision, "domestic violence" has the same meaning as in Section 6211 of the Family Code.

(2) For the purposes of this subdivision, "foster youth" has the same meaning as in Section 42238.01 of the Education Code.

(3) For the purposes of this subdivision, "dependent adult" has the same meaning as in Section 15610.23 of the Welfare and Institutions Code.

(4) For the purposes of this subdivision, "elder" has the same meaning as in Section 15610.27 of the Welfare and Institutions Code.

(e) "Debtor" means a person who owes or is otherwise liable for coerced debt.

(f) "Fraud" means an initial fraudulent act that is perpetrated against the debtor.

(g) "Immediate family member" has the same meaning as defined in paragraph (3) of subdivision (h) of Section 1946.7.

(h) "Person" means a natural person.

(i) "Qualified third-party professional" means any of the following:

(1) A domestic violence counselor, as defined in Section 1037.1 of the Evidence Code.

(2) A sexual assault counselor, as defined in Section 1035.2 of the Evidence Code.

(3) A Court-Appointed Special Advocate, as defined in Section 101 of the Welfare and Institutions Code.

(4) A court-appointed attorney, as defined in subdivision (e) of Section 317 of the Welfare and Institutions Code.

(5) A board certified psychiatrist or psychologist.

(6) A licensed marriage and family therapist.

(7) A licensed professional clinical counselor.

(8) A licensed clinical social worker.

(9) A social worker or caseworker employed by an adult protective service agency for the purposes described in Chapter 13 (commencing with Section 15750) of Part 3 of Division 9 of the Welfare and Institutions Code.

(10) A social worker who has completed the child welfare training program described in Article 2 (commencing with Section 16205) of Chapter 3 of Part 4 of Division 9 of the Welfare and Institutions Code.

(j)(1) "Sworn written certification" means a document in which the author declares under penalty of perjury as true any material fact, and which is accompanied by the following, to the extent that an item listed below is relevant to the debtor's allegation that the debt is coerced debt:

(A) A copy of the debtor's driver's license or identification card, as issued by the state.

(B) Any other identification document that supports the statement that the particular debt, or portion thereof, is coerced debt.

(C) An express statement that the debtor did not willingly authorize the use of the debtor's name or personal information for incurring the coerced debt, and specific facts supporting the claim of coerced debt, if available, and, if not all of the debt was coerced, a statement identifying the portion thereof that was coerced.

(D) Any available correspondence disputing the coerced debt after transaction information has been provided to the debtor.

(E) Information, if known by the debtor, including, but not limited to, a credit card number or loan number, that can be used by the claimant to identify the account associated with the coerced debt and the person or persons in whose name the debt was incurred.

(F) The identity of the person or persons who coerced the debtor into incurring the debt and contact information for that person or persons, if known by the debtor, unless the debtor signs a sworn statement that disclosing this information is likely to result in abuse, as defined in Section 6203 of the Family Code, to the debtor or an immediate family member of the debtor.

(G) A telephone number for contacting the person signing the certification concerning any additional information or questions, or direction that further communications to the debtor be in writing only, with the mailing address specified in the statement.

(2) The certification required by this subdivision shall be sufficient if it is in substantially the following form:

"I declare under penalty of perjury that the representations made herein are true, correct, and contain no material omissions of fact.

_____
(Date and Place)

_____
(Signature)"

Leg.H. Added Stats 2022 ch 989 §2 (SB 975), effective January 1, 2023.

§ 1798.97.2. Causing another person to incur coerced debt; Civil liability; Collection activities

(a) A person shall not cause another person to incur a coerced debt. A person who causes another person to incur a coerced debt in violation of this subdivision shall be civilly liable to the claimant for the amount of the debt, or portion thereof, determined by a court to be coerced debt, plus the claimant's attorney's fees and costs.

(b) Upon receipt of both of the following, a claimant shall cease collection activities until completion of the review provided in subdivision (d):

(1) Adequate documentation.

(2) The debtor's sworn written certification that a particular debt, or portion thereof, being collected is coerced debt.

(c) If a debtor notifies a claimant orally that a particular debt, or portion thereof, being collected is coerced debt, the claimant shall notify the debtor, orally or in writing, that the debtor's notification must be in writing. If a debtor notifies a claimant in writing that a particular debt, or portion thereof, being collected is coerced debt, but omits information required by subdivision (b), and if the claimant does not cease collection activities, the claimant shall provide written notice to the debtor of the additional information that is required.

(d)(1) Within 10 business days of receiving the complete statement and information described in subdivision (b), the claimant shall, if the claimant furnished adverse information about the debtor to a consumer credit reporting agency, notify the consumer credit reporting agency that the account is disputed.

(2) The claimant shall initiate a review considering all of the information provided by the debtor and other information available to the claimant in its file.

(3) Within 10 business days of completing the review, the claimant shall notify the debtor in writing of the claimant's determination and the good faith basis for that determination.

(4) The claimant shall not recommence collection activities until the debtor has been notified in writing of the good faith determination that the information does not establish that the particular debt, or portion thereof, is coerced debt.

(e) No inference or presumption that the debt is valid or invalid, or that the debtor is liable or not liable for the particular debt, or portion thereof, shall arise if the claimant decides after the review described in subdivision (d) to cease or recommence collection activities. The exercise or nonexercise of rights under this section is not a waiver of any other right or defense of the debtor or claimant.

(f)(1) At least 30 days before filing an action pursuant to paragraph (2) of subdivision (a) of Section 1798.97.3 or other action against a claimant in connection with an allegedly coerced debt, a debtor shall submit notice of the debtor's intent to file an action against the claimant and documents that comply with subdivision (b) in writing to the claimant.

(2) The written notice described in paragraph (1) shall be sent by certified mail, overnight delivery, or other method that allows for confirmation of the delivery date.

(3) The written notice described in paragraph (1) shall be sent to an address made available to the debtor by the claimant for receipt of the notice, or, if an address has not been identified by the claimant, to the claimant's principal place of business as identified by the Secretary of State. If an address is unavailable through the Secretary of State's website, the debtor may use the correspondence address of the claimant, or in the case of a debt collector, the address on file with the Department of Financial Protection and Innovation for licensing purposes.

(4)(A) The debtor shall not commence an action described in subdivision (a) of Section 1798.97.3 or other action against a claimant in connection with an allegedly coerced debt if the claimant informs the debtor that it has ceased all efforts to collect on the particular debt, or portion thereof, identified in the written notice pursuant to paragraph (1) and the debtor receives written notice of this cessation before the expiration of the 30-day period.

(B) The debtor may commence an action described in subdivision (a) of Section 1798.97.3 or other action against a claimant in connection with an allegedly coerced debt if either of the following conditions is satisfied:

(i) The 30-day period described in paragraph (1) expires and the collection activities have not ceased or the debtor has not received written notice that collection activities have ceased.

(ii) The debtor receives written notice pursuant to paragraph (4) of subdivision (d) of the claimant's good faith determination that the information does not establish that the particular debt, or portion thereof, is coerced debt.

(5) For purposes of this subdivision, the 30-day period shall begin to run when the claimant receives the written notice.

(g) A claimant that ceases collection activities under this section and does not recommence those collection activities shall do both of the following:

(1) If the claimant has furnished adverse information to a consumer credit reporting agency regarding the debtor and a particular debt, or portion thereof, notify the agency to delete that information no later than 10 business days after making its determination.

(2) If the claimant is a debt collector, notify the creditor no later than 10 business days after making its determination that collection activities have been terminated based upon the debtor's assertion that a particular debt, or portion thereof, being collected is coerced debt.

(h) A claimant that has possession of documents that the debtor is entitled to request from a creditor pursuant to Section 530.8 of the Penal Code may provide those documents to the debtor. **Leg.H.** Added Stats 2022 ch 989 §2 (SB 975), effective January 1, 2023.

§ 1798.97.3. Action to establish debt as coerced

(a)(1) A debtor may bring an action against a claimant to establish that a particular debt, or portion thereof, is coerced debt.

(2) In an action brought by a claimant to recover a particular debt against the debtor, the debtor may file a cross-complaint to establish that the particular debt, or portion thereof, is coerced debt. The notice described in subdivision (f) of Section 1798.97.2 shall not be required as a prerequisite to filing a cross-complaint.

(3) A debtor shall plead the allegations of coerced debt with particularity and shall do either of the following:

(A) Attach the documents provided to the claimant pursuant to subdivision (b) of Section 1798.97.2 to any complaint.

(B) Attach the documents identified in subdivision (b) of Section 1798.97.2 to any cross-complaint.

(b) If the debtor establishes by a preponderance of the evidence in an action described in subdivision (a) that the particular debt, or portion thereof, is coerced debt, the debtor shall be entitled to the following relief:

(1) A declaratory judgment that the debtor is not obligated to the claimant on the particular debt, or portion thereof, that is coerced debt.

(2) An injunction prohibiting the claimant from holding or attempting to hold the debtor personally liable on the particular debt, or portion thereof, that is coerced debt, and prohibiting the claimant from enforcing a judgment related to the particular debt, or portion thereof, that is coerced debt against the debtor.

(3) An order dismissing any cause of action brought by the claimant to enforce or collect on the particular debt from the debtor or, if only a portion of the debt is established as coerced debt, an order directing that the complaint and judgment, if any, in the action be amended to reflect only the portion of the particular debt that is not coerced debt.

(c)(1) If the debtor establishes by a preponderance of the evidence in an action described in subdivision (a) that the particular debt, or portion thereof, is coerced debt, the court shall issue a judgment in favor of the claimant against the person or persons who coerced the debtor into incurring the debt in the amount of the debt, or portion thereof, that is coerced debt, provided that the person or persons who coerced the debtor into incurring the debt or debts has been brought within the jurisdiction of the court and joined as a party to the action and the evidence supports such a judgment.

(2) The court presiding over the action shall take appropriate steps necessary to prevent abuse, as defined in Section 6203 of the Family Code, of the debtor or an immediate family member of the debtor, including, but not limited to, sealing court records, redacting personally identifiable information about the debtor and any immediate family member of the debtor, and directing that any deposition or evidentiary hearing be conducted remotely.

(d) A debtor who files knowingly false motions, pleadings, or other papers or engages in other tactics that are frivolous or intended to cause unnecessary delay against a claimant shall be liable for the claimant's attorney's fees and costs in defending the lawsuit.

(e) The claimant may move the court to make written findings regarding evidence related to the person who caused the coerced debt to be incurred.

(f) Where some or all of a claim is established as having arisen from coerced debt, a claimant shall have standing, and may use all rights and remedies, to collect by any lawful means that claim, or portion thereof, from the person or persons determined to have coerced the debt, or against a person who used or possessed money, goods, services, or property obtained through coerced debt.

(g) The statute of limitations for a claimant to bring an action to collect coerced debt from any person determined to have coerced the debt shall run from the date of the court's determination that the person caused the duress, intimidation, threat of force, force, fraud, or undue influence giving rise to the coerced debt at issue and shall be brought within five years of that determination. **Leg.H.** Added Stats 2022 ch 989 §2 (SB 975), effective January 1, 2023.

§ 1798.97.4. Applicability and effect of title

(a) This title does not apply to secured debts.

(b) This title does not require a court to order a claimant to refund any moneys already paid on a debt that is determined to be coerced.

(c) This title does not diminish the rights of a claimant to recover payment for a coerced debt from the person or persons who coerced a debtor into incurring that debt.

(d) This title does not reduce or eliminate any other rights or defenses available to a debtor or claimant pursuant to any other law. **Leg.H.** Added Stats 2022 ch 989 §2 (SB 975), effective January 1, 2023.

§ 1798.97.5. Applicability of title to debts incurred on or after July 1, 2023

(a) Except as set forth in subdivision (b), this title applies only to debts incurred on or after July 1, 2023.

(b) Notwithstanding subdivision (a), a debtor may file a cross-complaint described by paragraph (2) of subdivision (a) of Section 1798.97.3 in an action filed by a claimant to collect a debt incurred prior to July 1, 2023, in which case, this title applies to that action, unless a final judgment has been entered in that action. **Leg.H.** Added Stats 2022 ch 989 §2 (SB 975), effective January 1, 2023.

§ 1798.97.6. Severability of title provisions

If any provision of this title or the application thereof to any person or circumstances is held invalid, such invalidity shall not affect other provisions or applications of this title that can be given effect without the invalid provision or application, and to this end the provisions of this title are severable. **Leg.H.** Added Stats 2022 ch 989 §2 (SB 975), effective January 1, 2023.

TITLE 1.81.4
PRIVACY OF CUSTOMER ELECTRICAL OR NATURAL GAS USAGE DATA

Definitions; Rules for disclosure of customer's data. §1798.98.
Customers' remedies. §1798.99.

§1798.98. Definitions; Rules for disclosure of customer's data

(a) For the purposes of this title, the following definitions shall apply:

(1) "Business" means a sole proprietorship, partnership, corporation, association, or other group, however organized and whether or not organized to operate at a profit, including a financial institution organized, chartered, or holding a license or authorization certificate under the law of this state, any other state, the United States, or of any other country, or the parent or the subsidiary of a financial institution.

(2) "Customer" means a customer of an electrical or gas corporation or a local publicly owned electric utility that permits a business to have access to data in association with purchasing or leasing a product or obtaining a service from the business.

(3) "Data" means a customer's electrical or natural gas usage that is made available to the business as part of an advanced metering infrastructure provided by an electrical corporation, a gas corporation, or a local publicly owned electric utility, and includes the name, account number, or physical address of the customer.

(4) "Electrical corporation" has the same meaning as in Section 218 of the Public Utilities Code.

(5) "Gas corporation" has the same meaning as in Section 222 of the Public Utilities Code.

(6) "Local publicly owned electric utility" has the same meaning as in Section 224.3 of the Public Utilities Code.

(b) Unless otherwise required or authorized by federal or state law, a business shall not share, disclose, or otherwise make accessible to any third party a customer's data without obtaining the express consent of the customer and conspicuously disclosing to whom the disclosure will be made and how the data will be used.

(c) A business that discloses data, with the express consent of the customer, pursuant to a contract with a nonaffiliated third party, shall require by contract that the third party implement and maintain reasonable security procedures and practices appropriate to the nature of the information, to protect the data from unauthorized access, destruction, use, modification, or disclosure.

(d) A business shall implement and maintain reasonable security procedures and practices appropriate to the nature of the information to protect the data from unauthorized access, destruction, use, modification, or disclosure.

(e) A business shall not provide an incentive or discount to the customer for accessing the data without the prior consent of the customer.

(f) A business shall take all reasonable steps to dispose, or arrange for the disposal, of customer data within its custody or control when the records are no longer to be retained by the business by (1) shredding, (2) erasing, or (3) otherwise modifying the data in those records to make it unreadable or undecipherable through any means.

(g) The provisions of this section do not apply to an electrical corporation, a gas corporation, or a local publicly owned electric utility or a business that secures the data as a result of a contract with an electrical or gas corporation or a local publicly owned electric utility under the provisions of subdivision (f) of Section 8380 or subdivision (f) of 8381 of the Public Utilities Code. **Leg.H.** Added Stats 2013 ch 597 §1 (AB 1274), effective January 1, 2014. Amended Stats 2020 ch 188 §1 (AB 2788), effective January 1, 2021.

§1798.99. Customers' remedies

(a) A customer harmed by the release or unauthorized use of his or her customer data, in violation of Section 1798.98, may bring a civil action to recover actual damages in an amount not to exceed five hundred dollars ($500) for each willful violation.

(b) The rights, remedies, and penalties established by this title are in addition to the rights, remedies, or penalties established under any other law.

(c) Nothing in this title shall abrogate any authority of the Attorney General to enforce existing law. **Leg.H.** Added Stats 2013 ch 597 §1 (AB 1274), effective January 1, 2014.

TITLE 1.81.45
PARENT ACCOUNTABILITY AND CHILD PROTECTION

Proof of age; Sale of age restricted products or services. §1798.99.1.

§1798.99.1. Proof of age; Sale of age restricted products or services

(a)(1) A person or business that conducts business in California, and that seeks to sell any product or service in or into California that is illegal under state law to sell to a minor, as described in subdivisions (b) and (c), shall, notwithstanding any general term or condition, take reasonable steps to ensure that the purchaser is of legal age at the time of purchase or delivery, including, but not limited to, verifying the age of the purchaser.

(2) Reasonable steps as used in paragraph (1) for the purchase of items described in subdivision (b) include, but are not limited to, any of the following:

(A) Requiring the purchaser or recipient to input, scan, provide, or display a government-issued identification, provided that the person or business complies with all laws governing the retention, use, and disclosure of personally identifiable information, including, but not limited to, subdivision (a) of Section 1749.65, paragraphs (3) to (7), inclusive, of subdivision (b) of, and subdivisions (c) to (f), inclusive, of, Section 1798.90, paragraph (1) of subdivision (a) of Section 1798.90.1, Sections 1798.29, 1798.81.5, and 1798.82, and Sections 22575 to 22579, inclusive, of the Business and Professions Code.

(B) Requiring the purchaser to use a nonprepaid credit card for an online purchase.

(C) Implementing a system that restricts individuals with accounts designated as minor accounts from purchasing the products listed in subdivision (b).

(D) Shipping the product or service to an individual who is of legal age.

(3) Reasonable steps as used in paragraph (1) for the purchase of items described in subdivision (c) include, but are not limited to, any of the following:

(A) Requiring the purchaser or recipient to input, scan, provide, or display a government-issued identification, provided that the person or business complies with all laws governing the retention, use, and disclosure of personally identifiable information, including, but not limited to, subdivision (a) of Section 1749.65, paragraphs (3) to (7), inclusive, of subdivision (b) of, and subdivisions (c) to (f), inclusive, of, Section 1798.90, paragraph (1) of subdivision (a) of Section 1798.90.1, Sections 1798.29, 1798.81.5, and 1798.82, and Sections 22575 to 22579, inclusive, of the Business and Professions Code.

(B) Shipping the product or service to an individual who is of legal age.

(4) Reasonable steps as used in paragraph (1) shall not include consent obtained through the minor.

(5) A seller's reasonable and good faith reliance on bona fide evidence of the purchaser or recipient's age shall constitute an affirmative defense to any action under this subdivision.

(6) A person or business required to comply with this section shall not retain, use, or disclose any information it receives from a purchaser or recipient in an effort to verify age pursuant to this section for any purpose other than as required to comply with, or as needed to demonstrate compliance with, this section, California law, or a state or federal court order.

(b) Products or services that are illegal to sell to a minor under state law that are subject to subdivision (a) include all of the following:

(1) An aerosol container of paint that is capable of defacing property, as referenced in Section 594.1 of the Penal Code.

(2) Etching cream that is capable of defacing property, as referenced in Section 594.1 of the Penal Code.

(3) Dangerous fireworks, as referenced in Sections 12505 and 12689 of the Health and Safety Code.

(4) Tanning in an ultraviolet tanning device, as referenced in Sections 22702 and 22706 of the Business and Professions Code.

(5) Dietary supplement products containing ephedrine group alkaloids, as referenced in Section 110423.2 of the Health and Safety Code.

(6) Body branding, as referenced in Sections 119301 and 119302 of the Health and Safety Code.

(c) Products or services that are illegal to sell to a minor under state law that are subject to subdivision (a) include all of the following:

(1) Firearms or handguns, as referenced in Sections 16520, 16640, and 27505 of the Penal Code.

(2) A BB device, as referenced in Sections 16250 and 19910 of the Penal Code.

(3) Ammunition or reloaded ammunition, as referenced in Sections 16150 and 30300 of the Penal Code.

(4) Any tobacco, cigarette, cigarette papers, blunt wraps, any other preparation of tobacco, any other instrument or paraphernalia that is designed for the smoking or ingestion of tobacco, products prepared from tobacco, or any controlled substance, as referenced in Division 8.5 (commencing with Section 22950) of the Business and Professions Code, and Sections 308, 308.1, 308.2, and 308.3 of the Penal Code.

(5) Electronic cigarettes, as referenced in Section 119406 of the Health and Safety Code.

(6) A less lethal weapon, as referenced in Sections 16780 and 19405 of the Penal Code.

(d) In an action brought by a public prosecutor, a business or person that violates this section shall be subject to a civil penalty not exceeding seven thousand five hundred dollars ($7,500) for each violation.

(e) The provisions of this section do not apply to a business that is regulated by state or federal law providing greater protection to personal information or requiring greater age verification than provided by this section in regard to the subjects addressed by this section. Compliance with state or federal law shall be deemed compliance with this section with regard to those subjects. This subdivision does not relieve a business from a duty to comply with any other requirements of other state and federal law regarding the protection and privacy of personal information or age verification.

(f) For purposes of this section, a government-issued identification means any of the following:

(1) A document issued by a federal, state, county, or municipal government, or subdivision or agency thereof, including, but not limited to, an identification card or a valid motor vehicle operator's license, including licenses or identification cards issued pursuant to Section 12801.9 of the Vehicle Code, that contains the name, date of birth, description, and picture of the person.

(2) A valid passport issued by the United States or by a foreign government.

(3) A valid identification card issued to a member of the United States Armed Forces that includes the date of birth and picture of the person.

(4) A valid consular identification document.

(5) An identification card issued by a federally recognized tribal government.

(g) This section shall become operative on January 1, 2020. **Leg.H.** Added Stats 2018 ch 872 §1 (AB 2511), effective January 1, 2019, operative January 1, 2020. Amended Stats 2022 ch 482 §1 (AB 1766), effective January 1, 2023.

TITLE 1.81.46
ONLINE VIOLENCE PREVENTION ACT

Definitions. § 1798.99.20.
Reporting mechanism for violent posts. § 1798.99.21.
Action to remove violent post. § 1798.99.22.
Applicability of title. §1798.99.23.

§ 1798.99.20.   Definitions

For purposes of this section:

(a)(1) "Content" means statements or comments made by users and media that are created, posted, shared, or otherwise interacted with by users on an internet-based service or application.

(2) "Content" does not include media put on a service or application exclusively for the purpose of cloud storage, transmitting files, or file collaboration.

(b) "Social media platform" means a public or semipublic internet-based service or application that has users in California and that meets both of the following criteria:

(1)(A) A substantial function of the service or application is to connect users in order to allow users to interact socially with each other within the service or application.

(B) A service or application that provides email or direct messaging services shall not be considered to meet this criterion on the basis of that function alone.

(2) The service or application allows users to do all of the following:

(A) Construct a public or semipublic profile for purposes of signing into and using the service or application.

(B) Populate a list of other users with whom an individual shares a social connection within the system.

(C) Create or post content viewable by other users, including, but not limited to, on message boards, in chat rooms, or through a landing page or main feed that presents the user with content generated by other users.

(c) "Public or semipublic internet-based service or application" does not include a service or application used to facilitate communication with a business or enterprise among employees or affiliates of the business or enterprise, provided that access to the service or application is restricted to employees or affiliates of the business or enterprise using the service or application.

(d) "User" means a person with an account on a social media platform.

(e) "Violent post" means content on a social media platform that contains a true threat against a specific person that is not protected by the First Amendment to the United States Constitution. **Leg.H.** Added Stats 2022 ch 881 §1 (SB 1056), effective January 1, 2023.

§ 1798.99.21.   Reporting mechanism for violent posts

(a) A social media platform shall clearly and conspicuously state whether it has a mechanism for reporting violent posts that is available to users and nonusers of the platform.

(b) If the social media platform has a reporting mechanism, the statement required by this subdivision shall include a link to the reporting mechanism. **Leg.H.** Added Stats 2022 ch 881 §1 (SB 1056), effective January 1, 2023.

§ 1798.99.22.   Action to remove violent post

(a)(1)(A) A person who is the target of a violent post, or reasonably believes the person is the target of a violent post, may seek an order requiring the social media platform to remove the violent post and any related violent post the court determines shall be removed in the interests of justice.

(B)(i) A person may bring an action pursuant to this paragraph before 48 hours have passed since providing notice to a social media platform pursuant to paragraph (2), but the court shall not rule on the request for an order until 48 hours have passed from the provision of notice.

(ii) The court may dismiss an action described by clause (i) if the social media platform deletes the post before 48 hours have passed from the provision of notice.

(C) Except as provided in subparagraph (D), a person may bring an action pursuant to this paragraph at any time, and the court may rule on the request at any time, if the social media platform does not have a reporting mechanism described in Section 1798.99.21.

(D) A person shall not bring an action pursuant to this paragraph, nor shall a court issue an order requiring a social medial platform to remove a violent post or any related violent post, based upon content containing a true threat against a specific person if the date and time when the true threat that was threatened to occur has passed.

(2) If the social media platform has a reporting mechanism described in Section 1798.99.21, a person shall not bring an action pursuant to paragraph (1) until the person has notified the social media platform of the violent post and requested that it be removed through the reporting mechanism.

(b)(1) A court shall award court costs and reasonable attorney's fees to a prevailing plaintiff in an action brought pursuant to this section.

(2) Reasonable attorney's fees may be awarded to a prevailing defendant upon a finding by the court that the plaintiff's prosecution of the

action was not in good faith. **Leg.H.** Added Stats 2022 ch 881 §1 (SB 1056), effective January 1, 2023.

1798.99.23. Applicability of title

This title does not apply to a social media platform with fewer than 1,000,000 discrete monthly users. **Leg.H.** Added Stats 2022 ch 881 §1 (SB 1056), effective January 1, 2023.

TITLE 1.81.47
THE CALIFORNIA AGE-APPROPRIATE DESIGN CODE ACT

Citation of title. § 1798.99.28.
Legislative findings and declarations. § 1798.99.29.
Definitions. § 1798.99.30.
Requirements for business that provides online services, products, or features likely to be accessed by children. § 1798.99.31.
California Children's Data Protection Working Group [Repealed January 1, 2030]. § 1798.99.32.
Data Protection Impact Assessment completion deadline. § 1798.99.33.
Penalties; Deposit of moneys collected; Substantial compliance; No private right of action; Regulations. § 1798.99.35.
Applicability of title. § 1798.99.40.

§ 1798.99.28. Citation of title

This title shall be known, and may be cited, as the California Age-Appropriate Design Code Act. **Leg.H.** Added Stats 2022 ch 320 §2 (AB 2273), effective January 1, 2023.

§ 1798.99.29. Legislative findings and declarations

The Legislature declares that children should be afforded protections not only by online products and services specifically directed at them but by all online products and services they are likely to access and makes the following findings:

(a) Businesses that develop and provide online services, products, or features that children are likely to access should consider the best interests of children when designing, developing, and providing that online service, product, or feature.

(b) If a conflict arises between commercial interests and the best interests of children, companies should prioritize the privacy, safety, and well-being of children over commercial interests. **Leg.H.** Added Stats 2022 ch 320 §2 (AB 2273), effective January 1, 2023.

§ 1798.99.30. Definitions

(a) For purposes of this title, the definitions in Section 1798.140 shall apply unless otherwise specified in this title.

(b) For the purposes of this title:

(1) "Child" or "children," unless otherwise specified, means a consumer or consumers who are under 18 years of age.

(2) "Data Protection Impact Assessment" means a systematic survey to assess and mitigate risks that arise from the data management practices of the business to children who are reasonably likely to access the online service, product, or feature at issue that arises from the provision of that online service, product, or feature.

(3) "Default" means a preselected option adopted by the business for the online service, product, or feature.

(4) "Likely to be accessed by children" means it is reasonable to expect, based on the following indicators, that the online service, product, or feature would be accessed by children:

(A) The online service, product, or feature is directed to children as defined by the Children's Online Privacy Protection Act (15 U.S.C. Sec. 6501 et seq.).

(B) The online service, product, or feature is determined, based on competent and reliable evidence regarding audience composition, to be routinely accessed by a significant number of children.

(C) An online service, product, or feature with advertisements marketed to children.

(D) An online service, product, or feature that is substantially similar or the same as an online service, product, or feature subject to subparagraph (B).

(E) An online service, product, or feature that has design elements that are known to be of interest to children, including, but not limited to, games, cartoons, music, and celebrities who appeal to children.

(F) A significant amount of the audience of the online service, product, or feature is determined, based on internal company research, to be children.

(5) "Online service, product, or feature" does not mean any of the following:

(A) A broadband internet access service, as defined in Section 3100.

(B) A telecommunications service, as defined in Section 153 of Title 47 of the United States Code.

(C) The delivery or use of a physical product.

(6) "Profiling" means any form of automated processing of personal information that uses personal information to evaluate certain aspects relating to a natural person, including analyzing or predicting aspects concerning a natural person's performance at work, economic situation, health, personal preferences, interests, reliability, behavior, location, or movements. **Leg.H.** Added Stats 2022 ch 320 §2 (AB 2273), effective January 1, 2023.

§ 1798.99.31. Requirements for business that provides online services, products, or features likely to be accessed by children

(a) A business that provides an online service, product, or feature likely to be accessed by children shall take all of the following actions:

(1)(A) Before any new online services, products, or features are offered to the public, complete a Data Protection Impact Assessment for any online service, product, or feature likely to be accessed by children and maintain documentation of this assessment as long as the online service, product, or feature is likely to be accessed by children. A business shall biennially review all Data Protection Impact Assessments.

(B) The Data Protection Impact Assessment required by this paragraph shall identify the purpose of the online service, product, or feature, how it uses children's personal information, and the risks of material detriment to children that arise from the data management practices of the business. The Data Protection Impact Assessment shall address, to the extent applicable, all of the following:

(i) Whether the design of the online product, service, or feature could harm children, including by exposing children to harmful, or potentially harmful, content on the online product, service, or feature.

(ii) Whether the design of the online product, service, or feature could lead to children experiencing or being targeted by harmful, or potentially harmful, contacts on the online product, service, or feature.

(iii) Whether the design of the online product, service, or feature could permit children to witness, participate in, or be subject to harmful, or potentially harmful, conduct on the online product, service, or feature.

(iv) Whether the design of the online product, service, or feature could allow children to be party to or exploited by a harmful, or potentially harmful, contact on the online product, service, or feature.

(v) Whether algorithms used by the online product, service, or feature could harm children.

(vi) Whether targeted advertising systems used by the online product, service, or feature could harm children.

(vii) Whether and how the online product, service, or feature uses system design features to increase, sustain, or extend use of the online product, service, or feature by children, including the automatic playing of media, rewards for time spent, and notifications.

(viii) Whether, how, and for what purpose the online product, service, or feature collects or processes sensitive personal information of children.

(2) Document any risk of material detriment to children that arises from the data management practices of the business identified in the Data Protection Impact Assessment required by paragraph (1) and create a timed plan to mitigate or eliminate the risk before the online service, product, or feature is accessed by children.

(3) Within three business days of a written request by the Attorney General, provide to the Attorney General a list of all Data Protection Impact Assessments the business has completed.

(4)(A) For any Data Protection Impact Assessment completed pursuant to paragraph (1), make the Data Protection Impact Assessment available, within five business days, to the Attorney General pursuant to a written request.

(B) Notwithstanding any other law, a Data Protection Impact Assessment is protected as confidential and shall be exempt from public disclosure, including under the California Public Records Act ([1] **Division 10** (commencing with **Section 7920.000**) [2] of Division 7 of Title 1 of the Government Code).

(C) To the extent any information contained in a Data Protection Impact Assessment disclosed to the Attorney General includes information subject to attorney-client privilege or work product protection, disclosure pursuant to this paragraph shall not constitute a waiver of that privilege or protection.

(5) Estimate the age of child users with a reasonable level of certainty appropriate to the risks that arise from the data management practices of the business or apply the privacy and data protections afforded to children to all consumers.

(6) Configure all default privacy settings provided to children by the online service, product, or feature to settings that offer a high level of privacy, unless the business can demonstrate a compelling reason that a different setting is in the best interests of children.

(7) Provide any privacy information, terms of service, policies, and community standards concisely, prominently, and using clear language suited to the age of children likely to access that online service, product, or feature.

(8) If the online service, product, or feature allows the child's parent, guardian, or any other consumer to monitor the child's online activity or track the child's location, provide an obvious signal to the child when the child is being monitored or tracked.

(9) Enforce published terms, policies, and community standards established by the business, including, but not limited to, privacy policies and those concerning children.

(10) Provide prominent, accessible, and responsive tools to help children, or if applicable their parents or guardians, exercise their privacy rights and report concerns.

(b) A business that provides an online service, product, or feature likely to be accessed by children shall not take any of the following actions:

(1) Use the personal information of any child in a way that the business knows, or has reason to know, is materially detrimental to the physical health, mental health, or well-being of a child.

(2) Profile a child by default unless both of the following criteria are met:

(A) The business can demonstrate it has appropriate safeguards in place to protect children.

(B) Either of the following is true:

(i) Profiling is necessary to provide the online service, product, or feature requested and only with respect to the aspects of the online service, product, or feature with which the child is actively and knowingly engaged.

(ii) The business can demonstrate a compelling reason that profiling is in the best interests of children.

(3) Collect, sell, share, or retain any personal information that is not necessary to provide an online service, product, or feature with which a child is actively and knowingly engaged, or as described in subparagraphs (A) to (D), inclusive, of paragraph (1) of subdivision (a) of Section 1798.145, unless the business can demonstrate a compelling reason that the collecting, selling, sharing, or retaining of the personal information is in the best interests of children likely to access the online service, product, or feature.

(4) If the end user is a child, use personal information for any reason other than a reason for which that personal information was collected, unless the business can demonstrate a compelling reason that use of the personal information is in the best interests of children.

(5) Collect, sell, or share any precise geolocation information of children by default unless the collection of that precise geolocation information is strictly necessary for the business to provide the service, product, or feature requested and then only for the limited time that the collection of precise geolocation information is necessary to provide the service, product, or feature.

(6) Collect any precise geolocation information of a child without providing an obvious sign to the child for the duration of that collection that precise geolocation information is being collected.

(7) Use dark patterns to lead or encourage children to provide personal information beyond what is reasonably expected to provide that online service, product, or feature to forego privacy protections, or to take any action that the business knows, or has reason to know, is materially detrimental to the child's physical health, mental health, or well-being.

(8) Use any personal information collected to estimate age or age range for any other purpose or retain that personal information longer than necessary to estimate age. Age assurance shall be proportionate to the risks and data practice of an online service, product, or feature.

(c)(1) A Data Protection Impact Assessment conducted by a business for the purpose of compliance with any other law complies with this section if the Data Protection Impact Assessment meets the requirements of this title.

(2) A single data protection impact assessment may contain multiple similar processing operations that present similar risks only if each relevant online service, product, or feature is addressed.

(d) This section shall become operative on July 1, 2024. **Leg.H.** Added Stats 2022 ch 320 §2 (AB 2273), effective January 1, 2023, operative July 1, 2024. Amended Stats 2023 ch 131 §13 (AB 1754), effective January 1, 2024, operative July 1, 2024; Stats 2023 ch 567 §1 (AB 1194), effective January 1, 2024, operative July 1, 2024 (ch 567 prevails); Stats 2024 ch 80 §21 (SB 1525), effective January 1, 2025, operative July 1, 2024.

§ 1798.99.31. 2024 Deletes. [1] Chapter 3.5 [2] Section 6250)

§ 1798.99.32. California Children's Data Protection Working Group [Repealed January 1, 2030]

(a) The California Children's Data Protection Working Group is hereby created within the Office of the Attorney General to deliver a report to the Legislature, pursuant to subdivision (e), regarding best practices for the implementation of this title.

(b) Working group members shall consist of Californians with expertise in at least two of the following areas:

(1) Children's data privacy.

(2) Physical health.

(3) Mental health and well-being.

(4) Computer science.

(5) Children's rights.

(c) The working group shall select a chair and a vice chair from among its members and shall consist of the following nine members:

(1) Two appointees by the Governor.

(2) Two appointees by the President Pro Tempore of the Senate.

(3) Two appointees by the Speaker of the Assembly.

(4) Two appointees by the Attorney General.

(5) One appointee by the California Privacy Protection Agency.

(d) The working group shall take input from a broad range of stakeholders, including from academia, consumer advocacy groups, and small, medium, and large businesses affected by data privacy policies and shall make recommendations to the Legislature on best practices regarding, at minimum, all of the following:

(1) Identifying online services, products, or features likely to be accessed by children.

(2) Evaluating and prioritizing the best interests of children with respect to their privacy, physical health, and mental health and well-being and evaluating how those interests may be furthered by the design, development, and implementation of an online service, product, or feature.

(3) Ensuring that age assurance methods used by businesses that provide online services, products, or features likely to be accessed by children are proportionate to the risks that arise from the data management practices of the business, privacy protective, and minimally invasive.

(4) Assessing and mitigating risks to children that arise from the use of an online service, product, or feature.

(5) Publishing privacy information, policies, and standards in concise, clear language suited for the age of children likely to access an online service, product, or feature.

(6) How the working group and the Department of Justice may leverage the substantial and growing expertise of the California Privacy Protection Agency in the long-term development of data privacy policies that affect the privacy, rights, and safety of children online.

(e) On or before July 1, 2024, and every two years thereafter, the working group shall submit, pursuant to Section 9795 of the Government Code, a report to the Legislature regarding the recommendations described in subdivision (d).

(f) A meeting of the members of the working group may be conducted, in whole or in part, by electronic transmission, electronic video screen communication, conference telephone, or other means of remote communication.

(g) The members of the working group shall serve without compensation but shall be reimbursed for all necessary expenses actually incurred in the performance of their duties.

(h) This section shall remain in effect until January 1, 2030, and as of that date is repealed. **Leg.H.** Added Stats 2022 ch 320 §2 (AB 2273), effective January 1, 2023, repealed January 1, 2030. Amended Stats 2023 ch 45 §1 (AB 127), effective July 10, 2023, repealed January 1, 2030.

§ 1798.99.33. Data Protection Impact Assessment completion deadline

(a) A business shall complete a Data Protection Impact Assessment on or before July 1, 2024, for any online service, product, or feature likely to be accessed by children offered to the public before July 1, 2024.

(b) This section does not apply to an online service, product, or feature that is not offered to the public on or after July 1, 2024. **Leg.H.** Added Stats 2022 ch 320 §2 (AB 2273), effective January 1, 2023.

§ 1798.99.35. Penalties; Deposit of moneys collected; Substantial compliance; No private right of action; Regulations

(a) Any business that violates this title shall be subject to an injunction and liable for a civil penalty of not more than two thousand five hundred dollars ($2,500) per affected child for each negligent violation or not more than seven thousand five hundred dollars ($7,500) per affected child for each intentional violation, which shall be assessed and recovered only in a civil action brought in the name of the people of the State of California by the Attorney General.

(b) Any penalties, fees, and expenses recovered in an action brought under this title shall be deposited in the Consumer Privacy Fund, created within the General Fund pursuant to subdivision (a) of Section 1798.160, with the intent that they be used to fully offset costs incurred by the Attorney General in connection with this title.

(c)(1) If a business is in substantial compliance with the requirements of paragraphs (1) through (4), inclusive, of subdivision (a) of Section 1798.99.31, the Attorney General shall provide written notice to the business, before initiating an action under this title, identifying the specific provisions of this title that the Attorney General alleges have been or are being violated.

(2) If, within 90 days of the notice required by this subdivision, the business cures any noticed violation and provides the Attorney General a written statement that the alleged violations have been cured, and sufficient measures have been taken to prevent future violations, the business shall not be liable for a civil penalty for any violation cured pursuant to this subdivision.

(d) Nothing in this title shall be interpreted to serve as the basis for a private right of action under this title or any other law.

(e) The Attorney General may solicit broad public participation and adopt regulations to clarify the requirements of this title. **Leg.H.** Added Stats 2022 ch 320 §2 (AB 2273), effective January 1, 2023.

§ 1798.99.40. Applicability of title

This title does not apply to the information or entities described in subdivision (c) of Section 1798.145. **Leg.H.** Added Stats 2022 ch 320 §2 (AB 2273), effective January 1, 2023.

TITLE 1.81.48
DATA BROKER REGISTRATION

Definitions. §1798.99.80.
Data Brokers' Registry Fund. §1798.99.81.
Annual registration; Fees; Penalties. §1798.99.82.
Internet website page. §1798.99.84.
Actions required of data broker. § 1798.99.85.
Accessible deletion mechanism. § 1798.99.86.
Adoption of regulations by the California Privacy Protection Agency. § 1798.99.87.
Construction with California Consumer Privacy Act of 2018. §1798.99.88.
Statute of limitations for administrative actions. § 1798.99.89.

§1798.99.80. Definitions

For purposes of this title:

(a) The definitions in Section 1798.140 shall apply unless otherwise specified in this title.

(b) "Authorized agent" has the same meaning as used in Chapter 1 (commencing with Section 7000) of Division 6 of Title 11 of the California Code of Regulations.

(c) "Data broker" means a business that knowingly collects and sells to third parties the personal information of a consumer with whom the business does not have a direct relationship. "Data broker" does not include any of the following:

(1) An entity to the extent that it is covered by the federal Fair Credit Reporting Act (15 U.S.C. Sec. 1681 et seq.).

(2) An entity to the extent that it is covered by the Gramm-Leach-Bliley Act (Public Law 106-102) and implementing regulations.

(3) An entity to the extent that it is covered by the Insurance Information and Privacy Protection Act (Article 6.6 (commencing with Section 791) of Chapter 1 of Part 2 of Division 1 of the Insurance Code).

(4) An entity, or a business associate of a covered entity, to the extent their processing of personal information is exempt under Section 1798.146. For purposes of this paragraph, "business associate" and "covered entity" have the same meanings as defined in Section 1798.146. **Leg.H.** Added Stats 2019 ch 753 §2 (AB 1202), effective January 1, 2020. Amended Stats 2022 ch 420 §10 (AB 2960), effective January 1, 2023; Stats 2023 ch 709 §1 (SB 362), effective January 1, 2024.

§1798.99.81. Data Brokers' Registry Fund

A fund to be known as the "Data Brokers' Registry Fund" is hereby created within the State Treasury. The fund shall be administered by the California Privacy Protection Agency. All moneys collected or received by the California Privacy Protection Agency and the Department of Justice under this title shall be deposited into the Data Brokers' Registry Fund, to be available for expenditure by the California Privacy Protection Agency, upon appropriation by the Legislature, to offset all of the following costs:

(a) The reasonable costs of establishing and maintaining the informational internet website described in Section 1798.99.84.

(b) The costs incurred by the state courts and the California Privacy Protection Agency in connection with enforcing this title, as specified in Section 1798.99.82.

(c) The reasonable costs of establishing, maintaining, and providing access to the accessible deletion mechanism described in Section 1798.99.86. **Leg.H.** Added Stats 2020 ch 14 §3 (AB 82), effective June 29, 2020. Amended Stats 2023 ch 709 §2 (SB 362), effective January 1, 2024.

§1798.99.82. Annual registration; Fees; Penalties

(a) On or before January 31 following each year in which a business meets the definition of data broker as provided in this title, the business shall register with the California Privacy Protection Agency pursuant to the requirements of this section.

(b) In registering with the California Privacy Protection Agency, as described in subdivision (a), a data broker shall do all of the following:

(1) Pay a registration fee in an amount determined by the California Privacy Protection Agency, not to exceed the reasonable costs of establishing and maintaining the informational internet website described in Section 1798.99.84 and the reasonable costs of establishing, maintaining, and providing access to the accessible deletion mechanism described in Section 1798.99.86. Registration fees shall be deposited in the Data Brokers' Registry Fund, created within the State Treasury pursuant to Section 1798.99.81, and used for the purposes outlined in this paragraph.

(2) Provide the following information:

(A) The name of the data broker and its primary physical, email, and internet website addresses.

(B) The metrics compiled pursuant to paragraphs (1) and (2) of subdivision (a) of Section 1798.99.85.

(C) Whether the data broker collects the personal information of minors.

(D) Whether the data broker collects consumers' precise geolocation.

(E) Whether the data broker collects consumers' reproductive health care data.

(F) Beginning January 1, 2029, whether the data broker has undergone an audit as described in subdivision (e) of Section 1798.99.86, and, if so, the most recent year that the data broker has submitted a report resulting from the audit and any related materials to the California Privacy Protection Agency.

(G) A link to a page on the data broker's internet website that does both of the following:

(i) Details how consumers may exercise their privacy rights by doing all of the following:

(I) Deleting personal information, as described in Section 1798.105.

(II) Correcting inaccurate personal information, as described in Section 1798.106.

(III) Learning what personal information is being collected and how to access that personal information, as described in Section 1798.110.

(IV) Learning what personal information is being sold or shared and to whom, as described in Section 1798.115.

(V) Learning how to opt out of the sale or sharing of personal information, as described in Section 1798.120.

(VI) Learning how to limit the use and disclosure of sensitive personal information, as described in Section 1798.121.

(ii) Does not make use of any dark patterns.

(H) Whether and to what extent the data broker or any of its subsidiaries is regulated by any of the following:

(i) The federal Fair Credit Reporting Act (15 U.S.C. Sec. 1681 et seq.).

(ii) The Gramm-Leach-Bliley Act (Public Law 106-102) and implementing regulations.

(iii) The Insurance Information and Privacy Protection Act (Article 6.6 (commencing with Section 791) of Chapter 1 of Part 2 of Division 1 of the Insurance Code).

(iv) The Confidentiality of Medical Information Act (Part 2.6 (commencing with Section 56) of Division 1) or the privacy, security, and breach notification rules issued by the United States Department of Health and Human Services, Parts 160 and 164 of Title 45 of the Code of Federal Regulations, established pursuant to the federal Health Insurance Portability and Accountability Act of 1996 (Public Law 104-191).

(I) Any additional information or explanation the data broker chooses to provide concerning its data collection practices.

(c) A data broker that fails to register as required by this section is liable for administrative fines and costs in an administrative action brought by the California Privacy Protection Agency as follows:

(1) An administrative fine of two hundred dollars ($200) for each day the data broker fails to register as required by this section.

(2) An amount equal to the fees that were due during the period it failed to register.

(3) Expenses incurred by the California Privacy Protection Agency in the investigation and administration of the action as the court deems appropriate.

(d) A data broker required to register under this title that fails to comply with the requirements of Section 1798.99.86 is liable for administrative fines and costs in an administrative action brought by the California Privacy Protection Agency as follows:

(1) An administrative fine of two hundred dollars ($200) for each deletion request for each day the data broker fails to delete information as required by Section 1798.99.86.

(2) Reasonable expenses incurred by the California Privacy Protection Agency in the investigation and administration of the action.

(e) Any penalties, fines, fees, and expenses recovered in an action prosecuted under subdivision (c) or (d) shall be deposited in the Data Brokers' Registry Fund, created within the State Treasury pursuant to Section 1798.99.81, with the intent that they be used to fully offset costs incurred by the state courts and the California Privacy Protection Agency in connection with this title. **Leg.H.** Added Stats 2019 ch 753 §2 (AB 1202), effective January 1, 2020. Amended Stats 2020 ch 14 §4 (AB 82), effective June 29, 2020; Stats 2023 ch 709 §3 (SB 362), effective January 1, 2024.

§1798.99.84. Internet website page

The California Privacy Protection Agency shall create a page on its internet website where the registration information provided by data brokers described in paragraph (2) of subdivision (b) of Section 1798.99.82 and the accessible deletion mechanism described in Section 1798.99.86 shall be accessible to the public. **Leg.H.** Added Stats 2019 ch 753 §2 (AB 1202), effective January 1, 2020. Amended Stats 2023 ch 709 §4 (SB 362), effective January 1, 2024.

§1798.99.85. Actions required of data broker

(a) On or before July 1 following each calendar year in which a business meets the definition of a data broker as provided in this title, the business shall do all of the following:

(1) Compile the number of requests pursuant to subdivision (c) of Section 1798.99.86 and Sections 1798.105, 1798.110, 1798.115, 1798.120, and 1798.121 that the data broker received, complied with in whole or in part, and denied during the previous calendar year.

(2) Compile the median and the mean number of days within which the data broker substantively responded to requests pursuant to subdivision (c) of Section 1798.99.86 and Sections 1798.105, 1798.110, 1798.115, 1798.120, and 1798.121 that the data broker received during the previous calendar year.

(3) Disclose the metrics compiled pursuant to paragraphs (1) and (2) within the data broker's privacy policy posted on their internet website and accessible from a link included in the data broker's privacy policy.

(b) In its disclosure pursuant to paragraph (3) of subdivision (a) regarding requests made pursuant to subdivision (c) of Section 1798.99.86, a data broker shall disclose the number of requests that the data broker denied in whole or in part because of any of the following:

(1) The request was not verifiable.

(2) The request was not made by a consumer.

(3) The request called for information exempt from deletion.

(4) The request was denied on other grounds.

(c) In its disclosure pursuant to paragraph (3) of subdivision (a), a data broker shall, for each provision of Section 1798.145 or 1798.146 under which deletion was not required, specify the number of requests in which deletion was not required in whole, or in part, under that provision. **Leg.H.** Added Stats 2023 ch 709 §5 (SB 362), effective January 1, 2024.

§ 1798.99.86. Accessible deletion mechanism

(a) By January 1, 2026, the California Privacy Protection Agency shall establish an accessible deletion mechanism that does all of the following:

(1) Implements and maintains reasonable security procedures and practices, including, but not limited to, administrative, physical, and technical safeguards appropriate to the nature of the information and the purposes for which the personal information will be used and to protect consumers' personal information from unauthorized use, disclosure, access, destruction, or modification.

(2) Allows a consumer, through a single verifiable consumer request, to request that every data broker that maintains any personal information delete any personal information related to that consumer held by the data broker or associated service provider or contractor.

(3) Allows a consumer to selectively exclude specific data brokers from a request made under paragraph (2).

(4) Allows a consumer to make a request to alter a previous request made under this subdivision after at least 45 days have passed since the consumer last made a request under this subdivision.

(b) The accessible deletion mechanism established pursuant to subdivision (a) shall meet all of the following requirements:

(1) The accessible deletion mechanism shall allow a consumer to request the deletion of all personal information related to that consumer through a single deletion request.

(2) The accessible deletion mechanism shall permit a consumer to securely submit information in one or more privacy-protecting ways determined by the California Privacy Protection Agency to aid in the deletion request.

(3) The accessible deletion mechanism shall allow data brokers registered with the California Privacy Protection Agency to determine whether an individual has submitted a verifiable consumer request to delete the personal information related to that consumer as described in paragraph (1) and shall not allow the disclosure of any additional personal information when the data broker accesses the accessible deletion mechanism unless otherwise specified in this title.

(4) The accessible deletion mechanism shall allow a consumer to make a request described in paragraph (1) using an internet service operated by the California Privacy Protection Agency.

(5) The accessible deletion mechanism shall not charge a consumer to make a request described in paragraph (1).

(6) The accessible deletion mechanism shall allow a consumer to make a request described in paragraph (1) in any language spoken by any consumer for whom personal information has been collected by data brokers.

(7) The accessible deletion mechanism shall be readily accessible and usable by consumers with disabilities.

(8) The accessible deletion mechanism shall support the ability of a consumer's authorized agents to aid in the deletion request.

(9) The accessible deletion mechanism shall allow the consumer, or their authorized agent, to verify the status of the consumer's deletion request.

(10) The accessible deletion mechanism shall provide a description of all of the following:

(A) The deletion permitted by this section, including, but not limited to, the actions required by subdivisions (c) and (d).

(B) The process for submitting a deletion request pursuant to this section.

(C) Examples of the types of information that may be deleted.

(c)(1) Beginning August 1, 2026, a data broker shall access the accessible deletion mechanism established pursuant to subdivision (a) at least once every 45 days and do all of the following:

(A) Within 45 days after receiving a request made pursuant to this section, process all deletion requests made pursuant to this section and delete all personal information related to the consumers making the requests consistent with the requirements of this section.

(B) In cases where a data broker denies a consumer request to delete under this title because the request cannot be verified, process the request as an opt-out of the sale or sharing of the consumer's personal information, as provided for under Section 1798.120 and limited by Sections 1798.105, 1798.145, and 1798.146.

(C) Direct all service providers or contractors associated with the data broker to delete all personal information in their possession related to the consumers making the requests described in subparagraph (A).

(D) Direct all service providers or contractors associated with the data broker to process a request described by subparagraph (B) as an opt-out of the sale or sharing of the consumer's personal information, as provided for under Section 1798.120 and limited by Sections 1798.105, 1798.145, and 1798.146.

(2) Notwithstanding paragraph (1), a data broker shall not be required to delete a consumer's personal information if either of the following apply:

(A) It is reasonably necessary for the data broker to maintain the personal information to fulfill a purpose described in subdivision (d) of Section 1798.105.

(B) The deletion is not required pursuant to Section 1798.145 or 1798.146.

(3) Personal information described in paragraph (2) shall only be used for the purposes described in paragraph (2) and shall not be used or disclosed for any other purpose, including, but not limited to, marketing purposes.

(d)(1) Beginning August 1, 2026, after a consumer has submitted a deletion request and a data broker has deleted the consumer's data pursuant to this section, the data broker shall delete all personal information of the consumer at least once every 45 days pursuant to this section unless the consumer requests otherwise or the deletion is not required pursuant to paragraph (2) of subdivision (c).

(2) Beginning August 1, 2026, after a consumer has submitted a deletion request and a data broker has deleted the consumer's data pursuant to this section, the data broker shall not sell or share new personal information of the consumer unless the consumer requests otherwise or selling or sharing the personal information is permitted under Section 1798.145 or 1798.146.

(e)(1) Beginning January 1, 2028, and every three years thereafter, a data broker shall undergo an audit by an independent third party to determine compliance with this section.

(2) For an audit completed pursuant to paragraph (1), the data broker shall submit a report resulting from the audit and any related materials to the California Privacy Protection Agency within five business days of a written request from the California Privacy Protection Agency.

(3) A data broker shall maintain the report and materials described in paragraph (2) for at least six years.

(f)(1) The California Privacy Protection Agency may charge an access fee to a data broker when the data broker accesses the accessible deletion mechanism pursuant to subdivision [1] (c) that does not exceed the reasonable costs of providing that access.

(2) A fee collected by the California Privacy Protection Agency pursuant to paragraph (1) shall be deposited in the Data Brokers' Registry Fund. **Leg.H.** Added Stats 2023 ch 709 §6 (SB 362), effective January 1, 2024. Amended Stats 2024 ch 80 §22 (SB 1525), effective January 1, 2025.

§ 1798.99.86. 2024 Deletes. [1] (d)

§1798.99.87. Adoption of regulations by the California Privacy Protection Agency

(a) Except as provided in subdivision (b), the California Privacy Protection Agency may adopt regulations pursuant to the Administrative Procedure Act (Chapter 3.5 (commencing with Section 11340) of Part 1 of Division 3 of Title 2 of the Government Code) to implement and administer this title.

(b) Notwithstanding subdivision (a), any regulation adopted by the California Privacy Protection Agency to establish fees authorized by this title shall be exempt from the Administrative Procedure Act (Chapter 3.5 (commencing with Section 11340) of Part 1 of Division 3 of Title 2 of the Government Code). **Leg.H.** Added Stats 2023 ch 709 §7 (SB 362), effective January 1, 2024.

§1798.99.88. Construction with California Consumer Privacy Act of 2018

Nothing in this title shall be construed to supersede or interfere with the operation of the California Consumer Privacy Act of 2018 (Title 1.81.5 (commencing with Section 1798.100)). **Leg.H.** Added Stats 2019 ch 753 §2 (AB 1202), effective January 1, 2020.

§1798.99.89. Statute of limitations for administrative actions

No administrative action brought pursuant to this title alleging a violation of any of the provisions of this title shall be commenced more than five years after the date on which the violation occurred. **Leg.H.** Added Stats 2023 ch 709 §8 (SB 362), effective January 1, 2024.

TITLE 1.81.49
FAMILY PLANNING CENTER LOCATION DATA

Personal information restrictions of persons at family planning centers; Right of action. § 1798.99.90.

§ 1798.99.90. Personal information restrictions of persons at family planning centers; Right of action

(a) A person or business shall not collect, use, disclose, or retain the personal information of a person who is physically located at, or within a precise geolocation of, a family planning center, except as specified in subdivision (c).

(b) For purposes of this section, the following definitions apply:

(1) "Business" means the same as defined in subdivision (c) of Section 1798.140.

(2) "Collect" means the same as defined in subdivision (f) of Section 1798.140.

(3) "Family planning center" means a business categorized as a family planning center by the North American Industry Classification System adopted by the United States Census Bureau, including, but not limited to, a clinic or center that provides reproductive health care services as defined in Section 1798.300 of the Civil Code.

(4) "Personal information" has the same definition as that term is defined in subdivision (v) of Section 1798.140, except as applied to all persons and not limited to consumers and households, as those terms are defined in subdivisions (i) and (q), respectively, of that section.

(5) "Precise geolocation" means a geographic area that is equal to or less than the area of a circle with a radius of 1,850 feet as derived from a device that is used or intended to be used to locate a person.

(6) "Sell" means the same as defined in subdivision (ad) of Section 1798.140.

(7) "Share" means the same as defined in subdivision (ah) of Section 1798.140.

(c) A person or business shall not collect, use, disclose, or retain the personal information of a person who is physically located at, or within a precise geolocation of, a family planning center, except only as necessary to perform the services or provide the goods requested by the person. A person or business shall not sell or share this personal information.

(d)(1) An aggrieved person or entity, including a family planning center, may institute and prosecute a civil action against any person or business who violates this section for injunctive and monetary relief and attorney's fees within three years of discovery of the violation.

(2) If the court finds for the petitioner in an action authorized by paragraph (1), recovery shall be in the amount of three times the amount of actual damages and any other expenses, costs, or reasonable attorney's fees incurred in connection with the litigation.

(e) This section does not apply to a provider of health care, a health care service plan, or contractor, as those terms are defined in Section

56.05. **Leg.H.** Added Stats 2023 ch 260 §5 (SB 345), effective January 1, 2024.

TITLE 1.81.5
CALIFORNIA CONSUMER PRIVACY ACT OF 2018

General Duties of Businesses that Collect Personal Information. §1798.100.
Consumers' Right to Delete Personal Information. §1798.105.
Consumers' Right to Correct Inaccurate Personal Information. § 1798.106.
Consumers' Right to Know What Personal Information is Being Collected. Right to Access Personal Information. §1798.110.
Consumers' Right to Know What Personal Information is Sold or Shared and to Whom. §1798.115.
Consumers' Right to Opt Out of Sale or Sharing of Personal Information. §1798.120.
Consumers' Right to Limit Use and Disclosure of Sensitive Personal Information. § 1798.121.
Consumers' Right of No Retaliation Following Opt Out or Exercise of Other Rights. §1798.125.
Notice, Disclosure, Correction, and Deletion Requirements. §1798.130.
Methods of Limiting Sale, Sharing, and Use of Personal Information and Use of Sensitive Personal Information. §1798.135.
Definitions. §1798.140.
Exemptions. §1798.145.
Inapplicability of title to certain information and entities. §1798.146.
Reidentification of certain information prohibited; Exceptions. §1798.148.
Personal Information Security Breaches. §1798.150.
Administrative Enforcement. §1798.155.
Consumer Privacy Fund. §1798.160.
Conflicting Provisions. §1798.175.
Preemption. §1798.180.
Regulations. §1798.185.
Anti-Avoidance. §1798.190.
Waiver. §1798.192.
Construction of title. §1798.194.
Conflict with federal law or U.S. or California Constitution. §1798.196.
Operative date of title. §1798.198.
Operative date of Section 1798.180. §1798.199.
Establishment of California Privacy Protection Agency. § 1798.199.10.
Agency board membership. § 1798.199.15.
Term of service. § 1798.199.20.
Member compensation. § 1798.199.25.
Appointment of executive director, officers, counsel and employees. § 1798.199.30.
Delegation of authority to Chair or executive director. § 1798.199.35.
Agency functions. § 1798.199.40.
Investigation of violations. § 1798.199.45.
Notice of violation. § 1798.199.50.
Hearing on violation; Order. § 1798.199.55.
Rejection of Administrative Law Judge decision. § 1798.199.60.
Agency subpoena and audit powers. § 1798.199.65.
Administrative actions time limitations. § 1798.199.70.
Unpaid administrative fines. § 1798.199.75.
Application for judgment upon exhaustion or expiration of judicial review. § 1798.199.80.
Judicial review; Standard of review. § 1798.199.85.
Injunction; Penalties; Stay of action or investigation at Attorney General request. § 1798.199.90.
Appropriations; Staff support. § 1798.199.95.
Consideration of good faith and cooperation. § 1798.199.100.

§1798.100. General Duties of Businesses that Collect Personal Information

(a) A business that controls the collection of a consumer's personal information shall, at or before the point of collection, inform consumers of the following:

(1) The categories of personal information to be collected and the purposes for which the categories of personal information are collected or used and whether that information is sold or shared. A business shall not collect additional categories of personal information or use personal information collected for additional purposes that are incompatible with the disclosed purpose for which the personal information was collected without providing the consumer with notice consistent with this section.

(2) If the business collects sensitive personal information, the categories of sensitive personal information to be collected and the purposes for which the categories of sensitive personal information are collected or used, and whether that information is sold or shared. A business shall not collect additional categories of sensitive personal information or use sensitive personal information collected for additional purposes that are incompatible with the disclosed purpose for which the sensitive personal information was collected without providing the consumer with notice consistent with this section.

(3) The length of time the business intends to retain each category of personal information, including sensitive personal information, or if that is not possible, the criteria used to determine that period provided that a business shall not retain a consumer's personal information or sensitive personal information for each disclosed purpose for which the personal information was collected for longer than is reasonably necessary for that disclosed purpose.

(b) A business that, acting as a third party, controls the collection of personal information about a consumer may satisfy its obligation under subdivision (a) by providing the required information prominently and conspicuously on the homepage of its internet website. In addition, if a business acting as a third party controls the collection of personal information about a consumer on its premises, including in a vehicle, then the business shall, at or before the point of collection, inform consumers as to the categories of personal information to be collected and the purposes for which the categories of personal information are used, and whether that personal information is sold, in a clear and conspicuous manner at the location.

(c) A business' collection, use, retention, and sharing of a consumer's personal information shall be reasonably necessary and proportionate to achieve the purposes for which the personal information was collected or processed, or for another disclosed purpose that is compatible with the context in which the personal information was collected, and not further processed in a manner that is incompatible with those purposes.

(d) A business that collects a consumer's personal information and that sells that personal information to, or shares it with, a third party or that discloses it to a service provider or contractor for a business purpose shall enter into an agreement with the third party, service provider, or contractor, that:

(1) Specifies that the personal information is sold or disclosed by the business only for limited and specified purposes.

(2) Obligates the third party, service provider, or contractor to comply with applicable obligations under this title and obligate those persons to provide the same level of privacy protection as is required by this title.

(3) Grants the business rights to take reasonable and appropriate steps to help ensure that the third party, service provider, or contractor uses the personal information transferred in a manner consistent with the business' obligations under this title.

(4) Requires the third party, service provider, or contractor to notify the business if it makes a determination that it can no longer meet its obligations under this title.

(5) Grants the business the right, upon notice, including under paragraph (4), to take reasonable and appropriate steps to stop and remediate unauthorized use of personal information.

(e) A business that collects a consumer's personal information shall implement reasonable security procedures and practices appropriate to the nature of the personal information to protect the personal information from unauthorized or illegal access, destruction, use, modification, or disclosure in accordance with Section 1798.81.5.

(f) Nothing in this section shall require a business to disclose trade secrets, as specified in regulations adopted pursuant to paragraph (3) of subdivision (a) of Section 1798.185. **Leg.H.** Added Stats 2018 ch 55 §3 (AB 375), effective January 1, 2019, operative January 1, 2020. Amended Stats 2018 ch 735 §1 (SB 1121), effective September 23, 2018, operative January 1, 2020; Stats 2019 ch 757 §1 (AB 1355), effective January 1, 2020, operative January 1, 2020; Amendment approved by voters as Proposition 24 §4 (2020 Bill Text CA V. 9) on November 3, 2020, effective December 16, 2020, operative January 1, 2023.

2018 Notes: This measure shall be known and may be cited as "The California Consumer Privacy Act of 2018." Stats 2018 ch 55 §1 (AB 375).

For operative date of title, see CC §1798.198.

§1798.105. Consumers' Right to Delete Personal Information

(a) A consumer shall have the right to request that a business delete any personal information about the consumer which the business has collected from the consumer.

(b) A business that collects personal information about consumers shall disclose, pursuant to Section 1798.130, the consumer's rights to request the deletion of the consumer's personal information.

(c)(1) A business that receives a verifiable consumer request from a consumer to delete the consumer's personal information pursuant to subdivision (a) of this section shall delete the consumer's personal information from its records, notify any service providers or contractors to delete the consumer's personal information from their records, and notify all third parties to whom the business has sold or shared the personal information to delete the consumer's personal information unless this proves impossible or involves disproportionate effort.

(2) The business may maintain a confidential record of deletion requests solely for the purpose of preventing the personal information of a consumer who has submitted a deletion request from being sold, for compliance with laws or for other purposes, solely to the extent permissible under this title.

(3) A service provider or contractor shall cooperate with the business in responding to a verifiable consumer request, and at the direction of the business, shall delete, or enable the business to delete and shall notify any of its own service providers or contractors to delete personal information about the consumer collected, used, processed, or retained by the service provider or the contractor. The service provider or contractor shall notify any service providers, contractors, or third parties who may have accessed personal information from or through the service provider or contractor, unless the information was accessed at the direction of the business, to delete the consumer's personal information unless this proves impossible or involves disproportionate effort. A service provider or contractor shall not be required to comply with a deletion request submitted by the consumer directly to the service provider or contractor to the extent that the service provider or contractor has collected, used, processed, or retained the consumer's personal information in its role as a service provider or contractor to the business.

(d) A business, or a service provider or contractor acting pursuant to its contract with the business, another service provider, or another contractor, shall not be required to comply with a consumer's request to delete the consumer's personal information if it is reasonably necessary for the business, service provider, or contractor to maintain the consumer's personal information in order to:

(1) Complete the transaction for which the personal information was collected, fulfill the terms of a written warranty or product recall conducted in accordance with federal law, provide a good or service requested by the consumer, or reasonably anticipated by the consumer within the context of a business' ongoing business relationship with the consumer, or otherwise perform a contract between the business and the consumer.

(2) Help to ensure security and integrity to the extent the use of the consumer's personal information is reasonably necessary and proportionate for those purposes.

(3) Debug to identify and repair errors that impair existing intended functionality.

(4) Exercise free speech, ensure the right of another consumer to exercise that consumer's right of free speech, or exercise another right provided for by law.

(5) Comply with the California Electronic Communications Privacy Act pursuant to Chapter 3.6 (commencing with Section 1546) of Title 12 of Part 2 of the Penal Code.

(6) Engage in public or peer-reviewed scientific, historical, or statistical research that conforms or adheres to all other applicable ethics and privacy laws, when the business' deletion of the information is likely to render impossible or seriously impair the ability to complete such research, if the consumer has provided informed consent.

(7) To enable solely internal uses that are reasonably aligned with the expectations of the consumer based on the consumer's relationship with the business and compatible with the context in which the consumer provided the information.

(8) Comply with a legal obligation. **Leg.H.** Added Stats 2018 ch 55 §3 (AB 375), effective January 1, 2019, operative January 1, 2020. Amended Stats 2018 ch 735 §2 (SB 1121), effective September 23, 2018, operative January 1, 2020; Stats 2019 ch 751 §1 (AB 1146), effective January 1, 2020, operative January 1, 2020; Amendment approved by voters, Prop. 24 §5 (2020 Bill Text CA V. 9), on November 3, 2020, effective December 16, 2020, operative January 1, 2023.

2018 Notes: For citation of act, see the 2018 Note following CC §1798.100. For operative date of title, see CC §1798.198.

§ 1798.106 Consumers' Right to Correct Inaccurate Personal Information

(a) A consumer shall have the right to request a business that maintains inaccurate personal information about the consumer to correct that inaccurate personal information, taking into account the nature of the personal information and the purposes of the processing of the personal information.

(b) A business that collects personal information about consumers shall disclose, pursuant to Section 1798.130, the consumer's right to request correction of inaccurate personal information.

(c) A business that receives a verifiable consumer request to correct inaccurate personal information shall use commercially reasonable efforts to correct the inaccurate personal information as directed by the consumer, pursuant to Section 1798.130 and regulations adopted pursuant to paragraph [1] **(7)** of subdivision (a) of Section 1798.185. **Leg.H.** Adopted by voters, Prop. 24 §6 (2020 Bill Text CA V. 9), on November 3, 2020, effective December 16, 2020, operative January 1, 2023; Stats 2024 ch 121 §1 (AB 3286), effective January 1, 2025.

§ 1798.106 2024 Deletes. [1] (8)

§1798.110. Consumers' Right to Know What Personal Information is Being Collected. Right to Access Personal Information

(a) A consumer shall have the right to request that a business that collects personal information about the consumer disclose to the consumer the following:

(1) The categories of personal information it has collected about that consumer.

(2) The categories of sources from which the personal information is collected.

(3) The business or commercial purpose for collecting, selling, or sharing personal information.

(4) The categories of third parties to whom the business discloses personal information.

(5) The specific pieces of personal information it has collected about that consumer.

(b) A business that collects personal information about a consumer shall disclose to the consumer, pursuant to subparagraph (B) of paragraph (3) of subdivision (a) of Section 1798.130, the information specified in subdivision (a) upon receipt of a verifiable consumer request from the consumer, provided that a business shall be deemed to be in compliance with paragraphs (1) to (4), inclusive, of subdivision (a) to the extent that the categories of information and the business or commercial purpose for collecting, selling, or sharing personal information it would be required to disclose to the consumer pursuant to paragraphs (1) to (4), inclusive, of subdivision (a) is the same as the information it has disclosed pursuant to paragraphs (1) to (4), inclusive, of subdivision (c).

(c) A business that collects personal information about consumers shall disclose, pursuant to subparagraph (B) of paragraph (5) of subdivision (a) of Section 1798.130:

(1) The categories of personal information it has collected about consumers.

(2) The categories of sources from which the personal information is collected.

(3) The business or commercial purpose for collecting, selling, or sharing personal information.

(4) The categories of third parties to whom the business discloses personal information.

(5) That a consumer has the right to request the specific pieces of personal information the business has collected about that consumer. **Leg.H.** Added Stats 2018 ch 55 §3 (AB 375), effective January 1, 2019, operative January 1, 2020. Amended Stats 2018 ch 735 §3 (SB 1121), effective September 23, 2018, operative January 1, 2020; Stats 2019 ch 757 §2 (AB 1355), effective January 1, 2020, operative January 1, 2020; Amendment approved by voters, Prop. 24 §7 (2020 Bill Text CA V. 9), on November 3, 2020, effective December 16, 2020, operative January 1, 2023.

2018 Notes: For citation of act, see the 2018 Note following CC §1798.100. For operative date of title, see CC §1798.198.

§1798.115. Consumers' Right to Know What Personal Information is Sold or Shared and to Whom

(a) A consumer shall have the right to request that a business that sells or shares the consumer's personal information, or that discloses it for a business purpose, disclose to that consumer:

(1) The categories of personal information that the business collected about the consumer.

(2) The categories of personal information that the business sold or shared about the consumer and the categories of third parties to whom the personal information was sold or shared, by category or categories of personal information for each category of third parties to whom the personal information was sold or shared.

(3) The categories of personal information that the business disclosed about the consumer for a business purpose and the categories of persons to whom it was disclosed for a business purpose.

(b) A business that sells or shares personal information about a consumer, or that discloses a consumer's personal information for a business purpose, shall disclose, pursuant to paragraph (4) of subdivision (a) of Section 1798.130, the information specified in subdivision (a) to the consumer upon receipt of a verifiable consumer request from the consumer.

(c) A business that sells or shares consumers' personal information, or that discloses consumers' personal information for a business purpose, shall disclose, pursuant to subparagraph (C) of paragraph (5) of subdivision (a) of Section 1798.130:

(1) The category or categories of consumers' personal information it has sold or shared, or if the business has not sold or shared consumers' personal information, it shall disclose that fact.

(2) The category or categories of consumers' personal information it has disclosed for a business purpose, or if the business has not disclosed consumers' personal information for a business purpose, it shall disclose that fact.

(d) A third party shall not sell or share personal information about a consumer that has been sold to, or shared with, the third party by a business unless the consumer has received explicit notice and is provided an opportunity to exercise the right to opt-out pursuant to Section 1798.120. **Leg.H.** Added Stats 2018 ch 55 §3 (AB 375), effective January 1, 2019, operative January 1, 2020. Amended Stats 2018 ch 735 §4 (SB 1121), effective September 23, 2018, operative January 1, 2020; Stats 2019 ch 757 §3 (AB 1355), effective January 1, 2020, operative January 1, 2020; Amendment approved by voters, Prop. 24 §8 (2020 Bill Text CA V. 9), on November 3, 2020, effective December 16, 2020, operative January 1, 2023.

2018 Notes: For citation of act, see the 2018 Note following CC §1798.100. For operative date of title, see CC §1798.198.

§1798.120. Consumers' Right to Opt Out of Sale or Sharing of Personal Information

(a)(1) A consumer shall have the right, at any time, to direct a business that sells or shares personal information about the consumer to third parties not to sell or share the consumer's personal information. This right may be referred to as the right to [1] **opt out** of sale or sharing.

(2) A business to which another business transfers the personal information of a consumer as an asset that is part of a merger, acquisition, bankruptcy, or other transaction in which the transferee assumes control of all of, or part of, the transferor shall comply with a consumer's direction to the transferor made pursuant to this subdivision.

(b) A business that sells consumers' personal information to, or shares it with, third parties shall provide notice to consumers, pursuant to subdivision (a) of Section 1798.135, that this information may be sold or shared and that consumers have the "right to [2] **opt out**" of the sale or sharing of their personal information.

(c) Notwithstanding subdivision (a), a business shall not sell or share the personal information of consumers if the business has actual knowledge that the consumer is less than 16 years of age, unless the consumer, in the case of consumers at least 13 years of age and less than 16 years of age, or the consumer's parent or guardian, in the case of consumers who are less than 13 years of age, has affirmatively authorized the sale or sharing of the consumer's personal information. A business that willfully disregards the consumer's age shall be deemed to have had actual knowledge of the consumer's age.

(d) A business that has received direction from a consumer not to sell or share the consumer's personal information or, in the case of a minor, consumer's personal information has not received consent to sell or share the minor consumer's personal information, shall be prohibited, pursuant to paragraph (4) of subdivision (c) of Section 1798.135, from selling or sharing the consumer's personal information after its receipt of the consumer's direction, unless the consumer subsequently provides consent, for the sale or sharing of the consumer's personal information. **Leg.H.** Added Stats 2018 ch 55 §3 (AB 375), effective January 1, 2019, operative January 1, 2020. Amended Stats 2018 ch 735 §5 (SB 1121), effective September 23, 2018, operative January 1, 2020; Stats 2019 ch 757 §4 (AB 1355), effective January 1, 2020, operative January 1, 2020; Amendment approved by voters, Prop. 24 §9 (2020 Bill Text CA V. 9), on November 3, 2020, effective December 16, 2020, operative January 1, 2023; Stats 2024 ch 940 §1 (AB 1824), effective January 1, 2025.

§1798.120. 2024 Deletes. [1] opt-out [2] opt-out

2018 Notes: For citation of act, see the 2018 Note following CC §1798.100. For operative date of title, see CC §1798.198.

§ 1798.121. Consumers' Right to Limit Use and Disclosure of Sensitive Personal Information

(a) A consumer shall have the right, at any time, to direct a business that collects sensitive personal information about the consumer to limit its use of the consumer's sensitive personal information to that use which is necessary to perform the services or provide the goods reasonably expected by an average consumer who requests those goods or services, to perform the services set forth in paragraphs (2), (4), (5), and (8) of subdivision (e) of Section 1798.140, and as authorized by regulations adopted pursuant to subparagraph (C) of paragraph [1] **(18)** of subdivision (a) of Section 1798.185. A business that uses or discloses a consumer's sensitive personal information for purposes other than those specified in this subdivision shall provide notice to consumers, pursuant to subdivision (a) of Section 1798.135, that this information may be used, or disclosed to a service provider or contractor, for additional, specified purposes and that consumers have the right to limit the use or disclosure of their sensitive personal information.

(b) A business that has received direction from a consumer not to use or disclose the consumer's sensitive personal information, except as authorized by subdivision (a), shall be prohibited, pursuant to paragraph (4) of subdivision (c) of Section 1798.135, from using or disclosing the consumer's sensitive personal information for any other purpose after its receipt of the consumer's direction unless the consumer subsequently provides consent for the use or disclosure of the consumer's sensitive personal information for additional purposes.

(c) A service provider or contractor that assists a business in performing the purposes authorized by subdivision (a) may not use the sensitive personal information after it has received instructions from the business and to the extent it has actual knowledge that the personal information is sensitive personal information for any other purpose. A service provider or contractor is only required to limit its use of sensitive personal information received pursuant to a written contract with the business in response to instructions from the business and only with respect to its relationship with that business.

(d) Sensitive personal information that is collected or processed without the purpose of inferring characteristics about a consumer is not subject to this section, as further defined in regulations adopted pursuant to subparagraph (C) of paragraph [2] **(18)** of subdivision (a) of Section 1798.185, and shall be treated as personal information for purposes of all other sections of this act, including Section 1798.100. **Leg.H.** Adopted by voters, Prop. 24 §10 (2020 Bill Text CA V. 9), on November 3, 2020, effective December 16, 2020, operative January 1, 2023; Stats 2024 ch 121 §2 (AB 3286), effective January 1, 2025.

§ 1798.121. 2024 Deletes. [1] (19) [2] (19)

§1798.125. Consumers' Right of No Retaliation Following Opt Out or Exercise of Other Rights

(a)(1) A business shall not discriminate against a consumer because the consumer exercised any of the consumer's rights under this title, including, but not limited to, by:

(A) Denying goods or services to the consumer.

(B) Charging different prices or rates for goods or services, including through the use of discounts or other benefits or imposing penalties.

(C) Providing a different level or quality of goods or services to the consumer.

(D) Suggesting that the consumer will receive a different price or rate for goods or services or a different level or quality of goods or services.

(E) Retaliating against an employee, applicant for employment, or independent contractor, as defined in subparagraph (A) of paragraph (2) of subdivision (m) of Section 1798.145, for exercising their rights under this title.

(2) Nothing in this subdivision prohibits a business, pursuant to subdivision (b), from charging a consumer a different price or rate, or from providing a different level or quality of goods or services to the consumer, if that difference is reasonably related to the value provided to the consumer by the consumer's data.

(3) This subdivision does not prohibit a business from offering loyalty, rewards, premium features, discounts, or club card programs consistent with this title.

(b)(1) A business may offer financial incentives, including payments to consumers as compensation, for the collection of personal information, the sale of personal information, or the retention of personal information. A business may also offer a different price, rate, level, or quality of goods or services to the consumer if that price or difference is reasonably related to the value provided to the business by the consumer's data.

(2) A business that offers any financial incentives pursuant to this subdivision shall notify consumers of the financial incentives pursuant to Section 1798.130.

(3) A business may enter a consumer into a financial incentive program only if the consumer gives the business prior opt-in consent pursuant to Section 1798.130 that clearly describes the material terms of the financial incentive program, and which may be revoked by the consumer at any time. If a consumer refuses to provide opt-in consent, then the business shall wait for at least 12 months before next requesting that the consumer provide opt-in consent, or as prescribed by regulations adopted pursuant to Section 1798.185.

(4) A business shall not use financial incentive practices that are unjust, unreasonable, coercive, or usurious in nature. **Leg.H.** Added Stats 2018 ch 55 §3 (AB 375), effective January 1, 2019, operative January 1, 2020. Amended Stats 2018 ch 735 §6 (SB 1121), effective September 23, 2018, operative January 1, 2020; Stats 2019 ch 757 §5 (AB 1355), effective January 1, 2020, operative January 1, 2020; Amendment approved by voters, Prop. 24 §11 (2020 Bill Text CA V. 9), on November 3, 2020, effective December 16, 2020, operative January 1, 2023.

2018 Notes: For citation of act, see the 2018 Note following CC §1798.100. For operative date of title, see CC §1798.198.

§1798.130. Notice, Disclosure, Correction, and Deletion Requirements

(a) In order to comply with Sections 1798.100, 1798.105, 1798.106, 1798.110, 1798.115, and 1798.125, a business shall, in a form that is reasonably accessible to consumers:

(1)(A) Make available to consumers two or more designated methods for submitting requests for information required to be disclosed pursuant to Sections 1798.110 and 1798.115, or requests for deletion or correction pursuant to Sections 1798.105 and 1798.106, respectively, including, at a minimum, a toll-free telephone number. A business that operates exclusively online and has a direct relationship with a consumer from whom it collects personal information shall only be required to provide an email address for submitting requests for information required to be disclosed pursuant to Sections 1798.110 and 1798.115, or for requests for deletion or correction pursuant to Sections 1798.105 and 1798.106, respectively.

(B) If the business maintains an internet website, make the internet website available to consumers to submit requests for information required to be disclosed pursuant to Sections 1798.110 and 1798.115, or requests for deletion or correction pursuant to Sections 1798.105 and 1798.106, respectively.

(2)(A) Disclose and deliver the required information to a consumer free of charge, correct inaccurate personal information, or delete a consumer's personal information, based on the consumer's request, within 45 days of receiving a verifiable consumer request from the consumer. The business shall promptly take steps to determine whether the request is a verifiable consumer request, but this shall not extend the [1] **business'** duty to disclose and deliver the information, to correct inaccurate personal information, or to delete personal information within 45 days of receipt of the consumer's request. The time period to provide the required information, to correct inaccurate personal information, or to delete personal information may be extended once by an additional 45 days when reasonably necessary, provided the consumer is provided notice of the extension within the first 45-day period. The disclosure of the required information shall be made in writing and delivered through the consumer's account with the business, if the consumer maintains an account with the business, or by mail or electronically at the consumer's option if the consumer does not maintain an account with the business, in a readily useable format that allows the consumer to transmit this information from one entity to another entity without hindrance. The business may require authentication of the consumer that is reasonable in light of the nature of the personal information requested, but shall not require the consumer to create an account with the business in order to make a verifiable consumer request provided that if the consumer, has an account with the business, the business may require the consumer to use that account to submit a verifiable consumer request.

(B) The disclosure of the required information shall cover the 12-month period preceding the business' receipt of the verifiable consumer request provided that, upon the adoption of a regulation pursuant to paragraph [2] **(8)** of subdivision (a) of Section 1798.185, a consumer may request that the business disclose the required information beyond the 12-month period, and the business shall be required to provide that information unless doing so proves impossible or would involve a disproportionate effort. A consumer's right to request required information beyond the 12-month period, and a [3] **business'** obligation to provide that information, shall only apply to personal information collected on or after January 1, 2022. Nothing in this subparagraph shall require a business to keep personal information for any length of time.

(3)(A) A business that receives a verifiable consumer request pursuant to Section 1798.110 or 1798.115 shall disclose any personal information it has collected about a consumer, directly or indirectly, including through or by a service provider or contractor, to the consumer. A service provider or contractor shall not be required to comply with a verifiable consumer request received directly from a consumer or a consumer's authorized agent, pursuant to Section 1798.110 or 1798.115, to the extent that the service provider or contractor has collected personal information about the consumer in its role as a service provider or contractor. A service provider or contractor shall provide assistance to a business with which it has a contractual relationship with respect to the business' response to a verifiable consumer request, including, but not limited to, by providing to the business the consumer's personal information in the service provider or contractor's possession, which the service provider or contractor obtained as a result of providing services to the business, and by correcting inaccurate information or by enabling the business to do the same. A service provider or contractor that collects personal information pursuant to a written contract with a business shall be required to assist the business through appropriate technical and organizational measures in complying with the requirements of subdivisions (d) to (f), inclusive, of Section 1798.100, taking into account the nature of the processing.

(B) For purposes of subdivision (b) of Section 1798.110:

(i) To identify the consumer, associate the information provided by the consumer in the verifiable consumer request to any personal information previously collected by the business about the consumer.

(ii) Identify by category or categories the personal information collected about the consumer for the applicable period of time by reference to the enumerated category or categories in subdivision (c) that most closely describes the personal information collected; the categories of sources from which the consumer's personal information was collected; the business or commercial purpose for collecting, selling, or sharing the consumer's personal information; and the categories of third parties to whom the business discloses the consumer's personal information.

(iii) Provide the specific pieces of personal information obtained from the consumer in a format that is easily understandable to the average consumer, and to the extent technically feasible, in a structured, commonly used, machine-readable format that may also be transmitted to another entity at the consumer's request without hindrance. "Specific pieces of information" do not include data generated to help ensure security and integrity or as prescribed by regulation. Personal information is not considered to have been disclosed by a business when a consumer instructs a business to transfer the consumer's personal information from one business to another in the context of switching services.

(4) For purposes of subdivision (b) of Section 1798.115:

(A) Identify the consumer and associate the information provided by the consumer in the verifiable consumer request to any personal information previously collected by the business about the consumer.

(B) Identify by category or categories the personal information of the consumer that the business sold or shared during the applicable period of time by reference to the enumerated category in subdivision (c) that most closely describes the personal information, and provide the categories of third parties to whom the consumer's personal information was sold or shared during the applicable period of time by reference to the enumerated category or categories in subdivision (c) that most closely describes the personal information sold or shared. The business shall disclose the information in a list that is separate from a list generated for the purposes of subparagraph (C).

(C) Identify by category or categories the personal information of the consumer that the business disclosed for a business purpose during the applicable period of time by reference to the enumerated category or categories in subdivision (c) that most closely describes the personal information, and provide the categories of persons to whom the consumer's personal information was disclosed for a business purpose during the applicable period of time by reference to the enumerated category or categories in subdivision (c) that most closely describes the personal information disclosed. The business shall disclose the information in a list that is separate from a list generated for the purposes of subparagraph (B).

(5) Disclose the following information in its online privacy policy or policies if the business has an online privacy policy or policies and in any California-specific description of consumers' privacy rights, or if the business does not maintain those policies, on its internet website, and update that information at least once every 12 months:

(A) A description of a consumer's rights pursuant to Sections 1798.100, 1798.105, 1798.106, 1798.110, 1798.115, and 1798.125 and two or more designated methods for submitting requests, except as provided in subparagraph (A) of paragraph (1) of subdivision (a).

(B) For purposes of subdivision (c) of Section 1798.110:

(i) A list of the categories of personal information it has collected about consumers in the preceding 12 months by reference to the enumerated category or categories in subdivision (c) that most closely describe the personal information collected.

(ii) The categories of sources from which consumers' personal information is collected.

(iii) The business or commercial purpose for collecting, selling, or sharing consumers' personal information.

(iv) The categories of third parties to whom the business discloses consumers' personal information.

(C) For purposes of paragraphs (1) and (2) of subdivision (c) of Section 1798.115, two separate lists:

(i) A list of the categories of personal information it has sold or shared about consumers in the preceding 12 months by reference to the enumerated category or categories in subdivision (c) that most closely describe the personal information sold or shared, or if the business has not sold or shared consumers' personal information in the preceding 12 months, the business shall prominently disclose that fact in its privacy policy.

(ii) A list of the categories of personal information it has disclosed about consumers for a business purpose in the preceding 12 months by reference to the enumerated category in subdivision (c) that most closely describes the personal information disclosed, or if the business has not disclosed consumers' personal information for a business purpose in the preceding 12 months, the business shall disclose that fact.

(6) Ensure that all individuals responsible for handling consumer inquiries about the business' privacy practices or the business' compliance with this title are informed of all requirements in Sections 1798.100, 1798.105, 1798.106, 1798.110, 1798.115, 1798.125, and this section, and how to direct consumers to exercise their rights under those sections.

(7) Use any personal information collected from the consumer in connection with the business' verification of the consumer's request solely for the purposes of verification and shall not further disclose the personal information, retain it longer than necessary for purposes of verification, or use it for unrelated purposes.

(b) A business is not obligated to provide the information required by Sections 1798.110 and 1798.115 to the same consumer more than twice in a 12-month period.

(c) The categories of personal information required to be disclosed pursuant to Sections 1798.100, 1798.110, and 1798.115 shall follow the definitions of personal information and sensitive personal information in Section 1798.140 by describing the categories of personal information using the specific terms set forth in subparagraphs (A) to (K), inclusive, of paragraph (1) of subdivision (v) of Section 1798.140 and by describing the categories of sensitive personal information using the specific terms set forth in paragraphs (1) to (9), inclusive, of subdivision (ae) of Section 1798.140. **Leg.H.** Added Stats 2018 ch 55 §3 (AB 375), effective January 1, 2019, operative January 1, 2020. Amended Stats 2018 ch 735 §7 (SB 1121), effective September 23, 2018, operative January 1, 2020; Stats 2019 ch 757 §6 (AB 1355), effective January 1, 2020; Stats 2019 ch 759 §1 (AB 1564), effective January 1, 2020; Stats 2019 ch 763 §1.3 (AB 25), effective January 1, 2020, operative January 1, 2020 (ch 763 prevails); Stats 2020 ch 172 §1 (AB 713), effective September 25, 2020; Amendment approved by voters, Prop. 24 §12 (2020 Bill Text CA V. 9), on November 3, 2020, effective December 16, 2020, operative January 1, 2023; Amended Stats 2024 ch 121 §3 (AB 3286), effective January 1, 2025.

§1798.130. 2024 Deletes. [1] business's [2] (9) [3] business's

2018 Notes: For citation of act, see the 2018 Note following CC §1798.100. For operative date of title, see CC §1798.198.

§1798.135. Methods of Limiting Sale, Sharing, and Use of Personal Information and Use of Sensitive Personal Information

(a) A business that sells or shares consumers' personal information or uses or discloses consumers' sensitive personal information for purposes other than those authorized by subdivision (a) of Section 1798.121 shall, in a form that is reasonably accessible to consumers:

(1) Provide a clear and conspicuous link on the [1] **business'** internet homepages, titled "Do Not Sell or Share My Personal Information," to an internet web page that enables a consumer, or a person authorized by the consumer, to [2] **opt out** of the sale or sharing of the consumer's personal information.

(2) Provide a clear and conspicuous link on the business' internet homepages, titled "Limit the Use of My Sensitive Personal Information," that enables a consumer, or a person authorized by the consumer, to limit the use or disclosure of the consumer's sensitive personal information to those uses authorized by subdivision (a) of Section 1798.121.

(3) At the business' discretion, utilize a single, clearly labeled link on the business' internet homepages, in lieu of complying with paragraphs (1) and (2), if that link easily allows a consumer to opt out of the sale or sharing of the consumer's personal information and to limit the use or disclosure of the consumer's sensitive personal information.

(4) In the event that a business responds to opt-out requests received pursuant to paragraph (1), (2), or (3) by informing the consumer of a charge for the use of any product or service, present the terms of any financial incentive offered pursuant to subdivision (b) of Section 1798.125 for the retention, use, sale, or sharing of the consumer's personal information.

(b)(1) A business shall not be required to comply with subdivision (a) if the business allows consumers to opt out of the sale or sharing of their personal information and to limit the use of their sensitive personal information through an opt-out preference signal sent with the consumer's consent by a platform, technology, or mechanism, based on technical specifications set forth in regulations adopted pursuant to paragraph [3] **(19)** of subdivision (a) of Section 1798.185, to the business indicating the consumer's intent to opt out of the business' sale or sharing of the consumer's personal information or to limit the use or disclosure of the consumer's sensitive personal information, or both.

(2) A business that allows consumers to opt out of the sale or sharing of their personal information and to limit the use of their sensitive personal information pursuant to paragraph (1) may provide a link to a web page that enables the consumer to consent to the business ignoring the opt-out preference signal with respect to that business' sale or sharing of the consumer's personal information or the use of the consumer's sensitive personal information for additional purposes provided that:

(A) The consent web page also allows the consumer or a person authorized by the consumer to revoke the consent as easily as it is affirmatively provided.

(B) The link to the web page does not degrade the consumer's experience on the web page the consumer intends to visit and has a similar look, feel, and size relative to other links on the same web page.

(C) The consent web page complies with technical specifications set forth in regulations adopted pursuant to paragraph [4] **(19)** of subdivision (a) of Section 1798.185.

(3) A business that complies with subdivision (a) is not required to comply with subdivision (b). For the purposes of clarity, a business may elect whether to comply with subdivision (a) or subdivision (b).

(c) A business that is subject to this section shall:

(1) Not require a consumer to create an account or provide additional information beyond what is necessary in order to direct the business not to sell or share the consumer's personal information or to limit use or disclosure of the consumer's sensitive personal information.

(2) Include a description of a consumer's rights pursuant to Sections 1798.120 and 1798.121, along with a separate link to the "Do Not Sell or Share My Personal Information" internet web page and a separate link to the "Limit the Use of My Sensitive Personal Information" internet web page, if applicable, or a single link to both choices, or a statement that the business responds to and abides by opt-out preference signals sent by a platform, technology, or mechanism in accordance with subdivision (b), in:

(A) Its online privacy policy or policies if the business has an online privacy policy or policies.

(B) Any California-specific description of consumers' privacy rights.

(3) Ensure that all individuals responsible for handling consumer inquiries about the [5] **business'** privacy practices or the [6] **business'** compliance with this title are informed of all requirements in Sections 1798.120, 1798.121, and this section and how to direct consumers to exercise their rights under those sections.

(4) For consumers who exercise their right to [7] **opt out** of the sale or sharing of their personal information or limit the use or disclosure of their sensitive personal information, refrain from selling or sharing the consumer's personal information or using or disclosing the consumer's sensitive personal information and wait for at least 12 months before requesting that the consumer authorize the sale or sharing of the consumer's personal information or the use and disclosure of the consumer's sensitive personal information for additional purposes, or as authorized by regulations.

(5) For consumers under 16 years of age who do not consent to the sale or sharing of their personal information, refrain from selling or sharing the personal information of the consumer under 16 years of age and wait for at least 12 months before requesting the consumer's consent again, or as authorized by regulations or until the consumer attains 16 years of age.

(6) Use any personal information collected from the consumer in connection with the submission of the consumer's opt-out request solely for the purposes of complying with the opt-out request.

(d) Nothing in this title shall be construed to require a business to comply with the title by including the required links and text on the homepage that the business makes available to the public generally, if the business maintains a separate and additional homepage that is dedicated to California consumers and that includes the required links and text, and the business takes reasonable steps to ensure that California consumers are directed to the homepage for California consumers and not the homepage made available to the public generally.

(e) A consumer may authorize another person to [8] **opt out** of the sale or sharing of the consumer's personal information and to limit the use of the consumer's sensitive personal information on the consumer's behalf, including through an opt-out preference signal, as defined in paragraph (1) of subdivision (b), indicating the consumer's intent to opt out, and a business shall comply with an opt-out request received from a person authorized by the consumer to act on the consumer's behalf, pursuant to regulations adopted by the Attorney General regardless of whether the business has elected to comply with subdivision (a) or (b). For purposes of clarity, a business that elects to comply with subdivision (a) may respond to the consumer's opt-out [9] **request consistently** with Section 1798.125.

(f) If a business communicates a consumer's opt-out request to any person authorized by the business to collect personal information, the person shall thereafter only use that consumer's personal information for a business purpose specified by the business, or as otherwise permitted by this title, and shall be prohibited from:

(1) Selling or sharing the personal information.

(2) Retaining, using, or disclosing that consumer's personal information.

(A) For any purpose other than for the specific purpose of performing the services offered to the business.

(B) Outside of the direct business relationship between the person and the business.

(C) For a commercial purpose other than providing the services to the business.

(g) A business that communicates a consumer's opt-out request to a person pursuant to subdivision (f) shall not be liable under this title if the person receiving the opt-out request violates the restrictions set forth in the title provided that, at the time of communicating the opt-out request, the business does not have actual knowledge, or reason to believe, that the person intends to commit such a violation. Any provision of a contract or agreement of any kind that purports to waive or limit in any way this subdivision shall be void and unenforceable. **Leg.H.** Added Stats 2018 ch 55 §3 (AB 375), effective January 1, 2019, operative January 1, 2020. Amended Stats 2018 ch 735 §8 (SB 1121), effective September 23, 2018, operative January 1, 2020; Amendment approved by voters, Prop. 24 §13 (2020 Bill Text CA V. 9), on November 3, 2020, effective December 16, 2020, operative January 1, 2023; Stats 2024 ch 121 §4 (AB 3286), effective January 1, 2025.

§1798.135. 2024 Deletes. [1] business's [2] opt-out [3] (20) [4] (20) [5] business's [6] business's [7] opt-out [8] opt-out [9] consistent

2018 Notes: For citation of act, see the 2018 Note following CC §1798.100. For operative date of title, see CC §1798.198.

§1798.140. Definitions

For purposes of this title:

(a) "Advertising and marketing" means a communication by a business or a person acting on the business' behalf in any medium intended to induce a consumer to obtain goods, services, or employment.

(b) "Aggregate consumer information" means information that relates to a group or category of consumers, from which individual consumer identities have been removed, that is not linked or reasonably linkable to any consumer or household, including via a device. "Aggregate consumer information" does not mean one or more individual consumer records that have been deidentified.

(c) "Biometric information" means an individual's physiological, biological, or behavioral characteristics, including information pertaining to an individual's deoxyribonucleic acid (DNA), that is used or is intended to be used singly or in combination with each other or with other identifying data, to establish individual identity. Biometric information includes, but is not limited to, imagery of the iris, retina, fingerprint, face, hand, palm, vein patterns, and voice recordings, from which an identifier template, such as a faceprint, a minutiae template, or a voiceprint, can be extracted, and keystroke patterns or rhythms, gait patterns or rhythms, and sleep, health, or exercise data that contain identifying information.

(d) "Business" means:

(1) A sole proprietorship, partnership, limited liability company, corporation, association, or other legal entity that is organized or operated for the profit or financial benefit of its shareholders or other owners, that collects consumers' personal information, or on the behalf of which such information is collected and that alone, or jointly with others, determines the purposes and means of the processing of consumers' personal information, that does business in the State of California, and that satisfies one or more of the following thresholds:

(A) As of January 1 of the calendar year, had annual gross revenues in excess of twenty-five million dollars ($25,000,000) in the preceding calendar year, as adjusted pursuant to [1] **subdivision (d)** of Section [2] **1798.199.95**.

(B) Alone or in combination, annually buys, sells, or shares the personal information of 100,000 or more consumers or households.

(C) Derives 50 percent or more of its annual revenues from selling or sharing consumers' personal information.

(2) Any entity that controls or is controlled by a business, as defined in paragraph (1), and that shares common branding with the business and with whom the business shares consumers' personal information. "Control" or "controlled" means ownership of, or the power to vote, more than 50 percent of the outstanding shares of any class of voting security of a business; control in any manner over the election of a majority of the directors, or of individuals exercising similar functions; or the power to exercise a controlling influence over the management of a company. "Common branding" means a shared name, servicemark, or trademark that the average consumer would understand that two or more entities are commonly owned.

(3) A joint venture or partnership composed of businesses in which each business has at least a 40 percent interest. For purposes of this title, the joint venture or partnership and each business that composes the joint venture or partnership shall separately be considered a single business, except that personal information in the possession of each business and disclosed to the joint venture or partnership shall not be shared with the other business.

(4) A person that does business in California, that is not covered by paragraph (1), (2), or (3), and that voluntarily certifies to the California Privacy Protection Agency that it is in compliance with, and agrees to be bound by, this title.

(e) "Business purpose" means the use of personal information for the business' operational purposes, or other notified purposes, or for the service provider or contractor's operational purposes, as defined by regulations adopted pursuant to paragraph [3] **(10)** of subdivision (a) of Section 1798.185, provided that the use of personal information shall be reasonably necessary and proportionate to achieve the purpose for which the personal information was collected or processed or for another purpose that is compatible with the context in which the personal information was collected. Business purposes are:

(1) Auditing related to counting ad impressions to unique visitors, verifying positioning and quality of ad impressions, and auditing compliance with this specification and other standards.

(2) Helping to ensure security and integrity to the extent the use of the consumer's personal information is reasonably necessary and proportionate for these purposes.

(3) Debugging to identify and repair errors that impair existing intended functionality.

(4) Short-term, transient use, including, but not limited to, nonpersonalized advertising shown as part of a consumer's current interaction with the business, provided that the consumer's personal information is not disclosed to another third party and is not used to build a profile about the consumer or otherwise alter the consumer's experience outside the current interaction with the business.

(5) Performing services on behalf of the business, including maintaining or servicing accounts, providing customer service, processing or fulfilling orders and transactions, verifying customer information, processing payments, providing financing, providing analytic services, providing storage, or providing similar services on behalf of the business.

(6) Providing advertising and marketing services, except for cross-context behavioral advertising, to the consumer provided that, for the purpose of advertising and marketing, a service provider or contractor shall not combine the personal information of opted-out consumers that the service provider or contractor receives from, or on behalf of, the business with personal information that the service provider or contractor receives from, or on behalf of, another person or persons or collects from its own interaction with consumers.

(7) Undertaking internal research for technological development and demonstration.

(8) Undertaking activities to verify or maintain the quality or safety of a service or device that is owned, manufactured, manufactured for, or controlled by the business, and to improve, upgrade, or enhance the service or device that is owned, manufactured, manufactured for, or controlled by the business.

(f) "Collects," "collected," or "collection" means buying, renting, gathering, obtaining, receiving, or accessing any personal information pertaining to a consumer by any means. This includes receiving information from the consumer, either actively or passively, or by observing the consumer's behavior.

(g) "Commercial purposes" means to advance a person's commercial or economic interests, such as by inducing another person to buy, rent, lease, join, subscribe to, provide, or exchange products, goods, property, information, or services, or enabling or effecting, directly or indirectly, a commercial transaction.

(h) "Consent" means any freely given, specific, informed, and unambiguous indication of the consumer's wishes by which the consumer, or the consumer's legal guardian, a person who has power of attorney, or a person acting as a conservator for the consumer, including by a statement or by a clear affirmative action, signifies agreement to the processing of personal information relating to the consumer for a narrowly defined particular purpose. Acceptance of a general or broad terms of use, or similar document, that contains descriptions of personal information processing along with other, unrelated information, does not constitute consent. Hovering over, muting, pausing, or closing a given piece of content does not constitute consent. Likewise, agreement obtained through use of dark patterns does not constitute consent.

(i) "Consumer" means a natural person who is a California resident, as defined in Section 17014 of Title 18 of the California Code of Regulations, as that section read on September 1, 2017, however identified, including by any unique identifier.

(j)(1) "Contractor" means a person to whom the business makes available a consumer's personal information for a business purpose, pursuant to a written contract with the business, provided that the contract:

(A) Prohibits the contractor from:

(i) Selling or sharing the personal information.

(ii) Retaining, using, or disclosing the personal information for any purpose other than for the business purposes specified in the contract, including retaining, using, or disclosing the personal information for a commercial purpose other than the business purposes specified in the contract, or as otherwise permitted by this title.

(iii) Retaining, using, or disclosing the information outside of the direct business relationship between the contractor and the business.

(iv) Combining the personal information that the contractor receives pursuant to a written contract with the business with personal information that it receives from or on behalf of another person or persons, or collects from its own interaction with the consumer, provided that the contractor may combine personal information to perform any business purpose as defined in regulations adopted pursuant to paragraph [4] **(9)** of subdivision (a) of Section 1798.185, except as provided for in paragraph (6) of subdivision (e) and in regulations adopted by the California Privacy Protection Agency.

(B) Includes a certification made by the contractor that the contractor understands the restrictions in subparagraph (A) and will comply with them.

(C) Permits, subject to agreement with the contractor, the business to monitor the contractor's compliance with the contract through measures, including, but not limited to, ongoing manual reviews and automated scans and regular assessments, audits, or other technical and operational testing at least once every 12 months.

(2) If a contractor engages any other person to assist it in processing personal information for a business purpose on behalf of the business, or if any other person engaged by the contractor engages another person to assist in processing personal information for that business purpose, it shall notify the business of that engagement, and the engagement shall be pursuant to a written contract binding the other person to observe all the requirements set forth in paragraph (1).

(k) "Cross-context behavioral advertising" means the targeting of advertising to a consumer based on the consumer's personal information obtained from the consumer's activity across businesses, [5] **distinctly branded internet** websites, applications, or services, other than the business, [6] **distinctly branded internet** website, application, or service with which the consumer intentionally interacts.

(*l*) "Dark pattern" means a user interface designed or manipulated with the substantial effect of subverting or impairing user autonomy, decision-making, or choice, as further defined by regulation.

(m) "Deidentified" means information that cannot reasonably be used to infer information about, or otherwise be linked to, a particular consumer provided that the business that possesses the information:

(1) Takes reasonable measures to ensure that the information cannot be associated with a consumer or household.

(2) Publicly commits to maintain and use the information in deidentified form and not to attempt to reidentify the information, except that the business may attempt to reidentify the information solely for the purpose of determining whether its deidentification processes satisfy the requirements of this subdivision.

(3) Contractually obligates any recipients of the information to comply with all provisions of this subdivision.

(n) "Designated methods for submitting requests" means a mailing address, email address, internet web page, internet web portal, toll-free telephone number, or other applicable contact information, whereby consumers may submit a request or direction under this title, and any new, consumer-friendly means of contacting a business, as approved by the Attorney General pursuant to Section 1798.185.

(o) "Device" means any physical object that is capable of connecting to the [7] **internet**, directly or indirectly, or to another device.

(p) "Homepage" means the introductory page of an internet website and any internet web page where personal information is collected. In the case of an online service, such as a mobile application, homepage means the application's platform page or download page, a link within the application, such as from the application configuration, "About," "Information," or settings page, and any other location that allows consumers to review the notices required by this title, including, but not limited to, before downloading the application.

(q) "Household" means a group, however identified, of consumers who cohabitate with one another at the same residential address and share use of common devices or services.

(r) "Infer" or "inference" means the derivation of information, data, assumptions, or conclusions from facts, evidence, or another source of information or data.

(s) "Intentionally interacts" means when the consumer intends to interact with a person, or disclose personal information to a person, via one or more deliberate interactions, including visiting the person's **internet** website or purchasing a good or service from the person. Hovering over, muting, pausing, or closing a given piece of content does not constitute a consumer's intent to interact with a person.

(t) "Nonpersonalized advertising" means advertising and marketing that is based solely on a consumer's personal information derived from the consumer's current interaction with the business with the exception of the consumer's precise geolocation.

(u) "Person" means an individual, proprietorship, firm, partnership, joint venture, syndicate, business trust, company, corporation, limited liability company, association, committee, and any other organization or group of persons acting in concert.

(v)(1) "Personal information" means information that identifies, relates to, describes, is reasonably capable of being associated with, or could reasonably be linked, directly or indirectly, with a particular consumer or household. Personal information includes, but is not limited to, the following if it identifies, relates to, describes, is reasonably capable of being associated with, or could be reasonably linked, directly or indirectly, with a particular consumer or household:

(A) Identifiers such as a real name, alias, postal address, unique personal identifier, online identifier, Internet Protocol address, email address, account name, social security number, driver's license number, passport number, or other similar identifiers.

(B) Any personal information described in subdivision (e) of Section 1798.80.

(C) Characteristics of protected classifications under California or federal law.

(D) Commercial information, including records of personal property, products or services purchased, obtained, or considered, or other purchasing or consuming histories or tendencies.

(E) Biometric information.

(F) Internet or other electronic network activity information, including, but not limited to, browsing history, search history, and information regarding a consumer's interaction with an internet website application, or advertisement.

(G) Geolocation data.

(H) Audio, electronic, visual, thermal, olfactory, or similar information.

(I) Professional or employment-related information.

(J) Education information, defined as information that is not publicly available personally identifiable information as defined in the Family Educational Rights and Privacy Act (20 U.S.C. Sec. 1232g; 34 C.F.R. Part 99).

(K) Inferences drawn from any of the information identified in this subdivision to create a profile about a consumer reflecting the consumer's preferences, characteristics, psychological trends, predispositions, behavior, attitudes, intelligence, abilities, and aptitudes.

(L) Sensitive personal information.

(2)(A) **"Personal information" does not include publicly available information or lawfully obtained, truthful information that is a matter of public concern.**

(B)(i) **For purposes of this paragraph, "publicly available" means any of the following:**

(I) **Information that is lawfully made available from federal, state, or local government records.**

(II) **Information that a business has a reasonable basis to believe is lawfully made available to the general public by the consumer or from widely distributed media.**

[8] (III) [9] **Information** made available by a person to whom the consumer has disclosed the information if the consumer has not restricted the information to a specific audience. [10]

(ii) **"Publicly available" does not mean biometric information collected by a business about a consumer without the consumer's knowledge.**

(3) "Personal information" does not include consumer information that is deidentified or aggregate consumer information.

(4) **"Personal information" can exist in various formats, including, but not limited to, all of the following:**

(A) **Physical formats, including paper documents, printed images, vinyl records, or video tapes.**

(B) **Digital formats, including text, image, audio, or video files.**

(C) **Abstract digital formats, including compressed or encrypted files, metadata, or artificial intelligence systems that are capable of outputting personal information.**

(w) "Precise geolocation" means any data that is derived from a device and that is used or intended to be used to locate a consumer within a geographic area that is equal to or less than the area of a circle with a radius of 1,850 feet, except as prescribed by regulations.

(x) "Probabilistic identifier" means the identification of a consumer or a consumer's device to a degree of certainty of more probable than not based on any categories of personal information included in, or similar to, the categories enumerated in the definition of personal information.

(y) "Processing" means any operation or set of operations that are performed on personal information or on sets of personal information, whether or not by automated means.

(z) "Profiling" means any form of automated processing of personal information, as further defined by regulations pursuant to paragraph [11] **(15)** of subdivision (a) of Section 1798.185, to evaluate certain personal aspects relating to a natural person and in particular to analyze or predict aspects concerning that natural person's performance at work, economic situation, health, personal preferences, interests, reliability, behavior, location, or movements.

(aa) "Pseudonymize" or "Pseudonymization" means the processing of personal information in a manner that renders the personal information no longer attributable to a specific consumer without the use of additional information, provided that the additional information is kept separately and is subject to technical and organizational measures to ensure that the personal information is not attributed to an identified or identifiable consumer.

(ab) "Research" means scientific analysis, systematic study, and observation, including basic research or applied research that is designed to develop or contribute to public or scientific knowledge and that adheres or otherwise conforms to all other applicable ethics and privacy laws, including, but not limited to, studies conducted in the public interest in the area of public health. Research with personal information that may have been collected from a consumer in the course of the consumer's interactions with a business' service or device for other purposes shall be:

(1) Compatible with the business purpose for which the personal information was collected.

(2) Subsequently pseudonymized and deidentified, or deidentified and in the aggregate, such that the information cannot reasonably identify, relate to, describe, be capable of being associated with, or be linked, directly or indirectly, to a particular consumer, by a business.

(3) Made subject to technical safeguards that prohibit reidentification of the consumer to whom the information may pertain, other than as needed to support the research.

(4) Subject to business processes that specifically prohibit reidentification of the information, other than as needed to support the research.

(5) Made subject to business processes to prevent inadvertent release of deidentified information.

(6) Protected from any reidentification attempts.

(7) Used solely for research purposes that are compatible with the context in which the personal information was collected.

(8) Subjected by the business conducting the research to additional security controls that limit access to the research data to only those individuals as are necessary to carry out the research purpose.

(ac) "Security and integrity" means the ability of:

(1) Networks or information systems to detect security incidents that compromise the availability, authenticity, integrity, and confidentiality of stored or transmitted personal information.

(2) Businesses to detect security incidents, resist malicious, deceptive, fraudulent, or illegal actions and to help prosecute those responsible for those actions.

(3) Businesses to ensure the physical safety of natural persons.

(ad)(1) "Sell," "selling," "sale," or "sold," means selling, renting, releasing, disclosing, disseminating, making available, transferring, or otherwise communicating orally, in writing, or by electronic or other means, a consumer's personal information by the business to a third party for monetary or other valuable consideration.

(2) For purposes of this title, a business does not sell personal information when:

(A) A consumer uses or directs the business to intentionally:

(i) Disclose personal information.

(ii) Interact with one or more third parties.

(B) The business uses or shares an identifier for a consumer who has opted out of the sale of the consumer's personal information or limited the use of the consumer's sensitive personal information for the purposes of alerting persons that the consumer has opted out of the sale of the consumer's personal information or limited the use of the consumer's sensitive personal information.

(C) The business transfers to a third party the personal information of a consumer as an asset that is part of a merger, acquisition, bankruptcy, or other transaction in which the third party assumes control of all or part of the business, provided that information is used or shared consistently with this title. If a third party materially alters how it uses or shares the personal information of a consumer in a manner that is materially inconsistent with the promises made at the time of collection, it shall provide prior notice of the new or changed practice to the consumer. The notice shall be sufficiently prominent and robust to ensure that existing consumers can easily exercise their choices consistently with this title. This subparagraph does not authorize a business to make material, retroactive privacy policy changes or make other changes in their privacy policy in a manner that would violate the Unfair and Deceptive Practices Act (Chapter 5 (commencing with Section 17200) of Part 2 of Division 7 of the Business and Professions Code).

(ae) "Sensitive personal information" means:

(1) Personal information that reveals:

(A) A consumer's social security, driver's license, state identification card, or passport number.

(B) A consumer's account log-in, financial account, debit card, or credit card number in combination with any required security or access code, password, or credentials allowing access to an account.

(C) A consumer's precise geolocation.

(D) A consumer's racial or ethnic origin, citizenship or immigration status, religious or philosophical beliefs, or union membership.

(E) The contents of a consumer's mail, email, and text messages unless the business is the intended recipient of the communication.

(F) A consumer's genetic data.

(G)(i) A consumer's neural data.

(ii) "Neural data" means information that is generated by measuring the activity of a consumer's central or peripheral nervous system, and that is not inferred from nonneural information.

(2)(A) The processing of biometric information for the purpose of uniquely identifying a consumer.

(B) Personal information collected and analyzed concerning a consumer's health.

(C) Personal information collected and analyzed concerning a consumer's sex life or sexual orientation.

(3) Sensitive personal information that is "publicly available" pursuant to paragraph (2) of subdivision (v) shall not be considered sensitive personal information or personal information.

(af) "Service" or "services" means work, labor, and services, including services furnished in connection with the sale or repair of goods.

(ag)(1) "Service provider" means a person that processes personal information on behalf of a business and that receives from or on behalf of the business consumer's personal information for a business purpose pursuant to a written contract, provided that the contract prohibits the person from:

(A) Selling or sharing the personal information.

(B) Retaining, using, or disclosing the personal information for any purpose other than for the business purposes specified in the contract for the business, including retaining, using, or disclosing the personal information for a commercial purpose other than the business purposes specified in the contract with the business, or as otherwise permitted by this title.

(C) Retaining, using, or disclosing the information outside of the direct business relationship between the service provider and the business.

(D) Combining the personal information that the service provider receives from, or on behalf of, the business with personal information that it receives from, or on behalf of, another person or persons, or collects from its own interaction with the consumer, provided that the service provider may combine personal information to perform any business purpose as defined in regulations adopted pursuant to paragraph [12] **(9)** of subdivision (a) of Section 1798.185, except as provided for in paragraph (6) of subdivision (e) of this section and in regulations adopted by the California Privacy Protection Agency. The contract may, subject to agreement with the service provider, permit the business to monitor the service provider's compliance with the contract through measures, including, but not limited to, ongoing manual reviews and automated scans and regular assessments, audits, or other technical and operational testing at least once every 12 months.

(2) If a service provider engages any other person to assist it in processing personal information for a business purpose on behalf of the business, or if any other person engaged by the service provider engages another person to assist in processing personal information for that business purpose, it shall notify the business of that engagement, and the engagement shall be pursuant to a written contract binding the other person to observe all the requirements set forth in paragraph (1).

(ah)(1) "Share," "shared," or "sharing" means sharing, renting, releasing, disclosing, disseminating, making available, transferring, or otherwise communicating orally, in writing, or by electronic or other means, a consumer's personal information by the business to a third party for cross-context behavioral advertising, whether or not for monetary or other valuable consideration, including transactions between a business and a third party for cross-context behavioral advertising for the benefit of a business in which no money is exchanged.

(2) For purposes of this title, a business does not share personal information when:

(A) A consumer uses or directs the business to intentionally disclose personal information or intentionally interact with one or more third parties.

(B) The business uses or shares an identifier for a consumer who has opted out of the sharing of the consumer's personal information or limited the use of the consumer's sensitive personal information for the purposes of alerting persons that the consumer has opted out of the sharing of the consumer's personal information or limited the use of the consumer's sensitive personal information.

(C) The business transfers to a third party the personal information of a consumer as an asset that is part of a merger, acquisition, bankruptcy, or other transaction in which the third party assumes control of all or part of the business, provided that information is used or shared consistently with this title. If a third party materially alters how it uses or shares the personal information of a consumer in a manner that is materially inconsistent with the promises made at the time of collection, it shall provide prior notice of the new or changed practice to the consumer. The notice shall be sufficiently prominent and robust to ensure that existing consumers can easily exercise their choices consistently with this title. This subparagraph does not authorize a business to make material, retroactive privacy policy changes or make other changes in their privacy policy in a manner that would violate the Unfair and Deceptive Practices Act (Chapter 5 (commencing with Section 17200) of Part 2 of Division 7 of the Business and Professions Code).

(ai) "Third party" means a person who is not any of the following:

(1) The business with whom the consumer intentionally interacts and that collects personal information from the consumer as part of the consumer's current interaction with the business under this title.

(2) A service provider to the business.

(3) A contractor.

(aj) "Unique identifier" or "unique personal identifier" means a persistent identifier that can be used to recognize a consumer, a family, or a device that is linked to a consumer or family, over time and across different services, including, but not limited to, a device identifier; an Internet Protocol address; cookies, beacons, pixel tags, mobile ad identifiers, or similar technology; customer number, unique pseudonym, or user alias; telephone numbers, or other forms of persistent or probabilistic identifiers that can be used to identify a particular consumer or device that is linked to a consumer or family. For purposes of this subdivision, "family" means a custodial parent or guardian and any children under 18 years of age over which the parent or guardian has custody.

(ak) "Verifiable consumer request" means a request that is made by a consumer, by a consumer on behalf of the consumer's minor child, by a natural person or a person registered with the Secretary of State, authorized by the consumer to act on the consumer's behalf, or by a person who has power of attorney or is acting as a conservator for the consumer, and that the business can verify, using commercially reasonable methods, pursuant to regulations adopted by the Attorney General pursuant to paragraph [13] **(6)** of subdivision (a) of Section 1798.185 to be the consumer about whom the business has collected personal information. A business is not obligated to provide information to the consumer pursuant to Sections 1798.110 and 1798.115, to delete personal information pursuant to Section 1798.105, or to correct inaccurate personal information pursuant to Section 1798.106, if the business cannot verify, pursuant to this subdivision and regulations adopted by the Attorney General pursuant to paragraph [14] **(6)** of subdivision (a) of Section 1798.185, that the consumer making the request is the consumer about whom the business has collected information or is a person authorized by the consumer to act on such consumer's behalf. **Leg.H.** Added Stats 2018 ch 55 §3 (AB 375), effective January 1, 2019, operative January 1, 2020. Amended Stats 2018 ch 735 §9 (SB 1121), effective September 23, 2018, operative January 1, 2020; Stats 2019 ch 748 §1 (AB 874), effective January 1, 2020; Stats 2019 ch 757 §7.5 (AB 1355), effective January 1, 2020, operative January 1, 2020 (ch 757 prevails); Stats 2020 ch 370 §30 (SB 1371), effective January 1, 2021; Amendment approved by voters, Prop. 24 §14 (2020 Bill Text CA V. 9), on November 3, 2020, effective December 16, 2020, operative January 1, 2023; Amended Stats 2021 ch 525 §3 (AB 694), effective January 1, 2022, operative January 1, 2023; Stats 2023 ch 551 §1 (AB 947), effective January 1, 2024; Stats 2024 ch 121 §5 (AB 3286), effective January 1, 2025; Stats 2024 ch 802 §1 (AB 1008), effective January 1, 2025; Stats 2024 ch 887 §1.5 (SB 1223), effective January 1, 2025 (ch 887 prevails); §5; Stats 2024 ch 802 §1 (AB 1008), effective January 1, 2025; Stats 2024 ch 887 §1.5 (SB 1223), effective January 1, 2025 (ch 887 prevails).

§1798.140. 2024 Deletes. [1] paragraph (5) of subdivision (a) **[2]** 1798.185 **[3]** (11) **[4]** (10) **[5] distinctly-branded [6] distinctly-branded [7]** Internet **[8]** (2) **[9]** "Personal information" does not include publicly available information or lawfully obtained, truthful information that is a matter of public concern. For purposes of this paragraph, "publicly available" means: information that is lawfully made available from federal, state, or local government records, or information that a business has a reasonable basis to believe is lawfully made available to the general public by the consumer or from widely distributed media; or information **[10]** "Publicly available" does not mean biometric information collected by a business about a consumer without the consumer's knowledge. **[11]** (16) **[12]** (10) **[13]** (7) **[14]** (7)

2018 Notes: For citation of act, see the 2018 Note following CC §1798.100. For operative date of title, see CC §1798.198.

§1798.145. Exemptions

(a)(1) The obligations imposed on businesses by this title shall not restrict a business's ability to:

(A) Comply with federal, state, or local laws or comply with a court order or subpoena to provide information.

(B) Comply with a civil, criminal, or regulatory inquiry, investigation, subpoena, or summons by federal, state, or local authorities. Law enforcement agencies, including police and sheriff's departments, may direct a business pursuant to a law enforcement agency-approved investigation with an active case number not to delete a consumer's personal information, and, upon receipt of that direction, a business shall not delete the personal information for 90 days in order to allow the law enforcement agency to obtain a court-issued subpoena, order, or warrant to obtain a consumer's personal information. For good cause and only to the extent necessary for investigatory purposes, a law enforcement agency may direct a business not to delete the consumer's personal information for additional 90-day periods. A business that has received direction from a law enforcement agency not to delete the personal information of a consumer who has requested deletion of the consumer's personal information shall not use the consumer's personal information for any purpose other than retaining it to produce to law enforcement in response to a court-issued subpoena, order, or warrant unless the consumer's deletion request is subject to an exemption from deletion under this title.

(C) Cooperate with law enforcement agencies concerning conduct or activity that the business, service provider, or third party reasonably and in good faith believes may violate federal, state, or local law.

(D)(i) Cooperate with a government agency request for emergency access to a consumer's personal information if a natural person is at risk or danger of death or serious physical injury provided that:

(I) The request is approved by a high-ranking agency officer for emergency access to a consumer's personal information.

(II) The request is based on the agency's good faith determination that it has a lawful basis to access the information on a nonemergency basis.

(III) The agency agrees to petition a court for an appropriate order within three days and to destroy the information if that order is not granted.

(ii) For purposes of this subparagraph, a consumer accessing, procuring, or searching for services regarding contraception, pregnancy care, and perinatal care, including, but not limited to, abortion services, shall not constitute a natural person being at risk or danger of death or serious physical injury.

(E) Exercise or defend legal claims.

(F) Collect, use, retain, sell, share, or disclose consumers' personal information that is deidentified or aggregate consumer information.

(G) Collect, sell, or share a consumer's personal information if every aspect of that commercial conduct takes place wholly outside of California. For purposes of this title, commercial conduct takes place wholly outside of California if the business collected that information while the consumer was outside of California, no part of the sale of the consumer's personal information occurred in California, and no personal information collected while the consumer was in California is sold. This paragraph shall not prohibit a business from storing, including on a device, personal information about a consumer when the consumer is in California and then collecting that personal information when the consumer and stored personal information is outside of California.

(2)(A) This subdivision shall not apply if the consumer's personal information contains information related to accessing, procuring, or searching for services regarding contraception, pregnancy care, and perinatal care, including, but not limited to, abortion services.

(B) This paragraph does not alter the use of aggregated or deidentified personal information consistent with a business purpose as defined in paragraphs (1), (2), (3), (4), (5), (7), or (8) of subdivision (e) of Section 1798.140, provided that the personal information is only retained in aggregated and deidentified form and is not sold or shared.

(C) This paragraph does not alter the duty of a business to preserve or retain evidence pursuant to California or federal law in an ongoing civil proceeding.

(b) The obligations imposed on businesses by Sections 1798.110, 1798.115, 1798.120, 1798.121, 1798.130, and 1798.135 shall not apply where compliance by the business with the title would violate an evidentiary privilege under California law and shall not prevent a business from providing the personal information of a consumer to a person covered by an evidentiary privilege under California law as part of a privileged communication.

(c)(1) This title shall not apply to any of the following:

(A) Medical information governed by the Confidentiality of Medical Information Act (Part 2.6 (commencing with Section 56) of Division 1) or protected health information that is collected by a covered entity or business associate governed by the privacy, security, and breach notification rules issued by the United States Department of Health and Human Services, Parts 160 and 164 of Title 45 of the Code of Federal Regulations, established pursuant to the Health Insurance Portability and Accountability Act of 1996 (Public Law 104-191) and the Health Information Technology for Economic and Clinical Health Act (Public Law 111-5).

(B) A provider of health care governed by the Confidentiality of Medical Information Act (Part 2.6 (commencing with Section 56) of Division 1) or a covered entity governed by the privacy, security, and breach notification rules issued by the United States Department of Health

(3) Maintain information in identifiable, linkable, or associable form, or collect, obtain, retain, or access any data or technology, in order to be capable of linking or associating a verifiable consumer request with personal information.

(k) The rights afforded to consumers and the obligations imposed on the business in this title shall not adversely affect the rights and freedoms of other natural persons. A verifiable consumer request for specific pieces of personal information pursuant to Section 1798.110, to delete a consumer's personal information pursuant to Section 1798.105, or to correct inaccurate personal information pursuant to Section 1798.106, shall not extend to personal information about the consumer that belongs to, or the business maintains on behalf of, another natural person. A business may rely on representations made in a verifiable consumer request as to rights with respect to personal information and is under no legal requirement to seek out other persons that may have or claim to have rights to personal information, and a business is under no legal obligation under this title or any other provision of law to take any action under this title in the event of a dispute between or among persons claiming rights to personal information in the business's possession.

(*l*) The rights afforded to consumers and the obligations imposed on any business under this title shall not apply to the extent that they infringe on the noncommercial activities of a person or entity described in subdivision (b) of Section 2 of Article I of the California Constitution.

(m)(1) This title shall not apply to any of the following:

(A) Personal information that is collected by a business about a natural person in the course of the natural person acting as a job applicant to, an employee of, owner of, director of, officer of, medical staff member of, or independent contractor of, that business to the extent that the natural person's personal information is collected and used by the business solely within the context of the natural person's role or former role as a job applicant to, an employee of, owner of, director of, officer of, medical staff member of, or an independent contractor of, that business.

(B) Personal information that is collected by a business that is emergency contact information of the natural person acting as a job applicant to, an employee of, owner of, director of, officer of, medical staff member of, or independent contractor of, that business to the extent that the personal information is collected and used solely within the context of having an emergency contact on file.

(C) Personal information that is necessary for the business to retain to administer benefits for another natural person relating to the natural person acting as a job applicant to, an employee of, owner of, director of, officer of, medical staff member of, or independent contractor of, that business to the extent that the personal information is collected and used solely within the context of administering those benefits.

(2) For purposes of this subdivision:

(A) "Independent contractor" means a natural person who provides any service to a business pursuant to a written contract.

(B) "Director" means a natural person designated in the articles of incorporation as director, or elected by the incorporators and natural persons designated, elected, or appointed by any other name or title to act as directors, and their successors.

(C) "Medical staff member" means a licensed physician and surgeon, dentist, or podiatrist, licensed pursuant to Division 2 (commencing with Section 500) of the Business and Professions Code and a clinical psychologist as defined in Section 1316.5 of the Health and Safety Code.

(D) "Officer" means a natural person elected or appointed by the board of directors to manage the daily operations of a corporation, including a chief executive officer, president, secretary, or treasurer.

(E) "Owner" means a natural person who meets one of the following criteria:

(i) Has ownership of, or the power to vote, more than 50 percent of the outstanding shares of any class of voting security of a business.

(ii) Has control in any manner over the election of a majority of the directors or of individuals exercising similar functions.

(iii) Has the power to exercise a controlling influence over the management of a company.

(3) This subdivision shall not apply to subdivision (a) of Section 1798.100 or Section 1798.150.

(4) This subdivision shall become inoperative on January 1, 2023.

(n)(1) The obligations imposed on businesses by Sections 1798.100, 1798.105, 1798.106, 1798.110, 1798.115, 1798.121, 1798.130, and 1798.135 shall not apply to personal information reflecting a written or verbal communication or a transaction between the business and the consumer, where the consumer is a natural person who acted or is acting as an employee, owner, director, officer, or independent contractor of a company, partnership, sole proprietorship, nonprofit, or government agency and whose communications or transaction with the business occur solely within the context of the business conducting due diligence regarding, or providing or receiving a product or service to or from such company, partnership, sole proprietorship, nonprofit, or government agency.

(2) For purposes of this subdivision:

(A) "Independent contractor" means a natural person who provides any service to a business pursuant to a written contract.

(B) "Director" means a natural person designated in the articles of incorporation as such or elected by the incorporators and natural persons designated, elected, or appointed by any other name or title to act as directors, and their successors.

(C) "Officer" means a natural person elected or appointed by the board of directors to manage the daily operations of a corporation, such as a chief executive officer, president, secretary, or treasurer.

(D) "Owner" means a natural person who meets one of the following:

(i) Has ownership of, or the power to vote, more than 50 percent of the outstanding shares of any class of voting security of a business.

(ii) Has control in any manner over the election of a majority of the directors or of individuals exercising similar functions.

(iii) Has the power to exercise a controlling influence over the management of a company.

(3) This subdivision shall become inoperative on January 1, 2023.

(o)(1) Sections 1798.105 and 1798.120 shall not apply to a commercial credit reporting agency's collection, processing, sale, or disclosure of business controller information to the extent the commercial credit reporting agency uses the business controller information solely to identify the relationship of a consumer to a business that the consumer owns or contact the consumer only in the consumer's role as the owner, director, officer, or management employee of the business.

(2) For the purposes of this subdivision:

(A) "Business controller information" means the name or names of the owner or owners, director, officer, or management employee of a business and the contact information, including a business title, for the owner or owners, director, officer, or management employee.

(B) "Commercial credit reporting agency" has the meaning set forth in subdivision (b) of Section 1785.42.

(C) "Owner" means a natural person that meets one of the following:

(i) Has ownership of, or the power to vote, more than 50 percent of the outstanding shares of any class of voting security of a business.

(ii) Has control in any manner over the election of a majority of the directors or of individuals exercising similar functions.

(iii) Has the power to exercise a controlling influence over the management of a company.

(D) "Director" means a natural person designated in the articles of incorporation of a business as director, or elected by the incorporators and natural persons designated, elected, or appointed by any other name or title to act as directors, and their successors.

(E) "Officer" means a natural person elected or appointed by the board of directors of a business to manage the daily operations of a corporation, including a chief executive officer, president, secretary, or treasurer.

(F) "Management employee" means a natural person whose name and contact information is reported to or collected by a commercial credit reporting agency as the primary manager of a business and used solely within the context of the natural person's role as the primary manager of the business.

(p) The obligations imposed on businesses in Sections 1798.105, 1798.106, 1798.110, and 1798.115 shall not apply to household data.

(q)(1) This title does not require a business to comply with a verifiable consumer request to delete a consumer's personal information under Section 1798.105 to the extent the verifiable consumer request applies to a student's grades, educational scores, or educational test results that the business holds on behalf of a local educational agency, as defined in subdivision (d) of Section 49073.1 of the Education Code, at which the student is currently enrolled. If a business does not comply with a request pursuant to this section, it shall notify the consumer that it is acting pursuant to this exception.

and Human Services, Parts 160 and 164 of Title 45 of the Code of Federal Regulations, established pursuant to the Health Insurance Portability and Accountability Act of 1996 (Public Law 104-191), to the extent the provider or covered entity maintains patient information in the same manner as medical information or protected health information as described in subparagraph (A) of this section.

(C) Personal information collected as part of a clinical trial or other biomedical research study subject to, or conducted in accordance with, the Federal Policy for the Protection of Human Subjects, also known as the Common Rule, pursuant to good clinical practice guidelines issued by the International Council for Harmonisation or pursuant to human subject protection requirements of the United States Food and Drug Administration, provided that the information is not sold or shared in a manner not permitted by this subparagraph, and, if it is inconsistent, that participants be informed of that use and provide consent.

(2) For purposes of this subdivision, the definitions of "medical information" and "provider of health care" in Section 56.05 shall apply and the definitions of "business associate," "covered entity," and "protected health information" in Section 160.103 of Title 45 of the Code of Federal Regulations shall apply.

(d)(1) This title shall not apply to an activity involving the collection, maintenance, disclosure, sale, communication, or use of any personal information bearing on a consumer's creditworthiness, credit standing, credit capacity, character, general reputation, personal characteristics, or mode of living by a consumer reporting agency, as defined in subdivision (f) of Section 1681a of Title 15 of the United States Code, by a furnisher of information, as set forth in Section 1681s-2 of Title 15 of the United States Code, who provides information for use in a consumer report, as defined in subdivision (d) of Section 1681a of Title 15 of the United States Code, and by a user of a consumer report as set forth in Section 1681b of Title 15 of the United States Code.

(2) Paragraph (1) shall apply only to the extent that such activity involving the collection, maintenance, disclosure, sale, communication, or use of such information by that agency, furnisher, or user is subject to regulation under the Fair Credit Reporting Act, Section 1681 et seq., Title 15 of the United States Code and the information is not collected, maintained, used, communicated, disclosed, or sold except as authorized by the Fair Credit Reporting Act.

(3) This subdivision shall not apply to Section 1798.150.

(e) This title shall not apply to personal information collected, processed, sold, or disclosed subject to the federal Gramm-Leach-Bliley Act (Public Law 106-102), and implementing regulations, or the California Financial Information Privacy Act (Division 1.4 (commencing with Section 4050) of the Financial Code), or the federal Farm Credit Act of 1971 (as amended in 12 U.S.C. 2001-2279cc and implementing regulations, 12 C.F.R. 600, et seq.). This subdivision shall not apply to Section 1798.150.

(f) This title shall not apply to personal information collected, processed, sold, or disclosed pursuant to the Driver's Privacy Protection Act of 1994 (18 U.S.C. Sec. 2721 et seq.). This subdivision shall not apply to Section 1798.150.

(g)(1) Section 1798.120 shall not apply to vehicle information or ownership information retained or shared between a new motor vehicle dealer, as defined in Section 426 of the Vehicle Code, and the vehicle's manufacturer, as defined in Section 672 of the Vehicle Code, if the vehicle information or ownership information is shared for the purpose of effectuating, or in anticipation of effectuating, a vehicle repair covered by a vehicle warranty or a recall conducted pursuant to Sections 30118 to 30120, inclusive, of Title 49 of the United States Code, provided that the new motor vehicle dealer or vehicle manufacturer with which that vehicle information or ownership information is shared does not sell, share, or use that information for any other purpose.

(2) Section 1798.120 shall not apply to vessel information or ownership information retained or shared between a vessel dealer and the vessel's manufacturer, as defined in Section 651 of the Harbors and Navigation Code, if the vessel information or ownership information is shared for the purpose of effectuating, or in anticipation of effectuating, a vessel repair covered by a vessel warranty or a recall conducted pursuant to Section 4310 of Title 46 of the United States Code, provided that the vessel dealer or vessel manufacturer with which that vessel information or ownership information is shared does not sell, share, or use that information for any other purpose.

(3) For purposes of this subdivision:

(A) "Ownership information" means the name or names of the registered owner or owners and the contact information for the owner or owners.

(B) "Vehicle information" means the vehicle information number, make, model, year, and odometer reading.

(C) "Vessel dealer" means a person who is engaged, wholly or in part, in the business of selling or offering for sale, buying or taking in trade for the purpose of resale, or exchanging, any vessel or vessels, as defined in Section 651 of the Harbors and Navigation Code, and receives or expects to receive money, profit, or any other thing of value.

(D) "Vessel information" means the hull identification number, model, year, month and year of production, and information describing any of the following equipment as shipped, transferred, or sold from the place of manufacture, including all attached parts and accessories:

(i) An inboard engine.

(ii) An outboard engine.

(iii) A stern drive unit.

(iv) An inflatable personal floatation device approved under Section 160.076 of Title 46 of the Code of Federal Regulations.

(h) Notwithstanding a business's obligations to respond to and honor consumer rights requests pursuant to this title:

(1) A time period for a business to respond to a consumer for any verifiable consumer request may be extended by up to a total of 90 days where necessary, taking into account the complexity and number of the requests. The business shall inform the consumer of any such extension within 45 days of receipt of the request, together with the reasons for the delay.

(2) If the business does not take action on the request of the consumer, the business shall inform the consumer, without delay and at the latest within the time period permitted of response by this section, of the reasons for not taking action and any rights the consumer may have to appeal the decision to the business.

(3) If requests from a consumer are manifestly unfounded or excessive, in particular because of their repetitive character, a business may either charge a reasonable fee, taking into account the administrative costs of providing the information or communication or taking the action requested, or refuse to act on the request and notify the consumer of the reason for refusing the request. The business shall bear the burden of demonstrating that any verifiable consumer request is manifestly unfounded or excessive.

(i)(1) A business that discloses personal information to a service provider or contractor in compliance with this title shall not be liable under this title if the service provider or contractor receiving the personal information uses it in violation of the restrictions set forth in the title, provided that, at the time of disclosing the personal information, the business does not have actual knowledge, or reason to believe, that the service provider or contractor intends to commit such a violation. A service provider or contractor shall likewise not be liable under this title for the obligations of a business for which it provides services as set forth in this title provided that the service provider or contractor shall be liable for its own violations of this title.

(2) A business that discloses personal information of a consumer, with the exception of consumers who have exercised their right to opt out of the sale or sharing of their personal information, consumers who have limited the use or disclosure of their sensitive personal information, and minor consumers who have not opted in to the collection or sale of their personal information, to a third party pursuant to a written contract that requires the third party to provide the same level of protection of the consumer's rights under this title as provided by the business shall not be liable under this title if the third party receiving the personal information uses it in violation of the restrictions set forth in this title provided that, at the time of disclosing the personal information, the business does not have actual knowledge, or reason to believe, that the third party intends to commit such a violation.

(j) This title shall not be construed to require a business, service provider, or contractor to:

(1) Reidentify or otherwise link information that, in the ordinary course of business, is not maintained in a manner that would be considered personal information.

(2) Retain any personal information about a consumer if, in the ordinary course of business, that information about the consumer would not be retained.

(2) This title does not require, in response to a request pursuant to Section 1798.110, that a business disclose on educational standardized assessment or educational assessment or a consumer's specific responses to the educational standardized assessment or educational assessment if consumer access, possession, or control would jeopardize the validity and reliability of that educational standardized assessment or educational assessment. If a business does not comply with a request pursuant to this section, it shall notify the consumer that it is acting pursuant to this exception.

(3) For purposes of this subdivision:

(A) "Educational standardized assessment or educational assessment" means a standardized or nonstandardized quiz, test, or other assessment used to evaluate students in or for entry to kindergarten and grades 1 to 12, inclusive, schools, postsecondary institutions, vocational programs, and postgraduate programs that are accredited by an accrediting agency or organization recognized by the State of California or the United States Department of Education, as well as certification and licensure examinations used to determine competency and eligibility to receive certification or licensure from a government agency or government certification body.

(B) "Jeopardize the validity and reliability of that educational standardized assessment or educational assessment" means releasing information that would provide an advantage to the consumer who has submitted a verifiable consumer request or to another natural person.

(r) Sections 1798.105 and 1798.120 shall not apply to a business's use, disclosure, or sale of particular pieces of a consumer's personal information if the consumer has consented to the business's use, disclosure, or sale of that information to produce a physical item, including a school yearbook containing the consumer's photograph if:

(1) The business has incurred significant expense in reliance on the consumer's consent.

(2) Compliance with the consumer's request to opt out of the sale of the consumer's personal information or to delete the consumer's personal information would not be commercially reasonable.

(3) The business complies with the consumer's request as soon as it is commercially reasonable to do so. **Leg.H.** Amended Stats 2018 ch 735 §10 (SB 1121), effective September 23, 2018, operative January 1, 2020. Added Stats 2018 ch 55 §3 (AB 375), effective January 1, 2019, operative January 1, 2020. Amended Stats 2019 ch 751 §2 (AB 1146), effective January 1, 2020; Stats 2019 ch 757 §8 (AB 1355), effective January 1, 2020; Stats 2019 ch 763 §2.3 (AB 25), effective January 1, 2020, operative January 1, 2020 (ch 763 prevails); Stats 2020 ch 268 §1 (AB 1281), effective January 1, 2021; Stats 2020 ch 370 §31 (SB 1371), effective January 1, 2021; Amendment approved by voters, Prop. 24 §15 (2020 Bill Text CA V. 9), on November 3, 2020, effective December 16, 2020, operative January 1, 2023; Amended Stats 2021 ch 525 §4 (AB 694), effective January 1, 2022; Stats 2021 ch 700 §2.5 (AB 335), effective January 1, 2022, operative January 1, 2023 (ch 700 prevails); Stats 2023 ch 567 §2 (AB 1194), effective January 1, 2024; §1.

2018 Notes: For citation of act, see the 2018 Note following CC §1798.100. For operative date of title, see CC §1798.198.

§1798.146. Inapplicability of title to certain information and entities

(a) This title shall not apply to any of the following:

(1) Medical information governed by the Confidentiality of Medical Information Act (Part 2.6 (commencing with Section 56) of Division 1) or protected health information that is collected by a covered entity or business associate governed by the privacy, security, and breach notification rules issued by the United States Department of Health and Human Services, Parts 160 and 164 of Title 45 of the Code of Federal Regulations, established pursuant to the federal Health Insurance Portability and Accountability Act of 1996 (Public Law 104-191) and the federal Health Information Technology for Economic and Clinical Health Act, Title XIII of the federal American Recovery and Reinvestment Act of 2009 (Public Law 111-5).

(2) A provider of health care governed by the Confidentiality of Medical Information Act (Part 2.6 (commencing with Section 56) of Division 1) or a covered entity governed by the privacy, security, and breach notification rules issued by the United States Department of Health and Human Services, Parts 160 and 164 of Title 45 of the Code of Federal Regulations, established pursuant to the federal Health Insurance Portability and Accountability Act of 1996 (Public Law 104-191), to the extent the provider or covered entity maintains, uses, and discloses patient information in the same manner as medical information or protected health information as described in paragraph (1).

(3) A business associate of a covered entity governed by the privacy, security, and data breach notification rules issued by the United States Department of Health and Human Services, Parts 160 and 164 of Title 45 of the Code of Federal Regulations, established pursuant to the federal Health Insurance Portability and Accountability Act of 1996 (Public Law 104-191) and the federal Health Information Technology for Economic and Clinical Health Act, Title XIII of the federal American Recovery and Reinvestment Act of 2009 (Public Law 111-5), to the extent that the business associate maintains, uses, and discloses patient information in the same manner as medical information or protected health information as described in paragraph (1).

(4)(A) Information that meets both of the following conditions:

(i) It is deidentified in accordance with the requirements for deidentification set forth in Section 164.514 of Part 164 of Title 45 of the Code of Federal Regulations.

(ii) It is derived from patient information that was originally collected, created, transmitted, or maintained by an entity regulated by the Health Insurance Portability and Accountability Act, the Confidentiality Of Medical Information Act, or the Federal Policy for the Protection of Human Subjects, also known as the Common Rule.

(B) Information that met the requirements of subparagraph (A) but is subsequently reidentified shall no longer be eligible for the exemption in this paragraph, and shall be subject to applicable federal and state data privacy and security laws, including, but not limited to, the Health Insurance Portability and Accountability Act, the Confidentiality Of Medical Information Act, and this title.

(5) Information that is collected, used, or disclosed in research, as defined in Section 164.501 of Title 45 of the Code of Federal Regulations, including, but not limited to, a clinical trial, and that is conducted in accordance with applicable ethics, confidentiality, privacy, and security rules of Part 164 of Title 45 of the Code of Federal Regulations, the Federal Policy for the Protection of Human Subjects, also known as the Common Rule, good clinical practice guidelines issued by the International Council for Harmonisation, or human subject protection requirements of the United States Food and Drug Administration.

(b) For purposes of this section, all of the following shall apply:

(1) "Business associate" has the same meaning as defined in Section 160.103 of Title 45 of the Code of Federal Regulations.

(2) "Covered entity" has the same meaning as defined in Section 160.103 of Title 45 of the Code of Federal Regulations.

(3) "Identifiable private information" has the same meaning as defined in Section 46.102 of Title 45 of the Code of Federal Regulations.

(4) "Individually identifiable health information" has the same meaning as defined in Section 160.103 of Title 45 of the Code of Federal Regulations.

(5) "Medical information" has the same meaning as defined in Section 56.05.

(6) "Patient information" shall mean identifiable private information, protected health information, individually identifiable health information, or medical information.

(7) "Protected health information" has the same meaning as defined in Section 160.103 of Title 45 of the Code of Federal Regulations.

(8) "Provider of health care" has the same meaning as defined in Section 56.05. **Leg.H.** Added Stats 2020 ch 172 §2 (AB 713), effective September 25, 2020.

§1798.148. Reidentification of certain information prohibited; Exceptions

(a) A business or other person shall not reidentify, or attempt to reidentify, information that has met the requirements of paragraph (4) of subdivision (a) of Section 1798.146, except for one or more of the following purposes:

(1) Treatment, payment, or health care operations conducted by a covered entity or business associate acting on behalf of, and at the written direction of, the covered entity. For purposes of this paragraph, "treatment," "payment," "health care operations," "covered entity," and "business associate" have the same meaning as defined in Section 164.501 of Title 45 of the Code of Federal Regulations.

(2) Public health activities or purposes as described in Section 164.512 of Title 45 of the Code of Federal Regulations.

(3) Research, as defined in Section 164.501 of Title 45 of the Code of Federal Regulations, that is conducted in accordance with Part 46 of Title 45 of the Code of Federal Regulations, the Federal Policy for the Protection of Human Subjects, also known as the Common Rule.

(4) Pursuant to a contract where the lawful holder of the deidentified information that met the requirements of paragraph (4) of subdivision (a) of Section 1798.146 expressly engages a person or entity to attempt to reidentify the deidentified information in order to conduct testing, analysis, or validation of deidentification, or related statistical techniques, if the contract bans any other use or disclosure of the reidentified information and requires the return or destruction of the information that was reidentified upon completion of the contract.

(5) If otherwise required by law.

(b) In accordance with paragraph (4) of subdivision (a) of Section 1798.146, information reidentified pursuant this section shall be subject to applicable federal and state data privacy and security laws including, but not limited to, the Health Insurance Portability and Accountability Act, the Confidentiality of Medical Information Act, and this title.

(c) Beginning January 1, 2021, any contract for the sale or license of deidentified information that has met the requirements of paragraph (4) of subdivision (a) of Section 1798.146, where one of the parties is a person residing or doing business in the state, shall include the following, or substantially similar, provisions:

(1) A statement that the deidentified information being sold or licensed includes deidentified patient information.

(2) A statement that reidentification, and attempted reidentification, of the deidentified information by the purchaser or licensee of the information is prohibited pursuant to this section.

(3) A requirement that, unless otherwise required by law, the purchaser or licensee of the deidentified information may not further disclose the deidentified information to any third party unless the third party is contractually bound by the same or stricter restrictions and conditions.

(d) For purposes of this section, "reidentify" means the process of reversal of deidentification techniques, including, but not limited to, the addition of specific pieces of information or data elements that can, individually or in combination, be used to uniquely identify an individual or usage of any statistical method, contrivance, computer software, or other means that have the effect of associating deidentified information with a specific identifiable individual. **Leg.H.** Added Stats 2020 ch 172 §3 (AB 713), effective September 25, 2020.

§1798.150. Personal Information Security Breaches

(a)(1) Any consumer whose nonencrypted and nonredacted personal information, as defined in subparagraph (A) of paragraph (1) of subdivision (d) of Section 1798.81.5, or whose email address in combination with a password or security question and answer that would permit access to the account is subject to an unauthorized access and exfiltration, theft, or disclosure as a result of the [1] **business'** violation of the duty to implement and maintain reasonable security procedures and practices appropriate to the nature of the information to protect the personal information may institute a civil action for any of the following:

(A) To recover damages in an amount not less than one hundred dollars ($100) and not greater than seven hundred and fifty ($750) per consumer per incident or actual damages, whichever is greater. **The amounts in this subdivision shall be adjusted pursuant to subdivision (d) of Section 1798.199.95.**

(B) Injunctive or declaratory relief.

(C) Any other relief the court deems proper.

(2) In assessing the amount of statutory damages, the court shall consider any one or more of the relevant circumstances presented by any of the parties to the case, including, but not limited to, the nature and seriousness of the misconduct, the number of violations, the persistence of the misconduct, the length of time over which the misconduct occurred, the willfulness of the defendant's misconduct, and the defendant's assets, liabilities, and net worth.

(b) Actions pursuant to this section may be brought by a consumer if, prior to initiating any action against a business for statutory damages on an individual or class-wide basis, a consumer provides a business 30 days' written notice identifying the specific provisions of this title the consumer alleges have been or are being violated. In the event a cure is possible, if within the 30 days the business actually cures the noticed violation and provides the consumer an express written statement that the violations have been cured and that no further violations shall occur, no action for individual statutory damages or class-wide statutory damages may be initiated against the business. The implementation and maintenance of reasonable security procedures and practices pursuant to Section 1798.81.5 following a breach does not constitute a cure with respect to that breach. No notice shall be required prior to an individual consumer initiating an action solely for actual pecuniary damages suffered as a result of the alleged violations of this title. If a business continues to violate this title in breach of the express written statement provided to the consumer under this section, the consumer may initiate an action against the business to enforce the written statement and may pursue statutory damages for each breach of the express written statement, as well as any other violation of the title that postdates the written statement.

(c) The cause of action established by this section shall apply only to violations as defined in subdivision (a) and shall not be based on violations of any other section of this title. Nothing in this title shall be interpreted to serve as the basis for a private right of action under any other law. This shall not be construed to relieve any party from any duties or obligations imposed under other law or the United States or California Constitution. **Leg.H.** Added Stats 2018 ch 55 §3 (AB 375), effective January 1, 2019, operative January 1, 2020. Amended Stats 2018 ch 735 §11 (SB 1121), effective September 23, 2018, operative January 1, 2020; Stats 2019 ch 757 §9 (AB 1355), effective January 1, 2020, operative January 1, 2020; Amendment approved by voters, Prop. 24 §16 (2020 Bill Text CA V. 9), on November 3, 2020, effective December 16, 2020, operative January 1, 2023; Stats 2024 ch 121 §6 (AB 3286), effective January 1, 2025.

§1798.150. 2024 Deletes. [1] business's

2018 Notes: For citation of act, see the 2018 Note following CC §1798.100. For operative date of title, see CC §1798.198.

§1798.155. Administrative Enforcement

(a) Any business, service provider, contractor, or other person that violates this title shall be liable for an administrative fine of not more than two thousand five hundred dollars ($2,500) for each violation or seven thousand five hundred dollars ($7,500) for each intentional violation or violations involving the personal information of consumers whom the business, service provider, contractor, or other person has actual knowledge are under 16 years of age, as adjusted pursuant to [1] **subdivision (d)** of Section [2] **1798.199.95**, in an administrative enforcement action brought by the California Privacy Protection Agency.

(b) Any administrative fine assessed for a violation of this title, and the proceeds of any settlement of an action brought pursuant to subdivision (a), shall be deposited in the Consumer Privacy Fund, created within the General Fund pursuant to subdivision (a) of Section 1798.160 with the intent to fully offset any costs incurred by the state courts, the Attorney General, and the California Privacy Protection Agency in connection with this title. **Leg.H.** Added Stats 2018 ch 55 §3 (AB 375), effective January 1, 2019, operative January 1, 2020. Amended Stats 2018 ch 735 §12 (SB 1121), effective September 23, 2018, operative January 1, 2020; Amendment approved by voters, Prop. 24 §17 (2020 Bill Text CA V. 9), on November 3, 2020, effective December 16, 2020, operative January 1, 2023; Stats 2024 ch 121 §7 (AB 3286), effective January 1, 2025.

§1798.155. 2024 Deletes. [1] paragraph (5) of subdivision (a) [2] 1798.185

2018 Notes: For citation of act, see the 2018 Note following CC §1798.100. For operative date of title, see CC §1798.198.

§1798.160. Consumer Privacy Fund

(a) A special fund to be known as the "Consumer Privacy Fund" is hereby created within the General Fund in the State Treasury, and is available upon appropriation by the Legislature first to offset any costs incurred by the state courts in connection with actions brought to enforce this title, the costs incurred by the **California Privacy Protection Agency in carrying out its duties under this title, the costs incurred by the** Attorney General in carrying out the Attorney General's duties under this title, and then for the purposes of establishing an investment fund in the State Treasury, with any earnings or interest from the fund to be deposited in the General Fund, and making grants to promote and protect consumer privacy, educate children in the area of online privacy, and fund cooperative programs with international law enforcement organizations to combat fraudulent activities with respect to consumer data breaches.

(b) Funds transferred to the Consumer Privacy Fund shall be used exclusively as follows:

(1) To offset any costs incurred by the state courts, **the California Privacy Protection Agency,** and the Attorney General in connection with this title.

(2) After satisfying the obligations under paragraph (1), the remaining funds shall be allocated each fiscal year as follows:

(A) Ninety-one percent shall be invested by the Treasurer in financial assets with the goal of maximizing [1] **long-term** yields consistent with a prudent level of risk. The principal shall not be subject to transfer or appropriation, provided that any interest and earnings shall be transferred on an annual basis to the General Fund for appropriation by the Legislature for General Fund purposes.

(B) [2] **Subject to subdivision (d), 9** percent shall be made available to the California Privacy Protection Agency for the purposes of making grants in California, with 3 percent allocated to each of the following grant recipients:

(i) Nonprofit organizations to promote and protect consumer privacy.

(ii) Nonprofit organizations and public agencies, including school districts, to educate children in the area of online privacy.

(iii) State and local law enforcement agencies to fund cooperative programs with international law enforcement organizations to combat fraudulent activities with respect to consumer data breaches.

(c) Funds in the Consumer Privacy Fund shall not be subject to appropriation or transfer by the Legislature for any other purpose.

(d)(1) The California Privacy Protection Agency shall begin administering the grant program described in subparagraph (B) of paragraph (2) of subdivision (b) when the amount of grant funds available after all other distributions have been made in accordance with this section exceeds three hundred thousand dollars ($300,000).

(2) In a fiscal year in which the amount of funds available for grants pursuant to subparagraph (B) of paragraph (2) of subdivision (b) are equal to or less than three hundred thousand dollars ($300,000), the funds shall remain in the Consumer Privacy Fund and that amount shall be reserved for future year appropriations for the purpose of making grants pursuant to subparagraph (B) of paragraph (2) of subdivision (b) until the total funds accrued for that purpose after all other distributions have been made exceeds three hundred thousand dollars ($300,000). Leg.H. Added Stats 2018 ch 55 §3 (AB 375), effective January 1, 2019, operative January 1, 2020. Amendment approved by voters, Prop. 24 §18 (2020 Bill Text CA V. 9), on November 3, 2020, effective December 16, 2020; Stats 2024 ch 121 §8 (AB 3286), effective January 1, 2025.

§1798.160. 2024 Deletes. [1] long term **[2]** Nine

2018 Notes: For citation of act, see the 2018 Note following CC §1798.100. For operative date of title, see CC §1798.198.

§1798.175. Conflicting Provisions

This title is intended to further the constitutional right of privacy and to supplement existing laws relating to consumers' personal information, including, but not limited to, Chapter 22 (commencing with Section 22575) of Division 8 of the Business and Professions Code and Title 1.81 (commencing with Section 1798.80). The provisions of this title are not limited to information collected electronically or over the Internet, but apply to the collection and sale of all personal information collected by a business from consumers. Wherever possible, law relating to consumers' personal information should be construed to harmonize with the provisions of this title, but in the event of a conflict between other laws and the provisions of this title, the provisions of the law that afford the greatest protection for the right of privacy for consumers shall control. **Leg.H.** Added Stats 2018 ch 55 §3 (AB 375), effective January 1, 2019, operative January 1, 2020. Reenacted by voters, Prop. 24 §19 (2020 Bill Text CA V. 9), on November 3, 2020, effective December 16, 2020, operative January 1, 2023.

2018 Notes: For citation of act, see the 2018 Note following CC §1798.100. For operative date of title, see CC §1798.198.

§1798.180. Preemption

This title is a matter of statewide concern and supersedes and preempts all rules, regulations, codes, ordinances, and other laws adopted by a city, county, city and county, municipality, or local agency regarding the collection and sale of consumers' personal information by a business. **Leg.H.** Added Stats 2018 ch 55 §3 (AB 375), effective January 1, 2019, operative September 23, 2018. Reenacted by voters, Prop. 24 §20 (2020 Bill Text CA V. 9), on November 3, 2020, operative January 1, 2023.

2018 Notes: For citation of act, see the 2018 Note following CC §1798.100. For operative date of title, see CC §1798.198.

§1798.185. Regulations

(a) On or before July 1, 2020, the Attorney General shall solicit broad public participation and adopt regulations to further the purposes of this title, including, but not limited to, the following areas:

(1) Updating or adding categories of personal information to those enumerated in subdivision (c) of Section 1798.130 and subdivision (v) of Section 1798.140, and updating or adding categories of sensitive personal information to those enumerated in subdivision (ae) of Section 1798.140 in order to address changes in technology, data collection practices, obstacles to implementation, and privacy concerns.

(2) Updating as needed the definitions of "deidentified" and "unique identifier" to address changes in technology, data collection, obstacles to implementation, and privacy concerns, and adding, modifying, or deleting categories to the definition of designated methods for submitting requests to facilitate a consumer's ability to obtain information from a business pursuant to Section 1798.130. The authority to update the definition of "deidentified" shall not apply to deidentification standards set forth in Section 164.514 of Title 45 of the Code of Federal Regulations, where such information previously was "protected health information" as defined in Section 160.103 of Title 45 of the Code of Federal Regulations.

(3) Establishing any exceptions necessary to comply with state or federal law, including, but not limited to, those relating to trade secrets and intellectual property rights, within one year of passage of this title and as needed thereafter, with the intention that trade secrets should not be disclosed in response to a verifiable consumer request.

(4) Establishing rules and procedures for the following:

(A) To facilitate and govern the submission of a request by a consumer to opt out of the sale or sharing of personal information pursuant to Section 1798.120 and to limit the use of a consumer's sensitive personal information pursuant to Section 1798.121 to ensure that consumers have the ability to exercise their choices without undue burden and to prevent business from engaging in deceptive or harassing conduct, including in retaliation against consumers for exercising their rights, while allowing businesses to inform consumers of the consequences of their decision to opt out of the sale or sharing of their personal information or to limit the use of their sensitive personal information.

(B) To govern business compliance with a consumer's opt-out request.

(C) For the development and use of a recognizable and uniform opt-out logo or button by all businesses to promote consumer awareness of the opportunity to opt out of the sale of personal information.

[1]

(5) Establishing rules, procedures, and any exceptions necessary to ensure that the notices and information that businesses are required to provide pursuant to this title are provided in a manner that may be easily understood by the average consumer, are accessible to consumers with disabilities, and are available in the language primarily used to interact with the consumer, including establishing rules and guidelines regarding financial incentives within one year of passage of this title and as needed thereafter.

[2] **(6)** Establishing rules and procedures to further the purposes of Sections 1798.105, 1798.106, 1798.110, and 1798.115 and to facilitate a consumer's or the consumer's authorized agent's ability to delete personal information, correct inaccurate personal information pursuant to Section 1798.106, or obtain information pursuant to Section 1798.130, with the goal of minimizing the administrative burden on consumers, taking into account available technology, security concerns, and the burden on the business, to govern a [3] **business'** determination that a request for information received from a consumer is a verifiable consumer request, including treating a request submitted through a password-protected account maintained by the consumer with the business while the consumer is logged into the account as a verifiable consumer request and providing a mechanism for a consumer who does not maintain an account with the business to request information through the [4] **business'** authentication of the consumer's identity, within one year of passage of this title and as needed thereafter.

[5] **(7)** Establishing how often, and under what circumstances, a consumer may request a correction pursuant to Section 1798.106, including standards governing the following:

(A) How a business responds to a request for correction, including exceptions for requests to which a response is impossible or would involve disproportionate effort, and requests for correction of accurate information.

(B) How concerns regarding the accuracy of the information may be resolved.

(C) The steps a business may take to prevent fraud.

(D) If a business rejects a request to correct personal information collected and analyzed concerning a consumer's health, the right of a consumer to provide a written addendum to the business with respect to any item or statement regarding any such personal information that the consumer believes to be incomplete or incorrect. The addendum shall be limited to 250 words per alleged incomplete or incorrect item and shall clearly indicate in writing that the consumer requests the addendum to be made a part of the consumer's record.

[6] **(8)** Establishing the standard to govern a [7] **business'** determination, pursuant to subparagraph (B) of paragraph (2) of subdivision (a) of Section 1798.130, that providing information beyond the 12-month period in a response to a verifiable consumer request is impossible or would involve a disproportionate effort.

[8] **(9)** Issuing regulations further defining and adding to the business purposes, including other notified purposes, for which businesses, service providers, and contractors may use consumers' personal information consistent with consumers' expectations, and further defining the business purposes for which service providers and contractors may combine consumers' personal information obtained from different sources, except as provided for in paragraph (6) of subdivision (e) of Section 1798.140.

[9] **(10)** Issuing regulations identifying those business purposes, including other notified purposes, for which service providers and contractors may use consumers' personal information received pursuant to a written contract with a business, for the service provider or contractor's own business purposes, with the goal of maximizing consumer privacy.

[10] **(11)** Issuing regulations to further define "intentionally interacts," with the goal of maximizing consumer privacy.

[11] **(12)** Issuing regulations to further define "precise geolocation," including if the size defined is not sufficient to protect consumer privacy in sparsely populated areas or when the personal information is used for normal operational purposes, including billing.

[12] **(13)** Issuing regulations to define the term "specific pieces of information obtained from the consumer" with the goal of maximizing a consumer's right to access relevant personal information while minimizing the delivery of information to a consumer that would not be useful to the consumer, including system log information and other technical data. For delivery of the most sensitive personal information, the regulations may require a higher standard of authentication provided that the agency shall monitor the impact of the higher standard on the right of consumers to obtain their personal information to ensure that the requirements of verification do not result in the unreasonable denial of verifiable consumer requests.

[13] **(14)** Issuing regulations requiring businesses whose processing of consumers' personal information presents significant risk to consumers' privacy or security, to:

(A) Perform a cybersecurity audit on an annual basis, including defining the scope of the audit and establishing a process to ensure that audits are thorough and independent. The factors to be considered in determining when processing may result in significant risk to the security of personal information shall include the size and complexity of the business and the nature and scope of processing activities.

(B) Submit to the California Privacy Protection Agency on a regular basis a risk assessment with respect to their processing of personal information, including whether the processing involves sensitive personal information, and identifying and weighing the benefits resulting from the processing to the business, the consumer, other stakeholders, and the public, against the potential risks to the rights of the consumer associated with that processing, with the goal of restricting or prohibiting the processing if the risks to privacy of the consumer outweigh the benefits resulting from processing to the consumer, the business, other stakeholders, and the public. Nothing in this section shall require a business to divulge trade secrets.

[14] **(15)** Issuing regulations governing access and opt-out rights with respect to [15] **a business'** use of automated decisionmaking technology, including profiling and requiring [16] **a business'** response to access requests to include meaningful information about the logic involved in those decisionmaking processes, as well as a description of the likely outcome of the process with respect to the consumer.

[17] **(16)** Issuing regulations to further define a "law enforcement agency-approved investigation" for purposes of the exception in subparagraph (B) of paragraph (1) of subdivision (a) of Section 1798.145.

[18] **(17)** Issuing regulations to define the scope and process for the exercise of the agency's audit authority, to establish criteria for selection of persons to audit, and to protect consumers' personal information from disclosure to an auditor in the absence of a court order, warrant, or subpoena.

[19] **(18)**(A) Issuing regulations to define the requirements and technical specifications for an opt-out preference signal sent by a platform, technology, or mechanism, to indicate a consumer's intent to opt out of the sale or sharing of the consumer's personal information and to limit the use or disclosure of the consumer's sensitive personal information. The requirements and specifications for the opt-out preference signal should be updated from time to time to reflect the means by which consumers interact with businesses, and should:

(i) Ensure that the manufacturer of a platform or browser or device that sends the opt-out preference signal cannot unfairly disadvantage another business.

(ii) Ensure that the opt-out preference signal is consumer-friendly, clearly described, and easy to use by an average consumer and does not require that the consumer provide additional information beyond what is necessary.

(iii) Clearly represent a consumer's intent and be free of defaults constraining or presupposing that intent.

(iv) Ensure that the opt-out preference signal does not conflict with other commonly used privacy settings or tools that consumers may employ.

(v) Provide a mechanism for the consumer to selectively consent to a [20] **business'** sale of the consumer's personal information, or the use or disclosure of the consumer's sensitive personal information, without affecting the consumer's preferences with respect to other businesses or disabling the opt-out preference signal globally.

(vi) State that in the case of a page or setting view that the consumer accesses to set the opt-out preference signal, the consumer should see up to three choices, including:

(I) Global opt out from sale and sharing of personal information, including a direction to limit the use of sensitive personal information.

(II) Choice to "Limit the Use of My Sensitive Personal Information."

(III) Choice titled "Do Not Sell/Do Not Share My Personal Information for Cross-Context Behavioral Advertising."

(B) Issuing regulations to establish technical specifications for an opt-out preference signal that allows the consumer, or the consumer's parent or guardian, to specify that the consumer is less than 13 years of age or at least 13 years of age and less than 16 years of age.

(C) Issuing regulations, with the goal of strengthening consumer privacy while considering the legitimate operational interests of businesses, to govern the use or disclosure of a consumer's sensitive personal information, notwithstanding the consumer's direction to limit the use or disclosure of the consumer's sensitive personal information, including:

(i) Determining any additional purposes for which a business may use or disclose a consumer's sensitive personal information.

(ii) Determining the scope of activities permitted under paragraph (8) of subdivision (e) of Section 1798.140, as authorized by subdivision (a) of Section 1798.121, to ensure that the activities do not involve health-related research.

(iii) Ensuring the functionality of the [21] **business'** operations.

(iv) Ensuring that the exemption in subdivision (d) of Section 1798.121 for sensitive personal information applies to information that is collected or processed incidentally, or without the purpose of inferring characteristics about a consumer, while ensuring that businesses do not use the exemption for the purpose of evading consumers' rights to limit the use and disclosure of their sensitive personal information under Section 1798.121.

[22] **(19)** Issuing regulations to govern how a business that has elected to comply with subdivision (b) of Section 1798.135 responds to the opt-out preference signal and provides consumers with the opportunity subsequently to consent to the sale or sharing of their personal information or the use and disclosure of their sensitive personal information for

purposes in addition to those authorized by subdivision (a) of Section 1798.121. The regulations should:

(A) Strive to promote competition and consumer choice and be technology neutral.

(B) Ensure that the business does not respond to an opt-out preference signal by:

(i) Intentionally degrading the functionality of the consumer experience.

(ii) Charging the consumer a fee in response to the consumer's opt-out preferences.

(iii) Making any products or services not function properly or fully for the consumer, as compared to consumers who do not use the opt-out preference signal.

(iv) Attempting to coerce the consumer to opt in to the sale or sharing of the consumer's personal information, or the use or disclosure of the consumer's sensitive personal information, by stating or implying that the use of the opt-out preference signal will adversely affect the consumer as compared to consumers who do not use the opt-out preference signal, including stating or implying that the consumer will not be able to use the [23] **business'** products or services or that those products or services may not function properly or fully.

(v) Displaying any notification or pop-up in response to the consumer's opt-out preference signal.

(C) Ensure that any link to a web page or its supporting content that allows the consumer to consent to opt in:

(i) Is not part of a popup, notice, banner, or other intrusive design that obscures any part of the web page the consumer intended to visit from full view or that interferes with or impedes in any way the consumer's experience visiting or browsing the web page or **internet** website the consumer intended to visit.

(ii) Does not require or imply that the consumer must click the link to receive full functionality of any products or services, including the **internet** website.

(iii) Does not make use of any dark patterns.

(iv) Applies only to the business with which the consumer intends to interact.

(D) Strive to curb coercive or deceptive practices in response to an opt-out preference signal but should not unduly restrict businesses that are trying in good faith to comply with Section 1798.135.

[24] **(20)** Review existing Insurance Code provisions and regulations relating to consumer privacy, except those relating to insurance rates or pricing, to determine whether any provisions of the Insurance Code provide greater protection to consumers than the provisions of this title. Upon completing its review, the agency shall adopt a regulation that applies only the more protective provisions of this title to insurance companies. For the purpose of clarity, the Insurance Commissioner shall have jurisdiction over insurance rates and pricing.

[25] **(21)** Harmonizing the regulations governing opt-out mechanisms, notices to consumers, and other operational mechanisms in this title to promote clarity and the functionality of this title for consumers.

(b) The Attorney General may adopt additional regulations as necessary to further the purposes of this title.

(c) The Attorney General shall not bring an enforcement action under this title until six months after the publication of the final regulations issued pursuant to this section or July 1, 2020, whichever is sooner.

(d) Notwithstanding subdivision (a), the timeline for adopting final regulations required by the act adding this subdivision shall be July 1, 2022. Beginning the later of July 1, 2021, or six months after the agency provides notice to the Attorney General that it is prepared to begin rulemaking under this title, the authority assigned to the Attorney General to adopt regulations under this section shall be exercised by the California Privacy Protection Agency. Notwithstanding any other law, civil and administrative enforcement of the provisions of law added or amended by this act shall not commence until July 1, 2023, and shall only apply to violations occurring on or after that date. Enforcement of provisions of law contained in the California Consumer Privacy Act of 2018 amended by this act shall remain in effect and shall be enforceable until the same provisions of this act become enforceable. **Leg.H.** Added Stats 2018 ch 55 §3 (AB 375), effective January 1, 2019, operative January 1, 2020. Amended Stats 2018 ch 735 §13 (SB 1121), effective September 23, 2018, operative January 1, 2020; Stats 2019 ch 757 §10 (AB 1355), effective January 1, 2020, operative January 1, 2020; Amendment approved by voters, Prop. 24 §21 (2020 Bill Text CA V. 9), on November 3, 2020, effective December 16, 2020; Stats 2023 ch 567 §3 (AB 1194), effective January 1, 2024; Stats 2024 ch 121 §9 (AB 3286), effective January 1, 2025.

§1798.185. 2024 Deletes. [1] (5) Adjusting the monetary thresholds, in January of every odd-numbered year to reflect any increase in the Consumer Price Index, in: subparagraph (A) of paragraph (1) of subdivision (d) of Section 1798.140; subparagraph (A) of paragraph (1) of subdivision (a) of Section 1798.150; subdivision (a) of Section 1798.155; Section 1798.199.25; and subdivision (a) of Section 1798.199.90. (6) [2] (7) [3] business's [4] business's [5] (8) [6] (9) [7] business's [8] (10) [9] (11) [10] (12) [11] (13) [12] (14) [13] (15) [14] (16) [15] businesses' [16] businesses' [17] (17) [18] (18) [19] (19) [20] business's [21] business's [22] (20) [23] business's [24] (21) [25] (22)

2018 Notes: For citation of act, see the 2018 Note following CC §1798.100. For operative date of title, see CC §1798.198.

1798.190. Anti-Avoidance

A court or the agency shall disregard the intermediate steps or transactions for purposes of effectuating the purposes of this title:

(a) If a series of steps or transactions were component parts of a single transaction intended from the beginning to be taken with the intention of avoiding the reach of this title, including the disclosure of information by a business to a third party in order to avoid the definition of sell or share.

(b) If steps or transactions were taken to purposely avoid the definition of sell or share by eliminating any monetary or other valuable consideration, including by entering into contracts that do not include an exchange for monetary or other valuable consideration, but where a party is obtaining something of value or use. **Leg.H.** Added Stats 2018 ch 55 §3 (AB 375), effective January 1, 2019, operative January 1, 2020. Amendment approved by voters, Prop. 24 §22 (2020 Bill Text CA V. 9), on November 3, 2020, effective December 16, 2020, operative January 1, 2023.

2018 Notes: For citation of act, see the 2018 Note following CC §1798.100. For operative date of title, see CC §1798.198.

§1798.192. Waiver

Any provision of a contract or agreement of any kind, including a representative action waiver, that purports to waive or limit in any way a consumer's rights under this title, including, but not limited to, any right to a remedy or means of enforcement, shall be deemed contrary to public policy and shall be void and unenforceable. This section shall not prevent a consumer from declining to request information from a business, declining to opt out of a business's sale of the consumer's personal information, or authorizing a business to sell or share the consumer's personal information after previously opting out. **Leg.H.** Added Stats 2018 ch 55 §3 (AB 375), effective January 1, 2019, operative January 1, 2020. Amended Stats 2018 ch 735 §14 (SB 1121), effective September 23, 2018, operative January 1, 2020; Amendment approved by voters, Prop. 24 §23 (2020 Bill Text CA V. 9), on November 3, 2020, effective on the fifth day after Secretary of State files final Statement of Vote, operative January 1, 2023.

2018 Notes: For citation of act, see the 2018 Note following CC §1798.100. For operative date of title, see CC §1798.198.

§1798.194. Construction of title

This title shall be liberally construed to effectuate its purposes. **Leg.H.** Added Stats 2018 ch 55 §3 (AB 375), effective January 1, 2019, operative January 1, 2020.

2018 Notes: For citation of act, see the 2018 Note following CC §1798.100. For operative date of title, see CC §1798.198.

§1798.196. Conflict with federal law or U.S. or California Constitution

This title is intended to supplement federal and state law, if permissible, but shall not apply if such application is preempted by, or in conflict with, federal law or the United States or California Constitution. **Leg.H.** Added Stats 2018 ch 55 §3 (AB 375), effective January 1, 2019, operative January 1, 2020. Amended Stats 2018 ch 735 §15 (SB 1121), effective September 23, 2018, operative January 1, 2020.

2018 Notes: For citation of act, see the 2018 Note following CC §1798.100. For operative date of title, see CC §1798.198.

§1798.198. Operative date of title

(a) Subject to limitation provided in subdivision (b), and in Section 1798.199, this title shall be operative January 1, 2020.

(b) This title shall become operative only if initiative measure No. 17-0039, The Consumer Right to Privacy Act of 2018, is withdrawn from the ballot pursuant to Section 9604 of the Elections Code. **Leg.H.** Added Stats 2018 ch 55 §3 (AB 375), effective January 1, 2019, operative January 1, 2020. Amended Stats 2018 ch 735 §16 (SB 1121), effective September 23, 2018, operative January 1, 2020.

2018 Notes: For citation of act, see the 2018 Note following CC §1798.100. For operative date of title, see CC §1798.198.

§1798.199. Operative date of Section 1798.180

Notwithstanding Section 1798.198, Section 1798.180 shall be operative on the effective date of the act adding this section. **Leg.H.** Added Stats 2018 ch 735 §17 (SB 1121), effective September 23, 2018.

§ 1798.199.10. Establishment of California Privacy Protection Agency

(a) There is hereby established in state government the California Privacy Protection Agency, which is vested with full administrative power, authority, and jurisdiction to implement and enforce the California Consumer Privacy Act of 2018. The agency shall be governed by a five-member board, including the chairperson. The chairperson and one member of the board shall be appointed by the Governor. The Attorney General, Senate Rules Committee, and Speaker of the Assembly shall each appoint one member. These appointments should be made from among Californians with expertise in the areas of privacy, technology, and consumer rights.

(b) The initial appointments to the agency shall be made within 90 days of the effective date of the act adding this section. **Leg.H.** Adopted by voters, Prop. 24 §24.1 (2020 Bill Text CA V. 9), on November 3, 2020, effective December 16, 2020.

§ 1798.199.15. Agency board membership

(a) Have qualifications, experience, and skills, in particular in the areas of privacy and technology, required to perform the duties of the agency and exercise its powers.

(b) Maintain the confidentiality of information which has come to their knowledge in the course of the performance of their tasks or exercise of their powers, except to the extent that disclosure is required by the Public Records Act.

(c) Remain free from external influence, whether direct or indirect, and shall neither seek nor take instructions from another.

(d) Refrain from any action incompatible with their duties and engaging in any incompatible occupation, whether gainful or not, during their term.

(e) Have the right of access to all information made available by the agency to the chairperson.

(f) Be precluded, for a period of one year after leaving office, from accepting employment with a business that was subject to an enforcement action or civil action under this title during the member's tenure or during the five-year period preceding the member's appointment.

(g) Be precluded for a period of two years after leaving office from acting, for compensation, as an agent or attorney for, or otherwise representing, any other person in a matter pending before the agency if the purpose is to influence an action of the agency. **Leg.H.** Adopted by voters, Prop. 24 §24.2 (2020 Bill Text CA V. 9), on November 3, 2020, effective December 16, 2020.

§ 1798.199.20. Term of service

Members of the agency board, including the chairperson, shall serve at the pleasure of their appointing authority but shall serve for no longer than eight consecutive years. **Leg.H.** Adopted by voters, Prop. 24 §24.3 (2020 Bill Text CA V. 9), on November 3, 2020, effective December 16, 2020.

§ 1798.199.25. Member compensation

For each day on which they engage in official duties, members of the agency board shall be compensated at the rate of one hundred dollars ($100), adjusted [1] **pursuant to subdivision (d) of Section 1798.199.95**, and shall be reimbursed for expenses incurred in performance of their official duties. **Leg.H.** Adopted by voters, Prop. 24 §24.4 (2020 Bill Text CA V. 9), on November 3, 2020, effective December 16, 2020; Stats 2024 ch 121 §10 (AB 3286), effective January 1, 2025.

§ **1798.199.25. 2024 Deletes.** [1] biennially to reflect changes in the cost of living

§ 1798.199.30. Appointment of executive director, officers, counsel and employees

The agency board shall appoint an executive director who shall act in accordance with agency policies and regulations and with applicable law. The agency shall appoint and discharge officers, counsel, and employees, consistent with applicable civil service laws, and shall fix the compensation of employees and prescribe their duties. The agency may contract for services that cannot be provided by its employees. **Leg.H.** Adopted by voters, Prop. 24 §24.5 (2020 Bill Text CA V. 9), on November 3, 2020, effective December 16, 2020.

§ 1798.199.35. Delegation of authority to Chair or executive director

The agency board may delegate authority to the chairperson or the executive director to act in the name of the agency between meetings of the agency, except with respect to resolution of enforcement actions and rulemaking authority. **Leg.H.** Adopted by voters, Prop. 24 §24.6 (2020 Bill Text CA V. 9), on November 3, 2020, effective December 16, 2020.

§ 1798.199.40. Agency functions

The agency shall perform the following functions:

(a) Administer, implement, and enforce through administrative actions this title.

(b) On and after the later of July 1, 2021, or within six months of the agency providing the Attorney General with notice that it is prepared to assume rulemaking responsibilities under this title, adopt, amend, and rescind regulations pursuant to Section 1798.185 to carry out the purposes and provisions of the California Consumer Privacy Act of 2018, including regulations specifying recordkeeping requirements for businesses to ensure compliance with this title.

(c) Through the implementation of this title, protect the fundamental privacy rights of natural persons with respect to the use of their personal information.

(d) Promote public awareness and understanding of the risks, rules, responsibilities, safeguards, and rights in relation to the collection, use, sale, and disclosure of personal information, including the rights of minors with respect to their own information, and provide a public report summarizing the risk assessments filed with the agency pursuant to paragraph [1] **(14)** of subdivision (a) of Section 1798.185 while ensuring that data security is not compromised.

(e) Provide guidance to consumers regarding their rights under this title.

(f) Provide guidance to businesses regarding their duties and responsibilities under this title and appoint a Chief Privacy Auditor to conduct audits of businesses to ensure compliance with this title pursuant to regulations adopted pursuant to paragraph [2] **(17)** of subdivision (a) of Section 1798.185.

(g) Provide technical assistance and advice to the Legislature, upon request, with respect to privacy-related legislation.

(h) Monitor relevant developments relating to the protection of personal information and, in particular, the development of information and communication technologies and commercial practices.

(i) Cooperate with other agencies with jurisdiction over privacy laws and with data processing authorities in California, other states, territories, and countries to ensure consistent application of privacy protections.

(j) Establish a mechanism pursuant to which persons doing business in California that do not meet the definition of business set forth in paragraph (1), (2), or (3) of subdivision (d) of Section 1798.140 may voluntarily certify that they are in compliance with this title, as set forth in paragraph (4) of subdivision (d) of Section 1798.140, and make a list of those entities available to the public.

(k) Solicit, review, and approve applications for grants to the extent funds are available pursuant to paragraph (2) of subdivision (b) of Section 1798.160.

(*l*) Perform all other acts necessary or appropriate in the exercise of its power, authority, and jurisdiction and seek to balance the goals of strengthening consumer privacy while giving attention to the impact on businesses. **Leg.H.** Adopted by voters, Prop. 24 §24.7 (2020 Bill Text CA V. 9), on November 3, 2020, effective on the fifth day after Secretary of State files final Statement of Vote December 16, 2020; Amended Stats 2021 ch 525 §5 (AB 694), effective January 1, 2022; Stats 2024 ch 121 §11 (AB 3286), effective January 1, 2025.

§ **1798.199.40. 2024 Deletes.** [1] (15) [2] (18)

§ 1798.199.45. Investigation of violations

(a) Upon the sworn complaint of any person or on its own initiative, the agency may investigate possible violations of this title relating to any business, service provider, contractor, or person. The agency may decide not to investigate a complaint or decide to provide a business with a time period to cure the alleged violation. In making a decision not to investigate or provide more time to cure, the agency may consider the following:

(1) Lack of intent to violate this title.

(2) Voluntary efforts undertaken by the business, service provider, contractor, or person to cure the alleged violation prior to being notified by the agency of the complaint.

(b)(1) The agency shall notify in writing the person who made the complaint of the action, if any, the agency has taken or plans to take on the complaint, together with the reasons for that action or nonaction.

(2) The written notification required by this subdivision shall not include information that is subject to law enforcement exemptions and privileges, including, but not limited to, confidential information related to an investigation and information that is privileged under the Evidence Code and the Government Code. Leg.H. Adopted by voters, Prop. 24 §24.8 (2020 Bill Text CA V. 9), on November 3, 2020, effective December 16, 2020, operative January 1, 2023.; Stats 2024 ch 121 §12 (AB 3286), effective January 1, 2025.

§ 1798.199.50. Notice of violation

No finding of probable cause to believe this title has been violated shall be made by the agency unless, at least 30 days prior to the agency's consideration of the alleged violation, the business, service provider, contractor, or person alleged to have violated this title is notified of the violation by service of process or registered mail with return receipt requested, provided with a summary of the evidence, and informed of their right to be present in person and represented by counsel at any proceeding of the agency held for the purpose of considering whether probable cause exists for believing the person violated this title. Notice to the alleged violator shall be deemed made on the date of service, the date the registered mail receipt is signed, or if the registered mail receipt is not signed, the date returned by the post office. A proceeding held for the purpose of considering probable cause shall be private unless the alleged violator files with the agency a written request that the proceeding be public. **Leg.H.** Adopted by voters, Prop. 24 §24.9 (2020 Bill Text CA V. 9), on November 3, 2020, effective December 16, 2020, operative January 1, 2023.

§ 1798.199.55. Hearing on violation; Order

(a) When the agency determines there is probable cause for believing this title has been violated, it shall hold a hearing to determine if a violation has or violations have occurred. Notice shall be given and the hearing conducted in accordance with the Administrative Procedure Act (Chapter 5 (commencing with Section 11500), Part 1, Division 3, Title 2, Government Code). The agency shall have all the powers granted by that chapter. If the agency determines on the basis of the hearing conducted pursuant to this subdivision that a violation or violations have occurred, it shall issue an order that may require the violator to do all or any of the following:

(1) Cease and desist violation of this title.

(2) Subject to Section 1798.155, pay an administrative fine of up to two thousand five hundred dollars ($2,500) for each violation, or up to seven thousand five hundred dollars ($7,500) for each intentional violation and each violation involving the personal information of minor consumers to the Consumer Privacy Fund within the General Fund of the state. When the agency determines that no violation has occurred, it shall publish a declaration so stating.

(b) If two or more persons are responsible for any violation or violations, they shall be jointly and severally liable. **Leg.H.** Adopted by voters, Prop. 24 §24.10 (2020 Bill Text CA V. 9), on November 3, 2020, effective December 16, 2020, operative January 1, 2023.

§ 1798.199.60. Rejection of Administrative Law Judge decision

Whenever the agency rejects the decision of an administrative law judge made pursuant to Section 11517 of the Government Code, the agency shall state the reasons in writing for rejecting the decision. **Leg.H.** Adopted by voters, Prop. 24 §24.11 (2020 Bill Text CA V. 9), on November 3, 2020, effective December 16, 2020, operative January 1, 2023.

§ 1798.199.65. Agency subpoena and audit powers

The agency may subpoena witnesses, compel their attendance and testimony, administer oaths and affirmations, take evidence and require by subpoena the production of any books, papers, records, or other items material to the performance of the agency's duties or exercise of its powers, including, but not limited to, its power to audit a business' compliance with this title. **Leg.H.** Adopted by voters, Prop. 24 §24.12 (2020 Bill Text CA V. 9), on November 3, 2020, effective December 16, 2020, operative January 1, 2023.

§ 1798.199.70. Administrative actions time limitations

No administrative action brought pursuant to this title alleging a violation of any of the provisions of this title shall be commenced more than five years after the date on which the violation occurred.

(a) The service of the probable cause hearing notice, as required by Section 1798.199.50, upon the person alleged to have violated this title shall constitute the commencement of the administrative action.

(b) If the person alleged to have violated this title engages in the fraudulent concealment of the person's acts or identity, the five-year period shall be tolled for the period of the concealment. For purposes of this subdivision, "fraudulent concealment" means the person knows of material facts related to the person's duties under this title and knowingly conceals them in performing or omitting to perform those duties for the purpose of defrauding the public of information to which it is entitled under this title.

(c) If, upon being ordered by a superior court to produce any documents sought by a subpoena in any administrative proceeding under this title, the person alleged to have violated this title fails to produce documents in response to the order by the date ordered to comply therewith, the five-year period shall be tolled for the period of the delay from the date of filing of the motion to compel until the date the documents are produced. **Leg.H.** Adopted by voters, Prop. 24 §24.13 (2020 Bill Text CA V. 9), on November 3, 2020, effective December 16, 2020, operative January 1, 2023.

§ 1798.199.75. Unpaid administrative fines

(a) In addition to any other available remedies, the agency may bring a civil action and obtain a judgment in superior court for the purpose of collecting any unpaid administrative fines imposed pursuant to this title after exhaustion of judicial review of the agency's action. The action may be filed as a small claims, limited civil, or unlimited civil case depending on the jurisdictional amount. The venue for this action shall be in the county where the administrative fines were imposed by the agency. In order to obtain a judgment in a proceeding under this section, the agency shall show, following the procedures and rules of evidence as applied in ordinary civil actions, all of the following:

(1) That the administrative fines were imposed following the procedures set forth in this title and implementing regulations.

(2) That the defendant or defendants in the action were notified, by actual or constructive notice, of the imposition of the administrative fines.

(3) That a demand for payment has been made by the agency and full payment has not been received.

(b) A civil action brought pursuant to subdivision (a) shall be commenced within four years after the date on which the administrative fines were imposed. **Leg.H.** Adopted by voters, Prop. 24 §24.14 (2020 Bill Text CA V. 9), on November 3, 2020, effective December 16, 2020, operative January 1, 2023.

§ 1798.199.80. Application for judgment upon exhaustion or expiration of judicial review

(a) If the time for judicial review of a final agency order or decision has lapsed, or if all means of judicial review of the order or decision have been exhausted, the agency may apply to the clerk of the court for a judgment to collect the administrative fines imposed by the order or decision, or the order as modified in accordance with a decision on judicial review.

(b) The application, which shall include a certified copy of the order or decision, or the order as modified in accordance with a decision on judicial review, and proof of service of the order or decision, constitutes a sufficient showing to warrant issuance of the judgment to collect the administrative fines. The clerk of the court shall enter the judgment immediately in conformity with the application.

(c) An application made pursuant to this section shall be made to the clerk of the superior court in the county where the administrative fines were imposed by the agency.

(d) A judgment entered in accordance with this section has the same force and effect as, and is subject to all the provisions of law relating to, a judgment in a civil action and may be enforced in the same manner as any other judgment of the court in which it is entered.

(e) The agency may bring an application pursuant to this section only within four years after the date on which all means of judicial review of the order or decision have been exhausted.

(f) The remedy available under this section is in addition to those available under any other law. **Leg.H.** Adopted by voters, Prop. 24 §24.15 (2020 Bill Text CA V. 9), on November 3, 2020, effective December 16, 2020, operative January 1, 2023.

§ 1798.199.85. Judicial review; Standard of review

Any decision of the agency with respect to a complaint or administrative fine shall be subject to judicial review in an action brought by an interested party to the complaint or administrative fine and shall be subject to an abuse of discretion standard. **Leg.H.** Adopted by voters, Prop. 24 §24.16 (2020 Bill Text CA V. 9), on November 3, 2020, effective December 16, 2020, operative January 1, 2023.

§ 1798.199.90. Injunction; Penalties; Stay of action or investigation at Attorney General request

(a) Any business, service provider, contractor, or other person that violates this title shall be subject to an injunction and liable for a civil penalty of not more than two thousand five hundred dollars ($2,500) for each violation or seven thousand five hundred dollars ($7,500) for each intentional violation and each violation involving the personal information of minor consumers, as adjusted pursuant to [1] **subdivision (d)** of Section [2] **1798.199.95**, which shall be assessed and recovered in a civil action brought in the name of the people of the State of California by the Attorney General. The court may consider the good faith cooperation of the business, service provider, contractor, or other person in determining the amount of the civil penalty.

(b) Any civil penalty recovered by an action brought by the Attorney General for a violation of this title, and the proceeds of any settlement of any said action, shall be deposited in the Consumer Privacy Fund.

(c) The agency shall, upon request by the Attorney General, stay an administrative action or investigation under this title to permit the Attorney General to proceed with an investigation or civil action and shall not pursue an administrative action or investigation, unless the Attorney General subsequently determines not to pursue an investigation or civil action. The agency may not limit the authority of the Attorney General to enforce this title.

(d) No civil action may be filed by the Attorney General under this section for any violation of this title after the agency has issued a decision pursuant to Section 1798.199.85 or an order pursuant to Section 1798.199.55 against that person for the same violation.

(e) This section shall not affect the private right of action provided for in Section 1798.150. **Leg.H.** Adopted by voters, Prop. 24 §24.17 (2020 Bill Text CA V. 9), on November 3, 2020, effective December 16, 2020, operative January 1, 2023.; Stats 2024 ch 121 §13 (AB 3286), effective January 1, 2025.

§ 1798.199.90. 2024 Deletes. [1] paragraph (5) of subdivision (a) [2] 1798.185

§ 1798.199.95. Appropriations; Staff support

(a) There is hereby appropriated from the General Fund of the state to the agency the sum of five million dollars ($5,000,000) during the fiscal year 2020- [1] **21**, and the sum of ten million dollars ($10,000,000) adjusted for cost-of-living changes, during each fiscal year thereafter, for expenditure to support the operations of the agency pursuant to this title. The expenditure of funds under this appropriation shall be subject to the normal administrative review given to other state appropriations. The Legislature shall appropriate those additional amounts to the commission and other agencies as may be necessary to carry out the provisions of this title.

(b) The Department of Finance, in preparing the state budget and the Budget Act bill submitted to the Legislature, shall include an item for the support of this title that shall indicate all of the following:

(1) The amounts to be appropriated to other agencies to carry out their duties under this title, which amounts shall be in augmentation of the support items of those agencies.

(2) The additional amounts required to be appropriated by the Legislature to the agency to carry out the purposes of this title, as provided for in this section.

(3) In parentheses, for informational purposes, the continuing appropriation during each fiscal year of ten million dollars ($10,000,000), adjusted for cost-of-living changes made pursuant to this section.

(c) The Attorney General shall provide staff support to the agency until the agency has hired its own staff. The Attorney General shall be reimbursed by the agency for these services.

(d)(1) On January 1, 2025, and on January 1 of any odd-numbered year thereafter, the California Privacy Protection Agency shall adjust the monetary thresholds in subparagraph (A) of paragraph (1) of subdivision (d) of Section 1798.140, subparagraph (A) of paragraph (1) of subdivision (a) of Section 1798.150, subdivision (a) of Section 1798.155, Section 1798.199.25, and subdivision (a) of Section 1798.199.90 to reflect any increase in the Consumer Price Index.

(2) The agency shall use the Consumer Price Index (CPI) - California, All Items, All Urban Consumers percentage change from the previous two years' reports, published by the Department of Industrial Relations, Office of the Director-Research. The agency shall apply the percentage change in the CPI for the August-to-August point in time of the prior two years. The increase in the thresholds shall be rounded to the nearest whole dollar.

(3) The agency shall post the adjusted monetary thresholds on its internet website no later than January 15 of the year in which the adjustment becomes effective.

(4) Notwithstanding any other law, adjustments to monetary thresholds and their publication on the agency's internet website pursuant to this subdivision are not subject to the rulemaking provisions of the Administrative Procedure Act (Chapter 3.5 (commencing with Section 11340) of Part 1 of Division 3 of Title 2 of the Government Code). **Leg.H.** Adopted by voters, Prop. 24 §24.18 (2020 Bill Text CA V. 9), on November 3, 2020, effective December 16, 2020; Stats 2024 ch 121 §14 (AB 3286), effective January 1, 2025.

§ 1798.199.95. 2024 Deletes. [1] 2021

§ 1798.199.100. Consideration of good faith and cooperation

The agency and any court, as applicable, shall consider the good faith cooperation of the business, service provider, contractor, or other person in determining the amount of any administrative fine or civil penalty for a violation of this title. A business shall not be required by the agency, a court, or otherwise to pay both an administrative fine and a civil penalty for the same violation. **Leg.H.** Adopted by voters, Prop. 24 §24.19 (2020 Bill Text CA V. 9), on November 3, 2020, effective December 16, 2020, operative January 1, 2023.

TITLE 1.81.6
IDENTITY THEFT IN BUSINESS ENTITY FILINGS

Definitions. §1798.200.
Petition for determination of unlawful use of personal identifying information. §1798.201.
Evidence considered to determine petition; Order. §1798.202.
Personal identifying information. § 1798.203.

§1798.200. Definitions

For purposes of this title, the following terms are defined as follows:

(a) "Business entity filing" means a document required by law to be filed with the Secretary of State pursuant to the Corporations Code, the Financial Code, or the Insurance Code.

(b) "Personal identifying information" has the same meaning as defined in subdivision (b) of Section 530.55 of the Penal Code.

(c) "Person" means a natural person, firm, association, organization, partnership, business trust, company, corporation, limited liability company, or public entity. **Leg.H.** Added Stats 2018 ch 696 §1 (SB 1196), effective January 1, 2019.

§1798.201. Petition for determination of unlawful use of personal identifying information

A person who has learned or reasonably suspects that his or her personal identifying information has been used unlawfully, as described in subdivision (a) of Section 530.5 of the Penal Code, in a business entity filing, and has initiated a law enforcement investigation in accordance with subdivision (a) of Section 530.6 of the Penal Code, may petition the superior court in the county in which the person resides for an order, which may be granted ex parte, directing the alleged perpetrator of the act described in paragraph (1) of subdivision (c) of Section 530.5 of the Penal Code, if known, and the person using the personal identifying information in the business entity filing to appear at a hearing before the court and show cause for both of the following:

(a) Why the personal identifying information should not be labeled to show the information is impersonated and does not reflect the person's identity.

(b) Why the personal identifying information should be associated with the business entity. **Leg.H.** Added Stats 2018 ch 696 §1 (SB 1196), effective January 1, 2019.

§1798.202. Evidence considered to determine petition; Order

(a) A petition filed pursuant to Section 1798.201 shall be heard and determined based on declarations, affidavits, police reports, or other material, relevant, and reliable information submitted by the parties or ordered to be made part of the record by the court.

(b) If the court determines the petition is meritorious and there is no reasonable cause to believe that the victim's personal identifying information has been used lawfully in the business entity filing, the court shall make a finding that the victim's personal identifying information has been used unlawfully in the business entity filing and shall issue an order certifying this determination.

(c) Upon making a determination pursuant to subdivision (b), the court shall do the following:

(1) Order the name and associated personal identifying information in the business entity filing to be redacted or labeled to show that the data is impersonated and does not reflect the victim's identity.

(2) Order the data to be removed from publicly accessible electronic indexes and databases.

(d) A determination made pursuant to subdivision (b) may be vacated at any time if the petition or any information submitted in support of the petition is found to contain any material misrepresentation or was obtained by fraud.

(e) The Judicial Council shall develop a form for issuing an order of determination pursuant to this section.

(f) An order issued pursuant to subdivision (c) shall be filed with the Secretary of State.

(g) If an order has been filed pursuant to subdivision (f) within the record of a limited liability company or a corporation, the Secretary of State may cancel the business entity that is the subject of the order if, after 60 days, an updated statement of information has not been filed on behalf of the entity with the Secretary of State. The statement of information shall not contain any information ordered to be redacted pursuant to subdivision (c). Leg.H. Added Stats 2018 ch 696 §1 (SB 1196), effective January 1, 2019. Amended Stats 2024 ch 783 §1 (SB 1168), effective January 1, 2025.

§ 1798.203. Personal identifying information

(a) In addition to any of the other remedies provided under this title, a person who has learned that their personal identifying information has been used unlawfully, as described in subdivision (a) of Section 530.5 of the Penal Code, in a business entity filing may file with the Secretary of State a disclaimer of proper authority, as described in subdivision (b) and on a form prescribed by the Secretary of State, so long as the business entity has not been dissolved or terminated at the time of filing the disclaimer.

(b) A disclaimer of proper authority shall be signed and verified under penalty of perjury by the person claiming their personal identifying information was unlawfully used in the business entity filing as described in subdivision (a) and shall contain all of the following information:

(1) The name of the corporation, limited liability company, or limited partnership as it appears on the records of the Secretary of State.

(2) The Secretary of State file number for the corporation, limited liability company, or limited partnership.

(3) The entity type.

(4) The date the business entity document containing their personal identifying information was filed.

(5) The title of the business entity document that contained their personal identifying information.

(6) A description of the type of personal identifying information that the person claims was used unlawfully in the business entity filing.

(7) A statement that the person signing the disclaimer of proper authority did not authorize the use of their personal identifying information within the business entity document and that they reasonably suspect that their personal identifying information was included in furtherance of an unlawful purpose, as described in subdivision (a) of Section 530.5 of the Penal Code.

(8) A statement that the disclaimer of proper authority does not constitute a determination of any court or law enforcement investigation surrounding the facts and circumstances of the use of the information within the business entity document.

(c) The fee for filing a disclaimer of proper authority pursuant to this section shall be thirty dollars ($30) to cover the reasonable costs to the Secretary of State of processing that form. **Leg.H.** Added Stats 2024 ch 783 §2 (SB 1168), effective January 1, 2025.

TITLE 1.81.7
REPRODUCTIVE AND GENDER-AFFIRMING HEALTH CARE SERVICES

Definitions. § 1798.300.
Constitutional rights to reproductive health care services, gender-affirming health care services, and gender-affirming mental health care services. § 1798.301.
Interference of rights by foreign jurisdiction. § 1798.302.
Cause of action in response to abusive litigation infringing on legally protected health care activity. § 1798.303.
Motion to modify or quash subpoena related to abusive litigation. § 1798.304.
Damages. § 1798.305.
Jurisdiction. § 1798.306.
California laws applicable. § 1798.307.
Jurisdiction over state resident in out-of-state forum. § 1798.308.

§ 1798.300. Definitions

As used in this title, the following definitions apply:

(a) "Abusive litigation" means litigation or other legal action to deter, prevent, sanction, or punish a person engaging in legally protected health care activity by either of the following:

(1) Filing or prosecuting an action in a state other than California where liability, in whole or part, directly or indirectly, is based on a legally protected health care activity that was legal in the state in which it occurred, including an action in which liability is based on a theory of vicarious, joint, or several liability.

(2) Attempting to enforce an order or judgment issued in connection with an action described in paragraph (1) by a party to that action or a person acting on behalf of a party to that action. An action shall be considered to be based on conduct that was legal in the state in which it occurred if a part of an act or omission involved in the course of conduct that forms the basis for liability in the action occurs or is initiated in a state in which the health care was legal, whether or not the act or omission is alleged or included in a pleading or other filing in the lawsuit.

(b) "Aggrieved person, provider, or other entity" includes, but is not limited to, a person who resides in California, a business or entity doing business in the state or located in the state, a health care service plan, a health insurer, a person or entity that provided a legally protected health care activity in California, a person who received a legally protected health care activity from a provider licensed in California, a person or entity that is licensed in California to provide a legally protected health care activity, including a provider, clinic, or a person who assisted a person or entity that received or provided a legally protected health care activity in California.

(c) "Gender-affirming health care services" and "gender-affirming mental health care services" have the same meaning as defined in paragraph (3) of subdivision (b) of Section 16010.2 of the Welfare and Institutions Code.

(d)(1) "Legally protected health care activity" means any of the following:

(A) The exercise and enjoyment, or attempted exercise and enjoyment, by a person of rights to reproductive health care services, gender-affirming health care services, or gender-affirming mental health care services secured by the Constitution or laws of California or the provision by a health care service plan contract or a policy, or a certificate of health insurance, that provides for such services.

(B) An act or omission undertaken to aid or encourage, or attempt to aid or encourage, a person in the exercise and enjoyment or attempted exercise and enjoyment of rights to reproductive health care services, gender-affirming health care services, or gender-affirming mental health care services secured by the Constitution or laws of California.

(C) The provision of reproductive health care services, gender-affirming health care services, or gender-affirming mental health care services by a person duly licensed under the laws of California or the coverage of, and reimbursement for, such services or care by a health care service plan or a health insurer, if the service or care is lawful under the laws of California, regardless of the patient's location.

(2) "Legally protected health care activity" does not include any activity that would be deemed unprofessional conduct or that would violate antidiscrimination laws of California.

(e) "Reproductive health care services" means and includes all services, care, or products of a medical, surgical, psychiatric, therapeutic, diagnostic, mental health, behavioral health, preventative, rehabilitative, supportive, consultative, referral, prescribing, or dispensing nature relating to the human reproductive system provided in accordance with the constitution and laws of this state, whether provided in person or by means of telehealth services which includes, but is not limited to, all services, care, and products relating to pregnancy, the termination of a pregnancy, assisted reproduction, or contraception. **Leg.H.** Added Stats 2023 ch 260 §6 (SB 345), effective January 1, 2024.

§ 1798.301. Constitutional rights to reproductive health care services, gender-affirming health care services, and gender-affirming mental health care services

Reproductive health care services, gender-affirming health care services, and gender-affirming mental health care services are rights secured by the Constitution and laws of California. Interference with these rights, whether or not under the color of law, is against the public policy of California. **Leg.H.** Added Stats 2023 ch 260 §6 (SB 345), effective January 1, 2024.

§ 1798.302. Interference of rights by foreign jurisdiction

A public act or record of a foreign jurisdiction that prohibits, criminalizes, sanctions, authorizes a person to bring a civil action against, or otherwise interferes with a person, provider, or other entity in California that seeks, receives, causes, aids in access to, aids, abets, provides, or attempts or intends to seek, receive, cause, aid in access to, aid, abet, or provide, reproductive health care services, gender-affirming health care services, or gender-affirming mental health care services shall be an interference with the exercise and enjoyment of the rights secured by the Constitution and laws of California and shall be a violation of the public policy of California. **Leg.H.** Added Stats 2023 ch 260 §6 (SB 345), effective January 1, 2024.

§ 1798.303. Cause of action in response to abusive litigation infringing on legally protected health care activity

If a person, whether or not acting under color of law, engages or attempts to engage in abusive litigation that infringes on or interferes with, or attempts to infringe on or interfere with, a legally protected health care activity, then an aggrieved person, provider, carrier, or other entity, including a defendant in the abusive litigation, may institute a civil action for injunctive, monetary, or other appropriate relief within three years after the cause of action accrues. **Leg.H.** Added Stats 2023 ch 260 §6 (SB 345), effective January 1, 2024.

§ 1798.304. Motion to modify or quash subpoena related to abusive litigation

An aggrieved person, provider, or other entity, including a defendant in abusive litigation, may move to modify or quash a subpoena issued in connection with abusive litigation on the grounds that the subpoena is unreasonable, oppressive, or inconsistent with the public policy of California. **Leg.H.** Added Stats 2023 ch 260 §6 (SB 345), effective January 1, 2024.

§ 1798.305. Damages

If the court finds for the petitioner in an action authorized by Section 1798.303, recovery shall be in the amount of three times the amount of actual damages, which shall include damages for the amount of a judgment issued in connection with an abusive litigation, and any other expenses, costs, or reasonable attorney's fees incurred in connection with the abusive litigation. **Leg.H.** Added Stats 2023 ch 260 §6 (SB 345), effective January 1, 2024.

§ 1798.306. Jurisdiction

(a) A court may exercise jurisdiction over a person in an action authorized by Section 1798.303 if any of the following apply:

(1) Personal jurisdiction is found under Section 410.10 of the Code of Civil Procedure.

(2) The person has commenced an action in a court in California and, during the pendency of that action or an appeal therefrom, a summons and complaint is served on the person or the attorney appearing on the person's behalf in that action or as otherwise permitted by law.

(3) The exercise of jurisdiction is permitted under the Constitution of the United States.

(b) This section does not apply to a lawsuit or judgment entered in another state that is based on conduct for which a cause of action exists under the laws of California, including a contract, tort, common law, or statutory claim. **Leg.H.** Added Stats 2023 ch 260 §6 (SB 345), effective January 1, 2024.

§ 1798.307. California laws applicable

Notwithstanding any other law, the laws of California shall govern in a case or controversy heard in California related to reproductive health care services, gender-affirming health care services, or gender-affirming mental health care services, except as may be required by federal law. **Leg.H.** Added Stats 2023 ch 260 §6 (SB 345), effective January 1, 2024.

§ 1798.308. Jurisdiction over state resident in out-of-state forum

This title shall not be construed to provide jurisdiction over a California resident in an out-of-state forum when the California resident has not availed themselves of that forum. **Leg.H.** Added Stats 2023 ch 260 §6 (SB 345), effective January 1, 2024.

TITLE 1.82
BUSINESS RECORDS

Chapter 1. Definitions.
Chapter 2. Disclosures.
Chapter 3. Civil Remedies.

CHAPTER 1
DEFINITIONS

Definitions. §1799.

§1799. Definitions

As used in this title:

(a) The term "bookkeeping services" means keeping books, making trial balances, preparing statements, making audits, or preparing reports, all as a part of bookkeeping operations, provided that such trial balances, statements, or reports are not issued over the name of such person as having been prepared or examined by a certified public accountant or public accountant.

(b) The term "business entity" means a sole proprietorship, partnership, corporation, association or other group, however organized and whether or not organized to operate at a profit, but does not mean a financial institution organized, chartered, or holding a license or authorization certificate under a law of this State or the United States to make loans or extend credit and subject to supervision by an official or agency of this State or the United States, nor the parent of any such financial institution, nor any subsidiary of any such financial institution or parent.

(c) The term "individual" means a natural person.

(d) The term "person" means any natural person, corporation, partnership, limited liability company, firm, association, or governmental entity.

(e) The term "record" means any item, collection, or grouping of information about an individual or business entity. **Leg.H.** Added Stats 1977 ch 221 §1. Amended Stats 1994 ch 1010 §41 (SB 2053).

Prior Law: Former §1799 was added Stats 1931 ch 1070 §1, and repealed Stats 1963 ch 819 §2, effective January 1, 1965.

CHAPTER 2
DISCLOSURES

Prohibited disclosures; Exceptions. §1799.1.
Disclosure of information on tax return or schedule. §1799.1a.
Procedure and notice on change of address request by holder of credit card. §1799.1b.

§1799.1. Prohibited disclosures; Exceptions

(a) No business entity which performs bookkeeping services shall disclose in whole or in part the contents of any record, including the disclosure of information in the record in any composite of information, which is prepared or maintained by such business entity to any person, other than the individual or business entity which is the subject of the record, without the express written consent of such individual or business entity.

(b) This section shall not apply to the following:

(1) To a disclosure to any person pursuant to a subpoena or court order.

(2) To a disclosure which is discoverable.

(3) To a disclosure to any person acting pursuant to a lawful search warrant.

(4) To a disclosure to a law enforcement agency when required for investigations of criminal activity, unless such disclosure is prohibited by law.

(5) To a disclosure to a taxing agency for purposes of tax administration. **Leg.H.** Added Stats 1977 ch 221 §1.

§1799.1a. Disclosure of information on tax return or schedule

(a) No person, including an individual, firm, corporation, association, partnership, or joint venture, or any employee or agent thereof, shall disclose information obtained from a federal or state income tax return or any information obtained from a tax schedule submitted with the return by a consumer in connection with a financial or other business-related transaction unless the disclosure is within any of the following:

(1) Consented to in writing by the consumer in a separate document that states to whom the disclosure will be made and how the information will be used. If the consumer agrees, this separate consent document may be in the form of an electronic record, executed by an electronic signature as provided by Title 2.5 (commencing with Section 1633.1) of Part 2 of Division 3 of the Civil Code.

(2) Authorized or required by state or federal law.

(3) Necessary to complete or service the financial or business-related transaction or to effect, administer, or enforce a financial or business-related transaction requested by the consumer.

(4) Pursuant to court order.

(5) Required to complete any of the transactions described in subparagraphs (A) to (D), inclusive, by a person, including an individual, firm, corporation, association, partnership or joint venture, if the disclosure is made solely for that purpose. The provisions of this section apply to any person, including an individual, firm, corporation, association, partnership, or joint venture, and any employee or agent thereof, receiving information as a result of a disclosure authorized by this paragraph.

(A) A proposed or actual sale, merger, transfer, or exchange of all or a portion of a business or operating unit.

(B) A proposed or actual securitization or secondary market sale, including the sale of servicing rights.

(C) To provide information to insurance rate advisory organizations, guaranty funds or agencies, rating agencies, and other persons assessing compliance with industry standards.

(D) To protect against or to prevent actual or potential fraud and unauthorized transactions and claims and for institutional risk control activities.

(b) No unrelated use shall be made of a federal or state tax return or any information obtained therefrom or any information submitted with the return by a consumer in connection with a financial or other business-related transaction. "Unrelated use" means any use that is not necessary to effect, administer, or enforce the financial or other business-related transaction with the consumer or that is beyond the scope of the stated purpose to which the consumer consented for the use of the return or any other information he or she submitted.

(c)(1) For purposes of this section, the following definitions shall apply:

(A) "Affiliate" means any entity that, directly or indirectly, through one or more intermediaries, controls, is controlled by, or is under common control with, another entity.

(B) "Consumer" means an individual who requests or obtains financial or other business-related services.

(C) "Tax return" means a return, declaration, statement, refund claim, or other document required to be made or to be filed in connection with state or federal income taxes or state bank and corporation franchise taxes.

(2) A disclosure prohibited by this section includes a disclosure made internally within the entity or by that entity to any of its subsidiaries or affiliates.

(3) The information described in subdivision (a) includes that information obtained through an electronic medium.

(d) No person, including an individual, firm, corporation, association, partnership, or joint venture, or any employee or agent thereof, shall dispose of any of the information described in subdivision (a) in a manner in which the identity of the consumer may be determined from the disposed information alone or in combination with other publicly available information. This subdivision shall not become operative if Assembly Bill 2246 of the 1999–2000 Regular Session is enacted and becomes effective on or before January 1, 2001.

(e) The civil remedies in Chapter 3 (commencing with Section 1799.2) shall be applicable to a violation of this section. Each violation of this section shall constitute a separate cause of action for which damages are recoverable.

(f) The treatment of tax returns by tax preparers, as defined in Section 22251 of the Business and Professions Code, shall be governed by Section 17530.5 of the Business and Professions Code. **Leg.H.** Added Stats 2000 ch 1084 §5 (SB 1724).

§1799.1b. Procedure and notice on change of address request by holder of credit card

(a) Any credit card issuer that receives a change of address request, other than for a correction of a typographical error, from a cardholder who orders a replacement credit card within 60 days before or after that request is received shall send to that cardholder a change of address notification that is addressed to the cardholder at the cardholder's previous address of record. If the replacement credit card is requested prior to the effective date of the change of address, the notification shall be sent within 30 days of the change of address request. If the replacement credit card is requested after the effective date of the change of address, the notification shall be sent within 30 days of the request for the replacement credit card.

(b) Any business entity that provides telephone accounts that receives a change of address request, other than for a correction of a typographical error, from an accountholder who orders new service, shall send to that accountholder a change of address notification that is addressed to the accountholder at the accountholder's previous address of record. The notification shall be sent within 30 days of the request for new service.

(c) The notice required pursuant to subdivision (a) or (b) may be given by telephone or e-mail communication if the credit card issuer or business entity that provides telephone accounts reasonably believes that it has the current telephone number or e-mail address for the accountholder or cardholder who has requested a change of address. If the notification is in writing it may not contain the consumer's account number, social security number, or other personal identifying information, but may contain the consumer's name, previous address, and new address of record. For business entities described in subdivision (b), the notification may also contain the accountholder's telephone number.

(d) A credit card issuer or a business entity that provides telephone accounts is not required to send a change of address notification when a change of address request is made in person by a consumer who has presented valid identification, or is made by telephone and the requester has provided a unique alpha-numeric password.

(e) The following definitions shall apply to this section:

(1) "Credit account" has the same meaning as "credit card," as defined in subdivision (a) of Section 1747.02.

(2) "Telephone account" means an account with a telephone corporation, as defined in Section 234 of the Public Utilities Code. **Leg.H.** Added Stats 2003 ch 533 §5 (SB 602). Amended Stats 2004 ch 183 §36 (AB 3082).

CHAPTER 3
CIVIL REMEDIES

Action for damages; Jurisdiction; Time limitation. §1799.2.
Disclosure of video recording sales or rental information. §1799.3.

§1799.2. Action for damages; Jurisdiction; Time limitation

(a) A person may initiate a civil action against a business entity in accordance with state law whenever a business entity violates the provisions of Section 1799.1.

(b) In any suit brought pursuant to the provisions of subdivision (a) a business entity which has violated Section 1799.1 shall be liable to the person in an amount equal to the actual damages sustained by the person as a result of such violation, but in no case less than five hundred dollars ($500), and the attendant court costs and reasonable attorneys' fees.

(c) An action to enforce any liability created under this section may be brought in any court of competent jurisdiction within two years from the date on which the cause of action arose. **Leg.H.** Added Stats 1977 ch 221 §1.

§1799.3. Disclosure of video recording sales or rental information

(a) No person providing video recording sales or rental services shall disclose any personal information or the contents of any record, including sales or rental information, which is prepared or maintained by that person, to any person, other than the individual who is the subject of the record, without the written consent of that individual.

(b) This section does not apply to any of the following:

(1) To a disclosure to any person pursuant to a subpoena or court order.

(2) To a disclosure that is in response to the proper use of discovery in a pending civil action.

(3) To a disclosure to any person acting pursuant to a lawful search warrant.

(4) To a disclosure to a law enforcement agency when required for investigations of criminal activity, unless that disclosure is prohibited by law.

(5) To a disclosure to a taxing agency for purposes of tax administration.

(6) To a disclosure of names and addresses only for commercial purposes.

(c) Any willful violation of this section shall be subject to a civil penalty not to exceed five hundred dollars ($500) for each violation, which may be recovered in a civil action brought by the person who is the subject of the records.

(d)(1) Any person who willfully violates this section on three or more occasions in any six-month period shall, in addition, be subject to a civil penalty not to exceed five hundred dollars ($500) for each violation, which may be assessed and recovered in a civil action brought in the name of the people of the State of California by the Attorney General, by any district attorney or city attorney, or by a city prosecutor in any city or city and county having a full-time city prosecutor, in any court of competent jurisdiction.

(2) If the action is brought by the Attorney General, one-half of the penalty collected shall be paid to the treasurer of the county in which the judgment was entered, and one-half to the General Fund. If the action is brought by a district attorney, the penalty collected shall be paid to the treasurer of the county in which the judgment was entered. If the action is brought by a city attorney or city prosecutor, one-half of the penalty shall be paid to the treasurer of the city in which the judgment was entered, and one-half to the treasurer of the county in which the judgment was entered.

(e) The penalty provided by this section is not an exclusive remedy, and does not affect any other relief or remedy provided by law. **Leg.H.** Added Stats 1988 ch 1050 §1. Amended Stats 2009 ch 88 §14 (AB 176), effective January 1, 2010.

TITLE 1.83
PRECOMPUTED INTEREST

Definitions; Application of title. §1799.5.
Waiver of provisions of title void. §1799.6.

§1799.5. Definitions; Application of title

(a) "Precomputed interest" means interest, as that term is contemplated by the Truth in Lending Act, 15 United States Code 1605(a)(1), which is (1) computed by multiplying the original balance of the loan by a rate and multiplying that product by the number of payment periods elapsing between the date of the loan and the date of the last scheduled payment and (2) either added to the original principal balance of the loan in advance or subtracted from the loan proceeds.

(b) No loan which is made to a natural person primarily for personal, family, or household purposes shall provide for the payment of precomputed interest if the date on which the final installment is due, according to the original terms of the loan, is more than 62 months after the date of the loan.

(c) For purposes of determining whether a loan is covered by this title, the lender may conclusively rely on any written statement of intended purpose signed by the borrower. Such written statement may be a separate statement signed by the borrower or may be contained in a loan application or other document signed by the borrower.

(d) For purposes of this title, the term "loan" does not include the forbearance of a debt arising from a sale or lease of property and does not include any loan arising under an open end credit plan.

(e) This title shall apply only to loans made on or after January 1, 1983. **Leg.H.** Added Stats 1979 ch 805 §1. Amended Stats 1980 ch 1380 §2, effective October 1, 1980.

§1799.6. Waiver of provisions of title void

Any waiver of the provisions of this title is contrary to public policy, and is void and unenforceable. **Leg.H.** Added Stats 2002 ch 815 §17 (AB 2331).

TITLE 1.84
PRECOMPUTED FINANCE CHARGE CONTRACT

"Precomputed finance charge"; "Contract"; Application of title. §1799.8.
Waiver of provisions of title void. §1799.85.

§1799.8. "Precomputed finance charge"; "Contract"; Application of title

(a) "Precomputed finance charge" means a finance charge which is (1) computed by multiplying the original contract balance by a rate and multiplying that product by the number of payment periods elapsing between the date of the contract and the date of the last scheduled payment and (2) either added to the original contract balance in advance or subtracted from the contract balance.

(b) "Contract" means any agreement (1) providing for the construction, sale, or construction and sale of an entire residence, with or without a parcel of real property or an interest therein, or for the sale of a lot or parcel of real property, including any site preparation incidental to such sale, and (2) where the purchaser is a natural person who enters into such agreement primarily for personal, family, or household purposes.

(c) No contract as defined in subdivision (b) shall provide for the payment of a precomputed finance charge if the date on which the final installment is due, according to the original terms of the contract, is more than 62 months after the date of the contract.

(d) For purposes of determining whether a contract is covered by this title, the seller may conclusively rely on any written statement of intended purpose signed by the purchaser. Such written statement may be a separate statement signed by the purchaser or may be contained in a credit application or other document signed by the purchaser.

(e) This title shall apply only to contracts entered into on or after January 1, 1983. **Leg.H.** Added Stats 1979 ch 805 §2.

§1799.85. Waiver of provisions of title void

Any waiver of the provisions of this title is contrary to public policy, and is void and unenforceable. **Leg.H.** Added Stats 2002 ch 815 §18 (AB 2331).

TITLE 1.85
CONSUMER CREDIT CONTRACTS

Definitions. §1799.90.
Notice required. §1799.91.
Placement and form of notice. §1799.92.
Blank spaces in contract; Delivery of documents. §1799.93.
Construction of text of notice. §1799.94.
Effect of failure to give notice. §1799.95.
Federally sanctioned notices. §1799.96.
Security interest in religious materials. §1799.97.
Effect on other code provisions. §1799.98.
Notice required in other transactions. §1799.99.
Security interest in household goods or certain personal property; Damages; Definitions. §1799.100.
Additional definitions. §1799.101.
Cosigner's action to recover damages and attorney fees; Notice of intent. §1799.102.
Conditions for security interest in investment property that is pledged as collateral. §1799.103.
Waiver of provisions of title void. §1799.104.

§1799.90. Definitions

As used in this title:

(a) "Consumer credit contract" means any of the following obligations to pay money on a deferred payment basis, where the money, property, services or other consideration which is the subject matter of the contract is primarily for personal, family or household purposes:

(1) Retail installment contracts, as defined in Section 1802.6.

(2) Retail installment accounts, as defined in Section 1802.7.

(3) Conditional sales contracts, as defined in Section 2981.

(4) Loans or extensions of credit secured by other than real property, or unsecured, for use primarily for personal, family or household purposes.

(5) Loans or extensions of credit for use primarily for personal, family or household purposes where such loans or extensions of credit are subject to the provisions of Article 7 (commencing with Section 10240) of Chapter 3 of Part I of Division 4 of the Business and Professions Code, Division 7 (commencing with Section 18000), Division 9 (commencing with Section 22000), or Division 10 (commencing with Section 24000) of the Financial Code, whether secured by real property or otherwise.

(6) Lease contracts, as defined in Section 2985.7.

(b) "Creditor" means an individual, partnership, corporation, association or other entity, however designated, who enters into or arranges for consumer credit contracts in the ordinary course of business. **Leg.H.** Added Stats 1975 ch 847 §1, operative April 1, 1976. Amended Stats 1984 ch 890 §1; Stats 1997 ch 800 §1 (SB 1291).

§1799.91. Notice required

(a) Each creditor who obtains the signature of more than one person on a consumer credit contract shall deliver to each person who does not in fact receive any of the money, property, or services which are the subject matter of the consumer credit contract, prior to that person's becoming obligated on the consumer credit contract, a notice in English and the languages set forth in subdivision (b) of Section 1632 in a clear and conspicuous manner in at least 10-point Arial equivalent type as follows:

NOTICE TO COSIGNER

You are being asked to guarantee this debt. Think carefully before you do. If the borrower doesn't pay the debt, you will have to. Be sure you can afford to pay if you have to, and that you want to accept this responsibility.

You may have to pay up to the full amount of the debt if the borrower does not pay. You may also have to pay late fees or collection costs, which increase this amount.

The creditor can collect this debt from you without first trying to collect from the borrower. The creditor can use the same collection methods against you that can be used against the borrower, such as suing you, garnishing your wages, etc. If this debt is ever in default, that fact may become a part of your credit record.

This notice is not the contract that makes you liable for the debt.

(b) Whenever notice is required to be given under subdivision (a) or (d) and the consumer credit contract is written in a language other than English or a language set forth in subdivision (b) of Section 1632, the creditor shall deliver the notice as required in subdivision (a) or (d) in English and in the language in which the consumer contract is written.

(c) The requirements of subdivisions (a) and (b) do not apply to a creditor offering or extending open-end credit, as defined in Regulation Z, to joint applicants if all of the following conditions are satisfied:

(1) The application or agreement signed by each applicant clearly and conspicuously discloses that after credit approval each applicant shall have the right to use the open-end credit plan to the extent of any limit set by the creditor and may be liable for all amounts extended under the plan to any joint applicant.

(2) After credit approval, the creditor issues for the use of each applicant any credit device such as a credit card which may be used to obtain credit under the open-end credit plan and sends the credit device to the address specified in the application or otherwise delivers the credit device in a manner specified in the application or agreement signed by each applicant.

This paragraph does not apply to a creditor who does not issue a credit card or other credit device in order to obtain credit under the creditor's open-end credit plan.

(d) A lessor under a lease shall deliver to each person who does not in fact receive the vehicle which is the subject of the lease contract, prior to that person becoming liable on the lease contract, the following notice in English and the languages set forth in subdivision (b) of Section 1632 in a clear and conspicuous manner in at least 10-point Arial equivalent type in lieu of the notice required by subdivision (a):

NOTICE TO COSIGNER

You are being asked to guarantee this lease. Think carefully before you do. If the lessee doesn't pay, you will have to. Be sure you can afford to pay if you have to, and that you want to accept this responsibility.

You may have to pay up to the full amount owed on the lease if the lessee does not pay. You may also have to pay late fees or other collection costs, which increase this amount.

The lessor can collect on the lease from you without first trying to collect from the lessee. The lessor can use the same collection methods against you that can be used against the lessee, such as suing you, garnishing your wages, etc. If this lease is ever in default, that fact may become part of your credit record.

This notice is not the contract that makes you liable for the lease obligation.

(e) "Regulation Z" has the meaning set forth in Section 1802.18.

(f) The word "your" in the last sentence of the third paragraph of the notice in English set forth in subdivisions (a) and (d) shall be italicized.

(g)(1) On or before January 1, 2023, the Department of Financial Protection and Innovation shall make available for download on its internet website translations of the notices set forth in subdivisions (a) and (d), which may be used to satisfy the requirements of this section.

(2) If additional languages are added to Section 1632 by subsequent amendment, the department shall make available for download on its internet website translations of the notices set forth in subdivisions (a) and (d) in the new language. **Leg.H.** Added Stats 1975 ch 847 §1, operative April 1, 1976. Amended Stats 1985 ch 987 §1; Stats 1986 ch 280 §1; Stats 1987 ch 295 §1, effective July 30, 1987; Stats 1997 ch 800 §2 (SB 1291); Stats 2022 ch 149 §1 (SB 633), effective January 1, 2023.

§1799.92. Placement and form of notice

(a) The notice required by Section 1799.91 shall be provided on a separate sheet that meets the following requirements:

(1) It shall not contain any other text except as is necessary to identify the creditor and consumer credit contract or lessor and lease to which the statement refers.

(2) It shall provide for the date and the person's acknowledgment of receipt.

(3) It shall be attached to and precede the consumer credit contract or lease.

(b) The creditor or lessor may develop the separate sheet described in subdivision (a) so long as it conforms to the requirements of this title. **Leg.H.** Added Stats 1975 ch 847 §1, operative April 1, 1976. Amended Stats 1985 ch 987 §2; Stats 2022 ch 149 §2 (SB 633), effective January 1, 2023.

§1799.93. Blank spaces in contract; Delivery of documents

(a) The creditor shall not obtain the signature of any person entitled to notice under Section 1799.91 if the consumer credit contract contains blank spaces to be filled in after the person's signature has been obtained.

(b) The creditor shall give each person entitled to notice under Section 1799.91 a copy of the debt instrument and security agreement or deed of trust, if any, evidencing the consumer credit contract and, if separate therefrom, a copy of the notice required by Section 1799.91 and a copy of the document evidencing that person's obligations. **Leg.H.** Added Stats 1975 ch 847 §1, operative April 1, 1976. Amended Stats 1985 ch 987 §3.

§1799.94. Construction of text of notice

The text of the statement required by Section 1799.91 of this title shall not be construed to alter or affect the rights and obligations of the parties to any consumer credit contract. **Leg.H.** Added Stats 1975 ch 847 §1, operative April 1, 1976.

§1799.95. Effect of failure to give notice

No action shall be brought, nor shall any security interest be enforced, by any creditor or any assignee of a creditor on any consumer credit contract which fails to comply with this title against any person, however designated, who is entitled to notice under Section 1799.91 and who does not in fact receive any of the money, property or services which are the subject matter of the consumer credit contract.

Nothing herein shall affect the rights of any bona fide purchaser for value of property sold pursuant to the enforcement of a security interest if the purchase was made without notice of any facts constituting a violation of this title. **Leg.H.** Added Stats 1975 ch 847 §1, operative April 1, 1976. Amended Stats 1985 ch 987 §4.

§1799.96. Federally sanctioned notices

If federal law or regulations require or permit the use of a notice substantially similar to that required by Section 1799.91, the use of such federally sanctioned notice and an accurate translation thereof into the languages set forth in subdivision (b) of Section 1632 shall constitute compliance with Section 1799.91. However, the other provisions of this title shall remain unaffected. **Leg.H.** Added Stats 1975 ch 847 §1, operative April 1, 1976. Amended Stats 2022 ch 149 §3 (SB 633), effective January 1, 2023.

§1799.97. Security interest in religious materials

(a) No consumer credit contract shall provide for a security interest in any religious books, religious artifacts, or religious materials, valued at less than five hundred dollars ($500), unless the religious books, artifacts, or materials are specifically pledged as collateral.

(b) Any provision in any contract which provides for a security interest in violation of subdivision (a) shall be void and unenforceable. **Leg.H.** Added Stats 1984 ch 732 §1.

§1799.98. Effect on other code provisions

(a) Nothing in this title shall be construed to make applicable or affect or operate as a waiver of any of the provisions of any of the following:

(1) Title 13 (commencing with Section 2787) of Part 4 of Division 3 of this code.

(2) Parts 1 (commencing with Section 700), 2 (commencing with Section 760), 3 (commencing with Section 900), and 4 (commencing with Section 1100) of Division 4 of the Family Code.

(3) Sections 4301 and 4302 of the Family Code.

(b) The delivery of notice pursuant to Section 1799.91 is not evidence that the person to whom the notice was delivered entered or did not enter the transaction in the capacity of a surety. **Leg.H.** Added Stats 1985 ch 987 §5. Amended Stats 1992 ch 163 §10 (AB 2641), operative January 1, 1994; Stats 1993 ch 219 §28.5 (AB 1500).

§1799.99. Notice required in other transactions

(a) This section applies to transactions, other than consumer credit contracts as defined in Section 1799.90, which are subject to 16 C.F.R. 444.3, 12 C.F.R. 227.14, or 12 C.F.R. 535.3, whichever is applicable to the creditor.

(b) Unless the persons who are obligated under the transaction are married to each other, no action shall be brought, nor shall any security interest be enforced, against any person entitled to receive notice under 16 C.F.R. 444.3, 12 C.F.R. 227.14, or 12 C.F.R. 535.3, whichever is applicable to the creditor, if that person did not receive the notice in the manner prescribed by the applicable regulation and an accurate Spanish translation of the notice. **Leg.H.** Added Stats 1985 ch 987 §6. Amended Stats 1988 ch 160 §15.

§1799.100. Security interest in household goods or certain personal property; Damages; Definitions

(a) It is unlawful for any person to take a security interest in any household goods, as defined in subdivision (g), in connection with a consumer credit contract or other credit obligation incurred primarily for personal, family, or household purposes unless (1) the person takes possession of the household goods or (2) the purchase price of the household goods was financed through the consumer credit contract or credit obligation.

(b) An agreement or other document creating a nonpossessory security interest in personal property as defined in subdivision (d) in connection with a consumer credit contract or other credit obligation incurred primarily for personal, family, or household purposes shall contain a statement of description reviewed and signed by the consumer indicating each specific item of the personal property in which the security interest is taken. A consumer credit contract or other credit obligation subject to the Unruh Act (Chapter 1 (commencing with Section 1801) of Title 2) that complies with the provisions of subdivision (a) of Section 1803.3, or of subdivision (f) of Section 1810.1, shall be deemed to comply with this subdivision.

(c) Notwithstanding any other provision of law, a person who has a nonpossessory security interest in personal property, described in subdivision (d), taken in connection with a consumer credit contract or other credit obligation incurred primarily for personal, family, or household purposes shall only enforce the security interest by judicial action unless the property is abandoned or freely and voluntarily surrendered by the consumer.

(d) The provisions of subdivisions (b) and (c) apply only to the following types of personal property:

(1) Any goods, as defined in paragraph (44) of subdivision (a) of Section 9102 of the Commercial Code, except for vessels, vehicles, and aircraft, that are used or bought for use primarily for personal, family, or household purposes and that has a fair market value of less than one thousand dollars ($1,000) per individual item at the time the security interest is created.

(2) The property described in Section 704.050 and subdivision (a) of Section 704.060 of the Code of Civil Procedure, except for vessels, vehicles, and aircraft.

(e) Any security interest taken in violation of either subdivision (a) or (b) is void and unenforceable.

(f) Any person injured by a violation of this section may bring a civil action for the recovery of damages, equitable relief, and attorney's fees and costs.

(g) For the purpose of this section:

(1) "Household goods" means and includes clothing, furniture, appliances, one radio, one television, linens, china, crockery, kitchenware, personal effects, and wedding rings. "Household goods" does not include works of art, electronic entertainment equipment (except one radio and one television), items acquired as antiques, and jewelry (except wedding rings).

(2) "Antique" means any item over one hundred years of age, including such items that have been repaired or renovated without changing their original form or character. **Leg.H.** Added Stats 1989 ch 525 §1. Amended Stats 1990 ch 31 §1 (AB 1259), effective March 26, 1990; Stats 1999 ch 991 §3.5 (SB 45), operative July 1, 2001.

1990 Note: Nothing contained in Section 1799.100 of the Civil Code, as currently or heretofore in effect, is intended to, nor does it, affect in any way the rights, remedies, or obligations of a person taking or enforcing a security interest on or after January 1, 1990, in personal property other than household goods or personal property described in subdivision (d) of Section 1799.100 of the Civil Code. Stats 1990 ch 31 §10.

§1799.101. Additional definitions

(a) For the purposes of this section, the following terms are defined as follows:

(1) "Adverse information" means information directly or indirectly indicating that a delinquency has occurred, because a cosigner has not complied with the contractual provisions of a consumer credit contract.

(2) "Collection action" means requesting a cosigner to pay all or part of the obligation on a consumer credit contract.

(3) "Cosigner" means a natural person, other than the primary obligor or the spouse of the primary obligor, who renders himself or herself liable for the obligation on a consumer credit contract without compensation. The term includes a person whose signature is requested by a creditor as a condition to granting credit to another person. A person who does not receive goods, services, or money in return for executing a consumer credit contract does not receive compensation within the meaning of this section. "Cosigner" does not include a joint applicant for open-end credit pursuant to subdivision (c) of Section 1799.91. A person is a cosigner within the meaning of this section whether or not he or she is designated as such on a consumer credit contract or other document creating the consumer credit contract obligation for the cosigner.

(4) "Delinquency" means a failure to make timely payment to the creditor of all or a portion of any installment under a consumer credit contract.

(5) "Notice" means a writing which describes, recites, or otherwise refers to a delinquency.

(6) "Obligation" means an indebtedness incurred by an individual for personal, family, or household purposes.

(7) "Person" means an individual, firm, partnership, association, limited liability company, or corporation.

(8) "Primary obligor" means one or more persons, other than a cosigner, who sign a consumer credit contract and assume an obligation as debtor under that contract.

(b) Except as provided in subdivisions (d) and (e), no creditor shall provide any adverse information with respect to any cosigner, to a consumer credit reporting agency regarding a delinquency on a consumer credit contract entered into on or after July 1, 1992, unless, at or before the time the information is provided to the consumer credit reporting agency, written notice of the delinquency is provided to the cosigner.

(c) No creditor shall provide any information regarding the cosigner's obligation on a consumer credit contract to a debt collector, as defined in subdivision (c) of Section 1788.2, until notice has been provided to the cosigner under subdivision (b).

(d) The notice requirements of subdivisions (b) and (c) do not apply to any cosigner whose address, as shown in the creditor's records respecting the consumer credit contract, is the same as the primary obligor.

(e) The notice requirements of subdivisions (b) and (c) shall be satisfied by mailing a copy of the required notice to the cosigner at the cosigner's address, as shown in the creditor's records respecting the consumer credit contract. However, if more than one cosigner reside at the same address, as shown in the creditor's records respecting the consumer credit contract, a notice addressed to any cosigner at that address shall be deemed notice to all the cosigners residing at that address.

(f) Nothing in this section shall require any particular form or language with respect to a notice of delinquency sent to either a primary obligor or cosigner.

(g) Within a reasonable time after a creditor has reported to a credit reporting agency that a delinquency or delinquencies that have been reported to the consumer credit reporting agency and included in the cosigner's file maintained by the consumer credit reporting agency have been cured, the consumer credit reporting agency shall indicate in the file that the payment was made.

(h) Nothing in this section shall be construed to require notice of a delinquency to be provided to a cosigner in any instance not expressly specified in this section, or to provide notice to persons other than cosigners.

(i) This section shall become operative on July 1, 1992. **Leg.H.** Added Stats 1990 ch 1549 §1 (AB 2729), operative July 1, 1992. Amended Stats 1991 ch 131 §1 (AB 956), operative July 1, 1992; Stats 1994 ch 1010 §42 (SB 2053).

§1799.102. Cosigner's action to recover damages and attorney fees; Notice of intent

(a) A cosigner who suffers a loss as a result of a violation of Section 1799.101 may bring an action to recover actual damages or two hundred fifty dollars ($250), whichever is greater, and reasonable attorney fees.

(b) The cosigner shall, not less than 30 days prior to bringing an action pursuant to subdivision (a), notify the person alleged to have violated Section 1799.101 of the cosigner's intention to bring an action. The notice shall include a statement of the specific evidence that proves the loss suffered by the cosigner. If within 25 days after the date of receiving the notice, the person alleged to have violated Section 1799.101 tenders to the cosigner an amount equal to the loss, or otherwise resolves the matter to the cosigner's satisfaction, the cosigner shall be barred from further recovery of that loss, including reasonable attorney fees.

(c) This section shall become operative on July 1, 1992. **Leg.H.** Added Stats 1990 ch 1549 §2 (AB 2729), operative July 1, 1992.

§1799.103. Conditions for security interest in investment property that is pledged as collateral

No consumer credit contract or guarantee of a consumer credit contract shall provide for a security interest in any investment property, as defined in paragraph (49) of subdivision (a) of Section 9102 of the Commercial Code, that is pledged as collateral, unless (a) the contract either specifically identifies the investment property as collateral or (b) the secured party is a securities intermediary, as defined in paragraph (14) of subdivision (a) of Section 8102 of the Commercial Code, or commodity intermediary, as defined in paragraph (17) of subdivision (a) of Section 9102 of the Commercial Code, with respect to the investment property. The identification of an account shall include the name of the holder, account number, and name of the institute holding the investment property. In the event that a consumer credit contract or guarantee does not comply with this section, the security interest in the investment property is void. **Leg.H.** Added Stats 1996 ch 497 §1 (SB 1591). Amended Stats 1999 ch 991 §4 (SB 45), operative July 1, 2001.

§1799.104. Waiver of provisions of title void

Any waiver of the provisions of this title is contrary to public policy, and is void and unenforceable. **Leg.H.** Added Stats 2002 ch 815 §19 (AB 2331).

TITLE 1.86
CONSUMER CONTRACT AWARENESS ACT OF 1990

Citation of act. §1799.200.
Definitions. §1799.201.
Delivery of copy of contract to consumer. §1799.202.
Compliance with delivery requirements; Exceptions. §1799.203.
Compliance if more than one consumer signed contract. §1799.204.
Penalty for failure to comply. §1799.205.
Guaranty; Penalty for failure to comply. §1799.206.
Waiver of provisions of title void. §1799.207.
Restrictions on Out-of-State Arbitration and Choice of Law for California Consumers. § 1799.208.
Small Claims Act Option for Consumer Arbitration. § 1799.209.

§1799.200. Citation of act

This title shall be known and may be cited as the Consumer Contract Awareness Act of 1990. **Leg.H.** Added Stats 1990 ch 1079 §1 (SB 1107), operative July 1, 1991.

§1799.201. Definitions

As used in this title:

(a) "Consumer" means a natural person who has entered into a consumer contract with a seller.

(b) "Consumer contract" means a writing prepared by a seller and, except as provided in subdivision (c) of Section 1799.202, signed, or to be signed, by a consumer, which provides (1) for the sale or lease of goods or services that are purchased or leased primarily for personal, family, or household purposes, or (2) for extension of credit, the proceeds of which are used primarily for personal, family, or household purposes. Without affecting the enforceability of any incidental provision contained therein, an application for credit shall not be considered to be a consumer contract for purposes of this section even if it contains incidental provisions, such as the consumer's consent to a credit review, a certification of the accuracy of the information furnished, or the consumer's agreement to the terms that will be furnished to the consumer pursuant to this title.

(c) "Consumer contract guaranty" means a writing prepared by a seller and signed, or to be signed, by a guarantor which guarantees the obligation of a consumer under a consumer contract.

(d) "Copy" means a reproduction, facsimile, or duplicate.

(e) "Days" means calendar days.

(f) "Goods" means tangible and intangible personal property.

(g) "Guarantor" means a person who guarantees the obligation of a consumer under a consumer contract by signing a consumer contract guaranty.

(h) "Seller" means a person who has entered into a consumer contract with a consumer.

(i) "Services" means work, labor, and services, including depository services and other banking services.

(j) "Financial institution" means any commercial bank, trust company, savings and loan association, credit union, industrial loan company, insurance company, or person engaged in the business of lending money. **Leg.H.** Added Stats 1990 ch 1079 §1 (SB 1107), operative July 1, 1991. Amended Stats 1991 ch 1129 §1 (SB 108); Stats 1992 ch 879 §1 (AB 3468).

§1799.202. Delivery of copy of contract to consumer

(a) Except as otherwise provided in this title, a seller shall deliver a copy of a consumer contract to the consumer at the time it is signed by the consumer if the consumer contract is signed at a place of business of the seller. If the consumer contract is not signed by the consumer at a place of business of the seller, and the seller has not provided a copy of the consumer contract for the consumer which the consumer is instructed to keep, the seller shall mail or deliver a copy of it to the consumer within 10 calendar days after the seller receives the signed consumer contract. In any case, the copy of the contract provided to the consumer shall not contain any blank spaces to be completed after the consumer signs the contract, shall contain the signature of the seller if it provides for that signature, and may also contain the signature of the consumer.

(b) A seller that is a financial institution need not deliver to the consumer, pursuant to subdivision (a), any writing which the consumer contract incorporates by reference if either of the following conditions apply:

(1) The writing was previously delivered or mailed to the consumer.
(2) The writing was not prepared by the seller.

(c) If the consumer contract (1) is wholly or partly contained on a card or other writing which is used to identify the consumer in connection with a deposit account, safe deposit box, safekeeping agreement, or other service offered by a financial institution, and (2) contains information particular to the consumer's account, box, or other arrangement that, if known by a third party, could be used by the third party to cause loss to the consumer or financial institution, the copy of the contract furnished to the consumer need not contain the consumer's signature or any of the identifying information particular to the consumer's account, box, or other arrangement.

For purposes of this subdivision, a document which includes the same terms as those contained in the consumer contract shall be deemed a copy.

(d) Within a reasonable time after receipt of a written request from a consumer, a seller or financial institution shall mail a copy of the consumer's completed consumer credit application, which may, but need not, contain any information completed or added by the seller or financial institution, to the consumer at the address indicated on the request. By making a written request, the consumer shall conclusively be deemed to have waived any action against the seller or financial institution, as well as its employees or agents, on any theory, at law or in equity, arising directly or indirectly out of the mailing or other delivery of the copy, including any information added to the application by the seller or financial institution and included in the copy. The seller or financial institution may specify the address to which such a request may be sent, may charge the consumer a reasonable copying fee, and shall not be obligated to provide the copy until the fee is paid. **Leg.H.** Added Stats 1990 ch 1079 §1 (SB 1107), operative July 1, 1991. Amended Stats 1991 ch 1129 §2 (SB 108); Stats 1992 ch 879 §2 (AB 3468).

§1799.203. Compliance with delivery requirements; Exceptions

(a) It shall be deemed compliance with Section 1799.202 if a copy of any consumer contract which is subject to Article 10 (commencing with Section 1810.1) of Chapter 1 of Title 2, or which is an open-end consumer credit plan subject to Section 127 of the federal Truth in Lending Act (15 U.S.C. 1637), is delivered or mailed to the consumer before the consumer enters into a transaction covered and permitted by the consumer contract.

(b) Section 1799.202 does not apply to any of the following:
(1) A consumer contract for the purchase of goods by mail if the seller permits the consumer to examine the goods for seven calendar days and cancel the consumer contract and receive a full refund within 30 calendar days for returned unused and undamaged goods.
(2) A written contract created by, and consisting of, an exchange of letters by mail.
(3) Any consumer contract which is required to be mailed or delivered at a time prescribed by another law of this state or the United States. **Leg.H.** Added Stats 1990 ch 1079 §1 (SB 1107), operative July 1, 1991. Amended Stats 1991 ch 1129 §3 (SB 108).

§1799.204. Compliance if more than one consumer signed contract

If more than one consumer has signed a consumer contact, the seller may comply with Section 1799.202 by mailing or delivering the copy to any one of the consumers who reside at the same address. A copy shall also be mailed or delivered to any other consumer who has signed the consumer contract and who does not reside at the same address. **Leg.H.** Added Stats 1990 ch 1079 §1 (SB 1107), operative July 1, 1991.

1990 Note: It appears that the Legislature inadvertently substituted "contact" for the word "contract."

§1799.205. Penalty for failure to comply

(a) A seller who fails to comply with Section 1799.202 is liable to the consumer for any actual damages suffered by the consumer as the result of that failure. The remedy provided by this subdivision is nonexclusive and is in addition to any other remedies or penalties available under other laws of this state.

(b) Failure to comply with Section 1799.202 does not create an independent basis for the rescission, but is admissible to establish a basis for the rescission of the contract otherwise authorized by law. **Leg.H.** Added Stats 1990 ch 1079 §1 (SB 1107), operative July 1, 1991. Amended Stats 1991 ch 1129 §4 (SB 108).

§1799.206. Guaranty; Penalty for failure to comply

(a) Except as otherwise provided in this section, a seller shall deliver a copy of the consumer contract guaranty to the guarantor at the time the consumer contract guaranty is signed by the guarantor if the consumer contract guaranty is signed by the guarantor at a place of business of the seller. If the consumer contract guaranty is not signed by the guarantor at a place of business of the seller, and the seller has not provided a copy of the consumer contract guaranty for the guarantor which the guarantor is able to keep, the seller shall mail or deliver a copy of the consumer contract guaranty to the guarantor within 10 calendar days after the seller receives the signed consumer contract guaranty. In any case, the copy of the consumer contract guaranty provided to the guarantor shall not contain any blank spaces to be completed after the guarantor signs the guaranty, shall contain the signature of the seller if it provides for that signature, and may also contain the signature of the guarantor.

(b) If more than one guarantor has signed the consumer contract guaranty, the seller may comply with subdivision (a) by mailing or delivering the copy to any one of the guarantors who reside at the same address. A copy shall also be mailed or delivered to any guarantor who has signed the consumer contract guaranty and who does not reside at the same address.

(c) A seller that fails to comply with this section is liable to the guarantor for any actual damages suffered by the guarantor as the result of that failure. The remedy provided by this subdivision is nonexclusive and in addition to any other remedies or penalties available under other laws of this state.

(d) Failure to comply with this section does not create a new basis for rescission, but is admissible to establish a basis for rescission of the consumer contract guaranty otherwise authorized by law. **Leg.H.** Added Stats 1990 ch 1079 §1 (SB 1107), operative July 1, 1991. Amended Stats 1991 ch 1129 §5 (SB 108); Stats 1992 ch 879 §3 (AB 3468).

§1799.207. Waiver of provisions of title void

Any waiver of the provisions of this title is contrary to public policy, and is void and unenforceable. **Leg.H.** Added Stats 2002 ch 815 §20 (AB 2331).

§1799.208. Restrictions on Out-of-State Arbitration and Choice of Law for California Consumers

(a) A seller shall not require a consumer to agree to a provision that would do either of the following:
(1) Require the consumer to arbitrate outside of California a claim arising in California.
(2) Require the consumer to arbitrate a controversy arising in California under the substantive law of a state other than California.

(b) Any provision of a contract that violates subdivision (a) is voidable by the consumer, and if a provision is rendered void at the request of the consumer, the matter shall be adjudicated in California and California law shall govern the dispute.

(c) In addition to injunctive relief and any other remedies available, a court may award a consumer who is enforcing their rights under this section reasonable attorney's fees incurred in enforcing those rights.

(d) For purposes of this section, adjudication includes litigation and arbitration.

(e) This section applies to a contract entered into, modified, or extended on or after January 1, 2025. **Leg.H.** Added Stats 2024 ch 986 §2 (SB 940), effective January 1, 2025.

§ 1799.209. Small Claims Act Option for Consumer Arbitration

(a) If a consumer contract requires a dispute under the contract to be arbitrated and the dispute may be adjudicated pursuant to the Small Claims Act (Chapter 5.5 (commencing with Section 116.110) of Title 1 of Part 1 of the Code of Civil Procedure), the consumer shall be given the option to have the dispute adjudicated pursuant to that act.

(b) This section applies to a contract entered into, modified, or extended on or after January 1, 2025. **Leg.H.** Added Stats 2024 ch 986 §3 (SB 940), effective January 1, 2025.

§1800. [Section repealed 1965]

Leg.H. Added Stats 1931 ch 1070 §1. Repealed Stats 1963 ch 819 §2, effective January 1, 1965. The repealed section related to citation of title as the uniform sales act.

TITLE 1.90
COMMERCIAL FINANCING TRANSACTIONS WITH SMALL BUSINESSES

Definitions. § 1799.300.
Exceptions. § 1799.301.
Forbidden fees involving commercial financing transaction with small business or small business owner. § 1799.302.
Available relief for violation of Section 1799.302. § 1799.303.
Waiver void and unenforceable. § 1799.304.

§ 1799.300. Definitions

For purposes of this title, the following definitions apply:

(a) "Automated clearinghouse" means any federal reserve bank, or an organization established in agreement with the National Automated Clearing House Association, that operates as a clearinghouse for transmitting or receiving entries between banks or bank accounts and authorizes an electronic transfer of funds between these banks or bank accounts.

(b)(1) "Broker" means a person who is engaged in the business of performing any of the following acts in connection with commercial financing made by a provider:

(A) Transmitting confidential data about a prospective recipient to a provider with the expectation of compensation in connection with making a referral.

(B) Making a referral to a provider under an agreement with the provider that a prospective recipient referred by the person to the provider meet certain criteria involving confidential data.

(C) Participating in a negotiation of commercial financing between a provider and prospective recipient.

(D) Counseling, advising, or making recommendations to a prospective recipient about a commercial financing transaction based on the prospective recipient's confidential data.

(E)(i) Participating in the preparation of any commercial financing documents, including, but not limited to, commercial financing applications, other than providing a prospective recipient blank copies of commercial financing documents.

(ii) Notwithstanding clause (i), transmitting information that is not confidential data to a provider at the request of a prospective recipient shall not, by itself, constitute participation in the preparation of commercial financing documents.

(F) Communicating to a prospective recipient a provider's approval decisions related to a commercial financing transaction.

(G) Charging a fee to a prospective recipient for any services related to a prospective recipient's application for a commercial financing transaction from a provider.

(2) Notwithstanding paragraph (1), a person is not a "broker" under this title solely because they take any of the following acts:

(A) Performing support tasks, including, but not limited to, typing, word processing, data entry, filing, billing, answering phone calls, taking and receiving messages, and scheduling, in support of the performance by a broker of any of the activities described in subparagraphs (E) to (G), inclusive, of paragraph (1).

(B) Furnishing a consumer report to a covered entity by a consumer reporting agency in accordance with subsection (a) or (c) of Section 1681b of Title 15 of the United States Code.

(C) Furnishing a consumer credit report, as defined in Section 1785.3, to a covered entity by a consumer credit reporting agency in accordance with subdivision (a) or paragraph (1) of subdivision (b) of Section 1785.11.

(D) Furnishing a prequalifying report, as defined in Section 1785.3, to a covered entity by a consumer credit reporting agency in accordance with paragraph (2) of subdivision (b) of Section 1785.11.

(E) Distributing or disseminating to a prospective recipient of a provider's marketing materials or factual information about the provider, its lending activities, or its loan products, including, but not limited to, the provider's interest rates, the provider's minimum or maximum loan amounts or loan periods, or a general description of the provider's underwriting criteria.

(c) "Commercial financing" has the same meaning as defined in Section 22800 of the Financial Code.

(d) "Confidential data" means any of the following:

(1) A bank account number.
(2) A bank statement.
(3) A credit or debit card account number.
(4) A credit score, as defined in Section 1785.15.1.
(5) All or a portion of a social security number.
(6) Personal or business income information, including information self-reported by the person.
(7) A taxpayer or employer identification number.

(e) "Covered entity" means either of the following:
(1) A provider.
(2) A broker.

(f) "Depository institution" means any of the following:

(1) A bank, trust company, or industrial loan company doing business under the authority of, or in accordance with, a license, certificate, or charter issued by the United States, this state, or any other state, district, territory, or commonwealth of the United States that is authorized to transact business in this state.

(2) A federally chartered savings and loan association, federal savings bank, or federal credit union that is authorized to transact business in this state.

(3) A savings and loan association, savings bank, or credit union organized under the laws of this or any other state that is authorized to transact business in this state.

(g) "Provider" means a person who extends a specific offer of commercial financing to a recipient, including, but not limited to, a nondepository institution that enters into a written agreement with a depository institution to arrange for the extension of commercial financing by the depository institution to a recipient via an online lending platform administered by the nondepository institution. The fact that a provider extends a specific offer of commercial financing or lending on behalf of a depository institution shall not be construed to mean that the provider engaged in lending or originated that loan or financing.

(h) "Recipient" means a person who is presented a specific commercial financing offer by a provider that is equal to or less than five hundred thousand dollars ($500,000).

(i) "Referral" means the introduction of a prospective recipient to a provider or the delivery of a prospective recipient's contact information to a provider for the purpose of making an introduction.

(j) "Small business" means an independently owned and operated business that is not dominant in its field of operation, the principal office of which is located in California, the officers of which are domiciled in California, and that, together with affiliates, has 100 or fewer employees and average annual gross receipts of fifteen million dollars ($15,000,000) or less over the previous three years. **Leg.H.** Added Stats 2023 ch 881 §1 (SB 666), effective January 1, 2024.

§ 1799.301. Exceptions

This title does not apply to any of the following:

(a) A provider that is a depository institution.

(b) A provider that is a lender regulated under the federal Farm Credit Act of 1971 (12 U.S.C. Sec. 2001 et seq.).

(c) A commercial financing transaction secured by real property.

(d) A person who makes no more than one commercial financing transaction in California in a 12-month period.

(e) A person who makes five or fewer commercial financing transactions in California in a 12-month period that are incidental to the business of that person.

(f) A commercial financing transaction in which the recipient is a dealer, as defined by Section 285 of the Vehicle Code, or an affiliate of the dealer, pursuant to a specific commercial financing offer or commercial open-end credit plan of at least fifty thousand dollars ($50,000), including, but not limited to, a commercial loan made pursuant to that commercial financing transaction.

(g) A commercial financing transaction in which the recipient is a vehicle rental company, or an affiliate of the vehicle rental company, pursuant to a specific commercial financing offer or commercial open-end credit plan of at least fifty thousand dollars ($50,000), including, but not limited to, a commercial loan made pursuant to that commercial financing transaction. **Leg.H.** Added Stats 2023 ch 881 §1 (SB 666), effective January 1, 2024.

§ 1799.302. Forbidden fees involving commercial financing transaction with small business or small business owner

A covered entity shall not charge any of the following in connection with a commercial financing transaction with a small business or small business owner:

(a) A fee for accepting or processing a payment required by the terms of the commercial financing contract as an automated clearinghouse transfer debit, except for a fee imposed for a payment by an automated clearinghouse transfer that fails because of insufficient funds in the transferor's account.

(b) A fee for providing a small business with documentation prepared by the covered entity that contains a statement of the amount due to satisfy the remaining amount owed, including, but not limited to, interest accrued to the date the statement is prepared and a means of calculating per diem interest accruing thereafter.

(c) A fee in addition to an origination fee that does not have a clear corresponding service provided for the fee, including, but not limited to, a risk assessment, due diligence, or platform fee.

(d)(1) A fee for monitoring the small [1] **business' collateral**.

(2) Paragraph (1) does not apply if any of the following are true:

(A) The commercial financing transaction is an asset-based loan or factoring, and the fee is intended to compensate the covered entity for actions taken to validate the collateral with the intended purpose of maximizing the amount of financing provided to the small business or small business owner under the financing contract pursuant to which the fee is charged.

(B) The fee is expressed as a dollar amount or a percentage of an identifiable base, and the fee is deemed a finance charge, as described in Section 943 of Subchapter 3 of Chapter 3 of Title 10 of the California Code of Regulations.

(C) The commercial financing transaction is delinquent for more than 60 days.

(e) A fee for filing or terminating a lien filed in accordance with the provisions of the Uniform Commercial Code against the [2] **business'** assets that exceeds 150 percent of the cost of the filing or termination. **Leg.H.** Added Stats 2023 ch 881 §1 (SB 666), effective January 1, 2024. Amended Stats 2024 ch 194 §1 (SB 1521), effective January 1, 2025.

§ 1799.302. 2024 Deletes. [1] business's collateral, unless the underlying commercial financing transaction is delinquent for more than 60 days [2] business's

§ 1799.303. Available relief for violation of Section 1799.302

(a) If a covered entity violates Section 1799.302, the recipient shall be entitled to all of the following relief:

(1) Actual damages sustained as a result of the violation, including, but not limited to, the amount of fees paid by the recipient that are prohibited by Section 1799.302.

(2) Statutory damages of at least five hundred dollars ($500) but not greater than two thousand five hundred dollars ($2,500).

(3) Injunctive relief.

(4) Attorney's fees and costs.

(5) Any other relief that the court deems proper.

(b) A court may award a covered entity that is the prevailing party in an action brought pursuant to this section reasonable attorney's fees upon a finding that the recipient brought the action in bad faith. **Leg.H.** Added Stats 2023 ch 881 §1 (SB 666), effective January 1, 2024.

§ 1799.304. Waiver void and unenforceable

A waiver of the provisions of this title is contrary to public policy and is void and unenforceable. **Leg.H.** Added Stats 2023 ch 881 §1 (SB 666), effective January 1, 2024.

TITLE 2
CREDIT SALES

Chapter 1. Retail Installment Sales.
Chapter 2. Credit Transactions Regarding Women.

CHAPTER 1
RETAIL INSTALLMENT SALES

Article 1. General Provisions.
Article 2. Definitions.
Article 3. Provisions of Retail Installment Contracts.
Article 4. Restrictions on Retail Installment Contracts.
Article 5. Finance Charge Limitation.
Article 6. Payments.
Article 7. Refinancing and Consolidation.
Article 8. Add-on Sales.
Article 9. Terms of Purchase by Financing Agency.
Article 10. Retail Installment Accounts.
Article 10.5. Retail Installment Account Credit Card Periodic Rate Disclosures.
Article 11. Attorney's Fees and Court Costs.
Article 12.1. Repossession and Resale.
Article 12.2. Penalties.
Article 12.3. Actions.
Article 12.4. Financing Retail Purchases.

ARTICLE 1
General Provisions

Statutory citation. §1801.
Invalidity of waiver of statutory provisions. §1801.1.
Saving clause. §1801.2.
Application of chapter to contracts for construction or sale of particular property. §1801.4.
Disclosures in Regulation Z terms; Additional disclosures. §1801.5.
Characterization of credit transaction. §1801.6.
Inapplicability of provisions to premium finance agreement entered into by industrial loan company. §1801.7.

§1801. Statutory citation

This chapter may be cited as the "Unruh Act." **Leg.H.** Added Stats 1959 ch 201 §1, operative January 1, 1960.

§1801.1. Invalidity of waiver of statutory provisions

Any waiver by the buyer of the provisions of this chapter shall be deemed contrary to public policy and shall be unenforceable and void. **Leg.H.** Added Stats 1959 ch 201 §1, operative January 1, 1960. Amended Stats 1963 ch 1603 §1.

§1801.2. Saving clause

If any provision of this chapter or the application thereof to any person or circumstances is held unconstitutional, the remainder of the chapter and the application of such provision to other persons or circumstances shall not be affected thereby. **Leg.H.** Added Stats 1959 ch 201 §1, operative January 1, 1960.

§1801.3. [Section repealed 1963]

Leg.H. Added Stats 1959 ch 201 §1, operative January 1, 1960. Repealed Stats 1963 ch 1603 §2. The repealed section related to applicability of chapter.

§1801.4. Application of chapter to contracts for construction or sale of particular property

The provisions of this chapter shall not apply to any contract or series of contracts providing for: (a) the construction, sale, or construction and sale of an entire residence, including a mobilehome, or all or part of a structure designed for commercial or industrial occupancy, with or without a parcel of real property or an interest therein, (b) for the sale of a lot or parcel of real property, including any site preparation incidental to such sale, (c) the sale of any aircraft required to be registered under the Federal Aviation Act of 1958, or (d) the sale of any vessel as defined in subdivision (a) of Section 9840 of the Vehicle Code if the cash price of such vessel, including accessories and equipment sold in conjunction therewith, exceeds twenty-five thousand dollars ($25,000). **Leg.H.** Added Stats 1969 ch 554 §1. Amended Stats 1980 ch 437 §1, ch 1149 §6.

§1801.5. Disclosures in Regulation Z terms; Additional disclosures

Notwithstanding any other provision of this chapter to the contrary, any information required to be disclosed in a retail installment contract or other document under this chapter may be disclosed in any manner, method, or terminology required or permitted under Regulation Z, as in effect at the time such disclosure is made, except that permitted by paragraph (2) of subdivision (c) of Section 226.18 of Regulation Z, provided that all of the requirements and limitations set forth in subdivision (b) of Section 1803.3 are satisfied. Nothing contained in this chapter shall be deemed to prohibit the disclosure in such contract or other document of additional information required or permitted under Regulation Z, as in effect at the time such disclosure is made. **Leg.H.** Added Stats 1970 ch 546 §1. Amended Stats 1979 ch 805 §3; Stats 1981 ch 1075 §1, operative October 1, 1982.

§1801.6. Characterization of credit transaction

(a) The Legislature finds that the decisional law of this state regarding the characterization of credit transactions as either loans or credit sales has been made unclear by the holding in King v. Central Bank, 18 Cal. 3d 840. It is the purpose of subdivision (b) to clarify such law by establishing standards for determining whether a transaction is subject to the Unruh Act. However, subdivision (b) is not intended to abrogate the judicial principle that the substance of a transaction rather than its form is determinative of its characterization as a loan or credit sale as exemplified by such decisions as Verbeck v. Clymer, 202 Cal. 557, Milana v. Credit Discount Co., 27 Cal. 2d 335, and Boerner v. Colwell Co., 21 Cal. 3d 37. Subdivision (b) also is not intended to abrogate the decision in Morgan v. Reasor Corp., 69 Cal. 2d 881, to the extent such decision has not been modified by Chapter 554 of the Statutes of 1969 or other legislative amendments to the Unruh Act.

(b) The provisions of this chapter shall not apply to any transaction in the form of a loan made by a supervised financial organization to a buyer of goods or services where all or a portion of the loan proceeds are used to purchase such goods or services, whether or not the seller of such goods or services arranges the loan or participates in the preparation of the loan documents, unless the supervised financial organization and the seller:

(1) Are related by common ownership and control and the relationship was a material factor in the loan transaction; or

(2) Share in the profits and losses of either or both the sale and the loan.

(c) For purposes of this section:

(1) The term "supervised financial organization" means a person organized, chartered, or holding a license or authorization certificate to make loans pursuant to the laws of this state or the United States who is subject to supervision by an official or agency of this state or the United States.

(2) Receipt of a loan commission, brokerage or referral fee by a seller from a supervised financial organization shall not constitute a sharing of profits of the supervised financial organization, provided that such payment (i) is reasonable under the circumstances existing at the time the loan is consummated, and (ii) is not refundable or is wholly or partly refundable only if the loan is voluntarily paid in full prior to its scheduled maturity. For purposes of this paragraph, a loan commission, brokerage or referral fee not exceeding the greater of 1 percent of the amount financed (as that term is defined by Regulation Z with respect to loans), or twenty dollars ($20), is reasonable under the circumstances existing at the time the loan is consummated.

(3) Payment of money by a seller to a supervised financial organization pursuant to an actual or alleged contractual or statutory obligation to indemnify a supervised financial organization for losses incurred as a result of the assertion by a buyer of claims or defenses with respect to goods or services purchased with loan proceeds shall not constitute participation in or sharing of loan losses by the seller. **Leg.H.** Added Stats 1979 ch 1151 §1. Amended Stats 1980 ch 438 §1.

§1801.7. Inapplicability of provisions to premium finance agreement entered into by industrial loan company

The provisions of this chapter shall not apply to any premium finance agreement entered into by an industrial loan company pursuant to Chapter 8 (commencing with Section 18560) of Division 7 of the Financial Code. **Leg.H.** Added Stats 1979 ch 1151 §2.

ARTICLE 2
Definitions

Application of definitions. §1802.
"Goods". §1802.1.
"Services". §1802.2.
"Retail seller" or "seller". §1802.3.
"Retail buyer" or "buyer". §1802.4.
"Retail installment sale" or "sale". §1802.5.
"Retail installment contract" or "contract". §1802.6.
"Retail installment account" or "installment account" or "revolving account". §1802.7.
"Cash price". §1802.8.
"Total sale price". §1802.9.
"Finance charge". §1802.10.
"Amount financed;" "Unpaid balance". §1802.11.
"Total of payments". §1802.12.
"Holder". §1802.13.
"Official fees". §1802.14.
"Person". §1802.15.
"Financing agency". §1802.16.
"Billing cycle". §1802.17.
"Regulation Z". §1802.18.
Transactions subject to chapter. §1802.19.
"Simple-interest basis". §1802.20.
"Precomputed basis". §1802.21.

§1802. Application of definitions

Unless the context or subject matter otherwise requires, the definitions given in this article govern the construction of this chapter. **Leg.H.** Added Stats 1959 ch 201 §1, operative January 1, 1960.

§1802.1. "Goods"

"Goods" means tangible chattels bought for use primarily for personal, family or household purposes, including certificates or coupons exchangeable for such goods, and including goods which, at the time of the sale or subsequently are to be so affixed to real property as to become a part of such real property whether or not severable therefrom, but does not include any vehicle required to be registered under the Vehicle Code, nor any goods sold or leased with such a vehicle if sold under a contract governed by Section 2982 or leased under a contract governed by Section 2985.7. "Goods" also includes a trailer which is sold in conjunction with a vessel, as defined in subdivision (a) of Section 9840 of the Vehicle Code, unless the sales transaction is exempted under Section 1801.4. As used in this section, "trailer" means a vehicle designed solely for carrying vessels. **Leg.H.** Added Stats 1959 ch 201 §1, operative January 1, 1960. Amended Stats 1984 ch 1114 §1; Stats 1985 ch 1186 §1.

§1802.2. "Services"

"Services" means work, labor and services, for other than a commercial or business use, including services furnished in connection with the sale or repair of goods as defined in Section 1802.1 or furnished in connection with the repair of motor vehicles (except for service contracts as defined by subdivision (p) of Section 2981 which are sold in conjunction with the sale or lease of a vehicle required to be registered under the Vehicle Code) or in connection with the improvement of real property or the providing of insurance, but does not include the services of physicians or dentists, nor services for which the tariffs, rates, charges, costs or expenses, including in each instance the deferred payment price, are required by law to be filed with and approved by the federal government or any official, department, division, commission or agency of the United States. **Leg.H.** Added Stats 1959 ch 201 §1, operative January 1, 1960. Amended Stats 1968 ch 48 §1; Stats 1970 ch 546 §2; Stats 1980 ch 1380 §3, effective October 1, 1980; Stats 1981 ch 1075 §1.5, operative October 1, 1982; Stats 1984 ch 1114 §2.

§1802.3. "Retail seller" or "seller"

"Retail seller" or "seller" means a person engaged in the business of selling goods or furnishing services to retail buyers. **Leg.H.** Added Stats 1959 ch 201 §1, operative January 1, 1960.

§1802.4. "Retail buyer" or "buyer"

"Retail buyer" or "buyer" means a person who buys goods or obtains services from a retail seller in a retail installment sale and not principally for the purpose of resale. **Leg.H.** Added Stats 1959 ch 201 §1, operative January 1, 1960.

§1802.5. "Retail installment sale" or "sale"

"Retail installment sale" or "sale" means the sale of goods or the furnishing of services by a retail seller to a retail buyer for a deferred payment price payable in installments. **Leg.H.** Added Stats 1959 ch 201 §1, operative January 1, 1960. Amended Stats 1970 ch 546 §3.

§1802.6. "Retail installment contract" or "contract"

"Retail installment contract" or "contract" means any contract for a retail installment sale between a buyer and seller, entered into or performed in this state, which provides for (a) repayment in installments, whether or not such contract contains a title retention provision, and in which the buyer agrees to pay a finance charge, or in which the buyer does not agree to pay a finance charge but the goods or services are available at a lesser price if paid for by either cash or credit card, or in which the buyer would have received any additional goods or services or any higher quality goods or services at no added cost over the total amount payable in installments if the sale had been for cash, or (b) which provides for payment in more than four installments. When taken or given in connection with a retail installment sale, the term includes but is not limited to a security agreement and a contract for the bailment or leasing of goods by which the bailee or lessee contracts to pay as compensation for their use a sum substantially equivalent to or in excess of their value and by which it is agreed that the bailee or lessee will become, or for no other or for a nominal consideration has the option of becoming, the owner of the goods upon full compliance with the terms of the contract. **Leg.H.** Added Stats 1959 ch 201 §1, operative January 1, 1960. Amended Stats 1961 ch 1214 §1; Stats 1963 ch 819 §6, effective January 1, 1965; Stats 1969 ch 1192 §1; Stats 1970 ch 546 §4; Stats 1979 ch 805 §4.

§1802.7. "Retail installment account" or "installment account" or "revolving account"

"Retail installment account" or "installment account" or "revolving account" means an account established by an agreement entered into in this state, pursuant to which the buyer promises to pay, in installments, to a retail seller, his outstanding balance incurred in retail installment sales, whether or not a security interest in the goods sold is retained by the seller, and which provides for a finance charge which is expressed as a percent of the periodic balances to accrue thereafter providing such charge is not capitalized or stated as a dollar amount in such agreement. **Leg.H.** Added Stats 1959 ch 201 §1, operative January 1, 1960. Amended Stats 1970 ch 546 §5.

§1802.8. "Cash price"

"Cash price" means the cash price stated in a retail installment contract for which the seller would sell or furnish to the buyer and the buyer would buy or obtain from the seller the goods or services which are the subject matter of a retail installment contract if the sale were a sale for cash instead of a retail installment sale. The cash price shall include any taxes and cash prices for accessories and services, if any, included in a retail installment sale. **Leg.H.** Added Stats 1959 ch 201 §1, operative January 1, 1960. Amended Stats 1969 ch 625 §1; Stats 1981 ch 1075 §2, operative October 1, 1982.

§1802.9. "Total sale price"

"Total sale price" means the total of the cash price of the goods or services, the amounts, if any, included for insurance, official fees, and the finance charge. **Leg.H.** Added Stats 1959 ch 201 §1, operative January 1, 1960. Amended Stats 1969 ch 625 §2; Stats 1970 ch 546 §6; Stats 1981 ch 1075 §3, operative October 1, 1982.

§1802.10. "Finance charge"

"Finance charge" means the amount however denominated or expressed which the retail buyer contracts to pay or pays for the privilege of purchasing goods or services to be paid for by the buyer in installments. "Finance charge" does not include the amounts, if any, charged for insurance premiums, including premiums of the kind and to the extent described in paragraph (2) of subsection (e) of Section 226.4 of Regulation Z, delinquency charges, attorney's fees, court costs, collection expenses, official fees, extension or deferral agreement charges as provided by Section 1807.1, or amounts for insurance, repairs to or preservation of the goods, or preservation of the holder's security interest therein advanced by the holder subsequent to the execution of a contract. **Leg.H.** Added Stats 1959 ch 201 §1, operative January 1, 1960. Amended Stats 1969 ch 625 §3; Stats 1970 ch 546 §7; Stats 1980 ch 1380 §4, effective October 1, 1980; Stats 1984 ch 199 §1.

§1802.11. "Amount financed;" "Unpaid balance"

(a) "Amount financed" means the amount required to be disclosed pursuant to paragraph (7) of subdivision (c) of Section 1803.3.

(b) "Unpaid balance" means the cash price of the goods or services which are the subject matter of the retail installment sale, plus the amounts, if any, included in a retail installment sale for insurance and official fees, minus the amount of the buyer's downpayment in money or goods. **Leg.H.** Added Stats 1959 ch 201 §1, operative January 1, 1960. Amended Stats 1969 ch 625 §4; Stats 1970 ch 546 §8; Stats 1980 ch 1380 §5, effective October 1, 1980; Stats 1981 ch 1075 §4, operative October 1, 1982.

§1802.12. "Total of payments"

"Total of payments" means the amount required to be disclosed pursuant to subdivision (h) of Section 226.18 of Regulation Z. The term includes any portion of the downpayment deferred until not later than the second otherwise scheduled payment and which is not subject to a finance charge. **Leg.H.** Added Stats 1959 ch 201 §1, operative January 1, 1960. Amended Stats 1970 ch 546 §9; Stats 1981 ch 1075 §5, operative October 1, 1982.

§1802.13. "Holder"

"Holder" means the retail seller who acquires a retail installment contract or installment account executed, incurred or entered into by a retail buyer, or if the contract or installment account is purchased by a financing agency or other assignee, the financing agency or other assignee. The term does not include the pledgee of or the holder of a security interest in an aggregate number of such contracts or installment accounts to secure a bona fide loan thereon. **Leg.H.** Added Stats 1959 ch 201 §1, operative January 1, 1960.

§1802.14. "Official fees"

"Official fees" means the fees required by law and actually to be paid to the appropriate public officer to perfect a lien or other security interest, on or in goods, retained or taken by a seller under a retail installment contract or installment account, and license, certificate of title, and registration fees imposed by law. **Leg.H.** Added Stats 1959 ch 201 §1, operative January 1, 1960. Amended Stats 1970 ch 546 §10.

§1802.15. "Person"

"Person" means an individual, partnership, corporation, limited liability company, association or other group, however organized. **Leg.H.** Added Stats 1959 ch 201 §1, operative January 1, 1960. Amended Stats 1994 ch 1010 §43 (SB 2053).

§1802.16. "Financing agency"

"Financing agency" means a person engaged in this State in whole or in part in the business of purchasing retail installment contracts, or installment accounts from one or more retail sellers. The term includes but is not limited to a bank, trust company, private banker, or investment company, if so engaged. **Leg.H.** Added Stats 1959 ch 201 §1, operative January 1, 1960.

§1802.17. "Billing cycle"

"Billing cycle" means the time interval between regular monthly billing statement dates. **Leg.H.** Added Stats 1970 ch 546 §12.

Prior Law: Former §1802.17, relating to meaning of "retail installment account", was added Stats 1969 ch 625 §5 and repealed Stats 1970 ch 546 §11.

§1802.18. "Regulation Z"

"Regulation Z" means any rule, regulation, or interpretation promulgated by the Board of Governors of the Federal Reserve System ("Board") under the Federal Truth in Lending Act, as amended (15 U.S.C. 1601, et seq.), and any interpretation or approval issued by an official or employee of the Federal Reserve System duly authorized by the board under the Truth in Lending Act, as amended, to issue such interpretations or approvals. **Leg.H.** Added Stats 1970 ch 546 §13. Amended Stats 1979 ch 805 §5.

§1802.19. Transactions subject to chapter

(a) For the purposes of this chapter, a retail installment contract, contract, retail installment account, installment account, or revolving account shall be deemed to have been made in this state and, therefore, subject to the provisions of this chapter, if either the seller offers or agrees in this state to sell to a buyer who is a resident of this state or if such buyer accepts or makes the offer in this state to buy, regardless of the situs of the contract as specified therein.

(b) Any solicitation or communication to sell, oral or written, originating outside of this state, but forwarded to, and received in this state by, a buyer who is a resident of this state, shall be deemed to be an offer or agreement to sell in this state.

(c) Any solicitation or communication to buy, oral or written, originating within this state, from a buyer who is a resident of this state, but forwarded to, and received by, a retail seller outside of this state, shall be deemed to be a an acceptance or offer to buy in this state. **Leg.H.** Added Stats 1976 ch 508 §1.

§1802.20. "Simple-interest basis"

"Simple-interest basis" means the determination of a finance charge, other than an administrative finance charge, by applying a constant rate to the unpaid balance as it changes from time to time, either:

(a) Calculated on the basis of a 365-day year and actual days elapsed (although the seller may, but need not, adjust its calculations to account for leap years); reference in this chapter to the "365-day basis" shall mean this method of determining the finance charge, or

(b) For contracts entered into prior to January 1, 1988, calculated on the basis of a 360-day year consisting of 12 months of 30 days each and on the assumption that all payments will be received by the seller on their respective due dates; reference in this chapter to the "360-day basis" shall mean this method of determining the finance charge. **Leg.H.** Added Stats 1979 ch 805 §6.

§1802.21. "Precomputed basis"

"Precomputed basis" means the determination of a finance charge by multiplying the original unpaid balance of the contract by a rate and multiplying that product by the number of payment periods elapsing between the date on which the finance charge begins to be assessed and the date of the last scheduled payment. **Leg.H.** Added Stats 1979 ch 805 §7.

ARTICLE 3
Provisions of Retail Installment Contracts

Form. §1803.1.
Contents. §1803.2.
Disclosures. §1803.3.
Blank spaces. §1803.4.
Cost of insurance. §1803.5.
Charges and costs. §1803.6.
Delivery and acknowledgment. §1803.7.
Mail or telephone sales. §1803.8.
Rescission. §1803.9.
Inducements. §1803.10.
Periodic rate. §1803.11.

§1803.1. Form

A retail installment contract shall be dated and in writing; the printed portion thereof shall be in at least eight-point type. **Leg.H.** Added Stats 1959 ch 201 §1, operative January 1, 1960.

§1803.2. Contents

Except as provided in Section 1808.3, every retail installment contract shall be contained in a single document that shall contain:

(a) The entire agreement of the parties with respect to the cost and terms of payment for the goods and services, including any promissory notes or any other evidences of indebtedness between the parties relating to the transaction.

(b)(1) At the top of the contract the words "Security Agreement" shall appear in at least 12-point bold type where a security interest in the goods is retained or a security interest on other goods or realty is obtained by the seller as security for the goods or services purchased.

(2) At the top of the contract the words "Retail Installment Contract" shall appear in at least 12-point bold type where a security interest is not retained or obtained by the seller as security for the goods or services purchased.

(3) Any contract for goods or services that provides for a security interest in real property shall also provide the following notice, written in the same language, e.g., Spanish, as used in the contract: "WARNING TO BUYER: IF YOU SIGN THIS CONTRACT, YOU WILL BE PUTTING UP YOUR HOME AS SECURITY. THIS MEANS THAT YOUR HOME COULD BE SOLD WITHOUT YOUR PERMISSION AND WITHOUT ANY COURT ACTION IF YOU MISS ANY PAYMENT AS REQUIRED BY THIS CONTRACT." This notice shall be printed in at least 14-point boldface type, shall be set apart from the rest of the contract by a border, and shall appear directly above the space reserved for the signature of the buyer. A security interest created in any contract described in this paragraph that does not provide the notice as required by this paragraph shall be void and unenforceable.

As used in this subdivision, the term "security interest" refers to a contractual interest in property and not to a mechanic's lien or other interest in property arising by operation of law.

(c) Where the contract includes a finance charge that is determined on the precomputed basis and provides that the unearned portion of the finance charge to be refunded upon full prepayment of the contract is to be determined by a method other than actuarial, a notice in at least 10-point bold type if the contract is printed reading as follows: "Notice to buyer: (1) Do not sign this agreement before you read it or if it contains any blank spaces to be filled in. (2) You are entitled to a completely filled-in copy of this agreement. (3) You can prepay the full amount due under this agreement at any time and obtain a partial refund of the finance charge if it is $1 or more. Because of the way the amount of this refund will be figured, the time when you prepay could increase the ultimate cost of credit under this agreement. (4) If you desire to pay off in advance the full amount due, the amount of the refund you are entitled to, if any, will be furnished upon request."

(d) Where the contract includes a finance charge that is determined on the precomputed basis and provides for the actuarial method for computing the unearned portion of the finance charge upon prepayment in full, a notice in at least 10-point bold type if the contract is printed reading as follows: "Notice to buyer: (1) Do not sign this agreement before you read it or if it contains any blank spaces to be filled in. (2) You are entitled to a completely filled-in copy of this agreement. (3) You can prepay the full amount due under this agreement at any time and obtain a partial refund of the finance charge if it is $1 or more. (4) If you desire to pay off in advance the full amount due, the amount of the refund you are entitled to, if any, will be furnished upon request."

(e) Where the contract includes a finance charge that is determined on the simple-interest basis, a notice in at least 10-point bold type if the contract is printed reading as follows: "Notice to buyer: (1) Do not sign this agreement before you read it or if it contains any blank spaces to be filled in. (2) You are entitled to a completely filled-in copy of this agreement. (3) You can prepay the full amount due under this agreement at any time. (4) If you desire to pay off in advance the full amount due, the amount which is outstanding will be furnished upon request."

(f) This section shall become operative on October 1, 1995.

(g) The form specified in this section may be used before October 1, 1995, to comply with the provisions of this section as amended and repealed by Section 2 of Chapter 888 of the Statutes of 1994. **Leg.H.** Added Stats 1994 ch 888 §3 (AB 3269), operative October 1, 1995. Amended Stats 1995 ch 91 §17 (SB 975) (ch 153 prevails), ch 153 §1 (AB 1635), effective July 24, 1995, operative October 1, 1995.

Prior Law: Former §1803.2, similar to the present section, was added Stats 1979 ch 805 §7.5, amended Stats 1980 ch 1380 §7, effective October 1, 1980, Stats 1981 ch 107 §2, effective June 29, 1981, Stats 1982 ch 129 §2, effective March 24, 1982, operative October 1, 1982, Stats 1994 ch 888 §2, operative until October 1, 1995, and repealed, operative October 1, 1995, by its own terms.

Former §1803.2, similar to the present section, was added Stats 1959 ch 201 §1, operative January 1, 1960, amended Stats 1961 ch 1214 §2, Stats 1963 ch 819 §7, ch 1603 §3, Stats 1968 ch 452 §1, Stats 1969 ch 61 §1, ch 625 §5.5, Stats 1970 ch 546 §14, Stats 1971 ch 1061 §1, operative July 1, 1972, Stats 1979 ch 805 §7.3, Stats 1980 ch 1380 §6, effective October 1, 1980, Stats 1981 ch 107 §1, effective June 29, 1981, Stats 1982 ch 129 §1, effective March 24, 1982, and repealed, effective October 1, 1982, by its own terms.

§1803.3. Disclosures

Except as provided in Article 8 (commencing with Section 1808.1) of this chapter, a contract shall contain the following:

(a) The names of the seller and the buyer, the place of business of the seller, the residence or place of business of the buyer as specified by the buyer and a description of the goods or services sufficient to identify them. Services or multiple items of goods may be described in general terms and may be described in detail sufficient to identify them in a separate writing.

(b) Every contract subject to this chapter shall contain the disclosures required by Regulation Z whether or not Regulation Z applies to the transaction. In addition, to the extent applicable, the contract shall contain the other disclosures and notices required by, and shall satisfy the requirements and limitations of, this section. The disclosures required by subdivision (c) may be itemized or subtotaled to a greater extent than as required by that subdivision and shall be made together and in the sequence set forth in that subdivision. No particular terminology is required to disclose the items set forth in subdivision (c) except as therein expressly provided. Except as otherwise provided by this subdivision (b), these disclosures and notices may appear in the contract in any location or sequence and may be combined or interspersed with other provisions of the contract.

(c) The contract shall contain the following disclosures, as applicable, which shall be labeled "itemization of the amount financed":

(1)(A) The cash price, exclusive of taxes imposed on the sale.
(B) Taxes imposed on the sale.
(C) The total of the above.

(2) An itemization of the amount to be paid to any public officer for official fees.

(3) The aggregate amount of premiums agreed, upon execution of the contract, to be paid for policies of insurance included in the contract, excluding the amount of any insurance premium included in the finance charge.

(4) A subtotal representing the sum of the foregoing items.

(5) The amount of the buyer's downpayment, which downpayment shall not include any administrative finance charge charged, received, or

collected by the seller pursuant to subdivision (c) of Section 1805.1 and as shown as item (6), itemized to show the following:

(A) The net agreed value of the property being traded in.

(B) The amount of any portion of downpayment to be deferred until not later than the due date of the second regularly scheduled installment under the contract and which is not subject to a finance charge.

(C) The amount of any manufacturer's rebate applied or to be applied to the downpayment.

(D) The remaining amount paid or to be paid by the buyer as a downpayment.

(6) The amount of any administrative finance charge, labeled "prepaid finance charge."

(7) The difference between item (4) and the sum of items (5) and (6), labeled "amount financed."

(d) If the payment of all or a portion of the downpayment is to be deferred, the deferred payment shall be reflected in the payment schedule disclosed pursuant to Regulation Z.

(e) If the downpayment includes property being traded in, the contract shall contain a brief description of that property.

(f)(1) Where the contract includes a finance charge determined on the precomputed basis, the contract shall identify the method of computing the unearned portion of the finance charge in the event of prepayment in full of the buyer's obligation and contain a statement of the amount or method of computation of any charge that may be deducted from the amount of any such unearned finance charge in computing the amount that will be credited to the obligation or refunded to the buyer. Reference to the Rule of 78's, the sum of the digits, the sum of the periodic time balances or the actuarial method shall constitute a sufficient identification of the method of computing the unearned portion of the finance charge.

(2) Where the contract includes a finance charge which is determined on the simple-interest basis but provides for a minimum finance charge in the event of prepayment in full, the contract shall contain a statement of that fact and the amount of the minimum finance charge or its method of calculation.

(g) The contract shall contain an itemization of any insurance included as part of the amount financed disclosed pursuant to paragraph (3) of subdivision (c) and of any insurance included as part of the finance charge. The itemization shall identify the type of insurance coverage and the premium charged therefor, and, if the insurance expires before the date of the last scheduled installment included in the repayment schedule, the term of the insurance shall be stated. **Leg.H.** Added Stats 1959 ch 201 §1, operative January 1, 1960. Amended Stats 1969 ch 625 §6; 1970 ch 546 §15; Stats 1979 ch 805 §8; Stats 1980 ch 1380 §8, effective October 1, 1980; Stats 1981 ch 1075 §6, operative October 1, 1982.

§1803.4. Blank spaces

The seller shall not obtain the signature of the buyer to a contract when it contains blank spaces to be filled in after it has been signed. **Leg.H.** Added Stats 1959 ch 201 §1, operative January 1, 1960.

§1803.5. Cost of insurance

If the cost of any insurance is included in the contract and a separate charge is made to the buyer for such insurance:

(a) The contract shall state whether the insurance is to be procured by the buyer or the seller.

(b) The amount, included for such insurance, shall not exceed the premiums chargeable in accordance with rate fixed for such insurance by the insurer.

(c) If the insurance is to be procured by the seller or holder, he shall, within 45 days after delivery of the goods or furnishing of the services under the contract, deliver, mail or cause to be mailed to the buyer, at his address as specified in the contract, a notice thereof or a copy of the policy or policies of insurance or a certificate or certificates of the insurance so procured.

(d) The provisions of Insurance Code Section 1668 shall apply to any violation of this section. **Leg.H.** Added Stats 1959 ch 201 §1, operative January 1, 1960.

§1803.6. Charges and costs

(a) A contract may provide that for each installment in default the buyer shall pay a delinquency charge not in excess of one of the following amounts:

(1) For a period in default of not less than 10 days, an amount not in excess of ten dollars ($10).

(2) For a period in default of not less than 15 days, an amount not in excess of fifteen dollars ($15).

(b) Only one delinquency charge may be collected on any installment regardless of the period during which it remains in default. Payments timely received by the seller under a written extension or deferral agreement shall not be subject to any delinquency charge. The contract may also provide for payment of any actual and reasonable costs of collection occasioned by removal of the goods from the state without written permission of the holder, or by the failure of the buyer to notify the holder of any change of residence, or by the failure of the buyer to communicate with the holder for a period of 45 days after any default in making payments due under the contract. **Leg.H.** Added Stats 1959 ch 201 §1, operative January 1, 1960. Amended Stats 1980 ch 1380 §9, effective October 1, 1980; Stats 1994 ch 168 §1 (SB 1583); Stats 1996 ch 301 §1 (SB 2050).

§1803.7. Delivery and acknowledgment

The seller shall deliver to the buyer at the time of the buyer's signature a legible copy of the contract or of any other document which the seller has required or requested the buyer to sign, and which he has signed, during the contract negotiation. In addition to the penalties provided under Article 12.2 (commencing with Section 1812.6) of this chapter, until the seller delivers such documents the buyer shall be obligated to pay only the cash price. Any acknowledgment by the buyer of delivery of a copy of such documents shall be printed or written in a size equal to at least 10-point bold type and, if contained in the contract shall also appear directly above the space reserved for the buyer's signature. The buyer's written acknowledgment, conforming to the requirements of this section of delivery of a copy of such documents shall be a rebuttable presumption of such delivery and of compliance with this section and Section 1803.4, in any action or proceeding by or against an assignee of the contract without knowledge to the contrary when he purchases the contract. If the holder furnishes the buyer a copy of such documents, or a notice containing the items required by Section 1803.3 and stating that the buyer should notify the holder in writing within 30 days if he was not furnished a copy of the contract or of any other document which the seller had required or requested the buyer to sign, and which he did sign, during the contract negotiation, and no such notification is given, it shall be conclusively presumed in favor of the third party that copies of such documents were furnished as required by Sections 1803.4 and 1803.7. **Leg.H.** Added Stats 1959 ch 201 §1, operative January 1, 1960. Amended Stats 1961 ch 1214 §3; Stats 1969 ch 353 §1; Stats 1970 ch 546 §16.

§1803.8. Mail or telephone sales

Retail installment sales negotiated and entered into by mail or telephone without personal solicitation by a salesman or other representative of the seller, where the seller's cash and deferred payment prices and other terms are clearly set forth in a catalog or other printed solicitation of business which is generally available to the public, may be made as hereinafter provided. All of the provisions of this chapter shall apply to such sales except that the seller shall not be required to deliver a copy of the contract to the buyer as provided in Section 1803.7, and if, when the proposed retail installment sale contract is received by the seller from the buyer, there are blank spaces to be filled in, the seller may insert in the appropriate blank spaces the amounts of money and other terms which are set forth in the seller's catalog which is then in effect. In lieu of the copy of the contract provided for in Section 1803.7 the seller shall, within 15 days from the date of shipment of goods, furnish to the buyer a written statement of the items inserted in such blank spaces. **Leg.H.** Added Stats 1959 ch 201 §1, operative January 1, 1960.

§1803.9. Rescission

If it is explicitly understood between the seller and the buyer that all or any part of the cash price will be paid from the proceeds of a loan to be obtained by the buyer from a third party, the contract of sale or purchase order may be rescinded at the election of the buyer, and all considerations thereupon shall be returned by the respective parties without further demand, if the buyer is unable to obtain such third-party financing upon reasonable terms after having made a reasonable effort to obtain it, and buyer notifies the seller of the rescission within three business days. **Leg.H.** Added Stats 1979 ch 1151 §3.

Prior Law: Former §1803.9, relating to sales of $50 dollars or less, was added Stats 1963 §4 and repealed Stats 1968 ch 984 §1.

§1803.10. Inducements

It shall be unlawful for any seller to induce or attempt to induce any person to enter into a contract subject to this act by offering a rebate, discount, commission, or other consideration, contingent upon the happening of a future event, on the condition that the buyer either sells, or gives information or assistance for the purpose of leading to a sale by the seller of, the same or related goods. **Leg.H.** Added Stats 1968 ch 452 §2.

§1803.11. Periodic rate

It shall be unlawful for any seller to solicit buyers, in any advertisement, to enter into a retail installment contract with it if the seller does not intend to sell that retail installment contract to a financing agency or other assignee, unless the advertisement clearly states the periodic rate or range of periodic rates, expressed as an annual percentage rate or a range of annual percentage rates that will be used to determine the finance charge imposed on the retail installment contract. **Leg.H.** Added Stats 1991 ch 819 §1 (SB 1105).

§1804. [Section repealed 1931]

Leg.H. Enacted Stats 1872. Repealed Stats 1931 ch 1070 §1.

ARTICLE 4
Restrictions on Retail Installment Contracts

Prohibited contractual provisions. §1804.1.
Assignee of seller. §1804.2.
Security interests. §1804.3.
Effect of prohibited provision in contract. §1804.4.

§1804.1. Prohibited contractual provisions

No contract or obligation shall contain any provision by which:

(a) The buyer agrees not to assert against a seller a claim or defense arising out of the sale or agrees not to assert against an assignee such a claim or defense other than as provided in Section 1804.2.

(b) In the absence of the buyer's default in the performance of any of his or her obligations, the holder may accelerate the maturity of any part or all of the amount owing thereunder.

(c) A power of attorney is given to confess judgment in this state, or an assignment of wages is given; provided, that nothing herein contained shall prohibit the giving of an assignment of wages contained in a separate instrument, executed pursuant to Section 300 of the Labor Code.

(d) The seller or holder of the contract or other person acting on his or her behalf is given authority to enter upon the buyer's premises unlawfully or to commit any breach of the peace in the repossession of goods.

(e) The buyer waives any right of action against the seller or holder of the contract or other person acting on his or her behalf, for any illegal act committed in the collection of payments under the contract or in the repossession of goods.

(f) The buyer executes a power of attorney appointing the seller or holder of the contract, or other person acting on his or her behalf, as the buyer's agent in collection of payments under the contract or in the repossession of goods.

(g) The buyer relieves the seller from liability for any legal remedies which the buyer may have against the seller under the contract or any separate instrument executed in connection therewith.

(h) The buyer agrees to the payment of any charge by reason of the exercise of his or her right to rescind or void the contract.

(i) The seller or holder of the contract is given the right to commence an action on a contract under the provisions of this chapter in a county other than the county in which the contract was in fact signed by the buyer, the county in which the buyer resides at the commencement of the action, the county in which the buyer resided at the time that the contract was entered into, or in the county in which the goods purchased pursuant to the contract have been so affixed to real property as to become a part of such real property.

(j) The seller takes a security interest, other than a mechanics' lien, in the buyer's real property which is the buyer's primary residence where the buyer is a person who is 65 years of age or older and the contract is for a home improvement, as defined in Section 7151.2 of the Business and Professions Code. **Leg.H.** Added Stats 1959 ch 201 §1, operative January 1, 1960. Amended Stats 1961 ch 1214 §4; Stats 1963 ch 1310 §1; Stats 1965 ch 776 §1; Stats 1999 ch 512 §2 (SB 187).

§1804.2. Assignee of seller

(a) An assignee of the seller's rights is subject to all equities and defenses of the buyer against the seller arising out of the sale, notwithstanding an agreement to the contrary, but the assignee's liability may not exceed the amount of the debt owing to the assignee at the time of the assignment.

(b) The assignee shall have recourse against the seller to the extent of any liability incurred by the assignee pursuant to this section regardless of whether the assignment was with or without recourse. **Leg.H.** Added Stats 1967 ch 1294 §2. Amended Stats 1971 ch 999 §1; Stats 1975 ch 66 §1.

Prior Law: Former §1804.2, relating to notice of assignment, was added Stats 1959 ch 201 §1, operative January 1, 1960, amended Stats 1963 ch 1602 §1, and repealed Stats 1967 ch 1294 §1.

§1804.3. Security interests

(a) No contract other than one for services shall provide for a security interest in any goods theretofore fully paid for or which have not been sold by the seller.

(b) Any contract for goods which provides for a security interest in real property where the primary goods sold are not to be attached to the real property shall be a violation of this chapter and subject to the penalties set forth in Article 12.2 (commencing with Section 1812.6).

(c) This section shall become operative October 1, 1982. **Leg.H.** Added Stats 1980 ch 1380 §11, effective October 1, 1980, operative July 1, 1981. Amended Stats 1981 ch 107 §4, effective June 29, 1981, operative April 1, 1982; Stats 1982 ch 129 §4, effective March 25, 1982, operative October 1, 1982.

Prior Law: Former §1804.3, similar to the present section, was added Stats 1959 ch 201 §1, operative July 1, 1960, amended Stats 1970 ch 1483 §1, Stats 1979 ch 1012 §7, Stats 1980 ch 1380 §10, effective October 1, 1980, operative until July 1, 1981, Stats 1981 ch 107 §3, effective June 29, 1981, operative until April 1, 1982, Stats 1982 ch 129 §3, effective March 24, 1982, operative until October 1, 1982, and repealed, operative October 1, 1982, by its own terms.

§1804.4. Effect of prohibited provision in contract

Any provision in a contract which is prohibited by this chapter shall be void but shall not otherwise affect the validity of the contract. **Leg.H.** Added Stats 1959 ch 201 §1, operative January 1, 1960.

§1805. [Section repealed 1931]

Leg.H. Enacted Stats 1872. Repealed Stats 1931 ch 1070 §1.

ARTICLE 5
Finance Charge Limitation

Maximum finance charge; Annual fee or charge. §1805.1.
Authorized installments. §1805.2.
Included fees, expenses and charges; Fee for dishonored check. §1805.4.
Undelivered goods; Home improvement contract. §1805.6.
Calculation of finance charge for contracts after January 1, 1983. §1805.7.
Maximum rate of finance charge. §1805.8.
Finance charges determined by more than one basis. §1805.9.

§1805.1. Maximum finance charge; Annual fee or charge

The holder of the contract shall not charge, collect, or receive a finance charge which exceeds the dollar amount shown pursuant to subdivision (b) of Section 1803.3, except to the extent (a) caused by the holder's receipt of one or more payments under a contract which provides for determination of the finance charge or a portion thereof on the 365-day basis at a time or times other than as originally scheduled, whether or not the parties enter into an agreement pursuant to Section 1807.1, (b) permitted by paragraph (2), (3), or (4) of subdivision (c) of Section 226.17 of Regulation Z, or (3) permitted by Section 1805.8.

No annual fee or charge shall be made in any retail installment contract. **Leg.H.** Added Stats 1982 ch 129 §10 effective March 25, 1982. Amended Stats 1982 ch 1611 §2, effective September 30, 1982, operative January 1, 1984; Stats 1983 ch 1157 §2, operative January 1, 1986; Stats 1985 ch 227 §2, operative January 1, 1988; Stats 1988 ch 479 §1, operative until January 1, 1992; Stats 1991 ch 819 §2 (SB 1105).

Prior Law: Former §1805.1, similar to the present section, was added Stats 1982 ch 129 §9, effective March 25, 1982, amended Stats 1982 ch 1611 §1, effective September 30, 1982, ch 1613 §1.7, effective September 30, 1982, and repealed Stats 1982 ch 1614 §2.5.

Former §1805.1, similar to the present section, was added Stats 1982 ch 129 §8, effective March 25, 1982, amended Stats 1982 ch 1613 §1, effective September 30, 1982, and repealed, effective October 1, 1982, by its own terms.

Former §1805.1, similar to the present section, was added Stats 1980 ch 1381 §4, operative April 1, 1982, amended Stats 1981 ch 1146 §2.5, and repealed Stats 1982 ch 129 §7, effective March 25, 1982.

Former §1805.1, similar to the present section, was added Stats 1979 ch 805 §10, amended Stats 1980 ch 1380 §12, effective October 1, 1980, ch 1381 §2, Stats 1981 ch 1146 §§1, 1.5, and repealed Stats 1982 ch 129 §§5, 6, effective March 25, 1982.

Former §1805.1, similar to the present section, was added Stats 1959 ch 201 §1, operative January 1, 1960, amended Stats 1970 ch 546 §18, and repealed Stats 1979 ch 805 §9.

There was another section of this number, similar to the present section, added Stats 1988 ch 479 §1.5, operative January 1, 1992, and repealed Stats 1991 ch 819 §3 (SB 1105).

§1805.1a. [Section repealed 1991]

Leg.H. Added Stats 1988 ch 479 §2.5, operative January 1, 1992. Repealed Stats 1991 ch 819 §4 (SB 1105). The repealed section related to "household, furniture, furnishings, or appliances".

Prior Law: Former section, relating to household, furniture, furnishings, or appliances, was added Stats 1982 ch 374 §1, effective July 2, 1982, and repealed Stats 1988 ch 479 §2.

§1805.2. Authorized installments

Contracts may be payable in successive monthly, semimonthly or weekly installments. **Leg.H.** Added Stats 1959 ch 201 §1, operative January 1, 1960.

§1805.3. [Section repealed 1991]

Leg.H. Added Stats 1988 ch 479 §3.5, operative January 1, 1992. Repealed Stats 1991 ch 819 §5 (SB 1105). The repealed section related to finance charge rate for unequal installments.

Prior Law: Former section, relating to finance charge rate for unequal installments, was added Stats 1959 ch 201 §1, operative January 1, 1960, amended Stats 1970 ch 546 §19, and repealed Stats 1988 ch 479 §3.

§1805.4. Included fees, expenses and charges; Fee for dishonored check

The finance charge shall be inclusive of all charges incident to investigating and making the contract and for the extension of the credit provided for in the contract, and no fee, expense or other charge whatsoever shall be taken, received, reserved or contracted for except as otherwise provided in this chapter.

The seller or holder of a retail installment contract may charge and collect a fee not to exceed fifteen dollars ($15) for the return by a depository institution of a dishonored check, negotiable order of withdrawal, or share draft issued in connection with the retail installment contract. The fee is not included in charges as defined in this chapter or in determining the applicable charges which may be made under this chapter. **Leg.H.** Added Stats 1959 ch 201 §1, operative January 1, 1960. Amended Stats 1970 ch 546 §20; Stats 1982 ch 512 §1; Stats 1993 ch 101 §1 (SB 329).

§1805.5. [Section repealed 1991]

Leg.H. Added Stats 1988 ch 479 §4.5, operative January 1, 1992. Repealed Stats 1991 ch 819 §6 (SB 1105). The repealed section related to prohibition against splitting sales transaction to receive higher rate of finance charge.

Prior Law: Former section, relating to prohibition against splitting sales transaction to receive higher rate of finance charge, was added Stats 1959 ch 201 §1, operative January 1, 1906, amended Stats 1968 ch 48 §2, Stats 1970 ch 546 §21, and repealed Stats 1988 ch 479 §4.

§1805.6. Undelivered goods; Home improvement contract

(a) Notwithstanding the provisions of any contract to the contrary, except as provided in subdivision (b) or (c), no retail seller shall assess any finance charge for goods purchased under a retail installment contract until the goods are in the buyer's possession.

(b) A finance charge may be assessed for such undelivered goods, as follows:

(1) From the date when such goods are available for pickup by the buyer and the buyer is notified of their availability, or

(2) From the date of purchase, when such goods are delivered or available for pickup by the buyer within 10 days of the date of purchase.

(c) In the case of a home improvement contract as defined in Section 7151.2 of the Business and Professions Code, a finance charge may be assessed from the approximate date of commencement of the work as set forth in the home improvement contract. **Leg.H.** Added Stats 1975 ch 1041 §1. Amended Stats 1976 ch 1271 §3, effective September 28, 1976; Stats 1977 ch 868 §3; Stats 1979 ch 1000 §4; Stats 1980 ch 1380 §15, effective October 1, 1980; Stats 1981 ch 1075 §8, operative October 1, 1982.

Prior Law: There was another section of this number, similar to the present section, which was added Stats 1976 ch 1271 §4, effective September 18, 1976, operative January 1, 1980, amended Stats 1977 ch 868 §4, and repealed Stats 1979 ch 1000 §3.

§1805.7. Calculation of finance charge for contracts after January 1, 1983

All contracts entered into between a buyer and a seller on or after January 1, 1983, shall provide for the calculation of the finance charge contemplated by item (1) of subdivision (a) of Section 1805.1 on the simple-interest basis if the date on which the final installment is due, according to the original terms of the contract, is more than 62 months after the date of the contract. **Leg.H.** Added Stats 1979 ch 805 §11.

§1805.8. Maximum rate of finance charge

The maximum rate of finance charge which may be imposed on amounts advanced by the holder subsequent to the execution of the contract for insurance, repairs to or preservation of the goods, or preservation of the holder's security interest therein, shall not exceed the annual percentage rate disclosed pursuant to item (b) of Section 1803.3. **Leg.H.** Added Stats 1979 ch 805 §11.5. Amended Stats 1981 ch 1075 §9, operative October 1, 1982.

§1805.9. Finance charges determined by more than one basis

No contract shall provide for a finance charge which is determined in part by the precomputed basis and in part by the simple-interest basis, except for any finance charge permitted by Section 1805.8. **Leg.H.** Added Stats 1979 ch 805 §11.7.

§1806. [Section repealed 1931]

Leg.H. Enacted Stats 1872. Repealed Stats 1931 ch 1070 §1.

ARTICLE 6
Payments

Buyer's payment to last known holder as discharge. §1806.1.
Statement of amount due. §1806.2.
Payment of entire indebtedness before maturity. §1806.3.
Acknowledgment of payment in full. §1806.4.

§1806.1. Buyer's payment to last known holder as discharge

Unless the buyer has notice of actual or intended assignment of a contract or installment account, payment thereunder made by the buyer to the last known holder of such contract or installment account, shall to the extent of the payment, discharge the buyer's obligation. **Leg.H.** Added Stats 1959 ch 201 §1, operative January 1, 1960.

§1806.2. Statement of amount due

At any time after its execution, but not later than one year after the last payment thereunder, the holder of a contract shall, upon written request of the buyer made in good faith, promptly give or forward to the buyer a detailed written statement which will state with accuracy the total amount, if any, unpaid thereunder. Such a statement shall be supplied by the holder once each year without charge; if any additional statement is requested by the buyer, the holder shall supply such statement to the buyer at a charge not exceeding one dollar ($1) for each additional statement supplied to the buyer. The provisions of this section shall apply only to those transactions wherein, instead of periodic statements of account, the buyer is provided with a passbook or payment book in which all payments, credits, charges and the unpaid balance is entered. **Leg.H.** Added Stats 1959 ch 201 §1, operative January 1, 1960. Amended Stats 1969 ch 625 §7.

§1806.3. Payment of entire indebtedness before maturity

(a) Notwithstanding any provision of a contract to the contrary, the buyer may pay at any time before maturity the entire indebtedness evidenced by the contract without penalty. In the event of prepayment in full:

(1) If the finance charge was determined on the precomputed basis, the amount required to repay the contract shall be the outstanding contract balance as of that date, provided, however, that the buyer shall be entitled to a refund credit in the amount of the unearned portion of the finance charge. The amount of the unearned portion of the finance charge shall be at least as great a proportion of the finance charge, or if the contract has

been extended, deferred, or refinanced, of the additional charge therefor, as the sum of the periodic monthly time balances payable more than 15 days after the date of prepayment bears to the sum of all the periodic monthly time balances under the schedule of installments in the contract or, if the contract has been extended, deferred or refinanced, as so extended, deferred or refinanced. Where the amount of the refund credit is less than one dollar ($1), no refund credit need be made by the holder. Any refund credit in the amount of one dollar ($1) or more may be made in cash or credited to the outstanding obligations of the buyer under the contract.

(2) If the finance charge or a portion thereof was determined on the simple-interest basis, the amount required to prepay the contract shall be the outstanding contract balance as of that date, including any earned finance charges which are unpaid as of that date, and provided further that in cases where the finance charge or a portion thereof is determined on the 360-day basis, the payments theretofore received will be assumed to have been received on their respective due dates regardless of the actual dates on which those payments were received.

(b) Notwithstanding any provision of a contract to the contrary, whenever the indebtedness created by any retail installment contract is satisfied prior to its maturity through surrender of the collateral, repossession of the collateral, redemption of the collateral after repossession, or any judgment, the outstanding obligation of the buyer shall be determined as provided in subdivision (a); provided further that the buyer's outstanding obligation shall be computed by the holder as of the date the holder recovers the value of the collateral through disposition thereof or judgment is entered or, if the holder elects to keep the collateral in satisfaction of the buyer's indebtedness, as of the date the holder takes possession of the collateral.

(c) This section does not preclude the collection or retention by the holder of any delinquency charge made pursuant to Section 1803.6. **Leg.H.** Added Stats 1959 ch 201 §1, operative January 1, 1960. Amended Stats 1970 ch 546 §22; Stats 1973 ch 793 §1; Stats 1979 ch 805 §12; Stats 1980 ch 1380 §16, effective October 1, 1980; Stats 1988 ch 479 §5, operative until January 1, 1992; Stats 1991 ch 819 §7 (SB 1105).

Prior Law: There was another section of this number, similar to the present section, which was added Stats 1988 ch 479 §5.5, operative January 1, 1992, and repealed Stats 1991 ch 819 §8 (SB 1105).

§1806.4. Acknowledgment of payment in full

After the payment of all sums for which the buyer is obligated under a contract and upon demand made by the buyer, the holder shall deliver, or mail to the buyer at his last known address, such one or more good and sufficient instruments as may be necessary to acknowledge payment in full and to release all security in the goods under such contract. **Leg.H.** Added Stats 1959 ch 201 §1, operative January 1, 1960.

§1807. [Section repealed 1931]

Leg.H. Enacted Stats 1872. Repealed Stats 1931 ch 1070 §1.

ARTICLE 7
Refinancing and Consolidation

Extension of due date or deferral of payment of installment. §1807.1.
Refinancing payment. §1807.2.
Right of buyer to obtain new payment schedule upon default of balloon payment. §1807.3.

§1807.1. Extension of due date or deferral of payment of installment

(a) The holder of a retail installment contract may, upon agreement with the buyer, extend the scheduled due date or defer the scheduled payment of all or of any part of any installment or installments payable thereunder. No charge shall be made for any such extension or deferment unless the agreement for such extension or deferment is in writing and signed by the parties thereto.

(b) Where the contract includes a finance charge determined on the precomputed basis, the holder may charge and contract for the payment of an extension or deferral agreement charge by the buyer and collect and receive the same, but such charge may not exceed an amount equal to 1 percent per month simple interest on the amount of the installment or installments, or part thereof, extended or deferred for the period of extension or deferral. Such period shall not exceed the period from the date when such extended or deferred installment or installments, or part thereof, would have been payable in the absence of such extension or deferral, to the date when such installment or installments, or part thereof, are made payable under the agreement of extension or deferment; except that a minimum charge of one dollar ($1) for the period of extension or deferral may be made in any case where the extension or deferral agreement charge, when computed at such rate, amounts to less than one dollar ($1).

(c) Where the contract includes a finance charge determined on the simple-interest basis, the holder may charge and contract for the payment of an extension or deferral agreement charge by the buyer and collect and receive the same, but the charge for the extension or deferral agreement may not exceed the lesser of twenty-five dollars ($25) or 10 percent of the then unpaid balance of the contract. Such charge shall be in addition to any finance charges which accrue because such extended or deferred payments are received at a time other than as originally scheduled.

(d) An extension or deferral agreement may also provide for the payment by the buyer of the additional cost to the holder of the contract of premiums for continuing in force, until the end of such period of extension or deferral, any insurance coverages provided for in the contract, subject to the provisions of Section 1803.5. **Leg.H.** Added Stats 1959 ch 201 §1, operative January 1, 1960. Amended Stats 1980 ch 1380 §17, effective October 1, 1980.

§1807.2. Refinancing payment

The holder of a retail installment contract or contracts may, upon agreement in writing with the buyer, refinance the remaining amount owing on the contract or contracts by providing for a new schedule of installment payments. The holder may charge and contract for the payment of a refinance charge by the buyer and collect and receive the same, but such refinance charge shall be based upon the amount refinanced, plus any additional cost of insurance and of official fees incident to the refinancing, after the deduction of a refund credit in an amount equal to that to which the buyer would have been entitled under Section 1806.3 if he or she had prepaid in full his or her obligations under the contract or contracts. The agreement for refinancing may also provide for the payment by the buyer of the additional cost to the holder of the contract or contracts of premiums for continuing in force, until the maturity of the contract or contracts as refinanced, any insurance coverages provided for therein, subject to Section 1803.5. The refinancing agreement shall set forth:

(a) The amount of the existing outstanding balance to be refinanced, which consists of the remaining amount owing to be refinanced.

(b) The amount of any refund credit.

(c) The difference between subdivisions (a) and (b), which is the net outstanding balance to be refinanced.

(d) Any additional cost of insurance and of official fees to the buyer.

(e) The sum of subdivisions (c) and (d), which is the amount financed.

(f) The finance charge (1) as expressed as the annual percentage rate as defined in Regulation Z and (2) expressed in dollars.

(g) The number amount, and due dates or periods of payments scheduled to repay the indebtedness and the sum of those payments.

The items need not be stated in the sequence or order set forth above; additional items may be included to explain the computations made in determining the amount to be paid by the buyer. Where there is a consolidation of two or more contracts then Sections 1808.1 and 1808.2 shall apply. If the finance charge or any portion thereof is calculated on the 365-day basis, the amount of the finance charge shown pursuant to subdivision (f) shall be that amount which will be incurred by the buyer if all payments are received by the seller on their respective due dates. **Leg.H.** Added Stats 1959 ch 201 §1, operative January 1, 1960. Amended Stats 1970 ch 546 §23; Stats 1979 ch 805 §13; Stats 1981 ch 1075 §10, operative October 1, 1982; Stats 1988 ch 479 §6, operative until January 1, 1992; Stats 1991 ch 819 §9 (SB 1105).

Prior Law: There was another section of this number, similar to the present section, which was added Stats 1988 ch 479 §6.5, operative January 1, 1992, and repealed Stats 1991 ch 819 §10 (SB 1105).

§1807.3. Right of buyer to obtain new payment schedule upon default of balloon payment

(a) If any payment, other than a deferred downpayment, under a contract or refinancing agreement is more than twice the amount of an otherwise regularly scheduled equal payment, the contract or refinancing agreement shall contain the following provision:

"The payment schedule contained in this contract requires that you make a balloon payment of $_____ (Amount of balloon payment) which is a payment more than double the amount of the regular payments. You have an absolute right to obtain a new payment schedule if you default in the payment of any balloon payment."

(b) If the buyer defaults in the payment of any balloon payment, he or she shall be given an absolute right to obtain a new payment schedule. Unless agreed to by the buyer, the periodic payments under the new schedule shall not be substantially greater than the average of the preceding installments. **Leg.H.** Added Stats 1959 ch 201 §1, operative January 1, 1960. Amended Stats 1969 ch 625 §8; Stats 1970 ch 546 §23.5; Stats 1981 ch 1075 §11, operative October 1, 1982.

ARTICLE 8
Add-on Sales

Provisions for subsequent purchases. §1808.1.
Allocation of payments when subsequent purchase is made. §1808.2.
Memorandum when subsequent purchase made. §1808.3.
Limitation on buyer's obligation until memorandum delivered. §1808.4.
Determination of finance charge. §1808.5.

§1808.1. Provisions for subsequent purchases

A retail installment contract, which otherwise conforms to the requirements of this chapter, may contain the provision that the seller may at his option add subsequent purchases made by the buyer to the contract, and that the total price of the goods or services covered by the contract shall be increased by the price of such additional goods or services, and that all finance charges and installment payments may at the seller's option be increased proportionately, and that all terms and conditions of the contract shall apply equally to such additional goods or services. The contract may also provide that the goods purchased under the previous contract or contracts shall be security for the goods purchased under the subsequent contract but only until such time as the total of payments under the previous contract or contracts is fully paid. **Leg.H.** Added Stats 1959 ch 201 §1, operative January 1, 1960. Amended Stats 1969 ch 625 §9; Stats 1970 ch 546 §24.

§1808.2. Allocation of payments when subsequent purchase is made

When a subsequent purchase is made, the entire amount of all payments made previous thereto shall be deemed to have been applied toward the payment of the previous deferred payment price or deferred payment prices. Each payment thereafter received shall be deemed to be allocated to all of the various deferred payment prices in the same proportion or ratio as the original cash sale prices of the various purchases bear to one another; where the amount of each installment payment is increased in connection with the subsequent purchase, the subsequent payments (at the seller's election) may be deemed to be allocated as follows: an amount equal to the original payment to the previous deferred payment price, and an amount equal to the increase, to the subsequent deferred payment price. However, the amount of any initial or downpayment on the subsequent purchase shall be deemed to be allocated in its entirety to such purchase.

When a subsequent purchase is made under this section the seller shall deliver to the buyer, prior to the due date of the first installment, a memorandum which shall set forth the following:

(a) The names of the seller and the buyer, the place of business of the seller, the residence or place of business of the buyer as specified by the buyer and a description of the goods and services sufficient to identify them. Services or multiple items of goods may be described in general terms and may be described in detail in a separate writing.

(b) The cash price of the goods, services and accessories which are the subject matter of the new retail installment sale.

(c) The amount of the buyer's downpayment, itemizing the amounts paid in money and in goods and containing a brief description of the goods, if any, traded in.

(d) The difference between item (b) and item (c) which is the unpaid balance of cash price.

(e) The amount of the existing outstanding balance to be consolidated, which consists of the unpaid time balance or balances of the prior contract or contracts to be consolidated.

(f) The amount of any unearned finance charge, determined by deducting from the amount of item (e) any then unearned finance charge in an amount not less than the refund credit provided for in Article 6 (commencing with Section 1806.1) of this chapter (computed, however, without the allowance of any minimum earned finance charge).

(g) The difference between items (e) and (f), which is the net outstanding balance to be consolidated.

(h) The amount, if any, included for insurance, specifying the coverages.

(i) The amount, if any, of official fees.

(j) The unpaid balance, which is the sum of items (d), (g), (h) and (i).

(k) The finance charge (1) expressed as the annual percentage rate as defined in Regulation Z and (2) expressed in dollars, and computed in conformity with Section 1808.5.

(l) The number, amount, and due dates or periods of payment scheduled to repay the indebtedness and the sum of such payments.

(m) Any "balloon payments" as described in Section 1807.3.

The items need not be stated in the sequence or order set forth above; additional items may be included to explain the computations made in determining the amount to be paid by the buyer. If the finance charge or any portion thereof is calculated on the 365-day basis, the amount of the finance charge shown pursuant to item (k) shall be that amount which will be incurred by the buyer if all payments are received by the seller on their respective due dates. **Leg.H.** Added Stats 1959 ch 201 §1, operative January 1, 1960. Amended 1969 ch 625 §10; Stats 1970 ch 546 §25; Stats 1979 ch 805 §14.

§1808.3. Memorandum when subsequent purchase made

If a credit sale is one of a series of transactions made pursuant to an agreement providing for the addition of the amount financed plus the finance charge for the current sale to an existing outstanding balance, and the disclosures required under this article for the initial sale and each subsequent sale are delayed until some date prior to the date the first payment for that particular sale is due; and

(1) The customer has approved in writing both the annual percentage rate or rates and the method of treating any unearned finance charge on an existing outstanding balance in computing the finance charge or charges; and

(2) The seller retains no security interest in any property as to which he has received payments aggregating the amount of the sale price including any finance charges attributable thereto; then, for the purposes of this section, in the case of items purchased on different dates, the first purchased shall be deemed first paid for, and in the case of items purchased on the same date the lowest priced shall be deemed first paid for.

When a credit sale under this section is made, the seller shall deliver to the buyer, prior to the due date of the first installment, a memorandum which shall set forth the following:

(a) The names of the seller and the buyer, the place of business of the seller, the residence or place of business of the buyer as specified by the buyer and a description of the goods and services sufficient to identify them. Services or multiple items of goods may be described in general terms and may be described in detail in a separate writing.

(b) The cash price of the goods, services and accessories which are the subject matter of the new retail installment sale.

(c) The amount of the buyer's downpayment, itemizing the amounts paid in money and in goods and containing a brief description of the goods, if any, traded in.

(d) The difference between item (b) and item (c), which is the unpaid balance of cash price.

(e) The amount, if any, included for insurance, specifying the coverages.

(f) The amount, if any, of official fees.

(g) The amount financed, which is the sum of items (d), (e) and (f).

(h) The amount of the finance charge (1) expressed as the annual percentage rate as defined in Regulation Z and (2) expressed in dollars, which is to be computed in accordance with this chapter.

(i) The deferred payment price, which is the sum of the amounts determined under items (b), (e), (f) and (h).

(j) The previous balance, which is the amount owing on prior purchases.

(k) The number, amount, and due dates or periods of payments scheduled to repay the indebtedness and the sum of such payments.

(l) Any "balloon payments," as described in Section 1807.3.

The items need not be stated in the sequence or order set forth above; additional items may be included to explain the computations made in determining the amount to be paid by the buyer. If the finance charge or any portion thereof is calculated on the 365-day basis, the amount of the finance charge shown pursuant to item (h) shall be that amount which will be incurred by the buyer if all payments are received by the seller on their respective due dates. **Leg.H.** Added Stats 1959 ch 201 §1, operative January 1, 1960. Amended Stats 1969 ch 625 §11; Stats 1970 ch 546 §26; Stats 1979 ch 805 §15.

§1808.4. Limitation on buyer's obligation until memorandum delivered

Until the seller delivers to the buyer the memorandum as provided in Sections 1808.2 and 1808.3, the buyer shall be obligated to pay only the cash price of the subsequent purchase. **Leg.H.** Added Stats 1959 ch 201 §1, operative January 1, 1960. Amended Stats 1970 ch 546 §27.

§1808.5. Determination of finance charge

Subject to the other provisions of Article 5 (commencing with Section 1805.1), the finance charge to be included in a consolidated total of payments under subdivision (l) of Section 1808.2 shall be determined by applying the finance charge at the applicable rate to the unpaid balance under subdivision (j) of Section 1808.2, for the period from the date of the consolidation to and including the date when the final installment of the consolidated total is payable. **Leg.H.** Added Stats 1959 ch 201 §1, operative January 1, 1960. Amended Stats 1970 ch 546 §28; Stats 1979 ch 805 §16; Stats 1988 ch 479 §7, operative until January 1, 1992; Stats 1991 ch 819 §11 (SB 1105).

Prior Law: There was another section of this number, similar to the present section, which was added Stats 1988 ch 479 §7.5, operative January 1, 1992, and repealed Stats 1991 ch 819 §12 (SB 1105).

§1808.6. [Section repealed 1991]

Leg.H. Added Stats 1988 ch 479 §8.5, operative January 1, 1992. Repealed Stats 1991 ch 819 §13 (SB 1105). The repealed section related to minimum finance charges.

Prior Law: Former section, relating to minimum finance charges, was added Stats 1959 ch 201 §1, operative January 1, 1960, amended Stats 1979 ch 805 §17, Stats 1980 ch 1380 §18, effective October 1, 1980, and repealed Stats 1988 ch 479 §8.

ARTICLE 9
Terms of Purchase by Financing Agency

Rights; Notice. §1809.1.

§1809.1. Rights; Notice

Notwithstanding any contrary provision of this title a financing agency may purchase a retail installment contract or installment account from a seller on such terms and conditions and for such price as may be mutually agreed upon. No filing of notice or of the assignment, no notice to the buyer of the assignment, and no requirement that the seller be deprived of dominion over payments upon the contract or installment account or over the goods if repossessed by the seller, shall be necessary to the validity of a written assignment of a contract or installment account as against creditors, subsequent purchasers, pledgees, mortgagees or encumbrancers of the seller, except as may otherwise be required by law. **Leg.H.** Added Stats 1959 ch 201 §1, operative January 1, 1960.

ARTICLE 10
Retail Installment Accounts

Acts constituting acceptance by buyer in retail installment account agreement. §1810.
Required disclosures. §1810.1.
Finance charge. §1810.2.
Statement of account. §1810.3.
Charges and fees. §1810.4.
Cost of insurance. §1810.5.
Security interest in goods sold. §1810.6.
Protection of third party rights. §1810.7.
Application of provisions governing credit sales payments. §1810.8.
Charge for undelivered goods. §1810.10.
Statement of finance charges. §1810.11.
Delinquency and collection charges. §1810.12.

§1810. Acts constituting acceptance by buyer in retail installment account agreement

For the purposes of this article, a retail installment account agreement shall be deemed to be accepted by the buyer if (1) the buyer signs the agreement, including signing an application containing the terms of the agreement, or (2) the account is used by the buyer or a person who has been authorized by the buyer to use the account, and the buyer has been notified in writing that the use of the credit card will mean that the agreement has been accepted by the buyer. The agreement shall not become effective unless and until the buyer has been given or provided with the disclosures required pursuant to Section 1810.1, and has accepted the agreement as provided in this section. A subsequent change in any term of the agreement shall not become effective until the seller has given notice of the change and complies with the provisions of subdivision (d) of Section 1810.3. **Leg.H.** Added Stats 1995 ch 566 §1 (SB 538).

§1810.1. Required disclosures

Notwithstanding any other provisions of this article to the contrary, before the first transaction is made on any retail installment account, the seller shall disclose to the buyer in a single written statement, which the buyer may retain, in terminology consistent with the requirements of Section 1810.3, each of the following items, to the extent applicable:

(a) The conditions under which a finance charge may be imposed, including an explanation of the time period, if any, within which any credit extended may be paid without incurring a finance charge.

(b) The method of determining the balance upon which a finance charge may be imposed.

(c) The method of determining the amount of the finance charge, including the method of determining any minimum, the charge which may be imposed as a finance charge.

(d) Where one or more periodic rates may be used to compute the finance charge, each such rate, the range of balances to which it is applicable, and the corresponding annual percentage rate determined by multiplying the periodic rate by the number of periods in a year.

(e) The conditions under which any other charges may be imposed, and the method by which they will be determined.

(f) The conditions under which the creditor may retain or acquire any security interest in any property to secure the payment of any credit extended on the account, and a description or identification of the type of the interest or interests which may be so retained or acquired.

(g) The minimum periodic payment required.

In addition to the penalties provided under Article 12.2 (commencing with Section 1812.6) of this chapter, until the seller delivers the written statement required by this section, the buyer shall be obligated to pay only the cash price of the goods or services. **Leg.H.** Added Stats 1969 ch 625 §13. Amended Stats 1970 ch 304 §1, operative January 1, 1971, ch 546 §29.5, operative January 1, 1971.

Prior Law: Former §1810.1, similar to the present section, was added Stats 1959 ch 201 §1, operative January 1, 1960, amended Stats 1965 ch 1529 §1, operative July 1, 1966, and repealed Stats 1969 ch 625 §12.

§1810.2. Finance charge

Subject to the other provisions of this article, the seller or holder of a retail installment account may charge, receive and collect a finance charge as disclosed to the buyer pursuant to Section 1810.3. **Leg.H.** Added Stats 1980 ch 1381 §6. Amended Stats 1981 ch 26 §2; Stats 1982 ch 1611 §4, effective September 30, 1982, operative January 1, 1984; Stats 1983 ch 1157 §4, operative January 1, 1986; Stats 1985 ch 227 §4, operative January 1, 1988; Stats 1988 ch 479 §9, operative until January 1, 1992; Stats 1991 ch 819 §14 (SB1105).

Prior Law: Former §1810.2, relating to seller's confirmation of his acceptance of buyer's credit, was added Stats 1959 ch 201 §1, operative January 1, 1960, amended Stats 1965 ch 1529 §2, operative July 1, 1966, and repealed Stats 1969 ch 625 §14.

Former §1810.2, similar to the present section, was added Stats 1959 ch 201 §1 as §1810.4, renumbered and amended by Stats 1969 ch 625 §16, amended Stats 1970 ch 546 §30, Stats 1980 ch 1381 §5, Stats 1981 ch 26 §1, ch 1146 §3, Stats 1982 ch 1611 §3, effective September 30, 1982, ch 1613 §2.5, effective September 30, 1982, and repealed Stats 1982 ch 1614 §6.5.

There was another section of this number, similar to the present section, which was added Stats 1988 ch 479 §6.5, operative January 1, 1992, and repealed Stats 1991 ch 819 §15 (SB 1105).

There was another section of this number which was added Stats 1982 ch 1614 §7, amended Stats 1983 ch 1157 §3, Stats 1985 ch 227 §3, and repealed, effective January 1, 1988, by its own terms.

§1810.3. Statement of account

(a) Except in the case of an account which the seller deems to be uncollectible or with respect to which delinquency collection procedures have been instituted, the seller of any retail installment account shall mail or deliver to the buyer for each billing cycle at the end of which there is an outstanding debit balance in excess of one dollar ($1) in that account or with respect to which a finance charge is imposed, a statement or statements which the buyer may retain, setting forth in accordance with subdivision (c) each of the following items to the extent applicable:

(1) The outstanding balance in the account at the beginning of the billing cycle, using the term "previous balance."

(2) The amount and date of each extension of credit or the date the extension of credit is debited to the account during the billing cycle and, unless previously furnished, a brief identification of any goods or services purchased or other extension of credit.

(3) The total amounts credited to the account during the billing cycle for payments, using the term "payment," and for other credits, including returns, rebates of finance charges, and adjustments, using the term "credits," and unless previously furnished, a brief identification of each of the items included in the other credits.

(4) The amount of any finance charge, using the term "finance charge," debited to the account during the billing cycle, itemized and identified to show the amounts, if any, due to the application of periodic rates and the amount of any other charge included in the finance charge, such as a minimum charge, using appropriate descriptive terminology.

(5) Each periodic rate, using the term "periodic rate" (or "rates"), that may be used to compute the finance charge (whether or not applied during the billing cycle), and the range of balances to which it is applicable.

(6) The balance on which the finance charge was computed, and a statement of how that balance was determined. If any balance is determined without first deducting all credits during the billing cycle, that fact and the amount of the credits shall also be disclosed.

(7) The closing date of the billing cycle and the outstanding balance in the account on that date, using the term "new balance," accompanied by the statement of the date by which, or the period, if any, within which, payment must be made to avoid additional finance charges.

(b) The seller shall mail or deliver the statements required by subdivision (a) at least 14 days prior to any date or the end of any time period required to be disclosed under paragraph (7) of subdivision (a) in order for the consumer to avoid an additional finance or other charge. A seller that fails to meet this requirement shall not collect any finance or other charges imposed as a result of the failure.

(c) The disclosures required by subdivision (a) may be made on the face of the periodic statement or on its reverse side. In addition, the disclosures required by subdivision (a) may be made on the periodic statement supplemented by separate statement forms if they are enclosed together and delivered to the customer at the same time and if all of the following conditions are met:

(1) The disclosures required by paragraph (1) of subdivision (a) shall appear on the face of the periodic statement. If the amounts and dates of the charges and credits required to be disclosed under paragraphs (2) and (3) of subdivision (a) are not itemized on the face or reverse side of the periodic statement, they shall be disclosed on a separate statement or separate slips which shall accompany the periodic statement and identify each charge and credit and show the date and amount thereof. Identification of goods or services purchased may be made on an accompanying slip or by symbol relating to an identification list printed on the statement. If the disclosures required under paragraph (4) of subdivision (a) are not itemized on the face or reverse side of the periodic statement, they shall be disclosed on a separate statement which shall accompany the periodic statement.

(2) The disclosures required by paragraph (5) of subdivision (a) and a reference to the amounts required to be disclosed under paragraphs (4) and (6) of subdivision (a), if not disclosed together on the face or the reverse side of the periodic statement, shall appear together on the face of a single supplemental statement which shall accompany the periodic statement.

(3) The face of the periodic statement shall contain one of the following notices, as applicable: "NOTICE: See reverse side for important information" or "NOTICE: See accompanying statement(s) for important information" or "NOTICE: See reverse side and accompanying statement(s) for important information."

(4) The disclosures shall not be separated so as to confuse or mislead the customer, or to obscure or detract attention from the information required to be disclosed.

(d) If any change is to be made in terms of a retail installment account previously disclosed to the buyer, the seller shall mail or deliver to the buyer written disclosure of the proposed change not less than 30 days prior to the effective date of the change or 30 days prior to the beginning of the billing cycle within which the change will become effective, whichever is the earlier date. When the change involves a reduction of any component of a finance charge or other charge, the notice shall be sufficient if it appears on or accompanies the periodic statements mailed or delivered to buyers receiving periodic statements in the ordinary course of business. When the change involves an increase in any component of a finance charge, as defined in Section 1802.10, or involves a change in a charge permitted by Section 1810.4 or a change in the attorney's fee provision in the agreement pursuant to Section 1810.4, the change shall be effective only with respect to purchases made on or after the effective date of the change.

(e)(1) If any outstanding credit balance in excess of one dollar ($1) exists in a retail installment account, the seller shall mail or deliver to the buyer at the end of the billing cycle in which the credit balance is created either of the following:

(A) A cash refund in the amount of the outstanding credit.

(B) A statement setting forth the credit balance, and thereafter shall mail or deliver to the buyer a statement setting forth the credit balance no fewer than two additional times during the six-month period following creation of the credit balance.

(2) If the credit balance exists for a period of 90 days, the seller shall, at his or her option, do either of the following:

(A) Notify the buyer of his or her right to request and receive a cash refund in the amount of the outstanding credit balance in two successive statements covering, respectively, each of the two successive billing cycles immediately following the 90-day period. The notice is to be accomplished by a clear and conspicuous disclosure on or enclosed with each of the two successive statements, each of which shall be accompanied by a self-addressed return envelope. The disclosure shall contain the following information and may be in the following form:

"We owe owe you _____. Your credit balance will be refunded on request. If you don't request a refund, six months from the first appearance of a "credit balance" on your bill, your credit balance will be refunded automatically.

"If your credit balance is $1.00 or less, it will not be refunded unless requested, and after 6 months, it will not be credited against future purchases.

"You may obtain a refund of your credit balance by mail by presenting your statement at our store or by returning the top half of your statement in the enclosed envelope."

If between the sending of the first notice and the sending of the second notice required by this subparagraph, the outstanding credit balance is refunded to the buyer or otherwise disposed of, the sending of the second notice shall not be required.

(B) Refund to the buyer the outstanding credit balance at any time after the credit balance is created in the buyer's account and prior to the date by which the first notice of the outstanding balance would have been sent had the seller elected to proceed under subparagraph (A).

(f)(1) If a retail installment account with an outstanding credit balance in excess of one dollar ($1) which has been determined to be correct by the seller is dormant for a period of 180 days after the credit balance is created in the buyer's account, the seller shall mail or deliver a refund in the amount of the outstanding credit balance to the buyer at the buyer's last known address.

(2) If any refund is returned to the seller with a notification to the effect that the addressee is not located at the address to which it was sent, the seller shall make one remailing of the refund with an address correction request, and shall mail the refund to the corrected address, if it is obtained.

(3) If the refund reflecting an outstanding credit balance in excess of twenty-five dollars ($25) is again returned, the seller shall reinstate the full amount of the outstanding credit balance on the buyer's account to be retained and credited against future purchases for one year from the date on which the remailed refund was returned. The seller may continue to attempt to obtain a current mailing address for the buyer by whatever means the seller deems appropriate. Except as provided in subdivision (g), the seller shall not be required to take any further action with respect to sending any statement of the credit balance or otherwise with respect to the credit balance, unless the buyer of the account thereafter requests a

refund of the credit balance, in which event the seller shall either make the refund or provide a written explanation as provided in paragraph (5) of this subdivision.

(4) If a remailed refund reflecting an outstanding credit balance of twenty-five dollars ($25) or less is again returned, the seller, except as provided in subdivision (g), shall not be required to take any further action with respect to sending any statement of the credit balance to the buyer or otherwise with respect to the credit balance, unless the buyer of the account thereafter requests a refund of the credit balance, in which event the seller shall either make the refund or provide a written explanation as provided in paragraph (5) of this subdivision.

(5) If a buyer requests, in person or by mail, a refund of a credit balance in any amount which has been reflected at any time on the buyer's account, the seller shall, within 30 days of receipt of the request, either refund the amount requested, or furnish the customer with a written explanation, with supporting documentation when available, of the reasons for refusing to refund the amount requested.

(6) If a buyer, in writing, requests a seller to retain an outstanding credit balance on his or her account, the seller shall not be required to give notification as otherwise required by subdivisions (e) and (f).

(g) If an outstanding credit balance remains unrefundable for three years from the date it was created in the buyer's account, then the amount of the buyer's outstanding credit balance shall escheat to the state as property included within Section 1520 of the Code of Civil Procedure. Those funds shall be paid or delivered to the Controller, and may thereafter be claimed, as specified in Chapter 7 (commencing with Section 1500) of Title 10 of Part 4 of the Code of Civil Procedure.

(h) For the purposes of this section, an outstanding credit balance is created at the end of the billing cycle in which the credit balance is first recorded on a buyer's account and is created anew at the end of the billing cycle in which the recorded amount of an existing credit balance is changed because of the buyer's use of his or her account. **Leg.H.** Added Stats 1959 ch 201 §1, operative January 1, 1960, as §1810.5. Renumbered and amended by Stats 1969 ch 625 §17. Amended Stats 1970 ch 546 §31; Stats 1975 ch 947 §1; Stats 1981 ch 452 §1; Stats 1988 ch 1402 §1; Stats 1995 ch 566 §2 (SB 538); Stats 1996 ch 762 §1 (SB 2014).

Prior Law: Former CC §1810.3, relating to seller's display of statement as to authorized service charge rates, was added Stats 1959 ch 201 §1, operative January 1, 1960, and repealed Stats 1969 ch 625 §15.

§1810.4. Charges and fees

The finance charge shall include all charges incident to investigating and making the retail installment account. No fee, expense, delinquency, collection, or other charge whatsoever shall be taken, received, reserved, or contracted by the seller or holder of a retail installment account except as provided in this section. A seller may, however, in an agreement which is accepted by the buyer and of which a copy is given or furnished to the buyer provide for the payment of attorney's fees and costs in conformity with Article 11 (commencing with Section 1811.1). Any subsequent change in any term of the agreement shall not become effective until the seller has given notice of the change and complies with the provisions of subdivision (d) of Section 1810.3. When credit cards are issued in connection with a retail installment account, the seller, either in the agreement or after giving the notice required by subdivision (d) of Section 1810.3, may require the payment of an annual fee of not more than fifteen dollars ($15) for membership in the credit card plan, which fee shall not be deemed a finance charge or interest for any purpose of the law.

The seller or holder of a retail installment account may charge and collect a fee not to exceed fifteen dollars ($15) for the return by a depository institution of a dishonored check, negotiable order of withdrawal, or share draft issued in connection with the retail installment account. The fee is not included in charges as defined in this chapter or in determining the applicable charges which may be made under this chapter. **Leg.H.** Added Stats 1959 ch 201 §1, operative January 1, 1960, as §1810.6. Renumbered and amended by Stats 1969 ch 625 §18. Amended Stats 1970 ch 546 §32; Stats 1982 ch 371 §1, ch 512 §3; Stats 1993 ch 101 §2 (SB 329); Stats 1995 ch 566 §3 (SB 538).

Prior Law: Former §1810.4 was added Stats 1959 ch 201 §1, operative January 1, 1960, and renumbered CC §1810.2 by Stats 1969 ch 625 §16.

§1810.5. Cost of insurance

If the cost of any insurance is to be separately charged to the buyer, there shall be an agreement to this effect, signed by both the buyer and the seller, a copy of which shall be given or furnished to the buyer. Such agreement shall state whether the insurance is to be procured by the buyer or the seller or holder. If the insurance is to be procured by the seller or holder, the seller or holder shall comply with the provisions of Section 1803.5. **Leg.H.** Added Stats 1959 ch 201 §1, operative January 1, 1960, as §1810.7. Renumbered by Stats 1969 ch 625 §19.

Prior Law: Former §1810.5 was added Stats 1959 ch 201 §1, operative January 1, 1960, and amended and renumbered §1810.3 by Stats 1969 ch 625 §17.

§1810.6. Security interest in goods sold

Nothing in this article prohibits the execution of an agreement between a buyer and seller whereby the seller retains a security interest in goods sold to the buyer until full payment therefor has been made. For purposes of release of the security interests, in the case of goods or services purchased on different dates, the first purchased shall be deemed first paid for, and in the case of goods or services purchased on the same date, the lowest priced shall be deemed first paid for, and all amounts allocated to payment of these goods or services shall be applied to accomplish that result. However, any downpayment on a specific purchase shall be deemed to be allocated in its entirety to such purchase. **Leg.H.** Added Stats 1959 ch 201 §1, operative January 1, 1960, as §1810.8. Renumbered by Stats 1969 ch 625 §20. Amended Stats 1974 ch 563 §1; Stats 1981 ch 26 §3, effective April 30, 1981.

Prior Law: Former §1810.6 was added Stats 1959 ch 201 §1, operative January 1, 1960, and amended and renumbered CC §1810.4 by Stats 1969 ch 625 §18.

§1810.7. Protection of third party rights

No retail installment account shall require or entail the execution of any note or series of notes by the buyer which when separately negotiated will cut off as to third parties any right of action or defense which the buyer may have against the seller. **Leg.H.** Added Stats 1959 ch 201 §1, operative January 1, 1960, as §1810.9. Renumbered by Stats 1969 ch 625 §21.

Prior Law: Former §1810.7 was added Stats 1959 ch 201 §1, operative January 1, 1960, and renumbered CC §1810.5 by Stats 1969 ch 625 §19.

§1810.8. Application of provisions governing credit sales payments

The provisions of Sections 1806.1 and 1806.4 shall be applicable to retail installment accounts. **Leg.H.** Added Stats 1959 ch 201 §1, operative January 1, 1960, as §1810.10. Renumbered by Stats 1969 ch 625 §22.

Prior Law: Former §1810.8 was added Stats 1959 ch 201 §1, operative January 1, 1960, and renumbered CC §1810.6 by Stats 1969 ch 625 §20.

§1810.9. [Section repealed 1988]

Leg.H. Added Stats 1959 ch 201 §1, operative January 1, 1960, as §1810.11. Renumbered by Stats 1969 ch 625 §23. Repealed Stats 1988 ch 1402 §2. The repealed section related to absence of effect of statute on agreements entered into prior to statute's effective date.

Prior Law: Former §1810.9 was added Stats 1959 ch 201 §1, operative January 1, 1960, and renumbered CC §1810.7 by Stats 1969 ch 625 §21.

§1810.10. Charge for undelivered goods

(a) Notwithstanding the provision of any contract to the contrary, except as provided in subdivision (b) or (c), no retail seller shall assess any finance charge against the outstanding balance for goods purchased under a retail installment account until the goods are in the buyer's possession.

(b) A finance charge may be assessed against the outstanding balance for such undelivered goods, as follows:

(1) From the date when such goods are available for pickup by the buyer and the buyer is notified of their availability, or

(2) From the date of purchase, when such goods are delivered or available for pickup by the buyer within 10 days of the date of purchase.

(c) In the case of a home improvement contract as defined in Section 7151.2 of the Business and Professions Code, a finance charge may be assessed against the amount financed from the approximate date of commencement of the work as set forth in the home improvement contract. **Leg.H.** Added Stats 1975 ch 1041 §2. Amended Stats 1976 ch 1271 §5, effective September 28, 1976; Stats 1977 ch 868 §5; Stats 1979 ch 1000 §6.

Prior Law: Former §1810.10 was added Stats 1959 ch 201 §1, operative January 1, 1960, and renumbered CC §1810.8 by Stats 1969 ch 625 §22.

There was another section of this number, similar to the present section, which was added Stats 1976 ch 1271 §6, effective September 28, 1976, operative January 1, 1980, amended Stats 1977 ch 686 §6, and repealed Stats 1979 ch 1000 §5.

§1810.11. Statement of finance charges

The buyer may request, not more frequently than once a year, that the seller inform the buyer of the total amount of finance charges assessed on the account during the preceding calendar year and the seller shall provide that information to the buyer within 30 days of receiving the request, without charge.

If the buyer's request for the information is made in writing, the seller shall provide the information in writing, provided, however, that if the seller is required to furnish the buyer with a periodic billing or periodic statement of account or furnishes the billing or statement of account, the requested statement of finance charges may be furnished along with the periodic billing or periodic statement of account. "Seller," for the purposes of this section, means a person engaged in the business of selling goods or furnishing services to retail buyers whose annual sales pursuant to retail installment accounts in California have exceeded one hundred fifty million dollars ($150,000,000) in the seller's last two consecutive years. **Leg.H.** Added Stats 1995 ch 693 §2 (SB 539).

Prior Law: Former §1810.11, similar to the present section, was added Stats 1976 ch 82 §1 and repealed Stats 1995 ch 693 §1.

Former §1810.11 was added Stats 1959 ch 201 §1, operative January 1, 1960, and renumbered CC §1810.9 by Stats 1969 ch 625 §23.

§1810.12. Delinquency and collection charges

(a) Notwithstanding Section 1810.4, a seller or holder of a retail installment account may, subject to subdivision (d) of Section 1810.3, provide that for each installment in default the buyer shall pay a delinquency charge not in excess of one of the following amounts:

(1) For a period in default of not less than 10 days, an amount not in excess of ten dollars ($10).

(2) For a period in default of not less than 15 days, an amount not in excess of fifteen dollars ($15).

(b) Only one delinquency charge may be collected on any installment regardless of the period during which it remains in default. No delinquency charge shall be imposed for any default of payment on any payment due prior to the mailing or delivery to the buyer of the written disclosure concerning the delinquency charge provided by the seller or holder of a retail installment account pursuant to subdivision (d) of Section 1810.3. Payments timely received by the seller under a written extension or deferral agreement shall not be subject to any delinquency charge. The agreement may also provide for payment of any actual and reasonable costs of collection occasioned by removal of the goods from the state without written permission of the holder, or by the failure of the buyer to notify the holder of any change of residence, or by the failure of the buyer to communicate with the holder for a period of 45 days after any default in making payments due under the agreement.

(c) Notwithstanding subdivision (b) of Section 1810.3, the seller or holder of a retail installment account shall provide a minimum of 20 days between the monthly billing date and the date upon which the minimum payment is due, exclusive of the applicable grace period provided in subdivision (a). **Leg.H.** Added Stats 1983 ch 763 §1. Amended Stats 1988 ch 1402 §3; Stats 1994 ch 168 §2 (SB 1583); Stats 1996 ch 301 §2 (SB 2050).

ARTICLE 10.5
Retail Installment Account Credit Card Periodic Rate Disclosures

Citation of article. §1810.20.
Solicitations. §1810.21.

§1810.20. Citation of article

This article shall be known and may be cited as the "Areias Retail Installment Account Full Disclosure Act of 1986." **Leg.H.** Added Stats 1986 ch 1397 §4. Amended Stats 2000 ch 375 §6 (AB 1331).

§1810.21. Solicitations

(a) Any application form or preapproved written solicitation for a credit card issued in connection with a retail installment account that is mailed on or after October 1, 1987, to a retail buyer residing in this state by or on behalf of a retail seller, whether or not the retail seller is located in this state, other than an application form or solicitation included in a magazine, newspaper, or other publication distributed by someone other than the retail seller, shall contain or be accompanied by either of the following disclosures:

(1) A disclosure of each of the following, if applicable:

(A) Any periodic rate or rates that will be used to determine the finance charge imposed on the balance due under the terms of a retail installment account, expressed as an annual percentage rate or rates.

(B) Any membership or participation fee that will be imposed for availability of a retail installment account in connection with which a credit card is issued expressed as an annualized amount.

(C) If the retail seller provides a period during which the retail buyer may repay the full balance reflected on a billing statement that is attributable to purchases of goods or services from the retail seller without the imposition of additional finance charges, the retail seller shall either disclose the minimum number of days of that period, calculated from the closing date of the prior billing cycle to the date designated in the billing statement sent to the retail buyer as the date by which that payment must be received to avoid additional finance charges, or describe the manner in which the period is calculated. For purposes of this section, the period shall be referred to as the "free period" or "free-ride period." If the retail seller does not provide this period for purchases, the disclosure shall so indicate.

(2) A disclosure that satisfies the initial disclosure statement requirements of Regulation Z (12 C.F.R. 226.6).

(b) In the event that an unsolicited application form is mailed or otherwise delivered to retail buyers in more than one state, the requirements of subdivision (a) shall be satisfied if on the application form or the soliciting material there is a notice that credit terms may vary from state to state and that provides either the disclosures required by subdivision (a) or an address or phone number for the customer to use to obtain the disclosure. The notice shall be in boldface type no smaller than the largest type used in the narrative portion, excluding headlines, of the material soliciting the application. Any person responding to the notice shall be given the disclosures required by subdivision (a).

(c) A retail seller need not present the disclosures required by paragraph (1) of subdivision (a) in chart form or use any specific terminology, except as expressly provided in this section. The following chart shall not be construed in any way as a standard by which to determine whether a retail seller who elects not to use the chart has provided the required disclosures in a manner which satisfies paragraph (1) of subdivision (a). However, disclosures shall be conclusively presumed to satisfy the requirements of paragraph (1) of subdivision (a) if a chart with captions substantially as follows is completed with the applicable terms offered by the retail seller, or if the retail seller presents the applicable terms in tabular, list, or narrative format using terminology substantially similar to the captions included in the following chart:

THE FOLLOWING INFORMATION IS PROVIDED
PURSUANT TO THE AREIAS RETAIL
INSTALLMENT ACCOUNT FULL DISCLOSURE
ACT OF 1986:

CREDIT CARD TERMS VARY AMONG RETAIL
SELLERS—SELECTED TERMS FOR PURCHASES
UNDER THIS RETAIL INSTALLMENT ACCOUNT
ARE SET OUT BELOW

PERIODIC RATES (as APRs)	ANNUAL FEES	FREE-RIDE PERIOD

(d) For purposes of this section, "Regulation Z" has the meaning attributed to it under Section 1802.18, and all of the terms used in this section have the same meaning as attributed to them in federal Regulation Z (12 C.F.R. 226.1 et seq.).

(e) Nothing in this section shall be deemed or construed to prohibit a retail seller from disclosing additional terms, conditions, or information, whether or not relating to the disclosures required under this section, in conjunction with the disclosures required by this section. Notwithstanding subdivision (g) of Section 1748.11, a retail seller that complies with the requirements of Section 1748.11 shall be deemed to have complied with the requirements of this section.

(f) If a retail seller is required under federal law to make any disclosure of the terms applicable to a retail installment account in connection with application forms or solicitations, the retail seller shall be deemed to have complied with the requirements of paragraph (1) of subdivision (a) with respect to those application forms or solicitations if the retail seller complies with the federal disclosure requirement.

(g) If the disclosure required by this section does not otherwise appear on an application form or an accompanying retail installment agreement distributed in this state on or after October 1, 1987, other than by mail, the application form shall include a statement in substantially the following form:

"If you wish to receive disclosure of the terms of this retail installment account, pursuant to the Areias Retail Installment Account Full Disclosure Act of 1986, check here and return to the address on this form."

A box shall be printed in or next to this statement for placing such a checkmark.

(h) This article does not apply to (1) any application form or preapproved written solicitation for a retail installment account credit card where the credit to be extended will be secured by a lien on real or personal property, or both real and personal property, (2) any application form or written solicitation that invites a person or persons to apply for a retail installment account credit card and which is included as part of a catalog which is sent to one or more persons by a creditor in order to facilitate a credit sale of goods offered in the catalog, (3) any advertisement which does not invite, directly or indirectly, an application for a retail installment account credit card, and (4) any application form or written advertisement included in a magazine, newspaper, or other publication distributed in more than one state by someone other than the creditor. **Leg.H.** Added Stats 1986 ch 1397 §4. Amended Stats 2000 ch 375 §7 (AB 1331); Stats 2001 ch 159 §34 (SB 662).

ARTICLE 11
Attorney's Fees and Court Costs

Award. §1811.1.

§1811.1. Award

Reasonable attorney's fees and costs shall be awarded to the prevailing party in any action on a contract or installment account subject to the provisions of this chapter regardless of whether such action is instituted by the seller, holder or buyer. Where the defendant alleges in his answer that he tendered to the plaintiff the full amount to which he was entitled, and thereupon deposits in court, for the plaintiff, the amount so tendered, and the allegation is found to be true, then the defendant is deemed to be a prevailing party within the meaning of this article. **Leg.H.** Added Stats 1959 ch 201 §1, operative January 1, 1960. Amended Stats 1961 ch 1214 §6.

ARTICLE 12
Attachment [Repealed]

§1812. [Section repealed 1974]

Leg.H. Added Stats 1969 ch 669 §1. Repealed Stats 1974 ch 1516 §2, operative January 1, 1977. The repealed section related to protecting consumers in actions arising out of retail sales.

§1812.1. [Section repealed 1970]

Leg.H. Added Stats 1959 ch 201 §1, operative January 1, 1960. Repealed Stats 1970 ch 1523 §1. The repealed section related to attachments.

ARTICLE 12.1
Repossession and Resale

Procedure. §1812.2.
Notice. §1812.3.
Application of proceeds. §1812.4.
Deficiency judgment. §1812.5.

§1812.2. Procedure

In the event of any default by the buyer in the performance of his obligations under a contract or installment account, the holder, pursuant to any rights granted therein, may proceed to recover judgment for the balance due without retaking the goods, or he may retake the goods and proceed as hereinafter provided. If he retakes the goods, he shall, within 10 days, give notice to the buyer of his intention to sell the goods at public sale or give notice to the buyer of his intention to retain the goods in satisfaction of the balance due. The notice must state the amount of the overdue payments, that the buyer must pay, if he pays within 10 days of the notice, in order to redeem the goods. In either case the buyer shall have an absolute right to redeem the goods within 10 days after the notice is given by paying or tendering the amount owing under the contract. If the holder gives notice of election to sell the goods the buyer shall also have the absolute right to redeem the goods at any time before sale by paying or tendering the amounts specified above and also any expense reasonably incurred by the seller or holder in good faith in repairing, reconditioning the goods or preparing them for sale. If the holder gives notice of his intention to retain the goods in satisfaction of the indebtedness he shall be deemed to have done so at the end of the 10-day period if the goods are not redeemed; at the time the notice is given, the holder shall furnish the buyer a written statement of the sum due under the contract and the expenses provided for in this section. For failure to render such a statement the holder shall forfeit to the buyer ten dollars ($10) and also be liable to him for all damages suffered because of such failure. **Leg.H.** Added Stats 1959 ch 201 §1, operative January 1, 1960. Amended Stats 1961 ch 1214 §7; Stats 1963 ch 1952 §1.

§1812.3. Notice

The notice provided for in Section 1812.2 shall be given to the buyer and any other person liable by causing it to be delivered personally or to be deposited in the United States mail addressed to the buyer or to such other person at his last known address and shall advise the buyer or such other person of his right to redeem as provided for in Section 1812.2. If the holder determines to sell the goods at public sale he shall give notice of the time and place of sale at least 10 days before the date of sale by delivering a copy of the notice personally to the buyer or other person liable or depositing the same in the United States mail addressed to the buyer or such other person at his last known address. **Leg.H.** Added Stats 1959 ch 201 §1, operative January 1, 1960. Amended Stats 1961 ch 1214 §8.

§1812.4. Application of proceeds

The proceeds of a resale shall be applied (1) to the payment of the expenses thereof, (2) to the payment of any expenses of retaking, including reasonable attorney's fees actually incurred, and of any expenses of keeping, storing, repairing, reconditioning or preparing the goods for sale to which the holder may be entitled, (3) to the satisfaction of the balance due under the contract. Any sum remaining after the satisfaction of such claims shall be paid to the buyer. **Leg.H.** Added Stats 1959 ch 201 §1, operative January 1, 1960.

§1812.5. Deficiency judgment

If the proceeds of the sale are not sufficient to cover items (1), (2) and (3) of Section 1812.4, the holder may not recover the deficiency from the buyer or from anyone who has succeeded to the obligations of the buyer. **Leg.H.** Added Stats 1959 ch 201 §1, operative January 1, 1960. Amended Stats 1963 ch 1952 §2.

ARTICLE 12.2
Penalties

Criminal offense. §1812.6.
Bar to recovery. §1812.7.
Correction of violation. §1812.8.
Treble damages. §1812.9.

§1812.6. Criminal offense

Any person who shall willfully violate any provision of this chapter shall be guilty of a misdemeanor. **Leg.H.** Added Stats 1959 ch 201 §1, operative January 1, 1960.

§1812.7. Bar to recovery

In case of failure by any person to comply with the provisions of this chapter, such person or any person who acquires a contract or installment account with knowledge of such noncompliance is barred from recovery of any finance charge or of any delinquency, collection, extension, deferral or refinance charge imposed in connection with such contract or installment account and the buyer shall have the right to recover from such person an amount equal to any of such charges paid by the buyer. **Leg.H.** Added Stats 1959 ch 201 §1, operative January 1, 1960. Amended Stats 1970 ch 546 §33.

§1812.8. Correction of violation

Notwithstanding the provisions of this article, any failure to comply with any provision of this chapter may be corrected by the holder in accordance with the provisions of this section, provided that a willful violation may not be corrected, and a correction which will increase the amount owed by the buyer or the amount of any payment shall not be effective unless the buyer concurs in writing to the correction. If a violation is corrected by the holder in accordance with the provisions of this section, neither the seller nor the holder shall be subject to any penalty under this article. The correction shall be made by delivery to the buyer of a corrected copy of the contract within 30 days of the execution of the original contract by the buyer. Any amount improperly collected from the buyer shall be credited against the indebtedness evidenced by the contract. **Leg.H.** Added Stats 1959 ch 201 §1, operative January 1, 1960. Amended Stats 1961 ch 1214 §9.

§1812.9. Treble damages

In any case in which a person willfully violates any provision of this chapter in connection with the imposition, computation or disclosures of or relating to a finance charge on a consolidated total of two or more contracts under the provisions of Article 8 (commencing with Section 1808.1) of this chapter, the buyer may recover from such person an amount equal to three times the total of the finance charges and any delinquency, collection, extension, deferral or refinance charges imposed, contracted for or received on all contracts included in the consolidated total and the seller shall be barred from the recovery of any such charges. **Leg.H.** Added Stats 1959 ch 201 §1, operative January 1, 1960. Amended Stats 1961 ch 1214 §10; Stats 1970 ch 546 §34.

ARTICLE 12.3
Actions

Jurisdiction and venue. §1812.10.

§1812.10. Jurisdiction and venue

(a) An action on a contract or installment account under this chapter shall be tried in the superior court in the county where the contract was in fact signed by the buyer, where the buyer resided at the time the contract was entered into, where the buyer resides at the commencement of the action, or where the goods purchased pursuant to the contract have been so affixed to real property as to become a part of that real property.

(b) In the superior court designated as the proper court in subdivision (a), the proper court location for trial of an action under this chapter is the location where the court tries that type of action that is nearest or most accessible to where the contract was in fact signed by the buyer, where the buyer resided at the time the contract was entered into, where the buyer resides at the commencement of the action, or where the goods purchased pursuant to the contract have been so affixed to real property as to become a part of that real property. Otherwise, any location of the superior court designated as the proper court in subdivision (a) is the proper court location for the trial of the action. The court may specify by local rule the nearest or most accessible court location where the court tries that type of case.

(c) In any action subject to this section, concurrently with the filing of the complaint, the plaintiff shall file an affidavit stating facts showing that the action has been commenced in a superior court and court location described in this section as a proper place for the trial of the action. Those facts may be stated in a verified complaint and shall not be stated on information or belief. When that affidavit is filed with the complaint, a copy thereof shall be served with the summons. If a plaintiff fails to file the affidavit or state facts in a verified complaint required by this section, no further proceedings may occur, but the court shall, upon its own motion or upon motion of any party, dismiss the action without prejudice. The court may, on terms that are just, permit the affidavit to be filed subsequent to the filing of the complaint and a copy of the affidavit shall be served on the defendant. The time to answer or otherwise plead shall date from that service. **Leg.H.** Added Stats 1965 ch 792 §1. Amended Stats 1968 ch 743 §1; Stats 1969 ch 186 §1; Stats 1970 ch 725 §1; Stats 1971 ch 1529 §1; Stats 1998 ch 931 §16 (SB 2139), effective September 28, 1998; Stats 2002 ch 806 §1 (AB 3027).

ARTICLE 12.4
Financing Retail Purchases

Requiring financing from particular source. §1812.20.

§1812.20. Requiring financing from particular source

Notwithstanding Section 1801.6, no person shall require a purchaser of goods or services to obtain financing from any particular source. Any person who violates this section shall be subject to the penalty provided in Section 1812.6. **Leg.H.** Added Stats 1979 ch 1151 §4.

CHAPTER 2
CREDIT TRANSACTIONS REGARDING WOMEN

Credit and credit reporting. §1812.30.
Damages. §1812.31.
Injunction. §1812.32.
Penalty for violation of injunction. §1812.33.
Costs and fees. §1812.34.
Limitation of actions. §1812.35.

§1812.30. Credit and credit reporting

(a) No person, regardless of marital status, shall be denied credit in his or her own name if the earnings and other property over which he or she has management and control are such that a person of the opposite sex managing and controlling the same amount of earnings and other property would receive credit.

(b) No person, regardless of marital status, managing and controlling earnings and other property shall be offered credit on terms less favorable than those offered to a person of the opposite sex seeking the same type of credit and managing and controlling the same amount of earnings and other property.

(c) No unmarried person shall be denied credit if his or her earnings and other property are such that a married person managing and controlling the same amount of earnings and other property would receive credit.

(d) No unmarried person shall be offered credit on terms less favorable than those offered to a married person managing and controlling the same amount of earnings and other property.

(e) For accounts established after January 1, 1977 or for accounts in existence on January 1, 1977 where information on that account is received after January 1, 1977, a credit reporting agency which in its normal course of business receives information on joint credit accounts identifying the persons responsible for such accounts, or receives information which reflects the participation of both spouses, shall: (1) at the time such information is received file such information separately under the names of each person or spouse, or file such information in another manner which would enable either person or spouse to automatically gain access to the credit history without having in any way to list or refer to the name of the other person, and (2) provide access to all information about the account in the name of each person or spouse.

(f) For all accounts established prior to January 1, 1977, a credit reporting agency shall at any time upon the written or personal request of a person who is or has been married, verify the contractual liability, liability by operation of law, or authorized use by such person, of joint credit accounts appearing in the file of the person's spouse or former spouse, and, if applicable, shall file such information separately and thereafter continue to do so under the names of each person responsible for the joint account or in another manner which would enable either person responsible for the joint account to automatically gain access to the credit history without having in any way to list or refer to the name of the other person.

(g) For the purposes of this chapter "credit" means obtainment of money, property, labor, or services on a deferred-payment basis.

(h) For the purposes of this chapter, earnings shall include, but not be limited to, spousal, family, and child support payments, pensions, social security, disability or survivorship benefits. Spousal, family, and child support payments shall be considered in the same manner as earnings from salary, wages, or other sources where the payments are received pursuant to a written agreement or court decree to the extent that the reliability of such payments is established. The factors which a creditor may consider in evaluating the reliability of such payments are the length of time payments have been received; the regularity of receipt; and whether full or partial payments have been made.

(i) Nothing in this chapter shall be construed to prohibit a person from: (1) utilizing an evaluation of the reliability of earnings provided that such an evaluation is applied to persons without regard to their sex or marital status; or (2) inquiring into and utilizing an evaluation of the obligations for which community property is liable pursuant to the Family Code for the sole purpose of determining the creditor's rights and remedies with respect to the particular extension of credit, provided that such is done with respect to all applicants without regard to their sex; or (3) utilizing any other relevant factors or methods in determining whether to extend credit to an applicant provided that such factors or methods are applicable to all applicants without regard to their sex or marital status. For the purpose of this subdivision, the fact that an applicant is of childbearing age is not a relevant factor.

(j) Credit applications for the obtainment of money, goods, labor, or services shall clearly specify that the applicant, if married, may apply for a separate account. **Leg.H.** Added Stats 1973 ch 999 §1. Amended Stats 1975 ch 332 §1; Stats 1976 ch 1361 §1; Stats 1992 ch 163 §11 (AB 2641), operative January 1, 1994.

§1812.31. Damages

(a) Whoever violates Section 1812.30 shall be liable to the aggrieved person in an amount equal to the sum of any actual damages sustained by such person acting either in an individual capacity or as a representative of a class.

(b) Whoever violates Section 1812.30 shall be liable to the aggrieved person for punitive damages in an amount not greater than ten thousand dollars ($10,000), as determined by the court, in addition to any actual damages provided in subdivision (a); provided, however, that in pursuing the recovery allowed under this subdivision, the aggrieved person may proceed only in an individual capacity and not as a representative of a class.

(c) Notwithstanding subdivision (b), whoever violates Section 1812.30 may be liable for punitive damages in the case of a class action in such amount as the court may allow, except that as to each member of the class no minimum recovery shall be applicable, and the total recovery in such action shall not exceed the lesser of one hundred thousand dollars ($100,000) or one percent (1%) of the net worth of the creditor. In determining the amount of the award in any class action, the court shall consider, among other relevant factors, the amount of any actual damages awarded, the frequency and persistence of violations, the resources of the creditor, the number of persons adversely affected, and the extent to which the creditor's violation was intentional. **Leg.H.** Added Stats 1973 ch 999 §1. Amended Stats 1975 ch 332 §2.

§1812.32. Injunction

Any person, corporation, firm, partnership, joint stock company, or any other association or organization which violates or proposes to violate this chapter may be enjoined by any court of competent jurisdiction. Actions for injunction under this section may be prosecuted by the Attorney General or any district attorney, county counsel, city attorney, or city prosecutor in this state in the name of the people of the State of California or by any person denied credit or offered credit in violation of Section 1812.30. **Leg.H.** Added Stats 1975 ch 332 §3.

§1812.33. Penalty for violation of injunction

(a) Any person who intentionally violates any injunction issued pursuant to this chapter shall be liable for a civil penalty not to exceed two thousand five hundred dollars ($2,500) for each day that such person violates the injunction.

(b) The civil penalty prescribed by this section shall be assessed and recovered in a civil action brought in the name of the people of the State of California by the Attorney General or by any district attorney, county counsel, or city attorney in any court of competent jurisdiction. An action brought pursuant to this section to recover such civil penalties shall take special precedence over all civil matters on the calendar of the court except those matters to which equal precedence on the calendar is granted by law.

(c) If such an action is brought by the Attorney General, one-half of the penalty collected pursuant to this section shall be paid to the treasurer of the county in which the judgment was entered, and one-half to the State Treasurer. If brought by a district attorney or county counsel, the entire amount of the penalty collected shall be paid to the treasurer of the county in which the judgment was entered. If brought by a city attorney or city prosecutor, one-half of the penalty shall be paid to the treasurer of the county in which the judgment was entered and one-half to the city. **Leg.H.** Added Stats 1975 ch 332 §4.

§1812.34. Costs and fees

Any person denied credit or offered credit in violation of Section 1812.30 who brings an action pursuant to Section 1812.31 or 1812.32 of this code may petition the court for award of costs and reasonable attorney's fees which the court shall award if the action is successful. **Leg.H.** Added Stats 1975 ch 332 §5.

§1812.35. Limitation of actions

Any action commenced pursuant to Section 1812.31 shall be commenced within two years from the date on which the person is denied credit or is offered credit in violation of Section 1812.30. **Leg.H.** Added Stats 1975 ch 332 §6.

CHAPTER 3
RETAIL CREDIT ADVISORY COMMITTEE
[REPEALED]

§1812.40. [Section repealed 2004]

Leg.H. Added Stats 1980 ch 1381 §7. Repealed Stats 2004 ch 193 §10 (SB 111). The repealed section related to members.

§1812.41. [Section repealed 2004]

Leg.H. Added Stats 1980 ch 1381 §7. Amended Stats 1981 ch 26 §4, effective April 30, 1981, ch 1146 §4. Repealed Stats 2004 ch 193 §10 (SB 111). The repealed section related to authority and duties.

TITLE 2.4
CONTRACTS FOR DANCE STUDIO LESSONS AND OTHER SERVICES

Findings and declarations. §1812.50.
Definitions. §1812.51.
Form; Delivery. §1812.52.
Payments. §1812.53.
Contents. §1812.54.
Third party rights. §1812.55.
Assignment. §1812.56.
Death or disability; Installment payments. §1812.57.
Applicability of other provisions of law. §1812.58.
Noncomplying contracts. §1812.59.
Fraudulently induced contracts. §1812.60.
Waiver of provisions. §1812.61.
Civil actions. §1812.62.
Criminal violations. §1812.63.
Bond. §1812.64.
Beneficiary of bond. §1812.65.
Exceptions to bond requirements. §1812.67.
Severability of provisions. §1812.68.
Filing of bonds. §1812.69.

§1812.50. Findings and declarations

(a) The Legislature finds that there exists in connection with a substantial number of contracts for dance studio lessons and other services, sales practices, and business and financing methods which have worked a fraud, deceit, imposition, and financial hardship upon the people of this state; that existing legal remedies are inadequate to correct these abuses; that the dance studio industry has a significant impact upon the economy and well-being of this state and its local communities; and that the provisions of this title relating to these contracts are necessary for the public welfare.

(b) The Legislature declares that the purpose of this title is to safeguard the public against fraud, deceit, imposition, and financial hardship, and to foster and encourage competition, fair dealing, and prosperity in the field of dance studio lessons and other services by prohibiting or restricting false or misleading advertising, onerous contract terms, harmful financial practices, and other unfair, dishonest, deceptive, destructive, unscrupulous, fraudulent, and discriminatory practices by which the public has been injured in connection with contracts for dance studio lessons and other services. **Leg.H.** Added Stats 1969 ch 1571 §1. Amended Stats 1987 ch 449 §2; Stats 1988 ch 1043 §2.

§1812.51. Definitions

As used in this title, "contract for dance studio lessons and other services" means a contract for instruction in ballroom or other types of dancing, and includes lessons and other services, whether given to students individually or in groups. This title does not include contracts for professional services rendered or furnished by a person licensed under Division 2 (commencing with Section 500) of the Business and Professions Code, or contracts for instruction at schools operating pursuant to the Education Code. **Leg.H.** Added Stats 1969 ch 1571 §1. Amended Stats 1987 ch 449 §3; Stats 1988 ch 1043 §3.

§1812.51a. [Section repealed 1988]
Leg.H. Added Stats 1987 ch 449 §4. Repealed Stats 1988 ch 1043 §4. The repealed section related to definition of "educational dance instruction".

§1812.52. Form; Delivery
Every contract for dance studio lessons and other services shall be in writing and shall be subject to this title. A copy of the written contract shall be given to the customer at the time he or she signs the contract. **Leg.H.** Added Stats 1969 ch 1571 §1. Amended Stats 1987 ch 449 §5; Stats 1988 ch 1043 §5.

§1812.53. Payments
(a) No contract for dance studio lessons and other services shall require payments or financing by the buyer over a period in excess of one year from the date the contract is entered into, nor shall the term of any contract be measured by the life of the buyer. However, the lessons and other services to be rendered to the buyer under the contract may extend over a period not to exceed seven years from the date the contract is entered into.

(b) All contracts for dance studio lessons and other services that may be in effect between the same seller and the same buyer, the terms of which overlap for any period, shall be considered as one contract for the purposes of this title. **Leg.H.** Added Stats 1969 ch 1571 §1. Amended Stats 1983 ch 259 §1; Stats 1987 ch 449 §6; Stats 1988 ch 1043 §6; Stats 1999 ch 1024 §1 (AB 648).

§1812.54. Contents
(a) Every contract for dance studio lessons and other services shall provide that performance of the agreed-upon lessons will begin within six months from the date the contract is entered into.

(b) A contract for dance studio lessons and other services may be canceled by the student at any time provided he or she gives written notice to the dance studio at the address specified in the contract. When a contract for dance studio lessons and other services is canceled the dance studio shall calculate the refund on the contract, if any, on a pro rata basis. The dance studio shall refund any moneys owed to the student within 10 days of receiving the cancellation notice, unless the student owes the dance studio money for studio lessons or other services received prior to the cancellation, in which case any moneys owed the dance studio shall be deducted by the dance studio from the refund owed to the student and the balance, if any, shall be refunded as specified above. A dance studio shall not charge a cancellation fee, or other fee, for cancellation of the contract by the student.

(c) Every contract for dance studio lessons and other services shall contain a written statement of the hourly rate charged for each type of lesson for which the student has contracted. If the contract includes dance studio lessons that are sold at different per-hour rates, the contract shall contain separate hourly rates for each different type of lesson sold. All other services for which the student has contracted that are not capable of a per-hour charge shall be set forth in writing in specific terms. The statement shall be contained in the dance studio contract before the contract is signed by the buyer.

(d) Every dance studio subject to Sections 1812.64 and 1812.65 shall include in every contract for dance studio lessons or other services a statement that the studio is bonded and that information concerning the bond may be obtained by writing to the office of the Secretary of State. **Leg.H.** Added Stats 1969 ch 1571 §1. Amended Stats 1976 ch 1200 §1; Stats 1982 ch 517 §58; Stats 1983 ch 259 §2; Stats 1987 ch 449 §7; Stats 1988 ch 1043 §7; Stats 1997 ch 112 §1 (SB 338); Stats 1998 ch 829 §7 (SB 1652); Stats 1999 ch 1024 §2 (AB 648).

§1812.55. Third party rights
No contract for dance studio lessons and other services shall require or entail the execution of any note or series of notes by the buyer which, when separately negotiated, will cut off as to third parties any right of action or defense which the buyer may have against the seller. **Leg.H.** Added Stats 1969 ch 1571 §1. Amended Stats 1987 ch 449 §8; Stats 1988 ch 1043 §8.

§1812.56. Assignment
No right of action or defense arising out of a contract for dance studio lessons and other services which the buyer has against the seller, and which would be cut off by assignment, shall be cut off by assignment of the contract to any third party whether or not he or she acquires the contract in good faith and for value unless the assignee gives notice of the assignment to the buyer as provided in this section and, within 30 days of the mailing of notice, receives no written notice of the facts giving rise to the claim or defense of the buyer. A notice of assignment shall be in writing addressed to the buyer at the address shown on the contract and shall identify the contract and inform the buyer that he or she shall, within 30 days of the date of mailing of the notice, notify the assignee in writing of any facts giving rise to a claim or defense which he or she may have. The notice of assignment shall state the name of the seller and buyer, a description of the lessons and other services, the contract balance, and the number and amount of the installments. **Leg.H.** Added Stats 1969 ch 1571 §1. Amended Stats 1987 ch 449 §9; Stats 1988 ch 1043.

§1812.57. Death or disability; Installment payments
(a) Every contract for dance studio lessons and other services shall contain a clause providing that if, by reason of death or disability, the person agreeing to receive lessons and other services is unable to receive all lessons and other services for which he or she has contracted, the person and his or her estate shall be relieved from the obligation of making payment for lessons and other services other than those received prior to death or the onset of disability, and that if the buyer has prepaid any sum for lessons and other services so much of that sum as is allocable to lessons and other services he or she has not taken shall be promptly refunded to the buyer or his or her representative.

(b) Notwithstanding the provisions of any contract to the contrary, whenever the contract price is payable in installments and the buyer is relieved from making further payments or entitled to a refund under this section, the buyer shall be entitled to receive a refund or refund credit of so much of the cash price as is allocable to the lessons or other services not actually received by the buyer. The refund of the finance charge shall be computed according to the "sum of the balances method," also known as the "Rule of 78". **Leg.H.** Added Stats 1969 ch 1571 §1. Amended Stats 1976 ch 1200 §2; Stats 1987 ch 449 §10; Stats 1988 ch 1043 §10.

§1812.58. Applicability of other provisions of law
The provisions of this title are not exclusive and do not relieve the parties or the contracts subject thereto from compliance with all other applicable provisions of law. **Leg.H.** Added Stats 1969 ch 1571 §1 p 3190.

§1812.59. Noncomplying contracts
Any contract for dance studio lessons and other services which does not comply with the applicable provisions of this title shall be void and unenforceable as contrary to public policy. **Leg.H.** Added Stats 1969 ch 1571 §1. Amended Stats 1987 ch 449 §11; Stats 1988 ch 1043 §11.

§1812.60. Fraudulently induced contracts
Any contract for dance studio lessons and other services entered into in reliance upon any willful and false, fraudulent, or misleading information, representation, notice, or advertisement of the seller shall be void and unenforceable. **Leg.H.** Added Stats 1969 ch 1571 §1. Amended Stats 1987 ch 449 §12; Stats 1988 ch 1043 §12.

§1812.61. Waiver of provisions
Any waiver of the buyer of the provisions of this title shall be deemed contrary to public policy and shall be void and unenforceable. **Leg.H.** Added Stats 1969 ch 1571 §1.

§1812.62. Civil actions
(a) Any buyer injured by a violation of this title may bring an action for the recovery of damages. Judgment may be entered for three times the amount at which the actual damages are assessed plus reasonable attorney fees.

(b) Notwithstanding the provisions of this title, any failure to comply with any provision of this title may be corrected within 30 days after the execution of the contract by the buyer, and, if so corrected, neither the seller nor the holder shall be subject to any penalty under this title, provided that any correction which increases any monthly payment, the number of payments, or the total amount due, must be concurred in, in writing, by the buyer. "Holder" includes the seller who acquires the contract, of, if the contract is purchased by a financing agency or other assignee, the financing agency or other assignee. **Leg.H.** Added Stats 1969 ch 1571 §1.

§1812.63. Criminal violations
Any person who violates any provision of this title relating to dance studio contracts is guilty of a misdemeanor. Any superior court of this

state has jurisdiction in equity to restrain and enjoin the violation of any of the provisions of this title relating to dance studio contracts.

The duty to institute actions for violation of those provisions of this title, including equity proceedings to restrain and enjoin violations, is hereby vested in the Attorney General, district attorneys, and city attorneys. The Attorney General, any district attorney, or any city attorney may prosecute misdemeanor actions or institute equity proceedings, or both.

This section shall not be deemed to prohibit the enforcement by any person of any right provided by this or any other law. **Leg.H.** Added Stats 1969 ch 1571 §1. Amended Stats 1987 ch 449 §13; Stats 1988 ch 1043 §13.

§1812.64. Bond

Every dance studio shall maintain a bond issued by a surety company admitted to do business in this state. The principal sum of the bond shall be 25 percent of the dance studio's gross income from the studio business in this state during the studio's last fiscal year, except that the principal sum of the bond shall not be less than twenty-five thousand dollars ($25,000) in the first or any subsequent year of operation.

A copy of the bond shall be filed with the Secretary of State, together with a declaration under penalty of perjury signed by the owner of the studio stating the dance studio's gross income from the dance studio business in this state during the last fiscal year. The information contained in the declaration shall not be subject to public inspection. If the person in whose name the bond is issued severs his or her relationship with the bonded dance studio, the new owner shall, as a condition of doing business, notify the Secretary of State of the change of ownership and of proof of compliance with Sections 1812.64 and 1812.65. **Leg.H.** Added Stats 1969 ch 1571 §1. Amended Stats 1976 ch 1200 §3; Stats 1987 ch 449 §14; Stats 1988 ch 1043 §14; Stats 1999 ch 1024 §3 (AB 648).

§1812.65. Beneficiary of bond

The bond required by Section 1812.64 shall be in favor of the State of California for the benefit of any person who, after entering into a contract for dance studio lessons and other services with the dance studio, is damaged by fraud or dishonesty or failure to provide the services of the studio in performance of the contract. **Leg.H.** Added Stats 1969 ch 1571 §1. Amended Stats 1982 ch 517 §59; Stats 1987 ch 449 §15; Stats 1988 ch 1043 §15.

§1812.66. [Section repealed 1999]

Leg.H. Added Stats 1984 ch 545 §2. Amended Stats 1996 ch 633 §6 (SB 1978); Stats 1998 ch 829 §8 (SB 1652). Repealed Stats 1999 ch 1024 §4 (AB 648). The repealed section related to claims against deposits in lieu of bond.

Prior Law: Former §1812.66, relating to cash deposit in lieu of bond, was added Stats 1969 ch 1571 §1, amended Stats 1971 ch 903 §1, Stats 1976 ch 1200 §3, and repealed Stats 1982 ch 517 §60.

§1812.67. Exceptions to bond requirements

(a) Sections 1812.64 and 1812.65 do not apply to any dance studio which requires or receives less than fifty dollars ($50) in advance payments from or on behalf of each student for dance studio lessons or other services which are to be rendered by the studio in the future and such advance payments are not required or received by the studio from each student more frequently than once every 30 days.

(b) Sections 1812.53, 1812.54, 1812.64, and 1812.65 do not apply to a dance studio which only offers instruction in ballet, modern, jazz, tap dance, or any combination thereof, to persons under 21 years of age pursuant to a contract for dance studio lessons that provides all of the following: (1) a total payment of less than five hundred dollars ($500), (2) that all agreed-upon lessons will be offered within four months from the date the contract is entered, and (3) that the contract may be canceled and all money paid for instruction not yet received will be refunded within 10 days of cancellation, if the dance student cancels within three days after receiving the first lesson, or if the dance student cancels at any time after moving his or her residence to a location more than 15 miles from the location of the dance studio.

(c) Sections 1812.53, 1812.54, 1812.64, and 1812.65 do not apply to any organization that has qualified for a tax exemption under Section 501 (c) (3) of the Internal Revenue Code and which receives a direct grant of funds from the California Arts Council. **Leg.H.** Added Stats 1969 ch 1571 §1. Amended Stats 1971 ch 903 §2; Stats 1976 ch 1200 §4; Stats 1982 ch 517 §61; Stats 1987 ch 449 §16; Stats 1988 ch 1043 §16.

§1812.68. Severability of provisions

If any provision of this title or the application thereof to any person or circumstances is held unconstitutional, the remainder of the title and the application of such provision to other persons and circumstances shall not be affected thereby. **Leg.H.** Added Stats 1969 ch 1571 §1.

§1812.69. Filing of bonds

(a) The Secretary of State shall enforce the provisions of this title that govern the filing and maintenance of bonds.

(b) The Secretary of State shall charge a filing fee not to exceed the cost of filing the bond. **Leg.H.** Added Stats 1996 ch 633 §7 (SB 1978). Amended Stats 1999 ch 1024 §5 (AB 648).

TITLE 2.5
CONTRACTS FOR HEALTH STUDIO SERVICES

Findings and declarations. §1812.80.
Definitions. §1812.81.
Form; Delivery. §1812.82.
Contracts between same parties. §1812.83.
Term limits; Disclosure statement requirements. §1812.84.
Contents. §1812.85.
Maximum payments. §1812.86.
Third party rights. §1812.87.
Assignment. §1812.88.
Death or disability; Installments. §1812.89.
Applicability of other provisions. §1812.90.
Noncomplying contracts. §1812.91.
Fraudulently induced contracts. §1812.92.
Waiver of provisions. §1812.93.
Civil actions. §1812.94.
Severability. §1812.95.
Health studio not yet open for business. §1812.96.
Month-to-month contracts permitted. §1812.98.

§1812.80. Findings and declarations

(a) The Legislature finds that the health studio industry has a significant impact upon the economy and well-being of this state and its local communities; and that the provisions of this title relating to contracts for health studio services are necessary for the public welfare.

(b) The Legislature declares that the purpose of this title is to safeguard the public against fraud, deceit, imposition and financial hardship, and to foster and encourage competition, fair dealing, and prosperity in the field of health studio services by prohibiting or restricting false or misleading advertising, onerous contract terms, harmful financial practices, and other unfair, dishonest, deceptive, destructive, unscrupulous, fraudulent, and discriminatory practices by which the public has been injured in connection with contracts for health studio services. **Leg.H.** Added Stats 1961 ch 1675 §1. Amended Stats 1969 ch 1571 §3; Stats 2005 ch 439 §1 (SB 581), effective January 1, 2006.

§1812.81. Definitions

As used in this title, "contract for health studio services" means a contract for instruction, training or assistance in physical culture, body building, exercising, reducing, figure development, or any other such physical skill, or for the use by an individual patron of the facilities of a health studio, gymnasium or other facility used for any of the above purposes, or for membership in any group, club, association or organization formed for any of the above purposes; but does not include (a) contracts for professional services rendered or furnished by a person licensed under the provisions of Division 2 (commencing with Section 500) of the Business and Professions Code,(b)contracts for instruction at schools operating pursuant to the provisions of the Education Code, or (c) contracts for instruction, training, or assistance relating to diet or control of eating habits not involving physical culture, body building, exercising, figure development, or any other such physical skill. **Leg.H.** Added Stats 1961 ch 1675 §1. Amended Stats 1969 ch 1571 §4; Stats 1980 ch 690 §1.

§1812.82. Form; Delivery

Every contract for health studio services shall be in writing and shall be subject to the provisions of this title. A copy of the written contract shall be physically given to or delivered by email to the customer at the time he or she signs the contract. **Leg.H.** Added Stats 1961 ch 1675 §1. Amended

Stats 1969 ch 611 §1, ch 1571 §5; Stats 2016 ch 189 §1 (AB 2810), effective January 1, 2017.

§1812.83. Contracts between same parties

All contracts for health studio services, which may be in effect between the same seller and the same buyer, the terms of which overlap for any period, shall be considered as one contract for the purposes of this title. **Leg.H.** Added Stats 1961 ch 1675 §1. Amended Stats 1969 ch 1571 §6.

§1812.84. Term limits; Disclosure statement requirements

(a) A contract for health studio services may not require payments or financing by the buyer to exceed the term of the contract, nor may the term of the contract exceed three years. This subdivision does not apply to a member's obligation to pay valid, outstanding moneys due under the contract, including moneys to be paid pursuant to a termination notice period in the contract in which the termination notice period does not exceed 30 days.

(b) A contract for health studio services shall include a statement printed in a size at least 14-point type or presented in an equally legible electronic format that discloses the initial or minimum length of the term of the contract. This statement shall be placed above the space reserved for the signature of the buyer.

(c) At any time a cancellation is authorized by this title, a contract for health studio services may be canceled by the buyer in person, via email from an email address on file with the health studio, or via first-class mail. **Leg.H.** Added Stats 1961 ch 1675 §1. Amended Stats 1969 ch 1571 §7; Stats 1980 ch 651 §1; Stats 1993 ch 339 §1 (AB 626); Stats 2001 ch 233 §1 (SB 85); Stats 2005 ch 439 §2 (SB 581), effective January 1, 2006; Stats 2006 ch 219 §1 (AB 2664), effective January 1, 2007; Stats 2016 ch 189 §2 (AB 2810), effective January 1, 2017.

§1812.85. Contents

(a) Every contract for health studio services shall provide that performance of the agreed-upon services will begin within six months after the date the contract is entered into. The consumer may cancel the contract and receive a pro rata refund if the health studio fails to provide the specific facilities advertised or offered in writing by the time indicated. If no time is indicated in the contract, the consumer may cancel the contract within six months after the execution of the contract and shall receive a pro rata refund. If a health studio fails to meet a timeline set forth in this section, the consumer may cancel the contract at any time after the expiration of the timeline. However, if following the expiration of the timeline, the health studio provides the advertised or agreed-upon services, the consumer may cancel the contract up to 10 days after those services are provided.

(b)(1) Every contract for health studio services shall, in addition, contain on its face, and in close proximity to the space reserved for the signature of the buyer, a conspicuous statement in a size equal to at least 10-point boldface type, as follows:

"You, the buyer, may choose to cancel this agreement at any time prior to midnight of the fifth business day of the health studio after the date of this agreement, excluding Sundays and holidays. To cancel this agreement, mail, email, or deliver a signed and dated notice that states that you, the buyer, are canceling this agreement, or words of similar effect. The notice shall be sent via first-class mail, via email from an email address on file with the health studio, or delivered in person to

_____
(Name of health studio operator)
at _____
(Address and email address of health studio operator)."

(2) The contract for health studio services shall contain on the first page, in a type size no smaller than that generally used in the body of the document, the following: (A) the name and mailing address of the health studio operator to which the notice of cancellation is to be mailed, and (B) the email address of the health studio operator to which a notice of cancellation email is to be sent, and (C) the date the buyer signed the contract.

(3) The contract shall provide a description of the services, facilities, and hours of access to which the consumer is entitled or state where that information is available on the health studio operator's Internet Web site. Any services, facilities, and hours of access that are not described in the contract or on the health studio operator's Internet Web site shall be considered optional services, and these optional services shall be considered as separate contracts for the purposes of this title and Section 1812.83.

(4) Until the health studio operator has complied with this section, the buyer may cancel the contract for health studio services.

(5) All moneys paid pursuant to a contract for health studio services shall be refunded within 10 days after receipt of the notice of cancellation, except that payment shall be made for any health studio services received prior to cancellation.

(c) If at any time during the term of the contract, including a transfer of the contractual obligation, the health studio eliminates or substantially reduces the scope of the facilities, such as swimming pools or tennis courts, that were described in the contract, in an advertisement relating to the specific location, or in a written offer, and available to the consumer upon execution of the contract, the consumer may cancel the contract and receive a pro rata refund. The consumer may not cancel the contract pursuant to this subdivision if the health studio, after giving reasonable notice to its members, temporarily takes facilities out of operation for reasonable repairs, modifications, substitutions, or improvements. This subdivision shall not be interpreted to give the consumer the right to cancel a contract because of changes to the type or quantity of classes or equipment offered, provided the consumer is informed in the contract that the health studio reserves the right to make changes to the type or quantity of classes or equipment offered and the changes to the type or quantity of classes or equipment offered are reasonable under the circumstances.

(d)(1) If a contract for health studio services requires payment of one thousand five hundred dollars ($1,500) to two thousand dollars ($2,000), inclusive, including initiation fees or initial membership fees, by the person receiving the services or the use of the facility, the person shall have the right to cancel the contract within 20 days after the contract is executed.

(2) If a contract for health studio services requires payment of two thousand one dollars ($2,001) to two thousand five hundred dollars ($2,500), inclusive, including initiation fees or initial membership fees, by the person receiving the services or the use of the facility, the person shall have the right to cancel the contract within 30 days after the contract is executed.

(3) If a contract for health studio services requires payment of two thousand five hundred one dollars ($2,501) or more, including initiation fees or initial membership fees, by the person receiving the services or the use of the facility, the person shall have the right to cancel the contract within 45 days after the contract is executed.

(4) The right of cancellation provided in this subdivision shall be set out in the membership contract.

(5) The rights and remedies under this paragraph are cumulative to any rights and remedies under other law.

(6) A health studio entering into a contract for health studio services that requires a payment of less than one thousand five hundred dollars ($1,500), including initiation or initial membership fees and exclusive of interest or finance charges, by the person receiving the services or the use of the facilities, is not required to comply with paragraph (1), (2), or (3).

(e) Upon cancellation, the consumer shall be liable only for that portion of the total contract payment, including initiation fees and other charges however denominated, that has been available for use by the consumer, based upon a pro rata calculation over the term of the contract. The remaining portion of the contract payment shall be returned to the consumer by the health studio. **Leg.H.** Added Stats 1961 ch 1675 §1. Amended Stats 1967 ch 1613 §1; Stats 1969 ch 611 §2, ch 1571 §8; Stats 1980 ch 651 §2; Stats 2005 ch 439 §3 (SB 581), effective January 1, 2006; Stats 2006 ch 219 §2 (AB 2664), (ch 219 prevails), ch 538 §48 (SB 1852), effective January 1, 2007; Stats 2016 ch 189 §3 (AB 2810), effective January 1, 2017.

§1812.86. Maximum payments

(a) No contract for health studio services shall require payment by the person receiving the services or the use of the facilities of a total amount in excess of the amount specified in subdivision (b) or (c).

(b) The limit specified in subdivision (a) shall, on and after January 1, 2006, be three thousand dollars ($3,000), inclusive of initiation or initial membership fees and exclusive of interest or finance charges.

(c) The limit in subdivision (a) shall, on and after January 1, 2010, be four thousand four hundred dollars ($4,400), inclusive of initiation or initial membership fees and exclusive of interest or finance charges.

Leg.H. Added Stats 1961 ch 1675 §1. Amended Stats 1967 ch 1613 §2; Stats 1969 ch 1571 §9; Stats 1980 ch 651 §3; Stats 2005 ch 439 §4 (SB 581), effective January 1, 2006.

§1812.87. Third party rights

No contract for health studio services shall require or entail the execution of any note or series of notes by the buyer which when separately negotiated will cut off as to third parties any right of action or defense which the buyer may have against the seller. **Leg.H.** Added Stats 1961 ch 1675 §1. Amended Stats 1969 ch 1571 §10.

§1812.88. Assignment

No right of action or defense arising out of a contract for health studio services which the buyer has against the seller, and which would be cut off by assignment, shall be cut off by assignment of the contract to any third party whether or not he acquires the contract in good faith and for value unless the assignee gives notice of the assignment to the buyer as provided in this section and within 30 days of the mailing of notice receives no written notice of the facts giving rise to the claim or defense of the buyer. A notice of assignment shall be in writing addressed to the buyer at the address shown on the contract and shall identify the contract and inform the buyer that he must, within 30 days of the date of mailing of the notice, notify the assignee in writing of any facts giving rise to a claim or defense which he may have. The notice of assignment shall state the name of the seller and buyer, a description of the services, the contract balance and the number and amount of the installments. **Leg.H.** Added by Stats 1961 ch 1675 §1. Amended Stats 1969 ch 1675 §1.

§1812.89. Death or disability; Installments

(a)(1) Every contract for health studio services shall contain a clause providing that if, by reason of death or disability, the person agreeing to receive services is unable to receive all services for which he has contracted, he and his estate shall be relieved from the obligation of making payment for services other than those received prior to death or the onset of disability, and that if he has prepaid any sum for services, so much of such sum as is allocable to services he has not taken shall be promptly refunded to him or his representative.

(2) In every case in which a person has prepaid a sum for services under a contract for health studio services, and by reason of death or disability, is unable to receive all such services, the party agreeing to furnish such services shall, on request, immediately refund to such person or his personal representative such amount of the sum prepaid as is proportionate to the amount of services not received.

(3) For the purposes of this section, "disability" means a condition which precludes the buyer from physically using the facilities and the condition is verified by a physician.

(4) Notwithstanding the provisions of any contract to the contrary, whenever the contract price is payable in installments and the buyer is relieved from making further payments or entitled to a refund under this section, the amount of the contract price allocable to services not received shall represent at least as great a proportion of the total contract price as the sum of the periodic monthly balances not yet due bears to the sum of all the periodic monthly balances under the schedule of installments in the contract.

(b)(1) Except as provided in paragraph (2), every contract for health studio services shall contain a clause providing that if the person agreeing to receive health studio services moves further than 25 miles from the health studio and is unable to transfer the contract to a comparable facility, such person shall be relieved from the obligation of making payment for services other than those received prior to the move, and if such person has prepaid any sum for health studio services, so much of such sum as is allocable to services he or she has not taken shall be promptly refunded.

(2) Notwithstanding paragraph (1), a contract for health studio services may contain a clause providing that if the person agreeing to receive health studio services moves further than 25 miles from the health studio and is unable to transfer the contract to a comparable facility, such person may be charged a predetermined fee not exceeding one hundred dollars ($100), or, if more than half the life of the contract has expired, such person may be charged a predetermined fee not exceeding fifty dollars ($50). **Leg.H.** Added Stats 1961 ch 1675 §1. Amended Stats 1969 ch 1571 §12; Stats 1980 ch 651 §4.

§1812.90. Applicability of other provisions

The provisions of this title are not exclusive and do not relieve the parties or the contracts subject thereto from compliance with all other applicable provisions of law. **Leg.H.** Added Stats 1961 ch 1675 §1.

§1812.91. Noncomplying contracts

Any contract for health studio services which does not comply with the applicable provisions of this title shall be void and unenforceable as contrary to public policy. **Leg.H.** Added Stats 1961 ch 1675 §1. Amended Stats 1969 ch 1571 §13.

§1812.92. Fraudulently induced contracts

Any contract for health studio services entered into in reliance upon any willful and false, fraudulent, or misleading information, representation, notice or advertisement of the seller shall be void and unenforceable. **Leg.H.** Added Stats 1961 ch 1675 §1. Amended Stats 1969 ch 1571 §14.

§1812.93. Waiver of provisions

Any waiver of the buyer of the provisions of this title shall be deemed contrary to public policy and shall be void and unenforceable. **Leg.H.** Added Stats 1961 ch 1675 §1.

§1812.94. Civil actions

(a) Any buyer injured by a violation of this title may bring an action for the recovery of damages. Judgment may be entered for three times the amount at which the actual damages are assessed plus reasonable attorney fees.

(b) Notwithstanding the provisions of this title, any failure to comply with any provision of this title may be corrected within 30 days after the execution of the contract by the buyer, and, if so corrected, neither the seller nor the holder shall be subject to any penalty under this title, provided that any correction which increases any monthly payment, the number of payments, or the total amount due, must be concurred in, in writing, by the buyer. "Holder" includes the seller who acquires the contract or, if the contract is purchased by a financing agency or other assignee, the financing agency or other assignee. **Leg.H.** Added Stats 1961 ch 1675 §1. Amended Stats 1963 ch 299 §1.

§1812.95. Severability

If any provision of this title or the application thereof to any person or circumstances is held unconstitutional, the remainder of the title and the application of such provision to other persons and circumstances shall not be affected thereby. **Leg.H.** Added Stats 1961 ch 1675 §1.

§1812.96. Health studio not yet open for business

(a) Except as provided in subdivision (c) or (d), all money received by the seller of health studio services from a consumer for a health studio facility that has not yet opened for business shall be held in trust and shall be deposited in a trust account established in a state or federally chartered bank or savings association. The seller shall not draw, transfer, or encumber any of the money held in trust until five business days after the health studio facility has opened and the seller has fully paid refunds to consumers who canceled their contracts as provided in subdivision (b) or in Section 1812.85.

(b) In addition to any other cancellation rights, a consumer who pays any money under a contract for health studio services for a health studio facility that has not yet opened for business has the right to cancel the contract and receive a full refund at any time prior to midnight of the fifth business day after the date the health studio opens for business. The cancellation right shall be set forth in the contract. The refund shall be paid within 10 days of receipt of notice of cancellation.

(c) Notwithstanding subdivision (a), a seller of health studio services may draw on money held in trust to pay refunds or may draw, transfer, or encumber funds to the extent that the amount is offset by a bond of equal or greater amount that satisfies this subdivision. The bond shall be issued by a surety insurer admitted to do business in this state and shall be filed with the Secretary of State. The bond shall be in favor of the State of California for the benefit of consumers harmed by a violation of this title.

(d) Subdivision (a) does not apply to a seller of health studio services that is, at the time money is received from the consumer, operating at least five health studio facilities in this state that have been in operation for a period of at least five years, and that has an excess of current assets over current liabilities of at least one million dollars ($1,000,000). **Leg.H.** Added Stats 2005 ch 439 §5 (SB 581).

Prior Law: Former CC §1812.96, similar to the present section, was added Stats 1967 ch 1613 §3 and repealed Stats 1969 ch 1571 §15. See CC §1812.63.

§1812.98 Month-to-month contracts permitted

Nothing in this title is intended to prohibit month-to-month contracts. This section is declaratory of existing law. **Leg.H.** Added Stats 2005 ch

439 §6 (SB 581), effective January 1, 2006, as CC §1812.97. Renumbered by Stats 2006 ch 538 §49 (1852), effective January 1, 2007.

Prior Law: Former §1812.98 was added Stats 1967 ch 1613 §§5, 6 and repealed Stats 1969 ch 1571 §§17, 18. See CC §1812.63.

§1812.99.   [Section repealed 1969]

Leg.H. Added Stats 1967 ch 1613 §§5, 6. Repealed Stats 1969 ch 1571 §§17, 18. See CC §1812.63.

§1812.995   [Section repealed 1969]

Leg.H. Added Stats 1967 ch 1613 §7. Repealed Stats 1969 ch 1571 §19. See CC §1812.63.

TITLE 2.55
CONTRACTS FOR THE LEASE OR RENTAL OF ATHLETIC FACILITIES

Required warnings regarding steroids. §1812.97.

§1812.97.   Required warnings regarding steroids

(a) Every contract which has as its purpose the lease or rental of athletic facilities for instruction, training, or assistance in physical culture, body building, exercising, reducing, figure development, or any other related physical skill, or for baseball, football, tennis, basketball, gymnastics, track and field, hockey, ice skating, weightlifting, wrestling, or bicycling shall contain the following warning statement in 10-point bold type:

Warning: Use of steroids to increase strength or growth can cause serious health problems. Steroids can keep teenagers from growing to their full height; they can also cause heart disease, stroke, and damaged liver function. Men and women using steroids may develop fertility problems, personality changes, and acne. Men can also experience premature balding and development of breast tissue. These health hazards are in addition to the civil and criminal penalties for unauthorized sale, use, or exchange of anabolic steroids.

(b) Commencing June 1, 1990, the warning statement required pursuant to subdivision (a) shall be conspicuously posted in all athletic facilities in this state which have locker rooms. At least one warning statement shall be posted in every locker room of the athletic facility.

(c) As used in this section, "athletic facilities" includes a health studio regulated pursuant to Title 2.5 (commencing with Section 1812.80), a professional boxers' training gymnasium, as defined in Section 18685 of the Business and Professions Code, any privately owned sports facility or stadium in this state which is open to the general public, and any publicly owned sports facility or stadium in this state, including facilities in institutions of higher learning and schools that include any or all grades 7 to 12, inclusive.

(d) As used in this section, "anabolic steroids" include, but are not limited to, the following:

(1) Dianabol (methandrostenelone).
(2) Winstrol (stabozalol).
(3) Maxibolin (ethyl estrenol).
(4) Durabolin (nandrolone phenpropionate).
(5) Deca-Durabolin (nandrolone decanote).
(6) Testosterone propionate.
(7) Pregnyl (chorionic gonadotropin).
(8) Anavar (toxandroprione).

(e) When an athletic facility seeks to renew an operating license, if it can be demonstrated by a preponderance of the evidence that an athletic facility has not posted the sign required pursuant to this section, the licensing agency may impose a fine in the amount of fifty dollars ($50) per day for each day that the violation occurred, as a condition of obtaining the license renewal. **Leg.H.** Added Stats 1986 ch 565 §1. Amended Stats 1989 ch 807 §2, operative June 1, 1990.

Prior Law: Former §1812.97, similar to present CC §§1812.63–1812.67, was added Stats 1967 ch 1613 §4 and repealed Stats 1969 ch 1571 §16.

There was another section of this number which was added Stats 2005 ch 439 §6 (SB 581), effective January 1, 2006, and renumbered CC §1812.98 by Stats 2006 ch 538 §49 (SB 1852), effective January 1, 2007. CC §1812.98 appears in Title 2.5, "Contracts for Health Studio Services."

TITLE 2.6
CONTRACTS FOR DISCOUNT BUYING SERVICES

Findings and declarations. §1812.100.
Definitions. §1812.101.
Bond. §1812.103.
Beneficiary of bond; Liability of surety. §1812.104.
Claims against deposits in lieu of bond. §1812.105.
Required disclosures. §1812.106.
Contract requirements. §1812.107.
Overlapping terms. §1812.108.
Limitation on contract term. §1812.109.
Limitation on waiting period. §1812.110.
Third party rights. §1812.113.
Assignment. §1812.114.
Delayed delivery or nondelivery. §1812.116.
Exemption from trust account provisions for certain affiliate discount buying organizations. §1812.117.
Right to cancel. §1812.118.
Noncomplying contracts. §1812.119.
Fraudulently induced contracts. §1812.120.
Removal of business; Discontinuance of goods or services. §1812.121.
Transfer of duty or obligation by buying service. §1812.122.
Civil actions. §1812.123.
Criminal violations. §1812.125.
Applicability of other provisions. §1812.126.
Waiver of provisions. §1812.127.
Separability of provisions. §1812.128.
Filing of bonds. §1812.129.

§1812.100.   Findings and declarations

(a) The Legislature finds that there exist in connection with a substantial number of contracts for discount buying services, sales practices and business and financing practices which result in fraud, deceit, and financial hardships being perpetrated on the people of the state; that existing legal remedies are inadequate to correct these abuses; that the discount buying industry has a significant impact upon the economy and well-being of the state and its local communities; and that the provisions of this title relating to such contracts are necessary for the public welfare.

(b) The purpose of this title is to safeguard the public against fraud, deceit, and financial hardship, and to foster and encourage competition, fair dealing, and prosperity in the field of discount buying services by prohibiting or restricting false or misleading advertising, unfair contract terms, harmful financial practices, and other unfair, deceptive, destructive, unscrupulous, fraudulent and discriminatory practices by which the public has been endangered and by which the public may in the future be harmed in connection with contracts for discount buying services. This title shall be construed liberally in order to achieve the foregoing purposes. **Leg.H.** Added Stats 1976 ch 237 §1.

§1812.101.   Definitions

For the purpose of this title, the following definitions shall be used:

(a) "Discount buying organization" means any person or persons, corporation, unincorporated association, or other organization which, for a consideration, provides or purports to provide its clients or the clients or members of any other discount buying organization with the ability to purchase goods or services at discount prices, except that a discount buying organization does not include any of the following:

(1) Any discount buying organization in which the total consideration paid by each client or member in any manner whatsoever for the purchase of discount buying services from the organization that either:

(A) Does not exceed a one-time fee of fifty dollars ($50) or an annual fee of twenty-five dollars ($25) to be paid on a yearly basis.

(B) Does not exceed a one-time or annual fee of fifty dollars ($50) and the organization provides a majority of the goods and services through purchases by members who walk in to a fixed location operated by the organization.

(2) Any discount buying organization in which the total consideration paid by each client or member in any manner whatsoever for the purchase of discount buying services from the organization does not exceed a one-time or annual fee of one hundred dollars ($100) and the organization does all of the following in subparagraphs (A) to (F), inclusive, and subject to subparagraph (G):

(A) Offers buying services to clients or members through toll-free telephone access, computer access, or video shopping terminals.

(B)(i) During the first year of membership of each member, upon the request of the member, provides a full refund of membership fees, exclusive of any fees, however designated, not exceeding ten dollars ($10) in the aggregate, without conditions other than the surrender or destruction of materials which allow the member to access or use the service.

(ii)(I) The organization shall establish an escrow account of fifty thousand dollars ($50,000) for the purpose of providing refunds to members, pursuant to clause (i). If the fifty thousand dollars ($50,000) deposited in escrow is depleted during the first year of the existence of the escrow account, the organization shall within three business days of depletion replenish the account in the amount of fifty thousand dollars ($50,000). For each calendar year thereafter, the organization shall deposit in the account an amount equal to refunds made from the account in the prior calendar year, but not less than fifty thousand dollars ($50,000). At any time the balance in the escrow account decreases to 50 percent of the amount funded that year, the organization shall within three business days replenish the account back to the balance required at the beginning of that calendar year. The organization shall provide proof of the establishment of the escrow account to the Secretary of State and shall maintain records of all member requests for refunds and refunds made pursuant to this clause. The records shall be made available for review upon request by the Attorney General, any district attorney, or the Department of Justice.

(II) The escrow account shall be established and maintained at a federally insured bank or federally insured financial institution independent of the organization with escrow instructions making the bank or financial institution or an officer or employee thereof the escrow trustee.

(III) Refunds shall be made from the escrow account to any member who provides proof of membership while a California resident and requests, in writing, a membership refund, and has not previously been refunded his or her membership fee. The escrow trustee shall issue the refund within 10 days of the date the written request is received by the escrow trustee. In addition, requests for refunds may be made directly to and paid directly by the organization.

(IV) Proof of creation of the escrow account, and membership refund information, shall be provided to the members in the following form:

"The ____ (organization) has established an escrow account for the refund of membership fees at ____ (financial institution). Refunds from the escrow account may, in addition to other remedies and sources available to you, be obtained by mailing a written request along with proof of membership to ____ (escrow trustee). This refund request shall not affect or limit any other remedy at law available to you."

(C) Provides at least 15 toll-free service lines to California consumers devoted exclusively to customer service questions and complaints.

(D) Maintains a bond which meets the requirements of Sections 1812.103 and 1812.104, except that the principal sum of the bond need only be twenty thousand dollars ($20,000).

(E)(i) Possesses an unrevoked acknowledgment from the Attorney General that the organization has provided to the Attorney General, to the Attorney General's reasonable satisfaction, marketing procedures and documents that clearly explain membership fee cancellation and refund terms which include:

(I) The amount of the initial membership fee and how and when it will be collected.

(II) If applicable, that a member must be advised, before any charges are applied, that they need not provide billing information in order to be charged a membership fee, in circumstances in which the telemarketing firm has prior access to the member's billing information.

(III) In the case of trial membership offers, the duration of the trial period and that if the member does not cancel within the trial period he or she will automatically be charged the membership fee.

(IV) Specifically how the member may cancel membership.

(V) The written disclosure, printed in capital letters with a minimum 14-point boldface type, indicating who to contact, both directly through the company and through the escrow account, for a refund.

(VI) The written disclosure made at the time of solicitation and at the time an enrollment package is sent to consumers.

(ii) When an organization provides documentation that clearly explains membership fee cancellation and refund terms to the Attorney General's reasonable satisfaction, which includes the information required by subclauses (I) to (VI), inclusive, of clause (i) of subparagraph (E), the Attorney General shall issue a revocable acknowledgment to the organization for it to obtain this exception. The acknowledgment issued by the Attorney General is not evidence of the adequacy or accuracy of the organization's actual disclosures and representations provided to consumers. No organization in any marketing to consumers may make any reference to an acknowledgment issued by the Attorney General under this clause.

(F) Provides the disclosures listed in subclauses (I) to (VI), inclusive, of clause (i) of subparagraph (E) to every prospective member.

(G) The exemption is null and void if the organization fails to comply with the conditions set forth in this section or if the Attorney General's office revokes the exemption due to a organization not being in full compliance with all of the provisions of this section.

(3) Any discount buying organization in which persons receive discount buying services incidentally as part of a package of services provided to or available to the individual on account of his or her membership in the organization, which is not organized for the profit of any person or organization, and which does not have as one of its primary purposes or businesses, the provision of discount buying services.

(4) Any person, corporation, unincorporated association, or other organization, which, for a consideration collected from another entity, provides or purports to provide the clients of the other entity with the ability to purchase goods or services at discount prices, if the clients of the other entity do not order from, or pay any money to, that person, corporation, unincorporated association, or other organization; however, the entity, from which the customer purchases the right to obtain goods or services at discount prices, shall comply with the requirements of this title.

(b) "Contract for discount buying services" means a contract between one party (hereinafter referred to as the "buyer") who is purchasing the service for personal or family use, and a discount buying organization, whereby the buyer for a consideration receives the right to obtain goods or services from the discount buying organization, or to utilize the discount buying organization services in obtaining goods and services, at discount prices.

(c) "Discount prices" means prices which are represented to be lower on most or all offered goods or services than those generally charged for the items in the locality in which the representation is made.

This definition is not intended to affect the degree of savings which must be offered on an item or selection of items in order to truthfully and without misleading consumers represent an item, selection of items, or entire store as being "discount" or "discounted." **Leg.H.** Added Stats 1976 ch 237 §1. Amended Stats 1985 ch 558 §1; Stats 1986 ch 345 §1, effective July 15, 1986; Stats 1992 ch 304 §1 (AB 2859); Stats 2001 ch 178 §1 (SB 916).

§1812.103. Bond

Every discount buying organization shall maintain a bond issued by a surety company admitted to do business in this state. The principal sum of the bond shall be twenty thousand dollars ($20,000). A copy of such bond shall be filed with the Secretary of State. **Leg.H.** Added Stats 1976 ch 237 §1. Amended Stats 1996 ch 633 §8 (SB 1978).

§1812.104. Beneficiary of bond; Liability of surety

The bond required by Section 1812.103 shall be in favor of the State of California for the benefit of any person who is damaged by any violation of this title or by fraud or dishonesty or failure to provide the services of the discount buying organization in performance of the contract. The surety shall be liable only for the actual damages plus restitution and not the treble damages permitted under subdivision (a) of Section 1812.123. **Leg.H.** Added Stats 1976 ch 237 §1. Amended Stats 1982 ch 517 §62.

§1812.105. Claims against deposits in lieu of bond

(a) When a deposit has been made in lieu of a bond pursuant to Section 995.710 of the Code of Civil Procedure, the person asserting a claim against the deposit shall, in lieu of Section 996.430 of the Code of Civil Procedure, establish the claim by furnishing evidence to the Secretary of State of a money judgment entered by a court together with evidence that the claimant is a person described in Section 1812.104.

(b) When a person has established the claim with the Secretary of State, the Secretary of State shall review and approve the claim and enter the date of approval on the claim. The claim shall be designated an "approved claim."

(c) When the first claim against a particular deposit has been approved, it shall not be paid until the expiration of a period of 240 days after the date of its approval by the Secretary of State. Subsequent claims that are approved by the Secretary of State within the same 240-day period shall similarly not be paid until the expiration of the 240-day period. Upon the expiration of the 240-day period, the Secretary of State shall pay all approved claims from that 240-day period in full unless the deposit is insufficient, in which case each approved claim shall be paid a pro rata share of the deposit.

(d) When the Secretary of State approves the first claim against a particular deposit after the expiration of a 240-day period, the date of approval of that claim shall begin a new 240-day period to which subdivision (c) shall apply with respect to the amount remaining in the deposit.

(e) After a deposit is exhausted, no further claims shall be paid by the Secretary of State. Claimants who have had their claims paid in full or in part pursuant to subdivisions (c) and (d) shall not be required to return funds received from the deposit for the benefit of other claimants.

(f) When a deposit has been made in lieu of a bond, the amount of the deposit shall not be subject to attachment, garnishment, or execution with respect to an action or judgment against the discount buying organization, other than as to an amount as no longer needed or required for the purpose of this title that would otherwise be returned to the discount buying organization by the Secretary of State.

(g) The Secretary of State shall retain a cash deposit for two years from the date the Secretary of State receives written notification from the assignor of the deposit that the assignor has ceased to engage in the business of a discount buying organization or has filed a bond pursuant to Section 1812.103, provided that there are no outstanding claims against the deposit. This written notice shall include all of the following: (1) name, address, and telephone number of the assignor; (2) name, address, and telephone number of the bank at which the deposit is located; (3) account number of the deposit; and (4) a statement whether the assignor is ceasing to engage in the business of a discount buying organization or has filed a bond with the Secretary of State. The Secretary of State shall forward an acknowledgment of receipt of the written notice to the assignor at the address indicated therein, specifying the date of receipt of the written notice and anticipated date of release of the deposit, provided there are no outstanding claims against the deposit.

(h) A judge of a superior court may order the return of the deposit prior to the expiration of two years upon evidence satisfactory to the judge that there are no outstanding claims against the deposit or order the Secretary of State to retain the deposit for a sufficient period beyond the two years specified in subdivision (g) to resolve outstanding claims against the deposit. **Leg.H.** Added Stats 1984 ch 545 §3. Amended Stats 1996 ch 633 §9 (SB 1978); Stats 1998 ch 829 §9 (SB 1652); Stats 2002 ch 784 §14 (SB 1316).

Prior Law: Former §1812.105, relating to cash deposit in lieu of bond, was added Stats 1976 ch 237 §1 and repealed Stats 1982 ch 517 §63.

§1812.106. Required disclosures

Every discount buying organization, before obtaining the signature of a potential buyer on any application or contract for discount buying services, shall provide to the buyer, and shall allow the buyer to retain, the following written disclosures:

(a) The exact nature of the services it provides, specifying the general categories of goods that are available at the discount buying organization's place of business or warehouse, those categories of goods, if any, that must be ordered or obtained through stores to which the discount buying organization will refer the customer, and those categories of goods, if any, that must be ordered or obtained through the mail.

(b) A list, current within the previous 60 days, of at least 100 items that are sold by or through the organization or available to those who contract with the organization, identified by brand name, model, and total price including a reasonable estimate of freight charges, if any are to be imposed; a reasonable estimate of delivery charges, if any are to be imposed; a reasonable estimate of setup charges, if any are to be imposed; the discount buying organization's price markup; and a reasonable estimate of any other charges the discount buying organization imposes. These items shall be reasonably representative as to the type of goods available. In lieu of providing this list, the discount buying organization shall provide and allow the buyer to retain a list of at least 100 items that were purchased by its members through the discount buying organization during the preceding 60 days. This list shall identify the items by brand name, model, and total selling price including freight charges, if any; delivery charges, if any; setup charges, if any; the discount buying organization's price markup; and any other charges imposed by the discount buying organization, and shall be representative as to the type of goods sold and the prices charged for the listed goods sold during that period. If the maximum number of items available through a discount buying organization is fewer than 100 in number, it may comply with this section by furnishing a list of the total items available, identified as described above with a statement that those are the only goods presently available. Any list required by this subdivision shall state the date on which it was prepared.

(c) A statement of the discount buying organization's policy with respect to warranties or guarantees on goods ordered, and the policy with respect to the return of ordered goods, cancellation of orders by the buyer, and refunds for cancellation or return.

(d) A description of any charges, such as freight charges, delivery charges, setup charges, seller's markup, and any other charges that are incidental to the purchase of goods through the discount buying organization and are to be paid by the buyer. A disclosure of these costs in specific monetary amounts shall also be made on each order placed through the discount buying organization.

(e) If any stockholder, director, officer, or general or limited partner of the discount buying organization, as the case may be:

(1) Has been convicted of a felony or misdemeanor or pleaded nolo contendere to a felony or misdemeanor charge, if the felony or misdemeanor involved fraud, embezzlement, fraudulent conversion, misappropriation of property, or a violation of this title.

(2) Has been held liable in a civil action by final judgment or consented to the entry of a stipulated judgment if the civil action alleged fraud, embezzlement, fraudulent conversion, or misappropriation of property, a violation of this title, the use of untrue or misleading representations in an attempt to sell or dispose of real or personal property, or the use of unfair, unlawful, or deceptive business practices.

(3) Is subject to any currently effective injunction or restrictive order relating to business activity as the result of an action brought by a public agency or department, including, but not limited to, an action affecting any vocational license, a statement so stating, and including the name of the court, the date of the conviction, judgment, order, or injunction and, if applicable, the name of the governmental agency that filed the action resulting in the conviction, judgment, order, or injunction. **Leg.H.** Added Stats 1976 ch 237 §1. Amended Stats 1980 ch 1001 §1, effective September 21, 1980; Stats 2006 ch 538 §50 (SB 1852), effective January 1, 2007.

§1812.107. Contract requirements

Every contract for discount buying services shall be in writing and shall be subject to the provisions of this title. The address of the seller's discount buying facility and the residence address of the buyer shall be clearly indicated on the face of the contract. A copy of the written contract shall be given to the buyer at the time he signs the contract. All blank spaces in the contract shall be filled in before the contract is signed by the buyer. Provisions or terms written by hand on the buyer's copy shall be legible. The contract shall disclose that a bond has been obtained by the discount buying organization and that a copy of such bond is on file with the Secretary of State. The contract shall be specific as to the period of time for which the discount buying services will be available to the buyer. This time period shall not be measured by the life of the buyer. **Leg.H.** Added Stats 1976 ch 237 §1.

§1812.108. Overlapping terms

All contracts for discount buying services, which may be in effect between a seller or related sellers and a buyer, the terms of which overlap for any period of time, shall be considered as one contract for the purpose of this title. **Leg.H.** Added Stats 1976 ch 237 §1.

§1812.109. Limitation on contract term

No contract for discount buying services shall require payments or financing by the buyer over a period in excess of two years from the date the contract was entered into. **Leg.H.** Added Stats 1976 ch 237 §1.

§1812.110. Limitation on waiting period

Every contract for discount buying services shall provide that the buying services shall become available to the buyer within seven days from the date the contract was entered into. **Leg.H.** Added Stats 1976 ch 237 §1.

§1812.113. Third party rights

No contract for discount buying services shall require or entail the execution of any note or series of notes by the buyer which, when separately negotiated, will cut off as to any third party any right of action or defense which the buyer may have against the seller. **Leg.H.** Added Stats 1976 ch 237 §1.

§1812.114. Assignment

No right of action or defense arising out of a contract for discount buying services which the buyer has against the discount buying organization shall be cut off by assignment or transfer of the contract to any third party. **Leg.H.** Added Stats 1976 ch 237 §1.

§1812.116. Delayed delivery or nondelivery

(a) Every contract for discount buying services shall provide that if any goods ordered by the buyer from the seller are not delivered to the buyer or available for pickup by the buyer at a location within his county of residence within six weeks from the date the buyer placed an order for such goods, then any moneys paid by the buyer for such goods in advance of delivery shall, upon the buyer's request, be fully refunded unless a predetermined delivery date has been furnished to the buyer in writing at the time he ordered such goods and the goods are delivered to the buyer or are available for pickup by that date.

(b) Prior to receiving from a buyer any payments pursuant to the terms of a contract for discount buying services, the discount buying organization shall establish a trust account at a federally insured bank or savings and loan association for the deposit, except for the first fifty dollars ($50) of a downpayment, of the contract payments as they are received.

If the discount buying organization sells or assigns the contract for discount buying services to a third party and such third party pays the discount buying organization as consideration an amount which is commercially reasonable for the sale or assignment of the contract, the discount buying organization shall deposit all funds received from the third party into the trust account.

If the discount buying organization in any manner transfers the contract for discount buying services to a third party which is to act as the recipient of contract payments from the buyer and such third party does not pay the discount buying organization as consideration for such transfer an amount which is commercially reasonable, then all sums received by the third party from the buyer shall be deposited in the discount buying organization's trust account for contract payments.

As to each buyer, during the first one-fourth or first six months of the buyer's membership period, whichever is shorter, funds representing no more than one-fourth of the contract price may be withdrawn from the trust account. During each subsequent one-fourth or six-month period, whichever is shorter, funds representing an additional one-fourth of the contract price may be withdrawn from the trust account.

(c)(1) Prior to receiving funds for an order of goods or services from any buyer, the discount buying organization shall establish a trust account at a federally insured bank or savings and loan association for the deposit of the funds. The discount buying organization shall deposit into the account all funds received from buyers for orders of goods or services regardless of how the funds are styled, including but not limited to, down payment, partial payment, payment in full, freight charge, or any other terms. If the total cost of goods or services ordered by a buyer on any one day does not exceed fifty dollars ($50), including taxes, freight charges, delivery charges, markup and all other charges collected by the discount buying organization, then the funds received from the buyer need not be deposited in the trust account.

(2) The trust account required by this section shall be created and maintained for the benefit of buyers who order goods or services from or through the discount buying organization. The discount buying organization shall not in any manner encumber the corpus of the account and shall not withdraw money deposited therein on behalf of a buyer except: (i) in partial or full payment to the discount buying organization's source for the goods or services ordered by the buyer, or (ii) to make a refund to the buyer. After the withdrawal of money from a buyer's deposit pursuant to (i) or (ii) above, only that portion of the remainder of the deposit which represents compensation to the discount buying organization may be withdrawn. **Leg.H.** Added Stats 1976 ch 237 §1. Amended Stats 1980 ch 1001 §2, effective September 21, 1980.

§1812.117. Exemption from trust account provisions for certain affiliate discount buying organizations

(a) An affiliate discount buying organization may, at its option, and with the express written consent of its parent, comply with the trust account withdrawal provisions set forth in subdivision (b), in lieu of those contained in subdivision (b) of Section 1812.116.

(b) The affiliate shall comply with the trust account provisions of subdivision (b) of Section 1812.116, except that:

(1) As to each buyer, during the first one-fourth or first six months of the buyer's membership period, whichever is shorter, funds representing no more than one-half of the contract price may be withdrawn from the trust account.

(2) During the subsequent one-fourth or six-month period of the buyer's membership period, whichever is shorter, the remaining balance of the contract price may be withdrawn from the trust account.

(c) To qualify for the provisions set forth in subdivision (b), (1) the affiliate shall maintain a surety bond of two hundred fifty thousand dollars ($250,000), and (2) the parent shall maintain an aggregate surety bond of two million five hundred thousand dollars ($2,500,000) and a letter of credit, as set forth in subdivision (d), for all of its affiliates that qualify for the withdrawal provisions of subdivision (b). The bonds shall be issued by a surety company admitted to do business in this state. A copy of each bond shall be filed with the Secretary of State, with a copy provided to the Attorney General. The affiliate's bond shall be in lieu of the bond required by subdivision (a) of Section 1812.103. The surety bonds shall comply with the requirements of this section and shall be in favor of the State of California for the benefit of consumers harmed by any violation of this title by the affiliate, the failure of the affiliate to comply with the terms of its membership contracts with consumers, and the failure of the affiliate to comply with the terms of any agreement with consumers for the purchase of goods or services, provided the bonds shall cover only pecuniary loss and not exemplary damages or treble damages permitted under subdivision (a) of Section 1812.123, and provided further the parent's bond shall not be drawn on until the affiliate's bond is exhausted.

(d) The parent shall continuously maintain and provide to the Attorney General as beneficiary an irrevocable letter of credit issued by a California state chartered bank or a national bank with its principal place of business in the State of California, in the amount of one million dollars ($1,000,000), in a form satisfactory to the Attorney General. After the bonds described in subdivision (c) have been exhausted, only the Attorney General, by and through the Attorney General's deputy or assistant, may draw on the letter of credit for the satisfaction of any final judgments based on any violation of this title by the affiliate, the failure of the affiliate to comply with the terms of its membership contracts with consumers, or the failure of an affiliate to comply with the terms of any agreement with consumers for the purchase of goods or services, provided the liability is established by final judgment of a court of competent jurisdiction and the time for appeal has expired or, if an appeal is taken, the appeal is finally determined and the judgment is affirmed, and provided further the letter of credit shall cover only pecuniary loss and not exemplary damages or treble damages permitted under subdivision (a) of Section 1812.123. The letter of credit shall provide that payment shall be made to the Attorney General upon presentation to the issuer of a sight draft stating only the amount drawn and signed by the Attorney General or by an Assistant or Deputy Attorney General. Any amount received by the Attorney General under the letter of credit shall be used exclusively to satisfy final judgments as described in this subdivision. The Attorney General may apply to the court for orders as desired or needed to carry out the provisions of this subdivision.

(e) In addition to other lawful means for the enforcement of the surety's liability on the bonds required by this section, the surety's liability may be enforced by motion after a final judgment has been obtained against an affiliate based on any violation of this title by the affiliate, the failure of the affiliate to comply with the terms of its membership contracts with consumers, or the failure of the affiliate to comply with the terms of any agreement with consumers for the purchase of goods or services. The bond of the parent shall not be drawn on until the bond of the affiliate has been exhausted, as provided in subdivisions (c) and (d). The motion may be filed by the Attorney General, a public prosecutor, or any person who obtained the judgment without first attempting to enforce the judgment against any party liable under the judgment. The notice of motion, motion, and a copy of the judgment shall be served on the surety as provided in Chapter 5 (commencing with Section 1010) of Title 14 of Part 2 of the Code of Civil Procedure. The notice shall set forth the amount of the claim, a brief statement indicating that the claim is covered by the bond, and, if the motion is to enforce liability under the bond provided by the parent, a statement that the bond provided by the affiliate has been exhausted or will be exhausted if the motion is granted. Service shall also be made on the Attorney General directed to the Consumer [1] **Protection Section**. The court shall grant the motion unless the surety establishes that the claim is not covered by the bond or unless the court sustains an objection made by the Attorney General that the grant of the motion might impair the rights of actual or potential claimants or is not in the public interest. The court may, in the interest of justice, order a pro rata or other equitable distribution of the bond proceeds.

(f)(1) The bond required by subdivision (c) for an affiliate shall be continuously maintained by the affiliate until the date the affiliate ceases to make the election under subdivision (a) or ceases to engage in the business of a discount buying organization. The bond required by subdivision (c) for the parent shall be continuously maintained by the parent until the date all affiliates cease to make the election under subdivision (a) or all affiliates cease to engage in the business of a discount buying organization.

(2) Notwithstanding the expiration or termination of any bond required under this section, the bond remains in full force and effect for all liabilities incurred before, and for acts, omissions, and causes existing or which arose before, the expiration or termination of the bond. Legal proceedings may be had therefor in all respects as though the bond were in effect.

(3) The letter of credit required under subdivisions (c) and (d) shall be continuously maintained for a period of four years after all affiliates cease to make the election under subdivision (a) or cease to engage in the business of a discount buying organization, provided the period shall be extended until there is a final judgment, as described in subdivision (d), entered in each action seeking relief that may be covered by the letter of credit if the action was filed before the expiration of the four-year period.

(g) Subdivision (a) of Section 1812.121 does not apply to a discount buying organization that offers substantially equivalent alternative at-home ordering service through other generally available channels of communications, such as the [2] **internet**, for the same categories of goods and services, provided the ordered goods are shipped either to the home or to a freight receiver within 20 miles of the buyer's residence at the time the buyer entered into the contract for discount buying services.

(h) For purposes of this section, the following terms apply:

(1) "Affiliate" or "affiliate discount buying organization" means a discount buying organization that is a subsidiary of a parent, as defined in paragraph (4), or operates under a franchise, as defined in paragraph (3), granted by a parent.

(2) "Consumer" or "buyer" means and includes a client or member of an affiliate discount buying organization.

(3) "Franchise" has the same meaning as in Section 31005 of the Corporations Code.

(4) "Parent" means a business entity that directly or indirectly has franchised or operated 25 or more discount buying organizations for 10 years or more. **Leg.H.** Added Stats 2004 ch 451 §1 (AB 2613). Amended Stats 2024 ch 853 §15 (AB 3281), effective January 1, 2025.

§1812.117. 2024 Deletes. [1] Law section [2] Internet

§1812.118. Right to cancel

Every contract for discount buying services shall further provide that such contract may be canceled at any time within three days after the date of receipt by the buyer of a copy of the contract by written notice to the seller at the address specified in the contract. If such cancellation is made, all moneys paid pursuant to the contract shall be refunded. Every contract for discount buying services shall be subject to the cancellation privileges and comply with the requirements of Sections 1689.6 and 1689.7 of this code. **Leg.H.** Added Stats 1976 ch 237 §1.

§1812.119. Noncomplying contracts

(a) Any contract for discount buying services which does not comply with the applicable provisions of this title shall be voidable by the buyer.

(b) No discount buying organization shall make or authorize the making of any reference to its compliance with this title. **Leg.H.** Added Stats 1976 ch 237 §1. Amended Stats 1980 ch 1001 §3, effective September 21, 1980.

§1812.120. Fraudulently induced contracts

Any untrue or misleading information, representation, notice or advertisement of the seller which has been received by or made to the buyer prior to his signing a contract for discount buying services shall render the contract for discount buying services void and unenforceable by the seller. No seller shall make or disseminate such information, representations, notices or advertisements. The phrase "untrue or misleading information, representation, notice, or advertisement" shall include any acts which constitute violations of Chapter 1 (commencing with Section 17500) of Part 3 of Division 7 of the Business and Professions Code. However, neither this section nor any other section of this title shall operate to exempt discount buying services from any other provisions of law, including the penalty provisions of Section 17536 of the Business and Professions Code and Section 3370.1 of this code. **Leg.H.** Added Stats 1976 ch 237 §1.

§1812.121. Removal of business; Discontinuance of goods or services

(a) If a discount buying organization removes its place of business or, if it conducts business at more than one location, that place of business which is geographically closest to the buyer's residence indicated on the face of the contract, more than 20 miles farther from the buyer's residence than it was at the time the contract for discount buying services was entered into, the organization shall offer rescission and a pro rata refund to each buyer affected, based upon the amount of time for which the buyer has been a member of the organization.

(b) If a discount buying organization discontinues providing any category of goods or services disclosed in compliance with Section 1812.106 or otherwise represented to the buyer to be available at or before the buyer's signing of the contract for discount buying services, the organization shall offer rescission and a pro rata refund based upon the amount of time for which the buyer has been a member of the organization, to each buyer who was informed of the availability of the category of goods or services to be discontinued and signed a contract for discount buying services within the six months immediately preceding the discontinuance of said category of goods or services. **Leg.H.** Added Stats 1976 ch 237 §1.

§1812.122. Transfer of duty or obligation by buying service

Any transfer by a discount buying organization of its duty or obligation to provide services to buyers under its contracts for discount buying services to another individual, corporation, or other business entity, as a result of which a buyer shall have available substantially fewer goods and services, shall constitute a complete defense to an action for further enforcement of or collection on such a contract for discount buying services which may be asserted by any buyer who did not consent in writing, after a full and fair disclosure of the categories of goods and services to be provided by the new discount buying organization, to such transfer of the duty or obligation of performance, and shall entitle such a nonconsenting individual to rescind the contract and obtain a pro rata refund from the transferor. **Leg.H.** Added Stats 1976 ch 237 §1.

§1812.123. Civil actions

(a) Any buyer injured by a violation of this title may bring an action for the recovery of damages and return of all moneys paid by the buyer to the seller. Judgment shall be entered for three times the amount at which the actual damages, plus such restitution, are assessed plus reasonable attorney's fees and costs. In the event that the court finds a violation of Section 1812.120 relating to untrue or misleading statements, judgment shall be entered for one thousand dollars ($1,000) plus reasonable attorney's fees or three times the amount of actual damages plus restitution plus reasonable attorney's fees, whichever is greater.

(b) Notwithstanding any other provision of this title, any failure to comply with any provision of this title except Section 1812.120 may be corrected within 30 days after the execution of the contract by the buyer, and if so corrected, neither the seller nor his transferee shall be subject to any liability under this title except that of a suit for actual damages plus reasonable attorney's fees and costs, provided that any correction must be concurred in, in writing, by the buyer, or the contract shall be void and unenforceable by the seller, who shall forthwith tender to the buyer a full refund. "Transferee" includes holders and assignees. **Leg.H.** Added Stats 1976 ch 237 §1.

§1812.125. Criminal violations

(a) Any person who violates subdivision (b) or (c) of Section 1812.116 shall, upon conviction, be fined not more than ten thousand dollars ($10,000) for each violation, or imprisoned pursuant to subdivision (h) of Section 1170 of the Penal Code, or imprisoned in a county jail for not more than one year, or be punished by both that fine and imprisonment.

(b) Any person who violates any other provision of this title shall be guilty of a misdemeanor. **Leg.H.** Added Stats 1976 ch 237 §1. Amended Stats 1980 ch 1001 §4, effective September 21, 1980; Stats 2011 ch 15 §33 (AB 109), effective April 4, 2011, operative October 1, 2011.

2011 Notes: This act is titled and may be cited as the 2011 Realignment Legislation addressing public safety. Stats 2011 ch 15 (AB 109) §1.

This act will become operative no earlier than October 1, 2011, and only upon creation of a community corrections grant program to assist in implementing this act and upon an appropriation to fund the grant program. Stats 2011 ch 15 (AB 109) §636; Stats 2011 ch 39 (AB 117) §68.

The Community Corrections Grant Program referred to in Stats 2011 ch 15 (AB 109) §636, as amended by Stats 2011 ch 39 (AB 117) §68, was created by Stats 2011 ch 40 (AB 118) §3, operative October 1, 2011.

§1812.126. Applicability of other provisions

The prohibitions of this title are not exclusive and do not relieve the parties or the contracts subject thereto from compliance with any other applicable provision of law. **Leg.H.** Added Stats 1976 ch 237 §1.

§1812.127. Waiver of provisions

Any waiver by the buyer of the provisions of this title shall be deemed contrary to public policy and shall be void and unenforceable. **Leg.H.** Added Stats 1976 ch 237 §1.

§1812.128. Separability of provisions

If any provision of this title or the application thereof to any person or circumstances is held invalid, such invalidity shall not affect other provisions or applications of the title which can be given effect without the invalid provision or application, and to this end the provisions of this title are severable. **Leg.H.** Added Stats 1976 ch 237 §1.

§1812.129. Filing of bonds

(a) The Secretary of State shall enforce the provisions of this title that govern the filing and maintenance of bonds and deposits in lieu of bonds.

(b) The Secretary of State shall charge a filing fee not to exceed the cost of filing the bond or the deposit in lieu of a bond pursuant to Section 995.710 of the Code of Civil Procedure. **Leg.H.** Added Stats 1996 ch 633 §10 (SB 1978). Amended Stats 1998 ch 829 §10 (SB 1652).

TITLE 2.7
CONTRACTS FOR SELLER ASSISTED MARKETING PLANS

Findings and declarations. §1812.200.
Definitions. §1812.201.
Offer to sell or lease. §1812.202.
Filing and updating disclosure statements. §1812.203.
Prohibitions and restrictions on disclosure statements. §1812.204.
First communication Disclosures. §1812.205.
Information sheets. §1812.206.
Contracts requirements. §1812.207.
Contract cancellation. §1812.208.
Contracts provisions. §1812.209.
Third party rights; Downpayments. §1812.210.
Assignments. §1812.211.
Reference to compliance with statute. §1812.212.
Records. §1812.213.
Service of process; Bond; Accounts. §1812.214.
Fraudulently induced contracts. §1812.215.
Waiver of provisions. §1812.216.
Criminal violations. §1812.217.
Civil actions. §1812.218.
Exclusivity of provisions. §1812.219.
Severability of provisions. §1812.220.
Civil actions. §1812.221.

§1812.200. Findings and declarations

(a) The Legislature finds and declares that the widespread sale of seller assisted marketing plans, often connected with the sale of vending machines, racks or work-at-home paraphernalia, has created numerous problems in California for purchasers which are inimical to good business practice. Often purchasers of seller assisted marketing plans are individuals inexperienced in business matters who use their life savings to purchase the seller assisted marketing plan in the hope that they will earn enough money in addition to retirement income or salary to become or remain self-sufficient. Many purchasers are the elderly who are seeking a way to supplement their fixed incomes. The initial payment is usually in the form of a purchase of overpriced equipment or products. California purchasers have suffered substantial losses when they have failed to receive full and complete information regarding the seller assisted marketing plan, the amount of money they can reasonably expect to earn, and the previous experience of the seller assisted marketing plan seller. Seller assisted marketing plan sellers have a significant impact upon the economy and well-being of this state and its local communities. The provisions of this title relating to seller assisted marketing plans are necessary for the public welfare.

(b) It is the intent of this title to provide each prospective seller assisted marketing plan purchaser with the information necessary to make an intelligent decision regarding seller assisted marketing plans being offered; to safeguard the public against deceit and financial hardship; to insure, foster and encourage competition and fair dealing in the sale of seller assisted marketing plans by requiring adequate disclosure; to prohibit representations that tend to mislead; and to prohibit or restrict unfair contract terms. This title shall be construed liberally in order to achieve the foregoing purposes. **Leg.H.** Added Stats 1978 ch 876 §1.

§1812.201. Definitions

For the purposes of this title, the following definitions shall apply:

(a) "Seller assisted marketing plan" means any sale or lease or offer to sell or lease any product, equipment, supplies, or services that requires a total initial payment exceeding five hundred dollars ($500), but requires an initial cash payment of less than fifty thousand dollars ($50,000), that will aid a purchaser or will be used by or on behalf of the purchaser in connection with or incidental to beginning, maintaining, or operating a business when the seller assisted marketing plan seller has advertised or in any other manner solicited the purchase or lease of the seller assisted marketing plan and done any of the following acts:

(1) Represented that the purchaser will earn, is likely to earn, or can earn an amount in excess of the initial payment paid by the purchaser for participation in the seller assisted marketing plan.

(2) Represented that there is a market for the product, equipment, supplies, or services, or any product marketed by the user of the product, equipment, supplies, or services sold or leased or offered for sale or lease to the purchaser by the seller, or anything, be it tangible or intangible, made, produced, fabricated, grown, bred, modified, or developed by the purchaser using, in whole or in part, the product, supplies, equipment, or services that were sold or leased or offered for sale or lease to the purchaser by the seller assisted marketing plan seller.

(3) Represented that the seller will buy back or is likely to buy back any product made, produced, fabricated, grown, or bred by the purchaser using, in whole or in part, the product, supplies, equipment, or services that were initially sold or leased or offered for sale or lease to the purchaser by the seller assisted marketing plan seller.

(b) A "seller assisted marketing plan" shall not include:

(1) A security, as defined in the Corporate Securities Law of 1968 (Division 1 (commencing with Section 25000) of Title 4 of the Corporations Code), that has been qualified for sale by the Department of Financial Protection and Innovation, or is exempt under Chapter 1 (commencing with Section 25100) of Part 2 of Division 1 of Title 4 of the Corporations Code from the necessity to qualify.

(2) A franchise defined by the Franchise Investment Law (Division 5 (commencing with Section 31000) of Title 4 of the Corporations Code) that is registered with the Department of Financial Protection and Innovation or is exempt under Chapter 1 (commencing with Section 31100) of Part 2 of Division 5 of Title 4 of the Corporations Code from the necessity of registering.

(3) Any transaction in which either the seller or purchaser or the lessor or lessee is licensed pursuant to and the transaction is governed by the Real Estate Law, Division 4 (commencing with Section 10000) of the Business and Professions Code.

(4) A license granted by a general merchandise retailer that allows the licensee to sell goods, equipment, supplies, products, or services to the general public under the retailer's trademark, trade name, or service mark if all of the following criteria are satisfied:

(A) The general merchandise retailer has been doing business in this state continually for five years prior to the granting of the license.

(B) The general merchandise retailer sells diverse kinds of goods, equipment, supplies, products, or services.

(C) The general merchandise retailer also sells the same goods, equipment, supplies, products, or services directly to the general public.

(D) During the previous 12 months the general merchandise retailer's direct sales of the same goods, equipment, supplies, products, or services to the public account for at least 50 percent of its yearly sales of these goods, equipment, supplies, products, or services made under the retailer's trademark, trade name, or service mark.

(5) A newspaper distribution system distributing newspapers as defined in Section 6362 of the Revenue and Taxation Code.

(6) A sale or lease to an existing or beginning business enterprise that also sells or leases equipment, products, supplies, or performs services that are not supplied by the seller and that the purchaser does not utilize with the equipment, products, supplies, or services of the seller, if the equipment, products, supplies, or services not supplied by the seller account for more than 25 percent of the purchaser's gross sales.

(7) The sale in the entirety of an "ongoing business." For purposes of this paragraph, an "ongoing business" means a business that for at least six months previous to the sale has been operated from a particular specific location, has been open for business to the general public, and has had all equipment and supplies necessary for operating the business located at that location. The sale shall be of the entire "ongoing business" and not merely a portion of the ongoing business.

(8) A sale or lease or offer to sell or lease to a purchaser (A) who has for a period of at least six months previously bought products, supplies, services, or equipment that were sold under the same trademark or trade name or that were produced by the seller and, (B) who has received on resale of the product, supplies, services, or equipment an amount that is at least equal to the amount of the initial payment.

(9) The renewal or extension of an existing seller assisted marketing plan contract.

(10) A product distributorship that meets each of the following requirements:

(A) The seller sells products to the purchaser for resale by the purchaser, and it is reasonably contemplated that substantially all of the purchaser's sales of the product will be at wholesale.

(B) The agreement between the parties does not require that the purchaser pay the seller, or any person associated with the seller, a fee or any other payment for the right to enter into the agreement, and does not require the purchaser to buy a minimum or specified quantity of the products, or to buy products for a minimum or specified period of time. For purposes of this paragraph, a "person associated with the seller" means a person, including an individual or a business entity, controlling, controlled by, or under the same control as the seller.

(C) The seller is a corporation, partnership, limited liability company, joint venture, or any other business entity.

(D) The seller has a net worth of at least ten million dollars ($10,000,000) according to audited financial statements of the seller done during the 18 months preceding the date of the initial sale of products to the purchaser. Net worth may be determined on a consolidated basis if the seller is a subsidiary of another business entity that is permitted by generally accepted accounting standards to prepare financial statements on a consolidated basis and that business entity absolutely and irrevocably agrees in writing to guarantee the seller's obligations to the purchaser. The seller's net worth shall be verified by a certification to the Attorney General from an independent certified public accountant that the audited financial statement reflects a net worth of at least ten million dollars ($10,000,000). This certification shall be provided within 30 days following receipt of a written request from the Attorney General.

(E) The seller grants the purchaser a license to use a trademark that is registered under federal law.

(F) It is not an agreement or arrangement encouraging a distributor to recruit others to participate in the program and compensating the distributor for recruiting others into the program or for sales made by others recruited into the program.

(c) "Person" includes an individual, corporation, partnership, limited liability company, joint venture, or any business entity.

(d) "Seller" means a person who sells or leases or offers to sell or lease a seller assisted marketing plan and who meets either of the following conditions:

(1) Has sold or leased or represents or implies that the seller has sold or leased, whether in California or elsewhere, at least five seller assisted marketing plans within 24 months prior to a solicitation.

(2) Intends or represents or implies that the seller intends to sell or lease, whether in California or elsewhere, at least five seller assisted marketing plans within 12 months following a solicitation.

For purposes of this title, the seller is the person to whom the purchaser becomes contractually obligated. A "seller" does not include a licensed real estate broker or salesman who engages in the sale or lease of a "business opportunity" as that term is used in Sections 10000 to 10030, inclusive, of the Business and Professions Code, or elsewhere in Chapter 1 (commencing with Section 10000), Chapter 2 (commencing with Section 10050), or Chapter 6 (commencing with Section 10450) of Part 1 of Division 4 of the Business and Professions Code.

(e) "Purchaser" means a person who is solicited to become obligated or does become obligated on a seller assisted marketing plan contract.

(f) "Equipment" includes machines, all electrical devices, video or audio devices, molds, display racks, vending machines, coin operated game machines, machines that dispense products, and display units of all kinds.

(g) "Supplies" includes any and all materials used to produce, grow, breed, fabricate, modify, develop, or make any product or item.

(h) "Product" includes any tangible chattel, including food or living animals, that the purchaser intends to:

(1) Sell or lease.

(2) Use to perform a service.

(3) Resell or attempt to resell to the seller assisted marketing plan seller.

(4) Provide or attempt to provide to the seller assisted marketing plan seller or to any other person whom the seller suggests the purchaser contact so that the seller assisted marketing plan seller or that other person may assist, either directly or indirectly, the purchaser in distributing, selling, leasing, or otherwise disposing of the product.

(i) "Services" includes any assistance, guidance, direction, work, labor, or services provided by the seller to initiate or maintain or assist in the initiation or maintenance of a business.

(j) "Seller assisted marketing plan contract" or "contract" means any contract or agreement that obligates a purchaser to a seller.

(k) "Initial payment" means the total amount a purchaser is obligated to pay to the seller under the terms of the seller assisted marketing plan contract prior to or at the time of delivery of the equipment, supplies, products, or services or within six months of the purchaser commencing operation of the seller assisted marketing plan. If the contract sets forth a specific total sale price for purchase of the seller assisted marketing plan which total price is to be paid partially as a downpayment and then in specific monthly payments, the "initial payment" means the entire total sale price.

(l) "Initial cash payment" or "downpayment" means that portion of the initial payment that the purchaser is obligated to pay to the seller prior to or at the time of delivery of equipment, supplies, products, or services. It does not include any amount financed by or for which financing is to be obtained by the seller, or financing that the seller assists in obtaining.

(m) "Buy-back" or "secured investment" means any representation that implies in any manner that the purchaser's initial payment is protected from loss. These terms include a representation or implication of any of the following:

(1) That the seller may repurchase either all or part of what it sold to the purchaser.

(2) That the seller may at some future time pay the purchaser the difference between what has been earned and the initial payment.

(3) That the seller may in the ordinary course buy from the purchaser items made, produced, fabricated, grown, bred, modified, or developed by the purchaser using, in whole or in part, the product, supplies, equipment, or services that were initially sold or leased to the purchaser by the seller.

(4) That the seller or a person to whom the seller will refer the purchaser may in the ordinary course sell, lease, or distribute the items the purchaser has for sale or lease. **Leg.H.** Added Stats 1978 ch 876 §1. Amended Stats 1980 ch 567 §1; Stats 1981 ch 258 §1; Stats 1989 ch 1021 §1; Stats 1990 ch 216 §6 (SB 2510); Stats 1994 ch 1010 §44 (SB 2053); Stats 2000 ch 413 §1 (AB 2699); Stats 2015 ch 190 §5 (AB 1517), effective January 1, 2016; Stats 2022 ch 452 §26 (SB 1498), effective January 1, 2023.

§1812.202. Offer to sell or lease

(a) An offer to sell or offer to lease a seller assisted marketing plan shall occur in this state whenever:

(1) The offer to sell or offer to lease is made in this state;

(2) The purchaser resides in this state at the time of the offer; or

(3) The offer to sell or offer to lease either originates from this state or is directed by the seller or lessor to this state and received at the place to which it is directed.

(b) A sale or lease of a seller assisted marketing plan shall occur in this state whenever:

(1) The offer to sell or offer to lease is accepted in this state;

(2) The purchaser resides in this state at the time of the sale; or

(3) The acceptance is communicated to a seller situated in this state.

Leg.H. Added Stats 1978 ch 876 §1.

§1812.203. Filing and updating disclosure statements

(a) The seller of any seller assisted marketing plan shall pay an annual fee in the amount of one hundred dollars ($100) and annually file with the Attorney General a copy of the disclosure statements required under Sections 1812.205 and 1812.206, as well as a list of the names and resident addresses of those individuals who sell the seller assisted marketing plan on behalf of the seller. The first filing shall be made at least 30 days prior to placing any advertisement or making any other representations to prospective purchasers. The first filing shall not be deemed to be effective until a notice of filing has been issued by the Attorney General. The seller may not make any advertisement or other representation to prospective purchasers until a notice of filing has been issued by the Attorney General. The disclosure statements on file shall be updated through a new filing and payment of a fee in the amount of thirty dollars ($30), whenever material changes occur during the year following the annual filing and the updated filing shall include all disclosure statements required by Sections 1812.205 and 1812.206 and a list of the names and resident addresses of all current salespersons and all salespersons who have acted on behalf of the seller since the previous filing, whether the annual filing or an updated filing, indicating which salespersons are still active and which no longer act on behalf of the seller. Each seller of a seller assisted marketing plan shall file the annual renewal filing, whether or not any update filings have been made, at least 10 days before one year has elapsed from the date of the notice of filing issued by the Attorney General, and at least 10 days before the same date every year thereafter. The annual renewal filing shall include all disclosure statements required by Sections 1812.205 and 1812.206 and a list of the names and addresses of the residences of all current salespersons and all salespersons who have acted on behalf of the seller since the previous filing (whether the annual filing or an updated filing), indicating which salespersons are still active and which no longer act on behalf of the seller. The annual renewal filing fee shall be one hundred dollars ($100). If an annual renewal filing is not filed as required, the previous filing shall be deemed to have lapsed and the seller shall be prohibited from placing any seller assisted marketing plan advertisements or making any other representations to prospective purchasers of seller assisted marketing plan until a new annual filing is made and a new notice of filing has been issued by the Attorney General.

(b) The Attorney General may send by certified mail to the address set forth in the seller assisted marketing plan filing an intent to issue a stop order denying the effectiveness of or suspending or revoking the effectiveness of any filing if he or she finds the following:

(1) That there has been a failure to comply with any of the provisions of this title.

(2) That the offer or sale of the seller assisted marketing plan would constitute a misrepresentation to, or deceit of, or fraud on, the purchaser.

(3) That any person identified in the filing has been convicted of an offense under paragraph (1) of subdivision (b) of Section 1812.206, or is subject to an order or has had a civil judgment entered against him or her as described in paragraphs (2) and (3) of subdivision (b) of Section 1812.206, and the involvement of that person in the sale or management of the seller assisted marketing plan creates an unreasonable risk to prospective purchasers.

(c) The notice referred to shall include facts supporting a suspension or revocation. If the seller assisted marketing plan does not submit to the Attorney General, under penalties of perjury signed by an owner or officer of the seller assisted marketing plan, within 10 days of receipt of the intent to issue a stop order, a refutation of each and every supporting fact set forth in the notice, and each fact not refuted shall be deemed, for purposes of issuance of the order, an admission that the fact is true. If, in the opinion of the Attorney General, and based upon supporting facts not refuted by the seller assisted marketing plan, the plan is offered to the public without compliance with this title, the Attorney General may order the seller to desist and refrain from the further sale or attempted sale of the seller assisted marketing plan unless and until a notice of filing has been issued pursuant to this section. Until that time, the registration shall be void. The order shall be in effect until and unless the seller assisted marketing plan files a proceeding in superior court pursuant to Section 1085 or 1094.5 of the Code of Civil Procedure or seeks other judicial relief and serves a copy of the proceeding upon the Attorney General. **Leg.H.** Added Stats 1978 ch 876 §1. Amended Stats 1989 ch 1021 §2; Stats 1990 ch 1491 §2 (AB 3765); Stats 1998 ch 595 §1 (AB 1830).

§1812.204. Prohibitions and restrictions on disclosure statements

In selling, leasing, or offering to sell or lease a seller assisted marketing plan in this state, sellers shall not:

(a) Use the phrase "buy-back" or "secured investment" or similar phrase orally or in writing when soliciting, offering, leasing, or selling a seller assisted marketing plan if the "security" is the value of the equipment, supplies, products or services supplied by the seller to the purchaser.

(b) Use the phrase "buy-back" or "secured investment" or similar phrase orally or in writing when soliciting, offering, leasing, or selling a seller assisted marketing plan unless there are no restrictions or qualifications whatsoever preventing or limiting a purchaser from being able to invoke the "buy-back" or "secured" portion of the seller assisted marketing plan contract at any time the purchaser desires during the one-year period following the contract date. Upon invocation of the "buy-back" or "security" provision, the minimum amount a purchaser shall be entitled to have returned to him is the full amount of his initial payment, less the amount actually received by him from the operation of the seller assisted marketing plan. The "amount actually received" means either the amount the purchaser actually obtained from the seller for any product resold to the seller or the amount of money the purchaser received for use of the purchaser's product, equipment, supplies or services, less any amount: (1) the purchaser has paid the owner or manager of the location at which the purchaser's products, equipment, supplies or services are placed; and (2) the purchaser has paid to obtain other items needed in order to sell, make, produce, fabricate, grow, breed, modify, or develop the item which the seller assisted marketing plan purchaser intends to sell, lease, distribute, or otherwise dispose of.

(c) Represent that a purchaser's initial payment is "secured" in any manner or to any degree or that the seller provides a "buy-back" arrangement unless the seller has, in conformity with subdivision (b) of Section 1812.214, either obtained a surety bond issued by a surety company admitted to do business in this state or established a trust account at a federally insured bank or savings and loan association located in this state.

(d) Represent that the seller assisted marketing plan provides income or earning potential of any kind unless the seller has data to substantiate the claims of income or earning potential and discloses this data to the purchaser at the time the claim is made, if made in person, or if made through written or telephonic communication, at the first in-person communication thereafter and, when disclosed, the data is left with the purchaser. A mathematical computation of the number of sales multiplied by the amount of profit per sale to reach a projected income figure is not sufficient data to substantiate an income or earning potential claim. Income or earning potential claims cannot be made or implied at all unless they are based on the experience of at least 10 purchasers from the seller assisted marketing plan being offered. The data left by the seller must, at a minimum, disclose:

(1) The length of time the seller has been selling the particular seller assisted marketing plan being offered;

(2) The number of purchasers from the seller known to the seller to have made at least the same sales, income or profits as those represented; and

(3) The percentage the number represents of the total number of purchasers from the seller.

(e) Use the trademark, service mark, trade name, logotype, advertising or other commercial symbol of any business which does not either control the ownership interest in the seller or accept responsibility for all representations made by the seller in regard to the seller assisted marketing plan, unless the nature of the seller's relationship to such other business entity is set forth immediately adjacent to and in type size equal to or larger than that used to depict the commercial symbol of such other business. If a member of a trade association, the seller may use the logo or registration mark of the trade association in advertisements and materials without regard to this subdivision.

(f) Place or cause to be placed any advertisement for a seller assisted marketing plan which does not include the actual business name of the seller, and if it differs, the name under which the seller assisted marketing plan is operated and the street address of the principal place of business of the seller. **Leg.H.** Added Stats 1978 ch 876 §1. Amended Stats 1981 ch 258 §2.

§1812.205. First communication Disclosures

At the first in-person communication with a potential purchaser or in the first written response to an inquiry by a potential purchaser, whichever occurs first, wherein the seller assisted marketing plan is described, the seller or his or her representative shall provide the prospective purchaser a written document, the cover sheet of which is entitled in at least 16-point boldface capital letters "DISCLOSURE REQUIRED BY CALIFORNIA LAW." Under the title shall appear in boldface of at least 10-point type, the statement: "The State of California has not reviewed and does not approve, recommend, endorse or sponsor any seller assisted marketing plan. The information contained in this disclosure has not been checked by the state. If you have any questions about this purchase, see an attorney or other financial adviser before you sign a contract or agreement." Nothing shall appear on the cover sheet except the title and the statement required above. The disclosure document shall contain the following information:

(a) The name of the seller, the name under which the seller is doing or intends to do business and the name of any parent or affiliated company that will engage in business transactions with purchasers or accept responsibility for statements made by the seller.

(b) A statement of the initial payment to be paid by the purchaser to the seller, or when not known, a statement of the approximate initial payment charged, the amount of the initial payment to be paid to a person inducing, directly or indirectly, a purchaser to contract for the seller assisted marketing plan.

(c) A full and detailed description of the actual services the seller will undertake to perform for the purchaser.

(d) When the seller makes any statement concerning earnings or range of earnings that may be made through the seller assisted marketing plan, he must comply with subdivision (d) of Section 1812.204 and set forth in complete form in this disclosure statement the following:

"No guarantee of earnings or ranges of earnings can be made. The number of purchasers who have earned through this business an amount in excess of the amount of their initial payment is at least _____ which represents _____ percent of the total number of purchasers of this seller assisted marketing plan."

(e) If training of any type is promised by the seller, a complete description of the training and the length of the training.

(f) If the seller promises services to be performed in connection with the placement of the equipment, product or supplies at a location from which they will be sold or used, the full nature of those services as well as the nature of the agreements to be made with the owner or manager of the location at which the purchaser's equipment, product or supplies will be placed, must be set forth.

(g) If the seller represents orally or in writing when soliciting or offering for sale or lease or selling or leasing a seller assisted marketing plan that there is a "buy-back" arrangement or that the initial payment is in some manner protected from loss or "secured," the entire and precise nature of the "buy-back", "protection" or "security" arrangement shall be completely and clearly disclosed. **Leg.H.** Added Stats 1978 ch 876 §1. Amended Stats 1981 ch 258 §3.

§1812.206. Information sheets

At least 48 hours prior to the execution of a seller assisted marketing plan contract or agreement or at least 48 hours prior to the receipt of any consideration, whichever occurs first, the seller or his or her representative shall provide to the prospective purchaser in writing a document entitled "SELLER ASSISTED MARKETING PLAN INFORMATION SHEET." The seller may combine the information required under this section with the information required under Section 1812.205 and, if done, shall utilize the single title "DISCLOSURES REQUIRED BY CALIFORNIA LAW," and the title page required by Section 1812.205. If a combined document is used, it shall be given at the time required by Section 1812.205, provided that this time meets the 48-hour test of this section. The information sheet required by this section shall contain the following:

(a) The name of and the office held by the seller's owners, officers, directors, trustees and general or limited partners, as the case may be, and the names of those individuals who have management responsibilities in connection with the seller's business activities.

(b) A statement whether the seller, any person identified in subdivision (a), and any other company managed by a person identified in subdivision (a):

(1) Has been convicted of a felony or misdemeanor or pleaded nolo contendere to a felony or misdemeanor charge if the felony or misdemeanor involved an alleged violation of this title, fraud, embezzlement, fraudulent conversion or misappropriation of property.

(2) Has been held liable in a civil action by final judgment or consented to the entry of a stipulated judgment if the civil action alleged a violation of this title, fraud, embezzlement, fraudulent conversion or misappropriation of property or the use of untrue or misleading representations in an attempt to sell or dispose of real or personal property or the use of unfair, unlawful or deceptive business practices.

(3) Is subject to any currently effective agreement, injunction, or restrictive order, including, but not limited to, a "cease and desist" order, an "assurance of discontinuance," or other comparable agreement or order, relating to business activity as the result of an action or investigation brought by a public agency or department, including, but not limited to, an action affecting any vocational license.

The statements required by paragraphs (1), (2) and (3) of this subdivision shall set forth the terms of the agreement, or the court, the docket number of the matter, the date of the conviction or of the judgment and, when involved, the name of the governmental agency that initiated the investigation or brought the action resulting in the conviction or judgment.

(4) Has at any time during the previous seven fiscal years been the subject of an order for relief in bankruptcy, been reorganized due to insolvency, or been a principal, director, officer, trustee, general or limited partner, or had management responsibilities of any other person, as defined in subdivision (b) of Section 1812.201, that has so filed or was so reorganized, during or within one year after the period that the individual held that position. If so, the name and location of the person having so filed, or having been so reorganized, the date thereof, the court which exercised jurisdiction, and the docket number of the matter shall be set forth.

(c) The length of time the seller:

(1) Has sold seller assisted marketing plans.

(2) Has sold the specific seller assisted marketing plan being offered to the purchaser.

(d) If the seller is required to secure a bond or establish a trust account pursuant to the requirements of Section 1812.204, the information sheet shall state either:

(1) "Seller has secured a bond issued by

_____,

(name and address of surety company)

a surety company admitted to do business in this state. Before signing a contract to purchase this seller assisted marketing plan, you should check with the surety company to determine the bond's current status," or

(2) "Seller has deposited with the office of the Attorney General information regarding its trust account. Before signing a contract to purchase this seller assisted marketing plan, you should check with the Attorney General to determine the current status of the trust account."

(e) A copy of a recent, not more than 12 months old, financial statement of the seller, together with a statement of any material changes in the financial condition of the seller from the date thereof. That financial statement shall either be audited or be under penalty of perjury signed by one of the seller's officers, directors, trustees or general or limited partners. The declaration under penalty of perjury shall indicate that to the best of the signatory's knowledge and belief the information in the financial statement is true and accurate; the date of signature and the location where signed shall also be indicated. Provided, however, that where a seller is a subsidiary of another corporation which is permitted by generally accepted accounting standards to prepare financial statements on a consolidated basis, the above information may be submitted in the same manner for the parent if the corresponding financial statement of the seller is also provided and the parent absolutely and irrevocably has agreed to guarantee all obligations of the seller.

(f) An unexecuted copy of the entire seller assisted marketing plan contract.

(g) For purposes of this section, "seller's owners" means any individual who holds an equity interest of at least 10 percent in the seller. **Leg.H.** Added Stats 1978 ch 876 §1. Amended Stats 1981 ch 258 §4; Stats 1989 ch 1021 §3; Stats 1997 ch 377 §1 (AB 1548); Stats 1998 ch 595 §2 (AB 1830); Stats 2009 ch 500 §13 (AB 1059), effective January 1, 2010.

§1812.207. Contracts requirements

Every contract for sale or lease of a seller assisted marketing plan in this state shall be in writing and shall be subject to the provisions of this title. A copy of the fully completed contract and all other documents the seller requires the purchaser to sign shall be given to the purchaser at the time they are signed. **Leg.H.** Added Stats 1978 ch 876 §1.

§1812.208. Contract cancellation

The purchaser shall have the right to cancel a seller assisted marketing plan contract for any reason at any time within three business days of the date the purchaser and the seller sign the contract. The notice of the right to cancel and the procedures to be followed when a contract is canceled shall comply with Section 1812.209. **Leg.H.** Added Stats 1978 ch 876 §1.

§1812.209. Contracts provisions

Every seller assisted marketing plan contract shall set forth in at least 10-point type or equivalent size if handwritten, all of the following:

(a) The terms and conditions of payment including the initial payment, additional payments, and downpayment required. If the contract provides for the seller to receive more than 20 percent of the initial payment before delivery to the purchaser of the equipment, supplies or products or services to be furnished under the terms of the contract, the contract shall clearly set forth for the escrow account established pursuant to subdivision (b) of Section 1812.210 and the name and address of the escrow account holder, as well as the institution, branch, and account number of the escrow account. If the contract provides for payment of any amount in excess of 20 percent of the initial payment prior to delivery of the equipment, supplies or products or services to be furnished under the terms of the contract, the contract shall set forth that payment of the amount in excess of 20 percent shall be by separate instrument made payable to the escrow account.

(b) Immediately above the place at which the purchaser signs the contract the following notification, in boldface type, of the purchaser's right to cancel the contract:

"You have three business days in which you may cancel this contract for any reason by mailing or delivering written notice to the seller assisted marketing plan seller. The three business days shall expire on

_____
(last date to mail or deliver notice)
and notice of cancellation should be mailed or delivered to

_____
(seller assisted marketing plan seller's name and business street address).

If you choose to mail your notice, it must be placed in the United States mail properly addressed, first-class postage prepaid, and postmarked before midnight of the above date. If you choose to deliver your notice to the seller directly, it must be delivered to him by the end of his normal business day on the above date. Within five business days of receipt of the notice of cancellation, the seller shall return to the purchaser all sums paid by the purchaser to the seller pursuant to this contract. Within five business days after receipt of all such sums, the purchaser shall make available at his address or at the place at which they were caused to be located, all equipment, products and supplies provided to the purchaser pursuant to this contract. Upon demand of the seller, such equipment, products and supplies shall be made available at the time the purchaser receives full repayment by cash, money order or certified check."

(c) A full and detailed description of the acts or services the seller will undertake to perform for the purchaser.

(d) The seller's principal business address and the name and the address of its agent, other than the Secretary of State, in the State of California authorized to receive service of process.

(e) The business form of the seller, whether corporate, partnership or otherwise.

(f) The delivery date or, when the contract provides for a staggered delivery of items to the purchaser, the approximate delivery date of those products, equipment or supplies the seller is to deliver to the purchaser to enable the purchaser to begin or maintain his business and whether the products, equipment or supplies are to be delivered to the purchaser's home or business address or are to be placed or caused to be placed by the seller at locations owned or managed by persons other than the purchaser.

(g) A complete description of the nature of the "buy-back", "protection", or "security" arrangement, if the seller has represented orally or in writing when selling or leasing, soliciting or offering a seller assisted marketing plan that there is a "buy-back" or that the initial payment or any part of it is "protected" or "secured."

(h) A statement which accurately sets forth a purchaser's right to void the contract under the circumstances and in the manner set forth in subdivisions (a) and (b) of Section 1812.215.

(i) The name of the supplier and the address of such supplier of the products, equipment, or supplies the seller is to deliver to the purchaser to enable the purchaser to begin or maintain his business. **Leg.H.** Added Stats 1978 ch 876 §1. Amended Stats 1981 ch 258 §5; Stats 1989 ch 1021 §4.

§1812.210. Third party rights; Downpayments

(a) No seller assisted marketing plan contract shall require or entail the execution of any note or series of notes by the purchaser which, when separately negotiated, will cut off as to third parties any right of action or defense which the purchaser may have against the seller.

(b) If the contract referred to in Section 1812.209 provides for a downpayment to be paid to the seller, the downpayment shall not exceed 20 percent of the initial payment amount. In no event shall the contract payment schedule provide for the seller to receive more than 20 percent of the initial payment before delivery to the purchaser, or to the place at which they are to be located, the equipment, supplies or products, unless all sums in excess of 20 percent are placed in an escrow account as provided for in subdivision (c) of Section 1812.214. Funds placed in an escrow account shall not be released until the purchaser notifies the escrow holder in writing of the delivery of such equipment, supplies or products within the time limits set forth in the seller assisted marketing plan contract. Notification of delivery by the purchaser to the escrow holder shall not be unreasonably withheld. **Leg.H.** Added Stats 1978 ch 876 §1. Amended Stats 1981 ch 258 §6; Stats 1989 ch 1021 §5.

§1812.211. Assignments

Any assignee of the seller assisted marketing plan contract or the seller's rights is subject to all equities, rights and defenses of the purchaser against the seller. **Leg.H.** Added Stats 1978 ch 876 §1.

§1812.212. Reference to compliance with statute

No seller shall make or authorize the making of any reference to its compliance with this title. **Leg.H.** Added Stats 1978 ch 876 §1.

§1812.213. Records

Every seller shall at all times keep and maintain a complete set of books, records and accounts of seller assisted marketing plan sales made by the seller. All documents relating to each specific seller assisted marketing plan sold or leased shall be maintained for four years after the date of the seller assisted marketing plan contract. **Leg.H.** Added Stats 1978 ch 876 §1.

§1812.214. Service of process; Bond; Accounts

(a) Every seller of seller-assisted marketing plans other than a California corporation shall file with the Attorney General an irrevocable consent appointing the Secretary of State or successor in office to act as the seller's attorney to receive service or any lawful process in any noncriminal suit, action or proceeding against the seller or the seller's successor, executor or administrator, which may arise under this title. When service is made upon the Secretary of State, it shall have the same force and validity as if served personally on the seller. Service may be made by leaving a copy of the process in the office of the Secretary of State, but it shall not be effective unless:

(1) The plaintiff forthwith sends by first-class mail a notice of the service upon the Secretary of State and a copy of the process to the defendant or respondent at the last address on file with the Attorney General; and

(2) The plaintiffs affidavit of compliance with this section is filed in the case on or before the return date of the process, if any, or within such further time as the court allows.

(b) If, pursuant to subdivision (c) of Section 1812.204, a seller must obtain a surety bond or establish a trust account, the following procedures apply:

(1) If a bond is obtained, a copy of it shall be filed with the Attorney General; if a trust account is established, notification of the depository, the trustee and the account number shall be filed with the Attorney General.

(2) The bond or trust account required shall be in favor of the State of California for the benefit of any person who is damaged by any violation of this title or by the seller's breach of a contract subject to this title or of any obligation arising therefrom. The trust account shall also be in favor of any person damaged by these practices.

(3) Any person claiming against the trust account for a violation of this title may maintain an action at law against the seller and the trustee. The surety or trustee shall be liable only for actual damages and not the punitive damages permitted under Section 1812.218. The aggregate liability of the trustee to all persons damaged by a seller's violation of this title shall in no event exceed the amount of the trust account.

(4) The bond or the trust account shall be in an amount equal to the total amount of the "initial payment" section of all seller-assisted marketing plan contracts the seller has entered into during the previous year or three hundred thousand dollars ($300,000), whichever is less, but in no case shall the amount be less than fifty thousand dollars ($50,000). The amount required shall be adjusted twice a year, no later than the tenth day of the first month of the seller's fiscal year and no later than the tenth day of the seventh month of the seller's fiscal year. A seller need only establish a bond or trust account in the amount of fifty thousand dollars ($50,000) at the commencement of business and during the first six months the seller is in business. By the tenth day of the seller's seventh month in business, the amount of the bond or trust account shall be established as provided for herein as if the seller had been in business for a year.

(c) If, pursuant to subdivision (b) of Section 1812.210, a seller utilizes an escrow account to receive those portions of the downpayment in excess of 20 percent of the initial payment before delivery to the purchaser of the equipment, supplies or products or services to be furnished under the terms of the contract, the following procedures shall apply:

(1) The holder of the escrow account shall be independent of the seller, and the seller shall not have any authority to direct disbursements from the escrow account by the holder except upon written notification by the purchaser to the holder of the escrow account of the delivery of the equipment, supplies, or products as required by and within the time limits set forth in the seller assisted marketing plan contract.

(2) The name and address of the escrow account holder, the name of the institution, the branch and account number of the escrow account shall be reported to the Attorney General by the seller.

(3) Any person claiming against the escrow account for a violation of this title may maintain an action at law against the seller and the escrow account holder. The escrow account holder shall be liable only for actual damages and not the punitive damages permitted under Section 1812.218. The aggregate liability of the escrow account holder to all persons damaged by a seller's violation of this title shall in no event exceed the amount of the escrow account. **Leg.H.** Added Stats 1978 ch 876 §1. Amended Stats 1981 ch 258 §7; Stats 1982 ch 517 §64; Stats 1989 ch 1021 §6; Stats 1990 ch 1491 §3 (AB 3765).

§1812.215. Fraudulently induced contracts

(a) If a seller uses any untrue or misleading statements to sell or lease a seller assisted marketing plan, or fails to comply with Section 1812.203, or fails to give the disclosure documents or disclose any of the information required by Sections 1812.205 and 1812.206, or the contract does not comply with the requirements of this title, then within one year of the date of the contract at the election of the purchaser upon written notice to the seller, the contract shall be voidable by the purchaser and unenforceable by the seller or his assignee as contrary to public policy and the purchaser shall be entitled to receive from the seller all sums paid to the seller when the purchaser is able to return all equipment, supplies or products delivered by the seller; when such complete return cannot be made, the purchaser shall be entitled to receive from the seller all sums paid to the seller less the fair market value at the time of delivery of the equipment, supplies or products not returned by the purchaser, but delivered by the seller. Upon the receipt of such sums, the purchaser shall make available to the seller at the purchaser's address or at the places at which they are located at the time the purchaser gives notice pursuant to this section, the products, equipment or supplies received by the purchaser from the seller. Provided, however, if the seller inadvertently has failed to make any of the disclosures required by Section 1812.205 or 1812.206 or the contract inadvertently fails to comply with the requirements of this title, the seller may cure such inadvertent defect by providing the purchaser with the correct disclosure statements or contract if at the time of providing such correct disclosures or contract the seller also informs the purchaser in writing that because of the seller's error, the purchaser has an additional 15-day period after receipt of the correct disclosures or contract within which to cancel the contract and receive a full return of all moneys paid in exchange for return of whatever equipment, supplies or products the purchaser has. If the purchaser does not cancel the contract within 15 days after receipt of the correct disclosures or contract, he may not in the future exercise his right to void the contract under this section due to such noncompliance with the disclosure or contract requirements of this title.

(b) If a seller fails to deliver the equipment, supplies or product within 30 days of the delivery date stated in the contract, unless such delivery delay is beyond the control of the seller, then at any time prior to delivery or within 30 days after delivery, at the election of the purchaser upon written notice to the seller, the contract shall be voidable by the purchaser and unenforceable by the seller or his assignee as contrary to public policy.

The rights of the purchaser set forth in this section shall be cumulative to all other rights under this title or otherwise. **Leg.H.** Added Stats 1978 ch 876 §1. Amended Stats 1981 ch 258 §8.

§1812.216. Waiver of provisions

(a) Any waiver by a purchaser of the provisions of this title shall be deemed contrary to public policy and shall be void and unenforceable. Any attempt by a seller to have a purchaser waive rights given by this title shall be a violation of this title.

(b) In any proceeding involving this title, the burden of proving an exemption or an exception from a definition is upon the person claiming it. **Leg.H.** Added Stats 1978 ch 876 §1. Amended Stats 1981 ch 258 §9.

§1812.217. Criminal violations

Any person, including, but not limited to, the seller, a salesman, agent or representative of the seller or an independent contractor who attempts to sell or lease or sells or leases a seller assisted marketing plan, who willfully violates any provision of this title or employs, directly or indirectly, any device, scheme or artifice to deceive in connection with the offer or sale of any seller assisted marketing plan, or willfully engages, directly or indirectly, in any act, practice or course of business which operates or would operate as a fraud or deceit upon any person in connection with the offer, purchase, lease or sale of any seller assisted marketing plan shall, upon conviction, be fined not more than ten thousand dollars ($10,000) for each unlawful transaction, or imprisoned pursuant to subdivision (h) of Section 1170 of the Penal Code, or imprisoned in a county jail for not more than one year, or be punished by both that fine and imprisonment. **Leg.H.** Added Stats 1978 ch 876 §1. Amended Stats 2011 ch 15 §34 (AB 109), effective April 4, 2011, operative October 1, 2011.

2011 Notes: This act is titled and may be cited as the 2011 Realignment Legislation addressing public safety. Stats 2011 ch 15 (AB 109) §1.

This act will become operative no earlier than October 1, 2011, and only upon creation of a community corrections grant program to assist in implementing this act and upon an appropriation to fund the grant program. Stats 2011 ch 15 (AB 109) §636; Stats 2011 ch 39 (AB 117) §68.

The Community Corrections Grant Program referred to in Stats 2011 ch 15 (AB 109) §636, as amended by Stats 2011 ch 39 (AB 117) §68, was created by Stats 2011 ch 40 (AB 118) §3, operative October 1, 2011.

§1812.218. Civil actions

Any purchaser injured by a violation of this title or by the seller's breach of a contract subject to this title or of any obligation arising from the sale or lease of the seller assisted marketing plan may bring any action for recovery of damages. Judgment shall be entered for actual damages, plus reasonable attorney's fees and costs, but in no case shall the award of damages be less than the amount of the initial payment provided the purchaser is able to return all the equipment, supplies or products delivered by the seller; when such complete return cannot be made, the minimum award shall be no less than the amount of the initial payment less the fair market value at the time of delivery of the equipment, supplies or products that cannot be returned but were actually delivered by the seller. An award, if the trial court deems it proper, may be entered for punitive damages. **Leg.H.** Added Stats 1978 ch 876 §1.

§1812.219. Exclusivity of provisions

The provisions of this title are not exclusive. The remedies provided herein for violation of any section of this title or for conduct proscribed by any section of this title shall be in addition to any other procedures or remedies for any violation or conduct provided for in any other law.

Nothing in this title shall limit any other statutory or any common law rights of the Attorney General, any district attorney or city attorney, or any other person. If any act or practice proscribed under this title also constitutes a cause of action in common law or a violation of another statute, the purchaser may assert such common law or statutory cause of action under the procedures and with the remedies provided for in such other law. **Leg.H.** Added Stats 1978 ch 876 §1.

§1812.220. Severability of provisions

If any provision of this act or if any application thereof to any person or circumstance is held unconstitutional, the remainder of the title and the application of such provision to other persons and circumstances shall not be affected thereby. **Leg.H.** Added Stats 1978 ch 876 §1.

§1812.221. Civil actions

(a) When a deposit has been made in lieu of bond pursuant to paragraph (1) of subdivision (b) of Section 1812.214 and Section 995.710 of the Code of Civil Procedure, the person asserting a claim against the deposit shall, in lieu of the provisions of Section 996.430 of the Code of Civil Procedure, establish the claim by furnishing evidence to the Attorney General of a money judgment entered by a court together with evidence that the claimant is a person described in paragraph (2) of subdivision (b) of Section 1812.214.

(b) When a person has completely established the claim with the Attorney General, the Attorney General shall forthwith review and approve the claim and enter the date of approval thereon. The claim shall be designated an "approved claim."

(c) When the first claim against a particular deposit account has been approved, it shall not be paid until the expiration of a period of 240 days after the date of its approval by the Attorney General. Subsequent claims which are approved by the Attorney General within the same 240-day period shall similarly not be paid until the expiration of the 240-day period. Forthwith upon the expiration of the 240-day period, the Attorney General shall pay all approved claims from that 240-day period in full unless there are insufficient funds in the deposit account in which case each approved claim shall be paid a proportionate amount to exhaust the deposit account.

(d) When the Attorney General approves the first claim against a particular deposit account after the expiration of a 240-day period, the date of approval of that claim shall begin a new 240-day period to which subdivision (c) shall apply with respect to the amount remaining in the deposit account.

(e) After a deposit account is exhausted, no further claims shall be paid by the Attorney General. Claimants who have had their claims paid in full or in part pursuant to subdivisions (c) and (d) shall not be required to make a contribution back to the deposit account for the benefit of other claimants.

(f) When a deposit has been made in lieu of bond, the amount of the deposit shall not be subject to attachment, garnishment, or execution with respect to an action or judgment against the seller, other than as to an amount as no longer needed or required for the purpose of this title which would otherwise be returned to the seller by the Attorney General. **Leg.H.** Added Stats 1984 ch 545 §4. Amended Stats 1989 ch 1021 §7.

TITLE 2.8
MEMBERSHIP CAMPING CONTRACTS

Definitions. §1812.300.
Applicability of other provisions. §1812.301.
Disclosures. §1812.302.
Language; Notice of cancellation. §1812.303.
Notice of cancellation without inspection. §1812.304.
Exemptions. §1812.305.
Purchaser's remedies; Corrections by camping operator. §1812.306.
Conditions for withdrawal of campgrounds. §1812.307.
Transfer of interest in campground. §1812.308.
Representation of availability for use. §1812.309.
Brokers. §1812.314.
Severability. §1812.315.
Waiver of provisions of title void. §1812.316.

§1812.300. Definitions

For the purposes of this title:

(a) "Membership camping operator" means any enterprise, other than one that is tax exempt under Section 501(c) (3) of the Internal Revenue Code of 1954, as amended, that has as one of its purposes the ownership or operation of campgrounds which include or may include use of camping sites, that solicits membership paid for by a fee or periodic payments, such as annual dues, and the contractual members are the primary intended users. "Membership camping operator" does not include camping or recreational trailer parks, as defined in Section 18215 of the Health and Safety Code, which are open to the general public and which contain camping sites rented for a per use fee, or a "mobilehome park," as defined in either Section 798.4 of the Civil Code or Section 18214 of the Health and Safety Code.

As used in this title, "seller" means membership camping operator.

(b) "Membership camping contract" means an agreement offered or sold within the State of California by a membership camping operator or membership camping broker evidencing a purchaser's right or license to use for more than 14 days in a year, the campgrounds of a membership camping operator and includes a membership which provides for this use.

(c) "Camping site" means a space designed and promoted for the purpose of locating a trailer, tent, tent trailer, pickup camper, or other similar device used for camping.

(d) "Offer" means any solicitation reasonably designed to result in entering into a membership camping contract.

(e) "Person" means any individual, corporation, partnership, limited liability company, trust, association, or other organization other than a government or a subdivision thereof.

(f) "Purchaser" means a person who enters into a membership camping contract and thereby obtains the right to use the campgrounds of a membership camping operator.

(g) "Sale" or "sell" means entering into, or other disposition, of a membership camping contract for value. The term "value" does not include a reasonable fee to offset the administrative costs of transfer of a membership camping contract.

(h) "Campground" means real property within this state owned or operated by a membership camping operator and designated in whole or in part by the membership camping operator as available for camping or outdoor recreation by purchasers of membership camping contracts.

(i) "Blanket encumbrance" means any mortgage, deed of trust, option to purchase, vendor's lien or interest under a contract or agreement of sale, or other financing lien or encumbrance granted by the membership camping operator or affiliate which secures or evidences the obligation to pay money or to sell or convey any campgrounds made available to purchasers by the membership camping operator or any portion thereof, and which authorizes, permits, or requires the foreclosure or other disposition of the campground.

(j) "Nondisturbance agreement" means an instrument in recordable form by which the holder of a blanket encumbrance agrees to all of the following:

(1) The holder's rights in any campground made available to purchasers, prior or subsequent to the agreement, by the membership camping operator shall be subordinate to the rights of purchasers from and after the recordation of the nondisturbance agreement.

(2) The holder and all successors and assignees of the holder, and any person who acquires the campground through foreclosure or by deed in lieu of foreclosure of the blanket encumbrance shall take the campground subject to the rights of purchasers.

(3) The holder or any successor acquiring the campground through the blanket encumbrance shall not use or cause the campground to be used in a manner which would materially prevent purchasers from using or occupying the campground in a manner contemplated by the purchasers' membership camping contracts. However, the holder shall have no obligation to, and no liability for failure to assume the responsibilities or obligations of, the membership camping operator under the membership camping contracts.

(k) "Membership camping contract broker" means a person who, for compensation, resells or offers to resell a membership camping contract to a new purchaser on behalf of a prior purchaser. Membership camping contract broker does not include a membership camping operator or its employees or agents. **Leg.H.** Added Stats 1983 ch 847 §1. Amended Stats 1990 ch 1529 §4 (SB 2203); Stats 1994 ch 1010 §45 (SB 2053).

§1812.301. Applicability of other provisions

The membership camping contracts and persons covered by this title shall be subject to Chapter 5 (commencing with Section 17200) of Part 2 of Division 7 and Article 1 (commencing with Section 17500) of Chapter 1 of Part 3 of Division 7 of the Business and Professions Code and the Unruh Act (Chapter 1 (commencing with Section 1801) of Title 2 of Part 4 of Division 3). **Leg.H.** Added Stats 1983 ch 847 §1. Amended Stats 1990 ch 1529 §5 (SB 2203).

§1812.302. Disclosures

A membership camping operator shall provide to a purchaser the following written disclosures in any format which clearly communicates the following reasonably current information before the purchaser signs a membership camping contract, or gives any money or thing of value for the purchase of a membership camping contract. The written disclosures shall be included in or attached to the contract before the time the contract is signed. The following information shall be updated once a year.

(a) The name and address of the membership camping operator and any material affiliate membership camping operator.

(b) A brief description of the membership camping operator's experience in the membership camping business, including the number of years the operator has been in the membership camping business; a brief description of the past five years' business experience of the chairman, the president and chief executive officer, and if other than the foregoing, the person in charge of marketing of the membership camping operator, or persons in comparable positions in noncorporate operators, including the number of other membership camping operators with which the executive has been associated and the length of time with each.

(c) A brief description of the nature of the purchaser's right or license to use the membership camping operator's property or facilities.

(d) The location of each of the membership camping operator's campgrounds and a brief description for each campground of the significant facilities then available for use by purchasers and those which are represented to purchasers as being planned, together with a brief description of any significant facilities that are or will be available to nonpurchasers or nonmembers.

"Significant facilities" shall include, but are not limited to, each of the following: the number of campsites, in each campground; the number of campsites in each campground with full or partial hookups; swimming pools; tennis courts; recreation buildings; restrooms and showers; laundry rooms; trading posts; or grocery stores. "Partial hookups" mean those hookups with at least one of the following connections: electricity, water, or sewer connections.

Following such description there shall appear in 10-point bold type the following disclosure:

NOTICE: PURCHASE A MEMBERSHIP CAMPING CONTRACT ONLY ON THE BASIS OF EXISTING FACILITIES. CONSTRUCTION OF PLANNED FACILITIES IS SOMETIMES DEFERRED OR REVISED FOR A VARIETY OF REASONS. SHOULD THE SALESPERSON DESCRIBE A SIGNIFICANT FACILITY WHICH IS NEITHER LISTED AS EXISTING NOR PLANNED, TELEPHONE COLLECT OR TOLL FREE DURING WEEKDAY BUSINESS HOURS TO [insert headquarter's telephone number] TO VERIFY THE OPERATOR'S PLAN FOR SUCH A FACILITY.

(e) A brief description of the membership camping operator's ownership of, or other right to use, the campgrounds represented to be available for use by purchasers, together with the duration and expiration date of any lease, license, franchise, or reciprocal agreement entitling the membership camping operator to use the campgrounds, and any material provisions of any agreements, land use permits, or operating licenses which could materially restrict a purchaser's use of the campgrounds under the terms of the purchaser's camping contract.

(f) A summary or copy of the rules, restrictions, or covenants regulating the purchaser's use of the membership camping operator's properties, including a statement of whether and how the rules, restrictions, or covenants may be changed.

(g) A brief description of all payments of a purchaser under a membership camping contract, including initial fees and any further fees, charges, or assessments, together with any provisions for changing the payments.

(h) A description of any restraints on the transfer of the membership camping contract.

(i) A brief description of the policies relating to the availability of camping sites and whether reservations are required.

(j) A brief description of any grounds for forfeiture of a purchaser's membership camping contract.

(k) A copy of the membership camping contract form. **Leg.H.** Added Stats 1983 ch 847 §1. Amended Stats 1990 ch 1529 §6 (SB 2203).

§1812.303. Language; Notice of cancellation

(a) A membership camping contract shall be written in the same language as that principally used in any oral sales presentation (e.g., Spanish). A membership camping contract shall be dated, signed by the purchaser, and contain, in immediate proximity to the space reserved for the signature of the purchaser, a conspicuous statement in a size equal to at least 10-point bold type, as follows: "You, the purchaser, may cancel this contract at any time prior to midnight of the third business day after the date of the transaction. See an explanation of this right as set forth in this contract or on the attached notice of cancellation form." In the alternative the notice of cancellation as set forth in subdivision (b) may be placed in immediate proximity to the signature line of the contract in lieu of the foregoing statement.

(b) The contract shall be accompanied by a completed form in duplicate, captioned "Notice of Cancellation", which shall be attached to the contract and easily detachable. In the alternative, the seller may include all of the cancellation information on the contract and provide the consumer with a carbon copy which may be retained after cancellation. Both shall contain, in type of at least 10-point, the following statement written in the same language as used in the contract:

"Notice of Cancellation"

"You may cancel this contract, without any penalty or obligation, within three business days from the date the contract is executed.

"To cancel this contract, mail or deliver a signed and dated copy of this cancellation notice or a copy of this contract if it contains the cancellation instructions, or any other written notice, or send a telegram to _____ (Name of seller) at

_____
(Address of seller's place of business)
not later than midnight of _____. (Date)
I hereby cancel this transaction _____. (Date)

_____
(Purchaser's signature)

"With the notice of cancellation, or separately if a telegram is sent, you must return the original membership camping contract, membership card and all other evidence of membership to the seller. You should promptly return these documents with the notice of cancellation, or separately if a telegram is sent. Failure to send the documents promptly could delay your refund. You should retain for your records one copy of the cancellation notice, or a carbon of the contract when it provides the cancellation information, oil other writing showing intent to cancel. Mailing by ordinary mail is adequate but certified mail return receipt requested is recommended."

(c) On the date of purchase the membership camping operator shall provide the purchaser with a copy of the contract and duplicate of the notice of cancellation. The membership camping operator shall inform the purchaser orally of the right to cancel at the time the contract is executed.

(d) Within 20 days after the membership camping operator receives a notice of cancellation, the membership camping contract, the membership card and all other evidence of purchase or membership, the membership camping operator shall refund to the purchaser any sums paid as a deposit, downpayment or other payment therefor. If the purchaser does not promptly return the evidence of membership, the 20-day period shall be extended until such evidence of membership is returned.

(e) Until the membership camping operator has complied with this section, the purchaser shall have the right to cancel the contract.

(f) "Business day" means any calendar day except Sunday, or the following business holidays: New Year's Day, Washington's Birthday, Memorial Day, Independence Day, Labor Day, Columbus Day, Veteran's Day, Thanksgiving Day, and Christmas Day. **Leg.H.** Added Stats 1983 ch 847 §1. Amended Stats 1990 ch 1529 §7 (SB 2203).

§1812.304. Notice of cancellation without inspection

(a) If the purchaser has not inspected at least one of the membership camping operator's campgrounds prior to purchase of a membership camping contract, the notice shall contain the following additional language:

"If you sign this contract without having first inspected one of the membership camping operator's campgrounds, you may also cancel this contract at any time prior to midnight of the 10th business day after date of purchase by mailing or delivering the signed and dated attached written notice of cancellation or a copy of the contract when that contains the cancellation instructions together with the original camping club contract, membership card and any other evidence of membership."

(b) The seller shall return any payment made by the purchaser under the contract or offer to purchase, and any negotiable instrument executed by the purchaser, within 10 days of the return of evidence of membership and cancellation of the contract by the purchaser. If the purchaser does not promptly return the evidence of membership, the 10-day period shall be extended until the evidence of membership is returned. **Leg.H.** Added Stats 1983 ch 847 §1. Amended Stats 1990 ch 1529 §8 (SB 2203).

§1812.305. Exemptions

The following transactions are exempt from the provisions of this title.

(a) An offer, sale or transfer by any one person of not more than one membership camping contract for any given membership camping operator in any 12-month period.

(b) An offer or sale by a government or governmental agency.

(c) A bona fide pledge of a membership camping contract. **Leg.H.** Added Stats 1983 ch 847 §1.

§1812.306. Purchaser's remedies; Corrections by camping operator

(a) A purchaser's remedy for errors in or omissions from the membership camping contract of any of the disclosures or requirements of Sections 1812.302 to 1812.304, inclusive, shall be limited to a right of rescission and refund. Reasonable attorney's fees shall be awarded to the prevailing party in any action under this title. This limitation does not apply to errors or omissions from the contract, or disclosures or other requirements of this title, which are a part of a scheme to willfully misstate or omit the information required, or other requirements imposed by this title.

(b) Any failure, except a willful or material failure, to comply with any provision of Sections 1812.302 to 1812.304, inclusive, may be corrected within 30 days after receipt of written notice to the membership camping operator from the purchaser, and, if so corrected, there shall be no right of rescission. The membership camping operator or the holder shall not be subject to any penalty under this title. However, there can be no correction that increases any monthly payment, the number of payments, or the total amount due, unless concurred to, in writing, by the purchaser. "Holder" includes the seller who acquires the contract, or if the contract is purchased, a financing agency or other assignee who purchases the contract. **Leg.H.** Added Stats 1983 ch 847 §1. Amended Stats 2006 ch 538 §51 (SB 1852), effective January 1, 2007.

§1812.307. Conditions for withdrawal of campgrounds

No membership camping operator shall withdraw from the use by purchasers of membership camping contracts any campground unless one of the following conditions is satisfied:

(a) Adequate provision is made to provide within a reasonable time, a substitute campground in the same general area that is as desirable for the purpose of camping and outdoor recreation.

(b) The campground is withdrawn from use because, despite good faith efforts by the membership camping operator, a person not affiliated with the membership camping operator has exercised a superior right to possession (such as the right of a lessor to take possession following expiration of a lease of the property) and the terms and date of the withdrawal were disclosed in writing to all purchasers at or prior to the time of any sale of a membership camping contract after the membership camping operator represented to purchasers that the campground would be available for camping or recreation purposes.

(c) The rights of all purchasers of membership camping contracts who are entitled to use the campground have expired or have been lawfully terminated. **Leg.H.** Added Stats 1990 ch 1529 §10 (SB 2203).

Prior Law: Former §1812.307 was added Stats 1983 ch 847 §1 and amended and renumbered CC §1812.314 by Stats 1990 ch 1529 §9 (SB 2203).

§1812.308. Transfer of interest in campground

(a) Except in the case of a membership camping operator substituting a campground in accordance with Section 1812.307, no membership camping operator or owner of the underlying fee shall sell, lease, assign, or otherwise transfer his or her interest in a campground except by an instrument evidencing the transfer recorded in the office of the county recorder for the county in which the campground is located. The instrument shall be in recordable form and be executed by both the transferor and transferee and shall state each of the following:

(1) That the instrument is intended to protect the rights of all purchasers of membership camping contracts.

(2) That its terms may be enforced by any prior or subsequent purchaser so long as that purchaser is not in default on his or her obligations under the membership camping contract.

(3) That the transferee shall fully honor the rights of the purchasers to occupy and use the campground as provided in the purchaser's original membership camping contracts.

(4) That the transferee shall fully honor all rights of purchasers to cancel their contracts and receive appropriate refunds.

(5) That the obligations of the transferee under the instrument will continue to exist despite any cancellation or rejection of the contracts between the membership camping operator and purchaser arising out of bankruptcy proceedings.

(b) If any transfer of the interest of the membership camping operator or owner of the underlying fee occurs in a manner which is not in compliance with this section, the terms set forth in this section shall be presumed to be a part of the transfer and shall be deemed to be included in the instrument of transfer. Notice of the transfer shall be mailed to each purchaser within 30 days of the transfer. Persons who hold blanket encumbrances on a campground shall not be considered transferees for the purposes of this section. **Leg.H.** Added Stats 1990 ch 1529 §12 (SB 2203).

Prior Law: Former §1812.308 was added Stats 1983 ch 847 §1 and amended and renumbered CC §1812.315 by Stats 1990 ch 1529 §11 (SB 2203).

§1812.309. Representation of availability for use

(a) Campgrounds subject to this section include any campground which is offered or made available by an operator for the first time after January 1, 1991, or any campground which becomes subject to a new or refinanced blanket encumbrance after January 1, 1991. A membership camping operator shall not offer or represent that any campground subject to this section is available for use by the purchasers of its camping contracts unless one of the following conditions has been satisfied:

(1) The membership camping operator obtains and records a nondisturbance agreement from each holder of a blanket encumbrance. The nondisturbance agreement is executed by the membership camping operator and each holder of the blanket encumbrance and includes the provisions set forth in subdivision (j) of Section 1812.300 and each of the following:

(A) The instrument may be enforced by purchasers of membership camping contracts. If the membership camping operator is not in default under its obligations to the holder of the blanket encumbrance, the agreement may be enforced by both the membership camping operator and the purchasers.

(B) The nondisturbance agreement is effective as between each purchaser and the holder of the blanket encumbrance despite any rejection or cancellation of the purchaser's contract during any bankruptcy proceedings of the membership camping operator.

(C) The agreement is binding upon the successors in the interest of both the membership camping operator and the holder of the blanket encumbrance.

(D) A holder of the blanket encumbrance who obtains title or possession, or who causes a change in title or possession in a campground by foreclosure or otherwise, and who does not continue to operate the campground upon conditions no less favorable to members than existed prior to the change of title or possession shall either:

(i) Offer the title or possession of the campground to an association of members to operate the campground.

(ii) Obtain a commitment from another entity which obtains title or possession to undertake the responsibility of operating the campground.

(2) The membership camping operator posts a surety bond or irrevocable letter of credit with a trustee in favor of purchasers and which

guarantees that the payments on the blanket encumbrance are made as they become due. A trustee shall be either a corporate trustee or an attorney licensed to practice law in this state.

(3) The membership camping operator delivers to a trustee an encumbrance trust agreement which contains each of the following provisions:

(A) The membership camping operator shall collaterally assign to the trustee all of its membership camping contracts receivable or other receivables of the membership camping operator in an amount calculated in accordance with subparagraph (B). The membership camping operator shall provide the trustee with a security interest in the receivables and all proceeds therefrom. For purposes of this section, the membership camping operator shall be credited with 100 percent of the outstanding principal balance of each receivable assigned to the trustee. All proceeds of the receivables shall be held in a trust account by the trustee subject to this section for the use and benefit of the purchasers to make the payments of principal and interest due under the blanket encumbrance. However, if the proceeds of the receivables during any calendar year exceed the amount due under the blanket encumbrance in the following calendar quarter, these excess funds shall be returned by the trustee to the membership camping operator.

(B) The amount of membership camping contracts receivable or other receivables to be collaterally assigned as described in subparagraph (A) shall be calculated based upon the maximum number of contracts per camping site to be offered on or after January 1, 1991, in connection with the campground in question, which number of contracts per camping site shall not exceed 15 multiplied by the total number of camping sites available at the campground thereby yielding the anticipated total number of contracts to be sold in connection with the campground. The outstanding balance due under the blanket encumbrance shall then be divided by the anticipated total number of contracts to arrive at the amount per contract sold to be paid over to the trustee in the form of collaterally assigned receivables as described in subparagraph (A). The membership camping operator shall make the required collateral assignments to the trustee on a quarterly basis based upon the actual sales of contracts at the campground in question during the previous calendar quarter. However, the membership camping operator's obligation to collaterally assign receivables to the trustee shall cease when the membership camping operator has collaterally assigned to the trustee an aggregate principal amount of receivables equal to 100 percent of the aggregate principal indebtedness remaining due under the blanket encumbrance.

(C) If the outstanding balance due under the blanket encumbrance at the time of execution of the encumbrance trust agreement exceeds the anticipated gross revenue based upon the membership camping operator's price list to be generated by the sale of the anticipated total number of contracts as calculated in subparagraph (B), the membership camping operator shall meet the conditions specified in paragraph (1), (2), or (4) of this subdivision as to the full amount of the excess.

(D) It may be terminated by the membership camping operator if the membership camping operator has satisfied the obligation secured by the blanket encumbrance in full or has complied with paragraph (1), (2), or (4) of this subdivision. Upon termination of the agreement, all receivables and proceeds thereof held by the trustee shall be immediately assigned and delivered to the membership camping operator. All costs of administering this trust, filing, and perfecting the security interest, and foreclosing the lien shall be borne by the membership camping operator.

(4) Any financial institution which has made a hypothecation loan to the membership camping operator (a "hypothecation lender") shall have a lien on, or security interest in, the membership camping operator's interest in the campground, and the hypothecation lender shall have executed and recorded a nondisturbance agreement at the county recorder's office for the county in which the campground is located. Each person holding an interest in a blanket encumbrance superior to the interest held by the hypothecation lender shall execute and record at the county recorder's office, an instrument stating that the person shall give the hypothecation lender notice of, and at least 30 days to cure, any default under the blanket encumbrance before the person commences any foreclosure action affecting the campground. For the purposes of this paragraph, a "hypothecation loan to a membership camping operator" means a loan or line of credit secured by membership camping contracts receivable arising from the sale of membership camping contracts by the membership camping operator, which exceeds in the aggregate all outstanding indebtedness secured by blanket encumbrances superior to the interest held by the hypothecation lender.

A hypothecation lender who obtains title or possession, or who causes a change in title or possession, in a campground, by foreclosure or otherwise, and who does not continue to operate the campground upon conditions no less favorable to purchasers than existed prior to the change of title or possession shall either:

(A) Offer the title or possession to an association of members to operate the campground.

(B) Obtain a commitment from another entity which obtains title to, or possession of, the campground to undertake the responsibility of operating the campground.

(b) Any membership camping operator which does not comply at all times with subdivision (a) with regard to any blanket encumbrance in connection with any campground subject to that subdivision is prohibited from offering any membership camping contracts for sale during the period of noncompliance. **Leg.H.** Added Stats 1990 ch 1529 §13 (SB 2203).

§1812.314. Brokers

(a) All money received from the owner of a membership camping contract or the prospective purchaser thereof, by a membership camping contract broker in advance of the completion of any membership camping contract resale, including, but not limited to, listing fees, and fees for services, shall be deposited into an escrow account. The money shall not be disbursed until the transaction is complete, or until the escrow agent has received written instructions to disburse the funds signed by the owner of the membership camping contract or the prospective purchaser and the broker. For purposes of this section, a transaction is complete when ownership of the membership camping contract has been transferred from the prior purchaser to the new purchaser in the manner required by the terms of the membership camping contract, all documents necessary to complete the transfer have been fully executed, and the new purchaser has not exercised the right to cancel provided in paragraph (2) of subdivision (c).

(b) The broker shall inform the new purchaser in writing of the following:

(1) The risks of purchasing a membership camping contract without visiting at least one of the membership camping operator's campgrounds.

(2) That the membership camping operator may have a valid reason for not transferring the contract to the new purchaser such as a default in payment on contract or annual dues, or that the new purchaser does not meet the same credit standards applied to other new purchasers.

(3) That there may have been changes in the rules or regulations concerning the rights and obligations of the membership camping operator or its members including changes with respect to annual dues, fees, assessments, use restrictions or that some campgrounds may have been withdrawn.

(4) Any material changes or risks to the purchaser known to the broker.

(c)(1) Every broker shall provide in writing the following notice of cancellation to the new purchaser:

"You may cancel your contract of purchase, without any penalty or obligation, within 10 business days from the above date of purchase by mailing notice of cancellation together with the membership camping contract, if any, any contract for transfer, membership card or other evidence of membership to

_____
(Name and address of broker)
the membership camping operator
_____
(Name and address of membership camping operator)
and the escrow company
_____
(Name and address of escrow company)
if any, not later than midnight of _____ (Date).
I hereby cancel this transaction _____ (Purchaser's signature) _____ (Date).
Notice by ordinary mail is adequate but certified mail return receipt requested is recommended."

(2) Any escrow company which receives a notice of cancellation from a purchaser shall, within 72 hours of receipt of the notice, notify the membership camping operator of the cancellation and shall refund any

sums paid by the purchaser of the contract within 10 days of receipt of the notice of the cancellation and other documents. The escrow company shall incur no liability to the seller, purchaser, or broker as a result of its compliance with this section. **Leg.H.** Added Stats 1983 ch 847 §1 as §1812.307. Amended and renumbered by Stats 1990 ch 1529 §9 (SB 2203).

§1812.315. Severability

If any provision of this title or the application thereof to any person or circumstances is held invalid, the invalidity shall not affect other provisions or applications of this title which can be given effect without the invalid provision or application, and to this end the provisions of this title are severable. **Leg.H.** Added Stats 1983 ch 847 §1 as §1812.308. Amended and renumbered by Stats 1990 ch 1529 §11 (SB 2203).

§1812.316. Waiver of provisions of title void

Any waiver of the provisions of this title is contrary to public policy, and is void and unenforceable. **Leg.H.** Added Stats 2002 ch 815 §21 (AB 2331).

TITLE 2.9
CREDITOR REMEDIES: DISABILITY INSURANCE

Legislative findings and declarations. §1812.400.
Definitions. §1812.401.
Creditor remedies during disability. §1812.402.
Time for invoking creditor's remedy. §1812.403.
Remedies of creditor providing of insurance. §1812.404.
Open-end credit plans. §1812.405.
Key person insurance; Secured loan. §1812.406.
Nonpayment of sums due on or after April 1, 1984. §1812.407.
Waiver. §1812.408.
Interests of bona fide purchaser. §1812.409.
Severability. §1812.410.

§1812.400. Legislative findings and declarations

The Legislature finds and declares that it is unfair for a creditor who has directly participated in, arranged, or received a commission or other compensation for the sale of credit disability insurance to the debtor, or that creditor's successor in interest, to invoke a creditor's remedy because of a debtor's nonpayment of any sum which has become due during a period of disability until a reasonable time has passed for the disability insurance claim to be filed, verified and processed. **Leg.H.** Added Stats 1983 ch 973 §1.

§1812.401. Definitions

For the purposes of this title:

(a) "Credit disability insurance" means insurance of a debtor to provide indemnity for payments becoming due on a specific loan or other credit transaction while the debtor is disabled as defined in the policy.

(b) "Creditor" means the lender of money or vendor or lessor of goods, services, property, rights, or privileges, for which payment is arranged through a credit transaction, who has directly participated in, arranged, or received a commission or other compensation for the sale of credit disability insurance to the debtor, or any successor to the right, title, or interest of any such lender, vendor, or lessor, and an affiliate, associate, or subsidiary of any of them or any director, officer, or employee of any of them, or any other person in any way associated with any of them.

(c) "Debtor" means a borrower of money or a purchaser or lessee of goods, services, property, rights, or privileges for which payment is arranged through a credit transaction.

(d) "Creditor's remedy" means and includes the imposition of any late charge or penalty, the acceleration of the maturity of all or any part of the indebtedness, the collection or assignment for the collection of all or any part of the indebtedness, the commencement of any action or special proceeding, or the enforcement of any security interest in any manner, including, but not limited to, repossession, foreclosure, or the exercise of a power of sale contained in a deed of trust or mortgage.

(e) "Disability claim period" or "claim period" means the period beginning on the due date of the first payment not paid by the debtor for which the debtor claims disability coverage arising from a then current disability and continuing until three calendar months thereafter or until the insurer pays or rejects the claim, whichever occurs sooner.

(f) "Notice" to a creditor means written notice deposited in the United States mail, postage prepaid, addressed to the creditor at the location where payments on the loan or credit transaction are normally required to be sent by the debtor. A creditor may elect to require that written notice, otherwise complying with the requirements of this subdivision, be sent to a different location or may elect to accept telephonic notice to a telephone number specified by the creditor, in either case in lieu of notice being sent to the location where payments are regularly required to be sent, if that location or telephone number is clearly and conspicuously disclosed as the proper place to direct any notice to the creditor relating to any claim of disability on each monthly billing, or on or in each payment coupon book (by adhesive attachment, republication, or otherwise), as the case may be, or (if payments are automatically deducted from an account of the debtor) on the annual statement of loan activity. In any particular instance a creditor may waive the requirement that notice be in writing and accept oral notice. **Leg.H.** Added Stats 1983 ch 973 §1. Amended Stats 1984 ch 1200 §1, effective September 17, 1984.

§1812.402. Creditor remedies during disability

(a) No creditor, as defined in Section 1812.401, shall invoke any creditor's remedy against a debtor because of the debtor's nonpayment of any sum which becomes due during any disability claim period and for which credit disability insurance coverage, subject to this title, is provided.

(b) Upon initially receiving notice, as defined in subdivision (f) of Section 1812.401, of the debtor's claim of disability, the creditor shall inform the debtor in writing of the name, address, and telephone number of the insurer or its designated representative from whom the debtor may obtain claim forms. Upon receiving notice of the disability claim, the insurer or its designated representative shall send necessary claim forms to the debtor. The debtor shall submit the claim to the insurer or its designated representative and shall notify the creditor, as specified in subdivision (f) of Section 1812.401, that a claim has been submitted.

This subdivision shall apply to the original creditor who sold the disability insurance and shall not apply to that creditor's successor in interest if the successor in interest (1) is not related by common ownership or control to that creditor and (2) has no information regarding the name, address, and telephone number of the insurer or its designated representative.

(c) Nothing in this section prohibits a creditor from invoking any creditor's remedy during or after the claim period for the debtor's nonpayment of any sum due prior to the claim period, whether or not the nonpayment is related to the claimed disability, or for the debtor's nonpayment of any interest, finance charge, or late charge accruing during the claim period of any sum due prior to the period.

(d) Nothing in this section prohibits a creditor from foreclosing a lien on any property to protect that creditor's security interest if a senior lienholder on that property (1) has initiated the foreclosure of its lien, (2) is not prohibited from continuing the foreclosure by any law or order of court, or (3) will not otherwise suspend or delay its foreclosure proceeding until after the disability claim period.

(e) If the insurer pays the claim within the disability claim period, the creditor shall treat each payment made by the insurer as though it were timely made by the debtor. If the insurer rejects the claim within the disability claim period or accepts the claim within the claim period as a partial disability which results in a payment of less than the full benefit which would be paid for the total disability, the debtor shall have the opportunity to pay the entire amount which became due during the claim period or the difference between the amount which became due during the claim period and the amount paid by the insurer for the partial disability without being subject to any creditor's remedy, except the imposition of late charges, for 35 days following the date on which the insurer sends notice of the rejection of the claim or acceptance of the claim as a partial disability. In the event the debtor does not pay the entire amount which became due during the claim period plus any accrued late charges within 35 days from that date, the creditor may then invoke any creditor's remedy.

(f) The obligations of the creditor and debtor pursuant to this section shall be disclosed in writing in at least 10-point type by the creditor to the debtor at the time the creditor sells the insurance, in the manner provided in paragraph (1), and by the insurer to the debtor at the time the insurer sends claim forms pursuant to subdivision (b), in the manner provided in paragraph (2).

(1) The disclosure required by the creditor shall be substantially in the following form:

CLAIM PROCEDURE

If you become disabled, tell us (your creditor) right away. (We advise you to send this information to the same address to which you are normally required to send your payments, unless a different address or telephone number is given to you in writing by us as the location where we would like to be notified.) We will tell you where to get claim forms. Send in the completed form to the insurance company as soon as possible and tell us as soon as you do.

If your disability insurance covers all of your missed payment, WE CANNOT TRY TO COLLECT WHAT YOU OWE OR FORECLOSE UPON OR REPOSSESS ANY COLLATERAL UNTIL THREE CALENDAR MONTHS AFTER your first missed payment is due or until the insurance company pays or rejects your claim, whichever comes first. We can, however, try to collect, foreclose, or repossess if you have money due and owing us or are otherwise in default when your disability claim is made or if a senior mortgage or lien holder is foreclosing.

If the insurance company pays the claim within the three calendar months, we must accept the money as though you paid on time. If the insurance company rejects the claim within the three calendar months or accepts the claim within the three calendar months as a partial disability and pays less than for a total disability, you will have 35 days from the date that the rejection or the acceptance of the partial disability claim is sent to pay past due payments, or the difference between past due payments and what the insurance company pays for the partial disability, plus late charges. You can contact us, and we will tell you how much you owe. After that time, we can take action to collect or foreclose or repossess any collateral you may have given.

If the insurance company accepts your claim but requires that you send in additional forms to remain eligible for continued payments, you should send in these completed additional forms no later than required. If you do not send in these forms on time, the insurance company may stop paying, and we will then be able to take action to collect or foreclose or repossess any collateral you may have given.

(2) The disclosure required by the insurer shall be substantially in the following form:

CLAIM PROCEDURE

Send in the completed form to the insurance company as soon as possible and tell your creditor as soon as you do. (Your creditor has already advised you of the address or telephone number to use to confirm that you have submitted your completed form to the insurance company.)

If your disability insurance covers all of your missed payments, YOUR CREDITOR CANNOT TRY TO COLLECT WHAT YOU OWE OR FORECLOSE UPON OR REPOSSESS ANY COLLATERAL UNTIL THREE CALENDAR MONTHS AFTER your first missed payment is due or until the insurance company pays or rejects your claim, whichever comes first. Your creditor can, however, try to collect, foreclose, or repossess if you have money due and owing or are otherwise in default when your disability claim is made or if a senior mortgage or lienholder is foreclosing.

If the insurance company pays the claim within the three calendar months, your creditor must accept the money as though you paid on time. If the insurance company rejects the claim within the three calendar months or accepts the claim within the three calendar months as a partial disability and pays less than for a total disability, you will have 35 days from the date that the rejection or the acceptance of the partial disability claim was sent to pay past due payments, or the difference between past due payments and what the insurance company pays for the partial disability, plus late charges. You can contact your creditor who will tell you how much you owe. After that time, your creditor can take action to collect or foreclose or repossess any collateral you may have given.

If the insurance company accepts your claim, but requires that you send in additional forms to remain eligible for continued payments, you should send in these completed additional forms no later than required. If you do not send in these forms on time, the insurance company may stop paying, and your creditor will then be able to take action to collect or foreclose or repossess any collateral you have given.

(g) If a debtor does not make a payment for which the debtor claims disability coverage arising from a then current disability and if the creditor, after sending the debtor notice of the debtor's delinquency, invokes any creditor's remedy because of the nonpayment without knowledge of the debtor's claim of disability coverage, subject to this title, the following provisions apply:

(1) Upon receiving notice of the debtor's claim, the creditor shall not invoke any further creditor's remedy during the remainder of the claim period and the period provided in subdivision (e).

(2) Upon receiving notice, as specified in subdivision (f) of Section 1812.401, of the debtor's claim, the creditor shall rescind every creditor's remedy that has been invoked relating to the delinquency for which coverage is claimed, except that the creditor shall not be obligated to restore property which has been sold in a bona fide lawful sale to any person not related by common ownership or control to the creditor.

(3) The debtor shall be liable for costs and expenses actually incurred in connection with the invocation or rescission of any creditor's remedy.

(4) The creditor shall not be in violation of this title and shall not be liable under subdivision (i) provided the creditor complies with paragraphs (1) and (2) of this subdivision.

(h) The rights and remedies afforded debtors by this title shall be cumulative to each other and to all other rights and remedies which the debtors may have under other laws.

(i) The debtor may bring an action for damages, equitable relief, or other relief for any violation of this title. **Leg.H.** Added Stats 1983 ch 973 §1. Amended Stats 1984 ch 1200 §2, effective September 17, 1984.

§1812.403. Time for invoking creditor's remedy

A creditor may invoke any creditor's remedy 15 days after receiving notice that the insurer has ceased making payments on a credit disability insurance claim because of the debtor's failure to timely submit any forms required by the insurer for recertification of a temporary disability. **Leg.H.** Added Stats 1983 ch 973 §1.

§1812.404. Remedies of creditor providing of insurance

This title shall apply to a creditor only if the creditor, the predecessor to the right, title, or interest of the creditor, or the representative of either of them directly arranges or participates in the sale or receives a commission or other compensation for the sale of credit disability insurance to the debtor. **Leg.H.** Added Stats 1983 ch 973 §1.

§1812.405. Open-end credit plans

This title shall not prohibit a creditor from invoking any creditor's remedy as a result of a debtor's nonpayment when due of any amount obtained under an open-end credit plan, as hereafter defined, after the debtor has given notice of a disability claim unless the nonpayment is related to a covered disability then affecting the debtor other than the disability previously claimed. The creditor's termination of the open-end credit plan because the debtor does not meet the creditor's customary credit standards at the time the debtor notifies the creditor of the disability claim is not a creditor's remedy.

An "open-end credit plan" means credit extended by a creditor under a plan in which the creditor reasonably contemplates repeated transactions, the creditor may impose a finance charge from time to time on an outstanding unpaid balance, and the amount of credit that may be extended to the debtor during the term of the plan (up to any limit set by the creditor) is generally made available to the extent that any outstanding balance is repaid. **Leg.H.** Added Stats 1983 ch 973 §1.

§1812.406. Key person insurance; Secured loan

(a) This title does not apply to credit disability insurance covering a key person, as hereinafter defined, which a creditor requires as a condition to making a loan of at least twenty-five thousand dollars ($25,000) to be used in the operation of a business in which the key person is employed or has an ownership interest.

For the purposes of this subdivision, a "key person" is a person who the creditor and the debtor or debtors mutually agree must be involved in the operation of the business to assure its success.

(b) This title does not apply to a loan or other credit transaction (including an open line of credit) of more than 10 years' duration which is secured by a mortgage or deed of trust unless (1) the principal purpose of the loan or credit transaction is for the construction (other than initial construction), rehabilitation, or improvement (including "home improvement" as defined in Section 7151 of the Business and Professions Code) of real property consisting of four or fewer residential units, and (2) any document incident to the loan or credit transaction at the time the loan or extension of credit is made, or any course of dealing between the creditor and a contractor or material supplier assisting the borrower in obtaining the loan or extension of credit, would indicate that purpose.

(c) Subdivision (b) shall not apply to debtors who were entitled to receive notice from the creditor pursuant to subdivision (f) of Section 1812.402 on or after January 1, 1984, and prior to the effective date of the act which added this subdivision, unless the debtor receives written notice that the remedies provided in this title are revoked, the debtor is given an opportunity to cancel the coverage, and no claim has been made or notice provided as specified in Section 1812.401. If the debtor fails to cancel the insurance following receipt of the notice required under this subdivision, subdivision (b) shall apply to that policy upon payment by the debtor of the next installment of premium, whether to the insurer or to a creditor pursuant to a premium finance agreement. **Leg.H.** Added Stats 1983 ch 973 §1. Amended Stats 1984 ch 1200 §3, effective September 17, 1984.

§1812.407. Nonpayment of sums due on or after April 1, 1984

The provisions of this title shall apply to the nonpayment of any sum which becomes due on or after April 1, 1984, and for which the debtor claims disability coverage. **Leg.H.** Added Stats 1983 ch 973 §1.

§1812.408. Waiver

Any waiver by the debtor of the provisions of this title shall be void and unenforceable. **Leg.H.** Added Stats 1983 ch 973 §1.

§1812.409. Interests of bona fide purchaser

This title shall not affect or defeat an interest in the debtor's property, acquired after the creditor invokes a creditor's remedy in violation of this title, by a bona fide purchaser or encumbrancer for value and without notice of facts that constitute a violation of this title. **Leg.H.** Added Stats 1984 ch 1200 §4, effective September 17, 1984.

Prior Law: Former §1812.409 was added Stats 1983 ch 973 §1 and amended and renumbered CC §1812.410 by Stats 1984 ch 1200 §5, effective September 17, 1984.

§1812.410. Severability

If any provision of this title or the application thereof to any person or circumstance is held to be unconstitutional, the remainder of the title and the application of the provision to other persons and circumstances shall not be affected thereby. **Leg.H.** Added Stats 1983 ch 973 §1 as §1812.409. Amended and renumbered by Stats 1984 ch 1200 §5, effective September 17, 1984.

TITLE 2.91
EMPLOYMENT AGENCY, EMPLOYMENT COUNSELING, AND JOB LISTING SERVICES ACT

Chapter 1. General Provisions.
Chapter 2. Employment Agencies.
Chapter 3. Employment Counseling Services.
Chapter 4. Job Listing Services.
Chapter 5. Records.
Chapter 6. Remedies and Enforcement.
Chapter 7. Nurses' Registries.
Chapter 8. Long-Term Care Facilities.

CHAPTER 1
GENERAL PROVISIONS

Citation of title. §1812.500.
Definitions. §1812.501.
Exemptions from title. §1812.502.

§1812.500. Citation of title

This title shall be known and cited as the Employment Agency, Employment Counseling, and Job Listing Services Act. **Leg.H.** Added Stats 1989 ch 704 §2.

§1812.501. Definitions

(a)(1) "Employment agency" or "agency" means:

(A) Any person who, for a fee or other valuable consideration to be paid, directly or indirectly by a jobseeker, performs, offers to perform, or represents it can or will perform any of the following services:

(i) Procures, offers, promises, or attempts to procure employment or engagements for others or employees for employers.

(ii) Registers persons seeking to procure or retain employment or engagement.

(iii) Gives information as to where and from whom this help, employment, or engagement may be procured.

(iv) Provides employment or engagements.

(B) Any person who offers, as one of its main objects or purposes, to procure employment for any person who will pay for its services, or that collects dues, tuition, or membership or registration fees of any sort, if the main object of the person paying those fees is to secure employment.

(C) Any person who, for a fee or other valuable consideration, procures, offers, promises, provides, or attempts to procure babysitting or domestic employment for others or domestics or babysitters for others.

(2) "Employment agency" or "agency" shall not include any employment counseling service or any job listing service.

(b)(1) "Employment counseling service" means any person who offers, advertises, or represents it can or will provide any of the following services for a fee: career counseling, vocational guidance, aptitude testing, executive consulting, personnel consulting, career management, evaluation, or planning, or the development of résumés and other promotional materials relating to the preparation for employment. "Employment counseling service" shall not include persons who provide services strictly on an hourly basis with no financial obligation required of the consumer beyond the hourly fee for services rendered. An "employment counseling service" does not include the functions of an "employment agency" as defined in subdivision (a).

(2) "Employment counseling service" does not include:

(A) Businesses that are retained by, act solely on behalf of, and are compensated solely by prior or current employers that do not require any "customer" to sign a contract and do not in any way hold any "customer" liable for fees.

(B)(i) Any provider of vocational rehabilitation in which the counseling services are paid for by insurance benefits, if the counseling is provided as a result of marital dissolution or separation proceedings to prepare one of the spouses for reentry into the job market and if the fees are paid by some party other than the person receiving the counseling services.

(ii) The exemption provided in this subparagraph does not apply to any vocational rehabilitation counselor who receives any payments directly from the individual customer receiving the counseling.

(C) Any person who engages solely in the preparation of résumés and cover letters, provided that the résumé writing service does not advertise or hold itself out as offering other job seeking or placement services and does not charge more than three hundred dollars ($300) for any résumé, cover letter, or combination of both to any single customer in any individual transaction.

(D) Any public educational institution.

(E) Any private educational institution established solely for educational purposes that, as a part of its curriculum, offers employment counseling to its student body and conforms to the requirements of Article 3.5 (commencing with Section 94760) of Chapter 7 of Part 59 of the Education Code.

(F) A psychologist or psychological corporation licensed pursuant to Chapter 6.6 (commencing with Section 2900) of Division 2 of the Business and Professions Code, providing psychological assessment, career or occupational counseling, or consultation and related professional services within his, her, or its scope of practice.

(G) An educational psychologist licensed pursuant to Article 5 (commencing with Section 4986) of Chapter 13 of Division 2 of the Business and Professions Code, providing counseling services within his or her scope of practice.

(c) "Job listing service" means any person who provides, offers, or represents it can or will provide any of the following services, for a fee or other valuable consideration to be paid, directly or indirectly, by the jobseeker in advance of, or contemporaneously with, performance of these services: matches jobseekers with employment opportunities, providing or offering to provide jobseekers lists of employers or lists of job openings or like publications, or preparing résumés or lists of jobseekers for distribution to potential employers.

(d) A "nurses' registry" as defined in subdivision (b) of Section 1812.524 is an employment agency. However, unless otherwise provided for in this title, a nurses' registry shall not be required to comply with Chapter 2 (commencing with Section 1812.503) regulating employment agencies but, instead, shall be required to comply with Chapter 7 (commencing with Section 1812.524).

(e) "Jobseeker" means a person seeking employment.

(f) "Employer" means any individual, company, partnership, association, corporation, agent, employee, or representative for whom or for which an employment agency or job listing service attempts to obtain an employee or to place a jobseeker.

(g) "Job order" means any written or oral instruction, direction, or permission granted by an employer or its agent to an employment agency or job listing service to refer jobseekers for a specified job.

(h) "Domestic agency" means any agency that provides, or attempts to provide, employment by placement of domestic help in private homes.

(i) "Deposit" means any money or valuable consideration received by an employment agency or job listing service from a jobseeker for referring the jobseeker to a position of employment prior to the jobseeker's acceptance of a position.

(j) "Fee" means:

(1) Any money or other valuable consideration paid, or promised to be paid, for services rendered or to be rendered by any person conducting an employment agency, employment counseling service, or job listing service under this title.

(2) Any money received by any person in excess of that which has been paid out by him or her for transportation, transfer of baggage, or board and lodging for any applicant for employment.

(k) "Registration fee" means any charge made, or attempted to be made, by an employment agency for registering or listing an applicant for employment, for letter writing, or any charge of a like nature made, or attempted to be made without having a bona fide order for the placement of the applicant in a position.

(*l*) "Person" means any individual, corporation, partnership, limited liability company, trust, association, or other organization.

(m) This section shall become operative on January 1, 1997. **Leg.H.** Added Stats 1995 ch 758 §8.5 (AB 446), operative January 1, 1997. Amended Stats 2006 ch 538 §52 (SB 1852), effective January 1, 2007.

Prior Law: Former §1812.501, similar to the present section, was added Stats 1989 ch 704 §2, amended Stats 1990 ch 1256 §3, Stats 1994 ch 1010 §46, Stats 1995 ch 758 §8, operative until January 1, 1997, and repealed, operative January 1, 1997, by its own terms.

Former CC §1812.501, similar to the present section, was added Stats 1989 ch 704 §2 and repealed operative January 1, 1997, by its own provisions. Stats 1995 ch 758 §8.

§1812.502. Exemptions from title

(a) This title does not apply to any person who provides any of the services described in subdivision (a) of Section 1812.501 and who charges fees exclusively to employers for those services. The exemption from regulation provided by this subdivision does not apply to any person who provides babysitting or domestic employment for others. This subdivision does not apply to an employment counseling service as defined in subdivision (b) of Section 1812.501.

(b) This title shall not apply to any nonprofit corporation, organized for the purpose of economic adjustment, civic betterment, and the giving of vocational guidance and placement to its members, or others, including employment counseling services, when all of the following conditions exist:

(1) None of the directors, officers, or employees thereof receive any profit other than a nominal salary for services performed for the organization or corporation.

(2) No fee is charged for those services, though a voluntary contribution may be requested.

(3) Membership dues or fees charged are used solely for maintenance of the organization or corporation.

(c) Nothing in this title shall apply to a nonprofit corporation which has been formed in good faith for the promotion and advancement of the general professional interests of its members and which maintains a placement service principally engaged in securing employment for such members with the state or any county, city, district or other public agency under contracts providing employment for one year or longer, or any nonprofit corporation exempted by subdivision (b).

(d) This title shall not apply to a labor organization as defined in Section 1117 of the Labor Code, a newspaper of general circulation, bona fide newsletter, magazine, trade or professional journal, or other publication of general circulation, the main purpose of which is dissemination of news, reports, trade or professional information, or information not intended to assist in locating, securing, or procuring employment or assignments for others.

(e) As used in this title, "employment agency" or "agency" does not include a nursing school, business school, or vocational school, except that if such a school charges a fee for placement, the school shall be an employment agency within the meaning of this title.

(f)(1) A job listing service which meets the requirements specified in paragraph (2) or (3) shall not be subject to any of the following: Sections 1812.515, 1812.516, 1812.517, and 1812.518; subdivisions (a) and (b), and paragraph (3) of subdivision (c), and subdivision (d) of Section 1812.519; paragraph (2) of subdivision (b), and subdivisions (c), (d), (e), and (f) of Section 1812.520; and Section 1812.521.

(2) A job listing service shall be exempt pursuant to paragraph (1) if it complies with all of the following:

(A) Does not provide, offer, or imply the offer of, services related to employment.

(B) Does not offer or sell lists of employers or job openings to jobseekers on an in-person basis.

(C) Maintains records of all its advertisements identified by date and publication, and the sources of information used for the preparation of lists of employers and job openings, from which can be determined the accuracy of any statistics regarding success rate or similar statistics used in its advertising, promotional materials, or oral or written statements to jobseekers.

(D) Identifies, on each list of employers and job openings, its general source of information for jobs included on that list when the source of information is a publication or other public record.

(E) Provides, at or before the time of delivery of the list, a prominent written statement to the jobseeker granting the jobseeker a right to return the list for an immediate refund of the purchase price during a stated period of time which expires not less than 10 days from the date of delivery of the list. The list shall be deemed returned upon delivery to the address from which it was obtained or upon deposit in the mail properly addressed to that address, with postage prepaid.

(3) A job listing service shall be exempt pursuant to paragraph (1) if it complies with all of the following:

(A) A majority interest in the job listing service is owned by one or more colleges or universities, or alumni associations affiliated therewith, and each college or university is accredited by both (i) an accrediting agency recognized as such by the United States Department of Education and (ii) a member organization of the Council of Postsecondary Accreditation.

(B) The job listing service provides services related to employment exclusively for jobseekers who are the alumni of colleges or universities specified in subparagraph (A).

(C) The job listing service does not require, as a condition to receiving employment services, that the applicant have completed courses or examinations beyond the requirements for graduation from the college or university specified in subparagraph (A).

(D) More than 50 percent of the annual revenues received by the job listing service are derived from paid subscriptions of prospective employers. **Leg.H.** Added Stats 1989 ch 704 §2. Amended Stats 1990 ch 1256 §4 (AB 2649).

CHAPTER 2
EMPLOYMENT AGENCIES

Bonds. §1812.503.
Contracts. §1812.504.
Fees. §1812.505.
Refund of deposit or fee. §1812.506.
Job orders; Referrals. §1812.507.
Advertisements; Records. §1812.508.
Restrictions and disclosures. §1812.509.
Information agency must supply to employer when referring child care provider to employer that is not required to be licensed child day care facility. §1812.5093.
Domestic workers. §1812.5095.

§1812.503. Bonds

(a) Every employment agency subject to this title shall maintain a bond issued by a surety company admitted to do business in this state. The principal sum of the bond shall be three thousand dollars ($3,000). A copy of the bond shall be filed with the Secretary of State.

(b) The bond required by this section shall be in favor of, and payable to, the people of the State of California and shall be conditioned that the person obtaining the bond will comply with this title and will pay all sums due any individual or group of individuals when the person or his or her representative, agent, or employee has received those sums. The bond shall be for the benefit of any person or persons damaged by any violation of this title or by fraud, dishonesty, misstatement, misrepresentation, deceit, unlawful acts or omissions, or failure to provide the services of the employment agency in performance of the contract with the jobseeker, by the employment agency or its agents, representatives, or employees while acting within the scope of their employment.

(c)(1) No employment agency shall conduct any business without having a current surety bond in the amount prescribed by this title and filing a copy of the bond with the Secretary of State.

(2) Thirty days prior to the cancellation or termination of any surety bond required by this section, the surety shall send a written notice of that cancellation or termination to both the employment agency and the Secretary of State, identifying the bond and the date of cancellation or termination.

(3) If any employment agency fails to obtain a new bond and file a copy of that bond with the Secretary of State by the effective date of the cancellation or termination of the former bond, the employment agency shall cease to conduct any business unless and until a new surety bond is obtained and a copy of that bond is filed with the Secretary of State.

(d) When a deposit has been made in lieu of the bond pursuant to Section 995.710 of the Code of Civil Procedure, the person asserting a claim against the deposit shall, in lieu of Section 996.430 of the Code of Civil Procedure, establish the claim by furnishing evidence to the Secretary of State of a money judgment entered by a court together with evidence that the claimant is a person described in subdivision (b).

(e) When a claimant has established the claim with the Secretary of State, the Secretary of State shall review and approve the claim and enter the date of approval thereon. The claim shall be designated an "approved claim."

(f) When the first claim against a particular deposit has been approved, it shall not be paid until the expiration of a period of 240 days after the date of its approval by the Secretary of State. Subsequent claims that are approved by the Secretary of State within the same 240-day period shall similarly not be paid until the expiration of the 240-day period. Upon the expiration of the 240-day period, the Secretary of State shall pay all approved claims from that 240-day period in full unless the deposit is insufficient, in which case each approved claim shall be paid a pro rata share of the deposit.

(g) When the Secretary of State approves the first claim against a particular deposit after the expiration of a 240-day period, the date of approval of that claim shall begin a new 240-day period to which subdivision (f) shall apply with respect to any amount remaining in the deposit.

(h) After a deposit is exhausted, no further claims shall be paid by the Secretary of State. Claimants who have had their claims paid in full or in part pursuant to subdivision (f) or (g) shall not be required to return funds received from the deposit for the benefit of other claimants.

(i) When a deposit has been made in lieu of a bond, the amount of the deposit shall not be subject to attachment, garnishment, or execution with respect to an action or judgment against the employment agency, other than as to an amount as no longer needed or required for the purpose of this title that would otherwise be returned to the employment agency by the Secretary of State.

(j) The Secretary of State shall retain a cash deposit for two years from the date the Secretary of State receives written notification from the assignor of the deposit that the assignor has ceased to engage in the business of an employment agency or has filed a bond pursuant to subdivision (a), provided that there are no outstanding claims against the deposit. This written notice shall include all of the following: (1) name, address, and telephone number of the assignor; (2) name, address, and telephone number of the bank at which the deposit is located; (3) account number of the deposit; and (4) a statement whether the assignor is ceasing to engage in the business of an employment agency or has filed a bond with the Secretary of State. The Secretary of State shall forward an acknowledgment of receipt of the written notice to the assignor at the address indicated therein, specifying the date of receipt of the written notice and anticipated date of release of the deposit, provided there are no outstanding claims against the deposit.

(k) A judge of a superior court may order the return of the deposit prior to the expiration of two years upon evidence satisfactory to the judge that there are no outstanding claims against the deposit or order the Secretary of State to retain the deposit for a sufficient period beyond the two years pursuant to subdivision (j) to resolve outstanding claims against the deposit account.

(*l*) The Secretary of State shall charge a filing fee not to exceed the cost of filing the bond or deposit filed in lieu of a bond as set forth in Section 995.710 of the Code of Civil Procedure.

(m) The Secretary of State shall enforce the provisions of this chapter that govern the filing and maintenance of bonds and deposits in lieu of bonds. **Leg.H.** Added Stats 1989 ch 704 §2. Amended Stats 1996 ch 633 §11 (SB 1978); Stats 1998 ch 829 §11 (SB 1652); Stats 2002 ch 784 §15 (SB 1316).

§1812.504. Contracts

(a) Every employment agency shall give a written contract to every jobseeker from whom a fee or deposit is to be received, whether directly or indirectly. The original of the contract shall be given to the jobseeker at the time the jobseeker signs the contract and before the employment agency accepts any fee or deposit or the jobseeker becomes obligated to pay any such fee or deposit. The contract shall contain all of the following:

(1) The name, address, and telephone number of the employment agency, and, if the employment agency has more than one office or location, the address and telephone number of the principal office or location providing services to the jobseeker.

(2) The name and address of the person giving the order for help, the date and consecutive number of the receipt of the order by the agency, and its manner of transmission.

(3) The name of the jobseeker, the name and address of the person to whom the jobseeker is sent for employment, and the address where the jobseeker is to report for employment.

(4) The date and consecutive number of the contract.

(5) The amount of the fee to be charged and to be collected from the jobseeker, including a statement that if the employment is terminated, the fee may not exceed gross earnings of the jobseeker in that employment, and the amount of the fee paid or advanced by the prospective employer and by whom paid or advanced.

(6) The kind of work or employment.

(7) The daily hours of work; the wages or salary, including any consideration or privilege; the benefits; and any other conditions of employment.

(8) If any labor trouble exists at the place of employment, that fact shall be stated in the contract.

(9) A contract expiration date which shall not be later than 180 days from the date of the referral or signing of the contract, whichever occurs first; however, a domestic agency operating as a registry may enter into a continuing contract subject to termination by written notice by either the domestic worker or the agency.

(10) Any other term, condition, or understanding agreed upon between the agency and the jobseeker.

(11) The following statement, with the caption in type no smaller than 10-point boldfaced type and the remainder in a size no smaller than that generally used throughout the contract, and in full capitals, boldface, or italics:

RIGHT TO REFUND

"If you pay all or any portion of a fee and fail to accept employment, the employment agency shall, upon your request, return the amount paid to you within 48 hours after your request for a refund.

"If you leave employment for just cause or are discharged for reasons other than misconduct connected with your work within 90 days from the starting date of employment, the agency shall reduce your fee to that payable for temporary employment and shall refund any excess paid within 10 days of your request for a refund.

"No fee larger than that for temporary employment may be charged to you for employment lasting 90 days or less unless the agency's fee schedules, contracts, and agreements provide for a further charge if you leave employment without just cause or are discharged for misconduct in connection with your work.

"If any refund due is not made within the time limits set forth above, the employment agency shall pay you an additional sum equal to the amount of the refund."

(b) All contracts shall be dated and shall be made and numbered consecutively, both copies to be signed by the jobseeker and the person acting for the employment agency. The original shall be given to the jobseeker and one copy shall be kept on file at the employment agency.

(c) The full agreement between the parties shall be contained in a single document containing those elements set forth in this section.

(d) When a referral is made by telephone the agency shall execute the contract or receipt in triplicate and shall mail the original and duplicate to the jobseeker on the day the referral is made, with instructions that they be signed by the jobseeker and the duplicate returned to the agency. The date of mailing the contract or receipt to the jobseeker shall be entered thereon by the agency. The same contract or receipt shall not be used for more than one referral.

(e) For purposes of this section, a "domestic agency operating as a registry" means a domestic agency that engages in the business of obtaining and filling commitments for domestic help. **Leg.H.** Added Stats 1989 ch 704 §2. Amended Stats 1996 ch 102 §1 (SB 2030).

§1812.505. Fees

(a)(1) An employment agency shall provide a copy of the agency's jobseeker fee schedule and payment terms to any jobseeker from whom a fee or deposit is to be received, prior to the jobseeker being interviewed by a counselor. The jobseeker fee schedule shall indicate the percentage of both the projected annual and first month's total gross earnings represented by those fees.

(2) In the schedule, the various employments or salary ranges by which the fee is to be computed or determined shall be classified, and in each class the maximum fee shall be fixed and shall include the charges of every kind rendered by the agency in each case or transaction on behalf of the prospective employee. Changes in the schedule may be made, but no change shall become effective until posted for not less than seven days in a conspicuous place in the agency.

(3) A copy of the schedule in effect shall be kept posted in the employment agency in a conspicuous place, and the posted schedule and the changes therein shall be in lettering or printing of not less than standard pica capitals. The date of the taking effect of the schedule and of each change therein shall appear on the posted copies.

(4) A copy of all fee schedules, and of all changes therein, shall be kept on file at the employment agency, retrospectively, for a period of one year.

(b) No fee charged or collected shall be in excess of the fee as scheduled.

(c) No employment agency shall accept, directly or indirectly, a registration fee of any kind.

(d) No employment agency may take from a jobseeker a confession of judgment, a promissory note or notes, or an assignment of wages to cover its fees.

(e) The employment agency shall give a receipt to every jobseeker from whom a deposit is received. No other deposit or prepayment of any kind may be required by an agency. If the jobseeker accepts employment, the deposit shall be applied to the fee to be paid by the jobseeker.

(f)(1) If a jobseeker leaves employment for just cause or is discharged for reasons other than misconduct connected with the jobseeker's work within 90 days from the starting date of employment, the agency shall reduce the fee payable by the jobseeker to that payable for temporary employment under subdivision (g) and shall refund any fee paid in excess of that amount.

(2) No charge may be made to or obligation to pay incurred by any jobseeker beyond that authorized by subdivision (g) for employment lasting 90 days or less, unless the agency's fee schedules, contracts, and agreements specifically provide for a further charge if the jobseeker leaves employment without just cause or is discharged for misconduct in connection with his or her work, and then only if lack of just cause or misconduct exists. Otherwise, the agency shall retain or charge only the fee for temporary employment for any employment lasting 90 days or less from the starting date of employment.

(3) Notwithstanding subdivision (a) and this subdivision, in no instance in which the employment accepted is subsequently terminated shall the fee charged or obligation to pay incurred by a jobseeker be greater than the total gross earnings of the jobseeker in that employment. This provision shall be stated in all agency contracts issued pursuant to Section 1812.504.

(g) The fee payable by the jobseeker for temporary employment shall not exceed $1/_{90}$ of the fee for permanent employment for each consecutive calendar day during the period that the jobseeker is employed or compensated as though employed.

(h)(1) If a jobseeker accepts employment in which the jobseeker is to be paid on the basis of straight commissions, or a drawing account against commissions, or either a drawing account or salary plus commissions, the fee payable by the jobseeker may be predicated upon the projected total gross earnings during the first year of employment as estimated by the employer.

(2) Upon the conclusion of a jobseeker's first 12 months of employment, a computation of his or her actual total gross earnings may be provided by the jobseeker to the agency, and, predicated upon appropriate proof of earnings, an adjustment in the fee shall be made in which either the agency shall refund to the jobseeker any excess fee paid by him or her or the jobseeker shall pay to the agency any deficiency thereon.

(3) If the jobseeker's employment is terminated prior to the conclusion of the first 12 months of employment, the actual total gross earnings of the jobseeker for the period of employment shall be projected to 12 months on a pro rata basis as though the jobseeker had been employed for the entire period of 12 months, and a computation shall be made thereon. The fee paid or payable by the jobseeker shall be predicated upon that computation as though the jobseeker had been so employed.

(i) If an employment agency sends a jobseeker for employment and the jobseeker accepts employment other than that position specified in the bona fide order for employment to which the jobseeker was sent, but with the same employer, then the agency shall be entitled to a fee for the employment of the jobseeker, payable by the jobseeker, computed under the terms of the fee schedule in effect in the agency at the time of referral, provided that the jobseeker accepts employment within 180 days of the date of referral. The expiration date of the referral shall be stated in the contract.

In interagency disputes concerning the earning of a fee for placement of a jobseeker, the fee shall be earned by the agency responsible for the jobseeker being placed. A reasonable effort shall be made by the billing agency that it is entitled to the fee. The jobseeker shall be responsible for only one full fee for any single placement, and that fact shall be so stated in the contract.

(j)(1) No employment agency shall divide fees with an employer, an agent, or other employee of an employer or person to whom help is furnished.

(2) No employment agency shall charge any jobseeker a fee for accepting employment with such employment agency or any subsidiary of that agency.

(3) No employment agency shall charge any jobseeker a fee when help is furnished to an employer, an agent, any employee of an employer, a member, or person who has a financial interest in the employment agency. **Leg.H.** Added Stats 1989 ch 704 §2.

§1812.506. Refund of deposit or fee

(a) If a jobseeker paying or becoming obligated to pay a fee, or making a deposit on a fee for placement fails to accept employment, the employment agency shall, upon request by the jobseeker, repay the amount of the deposit or fee to the jobseeker. Unless the deposit is returned within 48 hours after request, the employment agency shall pay to the jobseeker an additional sum equal to the amount of the deposit. A notice to this effect shall be inserted in all contracts between the agency and the jobseeker, and in all receipts given to the jobseeker for cash payment in advance of employment, and in the schedule of fees posted in the office of the agency.

(b)(1) All employment provided by any employment agency to any jobseeker from whom a fee is to be received shall be considered permanent only if it lasts longer than 90 days. If a jobseeker leaves the job or is discharged within the first 90 days of employment, the agency shall make a refund or reduction of the fee to the temporary fee amount unless the agency's fee schedules, contracts, and agreements specifically provide for a further charge if the jobseeker leaves employment without just cause or is discharged for misconduct in connection with his or her work.

(2) "Just cause" or "discharge for reasons other than misconduct" includes, but is not limited to, the following:

(A) Wages or salary less than that agreed upon between the jobseeker and the employer.

(B) Receiving a payroll check which is not honored by the bank upon which it was drawn.

(C) Working hours, working days, or working shifts significantly different than those agreed upon between the jobseeker and the employer.

(D) Receiving a work assignment, subsequent to accepting the job, which is substantially different from that agreed upon between the jobseeker and the employer.

(E) Being assigned to a job location different from that which was agreed upon between the jobseeker and the employer.

(F) The jobseeker's lack of physical ability to perform duties connected with the position agreed upon between the jobseeker and the employer unless the provisions of subparagraph (E) of paragraph (3) apply.

(G) A lockout or strike causing loss of pay.

(H) The jobseeker's lack of physical ability to perform duties connected with the position unless the provisions of subparagraph (E) of paragraph (3) apply.

(J) The jobseeker's entry into active service in the armed forces.

(K) Physical or economic destruction of the business.

(L) The death of the jobseeker (any refund in that case shall be paid to the estate of the jobseeker).

(3) "Lack of just cause" or a discharge for "misconduct" includes, but is not limited to:

(A) Abandonment of the job by the jobseeker.

(B) Conviction of the jobseeker, subsequent to employment, of a crime when conviction temporarily or permanently prevents the jobseeker from fulfilling the terms of employment.

(C) Willful violation of lawful company policies or rules by the jobseeker.

(D) Willful failure to perform lawful duties appropriate to employment by the jobseeker.

(E) Acts of the jobseeker constituting misrepresentation or withholding of information directly related to education, work experience, responsibility, physical ability, or training, that would have caused the employer to refuse employment.

(c)(1) Except as otherwise provided in subdivision (a), a refund when due shall be made within 10 working days after request therefor from the jobseeker.

(2) Alternatively, if the decision of the agency is not to make a refund, the agency shall notify the jobseeker in writing, within the 10-day working period specified in paragraph (1), as to the specific reasons why the refund is not being made.

(3) If the agency fails to properly notify the jobseeker pursuant to paragraph (2) or fails to tender a refund within the time allowed, the agency shall be liable to the jobseeker in the amount of an additional sum equal to the amount of the refund. **Leg.H.** Added Stats 1989 ch 704 §2.

1989 Note: It appears that the Legislature inadvertently omitted subsection (b)(2)(I) of Section 1812.506.

§1812.507. Job orders; Referrals

(a) No employment agency shall accept a fee from any jobseeker, or send any jobseeker for employment, without having obtained, orally or in writing, a bona fide job order for employment.

(b) An agency shall identify itself as an employment agency to the employer in all instances in which it contacts an employer for the purpose of soliciting a job order. All job orders shall be recorded in writing. A job order for employment shall be considered to have been given by an employer to an employment agency under the following conditions:

(1) The employer, or his or her agent, orally or in writing, registers a request or gives permission that the agency recruit or refer jobseekers who meet the employer's stated job specifications and the employer furnishes such information as required by subdivision (a) of Section 1812.504. A job order is valid for the referral of any qualified jobseeker until it is filled or canceled by the employer, and may serve as the basis for agency advertising. The agency is required to recontact the employer within 30 days to ensure that the position is still vacant prior to any additional advertising or referral of jobseekers.

(2) When an agency has brought the qualifications of a specific jobseeker to the attention of an employer and the employer has expressed interest in that jobseeker either by agreeing to interview the jobseeker, or by requesting that the agency furnish him or her with the jobseeker's resumé or other written history or data, or by initiating direct contact with the jobseeker as a result of information furnished by the agency, that action by the employer shall constitute a job order only for the jobseeker discussed and is not valid for advertisement, unless the contact by the agency resulted in a job order for a specific position sufficient under paragraph (1). If the employer has no position open but merely wishes to explore the possible employment of the jobseeker and the jobseeker is to be responsible for the placement fee, that fact shall be indicated on the jobseeker's referral contract.

(c) No employment agency shall refer a jobseeker to a job knowing or having reason to know that:

(1) The job does not exist or the jobseeker is not qualified for the job.

(2) The job has been described or advertised by or on behalf of the agency in a false, misleading, or deceptive manner.

(3) The agency has not obtained written or oral permission to list the job from the employer or an authorized agent of the employer. **Leg.H.** Added Stats 1989 ch 704 §2.

§1812.508. Advertisements; Records

(a) No employment agency shall make, or cause to be made, any false, misleading, or deceptive advertisements or representations concerning the services that the agency will provide to jobseekers.

(b)(1) No employment agency shall publish or cause to be published any false, fraudulent, or misleading information, representation, notice, or advertisements.

(2) All advertisements of an employment agency shall contain the correct name of the employment agency and one of the following:

(A) The street address of the agency's place of business.

(B) The correct telephone number of the agency at its place of business.

(3) Every employment agency, except a nurses registry shall use, as part of its name, either the designation "agency" or personnel service."

(4) No employment agency shall give any false information or make any false promises or representations concerning an engagement or employment to any jobseeker who registers or applies for an engagement or employment or help.

(5) No employment agency shall, by its name, advertisement, or any other representation, represent itself to be a home health agency, as defined by subdivision (a) of Section 1727 of the Health and Safety Code, or to perform the services of a home health agency. An employment agency shall provide a written disclosure to each individual receiving nursing services in his or her place of residence stating that it does not perform the services of a home health agency and clearly describing that it is an employment agency only and that any complaints against personnel providing nursing services who are neither licensed nor certified shall be submitted to the local district attorney, complaints against certified nursing assistants and certified home health aides providing nursing services shall be submitted to the local district attorney and the State Department of Health Services, and complaints against licensed personnel providing nursing services shall be submitted to the local district attorney and the Department of Consumer Affairs. The address and telephone number of each agency and board to which complaints are required to be submitted shall be provided by the employment agency to all patients prior to the time they are under the care of any nursing services personnel.

(6) Any person may refer complaints concerning employment agencies to the proper law enforcement agency for action.

(c)(1) Where an employment agency job advertisement includes a description of the placement fee associated with the advertised job, the employment agency shall describe the placement fee in a manner which either clearly indicates whether or not a jobseeker shall be responsible for the placement fee or in accordance with the following terms and provisions:

(A) "FEE" means the jobseeker pays the entire placement fee.

(B) "NO FEE" means the jobseeker pays no portion of the placement fee.

(2) Where "NO FEE" jobs are advertised and the agency also administers placement for "FEE" jobs, the advertisement shall state "ALSO FEE JOBS" in type of equal size, prominence, and boldness as "NO FEE" notations.

(3) A group job advertisement which includes a description of the placement fee shall describe the placement fee either separately for each

job, or by use of the proper term as a heading under which all applicable jobs shall be listed. All those headings shall be in type and of the same size, prominence, and boldness.

(d) Special requirements not usually associated with a job shall be specified in any advertisement. When the location of the position advertised is more than 50 miles from the employment agency office responsible for the advertisement, it shall state either the location or that the job is "nonlocal." Special benefits of the job, if advertised, shall be specifically described and substitute terms or symbols such as "extras" or "+" shall not be sufficient.

(e) An advertised salary shall be based upon the starting salary contained in the job order. An advertised range of starting salaries shall be specified by preceding the minimum salary and maximum salary by the terms "from" and "to" respectively. When the job order contains only the maximum amount of a salary range, that advertised salary shall be preceded by the word "to." If a maximum salary is dependent upon the jobseeker's experience, the advertised salary may be described by listing the minimum salary and the term "up Depending on Experience" or "up D.O.E." The words "open" and "negotiable" or words or symbols of like import shall not be used as a substitute for the salary. If an advertised salary is based in whole or in part on commissions, that fact shall be indicated in the advertisement.

(f) All employment agencies shall maintain a record of all advertised jobs, correlated to show the date and the publication in which the advertisement appeared and the job order number of each job advertised, retrospectively for a period of one year. **Leg.H.** Added Stats 1989 ch 704 §2. Amended Stats 1990 ch 761 §1 (AB 3924).

§1812.509. Restrictions and disclosures

(a) No employment agency shall, when employment would be in violation of Chapter 1 (commencing with Section 1171) of Part 4 of Division 2 of the Labor Code or Part 27 (commencing with Section 48000) of the Education Code, accept any application for employment made by, or on behalf of, any minor, or place or assist in placing any minor in that employment.

(b) Every employment agency shall notify each jobseeker before sending the jobseeker in response to a request for employment whether a labor contract is in existence at the establishment to which the jobseeker is being sent, and whether union membership is required.

(c) No employment agency shall send a jobseeker to any place where a strike, lockout, or other labor trouble exists without notifying the jobseeker of that fact and shall in addition thereto enter a statement of those conditions upon the contract or receipt given to the jobseeker.

(d) No babysitting, domestic, or other employment agency which procures babysitting or domestic employment for employers shall refer babysitters or domestics for any employment without first conducting a personal interview of the jobseeker and making a reasonable effort to verify the experience or training of the jobseeker.

(e) No employment agency that procures temporary employment for long-term health care employers shall refer certified nurse assistants or licensed nursing staff as defined in Section 1812.540, for any employment without first conducting a personal interview of the individual, verifying the experience, training, and references of the individual, and verifying that the individual is in good standing with the appropriate licensing or certification board, including verification that the individual has successfully secured a criminal record clearance. **Leg.H.** Added Stats 1989 ch 704 §2. Amended Stats 1990 ch 1256 §5 (AB 2649); Stats 2001 ch 326 §1 (AB 1643).

§1812.5093. Information agency must supply to employer when referring child care provider to employer that is not required to be licensed child day care facility

(a) Every employment agency that refers a child care provider to an employer who is not required to be a licensed child day care facility pursuant to Section 1596.792 of the Health and Safety Code shall provide the employer with all the following:

(1) A description of the child care provider trustline registry established pursuant to Chapter 3.35 (commencing with Section 1596.60) of Division 2 of the Health and Safety Code that provides criminal history checks on child care providers.

(2) An explanation of how an employer may obtain more information about the child care provider trustline registry.

(3) A statement that an employment agency is prohibited by law from placing a child care provider unless the provider is a trustline applicant or a registered child care provider.

(4) An explanation of how the employer may verify the prospective child care provider's trustline registry registration.

(b) Receipt of the information required to be provided pursuant to subdivision (a) shall be verified in writing by the employer. **Leg.H.** Added Stats 1998 ch 287 §1 (AB 2001).

§1812.5095. Domestic workers

(a) For purposes of this section, the term "employment agency" means an employment agency, as defined in paragraph (3) of subdivision (a) of Section 1812.501, or a domestic agency, as defined in subdivision (h) of Section 1812.501.

(b) An employment agency is not the employer of a domestic worker for whom it procures, offers, refers, provides, or attempts to provide work, if all of the following factors characterize the nature of the relationship between the employment agency and the domestic worker for whom the agency procures, offers, refers, provides, or attempts to provide domestic work:

(1) There is a signed contract or agreement between the employment agency and the domestic worker that contains, at a minimum, provisions that specify all of the following:

(A) That the employment agency shall assist the domestic worker in securing work.

(B) How the employment agency's referral fee shall be paid.

(C) That the domestic worker is free to sign an agreement with other employment agencies and to perform domestic work for persons not referred by the employment agency.

(2) The domestic worker informs the employment agency of any restrictions on hours, location, conditions, or type of work he or she will accept and the domestic worker is free to select or reject any work opportunity procured, offered, referred, or provided by the employment agency.

(3) The domestic worker is free to renegotiate with the person hiring him or her the amount proposed to be paid for the work.

(4) The domestic worker does not receive any training from the employment agency with respect to the performance of domestic work. However, an employment agency may provide a voluntary orientation session in which the relationship between the employment agency and the domestic worker, including the employment agency's administrative and operating procedures, and the provisions of the contract or agreement between the employment agency and the domestic worker are explained.

(5) The domestic worker performs domestic work without any direction, control, or supervision exercised by the employment agency with respect to the manner and means of performing the domestic work. An employment agency shall not be deemed to be exercising direction, control, or supervision when it takes any of the following actions:

(A) Informs the domestic worker about the services to be provided and the conditions of work specified by the person seeking to hire a domestic worker.

(B) Contacts the person who has hired the domestic worker to determine whether that person is satisfied with the agency's referral service.

(C) Informs the domestic worker of the time during which new referrals are available.

(D) Requests the domestic worker to inform the employment agency if the domestic worker is unable to perform the work accepted.

(6) The employment agency does not provide tools, supplies, or equipment necessary to perform the domestic work.

(7) The domestic worker is not obligated to pay the employment agency's referral fee, and the employment agency is not obligated to pay the domestic worker if the person for whom the services were performed fails or refuses to pay for the domestic work.

(8) Payments for domestic services are made directly to either the domestic worker or to the employment agency. Payments made directly to the employment agency shall be deposited into a trust account until payment can be made to the domestic worker.

(9) The relationship between a domestic worker and the person for whom the domestic worker performs services may only be terminated by either of those parties and not by the employment agency that referred the domestic worker. However, an employment agency may decline to make

additional referrals to a particular domestic worker, and the domestic worker may decline to accept a particular referral.

(c) The fee charged by an employment agency for its services shall be reasonable, negotiable, and based on a fixed percentage of the job cost.

(d) An employment agency referring a domestic worker to a job shall inform that domestic worker, in writing, on or before the signing of the contract pursuant to paragraph (1) of subdivision (b), that the domestic worker may be obligated to obtain business permits or licenses, where required by any state or local law, ordinance, or regulation, and that he or she is not eligible for unemployment insurance, state disability insurance, social security, or workers' compensation benefits through an employment agency complying with subdivision (b). The employment agency referring a domestic worker shall also inform that domestic worker, if the domestic worker is self-employed, that he or she is required to pay self-employment tax, state tax, and federal income taxes.

(e) An employment agency referring a domestic worker to a job shall verify the worker's legal status or authorization to work prior to providing referral services in accordance with procedures established under federal law.

(f) An employment agency referring a domestic worker to a job shall orally communicate to the person seeking domestic services the disclosure set forth below prior to the referral of the domestic worker the following disclosure statement:

"(Name of agency) is not the employer of the domestic worker it referred to you. Depending on your arrangement with the domestic worker, you may have employer responsibilities."

Within three business days after the employment agency refers a domestic worker to the person seeking domestic services, the following statement printed in not less than 10-point type shall be mailed to the person seeking domestic services:

"(Name of agency) is not the employer of the domestic worker it referred to you. The domestic worker may be your employee or an independent contractor depending on the relationship you have with him or her. If you direct and control the manner and means by which the domestic worker performs his or her work you may have employer responsibilities, including employment taxes and workers' compensation, under state and federal law. For additional information contact your local Employment Development Department and the Internal Revenue Service."

(g) An employment agency referring a domestic worker to a job shall not specify that a worker is self-employed or an independent contractor in any notice, advertisement, or brochure provided to either the worker or the customer.

(h) Every employment agency referring a domestic worker to a job and who is not the employer of the domestic worker being referred, shall in any paid telephone directory advertisement or any other promotional literature or advertising distributed or placed by such an employment agency, on or after January 1, 1995, insert the following statement, in no less than 6-point type which shall be in print which contrasts with the background of the advertisement so as to be easily legible:

"(Name of agency)is a referral agency."

(i) An employment agency may not refer, in its advertising, soliciting, or other presentments to the public, to any bond required to be filed pursuant to this chapter.

(j) An employment agency may not refer, in its advertising, soliciting, or other presentments to the public, to any licensure acquired by the agency.

(k) Any violation of this section with the intent to directly or indirectly mislead the public on the nature of services provided by an employment agency shall constitute unfair competition which includes any unlawful, unfair, or fraudulent business acts or practices and unfair, deceptive, untrue, or misleading advertising. Any person or entity that engages in unfair competition shall be liable for a civil penalty not to exceed two thousand five hundred dollars ($2,500) for each violation. **Leg.H.** Added Stats 1993 ch 1275 §1 (AB 1370). Amended Stats 1994 ch 1081 §1 (SB 1418).

CHAPTER 3
EMPLOYMENT COUNSELING SERVICES

Bonds for employment service. §1812.510.
Contracts. §1812.511.
Fees. §1812.512.
Advertisements; Record. §1812.513.

§1812.510. Bonds for employment service

(a) Every employment counseling service subject to this title shall maintain a bond issued by a surety company admitted to do business in this state. The principal sum of the bond shall be ten thousand dollars ($10,000). A copy of the bond shall be filed with the Secretary of State.

(b) The bond required by this section shall be in favor of, and payable to, the people of the State of California, and shall be conditioned that the person obtaining the bond will comply with this title and will pay all sums due any individual or group of individuals when the person or his or her representative, agent, or employee has received those sums. The bond shall be for the benefit of any person or persons damaged by any violation of this title or by fraud, dishonesty, misstatement, misrepresentation, deceit, unlawful acts or omissions, or failure to provide the services of the employment counseling service in performance of the contract with the customer by the employment counseling service or its agents, representatives, or employees while acting within the scope of their employment.

(c)(1) No employment counseling service shall conduct any business without having a current surety bond in the amount prescribed by this title and filing a copy of the bond with the Secretary of State.

(2) Thirty days prior to the cancellation or termination of any surety bond required by this section, the surety shall send a written notice of that cancellation or termination to both the employment counseling service and the Secretary of State, identifying the bond and the date of cancellation or termination.

(3) If any employment counseling service fails to obtain a new bond and file a copy of that bond with the Secretary of State by the effective date of the cancellation or termination of the former bond, the employment counseling service shall cease to conduct any business unless and until a new surety bond is obtained and a copy of that bond is filed with the Secretary of State.

(d) When a deposit has been made in lieu of the bond pursuant to Section 995.710 of the Code of Civil Procedure, the person asserting a claim against the deposit shall, in lieu of Section 996.430 of the Code of Civil Procedure, establish the claim by furnishing evidence to the Secretary of State of a money judgment entered by a court together with evidence that the claimant is a person described in subdivision (b).

(e) When a person has established the claim with the Secretary of State, the Secretary of State shall immediately review and approve the claim and enter the date of approval on the claim. The claim shall be designated an "approved claim."

(f) When the first claim against a particular deposit has been approved, it shall not be paid until the expiration of a period of 240 days after the date of its approval by the Secretary of State. Subsequent claims that are approved by the Secretary of State within the same 240-day period shall similarly not be paid until the expiration of the 240-day period. Upon the expiration of the 240-day period, the Secretary of State shall pay all approved claims from that 240-day period in full unless the deposit is insufficient, in which case each approved claim shall be paid a pro rata share of the deposit.

(g) When the Secretary of State approves the first claim against a particular deposit account after the expiration of the 240-day period, the date of approval of that claim shall begin a new 240-day period to which subdivision (f) shall apply with respect to the amount remaining in the deposit account.

(h) After a deposit account is exhausted, no further claims shall be paid by the Secretary of State. Claimants who have had their claims paid in full or in part pursuant to subdivisions (f) and (g) shall not be required to return funds received from the deposit for the benefit of other claimants.

(i) When a deposit has been made in lieu of a bond, the amount of the deposit shall not be subject to attachment, garnishment, or execution with respect to an action or judgment against the employment counseling service, other than as to an amount as no longer needed or required for the purpose of this title that would otherwise be returned to the employment counseling service by the Secretary of State.

(j) The Secretary of State shall retain a cash deposit for two years from the date the Secretary of State receives written notification from the assignor of the deposit that the assignor has ceased to engage in the business of a counseling service or has filed a bond pursuant to subdivision (a), provided that there are no outstanding claims against the deposit. Written notification to the Secretary of State shall include all of the following: (1) name, address, and telephone number of the assignor;

(2) name, address, and telephone number of the bank at which the deposit is located; (3) account number of the deposit; and (4) a statement whether the assignor is ceasing to engage in the business of a counseling service or has filed a bond with the Secretary of State. The Secretary of State shall forward an acknowledgment of receipt of the written notice to the assignor at the address indicated in the notice, specifying the date of receipt of the written notice and anticipated date of release of the deposit, provided there are no outstanding claims against the deposit account.

(k) A judge of a superior court may order the return of the deposit prior to the expiration of two years upon evidence satisfactory to the judge that there are no outstanding claims against the deposit or order the Secretary of State to retain the deposit for a sufficient period beyond the two years pursuant to subdivision (j) to resolve outstanding claims against the deposit account.

(*l*) The Secretary of State shall charge a filing fee not to exceed the cost of filing the bond or the deposit filed in lieu of a bond pursuant to Section 995.710 of the Code of Civil Procedure.

(m) The Secretary of State shall enforce the provisions of this chapter that govern the filing and maintenance of bonds and deposits in lieu of bonds. **Leg.H.** Added Stats 1989 ch 704 §2. Amended Stats 1996 ch 633 §12 (SB 1978); Stats 1998 ch 829 §12 (SB 1652); Stats 2002 ch 784 §16 (SB 1316).

§1812.511. Contracts

(a) Every contract for employment counseling services shall be in writing. An original and one copy of the contract shall be given to the customer at the time the customer signs the contract and before the employment counseling service accepts any fee or deposit or the customer becomes obligated to pay any such fee or deposit. The contract shall contain all of the following:

(1) The name, address, and telephone number of the employment counseling service.

(2) The name and address of the person signing the contract and the person to whom the employment counseling services are to be provided.

(3) A description of the services to be provided; a statement when those services are to be provided; the duration of the contract; and refund provisions as appropriate, to be applicable if the described services are not provided according to the contract.

(4) The amount of the fee to be charged to or collected from the person receiving the services or any other person, and the date or dates when that fee is required to be paid.

(5) The following statement, in type no smaller than 10-point bold-faced type:

"No verbal or written promise or guarantee of any job or employment is made or implied under the terms of this contract."

(6) The following statement, in immediate proximity to the space reserved for the customer's signature, in type no smaller than 10-point boldfaced type:

YOUR RIGHT TO CANCEL

/enter date of transaction/

"You may cancel this contract for employment counseling services, without any penalty or obligation, if notice of cancellation is given, in writing, within three business days from the above date.

"To cancel this contract, just mail or deliver a signed and dated copy of the following cancellation notice or any other written notice of cancellation, or send a telegram containing a notice of cancellation, to (name of employment counseling service) at (address of its place of business), NOT LATER THAN MIDNIGHT OF /date/."

CANCELLATION NOTICE

I hereby cancel this contract.
Dated: _____

_____ Customer's Signature"

Until the employment counseling service has complied with this section the customer may cancel the employment counseling services contract.

(b) All contracts shall be dated and shall be made and numbered consecutively in triplicate, the original and each copy to be signed by the customer and the person acting for the employment counseling service. The original and one copy shall be given to the customer and the other copy shall be kept on file at the employment counseling service.

(c) The full agreement between the parties shall be contained in a single document containing those elements set forth in this section. **Leg.H.** Added Stats 1989 ch 704 §2.

§1812.512. Fees

(a)(1) An employment counseling service shall provide a copy of its fee schedule and payment terms to any customer from whom a fee or deposit is to be received, prior to the customer being interviewed by a counselor, agent, or employee.

(2) In the schedule, the maximum fee shall be fixed and shall include the charges of every kind rendered by the employment counseling service in each case or transaction on behalf of the prospective employee. Changes in the fee schedule may be made, but no change shall become effective until posted for not less than seven days in a conspicuous place in the employment counseling service.

(3) A copy of the schedule in effect shall be kept posted in the employment counseling service in a conspicuous place, and the posted schedule and the changes therein shall be in lettering or printing of not less than standard pica capitals. The date of the taking effect of the schedule and of each change therein shall appear on the posted copies.

(4) A copy of all fee schedules, and of all changes therein, shall be kept on file at the employment counseling service, retrospectively for a period of one year.

(b) No fee charged or collected shall be in excess of the fee as scheduled.

(c) No employment counseling service shall accept, directly or indirectly, a registration fee of any kind.

(d) No employment counseling service may take from a customer a confession of judgment, a promissory note or notes, or an assignment of wages to cover its fees. **Leg.H.** Added Stats 1989 ch 704 §2.

§1812.513. Advertisements; Record

(a) No employment counseling service shall make or cause to be made any false, misleading, or deceptive advertisements or representations concerning the services that the employment counseling service will provide to customers.

(b)(1) No employment counseling service shall publish or cause to be published any false, fraudulent, or misleading information, representation, notice, or advertisements.

(2) All advertisements of an employment counseling service shall contain the correct name of the employment counseling service and one of the following:

(A) The street address of the employment counseling service's place of business.

(B) The correct telephone number of the employment counseling service at its place of business.

(c) No employment counseling service shall give any false information or make any false promises or representations concerning engagement or employment to any customer, or make any verbal or written promise or guarantee of any job or employment.

(d) An employment counseling service shall maintain a record of all advertisements for the service, correlated to show the date and the publication in which the advertisement appeared, retrospectively, for a period of one year.

(e) No employment counseling service shall, by its choice of name or by advertisement or representation, represent itself to be an employment agency or to perform the job placement services of an employment agency. **Leg.H.** Added Stats 1989 ch 704 §2.

CHAPTER 4
JOB LISTING SERVICES

Bonds for job listing service. §1812.515.
Contracts. §1812.516.
Fees. §1812.517.
Refund of fees. §1812.518.
Job orders; Referrals. §1812.519.
Advertisements; Record. §1812.520.
Restrictions and disclosures. §1812.521.

§1812.515. Bonds for job listing service

(a) Every job listing service subject to this title shall maintain a bond issued by a surety company admitted to do business in this state. The principal sum of the bond shall be ten thousand dollars ($10,000) for each location. A copy of the bond shall be filed with the Secretary of State.

(b) The bond required by this section shall be in favor of, and payable to, the people of the State of California, and shall be conditioned that the person obtaining the bond will comply with this title and will pay all sums due any individual or group of individuals when the person or his or her representative, agent, or employee has received those sums. The bond shall be for the benefit of any person or persons damaged by any violation of misrepresentation, deceit, unlawful acts of omissions, or failure to provide the services of the job listing service in performance of the contract with the jobseeker, by the job listing service or its agent, representatives, or employees while acting within the scope of their employment.

(c)(1) No job listing service shall conduct any business without having a current surety bond in the amount prescribed by this chapter and filing a copy of the bond with the Secretary of State, identifying the bond and the date of cancellation or termination.

(2) Thirty days prior to the cancellation or termination of any surety bond required by this section, the surety shall send a written notice of that cancellation or termination to both the job listing service and the Secretary of State, identifying the bond and the date of cancellation or termination.

(3) If any job listing service fails to obtain a new bond and file a copy of that bond with the Secretary of State by the effective date of the cancellation or termination of the former bond, the job listing service shall cease to conduct any business unless and until a new surety bond is obtained and a copy of that bond is filed with the Secretary of State.

(d) When a deposit has been made in lieu of a bond pursuant to Section 995.710 of the Code of Civil Procedure, the person asserting a claim against the deposit shall, in lieu of Section 996.430 of the Code of Civil Procedure, establish the claim by furnishing evidence to the Secretary of State of a money judgment entered by a court together with evidence that the claimant is a person described in subdivision (b).

(e) When a person has established the claim with the Secretary of State, the Secretary of State shall review and approve the claim and enter the date of approval on the claim. The claim shall be designated an "approved claim."

(f) When the first claim against a particular deposit has been approved, it shall not be paid until the expiration of a period of 240 days after the date of its approval by the Secretary of State. Subsequent claims that are approved by the Secretary of State within the same 240-day period shall similarly not be paid until the expiration of the 240-day period. Upon the expiration of the 240-day period, the Secretary of State shall pay all approved claims from that 240-day period in full unless the deposit is insufficient, in which case each approved claim shall be paid in a pro rata share of the deposit.

(g) When the Secretary of State approves the first claim against a particular deposit after the expiration of the 240-day period, the date of approval of that claim shall begin a new 240-day period to which subdivision (f) shall apply with respect to the amount remaining in the deposit.

(h) After a deposit is exhausted, no further claims shall be paid by the Secretary of State. Claimants who have had their claims paid in full or in part pursuant to subdivisions (f) and (g) shall not be required to return funds received from the deposit for the benefit of other claimants.

(i) When a deposit has been made in lieu of a bond, the amount of the deposit shall not be subject to attachment, garnishment, or execution with respect to an action or judgment against the job listing service, other than as to an amount as no longer needed or required for the purpose of this title that would otherwise be returned to the job listing service by the Secretary of State.

(j) The Secretary of State shall retain a cash deposit for two years from the date the Secretary of State receives written notification from the assignor of the deposit that the assignor has ceased to engage in the business of a job listing service or has filed a bond pursuant to subdivision (a), provided that there are no outstanding claims against the deposit. Written notification to the Secretary of State shall include all of the following: (1) name, address, and telephone number of the assignor; (2) name, address, and telephone number of the bank at which the deposit is located; (3) account number of the deposit; and (4) a statement whether the assignor is ceasing to engage in the business of a job listing service or has filed a bond with the Secretary of State. The Secretary of State shall forward an acknowledgment of receipt of the written notice to the assignor at the address indicated therein, specifying the date of receipt of the written notice and anticipated date of release of the deposit, provided there are no outstanding claims against the deposit.

(k) A judge of a superior court may order the return of the deposit prior to the expiration of two years upon evidence satisfactory to the judge that there are no outstanding claims against the deposit or order the Secretary of State to retain the deposit for a specified period beyond the two years pursuant to subdivision (j) to resolve outstanding claims against the deposit account.

(*l*) The Secretary of State shall charge a filing fee not to exceed the cost of filing the bond or deposit filed in lieu of a bond pursuant to Section 995.710 of the Code of Civil Procedure.

(m) The Secretary of State shall enforce the provisions of this chapter that govern the filing and maintenance of bonds and deposits in lieu of bonds. **Leg.H.** Added Stats 1989 ch 704 §2. Amended Stats 1996 ch 633 §13 (SB 1978); Stats 1998 ch 829 §13 (SB 1652); Stats 2002 ch 784 §17 (SB 1316).

§1812.516. Contracts

(a) Every job listing service shall give a written contract to every jobseeker from whom a fee or deposit is to be received, whether directly or indirectly. The original and one copy of the contract shall be given to the jobseeker at the time the jobseeker signs the contract and before the job listing service accepts any fee or deposit or the jobseeker becomes obligated to pay any such fee or deposit. The contract shall contain all of the following:

(1) The name of the job listing service and the addresses and telephone numbers of the principal office of the job listing service and the location providing the listing services to the jobseeker.

(2) The amount of the fee to be charged and to be collected from the jobseeker.

(3) A description of the service to be performed by the job listing service, including significant conditions, restrictions, and limitations where applicable.

(4) A description of the jobseeker's specifications for the employment opportunity in clear language understandable to the jobseeker, including, but not limited to, the following:

(A) Kind of work or employment.

(B) Interests of jobseeker.

(C) Qualifications of jobseeker.

(D) Daily hours of work, the wages or salary, benefits, and other conditions of employment.

(E) Location of job.

(5) The contract expiration date, which shall not be later than 90 days from the date of execution of the contract.

(6) The following statement, in immediate proximity to the space reserved for the jobseeker's signature, in type no smaller than 10-point boldfaced type:

YOUR RIGHT TO CANCEL

/enter date of transaction/

"You may cancel this contract for job listing services without any penalty or obligation, if notice of cancellation is given, in writing, within three business days from the above date.

"To cancel this contract, just mail or deliver a signed and dated copy of the following cancellation notice or any other written notice of cancellation, to (name of job listing service) at (address of its place of business), NOT LATER THAN MIDNIGHT OF /date/."

CANCELLATION NOTICE

I hereby cancel this contract.
Dated: _____

_____ Customer's Signature"

Until the job listing service has complied with this section the jobseeker may cancel the job listing service's contract.

(7) The following statement, with the caption in type no smaller than 10-point boldfaced type and the remainder in a size no smaller than that generally used throughout the contract, and in full capitals, boldface, or italics:

"RIGHT TO REFUND"

"If, within seven business days after payment of a fee or deposit, the job listing service has not supplied you with at least three available employment opportunities meeting the specifications of the contract as to type of job; interests of jobseeker; qualifications of jobseeker; hours, salary, benefits, and other conditions of employment; location of job; and any other specifications expressly set forth in the contract, the full amount of the fee or deposit paid shall be refunded to you upon your request.

"If you do not obtain a job through the services of the job listing service, or if you obtain employment which lasts less than 90 days, any amount paid in fees or deposits in excess of a twenty-five dollar ($25) service charge shall be refunded to you, upon your request after expiration of the contract.

"Any refund due must be made to you within 10 days of your request. If the refund is not made in that time, the job listing service must pay to you an additional sum equal to the amount of your fee or deposit."

(8) If any labor trouble exists at the place of employment, that fact shall be stated in the listing of that employment provided to the jobseeker.

(b) All contracts shall be dated and shall be made and numbered consecutively in triplicate, the original and each copy to be signed by the jobseeker and the person acting for the job listing service. The original and one copy shall be given to the jobseeker and the other copy shall be kept on file at the job listing service.

(c) The full agreement between the parties shall be contained in a single document containing those elements set forth in this section. **Leg.H.** Added Stats 1989 ch 704 §2. Amended Stats 1990 ch 1256 §6 (AB 2649).

§1812.517. Fees

(a)(1) A job listing service shall provide a copy of the service's fee schedule and payment terms to any jobseeker from whom a fee or deposit is to be received, prior to the jobseeker being interviewed by a counselor or other agent or employee.

(2) In the schedule, the maximum fee shall be fixed and shall include the charges of every kind rendered by the job listing service in each case or transaction on behalf of the prospective employee. Changes in the fee schedule may be made, but no change shall become effective until posted for not less than seven days in a conspicuous place in the job listing service.

(3) A copy of the schedule in effect shall be kept posted in the job listing service in a conspicuous place, and the posted schedule and the changes therein shall be in lettering or printing of not less than standard pica capitals. The date of the taking effect of the schedule and of each change therein shall appear on the posted copies.

(4) A copy of all fee schedules, and of all changes therein, shall be kept on file at the job listing service, retrospectively, for a period of one year.

(b) No fee charged or collected shall be in excess of the fee as scheduled.

(c) No job listing service may take from a jobseeker a confession of judgment, a promissory note or notes, or an assignment of wages to cover its fees.

(d) The fee charged shall not be based on a portion or percentage of the salary or wages earned or to be earned in the employment obtained through use of the job listing service.

(e)(1) No job listing service shall divide fees with an employer, an agent, or other employee of any employer or person to whom help is furnished.

(2) No job listing service shall charge any jobseeker a fee for accepting employment with that job listing service or any subsidiary of that service.

(3) No job listing service shall charge any jobseeker a fee when help is furnished to an employer, an agent, any employee of any employer, a member, or person who has a financial interest in the job listing service. **Leg.H.** Added Stats 1989 ch 704 §2.

§1812.518. Refund of fees

(a)(1) A job listing service shall refund in full any advance fee paid and cancel any other obligation incurred by the jobseeker if the job listing service does not, within seven business days after execution of the contract, supply at least three employment opportunities then available to the jobseeker and meeting the specifications of the contract.

(2) A job listing service will be deemed to have supplied information meeting the specifications of the jobseeker if the information supplied meets the contract specifications with reference to: type of job; interests of jobseeker; qualifications of jobseeker; hours, salary, benefits, and other conditions of employment; location of job; and any other specifications expressly set forth in the contract.

(b) A job listing service shall refund any amount over and above a twenty-five dollar ($25) service charge and cancel any other obligation incurred by the jobseeker if the jobseeker does not obtain a job, or if employment, once obtained, lasts less than 90 days.

(c) A job listing service shall make all refunds required under this section within 10 days after the jobseeker requests such refund. Unless the refund is made within that time, the job listing service shall pay the jobseeker an additional sum equal to the amount of the deposit. **Leg.H.** Added Stats 1989 ch 704 §2.

§1812.519. Job orders; Referrals

(a) No job listing service shall accept a fee from any jobseeker, or send any jobseeker for employment, without having obtained, in writing, a bona fide job order for employment.

(b) A job listing service shall identify itself as a job listing service to the employer in all instances in which it contacts an employer for the purposes of soliciting a job order. All job orders shall be recorded in writing. A job order for employment shall be considered to have been given by an employer to a job listing service under the following conditions:

(1) The employer, or his or her agent, in writing, registers a request or gives permission that the job listing service recruit or refer jobseekers who meet the employer's stated job specifications and the employer furnishes such information as required by subdivision (a) of Section 1812.516.

(2) A job order is valid for the referral of any qualified jobseeker until it is filled or canceled by the employer, and may serve as the basis for job listing service advertising. The job listing service is required to recontact the employer within the four-day period immediately preceding dissemination of the job listing information to ensure that the position is still vacant prior to any additional advertising or referral of jobseekers.

(c) No job listing service shall refer a jobseeker to a job knowing or having reason to know that:

(1) The job does not exist or the jobseeker is not qualified for the job.

(2) The job has been described or advertised by or on behalf of the job listing service in a false, misleading, or deceptive manner.

(3) The job listing service has not obtained written permission to list the job from the employer or an authorized agent of the employer.

(d) No job listing service shall exchange job orders with an employment agency which charges a placement fee. **Leg.H.** Added Stats 1989 ch 704 §2. Amended Stats 1991 ch 654 §51 (AB 1893).

§1812.520. Advertisements; Record

(a) No job listing service shall make or cause to be made any false, misleading or deceptive advertisements or representations concerning the services that the job listing service will provide to jobseekers.

(b)(1) No job listing service shall publish or cause to be published any false, fraudulent, or misleading information, representation, notice, or advertisements.

(2) All advertisements of a job listing service shall contain the correct name of the job listing service and one of the following:

(A) The street address of the job listing service's place of business.

(B) The correct telephone number of the job listing service at its place of business.

(3) No job listing service shall give any false information or make any false promises or representations concerning an engagement or employment to any jobseeker.

(4) No job listing service shall, by its choice of name or by advertisement or representation, represent itself to be an employment agency or to perform the services of an employment agency.

(c) Special requirements not usually associated with a job shall be specified in any advertisement. When the location of the position advertised is more than 50 miles from the job listing service office responsible for the advertisement, it shall state either the location or that the job is "nonlocal." Special benefits of the job, if advertised, shall be specifically described and substitute terms or symbols such as "extras" or "+" shall not be sufficient.

(d) An advertised salary shall be based upon the starting salary contained in the job order. An advertised range of starting salaries shall be specified by preceding the minimum salary and maximum salary by terms "from" and "to" respectively. When the job order contains only the maximum amount of a salary range, that advertised salary shall be preceded by the word "to." If a maximum salary is dependent upon the jobseeker's experience, the advertised salary may be described by listing the minimum salary and the term "up Depending on Experience" or "up D.O.E." The words "open" and "negotiable" or words or symbols of like import shall not be used as a substitute for the salary. If an advertised salary is based in whole or in part on commissions, that fact shall be indicated in the advertisement.

(e) All job listing services shall maintain a record of all advertised jobs, correlated to show the date and the publication in which the advertisement appeared and the job order number of each job advertised, retrospectively for a period of one year. **Leg.H.** Added Stats 1989 ch 704 §2. Amended Stats 1990 ch 1256 §7 (AB 2649).

§1812.521. Restrictions and disclosures

(a) No job listing service shall, when employment would be in violation of Chapter 1 (commencing with Section 1171) of Part 4 of Division 2 of the Labor Code or Part 27 (commencing with Section 48000) of the Education Code, accept any application for employment made by, or on behalf of, any minor, or place or assist in placing any minor in that employment.

(b) Every job listing service shall notify each jobseeker before sending the jobseeker in response to a request for employment whether a labor contract is in existence at the establishment to which the jobseeker is being sent, and whether union membership is required.

(c) No job listing service shall send a jobseeker to any place where a strike, lockout, or other labor trouble exists without notifying the jobseeker of that fact and shall in addition thereto enter a statement of those conditions upon the contract or receipt given to the jobseeker. **Leg.H.** Added Stats 1989 ch 704 §2. Amended Stats 1990 ch 1256 §8 (AB 2649).

CHAPTER 5
RECORDS

Inspection; Copies furnished upon request. §1812.522.

§1812.522. Inspection; Copies furnished upon request

(a) All books, records, files, the schedules, and other papers required by this title to be kept by any employment agency, employment counseling service, or job listing service shall be open at all reasonable hours to the inspection of the representative of the Attorney General, any district attorney, or any city attorney. Every employment agency, employment counseling service, and job listing service shall furnish to the representative of the Attorney General, any district attorney, or any city attorney upon request a true copy of those books, records, files, the schedules, and papers or any portion thereof, and shall make such reports as the Attorney General prescribes.

(b) If any employment agency, employment counseling service, or job listing service also engages in any other business which is not subject to this title, the records of the agency or service pertaining to matters under the jurisdictions of this title shall be kept separate and apart from the records of that other business. **Leg.H.** Added Stats 1989 ch 704 §2.

CHAPTER 6
REMEDIES AND ENFORCEMENT

Criminal and civil remedies. §1812.523.

§1812.523. Criminal and civil remedies

(a) Any person who violates any provision of this title is guilty of a misdemeanor. The Attorney General, any district attorney, or any city attorney may prosecute misdemeanor actions.

(b) Actions for violation of this title, including, but not limited to, equity proceedings to restrain and enjoin such a violation, may be instituted by the Attorney General, any district attorney, or any city attorney. This section shall not be deemed to prohibit the enforcement by any person of any right provided by this or any other law.

(c) If any person uses any untrue or misleading statement, information, or advertisement to sell its services or fails to comply with the applicable provisions of this title, or the contract does not comply with the applicable provisions of this title, then the contract shall be void and unenforceable as contrary to public policy and the jobseeker, customer, or nurse shall be entitled to the return of all sums paid.

(d) Any person who is injured by any violation of this title or by the breach of a contract subject to this title may bring an action for the recovery of damages, an equity proceeding to restrain and enjoin those violations, or both. The amount awarded may be up to three times the damages actually incurred, but in no event less than the amount paid by the jobseeker, customer, or nurse to the person subject to this title. If the person subject to this title refuses or is unwilling to pay the damages awarded, the amount awarded may be satisfied out of the security required by this title. If the plaintiff prevails, the plaintiff shall be awarded a reasonable attorney's fee and costs. If the court determines that the breach or violation was willful, by clear and convincing evidence, the court, in its discretion, may award punitive damages in addition to the amounts set forth above.

(e) The provisions of this title are not exclusive and do not relieve the parties subject to this title from the duty to comply with all other applicable laws.

(f) The remedies provided in this title are not exclusive and shall be in addition to any other remedies or procedures provided in any other law.

(g) Any waiver by the consumer, jobseeker, or nurse of the provisions of this title shall be deemed contrary to public policy and shall be void and unenforceable. Any attempt by a person subject to this title to have a jobseeker, customer, or nurse waive rights given by this title shall constitute a violation of this title.

(h) If any provisions of this title or the application thereof to any person or circumstances is held unconstitutional, the remainder of the title and the application of that provision to other persons and circumstances shall not be affected thereby. **Leg.H.** Added Stats 1989 ch 704 §2.

CHAPTER 7
NURSES' REGISTRIES

Definitions. §1812.524.
Bonds for nurses' registry. §1812.525.
Contracts. §1812.526.
Fees. §1812.527.
Verification of qualifications. §1812.528.
Log sheets and other records. §1812.529.
Restrictions on acceptance of fees. §1812.530.
Division of fees. §1812.531.
Repayment of fees and expenses. §1812.532.
Advertisements; Record. §1812.533.

§1812.524. Definitions

(a) "Nursing service" means the assignment of a nurse, as a private duty, self-employed, licensed registered nurse, licensed vocational nurse, or practical nurse to render service to a patient under the direction or supervision of a physician or surgeon registered to practice in this state.

(b) "Nurses' registry" means a person who engages in the business of obtaining and filling commitments for nursing service. A nurses' registry which makes or plans to make referrals for nurses' employment other than private duty nursing shall comply with Chapters 1 (commencing with Section 1812.500) and 2 (commencing with Section 1812.503) of this title with respect to those referrals.

(c) "Private duty nurse" means a self-employed nurse rendering service in the care of either a physically or mentally ill patient under the direction of a physician or surgeon, but who is paid by either the patient or the designated agent of the patient and who accepts the responsibilities of a self-employed private contractor. **Leg.H.** Added Stats 1989 ch 704 §2. Amended Stats 1990 ch 1256 §9 (AB 2649).

§1812.525. Bonds for nurses' registry

(a) Every nurses' registry subject to this title shall maintain a bond issued by a surety company admitted to do business in this state. The principal sum of the bond shall be three thousand dollars ($3,000). A copy of the bond shall be filed with the Secretary of State.

(b) The bond required by this section shall be in favor of, and payable to, the people of the State of California, and shall be conditioned that the person obtaining the bond will comply with this title and will pay all sums due any individual or group of individuals when the person or his or her representative, agent, or employee has received those sums. The bond shall be for the benefit of any person or persons damaged by any violation of this title or by fraud, dishonesty, misstatement, misrepresentation, deceit, unlawful acts or omissions, or failure to provide the services of the nurses' registry in performance of the contract with the nurse by the nurses' registry or its agents, representatives, or employees while acting within the scope of their employment.

(c)(1) No nurses' registry shall conduct any business without having a current surety bond in the amount prescribed by this title and filing a copy of the bond with the Secretary of State.

(2) Thirty days prior to the cancellation or termination of any surety bond required by this section, the surety shall send a written notice of that cancellation or termination to both the nurses' registry and the Secretary of State, identifying the bond and the date of cancellation or termination.

(3) If any nurses' registry fails to obtain a new bond and file a copy of that bond with the Secretary of State by the effective date of the cancellation or termination of the former bond, the nurses' registry shall cease to conduct any business unless and until a new surety bond is obtained and a copy of that bond is filed with the Secretary of State.

(d) When a deposit has been made in lieu of a bond pursuant to Section 995.710 of the Code of Civil Procedure, the person asserting a claim against the deposit shall, in lieu of Section 996.430 of the Code of Civil Procedure, establish the claim by furnishing evidence to the Secretary of State of a money judgment entered by a court together with evidence that the claimant is a person described in subdivision (b).

(e) When a person has established the claim with the Secretary of State, the Secretary of State shall review and approve the claim and enter the date of approval on the claim. The claim shall be designated an "approved claim."

(f) When the first claim against a particular deposit has been approved, it shall not be paid until the expiration of a period of 240 days after the date of its approval by the Secretary of State. Subsequent claims that are approved by the Secretary of State within the same 240-day period shall similarly not be paid until the expiration of the 240-day period. Upon the expiration of the 240-day period, the Secretary of State shall pay all approved claims from that 240-day period in full unless the deposit is insufficient, in which case each approved claim shall be paid a pro rata share of the deposit.

(g) When the Secretary of State approves the first claim against a particular deposit after the expiration of a 240-day period, the date of approval of that claim shall begin a new 240-day period to which subdivision (f) shall apply with respect to the amount remaining in the deposit.

(h) After a deposit is exhausted, no further claims shall be paid by the Secretary of State. Claimants who have had their claims paid in full or in part pursuant to subdivisions (f) and (g) shall not be required to return funds received from the deposit for the benefit of other claimants.

(i) When a deposit has been made in lieu of a bond, the amount of the deposit shall not be subject to attachment, garnishment, or execution with respect to an action or judgment against the nurses' registry, other than as to an amount as no longer needed or required for the purpose of this title that would otherwise be returned to the nurses' registry by the Secretary of State.

(j) The Secretary of State shall retain a cash deposit for two years from the date the Secretary of State receives written notification from the assignor of the deposit that the assignor has ceased to engage in the business of a nurses' registry or has filed a bond pursuant to subdivision (a), provided that there are no outstanding claims against the deposit. The written notice to the Secretary of State shall include all of the following: (1) name, address, and telephone number of the assignor; (2) name, address, and telephone number of the bank at which the deposit is located; (3) account number of the deposit; and (4) a statement whether the assignor is ceasing to engage in the business of a nurses' registry or has filed a bond with the Secretary of State. The Secretary of State shall forward an acknowledgment of receipt of the written notice to the assignor at the address indicated therein, specifying the date of receipt of the written notice and anticipated date of release of the deposit, provided there are no outstanding claims against the deposit.

(k) A judge of a superior court may order the return of the deposit prior to the expiration of two years upon evidence satisfactory to the judge that there are no outstanding claims against the deposit or order the Secretary of State to retain the deposit for a specified period beyond the two years pursuant to subdivision (j) to resolve outstanding claims against the deposit.

(l) The Secretary of State shall charge a filing fee not to exceed the cost of filing the bond or deposit filed in lieu of a bond pursuant to Section 995.710 of the Code of Civil Procedure.

(m) The Secretary of State shall enforce the provisions of this chapter that govern the filing and maintenance of bonds and deposits in lieu of bonds. **Leg.H.** Added Stats 1989 ch 704 §2. Amended Stats 1996 ch 633 §14 (SB 1978); Stats 1998 ch 829 §14 (SB 1652); Stats 2002 ch 784 §18 (SB 1316).

§1812.526. Contracts

Nurses' registries may enter into a continuing contract with private duty nurses covering the assignment of those nurses by the nurses' registries. The continuing contract shall state:

(a) The name, address, and telephone number of the nurses registry.
(b) The name, address, and telephone number of the nurse.
(c) The current fee schedule of the nurses' registry.
(d) The date of its execution by the nurses' registry and the nurse.
(e) The contract shall specify that the provisions thereof are to govern only the assignment of private duty nurses and shall do all of the following:

(1) Designate the nurses' registry as the continuous agent of the nurse for purposes of assignment.

(2) Provide that the contract in effect may be terminated at any time by written notice given by one to the other for any future assignment.

(3) Provide for delivery to the nurse at the time of the execution of the contract a written schedule of the rates of nurses' charges currently agreed to between the nurses registry and the nurse for the nurse's services to the patient.

(4) State that the nurses registry will immediately notify the nurse in writing of all subsequent changes in the rates to be charged the patient for services, and that the nurse shall agree to abide by these rates.

(5) Contain express undertakings by the nurses registry that it shall continuously maintain true and correct records of orders and assignments as provided in this title.

(6) Provide that the nurses' registry shall periodically and at least once each month render to the nurse a written statement of all fees claimed to be due the nurses registry, and further that the statement shall adequately identify each assignment as to the inception date and period of service covered by the claim, including the name of the patient and the amount of service fee claimed.

(7) Contain appropriate wording advising the nurse of his or her right to dispute the correctness of any service fee claimed by the nurses registry in the written statement referred to above, and that in the absence of objections within a reasonable time, any such service fee may be presumed to be correctly charged.

(8) Include any other term, condition, or understanding agreed upon between the nurses' registry and the nurse.

(f) Each contract shall be numbered consecutively in original and duplicate, both to be signed by the nurse and the nurses registry. The original shall be given to the nurse and the duplicate shall be kept on file at the nurses' registry within the nurse's records.

(g) The full agreement between the parties shall be contained in a single document containing those elements set forth in this section.
Leg.H. Added Stats 1989 ch 704 §2. Amended Stats 1990 ch 1256 §10 (AB 2649).

§1812.527. Fees

(a)(1) A nurses' registry shall provide a copy of the registry's fee schedule and payment terms to any nurse from whom a fee or deposit is to be received, prior to the nurse being interviewed by the registry.

(2) In the schedule, the maximum fee shall be fixed and shall include the charges of every kind rendered by the nurses' registry in each case or transaction on behalf of the nurse. Changes in the fee schedule may be made, but no change shall become effective until posted for not less than seven days in a conspicuous place in the nurses' registry.

(3) A copy of the schedule in effect shall be kept posted in the nurses' registry in a conspicuous place, and the posted schedule and the changes therein shall be in lettering or printing of not less than standard pica capitals. The date of the taking effect of the schedule and of each change therein shall appear on the posted copies.

(4) A copy of all fee schedules, and of all changes therein, shall be kept on file at the nurses' registry, retrospectively for a period of one year.
Leg.H. Added Stats 1989 ch 704 §2.

§1812.528. Verification of qualifications

It shall be the duty of the nurses' registry to verify in writing the claims as to the experience or training listed on the application and to keep a file of those records in the nurse's folder within the nurses' registry. It shall also be the duty of the person interviewing the jobseeker to require the jobseeker to exhibit his or her license as issued by the Board of Registered Nursing or the Board of Vocational Nurse and Psychiatric Technician Examiners, with a notation to be made on the application by the interviewer that the license has been inspected and the date of expiration of the license. **Leg.H.** Added Stats 1989 ch 704 §2.

§1812.529. Log sheets and other records

Each nurses' registry shall continuously maintain in its offices true and correct permanent log sheets and other records which shall disclose, in addition to the other information required, the date and hour of the receipt by the nurses' registry of each order for a private duty nurse, and the date and hour of the making or giving of each assignment to the nurse by the nurses' registry, the name of the nurse assigned, the name of the patient and the address where the nurse is assigned, the name of the attending physician, the date the assignment is to start, the period of actual service for each assignment, and the amount of the fee charged for each assignment. No nurses' registry, his or her agent or employees, shall make any false entry in those records. The nurses' registry shall maintain the log sheets and records required by this section respectively for a period of one year. **Leg.H.** Added Stats 1989 ch 704 §2.

§1812.530. Restrictions on acceptance of fees

(a) No nurses' registry shall accept, directly or indirectly, a registration fee of any kind.

(b) No nurses' registry may take from a nurse a confession of judgment, or promissory note, or an assignment of wages to cover its fees. **Leg.H.** Added Stats 1989 ch 704 §2.

§1812.531. Division of fees

No nurses' registry shall divide fees with any physician and surgeon, nurse, hospital, patient, or any agent or employee of any of these. **Leg.H.** Added Stats 1989 ch 704 §2.

§1812.532. Repayment of fees and expenses

In the event that a nurses' registry collects from a nurse a fee or expenses for an assignment, and the nurse fails to obtain the assignment, or the nurse fails to be paid for the assignment, the nurses' registry shall upon demand therefor, repay to the nurse the fee and expenses so collected. Unless repayment is made within 48 hours after demand, the nurses' registry shall pay to the nurse an additional sum equal to the amount of the fee. **Leg.H.** Added Stats 1989 ch 704 §2.

§1812.533. Advertisements; Record

(a) No nurses' registry shall make, or cause to be made, any false, misleading, or deceptive advertisements or representations concerning the services that registry will provide to nurses.

(b)(1) No nurses' registry shall publish or cause to be published any false, fraudulent, or misleading information, representation, notice, or advertisements.

(2) All advertisements of a nurses registry shall contain the correct name of the nurses' registry and one of the following:

(A) The street address of the registry's place of business.

(B) The correct telephone number of the registry at its place of business.

(3) No nurses registry shall give any false information or make any false promises or representations concerning an assignment or employment to any nurse who registers or applies for an assignment or employment.

(4) No nurses' registry shall, by its name, advertisement, or any other representation, represent itself to be a home health agency, as defined by subdivision (a) of Section 1727 of the Health and Safety Code, or to perform the services of a home health agency. A nurses' registry shall provide a written disclosure to each individual receiving nursing services, as defined in subdivision (a) of Section 1812.524, in his or her place of residence stating that it does not perform the services of a home health agency and clearly describing that it is a nurses' registry only and that any complaints against licensed personnel providing a nursing service shall be brought to the local district attorney and the Department of Consumer Affairs. The address and telephone number of each agency and board to which complaints are required to be submitted shall be provided to all patients prior to the time they are under the care of any nursing services personnel.

(5) Any person may refer complaints concerning nurses' registries to the proper law enforcement agency for action.

(c) Every nurses' registry shall maintain a record of all advertisements, correlated to show the date and the publication in which the advertisement appeared, retrospectively for a period of one year. **Leg.H.** Added Stats 1989 ch 704 §2. Amended Stats 1990 ch 761 §2 (AB 3924).

CHAPTER 8
LONG-TERM CARE FACILITIES

Definitions. §1812.540.
Requirements of agency referring temporary certified nurse assistants. §1812.541.
Requirements of agency referring temporary licensed nursing staff. §1812.542.
Adoption of policies and procedures; Agency duties. §1812.543.
Advertising records; Advertising restrictions; Complaint referral procedure. §1812.544.

§1812.540. Definitions

For purposes of this chapter, the following definitions shall apply:

(a) "Direct care service" means the temporary assignment of certified nurse assistants to render basic care services directed at the safety, comfort, personal hygiene, or protection of a patient who is a resident of a long-term health care facility.

(b) "Nursing service" means the temporary assignment of a licensed registered nurse, licensed vocational nurse, or psychiatric technician to render nursing and basic care services to a patient who is a resident of a long-term health care facility.

(c) "Licensed nursing staff" means a licensed registered nurse, licensed vocational nurse, or psychiatric technician.

(d) "Long-term health care facility" means a licensed facility, as defined in Section 1418 of the Health and Safety Code. **Leg.H.** Added Stats 2001 ch 326 §2 (AB 1643).

§1812.541. Requirements of agency referring temporary certified nurse assistants

Every employment agency that refers temporary certified nurse assistants to an employer that is a long-term health care facility shall provide the employer with all of the following:

(a) Written verification that the employment agency has verified that any certified nurse assistant referred by the agency is registered on the state registry of certified nurse assistants and is in good standing. The employment agency shall provide to the employer the certified nurse assistant's professional certification number and date of expiration.

(b) A statement that the certified nurse assistant has at least six months of experience working in a long-term health care facility.

(c) A statement that the certified nurse assistant has had a health examination within 90 days prior to employment with the employment agency or seven days after employment with the employment agency and at least annually thereafter by a person lawfully authorized to perform that procedure. Each examination shall include a medical history and physical evaluation. The employment agency shall also provide verification that the individual has had tuberculosis screening within 90 days prior to employment and annually thereafter.

(d) A statement that the certified nurse assistant will participate in the facility's orientation program and any in-service training programs at the request of the long-term health care employer.

(e) A statement that a certified nurse assistant is in compliance with the in-service training requirements of paragraph (1) of subdivision (a) of Section 1337.6 of the Health and Safety Code. **Leg.H.** Added Stats 2001 ch 326 §2 (AB 1643).

§1812.542. Requirements of agency referring temporary licensed nursing staff

Every employment agency that refers temporary licensed nursing staff to an employer who is a licensed long-term health care facility shall provide the employer with all of the following:

(a) Written verification that the individual is in good standing with the Board of Registered Nursing or the Board of Vocational Nursing and Psychiatric Technicians, as applicable, and has successfully secured a criminal record clearance. The employment agency shall provide to the employer the individual's professional license and registration number and date of expiration.

(b) A statement that the licensed nursing staff person has had a health examination within 90 days prior to employment with the employment agency or seven days after employment with the employment agency and at least annually thereafter by a person lawfully authorized to perform that procedure. Each examination shall include a medical history and physical evaluation. The employment agency shall also provide verification that the individual has had tuberculosis screening within 90 days prior to employment and annually thereafter. **Leg.H.** Added Stats 2001 ch 326 §2 (AB 1643).

§1812.543. Adoption of policies and procedures; Agency duties

(a) An employment agency that makes referrals of licensed nursing staff or certified nurse assistants for temporary employment in a long-term health care facility shall adopt policies and procedures regarding prevention of resident or patient abuse by temporary staff.

(b) The employment agency shall provide written verification to the long-term health care facility that any certified nurse assistants or licensed nursing staff referred by the agency do not have any unresolved allegations against them involving the mistreatment, neglect, or abuse of a patient, including injuries of unknown source and misappropriation of resident property.

(c) No temporary staff person referred by an employment agency may be solely responsible for a unit unless that person has received a full orientation to the facility and the applicable unit for which he or she is assigned.

(d) Upon the request of the State Department of Health Services, an employment agency shall provide a list of temporary employees who have been referred to a specified facility during the period in which the facility is involved in a labor action.

(e) An employment agency shall require that any employee referred to a long-term care facility be identified as a temporary staff person in the facility's daily staffing levels required to be posted in accordance with the standards set forth in Section 941 of Appendix F of Public Law 106-554 (42 U.S.C. Sec. 1395i-3(b)(8) and 42 U.S.C. Sec. 1395r(b)(8)). **Leg.H.** Added Stats 2001 ch 326 §2 (AB 1643).

§1812.544. Advertising records; Advertising restrictions; Complaint referral procedure

(a) Every employment agency that makes referrals of licensed nursing staff or certified nurse assistants for temporary employment in a long-term health care facility shall maintain a record of all advertisements, showing the date of publication and the publication in which the advertisement appeared, for a period of one year from the date of the advertisement.

(b) No employment agency that makes referrals for employment to a long-term health care facility shall, by its name, advertisement, or any other representation, represent itself to be a home health agency, as defined by subdivision (a) of Section 1727 of the Health and Safety Code, or to perform the services of a home health agency. The employment agency shall provide a written disclosure to each employer stating that it does not perform the services of a home health agency and clearly describing that it is an employment agency only.

(c) Any facility or individual may refer complaints concerning employment agencies which place licensed nursing staff or certified nurse assistants in long-term health care facilities to the appropriate licensing, certification, ombudsman, adult protective services, or proper law enforcement agency for action. **Leg.H.** Added Stats 2001 ch 326 §2 (AB 1643).

TITLE 2.95
AUCTIONEER AND AUCTION COMPANIES

Bonds for auctioneers. §1812.600.
Definitions. §1812.601.
Injunctions. §1812.602.
Restitution. §1812.603.
Criminal violations. §1812.604.
Ethical duties of auctioneer, auction company, and others. §1812.605.
Responsibility for violations. §1812.606.
Disclosures. §1812.607.
Prohibited activities. §1812.608.
Waiver of provisions of title void. §1812.609.
Auctions including sale of real property; Bids meant for sole purpose to increase sale price. §1812.610.

§1812.600. Bonds for auctioneers

(a) Every auctioneer and auction company shall maintain a bond issued by a surety company admitted to do business in this state. The principal sum of the bond shall be twenty thousand dollars ($20,000). A copy of the bond shall be filed with the Secretary of State.

(b) The bond required by this section shall be in favor of, and payable to, the people of the State of California and shall be for the benefit of any person or persons damaged by any fraud, dishonesty, misstatement, misrepresentation, deceit, unlawful acts or omissions, or failure to provide the services of the auctioneer or auction company in performance of the auction by the auctioneer or auction company or its agents, representatives, or employees while acting within the scope of their employment.

(c)(1) No auctioneer or auction company shall conduct any business without having a current surety bond in the amount prescribed by this section and without filing a copy of the bond with the Secretary of State.

(2) Thirty days prior to the cancellation or termination of any surety bond required by this section, the surety shall send a written notice of that cancellation or termination to both the auctioneer or auction company and the Secretary of State, identifying the bond and the date of cancellation or termination.

(3) If any auctioneer or auction company fails to obtain a new bond and file a copy of that bond with the Secretary of State by the effective date of the cancellation or termination of the former bond, the auctioneer or auction company shall cease to conduct any business unless and until that time as a new surety bond is obtained and a copy of that bond is filed with the Secretary of State.

(d) A deposit may be made in lieu of a bond as set forth in Section 995.710 of the Code of Civil Procedure. When a deposit is made in lieu of the bond, the person asserting the claim against the deposit shall establish the claim by furnishing evidence to the Secretary of State of a money judgment entered by a court together with evidence that the claimant is a person described in subdivision (b).

(e) When a claimant has established the claim with the Secretary of State, the Secretary of State shall review and approve the claim and enter the date of approval on the claim. The claim shall be designated an "approved claim."

(f) When the first claim against a particular deposit has been approved, it shall not be paid until the expiration of a period of 240 days after the date of its approval by the Secretary of State. Subsequent claims that are approved by the Secretary of State within the same 240-day period shall similarly not be paid until the expiration of the 240-day period. Upon expiration of the 240-day period, the Secretary of State shall pay all approved claims from that 240-day period in full unless the deposit is insufficient, in which case each approved claim shall be paid a pro rata share of the deposit.

(g) When the Secretary of State approves the first claim against a particular deposit after the expiration of a 240-day period, the date of approval of that claim shall begin a new 240-day period to which subdivision (f) shall apply with respect to any amount remaining in the deposit.

(h) After a deposit is exhausted, no further claims shall be paid by the Secretary of State. Claimants who have had their claims paid in full or in part pursuant to subdivision (f) or (g) shall not be required to return funds received from the deposit for the benefit of other claimants.

(i) When a deposit has been made in lieu of a bond, the amount of the deposit shall not be subject to attachment, garnishment, or execution with respect to an action or judgment against the auctioneer or auction company, other than as to that amount that is no longer needed or required for the purpose of this section that otherwise would be returned to the auctioneer or auction company by the Secretary of State.

(j) The Secretary of State shall retain a cash deposit for two years from the date the Secretary of State receives written notification from the assignor of the deposit that the assignor has ceased to engage in the business of an auctioneer or auction company or has filed a bond pursuant to subdivision (a), provided that there are no outstanding claims against the deposit. Written notification to the Secretary of State shall include all of the following: (1) name, address, and telephone number of the assignor; (2) name, address, and telephone number of the bank at which the deposit is located; (3) account number of the deposit; and (4) a statement whether the assignor is ceasing to engage in the business of an auctioneer or auction company or has filed a bond with the Secretary of State. The Secretary of State shall forward an acknowledgment of receipt of the written notice to the assignor at the address indicated in the notice, specifying the date of receipt of the written notice and anticipated date of release of the deposit, provided there are no outstanding claims against the deposit.

(k) A judge of a superior court may order the return of the deposit prior to the expiration of two years upon evidence satisfactory to the judge that there are no outstanding claims against the deposit or order the Secretary of State to retain the deposit for a specified period beyond the two years pursuant to subdivision (j) to resolve outstanding claims against the deposit.

(*l*) If an auctioneer or auction company fails to perform any of the duties specifically imposed upon him or her pursuant to this title, any person may maintain an action for enforcement of those duties or to recover a civil penalty in the amount of one thousand dollars ($1,000), or for both enforcement and recovery.

(m) In any action to enforce these duties or to recover civil penalties, or for both enforcement and recovery, the prevailing plaintiff shall be entitled to reasonable attorney's fees and costs, in addition to the civil penalties provided under subdivision (*l*).

(n) Notwithstanding the repeal of Chapter 3.7 (commencing with Section 5700) of Division 3 of the Business and Professions Code by the act adding this chapter, any cash security in lieu of the surety bond formerly required and authorized by former Chapter 3.7 (commencing with Section 5700) of Division 3 of the Business and Professions Code, shall be transferred to, and maintained by, the Secretary of State.

(o) The Secretary of State shall charge and collect a filing fee not to exceed the cost of filing the bond or deposit filed in lieu of a bond as set forth in Section 995.710 of the Code of Civil Procedure.

(p) The Secretary of State shall enforce the provisions of this chapter that govern the filing and maintenance of bonds and deposits in lieu of bonds. **Leg.H.** Added Stats 1993 ch 1170 §2 (AB 259), effective October 11, 1993. Amended Stats 1996 ch 633 §15 (SB 1978); Stats 1998 ch 829 §15 (SB 1652); Stats 2002 ch 784 §19 (SB 1316).

§1812.601. Definitions

(a) "Advertisement" means any of the following:

(1) Any written or printed communication for the purpose of soliciting, describing, or offering to act as an auctioneer or provide auction company services, including any brochure, pamphlet, newspaper, periodical, or publication.

(2) A telephone or other directory listing caused or permitted by an auctioneer or auction company to be published that indicates the offer to practice auctioneering or auction company services.

(3) A radio, television, or similar airwave transmission that solicits or offers the practice of auctioneering or auction company services.

(b) "Auction" means a sale transaction conducted by means of oral or written exchanges, which include exchanges made in person or through electronic media, between an auctioneer and the members of his or her audience, which exchanges consist of a series of invitations for offers for the purchase of goods made by the auctioneer and offers to purchase made by members of the audience and culminate in the acceptance by the auctioneer of the highest or most favorable offer made by a member of the participating audience. However, auction does not include either of the following:

(1) A wholesale motor vehicle auction subject to regulation by the Department of Motor Vehicles.

(2) A sale of real estate or a sale in any sequence of real estate with personal property or fixtures or both in a unified sale pursuant to subparagraph (B) of paragraph (1) of subdivision (a) of Section 9604 of the Commercial Code.

(c) "Auction company" means any person who arranges, manages, sponsors, advertises, accounts for the proceeds of, or carries out auction sales at locations, including, but not limited to, any fixed location, including an auction barn, gallery place of business, sale barn, sale yard, sale pavilion, and the contiguous surroundings of each.

(d) "Auctioneer" means any individual who is engaged in, or who by advertising or otherwise holds himself or herself out as being available to engage in, the calling for, the recognition of, and the acceptance of, offers for the purchase of goods at an auction.

(e) "Employee" means an individual who works for an employer, is listed on the employer's payroll records, and is under the employer's control.

(f) "Employer" means a person who employs an individual for wages or salary, lists the individual on the person's payroll records, and withholds legally required deductions and contributions.

(g) "Goods" means any goods, wares, chattels, merchandise, or other personal property, including domestic animals and farm products.

(h) "Person" means an individual, corporation, partnership, trust, including a business trust, firm, association, organization, or any other form of business enterprise. **Leg.H.** Added Stats 1993 ch 1170 §2 (AB 259), effective October 11, 1993. Amended Stats 1994 ch 180 §2 (AB 375), effective July 9, 1994, ch 1010 §46.1 (SB 2053) (ch 180 prevails); Stats 1999 ch 991 §5 (SB 45), operative July 1, 2001; Stats 2004 ch 194 §1 (SB 1832).

§1812.602. Injunctions

The superior court for the county in which any person has engaged or is about to engage in any act that constitutes a violation of this title may, upon a petition filed by any person, issue an injunction or other appropriate order restraining the violative conduct. Proceedings under this section shall be governed by Chapter 3 (commencing with Section 525) of Title 7 of Part 2 of the Code of Civil Procedure, except that no undertaking shall be required. **Leg.H.** Added Stats 1993 ch 1170 §2 (AB 259), effective October 11, 1993.

§1812.603. Restitution

(a) The superior court for the county in which any person has engaged in any act that constitutes a violation of this title may, upon a petition filed by any person, order the person who committed the violation to make restitution to any person injured as a result of the violation.

(b) The court may order any person against whom an injunction or restraining order pursuant to subdivision (a), or an order requiring restitution pursuant to subdivision (b), is directed, to reimburse the petitioner for expenses incurred in the investigation related to its petition.

(c) The remedies set forth in this section are in addition to, and not a limitation on, the authority provided for in any other section of this code. **Leg.H.** Added Stats 1993 ch 1170 §2 (AB 259), effective October 11, 1993.

§1812.604. Criminal violations

Except as otherwise provided in this title, any person who violates any provision of this title is guilty of a misdemeanor, which offense is punishable by a fine not exceeding one thousand dollars ($1,000), or by imprisonment in a county jail for not more than one year, or by both that fine and imprisonment. In addition, upon a conviction of any violation of this chapter, or of any crime related to the conduct of an auctioneer, the court may issue an injunction and prohibit the convicted person from acting as an auctioneer or an auction company in this state, in which case the court shall inform the Secretary of State of that action. **Leg.H.** Added Stats 1993 ch 1170 §2 (AB 259), effective October 11, 1993.

§1812.605. Ethical duties of auctioneer, auction company, and others

In conducting the business of auctioneering, each auctioneer and auction company, and the company's owners, partners, officers, agents, and employees, shall do all of the following:

(a) Follow all lawful requests of the owner or consignor of the goods being sold at auction with regard to the sale of those goods.

(b) Perform his or her duties so that the highest or most favorable offer made by a member of his or her audience is accepted, except to the extent that any item or sale is offered with reserve or subject to confirmation.

(c) Truthfully represent the goods to be auctioned.

(d) Otherwise perform his or her duties in accordance with the laws of this state. **Leg.H.** Added Stats 1993 ch 1170 §2 (AB 259), effective October 11, 1993.

§1812.606. Responsibility for violations

Every auctioneer who operates his or her own auction company as a sole proprietor, and every auction company, together with its owners, partners, and officers, that employs an auctioneer, shall be responsible for all violations committed by the auctioneer or by any company employee in the conduct of auction business. An auctioneer who is employed by an auctioneer or auction company shall be responsible for all violations committed by him or her in the conduct of auction business.

It is a violation of this title for any auctioneer or auction company, or the company's owners, partners, and officers, to direct or knowingly permit any violation of this title by any auctioneer employed by or under contract with that auctioneer or auction company, or by any owner, partner, officer, agent, or employee of the auction company. **Leg.H.** Added Stats 1993 ch 1170 §2 (AB 259), effective October 11, 1993.

§1812.607. Disclosures

Every auction company and auctioneer shall do all of the following:

(a) Disclose his or her name, trade or business name, telephone number, and bond number in all advertising of auctions. A first violation of this subdivision is an infraction subject to a fine of fifty dollars ($50);

a second violation is subject to a fine of seventy-five dollars ($75); and a third or subsequent violation is subject to a fine of one hundred dollars ($100). This section shall not apply to business cards, business stationery, or to any advertisement that does not specify an auction date.

(b) Post a sign, the dimensions of which shall be at least 18 inches by 24 inches, at the main entrance to each auction, stating that the auction is being conducted in compliance with Section 2328 of the Commercial Code, Section 535 of the Penal Code, and the provisions of the California Civil Code. A first violation of this subdivision is an infraction subject to a fine of fifty dollars ($50); a second violation is subject to a fine of seventy-five dollars ($75); and a third or subsequent violation is subject to a fine of one hundred dollars ($100).

(c) Post or distribute to the audience the terms, conditions, restrictions, and procedures whereby goods will be sold at the auction, and announce any changes to those terms, conditions, restrictions, and procedures prior to the beginning of the auction sale. A first violation of this subdivision is an infraction subject to a fine of fifty dollars ($50); a second violation is subject to a fine of one hundred dollars ($100); and a third or subsequent violation is subject to a fine of two hundred fifty dollars ($250).

(d) Notify the Secretary of State of any change in address of record within 30 days of the change. A violation of this subdivision is an infraction subject to a fine of fifty dollars ($50).

(e) Notify the Secretary of State of any change in the officers of a corporate license within 30 days of the change. A violation of this subdivision is an infraction subject to a fine of fifty dollars ($50).

(f) Notify the Secretary of State of any change in the business or trade name of the auctioneer or auction company within 30 days of the change. A violation of this subdivision is an infraction subject to a fine of fifty dollars ($50).

(g) Keep and maintain, at the auctioneer's or auction company's address of record, complete and correct records and accounts pertaining to the auctioneer's or auction company's activity for a period of not less than two years. The records shall include the name and address of the owner or consignor and of any buyer of goods at any auction sale engaged in or conducted by the auctioneer or auction company, a description of the goods, the terms and conditions of the acceptance and sale of the goods, all written contracts with owners and consignors, and accounts of all moneys received and paid out, whether on the auctioneer's or auction company's own behalf or as agent, as a result of those activities. A first violation of this subdivision is a misdemeanor subject to a fine of five hundred dollars ($500); and a second or subsequent violation is subject to a fine of one thousand dollars ($1,000).

(h) Within 30 working days after the sale transaction, provide, or cause to be provided, an account to the owner or consignor of all goods that are the subject of an auction engaged in or conducted by the auctioneer or auction company. A first violation of this subdivision is a misdemeanor subject to a fine of five hundred dollars ($500); and a second or subsequent violation is subject to a fine of one thousand dollars ($1,000).

(i) Within 30 working days after a sale transaction of goods, pay or cause to be paid all moneys and proceeds due to the owner or the consignor of all goods that were the subject of an auction engaged in or conducted by the auctioneer or auction company, unless delay is compelled by legal proceedings or the inability of the auctioneer or auction company, through no fault of his or her own, to transfer title to the goods or to comply with any provision of this chapter, the Commercial Code, or the Code of Civil Procedure, or with any other applicable provision of law. A first violation of this subdivision is a misdemeanor subject to a fine of one thousand dollars ($1,000); a second violation is subject to a fine of one thousand five hundred dollars ($1,500); and a third or subsequent violation is subject to a fine of two thousand dollars ($2,000).

(j) Maintain the funds of all owners, consignors, buyers, and other clients and customers separate from his or her personal funds and accounts. A violation of this subdivision is an infraction subject to a fine of two hundred fifty dollars ($250).

(k) Immediately prior to offering any item for sale, disclose to the audience the existence and amount of any liens or other encumbrances on the item, unless the item is sold as free and clear. For the purposes of this subdivision, an item is "free and clear" if all liens and encumbrances on the item are to be paid prior to the transfer of title. A violation of this subdivision is an infraction subject to a fine of two hundred fifty dollars ($250) in addition to the requirement that the buyer be refunded, upon demand, the amount paid for any item that is the subject of the violation.

(l) Within two working days after an auction sale, return the blank check or deposit of each buyer who purchased no goods at the sale. A first violation of this subdivision is an infraction subject to a fine of one hundred dollars ($100); and a second or subsequent violation is subject to a fine of two hundred fifty dollars ($250).

(m) Within 30 working days of any auction sale, refund that portion of the deposit of each buyer that exceeds the cost of the goods purchased, unless delay is compelled by legal proceedings or the inability of the auctioneer or auction company, through no fault of his or her own, to transfer title to the goods or to comply with any provision of this chapter, the Commercial Code, or the Code of Civil Procedure, or with other applicable provisions of law, or unless the buyer violated the terms of a written agreement that he or she take possession of purchased goods within a specified period of time. A first violation of this subdivision is an infraction subject to a fine of one hundred dollars ($100); and a second or subsequent violation is subject to a fine of two hundred fifty dollars ($250). **Leg.H.** Added Stats 1993 ch 1170 §2 (AB 259), effective October 11, 1993, as CC §1861.607. Amended and renumbered by Stats 1997 ch 17 §16 (SB 947).

§1812.608. Prohibited activities

In addition to other requirements and prohibitions of this title, it is a violation of this title for any person to do any of the following:

(a) Fail to comply with any provision of this code, or with any provision of the Vehicle Code, the Commercial Code, any regulation of the Secretary of State, the Code of Civil Procedure, the Penal Code, or any law administered by the State Board of Equalization, relating to the auctioneering business, including, but not limited to, sales and the transfer of title of goods.

(b) Aid or abet the activity of any other person that violates any provision of this title. A violation of this subdivision is a misdemeanor subject to a fine of one thousand dollars ($1,000).

(c) Place or use any misleading or untruthful advertising or statements or make any substantial misrepresentation in conducting auctioneering business. A first violation of this subdivision is a misdemeanor subject to a fine of five hundred dollars ($500); and a second or subsequent violation is subject to a fine of one thousand dollars ($1,000).

(d) Sell goods at auction before the auctioneer or auction company involved has first entered into a written contract with the owner or consignor of the goods, which contract sets forth the terms and conditions upon which the auctioneer or auction company accepts the goods for sale. The written contract shall include all of the following:

(1) The auctioneer's or auction company's name, trade or business name, business address, and business telephone number.

(2) An inventory of the item or items to be sold at auction.

(3) A description of the services to be provided and the agreed consideration for the services, which description shall explicitly state which party shall be responsible for advertising and other expenses.

(4) The approximate date or dates when the item or items will be sold at auction.

(5) A statement as to which party shall be responsible for insuring the item or items against loss by theft, fire, or other means.

(6) A disclosure that the auctioneer or auction company has a bond on file with the Secretary of State. A first violation of this subdivision is an infraction subject to a fine of two hundred fifty dollars ($250); a second violation is subject to a fine of five hundred dollars ($500); and a third or subsequent violation is subject to a fine of one thousand dollars ($1,000).

(e) Sell goods at auction before the auctioneer or auction company involved has first entered into a written contract with the auctioneer who is to conduct the auction. A first violation of this subdivision is an infraction subject to a fine of one hundred dollars ($100); and a second or subsequent violation is subject to a fine of two hundred fifty dollars ($250).

(f) Fail to reduce to writing all amendments or addenda to any written contract with an owner or consignor or an auctioneer. A first violation of this subdivision is an infraction subject to a fine of one hundred dollars ($100); and a second or subsequent violation is subject to a fine of two hundred fifty dollars ($250).

(g) Fail to abide by the terms of any written contract required by this section. A first violation of this subdivision is an infraction subject to a fine of one hundred dollars ($100); and a second or subsequent violation is subject to a fine of two hundred fifty dollars ($250).

(h) Cause or allow any person to bid at a sale for the sole purpose of increasing the bid on any item or items being sold by the auctioneer, except as authorized by Section 2328 of the Commercial Code or by this title. A violation of this subdivision includes, but is not limited to, either of the following:

(1) Stating any increased bid greater than that offered by the last highest bidder when, in fact, no person has made such a bid.

(2) Allowing the owner, consignor, or agent thereof, of any item or items to bid on the item or items, without disclosing to the audience that the owner, consignor, or agent thereof has reserved the right to so bid.

A violation of this subdivision is an infraction subject to a fine of one hundred dollars ($100).

(i) Knowingly misrepresent the nature of any item or items to be sold at auction, including, but not limited to, age, authenticity, value, condition, or origin. A violation of this subdivision is an infraction subject to a fine of two hundred fifty dollars ($250). In addition, it shall be required that the buyer of the misrepresented item be refunded the purchase price of the item or items within 24 hours of return to the auctioneer or auction company of the item by the buyer, provided that the item is returned within five days after the date of the auction sale.

(j) Misrepresent the terms, conditions, restrictions, or procedures under which goods will be sold at auction. A violation of this subdivision is an infraction subject to a fine of seventy-five dollars ($75).

(k) Sell any item subject to sales tax without possessing a valid and unrevoked seller's permit from the State Board of Equalization. A violation of this subdivision is an infraction subject to a fine of five hundred dollars ($500). **Leg.H.** Added Stats 1993 ch 1170 §2 (AB 259), effective October 11, 1993, as CC §1861.608. Amended and renumbered by Stats 1997 ch 17 §17 (SB 947).

§1812.609. Waiver of provisions of title void

Any waiver of the provisions of this title is contrary to public policy, and is void and unenforceable. **Leg.H.** Added Stats 2002 ch 815 §22 (AB 2331).

§1812.610. Auctions including sale of real property; Bids meant for sole purpose to increase sale price

(a) Notwithstanding Section 1812.601, for purposes of this section, an auction includes the sale of real property and an "auctioneer" means any individual who is engaged in, or who by advertising or otherwise holds himself or herself out as being available to engage in, the calling for, the recognition of, and the acceptance of, offers for the purchase of real property at an auction.

(b) An auctioneer shall not state at an auction that an increased bid greater than that offered by the last highest bidder has been made when, in fact, no person has made an increased bid. Notwithstanding the foregoing, an auctioneer or another authorized person may place a bid on the seller's behalf during an auction of real property that would not result in a sale of the real property, if both of the following are true:

(1) Notice is given to all auction participants, including all other bidders, that liberty for that type of bidding is reserved and that type of bid will not result in the sale of the real property.

(2) The person placing that type of bid contemporaneously discloses to all auction participants, including all other bidders, that the particular bid has been placed on behalf of the seller.

(c) For the purpose of the conduct of online auctions of real property, "notice" means a statement of the information required to be given under paragraph (1) of subdivision (b) within the end user license agreement, terms of service, or equivalent policy posted on, or provided by, the operator of an Internet Web site, online service, online application, or mobile application, and by conspicuously posting the information required to be given under paragraph (1) of subdivision (b) in any of the following ways:

(1) Upon the Internet Web page or its equivalent through which a user directly interacts with the site, service, or application during the online auction.

(2) With an icon that hyperlinks to an Internet Web page or its equivalent upon which the required information is posted, if the icon is located on the Internet Web page or its equivalent through which a user directly interacts with the site, service, or application during the online auction. The icon shall use a color that contrasts with the background color of the Internet Web page or is otherwise readily distinguishable.

(3) With a text link that hyperlinks to an Internet Web page or its equivalent upon which the required information is posted, if the text link is located on the Internet Web page or its equivalent through which a user directly interacts with the site, service, or application during the online auction. The text link shall be written in capital letters that are in larger type than the surrounding text, or shall be written in contrasting type, font, or color to the surrounding text of the same size, or shall be set off from the surrounding text of the same size by symbols or other marks that call attention to the language.

(4) With any other functional hyperlink or its equivalent that is displayed on the site, service, or application through which a user directly interacts with the site, service, or application during the online auction so that a reasonable person would notice it and understand it to hyperlink to the required information. **Leg.H.** Added Stats 2014 ch 893 §1 (AB 2039), effective January 1, 2015, operative July 1, 2015. Amended Stats 2015 ch 354 §1 (SB 474), effective September 28, 2015.

TITLE 2.96
CALIFORNIA RENTAL-PURCHASE ACT

Citation of title. §1812.620.
Legislative findings and declarations. §1812.621.
Definitions. §1812.622.
Contents of rental-purchase agreement. §1812.623.
Prohibited provisions. §1812.624.
Security deposit. §1812.625.
Late payment fee. §1812.626.
Liability for loss or damage to property. §1812.627.
Agreement deemed home solicitation contract or offer. §1812.628.
Information and copies of documents to consumer. §1812.629.
Advertisements. §1812.630.
Default by consumer. §1812.631.
Right to acquire ownership of property. §1812.632.
Maintenance of property by lessor. §1812.633.
Transfer of warranties. §1812.634.
Service contracts. §1812.635.
Damages for violation of provisions. §1812.636.
Written notice of error by lessor. §1812.637.
Collection of payment or repossession of property. §1812.638.
Unfair or illegal conduct; Misleading statements. §1812.639.
Report to credit agency. §1812.640.
Solicitation or promotional material to person used as reference. §1812.641.
Discrimination against consumer. §1812.642.
Notice. §1812.643.
Total of payments; Cash price. §1812.644.
Venue. §1812.645.
Waiver or modification. §1812.646.
Violations; Misdemeanor. §1812.647.
Cumulative remedies. §1812.648.
Severability of provisions. §1812.649.
Electronic devices with geophysical location tracking, monitoring and remote assistance technology; Proper use; Notice and consent requirements; Privacy of consumer's information; Exceptions. §1812.650.

§1812.620. Citation of title

This title shall be known and may be cited as the Karnette Rental-Purchase Act. **Leg.H.** Added Stats 1994 ch 1026 §1 (AB 722).

§1812.621. Legislative findings and declarations

The Legislature hereby finds and declares that consumers enter into rental-purchase contracts that do not adequately disclose the actual terms and cost of the transaction or the consumer's liability for certain breaches of the contract, and that contain unfair provisions, including unfair terms related to fees and charges, the exercise or the termination of purchase option rights, property loss and damage, and the repair or replacement of improperly functioning rental property.

It is, therefore, the intent of the Legislature in enacting this title to ensure that consumers are protected from misrepresentations and unfair dealings by ensuring that consumers are adequately informed of all relevant terms, including the cash price, periodic payments, total purchase price, and other applicable charges or fees, before they enter into rental-purchase contracts.

It is further the intent of the Legislature to (a) prohibit unfair or unconscionable conduct toward consumers in connection with rental-purchase transactions, (b) prohibit unfair contract terms, including unreasonable charges, (c) prevent the forfeiture of contract rights by consumers, (d) provide a right of reinstatement and a reasonable formula for the exercise of purchase option rights under a rental-purchase contract, (e) provide reasonable requirements for the servicing, repair, and replacement of improperly functioning rental property, and (f) cover rental-purchase transactions under existing laws, including laws governing debt collection, cosigners, home solicitation contracts, and warranties. This title shall be liberally construed to achieve its remedial objectives. **Leg.H.** Added Stats 1994 ch 1026 §1 (AB 722).

§1812.622. Definitions

As used in this title:

(a) "Advertisement" means a commercial message in any medium that directly or indirectly solicits or promotes one or more specific rental-purchase transactions, excluding instore merchandising aids. This definition does not limit or alter the application of other laws, including Chapter 5 (commencing with Section 17200) of Part 2 and Chapter 1 (commencing with Section 17500) of Part 3, of Division 7 of the Business and Professions Code, to rental-purchase transactions.

(b) "Consumer" means a natural person or persons who rent or lease personal property from a lessor pursuant to a rental-purchase agreement or to whom a lessor offers personal property for use pursuant to a rental-purchase agreement.

(c) "Lessor" means any person or entity that provides or offers to provide personal property for use by consumers pursuant to a rental-purchase agreement.

(d) "Rental-purchase agreement," except as otherwise provided in this subdivision, means an agreement between a lessor and a consumer pursuant to which the lessor rents or leases, for valuable consideration, personal property for use by a consumer for personal, family, or household purposes for an initial term not exceeding four months that may be renewed or otherwise extended, if under the terms of the agreement the consumer acquires an option or other legally enforceable right to become owner of the property. A rental-purchase agreement is a lease subject to Title 1.5 (commencing with Section 1750) and Title 1.7 (commencing with Section 1790).

"Rental-purchase agreement" shall not be construed to be, nor be governed by, and shall not apply to, any of the following:

(1) A retail installment sale, as defined in Section 1802.5.

(2) A retail installment contract, as defined in Section 1802.6.

(3) A retail installment account, as defined in Section 1802.7.

(4) A lease or agreement that constitutes a security interest, as defined in Section 1201 of the Commercial Code.

(5) A consumer credit contract, as defined in Section 1799.90.

(e) "Cash price" means the price of the personal property described in the rental-purchase agreement that the consumer may pay in cash to the lessor at the inception of the rental-purchase agreement to acquire ownership of that personal property.

(f) "Cost of rental" means the difference between the total of all periodic payments necessary to acquire ownership under the rental-purchase agreement and the cash price of the rental property that is subject to the rental-purchase agreement.

(g) "Fee" means any payment, charge, fee, cost, or expense, however denominated, other than a rental payment.

(h) "Appliance" means and includes any refrigerator, freezer, range including any cooktop or oven, microwave oven, washer, dryer, dishwasher, or room air-conditioner or air purifier.

(i) "Electronic set" means and includes any television, radio, camera, video game, or any type of device for the recording, storage, copying, printing, transmission, display, or playback of any sound or image, but does not include any item that is part of a computer system.

(j) "Computer system" means a computer processor and a video monitor, printer, and peripheral items primarily designed for use with a computer. Audio and video devices, which are commonly used for entertainment and into which data may be downloaded from a computer, are not part of a computer system.

(k) "Lessor's cost" means the documented actual cost, including actual freight charges, of the rental property to the lessor from a wholesaler, distributor, supplier, or manufacturer and net of any discounts, rebates, and incentives.

(*l*) "Total of payments" means the total amount of periodic payments necessary to acquire ownership of the property that is the subject of the rental-purchase agreement if the consumer makes all regularly scheduled payments.

(m) "Electronic device" means a desktop or laptop computer, handheld device, tablet, smartphone, or other electronic product or device that has a platform on which to download, install, or run any software program, code, script, or other content.

(n) "Geophysical location tracking technology" means hardware, software, or an application that collects and reports data or information that identifies the precise geophysical location of an item, including technologies that report the GPS coordinates of an electronic device, the WiFi signals available to or actually used by an electronic device to access the Internet, the telecommunication towers or connections available to or actually used by an electronic device, the processing of any reported data or information through geolocation lookup services, or any information derived from any combination of the foregoing.

(o) "Monitoring technology" means any hardware, software, or application utilized in conjunction with an electronic device that can cause the electronic device to capture, monitor, record, or report information about user activities with or without the user's knowledge.

(p) "Remote technical assistance" means collaborative access by the user and technician to connect to an electronic device for the purpose of providing technical support to the user.

(q) "Express consent" means the affirmative agreement to any use or installation of geophysical location tracking technology or remote technical assistance. Express consent does not include consent given when either option is highlighted or preselected as a default setting. **Leg.H.** Added Stats 1994 ch 1026 §1 (AB 722). Amended Stats 2006 ch 254 §2 (SB 1481), effective January 1, 2007, ch 410 §1 (AB 594), effective January 1, 2007; Stats 2014 ch 426 §1 (AB 2667), effective January 1, 2015.

2006 Note: On and after June 1, 2006 to December 31, 2006, inclusive, a lessor may comply with Sections 1812.622, 1812.623, 1812.624, 1812.632, and 1812.644 of the Civil Code as amended by this act in lieu of complying with those sections as they were in effect before the effective date of this act without incurring any liability for doing so. Stats 2006 ch 410 (AB 594) §6.

§1812.623. Contents of rental-purchase agreement

(a) Every rental-purchase agreement shall be contained in a single document which shall set forth all of the agreements of the lessor and the consumer with respect to the rights and obligations of each party. Every rental-purchase agreement shall be written in at least 10-point type in the same language as principally used in any oral sales presentation or negotiations leading to the execution of the agreement, and shall clearly and conspicuously disclose all of the following:

(1) The names of the lessor and the consumer, the lessor's business address and telephone number, the consumer's address, the date on which the agreement is executed, and a description of the property sufficient to identify it.

(2) Whether the property subject to the rental-purchase agreement is new or used. If the property is new, the lessor shall disclose the model year or, if the model year is not known by the lessor, the date of the lessor's acquisition of the property. If the property is used, the age or the model year shall be disclosed if known by the lessor.

(3) The minimum period for which the consumer is obligated under the rental-purchase agreement; the duration of the rental-purchase agreement if all regularly scheduled periodic payments are made, designated as the "rental period"; and the amount of each periodic payment.

(4) The total of payments and the total number of periodic payments necessary to acquire ownership of the property if the renter makes all regularly scheduled periodic payments.

(5) The cash price of the property subject to the rental purchase agreement.

(6) The cost of rental.

(7) The amount and purpose of any other payment or fee permitted by this title in addition to those specified pursuant to paragraphs (3) and (4), including any late payment fee.

(8) A statement that the total number and dollar amount of payments necessary to acquire ownership of the rental property disclosed under paragraph (4) does not include other fees permitted by this title, such as late payment fees, and that the consumer should read the rental-purchase agreement for an explanation of any applicable additional fees.

(9) Whether the consumer is liable for loss or damage to the rental property and, if so, the maximum amount for which the consumer may be liable as provided in subdivision (a) of Section 1812.627.

(10) The following notice:

NOTICE

You are renting this property. You will not own it until you make all of the regularly scheduled payments or you use the early purchase option.

You do not have the right to keep the property if you do not make required payments or do not use the early purchase option. If you miss a payment, the lessor can repossess the property, but, you may have the right to the return of the same or similar property.

See the contract for an explanation of your rights.

(11) A description of the consumer's right to acquire ownership of the property before the end of the rental period as provided in subdivisions (a) and (b) of Section 1812.632.

(12) A description of the consumer's reinstatement rights as provided in Section 1812.631.

(13) If warranty coverage is transferable to a consumer who acquires ownership of the property, a statement that the unexpired portion of all warranties provided by the manufacturer, distributor, or seller of the property that is the subject of the rental-purchase agreement will be transferred by the lessor to the consumer at the time the consumer acquires ownership of the property from the lessor.

(14) A description of the lessor's obligation to maintain the rental property and to repair or replace rental property that is not operating properly, as provided in Section 1812.633.

(b)(1) The disclosures required by paragraphs (3), (4), (5), and (6) of subdivision (a) shall be printed in at least 10-point boldface type or capital letters if typed and shall be grouped together in a box formed by a heavy line in the following form:

TOTAL OF PAYMENTS	COST OF RENTAL	CASH PRICE	
$	$ Amount over cash price you will pay if you make all regular payments.	$ Property available at this price for cash from the lessor. See about your early purchase option rights.	
You must pay this amount to own the property if you make all the regular payments. You can buy the property for less under the early purchase option.	AMOUNT OF EACH PAYMENT $ per _____ (insert period)	NUMBER OF PAYMENTS	RENTAL PERIOD

(2) The box described in paragraph (1) shall appear immediately above the space reserved for the buyer's signature.

(c) The disclosures required by paragraphs (3), (4), (5), and (6) of subdivision (a) shall be grouped together in a box formed by a heavy line in the form prescribed in subdivision (b) and shall be clearly and conspicuously placed on a tag or sticker affixed to the property available for rental-purchase. If the property available for rental-purchase is not displayed at the lessor's place of business but appears in a photograph or catalog shown to consumers, a tag or sticker shall be affixed to the photograph of the property or catalog shown to consumers or shall be given to consumers. The disclosure required by paragraph (2) of subdivision (a) also shall be clearly and conspicuously placed on the tag or sticker.

(d) All disclosures required by this section shall be printed or typed in a color or shade that clearly contrasts with the background. **Leg.H.** Added Stats 1994 ch 1026 §1. Amended Stats 1997 ch 112 §2 (SB 338); Stats 2006 ch 410 §2 (AB 594), effective January 1, 2007.

2006 Note: On and after June 1, 2006 to December 31, 2006, inclusive, a lessor may comply with Sections 1812.622, 1812.623, 1812.624, 1812.632, and 1812.644 of the Civil Code as amended by this act in lieu of complying with those sections as they were in effect before the effective date of this act without incurring any liability for doing so. Stats 2006 ch 410 §6.

§1812.624. Prohibited provisions

(a) No rental-purchase agreement or any document that the lessor requests the consumer to sign shall contain any provision by which:

(1) A power of attorney is given to confess judgment in this state or to appoint the lessor, its agents, or its successors in interest as the consumer's agent in the collection of payments or the repossession of the rental property.

(2) The consumer authorizes the lessor or its agent to commit any breach of the peace in repossessing the rental property or to enter the consumer's dwelling or other premises without obtaining the consumer's consent at the time of entry.

(3) The consumer agrees to purchase from the lessor insurance or a liability waiver against loss or damage to the rental property.

(4) The consumer waives or agrees to waive any defense, counterclaim, or right the consumer may have against the lessor, its agent, or its successor in interest.

(5) The consumer is required to pay any fee in connection with reinstatement except as provided in Section 1812.631.

(6) The consumer is required to pay a fee in connection with the pickup of the property or the termination or rescission of the rental-purchase agreement.

(7) The consumer is required to pay any fee permitted by the rental-purchase agreement and this title that is not reasonable and actually incurred by the lessor. The lessor has the burden of proof to establish that a fee was reasonable and was an actual cost incurred by the lessor.

(8) The consumer is required to pay a downpayment, more than one advance periodic rental payment, or any other payment except a security deposit permitted under Section 1812.625.

(9) Except to the extent permitted by subdivision (b) of Section 1812.627, the consumer waives any rights under Sections 1928 or 1929.

(10) The consumer grants a security interest in any property.

(11) The consumer's liability for loss or damage to the property which is the subject of the rental-purchase agreement may exceed the maximum described in subdivision (a) of Section 1812.627.

(12) Except under the circumstances authorized by subdivision (a) or (b) of Section 1812.632, the consumer is obligated to make any balloon payment. A "balloon payment" is any payment for the purchase or use of the rental property which is more than the regularly scheduled periodic payment amount.

(13) The consumer is required to pay a late payment fee that is not permitted under Section 1812.626.

(14) The consumer is required to pay both a late payment fee and a fee for the lessor's collection of a past due payment at the consumer's home or other location.

(15) The consumer waives or offers to waive any right or remedy against the lessor, its agents, or its successors in interest for any violation of this title or any other illegal act. This subdivision does not apply to a document executed in connection with the bona fide settlement, compromise, or release of a specific disputed claim.

(16) The lessor, its agents, or its successors in interest may commence any judicial action against the consumer in a county other than the county in which (A) the rental-purchase agreement was signed or (B) the consumer resides at the time the action is commenced.

(17) The amount stated as the cash price for any item of personal property exceeds the cash price permitted under Section 1812.644.

(18) The total of payments exceeds the amount permitted under Section 1812.644.

(b) Any provision in a rental-purchase agreement that is prohibited by this title shall be void and unenforceable and a violation of this title. A rental-purchase agreement which contains any provision that is prohibited by this title is voidable by the consumer. **Leg.H.** Added Stats 1994 ch 1026 §1 (AB 722). Amended Stats 2006 ch 410 §3 (AB 594), effective January 1, 2007.

2006 Note: On and after June 1, 2006 to December 31, 2006, inclusive, a lessor may comply with Sections 1812.622, 1812.623, 1812.624, 1812.632, and 1812.644 of the Civil Code as amended by this act in lieu of complying with those sections as they were in effect before the effective date of this act without incurring any liability for doing so. Stats 2006 ch 410 (AB 594) §6.

§1812.625. Security deposit

(a) The lessor may require the consumer to pay a security deposit, however denominated, in an amount not to exceed the equivalent of one month's rental only for the purpose of satisfying any lawful claim by the lessor, up to the maximum described in subdivision (a) of Section 1812.627, for those amounts reasonably necessary to pay for the loss of the property or the repair of damage, exclusive of reasonable wear and tear.

(b) Within two weeks after the lessor has taken possession of the property from the consumer, the lessor shall deliver to the consumer the amount of the security deposit less the amount, if any, deducted for loss or repair as permitted by this title. If any amount is deducted, the lessor shall also deliver to the consumer at that time a copy of an itemized statement indicating the amount of the security deposit, the amount deducted for loss or repair, and a detailed statement of the basis for the deduction. Delivery may be made by personal delivery or by first-class mail, postage prepaid. **Leg.H.** Added Stats 1994 ch 1026 §1 (AB 722).

§1812.626. Late payment fee

(a) The lessor may assess a late payment fee if the late payment fee is specified in the rental-purchase agreement and is permitted by this section.

(b) No fee shall be assessed for a payment which is less than three days late if the rental-purchase agreement specifies weekly periodic payments.

(c) No fee shall be assessed for a payment which is less than 7 days late if the rental-purchase agreement specifies longer than weekly periodic payments.

(d) The lessor may assess more than one late fee for a particular late payment if the total of all fees assessed for that late payment does not exceed the maximum provided in subdivision (e). If the maximum total late payment fee has been imposed for a particular payment, no additional late payment fee may be imposed for that payment.

(e) The total of all fees for a late payment shall not exceed the lesser of 5 percent of the payment or five dollars ($5), except that a minimum total fee of two dollars ($2) may be required. **Leg.H.** Added Stats 1994 ch 1026 §1 (AB 722).

§1812.627. Liability for loss or damage to property

(a) The consumer's liability for loss or damage to the property which is the subject of the rental-purchase agreement shall in no event exceed the lesser of (1) the fair market value at the time of the loss or damage or (2) the amount that would be necessary for the renter to exercise the purchase option provided in subdivision (a) of Section 1812.632.

(b) A lessor and a consumer may agree that the consumer may be liable for loss only up to the maximum amount described in subdivision (a) and only for one of the following:

(1) Loss caused by the consumer's negligent, reckless, or intentional acts.

(2) Loss caused by the theft of the property subject to the rental-purchase agreement unless one of the following is applicable:

(A) There is evidence of a burglary of the premises in which the property is located, such as physical evidence or an official report filed by the consumer with the police or other law enforcement agency.

(B) The consumer establishes by the preponderance of the evidence that the consumer has not committed or aided or abetted in the commission of the theft of the property. **Leg.H.** Added Stats 1994 ch 1026 §1 (AB 722).

§1812.628. Agreement deemed home solicitation contract or offer

(a) In addition to the circumstances described in subdivision (a) of Section 1689.5, a rental-purchase agreement regardless of the amount involved shall be deemed a home solicitation contract or offer if the rental-purchase agreement has an initial term that exceeds one week and was made at other than appropriate trade premises, as defined in subdivision (b) of Section 1689.5.

(b) In addition to any other right of cancellation, a consumer has the right to cancel a rental-purchase agreement, without penalty or obligation if the consumer has not taken possession of the property. **Leg.H.** Added Stats 1994 ch 1026 §1 (AB 722).

§1812.629. Information and copies of documents to consumer

(a) Upon the request of the consumer, the lessor shall provide the information as required by subdivision (b) of Section 1812.623 in an exemplar of the rental-purchase agreement covering the property specified by the consumer and shall provide the consumer with a copy of the proposed rental-purchase agreement prior to its execution. The consumer may take this copy from the lessor's premises.

(b) The lessor shall not obtain the consumer's signature to a rental-purchase agreement if it contains blank spaces to be filled in after it has been signed.

(c) A copy of the fully completed rental-purchase agreement and all other documents which the lessor requests the consumer to sign shall be given to the consumer at the time they are signed. The rental-purchase agreement shall not be enforceable against the consumer until the consumer has received a signed copy.

(d) The lessor shall deliver to the consumer a written receipt for each payment made by the consumer. **Leg.H.** Added Stats 1994 ch 1026 §1 (AB 722).

§1812.630. Advertisements

(a)(1) Any advertisement of a rental-purchase agreement that states the amount of any payment shall clearly and conspicuously disclose all of the following in the same language used in the advertisement:

(A) That the agreement advertised is a rental-purchase agreement.

(B) That the property is used if that is the case.

(C) That ownership is not acquired until all of the payments necessary to acquire ownership have been made.

(D) The total amount and number of periodic payments necessary to acquire ownership.

(2) If more than one item is advertised in one print advertisement, the lessor may comply with paragraph (1) by clearly and conspicuously including in the advertisement a table or schedule sufficient in detail to permit determination of the total amount and number of periodic payments necessary to acquire ownership of the items advertised having the highest and lowest total amount of periodic payments necessary to acquire ownership.

(b) A lessor who advertises "no credit check" or otherwise states or implies that no inquiry will be made of a consumer's credit history or creditworthiness shall not (1) make any inquiry or request a consumer to complete any document concerning the consumer's assets or credit history, (2) obtain a consumer credit report as defined in subdivision (c) of Section 1785.3, or (3) obtain an investigative consumer report as defined in subdivision (c) of Section 1786.2. **Leg.H.** Added Stats 1994 ch 1026 §1 (AB 722).

§1812.631. Default by consumer

(a) A consumer may be deemed in default under the rental-purchase agreement if either of the following applies:

(1) The rental-purchase agreement requires weekly periodic rental payments and the consumer has not made a payment by the end of the seventh day after its due date.

(2) The rental-purchase agreement requires rental payments in periodic intervals longer than one week and the consumer has not made a payment by the end of the 10th day after its due date.

(b) A consumer who is in default under a rental-purchase agreement requiring weekly periodic rental payments may reinstate the rental-purchase agreement, without losing any rights or options under that agreement, by paying all past due payments including late payment fees, by the end of the seventh day after the due date of the payment in default if the consumer retains possession of the property and within one year after the due date of the payment in default if the consumer returns or tenders the property to the lessor, unless the lessor permits the consumer to retain the property during this period.

(c) A consumer who is in default under a rental-purchase agreement requiring rental payments in periodic intervals longer than one week may reinstate the rental-purchase agreement, without losing any rights or options under that agreement, by paying all past due payments, including late payment fees, by the end of the 10th day after the due date of the payment in default if the consumer retains possession of the property and within one year after the due date of the payment in default if the consumer returns or tenders the property to the lessor, unless the lessor permits the consumer to retain the property during this period.

(d) Upon reinstatement, the lessor shall provide the consumer with the same rental property, if available, or substitute property of the same brand, if available, and comparable quality, age, condition, and warranty coverage. If substitute property is provided, the lessor shall provide the lessee with the disclosures required in paragraph (2) of subdivision (a) of Section 1812.623.

(e)(1) Except as provided in paragraph (2), a lessor shall not deny a consumer the right of reinstatement provided in this section.

(2) This section does not apply to a consumer who has (A) stolen or unlawfully disposed of the property, (B) damaged the property as the result of the consumer's intentional, willful, wanton, or reckless conduct,

or (C) defaulted in making payments as described in subdivision (a) on three consecutive occasions.

(3) If the lessor denies a consumer the right to reinstate pursuant to paragraph (2), the lessor has the burden of proof to establish that the denial was in good faith and was permitted under paragraph (2).

(f) Nothing in this subdivision prohibits the lessor from contacting the consumer provided that the lessor does not violate Section 1812.638. **Leg.H.** Added Stats 1994 ch 1026 §1 (AB 722).

§1812.632. Right to acquire ownership of property

(a)(1) The consumer has the right to acquire ownership of the property within three months of the date on which the consumer executed the rental-purchase agreement by tendering to the lessor an amount equal to the cash price and any past due fees less all periodic payments that the consumer has paid.

(2) Within 10 days after the consumer executes the rental purchase agreement, the lessor shall personally deliver or send by first-class mail to the consumer a notice informing the consumer of the right described in paragraph (1), including the amount the consumer must pay to acquire ownership and the date by which payment must be made. The statement shall not be accompanied by any other written information including solicitations for other rental-purchase agreements.

(b) After the expiration of the three-month period following the execution of the rental-purchase agreement, the consumer has the right to acquire ownership of the property at any time by tendering to the lessor all past due payments and fees and an amount equal to the cash price stated in the rental-purchase agreement multiplied by a fraction that has as its numerator the number of periodic payments remaining under the agreement and that has as its denominator the total number of periodic payments.

(c)(1) The lessor shall, in connection with a consumer's rights under subdivision (b), provide the consumer with a written statement in the manner set forth in paragraph (2) below that clearly states (A) the total amount the consumer would have to pay to acquire ownership of the rental property if the consumer makes all regularly scheduled payments remaining under the rental-purchase agreement and (B) the total amount the consumer would have to pay to acquire ownership of that property pursuant to subdivision (a).

(2) The statement required by paragraph (1) shall be personally delivered or sent by first-class mail to the consumer within seven days after (A) the date the consumer requests information about the amount required to purchase the rental property and (B) the date the consumer has made one-half of the total number of periodic payments required to acquire ownership of the rental property. The statement shall not be accompanied by any other written information including solicitations for other rental-purchase agreements.

(d)(1) Subject to paragraph (2), if any consumer who has signed the rental-purchase agreement has experienced an interruption or reduction of 25 percent or more of income due to involuntary job loss, involuntary reduced employment, illness, pregnancy, or disability after one-half or more of the total amount of the periodic payments necessary to acquire ownership under the agreement has been paid, the lessor shall reduce the amount of each periodic rental payment by (A) the percentage of the reduction in the consumer's income or (B) 50 percent, whichever is less, for the period during which the consumer's income is interrupted or reduced. If payments are reduced, the total dollar amount of payments necessary to acquire ownership shall not be increased, and the rights and duties of the lessor and the consumer shall not otherwise be affected. When the consumer's income is restored, the lessor may increase the amount of rental payments, but in no event shall rental payments exceed the originally scheduled amount of rental payments.

(2) Paragraph (1) applies only after the consumer provides to the lessor some evidence of the amount and cause of the interruption or reduction of income. **Leg.H.** Added Stats 1994 ch 1026 §1 (AB 722). Amended Stats 2006 ch 410 §4 (AB 594), effective January 1, 2007.

2006 Note: On and after June 1, 2006 to December 31, 2006, inclusive, a lessor may comply with Sections 1812.622, 1812.623, 1812.624, 1812.632, and 1812.644 of the Civil Code as amended by this act in lieu of complying with those sections as they were in effect before the effective date of this act without incurring any liability for doing so. Stats 2006 ch 410 §6.

§1812.633. Maintenance of property by lessor

(a) The lessor shall maintain the property subject to the rental-purchase agreement in good working order while the agreement is in effect without charging any fee to the consumer in addition to the regularly scheduled rental payments set forth in the rental-purchase agreement.

(b) By the end of the second business day following the day on which the lessor received notice from the consumer that the property is not operating properly, the lessor shall repair or replace the property without any fee to the consumer in addition to the regularly scheduled rental payments set forth in the rental-purchase agreement.

(c) If a repair or replacement cannot be immediately effected, the lessor shall temporarily substitute property of comparable quality and condition while repairs are being effected. If repairs cannot be completed to the reasonable satisfaction of the consumer within 30 days after the lessor receives notice from the consumer or within a longer period voluntarily agreed to by the consumer, the lessor shall permanently replace the property.

(d) All replacement property shall be the same brand, if available, and comparable in quality, age, condition, and warranty coverage to the replaced property. If the same brand is not available, the brand of the replacement property shall be agreeable to the consumer.

(e) All of the consumer's and lessor's rights and obligations under the rental-purchase agreement and this title that applied to the property originally subject to the rental-purchase agreement shall apply to any replacement property.

(f) The consumer shall not be charged, or held liable for, any rental fee for any period of time during which the property that is the subject of the rental-purchase agreement or any property substituted for it pursuant to this section is not in good working order.

(g) This section does not apply to the repair of damage resulting from the consumer's intentional, willful, wanton, reckless, or negligent conduct. If the lessor does not comply with this section because of this subdivision, the lessor has the burden of proof to establish that noncompliance was justified and in good faith.

(h) A lessor shall not deliver to a consumer any property which the lessor knows or has reason to know is defective. **Leg.H.** Added Stats 1994 ch 1026 §1 (AB 722).

§1812.634. Transfer of warranties

When the lessor transfers ownership of the rental property, the lessor shall also transfer to the consumer the unexpired portion of any transferable warranties provided by the manufacturer, distributor, or seller of the rental property, and these warranties shall apply as if the consumer were the original purchaser of the goods. **Leg.H.** Added Stats 1994 ch 1026 §1 (AB 722).

§1812.635. Service contracts

(a) A lessor shall not sell, or offer for sale, a service contract for the rental property if that service contract provides any coverage while the rental-purchase agreement is in effect.

(b) A lessor may sell, or offer for sale, a service contract providing coverage for the rental property after the consumer acquires ownership of that property, if both of the following conditions are satisfied:

(1) The lessor does not sell, or offer to sell, the service contract before (A) the consumer pays at least one-half of the total number of periodic payments necessary to acquire ownership of the property or (B) the consumer acquires ownership of the property, as provided in Section 1812.632, whichever occurs first.

(2) The lessor clearly and conspicuously indicates to the consumer in writing before the consumer's purchase of the service contract that the purchase is optional.

(c) If the consumer chooses to purchase a service contract before the expiration of the rental-purchase agreement and defaults or otherwise does not make all payments necessary to acquire ownership within the rental period specified in the agreement, the lessor shall refund all consideration paid for the service contract to the consumer within two weeks after the lessor has received the consumer's last rental payment. This subdivision does not limit or alter any of the consumer's cancellation or refund rights under the service contract or under other provisions of law.

(d) "Service contract" has the meaning set forth in subdivision (o) of Section 1791. **Leg.H.** Added Stats 1994 ch 1026 §1 (AB 722).

§1812.636. Damages for violation of provisions

(a) A consumer damaged by a violation of this title by a lessor is entitled to recover all of the following:

(1) Actual damages.

(2) Twenty-five percent of an amount equal to the total amount of payments required to obtain ownership if all payments were made under the rental-purchase agreement, but not less than one hundred dollars ($100) nor more than one thousand dollars ($1,000).

(3) The consumer's reasonable attorney's fees and court costs.

(4) Exemplary damages, in the amount the court deems proper, for intentional or willful violations of this title.

(5) Equitable relief as the court deems proper.

(b) Where more than one consumer is a party to a rental-purchase agreement, the limitations of subdivision (a) shall apply to all those consumers in the aggregate, and no more than one recovery shall be permitted for each violation. **Leg.H.** Added Stats 1994 ch 1026 §1 (AB 722).

§1812.637. Written notice of error by lessor

(a) A lessor is not liable for a violation of this title if, before the 30th calendar day after the date the lessor discovers a bona fide error and before an action under this title is filed or written notice of the error is received by the lessor from the consumer, the lessor gives the consumer written notice of the error. "Bona fide error," as used in this section, means a violation that was not intentional and resulted from a bona fide error notwithstanding the maintenance of procedures reasonably adapted to avoid that error. Examples of a bona fide error include clerical errors, calculation errors, errors due to unintentionally improper computer programming or data entry, and printing errors, but does not include an error of legal judgment with respect to a lessor's obligations under this title.

(b) Notwithstanding subdivision (a), if the lessor notifies the consumer of a bona fide error the correction of which would increase the amount of any payment, the lessor may not collect the amount of the increase, and the consumer may enforce the rental-purchase agreement as initially written.

(c) Notwithstanding subdivision (a), if the lessor notifies the consumer of a bona fide error the correction of which would lower the amount of any payment, the lessor shall immediately refund to the consumer the difference between what the consumer paid and what the consumer should have paid if the agreement were correct at the inception of the transaction. **Leg.H.** Added Stats 1994 ch 1026 §1 (AB 722).

§1812.638. Collection of payment or repossession of property

(a) A lessor shall not engage in any unfair, unlawful, or deceptive conduct, or make any untrue or misleading statement in connection with the collection of any payment owed by a consumer or the repossession of any property or attempt to collect or collect any payment in a manner that would be unlawful to collect a debt pursuant to Title 1.6C (commencing with Section 1788).

(b) All of the following apply to any communication by a lessor with any person other than the consumer for the purpose of acquiring information about the location of a consumer or of any rental property:

(1) The lessor shall identify itself and state that the lessor is confirming or correcting location information concerning the consumer.

(2) The lessor shall not communicate with any person more than once unless requested to do so by the person or unless the lessor reasonably believes that the earlier response is erroneous or incomplete and that the person now has correct or complete location information.

(3) The lessor shall not communicate by postcard.

(4) The lessor shall not use any language or symbol on any envelope or in the contents of any communication that indicates that the communication relates to the collection of any payment or the recovery or repossession of rental property.

(5) The lessor shall not communicate with any person other than the consumer's attorney, after the lessor knows the consumer is represented by an attorney with regard to the rental-purchase agreement and has knowledge of, or can readily ascertain, the attorney's name and address, unless the attorney fails to respond within a reasonable period of time to communication from the lessor or unless the attorney consents to direct communication with the consumer.

(c) Without the prior consent of the consumer given directly to the lessor or the express permission of a court of competent jurisdiction, a lessor shall not communicate with a consumer in connection with the collection of any payment or the recovery or repossession of rental property at any of the following:

(1) The consumer's place of employment.

(2) Any unusual time or place or a time or place known or that should be known to be inconvenient to the consumer. In the absence of knowledge of circumstances to the contrary, a lessor shall assume that the convenient time for communicating with a consumer is after 8 a.m. and before 9 p.m., local time at the consumer's location.

(d) A lessor shall not communicate, in connection with the rental-purchase agreement, with any person other than the consumer, the consumer's attorney, or the lessor's attorney, except to the extent the communication is any of the following:

(1) Reasonably necessary to acquire location information concerning the consumer or the rental property, as provided in subdivision (b).

(2) Upon the prior consent of the consumer given directly to the lessor.

(3) Upon the express permission of a court of competent jurisdiction.

(4) Reasonably necessary to effectuate a postjudgment judicial remedy.

(e) If a consumer notifies the lessor in writing that the consumer wishes the lessor to cease further communication with the consumer, the lessor shall not communicate further with the consumer with respect to the rental-purchase agreement, except for any of the following:

(1) To advise the consumer that the lessor's further efforts are being terminated.

(2) To notify the consumer that the lessor may invoke specified remedies allowable by law which are ordinarily invoked by the lessor.

(3) Where necessary to effectuate any postjudgment remedy.

(f) A lessor shall not harass, oppress, or abuse any person in connection with a rental-purchase agreement, including engaging in any of the following conduct:

(1) Using or threatening the use of violence or any criminal means to harm the physical person, reputation, or property of any person.

(2) Using obscene, profane, or abusive language.

(3) Causing a telephone to ring, or engaging any person in telephone conversation repeatedly or continuously with intent to annoy, abuse, or harass any person.

(4) Placing telephone calls without disclosure of the caller's identity.
Leg.H. Added Stats 1994 ch 1026 §1 (AB 722).

§1812.639. Unfair or illegal conduct; Misleading statements

A lessor shall not engage in any unfair, unlawful, or deceptive conduct or make any untrue or misleading statement in connection with a rental-purchase agreement, including any violation of this title. **Leg.H.** Added Stats 1994 ch 1026 §1 (AB 722).

§1812.640. Report to credit agency

A lessor shall not report any late payment, default, or repossession to a consumer credit reporting agency, as defined in subdivision (d) of Section 1785.3, or to an investigative consumer reporting agency, as defined in subdivision (d) of Section 1786.2 if the lessor (a) advertises "no credit check" or otherwise states or implies that no inquiry will be made of a consumer's credit history or creditworthiness or (b) does not obtain a consumer credit report or investigative consumer report on a consumer before entering into a rental-purchase agreement with that consumer. **Leg.H.** Added Stats 1994 ch 1026 §1 (AB 722).

§1812.641. Solicitation or promotional material to person used as reference

(a) A lessor shall not send any solicitation or other promotional material to a person identified by the consumer as a reference to verify the consumer's income, assets, credit history, or residence unless all of the following occur:

(1) The lessor clearly discloses in the rental-purchase agreement or application that (A) the lessor may send solicitations or other promotional material to references provided by the consumer unless the consumer objects and (B) the consumer has the right to object without incurring any additional rental charge or fee or any loss of contractual rights.

(2) A space on the rental-purchase agreement or application adjacent to the disclosure described in paragraph (1) is provided for the consumer to indicate the consumer's approval or disapproval of the lessor's sending solicitations or other promotional material.

(3) The consumer affirmatively indicates approval.

(4) The lessor does not vary any term required to be disclosed pursuant to Section 1812.623 depending on whether the consumer approves or disapproves of the lessor's sending of solicitations or other promotional material to references.

(b) The first solicitation or other promotional material directed to a person whom the consumer has identified as a reference shall clearly offer the reference the opportunity, without cost, to instruct the lessor to refrain from sending further solicitations or other promotional material to the reference. If so instructed, the lessor shall not send any further solicitations or other promotional material to the reference and shall remove the reference's name and address from the lessor's mailing list.

(c) This section shall not apply to solicitations or other promotional material sent generally to people solely on the basis of demographic, geographic, or postal zip code criteria and without regard to whether the people have been identified as references by consumers. **Leg.H.** Added Stats 1994 ch 1026 §1 (AB 722).

§1812.642. Discrimination against consumer

A lessor shall not discriminate against a prospective consumer on any ground that would be a prohibited basis for a creditor to discriminate against an applicant for credit as provided in the Equal Credit Opportunity Act (15 U.S.C. Sec. 1691 et seq.) and Regulation B (12 C.F.R. Part 202) as if they applied to a rental-purchase agreement. Nothing in this section shall be construed in any manner to mean that a rental-purchase agreement is a credit transaction. **Leg.H.** Added Stats 1994 ch 1026 §1 (AB 722).

§1812.643. Notice

(a) Except as provided in subdivision (b), a lessor who obtains the signature of more than one person on a rental-purchase agreement shall deliver the notice set forth in subdivision (c) to each person before that person signs the agreement.

(b) This section does not apply if the persons signing the agreement are married to each other or in fact receive possession of the property described in the agreement.

(c) The notice required by this section is as follows:

"NOTICE TO COSIGNER

If you sign this contract, you will have the same responsibility for the property and the same obligation to make payments that every renter has.

If any renter does not pay, you may have to pay the full amount owed, including late fees, and you may have to pay for certain loss or damage to the property.

The lessor may collect from you without first trying to collect from any other renter. The lessor can use the same collection methods against you that can be used against any renter, such as suing you or garnishing your wages.

This notice is not the contract that makes you responsible.

Before you sign, be sure you can afford to pay if you have to, and that you want to accept this responsibility."

(d) The notice required by subdivision (c) shall be printed in at least 10-point boldface type in English and Spanish. If the rental-purchase agreement is required to be written in a language other than English or Spanish, the notice shall be written in English and, in addition or in lieu of Spanish, in that other language.

(e) If the notice set forth in subdivision (c) is included with the text of the rental-purchase agreement, the notice shall appear immediately above or adjacent to the disclosures required by subdivision (b) of Section 1812.623. If the notice is not included with the text of the agreement, the notice shall be on a separate sheet which shall not contain any other text except as is necessary to identify the lessor and agreement to which the notice refers and to provide for the date and the person's acknowledgment of receipt.

(f) The lessor shall give each person entitled to notice under this section a copy of the completed rental-purchase agreement before obtaining that person's signature.

(g) If a person entitled to receive notice and a copy of the rental-purchase agreement under this section does not receive the notice or agreement in the manner required, that person has no liability in connection with the rental-purchase transaction. **Leg.H.** Added Stats 1994 ch 1026 §1 (AB 722).

§1812.644. Total of payments; Cash price

(a) A lessor shall maintain records that establish the lessor's cost, as defined in subdivision (k) of Section 1812.622, for each item of personal property that is the subject of the rental-purchase agreement. A copy of each rental-purchase agreement and of the records required by this subdivision shall be maintained for two years following the termination of the agreement.

(b) The maximum cash price for the lessor's first rental of the property that is the subject of the rental-purchase agreement may not exceed 1.65 times the lessor's cost for computer systems and appliances, 1.7 times the lessor's cost for electronic sets, 1.9 times the lessor's cost for automotive accessories, furniture, jewelry, and musical instruments, and 1.65 times the lessor's cost for all other items.

(c) The maximum total of payments may not exceed 2.25 times the maximum cash price that could have been charged for the first rental of the property under subdivision (b).

(d) The maximum total of payments for the lessor's second and subsequent rental of the property that is the subject of the rental-purchase agreement may not exceed the maximum total of payments permitted under subdivision (c) for the first rental of that property less (1) for appliances and electronic sets, one-third the amount of all rental payments paid to the lessor by consumers who previously rented that property or (2) for furniture, computer systems, and all other items, one-half the amount of all rental payments paid to the lessor by consumers who previously rented that property.

(e) The maximum cash price for property on its second or subsequent rental may not exceed the maximum total of payments for that property as permitted under subdivision (d) divided by 2.25.

(f) Upon the written request of the Attorney General, any district attorney or city attorney, or the Director of the Department of Consumer Affairs, a lessor shall provide copies of the records described in this section.

(g) If a lessor willfully discloses a cash price or a total of payments that exceeds the amount permitted by this section, the rental-purchase agreement is void, the consumer shall retain the property without any obligation, and the lessor shall refund to the consumer all amounts paid. **Leg.H.** Added Stats 1994 ch 1026 §1 (AB 722). Amended Stats 2006 ch 410 §5 (AB 594), effective January 1, 2007.

2006 Note: On and after June 1, 2006 to December 31, 2006, inclusive, a lessor may comply with Sections 1812.622, 1812.623, 1812.624, 1812.632, and 1812.644 of the Civil Code as amended by this act in lieu of complying with those sections as they were in effect before the effective date of this act without incurring any liability for doing so. Stats 2006 ch 410 §6.

§1812.645. Venue

An action on a rental-purchase agreement shall be tried in the county in which the rental-purchase agreement was signed or the consumer resides at the time the action is commenced. **Leg.H.** Added Stats 1994 ch 1026 §1 (AB 722).

§1812.646. Waiver or modification

Any waiver or modification of the provisions of this title by the consumer or lessor shall be void and unenforceable as contrary to public policy. **Leg.H.** Added Stats 1994 ch 1026 §1 (AB 722).

§1812.647. Violations; Misdemeanor

Any person who willfully violates any provision of this title is guilty of a misdemeanor. **Leg.H.** Added Stats 1994 ch 1026 §1 (AB 722).

§1812.648. Cumulative remedies

The rights, remedies, and penalties established by this title are cumulative to the rights, remedies, or penalties established under other laws. **Leg.H.** Added Stats 1994 ch 1026 §1 (AB 722).

§1812.649. Severability of provisions

If any provision of this title or the application thereof to any person or circumstances is held invalid, that invalidity shall not affect other provisions or applications of the title that can be given effect without the invalid provision or application, and to this end the provisions of this title are severable. **Leg.H.** Added Stats 1994 ch 1026 §1 (AB 722).

§1812.650. Electronic devices with geophysical location tracking, monitoring and remote assistance technology; Proper use; Notice and consent requirements; Privacy of consumer's information; Exceptions

(a) A lessor shall provide clear and prominent notice to a consumer and obtain express consent from the consumer at the time the lessor and consumer enter into a rental-purchase agreement for an electronic device if that device has geophysical location tracking technology installed by the lessor, and at any time the geophysical location tracking technology is activated or used by the lessor.

(b) For purposes of this section, "clear and prominent notice" means notice presented in an understandable language and syntax, in the predominantly used language for that communication, and that:

(1) In textual communications, the required disclosures are separate and apart from a privacy policy, data use policy, terms of service, end-user license agreement, lease agreement, or other similar document, and of a type, size, and location sufficiently noticeable for an ordinary consumer to read and comprehend in print that contrasts highly with the background on which they appear.

(2) In communications disseminated orally or through audible means, the required disclosures are unavoidable and delivered in a volume and cadence sufficient for an ordinary consumer to hear and comprehend.

(3) In communications disseminated through video means, the required disclosures are in writing in a form consistent with paragraph (1) and appear on the screen for a duration sufficient for an ordinary consumer to read and comprehend them.

(4) In communications made through interactive media, including the Internet, online services, and software, the required disclosures are unavoidable and presented in a form consistent with paragraph (1), in addition to any audio or video presentation.

(c) A lessor shall not use, sell, or share geophysical location tracking technology on an electronic device for any purpose other than the repossession of the electronic device when there is a violation of the rental-purchase agreement, pursuant to law, or when requested by the consumer.

(d) Clear and prominent notification shall be displayed on an electronic device if geophysical location tracking technology is activated or used by the lessor. This notification requirement shall be suspended if the consumer or lessor reports that the electronic device has been stolen and has filed a police report stating that the electronic device has been stolen. For purposes of this subdivision, "filing a police report" means the filing of a consumer's or lessor's complaint with the police department in any form recognized by that jurisdiction.

(e) A lessor shall provide that any geophysical location tracking technology that has been installed by the lessor on an electronic device, or can be activated by the lessor, expires upon the first instance the electronic device connects to the Internet after completion of the purchase of the electronic device.

(f) A lessor shall not use or install monitoring technology on an electronic device for any purpose other than to provide remote technical assistance when requested by the consumer.

(g) A lessor shall provide clear and prominent notice to a consumer and obtain express consent from the consumer for the installation or use of any software that allows the lessor to provide remote technical assistance and upon the activation and deactivation of any remote technical assistance when requested by the consumer.

(h) A lessor shall not acquire any data when providing remote technical assistance beyond what is necessary to provide assistance to the user and beyond what the user has consented to. Any data acquired during the period of consumer consented technical assistance shall not be retained, used, or sold for any purpose.

(i) This section shall not be interpreted to require a lessor to enter into a rental-purchase agreement with any consumer who does not provide express consent to the above-described provisions of the rental-purchase agreement. **Leg.H.** Added Stats 2014 ch 426 §2 (AB 2667), effective January 1, 2015.

TITLE 2.97
CONSUMER COLLECTION NOTICE

Description of debtor rights; Language other than English. §1812.700.
When notice may be changed; Type size in disclosure. §1812.701.
Violations. §1812.702.

§1812.700. Description of debtor rights; Language other than English

(a) In addition to the requirements imposed by Article 2 (commencing with Section 1788.10) of Title 1.6C, third-party debt collectors subject to the federal Fair Debt Collection Practices Act (15 U.S.C. Sec. 1692 et seq.), shall provide a notice to debtors that shall include the following description of debtor rights:

"The state Rosenthal Fair Debt Collection Practices Act and the federal Fair Debt Collection Practices Act require that, except under unusual circumstances, collectors may not contact you before 8 a.m. or after 9 p.m. They may not harass you by using threats of violence or arrest or by using obscene language. Collectors may not use false or misleading statements or call you at work if they know or have reason to know that you may not receive personal calls at work. For the most part, collectors may not tell another person, other than your attorney or spouse, about your debt. Collectors may contact another person to confirm your location or enforce a judgment. For more information about debt collection activities, you may contact the Federal Trade Commission at 1-877-FTC-HELP or www.ftc.gov."

(b) The notice shall be included with the first written notice initially addressed to a California address of a debtor in connection with collecting the debt by the third-party debt collector.

(c) If a language other than English is principally used by the third-party debt collector in the initial oral contact with the debtor, a notice shall be provided to the debtor in that language within five working days. **Leg.H.** Added Stats 2003 ch 259 §1 (SB 1022), operative July 1, 2004.

§1812.701. When notice may be changed; Type size in disclosure

(a) The notice required in this title may be changed only as necessary to reflect changes under the federal Fair Debt Collection Practices Act (15 U.S.C. Sec. 1692 et seq.) that would otherwise make the disclosure inaccurate.

(b) The type-size used in the disclosure shall be at least the same type-size as that used to inform the debtor of his or her specific debt, but is not required to be larger than 12-point type. **Leg.H.** Added Stats 2003 ch 259 §1 (SB 1022), operative July 1, 2004. Amended Stats 2004 ch 183 §37 (AB 3082).

§1812.702. Violations

Any violation of this act shall be considered a violation of the Rosenthal Fair Debt Collection Practices Act (Title 1.6C (commencing with Section 1788)). **Leg.H.** Added Stats 2003 ch 259 §1 (SB 1022), operative July 1, 2004.

TITLE 3
DEPOSIT

Chapter 1. Deposit in General.
Chapter 2. Deposit for Keeping.
Chapter 3. Deposit for Exchange.
Chapter 4. Private Bulk Storage of Grain.

CHAPTER 1
DEPOSIT IN GENERAL

Article 1. Nature and Creation of Deposit.
Article 2. Obligations of the Depositary.

ARTICLE 1
Nature and Creation of Deposit

Deposit, kinds of. §1813.
Voluntary deposit, how made. §1814.
Making of involuntary deposit. §1815.
Duty of involuntary depositary with regard to property and abandoned animals. §1816.
Deposit for keeping, what. §1817.
Deposit for exchange, what. §1818.
[Section renumbered 1981]. §1821.23.

§1813. Deposit, kinds of

A deposit may be voluntary or involuntary; and for safekeeping or for exchange. **Leg.H.** Enacted Stats 1872.

§1814. Voluntary deposit, how made

A voluntary deposit is made by one giving to another, with his consent, the possession of personal property to keep for the benefit of the former, or of a third party. The person giving is called the depositor, and the person receiving the depositary. **Leg.H.** Enacted Stats 1872.

§1815. Making of involuntary deposit

An involuntary deposit is made:

(a) By the accidental leaving or placing of personal property in the possession of any person, without negligence on the part of its owner.

(b) In cases of fire, shipwreck, inundation, insurrection, riot, or like extraordinary emergencies, by the owner of personal property committing it, out of necessity, to the care of any person.

(c) By the delivery to, or picking up by, and the holding of, a stray live animal by any person or public or private entity.

(d) By the abandonment or leaving of a live animal, as proscribed by Section 597.1 of the Penal Code, in or about any premises or real property that has been vacated upon, or immediately preceding, the termination of a lease or other rental agreement or foreclosure of the property. **Leg.H.** Enacted Stats 1872. Amended Stats 1998 ch 752 §2 (SB 1785); Stats 1999 ch 83 §22 (SB 966); Stats 2008 ch 265 §1 (AB 2949), effective January 1, 2009.

§1816. Duty of involuntary depositary with regard to property and abandoned animals

(a) The person or private entity with whom a thing is deposited in the manner described in Section 1815 is bound to take charge of it, if able to do so.

(b) Any person or private entity with whom a live animal is deposited in the manner described in subdivision (d) of Section 1815 shall immediately notify animal control officials for the purpose of retrieving the animal pursuant to Section 597.1 of the Penal Code. Animal control officers who respond shall be entitled to exercise the right afforded them pursuant to that section to secure a lien for the purpose of recovering the costs of attempting to rescue the animal. Nothing in this subdivision shall impose any new or additional civil or criminal liability upon a depositary who complies with this subdivision.

(c) A public agency or shelter with whom an abandoned animal is deposited in the manner described in Section 1815 is bound to take charge of it, as provided in Section 597.1 of the Penal Code.

(d) The person in possession of the abandoned animal is subject to all local ordinances and state laws that govern the proper care and treatment of those animals.

(e) For purposes of this section, the person or private entity that notifies animal control officials to retrieve the animal or the successor property owner shall not be considered the keeper of the animal or the agent of the animal's owner as those terms are used in Section 597.1 of the Penal Code. **Leg.H.** Enacted Stats 1872. Amended Stats 1998 ch 752 §3 (SB 1785); Stats 2008 ch 265 §2 (AB 2949), effective January 1, 2009.

§1817. Deposit for keeping, what

A deposit for keeping is one in which the depositary is bound to return the identical thing deposited. **Leg.H.** Enacted Stats 1872.

§1818. Deposit for exchange, what

A deposit for exchange is one in which the depositary is only bound to return a thing corresponding in kind to that which is deposited. **Leg.H.** Enacted Stats 1872.

§1821.23. [Section renumbered 1981]

Leg.H. Added Stats 1979 ch 964 §20. Renumbered CC §1861.23 by Stats 1981 ch 714 §53.

ARTICLE 2
Obligations of the Depositary

Depositary must deliver on demand. §1822.
No obligation to deliver without demand. §1823.
Place of delivery. §1824.
Notice to owner of adverse claim. §1825.
Notice to owner of thing wrongfully detained. §1826.
Delivery of thing owned jointly, etc. §1827.
Joint deposit by more than one person. §1828.

§1822. Depositary must deliver on demand

A depositary must deliver the thing to the person for whose benefit it was deposited, on demand, whether the deposit was made for a specific time or not, unless he has a lien upon the thing deposited, or has been forbidden or prevented from doing so by the real owner thereof, or by the act of the law, and has given the notice required by Section 1825. **Leg.H.** Enacted Stats 1872.

§1823. No obligation to deliver without demand

A depositary is not bound to deliver a thing deposited without demand, even where the deposit is made for a specified time. **Leg.H.** Enacted Stats 1872.

§1824. Place of delivery

A depositary must deliver the thing deposited at his residence or place of business, as may be most convenient for him. **Leg.H.** Enacted Stats 1872.

§1825. Notice to owner of adverse claim

A depositary must give prompt notice to the person for whose benefit the deposit was made, of any proceedings taken adversely to his interest in the thing deposited, which may tend to excuse the depositary from delivering the thing to him. **Leg.H.** Enacted Stats 1872.

§1826. Notice to owner of thing wrongfully detained

A depositary, who believes that a thing deposited with him is wrongfully detained from its true owner, may give him notice of the deposit; and if within a reasonable time afterwards he does not claim it, and sufficiently establish his right thereto, and indemnify the depositary against the claim of the depositor, the depositary is exonerated from liability to the person to whom he gave the notice, upon returning the thing to the depositor, or assuming, in good faith, a new obligation changing his position in respect to the thing, to his prejudice. **Leg.H.** Enacted Stats 1872.

§1827. Delivery of thing owned jointly, etc.

If a thing deposited is owned jointly or in common by persons who cannot agree upon the manner of its delivery, the depositary may deliver to each his proper share thereof, if it can be done without injury to the thing. **Leg.H.** Enacted Stats 1872.

§1828. Joint deposit by more than one person

When a deposit is made in the name of two or more persons, deliverable or payable to either or to their survivor or survivors, such deposit or any part thereof, or increase thereof, may be delivered or paid to either of said persons or to the survivor or survivors in due course of business. **Leg.H.** Added Stats 1907 ch 75 §1.

CHAPTER 2
DEPOSIT FOR KEEPING

Article 1. General Provisions.
Article 2. Gratuitous Deposit.
Article 3. Storage.
Article 3.5. Deposits for Repair, Alteration or Sale.
Article 4. Innkeepers.

ARTICLE 1
General Provisions

Depositor must indemnify depositary. §1833.
Duties of depositary of living animals. §1834.
Policy against euthanization of adoptable or treatable animals. §1834.4.
Abandonment of animal delivered to veterinarian. §1834.5.
Animal shelter entities; Required statement regarding use of euthanized animals; Prohibition against euthanizing animal for transfer of carcass to research facility or animal dealer; Prohibition against transfer or receipt of living animal for purpose of research, experimentation, or testing; Violation. §1834.7.
Horses sold for slaughter at public auction or sale; Notice. §1834.8.
Use of alternative nonanimal test method or strategy by manufacturer and contract testing facility. §1834.9.
Canine and feline toxicological experiments regarding pesticides or chemical substances; Remedies for violation. § 1834.9.3.
Cosmetic developed or manufactured using animal test prohibited; Exceptions; Penalty for violation, §1834.9.5.
Obligations as to use of thing deposited. §1835.
Liability for damage arising from wrongful use. §1836.
Sale of thing in danger of perishing. §1837.
Injury to, or loss of thing deposited. §1838.
Service rendered by depositary. §1839.
Liability of depositary. §1840.

§1833. Depositor must indemnify depositary

A depositor must indemnify the depositary:

1. For all damage caused to him by the defects or vices of the thing deposited; and,

2. For all expenses necessarily incurred by him about the thing, other than such as are involved in the nature of the undertaking. **Leg.H.** Enacted Stats 1872.

§1834. Duties of depositary of living animals

A depositary of living animals shall provide the animals with necessary and prompt veterinary care, nutrition, and shelter, and treat them kindly. Any depositary that fails to perform these duties may be liable for civil damages as provided by law. **Leg.H.** Enacted Stats 1872. Amended Stats 1998 ch 752 §4 (SB 1785).

§1834.4. Policy against euthanization of adoptable or treatable animals

(a) It is the policy of the state that no adoptable animal should be euthanized if it can be adopted into a suitable home. Adoptable animals include only those animals eight weeks of age or older that, at or subsequent to the time the animal is impounded or otherwise taken into possession, have manifested no sign of a behavioral or temperamental defect that could pose a health or safety risk or otherwise make the animal unsuitable for placement as a pet, and have manifested no sign of disease, injury, or congenital or hereditary condition that adversely affects the health of the animal or that is likely to adversely affect the animal's health in the future.

(b) It is the policy of the state that no treatable animal should be euthanized. A treatable animal shall include any animal that is not adoptable but that could become adoptable with reasonable efforts. This subdivision, by itself, shall not be the basis of liability for damages regarding euthanasia. **Leg.H.** Added Stats 1998 ch 752 §5 (SB 1785).

§1834.5. Abandonment of animal delivered to veterinarian

(a) Notwithstanding any other provision of law, whenever an animal is delivered to a veterinarian, dog kennel, cat kennel, pet-grooming parlor, animal hospital, or any other animal care facility pursuant to a written or oral agreement entered into after the effective date of this section, and the owner of the animal does not pick up the animal within 14 calendar days after the day the animal was initially due to be picked up, the animal shall be deemed to be abandoned. The person into whose custody the animal was placed for care shall first try for a period of not less than 10 days to find a new owner for the animal or turn the animal over to a public animal control agency or shelter, society for the prevention of cruelty to animals shelter, humane society shelter, or nonprofit animal rescue group, provided that the shelter or rescue group has been contacted and has agreed to take the animal. If unable to place the animal with a new owner, shelter, or rescue group, the animal care facility may have the abandoned animal euthanized.

(b) If an animal so abandoned was left with a veterinarian or with a facility that has a veterinarian, and a new owner cannot be found pursuant to this section, the veterinarian may euthanize the animal.

(c) Nothing in this section shall be construed to require an animal care facility or a veterinarian to euthanize an abandoned animal upon the expiration of the 10-day period described in subdivision (a).

(d) There shall be a notice posted in a conspicuous place, or in conspicuous type in a written receipt given, to warn a person depositing an animal at an animal care facility of the provisions of this section.

(e) An abandoned animal shall not be used for scientific or any other type of experimentation. **Leg.H.** Added Stats 1969 ch 1138 §1. Amended Stats 1970 ch 1166 §1; Stats 1971 ch 477 §1; Stats 2014 ch 86 §1 (AB 1810), effective January 1, 2015.

§1834.6. [Section repealed 2015]

Leg.H. Added Stats 1969 ch 1138 §2. Repealed Stats 2014 ch 86 §2 (AB 1810), effective January 1, 2015. The repealed section related to use of abandoned animal for scientific experimentation. For present similar provisions, see CC §1834.5.

§1834.7 Animal shelter entities; Required statement regarding use of euthanized animals; Prohibition against euthanizing animal for transfer of carcass to research facility or animal dealer; Prohibition against transfer or receipt of living animal for purpose of research, experimentation, or testing; Violation

(a) For purposes of this section:

(1) "Animal dealer" means a person who, in commerce, for compensation or profit, delivers for transportation, or transports, except as a carrier, or who buys, sells, or negotiates the purchase or sale of any animal, whether alive or dead, for research, teaching, exhibition, or biological supply.

(2) "Animal shelter entity" includes, but is not limited to, an animal regulation agency, humane society, society for the prevention of cruelty to animals, or other private or public animal shelter.

(3) "Person" means an individual, partnership, firm, limited liability company, joint-stock company, corporation, association, trust, estate, governmental agency, or other legal entity.

(4) "Research facility" means a research facility as defined by Section 2132 of Title 7 of the United States Code, effective February 7, 2014.

(b)(1) An animal shelter entity where dead animals are turned over to a biological supply facility or a research facility for research purposes or to supply blood, tissue, or other biological products shall post a sign as described by this paragraph in a place where it will be clearly visible to a majority of persons when turning animals over to the shelter. The sign shall measure a minimum of 28 x 21 cm– 11 x 8½ inches –with lettering of a minimum of 3.2 cm high and 1.2 cm wide– 1¼ x ½ inch –(91 point) and shall state:

"Animals Euthanized at This Shelter May Be Used for Research Purposes or to Supply Blood, Tissue, or Other Biological Products"

(2) The statement in paragraph (1) shall also be included on owner surrender forms.

(3) An animal shelter or other person shall not euthanize an animal for the purpose of transferring the carcass to a research facility or animal dealer.

(c)(1) An animal shelter entity or other person that accepts animals from the public or takes in stray or unwanted animals shall not sell, give, or otherwise transfer a living animal to a research facility, an animal dealer, or other person for the purpose of research, experimentation, or testing.

(2) A research facility, animal dealer, or other person shall not procure, purchase, receive, accept, or use a living animal for the purpose of research, experimentation, or testing if that animal is transferred from, or received from, an animal shelter entity or other person that accepts animals from the public or takes in stray or unwanted animals.

(d) Nothing in this section shall prohibit a research facility from working in collaboration with an animal shelter to investigate problems and provide services to shelter animals.

(e) A violation of this section is subject to a civil penalty of one thousand dollars ($1,000) in an action to be brought by the district attorney or city attorney of the county or city where the violation occurred. When collected, the civil penalty shall be payable to the general fund of the governmental entity that brought the action to assess the penalty. **Leg.H.** Added Stats 2016 ch 568 §2 (AB 2269), effective January 1, 2017.

Prior Law: Former CC §1834.7, similar to the present section, was added Stats 1978 ch 777 §1, amended Stats 1980 ch 676 §50, Stats 2001 ch 139 §1 (SB 338), operative July 1, 2002, and repealed Stats 2016 ch 568 §1 (AB 2269), effective January 1, 2017.

Former CC §1834.7, similar to the present section, was added Stats 1978 ch 777 §1 and repealed Stats 2016 ch 568 §1 (AB 2269), effective January 1, 2017.

§1834.8. Horses sold for slaughter at public auction or sale; Notice

(a) At any public auction or sale where equines are sold, the management of the auction or sale shall post a sign (measuring a minimum of 15 x 9 inches with lettering of a minimum of 1¼ x ½ (91 point)) or shall insert into its consignment agreement with the seller in boldface type the notice stated in subdivision (b). If a sign is posted, it shall be posted in a conspicuous place so that it will be clearly visible to a majority of persons attending the sale. If the notice is inserted into the consignment agreement, space shall be provided adjacent to the notice for the seller to initial their acknowledgment of the notice.

(b) The notice required by subdivision (a) shall read as follows:

"WARNING
The sale of horses in California for slaughter for human consumption is a felony."

(c) For the purposes of this section, the management of the auction or sale shall post current slaughter prices or make them available to sellers upon request. **Leg.H.** Added Stats 1995 ch 99 §1 (SB 1219). Amended Stats 2006 ch 538 §53 (SB 1852), effective January 1, 2007; Stats 2019 ch 765 §2 (AB 128), effective January 1, 2020.

Prior Law: There was another section of this number which was added Stats 2000 ch 476 §1 and amended and renumbered CC §1834.9 by Stats 2001 ch 159 §34.5.

Former Sections: Former CC §1834.8 was added Stats 2000 ch 476 §1 and amended and renumbered to CC §1834.9 by Stats 2001 ch 159 §34.5.

§1834.9. Use of alternative nonanimal test method or strategy by manufacturer and contract testing facility

(a) Manufacturers and contract testing facilities shall not use traditional animal test methods within this state for which an appropriate alternative test method or strategy exists, or a waiver has been granted by the agency responsible for regulating the specific product or activity for which the test is being conducted. When there is no appropriate alternative test method or strategy available, manufacturers and contract testing facilities shall use a traditional animal test method using the fewest number of animals possible and reducing the level of pain, suffering, and stress of an animal used for testing.

(b) This section does not prohibit the use of any nonanimal test method or strategy for the testing of any product, product formulation, chemical, drug, medical device, vaccine, or ingredient that is not described in paragraph (1) of subdivision (g).

(c)(1) This section does not prohibit the use of traditional animal test methods to comply with requirements of state or federal agencies.

(2) This section does not prohibit the use of traditional animal test methods to comply with requests from state or federal agencies when the agency has approved an alternative nonanimal test method or strategy pursuant to subdivision (a), but concludes that a traditional animal test method is needed to fully assess the impacts on the health or safety of consumers.

(d) This section shall be enforced in a civil action for injunctive relief brought by the Attorney General, the district attorney of the county in which the violation is alleged to have occurred, or a city attorney of a city or a city and county having a population in excess of 750,000 and in which the violation is alleged to have occurred. If the court determines that the Attorney General or district attorney is the prevailing party in the enforcement action, the official may also recover costs, attorney's fees, and a civil penalty not to exceed five thousand dollars ($5,000) in that action.

(e) This section shall not apply to any traditional animal test methods performed for the purpose of medical research.

(f)(1) Starting January 1, 2027, and annually thereafter, a manufacturer or contract testing facility in this state using traditional animal test methods, except for those traditional animal test methods exempt under subdivision (e), shall report to the department the number and species of animals used, the type and number of alternative test methods or strategies used, the number of waivers used, and the purpose of the use of the traditional animal tests, alternative test methods or strategies, and waivers.

(2) The department shall develop and maintain a portal on its internet website to receive the information required by paragraph (1) and make the information collected publicly available on its internet website. The department shall ensure that information made available to the public does not include personally identifiable information or proprietary information.

(g) For the purposes of this section, the following terms apply:

(1) "Alternative test method or strategy" means a test method, including a new or revised method, that fulfills all of the following criteria:

(A) Does not use animals.

(B) Provides information of equivalent or better scientific quality and relevance compared to traditional animal test methods, and includes, but is not limited to, computational toxicology and bioinformatics, high-throughput screening methods, testing of categories of chemical substances, tiered testing methods, in vitro studies, and systems biology.

(C) Has been identified and accepted for use by a federal agency or program within an agency responsible for regulating the specific product or activity for which the test is being conducted.

(2) "Animal" means vertebrate nonhuman animal.

(3) "Contract testing facility" means any partnership, corporation, association, or other legal relationship that tests chemicals, ingredients, product formulations, or products in this state.

(4) "Department" means the State Department of Public Health.

(5) "Manufacturer" means any partnership, corporation, association, or other legal relationship that produces chemicals, ingredients, product formulations, or products in this state.

(6) "Medical research" means research related to the causes, diagnosis, treatment, control, or prevention of physical or mental diseases and impairments of humans and animals or related to the development of biomedical products, devices, or drugs as defined in Section 321(g)(1) of Title 21 of the United States Code. Medical research does not include the testing of an ingredient that was formerly used in a drug, tested for the drug use with traditional animal methods to characterize the ingredient and to substantiate its safety for human use, and is now proposed for use in a product other than a biomedical product, medical device, or drug.

(7) "Person" means an individual with managerial control, or a partnership, corporation, association, or other legal relationship.

(8) "Traditional animal test method" means a process or procedure using animals to obtain information on the characteristics of a chemical or agent and that generates information regarding the ability of a chemical or agent to produce a specific biological effect under specified conditions.

Leg.H. Added Stats 2000 ch 476 §1 (SB 2082) as CC §1834.8. Amended and renumbered Stats 2001 ch 159 §34.5 (SB 662); Stats 2023 ch 430 §1 (AB 357), effective January 1, 2024.

§1834.9.3. Canine and feline toxicological experiments regarding pesticides or chemical substances; Remedies for violation

(a) For purposes of this section, the following definitions apply:

(1) "Alternative test method" means a test method that does not use animals, or in some cases reduces or refines the use of animals, for which the reliability and relevance for a specific purpose has been established by validation bodies, including, but not limited to, the Interagency Coordinating Committee for the Validation of Alternative Methods and the Organization for Economic Co-operation and Development. Alternative test methods include, but are not limited to, high-throughput screening methods, testing of categories of chemical substances, tiered testing methods, in vitro studies, and systems biology.

(2) "Canine or feline toxicological experiment" means any test or study of any duration that seeks to determine the effect, if any, of the application or exposure, whether internal or external, of any amount of a chemical substance on a dog or cat. "Application or exposure" includes, but is not limited to, oral ingestion, skin or eye contact, or inhalation.

(3) "Cat" means any member of the species Felis catus.

(4) "Chemical substance" shall have the same meaning as that term is defined under subsection (2) of Section 2602 of Title 15 of the United States Code, except that for purposes of this section, such term shall include any pesticide, as defined under subsection (u) of Section 136 of Title 7 of the United States Code, and any food additive, as defined under subsection (s) of Section 321 of Title 21 of the United States Code.

(5) "Dog" means any member of the species Canis familiaris.

(6) "Food additive" shall have the same meaning as that term is defined in subsection (s) of Section 321 of Title 21 of the United States Code.

(7) "Medical research" means research related to the causes, diagnosis, treatment, control, or prevention of physical or mental diseases and impairments of humans and animals or related to the development of biomedical drugs or devices as those terms are defined in subsections (g) and (h), inclusive, of Section 321 of Title 21 of the United States Code. Medical research does not include experimentation or testing of a chemical substance or ingredient proposed for use in a product other than a biomedical drug or device as those terms are defined in the Federal Food, Drug, and Cosmetic Act (21 U.S.C. Sec. 321).

(8) "Pesticide" shall have the same meaning as that term is defined in subsection (u) of Section 136 of Title 7 of the United States Code.

(9) "Testing facility" means any partnership, corporation, association, school, institution, organization, or other legal relationship, whether privately or government owned, leased, or operated, that tests chemicals, ingredients, product formulations, or products in this state.

(b) Notwithstanding any other law, and in addition to the prohibitions set forth in Sections 1834.9 and 1834.9.5, a testing facility shall not conduct a canine or feline toxicological experiment in this state to achieve discovery, approval, maintenance of approval, notification, registration, or maintenance of a pesticide or chemical substance, unless the experiment is conducted pursuant to any of the following:

(1) To satisfy an express requirement imposed by the United States Environmental Protection Agency (EPA) under the authority of the Federal Insecticide, Fungicide, and Rodenticide Act (7 U.S.C. Sec. 136 et seq.) and the Toxic Substances Control Act (15 U.S.C. Sec. 2601 et seq.), including any EPA rule, regulation, or order.

(2) To support an application to the EPA for a waiver from the requirements in paragraph (1), provided that testing is conducted solely to reduce the total number of animals needed for experiments to achieve discovery, approval, maintenance of approval, notification, registration, or maintenance of a pesticide or chemical substance.

(3) To satisfy an express requirement imposed by the Food and Drug Administration (FDA) per the Federal Food, Drug, and Cosmetic Act (21 U.S.C. Sec. 301 et seq.) or any binding agency regulation promulgated upon notice and comment thereunder.

(c)(1) Notwithstanding any other law, the Attorney General, the district attorney of the county in which the violation is alleged to have occurred, or a city attorney of a city or city and county having a population in excess of 750,000 and in which the violation is alleged to have occurred, may bring a civil action for injunctive relief pursuant to this paragraph. If the court determines that the Attorney General, district attorney, or city attorney is the prevailing party in the enforcement action, the official may also recover costs, attorney fees, and a civil penalty not to exceed five thousand dollars ($5,000) for each day that each dog or each cat is used in a canine or feline toxicological experiment in violation of this section.

(2) The procedure set forth in paragraph (1) is the exclusive remedy for enforcing this section.

(d) The prohibition in subdivision (b) shall not apply to either of the following:

(1) Medical research.

(2) Testing or experimentation conducted for the purpose of developing, manufacturing, or marketing any product intended for beneficial use in dogs or cats. **Leg.H.** Added Stats 2022 ch 551 §2 (SB 879), effective January 1, 2023.

§1834.9.5. Cosmetic developed or manufactured using animal test prohibited; Exceptions; Penalty for violation

(a) Notwithstanding any other law, it is unlawful for a manufacturer to import for profit, sell, or offer for sale in this state, any cosmetic, if the cosmetic was developed or manufactured using an animal test that was conducted or contracted by the manufacturer, or any supplier of the manufacturer, on or after January 1, 2020.

(b) For purposes of this section, the following terms apply:

(1) "Animal test" means the internal or external application of a cosmetic, either in its final form or any ingredient thereof, to the skin, eyes, or other body part of a live, nonhuman vertebrate.

(2) "Cosmetic" means any article intended to be rubbed, poured, sprinkled, or sprayed on, introduced into, or otherwise applied to the human body or any part thereof for cleansing, beautifying, promoting attractiveness, or altering the appearance, including, but not limited to, personal hygiene products such as deodorant, shampoo, or conditioner.

(3) "Ingredient" means any component of a cosmetic as defined by Section 700.3 of Title 21 of the Code of Federal Regulations.

(4) "Manufacturer" means any person whose name appears on the label of a cosmetic product pursuant to the requirements of Section 701.12 of Title 21 of the Code of Federal Regulations.

(5) "Supplier" means any entity that supplies, directly or through a third party, any ingredient used in the formulation of a manufacturer's cosmetic.

(c) The prohibitions in subdivision (a) do not apply to the following:

(1) An animal test of any cosmetic that is required by a federal or state regulatory authority if all of the following apply:

(A) The ingredient is in wide use and cannot be replaced by another ingredient capable of performing a similar function.

(B) A specific human health problem is substantiated and the need to conduct animal tests is justified and is supported by a detailed research protocol proposed as the basis for the evaluation.

(C) There is not a nonanimal alternative method accepted for the relevant endpoint by the relevant federal or state regulatory authority.

(2) An animal test that was conducted to comply with a requirement of a foreign regulatory authority, if no evidence derived from the test was relied upon to substantiate the safety of the cosmetic sold in California by the manufacturer.

(3) An animal test that was conducted on any product or ingredient subject to the requirements of Chapter V of the Federal Food, Drug, and Cosmetic Act (21 U.S.C. 351 et seq.).

(4) An animal test that was conducted for noncosmetic purposes in response to a requirement of a federal, state, or foreign regulatory authority, if no evidence derived from the test was relied upon to substantiate the safety of the cosmetic sold in California by the manufacturer. A manufacturer is not prohibited from reviewing, assessing, or retaining evidence from an animal test conducted pursuant to this paragraph.

(d) A violation of this section shall be punishable by a fine of five thousand dollars ($5,000) and an additional one thousand dollars ($1,000) for each day the violation continues.

(e) A violation of this section may be enforced by the district attorney of the county in which the violation occurred, or by the city attorney of the city in which the violation occurred. The civil fine shall be paid to the entity that is authorized to bring the action.

(f) A district attorney or city attorney may, upon a determination that there is a reasonable likelihood of a violation of this section, review the testing data upon which a cosmetic manufacturer has relied in the development or manufacturing of the relevant cosmetic product sold in the state. Information provided under this section shall be protected as a trade secret as defined in subdivision (d) of Section 3426.1. Consistent with the procedures described in Section 3426.5, a district attorney or city attorney shall enter a protective order with a manufacturer before receipt of information from a manufacturer pursuant to this section, and shall take other appropriate measures necessary to preserve the confidentiality of information provided pursuant to this section.

(g) This section shall not apply to either of the following:

(1) A cosmetic, if the cosmetic, in its final form, was sold in California or tested on animals prior to January 1, 2020, even if the cosmetic is manufactured after that date.

(2) An ingredient, if the ingredient was sold in California or tested on animals prior to January 1, 2020, even if the ingredient is manufactured after that date.

(h) Notwithstanding any other provision of this section, cosmetic inventory found to be in violation of this section may be sold for a period of 180 days.

(i) No county or political subdivision of the state may establish or continue any prohibition on or relating to animal tests, as defined in this section, that is not identical to the prohibitions set forth in this section and that does not include the exemptions contained in subdivision (c).

(j) This section shall become operative on January 1, 2020. **Leg.H.** Added Stats 2018 ch 899 §1 (SB 1249), effective January 1, 2019, operative January 1, 2020.

§1835. Obligations as to use of thing deposited

A depositary may not use the thing deposited, or permit it to be used, for any purpose, without the consent of the depositor. He may not, if it is purposely fastened by the depositor, open it without the consent of the latter, except in case of necessity. **Leg.H.** Enacted Stats 1872.

§1836. Liability for damage arising from wrongful use

A depositary is liable for any damage happening to the thing deposited, during his wrongful use thereof, unless such damage must inevitably have happened though the property had not been thus used. **Leg.H.** Enacted Stats 1872.

§1837. Sale of thing in danger of perishing

If a thing deposited is in actual danger of perishing before instructions can be obtained from the depositor, the depositary may sell it for the best price obtainable, and retain the proceeds as a deposit, giving immediate notice of his proceedings to the depositor. **Leg.H.** Enacted Stats 1872.

§1838. Injury to, or loss of thing deposited

If a thing is lost or injured during its deposit, and the depositary refuses to inform the depositor of the circumstances under which the loss or injury occurred, so far as he has information concerning them, or willfully misrepresents the circumstances to him, the depositary is presumed to have willfully, or by gross negligence, permitted the loss or injury to occur. **Leg.H.** Enacted Stats 1872.

§1839. Service rendered by depositary

So far as any service is rendered by a depositary, or required from him, his duties and liabilities are prescribed by the title on employment and service. **Leg.H.** Enacted Stats 1872.

§1840. Liability of depositary

The liability of a depositary for negligence cannot exceed the amount which he is informed by the depositor, or has reason to suppose, the thing deposited to be worth. **Leg.H.** Enacted Stats 1872. Amended Stats 1873–74 ch 612 §200.

ARTICLE 2
Gratuitous Deposit

Gratuitous deposit, what. §1844.
Nature of involuntary deposit. §1845.
Degree of care required of gratuitous depositary. §1846.
Cessation of gratuitous depositary's duties. §1847.

§1844. Gratuitous deposit, what

Gratuitous deposit is a deposit for which the depositary receives no consideration beyond the mere possession of the thing deposited. **Leg.H.** Enacted Stats 1872.

§1845. Nature of involuntary deposit

An involuntary deposit is gratuitous, the depositary being entitled to no reward. However, an involuntary depositary of any live animal may accept advertised rewards or rewards freely offered by the owner of the animal. **Leg.H.** Enacted Stats 1872. Amended Stats 1998 ch 752 §6 (SB 1785).

§1846. Degree of care required of gratuitous depositary

(a) A gratuitous depositary must use, at least, slight care for the preservation of the thing deposited.

(b) A gratuitous depositary of a living animal shall provide the animal with necessary and prompt veterinary care, adequate nutrition and water, and shelter, and shall treat it humanely and, if the animal has any identification, make reasonable attempts to notify the owner of the animal's location. Any gratuitous depositary that does not have sufficient resources or desire to provide that care shall promptly turn the animal over to an appropriate care facility.

(c) If the gratuitous depositary of a living animal is a public animal shelter, shelter operated by a society for the prevention of cruelty to animals, or humane shelter, the depositary shall comply with all other requirements of the Food and Agricultural Code regarding the impounding of live animals. **Leg.H.** Enacted Stats 1872. Amended Stats 1998 ch 752 §7 (SB 1785); Stats 2019 ch 7 §2 (AB 1553), effective January 1, 2020.

§1847. Cessation of gratuitous depositary's duties

The duties of a gratuitous depositary cease:

(a) Upon restoration by the depositary of the thing deposited to its owner.

(b) Upon reasonable notice given by the depositary to the owner to remove it, and the owner failing to do so within a reasonable time. But an involuntary depositary, under subdivision (b) of Section 1815, may not give notice until the emergency that gave rise to the deposit is past. This subdivision shall not apply to a public animal shelter, a shelter operated by a society for the prevention of cruelty to animals, or a humane shelter. The duty to provide care, as required by Section 1846, continues until the public or private animal shelter is lawfully relieved of responsibility for the animal. **Leg.H.** Enacted Stats 1872. Amended Stats 1998 ch 752 §8 (SB 1785); Stats 2019 ch 7 §3 (AB 1553), effective January 1, 2020.

ARTICLE 3
Storage

Deposit for hire. §1851.
Degree of care required of depositary for hire. §1852.
Rate of compensation for fraction of a week, etc. §1853.
Termination of deposit. §1854.
Same. §1855.
Lien for storage charges, advances, insurance, and expenses. §1856.
Storage property to be sold. §1857.

§1851. Deposit for hire

A deposit not gratuitous is called storage. The depositary in such case is called a depositary for hire. **Leg.H.** Enacted Stats 1872.

§1852. Degree of care required of depositary for hire

A depositary for hire must use at least ordinary care for the preservation of the thing deposited. **Leg.H.** Enacted Stats 1872.

§1853. Rate of compensation for fraction of a week, etc.

In the absence of a different agreement or usage, a depositary for hire is entitled to one week's hire for the sustenance and shelter of living animals during any fraction of a week, and to half a month's hire for the storage of any other property during any fraction of a half-month. **Leg.H.** Enacted Stats 1872.

§1854. Termination of deposit

In the absence of an agreement as to the length of time during which a deposit is to continue, it may be terminated by the depositor at any time, and by the depositary upon reasonable notice. **Leg.H.** Enacted Stats 1872.

§1855. Same

Notwithstanding an agreement respecting the length of time during which a deposit is to continue, it may be terminated by the depositor on paying all that would become due to the depositary in case of the deposit so continuing. **Leg.H.** Enacted Stats 1872.

§1856. Lien for storage charges, advances, insurance, and expenses

A depositary for hire has a lien for storage charges and for advances and insurance incurred at the request of the bailor, and for money necessarily expended in and about the care, preservation and keeping of the property stored, and he also has a lien for money advanced at the request of the bailor, to discharge a prior lien, and for the expenses of a sale where default has been made in satisfying a valid lien. The rights of the depositary for hire to such lien are regulated by the title on liens. **Leg.H.** Added Stats 1891 ch 249 §1. Amended Stats 1909 ch 664 §1.

§1857. Storage property to be sold

If from any cause other than want of ordinary care and diligence on his part, a depositary for hire is unable to deliver perishable property, baggage, or luggage received by him for storage, or to collect his charges for storage due thereon, he may cause such property to be sold, in open market, to satisfy his lien for storage; provided, that no property except perishable property shall be sold, under the provisions of this section, upon which storage charges shall not be due and unpaid for one year at the time of such sale. **Leg.H.** Added Stats 1891 ch 249 §2.

ARTICLE 3.5
Deposits for Repair, Alteration or Sale

"Customer"; "Depositary"; "Property". §1858.
Receipt; Recital property not insured. §1858.1.
Failure to furnish receipt; Misrepresentation; Liability. §1858.2.
Same; Notice of insurance not required. §1858.3.

§1858. "Customer"; "Depositary"; "Property"

As used in this article:

(a) "Customer" means a natural person who deals with a depositary.

(b) "Depositary" means a person who in the ordinary course of business regularly receives property from customers for the purpose of repair or alteration.

(c) "Property" means personal property used for or intended for personal, family, or household purposes, but does not include any motor vehicle within the meaning of Section 415 of the Vehicle Code. **Leg.H.** Added Stats 1970 ch 1185 §1. Amended Stats 1971 ch 180 §1, effective June 25, 1971.

Prior Law: Former §1858, similar to UCC §7207, was added Stats 1905 ch 452 §1 and repealed Stats 1963 ch 819 §2, effective January 1, 1965.

§1858.1. Receipt; Recital property not insured

Every depositary shall, upon accepting property from a customer, present the customer with written receipt which shall include a statement, if such is the case, that such deposited property is not insured or protected to the amount of the actual cash value thereof by the depositary against loss occasioned by theft, fire, and vandalism while such property remains with the depositary. **Leg.H.** Added Stats 1970 ch 1185 §1.

§1858.2. Failure to furnish receipt; Misrepresentation; Liability

Every depositary who fails to furnish the receipt, or a statement thereon as required by Section 1858.1, or who makes any misrepresentation in such receipt, shall be strictly liable to the customer for any loss occasioned by theft, fire, or vandalism while such property remains with the depositary and shall forfeit any lien or other right to hold the property arising from services rendered in holding, repairing, altering, or selling the property. When liability is imposed upon a depositary under this section it shall be deemed as having been imposed for the commission of a willful act for the purposes of Section 533 of the Insurance Code. **Leg.H.** Added Stats 1970 ch 1185 §1.

§1858.3. Same; Notice of insurance not required

If the depositary by insurance or by self-insurance does protect property deposited by customers for loss or damage occasioned by theft, fire or vandalism while such property remains with the depositary, such depositary need not make or deliver to customer any notice thereof. **Leg.H.** Added Stats 1970 ch 1185 §1.

ARTICLE 3A
Warehousemen [Repealed]

§§1858a–1858f. [Sections repealed 1963]

Leg.H. Added Stats 1905 ch 452 §1. Repealed Stats 1963 ch 819 §2, effective January 1, 1965. See UCC §§7104, 7202, 7204, 7207, 7501, 7504.

ARTICLE 3B
Warehouse Receipts Act [Repealed]

§§1858.01–1858.55. [Sections repealed 1963]

Leg.H. Added Stats 1953 ch 49 §1. Repealed Stats 1963 ch 819 §2, effective January 1, 1965. See UCC §§1102, 1103, 1201, 2705, 7102, 7104, 7201–7204, 7207–7209, 7307, 7401–7404, 7601–7603.

§1858.56. [Section repealed 1963]

Leg.H. Added Stats 1953 ch 49 §1. Amended Stats 1957 ch 492 §1, Stats 1959 ch 1822 §1. Repealed Stats 1963 ch 819 §2, effective January 1, 1965. See UCC §§7210, 7308.

§§1858.57–1858.85. [Sections repealed 1963]

Leg.H. Added Stats 1953 ch 49 §1. Repealed Stats 1963 ch 819 §2, effective January 1, 1965. See UCC §§2705, 7206, 7501–7507.

ARTICLE 3C
Warehouse Receipts for Goods Out-of-State [Repealed]

§§1858.90–1858.93. [Sections repealed 1963]

Leg.H. Added Stats 1953 ch 37 §3. Repealed Stats 1963 ch 819 §2, effective January 1, 1965.

ARTICLE 4
Innkeepers

Liability. §1859.
Notice of nonliability; Limitations of liability. §1860.
Lien of innkeepers; Enforcement; Exempt property. §1861.
Definitions. §1861.1.
Application for writ of possession; Contents. §1861.5.
Hearing and procedure; Conditions for issuance. §1861.6.
Service of documents and papers. §1861.7.
Notice of Application and Hearing. §1861.8.
Affidavits, authorities and evidence. §1861.9.
Issuance of writ. §1861.10.
Issuance of writ of possession. §1861.12.
Effect of defendant's failure to oppose issuance of writ of possession or rebut evidence produced in proceedings. §1861.13.
Effect of court's determinations on unrelated issues and other actions. §1861.14.
Redelivery of property and liability for damages of plaintiff who fails to recover judgment. §1861.15.
Temporary restraining order. §1861.16.
Conduct subject to restraining order. §1861.17.
Service of writ officer. §1861.18.
Taking and disposition of property. §1861.19.
Return of writ of possession. §1861.20.
Plaintiff's undertaking. §1861.21.
Defendant's undertaking. §1861.22.
Exception to sureties. §1861.23.
Sale of property. §1861.24.
Third-party claims as to property taken. §1861.25.
Requirements for affidavits. §1861.27.
Performance of judicial duties. §1861.28.
Apartment keeper's lien; Enforcement; Notice of sale; Proceeds; Exemptions. §1861a.
Sale of personal property found in or deposited with hospital. §1862.5.
Keeper to post rates of charges. §1863.
Duties of person or entity arranging for transient occupancies on behalf of others. §1864.
"Hotel"; "Guest"; Right to evict guest who fails to depart by posted checkout time; Rights with respect to minors. §1865.
Definitions; Right to evict guest of special occupancy park who fails to depart by posted checkout time; Conditions; Rights with respect to minors. §1866.
Right to require guest in special occupancy park to move from a space when danger imminent; Definitions. §1867.

§1859. Liability

The liability of an innkeeper, hotelkeeper, operator of a licensed hospital, rest home or sanitarium, furnished apartment house keeper, furnished bungalow court keeper, boardinghouse or lodginghouse keeper, for losses of or injuries to personal property, is that of a depositary for hire; provided, however, that in no case shall such liability exceed the sum of one thousand dollars ($1,000) in the aggregate. In no case shall liability exceed, for each item of described property, the respective sums of five hundred dollars ($500) for each trunk and its contents, two hundred fifty dollars ($250) for each valise or traveling bag and its contents, two hundred fifty dollars ($250) for each box, bundle or package and its contents, and two hundred fifty dollars ($250) for all other personal property of any kind, unless he shall have consented in writing with the owner thereof to assume a greater liability. **Leg.H.** Enacted Stats 1872. Amended Stats 1895 ch 47 §1; Stats 1921 ch 150 §1; Stats 1927 ch 593 §1; Stats 1931 ch 1190 §1; Stats 1943 ch 363 §1; Stats 1957 ch 1251 §1; Stats 1979 ch 705 §1.

§1860. Notice of nonliability; Limitations of liability

If an innkeeper, hotelkeeper, operator of a licensed hospital, rest home or sanitarium, boardinghouse or lodginghouse keeper, keeps a fireproof safe and gives notice to a guest, patient, boarder or lodger, either personally or by putting up a printed notice in a prominent place in the office or the room occupied by the guest, patient, boarder, or lodger, that he keeps such a safe and will not be liable for money, jewelry, documents, furs, fur coats and fur garments, or other articles of unusual value and small compass, unless placed therein, he is not liable, except so far as his own acts shall contribute thereto, for any loss of or injury to such articles, if not deposited with him to be placed therein, nor in any case for more than the sum of five hundred dollars ($500) for any or all such property of any individual guest, patient, boarder, or lodger, unless he shall have given a receipt in writing therefor to such guest, patient, boarder or lodger. **Leg.H.** Enacted Stats 1872. Amended Stats 1895 ch 47 §2; Stats 1921 ch 150 §1; Stats 1943 ch 363 §2; Stats 1957 ch 1251 §2; Stats 1979 ch 705 §2.

§1861. Lien of innkeepers; Enforcement; Exempt property

Hotel, motel, inn, boardinghouse, and lodginghouse keepers shall have a lien upon the baggage and other property belonging to or legally under the control of their guests, boarders, tenants, or lodgers which may be in such hotel, motel, inn, or boarding or lodging house for the proper charges due from such guests, boarders, tenants, or lodgers, for their accommodation, board and lodging and room rent, and such extras as are furnished at their request, and for all money paid for or advanced to such guests, boarders, tenants, or lodgers, and for the costs of enforcing such lien. The lien may be enforced only after final judgment in an action brought to recover such charges or moneys. During the pendency of the proceeding, the plaintiff may take possession of the baggage and property pursuant to a writ of possession as provided by Sections 1861.1 to 1861.27, inclusive. However, if any baggage or property becoming subject to the lien herein provided for does not belong to the guest, lodger, tenant, or boarder who incurred the charges or indebtedness secured thereby, at the time when such charges or indebtedness was incurred, and if the hotel, motel, inn, boarding or lodging house keeper entitled to such lien receives notice of such fact at any time before the sale of such baggage or property hereunder, then, and in that event, such baggage and property which is subject to said lien and did not belong to said guest, boarder, tenant, or lodger at the time when such charges or indebtedness was incurred shall not be subject to this lien.

Any property which is exempt from enforcement of a money judgment is not subject to the lien provided for in this section. **Leg.H.** Enacted Stats 1875–76 ch 486 §1. Amended Stats 1915 ch 650 §1; Stats 1939 ch 483 §1; Stats 1953 ch 261 §1; Stats 1957 ch 42 §1, ch 591 §1; Stats 1965 ch 1540 §1; Stats 1967 ch 1387 §1; Stats 1968 ch 1182 §1; Stats 1970 ch 1247 §1; Stats 1974 ch 546 §13; Stats 1979 ch 964 §1.5; Stats 1982 ch 497 §9, operative July 1, 1983.

§1861.1. Definitions

Definitions for purposes of Sections 1861 through 1861.27 include the following:

(a) "Hotel", "motel", "inn", "boardinghouse", and "lodginghouse keeper" means any person, corporation, partnership, unincorporated association, public entity, or agent of any of the aforementioned, who offers and accepts payment for rooms, sleeping accommodations, or board and lodging and retains the right of access to, and control of, the dwelling unit.

(b) "Levying officer" means the sheriff or marshal who is directed to execute a writ of possession issued pursuant to this article.

(c) "Plaintiff" means any party filing a complaint or cross complaint.

(d) "Probable validity" means that the plaintiff, more likely than not, will obtain a judgment against the defendant on the plaintiff's claim. **Leg.H.** Added Stats 1979 ch 964 §2. Amended Stats 1996 ch 872 §23 (AB 3472).

§1861.5. Application for writ of possession; Contents

(a) Upon the filing of a complaint, or at any time thereafter, the plaintiff may apply, pursuant to this article, for a writ of possession by filing an application for the writ with the court in which the action was filed.

(b) The application shall be executed under oath and shall include all of the following:

(1) A showing of the basis of the plaintiff's claim, including a showing that the plaintiff is entitled to possession of the property claimed pursuant to an innkeepers' lien.

(2) A general description of the property and a statement of its value.

(3) A statement of the amount of money claimed to be owed by the guest, lodger, tenant, or boarder.

(c) The requirements of subdivision (b) may be satisfied by one or more affidavits filed with the application. **Leg.H.** Added Stats 1979 ch 964 §3.

§1861.6. Hearing and procedure; Conditions for issuance

(a) Except as otherwise provided in this section, no writ shall be issued under this article except after a hearing on a noticed motion.

(b) A writ of possession may be issued ex parte pursuant to this subdivision, if probable cause appears that the following conditions exist:

(1) The property is not necessary for the support of the defendant or his family;

(2) There is an immediate danger that the property will become unavailable to levy, by reason of being transferred, concealed, or removed from the state, or the premises of the motel, hotel, inn, boardinghouse, or lodginghouse, or will become substantially impaired in value by acts of destruction or by failure to take care of the property in a reasonable manner; and

(3) The ex parte issuance of a writ of possession is necessary to protect the property.

(4) The plaintiff establishes the probable validity of the plaintiff's claim.

The plaintiff's application for the writ shall satisfy the requirements of Section 1861.5 and, in addition, shall include a showing that the conditions required by this subdivision exist. A writ of possession may issue if the court finds that the conditions required by this subdivision exist, and the requirements of Section 1861.5 are met. Where a writ of possession has been issued pursuant to this subdivision, a copy of the summons and complaint, a copy of the application and any affidavit in support thereof, and a notice which satisfies the requirements of subdivisions (b) and (c) of Section 1861.8 and informs the defendant of his rights under this subdivision shall be served upon the defendant, and any other person required by Section 1861.8 to be served with a writ of possession. Any defendant whose property has been taken pursuant to a writ of possession issued under this subdivision may apply for an order that the writ be quashed, and any property levied on pursuant to the writ be released. Such application shall be made by noticed motion, and the provisions of Section 1861.9 shall apply. Pending the hearing of the defendant's application, the court may order that delivery pursuant to Section 1861.19 of any property previously levied upon be stayed. If the court determines that the plaintiff is not entitled to a writ of possession, the court shall quash the writ of possession and order the release and redelivery of any property previously levied upon, and shall award the defendant any damages sustained by the defendant which were proximately caused by the levy of the writ of possession and the loss of possession of the property pursuant to such levy. **Leg.H.** Added Stats 1979 ch 964 §4.

§1861.7. Service of documents and papers

Prior to the hearing required by subdivision (a) of Section 1861.6, the defendant shall be served with all of the following:

(a) A copy of the summons and complaint.

(b) Notice of application and hearing.

(c) A copy of the application and any affidavit filed in support thereof. **Leg.H.** Added Stats 1979 ch 964 §5.

§1861.8. Notice of Application and Hearing

The "Notice of Application and Hearing" shall inform the defendant of all of the following:

(a) The hearing will be held at a place and at a time, to be specified in the notice, on plaintiff's application for writ of possession.

(b) The writ shall be issued if the court finds that the plaintiff's claim has probable validity and the other requirements for issuing the writ are established. The hearing is not for the purpose of determining whether the claim is actually valid; such determination shall be made in subsequent proceedings in the action.

(c) If the defendant desires to oppose the issuance of the writ, he shall file with the court either an affidavit providing evidence sufficient to defeat the plaintiff's right to issuance of the writ, or an undertaking to stay the delivery of the property in accordance with Section 1861.22.

(d) The notice shall contain the following statement in 10-point bold type:

"If you believe the plaintiff may not be entitled to possession of the property claimed, you may wish to seek the advice of an attorney. Such attorney should be consulted promptly so that he may assist you before the time set for the hearing." **Leg.H.** Added Stats 1979 ch 964 §6.

§1861.9. Affidavits, authorities and evidence

Each party shall file with the court and serve upon the other party within the time prescribed by rule, any affidavits and points and authorities intended to be relied upon at the hearing. At the hearing, the court shall make its determination upon the basis of the pleadings and other papers in the record; but, upon good cause shown, the court may receive and consider additional evidence and authority produced at the hearing, or may continue the hearing for the production of additional evidence, oral or documentary, and the filing of other affidavits or points and authorities. **Leg.H.** Added Stats 1979 ch 964 §7.

§1861.10. Issuance of writ

(a) At the hearing a writ of possession shall issue if all of the following are found:

(1) The plaintiff has established the probable validity of his claim to possession of the property of the tenant, boarder, or lodger.

(2) That the property which is described within the application for the writ is located on the premises of the motel, hotel, boardinghouse or lodginghouse.

(3) The plaintiff has provided an undertaking as required by Section 1861.21.

(b) No writ directing the levying officer to enter any premises to take possession of any property shall be issued unless the plaintiff has established that there is probable cause to believe that such property is located there. **Leg.H.** Added Stats 1979 ch 964 §8.

§1861.12. Issuance of writ of possession

The writ of possession shall meet all of the following requirements:

(a) Be directed to the levying officer within whose jurisdiction the property is located.

(b) Generally describe the property to be seized.

(c) Specify the apartment, motel, or other boarding premises that may be entered to take possession of the property, or some part of it.

(d) Direct the levying officer to levy on the property pursuant to Section 1861.18 if found on the described premises, and to retain custody of it until released or sold pursuant to Section 1861.19.

(e) Inform the defendant of the right to object to the plaintiff's undertaking, a copy of which shall be attached to the writ, or to obtain the delivery of the property by filing an undertaking as prescribed by Section 1861.22. **Leg.H.** Added Stats 1979 ch 964 §9. Amended Stats 1982 ch 517 §65.

§1861.13. Effect of defendant's failure to oppose issuance of writ of possession or rebut evidence produced in proceedings

Neither the failure of the defendant to oppose the issuance of a writ of possession under this article, nor his failure to rebut any evidence produced by the plaintiff in connection with proceedings under this article, shall constitute a waiver of any defense to the plaintiff's claim in the action, or any other action, or have any effect on the right of the defendant to produce or exclude evidence at the trial of any such action. **Leg.H.** Added Stats 1979 ch 964 §10.

§1861.14. Effect of court's determinations on unrelated issues and other actions

The determinations of the court under this article shall have no effect on the determination of any issues in the action, other than the issues relevant to proceedings under this article, nor shall they affect the rights of any party in any other action arising out of the same claim. The determinations of the court under this article shall not be given in evidence, or referred to in the trial. **Leg.H.** Added Stats 1979 ch 964 §11.

§1861.15. Redelivery of property and liability for damages of plaintiff who fails to recover judgment

If the plaintiff fails to recover judgment in the action, he shall redeliver the property to the defendant, and be liable for all damages sustained by the defendant, which are proximately caused by operation of the temporary restraining order and preliminary injunction, if any, the levy of the writ of possession, and the loss of possession of the property pursuant to the levy of the writ of possession. **Leg.H.** Added Stats 1979 ch 964 §12.

§1861.16. Temporary restraining order

(a) At or after the time he files an application for a writ of possession, the plaintiff may apply for a temporary restraining order by setting forth in the application a statement of grounds justifying the issuance of such order.

(b) A temporary restraining order may issue ex parte if all the following are found:

(1) The plaintiff has established the probable validity of his claim and entitlement to possession of the property, pursuant to an innkeepers' lien.

(2) The plaintiff has provided an undertaking as required by Section 1861.21.

(3) The plaintiff has established the probable validity that there is an immediate danger that the property claimed may become unavailable to levy by reason of being transferred, concealed, or removed, or may become substantially impaired in value.

(c) If at the hearing on the issuance of the writ of possession the court determines that the plaintiff is not entitled to a writ of possession, the court shall dissolve any temporary restraining order; otherwise, the court may issue a preliminary injunction to remain in effect until the property claimed is seized pursuant to the writ of possession. **Leg.H.** Added Stats 1979 ch 964 §13.

§1861.17. Conduct subject to restraining order

In the discretion of the court, the temporary restraining order may prohibit the defendant from doing any or all of the following:

(a) Transferring any interest in the property by sale, pledge, or grant of security interest, or otherwise disposing of, or encumbering, the property.

(b) Concealing or otherwise removing the property in such a manner as to make it less available to seizure by the levying officer.

(c) Impairing the value of the property either by acts of destruction or by failure to care for the property in a reasonable manner. **Leg.H.** Added Stats 1979 ch 964 §14.

§1861.18. Service of writ officer

(a) At the time of levy, the levying officer shall deliver to the person in possession of the property a copy of the writ of possession, with a copy of the plaintiff's undertaking attached.

(b) If no one is in possession of the property at the time of levy, the levying officer shall subsequently serve the writ and attached undertaking on the defendant. If the defendant has appeared in the action, service shall be accomplished in the manner provided by Chapter 5 (commencing with Section 1010) of Title 14 of Part 2. If the defendant has not appeared in the action, service shall be accomplished in the manner provided for the service of summons and complaint by Article 3 (commencing with Section 415.10) of Chapter 4 of Title 5 of Part 2. **Leg.H.** Added Stats 1979 ch 964 §15.

§1861.19. Taking and disposition of property

(a) After the levying officer takes possession pursuant to the writ of possession, the levying officer shall keep the property in a secure place. Except as otherwise provided in Section 1861.6:

(1) If notice of the filing of an undertaking for redelivery or notice of objection to the undertaking is not received by the levying officer within 10 days after levy of the writ of possession, the levying officer shall deliver the property to plaintiff, upon receiving the fees for taking, and necessary expenses for keeping, the property.

(2) If notice of the filing of an undertaking for redelivery is received by the levying officer within 10 days after levy of the writ of possession, and no objection is made to the defendant's undertaking, the levying officer shall redeliver the property to defendant upon expiration of the time to object, upon receiving the fees for taking and necessary expenses for keeping the property not already paid or advanced by the plaintiff.

(3) If notice of objection to the plaintiff's undertaking or notice of the filing of an undertaking for redelivery is received within 10 days after levy of the writ of possession, and objection is made to the defendant's undertaking, the levying officer shall not deliver or redeliver the property until the time provided in Section 1861.23.

(b) Notwithstanding subdivision (a), when not otherwise provided by contract, and where an undertaking for redelivery has not been filed, upon a showing that the property is perishable, or will greatly deteriorate or depreciate in value, or for some other reason that the interest of the parties will be best served thereby, the court may order that the property be sold and the proceeds deposited in the court to abide the judgment in the action. **Leg.H.** Added Stats 1979 ch 964 §16. Amended Stats 1982 ch 517 §66.

§1861.20. Return of writ of possession

The levying officer shall return the writ of possession, with his proceedings thereon, to the court in which the action is pending, within 30 days after a levy, but in no event more than 60 days after the writ is issued. **Leg.H.** Added Stats 1979 ch 964 §17.

§1861.21. Plaintiff's undertaking

The court shall not issue a temporary restraining order or a writ of possession until the plaintiff has filed with the court an undertaking. The undertaking shall provide that the sureties are bound to the defendant in the amount of the undertaking for the return of the property to the defendant, if the return thereof be ordered, and for the payment to the defendant of any sum recovered against plaintiff. The undertaking shall be in an amount not less than twice the value of the property. **Leg.H.** Added Stats 1979 ch 964 §18. Amended Stats 1982 ch 517 §67.

§1861.22. Defendant's undertaking

(a) The defendant may prevent the plaintiff from taking possession of property, pursuant to a writ of possession, or regain possession of property so taken, by filing with the court in which the action was brought an undertaking in an amount equal to the amount of the plaintiff's undertaking required by Section 1861.21. The undertaking shall state that, if the plaintiff recovers judgment on the action, the defendant shall pay all costs awarded to the plaintiff and all damages that the plaintiff may sustain by reason of the loss of possession of the property, not exceeding the amount of the undertaking.

(b) The defendant's undertaking may be filed at any time before or after the levy of the writ of possession. The defendant shall mail a copy of the undertaking to the levying officer.

(c) If an undertaking for redelivery is filed, and no objection is made to the undertaking, the levying officer shall deliver the property to the defendant, or, if the plaintiff has previously been given possession of the property, the plaintiff shall deliver the property to the defendant. If an undertaking for redelivery is filed and an objection to the undertaking is made, the provisions of Section 1861.23 apply. **Leg.H.** Added Stats 1979 ch 964 §19. Amended Stats 1982 ch 517 §68.

§1861.23. Exception to sureties

(a) The defendant may object to the plaintiff's undertaking not later than 10 days after levy of the writ of possession. The defendant shall mail notice of objection to the levying officer.

(b) The plaintiff may object to the defendant's undertaking not later than 10 days after the defendant's undertaking is filed. The plaintiff shall mail notice of objection to the levying officer.

(c) If the court determines that the plaintiff's undertaking is not sufficient and a sufficient undertaking is not given within the time provided by statute, the court shall vacate the temporary restraining order or preliminary injunction, if any, and the writ of possession and, if levy has occurred, order the levying officer or the plaintiff to return the property to the defendant. If the court determines that the plaintiff's undertaking is sufficient, the court shall order the levying officer to deliver the property to the plaintiff.

(d) If the court determines that the defendant's undertaking is not sufficient and a sufficient undertaking is not given within the time required by statute, the court shall order the levying officer to deliver the property to the plaintiff, or, if the plaintiff has previously been given possession of the property, the plaintiff shall retain possession. If the court determines the defendant's undertaking is sufficient, the court shall order the levying officer or the plaintiff to deliver the property to the defendant. **Leg.H.** Added Stats 1979 ch 964 §20 as §1821.23. Renumbered by Stats 1981 ch 714 §53. Amended Stats 1982 ch 517 §69.

§1861.24. Sale of property

Unless the judgment is paid within 30 days from the date it becomes final, the plaintiff may sell the baggage and property at public auction to the highest bidder, after giving notice of the sale by publication. The notice shall contain the name of the debtor, the amount due, a brief description of the property to be sold, and the time and place of sale, in the manner required by Section 6061 of the Government Code in the county in which the premises are situated. A copy of the notice shall be mailed, at least 15 days prior to the date of sale, to the tenant or guest at his or her residence or other known address, and if not known, to the tenant or guest at the place where the premises are situated. After satisfying the lien out of the proceeds of the sale, together with any reasonable costs that may have been incurred in enforcing the lien, the balance of the proceeds of the sale, if any, which have not been claimed by the tenant or guest shall, within 30 days from the date of the sale, be paid into the treasury of the county in which the sale took place. If that balance is not claimed by the owner thereof, or his legal representative, within one year thereafter, by making application to the treasurer or other official designated by the county, it shall be paid into the general fund of the county. Any sale conducted pursuant to this section shall be a bar to any action against the plaintiff for the recovery of the baggage or property, or of the value thereof, or for any damages arising out of the failure of the tenant or guest to receive the baggage or property. **Leg.H.** Added Stats 1979 ch 964 §21.

§1861.25. Third-party claims as to property taken

Where the property taken is claimed by a third person, the rules and proceedings applicable in cases of third-party claims under Division 4 (commencing with Section 720.010) of Title 9 of Part 2 of the Code of Civil Procedure apply. **Leg.H.** Added Stats 1982 ch 497 §10.5; operative July 1, 1983.

§1861.27. Requirements for affidavits

The facts stated in each affidavit filed pursuant to this article shall be set forth with particularity. Except where matters are specifically permitted by this article to be shown by information and belief, each affidavit shall show affirmatively that the affiant, if sworn as a witness, can testify competently to the facts stated therein. The affiant may be any person, whether or not a party to this action, who has knowledge of the facts. A verified complaint that satisfies the requirements of this section may be used in lieu of, or in addition to, an ordinary affidavit. **Leg.H.** Added Stats 1979 ch 964 §22.

§1861.28. Performance of judicial duties

The judicial duties to be performed under this article are "subordinate judicial duties" within the meaning of Section 22 of Article VI of the California Constitution, and may be performed by appointed officers such as court commissioners. **Leg.H.** Added Stats 1979 ch 964 §23.

§1861a. Apartment keeper's lien; Enforcement; Notice of sale; Proceeds; Exemptions

Keepers of furnished and unfurnished apartment houses, apartments, cottages, or bungalow courts shall have a lien upon the baggage and other property of value belonging to their tenants or guests, and upon all the right, title and interest of their tenants or guests in and to all property in the possession of such tenants or guests which may be in such apartment house, apartment, cottage, or bungalow court, for the proper charges due from such tenants or guests, for their accommodation, rent, services, meals, and such extras as are furnished at their request, and for all moneys expended for them, at their request, and for the costs of enforcing such lien.

Such lien may be enforced only after final judgment in an action brought to recover such charges or moneys. During the pendency of the proceeding, the plaintiff may take possession of such baggage and property upon an order issued by the court, where it appears to the satisfaction of the court from an affidavit filed by or on behalf of the plaintiff that the baggage or property is about to be destroyed, substantially devalued, or removed from the premises. Ten days written notice of the hearing on the motion for such order shall be served on the defendant and shall inform the defendant that the defendant may file affidavits on the defendant's behalf and present testimony in the defendant's behalf and that if the defendant fails to appear the plaintiff will apply to the court for such order. The plaintiff shall file an undertaking with good and sufficient sureties, to be approved by the court, in such sum as may be fixed by the court.

Upon such order, the plaintiff shall have the right to enter peaceably the unfurnished apartment house, apartment, cottage, or bungalow court used by the guest or tenant without liability to the guest or tenant, including any possible claim of liability for conversion, trespass, or forcible entry. The plaintiff shall have the same duties and liabilities as a depository for hire as to property which the plaintiff takes into possession. An entry shall be considered peaceable when accomplished with a key or passkey or through an unlocked door during the hours between sunrise and sunset. Unless the judgment shall be paid within 30 days from the date when it becomes final, the plaintiff may sell the baggage and property, at public auction to the highest bidder, after giving notice of such sale by publication of a notice containing the name of the debtor, the amount due, a brief description of the property to be sold, and the time and place of such sale, pursuant to Section 6064 of the Government Code in the county in which said apartment house, apartment, cottage, or bungalow court is situated, and after by mailing, at least 15 days prior to the date of sale, a copy of such notice addressed to such tenant or guest at the residence or other known address of the tenant or guest, and if not known, such notice shall be addressed to the tenant or guest at the place where such apartment house, apartment, cottage, or bungalow court is situated; and, after satisfying such lien out of the proceeds of such sale, together with any reasonable costs, that may have been incurred in enforcing said lien, the residue of said proceeds of sale, if any, shall, upon demand made within six months after such sale, be paid to such tenant or guest; and if not demanded within six months from the date of such sale, said residue, if any, shall be paid into the treasury of the county in which such sale took place; and if the same be not claimed by the owner thereof, or the owner's legal representative within one year thereafter, it shall be paid into the general fund of the county; and such sale shall be a perpetual bar to any action against said keeper for the recovery of such baggage or property, or of the value thereof, or for any damages, growing out of the failure of such tenant or guest to receive such baggage or property.

When the baggage and property are not in the possession of the keeper as provided herein, such lien shall be enforced only in the manner provided for enforcement of a money judgment.

Any property which is exempt from enforcement of a money judgment is not subject to the lien provided for in this section. **Leg.H.** Added Stats 1917 ch 794 §1. Amended Stats 1933 ch 900 §1; Stats 1939 ch 483 §2; Stats 1941 ch 515 §1; Stats 1953 ch 250 §1, ch 1453 §1; Stats 1957 ch 454 §1; Stats 1961 ch 2041 §1; Stats 1965 ch 1540 §1.5; Stats 1967 ch 1387 §2; Stats 1968 ch 1182 §2; Stats 1970 ch 1247 §2; Stats 1982 ch 517 §70 (ch 497 prevails), ch 497 §10, operative July 1, 1983.

§1862. [Section repealed 1974]

Leg.H. Enacted Stats 1875–76 ch 486 §1. Amended Stats 1927 ch 483 §1; Stats 1937 ch 355 §1; Stats 1961 ch 2041 §2; Stats 1965 ch 1540 §3. Repealed Stats 1974 ch 331 §1. The repealed section related to sale of unclaimed baggage.

§1862.5. Sale of personal property found in or deposited with hospital

Whenever any personal property has heretofore been found in or deposited with, or is hereafter found in or deposited with any licensed hospital and has remained or shall remain unclaimed for a period of 180 days following the departure of the owner from the hospital, such hospital may proceed to sell the same at public auction, and out of the proceeds of such sale may retain the charges for storage, if any, the reasonable expenses of sale thereof and all sums due the hospital from the last known owner. No such sale shall be made until the expiration of four weeks from the time written notice of such sale is given to the last known owner. Said notice shall contain a description of each item of personal property to be sold, the name of the last owner, the name of the hospital and the time and place of sale and may be sent by regular mail, postage prepaid, to the last known owner at his last known address. In case there should be any balance from such sale after the deductions herein provided for, and such balance shall not be claimed by the rightful owner or his legal representative within one week of said sale, the same shall be paid into the treasury of the county wherein said hospital is located; and if the same be not claimed by the owner thereof, or his legal representative within one year thereafter, the same shall be paid into the general fund of said county. Proceedings in substantial compliance with this section shall exonerate the hospital from any liability for property so sold. This section shall not be construed as limiting or in any way amending any other provision of law limiting the liabilities of any licensed hospital. **Leg.H.** Added Stats 1963 ch 810 §1.

§1863. Keeper to post rates of charges

(a) Every keeper of a hotel, inn, boardinghouse or lodginghouse, shall post in a conspicuous place in the office or public room, and in every bedroom of said hotel, boardinghouse, inn, or lodginghouse, a printed copy of this section, and a statement of rate or range of rates by the day for lodging.

(b) No charge or sum shall be collected or received for any greater sum than is specified in subdivision (a). For any violation of this subdivision, the offender shall forfeit to the injured party one hundred dollars ($100) or three times the amount of the sum charged in excess of what he is entitled to, whichever is greater. There shall be no forfeiture under this subdivision unless notice be given of the overcharge to such keeper within 30 days after payment of such charges and such keeper shall fail or refuse to make proper adjustment of such overcharge. **Leg.H.** Added Code Amdts 1875–76 ch 486 §1. Amended Stats 1969 ch 826 §1.

§1864. Duties of person or entity arranging for transient occupancies on behalf of others

Any person or entity, including a person employed by a real estate broker, who, on behalf of another or others, solicits or arranges, or accepts reservations or money, or both, for transient occupancies described in paragraphs (1) and (2) of subdivision (b) of Section 1940, in a dwelling unit in a common interest development, as defined in Section 4100, in a dwelling unit in an apartment building or complex, or in a single-family home, shall do each of the following:

(a) Prepare and maintain, in accordance with a written agreement with the owner, complete and accurate records and books of account, kept in accordance with generally accepted accounting principles, of all reservations made and money received and spent with respect to each dwelling unit. All money received shall be kept in a trust account maintained for the benefit of owners of the dwelling units.

(b) Render, monthly, to each owner of the dwelling unit, or to that owner's designee, an accounting for each month in which there are any deposits or disbursements on behalf of that owner, however, in no event shall this accounting be rendered any less frequently than quarterly.

(c) Make all records and books of account with respect to a dwelling unit available, upon reasonable advance notice, for inspection and copying by the dwelling unit's owner. The records shall be maintained for a period of at least three years.

(d) Comply fully with all collection, payment, and recordkeeping requirements of a transient occupancy tax ordinance, if any, applicable to the occupancy.

(e) In no event shall any activities described in this section subject the person or entity performing those activities in any manner to Part 1 (commencing with Section 10000) of Division 4 of the Business and Professions Code. However, a real estate licensee subject to this section may satisfy the requirements of this section by compliance with the Real Estate Law. **Leg.H.** Added Stats 1992 ch 134 §2 (AB 814). Amended Stats 2012 ch 181 §37 (AB 806), effective January 1, 2013, operative January 1, 2014.

Prior Law: Former §1864, similar to present §2080, was enacted Stats 1872, and repealed Stats 1967 ch 1512 §1.

§1865. "Hotel"; "Guest"; Right to evict guest who fails to depart by posted checkout time; Rights with respect to minors

(a) For purposes of this section, "hotel" means any hotel, motel, bed and breakfast inn, or other similar transient lodging establishment, but it shall not include any residential hotel as defined in Section 50519 of the Health and Safety Code. "Innkeeper" means the owner or operator of a hotel, or the duly authorized agent or employee of the owner or operator.

(b) For purposes of this section, "guest" means, and is specifically limited to, an occupant of a hotel whose occupancy is exempt, pursuant to subdivision (b) of Section 1940, from Chapter 2 (commencing with Section 1940) of Title 5 of Part 4 of Division 3.

(c) In addition to, and not in derogation of, any other provision of law, every innkeeper shall have the right to evict a guest in the manner specified in this subdivision if the guest refuses or otherwise fails to fully depart the guest room at or before the innkeeper's posted checkout time on the date agreed to by the guest, but only if both of the following conditions are met:

(1) If the guest is provided written notice, at the time that he or she was received and provided accommodations by the innkeeper, that the innkeeper needs that guest's room to accommodate an arriving person with a contractual right thereto, and that if the guest fails to fully depart at the time agreed to the innkeeper may enter the guest's guest room, take possession of the guest's property, re-key the door to the guest room, and make the guest room available to a new guest. The written notice shall be signed by the guest.

(2) At the time that the innkeeper actually undertakes to evict the guest as specified in this subdivision, the innkeeper in fact has a contractual obligation to provide the guest room to an arriving person.

In the above cases, the innkeeper may enter the guest's guest room, take possession of the guest's property, re-key the door to the guest room, and make the guest room available to a new guest. The evicted guest shall be entitled to immediate possession of his or her property upon request therefor, subject to the rights of the innkeeper pursuant to Sections 1861 to 1861.28, inclusive.

(d) As pertains to a minor, the rights of an innkeeper include, but are not limited to, the following:

(1) Where a minor unaccompanied by an adult seeks accommodations, the innkeeper may require a parent or guardian of the minor, or another responsible adult, to assume, in writing, full liability for any and all proper charges and other obligations incurred by the minor for accommodations, food and beverages, and other services provided by or through the innkeeper, as well as for any and all injuries or damage caused by the minor to any person or property.

(2) Where a minor is accompanied by an adult, the innkeeper may require the adult to agree, in writing, not to leave any minor 12 years of age or younger unattended on the innkeeper's premises at any time during their stay, and to control the minor's behavior during their stay so as to preserve the peace and quiet of the innkeeper's other guests and to prevent any injury to any person and damage to any property. **Leg.H.** Added Stats 1999 ch 354 §2 (SB 1171). Amended Stats 2004 ch 183 §38 (AB 3082).

Prior Law: Former §1865, relating to finding and disposition of personalty, was enacted Stats 1872, amended Stats 1905 ch 453 §1; Stats 1951 ch 1676 §4, and repealed Stats 1967 ch 1512 §1.

§1866. Definitions; Right to evict guest of special occupancy park who fails to depart by posted checkout time; Conditions; Rights with respect to minors

(a) For purposes of this section, the following definitions apply:

(1) "Camping cabin" has the same meaning as in Section 18862.5 of the Health and Safety Code.

(2) "Campsite" has the same meaning as in Section 18862.9 of the Health and Safety Code.

(3) "Guest" is interchangeable with "occupant" and has the same meaning as used in Chapter 2.6 (commencing with Section 799.20) of Title 2 of Part 2 of Division 1.

(4) "Lot" has the same meaning as in Section 18862.23 of the Health and Safety Code.

(5) "Motor vehicle" has the same meaning as in Section 415 of the Vehicle Code.

(6) "Occupant" is interchangeable with "guest" and has the same meaning as used in Chapter 2.6 (commencing with Section 799.20) of Title 2 of Part 2 of Division 1.

(7) "Park trailer" has the same meaning as in Section 18009.3 of the Health and Safety Code.

(8) "Recreational vehicle" has the same meaning as in Section 18010 of the Health and Safety Code.

(9) "Site" means the campsite, camping cabin, lot, or rental unit.

(10) "Special occupancy park" has the same meaning as in Section 18862.43 of the Health and Safety Code.

(11) "Tent" has the same meaning as in Section 18862.49 of the Health and Safety Code.

(b)(1) Notwithstanding any other provision of law, the park management of a special occupancy park shall have the right to evict a guest if the guest refuses or otherwise fails to fully depart from the campsite, camping cabin, lot, or other rental unit at the park management's posted checkout time on the date agreed to by the guest, but only if the following conditions are met:

(A) The guest is provided with written notice, at the time that he or she was provided accommodations by the park management, that the park management needs that guest's campsite, camping cabin, lot, or rental unit to accommodate an arriving person with a contractual right thereto, and that if the guest fails to fully depart at the time agreed to, the park management may take possession of the guest's property left in the site, subject to the limits of paragraph (2), including any tent, park trailer, or recreational vehicle, and make the campsite, camping cabin, lot, or rental unit available to new guests. The written notice shall be signed by the guest.

(B)(i) At the time that the park management actually undertakes to evict the guest as specified in this subdivision, the park management has a contractual obligation to provide the guest's campsite, camping cabin, lot, or rental unit to an arriving person and there are no other substantially similar campsites, camping cabins, lots, or rental units available for the arriving person.

(ii) Subject to the same requirements described in subparagraph (i), a guest may be provided with the notice described in subparagraph (A) subsequent to the time he or she was provided accommodations by park management, if the notice is provided at least 24 hours prior to the guest's scheduled checkout time. If park management provides a notice under this subparagraph in bad faith or with the knowledge that the contractual obligation is not a bona fide obligation, it shall be liable to the evicted guest for actual damages, plus a civil penalty of two hundred fifty dollars ($250).

(C) At the time that the park management actually undertakes to evict the guest as specified in this subdivision, the park management offers another campsite, camping cabin, lot, or rental unit to the guest, if one is available.

(2) In addition to the requirements of paragraph (1), in order for management to remove a recreational vehicle or motor vehicle, the park management shall do all of the following:

(A) Management shall have an oral, face-to-face communication with the registered guest after the guest has held over that does all of the following:

(i) Alerts the guest that he or she is in violation of the terms of the reservation because he or she has failed to depart the site at the agreed-upon time.

(ii) Reminds the guest that failure to remove a recreational vehicle, motor vehicle, or any other property from the space within two hours may result in the park management removing the recreational vehicle, motor vehicle, or any other property.

(iii) Discloses that the cost of towing a recreational vehicle or motor vehicle is substantial and that these costs will be incurred by the guest.

(iv) Identifies another location in the park to which the guest may temporarily move his or her recreational vehicle or motor vehicle.

(B) The park management gives the guest two hours after the park management has communicated with the guest, pursuant to subparagraph (A), to remove the guest's recreational vehicle, motor vehicle, or other property from the site.

(c) Except as provided in subdivision (f), if the conditions specified in subdivision (b) are met, the park management may take possession of the guest's property left at the site and have the guest's recreational vehicle or motor vehicle towed from the special occupancy park and make the guest's campsite, camping cabin, lot, or rental unit available to a new guest. Park management may enter a campsite, camping cabin, park trailer, lot, or rental unit owned by the park management to take possession of the guest's possessions. The evicted guest shall be entitled to immediate possession of his or her property upon request, subject to the enforcement rights of the park management, which are the same as those accorded to a hotel, motel, inn, boarding house, or lodging housekeeper, pursuant to Sections 1861 to 1861.28, inclusive. If a guest's recreational vehicle or motor vehicle has been towed from the premises, the guest shall be entitled to immediate possession of his or her vehicle upon request, subject to the conditions of the towing company.

(d) When the park management moves or causes the removal of a guest's recreational vehicle, motor vehicle, or other property, the management and the individual or entity that removes the recreational vehicle, motor vehicle, or other property shall exercise reasonable and ordinary care in removing the recreational vehicle, motor vehicle, or other property.

(e) This section does not apply to a manufactured home, as defined in Section 18007 of the Health and Safety Code, or a mobilehome, as defined in Section 18008 of the Health and Safety Code.

(f) In the event that a guest is incapable of removing his or her recreational vehicle or motor vehicle from the lot because of: (1) a physical incapacity, (2) the recreational vehicle or motor vehicle is not motorized and cannot be moved by the guest's vehicle, or (3) the recreational vehicle or motor vehicle is inoperable due to mechanical difficulties, the guest shall be provided with 72 hours in which to remove the vehicle. If the guest has not removed the vehicle within 72 hours, park management may remove the vehicle without further notice.

(g) As pertains to a minor, the rights of guests include, but are not limited to, the following:

(1) If a minor who is unaccompanied by an adult seeks accommodations, the park management may require a parent or guardian of the minor, or another responsible adult, to assume, in writing, full liability for any and all proper charges and other obligations incurred by the minor for accommodations, food and beverages, and other services provided by or through the park management, as well as for any and all injuries or damage caused by the minor to any person or property.

(2) If a minor is accompanied by an adult, the park management may require the adult to agree, in writing, not to leave any minor 12 years of age or younger unattended on the park management's premises at any time during their stay, and to control the minor's behavior during their stay so as to preserve the peace and quiet of the other guests and to prevent any injury to any person and damage to any property. **Leg.H.** Added Stats 2004 ch 530 §4 (AB 1964).

Prior Law: Former §1866, relating to finding and disposition of personalty, was enacted Stats 1872, and repealed Stats 1967 ch 1512 §1.

§1867. Right to require guest in special occupancy park to move from a space when danger imminent; Definitions

(a) The park management of a special occupancy park may require a guest to move from a space in the special occupancy park to a different space in the special occupancy park if an imminent danger is present, as determined by the park management. If possible, the park management shall offer to return the guest to his or her original space once the park management has determined that the imminent danger is removed or resolved.

(b) For purposes of this section, the following definitions apply:

(1) "Imminent danger" means a danger that poses an immediate and likely risk to the health or safety of a guest or guests in the special occupancy park.

(2) "Space" means any of the following:

(A) "Camping cabin," as defined in Section 18862.5 of the Health and Safety Code.

(B) "Campsite," as defined in Section 18862.9 of the Health and Safety Code.

(C) "Lot," as defined in Section 18862.23 of the Health and Safety Code, or other rental unit.

(3) "Special occupancy park" has the same meaning as in Section 18862.43 of the Health and Safety Code. **Leg.H.** Added Stats 2004 ch 530 §5 (AB 1964).

Prior Law: Former §1867, relating to finding and disposition of personalty, was enacted Stats 1872, and repealed Stats 1967 ch 1512 §1.

ARTICLE 5
Finding [Repealed]

§§1868–1875. [Sections repealed 1967]

Leg.H. Enacted Stats 1872. Amended Stats 1905 ch 453 §§1, 2; Stats 1947 ch 893 §1; Stats 1951 ch 159 §1, ch 1676 §4, operative January 1, 1952; Stats 1961 ch 816 §1; Stats 1963 ch 470 §1; Stats 1967 ch 477 §1, ch 951 §4. Repealed Stats 1967 ch 1512 §1; Stats 1968 ch 48 §3. See §§2080.3 et seq.

CHAPTER 3
DEPOSIT FOR EXCHANGE

Relations of the parties. §1878.

§1878. Relations of the parties

A deposit for exchange transfers to the depositary the title to the thing deposited, and creates between him and the depositor the relation of debtor and creditor merely. **Leg.H.** Enacted Stats 1872.

CHAPTER 4
PRIVATE BULK STORAGE OF GRAIN

Title of chapter. §1880.
Definitions. §1880.1.
Marking storage facilities. §1880.2.
Sale of grain without delivery. §1880.3.
Bill of sale; Requisites. §1880.4.
Additional provisions in bill of sale. §1880.5.

Passage of title to buyer and assignees. §1880.6.
Notice of sale; Posting; Contents. §1880.7.
Presentation of bill of sale on delivery of grain. §1880.8.
Presumption as to right of holder of bill of sale. §1880.9.
Storage of grain not removed or delivered. §1881.
Offenses; Sale as affected by lack of or irregularity in notice or posting thereof. §1881.1.
Depositary as warehouseman or storer for hire; Storage facility as warehouse or public storage place. §1881.2.

§1880. Title of chapter
This chapter may be cited as the Private Bulk Grain Storage Law. **Leg.H.** Added Stats 1944 4th Ex Sess ch 54 §1, effective June 21, 1944.

§1880.1. Definitions
As used in this chapter:

(a) "Grain" includes barley, corn, flax, hay, grain, sorghums, oats, rice, rye and wheat.

(b) "Seller" means a producer of grain who continues to store grain after sale thereof by him in storage facilities owned, operated, or controlled by him.

(c) "Storage facilities" means any bin, building, elevator, protected enclosure, or other structure owned, operated, or controlled by the seller of the grain stored therein.

(d) "Private bulk storage" means the storage of grain in storage facilities after sale of such grain by a seller.

(e) "Buyer" means a purchaser of grain which is thereafter stored in private bulk storage, and includes the assigns and successors in interest of such buyer.

(f) "Bill of sale" means a written instrument, conforming to the requirements of this chapter, which evidences a transfer of grain. **Leg.H.** Added Stats 1944 4th Ex Sess ch 54 §1, effective June 21, 1944.

§1880.2. Marking storage facilities
The seller shall conspicuously mark on all storage facilities "Private bulk storage only" and with a designating number on each such facility and such markings shall be maintained at all times during which grain remains in private bulk storage therein. **Leg.H.** Added Stats 1944 4th Ex Sess ch 54 §1, effective June 21, 1944.

§1880.3. Sale of grain without delivery
Grain in private bulk storage facilities may be sold in conformity with this chapter by bill of sale without delivery and no provision of Section 3440 of this code or of any other law requiring delivery or actual and continued change of possession shall be applicable to grain so sold. **Leg.H.** Added Stats 1944 4th Ex Sess ch 54 §1, effective June 21, 1944.

§1880.4. Bill of sale; Requisites
Upon sale of grain which is to remain in private bulk storage the seller shall execute and deliver to the buyer a bill of sale which shall contain all of the following:

(a) The date and place where made.

(b) the names of the seller and the buyer.

(c) A statement of the estimated quantity and kind of grain.

(d) A statement of the location and designating numbers of the storage facilities in which the grain is stored.

(e) A statement of the price per unit and a statement of the amount received by the seller. **Leg.H.** Added Stats 1944 4th Ex Sess ch 54 §1, effective June 21, 1944.

§1880.5. Additional provisions in bill of sale
The bill of sale may contain other provisions, including reference to or provision for any one or more of the following:

(a) Provision that the total price is based upon the estimated weight and that the total price may be adjusted in accordance with the outturn weight.

(b) A statement that the buyer may have free use of the designated storage facilities until a specified date and that any extension beyond the specified date granted by seller must be endorsed under the signature of seller on the bill of sale.

(c) A statement that seller has the legal right to extend to buyer the use of designated storage facilities.

(d) A statement that actual possession of the grain by the buyer is to be taken on board trucks at the storage facility, or on railroad cars, or in the storage facility, or as may be agreed upon.

(e) A statement that if actual possession be not taken within the time specified, due to any cause not chargeable to seller, the seller may consign the same at buyer's risk and expense to a specified destination. **Leg.H.** Added Stats 1944 4th Ex Sess ch 54 §1, effective June 21, 1944.

§1880.6. Passage of title to buyer and assignees
Execution and delivery by a seller of a bill of sale shall pass seller's title to the grain covered thereby to the buyer and such title passes to the assignees of the buyer upon further endorsement and delivery of the bill of sale. **Leg.H.** Added Stats 1944 4th Ex Sess ch 54 §1, effective June 21, 1944.

§1880.7. Notice of sale; Posting; Contents
Upon the issuance of any such bill of sale, the seller shall immediately post upon the storage facilities containing the grain a notice in substantially the following form:

"Notice of Sale

On this ____ day of ____, 19____, grain in this storage facility numbered ____, estimated to be ____ bushels of _____ (designating the kind of grain) was transferred and sold as follows:

Name of Seller _____ Name of original Buyer _____
Address of Seller _____ Address of Buyer _____

Grain to be removed by buyer on or before ____, 19____, (If date extended such fact and the date to which extended must appear on the notice.)"

Such notice shall be maintained by seller in a conspicuous place upon the storage facility at all times during which the grain involved continues to be stored therein.

Leg.H. Added Stats 1944 4th Ex Sess ch 54 §1, effective June 21, 1944.

§1880.8. Presentation of bill of sale on delivery of grain
No delivery shall be made of any portion of the grain so privately stored unless the bill of sale therefor is presented to the seller, or other person in charge of the storage facility, and the amount of grain so delivered plainly endorsed upon the bill of sale; but this provision shall not apply to any consignment of the grain by the seller to the buyer upon the expiration of the time for delivery specified in the bill of sale. **Leg.H.** Added Stats 1944 4th Ex Sess ch 54 §1, effective June 21, 1944.

§1880.9. Presumption as to right of holder of bill of sale
The presentment of the bill of sale by the holder to seller shall be presumptive evidence that the person presenting it is entitled to delivery of the grain described therein unless the seller has knowledge of facts or circumstances sufficient to place him on notice that the possession of the instrument by such person is unlawful. **Leg.H.** Added Stats 1944 4th Ex Sess ch 54 §1, effective June 21, 1944.

§1881. Storage of grain not removed or delivered
If any grain in private bulk storage is not removed or delivered on or before the original date of delivery specified in the bill of sale and in the notice of sale, it shall be lawful for the seller to continue to store such grain to the order of the buyer upon such terms as may be agreed upon. **Leg.H.** Added Stats 1944 4th Ex Sess ch 54 §1, effective June 21, 1944.

§1881.1. Offenses; Sale as affected by lack of or irregularity in notice or posting thereof
A seller who shall willfully fail to comply with the requirements of notice and posting as provided for in Section 1880.2 or in Section 1880.7 shall be guilty of a misdemeanor and punishable by imprisonment in the county jail not exceeding six months, or by fine not exceeding one thousand dollars ($1,000), or by both. No sale of grain shall be invalidated by reason of any lack or irregularity in connection with such notice or posting. **Leg.H.** Added Stats 1944 4th Ex Sess ch 54 §1, effective June 21, 1944. Amended Stats 1983 ch 1092 §66, effective September 27, 1983, operative January 1, 1984.

§1881.2. Depositary as warehouseman or storer for hire; Storage facility as warehouse or public storage place
The storage of grain pursuant to this chapter shall not constitute the depositary a warehouseman or storer of goods for hire and no storage facility shall be deemed to constitute a warehouse or public place of storage. **Leg.H.** Added Stats 1944 4th Ex Sess ch 54 §1, effective June 21, 1944.

§1881.3. [Section repealed 1953]
Leg.H. Added Stats 1944 4th Ex Sess ch 54 §1, effective June 21, 1944. Amended Stats 1945 ch 337 §1; Stats 1947 ch 537 §1; Stats 1949 ch 295

§1; Stats 1951 ch 820 §1. Repealed Stats 1953 ch 867 §1. The repealed section provided for termination of the chapter.

TITLE 3.5
UTILITY SERVICES

Definitions. §1882.
Actions. §1882.1.
Damages. §1882.2.
Presumption of violation. §1882.3.
Injunctive relief; Damages. §1882.4.
Requirement of monetary damages. §1882.5.
Effect of recovery of damages on rates. §1882.6.

§1882. Definitions

Unless the context requires otherwise, the following definitions govern the construction of this title:

(a) "Customer" means the person in whose name a utility service is provided.

(b) "Divert" means to change the intended course or path of electricity, gas, or water without the authorization or consent of the utility.

(c) "Person" means any individual, a partnership, firm, association, limited liability company, or corporation.

(d) "Reconnection" means the commencement of utility service to a customer or other person after service has been lawfully discontinued by the utility.

(e) "Tamper" means to rearrange, injure, alter, interfere with, or otherwise to prevent from performing normal or customary function.

(f) "Utility" means any electrical, gas, or water corporation as those terms are defined in the Public Utilities Code and includes any electrical, gas, or water system operated by any public agency.

(g) "Utility service" means the provision of electricity, gas, water, or any other service or commodity furnished by the utility for compensation. **Leg.H.** Added Stats 1981 ch 981 §1. Amended Stats 1994 ch 1010 §47 (SB 2053).

§1882.1. Actions

A utility may bring a civil action for damages against any person who commits, authorizes, solicits, aids, abets, or attempts any of the following acts:

(a) Diverts, or causes to be diverted, utility services by any means whatsoever.

(b) Makes, or causes to be made, any connection or reconnection with property owned or used by the utility to provide utility service without the authorization or consent of the utility.

(c) Prevents any utility meter, or other device used in determining the charge for utility services, from accurately performing its measuring function by tampering or by any other means.

(d) Tampers with any property owned or used by the utility to provide utility services.

(e) Uses or receives the direct benefit of all, or a portion, of the utility service with knowledge of, or reason to believe that, the diversion, tampering, or unauthorized connection existed at the time of the use, or that the use or receipt, was without the authorization or consent of the utility. **Leg.H.** Added Stats 1981 ch 981 §1.

§1882.2. Damages

In any civil action brought pursuant to Section 1882.1, the utility may recover as damages three times the amount of actual damages, if any, plus the cost of the suit and reasonable attorney's fees. **Leg.H.** Added Stats 1981 ch 981 §1.

§1882.3. Presumption of violation

There is a rebuttable presumption that there is a violation of Section 1882.1 if, on premises controlled by the customer or by the person using or receiving the direct benefit of utility service, there is either, or both, of the following:

(a) Any instrument, apparatus, or device primarily designed to be used to obtain utility service without paying the full lawful charge therefor.

(b) Any meter that has been altered, tampered with, or bypassed so as to cause no measurement or inaccurate measurement of utility services. **Leg.H.** Added Stats 1981 ch 981 §1.

§1882.4. Injunctive relief; Damages

A utility may, in accordance with Chapter 3 (commencing with Section 525) of Title 7 of Part 2 of the Code of Civil Procedure, bring an action to enjoin and restrain any of the acts specified in Section 1882.1. The utility may, in the same action, seek damages for any of the acts specified in Section 1882.1. **Leg.H.** Added Stats 1981 ch 981 §1.

§1882.5. Requirement of monetary damages

It is not a necessary prerequisite to an action pursuant to Section 1882.4 that the utility have suffered, or be threatened with, monetary damages. **Leg.H.** Added Stats 1981 ch 981 §1.

§1882.6. Effect of recovery of damages on rates

Any damages recovered pursuant to this title in excess of the actual damages sustained by the utility may be taken into account by the Public Utilities Commission or other applicable ratemaking agency in establishing utility rates. **Leg.H.** Added Stats 1981 ch 981 §1.

TITLE 4
LOAN

Chapter 1. Loan for Use.
Chapter 1.5. Loans to Museums for Indefinite or Long Terms.
Chapter 2. Loan for Exchange.
Chapter 3. Loan of Money.
Chapter 3.5. Shared Appreciation Loans.
Chapter 4. Shared Appreciation Loans of E.R.I.S.A. Pension Funds.
Chapter 5. Shared Appreciation Loans.
Chapter 6. Loans of E.R.I.S.A. Pension Funds.
Chapter 7. Shared Appreciation Loans For Seniors.
Chapter 7.5. Mortgage Loans.
Chapter 8. Reverse Mortgages.

CHAPTER 1
LOAN FOR USE

Loan, what. §1884.
Title to property lent. §1885.
Care required of borrower. §1886.
Same. §1887.
Degree of skill. §1888.
Borrower, when to repair injuries. §1889.
Use of thing lent. §1890.
Relending forbidden. §1891.
Borrower, when to bear expenses. §1892.
Lender liable for defects. §1893.
Lender may require return of thing lent. §1894.
When returnable without demand. §1895.
Place of return. §1896.

§1884. Loan, what

A loan for use is a contract by which one gives to another the temporary possession and use of personal property, and the latter agrees to return the same thing to him at a future time, without reward for its use. **Leg.H.** Enacted Stats 1872.

§1885. Title to property lent

A loan for use does not transfer the title to the thing; and all its increase during the period of the loan belongs to the lender. **Leg.H.** Enacted Stats 1872.

§1886. Care required of borrower

A borrower for use must use great care for the preservation in safety and in good condition of the thing lent. **Leg.H.** Enacted Stats 1872.

§1887. Same

One who borrows a living animal for use, must treat it with great kindness, and provide everything necessary and suitable for it. **Leg.H.** Enacted Stats 1872.

§1888. Degree of skill

A borrower for use is bound to have and to exercise such skill in the care of the thing lent as he causes the lender to believe him to possess. **Leg.H.** Enacted Stats 1872.

§1889. Borrower, when to repair injuries

A borrower for use must repair all deteriorations or injuries to the thing lent, which are occasioned by his negligence, however slight. **Leg.H.** Enacted Stats 1872.

§1890. Use of thing lent

The borrower of a thing for use may use it for such purposes only as the lender might reasonably anticipate at the time of lending. **Leg.H.** Enacted Stats 1872.

§1891. Relending forbidden
The borrower of a thing for use must not part with it to a third person, without the consent of the lender. **Leg.H.** Enacted Stats 1872.

§1892. Borrower, when to bear expenses
The borrower of a thing for use must bear all its expenses during the loan, except such as are necessarily incurred by him to preserve it from unexpected and unusual injury. For such expenses he is entitled to compensation from the lender, who may, however, exonerate himself by surrendering the thing to the borrower. **Leg.H.** Enacted Stats 1872.

§1893. Lender liable for defects
The lender of a thing for use must indemnify the borrower for damage caused by defects or vices in it, which he knew at the time of lending, and concealed from the borrower. **Leg.H.** Enacted Stats 1872.

§1894. Lender may require return of thing lent
The lender of a thing for use may at any time require its return, even though he lent it for a specified time or purpose. But if, on the faith of such an agreement, the borrower has made such arrangements that a return of the thing before the period agreed upon would cause him loss, exceeding the benefit derived by him from the loan, the lender must indemnify him for such loss, if he compels such return, the borrower not having in any manner violated his duty. **Leg.H.** Enacted Stats 1872.

§1895. When returnable without demand
If a thing is lent for use for a specified time or purpose, it must be returned to the lender without demand, as soon as the time has expired, or the purpose has been accomplished. In other cases it need not be returned until demanded. **Leg.H.** Enacted Stats 1872.

§1896. Place of return
The borrower of a thing for use must return it to the lender, at the place contemplated by the parties at the time of lending; or if no particular place was so contemplated by them, then at the place where it was at that time. **Leg.H.** Enacted Stats 1872.

CHAPTER 1.5
LOANS TO MUSEUMS FOR INDEFINITE OR LONG TERMS

Legislative findings and declarations. §1899.
Definitions. §1899.1.
Notices. §1899.2.
Obligations of museums. §1899.3.
Obligations of owners of loaned property. §1899.4.
Notice of intent to preserve interest. §1899.5.
Conservation or disposal of loaned property. §1899.6.
Publication of notice of injury or loss. §1899.7.
Limitation of action arising from loss of or injury to property. §1899.8.
Termination of loans. §1899.9.
Limitation of action to recover property. §1899.10.
Disposition of unclaimed property. §1899.11.

§1899. Legislative findings and declarations
The Legislature finds and declares as follows:

(a) Many museums have benefited greatly from having property loaned to them for study or display. Problems have arisen, however, in connection with loans for indefinite or long terms, when museums and lenders have failed to maintain contact. Many of these problems could be avoided by a clarification and regularization of the rights and obligations of the parties to loans for indefinite or long terms.

(b) An existing law, the Unclaimed Property Law (commencing with Section 1500 of the Code of Civil Procedure), is technically applicable to property on loan to a museum which has been left unclaimed by its owner for at least seven years.

(c) While the Unclaimed Property Law addresses problems similar to those which arise in the museum context when the parties to loans fail to maintain contact, there is need for an alternative method of dealing with unclaimed property in the hands of museums, one tailored to the unique circumstances of unclaimed loans to museums. These circumstances include the likelihood that the unclaimed property has significant scientific, historical, aesthetic, or cultural value but does not have great monetary value; that the public's interest in the intangible values of unclaimed property loaned to museums can best be realized if title is transferred to the museums holding the property; that often lenders intend eventually to donate property but place it on indefinite or long term loan initially for tax and other reasons; and that many museums have incurred unreimbursed expenses in caring for and storing unclaimed loaned property.

(d) There is an inherent tendency for the condition of tangible property to change over time. Loaned property often requires conservation work and conservation measures may be expensive or potentially detrimental to the property. Organic materials and specimens may serve as breeding grounds for insects, fungi, or diseases which threaten other more valuable property.

(e) Museums cannot reasonably be expected to make decisions regarding conservation or disposition of loaned property at their own risk and expense. Over time, however, lenders die or move, and museums and lenders lose contact. If a lender has failed to maintain contact with a museum, it is often impossible to locate the lender so that the lender can make decisions regarding conservation or disposition of loaned property.

(f) Since museums rarely relocate, it is easier for lenders, and those who claim through them, to notify museums of address or ownership changes so that museums can readily contact lenders when decisions must be made regarding conservation or disposition of loaned property.

(g) The best evidence of ownership of property on loan to a museum is generally the original loan receipt. The longer property remains on loan, the less likely it is that the original lender will claim it, and the more likely it is that any claim which is made will be made by someone who does not have the original loan receipt or other clear evidence of ownership. The state has a substantial interest in cutting off stale and uncertain claims to tangible personal property loaned to nonprofit and public museums.

(h) Most of the tangible personal property which escheats to the state under the Unclaimed Property Law is found in safe deposit boxes. Although 40-50 percent of the intangible property which escheats to the state is subsequently claimed, less than 1 percent of escheated tangible personal property is claimed. Of the few claims which are presented to the Controller for tangible personal property, most are presented within two years of the date the Controller gives notice of the escheat.

(i) The public interest is served by requiring lenders to notify museums of changes in address or ownership of loaned property, by establishing a uniform procedure for lenders to preserve their interests in property loaned to museums for indefinite or long terms, and by vesting title to unclaimed property on loan to museums in the museums which have custody of the property. **Leg.H.** Added Stats 1983 ch 61 §1.

§1899.1. Definitions
For the purposes of this chapter:

(a) A "museum" is an institution located in California and operated by a nonprofit corporation or public agency, primarily educational, scientific, or aesthetic in purpose, which owns, borrows, or cares for, and studies, archives, or exhibits property.

(b) A "lender's address" is the most recent address as shown on the museum's records pertaining to the property on loan from the lender.

(c) The terms "loan," "loaned," and "on loan" include all deposits of property with a museum which are not accompanied by a transfer of title to the property.

(d) "Property" includes all tangible objects, animate and inanimate, under a museum's care which have intrinsic value to science, history, art, or culture, except that it does not include botanical or zoological specimens loaned to a museum for scientific research purposes. **Leg.H.** Added Stats 1983 ch 61 §1.

§1899.2. Notices
(a) When a museum is required to give a lender notice pursuant to the provisions of this chapter, the museum shall be deemed to have given a lender notice if the museum mails the notice to the lender at the lender's address and proof of receipt is received by the museum within 30 days from the date the notice was mailed. If the museum does not have an address for the lender, or if proof of receipt is not received by the museum, notice shall be deemed given if the museum publishes notice at least once a week for three successive weeks in a newspaper of general circulation in both the county in which the museum is located and the county of the lender's address, if any.

(b) In addition to any other information prescribed in this chapter, notices given pursuant to it shall contain the lender's name, the lender's address, if known, the date of the loan and, if the notice is being given by the museum, the name, address, and telephone number of the appropriate office or official to be contacted at the museum for information regarding the loan.

(c) For the purposes of this section, a museum is "located" in the county of a branch of the museum to which a loan is made. In all other instances, a museum is located in the county in which it has its principal place of business. **Leg.H.** Added Stats 1983 ch 61 §1.

§1899.3. Obligations of museums

(a) If, on or after January 1, 1984, a museum accepts a loan of property for an indefinite term, or for a term in excess of seven years, the museum shall inform the lender in writing at the time of the loan of the provisions of this chapter. A copy of the form notice prescribed in Section 1899.5, or a citation to this chapter, is adequate for this purpose.

(b) Unless the loaned property is returned to the claimant, the museum shall retain for a period of not less than 25 years the original or an accurate copy of each notice filed by a claimant pursuant to Section 1899.4.

(c) The museum shall furnish anyone who files a notice of intent to preserve an interest in property on loan proof of receipt of the notice by mailing an original receipt or a copy of the receipt portion of the form notice prescribed in Section 1899.5 to the lender or other claimant at the address given on the notice within 30 days of receiving the notice.

(d) A museum shall give a lender prompt notice of any known injury to or loss of property on loan. **Leg.H.** Added Stats 1983 ch 61 §1.

§1899.4. Obligations of owners of loaned property

(a) It is the responsibility of the owner of property on loan to a museum to notify the museum promptly in writing of any change of address or change in ownership of the property. Failure to notify the museum of these changes may result in the owner's loss of rights in the property.

(b) The owner of property on loan to a museum may file with the museum a notice of intent to preserve an interest in the property as provided for in Section 1899.5. The filing of a notice of intent to preserve an interest in property on loan to a museum does not validate or make enforceable any claim which would be extinguished under the terms of a written loan agreement, or which would otherwise be invalid or unenforceable. **Leg.H.** Added Stats 1983 ch 61 §1.

§1899.5. Notice of intent to preserve interest

(a) A notice of intent to preserve an interest in property on loan to a museum filed pursuant to this chapter shall be in writing, shall contain a description of the property adequate to enable the museum to identify the property, shall be accompanied by documentation sufficient to establish the claimant as owner of the property, and shall be signed under penalty of perjury by the claimant or by a person authorized to act on behalf of the claimant.

(b) The museum need not retain a notice that does not meet the requirements set forth in subdivision (a). If, however, the museum does not intend to retain a notice for this reason, the museum shall promptly notify the claimant at the address given on the notice that it believes the notice is ineffective to preserve an interest, and the reasons therefor. The fact that the museum retains a notice shall not be construed to mean that the museum accepts the sufficiency or accuracy of the notice or that the notice is effective to preserve an interest in property on loan to the museum.

(c) A notice of intent to preserve an interest in property on loan to a museum which is in substantially the following form, and contains the information and attachments described, satisfies the requirements of subdivision (a):

(c) A notice of intent to preserve an interest in property on loan to a museum which is in substantially the following form, and contains the information and attachments described, satisfies the requirements of subdivision (a):

NOTICE OF INTENT TO PRESERVE AN INTEREST IN PROPERTY ON LOAN TO A MUSEUM

TO THE LENDER: Section 1899.4 of the California Civil Code requires that you notify the museum promptly in writing of any change of address or ownership of the property. If the museum is unable to contact you regarding your loan, you may lose rights in the loaned property. If you choose to file this form with the museum to preserve your interest in the property, the museum is required to maintain it, or a copy of it, for 25 years. For full details, see Section 1899, et seq. of the California Civil Code.

TO THE MUSEUM: You are hereby notified that the undersigned claims an interest in the property described herein.

Claimant
Name: _____
Address: _____

Telephone: _____
Social Security Number (optional): _____
Museum Name: _____
Date Property Loaned: _____
Interest in Property: _____

If you are not the original lender, describe the origin of your interest in the property and attach a copy of any document creating your interest:
_____
_____
_____

Description of Property:
Unless an accurate, legible copy of the original loan receipt is attached, give a detailed description of the claimed property, including its nature and general characteristics and the museum registration number assigned to the property, if known, and attach any documentary evidence you have establishing the loan:
Registration # _____
Description: _____
_____
_____
_____

(Attach additional sheets if necessary.)

I understand that I must promptly notify the museum in writing of any change of address or change in ownership of the loaned property.

I declare under penalty of perjury that to the best of my knowledge the information contained in this notice is true.
Signed: _____ Date: _____
      (claimant)

OR

I declare under penalty of perjury that I am authorized to act on behalf of the claimant and am informed and believe that the information contained in this notice is true.
Signed: _____ Date: _____
      (claimant's representative)

RECEIPT FOR NOTICE OF INTENT TO PRESERVE
AN INTEREST IN PROPERTY
(For use by the museum.)

Notice received by: _____
Date of receipt: _____
Copy of receipt returned to claimant: _____
  By _____
  Date: _____

(d) Notices of intent to preserve an interest in property on loan to a museum filed pursuant to this chapter are exempt from the disclosure requirements of the California Public Records Act (Division 10 (commencing with Section 7920.000) of the Government Code). **Leg.H.** Added Stats 1983 ch 61 §1. Amended Stats 2021 ch 615 §50 (AB 474), effective January 1, 2022.

§1899.6. Conservation or disposal of loaned property

(a) Unless there is a written loan agreement to the contrary, a museum may apply conservation measures to or dispose of property on loan to the museum without a lender's permission if:

(1) Immediate action is required to protect the property on loan or to protect other property in the custody of the museum, or because the property on loan has become a hazard to the health and safety of the public or of the museum's staff, and:

(A) The museum is unable to reach the lender at the lender's last address of record so that the museum and the lender can promptly agree upon a solution; or

(B) The lender will not agree to the protective measures the museum recommends, yet is unwilling or unable to terminate the loan and retrieve the property.

(2) In the case of a lender who cannot be contacted in person, the museum publishes a notice containing the information described in subdivision (a) of Section 1899.7 and there is no response for 120 days.

(b) If a museum applies conservation measures to or disposes of property pursuant to subdivision (a):

(1) The museum shall have a lien on the property and on the proceeds from any disposition thereof for the costs incurred by the museum; and

(2) The museum shall not be liable for injury to or loss of the property:

(A) If the museum had a reasonable belief at the time the action was taken that the action was necessary to protect the property on loan or other property in the custody of the museum, or that the property on loan constituted a hazard to the health and safety of the public or the museum's staff; and

(B) If the museum applied conservation measures, the museum exercised reasonable care in the choice and application of the conservation measures. **Leg.H.** Added Stats 1983 ch 61 §1.

§1899.7. Publication of notice of injury or loss

(a) Except as provided in subdivision (b), if a museum is unable to give the lender the notice required by subdivision (d) of Section 1899.3 of injury to or loss of property on loan by mail, the museum shall be deemed to have given the lender notice of any injury or loss if in addition to the information required by subdivision (b) of Section 1899.2 the published notice includes a statement containing substantially the following information:

"The records of _____
(name of museum)
indicate that you have property on loan to it. Your failure to notify it in writing of a change of address or ownership of property on loan or to contact it in writing regarding the loan may result in the loss of rights in the loaned property. See California Civil Code Sections 1899, et seq."

(b) If, within three years of giving notice of injury to or loss of loaned property by publishing the notice set forth in subdivision (a), the museum receives a notice from a claimant pursuant to Section 1899.4, the museum shall promptly advise the claimant in writing of the nature of the injury to or the fact of the loss of property on loan and the approximate date thereof. For the purposes of the limitation period in Section 1899.8, if the museum mails the information to the claimant within 30 days of the date the museum receives the notice from the claimant, the museum shall be deemed to have given the claimant notice of the injury to or loss of property on loan on the date notice by publication pursuant to subdivision (a) was completed. **Leg.H.** Added Stats 1983 ch 61 §1.

§1899.8. Limitation of action arising from loss of or injury to property

Effective January 1, 1985, no action shall be brought against a museum for damages because of injury to or loss of property loaned to the museum more than (1) three years from the date the museum gives the lender notice of the injury or loss, or (2) ten years from the date of the injury or loss, whichever occurs earlier. **Leg.H.** Added Stats 1983 ch 61 §1.

§1899.9. Termination of loans

(a) A museum may give the lender notice of the museum's intent to terminate a loan which was made for an indefinite term, or which was made on or after January 1, 1984, for a term in excess of seven years.

A notice of intent to terminate a loan given pursuant to this section shall include a statement containing substantially the following information:

"The records of _____
(name of museum)
indicate that you have property on loan to it. The institution wishes to terminate the loan. You must contact the institution, establish your ownership of the property, and make arrangements to collect the property. If you fail to do so promptly, you will be deemed to have donated the property to the institution. See California Civil Code Sections 1899, et seq."

(b) For the purposes of this chapter, a loan for a specified term becomes a loan for an indefinite term if the property remains in the custody of the museum when the specified term expires. **Leg.H.** Added Stats 1983 ch 61 §1.

§1899.10. Limitation of action to recover property

(a) The three-year limitation on actions to recover personal property prescribed in Code of Civil Procedure Section 338.3 shall run from the date the museum gives the lender notice of its intent to terminate the loan pursuant to Section 1899.9.

(b) Except as provided in subdivision (e), effective January 1, 1985, no action shall be brought against a museum to recover property on loan when more than 25 years have passed from the date of the last written contact between the lender and the museum, as evidenced in the museum's records.

(c) A lender shall be deemed to have donated loaned property to a museum if the lender fails to file an action to recover the property on loan to the museum within the periods specified in subdivisions (a) and (b).

(d) One who purchases property from a museum acquires good title to the property if the museum represents that it has acquired title to the property pursuant to subdivision (c).

(e) Notwithstanding subdivisions (b) and (c), a lender who was not given notice that the museum intended to terminate a loan and who proves that the museum received a notice of intent to preserve an interest in loaned property within the 25 years immediately preceding the date on which the lender's right to recover the property otherwise expired under subdivision (b) may recover the property or, if the property has been disposed of, the reasonable value of the property at the time the property was disposed of with interest at the rate on judgments set by the Legislature pursuant to Section 1 of Article XV of the California Constitution. **Leg.H.** Added Stats 1983 ch 61 §1. Amended Stats 1984 ch 541 §1, effective July 17, 1984.

§1899.11. Disposition of unclaimed property

(a) The provisions of this chapter supersede the provisions of the Unclaimed Property Law (commencing with Section 1500 of the Code of Civil Procedure) except that at its option, a museum may report property which has been on loan unclaimed by its owner for more than seven years to the Controller pursuant to Section 1530 of the Code of Civil Procedure for disposition in accordance with the provisions of the Unclaimed Property Law.

(b) Not less than six months or more than 12 months before reporting any loaned property to the Controller, a museum shall mail to the lender at the lender's address, if known, a notice of intent to report the property to the Controller. The notice shall include a statement containing substantially the following information:

"The records of _____
(name of museum)
indicate that you have property on loan to the institution. The institution wishes to terminate the loan. You must contact the institution, establish your ownership of the property and make arrangements to collect the property before _____ (fill in date) or the property will be disposed of in accordance with the provisions of the Unclaimed Property Law (commencing with Section 1500 of the Code of Civil Procedure)."

Leg.H. Added Stats 1983 ch 61 §1.

CHAPTER 2
LOAN FOR EXCHANGE

Loan for exchange, what. §1902.
Same. §1903.
Title to property lent. §1904.
Contract cannot be modified by lender. §1905.
Certain sections applicable. §1906.

§1902. Loan for exchange, what

A loan for exchange is a contract by which one delivers personal property to another, and the latter agrees to return to the lender a similar thing at a future time, without reward for its use. **Leg.H.** Enacted Stats 1872.

§1903. Same

A loan, which the borrower is allowed by the lender to treat as a loan for use, or for exchange, at his option, is subject to all the provisions of this chapter. **Leg.H.** Enacted Stats 1872.

§1904. Title to property lent

By loan for exchange the title to the thing lent is transferred to the borrower, and he must bear all its expenses, and is entitled to all its increase. **Leg.H.** Enacted Stats 1872.

§1905. Contract cannot be modified by lender

A lender for exchange cannot require the borrower to fulfill his obligations at a time, or in a manner, different from that which was originally agreed upon. **Leg.H.** Enacted Stats 1872.

§1906. Certain sections applicable

Sections 1893, 1895 and 1896 apply to loan for exchange. **Leg.H.** Enacted Stats 1872.

CHAPTER 3
LOAN OF MONEY

Loan of money defined. §1912.
Loan to be repaid in current money. §1913.
Loan presumed to be on interest. §1914.
Interest defined. §1915.
Annual rate. §1916.
[No sections of these numbers.] §§ 1916-1–1916-5.
Inapplicability of interest rate restrictions to secured loans made by licensed real estate broker. §1916.1.
Applicability to out-of-state public pension system. §1916.2.
Variable interest rate; Statement required; Definitions; Exceptions to applicability. §1916.5.
Periodic change in variable interest rate. §1916.6.
Adjustable-payment, adjustable-rate loan secured by residential real property; Disclosure statement to prospective borrowers. §1916.7.
Renegotiable rate mortgage loan. §1916.8.
Offering fixed rate mortgage loan with offer of renegotiable rate mortgage loan. §1916.9.
Lien of mortgage or deed of trust. §1916.11.
Loans upon security of residential real property. §1916.12.

§1912. Loan of money defined

A loan of money is a contract by which one delivers a sum of money to another, and the latter agrees to return at a future time a sum equivalent to that which he borrowed. A loan for mere use is governed by the chapter on loan for use. **Leg.H.** Enacted Stats 1872.

§1913. Loan to be repaid in current money

A borrower of money, unless there is an express contract to the contrary, must pay the amount due in such money as is current at the time when the loan becomes due, whether such money is worth more or less than the actual money lent. **Leg.H.** Enacted Stats 1872.

§1914. Loan presumed to be on interest

Whenever a loan of money is made, it is presumed to be made upon interest, unless it is otherwise expressly stipulated at the time in writing. **Leg.H.** Enacted Stats 1872. Amended Code Amdts 1873–74 ch 201.

§1915. Interest defined

Interest is the compensation allowed by law or fixed by the parties for the use, or forbearance, or detention of money. **Leg.H.** Enacted Stats 1872. Amended Code Amdts 1873–74 ch 612 §202.

§1916. Annual rate

When a rate of interest is prescribed by a law or contract, without specifying the period of time by which such rate is to be calculated, it is to be deemed an annual rate. **Leg.H.** Enacted Stats 1872.

§§ 1916-1–1916-5. [No sections of these numbers.]

See Cal Uncod Init Measures & Stats Deer 1919, 1919-1

§1916.1. Inapplicability of interest rate restrictions to secured loans made by licensed real estate broker

The restrictions upon rates of interest contained in Section 1 of Article XV of the California Constitution shall not apply to any loan [1], **or any forbearance, extension, or modification of a loan,** made or arranged by any person licensed as a real estate broker by the State of California, and secured, directly or collaterally, in whole or in part by liens on real property. For purposes of this section, a loan, **or forbearance, extension, or modification of a loan,** is arranged by a person licensed as a real estate broker when [2] **a** broker (1) acts for compensation or in expectation of compensation for soliciting, negotiating, or arranging the loan**, or forbearance, extension, or modification of the loan,** for another, (2) acts for compensation or in expectation of compensation for selling, buying, leasing, exchanging, or negotiating the sale, purchase, lease, or exchange of real property or a business for another and (A) arranges a loan to pay all or any portion of the purchase price of, or of an improvement to, that property or business or (B) arranges a forbearance, extension, **modification,** or refinancing of any loan in connection with that sale, purchase, lease, exchange of, or an improvement to, real property or a business, or (3) arranges or negotiates for another a forbearance, extension, **modification,** or refinancing of any loan secured by real property in connection with a past transaction in which [3] **a** broker had acted for compensation or in expectation of compensation for selling, buying, leasing, exchanging, or negotiating the sale, purchase, lease, or exchange of real property or a business. The term "made or arranged" includes any loan**, or any forbearance, extension, or modification of a loan,** made by a person licensed as a real estate broker as a principal or as an agent for others, and whether or not the person is acting within the course and scope of such license. **Leg.H.** Added Stats 1983 ch 307 §1. Amended Stats 1985 ch 489 §1; Stats 2024 ch 601 §1 (SB 1146), effective January 1, 2025.

§1916.1. 2024 Deletes. [1] or forbearance **[2]** the **[3]** the

NOTE: Sections 1 through 3, set out below, contain the uncodified provisions of Stats. 1919 p. 1xxxiii, an initiative measure approved by the voters at the general election November 5, 1918, effective December 10, 1918. Having never been codified, these provisions are cited in various ways, and citation to them should include the name of the code publisher [see Cal. Fms Pl. & Pr., "Usury"]. Provisions governing interest rates are also contained in Cal. Const Art XV §1, which supersede all other provisions of the Constitution and all laws enacted thereunder in conflict therewith [Cal. Const. Art. XV §1]. In addition, federal Public Law 96-221 §§501–529, suspends state usury laws on certain types of loans and transactions. The state law cannot override this federal preemption unless the law explicitly and by its terms preempts the federal law and specifically refers to the provisions to be overridden [see Cal. Fms Pl. & Pr., "Usury" (Supp)].

Section 1. Legal and Contract Interest Rates.

The rate of interest upon the loan or forbearance of any money, goods or things in action or on accounts after demand or judgments rendered in any court of this state, shall be seven dollars upon the one hundred dollars for one year and at that rate for a greater or less sum or for a longer or a shorter time; but it shall be competent for parties to contract for the payment and receipt of a rate of interest not exceeding twelve dollars on the one hundred dollars for one year and not exceeding that rate for a greater or less sum or for a longer or shorter time, in which case such rate exceeding seven dollars on one hundred dollars shall be clearly expressed in writing. **Leg.H.** 1919 p. 1xxxiii.

Section 2. Limit on Contract Rates.

No person, company, association or corporation shall directly or indirectly take or receive in money, goods or things in action, or in any other manner whatsoever, any greater sum or any greater value for the loan or forbearance of money, goods or things in action than at the rate of twelve dollars upon one hundred dollars for one year; and in the computation of interest upon any bond, note, or other instrument or agreement, interest shall not be compounded, nor shall the interest thereon be construed to bear interest unless an agreement to that effect is clearly expressed in writing and signed by the party to be charged therewith. Any agreement or contract of any nature in conflict with the provisions of this section shall be null and void as to any agreement or stipulation therein contained to pay interest and no action at law to recover interest in any sum shall be maintained and the debt cannot be declared due until the full period of time it was contracted for has elapsed. **Leg.H.** 1919 p. 1xxxiii.

Section 3. Civil and Criminal Penalties for Violation.

(a) Every person, company, association or corporation, who for any loan or forbearance of money, goods or things in action shall have paid or delivered any greater sum or value than is allowed to be received under the preceding sections, one and two, may either in person or his or its personal representative, recover in an action at law against the person, company, association or corporation who shall have taken or received the same, or his or its personal representative, treble the amount of the money so paid or value delivered in violation of said sections, providing such action shall be brought within one year after such payment or delivery.

(b) Any person who willfully makes or negotiates, for himself or another, a loan of money, credit, goods, or things in action, and who directly or indirectly charges, contracts for, or receives with respect to any such loan any interest or charge of any nature, the value of which is in excess of that allowed by law, is guilty of loan-sharking, a felony, and is punishable by imprisonment in the state prison for not more than five years or in the county jail for not more than one year. This subdivision shall not apply to any person licensed to make or negotiate, for himself or another, loans of money, credit, goods, or things in action, or expressly exempted from compliance by the laws of this state with respect to such licensure or interest or other charge, or to any agent or employee of such person when acting within the scope of his agency or employment. **Leg.H.** 1919 p. 1xxxiii, 1970 ch. 784 §1.

§1916.2. Applicability to out-of-state public pension system

The restrictions upon rates of interest contained in Section 1 of Article XV of the California Constitution do not apply to any loans made by, or forbearances of, a public retirement or pension system that is created, authorized, and regulated by the laws of a state other than California, or the laws of a local agency of a state other than California.

This section establishes as an exempt class of persons pursuant to Section 1 of Article XV of the California Constitution, any public retirement or pension system that is created, authorized, and regulated by the laws of a state other than California, or the laws of a local agency of a state other than California. **Leg.H.** Added Stats 1987 ch 764 §5.

§1916.5. Variable interest rate; Statement required; Definitions; Exceptions to applicability

(a) No increase in interest provided for in any provision for a variable interest rate contained in a security document, or evidence of debt issued in connection therewith, by a lender other than a supervised financial organization is valid unless that provision is set forth in the security document, and in any evidence of debt issued in connection therewith, and the document or documents contain the following provisions:

(1) A requirement that when an increase in the interest rate is required or permitted by a movement in a particular direction of a prescribed standard an identical decrease is required in the interest rate by a movement in the opposite direction of the prescribed standard.

(2) The rate of interest shall not change more often than once during any semiannual period, and at least six months shall elapse between any two changes.

(3) The change in the interest rate shall not exceed one-fourth of 1 percent in any semiannual period, and shall not result in a rate more than 2.5 percentage points greater than the rate for the first loan payment due after the closing of the loan.

(4) The rate of interest shall not change during the first semiannual period.

(5) The borrower is permitted to prepay the loan in whole or in part without a prepayment charge within 90 days of notification of any increase in the rate of interest.

(6) A statement attached to the security document and to any evidence of debt issued in connection therewith printed or written in a size equal to at least 10-point boldface type, consisting of the following language:

NOTICE TO BORROWER: THIS DOCUMENT CONTAINS PROVISIONS FOR A VARIABLE INTEREST RATE.

(b)(1) This section shall be applicable only to a mortgage contract, deed of trust, real estate sales contract, or any note or negotiable instrument issued in connection therewith, when its purpose is to finance the purchase or construction of real property containing four or fewer residential units or on which four or fewer residential units are to be constructed.

(2) This section does not apply to unamortized construction loans with an original term of two years or less or to loans made for the purpose of the purchase or construction of improvements to existing residential dwellings.

(c) Regulations setting forth the prescribed standard upon which variations in the interest rate shall be based may be adopted by the Commissioner of Financial Protection and Innovation with respect to savings associations and by the Insurance Commissioner with respect to insurers. Regulations adopted by the Commissioner of Financial Protection and Innovation shall apply to all loans made by savings associations pursuant to this section before January 1, 1990.

(d) As used in this section:

(1) "Supervised financial organization" means a state or federally regulated bank, savings association, savings bank, or credit union, or state regulated industrial loan company, a licensed finance lender under the California Financing Law, a licensed residential mortgage lender under the California Residential Mortgage Lending Act, or holding company, affiliate, or subsidiary thereof, or institution of the Farm Credit System, as specified in Section 2002 of Title 12 of the United States Code.

(2) "Insurer" includes, but is not limited to, a nonadmitted insurance company.

(3) "Semiannual period" means each of the successive periods of six calendar months commencing with the first day of the calendar month in which the instrument creating the obligation is dated.

(4) "Security document" means a mortgage contract, deed of trust, or real estate sales contract.

(5) "Evidence of debt" means a note or negotiable instrument.

(e) This section is applicable only to instruments executed on and after the effective date of this section.

(f) This section does not apply to nonprofit public corporations.

(g) This section is not intended to apply to a loan made where the rate of interest provided for is less than the then current market rate for a similar loan in order to accommodate the borrower because of a special relationship, including, but not limited to, an employment or business relationship, of the borrower with the lender or with a customer of the lender and the sole increase in interest provided for with respect to the loan will result only by reason of the termination of that relationship or upon the sale, deed, or transfer of the property securing the loan to a person not having that relationship. **Leg.H.** Added Stats 1970 ch 1584 §1. Amended Stats 1971 ch 1265 §1; Stats 1975 ch 338 §1; Stats 1980 ch 1139 §1; Stats 1982 ch 1307 §1; Stats 1984 ch 975 §1; Stats 1989 ch 188 §1; Stats 1990 ch 157 §1 (AB 2728); Stats 1996 ch 1064 §5 (AB 3351), operative July 1, 1997; Stats 2004 ch 939 §1 (AB 1979), ch 940 §3 (AB 2693); Stats 2019 ch 143 §15 (SB 251), effective January 1, 2020; Stats 2022 ch 452 §27 (SB 1498), effective January 1, 2023.

1990 Note: In order to accurately reflect the intent of the Legislature in enacting Assembly Bill 438 of the 1989–90 Regular Session as Chapter 188 of the Statutes of 1989, which was to exempt from the operation of Section 1916.5 of the Civil Code any security documents or evidences of indebtedness issued by state or federally regulated financial institutions under the authority of federal law, this act shall apply to any security document or evidence of debt issued on or after January 1, 1990. Stats 1990 ch 157 §2.

§1916.6. Periodic change in variable interest rate

A security document, or evidence of debt issued in connection therewith, executed pursuant to Section 1916.5 may provide that the rate of interest shall not change until five years after execution of such document or documents, and not more frequently then every five years thereafter. In every security document, or evidence of debt issued in connection therewith, executed pursuant to this section all the provisions of Section 1916.5 shall be applicable, except those provisions specifying the frequency of interest rate changes and limiting rate changes to one-fourth of 1 percent in any semiannual period. For the purposes of this section "five years" means each of the successive periods of five years commencing with the first day of the calendar month in which the instrument creating the obligation is dated. **Leg.H.** Added Stats 1977 ch 575 §1.

§1916.7. Adjustable-payment, adjustable-rate loan secured by residential real property; Disclosure statement to prospective borrowers

(a) Sections 1916.5, 1916.6, 1916.8, and 1916.9 of the Civil Code, and any other provision of law restricting or setting forth requirements for changes in the rate of interest on loans, shall not be applicable to loans made pursuant to this section.

(b) A mortgage loan made pursuant to the provisions of this section is an adjustable-payment, adjustable-rate loan, on the security of real property occupied or intended to be occupied by the borrower containing four or fewer residential units and incorporating terms substantially as follows:

(1) The term of the loan shall be not less than 29 years, repayable in monthly installments amortized over a period of not less than 30 years.

(2) Monthly payments may be adjusted to reflect changes in the variable interest rate of the loan. Changes in interest and monthly payment shall not occur more often than twice during any annual period and at least six months shall elapse between any two changes. The rate of interest and monthly payments shall not change during the first semiannual period. The amount of any increase in monthly payment shall not exceed 7.5 percent annually.

(3) Monthly payments may also be established on a graduated basis within the parameters of a loan originated pursuant to the provisions of this section. A graduated payment adjustable mortgage loan shall meet all the requirements of this section and shall set forth in the note, at the time of origination, limitations on the rate of increase in the scheduled payments due both to graduation and to changes in the interest rate.

(4) Whenever any monthly installment is less than the amount of interest accrued during the month with respect to which the installment is payable, the borrower shall have the option to select one, or any combination of, the following:

(A) Notwithstanding paragraph (2) of subdivision (b), increase the monthly installment in an amount which at least covers the increase in interest.

(B) Have the difference added to the principal of the loan as of the due date of the installment and thereafter shall bear interest as part of the principal. In no instance shall the difference which is added to the principal be an amount which causes the resulting loan-to-value ratio to exceed the loan-to-value ratio at the time of loan origination.

(C) Extend the term of the loan up to, but not exceeding, 40 years.

(5) Changes in the rate of interest on the loan shall reflect the movement, in reference to the date of the original loan, of a periodically published index selected by the lender which may be either of the following:

(A) The contract interest rate on the purchase of previously occupied homes in the most recent monthly national average mortgage rate index for all major lenders published periodically by the Federal Home Loan Bank Board.

(B) The weighted average cost of funds for California Associations of the Eleventh District Savings and Loan Associations as published periodically by the Federal Home Loan Bank of San Francisco.

(6) Any change in the interest rate shall not exceed the limit, specified by the lender in the loan contract, for rate increases in any semiannual period and shall not exceed the limit, specified by the lender in the loan contract, for rate increases greater than the base index rate.

(7) Notwithstanding any change in the interest rate indicated by a movement of the index, increases in the interest rate shall be optional with the lender, while decreases are mandatory. Such decreases, upon the option of the borrower, shall be used (1) to pay off any negative amortization accrued when the interest rate was increased, or (2) to decrease the monthly payment as reflected in the decrease in the interest rate.

(8) The borrower is permitted to prepay the loan in whole or in part without a prepayment charge at any time, and no fee or other charge may be required by the lender of the borrower as a result of any change in the interest rate or the exercise of any option or election extended to the borrower pursuant to this section.

(9) The borrower, after initiation of the loan, shall not be subsequently required to demonstrate his or her qualification for the loan, except that this paragraph shall not limit any remedy available to the lender by law for default or other breach of contract.

(10) In the event the remaining principal due on a loan made pursuant to this section will not be paid off during the current term, within 90 days of expiration of the term a borrower may elect in writing to repay the remaining balance in full or in substantially equal installments of principal and interest over an additional period not to exceed 10 years, during which period the interest rate shall remain fixed.

(c) An applicant for a loan originated pursuant to the provisions of this section must be given, at the time he or she requests an application, a disclosure notice in the following form:

NOTICE TO BORROWER
IMPORTANT INFORMATION ABOUT THE
ADJUSTABLE-PAYMENT, ADJUSTABLE-RATE LOAN
PLEASE READ CAREFULLY
(at least 10-point bold type)

You have received an application form for an adjustable-payment, adjustable-rate mortgage loan. This loan may differ from other mortgages with which you are familiar.

I. GENERAL DESCRIPTION OF ADJUSTABLE-PAYMENT, ADJUSTABLE-RATE LOAN

The adjustable-payment, adjustable-rate mortgage loan is a flexible loan instrument. This means that the interest, monthly payment and/or the length of the loan may be changed during the course of the loan contract.

The first flexible feature of this loan is the interest rate. The interest rate on the loan may be changed by the lender every six months. Changes in the interest rate must reflect the movement of an index that is selected by the lender. Changes in the interest rate may result in increases or decreases in your monthly payment, in the outstanding principal loan balance, in the loan term, or in all three.

The lender is required by law to limit the amount that the interest can change at any one time or over the life of the loan. The law does not specify what these limits are. That is a matter you should negotiate with the lender.

You may also want to make inquiries concerning the lending terms offered by other lenders on adjustable-payment, adjustable-rate mortgage loans to compare the terms and conditions.

Another flexible feature of the adjustable-payment, adjustable-rate mortgage loan is the monthly payment. The amount of the monthly payment may be increased or decreased by the lender every six months to reflect the changes in the interest rate. State law prohibits the lender from increasing your monthly payment by more than 7.5 percent per year. There may be circumstances, however, in which you, the borrower, may want to increase the amount of your monthly payment beyond the 7.5 percent limit. This option would be available to you whenever changes in the interest rate threaten to increase the outstanding principal loan balance on the loan.

A third flexible feature of the adjustable-payment, adjustable-rate mortgage loan is that the outstanding principal loan balance (the total amount you owe) may be increased from time to time. This situation, called "negative amortization," can occur when rising interest rates make the monthly payment too small to cover the interest due on the loan. The difference between the monthly payment and the actual amount due in interest is added to the outstanding loan balance.

Under the terms of this mortgage, you as a borrower would always have the option of either incurring additions to the amount you owe on the loan or voluntarily increasing your monthly payments beyond the 7.5 percent annual limit to an amount needed to pay off the rising interest costs.

Continual increases in the outstanding loan balance may cause a situation in which the loan balance is not entirely paid off at the end of the 30-year loan term. If this occurs, you may elect in writing to repay the outstanding principal all at once, or with a series of fixed payments at a fixed rate of interest for up to 10 years.

The final flexible feature of the adjustable-payment, adjustable-rate mortgage loan is that you may lengthen the loan term from 30 to up to 40 years. Extending the loan term will lower your monthly payment slightly less than they would have been had the loan term not been extended.

II. INDEX

Adjustments to the interest rate of an adjustable-payment, adjustable-rate mortgage loan must correspond directly to the movement of an index which is selected, but not controlled, by the lender. Any adjustments to the interest rate are subject to limitations provided in the loan contract.

If the index moves down, the lender must reduce the interest rate by at least the decrease in the index. If the index moves up, the lender has the right to increase the interest rate by that amount. Although making such an increase is optional by the lender, you should be aware that the lender has this right and may be contractually obligated to exercise it.

The index used is [Name and description of index to be used for applicant's loan, initial index value (if known) and date of initial index value, a source or sources where the index may be readily obtained by the borrower, and the high and low index rates during the previous calendar year].

III. KEY PROVISIONS OF [Name of Institution] ADJUSTABLE-PAYMENT, ADJUSTABLE-RATE MORTGAGE LOAN

The following information is a summary of the basic terms on the mortgage loan being offered to you. This summary is intended for reference purposes only. Important information relating specifically to your loan will be contained in the loan agreement.

[Provide a summary of basic terms of the loan, including the loan term, the frequency of rate changes, the frequency of payment changes, the maximum rate change at any one time, the maximum rate change over the life of the loan, the maximum annual payment change, and whether additions to the principal loan balance are possible, in the following format:]

LOAN TERM
FREQUENCY OF RATE CHANGES
FREQUENCY OF PAYMENT CHANGES

IV. HOW YOUR ADJUSTABLE-PAYMENT, ADJUSTABLE-RATE MORTGAGE LOAN WOULD WORK

A. INITIAL INTEREST RATE

The initial interest rate offered by [Name of Institution] on your adjustable-payment, adjustable-rate mortgage loan will be established and disclosed to you on [commitment date, etc.] based on market conditions at that time.

[Insert a short description of each of the key provisions of the loan to be offered to the borrower, using headings where appropriate.]

B. NOTICE OF PAYMENT ADJUSTMENTS

[Name of Institution] will send you notice of an adjustment to the payment amount at least 60 days before it becomes effective. [Describe what information the notice will contain.]

C. PREPAYMENT PENALTY

You may prepay your adjustable-payment, adjustable-rate mortgage in whole or in part without penalty at any time during the term of the loan.

D. FEES

You will be charged fees by [Name of Institution] and by other persons in connection with the origination of your loan. The association will give you an estimate of these fees after receiving your loan application.

However, you will not be charged any costs of fees in connection with any regularly scheduled adjustment to the interest rate, the payment, the outstanding principal loan balance, or the loan term.

V. EXAMPLE OF OPERATION OF YOUR ADJUSTABLE-PAYMENT, ADJUSTABLE-RATE MORTGAGE LOAN

[Set out an example of the operation of the mortgage loan, including the use of a table. In at least one of the examples, create a situation showing how negative amortization could occur.]

(d) At least 60 days prior to the due date of a monthly installment to be revised due to a change in the interest rate, notice shall be mailed to the borrower of the following:

(1) The base index.

(2) The most recently published index at the date of the change in the rate.

(3) The interest rate in effect as a result of the change.

(4) The amount of the unpaid principal balance.

(5) If the interest scheduled to be paid on the due date exceeds the amount of the installment, a statement to that effect, including the amount of excess and extent of borrower options as described in paragraph (4) of subdivision (b).

(6) The amount of the revised monthly installment.

(7) The borrower's right to prepayment under paragraph (8) of subdivision (b).

(8) The address and telephone number of the office of the lender to which inquiries may be made.

(e) As used in this section:

(1) "Base index" means the last published index at the date of the note.

(2) "Base index rate" means the interest rate initially applicable to the loan as specified in the note.

(3) "Graduated Payment Adjustable Mortgage Loan" means a loan on which the monthly payments begin at a level lower than that necessary to pay off the remaining principal balance over an amortization period of not less than 30 years. During a period the length of which is fixed at loan origination (the "graduation period"), the scheduled payments gradually rise to a level sufficient to pay off the remaining principal balance over the stipulated amortization period. Limitations on the rate of increase in the scheduled payments due both to graduation and to changes in the interest rate are also fixed at loan origination.

(4) "Note" means the note or other loan contract evidencing an adjustable-payment, adjustable-rate mortgage loan. **Leg.H.** Added Stats 1981 ch 1079 §1.

§1916.8. Renegotiable rate mortgage loan

Any lender may make, purchase or participate in a renegotiable rate mortgage loan under this section if the loan complies with the provisions of this section pertaining to one- to four-family home loans.

(a) For purposes of this section, a renegotiable rate mortgage loan is a loan issued for a term of three, four or five years, secured by a long-term mortgage or deed of trust of up to 30 years, and automatically renewable at equal intervals except as provided in paragraph (1) of subdivision (b). The loan must be repayable in equal monthly installments of principal and interest during the loan term, in an amount at least sufficient to amortize a loan with the same principal and at the same interest rate over the remaining term of the mortgage or deed of trust. Only one of the indices described in paragraph (1) of subdivision (b) shall be used and no other index shall be used during the term of the mortgage or deed of trust securing the loan. At renewal, no change other than in the interest rate may be made in the terms or conditions of the initial loan. Prepayment in full or in part of the loan balance secured by the mortgage or deed of trust may be made without penalty at any time after the beginning of the minimum notice period for the first renewal, or at any earlier time specified in the loan contract.

(b) Interest rate changes at renewal shall be determined as follows:

(1) Subject to the provisions of subdivision (a) the interest rate offered at renewal shall reflect the movement, in reference to the date of the original loan, of an index, which may be either (i) the contract interest rate on the purchase of previously occupied homes in the most recent monthly national average mortgage rate index for all major lenders published by the Federal Home Loan Bank Board, or (ii) the weighted average cost of funds for the 11th District Savings and Loan Associations as computed by the Federal Home Loan Bank of San Francisco; provided that a lender may extend the initial terms of loans for a period less than six months so that they may mature on the same date three, four or five years after the end of such period of extension, in which case the interest rate offered at renewal shall reflect the movement of the index from the end of such period so that loans may be grouped as though all loans of such group had originated at the end of the extension period.

(2) The maximum rate increase or decrease shall be ½ of 1 percentage point per year multiplied by the number of years in the loan term, with a maximum increase or decrease of 5 percentage points over the life of the mortgage or deed of trust. The lender may offer a borrower a renegotiable rate mortgage loan with maximum annual and total interest rate decreases smaller than the maximum set out in this paragraph, except that in such a case the maximum annual and total interest rate increases offered shall not exceed the maximum annual and total decreases set out in the loan contract.

(3) Interest rate decreases from the previous loan term shall be mandatory. Interest rate increases are optional with the lender, but the lender may obligate itself to a third party to take the maximum increase permitted by this paragraph.

(c) The borrower may not be charged any costs or fees in connection with the renewal of such loan.

(d) At least 90 days before the due date of the loan, the lender shall send written notification in the following form to the borrower:

NOTICE

Your loan with [name of lender], secured by a [mortgage/deed of trust] on property located at [address], is due and payable on [90 days from the date of notice].

If you do not pay by that date, your loan will be renewed automatically for ____ years, upon the same terms and conditions as the current loan, except that the interest rate will be ____%. (See accompanying Truth-In-Lending statement for further credit information.)

Your monthly payment, based on that rate, will be $_____, beginning with the payment due on ____, 19____.

You may pay off the entire loan or a part of it without penalty at any time. If you have questions about this notice, please contact [title and telephone number of lender's employee].

(e) An applicant for a renegotiable rate mortgage loan must be given, at the time he or she requests an application, a disclosure notice in the following form:

INFORMATION ABOUT THE RENEGOTIABLE-RATE MORTGAGE

You have received an application form for a renegotiable-rate mortgage ("RRM"). The RRM differs from the fixed-rate mortgage with which you may be familiar. In the fixed-rate mortgage the length of the loan and the length of the underlying mortgage a Truth-In-re the same, but in the RRM the loan is short-term (3–5 years) and is automatically renewable for a period equal to the mortgage (up to 30 years). Therefore, instead of having an interest rate that is set at the beginning of the mortgage and remains the same, the RRM has an interest rate that may increase or decrease at each renewal of the short-term loan. This means that the amount of your monthly payment may also increase or decrease.

The term of the RRM loan is ____ years, and the length of the underlying mortgage is ____ years. The initial loan term may be up to six months longer than later terms.

The lender must offer to renew the loan, and the only loan provision that may be changed at renewal is the interest rate. The interest rate offered at renewal is based on changes in an index rate. The index used is (either of the following statements shall be given): [computed monthly by the Federal Home Loan Bank Board, an agency of the federal government. The index is based on the national average contract rate for all major lenders for the purchase of previously occupied, single-family homes.] [the weighted average cost of savings, borrowings and Federal Home Loan Bank advances to California members of the Federal Home Loan Bank Board of San Francisco as computed from statistics tabulated by the Federal Home Loan Bank of San Francisco. The index used is computed by the Federal Home Loan Bank of San Francisco.]

At renewal, if the index has moved higher than it was at the beginning of the mortgage, the lender has the right to offer a renewal of the loan at an interest rate equaling the original interest rate plus the increase in the index rate. This is the maximum increase permitted to the lender. Although taking such an increase is optional with the lender, you should be aware that the lender has this right and may become contractually obligated to exercise it.

If the index has moved down, the lender must at renewal reduce the original interest rate by the decrease in the index rate. No matter how much the index rate increases or decreases, THE LENDER, AT RENEWAL, MAY NOT INCREASE OR DECREASE THE INTEREST RATE ON YOUR RRM LOAN BY AN AMOUNT GREATER THAN ____ OF ONE PERCENTAGE POINT PER YEAR OF THE LOAN, AND THE TOTAL INCREASE OR DECREASE OVER THE LIFE OF THE MORTGAGE MAY NOT BE MORE THAN ____ PERCENTAGE POINTS.

As the borrower, you have the right to decline the lender's offer of renewal. If you decide not to renew, you will have to pay off the remaining balance of the mortgage. Even if you decide to renew, you have the right to prepay the loan in part or in full without penalty at any time after the beginning of the minimum notice period for the first renewal. To give you enough time to make this decision, the lender, 90 days before renewal, will send a notice stating the due date of the loan, the new interest rate and the monthly payment amount. If you do not respond to the notice, the loan will be automatically renewed at the new rate. You will not have to pay any fees or charges at renewal time.

The maximum interest rate increase at the first renewal is ____ percentage points. On a $50,000 mortgage with a loan term of ____ years and an original interest rate of [lender's current commitment rate] percent, this rate change would increase the monthly payment (principal and interest) from $_____ to $_____. Using the same example, the highest rate you might have to pay over the life of the mortgage would be ____ percent, and the lowest would be ____ percent.

Leg.H. Added Stats 1980 ch 1139 §2.

§1916.9. Offering fixed rate mortgage loan with offer of renegotiable rate mortgage loan

(a) Every lender who offers a renegotiable rate mortgage loan pursuant to Section 1916.8 to a borrower who occupies or intends to occupy the property which is security for the loan shall also offer to such borrower a fixed rate mortgage loan in the same amount with a term of at least 29 years.

(b) Nothing in this section shall require that the terms of such alternative loans, including the rates of interest thereon, must be the same as those terms offered with regard to the fixed-payment adjustable-rate loan or the renegotiable rate mortgage loan also offered.

(c) This section does not apply to any lender who makes less than 10 loans per year. **Leg.H.** Added Stats 1980 ch 1139 §3.

§1916.10. [Section repealed 1983]

Leg.H. Added Stats 1981 ch 274 §1, effective August 27, 1981. Amended Stats 1981 ch 1079 §2. Repealed effective December 31, 1983, by its own provisions. The repealed section related to loans bearing other than fixed-rate of interest upon security of real property.

§1916.11. Lien of mortgage or deed of trust

Notwithstanding any other remedy a borrower may have based on an alleged failure to comply with Sections 1916.5 through 1916.9, the lien of the mortgage or deed of trust shall be valid. **Leg.H.** Added Stats 1981 ch 274 §2, effective August 27, 1981.

§1916.12. Loans upon security of residential real property

(a) The Legislature finds that the economic environment of financial institutions has become increasingly volatile as a result of regulatory revisions enacted by the United States Congress and federal agencies including, but not necessarily limited to, the Comptroller of the Currency, the Federal Home Loan Bank Board, Federal Reserve Board, and the Depository Institutions Deregulation Committee. The Legislature further finds that deposit rate ceilings are being phased out while the cost of and competition for funds have escalated. It is the purpose of this section to maintain the quality of competition between state-licensed and federally regulated financial institutions in the field of mortgage lending, as well as promote the convenience, advantage and best interests of California residents in their pursuit of adequate and available housing. In order to remain competitive and provide the optimum housing environment for the citizens of California, state institutions require the ability to respond in a timely manner to changes in mortgage lending parameters initiated at the federal level. Local regulatory guidelines must promote continued parity between the state and federal levels in order to avoid creation of discriminatory burdens upon state institutions and to protect interests held by California citizens. It is the intent of the Legislature to eliminate past and prevent future inequities between state and federal financial institutions doing business in the State of California by creating a sensitive and responsive mortgage parity procedure.

(b) The Secretary of the Business, Consumer Services, and Housing Agency, or the secretary's designee as defined by subdivision (c) of Section 1918.5 of the Civil Code, shall have the authority to prescribe rules and regulations extending to lenders who make loans upon the security of residential real property any right, power, privilege or duty relating to mortgage instruments that is equivalent to authority extended to federally regulated financial institutions by federal statute or regulation.

(c) In order to grant equivalent mortgage lending authority to state financial institutions to that which has been extended to federal financial institutions, the secretary or the secretary's designee shall adopt such regulations within 60 days of the effective date of the statute or regulation extending the comparable right, power, privilege, or duty to federally regulated financial institutions.

(d) The provisions of Sections 1916.5, 1916.6, 1916.7, 1916.8, and 1916.9, and any other provisions of law relating to the requirements for changes in the rate of interest on loans, shall not be applicable to loans made pursuant to the provisions of this section and regulations promulgated thereunder.

(e) Any regulations adopted pursuant to this section shall expire on January 1 of the second succeeding year following the end of the calendar year in which the regulation was promulgated. Subsequent amendments to these regulations cannot extend this expiration date.

(f) This section shall become operative on December 31, 1983. **Leg.H.** Added Stats 1981 ch 1079 §3, operative December 31, 1983. Amended Stats 2013 ch 353 §10 (SB 820), effective September 26, 2013, operative July 1, 2013.

Usury Law

An act, to be known as the usury law, relating to the rate of interest which may be charged for the loan or forbearance of money, goods or things in action, or on accounts after demand, or on judgments, providing penalties for the violation of the provisions hereof, and repealing sections one thousand nine hundred seventeen, one thousand nine hundred eighteen, one thousand nine hundred nineteen, and one thousand nine hundred twenty of the Civil Code and all acts and parts of acts in conflict with this act.

Section 1 of Article XV of the Constitution, as amended in 1979, fixes the legal rate of interest at seven per cent per annum and permits written contracts for a rate of interest not exceeding ten per cent per annum. This section of the Constitution supersedes provisions of this act that conflict with it. **Leg.H.** Enacted Stats 1919 p lxxxiii, initiative measure approved November 5, 1918. Amended by Stats 1970 ch 784, approved November 3, 1970.

§1916.12-1. Legal rate of interest; Contract rate

The rate of interest upon the loan or forbearance of any money, goods or things in action or on accounts after demand or judgments rendered in any court of this state, shall be seven dollars upon the one hundred dollars for one year and at that rate for a greater or less sum or for a longer or a shorter time; but it shall be competent for parties to contract for the payment and receipt of a rate of interest not exceeding twelve dollars on the one hundred dollars for one year and not exceeding that rate for a greater or less sum or for a longer or shorter time, in which case such rate exceeding seven dollars on one hundred dollars shall be clearly expressed in writing. **Leg.H.** Enacted Stats 1919 p lxxxiii, initiative measure approved November 5, 1918.

§1916.12-2. Limitations on contract rates

No person, company, association or corporation shall directly or indirectly take or receive in money, goods or things in action, or in any other manner whatsoever, any greater sum or any greater value for the loan or forbearance of money, goods or things in action than at the rate of twelve dollars upon one hundred dollars for one year; and in the computation of interest upon any bond, note, or other instrument or agreement, interest shall not be compounded, nor shall the interest thereon be construed to bear interest unless an agreement to that effect is clearly expressed in writing and signed by the party to be charged therewith. Any agreement or contract of any nature in conflict with the provisions of this section shall be null and void as to any agreement or stipulation therein contained to pay interest and no action at law to recover interest in any sum shall be maintained and the debt cannot be declared due until the full period of time it was contracted for has elapsed. **Leg.H.** Enacted Stats 1919 p lxxxiii, initiative measure approved November 5, 1918.

§1916.12-3. Rights of person paying illegal interest; Penalty for violations

(a) Every person, company, association or corporation, who for any loan or forbearance of money, goods or things in action shall have paid or delivered any greater sum or value than is allowed to be received under the preceding sections, one and two, may either in person or his or its personal representative, recover in an action at law against the person, company, association or corporation who shall have taken or received the same, or his or its personal representative, treble the amount of the money so paid or value delivered in violation of said sections, providing such action shall be brought within one year after such payment or delivery.

(b) Any person who willfully makes or negotiates, for himself or another, a loan of money, credit, goods, or things in action, and who directly or indirectly charges, contracts for, or receives with respect to any such loan any interest or charge of any nature, the value of which is in excess of that allowed by law, is guilty of loan-sharking, a felony, and is punishable by imprisonment in the state prison for not more than five years or in the county jail for not more than one year. This subdivision shall not apply to any person licensed to make or negotiate, for himself or another, loans of money, credit, goods, or things in action, or expressly exempted from compliance by the laws of this state with respect to such licensure or interest or other charge, or to any agent or employee of such person when acting within the scope of his agency or employment. **Leg.H.** Enacted Stats 1919 p lxxxiii, initiative measure approved November 5, 1918.

§1916.12-4. Repeal of Civil Code sections relating to interest

Sections one thousand nine hundred seventeen, one thousand nine hundred eighteen, one thousand nine hundred nineteen and one thousand nine hundred twenty of the Civil Code and all acts and parts of acts in conflict with this act are hereby repealed. **Leg.H.** Enacted Stats 1919 p lxxxiii, initiative measure approved November 5, 1918.

§1916.12-5. Title of act

This act whenever cited, referred to, or amended may be designated simply as the "usury law." **Leg.H.** Enacted Stats 1919 p lxxxiii, initiative measure approved November 5, 1918.

CHAPTER 3.5
SHARED APPRECIATION LOANS

Definitions. §1917.
Relationship of borrower and lender. §1917.001.
Application of other provisions. §1917.002.
Contents of lien of deed of trust. §1917.003.
Attachment of lien. §1917.004.
Exemption from usury laws. §1917.005.
"Shared appreciation loan"; "Local public entity"; "Owner-occupied residence". §1917.006.

§1917. Definitions

For purposes of this chapter:

(a) "Contingent deferred interest" means the sum a borrower is obligated to pay to a lender pursuant to the documentation of a shared appreciation loan as a share of (1) the appreciation in the value of the security property (2) rents and profits attributable to the subject property, or (3) both.

(b) A "shared appreciation loan" means any loan made upon the security of an interest in real property which additionally obligates the borrower to pay to the lender contingent deferred interest pursuant to the loan documentation. "Shared appreciation loan" does not include any loan made upon the security of an interest in real property containing one to four residential units at least one of which at the time the loan is made is or is to be occupied by the borrower. **Leg.H.** Added Stats 1987 ch 652 §1.

Prior Law: Former §1917, relating to interest rate, was enacted Stats 1872, amended Code Amdts 1873–74 ch 612 §203, Code Amdts 1877–78 ch 73 §1, and repealed by initiative act adopted November 5, 1918, Stats 1919 p lxxxiii.

§1917.001. Relationship of borrower and lender

The relationship of the borrower and the lender in a shared appreciation loan transaction is that of debtor and creditor and shall not be, or be construed to be, a joint venture, equity venture, partnership, or other relationship. **Leg.H.** Added Stats 1987 ch 652 §1.

§1917.002. Application of other provisions

A shared appreciation loan shall not be subject to any provisions of this code or the Financial Code which limits the interest rate or change of interest rate of variable, adjustable, or renegotiable interest instruments, or which requires particular language or provisions in security instruments securing variable, adjustable, or renegotiable rate obligations or in evidences of such debts except for those specifically imposed by Chapter 4 (commencing with Section 1917.010) or Chapter 7 (commencing with Section 1917.320) for loans subject to those chapters. This section is declaratory of existing law. **Leg.H.** Added Stats 1987 ch 652 §1.

§1917.003. Contents of lien of deed of trust

The lien or liens of a deed or deeds of trust securing a shared appreciation loan shall include and secure the principal amount of the shared appreciation loan, and all interest, whether accrued or to be accrued, including all amounts of contingent deferred interest. **Leg.H.** Added Stats 1987 ch 652 §1. Amended Stats 1989 ch 1416 §5.

§1917.004. Attachment of lien

(a) The lien of a shared appreciation loan, including the principle amount and all interest, whether accrued or to be accrued, and all amounts of contingent deferred interest, shall attach from the time of the recordation of the deed of trust securing the loan, and the lien, including the lien of the interest accrued, or to be accrued, and of the contingent deferred interest, shall have priority over any other lien or encumbrance affecting the property encumbered by the shared appreciation deed of trust which is recorded after the time of recordation of the shared appreciation deed of trust. Nothing in this section shall preclude a junior or subordinate lien to the deed of trust securing the shared appreciation loan.

(b) Any deed of trust that acts as security for a shared appreciation loan shall indicate on the document that the deed of trust secures a shared appreciation loan. **Leg.H.** Added Stats 1987 ch 652 §1.

1987 Note: It appears that the Legislature inadvertently substituted the word "principle" for the word "principal" in subsection (a).

§1917.005. Exemption from usury laws

Lenders shall be exempt from the usury provisions of Article XV of the California Constitution with respect to shared appreciation loan transactions. This section is declaratory of existing law. **Leg.H.** Added Stats 1987 ch 652 §1.

§1917.006. "Shared appreciation loan"; "Local public entity"; "Owner-occupied residence"

For purposes of this chapter:

(a) "Shared appreciation loan" means, in addition to the meaning defined in Section 1917, a loan that obligates the borrower to pay to the lender contingent deferred interest pursuant to the loan documentation and that is made upon the security of an interest in real property that is an owner-occupied residence in compliance with all of the following conditions:

(1) The loan is made by, and all contingent deferred interest paid with respect to the loan is used by, a local public entity to provide financial assistance in the acquisition of housing that is affordable to persons and families of low or moderate income, as defined in Section 50093 of the Health and Safety Code.

(2) The loan is made or acquired with assets of the local public entity other than the proceeds of a bond meeting the requirements of Section 143 of the United States Internal Revenue Code of 1986.

(3) The loan documentation assures that the obligation to pay contingent deferred interest is subject to a superior right of the borrower, upon termination of the loan, to receive repayment of money paid by the borrower for purchase of the security property (including downpayment, installment payments of mortgage principal, escrow fees, transfer taxes, recording fees, brokerage commissions and similar costs of acquisition actually paid by the borrower) and money paid by the borrower for capital improvements to the security property, plus not less than the legal rate of interest on those cash payments.

(4) The loan documentation assures that the amount of contingent deferred interest shall not exceed that percentage of the appreciation in appraised fair market value of the security property that equals the local public entity's proportionate share of the total initial equity in the security property. The amount of the total initial equity and of the local public entity's share of the initial equity shall be agreed upon by the borrower and the local public entity at the time of executing the shared appreciation loan and shall include the local public entity's cash investment, the difference between the price of land provided by the local public entity and the fair market value of the land, the amount of fees waived by the local public entity, and the value of in-kind contributions made by or on behalf of the local public entity. Funds borrowed by the borrower, the repayment of which are secured by the security property, shall not be included in the calculation of total initial equity of the borrower.

(5) At least 30 days in advance of executing the loan documentation, the borrower receives full disclosure of the terms and conditions of the loan, including the economic consequences to the borrower of the obligation to pay contingent deferred interest.

(b) "Local public entity" means a city and county, or a housing authority or redevelopment agency of a city and county.

(c) "Owner-occupied residence" means real property containing one to four residential units at least one of which at the time the loan is made is, or is to be, occupied by the borrower. **Leg.H.** Added Stats 1990 ch 1606 §1 (SB 2716).

CHAPTER 4
SHARED APPRECIATION LOANS OF E.R.I.S.A. PENSION FUNDS

Article 1. Legislative Findings and Declarations.
Article 2. Definitions.
Article 3. Terms and Conditions.
Article 4. Annual Appraisals.
Article 5. Improvements.
Article 6. General Provisions.
Article 7. Notices and Disclosures.

ARTICLE 1
Legislative Findings and Declarations

Legislative findings [Inoperative]. §1917.010.

§1917.010. Legislative findings [Inoperative]

The Legislature hereby finds and declares that:

(a) It is necessary and essential that the state provide and promote alternative means of supplying affordable housing to the citizens of the state.

(b) High interest rates have caused payment schedules for new long-term, fixed-rate and adjustable-rate mortgages to exceed affordable levels for the vast majority of the state's households.

(c) Because of current economic conditions, including high and volatile interest rates, alternative mortgage instruments must be developed to supplement the standard long-term, fixed-rate mortgage.

(d) Because the interest to which the lender is entitled under a shared appreciation mortgage includes a share of the appreciated value of the property securing the loan, the periodic payments under a shared appreciation mortgage are lower and, therefore, more affordable to borrowers than under a mortgage in which the lender's interest does not include a share of the appreciated value of the property. State authorization of the shared appreciation loan for pension fund lenders will serve the need to develop alternative and more affordable means of financing the construction of new housing and the subsequent marketing of new homes, and to create vitally needed jobs in the construction industry.

(e) Pension funds may find shared appreciation loans suited to their investment needs since yields are keyed to appreciation in property values, which may serve as a hedge against inflation. **Leg.H.** Added Stats 1982 ch 466 §11. Inoperative January 1, 1990, by the terms of Stats 1982 ch 466 §11.5.

ARTICLE 2
Definitions

Definitions [Inoperative]. §1917.020.

§1917.020. Definitions [Inoperative]

For purposes of this chapter:

(a) "Adjusted fair market value" means all of the following:

(1) The net sale price, in the case of a bona fide sale made in good faith prior to the maturity date of the shared appreciation loan, but excluding any sale upon a foreclosure or trustee's sale pursuant to Section 726 of the Code of Civil Procedure or Section 2924.

(2) In all other cases, the amount of value of the property specified in the most recent annual appraisal performed pursuant to Section 1917.040 or 1917.042.

(b) "Borrower's cost of the property" means the total cost to the borrower incident to the purchase of the property, including documentary transfer taxes, escrow and recording fees, and title insurance premiums.

(c) "Contingent deferred interest" means the sum resulting upon multiplying the net appreciated value by one-third.

(d) "Cost of capital improvements" means the amount of the credit, if any, determined pursuant to Article 5 (commencing with Section 1917.050).

(e) "Lender" means any person who makes a shared appreciation loan on behalf of a pension fund specified in Section 1917.030. Subsequent to an assignment of a shared appreciation loan to a pension fund pursuant to Section 1917.030, "lender" shall mean the pension fund assignee (or any subsequent assignee) and its agents designated to service the shared appreciation loan.

(f) "Net appreciated value" means the adjusted fair market value less the sum of the borrower's cost of the property and the cost of capital improvements.

(g) "Net sale price" means the gross sale price less expenses of sale actually paid by the borrower, including real estate commissions, advertising, documentary transfer taxes, legal, escrow and recording fees, and title insurance premiums.

(h) "Prevailing rate" means the weighted average yield accepted by the Federal National Mortgage Association in its most recent free market system auction for four-month conventional mortgage commitments or, if the Federal National Mortgage Association alters its free market system auction, then the system which is adopted by the Federal National Mortgage Association which substantially replaces or supersedes the present free market system auction for four-month commitments, or if no auction or equivalent thereof has been conducted within the six months immediately preceding the date the application for a shared appreciation mortgage loan is executed, the weighted average cost of funds for the 11th District Savings and Loan Associations as computed by the Federal Home Loan Bank of San Francisco.

(i) "Shared appreciation loan" means any loan made pursuant to this chapter upon the security of owner-occupied real property of a type specified in Section 1917.030, and in connection with which the lender has a right to receive a share of the appreciation in the value of the security property. "Shared appreciation loan" includes a deed of trust and any evidence of debt issued in connection with the loan. **Leg.H.** Added Stats 1982 ch 466 §11. Inoperative January 1, 1990, by the terms of Stats 1982 ch 466 §11.5.

ARTICLE 3
Terms and Conditions

Shared appreciation loans [Inoperative]. §1917.030.
Terms and conditions of loans [Inoperative]. §1917.031.
Prepayment of loans [Inoperative]. §1917.032.
Refinancing of loans [Inoperative]. §1917.033.
Obtaining other financing [Inoperative]. §1917.034.

§1917.030. Shared appreciation loans [Inoperative]

Lenders may make shared appreciation loans pursuant to this chapter for the purchase of real property improved with one- to four-family dwelling units, including structures ancillary to such dwelling units and including attached single-family dwelling units, single-family mobile-home units placed upon permanent foundations, residential condominium units and dwelling units within a planned unit development. Shared appreciation loans shall be made to finance only owner-occupied dwelling units, but in the case of two- to four-unit dwellings financed under this chapter only one of the units need be owner-occupied. The original recipient of a shared appreciation loan shall certify in writing to the lender that he or she will occupy the security property as his or her principal residence, provided that failure to so occupy the security property shall not void a shared appreciation loan, but at the option of the lender the loan may be accelerated in accordance with the terms and conditions provided in the shared appreciation loan. All shared appreciation loans shall be originated by the lender on behalf of a pension fund which is subject to the Employee Retirement Income Security Act of 1974 (P.L. 93-406, 88 Stat. 829), pursuant to a prior written commitment to purchase the loan. **Leg.H.** Added Stats 1982 ch 466 §11. Inoperative January 1, 1990, by the terms of Stats 1982 ch 466 §11.5.

§1917.031. Terms and conditions of loans [Inoperative]

A shared appreciation loan shall include the following terms and conditions:

(a) The term of the loan, excluding refinancing under Section 1917.033, shall be at least seven years, but not more than 30 years.

(b) The repayment schedule for the loan, excluding refinancing under Section 1917.033, shall be cast so that full amortization of the principal amount of the loan would occur in 30 years, regardless of the actual term of the loan. Any principal balance remaining at maturity shall be due and payable at that time, unless refinanced as provided in Section 1917.033. Monthly installment payments shall be equal in amount and in addition to amortization of principal, shall include fixed interest pursuant to subdivision (d).

(c) The loan shall be secured by a deed of trust or mortgage on the real property financed.

(d) The loan shall bear interest at a fixed rate, which shall be one-third below the prevailing rate in effect 90 days prior to the loan closing, or at another date between that date and the loan closing if mutually agreed by the lender and borrower.

(e) The borrower shall additionally be obligated to pay contingent deferred interest in the amount of one-third of the net appreciated value of the real property which secures the loan, at the time the property is sold (including a sale pursuant to a land sale contract), when title is transferred, other than a transfer specified in Section 2924.6, when a lease with an option to purchase is entered into, when a partnership is formed which in effect transfers the beneficial ownership to another person, when a trust is created which affects title to the property, upon a judicial or nonjudicial foreclosure sale, at the time the loan is prepaid in full, or upon the maturity of the loan, whichever first occurs. **Leg.H.** Added Stats 1982 ch 466 §11. Inoperative January 1, 1990, by the terms of Stats 1982 ch 466 §11.5.

§1917.032. Prepayment of loans [Inoperative]

(a) The borrower shall have the right to prepay, at any time, in full or in part, the principal loan balance of the shared appreciation loan, together with accrued interest, including deferred contingent interest.

(b) Nothing in this chapter shall prevent a borrower from obligating himself or herself, by an agreement in writing, to pay a prepayment charge, as authorized by this section, upon prepayment of the loan, in full or in part, within five years of the date of execution of the shared appreciation loan.

(c) Any prepayment charge imposed upon the prepayment of a shared appreciation loan shall not exceed the amount authorized and specified in subdivision (b) of Section 2954.9.

(d) No prepayment charge shall be imposed as to any portion of the contingent deferred interest. **Leg.H.** Added Stats 1982 ch 466 §11. Inoperative January 1, 1990, by the terms of Stats 1982 ch 466 §11.5.

§1917.033. Refinancing of loans [Inoperative]

(a) If the shared appreciation loan is not prepaid in full or the real property securing the loan is not sold or transferred prior to maturity of the loan, the lender shall offer to the original borrower refinancing of the unpaid balance of the loan and all contingent deferred interest.

(b) The term of the refinancing loan shall be at least 30 years from the date of the refinancing, provided that if the interest rate of the refinancing loan is not adjustable or variable during the term of such loan, the loan may contain a call provision giving the lender an option to accelerate the principal loan balance making it, together with accrued interest, payable in full at a date specified in the shared appreciation loan, which shall be no earlier than seven years following the date of refinancing under this section. If such a call provision is included in the refinancing loan, a concise description thereof shall be included in upper case print in the disclosures on refinancing required by Section 1917.071.

(c) The interest rate for the refinancing loan shall not exceed the prevailing rate existing at maturity of the shared appreciation loan.

(d) The lender may require as a condition of the refinancing loan that it be secured by a deed of trust or mortgage of first priority on the property financed.

(e) The terms and conditions of refinancing pursuant to this section shall be specified in the shared appreciation loan, shall be a part of the shared appreciation loan contract, and shall be subject to the applicable laws in effect on the date of execution of the shared appreciation loan. The refinancing shall be fully amortizing and the interest rate may be either fixed or adjustable as permitted by law for home financing offered by banks or savings and loan associations doing business in this state to the public for financing housing similar to the borrower's property, provided that nothing in this section shall preclude such other lawful refinancing terms as may be mutually acceptable to the borrower and lender. If the lender offers more than one form of refinancing, the borrower may select from among the types of refinancing offered by the lender. **Leg.H.** Added Stats 1982 ch 466 §11. Inoperative January 1, 1990, by the terms of Stats 1982 ch 466 §11.5.

§1917.034. Obtaining other financing [Inoperative]

Nothing in this chapter shall preclude the borrower from obtaining any other financing, in lieu of the refinancing provided for in Section 1917.033, including refinancing on other terms that are mutually agreeable to the borrower and lender. **Leg.H.** Added Stats 1982 ch 466 §11. Inoperative January 1, 1990, by the terms of Stats 1982 ch 466 §11.5.

ARTICLE 4
Annual Appraisals

Determining fair market value annually [Inoperative]. §1917.040.
Disputing the appraisal [Inoperative]. §1917.041.
Calculating the adjustment [Inoperative]. §1917.042.
Determination of fair market value [Inoperative]. §1917.043.
Qualifications of appraisers [Inoperative]. §1917.044.

§1917.040. Determining fair market value annually [Inoperative]

The fair market value of the real property securing a shared appreciation loan shall be determined annually as provided in this article. The lender shall select an independent appraiser annually to perform an appraisal of the property subject to a shared appreciation loan. The appraisal shall be performed within 30 days preceding the anniversary date of the loan and a copy of the current appraisal shall be sent by first-class mail to the borrower no later than five days following the anniversary date of the loan, together with a notice informing the borrower that the appraisal will constitute a final and conclusive determination of the value of the property for certain purposes and that if the borrower disputes the amount of the appraisal, the borrower may procure an independent appraisal as provided in Section 1917.041. The lender may require the borrower to pay for the cost of the appraisal. **Leg.H.** Added Stats 1982 ch 466 §11. Inoperative January 1, 1990, by the terms of Stats 1982 ch 466 §11.5.

§1917.041. Disputing the appraisal [Inoperative]

If the borrower disputes the amount of the appraisal, the borrower, within 30 days of the anniversary date of the loan, may procure an appraisal of the property at the borrower's expense by a qualified independent appraiser, and a copy of the appraisal shall be sent by first-class mail to the lender within the 30-day period. **Leg.H.** Added Stats 1982 ch 466 §11. Inoperative January 1, 1990, by the terms of Stats 1982 ch 466 §11.5.

§1917.042. Calculating the adjustment [Inoperative]

If the appraisal by the appraiser selected by the borrower is lower in amount than the appraisal by the appraiser selected by the lender, the amount to be used to calculate the annual adjustment shall be one-half of the sum of the two appraisals. **Leg.H.** Added Stats 1982 ch 466 §11. Inoperative January 1, 1990, by the terms of Stats 1982 ch 466 §11.5.

§1917.043. Determination of fair market value [Inoperative]

The appraisal amount, as determined pursuant to Section 1917.040 if the borrower does not dispute the appraisal amount, or 1917.042 if the borrower disputes the appraisal amount, shall constitute the value of the property from and after the anniversary date of the loan for the purpose of determining the property's adjusted fair market value under Section 1917.020. **Leg.H.** Added Stats 1982 ch 466 §11. Inoperative January 1, 1990, by the terms of Stats 1982 ch 466 §11.5.

§1917.044. Qualifications of appraisers [Inoperative]

The qualifications of the appraisers may be specified by the terms of the shared appreciation loan for purposes of this article and Article 5 (commencing with Section 1917.050). **Leg.H.** Added Stats 1982 ch 466 §11. Inoperative January 1, 1990, by the terms of Stats 1982 ch 466 §11.5.

ARTICLE 5
Improvements

Improvements [Inoperative]. §1917.050.

§1917.050. Improvements [Inoperative]

The borrower may have the cost of capital improvements to the security property completed within any 12-month period, and with an appraised value in excess of two thousand five hundred dollars ($2,500), added to the borrower's cost of the property, for purposes of determining the contingent deferred interest, but only if the procedures set forth in this article are followed.

(a) Within 60 days following the completion of the improvements, the borrower shall send by first-class mail a notice of the completion of the improvements to the lender and shall submit proof of cost of the improvements.

(b) Within 90 days following the completion of the improvements, the lender shall select an appraiser to perform an appraisal to determine the increase in value of the property, if any, by reason of the improvements. A copy of the appraisal shall be sent by first-class mail to the borrower, together with a notice informing the borrower that the appraisal will constitute a final and conclusive determination of the increase in the value of the property by reason of the improvement for purposes of computing the net appreciated value of the property, and that if the borrower disputes the amount of the appraisal, the borrower may procure an independent appraisal as provided in subdivision (c). The lender may require the borrower to pay for the cost of the appraisal.

(c) If the borrower disputes the amount of the appraisal, the borrower, within 120 days of the completion of the improvements, may secure at borrower's expense, a qualified, independent appraiser to perform an appraisal to determine the increase in value of the property, if any, by reason of the improvements, and a copy of the appraisal shall be sent by first-class mail to the lender within that period of time.

(d) If the appraisal of the appraiser selected by the borrower is greater in amount than the appraisal by the appraiser selected by the lender, the amount of the appraisal, for the purposes of this section, shall be one-half of the sum of the two appraisals.

(e) The lesser of the borrower's actual cost or the appraised increase in the value of the property by reason of the improvements shall be available as a credit to the buyer for purposes of determining net appreciated value, except as provided in subdivision (f).

(f) If 50 percent or more of the value of the labor or other work on the improvements was performed by the borrower, then the appraised increase in the value of the property by reason of the improvements shall be the cost of capital improvements for purposes of establishing the credit under this section. **Leg.H.** Added Stats 1982 ch 466 §11. Inoperative January 1, 1990, by the terms of Stats 1982 ch 466 §11.5.

ARTICLE 6
General Provisions

Relationship of borrower and lender [Inoperative]. §1917.060.
Waiver of right void and unenforceable [Inoperative]. §1917.061.
Acceleration of maturity date upon sale of transfer valid and enforceable [Inoperative]. §1917.062.
Terms and conditions of loan to conform to this chapter [Inoperative]. §1917.063.
Interest rate not limited [Inoperative]. §1917.064.
Elements of lien [Inoperative]. §1917.065.
Attachment of lien; Priority [Inoperative]. §1917.066.
Exemption from usury provisions [Inoperative]. §1917.067.
Qualification requirements do not apply [Inoperative]. §1917.068.
Reasonable fee allowed [Inoperative]. §1917.069.

§1917.060. Relationship of borrower and lender [Inoperative]

The relationship of the borrower and the lender, as to a shared appreciation loan, is that of debtor and creditor and shall not be, or be construed to be, a joint venture, equity venture, partnership, or other relationship. **Leg.H.** Added Stats 1982 ch 466 §11. Inoperative January 1, 1990, by the terms of Stats 1982 ch 466 §11.5.

§1917.061. Waiver of right void and unenforceable [Inoperative]

Any waiver of any right of a borrower under the provisions of this chapter shall be void and unenforceable. **Leg.H.** Added Stats 1982 ch 466 §11. Inoperative January 1, 1990, by the terms of Stats 1982 ch 466 §11.5.

§1917.062. Acceleration of maturity date upon sale of transfer valid and enforceable [Inoperative]

(a) Notwithstanding Section 711, a provision in a shared appreciation loan (not including the refinancing obligation) permitting the lender to accelerate the maturity date of the principal and accrued interest on the loan upon a sale or other transfer of the property, as specified in subdivision (e) of Section 1917.031, shall be valid and enforceable against the borrower, except as may be precluded by Section 2924.6.

(b) The Legislature finds and declares that potential exposure to liability for enforcement of a "due-on-sale" clause consistent with Section 711, as interpreted by the courts, makes use of such a provision impractical. Moreover, the additional risks to the lender inherent in shared appreciation financing are greater with longer loan terms (which are more desirable from the standpoint of housing affordability), but this risk is reduced with an enforceable "due-on-sale" clause. Therefore, in order to facilitate shared appreciation financing, it is necessary to establish the exception specified in subdivision (a). **Leg.H.** Added Stats 1982 ch 466 §11. Inoperative January 1, 1990, by the terms of Stats 1982 ch 466 §11.5.

§1917.063. Terms and conditions of loan to conform to this chapter [Inoperative]

This chapter facilitates the making of shared appreciation financing in this state which conforms to the provisions of this chapter. The terms and conditions of any shared appreciation loan made pursuant to this chapter shall be consistent with this chapter. This chapter does not, however, apply to or limit shared appreciation financing of real property of a type specified in Section 1917.030 that is made pursuant to other provisions of law, or which is not otherwise unlawful. Nothing in this chapter shall be construed to in any way affect shared appreciation financing of commercial property or residential property not meeting the criteria specified in Section 1917.030.

Nothing in this chapter precludes a pension fund specified in Section 1917.030 from providing shared appreciation financing pursuant to Chapter 5 (commencing with Section 1917.110) or any other provision of law, or which is not otherwise unlawful. **Leg.H.** Added Stats 1982 ch 466 §11. Inoperative January 1, 1990, by the terms of Stats 1982 ch 466 §11.5.

§1917.064. Interest rate not limited [Inoperative]

A shared appreciation loan shall not be subject to any provision of this code or the Financial Code which limits the interest rate or change of interest rate of variable, adjustable, or renegotiable interest instruments, or which requires particular language or provisions in security instruments securing variable, adjustable, or renegotiable rate obligations or in evidences of such debts.

This section is declaratory of existing law. **Leg.H.** Added Stats 1982 ch 466 §11. Inoperative January 1, 1990, by the terms of Stats 1982 ch 466 §11.5.

§1917.065. Elements of lien [Inoperative]

The lien of a deed of trust securing a shared appreciation loan shall include and secure the principal amount of the shared appreciation loan, and all interest, whether accrued or to be accrued, including all amounts of contingent deferred interest. **Leg.H.** Added Stats 1982 ch 466 §11. Inoperative January 1, 1990, by the terms of Stats 1982 ch 466 §11.5.

§1917.066. Attachment of lien; Priority [Inoperative]

The lien of a shared appreciation loan, including the principal amount and all interest, whether accrued or to be accrued, and all amounts of contingent deferred interest, shall attach from the time of the recordation of the deed of trust securing the loan, and the lien, including the lien of the interest accrued or to be accrued and of the contingent deferred interest, shall have priority over any other lien or encumbrance affecting the property secured by the shared appreciation instrument which is recorded after the time of recordation of the shared appreciation instrument. However, nothing in this section or Section 1917.165 shall preclude a junior lien or encumbrance subordinate to the obligation of the shared appreciation loan. **Leg.H.** Added Stats 1982 ch 466 §11. Inoperative January 1, 1990, by the terms of Stats 1982 ch 466 §11.5.

§1917.067. Exemption from usury provisions [Inoperative]

Lenders shall be exempt from the usury provisions of Article XV of the California Constitution with respect to shared appreciation loans made pursuant to this chapter.

This section is declaratory of existing law. **Leg.H.** Added Stats 1982 ch 466 §11. Inoperative January 1, 1990, by the terms of Stats 1982 ch 466 §11.5.

§1917.068. Qualification requirements do not apply [Inoperative]

The qualification requirements of Sections 25110, 25120, and 25130 of the Corporations Code shall not apply to a shared appreciation loan, provided (1) the loan obligation is evidenced by one promissory note secured by a deed of trust which is not one of a series of notes secured by interests in the same real property and (2) the loan obligation is not evidenced by fractional undivided interests in one promissory note secured by interests in the same real property. **Leg.H.** Added Stats 1982 ch 466 §11. Inoperative January 1, 1990, by the terms of Stats 1982 ch 466 §11.5.

§1917.069. Reasonable fee allowed [Inoperative]

The aggregate amount of any fee charged to the borrower for processing an application and preparing any necessary documents in connection with originating a shared appreciation loan shall not exceed the reasonable cost of providing the service. No prepaid interest shall be charged to the borrower, but nothing in this chapter shall preclude a lender from requiring a fee for providing commitments for shared appreciation loans to builders or others who will not be the ultimate borrower. **Leg.H.** Added Stats 1982 ch 466 §11. Inoperative January 1, 1990, by the terms of Stats 1982 ch 466 §11.5.

ARTICLE 7
Notices and Disclosures

Disclosures [Inoperative]. §1917.070.
Written information provided to borrower [Inoperative]. §1917.071.
Provision of disclosures required by Federal Reserve Board [Inoperative]. §1917.072.
Additional written statement provided to borrower [Inoperative]. §1917.073.
Required language on deed of trust in connection with shared appreciation loan [Inoperative]. §1917.074.
Disclosure of method of calculating contingent deferred interest [Inoperative]. §1917.075.

§1917.070. Disclosures [Inoperative]

(a) The disclosures made pursuant to this chapter, as required, shall be the only disclosures required to be made pursuant to state law for shared appreciation loans, notwithstanding any contrary provisions applicable to loans not made under this chapter, except those, if any, that may be required by reason of the application of Division 1 (commencing with Section 25000) of the Corporations Code, or Chapter 1 (commencing with Section 11000) of Part 2 of Division 4 of the Business and Professions Code. A lender may, but shall not be required to, supplement the disclosures required by this article with additional disclosures that are not inconsistent with the disclosures required by this article.

(b) When very specific language is prescribed by this chapter, substantially the same language shall be utilized if possible, but reasonably equivalent language may be used to the extent necessary or appropriate to achieve a clearer or more accurate disclosure. **Leg.H.** Added Stats 1982 ch 466 §11. Inoperative January 1, 1990, by the terms of Stats 1982 ch 466 §11.5.

§1917.071. Written information provided to borrower [Inoperative]

(a) Each lender offering shared appreciation loans shall furnish to a prospective borrower, on the earlier of the date on which the lender first provides written information concerning shared appreciation loans from such lender or provides a loan application form to the prospective borrower, a written disclosure as provided in this section.

(b) The disclosure shall be entitled "INFORMATION ABOUT THE (Name of Lender) SHARED APPRECIATION LOAN," and shall describe the operation and effect of the shared appreciation loan including a brief summary of its terms and conditions, together with a statement consisting of substantially the following language, to the extent applicable to such loan:

INFORMATION ABOUT THE (Name of Lender) SHARED APPRECIATION LOAN.

(Name of Lender) is pleased to offer you the opportunity to finance your home through a shared appreciation loan.

Because the shared appreciation loan differs from the usual mortgage loan, the law requires that you should read and understand before you sign the loan documents.

The loan will bear a stated rate of interest which will be one-third below the prevailing market interest rate. In exchange for a stated interest rate which is below the prevailing rate, you will be obligated to pay us additional interest later. This additional interest is called "contingent deferred interest."

Contingent Deferred Interest.

This loan provides that you, as borrower, must pay to us, as lender, as contingent deferred interest, one-third of the net appreciated value of the real property which secures the loan. This contingent interest is due and payable when the property is sold or transferred, when the loan is paid in full, upon any acceleration of the loan upon default, or at the end of the term of the loan, whichever first occurs. The dollar amount of contingent interest which you will be required to pay cannot be determined at this time. If the property does not appreciate, you will owe us nothing.

Your obligation to pay contingent interest will reduce the amount of the appreciation, if any, that you will realize on the property. This appreciation will not produce a real gain in your equity in the property, unless the appreciation rate exceeds the general inflation rate, but you will be required to pay a portion of the appreciation as contingent interest without regard to whether the appreciation has resulted in a real gain.

When you sell or refinance your home, you normally will receive enough cash to pay the shared appreciation loan balance, accrued interest, prepayment penalty (if applicable), the contingent interest, and expenses of sale. However, if you sell with only a small downpayment, you may possibly not receive enough cash to pay the contingent interest, and, in that event, it will be necessary for you to provide cash from other funds.

If you do not sell the property before the end of the term of this loan, you will need to refinance this loan at that time. The term of this loan is (duration) years. We will offer to refinance the outstanding obligation, including any contingent interest, at that time. If you refinance this loan, your monthly payments may increase substantially if the property appreciates significantly or if the interest rate on the refinancing loan is much higher than today's prevailing rates. In general, the more your property appreciated, the larger will be the amount of the contingent interest that you will have an obligation to pay or refinance.

The contingent interest will not become due if title to the property is transferred on your death to a spouse, or where a transfer results from a decree of dissolution of a marriage and a spouse becomes the sole owner.

Calculating the Contingent Interest.

Contingent interest will be calculated as follows:

	FAIR MARKET VALUE OF THE PROPERTY (Sale price or amount of value determined by appraisal.)
— (less)	BORROWER'S COST OF THE PROPERTY (This amount includes certain costs paid by you incident to the purchase.)
— (less)	COST OF CAPITAL IMPROVEMENTS MADE BY YOU IN ANY 12-MONTH PERIOD (Must exceed $2,500 in value. The actual amount may be the lesser of actual cost or appraised value.)
= (equals)	NET APPRECIATED VALUE
× (times)	ONE-THIRD PERCENTAGE OWED TO LENDER
= (equals)	TOTAL CONTINGENT INTEREST

Determining Net Appreciated Value.

We are entitled to receive one-third of the net appreciated value of the property as contingent interest. As explained above, net appreciated value equals (1) the fair market value of the property at the time of the sale or appraisal, less (2) your cost of the property, less (3) the value of any capital improvements for which you are entitled to credit.

Determining Fair Market Value.

Fair market value is the sale price of the property in the case of a bona fide sale of the property made before the maturity of the shared appreciation loan, excluding certain foreclosure related sales. In all other cases, fair market value is determined by our most recent annual appraisal of the property. If you desire to contest the amount of our annual appraisal, you may obtain another appraisal by a qualified independent appraiser within 30 days after the anniversary date of the loan and send a copy of the appraisal to us by first-class mail within that 30-day period. If your appraiser's appraisal is lower than our appraisal, the annual appraisal shall equal one-half the sum of the two appraisals.

Determining Value of Capital Improvements.

The cost or value of certain capital improvements (but no maintenance or repair costs) may be added to your cost of the property for the purpose of determining the net appreciated value, but only if the procedures set forth in the shared appreciation loan documents are followed. It is important to note that capital improvements completed and for which a credit is claimed in any 12-month period must cost or be appraised at more than two thousand five hundred dollars ($2,500). The lesser of the cost or appraised value will control. However, if you have performed at least half the value of the labor or other work involved, then the appraised value of the improvements will control. The appraised value of the improvements shall be considered to be the increase in the value of the property resulting from the improvements. You will receive no credit for improvements that are not appraised at more than two thousand five hundred dollars ($2,500).

Cost of Appraisals.

The terms of this loan call for annual appraisals of the property, and for additional appraisals to value improvements or in the event of a dispute regarding the value of the property or improvements. The cost of the appraisals will be paid as follows:

Your Right to Refinance This Loan.

If the property is not sold or transferred prior to the maturity of the loan, we will offer to refinance the outstanding obligation on the loan, including any contingent interest. We will offer refinancing at the then prevailing interest rate either directly or through another mortgage lender.

The terms of the refinancing loan will be like home loans offered at that time by banks or savings and loan associations, but you are assured that at least one of the options will be a fully amortizing 30-year loan. The interest rate on the refinancing loan may be either fixed or adjustable, as provided in your shared appreciation loan.

We will not be permitted to look to the forecast of your income in offering to refinance. The interest rate and monthly payment upon refinancing cannot be determined at this time. They may be either more or less burdensome to you than the currently prevailing rates and terms.

Tax Consequences.

Use of the shared appreciation loan will have income tax or estate planning consequences which will depend upon your own financial and tax situation. FOR FURTHER INFORMATION, YOU ARE URGED TO CONSULT YOUR OWN ACCOUNTANT, ATTORNEY OR OTHER FINANCIAL ADVISER. THE QUESTIONS YOU SHOULD DISCUSS INCLUDE THE TAX DEDUCTIBILITY OF THE CONTINGENT INTEREST PAYMENT, YOUR RIGHT TO UTILIZE THAT DEDUCTION IN YEARS OTHER THAN THE YEAR IT IS PAID, AND THE EFFECT OF THE LOSS OF TAX BENEFITS BEFORE THAT TIME.

Other Important Information.

(Here insert additional description, if necessary, of the operation and effect of the shared appreciation loan.)

The foregoing describes our shared appreciation loan, includes a summary of all of its important provisions, and informs you of some of the risks of a shared appreciation loan.

If your loan application is accepted by us, we will provide you with more information about your particular shared appreciation loan, which will include a comparison with conventional mortgages, an illustration of the possible increase in your monthly payments upon refinancing, and other important information.

Before you enter into a shared appreciation loan with us, we recommend that you and your attorney or tax accountant review the loan documents for the full text of all of the terms and conditions which will govern the loan. **Leg.H.** Added Stats 1982 ch 466 §11. Inoperative January 1, 1990, by the terms of Stats 1982 ch 466 §11.5.

§1917.072. Provision of disclosures required by Federal Reserve Board [Inoperative]

(a) Each lender making a shared appreciation loan shall also furnish to the prospective borrower, prior to the consummation of the loan, the disclosures required by Subpart C of Federal Reserve Board Regulation Z (12 CFR Part 226), including 12 CFR Section 226.18(f), to the extent applicable to the transaction.

(b) The disclosure made pursuant to paragraph (a) and Regulation Z shall be based on the fixed interest rate of the shared appreciation loan, and shall include a description of the shared appreciation feature, including (1) the conditions for its imposition, the time at which it would be collected, and the limitations on the lender's share, as required by the Federal Reserve Board in the information published by the Board at 46 Federal Register 20877 and 20878 (April 7, 1981), and (2) the lender's share of the net appreciated value and the prevailing interest rate as defined in Section 1917.120(h).

(c) The disclosure made pursuant to paragraph (a) and Regulation Z shall be accompanied by (1) one or more transaction-specific examples of the operation and effect the shared appreciation loan, and (2) the following charts, comparing the shared appreciation loan and a conventional loan made at the prevailing interest rate, and illustrating the possible increase in the monthly payments, and the possible annual percentage rate of finance charge, on the assumptions therein stated:

Chart 1

CONVENTIONAL MORTGAGE AT ____ %
If the same loan balance were financed under a conventional, 30-year, fixed-rate, level-payment mortgage, your monthly payments would be:
Years 1–30
$____ /mo.

Chart 2

IF YOU REFINANCE THIS TRANSACTION AT ____ %
If your property appreciates at 10% per year, and if your total loan balance (including contingent deferred interest due) at the end of ____ years is refinanced at ____ % (the prevailing market interest rate now), your monthly payments will be:
Years 1– ____ Refinancing loan
$____ /mo. $____ /mo.*
*Refinancing loan, assuming a conventional 30-year, fixed-rate, level-payment mortgage. Other mortgage instruments, e.g., graduated-payment or shared-appreciation, if available, may result in lower payments.

Chart 3

APR IF PROPERTY APPRECIATES AT 10%
If your property appreciates at 10% per year, the total finance charge on your shared appreciation loan (including contingent interest) will equal $____, and the annual percentage rate of the total finance charge (including contingent interest) will equal ____ %.

(d) The disclosures required by paragraph (c) shall be separated from the disclosures required by Regulation Z, and may be presented in the document containing the disclosures required by Regulation Z or in one or more separate documents.

(e) Except to the extent that this section requires disclosure of additional information not required by Regulation Z, compliance with the applicable credit disclosure requirements of Regulation Z shall constitute compliance with the requirements of this section.

(f) The disclosures prescribed in Section 1917.171 shall be physically attached to the disclosures required by this section and Regulation Z at the time such disclosures are furnished to the borrower.

(g) In the event federal law is amended so that this section is inconsistent therewith, the federal law shall prevail as to the disclosures required by this section. **Leg.H.** Added Stats 1982 ch 466 §11. Inoperative January 1, 1990, by the terms of Stats 1982 ch 466 §11.5.

§1917.073. Additional written statement provided to borrower [Inoperative]

Each lender making a shared appreciation loan shall additionally furnish to the prospective borrower, prior to the consummation of the loan, a statement containing the following information:

IMPORTANT INFORMATION ABOUT YOUR SHARED APPRECIATION LOAN.

You are being offered a shared appreciation loan. Before you decide to accept this loan read this statement, which is designed to provide important information that you should consider.

1. Prevailing interest rate: ____%.
2. Fixed interest rate on this loan: ____%.
3. Lender's share of net appreciated value: one-third.
4. Amount of this loan: $____.
5. Amount of the monthly payments: $____.
6. Term of this loan: ____ years.
7. Amortization period on which payments are calculated: 30 years.
8. Prepayment penalty (if any) ____. **Leg.H.** Added Stats 1982 ch 466 §11. Inoperative January 1, 1990, by the terms of Stats 1982 ch 466 §11.5.

§1917.074. Required language on deed of trust in connection with shared appreciation loan [Inoperative]

Each deed of trust and evidence of debt executed in connection with a shared appreciation loan shall contain a statement, printed or written in a size equal to at least 12-point bold type, consisting of substantially the following language: "THIS IS A (DURATION) SHARED APPRECIATION LOAN. THE LENDER'S INTEREST INCLUDES ONE-THIRD OF THE NET APPRECIATED VALUE OF THE PROPERTY. FOR

FURTHER INFORMATION, READ THE FLYER 'INFORMATION ABOUT THE (NAME OF LENDER) SHARED APPRECIATION LOAN.'" The notice required by this section shall be completed to state the term of the shared appreciation loan. **Leg.H.** Added Stats 1982 ch 466 §11. Inoperative January 1, 1990, by the terms of Stats 1982 ch 466 §11.5.

§1917.075. Disclosure of method of calculating contingent deferred interest [Inoperative]

Where, pursuant to any provision of law, the lender is required to disclose the amount of interest due or to be due under a shared appreciation loan and the amount of contingent deferred interest due or to be due is not known, the lender may disclose that fact and specify in the disclosure the method for calculating contingent deferred interest. **Leg.H.** Added Stats 1982 ch 466 §11. Inoperative January 1, 1990, by the terms of Stats 1982 ch 466 §11.5.

CHAPTER 5
SHARED APPRECIATION LOANS

Article 1. Legislative Findings and Declarations.
Article 2. Definitions.
Article 3. Terms and Conditions.
Article 4. Determination of Fair Market Value.
Article 5. Improvements.
Article 6. General Provisions.
Article 7. Notices and Disclosures.

ARTICLE 1
Legislative Findings and Declarations

Legislative findings and declarations [Inoperative]. §1917.110.

§1917.110. Legislative findings and declarations [Inoperative]

The Legislature hereby finds and declares that:

(a) It is necessary and essential that the state provide and promote alternative means of supplying affordable housing to the citizens of the state.

(b) Because of current economic conditions, including the unprecedented fluctuation in interest rates, alternative mortgage instruments must be developed to supplement the standard long-term, fixed-rate mortgage.

(c) State facilitation of the shared appreciation loan will serve the need to develop alternative means of financing housing, particularly new homes, and will help to create vitally needed jobs in the construction industry. **Leg.H.** Added Stats 1982 ch 466 §12. Inoperative January 1, 1987, by the terms of Stats 1982 ch 466 §12.5.

Prior Law: Former §1917.110, similar to the inoperative section, was added Stats 1981 ch 1144 §1 and repealed Stats 1982 ch 466 §10.

1982 Note: For continued application, see 1982 Note following Chapter 5 heading.

Former Sections: Former CC §1917.110, similar to the inoperative section, was added Stats 1981 ch 1144 §1 and repealed Stats 1982 ch 466 §10.

ARTICLE 2
Definitions

Definitions [Inoperative]. §1917.120.

§1917.120. Definitions [Inoperative]

For purposes of this chapter:

(a) "Borrower" means the recipient or recipients of a shared appreciation loan and includes any successor in interest to the borrower under a shared appreciation loan, to the extent such succession is permitted by law or by the terms of the shared appreciation loan.

(b) "Borrower's cost of the property" means the price paid by the borrower for the purchase of the property to be financed with a shared appreciation loan and also includes documentary transfer taxes, escrow and recording fees, title insurance premiums, and any other fees directly paid by the borrower as a necessary or customary cost of consummating acquisition of the property. However, if the purchase price to be paid for the property does not reasonably reflect the true value of the property, the borrower may request that, in lieu of the actual price paid, the "borrower's cost of the property" be established at an amount mutually agreed by the lender and borrower or be established by averaging two appraisals in the same manner as specified in Section 1917.142 for determination of fair market value. Nothing in this subdivision shall be construed to require a lender to make shared appreciation loans with the borrower's cost of the property established on the basis of appraisals.

(c) "Contingent deferred interest" means the lender's share of net appreciated value, calculated as the sum resulting upon multiplying the net appreciated value by a percentage agreed by the lender and borrower, not to exceed 50 percent.

(d) "Fair market value" means the highest price on the date of valuation that would be agreed to by a seller, being willing to sell but under no particular or urgent necessity for so doing, nor obliged to sell, and a buyer, being ready, willing, and able to buy but under no particular necessity for so doing, each dealing with the other with full knowledge of all the uses and purposes for which the property is reasonably adaptable and available.

Fair market value shall be determined pursuant to Article 4 (commencing with Section 1917.140).

(e) "Lender" means any person who makes a shared appreciation loan or the successor in interest to any such person.

(f) "Net appreciated value" means the fair market value less the sum of the borrower's cost of the property and the value of capital improvements. Nothing in this chapter shall, however, preclude a shared appreciation loan from additionally including a provision requiring deduction of any or all of the borrower's costs of selling the property from fair market value in determining, "net appreciated value," and if such a provision is included, the disclosures required by Section 1917.171 shall be modified accordingly.

(g) "Prevailing rate" means the weighted average yield accepted by the Federal National Mortgage Association in its most recent free market system auction for four-month conventional mortgage commitments. In the event that the Federal National Mortgage Association discontinues or substantially alters its free market system auction for conventional mortgages then the "prevailing rate" shall be the average yield established at the most recent immediate delivery auction of the Federal Home Loan Mortgage Corporation, or if the auction has been discontinued, then the "prevailing rate" shall be specified in the shared appreciation loan as either (1) the most recently published Federal Home Loan Bank Board mortgage contract rate or (2) the average single-family home mortgage rate for the 10 largest savings and loan associations with principal offices in this state.

(h) "Property" means the property financed by the shared appreciation loan.

(i) "Sale" means any transfer of title to the property and additionally includes the execution of an installment sale contract giving the purchaser a right to possess the property before transfer of title, refinancing, judicial sale on execution or other legal process of foreclosure or trustee's sale (regardless of whether initiated by the lender), but "sale" does not include a transfer specified in Section 2924.6.

(j) "Shared appreciation loan" means any loan made pursuant to this chapter upon the security of owner-occupied real property of a type specified in Section 1917.130, and in connection with which the lender has a right to receive a share of the appreciation in the value of the security property. "Shared appreciation loan" includes a deed of trust and any evidence of debt issued in connection with the loan.

(k) "Value of capital improvements" means the amount of the credit or credits for capital improvements, if any, determined pursuant to Article 5 (commencing with Section 1917.150). **Leg.H.** Added Stats 1982 ch 466 §12. Inoperative January 1, 1987, by the terms of Stats 1982 ch 466 §12.5.

Prior Law: Former §1917.120, similar to the inoperative section, was added Stats 1981 ch 1144 §1 and repealed Stats 1982 ch 466 §10.

1982 Note: For continued application, see 1982 Note following Chapter 5 heading.

Former Sections: Former CC §1917.120, similar to the inoperative section, was added Stats 1981 ch 1144 §1 and repealed Stats 1982 ch 466 §10.

ARTICLE 3
Terms and Conditions

Lenders authority to make shared appreciation loans [Inoperative]. §1917.130.
Terms and conditions of shared appreciation loans [Inoperative]. §1917.131.
Right of prepayment [Inoperative]. §1917.132.
Refinancing of unpaid balance of loan [Inoperative]. §1917.133.
Laws applicable to terms and conditions of refinancing [Inoperative]. §1917.134.
Refinancing on mutually agreeable terms [Inoperative]. §1917.135.

§1917.130. Lenders authority to make shared appreciation loans [Inoperative]

Lenders may make shared appreciation loans pursuant to this chapter for the purchase of real property improved with one- to four-dwelling units, including structures ancillary to such dwelling units and including attached single-family dwelling units, single-family mobilehome units placed upon permanent foundations, residential condominium units, and dwelling units within a planned unit development. Shared appreciation loans shall be made to finance only owner-occupied dwelling units, but in the case of two- to four-unit dwellings financed under this chapter only one of the units need be owner-occupied. A dwelling unit shall be conclusively deemed to be owner-occupied for purposes of this chapter if an original recipient of the shared appreciation loan certifies in writing to the lender at the time the loan is made that he or she will occupy the property. **Leg.H.** Added Stats 1982 ch 466 §12. Inoperative January 1, 1987, by the terms of Stats 1982 ch 466 §12.5.

Prior Law: Former §1917.130, similar to the inoperative section, was added Stats 1981 ch 1144 §1, and repealed Stats 1982 ch 466 §10.

1982 Note: For continued application, see 1982 Note following Chapter 5 heading.

Former Sections: Former CC §1917.130, similar to the inoperative section, was added Stats 1981 ch 1144 §1 and repealed Stats 1982 ch 466 §10.

§1917.131. Terms and conditions of shared appreciation loans [Inoperative]

A shared appreciation loan shall include the following terms and conditions:

(a) The term of the loan, excluding any refinancing under Section 1917.133, shall be at least seven years, but not more than 30 years.

(b) The repayment schedule for the loan, excluding any refinancing under Section 1917.133, shall be cast so that full amortization of the principal amount of the loan would occur in not less than 30 nor more than 40 years, regardless of the actual term of the loan. Any principal balance remaining at maturity shall be due and payable at that time, unless refinanced as provided in Section 1917.133. Monthly installment payments shall be equal in amount, except for the final payment when a principal balance is remaining at maturity, and in addition to amortization of principal shall include fixed interest pursuant to subdivision (d).

(c) The loan shall be secured by a deed of trust on the real property financed.

(d) The loan shall bear interest at a fixed rate, which shall be established in relation to the prevailing rate (1) in effect 90 days prior to the loan closing, (2) in effect at another date between that date and the loan closing if and as mutually agreed by the lender and borrower, or (3) in effect at the time of the lender's loan commitment given to the borrower or to the person from whom the borrower purchases the property. The percentage by which the fixed interest rate is reduced below the applicable prevailing rate shall be at least one-half the lender's percentage share of net appreciated value which is contingent deferred interest, except that if the shared appreciation loan is for less than 80 percent of the borrower's purchase price of the property, the percentage by which the fixed interest rate is reduced below the applicable prevailing rate shall be at least two-thirds the lender's percentage share of net appreciated value which is contingent deferred interest.

(e) The borrower shall additionally be obligated to pay to the lender contingent deferred interest (1) at the time of sale of the property if the lender accelerates the principal balance of the loan in accordance with a provision in the shared appreciation loan authorized by Section 1917.162, (2) at the time the loan is prepaid in full, upon acceleration of the loan upon default, or (3) upon the maturity of the loan, whichever first occurs.

(f) The aggregate amount of any fee charged to the borrower by the lender for processing an application, preparing any necessary documents, obtaining a credit report, or any other costs incurred by the lender in connection with originating a shared appreciation loan shall not exceed two percent of the principal amount of the loan or five hundred dollars ($500), whichever is greater. No prepaid interest shall be charged to the borrower, but nothing in this chapter shall preclude a lender from requiring a fee for providing commitments for shared appreciation loans to builders or others who purchase such commitments and who will not be the ultimate borrower. **Leg.H.** Added Stats 1982 ch 466 §12. Inoperative January 1, 1987, by the terms of Stats 1982 ch 466 §12.5.

Prior Law: Former §1917.131, similar to the inoperative section, was added Stats 1981 ch 1144 §1 and repealed Stats 1982 ch 466 §10.

1982 Note: For continued application, see 1982 Note following Chapter 5 heading.

Former Sections: Former CC §1917.131, similar to the inoperative section, was added Stats 1981 ch 1144 §1 and repealed Stats 1982 ch 466 §10.

§1917.132. Right of prepayment [Inoperative]

(a) The borrower shall have the right to prepay, at any time, in full or in part, the principal loan balance of the shared appreciation loan, together with accrued interest, including contingent deferred interest.

(b) Nothing in this chapter shall prevent a borrower from obligating himself or herself, by an agreement in writing, to pay a prepayment charge upon prepayment of the loan, in full or in part, made within five years of the date of execution of the shared appreciation loan.

(c) Any prepayment charge imposed upon the prepayment of a shared appreciation loan shall not exceed the amount authorized and specified in subdivision (b) of Section 2954.9.

(d) No prepayment charge shall be imposed as to any portion of the contingent deferred interest. **Leg.H.** Added Stats 1982 ch 466 §12. Inoperative January 1, 1987, by the terms of Stats 1982 ch 466 §12.5.

Prior Law: Former CC §1917.132, similar to the inoperative section, was added Stats 1981 ch 1144 §1 and repealed Stats 1982 ch 466 §10.

1982 Note: For continued application, see 1982 Note following Chapter 5 heading.

Former Sections: Former CC §1917.132, similar to the inoperative section, was added Stats 1981 ch 1144 §1 and repealed Stats 1982 ch 466 §10.

§1917.133. Refinancing of unpaid balance of loan [Inoperative]

(a) If a shared appreciation loan with an original term of less than 10 years is not prepaid in full or the property is not sold or transferred prior to maturity of the loan, and provided the borrower is not then in default, the lender shall offer or arrange for refinancing of the unpaid balance of the loan upon maturity and all contingent deferred interest. The refinancing may be provided directly by the lender or another mortgage lender, or the lender may arrange at the time of making the shared appreciation loan for the refinancing to be provided by a federally or state chartered bank or savings and loan association doing business in this state or by a qualified mortgage banker. As used in this section "qualified mortgage banker" means a lender (1) meeting the criteria established by the Government National Mortgage Association for lenders selling over ten million dollars ($10,000,000) in mortgage loans to that organization annually and (2) which either has conducted an ongoing business of mortgage lending in this state for not less than five years immediately preceding the making of the shared appreciation loans, or made over fifty million dollars ($50,000,000) in mortgage loans in this state during the 12 months immediately preceding the making of the shared appreciation loan. If a refinancing commitment is arranged by the lender upon origination of the shared appreciation loan, this fact shall be fully and fairly disclosed to the borrower, a copy of the lender's contract with the bank, savings and loan association or qualified mortgage banker making the commitment shall be supplied to the borrower at such time, and the contract shall be fully enforceable by the borrower as a third-party beneficiary thereto, but the lender shall not be a guarantor of the obligation of the bank, savings and loan association, or qualified mortgage banker to provide refinancing.

If the original lender is a bank or savings and loan association doing business in this state or a qualified mortgage banker, it may provide the refinancing commitment to the borrower required by this section and assignees or successors in interest of the original lender shall not be guarantors of the refinancing obligation, provided the shared appreciation loan contains this limitation, which is fully and fairly disclosed to the borrower, and the original lender's refinancing commitment is fully enforceable by the borrower.

(b) The term of the loan for refinancing shall be established so that the borrower's repayment schedule provides for the final installment payment not less than 30 years from the date of origination of the shared appreciation loan. However, if loans at that duration are not available, within the meaning of subdivision (d), the lender or other obligor shall give the borrower a choice of any form of loan and maturity for that type of loan which is available at the time of refinancing, within the meaning of subdivision (d). The lender or other obligor shall inform the borrower of the types of loans (and maturities) available for refinancing under this section not less than 60 days prior to maturity of the shared appreciation loan.

(c) The interest rate for the refinancing loan shall not exceed rates generally available in the market for the type of loan instrument provided under subdivision (d) at the time of maturity of the shared appreciation loan. No loan origination fees shall be required of the borrower, either as prepaid interest or for processing services, as a condition of obtaining a refinancing loan pursuant to this section, but the borrower may be required to pay the costs of obtaining a policy of title insurance in accordance with the lender's requirements. The refinancing loan need not be a fixed interest rate loan, subject to the limitations of subdivision (d).

(d) The refinancing loan may be any form of loan which, at the time of refinancing, is generally offered to and utilized by the public for financing housing like the borrower's property by banks or savings and loan associations doing business in this state.

(e) The lender may require as a condition of the refinancing loan that it be secured by a deed of trust having a lien of first priority. **Leg.H.** Added Stats 1982 ch 466 §12. Inoperative January 1, 1987, by the terms of Stats 1982 ch 466 §12.5.

Prior Law: Former §1917.133, similar to the inoperative section, was added Stats 1981 ch 1144 §1 and repealed Stats 1982 ch 466 §10.

1982 Note: For continued application, see 1982 Note following Chapter 5 heading.

Former Sections: Former CC §1917.133, similar to the inoperative section, was added Stats 1981 ch 1144 §1 and repealed Stats 1982 ch 466 §10.

§1917.134. Laws applicable to terms and conditions of refinancing [Inoperative]

Except as provided in this article, the terms and conditions of the refinancing loan shall be subject to all laws applicable to loans in effect on the date of refinancing. **Leg.H.** Added Stats 1982 ch 466 §12. Inoperative January 1, 1987, by the terms of Stats 1982 ch 466 §12.5.

Prior Law: Former §1917.134, similar to the inoperative section, was added Stats 1981 ch 1144 §1 and repealed Stats 1982 ch 466 §10.

1982 Note: For continued application, see 1982 Note following Chapter 5 heading.

Former Sections: Former CC §1917.134, similar to the inoperative section, was added Stats 1981 ch 1144 §1 and repealed Stats 1982 ch 466 §10.

§1917.135. Refinancing on mutually agreeable terms [Inoperative]

Nothing in this chapter shall preclude the borrower from obtaining any other financing, in lieu of the refinancing provided for in Section 1917.133, including refinancing on other terms mutually agreeable to the borrower and lender. **Leg.H.** Added Stats 1982 ch 466 §12. Inoperative January 1, 1987, by the terms of Stats 1982 ch 466 §12.5.

Prior Law: Former §1917.135, similar to the inoperative section, was added Stats 1981 ch 1144 §1 and repealed Stats 1982 ch 466 §10.

1982 Note: For continued application, see 1982 Note following Chapter 5 heading.

Former Sections: Former CC §1917.135, similar to the inoperative section, was added Stats 1981 ch 1144 §1 and repealed Stats 1982 ch 466 §10.

ARTICLE 4
Determination of Fair Market Value

Stipulation of fair market value [Inoperative]. §1917.140.
Contesting in writing reasonableness of sale price [Inoperative]. §1917.141.
Appraisals and costs [Inoperative]. §1917.142.

§1917.140. Stipulation of fair market value [Inoperative]

The borrower may, at any time for the purpose of facilitating a sale of the property, request the lender to stipulate the minimum amount which the lender considers to be the fair market value of the property for the purposes of this chapter. The lender shall advise the borrower within 10 working days of the receipt of such request of the lender's estimate of the minimum fair market value. The estimate shall remain effective for purposes of this section for 90 days. For the purposes of this section and Section 1917.141, a sale of the property shall be deemed to have occurred within the 90-day period if there is a valid contract entered by an offer and acceptance within the 90-day period for the sale of the property. The lender's stipulation shall remain effective for an additional 60 days following execution of the sale contract to permit completion of the sale and close of escrow.

The lender shall not be liable to the borrower or any other party on account of damages alleged as a result of providing the stipulation or estimate required by this section if such stipulation or estimate is made in good faith. Evidence of lack of good faith shall include, but not be limited to, a showing that the lender has willfully or repeatedly overrepresented the fair market value of other properties in similar situations, applying equitable principles to those determinations. The lender shall be conclusively presumed to have acted in good faith and no action may be brought or maintained against a lender which arises out of the provision by the lender of such stipulation or estimate, if the lender relied upon an appraisal of an independent appraiser approved by the Federal National Mortgage Association. **Leg.H.** Added Stats 1982 ch 466 §12. Inoperative January 1, 1987, by the terms of Stats 1982 ch 466 §12.5.

Prior Law: Former §1917.140, similar to the inoperative section, was added Stats 1981 ch 1144 §1 and repealed Stats 1982 ch 466 §10.

1982 Note: For continued application, see 1982 Note following Chapter 5 heading.

Former Sections: Former CC §1917.140, similar to the inoperative section, was added Stats 1981 ch 1144 §1 and repealed Stats 1982 ch 466 §10.

§1917.141. Contesting in writing reasonableness of sale price [Inoperative]

(a) In the case of a sale for cash within 90 days after the lender stipulates, under the provisions of Section 1917.140, a minimum amount which the lender considers to be the fair market value of the property, the fair market value shall be the gross sale price, unless the gross sales price is below the minimum amount stipulated by the lender and the lender contests in writing the reasonableness of the gross sale price in relation to the fair market value within 10 working days of the lender's receipt of notice of the gross sale price from borrower, in which case fair market value shall be the greater of gross sale price or the amount determined under Section 1917.142.

(b) In the case of a sale for cash where the borrower has not requested the lender under the provisions of Section 1917.140 to stipulate to the minimum amount which the lender considers to be the fair market value of the property or where the stipulated minimum amount was provided by the lender more than 90 days prior to the date of sale, fair market value shall be the gross sale price, unless lender contests in writing the reasonableness of the gross sale price in relation to the fair market value within 10 working days of the lender's receipt of notice of the gross sale price from borrower, in which case fair market value shall be the greater of gross sale price or the amount determined under Section 1917.142.

(c) In the case of a sale which includes consideration to the seller other than cash, fair market value shall be as determined under Section 1917.142.

(d) In the case the shared appreciation loan is prepaid in full, or upon acceleration of the shared appreciation loan upon default, or upon maturity of the shared appreciation loan, fair market value shall be as determined under Section 1917.142. **Leg.H.** Added Stats 1982 ch 466 §12. Inoperative January 1, 1987, by the terms of Stats 1982 ch 466 §12.5.

Prior Law: Former §1917.141, similar to the inoperative section, was added Stats 1981 ch 1144 §1 and repealed Stats 1982 ch 466 §10.

1982 Note: For continued application, see 1982 Note following Chapter 5 heading.

Former Sections: Former CC §1917.141, similar to the inoperative section, was added Stats 1981 ch 1144 §1 and repealed Stats 1982 ch 466 §10.

§1917.142. Appraisals and costs [Inoperative]

When Section 1917.141 requires the application of this section, the fair market value shall be determined as the average of two appraisals of the property performed as described in this section. If possible, the appraisals shall be based on the sale prices of comparable properties in the market area sold within the preceding three-month period. The appraisals shall be made upon request of the lender by two independent residential appraisers, one to be selected by the lender and one by the borrower. Each appraiser shall be approved by the Federal National Mortgage Association. The cost of the appraiser selected by the lender shall be borne by the lender, and the cost of the appraiser selected by the borrower shall be borne by the borrower, unless the average of the two appraisals equals or is less than the gross sale price of the property, in which case the lender shall also pay the fee of the borrower's appraiser up to two hundred dollars ($200). If either of the appraisers determines that the gross sale price does not reasonably reflect the fair market value of the property, or, in the case of a sale for which appraisal is required by this section, then the fair market value of the property shall be determined as the average of the two appraisals. If the borrower fails to select a qualified appraiser within 15 days after the lender has notified the borrower in writing of the lender's request for an appraisal of the property, the reasons therefor, and the borrower's option to select an independent appraiser within 15 days after the lender's request is submitted to the borrower, the lender may designate the second appraiser, provided the lender's request informs the borrower of this time limitation, and that the lender will select an appraiser on behalf of the borrower in the event the borrower fails to designate an appraiser, with consequent cost to the borrower. If pursuant to this section the lender designates the second appraiser, the cost of both appraisals shall be borne equally by the borrower and lender. If in any case the property has been damaged (other than normal wear and tear) and the damage has not been fully repaired, the determination of fair market value shall be based on the condition of the property not including the damage.

Nothing in this section shall preclude the borrower and lender from establishing the fair market value of the property by mutual agreement in lieu of appraisals pursuant to this section. **Leg.H.** Added Stats 1982 ch 466 §12. Inoperative January 1, 1987, by the terms of Stats 1982 ch 466 §12.5.

Prior Law: Former §1917.142, similar to the inoperative section, was added Stats 1981 ch 1144 §1 and repealed Stats 1982 ch 466 §10.

1982 Note: For continued application, see 1982 Note following Chapter 5 heading.

Former Sections: Former CC §1917.142, similar to the inoperative section, was added Stats 1981 ch 1144 §1 and repealed Stats 1982 ch 466 §10.

ARTICLE 5
Improvements

Addition of value of capital improvements to borrower's cost [Inoperative]. §1917.150.
Providing borrower with greater credit [Inoperative]. §1917.151.

§1917.150. Addition of value of capital improvements to borrower's cost [Inoperative]

The borrower may have the value of capital improvements added to the borrower's cost of the property, for purposes of determining net appreciated value and the amount of contingent deferred interest, but only if the procedures set forth in this article are followed.

(a) Within 60 days following the completion of capital improvements during any 12-month period with a cost in excess of two thousand five hundred dollars ($2,500), the borrower shall send by first-class mail a notice of the completion of the improvements to the lender and shall submit proof of cost and an estimate of the increase in value of the property by reason of the improvements.

(b) If, within 30 days of receipt of the notice, the lender questions the claimed increase in value of the property by reason of the improvements, the lender and the borrower may, by mutual agreement, establish the value of the capital improvements or the lender may require appraisal of the property. An appraisal shall be made to determine the increase in value of the property, if any, by reason of the improvements, by two appraisers selected in the same manner specified in Section 1917.142. If appraisals are performed, the increase in value resulting from the improvements for the purposes of this section, shall be one-half of the sum of the two appraisals. The cost of the appraiser selected by the borrower shall be borne by the borrower, and the cost of the appraiser selected by the lender shall be borne by the lender.

(c) A credit for the value of capital improvements shall be provided if the increase in value of the property resulting therefrom is determined pursuant to subdivision (b) to exceed two thousand five hundred dollars ($2,500).

(d) If 50 percent or more of the value of the labor or other work on the improvements was performed by the borrower, then the actual cost of the improvements need not exceed two thousand five hundred dollars ($2,500) for purposes of making application under subdivision (a). **Leg.H.** Added Stats 1982 ch 466 §12. Inoperative January 1, 1987, by the terms of Stats 1982 ch 466 §12.5.

Prior Law: Former §1917.150, similar to the inoperative section, was added Stats 1981 ch 1144 §1 and repealed Stats 1982 ch 466 §10.

1982 Note: For continued application, see 1982 Note following Chapter 5 heading.

Former Sections: Former CC §1917.150, similar to the inoperative section, was added Stats 1981 ch 1144 §1 and repealed Stats 1982 ch 466 §10.

§1917.151. Providing borrower with greater credit [Inoperative]

Nothing in this article shall preclude a shared appreciation loan from providing the borrower with a greater credit for improvements than specified in this article, provided the relevant disclosures required by Article 7 (commencing with Section 1917.170) are appropriately modified to accurately disclose the terms of the credit. **Leg.H.** Added Stats 1982 ch 466 §12. Inoperative January 1, 1987, by the terms of Stats 1982 ch 466 §12.5.

Prior Law: Former §1917.151, similar to the inoperative section, was added Stats 1981 ch 1144 §1 and repealed Stats 1982 ch 466 §10.

1982 Note: For continued application, see 1982 Note following Chapter 5 heading.

Former Sections: Former CC §1917.151, similar to the inoperative section, was added Stats 1981 ch 1144 §1 and repealed Stats 1982 ch 466 §10.

ARTICLE 6
General Provisions

Relationship of borrower and lender [Inoperative]. §1917.160.
Waiver of borrower's rights [Inoperative]. §1917.161.
Acceleration of maturity date [Inoperative]. §1917.162.
Application of chapter [Inoperative]. §1917.163.
Application of other provisions [Inoperative]. §1917.164.
Contents of lien of deed of trust [Inoperative]. §1917.165.
Attachment of lien. §1917.166.
Loan complying with usury provisions of Constitution [Inoperative]. §1917.167.
Exemption from corporate securities requirements [Inoperative]. §1917.168.

§1917.160. Relationship of borrower and lender [Inoperative]

The relationship of the borrower and the lender, as to a shared appreciation loan, is that of debtor and creditor and shall not be, or be construed to be, a joint venture, equity venture, partnership, or other relationship. **Leg.H.** Added Stats 1982 ch 466 §12. Inoperative January 1, 1987, by the terms of Stats 1982 ch 466 §12.5.

Prior Law: Former §1917.160, similar to present CC §1917.001, was added Stats 1981 ch 1144 §1 and repealed Stats 1982 ch 466 §10.

1982 Note: For continued application, see 1982 Note following Chapter 5 heading.

Former Sections: Former CC §1917.160, similar to the inoperative section, was added Stats 1981 ch 1144 §1 and repealed Stats 1982 ch 466 §10.

§1917.161. Waiver of borrower's rights [Inoperative]

Any waiver of any right of a borrower under the provisions of this chapter shall be void and unenforceable. **Leg.H.** Added Stats 1982 ch 466 §12. Inoperative January 1, 1987, by the terms of Stats 1982 ch 466 §12.5.

Prior Law: Former §1917.161, similar to the inoperative section, was added Stats 1981 ch 1144 §1 and repealed Stats 1982 ch 466 §10.

1982 Note: For continued application, see 1982 Note following Chapter 5 heading.

Former Sections: Former CC §1917.161, similar to the inoperative section, was added Stats 1981 ch 1144 §1 and repealed Stats 1982 ch 466 §10.

§1917.162. Acceleration of maturity date [Inoperative]

(a) Notwithstanding Section 711, a provision in a shared appreciation loan made pursuant to this chapter permitting the lender to accelerate the maturity date of the principal and accrued interest on the loan upon sale of the property shall be valid and enforceable against the borrower, except as may be precluded by Section 2924.6.

(b) The Legislature finds and declares that potential exposure to liability for enforcement of a "due-on-sale" clause consistent with Section 711, as interpreted by the courts, makes use of such a provision impractical. Moreover, the additional risks to the lender inherent in shared appreciation financing are greater with longer loan terms (which are more desirable from the standpoint of housing affordability), but this risk is reduced with an enforceable "due-on-sale" clause. Therefore, in order to facilitate shared appreciation financing, it is necessary to establish the exception specified in subdivision (a). **Leg.H.** Added Stats 1982 ch 466 §12. Inoperative January 1, 1987, by the terms of Stats 1982 ch 466 §12.5.

Prior Law: Former §1917.162, similar to the inoperative section, was added Stats 1981 ch 1144 §1 and repealed Stats 1982 ch 466 §10.

1982 Note: For continued application, see 1982 Note following Chapter 5 heading.

Former Sections: Former CC §1917.162, similar to the inoperative section, was added Stats 1981 ch 1144 §1 and repealed Stats 1982 ch 466 §10.

§1917.163. Application of chapter [Inoperative]

This chapter facilitates the making of shared appreciation financing in this state which conforms to the provisions of this chapter. The terms and conditions of any shared appreciation loan made pursuant to this chapter shall be consistent with this chapter. This chapter does not, however, apply to or limit shared appreciation financing of real property of a type specified in Section 1917.130 that is made pursuant to other provisions of law, or which is not otherwise unlawful. Nothing in this chapter shall be construed to in any way affect shared appreciation financing of commercial property or residential property not meeting the criteria specified in Section 1917.130. **Leg.H.** Added Stats 1982 ch 466 §12. Inoperative January 1, 1987, by the terms of Stats 1982 ch 466 §12.5.

Prior Law: Former §1917.163, similar to the inoperative section, was added Stats 1981 ch 1144 §1 and repealed Stats 1982 ch 466 §10.

1982 Note: For continued application, see 1982 Note following Chapter 5 heading.

Former Sections: Former CC §1917.163, similar to the inoperative section, was added Stats 1981 ch 1144 §1 and repealed Stats 1982 ch 466 §10.

§1917.164. Application of other provisions [Inoperative]

A shared appreciation loan shall not be subject to any provision of this code or the Financial Code which limits the interest rate or change of interest rate of variable interest rate or renegotiable interest instruments, or which requires particular language or provisions in security instruments securing variable or renegotiable rate obligations or in evidences of those debts.

This section is declaratory of existing law. **Leg.H.** Added Stats 1982 ch 466 §12. Inoperative January 1, 1987, by the terms of Stats 1982 ch 466 §12.5.

Prior Law: Former §1917.164, similar to present CC §1917.002, was added Stats 1981 ch 1144 §1 and repealed Stats 1982 ch 466 §10.

1982 Note: For continued application, see 1982 Note following Chapter 5 heading.

Former Sections: Former CC §1917.164, similar to present CC §1917.002, was added Stats 1981 ch 1144 §1 and repealed Stats 1982 ch 466 §10.

§1917.165. Contents of lien of deed of trust [Inoperative]

The lien of a deed of trust securing a shared appreciation loan shall include and secure the principal amount of the shared appreciation loan, and all interest, whether accrued or to be accrued, including all amounts of contingent deferred interest. **Leg.H.** Added Stats 1982 ch 466 §12. Inoperative January 1, 1987, by the terms of Stats 1982 ch 466 §12.5.

Prior Law: Former §1917.165, similar to present CC §1917.003, was added Stats 1981 ch 1144 §1 and repealed Stats 1982 ch 466 §10.

1982 Note: For continued application, see 1982 Note following Chapter 5 heading.

Former Sections: Former CC §1917.165, similar to present CC §1917.003, was added Stats 1981 ch 1144 §1 and repealed Stats 1982 ch 466 §10.

§1917.166. Attachment of lien

The lien of a shared appreciation loan, including the principal amount and all interest, whether accrued or to be accrued, and all amounts of contingent deferred interest, shall attach from the time of the recordation of the deed of trust securing the loan, and the lien, including the lien of the interest accrued or to be accrued and of the contingent deferred interest, shall have priority over any other lien or encumbrance affecting the property secured by the shared appreciation instrument, recorded after the time of recordation of the shared appreciation instrument. However, nothing in this section or Section 1917.165 shall preclude a junior lien or encumbrance subordinate to the obligation of the shared appreciation loan. In no case may a junior lien achieve priority over the lien securing the obligation of the shared appreciation loan, provided that nothing in this section shall be construed to supersede Section 8450. **Leg.H.** Added Stats 1982 ch 466 §12. Inoperative January 1, 1987, by the terms of Stats 1982 ch 466 §12.5. Amended Stats 2010 ch 697 §11 (SB 189), effective January 1, 2011, operative July 1, 2012.

Prior Law: Former §1917.166, similar to present CC §1917.004, was added Stats 1981 ch 1144 §1 and repealed Stats 1982 ch 466 §10.

2012 Note: The amendment by Stats 2010 ch 697 §11 superseded the inoperative version on July 1, 2012.

1982 Note: For continued application, see 1982 Note following Chapter 5 heading.

Former Sections: Former CC §1917.166, similar to present CC §1917.004, was added Stats 1981 ch 1144 §1 and repealed Stats 1982 ch 466 §10.

§1917.167. Loan complying with usury provisions of Constitution [Inoperative]

A shared appreciation loan which at origination bears a fixed interest rate complying with the usury provisions of Article XV of the California Constitution shall not be deemed to become usurious by reason of the payment of contingent deferred interest pursuant to this chapter. **Leg.H.** Added Stats 1982 ch 466 §12. Inoperative January 1, 1987, by the terms of Stats 1982 ch 466 §12.5.

Prior Law: Former §1917.167, similar to present CC §1917.005, was added Stats 1981 ch 1144 §1 and repealed Stats 1982 ch 466 §10.

1982 Note: For continued application, see 1982 Note following Chapter 5 heading.

Former Sections: Former CC §1917.167, similar to present CC §1917.005, was added Stats 1981 ch 1144 §1 and repealed Stats 1982 ch 466 §10.

§1917.168. Exemption from corporate securities requirements [Inoperative]

The qualification requirements of Sections 25110, 25120, and 25130 of the Corporations Code do not apply to a shared appreciation loan to the extent the exemption afforded by subdivision (p) of Section 25100 of that code is applicable. **Leg.H.** Added Stats 1982 ch 466 §12. Inoperative January 1, 1987, by the terms of Stats 1982 ch 466 §12.5.

Prior Law: Former §1917.168, similar to the inoperative section, was added Stats 1981 ch 1144 §1 and repealed Stats 1982 ch 466 §10.

1982 Note: For continued application, see 1982 Note following Chapter 5 heading.

Former Sections: Former CC §1917.168, similar to the inoperative section, was added Stats 1981 ch 1144 §1 and repealed Stats 1982 ch 466 §10.

ARTICLE 7
Notices and Disclosures

Required notices and disclosures [Inoperative]. §1917.170.
Form and time of disclosure [Inoperative]. §1917.171.
Disclosures required by federal regulation [Inoperative]. §1917.172.
Information to be given prospective borrower [Inoperative]. §1917.173.
Statement in deed of trust and evidence of debt executed in connection with loan [Inoperative]. §1917.174.
Disclosure of amount of interest [Inoperative]. §1917.175.

§1917.170. Required notices and disclosures [Inoperative]

(a) The disclosures made pursuant to this chapter, as required, shall be the only disclosures required to be made pursuant to state law for shared appreciation loans, notwithstanding any contrary provision applicable to loans not made under this chapter, except those, if any, that may be required by reason of the application of Division 1 (commencing with Section 25000) of the Corporations Code, or Chapter 1 (commencing with Section 11000) of Part 2 of Division 4 of the Business and Professions Code. However, a lender shall not be precluded from supplementing the disclosures required by this chapter with additional disclosures that are not inconsistent with the disclosures required by this chapter.

(b) Whenever specific language is prescribed by this chapter, substantially the same language shall be utilized if possible, but reasonably equivalent language may be used to the extent necessary or appropriate to achieve a clearer or more accurate disclosure. **Leg.H.** Added Stats 1982 ch 466 §12. Inoperative January 1, 1987, by the terms of Stats 1982 ch 466 §12.5.

Prior Law: Former §1917.170, similar to the inoperative section, was added Stats 1981 ch 1144 §1 and repealed Stats 1982 ch 466 §10.

1982 Note: For continued application, see 1982 Note following Chapter 5 heading.

Former Sections: Former CC §1917.170, similar to the inoperative section, was added Stats 1981 ch 1144 §1 and repealed Stats 1982 ch 466 §10.

§1917.171. Form and time of disclosure [Inoperative]

(a) Each lender offering shared appreciation loans shall furnish to a prospective borrower, on the earlier of the dates on which the lender first provides written information concerning shared appreciation loans from the lender or provides a loan application form to the prospective borrower, a written disclosure as provided in this section.

(b) The disclosure shall be entitled "INFORMATION ABOUT THE (Name of Lender) SHARED APPRECIATION LOAN," and shall describe the operation and effect of the shared appreciation loan including a brief summary of its terms and conditions, together with a statement consisting of substantially the following language, to the extent applicable to such loan:

INFORMATION ABOUT THE (Name of Lender) SHARED
APPRECIATION LOAN.

(Name of Lender) is pleased to offer you the opportunity to finance your home through a shared appreciation loan.

Because the shared appreciation loan differs from the usual mortgage loan, the law requires that you have a detailed explanation of the special features of the loan before you apply. Before you sign your particular shared appreciation loan documents, you will receive more information about your particular shared appreciation loan, which you should read and understand before you sign the loan documents.

The loan will bear a stated rate of interest which will be (percent) below the prevailing market interest rate. In exchange for a stated interest rate which is below the prevailing rate, you will be obligated to pay us additional interest later. This additional interest is called "contingent interest."

The loan will require a balloon payment at the end of the ____ year. Thus, if you do not sell the property before that time, you will need to refinance the loan at that time.

Contingent Interest.

This loan provides that you, as borrower, must pay to us, as lender, as contingent interest, (percent) of the net appreciated value of the real property which secures the loan. This contingent interest is due and payable when the property is sold or transferred, when the loan is paid in full, upon any acceleration of the loan upon default, or at the end of the term of the loan, whichever first occurs. The dollar amount of contingent interest, if any, which you will be required to pay cannot be determined at this time. If the property does not appreciate, you will owe us nothing. The contingent interest will not become due if title to the property is transferred on your death to a spouse, or where a transfer results from a decree of dissolution of a marriage and a spouse becomes the sole owner.

Your obligation to pay contingent interest will reduce the amount of the appreciation, if any, that you will realize on the property. This appreciation will not produce a real gain in your equity in the property, unless the appreciation rate exceeds the general inflation rate, but you will be required to pay a portion of the appreciation as contingent interest without regard to whether the appreciation has resulted in a real gain.

When you sell or refinance your home, you normally will receive enough cash to pay the shared appreciation loan balance, accrued interest, prepayment charge (if applicable), contingent interest, and expenses of sale. However, if you sell with only a small downpayment, you may possibly not receive enough cash to pay the contingent interest, and, in that event, it will be necessary for you to provide cash from other funds.

Calculating the Contingent Interest.

Contingent interest will be calculated as follows:

	FAIR MARKET VALUE OF THE PROPERTY (Sale price or appraisal value.)	
— (less)	BORROWER'S COST OF THE PROPERTY (This amount includes certain costs paid by you incident to the purchase.)	
— (less)	VALUE OF CAPITAL IMPROVEMENTS MADE BY YOU (Must exceed $2,500 in value. Must also exceed $2,500 in cost unless you perform more than 50% of the value of the labor or work on the improvement.)_____	
= (equals)	NET APPRECIATED VALUE	
× (times)	____ PERCENT OWED TO LENDER	
= (equals)	TOTAL CONTINGENT INTEREST	

Determining Fair Market Value.

If you sell your property for cash before maturity of your shared appreciation loan, the gross sale price will be the fair market value of the property, unless appraisals are requested by us and the appraisals average more than the gross sale price. However, at your request, we also will tell you what we consider to be the fair market value of the property. If you sell for cash for a gross sale price that equals or exceeds that amount, the gross sale price will control and appraisals will not be needed.

Fair market value is determined by appraisals in the event of sales involving a consideration other than cash, prepayment of the loan in full, or maturity of the loan.

When appraisals are required, fair market value is determined by averaging two independent appraisals of the property. You may select one of the two appraisers from a list approved by the Federal National Mortgage Association. If appraisals are requested by us, we will provide you with full information on how to select an appraiser.

In lieu of appraisals, we may establish fair market value at an agreed amount if an agreement can be reached between you and us.

Determining Value of Capital Improvements.

Capital improvements with a value exceeding $2,500 (but no maintenance or repair costs) may be added to your cost of the property for the purpose of determining the net appreciated value, but only if the procedures set forth in the shared appreciation loan documents are followed. It is important to note that capital improvements completed and claimed in any 12-month period must add more than $2,500 in value to the property and must generally also cost more than $2,500. However, if you have performed at least half the value of the labor or other work involved, then the cost of the improvements will not be considered. The appraised value of the improvements will be the increase in the value of the property resulting from the improvements. You will receive no credit for minor or major repairs or for improvements that are not appraised at more than $2,500, but the lender will acquire a share of any resulting appreciation in the value of the property.

Determining Net Appreciated Value.

We are entitled to receive ____ percent of the net appreciated value of the property as contingent interest. As shown in the chart above, net appreciated value equals (1) the fair market value of the property at the time of the sale or appraisal, less (2) your cost of the property, less (3) the value of any capital improvements for which you are entitled to credit.

Balloon Payment of Principal.

If you do not sell the property before the end of the term of this loan, you will need to refinance this loan at that time. The term of this loan is (duration) years. We (are not obligated to refinance either the unpaid balance of the loan or the contingent interest at that time; you alone will be responsible for obtaining refinancing) (will offer or arrange with another lender to refinance the outstanding obligation, including any contingent interest, at that time). If you refinance this loan, your monthly payments may increase substantially if the property appreciates significantly or if the interest rate on the refinancing loan is much higher than today's prevailing rates. In general, the more your property appreciates, the larger will be the amount of the contingent interest that you will have an obligation to pay or refinance.

Your Right to Refinance This Loan.
(For loans with a refinancing obligation).

If the property is not sold or transferred prior to the maturity of the loan, we will offer or arrange with another lender to refinance the outstanding obligation of the loan, including any contingent interest. The refinancing will be at the then prevailing interest rate.

The terms of the refinancing loan will be like those of home loans offered at that time by banks or savings and loan associations. If at the time of refinancing, banks or savings and loan associations in this state offer loans of sufficient duration, you are assured that the combined length of your shared appreciation loan and refinancing loan will be at least 30 years. However, if loans of sufficient duration are not then offered by banks or savings and loan associations, you may elect any type and maturity of loan then offered by banks or savings and loan associations.

We will not be permitted to look to the forecast of your income in offering or arranging for your refinancing loan. The interest rate and specific terms of any refinancing loan will be subject to then-prevailing market conditions. The interest rate and monthly payment upon refinancing cannot be determined at this time. They may be either more or less burdensome to you than the currently prevailing rates and terms.

Tax Consequences.
(For all loans).

USE OF THE SHARED APPRECIATION LOAN WILL HAVE INCOME TAX OR ESTATE PLANNING CONSEQUENCES WHICH WILL DEPEND UPON YOUR OWN FINANCIAL AND TAX SITUATION. FOR FURTHER INFORMATION, YOU ARE URGED TO CONSULT YOUR OWN ACCOUNTANT, ATTORNEY, OR OTHER FINANCIAL ADVISOR.

THE QUESTIONS YOU SHOULD DISCUSS INCLUDE THE TAX DEDUCTIBILITY OF THE CONTINGENT INTEREST PAYMENT, YOUR RIGHT TO UTILIZE THAT DEDUCTION IN YEARS OTHER

THAN THE YEAR IT IS PAID, AND THE EFFECT OF THE LOSS OF TAX BENEFITS BEFORE THAT TIME.

Other Important Information.

(Here insert additional description, if necessary, of the operation and effect of the shared appreciation loan.

The foregoing describes our shared appreciation loan, includes a summary of all of its important provisions, and informs you of some of the risks of a shared appreciation loan.

If your loan application is accepted by us, we will provide you with more information about your particular shared appreciation loan, which will include a comparison with conventional mortgages, an illustration of the possible increase in your monthly payments upon refinancing, and other important information.

Before you enter into a shared appreciation loan with us, we recommend that you and your attorney or tax accountant review the loan documents for the full text of all of the terms and conditions which will govern the loan. **Leg.H.** Added Stats 1982 ch 466 §12. Inoperative January 1, 1987, by the terms of Stats 1982 ch 466 §12.5.

Prior Law: Former §1917.171, similar to the inoperative section, was added Stats 1981 ch 1144 §1 and repealed Stats 1982 ch 466 §10.

1982 Note: For continued application, see 1982 Note following Chapter 5 heading.

Former Sections: Former CC §1917.171, similar to the inoperative section, was added Stats 1981 ch 1144 §1 and repealed Stats 1982 ch 466 §10.

§1917.172. Disclosures required by federal regulation [Inoperative]

(a) Each lender making a shared appreciation loan shall also furnish to the prospective borrower, prior to the consummation of the loan, the disclosures required by Subpart C of Federal Reserve Board Regulation Z (12 CFR Part 226), including 12 CFR Section 226.18(f), to the extent applicable to the transaction.

(b) The disclosure made pursuant to subdivision (a) and Regulation Z shall be based on the fixed interest rate of the shared appreciation loan, and shall include a description of the shared appreciation feature, including (1) the conditions for its imposition, the time at which it would be collected, and the limitations on the lender's share, as required by the Federal Reserve Board in the information published by the board in 46 Federal Register 20877-78 (April 7, 1981), and (2) the lender's share of the net appreciated value and the prevailing interest rate as defined in Section 1917.120 of the Civil Code.

(c) The disclosure made pursuant to subdivision (a) and Regulation Z shall be accompanied by (1) one or more transaction-specific examples of the operation and effect of the shared appreciation loan and (2) the following charts comparing the shared appreciation loan and a conventional loan made at the prevailing interest rate, and illustrating the possible increase in the monthly payments, and the possible annual percentage rate of finance charge, on the assumptions therein stated:

Chart 1

CONVENTIONAL MORTGAGE AT _____ %
If the same loan balance were financed under a conventional, 30-year, fixed-rate, level-payment mortgage, your monthly payments would be:
Years 1–30
$_____ /mo.

Chart 2

IF YOU REFINANCE THIS TRANSACTION AT _____ %
If your property appreciates at 10% per year, and if your total loan balance (including contingent interest due) at the end of _____ years is refinanced at _____ % (the prevailing market interest rate now), your monthly payments will be:

Years 1–	Refinancing loan
$_____ /mo.	$_____ /mo.*

* Refinancing loan, assuming a conventional 30-year, fixed-rate, level-payment mortgage. Other mortgage instruments, e.g., graduated-payment or shared-appreciation, if available, may result in lower payments.

Chart 3

APR IF PROPERTY APPRECIATES AT 10%
If your property appreciates at 10% per year, the total finance charge on your shared appreciation loan (including contingent interest) will equal $_____, and the annual percentage rate of the total finance charge

APR IF PROPERTY APPRECIATES AT 10%
(including contingent interest) will equal _____ %.

(d) The disclosures required by subdivision (c) shall be separate from the disclosures required by Regulation Z, and may be presented in the document containing the disclosures required by Regulation Z or in one or more separate documents.

(e) Except to the extent that this section requires disclosure of additional information not required by Regulation Z, compliance with the applicable credit disclosure requirements of Regulation Z shall constitute compliance with the requirements of this section.

(f) The disclosure prescribed in Section 1917.171 shall be physically attached to the disclosures required by this section and Regulation Z at the time the Regulation Z disclosures are furnished to the borrower.

(g) In the event federal law is amended so that this section is inconsistent therewith, the federal law shall prevail as to the disclosures required by this section. **Leg.H.** Added Stats 1982 ch 466 §12. Inoperative January 1, 1987, by the terms of Stats 1982 ch 466 §12.5.

Prior Law: Former §1917.172, similar to the inoperative section, was added Stats 1981 ch 1144 §1 and repealed Stats 1982 ch 466 §10.

1982 Note: For continued application, see 1982 Note following Chapter 5 heading.

Former Sections: Former CC §1917.172, similar to the inoperative section, was added Stats 1981 ch 1144 §1 and repealed Stats 1982 ch 466 §10.

§1917.173. Information to be given prospective borrower [Inoperative]

Each lender making a shared appreciation loan shall additionally furnish to the prospective borrower, prior to consummation of the loan, a statement containing the following information:

IMPORTANT INFORMATION ABOUT YOUR SHARED APPRECIATION LOAN

You are being offered a shared appreciation loan. Before you decide to accept this loan, read this statement, which is designed to provide important information you should consider.

1. Prevailing interest rate: ____%.
2. Interest rate on this loan: ____%.
3. Lender's share of net appreciated value: ____%.
4. Amount of this loan: $____.
5. Amount of the monthly payments: $____.
6. Term of this loan: ____ years.
7. Amortization period on which payments are calculated: ____ years.
8. Prepayment charge (if any): ____.

Leg.H. Added Stats 1982 ch 466 §12. Inoperative January 1, 1987, by the terms of Stats 1982 ch 466 §12.5.

Prior Law: Former §1917.173, similar to the inoperative section, was added Stats 1981 ch 1144 §1 and repealed Stats 1982 ch 466 §10.

1982 Note: For continued application, see 1982 Note following Chapter 5 heading.

Former Sections: Former CC §1917.173, similar to the inoperative section, was added Stats 1981 ch 1144 §1 and repealed Stats 1982 ch 466 §10.

§1917.174. Statement in deed of trust and evidence of debt executed in connection with loan [Inoperative]

Each deed of trust and evidence of debt executed in connection with a shared appreciation loan shall contain a statement, printed or written in a size equal to at least 12-point bold type, consisting of substantially the following language: "THIS IS A (DURATION) SHARED APPRECIATION LOAN. THE LENDER'S INTEREST INCLUDES (PERCENT) OF THE NET APPRECIATED VALUE OF THE PROPERTY. A BALLOON PAYMENT OF PRINCIPAL WILL BE REQUIRED. FOR FURTHER INFORMATION, READ THE FLYER ENTITLED "INFORMATION ABOUT THE (NAME OF LENDER) SHARED APPRECIATION LOAN." The notice required by this section shall be completed to state the terms of the shared appreciation loan and the lender's share of the net appreciated value. **Leg.H.** Added Stats 1982 ch 466 §12. Inoperative January 1, 1987, by the terms of Stats 1982 ch 466 §12.5.

Prior Law: Former §1917.174, similar to the inoperative section, was added Stats 1981 ch 1144 §1 and repealed Stats 1982 ch 466 §10.

1982 Note: For continued application, see 1982 Note following Chapter 5 heading.

Former Sections: Former CC §1917.174, similar to the inoperative section, was added Stats 1981 ch 1144 §1 and repealed Stats 1982 ch 466 §10.

§1917.175. Disclosure of amount of interest [Inoperative]

Where, pursuant to any provision of law, the lender is required to disclose the amount of interest due or to be due under a shared appreciation loan and the amount of contingent deferred interest due or to be due is not known, the lender may disclose that fact and specify in the disclosure the method for calculating contingent deferred interest. **Leg.H.** Added Stats 1982 ch 466 §12. Inoperative January 1, 1987, by the terms of Stats 1982 ch 466 §12.5.

Prior Law: Former §1917.175, similar to the inoperative section, was added Stats 1981 ch 1144 §1 and repealed Stats 1982 ch 466 §10.

1982 Note: For continued application, see 1982 Note following Chapter 5 heading.

Former Sections: Former CC §1917.175, similar to the inoperative section, was added Stats 1981 ch 1144 §1 and repealed Stats 1982 ch 466 §10.

CHAPTER 6
LOANS OF E.R.I.S.A. PENSION FUNDS

Licenses. §1917.210.
Rates of interest. §1917.220.

§1917.210. Licenses

Each pension fund or retirement system which is subject to the Employee Retirement Income Security Act of 1974 (P.L. 93-406), shall not be required to obtain any license or certificate in order to provide funds for any type of loan transaction permitted by law. **Leg.H.** Added Stats 1983 ch 557 §2.

§1917.220. Rates of interest

Pursuant to the authority contained in Section 1 of Article XV of the California Constitution, the restrictions upon rates of interest contained in Section 1 of Article XV of the California Constitution shall not apply to any obligation of, loan made by, or forbearance of, any pension fund or retirement system which is subject to the Employee Retirement Income Security Act of 1974 (P.L. 93-406).

This section creates and authorizes pension funds or retirement systems subject to the Employee Retirement Income Security Act of 1974 (P.L. 93-406) as an exempt class of persons pursuant to Section 1 of Article XV of the Constitution. **Leg.H.** Added Stats 1983 ch 557 §2.

CHAPTER 7
SHARED APPRECIATION LOANS FOR SENIORS

Article 1. Definitions.
Article 2. Terms and Conditions.
Article 3. Determination of Fair Market Value.
Article 4. Improvements.
Article 5. General Provisions.
Article 6. Notices and Disclosures.

ARTICLE 1
Definitions

Definitions and calculations. §1917.320.

§1917.320. Definitions and calculations

For the purposes of this chapter:

(a) "Actual contingent interest" means the lender's appreciation share of the net appreciated amount. In no event, however, shall the rate of appreciation upon which actual contingent interest is calculated at the end of the loan term exceed 2½ times the rate at which projected contingent interest had been calculated.

(b) "Actual life expectancy" shall be calculated based upon actuarial tables for women only, regardless of the sex of the borrower, and acceptable to both the state and the insurance industry.

(c) "Annuity base amount" means the projected loan amount less (1) the initial advance and (2) the projected contingent interest based on the reasonable appreciation rate used in calculating the projected loan amount.

(d) "Borrower" means the recipient or recipients of a shared appreciation loan for seniors who is obligated by execution of a promissory note and who is at least 65 years of age.

(e) "Borrower's life expectancy" means the actual life expectancy of the borrower plus no more than five years. In the case of a loan executed by two borrowers, the actual life expectancy shall be based upon the youngest of the two.

(f) "Cessation of occupancy" means the rental to a third party of the right of exclusive occupancy of the subject property, or the abandonment by all coborrowers of the property as his or her residence.

(g) "Lender" means any corporation organized as a public benefit corporation pursuant to the Nonprofit Corporation Law (Part 2 (commencing with Section 5110), Div. 2, Title 1, Corp. C.).

(h) "Lender's appreciation share" means a proportion not to exceed 25 percent of the appreciation of the property securing the loan calculated in accordance with this chapter.

(i) "Shared appreciation loan for seniors" means any loan made pursuant to this chapter upon the security of owner-occupied real property of a type specified in Section 1917.330, and in connection with which the lender has a right to receive a share of the appreciation in the value of the security property. "Shared appreciation loan" includes a deed of trust and any evidence of debt issued in connection with the loan.

(j) "Maturity event" means the earliest of any of the following:
(1) The death of the borrower. In the case of a married couple who are coborrowers, the death of the surviving spouse.
(2) The date of sale.
(3) The date a loan made pursuant to this chapter is refinanced or repaid in full.
(4) Cessation of occupancy.

(k) "Monthly annuity" means an amount paid in equal monthly installments to the borrower which, together with interest calculated at the stated rate, shall exhaust the annuity base amount during the borrower's life expectancy.

In the event that the calculated monthly annuity exceeds the cap or ceiling determined in accordance with this subdivision, the lender may limit the actual monthly annuity payment to an amount not lower than the cap. If the cap is imposed, the lender's appreciation share shall be limited to 25 percent times the ratio between the actual capped monthly payment and the monthly payment calculated in accordance with the first sentence of this subdivision. For example, if the monthly payment calculated in the first sentence is five thousand dollars ($5,000), but the lender applies a two thousand five hundred dollar ($2,500) ceiling, the lender's share of the home's appreciation shall be likewise reduced by 50 percent.

The minimum cap shall be two thousand five hundred dollars ($2,500) for loans made during the calendar year 1989. In subsequent calendar years, the minimum cap shall be two thousand five hundred dollars ($2,500) increased to reflect the proportional increase in the Consumer Price Index for the State of California, as determined by the United States Bureau of Labor Statistics, for the period from January 1, 1989, until the November monthly index figure for the year prior to the year in which the loan agreement is entered into.

(*l*) "Net advance" means any lump-sum advance of funds by the lender to the borrower made at the time of the loan closing. Net advance shall not exceed 15 percent of the projected loan amount.

(m) "Net appreciated value" means the difference between the fair market value of the property securing the loan at the time the loan is made and the fair market value of the property securing the loan at the time of the maturity event, less any credit for approved improvements made during the term of the loan.

(n) "Prevailing rate" means the yield of a 30-year mortgage commitment for delivery within 30 days for a standard conventional fixed rate mortgage of the Federal Home Loan Mortgage Corporation.

(o) "Projected contingent interest" means the lender's appreciation share of the projected appreciation of the property securing the loan from the date of the loan until the end of the borrower's life expectancy, using the same reasonable projection of annual appreciation used in determining the projected loan amount.

(p) "Projected loan amount" means not less than 75 percent of the estimated fair market value of the borrower's home at the end of the borrower's life expectancy, calculated by applying to the fair market value a reasonable projection of appreciation over the borrower's life expectancy based on a reasonable projected annual appreciation rate of the fair market value of the home.

(q) "Sale" means any transfer of title to the property and includes the execution of an installment sale contract giving the purchaser a right to possess the property before transfer of title, refinancing, judicial sale on execution, or other legal process of foreclosure or trustee's sale, but "sale" does not include a transfer specified in Section 2924.6 if any spouse to whom the property is transferred is also a coborrower.

(r) "Stated interest rate" means a total interest rate of not more than four-fifths of the prevailing rate.

(s) "Total loan obligation" means the net original loan and the sum total of all monthly annuity payments received by the borrower, with interest on all outstanding amounts calculated no more often than monthly at the stated interest rate, and actual contingent interest plus interest at the prevailing rate as disclosed to the borrower at the time the loan was entered into on all of the above amounts from the date of any maturity event until the outstanding loan obligation is repaid in full. In no event shall the total loan obligation exceed the actual fair market value of the home on the date of the maturity event. **Leg.H.** Added Stats 1984 ch 1701 §1. Amended Stats 1988 ch 1406 §1.

ARTICLE 2
Terms and Conditions

Eligible dwelling units. §1917.330.
Items that must be included in loan. §1917.331.
Discontinuation or termination of monthly annuity. §1917.332.
Prepayments. §1917.333.
Applicability of laws in effect on date of loan. §1917.334.

§1917.330. Eligible dwelling units

Lenders may make shared appreciation loans for seniors pursuant to this chapter for the refinancing of real property improved with one- to four-dwelling units, including structures ancillary to such dwelling units and including attached single-family dwelling units, single-family mobilehome units, residential condominium units, and dwelling units within a planned unit development. Shared appreciation loans shall be made to refinance only owner-occupied dwelling units, but in the case of two- to four-unit dwellings financed under this chapter, only one of the units need be owner-occupied. A dwelling unit shall be conclusively deemed to be owner-occupied for purposes of this chapter with respect to initial qualification for participation in the loan program if a borrower certifies in writing to the lender at the time the loan is made that he or she will occupy the property.

Nothing contained herein shall be deemed or interpreted to restrict a lender from providing a shared appreciation loan based solely upon the value of the real property upon which the borrower's dwelling is situated, secured only by that real property and not by the improvements thereon. In that case, the lender's actual contingent interest, and any other necessary calculations, shall be based upon the land value alone, not taking into account any improvements thereon. This paragraph is declaratory of existing law. **Leg.H.** Added Stats 1984 ch 1701 §1. Amended Stats 1988 ch 1406 §2.

§1917.331. Items that must be included in loan

(a) A shared appreciation loan for seniors shall include all of the following:

(1) The term of the loan shall be for an open-ended term, terminating upon the occurrence of a maturity event, or the failure of the borrower to meet the terms of a deed of trust granted by the borrower to the lender which are normally and customarily used by mortgage lenders in this state for loans secured by residential real property. However, if the maturity event is either cessation of occupancy of the property by the borrower or death of the borrower, the term shall be extended until the earlier of the sale or refinancing of the property or 12 months after the occurrence of the maturity event.

(2) An initial advance, if desired by the borrower.

(3) Monthly annuity payments which shall continue until the occurrence of a maturity event, or earlier termination in accordance with paragraph (1).

(4) Interest on (2) and (3), calculated no more often than monthly at the stated interest rate.

(5) Actual contingent interest.

(6) Interest on paragraphs (2) to (5), inclusive, compounded no more often than monthly, from the date of a maturity event until the loan is repaid in full.

(b) The loan shall be secured by a deed of trust on the real property financed.

(c) The aggregate amount of any fee charged to the borrower by the lender for processing an application, preparing any necessary documents, obtaining a credit report, or any other costs incurred by the lender in connection with originating a shared appreciation loan for seniors shall not exceed five hundred dollars ($500). No prepaid interest shall be charged to the borrower. **Leg.H.** Added Stats 1984 ch 1701 §1. Amended Stats 1988 ch 1406 §3.

§1917.332. Discontinuation or termination of monthly annuity

Any provision in any loan made pursuant to this chapter for the discontinuation or termination of a monthly annuity other than upon the occurrence of a maturity event is void and unenforceable. **Leg.H.** Added Stats 1984 ch 1701 §1.

§1917.333. Prepayments

(a) The borrower shall have the right to prepay, at any time, in full or in part, the total loan obligation. **Leg.H.** Added Stats 1984 ch 1701 §1.

1984 Note: Section 1917.333 consists of only subsection (a).

§1917.334. Applicability of laws in effect on date of loan

Except as provided in this article, the terms and conditions of the shared appreciation loan for seniors shall be subject to all laws applicable to loans in effect on the date the loan is made. **Leg.H.** Added Stats 1984 ch 1701 §1.

ARTICLE 3
Determination of Fair Market Value

Request for stipulation of minimum fair market value. §1917.410.
Sale for cash; Sale including consideration other than cash. §1917.411.
Appraisals. §1917.412.

§1917.410. Request for stipulation of minimum fair market value

The borrower, at any time for the purpose of facilitating a sale of the property or prepaying or refinancing the loan, may request the lender to stipulate the minimum amount which the lender considers to be the fair market value of the property for the purposes of this chapter. The lender shall advise the borrower within 10 working days of the receipt of such request of the lender's estimate of the minimum fair market value. The estimate shall remain effective for purposes of this section for 90 days. For the purposes of this section and Section 1917.411, a sale of the property shall be deemed to have occurred within the 90-day period if there is a valid contract entered by an offer and acceptance within the 90-day period for the sale of the property. The lender's stipulation shall remain effective for an additional 60 days following execution of the sale contract to permit completion of the sale and close of escrow.

The lender shall not be liable to the borrower or any other party on account of damages alleged as a result of providing the stipulation or estimate required by this section if such stipulation or estimate is made in good faith. Evidence of lack of good faith shall include, but not be limited to, a showing that the lender has willfully or repeatedly overrepresented the fair market value of other properties in similar situations, applying equitable principles to those determinations. The lender shall be conclusively presumed to have acted in good faith and no action may be brought or maintained against a lender which arises out of the provision by the lender of such stipulation or estimate, if the lender relied upon an appraisal of an independent appraiser approved by the Federal National Mortgage Association. **Leg.H.** Added Stats 1984 ch 1701 §1.

§1917.411. Sale for cash; Sale including consideration other than cash

(a) In the case of a sale for cash within 90 days after the lender stipulates, under the provisions of Section 1917.410, a minimum amount which the lender considers to be the fair market value of the property, the fair market value shall be the gross sale price, unless the gross sale price is below the minimum amount stipulated by the lender and the lender contests in writing the reasonableness of the gross sale price in relation to the fair market value within 10 working days of the lender's receipt of notice of the gross sale price from the borrower, in which case fair market value shall be the greater of gross sale price or the amount determined under Section 1917.412.

(b) In the case of a sale for cash where the borrower has not requested the lender under the provisions of Section 1917.410 to stipulate to the minimum amount which the lender considers to be the fair market value of the property or where the stipulated minimum amount was provided by the lender more than 90 days prior to the date of sale, fair market value shall be the gross sale price, unless the lender contests in writing the reasonableness of the gross sale price in relation to the fair market value within 10 working days of the lender's receipt of notice of the gross sale price from borrower, in which case fair market value shall be the greater of the gross sale price or the amount determined under Section 1917.412.

(c) In the case of a sale which includes consideration to the seller other than cash, fair market value shall be as determined under Section 1917.412.

(d) If the shared appreciation loan is prepaid in full, or upon the occurrence of a maturity event, fair market value shall be as determined under Section 1917.412. **Leg.H.** Added Stats 1984 ch 1701 §1.

§1917.412. Appraisals

When Section 1917.411 requires the application of this section, the fair market value shall be determined by averaging two appraisals of the property performed as described in this section. If possible, the appraisals shall be based on the sale prices of comparable properties in the market area sold within the preceding three-month period. The appraisals shall be made upon request of the lender by two independent residential appraisers, one to be selected by the lender and one by the borrower. Each appraiser shall be approved by the Federal National Mortgage Association. The cost of the appraiser selected by the lender shall be borne by the lender, and the cost of the appraiser selected by the borrower shall be borne by the borrower, unless the average of the two appraisals equals or is less than the gross sale price of the property, in which case the lender shall also pay the fee of the borrower's appraiser up to two hundred dollars ($200). If either of the appraisers determines that the gross sale price does not reasonably reflect the fair market value of the property, or, in the case of a sale for which appraisal is required by this section, then the fair market value of the property shall be determined as the average of the two appraisals. If the borrower fails to select a qualified appraiser within 15 days after the lender has notified the borrower in writing of the lender's request for an appraisal of the property, the reasons therefor, and the borrower's option to select an independent appraiser within 15 days after the lender's request is submitted to the borrower, the lender may designate the second appraiser, provided the lender's request informs the borrower of this time limitation, and that the lender will select an appraiser on behalf of the borrower in the event the borrower fails to designate an appraiser, with consequent cost to the borrower. If pursuant to this section the lender designates the second appraiser, the cost of both appraisals shall be borne equally by the borrower and lender. If in any case the property has been damaged (other than normal wear and tear) and the damage has not been fully repaired, the determination of fair market value shall be based on the condition of the property not including the damage.

Nothing in this section shall preclude the borrower and lender from establishing the fair market value of the property by mutual agreement in lieu of appraisals pursuant to this section. **Leg.H.** Added Stats 1984 ch 1701 §1.

ARTICLE 4
Improvements

Addition to fair market value; Requirements. §1917.510.
Greater credit for improvements than specified in article. §1917.511.

§1917.510. Addition to fair market value; Requirements

The borrower may have the value of capital improvements added to the fair market value of the borrower's property, for purposes of determining the total loan obligation, but only if the procedures set forth in this article are followed.

(a) Within 60 days following the completion of capital improvements during any 12-month period with a cost in excess of one thousand dollars ($1,000), the borrower shall send by first-class mail a notice of the completion of the improvements to the lender and shall submit proof of cost and an estimate of the increase in value of the property by reason of the improvements.

(b) If, within 30 days of receipt of the notice, the lender questions the claimed increase in value of the property by reason of the improvements, the lender and the borrower may, by mutual agreement, establish the value of the capital improvements or the lender may require appraisal of the property. An appraisal shall be made to determine the increase in value of the property, if any, by reason of the improvements, by two appraisers selected in the same manner specified in Section 1917.412. If appraisals are performed, the increase in value resulting from the improvements for the purposes of this section, shall be one-half of the sum of the two appraisals. The cost of the appraiser selected by the borrower shall be borne by the borrower, and the cost of the appraiser selected by the lender shall be borne by the lender.

(c) A credit for the value of capital improvements shall be provided if the increase in value of the property resulting therefrom is determined pursuant to subdivision (b) to exceed one thousand dollars ($1,000).

(d) If 50 percent or more of the value of the labor or other work on the improvements was performed by the borrower, then the actual cost of the improvements need not exceed one thousand dollars ($1,000) for purposes of making application under subdivision (a). **Leg.H.** Added Stats 1984 ch 1701 §1.

§1917.511. Greater credit for improvements than specified in article

Nothing in this article shall preclude a shared appreciation loan for seniors from providing the borrower with a greater credit for improvements than specified in this article, provided the relevant disclosures required by Article 7 (commencing with Section 1917.710) are appropriately modified to accurately disclose the terms of the credit. **Leg.H.** Added Stats 1984 ch 1701 §1.

ARTICLE 5
General Provisions

Debtor and creditor relationship. §1917.610.
Waiver of rights. §1917.611.
Financing methods. §1917.612.
Applicability of other provisions. §1917.613.
Lien of deed of trust. §1917.614.
Lien of shared appreciation loan; Attachment; Priority. §1917.615.
Compliance with usury provisions. §1917.616.
Applicability of qualification requirements of Corporations Code. §1917.617.
Deficiency judgments. §1917.618.
Exemption from restrictions on interest rates. §1917.619.

§1917.610. Debtor and creditor relationship

The relationship of the borrower and the lender of a shared appreciation loan for seniors is that of debtor and creditor and shall not be, or be construed to be, a joint venture, an equity venture, a partnership, or other relationship. **Leg.H.** Added Stats 1984 ch 1701 §1.

§1917.611. Waiver of rights

Any waiver of any right of a borrower under the provisions of this chapter shall be void and unenforceable. **Leg.H.** Added Stats 1984 ch 1701 §1.

§1917.612. Financing methods

This chapter facilitates one method of making shared appreciation loans to senior citizens in this state. The terms and conditions of any shared appreciation loan for seniors made pursuant to this chapter shall be consistent with this chapter. This chapter does not, however, apply to or limit shared appreciation financing of real property of a type made pursuant to other provisions of law, or which is not otherwise unlawful. Nothing in this chapter shall be construed in any way to affect shared appreciation financing of residential property of senior citizens not meeting the criteria specified in this chapter. **Leg.H.** Added Stats 1984 ch 1701 §1.

§1917.613. Applicability of other provisions

A shared appreciation loan for seniors shall not be subject to any provision of this code or the Financial Code which limits the interest rate or change of interest rate of variable interest rate or renegotiable interest instruments, or which requires particular language or provisions in security instruments securing variable or renegotiable rate obligations or in evidences of those debts.

This section is declaratory of existing law. **Leg.H.** Added Stats 1984 ch 1701 §1.

§1917.614. Lien of deed of trust

The lien of a deed of trust securing a shared appreciation loan for seniors shall include and secure the total loan obligation of the shared appreciation loan for seniors. **Leg.H.** Added Stats 1984 ch 1701 §1.

§1917.615. Lien of shared appreciation loan; Attachment; Priority

The lien of a shared appreciation loan for seniors, including the total loan obligation, shall attach from the time of the recordation of the deed of trust securing the loan, and the lien, including the lien of the total loan obligation accrued or to be accrued, shall have priority over any other lien or encumbrance affecting the property secured by the shared appreciation instrument and recorded after the time of recordation of the shared appreciation instrument. However, nothing in this section or Section 1917.614 shall preclude a junior lien or encumbrance subordinate to the total loan obligation of the shared appreciation loan for seniors. In no case may a junior lien achieve priority over the lien securing the total loan obligation of the shared appreciation loan, provided that nothing in this section shall be construed to supersede Section 8450. **Leg.H.** Added Stats 1984 ch 1701 §1. Amended Stats 2010 ch 697 §12 (SB 189), effective January 1, 2011, operative July 1, 2012.

§1917.616. Compliance with usury provisions

A shared appreciation loan for seniors which bears a fixed interest rate complying with the usury provisions of Article XV of the California Constitution shall not be deemed to become usurious by reason of the payment of actual contingent interest pursuant to this chapter; provided, however, that in no event may the amount of actual contingent interest received by the lender, plus the stated interest received by the lender, result in an annual percentage rate in excess of 1.5 times the applicable usury rate calculated pursuant to Article XV of the California Constitution, when all of such interest is applied over the actual term of the loan. **Leg.H.** Added Stats 1984 ch 1701 §1.

§1917.617. Applicability of qualification requirements of Corporations Code

The qualification requirements of Sections 25110, 25120, and 25130 of the Corporations Code do not apply to a shared appreciation loan for seniors to the extent the exemption afforded by subdivision (p) of Section 25100 of that code is applicable. **Leg.H.** Added Stats 1984 ch 1701 §1.

§1917.618. Deficiency judgments

Any loan made pursuant to this chapter shall be subject to Section 580b of the Code of Civil Procedure. **Leg.H.** Added Stats 1984 ch 1701 §1.

§1917.619. Exemption from restrictions on interest rates

Pursuant to the authority contained in Section 1 of Article XV of the California Constitution, the restrictions upon rates of interest contained in Section 1 of Article XV of the California Constitution shall not apply to any obligation of any loan made by any lender pursuant to this chapter.

This section creates and authorizes lenders under this chapter as an exempt class of persons pursuant to Section 1 of Article XV of the Constitution. **Leg.H.** Added Stats 1984 ch 1701 §1.

ARTICLE 6
Notices and Disclosures

Disclosures. §1917.710.
Notices. §1917.711.
Disclosures required by Regulation Z. §1917.712.
Rate and total loan obligation. §1917.713.
Term. §1917.714.

§1917.710. Disclosures

(a) The disclosures made pursuant to this chapter, as required, shall be the only disclosures required to be made pursuant to state law for shared appreciation loans for seniors, notwithstanding any contrary provision applicable to loans not made under this chapter, except those, if any, that may be required by reason of the application of Division 1 (commencing with Section 25000) of the Corporations Code, or Chapter 1 (commencing with Section 11000) of Part 2 of Division 4 of the Business and Professions Code. However, a lender shall not be precluded from supplementing the disclosures required by this chapter with additional disclosures that are not inconsistent with the disclosures required by this chapter.

(b) Whenever specific language is prescribed by this chapter, substantially the same language shall be utilized if possible, but reasonably equivalent language may be used to the extent necessary or appropriate to achieve a clearer or more accurate disclosure. **Leg.H.** Added Stats 1984 ch 1701 §1.

§1917.711. Notices

(a) Each lender offering shared appreciation loans for seniors shall furnish to a prospective borrower, on the earlier of the dates on which the lender first provides written information concerning shared appreciation loans for seniors by the lender or provides a loan application form to the prospective borrower, a written disclosure as provided in this section, in type of not less than 10 point.

(b) The disclosure shall be entitled "INFORMATION ABOUT THE (Name of Lender) SHARED APPRECIATION LOAN FOR SENIORS," and shall describe the operation and effect of the shared appreciation loan for seniors, including a brief summary of its terms and conditions, together with a statement consisting of substantially the following language, to the extent applicable to such loan:

INFORMATION ABOUT THE SHARED APPRECIATION LOANS FOR SENIORS

Your lender is pleased to offer you the opportunity to borrow against the equity in your home through a Shared Appreciation Loan for Seniors.

Because the Shared Appreciation Loan for Seniors differs from the usual mortgage loan, the law requires that you have a detailed explanation of the special features of the loan before you apply. Before you sign your particular Shared Appreciation Loan for Seniors documents, you will receive more information about your particular Shared Appreciation Loan for Seniors, which you should read and understand before you sign the loan documents.

Receipt of shared appreciation loan proceeds could be considered income, thereby reducing payments received under government benefit programs, such as Supplemental Security Income (SSI). If this income is accumulated, the payments will be considered a resource, and could terminate your eligibility for SSI or Medi-Cal. See your legal adviser for more information.

I
GENERAL TERMS

A Shared Appreciation Loan for Seniors will provide you with funds to pay off any existing indebtedness on your home and to pay the closing costs for the loan, and will then advance funds to you each month (monthly annuity) (1) for so long as you or your spouse who is a coborrower live; or (2) until you sell the house; or (3) until you decide to refinance the property and pay off your Shared Appreciation Loan for Seniors; or (4) until you cease to occupy the property as your residence, meaning either that the property has been rented out for exclusive use by a nonborrower, or the abandonment by all coborrowers of the property as their residence. Any of these four events are considered "maturity events," and will constitute the end of the obligation to advance funds to you. The maturity events are described more fully in the promissory note. Your monthly annuity is calculated according to the method described in Section II, below. You will also be required to fulfill any customary terms or conditions included in the deed of trust encumbering your property.

Each advance of funds you receive, including both initial advances (net original loan) and each monthly annuity, will be considered outstanding principal on your loan and will bear a stated interest rate which will be not more than 80 percent of the prevailing rate of interest in the locality in which you live. No payments on your total loan obligation need be made by you until the occurrence of one of the four maturity events described above.

In exchange for a stated interest rate which is below the prevailing rate, you will be obligated to pay us additional interest later, in the form of a share of the appreciation of your home between the time you execute the promissory note and the occurrence of a maturity event. This additional interest is called "actual contingent interest" and is described more fully below at Section III. Once a maturity event has occurred, interest at the prevailing rate compounded not more often than monthly shall accrue on the entire outstanding loan balance, including the actual contingent interest, until repayment in full of the loan.

Balloon Payment of Principal. If you do not sell the property before the occurrence of a maturity event, you or your successors will need to refinance or pay this loan at that time. The term of this loan is until occurrence of a maturity event. However, if the maturity event is cessation of occupancy or death of the borrowers, the term shall be extended until the earlier of the sale or refinancing of the property, or 12 months after occurrence of the maturity event. We will not refinance either the unpaid balance of the loan or the contingent interest at that time; you or your successors alone will be responsible for obtaining refinancing. If you refinance this loan, your monthly payments may increase substantially if the property has appreciated significantly or if the interest rate on the refinancing loan is much higher than today's prevailing rates. In general, the more your property appreciates, the larger will be the amount of the actual contingent interest that you will have an obligation to pay or refinance.

Tax and Estate Consequences. USE OF THE SHARED APPRECIATION LOAN FOR SENIORS WILL HAVE INCOME TAX OR ESTATE

PLANNING CONSEQUENCES WHICH WILL DEPEND UPON YOUR OWN FINANCIAL AND TAX SITUATION. FOR FURTHER INFORMATION, YOU ARE URGED TO CONSULT YOUR OWN ACCOUNTANT, ATTORNEY, OR OTHER FINANCIAL ADVISER.

THE QUESTIONS YOU SHOULD DISCUSS INCLUDE THE TAX DEDUCTIBILITY OF THE CONTINGENT INTEREST PAYMENT, YOUR RIGHT TO UTILIZE THAT DEDUCTION IN YEARS OTHER THAN THE YEAR IT IS PAID, AND THE EFFECT OF THE LOSS OF TAX BENEFITS BEFORE THAT TIME. BECAUSE YOU WILL BE BORROWING A SIGNIFICANT AMOUNT OF THE EQUITY IN YOUR HOME, WHEN A MATURITY EVENT OCCURS AND YOUR LOAN IS REPAID, LITTLE OR NO EQUITY MAY REMAIN FOR YOU OR YOUR HEIRS.

Determining Fair Market Value. If you sell your property, the gross sale price will be the fair market value of the property, unless appraisals are requested by us and the appraisals average more than the gross sale price. However, at your request, we also will tell you what we consider to be the fair market value of the property. If you sell for cash for a gross sale price that equals or exceeds that amount, the gross sale price will control and appraisals will not be needed.

Fair market value is determined by appraisals in the event of sales involving a consideration other than cash, prepayment of the loan in full, or any other maturity event.

When appraisals are required, fair market value is determined by averaging two independent appraisals of the property. You may select one of the two appraisers from a list approved by the Federal National Mortgage Association. If appraisals are requested by us, we will provide you with full information on how to select an appraiser.

In lieu of appraisals, we may establish fair market value at an agreed amount if an agreement can be reached between you and us.

Determining Value of Capital Improvements. Capital improvements with a value exceeding one thousand dollars ($1,000) (but no maintenance or repair costs) may be added to the value of the property for the purpose of determining the net appreciated value, but only if the procedures set forth in the shared appreciation loan documents are followed. It is important to note that capital improvements completed and claimed in any 12-month period must add more than one thousand dollars ($1,000) in value to the property and must generally also cost more than one thousand dollars ($1,000). However, if you have performed at least one-half the value of the labor or other work involved, then the cost of the improvements will not be considered. The appraised value of the improvements will be the increase in the value of the property resulting from the improvements. You will receive no credit for minor or major repairs or for improvements that are not appraised at more than one thousand dollars ($1,000), but the lender will acquire a share of any resulting appreciation in the value of the property.

II
CALCULATION OF MONTHLY ANNUITY

Your Shared Appreciation Loan for Seniors consists of two components: first, an initial advance to cover the cost of paying off any existing liens which you wish to pay off, and to cover closing costs; and second, a monthly annuity.

Your Shared Appreciation Loan for Seniors is designed to provide a monthly stream of funds for the remainder of the lives of the borrowers, with no payments on the loan due at any time during the lives of the borrowers unless the property is sold or the loan is refinanced or repaid in full or until you cease to occupy the property. In determining the amount that it is able to lend, the lender estimates what at least 75 percent of the value of the borrower's home is likely to be at the end of the borrower's life expectancy, based on a reasonable projected appreciation rate per year. Borrowers, estimated life spans are predicted on the basis of "actuarial tables" prepared by the government and the insurance industry; and are based only upon estimated female life span, plus up to five years, to avoid any discriminatory effect between the sexes in determining loan amounts and for conservative lending practices. Once the maximum amount which may be loaned has been determined, the amount necessary to pay off existing liens and for closing costs, plus interest at the stated interest rate on that amount for the borrower's life expectancy, is subtracted. The "projected contingent interest" that is predicted to have been earned at the end of the estimated life span is also subtracted. A monthly annuity is then calculated on the remaining amount, based on the stated interest and the borrower's life expectancy.

This complex calculation is illustrated by the following example:

Mr. and Mrs. Smith, who are 73 and 71 years of age, respectively, live in a home with a current value of one hundred fifty thousand dollars ($150,000), and apply for a Shared Appreciation Loan for Seniors. According to acceptable actuarial tables, Mrs. Smith, the younger of the two, has a remaining actuarial life span of 18 years. At the end of the 18 years, at a 4 percent per year projected appreciation rate, the house would be worth three hundred thousand dollars ($300,000), 80 percent of which equals two hundred forty thousand dollars ($240,000) (the lender could have based the calculation on as little as 75 percent of the three hundred thousand dollar ($300,000) projected value). The house currently has a fifteen thousand dollar ($15,000) first mortgage, and closing costs will be approximately two thousand dollars ($2,000), and the Smiths' wish to receive an initial advance to pay off the mortgage and to cover closing costs.

At the time the Smiths apply, the average of the 30-year fixed interest rate for home mortgages of the Federal Home Loan Mortgage Corporation is 13 percent, which is the "prevailing rate." The "stated interest rate" on the Smiths' loan will be 75 percent of the "prevailing rate," or 9¾ percent (the lender could have charged up to 80 percent of the prevailing rate).

The Smiths' payments will be calculated so that at the end of the projected loan term of 18 years, the total of all payments owed to the lender will be two hundred forty thousand dollars ($240,000), 80 percent of the estimated value of the Smiths' home after 18 years.

Two items must be subtracted from the two hundred forty thousand dollar ($240,000) future value before the Smiths' payment can be calculated:

(a) Since the Smiths' are requesting an advance of seventeen thousand dollars ($17,000) to pay off their existing mortgage and for closing costs, seventeen thousand dollars ($17,000), plus interest on seventeen thousand dollars ($17,000) at 9¾ percent for 18 years, for a total of ninety-six thousand fifty-seven dollars ($96,057), must be subtracted from the two hundred forty thousand dollars ($240,000) available for lending. This leaves one hundred forty-three thousand nine hundred forty-three dollars ($143,943).

(b) The lender's share of appreciation of the value of the home is also subtracted before calculating the monthly payment. Since the home is projected to increase in value by one hundred fifty thousand dollars ($150,000), the lender's share, 25 percent, equals thirty-seven thousand five hundred dollars ($37,500). When subtracted from one hundred forty-three thousand nine hundred forty-three dollars ($143,943), this leaves one hundred six thousand four hundred forty-three dollars ($106,443) for monthly payments.

The monthly payment is calculated on the basis of one hundred six thousand four hundred forty-three dollars ($106,443), over an 18-year term with interest at 9¾ percent. This equals one hundred eighty-four dollars ($184) per month. The Smiths' will receive one hundred eighty-four dollars ($184) per month until a maturity event occurs.

At the time of occurrence of a maturity event, the Smiths, or their successors, if they are both deceased, will owe the seventeen thousand dollars ($17,000) advanced initially, plus the sum of all the monthly payments of one hundred eighty-four dollars ($184) received by them until the occurrence of the maturity event, plus interest at 9¾ percent on all of the above from the time the funds were advanced until occurrence of the maturity event, plus actual contingent interest calculated as described in Section III below. Interest, compounded no more often than monthly, on all of the above shall accrue at the prevailing rate from the date of any maturity event until the loan is paid in full.

Because interest accumulates rapidly, when a large initial advance is received, or the projected loan term is relatively long, the monthly payment is significantly lower. For instance, if the Smiths' were 80 years old, and received no lump-sum advance, their monthly payment would be seven hundred forty-nine dollars ($749) per month.

The longer the loan has been in effect, of course, the greater the amount that will be owed, as monthly payments and interest accumulate, and as the home appreciates in value. Unless the borrowers choose to sell the home or refinance the loan, monthly payments will continue until both are deceased, no matter how long they live so long as they continue to occupy the property. Thus, the total loan obligation is not limited to the projected life span of the borrowers, nor to any set dollar amount, regardless of the projected maximum. Regardless of how much principal has been advanced by Shared Appreciation Loans for Seniors, and regardless of how much stated interest and actual contingent interest have accumulated or been earned, payments will continue. If the borrower lives substantially longer than the actuarial prediction, it is possible that the total of principal and acquired stated interest plus actual contingent interest, may exceed the value of the home. IN NO EVENT, HOWEVER, WILL A BORROWER OR A BORROWER'S ESTATE BE LIABLE ON THE SHARED APPRECIATION LOAN FOR SENIORS IN AN AMOUNT GREATER THAN THE VALUE OF THE HOME.

The Smith example can be illustrated as follows:

A.	$150,000	= Value of home at time of loan.
B.	$300,000	= Estimated value of home at end of life expectancy (18 years, 4% annual appreciation).
C.	$240,000	= Loan (80% of B)
D.	$150,000	= Total appreciation (B less A).
E.	$37,500	= Lender's share of appreciation (25% × D).
F.	$96,057	= Payoff of preexisting mortgage, plus interest.
G.	$106,443	= Amount from which monthly payment is calculated (C less E less F).
H.	$184	= Monthly payment (based on G) to the Smiths. At death or other maturity event, the sum of all monthly payments, plus interest, plus the lender's share of appreciation, plus the amount owing from payoff of the old mortgage, must be paid to the lender.

III
ACTUAL CONTINGENT INTEREST

This Shared Appreciation Loan for Seniors provides that you, as borrower, must pay to the lender, as actual contingent interest, a share of up to 25 percent of the net appreciated value of the real property which secures the loan. This actual contingent interest is due and payable whenever a maturity event occurs. The dollar amount of actual contingent interest, if any, which you will be required to pay cannot be determined at this time. If the property does not appreciate, you will owe us nothing as actual contingent interest, and will only have to repay principal and stated interest. Actual contingent interest will not become due if title to the property is transferred on your death to a spouse who is a coborrower, or where a transfer results from a decree of dissolution of a marriage and a spouse who is a coborrower becomes the sole owner.

Your obligation to pay actual contingent interest and stated interest will reduce the amount of the appreciation, if any, that you will realize on the property over and above its value today. Appreciation will not produce a real gain in your equity in the property unless the appreciation rate exceeds the general inflation rate, but you will be required to pay a portion of the appreciation as actual contingent interest without regard to whether the appreciation has resulted in a real gain.

When your home is sold or refinanced, you normally will receive enough cash to pay the total loan obligation. However, if you sell and provide financing to the buyer, you may possibly not receive enough cash to pay the actual contingent interest, and, in that event, it will be necessary for you to provide cash from other funds. In no event, however, will your total loan obligation exceed the value of your home at the time of occurrence of a maturity event, unless you have willfully caused damage to the property.

Calculating the actual contingent interest. Actual contingent interest will be calculated as follows:

	FAIR MARKET VALUE OF THE PROPERTY ON DATE OF MATURITY EVENT Sale Price or Appraised Value)
— (less)	CURRENT VALUE OF THE PROPERTY
— (less)	VALUE OF CAPITAL IMPROVEMENTS
	FAIR MARKET VALUE OF THE PROPERTY ON DATE OF MATURITY EVENT Sale Price or Appraised Value) MADE BY YOU (Must exceed $1,000 in cost.)
× (times)	LENDER'S APPRECIATION SHARE (up to 25%)
= (equals)	ACTUAL CONTINGENT INTEREST

Below are answers to two frequently asked questions about the Shared Appreciation Loans for Seniors program. If you have any further questions, feel free to call the lender at _____, or write to the lender at _____.

Question. What if I marry, or my spouse is not a coborrower?

Answer. Your Shared Appreciation Loan for Seniors will be due upon the death of the last surviving coborrower. Your lender will be happy to include a new or present spouse as a coborrower, provided the new spouse is over age _____ at the time he or she becomes a coborrower. Because the monthly payment annuity is based upon the projected life span of the youngest coborrower, the annuity will be readjusted if a new, younger coborrower is added. The annuity will be adjusted to reflect the annuity that would have existed had the new coborrower been a coborrower from the beginning of the loan period. Since the monthly annuity is based on a fixed "lendable amount" derived from projected appreciation of the home (see Section II, above), a longer projected loan period, because of the younger age of the new coborrower, will result in a decrease in the size of the monthly annuity.

Question. Can I obtain an additional advance for home improvements?

Answer. Yes, provided your lender approves of the improvement. Your lender will act reasonably in reviewing your request. At the time the advance is made, your lender will calculate the amount of interest at the stated interest rate that will accrue through the projected life of the loan, as it was determined at the time the loan was made. This amount will be deducted from the original lendable amount, and a new annuity calculated, based upon the calculations described in Section II. The effect is the same as if the advance had been made at the outset of the loan, except, of course, you will not be responsible for any interest until the funds are actually advanced. Your annuity will, however, be smaller. **Leg.H.** Added Stats 1984 ch 1701 §1. Amended Stats 1988 ch 1406 §4.

§1917.712. Disclosures required by Regulation Z

(a) Each lender making a shared appreciation loan for seniors shall also furnish to the prospective borrower, prior to the consummation of the loan, the disclosures required by Subpart C of Federal Reserve Board Regulation Z (12 C.F.R. Part 226), including 12 C.F.R. Section 226.18(f), to the extent applicable to the transaction.

(b) The disclosure made pursuant to subdivision (a) and Regulation Z shall be based on the fixed interest rate of the shared appreciation loan for seniors, and shall include a description of the shared appreciation feature, including (1) the conditions for its imposition, the time at which it would be collected, and the limitations on the lender's share, as required by the Federal Reserve Board in the information published by the board in 46 Federal Register 20877–78 (April 7, 1981), and (2) the lender's share of the appreciated value and the prevailing interest rate as defined in Section 1917.320.

(c) The disclosure made pursuant to subdivision (a) and Regulation Z shall be accompanied by (1) several transaction-specific examples of the operation and effect of the shared appreciation loan and (2) the following charts comparing the shared appreciation loan and a conventional loan made at the prevailing interest rate, and illustrating the possible increase in the monthly payments, and the possible annual percentage rate of finance charge, on the assumptions therein stated:

Chart 1
CONVENTIONAL MORTGAGE AT _____%
If the same loan balance were financed under a conventional, 30-year, fixed-rate, level-payment mortgage, your monthly payments would be:
Years 1–30
$_____/mo.

Chart 2
IF YOU REFINANCE THIS TRANSACTION AT _____%
If your property appreciates at 10% per year, and if your total loan obligation (including actual contingent interest due) at the end of ____

IF YOU REFINANCE THIS TRANSACTION AT ____%
years is refinanced at ____% (the prevailing market interest rate now), your monthly payments will be:
Years 1–   ____ Refinancing loan
$____/mo. $____/mo.*

* Refinancing loan, assuming a conventional 30-year, fixed-rate, level-payment mortgage. Other mortgage instruments, e.g., graduated-payment or shared-appreciation, if available, may result in lower payments.

Chart 3

APR IF PROPERTY APPRECIATES AT 10%
If your property appreciates at 10% per year, the total finance charge on your shared appreciation loan for seniors (including actual contingent interest) will equal $____, and the annual percentage rate of the total of finance charge (including actual contingent interest) will equal ____%.

(d) The disclosures required by subdivision (c) shall be separate from the disclosures required by Regulation Z, and may be presented in the document containing the disclosures required by Regulation Z or in one or more separate documents.

(e) Except to the extent that this section requires disclosure of additional information not required by Regulation Z, compliance with the applicable credit disclosure requirements of Regulation Z shall constitute compliance with the requirements of this section.

(f) The disclosure prescribed in Section 1917.711 shall be physically attached to the disclosures required by this section and Regulation Z at the time the Regulation Z disclosures are furnished to the borrower.

(g) In the event federal law is amended so that this section is inconsistent therewith, the federal law shall prevail as to the disclosures required by this section. **Leg.H.** Added Stats 1984 ch 1701 §1.

§1917.713. Rate and total loan obligation

Each lender making a shared appreciation loan for seniors shall additionally furnish to the prospective borrower, prior to consummation of the loan, a statement containing the following information:

IMPORTANT INFORMATION ABOUT YOUR SHARED APPRECIATION LOAN FOR SENIORS.

You are being offered a shared appreciation loan. Before you decide to accept this loan, read this statement, which is designed to provide important information you should consider.
1. Prevailing interest rate: ____%.
2. Stated interest rate on this loan: ____%.
3. Projected contingent interest: ____%.
4. Initial amount of this loan: $____.
5. Amount of the monthly annuity payments you will receive: $____.
6. Projected term of this loan: ____ years.
7. Projected total loan obligation you will have to pay, assuming the loan continues to the end of the "borrower's" life expectancy: $____.

Leg.H. Added Stats 1984 ch 1701 §1.

§1917.714. Term

Each deed of trust and evidence of debt executed in connection with a shared appreciation loan for seniors shall contain a statement, printed or written in a size equal to at least 12-point bold type, consisting of substantially the following language: "THIS IS A [DURATION] SHARED APPRECIATION LOAN FOR SENIORS. THE LENDER'S INTEREST INCLUDES [PERCENT] OF THE NET APPRECIATED VALUE OF THE PROPERTY. A BALLOON PAYMENT OF PRINCIPAL WILL BE REQUIRED. FOR FURTHER INFORMATION, READ THE FLYER ENTITLED 'INFORMATION ABOUT THE [NAME OF LENDER] SHARED APPRECIATION LOAN FOR SENIORS.' " The notice required by this section shall be completed to state the terms of the shared appreciation loan and the lender's share of the net appreciated value. **Leg.H.** Added Stats 1984 ch 1701 §1.

CHAPTER 7.5
MORTGAGE LOANS

Definitions. §1918.5.
Requirements of mortgage instrument. §1920.
Disclosure of information as to adjustable-rate loans. §1921.

§1918. [Section repealed 1997]

Leg.H. Added Stats 1981 ch 1079 §4, operative January 1, 1983. Repealed Stats 1997 ch 232 §22 (AB 447). The repealed section related to legislative findings and declarations regarding mortgage loans.

Prior Law: Former §1918, relating to interest rate, was enacted Stats 1872 and repealed by initiative act adopted November 5, 1918, Stats 1919.

§1918.5. Definitions

As used in this chapter:
(a) "Evidence of debt" means a note or negotiable instrument.
(b) "Secretary" means the Secretary of the Business, Consumer Services, and Housing.
(c) "Secretary's designee" means the director of a department within the agency that licenses or regulates the institutions, organizations, or persons engaged in a business related to or affecting compliance with this chapter.
(d) "Security document" means a mortgage contract, deed of trust, real estate sales contract, or any note or negotiable instrument issued in connection therewith, when its purpose is to finance the purchase or construction of real property occupied or intended to be occupied by the borrower, containing four or fewer residential units or on which four or fewer residential units are to be constructed. **Leg.H.** Added Stats 1981 ch 1079 §4, operative January 1, 1983. Amended Stats 2013 ch 353 §11 (SB 820), effective September 26, 2013, operative July 1, 2013.

§1919. [Section repealed 1997]

Leg.H. Added Stats 1981 ch 1079 §4, operative January 1, 1983. Repealed Stats 1997 ch 232 §23 (AB 447). The repealed section related to rules and regulations regarding mortgage loans.

Prior Law: Former §1919, relating to interest rate, was enacted Stats 1872 and repealed by initiative act adopted November 5, 1918, Stats 1919.

§1920. Requirements of mortgage instrument

Any mortgage instrument that is made pursuant to the provisions of this chapter shall meet the following requirements:

(a) Standards for the adjustment of interest rates or monthly payments shall consider factors which can reasonably be deemed to affect the ability of borrowers to meet their mortgage obligations.

(b) No change in interest provided for in any provision for a variable interest rate contained in a security document, or evidence of debt issued in connection therewith, shall be valid unless the provision is set forth in the security document, and in any evidence of debt issued in connection therewith, and the document or documents contain the following provisions:

(1) A statement attached to the security document and to any evidence of debt issued in connection therewith printed or written in a size equal to at least 10-point bold type, consisting of language authorized by the secretary or the secretary's designee notifying the borrower that the mortgage may provide for changes in interest, principal loan balance, payment, or the loan term.

(2) Before the due date of the first monthly installment following each change in the interest rate, notice shall be mailed to the borrower of the following:
(A) The base index.
(B) The most recently published index at the date of the change in the rate.
(C) The interest rate in effect as a result of the change.
(D) Any change in the monthly installment.
(E) The amount of the unpaid principal balance.
(F) If the interest scheduled to be paid on the due date exceeds the amount of the installment, a statement to that effect and the amount of the excess, and the address and telephone number of the office of the lender to which inquiries may be made.

(c) The borrower is permitted to prepay the loan in whole or in part without a prepayment charge at any time, and no fee or other charge may be required by the lender of the borrower as a result of any change in the interest rate, the payment, the outstanding principal loan balance, or the loan term.

(d) Changes in the rate of interest on the loan shall reflect the movement of an index, which shall be authorized by the secretary or the secretary's designee.

(e) To the extent that any monthly installment is less than the amount of interest accrued during the month with respect to which the installment is payable, the borrower shall be notified of such instance in a form and manner prescribed by the secretary or the secretary's designee. Such notice shall include, but not be limited to, the amount of interest exceeding the monthly installment, and any borrower options under these circumstances.

(f) The lender shall provide to the borrower, prior to the execution by the borrower of any mortgage payment instrument authorized pursuant to this chapter, full and complete disclosure, as specified by the secretary or the secretary's designee, of the nature and effect of the mortgage payment instrument, and all costs or savings attributed to the mortgage instrument. **Leg.H.** Added Stats 1981 ch 1079 §4, operative January 1, 1983. Amended Stats 1997 ch 232 §24 (AB 447).

Prior Law: Former §1920, relating to interest rate, was enacted Stats 1872, amended Code Amdts 1873–74 ch 612 §204, and repealed by initiative act adopted November 5, 1918, Stats 1919 p lxxxiii.

§1921. Disclosure of information as to adjustable-rate loans

(a) As used in this section:

(1) "Adjustable-rate residential mortgage loan" means any loan or credit sale which is primarily for personal, family, or household purposes which bears interest at a rate subject to change during the term of the loan, whether predetermined or otherwise, and which is made upon the security of real property containing not less than one nor more than four dwelling units.

(2) "Lender" means any person, association, corporation, partnership, limited partnership, or other business entity making, in any 12-month period, more than 10 loans or credit sales upon the security of residential real property containing not less than one nor more than four dwelling units.

(b) Any lender offering adjustable-rate residential mortgage loans shall provide to prospective borrowers a copy of the most recent available publication of the Federal Reserve Board that is designed to provide the public with descriptive information concerning adjustable-rate mortgages (currently entitled "Consumer Handbook on Adjustable Rate Mortgages"), either upon the prospective borrower's request or at the same time the lender first provides written information, other than direct-mail advertising, concerning any adjustable-rate residential mortgage loan or credit sale to the prospective borrower, whichever is earlier. Any lender who fails to comply with the requirements of this section may be enjoined by any court of competent jurisdiction and shall be liable for actual damages, the costs of the action, and reasonable attorney's fees as determined by the court. The court may make those orders as may be necessary to prevent future violations of this section.

(c) A lender that makes adjustable-rate mortgage loan disclosures pursuant to either Part 29 of Chapter I of, or Part 563 of Chapter V of, Title 12 of the Code of Federal Regulations, may comply with this section by providing the descriptive information required by subdivision (b) at the same time and under the same circumstances that it makes disclosures in accordance with those federal regulations. Such a lender shall also display and make the descriptive information available to the public in an area of the lender's office that is open to the public. **Leg.H.** Added Stats 1985 ch 1284 §1. Amended Stats 1987 ch 56 §19.

CHAPTER 8
REVERSE MORTGAGES

Criteria for reverse mortgage. §1923.
Requirements of reverse mortgage loan; Counseling. §1923.2.
Lien against property. §1923.3.
Owner-occupied property. §1923.4.
Notice to prospective borrower; Reverse mortgage worksheet guide. §1923.5.
Disclosure duty. §1923.6.
Failure to comply. §1923.7.
Treatment of payments and funds. §1923.9.
Applicability. §1923.10.

§1923. Criteria for reverse mortgage

For purposes of this chapter, "reverse mortgage" means a nonrecourse loan secured by real property that meets all of the following criteria:

(a) The loan provides cash advances to a borrower based on the equity or the value in a borrower's owner-occupied principal residence.

(b) The loan requires no payment of principal or interest until the entire loan becomes due and payable.

(c) The loan is made by a lender licensed or chartered pursuant to the laws of this state or the United States. **Leg.H.** Added Stats 1997 ch 797 §1 (AB 456).

§1923.2. Requirements of reverse mortgage loan; Counseling

A reverse mortgage loan shall comply with all of the following requirements:

(a) Prepayment, in whole or in part, shall be permitted without penalty at any time during the term of the reverse mortgage loan. For the purposes of this section, penalty does not include any fees, payments, or other charges that would have otherwise been due upon the reverse mortgage being due and payable.

(b) A reverse mortgage loan may provide for a fixed or adjustable interest rate or combination thereof, including compound interest, and may also provide for interest that is contingent on the value of the property upon execution of the loan or at maturity, or on changes in value between closing and maturity.

(c) A reverse mortgage may include costs and fees that are charged by the lender, or the lender's designee, originator, or servicer, including costs and fees charged upon execution of the loan, on a periodic basis, or upon maturity.

(d) If a reverse mortgage loan provides for periodic advances to a borrower, these advances shall not be reduced in amount or number based on any adjustment in the interest rate.

(e) A lender who fails to make loan advances as required in the loan documents, and fails to cure an actual default after notice as specified in the loan documents, shall forfeit to the borrower treble the amount wrongfully withheld plus interest at the legal rate.

(f) The reverse mortgage loan may become due and payable upon the occurrence of any one of the following events:

(1) The home securing the loan is sold or title to the home is otherwise transferred.

(2) All borrowers cease occupying the home as a principal residence, except as provided in subdivision (g).

(3) Any fixed maturity date agreed to by the lender and the borrower occurs.

(4) An event occurs which is specified in the loan documents and which jeopardizes the lender's security.

(g) Repayment of the reverse mortgage loan shall be subject to the following additional conditions:

(1) Temporary absences from the home not exceeding 60 consecutive days shall not cause the mortgage to become due and payable.

(2) Extended absences from the home exceeding 60 consecutive days, but less than one year, shall not cause the mortgage to become due and payable if the borrower has taken prior action which secures and protects the home in a manner satisfactory to the lender, as specified in the loan documents.

(3) The lender's right to collect reverse mortgage loan proceeds shall be subject to the applicable statute of limitations for written loan contracts. Notwithstanding any other provision of law, the statute of limitations shall commence on the date that the reverse mortgage loan becomes due and payable as provided in the loan agreement.

(4) The lender shall prominently disclose in the loan agreement any interest rate or other fees to be charged during the period that commences on the date that the reverse mortgage loan becomes due and payable, and that ends when repayment in full is made.

(h) The first page of any deed of trust securing a reverse mortgage loan shall contain the following statement in 10-point boldface type: "This deed of trust secures a reverse mortgage loan."

(i) A lender or any other person that participates in the origination of the mortgage shall not require an applicant for a reverse mortgage to purchase an annuity as a condition of obtaining a reverse mortgage loan.

(1) The lender or any other person that participates in the origination of the mortgage shall not do either of the following:

(A) Participate in, be associated with, or employ any party that participates in or is associated with any other financial or insurance activity, unless the lender maintains procedural safeguards designed to ensure that individuals participating in the origination of the mortgage shall have no involvement with, or incentive to provide the prospective borrower with, any other financial or insurance product.

(B) Refer the borrower to anyone for the purchase of an annuity or other financial or insurance product prior to the closing of the reverse mortgage or before the expiration of the right of the borrower to rescind the reverse mortgage agreement.

(2) This subdivision does not prevent a lender from offering or referring borrowers for title insurance, hazard, flood, or other peril insurance, or other similar products that are customary and normal under a reverse mortgage loan.

(3) A lender or any other person who participates in the origination of a reverse mortgage loan to which this subdivision would apply, and who complies with paragraph (1) of subsection (n), and with subsection (o), of Section 1715z-20 of Title 12 of the United States Code, and any regulations and guidance promulgated under that section, as amended from time to time, in offering the loan, regardless of whether the loan is originated pursuant to the program authorized under Section 1715z-20 of Title 12 of the United States Code, and any regulations and guidance promulgated under that section, shall be deemed to have complied with this subdivision.

(j) Prior to accepting a final and complete application for a reverse mortgage the lender shall provide the borrower with a list of not fewer than 10 counseling agencies that are approved by the United States Department of Housing and Urban Development to engage in reverse mortgage counseling as provided in Subpart B of Part 214 of Title 24 of the Code of Federal Regulation. The counseling agency shall not receive any compensation, either directly or indirectly, from the lender or from any other person or entity involved in originating or servicing the mortgage or the sale of annuities, investments, long-term care insurance, or any other type of financial or insurance product. This subdivision does not prevent a counseling agency from receiving financial assistance that is unrelated to the offering or selling of a reverse mortgage loan and that is provided by the lender as part of charitable or philanthropic activities.

(k) A lender shall not accept a final and complete application for a reverse mortgage loan from a prospective applicant or assess any fees upon a prospective applicant until the lapse of seven days from the date of counseling, as evidenced by the counseling certification, and without first receiving certification from the applicant or the applicant's authorized representative that the applicant has received counseling from an agency as described in subdivision (j) and that the counseling was conducted in person, unless the certification specifies that the applicant elected to receive the counseling in a manner other than in person. The certification shall be signed by the borrower and the agency counselor, and shall include the date of the counseling and the name, address, and telephone number of both the counselor and the applicant. Electronic facsimile copy of the housing counseling certification satisfies the requirements of this subdivision. The lender shall maintain the certification in an accurate, reproducible, and accessible format for the term of the reverse mortgage.

(*l*) A lender shall not make a reverse mortgage loan without first complying with, or in the case of brokered loans ensuring compliance with, the requirements of Section 1632, if applicable. **Leg.H.** Added Stats 1997 ch 797 §1 (AB 456). Amended Stats 2006 ch 202 §2 (SB 1609), effective January 1, 2007; Stats 2009 ch 236 §3 (AB 329), effective January 1, 2010; Stats 2012 ch 641 §1 (AB 2010), effective January 1, 2013; Stats 2014 ch 854 §2 (AB 1700), effective January 1, 2015.

2014 Note: See Note following §1923.5.
2009 Note: This act shall be known as the Reverse Mortgage Elder Protection Act of 2009. Stats 2009 ch 236 (AB 329) §1.

§1923.3. Lien against property

A reverse mortgage shall constitute a lien against the subject property to the extent of all advances made pursuant to the reverse mortgage and all interest accrued on these advances, and that lien shall have priority over any lien filed or recorded after recordation of a reverse mortgage loan. **Leg.H.** Added Stats 1997 ch 797 §1 (AB 456).

§1923.4. Owner-occupied property

For the purposes of this chapter, a property shall be deemed to be owner-occupied, notwithstanding that the legal title to the property is held in the name of a trust, provided that the occupant of the property is a beneficiary of that trust. **Leg.H.** Added Stats 1997 ch 797 §1 (AB 456).

§1923.5. Notice to prospective borrower; Reverse mortgage worksheet guide

(a) No reverse mortgage loan application shall be taken by a lender unless the loan applicant, prior to receiving counseling, has received from the lender the following plain language statement in conspicuous 16-point type or larger, advising the prospective borrower about counseling prior to obtaining the reverse mortgage loan:

IMPORTANT NOTICE TO REVERSE MORTGAGE LOAN APPLICANT

A REVERSE MORTGAGE IS A COMPLEX FINANCIAL TRANSACTION. IF YOU DECIDE TO OBTAIN A REVERSE MORTGAGE LOAN, YOU WILL SIGN BINDING LEGAL DOCUMENTS THAT WILL HAVE IMPORTANT LEGAL AND FINANCIAL IMPLICATIONS FOR YOU AND YOUR ESTATE. IT IS THEREFORE IMPORTANT TO UNDERSTAND THE TERMS OF THE REVERSE MORTGAGE AND ITS EFFECT ON YOUR FUTURE NEEDS. BEFORE ENTERING INTO THIS TRANSACTION, YOU ARE REQUIRED TO CONSULT WITH AN INDEPENDENT REVERSE MORTGAGE LOAN COUNSELOR TO DISCUSS WHETHER OR NOT A REVERSE MORTGAGE IS RIGHT FOR YOU. A LIST OF APPROVED COUNSELORS WILL BE PROVIDED TO YOU BY THE LENDER.

SENIOR CITIZEN ADVOCACY GROUPS ADVISE AGAINST USING THE PROCEEDS OF A REVERSE MORTGAGE TO PURCHASE AN ANNUITY OR RELATED FINANCIAL PRODUCTS. IF YOU ARE CONSIDERING USING YOUR PROCEEDS FOR THIS PURPOSE, YOU SHOULD DISCUSS THE FINANCIAL IMPLICATIONS OF DOING SO WITH YOUR COUNSELOR AND FAMILY MEMBERS.

(b)(1) In addition to the plain language notice described in subdivision (a), no reverse mortgage loan application shall be taken by a lender unless the lender provides the prospective borrower, prior to his or her meeting with a counseling agency on reverse mortgages, with a reverse mortgage worksheet guide, or in the event that the prospective borrower seeks counseling prior to requesting a reverse mortgage loan application from the reverse mortgage lender, the counseling agency shall provide the prospective borrower with the following plain language reverse mortgage worksheet guide in 14-point type or larger:

Reverse Mortgage Worksheet Guide—Is a Reverse Mortgage Right for Me?

To decide if a recommended purchase of a reverse mortgage is right for you, consider all of your goals, needs, and available options. This self-evaluation worksheet has five essential questions for you to consider when deciding if a reverse mortgage is right for you.

Directions: The State of California advises you to carefully read and complete this worksheet, and bring it with you to your counseling session. You may make notes on a separate piece of paper with questions you may have about whether a reverse mortgage is right for you. During the counseling session, you can speak openly and confidentially with a professional reverse mortgage counselor, independent of the lender, who can help you understand what it means for you to become involved with this particular loan.

1. What happens to others in your home after you die or move out?
Rule: When the borrower dies, moves, or is absent from the home for 12 consecutive months, the loan may become due.
Considerations: Having a reverse mortgage affects the future of all those living with you. If the loan cannot be paid off, then the home will have to be sold in order to satisfy the lender. To determine if this is an issue for you, ask yourself:
(A) Who is currently living in the home with you?
(B) What will they do when you die or permanently move from the home?
(C) Have you discussed this with all those living with you or any family members?
(D) Who will pay off the loan, and have you discussed this with them?
(E) If your heirs do not have enough money to pay off the loan, the home will pass into foreclosure.
Do you need to discuss this with your counselor? Yes or No

2. Do you know that you can default on a reverse mortgage?
Rule: There are three continuous financial obligations. If you fail to keep up with your insurance, property taxes, and home maintenance, you will go into default. Uncured defaults lead to foreclosures.
Considerations: Will you have adequate resources and income to support your financial needs and obligations once you have removed all of your available equity with a reverse mortgage? To determine if this is an issue for you, ask yourself:
(A) Are you contemplating a lump-sum withdrawal?
(B) What other resources will you have once you have reached your equity withdrawal limit?
(C) Will you have funds to pay for unexpected medical expenses?

(D) Will you have the ability to finance alternative living accommodations, such as independent living, assisted living, or a long-term care nursing home?

(E) Will you have the ability to finance routine or catastrophic home repairs, especially if maintenance is a factor that may determine when the mortgage becomes payable?

Do you need to discuss this with your counselor? Yes or No

3. Have you fully explored other options?

Rule: Less costly options may exist.

Consideration: Reverse mortgages are compounding-interest loans, and the debt to the lender increases as time goes on. You may want to consider using less expensive alternatives or other assets you may have before you commit to a reverse mortgage. To determine if this is an issue for you, consider:

(A) Alternative financial options for seniors may include, but are not limited to, less costly home equity lines of credit, property tax deferral programs, or governmental aid programs.

(B) Other types of lending arrangements may be available and less costly. You may be able to use your home equity to secure loans from family members, friends, or would-be heirs.

Do you need to discuss this with your counselor? Yes or No

4. Are you intending to use the reverse mortgage to purchase a financial product?

Rule: Reverse mortgages are interest-accruing loans.

Considerations: Due to the high cost and increasing debt incurred by reverse mortgage borrowers, using home equity to finance investments is not suitable in most instances. To determine if this is an issue for you, consider:

(A) The cost of the reverse mortgage loan may exceed any financial gain from any product purchased.

(B) Will the financial product you are considering freeze or otherwise tie up your money?

(C) There may be high surrender fees, service charges, or undisclosed costs on the financial products purchased with the proceeds of a reverse mortgage.

(D) Has the sales agent offering the financial product discussed suitability with you?

Do you need to discuss this with your counselor? Yes or No

5. Do you know that a reverse mortgage may impact your eligibility for government assistance programs?

Rule: Income received from investments will count against individuals seeking government assistance.

Considerations: Converting your home equity into investments may create nonexempt asset statuses. To determine if this is an issue for you, consider:

(A) There are state and federal taxes on the income investments financed through home equity.

(B) If you go into a nursing home for an extended period of time, the reverse mortgage loan will become due, the home may be sold, and any proceeds from the sale of the home may make you ineligible for government benefits.

(C) If the homeowner is a Medi-Cal beneficiary, a reverse mortgage may make it difficult to transfer ownership of the home, thus resulting in Medi-Cal recovery.

Do you need to discuss this with your counselor? Yes or No

(2) The reverse mortgage worksheet guide required in paragraph (1) shall be signed by the agency counselor, if the counseling is done in person, and by the prospective borrower and returned to the lender along with the certification of counseling required under subdivision (k) of Section 1923.2, and the loan application shall not be approved until the signed reverse mortgage worksheet guide is provided to the lender. A copy of the reverse mortgage worksheet guide shall be provided to the borrower. **Leg.H.** Added Stats 1997 ch 797 §1 (AB 456). Amended Stats 2006 ch 202 §3 (SB 1609), effective January 1, 2007; Stats 2009 ch 236 §4 (AB 329), effective January 1, 2010; Stats 2014 ch 854 §3 (AB 1700), effective January 1, 2015.

2014 Note: (a) A reverse mortgage is a loan that allows a homeowner to convert home equity into tax-free cash payments. More than 90 percent of all reverse mortgages are obtained through the Home Equity Conversion Mortgage (HECM) program sponsored by the United States Department of Housing and Urban Development. Many senior citizens use reverse mortgage payments to supplement retirement income or pay medical expenses. Although the HECM program has been in existence since 1989, the program has seen rapid growth only in the past few years. As the population ages, this growth rate is expected to accelerate. The growth rate is also expected to increase as sales agents and lenders turn from the declining subprime and conventional mortgage market to the rapidly growing market for reverse mortgages.

(b) Because reverse mortgage decisionmaking involves a number of complex issues, before committing to a loan every senior should contemplate possible negative consequences. Every prospective purchaser of a reverse mortgage should study and discuss with an HUD-approved reverse mortgage counselor the items in the reverse mortgage worksheet guide specified in subdivision (b) of Section 1923.5 of the Civil Code.

(c) In specifying these requirements, it is not the intent of the Legislature to discourage the use of reverse mortgages, which can provide substantial benefits to senior citizens. Rather, these requirements seek to ensure that senior citizens will make informed decisions and that persons who offer, sell, or arrange the sale of reverse mortgages to senior citizens will act in the best interest of reverse mortgage loan borrowers. Stats 2014 ch 854 (AB 1700) §1.

2009 Note: This act shall be known as the Reverse Mortgage Elder Protection Act of 2009. Stats 2009 ch 236 (AB 329) §1.

§1923.6. Disclosure duty

The lender shall be presumed to have satisfied any disclosure duty imposed by this chapter if the lender provides a disclosure statement in the same form as provided in this chapter. **Leg.H.** Added Stats 1997 ch 797 §1 (AB 456).

§1923.7. Failure to comply

No arrangement, transfer, or lien subject to this chapter shall be invalidated solely because of the failure of a lender to comply with any provision of this chapter. However, nothing in this section shall preclude the application of any other existing civil remedies provided by law. **Leg.H.** Added Stats 1997 ch 797 §1 (AB 456).

§1923.9. Treatment of payments and funds

(a) To the extent that implementation of this section does not conflict with federal law resulting in the loss of federal funding, reverse mortgage loan payments made to a borrower shall be treated as proceeds from a loan and not as income for the purpose of determining eligibility and benefits under means-tested programs of aid to individuals.

(b) Undisbursed reverse mortgage funds shall be treated as equity in the borrower's home and not as proceeds from a loan, resources, or assets for the purpose of determining eligibility and benefits under means-tested programs of aid to individuals.

(c) This section applies to any law or program relating to payments, allowances, benefits, or services provided on a means-tested basis, by this state, including, but not limited to, optional state supplements to the federal supplemental security income program, low-income energy assistance, property tax relief, general assistance, and medical assistance only to the extent this section does not conflict with Title 19 of the federal Social Security Act.

(d) For the purposes of this section, "means-tested programs and aid to individuals" includes, but is not limited to, programs set forth in Chapter 2 (commencing with Section 11200) of Part 3 of Division 9, and Part 5 (commencing with Section 17000) of Division 9, of the Welfare and Institutions Code. **Leg.H.** Added Stats 1997 ch 797 §1 (AB 456).

§1923.10. Applicability

This chapter shall only apply to those reverse mortgage loans executed on or after January 1, 1998. **Leg.H.** Added Stats 1997 ch 797 §1 (AB 456).

TITLE 4.5
APPRAISALS OF REAL PROPERTY
[REPEALED]

§1922. [Section repealed 1992]

Leg.H. Added Stats 1986 ch 372 §1, operative January 1, 1988. Repealed Stats 1990 ch 491 §2 (AB 527), as amended Stats 1991 ch 84 §6 (SB 1028), effective June 30, 1991, operative by January 1, 1992. The repealed section related to citation of title.

§1922.1. [Section repealed 1992]

Leg.H. Added Stats 1986 ch 372 §1, operative January 1, 1988. Amended Stats 1987 ch 420 §1. Repealed Stats 1990 ch 491 §2 (AB 527), as amended Stats 1991 ch 84 §6 (SB 1028), effective June 30, 1991, operative by January 1, 1992. The repealed section related to definitions.

§1922.2. [Section repealed 1992]

Leg.H. Added Stats 1986 ch 372 §1, operative January 1, 1988. Amended Stats 1987 ch 420 §2. Repealed Stats 1990 ch 491 §2 (AB 527), as amended Stats 1991 ch 84 §6 (SB 1028), effective June 30, 1991, operative by January 1, 1992. The repealed section related to duties of persons performing certified appraisals of real property.

§1922.4. [Section repealed 1992]

Leg.H. Added Stats 1986 ch 372 §1, operative January 1, 1988. Repealed Stats 1990 ch 491 §2 (AB 527), as amended Stats 1991 ch 84 §6 (SB 1028), effective June 30, 1991, operative by January 1, 1992. The repealed section related to additional duties.

§1922.6. [Section repealed 1992]

Leg.H. Added Stats 1986 ch 372 §1, operative January 1, 1988. Repealed Stats 1990 ch 491 §2 (AB 527), as amended Stats 1991 ch 84 §6 (SB 1028), effective June 30, 1991, operative by January 1, 1992. The repealed section related to certified appraisal report.

§1922.8. [Section repealed 1992]

Leg.H. Added Stats 1986 ch 372 §1, operative January 1, 1988. Repealed Stats 1990 ch 491 §2 (AB 527), as amended Stats 1991 ch 84 §6 (SB 1028), effective June 30, 1991, operative by January 1, 1992. The repealed section related to prohibitions.

§1922.10. [Section repealed 1992]

Leg.H. Added Stats 1986 ch 372 §1, operative January 1, 1988. Repealed Stats 1990 ch 491 §2 (AB 527), as amended Stats 1991 ch 84 §6 (SB 1028), effective June 30, 1991, operative by January 1, 1992. The repealed section related to retention of documents.

§1922.11. [Section repealed 1992]

Leg.H. Added Stats 1986 ch 372 §1, operative January 1, 1988. Repealed Stats 1990 ch 491 §2 (AB 527), as amended Stats 1991 ch 84 §6 (SB 1028), effective June 30, 1991, operative by January 1, 1992. The repealed section related to action for damages and equitable relief.

§1922.12. [Section repealed 1987]

Leg.H. Added Stats 1986 ch 372 §1, operative January 1, 1988. Repealed Stats 1987 ch 699 §1. The repealed section related to certified appraisal or certified appraisal report.

§1922.13. [Section repealed 1992]

Leg.H. Added Stats 1988 ch 179 §1. Repealed Stats 1990 ch 491 §2 (AB 527), as amended Stats 1991 ch 84 §6 (SB 1028), effective June 30, 1991, operative by January 1, 1992. The repealed section related to certified appraisal of property containing specified number of residential units.

§1922.14. [Section repealed 1992]

Leg.H. Added Stats 1986 ch 372 §1, operative January 1, 1988. Repealed Stats 1990 ch 491 §2 (AB 527), as amended Stats 1991 ch 84 §6 (SB 1028), effective June 30, 1991, operative by January 1, 1992. The repealed section related to severability.

TITLE 5
HIRING

Chapter 1. Hiring in General.
Chapter 1.5. Rental Passenger Vehicle Transactions.
Chapter 2. Hiring of Real Property.
Chapter 2.4. Occupancy in interim homelessness programs.
Chapter 2.5. Transitional Housing Participant Misconduct [First of two].
Chapter 2.5. Water Service [Second of two].
Chapter 2.6. Commercial Rental Control.
Chapter 2.7. Residential Rent Control.
Chapter 2.8. Bed Bug Infestations.
Chapter 3. Hiring of Personal Property.
Chapter 4. Identification of Property Owners.
Chapter 4.5. Disposition of Personal Property Upon Request of Tenant.
Chapter 5. Disposition of Personal Property Remaining on Premises at Termination of Tenancy.
Chapter 5.5. Disposition of Property Remaining on Premises at Termination of Commercial Tenancy.
Chapter 6. Assignment and Sublease.
Chapter 7. Use Restrictions.

CHAPTER 1
HIRING IN GENERAL

Hiring, what. §1925.
Products of thing. §1926.
Quiet possession. §1927.
Degree of care, etc., on part of hirer. §1928.
Duty to repair. §1929.
Thing let for a particular purpose. §1930.
When letter may terminate the hiring. §1931.
When hirer may terminate the hiring. §1932.
When hiring terminates. §1933.
When terminated by death, etc., of party. §1934.
Nursing or convalescent home accommodations terminated by death of patient. §1934.5.
Apportionment of hire. §1935.
Verification of inspection by Certified Access Specialist (CASp); Provision of CASp report to lessee or tenant; Provision of disability access inspection certificate and inspection report or specified statement. §1938.

§1925. Hiring, what

Hiring is a contract by which one gives to another the temporary possession and use of property, other than money, for reward, and the latter agrees to return the same to the former at a future time. **Leg.H.** Enacted Stats 1872.

§1926. Products of thing

The products of a thing hired, during the hiring, belong to the hirer. **Leg.H.** Enacted Stats 1872.

§1927. Quiet possession

An agreement to let upon hire binds the letter to secure to the hirer the quiet possession of the thing hired during the term of the hiring, against all persons lawfully claiming the same. **Leg.H.** Enacted Stats 1872.

§1928. Degree of care, etc., on part of hirer

The hirer of a thing must use ordinary care for its preservation in safety and in good condition. **Leg.H.** Enacted Stats 1872.

§1929. Duty to repair

The hirer of a thing must repair all deteriorations or injuries thereto occasioned by his want of ordinary care. **Leg.H.** Enacted Stats 1872. Amended Stats 1905 ch 454 §1.

§1930. Thing let for a particular purpose

When a thing is let for a particular purpose the hirer must not use it for any other purpose; and if he does, he is liable to the letter for all damages resulting from such use, or the letter may treat the contract as thereby rescinded. **Leg.H.** Enacted Stats 1872. Amended Stats 1905 ch 454 §2.

§1931. When letter may terminate the hiring

The letter of a thing may terminate the hiring and reclaim the thing before the end of the term agreed upon:

1. When the hirer uses or permits a use of the thing hired in a manner contrary to the agreement of the parties; or,

2. When the hirer does not, within a reasonable time after request, make such repairs as he is bound to make. **Leg.H.** Enacted Stats 1872.

§1932. When hirer may terminate the hiring

The hirer of a thing may terminate the hiring before the end of the term agreed upon:

1. When the letter does not, within a reasonable time after request, fulfill his obligations, if any, as to placing and securing the hirer in the quiet possession of the thing hired, or putting it into good condition, or repairing; or,

2. When the greater part of the thing hired, or that part which was and which the letter had at the time of the hiring reason to believe was the material inducement to the hirer to enter into the contract, perishes from any other cause than the want of ordinary care of the hirer. **Leg.H.** Enacted Stats 1872. Amended Stats 1905 ch 454 §3.

§1933. When hiring terminates

The hiring of a thing terminates:

1. At the end of the term agreed upon;
2. By the mutual consent of the parties;
3. By the hirer acquiring a title to the thing hired superior to that of the letter; or,
4. By the destruction of the thing hired. **Leg.H.** Enacted Stats 1872.

§1934. When terminated by death, etc., of party

If the hiring of a thing is terminable at the pleasure of one of the parties, it is terminated by notice to the other of his death or incapacity to contract. In other cases it is not terminated thereby. **Leg.H.** Enacted Stats 1872.

§1934.5. Nursing or convalescent home accommodations terminated by death of patient

Notwithstanding the provisions of Section 1934, the hiring of accommodations from month to month in a nursing or convalescent home shall be terminated by the death of the patient by or for whom the hiring was made. The hirer or his heir, legatee, or personal representative shall not be liable for any rent due for such accommodations under the hiring agreement beyond that rent due for the date on which such patient died. No advance payment of rent made by the hirer shall be subject to the claim of, or retention by, the nursing or convalescent home and shall be returned to the heir, legatee, or personal representative no later than two weeks after such patient has died. Any provision in the hiring agreement by which the hirer agrees to modify or waive any of his rights under this section shall be void as contrary to public policy.

The provisions of this section shall be applicable to all hiring agreements executed on or after January 1, 1979. **Leg.H.** Added Stats 1978 ch 628 §1.

§1935. Apportionment of hire

When the hiring of a thing is terminated before the time originally agreed upon, the hirer must pay the due proportion of the hire for such use as he has actually made of the thing, unless such use is merely nominal, and of no benefit to him. **Leg.H.** Enacted Stats 1872.

§1936. Liability for rented vehicle; Rental contract provisions; Rental rates; Foreign renter; Acceptance of service of process [Repealed]

Leg.H. Added Stats 1996 ch 992 §2 (SB 1070), operative January 1, 2002. Amended Stats 2001 ch 661 §1 (AB 491), operative January 1, 2002. Stats 2002 ch 948 §2 (AB 2457), repealed January 1, 2006; Stats 2004 ch 317 §1 (AB 2840), repealed January 1, 2006; Stats 2005 ch 82 §2 (AB 987), effective January 1, 2006; Stats 2007 ch 44 §1 (SB 641), effective January 1, 2008; Stats 2008 ch 179 §31 (SB 1498), ch 228 §1 (AB 2142), ch 620 §1 (SB 1510) (ch 620 prevails), effective January 1, 2009; Stats 2009 ch 140 §28 (AB 1164), effective January 1, 2010; Stats 2010 ch 642 §1 (SB 1192), effective January 1, 2011; Stats 2011 ch 531 §1 (AB 621), effective January 1, 2012, repealed January 1, 2015; Stats 2012 ch 32 §2 (SB 1006), effective June 27, 2012, repealed January 1, 2015; Stats 2013 ch 549 §1 (AB 359), effective January 1, 2014, repealed January 1, 2015; Stats 2014 ch 913 §5.2 (AB 2747), effective January 1, 2015, repealed January 1, 2020; Stats 2015 ch 333 §1 (AB 675), effective January 1, 2016; Repealed Stats 2016 ch 183 §1 (AB 2051), effective January 1, 2017.

Prior Law: Former CC §1936, similar to the present section, was added Stats 2011 ch 531 §2, effective January 1, 2012, operative January 1, 2015, amended Stats 2012 ch 32 §3, effective June 27, 2012, Stats 2013 ch 549 §2, effective January 1, 2014, operative January 1, 2015, Stats 2014 ch 417 §1, effective January 1, 2015, ch 913 §5.7, effective January 1, 2015, operative January 1, 2020, and repealed Stats 2015 ch 333 §2, effective January 1, 2016.

Former §1936, similar to the present section, was added Stats 1988 ch 1523 §1, amended Stats 1992 ch 1184 §1, Stats 1996 ch 992 §1, and repealed operative January 1, 2002, by its own terms.

There was another section of this number, similar to the present section, which was added Stats 2002 ch. 938 sec. 3, effective January 1, 2003, to become operative January 1, 2006, and was repealed prior to becoming operative Stats 2005 ch. 82, sec. 3.

Former CC §1936 was added in 2011 and repealed Stats 2015 ch 333 (AB 675) §2.

Former CC §1936 was added in 2002, operative January 1, 2006, and repealed Stats 2005 ch 82 (AB 987) §3.

Former CC §1936 was added in 1988 and repealed operative January 1, 2002, by its own provisions. Stats 1996 ch 992 §1.

§1936.01. [Section repealed 2016]

Leg.H. Added Stats 2006 ch 790 §1 (AB 2592), effective January 1, 2007. Amended Stats 2014 ch 401 §3 (AB 2763), effective January 1, 2015, ch 417 §2 (AB 1981), effective January 1, 2015. Repealed Stats 2015 ch 333 §3 (AB 675), effective January 1, 2016. The repealed section related to rental car rate advertising and permissible fees.

§1936.015. [Section repealed 2016]

Leg.H. Added Stats 2009-10 2nd Ex Sess ch 8 §1 (SBX2-10), effective May 21, 2009. Amended Stats 2009 ch 156 §1 (SB 348), effective August 21, 2009, operative term contingent; Stats 2014 ch 417 §3 (AB 1981), effective January 1, 2015. Repealed Stats 2015 ch 333 §4 (AB 675), effective January 1, 2016. The repealed section related to requirements of rental companies to include increased vehicle license fees in rental contract disclosures, reconciliation of increased vehicle license fees, and increased vehicle license recovery fees.

§1936.05. Definitions; Exception for renters of business program sponsors; Actions; Waiver; Compliance with Section 1936 [Repealed]

Leg.H. Added Stats 2004 ch 536 §1 (AB 2761). Amended Stats 2014 ch 417 §4 (AB 1981), effective January 1, 2015; Stats 2015 ch 333 §5 (AB 675), effective January 1, 2016. Repealed Stats 2016 ch 183 §2 (AB 2051), effective January 1, 2017.

§1936.1. Documentation related to danger of rollover crashes required for renters of 15-passenger vans [Repealed]

Leg.H. Added Stats 2004 ch 883 §1 (AB 2503). Repealed Stats 2016 ch 183 §3 (AB 2051), effective January 1, 2017.

§1936.5. Exception to rental requirements of Vehicle Code Section 14608 for certain rental companies [Repealed]

Leg.H. Added Stats 2012 ch 862 §1 (AB 2189), effective January 1, 2013. Repealed Stats 2016 ch 183 §4 (AB 2051), effective January 1, 2017.

Prior Law: Former CC §1936.5, relating to additional fees by rental car companies doing business with specified customers at San Jose International Airport, was added Stats 1999 ch 760 §1 (SB 1228), and repealed Stats 2007 ch 44 §2 (SB 641), effective January 1, 2008.

Former CC §1936.5, similar to the present section, was added Stats 2012 ch 406 §1, effective January 1, 2013, and repealed Stats 2015 ch 303 §27, effective January 1, 2016.

Former CC §1936.5 was added Stats 2012 ch 406 and repealed Stats 2015 ch 303 (AB 731) §27.

Former CC §1936.5 was added in 1999 and repealed Stats 2007 ch 44 (SB 641) §2.

§1938. Verification of inspection by Certified Access Specialist (CASp); Provision of CASp report to lessee or tenant; Provision of disability access inspection certificate and inspection report or specified statement

(a) A commercial property owner or lessor shall state on every lease form or rental agreement executed on or after January 1, 2017, whether or not the subject premises have undergone inspection by a Certified Access Specialist (CASp).

(b) If the subject premises have undergone inspection by a CASp and, to the best of the commercial property owner's or lessor's knowledge, there have been no modifications or alterations completed or commenced between the date of the inspection and the date of the lease or rental agreement that have impacted the subject premises' compliance with construction-related accessibility standards, the commercial property owner or lessor shall provide, prior to execution of the lease or rental agreement, a copy of any report prepared by the CASp with an agreement from the prospective lessee or tenant that information in the report shall remain confidential, except as necessary for the tenant to complete repairs and corrections of violations of construction-related accessibility standards that the lessee or tenant agrees to make.

(c) Making any repairs or modifications necessary to correct violations of construction-related accessibility standards that are noted in a CASp report is presumed to be the responsibility of the commercial property owner or lessor, unless otherwise mutually agreed upon by the commercial property owner or lessor and the lessee or tenant. The prospective lessee or tenant shall have the opportunity to review any CASp report prior to execution of the lease or rental agreement. If the report is not provided to the prospective lessee or tenant at least 48 hours prior to execution of the lease or rental agreement, the prospective lessee or tenant shall have the right to rescind the lease or rental agreement, based upon the information contained in the report, for 72 hours after execution of the agreement.

(d) If the subject premises have been issued an inspection report by a CASp, as described in paragraph (1) of subdivision (a) of Section 55.53, indicating that it meets applicable standards, as defined in paragraph (4) of subdivision (a) of Section 55.52, the commercial property owner or lessor shall provide a copy of the current disability access inspection certificate and any inspection report to the lessee or tenant not already provided pursuant to subdivision (b) within seven days of the date of the execution of the lease form or rental agreement.

(e) If the subject premises have not been issued a disability access inspection certificate, as described in subdivision (e) of Section 55.53, the commercial property owner or lessor shall state the following on the lease form or rental agreement:

"A Certified Access Specialist (CASp) can inspect the subject premises and determine whether the subject premises comply with all of the applicable construction-related accessibility standards under state law. Although state law does not require a CASp inspection of the subject premises, the commercial property owner or lessor may not prohibit the lessee or tenant from obtaining a CASp inspection of the subject premises for the occupancy or potential occupancy of the lessee or tenant, if requested by the lessee or tenant. The parties shall mutually agree on the arrangements for the time and manner of the CASp inspection, the payment of the fee for the CASp inspection, and the cost of making any repairs necessary to correct violations of construction-related accessibility standards within the premises."

(f) As used in this section, "commercial property" means property that is offered for rent or lease to persons operating, or intending to operate, a place of public accommodation as defined in Section 202 of Chapter 2 of Part 2 of Title 24 of the California Code of Regulations, or a facility to which the general public is invited, at those premises. **Leg.H.** Added Stats 2012 ch 383 §12 (SB 1186), effective September 19, 2012. Amended Stats 2016 ch 379 §1 (AB 2093), effective September 16, 2016; Stats 2017 ch 87 §1 (AB 1148), effective July 21, 2017; Stats 2018 ch 92 §37 (SB 1289), effective January 1, 2019.

CHAPTER 1.5
RENTAL PASSENGER VEHICLE TRANSACTIONS

Definitions. § 1939.01.
Renter responsibilities for rented vehicle. §1939.03.
Total amount of renter's liability from damage to rented vehicle. §1939.05.
Claims for damage or loss; Limits; mitigation of damages; Insurance coverage for renter; Chapter application. §1939.07.
Damage waiver; Contents; Application; Disclosure by rental company; Sale. §1939.09.
Purchase of damage waiver, Optional insurance. §1939.13.
Recovery of claim from damage or loss of vehicle by rental company. §1939.15.
Collection of customer facility charge. §1939.17.
Quotes, charges imposed by rental company; Mandatory charges; Rate advertisements. §1939.19.
Exclusion of rental vehicle charges pricing information disclosed to consumers not violation of Section 1770. § 1939.20.
Separate quotation and imposition of additional charges for renter of business program sponsor. §1939.21.
Electronic communications between rental company and renter. §1939.22.
Prohibition against use of electronic surveillance technology; Exceptions. §1939.23.
Action for violation of chapter; Attorney's fees. §1939.25.
Action for loss due to theft; Jurisdiction. §1939.27.
Waiver of provisions of chapter prohibited. §1939.29.
Disclosure requirements under rental company membership program. §1939.31.
Service of complaint by foreign renter. §1939.33.
Advisories for 15-passenger van renters. §1939.35.
Exceptions to rental company under Section 14608 of Vehicle Code. §1939.37.
Commercial airport facility customer facility charge. § 1939.38.
Personal vehicle sharing program vehicle certification. § 1939.39.

§1939.01. Definitions

For the purpose of this chapter, the following definitions shall apply:

(a) "Rental company" means a person or entity in the business of renting passenger vehicles to the public.

(b) "Renter" means any person in a manner obligated under a contract for the lease or hire of a passenger vehicle from a rental company for a period of less than 30 days.

(c) "Additional mandatory charges" means any separately stated charges that the rental company requires the renter to pay to hire or lease the vehicle for the period of time to which the rental rate applies, which are imposed by a governmental entity and specifically relate to the operation of a rental vehicle business, including, but not limited to, a customer facility charge, airport concession fee, tourism commission assessment, vehicle license recovery fee, or other government-imposed taxes or fees.

(d) "Airport concession fee" means a charge collected by a rental company from a renter that is the renter's proportionate share of the amount paid by the rental company to the owner or operator of an airport for the right or privilege of conducting a vehicle rental business on the airport's premises.

(e) "Authorized driver" means all of the following:
(1) The renter.
(2) The renter's spouse, if that person is a licensed driver and satisfies the rental company's minimum age requirement.
(3) The renter's employer or coworker, if the employer or coworker is engaged in business activity with the renter, is a licensed driver, and satisfies the rental company's minimum age requirement.
(4) A person expressly listed by the rental company on that renter's contract as an authorized driver.

(f) "Customer facility charge" means any fee, including an alternative fee, required by an airport to be collected by a rental company from a renter pursuant to Section 50474.21 of the Government Code.

(g) "Damage waiver" means a rental company's agreement not to hold a renter liable for all or any portion of any damage or loss related to the rented vehicle, any loss of use of the rented vehicle, or any storage, impound, towing, or administrative charges.

(h) "Electronic surveillance technology" means a technological method or system used to observe, monitor, or collect information, including telematics, Global Positioning System (GPS), wireless technology, or location-based technologies. "Electronic surveillance technology" does not include event data recorders (EDR), sensing and diagnostic modules (SDM), or other systems that are used either:

(1) For the purpose of identifying, diagnosing, or monitoring functions related to the potential need to repair, service, or perform maintenance on the rental vehicle.

(2) As part of the vehicle's airbag sensing and diagnostic system in order to capture safety systems-related data for retrieval after a crash has occurred or in the event that the collision sensors are activated to prepare the decisionmaking computer to make the determination to deploy or not to deploy the airbag.

(i) "Estimated time for replacement" means the number of hours of labor, or fraction thereof, needed to replace damaged vehicle parts as set forth in collision damage estimating guides generally used in the vehicle repair business and commonly known as "crash books."

(j) "Estimated time for repair" means a good faith estimate of the reasonable number of hours of labor, or fraction thereof, needed to repair damaged vehicle parts.

(k) "Membership program" means a service offered by a rental company that permits customers to bypass the rental counter and go directly to the vehicle previously reserved or select an alternate vehicle. A membership program shall meet all of the following requirements:

(1) The renter initiates enrollment by completing an application on which the renter can specify a preference for type of vehicle and acceptance or declination of optional services.

(2) The rental company fully discloses, prior to the enrollee's first rental as a participant in the program, all terms and conditions of the rental agreement as well as all required disclosures.

(3) The renter may terminate enrollment at any time.

(4) The rental company fully explains to the renter that designated preferences, as well as acceptance or declination of optional services, may be changed by the renter at any time for the next and future rentals.

(5) An employee is available at the lot where the renter takes possession of the vehicle, to receive any change in the rental agreement from the renter.

(*l*) "Passenger vehicle" or "vehicle" means a "passenger vehicle" as defined in Section 465 of the Vehicle Code.

(m) "Personal vehicle sharing program" means a person or entity that for monetary compensation facilitates sharing or renting passenger vehicles to the public, including via a peer-to-peer internet website, application, or other platform that connects a vehicle owner with a vehicle driver to facilitate sharing or renting a vehicle for consideration, and includes a personal vehicle sharing program as defined in Section 11580.24 of the Insurance Code.

(n) "Quote" means an estimated cost of rental provided by a rental company or a third party to a potential customer that is based on information provided by the potential customer and used to generate an estimated cost of rental, including, but not limited to, potential dates of rental, locations, or classes of vehicle.

(o) "Tourism commission assessment" means the charge collected by a rental company from a renter that has been established by the California Travel and Tourism Commission pursuant to Section 13995.65 of the Government Code.

(p) "Vehicle license fee" means the tax imposed pursuant to the Vehicle License Fee Law (Part 5 (commencing with Section 10701) of Division 2 of the Revenue and Taxation Code).

(q) "Vehicle registration fee" means any fee imposed pursuant to any provision of Chapter 6 (commencing with Section 9101) of Division 3 of the Vehicle Code or any other law that imposes a fee upon the registration of vehicles in this state.

(r) "Vehicle license recovery fee" means a charge that seeks to recover the amount of any vehicle license fee and vehicle registration fee paid by a rental company for the particular class of vehicle being rented. If imposed, the vehicle license recovery fee shall be separately stated as a single charge in the quote and rental contract. **Leg.H.** Added Stats 2016 ch 183 §5 (AB 2051), effective January 1, 2017. Amended Stats 2023 ch 547 §1 (AB 893), effective January 1, 2024.

§1939.03. Renter responsibilities for rented vehicle

Except as limited by Section 1939.05, a rental company and a renter may agree that the renter will be responsible for no more than all of the following:

(a) Physical or mechanical damage to the rented vehicle up to its fair market value, as determined in the customary market for the sale of that vehicle, resulting from collision regardless of the cause of the damage.

(b) Loss due to theft of the rented vehicle up to its fair market value, as determined in the customary market for the sale of that vehicle, provided that the rental company establishes by clear and convincing evidence that the renter or the authorized driver failed to exercise ordinary care while in possession of the vehicle. In addition, the renter shall be presumed to have no liability for any loss due to theft if (1) an authorized driver has possession of the ignition key furnished by the rental company or an authorized driver establishes that the ignition key furnished by the rental company was not in the vehicle at the time of the theft, and (2) an authorized driver files an official report of the theft with the police or other law enforcement agency within 24 hours of learning of the theft and reasonably cooperates with the rental company and the police or other law enforcement agency in providing information concerning the theft. The presumption set forth in this subdivision is a presumption affecting the burden of proof which the rental company may rebut by establishing that an authorized driver committed, or aided and abetted the commission of, the theft.

(c) Physical damage to the rented vehicle up to its fair market value, as determined in the customary market for the sale of that vehicle, resulting from vandalism occurring after, or in connection with, the theft of the rented vehicle. However, the renter shall have no liability for any damage due to vandalism if the renter would have no liability for theft pursuant to subdivision (b).

(d) Physical damage to the rented vehicle up to a total of five hundred dollars ($500) resulting from vandalism unrelated to the theft of the rented vehicle.

(e) Actual charges for towing, storage, and impound fees paid by the rental company if the renter is liable for damage or loss.

(f) An administrative charge, which shall include the cost of appraisal and all other costs and expenses incident to the damage, loss, repair, or replacement of the rented vehicle. **Leg.H.** Added Stats 2016 ch 183 §5 (AB 2051), effective January 1, 2017.

§1939.05. Total amount of renter's liability from damage to rented vehicle

(a) The total amount of the renter's liability to the rental company resulting from damage to the rented vehicle shall not exceed the sum of the following:

(1) The estimated cost of parts which the rental company would have to pay to replace damaged vehicle parts.

(2) The estimated cost of labor to replace damaged vehicle parts, which shall not exceed the product of (A) the rate for labor usually paid by the rental company to replace vehicle parts of the type that were damaged and (B) the estimated time for replacement.

(3) The estimated cost of labor to repair damaged vehicle parts, which shall not exceed the lesser of the following:

(A) The product of the rate for labor usually paid by the rental company to repair vehicle parts of the type that were damaged and the estimated time for repair.

(B) The sum of the estimated labor and parts costs determined under paragraphs (1) and (2) to replace the same vehicle parts.

(4) Actual charges for towing, storage, and impound fees paid by the rental company.

(b) For purposes of subdivision (a), all discounts and price reductions or adjustments that are or will be received by the rental company shall be subtracted from the estimate to the extent not already incorporated in the estimate, or otherwise promptly credited or refunded to the renter.

(c) For the purpose of converting the estimated time for repair into the same units of time in which the rental rate is expressed, a day shall be deemed to consist of eight hours.

(d) The administrative charge described in subdivision (f) of Section 1939.03 shall not exceed (1) fifty dollars ($50) if the total estimated cost for parts and labor is more than one hundred dollars ($100) up to and including five hundred dollars ($500), (2) one hundred dollars ($100) if the total estimated cost for parts and labor exceeds five hundred dollars ($500) up to and including one thousand five hundred dollars ($1,500), or (3) one hundred fifty dollars ($150) if the total estimated cost for parts and labor exceeds one thousand five hundred dollars ($1,500). An administrative charge shall not be imposed if the total estimated cost of parts and labor is one hundred dollars ($100) or less.

(e) The total amount of an authorized driver's liability to the rental company, if any, for damage occurring during the authorized driver's operation of the rented vehicle shall not exceed the amount of the renter's liability under this section.

(f) A rental company shall not recover from an authorized driver an amount exceeding the renter's liability under this section. **Leg.H.** Added Stats 2016 ch 183 §5 (AB 2051), effective January 1, 2017.

§1939.07. Claims for damage or loss; Limits; mitigation of damages; Insurance coverage for renter; Chapter application

(a) A claim against a renter resulting from damage or loss, excluding loss of use, to a rental vehicle shall be reasonably and rationally related to the actual loss incurred. A rental company shall mitigate damages where possible and shall not assert or collect a claim for physical damage which exceeds the actual costs of the repairs performed or the estimated cost of repairs, if the rental company chooses not to repair the vehicle, including all discounts and price reductions. However, if the vehicle is a total loss vehicle, the claim shall not exceed the total loss vehicle value established in accordance with procedures that are customarily used by insurance companies when paying claims on total loss vehicles, less the proceeds from salvaging the vehicle, if those proceeds are retained by the rental company.

(b) If insurance coverage exists under the renter's applicable personal or business insurance policy and the coverage is confirmed during regular business hours, the renter may require that the rental company submit any claims to the renter's applicable personal or business insurance carrier. The rental company shall not make any written or oral representations that it will not present claims or negotiate with the renter's insurance carrier. For purposes of this subdivision, confirmation of coverage includes telephone confirmation from insurance company representatives during regular business hours. Upon request of the renter and after confirmation of coverage, the amount of claim shall be resolved between the insurance carrier and the rental company. The renter shall remain responsible for payment to the rental company for any loss sustained that the renter's applicable personal or business insurance policy does not cover.

(c) A rental company shall not recover from an authorized driver for an item described in Section 1939.03 to the extent the rental company obtains recovery from another person.

(d) This chapter applies only to the maximum liability of an authorized driver to the rental company resulting from damage to the rented vehicle and not to the liability of another person. **Leg.H.** Added Stats 2016 ch 183 §5 (AB 2051), effective January 1, 2017.

§1939.09. Damage waiver; Contents; Application; Disclosure by rental company; Sale

(a)(1) Except as provided in subdivision (b), a damage waiver shall provide or, if not expressly stated in writing, shall be deemed to provide that the renter has no liability for damage, loss, loss of use, or a cost or expense incident thereto.

(2) Except as provided in subdivision (b), every limitation, exception, or exclusion to a damage waiver is void and unenforceable.

(b) A rental company may provide in the rental contract that a damage waiver does not apply under any of the following circumstances:

(1) Damage or loss results from an authorized driver's (A) intentional, willful, wanton, or reckless conduct, (B) operation of the vehicle under the influence of drugs or alcohol in violation of Section 23152 of the Vehicle Code, (C) towing or pushing anything, or (D) operation of the vehicle on an unpaved road if the damage or loss is a direct result of the road or driving conditions.

(2) Damage or loss occurs while the vehicle is (A) used for commercial hire, (B) used in connection with conduct that could be properly charged as a felony, (C) involved in a speed test or contest or in driver training activity, (D) operated by a person other than an authorized driver, or (E) operated outside the United States.

(3) An authorized driver who has (A) provided fraudulent information to the rental company, or (B) provided false information and the rental company would not have rented the vehicle if it had instead received true information.

(c)(1) A rental company that offers or provides a damage waiver for any consideration in addition to the rental rate shall clearly and conspicuously disclose the following information in the rental contract or holder in which the contract is placed and, also, in signs posted at the location where the renter signs the rental contract, and, for renters who are enrolled in the rental company's membership program, in a sign that shall be posted in a location clearly visible to those renters as they enter the location where their reserved rental vehicles are parked or near the exit of the bus or other conveyance that transports the enrollee to a reserved vehicle: (A) the nature of the renter's liability, such as liability for all collision damage regardless of cause, (B) the extent of the renter's liability, such as liability for damage or loss up to a specified amount, (C) the renter's personal insurance policy or the credit card used to pay for the vehicle rental transaction may provide coverage for all or a portion of the renter's potential liability, (D) the renter should consult with their insurer to determine the scope of insurance coverage, including the amount of the deductible, if any, for which the renter is obligated, (E) the renter may purchase an optional damage waiver to cover all liability, subject to whatever exceptions the rental company expressly lists that are permitted under subdivision (b), and (F) the range of charges for the damage waiver.

(2) In addition to the requirements of paragraph (1), a rental company that offers or provides a damage waiver shall orally disclose to all renters, except those who are participants in the rental company's membership program, that the damage waiver may be duplicative of coverage that the customer maintains under their own policy of motor vehicle insurance. The renter shall acknowledge receipt of the oral disclosure near that part of the contract where the renter indicates, by the renter's own initials, their acceptance or declination of the damage waiver. Adjacent to that same part, the contract also shall state that the damage waiver is optional. Further, the contract for these renters shall include a clear and conspicuous written disclosure that the damage waiver may be duplicative of coverage that the customer maintains under their own policy of motor vehicle insurance.

(3)(A) The following is an example, for purposes of illustration and not limitation, of a notice fulfilling the requirements of paragraph (1) for a rental company that imposes liability on the renter for collision damage to the full value of the vehicle:

NOTICE ABOUT YOUR FINANCIAL RESPONSIBILITY AND OPTIONAL DAMAGE WAIVER

You are responsible for all collision damage to the rented vehicle even if someone else caused it or the cause is unknown. You are responsible for the cost of repair up to the value of the vehicle, and towing, storage, and impound fees.

Your own insurance, or the issuer of the credit card you use to pay for the vehicle rental transaction, may cover all or part of your financial responsibility for the rented vehicle. You should check with your insurance company, or credit card issuer, to find out about your coverage and the amount of the deductible, if any, for which you may be liable.

Further, if you use a credit card that provides coverage for your potential liability, you should check with the issuer to determine if you must first exhaust the coverage limits of your own insurance before the credit card coverage applies.

The rental company will not hold you responsible if you buy a damage waiver. But a damage waiver will not protect you if (list exceptions).

(B) When the notice in subparagraph (A) is printed in the rental contract or holder in which the contract is placed, the following shall be printed immediately following the notice:

"The cost of an optional damage waiver is $_____ for every (day or week)."

(C) When the notice in subparagraph (A) appears on a sign, the following shall appear immediately adjacent to the notice:

"The cost of an optional damage waiver is $_____ to $_____ for every (day or week), depending upon the vehicle rented."

(d) Notwithstanding any other law, a rental company may sell a damage waiver for each full or partial 24-hour rental day for the damage waiver, subject to the following rate limitations:

(1) For rental vehicles that the rental company designates as an "economy car," "compact car," "intermediate car," "standard car," "full-size car," or another term having similar meaning to the five smallest body-size categories of vehicles established by the Association of Car Rental Industry Systems Standards for North America when offered for rental, the rate shall not exceed twenty-five dollars ($25).

(2) Starting January 1, 2023, and each January thereafter, the rate cap shall be increased based on the increase in the Consumer Price Index for All Urban Consumers (CPI-U) over the previous year as reported by the United States Bureau of Labor Statistics. **Leg.H.** Added Stats 2016 ch 183 §5 (AB 2051), effective January 1, 2017. Amended Stats 2021 ch 415 §1 (AB 901), effective January 1, 2022.

§1939.13. Purchase of damage waiver, Optional insurance

(a) A rental company shall not require the purchase of a damage waiver, optional insurance, or another optional good or service.

(b) A rental company shall not engage in any unfair, deceptive, or coercive conduct to induce a renter to purchase the damage waiver, optional insurance, or another optional good or service, including conduct such as, but not limited to, refusing to honor the renter's reservation, limiting the availability of vehicles, requiring a deposit, or debiting or blocking the renter's credit card account for a sum equivalent to a deposit if the renter declines to purchase the damage waiver, optional insurance, or another optional good or service. **Leg.H.** Added Stats 2016 ch 183 §5 (AB 2051), effective January 1, 2017.

§1939.15. Recovery of claim from damage or loss of vehicle by rental company

(a) In the absence of express permission granted by the renter subsequent to damage to, or loss of, the rented vehicle, a rental company shall not seek to recover any portion of a claim arising out of damage to, or loss of, the vehicle by processing a credit card charge or causing a debit or block to be placed on the renter's credit card account.

(b) A rental company shall not engage in any unfair, deceptive, or coercive tactics in attempting to recover or in recovering on any claim arising out of damage to, or loss of, the rented vehicle. **Leg.H.** Added Stats 2016 ch 183 §5 (AB 2051), effective January 1, 2017.

§1939.17. Collection of customer facility charge

A customer facility charge or alternative customer facility charge may be collected by a rental company pursuant to Section 50474.3 of the Government Code. **Leg.H.** Added Stats 2016 ch 183 §5 (AB 2051), effective January 1, 2017.

§1939.19. Quotes, charges imposed by rental company; Mandatory charges; Rate advertisements

(a) When providing a quote, or imposing charges for a rental, the rental company may separately state the rental rate, additional mandatory charges, if any, and a mileage charge, if any, that a renter must pay to hire or lease the vehicle for the period of time to which the rental rate applies. A rental company shall not charge in addition to the rental rate, additional mandatory charges, or a mileage charge, as those may be applicable, any other fee that is required to be paid by the renter as a condition of hiring or leasing the vehicle.

(b) If additional mandatory charges are imposed, the rental company shall do each of the following:

(1) At the time the quote is given, provide the person receiving the quote with a good faith estimate of the rental rate and all additional

mandatory charges, as well as the total charges for the entire rental. The total charges, if provided on an internet website page, shall be displayed in a typeface at least as large as any rental rate disclosed on that page and shall be provided on a page that the person receiving the quote may reach by following a link directly from the page on which the rental rate is first provided. The good faith estimate may exclude mileage charges and charges for optional items that cannot be determined prior to completing the reservation based upon the information provided by the person.

(2) At the time and place the rental commences, clearly and conspicuously disclose in the rental contract, or that portion of the contract that is provided to the renter, the total of the rental rate and additional mandatory charges, for the entire rental, exclusive of charges that cannot be determined at the time the rental commences. Charges imposed pursuant to this paragraph shall be no more than the amount of the quote provided in a confirmed reservation, unless the person changes the terms of the rental contract subsequent to making the reservation.

(3) Provide each person, other than those persons within the rental company, offering quotes to actual or prospective customers access to information about additional mandatory charges, as well as access to information about when those charges apply. Any person providing quotes to actual or prospective customers for the hire or lease of a vehicle from a rental company shall provide the quotes in the manner described in paragraph (1).

(c) In addition to the rental rate, taxes, additional mandatory charges, if any, and mileage charges, if any, a rental company may charge for an item or service provided in connection with a particular rental transaction if the renter could have avoided incurring the charge by choosing not to obtain or utilize the optional item or service. Items and services for which the rental company may impose an additional charge include, but are not limited to, optional insurance and accessories requested by the renter, service charges incident to the renter's optional return of the vehicle to a location other than the location where the vehicle was hired or leased, and charges for refueling the vehicle at the conclusion of the rental transaction in the event the renter did not return the vehicle with as much fuel as was in the fuel tank at the beginning of the rental. A rental company also may impose an additional charge based on reasonable age criteria established by the rental company.

(d) A rental company may charge a fee for an authorized driver, in addition to the rental charge for an individual renter, unless the authorized driver is either of the following:

(1) The renter's spouse, as described in paragraph (2) of subdivision (e) of Section 1939.01, the renter's child or person for whom the renter is a legal guardian, the renter's sibling, or the renter's parent or grandparent.

(2) The renter's employer or coworker, as described in paragraph (3) of subdivision (e) of Section 1939.01.

(e) In the event that a rental company learns that an additional driver who was not previously authorized in the rental agreement has driven the rental car, the rental company may charge up to twice the authorized driver fee.

(f) If a rental company states a rental rate in print advertisement or in a quotation, the rental company shall disclose clearly in that advertisement or quotation the terms of mileage conditions relating to the advertised or quoted rental rate, including, but not limited to, to the extent applicable, the amount of mileage and gas charges, the number of miles for which no charges will be imposed, and a description of geographic driving limitations within the United States and Canada.

(g) All rate advertisements shall include a disclaimer, which shall be prominently displayed, providing that additional mandatory charges may be imposed, including, but not limited to, airport fees, tourism fees, vehicle license recovery fees, or other government imposed taxes or fees, and indicating that this information, including an estimate of the total rental cost, is displayed on the rental company's internet website. All rate advertisements shall also include a statement that additional charges may apply if an optional good or service, such as a damage waiver, is purchased.

(h) If any person or entity other than a rental company, including a passenger carrier or a seller of travel services, advertises a rental rate for a vehicle rental that includes additional mandatory charges, that person or entity shall clearly disclose the existence and amount of the charges. If a rental company provides the person or entity with rental rate and additional mandatory charges information, the rental car company is not responsible for the failure of that person or entity to comply with this subdivision.

(i) If a rental company delivers a vehicle to a renter at a location other than the location where the rental company normally carries on its business, the rental company shall not charge the renter an amount for the rental for the period before the delivery of the vehicle. If a rental company picks up a rented vehicle from a renter at a location other than the location where the rental company normally carries on its business, the rental company shall not charge the renter an amount for the rental for the period after the renter notifies the rental company to pick up the vehicle.

(j) Except as otherwise permitted pursuant to the customer facility charge, a rental company shall not separately charge, in addition to the rental rate, a fee for transporting the renter to a location where the rented vehicle will be delivered to the renter. **Leg.H.** Added Stats 2016 ch 183 §5 (AB 2051), effective January 1, 2017. Amended Stats 2021 ch 415 §2 (AB 901), effective January 1, 2022.

§ 1939.20. Exclusion of rental vehicle charges pricing information disclosed to consumers not violation of Section 1770

(a) A rental company is not in violation of paragraph (29) of subdivision (a) of Section 1770 for excluding from the advertised, displayed, or offered price of a rental vehicle charges that are disclosed to the consumer in compliance with subdivisions (a), (b), and (g) of Section 1939.19.

(b) This section shall become operative on July 1, 2024. **Leg.H.** Added Stats 2023 ch 400 §4 (SB 478), effective January 1, 2024, operative July 1, 2024.

§1939.21. Separate quotation and imposition of additional charges for renter of business program sponsor

(a) For purposes of this section:

(1) "Additional charges" means charges other than a per period base rental rate established by the business program.

(2) "Business program" means either of the following:

(A) A contract between a rental company and a business program sponsor that has established the per period base rental rate, and any other material terms relating to additional charges, on which the rental company will rent passenger vehicles to persons authorized by the sponsor.

(B) A plan, program, or other arrangement established by a rental company at the request of, or with the consent of, a business program sponsor under which the rental company offers to rent passenger vehicles to persons authorized by the sponsor at per period base rental rates, and any other material terms relating to additional charges, that are not the same as those generally offered by the rental company to the public.

(3) "Business program sponsor" means a legal entity, other than a natural person, that is a corporation, limited liability company, or partnership.

(4) "Business renter" means, for any business program sponsor, a person who is authorized by the sponsor, through the use of an identifying number or program name or code, to enter into a rental contract under the sponsor's business program. In no case shall the term "business renter" include a person renting as any of the following:

(A) A nonemployee member of a not-for-profit organization.

(B) The purchaser of a voucher or other prepaid rental arrangement from a person, including a tour operator, engaged in the business of reselling those vouchers or prepaid rental arrangements to the general public.

(C) An individual whose vehicle rental is eligible for reimbursement in whole or in part as a result of the person being insured or provided coverage under a policy of insurance issued by an insurance company.

(D) An individual whose vehicle rental is eligible for reimbursement in whole or in part as a result of the person purchasing passenger vehicle repair services from a person licensed to perform such services.

(5) "Qualified business rental" under a business program established for a business program sponsor by a rental company means the rental of a passenger vehicle under the business program if either:(A) in the 12-month period ending on the date of the rental or in the calendar year immediately preceding the year in which the rental occurs, the rentals under all business programs established by the rental company for the business program sponsor and its affiliates produced gross rental revenues in excess of twenty-five thousand dollars ($25,000) or (B) the rental company in good faith estimates that rentals under all the business programs established by the rental company for the business program

sponsor and its affiliates will produce gross rental revenues in excess of twenty-five thousand dollars ($25,000) in the 12-month period commencing with the date of the rental or in the calendar year in which the rental occurs. The rental company has the burden of establishing by objectively verifiable evidence that the rental was a qualified business rental.

(6) "Quote" means telephonic, in-person, and computer-transmitted quotations.

(b) Notwithstanding any provision to the contrary contained in Section 1939.19 or 1939.23, a rental company may, in connection with the qualified business rental of a passenger vehicle to a business renter of a business program sponsor under the sponsor's business program, do both of the following:

(1) Separately quote additional charges for the rental if, at the time the quote is provided, the person receiving the quote is also provided a good faith estimate of the total of all the charges for the entire rental. The estimate may exclude mileage charges and charges for optional items and services that cannot be determined prior to completing the reservation based upon the information provided by the renter.

(2) Separately impose additional charges for the rental, if the rental contract, or another document provided to the business renter at the time and place the rental commences, clearly and conspicuously discloses the total of all the charges for the entire rental, exclusive of charges that cannot be determined at the time the rental commences.

(c) A renter may bring an action against a rental company for the recovery of damages and appropriate equitable relief for a violation of this section. The prevailing party shall be entitled to recover reasonable attorney's fees and costs.

(d) Any waiver of any of the provisions of this section shall be void and unenforceable as contrary to public policy.

(e) This section shall not be interpreted to mean that a rental company is not required to comply with the requirements of subdivisions (c) to (h), inclusive, of Section 1939.19. **Leg.H.** Added Stats 2016 ch 183 §5 (AB 2051), effective January 1, 2017.

§1939.22. Electronic communications between rental company and renter

A rental company shall send communications to a renter electronically if the renter agrees to that communication in the rental or lease agreement. A rental company shall not deny a rental or lease agreement if the renter chooses not to receive communications electronically. For purposes of this section, "electronically" does not include a cellular telephone. **Leg.H.** Added Stats 2018 ch 344 §1 (AB 2620), effective January 1, 2019.

§1939.23. Prohibition against use of electronic surveillance technology; Exceptions

(a) A rental company shall not use, access, or obtain any information relating to the renter's use of the rental vehicle that was obtained using electronic surveillance technology, except in the following circumstances:

(1)(A) When the equipment is used by the rental company only for the purpose of locating a stolen, abandoned, or missing rental vehicle after one of the following:

(i) The renter or law enforcement has informed the rental company that the vehicle is missing or has been stolen or abandoned.

(ii) **[1]** If the rental vehicle has not been returned following **[2] 24** hours after the contracted return date or by **[3] 24** hours following the end of an extension of that return date, the rental company may activate electronic surveillance technology. The rental company shall provide notice of activation of the electronic surveillance technology 24 hours **[4] before** activation, by telephone and electronically pursuant to Section 1939.22, unless the renter has not provided a telephone number or the renter has not agreed to electronic communication pursuant to Section 1939.22. The rental or lease agreement shall advise the renter that electronic surveillance technology may be activated if the rental vehicle has not been returned within **[5] 24** hours after the contracted return date or extension of the return date. The renter shall acknowledge this advisement in the rental or lease agreement by initials. The advisement shall also be made orally to the renter at the time of executing the rental or lease agreement **if the transaction is completed in person or by telephone**. The advisements are not required to be made to members of the rental company's membership program executing a rental or lease agreement **[6]**. However, a renter shall be given those advisements upon enrolling in the rental company's membership program.

(iii) Notwithstanding clause (ii), if the rental vehicle has not been returned following one week after the contracted return date or by one week following the end of an extension of that return date.

(iv) The rental company discovers the rental vehicle has been stolen or abandoned, and, if stolen, the rental company shall report the vehicle stolen to law enforcement by filing a stolen vehicle report, unless law enforcement has already informed the rental company that the vehicle is missing or has been stolen or abandoned.

(v) The rental vehicle is the subject of an AMBER Alert issued pursuant to Section 8594 of the Government Code. If the rental company uses the equipment in connection with this provision relating to an AMBER Alert, the rental company shall notify law enforcement that one of the rental company's vehicles is the subject of an AMBER Alert upon becoming aware of the situation, unless law enforcement has already informed the rental company that the vehicle was the subject of an AMBER Alert.

(B) If electronic surveillance technology is activated pursuant to subparagraph (A), a rental company shall maintain a record, in either electronic or written form, of information relevant to the activation of that technology. That information shall include the rental agreement, including the return date, and the date and time the electronic surveillance technology was activated. The record shall also include, if relevant, a record of written or other communication with the renter, including communications regarding extensions of the rental, police reports, or other written communication with law enforcement officials. The record shall be maintained for a period of at least 12 months from the time the record is created and shall be made available upon the renter's request. The rental company shall maintain and furnish explanatory codes necessary to read the record. A rental company shall not be required to maintain a record if electronic surveillance technology is activated to recover a rental vehicle that is stolen or missing at a time other than during a rental period.

(2) In response to a specific request from law enforcement pursuant to a subpoena or search warrant.

(b) Subdivision (a) does not prohibit a rental company from equipping rental vehicles with any of the following:

(1) GPS-based technology that provides navigation assistance to the occupants of the rental vehicle, if the rental company does not use, access, or obtain information relating to the renter's use of the rental vehicle that was obtained using that technology, except for the purposes of discovering or repairing a defect in the technology and the information may then be used only for that purpose.

(2) Electronic surveillance technology that allows for the remote locking or unlocking of the vehicle at the request of the renter, if the rental company does not use, access, or obtain information relating to the renter's use of the rental vehicle that was obtained using that technology, except as necessary to lock or unlock the vehicle.

(3) Electronic surveillance technology that allows the company to provide roadside assistance, such as towing, flat tire, or fuel services, at the request of the renter, if the rental company does not use, access, or obtain information relating to the renter's use of the rental vehicle that was obtained using that technology except as necessary to provide the requested roadside assistance.

(c) Subdivision (a) does not prohibit a rental company from obtaining, accessing, or using information from electronic surveillance technology for the sole purpose of determining the date and time the vehicle departs from and is returned to the rental company, and the total mileage driven and the vehicle fuel level of the returned vehicle. The information obtained or accessed from this electronic surveillance technology shall only be used for the purpose described in this subdivision.

(d) A rental company shall not use electronic surveillance technology to track a renter in order to impose fines or surcharges relating to the renter's use of the rental vehicle. **Leg.H.** Added Stats 2016 ch 183 §5 (AB 2051), effective January 1, 2017. Amended Stats 2017 ch 163 §1 (SB 466), effective January 1, 2018; Stats 2018 ch 344 §2 (AB 2620), effective January 1, 2019; Stats 2023 ch 478 §5 (AB 1756), effective January 1, 2024; Stats 2024 ch 970 §1 (AB 2741), effective January 1, 2025.

§1939.23. 2024 Deletes. [1] Until January 1, 2028, and for purposes of this clause, **[2]** 72 **[3]** 72 **[4]** prior to **[5]** 72 **[6]** ;

§1939.25. Action for violation of chapter; Attorney's fees

A renter may bring an action against a rental company for the recovery of damages and appropriate equitable relief for a violation of this chapter, except for Sections 1939.21, 1939.35, and 1939.37. The prevailing party shall be entitled to recover reasonable attorney's fees and costs. **Leg.H.** Added Stats 2016 ch 183 §5 (AB 2051), effective January 1, 2017.

§1939.27. Action for loss due to theft; Jurisdiction

A rental company that brings an action against a renter for loss due to theft of the vehicle shall bring the action in the county in which the renter resides or, if the renter is not a resident of this state, in the jurisdiction in which the renter resides. **Leg.H.** Added Stats 2016 ch 183 §5 (AB 2051), effective January 1, 2017.

§1939.29. Waiver of provisions of chapter prohibited

A waiver of any of the provisions of this chapter, except for Sections 1939.21, 1939.35, and 1939.37, shall be void and unenforceable as contrary to public policy. **Leg.H.** Added Stats 2016 ch 183 §5 (AB 2051), effective January 1, 2017.

§1939.31. Disclosure requirements under rental company membership program

(a) A rental company's disclosure requirements shall be satisfied for renters who are enrolled in the rental company's membership program if all of the following conditions are met:

(1) Prior to the enrollee's first rental as a participant in the program, the renter receives, in writing, the following:

(A) All of the disclosures required by paragraph (1) of subdivision (c) of Section 1939.09, including the terms and conditions of the rental agreement then in effect.

(B) An internet website address, as well as a contact number or address, where the enrollee can learn of changes to the rental agreement or to the laws of this state governing rental agreements since the effective date of the rental company's most recent restatement of the rental agreement and distribution of that restatement to its members.

(2) At the commencement of each rental period, the renter is provided, on the rental record or the folder in which it is inserted, with a printed notice stating that the renter had either previously selected or declined an optional damage waiver and that the renter has the right to change preferences.

(b) This section does not relieve the rental company from the disclosures required to be made within the text of a contract or holder in which the contract is placed; in or on an advertisement containing a rental rate; or in a telephonic, in-person, or computer-transmitted quotation or reservation. **Leg.H.** Added Stats 2016 ch 183 §5 (AB 2051), effective January 1, 2017. Amended Stats 2021 ch 415 §3 (AB 901), effective January 1, 2022.

§1939.33. Service of complaint by foreign renter

(a) When a rental company enters into a rental agreement in the state for the rental of a vehicle to any renter who is not a resident of this country and, as part of, or associated with, the rental agreement, the renter purchases liability insurance, as defined in subdivision (b) of Section 1758.85 of the Insurance Code, from the rental company in its capacity as a rental vehicle agent for an authorized insurer, the rental company shall be authorized to accept, and, if served as set forth in this section, shall accept, service of a summons and complaint and any other required documents against the foreign renter for any accident or collision resulting from the operation of the rental vehicle within the state during the rental period. If the rental company has a registered agent for service of process on file with the Secretary of State, process shall be served on the rental company's registered agent, either by first-class mail, return receipt requested, or by personal service.

(b) Within 30 days of acceptance of service of process, the rental company shall provide a copy of the summons and complaint and any other required documents served in accordance with this section to the foreign renter by first-class mail, return receipt requested.

(c) Any plaintiff, or his or her representative, who elects to serve the foreign renter by delivering a copy of the summons and complaint and any other required documents to the rental company pursuant to subdivision (a) shall agree to limit his or her recovery against the foreign renter and the rental company to the limits of the protection extended by the liability insurance.

(d) Notwithstanding the requirements of Sections 17450 to 17456, inclusive, of the Vehicle Code, service of process in compliance with subdivision (a) shall be deemed a valid and effective service.

(e) Notwithstanding any other law, the requirement that the rental company accept service of process pursuant to subdivision (a) shall not create any duty, obligation, or agency relationship other than that provided in subdivision (a). **Leg.H.** Added Stats 2016 ch 183 §5 (AB 2051), effective January 1, 2017.

§1939.35. Advisories for 15-passenger van renters

(a)(1) A rental company shall provide a renter of a 15-passenger van with a copy of the United States Department of Transportation, National Highway Traffic Safety Administration's consumer advisory for 15-passenger vans titled "Reducing the Risk of Rollover Crashes" or, if that advisory is updated, a copy of the updated advisory. The renter shall acknowledge receipt of that copy by signing an acknowledgment of receipt on the rental agreement or on an attached form.

(2) If the rental of that 15-passenger van is for a business purpose or use, the rental company shall also provide on the document described in paragraph (1) that only an employee with the proper licensing may drive that vehicle. The renter shall acknowledge the receipt thereof in the same manner as described in paragraph (1).

(b)(1) Except as provided in paragraph (2), for purposes of this section, a "15-passenger van" means any van manufactured to accommodate 15 passengers, including the driver, regardless of whether that van has been altered to accommodate fewer than 15 passengers.

(2) For purposes of this section, a "15-passenger van" does not mean a 15-passenger van with dual rear wheels that has a gross weight rating equal to, or greater than, 11,500 pounds. **Leg.H.** Added Stats 2016 ch 183 §5 (AB 2051), effective January 1, 2017.

§1939.37. Exceptions to rental company under Section 14608 of Vehicle Code

A rental company is not subject to the requirements of Section 14608 of the Vehicle Code if the rental is subject to the terms of a membership agreement that allows the renter to gain physical access to a vehicle without a key through use of a code, key card, or by other means that allow the vehicle to be accessed at a remote location, or at a business location of the rental company outside of that location's regular hours of operation. **Leg.H.** Added Stats 2016 ch 183 §5 (AB 2051), effective January 1, 2017.

§1939.38. Commercial airport facility customer facility charge

(a) Notwithstanding any other law, a commercial airport facility may regulate access to an airport and require any person or entity described in subdivision (m) of Section 1939.01 to collect a customer facility charge pursuant to Section 50474.21 of the Government Code.

(b)(1) Before facilitating the sharing or renting of vehicles, any program, person, or entity described in subdivision (m) of Section 1939.01 shall obtain a permit or other written authorization from the airport operator that sets forth the terms, standards, regulations, procedures, fees, and access requirements for the activity.

(2) For purposes of paragraph (1), "facilitating the sharing or renting of vehicles" includes listing, publishing, or advertising vehicles or motor vehicles parked on airport property or at airport facilities.

(c) This section shall not affect the authority of any political subdivision or the state to do any of the following:

(1) Regulate access to an airport it owns or operates.

(2) Enter into written agreements.

(3) Set access fees or permit requirements.

(4) Regulate existing airport access permits granted by an airport to personal vehicle sharing programs.

(d) This section shall become operative on July 1, 2024. **Leg.H.** Added Stats 2023 ch 547 §2 (AB 893), effective January 1, 2024, operative July 1, 2024.

§1939.39. Personal vehicle sharing program vehicle certification

On and after July 1, 2024, a personal vehicle sharing program shall not allow a vehicle to be placed on a digital network or software application of the personal vehicle sharing program for the purpose of making the vehicle available for rental through the personal vehicle sharing program unless the certification described in subdivision (a) or (b), as applicable, is fulfilled:

(a) If the request is to list a motor vehicle that was purchased in California, and that motor vehicle would first be made available for sharing on or after July 1, 2024, certification that one of the following occurred:

(1) All sales and use taxes were paid on the purchase price of the motor vehicle.

(2) The purchaser elected to have sales and use taxes collected on receipts from renting the motor vehicle in lieu of paying applicable taxes on the purchase price of the motor vehicle.

(3) The purchase of the motor vehicle was not subject to taxation due to an exemption available under law.

(b) If the request is to list a motor vehicle that was not purchased in California, and that motor vehicle would first be made available for sharing on or after July 1, 2024, certification that one of the following occurred:

(1) Applicable taxes were paid on the purchase price of the vehicle.

(2) Applicable taxes were not paid on the purchase price of the vehicle.

Leg.H. Added Stats 2023 ch 547 §3 (AB 893), effective January 1, 2024.

CHAPTER 2
HIRING OF REAL PROPERTY

Applicability of chapter; "Persons who hire" and "dwelling unit" defined. §1940.
"Immigration or citizenship status". §1940.05.
Application to residential hotels. §1940.1.
Acts of theft, extortion, or menacing conduct by landlord seeking to have tenant vacate dwelling; Civil action and penalty. §1940.2.
Prohibited acts based on immigration or citizenship status. §1940.3.
Landlord not to disclose immigration status; Violation and penalties. §1940.35.
Landlords shall not prohibit tenants from displaying political signs; Exceptions. §1940.4.
Tenant personal micromobility device. § 1940.41.
Restriction on religious items displayed on entry of dwelling not enforceable; Exceptions; Definitions. §1940.45.
Refusal to rent based on tenant's possession of waterbed. §1940.5.
Notice of application for permit to demolish residential dwelling. §1940.6.
Disclosure of former ordnance locations in neighborhood area. §1940.7.
Notice to new tenants of contracts for periodic pest control. §1940.8.
Notice to tenants of pesticide application without licensed pest control operator. §1940.8.5.
Disclosure required by landlord to tenant regarding gas and electric meters. §1940.9.
Personal agriculture; Definitions; Conditions for landlord to permit. §1940.10.
Tenant's use of clothesline or drying rack. §1940.20.
Lessor to make dwelling-house fit for its purpose. §1941.
Untenantable dwelling. §1941.1.
Effect of tenant's violations upon landlord's duties. §1941.2.
Landlord's obligation to install locks on doors and locks or security devices on windows; Tenant's obligation to give notice; Remedies; Exemptions. §1941.3.
Lessor's responsibility for telephone jacks and inside telephone wiring. §1941.4.
When person who is restrained from contact with protected tenant is not tenant of same dwelling unit as the protected tenant; Changing locks; Duties of landlord and protected tenant. § 1941.5.
When person who is restrained from contact with protected tenant is tenant of same dwelling unit as protected tenant; Changing locks; Duties of landlord and protected tenant; Liability. §1941.6.
Dilapidation relating to the presence of mold. §1941.7.
Repairs by lessee. §1942.
Waiver of tenant's rights; Arbitration. §1942.1.
Deduction of utility payment from rent. §1942.2.
Rebuttable presumption that landlord breached habitability requirements in Section 1941. §1942.3.
Liability of lessor demanding rent under specified conditions. §1942.4.
Prohibition against certain retaliatory acts by lessor against lessee for exercising rights; Timeframe; Civil action; Damages; Attorney's fees. § 1942.5.
Entry on property to provide information regarding tenants' rights or to participate in association as not constituting trespass. §1942.6.
Declawing or devocalization as condition of occupancy prohibited. §1942.7.
Fees or reduction of services related to COVID-19 rental debt. § 1942.9.
Term of hiring when no limit is fixed. §1943.
Hiring of lodgings for indefinite term. §1944.
Renewal of lease by lessee's continued possession. §1945.
Required printing of renewal provision. §1945.5.
Notice required to terminate tenancy. §1946.
Renewal at end of implied term absent written notice; Time and manner of notice. §1946.1.
Limitations on tenancy termination after twelve months continuous, lawful occupation; Opportunity to cure violation; Owner obligation in no-fault just cause termination; Notice [Repealed January 1, 2030]. § 1946.2.
Termination of room rental by lodger in owner occupied dwelling. §1946.5.
Terminating tenancy due to domestic violence or specified reason; Notice; Responsibility for rental payments; Prohibition on disclosure by landlord; Civil penalty. §1946.7.
Lease provision purporting to penalize or limit good faith summoning of law enforcement or emergency assistance void; Imposition or threat of penalties by landlord for such prohibited. §1946.8.
Restrictions on adverse actions in tenant screening. § 1946.9.
Rent, when payable. §1947.
Parking. § 1947.1.
Form of payment of rent or deposit of security; Payment of rent by third parties. §1947.3.
Smoking of cigarettes or other tobacco products; Authority of landlord; Changes to terms of lease or rental agreement. §1947.5.
Installation by lessor of electric vehicle charging station; When required; How requested; Costs; Exceptions; Liability. §1947.6.
Owner's "good faith" exemption from rent stabilization program fines and penalties. §1947.7.
Rent control program certification of permissible rent levels. §1947.8.
Levels of compensation for temporary displacement of tenant household; Construction. §1947.9.
Eviction based on owner's intention to occupy rent controlled unit. §1947.10.
Refund of rent in excess of controlled amount. §1947.11.
Limitations on gross rental rate increase; Notice of increase; Legislative report; Increases prior to operation date of section; Waivers void [Repealed January 1, 2030]. § 1947.12.
Limitations on rental rates upon expiration of rental restrictions [Repealed January 1, 2030]. §1947.13.
Professional expenses allowed owners of rent controlled property [Operation contingent]. §1947.15.
Attornment of a tenant to a stranger. §1948.
Tenant must deliver notice served on him. §1949.
Letting parts of rooms forbidden. §1950.
Reusable tenant screening report. § 1950.1.
Security for performance of rental agreement for residential property; Amount; Priority; What damages landlord may claim; Notice; Initial inspection and opportunity to remedy; Itemized statement; Documentation; Termination of landlord's interest; Liability for noncompliance. § 1950.5.
Application screening fee; Provision of consumer credit report to applicant. § 1950.6.
Security for performance of rental agreement for other than residential property; use; return of balance to tenant; transfer or return on termination of landlord's interest; penalty for bad faith retention. §1950.7.
Prohibited lease or rental agreement preparation fees; Civil penalty. §1950.8.
Requirements for charging qualified commercial tenants fees to recover building operating costs. § 1950.9.
"Rent"; "Lease". §1951.
Lessor's remedies upon breach by lessee; Indemnification. §1951.2.
Real property other than commercial real property; Procedure for establishing abandonment of leased property. §1951.3.
Commercial real property; Procedure for establishing abandonment of leased property. §1951.35.
Continuation of lease. §1951.4.
Liquidated damages. §1951.5.
Heads Advance payments to lessor; Notice on reletting. §1951.7.
Right to equitable relief. §1951.8.
Effect of other actions. §1952.
Leases affected. §1952.2.
Possession delivered to lessor before trial or judgment in unlawful detainer proceeding. §1952.3.
Agreement for exploration for or removal of natural resources as lease. §1952.4.
Leases involving public entities or nonprofit corporations; Exclusions. §1952.6.
Term in lease prohibiting installation of electric vehicle charging station is void; Installation by lessee; Requirements; Costs; Exceptions; Liability. §1952.7.
Lease of service station; Vapor control systems. §1952.8.
Public policy; Modification or waiver of lessee's rights. §1953.
Landlord's right of access to dwelling unit; Notice of entry. §1954.
Right of assignee for benefit of creditor to occupy business premises leased by assignor; Establishment of reasonable rental value recoverable by landlord. §1954.05.
Reporting of tenant's rental payments to consumer reporting agencies. § 1954.06.
Positive rental payment information reporting. § 1954.07.
Right of assignee for benefit of creditor to occupy business premises leased by assignor; Establishment of reasonable rental value recoverable by landlord [Renumbered]. §1954.1.

§1940. Applicability of chapter; "Persons who hire" and "dwelling unit" defined

(a) Except as provided in subdivision (b), this chapter shall apply to all persons who hire dwelling units located within this state including tenants, lessees, boarders, lodgers, and others, however denominated.

(b) The term "persons who hire" shall not include a person who maintains either of the following:

(1) Transient occupancy in a hotel, motel, residence club, or other facility when the transient occupancy is or would be subject to tax under Section 7280 of the Revenue and Taxation Code. The term "persons who hire" shall not include a person to whom this paragraph pertains if the person has not made valid payment for all room and other related charges owing as of the last day on which his or her occupancy is or would be subject to tax under Section 7280 of the Revenue and Taxation Code.

(2) Occupancy at a hotel or motel where the innkeeper retains a right of access to and control of the dwelling unit and the hotel or motel provides or offers all of the following services to all of the residents:

(A) Facilities for the safeguarding of personal property pursuant to Section 1860.

(B) Central telephone service subject to tariffs covering the same filed with the California Public Utilities Commission.

(C) Maid, mail, and room services.

(D) Occupancy for periods of less than seven days.

(E) Food service provided by a food establishment, as defined in Section 113780 of the Health and Safety Code, located on or adjacent to the premises of the hotel or motel and owned or operated by the innkeeper or owned or operated by a person or entity pursuant to a lease or similar relationship with the innkeeper or person or entity affiliated with the innkeeper.

(c) "Dwelling unit" means a structure or the part of a structure that is used as a home, residence, or sleeping place by one person who maintains a household or by two or more persons who maintain a common household.

(d) Nothing in this section shall be construed to limit the application of any provision of this chapter to tenancy in a dwelling unit unless the provision is so limited by its specific terms. **Leg.H.** Added Stats 1976 ch 712 §1. Amended Stats 1994 ch 680 §1 (SB 2088); Stats 1996 ch 1023 §28 (SB 1497), effective September 29, 1996.

§1940.05. "Immigration or citizenship status"

For purposes of this chapter, "immigration or citizenship status" includes a perception that the person has a particular immigration status or citizenship status, or that the person is associated with a person who has, or is perceived to have, a particular immigration status or citizenship status. **Leg.H.** Added Stats 2017 ch 489 §2 (AB 291), effective January 1, 2018.

§1940.1. Application to residential hotels

(a) No person may require an occupant of a residential hotel, as defined in Section 50519 of the Health and Safety Code, to move, or to check out and reregister, before the expiration of 30 days occupancy if a purpose is to have that occupant maintain transient occupancy status pursuant to paragraph (1) of subdivision (b) of Section 1940. Evidence that an occupant was required to check out and reregister shall create a rebuttable presumption, which shall affect solely the burden of producing evidence, of the purpose referred to in this subdivision.

(b) In addition to any remedies provided by local ordinance, any violation of subdivision (a) is punishable by a civil penalty of five hundred dollars ($500). In any action brought pursuant to this section, the prevailing party shall be entitled to reasonable attorney's fees.

(c) Nothing in this section shall prevent a local governing body from establishing inspection authority or reporting or recordkeeping requirements to ensure compliance with this section. **Leg.H.** Added Stats 1990 ch 1235 §1 (AB 3926). Amended Stats 1991 ch 245 §1 (AB 537), effective July 29, 1991; Stats 2004 ch 950 §1 (AB 2867).

§1940.2. Acts of theft, extortion, or menacing conduct by landlord seeking to have tenant vacate dwelling; Civil action and penalty

(a) It is unlawful for a landlord to do any of the following for the purpose of influencing a tenant to vacate a dwelling:

(1) Engage in conduct that violates subdivision (a) of Section 484 of the Penal Code.

(2) Engage in conduct that violates Section 518 of the Penal Code.

(3) Use, or threaten to use, force, willful threats, or menacing conduct constituting a course of conduct that interferes with the tenant's quiet enjoyment of the premises in violation of Section 1927 that would create an apprehension of harm in a reasonable person. Nothing in this paragraph requires a tenant to be actually or constructively evicted in order to obtain relief.

(4) Commit a significant and intentional violation of Section 1954.

(5) Threaten to disclose information regarding or relating to the immigration or citizenship status of a tenant, occupant, or other person known to the landlord to be associated with a tenant or occupant. This paragraph does not require a tenant to be actually or constructively evicted in order to obtain relief.

(b) A tenant who prevails in a civil action, including an action in small claims court, to enforce his or her rights under this section is entitled to a civil penalty in an amount not to exceed two thousand dollars ($2,000) for each violation.

(c) An oral or written warning notice, given in good faith, regarding conduct by a tenant, occupant, or guest that violates, may violate, or violated the applicable rental agreement, rules, regulations, lease, or laws, is not a violation of this section. An oral or written explanation of the rental agreement, rules, regulations, lease, or laws given in the normal course of business is not a violation of this section.

(d) This section does not enlarge or diminish a landlord's right to terminate a tenancy pursuant to existing state or local law; nor does this section enlarge or diminish any ability of local government to regulate or enforce a prohibition against a landlord's harassment of a tenant. **Leg.H.** Added Stats 2003 ch 542 §1 (AB 1059). Amended Stats 2017 ch 489 §3 (AB 291), effective January 1, 2018.

§1940.3. Prohibited acts based on immigration or citizenship status

(a) A public entity shall not, by ordinance, regulation, policy, or administrative action implementing any ordinance, regulation, policy, or administrative action, compel a landlord or any agent of the landlord to make any inquiry, compile, disclose, report, or provide any information, prohibit offering or continuing to offer, accommodations in the property for rent or lease, or otherwise take any action regarding or based on the immigration or citizenship status of a tenant, prospective tenant, occupant, or prospective occupant of residential rental property.

(b) A landlord, or any agent of the landlord, shall not do any of the following:

(1) Make any inquiry regarding or based on the immigration or citizenship status of a tenant, prospective tenant, occupant, or prospective occupant of residential rental property.

(2) Require that any tenant, prospective tenant, occupant, or prospective occupant of the rental property disclose or make any statement, representation, or certification concerning his or her immigration or citizenship status.

(3) Disclose to any person or entity information regarding or relating to the immigration or citizenship status of any tenant, prospective tenant, occupant, or prospective occupant of the rental property for the purpose of, or with the intent of, harassing or intimidating a tenant, prospective tenant, occupant, or prospective occupant, retaliating against a tenant or occupant for the exercise of his or her rights, influencing a tenant or occupant to vacate a dwelling, or recovering possession of the dwelling.

(c) This section does not prohibit a landlord from doing any of the following:

(1) Complying with any legal obligation under federal law, including, but not limited to, any legal obligation under any federal government program that provides for rent limitations or rental assistance to a qualified tenant, or a subpoena, warrant, or other order issued by a court.

(2) Requesting information or documentation necessary to determine or verify the financial qualifications of a prospective tenant, or to determine or verify the identity of a prospective tenant or prospective occupant.

(d) For purposes of this section, both of the following shall apply:

(1) "Public entity" includes the state, a city, county, city and county, district, public authority, public agency, and any other political subdivision or public corporation in the state.

(2) "State" includes any state office, department, division, bureau, board, or commission and the Trustees of the California State University and the California State University. **Leg.H.** Added Stats 2007 ch 403 §1 (AB 976), effective January 1, 2008. Amended Stats 2017 ch 489 §4 (AB 291), effective January 1, 2018; Stats 2017 ch 490 §1.5 (AB 299), effective January 1, 2018 (ch 490 prevails); Stats 2017 ch 489 §4 (AB 291), effective January 1, 2018.

§1940.35. Landlord not to disclose immigration status; Violation and penalties

(a) It is unlawful for a landlord to disclose to any immigration authority, law enforcement agency, or local, state, or federal agency information regarding or relating to the immigration or citizenship status of any tenant, occupant, or other person known to the landlord to be associated with a tenant or occupant, for the purpose of, or with the intent of, harassing or intimidating a tenant or occupant, retaliating against a tenant or occupant for the exercise of his or her rights, influencing a tenant or occupant to vacate a dwelling, or recovering possession of the dwelling, irrespective of whether the tenant or occupant currently resides in the dwelling.

(b) If a court of applicable jurisdiction finds a violation of this section in a proceeding initiated by a party or upon a motion of the court, the court shall do all of the following:

(1) For each person whose status was so disclosed, order the landlord to pay statutory damages in an amount to be determined in the court's discretion that is between 6 and 12 times the monthly rent charged for the dwelling in which the tenant or occupant resides or resided.

(2) Issue injunctive relief to prevent the landlord from engaging in similar conduct with respect to other tenants, occupants, and persons known to the landlord to be associated with the tenants or occupants.

(3) Notify the district attorney of the county in which the real property for hire is located of a potential violation of Section 519 of the Penal Code.

(c) A landlord is not in violation of this section if he or she is complying with any legal obligation under federal law, or subpoena, warrant, or order issued by a court.

(d) In making findings in a proceeding under this section, a court may take judicial notice under subdivision (d) of Section 452 of the Evidence Code of the proceedings and records of any federal removal, inadmissibility, or deportation proceeding.

(e) A court shall award to the prevailing party in an action under this section attorney's fees and costs.

(f) The remedies provided by this section shall be in addition to any other remedies provided by statutory or decisional law.

(g) Any waiver of a right under this section by a tenant, occupant, or person known to the landlord to be associated with a tenant or occupant shall be void as a matter of public policy.

(h) An action for injunctive relief pursuant to this section may be brought by a nonprofit organization exempt from federal income taxation under Section 501(c)(3) of the Internal Revenue Code, as amended. That organization shall be considered a party for purposes of this section. **Leg.H.** Added Stats 2017 ch 489 §5 (AB 291), effective January 1, 2018.

§1940.4. Landlords shall not prohibit tenants from displaying political signs; Exceptions

(a) Except as provided in subdivision (c), a landlord shall not prohibit a tenant from posting or displaying political signs relating to any of the following:

(1) An election or legislative vote, including an election of a candidate to public office.

(2) The initiative, referendum, or recall process.

(3) Issues that are before a public commission, public board, or elected local body for a vote.

(b) Political signs may be posted or displayed in the window or on the door of the premises leased by the tenant in a multifamily dwelling, or from the yard, window, door, balcony, or outside wall of the premises leased by a tenant of a single-family dwelling.

(c) A landlord may prohibit a tenant from posting or displaying political signs in the following circumstances:

(1) The political sign is more than six square feet in size.

(2) The posting or displaying would violate a local, state, or federal law.

(3) The posting or displaying would violate a lawful provision in a common interest development governing a document that satisfies the criteria of Section 1353.6.

(d) A tenant shall post and remove political signs in compliance with the time limits set by the ordinance for the jurisdiction where the premises are located. A tenant shall be solely responsible for any violation of a local ordinance. If no local ordinance exists or if the local ordinance does not include a time limit for posting and removing political signs on private property, the landlord may establish a reasonable time period for the posting and removal of political signs. A reasonable time period for this purpose shall begin at least 90 days prior to the date of the election or vote to which the sign relates and end at least 15 days following the date of the election or vote.

(e) Notwithstanding any other provision of law, any changes in the terms of a tenancy that are made to implement the provisions of this section and are noticed pursuant to Section 827 shall not be deemed to cause a diminution in housing services, and may be enforced in accordance with Section 1161 of the Code of Civil Procedure. **Leg.H.** Added Stats 2011 ch 383 §1 (SB 337), effective January 1, 2012.

2011 Note: It is the intent of the Legislature that the enactment of this bill shall not affect in any way other forms of noncommercial expression by a tenant when that expression is not associated with political signs. Stats 2011 ch 383 (SB 337) §2.

§ 1940.41. Tenant personal micromobility device

(a) For purposes of this section:

(1) "Personal micromobility device" means a device with both of the following characteristics:

(A) It is powered by the physical exertion of the rider or an electric motor.

(B) It is designed to transport one individual or one adult accompanied by up to three minors.

(2) "Secure, long-term storage" means a location with all of the following characteristics:

(A) Access is limited to residents of the same housing complex.

(B) It is located on the premises.

(C) It is reasonably protected against precipitation.

(D) It has a minimum of one standard electrical connection for each personal micromobility device that will be stored and recharged in that location.

(E) Tenants are not charged for its use.

(b) A landlord shall not prohibit a tenant from either of the following:

(1) Owning personal micromobility devices.

(2)(A) Storing and recharging up to one personal micromobility device in their dwelling unit for each person occupying the unit if the personal micromobility device meets one of the following:

(i) Is not powered by an electric motor.

(ii) Complies with the following safety standards:

(I) For e-bikes, UL 2849, the Standard for Electrical Systems for E-bikes, as recognized by the United States Consumer Product Safety Commission, or EN 15194, the European Standard for electrically powered assisted cycles (EPAC Bicycles).

(II) For e-scooters, UL 2272, the Standard for Electrical Systems for Personal E-Mobility Devices, as recognized by the United States Consumer Product Safety Commission, or EN 17128, the European Standard for personal light electric vehicles (PLEV).

(iii) Is insured by the tenant under an insurance policy covering storage of the device within the tenant's dwelling unit. The owner may prohibit the tenant from charging a device in the unit if the device does not meet the standards in subclauses (I) and (II) of clause (ii).

(B) Subparagraph (A) does not apply if the landlord provides the tenant secure, long-term storage for the tenant's personal micromobility devices.

(C) Subparagraphs (A) and (B) do not apply to circumstances in which an occupant of the unit requires the use of a personal micromobility device as an accommodation for a disability.

(c) This section does not require a landlord to modify or approve a tenant's request to modify a rental dwelling unit for the purpose of storing a micromobility device inside of the dwelling unit.

(d) This section does not prohibit a landlord from doing any of the following:

(1)(A) Prohibiting repair or maintenance on batteries and motors of personal micromobility devices within a dwelling unit.

(B) Subparagraph (A) does not prohibit a tenant from changing a flat tire or adjusting the brakes on a personal micromobility device within the unit.

(2) Requiring a tenant to store a personal micromobility device in compliance with applicable fire code.

(3) Requiring a tenant to store a personal micromobility device in compliance with the Office of State Fire Marshal Information Bulletin 23-003 regarding lithium-ion battery safety, issued April 3, 2023, or any

updated guidance issued by the Office of the State Fire Marshal regarding lithium-ion battery safety, if such bulletin or guidance is provided to the tenant by the landlord.

(e) This section does not limit the rights and remedies available to disabled persons under federal or state law. **Leg.H.** Added Stats 2023 ch 630 §1 (SB 712), effective January 1, 2024.

§1940.45. Restriction on religious items displayed on entry of dwelling not enforceable; Exceptions; Definitions

(a) Except as otherwise provided by this section, a property owner shall not enforce or adopt a restrictive covenant or any other restriction that prohibits one or more religious items from being displayed or affixed on any entry door or entry door frame of a dwelling.

(b) To the extent permitted by Article 1, Section 4, of the California Constitution and the First Amendment to the United States Constitution, this section does not prohibit the enforcement or adoption of a restrictive covenant or other restriction prohibiting the display or affixing of a religious item on any entry door or entry door frame to a dwelling that:

(1) Threatens the public health or safety.

(2) Hinders the opening or closing of any entry door.

(3) Violates any federal, state, or local law.

(4) Contains graphics, language or any display that is obscene or otherwise illegal.

(5) Individually or in combination with any other religious item displayed or affixed on any entry door or door frame that has a total size greater than 36 by 12 square inches, provided it does not exceed the size of the door.

(c) As used in this section, the following terms have the following meanings:

(1) "Property owner" means all of the following:

(A) An association, as that term is defined in Section 4080.

(B) A board, as that term is defined in Section 4085.

(C) A member, as that term is defined in Section 4160.

(D) A landlord, as that term is defined in Section 1940.8.5.

(E) A sublessor.

(2) "Religious item" means an item displayed because of sincerely held religious beliefs. **Leg.H.** Added Stats 2019 ch 154 §1 (SB 652), effective January 1, 2020.

§1940.5. Refusal to rent based on tenant's possession of waterbed

An owner or an owner's agent shall not refuse to rent a dwelling unit in a structure which received its valid certificate of occupancy after January 1, 1973, to an otherwise qualified prospective tenant or refuse to continue to rent to an existing tenant solely on the basis of that tenant's possession of a waterbed or other bedding with liquid filling material where all of the following requirements and conditions are met:

(a) A tenant or prospective tenant furnishes to the owner, prior to installation, a valid waterbed insurance policy or certificate of insurance for property damage. The policy shall be issued by a company licensed to do business in California and possessing a Best's Insurance Report rating of "B" or higher. The insurance policy shall be maintained in full force and effect until the bedding is permanently removed from the rental premises. The policy shall be written for no less than one hundred thousand dollars ($100,000) of coverage. The policy shall cover, up to the limits of the policy, replacement value of all property damage, including loss of use, incurred by the rental property owner or other caused by or arising out of the ownership, maintenance, use, or removal of the waterbed on the rental premises only, except for any damage caused intentionally or at the direction of the insured, or for any damage caused by or resulting from fire. The owner may require the tenant to produce evidence of insurance at any time. The carrier shall give the owner notice of cancellation or nonrenewal 10 days prior to this action. Every application for a policy shall contain the information as provided in subdivisions (a), (b), and (c) of Section 1962 and Section 1962.5.

(b) The bedding shall conform to the pounds-per-square foot weight limitation and placement as dictated by the floor load capacity of the residential structure. The weight shall be distributed on a pedestal or frame which is substantially the dimensions of the mattress itself.

(c) The tenant or prospective tenant shall install, maintain and remove the bedding, including, but not limited to, the mattress and frame, according to standard methods of installation, maintenance, and removal as prescribed by the manufacturer, retailer, or state law, whichever provides the higher degree of safety. The tenant shall notify the owner or owner's agent in writing of the intent to install, remove, or move the waterbed. The notice shall be delivered 24 hours prior to the installation, removal, or movement. The owner or the owner's agent may be present at the time of installation, removal, or movement at the owner's or the owner's agent's option. If the bedding is installed or moved by any person other than the tenant or prospective tenant, the tenant or prospective tenant shall deliver to the owner or to the owner's agent a written installation receipt stating the installer's name, address, and business affiliation where appropriate.

(d) Any new bedding installation shall conform to the owner's or the owner's agent's reasonable structural specifications for placement within the rental property and shall be consistent with floor capacity of the rental dwelling unit.

(e) The tenant or prospective tenant shall comply with the minimum component specification list prescribed by the manufacturer, retailer, or state law, whichever provides the higher degree of safety.

(f) Subject to the notice requirements of Section 1954, the owner, or the owner's agent, shall have the right to inspect the bedding installation upon completion, and periodically thereafter, to insure its conformity with this section. If installation or maintenance is not in conformity with this section, the owner may serve the tenant with a written notice of breach of the rental agreement. The owner may give the tenant three days either to bring the installation into conformity with those standards or to remove the bedding, unless there is an immediate danger to the structure, in which case there shall be immediate corrective action. If the bedding is installed by any person other than the tenant or prospective tenant, the tenant or prospective tenant shall deliver to the owner or to the owner's agent a written installation receipt stating the installer's name and business affiliation where appropriate.

(g) Notwithstanding Section 1950.5, an owner or owner's agent is entitled to increase the security deposit on the dwelling unit in an amount equal to one-half of one months' rent. The owner or owner's agent may charge a tenant, lessee, or sublessee a reasonable fee to cover administration costs. In no event does this section authorize the payment of a rebate of premium in violation of Article 5 (commencing with Section 750) of Chapter 1 of Part 2 of Division 1 of the Insurance Code.

(h) Failure of the owner, or owner's agent, to exercise any of his or her rights pursuant to this section does not constitute grounds for denial of an insurance claim.

(i) As used in this section, "tenant" includes any lessee, and "rental" means any rental or lease. **Leg.H.** Added Stats 1987 ch 1503 §1. Amended Stats 1996 ch 1137 §52 (SB 1077).

§1940.6. Notice of application for permit to demolish residential dwelling

(a) The owner of a residential dwelling unit or the owner's agent who applies to any public agency for a permit to demolish that residential dwelling unit shall give written notice of that fact to:

(1) A prospective tenant prior to the occurrence of any of the following actions by the owner or the owner's agent:

(A) Entering into a rental agreement with a prospective tenant.

(B) Requiring or accepting payment from the prospective tenant for an application screening fee, as provided in Section 1950.6.

(C) Requiring or accepting any other fees from a prospective tenant.

(D) Requiring or accepting any writings that would initiate a tenancy.

(2) A current tenant, including a tenant who has entered into a rental agreement but has not yet taken possession of the dwelling unit, prior to applying to the public agency for the permit to demolish that residential dwelling unit.

(b) The notice shall include the earliest possible approximate date on which the owner expects the demolition to occur and the approximate date on which the owner will terminate the tenancy. However, in no case may the demolition for which the owner or the owner's agent has applied occur prior to the earliest possible approximate date noticed.

(c) If a landlord fails to comply with subdivision (a) or (b), a tenant may bring an action in a court of competent jurisdiction. The remedies the court may order shall include, but are not limited to, the following:

(1) In the case of a prospective tenant who moved into a residential dwelling unit and was not informed as required by subdivision (a) or (b), the actual damages suffered, moving expenses, and a civil penalty not to exceed two thousand five hundred dollars ($2,500) to be paid by the landlord to the tenant.

(2) In the case of a current tenant who was not informed as required by subdivision (a) or (b), the actual damages suffered, and a civil penalty not to exceed two thousand five hundred dollars ($2,500) to be paid by the landlord to the tenant.

(3) In any action brought pursuant to this section, the prevailing party shall be entitled to reasonable attorney's fees.

(d) The remedies available under this section are cumulative to other remedies available under law.

(e) This section shall not be construed to preempt other laws regarding landlord obligations or disclosures, including, but not limited to, those arising pursuant to Chapter 12.75 (commencing with Section 7060) of Division 7 of Title 1 of the Government Code.

(f) For purposes of this section:

(1) "Residential dwelling unit" has the same meaning as that contained in Section 1940.

(2) "Public agency" has the same meaning as that contained in Section 21063 of the Public Resources Code. **Leg.H.** Added Stats 2002 ch 285 §1 (SB 1576).

§1940.7. Disclosure of former ordnance locations in neighborhood area

(a) The Legislature finds and declares that the December 10, 1983, tragedy in Tierra Santa, in which lives were lost as a result of a live munition exploding in a residential area that was formerly a military ordnance location, has demonstrated (1) the unique and heretofore unknown risk that there are other live munitions in former ordnance locations in California, (2) that these former ordnance locations need to be identified by the federal, state, or local authorities, and (3) that the people living in the neighborhood of these former ordnance locations should be notified of their existence. Therefore, it is the intent of the Legislature that the disclosure required by this section is solely warranted and limited by (1) the fact that these former ordnance locations cannot be readily observed or discovered by landlords and tenants, and (2) the ability of a landlord who has actual knowledge of a former ordnance location within the neighborhood of his or her rental property to disclose this information for the safety of the tenant.

(b) The landlord of a residential dwelling unit who has actual knowledge of any former federal or state ordnance locations in the neighborhood area shall give written notice to a prospective tenant of that knowledge prior to the execution of a rental agreement. In cases of tenancies in existence on January 1, 1990, this written notice shall be given to tenants as soon as practicable thereafter.

(c) For purposes of this section:

(1) "Former federal or state ordnance location" means an area identified by an agency or instrumentality of the federal or state government as an area once used for military training purposes and which may contain potentially explosive munitions.

(2) "Neighborhood area" means within one mile of the residential dwelling. **Leg.H.** Added Stats 1989 ch 294 §2.

§1940.7.5. [Section repealed 2006]

Leg.H. Added Stats 2001 ch 466 §2 (SB 189), repealed January 1, 2004. Amended Stats 2002 ch 664 §44 (AB 3034), repealed January 1, 2004; Stats 2003 ch 422 §2 (AB 24), repealed January 1, 2006. Repealed operative January 1, 2006, by its own provisions. The repealed section related to notice of illegal controlled substance releases on or beneath a residential dwelling unit prior to execution of the rental agreement.

§1940.8. Notice to new tenants of contracts for periodic pest control

A landlord of a residential dwelling unit shall provide each new tenant that occupies the unit with a copy of the notice provided by a registered structural pest control company pursuant to Section 8538 of the Business and Professions Code, if a contract for periodic pest control service has been executed. **Leg.H.** Added Stats 2000 ch 234 §2 (SB 2143).

§1940.8.5. Notice to tenants of pesticide application without licensed pest control operator

(a) For purposes of this section, the following terms have the following meanings:

(1) "Adjacent dwelling unit" means a dwelling unit that is directly beside, above, or below a particular dwelling unit.

(2) "Authorized agent" means an individual, organization, or other entity that has entered into an agreement with a landlord to act on the landlord's behalf in relation to the management of a residential rental property.

(3) "Broadcast application" means spreading pesticide over an area greater than two square feet.

(4) "Electronic delivery" means delivery of a document by electronic means to the electronic address at or through which a tenant, landlord, or authorized agent has authorized electronic delivery.

(5) "Landlord" means an owner of residential rental property.

(6) "Pest" means a living organism that causes damage to property or economic loss, or transmits or produces diseases.

(7) "Pesticide" means any substance, or mixture of substances, that is intended to be used for controlling, destroying, repelling, or mitigating any pest or organism, excluding antimicrobial pesticides as defined by the Federal Insecticide, Fungicide, and Rodenticide Act (7 U.S.C. Sec. 136(mm)).

(8) "Licensed pest control operator" means anyone licensed by the state to apply pesticides.

(b)(1) A landlord or authorized agent that applies any pesticide to a dwelling unit without a licensed pest control operator shall provide a tenant of that dwelling unit and, if making broadcast applications, or using total release foggers or aerosol sprays, any tenant in an adjacent dwelling unit that could reasonably be impacted by the pesticide use with written notice that contains the following statements and information using words with common and everyday meaning:

(A) The pest or pests to be controlled.

(B) The name and brand of the pesticide product proposed to be used.

(C) "State law requires that you be given the following information:

CAUTION - PESTICIDES ARE TOXIC CHEMICALS. The California Department of Pesticide Regulation and the United States Environmental Protection Agency allow the unlicensed use of certain pesticides based on existing scientific evidence that there are no appreciable risks if proper use conditions are followed or that the risks are outweighed by the benefits. The degree of risk depends upon the degree of exposure, so exposure should be minimized.

If within 24 hours following application of a pesticide, a person experiences symptoms similar to common seasonal illness comparable to influenza, the person should contact a physician, appropriate licensed health care provider, or the California Poison Control System (1-800-222-1222).

For further information, contact any of the following: for Health Questions - the County Health Department (telephone number) and for Regulatory Information - the Department of Pesticide Regulation (916-324-4100)."

(D) The approximate date, time, and frequency with which the pesticide will be applied.

(E) The following notification:

"The approximate date, time, and frequency of this pesticide application is subject to change."

(2) At least 24 hours prior to application of the pesticide to the dwelling unit, the landlord or authorized agent shall provide the notice to the tenant of the dwelling unit, as well as any tenants in adjacent units that are required to be notified pursuant to paragraph (1), in at least one of the following ways:

(A) First-class mail.

(B) Personal delivery to the tenant, someone of suitable age and discretion at the premises, or under the usual entry door of the premises.

(C) Electronic delivery, if an electronic mailing address has been provided by the tenant.

(D) Posting a written notice in a conspicuous place at the unit entry in a manner in which a reasonable person would discover the notice.

(3)(A) Upon receipt of written notification, the tenant may agree in writing, or if notification was electronically delivered, the tenant may agree through electronic delivery, to allow the landlord or authorized agent to apply a pesticide immediately or at an agreed upon time.

(B)(i) Prior to receipt of written notification, the tenant and the landlord or authorized agent may agree orally to an immediate pesticide application if a tenant requests that the pesticide be applied before 24-hour advance notice can be given. The oral agreement shall include the name and brand of the pesticide product proposed to be used.

(ii) With respect to a tenant entering into an oral agreement for immediate pesticide application, the landlord or authorized agent, no later than the time of pesticide application, shall leave the written notice specified in paragraph (1) in a conspicuous place in the dwelling unit, or at the entrance of the unit in a manner in which a reasonable person would discover the notice.

(iii) If any tenants in adjacent dwelling units are also required to be notified pursuant to this subdivision, the landlord or authorized agent shall provide those tenants with this notice as soon as practicable after the oral agreement is made authorizing immediate pesticide application, but in no case later than commencement of application of the pesticide.

(4)(A) This subdivision shall not be construed to require an association, as defined in Section 4080, to provide notice of pesticide use in a separate interest, as defined in Section 4185, within a common interest development, as defined in Section 4100.

(B) Notwithstanding subparagraph (A), an association, as defined in Section 4080, that has taken title to a separate interest, as defined in Section 4185, shall provide notification to tenants as specified in this subdivision.

(c)(1) A landlord or authorized agent that applies any pesticide to a common area without a licensed pest control operator, excluding routine pesticide applications described in subdivision (d), shall post written notice in a conspicuous place in the common area in which a pesticide is to be applied that contains the following statements and information using words with common and everyday meaning:

(A) The pest or pests to be controlled.

(B) The name and brand of the pesticide product proposed to be used.

(C) "State law requires that you be given the following information: CAUTION - PESTICIDES ARE TOXIC CHEMICALS. The California Department of Pesticide Regulation and the United States Environmental Protection Agency allow the unlicensed use of certain pesticides based on existing scientific evidence that there are no appreciable risks if proper use conditions are followed or that the risks are outweighed by the benefits. The degree of risk depends upon the degree of exposure, so exposure should be minimized.

If within 24 hours following application of a pesticide, a person experiences symptoms similar to common seasonal illness comparable to influenza, the person should contact a physician, appropriate licensed health care provider, or the California Poison Control System (1-800-222-1222).

For further information, contact any of the following: for Health Questions - the County Health Department (telephone number) and for Regulatory Information - the Department of Pesticide Regulation (916-324-4100)."

(D) The approximate date, time, and frequency with which the pesticide will be applied.

(2)(A) The notice shall be posted before a pesticide application in a common area and shall remain posted for at least 24 hours after the pesticide is applied.

(B) Landlords and their authorized agents are not liable for any notice removed from a common area without the knowledge or consent of the landlord or authorized agent.

(C) If the pest poses an immediate threat to health and safety, thereby making compliance with notification prior to the pesticide application required in subparagraph (A) unreasonable, a landlord or authorized agent shall post the notification as soon as practicable, but not later than one hour after the pesticide is applied.

(3) If a common area lacks a suitable place to post a notice, then the landlord shall provide the notice to each dwelling unit in at least one of the following ways:

(A) First-class mail.

(B) Personal delivery to the tenant, someone of suitable age and discretion at the premises, or under the usual entry door of the premises.

(C) Electronic delivery, if an electronic mailing address has been provided by the tenant.

(D) Posting a written notice in a conspicuous place at the unit entry in a manner in which a reasonable person would discover the notice.

(4) This subdivision shall not be construed to require any landlord or authorized agent, or an association, as defined in Section 4080, to provide notice of pesticide use in common areas within a common interest development, as defined in Section 4100.

(d)(1) A landlord or authorized agent that routinely applies pesticide in a common area on a set schedule without a licensed pest control operator shall provide a tenant in each dwelling unit with written notice that contains the following statements and information using words with common and everyday meaning:

(A) The pest or pests to be controlled.

(B) The name and brand of the pesticide product proposed to be used.

(C) "State law requires that you be given the following information: CAUTION - PESTICIDES ARE TOXIC CHEMICALS. The California Department of Pesticide Regulation and the United States Environmental Protection Agency allow the unlicensed use of certain pesticides based on existing scientific evidence that there are no appreciable risks if proper use conditions are followed or that the risks are outweighed by the benefits. The degree of risk depends upon the degree of exposure, so exposure should be minimized.

If within 24 hours following application of a pesticide, a person experiences symptoms similar to common seasonal illness comparable to influenza, the person should contact a physician, appropriate licensed health care provider, or the California Poison Control System (1-800-222-1222).

For further information, contact any of the following: for Health Questions - the County Health Department (telephone number) and for Regulatory Information - the Department of Pesticide Regulation (916-324-4100)."

(D) The schedule pursuant to which the pesticide will be routinely applied.

(2)(A) The landlord or authorized agent shall provide the notice to both of the following:

(i) Existing tenants prior to the initial pesticide application.

(ii) Each new tenant prior to entering into a lease agreement.

(B) The landlord or authorized agent shall provide the notice to the tenant in at least one of the following ways:

(i) First-class mail.

(ii) Personal delivery to the tenant, someone of suitable age and discretion at the premises, or under the usual entry door of the premises.

(iii) Electronic delivery, if an electronic mailing address has been provided by the tenant.

(iv) Posting a written notice in a conspicuous place at the unit entry in a manner in which a reasonable person would discover the notice.

(C) If the pesticide to be used is changed, a landlord or authorized agent shall provide a new notice pursuant to paragraph (1).

(D) This subdivision shall not be construed to require any landlord or authorized agent, or an association, as defined in Section 4080, to provide notice of pesticide use in common areas within a common interest development, as defined in Section 4100.

(e) Nothing in this section abrogates the responsibility of a registered structural pest control company to abide by the notification requirements of Section 8538 of the Business and Professions Code.

(f) Nothing in this section authorizes a landlord or authorized agent to enter a tenant's dwelling unit in violation of Section 1954.

(g) If a tenant is provided notice in compliance with this section, a landlord or authorized agent is not required to provide additional information, and the information shall be deemed adequate to inform the tenant regarding the application of pesticides. **Leg.H.** Added Stats 2015 ch 278 §2 (SB 328), effective January 1, 2016.

2015 Note: The Legislature finds and declares all of the following:

(a) Existing law requires licensed pest control operators to provide to tenants written notification that includes the pest to be targeted, the pesticide to be used, the frequency of its use, and a health and safety statement prior to a pesticide application.

(b) Landlords or authorized agents may apply pesticides without using the services of a licensed pest control operator. There is no requirement for landlords or authorized agents to notify tenants when pesticides are applied to their units or common areas.

(c) It is therefore the intent of this bill to ensure that when pesticides are about to be applied to rental property by the landlord or an authorized agent, rather than by a licensed pest control operator, potentially affected tenants are provided with substantially the same written notification that they would have received under existing law had the pesticides been applied by a pest control operator. Stats 2015 ch 278 (SB 328) §1.

§1940.9. Disclosure required by landlord to tenant regarding gas and electric meters

(a) If the landlord does not provide separate gas and electric meters for each tenant's dwelling unit so that each tenant's meter measures only the electric or gas service to that tenant's dwelling unit and the landlord or his or her agent has knowledge that gas or electric service provided through a tenant's meter serves an area outside the tenant's dwelling unit, the landlord, prior to the inception of the tenancy or upon discovery, shall explicitly disclose that condition to the tenant and shall do either of the following:

(1) Execute a mutual written agreement with the tenant for payment by the tenant of the cost of the gas or electric service provided through the tenant's meter to serve areas outside the tenant's dwelling unit.

(2) Make other arrangements, as are mutually agreed in writing, for payment for the gas or electric service provided through the tenant's meter to serve areas outside the tenant's dwelling unit. These arrangements may include, but are not limited to, the landlord becoming the customer of record for the tenant's meter, or the landlord separately metering and becoming the customer of record for the area outside the tenant's dwelling unit.

(b) If a landlord fails to comply with subdivision (a), the aggrieved tenant may bring an action in a court of competent jurisdiction. The remedies the court may order shall include, but are not limited to, the following:

(1) Requiring the landlord to be made the customer of record with the utility for the tenant's meter.

(2) Ordering the landlord to reimburse the tenant for payments made by the tenant to the utility for service to areas outside of the tenant's dwelling unit. Payments to be reimbursed pursuant to this paragraph shall commence from the date the obligation to disclose arose under subdivision (a).

(c) Nothing in this section limits any remedies available to a landlord or tenant under other provisions of this chapter, the rental agreement, or applicable statutory or common law. **Leg.H.** Added Stats 1989 ch 861 §1.

§1940.10. Personal agriculture; Definitions; Conditions for landlord to permit

(a) For the purposes of this section, the following definitions shall apply:

(1) "Private area" means an outdoor backyard area that is on the ground level of the rental unit.

(2) "Personal agriculture" means a use of land where an individual cultivates edible plant crops for personal use or donation.

(3) "Plant crop" means any crop in its raw or natural state, which comes from a plant that will bear edible fruits or vegetables. It shall not include marijuana or any unlawful crops or substances.

(b) A landlord shall permit a tenant to participate in personal agriculture in portable containers approved by the landlord in the tenant's private area if the following conditions are met:

(1) The tenant regularly removes any dead plant material and weeds, with the exception of straw, mulch, compost, and any other organic materials intended to encourage vegetation and retention of moisture in soil, unless the landlord and tenant have a preexisting or separate agreement regarding garden maintenance where the tenant is not responsible for removing or maintaining plant crop and weeds.

(2) The plant crop will not interfere with the maintenance of the rental property.

(3) The placement of the portable containers does not interfere with any tenant's parking spot.

(4) The placement and location of the portable containers may be determined by the landlord. The portable containers may not create a health and safety hazard, block doorways, or interfere with walkways or utility services or equipment.

(c) The cultivation of plant crops on the rental property other than that which is contained in portable containers shall be subject to approval from the landlord.

(d) A landlord may prohibit the use of synthetic chemical herbicides, pesticides, fungicides, rodenticides, insecticides, or any other synthetic chemical product commonly used in the growing of plant crops.

(e) A landlord may require the tenant to enter into a written agreement regarding the payment of any excess water and waste collection bills arising from the tenant's personal agriculture activities.

(f) Subject to the notice required by Section 1954, a landlord has a right to periodically inspect any area where the tenant is engaging in personal agriculture to ensure compliance with this section.

(g) This section shall only apply to residential real property that is improved with, or consisting of, a building containing not more than two units that are intended for human habitation. **Leg.H.** Added Stats 2014 ch 584 §2 (AB 2561), effective January 1, 2015.

§1940.20. Tenant's use of clothesline or drying rack

(a) For purposes of this section, the following definitions shall apply:

(1) "Clothesline" includes a cord, rope, or wire from which laundered items may be hung to dry or air. A balcony, railing, awning, or other part of a structure or building shall not qualify as a clothesline.

(2) "Drying rack" means an apparatus from which laundered items may be hung to dry or air. A balcony, railing, awning, or other part of a structure or building shall not qualify as a drying rack.

(3) "Private area" means an outdoor area or an area in the tenant's premises enclosed by a wall or fence with access from a door of the premises.

(b) A tenant may utilize a clothesline or drying rack in the tenant's private area if all of the following conditions are met:

(1) The clothesline or drying rack will not interfere with the maintenance of the rental property.

(2) The clothesline or drying rack will not create a health or safety hazard, block doorways, or interfere with walkways or utility service equipment.

(3) The tenant seeks the landlord's consent before affixing a clothesline to a building.

(4) Use of the clothesline or drying rack does not violate reasonable time or location restrictions imposed by the landlord.

(5) The tenant has received approval of the clothesline or drying rack, or the type of clothesline or drying rack, from the landlord. **Leg.H.** Added Stats 2015 ch 602 §1 (AB 1448), effective January 1, 2016.

§1941. Lessor to make dwelling-house fit for its purpose

The lessor of a building intended for the occupation of human beings must, in the absence of an agreement to the contrary, put it into a condition fit for such occupation, and repair all subsequent dilapidations thereof, which render it untenantable, except such as are mentioned in section nineteen hundred and twenty-nine. **Leg.H.** Enacted Stats 1872. Amended Code Amdts 1873–74 ch 612 §205.

§1941.1. Untenantable dwelling

(a) A dwelling shall be deemed untenantable for purposes of Section 1941 if it substantially lacks any of the following affirmative standard characteristics or is a residential unit described in Section 17920.3 or 17920.10 of the Health and Safety Code:

(1) Effective waterproofing and weather protection of roof and exterior walls, including unbroken windows and doors.

(2) Plumbing or gas facilities that conformed to applicable law in effect at the time of installation, maintained in good working order.

(3) A water supply approved under applicable law that is under the control of the tenant, capable of producing hot and cold running water, or a system that is under the control of the landlord, that produces hot and cold running water, furnished to appropriate fixtures, and connected to a sewage disposal system approved under applicable law.

(4) Heating facilities that conformed with applicable law at the time of installation, maintained in good working order.

(5) Electrical lighting, with wiring and electrical equipment that conformed with applicable law at the time of installation, maintained in good working order.

(6) Building, grounds, and appurtenances at the time of the commencement of the lease or rental agreement, and all areas under control of the landlord, kept in every part clean, sanitary, and free from all accumulations of debris, filth, rubbish, garbage, rodents, and vermin.

(7) An adequate number of appropriate receptacles for garbage and rubbish, in clean condition and good repair at the time of the commencement of the lease or rental agreement, with the landlord providing appropriate serviceable receptacles thereafter and being responsible for the clean condition and good repair of the receptacles under his or her control.

(8) Floors, stairways, and railings maintained in good repair.

(9) A locking mail receptacle for each residential unit in a residential hotel, as required by Section 17958.3 of the Health and Safety Code. This subdivision shall become operative on July 1, 2008.

(b) Nothing in this section shall be interpreted to prohibit a tenant or owner of rental properties from qualifying for a utility energy savings assistance program, or any other program assistance, for heating or hot water system repairs or replacement, or a combination of heating and hot water system repairs or replacements, that would achieve energy savings. **Leg.H.** Added Stats 1970 ch 1280 §1. Amended Stats 1979 ch 307 §1;

Stats 2002 ch 931 §1 (SB 460); Stats 2007 ch 599 §1 (AB 607), effective January 1, 2008; Stats 2012 ch 600 §1 (AB 1124), effective January 1, 2013.

§1941.2. Effect of tenant's violations upon landlord's duties

(a) No duty on the part of the landlord to repair a dilapidation shall arise under Section 1941 or 1942 if the tenant is in substantial violation of any of the following affirmative obligations, provided the tenant's violation contributes substantially to the existence of the dilapidation or interferes substantially with the landlord's obligation under Section 1941 to effect the necessary repairs:

(1) To keep that part of the premises which he occupies and uses clean and sanitary as the condition of the premises permits.

(2) To dispose from his dwelling unit of all rubbish, garbage and other waste, in a clean and sanitary manner.

(3) To properly use and operate all electrical, gas and plumbing fixtures and keep them as clean and sanitary as their condition permits.

(4) Not to permit any person on the premises, with his permission, to willfully or wantonly destroy, deface, damage, impair or remove any part of the structure or dwelling unit or the facilities, equipment, or appurtenances thereto, nor himself do any such thing.

(5) To occupy the premises as his abode, utilizing portions thereof for living, sleeping, cooking or dining purposes only which were respectively designed or intended to be used for such occupancies.

(b) Paragraphs (1) and (2) of subdivision (a) shall not apply if the landlord has expressly agreed in writing to perform the act or acts mentioned therein. **Leg.H.** Added Stats 1970 ch 1280 §2. Amended Stats 1979 ch 307 §2.

§1941.3. Landlord's obligation to install locks on doors and locks or security devices on windows; Tenant's obligation to give notice; Remedies; Exemptions

(a) On and after July 1, 1998, the landlord, or his or her agent, of a building intended for human habitation shall do all of the following:

(1) Install and maintain an operable dead bolt lock on each main swinging entry door of a dwelling unit. The dead bolt lock shall be installed in conformance with the manufacturer's specifications and shall comply with applicable state and local codes including, but not limited to, those provisions relating to fire and life safety and accessibility for the disabled. When in the locked position, the bolt shall extend a minimum of $^{13}/_{16}$ of an inch in length beyond the strike edge of the door and protrude into the doorjamb.

This section shall not apply to horizontal sliding doors. Existing dead bolts of at least one-half inch in length shall satisfy the requirements of this section. Existing locks with a thumb-turn deadlock that have a strike plate attached to the doorjamb and a latch bolt that is held in a vertical position by a guard bolt, a plunger, or an auxiliary mechanism shall also satisfy the requirements of this section. These locks, however, shall be replaced with a dead bolt at least $^{13}/_{16}$ of an inch in length the first time after July 1, 1998, that the lock requires repair or replacement.

Existing doors which cannot be equipped with dead bolt locks shall satisfy the requirements of this section if the door is equipped with a metal strap affixed horizontally across the midsection of the door with a dead bolt which extends $^{13}/_{16}$ of an inch in length beyond the strike edge of the door and protrudes into the doorjamb. Locks and security devices other than those described herein which are inspected and approved by an appropriate state or local government agency as providing adequate security shall satisfy the requirements of this section.

(2) Install and maintain operable window security or locking devices for windows that are designed to be opened. Louvered windows, casement windows, and all windows more than 12 feet vertically or six feet horizontally from the ground, a roof, or any other platform are excluded from this subdivision.

(3) Install locking mechanisms that comply with applicable fire and safety codes on the exterior doors that provide ingress or egress to common areas with access to dwelling units in multifamily developments. This paragraph does not require the installation of a door or gate where none exists on January 1, 1998.

(b) The tenant shall be responsible for notifying the owner or his or her authorized agent when the tenant becomes aware of an inoperable dead bolt lock or window security or locking device in the dwelling unit. The landlord, or his or her authorized agent, shall not be liable for a violation of subdivision (a) unless he or she fails to correct the violation within a reasonable time after he or she either has actual notice of a deficiency or receives notice of a deficiency.

(c) On and after July 1, 1998, the rights and remedies of tenant for a violation of this section by the landlord shall include those available pursuant to Sections 1942, 1942.4, and 1942.5, an action for breach of contract, and an action for injunctive relief pursuant to Section 526 of the Code of Civil Procedure. Additionally, in an unlawful detainer action, after a default in the payment of rent, a tenant may raise the violation of this section as an affirmative defense and shall have a right to the remedies provided by Section 1174.2 of the Code of Civil Procedure.

(d) A violation of this section shall not broaden, limit, or otherwise affect the duty of care owed by a landlord pursuant to existing law, including any duty that may exist pursuant to Section 1714. The delayed applicability of the requirements of subdivision (a) shall not affect a landlord's duty to maintain the premises in safe condition.

(e) Nothing in this section shall be construed to affect any authority of any public entity that may otherwise exist to impose any additional security requirements upon a landlord.

(f) This section shall not apply to any building which has been designated as historically significant by an appropriate local, state, or federal governmental jurisdiction.

(g) Subdivisions (a) and (b) shall not apply to any building intended for human habitation which is managed, directly or indirectly, and controlled by the Department of Transportation. This exemption shall not be construed to affect the duty of the Department of Transportation to maintain the premises of these buildings in a safe condition or abrogate any express or implied statement or promise of the Department of Transportation to provide secure premises. Additionally, this exemption shall not apply to residential dwellings acquired prior to July 1, 1997, by the Department of Transportation to complete construction of state highway routes 710 and 238 and related interchanges. **Leg.H.** Added Stats 1997 ch 537 §1 (SB 548).

§1941.4. Lessor's responsibility for telephone jacks and inside telephone wiring

The lessor of a building intended for the residential occupation of human beings shall be responsible for installing at least one usable telephone jack and for placing and maintaining the inside telephone wiring in good working order, shall ensure that the inside telephone wiring meets the applicable standards of the most recent California Electrical Code, and shall make any required repairs. The lessor shall not restrict or interfere with access by the telephone utility to its telephone network facilities up to the demarcation point separating the inside wiring.

"Inside telephone wiring" for purposes of this section, means that portion of the telephone wire that connects the telephone equipment at the customer's premises to the telephone network at a demarcation point determined by the telephone corporation in accordance with orders of the Public Utilities Commission. **Leg.H.** Added Stats 1991 ch 1001 §2 (SB 841). Amended Stats 2013 ch 183 §5 (SB 745), effective January 1, 2014.

§ 1941.5. When person who is restrained from contact with protected tenant is not tenant of same dwelling unit as the protected tenant; Changing locks; Duties of landlord and protected tenant

(a) This section shall apply if a person is alleged to have committed abuse or violence against the eligible tenant or the immediate family or household member of the eligible tenant and the person is not a tenant of the same dwelling unit as the eligible tenant.

(b) A landlord shall, at the landlord's own expense, change the locks of the eligible tenant's dwelling unit upon written request of the eligible tenant not later than 24 hours after the eligible tenant gives the landlord a form of documentation described in subdivision (d) and shall give the eligible tenant a key to the new locks.

(c)(1) If a landlord fails to change the locks within 24 hours, the eligible tenant may change the locks without the landlord's permission, notwithstanding any provision in the lease to the contrary.

(2) If the eligible tenant changes the locks pursuant to this subdivision, the following shall apply:

(A) No later than 21 days after the eligible tenant changes the locks, the landlord shall reimburse the eligible tenant for the expenses the eligible tenant incurred to change the locks.

(B) The eligible tenant shall do all of the following:

(i) Change the locks in a workmanlike manner with locks of similar or better quality than the original lock.

(ii) Notify the landlord within 24 hours that the locks have been changed.

(iii) Provide the landlord with a key by any reasonable method agreed upon by the landlord and eligible tenant.

(3) This subdivision shall apply to leases executed on or after January 1, 2011.

(d) A written request to change the locks pursuant to subdivision (b) shall include one of the following forms of documentation attached to the request:

(1) A copy of a temporary restraining order, emergency protective order, or protective order lawfully issued pursuant to Part 3 (commencing with Section 6240), Part 4 (commencing with Section 6300), or Part 5 (commencing with Section 6400) of Division 10 of the Family Code, Section 136.2 of the Penal Code, Section 527.6 of the Code of Civil Procedure, or Section 213.5 or 15657.03 of the Welfare and Institutions Code that protects the eligible tenant, household member, or immediate family member from abuse or violence.

(2) A copy of a written report by a peace officer employed by a state or local law enforcement agency acting in the peace officer's official capacity stating that the tenant, household member, or immediate family member has filed a report alleging that the tenant, the household member, or the immediate family member is a victim of abuse or violence.

(3)(A) Documentation from a qualified third party based on information received by that third party while acting in their professional capacity to indicate that the tenant, the tenant's immediate family member, or the tenant's household member is seeking assistance for physical or mental injuries or abuse resulting from an act of abuse or violence, which shall contain, in substantially the same form, the following:

Tenant Statement and Qualified Third Party Statement under Civil Code Section 1941.5

Part I. Statement By Tenant

I, [insert name of tenant], state as follows:

I, my immediate family member, or a member of my household, have been a victim of:

[insert one or more of the following: domestic violence, sexual assault, stalking, human trafficking, elder abuse, dependent adult abuse, or a crime that caused bodily injury or death, a crime that included the exhibition, drawing, brandishing, or use of a firearm or other deadly weapon or instrument, or a crime that included the use of force against the victim or a threat of force against the victim.]

The most recent incident(s) happened on or about:

[insert date or dates.]

The incident(s) was/were committed by the following person(s), with these physical description(s), if known and safe to provide:

[if known and safe to provide, insert name(s) and physical description(s).]

_____
(signature of tenant)
_____
(date)

Part II. Qualified Third Party Statement

I, [insert name of qualified third party], state as follows:

My business address and phone number are:

[insert business address and phone number.]

Check and complete one of the following:

_____ I meet the requirements for a sexual assault counselor provided in Section 1035.2 of the Evidence Code and I am either engaged in an office, hospital, institution, or center commonly known as a rape crisis center described in that section or employed by an organization providing the programs specified in Section 13835.2 of the Penal Code.

_____ I meet the requirements for a domestic violence counselor provided in Section 1037.1 of the Evidence Code and I am employed, whether financially compensated or not, by a domestic violence victim service organization, as defined in that section.

_____ I meet the requirements for a human trafficking caseworker provided in Section 1038.2 of the Evidence Code and I am employed, whether financially compensated or not, by an organization that provides programs specified in Section 18294 of the Welfare and Institutions Code or in Section 13835.2 of the Penal Code.

_____ I meet the definition of "victim of violent crime advocate" provided in Section 1946.7 of the Civil Code and I am employed, whether financially compensated or not, by an agency or organization that has a documented record of providing services to victims of violent crime or provides those services under the auspices or supervision of a court or a law enforcement or prosecution agency.

_____ I am licensed by the State of California as a:

[insert one of the following: physician and surgeon, osteopathic physician and surgeon, registered nurse, psychiatrist, psychologist, licensed clinical social worker, licensed marriage and family therapist, or licensed professional clinical counselor.] and I am licensed by, and my license number is:

[insert name of state licensing entity and license number.]

The person who signed the Statement By Tenant above stated to me that the person, or a member of their immediate family, or a member of their household, is a victim of:

[insert one or more of the following: domestic violence, sexual assault, stalking, human trafficking, elder abuse, dependent adult abuse, a crime that caused bodily injury or death, a crime that included the exhibition, drawing, brandishing, or use of a firearm or other deadly weapon or instrument, or a crime that included the use or threat of force against the victim.]

The person further stated to me the incident(s) occurred on or about the date(s) stated above.

_____
(signature of qualified third party)
_____
(date)

(B) The documentation may be signed by a person who meets the requirements for a sexual assault counselor, domestic violence counselor, a human trafficking caseworker, or a victim of violent crime advocate only if the documentation displays the letterhead of the office, hospital, institution, center, or organization, as appropriate, that engages or employs, whether financially compensated or not, this counselor, caseworker, or advocate.

(4) Any other form of documentation that reasonably verifies that the abuse or violence occurred, including, but not limited to, a signed statement from the eligible tenant.

(e) An eligible tenant satisfies the documentation requirements under subdivision (d) by providing one of the forms of documentation listed in subdivision (d), of the tenant's choosing.

(f) For the purposes of this section, the following definitions apply:

(1) "Abuse or violence" has the same meaning as defined in paragraph (1) of subdivision (a) of Section 1161.3 of the Code of Civil Procedure.

(2) "Eligible tenant" means either of the following:

(A) A tenant who is a victim of abuse or violence.

(B) A tenant who has an immediate family member or household member who is a victim of abuse or violence, if the tenant is not alleged to have committed the abuse or violence.

(3) "Health practitioner" means a physician and surgeon, osteopathic physician and surgeon, psychiatrist, psychologist, registered nurse, licensed clinical social worker, licensed marriage and family therapist, or a licensed professional clinical counselor.

(4) "Household member" has the same meaning as defined in paragraph (1) of subdivision (h) of Section 1946.7.

(5) "Immediate family member" has the same meaning as defined in paragraph (3) of subdivision (h) of Section 1946.7.

(6) "Locks" means any exterior lock that provides access to the dwelling.

(7) "Qualified third party" means a health practitioner, domestic violence counselor, as defined in subdivision (a) of Section 1037.1 of the Evidence Code, a sexual assault counselor, as defined in Section 1035.2 of the Evidence Code, a human trafficking caseworker, as defined in subdivision (c) of Section 1038.2 of the Evidence Code, or a victim of violent crime advocate.

(8) "Tenant" means tenant, subtenant, lessee, or sublessee.

(9) "Victim of violent crime advocate" has the same meaning as defined in paragraph (5) of subdivision (h) of Section 1946.7. **Leg.H.** Added Stats 2024 ch 75 §2 (SB 1051), effective January 1, 2025.

Prior Law Former CC §1941.5, similar to the present section, was added Stats 2010 ch 626 §2 (SB 782), effective January 1, 2011 and repealed Stats 2024 ch 75 §1 (SB 1051), effective January 1, 2025, by its own provision.

§1941.6. When person who is restrained from contact with protected tenant is tenant of same dwelling unit as protected tenant; Changing locks; Duties of landlord and protected tenant; Liability

(a) This section shall apply if a person who is restrained from contact with a protected tenant under a court order is a tenant of the same dwelling unit as the protected tenant.

(b) A landlord shall, **at the landlord's own expense,** change the locks of a protected tenant's dwelling unit upon written request of the protected tenant not later than 24 hours after the protected tenant gives the landlord a copy of a court order that excludes from the dwelling unit the restrained person referred to in subdivision (a). The landlord shall give the protected tenant a key to the new locks.

(c)(1) If a landlord fails to change the locks within 24 hours, the protected tenant may change the locks without the landlord's permission, notwithstanding any provision in the lease to the contrary.

(2) If the protected tenant changes the locks pursuant to this subdivision, [1] **both** of the following **shall apply**:

(A) No later than 21 days after the protected tenant changes the locks, the landlord shall reimburse the protected tenant for the expenses the protected tenant incurred to change the locks.

(B) The protected tenant shall do all of the following:

[2] **(i)** Change the locks in a workmanlike manner with locks of similar or better quality than the original lock.

[3] **(ii)** Notify the landlord within 24 hours that the locks have been changed.

[4] **(iii)** Provide the landlord with a key by any reasonable method agreed upon by the landlord and protected tenant.

(3) This subdivision shall apply to leases executed on or after [5] **January 1, 2011**.

(d) Notwithstanding Section 789.3, if the locks are changed pursuant to this section, the landlord is not liable to a person excluded from the dwelling unit pursuant to this section.

(e) A person who has been excluded from a dwelling unit under this section remains liable under the lease with all other tenants of the dwelling unit for rent as provided in the lease.

(f) For the purposes of this section, the following definitions shall apply:

(1) "Court order" means a court order lawfully issued within the last 180 days pursuant to Section 527.6 of the Code of Civil Procedure, Part 3 (commencing with Section 6240), Part 4 (commencing with Section 6300), or Part 5 (commencing with Section 6400) of Division 10 of the Family Code, Section 136.2 of the Penal Code, or Section 213.5 of the Welfare and Institutions Code.

(2) "Locks" means any exterior lock that provides access to the dwelling.

(3) "Protected tenant" means a tenant who has obtained a court order.

(4) "Tenant" means tenant, subtenant, lessee, or sublessee. **Leg.H.** Added Stats 2010 ch 626 §3 (SB 782), effective January 1, 2011. Amended Stats 2024 ch 75 §3 (SB 1051), effective January 1, 2025.

§1941.6. 2024 Deletes. [1] the protected tenant shall do all [2] (A) [3] (B) [4] (C) [5] the date the act that added this section takes effect

§1941.7. Dilapidation relating to the presence of mold

(a) An obligation shall not arise under Section 1941 or 1942 to repair a dilapidation relating to the presence of mold pursuant to paragraph (13) of subdivision (a) of Section 17920.3 of the Health and Safety Code until the lessor has notice of the dilapidation or if the tenant is in violation of Section 1941.2.

(b) A landlord may enter a dwelling unit to repair a dilapidation relating to the presence of mold pursuant to paragraph (13) of subdivision (a) of Section 17920.3 of the Health and Safety Code provided the landlord complies with the provisions of Section 1954. **Leg.H.** Added Stats 2015 ch 720 §1 (SB 655), effective January 1, 2016.

§1942. Repairs by lessee

(a) If within a reasonable time after written or oral notice to the landlord or his agent, as defined in subdivision (a) of Section 1962, of dilapidations rendering the premises untenantable which the landlord ought to repair, the landlord neglects to do so, the tenant may repair the same himself where the cost of such repairs does not require an expenditure more than one month's rent of the premises and deduct the expenses of such repairs from the rent when due, or the tenant may vacate the premises, in which case the tenant shall be discharged from further payment of rent, or performance of other conditions as of the date of vacating the premises. This remedy shall not be available to the tenant more than twice in any 12-month period.

(b) For the purposes of this section, if a tenant acts to repair and deduct after the 30th day following notice, he is presumed to have acted after a reasonable time. The presumption established by this subdivision is a rebuttable presumption affecting the burden of producing evidence and shall not be construed to prevent a tenant from repairing and deducting after a shorter notice if all the circumstances require shorter notice.

(c) The tenant's remedy under subdivision (a) shall not be available if the condition was caused by the violation of Section 1929 or 1941.2.

(d) The remedy provided by this section is in addition to any other remedy provided by this chapter, the rental agreement, or other applicable statutory or common law. **Leg.H.** Enacted Stats 1872. Amended Code Amdts 1873–74 ch 612 §206; Stats 1970 ch 1280 §3; Stats 1979 ch 307 §3.

§1942.1. Waiver of tenant's rights; Arbitration

Any agreement by a lessee of a dwelling waiving or modifying his rights under Section 1941 or 1942 shall be void as contrary to public policy with respect to any condition which renders the premises untenantable, except that the lessor and the lessee may agree that the lessee shall undertake to improve, repair or maintain all or stipulated portions of the dwelling as part of the consideration for rental.

The lessor and lessee may, if an agreement is in writing, set forth the provisions of Sections 1941 to 1942.1, inclusive, and provide that any controversy relating to a condition of the premises claimed to make them untenantable may by application of either party be submitted to arbitration, pursuant to the provisions of Title 9 (commencing with Section 1280), Part 3 of the Code of Civil Procedure, and that the costs of such arbitration shall be apportioned by the arbitrator between the parties. **Leg.H.** Added Stats 1970 ch 1280 §4.

§1942.2. Deduction of utility payment from rent

A tenant who has made a payment to a utility pursuant to Section 777, 777.1, 10009, 10009.1, 12822, 12822.1, 16481, or 16481.1 of the Public Utilities Code, or to a district pursuant to Section 60371 of the Government Code, may deduct the payment from the rent as provided in that section. **Leg.H.** Added Stats 2009 ch 560 §1 (SB 120), effective January 1, 2010. Amended Stats 2014 ch 913 §6 (AB 2747), effective January 1, 2015.

§1942.3. Rebuttable presumption that landlord breached habitability requirements in Section 1941

(a) In any unlawful detainer action by the landlord to recover possession from a tenant, a rebuttable presumption affecting the burden of producing evidence that the landlord has breached the habitability requirements in Section 1941 is created if all of the following conditions exist:

(1) The dwelling substantially lacks any of the affirmative standard characteristics listed in Section 1941.1, is deemed and declared substandard pursuant to Section 17920.3 of the Health and Safety Code, or contains lead hazards as defined in Section 17920.10 of the Health and Safety Code.

(2) A public officer or employee who is responsible for the enforcement of any housing law has notified the landlord, or an agent of the landlord, in a written notice issued after inspection of the premises which informs the landlord of his or her obligation to abate the nuisance or repair the substandard or unsafe conditions identified under the authority described in paragraph (1).

(3) The conditions have existed and have not been abated 60 days beyond the date of issuance of the notice specified in paragraph (2) and the delay is without good cause.

(4) The conditions were not caused by an act or omission of the tenant or lessee in violation of Section 1929 or 1941.2.

(b) The presumption specified in subdivision (a) does not arise unless all of the conditions set forth therein are proven, but failure to so establish the presumption shall not otherwise affect the right of the tenant to raise and pursue any defense based on the landlord's breach of the implied warranty of habitability.

(c) The presumption provided in this section shall apply only to rental agreements or leases entered into or renewed on or after January 1, 1986.

Leg.H. Added Stats 1985 ch 1279 §1. Amended Stats 2005 ch 595 §2 (SB 253), effective January 1, 2006.

§1942.4. Liability of lessor demanding rent under specified conditions

(a) A landlord of a dwelling may not demand rent, collect rent, issue a notice of a rent increase, or issue a three-day notice to pay rent or quit pursuant to subdivision (2) of Section 1161 of the Code of Civil Procedure, if all of the following conditions exist prior to the landlord's demand or notice:

(1) The dwelling substantially lacks any of the affirmative standard characteristics listed in Section 1941.1 or violates Section 17920.10 of the Health and Safety Code, or is deemed and declared substandard as set forth in Section 17920.3 of the Health and Safety Code because conditions listed in that section exist to an extent that endangers the life, limb, health, property, safety, or welfare of the public or the occupants of the dwelling.

(2) A public officer or employee who is responsible for the enforcement of any housing law, after inspecting the premises, has notified the landlord or the landlord's agent in writing of his or her obligations to abate the nuisance or repair the substandard conditions.

(3) The conditions have existed and have not been abated 35 days beyond the date of service of the notice specified in paragraph (2) and the delay is without good cause. For purposes of this subdivision, service shall be complete at the time of deposit in the United States mail.

(4) The conditions were not caused by an act or omission of the tenant or lessee in violation of Section 1929 or 1941.2.

(b)(1) A landlord who violates this section is liable to the tenant or lessee for the actual damages sustained by the tenant or lessee and special damages of not less than one hundred dollars ($100) and not more than five thousand dollars ($5,000).

(2) The prevailing party shall be entitled to recovery of reasonable attorney's fees and costs of the suit in an amount fixed by the court.

(c) Any court that awards damages under this section may also order the landlord to abate any nuisance at the rental dwelling and to repair any substandard conditions of the rental dwelling, as defined in Section 1941.1, which significantly or materially affect the health or safety of the occupants of the rental dwelling and are uncorrected. If the court orders repairs or corrections, or both, the court's jurisdiction continues over the matter for the purpose of ensuring compliance.

(d) The tenant or lessee shall be under no obligation to undertake any other remedy prior to exercising his or her rights under this section.

(e) Any action under this section may be maintained in small claims court if the claim does not exceed the jurisdictional limit of that court.

(f) The remedy provided by this section may be utilized in addition to any other remedy provided by this chapter, the rental agreement, lease, or other applicable statutory or common law. Nothing in this section shall require any landlord to comply with this section if he or she pursues his or her rights pursuant to Chapter 12.75 (commencing with Section 7060) of Division 7 of Title 1 of the Government Code. **Leg.H.** Added Stats 1985 ch 1279 §2. Amended Stats 1990 ch 1305 §1 (SB 2627); Stats 1992 ch 488 §1 (AB 2574); Stats 1993 ch 589 §23 (AB 2211); Stats 2003 ch 109 §1 (AB 647).

§1942.5. Prohibition against certain retaliatory acts by lessor against lessee for exercising rights; Timeframe; Civil action; Damages; Attorney's fees

(a) If the lessor retaliates against the lessee because of the exercise by the lessee of the lessee's rights under this chapter or because of the lessee's complaint to an appropriate agency as to tenantability of a dwelling, and if the lessee of a dwelling is not in default as to the payment of rent, the lessor may not recover possession of a dwelling in any action or proceeding, cause the lessee to quit involuntarily, increase the rent, or decrease any services within 180 days of any of the following:

(1) After the date upon which the lessee, in good faith, has given notice pursuant to Section 1942, has provided notice of a suspected bed bug infestation, or has made an oral complaint to the lessor regarding tenantability.

(2) After the date upon which the lessee, in good faith, has filed a written complaint, or an oral complaint which is registered or otherwise recorded in writing, with an appropriate agency, of which the lessor has notice, for the purpose of obtaining correction of a condition relating to tenantability.

(3) After the date of an inspection or issuance of a citation, resulting from a complaint described in paragraph (2) of which the lessor did not have notice.

(4) After the filing of appropriate documents commencing a judicial or arbitration proceeding involving the issue of tenantability.

(5) After entry of judgment or the signing of an arbitration award, if any, when in the judicial proceeding or arbitration the issue of tenantability is determined adversely to the lessor.

In each instance, the 180-day period shall run from the latest applicable date referred to in paragraphs (1) to (5), inclusive.

(b) A lessee may not invoke subdivision (a) more than once in any 12-month period.

(c) To report, or to threaten to report, the lessee or individuals known to the landlord to be associated with the lessee to immigration authorities is a form of retaliatory conduct prohibited under subdivision (a). This subdivision shall in no way limit the definition of retaliatory conduct prohibited under this section.

(d) Notwithstanding subdivision (a), it is unlawful for a lessor to increase rent, decrease services, cause a lessee to quit involuntarily, bring an action to recover possession, or threaten to do any of those acts, for the purpose of retaliating against the lessee because the lessee has lawfully organized or participated in a lessees' association or an organization advocating lessees' rights or has lawfully and peaceably exercised any rights under the law. In an action brought by or against the lessee pursuant to this subdivision, the lessee shall bear the burden of producing evidence that the lessor's conduct was, in fact, retaliatory.

(e) To report, or to threaten to report, the lessee or individuals known to the landlord to be associated with the lessee to immigration authorities is a form of retaliatory conduct prohibited under subdivision (d). This subdivision shall in no way limit the definition of retaliatory conduct prohibited under this section.

(f) This section does not limit in any way the exercise by the lessor of the lessor's rights under any lease or agreement or any law pertaining to the hiring of property or the lessor's right to do any of the acts described in subdivision (a) or (d) for any lawful cause. Any waiver by a lessee of the lessee's rights under this section is void as contrary to public policy.

(g) Notwithstanding subdivisions (a) to (f), inclusive, a lessor may recover possession of a dwelling and do any of the other acts described in subdivision (a) within the period or periods prescribed therein, or within subdivision (d), if the notice of termination, rent increase, or other act, and any pleading or statement of issues in an arbitration, if any, states the ground upon which the lessor, in good faith, seeks to recover possession, increase rent, or do any of the other acts described in subdivision (a) or (d). If the statement is controverted, the lessor shall establish its truth at the trial or other hearing.

(h) Any lessor or agent of a lessor who violates this section shall be liable to the lessee in a civil action for all of the following:

(1) The actual damages sustained by the lessee.

(2) Punitive damages in an amount of not less than one hundred dollars ($100) nor more than two thousand dollars ($2,000) for each retaliatory act where the lessor or agent has been guilty of fraud, oppression, or malice with respect to that act.

(i) In any action brought for damages for retaliatory eviction, the court shall award reasonable attorney's fees to the prevailing party if either party requests attorney's fees upon the initiation of the action.

(j) The remedies provided by this section shall be in addition to any other remedies provided by statutory or decisional law.

(k) A lessor does not violate subdivision (c) or (e) by complying with any legal obligation under any federal government program that provides for rent limitations or rental assistance to a qualified tenant.

(*l*) This section shall become operative on October 1, 2021. **Leg.H.** Added Stats 2020 ch 37 §7 (AB 3088), effective August 31, 2020, operative February 1, 2021. Amended Stats 2021 ch 2 §6 (SB 91), effective January 29, 2021, operative July 1, 2021; Stats 2021 ch 27 §5 (AB 832), effective June 28, 2021, operative October 1, 2021.

Prior Law Former CC §1942.5, similar to the present section, was added Stats 1979 ch 652 §2, amended Stats 2003 ch 542 §2 (AB 1059), Stats 2016 ch 599 §1 (AB 551), effective January 1, 2017, Stats 2016 ch 703 §2.5 (AB 2881), effective January 1, 2017, Stats 2017 ch 489 §6 (AB 291), effective January 1, 2018, Stats 2020 ch 37 §6 (AB 3088), effective August 31, 2020, repealed February 1, 2021, Stats 2021 ch 2 §5 (SB 91), effective January 29, 2021, repealed July 1, 2021, Stats

2021 ch 27 §4 (AB 832), effective June 28, 2021, and was repealed by its own terms October 1, 2021.

§1942.6. Entry on property to provide information regarding tenants' rights or to participate in association as not constituting trespass

Any person entering onto residential real property, upon the invitation of an occupant, during reasonable hours or because of emergency circumstances, for the purpose of providing information regarding tenants' rights or to participate in a lessees' association or association of tenants or an association that advocates tenants' rights shall not be liable in any criminal or civil action for trespass.

The Legislature finds and declares that this section is declaratory of existing law. Nothing in this section shall be construed to enlarge or diminish the rights of any person under existing law. **Leg.H.** Added Stats 1999 ch 590 §1 (SB 1098).

§1942.7. Declawing or devocalization as condition of occupancy prohibited

(a) A person or corporation that occupies, owns, manages, or provides services in connection with any real property, including the individual's or corporation's agents or successors in interest, and that allows an animal on the premises, shall not do any of the following:

(1) Advertise, through any means, the availability of real property for occupancy in a manner designed to discourage application for occupancy of that real property because an applicant's animal has not been declawed or devocalized.

(2) Refuse to allow the occupancy of any real property, refuse to negotiate the occupancy of any real property, or otherwise make unavailable or deny to any other person the occupancy of any real property because of that person's refusal to declaw or devocalize any animal.

(3) Require any tenant or occupant of real property to declaw or devocalize any animal allowed on the premises.

(b) For purposes of this section, the following definitions apply:

(1) "Animal" means any mammal, bird, reptile, or amphibian.

(2) "Application for occupancy" means all phases of the process of applying for the right to occupy real property, including, but not limited to, filling out applications, interviewing, and submitting references.

(3) "Claw" means a hardened keratinized modification of the epidermis, or a hardened keratinized growth, that extends from the end of the digits of certain mammals, birds, reptiles, and amphibians, often commonly referred to as a "claw," "talon," or "nail."

(4) "Declawing" means performing, procuring, or arranging for any procedure, such as an onychectomy, tendonectomy, or phalangectomy, to remove or to prevent the normal function of an animal's claw or claws.

(5) "Devocalizing" means performing, procuring, or arranging for any surgical procedure such as a vocal cordectomy, to remove an animal's vocal cords or to prevent the normal function of an animal's vocal cords.

(6) "Owner" means any person who has any right, title, or interest in real property.

(c)(1) A city attorney, district attorney, or other law enforcement prosecutorial entity has standing to enforce this section and may sue for declaratory relief or injunctive relief for a violation of this section, and to enforce the civil penalties provided in paragraphs (2) and (3).

(2) In addition to any other penalty allowed by law, a violation of paragraph (1) of subdivision (a) shall result in a civil penalty of not more than one thousand dollars ($1,000) per advertisement, to be paid to the entity that is authorized to bring the action under this section.

(3) In addition to any other penalty allowed by law, a violation of paragraph (2) or (3) of subdivision (a) shall result in a civil penalty of not more than one thousand dollars ($1,000) per animal, to be paid to the entity that is authorized to bring the action under this section. **Leg.H.** Added Stats 2012 ch 596 §2 (SB 1229), effective January 1, 2013.

§1942.8. Temporary residence by persons who are at risk of homelessness; Rights and obligations of tenant and landlord [Repealed]

Leg.H. Added Stats 2019 ch 339 §1 (AB 1188), effective January 1, 2020, repealed January 1, 2024.

§1942.9. Fees or reduction of services related to COVID-19 rental debt

(a) Notwithstanding any other law, a landlord shall not, with respect to a tenant who has COVID-19 rental debt, as that term is defined in Section 1179.02 of the Code of Civil Procedure, and who has submitted a declaration of COVID-19-related financial distress, as defined in Section 1179.02 of the Code of Civil Procedure, do either of the following:

(1) Charge a tenant, or attempt to collect from a tenant, fees assessed for the late payment of that COVID-19 rental debt.

(2) Increase fees charged to the tenant or charge the tenant fees for services previously provided by the landlord without charge.

(b) Notwithstanding any other law, a landlord who temporarily reduces or makes unavailable a service or amenity as the result of compliance with federal, state, or local public health orders or guidelines shall not be considered to have violated the rental or lease agreement, nor to have provided different terms or conditions of tenancy or reduced services for purposes of any law, ordinance, rule, regulation, or initiative measure adopted by a local governmental entity that establishes a maximum amount that a landlord may charge a tenant for rent. **Leg.H.** Added Stats 2021 ch 2 §7 (SB 91), effective January 29, 2021. Amended Stats 2021 ch 5 §6 (AB 81), effective February 23, 2021.

§1943. Term of hiring when no limit is fixed

A hiring of real property, other than lodgings and dwelling-houses, in places where there is no custom or usage on the subject, is presumed to be a month to month tenancy unless otherwise designated in writing; except that, in the case of real property used for agricultural or grazing purposes a hiring is presumed to be for one year from its commencement unless otherwise expressed in the hiring. **Leg.H.** Enacted Stats 1872. Amended Stats 1953 ch 1541 §1.

§1944. Hiring of lodgings for indefinite term

A hiring of lodgings or a dwelling-house for an unspecified term is presumed to have been made for such length of time as the parties adopt for the estimation of the rent. Thus a hiring at a monthly rate of rent is presumed to be for one month. In the absence of any agreement respecting the length of time or the rent, the hiring is presumed to be monthly. **Leg.H.** Enacted Stats 1872.

§1945. Renewal of lease by lessee's continued possession

If a lessee of real property remains in possession thereof after the expiration of the hiring, and the lessor accepts rent from him, the parties are presumed to have renewed the hiring on the same terms and for the same time, not exceeding one month when the rent is payable monthly, nor in any case one year. **Leg.H.** Enacted Stats 1872.

§1945.5. Required printing of renewal provision

Notwithstanding any other provision of law, any term of a lease executed after the effective date of this section for the hiring of residential real property which provides for the automatic renewal or extension of the lease for all or part of the full term of the lease if the lessee remains in possession after the expiration of the lease or fails to give notice of his intent not to renew or extend before the expiration of the lease shall be voidable by the party who did not prepare the lease unless such renewal or extension provision appears in at least eight-point boldface type, if the contract is printed, in the body of the lease agreement and a recital of the fact that such provision is contained in the body of the agreement appears in at least eight-point boldface type, if the contract is printed, immediately prior to the place where the lessee executes the agreement as against public policy. In such case, the presumption in Section 1945 of this code shall apply.

Any waiver of the provisions of this section is void as against public policy. **Leg.H.** Added Stats 1965 ch 1664 §1, operative June 30, 1966. Amended Stats 1976 ch 1107 §1.

§1946. Notice required to terminate tenancy

(a) A hiring of real property, for a term not specified by the parties, is deemed to be renewed as stated in Section 1945, at the end of the term implied by law unless one of the parties gives written notice to the other of that party's intention to terminate the same, at least as long before the expiration thereof as the term of the hiring itself, not exceeding 30 days; provided, however, that as to tenancies from month to month either of the parties may terminate the same by giving at least 30 days' written notice thereof at any time and the rent shall be due and payable to and including the date of termination. It shall be competent for the parties to provide by an agreement at the time the tenancy is created that a notice of the intention to terminate the same may be given at any time not less than seven days before the expiration of the term thereof. The notice herein required shall be given in the manner prescribed in Section 1162 of the

Code of Civil Procedure or by sending a copy by certified or registered mail addressed to the other party. In addition, the lessee may give the notice by sending a copy by certified or registered mail addressed to the agent of the lessor to whom the lessee has paid the rent for the month prior to the date of the notice or by delivering a copy to the agent personally. The notice given by the lessor shall also contain, in substantially the same form, the following:

"State law permits former tenants to reclaim abandoned personal property left at the former address of the tenant, subject to certain conditions. You may or may not be able to reclaim property without incurring additional costs, depending on the cost of storing the property and the length of time before it is reclaimed. In general, these costs will be lower the sooner you contact your former landlord after being notified that property belonging to you was left behind after you moved out."

(b) A landlord or its agent shall not charge a tenant a fee for serving, posting, or otherwise delivering any notice, as described in this section. **Leg.H.** Enacted Stats 1872. Amended Stats 1931 ch 643 §1; Stats 1937 ch 354 §1; Stats 1941 ch 784 §1; Stats 1947 ch 676 §2; Stats 1969 ch 442 §1; Stats 1973 ch 167 §10; Stats 2012 ch 560 §1 (AB 2521), effective January 1, 2013; Stats 2018 ch 104 §1 (AB 2847), effective January 1, 2019; Stats 2024 ch 287 §1 (SB 611), effective January 1, 2025.

§1946.1. Renewal at end of implied term absent written notice; Time and manner of notice

(a) Notwithstanding Section 1946, a hiring of residential real property **or commercial real property by a qualified commercial tenant** for a term not specified by the parties, is deemed to be renewed as stated in Section 1945, at the end of the term implied by law unless one of the parties gives written notice to the other of [1] **the party's** intention to terminate the tenancy, as provided in this section.

(b) An owner of a residential dwelling **or commercial real property hired by a qualified commercial tenant** giving notice pursuant to this section shall give notice at least 60 days prior to the proposed date of termination. A tenant giving notice pursuant to this section shall give notice for a period at least as long as the term of the periodic tenancy prior to the proposed date of termination.

(c) Notwithstanding subdivision (b), an owner of a residential dwelling **or commercial real property hired by a qualified commercial tenant** giving notice pursuant to this section shall give notice at least 30 days prior to the proposed date of termination if [2] a tenant or resident has resided in the dwelling **or occupied the property** for less than one year.

(d) Notwithstanding subdivision (b), an owner of a residential dwelling giving notice pursuant to this section shall give notice at least 30 days prior to the proposed date of termination if all of the following apply:

(1) The dwelling or unit is alienable separate from the title to any other dwelling unit.

(2) The owner has contracted to sell the dwelling or unit to a bona fide purchaser for value, and has established an escrow with a title insurer or an underwritten title company, as defined in Sections 12340.4 and 12340.5 of the Insurance Code, respectively, a licensed escrow agent, as defined in Sections 17004 and 17200 of the Financial Code, or a licensed real estate broker, as defined in Section 10131 of the Business and Professions Code.

(3) The purchaser is a natural person or persons.

(4) The notice is given no more than 120 days after the escrow has been established.

(5) Notice was not previously given to the tenant pursuant to this section.

(6) The purchaser in good faith intends to reside in the property for at least one full year after the termination of the tenancy.

(e) After an owner has given notice of [3] **the owner's** intention to terminate the tenancy pursuant to this section, a tenant may also give notice of [4] **the tenant's** intention to terminate the tenancy pursuant to this section, provided that the tenant's notice is for a period at least as long as the term of the periodic tenancy and the proposed date of termination occurs before the owner's proposed date of termination.

(f) The notices required by this section shall be given in the manner prescribed in Section 1162 of the Code of Civil Procedure or by sending a copy by certified or registered mail.

(g) This section may not be construed to affect the authority of a public entity that otherwise exists to regulate or monitor the basis for eviction.

(h) [5] **A** notice given by an owner pursuant to this section shall contain, in substantially the same form, the following:

"State law permits former tenants to reclaim abandoned personal property left at the former address of the tenant, subject to certain conditions. You may or may not be able to reclaim property without incurring additional costs, depending on the cost of storing the property and the length of time before it is reclaimed. In general, these costs will be lower the sooner you contact your former landlord after being notified that property belonging to you was left behind after you moved out."

(i) A landlord or its agent shall not charge a tenant a fee for serving, posting, or otherwise delivering any notice, as described in this section.

(j) A landlord of a commercial real property shall include in the notice required by this section information on the provisions of this section.

(k) For the purposes of this section, the following definitions apply:

(1) "Commercial real property" means all real property in this state, except dwelling units subject to this chapter, mobilehomes as defined in Section 798.3, and recreational vehicles as defined in Section 799.29.

(2) "Microenterprise" has the same meaning as that term is defined in subdivision (a) of Section 18000 of the Business and Professions Code.

(3) "Nonprofit organization" means any private, nonprofit organization that qualifies under Section 501(c)(3) of the United States Internal Revenue Code of 1986.

(4) "Qualified commercial tenant" means a tenant of commercial real property that meets both of the following requirements:

(A) The tenant is a microenterprise, a restaurant with fewer than 10 employees, or a nonprofit organization with fewer than 20 employees.

(B)(i) Subject to clause (ii), the tenant has provided the landlord, within the previous 12 months, a written notice that the tenant is a qualified commercial tenant and a self-attestation regarding the number of employees, at such time the protections under this section come into place.

(ii) Unless the tenancy is from week to week, month to month, or other period less than a month, the tenant provided the notice and self-attestation described in clause (i) before or upon execution of the lease, and annually thereafter, at such time the protections under this section come into place. **Leg.H.** Added Stats 2006 ch 842 §1 (AB 1169), effective January 1, 2007. Amended Stats 2009 ch 347 §1 (SB 290), effective January 1, 2010; Stats 2012 ch 560 §2 (AB 2521), effective January 1, 2013, ch 786 §2.5 (AB 2303), effective January 1, 2013; Stats 2024 ch 287 §2 (SB 611), effective January 1, 2025; Stats 2024 §3.5 (SB 1103), effective January 1, 2025 (ch 1015 prevails).

§1946.1. 2024 Deletes. [1] his or her [2] any [3] his or her [4] his or her [5] Any

Prior Law: Former CC §1946.1, similar to the present section, was added Stats 2001 ch 729 §1, repealed January 1, 2005, amended Stats 2002 ch 301 §1, repealed January 1, 2006; Stats 2003 ch 62 §17, repealed January 1, 2006 and repealed Stats January 1, 2006, by its own terms.

Former CC §1946.1, similar to the present section, was added Stats 2001 ch 729 §1 and repealed operative January 1, 2006, by its own provisions.

§ 1946.2. Limitations on tenancy termination after twelve months continuous, lawful occupation; Opportunity to cure violation; Owner obligation in no-fault just cause termination; Notice [Repealed January 1, 2030]

(a) Notwithstanding any other law, after a tenant has continuously and lawfully occupied a residential real property for 12 months, the owner of the residential real property shall not terminate a tenancy without just cause, which shall be stated in the written notice to terminate tenancy. If any additional adult tenants are added to the lease before an existing tenant has continuously and lawfully occupied the residential real property for 24 months, then this subdivision shall only apply if either of the following are satisfied:

(1) All of the tenants have continuously and lawfully occupied the residential real property for 12 months or more.

(2) One or more tenants have continuously and lawfully occupied the residential real property for 24 months or more.

(b) For purposes of this section, "just cause" means either of the following:

(1) At-fault just cause, which means any of the following:

(A) Default in the payment of rent.

(B) A breach of a material term of the lease, as described in paragraph (3) of Section 1161 of the Code of Civil Procedure, including, but not limited to, violation of a provision of the lease after being issued a written notice to correct the violation.

(C) Maintaining, committing, or permitting the maintenance or commission of a nuisance as described in paragraph (4) of Section 1161 of the Code of Civil Procedure.

(D) Committing waste as described in paragraph (4) of Section 1161 of the Code of Civil Procedure.

(E) The tenant had a written lease that terminated on or after January 1, 2020, or January 1, 2022, if the lease is for a tenancy in a mobilehome, and after a written request or demand from the owner, the tenant has refused to execute a written extension or renewal of the lease for an additional term of similar duration with similar provisions, provided that those terms do not violate this section or any other provision of law.

(F) Criminal activity by the tenant on the residential real property, including any common areas, or any criminal activity or criminal threat, as defined in subdivision (a) of Section 422 of the Penal Code, on or off the residential real property, that is directed at any owner or agent of the owner of the residential real property.

(G) Assigning or subletting the premises in violation of the tenant's lease, as described in paragraph (4) of Section 1161 of the Code of Civil Procedure.

(H) The tenant's refusal to allow the owner to enter the residential real property as authorized by Sections 1101.5 and 1954 of this code, and Sections 13113.7 and 17926.1 of the Health and Safety Code.

(I) Using the premises for an unlawful purpose as described in paragraph (4) of Section 1161 of the Code of Civil Procedure.

(J) The employee, agent, or licensee's failure to vacate after their termination as an employee, agent, or a licensee as described in paragraph (1) of Section 1161 of the Code of Civil Procedure.

(K) When the tenant fails to deliver possession of the residential real property after providing the owner written notice as provided in Section 1946 of the tenant's intention to terminate the hiring of the real property, or makes a written offer to surrender that is accepted in writing by the owner, but fails to deliver possession at the time specified in that written notice as described in paragraph (5) of Section 1161 of the Code of Civil Procedure.

(2) No-fault just cause, which means any of the following:

(A)(i) Intent to occupy the residential real property by the owner or the owner's spouse, domestic partner, children, grandchildren, parents, or grandparents for a minimum of 12 continuous months as that person's primary residence.

(ii) For leases entered into on or after July 1, 2020, or July 1, 2022, if the lease is for a tenancy in a mobilehome, clause (i) shall apply only if the tenant agrees, in writing, to the termination, or if a provision of the lease allows the owner to terminate the lease if the owner, or the owner's spouse, domestic partner, children, grandchildren, parents, or grandparents, unilaterally decides to occupy the residential real property. Addition of a provision allowing the owner to terminate the lease as described in this clause to a new or renewed rental agreement or fixed-term lease constitutes a similar provision for the purposes of subparagraph (E) of paragraph (1).

(iii) This subparagraph does not apply if the intended occupant occupies a rental unit on the property or if a vacancy of a similar unit already exists at the property.

(iv) The written notice terminating a tenancy for a just cause pursuant to this subparagraph shall contain the name or names and relationship to the owner of the intended occupant. The written notice shall additionally include notification that the tenant may request proof that the intended occupant is an owner or related to the owner as defined in subclause (II) of clause (viii). The proof shall be provided upon request and may include an operating agreement and other non-public documents.

(v) Clause (i) applies only if the intended occupant moves into the rental unit within 90 days after the tenant vacates and occupies the rental unit as a primary residence for at least 12 consecutive months.

(vi)(I) If the intended occupant fails to occupy the rental unit within 90 days after the tenant vacates or fails to occupy the rental unit as their primary residence for at least 12 consecutive months, the owner shall offer the unit to the tenant who vacated it at the same rent and lease terms in effect at the time the tenant vacated and shall reimburse the tenant for reasonable moving expenses incurred in excess of any relocation assistance that was paid to the tenant in connection with the written notice.

(II) If the intended occupant moves into the rental unit within 90 days after the tenant vacates, but dies before having occupied the rental unit as a primary residence for 12 months, as required by clause (vi), this will not be considered a failure to comply with this section or a material violation of this section by the owner as provided in subdivision (h).

(vii) For a new tenancy commenced during the time periods described in clause (v), the accommodations shall be offered and rented or leased at the lawful rent in effect at the time any notice of termination of tenancy is served.

(viii) As used in this subparagraph:

(I) "Intended occupant" means the owner of the residential real property or the owner's spouse, domestic partner, child, grandchild, parent, or grandparent, as described in clause (i).

(II) "Owner" means any of the following:

(ia) An owner who is a natural person that has at least a 25-percent recorded ownership interest in the property.

(ib) An owner who is a natural person who has any recorded ownership interest in the property if 100 percent of the recorded ownership is divided among owners who are related to each other as sibling, spouse, domestic partner, child, parent, grandparent, or grandchild.

(ic) An owner who is a natural person whose recorded interest in the property is owned through a limited liability company or partnership.

(III) For purposes of subclause (II), "natural person" includes any of the following:

(ia) A natural person who is a settlor or beneficiary of a family trust.

(ib) If the property is owned by a limited liability company or partnership, a natural person with a 25-percent ownership interest in the property.

(IV) "Family trust" means a revocable living trust or irrevocable trust in which the settlors and beneficiaries of the trust are persons who are related to each other as sibling, spouse, domestic partner, child, parent, grandparent, or grandchild.

(V) "Beneficial owner" means a natural person or family trust for whom, directly or indirectly and through any contract arrangement, understanding, relationship, or otherwise, and any of the following applies:

(ia) The natural person exercises substantial control over a partnership or limited liability company.

(ib) The natural person owns 25 percent or more of the equity interest of a partnership or limited liability company.

(ic) The natural person receives substantial economic benefits from the assets of a partnership

(B) Withdrawal of the residential real property from the rental market.

(C)(i) The owner complying with any of the following:

(I) An order issued by a government agency or court relating to habitability that necessitates vacating the residential real property.

(II) An order issued by a government agency or court to vacate the residential real property.

(III) A local ordinance that necessitates vacating the residential real property.

(ii) If it is determined by any government agency or court that the tenant is at fault for the condition or conditions triggering the order or need to vacate under clause (i), the tenant shall not be entitled to relocation assistance as outlined in paragraph (3) of subdivision (d).

(D)(i) Intent to demolish or to substantially remodel the residential real property.

(ii) For purposes of this subparagraph, "substantially remodel" means either of the following that cannot be reasonably accomplished in a safe manner that allows the tenant to remain living in the place and that requires the tenant to vacate the residential real property for at least 30 consecutive days:

(I) The replacement or substantial modification of any structural, electrical, plumbing, or mechanical system that requires a permit from a governmental agency.

(II) The abatement of hazardous materials, including lead-based paint, mold, or asbestos, in accordance with applicable federal, state, and local laws.

(iii) For purposes of this subparagraph, a tenant is not required to vacate the residential real property on any days where a tenant could continue living in the residential real property without violating health, safety, and habitability codes and laws. Cosmetic improvements alone, including painting, decorating, and minor repairs, or other work that can be performed safely without having the residential real property vacated, do not qualify as substantial remodel.

(iv) A written notice terminating a tenancy for a just cause pursuant to this subparagraph shall include all of the following information:

(I) A statement informing the tenant of the owner's intent to demolish the property or substantially remodel the rental unit property.

(II) The following statement:

"If the substantial remodel of your unit or demolition of the property as described in this notice of termination is not commenced or completed, the owner must offer you the opportunity to re-rent your unit with a rental agreement containing the same terms as your most recent rental agreement with the owner at the rental rate that was in effect at the time you vacated. You must notify the owner within thirty (30) days of receipt of the offer to re-rent of your acceptance or rejection of the offer, and, if accepted, you must reoccupy the unit within thirty (30) days of notifying the owner of your acceptance of the offer."

(III) A description of the substantial remodel to be completed, the approximate expected duration of the substantial remodel, or if the property is to be demolished, the expected date by which the property will be demolished, together with one of the following:

(ia) A copy of the permit or permits required to undertake the substantial remodel or demolition.

(ib) Only if a notice is issued pursuant to subclause (II) of clause (ii) and the remodel does not require any permit, a copy of the signed contract with the contractor hired by the owner to complete the substantial remodel, that reasonably details the work that will be undertaken to abate the hazardous materials as described in subclause (II) of clause (ii).

(IV) A notification that if the tenant is interested in reoccupying the rental unit following the substantial remodel, the tenant shall inform the owner of the tenant's interest in reoccupying the rental unit following the substantial remodel and provide to the owner the tenant's address, telephone number, and email address.

(c) Before an owner of residential real property issues a notice to terminate a tenancy for just cause that is a curable lease violation, the owner shall first give notice of the violation to the tenant with an opportunity to cure the violation pursuant to paragraph (3) of Section 1161 of the Code of Civil Procedure. If the violation is not cured within the time period set forth in the notice, a three-day notice to quit without an opportunity to cure may thereafter be served to terminate the tenancy.

(d)(1) For a tenancy for which just cause is required to terminate the tenancy under subdivision (a), if an owner of residential real property issues a termination notice based on a no-fault just cause described in paragraph (2) of subdivision (b), the owner shall, regardless of the tenant's income, at the owner's option, do one of the following:

(A) Assist the tenant to relocate by providing a direct payment to the tenant as described in paragraph (3).

(B) Waive in writing the payment of rent for the final month of the tenancy, prior to the rent becoming due.

(2) If an owner issues a notice to terminate a tenancy for no-fault just cause, the owner shall notify the tenant in the written termination notice of the tenant's right to relocation assistance or rent waiver pursuant to this section. If the owner elects to waive the rent for the final month of the tenancy as provided in subparagraph (B) of paragraph (1), the notice shall state the amount of rent waived and that no rent is due for the final month of the tenancy.

(3)(A) The amount of relocation assistance or rent waiver shall be equal to one month of the tenant's rent that was in effect when the owner issued the notice to terminate the tenancy. Any relocation assistance shall be provided within 15 calendar days of service of the notice.

(B) If a tenant fails to vacate after the expiration of the notice to terminate the tenancy, the actual amount of any relocation assistance or rent waiver provided pursuant to this subdivision shall be recoverable as damages in an action to recover possession.

(C) The relocation assistance or rent waiver required by this subdivision shall be credited against any other relocation assistance required by any other law.

(4) An owner's failure to strictly comply with this subdivision shall render the notice of termination void.

(e) This section shall not apply to the following types of residential real properties or residential circumstances:

(1) Transient and tourist hotel occupancy as defined in subdivision (b) of Section 1940.

(2) Housing accommodations in a nonprofit hospital, religious facility, extended care facility, licensed residential care facility for the elderly, as defined in Section 1569.2 of the Health and Safety Code, or an adult residential facility, as defined in Chapter 6 of Division 6 of Title 22 of the Manual of Policies and Procedures published by the State Department of Social Services.

(3) Dormitories owned and operated by an institution of higher education or a kindergarten and grades 1 to 12, inclusive, school.

(4) Housing accommodations in which the tenant shares bathroom or kitchen facilities with the owner who maintains their principal residence at the residential real property.

(5) Single-family owner-occupied residences, including both of the following:

(A) A residence in which the owner-occupant rents or leases no more than two units or bedrooms, including, but not limited to, an accessory dwelling unit or a junior accessory dwelling unit.

(B) A mobilehome.

(6) A property containing two separate dwelling units within a single structure in which the owner occupied one of the units as the owner's principal place of residence at the beginning of the tenancy, so long as the owner continues in occupancy, and neither unit is an accessory dwelling unit or a junior accessory dwelling unit.

(7) Housing that has been issued a certificate of occupancy within the previous 15 years, unless the housing is a mobilehome.

(8) Residential real property, including a mobilehome, that is alienable separate from the title to any other dwelling unit, provided that both of the following apply:

(A) The owner is not any of the following:

(i) A real estate investment trust, as defined in Section 856 of the Internal Revenue Code.

(ii) A corporation.

(iii) A limited liability company in which at least one member is a corporation.

(iv) Management of a mobilehome park, as defined in Section 798.2.

(B)(i) The tenants have been provided written notice that the residential property is exempt from this section using the following statement:

"This property is not subject to the rent limits imposed by Section 1947.12 of the Civil Code and is not subject to the just cause requirements of Section 1946.2 of the Civil Code. This property meets the requirements of Sections 1947.12 (d)(5) and 1946.2 (e)(8) of the Civil Code and the owner is not any of the following: (1) a real estate investment trust, as defined by Section 856 of the Internal Revenue Code; (2) a corporation; or (3) a limited liability company in which at least one member is a corporation."

(ii)(I) Except as provided in subclause (II), for a tenancy existing before July 1, 2020, the notice required under clause (i) may, but is not required to, be provided in the rental agreement.

(II) For a tenancy in a mobilehome existing before July 1, 2022, the notice required under clause (i) may, but is not required to, be provided in the rental agreement.

(iii)(I) Except as provided in subclause (II), for any tenancy commenced or renewed on or after July 1, 2020, the notice required under clause (i) must be provided in the rental agreement.

(II) For any tenancy in a mobilehome commenced or renewed on or after July 1, 2022, the notice required under clause (i) shall be provided in the rental agreement.

(iv) Addition of a provision containing the notice required under clause (i) to any new or renewed rental agreement or fixed-term lease constitutes a similar provision for the purposes of subparagraph (E) of paragraph (1) of subdivision (b).

(9) Housing restricted by deed, regulatory restriction contained in an agreement with a government agency, or other recorded document as affordable housing for persons and families of very low, low, or moderate income, as defined in Section 50093 of the Health and Safety Code, or subject to an agreement that provides housing subsidies for affordable housing for persons and families of very low, low, or moderate income, as defined in Section 50093 of the Health and Safety Code or comparable federal statutes.

(f) An owner of residential real property subject to this section shall provide notice to the tenant as follows:

(1)(A) Except as provided in subparagraph (B), for any tenancy commenced or renewed on or after July 1, 2020, as an addendum to the lease or rental agreement, or as a written notice signed by the tenant, with a copy provided to the tenant.

(B) For a tenancy in a mobilehome commenced or renewed on or after July 1, 2022, as an addendum to the lease or rental agreement, or as a written notice signed by the tenant, with a copy provided to the tenant.

(2)(A) Except as provided in subparagraph (B), for a tenancy existing prior to July 1, 2020, by written notice to the tenant no later than August 1, 2020, or as an addendum to the lease or rental agreement.

(B) For a tenancy in a mobilehome existing prior to July 1, 2022, by written notice to the tenant no later than August 1, 2022, or as an addendum to the lease or rental agreement.

(3) The notification or lease provision shall be in no less than 12-point type, and shall include the following:

"California law limits the amount your rent can be increased. See Section 1947.12 of the Civil Code for more information. California law also provides that after all of the tenants have continuously and lawfully occupied the property for 12 months or more or at least one of the tenants has continuously and lawfully occupied the property for 24 months or more, a landlord must provide a statement of cause in any notice to terminate a tenancy. See Section 1946.2 of the Civil Code for more information."

The notification or lease provision shall be subject to Section 1632.

(g) An owner's failure to comply with any provision of this section shall render the written termination notice void.

(h)(1) An owner who attempts to recover possession of a rental unit in material violation of this section shall be liable to the tenant in a civil action for all of the following:

(A) Actual damages.

(B) In the court's discretion, reasonable attorney's fees and costs.

(C) Upon a showing that the owner has acted willfully or with oppression, fraud, or malice, up to three times the actual damages. An award may also be entered for punitive damages for the benefit of the tenant against the owner.

(2) The Attorney General, in the name of the people of the State of California, and the city attorney or county counsel in the jurisdiction in which the rental unit is located, in the name of the city or county, may seek injunctive relief based on violations of this section.

(i)(1) This section does not apply to the following residential real property:

(A) Residential real property subject to a local ordinance requiring just cause for termination of a residential tenancy adopted on or before September 1, 2019, in which case the local ordinance shall apply.

(B) Residential real property subject to a local ordinance requiring just cause for termination of a residential tenancy adopted or amended after September 1, 2019, that is more protective than this section, in which case the local ordinance shall apply. For purposes of this subparagraph, an ordinance is "more protective" if it meets all of the following criteria:

(i) The just cause for termination of a residential tenancy under the local ordinance is consistent with this section.

(ii) The ordinance further limits the reasons for termination of a residential tenancy, provides for higher relocation assistance amounts, or provides additional tenant protections that are not prohibited by any other provision of law.

(iii) The local government has made a binding finding within their local ordinance that the ordinance is more protective than the provisions of this section.

(2) A residential real property shall not be subject to both a local ordinance requiring just cause for termination of a residential tenancy and this section.

(3) A local ordinance adopted after September 1, 2019, that is less protective than this section shall not be enforced unless this section is repealed.

(j) Any waiver of the rights under this section shall be void as contrary to public policy.

(k) For the purposes of this section, the following definitions shall apply:

(1) "Owner" includes any person, acting as principal or through an agent, having the right to offer residential real property for rent, and includes a predecessor in interest to the owner.

(2) "Residential real property" means any dwelling or unit that is intended for human habitation, including any dwelling or unit in a mobilehome park.

(3) "Tenancy" means the lawful occupation of residential real property and includes a lease or sublease.

(*l*) This section shall not apply to a homeowner of a mobilehome, as defined in Section 798.9.

(m) This section shall become operative on April 1, 2024.

(n) This section shall remain in effect only until January 1, 2030, and as of that date is repealed. **Leg.H.** Added Stats 2023 ch 290 §2 (SB 567), effective January 1, 2024, operative April 1, 2024, repealed January 1, 2030. Amended Stats 2024 ch 8 §1 (SB 479), effective March 25, 2024, operative April 1, 2024, repealed January 1, 2030.

Prior Law Former CC §1946.2, relating to the present section, added Stats 2019 ch 597 §2 (AB 1482), effective January 1, 2020, repealed January 1, 2030, amended Stats 2020 ch 37 §8 (AB 3088), effective August 31, 2020, repealed January 1, 2030; Stats 2020 ch 370 §32 (SB 1371), effective January 1, 2021, repealed January 1, 2030 (ch 37 prevails); Stats 2021 ch 125 §3 (AB 978), effective January 1, 2022, repealed January 1, 2030; Stats 2023 ch 290 §1 (SB 567), effective January 1, 2024, repealed April 1, 2024.

§ 1946.2. Limitations on tenancy termination after twelve months continuous, lawful occupation; Opportunity to cure violation; Owner obligation in no-fault just cause termination; Notice [Repealed January 1, 2030]

(a) Notwithstanding any other law, after a tenant has continuously and lawfully occupied a residential real property for 12 months, the owner of the residential real property shall not terminate a tenancy without just cause, which shall be stated in the written notice to terminate tenancy. If any additional adult tenants are added to the lease before an existing tenant has continuously and lawfully occupied the residential real property for 24 months, then this subdivision shall only apply if either of the following are satisfied:

(1) All of the tenants have continuously and lawfully occupied the residential real property for 12 months or more.

(2) One or more tenants have continuously and lawfully occupied the residential real property for 24 months or more.

(b) For purposes of this section, "just cause" means either of the following:

(1) At-fault just cause, which means any of the following:

(A) Default in the payment of rent.

(B) A breach of a material term of the lease, as described in paragraph (3) of Section 1161 of the Code of Civil Procedure, including, but not limited to, violation of a provision of the lease after being issued a written notice to correct the violation.

(C) Maintaining, committing, or permitting the maintenance or commission of a nuisance as described in paragraph (4) of Section 1161 of the Code of Civil Procedure.

(D) Committing waste as described in paragraph (4) of Section 1161 of the Code of Civil Procedure.

(E) The tenant had a written lease that terminated on or after January 1, 2020, or January 1, 2022, if the lease is for a tenancy in a mobilehome, and after a written request or demand from the owner, the tenant has refused to execute a written extension or renewal of the lease for an additional term of similar duration with similar provisions, provided that those terms do not violate this section or any other provision of law.

(F) Criminal activity by the tenant on the residential real property, including any common areas, or any criminal activity or criminal threat, as defined in subdivision (a) of Section 422 of the Penal Code, on or off the residential real property, that is directed at any owner or agent of the owner of the residential real property.

(G) Assigning or subletting the premises in violation of the tenant's lease, as described in paragraph (4) of Section 1161 of the Code of Civil Procedure.

(H) The tenant's refusal to allow the owner to enter the residential real property as authorized by Sections 1101.5 and 1954 of this code, and Sections 13113.7 and 17926.1 of the Health and Safety Code.

(I) Using the premises for an unlawful purpose as described in paragraph (4) of Section 1161 of the Code of Civil Procedure.

(J) The employee, agent, or licensee's failure to vacate after their termination as an employee, agent, or a licensee as described in paragraph (1) of Section 1161 of the Code of Civil Procedure.

(K) When the tenant fails to deliver possession of the residential real property after providing the owner written notice as provided in Section 1946 of the tenant's intention to terminate the hiring of the real property, or makes a written offer to surrender that is accepted in writing by the owner, but fails to deliver possession at the time specified in that written notice as described in paragraph (5) of Section 1161 of the Code of Civil Procedure.

(2) No-fault just cause, which means any of the following:

(A)(i) Intent to occupy the residential real property by the owner or the owner's spouse, domestic partner, children, grandchildren, parents, or grandparents for a minimum of 12 continuous months as that person's primary residence.

(ii) For leases entered into on or after July 1, 2020, or July 1, 2022, if the lease is for a tenancy in a mobilehome, clause (i) shall apply only if the tenant agrees, in writing, to the termination, or if a provision of the lease allows the owner to terminate the lease if the owner, or the owner's spouse, domestic partner, children, grandchildren, parents, or grandparents, unilaterally decides to occupy the residential real property. Addition of a provision allowing the owner to terminate the lease as described in this clause to a new or renewed rental agreement or fixed-term lease constitutes a similar provision for the purposes of subparagraph (E) of paragraph (1).

(iii) This subparagraph does not apply if the intended occupant occupies a rental unit on the property or if a vacancy of a similar unit already exists at the property.

(iv) The written notice terminating a tenancy for a just cause pursuant to this subparagraph shall contain the name or names and relationship to the owner of the intended occupant. The written notice shall additionally include notification that the tenant may request proof that the intended occupant is an owner or related to the owner as defined in subclause (II) of clause (viii). The proof shall be provided upon request and may include an operating agreement and other non-public documents.

(v) Clause (i) applies only if the intended occupant moves into the rental unit within 90 days after the tenant vacates and occupies the rental unit as a primary residence for at least 12 consecutive months.

(vi)(I) If the intended occupant fails to occupy the rental unit within 90 days after the tenant vacates or fails to occupy the rental unit as their primary residence for at least 12 consecutive months, the owner shall offer the unit to the tenant who vacated it at the same rent and lease terms in effect at the time the tenant vacated and shall reimburse the tenant for reasonable moving expenses incurred in excess of any relocation assistance that was paid to the tenant in connection with the written notice.

(II) If the intended occupant moves into the rental unit within 90 days after the tenant vacates, but dies before having occupied the rental unit as a primary residence for 12 months, as required by clause (vi), this will not be considered a failure to comply with this section or a material violation of this section by the owner as provided in subdivision (h).

(vii) For a new tenancy commenced during the time periods described in clause (v), the accommodations shall be offered and rented or leased at the lawful rent in effect at the time any notice of termination of tenancy is served.

(viii) As used in this subparagraph:

(I) "Intended occupant" means the owner of the residential real property or the owner's spouse, domestic partner, child, grandchild, parent, or grandparent, as described in clause (i).

(II) "Owner" means any of the following:

(ia) An owner who is a natural person that has at least a 25-percent recorded ownership interest in the property.

(ib) An owner who is a natural person who has any recorded ownership interest in the property if 100 percent of the recorded ownership is divided among owners who are related to each other as sibling, spouse, domestic partner, child, parent, grandparent, or grandchild.

(ic) An owner who is a natural person whose recorded interest in the property is owned through a limited liability company or partnership.

(III) For purposes of subclause (II), "natural person" includes any of the following:

(ia) A natural person who is a settlor or beneficiary of a family trust.

(ib) If the property is owned by a limited liability company or partnership, a natural person [1] **who is a beneficial owner with at least** a 25-percent ownership interest in the property.

(IV) "Family trust" means a revocable living trust or irrevocable trust in which the settlors and beneficiaries of the trust are persons who are related to each other as sibling, spouse, domestic partner, child, parent, grandparent, or grandchild.

(V) "Beneficial owner" means a natural person or family trust for whom, directly or indirectly and through any contract arrangement, understanding, relationship, or otherwise, and any of the following applies:

(ia) The natural person exercises substantial control over a partnership or limited liability company.

(ib) The natural person owns 25 percent or more of the equity interest of a partnership or limited liability company.

(ic) The natural person receives substantial economic benefits from the assets of a partnership.

(B) Withdrawal of the residential real property from the rental market.

(C)(i) The owner complying with any of the following:

(I) An order issued by a government agency or court relating to habitability that necessitates vacating the residential real property.

(II) An order issued by a government agency or court to vacate the residential real property.

(III) A local ordinance that necessitates vacating the residential real property.

(ii) If it is determined by any government agency or court that the tenant is at fault for the condition or conditions triggering the order or need to vacate under clause (i), the tenant shall not be entitled to relocation assistance as outlined in paragraph (3) of subdivision (d).

(D)(i) Intent to demolish or to substantially remodel the residential real property.

(ii) For purposes of this subparagraph, "substantially remodel" means either of the following that cannot be reasonably accomplished in a safe manner that allows the tenant to remain living in the place and that requires the tenant to vacate the residential real property for at least 30 consecutive days:

(I) The replacement or substantial modification of any structural, electrical, plumbing, or mechanical system that requires a permit from a governmental agency.

(II) The abatement of hazardous materials, including lead-based paint, mold, or asbestos, in accordance with applicable federal, state, and local laws.

(iii) For purposes of this subparagraph, a tenant is not required to vacate the residential real property on any days where a tenant could continue living in the residential real property without violating health, safety, and habitability codes and laws. Cosmetic improvements alone, including painting, decorating, and minor repairs, or other work that can be performed safely without having the residential real property vacated, do not qualify as substantial remodel.

(iv) A written notice terminating a tenancy for a just cause pursuant to this subparagraph shall include all of the following information:

(I) A statement informing the tenant of the owner's intent to demolish the property or substantially remodel the rental unit property.

(II) The following statement:

"If the substantial remodel of your unit or demolition of the property as described in this notice of termination is not commenced or completed, the owner must offer you the opportunity to re-rent your unit with a rental agreement containing the same terms as your most recent rental agreement with the owner at the rental rate that was in effect at the time you vacated. You must notify the owner within thirty (30) days of receipt of the offer to re-rent of your acceptance or rejection of the offer, and, if accepted, you must reoccupy the unit within thirty (30) days of notifying the owner of your acceptance of the offer."

(III) A description of the substantial remodel to be completed, the approximate expected duration of the substantial remodel, or if the property is to be demolished, the expected date by which the property will be demolished, together with one of the following:

(ia) A copy of the permit or permits required to undertake the substantial remodel or demolition.

(ib) Only if a notice is issued pursuant to subclause (II) of clause (ii) and the remodel does not require any permit, a copy of the signed contract with the contractor hired by the owner to complete the substantial remodel, that reasonably details the work that will be undertaken to abate the hazardous materials as described in subclause (II) of clause (ii).

(IV) A notification that if the tenant is interested in reoccupying the rental unit following the substantial remodel, the tenant shall inform the owner of the tenant's interest in reoccupying the rental unit following the substantial remodel and provide to the owner the tenant's address, telephone number, and email address.

(c) Before an owner of residential real property issues a notice to terminate a tenancy for just cause that is a curable lease violation, the owner shall first give notice of the violation to the tenant with an opportunity to cure the violation pursuant to paragraph (3) of Section 1161 of the Code of Civil Procedure. If the violation is not cured within the time period set forth in the notice, a three-day notice to quit without an opportunity to cure may thereafter be served to terminate the tenancy.

(d)(1) For a tenancy for which just cause is required to terminate the tenancy under subdivision (a), if an owner of residential real property issues a termination notice based on a no-fault just cause described in paragraph (2) of subdivision (b), the owner shall, regardless of the tenant's income, at the owner's option, do one of the following:

(A) Assist the tenant to relocate by providing a direct payment to the tenant as described in paragraph (3).

(B) Waive in writing the payment of rent for the final month of the tenancy, prior to the rent becoming due.

(2) If an owner issues a notice to terminate a tenancy for no-fault just cause, the owner shall notify the tenant in the written termination notice of the tenant's right to relocation assistance or rent waiver pursuant to this section. If the owner elects to waive the rent for the final month of the tenancy as provided in subparagraph (B) of paragraph (1), the notice shall state the amount of rent waived and that no rent is due for the final month of the tenancy.

(3)(A) The amount of relocation assistance or rent waiver shall be equal to one month of the tenant's rent that was in effect when the owner issued the notice to terminate the tenancy. Any relocation assistance shall be provided within 15 calendar days of service of the notice.

(B) If a tenant fails to vacate after the expiration of the notice to terminate the tenancy, the actual amount of any relocation assistance or rent waiver provided pursuant to this subdivision shall be recoverable as damages in an action to recover possession.

(C) The relocation assistance or rent waiver required by this subdivision shall be credited against any other relocation assistance required by any other law.

(4) An owner's failure to strictly comply with this subdivision shall render the notice of termination void.

(e) This section shall not apply to the following types of residential real properties or residential circumstances:

(1) Transient and tourist hotel occupancy as defined in subdivision (b) of Section 1940.

(2) Housing accommodations in a nonprofit hospital, religious facility, extended care facility, licensed residential care facility for the elderly, as defined in Section 1569.2 of the Health and Safety Code, or an adult residential facility, as defined in Chapter 6 of Division 6 of Title 22 of the Manual of Policies and Procedures published by the State Department of Social Services.

(3) Dormitories owned and operated by an institution of higher education or a kindergarten and grades 1 to 12, inclusive, school.

(4) Housing accommodations in which the tenant shares bathroom or kitchen facilities with the owner who maintains their principal residence at the residential real property.

(5) Single-family owner-occupied residences, including both of the following:

(A) A residence in which the owner-occupant rents or leases no more than two units or bedrooms, including, but not limited to, an accessory dwelling unit or a junior accessory dwelling unit.

(B) A mobilehome.

(6) A property containing two separate dwelling units within a single structure in which the owner occupied one of the units as the owner's principal place of residence at the beginning of the tenancy, so long as the owner continues in occupancy, and neither unit is an accessory dwelling unit or a junior accessory dwelling unit.

(7) Housing that has been issued a certificate of occupancy within the previous 15 years, unless the housing is a mobilehome.

(8) Residential real property, including a mobilehome, that is alienable separate from the title to any other dwelling unit, provided that both of the following apply:

(A) The owner is not any of the following:

(i) A real estate investment trust, as defined in Section 856 of the Internal Revenue Code.

(ii) A corporation.

(iii) A limited liability company in which at least one member is a corporation.

(iv) Management of a mobilehome park, as defined in Section 798.2.

(B)(i) The tenants have been provided written notice that the residential property is exempt from this section using the following statement:

"This property is not subject to the rent limits imposed by Section 1947.12 of the Civil Code and is not subject to the just cause requirements of Section 1946.2 of the Civil Code. This property meets the requirements of Sections 1947.12 (d)(5) and 1946.2 (e)(8) of the Civil Code and the owner is not any of the following: (1) a real estate investment trust, as defined by Section 856 of the Internal Revenue Code; (2) a corporation; or (3) a limited liability company in which at least one member is a corporation."

(ii)(I) Except as provided in subclause (II), for a tenancy existing before July 1, 2020, the notice required under clause (i) may, but is not required to, be provided in the rental agreement.

(II) For a tenancy in a mobilehome existing before July 1, 2022, the notice required under clause (i) may, but is not required to, be provided in the rental agreement.

(iii)(I) Except as provided in subclause (II), for any tenancy commenced or renewed on or after July 1, 2020, the notice required under clause (i) must be provided in the rental agreement.

(II) For any tenancy in a mobilehome commenced or renewed on or after July 1, 2022, the notice required under clause (i) shall be provided in the rental agreement.

(iv) Addition of a provision containing the notice required under clause (i) to any new or renewed rental agreement or fixed-term lease constitutes a similar provision for the purposes of subparagraph (E) of paragraph (1) of subdivision (b).

(9) Housing restricted by deed, regulatory restriction contained in an agreement with a government agency, or other recorded document as affordable housing for persons and families of very low, low, or moderate income, as defined in Section 50093 of the Health and Safety Code, or subject to an agreement that provides housing subsidies for affordable housing for persons and families of very low, low, or moderate income, as defined in Section 50093 of the Health and Safety Code or comparable federal statutes.

(f) An owner of residential real property subject to this section shall provide notice to the tenant as follows:

(1)(A) Except as provided in subparagraph (B), for any tenancy commenced or renewed on or after July 1, 2020, as an addendum to the lease or rental agreement, or as a written notice signed by the tenant, with a copy provided to the tenant.

(B) For a tenancy in a mobilehome commenced or renewed on or after July 1, 2022, as an addendum to the lease or rental agreement, or as a written notice signed by the tenant, with a copy provided to the tenant.

(2)(A) Except as provided in subparagraph (B), for a tenancy existing prior to July 1, 2020, by written notice to the tenant no later than August 1, 2020, or as an addendum to the lease or rental agreement.

(B) For a tenancy in a mobilehome existing prior to July 1, 2022, by written notice to the tenant no later than August 1, 2022, or as an addendum to the lease or rental agreement.

(3) The notification or lease provision shall be in no less than 12-point type, and shall include the following:

"California law limits the amount your rent can be increased. See Section 1947.12 of the Civil Code for more information. California law also provides that after all of the tenants have continuously and lawfully occupied the property for 12 months or more or at least one of the tenants has continuously and lawfully occupied the property for 24 months or more, a landlord must provide a statement of cause in any notice to terminate a tenancy. See Section 1946.2 of the Civil Code for more information."

The notification or lease provision shall be subject to Section 1632.

(g) An owner's failure to comply with any provision of this section shall render the written termination notice void.

(h)(1) An owner who attempts to recover possession of a rental unit in material violation of this section shall be liable to the tenant in a civil action for all of the following:

(A) Actual damages.

(B) In the court's discretion, reasonable attorney's fees and costs.

(C) Upon a showing that the owner has acted willfully or with oppression, fraud, or malice, up to three times the actual damages. An award may also be entered for punitive damages for the benefit of the tenant against the owner.

(2) The Attorney General, in the name of the people of the State of California, and the city attorney or county counsel in the jurisdiction in which the rental unit is located, in the name of the city or county, may seek injunctive relief based on violations of this section.

(i)(1) This section does not apply to the following residential real property:

(A) Residential real property subject to a local ordinance requiring just cause for termination of a residential tenancy adopted on or before September 1, 2019, in which case the local ordinance shall apply.

(B) Residential real property subject to a local ordinance requiring just cause for termination of a residential tenancy adopted or amended after September 1, 2019, that is more protective than this section, in which case the local ordinance shall apply. For purposes of this subparagraph, an ordinance is "more protective" if it meets all of the following criteria:

(i) The just cause for termination of a residential tenancy under the local ordinance is consistent with this section.

(ii) The ordinance further limits the reasons for termination of a residential tenancy, provides for higher relocation assistance amounts, or provides additional tenant protections that are not prohibited by any other provision of law.

(iii) The local government has made a binding finding within their local ordinance that the ordinance is more protective than the provisions of this section.

(2) A residential real property shall not be subject to both a local ordinance requiring just cause for termination of a residential tenancy and this section.

(3) A local ordinance adopted after September 1, 2019, that is less protective than this section shall not be enforced unless this section is repealed.

(j) Any waiver of the rights under this section shall be void as contrary to public policy.

(k) For the purposes of this section, the following definitions shall apply:

(1) "Owner" includes any person, acting as principal or through an agent, having the right to offer residential real property for rent, and includes a predecessor in interest to the owner.

(2) "Residential real property" means any dwelling or unit that is intended for human habitation, including any dwelling or unit in a mobilehome park.

(3) "Tenancy" means the lawful occupation of residential real property and includes a lease or sublease.

(*l*) This section shall not apply to a homeowner of a mobilehome, as defined in Section 798.9.

(m) This section shall become operative on April 1, 2024.

(n) This section shall remain in effect only until January 1, 2030, and as of that date is repealed. **Leg.H.** Added Stats 2023 ch 290 §2 (SB 567), effective January 1, 2024, operative April 1, 2024, repealed January 1, 2030. Amended Stats 2024 ch 8 §1 (SB 479), effective March 25, 2024, operative April 1, 2024, repealed January 1, 2030.

§ 1946.2. 2024 Deletes. [1] with

§1946.5. Termination of room rental by lodger in owner occupied dwelling

(a) The hiring of a room by a lodger on a periodic basis within a dwelling unit occupied by the owner may be terminated by either party giving written notice to the other of his or her intention to terminate the hiring, at least as long before the expiration of the term of the hiring as specified in Section 1946. The notice shall be given in a manner prescribed in Section 1162 of the Code of Civil Procedure or by certified or registered mail, restricted delivery, to the other party, with a return receipt requested.

(b) Upon expiration of the notice period provided in the notice of termination given pursuant to subdivision (a), any right of the lodger to remain in the dwelling unit or any part thereof is terminated by operation of law. The lodger's removal from the premises may thereafter be effected pursuant to the provisions of Section 602.3 of the Penal Code or other applicable provisions of law.

(c) As used in this section, "lodger" means a person contracting with the owner of a dwelling unit for a room or room and board within the dwelling unit personally occupied by the owner, where the owner retains a right of access to all areas of the dwelling unit occupied by the lodger and has overall control of the dwelling unit.

(d) This section applies only to owner-occupied dwellings where a single lodger resides. Nothing in this section shall be construed to determine or affect in any way the rights of persons residing as lodgers in an owner-occupied dwelling where more than one lodger resides. **Leg.H.** Added Stats 1986 ch 1010 §1.

§1946.7. Terminating tenancy due to domestic violence or specified reason; Notice; Responsibility for rental payments; Prohibition on disclosure by landlord; Civil penalty

(a) A tenant may notify the landlord that the tenant intends to terminate the tenancy if the tenant, a household member, or an immediate family member was the victim of an act that constitutes any of the following:

(1) Domestic violence as defined in Section 6211 of the Family Code.

(2) Sexual assault as defined in Section 261, 261.5, 286, 287, or 289 of the Penal Code.

(3) Stalking as defined in Section 1708.7.

(4) Human trafficking as defined in Section 236.1 of the Penal Code.

(5) Abuse of an elder or a dependent adult as defined in Section 15610.07 of the Welfare and Institutions Code.

(6) A crime that caused bodily injury or death.

(7) A crime that included the exhibition, drawing, brandishing, or use of a firearm or other deadly weapon or instrument.

(8) A crime that included the use of force against the victim or a threat of force against the victim.

(b) A notice to terminate a tenancy under this section shall be in writing, with one of the following attached to the notice:

(1) A copy of a temporary restraining order, emergency protective order, or protective order lawfully issued pursuant to Part 3 (commencing with Section 6240) or Part 4 (commencing with Section 6300) of Division 10 of the Family Code, Section 136.2 of the Penal Code, Section 527.6 of the Code of Civil Procedure, or Section 213.5 or 15657.03 of the Welfare and Institutions Code that protects the tenant, household member, or immediate family member from further domestic violence, sexual assault, stalking, human trafficking, abuse of an elder or a dependent adult, or any act or crime listed in subdivision (a).

(2) A copy of a written report by a peace officer employed by a state or local law enforcement agency acting in the peace officer's official capacity stating that the tenant, household member, or immediate family member has filed a report alleging that the tenant, the household member, or the immediate family member is a victim of an act or crime listed in subdivision (a).

(3)(A) Documentation from a qualified third party based on information received by that third party while acting in the third party's professional capacity to indicate that the tenant, household member, or immediate family member is seeking assistance for physical or mental injuries or abuse resulting from an act or crime listed in subdivision (a).

(B) The documentation shall contain, in substantially the same form, the following:

Tenant Statement and Qualified Third Party Statement under Civil Code Section 1946.7

Part I. Statement By Tenant
I, [insert name of tenant], state as follows:

I, or a member of my household or immediate family, have been a victim of:

[insert one or more of the following: domestic violence, sexual assault, stalking, human trafficking, elder abuse, dependent adult abuse, or a crime that caused bodily injury or death, a crime that included the exhibition, drawing, brandishing, or use of a firearm or other deadly weapon or instrument, or a crime that included the use of force against the victim or a threat of force against the victim.]

The most recent incident(s) happened on or about:

[insert date or dates.]

The incident(s) was/were committed by the following person(s), with these physical description(s), if known and safe to provide:

[if known and safe to provide, insert name(s) and physical description(s).]

_____ _____
(signature of tenant)   (date)

Part II. Qualified Third Party Statement

I, [insert name of qualified third party], state as follows:

My business address and phone number are:

[insert business address and phone number.]

Check and complete one of the following:

____ I meet the requirements for a sexual assault counselor provided in Section 1035.2 of the Evidence Code and I am either engaged in an office, hospital, institution, or center commonly known as a rape crisis center described in that section or employed by an organization providing the programs specified in Section 13835.2 of the Penal Code.

____ I meet the requirements for a domestic violence counselor provided in Section 1037.1 of the Evidence Code and I am employed, whether financially compensated or not, by a domestic violence victim service organization, as defined in that section.

____ I meet the requirements for a human trafficking caseworker provided in Section 1038.2 of the Evidence Code and I am employed, whether financially compensated or not, by an organization that provides programs specified in Section 18294 of the Welfare and Institutions Code or in Section 13835.2 of the Penal Code.

____ I meet the definition of "victim of violent crime advocate" provided in Section 1947.6 of the Civil Code and I am employed, whether financially compensated or not, by an agency or organization that has a documented record of providing services to victims of violent crime or provides those services under the auspices or supervision of a court or a law enforcement or prosecution agency.

____ I am licensed by the State of California as a:

[insert one of the following: physician and surgeon, osteopathic physician and surgeon, registered nurse, psychiatrist, psychologist, licensed clinical social worker, licensed marriage and family therapist, or licensed professional clinical counselor.] and I am licensed by, and my license number is:

[insert name of state licensing entity and license number.]

The person who signed the Statement By Tenant above stated to me that the person, or a member of the person's household or immediate family, is a victim of:

[insert one or more of the following: domestic violence, sexual assault, stalking, human trafficking, elder abuse, dependent adult abuse, or a crime that caused physical injury, emotional injury and the threat of physical injury, or death.]

The person further stated to me the incident(s) occurred on or about the date(s) stated above.

I understand that the person who made the Statement By Tenant may use this document as a basis for terminating a lease with the person's landlord.

_____ _____
(signature of qualified third party)   (date)

(C) The documentation may be signed by a person who meets the requirements for a sexual assault counselor, domestic violence counselor, a human trafficking caseworker, or a victim of violent crime advocate only if the documentation displays the letterhead of the office, hospital, institution, center, or organization, as appropriate, that engages or employs, whether financially compensated or not, this counselor, caseworker, or advocate.

(4) Any other form of documentation that reasonably verifies that the crime or act listed in subdivision (a) occurred.

(c) If the tenant is terminating tenancy pursuant to subdivision (a) because an immediate family member is a victim of an eligible act or crime listed in subdivision (a) and that tenant did not live in the same household as the immediate family member at the time of the act or crime, and no part of the act or crime occurred within the dwelling unit or within 1,000 feet of the dwelling unit of the tenant, the tenant shall attach to the notice and other documentation required by subdivision (b) a written statement stating all of the following:

(1) The tenant's immediate family member was a victim of an act or crime listed in subdivision (a).

(2) The tenant intends to relocate as a result of the tenant's immediate family member being a victim of an act or crime listed in subdivision (a).

(3) The tenant is relocating to increase the safety, physical well-being, emotional well-being, psychological well-being, or financial security of the tenant or of the tenant's immediate family member as a result of the act or crime.

(d) The notice to terminate the tenancy shall be given within 180 days of the date that any order described in paragraph (1) of subdivision (b) was issued, within 180 days of the date that any written report described in paragraph (2) of subdivision (b) was made, within 180 days of the date that an act or a crime described in subdivision (a) occurred, or within the time period described in Section 1946.

(e) If notice to terminate the tenancy is provided to the landlord under this section, the tenant shall be responsible for payment of rent for no more than 14 calendar days following the giving of the notice, or for any shorter appropriate period as described in Section 1946 or the lease or rental agreement. The tenant shall be released without penalty from any further rent or other payment obligation to the landlord under the lease or rental agreement. If the premises are relet to another party prior to the end of the obligation to pay rent, the rent owed under this subdivision shall be prorated.

(f) Notwithstanding any law, a landlord shall not, due to the termination, require a tenant who terminates a lease or rental agreement pursuant to this section to forfeit any security deposit money or advance rent paid. A tenant who terminates a rental agreement pursuant to this section shall not be considered for any purpose, by reason of the termination, to have breached the lease or rental agreement. In all other respects, the law governing the security deposit shall apply.

(g) This section does not relieve a tenant, other than the tenant who is, or who has a household member or immediate family member who is, a victim of an act or crime listed in subdivision (a) and members of that tenant's household, from their obligations under the lease or rental agreement.

(h) For purposes of this section, the following definitions apply:

(1) "Household member" means a member of the tenant's family who lives in the same residential unit as the tenant.

(2) "Health practitioner" means a physician and surgeon, osteopathic physician and surgeon, psychiatrist, psychologist, registered nurse, licensed clinical social worker, licensed marriage and family therapist, licensed professional clinical counselor, or a victim of violent crime advocate.

(3) "Immediate family member" means the parent, stepparent, spouse, child, child-in-law, stepchild, or sibling of the tenant, or any person living in the tenant's household at the time the crime or act listed in subdivision (a) occurred who has a relationship with the tenant that is substantially similar to that of a family member.

(4) "Qualified third party" means a health practitioner, domestic violence counselor, as defined in Section 1037.1 of the Evidence Code, a sexual assault counselor, as defined in Section 1035.2 of the Evidence Code, or a human trafficking caseworker, as defined in Section 1038.2 of the Evidence Code.

(5) "Victim of violent crime advocate" means a person who is employed, whether financially compensated or not, for the purpose of rendering advice or assistance to victims of violent crimes for an agency or organization that has a documented record of providing services to victims of violent crime or provides those services under the auspices or supervision of a court or a law enforcement or prosecution agency.

(i)(1) A landlord shall not disclose any information provided by a tenant under this section to a third party unless the disclosure satisfies one or more of the following:

(A) The tenant consents in writing to the disclosure.

(B) The disclosure is required by law or order of the court.

(2) A landlord's communication to a qualified third party who provides documentation under paragraph (3) of subdivision (b) to verify the contents of that documentation is not disclosure for purposes of this subdivision.

(j) An owner or an owner's agent shall not refuse to rent a dwelling unit to an otherwise qualified prospective tenant or refuse to continue to rent to an existing tenant solely on the basis that the tenant has previously exercised the tenant's rights under this section or has previously terminated a tenancy because of the circumstances described in subdivision (a).

(k) A landlord or agent of a landlord who violates this section shall be liable to the tenant in a civil action for both of the following:

(1) The actual damages sustained by the tenant.

(2)(A) Statutory damages of not less than one hundred dollars ($100) and not more than five thousand dollars ($5,000).

(B) Notwithstanding subparagraph (A), a landlord or agent of a landlord who violates this section shall not be liable for statutory damages if the tenant provided documentation of the crime or act to the landlord or the agent of the landlord pursuant to paragraph (4) of subdivision (b) only.

(*l*) The remedies provided by this section shall be in addition to any other remedy provided by law. **Leg.H.** Added Stats 2008 ch 440 §1 (AB 2052), effective September 27, 2008. Amended Stats 2011 ch 76 §1 (AB 588), effective January 1, 2012; Stats 2012 ch 516 §1 (SB 1403), effective January 1, 2013; Stats 2013 ch 130 §1 (SB 612), effective January 1, 2014, repealed January 1, 2016; Stats 2015 ch 70 §1 (AB 418), effective January 1, 2016; Stats 2018 ch 423 §6 (SB 1494), effective January 1, 2019; Stats 2019 ch 497 §26 (AB 991), effective January 1, 2020; Stats 2020 ch 205 §1 (SB 1190), effective January 1, 2021; Stats 2021 ch 626 §5 (AB 1171), effective January 1, 2022; Stats 2022 ch 28 §24 (SB 1380), effective January 1, 2023; Stats 2022 ch 558 §1 (SB 1017), effective January 1, 2023 (ch 558 prevails).

Prior Law: Former CC §1946.7, similar to the present section, was added Stats 2013 ch 130 §2, effective January 1, 2014, operative January 1, 2016, and repealed Stats 2015 ch 70 §2, effective January 1, 2016.

Former CC §1946.7, similar to the present section, was added Stats 2013 ch 130 §2, operative January 1, 2016, and repealed Stats 2015 ch 70 §2.

§1946.8. Lease provision purporting to penalize or limit good faith summoning of law enforcement or emergency assistance void; Imposition or threat of penalties by landlord for such prohibited

(a) For purposes of this section:

(1) "Individual in an emergency" means a person who believes that immediate action is required to prevent or mitigate the loss or impairment of life, health, or property.

(2) "Occupant" means a person residing in a dwelling unit with the tenant. "Occupant" includes lodgers as defined in Section 1946.5.

(3) "Penalties" means the following:

(A) The actual or threatened assessment of fees, fines, or penalties.

(B) The actual or threatened termination of a tenancy or the actual or threatened failure to renew a tenancy.

(C) Subjecting a tenant to inferior terms, privileges, and conditions of tenancy in comparison to tenants who have not sought law enforcement assistance or emergency assistance.

(4) "Resident" means a member of the tenant's household or any other occupant living in the dwelling unit with the consent of the tenant.

(5) "Victim of abuse" includes:

(A) A victim of domestic violence as defined in Section 6211 of the Family Code.

(B) A victim of elder or dependent adult abuse as defined in Section 15610.07 of the Welfare and Institutions Code.

(C) A victim of human trafficking as described in Section 236.1 of the Penal Code.

(D) A victim of sexual assault, meaning a victim of any act made punishable by Section 261, 264.1, 285, 286, 288, 288a, or 289 of the Penal Code.

(E) A victim of stalking as described in Section 1708.7 of this code or Section 646.9 of the Penal Code.

(6) "Victim of crime" means any victim of a misdemeanor or felony.

(b) Any provision in a rental or lease agreement for a dwelling unit that prohibits or limits, or threatens to prohibit or limit, a tenant's, resident's, or other person's right to summon law enforcement assistance or emergency assistance as, or on behalf of, a victim of abuse, a victim of crime, or an individual in an emergency, if the tenant, resident, or other person believes that the law enforcement assistance or emergency assistance is necessary to prevent or address the perpetration, escalation, or exacerbation of the abuse, crime, or emergency, shall be void as contrary to public policy.

(c) A landlord shall not impose, or threaten to impose, penalties on a tenant or resident who exercises the tenant's or resident's right to summon law enforcement assistance or emergency assistance as, or on behalf of, a victim of abuse, a victim of crime, or an individual in an emergency, based on the person's belief that the assistance is necessary, as described in subdivision (b). A landlord shall not impose, or threaten to impose, penalties on a tenant or resident as a consequence of a person who is not a resident or tenant summoning law enforcement assistance or emergency assistance on the tenant's, resident's, or other person's behalf, based on the person's belief that the assistance is necessary.

(d) Documentation is not required to establish belief for purposes of subdivision (b) or (c), but belief may be established by documents such as those described in Section 1161.3 of the Code of Civil Procedure.

(e) Any waiver of the provisions of this section is contrary to public policy and is void and unenforceable.

(f)(1) In an action for unlawful detainer, a tenant, resident, or occupant may raise, as an affirmative defense, that the landlord or owner violated this section.

(2) There is a rebuttable presumption that a tenant, resident, or occupant has established an affirmative defense under this subdivision if the landlord or owner files a complaint for unlawful detainer within 30 days of a resident, tenant, or other person summoning law enforcement assistance or emergency assistance and the complaint is based upon a notice that alleges that the act of summoning law enforcement assistance or emergency assistance as, or on behalf of, a victim of abuse, a victim of crime, or an individual in an emergency constitutes a rental agreement violation, lease violation, or a nuisance. A reference to a person summoning law enforcement in a notice that is the basis for a complaint for unlawful detainer that is necessary to describe conduct that is alleged to constitute a violation of a rental agreement or lease is not, in itself, an allegation for purposes of this paragraph.

(3) A landlord or owner may rebut the presumption described in paragraph (2) by demonstrating that a reason other than the summoning of law enforcement or emergency assistance as, or on behalf of, a victim of abuse, a victim of crime, or an individual in an emergency was a substantial motivating factor for filing the complaint.

(g) In addition to other remedies provided by law, a violation of this section entitles a tenant, a resident, or other aggrieved person to seek injunctive relief prohibiting the landlord from creating or enforcing policies in violation of this section, or from imposing or threatening to impose penalties against the tenant, resident, or other aggrieved person based on summoning law enforcement or emergency assistance as, or on behalf of, a victim of abuse, a victim of crime, or an individual in an emergency.

(h) This section does not permit an injunction to be entered that would prohibit the filing of an unlawful detainer action.

(i) This section does not limit a landlord's exercise of the landlord's other rights under a lease or rental agreement, or under other law pertaining to the hiring of property, with regard to matters that are not addressed by this section. **Leg.H.** Added Stats 2018 ch 190 §1 (AB 2413), effective January 1, 2019. Amended Stats 2021 ch 626 §6 (AB 1171), effective January 1, 2022.

§ 1946.9. Restrictions on adverse actions in tenant screening

(a) For the purposes of tenant screening, a landlord or a landlord's agent shall not make an adverse action based on any of the following:

(1) An allegation that the prospective tenant breached a lease or rental agreement if the alleged breach stemmed from an act of abuse or violence against a tenant, a tenant's immediate family member, or a tenant's household member, and the prospective tenant is not alleged to have committed the abuse or violence. The landlord shall accept any form of documentation evidencing abuse or violence against the tenant, the tenant's immediate family member, or the tenant's household member, as provided by subdivision (d) of Section 1941.5, as sufficient for the purposes of this paragraph.

(2) The prospective tenant having previously requested to have their locks changed pursuant to Section 1941.5 or 1941.6, regardless of whether the request was granted.

(3) The prospective tenant, or an immediate family member or household member of the prospective tenant, having been a victim of abuse or violence. A landlord or the landlord's agent may request that a prospective tenant provide documentation described in subdivision (d) of Section 1941.5 to establish if a prospective tenant, or an immediate family member or household member of the prospective member, has been a victim of abuse or violence for the purposes of this paragraph. If the prospective tenant provides documentation described in subdivision (d) of Section 1941.5, the landlord shall accept the documentation as sufficient to establish that a prospective tenant, or an immediate family member or household member of the prospective member, has been a victim of abuse or violence for the purposes of this paragraph.

(4) The prospective tenant, or a guest of the prospective tenant, having previously summoned law enforcement assistance or emergency assistance, as, or on behalf of a victim of abuse, a victim of crime, or an individual in an emergency, as provided in Section 1946.8.

(b) A landlord or agent of a landlord who violates this section shall be liable to the prospective or current tenant in a civil action for both of the following:

(1) The actual damages sustained by the prospective or current tenant.

(2) Statutory damages of not less than one hundred dollars ($100) and not more than five thousand dollars ($5,000).

(c) The remedies provided by this section shall be in addition to any other remedy provided by law.

(d) For the purposes of this section, the following definitions apply:

(1) "Abuse or violence" has the same meaning as defined in paragraph (1) of subdivision (a) of Section 1161.3 of the Code of Civil Procedure.

(2) "Adverse action" means either of the following:

(A) Denial of a prospective tenant's rental application.

(B) Approval of a prospective tenant's rental application, subject to terms or conditions different and less favorable to the prospective tenant than those included in any written notice, statement, or advertisement for the rental unit, including written communication sent directly from the landlord or landlord's agent to a prospective tenant.

(3) "Household member" has the same meaning as defined in paragraph (1) of subdivision (h) of Section 1946.7.

(4) "Immediate family member" has the same meaning as defined in paragraph (3) of subdivision (h) of Section 1946.7.

(5) "Tenant" means tenant, subtenant, lessee, or sublessee.

(6) "Tenant screening" means any process used by a landlord or landlord's agent to evaluate the fitness of a prospective tenant. **Leg.H.** Added Stats 2024 ch 75 §4 (SB 1051), effective January 1, 2025.

§1947. Rent, when payable

When there is no usage or contract to the contrary, rents are payable at the termination of the holding, when it does not exceed one year. If the holding is by the day, week, month, quarter, or year, rent is payable at termination of the respective periods, as it successively becomes due. **Leg.H.** Enacted Stats 1872.

§ 1947.1. Parking

(a) If an owner of a qualifying residential property provides parking with the qualifying residential property, they shall unbundle parking from the price of rent.

(b)(1) Off-street parking accessory to a qualifying residential property shall not be included in any residential rental agreement and shall be subject to a rental agreement addendum or provided in a separate rental agreement.

(2) All off-street parking spaces shall be unbundled from the qualifying residential property for the life of the property.

(c)(1) A tenant of a qualifying residential property shall have the right of first refusal to parking spaces built for their property. Remaining residential unbundled parking spaces that are not leased to tenants of the residential dwelling may be leased by the owner of the qualifying residential property to other on-site users or to off-site residential users on a month-to-month basis.

(2) If there are unavailable parking spaces on the residential property upon the occupancy of a new tenant, and parking spaces are subsequently built for the residential dwelling or otherwise becomes available on the qualifying residential property, the new tenant shall receive a right of first refusal to an available parking space.

(d)(1) A tenant's failure to pay the parking fee pursuant to a separately leased parking agreement shall not form the basis of any unlawful detainer action against the tenant.

(2) If a tenant fails to pay by the 45th day following the date payment is owed for a separately leased parking space, the property owner may revoke that tenant's right to lease that parking spot.

(e) For purposes of this section:

(1) "Owner of qualifying residential property" includes any person, acting as principal or through an agent, having the right to offer qualifying residential property for rent, and includes a predecessor in interest to the owner.

(2)(A) "Qualifying residential property" means any dwelling or unit that is intended for human habitation that meets all of the following criteria:

(i) The property is issued a certificate of occupancy on or after January 1, 2025.

(ii) The property consists of 16 or more residential units.

(iii) The property is located in one of the following counties:

(I) Alameda.

(II) Fresno.

(III) Los Angeles.

(IV) Riverside.

(V) Sacramento.

(VI) San Bernardino.

(VII) San Joaquin.

(VIII) Santa Clara.

(IX) Shasta.

(X) Ventura.

(B) "Qualifying residential property" does not include any of the following:

(i) A residential property or unit with an individual garage that is functionally a part of the property or unit, including, but not limited to, townhouses and row houses.

(ii) A housing development of which 100 percent of its units, exclusive of any manager's unit or units, are restricted by deed, regulatory restriction contained in an agreement with a governmental agency, or other recorded document as affordable housing for persons and families of low or moderate income, as defined in Section 50093 of the Health and Safety Code.

(iii) A housing development that receives low-income housing tax credits pursuant to Section 42 of the Internal Revenue Code (26 u.S.C. Sec. 42).

(iv) A housing development that is financed with tax-exempt bonds pursuant to a program administered by the California Housing Finance Agency.

(v) A residential unit that is leased to a tenant who receives a federal housing assistance voucher issued under Section 8 of the United States Housing Act of 1937 (42 U.S.C. Sec. 1437f), including a federal Department of Housing and Urban Development Veterans Affairs Supportive Housing voucher.

(3) "Unbundled parking" means the practice of selling or leasing parking spaces separate from the lease of the residential property. **Leg.H.** Added Stats 2023 ch 757 §1 (AB 1317), effective January 1, 2024. Amended Stats 2024 ch 420 §1 (AB 2898), effective January 1, 2025.

§1947.3. Form of payment of rent or deposit of security; Payment of rent by third parties

(a)(1) Except as provided in paragraph (2), a landlord or a landlord's agent shall allow a tenant to pay rent and deposit of security by at least one form of payment that is neither cash nor electronic funds transfer.

(2) A landlord or a landlord's agent may demand or require cash as the exclusive form of payment of rent or deposit of security if the tenant has previously attempted to pay the landlord or landlord's agent with a check drawn on insufficient funds or the tenant has instructed the drawee to stop payment on a check, draft, or order for the payment of money. The landlord may demand or require cash as the exclusive form of payment only for a period not exceeding three months following an attempt to pay with a check on insufficient funds or following a tenant's instruction to stop payment. If the landlord chooses to demand or require cash payment under these circumstances, the landlord shall give the tenant a written

notice stating that the payment instrument was dishonored and informing the tenant that the tenant shall pay in cash for a period determined by the landlord, not to exceed three months, and attach a copy of the dishonored instrument to the notice. The notice shall comply with Section 827 if demanding or requiring payment in cash constitutes a change in the terms of the lease.

(3) Subject to the limitations below, a landlord or a landlord's agent shall allow a tenant to pay rent through a third party.

(A) A landlord or landlord's agent is not required to accept the rent payment tendered by a third party unless the third party has provided to the landlord or landlord's agent a signed acknowledgment stating that they are not currently a tenant of the premises for which the rent payment is being made and that acceptance of the rent payment does not create a new tenancy with the third party.

(B) Failure by a third party to provide the signed acknowledgment to the landlord or landlord's agent shall void the obligation of a landlord or landlord's agent to accept a tenant's rent tendered by a third party.

(C) The landlord or landlord's agent may, but is not required to, provide a form acknowledgment to be used by third parties, as provided for in subparagraph (A), provided however that a landlord shall accept as sufficient for compliance with subparagraph (A) an acknowledgment in substantially the following form:

I, [insert name of third party], state as follows:
I am not currently a tenant of the premises located at [insert address of premises].
I acknowledge that acceptance of the rent payment I am offering for the premises does not create a new tenancy.

_____   _____
(signature of third party)   (date)

(D) A landlord or landlord's agent may require a signed acknowledgment for each rent payment made by the third party. A landlord or landlord's agent and the third party may agree that one acknowledgment shall be sufficient for when the third party makes more than one rent payment during a period of time.

(E) Nothing in this paragraph shall be construed to require a landlord or landlord's agent to enter into a contract in connection with a federal, state, or local housing assistance program, including, but not limited to, the federal housing assistance voucher programs under Section 8 of the United States Housing Act of 1937 (42 U.S.C. Sec. 1437f).

(4) Paragraphs (2) and (3) do not enlarge or diminish a landlord's or landlord's agent's legal right to terminate a tenancy. Nothing in paragraph (3) is intended to extend the due date for any rent payment or require a landlord or landlord's agent to accept tender of rent beyond the expiration of the period stated in paragraph (2) of Section 1161 of the Code of Civil Procedure.

(b) A landlord or its agent shall not charge a tenant any fee for payment by check for rent or security deposit as described in this section.

[1] **(c)** For the purposes of this section, the issuance of a money order or a cashier's check is direct evidence only that the instrument was issued.

[2] **(d)** For purposes of this section, "electronic funds transfer" means any transfer of funds, other than a transaction originated by check, draft, or similar paper instrument, that is initiated through an electronic terminal, telephonic instrument, computer, or magnetic tape so as to order, instruct, or authorize a financial institution to debit or credit an account. "Electronic funds transfer" includes, but is not limited to, point-of-sale transfers, direct deposits or withdrawals of funds, transfers initiated by telephone, transfers via an automated clearinghouse, transfers initiated electronically that deliver a paper instrument, and transfers authorized in advance to recur at substantially regular intervals.

[3] **(e)** Nothing in this section shall be construed to prohibit the tenant and landlord or agent to mutually agree that rent payments may be made in cash or by electronic funds transfer, so long as another form of payment is also authorized, subject to the requirements of subdivision (a).

[4] **(f)** A waiver of the provisions of this section is contrary to public policy, and is void and unenforceable. **Leg.H.** Added Stats 2004 ch 76 §1 (SB 115). Amended Stats 2012 ch 268 §1 (SB 1055), effective January 1, 2013; Stats 2018 ch 233 §1 (AB 2219), effective January 1, 2019; Stats 2024 ch 287 §3 (SB 611), effective January 1, 2025.

§1947.3. 2024 Deletes. [1] (b) [2] (c) [3] (d) [4] (e)

§1947.5. Smoking of cigarettes or other tobacco products; Authority of landlord; Changes to terms of lease or rental agreement

(a) A landlord of a residential dwelling unit, as defined in Section 1940, or his or her agent, may prohibit the smoking of a cigarette, as defined in Section 104556 of the Health and Safety Code, or other tobacco product on the property or in any building or portion of the building, including any dwelling unit, other interior or exterior area, or the premises on which it is located, in accordance with this article.

(b)(1) Every lease or rental agreement entered into on or after January 1, 2012, for a residential dwelling unit on property on any portion of which the landlord has prohibited the smoking of cigarettes or other tobacco products pursuant to this article shall include a provision that specifies the areas on the property where smoking is prohibited, if the lessee has not previously occupied the dwelling unit.

(2) For a lease or rental agreement entered into before January 1, 2012, a prohibition against the smoking of cigarettes or other tobacco products in any portion of the property in which smoking was previously permitted shall constitute a change of the terms of tenancy, requiring adequate notice in writing, to be provided in the manner prescribed in Section 827.

(c) A landlord who exercises the authority provided in subdivision (a) to prohibit smoking shall be subject to federal, state, and local requirements governing changes to the terms of a lease or rental agreement for tenants with leases or rental agreements that are in existence at the time that the policy limiting or prohibiting smoking is adopted.

(d) This section shall not be construed to preempt any local ordinance in effect on or before January 1, 2012, or any provision of a local ordinance in effect on or after January 1, 2012, that restricts the smoking of cigarettes or other tobacco products.

(e) A limitation or prohibition of the use of any tobacco product shall not affect any other term or condition of the tenancy, nor shall this section be construed to require statutory authority to establish or enforce any other lawful term or condition of the tenancy.

(f) For purposes of this section, "smoking" has the same meaning as in subdivision (c) of Section 22950.5 of the Business and Professions Code.

(g) For purposes of this section, "tobacco product" means a product or device as defined in subdivision (d) of Section 22950.5 of the Business and Professions Code. **Leg.H.** Added Stats 2011 ch 264 §2 (SB 332), effective January 1, 2012. Amended Stats 2016 2nd Ex Sess 2015–2016 ch 7 §8 (SBX2-5), effective June 9, 2016.

§1947.6. Installation by lessor of electric vehicle charging station; When required; How requested; Costs; Exceptions; Liability

(a) For any lease executed, extended, or renewed on and after July 1, 2015, a lessor of a dwelling shall approve a written request of a lessee to install an electric vehicle charging station at a parking space allotted for the lessee that meets the requirements of this section and complies with the lessor's procedural approval process for modification to the property.

(b) This section does not apply to residential rental properties where:

(1) Electric vehicle charging stations already exist for lessees in a ratio that is equal to or greater than 10 percent of the designated parking spaces.

(2) Parking is not provided as part of the lease agreement.

(3) There are fewer than five parking spaces.

(4) The dwelling is subject to a residential rent control ordinance. This paragraph shall not apply to a lease executed, extended, or renewed on and after January 1, 2019.

(5) The dwelling is subject to both a residential rent control ordinance and an ordinance, adopted on or before January 1, 2018, that requires the lessor to approve a lessee's written request to install an electric vehicle charging station at a parking space allotted to the lessee.

(c) For purposes of this section, "electric vehicle charging station" or "charging station" means any level of electric vehicle supply equipment station that is designed and built in compliance with Article 625 of the California Electrical Code, as it reads on the effective date of this section, and delivers electricity from a source outside an electric vehicle into a plug-in electric vehicle.

(d) A lessor shall not be obligated to provide an additional parking space to a lessee in order to accommodate an electric vehicle charging station.

(e) If the electric vehicle charging station has the effect of providing the lessee with a reserved parking space, the lessor may charge a monthly rental amount for that parking space.

(f) An electric vehicle charging station and all modifications and improvements to the property shall comply with federal, state, and local law, and all applicable zoning requirements, land use requirements, and covenants, conditions, and restrictions.

(g) A lessee's written request to make a modification to the property in order to install and use an electric vehicle charging station shall include, but is not limited to, the lessee's consent to enter into a written agreement that includes, but is not limited to, the following:

(1) Compliance with the lessor's requirements for the installation, use, maintenance, and removal of the charging station and installation, use, and maintenance of the infrastructure for the charging station.

(2) Compliance with the lessor's requirements for the lessee to provide a complete financial analysis and scope of work regarding the installation of the charging station and its infrastructure.

(3) A written description of how, when, and where the modifications and improvements to the property are proposed to be made consistent with those items specified in the "Permitting Checklist" of the "Zero-Emission Vehicles in California: Community Readiness Guidebook" published by the Office of Planning and Research.

(4) Obligation of the lessee to pay the lessor all costs associated with the lessor's installation of the charging station and its infrastructure prior to any modification or improvement being made to the leased property. The costs associated with modifications and improvements shall include, but are not limited to, the cost of permits, supervision, construction, and, solely if required by the contractor, consistent with its past performance of work for the lessor, performance bonds.

(5) Obligation of the lessee to pay as part of rent for the costs associated with the electrical usage of the charging station, and cost for damage, maintenance, repair, removal, and replacement of the charging station, and modifications or improvements made to the property associated with the charging station.

(h) The lessee and each successor lessee shall obtain personal liability coverage, as described in Section 108 of the Insurance Code, in an amount not to exceed 10 times the annual rent changed for the dwelling, covering property damage and personal injury proximately caused by the installation or operation of the electric vehicle charging station. The policy shall be maintained in full force and effect from the time of installation of the electric vehicle charging station until the electric vehicle charging station is removed or the lessee forfeits possession of the dwelling to the lessor.

(i) Notwithstanding subdivision (h), no insurance shall be required of a lessee installing an electric vehicle charging station if both of the following are satisfied:

(1) The electric vehicle charging station has been certified by a Nationally Recognized Testing Laboratory that is approved by the Occupational Safety and Health Administration of the United States Department of Labor.

(2) The electric vehicle charging station and any associated alterations to the dwelling's electrical system are performed by a licensed electrician.
Leg.H. Added Stats 2014 ch 529 §1 (AB 2565), effective January 1, 2015. Amended Stats 2018 ch 163 §1 (AB 1796), effective January 1, 2019; Stats 2019 ch 855 §1 (SB 638), effective January 1, 2020.

§1947.7. Owner's "good faith" exemption from rent stabilization program fines and penalties

(a) The Legislature finds and declares that the operation of local rent stabilization programs can be complex and that disputes often arise with regard to standards of compliance with the regulatory processes of those programs. Therefore, it is the intent of the Legislature to limit the imposition of penalties and sanctions against an owner of residential rental units where that person has attempted in good faith to fully comply with the regulatory processes.

(b) An owner of a residential rental unit who is in substantial compliance with an ordinance or charter that controls or establishes a system of controls on the price at which residential rental units may be offered for rent or lease and which requires the registration of rents, or any regulation adopted pursuant thereto, shall not be assessed a penalty or any other sanction for noncompliance with the ordinance, charter, or regulation.

Restitution to the tenant or recovery of the registration or filing fees due to the local agency shall be the exclusive remedies which may be imposed against an owner of a residential rental unit who is in substantial compliance with the ordinance, charter, or regulation.

"Substantial compliance," as used in this subdivision, means that the owner of a residential rental unit has made a good faith attempt to comply with the ordinance, charter, or regulation sufficient to reasonably carry out the intent and purpose of the ordinance, charter, or regulation, but is not in full compliance, and has, after receiving notice of a deficiency from the local agency, cured the defect in a timely manner, as reasonably determined by the local agency.

"Local agency," as used in this subdivision, means the public entity responsible for the implementation of the ordinance, charter, or regulation.

(c) For any residential unit which has been registered and for which a base rent has been listed or for any residential unit which an owner can show, by a preponderance of the evidence, a good faith attempt to comply with the registration requirements or who was exempt from registration requirements in a previous version of the ordinance or charter and for which the owner of that residential unit has subsequently found not to have been in compliance with the ordinance, charter, or regulation, all annual rent adjustments which may have been denied during the period of the owner's noncompliance shall be restored prospectively once the owner is in compliance with the ordinance, charter, or regulation.

(d) In those jurisdictions where, prior to January 1, 1990, the local ordinance did not allow the restoration of annual rent adjustment, once the owner is in compliance with this section the local agency may phase in any increase in rent caused by the restoration of the annual rent adjustments that is in excess of 20 percent over the rent previously paid by the tenant, in equal installments over three years, if the tenant demonstrates undue financial hardship due to the restoration of the full annual rent adjustments. This subdivision shall remain operative only until January 1, 1993, unless a later enacted statute which is chaptered by January 1, 1993, deletes or extends that date.

(e) For purposes of this subdivision, an owner shall be deemed in compliance with the ordinance, charter, or regulation if he or she is in substantial compliance with the applicable local rental registration requirements and applicable local and state housing code provisions, has paid all fees and penalties owed to the local agency which have not otherwise been barred by the applicable statute of limitations, and has satisfied all claims for refunds of rental overcharges brought by tenants or by the local rent control board on behalf of tenants of the affected unit.

(f) Nothing in this section shall be construed to grant to any public entity any power which it does not possess independent of this section to control or establish a system of control on the price at which accommodations may be offered for rent or lease, or to diminish any power to do so which that public entity may possess, except as specifically provided in this section.

(g) In those jurisdictions where an ordinance or charter controls, or establishes a system of controls on, the price at which residential rental units may be offered for rent or lease and requires the periodic registration of rents, and where, for purposes of compliance with subdivision (e) of Section 1954.53, the local agency requires an owner to provide the name of a present or former tenant, the tenant's name and any additional information provided concerning the tenant, is confidential and shall be treated as confidential information within the meaning of the Information Practices Act of 1977 (Chapter 1 (commencing with Section 1798) of Title 1.8 of this part). A local agency shall, to the extent required by this subdivision, be considered an "agency" as defined in subdivision (b) of Section 1798.3. For purposes of compliance with subdivision (e) of Section 1954.53, a local agency subject to this subdivision may request, but shall not compel, an owner to provide any information regarding a tenant other than the tenant's name. **Leg.H.** Added Stats 1986 ch 1199 §1. Amended Stats 1989 ch 987 §1; Stats 1996 ch 566 §1 (SB 1632).

§1947.8. Rent control program certification of permissible rent levels

(a) If an ordinance or charter controls or establishes a system of controls on the price at which residential rental units may be offered for rent or lease and requires the registration of rents, the ordinance or charter, or any regulation adopted pursuant thereto, shall provide for the establishment and certification of permissible rent levels for the registered rental units, and any changes thereafter to those rent levels, by the local agency as provided in this section.

(b) If the ordinance, charter, or regulation is in effect on January 1, 1987, the ordinance, charter, or regulation shall provide for the establishment and certification of permissible rent levels on or before January 1, 1988, including completion of all appeals and administrative proceedings connected therewith. After July 1, 1990, no local agency may maintain any action to recover excess rent against any property owner who has registered the unit with the local agency within the time limits set forth in this section if the initial certification of permissible rent levels affecting that particular property has not been completed, unless the delay is willfully and intentionally caused by the property owner or is a result of court proceedings or further administrative proceedings ordered by a court. If the ordinance, charter, or regulation is adopted on or after January 1, 1987, the ordinance, charter, or regulation shall provide for the establishment and certification of permissible rent levels within one year after it is adopted, including completion of all appeals and administrative proceedings connected therewith. Upon the request of the landlord or the tenant, the local agency shall provide the landlord and the tenant with a certificate or other documentation reflecting the permissible rent levels of the rental unit. A landlord may request a certificate of permissible rent levels for rental units that have a base rent established, but are vacant and not exempt from registration under this section. The landlord or the tenant may appeal the determination of the permissible rent levels reflected in the certificate. The permissible rent levels reflected in the certificate or other documentation shall, in the absence of intentional misrepresentation or fraud, be binding and conclusive upon the local agency unless the determination of the permissible rent levels is being appealed.

(c) After the establishment and certification of permissible rent levels under subdivision (b), the local agency shall, upon the request of the landlord or the tenant, provide the landlord and the tenant with a certificate of the permissible rent levels of the rental unit. The certificate shall be issued within five business days from the date of request by the landlord or the tenant. The permissible rent levels reflected in the certificate shall, in the absence of intentional misrepresentation or fraud, be binding and conclusive upon the local agency unless the determination of the permissible rent levels is being appealed. The landlord or the tenant may appeal the determination of the permissible rent levels reflected in the certificate. Any appeal of a determination of permissible rent levels as reflected in the certificate, other than an appeal made pursuant to subdivision (b), shall be filed with the local agency within 15 days from issuance of the certificate. The local agency shall notify, in writing, the landlord and the tenant of its decision within 60 days following the filing of the appeal.

(d) The local agency may charge the person to whom a certificate is issued a fee in the amount necessary to cover the reasonable costs incurred by the local agency in issuing the certificate.

(e) The absence of a certification of permissible rent levels shall not impair, restrict, abridge, or otherwise interfere with either of the following:

(1) A judicial or administrative hearing.

(2) Any matter in connection with a conveyance of an interest in property.

(f) The record of permissible rent levels is a public record for purposes of the California Public Records Act (Division 10 (commencing with Section 7920.000) of Title 1 of the Government Code).

(g) Any notice specifying the rents applicable to residential rental units that is given by an owner to a public entity or tenant in order to comply with Chapter 12.75 (commencing with Section 7060) of Division 7 of Title 1 of the Government Code shall not be considered a registration of rents for purposes of this section.

(h) "Local agency," as used in this section, means the public entity responsible for the implementation of the ordinance, charter, or regulation.

(i) Nothing in this section shall be construed:

(1) To grant to any public entity any power that it does not possess independent of this section to control or establish a system of control on the price at which accommodations may be offered for rent or lease, or to diminish any power of this type that the public entity may possess, except as specifically provided in this section.

(2) On and after January 1, 2016, to apply to tenancies commencing on or after January 1, 1999, for which the owner of residential property may establish the initial rent under Chapter 2.7 (commencing with Section 1954.50). However, for a tenancy that commenced on or after January 1, 1999, if a property owner has provided the local agency with the tenancy's initial rent in compliance with that agency's registration requirements in a writing signed under penalty of perjury, there shall be a rebuttable presumption that the statement of the initial rent is correct. **Leg.H.** Added Stats 1986 ch 1199 §2. Amended Stats 1989 ch 987 §2; Stats 2016 ch 83 §1 (SB 775), effective January 1, 2017; Stats 2021 ch 615 §51 (AB 474), effective January 1, 2022.

§1947.9. Levels of compensation for temporary displacement of tenant household; Construction

(a)(1) Notwithstanding any local law to the contrary, for those units governed by the local rent stabilization ordinance in the City and County of San Francisco, levels of compensation for the temporary displacement of a tenant household for less than 20 days shall be limited to both of the following:

(A) Temporary housing and living expenses, of two hundred seventy-five dollars ($275) per day per tenant household. This limit may be adjusted annually by the city and county in an amount equal to the Consumer Price Index, beginning on January 1, 2014.

(B) Actual moving expenses if it is necessary to move the possessions of the tenant household.

(2) The landlord shall have the option to provide a comparable dwelling unit and pay any actual moving expenses, in lieu of the compensation specified in subparagraph (A) of paragraph (1). The rental housing shall be comparable to the tenant household's existing housing in location, size, number of bedrooms, accessibility, type, and quality of construction, and proximity to services and institutions upon which the displaced tenant household depends.

(b) This section shall not be construed to do any of the following:

(1) To terminate, interrupt, or amend, in any way, a tenancy subject to the lease provisions, or the rights and obligations of either party, including, but not limited to, the payment of rent.

(2) To create or affect any grounds for displacement or requirements of a landlord seeking temporary displacement, except the payment of relocation fees pursuant to subdivision (a) for displacement not exceeding 20 days.

(3) To affect the authority of a public entity that may regulate or monitor the basis for eviction.

(c) If a federal or state law regarding relocation compensation is also applicable to the temporary displacement, the tenant may elect to be compensated under those other provisions, and subdivision (a) shall be inapplicable.

(d) This section shall affect only levels of compensation for a temporary displacement of less than 20 days, and does not affect any other local procedures governing temporary relocation. **Leg.H.** Added Stats 2012 ch 243 §1 (AB 1925), effective January 1, 2013.

§1947.10. Eviction based on owner's intention to occupy rent controlled unit

(a) After July 1, 1990, in any city, county, or city and county which administers a system of controls on the price at which residential rental units may be offered for rent or lease and which requires the registration of rents, any owner who evicts a tenant based upon the owner's or the owner's immediate relative's intention to occupy the tenant's unit, shall be required to maintain residence in the unit for at least six continuous months. If a court determines that the eviction was based upon fraud by the owner or the owner's immediate relative to not fulfill this six-month requirement, a court may order the owner to pay treble the cost of relocating the tenant from his or her existing unit back into the previous unit and may order the owner to pay treble the amount of any increase in rent which the tenant has paid. If the tenant decides not to relocate back into the previous unit, the court may order the owner to pay treble the amount of one month's rent paid by the tenant for the unit from which he or she was evicted and treble the amount of any costs incurred in relocating to a different unit. The prevailing party shall be awarded attorney's fees and court costs.

(b) The remedy provided by this section shall not be construed to prohibit any other remedies available to a any party affected by this section. **Leg.H.** Added Stats 1989 ch 987 §3.

1989 Note: It appears that the Legislature inadvertently included both articles "a" and "any" in subsection (b).

§1947.11. Refund of rent in excess of controlled amount

(a) In any city, county, or city and county which administers a system of controls on the price at which residential rental units may be offered for rent or lease and which requires the registration of rents, upon the establishment of a certified rent level, any owner who charges rent to a tenant in excess of the certified lawful rent ceiling shall refund the excess rent to the tenant upon demand. If the owner refuses to refund the excess rent and if a court determines that the owner willfully or intentionally charged the tenant rent in excess of the certified lawful rent ceiling, the court shall award the tenant a judgment for the excess amount of rent and may treble that amount. The prevailing party shall be awarded attorney's fees and court costs.

(b) The remedy provided by this section shall not be construed to prohibit any other remedies available to any party affected by this section.

(c) This section shall not be construed to extend the time within which actions are required to be brought beyond the otherwise applicable limitation set forth in the Code of Civil Procedure. **Leg.H.** Added Stats 1989 ch 987 §4. Amended Stats 1990 ch 216 §7 (SB 2510).

§ 1947.12. Limitations on gross rental rate increase; Notice of increase; Legislative report; Increases prior to operation date of section; Waivers void [Repealed January 1, 2030]

(a)(1) Subject to subdivision (b), an owner of residential real property shall not, over the course of any 12-month period, increase the gross rental rate for a dwelling or a unit more than 5 percent plus the percentage change in the cost of living, or 10 percent, whichever is lower, of the lowest gross rental rate charged for that dwelling or unit at any time during the 12 months prior to the effective date of the increase. In determining the lowest gross rental amount pursuant to this section, any rent discounts, incentives, concessions, or credits offered by the owner of such unit of residential real property and accepted by the tenant shall be excluded. The gross per-month rental rate and any owner-offered discounts, incentives, concessions, or credits shall be separately listed and identified in the lease or rental agreement or any amendments to an existing lease or rental agreement.

(2) If the same tenant remains in occupancy of a unit of residential real property over any 12-month period, the gross rental rate for the unit of residential real property shall not be increased in more than two increments over that 12-month period, subject to the other restrictions of this subdivision governing gross rental rate increase.

(b) For a new tenancy in which no tenant from the prior tenancy remains in lawful possession of the residential real property, the owner may establish the initial rental rate not subject to subdivision (a). Subdivision (a) is only applicable to subsequent increases after that initial rental rate has been established.

(c) A tenant of residential real property subject to this section shall not enter into a sublease that results in a total rent for the premises that exceeds the allowable rental rate authorized by subdivision (a). Nothing in this subdivision authorizes a tenant to sublet or assign the tenant's interest where otherwise prohibited.

(d) This section shall not apply to the following residential real properties:

(1) Housing restricted by deed, regulatory restriction contained in an agreement with a government agency, or other recorded document as affordable housing for persons and families of very low, low, or moderate income, as defined in Section 50093 of the Health and Safety Code, or subject to an agreement that provides housing subsidies for affordable housing for persons and families of very low, low, or moderate income, as defined in Section 50093 of the Health and Safety Code or comparable federal statutes.

(2) Dormitories owned and operated by an institution of higher education or a kindergarten and grades 1 to 12, inclusive, school.

(3) Housing subject to rent or price control through a public entity's valid exercise of its police power consistent with Chapter 2.7 (commencing with Section 1954.50) that restricts annual increases in the rental rate to an amount less than that provided in subdivision (a).

(4) Housing that has been issued a certificate of occupancy within the previous 15 years, unless the housing is a mobilehome.

(5) Residential real property that is alienable separate from the title to any other dwelling unit, including a mobilehome, provided that both of the following apply:

(A) The owner is not any of the following:

(i) A real estate investment trust, as defined in Section 856 of the Internal Revenue Code.

(ii) A corporation.

(iii) A limited liability company in which at least one member is a corporation.

(iv) Management of a mobilehome park, as defined in Section 798.2.

(B)(i) The tenants have been provided written notice that the residential real property is exempt from this section using the following statement:

"This property is not subject to the rent limits imposed by Section 1947.12 of the Civil Code and is not subject to the just cause requirements of Section 1946.2 of the Civil Code. This property meets the requirements of Sections 1947.12 (d)(5) and 1946.2 (e)(8) of the Civil Code and the owner is not any of the following: (1) a real estate investment trust, as defined by Section 856 of the Internal Revenue Code; (2) a corporation; or (3) a limited liability company in which at least one member is a corporation."

(ii) For a tenancy existing before July 1, 2020, or July 1, 2022, if the lease is for a tenancy in a mobilehome, the notice required under clause (i) may, but is not required to, be provided in the rental agreement.

(iii) For a tenancy commenced or renewed on or after July 1, 2020, or July 1, 2022, if the lease is for a tenancy in a mobilehome, the notice required under clause (i) must be provided in the rental agreement.

(iv) Addition of a provision containing the notice required under clause (i) to any new or renewed rental agreement or fixed-term lease constitutes a similar provision for the purposes of subparagraph (E) of paragraph (1) of subdivision (b) of Section 1946.2.

(6) A property containing two separate dwelling units within a single structure in which the owner occupied one of the units as the owner's principal place of residence at the beginning of the tenancy, so long as the owner continues in occupancy, and neither unit is an accessory dwelling unit or a junior accessory dwelling unit.

(e) An owner shall provide notice of any increase in the rental rate, pursuant to subdivision (a), to each tenant in accordance with Section 827.

(f)(1) On or before January 1, 2030, the Legislative Analyst's Office shall report to the Legislature regarding the effectiveness of this section and Section 1947.13. The report shall include, but not be limited to, the impact of the rental rate cap pursuant to subdivision (a) on the housing market within the state.

(2) The report required by paragraph (1) shall be submitted in compliance with Section 9795 of the Government Code.

(g) For the purposes of this section, the following definitions shall apply:

(1) "Consumer Price Index for All Urban Consumers for All Items" means the following:

(A) The Consumer Price Index for All Urban Consumers for All Items (CPI-U) for the metropolitan area in which the property is located, as published by the United States Bureau of Labor Statistics, which are as follows:

(i) The CPI-U for the Los Angeles-Long Beach-Anaheim metropolitan area covering the Counties of Los Angeles and Orange.

(ii) The CPI-U for the Riverside-San Bernardino-Ontario metropolitan area covering the Counties of Riverside and San Bernardino.

(iii) The CPI-U for the San Diego-Carlsbad metropolitan area covering the County of San Diego.

(iv) The CPI-U for the San Francisco-Oakland-Hayward metropolitan area covering the Counties of Alameda, Contra Costa, Marin, San Francisco, and San Mateo.

(v) Any successor metropolitan area index to any of the indexes listed in clauses (i) to (iv), inclusive.

(B) If the United States Bureau of Labor Statistics does not publish a CPI-U for the metropolitan area in which the property is located, the California Consumer Price Index for All Urban Consumers for All Items as published by the Department of Industrial Relations.

(C) On or after January 1, 2021, if the United States Bureau of Labor Statistics publishes a CPI-U index for one or more metropolitan areas not listed in subparagraph (A), that CPI-U index shall apply in those areas with respect to rent increases that take effect on or after August 1 of the calendar year in which the 12-month change in that CPI-U, as described in subparagraph (B) of paragraph (3), is first published.

(2) "Owner" includes any person, acting as principal or through an agent, having the right to offer residential real property for rent, and includes a predecessor in interest to the owner.

(3)(A) "Percentage change in the cost of living" means the percentage change, computed pursuant to subparagraph (B), in the applicable, as determined pursuant to paragraph (1), Consumer Price Index for All Urban Consumers for All Items.

(B)(i) For rent increases that take effect before August 1 of any calendar year, the following shall apply:

(I) The percentage change shall be the percentage change in the amount published for April of the immediately preceding calendar year and April of the year before that.

(II) If there is not an amount published in April for the applicable geographic area, the percentage change shall be the percentage change in the amount published for March of the immediately preceding calendar year and March of the year before that.

(ii) For rent increases that take effect on or after August 1 of any calendar year, the following shall apply:

(I) The percentage change shall be the percentage change in the amount published for April of that calendar year and April of the immediately preceding calendar year.

(II) If there is not an amount published in April for the applicable geographic area, the percentage change shall be the percentage change in the amount published for March of that calendar year and March of the immediately preceding calendar year.

(iii) The percentage change shall be rounded to the nearest one-tenth of 1 percent.

(4) "Residential real property" means any dwelling or unit that is intended for human habitation, including any dwelling or unit in a mobilehome park.

(5) "Tenancy" means the lawful occupation of residential real property and includes a lease or sublease.

(h)(1) This section shall apply to all rent increases subject to subdivision (a) occurring on or after March 15, 2019, except as provided in subdivision (i).

(2) In the event that an owner has increased the rent by more than the amount permissible under subdivision (a) between March 15, 2019, and January 1, 2020, both of the following shall apply:

(A) The applicable rent on January 1, 2020, shall be the rent as of March 15, 2019, plus the maximum permissible increase under subdivision (a).

(B) An owner shall not be liable to the tenant for any corresponding rent overpayment.

(3) An owner of residential real property subject to subdivision (a) who increased the rental rate on that residential real property on or after March 15, 2019, but prior to January 1, 2020, by an amount less than the rental rate increase permitted by subdivision (a) shall be allowed to increase the rental rate twice, as provided in paragraph (2) of subdivision (a), within 12 months of March 15, 2019, but in no event shall that rental rate increase exceed the maximum rental rate increase permitted by subdivision (a).

(i)(1) Notwithstanding subdivision (h), this section shall apply only to rent increases for a tenancy in a mobilehome subject to subdivision (a) occurring on or after February 18, 2021.

(2) In the event that an owner has increased the rent for a tenancy in a mobilehome by more than the amount permissible under subdivision (a) between February 18, 2021, and January 1, 2022, both of the following shall apply:

(A) The applicable rent on January 1, 2022, shall be the rent as of February 18, 2021, plus the maximum permissible increase under subdivision (a).

(B) An owner shall not be liable to the tenant for any corresponding rent overpayment.

(3) An owner of residential real property subject to subdivision (a) who increased the rental rate on that residential real property on or after February 18, 2021, but prior to January 1, 2022, by an amount less than the rental rate increase permitted by subdivision (a) shall be allowed to increase the rental rate twice, as provided in paragraph (2) of subdivision (a), within 12 months of February 18, 2021, but in no event shall that rental rate increase exceed the maximum rental rate increase permitted by subdivision (a).

(j) This section shall not apply to a homeowner of a mobilehome, as defined in Section 798.9.

(k)(1) An owner who demands, accepts, receives, or retains any payment of rent in excess of the maximum rent allowed by this section shall be liable in a civil action to the tenant from whom those payments are demanded, accepted, received, or retained for all of the following:

(A) Injunctive relief.

(B) Damages in the amount by which any payment demanded, accepted, received, or retained exceeds the maximum allowable rent.

(C) In the court's discretion, reasonable attorney's fees and costs.

(D) Upon a showing that the owner has acted willfully or with oppression, fraud, or malice, damages up to three times the amount by which any payment demanded, accepted, received, or retained exceeds the maximum allowable rent.

(2) The Attorney General, in the name of the people of the State of California, and the city attorney or county counsel in the jurisdiction in which the rental unit is located, in the name of the city or county, may do both of the following:

(A) Enforce the provisions of this section.

(B) Seek injunctive relief based on violations of this section.

(3) In an action pursuant to this subdivision for injunctive relief, it shall be presumed that a tenant suffers irreparable harm through violation of this section.

(4) An action pursuant to this subdivision shall not be brought after the date that is three years from the date on which the cause of action accrued.

(*l*) Any waiver of the rights under this section shall be void as contrary to public policy.

(m)(1) The Legislature finds and declares that the unique circumstances of the current housing crisis require a statewide response to address rent gouging by establishing statewide limitations on gross rental rate increases.

(2) It is the intent of the Legislature that this section should apply only for the limited time needed to address the current statewide housing crisis, as described in paragraph (1). This section is not intended to expand or limit the authority of local governments to establish local policies regulating rents consistent with Chapter 2.7 (commencing with Section 1954.50), nor is it a statement regarding the appropriate, allowable rental rate increase when a local government adopts a policy regulating rent that is otherwise consistent with Chapter 2.7 (commencing with Section 1954.50).

(3) Nothing in this section authorizes a local government to establish limitations on any rental rate increases not otherwise permissible under Chapter 2.7 (commencing with Section 1954.50), or affects the existing authority of a local government to adopt or maintain rent controls or price controls consistent with that chapter.

(n) This section shall become operative on April 1, 2024.

(o) This section shall remain in effect until January 1, 2030, and as of that date is repealed. **Leg.H.** Added Stats 2023 ch 290 §4 (SB 567), effective January 1, 2024, operative April 1, 2024, repealed January 1, 2030.

Prior Law Former CC §1947.12, similar to the present section, was added Stats 2019 ch 597 §3 (AB 1482), effective January 1, 2020, amended Stats 2020 ch 37 §9 (AB 3088), effective August 31, 2020, Stats 2021 ch 125 §4 (AB 978), effective January 1, 2022, and Stats 2023 ch 290 §3 (SB 567), effective January 1, 2024, and repealed April 1, 2024, by its own provision.

§1947.13. Limitations on rental rates upon expiration of rental restrictions [Repealed January 1, 2030]

(a) Notwithstanding subdivision (a) of Section 1947.12, upon the expiration of rental restrictions, the following shall apply:

(1) The owner of an assisted housing development who demonstrates, under penalty of perjury, compliance with all applicable provisions of Sections 65863.10, 65863.11, and 65863.13 of the Government Code and any other applicable federal, state, or local law or regulation may establish the initial unassisted rental rate for units in the applicable housing development. Any subsequent rent increase in the development shall be subject to Section 1947.12.

(2) The owner of a deed-restricted affordable housing unit or an affordable housing unit subject to a regulatory restriction contained in an agreement with a government agency limiting rental rates that is not within an assisted housing development may, subject to any applicable federal, state, or local law or regulation, establish the initial rental rate for the unit upon the expiration of the restriction. Any subsequent rent increase for the unit shall be subject to Section 1947.12.

(b) For purposes of this section:

(1) "Assisted housing development" has the same meaning as defined in paragraph (3) of subdivision (a) of Section 65863.10 of the Government Code.

(2) "Expiration of rental restrictions" has the same meaning as defined in paragraph (5) of subdivision (a) of Section 65863.10 of the Government Code.

(c) This section shall remain in effect until January 1, 2030, and as of that date is repealed.

(d) Any waiver of the rights under this section shall be void as contrary to public policy.

(e) This section shall not be construed to preempt any local law. **Leg.H.** Added Stats 2019 ch 597 §4 (AB 1482), effective January 1, 2020, repealed January 1, 2030. Amended Stats 2020 ch 37 §10 (AB 3088), effective August 31, 2020, repealed January 1, 2030.

§1947.15. Professional expenses allowed owners of rent controlled property [Operation contingent]

(a) The Legislature declares the purpose of this section is to:

(1) Ensure that owners of residential rental units that are subject to a system of controls on the price at which the units may be offered for rent or lease, or controls on the adjustment of the rent level, are not precluded or discouraged from obtaining a fair return on their properties as guaranteed by the United States Constitution and California Constitution because the professional expenses reasonably required in the course of the administrative proceedings, in order to obtain the rent increases necessary to provide a fair return, are not treated as a legitimate business expense.

(2) Encourage agencies which administer a system of controls on the price at which residential rental units may be offered for rent or lease, or controls the adjustment of the rent level, to enact streamlined administrative procedures governing rent adjustment petitions which minimize, to the extent possible, the cost and expense of these administrative proceedings.

(3) Ensure that the cost of professional services reasonably incurred and required by owners of residential rental units subject to a system of controls in the price at which the units may be offered for rent or lease, or controls on the adjustments of the rent level in the course of defending rights related to the rent control system, be treated as a legitimate business expense.

(b) Any city, county, or city and county, including a charter city, which administers an ordinance, charter provision, rule, or regulation that controls or establishes a system of controls on the price at which all or any portion of the residential rental units located within the city, county, or city and county, may be offered for rent or lease, or controls the adjustment of the rent level, and which does not include a system of vacancy decontrol, as defined in subdivision (i), shall permit reasonable expenses, fees, and other costs for professional services, including, but not limited to, legal, accounting, appraisal, bookkeeping, consulting, property management, or architectural services, reasonably incurred in the course of successfully pursuing rights under or in relationship to, that ordinance, charter provision, rule, or regulation, or the right to a fair return on an owner's property as protected by the United States Constitution or California Constitution, to be included in any calculation of net operating income and operating expenses used to determine a fair return to the owner of the property. All expenses, fees, and other costs reasonably incurred by an owner of property in relation to administrative proceedings for purposes specified in this subdivision shall be included in the calculation specified in this subdivision.

(c) Reasonable fees that are incurred by the owner in successfully obtaining a judicial reversal of an adverse administrative decision regarding a petition for upward adjustment of rents shall be assessed against the respondent public agency which issued the adverse administrative decision, and shall not be included in the calculations specified in subdivisions (b) and (d).

(d)(1) Notwithstanding subdivision (b), the city, county, or city and county, on the basis of substantial evidence in the record that the expenses reasonably incurred in the underlying proceeding will not reoccur annually, may amortize the expenses for a period not to exceed five years, except that in extraordinary circumstances, the amortization period may be extended to a period of eight years. The extended amortization period shall not apply to vacant units and shall end if the unit becomes vacant during the period that the expense is being amortized. An amortization schedule shall include a reasonable rate of interest.

(2) Any determination of the reasonableness of the expenses claimed, of an appropriate amortization period, or of the award of an upward adjustment of rents to compensate the owner for expenses and costs incurred shall be made as part of, or immediately following, the decision in the underlying administrative proceeding.

(e) Any and all of the following factors shall be considered in the determination of the reasonableness of the expenses, fees, or other costs authorized by this section:

(1) The rate charged for those professional services in the relevant geographic area.

(2) The complexity of the matter.

(3) The degree of administrative burden or judicial burden, or both, imposed upon the property owner.

(4) The amount of adjustment sought or the significance of the rights defended and the results obtained.

(5) The relationship of the result obtained to the expenses, fees, and other costs incurred (that is, whether professional assistance was reasonably related to the result achieved).

(f) This section shall not be applicable to any ordinance, rule, regulation, or charter provision of any city, county, or city and county, including a charter city, to the extent that the ordinance, rule, or regulation, or charter provision places a limit on the amount of rent that an owner may charge a tenant of a mobilehome park.

(g) For purposes of this section, the rights of a property owner shall be deemed to be successfully pursued or defended if the owner obtains an upward adjustment in rents, successfully defends his or her rights in an administrative proceeding brought by the tenant or the local rent board, or prevails in a proceeding, brought pursuant to Section 1947.8 concerning certification of maximum lawful rents.

(h)(1) If it is determined that a landlord petition assisted by attorneys or consultants is wholly without merit, the tenant shall be awarded a reduction in rent to compensate for the reasonable costs of attorneys or consultants retained by the tenant to defend the petition brought by the landlord. The reasonableness of the costs of the tenant's defense of the action brought by the landlord shall be determined pursuant to the same provisions established by this section for determining the reasonableness of the landlord's costs for the professional services. The determination of the reasonableness of the expenses claimed, an appropriate amortization period, and the award of a reduction in rents to compensate the tenant for costs incurred shall be made immediately following the decision in the underlying administrative proceeding.

(2) If it is determined that a landlord's appeal of an adverse administrative decision is frivolous or solely intended to cause unnecessary delay, the public agency which defended the action shall be awarded its reasonably incurred expenses, including attorney's fees, in defending the action. As used in this paragraph, "frivolous" means either (A) totally and completely without merit; or (B) for the sole purpose of harassing an opposing party.

(i) For purposes of this section, the following terms shall have the following meanings:

(1) "Vacancy decontrol" means a system of controls on the price at which residential rental units may be offered for rent or lease which permits the rent to be increased to its market level, without restriction, each time a vacancy occurs. "Vacancy decontrol" includes systems which reimpose controls on the price at which residential rental units may be offered for rent or lease upon rerental of the unit.

(2) "Vacancy decontrol" includes circumstances where the tenant vacates the unit of his or her own volition, or where the local jurisdiction permits the rent to be raised to market rate after an eviction for cause, as specified in the ordinance, charter provision, rule, or regulation.

(j) This section shall not be construed to affect in any way the ability of a local agency to set its own fair return standards or to limit other actions under its local rent control program other than those expressly set forth in this section.

(k) This section is not operative unless the Costa-Hawkins Rental Housing Act (Chapter 2.7 (commencing with Section 1954.50) of Title 5 of Part 4 of Division 3) is repealed. **Leg.H.** Added Stats 1993 ch 843 §1 (AB 264). Amended Stats 1996 ch 566 §2 (SB 1632); Stats 2002 ch 301 §2 (SB 1403).

2002 Note: The Costa-Hawkins Rental Housing Act was not repealed during the 2001-2002 legislative session.

§1948. Attornment of a tenant to a stranger

The attornment of a tenant to a stranger is void, unless it is made with the consent of the landlord, or in consequence of a judgment of a court of competent jurisdiction. **Leg.H.** Enacted Stats 1872.

§1949. Tenant must deliver notice served on him

Every tenant who receives notice of any proceeding to recover the real property occupied by him or her, or the possession of the real property, shall immediately inform his or her landlord of the proceeding, and also deliver to the landlord the notice, if in writing, and is responsible to the landlord for all damages which he or she may sustain by reason of any omission to inform the landlord of the notice, or to deliver it to him or her if in writing. **Leg.H.** Enacted Stats 1872. Amended Code Amdts 1873–74 ch 612 §207; Stats 1989 ch 1360 §11.

§1950. Letting parts of rooms forbidden

One who hires part of a room for a dwelling is entitled to the whole of the room, notwithstanding any agreement to the contrary; and if a landlord lets a room as a dwelling for more than one family, the person to whom he first lets any part of it is entitled to the possession of the whole room for the term agreed upon, and every tenant in the building, under the same landlord, is relieved from all obligation to pay rent to him while such double letting of any room continues. **Leg.H.** Enacted Stats 1872.

§ 1950.1. Reusable tenant screening report

(a) A reusable tenant screening report shall include all of the following information regarding an applicant:

(1) Name.

(2) Contact information.

(3) Verification of employment.

(4) Last known address.

(5) Results of an eviction history check in a manner and for a period of time consistent with applicable law related to the consideration of eviction history in housing.

(b) A reusable tenant screening report shall prominently state the date through which the information contained in the report is current.

(c) A landlord may elect to accept reusable tenant screening reports and may require an applicant to state that there has not been a material change to the information in the reusable tenant screening report.

(d) Notwithstanding Section 1950.6, if an applicant provides a reusable tenant screening report to a landlord that accepts reusable tenant screening reports, the landlord shall not charge the applicant either of the following:

(1) A fee for the landlord to access the report.

(2) An application screening fee.

(e) As used in this section:

(1) "Applicant" has the same meaning as defined in Section 1950.6.

(2) "Application screening fee" has the same meaning as defined in Section 1950.6.

(3) "Consumer report" has the same meaning as defined in Section 1681a of Title 15 of the United States Code.

(4) "Consumer reporting agency" means a person which, for monetary fees, dues, or on a cooperative nonprofit basis, regularly engages in whole or in part in the practice of assembling or evaluating consumer credit information or other information on consumers for the purpose of furnishing consumer reports to third parties and that uses any means or facility of interstate commerce for the purpose of preparing or furnishing consumer reports.

(5) "Landlord" means an owner of residential rental property or the owner's agent.

(6) "Reusable tenant screening report" means a consumer report that meets all of the following criteria:

(A) Was prepared within the previous 30 days by a consumer reporting agency at the request and expense of an applicant.

(B) Is made directly available to a landlord for use in the rental application process or is provided through a third-party website that regularly engages in the business of providing a reusable tenant screening report and complies with all state and federal laws pertaining to use and disclosure of information contained in a consumer report by a consumer reporting agency.

(C) Is available to the landlord at no cost to access or use.

(f) This section does not affect any other applicable law related to the consideration of criminal history information in housing, including, but not limited to, Article 24 (commencing with Section 12264) of Subchapter 7 of Chapter 5 of Division 4.1 of Title 2 of the California Code of Regulations and local ordinances governing the information that landlords may review and consider when determining to whom they will rent.

(g) If an ordinance, resolution, regulation, administrative action, initiative, or other policy adopted by a city, county, or city and county conflicts with this section, the policy that provides greater protections to applicants shall apply.

(h) This section does not require a landlord to accept reusable tenant screening reports. **Leg.H.** Added Stats 2022 ch 288 §1 (AB 2559), effective January 1, 2023.

§ 1950.5. Security for performance of rental agreement for residential property; Amount; Priority; What damages landlord may claim; Notice; Initial inspection and opportunity to remedy; Itemized statement; Documentation; Termination of landlord's interest; Liability for noncompliance

(a) This section applies to security for a rental agreement for residential property that is used as the dwelling of the tenant.

(b) As used in this section, "security" means any payment, fee, deposit, or charge, including, but not limited to, any payment, fee, deposit, or charge, except as provided in Section 1950.6, that is imposed at the beginning of the tenancy to be used to reimburse the landlord for costs associated with processing a new tenant or that is imposed as an advance payment of rent, used or to be used for any purpose, including, but not limited to, any of the following:

(1) The compensation of a landlord for a tenant's default in the payment of rent.

(2) The repair of damages to the premises, exclusive of ordinary wear and tear, caused by the tenant or by a guest or licensee of the tenant.

(3) The cleaning of the premises upon termination of the tenancy necessary to return the unit to the same level of cleanliness it was in at the inception of the tenancy. The amendments to this paragraph enacted by the act adding this sentence shall apply only to tenancies for which the tenant's right to occupy begins after January 1, 2003.

(4) To remedy future defaults by the tenant in any obligation under the rental agreement to restore, replace, or return personal property or appurtenances, exclusive of ordinary wear and tear, if the security deposit is authorized to be applied thereto by the rental agreement.

(c)(1) Except as provided in paragraph (2), (3), or (5), a landlord may not demand or receive security, however denominated, in an amount or value in excess of an amount equal to one month's rent, in addition to any rent for the first month paid on or before initial occupancy.

(2) This subdivision does not prohibit an advance payment of not less than six months' rent if the term of the lease is six months or longer.

(3) This subdivision does not preclude a landlord and a tenant from entering into a mutual agreement for the landlord, at the request of the tenant and for a specified fee or charge, to make structural, decorative, furnishing, or other similar alterations, if the alterations are other than cleaning or repairing for which the landlord may charge the previous tenant as provided by subdivision (e).

(4) On or after April 1, 2025, if a landlord or its agent charges a service member who rents residential property in which the service member will reside a higher than standard or advertised security pursuant to paragraph (1) due to the credit history, credit score, housing history, or other factor related to the tenant, the landlord shall provide the tenant with a written statement, on or before the date the lease is signed, of the amount of the higher security and an explanation why the higher security amount is being charged. The additional amount of security shall be returned to the tenant after no more than six months of residency if the tenant is not in arrears for any rent due during that period. The date for return of the additional amount of security shall be included in the lease agreement. For purposes of this paragraph, "service member" has the same meaning as in Section 400 of the Military and Veterans Code.

(5)(A) Notwithstanding paragraph (1), a landlord may not demand or receive security, however denominated, in an amount or value in excess of an amount equal to two months' rent, in addition to any rent for the first month paid on or before initial occupancy if the landlord meets both of the following requirements:

(i) The landlord is a natural person or a limited liability company in which all members are natural persons.

(ii) The landlord owns no more than two residential rental properties that collectively include no more than four dwelling units offered for rent.

(B) Subparagraph (A) shall not apply if the prospective tenant is a service member. A landlord shall not refuse to enter into a rental agreement for residential property with a prospective tenant who is a service member because this subparagraph prohibits the landlord from demanding or receiving a greater amount of security than that which is established in paragraph (1). For purposes of this subparagraph, "service member" has the same meaning as in Section 400 of the Military and Veterans Code.

(C) For purposes of this paragraph:

(i) "Natural person" includes any natural person who is a settlor or beneficiary of a family trust.

(ii) "Family trust" means a revocable living trust or irrevocable trust in which the settlors and beneficiaries of the trust are persons who are related to each other as sibling, spouse, domestic partner, child, parent, grandparent, or grandchild.

(6) This subdivision shall not apply to a security collected or demanded by the landlord before July 1, 2024.

(d) Any security shall be held by the landlord for the tenant who is party to the lease or agreement. The claim of a tenant to the security shall be prior to the claim of any creditor of the landlord.

(e) The landlord may claim of the security only those amounts as are reasonably necessary for the purposes specified in subdivision (b). The landlord may not assert a claim against the tenant or the security for damages to the premises or any defective conditions that preexisted the tenancy, for ordinary wear and tear or the effects thereof, whether the wear and tear preexisted the tenancy or occurred during the tenancy, or for the cumulative effects of ordinary wear and tear occurring during any one or more tenancies.

(f)(1) Within a reasonable time after notification of either party's intention to terminate the tenancy, or before the end of the lease term, the landlord shall notify the tenant in writing of the tenant's option to request an initial inspection and of the tenant's right to be present at the inspection. The requirements of this subdivision do not apply when the tenancy is terminated pursuant to subdivision (2), (3), or (4) of Section 1161 of the Code of Civil Procedure. At a reasonable time, but no earlier than two weeks before the termination or the end of lease date, the landlord, or an agent of the landlord, shall, upon the request of the tenant, make an initial inspection of the premises prior to any final inspection the landlord makes after the tenant has vacated the premises. The purpose of the initial inspection shall be to allow the tenant an opportunity to remedy identified deficiencies, in a manner consistent with the rights and obligations of the parties under the rental agreement, in order to avoid deductions from the security. If a tenant chooses not to request an initial inspection, the duties of the landlord under this subdivision are discharged. If an inspection is requested, the parties shall attempt to schedule the inspection at a mutually acceptable date and time. The landlord shall give at least 48 hours' prior written notice of the date and time of the inspection if either a mutual time is agreed upon, or if a mutually agreed time cannot be scheduled but the tenant still wishes an inspection. The tenant and landlord may agree to forgo the 48-hour prior written notice by both signing a written waiver. The landlord shall proceed with the inspection whether the tenant is present or not, unless the tenant previously withdrew their request for the inspection. Written notice by the landlord shall contain, in substantially the same form, the following:

"State law permits former tenants to reclaim abandoned personal property left at the former address of the tenant, subject to certain conditions. You may or may not be able to reclaim property without incurring additional costs, depending on the cost of storing the property and the length of time before it is reclaimed. In general, these costs will be lower the sooner you contact your former landlord after being notified that property belonging to you was left behind after you moved out."

(2) Based on the inspection, the landlord shall give the tenant an itemized statement specifying repairs or cleanings that are proposed to be the basis of any deductions from the security the landlord intends to make pursuant to paragraphs (1) to (4), inclusive, of subdivision (b). This statement shall also include the texts of paragraphs (1) to (4), inclusive, of subdivision (b). The statement shall be given to the tenant, if the tenant is present for the inspection, or shall be left inside the premises.

(3) The tenant shall have the opportunity during the period following the initial inspection until termination of the tenancy to remedy identified deficiencies, in a manner consistent with the rights and obligations of the parties under the rental agreement, in order to avoid deductions from the security.

(4) Nothing in this subdivision shall prevent a landlord from using the security for deductions itemized in the statement provided for in paragraph (2) that were not cured by the tenant so long as the deductions are for damages authorized by this section.

(5) Nothing in this subdivision shall prevent a landlord from using the security for any purpose specified in paragraphs (1) to (4), inclusive, of subdivision (b) that occurs between completion of the initial inspection and termination of the tenancy or was not identified during the initial inspection due to the presence of a tenant's possessions.

(g)(1) No later than 21 calendar days after the tenant has vacated the premises, but not earlier than the time that either the landlord or the tenant provides a notice to terminate the tenancy under Section 1946 or 1946.1, Section 1161 of the Code of Civil Procedure, or not earlier than 60 calendar days prior to the expiration of a fixed-term lease, the landlord shall furnish the tenant, by personal delivery or by first-class mail, postage prepaid, a copy of an itemized statement indicating the basis for, and the amount of, any security received and the disposition of the security, and shall return any remaining portion of the security to the tenant. After either the landlord or the tenant provides notice to terminate the tenancy, the landlord and tenant may mutually agree to have the landlord deposit any remaining portion of the security deposit electronically to a bank account or other financial institution designated by the tenant. After either the landlord or the tenant provides notice to terminate the tenancy, the landlord and the tenant may also agree to have the landlord provide a copy of the itemized statement along with the copies required by paragraph (2) to an email account provided by the tenant.

(2) Along with the itemized statement, the landlord shall also include copies of documents showing charges incurred and deducted by the landlord to repair or clean the premises, as follows:

(A) If the landlord or landlord's employee did the work, the itemized statement shall reasonably describe the work performed. The itemized statement shall include the time spent and the reasonable hourly rate charged.

(B) If the landlord or landlord's employee did not do the work, the landlord shall provide the tenant a copy of the bill, invoice, or receipt supplied by the person or entity performing the work. The itemized statement shall provide the tenant with the name, address, and telephone number of the person or entity, if the bill, invoice, or receipt does not include that information.

(C) If a deduction is made for materials or supplies, the landlord shall provide a copy of the bill, invoice, or receipt. If a particular material or supply item is purchased by the landlord on an ongoing basis, the landlord may document the cost of the item by providing a copy of a bill, invoice, receipt, vendor price list, or other vendor document that reasonably documents the cost of the item used in the repair or cleaning of the unit.

(3) If a repair to be done by the landlord or the landlord's employee cannot reasonably be completed within 21 calendar days after the tenant has vacated the premises, or if the documents from a person or entity providing services, materials, or supplies are not in the landlord's possession within 21 calendar days after the tenant has vacated the premises, the landlord may deduct the amount of a good faith estimate of the charges that will be incurred and provide that estimate with the itemized statement. If the reason for the estimate is because the documents from a person or entity providing services, materials, or supplies are not in the landlord's possession, the itemized statement shall include the name, address, and telephone number of the person or entity. Within 14 calendar days of completing the repair or receiving the documentation, the landlord shall complete the requirements in paragraphs (1) and (2) in the manner specified.

(4) The landlord need not comply with paragraph (2) or (3) if either of the following applies:

(A) The deductions for repairs and cleaning together do not exceed one hundred twenty-five dollars ($125).

(B) The tenant waived the rights specified in paragraphs (2) and (3). The waiver shall only be effective if it is signed by the tenant at the same time or after a notice to terminate a tenancy under Section 1946 or 1946.1 has been given, a notice under Section 1161 of the Code of Civil Procedure has been given, or no earlier than 60 calendar days prior to the expiration of a fixed-term lease. The waiver shall substantially include the text of paragraph (2).

(5) Notwithstanding paragraph (4), the landlord shall comply with paragraphs (2) and (3) when a tenant makes a request for documentation within 14 calendar days after receiving the itemized statement specified in paragraph (1). The landlord shall comply within 14 calendar days after receiving the request from the tenant.

(6) Any mailings to the tenant pursuant to this subdivision shall be sent to the address provided by the tenant. If the tenant does not provide an address, mailings pursuant to this subdivision shall be sent to the unit that has been vacated.

(h) Upon termination of the landlord's interest in the premises, whether by sale, assignment, death, appointment of receiver, or otherwise, the landlord or the landlord's agent shall, within a reasonable time, do one of the following acts, either of which shall relieve the landlord of further liability with respect to the security held:

(1) Transfer the portion of the security remaining after any lawful deductions made under subdivision (e) to the landlord's successor in interest. The landlord shall thereafter notify the tenant by personal delivery or by first-class mail, postage prepaid, of the transfer, of any claims made against the security, of the amount of the security deposited, and of the names of the successors in interest, their addresses, and their telephone numbers. If the notice to the tenant is made by personal delivery, the tenant shall acknowledge receipt of the notice and sign their name on the landlord's copy of the notice.

(2) Return the portion of the security remaining after any lawful deductions made under subdivision (e) to the tenant, together with an accounting as provided in subdivision (g).

(i) Prior to the voluntary transfer of a landlord's interest in the premises, the landlord shall deliver to the landlord's successor in interest a written statement indicating the following:

(1) The security remaining after any lawful deductions are made.

(2) An itemization of any lawful deductions from any security received.

(3) Their election under paragraph (1) or (2) of subdivision (h).

This subdivision does not affect the validity of title to the real property transferred in violation of this subdivision.

(j)(1) In the event of noncompliance with subdivision (h), the landlord's successors in interest shall be jointly and severally liable with the landlord for repayment of the security, or that portion thereof to which the tenant is entitled, when and as provided in subdivisions (e) and (g). A successor in interest of a landlord may not require the tenant to post any security to replace that amount not transferred to the tenant or successors in interest as provided in subdivision (h), unless and until the successor in interest first makes restitution of the initial security as provided in paragraph (2) of subdivision (h) or provides the tenant with an accounting as provided in subdivision (g).

(2) This subdivision does not preclude a successor in interest from recovering from the tenant compensatory damages that are in excess of the security received from the landlord previously paid by the tenant to the landlord.

(3) Notwithstanding this subdivision, if, upon inquiry and reasonable investigation, a landlord's successor in interest has a good faith belief that the lawfully remaining security deposit is transferred to the successor in interest or returned to the tenant pursuant to subdivision (h), the successor in interest is not liable for damages as provided in subdivision (*l*), or any security not transferred pursuant to subdivision (h).

(k) Upon receipt of any portion of the security under paragraph (1) of subdivision (h), the landlord's successors in interest shall have all of the rights and obligations of a landlord holding the security with respect to the security.

(*l*) The bad faith claim or retention by a landlord or the landlord's successors in interest of the security or any portion thereof in violation of this section, or the bad faith demand of replacement security in violation of subdivision (j), may subject the landlord or the landlord's successors in interest to statutory damages of up to twice the amount of the security, in addition to actual damages. The court may award damages for bad faith whenever the facts warrant that award, regardless of whether the injured party has specifically requested relief. In an action under this section, the landlord or the landlord's successors in interest shall have the burden of proof as to the reasonableness of the amounts claimed or the authority pursuant to this section to demand additional security deposits.

(m) No lease or rental agreement may contain a provision characterizing any security as "nonrefundable."

(n) An action under this section may be maintained in small claims court if the damages claimed, whether actual, statutory, or both, are within the jurisdictional amount allowed by Section 116.220 or 116.221 of the Code of Civil Procedure.

(o) Proof of the existence of and the amount of a security deposit may be established by any credible evidence, including, but not limited to, a canceled check, a receipt, a lease indicating the requirement of a deposit as well as the amount, prior consistent statements or actions of the landlord or tenant, or a statement under penalty of perjury that satisfies the credibility requirements set forth in Section 780 of the Evidence Code.

(p) The amendments to this section made during the 1985 portion of the 1985-86 Regular Session of the Legislature that are set forth in subdivision (e) are declaratory of existing law.

(q) The amendments to this section made during the 2003 portion of the 2003-04 Regular Session of the Legislature that are set forth in paragraph (1) of subdivision (f) are declaratory of existing law.

(r) This section shall become operative on July 1, 2024. **Leg.H.** Added Stats 2023 ch 733 §2 (AB 12), effective January 1, 2024, operative July 1, 2024. Amended Stats 2024 ch 280 §2 (AB 2801), effective January 1, 2025; Stats 2024 ch 287 §4 (SB 611), effective January 1, 2025 (ch 287 prevails).

Prior Law: Former §1950.5, similar to the present section, was added Stats 1970 ch 1317 §1 as CC §1951, amended and renumbered by Stats 1972 ch 618 §4, and repealed Stats 1977 ch 971 §1.

Former CC § 1950.5, similar to the present section, was added Stats 1977 ch 971 §2, amended Stats 1985 ch 1291 §1, ch 1555 §2; Stats 1986 ch 564 §1; Stats 1993 ch 755 §1 (SB 444); Stats 1994 ch 146 §13 (AB 3601); Stats 2002 ch 1061 §1 (AB 2330); Stats 2003 ch 335 §1 (SB 90), ch 576 §1.5 (AB 1384); Stats 2004 ch 568 §3 (SB 1145); Stats 2006 ch 167 §3 (AB 2618), effective January 1, 2007; Stats 2012 ch 557 §1 (AB 1679), effective January 1, 2013, ch 560 §3.5 (AB 2521), effective January 1, 2013; Stats 2013 ch 76 §12 (AB 383), effective January 1, 2014; Stats 2019 ch 602 §2 (SB 644), effective January 1, 2020; Stats 2023 ch 733 §1 (AB 12), effective January 1, 2024, and repealed July 1, 2024, by its own provision.

§ 1950.6. Application screening fee; Provision of consumer credit report to applicant

(a) Notwithstanding Section 1950.5, when a landlord or their agent receives a request to rent a residential property from an applicant, the landlord or their agent may charge, **pursuant to subdivision (c),** that applicant an application screening fee to cover the costs of obtaining information about the applicant. The information requested and obtained by the landlord or their agent may include, but is not limited to, personal reference checks and consumer credit reports produced by consumer credit reporting agencies as defined in Section 1785.3. A landlord or their agent may, but is not required to, accept and rely upon a consumer credit report presented by an applicant.

(b) The amount of the application screening fee shall not be greater than the actual out-of-pocket costs of gathering information concerning the applicant, including, but not limited to, the cost of using a tenant screening service or a consumer credit reporting service, and the reasonable value of time spent by the landlord or their agent in obtaining information on the applicant. In no case shall the amount of the application screening fee charged by the landlord or their agent be greater than thirty dollars ($30) per applicant. The thirty dollar ($30) application screening fee may be adjusted annually by the landlord or their agent commensurate with an increase in the Consumer Price Index, beginning on January 1, 1998.

(c) [1]

(1) A landlord or their agent [2] **shall** not charge an applicant an application screening fee when they know or should have known that no rental unit is available at that time or will be available within a reasonable period of time.

(2) A landlord or their agent may charge an applicant an application screening fee only if the landlord or their agent, at the time the application screening fee is collected, offers any of the following:

(A) An application screening process that complies with all of the following:

(i) Completed applications are considered, as provided for in the landlord's established screening criteria, in the order in which the completed applications were received. The landlord's screening criteria shall be provided to the applicant in writing together with the application form.

(ii) The first applicant who meets the landlord's established screening criteria is approved for tenancy.

(iii) Applicants are not charged an application screening fee unless or until their application is actually considered.

(iv) Clause (iii) shall not be considered violated if a landlord or their agent inadvertently collects an application screening fee from an applicant as the result of multiple concurrent application submissions, provided that the landlord or their agent issues a refund of the

application screening fee within 7 days to any applicant whose application is not considered. The landlord may offer, as an alternative to refunding the screening fee, the option, at the applicant's discretion, for the screening fee paid by the applicant to be applied to an application for another rental unit offered by the landlord. A landlord or their agent shall not be required to refund an application screening fee to an applicant whose application is denied, after consideration, because the applicant does not meet the landlord's established screening criteria.

(B) An application screening process in which the landlord or their agent returns the entire screening fee to any applicant who is not selected for tenancy, regardless of the reason, within 7 days of selecting an applicant for tenancy or 30 days of when the application was submitted, whichever occurs first.

(d) The landlord or their agent shall provide, personally, or by mail, the applicant with a receipt for the fee paid by the applicant, which receipt shall itemize the out-of-pocket expenses and time spent by the landlord or their agent to obtain and process the information about the applicant. The landlord or their agent and the applicant may agree to have the landlord provide a copy of the receipt for the fee paid by the applicant to an email account provided by the applicant.

(e) If the landlord or their agent does not perform a personal reference check or does not obtain a consumer credit report, the landlord or their agent shall return any amount of the screening fee that is not used for the purposes authorized by this section to the applicant.

(f) If an application screening fee has been paid by the [3], the landlord or their agent shall provide a copy of the consumer credit report to the applicant who is the subject of that **report by personal delivery, mail, or email within 7 days of the landlord or their agent receiving the report**.

(g) **Nothing in this section prevents a landlord from accepting a reusable screening report pursuant to Section 1950.1.**

[4] (h) As used in this section, "landlord" means an owner of residential rental property.

[5] (i) As used in this section, "application screening fee" means any nonrefundable payment of money charged by a landlord or their agent to an applicant, the purpose of which is to purchase a consumer credit report and to validate, review, or otherwise process an application for the rent or lease of residential rental property.

[6] (j) As used in this section, "applicant" means any entity or individual who makes a request to a landlord or their agent to rent a residential housing unit, or an entity or individual who agrees to act as a guarantor or cosignor on a rental agreement.

[7] (k) The application screening fee shall not be considered an "advance fee" as that term is used in Section 10026 of the Business and Professions Code, and shall not be considered "security" as that term is used in Section 1950.5.

[8] (l) This section is not intended to preempt any provisions or regulations that govern the collection of deposits and fees under federal or state housing assistance programs. **Leg.H.** Added Stats 1996 ch 525 §1 (AB 2263). Amended Stats 2023 ch 770 §2 (AB 1764), effective January 1, 2024; Stats 2024 ch 966 §1 (AB 2493), effective January 1, 2025.

§ 1950.6. 2024 Deletes. [1] Unless [2] may [3] applicant and if requested by the applicant [4] (g) [5] (h) [6] (i) [7] (j) [8] (k)

§1950.7. Security for performance of rental agreement for other than residential property; use; return of balance to tenant; transfer or return on termination of landlord's interest; penalty for bad faith retention

(a) Any payment or deposit of money the primary function of which is to secure the performance of a rental agreement for other than residential property or any part of the agreement, other than a payment or deposit, including an advance payment of rent, made to secure the execution of a rental agreement, shall be governed by the provisions of this section. With respect to residential property, the provisions of Section 1950.5 shall prevail.

(b) The payment or deposit of money shall be held by the landlord for the tenant who is party to the agreement. The claim of a tenant to the payment or deposit shall be prior to the claim of any creditor of the landlord, except a trustee in bankruptcy.

(c) The landlord may claim of the payment or deposit only those amounts as are reasonably necessary to remedy tenant defaults in the payment of rent, to repair damages to the premises caused by the tenant, or to clean the premises upon termination of the tenancy, if the payment or deposit is made for any or all of those specific purposes.

(1) If the claim of the landlord upon the payment or deposit is only for defaults in the payment of rent and the security deposit equals no more than one month's rent plus a deposit amount clearly described as the payment of the last month's rent, then any remaining portion of the payment or deposit shall be returned to the tenant at a time as may be mutually agreed upon by landlord and tenant, but in no event later than 30 days from the date the landlord receives possession of the premises.

(2) If the claim of the landlord upon the payment or deposit is only for defaults in the payment of rent and the security deposit exceeds the amount of one month's rent plus a deposit amount clearly described as the payment of the last month's rent, then any remaining portion of the payment or deposit in excess of an amount equal to one month's rent shall be returned to the tenant no later than two weeks after the date the landlord receives possession of the premises, with the remainder to be returned or accounted for within 30 days from the date the landlord receives possession of the premises.

(3) If the claim of the landlord upon the payment or deposit includes amounts reasonably necessary to repair damages to the premises caused by the tenant or to clean the premises, then any remaining portion of the payment or deposit shall be returned to the tenant at a time as may be mutually agreed upon by landlord and tenant, but in no event later than 30 days from the date the landlord receives possession of the premises.

(d) Upon termination of the landlord's interest in the unit in question, whether by sale, assignment, death, appointment of receiver or otherwise, the landlord or the landlord's agent shall, within a reasonable time, do one of the following acts, either of which shall relieve the landlord of further liability with respect to the payment or deposit:

(1) Transfer the portion of the payment or deposit remaining after any lawful deductions made under subdivision (c) to the landlord's successor in interest, and thereafter notify the tenant by personal delivery or certified mail of the transfer, of any claims made against the payment or deposit, and of the transferee's name and address. If the notice to the tenant is made by personal delivery, the tenant shall acknowledge receipt of the notice and sign his or her name on the landlord's copy of the notice.

(2) Return the portion of the payment or deposit remaining after any lawful deductions made under subdivision (c) to the tenant.

(e) Upon receipt of any portion of the payment or deposit under paragraph (1) of subdivision (d), the transferee shall have all of the rights and obligations of a landlord holding the payment or deposit with respect to the payment or deposit.

(f) The bad faith retention by a landlord or transferee of a payment or deposit or any portion thereof, in violation of this section, may subject the landlord or the transferee to damages not to exceed two hundred dollars ($200), in addition to any actual damages.

(g) This section is declarative of existing law and therefore operative as to all tenancies, leases, or rental agreements for other than residential property created or renewed on or after January 1, 1971. **Leg.H.** Added Stats 1977 ch 971 §3. Amended Stats 1981 ch 259 §1; Stats 2003 ch 89 §1 (AB 1361).

§1950.8. Prohibited lease or rental agreement preparation fees; Civil penalty

(a) This section applies only to commercial leases and nonresidential tenancies of real property.

(b) It shall be unlawful for any person to require, demand, or cause to make payable any payment of money, including, but not limited to, "key money," however denominated, or the lessor's attorney's fees reasonably incurred in preparing the lease or rental agreement, as a condition of initiating, continuing, or renewing a lease or rental agreement, unless the amount of payment is stated in the written lease or rental agreement

(c) Any person who requires, demands, or causes to make payable any payment in violation of subdivision (a), shall be subject to civil penalty of three times the amount of actual damages proximately suffered by the person seeking to obtain the lease or rental of real property, and the person so damaged shall be entitled to an award of costs, including reasonable attorney's fees, reasonable incurred in connection with obtaining the civil penalty.

(d) Nothing in this section shall prohibit the advance payment of rent, if the amount and character of the payment are clearly stated in a written lease or rental agreement.

(e) Nothing in this section shall prohibit any person from charging a reasonable amount for the purpose of conducting reasonable business activity in connection with initiating, continuing, or renewing a lease or rental agreement for nonresidential real property, including, but not limited to, verifying creditworthiness or qualifications of any person seeking to initiate, continue, or renew a lease or rental agreement for any use other than residential use, or cleaning fees, reasonably incurred in connection with the hiring of the real property.

(f) Nothing in this section shall prohibit a person from increasing a tenant's rent for nonresidential real property in order to recover building operating costs incurred on behalf of the tenant, if the right to the rent, the method of calculating the increase, and the period of time covered by the increase is stated in the lease or rental agreement. **Leg.H.** Added Stats 2001 ch 368 §1 (AB 533).

§ 1950.9. Requirements for charging qualified commercial tenants fees to recover building operating costs

(a) A landlord of a commercial real property shall not charge a qualified commercial tenant a fee to recover building operating costs unless all of the following apply:

(1) The building operating costs are allocated proportionately per tenant, by square footage, or another method as substantiated through supporting documentation provided by the landlord to the qualified commercial tenant.

(2) The building operating costs have been incurred within the previous 18 months, or are reasonably expected to be incurred within the next 12 months based on reasonable estimates.

(3) Before the execution of the lease, the landlord provides the prospective qualified commercial tenant a paper or electronic notice stating that the tenant may inspect any supporting documentation of building operating costs upon written request pursuant to paragraph (4).

(4) Within 30 days of a written request, the landlord provides the qualified commercial tenant supporting documentation of the previously incurred or reasonably expected building operating costs.

(5) The costs do not include expenses paid by a tenant directly to a third party.

(6) The costs do not include expenses for which a third party, tenant, or insurance reimbursed the landlord.

(b) A landlord of a commercial real property shall not charge a fee to recover any building operating costs from the qualified commercial tenant until the landlord provides the qualified commercial tenant supporting documentation.

(c) During the course of a commercial tenancy, the landlord shall not alter the method or formula used to allocate building operating costs to the qualified commercial tenant in a way that increases the qualified commercial tenant's share of those costs, unless the qualified commercial tenant is provided with written notice of the change in the method or formula with supporting documentation of the basis of the alteration.

(d) In an action for an unlawful detainer, ejectment, or other action to recover possession based on a failure to pay a fee to recover building operating costs, a qualified commercial tenant may raise, as an affirmative defense, that the landlord violated this section.

(e) A landlord of a commercial real property who violates this section shall be liable to a qualified commercial tenant in a civil action for all of the following:

(1) Actual damages.

(2) In the courts discretion, reasonable attorney's fees and costs.

(3) Upon showing that the landlord, lessor, or their agent has acted willfully or with oppression, fraud, or malice both of the following:

(A) Three times the amount of actual damages.

(B) Punitive damages.

(f) The district attorney, city attorney, or county counsel in the jurisdiction in which the commercial real property is located, in the name of the city or county, may seek injunctive relief based on a violation of this section.

(g) Any waiver of a right under this section by a qualified commercial tenant shall be void as a matter of public policy.

(h) For the purposes of this section, the following definitions apply:

(1) "Building operating costs" means costs that are incurred on behalf of a tenant for the operation, maintenance, or repair of the commercial real property, including, but not limited to, maintenance of common areas, utilities that are not separately metered, and taxes or assessments charged to the landlord pursuant to property ownership.

(2) "Commercial real property" means all real property in this state, except dwelling units subject to this chapter, mobilehomes, as defined in Section 798.3, and recreational vehicles, as defined in Section 799.29.

(3) "Microenterprise" has the same meaning as that term is defined in subdivision (a) of Section 18000 of the Business and Professions Code.

(4) "Nonprofit organization" means any private nonprofit organization that qualifies under Section 501(c)(3) of the United States Internal Revenue Code of 1986.

(5) "Qualified commercial tenant" means a tenant of commercial real property that meets both of the following requirements:

(A) The tenant is a microenterprise, a restaurant with fewer than 10 employees, or a nonprofit organization with fewer than 20 employees.

(B)(i) Subject to clause (ii), the tenant has provided the landlord, within the previous 12 months, a written notice that the tenant is a qualified commercial tenant and a self-attestation regarding the number of employees, at such time the protections under this section come into place.

(ii) Unless the tenancy is from week to week, month to month, or other period less than a month, the tenant provided the notice and self-attestation described in clause (i) before or upon execution of the lease, and annually thereafter, at such time the protections under this section come into place.

(6) "Supporting documentation" means a dated and itemized quote, contract, receipt, or invoice from a licensed contractor or a provider of services that includes, but is not limited to, both of the following:

(A) A tabulation showing how the costs are allocated among tenants in compliance with paragraph (1) of subdivision (a).

(B) A signed and dated attestation by the landlord that the documentation and costs are true and correct.

(i) This section shall only apply to the following:

(1) Leases executed or tenancies commenced or renewed on or after January 1, 2025.

(2) A tenancy that is from week to week, month to month, or other period less than a month.

(3) Leases executed or tenancies commenced before January 1, 2025, that do not contain a provision regarding building operating costs.

(j) This section does not apply to assessment levied pursuant to Part 7 (commencing with Section 36600) of Division 18 of the Streets and Highways Code. **Leg.H.** Added Stats 2024 ch 1015 §4 (SB 1103), effective January 1, 2025.

§1951. "Rent"; "Lease"

As used in Sections 1951.2 to 1952.6, inclusive:

(a) "Rent" includes charges equivalent to rent.

(b) "Lease" includes a sublease. **Leg.H.** Added Stats 1970 ch 89 §1, operative July 1, 1971.

Prior Law: There was another section of this number which was added Stats 1970 ch 1317 §1 and amended and renumbered §1950.5 by Stats 1972 ch 618 §4.

§1951.2. Lessor's remedies upon breach by lessee; Indemnification

(a) Except as otherwise provided in Section 1951.4, if a lessee of real property breaches the lease and abandons the property before the end of the term or if his right to possession is terminated by the lessor because of a breach of the lease, the lease terminates. Upon such termination, the lessor may recover from the lessee:

(1) The worth at the time of award of the unpaid rent which had been earned at the time of termination;

(2) The worth at the time of award of the amount by which the unpaid rent which would have been earned after termination until the time of award exceeds the amount of such rental loss that the lessee proves could have been reasonably avoided;

(3) Subject to subdivision (c), the worth at the time of award of the amount by which the unpaid rent for the balance of the term after the time of award exceeds the amount of such rental loss that the lessee proves could be reasonably avoided; and

(4) Any other amount necessary to compensate the lessor for all the detriment proximately caused by the lessee's failure to perform his obligations under the lease or which in the ordinary course of things would be likely to result therefrom.

(b) The "worth at the time of award" of the amounts referred to in paragraphs (1) and (2) of subdivision (a) is computed by allowing interest at such lawful rate as may be specified in the lease or, if no such rate is specified in the lease, at the legal rate. The worth at the time of award of the amount referred to in paragraph (3) of subdivision (a) is computed by discounting such amount at the discount rate of the Federal Reserve Bank of San Francisco at the time of award plus 1 percent.

(c) The lessor may recover damages under paragraph (3) of subdivision (a) only if:

(1) The lease provides that the damages he may recover include the worth at the time of award of the amount by which the unpaid rent for the balance of the term after the time of award, or for any shorter period of time specified in the lease, exceeds the amount of such rental loss for the same period that the lessee proves could be reasonably avoided; or

(2) The lessor relet the property prior to the time of award and proves that in reletting the property he acted reasonably and in a good-faith effort to mitigate the damages, but the recovery of damages under this paragraph is subject to any limitations specified in the lease.

(d) Efforts by the lessor to mitigate the damages caused by the lessee's breach of the lease do not waive the lessor's right to recover damages under this section.

(e) Nothing in this section affects the right of the lessor under a lease of real property to indemnification for liability arising prior to the termination of the lease for personal injuries or property damage where the lease provides for such indemnification. **Leg.H.** Added Stats 1970 ch 89 §2, operative July 1, 1971.

§1951.3. Real property other than commercial real property; Procedure for establishing abandonment of leased property

(a) This section applies to real property other than commercial real property, as defined in subdivision (d) of Section 1954.26.

(b) Real property shall be deemed abandoned by the lessee, within the meaning of Section 1951.2, and the lease shall terminate if the lessor gives written notice of belief of abandonment as provided in this section and the lessee fails to give the lessor written notice, prior to the date of termination specified in the lessor's notice, stating that the lessee does not intend to abandon the real property and stating an address at which the lessee may be served by certified mail in any action for unlawful detainer of the real property.

(c) The lessor may give a notice of belief of abandonment to the lessee pursuant to this section only where the rent on the property has been due and unpaid for at least 14 consecutive days and the lessor reasonably believes that the lessee has abandoned the property. The date of termination of the lease shall be specified in the lessor's notice and shall be not less than 15 days after the notice is served personally or, if mailed, not less than 18 days after the notice is deposited in the mail.

(d) The lessor's notice of belief of abandonment shall be personally delivered to the lessee or sent by first-class mail, postage prepaid, to the lessee at the lessee's last known address and, if there is reason to believe that the notice sent to that address will not be received by the lessee, also to any other address known to the lessor where the lessee may reasonably be expected to receive the notice.

(e) The notice of belief of abandonment shall be in substantially the following form:

Notice of Belief of Abandonment

To: _____ (Name of lessee/tenant)

_____ (Address of lessee/tenant)

This notice is given pursuant to Section 1951.3 of the Civil Code concerning the real property leased by you at _____ (state location of the property by address or other sufficient description). The rent on this property has been due and unpaid for 14 consecutive days and the lessor/landlord believes that you have abandoned the property.

The real property will be deemed abandoned within the meaning of Section 1951.2 of the Civil Code and your lease will terminate on _____ (here insert a date not less than 15 days after this notice is served personally or, if mailed, not less than 18 days after this notice is deposited in the mail) unless before that date the lessor/landlord receives at the address indicated below a written notice from you stating both of the following:

Your intent not to abandon the real property.

An address at which you may be served by certified mail in any action for unlawful detainer of the real property.

You are required to pay the rent due and unpaid on this real property as required by the lease, and your failure to do so can lead to a court proceeding against you.

Dated: _____

_____
(Signature of lessor/landlord)

_____
(Type or print name of lessor/landlord)

_____
(Address to which lessee/tenant is to send notice)

(f) The real property shall not be deemed to be abandoned pursuant to this section if the lessee proves any of the following:

(1) At the time the notice of belief of abandonment was given, the rent was not due and unpaid for 14 consecutive days.

(2) At the time the notice of belief of abandonment was given, it was not reasonable for the lessor to believe that the lessee had abandoned the real property. The fact that the lessor knew that the lessee left personal property on the real property does not, of itself, justify a finding that the lessor did not reasonably believe that the lessee had abandoned the real property.

(3) Before the date specified in the lessor's notice, the lessee gave written notice to the lessor stating the lessee's intent not to abandon the real property and stating an address at which the lessee may be served by certified mail in any action for unlawful detainer of the real property.

(4) During the period beginning 14 days before the time the notice of belief of abandonment was given and ending on the date the lease would have terminated pursuant to the notice, the lessee paid to the lessor all or a portion of the rent due and unpaid on the real property.

(g) Nothing in this section precludes the lessor or the lessee from otherwise proving that the real property has been abandoned by the lessee within the meaning of Section 1951.2.

(h) Nothing in this section precludes the lessor from serving a notice requiring the lessee to pay rent or quit as provided in Sections 1161 and 1162 of the Code of Civil Procedure at any time permitted by those sections, or affects the time and manner of giving any other notice required or permitted by law. The giving of the notice provided by this section does not satisfy the requirements of Sections 1161 and 1162 of the Code of Civil Procedure. **Leg.H.** Added Stats 1974 ch 332 §1. Amended Stats 2018 ch 104 §2 (AB 2847), effective January 1, 2019.

§1951.35. Commercial real property; Procedure for establishing abandonment of leased property

(a) This section applies only to commercial real property, as defined in subdivision (d) of Section 1954.26.

(b) Commercial real property shall be deemed abandoned by the lessee within the meaning of Section 1951.2 and the lease shall terminate if the lessor gives written notice of belief of abandonment pursuant to subdivision (c) and, prior to the date of termination specified in the lessor's notice of belief of abandonment, the lessee fails to give the lessor written notice stating that the lessee does not intend to abandon the commercial real property and provides an address at which the lessee may be served by certified mail in an action for unlawful detainer of real property.

(c) The lessor may give notice of belief of abandonment pursuant to this section only if the rent on the property has been due and unpaid for at least the number of days required for the lessor to declare a rent default under the terms of the lease, but in no case less than three days, and the lessor reasonably believes that the lessee has abandoned the property. The date of termination of the lease shall be specified in the notice and shall be not less than 15 days after the notice is served personally, sent to the lessee by an overnight courier service, or deposited in the mail.

(d) The lessor's notice of belief of abandonment shall be personally delivered to the lessee, sent by a recognized overnight carrier, or sent by first-class mail, postage prepaid, to the lessee at the lessee's last known address, and, if there is reason to believe that the notice sent to that address will not be received by the lessee, also to any other address known to the lessor where the lessee may reasonably be expected to receive the notice.

(e) The notice of belief of abandonment shall be in substantially the following form:

Notice of Belief of Abandonment

To: _____
(Name of lessee/tenant)

_____
(Address of lessee/tenant)

This notice is given pursuant to Section 1951.35 of the Civil Code concerning the real property leased by you at _____ (state location of the property by address or other sufficient description). The rent on this property has been due and unpaid for the number of days necessary to declare a rent default under your lease and the lessor/landlord believes that you have abandoned the property.

The real property will be deemed abandoned within the meaning of Section 1951.2 of the Civil Code and your lease will terminate on _____ (here insert a date not less than 15 days after this notice is served personally, sent by overnight courier service, or deposited in the mail) unless before that date the lessor/landlord receives at the address below a written notice from you stating both of the following:

(1) Your intent not to abandon the real property.

(2) An address at which you may be served by certified mail in any action for unlawful detainer of the real property.

You are required to pay the rent due and unpaid on this real property as required by the lease, and your failure to do so can lead to a court proceeding against you.

Dated: _____

_____
(Signature of lessor/landlord)

_____
(Type or print name of lessor/landlord)

_____
(Address to which lessee/tenant is to send notice)

(f) The real property shall not be deemed to be abandoned pursuant to this section if the lessee provides any of the following:

(1) At the time the notice of belief of abandonment was given, the rent was not due and unpaid for the time period necessary to declare a rent default under the lessee's lease.

(2) At the time the notice of belief of abandonment was given, it was not reasonable for the lessor to believe that the lessee had abandoned the real property. The fact that the lessor knew that the lessee left personal property on the real property does not, by itself, justify a finding that the lessor did not believe that the lessee had abandoned the real property.

(3) Before the date specified in the lessor's notice, the lessee gave written notice to the lessor stating the lessee's intent not to abandon the real property and provided an address at which the lessee may be served by certified mail in an action for unlawful detainer of real property.

(4) During the period beginning at the start of the applicable rent default period and ending on the date the lease would have terminated pursuant to the notice, the lessee paid to the lessor all or a portion of the rent due and unpaid on the real property.

(g) Nothing in this section precludes the lessor or the lessee from otherwise proving that the real property has been abandoned by the lessee within the meaning of Section 1951.2.

(h) Nothing in this section precludes the lessor from serving a notice requiring the lessee to pay rent or quit as provided in Section 1161 or 1162 of the Code of Civil Procedure at any time permitted by those sections, or affects the time and manner of giving any other notice required or permitted by law. Giving notice pursuant to this section does not satisfy the requirements of Section 1161 or 1162 of the Code of Civil Procedure. **Leg.H.** Added Stats 2018 ch 104 §3 (AB 2847), effective January 1, 2019.

§1951.4. Continuation of lease

(a) The remedy described in this section is available only if the lease provides for this remedy. In addition to any other type of provision used in a lease to provide for the remedy described in this section, a provision in the lease in substantially the following form satisfies this subdivision:

"The lessor has the remedy described in California Civil Code Section 1951.4 (lessor may continue lease in effect after lessee's breach and abandonment and recover rent as it becomes due, if lessee has right to sublet or assign, subject only to reasonable limitations)."

(b) Even though a lessee of real property has breached the lease and abandoned the property, the lease continues in effect for so long as the lessor does not terminate the lessee's right to possession, and the lessor may enforce all the lessor's rights and remedies under the lease, including the right to recover the rent as it becomes due under the lease, if any of the following conditions is satisfied:

(1) The lease permits the lessee, or does not prohibit or otherwise restrict the right of the lessee, to sublet the property, assign the lessee's interest in the lease, or both.

(2) The lease permits the lessee to sublet the property, assign the lessee's interest in the lease, or both, subject to express standards or conditions, provided the standards and conditions are reasonable at the time the lease is executed and the lessor does not require compliance with any standard or condition that has become unreasonable at the time the lessee seeks to sublet or assign. For purposes of this paragraph, an express standard or condition is presumed to be reasonable; this presumption is a presumption affecting the burden of proof.

(3) The lease permits the lessee to sublet the property, assign the lessee's interest in the lease, or both, with the consent of the lessor, and the lease provides that the consent shall not be unreasonably withheld or the lease includes a standard implied by law that consent shall not be unreasonably withheld.

(c) For the purposes of subdivision (b), the following do not constitute a termination of the lessee's right to possession:

(1) Acts of maintenance or preservation or efforts to relet the property.

(2) The appointment of a receiver upon initiative of the lessor to protect the lessor's interest under the lease.

(3) Withholding consent to a subletting or assignment, or terminating a subletting or assignment, if the withholding or termination does not violate the rights of the lessee specified in subdivision (b). **Leg.H.** Added Stats 1970 ch 89 §3, operative July 1, 1971. Amended Stats 1989 ch 982 §1; Stats 1991 ch 67 §1 (SB 256).

§1951.5. Liquidated damages

Section 1671, relating to liquidated damages, applies to a lease of real property. **Leg.H.** Added Stats 1970 ch 89 §4, operative July 1, 1971. Amended Stats 1977 ch 198 §8, operative July 1, 1978.

§1951.7. Heads Advance payments to lessor; Notice on reletting

(a) As used in this section, "advance payment" means moneys paid to the lessor of real property as prepayment of rent, or as a deposit to secure faithful performance of the terms of the lease, or another payment that is the substantial equivalent of either of these. A payment that is not in excess of the amount of one month's rent is not an advance payment for purposes of this section.

(b) The notice provided by subdivision (c) is required to be given only if all of the following apply:

(1) The lessee has made an advance payment.

(2) The lease is terminated pursuant to Section 1951.2.

(3) The lessee has made a request, in writing, to the lessor that he or she be given notice under subdivision (c).

(c) Upon the initial reletting of the property, the lessor shall send a written notice to the lessee stating that the property has been relet, the name and address of the new lessee, and the length of the new lease and the amount of the rent. The notice shall be delivered to the lessee personally, or be sent by regular mail to the lessee at the address shown on the request, not later than 30 days after the new lessee takes possession of the property. Notice is not required if the amount of the rent due and unpaid at the time of termination exceeds the amount of the advance payment. **Leg.H.** Added Stats 1970 ch 89 §5, operative July 1, 1971. Amended Stats 2008 ch 179 §32 (SB 1498), effective January 1, 2009.

§1951.8. Right to equitable relief

Nothing in Section 1951.2 or 1951.4 affects the right of the lessor under a lease of real property to equitable relief where such relief is appropriate. **Leg.H.** Added Stats 1970 ch 89 §6, operative July 1, 1971.

§1952. Effect of other actions

(a) Except as provided in subdivision (c), nothing in Sections 1951 to 1951.8, inclusive, affects the provisions of Chapter 4 (commencing with Section 1159) of Title 3 of Part 3 of the Code of Civil Procedure, relating to actions for unlawful detainer, forcible entry, and forcible detainer.

(b) Unless the lessor amends the complaint as provided in paragraph (1) of subdivision (a) of Section 1952.3 to state a claim for damages not recoverable in the unlawful detainer proceeding, the bringing of an action under the provisions of Chapter 4 (commencing with Section 1159) of Title 3 of Part 3 of the Code of Civil Procedure does not affect the lessor's right to bring a separate action for relief under Sections 1951.2, 1951.5, and 1951.8, but no damages shall be recovered in the subsequent action for any detriment for which a claim for damages was made and determined on the merits in the previous action.

(c) After the lessor obtains possession of the property under a judgment pursuant to Section 1174 of the Code of Civil Procedure, he is no longer entitled to the remedy provided under Section 1951.4 unless the lessee obtains relief under Section 1179 of the Code of Civil Procedure. **Leg.H.** Added Stats 1970 ch 89 §7, operative July 1, 1971. Amended Stats 1977 ch 49 §1.

§1952.2. Leases affected

Sections 1951 to 1952, inclusive, do not apply to:

(a) Any lease executed before July 1, 1971.

(b) Any lease executed on or after July 1, 1971, if the terms of the lease were fixed by a lease, option, or other agreement executed before July 1, 1971. **Leg.H.** Added Stats 1970 ch 89 §8, operative July 1, 1971.

§1952.3. Possession delivered to lessor before trial or judgment in unlawful detainer proceeding

(a) Except as provided in subdivisions (b) and (c), if the lessor brings an unlawful detainer proceeding and possession of the property is no longer in issue because possession of the property has been delivered to the lessor before trial or, if there is no trial, before judgment is entered, the case becomes an ordinary civil action in which:

(1) The lessor may obtain any relief to which he is entitled, including, where applicable, relief authorized by Section 1951.2; but, if the lessor seeks to recover damages described in paragraph (3) of subdivision (a) of Section 1951.2 or any other damages not recoverable in the unlawful detainer proceeding, the lessor shall first amend the complaint pursuant to Section 472 or 473 of the Code of Civil Procedure so that possession of the property is no longer in issue and to state a claim for such damages and shall serve a copy of the amended complaint on the defendant in the same manner as a copy of a summons and original complaint is served.

(2) The defendant may, by appropriate pleadings or amendments to pleadings, seek any affirmative relief, and assert all defenses, to which he is entitled, whether or not the lessor has amended the complaint; but subdivision (a) of Section 426.30 of the Code of Civil Procedure does not apply unless, after delivering possession of the property to the lessor, the defendant (i) files a cross-complaint or (ii) files an answer or an amended answer in response to an amended complaint filed pursuant to paragraph (1).

(b) The defendant's time to respond to a complaint for unlawful detainer is not affected by the delivery of possession of the property to the lessor; but, if the complaint is amended as provided in paragraph (1) of subdivision (a), the defendant has the same time to respond to the amended complaint as in an ordinary civil action.

(c) The case shall proceed as an unlawful detainer proceeding if the defendant's default (1) has been entered on the unlawful detainer complaint and (2) has not been opened by an amendment of the complaint or otherwise set aside.

(d) Nothing in this section affects the pleadings that may be filed, relief that may be sought, or defenses that may be asserted in an unlawful detainer proceeding that has not become an ordinary civil action as provided in subdivision (a). **Leg.H.** Added Stats 1977 ch 49 §2.

§1952.4. Agreement for exploration for or removal of natural resources as lease

An agreement for the exploration for or the removal of natural resources is not a lease of real property within the meaning of Sections 1951 to 1952.2, inclusive. **Leg.H.** Added Stats 1970 ch 89 §9, operative July 1, 1971.

§1952.6. Leases involving public entities or nonprofit corporations; Exclusions

(a) Sections 1951 to 1952.2, inclusive, shall not apply to any lease or agreement for a lease of real property between any public entity and any nonprofit corporation whose title or interest in the property is subject to reversion to or vesting in a public entity and which issues bonds or other evidences of indebtedness, the interest on which is exempt from federal income taxes for the purpose of acquiring, constructing, or improving the property or a building or other facility thereon, or between any public entity and any other public entity, unless the lease or the agreement shall specifically provide that Sections 1951 to 1952.2, inclusive, or any portions thereof, are applicable to the lease or the agreement.

(b) Except as provided in subdivision (a), a public entity lessee in a contract for a capital lease of real property involving the payment of rents of one million dollars ($1,000,000) or more may elect to waive any of the remedies for a breach of the lease provided in Sections 1951 to 1952.2, inclusive, and contract instead for any other remedy permitted by law. As used in this subdivision, "capital lease" refers to a lease entered into for the purpose of acquiring, constructing, or improving the property or a building or other facility thereon.

(c) As used in this section, "public entity" includes the state, a county, city and county, city, district, public authority, public agency, or any other political subdivision or public corporation. **Leg.H.** Added Stats 1970 ch 89 §10, operative July 1, 1971. Amended Stats 1971 ch 732 §1, effective August 24, 1971; Stats 1989 ch 613 §1.

§1952.7. Term in lease prohibiting installation of electric vehicle charging station is void; Installation by lessee; Requirements; Costs; Exceptions; Liability

(a)(1) Any term in a lease that is executed, renewed, or extended on or after January 1, 2015, that conveys any possessory interest in commercial property that either prohibits or unreasonably restricts the installation or use of an electric vehicle charging station in a parking space associated with the commercial property, or that is otherwise in conflict with the provisions of this section, is void and unenforceable.

(2) This subdivision does not apply to provisions that impose reasonable restrictions on the installation of electric vehicle charging stations. However, it is the policy of the state to promote, encourage, and remove obstacles to the use of electric vehicle charging stations.

(3) This subdivision shall not grant the holder of a possessory interest under the lease described in paragraph (1) the right to install electric vehicle charging stations in more parking spaces than are allotted to the leaseholder in his or her lease, or, if no parking spaces are allotted, a number of parking spaces determined by multiplying the total number of parking spaces located at the commercial property by a fraction, the denominator of which is the total rentable square feet at the property, and the numerator of which is the number of total square feet rented by the leaseholder.

(4) If the installation of an electric vehicle charging station has the effect of granting the leaseholder a reserved parking space and a reserved parking space is not allotted to the leaseholder in the lease, the owner of the commercial property may charge a reasonable monthly rental amount for the parking space.

(b) This section shall not apply to any of the following:

(1) A commercial property where charging stations already exist for use by tenants in a ratio that is equal to or greater than 2 available parking spaces for every 100 parking spaces at the commercial property.

(2) A commercial property where there are less than 50 parking spaces.

(c) For purposes of this section:

(1) "Electric vehicle charging station" or "charging station" means a station that is designed in compliance with Article 625 of the California Electrical Code, as it reads on the effective date of this section, and delivers electricity from a source outside an electric vehicle into one or more electric vehicles.

(2) "Reasonable costs" includes, but is not limited to, costs associated with those items specified in the "Permitting Checklist" of the "Zero-Emission Vehicles in California: Community Readiness Guidebook" published by the Office of Planning and Research.

(3) "Reasonable restrictions" or "reasonable standards" are restrictions or standards that do not significantly increase the cost of the electric vehicle charging station or its installation or significantly decrease the charging station's efficiency or specified performance.

(d) An electric vehicle charging station shall meet applicable health and safety standards and requirements imposed by state and local authorities as well as all other applicable zoning, land use, or other ordinances, or land use permit requirements.

(e) If lessor approval is required for the installation or use of an electric vehicle charging station, the application for approval shall not be willfully avoided or delayed. The approval or denial of an application shall be in writing.

(f) An electric vehicle charging station installed by a lessee shall satisfy the following provisions:

(1) If lessor approval is required, the lessee first shall obtain approval from the lessor to install the electric vehicle charging station and the lessor shall approve the installation if the lessee complies with the applicable provisions of the lease consistent with the provisions of this section and agrees in writing to do all of the following:

(A) Comply with the lessor's reasonable standards for the installation of the charging station.

(B) Engage a licensed contractor to install the charging station.

(C) Within 14 days of approval, provide a certificate of insurance that names the lessor as an additional insured under the lessee's insurance policy in the amount set forth in paragraph (3).

(2) The lessee shall be responsible for all of the following:

(A) Costs for damage to property and the charging station resulting from the installation, maintenance, repair, removal, or replacement of the charging station.

(B) Costs for the maintenance, repair, and replacement of the charging station.

(C) The cost of electricity associated with the charging station.

(3) The lessee at all times, shall maintain a lessee liability coverage policy in the amount of one million dollars ($1,000,000), and shall name the lessor as a named additional insured under the policy with a right to notice of cancellation and property insurance covering any damage or destruction caused by the charging station, naming the lessor as its interests may appear.

(g) A lessor may, in its sole discretion, create a new parking space where one did not previously exist to facilitate the installation of an electric vehicle charging station, in compliance with all applicable laws.

(h) Any installation by a lessor or a lessee of an electric vehicle charging station in a common interest development is also subject to all of the requirements of subdivision (f) of Section 4745. **Leg.H.** Added Stats 2014 ch 529 §2 (AB 2565), effective January 1, 2015. Amended Stats 2016 ch 714 §4 (SB 944), effective January 1, 2017.

§1952.8. Lease of service station; Vapor control systems

On and after the effective date of this section, no owner of a gasoline service station shall enter into a lease with any person for the leasing of the station for the purpose of operating a gasoline service station, unless (a) the station is equipped with a vapor control system for the control of gasoline vapor emissions during gasoline marketing operations, including storage, transport, and transfer operations, if such vapor control system is required by law or by any rule or regulation of the State Air Resources Board or of the air pollution control district in which the station is located or (b) no vapor control system has been certified by the board prior to the date of the lease.

A lease entered into in violation of this section shall be voidable at the option of the lessee. **Leg.H.** Added Stats 1976 ch 1030 §1, effective September 20, 1976.

§1953. Public policy; Modification or waiver of lessee's rights

(a) Any provision of a lease or rental agreement of a dwelling by which the lessee agrees to modify or waive any of the following rights shall be void as contrary to public policy:

(1) His rights or remedies under Section 1950.5 or 1954.

(2) His right to assert a cause of action against the lessor which may arise in the future.

(3) His right to a notice or hearing required by law.

(4) His procedural rights in litigation in any action involving his rights and obligations as a tenant.

(5) His right to have the landlord exercise a duty of care to prevent personal injury or personal property damage where that duty is imposed by law.

(b) Any provision of a lease or rental agreement of a dwelling by which the lessee agrees to modify or waive a statutory right, where the modification or waiver is not void under subdivision (a) or under Section 1942.1, 1942.5, or 1954, shall be void as contrary to public policy unless the lease or rental agreement is presented to the lessee before he takes actual possession of the premises. This subdivision does not apply to any provisions modifying or waiving a statutory right in agreements renewing leases or rental agreements where the same provision was also contained in the lease or rental agreement which is being renewed.

(c) This section shall apply only to leases and rental agreements executed on or after January 1, 1976. **Leg.H.** Added Stats 1975 ch 302 §1.

§1954. Landlord's right of access to dwelling unit; Notice of entry

(a) A landlord may enter the dwelling unit only in the following cases:

(1) In case of emergency.

(2) To make necessary or agreed repairs, decorations, alterations or improvements, supply necessary or agreed services, or exhibit the dwelling unit to prospective or actual purchasers, mortgagees, tenants, workers, or contractors or to make an inspection pursuant to subdivision (f) of Section 1950.5.

(3) When the tenant has abandoned or surrendered the premises.

(4) Pursuant to court order.

(5) For the purposes set forth in Chapter 2.5 (commencing with Section 1954.201).

(6) To comply with the provisions of Article 2.2 (commencing with Section 17973) of Chapter 5 of Part 1.5 of Division 13 of the Health and Safety Code.

(b) Except in cases of emergency or when the tenant has abandoned or surrendered the premises, entry may not be made during other than normal business hours unless the tenant consents to an entry during other than normal business hours at the time of entry.

(c) The landlord may not abuse the right of access or use it to harass the tenant.

(d)(1) Except as provided in subdivision (e), or as provided in paragraph (2) or (3), the landlord shall give the tenant reasonable notice in writing of his or her intent to enter and enter only during normal business hours. The notice shall include the date, approximate time, and purpose of the entry. The notice may be personally delivered to the tenant, left with someone of a suitable age and discretion at the premises, or, left on, near, or under the usual entry door of the premises in a manner in which a reasonable person would discover the notice. Twenty-four hours shall be presumed to be reasonable notice in absence of evidence to the contrary. The notice may be mailed to the tenant. Mailing of the notice at least six days prior to an intended entry is presumed reasonable notice in the absence of evidence to the contrary.

(2) If the purpose of the entry is to exhibit the dwelling unit to prospective or actual purchasers, the notice may be given orally, in person or by telephone, if the landlord or his or her agent has notified the tenant in writing within 120 days of the oral notice that the property is for sale and that the landlord or agent may contact the tenant orally for the purpose described above. Twenty-four hours is presumed reasonable notice in the absence of evidence to the contrary. The notice shall include the date, approximate time, and purpose of the entry. At the time of entry, the landlord or agent shall leave written evidence of the entry inside the unit.

(3) The tenant and the landlord may agree orally to an entry to make agreed repairs or supply agreed services. The agreement shall include the date and approximate time of the entry, which shall be within one week of the agreement. In this case, the landlord is not required to provide the tenant a written notice.

(e) No notice of entry is required under this section:

(1) To respond to an emergency.

(2) If the tenant is present and consents to the entry at the time of entry.

(3) After the tenant has abandoned or surrendered the unit. **Leg.H.** Added Stats 1975 ch 302 §2. Amended Stats 2002 ch 301 §3 (SB 1403), ch 1061 §2.5 (AB 2330); Stats 2003 ch 62 §18 (SB 600), ch 787 §1 (SB 345) (ch 787 prevails); Stats 2016 ch 623 §1 (SB 7), effective January 1, 2017; Stats 2018 ch 445 §1 (SB 721), effective January 1, 2019.

§1954.05. Right of assignee for benefit of creditor to occupy business premises leased by assignor; Establishment of reasonable rental value recoverable by landlord

In any general assignment for the benefit of creditors, as defined in Section 493.010 of the Code of Civil Procedure, the assignee shall have the right to occupy, for a period of up to 90 days after the date of the assignment, any business premises held under a lease by the assignor upon payment when due of the monthly rental reserved in the lease for the period of such occupancy, notwithstanding any provision in the lease, whether heretofore or hereafter entered into, for the termination thereof upon the making of the assignment or the insolvency of the lessee or other condition relating to the financial condition of the lessee. This section shall be construed as establishing the reasonable rental value of the premises recoverable by a landlord upon a holding-over by the tenant upon the termination of a lease under the circumstances specified herein.

Leg.H. Added Stats 1982 ch 35 §1, effective February 17, 1982. Renumbered from Cal Civ Code §1954.1 by Stats 2016 ch 599 §2 (AB 551), effective January 1, 2017.

§ 1954.06. Reporting of tenant's rental payments to consumer reporting agencies

(a) As specified in subdivision (b), and except as provided in subdivision (j), beginning July 1, 2021, any landlord of an assisted housing development shall offer the tenant or tenants obligated on the lease of each unit in that housing development the option of having the tenant's rental payment information reported to at least one nationwide consumer reporting agency that meets the definition in Section 603(p) of the federal Fair Credit Reporting Act (15 U.S.C. Section 1681a(p)) or any other consumer reporting agency that meets the definition in Section 603(f) of the federal Fair Credit Reporting Act (15 U.S.C. Section 1681a(f)) so long as the consumer reporting agency resells or otherwise furnishes rental payment information to a nationwide consumer reporting agency that meets the definition in Section 603(p) of the federal Fair Credit Reporting Act (15 U.S.C. Section 1681a(p)). A tenant's election to have rent reported under this subdivision shall be in writing, as described in subdivision (c).

(b) For leases entered into on and after July 1, 2021, the offer of rent reporting shall be made at the time of the lease agreement and at least once annually thereafter. For leases outstanding as of July 1, 2021, the offer of rent reporting shall be made no later than October 1, 2021, and at least once annually thereafter.

(c) **Upon the agreement of the tenant, the landlord may provide the offer of rent reporting to the tenant by first-class United States mail or email.** The offer of rent reporting shall include a written election of rent reporting that contains all of the following:

(1) A statement that reporting of the tenant's rental payment information is optional.

(2) Identification of each consumer reporting agency to which rental payment information will be reported.

(3) [1] **If applicable, a** statement that all of the tenant's rental payments will be reported, regardless of whether the payments are timely, late, or missed.

(4) The amount of any fee charged pursuant to subdivision (f).

(5) Instructions on how to submit the written election of rent reporting to the landlord by [2] **first-class United States mail or email**.

(6) A statement that the tenant may opt into rent reporting at any time following the initial offer by the landlord.

(7) A statement that the tenant may elect to stop rent reporting at any time, but that they will not be able to resume rent reporting for at least six months after their election to opt out.

(8) Instructions on how to opt out of reporting rental payment information.

(9) A signature block that the tenant shall date and sign in order to accept the offer of rent reporting.

(d) [3] **If** the offer of rent reporting is made **by first-class United States mail**, the landlord shall provide the tenant with a self-addressed, stamped envelope to return the written election of rent reporting.

(e) The written election to begin rent reporting shall not be accepted from the tenant at the time of the offer. A tenant may submit their completed written election of rent reporting at any time after they receive the offer of rent reporting from the landlord. A tenant may request and shall obtain additional copies of the written election of rent reporting form from the landlord at any time.

(f) If a tenant elects to have that tenant's rental payments reported to a consumer reporting agency under subdivision (a), the landlord may require that tenant to pay a fee not to exceed the lesser of the actual cost to the landlord to provide the service or ten dollars ($10) per month. The payment or nonpayment of this fee by the tenant shall not be reported to a consumer reporting agency.

(g) If a tenant fails to pay any fee required by the landlord pursuant to subdivision (f), all of the following shall apply:

(1) The failure to pay the fee shall not be cause for termination of the tenancy, whether pursuant to Section 1161 of the Code of Civil Procedure or otherwise.

(2) The landlord shall not deduct the unpaid fee from the tenant's security deposit.

(3) If the fee remains unpaid for 30 days or more, the landlord may stop reporting the tenant's rental payments and the tenant shall be unable to elect rent reporting again for a period of six months from the date on which the fee first became due.

(h) A tenant who elects to have rent reported as described in subdivision (a) may subsequently file a written request with their landlord to stop that reporting with which the landlord shall comply. A tenant who elects to stop reporting shall not be allowed to elect rent reporting again for a period of at least six months from the date of the tenant's written request to stop reporting.

(i) A tenant who elects to have rent reported does not forfeit any rights under Sections 1941 to 1942, inclusive. If a tenant makes deductions from rent or otherwise withholds rent as authorized by those sections, the deductions or withholding of rent shall not constitute a late rental payment. A tenant invoking the right to repair and deduct or withhold rent under those sections shall notify their landlord of the deduction or withholding prior to the date rent is due. This subdivision shall not be construed to relieve a housing provider of the obligation to maintain habitable premises.

(j) This section shall not apply to any landlord of an assisted housing development that contains 15 or fewer dwelling units, unless both of the following apply:

(1) The landlord owns more than one assisted housing development, regardless of the number of units in each assisted housing development.

(2) The landlord is one of the following:

(A) A real estate investment trust, as defined in Section 856 of Title 26 of the United States Code.

(B) A corporation.

(C) A limited liability company in which at least one member is a corporation.

(k) For purposes of this section, the following definitions shall apply:

(1) "Assisted housing development" has the same meaning as defined in Section 65863.10 of the Government Code.

(2) "Landlord" means an owner of residential real property containing five or more dwelling units.

[4] **Leg.H.** Added Stats 2020 ch 204 §1 (SB 1157), effective January 1, 2021, repealed July 1, 2025. Amended Stats 2022 ch 670 §1 (SB 1396), effective January 1, 2023, repealed July 1, 2025; Stats 2024 ch 519 §1 (SB 924), effective January 1, 2025.

§ 1954.06. 2024 Deletes. [1] A [2] mail [3] When [4] (l) An independent evaluator, upon appropriation by the Legislature for this purpose, shall be selected by the Department of Financial Protection and Innovation and shall be responsible for conducting an evaluation of the impact of rental payment reporting in this state pursuant to this section. (1) The evaluator shall be selected through a competitive process to be completed on or before March 1, 2024. (2) The evaluator shall conduct the evaluation of the impact of rental payment reporting in this state pursuant to this section from July 1, 2021, through June 30, 2024, or a later date chosen by the evaluator with the approval of the Department of Financial Protection and Innovation. (3) Based on the evaluation described in paragraph (2), the evaluator shall create a report that includes, but is not limited to, information about all of the following: (A) The estimated percentage of assisted housing developments in compliance with this section. (B) Any significant barriers to compliance with this section experienced by assisted housing developments. (C) The estimated number of participating tenants. (D) Any significant barriers to participation experienced by tenants. (E) The estimated impact of participation on the credit scores of participating tenants living in assisted housing developments. (F) Recommendations, if any, for changes to the rental payment reporting process established by this section that could positively impact tenants of assisted housing developments. (4) In complying with this subdivision, the Department of Financial Protection and Innovation and the evaluator may employ statistical probability methods and other sampling methods to provide estimates. (5) If the information required in paragraph (3) cannot be obtained due to an absence of data or other methodological constraints, the Department of Financial Protection and Innovation shall notify the Legislature by January 1, 2024. This notification shall describe in detail the actions taken to attempt to obtain the information, why the required information was unable to be obtained, and recommendations for statutory changes that could produce data to satisfy the requirements enumerated in paragraph (3). (6) On or before January 1, 2025, the annual report required pursuant to paragraph (3) shall be posted on the internet website of the Department of Financial Protection and Innovation and distributed to the appropriate policy committees of the Legislature for review. (m) This section shall remain in effect only until July 1, 2025, and as of that date is repealed, unless a later enacted statute that is enacted before July 1, 2025, deletes or extends that date.

§ 1954.07. Positive rental payment information reporting

(a) As specified in subdivision (b), and except as provided in subdivision (j), any landlord of a dwelling unit of residential real property shall offer any tenant obligated on the lease the option of having the tenant's positive rental payment information reported to at least one nationwide consumer reporting agency that meets the definition in Section 603(p) of the federal Fair Credit Reporting Act (15 U.S.C. Sec. 1681a(p)) or any other consumer reporting agency that meets the definition in Section 603(f) of the federal Fair Credit Reporting Act (15 U.S.C. Sec. 1681a(f)) as long as the consumer reporting agency resells or otherwise furnishes rental payment information to a nationwide consumer reporting agency that meets the definition in Section 603(p) of the federal Fair Credit Reporting Act (15 U.S.C. Sec. 1681a(p)).

(b) For leases entered into on and after April 1, 2025, the offer of positive rental payment information reporting shall be made at the time of the lease agreement and at least once annually thereafter. For leases outstanding as of January 1, 2025, the offer of positive rental payment information reporting shall be made no later than April 1, 2025, and at least once annually thereafter.

(c) A landlord may provide the offer of positive rental payment information reporting required by subdivision (a) to the tenant by first-class United States mail or email.

(d) The offer of positive rental payment information reporting shall include a written election of positive rental payment information reporting that contains all of the following:

(1) A statement that reporting of the tenant's positive rental payment information is optional.

(2) Identification of each consumer reporting agency to which positive rental payment information will be reported.

(3) The amount of any fee charged pursuant to subdivision (g).

(4) Instructions on how to submit the written election of positive rental payment information reporting to the landlord by first-class United States mail or email.

(5) A statement that the tenant may opt into positive rental payment information reporting at any time following the initial offer by the landlord.

(6) A statement that the tenant may elect to stop positive rental payment information reporting at any time, but that the tenant will not be able to resume positive rental payment information reporting for at least six months after the election to opt out.

(7) Instructions on how to opt out of positive rental payment information reporting.

(8) A signature block that the tenant shall date and sign in order to accept the offer of positive rental payment information reporting.

(e) If the offer of positive rental payment information reporting is made by first-class United States mail, the landlord shall provide the tenant with a self-addressed, stamped envelope to return the written election of positive rental payment information reporting.

(f)(1) A tenant may submit the tenant's completed written election of rent reporting at any time after the tenant receives the offer of positive rental payment information reporting from the landlord.

(2)(A) A tenant may request additional copies of the written election of positive rental payment information reporting from the landlord at any time.

(B) A landlord that receives a request from a tenant pursuant to this paragraph shall comply with the request.

(g)(1) If a tenant elects to have that tenant's positive rental payment information reported to a consumer reporting agency under subdivision (a), the landlord may require that tenant to pay a fee not to exceed the lesser of the actual cost to the landlord to provide the service or ten dollars ($10) per month. If the landlord does not incur any actual cost to report positive rental payment information, no amount shall be charged from the tenant. The payment or nonpayment of this fee by the tenant shall not be reported to a consumer reporting agency.

(2) An amount tendered in full or partial satisfaction of rent or any other obligation under the lease, however designated by the party tendering the payment, shall not be applied or credited to the fee authorized by this subdivision.

(h) If a tenant fails to pay any fee required by the landlord pursuant to subdivision (g), all of the following shall apply:

(1) The failure to pay the fee shall not be cause for termination of the tenancy, whether pursuant to Section 1161 of the Code of Civil Procedure or otherwise.

(2) The landlord shall not deduct the unpaid fee from the tenant's security deposit.

(3) If the fee remains unpaid for 30 days or more, the landlord may stop reporting the tenant's rental payments, and the tenant shall not elect positive rental payment information reporting again for a period of six months from the date on which the fee first became due.

(i) A tenant who elects to have positive rental payment information reported as described in subdivision (a) may subsequently file a written request with the tenant's landlord to stop that reporting with which the landlord shall comply. A tenant who elects to stop reporting shall not be allowed to elect positive rental payment information reporting again for a period of at least six months from the date of the tenant's written request to stop reporting.

(j) This section shall not apply to either of the following:

(1) A landlord of a residential rental building that contains 15 or fewer dwelling units, unless both of the following apply:

(A) The landlord owns more than one residential rental building, regardless of the number of units in each building.

(B) The landlord is one of the following:

(i) A real estate investment trust, as defined in Section 856 of Title 26 of the United States Code.

(ii) A corporation.

(iii) A limited liability company in which at least one member is a corporation.

(2) An assisted housing development, as defined in Section 65863.10 of the Government Code.

(k) A tenant who elects to have rent reported does not forfeit any rights under Sections 1941 to 1942, inclusive. If a tenant makes deductions from rent or otherwise withholds rent as authorized by those sections, the deductions or withholding of rent shall not constitute a late rental payment. A tenant invoking the right to repair and deduct or withhold rent under those sections shall notify the tenant's landlord of the deduction or withholding prior to the date rent is due. This subdivision shall not be construed to relieve a housing provider of the obligation to maintain habitable premises.

(l)(1) As used in this section, "positive rental payment information" means information regarding a tenant's complete, timely payments of rent.

(2) "Positive rental payment information" does not include an instance in which a tenant did not completely or timely make a rental payment.

Leg.H. Added Stats 2024 ch 279 §1 (AB 2747), effective January 1, 2025.

§1954.1. Right of assignee for benefit of creditor to occupy business premises leased by assignor; Establishment of reasonable rental value recoverable by landlord [Renumbered]

Leg.H. Added Stats 1982 ch 35 §1, effective February 17, 1982. Amended and renumbered to Civ C §1954.05 by Stats 2016 ch 599 §2 (AB 551), effective January 1, 2017.

CHAPTER 2.4
OCCUPANCY IN INTERIM HOMELESSNESS PROGRAMS

Definitions. § 1954.08.
New tenancy; Program requirements. § 1954.09.
Tenant rights. § 1954.091.
Nontransient hotel or motel. § 1954.092.

§ 1954.08. Definitions

For the purposes of this chapter, the following definitions apply:

(a) "Harm-reduction" means a set of strategies, policies, and practices aimed at mitigating the negative social and physical consequences associated with various human behaviors, including, but not limited to, substance use, and that do not rely on punitive measures to gain program compliance.

(b) "Motel or hotel" means [1] **any hotel, motel, bed and breakfast inn, or other similar transient lodging establishment.**
[2]

(c) **"Self-exit" means when a shelter program participant voluntarily leaves a shelter program, including for a reason unknown to the shelter program operator, and does not return to the site or make reasonable contact with the shelter program operator within 72 hours of leaving. The shelter program operator shall contact hospitals, jails, and any other relevant sites to make a good faith effort to determine** the location of the individual and if their exit from the program was voluntary.

[3] **(d)** "Shelter program" means a city-, county-, continuum of care-, state-, or federally funded shelter, interim housing, motel voucher, or emergency shelter program in which the city, county, continuum of care, state, or federal governmental entity retains an oversight and accountability role in ensuring compliance with program regulations and proper program administration.

[4] **(e)** "Shelter program administrator" means a city, county, or continuum of care entity that retains an oversight role in ensuring compliance with program regulations and proper program administration.

[5] **(f)** "Shelter program operator" means a service provider agency that is contracting with a shelter program administrator to carry out the operations of the shelter program. A "shelter program operator" may include community-based service providers as well as public government agencies carrying out program operations.

[6] **(g)** "Shelter program participant" means an occupant of a motel, hotel, or other shelter site whose occupancy is solely due to their participation in a shelter program.

[7] **(h)** "Trauma-informed" means a set of practices that promote safety, empowerment, and healing in recognition that program participants may have experienced trauma that informs their experiences and responses. **Leg.H.** Added Stats 2022 ch 645 §1 (AB 1991), effective January 1, 2023. Amended Stats 2024 ch 209 §1 (AB 2835), effective January 1, 2025.

§ 1954.08. 2024 Deletes. [1] a dwelling unit, as defined by subdivision (c) of Section 1940, that an innkeeper retains a right of access to and control of, and that provides or offers all of the following services to all of the residents: [2] (1) Facilities for the safeguarding of personal property pursuant to Section 1860. (2) Central telephone service subject to tariffs covering the same filed with the California Public Utilities Commission. (3) Maid, mail, and room services. [3] (c) [4] (d) [5] (e) [6] (f) [7] (g)

§ 1954.09. New tenancy; Program requirements

(a) Notwithstanding paragraph (1) of subdivision (b) of Section 1954.091, shelter program participants shall not have their continued occupancy in a motel, hotel, or shelter program constitute a new tenancy and shall not be considered persons who hire pursuant to Section 1940 for the purposes of Section 1161 of the Code of Civil Procedure, if the shelter program meets all of the following requirements:

(1) The shelter program adheres to the core components of Housing First, pursuant to subdivision (b) of Section 8255 of the Welfare and Institutions Code.

(2) The shelter program establishes, adopts, and clearly documents rules governing how and for what reasons a shelter program participant's enrollment may be terminated and the shelter program operator discloses the termination policy to program participants in writing, in plain language, at the commencement of their occupancy.

(A) Permissible reasons for termination shall include sexual assault, verbally or physically threatening behaviors, which rise to the level of a "direct threat" to persons or property, as defined in paragraph (3) of subdivision (b) of Section 12179 of Title 2 of the Code of California Regulations, physical violence to staff, **hotel guests,** or other program participants, direct observation of participant engaging in illegal activity onsite, or time limits established by the shelter program.

(B) Terminations for reasons not stated in subparagraph (A) and any operational policies negotiated prior to the commencement of the shelter program shall be approved by the shelter program administrator and shared with their shelter program participants in a clearly labeled document.

(C) The shelter program administrator shall endeavor to ensure terminations are performed by the shelter program operator in a trauma-informed manner utilizing a harm-reduction approach, and shall ensure that the termination policies and procedures of the hotel, motel, and shelter program, including the required grievance procedure, comply with all applicable disability laws, including requirements for reasonable accommodation.

(D) The shelter program operator is exempt from providing a 30-day notice pursuant to subparagraph (A) of paragraph (3) if the shelter program participant has self-exited from the program.

(E) If a shelter program participant will exit from the program due to time limits and the participant's stay is extended for a period of less than 30 days beyond the original termination date, the shelter program administrator or shelter program operator may issue an amended termination notice with an additional period of time equal to the number of days of the program extension.

(3) The shelter program administrator establishes procedures regarding how a shelter program participant will be provided a written termination notice if a termination occurs and the shelter program operator discloses those procedures to shelter program participants in writing at the commencement of their occupancy.

(A) The shelter program operator shall provide the termination notice to the participant at least 30 days prior to the proposed termination or, if the underlying cause for a proposed termination constitutes a "direct threat," as defined in paragraph (3) of subdivision (b) of Section 12179 of Title 2 of the Code of California Regulations, the shelter program operator may remove the participant from the premises immediately, provided that the operator advises the participant of their right to utilize the grievance process described in paragraph (5).

(B) The termination notice shall contain a clear, plain-language statement of the reason for the termination, shall notify the participant of their right to request a reasonable accommodation if they are a qualified person with a disability, and shall notify the participant of their right to utilize the grievance process described in [1] **paragraph (5)**.

(C) The established procedures developed regarding participant guideline violations shall include an escalation continuum that incorporates documented warnings and documented shelter program operator staff and participant problem solving methods prior to instituting terminations from the shelter program.

(4) The shelter program operator shall provide an exit plan upon termination of a shelter program participant that includes referrals to any available local shelter service for which the participant is eligible and the shelter program operator shall make a good faith, reasonable effort to facilitate an intake for that participant in an available bed or unit.

(A) The shelter program operator shall document good faith, reasonable efforts and shall make that documentation available upon request.

(B) The shelter program administrator, in cases where the grievance process is utilized, shall determine whether the shelter program operator's efforts constitute a good faith effort to facilitate a participant into an alternative available shelter site or program.

(C)(i) The shelter program administrator shall make good faith efforts to provide reasonable transportation accommodations upon termination of a shelter program participant from a program or upon transfer of a shelter program participant to an alternative available bed or unit.

(ii) In exigent circumstances that necessitate the presence of first responders, police, or fire department and render it infeasible to provide a termination letter at that time or coordinate a postexit plan, the shelter program operator shall create a termination letter that satisfies the above-described requirements and make that documentation available to participants within 24 hours of their request.

(5) The shelter program administrator shall establish a grievance process that complies with due process and the shelter program operator shall disclose the grievance process to occupants in writing, in plain language, at the commencement of their occupancy.

(A) The grievance process shall give shelter program participants a right to due process appeal through the shelter program administrator if the shelter program participant believes they were or are being wrongfully terminated from the program, and shall inform shelter program participants on how to access and initiate the grievance process.

(B)(i) Program participants shall be provided the opportunity to initiate the grievance process 30 days prior to their proposed termination date or at any point thereafter.

(ii) In cases where participants are subject to immediate removal based on circumstances that present a "direct threat," as defined in paragraph (3) of subdivision (b) of Section 12179 of Title 2 of the Code of California Regulations, participants shall be provided the opportunity to initiate the grievance process at the time of removal or at any point thereafter.

(C) If, following the grievance process, the proposed termination is not carried out, any participant already removed shall be granted the right to resume their participation in the program. If the shelter program operator is unable to place the individual in the original site, the shelter program operator shall facilitate a placement for the individual in an alternative available motel, hotel, or shelter site.

(b) Where a shelter program administrator is also the shelter program operator, the shelter program administrator is responsible for all of the duties described in subdivision (a).

(c) For properties that are being converted from use as a motel or hotel, or from use as a shelter, interim housing, emergency shelter, or other interim facility to a permanent housing site, paragraph (2) shall not apply to occupants of the site from the date that the site receives a certificate of occupancy as a permanent housing site. **Leg.H.** Added Stats 2022 ch 645 §1 (AB 1991), effective January 1, 2023. Amended Stats 2024 ch 209 §2 (AB 2835), effective January 1, 2025.

§ 1954.09. 2024 Deletes. [1] subparagraph (E)

§ 1954.091. Tenant rights

(a) Section 310.3 of Chapter 3 (commencing with Section 301.1) of Part 2 of Title 24 (the California Building Standards Code) of the California Code of Regulations shall not be interpreted to restrict the duration of occupancy for shelter program participants.

(b)(1) This chapter shall not be interpreted to either confer or deny any tenant rights or protections for persons who hire pursuant to Section 1940, or any rights that the tenant may otherwise be entitled to under any applicable federal, state, or local law.

(2) Notwithstanding paragraph (1), a shelter program participant of a shelter program that complies with the requirements described in Section 1954.09 shall be entitled to all of the following:

(A) A shelter program participant's continued occupancy in a motel or hotel does not constitute a new tenancy.

(B) A shelter program participant shall not be considered a person who hires pursuant to Section 1940 for the purposes of Section 1161 of the Code of Civil Procedure.

(C) Receipt of a written termination policy.

(D) Disclosure of a termination notice procedure.

(E) Thirty days' notice prior to termination, except as described in Section 1954.09.

(F) Right to appeal termination pursuant to the grievance policy required by Section 1954.09. **Leg.H.** Added Stats 2022 ch 645 §1 (AB 1991), effective January 1, 2023.

§ 1954.092. Nontransient hotel or motel

(a) A motel or hotel shall not be designated as a nontransient motel or a nontransient hotel pursuant to Section 310.4 of Chapter 3 (commencing with Section 301.1) of Part 2 of Title 24 (the California Building Standards Code) of the California Code of Regulations solely as a result of a shelter program participant's occupancy in the motel or hotel beyond a 30-day period.

(b) **Notwithstanding subparagraph (B) of paragraph (2) of subdivision (a) of Section 1954.09,** a hotel or motel shall not do either of the following:

(1)(A) Adopt termination policies specifically for motel or hotel occupants who are shelter program participants that do not apply to other motel or hotel occupants who are not participating in a shelter program, impose restrictions on the ability of program participants to freely enter or exit the property or access certain areas or amenities of the property that do not apply to other motel or hotel occupants, or levy charges and fees, including fees for room card replacements, that do not apply to other motel or hotel occupants.

(B) This paragraph sets minimum standards for shelter program terminations and shall not be construed to restrict shelter program operating standards that confer greater rights to participants with regard to shelter program terminations.

(2) Require shelter program participants to check out and reregister, move out of rooms or between rooms, or from the hotel or motel while actively enrolled in the shelter program for the purposes of preventing an occupant from establishing rights of tenancy. **Leg.H.** Added Stats 2022 ch 645 §1 (AB 1991), effective January 1, 2023. Amended Stats 2024 ch 209 §3 (AB 2835), effective January 1, 2025.

§ 1954.093. Repeal of chapter [Repealed]

Leg.H. Added Stats 2022 ch 645 §1 (AB 1991), effective January 1, 2023, repealed January 1, 2025. Repealed Stats 2024 ch 209 §4 (AB 2835), effective January 1, 2025.

CHAPTER 2.5
TRANSITIONAL HOUSING PARTICIPANT MISCONDUCT [FIRST OF TWO]

Article 1. General Provisions and Definitions.
Article 2. Temporary Restraining Order and Injunction.
Article 3. Recovery of Dwelling.

ARTICLE 1
General Provisions and Definitions

Citation of chapter. §1954.10.
Legislative intent. §1954.11.
Definitions. §1954.12.

§1954.10. Citation of chapter

This chapter shall be known and may be cited as the Transitional Housing Participant Misconduct Act. **Leg.H.** Added Stats 2016 ch 714 §5 (SB 944), effective January 1, 2017.

§1954.11. Legislative intent

In enacting this chapter, it is the intent of the Legislature to prevent the recurrence of acts of substantial disruption or violence by participants in transitional housing programs against other such participants, program staff, or immediate neighbors of the participants. **Leg.H.** Added Stats 2016 ch 714 §5 (SB 944), effective January 1, 2017.

§1954.12. Definitions

The following definitions shall govern the construction of this chapter:

(a) "Abuse" means intentionally or recklessly causing or attempting to cause bodily injury, or sexual assault or placing another person in reasonable apprehension of imminent serious bodily injury to himself, herself, or another, where the injured person is another participant, program operator's staff, or a person residing within 100 feet of the program site.

(b) "Homeless person" means an individual or family who, prior to participation in a transitional housing program, either lacked a fixed, regular, and adequate nighttime residence or had a primary nighttime residence, that was one of the following:

(1) A supervised publicly or privately operated shelter designed to provide temporary living accommodations, including, but not limited to, welfare hotels, congregate shelters, and transitional housing for the mentally ill.

(2) An institution that provides a temporary residence for individuals intended to be institutionalized.

(3) A public or private place not designed for, or ordinarily used as, a regular sleeping accommodation for human beings.

(c) "Participant" means a homeless person under contract with a program operator to participate in a transitional housing program and to use a dwelling unit in the program site. For the purposes of naming a defendant under this part, or a person to be protected under this part, "participant" shall include a person living with a participant at the program site. The contract shall specifically include the transitional housing program rules and regulations, a statement of the program operator's right of control over and access to the program unit occupied by the participant, and a restatement of the requirements and procedures of this chapter.

(d) "Program misconduct" means any intentional violation of the transitional housing program rules and regulations which (1) substantially interferes with the orderly operation of the transitional housing program, and (2) relates to drunkenness on the program site, unlawful use or sale of controlled substances, theft, arson, or destruction of the property of the program operator, persons living within 100 feet of the program site, program employees, or other participants, or (3) relates to violence or threats of violence, and harassment of persons living within 100 feet of the program site, program employees, or of other participants.

(e) "Program operator" means a governmental agency, or private nonprofit corporation receiving any portion of its transitional housing program funds from a governmental agency, which is operating a transitional housing program. "Program operator" also includes any other manager or operator hired by a governmental agency or nonprofit corporation to operate its transitional housing program.

(f) "Program site" means the real property containing a dwelling unit, the use of which is granted to a participant, and other locations where program activities or services are carried out or provided, subject to the participant's compliance with the transitional housing program rules and regulations.

(g) "Transitional housing program" means any program which is designed to assist homeless persons in obtaining skills necessary for independent living in permanent housing and which has all of the following components:

(1) Comprehensive social service programs which include regular individualized case management services and which may include alcohol and drug abuse counseling, self-improvement education, employment and training assistance services, and independent living skills development.

(2) Use of a program unit as a temporary housing unit in a structured living environment which use is conditioned upon compliance with the transitional housing program rules and regulations.

(3) A rule or regulation which specifies an occupancy period of not less than 30 days, but not more than 24 months. **Leg.H.** Added Stats 2016 ch 714 §5 (SB 944), effective January 1, 2017.

ARTICLE 2
Temporary Restraining Order and Injunction

Prohibition of abuse or program misconduct. §1954.13.
Transmittal of copy of temporary restraining order, injunction, modification, or termination; Willful disobedience of order or injunction; Contempt. §1954.14.
Violation of order as unlawful detainer. §1954.15.
Promulgation of forms by Judicial Council. §1954.16.

§1954.13. Prohibition of abuse or program misconduct

(a) The program operator may seek, on its own behalf or on behalf of other participants, project employees, or persons residing within 100 feet of the program site, a temporary restraining order and an injunction prohibiting abuse or program misconduct as provided in this chapter. A program operator may not seek a temporary restraining order, pursuant to this section, against a participant after the participant has been under contract with the program operator for at least six months or longer, except when an action is pending against the participant or a temporary restraining order is in effect and subject to further orders. Nothing in this section shall be construed to authorize a person residing within 100 feet of the program site to seek a temporary restraining order or injunction under this chapter.

(b) Upon filing a petition for an injunction under this chapter, the program operator may obtain a temporary restraining order in accordance with the provisions of this section. No temporary restraining order shall be issued without notice to the opposite party, unless it shall appear from the facts shown by the affidavit that great or irreparable harm would result to the program operator, a program participant, or an individual residing within 100 feet of the program site before the matter can be heard on notice. The program operator or the program operator's attorney shall state in an affidavit to the court (1) that within a reasonable time prior to the application for a temporary restraining order he or she informed the opposing party or his or her attorney at what time and where the application would be made, (2) that he or she in good faith attempted to so inform the opposing party and his or her attorney but was unable to so inform the opposing attorney or his or her party, specifying the efforts made to contact them, or (3) that for reasons specified he or she should not be required to inform the opposing party or his or her attorney.

A temporary restraining order may be granted upon an affidavit which, to the satisfaction of the court, shows reasonable proof of program misconduct or abuse by the participant, and that great or irreparable harm would result. A temporary restraining order granted under this section shall remain in effect, at the court's discretion, for a period not to exceed five days, unless otherwise modified, extended, or terminated by the court.

(c) The matter shall be made returnable on an order requiring cause to be shown why the injunction should not be granted, not later than five days from the date of the order. When the matter comes up for hearing, the party who obtained the temporary restraining order shall be ready to proceed and shall have personally served upon the opposite party at least two days prior to the hearing, a copy of the petition, a copy of the temporary restraining order, if any, the notice of hearing, copies of all affidavits to be used in the application, and a copy of any points and authorities in support of the petition. If the party who obtained the temporary restraining order is not ready, or if he or she fails to serve a copy of his or her petition, affidavits, and points and authorities, as herein required, the court shall dissolve the temporary restraining order. The court may, upon the filing of an affidavit by the program operator or his or her attorney, that the participant could not be served on time, reissue any temporary restraining order previously issued pursuant to this section and dissolved by the court for failure to serve the participant. An order reissued under this section shall state on its face the new date of expiration of the order. No fees shall be charged for the reissuance of any order under this section. The participant shall be entitled to a continuance, provided that the request is made on or before the hearing date and the hearing shall be set for a date within 15 days of the application, unless the participant requests a later date. The court may extend, or modify and extend, any temporary restraining order until the date and time upon which the hearing is held. The participant may file a response which explains, excuses, justifies, or denies the alleged conduct. No fee shall be charged for the filing of a response. At the hearing, the judge shall receive any testimony or evidence that is relevant, and may make an independent inquiry. If the judge finds by clear and convincing evidence that program misconduct or abuse exists, an injunction shall issue prohibiting that conduct. An injunction issued pursuant to this section shall have a duration of not more than one year. At any time within the three months before the expiration of the injunction, the program operator may apply for renewal of the injunction by filing a new petition for an injunction under this section.

(d) In addition to orders restraining abuse, the court may, upon clear and convincing evidence of abuse, issue an order excluding the participant from the program site, or restraining the participant from coming within 200 feet of the program site, upon an affidavit which, to the satisfaction of the court, shows clear and convincing evidence of abuse of a project employee, another participant, or a person who resides within 100 feet of the program site, by the participant and that great or irreparable injury would result to one of these individuals if the order is not issued. An order excluding the participant from the program site may be included in the temporary restraining order only in an emergency where it is necessary to protect another participant, a project employee, or an individual who lives within 100 feet of the project site from imminent serious bodily injury.

(e) Nothing in this chapter shall preclude either party from representation by private counsel or from appearing on his or her own behalf.

(f) The notice of hearing specified in subdivision (c) shall contain on its face the name and phone number of an office funded by the federal Legal Services Corporation which provides legal services to low-income persons in the county in which the action is filed. The notice shall indicate that this number may be called for legal advice concerning the filing of a response to the petition.

(g) Nothing in this chapter shall preclude the program operator's right to utilize other existing civil remedies. An order issued under this section shall not affect the rights of anyone not named in the order. **Leg.H.** Added Stats 2016 ch 714 §5 (SB 944), effective January 1, 2017.

§1954.14. Transmittal of copy of temporary restraining order, injunction, modification, or termination; Willful disobedience of order or injunction; Contempt

(a) The clerk shall transmit a copy of each temporary restraining order or injunction or modification or termination thereof, granted under this chapter, by the close of the business day on which the order was granted, to the law enforcement agencies having jurisdiction over the program site. Each law enforcement agency may make available information as to the existence and current status of these orders to law enforcement officers responding to the scene of reported abuse or program misconduct.

(b) Any willful disobedience of any temporary restraining order or injunction granted under this section shall be a misdemeanor pursuant to Section 166 of the Penal Code.

(c) If a participant is found in contempt of a court order issued pursuant to this section, the court may, in addition to any other punishment, modify the order to exclude the participant from the program site. **Leg.H.** Added Stats 2016 ch 714 §5 (SB 944), effective January 1, 2017.

§1954.15. Violation of order as unlawful detainer

If a participant has violated an order issued under Section 1954.13, the participant shall be considered to have failed to perform the conditions of the agreement under which the property is held as provided in subsection 3 of Section 1161 of the Code of Civil Procedure, which conditions cannot afterward be performed. **Leg.H.** Added Stats 2016 ch 714 §5 (SB 944), effective January 1, 2017.

§1954.16. Promulgation of forms by Judicial Council

The Judicial Council shall promulgate forms and related instructions to implement the procedures required by this chapter. The petition and response forms shall be simple and concise. **Leg.H.** Added Stats 2016 ch 714 §5 (SB 944), effective January 1, 2017.

ARTICLE 3
Recovery of Dwelling

Recovery after hearing without notice. §1954.17.
Participant's opportunity to remove property. §1954.18.

§1954.17. Recovery after hearing without notice

If, after hearing pursuant to this chapter, an order excluding the participant from the program site is issued, the program operator may, without further notice, take possession of the participant's dwelling unit on the program site. The program operator shall have the same rights to the dwelling unit as if it had been recovered after abandonment in accordance with Section 1951.3 and without objection of the participant. If other participants, including the defendant participant's family members, reside in the dwelling unit, the abandonment shall be deemed only to affect the rights of the individual or individuals against whom the order was issued. **Leg.H.** Added Stats 2016 ch 714 §5 (SB 944), effective January 1, 2017.

§1954.18. Participant's opportunity to remove property

If the program operator takes possession of the property, pursuant to this article, the program operator shall give the subject participant a reasonable opportunity to remove the participant's property from his or her dwelling unit on the program site, and, thereafter, the program operator may consider the remaining subject participant's property to be abandoned property pursuant to Chapter 5 (commencing with Section 1980). **Leg.H.** Added Stats 2016 ch 714 §5 (SB 944), effective January 1, 2017.

CHAPTER 2.5
WATER SERVICE [SECOND OF TWO]

Legislative intent. §1954.201.
Definitions. §1954.202.
Submeter requirements. §1954.203.
Disclosure requirements. §1954.204.
Billing; Calculation of charges. §1954.205.
Billing cycle; Statement. §1954.206.
Initial and final billing; Deduction for unpaid bill. §1954.207.
Fees or penalties. §1954.208.
Maintenance and provision by landlord of specified information. §1954.209.
Water fixture or water-saving device repair; Investigation of high water usage. §1954.210.
Authority to enter dwelling unit. §1954.211.
Billing; Calculation of charges if monthly reading unavailable. §1954.212.
Late fees; Partial payment; Termination of tenancy; Service shut off. §1954.213.
Local ordinance or regulation adopted prior to specified date. §1954.214.
Prohibition against waiver of rights or obligations. §1954.215.
Applicability of chapter. §1954.216.
Submetering system measuring only portion of dwelling unit's water usage. §1954.217.
Operative date of chapter. §1954.218.
Billing requirement for multiunit structures with individual submeters. §1954.219.

§1954.201. Legislative intent

It is the intent of the Legislature in enacting this chapter to do both of the following:

(a) To encourage the conservation of water in multifamily residential rental buildings through means either within the landlord's or the tenant's control.

(b) To establish that the practices involving the submetering of dwelling units for water service are just and reasonable, and include appropriate safeguards for both tenants and landlords. **Leg.H.** Added Stats 2016 ch 623 §2 (SB 7), effective January 1, 2017, operative January 1, 2018.

2016 Note: For operative date of chapter, see CC §1954.218.

§1954.202. Definitions

For the purposes of this chapter:

(a) "Billing agent" means a person or entity who contracts to provide submetering services to a landlord, including billing.

(b) "Landlord" means an owner of residential rental property. "Landlord" does not include a tenant who rents all or a portion of a dwelling unit to subtenants. "Landlord" does not include a common interest development, as defined in Section 4100 of the Civil Code.

(c) "Property" means real property containing two or more dwelling units that is served by a single master meter.

(d) "Ratio utility billing system" means the allocation of water and sewer costs to tenants based on the square footage, occupancy, or other physical factors of a dwelling unit.

(e) "Rental agreement" includes a fixed-term lease.

(f) "Renting" includes leasing, whether on a periodic or fixed-term basis.

(g) "Submeter" means a device that measures water consumption of an individual rental unit within a multiunit residential structure or mixed-use residential and commercial structure, and that is owned and operated by the landlord of the structure or the landlord's agent. As used in this section, "multiunit residential structure" and "mixed-use residential and commercial structure" mean real property containing two or more dwelling units.

(h) "Water service" includes any charges, whether presented for payment on local water purveyor bills, tax bills, or bills from other entities, related to water treatment, distribution, or usage, including, but not limited to, water, sewer, stormwater, and flood control.

(i) "Water purveyor" means a water purveyor as defined in Section 512 of the Water Code. Added Stats 2016 ch 623 §2 (SB 7), effective January 1, 2017, operative January 1, 2018.

2016 Note: For operative date of chapter, see CC §1954.218.

§1954.203. Submeter requirements

(a) Submeters used to separately bill tenants for water service shall satisfy each of the following requirements:

(1) The submeter shall be inspected, tested, and verified for commercial purposes pursuant to law, including, but not limited to, Section 12500.5 of the Business and Professions Code.

(2) The submeter shall conform to all laws regarding installation, maintenance, repair, and use, including, but not limited to, regulations established pursuant to Section 12107 of the Business and Professions Code.

(3) The submeter shall measure only water that is supplied for the exclusive use of the particular dwelling unit, and only to an area within the exclusive possession and control of the tenant of the dwelling unit.

(4) The submeter shall be capable of being accessed and read by the tenant of the dwelling unit and read by the landlord without entering the dwelling unit. A submeter installed before January 1, 2018, may be read by the landlord after entry into the unit, in accordance with this chapter and Section 1954.

(5) The submeter shall be reinspected and recalibrated within the time limits specified in law or regulation.

(b) This section does not require a water purveyor to assume responsibility for ensuring compliance with any law or regulation governing installation, certification, maintenance, and testing of submeters and associated onsite plumbing. **Leg.H.** Added Stats 2016 ch 623 §2 (SB 7), effective January 1, 2017, operative January 1, 2018.

2016 Note: For operative date of chapter, see CC §1954.218.

§1954.204. Disclosure requirements

Before executing a rental agreement, a landlord who intends to charge a tenant separately from rent for water service in a property with submeters shall clearly disclose the following information to the tenant, in writing, in at least 10-point type, which may be incorporated into the rental agreement:

(a) That the tenant will be billed for water service separately from the rent.

(b) An estimate of the monthly bill for water service for dwelling units at the property based on either of the following:

(1) The average or median bill for water service for comparative dwelling units at the property over any three of the past six months.

(2) The amount of the bill based upon average indoor water use of a family of four of approximately 200 gallons per day, and including all other monthly charges that will be assessed. Estimates for other gallons per day may also be included. The estimate shall include a statement that the average family of four uses about 200 gallons of water each day.

(c) The due dates and payment procedures for bills for water service.

(d) A mailing address, an email address, and a toll-free telephone number or a local telephone number for the tenant to contact the landlord or billing agent with questions regarding the water service billing and the days and hours for regular telephone service at either number.

(e) That the monthly bill for water service may only include the following charges:

(1) Payment due for the amount of usage as measured by the submeter and charged at allowable rates in accordance with subdivision (a) of Section 1954.205.

(2) Payment of a portion of the fixed fee charged by the water purveyors for water service.

(3) A fee for the landlord's or billing agent's costs in accordance with paragraph (3) of subdivision (a) of Section 1954.205.

(4) Any late fee, with the amounts and times assessed, in compliance with Section 1954.213.

(f) A statement that the tenant shall notify the landlord of any leaks, drips, water fixtures that do not shut off properly, including, but not limited to, a toilet, or other problems with the water system, including, but not limited to, problems with water-saving devices, and that the landlord is required to investigate, and, if necessary, repair these problems within 21 days, otherwise, the water bill will be adjusted pursuant to law.

(g) A mailing address, an email address, and a toll-free telephone number or a local telephone number for the tenant to use to contact the landlord, or an agent of the landlord, to report any leaks, drips, water fixtures that do not shut off properly, including, but not limited to, a toilet, or other problems with the water system, including, but not limited to, problems with water-saving devices.

(h) A statement that the landlord shall provide any of the following information if asked by the tenant:

(1) The location of the submeter.

(2) The calculations used to determine a monthly bill.

(3) The date the submeter was last certified for use, and the date it is next scheduled for certification, if known.

(i) A statement that if the tenant believes that the submeter reading is inaccurate or the submeter is malfunctioning, the tenant shall first notify the landlord in writing and request an investigation. A tenant shall be provided with notice that if an alleged submeter malfunction is not resolved by the landlord, a tenant may contact the local county sealer and request that the submeter be tested. Contact information for the county sealer shall be included in the disclosure to the tenant.

(j) A statement that this disclosure is only a general overview of the laws regarding submeters and that the laws can be found at Chapter 2.5 (commencing with Section 1954.201) of Title 5 of Part 4 of Division 3 of the Civil Code, available online or at most libraries. **Leg.H.** Added Stats 2016 ch 623 §2 (SB 7), effective January 1, 2017, operative January 1, 2018.

2016 Note: For operative date of chapter, see CC §1954.218.

§1954.205. Billing; Calculation of charges

(a) As part of the regular bill for water service, a landlord shall only bill a tenant for the following water service:

(1) A charge for volumetric usage, which may be calculated in any the following ways:

(A) The amount shall be calculated by first determining the proportion of the tenant's usage, as shown by the submeter, to the total usage as shown by the water purveyor's billing. The dollar amount billed to the tenant for usage shall be in that same proportion to the dollar amount for usage shown by the water purveyor's billing.

(B) If the water purveyor charges for volumetric usage based on a tiered rate schedule, the landlord may calculate the charge for a tenant's volumetric usage as described in subparagraph (A) or the landlord may instead divide each tier's volume evenly among the number of dwelling units, and the rate applicable to each block shall be applied to the consumption recorded for each dwelling unit.

(C) If the water purveyor charges the property rates on a per-dwelling unit basis, the tenants may be charged at those exact per unit rates.

(2) Any recurring fixed charge for water service billed to the property by the water purveyors that, at the landlord's discretion, shall be calculated by either of the following:

(A) The tenant's proportion of the total fixed charges charged to the property. The tenant's proportion shall be based on the percentage of the tenant's volumetric water use in relation to the total volumetric water use of the entire property, as shown on the property's water bill during that period.

(B) Dividing the total fixed charges charged to the property equally among the total number of residential units and nonresidential units at the property.

(3) A billing, administrative, or other fee for the landlord's and billing agent's costs, which shall be the lesser of an amount not to exceed four dollars and seventy-five cents ($4.75), as adjusted pursuant to this paragraph or 25 percent of the amount billed pursuant to paragraph (1). Beginning January 1, 2018, the maximum fee authorized by this paragraph may be adjusted each calendar year by the landlord, no higher than a commensurate increase in the Consumer Price Index based on a California fiscal year average for the previous fiscal year, for all urban consumers, as determined by the Department of Finance.

(4) A late charge as assessed pursuant to Section 1954.213.

(b) If a submeter reading for the beginning or end of a billing period is, in good faith, not available, the landlord shall bill the tenant according to Section 1954.212.

(c) This section does not prohibit a landlord or the landlord's billing agent from including any other lawful charges, including, but not limited to, rent, on the same bill. **Leg.H.** Added Stats 2016 ch 623 §2 (SB 7), effective January 1, 2017, operative January 1, 2018.

2016 Note: For operative date of chapter, see CC §1954.218.

§1954.206. Billing cycle; Statement

(a) Submeters shall be read within three days of the same point in each billing cycle.

(b) Payments shall be due at the same point in each billing cycle. A tenant may agree in writing to receive a bill electronically. A tenant may rescind authorization for electronic delivery of bills at any time. The landlord shall have 30 days to comply with any change in how a tenant requests to receive a bill. A tenant shall not be required to pay a bill electronically.

(c) A bill shall include and separately set forth the following information:

(1) The submeter reading for the beginning date and ending date of the billing cycle, the dates read, and the indicated consumption as determined by subtracting the amount of the beginning date submeter reading from the amount of the ending date submeter reading. If the unit of measure is in something other than gallons, the indicated consumption shall be expressed in gallons.

(2) The amounts charged pursuant to subdivision (a) of Section 1954.205.

(3) The rate or rates charged for the volumetric charge per unit of measure.

(4) The amount, if any, due from the previous month's bill.

(5) The amount, if any, due from bills prior to the previous month's bill.

(6) The late fee, if any, imposed on amounts specified in paragraph (4) or (5).

(7) The total amount due for the billing period.

(8) The due date for the payment.

(9) If a late fee is charged by the landlord, a statement of when the late fees would apply.

(10) The procedure to contact the landlord or billing agent with questions or concerns regarding the bill. Upon request of the tenant, the landlord or billing agent shall respond in writing to any questions or disputes from the tenant. If a billing agent is used, the name of the billing agent shall be disclosed. The tenant shall be provided a mailing address, email address, and telephone number, which shall be either a toll-free or a local number, and the time of regular telephone hours for contact regarding billing inquiries.

(11) A statement that the landlord or billing agent is not the water purveyor that includes the name of the local water purveyor providing the water service to the master meter.

(12) A mailing address, an email address, and a toll-free telephone number or a local telephone number for the tenant to use to contact the landlord, or an agent of the landlord, to report any leaks, drips, water fixtures that do not shut off properly, including, but not limited to, a toilet, or other problems with the water system, including, but not limited to, problems with water-saving devices.

(d) Notwithstanding paragraphs (4) and (5) of subdivision (c), a separate bill may be provided for past due amounts if past due amounts are not included on the current month's bill. **Leg.H.** Added Stats 2016 ch 623 §2 (SB 7), effective January 1, 2017, operative January 1, 2018.

2016 Note: For operative date of chapter, see CC §1954.218.

§1954.207. Initial and final billing; Deduction for unpaid bill

(a) At the beginning of a tenancy, a submeter shall be read after the tenant takes possession. If the regular reading occurs less than five days prior to the tenant taking possession, that reading may be substituted to establish usage. If the submeter is manually read, the first bill may be estimated based on the rate established in subdivision (b) of Section 1954.212.

(b) For a water-service bill at the end of a tenancy, the submeter shall be read within five days, if possible. If the submeter cannot be read within five days at the end of a tenancy, the bill amount for the final month shall be based on the bill amount for the previous month.

(c) The landlord may, at his or her discretion, deduct an unpaid water service bill from the security deposit during or upon termination of a tenancy, if the last water service bill showing the amount due is attached to the documentation required by Section 1950.5. **Leg.H.** Added Stats 2016 ch 623 §2 (SB 7), effective January 1, 2017, operative January 1, 2018.

2016 Note: For operative date of chapter, see CC §1954.218.

§1954.208. Fees or penalties

Unless it can be documented that a penalty is primarily the result of a tenant's or tenants' failure to comply with state or local water use regulations or restrictions, or both, regarding wasting of water, a landlord shall not charge, recover, or allow to be charged or recovered, fees incurred by the landlord from the water purveyors, billing agent, or any other person for any deposit, disconnection, reconnection, late payment by the landlord, or any other penalty assessed against the landlord. This section shall not prevent a landlord from charging a tenant for the tenant's late payment of any bill. **Leg.H.** Added Stats 2016 ch 623 §2 (SB 7), effective January 1, 2017, operative January 1, 2018.

2016 Note: For operative date of chapter, see CC §1954.218.

§1954.209. Maintenance and provision by landlord of specified information

The landlord shall maintain and make available in writing, at the tenant's written or electronic request, within seven days after the request, the following:

(a) The date the submeter was last inspected, tested, and verified, and the date by which it shall be reinspected, tested, and verified under law, if available. If this information is not available, the landlord shall disclose that the information is not available.

(b) The data used to calculate the tenant's bill, as follows:

(1) The most recent water bill for the property's master water meter showing the recurring fixed charge for water service billed to the property by the water purveyor, and the usage charges for the property, including any tiered amounts.

(2) Any other bills for water service, as defined in subdivision (h) of Section 1954.202, for the property.

(3) The number of dwelling units in the property used in the last billing period to calculate the tenant's water service charges.

(4) If not shown on the bill for the property, the per unit charges for volumetric water usage, including any tiered amounts.

(5) The formula used to calculate the charge for the tenant's volumetric water usage.

(c) The location of the submeter. **Leg.H.** Added Stats 2016 ch 623 §2 (SB 7), effective January 1, 2017, operative January 1, 2018.

2016 Note: For operative date of chapter, see CC §1954.218.

§1954.210. Water fixture or water-saving device repair; Investigation of high water usage

(a) If a tenant notifies the landlord of, or the landlord otherwise becomes aware of, a leak, a drip, a water fixture that does not shut off property, including, but not limited to, a toilet, a problem with a water-saving device, or other problem with the water system that causes constant or abnormally high water usage, or a submeter reading indicates constant or abnormal high water usage, the landlord shall have the condition investigated, and, if warranted, rectify the condition.

(b) A tenant shall not remove any water fixtures or water-saving devices that have been installed by the landlord.

(c) If the condition is rectified more than 21 days after the tenant provides notice to the landlord or the landlord otherwise becomes aware of a leak, a drip, a water fixture that does not shut off properly, including, but not limited to, a toilet, a problem with a water-saving device, or other problem with the water system that causes constant or abnormally high water usage, or a submeter reading indicates constant or abnormally high water usage, pursuant to subdivision (a), the tenant's volumetric usage for any month or months that include the period between 21 days after the initial investigation and the repair shall be deemed to be fifteen dollars ($15) or actual usage, whichever is less. At the landlord's option, if submeter readings are available to determine the usage at a point prior to investigation and a point following repair, usage shall be deemed to be fifty cents ($0.50) per day for those days between the two submeter readings or actual usage, whichever is less.

(d) If the condition remains unrectified for 180 days after investigation, no further volumetric usage charges may be imposed until the condition is repaired.

(e) If, in order to comply with subdivision (a), the landlord has provided notice pursuant to Section 1954, and the tenant has failed to provide access to the dwelling unit, then the charges shall not be determined pursuant to subdivisions (c) and (d).

(f) If the local water purveyor notifies the landlord of constant or abnormally high water usage at the property, the landlord shall investigate and, if possible, rectify the cause of the high water usage. **Leg.H.** Added Stats 2016 ch 623 §2 (SB 7), effective January 1, 2017, operative January 1, 2018.

2016 Note: For operative date of chapter, see CC §1954.218.

§1954.211. Authority to enter dwelling unit

The landlord may enter a dwelling unit as follows:

(a) For the purpose of installing, repairing, or replacing a submeter, or for the purpose of investigating or rectifying a condition causing constant or abnormally high water usage, as required by subdivision (a) of Section 1954.210, if the requirements of Section 1954 are met.

(b) To read a submeter, if the requirements of this chapter and Section 1954 are met. Notwithstanding paragraph (3) of subdivision (d) of Section 1954, notice shall be given only in writing. **Leg.H.** Added Stats 2016 ch 623 §2 (SB 7), effective January 1, 2017, operative January 1, 2018.

2016 Note: For operative date of chapter, see CC §1954.218.

§1954.212. Billing; Calculation of charges if monthly reading unavailable

(a) If a monthly submeter reading necessary to measure volumetric usage is unavailable, and the tenant has provided access to the submeter, the tenant may be charged 75 percent of the average amount billed for volumetric usage for the last three months for which complete billing information is available. The adjustment shall be disclosed on the bill.

(b) If no complete billing information is available for the prior three months, the volumetric usage charge shall be deemed to be fifty cents ($0.50) per day that the data is not available.

(c) If monthly submeter readings remain unavailable for more than six months, the volumetric usage charge shall be deemed to be zero for any subsequent month that the data is not available. **Leg.H.** Added Stats 2016 ch 623 §2 (SB 7), effective January 1, 2017, operative January 1, 2018.

2016 Note: For operative date of chapter, see CC §1954.218.

§1954.213. Late fees; Partial payment; Termination of tenancy; Service shut off

(a) A tenant may be charged a late fee for any water service bill not paid 25 days after mailing or other transmittal of the bill. If the 25th day falls on a Saturday, Sunday, or holiday, the late fee shall not be imposed until the day after the first business day following the 25th day.

(b)(1) A late fee of up to seven dollars ($7) may be imposed if any amount of a water service bill remains unpaid after the time described in subdivision (a). A late fee of up to ten dollars ($10) may be imposed in each subsequent bill if any amount remains unpaid.

(2) The total late fee imposed in any 12-month period upon the amount of a bill that remains unpaid shall not exceed 10 percent of the unpaid amount, exclusive of the administrative fee imposed pursuant to paragraph (3) of subdivision (a) of Section 1954.205 and the late fee imposed pursuant to paragraph (1).

(3) If any partial payments are made, they shall be credited against the bill that has been outstanding the longest.

(c) Notwithstanding subdivision (c) of Section 1954.207, if the water bill remains unpaid for 180 days after the date upon which it is due or the amount of the unpaid water bill equals or exceeds two hundred dollars ($200), the landlord may terminate the tenancy in accordance with Section 1161 of the Code of Civil Procedure with the service of a three-day notice to perform the conditions or covenants or quit upon the tenant.

(d) Water service charges under this chapter shall not constitute rent.

(e) The water service to a dwelling unit shall not be shut off or otherwise interfered with by the landlord for any reason, including nonpayment of a bill. Notwithstanding the foregoing, a landlord or its agent may shut off water service to a dwelling unit or the property, in order to make repairs, replacements of equipment, or perform other maintenance at the property. **Leg.H.** Added Stats 2016 ch 623 §2 (SB 7), effective January 1, 2017, operative January 1, 2018.

2016 Note: For operative date of chapter, see CC §1954.218.

§1954.214. Local ordinance or regulation adopted prior to specified date

This chapter does not preclude or preempt an ordinance or regulation adopted prior to January 1, 2013, that regulates the approval of submeter types or the installation, maintenance, reading, billing, or testing of submeters and associated onsite plumbing. **Leg.H.** Added Stats 2016 ch 623 §2 (SB 7), effective January 1, 2017, operative January 1, 2018.

2016 Note: For operative date of chapter, see CC §1954.218.

§1954.215. Prohibition against waiver of rights or obligations

The rights or obligations established under this chapter shall not be waived. Any purported waiver is void. **Leg.H.** Added Stats 2016 ch 623 §2 (SB 7), effective January 1, 2017, operative January 1, 2018.

2016 Note: For operative date of chapter, see CC §1954.218.

§1954.216. Applicability of chapter

(a) This chapter applies to the following:

(1) All dwelling units offered for rent or rented in a building where submeters were required to be installed pursuant to a building standard adopted in accordance with Section 17922.14 of the Health and Safety Code.

(2) All dwelling units where submeters are used to charge a tenant separately for water service.

(b) Nothing in this chapter shall be construed to apply to any dwelling units other than those described in subdivision (a).

(c) Nothing in this chapter shall be construed to apply or create a public policy or requirement that favors or disfavors the use of a ratio utility billing system. **Leg.H.** Added Stats 2016 ch 623 §2 (SB 7), effective January 1, 2017, operative January 1, 2018.

2016 Note: For operative date of chapter, see CC §1954.218.

§1954.217. Submetering system measuring only portion of dwelling unit's water usage

A submetering system that measures only a portion of a dwelling unit's water usage, including, but not limited to, a system that measures only hot water usage, shall not be subject to this chapter if the system was first put in service before January 1, 2018. **Leg.H.** Added Stats 2016 ch 623 §2 (SB 7), effective January 1, 2017, operative January 1, 2018.

2016 Note: For operative date of chapter, see CC §1954.218.

§1954.218. Operative date of chapter

This chapter shall become operative on January 1, 2018. **Leg.H.** Added Stats 2016 ch 623 §2 (SB 7), effective January 1, 2017, operative January 1, 2018.

§1954.219. Billing requirement for multiunit structures with individual submeters

Any property that is required to install individual submeters pursuant to Article 5 (commencing with Section 537) of Chapter 8 of Division 1 of the Water Code shall at all times be required to bill residents for water service pursuant to this chapter. **Leg.H.** Added Stats 2016 ch 623 §2 (SB 7), effective January 1, 2017, operative January 1, 2018.

2016 Note: For operative date of chapter, see CC §1954.218.

CHAPTER 2.6
COMMERCIAL RENTAL CONTROL

Legislative findings. §1954.25.
Definitions. §1954.26.
Enactment of rent control measures. §1954.27.
Application of chapter. §1954.28.
Effect of chapter. §1954.29.
Power and authority of public entities. §1954.30.
Enactment of rent control measures. §1954.31.

§1954.25. Legislative findings

The Legislature finds that the price charged for commercial real property is a matter of statewide concern. Price controls on commercial rents discourage expansion of commercial development and entrepreneurial enterprise. These controls also discourage competition in the open market by giving artificial price benefits to one enterprise to the disadvantage of another. Because the impact of these controls goes beyond the local boundaries within which the controls are imposed, the adverse economic consequences become statewide.

In order to prevent this statewide economic drain from occurring, the Legislature hereby enacts a uniform system with respect to commercial rents, which shall apply to every local jurisdiction in the state. This legislative action is needed to prevent the imposition of artificial barriers on commercial rents, as well as to define those areas not included within the definition of commercial real property.

In making these findings and in enacting this chapter, the Legislature expressly declares its intent that this chapter shall not apply or be interpreted to apply to local rental controls on residential real property. **Leg.H.** Added Stats 1987 ch 824 §2.

1987 Note: It appears the Legislature inadvertently substituted "consquences" for the word "consequences" in the first paragraph of this section.

§1954.26. Definitions

As used in this chapter, the following terms have the following meanings:

(a) "Owner" includes any person, acting as principal or through an agent, having the right to offer commercial real property for rent, and includes any predecessor in interest to the owner.

(b) "Price" includes any charge or fee, however denominated, for the hiring of commercial real property and includes any security or deposit subject to Section 1950.7.

(c) "Public entity" has the same meaning as defined in Section 811.2 of the Government Code.

(d) "Commercial real property" includes any part, portion, or unit thereof, and any related facilities, space, or services, except the following:

(1) Any dwelling or dwelling unit subject to the provisions of Section 1940.

(2) Any accommodation in any residential hotel, as defined in Section 50519 of the Health and Safety Code, or comparable accommodations which are specifically regulated by a public entity in structures where 20 percent or more of the accommodations are occupied by persons as their primary residence.

(3) Any hotel unit not otherwise specified in paragraph (1) or (2) that is located in a structure with 20 or more units or in which 20 percent or more of the accommodations were occupied as of August 5, 1987, by persons as their primary residence, if, in either circumstance, the unit was subject to rental controls on August 5, 1987, provided that any control exercised thereafter is in accordance with the system of controls in effect on August 5, 1987.

(4) Any space or dwelling unit in any mobilehome park, as defined in Section 18214 of the Health and Safety Code.

(e) "Rent" means to hire real property and includes a lease or sublease.

(f) "Commercial rental control" includes any action of a public entity taken by statute, charter, ordinance, resolution, administrative regulation, or any other governmental enactment to establish, continue, implement, or enforce any control or system of controls, on the price at which, or the term for which, commercial real property may be offered for rent, or control or system of controls which would select, mandate, dictate, or otherwise designate a specific tenant or specific person or entity with whom the owner must negotiate on the formation, extension, or renewal of a tenancy; or any other enactment which has such a purpose.

(g) "Tenant" includes a lessee, subtenant, and sublessee.

(h) "Term" means the period of time for which real property is rented or offered for rent, and includes any provision for a termination or extension of such a period or renewal thereof, except that nothing in this chapter supersedes the specific provisions of this code or of the Code of Civil Procedure which of themselves establish, prescribe, limit, or define the term for which real property may be rented.

(i) "Impasse notice" means a written notice which states either of the following:

(1) That the owner has not received from the tenant an offer of any terms for an extension or renewal of the lease which are acceptable to the

owner, or an acceptance by the tenant of any offer of terms by the owner, and that an impasse with respect to any agreement on a lease extension or renewal has been reached.

(2) That the owner is not willing to extend or renew the lease.

(j) "Negotiation notice" means a written notice by a tenant in privity of estate, and in privity of contract with the owner, stating either of the following:

(1) That the tenant offers to extend or renew the lease on terms set forth in the notice.

(2) That the tenant solicits an offer for the extension or renewal of the lease from the owner.

(k) "Deliver" means to deliver by personal service or by placing a copy of the notice in the mail, postage prepaid, by certified mail, return receipt requested, addressed to the party at the address for the receipt of notices under the lease.

(*l*) "Developer" means any person who enters into an agreement with a redevelopment agency for the purpose of developing specific commercial real property within a redevelopment project area with the intention of acquiring ownership of that property, even if that person does not own that property when the agreement is executed. **Leg.H.** Added Stats 1987 ch 824 §2.

§1954.27. Enactment of rent control measures

(a) No public entity shall enact any measure constituting commercial rental control, nor shall any public entity enforce any commercial rental control, whether enacted prior to or on or after January 1, 1988.

(b) However, nothing in this chapter shall be construed to do any of the following:

(1) Relieve any party to a commercial lease or rental agreement of the duty to perform any obligation thereunder.

(2) Preclude express establishment in a commercial lease or rental agreement of the price at which real property may be offered to a subtenant or sublessee.

(3) Impair any obligation of any contract entered into prior to January 1, 1988.

(4) Affect any provision of, or requirement for mitigation of damages under, Sections 1951 to 1952.6, inclusive.

(5) Limit any adjustment of price required or permitted by law due to constructive eviction.

(6) Enlarge or diminish in any way any power which a public entity may have with respect to regulation of rental rates or the ownership, conveyance, or use of any property specified in paragraph (1), (2), or (3) of subdivision (d) of Section 1954.26.

(7) Relieve any party of any requirement or mandate to arbitrate, or deprive any party of any right to arbitrate or compel arbitration, which mandate or right exists pursuant to Title 9 (commencing with Section 1280) of Part 3 of the Code of Civil Procedure, titled "Arbitration," Chapter 2.5 (commencing with Section 1141.10) of Title 3 of Part 3 of the Code of Civil Procedure, titled "Judicial Arbitration," Title 1 (commencing with Section 1823) of Part 3 of the Code of Civil Procedure, titled "Pilot Projects," or any other provision of state law.

(8) Affect in any way, or preclude the inclusion of, any provision in a lease creating any lawful option, right of first refusal, or any covenant to renew or extend the lease or sell the real property or any interest therein.

(9) Relieve any person of any duty or deprive any person of any right or cause of action which may exist pursuant to Section 51, 53, or 782. **Leg.H.** Added Stats 1987 ch 824 §2.

§1954.28. Application of chapter

Nothing in this chapter limits or affects public entities with respect to any of the following:

(a) The Eminent Domain Law, Title 7 (commencing with Section 1230.10) of Part 3 of the Code of Civil Procedure.

(b) Abatement of nuisances. However, except as to conditions expressly defined as nuisances by statute, authority to abate or bring actions to abate nuisances shall not be used to circumvent the limitations of this chapter with respect to conditions not manifesting the quantum and character of unreasonableness and injuriousness to constitute a nuisance under law.

(c) The Airport Approaches Zoning Law, Article 6.5 (commencing with Section 50485) of Chapter 2 of Part 1 of Division 1 of Title 5 of the Government Code.

(d) Any contract or agreement by which an owner agrees with a public entity to offer any real property for rent at a stipulated or maximum price or under a specified formula for ascertaining a stipulated or maximum price, in consideration for a direct financial contribution; any written contract between a redevelopment agency and an owner or developer of commercial real property within a redevelopment project area; or any written development agreement entered into pursuant to Article 2.5 (commencing with Section 65864) of Chapter 4 of Division 1 of Title 7 of the Government Code. Any contract or agreement specified in this subdivision is not enforceable against an owner who became an owner (1) without actual knowledge of the contract or agreement, and (2) more than 30 days prior to the recording with the county recorder of a written memorandum of the contract or agreement specifically describing its terms and identifying the real property and the owner. The county recorder shall index these memorandums in the grantor-grantee index.

(e) Article 2 (commencing with Section 5020) of Chapter 1 of Division 5 of the Public Resources Code, relating to historical resources.

(f) The Subdivision Map Act, Division 2 (commencing with Section 66410) of Title 7 of the Government Code.

(g) Any contract or agreement entered into by a public entity relating to the transfer, lease, or license of commercial real property owned or leased by that public entity, except any requirement enacted pursuant to Section 1954.31. **Leg.H.** Added Stats 1987 ch 824 §2.

§1954.29. Effect of chapter

Nothing in this chapter shall, with respect to a public entity:

(a) Grant, enlarge, or diminish any power (1) which it may possess under the provisions of, and for the purposes of, Division 1 (commencing with Section 65000) of Title 7 of the Government Code, (2) with respect to charter cities, planning, or zoning powers granted under Section 5 of Article XI of the California Constitution, or (3) any power which it may possess to mitigate the impact caused by the construction, reconstruction, demolition, or alteration of the size of any commercial real property. However, this subdivision does not apply to any actions taken for the clear or systematic purpose of circumventing this chapter.

(b) Grant, repeal, enlarge, or diminish any authority to require a business license, whether for regulation or revenue. **Leg.H.** Added Stats 1987 ch 824 §2.

§1954.30. Power and authority of public entities

Nothing in this chapter grants or augments any authority of a public entity which it does not possess independent of this chapter, nor diminish any power of a public entity except as expressly provided in this chapter. **Leg.H.** Added Stats 1987 ch 824 §2.

§1954.31. Enactment of rent control measures

A public entity may by enactment of a statute, charter or charter amendment, or ordinance, establish a requirement for notice relating to the termination of a lease of commercial real property due to the expiration of its term.

(a) The enactment shall contain provisions dealing with any or all of the following:

(1) The delivery of a negotiation notice by a tenant.

(2) A requirement for an owner to deliver an impasse notice at any time after delivery of the negotiation notice, except that:

(A) The requirement shall be inapplicable unless the tenant has been required to deliver a negotiation notice not less than 270 days before the expiration of the lease, and has done so.

(B) The mandate for delivery of an impasse notice shall not occur earlier than 180 days before expiration of the lease.

(C) No impasse notice shall be required if the parties have executed a renewal or extension of the lease.

(D) Provision shall be made that the notice will include, in a form of type which will distinguish it from the body of the text of the balance of the notice, a disclosure reading, either:

(i) The giving of this notice does not necessarily preclude further dialogue or negotiation on an extension or renewal of the lease if the parties choose to negotiate, but the delivery of this notice discharges all obligations of _____ (the owner) under provisions of _____ (the enactment) and Section 1954.31 of the Civil Code; or

(ii) By giving this notice _____ (the owner) declares that he or she does not intend to negotiate further on any extension or renewal of the lease.

(3) Establish that a bad faith failure to comply with the enactment is subject to a remedy for actual damages.

(4) Any remedy under the enactment or Section 1954.31 shall be available only by an action brought by the owner or the tenant.

(b) The enactment shall contain (or shall be deemed to contain), a provision that:

(1) A tenant may not exercise any right pursuant to the enactment or this chapter, unless the tenant has performed the terms of the lease in such manner as would entitle the tenant to exercise any option he or she might possess under the lease.

(2) No right or cause of action accruing to a tenant pursuant to the enactment or this chapter, may be assigned other than to a person who is a lawful assignee of the lease, is in lawful possession of the premises under the lease, and is in compliance with paragraph (1).

(3) Nothing in the enactment or this chapter creates or imposes, nor shall be construed to create or impose, a duty to extend or renew, or to negotiate on an extension or renewal, of any lease; nor shall the delivery or receipt of any notice provided for by the enactment or by this chapter, constitute a waiver of any rights to continued performance under the covenants under the lease or to actions for possession.

(4) The delivery of any notice pursuant to the enactment or this chapter shall create a rebuttable presumption affecting the burden of proof, that the notice has been properly given.

(c) No enactment shall provide, or be deemed to provide:

(1) For any extension of the term of any lease without the mutual, written consent of the owner and the tenant.

(2) For any requirement on either party to offer to extend or renew or to negotiate an extension or renewal of the lease.

(3) Bar any action brought to recover possession whether by ejectment, unlawful detainer, or other lawful means.

(4) Any remedy under the enactment or this chapter, other than that which may be provided pursuant to paragraph (3) of subdivision (a).

(d) The provisions of any enactment adopted pursuant to this section shall not apply to:

(1) Any lease or rental agreement which is not in writing, which constitutes a tenancy at will, which is for a term of less than one year or for an unspecified term, which is a month-to-month tenancy or a tenancy at sufferance.

(2) Any lease, the term of which expires within 270 days after the effective date of the enactment. **Leg.H.** Added Stats 1987 ch 824 §2.

CHAPTER 2.7
RESIDENTIAL RENT CONTROL

Citation of chapter. §1954.50.
Definitions. §1954.51.
Conditions for owner to establish rental rates. §1954.52.
Exceptions. § 1954.53.
Termination of agreement with government agency providing for rent limitations; Notice to tenants. §1954.535.

§1954.50. Citation of chapter

This chapter shall be known and may be cited as the Costa-Hawkins Rental Housing Act. **Leg.H.** Added Stats 1995 ch 331 §1 (AB 1164).

§1954.51. Definitions

As used in this chapter, the following terms have the following meanings:

(a) "Comparable units" means rental units that have approximately the same living space, have the same number of bedrooms, are located in the same or similar neighborhoods, and feature the same, similar, or equal amenities and housing services.

(b) "Owner" includes any person, acting as principal or through an agent, having the right to offer residential real property for rent, and includes a predecessor in interest to the owner, except that this term does not include the owner or operator of a mobilehome park, or the owner of a mobilehome or his or her agent.

(c) "Prevailing market rent" means the rental rate that would be authorized pursuant to 42 U.S.C.A. 1437 (f), as calculated by the United States Department of Housing and Urban Development pursuant to Part 888 of Title 24 of the Code of Federal Regulations.

(d) "Public entity" has the same meaning as set forth in Section 811.2 of the Government Code.

(e) "Residential real property" includes any dwelling or unit that is intended for human habitation.

(f) "Tenancy" includes the lawful occupation of property and includes a lease or sublease. **Leg.H.** Added Stats 1995 ch 331 §1 (AB 1164).

§1954.52. Conditions for owner to establish rental rates

(a) Notwithstanding any other provision of law, an owner of residential real property may establish the initial and all subsequent rental rates for a dwelling or a unit about which any of the following is true:

(1) It has a certificate of occupancy issued after February 1, 1995.

(2) It has already been exempt from the residential rent control ordinance of a public entity on or before February 1, 1995, pursuant to a local exemption for newly constructed units.

(3)(A) It is alienable separate from the title to any other dwelling unit or is a subdivided interest in a subdivision, as specified in subdivision (b), (d), or (f) of Section 11004.5 of the Business and Professions Code.

(B) This paragraph does not apply to either of the following:

(i) A dwelling or unit where the preceding tenancy has been terminated by the owner by notice pursuant to Section 1946.1 or has been terminated upon a change in the terms of the tenancy noticed pursuant to Section 827.

(ii) A condominium dwelling or unit that has not been sold separately by the subdivider to a bona fide purchaser for value. The initial rent amount of the unit for purposes of this chapter shall be the lawful rent in effect on May 7, 2001, unless the rent amount is governed by a different provision of this chapter. However, if a condominium dwelling or unit meets the criteria of paragraph (1) or (2) of subdivision (a), or if all the dwellings or units except one have been sold separately by the subdivider to bona fide purchasers for value, and the subdivider has occupied that remaining unsold condominium dwelling or unit as his or her principal residence for at least one year after the subdivision occurred, then subparagraph (A) of paragraph (3) shall apply to that unsold condominium dwelling or unit.

(C) Where a dwelling or unit in which the initial or subsequent rental rates are controlled by an ordinance or charter provision in effect on January 1, 1995, the following shall apply:

(i) An owner of real property as described in this paragraph may establish the initial and all subsequent rental rates for all existing and new tenancies in effect on or after January 1, 1999, if the tenancy in effect on or after January 1, 1999, was created between January 1, 1996, and December 31, 1998.

(ii) Commencing on January 1, 1999, an owner of real property as described in this paragraph may establish the initial and all subsequent rental rates for all new tenancies if the previous tenancy was in effect on December 31, 1995.

(iii) The initial rental rate for a dwelling or unit as described in this paragraph in which the initial rental rate is controlled by an ordinance or charter provision in effect on January 1, 1995, may not, until January 1, 1999, exceed the amount calculated pursuant to subdivision (c) of Section 1954.53. An owner of residential real property as described in this paragraph may, until January 1, 1999, establish the initial rental rate for a dwelling or unit only where the tenant has voluntarily vacated, abandoned, or been evicted pursuant to paragraph (2) of Section 1161 of the Code of Civil Procedure.

(b) Subdivision (a) does not apply where the owner has otherwise agreed by contract with a public entity in consideration for a direct financial contribution or any other forms of assistance specified in Chapter 4.3 (commencing with Section 65915) of Division 1 of Title 7 of the Government Code.

(c) Nothing in this section shall be construed to affect the authority of a public entity that may otherwise exist to regulate or monitor the basis for eviction.

(d) This section does not apply to any dwelling or unit that contains serious health, safety, fire, or building code violations, excluding those caused by disasters for which a citation has been issued by the appropriate governmental agency and which has remained unabated for six months or longer preceding the vacancy. **Leg.H.** Added Stats 1995 ch 331 §1 (AB 1164). Amended Stats 2001 ch 729 §2 (SB 985); Stats 2004 ch 568 §4 (SB 1145). Amendment approved by voters, Prop. 21 §5, effective November 3, 2020.

§1954.53. Exceptions

(a) Notwithstanding any other provision of law, an owner of residential real property may establish the initial rental rate for a dwelling or unit, except where any of the following applies:

(1) The previous tenancy has been terminated by the owner by notice pursuant to Section 1946.1 or has been terminated upon a change in the terms of the tenancy noticed pursuant to Section 827, except a change permitted by law in the amount of rent or fees. For the purpose of this paragraph, the owner's termination or nonrenewal of a contract or recorded agreement with a governmental agency that provides for a rent limitation to a qualified tenant, shall be construed as a change in the terms of the tenancy pursuant to Section 827.

(A) In a jurisdiction that controls by ordinance or charter provision the rental rate for a dwelling or unit, an owner who terminates or fails to renew a contract or recorded agreement with a governmental agency that provides for a rent limitation to a qualified tenant may not set an initial rent for three years following the date of the termination or nonrenewal of the contract or agreement. For any new tenancy established during the three-year period, the rental rate for a new tenancy established in that vacated dwelling or unit shall be at the same rate as the rent under the terminated or nonrenewed contract or recorded agreement with a governmental agency that provided for a rent limitation to a qualified tenant, plus any increases authorized after the termination or cancellation of the contract or recorded agreement.

(B) Subparagraph (A) does not apply to any new tenancy of 12 months or more duration established after January 1, 2000, pursuant to the owner's contract or recorded agreement with a governmental agency that provides for a rent limitation to a qualified tenant, unless the prior vacancy in that dwelling or unit was pursuant to a nonrenewed or canceled contract or recorded agreement with a governmental agency that provides for a rent limitation to a qualified tenant as set forth in that subparagraph.

(2) The owner has otherwise agreed by contract with a public entity in consideration for a direct financial contribution or any other forms of assistance specified in Chapter 4.3 (commencing with Section 65915) of Division 1 of Title 7 of the Government Code.

(3) The initial rental rate for a dwelling or unit whose initial rental rate is controlled by an ordinance or charter provision in effect on January 1, 1995, may not until January 1, 1999, exceed the amount calculated pursuant to subdivision (c).

(4)(A) Notwithstanding any other law, for a dwelling or unit subject to an ordinance or charter provision that controls the rental rate of the dwelling or unit, the jurisdiction that adopted the ordinance or charter provision may require the owner of the residential real property to permit a tenant who is not subject to eviction for nonpayment and who has a permanent physical disability as defined in subdivision (m) of Section 12926 of the Government Code and that is related to mobility to move to an available comparable or smaller unit located on an accessible floor of the property. An owner that is subject to a requirement established pursuant to this paragraph that is required to grant a tenant's request for a reasonable accommodation relating to the tenant's physical disability, after complying with any requirement to engage in an interactive process with the tenant, including Sections 12177 to 12180, inclusive, of Title 2 of the California Code of Regulations, shall allow the tenant to retain their lease at the same rental rate and terms of the existing lease if all of the following apply:

(i) The move is determined to be necessary to accommodate the tenant's physical disability related to mobility.

(ii) There is no operational elevator that serves the floor of the tenant's current dwelling or unit.

(iii) The new dwelling or unit is in the same building or on the same parcel with at least four other units and shares the same owner.

(iv) The new dwelling or unit does not require renovation to comply with applicable requirements of the Health and Safety Code.

(v) The applicable rent control board or authority determines that the owner will continue to receive a fair rate of return or offers an administrative procedure ensuring a fair rate of return for the new unit.

(vi) The tenant, who is not subject to eviction for nonpayment and who has a permanent physical disability as defined in subdivision (m) of Section 12926 of the Government Code and that is related to mobility, provides the owner a written request to move into an available comparable or smaller unit located on an accessible floor of the property prior to that unit becoming available.

(B) Any security deposit paid by the tenant in connection with their rental of the dwelling or unit being vacated shall be handled in accordance with Section 1950.5 upon the tenant's move pursuant to this paragraph.

(C) This paragraph shall not apply unless all of the tenants on the lease agree to move to the available comparable or smaller unit located on an accessible floor of the property pursuant to the request of the tenant with the physical disability.

(D) For purposes of this paragraph, "comparable or smaller unit" means a dwelling or unit that has the same or less than the number of bedrooms and bathrooms, square footage, and parking spaces as the unit being vacated.

(E) This paragraph shall not apply if the owner, or their spouse, domestic partner, children, grandchildren, parents, or grandparents, intend to occupy the available comparable or smaller unit located on an accessible floor of the property.

(F) The requirements of this paragraph shall be in addition to those of any other fair housing law, including, but not limited to, the California Fair Employment and Housing Act (Part 2.8 (commencing with Section 12900) of Division 3 of Title 2 of the Government Code), the Unruh Civil Rights Act (Section 51), the federal Fair Housing Act (42 U.S.C. Sec. 3601 et seq.), and any implementing regulations thereunder.

(G) This paragraph shall not be construed to prevent owners of residential real property from granting reasonable accommodations to change housing units and retain the existing lease at the same rental rate and terms in order to accommodate any disability, as defined in subdivision (m) of Section 12926 of the Government Code.

(b) Subdivision (a) applies to, and includes, renewal of the initial hiring by the same tenant, lessee, authorized subtenant, or authorized sublessee for the entire period of their occupancy at the rental rate established for the initial hiring.

(c) The rental rate of a dwelling or unit whose initial rental rate is controlled by ordinance or charter provision in effect on January 1, 1995, shall, until January 1, 1999, be established in accordance with this subdivision. Where the previous tenant has voluntarily vacated, abandoned, or been evicted pursuant to paragraph (2) of Section 1161 of the Code of Civil Procedure, an owner of residential real property may, no more than twice, establish the initial rental rate for a dwelling or unit in an amount that is no greater than 15 percent more than the rental rate in effect for the immediately preceding tenancy or in an amount that is 70 percent of the prevailing market rent for comparable units, whichever amount is greater.

The initial rental rate established pursuant to this subdivision may not substitute for or replace increases in rental rates otherwise authorized pursuant to law.

(d)(1) Nothing in this section or any other provision of law shall be construed to preclude express establishment in a lease or rental agreement of the rental rates to be applicable in the event the rental unit subject thereto is sublet. Nothing in this section shall be construed to impair the obligations of contracts entered into prior to January 1, 1996.

(2) If the original occupant or occupants who took possession of the dwelling or unit pursuant to the rental agreement with the owner no longer permanently reside there, an owner may increase the rent by any amount allowed by this section to a lawful sublessee or assignee who did not reside at the dwelling or unit prior to January 1, 1996.

(3) This subdivision does not apply to partial changes in occupancy of a dwelling or unit where one or more of the occupants of the premises, pursuant to the agreement with the owner provided for above, remains an occupant in lawful possession of the dwelling or unit, or where a lawful sublessee or assignee who resided at the dwelling or unit prior to January 1, 1996, remains in possession of the dwelling or unit. Nothing contained in this section shall be construed to enlarge or diminish an owner's right to withhold consent to a sublease or assignment.

(4) Acceptance of rent by the owner does not operate as a waiver or otherwise prevent enforcement of a covenant prohibiting sublease or assignment or as a waiver of an owner's rights to establish the initial rental rate, unless the owner has received written notice from the tenant that is party to the agreement and thereafter accepted rent.

(e) Nothing in this section shall be construed to affect any authority of a public entity that may otherwise exist to regulate or monitor the grounds for eviction.

(f) This section does not apply to any dwelling or unit if all the following conditions are met:

(1) The dwelling or unit has been cited in an inspection report by the appropriate governmental agency as containing serious health, safety, fire,

or building code violations, as defined by Section 17920.3 of the Health and Safety Code, excluding any violation caused by a disaster.

(2) The citation was issued at least 60 days prior to the date of the vacancy.

(3) The cited violation had not been abated when the prior tenant vacated and had remained unabated for 60 days or for a longer period of time. However, the 60-day time period may be extended by the appropriate governmental agency that issued the citation. **Leg.H.** Added Stats 1995 ch 331 §1 (AB 1164). Amended Stats 1996 ch 1031 §1 (AB 3244); Stats 1999 ch 590 §2 (SB 1098); Stats 2004 ch 568 §5 (SB 1145); Amendment approved by voters, Prop. 21 §6, effective November 3, 2020; Stats 2023 ch 767 §1 (AB 1620), effective January 1, 2024.

§1954.535. Termination of agreement with government agency providing for rent limitations; Notice to tenants

Where an owner terminates or fails to renew a contract or recorded agreement with a governmental agency that provides for rent limitations to a qualified tenant, the tenant or tenants who were the beneficiaries of the contract or recorded agreement shall be given at least 90 days' written notice of the effective date of the termination and shall not be obligated to pay more than the tenant's portion of the rent, as calculated under the contract or recorded agreement to be terminated, for 90 days following receipt of the notice of termination of nonrenewal of the contract. **Leg.H.** Added Stats 1999 ch 590 §3 (SB 1098).

CHAPTER 2.8
BED BUG INFESTATIONS

Legislative findings and declarations. §1954.600.
"Pest control operator". §1954.601.
Bed bug infestation; Showing, renting, or leasing of premises prohibited; Knowledge; Notice; Duty to inspect. §1954.602.
Prospective tenants; Bed bug information notice; Requirements. §1954.603.
Entry of dwelling by landlord for purpose of bed bug inspection. §1954.604.
Bed bug inspection; Findings; Notification of tenant by landlord. §1954.605.

§1954.600. Legislative findings and declarations

The Legislature finds and declares:

(a) Controlling bed bugs is uniquely challenging, as bed bug resistance to existing insecticidal control measures is significant. Cooperation among landlords, tenants, and pest control operators is required for successful control. With cooperation among landlords, tenants, and pest control operators, most bed bug infestations can be successfully controlled.

(b) Effective control is more likely to occur when landlords and tenants are informed of the best practices for bed bug control.

(c) Early detection and reporting of bed bugs is an important component required for preventing bed bug infestations. Tenants should not face retaliation for reporting a problem.

(d) Lack of cooperation by landlords and tenants can undermine pest control operator efforts to identify the presence of bed bugs and control an infestation. Depending on the treatment strategy, it is often critical that tenants cooperate with pest control operators by reducing clutter, washing clothes, or performing other activities. Likewise, inadequate or untimely response or planning by landlords may exacerbate an infestation.

(e) Pest control operators with knowledge and education in current best practices for bed bug management, such as those created by the National Pest Management Association (NPMA), are best equipped to help property owners and tenants eradicate bed bugs from their home.

(f) The Structural Pest Control Board should incorporate training in bed bug management based on the National Pest Management Association (NPMA) best practices for the issuance or renewal of a Branch 2 operator, field representative, or applicator license. **Leg.H.** Added Stats 2016 ch 599 §3 (AB 551), effective January 1, 2017.

§1954.601. "Pest control operator"

For purposes of this chapter, the term "pest control operator" means an individual holding a Branch 2 operator, field representative, or applicator license from the Structural Pest Control Board. **Leg.H.** Added Stats 2016 ch 599 §3 (AB 551), effective January 1, 2017.

§1954.602. Bed bug infestation; Showing, renting, or leasing of premises prohibited; Knowledge; Notice; Duty to inspect

(a) A landlord shall not show, rent, or lease to a prospective tenant any vacant dwelling unit that the landlord knows has a current bed bug infestation.

(b) This section does not impose a duty on a landlord to inspect a dwelling unit or the common areas of the premises for bed bugs if the landlord has no notice of a suspected or actual bed bug infestation. If a bed bug infestation is evident on visual inspection, the landlord shall be considered to have notice pursuant to this section. **Leg.H.** Added Stats 2016 ch 599 §3 (AB 551), effective January 1, 2017.

§1954.603. Prospective tenants; Bed bug information notice; Requirements

On and after July 1, 2017, prior to creating a new tenancy for a dwelling unit, a landlord shall provide a written notice to the prospective tenant as provided in this section. This notice shall be provided to all other tenants by January 1, 2018. The notice shall be in at least 10-point type and shall include, but is not limited to, the following:

(a) General information about bed bug identification, behavior and biology, the importance of cooperation for prevention and treatment, and the importance of and for prompt written reporting of suspected infestations to the landlord. The information shall be in substantially the following form:

Information about Bed Bugs

Bed bug Appearance: Bed bugs have six legs. Adult bed bugs have flat bodies about 1/4 of an inch in length. Their color can vary from red and brown to copper colored. Young bed bugs are very small. Their bodies are about 1/16 of an inch in length. They have almost no color. When a bed bug feeds, its body swells, may lengthen, and becomes bright red, sometimes making it appear to be a different insect. Bed bugs do not fly. They can either crawl or be carried from place to place on objects, people, or animals. Bed bugs can be hard to find and identify because they are tiny and try to stay hidden.

Life Cycle and Reproduction: An average bed bug lives for about 10 months. Female bed bugs lay one to five eggs per day. Bed bugs grow to full adulthood in about 21 days.

Bed bugs can survive for months without feeding.

Bed bug Bites: Because bed bugs usually feed at night, most people are bitten in their sleep and do not realize they were bitten. A person's reaction to insect bites is an immune response and so varies from person to person. Sometimes the red welts caused by the bites will not be noticed until many days after a person was bitten, if at all.

Common signs and symptoms of a possible bed bug infestation:

• Small red to reddish brown fecal spots on mattresses, box springs, bed frames, mattresses, linens, upholstery, or walls.

• Molted bed bug skins, white, sticky eggs, or empty eggshells.

• Very heavily infested areas may have a characteristically sweet odor.

• Red, itchy bite marks, especially on the legs, arms, and other body parts exposed while sleeping. However, some people do not show bed bug lesions on their bodies even though bed bugs may have fed on them.

For more information, see the Internet Web sites of the United States Environmental Protection Agency and the National Pest Management Association.

(b) The procedure to report suspected infestations to the landlord. **Leg.H.** Added Stats 2016 ch 599 §3 (AB 551), effective January 1, 2017.

§1954.604. Entry of dwelling by landlord for purpose of bed bug inspection

Entry to inspect a tenant's dwelling unit shall comply with Section 1954. Entry to inspect any unit selected by the pest control operator and to conduct followup inspections of surrounding units until bed bugs are eliminated is a necessary service for the purpose of Section 1954. Tenants shall cooperate with the inspection to facilitate the detection and treatment of bed bugs, including providing requested information that is necessary to facilitate the detection and treatment of bed bugs to the pest control operator. **Leg.H.** Added Stats 2016 ch 599 §3 (AB 551), effective January 1, 2017.

§1954.605. Bed bug inspection; Findings; Notification of tenant by landlord

The landlord shall notify the tenants of those units inspected by the pest control operator pursuant to Section 1954.604 of the pest control operator's findings. The notification shall be in writing and made within two business days of receipt of the pest control operator's findings. For confirmed infestations in common areas, all tenants shall be provided notice of the pest control operator's findings. **Leg.H.** Added Stats 2016 ch 599 §3 (AB 551), effective January 1, 2017.

CHAPTER 3
HIRING OF PERSONAL PROPERTY

Obligations of lessor of personal property. §1955.
Ordinary expenses. §1956.
Extraordinary expenses. §1957.
Return of thing hired. §1958.
Charter party, what. §1959.

§1955. Obligations of lessor of personal property

Except as otherwise agreed by the lessor and the lessee in lease agreements for a term of more than 20 days, one who leases personal property must deliver it to the lessee, secure his or her quiet enjoyment thereof against all lawful claimants, put it into a condition fit for the purpose for which he or she leases it, and repair all deteriorations thereof not occasioned by the fault of the lessee and not the natural result of its use. **Leg.H.** Enacted Stats 1872. Amended Stats 1982 ch 561 §1.

§1956. Ordinary expenses

Except as otherwise agreed by the lessor and lessee, a lessee of personal property must bear all such expenses concerning it as might naturally be foreseen to attend it during its use by him or her, and all other expenses must be borne by the lessor. **Leg.H.** Enacted Stats 1872. Amended Stats 1982 ch 561 §2.

§1957. Extraordinary expenses

If a lessor fails to fulfill his or her obligations, as prescribed by Section 1955, the lessee, after giving him or her notice to do so, if the notice can conveniently be given, may expend any reasonable amount necessary to make good the lessor's default, and may recover such amount from him or her. **Leg.H.** Enacted Stats 1872. Amended Stats 1982 ch 561 §3.

§1958. Return of thing hired

At the expiration of the term for which personal property is leased, the lessee must return it to the lessor at the place contemplated by the parties at the time of leasing; or, if no particular place was so contemplated by them, at the place at which it was at that time. **Leg.H.** Enacted Stats 1872. Amended Stats 1982 ch 561 §4.

§1959. Charter party, what

The contract by which a ship is let is termed a charter party. By it the owner may either let the capacity or burden of the ship, continuing the employment of the owner's master, crew, and equipments, or may surrender the entire ship to the charterer, who then provides them himself. The master or a part owner may be a charterer. **Leg.H.** Enacted Stats 1872.

CHAPTER 4
IDENTIFICATION OF PROPERTY OWNERS

Application of provisions. §1961.
Information required in rental agreement. §1962.
Alternative methods of disclosing information. §1962.5.
Service of process on noncomplying owner. §1962.7.

§1961. Application of provisions

This chapter shall apply to every dwelling structure containing one or more units offered to the public for rent or for lease for residential purposes. **Leg.H.** Added Stats 1972 ch 941 §1, operative July 1, 1973. Amended Stats 1987 ch 769 §1.

§1962. Information required in rental agreement

(a) Any owner of a dwelling structure specified in Section 1961 or a party signing a rental agreement or lease on behalf of the owner shall do all of the following:

(1) Disclose therein the name, telephone number, and usual street address at which personal service may be effected of each person who is:

(A) Authorized to manage the premises.

(B) An owner of the premises or a person who is authorized to act for and on behalf of the owner for the purpose of service of process and for the purpose of receiving and receipting for all notices and demands.

(2) Disclose therein the name, telephone number, and address of the person or entity to whom rent payments shall be made.

(A) If rent payments may be made personally, the usual days and hours that the person will be available to receive the payments shall also be disclosed.

(B) At the owner's option, the rental agreement or lease shall instead disclose the number of either:

(i) The account in a financial institution into which rent payments may be made, and the name and street address of the institution; provided that the institution is located within five miles of the rental property.

(ii) The information necessary to establish an electronic funds transfer procedure for paying the rent.

(3) Disclose therein the form or forms in which rent payments are to be made.

(4) Provide a copy of the rental agreement or lease to the tenant within 15 days of its execution by the tenant. Once each calendar year thereafter, upon request by the tenant, the owner or owner's agent shall provide an additional copy to the tenant within 15 days. If the owner or owner's agent does not possess the rental agreement or lease or a copy of it, the owner or owner's agent shall instead furnish the tenant with a written statement stating that fact and containing the information required by paragraphs (1), (2), and (3).

(b) In the case of an oral rental agreement, the owner, or a person acting on behalf of the owner for the receipt of rent or otherwise, shall furnish the tenant, within 15 days of the agreement, with a written statement containing the information required by paragraphs (1), (2), and (3) of subdivision (a). Once each calendar year thereafter, upon request by the tenant, the owner or owner's agent shall provide an additional copy of the statement to the tenant within 15 days.

(c) The information required by this section shall be kept current and this section shall extend to and be enforceable against any successor owner or manager, who shall comply with this section within 15 days of succeeding the previous owner or manager. A successor owner or manager shall not serve a notice pursuant to paragraph (2) of Section 1161 of the Code of Civil Procedure or otherwise evict a tenant for nonpayment of rent that accrued during the period of noncompliance by a successor owner or manager with this subdivision. Nothing in this subdivision shall relieve the tenant of any liability for unpaid rent.

(d) A party who enters into a rental agreement on behalf of the owner who fails to comply with this section is deemed an agent of each person who is an owner:

(1) For the purpose of service of process and receiving and receipting for notices and demands.

(2) For the purpose of performing the obligations of the owner under law and under the rental agreement.

(3) For the purpose of receiving rental payments, which may be made in cash, by check, by money order, or in any form previously accepted by the owner or owner's agent, unless the form of payment has been specified in the oral or written agreement, or the tenant has been notified by the owner in writing that a particular form of payment is unacceptable.

(e) Nothing in this section limits or excludes the liability of any undisclosed owner.

(f) If the address provided by the owner does not allow for personal delivery, then it shall be conclusively presumed that upon the mailing of any rent or notice to the owner by the tenant to the name and address provided, the notice or rent is deemed receivable by the owner on the date posted, if the tenant can show proof of mailing to the name and address provided by the owner. **Leg.H.** Added Stats 1972 ch 941 §1, operative July 1, 1973. Amended Stats 1987 ch 769 §2; Stats 2001 ch 729 §3 (SB 985); Stats 2012 ch 695 §1 (AB 1953), effective January 1, 2013.

§1962.5. Alternative methods of disclosing information

(a) Notwithstanding subdivisions (a) and (b) of Section 1962, the information required by paragraph (1) of subdivision (a) of Section 1962 to be disclosed to a tenant may, instead of being disclosed in the manner described in subdivisions (a) and (b) of Section 1962, be disclosed by the following method:

(1) In each dwelling structure containing an elevator a printed or typewritten notice containing the information required by paragraph (1) of subdivision (a) of Section 1962 shall be placed in every elevator and in one other conspicuous place.

(2) In each structure not containing an elevator, a printed or typewritten notice containing the information required by paragraph (1) of subdivision (a) of Section 1962 shall be placed in at least two conspicuous places.

(3) In the case of a single unit dwelling structure, the information to be disclosed under this section may be disclosed by complying with either paragraph (1) or (2).

(b) Except as provided in subdivision (a), all the provisions of Section 1962 shall be applicable. **Leg.H.** Added Stats 1972 ch 941 §1, operative

July 1, 1973. Amended Stats 1987 ch 769 §3; Stats 2001 ch 729 §4 (SB 985).

§1962.7. Service of process on noncomplying owner

In the event an owner, successor owner, manager, or agent specified in Section 1961 fails to comply with the requirements of this chapter, service of process by a tenant with respect to a dispute arising out of the tenancy may be made by registered or certified mail sent to the address at which rent is paid, in which case the provisions of Section 1013 of the Code of Civil Procedure shall apply. **Leg.H.** Added Stats 1987 ch 769 §4. Amended Stats 2001 ch 729 §5 (SB 985).

CHAPTER 4.5
DISPOSITION OF PERSONAL PROPERTY UPON REQUEST OF TENANT

Surrender of tenant's property by landlord; Terms and conditions; Penalties for violation of chapter. §1965.

§1965. Surrender of tenant's property by landlord; Terms and conditions; Penalties for violation of chapter

(a) A residential landlord shall not refuse to surrender, to a residential tenant or to a residential tenant's duly authorized representative, any personal property not owned by the landlord which has been left on the premises after the tenant has vacated the residential premises and the return of which has been requested by the tenant or by the authorized representative of the tenant if all of the following occur:

(1) The tenant requests, in writing, within 18 days of vacating the premises, the surrender of the personal property and the request includes a description of the personal property held by the landlord and specifies the mailing address of the tenant.

(2) The landlord or the landlord's agent has control or possession of the tenant's personal property at the time the request is received.

(3) The tenant, prior to the surrender of the personal property by the landlord and upon written demand by the landlord, tenders payment of all reasonable costs associated with the landlord's removal and storage of the personal property. The landlord's demand for payment of reasonable costs associated with the removal and storage of personal property shall be in writing and shall either be mailed to the tenant at the address provided by the tenant pursuant to paragraph (1) or shall be personally presented to the tenant or to the tenant's authorized representative, within five days after the actual receipt of the tenant's request for surrender of the personal property, unless the property is returned first. The demand shall itemize all charges, specifying the nature and amount of each item of cost.

(4) The tenant agrees to claim and remove the personal property at a reasonable time mutually agreed upon by the landlord and tenant but not later than 72 hours after the tender provided for under paragraph (3).

(b) For the purposes of this chapter, "reasonable costs associated with the landlord's removal and storage of the personal property" shall include, but not be limited to, each of the following:

(1) Reasonable costs actually incurred, or the reasonable value of labor actually provided, or both, in removing the personal property from its original location to the place of storage, including disassembly and transportation.

(2) Reasonable storage costs actually incurred, which shall not exceed the fair rental value of the space reasonably required for the storage of the personal property.

(c) This chapter shall not apply when disposition of the personal property has been initiated or completed pursuant to the procedure set forth in Chapter 5 (commencing with Section 1980) or the occupancy is one defined by subdivision (b) of Section 1940.

(d) A landlord who complies with this chapter shall not be liable to any person with respect to that person's personal property that is given to another person. In the event of conflicting demands, the first timely request for surrender of personal property received by the landlord shall prevail.

(e) Any landlord who retains personal property in violation of this chapter shall be liable to the tenant in a civil action for all the following:

(1) Actual damages not to exceed the value of the personal property, if the personal property is not surrendered by the later of either of the following: (A) within a reasonable time after the tenant's request for surrender of the personal property, or (B) if the landlord has demanded payment of reasonable costs associated with removal and storage and the tenant has complied with the requirements set forth in paragraphs (3) and (4) of subdivision (a), whichever is later. Three days is presumed to be a reasonable time in the absence of evidence to the contrary.

(2) An amount not to exceed two hundred fifty dollars ($250) for each bad faith violation of this section. In determining the amount of the award, the court shall consider proof of matters as justice may require.

(3) The court may award reasonable attorney's fees and cost to the prevailing party.

(f) The remedy provided by this chapter is not exclusive and shall not preclude either the landlord or the tenant from pursuing any other remedy provided by law. **Leg.H.** Added Stats 1988 ch 797 §2.

Prior Law: Former §1965, similar to Lab C §2750, was repealed 1937.

§§1966–1979. [Sections repealed 1937]

Leg.H. Enacted Stats 1872. Repealed 1937. See Lab C §§2750, 2800–2804, 2850–2854.

CHAPTER 5
DISPOSITION OF PERSONAL PROPERTY REMAINING ON PREMISES AT TERMINATION OF TENANCY

Definitions. §1980.
Application of chapter. §1980.5.
Application of provisions. §1981.
Property believed to be lost. §1982.
Notice to former tenant. §1983.
Form of notice to former tenant. §1984.
Form of notice to person other than former tenant. §1985.
Storage of abandoned property. §1986.
Release of property. §1987.
Sale or other disposition of unreleased property. §1988.
Limitation of liability. §1989.
Assessment of storage costs. §1990.
Notice combined with notice of belief of abandonment of leased real property. §1991.

§1980. Definitions

As used in this chapter:

(a) "Landlord" means any operator, keeper, lessor, or sublessor of any furnished or unfurnished premises for hire, or his or her agent or successor in interest.

(b) "Owner" means any person other than the landlord who has any right, title, or interest in personal property.

(c) "Premises" includes any common areas associated therewith.

(d) "Reasonable belief" means the actual knowledge or belief a prudent person would have without making an investigation (including any investigation of public records) except that, where the landlord has specific information indicating that such an investigation would more probably than not reveal pertinent information and the cost of such an investigation would be reasonable in relation to the probable value of the personal property involved, "reasonable belief" includes the actual knowledge or belief a prudent person would have if such an investigation were made.

(e) "Records" means any material, regardless of the physical form, on which information is recorded or preserved by any means, including in written or spoken words, graphically depicted, printed, or electromagnetically transmitted. "Records" does not include publicly available directories containing information an individual has voluntarily consented to have publicly disseminated or listed, such as name, address, or telephone number.

(f) "Tenant" includes any paying guest, lessee, or sublessee of any premises for hire. **Leg.H.** Added Stats 1974 ch 331 §2. Amended Stats 2009 ch 134 §4 (AB 1094), effective January 1, 2010.

Prior Law: Former §1980, similar to present Lab C §2855, was repealed 1937.

§1980.5. Application of chapter

(a) Except as provided in Section 1993.01, the provisions of this chapter shall not apply to commercial real property, as defined in subdivision (d) of Section 1954.26. For purposes of this section, commercial real property shall not include self-storage units.

(b) This chapter shall apply to self-storage units only to the extent that it does not conflict with Chapter 10 (commencing with Section 21700) of Division 8 of the Business and Professions Code. Leg.H. Added Stats 2008 ch 161 §1 (AB 2025). Amended Stats 2024 ch 91 §7 (AB 1916), effective January 1, 2025.

§1981. Application of provisions

(a) This chapter provides an optional procedure for the disposition of personal property that remains on the premises after a tenancy has terminated and the premises have been vacated by the tenant.

(b) This chapter does not apply whenever Section 1862.5, 2080.8, 2080.9, or 2081 to 2081.6, inclusive, applies. This chapter does not apply to property that exists for the purpose of providing utility services and is owned by a public utility, whether or not that property is actually in operation to provide those utility services.

(c) This chapter does not apply to any manufactured home as defined in Section 18007 of the Health and Safety Code, any mobilehome as defined in Section 18008 of the Health and Safety Code, or to any commercial coach as defined in Section 18001.8 of the Health and Safety Code, including attachments thereto or contents thereof, whether or not the manufactured home, mobilehome, or commercial coach is subject to registration under the Health and Safety Code.

(d) This chapter does not apply to the disposition of an animal to which subdivision (d) of Section 1815 or Chapter 7 (commencing with Section 17001) of Part 1 of Division 9 of the Food and Agricultural Code applies, and those animals shall be disposed of in accordance with those provisions.

(e) If the requirements of this chapter are not satisfied, nothing in this chapter affects the rights and liabilities of the landlord, former tenant, or any other person. **Leg.H.** Added Stats 1974 ch 331 §2. Amended Stats 1983 ch 1124 §5; Stats 1996 ch 653 §1 (AB 2605); Stats 2008 ch 265 §3 (AB 2949), effective January 1, 2009.

Prior Law: Former §1981, similar to present Lab C §2856, was amended Code Amdts 1873-74 ch 612 §208 and repealed 1937.

§1982. Property believed to be lost

(a) Personal property which the landlord reasonably believes to have been lost shall be disposed of pursuant to Article 1 (commencing with Section 2080) of Chapter 4 of Title 6. The landlord is not liable to the owner of the property if he complies with this subdivision.

(b) If the appropriate police or sheriff's department refuses to accept property pursuant to subdivision (a), the landlord may dispose of the property pursuant to this chapter. **Leg.H.** Added Stats 1974 ch 331 §2.

Prior Law: Former §1982, similar to present Lab C §2857, was repealed 1937.

§1983. Notice to former tenant

(a) Where personal property remains on the premises after a tenancy has terminated and the premises have been vacated by the tenant, the landlord shall give written notice to the tenant and to any other person the landlord reasonably believes to be the owner of the property. If the property consists of records, the tenant shall be presumed to be the owner of the records for the purposes of this chapter.

(b) The notice shall describe the property in a manner reasonably adequate to permit the owner of the property to identify it. The notice may describe all or a portion of the property, but the limitation of liability provided by Section 1989 does not protect the landlord from any liability arising from the disposition of property not described in the notice except that a trunk, valise, box, or other container which is locked, fastened, or tied in a manner which deters immediate access to its contents may be described as such without describing its contents. The notice shall advise the person to be notified that reasonable costs of storage may be charged before the property is returned, where the property may be claimed, and the date before which the claim must be made. The date specified in the notice shall be a date not less than 15 days after the notice is personally delivered or, if mailed, not less than 18 days after the notice is deposited in the mail.

(c) The notice shall be personally delivered to the person to be notified or sent by first-class mail, postage prepaid, to the person to be notified at his or her last known address and, if there is reason to believe that the notice sent to that address will not be received by that person, also to any other address known to the landlord where the person may reasonably be expected to receive the notice. If the notice is sent by mail to the former tenant, one copy shall be sent to the premises vacated by the tenant. If the former tenant provided the landlord with the tenant's email address, the landlord may also send the notice by email. **Leg.H.** Added Stats 1974 ch 331 §2. Amended Stats 2009 ch 134 §5 (AB 1094), effective January 1, 2010; Stats 2012 ch 560 §4 (AB 2521), effective January 1, 2013.

Prior Law: Former §1983, similar to present Lab C §2858, was repealed 1937.

§1984. Form of notice to former tenant

(a) A notice given to the former tenant which is in substantially the following form satisfies the requirements of Section 1983:

Notice of Right to Reclaim Abandoned Property

To: _____
(Name of former tenant)

_____
(Address of former tenant)

When you vacated the premises at _____
_____,
(Address of premises, including room or apartment number, if any) the following personal property remained:
_____
(Insert description of the personal property)
You may claim this property at _____
_____.
(Address where property may be claimed)

If you claim this property by _____ (insert date not less than 2 days after the former tenant vacated the premises), you may minimize the costs of storage. If you fail to claim this property by _____ (insert date not less than 2 days after the former tenant vacated the premises), unless you pay the landlord's reasonable cost of storage for all the above-described property, and take possession of the property which you claim, not later than _____ (insert date not less than 15 days after notice is personally delivered or, if mailed, not less than 18 days after notice is deposited in the mail) this property may be disposed of pursuant to Civil Code Section 1988.

(Insert here the statement required by subdivision (b) of this section)
Dated: _____ _____
(Signature of landlord)

_____
(Type or print name of landlord)

_____
(Telephone number)

_____
(Address)

(b) The notice set forth in subdivision (a) shall also contain one of the following statements:

(1) "If you fail to reclaim the property, it will be sold at a public sale after notice of the sale has been given by publication. You have the right to bid on the property at this sale. After the property is sold and the cost of storage, advertising, and sale is deducted, the remaining money will be paid over to the county. You may claim the remaining money at any time within one year after the county receives the money."

(2) "Because this property is believed to be worth less than $700, it may be kept, sold, or destroyed without further notice if you fail to reclaim it within the time indicated above." **Leg.H.** Added Stats 1974 ch 331 §2. Amended Stats 1984 ch 1249 §1; Stats 2012 ch 560 §5 (AB 2521), effective January 1, 2013.

Prior Law: Former §1984, similar to present Lab C §2859, was amended Code Amdts 1873-74 ch 612 §209 and repealed 1937.

§1985. Form of notice to person other than former tenant

A notice which is in substantially the following form given to a person (other than the former tenant) the landlord reasonably believes to be the owner of personal property satisfies the requirements of Section 1983:

Notice of Right to Reclaim Abandoned Property

To: _____
(Name)

_____
(Address)

When _____ vacated the premises at
(Name of former tenant)
_____,
(address of premises, including room or apartment number, if any) the following personal property remained:
_____
(insert description of the personal property)

If you own any of this property, you may claim it at _____
_____.
(address where property may be claimed)

If you claim this property by _____ (insert date not less than 2 days after the former tenant vacated the premises), you may minimize the costs of storage.

If you fail to claim this property by _____ (insert date not less than 2 days after the former tenant vacated the premises), unless you pay the landlord's reasonable cost of storage and take possession of the property to which you are entitled not later than _____ (insert date not less than 15 days after notice is personally delivered or, if mailed, not less than 18 days after notice is deposited in the mail) this property may be disposed of pursuant to Civil Code Section 1988.
Dated: _____
_____
(Signature of landlord)
_____
(Type or print name of landlord)
_____
(Telephone number)
_____
(Address)

Leg.H. Added Stats 1974 ch 331 §2. Amended Stats 2012 ch 560 §6 (AB 2521), effective January 1, 2013.

Prior Law: Former §1985, similar to present Lab C §2860, was repealed 1937.

§1986. Storage of abandoned property

The personal property described in the notice shall either be left on the vacated premises or be stored by the landlord in a place of safekeeping until the landlord either releases the property pursuant to Section 1987 or disposes of the property pursuant to Section 1988. The landlord shall exercise reasonable care in storing the property, but he is not liable to the tenant or any other owner for any loss not caused by his deliberate or negligent act. **Leg.H.** Added Stats 1974 ch 331 §2.

Prior Law: Former §1986, similar to present Lab C §2861, was repealed 1937.

§1987. Release of property

(a) The personal property described in the notice shall be released by the landlord to the former tenant or, at the landlord's option, to any person reasonably believed by the landlord to be its owner if that tenant or other person pays the reasonable cost of storage and takes possession of the property not later than the date specified in the notice for taking possession.

(b) Where personal property is not released pursuant to subdivision (a) and the notice stated that the personal property would be sold at a public sale, the landlord shall release the personal property to the former tenant if he or she claims it prior to the time it is sold and pays the reasonable cost of storage, advertising, and sale incurred prior to the time the property is withdrawn from sale.

(c) Notwithstanding subdivision (a), the landlord shall release the personal property described in the notice to the former tenant and shall not require the former tenant to pay the cost of storage if the property remained in the dwelling and the former tenant or other person reasonably believed by the landlord to be its owner reclaims the property within two days of vacating the dwelling. **Leg.H.** Added Stats 1974 ch 331 §2. Amended Stats 2012 ch 560 §7 (AB 2521), effective January 1, 2013.

Prior Law: Former §1987, similar to present Lab C §2862, was repealed 1937.

§1988. Sale or other disposition of unreleased property

(a) If the personal property described in the notice is not released pursuant to Section 1987, it shall be sold at public sale by competitive bidding. However, if the landlord reasonably believes that the total resale value of the property not released is less than seven hundred dollars ($700), the landlord may retain the property for his or her own use or dispose of it in any manner. Nothing in this section shall be construed to preclude the landlord or tenant from bidding on the property at the public sale.

(b) Notice of the time and place of the public sale shall be given by publication pursuant to Section 6066 of the Government Code in a newspaper of general circulation published in the county where the sale is to be held. The last publication shall be not less than five days before the sale is to be held. The notice of the sale shall not be published before the last of the dates specified for taking possession of the property in any notice given pursuant to Section 1983. The notice of the sale shall describe the property to be sold in a manner reasonably adequate to permit the owner of the property to identify it. The notice may describe all or a portion of the property, but the limitation of liability provided by Section 1989 does not protect the landlord from any liability arising from the disposition of property not described in the notice, except that a trunk, valise, box, or other container which is locked, fastened, or tied in a manner which deters immediate access to its contents may be described as such without describing its contents.

(c) After deduction of the costs of storage, advertising, and sale, any balance of the proceeds of the sale which is not claimed by the former tenant or an owner other than such tenant shall be paid into the treasury of the county in which the sale took place not later than 30 days after the date of sale. The former tenant or other owner may claim the balance within one year from the date of payment to the county by making application to the county treasurer or other official designated by the county. If the county pays the balance or any part thereof to a claimant, neither the county nor any officer or employee thereof is liable to any other claimant as to the amount paid. **Leg.H.** Added Stats 1974 ch 331 §2. Amended Stats 1982 ch 811 §1; Stats 2012 ch 560 §8 (AB 2521), effective January 1, 2013.

Prior Law: Former §1988, similar to present Lab C §2863, was amended Code Amdts 1873-74 ch 612 §210 and repealed 1937.

§1989. Limitation of liability

(a) Notwithstanding subdivision (c) of Section 1981, where the landlord releases to the former tenant property which remains on the premises after a tenancy is terminated, the landlord is not liable with respect to that property to any person.

(b) Where the landlord releases property pursuant to Section 1987 to a person (other than the former tenant) reasonably believed by the landlord to be the owner of the property, the landlord is not liable with respect to that property to:

(1) Any person to whom notice was given pursuant to Section 1983; or

(2) Any person to whom notice was not given pursuant to Section 1983 unless such person proves that, prior to releasing the property, the landlord believed or reasonably should have believed that such person had an interest in the property and also that the landlord knew or should have known upon reasonable investigation the address of such person.

(c) Where property is disposed of pursuant to Section 1988, the landlord is not liable with respect to that property to:

(1) Any person to whom notice was given pursuant to Section 1983; or

(2) Any person to whom notice was not given pursuant to Section 1983 unless such person proves that, prior to disposing of the property pursuant to Section 1988, the landlord believed or reasonably should have believed that such person had an interest in the property and also that the landlord knew or should have known upon reasonable investigation the address of such person. **Leg.H.** Added Stats 1974 ch 331 §2.

Prior Law: Former §1989, similar to present Lab C §2864, was repealed 1937.

§1990. Assessment of storage costs

(a) Costs of storage which may be required to be paid under this chapter shall be assessed in the following manner:

(1) Where a former tenant claims property pursuant to Section 1987, he or she may be required to pay the reasonable costs of storage for all the personal property remaining on the premises at the termination of the tenancy which are unpaid at the time the claim is made.

(2) Where an owner other than the former tenant claims property pursuant to Section 1987, he or she may be required to pay the reasonable costs of storage for only the property in which he or she claims an interest.

(b) In determining the costs to be assessed under subdivision (a), the landlord shall not charge more than one person for the same costs.

(c) If the landlord stores the personal property on the premises, the cost of storage shall be the fair rental value of the space reasonably required for that storage for the term of the storage. Costs shall not be assessed if the former tenant reclaims property stored on the premises within two days of having vacated the premises. **Leg.H.** Added Stats 1974 ch 331 §2. Amended Stats 2012 ch 560 §9 (AB 2521), effective January 1, 2013.

Prior Law: Former §1990, similar to present Lab C §2865, was repealed 1937.

§1991. Notice combined with notice of belief of abandonment of leased real property

Where a notice of belief of abandonment is given to a lessee pursuant to Section 1951.3, the notice to the former tenant given pursuant to

Section 1983 may, but need not, be given at the same time as the notice of belief of abandonment even though the tenancy is not terminated until the end of the period specified in the notice of belief of abandonment. If the notices are so given, the notices may, but need not, be combined in one notice that contains all the information required by the sections under which the notices are given. **Leg.H.** Added Stats 1974 ch 331 §2.

Prior Law: Former §1991 repealed 1937. See Lab C §2866.

§1992. [Section repealed 1937]

Leg.H. Enacted Stats 1872. Repealed Stats 1937.

CHAPTER 5.5
DISPOSITION OF PROPERTY REMAINING ON PREMISES AT TERMINATION OF COMMERCIAL TENANCY

Applicability; Definitions. §1993.
Applicability of requirements of Sections 1982, 1987, and 1990. §1993.01.
Optional procedure for disposition of property; Inapplicability. §1993.02.
Notice requirement; Service. §1993.03.
Form and contents of notice. §1993.04.
Notice to person other than former tenant that personal property remains on premises. §1993.05.
Storage of personal property. §1993.06.
Public sale of property; Possibility of retention; Notice of sale; Proceeds. §1993.07.
Liability of landlord. §1993.08.
Construction with notice of belief of abandonment provisions. §1993.09.

§1993. Applicability; Definitions

This chapter shall only apply to commercial real property. As used in this chapter:

(a) "Commercial real property" has the meaning specified in subdivision (d) of Section 1954.26. For purposes of this chapter, commercial real property shall not include self-storage units.

(b) "Landlord" means any operator, keeper, lessor, or sublessor of any furnished or unfurnished premises for hire, or his or her agent or successor in interest.

(c) "Owner" means any person other than the landlord who has any right, title, or interest in property.

(d) "Premises" includes any common areas associated therewith.

(e) "Reasonable belief" means the actual knowledge or belief a prudent person would have without making an investigation, including any investigation of public records, except that, if the landlord has specific information indicating that an investigation would more probably than not reveal pertinent information and the cost of an investigation would be reasonable in relation to the probable value of the property involved, "reasonable belief" includes the actual knowledge or belief a prudent person would have if an investigation were made.

(f) "Records" means any material, regardless of the physical form, on which information is recorded or preserved by any means, including in written or spoken words, graphically depicted, printed, or electromagnetically transmitted. "Records" does not include publicly available directories containing information an individual has voluntarily consented to have publicly disseminated or listed, such as name, address, or telephone number.

(g) "Tenant" includes any lessee or sublessee of any commercial real property and its premises for hire. **Leg.H.** Added Stats 2008 ch 161 §2 (AB 2025), effective January 1, 2009. Amended Stats 2009 ch 134 §6 (AB 1094) (ch 134 prevails), effective January 1, 2010, ch 140 §29 (AB 1164), effective January 1, 2010.

§1993.01. Applicability of requirements of Sections 1982, 1987, and 1990

Notwithstanding Section 1980.5, the requirements of Sections 1982, 1987, and 1990 shall apply to property that is subject to this chapter. **Leg.H.** Added Stats 2008 ch 161 §2 (AB 2025), effective January 1, 2009.

§1993.02. Optional procedure for disposition of property; Inapplicability

(a) This chapter provides an optional procedure for the disposition of property that remains on the premises after a tenancy of commercial real property has terminated and the premises have been vacated by the tenant.

(b) This chapter does not apply if Section 1862.5, 2080.8, or 2080.9, or Article 2 (commencing with Section 2081) of Chapter 4 of Title 6, apply. This chapter does not apply to property that exists for the purpose of providing utility services and is owned by a public utility, whether or not that property is actually in operation to provide those utility services.

(c) This chapter does not apply to a manufactured home, as defined in Section 18007 of the Health and Safety Code, a mobilehome, as defined in Section 18008 of the Health and Safety Code, or a commercial coach, as defined in Section 18001.8 of the Health and Safety Code, including any attachments or contents, whether or not the manufactured home, mobilehome, or commercial coach is subject to registration under the Health and Safety Code.

(d) This chapter does not apply to the disposition of animals subject to Chapter 7 (commencing with Section 17001) of Part 1 of Division 9 of the Food and Agricultural Code.

(e) This chapter does not apply to residential property or self-storage units.

(f) If the requirements of this chapter are not satisfied, nothing in this chapter affects the rights and liabilities of the landlord, former tenant, or any other person. **Leg.H.** Added Stats 2008 ch 161 §2 (AB 2025), effective January 1, 2009. Amended Stats 2009 ch 140 §30 (AB 1164), effective January 1, 2010.

§1993.03. Notice requirement; Service

(a) If property remains on the premises after a tenancy has terminated and the premises have been vacated by the tenant, the landlord shall give written notice to the tenant and to any other person the landlord reasonably believes to be the owner of the property. If the property consists of records, the tenant shall be presumed to be the owner of the records for the purposes of this chapter.

(b) The notice shall describe the property in a manner reasonably adequate to permit the owner of the property to identify it. The notice may describe all or a portion of the property, but the limitation of liability provided by Section 1993.08 does not protect the landlord from any liability arising from the disposition of property not described in the notice, except that a trunk, valise, box, safe, vault, or other container that is locked, fastened, or tied in a manner that deters immediate access to its contents may be described as such without describing its contents. The notice shall advise the person to be notified that reasonable costs of storage may be charged before the property is returned, where the property may be claimed, and the date before which the claim must be made. The date specified in the notice shall be a date not less than 15 days after the notice is personally delivered or, if mailed, not less than 18 days after the notice is deposited in the mail.

(c) The notice shall be personally delivered to the person to be notified or sent by first-class mail, postage prepaid, to the person to be notified at his or her last known address and, if there is reason to believe that the notice sent to that address will not be received by that person, also to any other address known to the landlord where the person may reasonably be expected to receive the notice. If the notice is sent by mail to the former tenant, one copy shall be sent to the premises vacated by the tenant. **Leg.H.** Added Stats 2008 ch 161 §2 (AB 2025), effective January 1, 2009. Amended Stats 2009 ch 134 §7 (AB 1094) (ch 134 prevails), effective January 1, 2010, ch 140 §31 (AB 1164), effective January 1, 2010.

§1993.04. Form and contents of notice

(a) A notice given to the former tenant that is in substantially the following form satisfies the requirements of Section 1993.03:

Notice of Right to Reclaim Abandoned Property

To: _____
(Name of Former tenant)

_____
(Address of former tenant)

When you vacated the premises at _____,
(Address of premises, including room, if any)
the following personal property remained:

_____
(Insert description of the personal property)
You may claim this property at _____.

(Address where property may be claimed)

Unless you pay the reasonable cost of storage for all the above-described property, and take possession of the property which you claim, not later than (insert date not less than 15 days after notice is personally delivered or, if mailed, not less than 18 days after notice is deposited in the mail) this property may be disposed of pursuant to Section 1993.07 of the Civil Code.

(Insert here the statement required by subdivision (b) of this section)
Dated: _____ _____
(Signature of landlord)

_____
(Type or print name of landlord)

_____
(Telephone number of landlord)

_____
(Address of landlord)

(b) The notice set forth in subdivision (a) shall also contain one of the following statements:

(1) "If you fail to reclaim the property, it will be sold at a public sale after notice of the sale has been given by publication. You have the right to bid on the property at this sale. After the property is sold and the cost of storage, advertising, and sale is deducted, the remaining money will be paid over to the county. You may claim the remaining money at any time within one year after the county receives the money."

(2) "Because you were a commercial tenant and this property is believed to be worth less than either two thousand five hundred dollars ($2,500) or an amount equal to one month's rent for the premises you occupied, whichever is greater, it may be kept, sold, or destroyed without further notice if you fail to reclaim it within the time indicated above." **Leg.H.** Added Stats 2008 ch 161 §2 (AB 2025), effective January 1, 2009. Amended Stats 2009 ch 140 §32 (AB 1164), effective January 1, 2010; Stats 2018 ch 74 §2 (AB 2173), effective January 1, 2019.

§1993.05. Notice to person other than former tenant that personal property remains on premises

A notice in substantially the following form given to a person (other than the former tenant) the landlord reasonably believes to be the owner of personal property satisfies the requirements of Section 1993.03:

Notice of Right to Reclaim Abandoned Property

To: _____
(Name of owner)

_____
(Address of owner)

When _____ vacated the premises at
(Name of former tenant)
_____,
(Address of premises, including room, if any)
the following personal property remained:
_____
(insert description of the personal property)
You may claim this property at _____
_____.
(Address where property may be claimed)

Unless you pay the reasonable cost of storage for all of the above-described property, and take possession of the property that you claim, not later than _____ (insert date not less than 15 days after notice is personally delivered or, if mailed, not less than 18 days after notice is deposited in the mail) this property may be disposed of pursuant to Section 1993.07 of the Civil Code.

(Insert here the statement required by subdivision (b) of this section)
Dated: _____ _____
(Signature of landlord)

_____
(Type or print name of landlord)

_____
(Telephone number of landlord)

_____
(Address of landlord)

Leg.H. Added Stats 2008 ch 161 §2 (AB 2025), effective January 1, 2009. Amended Stats 2009 ch 140 §33 (AB 1164), effective January 1, 2010.

§1993.06. Storage of personal property

The personal property described in the notice shall either be left on the vacated premises or be stored by the landlord in a place of safekeeping until the landlord either releases the property pursuant to Section 1987 or disposes of the property pursuant to Section 1993.07. The landlord shall exercise reasonable care in storing the property, but he or she is not liable to the tenant or any other owner for any loss not caused by his or her deliberate or negligent act. **Leg.H.** Added Stats 2008 ch 161 §2 (AB 2025), effective January 1, 2009.

§1993.07. Public sale of property; Possibility of retention; Notice of sale; Proceeds

(a)(1) The property described in the notice that is not released pursuant to Section 1987 shall be sold at public sale by competitive bidding except that, if the landlord reasonably believes that the total resale value of the property is less than the threshold amount, the landlord may retain the property for his or her own use or dispose of it in any manner.

(2) For the purposes of this section, "threshold amount" means either two thousand five hundred dollars ($2,500) or an amount equal to one month's rent for the premises occupied by the tenant, whichever is greater.

(b)(1) Notice of the time and place of the public sale shall be given by publication pursuant to Section 6066 of the Government Code in a newspaper of general circulation published in the county where the sale is to be held.

(2) The last publication shall be not less than five days before the sale is to be held.

(3) The notice of the sale shall not be published before the last of the dates specified for taking possession of the property in any notice given pursuant to Section 1993.03.

(4) The notice of the sale shall describe the property to be sold in a manner reasonably adequate to permit the owner of the property to identify it.

(5) The notice may describe all or a portion of the property, but the limitation of liability provided by Section 1993.08 does not protect the landlord from any liability arising from the disposition of property not described in the notice, except that a trunk, valise, box, safe, vault, or other container that is locked, fastened, or tied in a manner that deters immediate access to its contents may be described as such without describing its contents.

(c)(1) After deduction of the costs of storage, advertising, and sale, any balance of the proceeds of the sale that is not claimed by the former tenant or an owner other than the tenant shall be paid into the treasury of the county in which the sale took place not later than 30 days after the date of sale.

(2) The former tenant or other owner may claim the balance within one year from the date of payment to the county by making application to the county treasurer or other official designated by the county.

(3) If the county pays the balance or any part thereof to a claimant, neither the county nor any officer or employee thereof shall be liable to any other claimant as to the amount paid.

(d) Nothing in this section precludes a landlord or tenant from bidding on the property at the public sale. **Leg.H.** Added Stats 2008 ch 161 §2 (AB 2025), effective January 1, 2009. Amended Stats 2009 ch 140 §34 (AB 1164), effective January 1, 2010; Stats 2018 ch 74 §3 (AB 2173), effective January 1, 2019.

§1993.08. Liability of landlord

(a) Notwithstanding subdivision (c) of Section 1993.02, if the landlord releases to the former tenant property that remains on the premises after a tenancy is terminated, the landlord shall not be liable with respect to that property to any person.

(b) If the landlord releases property pursuant to Section 1987 to a person, other than the former tenant, who is reasonably believed by the landlord to be the owner of the property, the landlord shall not be liable with respect to that property to any of the following persons:

(1) A person to whom notice was given pursuant to Section 1993.03.

(2) A person to whom notice was not given pursuant to Section 1993.03, unless the person proves that, prior to releasing the property, the landlord believed or reasonably should have believed that the person had an interest in the property and also that the landlord knew or should have known upon reasonable investigation the address of the person.

(c) If property is disposed of pursuant to Section 1993.07, the landlord shall not be liable with respect to that property to any of the following persons:

(1) A person to whom notice was given pursuant to Section 1993.03.

(2) A person to whom notice was not given pursuant to Section 1993.03, unless the person proves that, prior to disposing of the property pursuant to Section 1993.07, the landlord believed or reasonably should have believed that the person had an interest in the property and also that the landlord knew or should have known upon reasonable investigation the address of the person. **Leg.H.** Added Stats 2008 ch 161 §2 (AB 2025), effective January 1, 2009. Amended Stats 2009 ch 140 §35 (AB 1164), effective January 1, 2010.

§1993.09. Construction with notice of belief of abandonment provisions

If a notice of belief of abandonment is given to a lessee pursuant to Section 1951.3, the notice to the former tenant given pursuant to Section 1993.03 maybe given at the same time as the notice of belief of abandonment, even though the tenancy is not terminated until the end of the period specified in the notice of belief of abandonment. The notices may be combined in one notice that contains all the information required by the sections under which the notices are given. **Leg.H.** Added Stats 2008 ch 161 §2 (AB 2025), effective January 1, 2009. Amended Stats 2009 ch 140 §36 (AB 1164), effective January 1, 2010.

CHAPTER 6
ASSIGNMENT AND SUBLEASE

Article 1. General Provisions.
Article 2. Restrictions on Transfer.
Article 3. Breach and Remedies.

ARTICLE 1
General Provisions

Applicability of chapter. §1995.010.
Definitions. §1995.020.
Retroactive effect. §1995.030.

§1995.010. Applicability of chapter

This chapter applies to transfer of a tenant's interest in a lease of real property for other than residential purposes. **Leg.H.** Added Stats 1989 ch 982 §2.

§1995.020. Definitions

As used in this chapter:
(a) "Landlord" includes a tenant who is a sublandlord under a sublease.
(b) "Lease" means a lease or sublease of real property for other than residential purposes, and includes modifications and other agreements affecting a lease.
(c) "Restriction on transfer" means a provision in a lease that restricts the right of transfer of the tenant's interest in the lease.
(d) "Tenant" includes a subtenant or assignee.
(e) "Transfer" of a tenant's interest in a lease means an assignment, sublease, or other voluntary or involuntary transfer or encumbrance of all or part of a tenant's interest in the lease. **Leg.H.** Added Stats 1989 ch 982 §2.

§1995.030. Retroactive effect

Except as provided in Section 1995.270, this chapter applies to a lease executed before, on, or after January 1, 1990. **Leg.H.** Added Stats 1989 ch 982 §2.

ARTICLE 2
Restrictions on Transfer

Inclusion in lease. §1995.210.
Construction. §1995.220.
Prohibition of transfer. §1995.230.
Standard or condition of transfer. §1995.240.
Requirement of landlord's consent. §1995.250.
Standard for giving or withholding consent. §1995.260.
Legislative findings and declarations. §1995.270.

§1995.210. Inclusion in lease

(a) Subject to the limitations in this chapter, a lease may include a restriction on transfer of the tenant's interest in the lease.
(b) Unless a lease includes a restriction on transfer, a tenant's rights under the lease include unrestricted transfer of the tenant's interest in the lease. **Leg.H.** Added Stats 1989 ch 982 §2.

§1995.220. Construction

An ambiguity in a restriction on transfer of a tenant's interest in a lease shall be construed in favor of transferability. **Leg.H.** Added Stats 1989 ch 982 §2.

§1995.230. Prohibition of transfer

A restriction on transfer of a tenant's interest in a lease may absolutely prohibit transfer. **Leg.H.** Added Stats 1989 ch 982 §2.

§1995.240. Standard or condition of transfer

A restriction on transfer of a tenant's interest in a lease may provide that the transfer is subject to any express standard or condition, including, but not limited to, a provision that the landlord is entitled to some or all of any consideration the tenant receives from a transferee in excess of the rent under the lease. **Leg.H.** Added Stats 1989 ch 982 §2.

§1995.250. Requirement of landlord's consent

A restriction on transfer of a tenant's interest in a lease may require the landlord's consent for transfer subject to any express standard or condition for giving or withholding consent, including, but not limited to, either of the following:
(a) The landlord's consent may not be unreasonably withheld.
(b) The landlord's consent may be withheld subject to express standards or conditions. **Leg.H.** Added Stats 1989 ch 982 §2.

§1995.260. Standard for giving or withholding consent

If a restriction on transfer of the tenant's interest in a lease requires the landlord's consent for transfer but provides no standard for giving or withholding consent, the restriction on transfer shall be construed to include an implied standard that the landlord's consent may not be unreasonably withheld. Whether the landlord's consent has been unreasonably withheld in a particular case is a question of fact on which the tenant has the burden of proof. The tenant may satisfy the burden of proof by showing that, in response to the tenant's written request for a statement of reasons for withholding consent, the landlord has failed, within a reasonable time, to state in writing a reasonable objection to the transfer. **Leg.H.** Added Stats 1989 ch 982 §2.

§1995.270. Legislative findings and declarations

(a) The Legislature finds and declares:
(1) It is the public policy of the state and fundamental to the commerce and economic development of the state to enable and facilitate freedom of contract by the parties to commercial real property leases.
(2) The parties to commercial real property leases must be able to negotiate and conduct their affairs in reasonable reliance on the rights and protections given them under the laws of the state.
(3) Until the case of Kendall v. Ernest Pestana, Inc., 40 Cal. 3d 488 (1985), and its predecessor, Cohen v. Ratinoff, 147 Cal. App. 3d 321 (1983), the parties to commercial real property leases could reasonably rely on the law of the state to provide that if a lease restriction requires the landlord's consent for transfer of the tenant's interest in the lease but provides no standard for giving or withholding consent, the landlord's consent may be unreasonably withheld.
(4) The Kendall and Cohen decisions reversed the law on which parties to commercial real property leases executed before September 23, 1983, the date of the Cohen decision, could reasonably rely, thereby frustrating the expectations of the parties, with the result of impairing commerce and economic development.
(b) Section 1995.260 applies to a restriction on transfer executed on or after September 23, 1983. If a restriction on transfer executed before September 23, 1983, requires the landlord's consent for the tenant's transfer but provides no standard for giving or withholding consent, the landlord's consent may be unreasonably withheld. For purposes of this subdivision, if the terms of a restriction on transfer are fixed by an option or other agreement, the restriction on transfer is deemed to be executed on the date of execution of the option or other agreement. **Leg.H.** Added Stats 1989 ch 982 §2.

ARTICLE 3
Breach and Remedies

Remedies subject to lease provisions and applicable defenses. §1995.300.
Remedies for unreasonable withholding of consent to transfer interest in lease. §1995.310.
Remedies for transfer of tenant's interest in violation of restriction in lease. §1995.320.
Liability of transferee; Landlord's right to terminate transfer without terminating lease. §1995.330.
Application of lease provision restricting transfer. §1995.340.

§1995.300. Remedies subject to lease provisions and applicable defenses

A remedy provided by law for violation of the rights of the tenant or of the landlord concerning transfer of a tenant's interest in a lease, including a remedy provided in this article, is (a) subject to an express provision in the lease that affects the remedy and (b) subject to any applicable defense, whether legal or equitable, including, but not limited to, waiver and estoppel. **Leg.H.** Added Stats 1991 ch 67 §2 (SB 256).

§1995.310. Remedies for unreasonable withholding of consent to transfer interest in lease

If a restriction on transfer of a tenant's interest in a lease requires the landlord's consent for transfer subject to an express or implied standard that the landlord's consent may not be unreasonably withheld, and the landlord unreasonably withholds consent to a transfer in violation of the tenant's rights under the lease, in addition to any other remedies provided by law for breach of a lease, the tenant has all the remedies provided for breach of contract, including, but not limited to, either or both of the following:

(a) The right to contract damages caused by the landlord's breach.

(b) The right to terminate the lease. **Leg.H.** Added Stats 1991 ch 67 §2 (SB 256).

§1995.320. Remedies for transfer of tenant's interest in violation of restriction in lease

If a tenant transfers the tenant's interest in a lease in violation of a restriction on transfer of the tenant's interest in the lease, in addition to any other remedies provided by law for breach of a lease, the landlord has all the remedies provided for breach of contract, including, but not limited to, either or both of the following:

(a) The right to contract damages caused by the tenant's breach.

(b) The right to terminate the lease. **Leg.H.** Added Stats 1991 ch 67 §2 (SB 256).

§1995.330. Liability of transferee; Landlord's right to terminate transfer without terminating lease

(a) An assignee who receives or makes a transfer in violation of a restriction on transfer of a tenant's interest in a lease is jointly and severally liable with the tenant for contract damages under Section 1995.320. For this purpose, the provisions of Section 1951.2 applicable to a lessee apply to an assignee.

(b) The landlord's right to terminate a lease under Section 1995.320 includes the right to terminate a transfer without terminating the lease. If the landlord terminates a transfer without terminating the lease, the assignee or subtenant in possession is guilty of unlawful detainer and the landlord may obtain possession from the assignee or subtenant without terminating the right to possession of the tenant. For this purpose, the landlord may use the procedure provided in Chapter 4 (commencing with Section 1159) of Title 3 of Part 3 of the Code of Civil Procedure, with the changes necessary to make the procedure applicable to this subdivision. **Leg.H.** Added Stats 1991 ch 67 §2 (SB 256).

§1995.340. Application of lease provision restricting transfer

(a) Subject to subdivision (b), a restriction on transfer of a tenant's interest in a lease applies to a subsequent transfer by a tenant, an assignee, or a subtenant notwithstanding the landlord's consent to a prior transfer or the landlord's waiver of a standard or condition for a prior transfer.

(b) Subdivision (a) does not apply if either of the following conditions is satisfied:

(1) The lease provides expressly that the restriction on transfer is limited to the original tenant.

(2) The landlord states expressly in writing that the consent or waiver applies to a subsequent transfer. **Leg.H.** Added Stats 1991 ch 67 §2 (SB 256).

§§1996, 1997. [Sections repealed 1937]

Leg.H. Enacted Stats 1872. Repealed Stats 1937. See Lab C §§2920, 2921.

CHAPTER 7
USE RESTRICTIONS

Article 1. General Provisions.
Article 2. Use Restrictions.

ARTICLE 1
General Provisions

Application of chapter. §1997.010.
Definitions. §1997.020.
Use of restrictions prohibited by law. §1997.030.
Computation of amount of rental loss; Availability of remedy. §1997.040.
Leases to which chapter applies. §1997.050.

§1997.010. Application of chapter

This chapter applies to a restriction on use of leased property by a tenant under a lease of real property for other than residential purposes. **Leg.H.** Added Stats 1991 ch 67 §3 (SB 256).

§1997.020. Definitions

As used in this chapter:

(a) "Landlord" includes a tenant who is a sublandlord under a sublease.

(b) "Lease" means a lease or sublease of real property for other than residential purposes, and includes modifications and other agreements affecting a lease.

(c) "Restriction on use" means a provision in a lease that restricts the use of leased property by a tenant, whether by limiting use to a specified purpose, mandating use for a specified purpose, prohibiting use for a specified purpose, limiting or prohibiting a change in use, or otherwise.

(d) "Tenant" includes a subtenant or assignee. **Leg.H.** Added Stats 1991 ch 67 §3 (SB 256).

§1997.030. Use of restrictions prohibited by law

Nothing in this chapter authorizes a restriction on use that is otherwise prohibited by law. **Leg.H.** Added Stats 1991 ch 67 §3 (SB 256).

§1997.040. Computation of amount of rental loss; Availability of remedy

(a) For the purpose of subdivision (a) of Section 1951.2 (damages on termination for breach), the amount of rental loss that could be or could have been reasonably avoided is computed by taking into account any reasonable use of the leased property. However, if the lease contains a restriction on use that is enforceable under this chapter, the computation shall take into account the restricted use of the property except to the extent the tenant proves that under all the circumstances enforcement of the restriction would be unreasonable. The circumstances include, but are not limited to, those involving both the leased property and any building or complex in which it is located.

(b) The remedy described in Section 1951.4 (continuation of lease after breach and abandonment) is available notwithstanding the presence in the lease of a restriction on use of the leased property. The restriction on use applies under Section 1951.4 if it is enforceable under this chapter except to the extent the tenant proves that under all the circumstances enforcement of the restriction would be unreasonable. The circumstances include, but are not limited to, those involving both the leased property and any building or complex in which it is located. **Leg.H.** Added Stats 1991 ch 67 §3 (SB 256).

§1997.050. Leases to which chapter applies

Except as provided in Section 1997.270, this chapter applies to a lease executed before, on, or after January 1, 1992. **Leg.H.** Added Stats 1991 ch 67 §3 (SB 256).

ARTICLE 2
Use Restrictions

Restriction on use; Tenant's rights in absence of restriction. §1997.210.
Construction of ambiguity in restriction. §1997.220.
Absolute prohibition of change in use. §1997.230.
Express standard or condition for change in use. §1997.240.
Consent for change in use. §1997.250.
Construction of restriction requiring consent for change in use. §1997.260.
Leases to which construction of provision applies. §1997.270.

§1997.210. Restriction on use; Tenant's rights in absence of restriction

(a) Subject to the limitations in this chapter, a lease may include a restriction on use of leased property by a tenant.

(b) Unless the lease includes a restriction on use, a tenant's rights under a lease include any reasonable use of leased property. **Leg.H.** Added Stats 1991 ch 67 §3 (SB 256).

§1997.220. Construction of ambiguity in restriction

An ambiguity in a restriction on use of leased property by a tenant shall be construed in favor of unrestricted use. **Leg.H.** Added Stats 1991 ch 67 §3 (SB 256).

§1997.230. Absolute prohibition of change in use

A restriction on use of leased property by a tenant may absolutely prohibit a change in use. **Leg.H.** Added Stats 1991 ch 67 §3 (SB 256).

§1997.240. Express standard or condition for change in use

A restriction on use of leased property by a tenant may provide that a change in use is subject to any express standard or condition. **Leg.H.** Added Stats 1991 ch 67 §3 (SB 256).

§1997.250. Consent for change in use

A restriction on use of leased property by a tenant may require the landlord's consent for a change in use subject to any express standard or condition for giving or withholding consent, including, but not limited to, either of the following:

(a) The landlord's consent may not be unreasonably withheld.

(b) The landlord's consent may be withheld subject to express standards or conditions. **Leg.H.** Added Stats 1991 ch 67 §3 (SB 256).

§1997.260. Construction of restriction requiring consent for change in use

If a restriction on use of leased property by a tenant requires the landlord's consent for a change in use but provides no standard for giving or withholding consent, the restriction shall be construed to include an implied standard that the landlord's consent may not be unreasonably withheld. Whether the landlord's consent has been unreasonably withheld in a particular case is a question of fact on which the tenant has the burden of proof. The tenant may satisfy the burden of proof by showing that, in response to the tenant's written request for a statement of reasons for withholding consent, the landlord has failed, within a reasonable time, to state in writing a reasonable objection to the change in use. **Leg.H.** Added Stats 1991 ch 67 §3 (SB 256).

§1997.270. Leases to which construction of provision applies

(a) Section 1997.260 applies to a restriction on use executed on or after January 1, 1992. If a restriction on use executed before January 1, 1992, requires the landlord's consent for a change in use of leased premises by a tenant, but provides no standard for giving or withholding consent, the landlord has sole and absolute discretion to give or withhold consent.

(b) For purposes of this section, if the terms of a restriction on change in use are fixed by an option or other agreement, the restriction on change in use is deemed to be executed on the date of execution of the option or other agreement. **Leg.H.** Added Stats 1991 ch 67 §3 (SB 256).

TITLE 6
SERVICE

Chapter 2. Particular Employments.
Chapter 3. Service Without Employment.
Chapter 4. Lost and Unclaimed Property.

CHAPTER 1
SERVICE WITH EMPLOYMENT [REPEALED]

CHAPTER 2
PARTICULAR EMPLOYMENTS

Article 2. Agents.
Article 3. Factors.

ARTICLE 1
Master and Servant [Repealed]

ARTICLE 2
Agents

Agent to conform to authority. §2019.
Must keep principal informed. §2020.
Collecting agent. §2021.
Responsibility of sub-agent. §2022.

§2019. Agent to conform to authority

An agent must not exceed the limits of his actual authority, as defined by the title on agency. **Leg.H.** Enacted 1872.

§2020. Must keep principal informed

An agent must use ordinary diligence to keep his principal informed of his acts in the course of the agency. **Leg.H.** Enacted 1872.

§2021. Collecting agent

An agent employed to collect a negotiable instrument must collect it promptly, and take all measures necessary to charge the parties thereto, in case of its dishonor; and, if it is a bill of exchange, must present it for acceptance with reasonable diligence. **Leg.H.** Enacted 1872.

§2022. Responsibility of sub-agent

A mere agent of an agent is not responsible as such to the principal of the latter. **Leg.H.** Enacted 1872.

ARTICLE 3
Factors

Factor, defined. §2026.
Obedience required from factor. §2027.
Sales on credit. §2028.
Liability of factor under guaranty commission. §2029.
Factor cannot relieve himself from liability. §2030.

§2026. Factor, defined

A factor is an agent who, in the pursuit of an independent calling, is employed by another to sell property for him, and is vested by the latter with the possession or control of the property, or authorized to receive payment therefor from the purchaser. **Leg.H.** Enacted 1872.

§2027. Obedience required from factor

A factor must obey the instructions of his principal to the same extent as any other employee, notwithstanding any advances he may have made to his principal upon the property consigned to him, except that if the principal forbids him to sell at the market price, he may, nevertheless, sell for his reimbursement, after giving to his principal reasonable notice of his intention to do so, and of the time and place of sale, and proceeding in all respects as a pledgee. **Leg.H.** Enacted 1872.

§2028. Sales on credit

A factor may sell property consigned to him on such credit as is usual; but, having once agreed with the purchaser upon the term of credit, may not extend it. **Leg.H.** Enacted 1872.

§2029. Liability of factor under guaranty commission

A factor who charges his principal with a guaranty commission upon a sale, thereby assumes absolutely to pay the price when it falls due, as if it were a debt of his own, and not as a mere guarantor for the purchaser; but he does not thereby assume any additional responsibility for the safety of his remittance of the proceeds. **Leg.H.** Enacted 1872.

§2030. Factor cannot relieve himself from liability

A factor who receives property for sale, under a general agreement or usage to guarantee the sales or the remittance of the proceeds, cannot relieve himself from responsibility therefor without the consent of his principal. **Leg.H.** Enacted 1872.

ARTICLE 4
Shipmasters [Repealed]

§§2034–2044. [Sections repealed]

ARTICLE 5
Mates and Seamen [Repealed]

§§2048–2066. [Sections repealed]

ARTICLE 6
Ships' Managers [Repealed]

§§2070–2072. [Sections repealed]

CHAPTER 3
SERVICE WITHOUT EMPLOYMENT

Article 1. Voluntary Interference with Property.
Article 2. Duty to Prospective Purchaser of Real Property.

ARTICLE 1
Voluntary Interference with Property

Voluntary interference with property. §2078.

§2078. Voluntary interference with property

One who officiously, and without the consent of the real or apparent owner of a thing, takes it into his possession for the purpose of rendering a service about it, must complete such service, and use ordinary care, diligence, and reasonable skill about the same. He is not entitled to any compensation for his service or expenses, except that he may deduct actual and necessary expenses incurred by him about such service from any profits which his service has caused the thing to acquire for its owner, and must account to the owner for the residue. **Leg.H.** Enacted 1872.

ARTICLE 2
Duty to Prospective Purchaser of Real Property

Duty of real estate broker to make visual inspection; Disclosure of material facts. §2079.

Application of provisions to leases and sales contracts. §2079.1.

Standard of care. §2079.2.

Inspection of inaccessible areas; Inspection of unit in planned development, condominium, or stock cooperative. §2079.3.

Limitation of actions. §2079.4.

Duty of buyer or prospective buyer. §2079.5.

Nonapplication of article to specified sales. §2079.6.

Provision of information concerning common environmental hazards affecting real property. §2079.7.

Exception to requirement regarding disclosures concerning geologic and seismic hazards in general. §2079.8.

Effect of delivery of Commercial Property Owner's Guide to Earthquake Safety. §2079.9.

Informational booklets about statewide home energy rating program and water conservation; Delivery to buyer. §2079.10.

Notice regarding gas and hazardous liquid transmission pipelines. §2079.10.5.

Real property disclosure; Registered sex offenders. §2079.10a.

Consumer information publications as in public domain; Availability of safety guide at cost. §2079.11.

Legislative findings and declarations. §2079.12.

Definitions. §2079.13.

Provision of disclosure form to buyer and seller; Acknowledgment of receipt. §2079.14.

Party's refusal to sign acknowledgment of receipt. §2079.15.

Contents of disclosure form. §2079.16.

Disclosure of exclusive or dual agency; Confirmation of relationship. §2079.17.

Payment of compensation; Effect on determination of particular agency relationship. §2079.19.

Selection of specific form of agency relationship as condition of employment. §2079.20.

Nondisclosure responsibilities of dual agents. §2079.21.

Combined seller's and buyer's agent. §2079.22.

Time for modification of agency contract; Imposing obligations to defend or indemnify lender or auction company. §2079.23.

Construction of article; Breach of fiduciary duty or duty of disclosure. §2079.24.

Applicability of Section 1102.1(d) to article. §2079.25.

§2079. Duty of real estate broker to make visual inspection; Disclosure of material facts

(a) It is the duty of a real estate broker or salesperson, licensed under Division 4 (commencing with Section 10000) of the Business and Professions Code, to a prospective buyer of residential real property improved with one to four dwelling units or a manufactured home as defined in Section 18007 of the Health and Safety Code, to conduct a reasonably competent and diligent visual inspection of the property offered for sale and to disclose to that prospective buyer all facts materially affecting the value or desirability of the property that an investigation would reveal, if that broker has a written contract with the seller to find or obtain a buyer or is a broker who acts in cooperation with that broker to find and obtain a buyer.

(b) It is the duty of a real estate broker or salesperson, licensed under Division 4 (commencing with Section 10000) of the Business and Professions Code, to comply with this section and any regulations imposing standards of professional conduct adopted pursuant to Section 10080 of the Business and Professions Code with reference to Sections 10176 and 10177 of the Business and Professions Code. **Leg.H.** Added Stats 1985 ch 223 §2. Amended Stats 1994 ch 339 §1; Stats 1996 ch 812 §2 (AB 2221); Stats 2018 ch 907 §30 (AB 1289), effective January 1, 2019; Stats 2019 ch 310 §8 (AB 892), effective January 1, 2020.

Prior Law: Former §2079, similar to present H & N C §534, was enacted 1872, amended Code Amdts 1873–74 ch 612 §212, and repealed Stats 1937 ch 368 (H & N C §10001).

§2079.1. Application of provisions to leases and sales contracts

The provisions of this article relating sale transactions of residential real property comprising one to four dwelling units apply with equal force to leases of that property that include an option to purchase, ground leases of land on which one to four dwelling units have been constructed, or real property sales contracts, as defined in Section 2985, for that property. **Leg.H.** Added Stats 1985 ch 223 §2.

§2079.2. Standard of care

The standard of care owed by a broker under this article is the degree of care that a reasonably prudent real estate licensee would exercise and is measured by the degree of knowledge through education, experience, and examination, required to obtain a license under Division 4 (commencing with Section 10000) of the Business and Professions Code. **Leg.H.** Added Stats 1985 ch 223 §2.

§2079.3. Inspection of inaccessible areas; Inspection of unit in planned development, condominium, or stock cooperative

The inspection to be performed pursuant to this article does not include or involve an inspection of areas that are reasonably and normally inaccessible to this type of an inspection, nor an affirmative inspection of areas off the site of the subject property or public records or permits concerning the title or use of the property, and, if the property comprises a unit in a planned development as defined in Section 11003 of the Business and Professions Code, a condominium as defined in Section 783, or a stock cooperative as defined in Section 11003.2 of the Business and Professions Code, does not include an inspection of more than the unit offered for sale, if the seller or the broker complies with the provisions of Sections 4525 to 4580, inclusive. **Leg.H.** Added Stats 1985 ch 223 §2. Amended Stats 1994 ch 339 §2; Stats 2012 ch 181 §38 (AB 806), effective January 1, 2013, operative January 1, 2014.

§2079.4. Limitation of actions

In no event shall the time for commencement of legal action for breach of duty imposed by this article exceed two years from the date of possession, which means the date of recordation, the date of close of escrow, or the date of occupancy, whichever occurs first. **Leg.H.** Added Stats 1985 ch 223 §2.

§2079.5. Duty of buyer or prospective buyer

Nothing in this article relieves a buyer or prospective buyer of the duty to exercise reasonable care to protect himself or herself, including those facts which are known to or within the diligent attention and observation of the buyer or prospective buyer. **Leg.H.** Added Stats 1985 ch 223 §2.

§2079.6. Nonapplication of article to specified sales

This article does not apply to sales which are required to be preceded by the furnishing, to a prospective buyer, of a copy of a public report pursuant to Section 11018.1 or Section 11234 of the Business and Professions Code and sales that can be made without a public report pursuant to Section 11010.4 of the Business and Professions Code, unless the property has been previously occupied. **Leg.H.** Added Stats 1988 ch 274 §1. Amended Stats 2015 ch 88 §3 (AB 905), effective January 1, 2016; Stats 2018 ch 907 §31 (AB 1289), effective January 1, 2019.

§2079.7. Provision of information concerning common environmental hazards affecting real property

(a) If a consumer information booklet described in Section 10084.1 of the Business and Professions Code is delivered to a buyer in connection with the sale of real property, including property specified in Section 1102 of the Civil Code, or manufactured housing, as defined in Section 18007 of the Health and Safety Code, a seller or broker is not required to provide additional information concerning, and the information shall be deemed to be adequate to inform the buyer regarding, common environmental hazards, as described in the booklet, that can affect real property.

(b) Notwithstanding subdivision (a), nothing in this section either increases or decreases the duties, if any, of sellers or brokers, including, but not limited to, the duties of a seller or broker under this article, Article 1.5 (commencing with Section 1102) of Chapter 2 of Title 4 of Part 4 of Division 2, or Section 78700 of the Health and Safety Code, or alters the duty of a seller or broker to disclose the existence of known environmental hazards on or affecting the real property. **Leg.H.** Added Stats 1989 ch 969 §2. Amended Stats 2018 ch 907 §32 (AB 1289), effective January 1, 2019; Stats 2022 ch 258 §5 (AB 2327), effective January 1, 2023, operative January 1, 2024.

§2079.8. Exception to requirement regarding disclosures concerning geologic and seismic hazards in general

(a) If a Homeowner's Guide to Earthquake Safety described in Section 10149 of the Business and Professions Code is delivered to a buyer in connection with the sale of real property, including property specified in

Section 1102 or under Chapter 7.5 (commencing with Section 2621) of Division 2 of the Public Resources Code, a seller or broker is not required to provide additional information concerning, and the information shall be deemed to be adequate to inform the buyer regarding, geologic and seismic hazards, in general, as described in the guide, that may affect real property and mitigating measures that the buyer or seller might consider.

(b) Notwithstanding subdivision (a), nothing in this section increases or decreases the duties, if any, of sellers or brokers, including, but not limited to, the duties of a seller or broker under this article, Article 1.5 (commencing with Section 1102) of Chapter 2 of Title 4 of Part 4 of Division 2, or under Chapter 7.5 (commencing with Section 2621) of Division 2 of the Public Resources Code, or alters the duty of a seller or broker to disclose the existence of known hazards on or affecting the real property. **Leg.H.** Added Stats 1990 ch 1499 §2 (AB 2959). Amended Stats 1991 ch 550 §2 (AB 29); Stats 2018 ch 907 §33 (AB 1289), effective January 1, 2019.

§2079.9. Effect of delivery of Commercial Property Owner's Guide to Earthquake Safety

(a) If a Commercial Property Owner's Guide to Earthquake Safety described in Section 10147 of the Business and Professions Code is delivered to a buyer in connection with the sale of real property, including property specified in Section 1102 or under Chapter 7.5 (commencing with Section 2621) of Division 2 of the Public Resources Code, a seller or broker is not required to provide additional information concerning, and the information shall be deemed to be adequate to inform the buyer regarding, geologic and seismic hazards, in general, as described in the guide, that may affect real property and mitigating measures that the buyer or seller might consider.

(b) Notwithstanding subdivision (a), nothing in this section increases or decreases the duties, if any, of sellers, their real estate brokers or agents under this article or under Chapter 7.5 (commencing with Section 2621) or Chapter 7.8 (commencing with Section 2690) of Division 2 of the Public Resources Code, or alters the duty of a seller, agent, or broker to disclose the existence of known hazards on or affecting the real property. **Leg.H.** Added Stats 1991 ch 859 §2 (AB 1968). Amended Stats 2018 ch 907 §34 (AB 1289), effective January 1, 2019.

§2079.10. Informational booklets about statewide home energy rating program and water conservation; Delivery to buyer

(a) If the informational booklet published pursuant to Section 25402.9 of the Public Resources Code, concerning the statewide home energy rating program adopted pursuant to Section 25942 of the Public Resources Code, is delivered to a buyer in connection with the sale of real property, including, but not limited to, property specified in Section 1102, manufactured homes as defined in Section 18007 of the Health and Safety Code, and property subject to Chapter 7.5 (commencing with Section 2621) of Division 2 of the Public Resources Code, the seller or broker is not required to provide information additional to that contained in the booklet concerning home energy ratings, and the information in the booklet shall be deemed to be adequate to inform the buyer about the existence of a statewide home energy rating program.

(b) Notwithstanding subdivision (a), nothing in this section alters any existing duty of the seller or broker under any other law including, but not limited to, the duties of a seller or broker under this article, Article 1.5 (commencing with Section 1102) of Chapter 2 of Title 4 of Part 4 of Division 2 of the Civil Code, or Chapter 7.5 (commencing with Section 2621) of Division 2 of the Public Resources Code, to disclose information concerning the existence of a home energy rating program affecting the real property.

(c) If the informational booklet or materials described in Section 375.5 of the Water Code concerning water conservation and water conservation programs are delivered to a buyer in connection with the sale of real property, including property described in subdivision (a), the seller or broker is not required to provide information concerning water conservation and water conservation programs that is additional to that contained in the booklet or materials, and the information in the booklet or materials shall be deemed to be adequate to inform the buyer about water conservation and water conservation programs. **Leg.H.** Added Stats 1992 ch 769 §2 (SB 1207). Amended Stats 2004 ch 111 §1 (AB 2470); Stats 2018 ch 907 §35 (AB 1289), effective January 1, 2019.

§2079.10.5. Notice regarding gas and hazardous liquid transmission pipelines

(a) Every contract for the sale of single-family residential real property entered into on or after July 1, 2013, shall contain, in not less than 8-point type, a notice as specified below:

NOTICE REGARDING GAS AND HAZARDOUS LIQUID TRANSMISSION PIPELINES

This notice is being provided simply to inform you that information about the general location of gas and hazardous liquid transmission pipelines is available to the public via the National Pipeline Mapping System (NPMS) Internet Web site maintained by the United States Department of Transportation at http://www.npms.phmsa.dot.gov/. To seek further information about possible transmission pipelines near the property, you may contact your local gas utility or other pipeline operators in the area. Contact information for pipeline operators is searchable by ZIP Code and county on the NPMS Internet Web site.

(b) Upon delivery of the notice to the buyer of the real property, the seller or broker is not required to provide information in addition to that contained in the notice regarding gas and hazardous liquid transmission pipelines in subdivision (a). The information in the notice shall be deemed to be adequate to inform the buyer about the existence of a statewide database of the locations of gas and hazardous liquid transmission pipelines and information from the database regarding those locations.

(c) Nothing in this section shall alter any existing duty under any other statute or decisional law imposed upon the seller or broker, including, but not limited to, the duties of a seller or broker under this article, or the duties of a seller or broker under Article 1.5 (commencing with Section 1102) of Chapter 2 of Title 4 of Part 4 of Division 2. **Leg.H.** Added Stats 2012 ch 91 §1 (AB 1511), effective January 1, 2013. Amended Stats 2018 ch 907 §36 (AB 1289), effective January 1, 2019.

§2079.10a. Real property disclosure; Registered sex offenders

(a) Every lease or rental agreement for single-family residential real property entered into on or after July 1, 1999, any leasehold interest in real property consisting of multiunit residential property with more than four dwelling units entered into after that date, and every contract for the sale of residential real property comprised of one to four dwelling units entered into on or after that date, shall contain, in not less than 8-point type, a notice as specified in paragraph (1), (2), or (3).

(1) A contract entered into by the parties on or after July 1, 1999, and before September 1, 2005, shall contain the following notice:

Notice: The California Department of Justice, sheriff's departments, police departments serving jurisdictions of 200,000 or more, and many other local law enforcement authorities maintain for public access a database of the locations of persons required to register pursuant to subdivision (a) of Section 290.4 of the Penal Code. The database is updated on a quarterly basis and is a source of information about the presence of these individuals in any neighborhood. The Department of Justice also maintains a Sex Offender Identification Line through which inquiries about individuals may be made. This is a "900" telephone service. Callers shall have specific information about individuals they are checking. Information regarding neighborhoods is not available through the "900" telephone service.

(2) A contract entered into by the parties on or after September 1, 2005, and before April 1, 2006, shall contain either the notice specified in paragraph (1) or the notice specified in paragraph (3).

(3) A contract entered into by the parties on or after April 1, 2006, shall contain the following notice:

Notice: Pursuant to Section 290.46 of the Penal Code, information about specified registered sex offenders is made available to the public via an Internet Web site maintained by the Department of Justice at www.meganslaw.ca.gov. Depending on an offender's criminal history, this information will include either the address at which the offender resides or the community of residence and ZIP Code in which the offender resides.

(b) Subject to subdivision (c), upon delivery of the notice to the lessee or buyer of the real property, the lessor, seller, or broker is not required to provide information in addition to that contained in the notice regarding the proximity of registered sex offenders. The information in the notice shall be deemed to be adequate to inform the lessee or buyer about the existence of a statewide database of the locations of registered sex offenders and information from the database regarding those locations.

The information in the notice shall not give rise to any cause of action against the disclosing party by a registered sex offender.

(c) Notwithstanding subdivisions (a) and (b), nothing in this section shall alter any existing duty of the lessor, seller, or broker under any other statute or decisional law including, but not limited to, the duties of a lessor, seller, or broker under this article, or the duties of a seller or broker under Article 1.5 (commencing with Section 1102) of Chapter 2 of Title 4 of Part 4 of Division 2. **Leg.H.** Added Stats 1998 ch 645 §1 (SB 1989). Amended Stats 1999 ch 876 §4 (AB 248); Stats 2005 ch 722 §1 (AB 1323), effective October 7, 2005; Stats 2018 ch 907 §37 (AB 1289), effective January 1, 2019.

2005 Note: The notice concerning sex offender information required by Section 2079.10a of the Civil Code is not expected to change immediately upon the effective date of this act or immediately upon the notification to the Secretary of State pursuant to Section 290.47 of the Penal Code, as added by this act. It is expected that forms accompanying real estate transactions may reflect the notice in the prior law for a reasonable period following those dates. Stats 2005 ch 722 (AB 1323) §12(c).

§2079.11. Consumer information publications as in public domain; Availability of safety guide at cost

(a) Except as provided in subdivision (b), to the extent permitted by law, the consumer information publications referred to in this article, including, but not limited to, the information booklets described in Section 10084.1 of the Business and Professions Code and Section 25402.9 of the Public Resources Code, shall be in the public domain and freely available.

(b) Notwithstanding subdivision (a), the Seismic Safety Commission's Homeowner's Guide to Earthquake Safety, published pursuant to Section 10149 of the Business and Professions Code, shall be made available to the public at cost and for reproduction at no cost to any vendor who wishes to publish the guide, provided the vendor agrees to submit the guide to the commission prior to publication for content approval. **Leg.H.** Added Stats 1994 ch 66 §1 (SB 1229). Amended Stats 1998 ch 65 §4 (AB 1195), effective June 9, 1998, operative June 1, 1998.

§2079.12. Legislative findings and declarations

(a) The Legislature hereby finds and declares all of the following:

(1) That the imprecision of terms in the opinion rendered in Easton v Strassburger, 152 Cal. App. 3d 90, and the absence of a comprehensive declaration of duties, standards, and exceptions, has caused insurers to modify professional liability coverage of real estate licensees and has caused confusion among real estate licensees as to the manner of performing the duty ascribed to them by the court.

(2) That it is necessary to resolve and make precise these issues in an expeditious manner.

(3) That it is desirable to facilitate the issuance of professional liability insurance as a resource for aggrieved members of the public.

(4) That Sections 2079 to 2079.6, inclusive, of this article should be construed as a definition of the duty of care found to exist by the holding of Easton v Strassburger, 152 Cal. App. 3d 90, and the manner of its discharge, and is declarative of the common law regarding this duty. However, nothing in this section is intended to affect the court's ability to interpret Sections 2079 to 2079.6, inclusive.

(b) It is the intent of the Legislature to codify and make precise the holding of Easton v Strassburger, 152 Cal. App. 3d 90. It is not the intent of the Legislature to modify or restrict existing duties owed by real estate licensees. **Leg.H.** Added Stats 1995 ch 428 §1 (SB 467). Amended Stats 1996 ch 124 §7 (AB 3470) (ch 476 prevails), ch 476 §1 (AB 2935).

§2079.13. Definitions

As used in this section and Sections 2079.7 and 2079.14 to 2079.24, inclusive, the following terms have the following meanings:

(a) "Agent" means a person acting under provisions of Title 9 (commencing with Section 2295) in a real property transaction, and includes a person who is licensed as a real estate broker under Chapter 3 (commencing with Section 10130) of Part 1 of Division 4 of the Business and Professions Code, and under whose license a listing is executed or an offer to purchase is obtained.

The agent in the real property transaction bears responsibility for that agent's salespersons or broker associates who perform as agents of the agent. When a salesperson or broker associate owes a duty to any principal, or to any buyer or seller who is not a principal, in a real property transaction, that duty is equivalent to the duty owed to that party by the broker for whom the salesperson or broker associate functions.

(b) "Buyer" means a transferee in a real property transaction, and includes a person who executes an offer to purchase real property from a seller through an agent, or who seeks the services of an agent in more than a casual, transitory, or preliminary manner, with the object of entering into a real property transaction. "Buyer" includes a vendee or lessee of real property.

(c) "Commercial real property" means all real property in the state, except (1) single-family residential real property, (2) dwelling units made subject to Chapter 2 (commencing with Section 1940) of Title 5, (3) a mobilehome, as defined in Section 798.3, (4) vacant land, or (5) a recreational vehicle, as defined in Section 799.29.

(d) "Dual agent" means an agent acting, either directly or through a salesperson or broker associate, as agent for both the seller and the buyer in a real property transaction.

(e) "Listing agreement" means a written contract between a seller of real property and an agent, by which the agent has been authorized to sell the real property or to find or obtain a buyer, including rendering other services for which a real estate license is required to the seller pursuant to the terms of the agreement.

(f) "Seller's agent" means a person who has obtained a listing of real property to act as an agent for compensation.

(g) "Listing price" is the amount expressed in dollars specified in the listing for which the seller is willing to sell the real property through the seller's agent.

(h) "Offering price" is the amount expressed in dollars specified in an offer to purchase for which the buyer is willing to buy the real property.

(i) "Offer to purchase" means a written contract executed by a buyer acting through a buyer's agent that becomes the contract for the sale of the real property upon acceptance by the seller.

(j) "Real property" means any estate specified by subdivision (1) or (2) of Section 761 in property, and includes (1) single-family residential property, (2) multiunit residential property with more than four dwelling units, (3) commercial real property, (4) vacant land, (5) a ground lease coupled with improvements, or (6) a manufactured home as defined in Section 18007 of the Health and Safety Code, or a mobilehome as defined in Section 18008 of the Health and Safety Code, when offered for sale or sold through an agent pursuant to the authority contained in Section 10131.6 of the Business and Professions Code.

(k) "Real property transaction" means a transaction for the sale of real property in which an agent is retained by a buyer, seller, or both a buyer and seller to act in that transaction, and includes a listing or an offer to purchase.

(*l*) "Single-family residential property" or "single-family residential real property" means any of the following:

(1) Real property improved with one to four dwelling units, including a leasehold exceeding one year's duration.

(2) A unit in a residential stock cooperative, condominium, or planned unit development.

(3) A mobilehome or manufactured home when offered for sale or sold through a real estate broker pursuant to Section 10131.6 of the Business and Professions Code.

(m) "Sell," "sale," or "sold" refers to a transaction for the transfer of real property from the seller to the buyer and includes exchanges of real property between the seller and buyer, transactions for the creation of a real property sales contract within the meaning of Section 2985, and transactions for the creation of a leasehold exceeding one year's duration.

(n) "Seller" means the transferor in a real property transaction and includes an owner who lists real property with an agent, whether or not a transfer results, or who receives an offer to purchase real property of which they are the owner from an agent on behalf of another. "Seller" includes both a vendor and a lessor of real property.

(o) "Buyer's agent" means an agent who represents a buyer in a real property transaction.

(p) "buyer-broker representation agreement" means a written contract between a buyer of real property and a buyer's agent by which the buyer's agent has been authorized by the buyer to provide services set forth in subdivision (a) of Section 10131 of the Business and Professions Code for or on behalf of the buyer for which a real estate license is required pursuant to the terms of the contract. Leg.H. Added Stats 1995 ch 428 §2 (SB 467). Amended Stats 2014 ch 200 §2 (SB

1171), effective January 1, 2015; Stats 2016 ch 125 §1 (AB 1750), effective January 1, 2017; Stats 2017 ch 561 §18 (AB 1516), effective January 1, 2018; Stats 2018 ch 907 §38 (AB 1289), effective January 1, 2019; Stats 2019 ch 310 §9 (AB 892), effective January 1, 2020; Stats 2024 ch 516 §3 (AB 2992), effective January 1, 2025.

§2079.14. Provision of disclosure form to buyer and seller; Acknowledgement of receipt

(a) A copy of the disclosure form specified in Section 2079.16 shall be provided in a real property transaction as follows:

(1) The seller's agent, if any, shall provide the disclosure form to the seller before entering into the listing agreement.

(2) The buyer's agent shall provide the disclosure form to the buyer as soon as practicable before execution of **a buyer-broker representation agreement and execution of** the buyer's offer to purchase. If the offer to purchase is not prepared by the buyer's agent, the buyer's agent shall present the disclosure form to the buyer not later than the next business day after receiving the offer to purchase from the buyer.

(b) The agent providing the disclosure form specified in Section 2079.16 shall obtain a signed acknowledgment of receipt from the buyer or seller except as provided in Section 2079.15. **Leg.H.** Added Stats 1995 ch 428 §3 (SB 467). Amended Stats 2018 ch 907 §39 (AB 1289), effective January 1, 2019; Stats 2019 ch 310 §10 (AB 892), effective January 1, 2020; Stats 2024 ch 516 §4 (AB 2992), effective January 1, 2025.

§2079.15. Party's refusal to sign acknowledgment of receipt

In any circumstance in which the seller or buyer refuses to sign an acknowledgment of receipt pursuant to Section 2079.14, the agent shall set forth, sign, and date a written declaration of the facts of the refusal. **Leg.H.** Added Stats 1995 ch 428 §4 (SB 467). Amended Stats 2018 ch 907 §40 (AB 1289), effective January 1, 2019.

§2079.16. Contents of disclosure form

The disclosure form required by Section 2079.14 shall have Sections 2079.13 to 2079.24, inclusive, excluding this section, printed on the back, and on the front of the disclosure form the following shall appear:

DISCLOSURE REGARDING REAL ESTATE AGENCY RELATIONSHIP
(As required by the Civil Code)

When you enter into a discussion with a real estate agent regarding a real estate transaction, you should from the outset understand what type of agency relationship or representation you wish to have with the agent in the transaction.

SELLER'S AGENT

A Seller's agent under a listing agreement with the Seller acts as the agent for the Seller only. A Seller's agent or a subagent of that agent has the following affirmative obligations:

To the Seller:
A fiduciary duty of utmost care, integrity, honesty, and loyalty in dealings with the Seller.

To the Buyer and the Seller:
(a) Diligent exercise of reasonable skill and care in performance of the agent's duties.
(b) A duty of honest and fair dealing and good faith.
(c) A duty to disclose all facts known to the agent materially affecting the value or desirability of the property that are not known to, or within the diligent attention and observation of, the parties.

An agent is not obligated to reveal to either party any confidential information obtained from the other party that does not involve the affirmative duties set forth above.

BUYER'S AGENT

A Buyer's agent can, with a Buyer's consent, agree to act as agent for the Buyer only. **This includes a Buyer's agent under a buyer-broker representation agreement with the Buyer.** In these situations, the agent is not the Seller's agent, even if by agreement the agent may receive compensation for services rendered, either in full or in part from the Seller. An agent acting only for a Buyer has the following affirmative obligations:

To the Buyer:
A fiduciary duty of utmost care, integrity, honesty, and loyalty in dealings with the Buyer.

To the Buyer and the Seller:
(a) Diligent exercise of reasonable skill and care in performance of the agent's duties.
(b) A duty of honest and fair dealing and good faith.
(c) A duty to disclose all facts known to the agent materially affecting the value or desirability of the property that are not known to, or within the diligent attention and observation of, the parties. An agent is not obligated to reveal to either party any confidential information obtained from the other party that does not involve the affirmative duties set forth above.

AGENT REPRESENTING BOTH SELLER AND BUYER

A real estate agent, either acting directly or through one or more salespersons and broker associates, can legally be the agent of both the Seller and the Buyer in a transaction, but only with the knowledge and consent of both the Seller and the Buyer.

In a dual agency situation, the agent has the following affirmative obligations to both the Seller and the Buyer:

(a) A fiduciary duty of utmost care, integrity, honesty, and loyalty in the dealings with either the Seller or the Buyer.

(b) Other duties to the Seller and the Buyer as stated above in their respective sections.

In representing both Seller and Buyer, a dual agent may not, without the express permission of the respective party, disclose to the other party confidential information, including, but not limited to, facts relating to either the Buyer's or Seller's financial position, motivations, bargaining position, or other personal information that may impact price, including the Seller's willingness to accept a price less than the listing price or the Buyer's willingness to pay a price greater than the price offered.

SELLER AND BUYER RESPONSIBILITIES

Either the purchase agreement or a separate document will contain a confirmation of which agent is representing you and whether that agent is representing you exclusively in the transaction or acting as a dual agent. Please pay attention to that confirmation to make sure it accurately reflects your understanding of your agent's role.

The above duties of the agent in a real estate transaction do not relieve a Seller or Buyer from the responsibility to protect [1] **their** own interests. You should carefully read all agreements to assure that they adequately express your understanding of the transaction. A real estate agent is a person qualified to advise about real estate. If legal or tax advice is desired, consult a competent professional.

If you are a Buyer, you have the duty to exercise reasonable care to protect yourself, including as to those facts about the property which are known to you or within your diligent attention and observation.

Both Sellers and Buyers should strongly consider obtaining tax advice from a competent professional because the federal and state tax consequences of a transaction can be complex and subject to change.

Throughout your real property transaction you may receive more than one disclosure form, depending upon the number of agents assisting in the transaction. The law requires each agent with whom you have more than a casual relationship to present you with this disclosure form. You should read its contents each time it is presented to you, considering the relationship between you and the real estate agent in your specific transaction.

This disclosure form includes the provisions of Sections 2079.13 to 2079.24, inclusive, of the Civil Code set forth on the reverse hereof. Read it carefully.

Agent (date)	Buyer/Seller (date)
	(Signature)
Salesperson or Broker Associate, if any (date) (Signature)	Buyer/Seller (date) (Signature)

Leg.H. Added Stats 1995 ch 428 §5 (SB 467). Amended Stats 1996 ch 240 §4 (AB 2383); Stats 2018 ch 907 §41 (AB 1289), effective January 1, 2019; Stats 2024 ch 516 §5 (AB 2992), effective January 1, 2025.

§2079.16. 2024 Deletes. [1] his or her

§2079.17. Disclosure of exclusive or dual agency; Confirmation of relationship

(a) As soon as practicable, the buyer's agent shall disclose to the buyer and seller whether the agent is acting in the real property transaction as the buyer's agent, or as a dual agent representing both the buyer and the seller. This relationship shall be confirmed in the contract to purchase and sell real property or in a separate writing executed or acknowledged by the seller, the buyer, and the buyer's agent prior to or coincident with execution of that contract by the buyer and the seller, respectively.

(b) As soon as practicable, the seller's agent shall disclose to the seller whether the seller's agent is acting in the real property transaction as the seller's agent, or as a dual agent representing both the buyer and seller. This relationship shall be confirmed in the contract to purchase and sell real property or in a separate writing executed or acknowledged by the seller and the seller's agent prior to or coincident with the execution of that contract by the seller.

(c) The confirmation required by subdivisions (a) and (b) shall be in the following form:

___

(Name of Seller's Agent, Brokerage firm and license number)
is the broker of (check one):
[ ] the seller; or
[ ] both the buyer and seller. (dual agent)

___

(Name of Seller's Agent and license number)
is (check one):
[ ] is the Seller's Agent. (salesperson or broker associate)
[ ] is both the Buyer's and Seller's Agent. (dual agent)

___

(Name of Buyer's Agent, Brokerage firm and license number)
is the broker of (check one):
[ ] the buyer; or
[ ] both the buyer and seller. (dual agent)

___

(Name of Buyer's Agent and license number)
is (check one):
[ ] the Buyer's Agent. (salesperson or broker associate)
[ ] both the Buyer's and Seller's Agent. (dual agent)

(d) The disclosures and confirmation required by this section shall be in addition to the disclosure required by Section 2079.14. An agent's duty to provide disclosure and confirmation of representation in this section may be performed by a real estate salesperson or broker associate affiliated with that broker. **Leg.H.** Added Stats 1995 ch 428 §6 (SB 467). Amended Stats 2018 ch 907 §42 (AB 1289), effective January 1, 2019.

§2079.18. Representation of buyer by selling and listing agent [Repealed]

Leg.H. Added Stats 1995 ch 428 §7 (SB 467). Repealed Stats 2018 ch 907 §43 (AB 1289), effective January 1, 2019.

§2079.19. Payment of compensation; Effect on determination of particular agency relationship

The payment of compensation or the obligation to pay compensation to an agent by the seller or buyer is not necessarily determinative of a particular agency relationship between an agent and the seller or buyer. A listing agent and a selling agent may agree to share any compensation or commission paid, or any right to any compensation or commission for which an obligation arises as the result of a real estate transaction, and the terms of any such agreement shall not necessarily be determinative of a particular relationship. **Leg.H.** Added Stats 1995 ch 428 §8 (SB 467).

§2079.20. Selection of specific form of agency relationship as condition of employment

Nothing in this article prevents an agent from selecting, as a condition of the agent's employment, a specific form of agency relationship not specifically prohibited by this article if the requirements of Section 2079.14 and Section 2079.17 are complied with. **Leg.H.** Added Stats 1995 ch 428 §9 (SB 467).

§2079.21. Nondisclosure responsibilities of dual agents

(a) A dual agent may not, without the express permission of the seller, disclose to the buyer any confidential information obtained from the seller.

(b) A dual agent may not, without the express permission of the buyer, disclose to the seller any confidential information obtained from the buyer.

(c) "Confidential information" means facts relating to the client's financial position, motivations, bargaining position, or other personal information that may impact price, such as the seller is willing to accept a price less than the listing price or the buyer is willing to pay a price greater than the price offered.

(d) This section does not alter in any way the duty or responsibility of a dual agent to any principal with respect to confidential information other than price. **Leg.H.** Added Stats 1995 ch 428 §10 (SB 467). Amended Stats 2018 ch 907 §44 (AB 1289), effective January 1, 2019.

§2079.22. Combined seller's and buyer's agent

Nothing in this article precludes a seller's agent from also being a buyer's agent. If a seller or buyer in a transaction chooses to not be represented by an agent, that does not, of itself, make that agent a dual agent. **Leg.H.** Added Stats 1995 ch 428 §11 (SB 467). Amended Stats 2018 ch 907 §45 (AB 1289), effective January 1, 2019.

§2079.23. Time for modification of agency contract; Imposing obligations to defend or indemnify lender or auction company

(a) A contract between the principal and agent may be modified or altered to change the agency relationship at any time before the performance of the act which is the object of the agency with the written consent of the parties to the agency relationship.

(b) A lender or an auction company retained by a lender to control aspects of a transaction of real property subject to this part, including validating the sales price, shall not require, as a condition of receiving the lender's approval of the transaction, the homeowner or listing agent to defend or indemnify the lender or auction company from any liability alleged to result from the actions of the lender or auction company. Any clause, provision, covenant, or agreement purporting to impose an obligation to defend or indemnify a lender or an auction company in violation of this subdivision is against public policy, void, and unenforceable. **Leg.H.** Added Stats 1995 ch 428 §12 (SB 467). Amended Stats 2014 ch 893 §2 (AB 2039), effective January 1, 2015.

§2079.24. Construction of article; Breach of fiduciary duty or duty of disclosure

Nothing in this article shall be construed to either diminish the duty of disclosure owed buyers and sellers by agents and their associate licensees, subagents, and employees or to relieve agents and their associate licensees, subagents, and employees from liability for their conduct in connection with acts governed by this article or for any breach of a fiduciary duty or a duty of disclosure. **Leg.H.** Added Stats 1995 ch 428 §13 (SB 467).

§2079.25. Applicability of Section 1102.1(d) to article

The provisions of subdivision (d) of Section 1102.1 shall apply to this article. **Leg.H.** Added Stats 2018 ch 907 §46 (AB 1289), effective January 1, 2019.

CHAPTER 4
LOST AND UNCLAIMED PROPERTY

Article 1. Lost Money and Goods.
Article 2. Unclaimed Property.
Article 3. Fees of Officers.

ARTICLE 1
Lost Money and Goods

Duty of finder; Compensation. §2080.
Unknown owner. §2080.1.
Time for claiming property by owner. §2080.2.
Notice; Vesting of title; Public sale. §2080.3.
Ordinances providing for care and disposition of unclaimed property. §2080.4.
Quick sale. §2080.5.
Public agency regulations. §2080.6.
Intentionally abandoned property. §2080.7.
Resolutions and regulations of Regents of University of California and Trustees of California State University. §2080.8.
Public agency responsibilities upon obtaining possession of personal property. §2080.10.

§2080. Duty of finder; Compensation

Any person who finds a thing lost is not bound to take charge of it, unless the person is otherwise required to do so by contract or law, but when the person does take charge of it he or she is thenceforward a depositary for the owner, with the rights and obligations of a depositary for hire. Any person or any public or private entity that finds and takes possession of any money, goods, things in action, or other personal property, or saves any domestic animal from harm, neglect, drowning, or starvation, shall, within a reasonable time, inform the owner, if known, and make restitution without compensation, except a reasonable charge for saving and taking care of the property. Any person who takes possession of a live domestic animal shall provide for humane treatment of the animal. **Leg.H.** Added Stats 1967 ch 1512 §3 p 3601. Amended Stats 1998 ch 752 §9 (SB 1785).

Prior Law: Former §2080, similar in part to present CC §§2080, 2080.1, was added Stats 1951 ch 656 §2, and repealed Stats 1967 ch 1512 §3.

§2080.1. Unknown owner

(a) If the owner is unknown or has not claimed the property, the person saving or finding the property shall, if the property is of the value of one hundred dollars ($100) or more, within a reasonable time turn the property over to the police department of the city or city and county, if found therein, or to the sheriff's department of the county if found outside of city limits, and shall make an affidavit, stating when and where he or she found or saved the property, particularly describing it. If the property was saved, the affidavit shall state:

(1) From what and how it was saved.

(2) Whether the owner of the property is known to the affiant.

(3) That the affiant has not secreted, withheld, or disposed of any part of the property.

(b) The police department or the sheriff's department shall notify the owner, if his or her identity is reasonably ascertainable, that it possesses the property and where it may be claimed. The police department or sheriff's department may require payment by the owner of a reasonable charge to defray costs of storage and care of the property. **Leg.H.** Added Stats 1967 ch 1512 §3 p 3601. Amended Stats 1992 ch 138 §1 (AB 2457).

Prior Law: Former §2080.1, similar in part to the present section, was added by Stats 1951 ch 656 §2 p 1866, amended by Stats 1953 ch 602 §1 p 1847, and repealed by Stats 1967 ch 1512 §3 p 3601.

§2080.2. Time for claiming property by owner

If the owner appears within 90 days, after receipt of the property by the police department or sheriff's department, proves his ownership of the property, and pays all reasonable charges, the police department or sheriff's department shall restore the property to him. **Leg.H.** Added Stats 1967 ch 1512 §3 p 3601.

Prior Law: Former §2080.2, relating to appraisers, was added by Stats 1951 ch 656 §2 p 1866, amended by Stats 1953 ch 602 §2 p 1847, and repealed by Stats 1967 ch 1512 §2 p 3601.

§2080.3. Notice; Vesting of title; Public sale

(a) If the reported value of the property is two hundred fifty dollars ($250) or more and no owner appears and proves his or her ownership of the property within 90 days, the police department or sheriff's department shall cause notice of the property to be published at least once in a newspaper of general circulation. If, after seven days following the first publication of the notice, no owner appears and proves his or her ownership of the property and the person who found or saved the property pays the cost of the publication, the title shall vest in the person who found or saved the property unless the property was found in the course of employment by an employee of any public agency, in which case the property shall be sold at public auction. Title to the property shall not vest in the person who found or saved the property or in the successful bidder at the public auction unless the cost of publication is first paid to the city, county, or city and county whose police or sheriff's department caused the notice to be published.

(b) If the reported value of the property is less than two hundred fifty dollars ($250) and no owner appears and proves his or her ownership of the property within 90 days, the title shall vest in the person who found or saved the property, unless the property was found in the course of employment by an employee of any public agency, in which case the property shall be sold at public auction. **Leg.H.** Added Stats 1967 ch 1512 §3 p 3601. Amended Stats 1970 ch 260 §1 p 524; Stats 1971 ch 1254 §1; Stats 1977 ch 250 §1; Stats 1992 ch 138 §2 (AB 2457).

Prior Law: Former §2080.3, relating to lists of valuation and description of property, was added by Stats 1951 ch 656 §2 p 1866, amended by Stats 1953 ch 602 §3 p 1847, and repealed by Stats 1967 ch 1512 §2 p 3601.

§2080.4. Ordinances providing for care and disposition of unclaimed property

Notwithstanding the provisions of Section 2080.3 or Section 2080.6, the legislative body of any city, city and county, or county may provide by ordinance for the care, restitution, sale or destruction of unclaimed property in the possession of the police department of such city or city and county or of the sheriff of such county. Any city, city and county, or county adopting such an ordinance shall provide therein (1) that such unclaimed property shall be held by the police department or sheriff for a period of at least three months, and (2) that thereafter such property will be sold at public auction to the highest bidder, with notice of such sale being given by the chief of police or sheriff at least five days before the time fixed therefor by publication once in a newspaper of general circulation published in the county, or that thereafter such property will be transferred to the local government purchasing and stores agency or other similar agency for sale to the public at public auction. If such property is transferred to a county purchasing agent it may be sold in the manner provided by Article 7 (commencing with Section 25500) of Chapter 5 of Part 2 of Division 2 of Title 3 of the Government Code for the sale of surplus personal property. If property is transferred to the local government purchasing and stores agency or other similar agency pursuant to this section, such property shall not be redeemable by the owner or other person entitled to possession. If the local government purchasing and stores agency or other similar agency determines that any such property transferred to it for sale is needed for a public use, such property may be retained by the agency and need not be sold. **Leg.H.** Added Stats 1967 ch 1512 §3 p 3601. Amended Stats 1969 ch 857 §1 p 1689; Stats 1983 ch 878 §1.

Prior Law: Former §2080.4, relating to filing and recording copy of list, was added by Stats 1951 ch 656 §2 p 1866, amended by Stats 1953 ch 602 §4 p 1847, and repealed by Stats 1967 ch 1512 §2 p 3601.

§2080.5. Quick sale

The police department or sheriff's department may sell such property by public auction, in the manner and upon the notice of sale of personal property under execution, if it is a thing which is commonly the subject of sale, when the owner cannot, with reasonable diligence, be found, or, being found, refuses upon demand to pay the lawful charges provided by Sections 2080 and 2080.1, in the following cases:

(1) When the thing is in danger of perishing, or of losing the greater part of its value; or,

(2) When the lawful charges provided by Sections 2080 and 2080.1 amount to two-thirds of its value. **Leg.H.** Added Stats 1967 ch 1512 §3 p 3601.

Prior Law: Former §2080.5, similar to present §2080.3, was added by Stats 1951 ch 656 §2 p 1867 and repealed by Stats 1967 ch 1512 §2 p 3601.

§2080.6. Public agency regulations

(a) Any public agency may elect to be governed by the provisions of this article with respect to disposition of personal property found or saved on property subject to its jurisdiction, or may adopt reasonable regulations for the care, restitution, sale or destruction of unclaimed property in its possession. Any public agency adopting such regulations shall provide therein (1) that such unclaimed property shall be held by such agency for a period of at least three months, (2) that thereafter such property will be sold at public auction to the highest bidder, and (3) that notice of such sale shall be given by the chief administrative officer of such agency at least five days before the time fixed therefor by publication once in a newspaper of general circulation published in the county in which such property was found. Any property remaining unsold after being offered at such public auction may be destroyed or otherwise disposed of by the public agency. In a county having a purchasing agent, the purchasing agent may conduct such sale, in which case the provisions of subdivisions (2) and (3) of this section shall not be applicable. Such sale shall be made by the county purchasing agent in the manner provided by Article 7 (commencing with Section 25500) of Chapter 5 of Part 2 of Division 2 of Title 3 of the Government Code for the sale of surplus personal property. If the public agency determines that any such property transferred to it for sale is needed for a public use, such property may be retained by the agency and need not be sold.

(b) "Public agency" as used in this section means any state agency, including the Department of General Services and the Department of Parks and Recreation, any city, county, city and county, special district, or other political subdivision. **Leg.H.** Added Stats 1967 ch 1512 §3. Amended Stats 1969 ch 857 §2; Stats 1988 ch 1282 §1.

Prior Law: Former §2080.6, similar to present §2080.3, was added Stats 1951 ch 656 §2 and repealed Stats 1967 ch 1512 §2.

§2080.7. Intentionally abandoned property

The provisions of this article have no application to things which have been intentionally abandoned by their owner. **Leg.H.** Added Stats 1967 ch 1512 §3 p 3601.

Prior Law: Former §2080.7, similar in part to present §2080.2, was added by Stats 1951 ch 656 §2 p 1867 and repealed by Stats 1967 ch 1512 §2 p 3601.

§2080.8. Resolutions and regulations of Regents of University of California and Trustees of California State University

(a) The Regents of the University of California and the Trustees of the California State University, as applicable, may provide by resolution or regulation for the care, restitution, sale, or destruction of unclaimed, lost, or abandoned property in the possession of the Regents of the University of California, the University of California Police Department, or any state university.

(b) Any resolution or regulation adopted pursuant to this section shall provide therein (1) that unclaimed, lost, or abandoned property valued at or above three hundred dollars ($300) shall be held by the Regents of the University of California, the University of California Police Department, or the particular state university for a period of at least three months, (2) that thereafter the property will be sold at public auction to the highest bidder, and (3) that notice of that sale shall be given by the Regents of the University of California, the University of California Police Department, or the Trustees of the California State University at least five days before the time therefor by publication once in a newspaper of general circulation published in the county in which the property is held.

(c) The Regents of the University of California or the Trustees of the California State University may dispose of any of that property upon which no bid is made at any sale. **Leg.H.** Added Stats 1967 ch 1512 §3 p 3601. Amended Stats 1969 ch 857 §3 p 1690; Stats 2010 ch 199 §1 (AB 1890), effective January 1, 2011.

Prior Law: Former §2080.8, relating to finder failing to make discovery pursuant to this article, was added by Stats 1951 ch 656 §2 p 1867 and repealed by Stats 1967 ch 1512 §2 p 3601.

§2080.9. [Section repealed 2011]

Leg.H. Added Stats 1967 ch 1512 §3. Amended Stats 1973 ch 167 §11; Stats 1983 ch 143 §2. Repealed Stats 2010 ch 199 §2 (AB 1890), effective January 1, 2011. The repealed section related to State University Trustees' regulations. For present similar provisions see CC §2080.8.

Prior Law: Former §2080.9, relating to proof made before clerk with whom list is filed, was added Stats 1951 ch 656 §2, and repealed Stats 1967 ch 1512 §2.

§2080.10. Public agency responsibilities upon obtaining possession of personal property

(a) When a public agency obtains possession of personal property from a person for temporary safekeeping, the public agency shall do all of the following:

(1) Take responsibility for the storage, documentation, and disposition of the property.

(2) Provide the person from whom the property was taken with a receipt and instructions for the retrieval of the property. The receipt and instructions shall either be given to the person from whom the property was taken at the time the public agency obtains the property or immediately mailed, by first-class mail, to the person from whom the property was taken.

(3) If the public agency has knowledge that the person from whom the property was taken is not the owner, the agency shall make reasonable efforts to identify the owner. If the owner is identified, the public agency shall mail, by first-class mail, a receipt and instructions for the retrieval of the property.

(b) The receipt and instructions shall notify the person from whom the property was taken that the property must be claimed within 60 days after the public agency obtains possession or the property will be disposed of in accordance with the disposal provisions of this article. Within 60 days, the person may do one of the following:

(1) Retrieve the property.

(2) Authorize in writing another person to retrieve the property.

(3) Notify the public agency in writing that he or she is unable to retrieve the property, because he or she is in custody, and request the public agency to hold the property. If a person notifies the public agency that he or she is unable to retrieve the property within 60 days, or have an authorized person retrieve the property, the public agency shall hold the property for not longer than 10 additional months.

(c) The public agency shall not be liable for damages caused by any official action performed with due care regarding the disposition of personal property pursuant to this section and the disposal provisions of this article.

(d) As used in this section, "public agency" means any state agency, any city, county, city and county, special district, or other political subdivision. **Leg.H.** Added Stats 1998 ch 540 §1 (SB 1707).

ARTICLE 2
Unclaimed Property

Retention of property pending payment of freight charges. §2081.
Sale at public auctions. §2081.1.
Disposition of surplus funds. §2081.2.
Unclaimed surplus. §2081.3.
Termination of responsibility. §2081.4.
Sale of property upon which advancements have been made. §2081.5.
Proceedings governed entirely by provisions of this article. §2081.6.

§2081. Retention of property pending payment of freight charges

When any goods, merchandise, or other property has been received by any railroad or express company, other common carrier, commission merchant, innkeeper, or warehouseman, for transportation or safekeeping, and is not delivered to the owner, consignee, or other authorized person, the carrier, commission merchant, innkeeper, or warehouseman may hold or store the property with some responsible person until the freight and all just and reasonable charges are paid. **Leg.H.** Added Stats 1951 ch 656 §2 p 1867.

§2081.1. Sale at public auctions

If within 60 days after its receipt no person calls for the property and pays the freight and charges upon it, the carrier, commission merchant, innkeeper, or warehouseman may sell the property, or so much of it as will pay freight and charges, to the highest bidder at public auction, after first causing such notice of sale to be given as is customary in sales of goods by auction at the place where the goods are held or stored. **Leg.H.** Added Stats 1951 ch 656 §2 p 1867.

§2081.2. Disposition of surplus funds

If any surplus remains after paying the freight, storage, expenses of sale, and other reasonable charges, the sum remaining shall be paid over to the owner of the property, upon his demand at any time within 60 days after the sale. **Leg.H.** Added Stats 1951 ch 656 §2 p 1867.

§2081.3. Unclaimed surplus

If the owner or his agent fails to demand the surplus within 60 days after the sale, it shall be paid into the county treasury subject to the order of the owner. **Leg.H.** Added Stats 1951 ch 656 §2 p 1867.

§2081.4. Termination of responsibility

After the storage of the property the responsibility of the carrier, commission merchant, innkeeper, or warehouseman ceases. The person with whom the property is stored is not liable for loss or damage on its account unless the loss or damage results from his negligence or want of proper care. **Leg.H.** Added Stats 1951 ch 656 §2 p 1868.

§2081.5. Sale of property upon which advancements have been made

When any commission merchant or warehouseman receives produce, merchandise, or other property on consignment and makes advances upon it, either to the owner or for freight and charges, if the advances are not paid to him within 60 days from the date made, he may cause the produce, merchandise, or property on which the advances were made, to be advertised and sold pursuant to this article. **Leg.H.** Added Stats 1951 ch 656 §2 p 1868.

§2081.6. Proceedings governed entirely by provisions of this article

All proceedings pursuant to this article are governed entirely by its provisions and are not controlled or affected by Article 2, Chapter 3, Title 7, Part 4, Division 3 of this code. **Leg.H.** Added Stats 1951 ch 656 §2 p 1868.

ARTICLE 3
Fees of Officers

Fees of officers. §2082.

§2082. **Fees of officers**
The fees of officers under this chapter are the same allowed by law for similar services, and shall be paid by the taker up or finder and recovered from the owner. **Leg.H.** Added Stats 1951 ch 656 §2 p 1868.

TITLE 7
CARRIAGE

Chapter 1. Carriage in General.
Chapter 2. Carriage of Persons.
Chapter 3. Carriage of Property.
Chapter 4. Carriage of Messages.
Chapter 5. Common Carriers.
Chapter 6. Carrier of Passengers Act of 2024.

CHAPTER 1
CARRIAGE IN GENERAL

Contract of carriage. §2085.
Different kinds of carriers. §2086.
Marine and inland carriers, what. §2087.
Carriers by sea. §2088.
Obligations of gratuitous carriers. §2089.
Obligations of gratuitous carrier who has begun to carry. §2090.

§2085. **Contract of carriage**
The contract of carriage is a contract for the conveyance of property, persons, or messages, from one place to another. **Leg.H.** Enacted 1872.

§2086. **Different kinds of carriers**
Carriage is either:
1. Inland; or,
2. Marine. **Leg.H.** Enacted 1872.

§2087. **Marine and inland carriers, what**
Carriers upon the ocean and upon arms of the sea are marine carriers. All others are inland carriers. **Leg.H.** Enacted 1872.

§2088. **Carriers by sea**
Rights and duties peculiar to carriers by sea are defined by Acts of Congress. **Leg.H.** Enacted 1872.

§2089. **Obligations of gratuitous carriers**
Carriers without reward are subject to the same rules as employees without reward, except so far as is otherwise provided by this title. **Leg.H.** Enacted 1872.

§2090. **Obligations of gratuitous carrier who has begun to carry**
A carrier without reward, who has begun to perform his undertaking, must complete it in like manner as if he had received a reward, unless he restores the person or thing carried to as favorable a position as before he commenced the carriage. **Leg.H.** Enacted 1872.

CHAPTER 2
CARRIAGE OF PERSONS

Article 1. Gratuitous Carriage of Persons.
Article 2. Carriage for Reward.

ARTICLE 1
Gratuitous Carriage of Persons

Degree of care required. §2096.

§2096. **Degree of care required**
A carrier of persons without reward must use ordinary care and diligence for their safe carriage. **Leg.H.** Enacted 1872.

ARTICLE 2
Carriage for Reward

General duties of carrier. §2100.
Vehicles. §2101.
Not to overload his vehicle. §2102.
Treatment of passengers. §2103.
Rate of speed and delays. §2104.

§2100. **General duties of carrier**
A carrier of persons for reward must use the utmost care and diligence for their safe carriage, must provide everything necessary for that purpose, and must exercise to that end a reasonable degree of skill. **Leg.H.** Enacted 1872.

§2101. **Vehicles**
A carrier of persons for reward is bound to provide vehicles safe and fit for the purposes to which they are put, and is not excused for default in this respect by any degree of care. **Leg.H.** Enacted 1872.

§2102. **Not to overload his vehicle**
A carrier of persons for reward must not overcrowd or overload his vehicle. **Leg.H.** Enacted 1872.

§2103. **Treatment of passengers**
A carrier of persons for reward must give to passengers all such accommodations as are usual and reasonable, and must treat them with civility and give them a reasonable degree of attention. **Leg.H.** Enacted 1872.

§2104. **Rate of speed and delays**
A carrier of persons for reward must travel at a reasonable rate of speed, and without any unreasonable delay, or deviation from his proper route. **Leg.H.** Enacted 1872.

CHAPTER 3
CARRIAGE OF PROPERTY

Article 1. General Definitions.
Article 2. Obligations of the Carrier.
Article 4. Freightage.
Article 5. General Average.

ARTICLE 1
General Definitions

Freight, consignor, etc., defined. §2110.

§2110. **Freight, consignor, etc., defined**
Property carried is called freight; the reward, if any, to be paid for its carriage is called freightage; the person who delivers the freight to the carrier is called the consignor; and the person to whom it is to be delivered is called the consignee. **Leg.H.** Enacted 1872.

ARTICLE 2
Obligations of the Carrier

Care and diligence required of carriers. §2114.
Obedience to directions. §2115.
Delivery of freight. §2118.
Place of delivery. §2119.
Nondelivery. §2120.
Nonacceptance. §2121.

§2114. **Care and diligence required of carriers**
A carrier of property for reward must use at least ordinary care and diligence in the performance of all his duties. A carrier without reward must use at least slight care and diligence. **Leg.H.** Enacted 1872.

§2115. **Obedience to directions**
Subject to Section 7303 of the Uniform Commercial Code, a carrier must comply with the directions of the consignor or consignee to the same extent that an employee is bound to comply with those of his employer. **Leg.H.** Enacted 1872. Amended Stats 1963 ch 819 §8 p 1999, effective January 1, 1965.

§2116. **[Section repealed 1963]**
Leg.H. Enacted 1872 and repealed by Stats 1963 ch 819 §9 p 1999, effective January 1, 1965. See UCC §7303.

§2117. **[Section repealed 1937]**
Leg.H. Enacted 1872 and repealed by Stats 1937 ch 368 (H & N C §10002) p 1002. See H & N C §423.

§2118. **Delivery of freight**
Subject to Section 7303 of the Uniform Commercial Code, a carrier of property must deliver it to the consignee, at the place to which it is addressed, in the manner usual at that place. **Leg.H.** Enacted 1872. Amended Stats 1963 ch 819 §10 p 1999, effective January 1, 1965.

§2119. **Place of delivery**
If there is no usage to the contrary at the place of delivery, freight must be delivered as follows:
1. If carried upon a railway owned or managed by the carrier, it may be delivered at the station nearest to the place to which it is addressed;
2. If carried by sea from a foreign country, it may be delivered at the wharf where the ship moors, within a reasonable distance from the place

of address; or, if there is no wharf, on board a lighter alongside the ship; or,

3. Subject to Section 7303 of the Uniform Commercial Code, in other cases, it must be delivered to the consignee or his agent, personally, if either can, with reasonable diligence, be found. **Leg.H.** Enacted 1872. Amended Stats 1963 ch 819 §11 p 1999, effective January 1, 1965.

§2120. Nondelivery

If, for any reason, a carrier does not deliver freight to the consignee or his agent personally, he must give notice to the consignee of its arrival, and keep the same in safety, upon his responsibility as a warehouseman, until the consignee has had a reasonable time to remove it. If the place of residence or business of the consignee be unknown to the carrier, he may give the notice by letter dropped in the nearest postoffice. **Leg.H.** Enacted 1872. Amended Code Amdts 1873–74 ch 612 §213 p 247.

§2121. Nonacceptance

If a consignee does not accept and remove freight within a reasonable time after the carrier has fulfilled his obligation to deliver, or duly offered to fulfill the same, the carrier may exonerate himself from further liability by placing the freight in a suitable warehouse, on storage, on account of the consignee, and giving notice thereof to him. **Leg.H.** Enacted 1872. Amended Code Amdts 1873–74 ch 612 §214 p 248.

§2122. [Section repealed]

Leg,H. Enacted 1872. Repealed by Code Amdts 1873–74 ch 612 §215 p 248.

ARTICLE 3
Bills of Lading [Repealed]

§§2126–2132c. [Sections repealed]

ARTICLE 4
Freightage

When freightage is to be paid. §2136.
Consignor, when liable for freightage. §2137.
Consignee, when liable. §2138.
Natural increase of freight. §2139.
Apportionment by contract. §2140.
Same. §2141.
Apportionment according to distance. §2142.
Freight carried further than agreed, etc. §2143.
Carrier's lien. §2144.

§2136. When freightage is to be paid

A carrier may require his freightage to be paid upon his receiving the freight; but if he does not demand it then, he cannot until he is ready to deliver the freight to the consignee. **Leg.H.** Enacted 1872.

§2137. Consignor, when liable for freightage

The consignor of freight is presumed to be liable for the freightage, but if the contract between him and the carrier provides that the consignee shall pay it, and the carrier allows the consignee to take the freight, he cannot afterward recover the freightage from the consignor. **Leg.H.** Enacted 1872.

§2138. Consignee, when liable

The consignee of freight is liable for the freightage, if he accepts the freight with notice of the intention of the consignor that he should pay it. **Leg.H.** Enacted 1872.

§2139. Natural increase of freight

No freightage can be charged upon the natural increase of freight. **Leg.H.** Enacted 1872.

§2140. Apportionment by contract

If freightage is apportioned by a bill of lading or other contract made between a consignor and carrier, the carrier is entitled to payment, according to the apportionment, for so much as he delivers. **Leg.H.** Enacted 1872.

§2141. Same

If a part of the freight is accepted by a consignee, without a specific objection that the rest is not delivered, the freightage must be apportioned and paid as to that part, though not apportioned in the original contract. **Leg.H.** Enacted 1872.

§2142. Apportionment according to distance

If a consignee voluntarily receives freight at a place short of the one appointed for delivery, the carrier is entitled to a just proportion of the freightage, according to distance. If the carrier, being ready and willing, offers to complete the transit, he is entitled to the full freightage. If he does not thus offer completion, and the consignee receives the freight only from necessity, the carrier is not entitled to any freightage. **Leg.H.** Enacted 1872.

§2143. Freight carried further than agreed, etc.

If freight is carried further, or more expeditiously, than was agreed upon by the parties, the carrier is not entitled to additional compensation, and cannot refuse to deliver it, on the demand of the consignee, at the place and time of its arrival. **Leg.H.** Enacted 1872.

§2144. Carrier's lien

A carrier has a lien for (a) freightage and for services rendered at request of shipper or consignee in and about the transportation of the property,(b) care and preservation of the property, (c) money advanced at request of shipper or consignee to discharge a prior lien, and (d), subject to the limitations specified in Section 3051.6, any fines, penalties, costs, expenses, and interest arising from the provision of false or erroneous certifications of gross cargo weight as required by Section 508 of Title 49 of the United States Code. The carrier's rights to this lien are regulated by the title on liens. **Leg.H.** Enacted 1872. Amended Stats 1909 ch 663 §1 p 1000; Stats 1993 ch 757 §1 (SB 619).

ARTICLE 5
General Average

§§2148–2155. [Sections repealed]

CHAPTER 4
CARRIAGE OF MESSAGES

Duties. §2161.
Degree of care. §2162.

§2161. Duties

A carrier of messages for reward, other than by telegraph or telephone, must deliver them at the place to which they are addressed, or to the person for whom they are intended. Such carrier, by telegraph or telephone, must deliver them at such place and to such person, provided the place of address, or the person for whom they are intended, is within a distance of two miles from the main office of the carrier in the city or town to which the messages are transmitted, and the carrier is not required, in making the delivery, to pay on his route toll or ferriage; but for any distance beyond one mile from such office, compensation may be charged for a messenger employed by the carrier. **Leg.H.** Enacted 1872. Amended Code Amdts 1873–74 ch 612 §216 p 248; Stats 1905 ch 469 §1 p 627.

§2162. Degree of care

A carrier of messages for reward, must use great care and diligence in the transmission and delivery of messages. **Leg.H.** Enacted 1872. Amended Code Amdts 1873–74 ch 612 §217 p 249.

CHAPTER 5
COMMON CARRIERS

Article 1. Common Carriers in General.
Article 2. Common Carriers of Persons.
Article 3. Common Carriers of Property.
Article 4. Common Carriers of Messages.
Article 5. Space Flight Liability and Immunity.

ARTICLE 1
Common Carriers in General

Definition. §2168.
Obligation to accept freight. §2169.
Obligation not to give preference. §2170.
What preferences he must give. §2171.
Starting. §2172.
Compensation. §2173.
Obligations of carrier altered only by agreement. §2174.
Certain agreements void. §2175.
Effect of written contract. §2176.
Loss of valuable letters. §2177.
Railroad baggage liability. §2178.

§2168. Definition

Everyone who offers to the public to carry persons, property, or messages, excepting only telegraphic messages, is a common carrier of whatever he thus offers to carry. **Leg.H.** Enacted 1872. Amended Code Amdts 1873–74 ch 612 §218 p 249.

§2169. Obligation to accept freight
A common carrier must, if able to do so, accept and carry whatever is offered to him, at a reasonable time and place, of a kind that he undertakes or is accustomed to carry. **Leg.H.** Enacted 1872.

§2170. Obligation not to give preference
A common carrier must not give preference in time, price, or otherwise, to one person over another. Every common carrier of passengers by railroad, or by vessel plying upon waters, lying wholly within this state, shall establish a schedule time for the starting of trains or vessel from their respective stations or wharves, of which public notice shall be given, and shall, weather permitting, except in case of accident or detention caused by connecting lines, start their said trains or vessel at or within ten minutes after the schedule time so established and notice given, under a penalty of two hundred and fifty dollars for each neglect so to do, to be recovered by action before any court of competent jurisdiction, upon complaint filed by the district attorney of the county in the name of the people, and paid into the common-school fund of the said county. **Leg.H.** Enacted 1872. Amended Code Amdts 1880 ch 37 §1 p 2.

§2171. What preferences he must give
A common carrier must always give a preference in time, and may give a preference in price, to the United States and to this state. **Leg.H.** Enacted 1872.

§2172. Starting
A common carrier must start at such time and place as he announces to the public, unless detained by accident or the elements, or in order to connect with carriers on other lines of travel. **Leg.H.** Enacted 1872. Amended Code Amdts 1873–74 ch 612 §219 p 249.

§2173. Compensation
A common carrier is entitled to a reasonable compensation and no more, which he may require to be paid in advance. If payment thereof is refused, he may refuse to carry. **Leg.H.** Enacted 1872.

§2174. Obligations of carrier altered only by agreement
The obligations of a common carrier cannot be limited by general notice on his part, but may be limited by special contract. **Leg.H.** Enacted 1872. Amended Code Amdts 1873–74 ch 612 §220 p 249.

§2175. Certain agreements void
A common carrier cannot be exonerated, by any agreement made in anticipation thereof, from liability for the gross negligence, fraud, or willful wrong of himself or his servants. **Leg.H.** Enacted 1872.

§2176. Effect of written contract
A passenger, consignor, or consignee, by accepting a ticket, bill of lading, or written contract for carriage, with a knowledge of its terms, assents to the rate of hire, the time, place, and manner of delivery therein stated; and also to the limitation stated therein upon the amount of the carrier's liability in case property carried in packages, trunks, or boxes, is lost or injured, when the value of such property is not named; and also to the limitation stated therein to the carrier's liability for loss or injury to live animals carried. But his assent to any other modification of the carrier's obligations contained in such instrument can be manifested only by his signature to the same. **Leg.H.** Enacted 1872. Amended Code Amdts 1873–74 ch 612 §221 p 249.

§2177. Loss of valuable letters
A common carrier is not responsible for loss or miscarriage of a letter, or package having the form of a letter, containing money or notes, bills of exchange, or other papers of value, unless he be informed at the time of its receipt of the value of its contents. **Leg.H.** Added Code Amdts 1873–74 ch 612 §222 p 250.

§2178. Railroad baggage liability
A common carrier of property by steam or electric railroad which accepts for transportation, storage, handling or safekeeping, as a part of or in connection with passenger transportation, property carried in trunks, valises, suitcases, traveling bags, boxes, bundles or packages, shall not be liable, in the event of loss of or injury to the same, for more than one hundred dollars for each trunk and contents, nor more than fifty dollars for each valise and contents, or suitcase and contents, or traveling bag and contents, nor more than ten dollars for each box, bundle or package and contents, unless the carrier shall have consented in writing to assume a greater liability. The term "common carrier" as used in this section shall include sleeping-car companies. **Leg.H.** Added Stats 1931 ch 614 §1 p 1323.

ARTICLE 2
Common Carriers of Persons

Duties with respect to baggage. §2180.
Luggage; Bicycles. §2181.
Liability for luggage. §2182.
Duties with respect to luggage. §2183.
Duties with respect to vehicles. §2184.
Duties with respect to seating passengers. §2185.
Regulations for conduct of business. §2186.
Fare, when payable. §2187.
Ejection of passengers. §2188.
Fare not payable after ejection. §2190.
Carrier's lien. §2191.

§2180. Duties with respect to baggage
A common carrier of persons, unless his vehicle is fitted for the reception of persons exclusively, must receive and carry a reasonable amount of baggage for each passenger without charge, except for an excess of weight over one hundred pounds to a passenger; if such carrier is a proprietor of a stage line, he need not receive and carry for each passenger by such stage line, without charge, more than sixty pounds of baggage. **Leg.H.** Enacted 1872. Amended Code Amdts 1877–78 ch 159 §1 p 87; Stats 1905 ch 455 §1 p 615.

§2181. Luggage; Bicycles
Luggage may consist of whatever the passenger takes with him for his personal use and convenience, according to the habits or wants of the particular class to which he belongs, either with reference to the important necessities or to the ultimate purposes of his journey. Luggage within the meaning of this section shall include the samples, case, wares, appliances and catalogues of commercial travelers or their employers, used by them for the purpose of transacting their business and carried with them solely for that purpose, when securely packed and locked in substantial trunks or sample cases of convenient shape and weight for handling. No crate, cover, or other protection shall be required for any bicycle carried as luggage, but no passenger shall be entitled to carry as luggage more than one bicycle. **Leg.H.** Enacted 1872. Amended Stats 1897 ch 4 §1 p 4; Stats 1911 ch 363 §1 p 638.

§2182. Liability for luggage
The liability of a carrier for luggage received by him with a passenger is the same as that of a common carrier of property. **Leg.H.** Enacted 1872.

§2183. Duties with respect to luggage
A common carrier must deliver every passenger's luggage, whether within the prescribed weight or not, immediately upon the arrival of the passenger at his destination; and, unless the vehicle would be overcrowded or overloaded thereby, must carry it on the same vehicle by which he carries the passenger to whom it belonged, except that where luggage is transported by rail, it must be checked and carried in a regular baggage-car; and whenever passengers neglect or refuse to have their luggage so checked and transported, it is carried at their risk. **Leg.H.** Enacted 1872. Amended Code Amdts 1873–74 ch 612 §223 p 250.

§2184. Duties with respect to vehicles
A common carrier of persons must provide a sufficient number of vehicles to accommodate all the passengers who can be reasonably expected to require carriage at any one time. This section shall not apply, however, to any passenger stage corporation or street railroad corporation, as defined in Sections 226 and 232, respectively, of the Public Utilities Code, which is subject to the jurisdiction of the Public Utilities Commission. **Leg.H.** Enacted 1872. Amended Stats 1957 ch 511 §1 p 1548.

§2185. Duties with respect to seating passengers
A common carrier of persons must provide every passenger with a seat. He must not overload his vehicle by receiving and carrying more passengers than its rated capacity allows. This section shall not apply, however, to any city, county, city and county that operates a transportation system, or to any passenger stage corporation or street railroad corporation, as defined in Sections 226 and 232, respectively, of the Public Utilities Code, which is subject to the jurisdiction of the Public Utilities

Commission. **Leg.H.** Enacted 1872. Amended Stats 1957 ch 511 §2 p 1549; Stats 1963 ch 1409 §1 p 2947.

§2186. Regulations for conduct of business
A common carrier of persons may make rules for the conduct of his business, and may require passengers to conform to them, if they are lawful, public, uniform in their application, and reasonable. **Leg.H.** Enacted 1872.

§2187. Fare, when payable
A common carrier may demand the fare of passengers, either at starting or at any subsequent time. **Leg.H.** Enacted 1872.

§2188. Ejection of passengers
A passenger who refuses to pay his fare or to conform to any lawful regulation of the carrier, may be ejected from the vehicle by the carrier. But this must be done with as little violence as possible, and at any usual stopping-place or near some dwelling-house. **Leg.H.** Enacted 1872.

§2189. [Section repealed 1951]
Leg.H. Enacted 1872 and repealed by Stats 1951 ch 764 (Pub U C §25003) p 2258. See Pub U C §7656.

§2190. Fare not payable after ejection
After having ejected a passenger, a carrier has no right to require the payment of any part of his fare. **Leg.H.** Enacted 1872.

§2191. Carrier's lien
A common carrier has a lien upon the luggage of a passenger for the payment of such fare as he is entitled to from him. This lien is regulated by the title on liens. **Leg.H.** Enacted 1872.

ARTICLE 3
Common Carriers of Property

Liability of inland carriers for loss. §2194.
Applicability of exemptions. §2195.
Liability for delay. §2196.
Storage or equipment rental charges. §2197.
Additional liability of consignee to motor carrier. §2197.5.
Liability with respect to valuables. §2200.
Carrier's services, other than carriage and delivery. §2203.
Sale of perishable property for freight. §2204.
Liability with respect to baggage. §2205.

§2194. Liability of inland carriers for loss
Unless the consignor accompanies the freight and retains exclusive control thereof, an inland common carrier of property is liable, from the time that he accepts until he relieves himself from liability pursuant to sections two thousand one hundred and eighteen to two thousand one hundred and twenty-two for the loss or injury thereof from any cause whatever, except:

1. An inherent defect, vice, or weakness, or a spontaneous action, of the property itself;
2. The act of a public enemy of the United States, or of this state;
3. The act of the law; or,
4. Any irresistible superhuman cause. **Leg.H.** Enacted 1872.

§2195. Applicability of exemptions
A common carrier is liable, even in the cases excepted by the last section, if his want of ordinary care exposes the property to the cause of the loss. **Leg.H.** Enacted 1872. Amended Stats 1905 ch 455 §2 p 615.

§2196. Liability for delay
A common carrier is liable for delay only when it is caused by his want of ordinary care and diligence. **Leg.H.** Enacted 1872. Amended Code Amdts 1873–74 ch 612 §224 p 251.

§2197. Storage or equipment rental charges
(a) Liability for storage or equipment rental charges assessed against a motor carrier by a railroad or steamship company shall be as follows if the charges arise out of a delay caused by the consignor or consignee of the freight:

(1) The consignor is liable to the motor carrier for the charges if the consignor caused the delay.

(2) The consignee is liable to the motor carrier for the charges if the consignee caused the delay.

(b) Nothing in this section shall affect the rights, duties, and obligations between a railroad or steamship company and a motor carrier. **Leg.H.** Added Stats 1988 ch 937 §1.

§2197.5. Additional liability of consignee to motor carrier
(a) In addition to the liability established by Section 2197, the consignee is liable to the motor carrier for the charges if the freight is shipped prepaid and the delay was caused by either the consignor or the consignee.

(b) Nothing in this section shall affect the rights, duties, and obligations between a railroad or steamship company and a motor carrier. **Leg.H.** Added Stats 1988 ch 937 §2, operative until January 1, 1993. Amended Stats 1992 ch 466 §1 (AB 2387).

§§2198, 2199. [Sections repealed 1937]
Leg.H. Enacted 1872 and repealed by Stats 1937 ch 368 (H & N C §10001) p 1002. See H & N C §§420–422.

§2200. Liability with respect to valuables
A common carrier of gold, silver, platina, or precious stones, or of imitations thereof, in a manufactured or unmanufactured state; of timepieces of any description; of negotiable paper or other valuable writings; of pictures, glass, or chinaware; of statuary, silk, or laces; or of plated ware of any kind, is not liable for more than fifty dollars upon the loss or injury of any one package of such articles, unless he has notice, upon his receipt thereof, by mark upon the package or otherwise, of the nature of the freight; nor is such carrier liable upon any package carried for more than the value of the articles named in the receipt or the bill of lading. **Leg.H.** Enacted 1872. Amended Code Amdts 1873–74 ch 612 §225 p 251.

§§2201, 2202. [Sections repealed 1963]
Leg.H. Enacted 1872 and repealed by Stats 1963 ch 819 §§12, 13, p 1999, effective January 1, 1965. See UCC §7302.

§2203. Carrier's services, other than carriage and delivery
In respect to any service rendered by a common carrier about freight, other than its carriage and delivery, his rights and obligations are defined by the title on deposit and service. **Leg.H.** Enacted 1872.

§2204. Sale of perishable property for freight
If, from any cause other than want of ordinary care and diligence on his part, a common carrier is unable to deliver perishable property transported by him, and collect his charges thereon, he may cause the property to be sold in open market to satisfy his lien for freightage. **Leg.H.** Added Code Amdts 1873–74 ch 612 §226 p 251.

§2205. Liability with respect to baggage
The liability of any stageline, transfer company, or other common carriers operating over the public highways for the loss of or for damage to any baggage shall not exceed the sum of five hundred dollars ($500) for each trunk and its contents; two hundred fifty dollars ($250) for each valise, suitcase or traveling bag and its contents; or two hundred fifty dollars ($250) for each box, bundle, or package and its contents, unless a higher valuation is declared at the time of delivery of such baggage to the carrier and assented thereto in writing by such carrier.

All baggage presented to the carrier for checking shall be appropriately tagged by the owner with his name and address. **Leg.H.** Added Stats 1925 ch 146 §1 p 299. Amended Stats 1965 ch 104 §1 p 324; Stats 1969 ch 982 §1 p 1950; Stats 1971 ch 1653 §1.

ARTICLE 4
Common Carriers of Messages

Order of transmission of telegraphic messages. §2207.
Order in other cases. §2208.
Damages when message is refused or postponed. §2209.

§2207. Order of transmission of telegraphic messages
A carrier of messages by telegraph must, if it is practicable, transmit every such message immediately upon its receipt. But if this is not practicable, and several messages, accumulate upon his hands, he must transmit them in the following order:

1. Messages from public agents of the United States or of this state, on public business;
2. Messages intended in good faith for immediate publication in newspapers, and not for any secret use;
3. Messages giving information relating to the sickness or death of any person;
4. Other messages in the order in which they were received. **Leg.H.** Enacted 1872.

§2208. Order in other cases

A common carrier of messages, otherwise than by telegraph, must transmit messages in the order in which he receives them, except messages from agents of the United States or of this state, on public business, to which he must always give priority. But he may fix upon certain times for the simultaneous transmission of messages previously received. **Leg.H.** Enacted 1872.

§2209. Damages when message is refused or postponed

Every person whose message is refused or postponed, contrary to the provisions of this chapter, is entitled to recover from the carrier his actual damages, and fifty dollars in addition thereto. **Leg.H.** Enacted 1872.

ARTICLE 5
Space Flight Liability and Immunity

Definitions. §2210.
Warning statement for space flight activities. §2211.
Liability for injury arising out of space flight activities. §2212.

§2210. Definitions

For purposes of this article:

(a) "Participant" means a space flight participant as defined in Section 50902 of Title 51 of the United States Code.

(b) "Participant injury" means a bodily injury, including death, emotional injury, or property damage, sustained by the participant.

(c) "Space flight activities" means launch services or reentry services as defined in Section 50902 of Title 51 of the United States Code.

(d) "Space flight entity" means any public or private entity that holds, either directly or through a corporate subsidiary or parent, a license, permit, or other authorization issued by the United States Federal Aviation Administration pursuant to the federal Commercial Space Launch Amendments Act of 2004 (51 U.S.C. Sec. 50905 et seq.), including, but not limited to, a safety approval and a payload determination. **Leg.H.** Added Stats 2012 ch 416 §2 (AB 2243), effective January 1, 2013.

2012 Note: This act shall be known and may be cited as the Space Flight Liability and Immunity Act. Stats 2012 ch 416 (AB 2243) §1.

§2211. Warning statement for space flight activities

(a) A space flight entity providing space flight activities to a participant shall have each participant sign a warning statement that shall contain, at a minimum, and in addition to any language required by federal law, the following notice:

"WARNING AND ACKNOWLEDGMENT: I understand and acknowledge that, under California law, there is limited civil liability for bodily injury, including death, emotional injury, or property damage, sustained by a participant as a result of the inherent risks associated with space flight activities provided by a space flight entity. I have given my informed consent to participate in space flight activities after receiving a description of the inherent risks associated with space flight activities, as required by federal law pursuant to Section 50905 of Title 51 of the United States Code and Section 460.45 of Title 14 of the Code of Federal Regulations. The consent that I have given acknowledges that the inherent risks associated with space flight activities include, but are not limited to, risk of bodily injury, including death, emotional injury, and property damage. I understand and acknowledge that I am participating in space flight activities at my own risk. I have been given the opportunity to consult with an attorney before signing this statement."

(b) Failure to comply with the requirements provided in this section shall prevent a space flight entity from invoking the privileges of immunity provided by Section 2212.

(c) Nothing in this section shall be construed to be contrary to the public policy of this state. **Leg.H.** Added Stats 2012 ch 416 §2 (AB 2243), effective January 1, 2013. Amended Stats 2014 ch 48 §1 (SB 415), effective January 1, 2015.

2012 Note: For citation of Stats 2012 ch 416 (AB 2243), see 2012 Note following §2210.

§2212. Liability for injury arising out of space flight activities

(a) Except as provided in subdivision (c), a space flight entity shall not be liable for participant injury arising out of space flight activities if both of the following apply:

(1) The participant has been informed of the risks associated with space flight activities as required by federal law and Section 2211.

(2) The participant has given his or her informed consent that he or she is voluntarily participating in space flight activities after having been informed of the risks associated with those activities, as required by federal law and Section 2211.

(b) If informed consent is given pursuant to subdivision (a), a participant, his or her representative, including the heirs, administrators, executors, assignees, next of kin, and estate of the participant, or any person who attempts to bring a claim on behalf of the participant for a participant injury, shall not be authorized to maintain an action against, or recover from, a space flight entity for a participant injury that resulted from the risks associated with space flight activities, except as provided in subdivision (c).

(c) Nothing in this section shall prevent or limit the liability of a space flight entity that does any of the following:

(1) Commits an act or omission that constitutes gross negligence or willful or wanton disregard for the safety of the participant, and that act or omission proximately causes a participant injury.

(2) Intentionally causes a participant injury.

(3) Has actual knowledge or reasonably should have known of a dangerous condition on the land or in the facilities or equipment used in space flight activities and the dangerous condition proximately causes injury, damage, or death to the participant.

(d) Any limitation on legal liability afforded by this section to a space flight entity is in addition to any other limitations of legal liability otherwise provided by law.

(e) Nothing in this section shall be construed to limit the liability of a manufacturer of a part or component used in space flight activities if a defective part or component proximately causes an injury to the participant. **Leg.H.** Added Stats 2012 ch 416 §2 (AB 2243), effective January 1, 2013.

2012 Note: For citation of Stats 2012 ch 416 (AB 2243), see 2012 Note following §2210.

CHAPTER 6
CARRIER OF PASSENGERS ACT OF 2024

Article 1. Title.
Article 2. Definitions.
Article 3. General Provisions.
Article 4. Civil Action and Penalties.
Article 5. Applicability.
Article 6. Severability.

ARTICLE 1
Title

Citation of chapter. § 2213.

§ 2213. Citation of chapter

This chapter shall be known, and may be cited, as the Carrier of Passengers Act of 2024. **Leg.H.** Added Stats 2024 ch 742 §1 (AB 2780), effective January 1, 2025.

ARTICLE 2
Definitions

Definitions. § 2214.

§ 2214. Definitions

For purposes of this chapter, the following definitions apply:

(a) "Carrier of passengers" means a motor carrier, passenger carrier, or charter-party carrier of passengers that operates a motor vehicle, on a commercial or for-hire basis, and engages in the embarkation and disembarkation of passengers.

(b) "Charter-party carrier of passengers" has the same meaning as used in Section 5360.

(c) "Disembarkation" means the physical discharge of passengers from a transportation service provided by a carrier of passengers at a geographic location within California.

(d) "Embarkation" means the physical commencement of a transportation service provided by a carrier of passengers.

(e) "Motor vehicle" has the same meaning as used in Section 5359 of the Public Utilities Code. **Leg.H.** Added Stats 2024 ch 742 §1 (AB 2780), effective January 1, 2025.

ARTICLE 3
General Provisions

Emergency shelter and other immediate services upon disembarkation; Electronic

§ 2215. Emergency shelter and other immediate services upon disembarkation; Electronic notice requirements; Location of disembarkation; Nondisclosure to immigration authority

(a)(1) This chapter applies to any carrier of passengers operating a motor vehicle who knows or reasonably should know that the motor vehicle will be transporting, from embarkation, 10 or more passengers who are likely to seek emergency shelter and other immediate services upon disembarkation.

(2) For purposes of this subdivision, "likely to seek emergency shelter and other immediate services upon disembarkation" may include, but is not limited to, any of the following:

(A) Temporary housing or shelter.
(B) Food.
(C) Clothing.
(D) Medical screenings.

(b) For purposes of this chapter, there is a presumption that passengers who have arrived in the United States within 30 days of embarkation are likely to seek emergency shelter and other immediate services upon disembarkation.

(c) At least 24 hours before embarkation, a carrier of passengers shall provide electronic notice to a designated point of contact at the governing body of the city, county, or city and county with jurisdiction at the geographic location of disembarkation. This electronic notice shall include all of the following information:

(1) The anticipated date and time of arrival of passengers at the geographic location of disembarkation and the address of the geographic location.

(2) The waybill or trip report, consistent with Section 5381.5 of the Public Utilities Code.

(3) The number of passengers on the motor vehicle who the carrier of passengers knows or reasonably should know arrived in the United States within 30 days of embarkation, and, if the carrier of passengers has relevant information, the number of these passengers that are likely to seek emergency shelter and other immediate services upon disembarkation.

(4) A description of the motor vehicle, including the color, the license plate number, and any logo or other information printed on the exterior of the motor vehicle to assist local officials in identifying the motor vehicle.

(d)(1) The governing body of the city, county, or city and county with jurisdiction at the geographic location of disembarkation may designate a specific location of disembarkation within the governing body's jurisdiction.

(2) A governing body described in paragraph (1) that elects to designate a specific location of disembarkation pursuant to paragraph (1) shall post notice of that location on the governing body's internet website. The carrier of passengers shall check the internet website before embarkation. If the location of disembarkation is not posted on the internet website, the carrier of passengers may disembark at the geographic location they specify pursuant to paragraph (1) of subdivision (c).

(e) If a governing body described in paragraph (1) of subdivision (d) elects to designate a specific location of disembarkation pursuant to paragraph (1) of subdivision (d), and has provided electronic notice of that location pursuant to paragraph (2) of subdivision (d) or posted notice of that location on the governing body's internet website pursuant to paragraph (2) of subdivision (d), disembarkation shall only occur at that location.

(f)(1) The location of disembarkation, including the city and county, shall be made known to, and agreed to by, each passenger before embarkation.

(2) If the passenger is a minor, then the location of disembarkation shall be made known to, and agreed to by, the minor passenger's parent or guardian before embarkation. The notice and agreement shall be done in the passenger's primary language.

(g) A governing body shall not share, disclose, or otherwise make accessible to any immigration authority, as defined in Section 7284.4 of the Government Code, any information shared or received pursuant to any provision of this chapter without a court-ordered subpoena or judicial warrant. **Leg.H.** Added Stats 2024 ch 742 §1 (AB 2780), effective January 1, 2025.

Prior Law Former CC §2215, relating to trusts classified, was enacted 1872, and repealed Stats 1986 ch 820 §7, operative July 1, 1987.

ARTICLE 4
Civil Action and Penalties

Civil action and penalties for violations. § 2216.

§ 2216. Civil action and penalties for violations

(a) Any of the following parties may bring a civil action seeking preventive relief, including for a permanent or temporary injunction, restraining order, or other order against the carrier of passengers, for one or more violations of this chapter:

(1) The Attorney General, a district attorney, or a city attorney.
(2) A passenger who was transported in violation of this chapter.
(3) A homeless service provider or shelter, a health care service provider, or a nonprofit social service provider that suffered a direct violation of this chapter.

(b) A carrier of passengers that violates this chapter, or whose employee violates this chapter, may be assessed a civil penalty of up to ten thousand dollars ($10,000) for each act of transporting a person that resulted in one or more violations of this chapter.

(c) Article 6 (commencing with Section 5411) of Chapter 8 of the Public Utilities Code does not apply for purposes of this chapter.

(d) The Attorney General, a district attorney, or a city attorney may bring the action described in subdivision (b).

(e) A prevailing plaintiff shall be entitled to attorney's fees and costs in any action brought pursuant to subdivision (a) or (b). **Leg.H.** Added Stats 2024 ch 742 §1 (AB 2780), effective January 1, 2025.

Prior Law Former CC §2216, relating to voluntary trust, was enacted 1872, and repealed Stats 1986 ch 820 §7, operative July 1, 1987.

ARTICLE 5
Applicability

Effect on local ordinance, code, regulation, or order; Consistency with federal law. § 2217.

§ 2217. Effect on local ordinance, code, regulation, or order; Consistency with federal law

(a) This chapter does not preempt, limit, prohibit, or otherwise affect the adoption, implementation, or enforcement of any local ordinance, code, regulation, or order related to carrier of passenger transportation services, except only to the extent that the local ordinance, code, regulation, or order is inconsistent with this chapter. Any local ordinance, code, regulation, or order is not inconsistent with this chapter if it affords greater protection to passengers than the requirements set forth in this chapter. Any local ordinance, code, regulation, or order that duplicates or supplements this chapter shall be construed as providing additional remedies to those set forth in this chapter, and shall not be construed to preempt, limit, prohibit, or otherwise affect this chapter.

(b) This chapter shall only be implemented to the extent that implementation is consistent with federal law. **Leg.H.** Added Stats 2024 ch 742 §1 (AB 2780), effective January 1, 2025.

Prior Law Former CC §2217, relating to involuntary trust, was enacted 1872, and repealed Stats 1986 ch 820 §7, operative July 1, 1987.

ARTICLE 6
Severability

Severability. § 2218.

§ 2218. Severability

(a) The provisions of this chapter are severable. If any provision of this chapter or its application is held invalid, that invalidity shall not affect other provisions or applications that can be given effect without the invalid provision or application. **Leg.H.** Added Stats 2024 ch 742 §1 (AB 2780), effective January 1, 2025.

Prior Law Former CC §2218, relating to involuntary trusts, was enacted 1872, and repealed Stats 1986 ch 820 §7, operative July 1, 1987. See Prob C §§24, 84.

TITLE 8
INVOLUNTARY TRUSTS

Who is involuntary trustee. §2223.
Involuntary trusts of wrongful gains. §2224.
Time limitation for action by Attorney General pursuant to Section 2223 or 2224. §2224.5.

Proceeds from sale of story of felony by convicted felon; Involuntary trust. §2225.

§2215. [Section repealed 1987]

Leg.H. Enacted 1872. Repealed Stats 1986 ch 820 §7, operative July 1, 1987. The repealed section related to trusts classified.

§2216. [Section repealed 1987]

Leg.H. Enacted 1872. Repealed Stats 1986 ch 820 §7, operative July 1, 1987. The repealed section related to voluntary trust.

§2217. [Section repealed 1987]

Leg.H. Enacted 1872. Repealed Stats 1986 ch 820 §7, operative July 1, 1987. The repealed section related to involuntary trust.

§2218. [Section repealed 1987]

Leg.H. Enacted 1872. Repealed Stats 1986 ch 820 §7, operative July 1, 1987. See Prob C §§24, 84.

§2219. [Section repealed 1987]

Leg.H. Enacted 1872. Repealed Stats 1986 ch 820 §7, operative July 1, 1987. The repealed section related to what constitutes one a trustee.

§2220. [Section repealed 1987]

Leg.H. Enacted 1872. Amended Stats 1929 ch 146 §1 p 282. Repealed Stats 1986 ch 820 §7, operative July 1, 1987. See Prob C §15203.

§2221. [Section repealed 1987]

Leg.H. Enacted 1872. Repealed Stats 1986 ch 820 §7, operative July 1, 1987. See Prob C §§15200–15207.

§2222. [Section repealed 1987]

Leg.H. Enacted 1872. Repealed Stats 1986 ch 820 §7, operative July 1, 1987. See Prob C §§15200–15207.

§2223. Who is involuntary trustee

One who wrongfully detains a thing is an involuntary trustee thereof, for the benefit of the owner. **Leg.H.** Added Stats 1986 ch 820 §8, operative July 1, 1987.

Prior Law: Former §2223, similar to the present section, was enacted 1872, and repealed by Stats 1986 ch 820 §7, operative July 1, 1987.

§2224. Involuntary trusts of wrongful gains

One who gains a thing by fraud, accident, mistake, undue influence, the violation of a trust, or other wrongful act, is, unless he or she has some other and better right thereto, an involuntary trustee of the thing gained, for the benefit of the person who would otherwise have had it. **Leg.H.** Added Stats 1986 ch 820 §8, operative July 1, 1987.

Prior Law: Former §2224, similar to the present section, was enacted 1872, and repealed by Stats 1986 ch 820 §7, operative July 1, 1987.

§2224.1. [Section repealed 1987]

Leg.H. Enacted Stats 1983 ch 1016 §2. Repealed Stats 1986 ch 820 §7, operative July 1, 1987. See CC §2225.

§2224.5. Time limitation for action by Attorney General pursuant to Section 2223 or 2224

An action brought by the Attorney General pursuant to Section 2223 or 2224 may be brought at any time within 10 years after the cause of action accrued. **Leg.H.** Added Stats 2015 ch 299 §2 (AB 556), effective January 1, 2016.

§2225. Proceeds from sale of story of felony by convicted felon; Involuntary trust

(a) As used in this section:

(1) "Convicted felon" means any person convicted of a felony, or found not guilty by reason of insanity of a felony committed in California, either by a court or jury trial or by entry of a plea in court.

(2) "Felony" means a felony defined by any California or United States statute.

(3)(A) "Representative of the felon" means any person or entity receiving proceeds or profits by designation of that felon, on behalf of that felon, or in the stead of that felon, whether by the felon's designation or by operation of law.

(B) "Profiteer of the felony" means any person who sells or transfers for profit any memorabilia or other property or thing of the felon, the value of which is enhanced by the notoriety gained from the commission of the felony for which the felon was convicted. This subparagraph shall not apply to any media entity reporting on the felon's story or on the sale of the materials, memorabilia, or other property or thing of the felon. Nor shall it apply to the sale of the materials, as the term is defined in paragraph (6), where the seller is exercising his or her first amendment rights. This subparagraph also shall not apply to the sale or transfer by a profiteer of any other expressive work protected by the First Amendment unless the sale or transfer is primarily for a commercial or speculative purpose.

(4)(A) "Beneficiary" means a person who, under applicable law, other than the provisions of this section, has or had a right to recover damages from the convicted felon for physical, mental, or emotional injury, or pecuniary loss proximately caused by the convicted felon as a result of the crime for which the felon was convicted.

(B) If a beneficiary described in subparagraph (A) has died, "beneficiary" also includes a person or estate entitled to recover damages pursuant to Chapter 4 (commencing with Section 377.10) of Title 3 of Part 2 of the Code of Civil Procedure.

(C) If a person has died and the death was proximately caused by the convicted felon as a result of the crime for which the felon was convicted, "beneficiary" also includes a person described in Section 377.60 of the Code of Civil Procedure and any beneficiary of a will of the decedent who had a right under that will to receive more than 25 percent of the value of the estate of the decedent.

(5) "Beneficiary's interest" means that portion of the proceeds or profits necessary to pay the following:

(A) In the case of a beneficiary described in subparagraph (A) or (B) of paragraph (4), those damages that, under applicable law, other than the provisions of this section, the beneficiary has or had a right to recover from the convicted felon for injuries proximately caused by the convicted felon as a result of the crime for which the felon was convicted.

(B) In the case of a beneficiary described in subparagraph (C) of paragraph (4), those damages that, under all the circumstances of the case, may be just.

(C) A beneficiary's interest shall be reduced by the following amount:

(i) Money paid to the beneficiary from the Restitution Fund because of the crime for which the felon was convicted.

(ii) Money paid to the beneficiary by the convicted felon because of a requirement of restitution imposed by a court in connection with the crime for which the felon was convicted.

(iii) Money paid to the beneficiary because of a judgment against the convicted felon based upon the crime for which the felon was convicted.

(D) In the case of an unsatisfied existing judgment or order of restitution against the convicted felon and in favor of a beneficiary, any money paid to the beneficiary pursuant to this section shall be applied to reduce the amount of the unsatisfied judgment or order.

(6) "Materials" means books, magazine or newspaper articles, movies, films, videotapes, sound recordings, interviews or appearances on television and radio stations, and live presentations of any kind.

(7) "Story" means a depiction, portrayal, or reenactment of a felony and shall not be taken to mean a passing mention of the felony, as in a footnote or bibliography.

(8) "Sale" includes lease, license, or any other transfer or alienation taking place in California or elsewhere.

(9) "Proceeds" means all fees, royalties, real property, or other consideration of any and every kind or nature received by or owing to a felon or his or her representatives for the preparation for the purpose of sale of materials, for the sale of the rights to materials, or the sale or distribution by the convicted felon of materials whether earned, accrued, or paid before or after the conviction. It includes any interest, earnings, or accretions upon proceeds, and any property received in exchange for proceeds.

(10) "Profits" means all income from anything sold or transferred by the felon, a representative of the felon, or a profiteer of the felony, including any right, the value of which thing or right is enhanced by the notoriety gained from the commission of a felony for which a convicted felon was convicted. This income may have been accrued, earned, or paid before or after the conviction. However, voluntary donations or contributions to a defendant to assist in the defense of criminal charges shall not be deemed to be "profits," provided the donation or contribution to that defense is not given in exchange for some material of value.

(b)(1) All proceeds from the preparation for the purpose of sale, the sale of the rights to, or the sale of materials that include or are based on the story of a felony for which a convicted felon was convicted, shall be subject to an involuntary trust for the benefit of the beneficiaries set forth in this section. That trust shall continue until five years after the time of payment of the proceeds to the felon or five years after the date of conviction, whichever is later. If an action is filed by a beneficiary to recover his or her interest in a trust within those time limitations, the trust character of the property shall continue until the conclusion of the action. At the end of the five-year trust period, any proceeds that remain in trust that have not been claimed by a beneficiary shall be transferred to the Controller, to be allocated to the Restitution Fund for the payment of claims pursuant to Section 13969 of the Government Code.

(2) All profits shall be subject to an involuntary trust for the benefit of the beneficiaries set forth in this section. That trust shall continue until five years after the time of payment of the profits to the felon or five years after the date of conviction, whichever is later. If an action is filed by a beneficiary to recover his or her interest in a trust within those time limitations, the trust character of the property shall continue until the conclusion of the action. At the end of the five-year trust period, any profits that remain in trust that have not been claimed by a beneficiary shall be transferred to the Controller, to be allocated to the Restitution Fund for the payment of claims pursuant to Section 13969 of the Government Code.

(3) Notwithstanding paragraph (2), in the case of a sale or transfer by a profiteer of the felony, the court in an action under subdivision (c) shall, upon an adequate showing by the profiteer of the felony, exclude from the involuntary trust that portion of the profits that represents the inherent value of the memorabilia, property, or thing sold or transferred and exclusive of the amount of the enhancement to the value due to the notoriety of the convicted felon.

(c)(1) Any beneficiary may bring an action against a convicted felon, representative of the felon, or a profiteer of a felony to recover his or her interest in the trust established by this section.

(2) That action may be brought in the superior court of the county in which the beneficiary resides, or of the county in which the convicted felon resides, or of the county in which proceeds or profits are located.

(3) If the court determines that a beneficiary is entitled to proceeds or profits pursuant to this section, the court shall order the payment from proceeds or profits that have been received, and, if that is insufficient, from proceeds or profits that may be received in the future.

(d) If there are two or more beneficiaries and if the available proceeds or profits are insufficient to pay all beneficiaries, the proceeds or profits shall be equitably apportioned among the beneficiaries taking into account the impact of the crime upon them.

Prior to any distribution of any proceeds to a beneficiary, the court shall determine whether the convicted felon has failed to pay any portion of a restitution fine or penalty fine imposed by a court, or any restitution imposed as a condition of probation. The court shall also determine whether the felon is obligated to reimburse a governmental entity for the costs of his or her defense and whether a portion of the proceeds is needed to cover his or her reasonable attorney's fees incurred in the criminal proceeding related to the felony, or any appeal or other related proceeding, or in the defense of the action brought under this section. The court shall order payment of these obligations prior to any payment to a beneficiary, except that 60 percent of the proceeds or profits shall be reserved for payment to the beneficiaries.

(e)(1) The Attorney General may bring an action to require proceeds or profits received by a convicted felon to be held in an express trust in a bank authorized to act as a trustee.

(2) An action may be brought under this subdivision within one year after the receipt of proceeds or profits by a convicted felon or one year after the date of conviction, whichever is later.

That action may be brought in the superior court of any county in which the Attorney General has an office.

(3) If the Attorney General proves that the proceeds or profits are proceeds or profits from the sale of a story or thing of value that are subject to an involuntary trust pursuant to this section, and that it is more probable than not that there are beneficiaries within the meaning of this section, the court shall order that all proceeds or profits be deposited in a bank and held by the bank as trustee of the trust until an order of disposition is made by a court pursuant to subdivision (d), or until the expiration of the period specified in subdivision (b).

(4) If the Attorney General prevails in an action under this subdivision, the court shall order the payment from the proceeds or profits to the Attorney General of reasonable costs and attorney's fees.

(f)(1) In any action brought pursuant to this section, upon motion of a party the court shall grant a preliminary injunction to prevent any waste of proceeds or profits if it appears that the proceeds or profits are subject to the provisions of this section, and that they may be subject to waste.

(2) Upon motion of the Attorney General or any potential beneficiary, the court shall grant a preliminary injunction against a person against whom an indictment or information for a felony has been filed in superior court to prevent any waste of proceeds or profits if there is probable cause to believe that the proceeds or profits would be subject to an involuntary trust pursuant to this section upon conviction of this person, and that they may be subject to waste.

(g) Any violation of an order of a court made pursuant to this section shall be punishable as contempt.

(h) The remedies provided by this section are in addition to other remedies provided by law.

No period of limitations, except those provided by this section, shall limit the right of recovery under this section. **Leg.H.** Added Stats 1986 ch 820 §8, operative July 1, 1987. Amended Stats 1992 ch 178 §2 (SB 1496); Stats 1994 ch 556 §1 (SB 1330), effective September 12, 1994; Stats 1995 ch 262 §1 (SB 287); Stats 2000 ch 261 §2 (SB 1565).

2000 Note: The provisions of this act are severable. If any provision of this act or its application is held invalid, that invalidity shall not affect other provisions or applications that can be given effect without the invalid provision or application. Stats 2000 ch 261 §3.

Prior Law: Former §2225, similar to present Prob C §§15001, 15206, 15209, was added Stats 1983 ch 138 §1, and repealed Stats 1986 ch 820 §7, operative July 1, 1987.

§2228. [Section repealed 1987]

Leg.H. Enacted 1872. Repealed Stats 1986 ch 820 §7, operative July 1, 1987. See Prob C §16002.

§2229. [Section repealed 1987]

Leg.H. Enacted 1872. Repealed Stats 1986 ch 820 §7, operative July 1, 1987. See Prob C §§16002, 16004.

§2230. [Section repealed 1987]

Leg.H. Enacted 1872. Repealed Stats 1986 ch 820 §7, operative July 1, 1987. See Prob C §§16004, 16463.

§2231. [Section repealed 1987]

Leg.H. Enacted 1872. Repealed Stats 1986 ch 820 §7, operative July 1, 1987. See Prob C §16002.

§2232. [Section repealed 1987]

Leg.H. Enacted 1872. Repealed Stats 1986 ch 820 §7, operative July 1, 1987. See Prob C §§16002, 16005.

§2233. [Section repealed 1987]

Leg.H. Enacted 1872. Repealed Stats 1986 ch 820 §7, operative July 1, 1987. See Prob C §§15642, 16002.

§2234. [Section repealed 1987]

Leg.H. Enacted 1872. Repealed Stats 1986 ch 820 §7, operative July 1, 1987. See Prob C §16400.

§2235. [Section repealed 1987]

Leg.H. Enacted 1872. Amended Stats 1963 ch 1215 §1 p 2733. Repealed Stats 1986 ch 820 §7, operative July 1, 1987. See Prob C §§16002, 16004.

§2236. [Section repealed 1987]

Leg.H. Enacted 1872. Amended Stats 1905 ch 456 §1 p 615. Repealed Stats 1986 ch 820 §7, operative July 1, 1987. See Prob C §§16009, 16420, 16440.

§2237. [Section repealed 1987]

Leg.H. Enacted 1872. Repealed Stats 1986 ch 820 §7, operative July 1, 1987. See Prob C §§16440, 16441.

§2238. [Section repealed 1987]

Leg.H. Enacted 1872. Amended Stats 1983 ch 99 §1. Repealed Stats 1986 ch 820 §7, operative July 1, 1987. See Prob C §§16420, 16440, 16462.

§2239. [Section repealed 1987]
Leg.H. Enacted 1872. Repealed Stats 1986 ch 820 §7, operative July 1, 1987. See Prob C §16402.

§2240. [Section repealed 1987]
Leg.H. Added Stats 1972 ch 1057 §8. Repealed Stats 1986 ch 820 §7, operative July 1, 1987. See Prob C §15620.

§2243. [Section repealed 1987]
Leg.H. Enacted 1872. Repealed Stats 1986 ch 820 §7, operative July 1, 1987. See Prob C §18100.

§2244. [Section repealed 1987]
Leg.H. Enacted 1872. Repealed Stats 1986 ch 820 §7, operative July 1, 1987. See Prob C §18101.

§2250. [Section repealed 1987]
Leg.H. Enacted 1872. Repealed Stats 1986 ch 820 §7, operative July 1, 1987. See Prob C §82.

§2251. [Section repealed 1987]
Leg.H. Enacted 1872. Repealed Stats 1986 ch 820 §7, operative July 1, 1987. See Prob C §§15200–15207, 15600.

§2252. [Section repealed 1987]
Leg.H. Enacted 1872. Repealed Stats 1986 ch 820 §7, operative July 1, 1987. The repealed section related to trustees appointed by court.

§2253. [Section repealed 1987]
Leg.H. Enacted 1872. Repealed Stats 1986 ch 820 §7, operative July 1, 1987. See Prob C §§15200, 15201.

§2254. [Section repealed 1987]
Leg.H. Enacted 1872. Repealed Stats 1986 ch 820 §7, operative July 1, 1987. The repealed section related to declaration of trust.

§2258. [Section repealed 1987]
Leg.H. Enacted 1872. Amended Stats 1983 ch 99 §2. Repealed Stats 1986 ch 820 §7, operative July 1, 1987. See Prob C §§15404, 16000, 16001, 16462.

§2259. [Section repealed 1987]
Leg.H. Enacted 1872. Repealed Stats 1986 ch 820 §7, operative July 1, 1987. See Prob C §§16040, 16041.

§2260. [Section repealed 1987]
Leg.H. Enacted 1872. Repealed Stats 1986 ch 820 §7, operative July 1, 1987. See Pro §§15641, 15660, 16000.

§2261. [Section repealed 1987]
Leg.H. Enacted 1872. Amended Stats 1943 ch 811 §1 p 2602; Stats 1967 ch 688 §1 p 2054, ch 1706 §1 p 4265; Stats 1968 ch 161 §1 p 385; Stats 1969 ch 259 §1 p 611; Stats 1984 ch 1372 §1. Repealed Stats 1986 ch 820 §7, operative July 1, 1987. See Prob C §§16040, 16047, 16200, 16226.

§2262. [Section repealed 1987]
Leg.H. Enacted 1872. Repealed Stats 1986 ch 820 §7, operative July 1, 1987. See Prob C §§16440, 16441.

§2263. [Section repealed 1987]
Leg.H. Enacted 1872. Repealed Stats 1986 ch 820 §7, operative July 1, 1987. See Prob C §16004.

§2264. [Section repealed 1987]
Leg.H. Added Stats 1966 1st Ex Sess ch 50 §2 p 364, effective May 4, 1966. Repealed Stats 1986 ch 820 §7, operative July 1, 1987. The repealed section related to transfer in trust of a pecuniary amount.

§2267. [Section repealed 1987]
Leg.H. Enacted 1872. Repealed Stats 1986 ch 820 §7, operative July 1, 1987. See Prob C §§16200, 18000, 18004.

§2268. [Section repealed 1987]
Leg.H. Enacted 1872. Repealed Stats 1986 ch 820 §7, operative July 1, 1987. See Prob C §15620.

§2269. [Section repealed 1987]
Leg.H. Enacted 1872. Amended Stats 1981 ch 1046 §1; Stats 1983 ch 99 §3. Repealed Stats 1986 ch 820 §7, operative July 1, 1987. See Prob C §§16080, 16081, 17200.

§2269.1. [Section repealed 1987]
Leg.H. Added Stats 1984 ch 1017 §2. Repealed Stats 1986 ch 820 §7, operative July 1, 1987. See Prob C §§16202, 16224.

§2270. [Section repealed 1987]
Leg.H. Added Stats 1939 ch 538 §3 p 1943. Repealed Stats 1986 ch 820 §7, operative July 1, 1987. See Prob C §16234.

§2271. [Section repealed 1987]
Leg.H. Added Stats 1971 ch 717 §1, effective August 24, 1971. Repealed Stats 1986 ch 820 §7, operative July 1, 1987. See Prob C §§16100–16102, 16104.

§2271.1. [Section repealed 1987]
Leg.H. Added Stats 1971 ch 717 §2, effective August 24, 1971. Repealed Stats 1986 ch 820 §7, operative July 1, 1987. See Prob C §§15001, 16100, 16102–16104.

§2271.2. [Section repealed 1987]
Leg.H. Added Stats 1971 ch 717 §3, effective August 24, 1971. Repealed Stats 1986 ch 820 §7, operative July 1, 1987. See Prob C §16105.

§2272. [Section repealed 1987]
Leg.H. Added Stats 1947 ch 506 §1 p 1493. Repealed Stats 1986 ch 820 §7, operative July 1, 1987. See Prob C §§16231, 18100.

§2273. [Section repealed 1987]
Leg.H. Enacted 1872. Repealed Stats 1986 ch 820 §7, operative July 1, 1987. See Prob C §15684.

§2274. [Section repealed 1987]
Leg.H. Enacted 1872. Amended Stats 1889 ch 224 §1 p 334; Stats 1909 ch 151 §1 p 252; Stats 1937 ch 536 §1 p 1347; Stats 1967 ch 661 §1 p 2030; Stats 1972 ch 937 §1. Repealed Stats 1986 ch 820 §7, operative July 1, 1987. See Prob C §§15680, 15681, 15683, 17000.

§2275. [Section repealed 1987]
Leg.H. Enacted 1872. Repealed Stats 1986 ch 820 §7, operative July 1, 1987. The repealed section related to involuntary trustee.

§2279. [Section repealed 1987]
Leg.H. Enacted 1872. Repealed Stats 1986 ch 820 §7, operative July 1, 1987. See Prob C §15407.

§2279.1. [Section repealed 1987]
Leg.H. Added Stats 1973 ch 506 §1. Repealed Stats 1986 ch 820 §7, operative July 1, 1987. See Prob C §§15002, 15408, 15410, 17206.

§2280. [Section repealed 1987]
Leg.H. Enacted 1872. Amended Stats 1931 ch 950 §1. Repealed Stats 1986 ch 820 §7, operative July 1, 1987. See Prob C §§15400, 15401, 15410.

§2281. [Section repealed 1987]
Leg.H. Enacted 1872. Amended Stats 1961 ch 1042 §1. Repealed Stats 1986 ch 820 §7, operative July 1, 1987. See Civ C §2934b; Pro C §§15643, 18102.

§2282. [Section repealed 1987]
Leg.H. Enacted 1872. Amended Stats 1883 ch 5 §1 p 3; Stats 1961 ch 1042 §2 p 2726; Stats 1983 ch 99 §4. Repealed Stats 1986 ch 820 §7, operative July 1, 1987. See Prob C §§15640, 15641, 16460, 16463.

§2283. [Section repealed 1987]
Leg.H. Enacted 1872. Amended Code Amdts 1880 ch 41 §23 p 8; Stats 1969 ch 272 §1 p 621. Repealed Stats 1986 ch 820 §7, operative July 1, 1987. See Prob C §§15640, 15642.

§2287. [Section repealed 1987]
Leg.H. Enacted 1872. Amended Code Amdts 1880 ch 41 §24 p 8; Stats 1911 ch 67 §1 p 79; Stats 1913 ch 237 §1 p 395; Stats 1933 ch 970 §1 p 2499. Repealed Stats 1986 ch 820 §7, operative July 1, 1987. See Prob C §15660.

§2288. [Section repealed 1987]

Leg.H. Enacted 1872. Repealed Stats 1986 ch 820 §7, operative July 1, 1987. See Prob C §15621.

§2289. [Section repealed 1987]

Leg.H. Enacted 1872. Amended Code Amdts 1880 ch 41 §25. Repealed Stats 1986 ch 820 §7, operative July 1, 1987. See Prob C §§15660, 17005.

§2290.1. [Section repealed 1987]

Leg.H. Added Stats 1973 ch 940 §1. Amended Stats 1974 ch 278 §1. Repealed Stats 1986 ch 820 §7, operative July 1, 1987. See Prob C §18501.

§2290.2. [Section repealed 1987]

Leg.H. Added Stats 1973 ch 950 §1. Amended Stats 1978 ch 806 §2. Repealed Stats 1986 ch 820 §7, operative July 1, 1987. See Prob C §18502.

§2290.3. [Section repealed 1987]

Leg.H. Added Stats 1973 ch 950 §2. Repealed Stats 1986 ch 820 §7, operative July 1, 1987. See Prob C §18503.

§2290.4. [Section repealed 1987]

Leg.H. Added Stats 1973 ch 950 §1. Repealed Stats 1986 ch 820 §7, operative July 1, 1987. See Prob C §18504.

§2290.5. [Section repealed 1987]

Leg.H. Added Stats 1973 ch 950 §1. Repealed Stats 1986 ch 820 §7, operative July 1, 1987. See Prob C §18505.

§2290.6. [Section repealed 1987]

Leg.H. Added Stats 1973 ch 950 §1. Repealed Stats 1986 ch 820 §7, operative July 1, 1987. See Prob C §18506.

§2290.7. [Section repealed 1987]

Leg.H. Added Stats 1973 ch 950 §1. Amended Stats 1974 ch 278 §2. Repealed Stats 1986 ch 820 §7, operative July 1, 1987. See Prob C §18507.

§2290.8. [Section repealed 1987]

Leg.H. Added Stats 1973 ch 950 §1. Repealed Stats 1986 ch 820 §7, operative July 1, 1987. The repealed section related to severability of provisions of chapter.

§2290.9. [Section repealed 1987]

Leg.H. Added Stats 1973 ch 950 §1. Repealed Stats 1986 ch 820 §7, operative July 1, 1987. The repealed section related to application and construction of chapter.

§2290.10. [Section repealed 1983]

Leg.H. Added Stats 1973 ch 950 §1. Amended Stats 1978 ch 806 §3. Repealed effective January 1, 1983, by its own provisions. The repealed section related to reports filed by institutions.

§2290.11. [Section repealed 1987]

Leg.H. Added Stats 1973 ch 950 §1. Repealed Stats 1986 ch 820 §7, operative July 1, 1987. See Prob C §18508.

§2290.12. [Section repealed 1987]

Leg.H. Added Stats 1973 ch 950 §1. Repealed Stats 1986 ch 820 §7, operative July 1, 1987. See Prob C §18500.

TITLE 9
AGENCY

Chapter 1. Agency in General.
Chapter 2. Particular Agencies.

CHAPTER 1
AGENCY IN GENERAL

Article 1. Definition of Agency.
Article 2. Authority of Agents.
Article 3. Mutual Obligations of Principals and Third Persons.
Article 4. Obligations of Agents to Third Persons.
Article 5. Delegation of Agency.
Article 6. Termination of Agency.

ARTICLE 1
Definition of Agency

Agency, what. §2295.
Who may appoint, and who may be an agent. §2296.
Agents, general or special. §2297.
Agency, actual or ostensible. §2298.
Actual agency. §2299.
Ostensible agency. §2300.

§2295. Agency, what

An agent is one who represents another, called the principal, in dealings with third persons. Such representation is called agency. **Leg.H.** Enacted 1872.

§2296. Who may appoint, and who may be an agent

Any person having capacity to contract may appoint an agent, and any person may be an agent. **Leg.H.** Enacted 1872.

§2297. Agents, general or special

An agent for a particular act or transaction is called a special agent. All others are general agents. **Leg.H.** Enacted 1872.

§2298. Agency, actual or ostensible

An agency is either actual or ostensible. **Leg.H.** Enacted 1872.

§2299. Actual agency

An agency is actual when the agent is really employed by the principal. **Leg.H.** Enacted 1872.

§2300. Ostensible agency

An agency is ostensible when the principal intentionally, or by want of ordinary care, causes a third person to believe another to be his agent who is not really employed by him. **Leg.H.** Enacted 1872.

ARTICLE 2
Authority of Agents

What authority may be conferred. §2304.
Agent may perform acts required of principal by code. §2305.
Agent cannot have authority to defraud principal. §2306.
Creation of agency. §2307.
Consideration unnecessary. §2308.
Form of authority. §2309.
Ratification of agent's act. §2310.
Ratification of part of a transaction. §2311.
When ratification void. §2312.
Ratification not to work injury to third persons. §2313.
Rescission of ratification. §2314.
Measure of agent's authority. §2315.
Actual authority, what. §2316.
Ostensible authority. §2317.
Agent's authority as to persons having notice of restrictions upon it. §2318.
Agent's necessary authority. §2319.
Agent's power to disobey instructions. §2320.
Authority to be construed by its specific, rather than by its general terms. §2321.
Authority of agent. §2322.
What included in authority to sell personal property. §2323.
What included in authority to sell real property. §2324.
Authority of general agent to receive price of property. §2325.
Authority of special agent to receive price. §2326.

§2304. What authority may be conferred

An agent may be authorized to do any acts which his principal might do, except those to which the latter is bound to give his personal attention. **Leg.H.** Enacted 1872.

§2305. Agent may perform acts required of principal by code

Every act which, according to this code, may be done by or to any person, may be done by or to the agent of such person for that purpose, unless a contrary intention clearly appears. **Leg.H.** Enacted 1872.

§2306. Agent cannot have authority to defraud principal

An agent can never have authority, either actual or ostensible, to do an act which is, and is known or suspected by the person with whom he deals, to be a fraud upon the principal. **Leg.H.** Enacted 1872.

§2307. Creation of agency

An agency may be created, and an authority may be conferred, by a precedent authorization or a subsequent ratification. **Leg.H.** Enacted 1872.

§2307.1. [Section repealed 1981]
Leg.H. Added Stats 1979 ch 234 §1. Repealed Stats 1981 ch 511 §1. The repealed section related to subsequent disability or incapacity of principal.

§2308. Consideration unnecessary
A consideration is not necessary to make an authority, whether precedent or subsequent, binding upon the principal. **Leg.H.** Enacted 1872.

§2309. Form of authority
An oral authorization is sufficient for any purpose, except that an authority to enter into a contract required by law to be in writing can only be given by an instrument in writing. **Leg.H.** Enacted 1872.

§2310. Ratification of agent's act
A ratification can be made only in the manner that would have been necessary to confer an original authority for the act ratified, or where an oral authorization would suffice, by accepting or retaining the benefit of the act, with notice thereof. **Leg.H.** Enacted 1872.

§2311. Ratification of part of a transaction
Ratification of part of an indivisible transaction is a ratification of the whole. **Leg.H.** Enacted 1872.

§2312. When ratification void
A ratification is not valid unless, at the time of ratifying the act done, the principal has power to confer authority for such an act. **Leg.H.** Enacted 1872.

§2313. Ratification not to work injury to third persons
No unauthorized act can be made valid, retroactively, to the prejudice of third persons, without their consent. **Leg.H.** Enacted 1872.

§2314. Rescission of ratification
A ratification may be rescinded when made without such consent as is required in a contract, or with an imperfect knowledge of the material facts of the transaction ratified, but not otherwise. **Leg.H.** Enacted 1872.

§2315. Measure of agent's authority
An agent has such authority as the principal, actually or ostensibly, confers upon him. **Leg.H.** Enacted 1872.

§2316. Actual authority, what
Actual authority is such as a principal intentionally confers upon the agent, or intentionally, or by want of ordinary care, allows the agent to believe himself to possess. **Leg.H.** Enacted 1872.

§2317. Ostensible authority
Ostensible authority is such as a principal, intentionally or by want of ordinary care, causes or allows a third person to believe the agent to possess. **Leg.H.** Enacted 1872.

§2318. Agent's authority as to persons having notice of restrictions upon it
Every agent has actually such authority as is defined by this Title, unless specially deprived thereof by his principal, and has even then such authority ostensibly, except as to persons who have actual or constructive notice of the restriction upon his authority. **Leg.H.** Enacted 1872.

§2319. Agent's necessary authority
An agent has authority:
1. To do everything necessary or proper and usual, in the ordinary course of business, for effecting the purpose of his agency; and,
2. To make a representation respecting any matter of fact, not including the terms of his authority, but upon which his right to use his authority depends, and the truth of which cannot be determined by the use of reasonable diligence on the part of the person to whom the representation is made. **Leg.H.** Enacted 1872.

§2320. Agent's power to disobey instructions
An agent has power to disobey instructions in dealing with the subject of the agency, in cases where it is clearly for the interest of his principal that he should do so, and there is not time to communicate with the principal. **Leg.H.** Enacted 1872.

§2321. Authority to be construed by its specific, rather than by its general terms
When an authority is given partly in general and partly in specific terms, the general authority gives no higher powers that those specifically mentioned. **Leg.H.** Enacted 1872.

§2322. Authority of agent
An authority expressed in general terms, however broad, does not authorize an agent to do any of the following:
(a) Act in the agent's own name, unless it is the usual course of business to do so.
(b) Define the scope of the agency.
(c) Violate a duty to which a trustee is subject under Section 16002, 16004, 16005, or 16009 of the Probate Code. **Leg.H.** Enacted 1872. Amended Stats 1986 ch 820 §9, operative July 1, 1987; Stats 1988 ch 113 §5, effective May 24, 1988.

§2323. What included in authority to sell personal property
An authority to sell personal property includes authority to warrant the title of the principal, and the quality and quantity of the property. **Leg.H.** Enacted 1872.

§2324. What included in authority to sell real property
An authority to sell and convey real property includes authority to give the usual covenants of warranty. **Leg.H.** Enacted 1872.

§2325. Authority of general agent to receive price of property
A general agent to sell, who is entrusted by the principal with the possession of the thing sold, has authority to receive the price. **Leg.H.** Enacted 1872.

§2326. Authority of special agent to receive price
A special agent to sell has authority to receive the price on delivery of the thing sold, but not afterwards. **Leg.H.** Enacted 1872.

ARTICLE 3
Mutual Obligations of Principals and Third Persons

Principal, how affected by acts of agent within the scope of his authority. §2330.
Principal, when bound by incomplete execution of authority. §2331.
Notice to agent, when notice to principal. §2332.
Obligation of principal when agent exceeds his authority. §2333.
For acts done under a merely ostensible authority. §2334.
When exclusive credit is given to agent. §2335.
Rights of person who deals with agent without knowledge of agency. §2336.
Instrument intended to bind principal does bind him. §2337.
Principal's responsibility for agent's negligence or omission. §2338.
Principal's responsibility for wrongs willfully committed by the agent. §2339.

§2330. Principal, how affected by acts of agent within the scope of his authority
An agent represents his principal for all purposes within the scope of his actual or ostensible authority, and all the rights and liabilities which would accrue to the agent from transactions within such limit, if they had been entered into on his own account, accrue to the principal. **Leg.H.** Enacted 1872.

§2331. Principal, when bound by incomplete execution of authority
A principal is bound by an incomplete execution of an authority, when it is consistent with the whole purpose and scope thereof, but not otherwise. **Leg.H.** Enacted 1872.

§2332. Notice to agent, when notice to principal
As against a principal, both principal and agent are deemed to have notice of whatever either has notice of, and ought, in good faith and the exercise of ordinary care and diligence, to communicate to the other. **Leg.H.** Enacted 1872.

§2333. Obligation of principal when agent exceeds his authority
When an agent exceeds his authority, his principal is bound by his authorized acts so far only as they can be plainly separated from those which are unauthorized. **Leg.H.** Enacted 1872.

§2334. For acts done under a merely ostensible authority
A principal is bound by acts of his agent, under a merely ostensible authority, to those persons only who have in good faith, and without want of ordinary care, incurred a liability or parted with value, upon the faith thereof. **Leg.H.** Enacted 1872. Amended Stats 1905 ch 467 §1.

§2335. When exclusive credit is given to agent
If exclusive credit is given to an agent by the person dealing with him, his principal is exonerated by payment or other satisfaction made by him

to his agent in good faith, before receiving notice of the creditor's election to hold him responsible. **Leg.H.** Enacted 1872.

§2336. Rights of person who deals with agent without knowledge of agency

One who deals with an agent without knowing or having reason to believe that the agent acts as such in the transaction, may set off against any claim of the principal arising out of the same, all claims which he might have set off against the agent before notice of the agency. **Leg.H.** Enacted 1872.

§2337. Instrument intended to bind principal does bind him

An instrument within the scope of his authority by which an agent intends to bind his principal, does bind him if such intent is plainly inferable from the instrument itself. **Leg.H.** Enacted 1872.

§2338. Principal's responsibility for agent's negligence or omission

Unless required by or under the authority of law to employ that particular agent, a principal is responsible to third persons for the negligence of his agent in the transaction of the business of the agency, including wrongful acts committed by such agent in and as a part of the transaction of such business, and for his willful omission to fulfill the obligations of the principal. **Leg.H.** Enacted 1872.

§2339. Principal's responsibility for wrongs willfully committed by the agent

A principal is responsible for no other wrongs committed by his agent than those mentioned in the last section, unless he has authorized or ratified them, even though they are committed while the agent is engaged in his service. **Leg.H.** Enacted 1872.

ARTICLE 4
Obligations of Agents to Third Persons

Warranty of authority. §2342.
Agent's responsibility to third persons. §2343.
Obligation of agent to surrender property to third person. §2344.
Code provisions governing. §2345.

§2342. Warranty of authority

One who assumes to act as an agent thereby warrants, to all who deal with him in that capacity, that he has the authority which he assumes. **Leg.H.** Enacted 1872.

§2343. Agent's responsibility to third persons

One who assumes to act as an agent is responsible to third persons as a principal for his acts in the course of his agency, in any of the following cases, and in no others:

1. When, with his consent, credit is given to him personally in a transaction;
2. When he enters into a written contract in the name of his principal, without believing, in good faith, that he has authority to do so; or,
3. When his acts are wrongful in their nature. **Leg.H.** Enacted 1872.

§2344. Obligation of agent to surrender property to third person

If an agent receives anything for the benefit of his principal, to the possession of which another person is entitled, he must, on demand, surrender it to such person, or so much of it as he has under his control at the time of demand, on being indemnified for any advance which he has made to his principal, in good faith, on account of the same; and is responsible therefor, if, after notice from the owner, he delivers it to his principal. **Leg.H.** Enacted 1872.

§2345. Code provisions governing

The provisions of this article are subject to the provisions of part one, division first, of this code. **Leg.H.** Enacted 1872.

ARTICLE 5
Delegation of Agency

Agent's delegation of his powers. §2349.
Agent's unauthorized employment of subagent. §2350.
Sub-agent rightfully appointed, represents principal. §2351.

§2349. Agent's delegation of his powers

An agent, unless specially forbidden by his principal to do so, can delegate his powers to another person in any of the following cases, and in no others:

1. When the act to be done is purely mechanical;
2. When it is such as the agent cannot himself, and the subagent can lawfully perform;
3. When it is the usage of the place to delegate such powers; or,
4. When such delegation is specially authorized by the principal. **Leg.H.** Enacted 1872.

§2350. Agent's unauthorized employment of subagent

If an agent employs a subagent without authority, the former is a principal and the latter his agent, and the principal of the former has no connection with the latter. **Leg.H.** Enacted 1872.

§2351. Sub-agent rightfully appointed, represents principal

A sub-agent, lawfully appointed, represents the principal in like manner with the original agent; and the original agent is not responsible to third persons for the acts of the sub-agent. **Leg.H.** Enacted 1872.

ARTICLE 6
Termination of Agency

Termination of agency. §2355.
Termination of agency not coupled with interest. §2356.
Absentee principal. §2357.

§2355. Termination of agency

An agency is terminated, as to every person having notice thereof, by any of the following:
(a) The expiration of its term.
(b) The extinction of its subject.
(c) The death of the agent.
(d) The agent's renunciation of the agency.
(e) The incapacity of the agent to act as such. **Leg.H.** Enacted 1872. Amended Stats 1972 ch 988 §1, effective August 16, 1972; Stats 1980 ch 246 §1; Stats 1983 ch 99 §5; Stats 1994 ch 307 §1 (SB 1907).

§2356. Termination of agency not coupled with interest

(a) Unless the power of an agent is coupled with an interest in the subject of the agency, it is terminated by any of the following:
(1) Its revocation by the principal.
(2) The death of the principal.
(3) The incapacity of the principal to contract.
(b) Notwithstanding subdivision (a), any bona fide transaction entered into with an agent by any person acting without actual knowledge of the revocation, death, or incapacity shall be binding upon the principal, his or her heirs, devisees, legatees, and other successors in interest.
(c) Nothing in this section shall affect the provisions of Section 1216.
(d) With respect to a proxy given by a person to another person relating to the exercise of voting rights, to the extent the provisions of this section conflict with or contravene any other provisions of the statutes of California pertaining to the proxy, the latter provisions shall prevail. **Leg.H.** Enacted 1872. Amended Stats 1943 ch 413 §1, effective May 13, 1943; Stats 1972 ch 988 §2, effective August 16, 1972; Stats 1979 ch 234 §2; Stats 1980 ch 246 §2; Stats 1981 ch 511 §2; Stats 1983 ch 1204 §1; Stats 1994 ch 307 §2 (SB 1907).

§2357. Absentee principal

For the purposes of subdivision (b) of Section 2356, in the case of a principal who is an absentee as defined in Section 1403 of the Probate Code, a person shall be deemed to be without actual knowledge of:
(a) The principal's death or incapacity while the absentee continues in missing status and until the person receives notice of the determination of the death of the absentee by the secretary concerned or the head of the department or agency concerned or the delegate of the secretary or head.
(b) Revocation by the principal during the period described in subdivision (a). **Leg.H.** Added Stats 1981 ch 511 §3. Amended Stats 1994 ch 307 §3 (SB 1907).

CHAPTER 2
PARTICULAR AGENCIES

Article 1. Auctioneers.
Article 2. Factors.
Article 3. Powers of Attorney Under Probate Code.

ARTICLE 1
Auctioneers

Auctioneer's authority from the seller. §2362.
Auctioneer's authority from the bidder. §2363.

§2362. Auctioneer's authority from the seller

An auctioneer, in the absence of special authorization or usage to the contrary, has authority from the seller, only as follows:

1. To sell by public auction to the highest bidder;
2. To sell for cash only, except such articles as are usually sold on credit at auction;
3. To warrant, in like manner with other agents to sell, according to section two thousand three hundred and twenty-three;
4. To prescribe reasonable rules and terms of sale;
5. To deliver the thing sold, upon payment of the price;
6. To collect the price; and,
7. To do whatever else is necessary, or proper and usual, in the ordinary course of business, for effecting these purposes. **Leg.H.** Enacted 1872.

§2363. Auctioneer's authority from the bidder

An auctioneer has authority from a bidder at the auction, as well as from the seller, to bind both by a memorandum of the contract, as prescribed in the title on sale. **Leg.H.** Enacted 1872.

ARTICLE 2
Factors

Factor, what. §2367.
Actual authority of factor. §2368.
Ostensible authority. §2369.

§2367. Factor, what

A factor is an agent, as defined by section two thousand and twenty-six. **Leg.H.** Enacted 1872.

§2368. Actual authority of factor

In addition to the authority of agents in general, a factor has actual authority from his principal, unless specially restricted:

1. To insure property consigned to him uninsured;
2. To sell, on credit, anything intrusted to him for sale, except such things as it is contrary to usage to sell on credit; but not to pledge, mortgage, or barter the same; and,
3. To delegate his authority to his partner or servant, but not to any person in an independent employment. **Leg.H.** Enacted 1872.

§2369. Ostensible authority

A factor has ostensible authority to deal with the property of his principal as his own, in transactions with persons not having notice of the actual ownership. **Leg.H.** Enacted 1872.

ARTICLE 2.5
Agency Relationships in Residential Real Property Transactions [Repealed]

§2373. [Section repealed 1995]

Leg.H. Added Stats 1986 ch 785 §2, operative January 1, 1988. Repealed Stats 1995 ch 428 §2 (SB 467). See CC §2079.13.

Prior Law: Former §2373 was enacted 1872, amended Code Amdts 1873–74 ch 612, and repealed Stats 1937 ch 368 (former H & N C §10001).

§2374. [Section repealed 1995]

Leg.H. Added Stats 1986 ch 785 §2, operative January 1, 1988. Repealed Stats 1995 ch 428 §2 (SB 467). See CC §2079.14.

Prior Law: Former §2374 was enacted 1872, amended Code Amdts 1873–74 ch 612, and repealed Stats 1937 ch 368 (former H & N C §10001).

§2374.5. [Section repealed 1995]

Leg.H. Added Stats 1986 ch 785 §2, operative January 1, 1988. Repealed Stats 1995 ch 428 §2 (SB 467). See CC §2079.15.

§2375. [Section repealed 1995]

Leg.H. Added Stats 1986 ch 785 §2, operative January 1, 1988. Amended Stats 1987 ch 56 §20. Repealed Stats 1995 ch 428 §2 (SB 467). See CC §2079.16.

Prior Law: Former §2375 was enacted 1872, amended Code Amdts 1873–74 ch 612, and repealed Stats 1937 ch 368 (former H & N C §10001).

§2375.5. [Section repealed 1995]

Leg.H. Added Stats 1986 ch 785 §2, operative January 1, 1988. Repealed Stats 1995 ch 428 §2 (SB 467). See CC §2079.17.

§2376. [Section repealed 1995]

Leg.H. Added Stats 1986 ch 785 §2, operative January 1, 1988. Repealed Stats 1995 ch 428 §2 (SB 467). See CC §2079.18.

Prior Law: Former §2376 was enacted 1872, amended Code Amdts 1873–74 ch 612, and repealed Stats 1937 ch 368 (former H & N C §10001).

§2377. [Section repealed 1995]

Leg.H. Added Stats 1986 ch 785 §2, operative January 1, 1988. Repealed Stats 1995 ch 428 §2 (SB 467). See CC §2079.19.

Prior Law: Former §2377 was enacted 1872, amended Code Amdts 1873–74 ch 612, and repealed Stats 1937 ch 368 (former H & N C §10001).

§2378. [Section repealed 1995]

Leg.H. Added Stats 1986 ch 785 §2, operative January 1, 1988. Repealed Stats 1995 ch 428 §2 (SB 467). See CC §2079.20.

Prior Law: Former §2378 was enacted 1872, amended Code Amdts 1873–74 ch 612, and repealed Stats 1937 ch 368 (former H & N C §10001).

§2379. [Section repealed 1995]

Leg.H. Added Stats 1986 ch 785 §2, operative January 1, 1988. Repealed Stats 1995 ch 428 §2 (SB 467). See CC §2079.21.

Prior Law: Former §2379 was enacted 1872, amended Code Amdts 1873–74 ch 612, and repealed Stats 1937 ch 368 (former H & N C §10001).

§2380. [Section repealed 1995]

Leg.H. Added Stats 1986 ch 785 §2, operative January 1, 1988. Repealed Stats 1995 ch 428 §2 (SB 467). See CC §2079.22.

Prior Law: Former §2380 was enacted 1872, amended Code Amdts 1873–74 ch 612, and repealed Stats 1937 ch 368 (former H & N C §10001).

§2381. [Section repealed 1995]

Leg.H. Added Stats 1986 ch 785 §2, operative January 1, 1988. Repealed Stats 1995 ch 428 §2 (SB 467). See CC §2079.23.

Prior Law: Former §2381 was enacted 1872, amended Code Amdts 1873–74 ch 612, and repealed Stats 1937 ch 368 (former H & N C §10001).

§2382. [Section repealed 1995]

Leg.H. Added Stats 1986 ch 785 §2, operative January 1, 1988. Repealed Stats 1995 ch 428 §2 (SB 467). See CC §2079.24.

Prior Law: Former §2382 was enacted 1872, amended Code Amdts 1873–74 ch 612, and repealed Stats 1937 ch 368 (former H & N C §10001).

§§2383–2384. [Sections repealed 1937]

Leg.H. Enacted 1872. Amended by Code Amdts 1873–74 ch 612. Repealed Stats 1937 ch 368 (former H & N C §10001).

§2385. [Section repealed 1937]

Leg.H. Enacted 1872. Amended by Code Amdts 1873–74 ch 612. Repealed Stats 1937 ch 368 (former H & N C §10001). See H & N C §424.

§§2388, 2389. [Sections repealed 1937]

Leg.H. Enacted 1872. Amended Code Amdts 1873–74 ch 612. Repealed Stats 1937 ch 368 (former H & N C §10001).

§§2395–2399. [Sections repealed 1949]

Leg.H. Added Stats 1929 ch 864 §1. Repealed Stats 1949 ch 383 §2 (Corp C §10002). See Corp C §§16101 et seq.

Prior Law: Former §§2395–2397, relating to partnerships, were enacted 1872 and repealed Stats 1929 ch 864 §1.

ARTICLE 3
Powers of Attorney Under Probate Code

Applicable law. §2400.

§2400. Applicable law

Powers of attorney are governed by the Power of Attorney Law (Division 4.5 (commencing with Section 4000) of the Probate Code) to the extent provided in that law. **Leg.H.** Added Stats 1994 ch 307 §5 (SB 1907).

Prior Law: Former §2400, similar to present Corp C §16202, was added Stats 1929 ch 864 §1 and repealed Stats 1949 ch 383 §2 (Corp C §100002).

Former §2400, similar to present Pro C §4124, was added Stats 1981 ch 511 §4, amended Stats 1985 ch 403 §1, and repealed Stats 1994 ch 307 §4 (SB 1907).

Original §2400, relating to partnerships, was enacted 1872 and repealed Stats 1929 ch 864 §1.

§2400.5. [Section repealed 1994]

Leg.H. Added Stats 1985 ch 403 §2. Repealed Stats 1994 ch 307 §4 (SB 1907). The repealed section related to vote by proxy.

§2401. [Section repealed 1994]

Leg.H. Added Stats 1981 ch 511 §4. Repealed Stats 1994 ch 307 §4 (SB 1907). See Prob C §4125.

Prior Law: Former §2401, similar to present Corp C §16202, was added Stats 1929 ch 864 §1 and repealed Stats 1949 ch 383 §2 (Corp C §100002).

Original §2401, relating to partnerships, was enacted 1872 and repealed Stats 1929 ch 864 §1.

§2402. [Section repealed 1994]

Leg.H. Added Stats 1981 ch 511 §4. Amended Stats 1983 ch 1204 §2. Repealed Stats 1994 ch 307 §4. See Prob C §4126.

Prior Law: Former §2402, similar to present Corp C §16204, was added Stats 1929 ch 864 §1, and repealed Stats 1949 ch 383 §2 (Corp C §100002).

Original §2402, relating to partnerships, was enacted 1872, and repealed Stats 1929 ch 864 §1.

§2403. [Section repealed 1994]

Leg.H. Added Stats 1981 ch 511 §4. Repealed Stats 1994 ch 307 §4 (SB 1907). See Prob C §4304.

Prior Law: Former §2403, similar to present Corp C §§16302, 16105, was added Stats 1929 ch 864 §1 and repealed Stats 1949 ch 383 §2 (Corp C §100002).

Original §2403, relating to partnerships, was enacted 1872 and repealed Stats 1929 ch 864 §1.

§2404. [Section repealed 1994]

Leg.H. Added Stats 1981 ch 511 §4. Repealed Stats 1994 ch 307 §4 (SB 1907). See Prob C §4305.

Prior Law: Former §2404, similar to present Corp C §§16302, 16105, was added Stats 1929 ch 864 §1 and repealed Stats 1949 ch 383 §2 (Corp C §100002).

Original §2404, relating to partnerships, was enacted 1872 and repealed Stats 1929 ch 864 §1.

§2405. [Section repealed 1994]

Leg.H. Added Stats 1981 ch 511 §4. Repealed Stats 1994 ch 307 §4 (SB 1907). The repealed section related to construction of article.

Prior Law: Former §2405, relating to admissions of partners binding the partnership, was added by Stats 1929 ch 864 §1 and repealed by Stats 1949 ch 383 §2 (Corp C §100002) p 697.

Original §2405, relating to partnerships, was enacted 1872 and repealed by Stats 1929 ch 864 §1.

§2406. [Section repealed 1994]

Leg.H. Added Stats 1981 ch 511 §4. Repealed Stats 1994 ch 307 §4 (SB 1907). See Prob C §4001.

Prior Law: Former §2406, similar to present Corp C §16102, was added by Stats 1929 ch 864 §1 and repealed by Stats 1949 ch 383 §2 (Corp C §100002) p 697.

Original §2406, relating to partnerships, was enacted 1872 and repealed by Stats 1929 ch 864 §1.

§2407. [Section repealed 1994]

Leg.H. Added Stats 1981 ch 511 §4. Repealed Stats 1994 ch 307 §4 (SB 1907). The repealed section related to severability.

Prior Law: Former §2407, similar to present Corp C §16305, was added by Stats 1929 ch 864 §1 and repealed by Stats 1949 ch 383 §2 (Corp C §100002) p 697.

§§2408, 2409. [Sections repealed 1949]

Leg.H. Added Stats 1929 ch 864 §1. Repealed Stats 1949 ch 383 §2 (Corp C §100002). See Corp C §§16305, 16306.

ARTICLE 4
Court Enforcement of Duties of Attorney in Fact
[Repealed]

§2410. [Section repealed 1994]

Leg.H. Added Stats 1981 ch 511 §4.5. Amended Stats 1983 ch 1204 §3; Stats 1984 ch 312 §1. Repealed Stats 1994 ch 307 §6. See Prob C §4010.

Prior Law: Former §2410, similar to present Corp C §16308, was added Stats 1929 ch 864 §1, and repealed Stats 1949 ch 383 §2 (Corp C §100002).

Original §2410, relating to partnerships, was enacted 1872, and repealed Stats 1929 ch 864 §1.

§2411. [Section repealed 1994]

Leg.H. Added Stats 1981 ch 511 §4.5. Amended Stats 1983 ch 1204 §4. Repealed Stats 1994 ch 307 §6 (SB 1907). See Prob C §§4540, 4765.

Prior Law: Former §2411, similar to present Corp C §16308, was added by Stats 1929 ch 864 §1 and repealed by Stats 1949 ch 383 §2 (Corp C §100002) p 697.

Original §2411, relating to partnerships, was enacted 1872 and repealed by Stats 1929 ch 864 §1.

§2412. [Section repealed 1994]

Leg.H. Added Stats 1981 ch 511 §4.5. Amended Stats 1983 ch 1204 §5; Stats 1992 ch 178 §3 (SB 1496). Repealed Stats 1994 ch 307 §6 (SB 1907). See Prob C §4941.

Prior Law: Former §2412, similar to present Corp C §16401, was added by Stats 1929 ch 864 §1 and repealed by Stats 1949 ch 383 §2 (Corp C §100002) p 697.

Original §2412, relating to partnerships, was enacted 1872 and repealed by Stats 1929 ch 864 §1.

§2412.5. [Section repealed 1994]

Leg.H. Added Stats 1983 ch 1204 §6. Repealed Stats 1994 ch 307 §6 (SB 1907). See Prob C §4766.

§2413. [Section repealed 1994]

Leg.H. Added Stats 1981 ch 511 §4.5. Amended Stats 1991 ch 1055 §8 (SB 271). Repealed Stats 1994 ch 307 §6 (SB 1907). See Prob C §§4520 and 4760.

Prior Law: Former §2413, similar to present Corp C §16403, was added Stats 1929 ch 864 §1 and repealed Stats 1949 ch 383 §2 (Corp C §100002).

Original §2413, relating to partnerships, was enacted 1872 and repealed Stats 1929 ch 864 §1.

§2414. [Section repealed 1994]

Leg.H. Added Stats 1981 ch 511 §4.5. Repealed Stats 1994 ch 307 §6 (SB 1907). See Prob C §§4523 and 4763.

Prior Law: Former §2414, similar to present Corp C §16403, was added by Stats 1929 ch 864 §1 and repealed by Stats 1949 ch 383 §2 (Corp C §100002) p 697.

§2415. [Section repealed 1994]

Leg.H. Added Stats 1981 ch 511 §4.5. Repealed Stats 1994 ch 307 §6 (SB 1907). See Prob C §§4542 and 4767.

Prior Law: Former §2415, similar to present Corp C §16404, was added by Stats 1929 ch 864 §1 and repealed by Stats 1949 ch 383 §2 (Corp C §100002) p 697.

§2416. [Section repealed 1994]

Leg.H. Added Stats 1981 ch 511 §4.5. Amended Stats 1984 ch 312 §2. Repealed Stats 1994 ch 307 §6 (SB 1907). See Prob C §§4543 and 4768.

Prior Law: Former §2416, similar to present Corp C §16406, was added by Stats 1929 ch 864 §1 and repealed by Stats 1949 ch 383 §2 (Corp C §100002) p 697.

§2417. [Section repealed 1994]

Leg.H. Added Stats 1981 ch 511 §4.5. Amended Stats 1983 ch 1204 §7; Stats 1988 ch 1199 §1, operative July 1, 1989. Repealed Stats 1994 ch 307 §6. See Prob C §§4544 and 4769.

Prior Law: Former §2417, similar to present Corp C §16406, was added Stats 1929 ch 864 §1, and repealed Stats 1949 ch 383 §2 (Corp C §100002).

Original §2417, relating to partnerships, was enacted 1872, and repealed Stats 1929 ch 864 §1.

§2418. [Section repealed 1994]

Leg.H. Added Stats 1981 ch 511 §4.5. Repealed Stats 1994 ch 307 §6 (SB 1907). The repealed section related to appointment of guardian ad litem.

Prior Law: Former §2418, relating to the property rights of a partner, was added by Stats 1929 ch 864 §1 and repealed by Stats 1949 ch 383 §2 (Corp C §100002) p 697.

Original §2418, relating to partnerships, was enacted 1872 and repealed by Stats 1929 ch 864 §1.

§2419. [Section repealed 1994]

Leg.H. Added Stats 1981 ch 511 §4.5. Amended Stats 1983 ch 1204 §8. Repealed Stats 1994 ch 307 §6 (SB 1907). See Prob C §1302.

Prior Law: Former §2419, similar to present Corp C §§16501, 16503, 16504, was added by Stats 1929 ch 864 §1 and repealed by Stats 1949 ch 383 §2 (Corp C §100002) p 697.

§2420. [Section repealed 1994]

Leg.H. Added Stats 1981 ch 511 §4.5. Repealed Stats 1994 ch 307 §6. See Prob C §§4501, 4751.

Prior Law: Former §2420, similar to present Corp C §§16501, 16502, was added Stats 1929 ch 864 §1, and repealed Stats 1949 ch 383 §2 (Corp C §100002).

§2421. [Section repealed 1994]

Leg.H. Added Stats 1981 ch 511 §4.5. Amended Stats 1983 ch 1204 §9; Stats 1984 ch 312 §3. Repealed Stats 1994 ch 307 §6 (SB 1907). See Prob C §§4503 and 4753.

Prior Law: Former §2421, similar to present Corp C §16503, was added by Stats 1929 ch 864 §1 and repealed by Stats 1949 ch 383 §2 (Corp C §100002) p 697.

§2422. [Section repealed 1994]

Leg.H. Added Stats 1981 ch 511 §4.5. Repealed Stats 1994 ch 307 §6. See Prob C §§4502 and 4752.

Prior Law: Former §2422, similar to present Corp C §16504, was added Stats 1929 ch 864 §1, and repealed Stats 1949 ch 383 §2 (Corp C §100002).

§2423. [Section repealed 1994]

Leg.H. Added Stats 1981 ch 511 §4.5. Repealed Stats 1994 ch 307 §6 (SB 1907). See Prob C §§4500 and 4750.

Prior Law: Former §2423, relating to definition of dissolution, was added by Stats 1929 ch 864 §1 and repealed by Stats 1949 ch 383 §2 (Corp C §100002) p 697.

§§2424–2429. [Sections repealed 1949]

Leg.H. Added Stats 1929 ch 864 §1. Repealed Stats 1949 ch 383 §2 (Corp C §100002). See Corp C §§16801 et seq.

Prior Law: Former §§2424, 2428, 2429, relating to partnerships, were enacted 1872 and repealed by Stats 1929 ch 864 §1.

ARTICLE 5
Durable Power of Attorney for Health Care [Repealed]

§2430. [Section repealed 1994]

Leg.H. Added Stats 1983 ch 1204 §10. Amended Stats 1988 ch 1543 §1. Repealed Stats 1994 ch 307 §7 (SB 1907) (ch 307 prevails). Amended Stats 1994 ch 1010 §48 (SB 2053). See Prob C §4603.

Prior Law: Former §2430, similar to present Corp C §16807, was added by Stats 1929 ch 864 §1 and repealed by Stats 1949 ch 383 §2 (Corp C §100002) p 697.

Original §2430, relating to partnerships, was enacted 1872 and repealed by Stats 1929 ch 864 §1.

§2431. [Section repealed 1994]

Leg.H. Added Stats 1983 ch 1204 §10. Repealed Stats 1994 ch 307 §7 (SB 1907). See Prob C §4671.

Prior Law: Former §2431, similar to present Corp C §16803, was added by Stats 1929 ch 864 §1 and repealed by Stats 1949 ch 383 §2 (Corp C §100002) p 697.

Original §2431, relating to partnerships, was enacted 1872 and repealed by Stats 1929 ch 864 §1.

§2432. [Section repealed 1994]

Leg.H. Added Stats 1983 ch 1204 §10. Amended Stats 1985 ch 403 §3; Stats 1988 ch 1543 §2; Stats 1990 ch 331 §1 (AB 835); Stats 1992 ch 470 §1 (AB 2697), effective August 7, 1992; Stats 1993 ch 141 §1 (AB 346), effective July 19, 1993. Repealed Stats 1994 ch 307 §7 (SB 1907). See Prob C §4700.

Prior Law: Former §2432, similar to present Corp C §16807, was added Stats 1929 ch 864 §1 and repealed Stats 1949 ch 383 §2 (Corp C §100002) p 697.

§2432.5. [Section repealed 1994]

Leg.H. Added Stats 1984 ch 312 §4. Amended Stats 1985 ch 403 §4; Stats 1988 ch 1543 §3. Repealed Stats 1994 ch 307 §7 (SB 1907). The repealed section related to designation of attorney-in-fact.

§2433. [Section repealed 1994]

Leg.H. Added Stats 1983 ch 1204 §10. Amended Stats 1984 ch 312 §5; Stats 1985 ch 403 §5; Stats 1991 ch 896 §1 (AB 793). Repealed Stats 1994 ch 307 §7 (SB 1907). The repealed section related to a printed form.

Prior Law: Former §2433, relating to effect of rescission of partnership contract on ground of fraud, was added by Stats 1929 ch 864 §1 and repealed by Stats 1949 ch 383 §2 (Corp C §100002) p 697.

§2434. [Section repealed 1994]

Leg.H. Added Stats 1983 ch 1204 §10. Amended Stats 1984 ch 312 §6. Repealed Stats 1994 ch 307 §7 (SB 1907). See Prob C §§4682 et seq.

Prior Law: Former §2434, similar to present Corp C §16807, was added by Stats 1929 ch 864 §1 and repealed by Stats 1949 ch 383 §2 (Corp C §100002) p 697.

§2435. [Section repealed 1994]

Leg.H. Added Stats 1983 ch 1204 §10. Repealed Stats 1994 ch 307 §7 (SB 1907). See Prob C §4652.

Prior Law: Former §2435, relating to liability of persons continuing business in certain cases, was added by Stats 1929 ch 864 §1 and repealed by Stats 1949 ch 383 §2 (Corp C §100002) p 697.

Original §2435, relating to partnerships, was enacted 1872 and repealed by Stats 1929 ch 864 §1.

§2436. [Section repealed 1994]

Leg.H. Added Stats 1983 ch 1204 §10. Repealed Stats 1994 ch 307 §7 (SB 1907). See Prob C §4678.

Prior Law: Former §2436, similar to present Corp C §16807, was added by Stats 1929 ch 864 §1 and repealed by Stats 1949 ch 383 §2 (Corp C §100002) p 697.

Original §2436, relating to partnerships, was enacted 1872 and repealed by Stats 1929 ch 864 §1.

§2436.5. [Section repealed 1994]

Leg.H. Added Stats 1983 ch 1204 §10. Amended Stats 1991 ch 896 §2 (AB 793). Repealed Stats 1994 ch 307 §7 (SB 1907). The repealed section related to expiration of durable power of attorney for health care.

§2437. [Section repealed 1994]

Leg.H. Added Stats 1983 ch 1204 §10. Amended Stats 1984 ch 312 §7. Repealed Stats 1994 ch 307 §7 (SB 1907). See Prob C §§4657, 4695, 4697, 4698, 4731, and 4740.

Prior Law: Former §2437, similar to present Corp C §16807, was added by Stats 1929 ch 864 §1 and repealed by Stats 1949 ch 383 §2 (Corp C §100002) p 697.

Original §2437, relating to partnerships, was enacted 1872 and repealed by Stats 1929 ch 864 §1.

§2438. [Section repealed 1994]

Leg.H. Added Stats 1983 ch 1204 §10. Repealed Stats 1994 ch 307 §7 (SB 1907). See Prob C §4740.

Prior Law: Former §2438, relating to general partnerships and general partners, was added by Stats 1929 ch 864 §1 and repealed by Stats 1949 ch 383 §2 (Corp C §100002) p 697.

Original §2438, relating to partnerships, was enacted 1872 and repealed by Stats 1929 ch 864 §1.

§2438.5. [Section repealed 1994]

Leg.H. Added Stats 1992 ch 470 §2 (AB 2697), effective August 7, 1992. Repealed Stats 1994 ch 307 §7 (SB 1907). See Prob C §4676.

§2439. [Section repealed 1994]

Leg.H. Added Stats 1983 ch 1204 §10. Repealed Stats 1994 ch 307 §7 (SB 1907). See Prob C §§4682 et seq.

Prior Law: Former §2439, similar to present Corp C §16109, was added by Stats 1929 ch 864 §1 and repealed by Stats 1949 ch 383 §2 (Corp C §100002) p 697.

§2440. [Section repealed 1994]

Leg.H. Added Stats 1983 ch 1204 §10. Amended Stats 1985 ch 403 §6. Repealed Stats 1994 ch 307 §7 (SB 1907). See Prob C §4689.

§2441. [Section repealed 1994]

Leg.H. Added Stats 1983 ch 1204 §10. Repealed Stats 1994 ch 307 §7 (SB 1907). See Prob C §4677.

§2442. [Section repealed 1994]

Leg.H. Added Stats 1983 ch 1204 §10. Repealed Stats 1994 ch 307 §7 (SB 1907). See Prob C §4743.

§2443. [Section repealed 1994]

Leg.H. Added Stats 1983 ch 1204 §10. Repealed Stats 1994 ch 307 §7 (SB 1907). See Prob C §§4653 and 4655.

Prior Law: Former §2443, relating to partnerships, was enacted 1872 and repealed by Stats 1929 ch 864 §1.

§2444. [Section repealed 1994]

Leg.H. Added Stats 1985 ch 403 §6.5. Amended Stats 1988 ch 1543 §4; Stats 1991 ch 896 §3 (AB 793). Repealed Stats 1994 ch 307 §7 (SB 1907). The repealed section related to sale or distribution of a printed form of a durable power of attorney.

Prior Law: Former §2444, relating to partnerships, was enacted 1872 and repealed by Stats 1929 ch 864 §1.

§2445. [Section repealed 1994]

Leg.H. Added Stats 1992 ch 470 §3 (AB 2697), effective August 7, 1992. Repealed Stats 1994 ch 307 §7 (SB 1907). See Prob C §4676.

Prior Law: Former §2445, relating to partnerships, was enacted 1872 and repealed by Stats 1929 ch 864 §1.

§2449. [Section repealed 1929]

Leg.H. Enacted 1872. Repealed Stats 1929 ch 864 §1. The repealed section related to partnerships.

CHAPTER 3
STATUTORY SHORT FORM POWER OF ATTORNEY [REPEALED]

§2450. [Section repealed 1994]

Leg.H. Added Stats 1990 ch 986 §2 (SB 1777). Repealed Stats 1994 ch 307 §8 (SB 1907). See Prob C §4409.

Prior Law: Former Corp C §2450, similar to present Prob C §4401, was added Stats 1984 ch 602 §1, amended Stats 1985 ch 403 §7, and repealed Stats 1990 ch 986 §1 (SB 1777).

Former CC §2450, relating to partnerships, was enacted 1872 and repealed Stats 1929 ch 864 §1.

§2451. [Section repealed 1990]

Leg.H. Added Stats 1984 ch 602 §1. Amended Stats 1985 ch 403 §8. Repealed Stats 1990 ch 986 §1 (SB 1777). See Prob C §4401.

Prior Law: Former §2451, relating to partnerships, was enacted 1872 and repealed Stats 1929 ch 864 §1.

§§2452–2456. [Sections repealed 1990]

Leg.H. Added Stats 1984 ch 602 §1. Repealed Stats 1990 ch 986 §1 (SB 1777). See Prob C §§4401, 4402, 4408.

Prior Law: Former §§2452, 2453, 2454, relating to partnerships, were enacted 1872 and repealed Stats 1929 ch 864 §1.

§2457. [Section repealed 1990]

Leg.H. Added Stats 1985 ch 403 §9. Repealed Stats 1990 ch 986 §1 (SB 1777). The repealed section related to use of form complying with prior law.

§§2458, 2459. [Sections repealed 1929]

Leg.H. Enacted 1872. Repealed Stats 1929 ch 864 §1. The repealed sections related to liquidation of partnerships.

§§2460–2466. [Sections repealed 1990]

Leg.H. Added Stats 1984 ch 602 §1. Repealed Stats 1990 ch 986 §1 (SB 1777). See Prob C §§4451 et seq.

Prior Law: Former §§2460, 2461, 2462, relating to partnerships, were enacted 1872 and repealed Stats 1929 ch 864 §1.

Former §2466, similar to present B & P C §§17900, 17910, 17913, 17915, 17917, was enacted 1872, amended Code Amdts 1873–84 ch 612 §231, Stats 1911 ch 262 §1, Stats 1923 ch 113 §1, Stats 1951 ch 48 §1, Stats 1955 ch 861 §1, and repealed Stats 1970 ch 618 §5, effective July 1, 1971.

§2467. [Section repealed 1990]

Leg.H. Added Stats 1984 ch 602 §1. Amended Stats 1986 ch 820 §10, operative July 1, 1987; Stats 1988 ch 113 §6, effective May 25, 1988, operative July 1, 1988. Repealed Stats 1990 ch 986 §1. See Prob C §4458.

Prior Law: Former §2467, relating to fictitious names, was enacted 1872, amended Code Amdts 1873–74 ch 612 §232, and repealed Stats 1970 ch 618 §5, operative July 1, 1971.

§§2468, 2469. [Sections repealed 1990]

Leg.H. Added Stats 1984 ch 602 §1. Repealed Stats 1990 ch 986 §1 (SB 1777). See Prob C §§4459, 4463.

Prior Law: Former §2468, similar to present B & P C §§17910, 17914, 17917–17919, was enacted 1872, amended Code Amdts 1873–74 ch 612 §233, Stats 1911 ch 263 §1, Stats 1951 ch 1103 §1, Stats 1967 ch 257 §1, and repealed Stats 1970 ch 618 §5, operative July 1, 1971.

Former §2469, similar to present B & P C §17923, was enacted 1872, amended Code Amdts 1873–74 ch 612 §234, and repealed Stats 1970 ch 618 §5, operative July 1, 1971.

§2469.1. [Section repealed 1971]

Leg.H. Added Stats 1949 ch 1210 §1. Amended Stats 1951 ch 48 §2; Stats 1953 ch 268 §1. Repealed Stats 1970 ch 618 §5, operative July 1, 1971. See B & P C §17922.

§2469.2. [Section repealed 1971]

Leg.H. Added Stats 1966 1st Ex Sess ch 120 §4. Amended Stats 1969 ch 114 §1. Repealed Stats 1970 ch 618 §5, operative July 1, 1971. See B & P C §§17910, 17917, 17920.

§2469.3. [Section repealed 1971]

Leg.H. Added Stats 1966 1st Ex Sess ch 120 §5. Repealed Stats 1970 ch 618 §5, operative July 1, 1971. See B & P C §17927.

§§2470, 2471. [Sections repealed 1990]

Leg.H. Added Stats 1984 ch 602 §1. Repealed Stats 1990 ch 986 §1 (SB 1777). See Prob C §§4460, 4461.

Prior Law: Former §2470, similar to present B & P C §§17922, 17925, was enacted 1872, amended Code Amdts 1873–74 ch 612 §235, Stats 1911 ch 261 §1, Stats 1949 ch 1210 §2, Stats 1st Ex Sess ch 120 §6, and repealed Stats 1970 ch 618 §5, operative July 1, 1971.

Former §2471, relating to fictitious names, was enacted 1872 and repealed Stats 1970 ch 618 §5, operative July 1, 1971.

§2472. [Section repealed 1990]

Leg.H. Added Stats 1984 ch 602 §1. Repealed Stats 1990 ch 986 §1 (SB 1777). The repealed section related to records, reports, and statements.

Prior Law: Former §2472, relating to process agents for certain foreign partnerships, was added Stats 1909 ch 626 §1, amended Stats 1947 ch 1324 §1, and repealed Stats 1949 ch 383 §2 (Corp C §100002) p 697.

§2473. [Section repealed 1990]

Leg.H. Added Stats 1984 ch 602 §1. Repealed Stats 1990 ch 986 §1 (SB 1777). The repealed section related to general authority for "all other matters".

CHAPTER 3.5
UNIFORM STATUTORY FORM POWER OF ATTORNEY ACT [REPEALED]

§2475. [Section repealed 1994]

Leg.H. Added Stats 1990 ch 986 §3 (SB 1777). Amended Stats 1991 ch 1090 §1 (AB 1484); Stats 1993 ch 141 §2 (AB 346), effective July 19, 1993. Repealed Stats 1994 ch 307 §9 (SB 1907). See Prob C §4401.

§2476. [Section repealed 1994]

Leg.H. Added Stats 1990 ch 986 §3 (SB 1777). Amended Stats 1992 ch 178 §3.5 (SB 1496). Repealed Stats 1994 ch 307 §9 (SB 1907). See Prob C §4402.

§2477. [Section repealed 1994]

Leg.H. Added Stats 1990 ch 986 §3 (SB 1777). Repealed Stats 1994 ch 307 §9 (SB 1907). See Prob C §4403.

Prior Law: Former §2477, similar to present Corp C §15501, was added Stats 1929 ch 865 §1 and repealed Stats 1949 ch 383 §2.

Former §2477, relating to special partnerships, was enacted 1872 and repealed Stats 1929 ch 865 §1.

§2478. [Section repealed 1994]

Leg.H. Added Stats 1990 ch 986 §3 (SB 1777). Repealed Stats 1994 ch 307 §9 (SB 1907). See Prob C §4404.

Prior Law: Former §2478, similar to present Corp C §15502, was added Stats 1929 ch 865 §1 and repealed Stats 1949 ch 383 §2.

Former §2478, relating to special partnerships, was enacted 1872 and repealed Stats 1929 ch 865 §1.

§2479. [Section repealed 1994]

Leg.H. Added Stats 1990 ch 986 §3 (SB 1777). Repealed Stats 1994 ch 307 §9 (SB 1907). See Prob C §4405.

Prior Law: Former §2479, similar to present Corp C §15503, was added Stats 1929 ch 865 §1 and repealed Stats 1949 ch 383 §2.

Former §2479, relating to special partnerships, was enacted 1872 and repealed Stats 1929 ch 865 §1.

§2480. [Section repealed 1994]

Leg.H. Added Stats 1990 ch 986 §3 (SB 1777). Repealed Stats 1994 ch 307 §9 (SB 1907). See Prob C §4407.

Prior Law: Former §2480, similar to present Corp C §15504, was added Stats 1929 ch 865 §1 and repealed Stats 1949 ch 383 §2.

Former §2480, relating to special partnerships, was enacted 1872 and repealed Stats 1929 ch 865 §1.

§2480.5. [Section repealed 1994]

Leg.H. Added Stats 1992 ch 178 §4 (SB 1496). Repealed Stats 1994 ch 307 §9 (SB 1907). See Prob C §4406.

§2481. [Section repealed 1994]

Leg.H. Added Stats 1990 ch 986 §3 (SB 1777). Repealed Stats 1994 ch 307 §9 (SB 1907). See Prob C §4408.

Prior Law: Former §2481, similar to present Corp C §15505, was added Stats 1929 ch 865 §1 and repealed Stats 1949 ch 383 §2.

Former §2481, relating to special partnerships, was enacted 1872 and repealed Stats 1929 ch 865 §1.

§2482. [Section repealed 1994]

Leg.H. Added Stats 1990 ch 986 §3 (SB 1777). Repealed Stats 1994 ch 307 §9 (SB 1907). See Prob C §4400.

Prior Law: Former §2482, similar to present Corp C §15506, was added Stats 1929 ch 865 §1, amended Stats 1935 ch 199 §1, and repealed Stats 1949 ch 383 §2.

Former §2482, relating to special partnerships, was enacted 1872 and repealed Stats 1929 ch 865 §1.

§2483. [Section repealed 1994]

Leg.H. Added Stats 1990 ch 986 §3 (SB 1777). Repealed Stats 1994 ch 307 §9 (SB 1907). The repealed section related to construction of chapter.

Prior Law: Former §2483, similar to present Corp C §15507, was added Stats 1929 ch 865 §1 and repealed Stats 1949 ch 383 §2.

Former §2483, relating to special partnerships, was enacted 1872 and repealed Stats 1929 ch 865 §1.

§2484. [Section repealed 1994]

Leg.H. Added Stats 1990 ch 986 §3 (SB 1777). Repealed Stats 1994 ch 307 §9 (SB 1907). The repealed section related to severability.

Prior Law: Former §2484, similar to present Corp C §15508, was added Stats 1929 ch 865 §1, amended Stats 1935 ch 199 §2, and repealed Stats 1949 ch 383 §2.

Former §2484, relating to special partnerships, was enacted 1872 and repealed Stats 1929 ch 865 §1.

§2485. [Section repealed 1994]

Leg.H. Added Stats 1990 ch 986 §3 (SB 1777). Repealed Stats 1994 ch 307 §9 (SB 1907). See Prob C §4450.

Prior Law: Former §2485, similar to present Corp C §15509, was added Stats 1929 ch 865 §1 and repealed Stats 1949 ch 383 §2.

Former §2485, relating to special partnerships, was enacted 1872 and repealed Stats 1929 ch 865 §1.

§2486. [Section repealed 1994]

Leg.H. Added Stats 1990 ch 986 §3 (SB 1777). Repealed Stats 1994 ch 307 §9 (SB 1907). See Prob C §4451.

Prior Law: Former §2486, similar to present Corp C §15510, was added Stats 1929 ch 865 §1 and repealed Stats 1949 ch 383 §2.

§2487. [Section repealed 1994]

Leg.H. Added Stats 1990 ch 986 §3 (SB 1777). Repealed Stats 1994 ch 307 §9 (SB 1907). See Prob C §4452.

Prior Law: Former §2487, similar to present Corp C §15511, was added Stats 1929 ch 865 §1 and repealed Stats 1949 ch 383 §2.

§2488. [Section repealed 1994]

Leg.H. Added Stats 1990 ch 986 §3 (SB 1777). Repealed Stats 1994 ch 307 §9 (SB 1907). See Prob C §4453.

Prior Law: Former §2488, similar to present Corp C §15512, was added Stats 1929 ch 865 §1 and repealed Stats 1949 ch 383 §2.

§2489. [Section repealed 1994]

Leg.H. Added Stats 1990 ch 986 §3 (SB 1777). Repealed Stats 1994 ch 307 §9 (SB 1907). See Prob C §4454.

Prior Law: Former §2489, similar to present Corp C §15513, was added Stats 1929 ch 865 §1 and repealed Stats 1949 ch 383 §2.

Former §2489, relating to special partnerships, was enacted 1872 and repealed Stats 1929 ch 865 §1.

§2490. [Section repealed 1994]

Leg.H. Added Stats 1990 ch 986 §3 (SB 1777). Repealed Stats 1994 ch 307 §9 (SB 1907). See Prob C §4455.

Prior Law: Former §2490, similar to present Corp C §15514, was added Stats 1929 ch 865 §1 and repealed Stats 1949 ch 383 §2.

Former §2490, relating to special partnerships, was enacted 1872 and repealed Stats 1929 ch 865 §1.

§2491. [Section repealed 1994]

Leg.H. Added Stats 1990 ch 986 §3 (SB 1777). Repealed Stats 1994 ch 307 §9 (SB 1907). See Prob C §4456.

Prior Law: Former §2491, similar to present Corp C §15515, was added Stats 1929 ch 865 §1 and repealed Stats 1949 ch 383 §2.

Former §2491, relating to special partnerships, was enacted 1872 and repealed Stats 1929 ch 865 §1.

§2492. [Section repealed 1994]

Leg.H. Added Stats 1990 ch 986 §3 (SB 1777). Repealed Stats 1994 ch 307 §9 (SB 1907). See Prob C §4457.

Prior Law: Former §2492, similar to present Corp C §15516, was added Stats 1929 ch 865 §1 and repealed Stats 1949 ch 383 §2.

Former §2492, relating to special partnerships, was enacted 1872 and repealed Stats 1929 ch 865 §1.

§2493. [Section repealed 1994]

Leg.H. Added Stats 1990 ch 986 §3 (SB 1777). Repealed Stats 1994 ch 307 §9 (SB 1907). See Prob C §4458.

Prior Law: Former §2493, similar to present Corp C §15517, was added Stats 1929 ch 865 §1 and repealed Stats 1949 ch 383 §2.

Former §2493, relating to special partnerships, was enacted 1872 and repealed Stats 1929 ch 865 §1.

§2494. [Section repealed 1994]

Leg.H. Added Stats 1990 ch 986 §3 (SB 1777). Repealed Stats 1994 ch 307 §9 (SB 1907). See Prob C §4459.

Prior Law: Former §2494, similar to present Corp C §15518, was added Stats 1929 ch 865 §1 and repealed Stats 1949 ch 383 §2.

Former §2494, relating to special partnerships, was enacted 1872 and repealed Stats 1929 ch 865 §1.

§2495. [Section repealed 1994]

Leg.H. Added Stats 1990 ch 986 §3 (SB 1777). Repealed Stats 1994 ch 307 §9 (SB 1907). See Prob C §4460.

Prior Law: Former §2495, similar to present Corp C §15519, was added Stats 1929 ch 865 §1 and repealed Stats 1949 ch 383 §2.

Former §2495, relating to special partnerships, was enacted 1872 and repealed Stats 1929 ch 865 §1.

§2496. [Section repealed 1994]

Leg.H. Added Stats 1990 ch 986 §3 (SB 1777). Repealed Stats 1994 ch 307 §9 (SB 1907). See Prob C §4461.

Prior Law: Former §2496, similar to present Corp C §15520, was added Stats 1929 ch 865 §1 and repealed Stats 1949 ch 383 §2.

Former §2496, relating to special partnerships, was enacted 1872 and repealed Stats 1929 ch 865 §1.

§2497. [Section repealed 1994]

Leg.H. Added Stats 1990 ch 986 §3 (SB 1777). Repealed Stats 1994 ch 307 §9 (SB 1907). See Pro C §4462.

Prior Law: Former §2497, similar to present Corp C §15521, was added Stats 1929 ch 865 §1 and repealed Stats 1949 ch 383 §2.

§2498. [Section repealed 1994]

Leg.H. Added Stats 1990 ch 986 §3 (SB 1777). Repealed Stats 1994 ch 307 §9 (SB 1907). See Prob C §4463.

Prior Law: Former §2498, similar to present Corp C §15522, was added Stats 1929 ch 865 §1 and repealed Stats 1949 ch 383 §2.

§2499. [Section repealed 1994]

Leg.H. Added Stats 1990 ch 986 §3 (SB 1777). Repealed Stats 1994 ch 307 §9 (SB 1907). See Prob C §4464.

Prior Law: Former §2499, similar to present Corp C §15523, was added Stats 1929 ch 865 §1 and repealed Stats 1949 ch 383 §2.

§2499.5. [Section repealed 1994]

Leg.H. Added Stats 1990 ch 986 §3 (SB 1777). Repealed Stats 1994 ch 307 §9 (SB 1907). See Prob C §4465.

CHAPTER 4
STATUTORY FORM DURABLE POWER OF ATTORNEY FOR HEALTH CARE [REPEALED]

CHAPTER 5
MISCELLANEOUS PROVISIONS RELATING TO POWERS OF ATTORNEY [REPEALED]

TITLE 10
RECORDING ARTIST CONTRACTS

Definitions. §2500.
Right of royalty recipient to audit records of royalty reporting party; Confidential information. §2501.

§2500. Definitions

As used in this title:

(a) "Royalty recipient" means a party to a contract for the furnishing of services in the production of sound recordings, as defined in Section 101 of Title 17 of the United States Code, who has the right to receive royalties under that contract.

(b) A "royalty reporting party" is the party obligated to pay royalties to the royalty recipient under the contract described in subdivision (a). **Leg.H.** Added Stats 2004 ch 150 §2 (SB 1034).

Prior Law: Former §2500, relating to statutory form for a durable power of attorney for health care, was added Stats 1984 ch 312 §8, amended Stats 1985 ch 403 §10, Stats 1988 ch 1543 §5, Stats 1990 ch 331 §2, Stats 1991 ch 896 §4, and repealed Stats 1994 ch 307 §10.

§2501. Right of royalty recipient to audit records of royalty reporting party; Confidential information

Notwithstanding any provision of a contract described in Section 2500:

(a) A royalty recipient may audit the books and records of the royalty reporting party to determine if the royalty recipient earned all of the royalties due the royalty recipient pursuant to the contract, subject to the following:

(1) A royalty recipient may conduct an audit not more than once per year.

(2) A royalty recipient shall request an audit within three years after the end of a royalty earnings period under the contract.

(3) A royalty recipient may not audit a particular royalty earnings period more than once.

(b) The royalty recipient shall retain a qualified royalty auditor of the royalty recipient's choice to conduct an audit described in this section.

(c) The royalty recipient may enter into a contingency fee agreement with the auditor described in subdivision (b).

(d) A qualified royalty auditor may conduct individual audits of the books and records of a royalty reporting party on behalf of different royalty recipients simultaneously.

(e) Except as required by law, a qualified royalty auditor shall not disclose any confidential information obtained solely during an audit without the express consent of the party or parties to whom that information is confidential. This subdivision shall not prohibit the auditor from disclosing to the royalty recipient, or an agent of the recipient, on behalf of whom the auditor is conducting the audit information directly pertaining to that royalty recipient's contract, as described in Section 2500.

(f) The provisions of subdivisions (a), (b), (c), (d), and (e) are in addition to any other rights provided by a contract, as described in Section 2500, between a royalty recipient and a royalty reporting party.

(g) Nothing in subdivision (a), (b), (c), (d), or (e) shall be deemed to extend any limitations period applicable to royalty accounting or payments not specifically addressed in this section.

(h) Nothing in subdivision (a), (b), (c), (d), or (e) shall be deemed to limit any rights provided by collective bargaining agreement or by applicable state or federal law. **Leg.H.** Added Stats 2004 ch 150 §2 (SB 1034).

Prior Law: Former §2501, relating to statements in the durable power of attorney for health care, was added Stats 1984 ch 312 §8 and repealed Stats 1994 ch 307 §10.

§2502. [Section repealed 1994]

Leg.H. Added Stats 1984 ch 312 §8. Amended Stats 1988 ch 113 §6.5, effective May 25, 1988, operative July 1, 1988. Repealed Stats 1994 ch 307 §10 (SB 1907). The repealed section related to requirements for the durable power of attorney for health care.

Prior Law: Former §2502, similar to present Corp C §15526, was added by Stats 1929 ch 865 §1 and repealed by Stats 1949 ch 383 §2 (Corp C §10002) p 697.

Original §2502, relating to special partnerships, was enacted 1872 and repealed by Stats 1929 ch 865 §1.

§2503. [Section repealed 1994]

Leg.H. Added Stats 1984 ch 312 §8. Repealed Stats 1994 ch 307 §10 (SB 1907). The repealed section related to when a power of attorney was a statutory form durable power of attorney for health care.

Prior Law: Former §2503, similar to present Corp C §15527, was added by Stats 1929 ch 864 §1 and repealed by Stats 1949 ch 383 §2 (Corp C §100002) p 697.

Original §2503, relating to special partnerships, was enacted 1872 and repealed by Stats 1929 ch 865 §1.

§2503.5. [Section repealed 1994]

Leg.H. Added Stats 1985 ch 403 §11. Amended Stats 1991 ch 896 §5 (AB 793). Repealed Stats 1994 ch 307 §10 (SB 1907). The repealed section related to validity of certain statutory form durable powers of attorney for health care.

§2504. [Section repealed 1994]

Leg.H. Added Stats 1984 ch 312 §8. Repealed Stats 1994 ch 307 §10 (SB 1907). The repealed section related to language conferring authority for health care decisions.

Prior Law: Former §2504, similar to present Corp C §15528, was added by Stats 1929 ch 865 §1 and repealed by Stats 1949 ch 383 §2 (Corp C §100002) p 697.

§2505. [Section repealed 1994]

Leg.H. Added Stats 1984 ch 312 §8. Repealed Stats 1994 ch 307 §10 (SB 1907). The repealed section related to execution of document by the attorney in fact.

Prior Law: Former §2505, similar to present Corp C §15529, was added by Stats 1929 ch 865 §1 and repealed by Stats 1949 ch 383 §2 (Corp C §100002) p 697.

§2506. [Section repealed 1994]

Leg.H. Added Stats 1984 ch 312 §8. Repealed Stats 1994 ch 307 §10 (SB 1907). The repealed section related to the power of the alternate agent to make health care decisions.

Prior Law: Former §2506, similar to present Corp C §15530, was added by Stats 1929 ch 865 §1 and repealed by Stats 1949 ch 383 §2 (Corp C §100002) p 697.

§2507. [Section repealed 1994]

Leg.H. Added Stats 1984 ch 312 §8. Repealed Stats 1994 ch 307 §10 (SB 1907). See Prob C §4700.

Prior Law: Former §2507, relating to special partnerships, was enacted 1872 and repealed by Stats 1929 ch 865 §1.

§2508. [Section repealed 1994]

Leg.H. Added Stats 1984 ch 312 §8. Repealed Stats 1994 ch 307 §10 (SB 1907). The repealed section related to the title of the chapter.

Prior Law: Former §2508, relating to special partnerships, was enacted 1872 and repealed by Stats 1929 ch 865 §1.

§2509. [Section repealed 1929]

Leg.H. Enacted 1872 and repealed by Stats 1929 ch 865 §1. The repealed section related to special partnerships.

§2510. [Section repealed 1994]

Leg.H. Added Stats 1985 ch 403 §12. Amended Stats 1990 ch 986 §4 (SB 1777). Repealed Stats 1994 ch 307 §11 (SB 1907). See Prob C §4128.

Prior Law: Former §2510, relating to special partnerships, was enacted 1872 and repealed by Stats 1929 ch 865 §1.

§2510.5. [Section repealed 1994]

Leg.H. Added Stats 1985 ch 403 §12. Repealed Stats 1994 ch 307 §11 (SB 1907). See Prob C §4102.

§2511. [Section repealed 1994]

Leg.H. Added Stats 1985 ch 403 §12. Amended Stats 1990 ch 331 §3 (AB 835), ch 986 §5.5 (SB 1777). Repealed Stats 1994 ch 307 §11 (SB 1907). See Prob C §4751.

Prior Law: Former §2511, relating to definition of a mining partnership, was enacted 1872 and repealed by Stats 1939 ch 93 (Pub Res C §10002) p 1215.

§2512. [Section repealed 1994]

Leg.H. Added Stats 1985 ch 403 §12. Repealed Stats 1994 ch 307 §11 (SB 1907). See Prob C §4303.

Prior Law: Former §2512, relating to necessity of expressed mining partnership agreements, was enacted 1872 and repealed by Stats 1939 ch 93 (Pub Res C §10002) p 1215.

§2513. [Section repealed 1994]

Leg.H. Added Stats 1985 ch 403 §12. Repealed Stats 1994 ch 307 §11 (SB 1907). See Prob C §4123.

Prior Law: Former §2513, relating to sharing of profits and losses by mining partnerships, was enacted 1872 and repealed by Stats 1939 ch 93 (Pub Res C §10002) p 1215.

§2514. [Section repealed 1994]

Leg.H. Added Stats 1990 ch 986 §6. Repealed Stats 1994 ch 307 §11. See Prob C §4010.

Prior Law: Former §2514, relating to members' liens against partnership property, was enacted 1872, and repealed Stats 1939 ch 93 (Pub Res C §100002).

§§2515–2520. [Sections repealed 1939]

Leg.H. Enacted 1872. Repealed Stats 1939 ch 93 (Pub Res C §100002) p 1215. See Pub Res C §§3940 et seq.

TITLE 10.1
SHARED MOBILITY DEVICES

Definitions; Agreements and permits for shared mobility devices; Insurance; Disclosure. § 2505.
Study and report to Legislature [Repealed January 1, 2027]. § 2505.5.
Required service provider identification sign. § 2506.

§ 2505. Definitions; Agreements and permits for shared mobility devices; Insurance; Disclosure

(a) For purposes of this title:

(1) "Assistive technology device" has the same meaning as in Section 7002 of Title 9 of the California Code of Regulations.

(2) "Shared mobility device" means an electrically motorized board as defined in Section 313.5 of the Vehicle Code, motorized scooter as defined in Section 407.5 of the Vehicle Code, electric bicycle as defined in Section 312.5 of the Vehicle Code, bicycle as defined in Section 231 of the Vehicle Code, or other similar personal transportation device, except as provided in subdivision (b) of Section 415 of the Vehicle Code, that is made available to the public by a shared mobility service provider for shared use and transportation in exchange for financial compensation via a digital application or other electronic or digital platform.

(3) "Shared mobility service provider" or "provider" means a person or entity that offers, makes available, or provides a shared mobility device in exchange for financial compensation or membership via a digital application or other electronic or digital platform.

(b)(1) Before distribution of a shared mobility device, a shared mobility service provider shall enter into an agreement with, or obtain a permit from, the city or county with jurisdiction over the area of use. The agreement or permit shall, at a minimum, require that the shared mobility service provider maintain commercial general liability insurance coverage with an admitted insurer, or a nonadmitted insurer that is eligible to insure a home state insured under Chapter 6 (commencing with Section 1760) of Part 2 of Division 1 of the Insurance Code, with limits not less than one million dollars ($1,000,000) for each occurrence for bodily injury or property damage, including contractual liability, personal injury, and product liability and completed operations, and not less than five million dollars ($5,000,000) aggregate for all occurrences during the policy period. The insurance shall not exclude coverage for injuries or damages caused by the shared mobility service provider to the shared mobility device user.

(2)(A)(i)(I) Notwithstanding any other law, effective July 1, 2023, the agreement or permit required pursuant to paragraph (1) shall require, in addition to the coverage required by paragraph (1), a shared mobility service provider to offer or make available, or to confirm the user of a shared mobility device maintains, insurance coverage for bodily injury or death suffered by a pedestrian when the injury or death involves, in whole or in part, the negligent conduct of the shared mobility device user, of ten thousand dollars ($10,000) for each occurrence of bodily injury to, or death of, one pedestrian in any one accident, and for property damage to an assistive technology device, of one thousand dollars ($1,000), for each occurrence. This paragraph shall not be interpreted to require coverage as provided in Division 7 (commencing with Section 16000) of the Vehicle Code.

(II) This clause shall not be interpreted to limit or supersede the requirement pursuant to paragraph (1) that the shared mobility service provider, in its agreement with or permit from the city or county with jurisdiction over the area of use, maintain commercial general liability insurance coverage with limits not less than five million dollars ($5,000,000) aggregate for all occurrences during the policy period.

(III) This clause shall not be interpreted to prohibit an aggregated cap on the insurance required by subclause (I).

(IV) Insurance coverage offered, made available, or confirmed pursuant to this clause shall not be considered a group insurance policy.

(ii) Notwithstanding clause (i) or any other law, a shared mobility service provider or user of a shared mobility device is not required to maintain insurance coverage, as described in clause (i), for injuries of, or death to, a pedestrian or property damage involving the following devices:

(I) A bicycle propelled exclusively by human power, as described in Section 231 of the Vehicle Code. For purposes of this paragraph, "bicycle" shall not include an electric bicycle.

(II) A class 1 electric bicycle as defined in paragraph (1) of subdivision (a) of Section 312.5 of the Vehicle Code.

(III) A class 2 electric bicycle as defined in paragraph (2) of subdivision (a) of Section 312.5 of the Vehicle Code.

(iii) The Legislature finds and declares that bicycles may be recognized as safer than motorized devices when in use, and recognizes there may remain a propensity for pedestrian injuries or death resulting from shared mobility bicycles and shared mobility electric bicycles being left negligently abandoned on pedestrian walkways.

(B) A shared mobility service provider may partner with an insurer to provide an option to its users via its digital application or other electronic platform where the user may purchase insurance coverage that meets or exceeds the requirements of subparagraph (A). The shared mobility service provider shall disclose via its digital application or other electronic platform the name, contact information, and location to make a claim with the insurer they chose to partner with. The shared mobility service provider may fund the cost of providing this coverage itself and pass the cost on in its standard fee to users, or through a separate charge to users. If a user of a shared mobility device does not maintain their own insurance policy, then that coverage shall be offered or made available by the shared mobility service provider. A shared mobility service provider shall not allow a user or individual to operate or utilize a shared mobility device without the coverage identified in subparagraph (A). If a user or individual gains access to a shared mobility device without obtaining coverage through the options outlined in this subparagraph or subparagraph (C), and uses or operates it uninsured, the shared mobility service provider shall be required to provide the insurance coverage identified in subparagraph (A).

(C)(i) A shared mobility service provider may enter into separate individual agreements with users maintaining their own liability insurance coverage that meets or exceeds the requirements of subparagraph (A), to exclude the user from the provider's insurance coverage required in subparagraph (A) when, in consideration for such an agreement, the user shall not pay a separate charge for the coverage or shall be refunded the portion of the provider's fee that pays for the provider's coverage. The agreement shall be null and void upon lapse, cancellation, or expiration of the user's policy. If a shared mobility device user entering into an agreement under this subparagraph misrepresents their maintenance of a policy or through an error or act of omission does not provide coverage, the shared mobility service provider shall be required to maintain the insurance to cover any claims resulting in injury, death, or property damage described in subparagraph (A).

(ii) It is the intent of the Legislature that, in enacting this subparagraph, shared mobility service providers have the flexibility to offer or make available insurance options to their users, while also ensuring the shared mobility service providers' insurance serves as the backstop to cover any pedestrian injuries or death, or property damage, should there be any unintended gaps in coverage as a result of users misrepresenting or not maintaining the insurance.

(D) A shared mobility service provider shall keep an up-to-date list of its users that maintain their own liability insurance coverage that meets or exceeds the requirements of subparagraph (A). The provider shall annually transmit information on the percentage of its total users in the state that maintain their own insurance coverage, in the same manner as proscribed in subdivision (b) of Section 2505.5 of the Civil Code, to the Department of Insurance.

(3) Effective July 1, 2023, nothing in this section shall prohibit a provider from requiring a user to enter into an indemnity contract whereby the user will indemnify the provider for the user's proportionate share of liability. The indemnity contract shall not require the user to defend or indemnify the provider for the provider's negligence or willful misconduct. This section shall not be waived or modified by contractual agreement, act, or omission of the parties.

(c)(1) A city or county that authorizes a provider to operate within its jurisdiction on or after January 1, 2021, shall adopt rules for the operation, parking, and maintenance of shared mobility devices before a provider may offer any shared mobility device for rent or use in the city or county by any of the following:

(A) Ordinance.
(B) Agreement.
(C) Permit terms.

(2) A city or county that authorized a provider to operate within its jurisdiction before January 1, 2021, and continues to provide that authorization shall adopt rules for the operation, parking, and maintenance of shared mobility devices by January 1, 2022, by any of the following:

(A) Ordinance.
(B) Agreement.
(C) Permit terms.

(3) A provider shall comply with all applicable rules, agreements, and permit terms established pursuant to this subdivision.

(d) Nothing in this section shall prohibit a city or county from adopting any ordinance or regulation that is not inconsistent with this title.

(e) On or before July 1, 2023, a shared mobility service provider shall disclose to its customers that the customer's existing homeowner's, renter's, or automobile insurance policies might not provide coverage for liability resulting from the use of shared mobility devices and that the customer should contact their insurance company or insurance agent to determine if coverage is provided, prior to allowing a user to initiate their first use of a device.

(1) The disclosure shall be made to, and acknowledged by, the customer via the provider's digital application or electronic platform and posted on the provider's internet website.

(2) The disclosure shall include the following language in capital letters:

"YOUR HOMEOWNER'S, RENTER'S, OR AUTOMOBILE INSURANCE POLICIES MIGHT NOT PROVIDE COVERAGE FOR ACCIDENTS INVOLVING THE USE OF THIS DEVICE. TO DETERMINE IF COVERAGE IS PROVIDED YOU SHOULD CONTACT YOUR INSURANCE COMPANY OR AGENT." **Leg.H.** Added Stats 2020 ch 91 §1 (AB 1286), effective January 1, 2021. Amended Stats 2022 ch 740 §1 (AB 371), effective January 1, 2023; Stats 2023 ch 440 §1 (AB 458), effective January 1, 2024.

Prior Law Former Civ C §2505, relating to execution of document by the attorney in fact, was added Stats 1984 ch 312 §8, and repealed Stats 1994 ch 307 §10 (SB 1907).

Former Civ C §2505, similar to present Corp C §15529, was added by Stats 1929 ch 865 §1 and repealed by Stats 1949 ch 383 §2 (Corp C §100002) p 697.

§ 2505.5. Study and report to Legislature [Repealed January 1, 2027]

(a) The Department of Insurance shall conduct a study and report the findings to the Legislature and the insurance committees of both houses no later than December 31, 2026, that does all of the following:

(1) In collaboration with a city or county with jurisdiction over areas of shared mobility device use and shared mobility device insurers and operators, assesses whether coverage requirements for shared mobility devices are appropriate to the risk of shared mobility device services and provide recommendations to update coverage requirements, if found to be necessary. The Department of Insurance may specify by bulletin the time periods and elements of data to be provided by admitted and nonadmitted insurers writing coverage pursuant to subdivision (b) of Section 2505.

(2) With input from shared mobility device providers, analyzes the process by which providers give users an option to purchase their own insurance coverage, and make recommendations, if necessary, on how to strengthen the market for individual mobility device liability coverage, including on ensuring agreements between a provider and user to remove the user from the provider's policy do not result in circumstances where there is a gap in coverage providing recovery for injured pedestrians.

(3)(A) In collaboration with a city or county with jurisdiction over areas of shared mobility device use and shared mobility device insurers and operators, assesses whether there is a need for insurance coverage for injuries to, or death of, a pedestrian or property damage to assistive technology devices when the injury, death, or property damage involves, in whole or in part, the following devices:

(i) A bicycle propelled exclusively by human power, as described in Section 231 of the Vehicle Code. For purposes of this paragraph, "bicycle" shall not include an electric bicycle.

(ii) A class 1 electric bicycle as defined in paragraph (1) of subdivision (a) of Section 312.5 of the Vehicle Code.

(iii) A class 2 electric bicycle as defined in paragraph (2) of subdivision (a) of Section 312.5 of the Vehicle Code.

(B) It is the intent of the Legislature that the assessment in subparagraph (A) of this section will provide data on the prevalence of injuries, death, or property damage resulting from the devices described in clauses (i), (ii), and (iii) of subparagraph (A), including, but not limited to, resulting from such devices being negligently abandoned on pedestrian walkways, and determine whether additional insurance coverage is necessary to account for such pedestrian injuries or death and property damage.

(b) Data collected by the Department of Insurance pursuant to this section shall not include information that identifies or describes an individual, including, but not limited to, an individual's name, social security number, home address, home telephone number, education, financial matters, medical or employment history, geolocation, or statements made by, or attributed to, the individual, or that may otherwise compromise the privacy of the individual under existing law.

(c)(1) A report to be submitted pursuant to this section shall be submitted in compliance with Section 9795 of the Government Code.

(2) Pursuant to Section 10231.5 of the Government Code, this section is repealed on January 1, 2027. **Leg.H.** Added Stats 2022 ch 740 §2 (AB 371), effective January 1, 2023, repealed January 1, 2027.

§ 2506. Required service provider identification sign

(a) A shared mobility service provider shall affix to each shared mobility device a readily accessible, single, and clearly displayed tactile sign containing raised characters and accompanying braille that complies with Section 11B-703 of the California Building Code, except that the raised characters shall be, at minimum, one-half inch high and in a color that contrasts with the signage background, in order to identify the device for the purpose of reporting illegal or negligent activity. The sign shall minimally consist of the company name and telephone number of the service provider that is visible from a minimum of five feet and not obfuscated by branding or other markings.

(b) This section shall become operative on January 1, 2024. **Leg.H.** Added Stats 2023 ch 36 §2 (AB 410), effective July 6, 2023, operative January 1, 2024.

Prior Law Former Civ C §2506, relating to required service provider identification sign, was added Stats 2022 ch 740 §3 (AB 371), effective January 1, 2023, and repealed Stats 2023 ch 36 §1 (AB 410), effective July 6, 2023.

Former Civ C §2506, relating to power of alternate agent to make health care decisions, was added Stats 1984 ch 312 §8, and repealed Stats 1994 ch 307 §10 (SB 1907).

Former Civ C §2506, similar to present Corp C §15530, was added by Stats 1929 ch 865 §1 and repealed by Stats 1949 ch 383 §2 (Corp C §100002) p 697.

TITLE 10A
UNINCORPORATED NONPROFIT ASSOCIATIONS AND THEIR MEMBERS [REPEALED]

§§2523–2525. [Sections repealed 1947]

Leg.H. Added Stats 1945 ch 144 §1. Repealed Stats 1947 ch 1038 (Corp C §100003) p 2441. See Corp C §§21000–21102.

TITLE 11
PHARMACEUTICAL SERVICES

Studies of fees for pharmaceutical dispensing services to private consumers; "Prescription drug claims processor". §2527.
Remedies for violation of Section 2527; Pharmacy owners' standing to sue. §2528.

§2527. Studies of fees for pharmaceutical dispensing services to private consumers; "Prescription drug claims processor"

(a) On or after January 1, 1984, no prescription drug claims processor, as defined in subdivision (b), shall enter into or perform any provision of any new contract, or perform any provision of any existing contract, with a licensed California pharmacy, or process or assist in the processing of any prescription drug claim submitted by or otherwise involving a service of a licensed California pharmacy unless the processor is in compliance with subdivisions (c) and (d).

(b) A "prescription drug claims processor," as used in this part, means any nongovernmental entity which has a contractual relationship with purchasers of prepaid or insured prescription drug benefits, and which processes, consults, advises on, or otherwise assists in the processing of prepaid or insured prescription drug benefit claims submitted by a licensed California pharmacy or patron thereof. A "prescription drug claims processor" shall not include insurers (as defined in Section 23 of the Insurance Code), health care service plans (as defined in subdivision (f) of Section 1345 of the Health and Safety Code), nonprofit hospital service plans (pursuant to Chapter 11A, (commencing with Section 11491) of Part 2 of Division 2 of the Insurance Code), pharmacy permitholders (pursuant to Section 4080 of the Business and Professions Code), employers, trusts, and other entities which assume the risks of pharmaceutical services for designated beneficiaries. Also, a "prescription drug claims processor" shall not include insurers, health care service plans, and nonprofit hospital service plans which process claims on a nonrisk basis for self-insured clients.

(c) On or before January 1, 1984, every prescription drug claims processor shall have conducted or obtained the results of a study or studies which identifies the fees, separate from ingredient costs, of all, or of a statistically significant sample, of California pharmacies, for pharmaceutical dispensing services to private consumers. The study or studies shall meet reasonable professional standards of the statistical profession. The determination of the pharmacy's fee made for purposes of the study or studies shall be computed by reviewing a sample of the pharmacy's usual charges for a random or other representative sample of commonly prescribed drug products, subtracting the average wholesale price of drug ingredients, and averaging the resulting fees by dividing the aggregate of the fees by the number of prescriptions reviewed. A study report shall include a preface, an explanatory summary of the results and findings including a comparison of the fees of California pharmacies by setting forth the mean fee and standard deviation, the range of fees and fee percentiles (10th, 20th, 30th, 40th, 50th, 60th, 70th, 80th, 90th). This study or these studies shall be conducted or obtained no less often than every 24 months.

(d) The study report or reports obtained pursuant to subdivision (c) shall be transmitted by certified mail by each prescription drug claims processor to the chief executive officer or designee, of each client for whom it performs claims processing services. Consistent with subdivision (c), the processor shall transmit the study or studies to clients no less often than every 24 months.

Nothing in this section shall be construed to require a prescription drug claims processor to transmit to its clients more than two studies meeting the requirements of subdivision (c) during any such 24-month period.

Effective January 1, 1986, a claims processor may comply with subdivision (c) and this subdivision, in the event that no new study or studies meeting the criteria of subdivision (c) have been conducted or obtained subsequent to January 1, 1984, by transmitting the same study or studies previously transmitted, with notice of cost-of-living changes as measured by the Consumer Price Index (CPI) of the United States Department of Labor. **Leg.H.** Added Stats 1982 ch 296 §1.

Prior Law: Former §2527, relating to insurance, was enacted 1872 and repealed by Stats 1979 ch 373 §45.

§2528. Remedies for violation of Section 2527; Pharmacy owners' standing to sue

A violation of Section 2527 may result only in imposition of a civil remedy, which includes, but is not limited to, imposition of statutory damages of not less than one thousand dollars ($1,000) or more than ten thousand dollars ($10,000) depending on the severity or gravity of the violation, plus reasonable attorney's fees and costs, declaratory and injunctive relief, and any other relief which the court deems proper. Any owner of a licensed California pharmacy shall have standing to bring an action seeking a civil remedy pursuant to this section so long as his or her pharmacy has a contractual relationship with, or renders pharmaceutical services to, a beneficiary of a client of the prescription drug claims processor, against whom the action is brought provided that no such action may be commenced by the owner unless he or she has notified the processor in writing as to the nature of the alleged violation and the processor fails to remedy the violation within 30 days from the receipt of the notice or fails to undertake steps to remedy the violation within that period and complete the steps promptly thereafter. **Leg.H.** Added Stats 1982 ch 296 §1.

§§2531–2769. [Sections repealed 1935]

Leg.H. Enacted 1872. Amended Code Amdts 1873–74 ch 612; Stats 1901 ch 177; Stats 1905 ch 458; Stats 1909 ch 602; Stats 1909 ch 604; Stats 1913 ch 332; Stats 1917 ch 695; Stats 1923 ch 347; Stats 1925 ch 187; Stats 1927 ch 658; Stats 1929 ch 28. Repealed Stats 1935 ch 145 (Ins C §13001) pp 778, 779.

TITLE 12
INDEMNITY

"Indemnity". §2772.
Indemnity for a future wrongful act void. §2773.
Indemnity for a past wrongful act valid. §2774.
Indemnity extends to acts of agents. §2775.
Indemnity to several. §2776.
Person indemnifying liable jointly or severally with person indemnified. §2777.
Rules for interpreting agreement of indemnity. §2778.
When person indemnifying is a surety. §2779.
Construction contracts; Agreements indemnifying promisee or relieving public agency from liability as void; Subcontractor's defense or indemnity obligation; Builder's or general contractor's rights to damages; Equitable indemnity. §2782.
Construction contract and amendments entered on or after January 1, 2013; Insertion of void or unenforceable provisions; Waiver or modification; Subcontractor's defense or indemnity obligation; General contractor's or construction manager's rights to damages; Construction. §2782.05.
Exemption as to responsibility under construction contract. §2782.1.
Exception for inspection services. §2782.2.
Allocation or limitation of liability. §2782.5.
Exception for professional engineer or geologist; "Hazardous materials". §2782.6.
Contracts for design professional services; Limitations on indemnity; Applicability. §2782.8.
Construction contracts on which wrap-up insurance policy applicable; Agreements indemnifying another from liability void; Equitable indemnity; Waiver or modification. §2782.9.
Provisions governing construction where wrap-up insurance policy covers private residential improvement; Disclosure; Bidding. §2782.95.

Provisions governing construction where wrap-up insurance policy covers public work; Calculations to be clearly delineated in bid document; Disclosure. §2782.96.

"Construction contract". §2783.

"Design defect". §2784.

Invalid indemnity provision in trucking or cartage contracts. §2784.5.

§2772. "Indemnity"

Indemnity is a contract by which one engages to save another from a legal consequence of the conduct of one of the parties, or of some other person. **Leg.H.** Enacted 1872.

§2773. Indemnity for a future wrongful act void

An agreement to indemnify a person against an act thereafter to be done, is void, if the act be known by such person at the time of doing it to be unlawful. **Leg.H.** Enacted 1872. Amended Code Amdts 1873–74 ch 612 §253.

§2774. Indemnity for a past wrongful act valid

An agreement to indemnify a person against an act already done, is valid, even though the act was known to be wrongful, unless it was a felony. **Leg.H.** Enacted 1872.

§2775. Indemnity extends to acts of agents

An agreement to indemnify against the acts of a certain person, applies not only to his acts and their consequences, but also to those of his agents. **Leg.H.** Enacted 1872.

§2776. Indemnity to several

An agreement to indemnify several persons applies to each, unless a contrary intention appears. **Leg.H.** Enacted 1872.

§2777. Person indemnifying liable jointly or severally with person indemnified

One who indemnifies another against an act to be done by the latter, is liable jointly with the person indemnified, and separately, to every person injured by such act. **Leg.H.** Enacted 1872.

§2778. Rules for interpreting agreement of indemnity

In the interpretation of a contract of indemnity, the following rules are to be applied, unless a contrary intention appears:

1. Upon an indemnity against liability, expressly, or in other equivalent terms, the person indemnified is entitled to recover upon becoming liable;

2. Upon an indemnity against claims, or demands, or damages, or costs, expressly, or in other equivalent terms, the person indemnified is not entitled to recover without payment thereof;

3. An indemnity against claims, or demands, or liability, expressly, or in other equivalent terms, embraces the costs of defense against such claims, demands, or liability incurred in good faith, and in the exercise of a reasonable discretion;

4. The person indemnifying is bound, on request of the person indemnified, to defend actions or proceedings brought against the latter in respect to the matters embraced by the indemnity, but the person indemnified has the right to conduct such defenses, if he chooses to do so;

5. If, after request, the person indemnifying neglects to defend the person indemnified, a recovery against the latter suffered by him in good faith, is conclusive in his favor against the former;

6. If the person indemnifying, whether he is a principal or a surety in the agreement, has not reasonable notice of the action or proceeding against the person indemnified, or is not allowed to control its defense, judgment against the latter is only presumptive evidence against the former;

7. A stipulation that a judgment against the person indemnified shall be conclusive upon the person indemnifying, is inapplicable if he had a good defense upon the merits, which by want of ordinary care he failed to establish in the action. **Leg.H.** Enacted 1872.

§2779. When person indemnifying is a surety

Where one, at the request of another, engages to answer in damages, whether liquidated or unliquidated, for any violation of duty on the part of the latter, he is entitled to be reimbursed in the same manner as a surety, for whatever he may pay. **Leg.H.** Enacted 1872.

§2780. [Section repealed 1982]

Leg.H. Enacted 1872. Repealed Stats 1982 ch 517 §71. The repealed section related to the description of bail.

§2781. [Section repealed 1982]

Leg.H. Enacted 1872. Repealed Stats 1982 ch 517 §72. The repealed section related to the obligations of bail.

§2782. Construction contracts; Agreements indemnifying promisee or relieving public agency from liability as void; Subcontractor's defense or indemnity obligation; Builder's or general contractor's rights to damages; Equitable indemnity

(a) Except as provided in Sections 2782.1, 2782.2, 2782.5, and 2782.6, provisions, clauses, covenants, or agreements contained in, collateral to, or affecting any construction contract and that purport to indemnify the promisee against liability for damages for death or bodily injury to persons, injury to property, or any other loss, damage or expense arising from the sole negligence or willful misconduct of the promisee or the promisee's agents, servants, or independent contractors who are directly responsible to the promisee, or for defects in design furnished by those persons, are against public policy and are void and unenforceable; provided, however, that this section shall not affect the validity of any insurance contract, workers' compensation, or agreement issued by an admitted insurer as defined by the Insurance Code.

(b)(1) Except as provided in Sections 2782.1, 2782.2, and 2782.5, provisions, clauses, covenants, or agreements contained in, collateral to, or affecting any construction contract with a public agency entered into before January 1, 2013, that purport to impose on the contractor, or relieve the public agency from, liability for the active negligence of the public agency are void and unenforceable.

(2) Except as provided in Sections 2782.1, 2782.2, and 2782.5, provisions, clauses, covenants, or agreements contained in, collateral to, or affecting any construction contract with a public agency entered into on or after January 1, 2013, that purport to impose on any contractor, subcontractor, or supplier of goods or services, or relieve the public agency from, liability for the active negligence of the public agency are void and unenforceable.

(c)(1) Except as provided in subdivision (d) and Sections 2782.1, 2782.2, and 2782.5, provisions, clauses, covenants, or agreements contained in, collateral to, or affecting any construction contract entered into on or after January 1, 2013, with the owner of privately owned real property to be improved and as to which the owner is not acting as a contractor or supplier of materials or equipment to the work, that purport to impose on any contractor, subcontractor, or supplier of goods or services, or relieve the owner from, liability are unenforceable to the extent of the active negligence of the owner, including that of its employees.

(2) For purposes of this subdivision, an owner of privately owned real property to be improved includes the owner of any interest therein, other than a mortgage or other interest that is held solely as security for performance of an obligation.

(3) This subdivision shall not apply to a homeowner performing a home improvement project on his or her own single family dwelling.

(d) For all construction contracts, and amendments thereto, entered into after January 1, 2009, for residential construction, as used in Title 7 (commencing with Section 895) of Part 2 of Division 2, all provisions, clauses, covenants, and agreements contained in, collateral to, or affecting any construction contract, and amendments thereto, that purport to insure or indemnify, including the cost to defend, the builder, as defined in Section 911, or the general contractor or contractor not affiliated with the builder, as described in subdivision (b) of Section 911, by a subcontractor against liability for claims of construction defects are unenforceable to the extent the claims arise out of, pertain to, or relate to the negligence of the builder or contractor or the builder's or contractor's other agents, other servants, or other independent contractors who are directly responsible to the builder, or for defects in design furnished by those persons, or to the extent the claims do not arise out of, pertain to, or relate to the scope of work in the written agreement between the parties. This section shall not be waived or modified by contractual agreement, act, or omission of the parties. Contractual provisions, clauses, covenants, or agreements not expressly prohibited herein are reserved to the agreement of the parties. Nothing in this subdivision shall prevent any party from exercising its rights under subdivision (a) of Section 910. This subdivision shall not affect the obligations of an insurance carrier under the holding of Presley Homes, Inc. v. American States Insurance Company (2001) 90 Cal.App.4th 571. Nor shall this subdivision affect the obligations of a builder or subcontractor pursuant to Title 7 (commencing with Section 895) of Part 2 of Division 2.

(e) Subdivision (d) does not prohibit a subcontractor and builder or general contractor from mutually agreeing to the timing or immediacy of the defense and provisions for reimbursement of defense fees and costs, so long as that agreement does not waive or modify the provisions of subdivision (d) subject, however, to paragraphs (1) and (2). A subcontractor shall owe no defense or indemnity obligation to a builder or general contractor for a construction defect claim unless and until the builder or general contractor provides a written tender of the claim, or portion thereof, to the subcontractor which includes all of the information provided to the builder or general contractor by the claimant or claimants, including, but not limited to, information provided pursuant to subdivision (a) of Section 910, relating to claims caused by that subcontractor's scope of work. This written tender shall have the same force and effect as a notice of commencement of a legal proceeding. If a builder or general contractor tenders a claim for construction defects, or a portion thereof, to a subcontractor in the manner specified by this provision, the subcontractor shall elect to perform either of the following, the performance of which shall be deemed to satisfy the subcontractor's defense obligation to the builder or general contractor:

(1) Defend the claim with counsel of its choice, and the subcontractor shall maintain control of the defense for any claim or portion of claim to which the defense obligation applies. If a subcontractor elects to defend under this paragraph, the subcontractor shall provide written notice of the election to the builder or general contractor within a reasonable time period following receipt of the written tender, and in no event later than 90 days following that receipt. Consistent with subdivision (d), the defense by the subcontractor shall be a complete defense of the builder or general contractor of all claims or portions thereof to the extent alleged to be caused by the subcontractor, including any vicarious liability claims against the builder or general contractor resulting from the subcontractor's scope of work, but not including claims resulting from the scope of work, actions, or omissions of the builder, general contractor, or any other party. Any vicarious liability imposed upon a builder or general contractor for claims caused by the subcontractor electing to defend under this paragraph shall be directly enforceable against the subcontractor by the builder, general contractor, or claimant.

(2) Pay, within 30 days of receipt of an invoice from the builder or general contractor, no more than a reasonable allocated share of the builder's or general contractor's defense fees and costs, on an ongoing basis during the pendency of the claim, subject to reallocation consistent with subdivision (d), and including any amounts reallocated upon final resolution of the claim, either by settlement or judgment. The builder or general contractor shall allocate a share to itself to the extent a claim or claims are alleged to be caused by its work, actions, or omissions, and a share to each subcontractor to the extent a claim or claims are alleged to be caused by the subcontractor's work, actions, or omissions, regardless of whether the builder or general contractor actually tenders the claim to any particular subcontractor, and regardless of whether that subcontractor is participating in the defense. Any amounts not collected from any particular subcontractor may not be collected from any other subcontractor.

(f) Notwithstanding any other provision of law, if a subcontractor fails to timely and adequately perform its obligations under paragraph (1) of subdivision (e), the builder or general contractor shall have the right to pursue a claim against the subcontractor for any resulting compensatory damages, consequential damages, and reasonable attorney's fees. If a subcontractor fails to timely perform its obligations under paragraph (2) of subdivision (e), the builder or general contractor shall have the right to pursue a claim against the subcontractor for any resulting compensatory and consequential damages, as well as for interest on defense and indemnity costs, from the date incurred, at the rate set forth in subdivision (g) of Section 3260, and for the builder's or general contractor's reasonable attorney's fees incurred to recover these amounts. The builder or general contractor shall bear the burden of proof to establish both the subcontractor's failure to perform under either paragraph (1) or (2) of subdivision (e) and any resulting damages. If, upon request by a subcontractor, a builder or general contractor does not reallocate defense fees to subcontractors within 30 days following final resolution of the claim as described above, the subcontractor shall have the right to pursue a claim against the builder or general contractor for any resulting compensatory and consequential damages, as well as for interest on the fees, from the date of final resolution of the claim, at the rate set forth in subdivision (g) of Section 3260, and the subcontractor's reasonable attorney's fees incurred in connection therewith. The subcontractor shall bear the burden of proof to establish both the failure to reallocate the fees and any resulting damages. Nothing in this section shall prohibit the parties from mutually agreeing to reasonable contractual provisions for damages if any party fails to elect for or perform its obligations as stated in this section.

(g) A builder, general contractor, or subcontractor shall have the right to seek equitable indemnity for any claim governed by this section.

(h) Nothing in this section limits, restricts, or prohibits the right of a builder, general contractor, or subcontractor to seek equitable indemnity against any supplier, design professional, or product manufacturer.

(i) As used in this section, "construction defect" means a violation of the standards set forth in Sections 896 and 897. **Leg.H.** Added Stats 1967 ch 1327 §1. Amended Stats 1980 ch 211 §1; Stats 1982 ch 386 §1; Stats 1985 ch 567 §1; Stats 1990 ch 814 §1 (SB 1922); Stats 2005 ch 394 §1 (AB 758), effective January 1, 2006; Stats 2007 ch 32 §1 (SB 138), effective January 1, 2008; Stats 2008 ch 467 §1 (AB 2738), effective January 1, 2009; Stats 2011 ch 707 §2 (SB 474), effective January 1, 2012.

§2782.05. Construction contract and amendments entered on or after January 1, 2013; Insertion of void or unenforceable provisions; Waiver or modification; Subcontractor's defense or indemnity obligation; General contractor's or construction manager's rights to damages; Construction

(a) Except as provided in subdivision (b), provisions, clauses, covenants, and agreements contained in, collateral to, or affecting any construction contract and amendments thereto entered into on or after January 1, 2013, that purport to insure or indemnify, including the cost to defend, a general contractor, construction manager, or other subcontractor, by a subcontractor against liability for claims of death or bodily injury to persons, injury to property, or any other loss, damage, or expense are void and unenforceable to the extent the claims arise out of, pertain to, or relate to the active negligence or willful misconduct of that general contractor, construction manager, or other subcontractor, or their other agents, other servants, or other independent contractors who are responsible to the general contractor, construction manager, or other subcontractor, or for defects in design furnished by those persons, or to the extent the claims do not arise out of the scope of work of the subcontractor pursuant to the construction contract. This section shall not be waived or modified by contractual agreement, act, or omission of the parties. Contractual provisions, clauses, covenants, or agreements not expressly prohibited herein are reserved to the agreement of the parties. This section shall not affect the obligations of an insurance carrier under the holding of Presley Homes, Inc. v. American States Insurance Company (2001) 90 Cal.App.4th 571, nor the rights of an insurance carrier under the holding of Buss v. Superior Court (1997) 16 Cal.4th 35.

(b) This section does not apply to:

(1) Contracts for residential construction that are subject to any part of Title 7 (commencing with Section 895) of Part 2 of Division 2.

(2) Direct contracts with a public agency that are governed by subdivision (b) of Section 2782.

(3) Direct contracts with the owner of privately owned real property to be improved that are governed by subdivision (c) of Section 2782.

(4) Any wrap-up insurance policy or program.

(5) A cause of action for breach of contract or warranty that exists independently of an indemnity obligation.

(6) A provision in a construction contract that requires the promisor to purchase or maintain insurance covering the acts or omissions of the promisor, including additional insurance endorsements covering the acts or omissions of the promisor during ongoing and completed operations.

(7) Indemnity provisions contained in loan and financing documents, other than construction contracts to which the contractor and a contracting project owner's lender are parties.

(8) General agreements of indemnity required by sureties as a condition of execution of bonds for construction contracts.

(9) The benefits and protections provided by the workers' compensation laws.

(10) The benefits or protections provided by the governmental immunity laws.

(11) Provisions that require the purchase of any of the following:

(A) Owners and contractors protective liability insurance.

(B) Railroad protective liability insurance.

(C) Contractors all-risk insurance.

(D) Builders all-risk or named perils property insurance.

(12) Contracts with design professionals.

(13) Any agreement between a promisor and an admitted surety insurer regarding the promisor's obligations as a principal or indemnitor on a bond.

(c) Notwithstanding any choice-of-law rules that would apply the laws of another jurisdiction, the law of California shall apply to every contract to which this section applies.

(d) Any waiver of the provisions of this section is contrary to public policy and is void and unenforceable.

(e) Subdivision (a) does not prohibit a subcontractor and a general contractor or construction manager from mutually agreeing to the timing or immediacy of the defense and provisions for reimbursement of defense fees and costs, so long as that agreement does not waive or modify the provisions of subdivision (a) subject, however, to paragraphs (1) and (2). A subcontractor shall owe no defense or indemnity obligation to a general contractor or construction manager for a claim unless and until the general contractor or construction manager provides a written tender of the claim, or portion thereof, to the subcontractor that includes the information provided by the claimant or claimants relating to claims caused by that subcontractor's scope of work. In addition, the general contractor or construction manager shall provide a written statement regarding how the reasonable allocated share of fees and costs was determined. The written tender shall have the same force and effect as a notice of commencement of a legal proceeding. If a general contractor or construction manager tenders a claim, or portion thereof, to a subcontractor in the manner specified by this subdivision, the subcontractor shall elect to perform either of the following, the performance of which shall be deemed to satisfy the subcontractor's defense obligation to the general contractor or construction manager:

(1) Defend the claim with counsel of its choice, and the subcontractor shall maintain control of the defense for any claim or portion of claim to which the defense obligation applies. If a subcontractor elects to defend under this paragraph, the subcontractor shall provide written notice of the election to the general contractor or construction manager within a reasonable time period following receipt of the written tender, and in no event later than 30 days following that receipt. Consistent with subdivision (a), the defense by the subcontractor shall be a complete defense of the general contractor or construction manager of all claims or portions thereof to the extent alleged to be caused by the subcontractor, including any vicarious liability claims against the general contractor or construction manager resulting from the subcontractor's scope of work, but not including claims resulting from the scope of work, actions, or omissions of the general contractor or construction manager, or any other party. Any vicarious liability imposed upon a general contractor or construction manager for claims caused by the subcontractor electing to defend under this paragraph shall be directly enforceable against the subcontractor by the general contractor, construction manager, or claimant. All information, documentation, or evidence, if any, relating to a subcontractor's assertion that another party is responsible for the claim shall be provided by that subcontractor to the general contractor or construction manager that tendered the claim.

(2) Pay, within 30 days of receipt of an invoice from the general contractor or construction manager, no more than a reasonable allocated share of the general contractor's or construction manager's defense fees and costs, on an ongoing basis during the pendency of the claim, subject to reallocation consistent with subdivision (a), and including any amounts reallocated upon final resolution of the claim, either by settlement or judgment. The general contractor or construction manager shall allocate a share to itself to the extent a claim or claims are alleged to be caused by its work, actions, or omissions, and a share to each subcontractor to the extent a claim or claims are alleged to be caused by the subcontractor's work, actions, or omissions, regardless of whether the general contractor or construction manager actually tenders the claim to any particular subcontractor, and regardless of whether that subcontractor is participating in the defense. Any amounts not collected from any particular subcontractor may not be collected from any other subcontractor.

(f) Notwithstanding any other provision of law, if a subcontractor fails to timely and adequately perform its obligations under paragraph (1) of subdivision (e), the general contractor or construction manager shall have the right to pursue a claim against the subcontractor for any resulting compensatory damages, consequential damages, and reasonable attorney's fees. If a subcontractor fails to timely perform its obligations under paragraph (2) of subdivision (e), the general contractor or construction manager shall have the right to pursue a claim against the subcontractor for any resulting compensatory damages, interest on defense and indemnity costs, from the date incurred, at the rate set forth in subdivision (g) of Section 3260, consequential damages, and reasonable attorney's fees incurred to recover these amounts. The general contractor or construction manager shall bear the burden of proof to establish both the subcontractor's failure to perform under either paragraph (1) or (2) of subdivision (e) and any resulting damages. If, upon request by a subcontractor, a general contractor or construction manager does not reallocate defense fees to subcontractors within 30 days following final resolution of the claim, the subcontractor shall have the right to pursue a claim against the general contractor or construction manager for any resulting compensatory damages with interest, from the date of final resolution of the claim, at the rate set forth in subdivision (g) of Section 3260. The subcontractor shall bear the burden of proof to establish both the failure to reallocate the fees and any resulting damages. Nothing in this section shall prohibit the parties from mutually agreeing to reasonable contractual provisions for damages if any party fails to elect for or perform its obligations as stated in this section.

(g) For purposes of this section, "construction manager" means a person or entity, other than a public agency or owner of privately owned real property to be improved, who is contracted by a public agency or the owner of privately owned real property to be improved to direct, schedule, or coordinate the work of contractors for a work of improvement, but does not itself perform the work.

(h) For purposes of this section, "general contractor," in relation to a given subcontractor, means a person who has entered into a construction contract and who has entered into a subcontract with that subcontractor under which the subcontractor agrees to perform a portion of that scope of work. Where a subcontractor has itself subcontracted a portion of its work, that subcontractor, along with its general contractor, shall be considered a general contractor as to its subcontractors.

(i) For purposes of this section, "subcontractor" means a person who has entered into a construction contract either with a contractor to perform a portion of that contractor's work under a construction contract or with any person to perform a construction contract subject to the direction or control of a general contractor or construction manager.

(j) A general contractor, construction manager, or subcontractor shall have the right to seek equitable indemnity for any claim governed by this section.

(k) Nothing in this section limits, restricts, or prohibits the right of a general contractor, construction manager, or subcontractor to seek equitable indemnity against any supplier, design professional, product manufacturer, or other independent contractor or subcontractor.

(*l*) This section shall not affect the validity of any existing insurance contract or agreement, including, but not limited to, a contract or agreement for workers' compensation or an agreement issued on or before January 1, 2012, by an admitted insurer, as defined in the Insurance Code.

(m) Nothing in this section shall be construed to affect the obligation, if any, of either a contractor or construction manager to indemnify, including defending or paying the costs to defend, a public agency against any claim arising from the alleged active negligence of the public agency under subdivision (b) of Section 2782 or to indemnify, including defending or paying the costs to defend, an owner of privately owned real property to be improved against any claim arising from the alleged active negligence of the owner under subdivision (c) of Section 2782.

(n) Nothing in this section shall be construed to affect the obligation, if any, of either a contractor or construction manager to provide or maintain insurance covering the acts or omissions of the promisor, including additional insurance endorsements covering the acts or omissions of the promisor during ongoing and completed operations pursuant to a construction contract with a public agency under subdivision (b) of Section 2782 or an owner of privately owned real property to be improved under subdivision (c) of Section 2782. **Leg.H.** Added Stats 2011 ch 707 §3 (SB 474), effective January 1, 2012.

§2782.1. Exemption as to responsibility under construction contract

Nothing contained in Section 2782 shall prevent a contractor responsible for the performance of a construction contract, as defined in Section 2783, from indemnifying fully a person, firm, corporation, state or other agency for whose account the construction contract is not being performed but who, as an accommodation, enters into an agreement with the contractor permitting such contractor to enter upon or adjacent to its property for the purpose of performing such construction contract for others. **Leg.H.** Added Stats 1968 ch 466 §1 p 1097.

§2782.2. Exception for inspection services

(a) Nothing contained in subdivision (a) of Section 2782 prevents an agreement to indemnify a professional engineer against liability for the negligence of the engineer, or the engineer's agents or employees, in providing inspection services to plants or other facilities if all the following criteria are satisfied:

(1) The promisor is the owner of the plants or facilities inspected.

(2) The promisor is audited annually by an independent certified public accountant, public accountant, or accounting licentiate of another state authorized by the laws of that state to perform the audit.

(3) The net worth of the promisor exceeds ten million dollars ($10,000,000), as determined by the promisor's most recent annual independent audit. The requirement of this paragraph shall be satisfied at the time the contract for indemnification is entered, and a subsequent reduction of the promisor's net worth shall not void the obligation to indemnify.

(4) The promisor is self-insured with respect to liability arising from ownership of the plant or facility.

(5) The indemnification shall not be applicable to the first two hundred fifty thousand dollars ($250,000) of liability.

(b) Subdivision (a) does not authorize contracts for indemnification of liability arising from willful misconduct. **Leg.H.** Added Stats 1985 ch 567 §2.

§2782.5. Allocation or limitation of liability

Nothing contained in Section 2782 shall prevent a party to a construction contract and the owner or other party for whose account the construction contract is being performed from negotiating and expressly agreeing with respect to the allocation, release, liquidation, exclusion, or limitation as between the parties of any liability (a) for design defects, or (b) of the promisee to the promisor arising out of or relating to the construction contract. **Leg.H.** Added Stats 1967 ch 1327 §2. Amended Stats 1980 ch 211 §2.

§2782.6. Exception for professional engineer or geologist; "Hazardous materials"

(a) Nothing in subdivision (a) of Section 2782 prevents an agreement to indemnify a professional engineer or geologist or the agents, servants, independent contractors, subsidiaries, or employees of that engineer or geologist from liability as described in Section 2782 in providing hazardous materials identification, evaluation, preliminary assessment, design, remediation services, or other services of the types described in Sections 78125 and 78135 of the Health and Safety Code or the federal National Oil and Hazardous Substances Pollution Contingency Plan (40 C.F.R. Sec. 300.1 et seq.), if all of the following criteria are satisfied:

(1) The services in whole or in part address subterranean contamination or other concealed conditions caused by the hazardous materials.

(2) The promisor is responsible, or potentially responsible, for all or part of the contamination.

(b) The indemnification described in this section is valid only for damages arising from, or related to, subterranean contamination or concealed conditions, and is not applicable to the first two hundred fifty thousand dollars ($250,000) of liability or a greater amount as is agreed to by the parties.

(c) This section does not authorize contracts for indemnification, by promisors specified in paragraph (2) of subdivision (a), of any liability of a promisee arising from the gross negligence or willful misconduct of the promisee.

(d) "Hazardous materials," as used in this section, means any hazardous or toxic substance, material, or waste that is or becomes subject to regulation by any agency of the state, any municipality or political subdivision of the state, or the United States. "Hazardous materials" includes, but is not limited to, any material or substance that is any of the following:

(1) A hazardous substance, as defined in subdivision (a) of Section 78075 of the Health and Safety Code.

(2) Hazardous material, as defined in subdivision (n) of Section 25501 of the Health and Safety Code.

(3) A regulated substance, as defined in subdivision (i) of Section 25532 of the Health and Safety Code.

(4) Hazardous waste, as defined in Section 25117 of the Health and Safety Code.

(5) Extremely hazardous waste, as defined in Section 25115 of the Health and Safety Code.

(6) Petroleum.

(7) Asbestos.

(8) Designated as a hazardous substance for purposes of Section 311 of the Federal Water Pollution Control Act, as amended (33 U.S.C. Sec. 1321).

(9) Hazardous waste, as defined by subsection (5) of Section 1004 of the federal Resource Conservation and Recovery Act of 1976, as amended (42 U.S.C. Sec. 6903).

(10) A hazardous substance, as defined by subsection (14) of Section 101 of the federal Comprehensive Environmental Response, Compensation, and Liability Act of 1980, as amended (42 U.S.C. Sec. 9601).

(11) A regulated substance, as defined by subsection (7) of Section 9001 of the federal Solid Waste Disposal Act, as amended (42 U.S.C. Sec. 6991).

(e) Nothing in this section shall be construed to alter, modify, or otherwise affect the liability of the promisor or promisee, under an indemnity agreement meeting the criteria of this section, to third parties for damages for death or bodily injury to persons, injury to property, or any other loss, damage, or expense.

(f) This section does not apply to public entities, as defined by Section 811.2 of the Government Code. **Leg.H.** Added Stats 1990 ch 814 §2 (SB 1922). Amended Stats 2018 ch 59 §1 (SB 1502), effective January 1, 2019; Stats 2021 ch 115 §1 (AB 148), effective July 22, 2021; Stats 2022 ch 258 §6 (AB 2327), effective January 1, 2023, operative January 1, 2024.

§2782.8. Contracts for design professional services; Limitations on indemnity; Applicability

(a) For all contracts, and amendments thereto, entered into on or after January 1, 2018, for design professional services, all provisions, clauses, covenants, and agreements contained in, collateral to, or affecting any such contract, and amendments thereto, that purport to indemnify, including the duty and the cost to defend, the indemnitee by a design professional against liability for claims against the indemnitee, are unenforceable, except to the extent that the claims against the indemnitee arise out of, pertain to, or relate to the negligence, recklessness, or willful misconduct of the design professional. In no event shall the cost to defend charged to the design professional exceed the design professional's proportionate percentage of fault. However, notwithstanding the previous sentence, in the event one or more defendants is unable to pay its share of defense costs due to bankruptcy or dissolution of the business, the design professional shall meet and confer with other parties regarding unpaid defense costs. The duty to indemnify, including the duty and the cost to defend, is limited as provided in this section. This section shall not be waived or modified by contractual agreement, act, or omission of the parties. Contractual provisions, clauses, covenants, or agreements not expressly prohibited herein are reserved to the agreement of the parties.

(b) All contracts and all solicitation documents, including requests for proposal, invitations for bid, and other solicitation documents for design professional services are deemed to incorporate by reference the provisions of this section.

(c) For purposes of this section, "design professional" includes all of the following:

(1) An individual licensed as an architect pursuant to Chapter 3 (commencing with Section 5500) of Division 3 of the Business and Professions Code, and a business entity offering architectural services in accordance with that chapter.

(2) An individual licensed as a landscape architect pursuant to Chapter 3.5 (commencing with Section 5615) of Division 3 of the Business and

Professions Code, and a business entity offering landscape architectural services in accordance with that chapter.

(3) An individual registered as a professional engineer pursuant to Chapter 7 (commencing with Section 6700) of Division 3 of the Business and Professions Code, and a business entity offering professional engineering services in accordance with that chapter.

(4) An individual licensed as a professional land surveyor pursuant to Chapter 15 (commencing with Section 8700) of Division 3 of the Business and Professions Code, and a business entity offering professional land surveying services in accordance with that chapter.

(d) This section shall apply only to a professional service contract, or any amendment thereto, entered into on or after January 1, 2018.

(e) The provisions of this section pertaining to the duty and cost to defend shall not apply to either of the following:

(1) Any contract for design professional services, or amendments thereto, where a project-specific general liability policy insures all project participants for general liability exposures on a primary basis and also covers all design professionals for their legal liability arising out of their professional services on a primary basis.

(2) A design professional who is a party to a written design-build joint venture agreement.

(f) Nothing in this section shall abrogate the provisions of Section 1104 of the Public Contract Code.

(g) Indemnitee, for purposes of this section, does not include any agency of the state. **Leg.H.** Added Stats 2006 ch 455 §1 (AB 573), effective January 1, 2007. Amended Stats 2010 ch 510 §1 (SB 972), effective January 1, 2011; Stats 2017 ch 8 §1 (SB 496), effective January 1, 2018.

§2782.9. Construction contracts on which wrap-up insurance policy applicable; Agreements indemnifying another from liability void; Equitable indemnity; Waiver or modification

(a) All contracts, provisions, clauses, amendments, or agreements contained therein entered into after January 1, 2009, for a residential construction project on which a wrap-up insurance policy, as defined in subdivision (b) of Section 11751.82 of the Insurance Code, or other consolidated insurance program, is applicable, that require an enrolled and participating subcontractor or other participant to indemnify, hold harmless, or defend another for any claim or action covered by that program, arising out of that project are unenforceable.

(b) To the extent any contractual provision is deemed unenforceable pursuant to this section, any party may pursue an equitable indemnity claim against another party for a claim or action unless there is coverage for the claim or action under the wrap-up policy or policies. Nothing in this section shall prohibit a builder or general contractor from requiring a reasonably allocated contribution from a subcontractor or other participant to the self-insured retention or deductible required under the wrap-up policy or other consolidated insurance program, if the maximum amount and method of collection of the participant's contribution is disclosed in the contract with the participant and the contribution is reasonably limited so that each participant may have some financial obligation in the event of a claim alleged to be caused by that participant's scope of work. The contribution shall only be collected when and as any such self-insured retention or deductible is incurred by the builder or general contractor and in an amount that bears a reasonable and proportionate relationship to the alleged liability arising from the claim or claims alleged to be caused by the participant's scope of work, when viewed in the context of the entirety of the alleged claim or claims. Any contribution shall only be collected from a participant after written notice to the participant of the amount of and basis for the contribution. In no event shall the total amount of contributions collected from participants exceed the amount of any self-insured retention or deductible due and payable by the builder or general contractor for the claim or claims. However, this requirement does not prohibit any legally permissible recovery of costs and legal fees to collect a participant's contribution if the contribution satisfies the requirements of this subdivision and is not paid by the participant when due.

(c) This section shall not be waived or modified by contractual agreement, act, or omission of the parties. **Leg.H.** Added Stats 2008 ch 467 §2 (AB 2738), effective January 1, 2009.

§2782.95. Provisions governing construction where wrap-up insurance policy covers private residential improvement; Disclosure; Bidding

For any wrap-up insurance policy or other consolidated insurance program that insures a private residential (as that term is used in Title 7 (commencing with Section 895) of Part 2 of Division 2) work of improvement that first commences construction after January 1, 2009, the following shall apply:

(a) The owner, builder, or general contractor obtaining the wrap-up insurance policy or other consolidated insurance program shall disclose the total amount or method of calculation of any credit or compensation for premium required from a subcontractor or other participant for that wrap-up policy in the contract documents.

(b) The contract documents shall disclose, if and to the extent known:

(1) The policy limits.

(2) The scope of policy coverage.

(3) The policy term.

(4) The basis upon which the deductible or occurrence is triggered by the insurance carrier.

(5) If the policy covers more than one work of improvement, the number of units, if any, indicated on the application for the insurance policy.

(6) A good faith estimate of the amount of available limits remaining under the policy as of a date indicated in the disclosure obtained from the insurer.

(7) Disclosures made pursuant to paragraphs (5) and (6) are recognized to be based upon information at a given moment in time and may not accurately reflect the actual number of units covered by the policy nor the amount of insurance available, if any, when a later claim is made. These disclosures are presumptively made in good faith if the disclosure pursuant to paragraph (5) is the same as that contained in the application to the wrap-up insurer and the disclosure pursuant to paragraph (6) was obtained from the wrap-up insurer or broker. The presumptions stated above shall be overcome only by a showing that the insurer, broker, builder, or general contractor intentionally misrepresented the facts identified in paragraphs (5) or (6).

(c) Upon the written request of any participant, a copy of the insurance policy shall be provided, if available, that shows the coverage terms and items in paragraphs (1) to (4), inclusive, of subdivision (b) above. If the policy is not available at the time of the request, a copy of the insurance binder or declaration of coverage may be provided in lieu of the actual policy. Paragraphs (1) to (4), inclusive, of subdivision (b) may be satisfied by providing the participant with a copy of the binder or declaration. Any party receiving a copy of the policy, binder, or declaration shall not disclose it to third parties other than the participant's insurance broker or attorney unless required to do so by law. The participant's insurance broker or attorney may not disclose the policy, binder, or declaration to any third party unless required to do so by law.

(d) If the owner, builder, or general contractor obtaining the wrap-up insurance policy or other consolidated insurance program does not disclose the total amount or method of calculation of the premium credit or compensation to be charged to the participant prior to the time the participant submits its bid, the participant shall not be legally bound by the bid unless that participant has the right to increase the bid up to the amount equal to the difference between the amount the participant included, if any, for insurance in the original bid and the amount of the actual bid credit required by the owner, builder, or general contractor obtaining the wrap-up insurance policy or other consolidated insurance program. This subdivision shall not apply if the owner, builder, or general contractor obtaining the wrap-up insurance policy or other consolidated insurance program did not require the subcontractor to offset the original bid amount with a deduction for the wrap-up insurance policy or program. **Leg.H.** Added Stats 2008 ch 467 §3 (AB 2738), effective January 1, 2009.

§2782.96. Provisions governing construction where wrap-up insurance policy covers public work; Calculations to be clearly delineated in bid document; Disclosure

If an owner, builder, or general contractor obtains a wrap-up insurance policy or other consolidated insurance program for a public work as defined in Section 1720 of the Labor Code or any other project other than residential construction, as that term is used in Title 7 (commencing with Section 895) of Part 2 of Division 2, that is put out for bid after January 1, 2009, the following shall apply:

(a) The total amount or method of calculation of any credit or compensation for premium required from a subcontractor or other participant for that policy shall be clearly delineated in the bid documents.

(b) The named insured, to the extent known, shall disclose to the subcontractor or other participant in the contract documents the policy limits, known exclusions, and the length of time the policy is intended to remain in effect. In addition, upon written request, once available, the named insured shall provide copies of insurance policies to all those who are covered by the policy. Until such time as the policies are available, the named insured may also satisfy the disclosure requirements of this subdivision by providing the subcontractor or other participant with a copy of the insurance binder or declaration of coverage. Any party receiving a copy of the policy, binder, or declaration shall not disclose it to third parties other than the participant's insurance broker or attorney unless required to do so by law. The participant's insurance broker or attorney may not disclose the policy, binder, or declaration to any third party unless required to do so by law.

(c) The disclosure requirements in subdivisions (a) and (b) do not apply to an insurance policy purchased by an owner, builder, or general contractor that provides additional coverage beyond what was contained in the original wrap-up policy or other consolidated insurance program if no credit or compensation for premium is required of the subcontractor for the additional insurance policy. **Leg.H.** Added Stats 2008 ch 467 §4 (AB 2738), effective January 1, 2009. Amended Stats 2009 ch 140 §37 (AB 1164), effective January 1, 2010.

§2783. "Construction contract"

As used in Sections 2782 and 2782.5, "construction contract" is defined as any agreement or understanding, written or oral, respecting the construction, surveying, design, specifications, alteration, repair, improvement, renovation, maintenance, removal of or demolition of any building, highway, road, parking facility, bridge, water line, sewer line, oil line, gas line, electric utility transmission or distribution line, railroad, airport, pier or dock, excavation or other structure, appurtenance, development or other improvement to real or personal property, or an agreement to perform any portion thereof or any act collateral thereto, or to perform any service reasonably related thereto, including, but not limited to, the erection of all structures or performance of work in connection therewith, electrical power line clearing, tree trimming, vegetation maintenance, the rental of all equipment, all incidental transportation, moving, lifting, crane and rigging service and other goods and services furnished in connection therewith. **Leg.H.** Added Stats 1967 ch 1327 §3. Amended Stats 2011 ch 707 §4 (SB 474), effective January 1, 2012.

§2784. "Design defect"

As used in Sections 2782 and 2782.5, a "design defect" is defined as a condition arising out of its design which renders a structure, item of equipment or machinery or any other similar object, movable or immovable, when constructed substantially in accordance with its design, inherently unfit, either wholly or in part, for its intended use or which impairs or renders the use of such structure, equipment, machinery or property dangerous. **Leg.H.** Added Stats 1967 ch 1327 §4.

§2784.5. Invalid indemnity provision in trucking or cartage contracts

Any provision, promise, agreement, clause, or covenant contained in, collateral to, or affecting any hauling, trucking, or cartage contract or agreement is against public policy, void and unenforceable if it purports to indemnify the promisee against liability for any of the following damages which are caused by the sole negligence or willful misconduct of the promisee, agents, servants, or the independent contractors directly responsible to the promisee, except when such agents, servants, or independent contractors are under the direct supervision and control of the promisor:

(a) Damages arising out of bodily injury or death to persons.

(b) Damage to property.

(c) Any other damage or expense arising under either (a) or (b).

This section shall not affect the validity of any insurance contract, workmen's compensation insurance contract, or agreement issued by an admitted insurer as defined by Sections 23 and 24 of the Insurance Code or insurance effected by surplus line brokers under Sections 1760 through 1780 of the Insurance Code. **Leg.H.** Added Stats 1967 ch 1314 §1.

TITLE 13
SURETYSHIP

Article 1. Definition of Suretyship.
Article 2. Creation of Suretyship.
Article 3. Interpretation of Suretyship.
Article 4. Liability of Sureties.
Article 5. Continuing Guaranty.
Article 6. Exoneration of Sureties.
Article 7. Position of Sureties.

ARTICLE 1
Definition of Suretyship

Former distinctions abolished; Surety or guarantor defined; Guaranties of collection; Continuing guaranties. §2787.
Creation of suretyship not dependent upon knowledge or consent of principal. §2788.

§2787. Former distinctions abolished; Surety or guarantor defined; Guaranties of collection; Continuing guaranties

The distinction between sureties and guarantors is hereby abolished. The terms and their derivatives, wherever used in this code or in any other statute or law of this state now in force or hereafter enacted, shall have the same meaning as defined in this section. A surety or guarantor is one who promises to answer for the debt, default, or miscarriage of another, or hypothecates property as security therefor. Guaranties of collection and continuing guaranties are forms of suretyship obligations, and except in so far as necessary in order to give effect to provisions specially relating thereto, shall be subject to all provisions of law relating to suretyships in general. A letter of credit is not a form of suretyship obligation. For purposes of this section, the term "letter of credit" means a "letter of credit" as defined in paragraph (10) of subdivision (a) of Section 5102 of the Commercial Code whether or not the engagement is governed by Division 5 (commencing with Section 5101) of the Commercial Code. **Leg.H.** Enacted 1872. Amended Stats 1939 ch 453 §10; Stats 1994 ch 611 §1 (SB 1612), effective September 15, 1994; Stats 1996 ch 176 §1 (SB 1599).

§2788. Creation of suretyship not dependent upon knowledge or consent of principal

A person may become surety even without the knowledge or consent of the principal. **Leg.H.** Enacted 1872. Amended Stats 1939 ch 453 §12.

ARTICLE 2
Creation of Suretyship

Necessity for consideration. §2792.
Obligations required to be in writing. §2793.
Obligations not required to be in writing. §2794.
Acceptance of offer to become surety; Notice of acceptance. §2795.

§2792. Necessity for consideration

Where a suretyship obligation is entered into at the same time with the original obligation, or with the acceptance of the latter by the creditor, and forms with that obligation a part of the consideration to him, no other consideration need exist. In all other cases there must be a consideration distinct from that of the original obligation. **Leg.H.** Enacted 1872. Amended Stats 1939 ch 453 §12.

§2793. Obligations required to be in writing

Except as prescribed by the next section, a suretyship obligation must be in writing, and signed by the surety; but the writing need not express a consideration. **Leg.H.** Enacted 1872. Amended Stats 1939 ch 453 §13.

§2794. Obligations not required to be in writing

A promise to answer for the obligation of another, in any of the following cases, is deemed an original obligation of the promisor, and need not be in writing:

(1) Where the promise is made by one who has received property of another upon an undertaking to apply it pursuant to such promise; or by one who has received a discharge from an obligation in whole or in part, in consideration of such promise;

(2) Where the creditor parts with value, or enters into an obligation, in consideration of the obligation in respect to which the promise is made, in terms or under circumstances such as to render the party making the promise the principal debtor and the person in whose behalf it is made, his surety;

(3) Where the promise, being for an antecedent obligation of another, is made upon the consideration that the party receiving it cancels the antecedent obligation, accepting the new promise as a substitute therefor; or upon the consideration that the party receiving it releases the property of another from a levy, or his person from imprisonment under an execution on a judgment obtained upon the antecedent obligation;

(4) Where the promise is upon a consideration beneficial to the promisor, whether moving from either party to the antecedent obligation, or from another person;

(5) Where a factor undertakes, for a commission, to sell merchandise and act as surety in connection with the sale;

(6) Where the holder of an instrument for the payment of money, upon which a third person is or may become liable to him, transfers it in payment of a precedent debt of his own, or for a new consideration, and in connection with such transfer enters into a promise respecting such instrument. **Leg.H.** Enacted 1872. Amended Stats 1939 ch 453 §14.

§2795. Acceptance of offer to become surety; Notice of acceptance

Unless notice of acceptance is expressly required, an offer to become a surety may be accepted by acting upon it, or by acceptance upon other consideration. An absolute suretyship obligation is binding upon the surety without notice of acceptance. **Leg.H.** Enacted 1872. Amended Stats 1939 ch 453 §15.

ARTICLE 3
Interpretation of Suretyship

Implication of risks of surety under uncompleted contract. §2799.
Guaranty that an obligation is good or collectible. §2800.
Recovery upon such guaranty. §2801.
Guarantor's liability upon such guaranty. §2802.

§2799. Implication of risks of surety under uncompleted contract

In an assumption of liability as surety in connection with a contract, the terms of which are not then settled, it is implied that its terms shall be such as will not expose the surety to greater risks than he would incur under those terms which are most common in similar contracts at the place where the principal contract is to be performed. **Leg.H.** Enacted 1872. Amended Stats 1939 ch 453 §16.

§2800. Guaranty that an obligation is good or collectible

A guaranty to the effect that an obligation is good, or is collectible, imports that the debtor is solvent, and that the demand is collectible by the usual legal proceedings, if taken with reasonable diligence. **Leg.H.** Enacted 1872.

§2801. Recovery upon such guaranty

A guaranty, such as is mentioned in the last section, is not discharged by an omission to take proceedings upon the principal debt, or upon any collateral security for its payment, if no part of the debt could have been collected thereby. **Leg.H.** Enacted 1872.

§2802. Guarantor's liability upon such guaranty

In the cases mentioned in section two thousand eight hundred, the removal of the principal from the state, leaving no property therein from which the obligation might be satisfied, is equivalent to the insolvency of the principal in its effect upon the rights and obligations of the guarantor. **Leg.H.** Enacted 1872.

ARTICLE 4
Liability of Sureties

Construction of suretyship obligation. §2806.
Necessity for demand or notice; Surety for payment or performance. §2807.
Surety upon conditional obligation. §2808.
Measure of liability; Generally. §2809.
Disability of principal. §2810.
Deposit of money held by bonded fiduciaries; Agreements authorized. §2811.

§2806. Construction of suretyship obligation

A suretyship obligation is to be deemed unconditional unless its terms import some condition precedent to the liability of the surety. **Leg.H.** Enacted 1872. Amended Stats 1939 ch 453 §17.

§2807. Necessity for demand or notice; Surety for payment or performance

A surety who has assumed liability for payment or performance is liable to the creditor immediately upon the default of the principal, and without demand or notice. **Leg.H.** Enacted 1872. Amended Stats 1939 ch 453 §18.

§2808. Surety upon conditional obligation

Where one assumes liability as surety upon a conditional obligation, his liability is commensurate with that of the principal, and he is not entitled to notice of the default of the principal, unless he is unable, by the exercise of reasonable diligence, to acquire information of such default, and the creditor has actual notice thereof. **Leg.H.** Enacted 1872. Amended Stats 1939 ch 453 §19.

§2809. Measure of liability; Generally

The obligation of a surety must be neither larger in amount nor in other respects more burdensome than that of the principal; and if in its terms it exceeds it, it is reducible in proportion to the principal obligation. **Leg.H.** Enacted 1872. Amended Stats 1939 ch 453 §20.

§2810. Disability of principal

A surety is liable, notwithstanding any mere personal disability of the principal, though the disability be such as to make the contract void against the principal; but he is not liable if for any other reason there is no liability upon the part of the principal at the time of the execution of the contract, or the liability of the principal thereafter ceases, unless the surety has assumed liability with knowledge of the existence of the defense. Where the principal is not liable because of mere personal disability, recovery back by the creditor of any res which formed all or part of the consideration for the contract shall have the effect upon the liability of the surety which is attributed to the recovery back of such a res under the law of sales generally. **Leg.H.** Enacted 1872. Amended Stats 1939 ch 453 §21.

§2811. Deposit of money held by bonded fiduciaries; Agreements authorized

Any party required to give a bond undertaking or other obligation may agree with his surety for the deposit of any money and assets for which the surety is responsible with a bank, savings bank, safe deposit, or trust company authorized by law to do business as such, or other depository approved by the court or a judge thereof, if such deposit is otherwise proper, for the safekeeping of such money and assets and in such manner as to prevent the withdrawal of any or all such money and assets without the written consent of the surety, or an order of court or a judge thereof, made on such notice to the surety as the court or judge may direct. Such agreement shall not in any manner release, or change the liability of, the principal or surety as established by the terms of the bond. **Leg.H.** Added Stats 1953 ch 37 §4.

ARTICLE 5
Continuing Guaranty

Continuing guaranty, what. §2814.
Revocation. §2815.

§2814. Continuing guaranty, what

A guaranty relating to a future liability of the principal, under successive transactions, which either continue his liability or from time to time renew it after it has been satisfied, is called a continuing guaranty. **Leg.H.** Enacted 1872.

§2815. Revocation

A continuing guaranty may be revoked at any time by the guarantor, in respect to future transactions, unless there is a continuing consideration as to such transactions which he does not renounce. **Leg.H.** Enacted 1872.

ARTICLE 6
Exoneration of Sureties

Acts operating to exonerate generally. §2819.
Void or voidable promise by creditor. §2820.
Rescission of agreement altering original obligation. §2821.
Acceptance of part performance. §2822.
Delay in proceeding against principal. §2823.
Release of principal, etc., after indemnification of surety. §2824.
Discharge of principal by operation of law. §2825.

§2819. Acts operating to exonerate generally

A surety is exonerated, except so far as he or she may be indemnified by the principal, if by any act of the creditor, without the consent of the surety the original obligation of the principal is altered in any respect, or the remedies or rights of the creditor against the principal, in respect thereto, in any way impaired or suspended. However, nothing in this section shall be construed to supersede subdivision (b) of Section 2822. **Leg.H.** Enacted 1872. Amended Stats 1939 ch 453 §22; Stats 1993 ch 149 §1 (AB 1402), effective July 16, 1993.

§2820. Void or voidable promise by creditor

That a promise by a creditor is for any cause void, or voidable by him at his option, shall not prevent it from altering the obligation or suspending or impairing the remedy within the meaning of the last section. **Leg.H.** Enacted 1872. Amended Stats 1939 ch 453 §34.

§2821. Rescission of agreement altering original obligation

The rescission of an agreement altering the original obligation of a debtor, or impairing the remedy of a creditor, does not restore the liability of a surety who has been exonerated by such agreement. **Leg.H.** Enacted 1872. Amended Stats 1939 ch 453 §23.

§2822. Acceptance of part performance

(a) The acceptance, by a creditor, of anything in partial satisfaction of an obligation, reduces the obligation of a surety thereof, in the same measure as that of the principal, but does not otherwise affect it. However, if the surety is liable upon only a portion of an obligation and the principal provides partial satisfaction of the obligation, the principal may designate the portion of the obligation that is to be satisfied.

(b) For purposes of this section and Section 2819, an agreement by a creditor to accept from the principal debtor a sum less than the balance owed on the original obligation, without the prior consent of the surety and without any other change to the underlying agreement between the creditor and principal debtor, shall not exonerate the surety for the lesser sum agreed upon by the creditor and principal debtor. **Leg.H.** Enacted 1872. Amended Stats 1939 ch 453 §23; Stats 1993 ch 149 §2 (AB 1402), effective July 16, 1993.

§2823. Delay in proceeding against principal

Mere delay on the part of a creditor to proceed against the principal, or to enforce any other remedy, does not exonerate a surety. **Leg.H.** Enacted 1872. Amended Stats 1939 ch 453 §25.

§2824. Release of principal, etc., after indemnification of surety

A surety, who has been indemnified by the principal, is liable to the creditor to the extent of the indemnity, notwithstanding that the creditor, without the assent of the surety, may have modified the contract or released the principal. **Leg.H.** Enacted 1872. Amended Stats 1939 ch 453 §26.

§2825. Discharge of principal by operation of law

A surety is not exonerated by the discharge of his principal by operation of law, without the intervention or omission of the creditor. **Leg.H.** Enacted 1872. Amended Stats 1939 ch 453 §27.

ARTICLE 7
Position of Sureties

Apparent principal may show that he is surety. §2832.
Rules of interpretation. §2837.
Judgment against surety does not alter the relation. §2838.
Surety exonerated by performance or offer of performance. §2839.
Surety may require creditor to proceed against principal; Effect of neglect to proceed. §2845.
Surety may compel principal to perform obligations, when due. §2846.
A principal bound to reimburse his surety. §2847.
The surety acquires the right of the creditor. §2848.
Surety entitled to benefit of securities held by creditor. §2849.
The property of principal to be taken first. §2850.
Creditors entitled to benefit of securities held by surety. §2854.
Arbitration award against principal not award against surety. §2855.
Waiver. §2856.

§2831. [Section repealed 1939]

Leg.H. Enacted 1872. Repealed Stats 1939 ch 453 §31. See CC §2787.

§2832. Apparent principal may show that he is surety

One who appears to be a principal, whether by the terms of a written instrument or otherwise, may show that he is in fact a surety, except as against persons who have acted on the faith of his apparent character of principal. It is not necessary for him to show that the creditor accepted him as surety. **Leg.H.** Enacted 1872. Amended Stats 1939 ch 453 §28.

§2836. [Section repealed 1939]

Leg.H. Enacted 1872. Repealed Stats 1939 ch 453 §31. See CC §2809.

§2837. Rules of interpretation

In interpreting the terms of a contract of suretyship, the same rules are to be observed as in the case of other contracts. Except as provided in section 2794, the position of a surety to whom consideration moves is the same as that of one who is gratuitous. **Leg.H.** Enacted 1872. Amended Stats 1939 ch 453 §29.

§2838. Judgment against surety does not alter the relation

Notwithstanding the recovery of judgment by a creditor against a surety, the latter still occupies the relation of surety. **Leg.H.** Enacted 1872.

§2839. Surety exonerated by performance or offer of performance

Performance of the principal obligation, or an offer of such performance, duly made as provided in this code, exonerates a surety. **Leg.H.** Enacted 1872. Amended Code Amdts 1873–74 ch 612 §254.

§2840. [Section repealed 1939]

Leg.H. Enacted 1872. Repealed Stats 1939 ch 453 §31. See CC §§2819 et seq.

§2844. [Section repealed 1939]

Leg.H. Enacted 1872. Repealed Stats 1939 ch 453 §31. See CC §§2787, 2845 et seq.

§2845. Surety may require creditor to proceed against principal; Effect of neglect to proceed

A surety may require the creditor, subject to Section 996.440 of the Code of Civil Procedure, to proceed against the principal, or to pursue any other remedy in the creditor's power which the surety cannot pursue, and which would lighten the surety's burden; and if the creditor neglects to do so, the surety is exonerated to the extent to which the surety is thereby prejudiced. **Leg.H.** Enacted 1872. Amended Stats 1939 ch 453 §30; Stats 1972 ch 391 §1; Stats 1982 ch 517 §73.

§2846. Surety may compel principal to perform obligations, when due

A surety may compel his principal to perform the obligation when due. **Leg.H.** Enacted 1872.

§2847. A principal bound to reimburse his surety

If a surety satisfies the principal obligation, or any part thereof, whether with or without legal proceedings, the principal is bound to reimburse what he has disbursed, including necessary costs and expenses; but the surety has no claim for reimbursement against other persons, though they may have been benefited by his act, except as prescribed by the next section. **Leg.H.** Enacted 1872.

§2848. The surety acquires the right of the creditor

A surety, upon satisfying the obligation of the principal, is entitled to enforce every remedy which the creditor then has against the principal to the extent of reimbursing what he has expended, and also to require all his co-sureties to contribute thereto, without regard to the order of time in which they became such. **Leg.H.** Enacted 1872.

§2849. Surety entitled to benefit of securities held by creditor

A surety is entitled to the benefit of every security for the performance of the principal obligation held by the creditor, or by a co-surety at the time of entering into the contract of suretyship, or acquired by him afterwards, whether the surety was aware of the security or not. **Leg.H.** Enacted 1872.

§2850. The property of principal to be taken first

Whenever property of a surety is hypothecated with property of the principal, the surety is entitled to have the property of the principal first applied to the discharge of the obligation. **Leg.H.** Enacted 1872.

§2851. [Section repealed 1982]

Leg.H. Added Stats 1939 ch 622 §1. Repealed Stats 1982 ch 517 §74. The repealed section related to notice of termination of bond and relief of surety from liability.

§2852. [Section repealed 1982]

Leg.H. Added Stats 1939 ch 622 §2. Repealed Stats 1982 ch 517 §75. The repealed section related to the requisites of a bond given on behalf of a licensee or permittee.

§2854. Creditors entitled to benefit of securities held by surety

A creditor is entitled to the benefit of everything which a surety has received from the debtor by way of security for the performance of the obligation, and may, upon the maturity of the obligation, compel the application of such security to its satisfaction. **Leg.H.** Enacted 1872.

§2855. Arbitration award against principal not award against surety

An arbitration award rendered against a principal alone shall not be, be deemed to be, or be utilized as, an award against his surety.

The intent of this legislation is to apply existing law to arbitration awards. **Leg.H.** Added Stats 1979 ch 346 §1.

§2856. Waiver

(a) Any guarantor or other surety, including a guarantor of a note or other obligation secured by real property or an estate for years, may waive any or all of the following:

(1) The guarantor or other surety's rights of subrogation, reimbursement, indemnification, and contribution and any other rights and defenses that are or may become available to the guarantor or other surety by reason of Sections 2787 to 2855, inclusive.

(2) Any rights or defenses the guarantor or other surety may have in respect of his or her obligations as a guarantor or other surety by reason of any election of remedies by the creditor.

(3) Any rights or defenses the guarantor or other surety may have because the principal's note or other obligation is secured by real property or an estate for years. These rights or defenses include, but are not limited to, any rights or defenses that are based upon, directly or indirectly, the application of Section 580a, 580b, 580d, or 726 of the Code of Civil Procedure to the principal's note or other obligation.

(b) A contractual provision that expresses an intent to waive any or all of the rights and defenses described in subdivision (a) shall be effective to waive these rights and defenses without regard to the inclusion of any particular language or phrases in the contract to waive any rights and defenses or any references to statutory provisions or judicial decisions.

(c) Without limiting any rights of the creditor or any guarantor or other surety to use any other language to express an intent to waive any or all of the rights and defenses described in paragraphs (2) and (3) of subdivision (a), the following provisions in a contract shall effectively waive all rights and defenses described in paragraphs (2) and (3) of subdivision (a):

The guarantor waives all rights and defenses that the guarantor may have because the debtor's debt is secured by real property. This means, among other things:

(1) The creditor may collect from the guarantor without first foreclosing on any real or personal property collateral pledged by the debtor.

(2) If the creditor forecloses on any real property collateral pledged by the debtor:

(A) The amount of the debt may be reduced only by the price for which that collateral is sold at the foreclosure sale, even if the collateral is worth more than the sale price.

(B) The creditor may collect from the guarantor even if the creditor, by foreclosing on the real property collateral, has destroyed any right the guarantor may have to collect from the debtor. This is an unconditional and irrevocable waiver of any rights and defenses the guarantor may have because the debtor's debt is secured by real property. These rights and defenses include, but are not limited to, any rights or defenses based upon Section 580a, 580b, 580d, or 726 of the Code of Civil Procedure.

(d) Without limiting any rights of the creditor or any guarantor or other surety to use any other language to express an intent to waive all rights and defenses of the surety by reason of any election of remedies by the creditor, the following provision shall be effective to waive all rights and defenses the guarantor or other surety may have in respect of his or her obligations as a surety by reason of an election of remedies by the creditor:

The guarantor waives all rights and defenses arising out of an election of remedies by the creditor, even though that election of remedies, such as a nonjudicial foreclosure with respect to security for a guaranteed obligation, has destroyed the guarantor's rights of subrogation and reimbursement against the principal by the operation of Section 580d of the Code of Civil Procedure or otherwise.

(e) Subdivisions (b), (c), and (d) shall not apply to a guaranty or other type of suretyship obligation made in respect of a loan secured by a deed of trust or mortgage on a dwelling for not more than four families when the dwelling is occupied, entirely or in part, by the borrower and that loan was in fact used to pay all or part of the purchase price of that dwelling.

(f) The validity of a waiver executed before January 1, 1997, shall be determined by the application of the law that existed on the date that the waiver was executed. **Leg.H.** Added Stats 1996 ch 1013 §2 (AB 2585).

Prior Law: Former §2856, similar to the present section, was added Stats 1994 ch 1204 §1, and repealed Stats 1996 ch 1013 §1.

1996 Note: It is the intent of the Legislature that the types of waivers described in Section 2856 of the Civil Code do not violate the public policy of this state. Additionally, the Legislature, by enacting subdivisions (b), (c), and (d) of Section 2856 of the Civil Code, does not intend to address the legal requirements for waivers in a guaranty or other suretyship contract in connection with the types of transactions described in subdivision (e) of Section 2856 of the Civil Code. No inference of any kind should be drawn from the exclusion of these transactions from the application of subdivisions (b), (c), and (d) of Section 2856 of the Civil Code. These amendments are not intended to limit or otherwise affect any rights or protections currently afforded to borrowers under Section 580a, 580b, 580d, or 726 of the Code of Civil Procedure. Stats 1996 ch 1013 §3.

ARTICLE 8
Letter of Credit [Repealed]

§2858. [Section repealed 1965]

Leg.H. Enacted 1872. Repealed Stats 1963 ch 819 §2, effective January 1, 1965. See UCC §§5103, 5104.

§§2859–2866. [Sections repealed 1965]

Leg.H. Enacted 1872. Repealed Stats 1963 ch 819 §2, effective January 1, 1965.

TITLE 13.5
OBLIGATION TO DEFEND ACTION

Provision of independent counsel to insured; Conflicts of interest; Selection of counsel; Waiver of right to counsel. §2860.

§2860. Provision of independent counsel to insured; Conflicts of interest; Selection of counsel; Waiver of right to counsel

(a) If the provisions of a policy of insurance impose a duty to defend upon an insurer and a conflict of interest arises which creates a duty on the part of the insurer to provide independent counsel to the insured, the insurer shall provide independent counsel to represent the insured unless, at the time the insured is informed that a possible conflict may arise or does exist, the insured expressly waives, in writing, the right to independent counsel. An insurance contract may contain a provision which sets forth the method of selecting that counsel consistent with this section.

(b) For purposes of this section, a conflict of interest does not exist as to allegations or facts in the litigation for which the insurer denies coverage; however, when an insurer reserves its rights on a given issue and the outcome of that coverage issue can be controlled by counsel first retained by the insurer for the defense of the claim, a conflict of interest may exist. No conflict of interest shall be deemed to exist as to allegations of punitive damages or be deemed to exist solely because an insured is sued for an amount in excess of the insurance policy limits.

(c) When the insured has selected independent counsel to represent him or her, the insurer may exercise its right to require that the counsel selected by the insured possess certain minimum qualifications which may include that the selected counsel have (1) at least five years of civil litigation practice which includes substantial defense experience in the subject at issue in the litigation, and (2) errors and omissions coverage. The insurer's obligation to pay fees to the independent counsel selected by the insured is limited to the rates which are actually paid by the insurer to attorneys retained by it in the ordinary course of business in the defense of similar actions in the community where the claim arose or is being defended. This subdivision does not invalidate other different or additional policy provisions pertaining to attorney's fees or providing for methods of settlement of disputes concerning those fees. Any dispute concerning attorney's fees not resolved by these methods shall be resolved by final and binding arbitration by a single neutral arbitrator selected by the parties to the dispute.

(d) When independent counsel has been selected by the insured, it shall be the duty of that counsel and the insured to disclose to the insurer all information concerning the action except privileged materials relevant to coverage disputes, and timely to inform and consult with the insurer on all matters relating to the action. Any claim of privilege asserted is subject to in camera review in the appropriate law and motion department of the superior court. Any information disclosed by the insured or by independent counsel is not a waiver of the privilege as to any other party.

(e) The insured may waive its right to select independent counsel by signing the following statement: "I have been advised and informed of my right to select independent counsel to represent me in this lawsuit. I have considered this matter fully and freely waive my right to select independent counsel at this time. I authorize my insurer to select a defense attorney to represent me in this lawsuit."

(f) Where the insured selects independent counsel pursuant to the provisions of this section, both the counsel provided by the insurer and independent counsel selected by the insured shall be allowed to participate in all aspects of the litigation. Counsel shall cooperate fully in the exchange of information that is consistent with each counsel's ethical and legal obligation to the insured. Nothing in this section shall relieve the insured of his or her duty to cooperate with the insurer under the terms of the insurance contract. **Leg.H.** Added Stats 1987 ch 1498 §4. Amended Stats 1988 ch 1114 §1.

TITLE 13.7
OBLIGATION TO SETTLE INSURANCE CLAIMS FAIRLY [INOPERATIVE]

TITLE 14
LIEN

Chapter 1. Liens in General.
Chapter 2. Mortgage.
Chapter 2a. Home Equity Loan Disclosure Act.
Chapter 2b. Automobile Sales Finance Act.
Chapter 2c. Real Property Sales Contracts.
Chapter 2d. Vehicle Leasing Act.
Chapter 2e. Controlled Escrows.
Chapter 3.5. Health Care Liens.
Chapter 4. Hospital Liens.
Chapter 6. Other Liens.
Chapter 6.5. Liens on Vehicles.
Chapter 6.7. Livestock Service Lien.
Chapter 7. Stoppage in Transit.

CHAPTER 1
LIENS IN GENERAL

Article 1. Definition of Liens.
Article 2. Creation of Liens.
Article 3. Effect of Liens.
Article 4. Priority of Liens.
Article 5. Redemption From Liens.
Article 6. Extinction of Liens.

ARTICLE 1
Definition of Liens

Lien, what. §2872.
Liens, general or special. §2873.
General lien defined. §2874.
Special lien, what. §2875.
Prior liens. §2876.
Contracts subject to provisions of this chapter. §2877.

§2872. Lien, what
A lien is a charge imposed in some mode other than by a transfer in trust upon specific property by which it is made security for the performance of an act. **Leg.H.** Enacted 1872. Amended Code Amdts 1877–78 ch 74 §1.

§2873. Liens, general or special
Liens are either general or special. **Leg.H.** Enacted 1872.

§2874. General lien defined
A general lien is one which the holder thereof is entitled to enforce as a security for the performance of all the obligations, or all of a particular class of obligations, which exist in his favor against the owner of the property. **Leg.H.** Enacted 1872.

§2875. Special lien, what
A special lien is one which the holder thereof can enforce only as security for the performance of a particular act or obligation, and of such obligations as may be incidental thereto. **Leg.H.** Enacted 1872.

§2876. Prior liens
Where the holder of a special lien is compelled to satisfy a prior lien for his own protection, he may enforce payment of the amount so paid by him, as a part of the claim for which his own lien exists. **Leg.H.** Enacted 1872.

§2877. Contracts subject to provisions of this chapter
Contracts of mortgage, pledge, bottomry, or respondentia are subject to all of the provisions of this chapter. **Leg.H.** Enacted 1872. Amended Stats 2013 ch 76 §13 (AB 383), effective January 1, 2014.

ARTICLE 2
Creation of Liens

Lien, how created. §2881.
No lien for claim not due. §2882.
Lien on future interest. §2883.
Lien may be created by contract. §2884.
Notice of recordation of tax lien. §2885.

§2881. Lien, how created
A lien is created:
1. By contract of the parties; or,
2. By operation of law. **Leg.H.** Enacted 1872.

§2882. No lien for claim not due
No lien arises by mere operation of law until the time at which the act to be secured thereby ought to be performed. **Leg.H.** Enacted 1872.

§2883. Lien on future interest
(a) An agreement may be made to create a lien upon property not yet acquired by the party agreeing to give the lien, or not yet in existence. In that case the lien agreed for attaches from the time when the party agreeing to give it acquires an interest in the thing, to the extent of such interest.

(b) For purposes of subdivision (a), an agreement by a beneficiary of an estate that is subject to administration, as provided in Division 7 (commencing with Section 7000) of the Probate Code, to create a lien upon real property in the estate that is undistributed at the time the agreement is entered into, shall create no lien upon the real property unless and until the real property is distributed to that beneficiary. Upon recordation of an order confirming the sale of the real property pursuant to Section 10313 of the Probate Code and the recording of a duly executed deed in accordance therewith, any expectancy of a lien in the real property under the agreement shall be extinguished. **Leg.H.** Enacted 1872. Amended Stats 1993 ch 382 §1 (SB 848), ch 527 §1 (AB 908).

§2884. Lien may be created by contract
A lien may be created by contract, to take immediate effect, as security for the performance of obligations not then in existence. **Leg.H.** Enacted 1872.

§2885. Notice of recordation of tax lien
Any state agency, upon recording a state tax lien against real property, shall mail written notice of the recordation to the tax debtor, unless previous correspondence mailed to the address of record was returned undelivered with no forwarding address. Failure to notify the tax debtor shall not affect the constructive notice otherwise imparted by recordation, nor shall it affect the force, effect, or priority otherwise accorded such tax lien. **Leg.H.** Added Stats 1980 ch 1281 §1. Amended Stats 1983 ch 643 §1, effective September 1, 1983.

ARTICLE 3
Effect of Liens

Lien, or contract for lien, transfers no title. §2888.
Certain contracts void. §2889.
Creation of lien does not imply personal obligation. §2890.
Extent of lien. §2891.
Holder of lien not entitled to compensation. §2892.

§2888. Lien, or contract for lien, transfers no title
Notwithstanding an agreement to the contrary, a lien, or a contract for a lien, transfers no title to the property subject to the lien. **Leg.H.** Enacted 1872.

§2889. Certain contracts void
All contracts for the forfeiture of property subject to a lien, in satisfaction of the obligation secured thereby, and all contracts in restraint of the right of redemption from a lien, are void. **Leg.H.** Enacted 1872.

§2890. Creation of lien does not imply personal obligation
The creation of a lien does not of itself imply that any person is bound to perform the act for which the lien is a security. **Leg.H.** Enacted 1872.

§2891. Extent of lien
The existence of a lien upon property does not of itself entitle the person in whose favor it exists to a lien upon the same property for the performance of any other obligation than that which the lien originally secured. **Leg.H.** Enacted 1872.

§2892. Holder of lien not entitled to compensation
One who holds property by virtue of a lien thereon, is not entitled to compensation from the owner thereof for any trouble or expense which he incurs respecting it, except to the same extent as a borrower, under sections eighteen hundred and ninety-two and eighteen hundred and ninety-three. **Leg.H.** Enacted 1872.

ARTICLE 4
Priority of Liens

Priority of liens. §2897.
Purchase money mortgages and deeds of trust. §2898.
Order of resort to different funds. §2899.

§2897. Priority of liens
Other things being equal, different liens upon the same property have priority according to the time of their creation, except in cases of bottomry and respondentia. **Leg.H.** Enacted 1872.

§2898. Purchase money mortgages and deeds of trust
(a) A mortgage or deed of trust given for the price of real property, at the time of its conveyance, has priority over all other liens created against the purchaser, subject to the operation of the recording laws.

(b) The priority of the lien of a mortgage or deed of trust on an estate for years in real property shall be determined in the same manner as for determining the priority of a lien of a mortgage or deed of trust on real property. **Leg.H.** Enacted 1872. Amended Stats 1939 ch 520 §1; Stats 1989 ch 698 §3.

§2899. Order of resort to different funds
Where one has a lien upon several things, and other persons have subordinate liens upon, or interests in, some but not all of the same things, the person having the prior lien, if he can do so without risk of loss to himself, or of injustice to other persons, must resort to the property in the following order, on the demand of any party interested:

1. To the things upon which he has an exclusive lien;
2. To the things which are subject to the fewest subordinate liens;
3. In like manner inversely to the number of subordinate liens upon the same thing; and,
4. When several things are within one of the foregoing classes, and subject to the same number of liens, resort must be had—
   (1) To the things which have not been transferred since the prior lien was created;
   (2) To the things which have been so transferred without a valuable consideration; and,
   (3) To the things which have been so transferred for a valuable consideration in the inverse order of the transfer. **Leg.H.** Enacted 1872.

ARTICLE 5
Redemption From Liens

Right to redeem; Subrogation. §2903.
Rights of inferior lienor. §2904.
Redemption from lien, how made. §2905.
Priority of option granted to secured party. §2906.

§2903. Right to redeem; Subrogation
Every person, having an interest in property subject to a lien, has the right to redeem it from the lien, at any time after the claim is due, and before his right of redemption is foreclosed, and, by such redemption, becomes subrogated to all the benefits of the lien, as against all owners of other interests in the property, except in so far as he was bound to make such redemption for their benefit. **Leg.H.** Enacted 1872. Amended Stats 1905 ch 459 §1.

§2904. Rights of inferior lienor
One who has a lien inferior to another, upon the same property, has a right:
1. To redeem the property in the same manner as its owner might, from the superior lien; and,
2. To be subrogated to all the benefits of the superior lien, when necessary for the protection of his interests, upon satisfying the claim secured thereby. **Leg.H.** Enacted 1872.

§2905. Redemption from lien, how made
Redemption from a lien is made by performing, or offering to perform, the act for the performance of which it is a security, and paying, or offering to pay, the damages, if any, to which the holder of the lien is entitled for delay. **Leg.H.** Enacted 1872.

§2906. Priority of option granted to secured party
An option granted to a secured party by a debtor to acquire an interest in real property collateral takes priority as of its recording and is effective according to its terms if the right to exercise the option is not dependent upon the occurrence of a default with respect to the security agreement and, where the real property which is the subject of the option is other than residential real property containing four or fewer units, shall not be deemed invalid or ineffective on the basis that the secured party has impaired the debtor's equity of redemption in violation of common law or Section 2889. This section shall not be construed to make valid or effective an otherwise unlawful option nor shall any inference be drawn from this section as to the validity or application of common law with respect to residential real property containing four or fewer units. **Leg.H.** Added Stats 1984 ch 565 §1.

ARTICLE 6
Extinction of Liens

Lien deemed accessory to the act whose performance it secures. §2909.
Extinction by sale or conversion. §2910.
Extinguishment by lapse of time; Presumption as to improvement liens. §2911.
Apportionment of lien. §2912.
Extinguishment of possessory lien by restoration of property. §2913.
Inapplicability of chapter to matters governed by Commercial Code. §2914.

§2909. Lien deemed accessory to the act whose performance it secures
A lien is to be deemed accessory to the act for the performance of which it is a security, whether any person is bound for such performance or not, and is extinguishable in like manner with any other accessory obligation. **Leg.H.** Enacted 1872.

§2910. Extinction by sale or conversion
The sale of any property on which there is a lien, in satisfaction of the claim secured thereby, or in case of personal property, its wrongful conversion by the person holding the lien, extinguishes the lien thereon. **Leg.H.** Enacted 1872.

§2911. Extinguishment by lapse of time; Presumption as to improvement liens
A lien is extinguished by the lapse of time within which, under the provisions of the Code of Civil Procedure, either:
1. An action can be brought upon the principal obligation, or
2. A treasurer, street superintendent or other public official may sell any real property to satisfy a public improvement assessment or any bond issued to represent such assessment and which assessment is secured by a lien upon said real property; whichever is later.

Anything to the contrary notwithstanding, any lien heretofore existing or which may hereafter exist upon real property to secure the payment of a public improvement assessment shall be presumed to have been extinguished at the expiration of four years after the due date of such assessment or the last installment thereof, or four years after the date the lien attaches, or on January 1, 1947, whichever is later, or in the event bonds were or shall be issued to represent such assessment, the lien shall then be presumed to have been extinguished at the expiration of four years after the due date of said bonds or of the last installment thereof or of the last principal coupon attached thereto, or on January 1, 1947, whichever is later. The presumptions mentioned in this paragraph shall be conclusive in favor of a bona fide purchaser for value of said property after such dates. **Leg.H.** Enacted 1872. Amended Stats 1945 ch 361 §1.

§2912. Apportionment of lien
The partial performance of an act secured by a lien does not extinguish the lien upon any part of the property subject thereto, even if it is divisible. **Leg.H.** Enacted 1872.

§2913. Extinguishment of possessory lien by restoration of property
The voluntary restoration of property to its owner by the holder of a lien thereon dependent upon possession extinguishes the lien as to such property, unless otherwise agreed by the parties, and extinguishes it,

notwithstanding any such agreement, as to creditors of the owner and persons, subsequently acquiring a title to the property or a lien thereon, in good faith, and for value. **Leg.H.** Enacted 1872. Amended Code Amdts 1873–74 ch 612 §255; Stats 1905 ch 459 §2.

§2914. Inapplicability of chapter to matters governed by Commercial Code

None of the provisions of this chapter apply to any transaction or security interest governed by the Uniform Commercial Code. **Leg.H.** Added Stats 1963 ch 819 §14, effective January 1, 1965.

CHAPTER 2
MORTGAGE

Article 1. Mortgages in General.
Article 1.5. Mortgage Foreclosure Consultants.
Article 2. Mortgage of Real Property.
Article 3. Disclosures on Purchase Money Liens on Residential Property.
Article 4. State of Emergency.

ARTICLE 1
Mortgages in General

"Mortgage". §2920.
Definitions. §2920.5.
Property adversely held may be mortgaged. §2921.
To be in writing. §2922.
Lien of a mortgage, when special. §2923.
Mortgage broker a fiduciary. §2923.1.
Recorded notice of default; Recorded notice of sale. §2923.3.
Purpose of Act; Loss mitigation options; Construction. §2923.4.
Notice of default, grace period; Contact to assess borrower's financial situation; Due diligence requirement; Discussion of options to avoid foreclosure; Applicability. §2923.5.
Recordation of notice of default; Requirements; Declaration regarding contact; "Due diligence"; Applicability. §2923.55.
Legislative findings and declarations and intent regarding loan modification or workout plan; Prohibition against recording notice of default or sale or conducting trustee's sale while pending first lien loan modification application; Denial of first lien loan modification application; Applicability. §2923.6.
Responsibilities of single point of contact; Applicability. §2923.7.
Transfer as security deemed mortgage or pledge; Exercise of power of sale; No liability for good faith error; Recital of acts as prima facie evidence; Privileged communications; Rebuttable presumption. §2924.
Recordation of transfer of property in common interest development. §2924.1.
Notice by agent collecting payments from obligor. §2924.3.
Recitation of acceleration clause in instruments encumbering small residential properties. §2924.5.
Limitations on acceleration. §2924.6.
Enforcement of acceleration of maturity date of principal and interest or disbursement of proceeds of property insurance by beneficiary, trustee, mortgagee, or agent. §2924.7.
Posting of notice of pending foreclosure sale; Infraction to destroy notice; Translations; Applicability. § 2924.8.
Written communication to borrower after mortgage servicer offering foreclosure prevention alternative records notice of default pursuant to Section 2924; Applicability. §2924.9.
Written acknowledgment of receipt of first lien loan modification application or documentation; Applicability. §2924.10.
Approved foreclosure prevention alternative; Prohibition against recording notice of default or sale or conducting trustee's sale; Rescission or cancellation; Fees; Subsequent mortgage servicer; Applicability. §2924.11.
Actions concerning trustee's deed upon sale; Injunctive relief; Liability; Damages; Violations; Attorney's fees and costs. §2924.12.
Applicability of specified code sections to first lien mortgages or deeds of trust secured by owner-occupied residential real property containing no more than four dwelling units. § 2924.15.
Recording or filing of certain documents; Review of evidence to substantiate borrower's default and right to foreclose; Uncorrected violations; Civil penalties. §2924.17.
Pending first lien loan modification application or approved foreclosure prevention alternative; Prohibition against recording notice of default or sale or conducting trustee's sale; Applicability to depository institutions and specified licensed persons that foreclosed on 175 or fewer residential real properties; Notifications; Subsequent mortgage servicer; Applicability to specified mortgages or deeds of trust. §2924.18.
Actions concerning trustee's deed; Injunctive relief; Liability; Damages; Violations; Attorney's fees and costs; Applicability. §2924.19.
Adoption of regulations; Enforcement. §2924.20.
Initiation of claim of surplus. § 2924.21.
Liability of title company for violation of specified Civil Code sections if notice of default or sale recorded at request of trustee, substitute trustee, or beneficiary. §2924.26.
Conduct of sale by attorney for trustee. §2924a.
Request for copy of notice of default or sale; Recordation; Duty of mortgagee, trustee, etc. §2924b.
Curing default; Notice of default; Limitation on costs and expenses; Trustee's or attorney's fees; Reinstatement of default. §2924c.
Right to reimbursement for costs and expenses of enforcement; Trustee's or attorney's fees; Prohibition against kickbacks [Repealed January 1, 2031]. §2924d.
Right to reimbursement for costs and expenses of enforcement; Trustee's or attorney's fees; Prohibition against kickbacks [Operative January 1, 2031]. § 2924d.
Junior mortgagee's request to senior lienor for notice of delinquencies; Liability for failure to give notice. §2924e.
Notice of sale; Posting, publication, and recording; Contents; Place of sale; Bids prior to sale; Postponement of sale [Repealed January 1, 2031]. §2924f.
Notice of sale; Posting, publication, and recording; Contents; Place of sale; Bids prior to sale; Postponement of sale [Operative January 1, 2031]. § 2924f.
Time and place of sale; Postponement; Conduct of sale [Repealed January 1, 2031]. §2924g.
Time and place of sale; Postponement; Conduct of sale [Operative January 1, 2031]. § 2924g.
Bidding; Penalties [Repealed January 1, 2031]. §2924h.
Bidding; Penalties [Operative January 1, 2031]. § 2924h.
Notice regarding final payment on balloon payment loan. §2924i.
Notice when surplus proceeds remain; Determination of priority of written claims; Declaration of unresolved claims; Deposit of funds; Consideration by court; Interpleader action; Unclaimed Property Law. §2924j.
Priority of order of distribution of proceeds; Trustee's costs and expenses. §2924k.
Declaration of nonmonetary status by trustee of deed of trust named in action. §2924l.
Conditions for sale to be deemed final; Procedures in the event sale not final [Repealed January 1, 2031]. § 2924m.
Article not to affect eviction rights and duties. § 2924n.
Requirements of recorded covenants for real property purchased pursuant to Section 2924m [Repealed January 1, 2031]. § 2924o.
Purchase of properties acquired through foreclosure by prospective owner-occupants and eligible bidders. § 2924p.
Transfer made subject to defeasance may be proved. §2925.
Mortgage, on what a lien. §2926.
Mortgage does not entitle mortgagee to possession. §2927.
Mortgage not a personal obligation. §2928.
Waste. §2929.
Duty of foreclosure purchaser to maintain vacant property; Notice of violation; Fines and penalties; Relation to local ordinances. §2929.3.
Notice of violation for failing to maintain vacant property; Applicability. §2929.4.
Assessment or lien to recover costs of nuisance abatement. §2929.45.
Secured lender's right of entry and inspection. §2929.5.
Subsequently acquired title inures to mortgagee. §2930.
Foreclosure. §2931.
Joinder of state agency in specified actions; Jurisdiction of court; Complaint or petition; Representation by Attorney General. §2931a.
Power of Attorney General to bid at sale. §2931b.
Action by Attorney General to enforce tax lien. §2931c.
Power of sale. §2932.
Residential real property containing more than four dwelling units; Written disclosure; Notice of default and notice of sale. § 2932.2.
Power of sale under assigned mortgage. §2932.5.
Repair of residential real property acquired through foreclosure. §2932.6.
Power of attorney to execute. §2933.
Recording of assignment or subordination instrument as constructive notice of contents. §2934.
Substitution of trustee under trust deed. §2934a.
Vacation of office of trustee under deed of trust. §2934b.
Record of assignment as notice to debtor. §2935.
Mortgage passes by assignment of debt. §2936.
Transfer of servicing of indebtedness on single family residential real property; Notice; Insurance policy information; Payments made prior to notice. §2937.
Effect of service of process to trustee. §2937.7.
Written assignment of interest to create security interest; Demand to pay rent to party other than landlord. §2938.
Discharge of recorded mortgage. §2939.
[Section renumbered 1979]. §2939½.
Satisfaction by foreign executors. §2939.5.
Recording of certificate of discharge. §2940.
Certificate of discharge; Request for full reconveyance; Damages for violations; Fee for services connected with reconveyance; "Original" as including optically imaged reproduction. §2941.

Reconveyance fee where no payoff demand statement issued. §2941.1.
Criminal penalties. §2941.5.
Discharge when mortgagee or beneficiary cannot be located or refuses to execute. §2941.7.
Holders of more than fifty percent. §2941.9.
Provisions of this chapter do not affect bottomry or respondentia. §2942.
Beneficiary's obligation to furnish beneficiary statement or payoff demand statement; Liability for noncompliance. §2943.
Borrower's instruction to suspend and close equity line of credit. §2943.1.
Application of chapter to matters governed by Commercial Code. §2944.
Refusal to accept policy issued by admitted insurer for continuous period without fixed expiration date. §2944.5.
Notice provided to borrower; Translation; Fine; Applicability. §2944.6.
Unlawful activities in conjunction with mortgage loan modification; Penalties; Civil action; Permissible activities; Applicability. §2944.7.
Unlawful activities in conjunction with mortgage loan modification where victim is senior citizen or disabled. §2944.8.
Unlawful activities in conjunction with mortgage loan modification; Time limitation. §2944.10.

§2920. "Mortgage"

(a) A mortgage is a contract by which specific property, including an estate for years in real property, is hypothecated for the performance of an act, without the necessity of a change of possession.

(b) For purposes of Sections 2924 to 2924h, inclusive, "mortgage" also means any security device or instrument, other than a deed of trust, that confers a power of sale affecting real property or an estate for years therein, to be exercised after breach of the obligation so secured, including a real property sales contract, as defined in Section 2985, which contains such a provision. **Leg.H.** Enacted 1872. Amended Stats 1986 ch 1385 §1; Stats 1989 ch 698 §4.

§2920.5. Definitions

For purposes of this article, the following definitions apply:

(a) "Mortgage servicer" means a person or entity who directly services a loan, or who is responsible for interacting with the borrower, managing the loan account on a daily basis including collecting and crediting periodic loan payments, managing any escrow account, or enforcing the note and security instrument, either as the current owner of the promissory note or as the current owner's authorized agent. "Mortgage servicer" also means a subservicing agent to a master servicer by contract. "Mortgage servicer" shall not include a trustee, or a trustee's authorized agent, acting under a power of sale pursuant to a deed of trust.

(b) "Foreclosure prevention alternative" means a first lien loan modification or another available loss mitigation option.

(c)(1) Unless otherwise provided and for purposes of Sections 2923.4, 2923.5, 2923.55, 2923.6, 2923.7, 2924.9, 2924.10, 2924.11, 2924.18, and 2924.19, "borrower" means any natural person who is a mortgagor or trustor and who is potentially eligible for any federal, state, or proprietary foreclosure prevention alternative program offered by, or through, his or her mortgage servicer.

(2) For purposes of the sections listed in paragraph (1), "borrower" shall not include any of the following:

(A) An individual who has surrendered the secured property as evidenced by either a letter confirming the surrender or delivery of the keys to the property to the mortgagee, trustee, beneficiary, or authorized agent.

(B) An individual who has contracted with an organization, person, or entity whose primary business is advising people who have decided to leave their homes on how to extend the foreclosure process and avoid their contractual obligations to mortgagees or beneficiaries.

(C) An individual who has filed a case under Chapter 7, 11, 12, or 13 of Title 11 of the United States Code and the bankruptcy court has not entered an order closing or dismissing the bankruptcy case, or granting relief from a stay of foreclosure.

(d) "First lien" means the most senior mortgage or deed of trust on the property that is the subject of the notice of default or notice of sale. **Leg.H.** Added Stats 2012 ch 87 §2 (SB 900), effective January 1, 2013.

Prior Law: Former CC §2920.5, similar to the present section, was added Stats 2012 ch 86 §2 (AB 278), effective January 1, 2013, and repealed Stats 2018 ch 404 §1 (SB 818), effective January 1, 2019.

Former Sections: Former CC §2920.5, similar to the present section, was added Stats 2012 ch 86 §2 (AB 278) and repealed Stats 2018 ch 404 §1 (SB 818).

§2920.7. Notice of default; Requirements of mortgage servicer prior to recording when notified of borrower's death; Applicability [Repealed]

Leg.H. Added Stats 2016 ch 838 §2 (SB 1150), effective January 1, 2017, repealed January 1, 2020. Amended Stats 2018 ch 136 §1 (SB 1183), effective January 1, 2019, repealed January 1, 2020; Stats 2019 ch 497 §27 (AB 991), effective January 1, 2020, repealed January 1, 2020.

§2921. Property adversely held may be mortgaged

A mortgage may be created upon property held adversely to the mortgagor. **Leg.H.** Enacted 1872.

§2922. To be in writing

A mortgage can be created, renewed, or extended, only by writing, executed with the formalities required in the case of a grant of real property. **Leg.H.** Enacted 1872.

§2923. Lien of a mortgage, when special

The lien of a mortgage is special, unless otherwise expressly agreed, and is independent of possession. **Leg.H.** Enacted 1872.

§2923.1. Mortgage broker a fiduciary

(a) A mortgage broker providing mortgage brokerage services to a borrower is the fiduciary of the borrower, and any violation of the broker's fiduciary duties shall be a violation of the mortgage broker's license law. This fiduciary duty includes a requirement that the mortgage broker place the economic interest of the borrower ahead of his or her own economic interest. A mortgage broker who provides mortgage brokerage services to the borrower owes this fiduciary duty to the borrower regardless of whether the mortgage broker is acting as an agent for any other party in connection with the residential mortgage loan transaction.

(b) For purposes of this section, the following definitions apply:

(1) "Licensed person" means a real estate broker licensed under the Real Estate Law (Part 1 (commencing with Section 10000) of Division 4 of the Business and Professions Code), a finance lender or broker licensed under the California Finance Lenders Law (Division 9 (commencing with Section 22000) of the Financial Code), a residential mortgage lender licensed under the California Residential Mortgage Lending Act (Division 20 (commencing with Section 50000) of the Financial Code), a commercial or industrial bank organized under the Banking Law (Division 1 (commencing with Section 99) of the Financial Code), a savings association organized under the Savings Association Law (Division 2 (commencing with Section 5000) of the Financial Code), and a credit union organized under the California Credit Union Law (Division 5 (commencing with Section 14000) of the Financial Code).

(2) "Mortgage broker" means a licensed person who provides mortgage brokerage services. For purposes of this section, a licensed person who makes a residential mortgage loan is a "mortgage broker," and subject to the requirements of this section applicable to mortgage brokers, only with respect to transactions in which the licensed person provides mortgage brokerage services.

(3) "Mortgage brokerage services" means arranging or attempting to arrange, as exclusive agent for the borrower or as dual agent for the borrower and lender, for compensation or in expectation of compensation, paid directly or indirectly, a residential mortgage loan made by an unaffiliated third party.

(4) "Residential mortgage loan" means a consumer credit transaction that is secured by residential real property that is improved by four or fewer residential units.

(c) The duties set forth in this section shall not be construed to limit or narrow any other fiduciary duty of a mortgage broker. **Leg.H.** Added Stats 2009 ch 629 §2 (AB 260), effective January 1, 2010.

§2923.3. Recorded notice of default; Recorded notice of sale

(a) With respect to residential real property containing no more than four dwelling units, a mortgagee, trustee, beneficiary, or authorized agent shall provide to the mortgagor or trustor a copy of the recorded notice of default with an attached separate summary document of the notice of default in English and the languages described in Section 1632, as set forth in subdivision (c), and a copy of the recorded notice of sale with an attached separate summary document of the information required to be contained in the notice of sale in English and the languages described in Section 1632, as set forth in subdivision (d). These summaries are not required to be recorded or published. This subdivision shall become operative on April 1, 2013, or 90 days following the issuance of the translations by the Department of Financial Protection and Innovation pursuant to subdivision (b), whichever is later.

(b)(1) The Department of Financial Protection and Innovation shall provide a standard translation of the statement in paragraph (1) of subdivision (c), and of the summary of the notice of default, as set forth in paragraph (2) of subdivision (c) in the languages described in Section 1632.

(2) The Department of Financial Protection and Innovation shall provide a standard translation of the statement in paragraph (1) of subdivision (d), and of the summary of the notice of sale, as set forth in paragraph (2) of subdivision (d).

(3) The department shall make the translations described in paragraphs (1) and (2) available without charge on its internet website. Any mortgagee, trustee, beneficiary, or authorized agent who provides the department's translations in the manner prescribed by this section shall be in compliance with this section.

(c)(1) The following statement shall appear in the languages described in Section 1632 at the beginning of the notice of default:

NOTE: THERE IS A SUMMARY OF THE INFORMATION IN THIS DOCUMENT ATTACHED.

(2) The following summary of key information shall be attached to the copy of the notice of default provided to the mortgagor or trustor:

SUMMARY OF KEY INFORMATION

The attached notice of default was sent to [name of the trustor], in relation to [description of the property that secures the mortgage or deed of trust in default]. This property may be sold to satisfy your obligation and any other obligation secured by the deed of trust or mortgage that is in default. [Trustor] has, as described in the notice of default, breached the mortgage or deed of trust on the property described above.

IMPORTANT NOTICE: IF YOUR PROPERTY IS IN FORECLOSURE BECAUSE YOU ARE BEHIND IN YOUR PAYMENTS, IT MAY BE SOLD WITHOUT ANY COURT ACTION, and you may have the legal right to bring your account in good standing by paying all of your past due payments plus permitted costs and expenses within the time permitted by law for reinstatement of your account, which is normally five business days prior to the date set for the sale of your property. No sale date may be set until approximately 90 days from the date the attached notice of default may be recorded (which date of recordation appears on the notice). This amount is _____ as of _____(date) and will increase until your account becomes current.

While your property is in foreclosure, you still must pay other obligations (such as insurance and taxes) required by your note and deed of trust or mortgage. If you fail to make future payments on the loan, pay taxes on the property, provide insurance on the property, or pay other obligations as required in the note and deed of trust or mortgage, the beneficiary or mortgagee may insist that you do so in order to reinstate your account in good standing. In addition, the beneficiary or mortgagee may require as a condition to reinstatement that you provide reliable written evidence that you paid all senior liens, property taxes, and hazard insurance premiums.

Upon your written request, the beneficiary or mortgagee will give you a written itemization of the entire amount you must pay. You may not have to pay the entire unpaid portion of your account, even though full payment was demanded, but you must pay all amounts in default at the time payment is made. However, you and your beneficiary or mortgagee may mutually agree in writing prior to the time the notice of sale is posted (which may not be earlier than three months after this notice of default is recorded) to, among other things, (1) provide additional time in which to cure the default by transfer of the property or otherwise; or (2) establish a schedule of payments in order to cure your default; or both (1) and (2). Following the expiration of the time period referred to in the first paragraph of this notice, unless the obligation being foreclosed upon or a separate written agreement between you and your creditor permits a longer period, you have only the legal right to stop the sale of your property by paying the entire amount demanded by your creditor.

To find out the amount you must pay, or to arrange for payment to stop the foreclosure, or if your property is in foreclosure for any other reason, contact:

_____

(Name of beneficiary or mortgagee)

_____

(Mailing address)

_____

(Telephone)

If you have any questions, you should contact a lawyer or the governmental agency which may have insured your loan.

Notwithstanding the fact that your property is in foreclosure, you may offer your property for sale, provided the sale is concluded prior to the conclusion of the foreclosure.

Remember, YOU MAY LOSE LEGAL RIGHTS IF YOU DO NOT TAKE PROMPT ACTION.

If you would like additional copies of this summary, you may obtain them by calling [insert telephone number].

(d)(1) The following statement shall appear in the languages described in Section 1632 at the beginning of the notice of sale:

NOTE: THERE IS A SUMMARY OF THE INFORMATION IN THIS DOCUMENT ATTACHED.

(2) The following summary of key information shall be attached to the copy of the notice of sale provided to the mortgagor or trustor:

SUMMARY OF KEY INFORMATION

The attached notice of sale was sent to [trustor], in relation to [description of the property that secures the mortgage or deed of trust in default].

YOU ARE IN DEFAULT UNDER A (Deed of trust or mortgage) DATED _____. UNLESS YOU TAKE ACTION TO PROTECT YOUR PROPERTY, IT MAY BE SOLD AT A PUBLIC SALE.

IF YOU NEED AN EXPLANATION OF THE NATURE OF THE PROCEEDING AGAINST YOU, YOU SHOULD CONTACT A LAWYER.

The total amount due in the notice of sale is _____

Your property is scheduled to be sold on [insert date and time of sale] at [insert location of sale].

However, the sale date shown on the attached notice of sale may be postponed one or more times by the mortgagee, beneficiary, trustee, or a court, pursuant to Section 2924g of the California Civil Code. The law requires that information about trustee sale postponements be made available to you and to the public, as a courtesy to those not present at the sale. If you wish to learn whether your sale date has been postponed, and, if applicable, the rescheduled time and date for the sale of this property, you may call [telephone number for information regarding the trustee's sale] or visit this internet website [internet website address for information regarding the sale of this property], using the file number assigned to this case [case file number]. Information about postponements that are very short in duration or that occur close in time to the scheduled sale may not immediately be reflected in the telephone information or on the internet website. The best way to verify postponement information is to attend the scheduled sale.

If you would like additional copies of this summary, you may obtain them by calling [insert telephone number].

(e) Failure to provide these summaries to the mortgagor or trustor shall have the same effect as if the notice of default or notice of sale were incomplete or not provided.

(f) This section sets forth a requirement for translation in languages other than English, and a document complying with the provisions of this section may be recorded pursuant to subdivision (b) of Section 27293 of the Government Code. A document that complies with this section shall not be rejected for recordation on the ground that some part of the document is in a language other than English. **Leg.H.** Added Stats 2012 ch 556 §1 (AB 1599), effective January 1, 2013. Amended Stats 2015 ch 190 §6 (AB 1517), effective January 1, 2016; Stats 2022 ch 452 §28 (SB 1498), effective January 1, 2023.

§2923.4. Purpose of Act; Loss mitigation options; Construction

The purpose of the act that added this section is to ensure that, as part of the nonjudicial foreclosure process, borrowers are considered for, and have a meaningful opportunity to obtain, available loss mitigation options, if any, offered by or through the borrower's mortgage servicer, such as loan modifications or other alternatives to foreclosure. Nothing in the act that added this section, however, shall be interpreted to require a particular result of that process. **Leg.H.** Added Stats 2012 ch 87 §3 (SB 900), effective January 1, 2013. Amended Stats 2018 ch 404 §2 (SB 818), effective January 1, 2019.

Prior Law: Former CC §2923.4, similar to the present section, was added Stats 2012 ch 86 §3 (AB 278), effective January 1, 2013, and repealed Stats 2018 ch 404 §3 (SB 818), effective January 1, 2019.

2018 Notes: The amendment, addition, or repeal of a section, or part of a section, by this act shall not have the effect to release, extinguish, or change, in whole or in part, any liability that shall have been incurred under that section, unless the amendment, addition, or repeal expressly so provides. The section, or part of a section, that is amended, added, or repealed shall be treated as still remaining in force for the purpose of sustaining any proper action, suit, proceeding, or prosecution, for the enforcement of a penalty, forfeiture, or liability, as well as for the purpose of sustaining any judgment, decree, or order. Stats 2018 ch 404 §25 (SB 818).

It is the intent of the Legislature that any amendment, addition, or repeal of a section or part of a section enacted by Senate Bill 900 (Chapter 87 of the Statutes of 2012) and Assembly Bill 278 (Chapter 86 of the Statutes of 2012), commonly known as the California Homeowner Bill of Rights, that took effect as of January 1, 2018, shall not have the effect to release, extinguish, or change, in whole or in part, any liability that shall have been incurred under that section, or part of a section, prior to January 1, 2018, unless the amendment, addition, or repeal expressly so provides. The section, or part of a section, that was amended, added, or repealed shall be treated as still remaining in force for the purpose of sustaining any proper action, suit, or proceeding for the enforcement of such a liability, as well as for the purpose of sustaining any judgment, decree, or order. Stats 2018 ch 404 §26 (SB 818).

Former Sections: Former CC §2923.4, similar to the present section, was added Stats 2012 ch 86 §3 (AB 278) and repealed Stats 2018 ch 404 §3 (SB 818).

§2923.5. Notice of default, grace period; Contact to assess borrower's financial situation; Due diligence requirement; Discussion of options to avoid foreclosure; Applicability

(a)(1) A mortgage servicer, mortgagee, trustee, beneficiary, or authorized agent shall not record a notice of default pursuant to Section 2924 until both of the following:

(A) Either 30 days after initial contact is made as required by paragraph (2) or 30 days after satisfying the due diligence requirements as described in subdivision (e).

(B) The mortgage servicer complies with paragraph (1) of subdivision (a) of Section 2924.18, if the borrower has provided a complete application as defined in subdivision (d) of Section 2924.18.

(2)(A) A mortgage servicer shall contact the borrower in person or by telephone in order to assess the borrower's financial situation and explore options for the borrower to avoid foreclosure. During the initial contact, the mortgage servicer shall advise the borrower that [1] **the borrower** has the right to request a subsequent meeting and, if requested, the mortgage servicer shall schedule the meeting to occur within 14 days. The assessment of the borrower's financial situation and discussion of options may occur during the first contact, or at the subsequent meeting scheduled for that purpose. In either case, the borrower shall be provided the toll-free telephone number made available by the United States Department of Housing and Urban Development (HUD) to find a HUD-certified housing counseling agency. Any meeting may occur telephonically.

(B) The mortgage servicer shall notify the borrower during the initial contact required pursuant to subparagraph (A) that a third party, such as a family member, HUD-certified housing counselor, or attorney, may record a request to receive copies of any notice of default and notice of sale pursuant to the process described in Section 2924b and that receiving a copy of these documents may allow the third party to assist the borrower in avoiding foreclosure.

(b) A notice of default recorded pursuant to Section 2924 shall include a declaration that the mortgage servicer has contacted the borrower, has tried with due diligence to contact the borrower as required by this section, or that no contact was required because the individual did not meet the definition of "borrower" pursuant to subdivision (c) of Section 2920.5.

(c) A mortgage servicer's loss mitigation personnel may participate by telephone during any contact required by this section.

(d) A borrower may designate, with consent given in writing, a HUD-certified housing counseling agency, attorney, or other advisor to discuss with the mortgage servicer, on the borrower's behalf, the borrower's financial situation and options for the borrower to avoid foreclosure. That contact made at the direction of the borrower shall satisfy the contact requirements of paragraph (2) of subdivision (a). Any loan modification or workout plan offered at the meeting by the mortgage servicer is subject to approval by the borrower.

(e) A notice of default may be recorded pursuant to Section 2924 when a mortgage servicer has not contacted a borrower as required by paragraph (2) of subdivision (a) provided that the failure to contact the borrower occurred despite the due diligence of the mortgage servicer. For purposes of this section, "due diligence" shall require and mean all of the following:

(1)(A) A mortgage servicer shall first attempt to contact a borrower by sending a first-class letter that includes the toll-free telephone number made available by HUD to find a HUD-certified housing counseling agency.

(B) The mortgage servicer shall notify the borrower in the first-class letter described in subparagraph (A) that a third party, such as a family member, HUD-certified housing counselor, or attorney, may record a request to receive copies of any notice of default and notice of sale pursuant to the process described in Section 2924b and that receiving a copy of these documents may allow the third party to assist the borrower in avoiding foreclosure.

(2)(A) After the letter has been sent, the mortgage servicer shall attempt to contact the borrower by telephone at least three times at different hours and on different days. Telephone calls shall be made to the primary telephone number on file.

(B) A mortgage servicer may attempt to contact a borrower using an automated system to dial borrowers, provided that, if the telephone call is answered, the call is connected to a live representative of the mortgage servicer.

(C) A mortgage servicer satisfies the telephone contact requirements of this paragraph:

(i) If it determines, after attempting contact pursuant to this paragraph, that the borrower's primary telephone number and secondary telephone number or numbers on file, if any, have been disconnected.

(ii) If the borrower or [2] **the borrower's** authorized agent notifies the mortgage servicer in writing to cease further communication with the borrower. The cease communication notification shall explicitly pertain to the mortgage loan account to be effective. The cease communication notification shall be effective until the borrower or [3] **the borrower's** authorized agent rescinds it in writing.

(3) If the borrower does not respond within two weeks after the telephone call requirements of paragraph (2) have been satisfied, the mortgage servicer shall then send a certified letter, with return receipt requested.

(4) The mortgage servicer shall provide a means for the borrower to contact it in a timely manner, including a toll-free telephone number that will provide access to a live representative during business hours.

(5) The mortgage servicer has posted a prominent link on the [4] **home page** of its [5] **internet website**, if any, to the following information:

(A) Options that may be available to borrowers who are unable to afford their mortgage payments and who wish to avoid foreclosure, and instructions to borrowers advising them on steps to take to explore those options.

(B) A list of financial documents borrowers should collect and be prepared to present to the mortgage servicer when discussing options for avoiding foreclosure.

(C) A toll-free telephone number for borrowers who wish to discuss options for avoiding foreclosure with their mortgage servicer.

(D) The toll-free telephone number made available by HUD to find a HUD-certified housing counseling agency.

(f) This section shall apply only to mortgages or deeds of trust described in Section 2924.15.

(g) This section shall apply only to entities described in subdivision (b) of Section 2924.18. **Leg.H.** Added Stats 2012 ch 87 §5 (SB 900), effective January 1, 2013, operative January 1, 2018. Amended Stats 2018 ch 404 §4 (SB 818), effective January 1, 2019; Stats 2024 ch 311 §1 (AB 2424), effective January 1, 2025.

§2923.5. 2024 Deletes. [1] he or she [2] his or her [3] his or her [4] homepage [5] Internet Web site

2018 Note: For effect of Stats 2018 ch 404 and legislative intent, see the 2018 Notes following CC §2923.4.

Former Sections: Former CC §2923.5, similar to the present section, was added Stats 2012 ch 86 §5 (AB 278), operative January 1, 2018, and repealed Stats 2018 ch 404 §5 (SB 818).

Former CC §2923.5, similar to the present section, was added Stats 2008 ch 69 §2 (SB 1137), effective July 8, 2008, operative September 6, 2008, and repealed operative January 1, 2018, by its own provisions.

Prior Law: Former CC §2923.5, similar to the present section, was added Stats 2008 ch 69 §2 (SB 1137), effective July 8, 2008, operative September 6, 2008, repealed January 1, 2013, amended Stats 2009 ch 43 §1 (SB 306), effective January

1, 2010, repealed January 1, 2013, Stats 2012 ch 86 §4 (AB 278), effective January 1, 2013, repealed January 1, 2018, Stats 2012 ch 87 §4 (SB 900), effective January 1, 2013, and repealed January 1, 2018, by its own terms.

Former CC §2923.5, similar to the present section, was added Stats 2012 ch 86 §5 (AB 278), effective January 1, 2013, operative January 1, 2018, and repealed Stats 2018 ch 404 §5 (SB 818), effective January 1, 2019.

§2923.52. [Section repealed 2011]

Leg.H. Added 2009 2nd Ex Sess Stats 2009–2010 ch 5 §3 (ABX2-7), effective May 21, 2009, repealed January 1, 2011. Repealed operative January 1, 2011, by its own provisions. The repealed section related to delayed notification of default and exercise of power of sale, conditions, and application of section.

Former Sections: Former CC §2923.52 was added Stats 2009–10 2d Ex Sess ch 4 §3 (SBX2 7), effective May 21, 2009, and repealed operative January 1, 2011, by its own provisions.

§2923.53. [Section repealed 2011]

Leg.H. Added 2009 2nd Ex Sess Stats 2009–2010 ch 5 §4 (ABX2-7), effective May 21, 2009, repealed January 1, 2011. Repealed operative January 1, 2011, by its own provisions. The repealed section related to exemption from provisions of CC §2923.52 upon implementation of comprehensive loan modification program, required features of program, application for exemption order, and violation of provisions.

Former Sections: Former CC §2923.53 was added Stats 2009–10 2d Ex Sess ch 4 §4 (SBX2 7), effective May 21, 2009, and repealed operative January 1, 2011, by its own provisions.

§2923.54. [Section repealed 2011]

Leg.H. Added 2009 2nd Ex Sess Stats 2009–2010 ch 5 §5 (ABX2-7), effective May 21, 2009, repealed January 1, 2011. Repealed operative January 1, 2011, by its own provisions. The repealed section related to required statements from mortgage loan servicer in the notice of sale.

Former Sections: Former CC §2923.54 was added Stats 2009–10 2d Ex Sess ch 4 §5 (SBX2 7), effective May 21, 2009, and repealed operative January 1, 2011, by its own provisions.

§2923.55. Recordation of notice of default; Requirements; Declaration regarding contact; "Due diligence"; Applicability

(a) A mortgage servicer, mortgagee, trustee, beneficiary, or authorized agent shall not record a notice of default pursuant to Section 2924 until all of the following:

(1) The mortgage servicer has satisfied the requirements of paragraph (1) of subdivision (b).

(2) Either 30 days after initial contact is made as required by paragraph (2) of subdivision (b) or 30 days after satisfying the due diligence requirements as described in subdivision (f).

(3) The mortgage servicer complies with subdivision (c) of Section 2923.6, if the borrower has provided a complete application as defined in subdivision (h) of Section 2923.6.

(b)(1) As specified in subdivision (a), a mortgage servicer shall send the following information in writing to the borrower:

(A) A statement that if the borrower is a servicemember or a dependent of a servicemember, [1] **the borrower** may be entitled to certain protections under the federal Servicemembers Civil Relief Act (50 U.S.C. Sec. 3901 et seq.) regarding the servicemember's interest rate and the risk of foreclosure, and counseling for covered servicemembers that is available at agencies such as Military OneSource and Armed Forces Legal Assistance.

(B) A statement that the borrower may request the following:

(i) A copy of the borrower's promissory note or other evidence of indebtedness.

(ii) A copy of the borrower's deed of trust or mortgage.

(iii) A copy of any assignment, if applicable, of the borrower's mortgage or deed of trust required to demonstrate the right of the mortgage servicer to foreclose.

(iv) A copy of the borrower's payment history since the borrower was last less than 60 days past due.

(2)(A) A mortgage servicer shall contact the borrower in person or by telephone in order to assess the borrower's financial situation and explore options for the borrower to avoid foreclosure. During the initial contact, the mortgage servicer shall advise the borrower that [2] **the borrower** has the right to request a subsequent meeting and, if requested, the mortgage servicer shall schedule the meeting to occur within 14 days. The assessment of the borrower's financial situation and discussion of options may occur during the first contact, or at the subsequent meeting scheduled for that purpose. In either case, the borrower shall be provided the toll-free telephone number made available by the United States Department of Housing and Urban Development (HUD) to find a HUD-certified housing counseling agency. Any meeting may occur telephonically.

(B) The mortgage servicer shall notify the borrower during the initial contact required pursuant to subparagraph (A) that a third party, such as a family member, HUD-certified housing counselor, or attorney, may record a request to receive copies of any notice of default and notice of sale pursuant to the process described in Section 2924b and that receiving a copy of these documents may allow the third party to assist the borrower in avoiding foreclosure.

(c) A notice of default recorded pursuant to Section 2924 shall include a declaration that the mortgage servicer has contacted the borrower, has tried with due diligence to contact the borrower as required by this section, or that no contact was required because the individual did not meet the definition of "borrower" pursuant to subdivision (c) of Section 2920.5.

(d) A mortgage servicer's loss mitigation personnel may participate by telephone during any contact required by this section.

(e) A borrower may designate, with consent given in writing, a HUD-certified housing counseling agency, attorney, or other adviser to discuss with the mortgage servicer, on the borrower's behalf, the borrower's financial situation and options for the borrower to avoid foreclosure. That contact made at the direction of the borrower shall satisfy the contact requirements of paragraph (2) of subdivision (b). Any foreclosure prevention alternative offered at the meeting by the mortgage servicer is subject to approval by the borrower.

(f) A notice of default may be recorded pursuant to Section 2924 when a mortgage servicer has not contacted a borrower as required by paragraph (2) of subdivision (b), provided that the failure to contact the borrower occurred despite the due diligence of the mortgage servicer. For purposes of this section, "due diligence" shall require and mean all of the following:

(1)(A) A mortgage servicer shall first attempt to contact a borrower by sending a first-class letter that includes the toll-free telephone number made available by HUD to find a HUD-certified housing counseling agency.

(B) The mortgage servicer shall notify the borrower in the first-class letter described in subparagraph (A) that a third party, such as a family member, HUD-certified housing counselor, or attorney, may record a request to receive copies of any notice of default and notice of sale pursuant to the process described in Section 2924b and that receiving a copy of these documents may allow the third party to assist the borrower in avoiding foreclosure.

(2)(A) After the letter has been sent, the mortgage servicer shall attempt to contact the borrower by telephone at least three times at different hours and on different days. Telephone calls shall be made to the primary telephone number on file.

(B) A mortgage servicer may attempt to contact a borrower using an automated system to dial borrowers, provided that, if the telephone call is answered, the call is connected to a live representative of the mortgage servicer.

(C) A mortgage servicer satisfies the telephone contact requirements of this paragraph:

(i) If it determines, after attempting contact pursuant to this paragraph, that the borrower's primary telephone number and secondary telephone number or numbers on file, if any, have been disconnected.

(ii) If the borrower or [3] **the borrower's** authorized agent notifies the mortgage servicer in writing to cease further communication with the borrower. The cease communication notification shall explicitly pertain to the mortgage loan account to be effective. The cease communication notification shall be effective until the borrower or [4] **the borrower's** authorized agent rescinds it in writing.

(3) If the borrower does not respond within two weeks after the telephone call requirements of paragraph (2) have been satisfied, the mortgage servicer shall then send a certified letter, with return receipt requested, that includes the toll-free telephone number made available by HUD to find a HUD-certified housing counseling agency.

(4) The mortgage servicer shall provide a means for the borrower to contact it in a timely manner, including a toll-free telephone number that will provide access to a live representative during business hours.

(5) The mortgage servicer has posted a prominent link on the [5] **home page** of its [6] **internet website**, if any, to the following information:

(A) Options that may be available to borrowers who are unable to afford their mortgage payments and who wish to avoid foreclosure, and instructions to borrowers advising them on steps to take to explore those options.

(B) A list of financial documents borrowers should collect and be prepared to present to the mortgage servicer when discussing options for avoiding foreclosure.

(C) A toll-free telephone number for borrowers who wish to discuss options for avoiding foreclosure with their mortgage servicer.

(D) The toll-free telephone number made available by HUD to find a HUD-certified housing counseling agency.

(g) This section shall not apply to entities described in subdivision (b) of Section 2924.18.

(h) This section shall apply only to mortgages or deeds of trust described in Section 2924.15. **Leg.H.** Added Stats 2018 ch 404 §6 (SB 818), effective January 1, 2019. Amended Stats 2024 ch 311 §2 (AB 2424), effective January 1, 2025.

§2923.55. 2024 Deletes. [1] he or she [2] he or she [3] his or her [4] his or her [5] homepage [6] Internet Web site

Prior Law: Former CC §2923.55, similar to the present section, was added Stats 2012 ch 87 §6 (SB 900), effective January 1, 2013, repealed January 1, 2018, amended Stats 2013 ch 76 §15 (AB 383), effective January 1, 2014, and repealed January 1, 2018, by its own terms.

Former CC §2923.55, similar to the present section, was added Stats 2012 ch 86 §6 (AB 278), effective January 1, 2013, amended Stats 2013 ch 76 §14 (AB 383), effective January 1, 2014, and repealed Stats 2015 ch 303 §28 (AB 731), effective January 1, 2016.

Former CC §2923.55, relating to specified conditions for which CC §2923.52 is inapplicable, was added Stats 2009–2010 2d Ex Sess ch 4 §6 (SBX2 7), effective May 21, 2009, Stats 2009–2010 2d Ex Sess ch 5 §6 (ABX2 7), effective May 21, 2009, and repealed January 1, 2011, by its own terms.

2018 Note: For effect of Stats 2018 ch 404 and legislative intent, see the 2018 Notes following CC §2923.4.

Former Sections: Former CC §2923.55, similar to the present section, was added Stats 2012 ch 86 §6 (AB 278) and repealed Stats 2015 ch 303 §28 (AB 731).

Former CC §2923.55, relating to specified conditions for which CC §2923.52 is inapplicable, was added Stats 2009–2010 2d Ex Sess ch 4 §6 (SBX2 7), effective May 21, 2009, Stats 2009–2010 2d Ex Sess ch 5 §6 (ABX2 7), effective May 21, 2009, and repealed January 1, 2011, by its own terms.

§2923.6. Legislative findings and declarations and intent regarding loan modification or workout plan; Prohibition against recording notice of default or sale or conducting trustee's sale while pending first lien loan modification application; Denial of first lien loan modification application; Applicability

(a) The Legislature finds and declares that any duty mortgage servicers may have to maximize net present value under their pooling and servicing agreements is owed to all parties in a loan pool, or to all investors under a pooling and servicing agreement, not to any particular party in the loan pool or investor under a pooling and servicing agreement, and that a mortgage servicer acts in the best interests of all parties to the loan pool or investors in the pooling and servicing agreement if it agrees to or implements a loan modification or workout plan for which both of the following apply:

(1) The loan is in payment default, or payment default is reasonably foreseeable.

(2) Anticipated recovery under the loan modification or workout plan exceeds the anticipated recovery through foreclosure on a net present value basis.

(b) It is the intent of the Legislature that the mortgage servicer offer the borrower a loan modification or workout plan if such a modification or plan is consistent with its contractual or other authority.

(c) If a borrower submits a complete application for a first lien loan modification offered by, or through, the borrower's mortgage servicer at least five business days before a scheduled foreclosure sale, a mortgage servicer, mortgagee, trustee, beneficiary, or authorized agent shall not record a notice of default or notice of sale, or conduct a trustee's sale, while the complete first lien loan modification application is pending. A mortgage servicer, mortgagee, trustee, beneficiary, or authorized agent shall not record a notice of default or notice of sale or conduct a trustee's sale until any of the following occurs:

(1) The mortgage servicer makes a written determination that the borrower is not eligible for a first lien loan modification, and any appeal period pursuant to subdivision (d) has expired.

(2) The borrower does not accept an offered first lien loan modification within 14 days of the offer.

(3) The borrower accepts a written first lien loan modification, but defaults on, or otherwise breaches the borrower's obligations under, the first lien loan modification.

(d) If the borrower's application for a first lien loan modification is denied, the borrower shall have at least 30 days from the date of the written denial to appeal the denial and to provide evidence that the mortgage servicer's determination was in error.

(e) If the borrower's application for a first lien loan modification is denied, the mortgage servicer, mortgagee, trustee, beneficiary, or authorized agent shall not record a notice of default or, if a notice of default has already been recorded, record a notice of sale or conduct a trustee's sale until the later of:

(1) Thirty-one days after the borrower is notified in writing of the denial.

(2) If the borrower appeals the denial pursuant to subdivision (d), the later of 15 days after the denial of the appeal or 14 days after a first lien loan modification is offered after appeal but declined by the borrower, or, if a first lien loan modification is offered and accepted after appeal, the date on which the borrower fails to timely submit the first payment or otherwise breaches the terms of the offer.

(f) Following the denial of a first lien loan modification application, the mortgage servicer shall send a written notice to the borrower identifying the reasons for denial, including the following:

(1) The amount of time from the date of the denial letter in which the borrower may request an appeal of the denial of the first lien loan modification and instructions regarding how to appeal the denial.

(2) If the denial was based on investor disallowance, the specific reasons for the investor disallowance.

(3) If the denial is the result of a net present value calculation, the monthly gross income and property value used to calculate the net present value and a statement that the borrower may obtain all of the inputs used in the net present value calculation upon written request to the mortgage servicer.

(4) If applicable, a finding that the borrower was previously offered a first lien loan modification and failed to successfully make payments under the terms of the modified loan.

(5) If applicable, a description of other foreclosure prevention alternatives for which the borrower may be eligible, and a list of the steps the borrower must take in order to be considered for those options. If the mortgage servicer has already approved the borrower for another foreclosure prevention alternative, information necessary to complete the foreclosure prevention alternative.

(g) In order to minimize the risk of borrowers submitting multiple applications for first lien loan modifications for the purpose of delay, the mortgage servicer shall not be obligated to evaluate applications from borrowers who have been evaluated or afforded a fair opportunity to be evaluated consistent with the requirements of this section, unless there has been a material change in the borrower's financial circumstances since the date of the borrower's previous application and that change is documented by the borrower and submitted to the mortgage servicer.

(h) For purposes of this section, an application shall be deemed "complete" when a borrower has supplied the mortgage servicer with all documents required by the mortgage servicer within the reasonable timeframes specified by the mortgage servicer.

(i) Subdivisions (c) to (h), inclusive, shall not apply to entities described in subdivision (b) of Section 2924.18.

(j) This section shall apply only to mortgages or deeds of trust described in Section 2924.15. **Leg.H.** Added Stats 2012 ch 87 §8 (SB 900), effective January 1, 2013, operative January 1, 2018. Amended Stats 2018 ch 404 §7 (SB 818), effective January 1, 2019.

2018 Note: For effect of Stats 2018 ch 404 and legislative intent, see the 2018 Notes following CC §2923.4.

Former Sections: Former CC §2923.6, similar to the present section, was added Stats 2012 ch 86 §8 (AB 278), operative January 1, 2018, and repealed Stats 2018 ch 404 §8 (SB 818).

Former CC §2923.6, similar to the present section, was added Stats 2008 ch 69 §3 (SB 1137), effective July 8, 2008, and repealed operative January 1, 2018, by its own provisions. Stats 2012 chs 86 (AB 278) §7, 87 (SB 900) §7.

Prior Law: Former CC § 2923.6, similar to the present section, was added Stats 2008 ch 69 §3 (SB 1137), effective July 8, 2008, repealed January 1, 2013, amended Stats 2009 ch 43 §2 (SB 306), effective January 1, 2010, repealed January 1, 2013, Stats 2012 ch 86 §7 (AB 278), effective January 1, 2013, repealed January 1, 2018, Stats 2012 ch 87 §7 (SB 900), effective January 1, 2013, and repealed January 1, 2018, by its own terms.

Former CC §2923.6, similar to the present section, was added Stats 2012 ch 86 §8 (AB 278), effective January 1, 2013, operative January 1, 2018, and repealed Stats 2018 ch 404 §8 (SB 818), effective January 1, 2019.

§2923.7. Responsibilities of single point of contact; Applicability

(a) When a borrower requests a foreclosure prevention alternative, the mortgage servicer shall promptly establish a single point of contact and provide to the borrower one or more direct means of communication with the single point of contact.

(b) The single point of contact shall be responsible for doing all of the following:

(1) Communicating the process by which a borrower may apply for an available foreclosure prevention alternative and the deadline for any required submissions to be considered for these options.

(2) Coordinating receipt of all documents associated with available foreclosure prevention alternatives and notifying the borrower of any missing documents necessary to complete the application.

(3) Having access to current information and personnel sufficient to timely, accurately, and adequately inform the borrower of the current status of the foreclosure prevention alternative.

(4) Ensuring that a borrower is considered for all foreclosure prevention alternatives offered by, or through, the mortgage servicer, if any.

(5) Having access to individuals with the ability and authority to stop foreclosure proceedings when necessary.

(c) The single point of contact shall remain assigned to the borrower's account until the mortgage servicer determines that all loss mitigation options offered by, or through, the mortgage servicer have been exhausted or the borrower's account becomes current.

(d) The mortgage servicer shall ensure that a single point of contact refers and transfers a borrower to an appropriate supervisor upon request of the borrower, if the single point of contact has a supervisor.

(e) For purposes of this section, "single point of contact" means an individual or team of personnel each of whom has the ability and authority to perform the responsibilities described in subdivisions (b) to (d), inclusive. The mortgage servicer shall ensure that each member of the team is knowledgeable about the borrower's situation and current status in the alternatives to foreclosure process.

(f) This section shall apply only to mortgages or deeds of trust described in Section 2924.15.

(g)(1) **This section shall not apply to either of the following:**

(A) [1] A depository institution chartered under state or federal law, a person licensed pursuant to Division 9 (commencing with Section 22000) or Division 20 (commencing with Section 50000) of the Financial Code, or a person licensed pursuant to Part 1 (commencing with Section 10000) of Division 4 of the Business and Professions Code, that, during its immediately preceding annual reporting period, as established with its primary regulator, foreclosed on 175 or fewer residential real properties, containing no more than four dwelling units, that are located in California.

(B) A person or entity that makes and services seven or fewer loans for the purchase of residential real property in a calendar year.

(2) Within three months after the close of any calendar year or annual reporting period as established with its primary regulator during which an entity or person described in **subparagraph (A) of** paragraph (1) exceeds the threshold of 175 specified in **subparagraph (A) of** paragraph (1), that entity shall notify its primary regulator, in a manner acceptable to its primary regulator, and any mortgagor or trustor who is delinquent on a residential mortgage loan serviced by that entity of the date on which that entity will be subject to this section, which date shall be the first day of the first month that is six months after the close of the calendar year or annual reporting period during which that entity exceeded the threshold.

Leg.H. Added Stats 2012 ch 87 §9 (SB 900), effective January 1, 2013. Amended Stats 2018 ch 404 §9 (SB 818), effective January 1, 2019; Stats 2024 ch 601 §2 (SB 1146), effective January 1, 2025.

§2923.7. 2024 Deletes. [1] This section shall not apply to a

Prior Law: Former CC §2923.7, similar to the present section, was added Stats 2012 ch 86 §9 (AB 278), effective January 1, 2013, and repealed Stats 2018 ch 404 §10 (SB 818), effective January 1, 2019.

2018 Note: For effect of Stats 2018 ch 404 and legislative intent, see the 2018 Notes following CC §2923.4.

Former Sections: Former CC §2923.7, similar to the present section, was added Stats 2012 ch 86 §9 (AB 278) and repealed Stats 2018 ch 404 §10 (SB 818).

§2924. Transfer as security deemed mortgage or pledge; Exercise of power of sale; No liability for good faith error; Recital of acts as prima facie evidence; Privileged communications; Rebuttable presumption

(a) Every transfer of an interest in property, other than in trust, made only as a security for the performance of another act, is to be deemed a mortgage, except when in the case of personal property it is accompanied by actual change of possession, in which case it is to be deemed a pledge. If, by a mortgage created after July 27, 1917, of any estate in real property, other than an estate at will or for years, less than two, or in any transfer in trust made after July 27, 1917, of a like estate to secure the performance of an obligation, a power of sale is conferred upon the mortgagee, trustee, or any other person, to be exercised after a breach of the obligation for which that mortgage or transfer is a security, the power shall not be exercised except where the mortgage or transfer is made pursuant to an order, judgment, or decree of a court of record, or to secure the payment of bonds or other evidences of indebtedness authorized or permitted to be issued by the Commissioner of Financial Protection and Innovation, or is made by a public utility subject to the provisions of the Public Utilities Act, until all of the following apply:

(1) The trustee, mortgagee, or beneficiary, or any of their authorized agents shall first file for record, in the office of the recorder of each county wherein the mortgaged or trust property or some part or parcel thereof is situated, a notice of default. That notice of default shall include all of the following:

(A) A statement identifying the mortgage or deed of trust by stating the name or names of the trustor or trustors and giving the book and page, or instrument number, if applicable, where the mortgage or deed of trust is recorded or a description of the mortgaged or trust property.

(B) A statement that a breach of the obligation for which the mortgage or transfer in trust is security has occurred.

(C) A statement setting forth the nature of each breach actually known to the beneficiary and of the beneficiary's election to sell or cause to be sold the property to satisfy that obligation and any other obligation secured by the deed of trust or mortgage that is in default.

(D) If the default is curable pursuant to Section 2924c, the statement specified in paragraph (1) of subdivision (b) of Section 2924c.

(2) Not less than three months shall elapse from the filing of the notice of default.

(3) Except as provided in paragraph (4), after the lapse of the three months described in paragraph (2), the mortgagee, trustee, or other person authorized to take the sale shall give notice of sale, stating the time and place thereof, in the manner and for a time not less than that set forth in Section 2924f.

(4) Notwithstanding paragraph (3), the mortgagee, trustee, or other person authorized to take sale may record a notice of sale pursuant to Section 2924f up to [1] **5** days before the lapse of the three-month period described in paragraph (2), provided that the date of sale is no earlier than three months and 20 days after the recording of the notice of default.

(5) Whenever a sale is postponed for a period of at least 10 business days pursuant to Section 2924g, a mortgagee, beneficiary, or authorized agent shall provide written notice to a borrower regarding the new sale date and time, within [2] **5** business days following the postponement. Information provided pursuant to this paragraph shall not constitute the public declaration required by subdivision (d) of Section 2924g. Failure to comply with this paragraph shall not invalidate any sale that would otherwise be valid under Section 2924f.

(6) An entity shall not record or cause a notice of default to be recorded or otherwise initiate the foreclosure process unless it is the holder of the beneficial interest under the mortgage or deed of trust, the original trustee or the substituted trustee under the deed of trust, or the designated agent of the holder of the beneficial interest. An agent of the holder of the beneficial interest under the mortgage or deed of trust, original trustee, or

substituted trustee under the deed of trust shall not record a notice of default or otherwise commence the foreclosure process except when acting within the scope of authority designated by the holder of the beneficial interest.

(b) In performing acts required by this article **or responding to requests for payoff or reinstatement information**, the trustee shall **not** incur [3] liability for any good faith error resulting from reliance on information provided in good faith by the beneficiary regarding the nature and the amount of the default under the secured obligation, deed of trust, or mortgage. In performing the acts required by this article **or responding to requests for payoff or reinstatement information**, a trustee shall not be subject to Title 1.6c (commencing with Section 1788) of Part 4.

(c) A recital in the deed executed pursuant to the power of sale of compliance with all requirements of law regarding the mailing of copies of notices or the publication of a copy of the notice of default or the personal delivery of the copy of the notice of default or the posting of copies of the notice of sale or the publication of a copy thereof shall constitute prima facie evidence of compliance with these requirements and conclusive evidence thereof in favor of bona fide purchasers and encumbrancers for value and without notice.

(d) All of the following shall constitute privileged communications pursuant to Section 47:

(1) The mailing, publication, and delivery of notices as required by this section.

(2) Performance of the procedures set forth in this article.

(3) Performance of the functions and procedures set forth in this article if those functions and procedures are necessary to carry out the duties described in Sections 729.040, 729.050, and 729.080 of the Code of Civil Procedure.

(e) There is a rebuttable presumption that the beneficiary actually knew of all unpaid loan payments on the obligation owed to the beneficiary and secured by the deed of trust or mortgage subject to the notice of default. However, the failure to include an actually known default shall not invalidate the notice of sale and the beneficiary shall not be precluded from asserting a claim to this omitted default or defaults in a separate notice of default.

(f) With respect to residential real property containing no more than four dwelling units, a separate document containing a summary of the notice of default information in English and the languages described in Section 1632 shall be attached to the notice of default provided to the mortgagor or trustor pursuant to Section 2923.3. **Leg.H.** Added 2009 2nd Ex Sess Stats 2009–2010 ch 4 §8 (SBX2-7), effective May 21, 2009, operative January 1, 2011. Amended Stats 2010 ch 180 §1 (SB 1221), effective January 1, 2011, operative January 1, 2011; Stats 2012 ch 86 §10 (AB 278), effective January 1, 2013, ch 87 §10 (SB 900), effective January 1, 2013, ch 556 §2.5 (AB 1599), effective January 1, 2013; Stats 2018 ch 404 §11 (SB 818), effective January 1, 2019; Stats 2019 ch 143 §16 (SB 251), effective January 1, 2020; Stats 2022 ch 452 §29 (SB 1498), effective January 1, 2023; Stats 2024 ch 142 §1 (AB 295), effective July 18, 2024.

§2924. 2024 Deletes. [1] five [2] five [3] no

Prior Law: Former CC 2924, similar to the present section, was added Stats 2009-2010 2d Ex Sess ch 5 §8 (AB 7XX), effective May 21, 2009, operative January 1, 2011, amended Stats 2010 ch 180 §2 (SB 1221), effective January 1, 2011, operative January 1, 2011, and repealed Stats 2012 ch 86 §11 (AB 278), effective January 1, 2013, ch 87 §11 (SB 900), effective January 1, 2013, and ch 556 §3 (AB 1599), effective January 1, 2013.

Former §2924, similar to the present section, was enacted 1872, amended Code Amdts 1873-74 ch 612 §256; Stats 1917 ch 204 §1; Stats 1923 ch 374 §1; Stats 1931 ch 764 §1; Stats 1933 ch 642 §1, reenacted Stats 1935 ch 650 §1, amended Stats 1939 ch 983 §1; Stats 1959 ch 1890 §1; Stats 1972 ch 1056 §1; Stats 1973 ch 817 §1, operative July 1, 1974; Stats 1981 ch 427 §1, Stats 1990 ch 637 §1; Stats 1993 ch 686 §2; Stats 1995 ch 752 §1; Stats 1996 ch 483 §1; Stats 1999 ch 974 §8; Stats 2000 ch 636 §6; Stats 2006 ch 575 §4, effective January 1, 2007; Stats 2009-2010 2d Ex Sess ch 4 §7, effective May 21, 2009, ch 5 §7, effective May 21, 2009, repealed January 1, 2011, and repealed January 1, 2011, by its own terms.

2018 Note: For effect of Stats 2018 ch 404 and legislative intent, see the 2018 Notes following CC §2923.4.

2009 Note: This act shall be known as the California Foreclosure Prevention Act. Stats 2009–10 ch 4 (Second Extra. Sess.) (SB 7 (Second Extra. Sess.)) §1.

Former Sections: Former CC §2924, similar to the present section, was added Stats 2009–10 2d Ex Sess ch 5 §8 (ABX2 7), effective May 21, 2009, operative January 1, 2011, and repealed Stats 2012 ch 86 §11 (AB 278), ch 87 §11 (SB 900), and ch 556 §3 (AB 1599).

Former CC §2924, similar to the present section, was enacted in 1872 and repealed operative January 1, 2011, by its own provisions.

§2924.1. Recordation of transfer of property in common interest development

(a) Notwithstanding any other law, the transfer, following the sale, of property in a common interest development, as defined by Section 1351, executed under the power of sale contained in any deed of trust or mortgage, shall be recorded within 30 days after the date of sale in the office of the county recorder where the property or a portion of the property is located.

(b) Any failure to comply with the provisions of this section shall not affect the validity of a trustee's sale or a sale in favor of a bona fide purchaser. **Leg.H.** Added Stats 2012 ch 255 §1 (AB 2273), effective January 1, 2013.

§2924.3. Notice by agent collecting payments from obligor

(a) Except as provided in subdivisions (b) and (c), a person who has undertaken as an agent of a mortgagee, beneficiary, or owner of a promissory note secured directly or collaterally by a mortgage or deed of trust on real property or an estate for years therein, to make collections of payments from an obligor under the note, shall mail the following notices, postage prepaid, to each mortgagee, beneficiary or owner for whom the agent has agreed to make collections from the obligor under the note:

(1) A copy of the notice of default filed in the office of the county recorder pursuant to Section 2924 on account of a breach of obligation under the promissory note on which the agent has agreed to make collections of payments, within 15 days after recordation.

(2) Notice that a notice of default has been recorded pursuant to Section 2924 on account of a breach of an obligation secured by a mortgage or deed of trust against the same property or estate for years therein having priority over the mortgage or deed of trust securing the obligation described in paragraph (1), within 15 days after recordation or within three business days after the agent receives the information, whichever is later.

(3) Notice of the time and place scheduled for the sale of the real property or estate for years therein pursuant to Section 2924f under a power of sale in a mortgage or deed of trust securing an obligation described in paragraphs (1) or (2), not less than 15 days before the scheduled date of the sale or not later than the next business day after the agent receives the information, whichever is later.

(b) An agent who has undertaken to make collections on behalf of mortgagees, beneficiaries or owners of promissory notes secured by mortgages or deeds of trust on real property or an estate for years therein shall not be required to comply with the provisions of subdivision (a) with respect to a mortgagee, beneficiary or owner who is entitled to receive notice pursuant to subdivision (c) of Section 2924b or for whom a request for notice has been recorded pursuant to subdivision (b) of Section 2924b if the agent reasonably believes that the address of the mortgagee, beneficiary, or owner described in Section 2924b is the current business or residence address of that person.

(c) An agent who has undertaken to make collections on behalf of mortgagees, beneficiaries or owners of promissory notes secured by mortgages or deeds of trust on real property or an estate for years therein shall not be required to comply with the provisions of paragraph (1) or (2) of subdivision (a) if the agent knows or reasonably believes that the default has already been cured by or on behalf of the obligor.

(d) Any failure to comply with the provisions of this section shall not affect the validity of a sale in favor of a bona fide purchaser or the rights of an encumbrancer for value and without notice. **Leg.H.** Added Stats 1982 ch 711 §4. Amended Stats 1989 ch 698 §7; Stats 1998 ch 932 §10 (AD 1094).

§2924.5. Recitation of acceleration clause in instruments encumbering small residential properties

No clause in any deed of trust or mortgage on property containing four or fewer residential units or on which four or fewer residential units are to be constructed or in any obligation secured by any deed of trust or mortgage on property containing four or fewer residential units or on which four or fewer residential units are to be constructed that provides for the acceleration of the due date of the obligation upon the sale, conveyance, alienation, lease, succession, assignment or other transfer of the property subject to the deed of trust or mortgage shall be valid unless the clause is set forth, in its entirety in both the body of the deed of trust or mortgage and the promissory note or other document evidencing the secured obligation. This section shall apply to all such deeds of trust, mortgages, and obligations secured thereby executed on or after July 1, 1972. **Leg.H.** Added Stats 1971 ch 429 §1. Amended Stats 1972 ch 216 §1, effective June 30, 1972.

§2924.6. Limitations on acceleration

(a) An obligee may not accelerate the maturity date of the principal and accrued interest on any loan secured by a mortgage or deed of trust on residential real property solely by reason of any one or more of the following transfers in the title to the real property:

(1) A transfer resulting from the death of an obligor where the transfer is to the spouse who is also an obligor.

(2) A transfer by an obligor where the spouse becomes a coowner of the property.

(3) A transfer resulting from a decree of dissolution of the marriage or legal separation or from a property settlement agreement incidental to such a decree which requires the obligor to continue to make the loan payments by which a spouse who is an obligor becomes the sole owner of the property.

(4) A transfer by an obligor or obligors into an inter vivos trust in which the obligor or obligors are beneficiaries.

(5) Such real property or any portion thereof is made subject to a junior encumbrance or lien.

(b) Any waiver of the provisions of this section by an obligor is void and unenforceable and is contrary to public policy.

(c) For the purposes of this section, "residential real property" means any real property which contains at least one but not more than four housing units.

(d) This act applies only to loans executed or refinanced on or after January 1, 1976. **Leg.H.** Added Stats 1975 ch 850 §1.

§2924.7. Enforcement of acceleration of maturity date of principal and interest or disbursement of proceeds of property insurance by beneficiary, trustee, mortgagee, or agent

(a) The provisions of any deed of trust or mortgage on real property which authorize any beneficiary, trustee, mortgagee, or his or her agent or successor in interest, to accelerate the maturity date of the principal and interest on any loan secured thereby or to exercise any power of sale or other remedy contained therein upon the failure of the trustor or mortgagor to pay, at the times provided for under the terms of the deed of trust or mortgage, any taxes, rents, assessments, or insurance premiums with respect to the property or the loan, or any advances made by the beneficiary, mortgagee, or his or her agent or successor in interest shall be enforceable whether or not impairment of the security interest in the property has resulted from the failure of the trustor or mortgagor to pay the taxes, rents, assessments, insurance premiums, or advances.

(b) The provisions of any deed of trust or mortgage on real property which authorize any beneficiary, trustee, mortgagee, or his or her agent or successor in interest, to receive and control the disbursement of the proceeds of any policy of fire, flood, or other hazard insurance respecting the property shall be enforceable whether or not impairment of the security interest in the property has resulted from the event that caused the proceeds of the insurance policy to become payable. **Leg.H.** Added Stats 1988 ch 179 §2.

1988 Note: The Legislature hereby declares that the enactment of 2924.7 is not intended to abrogate the holding in the case of Schoolcraft v. Ross (81 Cal. App. 3d 75) insofar as it provides that a lender may not prohibit the use of insurance proceeds for the restoration of the security property absent a showing that the lender's security interest in the property has been impaired. It is the intent of the Legislature to abrogate the holdings in cases such as Kreshek v. Sperling (157 Cal. App. 3d 279) and Freeman v. Lind (181 Cal. App. 3d 791) to the extent those holdings in any way restrict the right of a beneficiary or mortgagee under a deed of trust or mortgage on real property to enforce the express provisions of the deed of trust or mortgage. Stats 1988 ch 179 §3.

§ 2924.8. Posting of notice of pending foreclosure sale; Infraction to destroy notice; Translations; Applicability

(a) Upon posting a notice of sale pursuant to Section 2924f, a trustee or authorized agent shall also post the following notice, in the manner required for posting the notice of sale on the property to be sold, and a mortgagee, trustee, beneficiary, or authorized agent, concurrently with the mailing of the notice of sale pursuant to Section 2924b, shall send by first-class mail in an envelope addressed to the "Resident of property subject to foreclosure sale" the following notice in English and the languages described in Section 1632:

Foreclosure process has begun on this property, which may affect your right to continue to live in this property. Twenty days or more after the date of this notice, this property may be sold at foreclosure. If you are renting this property, the new property owner may either give you a new lease or rental agreement or provide you with a 90-day eviction notice. You may have a right to stay in your home for longer than 90 days. If you have a fixed-term lease, the new owner must honor the lease unless the new owner will occupy the property as a primary residence or in other limited circumstances. Also, in some cases and in some cities with a "just cause for eviction" law, you may not have to move at all. All rights and obligations under your lease or tenancy, including your obligation to pay rent, will continue after the foreclosure sale. You may wish to contact a lawyer or your local legal aid office or housing counseling agency to discuss any rights you may have.

(b) It is an infraction to tear down the notice described in subdivision (a) within 72 hours of posting. Violators shall be subject to a fine of one hundred dollars ($100).

(c) The Department of Financial Protection and Innovation and the Department of Real Estate shall make available translations of the notice described in subdivision (a) which may be used by a mortgagee, trustee, beneficiary, or authorized agent to satisfy the requirements of this section.

(d) This section shall only apply to loans secured by residential real property, and if the billing address for the mortgage note is different than the property address.

(e) This section shall become operative on March 1, 2021. **Leg.H.** Added Stats 2020 ch 36 §14 (AB 3364), effective January 1, 2021, operative March 1, 2021. Amended Stats 2022 ch 452 §30 (SB 1498), effective January 1, 2023.

Prior Law: Former Civ C §2924.8, similar to the present section, was added Stats 2008 ch 69 §4 (SB 1137), effective July 8, 2008, operative September 6, 2008, repealed January 1, 2013, amended Stats 2009 ch 43 §3 (SB 306), effective January 1, 2010, repealed January 1, 2013, Stats 2012 ch 562 §1 (AB 2610), effective January 1, 2013, repealed December 31, 2019, Stats 2013 ch 76 §16 (AB 383), effective January 1, 2014, and repealed December 31, 2019, by its own terms.

§2924.85. Disclosure notice of default; Rights and remedies [Repealed]

Leg.H. Added Stats 2012 ch 566 §1 (SB 1191), effective January 1, 2013. Repealed January 1, 2018, by its own terms.

§2924.9. Written communication to borrower after mortgage servicer offering foreclosure prevention alternative records notice of default pursuant to Section 2924; Applicability

(a) Unless a borrower has previously exhausted the first lien loan modification process offered by, or through, his or her mortgage servicer described in Section 2923.6, within five business days after recording a notice of default pursuant to Section 2924, a mortgage servicer that offers one or more foreclosure prevention alternatives shall send a written communication to the borrower that includes all of the following information:

(1) That the borrower may be evaluated for a foreclosure prevention alternative or, if applicable, foreclosure prevention alternatives.

(2) Whether an application is required to be submitted by the borrower in order to be considered for a foreclosure prevention alternative.

(3) The means and process by which a borrower may obtain an application for a foreclosure prevention alternative.

(b) This section shall not apply to entities described in subdivision (b) of Section 2924.18.

(c) This section shall apply only to mortgages or deeds of trust described in Section 2924.15. **Leg.H.** Added Stats 2018 ch 404 §12 (SB 818), effective January 1, 2019.

Prior Law: Former CC §2924.9, similar to the present section, was added Stats 2012 ch 87 §12 (SB 900), effective January 1, 2013, and repealed January 1, 2018, by its own terms.

Former CC §2924.9, similar to the present section, was added Stats 2012 ch 86 §12 (AB 278), effective January 1, 2013, and repealed January 1, 2018, by its own terms.

2018 Note: For effect of Stats 2018 ch 404 and legislative intent, see the 2018 Notes following CC §2923.4.

Former Sections: Former CC §2924.9, similar to the present section, was added Stats 2012 ch 87 §12 (SB 900) and repealed operative January 1, 2018, by its own terms.

Former CC §2924.9, similar to the present section, was added Stats 2012 ch 86 §12 (AB 278) and repealed operative January 1, 2018, by its own terms.

§2924.10. Written acknowledgment of receipt of first lien loan modification application or documentation; Applicability

(a) When a borrower submits a complete first lien modification application or any document in connection with a first lien modification application, the mortgage servicer shall provide written acknowledgment of the receipt of the documentation within five business days of receipt. In its initial acknowledgment of receipt of the loan modification application, the mortgage servicer shall include the following information:

(1) A description of the loan modification process, including an estimate of when a decision on the loan modification will be made after a complete application has been submitted by the borrower and the length of time the borrower will have to consider an offer of a loan modification or other foreclosure prevention alternative.

(2) Any deadlines, including deadlines to submit missing documentation, that would affect the processing of a first lien loan modification application.

(3) Any expiration dates for submitted documents.

(4) Any deficiency in the borrower's first lien loan modification application.

(b) For purposes of this section, a borrower's first lien loan modification application shall be deemed to be "complete" when a borrower has supplied the mortgage servicer with all documents required by the mortgage servicer within the reasonable timeframes specified by the mortgage servicer.

(c) This section shall not apply to entities described in subdivision (b) of Section 2924.18.

(d) This section shall apply only to mortgages or deeds of trust described in Section 2924.15. **Leg.H.** Added Stats 2018 ch 404 §13 (SB 818), effective January 1, 2019.

Prior Law: Former CC §2924.10, similar to the present section, was added Stats 2012 ch 87 §13 (SB 900), effective January 1, 2013, and repealed January 1, 2018, by its own terms.

Former CC §2924.10, similar to the present section, was added Stats 2012 ch 86 §13 (AB 278), effective January 1, 2013, and repealed January 1, 2018, by its own terms.

2018 Note: For effect of Stats 2018 ch 404 and legislative intent, see the 2018 Notes following CC §2923.4.

Former Sections: Former CC §2924.10, similar to the present section, was added Stats 2012 ch 87 §13 (SB 900) and repealed operative January 1, 2018, by its own terms.

Former CC §2924.10, similar to the present section, was added Stats 2012 ch 86 §13 (AB 278) and repealed operative January 1, 2018, by its own terms.

§2924.11. Approved foreclosure prevention alternative; Prohibition against recording notice of default or sale or conducting trustee's sale; Rescission or cancellation; Fees; Subsequent mortgage servicer; Applicability

(a) If a foreclosure prevention alternative is approved in writing prior to the recordation of a notice of default, a mortgage servicer, mortgagee, trustee, beneficiary, or authorized agent shall not record a notice of default under either of the following circumstances:

(1) The borrower is in compliance with the terms of a written trial or permanent loan modification, forbearance, or repayment plan.

(2) A foreclosure prevention alternative has been approved in writing by all parties, including, for example, the first lien investor, junior lienholder, and mortgage insurer, as applicable, and proof of funds or financing has been provided to the servicer.

(b) If a foreclosure prevention alternative is approved in writing after the recordation of a notice of default, a mortgage servicer, mortgagee, trustee, beneficiary, or authorized agent shall not record a notice of sale or conduct a trustee's sale under either of the following circumstances:

(1) The borrower is in compliance with the terms of a written trial or permanent loan modification, forbearance, or repayment plan.

(2) A foreclosure prevention alternative has been approved in writing by all parties, including, for example, the first lien investor, junior lienholder, and mortgage insurer, as applicable, and proof of funds or financing has been provided to the servicer.

(c) When a borrower accepts an offered first lien loan modification or other foreclosure prevention alternative, the mortgage servicer shall provide the borrower with a copy of the fully executed loan modification agreement or agreement evidencing the foreclosure prevention alternative following receipt of the executed copy from the borrower.

(d) A mortgagee, beneficiary, or authorized agent shall record a rescission of a notice of default or cancel a pending trustee's sale, if applicable, upon the borrower executing a permanent foreclosure prevention alternative. In the case of a short sale, the cancellation of the pending trustee's sale shall occur when the short sale has been approved by all parties and proof of funds or financing has been provided to the mortgagee, beneficiary, or authorized agent.

(e) The mortgage servicer shall not charge any application, processing, or other fee for a first lien loan modification or other foreclosure prevention alternative.

(f) The mortgage servicer shall not collect any late fees for periods during which a complete first lien loan modification application is under consideration or a denial is being appealed, the borrower is making timely modification payments, or a foreclosure prevention alternative is being evaluated or exercised.

(g) If a borrower has been approved in writing for a first lien loan modification or other foreclosure prevention alternative, and the servicing of that borrower's loan is transferred or sold to another mortgage servicer, the subsequent mortgage servicer shall continue to honor any previously approved first lien loan modification or other foreclosure prevention alternative, in accordance with the provisions of the act that added this section.

(h) This section shall apply only to mortgages or deeds of trust described in Section 2924.15.

(i) This section shall not apply to entities described in subdivision (b) of Section 2924.18. **Leg.H.** Added Stats 2018 ch 404 §16 (SB 818), effective January 1, 2019.

Prior Law: Former CC §2924.11, similar to the present section and present CC §2923.6, was added Stats 2012 ch 87 §15 (SB 900), effective January 1, 2013, operative January 1, 2018, and repealed Stats 2018 ch 404 §15 (SB 818), effective January 1, 2019.

Former CC §2924.11, similar to the present section and present CC §2923.6, was added Stats 2012 ch 86 §15 (AB 278), effective January 1, 2013, operative January 1, 2018, and repealed Stats 2018 ch 404 §14 (SB 818), effective January 1, 2019.

Former CC §2924.11, similar to the present section, was added Stats 2012 ch 86 §14 (AB 278), effective January 1, 2013, repealed January 1, 2018, amended Stats 2016 ch 170 §1 (SB 983), effective January 1, 2017, and repealed January 1, 2018, by its own terms.

Former CC §2924.11, similar to the present section, was added Stats 2012 ch 87 §14 (SB 900), effective January 1, 2013, repealed January 1, 2018, and repealed Stats 2016 ch 170 §2 (SB 983), effective January 1, 2017.

2018 Note: For effect of Stats 2018 ch 404 and legislative intent, see the 2018 Notes following CC §2923.4.

Former Sections: Former CC §2924.11, similar to the present section and present CC §2923.6, was added Stats 2012 ch 87 §15 (SB 900), operative January 1, 2018, and repealed Stats 2018 ch 404 §15 (SB 818).

Former CC §2924.11, similar to the present section and present CC §2923.6, was added Stats 2012 ch 86 §15 (AB 278), operative January 1, 2018, and repealed Stats 2018 ch 404 §14 (SB 818).

Former CC §2924.11, similar to the present section, was added Stats 2012 ch 86 §14 (AB 278) and repealed January 1, 2018, by its own terms.

Former CC §2924.11, similar to the present section, was added Stats 2012 ch 87 §14 (SB 900) and repealed Stats 2016 ch 170 §2 (SB 983).

§2924.12. Actions concerning trustee's deed upon sale; Injunctive relief; Liability; Damages; Violations; Attorney's fees and costs

(a)(1) If a trustee's deed upon sale has not been recorded, a borrower may bring an action for injunctive relief to enjoin a material violation of Section 2923.55, 2923.6, 2923.7, 2924.9, 2924.10, 2924.11, or 2924.17.

(2) Any injunction shall remain in place and any trustee's sale shall be enjoined until the court determines that the mortgage servicer, mortgagee, trustee, beneficiary, or authorized agent has corrected and remedied the violation or violations giving rise to the action for injunctive relief. An enjoined entity may move to dissolve an injunction based on a showing that the material violation has been corrected and remedied.

(b) After a trustee's deed upon sale has been recorded, a mortgage servicer, mortgagee, trustee, beneficiary, or authorized agent shall be liable to a borrower for actual economic damages pursuant to Section 3281, resulting from a material violation of Section 2923.55, 2923.6, 2923.7, 2924.9, 2924.10, 2924.11, or 2924.17 by that mortgage servicer, mortgagee, trustee, beneficiary, or authorized agent where the violation was not corrected and remedied prior to the recordation of the trustee's deed upon sale. If the court finds that the material violation was intentional or reckless, or resulted from willful misconduct by a mortgage servicer, mortgagee, trustee, beneficiary, or authorized agent, the court may award the borrower the greater of treble actual damages or statutory damages of fifty thousand dollars ($50,000).

(c) A mortgage servicer, mortgagee, trustee, beneficiary, or authorized agent shall not be liable for any violation that it has corrected and remedied prior to the recordation of the trustee's deed upon sale, or that has been corrected and remedied by third parties working on its behalf prior to the recordation of the trustee's deed upon sale.

(d) A violation of Section 2923.55, 2923.6, 2923.7, 2924.9, 2924.10, 2924.11, or 2924.17 by a person licensed by the Department of Financial Protection and Innovation or the Department of Real Estate shall be deemed to be a violation of that person's licensing law.

(e) No violation of this article shall affect the validity of a sale in favor of a bona fide purchaser and any of its encumbrancers for value without notice.

(f) A third-party encumbrancer shall not be relieved of liability resulting from violations of Section 2923.55, 2923.6, 2923.7, 2924.9, 2924.10, 2924.11, or 2924.17 committed by that third-party encumbrancer, that occurred prior to the sale of the subject property to the bona fide purchaser.

(g) The rights, remedies, and procedures provided by this section are in addition to and independent of any other rights, remedies, or procedures under any other law. Nothing in this section shall be construed to alter, limit, or negate any other rights, remedies, or procedures provided by law.

(h) A court may award a prevailing borrower reasonable attorney's fees and costs in an action brought pursuant to this section. A borrower shall be deemed to have prevailed for purposes of this subdivision if the borrower obtained injunctive relief or was awarded damages pursuant to this section.

(i) This section shall not apply to entities described in subdivision (b) of Section 2924.18. **Leg.H.** Added Stats 2012 ch 87 §17 (SB 900), effective January 1, 2013, operative January 1, 2018. Amended Stats 2014 ch 401 §7 (AB 2763), effective January 1, 2015, operative January 1, 2018; Stats 2018 ch 404 §17 (SB 818), effective January 1, 2019; Stats 2022 ch 452 §31 (SB 1498), effective January 1, 2023.

Prior Law: Former CC §2924.12, similar to the present section, was added Stats 2012 ch 86 §17 (AB 278), effective January 1, 2013, operative January 1, 2018, amended Stats 2014 ch 401 §6 (AB 2763), effective January 1, 2015, operative January 1, 2018, and repealed Stats 2018 ch 404 §18 (SB 818), effective January 1, 2019.

Former CC §2924.12, similar to the present section, was added Stats 2012 ch 87 §16 (SB 900), effective January 1, 2013, repealed January 1, 2018, amended Stats 2014 ch 401 §5 (AB 2763), effective January 1, 2015, and repealed January 1, 2018, by its own terms.

Former CC §2924.12, similar to the present section, was added Stats 2012 ch 86 §16 (AB 278), effective January 1, 2013, repealed January 1, 2018, amended Stats 2014 ch 401 §4 (AB 2763), effective January 1, 2015, and repealed January 1, 2018, by its own terms.

2018 Note: For effect of Stats 2018 ch 404 and legislative intent, see the 2018 Notes following CC §2923.4.

Former Sections: Former CC §2924.12, similar to the present section, was added Stats 2012 ch 86 §17 (AB 278), operative January 1, 2018, and repealed Stats 2018 ch 404 §18 (SB 818).

Former CC §2924.12, similar to the present section, was added Stats 2012 ch 87 §16 (SB 900) and repealed operative January 1, 2018, by its own terms.

Former CC §2924.12, similar to the present section, was added Stats 2012 ch 86 §16 (AB 278) and repealed operative January 1, 2018, by its own terms.

§ 2924.15. Applicability of specified code sections to first lien mortgages or deeds of trust secured by owner-occupied residential real property containing no more than four dwelling units

(a) Unless otherwise provided, paragraph (5) of subdivision (a) of Section 2924 and Sections 2923.5, 2923.55, 2923.6, 2923.7, 2924.9, 2924.10, 2924.11, and 2924.18 shall apply only to a first lien mortgage or deed of trust that [1] **is secured by owner-occupied residential real property containing no more than four dwelling units.**

[2]

(b) For purposes of this [3] **section**, "owner-occupied" means that the property is the principal residence of the borrower and is security for a loan made for personal, family, or household purposes. [4] **Leg.H.** Added Stats 2020 ch 37 §12 (AB 3088), effective August 31, 2020, operative January 1, 2023. Amended Stats 2021 ch 360 §5 (AB 1584), effective January 1, 2022, operative January 1, 2023; Stats 2024 ch 601 §3 (SB 1146), effective January 1, 2025.

§ 2924.15. 2024 Deletes. [1] meets either of the following conditions: **[2]** (1) (A) The first lien mortgage or deed of trust is secured by owner-occupied residential real property containing no more than four dwelling units. (B) For purposes of this paragraph, "owner-occupied" means that the property is the principal residence of the borrower and is security for a loan made for personal, family, or household purposes. (2) The first lien mortgage or deed of trust is secured by residential real property that is occupied by a tenant and that contains no more than four dwelling units and meets all of the conditions described in subparagraph (B) and one of the conditions described in subparagraph (C). (A) For purposes of this paragraph: (i) "Applicable lease" means a lease entered pursuant to an arm's length transaction before, and in effect on, March 4, 2020. (ii) "Arm's length transaction" means a lease entered into in good faith and for valuable consideration that reflects the fair market value in the open market between informed and willing parties. (iii) "Occupied by a tenant" means that the property is the principal residence of a tenant. (B) To meet the conditions of this paragraph, a first lien mortgage or deed of trust shall have all of the following characteristics: (i) The property is owned by an individual who owns no more than three residential real properties, each of which contains no more than four dwelling units. (ii) The property shall have been occupied by a tenant pursuant to an applicable lease. (iii) A tenant occupying the property shall have been unable to pay rent due to a reduction in income resulting from COVID-19. (C) For a first lien mortgage or deed of trust to meet the conditions of this paragraph, the borrower shall satisfy either of the following characteristics: (i) The borrower has been approved in writing for a first lien loan modification or other foreclosure prevention alternative before January 1, 2023. (ii) The borrower submits a completed application for a first lien loan modification before January 1, 2023, and, as of January 1, 2023, either the mortgage servicer has not yet determined whether the applicant is eligible for a first lien loan modification, or the appeal period for the mortgage servicer's denial of the application has not yet expired. (D) Relief shall be available pursuant to subdivision (a) of Section 2924 and Sections 2923.5 2923.55,2923,6,2923,7,2924.9,2924.10,2924.11, and 2924.18 for so long as the property remains occupied by a tenant pursuant to a lease entered into an arm's length transaction. (B) **[3]** paragraph **[4]** (b) This section shall become operative on January 1, 2023.

Prior Law: Former CC §2924.15, similar to the present section, was added Stats 2012 ch 87 §18 (SB 900), effective January 1, 2013, and repealed January 1, 2018, by its own terms.

Former CC §2924.15, similar to the present section, was added Stats 2012 ch 86 §18 (AB 278), effective January 1, 2013, and repealed January 1, 2018, by its own terms.

Former CC §2924.15, similar to the present section, was added Stats 2012 ch 86 §19 (AB 278), effective January 1, 2013, operative January 1, 2018, and repealed Stats 2018 ch 404 §20 (SB 818), effective January 1, 2019.

Former CC §2924.15, similar to the present section, was added Stats 2012 ch 87 §19 (SB 900), effective January 1, 2013, operative January 1, 2018, amended Stats 2018 ch 404 §19 (SB 818), effective January 1, 2019; Stats 2020 ch 37 §11 (AB 3088), effective August 31, 2020, repealed January 1, 2023; and Stats 2021 ch 360 §4 (AB1584), effective January 1, 2022, and was repealed by its own terms January 1, 2023.

§2924.17. Recording or filing of certain documents; Review of evidence to substantiate borrower's default and right to foreclose; Uncorrected violations; Civil penalties

(a) A declaration recorded pursuant to Section 2923.5 or pursuant to Section 2923.55, a notice of default, notice of sale, assignment of a deed of trust, or substitution of trustee recorded by or on behalf of a mortgage servicer in connection with a foreclosure subject to the requirements of Section 2924, or a declaration or affidavit filed in any court relative to a foreclosure proceeding shall be accurate and complete and supported by competent and reliable evidence.

(b) Before recording or filing any of the documents described in subdivision (a), a mortgage servicer shall ensure that it has reviewed competent and reliable evidence to substantiate the borrower's default and the right to foreclose, including the borrower's loan status and loan information.

(c) Any mortgage servicer that engages in multiple and repeated uncorrected violations of subdivision (b) in recording documents or filing documents in any court relative to a foreclosure proceeding shall be liable for a civil penalty of up to seven thousand five hundred dollars ($7,500) per mortgage or deed of trust in an action brought by a government entity identified in Section 17204 of the Business and Professions Code, or in an administrative proceeding brought by the Department of Financial Protection and Innovation or the Department of Real Estate against a respective licensee, in addition to any other remedies available to these entities. **Leg.H.** Added Stats 2012 ch 87 §20 (SB 900), effective January 1, 2013. Amended Stats 2014 ch 401 §9 (AB 2763), effective January 1, 2015; Stats 2018 ch 404 §21 (SB 818), effective January 1, 2019; Stats 2022 ch 452 §32 (SB 1498), effective January 1, 2023.

Prior Law: Former CC §2924.17, similar to the present section, was added Stats 2012 ch 86 §20 (AB 278), effective January 1, 2013, amended Stats 2014 ch 401 §8 (AB 2763), effective January 1, 2015, and repealed Stats 2018 ch 404 §22 (SB 818), effective January 1, 2019.

2018 Note: For effect of Stats 2018 ch 404 and legislative intent, see the 2018 Notes following CC §2923.4.

Former Sections: Former CC §2924.17, similar to the present section, was added Stats 2012 ch 86 §20 (AB 278) and repealed Stats 2018 ch 404 §22 (SB 818).

§2924.18. Pending first lien loan modification application or approved foreclosure prevention alternative; Prohibition against recording notice of default or sale or conducting trustee's sale; Applicability to depository institutions and specified licensed persons that foreclosed on 175 or fewer residential real properties; Notifications; Subsequent mortgage servicer; Applicability to specified mortgages or deeds of trust

(a)(1) If a borrower submits a complete application for a first lien loan modification offered by, or through, the borrower's mortgage servicer at least five business days before a scheduled foreclosure sale, a mortgage servicer, trustee, mortgagee, beneficiary, or authorized agent shall not record a notice of default, notice of sale, or conduct a trustee's sale while the complete first lien loan modification application is pending, and until the borrower has been provided with a written determination by the mortgage servicer regarding that borrower's eligibility for the requested loan modification.

(2) If a foreclosure prevention alternative has been approved in writing prior to the recordation of a notice of default, a mortgage servicer, mortgagee, trustee, beneficiary, or authorized agent shall not record a notice of default under either of the following circumstances:

(A) The borrower is in compliance with the terms of a written trial or permanent loan modification, forbearance, or repayment plan.

(B) A foreclosure prevention alternative has been approved in writing by all parties, including, for example, the first lien investor, junior lienholder, and mortgage insurer, as applicable, and proof of funds or financing has been provided to the servicer.

(3) If a foreclosure prevention alternative is approved in writing after the recordation of a notice of default, a mortgage servicer, mortgagee, trustee, beneficiary, or authorized agent shall not record a notice of sale or conduct a trustee's sale under either of the following circumstances:

(A) The borrower is in compliance with the terms of a written trial or permanent loan modification, forbearance, or repayment plan.

(B) A foreclosure prevention alternative has been approved in writing by all parties, including, for example, the first lien investor, junior lienholder, and mortgage insurer, as applicable, and proof of funds or financing has been provided to the servicer.

(b) This section shall apply to both of the following:

(1) [1] A depository institution chartered under state or federal law, a person licensed pursuant to Division 9 (commencing with Section 22000) or Division 20 (commencing with Section 50000) of the Financial Code, or a person licensed pursuant to Part 1 (commencing with Section 10000) of Division 4 of the Business and Professions Code, that, during its immediately preceding annual reporting period, as established with its primary regulator, foreclosed on 175 or fewer residential real properties, containing no more than four dwelling units, that are located in California.

(2) A person or entity that makes and services seven or fewer loans for the purchase of residential real property in a calendar year.

(c) Within three months after the close of any calendar year or annual reporting period as established with its primary regulator during which an entity or person described in **paragraph (1) of** subdivision (b) exceeds the threshold of 175 specified in **paragraph (1) of** subdivision (b), that entity shall notify its primary regulator, in a manner acceptable to its primary regulator, and any mortgagor or trustor who is delinquent on a residential mortgage loan serviced by that entity of the date on which that entity will be subject to Sections 2923.55, 2923.6, 2923.7, 2924.9, 2924.10, 2924.11, and 2924.12, which date shall be the first day of the first month that is six months after the close of the calendar year or annual reporting period during which that entity exceeded the threshold.

(d) For purposes of this section, an application shall be deemed "complete" when a borrower has supplied the mortgage servicer with all documents required by the mortgage servicer within the reasonable timeframes specified by the mortgage servicer.

(e) If a borrower has been approved in writing for a first lien loan modification or other foreclosure prevention alternative, and the servicing of the borrower's loan is transferred or sold to another mortgage servicer, the subsequent mortgage servicer shall continue to honor any previously approved first lien loan modification or other foreclosure prevention alternative, in accordance with the provisions of the act that added this section.

(f) This section shall apply only to mortgages or deeds of trust described in Section 2924.15. **Leg.H.** Added Stats 2018 ch 404 §23 (SB 818), effective January 1, 2019. Amended Stats 2024 ch 601 §4 (SB 1146), effective January 1, 2025.

§2924.18. 2024 Deletes. [1] This section shall apply only to a

Prior Law: Former CC §2924.18, similar to the present section, was added Stats 2012 ch 86 §21 (AB 278), effective January 1, 2013, and repealed January 1, 2018, by its own terms.

Former CC §2924.18, similar to the present section, was added Stats 2012 ch 87 §21 (SB 900), effective January 1, 2013, and repealed January 1, 2018, by its own terms.

2018 Note: For effect of Stats 2018 ch 404 and legislative intent, see the 2018 Notes following CC §2923.4.

Former Sections: Former CC §2924.18, similar to the present section, was added Stats 2012 ch 87 §21 (SB 900) and repealed January 1, 2018, by its own terms.

Former CC §2924.18, similar to the present section, was added Stats 2012 ch 86 §21 (AB 278) and repealed January 1, 2018, by its own terms.

§2924.19. Actions concerning trustee's deed; Injunctive relief; Liability; Damages; Violations; Attorney's fees and costs; Applicability

(a)(1) If a trustee's deed upon sale has not been recorded, a borrower may bring an action for injunctive relief to enjoin a material violation of Section 2923.5, 2924.17, or 2924.18.

(2) An injunction shall remain in place and any trustee's sale shall be enjoined until the court determines that the mortgage servicer, mortgagee, beneficiary, or authorized agent has corrected and remedied the violation or violations giving rise to the action for injunctive relief. An enjoined entity may move to dissolve an injunction based on a showing that the material violation has been corrected and remedied.

(b) After a trustee's deed upon sale has been recorded, a mortgage servicer, mortgagee, beneficiary, or authorized agent shall be liable to a borrower for actual economic damages pursuant to Section 3281, resulting from a material violation of Section 2923.5, 2924.17, or 2924.18 by that mortgage servicer, mortgagee, beneficiary, or authorized agent where the violation was not corrected and remedied prior to the recordation of the trustee's deed upon sale. If the court finds that the material violation was intentional or reckless, or resulted from willful misconduct by a mortgage servicer, mortgagee, beneficiary, or authorized agent, the court may award the borrower the greater of treble actual damages or statutory damages of fifty thousand dollars ($50,000).

(c) A mortgage servicer, mortgagee, beneficiary, or authorized agent shall not be liable for any violation that it has corrected and remedied prior to the recordation of the trustee's deed upon sale, or that has been corrected and remedied by third parties working on its behalf prior to the recordation of the trustee's deed upon sale.

(d) A violation of Section 2923.5, 2924.17, or 2924.18 by a person licensed by the Department of Financial Protection and Innovation or the Department of Real Estate shall be deemed to be a violation of that person's licensing law.

(e) A violation of this article shall not affect the validity of a sale in favor of a bona fide purchaser and any of its encumbrancers for value without notice.

(f) A third-party encumbrancer shall not be relieved of liability resulting from violations of Section 2923.5, 2924.17, or 2924.18, committed by that third-party encumbrancer, that occurred prior to the sale of the subject property to the bona fide purchaser.

(g) The rights, remedies, and procedures provided by this section are in addition to and independent of any other rights, remedies, or procedures under any other law. Nothing in this section shall be construed to alter, limit, or negate any other rights, remedies, or procedures provided by law.

(h) A court may award a prevailing borrower reasonable attorney's fees and costs in an action brought pursuant to this section. A borrower shall be deemed to have prevailed for purposes of this subdivision if the borrower obtained injunctive relief or damages pursuant to this section.

(i) This section shall apply only to entities described in subdivision (b) of Section 2924.18. **Leg.H.** Added Stats 2018 ch 404 §24 (SB 818), effective January 1, 2019. Amended Stats 2022 ch 452 §33 (SB 1498), effective January 1, 2023.

Prior Law: Former CC §2924.18, similar to the present section, was added Stats 2012 ch 87 §21 (SB 900), effective January 1, 2013, and repealed January 1, 2018, by its own terms.

Former CC §2924.18, similar to the present section, was added Stats 2012 ch 86 §21 (AB 278), effective January 1, 2013, and repealed January 1, 2018, by its own terms.

2018 Note: For effect of Stats 2018 ch 404 and legislative intent, see the 2018 Notes following CC §2923.4.

Former Sections: Former CC §2924.19, similar to the present section, was added Stats 2012 ch 87 §22 (SB 900) and repealed January 1, 2018, by its own terms.

Former CC §2924.19, similar to the present section, was added Stats 2012 ch 86 §22 (AB 278) and repealed Stats 2015 ch 303 §29 (AB 731).

§2924.20. Adoption of regulations; Enforcement

Consistent with their general regulatory authority, and notwithstanding subdivisions (b) and (c) of Section 2924.18, the Department of Financial Protection and Innovation and the Bureau of Real Estate may adopt regulations applicable to any entity or person under their respective jurisdictions that are necessary to carry out the purposes of the act that added this section. A violation of the regulations adopted pursuant to this section shall only be enforceable by the regulatory agency. **Leg.H.** Added Stats 2012 ch 87 §23 (SB 900), effective January 1, 2013. Amended Stats 2014 ch 401 §13 (AB 2763), effective January 1, 2015; Stats 2022 ch 452 §34 (SB 1498), effective January 1, 2023.

Prior Law: Former CC §2924.20, similar to the present section, was added Stats 2012 ch 86 §23, effective January 1, 2013, amended Stats 2014 ch 401 §12, effective January 1, 2015, and repealed Stats 2015 ch 303 §30, effective January 1, 2016.

Former CC §2924.20, similar to the present section, was added Stats 2012 ch 86 §23 and repealed Stats 2015 ch 303 §30, effective January 1, 2016.

§ 2924.21. Initiation of claim of surplus

A person shall not contact, solicit, or initiate communication with an owner to claim the surplus funds from a foreclosure sale of the owner's residence before 90 days after the trustee's deed has been recorded. **Leg.H.** Added Stats 2024 ch 142 §2 (AB 295), effective July 18, 2024.

§2924.25. Liability of title company for violation of specified Civil Code sections if notice of default or sale recorded at request of trustee, substitute trustee, or beneficiary [Repealed]

Leg.H. Added Stats 2013 ch 251 §1 (SB 310), effective January 1, 2014. Repealed January 1, 2018, by its own provisions. See CC §2924.26.

§2924.26. Liability of title company for violation of specified Civil Code sections if notice of default or sale recorded at request of trustee, substitute trustee, or beneficiary

(a) Unless acting in the capacity of a trustee, a licensed title company or underwritten title company shall not be liable for a violation of Section 2923.5 or 2924.11 if it records or causes to record a notice of default or notice of sale at the request of a trustee, substitute trustee, or beneficiary, in good faith and in the normal course of its business activities.

(b) This section shall become operative on January 1, 2018. **Leg.H.** Added Stats 2013 ch 251 §2 (SB 310), effective January 1, 2014, operative January 1, 2018.

2013 Note: Sections 2924.25 and 2924.26 shall not be construed to affect the liability of a trustee, substitute trustee, or beneficiary that requests a licensed title company or underwritten title company to record a notice of default or notice of sale. Stats 2013 ch 251 (SB 310) §3.

§2924a. Conduct of sale by attorney for trustee

If, by the terms of any trust or deed of trust a power of sale is conferred upon the trustee, the attorney for the trustee, or any duly authorized agent, may conduct the sale and act in the sale as the auctioneer for the trustee. **Leg.H.** Added Stats 1929 ch 610 §1. Amended Stats 2006 ch 575 §5 (AB 2624), effective January 1, 2007.

§2924b. Request for copy of notice of default or sale; Recordation; Duty of mortgagee, trustee, etc.

(a) Any person desiring a copy of any notice of default and of any notice of sale under any deed of trust or mortgage with power of sale upon real property or an estate for years therein, as to which deed of trust or mortgage the power of sale cannot be exercised until these notices are given for the time and in the manner provided in Section 2924 may, at any time subsequent to recordation of the deed of trust or mortgage and prior to recordation of notice of default thereunder, cause to be filed for record in the office of the recorder of any county in which any part or parcel of the real property is situated, a duly acknowledged request for a copy of the notice of default and of sale. This request shall be signed and acknowledged by the person making the request, specifying the name and address of the person to whom the notice is to be mailed, shall identify the deed of trust or mortgage by stating the names of the parties thereto, the date of recordation thereof, and the book and page where the deed of trust or mortgage is recorded or the recorder's number, and shall be in substantially the following form:

"In accordance with Section 2924b, Civil Code, request is hereby made that a copy of any notice of default and a copy of any notice of sale under the deed of trust (or mortgage) recorded ____, ____, in Book ____ page ____ records of _____ County, (or filed for record with recorder's serial number ____, _____ County) California, executed by _____ as trustor (or mortgagor) in which _____ is named as beneficiary (or mortgagee) and _____ as trustee be mailed to _____ at _____
Name   Address
NOTICE: A copy of any notice of default and of any notice of sale will be sent only to the address contained in this recorded request. If your address changes, a new request must be recorded.
                                        Signature _____"

Upon the filing for record of the request, the recorder shall index in the general index of grantors the names of the trustors (or mortgagors) recited therein and the names of persons requesting copies.

(b) The mortgagee, trustee, or other person authorized to record the notice of default or the notice of sale shall do each of the following:

(1) Within 10 business days following recordation of the notice of default, deposit or cause to be deposited in the United States mail an envelope, sent by registered or certified mail with postage prepaid, containing a copy of the notice with the recording date shown thereon, addressed to each person whose name and address are set forth in a duly recorded request therefor, directed to the address designated in the request and to each trustor or mortgagor at his or her last known address if different than the address specified in the deed of trust or mortgage with power of sale.

(2) At least 20 days before the date of sale, deposit or cause to be deposited in the United States mail an envelope, sent by registered or certified mail with postage prepaid, containing a copy of the notice of the time and place of sale, addressed to each person whose name and address are set forth in a duly recorded request therefor, directed to the address designated in the request and to each trustor or mortgagor at his or her last known address if different than the address specified in the deed of trust or mortgage with power of sale.

(3) As used in paragraphs (1) and (2), the "last known address" of each trustor or mortgagor means the last business or residence physical address actually known by the mortgagee, beneficiary, trustee, or other person authorized to record the notice of default. For the purposes of this subdivision, an address is "actually known" if it is contained in the original deed of trust or mortgage, or in any subsequent written notification of a change of physical address from the trustor or mortgagor pursuant to the deed of trust or mortgage. For the purposes of this subdivision, "physical address" does not include an email or any form of electronic address for a trustor or mortgagor. The beneficiary shall inform the trustee of the trustor's last address actually known by the beneficiary.

However, the trustee shall incur no liability for failing to send any notice to the last address unless the trustee has actual knowledge of it.

(4) A "person authorized to record the notice of default or the notice of sale" shall include an agent for the mortgagee or beneficiary, an agent of the named trustee, any person designated in an executed substitution of trustee, or an agent of that substituted trustee.

(c) The mortgagee, trustee, or other person authorized to record the notice of default or the notice of sale shall do the following:

(1) Within one month following recordation of the notice of default, deposit or cause to be deposited in the United States mail an envelope, sent by registered or certified mail with postage prepaid, containing a copy of the notice with the recording date shown thereon, addressed to each person set forth in paragraph (2), provided that the estate or interest of any person entitled to receive notice under this subdivision is acquired by an instrument sufficient to impart constructive notice of the estate or interest in the land or portion thereof that is subject to the deed of trust or mortgage being foreclosed, and provided the instrument is recorded in the office of the county recorder so as to impart that constructive notice prior to the recording date of the notice of default and provided the instrument as so recorded sets forth a mailing address that the county recorder shall use, as instructed within the instrument, for the return of the instrument after recording, and which address shall be the address used for the purposes of mailing notices herein.

(2) The persons to whom notice shall be mailed under this subdivision are:

(A) The successor in interest, as of the recording date of the notice of default, of the estate or interest or any portion thereof of the trustor or mortgagor of the deed of trust or mortgage being foreclosed.

(B) The beneficiary or mortgagee of any deed of trust or mortgage recorded subsequent to the deed of trust or mortgage being foreclosed, or recorded prior to or concurrently with the deed of trust or mortgage being foreclosed but subject to a recorded agreement or a recorded statement of subordination to the deed of trust or mortgage being foreclosed.

(C) The assignee of any interest of the beneficiary or mortgagee described in subparagraph (B), as of the recording date of the notice of default.

(D) The vendee of any contract of sale, or the lessee of any lease, of the estate or interest being foreclosed that is recorded subsequent to the deed of trust or mortgage being foreclosed, or recorded prior to or concurrently with the deed of trust or mortgage being foreclosed but subject to a recorded agreement or statement of subordination to the deed of trust or mortgage being foreclosed.

(E) The successor in interest to the vendee or lessee described in subparagraph (D), as of the recording date of the notice of default.

(F) The office of the Controller, Sacramento, California, where, as of the recording date of the notice of default, a "Notice of Lien for Postponed Property Taxes" has been recorded against the real property to which the notice of default applies.

(3) At least 20 days before the date of sale, deposit or cause to be deposited in the United States mail an envelope, sent by registered or certified mail with postage prepaid, containing a copy of the notice of the time and place of sale addressed to each person to whom a copy of the notice of default is to be mailed as provided in paragraphs (1) and (2), and addressed to the office of any state taxing agency, Sacramento, California, that has recorded, subsequent to the deed of trust or mortgage being foreclosed, a notice of tax lien prior to the recording date of the notice of default against the real property to which the notice of default applies.

(4) Provide a copy of the notice of sale to the Internal Revenue Service, in accordance with Section 7425 of the Internal Revenue Code and any applicable federal regulation, if a "Notice of Federal Tax Lien under Internal Revenue Laws" has been recorded, subsequent to the deed of trust or mortgage being foreclosed, against the real property to which the notice of sale applies. The failure to provide the Internal Revenue Service with a copy of the notice of sale pursuant to this paragraph shall be sufficient cause to rescind the trustee's sale and invalidate the trustee's deed, at the option of either the successful bidder at the trustee's sale or the trustee, and in either case with the consent of the beneficiary. Any option to rescind the trustee's sale pursuant to this paragraph shall be exercised prior to any transfer of the property by the successful bidder to a bona fide purchaser for value. A rescission of the trustee's sale pursuant to this paragraph may be recorded in a notice of rescission pursuant to Section 1058.5.

(5) The mailing of notices in the manner set forth in paragraph (1) shall not impose upon any licensed attorney, agent, or employee of any person entitled to receive notices as herein set forth any duty to communicate the notice to the entitled person from the fact that the mailing address used by the county recorder is the address of the attorney, agent, or employee.

(d) Any deed of trust or mortgage with power of sale hereafter executed upon real property or an estate for years therein may contain a request that a copy of any notice of default and a copy of any notice of sale thereunder shall be mailed to any person or party thereto at the address of the person given therein, and a copy of any notice of default and of any notice of sale shall be mailed to each of these at the same time and in the same manner required as though a separate request therefor had been filed by each of these persons as herein authorized. If any deed of trust or mortgage with power of sale executed after September 19, 1939, except a deed of trust or mortgage of any of the classes excepted from the provisions of Section 2924, does not contain a mailing address of the trustor or mortgagor therein named, and if no request for special notice by the trustor or mortgagor in substantially the form set forth in this section has subsequently been recorded, a copy of the notice of default shall be published once a week for at least four weeks in a newspaper of general circulation in the county in which the property is situated, the publication to commence within 10 business days after the filing of the notice of default. In lieu of publication, a copy of the notice of default may be delivered personally to the trustor or mortgagor within the 10 business days or at any time before publication is completed, or by posting the notice of default in a conspicuous place on the property and mailing the notice to the last known address of the trustor or mortgagor.

(e) Any person required to mail a copy of a notice of default or notice of sale to each trustor or mortgagor pursuant to subdivision (b) or (c) by registered or certified mail shall simultaneously cause to be deposited in the United States mail, with postage prepaid and mailed by first-class mail, an envelope containing an additional copy of the required notice addressed to each trustor or mortgagor at the same address to which the notice is sent by registered or certified mail pursuant to subdivision (b) or (c). The person shall execute and retain an affidavit identifying the notice mailed, showing the name and residence or business address of that person, that he or she is over 18 years of age, the date of deposit in the mail, the name and address of the trustor or mortgagor to whom sent, and that the envelope was sealed and deposited in the mail with postage fully prepaid. In the absence of fraud, the affidavit required by this subdivision shall establish a conclusive presumption of mailing.

(f)(1) Notwithstanding subdivision (a), with respect to separate interests governed by an association, as defined in Section 4080 or 6528, the association may cause to be filed in the office of the recorder in the county in which the separate interests are situated a request that a mortgagee, trustee, or other person authorized to record a notice of default regarding any of those separate interests mail to the association a copy of any trustee's deed upon sale concerning a separate interest. The request shall include a legal description or the assessor's parcel number of all the separate interests. A request recorded pursuant to this subdivision shall include the name and address of the association and a statement that it is an association as defined in Section 4080 or 6528. Subsequent requests of an association shall supersede prior requests. A request pursuant to this subdivision shall be recorded before the filing of a notice of default. The mortgagee, trustee, or other authorized person shall mail the requested information to the association within 15 business days following the date of the trustee's sale. Failure to mail the request, pursuant to this subdivision, shall not affect the title to real property.

(2) A request filed pursuant to paragraph (1) does not, for purposes of Section 27288.1 of the Government Code, constitute a document that either effects or evidences a transfer or encumbrance of an interest in real property or that releases or terminates any interest, right, or encumbrance of an interest in real property.

(g) No request for a copy of any notice filed for record pursuant to this section, no statement or allegation in the request, and no record thereof shall affect the title to real property or be deemed notice to any person that any person requesting copies of notice has or claims any right, title, or interest in, or lien or charge upon the property described in the deed of trust or mortgage referred to therein.

(h) "Business day," as used in this section, has the meaning specified in Section 9. **Leg.H.** Added Stats 1933 ch 642 §2. Reenacted Stats 1935 ch 650 §2. Amended Stats 1939 ch 983 §2; Stats 1951 ch 417 §2; Stats

1957 ch 1865 §11; Stats 1959 ch 425 §1, ch 1890 §2; Stats 1961 ch 2218 §1; Stats 1976 ch 1149 §1, operative July 1, 1977; Stats 1977 ch 1242 §2, effective October 1, 1977; Stats 1978 ch 43 §1, effective March 16, 1978; Stats 1979 ch 1015 §1; Stats 1980 ch 925 §1, effective September 18, 1980; Stats 1985 ch 154 §1, ch 1206 §1; Stats 1986 ch 1361 §3, ch 1385 §2.5; Stats 1989 ch 698 §5; Stats 1992 ch 351 §1 (AB 2981); Stats 1993 ch 686 §3 (AB 1219); Stats 2001 ch 438 §2 (SB 958), effective October 2, 2001; Stats 2002 ch 809 §1 (SB 1504); Stats 2004 ch 177 §1 (SB 1277); Stats 2005 ch 224 §1 (AB 885), effective January 1, 2006; Stats 2008 ch 527 §1 (SB 1511), effective January 1, 2009; Stats 2010 ch 133 §1 (AB 2016), effective January 1, 2011; Stats 2012 ch 181 §39 (AB 806), effective January 1, 2013, ch 255 §2 (AB 2273), effective January 1, 2013; Stats 2013 ch 183 §6 (SB 745), effective January 1, 2014, ch 605 §17 (SB 752), effective January 1, 2014.

§2924c. Curing default; Notice of default; Limitation on costs and expenses; Trustee's or attorney's fees; Reinstatement of default

(a)(1) Whenever all or a portion of the principal sum of any obligation secured by deed of trust or mortgage on real property or an estate for years therein hereafter executed has, prior to the maturity date fixed in that obligation, become due or been declared due by reason of default in payment of interest or of any installment of principal, or by reason of failure of trustor or mortgagor to pay, in accordance with the terms of that obligation or of the deed of trust or mortgage, taxes, assessments, premiums for insurance, or advances made by beneficiary or mortgagee in accordance with the terms of that obligation or of the deed of trust or mortgage, the trustor or mortgagor or their successor in interest in the mortgaged or trust property or any part thereof, or any beneficiary under a subordinate deed of trust or any other person having a subordinate lien or encumbrance of record thereon, at any time within the period specified in subdivision (e), if the power of sale therein is to be exercised, or, otherwise at any time prior to entry of the decree of foreclosure, may pay to the beneficiary or the mortgagee or their successors in interest, respectively, the entire amount due, at the time payment is tendered, with respect to (A) all amounts of principal, interest, taxes, assessments, insurance premiums, or advances actually known by the beneficiary to be, and that are, in default and shown in the notice of default, under the terms of the deed of trust or mortgage and the obligation secured thereby, (B) all amounts in default on recurring obligations not shown in the notice of default, and (C) all reasonable costs and expenses, subject to subdivision (c), that are actually incurred, or will be incurred as a direct result of the payment being tendered, in enforcing the terms of the obligation, deed of trust, or mortgage, and trustee's or attorney's fees, subject to subdivision (d), other than the portion of principal as would not then be due had no default occurred, and thereby cure the default theretofore existing, and thereupon, all proceedings theretofore had or instituted shall be dismissed or discontinued and the obligation and deed of trust or mortgage shall be reinstated and shall be and remain in force and effect, the same as if the acceleration had not occurred. This section does not apply to bonds or other evidences of indebtedness authorized or permitted to be issued by the Department of Financial Protection and Innovation or made by a public utility subject to the Public Utilities Code. For the purposes of this subdivision, the term "recurring obligation" means all amounts of principal and interest on the loan, or rents, subject to the deed of trust or mortgage in default due after the notice of default is recorded; all amounts of principal and interest or rents advanced on senior liens or leaseholds that are advanced after the recordation of the notice of default; and payments of taxes, assessments, and hazard insurance advanced after recordation of the notice of default. If the beneficiary or mortgagee has made no advances on defaults that would constitute recurring obligations, the beneficiary or mortgagee may require the trustor or mortgagor to provide reliable written evidence that the amounts have been paid prior to reinstatement.

(2) If the trustor, mortgagor, or other person authorized to cure the default pursuant to this subdivision does cure the default, the beneficiary or mortgagee or the agent for the beneficiary or mortgagee shall, within 21 days following the reinstatement, execute and deliver to the trustee a notice of rescission that rescinds the declaration of default and demand for sale and advises the trustee of the date of reinstatement. The trustee shall cause the notice of rescission to be recorded within 30 days of receipt of the notice of rescission and of all allowable fees and costs, **unless the mortgage or deed of trust is paid in full and a full reconveyance or certificate of discharge is properly recorded**.

No charge, except for the recording fee, shall be made against the trustor or mortgagor for the execution and recordation of the notice which rescinds the declaration of default and demand for sale.

(b)(1) The notice, of any default described in this section, recorded pursuant to Section 2924, and mailed to any person pursuant to Section 2924b, shall begin with the following statement, printed or typed thereon:

> IMPORTANT NOTICE [14-point boldface type if printed or in capital letters if typed]
>
> IF YOUR PROPERTY IS IN FORECLOSURE BECAUSE YOU ARE BEHIND IN YOUR PAYMENTS, IT MAY BE SOLD WITHOUT ANY COURT ACTION, [14-point boldface type if printed or in capital letters if typed] and you may have the legal right to bring your account in good standing by paying all of your past due payments plus permitted costs and expenses within the time permitted by law for reinstatement of your account, which is normally five business days prior to the date set for the sale of your property. No sale date may be set until approximately 90 days from the date this notice of default may be recorded (which date of recordation appears on this notice).
>
> This amount is _____ as of _____ and will increase (Date) until your account becomes current.
>
> While your property is in foreclosure, you still must pay other obligations (such as insurance and taxes) required by your note and deed of trust or mortgage. If you fail to make future payments on the loan, pay taxes on the property, provide insurance on the property, or pay other obligations as required in the note and deed of trust or mortgage, the beneficiary or mortgagee may insist that you do so in order to reinstate your account in good standing. In addition, the beneficiary or mortgagee may require as a condition to reinstatement that you provide reliable written evidence that you paid all senior liens, property taxes, and hazard insurance premiums.
>
> Upon your written request, the beneficiary or mortgagee will give you a written itemization of the entire amount you must pay. You may not have to pay the entire unpaid portion of your account, even though full payment was demanded, but you must pay all amounts in default at the time payment is made. However, you and your beneficiary or mortgagee may mutually agree in writing prior to the time the notice of sale is posted (which may not be earlier than three months after this notice of default is recorded) to, among other things, (1) provide additional time in which to cure the default by transfer of the property or otherwise; or (2) establish a schedule of payments in order to cure your default; or both (1) and (2).
>
> Following the expiration of the time period referred to in the first paragraph of this notice, unless the obligation being foreclosed upon or a separate written agreement between you and your creditor permits a longer period, you have only the legal right to stop the sale of your property by paying the entire amount demanded by your creditor.
>
> To find out the amount you must pay, or to arrange for payment to stop the foreclosure, or if your property is in foreclosure for any other reason, contact:
>
> _____
> (Name of beneficiary or mortgagee)
> _____
> (Mailing address)
> _____
> (Telephone)
>
> If you have any questions, you should contact a lawyer or the governmental agency that may have insured your loan.
>
> Notwithstanding the fact that your property is in foreclosure, you may offer your property for sale, provided the sale is concluded prior to the conclusion of the foreclosure.
>
> Remember, YOU MAY LOSE LEGAL RIGHTS IF YOU DO NOT TAKE PROMPT ACTION. [14-point boldface type if printed or in capital letters if typed]

Unless otherwise specified, the notice, if printed, shall appear in at least 12-point boldface type.

If the obligation secured by the deed of trust or mortgage is a contract or agreement described in paragraph (1) or (4) of subdivision (a) of Section 1632, the notice required herein shall be in Spanish if the trustor requested a Spanish language translation of the contract or agreement pursuant to Section 1632. If the obligation secured by the deed of trust or mortgage is contained in a home improvement contract, as defined in Sections 7151.2 and 7159 of the Business and Professions Code, which is subject to Title 2 (commencing with Section 1801), the seller shall specify on the contract whether or not the contract was principally negotiated in Spanish and if the contract was principally negotiated in Spanish, the notice required herein shall be in Spanish. No assignee of the contract or person authorized to record the notice of default shall incur any obligation or liability for failing to mail a notice in Spanish unless Spanish is specified in the contract or the assignee or person has actual knowledge that the secured obligation was principally negotiated in Spanish. Unless specified in writing to the contrary, a copy of the notice required by subdivision (c) of Section 2924b shall be in English.

(2) Any failure to comply with the provisions of this subdivision shall not affect the validity of a sale in favor of a bona fide purchaser or the rights of an encumbrancer for value and without notice.

(c) Costs and expenses that may be charged pursuant to Sections 2924 to 2924i, inclusive, shall be limited to the costs incurred for recording, mailing, including certified and express mail charges, publishing, and posting notices required by Sections 2924 to 2924i, inclusive, recording a notice of rescission under this section, postponement pursuant to Section 2924g not to exceed one hundred dollars ($100) per postponement and a fee for a trustee's sale guarantee or, in the event of judicial foreclosure, a litigation guarantee. For purposes of this subdivision, a trustee or beneficiary may purchase a trustee's sale guarantee at a rate meeting the standards contained in Sections 12401.1 and 12401.3 of the Insurance Code.

(d)(1) Trustee's or attorney's fees that may be charged pursuant to subdivision (a), or until the notice of sale is deposited in the mail to the trustor as provided in Section 2924b, if the sale is by power of sale contained in the deed of trust or mortgage, or, otherwise at any time prior to the decree of foreclosure, are hereby authorized to be in an amount as follows:

(A) If the unpaid principal sum secured is fifty thousand dollars ($50,000) or less, then in a base amount that does not exceed three hundred fifty dollars ($350).

(B) If the unpaid principal sum secured is greater than fifty thousand dollars ($50,000) but does not exceed one hundred fifty thousand dollars ($150,000), then in a base amount that does not exceed three hundred fifty dollars ($350) plus one-half of 1 percent of the unpaid principal sum secured exceeding fifty thousand dollars ($50,000).

(C) If the unpaid principal sum secured is greater than one hundred fifty thousand dollars ($150,000) but does not exceed five hundred thousand dollars ($500,000), then in a base amount that does not exceed three hundred dollars ($300) plus one-half of 1 percent of the unpaid principal sum secured exceeding fifty thousand dollars ($50,000) up to and including one hundred fifty thousand dollars ($150,000) plus one-quarter of 1 percent of any portion of the unpaid principal sum secured exceeding one hundred fifty thousand dollars ($150,000).

(D) If the unpaid principal sum secured is greater than five hundred thousand dollars ($500,000), then in a base amount that does not exceed three hundred dollars ($300) plus one-half of 1 percent of the unpaid principal sum secured exceeding fifty thousand dollars ($50,000) up to and including one hundred fifty thousand dollars ($150,000) plus one-quarter of 1 percent of any portion of the unpaid principal sum secured exceeding one hundred fifty thousand dollars ($150,000) up to and including five hundred thousand dollars ($500,000) plus one-eighth of 1 percent of any portion of the unpaid principal sum secured exceeding five hundred thousand dollars ($500,000).

(2) Any charge for trustee's or attorney's fees authorized by this subdivision shall be conclusively presumed to be lawful and valid where the charge does not exceed the amounts authorized in this subdivision. For purposes of this subdivision, the unpaid principal sum secured shall be determined as of the date the notice of default is recorded.

(e) Reinstatement of a monetary default under the terms of an obligation secured by a deed of trust, or mortgage may be made at any time within the period commencing with the date of recordation of the notice of default until five business days prior to the date of sale set forth in the initial recorded notice of sale.

In the event the sale does not take place on the date set forth in the initial recorded notice of sale or a subsequent recorded notice of sale is required to be given, the right of reinstatement shall be revived as of the date of recordation of the subsequent notice of sale, and shall continue from that date until five business days prior to the date of sale set forth in the subsequently recorded notice of sale.

In the event the date of sale is postponed on the date of sale set forth in either an initial or any subsequent notice of sale, or is postponed on the date declared for sale at an immediately preceding postponement of sale, and, the postponement is for a period that exceeds five business days from the date set forth in the notice of sale, or declared at the time of postponement, then the right of reinstatement is revived as of the date of postponement and shall continue from that date until five business days prior to the date of sale declared at the time of the postponement.

Nothing contained herein shall give rise to a right of reinstatement during the period of five business days prior to the date of sale, whether the date of sale is noticed in a notice of sale or declared at a postponement of sale.

Pursuant to the terms of this subdivision, no beneficiary, trustee, mortgagee, or their agents or successors shall be liable in any manner to a trustor, mortgagor, their agents or successors or any beneficiary under a subordinate deed of trust or mortgage or any other person having a subordinate lien or encumbrance of record thereon for the failure to allow a reinstatement of the obligation secured by a deed of trust or mortgage during the period of five business days prior to the sale of the security property, and no such right of reinstatement during this period is created by this section. Any right of reinstatement created by this section is terminated five business days prior to the date of sale set forth in the initial date of sale, and is revived only as prescribed herein and only as of the date set forth herein.

As used in this subdivision, the term "business day" has the same meaning as specified in Section 9. **Leg.H.** Added Stats 1933 ch 642 §3. Reenacted Stats 1935 ch 650 §3. Amended Stats 1949 ch 1437 §1; Stats 1951 ch 417 §11; Stats 1957 ch 362 §1; Stats 1973 ch 817 §2, operative July 1, 1974; Stats 1974 ch 308 §1, effective May 31, 1974, operative July 1, 1974; Stats 1979 ch 655 §4, effective September 14, 1979, operative January 1, 1980, ch 1015 §2; Stats 1980 ch 423 §12, effective July 11, 1980, ch 1380 §18.5, effective October 1, 1980, operative January 1, 1981; Stats 1981 ch 427 §2; Stats 1983 ch 112 §1, ch 1217 §1; Stats 1984 ch 919 §1, ch 1730 §1, ch 1730 §1.5, operative July 1, 1985; Stats 1985 ch 1206 §2; Stats 1986 ch 1385 §3; Stats 1989 ch 698 §6; Stats 1990 ch 657 §2 (SB 2339); Stats 1992 ch 351 §2 (AB 2981); Stats 1993 ch 686 §4 (AB 1219); Stats 1996 ch 483 §2 (SB 1488); Stats 1997 ch 74 §2 (SB 665); Stats 1998 ch 485 §39 (AB 2803), Stats 1998 ch 932 §8 (AB 1094) (ch 932 prevails); Stats 1999 ch 974 §9 (AB 431); Stats 2000 ch 135 §13 (AB 2539); Stats 2001 ch 438 §3 (SB 958), effective October 2, 2001, operative January 1, 2002; Stats 2010 ch 180 §3 (SB 1221), effective January 1, 2011; Stats 2016 ch 170 §3 (SB 983), effective January 1, 2017; Stats 2017 ch 217 §1 (SB 479), effective January 1, 2018; Stats 2022 ch 452 §35 (SB 1498), effective January 1, 2023; Stats 2024 ch 142 §3 (AB 295), effective July 18, 2024; Stats 2024 ch 601 §5 (SB 1146), effective January 1, 2025.

1990 Note: See note following §2924.

§2924d. Right to reimbursement for costs and expenses of enforcement; Trustee's or attorney's fees; Prohibition against kickbacks [Repealed January 1, 2031]

(a)(1) Commencing with the date that the notice of sale is deposited in the mail, as provided in Section 2924b, and until the property is sold pursuant to the power of sale contained in the mortgage or deed of trust, a beneficiary, trustee, mortgagee, or their agent or successor in interest may demand and receive from a trustor, mortgagor, or their agent or successor in interest or any beneficiary under a subordinate deed of trust, or any other person having a subordinate lien or encumbrance of record those reasonable costs and expenses, to the extent allowed by subdivision (c) of Section 2924c, that are actually incurred in enforcing the terms of the obligation and trustee's or attorney's fees that are hereby authorized to be in an amount as follows:

(A) If the unpaid principal sum secured is fifty thousand dollars ($50,000) or less, then in a base amount that does not exceed four hundred seventy-five dollars ($475).

(B) If the unpaid principal sum secured is greater than fifty thousand dollars ($50,000) but does not exceed one hundred fifty thousand dollars ($150,000), then in a base amount that does not exceed four hundred seventy-five dollars ($475) plus 1 percent of the unpaid principal sum secured exceeding fifty thousand dollars ($50,000).

(C) If the unpaid principal sum secured is greater than one hundred fifty thousand dollars ($150,000) but does not exceed five hundred thousand dollars ($500,000), then in a base amount that does not exceed four hundred ten dollars ($410) plus 1 percent of the unpaid principal sum secured exceeding fifty thousand dollars ($50,000) up to and including one hundred fifty thousand dollars ($150,000), plus one-half of 1 percent of any portion of the unpaid principal sum secured exceeding one hundred fifty thousand dollars ($150,000).

(D) If the unpaid principal sum secured exceeds five hundred thousand dollars ($500,000), then in a base amount that does not exceed four hundred ten dollars ($410) plus 1 percent of the unpaid principal sum secured exceeding fifty thousand dollars ($50,000) up to and including one hundred fifty thousand dollars ($150,000), plus one-half of 1 percent of any portion of the unpaid principal sum secured exceeding one hundred fifty thousand dollars ($150,000) up to and including five hundred thousand dollars ($500,000), plus one-quarter of 1 percent of any portion of the unpaid principal sum secured exceeding five hundred thousand dollars ($500,000).

(2) For purposes of this subdivision, the unpaid principal sum secured shall be determined as of the date the notice of default is recorded. Any charge for trustee's or attorney's fees authorized by this subdivision shall be conclusively presumed to be lawful and valid where that charge does not exceed the amounts authorized in this subdivision. Any charge for trustee's or attorney's fees made pursuant to this subdivision shall be in lieu of and not in addition to those charges authorized by subdivision (d) of Section 2924c.

(b)(1) Upon the sale of property pursuant to a power of sale, a trustee, or their agent or successor in interest, may demand and receive from a beneficiary, or their agent or successor in interest, or may deduct from the proceeds of the sale, those reasonable costs and expenses, to the extent allowed by subdivision (c) of Section 2924c, that are actually incurred in enforcing the terms of the obligation and trustee's or attorney's fees that are hereby authorized to be in an amount which does not exceed four hundred seventy-five dollars ($475) or 1 percent of the unpaid principal sum secured, whichever is greater. For purposes of this subdivision, the unpaid principal sum secured shall be determined as of the date the notice of default is recorded.

(2) In addition to the amounts authorized under paragraph (1), if at least one eligible tenant buyer or eligible bidder submits to the trustee either a bid or a nonbinding written notice of intent to place a bid pursuant to paragraph (2) of subdivision (c) of Section 2924m, the trustee may deduct from the proceeds of the sale trustee's or attorney's fees for providing services pursuant to Section 2924m that are hereby authorized to be in an amount which does not exceed two hundred dollars ($200) or one-sixth of 1 percent of the unpaid principal sum secured, whichever is greater.

(3) Any charge for trustee's or attorney's fees authorized by this subdivision shall be conclusively presumed to be lawful and valid where that charge does not exceed the amount authorized herein. Any charges for trustee's or attorney's fees made pursuant to this subdivision shall be in lieu of and not in addition to those charges authorized by subdivision (a) of this section and subdivision (d) of Section 2924c.

(c)(1) No person shall pay or offer to pay or collect any rebate or kickback for the referral of business involving the performance of any act required by this article.

(2) Any person who violates this subdivision shall be liable to the trustor for three times the amount of any rebate or kickback, plus reasonable attorney's fees and costs, in addition to any other remedies provided by law.

(3) No violation of this subdivision shall affect the validity of a sale in favor of a bona fide purchaser or the rights of an encumbrancer for value without notice.

(d) It shall not be unlawful for a trustee to pay or offer to pay a fee to an agent or subagent of the trustee for work performed by the agent or subagent in discharging the trustee's obligations under the terms of the deed of trust. Any payment of a fee by a trustee to an agent or subagent of the trustee for work performed by the agent or subagent in discharging the trustee's obligations under the terms of the deed of trust shall be conclusively presumed to be lawful and valid if the fee, when combined with other fees of the trustee, does not exceed in the aggregate the trustee's fee authorized by subdivision (d) of Section 2924c or subdivision (a) or (b) of this section.

(e) When a court issues a decree of foreclosure, it shall have discretion to award attorney's fees, costs, and expenses as are reasonable, if provided for in the note, deed of trust, or mortgage, pursuant to Section 580c of the Code of Civil Procedure.

(f) This section shall remain in effect only until January 1, 2031, and as of that date is repealed. **Leg.H.** Added Stats 1983 ch 1217 §2. Amended Stats 1984 ch 1730 §2; Stats 1985 ch 560 §1, ch 1206 §4; Stats 1993 ch 686 §5 (AB 1219); Stats 1997 ch 74 §3 (SB 665); Stats 2001 ch 438 §4 (SB 958), effective October 2, 2001, operative January 1, 2002; Stats 2016 ch 170 §4 (SB 983), effective January 1, 2017; Stats 2017 ch 217 §2 (SB 479), effective January 1, 2018; Stats 2022 ch 642 §1 (AB 1837), effective January 1, 2023, repealed January 1, 2031.

Prior Law: Former CC §2924d, relating to cure of defects in chattel mortgages, purchase contracts, etc., was added Stats 1941 ch 135 §1, effective April 17, 1941, and repealed Stats 1972 ch 1056 §2.

§ 2924d. Right to reimbursement for costs and expenses of enforcement; Trustee's or attorney's fees; Prohibition against kickbacks [Operative January 1, 2031]

(a)(1) Commencing with the date that the notice of sale is deposited in the mail, as provided in Section 2924b, and until the property is sold pursuant to the power of sale contained in the mortgage or deed of trust, a beneficiary, trustee, mortgagee, or their agent or successor in interest may demand and receive from a trustor, mortgagor, or their agent or successor in interest or any beneficiary under a subordinate deed of trust, or any other person having a subordinate lien or encumbrance of record those reasonable costs and expenses, to the extent allowed by subdivision (c) of Section 2924c, that are actually incurred in enforcing the terms of the obligation and trustee's or attorney's fees that are hereby authorized to be in an amount as follows:

(A) If the unpaid principal sum secured is fifty thousand dollars ($50,000) or less, then in a base amount that does not exceed four hundred seventy-five dollars ($475).

(B) If the unpaid principal sum secured is greater than fifty thousand dollars ($50,000) but does not exceed one hundred fifty thousand dollars ($150,000), then in a base amount that does not exceed four hundred seventy-five dollars ($475) plus 1 percent of the unpaid principal sum secured exceeding fifty thousand dollars ($50,000).

(C) If the unpaid principal sum secured is greater than one hundred fifty thousand dollars ($150,000) but does not exceed five hundred thousand dollars ($500,000), then in a base amount that does not exceed four hundred ten dollars ($410) plus 1 percent of the unpaid principal sum secured exceeding fifty thousand dollars ($50,000) up to and including one hundred fifty thousand dollars ($150,000), plus one-half of 1 percent of any portion of the unpaid principal sum secured exceeding one hundred fifty thousand dollars ($150,000).

(D) If the unpaid principal sum secured exceeds five hundred thousand dollars ($500,000), then in a base amount that does not exceed four hundred ten dollars ($410) plus 1 percent of the unpaid principal sum secured exceeding fifty thousand dollars ($50,000) up to and including one hundred fifty thousand dollars ($150,000), plus one-half of 1 percent of any portion of the unpaid principal sum secured exceeding one hundred fifty thousand dollars ($150,000) up to and including five hundred thousand dollars ($500,000), plus one-quarter of 1 percent of any portion of the unpaid principal sum secured exceeding five hundred thousand dollars ($500,000).

(2) For purposes of this subdivision, the unpaid principal sum secured shall be determined as of the date the notice of default is recorded. Any charge for trustee's or attorney's fees authorized by this subdivision shall be conclusively presumed to be lawful and valid where that charge does not exceed the amounts authorized in this subdivision. Any charge for trustee's or attorney's fees made pursuant to this subdivision shall be in lieu of and not in addition to those charges authorized by subdivision (d) of Section 2924c.

(b) Upon the sale of property pursuant to a power of sale, a trustee, or their agent or successor in interest, may demand and receive from a beneficiary, or their agent or successor in interest, or may deduct from the proceeds of the sale, those reasonable costs and expenses, to the extent allowed by subdivision (c) of Section 2924c, that are actually incurred in enforcing the terms of the obligation and trustee's or attorney's fees that are hereby authorized to be in an amount which does not exceed four hundred seventy-five dollars ($475) or 1 percent of the unpaid principal sum secured, whichever is greater. For purposes of this subdivision, the unpaid principal sum secured shall be determined as of the date the notice of default is recorded. Any charge for trustee's or attorney's fees authorized by this subdivision shall be conclusively presumed to be lawful and valid where that charge does not exceed the amount authorized herein. Any charges for trustee's or attorney's fees made pursuant to this subdivision shall be in lieu of and not in addition to those charges authorized by subdivision (a) of this section and subdivision (d) of Section 2924c.

(c)(1) No person shall pay or offer to pay or collect any rebate or kickback for the referral of business involving the performance of any act required by this article.

(2) Any person who violates this subdivision shall be liable to the trustor for three times the amount of any rebate or kickback, plus reasonable attorney's fees and costs, in addition to any other remedies provided by law.

(3) No violation of this subdivision shall affect the validity of a sale in favor of a bona fide purchaser or the rights of an encumbrancer for value without notice.

(d) It shall not be unlawful for a trustee to pay or offer to pay a fee to an agent or subagent of the trustee for work performed by the agent or subagent in discharging the trustee's obligations under the terms of the deed of trust. Any payment of a fee by a trustee to an agent or subagent of the trustee for work performed by the agent or subagent in discharging the trustee's obligations under the terms of the deed of trust shall be conclusively presumed to be lawful and valid if the fee, when combined with other fees of the trustee, does not exceed in the aggregate the trustee's fee authorized by subdivision (d) of Section 2924c or subdivision (a) or (b) of this section.

(e) When a court issues a decree of foreclosure, it shall have discretion to award attorney's fees, costs, and expenses as are reasonable, if provided for in the note, deed of trust, or mortgage, pursuant to Section 580c of the Code of Civil Procedure.

(f) This section shall be operative January 1, 2031. **Leg.H.** Added Stats 2022 ch 642 §2 (AB 1837), effective January 1, 2023, operative January 1, 2031.

§2924e. Junior mortgagee's request to senior lienor for notice of delinquencies; Liability for failure to give notice

(a) The beneficiary or mortgagee of any deed of trust or mortgage on real property either containing one to four residential units or given to secure an original obligation not to exceed three hundred thousand dollars ($300,000) may, with the written consent of the trustor or mortgagor that is either effected through a signed and dated agreement which shall be separate from other loan and security documents or disclosed to the trustor or mortgagor in at least 10-point type, submit a written request by certified mail to the beneficiary or mortgagee of any lien which is senior to the lien of the requester, for written notice of any or all delinquencies of four months or more, in payments of principal or interest on any obligation secured by that senior lien notwithstanding that the loan secured by the lien of the requester is not then in default as to payments of principal or interest.

The request shall be sent to the beneficiary or mortgagee, or agent which it might designate for the purpose of receiving loan payments, at the address specified for the receipt of these payments, if known, or, if not known, at the address shown on the recorded deed of trust or mortgage.

(b) The request for notice shall identify the ownership or security interest of the requester, the date on which the interest of the requester will terminate as evidenced by the maturity date of the note of the trustor or mortgagor in favor of the requester, the name of the trustor or mortgagor and the name of the current owner of the security property if different from the trustor or mortgagor, the street address or other description of the security property, the loan number (if available to the requester) of the loan secured by the senior lien, the name and address to which notice is to be sent, and shall include or be accompanied by the signed written consent of the trustor or mortgagor, and a fee of forty dollars ($40). For obligations secured by residential properties, the request shall remain valid until withdrawn in writing and shall be applicable to all delinquencies as provided in this section, which occur prior to the date on which the interest of the requester will terminate as specified in the request or the expiration date, as appropriate. For obligations secured by nonresidential properties, the request shall remain valid until withdrawn in writing and shall be applicable to all delinquencies as provided in this section, which occur prior to the date on which the interest of the requester will terminate as specified in the request or the expiration date, as appropriate. The beneficiary or mortgagee of obligations secured by nonresidential properties that have sent five or more notices prior to the expiration of the effective period of the request may charge a fee up to fifteen dollars ($15) for each subsequent notice. A request for notice shall be effective for five years from the mailing of the request or the recording of that request, whichever occurs later, and may be renewed within six months prior to its expiration date by sending the beneficiary or mortgagee, or agent, as the case may be, at the address to which original requests for notice are to be sent, a copy of the earlier request for notice together with a signed statement that the request is renewed and a renewal fee of fifteen dollars ($15). Upon timely submittal of a renewal request for notice, the effectiveness of the original request is continued for five years from the time when it would otherwise have lapsed. Succeeding renewal requests may be submitted in the same manner. The request for notice and renewals thereof shall be recorded in the office of the county recorder of the county in which the security real property is situated. The rights and obligations specified in this section shall inure to the benefit of, or pass to, as the case may be, successors in interest of parties specified in this section. Any successor in interest of a party entitled to notice under this section shall file a request for that notice with any beneficiary or mortgagee of the senior lien and shall pay a processing fee of fifteen dollars ($15). No new written consent shall be required from the trustor or mortgagor.

(c) Unless the delinquency has been cured, within 15 days following the end of four months from any delinquency in payments of principal or interest on any obligation secured by the senior lien which delinquency exists or occurs on or after 10 days from the mailing of the request for notice or the recording of that request, whichever occurs later, the beneficiary or mortgagee shall give written notice to the requester of the fact of any delinquency and the amount thereof.

The notice shall be given by personal service, or by deposit in the mail, first-class postage paid. Following the recording of any notice of default pursuant to Section 2924 with respect to the same delinquency, no notice or further notice shall be required pursuant to this section.

(d) If the beneficiary or mortgagee of any such senior lien fails to give notice to the requester as required in subdivision (c), and a subsequent foreclosure or trustee's sale of the security property occurs, the beneficiary or mortgagee shall be liable to the requester for any monetary damage due to the failure to provide notice within the time period specified in subdivision (c) which the requester has sustained from the date on which notice should have been given to the earlier of the date on which the notice is given or the date of the recording of the notice of default under Section 2924, and shall also forfeit to the requester the sum of three hundred dollars ($300). A showing by the beneficiary or mortgagee by a preponderance of the evidence that the failure to provide timely notice as required by subdivision (c) resulted from a bona fide error notwithstanding the maintenance of procedures reasonably adapted to avoid any such error shall be a defense to any liability for that failure.

(e) If any beneficiary or mortgagee, or agent which it had designated for the purpose of receiving loan payments, has been succeeded in interest by any other person, any request for notice received pursuant to this section shall be transmitted promptly to that person.

(f) Any failure to comply with the provisions of this section shall not affect the validity of a sale in favor of a bona fide purchaser or the rights of an encumbrancer for value and without notice.

(g) Upon satisfaction of an obligation secured by a junior lien with respect to which a notice request was made pursuant to this section, the beneficiary or mortgagee that made the request shall communicate that fact in writing to the senior lienholder to whom the request was made. The communication shall specify that provision of notice pursuant to the prior request under this section is no longer required. **Leg.H.** Added Stats 1984 ch 1331 §1, operative July 1, 1985. Amended Stats 1986 ch 618 §1; Stats 1988 ch 510 §1; Stats 1990 ch 788 §1 (SB 2042).

§2924f. Notice of sale; Posting, publication, and recording; Contents; Place of sale; Bids prior to sale; Postponement of sale [Repealed January 1, 2031]

(a) As used in this section and Sections 2924g and 2924h, "property" means real property or a leasehold estate therein, and "calendar week" means Monday through Saturday, inclusive.

(b)(1) Except as provided in subdivision (c), before any sale of property can be made under the power of sale contained in any deed of trust or mortgage, or any resale resulting from a rescission for a failure of consideration pursuant to subdivision (c) of Section 2924h, notice of the sale thereof shall be given by posting a written notice of the time of sale and of the street address and the specific place at the street address where the sale will be held, and describing the property to be sold, at least 20 days before the date of sale in one public place in the city where the property is to be sold, if the property is to be sold in a city, or, if not, then in one public place in the county seat of the county where the property is to be sold, and publishing a copy once a week for three consecutive calendar weeks.

(2) The first publication to be at least 20 days before the date of sale, in a newspaper of general circulation published in the public notice district in which the property or some part thereof is situated, or in case no newspaper of general circulation is published in the public notice district, in a newspaper of general circulation published in the county in which the property or some part thereof is situated, or in case no newspaper of general circulation is published in the public notice district or county, as the case may be, in a newspaper of general circulation published in the county in this state that is contiguous to the county in which the property or some part thereof is situated and has, by comparison with all similarly contiguous counties, the highest population based upon total county population as determined by the most recent federal decennial census published by the Bureau of the Census. For the purposes of this section, publication of notice in a public notice district is governed by Chapter 1.1 (commencing with Section 6080) of Division 7 of Title 1 of the Government Code.

(3) A copy of the notice of sale shall also be posted in a conspicuous place on the property to be sold at least 20 days before the date of sale, where possible and where not restricted for any reason. If the property is a single-family residence the posting shall be on a door of the residence, but, if not possible or restricted, then the notice shall be posted in a conspicuous place on the property; however, if access is denied because a common entrance to the property is restricted by a guard gate or similar impediment, the property may be posted at that guard gate or similar impediment to any development community.

(4) The notice of sale shall conform to the minimum requirements of Section 6043 of the Government Code and be recorded with the county recorder of the county in which the property or some part thereof is situated at least 20 days prior to the date of sale.

(5) The notice of sale shall contain the name, street address in this state, which may reflect an agent of the trustee, and either a toll-free telephone number or telephone number in this state of the trustee, and the name of the original trustor, and also shall contain the statement required by paragraph (3) of subdivision (c). In addition to any other description of the property, the notice shall describe the property by giving its street address, if any, or other common designation, if any, and a county assessor's parcel number; but if the property has no street address or other common designation, the notice shall contain a legal description of the property, the name and address of the beneficiary at whose request the sale is to be conducted, and a statement that directions may be obtained pursuant to a written request submitted to the beneficiary within 10 days from the first publication of the notice. Directions shall be deemed reasonably sufficient to locate the property if information as to the location of the property is given by reference to the direction and approximate distance from the nearest crossroads, frontage road, or access road. If a legal description or a county assessor's parcel number and either a street address or another common designation of the property is given, the validity of the notice and the validity of the sale shall not be affected by the fact that the street address, other common designation, name and address of the beneficiary, or the directions obtained therefrom are erroneous or that the street address, other common designation, name and address of the beneficiary, or directions obtained therefrom are omitted.

(6) The term "newspaper of general circulation," as used in this section, has the same meaning as defined in Article 1 (commencing with Section 6000) of Chapter 1 of Division 7 of Title 1 of the Government Code.

(7) The notice of sale shall contain a statement of the total amount of the unpaid balance of the obligation secured by the property to be sold and reasonably estimated costs, expenses, advances at the time of the initial publication of the notice of sale, and, if republished pursuant to a cancellation of a cash equivalent pursuant to subdivision (d) of Section 2924h, a reference of that fact; provided, that the trustee shall incur no liability for any good faith error in stating the proper amount, including any amount provided in good faith by or on behalf of the beneficiary. An inaccurate statement of this amount shall not affect the validity of any sale to a bona fide purchaser for value, nor shall the failure to post the notice of sale on a door as provided by this subdivision affect the validity of any sale to a bona fide purchaser for value.

(8)(A) On and after April 1, 2012, if the deed of trust or mortgage containing a power of sale is secured by real property containing from one to four single-family residences, the notice of sale shall contain substantially the following language, in addition to the language required pursuant to paragraphs (1) to (7), inclusive:

NOTICE TO POTENTIAL BIDDERS: If you are considering bidding on this property lien, you should understand that there are risks involved in bidding at a trustee auction. You will be bidding on a lien, not on the property itself. Placing the highest bid at a trustee auction does not automatically entitle you to free and clear ownership of the property. You should also be aware that the lien being auctioned off may be a junior lien. If you are the highest bidder at the auction, you are or may be responsible for paying off all liens senior to the lien being auctioned off, before you can receive clear title to the property. You are encouraged to investigate the existence, priority, and size of outstanding liens that may exist on this property by contacting the county recorder's office or a title insurance company, either of which may charge you a fee for this information. If you consult either of these resources, you should be aware that the same lender may hold more than one mortgage or deed of trust on the property.

NOTICE TO PROPERTY OWNER: The sale date shown on this notice of sale may be postponed one or more times by the mortgagee, beneficiary, trustee, or a court, pursuant to Section 2924g of the California Civil Code. The law requires that information about trustee sale postponements be made available to you and to the public, as a courtesy to those not present at the sale. If you wish to learn whether your sale date has been postponed, and, if applicable, the rescheduled time and date for the sale of this property, you may call [telephone number for information regarding the trustee's sale] or visit this internet website [internet website address for information regarding the sale of this property], using the file number assigned to this case [case file number]. Information about postponements that are very short in duration or that occur close in time to the scheduled sale may not immediately be reflected in the telephone information or on the internet website. The best way to verify postponement information is to attend the scheduled sale.

NOTICE TO TENANT: You may have a right to purchase this property after the trustee auction pursuant to Section 2924m of the California Civil Code. If you are an "eligible tenant buyer," you can purchase the property if you match the last and highest bid placed at the trustee auction. If you are an "eligible bidder," you may be able to purchase the property if you exceed the last and highest bid placed at the trustee auction. There are three steps to exercising this right of purchase. First, 48 hours after the date of the trustee sale, you can call [telephone number for information regarding the trustee's sale], or visit this internet website [internet website address for information regarding the sale of this property], using the file number assigned to this case [case file number] to find the date on which the trustee's sale was held, the amount of the last and highest bid, and the address of the trustee. Second, you must send a written notice of intent to place a bid so that the trustee receives it no more than 15 days after the trustee's sale. Third, you must submit a bid so that the trustee receives it no more than 45 days after the trustee's sale. If you think you may qualify as an "eligible tenant buyer" or "eligible bidder," you should consider contacting an attorney or appropriate real estate professional immediately for advice regarding this potential right to purchase.

(B) A mortgagee, beneficiary, trustee, or authorized agent shall make a good faith effort to provide up-to-date information regarding sale dates and postponements to persons who wish this information. This information shall be made available free of charge. It may be made available via an internet website, a telephone recording that is accessible 24 hours a day, seven days a week, or through any other means that allows 24 hours a day, seven days a week, no-cost access to updated information. A disruption of any of these methods of providing sale date and postponement information to allow for reasonable maintenance or due to a service outage shall not be deemed to be a violation of the good faith standard.

(C) Except as provided in subparagraph (B), nothing in the wording of the notices required by subparagraph (A) is intended to modify or create any substantive rights or obligations for any person providing, or specified in, either of the required notices. Failure to comply with subparagraph (A) or (B) shall not invalidate any sale that would otherwise be valid under this section.

(D) Information provided pursuant to subparagraph (A) does not constitute the public declaration required by subdivision (d) of Section 2924g.

(E) For purposes of a property subject to this paragraph and of satisfying the requirements of Section 2924m, a trustee or an authorized agent shall maintain an internet website and a telephone number to provide information on applicable properties to persons who wish the information. In addition to any other information required by subparagraph (B), a trustee or an authorized agent shall provide information regarding the sale date, amount of the last and highest bid, and the trustee's address, to be accessible using the file number assigned to the case and listed on the NOTICE TO TENANT required by subparagraph (A). This information shall be made available free of charge and shall be available 24 hours a day, seven days a week.

(9) If the sale of the property is to be a unified sale as provided in subparagraph (B) of paragraph (1) of subdivision (a) of Section 9604 of the Commercial Code, the notice of sale shall also contain a description of the personal property or fixtures to be sold. In the case where it is contemplated that all of the personal property or fixtures are to be sold, the description in the notice of the personal property or fixtures shall be sufficient if it is the same as the description of the personal property or fixtures contained in the agreement creating the security interest in or encumbrance on the personal property or fixtures or the filed financing statement relating to the personal property or fixtures. In all other cases, the description in the notice shall be sufficient if it would be a sufficient description of the personal property or fixtures under Section 9108 of the Commercial Code. Inclusion of a reference to or a description of personal property or fixtures in a notice of sale hereunder shall not constitute an election by the secured party to conduct a unified sale pursuant to subparagraph (B) of paragraph (1) of subdivision (a) of Section 9604 of the Commercial Code, shall not obligate the secured party to conduct a unified sale pursuant to subparagraph (B) of paragraph (1) of subdivision (a) of Section 9604 of the Commercial Code, and in no way shall render defective or noncomplying either that notice or a sale pursuant to that notice by reason of the fact that the sale includes none or less than all of the personal property or fixtures referred to or described in the notice. This paragraph shall not otherwise affect the obligations or duties of a secured party under the Commercial Code.

(c)(1) This subdivision applies only to deeds of trust or mortgages which contain a power of sale and which are secured by real property containing a single-family, owner-occupied residence, where the obligation secured by the deed of trust or mortgage is contained in a contract for goods or services subject to the provisions of the Unruh Act (Chapter 1 (commencing with Section 1801) of Title 2 of Part 4 of Division 3).

(2) Except as otherwise expressly set forth in this subdivision, all other provisions of law relating to the exercise of a power of sale shall govern the exercise of a power of sale contained in a deed of trust or mortgage described in paragraph (1).

(3) If any default of the obligation secured by a deed of trust or mortgage described in paragraph (1) has not been cured within 30 days after the recordation of the notice of default, the trustee or mortgagee shall mail to the trustor or mortgagor, at their last known address, a copy of the following statement:

YOU ARE IN DEFAULT UNDER A
_____
(Deed of trust or mortgage)
DATED _____. UNLESS YOU TAKE ACTION TO PROTECT YOUR PROPERTY, IT MAY BE SOLD AT A PUBLIC SALE. IF YOU NEED AN EXPLANATION OF THE NATURE OF THE PROCEEDING AGAINST YOU, YOU SHOULD CONTACT A LAWYER.

(4) All sales of real property pursuant to a power of sale contained in any deed of trust or mortgage described in paragraph (1) shall be held in the county where the residence is located and shall be made to the person making the highest offer. The trustee may receive offers during the 10-day period immediately prior to the date of sale and if any offer is accepted in writing by both the trustor or mortgagor and the beneficiary or mortgagee prior to the time set for sale, the sale shall be postponed to a date certain and prior to which the property may be conveyed by the trustor to the person making the offer according to its terms. The offer is revocable until accepted. The performance of the offer, following acceptance, according to its terms, by a conveyance of the property to the offeror, shall operate to terminate any further proceeding under the notice of sale and it shall be deemed revoked.

(5) In addition to the trustee fee pursuant to Section 2924c, the trustee or mortgagee pursuant to a deed of trust or mortgage subject to this subdivision shall be entitled to charge an additional fee of fifty dollars ($50).

(6) This subdivision applies only to property on which notices of default were filed on or after the effective date of this subdivision.

(d) With respect to residential real property containing no more than four dwelling units, a separate document containing a summary of the notice of sale information in English and the languages described in Section 1632 shall be attached to the notice of sale provided to the mortgagor or trustor pursuant to Section 2923.3.

(e)(1) With respect to residential real property containing no more than four dwelling units that is subject to a power of sale contained in any deed of trust or mortgage, a sale of the property under the power of sale shall not be conducted until the expiration of an additional 45 days following the scheduled date of sale pursuant to subdivision (a) or (c) of Section 2924g if the trustee receives, at least five business days before the scheduled date of sale, from the mortgagor or trustor, by certified mail with the United States Postal Service or by another overnight mail courier service with tracking information that confirms the recipient's signature and the date and time of receipt and delivery, a listing agreement with a California licensed real estate broker to be placed in a publicly available marketing platform for the sale of the property at least five business days before the scheduled date of sale. The provisions of this paragraph shall not be used to postpone the scheduled sale date more than once.

(2) If a scheduled date of sale is postponed pursuant to paragraph (1), the trustor's or mortgagor's right to reinstate the account shall be extended, calculated pursuant to subdivision (e) of Section 2924c based on the new scheduled date of sale.

(3) If a scheduled date of sale has been postponed pursuant to paragraph (1) and the trustee receives, at least five business days before the scheduled date of sale, from the mortgagor or trustor, by certified mail with the United States Postal Service or by another overnight mail courier service with tracking information that confirms the recipient's signature and the date and time of receipt and delivery, a copy of a purchase agreement for the sale of the property at least five business days before the scheduled sale, the trustee shall postpone the scheduled date of sale to a date that is at least 45 days after the date on which the purchase agreement was received by the trustee. The provisions of this paragraph shall not be used to postpone the scheduled sale date more than once.

(4) For purposes of this subdivision, "purchase agreement" means a bona fide and fully executed contract for the sale of the property that is subject to a power of sale with a purchase price amount equal to or greater than the amount of the unpaid balance of all obligations of record secured by the property that includes the name of the buyer, the sales price, the agreed closing date, and acceptance by the designated escrow agent.

(f)(1) With respect to residential real property containing no more than four dwelling units that is subject to a power of sale contained in a first lien deed of trust or mortgage, the mortgagee, beneficiary, or authorized agent shall provide to the trustee a fair market value of the property at least 10 days prior to the initially scheduled date of sale, and the trustee shall not sell the property at the initially scheduled date of sale for less than 67 percent of that fair market value of the property. The trustee may rely on the fair market value provided pursuant to this paragraph, and shall not have a duty to verify the source or accuracy of the valuation.

(2) If the property remains unsold after the initial trustee's sale pursuant to paragraph (1), then the trustee shall postpone the sale for at least seven days, and the property may be sold to the highest bidder.

(3) For purposes of this subdivision, "fair market value of the property" means an estimate of the fair market value of the property

made within six months of the initially scheduled date of sale and determined by an opinion of a licensed real estate broker, an appraisal from a licensed appraiser, a value from a commercially utilized automated valuation model, or a value from a computerized property valuation system that is used to derive a real property value.

(4) A failure to comply with the provisions of paragraph (1) shall not affect the validity of a trustee's sale or a sale to a bona fide purchaser for value.

(5) The provisions of this subdivision shall apply to the initial trustee's sale for each notice of sale issued pursuant to subdivision (b) of Section 2924f.

[1] **(g)** This section shall remain in effect only until January 1, 2031, and as of that date is repealed, unless a later enacted statute that is enacted before January 1, 2031, deletes or extends that date. **Leg.H.** Added Stats 2010 ch 597 §2 (AB 2347), effective January 1, 2011, operative January 1, 2013. Amended Stats 2011 ch 229 §2 (SB 4), effective January 1, 2012, operative January 1, 2013; Stats 2012 ch 556 §4 (AB 1599), effective January 1, 2013; Stats 2016 ch 703 §3 (AB 2881), effective January 1, 2017; Stats 2020 ch 202 §1 (SB 1079), effective January 1, 2021, repealed January 1, 2026; Stats 2020 ch 203 §1.3 (SB 1148), effective January 1, 2021, repealed January 1, 2026 (ch 203 prevails); Stats 2022 ch 642 §3 (AB 1837), effective January 1, 2023, repealed January 1, 2031; Stats 2023 ch 131 §14 (AB 1754), effective January 1, 2024, repealed January 1, 2031; Stats 2024 ch 311 §3 (AB 2424), effective January 1, 2025, repealed January 1, 2031.

§2924f. 2024 Deletes. [1] (e)

Prior Law: Former CC §2924f was enacted in 1972 and repealed operative January 1, 2013, by its own provisions. Stats 2011 ch 229 (SB 4) §1.

§ 2924f. Notice of sale; Posting, publication, and recording; Contents; Place of sale; Bids prior to sale; Postponement of sale [Operative January 1, 2031]

(a) As used in this section and Sections 2924g and 2924h, "property" means real property or a leasehold estate therein, and "calendar week" means Monday through Saturday, inclusive.

(b)(1) Except as provided in subdivision (c), before any sale of property can be made under the power of sale contained in any deed of trust or mortgage, or any resale resulting from a rescission for a failure of consideration pursuant to subdivision (c) of Section 2924h, notice of the sale thereof shall be given by posting a written notice of the time of sale and of the street address and the specific place at the street address where the sale will be held, and describing the property to be sold, at least 20 days before the date of sale in one public place in the city where the property is to be sold, if the property is to be sold in a city, or, if not, then in one public place in the county seat of the county where the property is to be sold, and publishing a copy once a week for three consecutive calendar weeks.

(2) The first publication to be at least 20 days before the date of sale, in a newspaper of general circulation published in the public notice district in which the property or some part thereof is situated, or in case no newspaper of general circulation is published in the public notice district, in a newspaper of general circulation published in the county in which the property or some part thereof is situated, or in case no newspaper of general circulation is published in the public notice district or county, as the case may be, in a newspaper of general circulation published in the county in this state that is contiguous to the county in which the property or some part thereof is situated and has, by comparison with all similarly contiguous counties, the highest population based upon total county population as determined by the most recent federal decennial census published by the Bureau of the Census. For the purposes of this section, publication of notice in a public notice district is governed by Chapter 1.1 (commencing with Section 6080) of Division 7 of Title 1 of the Government Code.

(3) A copy of the notice of sale shall also be posted in a conspicuous place on the property to be sold at least 20 days before the date of sale, where possible and where not restricted for any reason. If the property is a single-family residence the posting shall be on a door of the residence, but, if not possible or restricted, then the notice shall be posted in a conspicuous place on the property; however, if access is denied because a common entrance to the property is restricted by a guard gate or similar impediment, the property may be posted at that guard gate or similar impediment to any development community.

(4) The notice of sale shall conform to the minimum requirements of Section 6043 of the Government Code and be recorded with the county recorder of the county in which the property or some part thereof is situated at least 20 days prior to the date of sale.

(5) The notice of sale shall contain the name, street address in this state, which may reflect an agent of the trustee, and either a toll-free telephone number or telephone number in this state of the trustee, and the name of the original trustor, and also shall contain the statement required by paragraph (3) of subdivision (c). In addition to any other description of the property, the notice shall describe the property by giving its street address, if any, or other common designation, if any, and a county assessor's parcel number; but if the property has no street address or other common designation, the notice shall contain a legal description of the property, the name and address of the beneficiary at whose request the sale is to be conducted, and a statement that directions may be obtained pursuant to a written request submitted to the beneficiary within 10 days from the first publication of the notice. Directions shall be deemed reasonably sufficient to locate the property if information as to the location of the property is given by reference to the direction and approximate distance from the nearest crossroads, frontage road, or access road. If a legal description or a county assessor's parcel number and either a street address or another common designation of the property is given, the validity of the notice and the validity of the sale shall not be affected by the fact that the street address, other common designation, name and address of the beneficiary, or the directions obtained therefrom are erroneous or that the street address, other common designation, name and address of the beneficiary, or directions obtained therefrom are omitted.

(6) The term "newspaper of general circulation," as used in this section, has the same meaning as defined in Article 1 (commencing with Section 6000) of Chapter 1 of Division 7 of Title 1 of the Government Code.

(7) The notice of sale shall contain a statement of the total amount of the unpaid balance of the obligation secured by the property to be sold and reasonably estimated costs, expenses, advances at the time of the initial publication of the notice of sale, and, if republished pursuant to a cancellation of a cash equivalent pursuant to subdivision (d) of Section 2924h, a reference of that fact; provided, that the trustee shall incur no liability for any good faith error in stating the proper amount, including any amount provided in good faith by or on behalf of the beneficiary. An inaccurate statement of this amount shall not affect the validity of any sale to a bona fide purchaser for value, nor shall the failure to post the notice of sale on a door as provided by this subdivision affect the validity of any sale to a bona fide purchaser for value.

(8)(A) On and after April 1, 2012, if the deed of trust or mortgage containing a power of sale is secured by real property containing from one to four single-family residences, the notice of sale shall contain substantially the following language, in addition to the language required pursuant to paragraphs (1) to (7), inclusive:

NOTICE TO POTENTIAL BIDDERS: If you are considering bidding on this property lien, you should understand that there are risks involved in bidding at a trustee auction. You will be bidding on a lien, not on the property itself. Placing the highest bid at a trustee auction does not automatically entitle you to free and clear ownership of the property. You should also be aware that the lien being auctioned off may be a junior lien. If you are the highest bidder at the auction, you are or may be responsible for paying off all liens senior to the lien being auctioned off, before you can receive clear title to the property. You are encouraged to investigate the existence, priority, and size of outstanding liens that may exist on this property by contacting the county recorder's office or a title insurance company, either of which may charge you a fee for this information. If you consult either of these resources, you should be aware that the same lender may hold more than one mortgage or deed of trust on the property.

NOTICE TO PROPERTY OWNER: The sale date shown on this notice of sale may be postponed one or more times by the mortgagee, beneficiary, trustee, or a court, pursuant to Section 2924g of the California Civil Code. The law requires that information about trustee sale postponements be made available to you and to the public, as a courtesy to those not present at the sale. If you wish to learn whether your sale date has been postponed, and, if applicable, the rescheduled time and date for the sale of this property, you may call [telephone number for information regarding the trustee's sale] or visit this internet website [internet website address for information regarding the sale of this property], using the file number assigned to this case [case file number]. Information about postponements that are very short in duration or that occur close in time to the scheduled sale may not immediately be reflected in the telephone information or on the internet website. The best way to verify postponement information is to attend the scheduled sale.

(B) A mortgagee, beneficiary, trustee, or authorized agent shall make a good faith effort to provide up-to-date information regarding sale dates and postponements to persons who wish this information. This information shall be made available free of charge. It may be made available via an internet website, a telephone recording that is accessible 24 hours a day, seven days a week, or through any other means that allows 24 hours a day, seven days a week, no-cost access to updated information. A disruption of any of these methods of providing sale date and postponement information to allow for reasonable maintenance or due to a service outage shall not be deemed to be a violation of the good faith standard.

(C) Except as provided in subparagraph (B), nothing in the wording of the notices required by subparagraph (A) is intended to modify or create any substantive rights or obligations for any person providing, or specified in, either of the required notices. Failure to comply with subparagraph (A) or (B) shall not invalidate any sale that would otherwise be valid under this section.

(D) Information provided pursuant to subparagraph (A) does not constitute the public declaration required by subdivision (d) of Section 2924g.

(9) If the sale of the property is to be a unified sale as provided in subparagraph (B) of paragraph (1) of subdivision (a) of Section 9604 of the Commercial Code, the notice of sale shall also contain a description of the personal property or fixtures to be sold. In the case where it is contemplated that all of the personal property or fixtures are to be sold, the description in the notice of the personal property or fixtures shall be sufficient if it is the same as the description of the personal property or fixtures contained in the agreement creating the security interest in or encumbrance on the personal property or fixtures or the filed financing statement relating to the personal property or fixtures. In all other cases, the description in the notice shall be sufficient if it would be a sufficient description of the personal property or fixtures under Section 9108 of the Commercial Code. Inclusion of a reference to or a description of personal property or fixtures in a notice of sale hereunder shall not constitute an election by the secured party to conduct a unified sale pursuant to subparagraph (B) of paragraph (1) of subdivision (a) of Section 9604 of the Commercial Code, shall not obligate the secured party to conduct a unified sale pursuant to subparagraph (B) of paragraph (1) of subdivision (a) of Section 9604 of the Commercial Code, and in no way shall render defective or noncomplying either that notice or a sale pursuant to that notice by reason of the fact that the sale includes none or less than all of the personal property or fixtures referred to or described in the notice. This paragraph shall not otherwise affect the obligations or duties of a secured party under the Commercial Code.

(c)(1) This subdivision applies only to deeds of trust or mortgages which contain a power of sale and which are secured by real property containing a single-family, owner-occupied residence, where the obligation secured by the deed of trust or mortgage is contained in a contract for goods or services subject to the provisions of the Unruh Act (Chapter 1 (commencing with Section 1801) of Title 2 of Part 4 of Division 3).

(2) Except as otherwise expressly set forth in this subdivision, all other provisions of law relating to the exercise of a power of sale shall govern the exercise of a power of sale contained in a deed of trust or mortgage described in paragraph (1).

(3) If any default of the obligation secured by a deed of trust or mortgage described in paragraph (1) has not been cured within 30 days after the recordation of the notice of default, the trustee or mortgagee shall mail to the trustor or mortgagor, at their last known address, a copy of the following statement:

YOU ARE IN DEFAULT UNDER A

_____,

(Deed of trust or mortgage)
DATED . UNLESS YOU TAKE ACTION TO PROTECT YOUR PROPERTY, IT MAY BE SOLD AT A PUBLIC SALE. IF YOU NEED AN EXPLANATION OF THE NATURE OF THE PROCEEDING AGAINST YOU, YOU SHOULD CONTACT A LAWYER.

(4) All sales of real property pursuant to a power of sale contained in any deed of trust or mortgage described in paragraph (1) shall be held in the county where the residence is located and shall be made to the person making the highest offer. The trustee may receive offers during the 10-day period immediately prior to the date of sale and if any offer is accepted in writing by both the trustor or mortgagor and the beneficiary or mortgagee prior to the time set for sale, the sale shall be postponed to a date certain and prior to which the property may be conveyed by the trustor to the person making the offer according to its terms. The offer is revocable until accepted. The performance of the offer, following acceptance, according to its terms, by a conveyance of the property to the offeror, shall operate to terminate any further proceeding under the notice of sale and it shall be deemed revoked.

(5) In addition to the trustee fee pursuant to Section 2924c, the trustee or mortgagee pursuant to a deed of trust or mortgage subject to this subdivision shall be entitled to charge an additional fee of fifty dollars ($50).

(6) This subdivision applies only to property on which notices of default were filed on or after the effective date of this subdivision.

(d) With respect to residential real property containing no more than four dwelling units, a separate document containing a summary of the notice of sale information in English and the languages described in Section 1632 shall be attached to the notice of sale provided to the mortgagor or trustor pursuant to Section 2923.3.

(e)(1) With respect to residential real property containing no more than four dwelling units that is subject to a power of sale contained in any deed of trust or mortgage, a sale of the property under the power of sale shall not be conducted until the expiration of an additional 45 days following the scheduled date of sale pursuant to subdivision (a) or (c) of Section 2924g if the trustee receives, at least five business days before the scheduled date of sale, from the mortgagor or trustor, by certified mail with the United States Postal Service or by another overnight mail courier service with tracking information that confirms the recipient's signature and the date and time of receipt and delivery, a listing agreement with a California licensed real estate broker to be placed in a publicly available marketing platform for the sale of the property at least five business days before the scheduled date of sale. The provisions of this paragraph shall not be used to postpone the scheduled sale date more than once.

(2) If a scheduled date of sale is postponed pursuant to paragraph (1), the trustor's or mortgagor's right to reinstate the account shall be extended, calculated pursuant to subdivision (e) of Section 2924c based on the new scheduled date of sale.

(3) If a scheduled date of sale has been postponed pursuant to paragraph (1) and the trustee receives, at least five business days before the scheduled date of sale, from the mortgagor or trustor, by certified mail with the United States Postal Service or by another overnight mail courier service with tracking information that confirms the recipient's signature and the date and time of receipt and delivery, a copy of a purchase agreement for the sale of the property at least five business days before the scheduled sale, the trustee shall postpone the scheduled date of sale to a date that is at least 45 days after the date on which the purchase agreement was received by the trustee. The provisions of this paragraph shall not be used to postpone the scheduled sale date more than once.

(4) For purposes of this subdivision, "purchase agreement" means a bona fide and fully executed contract for the sale of the property that is subject to a power of sale with a purchase price amount equal to or greater than the amount of the unpaid balance of all obligations of record secured by the property that includes the name of the buyer, the sales price, the agreed closing date, and acceptance by the designated escrow agent.

(f)(1) With respect to residential real property containing no more than four dwelling units that is subject to a power of sale contained in a first lien deed of trust or mortgage, the mortgagee, beneficiary, or authorized agent shall provide to the trustee a fair market value of the property at least 10 days prior to the initially scheduled date of sale, and the trustee shall not sell the property at the initially scheduled date of sale for less than 67 percent of that fair market value of the property. The trustee may rely on the fair market value provided pursuant to this paragraph, and shall not have a duty to verify the source or accuracy of the valuation.

(2) If the property remains unsold after the initial trustee's sale pursuant to paragraph (1), then the trustee shall postpone the sale for

at least seven days, and the property may be sold to the highest bidder.

(3) For purposes of this subdivision, "fair market value of the property" means an estimate of the fair market value of the property made within six months of the initially scheduled date of sale and determined by an opinion of a licensed real estate broker, an appraisal from a licensed appraiser, a value from a commercially utilized automated valuation model, or a value from a computerized property valuation system that is used to derive a real property value.

(4) A failure to comply with the provisions of paragraph (1) shall not affect the validity of a trustee's sale or a sale to a bona fide purchaser for value.

(5) The provisions of this subdivision shall apply to the initial trustee's sale for each notice of sale issued pursuant to subdivision (b) of Section 2924f.

[1] **(g)** This section shall be operative January 1, 2031. **Leg.H.** Added Stats 2020 ch 203 §1.5 (SB 1148), effective January 1, 2021, operative January 1, 2026. Amended Stats 2022 ch 642 §4 (AB 1837), effective January 1, 2023, operative January 1, 2031; Stats 2023 ch 131 §15 (AB 1754), effective January 1, 2024, operative January 1, 2031; Stats 2024 ch 311 §4 (AB 2424), effective January 1, 2025, operative January 1, 2031, repealed January 1, 2031.

§ 2924f. 2024 Deletes. [1] (e)

§2924g. Time and place of sale; Postponement; Conduct of sale [Repealed January 1, 2031]

(a)(1) All sales of property under the power of sale contained in any deed of trust or mortgage shall be held in the county where the property or some part thereof is situated, and shall be made at auction, to the highest bidder, between the hours of 9 a.m. and 5 p.m. on any business day, Monday through Friday.

(2)(A) The sale shall commence at the time and location specified in the notice of sale. Any postponement shall be announced at the time and location specified in the notice of sale for commencement of the sale or pursuant to paragraph (1) of subdivision (c).

(B) A sale that is postponed pursuant to subparagraph (E) of paragraph (1) of subdivision (c) shall be postponed seven calendar days at the same time and location.

(3) If the sale of more than one parcel of real property has been scheduled for the same time and location by the same trustee, (A) any postponement of any of the sales shall be announced at the time published in the notice of sale, (B) the first sale shall commence at the time published in the notice of sale or immediately after the announcement of any postponement, and (C) each subsequent sale shall take place as soon as possible after the preceding sale has been completed.

(4) Notwithstanding any other law, a sale of property under the power of sale contained in any deed of trust or mortgage shall be subject to the following restriction: a trustee shall not bundle properties for the purpose of sale and each property shall be bid on separately, unless the deed of trust or mortgage requires otherwise.

(b) When the property consists of several known lots or parcels, they shall be sold separately unless the deed of trust or mortgage provides otherwise. When a portion of the property is claimed by a third person, who requires it to be sold separately, the portion subject to the claim may be thus sold. The trustor, if present at the sale, may also, unless the deed of trust or mortgage otherwise provides, direct the order in which property shall be sold, when the property consists of several known lots or parcels which may be sold to advantage separately, and the trustee shall follow that direction. After sufficient property has been sold to satisfy the indebtedness, no more can be sold.

If the property under power of sale is in two or more counties, the public auction sale of all of the property under the power of sale may take place in any one of the counties where the property or a portion thereof is located.

(c)(1) There may be a postponement or postponements of the sale proceedings, including a postponement upon instruction by the beneficiary to the trustee that the sale proceedings be postponed, at any time prior to the completion of the sale for any period of time not to exceed a total of 365 days from the date set forth in the notice of sale. The trustee shall postpone the sale in accordance with any of the following:

(A) Upon the order of any court of competent jurisdiction.

(B) If stayed by operation of law.

(C) By mutual agreement, whether oral or in writing, of any trustor and any beneficiary or any mortgagor and any mortgagee.

(D) At the discretion of the trustee.

(E) If an act of force majeure prevents access to the sale location at the time of the sale.

(2) In the event that the sale proceedings are postponed for a period or periods totaling more than 365 days, the scheduling of any further sale proceedings shall be preceded by giving a new notice of sale in the manner prescribed in Section 2924f. New fees incurred for the new notice of sale shall not exceed the amounts specified in Sections 2924c and 2924d, and shall not exceed reasonable costs that are necessary to comply with this paragraph.

(d)(1) The notice of each postponement and the reason therefor shall be given by public declaration by the trustee at the time and place last appointed for sale. A public declaration of postponement shall also set forth the new date, time, and place of sale and the place of sale shall be the same place as originally fixed by the trustee for the sale. No other notice of postponement need be given. However, the sale shall be conducted no sooner than on the seventh day after the earlier of (1) dismissal of the action or (2) expiration or termination of the injunction, restraining order, or stay that required postponement of the sale, whether by entry of an order by a court of competent jurisdiction, operation of law, or otherwise, unless the injunction, restraining order, or subsequent order expressly directs the conduct of the sale within that seven-day period. For purposes of this subdivision, the seven-day period shall not include the day on which the action is dismissed, or the day on which the injunction, restraining order, or stay expires or is terminated. If the sale had been scheduled to occur, but this subdivision precludes its conduct during that seven-day period, a new notice of postponement shall be given if the sale had been scheduled to occur during that seven-day period. The trustee shall maintain records of each postponement and the reason therefor.

(2) The public declaration described in paragraph (1) shall not be required if the sale is postponed because an act of force majeure prevented access to the sale location.

(e) Notwithstanding the time periods established under subdivision (d), if postponement of a sale is based on a stay imposed by Title 11 of the United States Code (bankruptcy), the sale shall be conducted no sooner than the expiration of the stay imposed by that title and the seven-day provision of subdivision (d) shall not apply.

(f) For purposes of this section, "an act of force majeure" means an event that was unforeseeable at the time the sale was scheduled that is outside of the trustee's control and renders completion of the sale impossible or impractical.

[1] **(g)** This section shall remain in effect only until January 1, 2031, and as of that date is repealed, unless a later enacted statute that is enacted before January 1, 2031, deletes or extends that date. **Leg.H.** Added Stats 1972 ch 1056 §4, Amended Stats 1979 ch 1015 §4; Stats 1980 ch 423 §14, effective July 11, 1980; Stats 1984 ch 1730 §4; Stats 1985 ch 1206 §5; Stats 1986 ch 1385 §4; Stats 1992 ch 351 §4 (AB 2981); Stats 1993 ch 686 §7 (AB 1219); Stats 1994 ch 587 §1.2 (AB 3600); Stats 1997 ch 74 §5 (SB 665); Stats 2000 ch 636 §7 (AB 2284); Stats 2001 ch 438 §5 (SB 958), effective October 2, 2001, operative January 1, 2002; Stats 2005 ch 224 §2 (AB 885), effective January 1, 2006; Stats 2020 ch 202 §3 (SB 1079), effective January 1, 2021, repealed January 1, 2026; Stats 2022 ch 642 §5 (AB 1837), effective January 1, 2023, repealed January 1, 2031; Stats 2024 ch 601 §6 (SB 1146), effective January 1, 2025, repealed January 1, 2031.

§2924g. 2024 Deletes. [1] (f)

§ 2924g. Time and place of sale; Postponement; Conduct of sale [Operative January 1, 2031]

(a)(1) All sales of property under the power of sale contained in any deed of trust or mortgage shall be held in the county where the property or some part thereof is situated, and shall be made at auction, to the highest bidder, between the hours of 9 a.m. and 5 p.m. on any business day, Monday through Friday.

(2) The sale shall commence at the time and location specified in the notice of sale. Any postponement shall be announced at the time and location specified in the notice of sale for commencement of the sale or pursuant to paragraph (1) of subdivision (c).

(3) If the sale of more than one parcel of real property has been scheduled for the same time and location by the same trustee, [1] **all of the following conditions apply:**

[2] **(A)** Any postponement of any of the sales shall be announced at the time published in the notice of sale [3].

[4] **(B)** The first sale shall commence at the time published in the notice of sale or immediately after the announcement of any postponement [5].

[6] **(C)** Each subsequent sale shall take place as soon as possible after the preceding sale has been completed.

(4) A sale that is postponed pursuant to subparagraph (E) of paragraph (1) of subdivision (c) shall be postponed seven calendar days at the same time and location.

(b) When the property consists of several known lots or parcels, they shall be sold separately unless the deed of trust or mortgage provides otherwise. When a portion of the property is claimed by a third person, who requires it to be sold separately, the portion subject to the claim may be thus sold. The trustor, if present at the sale, may also, unless the deed of trust or mortgage otherwise provides, direct the order in which property shall be sold, when the property consists of several known lots or parcels which may be sold to advantage separately, and the trustee shall follow that direction. After sufficient property has been sold to satisfy the indebtedness, no more can be sold.

If the property under power of sale is in two or more counties, the public auction sale of all of the property under the power of sale may take place in any one of the counties where the property or a portion thereof is located.

(c)(1) There may be a postponement or postponements of the sale proceedings, including a postponement upon instruction by the beneficiary to the trustee that the sale proceedings be postponed, at any time prior to the completion of the sale for any period of time not to exceed a total of 365 days from the date set forth in the notice of sale. The trustee shall postpone the sale in accordance with any of the following:

(A) Upon the order of any court of competent jurisdiction.

(B) If stayed by operation of law.

(C) By mutual agreement, whether oral or in writing, of any trustor and any beneficiary or any mortgagor and any mortgagee.

(D) At the discretion of the trustee.

(E) If an act of force majeure prevents access to the sale location at the time of the sale.

(2) In the event that the sale proceedings are postponed for a period or periods totaling more than 365 days, the scheduling of any further sale proceedings shall be preceded by giving a new notice of sale in the manner prescribed in Section 2924f. New fees incurred for the new notice of sale shall not exceed the amounts specified in Sections 2924c and 2924d, and shall not exceed reasonable costs that are necessary to comply with this paragraph.

(d)(1) The notice of each postponement and the reason therefor shall be given by public declaration by the trustee at the time and place last appointed for sale. A public declaration of postponement shall also set forth the new date, time, and place of sale and the place of sale shall be the same place as originally fixed by the trustee for the sale. No other notice of postponement need be given. However, the sale shall be conducted no sooner than on the seventh day after the earlier of (1) dismissal of the action or (2) expiration or termination of the injunction, restraining order, or stay that required postponement of the sale, whether by entry of an order by a court of competent jurisdiction, operation of law, or otherwise, unless the injunction, restraining order, or subsequent order expressly directs the conduct of the sale within that seven-day period. For purposes of this subdivision, the seven-day period shall not include the day on which the action is dismissed, or the day on which the injunction, restraining order, or stay expires or is terminated. If the sale had been scheduled to occur, but this subdivision precludes its conduct during that seven-day period, a new notice of postponement shall be given if the sale had been scheduled to occur during that seven-day period. The trustee shall maintain records of each postponement and the reason therefor.

(2) The public declaration described in paragraph (1) shall not be required if the sale is postponed because an act of force majeure prevented access to the sale location.

(e) Notwithstanding the time periods established under subdivision (d), if postponement of a sale is based on a stay imposed by Title 11 of the United States Code (bankruptcy), the sale shall be conducted no sooner than the expiration of the stay imposed by that title and the seven-day provision of subdivision (d) shall not apply.

(f) For purposes of this section, "an act of force majeure" means an event that was unforeseeable at the time the sale was scheduled that is outside of the trustee's control and renders completion of the sale impossible or impractical.

[7] **(g)** This section shall be operative January 1, 2031. **Leg.H.** Added Stats 2020 ch 202 §4 (SB 1079), effective January 1, 2021, operative January 1, 2026. Amended Stats 2022 ch 642 §6 (AB 1837), effective January 1, 2023, operative January 1, 2031; Stats 2024 ch 601 §7 (SB 1146), effective January 1, 2025, operative January 1, 2031.

§ 2924g. 2024 Deletes. [1] (1) any postponement of any of the sales shall be announced at the time published in the notice of sale, (2) the first sale shall commence at the time published in the notice of sale or immediately after the announcement of any postponement, and (3) each subsequent sale shall take place as soon as possible after the preceding sale has been completed. [2] (1) [3] , [4] (2) [5] , and [6] (3) [7] (f)

§2924h. Bidding; Penalties [Repealed January 1, 2031]

(a) Each and every bid made by a bidder at a trustee's sale under a power of sale contained in a deed of trust or mortgage shall be deemed to be an irrevocable offer by that bidder to purchase the property being sold by the trustee under the power of sale for the amount of the bid. Any second or subsequent bid by the same bidder or any other bidder for a higher amount shall be a cancellation of the prior bid.

(b) At the trustee's sale, the trustee shall have the right to require any of the following:

(1) Every bidder to show evidence of the bidder's ability to deposit with the trustee the full amount of their final bid in cash, a cashier's check drawn on a state or national bank, a check drawn by a state or federal credit union, or a check drawn by a state or federal savings and loan association, savings association, or savings bank specified in Section 5102 of the Financial Code and authorized to do business in this state, or a cash equivalent which has been designated in the notice of sale as acceptable to the trustee prior to, and as a condition to, the recognizing of the bid, and to conditionally accept and hold these amounts for the duration of the sale.

(2) Any bid that is not cash to be made directly payable to the trustee, if the requirement is set forth by the trustee in the notice of sale.

[1] **(3)** [2] **The** last and highest bidder to deposit, if not deposited previously, the full amount of the bidder's final bid in cash, a cashier's check drawn on a state or national bank, a check drawn by a state or federal credit union, or a check drawn by a state or federal savings and loan association, savings association, or savings bank specified in Section 5102 of the Financial Code and authorized to do business in this state, or a cash equivalent which has been designated in the notice of sale as acceptable to the trustee, immediately prior to the completion of the sale, the completion of the sale being so announced by the fall of the hammer or in another customary manner. The present beneficiary of the deed of trust under foreclosure shall have the right to offset their bid or bids only to the extent of the total amount due the beneficiary including the trustee's fees and expenses.

(c) In the event the trustee accepts a check drawn by a credit union or a savings and loan association pursuant to this subdivision or a cash equivalent designated in the notice of sale, the trustee may withhold the issuance of the trustee's deed to the successful bidder submitting the check drawn by a state or federal credit union or savings and loan association or the cash equivalent until funds become available to the payee or endorsee as a matter of right. **The trustee may require the successful bidder to replace the check drawn by a credit union or a savings and loan association or cash equivalent pursuant to this subdivision with a check drawn by a credit union or a savings and loan association or cash equivalent to this subdivision made directly payable to the trustee if necessary for the funds to be made available to the trustee.**

For the purposes of this subdivision, the trustee's sale shall be deemed final upon the acceptance of the last and highest bid, and shall be deemed perfected as of 8 a.m. on the actual date of sale if the trustee's deed is recorded within 21 calendar days after the sale, or the next business day following the 21st day if the county recorder in which the property is located is closed on the 21st day. If an eligible bidder submits a written notice of intent to bid pursuant to paragraph (2) of subdivision (c) of Section 2924m, the trustee's sale shall be deemed perfected as of 8 a.m. on the actual date of sale if the trustee's deed is recorded within 60 calendar days after the sale or the next business day following the 60th day if the county recorder in which the property is located is closed on the 60th day. However, the sale is subject to an automatic rescission for a failure of consideration in the event the funds are not "available for withdrawal" as defined in Section 12413.1 of the Insurance Code. The trustee shall send a notice of rescission for a failure of consideration to the last and highest bidder submitting the check or alternative instrument, if the address of the last and highest bidder is known to the trustee.

If a sale results in an automatic right of rescission for failure of consideration pursuant to this subdivision, the interest of any lienholder shall be reinstated in the same priority as if the previous sale had not occurred.

(d) If the trustee has not required the last and highest bidder to deposit the cash, a cashier's check drawn on a state or national bank, a check drawn by a state or federal credit union, or a check drawn by a state or federal savings and loan association, savings association, or savings bank specified in Section 5102 of the Financial Code and authorized to do business in this state, or a cash equivalent which has been designated in the notice of sale as acceptable to the trustee in the manner set forth in paragraph (2) of subdivision (b), the trustee shall complete the sale. If the last and highest bidder then fails to deliver to the trustee, when demanded, the amount of their final bid in cash, a cashier's check drawn on a state or national bank, a check drawn by a state or federal credit union, or a check drawn by a state or federal savings and loan association, savings association, or savings bank specified in Section 5102 of the Financial Code and authorized to do business in this state, or a cash equivalent which has been designated in the notice of sale as acceptable to the trustee, that bidder shall be liable to the trustee for all damages which the trustee may sustain by the refusal to deliver to the trustee the amount of the final bid, including any court costs and reasonable attorney's fees.

If the last and highest bidder willfully fails to deliver to the trustee the amount of their final bid in cash, a cashier's check drawn on a state or national bank, a check drawn by a state or federal credit union, or a check drawn by a state or federal savings and loan association, savings association, or savings bank specified in Section 5102 of the Financial Code and authorized to do business in this state, or a cash equivalent which has been designated in the notice of sale as acceptable to the trustee, or if the last and highest bidder cancels a cashier's check drawn on a state or national bank, a check drawn by a state or federal credit union, or a check drawn by a state or federal savings and loan association, savings association, or savings bank specified in Section 5102 of the Financial Code and authorized to do business in this state, or a cash equivalent that has been designated in the notice of sale as acceptable to the trustee, that bidder shall be guilty of a misdemeanor punishable by a fine of not more than two thousand five hundred dollars ($2,500).

In the event the last and highest bidder cancels an instrument submitted to the trustee as a cash equivalent, the trustee shall provide a new notice of sale in the manner set forth in Section 2924f and shall be entitled to recover the costs of the new notice of sale as provided in Section 2924c.

(e) Any postponement or discontinuance of the sale proceedings shall be a cancellation of the last bid.

(f) Except as specifically provided in Section 2924m, in the event that this section conflicts with any other statute, then this section shall prevail.

(g) It shall be unlawful for any person, acting alone or in concert with others, (1) to offer to accept or accept from another, any consideration of any type not to bid, or (2) to fix or restrain bidding in any manner, at a sale of property conducted pursuant to a power of sale in a deed of trust or mortgage. However, it shall not be unlawful for any person, including a trustee, to state that a property subject to a recorded notice of default or subject to a sale conducted pursuant to this chapter is being sold in an "as-is" condition.

In addition to any other remedies, any person committing any act declared unlawful by this subdivision or any act which would operate as a fraud or deceit upon any beneficiary, trustor, or junior lienor shall, upon conviction, be fined not more than ten thousand dollars ($10,000) or imprisoned in the county jail for not more than one year, or be punished by both that fine and imprisonment.

(h) This section shall remain in effect only until January 1, 2031, and as of that date is repealed, unless a later enacted statute that is enacted before January 1, 2031, deletes or extends that date.

(i) The amendments made to this section by the bill adding this subdivision shall become operative on January 1, 2022.

(j) The amendments made to this section by the act adding this subdivision are declaratory of existing law. **Leg.H.** Added Stats 1972 ch 1056 §5. Amended Stats 1979 ch 1015 §5; Stats 1981 ch 427 §3; Stats 1986 ch 1385 §6; Stats 1987 ch 725 §2; Stats 1992 ch 351 §5 (AB 2981); Stats 1993 ch 724 §3 (AB 1196); Stats 1995 ch 752 §3 (AB 1695); Stats 2004 ch 177 §2 (SB 1277); Stats 2020 ch 202 §5 (SB 1079), effective January 1, 2021, repealed January 1, 2026; Stats 2021 ch 255 §1 (AB 175), effective September 23, 2021, operative January 1, 2022, repealed January 1, 2026; Stats 2022 ch 642 §7 (AB 1837), effective January 1, 2023, repealed January 1, 2031; Stats 2024 ch 142 §4 (AB 295), effective July 18, 2024, repealed January 1, 2031; Stats 2024 ch 601 §8 (SB 1146), effective January 1, 2025, repealed January 1, 2031.

§2924h. 2024 Deletes. [1] (b) **[2]** At the trustee's sale the trustee shall have the right (1) to require every bidder to show evidence of the bidder's ability to deposit with the trustee the full amount of their final bid in cash, a cashier's check drawn on a state or national bank, a check drawn by a state or federal credit union, or a check drawn by a state or federal savings and loan association, savings association, or savings bank specified in Section 5102 of the Financial Code and authorized to do business in this state, or a cash equivalent which has been designated in the notice of sale as acceptable to the trustee prior to, and as a condition to, the recognizing of the bid, and to conditionally accept and hold these amounts for the duration of the sale, and (2) to require the

§ 2924h. Bidding; Penalties [Operative January 1, 2031]

(a) Each and every bid made by a bidder at a trustee's sale under a power of sale contained in a deed of trust or mortgage shall be deemed to be an irrevocable offer by that bidder to purchase the property being sold by the trustee under the power of sale for the amount of the bid. Any second or subsequent bid by the same bidder or any other bidder for a higher amount shall be a cancellation of the prior bid.

(b) At the trustee's sale, the trustee shall have the right to require any of the following:

(1) Every bidder to show evidence of the bidder's ability to deposit with the trustee the full amount of their final bid in cash, a cashier's check drawn on a state or national bank, a check drawn by a state or federal credit union, or a check drawn by a state or federal savings and loan association, savings association, or savings bank specified in Section 5102 of the Financial Code and authorized to do business in this state, or a cash equivalent which has been designated in the notice of sale as acceptable to the trustee prior to, and as a condition to, the recognizing of the bid, and to conditionally accept and hold these amounts for the duration of the sale.

(2) Any bid that is not cash to be made directly payable to the trustee, if the requirement is set forth by the trustee in the notice of sale.

[1] (3) [2] The last and highest bidder to deposit, if not deposited previously, the full amount of the bidder's final bid in cash, a cashier's check drawn on a state or national bank, a check drawn by a state or federal credit union, or a check drawn by a state or federal savings and loan association, savings association, or savings bank specified in Section 5102 of the Financial Code and authorized to do business in this state, or a cash equivalent which has been designated in the notice of sale as acceptable to the trustee, immediately prior to the completion of the sale, the completion of the sale being so announced by the fall of the hammer or in another customary manner. The present beneficiary of the deed of trust under foreclosure shall have the right to offset their bid or bids only to the extent of the total amount due the beneficiary including the trustee's fees and expenses.

(c) In the event the trustee accepts a check drawn by a credit union or a savings and loan association pursuant to this subdivision or a cash equivalent designated in the notice of sale, the trustee may withhold the issuance of the trustee's deed to the successful bidder submitting the check drawn by a state or federal credit union or savings and loan association or the cash equivalent until funds become available to the payee or endorsee as a matter of right. **The trustee may require the successful bidder to replace the check drawn by a credit union or a savings and loan association or cash equivalent pursuant to this subdivision with a check drawn by a credit union or a savings and loan association or cash equivalent to this subdivision made directly payable to the trustee if necessary for the funds to be made available to the trustee.**

For the purposes of this subdivision, the trustee's sale shall be deemed final upon the acceptance of the last and highest bid, and shall be deemed perfected as of 8 a.m. on the actual date of sale if the trustee's deed is recorded within 15 calendar days after the sale, or the next business day following the 15th day if the county recorder in which the property is located is closed on the 15th day. However, the sale is subject to an automatic rescission for a failure of consideration in the event the funds are not "available for withdrawal" as defined in Section 12413.1 of the Insurance Code. The trustee shall send a notice of rescission for a failure of consideration to the last and highest bidder submitting the check or alternative instrument, if the address of the last and highest bidder is known to the trustee.

If a sale results in an automatic right of rescission for failure of consideration pursuant to this subdivision, the interest of any lienholder shall be reinstated in the same priority as if the previous sale had not occurred.

(d) If the trustee has not required the last and highest bidder to deposit the cash, a cashier's check drawn on a state or national bank, a check drawn by a state or federal credit union, or a check drawn by a state or federal savings and loan association, savings association, or savings bank specified in Section 5102 of the Financial Code and authorized to do business in this state, or a cash equivalent which has been designated in the notice of sale as acceptable to the trustee in the manner set forth in paragraph (2) of subdivision (b), the trustee shall complete the sale. If the last and highest bidder then fails to deliver to the trustee, when demanded, the amount of their final bid in cash, a cashier's check drawn on a state or national bank, a check drawn by a state or federal credit union, or a check drawn by a state or federal savings and loan association, savings association, or savings bank specified in Section 5102 of the Financial Code and authorized to do business in this state, or a cash equivalent which has been designated in the notice of sale as acceptable to the trustee, that bidder shall be liable to the trustee for all damages which the trustee may sustain by the refusal to deliver to the trustee the amount of the final bid, including any court costs and reasonable [3] **attorney's** fees.

If the last and highest bidder willfully fails to deliver to the trustee the amount of their final bid in cash, a cashier's check drawn on a state or national bank, a check drawn by a state or federal credit union, or a check drawn by a state or federal savings and loan association, savings association, or savings bank specified in Section 5102 of the Financial Code and authorized to do business in this state, or a cash equivalent which has been designated in the notice of sale as acceptable to the trustee, or if the last and highest bidder cancels a [4] **cashier's** check drawn on a state or national bank, a check drawn by a state or federal credit union, or a check drawn by a state or federal savings and loan association, savings association, or savings bank specified in Section 5102 of the Financial Code and authorized to do business in this state, or a cash equivalent that has been designated in the notice of sale as acceptable to the trustee, that bidder shall be guilty of a misdemeanor punishable by a fine of not more than two thousand five hundred dollars ($2,500).

In the event the last and highest bidder cancels an instrument submitted to the trustee as a cash equivalent, the trustee shall provide a new notice of sale in the manner set forth in Section 2924f and shall be entitled to recover the costs of the new notice of sale as provided in Section 2924c.

(e) Any postponement or discontinuance of the sale proceedings shall be a cancellation of the last bid.

(f) In the event that this section conflicts with any other statute, then this section shall prevail.

(g) It shall be unlawful for any person, acting alone or in concert with others, (1) to offer to accept or accept from another, any consideration of any type not to bid, or (2) to fix or restrain bidding in any manner, at a sale of property conducted pursuant to a power of sale in a deed of trust or mortgage. However, it shall not be unlawful for any person, including a trustee, to state that a property subject to a recorded notice of default or subject to a sale conducted pursuant to this chapter is being sold in an "as-is" condition.

In addition to any other remedies, any person committing any act declared unlawful by this subdivision or any act which would operate as a fraud or deceit upon any beneficiary, trustor, or junior lienor shall, upon conviction, be fined not more than ten thousand dollars ($10,000) or imprisoned in the county jail for not more than one year, or be punished by both that fine and imprisonment.

(h) This section shall be operative January 1, 2031. **Leg.H.** Added Stats 2020 ch 202 §6 (SB 1079), effective January 1, 2021, operative January 1, 2026. Amended Stats 2022 ch 642 §8 (AB 1837), effective January 1, 2023, operative January 1, 2031; Stats 2024 ch 601 §9 (SB 1146), effective January 1, 2025, operative January 1, 2031.

§ 2924h. 2024 Deletes. [1] (b) **[2]** At the trustee's sale the trustee shall have the right (1) to require every bidder to show evidence of the bidder's ability to deposit with the trustee the full amount of their final bid in cash, a cashier's check drawn on a state or national bank, a check drawn by a state or federal credit union, or a check drawn by a state or federal savings and loan association, savings association, or savings bank specified in Section 5102 of the Financial Code and authorized to do business in this state, or a cash equivalent which has been designated in the notice of sale as acceptable to the trustee prior to, and as a condition to, the recognizing of the bid, and to conditionally accept and hold these amounts for the duration of the sale, and (2) to require the **[3]** attorneys' **[4]** cashiers

§2924i. Notice regarding final payment on balloon payment loan

(a) This section applies to loans secured by a deed of trust or mortgage on real property containing one to four residential units at least one of which at the time the loan is made is or is to be occupied by the borrower if the loan is for a period in excess of one year and is a balloon payment loan.

(b) This section shall not apply to (1) open end credit as defined in Regulation Z, whether or not the transaction is otherwise subject to Regulation Z, (2) transactions subject to Section 2956, or (3) loans made for the principal purpose of financing the construction of one or more residential units.

(c) At least 90 days but not more than 150 days prior to the due date of the final payment on a loan that is subject to this section, the holder of the loan shall deliver or mail by first-class mail, with a certificate of mailing obtained from the United States Postal Service, to the trustor, or his or her successor in interest, at the last known address of that person, a written notice which shall include all of the following:

(1) A statement of the name and address of the person to whom the final payment is required to be paid.

(2) The date on or before which the final payment is required to be paid.

(3) The amount of the final payment, or if the exact amount is unknown, a good faith estimate of the amount thereof, including unpaid principal, interest and any other charges, such amount to be determined assuming timely payment in full of all scheduled installments coming due between the date the notice is prepared and the date when the final payment is due.

(4) If the borrower has a contractual right to refinance the final payment, a statement to that effect.

If the due date of the final payment of a loan subject to this section is extended prior to the time notice is otherwise required under this subdivision, this notice requirement shall apply only to the due date as extended (or as subsequently extended).

(d) For purposes of this section:

(1) A "balloon payment loan" is a loan which provides for a final payment as originally scheduled which is more than twice the amount of any of the immediately preceding six regularly scheduled payments or which contains a call provision; provided, however, that if the call provision is not exercised by the holder of the loan, the existence of the unexercised call provision shall not cause the loan to be deemed to be a balloon payment loan.

(2) "Call provision" means a loan contract term that provides the holder of the loan with the right to call the loan due and payable either after a specified period has elapsed following closing or after a specified date.

(3) "Regulation Z" means any rule, regulation, or interpretation promulgated by the Board of Governors of the Federal Reserve System under the Federal Truth in Lending Act, as amended (15 U.S.C. Sec. 1601 et seq.), and any interpretation or approval thereof issued by an official or employee of the Federal Reserve System duly authorized by the board under the Truth in Lending Act, as amended, to issue such interpretations or approvals.

(e) Failure to provide notice as required by subdivision (a) does not extinguish any obligation of payment by the borrower, except that the due date for any balloon payment shall be the date specified in the balloon payment note, or 90 days from the date of delivery or mailing of the notice required by subdivision (a), or the due date specified in the notice required by subdivision (a), whichever date is later. If the operation of this section acts to extend the term of any note, interest shall continue to accrue for the extended term at the contract rate and payments shall continue to be due at any periodic interval and on any payment schedule specified in the note and shall be credited to principal or interest under the terms of the note. Default in any extended periodic payment shall be considered a default under terms of the note or security instrument.

(f)(1) The validity of any credit document or of any security document subject to the provisions of this section shall not be invalidated solely because of the failure of any person to comply with this section. However, any person who willfully violates any provision of this section shall be liable in the amount of actual damages suffered by the debtor as the proximate result of the violation, and, if the debtor prevails in any suit to recover that amount, for reasonable attorney's fees.

(2) No person may be held liable in any action under this section if it is shown by a preponderance of the evidence that the violation was not intentional and resulted from a bona fide error notwithstanding the maintenance of procedures reasonably adopted to avoid any such error.

(g) The provisions of this section shall apply to any note executed on or after January 1, 1984. **Leg.H.** Added Stats 1983 ch 1094 §1. Amended Stats 1986 ch 1360 §1.

§2924j. Notice when surplus proceeds remain; Determination of priority of written claims; Declaration of unresolved claims; Deposit of funds; Consideration by court; Interpleader action; Unclaimed Property Law

(a) Unless an interpleader action has been filed, within 30 days of the execution of the trustee's deed resulting from a sale in which there are proceeds remaining after payment of the amounts required by paragraphs (1) and (2) of subdivision (a) of Section 2924k, the trustee shall send written notice to all persons with recorded interests in the real property as of the date immediately prior to the trustee's sale who would be entitled to notice pursuant to subdivisions (b) and (c) of Section 2924b. The notice shall be sent by first-class mail in the manner provided in paragraph (1) of subdivision (c) of Section 2924b and inform each entitled person of each of the following:

(1) That there has been a trustee's sale of the described real property.

(2) That the noticed person may have a claim to all or a portion of the sale proceeds remaining after payment of the amounts required by paragraphs (1) and (2) of subdivision (a) of Section 2924k.

(3) The noticed person may contact the trustee at the address provided in the notice to pursue any potential claim.

(4) That before the trustee can act, the noticed person may be required to present proof that the person holds the beneficial interest in the obligation and the security interest therefor. In the case of a promissory note secured by a deed of trust, proof that the person holds the beneficial interest may include the original promissory note and assignment of beneficial interests related thereto. The noticed person shall also submit a written claim to the trustee, executed under penalty of perjury, stating the following:

(A) The amount of the claim to the date of trustee's sale.

(B) An itemized statement of the principal, interest, and other charges.

(C) That claims must be received by the trustee at the address stated in the notice no later than 30 days after the date the trustee sends notice to the potential claimant.

(b) The trustee shall exercise due diligence to determine the priority of the written claims received by the trustee to the trustee's sale surplus proceeds from those persons to whom notice was sent pursuant to subdivision (a). In the event there is no dispute as to the priority of the written claims submitted to the trustee, proceeds shall be paid within 30 days after the conclusion of the notice period. If the trustee has failed to determine the priority of written claims within 90 days following the 30-day notice period, then within 10 days thereafter the trustee shall deposit the funds with the clerk of the court pursuant to subdivision (c) or file an interpleader action pursuant to subdivision (e). Nothing in this section shall preclude any person from pursuing other remedies or claims as to surplus proceeds.

(c) If, after due diligence, the trustee is unable to determine the priority of the written claims received by the trustee to the trustee's sale surplus of multiple persons or if the trustee determines there is a conflict between potential claimants, the trustee may file a declaration of the unresolved claims and deposit with the clerk of the superior court of the county in which the sale occurred, that portion of the sales proceeds that cannot be distributed, less any fees charged by the clerk pursuant to this subdivision. The declaration shall specify the date of the trustee's sale, a description of the property, the names and addresses of all persons sent notice pursuant to subdivision (a), a statement that the trustee exercised due diligence pursuant to subdivision (b), that the trustee provided written notice as required by subdivisions (a) and (d), and the amount of the sales proceeds deposited by the trustee with the court. Further, the trustee shall submit a copy of the trustee's sales guarantee and any information relevant to the identity, location, and priority of the potential claimants with the court and shall file proof of service of the notice required by subdivision (d) on all persons described in subdivision (a).

The clerk shall deposit the amount with the county treasurer or, if a bank account has been established for moneys held in trust under paragraph (2) of subdivision (a) of Section 77009 of the Government Code, in that account, subject to order of the court upon the application of any interested party. The clerk may charge a reasonable fee for the performance of activities pursuant to this subdivision equal to the fee for filing an interpleader action pursuant to Chapter 5.8 (commencing with Section 70600) of Title 8 of the Government Code. Upon deposit of that portion of the sale proceeds that cannot be distributed by due diligence, the trustee shall be discharged of further responsibility for the disbursement of sale proceeds. A deposit with the clerk of the court pursuant to this subdivision may be either for the total proceeds of the trustee's sale, less any fees charged by the clerk, if a conflict or conflicts exist with respect to the total proceeds, or that portion that cannot be distributed after due diligence, less any fees charged by the clerk.

(d) Before the trustee deposits the funds with the clerk of the court pursuant to subdivision (c), the trustee shall send written notice by first-class mail, postage prepaid, to all persons described in subdivision (a) informing them that the trustee intends to deposit the funds with the clerk of the court and that a claim for the funds must be filed with the court within 30 days from the date of the notice, providing the address of the court in which the funds were deposited, and a telephone number for obtaining further information.

Within 90 days after deposit with the clerk, the court shall consider all claims filed at least 15 days before the date on which the hearing is scheduled by the court, the clerk shall serve written notice of the hearing by first-class mail on all claimants identified in the trustee's declaration at the addresses specified therein. Where the amount of the deposit is thirty-five thousand dollars ($35,000) or less, a proceeding pursuant to this section is a limited civil case. The court shall distribute the deposited funds to any and all claimants entitled thereto.

(e) Nothing in this section restricts the ability of a trustee to file an interpleader action in order to resolve a dispute about the proceeds of a trustee's sale. Once an interpleader action has been filed, thereafter the provisions of this section do not apply.

(f) "Due diligence," for the purposes of this section means that the trustee researched the written claims submitted or other evidence of conflicts and determined that a conflict of priorities exists between two or more claimants which the trustee is unable to resolve.

(g) To the extent required by the Unclaimed Property Law, a trustee in possession of surplus proceeds not required to be deposited with the court pursuant to subdivision (b) shall comply with the Unclaimed Property Law (Chapter 7 (commencing with Section 1500) of Title 10 of Part 3 of the Code of Civil Procedure).

(h) The trustee, beneficiary, or counsel to the trustee or beneficiary, is not liable for providing to any person who is entitled to notice pursuant to this section, information set forth in, or a copy of, subdivision (h) of Section 2945.3. **Leg.H.** Added Stats 1989 ch 849 §1. Amended Stats 1990 ch 287 §1 (AB 3078); Stats 1992 ch 351 §6 (AB 2981); Stats 1998 ch 932 §9 (AB 1094); Stats 1999 ch 974 §11 (AB 431); Stats 2002 ch 784 §20 (SB 1316); Stats 2003 ch 62 §19 (SB 600); Stats 2004 ch 177 §3 (SB 1277); Stats 2005 ch 75 §15 (AB 145), effective July 19, 2005, operative January 1, 2006; Stats 2023 ch 861 §1 (SB 71), effective January 1, 2024.

Prior Law: Former CC §2924j, relating to prohibition against issuance of trustee's deed in enjoined or stayed nonjudicial foreclosure, was added Stats 1986 ch 943 §1 and repealed Stats 1987 ch 97 §1, effective July 2, 1987.

§2924k. Priority of order of distribution of proceeds; Trustee's costs and expenses

(a) The trustee, or the clerk of the court upon order to the clerk pursuant to subdivision (d) of Section 2924j, shall distribute the proceeds, or a portion of the proceeds, as the case may be, of the trustee's sale conducted pursuant to Section 2924h in the following order of priority:

(1) To the costs and expenses of exercising the power of sale and of sale, including the payment of the trustee's fees and attorney's fees permitted pursuant to subdivision (b) of Section 2924d and subdivision (b) of this section.

(2) To the payment of the obligations secured by the deed of trust or mortgage which is the subject of the trustee's sale.

(3) To satisfy the outstanding balance of obligations secured by any junior liens or encumbrances in the order of their priority.

(4) To the trustor or the trustor's successor in interest. In the event the property is sold or transferred to another, to the vested owner of record at the time of the trustee's sale.

(b) A trustee may charge costs and expenses incurred for such items as mailing and a reasonable fee for services rendered in connection with the distribution of the proceeds from a trustee's sale, including, but not limited to, the investigation of priority and validity of claims and the disbursement of funds. If the fee charged for services rendered pursuant to this subdivision does not exceed one hundred dollars ($100), or one hundred twenty-five dollars ($125) where there are obligations specified in paragraph (3) of subdivision (a), the fee is conclusively presumed to be reasonable. **Leg.H.** Added Stats 1990 ch 287 §2 (AB 3078). Amended Stats 1999 ch 974 §12 (AB 431).

§2924*l*. Declaration of nonmonetary status by trustee of deed of trust named in action

(a) In the event that a trustee under a deed of trust is named in an action or proceeding in which that deed of trust is the subject, and in the event that the trustee maintains a reasonable belief that it has been named in the action or proceeding solely in its capacity as trustee, and not arising out of any wrongful acts or omissions on its part in the performance of its duties as trustee, then, at any time, the trustee may file a declaration of nonmonetary status. The declaration shall be served on the parties in the manner set forth in Chapter 5 (commencing with Section 1010) of Title 14 of the Code of Civil Procedure.

(b) The declaration of nonmonetary status shall set forth the status of the trustee as trustee under the deed of trust that is the subject of the action or proceeding, that the trustee knows or maintains a reasonable belief that it has been named as a defendant in the proceeding solely in its capacity as a trustee under the deed of trust, its reasonable belief that it has not been named as a defendant due to any acts or omissions on its part in the performance of its duties as trustee, the basis for that knowledge or reasonable belief, and that it agrees to be bound by whatever order or judgment is issued by the court regarding the subject deed of trust.

(c) The parties who have appeared in the action or proceeding shall have 15 days from the service of the declaration by the trustee in which to object to the nonmonetary judgment status of the trustee. Any objection shall set forth the factual basis on which the objection is based and shall be served on the trustee.

(d) In the event that no objection is served within the 15-day objection period, the trustee shall not be required to participate any further in the action or proceeding, shall not be subject to any monetary awards as and for damages, attorneys' fees or costs, shall be required to respond to any discovery requests as a nonparty, and shall be bound by any court order relating to the subject deed of trust that is the subject of the action or proceeding.

(e) In the event of a timely objection to the declaration of nonmonetary status, the trustee shall thereafter be required to participate in the action or proceeding.

Additionally, in the event that the parties elect not to, or fail to, timely object to the declaration of nonmonetary status, but later through discovery, or otherwise, determine that the trustee should participate in the action because of the performance of its duties as a trustee, the parties may file and serve on all parties and the trustee a motion pursuant to Section 473 of the Code of Civil Procedure that specifies the factual basis for the demand. Upon the court's granting of the motion, the trustee shall thereafter be required to participate in the action or proceeding, and the court shall provide sufficient time prior to trial for the trustee to be able to respond to the complaint, to conduct discovery, and to bring other pretrial motions in accordance with the Code of Civil Procedure.

(f) Upon the filing of the declaration of nonmonetary status, the time within which the trustee is required to file an answer or other responsive pleading shall be tolled for the period of time within which the opposing parties may respond to the declaration. Upon the timely service of an objection to the declaration on nonmonetary status, the trustee shall have 30 days from the date of service within which to file an answer or other responsive pleading to the complaint or cross-complaint.

(g) For purposes of this section, "trustee" includes any agent or employee of the trustee who performs some or all of the duties of a trustee under this article, and includes substituted trustees and agents of the beneficiary or trustee.

(h) A fee shall not be charged for the filing of a declaration of nonmonetary status pursuant to this section. **Leg.H.** Added Stats 1995 ch 752 §4 (AB 1695). Amended Stats 1997 ch 74 §6 (SB 665); Stats 1999 ch 974 §13 (AB 431); Stats 2004 ch 177 §4 (SB 1277); Stats 2020 ch 203 §2 (SB 1148), effective January 1, 2021.

§ 2924m. Conditions for sale to be deemed final; Procedures in the event sale not final [Repealed January 1, 2031]

(a) For purposes of this section:

(1) "Prospective owner-occupant" means a natural person who presents to the trustee an affidavit or declaration, pursuant to Section 2015.5 of the Code of Civil Procedure, that:

(A) They will occupy the property as their primary residence within 60 days of the trustee's deed being recorded.

(B) They will maintain their occupancy for at least one year.

(C) They are not any of the following:

(i) The mortgagor or trustor.

(ii) The child, spouse, or parent of the mortgagor or trustor.

(iii) The grantor of a living trust that was named in the title to the property when the notice of default was recorded.

(iv) An employee, officer, or member of the mortgagor or trustor.

(v) A person with an ownership interest in the mortgagor, unless the mortgagor is a publicly traded company.

(D) They are not acting as the agent of any other person or entity in purchasing the real property.

(2) "Eligible tenant buyer" means a natural person who at the time of the trustee's sale:

(A) Is occupying the real property as their primary residence.

(B) Is occupying the real property under a rental or lease agreement entered into as the result of an arm's-length transaction with the mortgagor or trustor, or with the mortgagor or trustor's predecessor in interest, on a date prior to the recording of the notice of default against the property, and who attaches evidence demonstrating the existence of the tenancy to the affidavit or declaration required pursuant to subparagraph (B) of paragraph (2) of subdivision (c).

(C) Is not the mortgagor or trustor, or the child, spouse, or parent of the mortgagor or trustor.

(D) Is not acting as the agent of any other person or entity in purchasing the real property. Submission of a bid pursuant to paragraph (3) of subdivision (c) does not violate this subparagraph.

(E) Has not filed a petition under Chapter 7, 11, 12, or 13 of Title 11 of the United States Code at any time during the period from the date of the trustee's sale of the property to the 45th day after the trustee's sale, or the next business day following the 45th day if the 45th day is a weekend or holiday.

(3) "Eligible bidder" means any of the following:

(A) An eligible tenant buyer.

(B) A prospective owner-occupant.

(C) A nonprofit association, nonprofit corporation, or cooperative corporation in which an eligible tenant buyer is a voting member or director.

(D) An eligible nonprofit corporation with all of the following attributes:

(i) It has a determination letter from the Internal Revenue Service affirming its tax-exempt status pursuant to Section 501(c)(3) of the Internal Revenue Code and is not a private foundation as that term is defined in Section 509 of the Internal Revenue Code.

(ii) It has its principal place of business in California.

(iii) The primary residences of all board members are located in California.

(iv) One of its primary activities is the development and preservation of affordable rental or home ownership housing in California.

(v) It is registered and in good standing with the Attorney General's Registry of Charities and Fundraisers, pursuant to the Supervision of

Trustees and Fundraisers for Charitable Purposes Act (Article 7 (commencing with Section 12580) of Chapter 6 of Part 2 of Division 3 of Title 2 of the Government Code).

(E) A limited liability company wholly owned by one or more eligible nonprofit corporations as described in subparagraph (C) or (D).

(F) A community land trust, as defined in clause (ii) of subparagraph (C) of paragraph (11) of subdivision (a) of Section 402.1 of the Revenue and Taxation Code.

(G) A limited-equity housing cooperative as defined in Section 817.

(H) The state, the Regents of the University of California, a county, city, district, public authority, or public agency, and any other political subdivision or public corporation in the state.

(4) "Evidence demonstrating the existence of the tenancy" means a copy of the dated and signed rental or lease agreement or, if a copy of the dated and signed rental or lease agreement is not available, then one of the following:

(A) Evidence of rent payments made for the property by the person asserting that they are an eligible tenant buyer for the six months prior to the recording of the notice of default.

(B) Copies of utility bills for the property payable by the person asserting that they are an eligible tenant buyer for the six months prior to the recording of the notice of default.

(b) This section does not prevent an eligible tenant buyer who meets the conditions set forth in paragraph (1) of subdivision (a) from being deemed a prospective owner-occupant.

(c) A trustee's sale of property under a power of sale contained in a deed of trust or mortgage on real property containing one to four residential units pursuant to Section 2924g shall not be deemed final until the earliest of the following:

(1) If a prospective owner-occupant is the last and highest bidder at the trustee's sale, the date upon which the conditions set forth in Section 2924h for the sale to become final are met. The prospective owner-occupant shall submit to the trustee the affidavit or declaration described in paragraph (1) of subdivision (a) at the trustee's sale or to the trustee by 5 p.m. on the next business day following the trustee's sale.

(2) Fifteen days after the trustee's sale unless at least one eligible tenant buyer or eligible bidder submits to the trustee either a bid pursuant to paragraph (3) or (4) or a nonbinding written notice of intent to place such a bid. The bid or written notice of intent to place a bid shall:

(A) Be sent to the trustee by certified mail, overnight delivery, or [1] **another** method that allows for confirmation of the delivery date.

(B) Be accompanied by an affidavit or declaration, pursuant to Section 2015.5 of the Code of Civil Procedure, identifying the category set forth in paragraph (3) of subdivision (a) to which the person or entity submitting the bid or nonbinding written notice of intent belongs and stating that the person meets the criteria for that category. If the winning bid is placed by an eligible bidder described in subparagraphs (C) to (G), inclusive, of paragraph (3) of subdivision (a), the affidavit or declaration shall affirm the bidder's duty to comply with subdivision (a) of Section 2924o for the benefit of tenants occupying the property.

(C) Be received by the trustee no later than 5 p.m. on the 15th day after the trustee's sale, or the next business day following the 15th day if the 15th day is a weekend or holiday.

(D) Contain a current telephone number and return mailing address for the person submitting the bid or nonbinding written notice of intent.

(3)(A) The date upon which a representative of all of the eligible tenant buyers submits to the trustee a bid in an amount equal to the full amount of the last and highest bid at the trustee's sale, in the form of cash, a cashier's check drawn on a state or national bank, a cashier's check drawn by a state or federal credit union, or a cashier's check drawn by a state or federal savings and loan association, savings association, or savings bank specified in Section 5102 of the Financial Code and authorized to do business in this state. This bid shall:

(i) Be sent to the trustee by certified mail, overnight delivery, or [2] **another** method that allows for confirmation of the delivery date.

(ii) Be accompanied by an affidavit or declaration, pursuant to Section 2015.5 of the Code of Civil Procedure, stating that the persons represented meet the criteria set forth in paragraph (2) of subdivision (a), and that the persons represented are all of the eligible tenant buyers.

(iii) Meet either of the following criteria:

(I) Be received by the trustee no later than 5 p.m. on the 15th day after the trustee's sale, or the next business day following the 15th day if the 15th day is a weekend or holiday.

(II) Be received by the trustee no later than 5 p.m. on the 45th day after the trustee's sale, or the next business day following the 45th day if the 45th day is a weekend or holiday, if at least one of the eligible tenant buyers submitted a nonbinding written notice of intent to place a bid pursuant to paragraph (2).

(iv) Contain a current telephone number and return mailing address for the person submitting the bid.

(B) If the conditions in this paragraph are satisfied, the eligible tenant buyers shall be deemed the last and highest bidder pursuant to the power of sale.

(4)(A) Forty-five days after the trustee's sale, except that during the 45-day period, an eligible bidder may submit to the trustee a bid in an amount that exceeds the last and highest bid at the trustee's sale, in the form of cash, a cashier's check drawn on a state or national bank, a cashier's check drawn by a state or federal credit union, or a cashier's check drawn by a state or federal savings and loan association, savings association, or savings bank specified in Section 5102 of the Financial Code and authorized to do business in this state. The bid shall:

(i) Be sent to the trustee by certified mail, overnight delivery, or [3] **another** method that allows for confirmation of the delivery date.

(ii) Be accompanied by an affidavit or declaration, pursuant to Section 2015.5 of the Code of Civil Procedure, identifying the category set forth in paragraph (3) of subdivision (a) to which the eligible bidder belongs and stating that the eligible bidder meets the criteria for that category.

(iii) Be received by the trustee no later than 5 p.m. on the 45th day after the trustee's sale, or the next business day following the 45th day if the 45th day is a weekend or holiday, if the eligible bidder submitted a nonbinding written notice of intent to bid pursuant to paragraph (2). Notwithstanding clause (i), on the last day that bids are eligible to be received by the trustee under this clause, the trustee shall not receive any bid that is not sent by certified mail [4] **with the United States Postal Service or by another overnight mail courier service with tracking information that confirms the recipient's signature and the date and time of receipt and delivery.**

(iv) Contain a current telephone number and return mailing address for the person submitting the bid.

(v) Be limited to a single bid amount and not contain instructions for successive bid amounts.

(B) As of 5 p.m. on the 45th day after the trustee's sale, if one or more eligible bidders has submitted a bid that meets the conditions in this paragraph, the eligible bidder that submitted the highest bid shall be deemed the last and highest bidder pursuant to the power of sale. The trustee shall return any losing bid to the eligible bidder that submitted it.

(d) The trustee may reasonably rely on affidavits and declarations regarding bidder eligibility received under this section. The affidavit or declaration of the winning bidder shall be attached as an exhibit to the trustee's deed and recorded. If the winning bidder is not required to submit an affidavit or declaration pursuant to this section, the trustee shall attach as an exhibit to the trustee's deed a statement that no affidavit or declaration is required by this section, and the lack of an affidavit or declaration shall not prevent the deed from being recorded and shall not invalidate the transfer of title pursuant to the trustee's deed.

(e) If the conditions set forth in paragraph (1) of subdivision (c) for a sale to be deemed final are not met, then:

(1) Not later than 48 hours after the trustee's sale of property under Section 2924g, the trustee or an authorized agent shall post on the internet website set forth on the notice of sale, as required under paragraph (8) of subdivision (b) of Section 2924f, the following information:

(A) The date on which the trustee's sale took place.

(B) The amount of the last and highest bid at the trustee's sale.

(C) An address at which the trustee can receive documents sent by United States mail and by a method of delivery providing for overnight delivery.

(2) The information required to be posted on the internet website under paragraph (1) shall also be made available not later than 48 hours after the trustee's sale of property under Section 2924g by calling the telephone number set forth on the notice of sale as required under paragraph (8) of subdivision (b) of Section 2924f.

(3) The information required to be provided under paragraphs (1) and (2) shall be made available using the file number assigned to the case that is set forth on the notice of sale as required under paragraph (8) of subdivision (b) of Section 2924f.

(4) The information required to be provided under paragraphs (1) and (2) shall be made available for a period of not less than 45 days after the sale of property under Section 2924g.

(5) A disruption of any of these methods of providing the information required under paragraphs (1) and (2) to allow for reasonable maintenance or due to a service outage shall not be deemed to be a violation of this subdivision.

(6) The information to be provided by the trustee to eligible bidders or to persons considering whether to submit a bid or notice of intent to bid pursuant to this section is limited to the information set forth in paragraph (1).

(f) Title to the property shall remain with the mortgagor or trustor or successor in interest until the property sale is deemed final as provided in this section.

(g) A prospective owner-occupant shall not be in violation of this section if a legal owner's compliance with the requirements of Section 2924n renders them unable to occupy the property as their primary residence within 60 days of the trustee's deed being recorded.

(h) This section shall prevail over any conflicting provision of Section 2924h.

(i) For trustee's sales where the winning bidder is an eligible bidder under this section, the trustee or an authorized agent shall electronically send the following information to the office of the Attorney General within 15 days of the sale being deemed final:

(1) The dates when the trustee's sale took place and when it was deemed final.

(2) The name of the winning bidder.

(3) The street address and assessor's parcel number of the subject property.

(4) A copy of the trustee's deed, as executed, including the attached affidavit or declaration of the winning bidder.

(5) The category set forth in paragraph (3) of subdivision (a) to which the eligible bidder belongs.

(j) The Attorney General, a county counsel, a city attorney, or a district attorney may bring an action for specific performance or any other remedy at equity or at law to enforce this section.

(k) The Department of Justice shall include a summary of information contained in the reports received pursuant to subdivision (i) in a searchable repository on its official internet website.

(*l*) The pendency of a determination of finality under subdivision (c) shall not cause termination of any hazard insurance coverage in effect at the time of the trustee's sale.

(m) This section shall remain in effect only until January 1, 2031, and as of that date is repealed, unless a later enacted statute that is enacted before January 1, 2031, deletes or extends that date. **Leg.H.** Added Stats 2020 ch 202 §7 (SB 1079), effective January 1, 2021, repealed January 1, 2026. Amended Stats 2021 ch 255 §2 (AB 175), effective September 23, 2021, operative January 1, 2022, repealed January 1, 2026; Stats 2022 ch 642 §9 (AB 1837), effective January 1, 2023, repealed January 1, 2031; Stats 2023 ch 478 §6 (AB 1756), effective January 1, 2024, repealed January 1, 2031; Stats 2024 ch 142 §5 (AB 295), effective July 18, 2024, repealed January 1, 2031; Stats 2024 ch 601 §10 (SB 1146), effective January 1, 2025, repealed January 1, 2031.

§ 2924m. 2024 Deletes. [1] other [2] other [3] other [4] or overnight mail

§ 2924n. Article not to affect eviction rights and duties

Nothing in this article shall relieve a person deemed the legal owner of real property when the trustee's deed is recorded from complying with applicable law regarding the eviction or displacement of tenants, including, but not limited to, notice requirements, requirements for the provision of temporary or permanent relocation assistance, the right to return, and just cause eviction requirements. **Leg.H.** Added Stats 2020 ch 202 §8 (SB 1079), effective January 1, 2021.

§ 2924o. Requirements of recorded covenants for real property purchased pursuant to Section 2924m [Repealed January 1, 2031]

(a) On and after January 1, 2023, in the case of any real property purchased pursuant to Section 2924m by an eligible bidder described in subparagraphs (C) to (G), inclusive, of paragraph (3) of subdivision (a) of that section, the property shall be subject to a recorded covenant that ensures the property shall be sold at an affordable housing cost, as defined in Section 50052.5 of the Health and Safety Code, or rented at an affordable rent, as defined in Section 50053 of the Health and Safety Code, for lower income households for 30 years from the date the trustee's deed is issued, or a greater period of time if any of the following apply:

(1) The terms of a federal, state, or local grant, tax credit, or other source of project financing funding the purchase or maintenance of the property by an eligible bidder require a longer term.

(2) The property becomes subject to a contract as described in paragraph (11) of subdivision (a) of Section 402.1 of the Revenue and Taxation Code.

(b) Tenants, if any, of a property purchased pursuant to Section 2924m by an eligible bidder described in subparagraphs (C) to (G), inclusive, of paragraph (3) of subdivision (a) of that section may exercise any rights available at equity or in law, including, without limitation, to defend an unlawful detainer or institute an action to enforce this section.

(c) For purposes of this section, "lower income households" has the same meaning as described in Section 50079.5 of the Health and Safety Code.

(d) This section shall remain in effect only until January 1, 2031, and as of that date is repealed, unless a later enacted statute that is enacted before January 1, 2031, deletes or extends that date. **Leg.H.** Added Stats 2022 ch 642 §10 (AB 1837), effective January 1, 2023, repealed January 1, 2031.

§ 2924p. Purchase of properties acquired through foreclosure by prospective owner-occupants and eligible bidders

(a) For purposes of this section, it is the intent of the Legislature to do all of the following:

(1) Allow for prospective owner-occupants and eligible bidders to have the first opportunity to purchase properties that have been acquired through the foreclosure process by an entity that annually forecloses on 175 or more residential real properties in California.

(2) Promote owner occupancy by enacting legislation consistent with the provisions of the federal First Look program that provides owner-occupants and affordable housing providers an opportunity for their offers to be considered on foreclosed properties prior to other offers.

(3) Ensure that the requirements of this section are consistent with the original stated goals of the federal First Look program, which were to expand home ownership opportunities, strengthen neighborhoods and communities, while also providing that sellers are required to respond to offers received during the first look period before accepting or considering investor offers to purchase single-family homes.

(b) For purpose of this section:

(1) "Bundled sale" means the sale of two or more parcels of real property containing one to four residential dwelling units, inclusive, at least two of which have been acquired through foreclosure under a mortgage or deed of trust.

(2) "Eligible bidder" means any of the following:

(A) A prospective owner-occupant.

(B) A nonprofit corporation that meets all of the following requirements:

(i) The nonprofit corporation has a determination letter from the Internal Revenue Service affirming its tax-exempt status pursuant to Section 501(c)(3) of the Internal Revenue Code and is not a private foundation as that term is defined in Section 509 of the Internal Revenue Code.

(ii) The nonprofit corporation is based in California.

(iii) All of the board members of the nonprofit corporation have their primary residence in California.

(iv) The primary activity of the nonprofit corporation is the development and preservation of affordable rental or home ownership housing in California.

(C) A community land trust based in California, as defined in clause (ii) of subparagraph (C) of paragraph (11) of subdivision (a) of Section 402.1 of the Revenue and Taxation Code, **as amended by the act amending this subparagraph.**

(D) A limited-equity housing cooperative, as defined in Section 817, that is based in California.

(E) The state, the Regents of the University of California, a county, city, district, public authority, or public agency, and any other political subdivision or public corporation in the state.

(3) "Institution" means any of the following, if that person or entity, during its immediately preceding annual reporting period, as established

with its primary regulator, foreclosed on 175 or more residential real properties, containing no more than 4 dwelling units:

(A) A depository institution chartered under state or federal law.

(B) A person licensed pursuant to Division 9 (commencing with Section 22000) or Division 20 (commencing with Section 50000) of the Financial Code.

(C) A person licensed pursuant to Part 1 (commencing with Section 10000) of Division 4 of the Business and Professions Code.

(4) "Prospective owner-occupant" means a natural person whose affidavit or declaration under paragraph (2) of subdivision (c) states all of the following:

(A) They will occupy the property as their primary residence within 60 days of the trustee's deed being recorded.

(B) They will maintain their occupancy for at least one year.

(C) They are not any of the following:

(i) The mortgagor or trustor.

(ii) The child, spouse, or parent of the mortgagor or trustor.

(iii) The grantor of a living trust that was named in the title to the property when the notice of default was recorded.

(iv) An employee, officer, or member of the mortgagor or trustor.

(v) A person with an ownership interest in the mortgagor, unless the mortgagor is a publicly traded company.

(D) They are not acting as the agent of any other person or entity in purchasing the real property.

(c) All of the following shall apply to sales of real property containing one to four residential dwelling units, inclusive, that is acquired through foreclosure under a mortgage or deed of trust by an institution or that is acquired at a foreclosure sale by an institution:

(1) During the first 30 days after the property is listed for sale, the institution shall only accept offers from eligible bidders.

(2) An eligible bidder shall submit with their offer to the institution an affidavit or declaration, pursuant to Section 2015.5 of the Code of Civil Procedure, that states they are either of the following:

(A) An eligible bidder pursuant to subparagraphs (B) through (E) of paragraph (2) of subdivision (b).

(B) A prospective owner-occupant purchasing the property as a primary residence pursuant to this subdivision.

(3) Any fraudulent statements may be subject to criminal or civil liability.

(4) The institution shall respond, in writing, to all offers received from eligible bidders during the first 30 days after the property is listed for sale before considering any other offers.

(5) Notwithstanding any other law, an institution shall not conduct a bundled sale.

(d) The provisions of this section are severable. If any provision of this section or its application is held invalid, that invalidity shall not affect other provisions or applications that can be given effect without the invalid provision or application. **Leg.H.** Added Stats 2022 ch 865 §1 (AB 2170), effective January 1, 2023. Amended Stats 2024 ch 580 §1 (AB 2897), effective January 1, 2025.

§2924½. [Section repealed 1959]

Leg.H. Added Stats 1933 ch 642 §8. Amended Stats 1935 ch 669 §1. Repealed Stats 1959 ch 593 §3. The repealed section related to deficiency judgment limitations.

§2925. Transfer made subject to defeasance may be proved

The fact that a transfer was made subject to defeasance on a condition, may, for the purpose of showing such transfer to be a mortgage, be proved (except as against a subsequent purchaser or incumbrancer for value and without notice), though the fact does not appear by the terms of the instrument. **Leg.H.** Enacted 1872.

§2926. Mortgage, on what a lien

A mortgage is a lien upon everything that would pass by a grant of the property. **Leg.H.** Enacted 1872.

§2927. Mortgage does not entitle mortgagee to possession

A mortgage does not entitle the mortgagee to the possession of the property, unless authorized by the express terms of the mortgage; but after the execution of the mortgage the mortgagor may agree to such change of possession without a new consideration. **Leg.H.** Enacted 1872.

§2928. Mortgage not a personal obligation

A mortgage does not bind the mortgagor personally to perform the act for the performance of which it is a security, unless there is an express covenant therein to that effect. **Leg.H.** Enacted 1872.

§2929. Waste

No person whose interest is subject to the lien of a mortgage may do any act which will substantially impair the mortgagee's security. **Leg.H.** Enacted 1872.

§2929.3. Duty of foreclosure purchaser to maintain vacant property; Notice of violation; Fines and penalties; Relation to local ordinances

(a)(1) A legal owner shall maintain vacant residential property purchased by that owner at a foreclosure sale once that sale is deemed final, or acquired by that owner through foreclosure under a mortgage or deed of trust. A governmental entity may impose a civil fine upon the legal owner of the property for a violation as set forth in this section. The governmental entity is not required to impose a civil fine if the violation is not remedied.

(2) If the governmental entity chooses to impose a fine pursuant to this section, it shall give the legal owner, prior to the imposition of the fine, a notice containing the following information:

(A) Notice of the alleged violation, including a detailed description of the conditions that gave rise to the allegation.

(B) Notice of the entity's intent to assess a civil fine if the legal owner does not do both of the following:

(i) Within a period determined by the entity, consisting of not less than 14 business days following the date of the notice, commence action to remedy the violation and notify the entity of that action. This time period shall be extended by an additional 10 business days if requested by the legal owner in order to clarify with the entity the actions necessary to remedy the violation.

(ii) Complete the action described in clause (i) within a period of no less than 16 business days following the end of the period set forth in clause (i).

(C) The notice required under this paragraph shall be mailed to the address provided in the deed or other instrument as specified in subdivision (a) of Section 27321.5 of the Government Code, or, if none, to the return address provided on the deed or other instrument.

(3) The governmental entity shall provide a period of not less than the time set forth in clauses (i) and (ii) of subparagraph (B) of paragraph (2) to remedy the violation prior to imposing a civil fine and shall allow for a hearing and opportunity to contest any fine imposed. In determining the amount of the fine, the governmental entity shall take into consideration any timely and good faith efforts by the legal owner to remedy the violation. The maximum civil fine authorized by this section for each day that the owner fails to maintain the property, commencing on the day following the expiration of the period to remedy the violation established by the governmental entity, is as follows:

(A) Up to a maximum of two thousand dollars ($2,000) per day for the first 30 days.

(B) Up to a maximum of five thousand dollars ($5,000) per day thereafter.

(4) Subject to the provisions of this section, a governmental entity may establish different compliance periods for different conditions on the same property in the notice of alleged violation mailed to the legal owner.

(b) For purposes of this section, "failure to maintain" means failure to care for the exterior of the property, including, but not limited to, permitting excessive foliage growth that diminishes the value of surrounding properties, failing to take action to prevent trespassers or squatters from remaining on the property, or failing to take action to prevent mosquito larvae from growing in standing water or other conditions that create a public nuisance.

(c) Notwithstanding subdivisions (a) and (b), a governmental entity may provide less than 30 days' notice to remedy a condition before imposing a civil fine if the entity determines that a specific condition of the property threatens public health or safety and provided that notice of that determination and time for compliance is given.

(d) Fines and penalties collected pursuant to this section shall be directed to local nuisance abatement programs, including, but not limited to, legal abatement proceedings.

(e) A governmental entity may not impose fines on a legal owner under both this section and a local ordinance.

(f) These provisions shall not preempt any local ordinance.

(g) This section shall only apply to residential real property.

(h) The rights and remedies provided in this section are cumulative and in addition to any other rights and remedies provided by law. **Leg.H.** Added Stats 2008 ch 69 §5 (SB 1137), effective July 8, 2008, repealed January 1, 2013. Amended Stats 2012 ch 201 §1 (AB 2314), effective January 1, 2013; Stats 2020 ch 202 §9 (SB 1079), effective January 1, 2021.

2008 Note: Nothing in this act is intended t affect any local just-cause eviction ordinance. This act does not, and shall not be construed to, affect the authority of a public entity that otherwise exists to regulate or monitor the basis for eviction. Stats 2008 ch 69 (SB 1137) §7.

§2929.4. Notice of violation for failing to maintain vacant property; Applicability

(a) Prior to imposing a fine or penalty for failure to maintain a vacant property that is subject to a notice of default, that is purchased at a foreclosure sale, or that is acquired through foreclosure under a mortgage or deed of trust, a governmental entity shall provide the owner of that property with a notice of the violation and an opportunity to correct that violation.

(b) This section shall not apply if the governmental entity determines that a specific condition of the property threatens public health or safety. **Leg.H.** Added Stats 2010 ch 527 §1 (SB 1427), effective January 1, 2011.

§2929.45. Assessment or lien to recover costs of nuisance abatement

(a) An assessment or lien to recover the costs of nuisance abatement measures taken by a governmental entity with regard to property that is subject to a notice of default, that is purchased at a foreclosure sale, or that is acquired through foreclosure under a mortgage or deed of trust, shall not exceed the actual and reasonable costs of nuisance abatement.

(b) A governmental entity shall not impose an assessment or lien unless the costs that constitute the assessment or lien have been adopted by the elected officials of that governmental entity at a public hearing. **Leg.H.** Added Stats 2010 ch 527 §2 (SB 1427), effective January 1, 2011.

§2929.5. Secured lender's right of entry and inspection

(a) A secured lender may enter and inspect the real property security for the purpose of determining the existence, location, nature, and magnitude of any past or present release or threatened release of any hazardous substance into, onto, beneath, or from the real property security on either of the following:

(1) Upon reasonable belief of the existence of a past or present release or threatened release of any hazardous substance into, onto, beneath, or from the real property security not previously disclosed in writing to the secured lender in conjunction with the making, renewal, or modification of a loan, extension of credit, guaranty, or other obligation involving the borrower.

(2) After the commencement of nonjudicial or judicial foreclosure proceedings against the real property security.

(b) The secured lender shall not abuse the right of entry and inspection or use it to harass the borrower or tenant of the property. Except in case of an emergency, when the borrower or tenant of the property has abandoned the premises, or if it is impracticable to do so, the secured lender shall give the borrower or tenant of the property reasonable notice of the secured lender's intent to enter, and enter only during the borrower's or tenant's normal business hours. Twenty-four hours' notice shall be presumed to be reasonable notice in the absence of evidence to the contrary.

(c) The secured lender shall reimburse the borrower for the cost of repair of any physical injury to the real property security caused by the entry and inspection.

(d) If a secured lender is refused the right of entry and inspection by the borrower or tenant of the property, or is otherwise unable to enter and inspect the property without a breach of the peace, the secured lender may, upon petition, obtain an order from a court of competent jurisdiction to exercise the secured lender's rights under subdivision (a), and that action shall not constitute an action within the meaning of subdivision (a) of Section 726 of the Code of Civil Procedure.

(e) For purposes of this section:

(1) "Borrower" means the trustor under a deed of trust, or a mortgagor under a mortgage, where the deed of trust or mortgage encumbers real property security and secures the performance of the trustor or mortgagor under a loan, extension of credit, guaranty, or other obligation. The term includes any successor-in-interest of the trustor or mortgagor to the real property security before the deed of trust or mortgage has been discharged, reconveyed, or foreclosed upon.

(2) "Hazardous substance" includes all of the following:

(A) Any "hazardous substance" as defined in subdivision (h) of Section 25281 of the Health and Safety Code.

(B) Any "waste" as defined in subdivision (d) of Section 13050 of the Water Code.

(C) Petroleum, including crude oil or any fraction thereof, natural gas, natural gas liquids, liquefied natural gas, or synthetic gas usable for fuel, or any mixture thereof.

(3) "Real property security" means any real property and improvements, other than a separate interest and any related interest in the common area of a residential common interest development, as the terms "separate interest," "common area," and "common interest development" are defined in Sections 4095, 4100, and 4185, or real property consisting of one acre or less which contains 1 to 15 dwelling units.

(4) "Release" means any spilling, leaking, pumping, pouring, emitting, emptying, discharging, injecting, escaping, leaching, dumping, or disposing into the environment, including continuing migration, of hazardous substances into, onto, or through soil, surface water, or groundwater.

(5) "Secured lender" means the beneficiary under a deed of trust against the real property security, or the mortgagee under a mortgage against the real property security, and any successor-in-interest of the beneficiary or mortgagee to the deed of trust or mortgage. **Leg.H.** Added Stats 1991 ch 1167 §1 (AB 1735). Amended Stats 1992 ch 167 §1 (AB 2750); Stats 2002 ch 999 §2 (AB 2481); Stats 2012 ch 181 §40 (AB 806), effective January 1, 2013, operative January 1, 2014.

§2930. Subsequently acquired title inures to mortgagee

Title acquired by the mortgagor subsequent to the execution of the mortgage, inures to the mortgagee as security for the debt in like manner as if acquired before the execution. **Leg.H.** Enacted 1872. Amended Code Amdts 1873–74 ch 612 §257.

§2931. Foreclosure

A mortgagee may foreclose the right of redemption of the mortgagor in the manner prescribed by the Code of Civil Procedure. **Leg.H.** Enacted 1872.

§2931a. Joinder of state agency in specified actions; Jurisdiction of court; Complaint or petition; Representation by Attorney General

In any action brought to determine conflicting claims to real property, or for partition of real property or an estate for years therein, or to foreclose a deed of trust, mortgage, or other lien upon real property, or in all eminent domain proceedings under Section 1250.110 et seq., of the Code of Civil Procedure against real property upon which exists a lien to secure the payment of taxes or other obligations to an agency of the State of California, other than ad valorem taxes upon the real property, the state agency charged with the collection of the tax obligation may be made a party. In such an action, the court shall have jurisdiction to determine the priority and effect of the liens described in the complaint in or upon the real property or estate for years therein, but the jurisdiction of the court in the action shall not include a determination of the validity of the tax giving rise to the lien or claim of lien. The complaint or petition in the action shall contain a description of the lien sufficient to enable the tax or other obligation, payment of which it secures, to be identified with certainty, and shall include the name and address of the person owing the tax or other obligation, the name of the state agency that recorded the lien, and the date and place where the lien was recorded. Services of process in the action shall be made upon the agency, officer, board, commission, department, division, or other body charged with the collection of the tax or obligation. It shall be the duty of the Attorney General to represent the state agency in the action. **Leg.H.** Added Stats 1935 ch 464 §1. Amended Stats 1941 ch 1193 §1; Stats 1980 ch 44 §2; Stats 1986 ch 81 §1; Stats 1989 ch 698 §8.

§2931b. Power of Attorney General to bid at sale

In all actions in which the State of California is named a party pursuant to the provisions of Section 2931a and in which real property or an estate for years therein is sought to be sold, the Attorney General may, with the consent of the Department of Finance, bid upon and purchase that real property or estate for years. **Leg.H.** Added Stats 1953 ch 1675 §1. Amended Stats 1989 ch 698 §9.

§2931c. Action by Attorney General to enforce tax lien

The Attorney General may bring an action in the courts of this or any other state or of the United States to enforce any lien to secure the payment of taxes or other obligations to the State of California under the Unemployment Insurance Code, the Revenue and Taxation Code, or Chapter 6 (commencing with Section 16180) of Part 1 of Division 4 of Title 2 of the Government Code or to subject to payment of the liability giving rise to the lien any property in which the debtor has any right, title, or interest. In any action brought under this section the court shall have jurisdiction to determine the priority and effect of the lien in or upon the property, but the jurisdiction of the court in such action shall not extend to a determination of the validity of the liability giving rise to the lien. **Leg.H.** Added Stats 1963 ch 1308 §1. Amended Stats 1977 ch 1242 §3, effective October 1, 1977.

§2932. Power of sale

A power of sale may be conferred by a mortgage upon the mortgagee or any other person, to be exercised after a breach of the obligation for which the mortgage is a security. **Leg.H.** Enacted 1872.

§2932.2. Residential real property containing more than four dwelling units; Written disclosure; Notice of default and notice of sale

With respect to residential real property containing no more than four dwelling units, a mortgagee, beneficiary, or authorized agent shall provide to the mortgagor or trustor, before the mortgagor or trustor signs the mortgage or deed of trust, a written disclosure that a third party, such as a family member, HUD-certified housing counselor, or attorney, may record a request to receive copies of any notice of default and notice of sale. A request for notice under this section shall comply with Section 2924b. **Leg.H.** Added Stats 2024 ch 311 §5 (AB 2424), effective January 1, 2025.

§2932.5. Power of sale under assigned mortgage

Where a power to sell real property is given to a mortgagee, or other encumbrancer, in an instrument intended to secure the payment of money, the power is part of the security and vests in any person who by assignment becomes entitled to payment of the money secured by the instrument. The power of sale may be exercised by the assignee if the assignment is duly acknowledged and recorded. **Leg.H.** Added Stats 1986 ch 820 §11, operative July 1, 1987.

§2932.6. Repair of residential real property acquired through foreclosure

(a) Notwithstanding any other provision of law, a financial institution may undertake to repair any property acquired through foreclosure under a mortgage or deed of trust.

(b) As used in this section, the term "financial institution" includes, but is not limited to, banks, savings associations, credit unions, and industrial loan companies.

(c) The rights granted to a financial institution by this section are in addition to, and not in derogation of, the rights of a financial institution which otherwise exist. **Leg.H.** Added Stats 1987 ch 187 §1. Amended Stats 1988 ch 125 §1.

§2933. Power of attorney to execute

A power of attorney to execute a mortgage must be in writing, subscribed, acknowledged, or proved, certified, and recorded in like manner as powers of attorney for grants of real property. **Leg.H.** Enacted 1872.

§2934. Recording of assignment or subordination instrument as constructive notice of contents

Any assignment of a mortgage and any assignment of the beneficial interest under a deed of trust may be recorded, and from the time the same is filed for record operates as constructive notice of the contents thereof to all persons; and any instrument by which any mortgage or deed of trust of, lien upon or interest in real property (or by which any mortgage of, lien upon or interest in personal property a document evidencing or creating which is required or permitted by law to be recorded), is subordinated or waived as to priority may be recorded, and from the time the same is filed for record operates as constructive notice of the contents thereof, to all persons. **Leg.H.** Enacted 1872. Amended Code Amdts 1873–74 ch 612 §258; Stats 1931 ch 80 §1; Stats 1935 ch 818 §1.

§2934a. Substitution of trustee under trust deed

(a)(1) The trustee under a trust deed upon real property or an estate for years given to secure an obligation to pay money and conferring no other duties upon the trustee than those which are incidental to the exercise of the power of sale therein conferred, may be substituted by the recording in the county in which the property is located of a substitution executed and acknowledged by either of the following:

(A) All of the beneficiaries under the trust deed, or their successors in interest, and the substitution shall be effective notwithstanding any contrary provision in any trust deed executed on or after January 1, 1968.

(B) The holders of more than 50 percent of the record beneficial interest of a series of notes secured by the same real property or of undivided interests in a note secured by real property equivalent to a series transaction, exclusive of any notes or interests of a licensed real estate broker that is the issuer or servicer of the notes or interests or of any affiliate of that licensed real estate broker.

(2) A substitution executed pursuant to subparagraph (B) of paragraph (1) is not effective unless all the parties signing the substitution sign, under penalty of perjury, a separate written document stating the following:

(A) The substitution has been signed pursuant to subparagraph (B) of paragraph (1).

(B) None of the undersigned is a licensed real estate broker or an affiliate of the broker that is the issuer or servicer of the obligation secured by the deed of trust.

(C) The undersigned together hold more than 50 percent of the record beneficial interest of a series of notes secured by the same real property or of undivided interests in a note secured by real property equivalent to a series transaction.

(D) Notice of the substitution was sent by certified mail, postage prepaid, with return receipt requested to each holder of an interest in the obligation secured by the deed of trust who has not joined in the execution of the substitution or the separate document.

The separate document shall be attached to the substitution and recorded in the office of the county recorder of each county in which the real property described in the deed of trust is located. Once the document is recorded, it shall constitute conclusive evidence of compliance with the requirements of this paragraph in favor of substituted trustees acting pursuant to this section, subsequent assignees of the obligation secured by the deed of trust and subsequent bona fide purchasers or encumbrancers for value of the real property described therein.

(3) For purposes of this section, "affiliate of the licensed real estate broker" includes any person as defined in Section 25013 of the Corporations Code that is controlled by, or is under common control with, or who controls, a licensed real estate broker. "Control" means the possession, direct or indirect, of the power to direct or cause the direction of management and policies.

(4) The substitution shall contain the date of recordation of the trust deed, the name of the trustor, the book and page or instrument number where the trust deed is recorded, and the name of the new trustee. From the time the substitution is filed for record, the new trustee shall succeed to all the powers, duties, authority, and title granted and delegated to the trustee named in the deed of trust. A substitution may be accomplished, with respect to multiple deeds of trust that are recorded in the same county in which the substitution is being recorded and that all have the same trustee and beneficiary or beneficiaries, by recording a single document, complying with the requirements of this section, substituting trustees for all those deeds of trust.

(b) If the substitution is executed, but not recorded, prior to or concurrently with the recording of the notice of default, the beneficiary or beneficiaries or their authorized agents shall mail notice of the substitution before or concurrently with the recording thereof, in the manner provided in Section 2924b, to all persons to whom a copy of the notice of default would be required to be mailed by Section 2924b. An affidavit shall be attached to the substitution that notice has been given to those persons, as required by this subdivision.

(c) If the substitution is effected after a notice of default has been recorded but prior to the recording of the notice of sale, the beneficiary or beneficiaries or their authorized agents shall mail a copy of the substitution, before, or concurrently with, the recording thereof, as provided in

Section 2924b, to the trustee then of record and to all persons to whom a copy of the notice of default would be required to be mailed by Section 2924b. An affidavit shall be attached to the substitution that notice has been given to those persons, as required by this subdivision.

(d)(1) A trustee named in a recorded substitution of trustee shall be deemed to be authorized to act as the trustee under the mortgage or deed of trust for all purposes from the date the substitution is executed by the mortgagee, beneficiaries, or by their authorized agents. A trustee under a recorded substitution is not required to accept the substitution, and may either resign or refuse to accept appointment as trustee pursuant to this subdivision.

(2)(A) A trustee named in a recorded substitution of trustee may resign or refuse to accept appointment as trustee at that trustee's own election without the consent of the beneficiary or beneficiaries or their authorized agents. The trustee shall give prompt written notice of that resignation or refusal to accept appointment as trustee to the beneficiary or beneficiaries or their authorized agents by doing both of the following:

(i) Depositing or causing to be deposited in the United States mail an envelope containing a notice of resignation of trustee, sent by registered or certified mail with postage prepaid, to all beneficiaries or their authorized agents at the address shown on the last-recorded substitution of trustee for that real property or estate for years in that county.

(ii) Recording the notice of resignation of trustee, mailed in the manner described in clause (i), in each county in which the substitution of trustee under which the trustee was appointed is recorded. An affidavit stating that notice has been mailed to all beneficiaries and their authorized agents in the manner provided in clause (i) shall be attached to the recorded notice of resignation of trustee.

(B) The resignation of the trustee or refusal to accept appointment as trustee pursuant to this subdivision shall become effective upon the recording of the notice of resignation of trustee in each county in which the substitution of trustee under which the trustee was appointed is recorded.

(C) The resignation of the trustee or refusal to accept appointment as trustee pursuant to this subdivision does not affect the validity of the mortgage or deed of trust, except that no action required to be performed by the trustee under this chapter or under the mortgage or deed of trust may be taken until a substituted trustee is appointed pursuant to this section. If a trustee is not designated in the deed of trust, or upon the resignation, incapacity, disability, absence or death of the trustee, or the election of the beneficiary or beneficiaries to replace the trustee, the beneficiary or beneficiaries or their authorized agents shall appoint a trustee or a successor trustee.

(D) A notice of resignation of trustee mailed and recorded pursuant to this paragraph shall set forth the intention of the trustee to resign or refuse appointment as trustee and the recording date and instrument number of the recorded substitution of trustee under which the trustee was appointed.

(E) A notice of resignation of trustee mailed and recorded pursuant to this paragraph shall contain an address at which the trustee and any successor in interest will be available for service of process for at least five years after the date that the notice of resignation is recorded.

(F) For at least five years after a notice of resignation of trustee is mailed and recorded pursuant to this paragraph, the trustee and any successor in interest to that trustee shall retain and preserve every writing, as that term is defined in Section 250 of the Evidence Code, relating to the trust deed or estate for years under which the trustee was appointed.

(3) For purposes of this section, paragraph (2) sets forth the exclusive procedure for a trustee to either resign or refuse to accept appointment as trustee.

(4) Once recorded, the substitution shall constitute conclusive evidence of the authority of the substituted trustee or their authorized agents to act pursuant to this section, unless prompt written notice of resignation of trustee has been given in accordance with the procedures set forth in paragraph (2).

(e) Notwithstanding any provision of this section or any provision in any deed of trust, unless a new notice of sale containing the name, street address, and telephone number of the substituted trustee is given pursuant to Section 2924f after execution of the substitution, any sale conducted by the substituted trustee shall be void. **Leg.H.** Added Stats 1993 ch 754 §2.5 (SB 313), effective October 2, 1993, operative January 1, 1998. Amended Stats 1996 ch 839 §2 (SB 1638), effective January 1, 1997, operative January 1, 1998; Stats 1999 ch 974 §14 (AB 431), effective January 1, 2000; Stats 2004 ch 177 §5 (SB 1277), effective January 1, 2005; Stats 2019 ch 474 §1 (SB 306), effective January 1, 2020.

Prior Law: Former CC §2934a, similar to the present section, was added Stats 1935 ch 609 §1, amended Stats 1957 ch 914 §1, Stats 1967 ch 1163 §1, Stats 1979 ch 1015 §6, Stats 1982 ch 521 §1, Stats 1984 ch 1730 §5, Stats 1984 ch 1730 §5, Stats 1989 ch 698 §10 (SB 1598), Stats 1993 ch 686 §8 (AB 1219), Stats 1993 ch 754 §1 (SB 313), effective October 2, 1993, operative until January 1, 1994, §1.5, effective October 2, 1993, operative January 1, 1994, Stats 1996 ch 839 §1 (SB 1638), effective January 1, 1997, inoperative January 1, 1998, and repealed Stats 2015 ch 303 §31 (AB 731), effective January 1, 2016.

Former CC §2934a, similar to the present section, was added Stats 1935 ch 609 §1 and repealed Stats 2015 ch 303 §31 (AB 731).

§2934b. Vacation of office of trustee under deed of trust

Sections 15643 and 18102 of the Probate Code apply to trustees under deeds of trust given to secure obligations. **Leg.H.** Added Stats 1986 ch 820 §12, operative July 1, 1987.

§2935. Record of assignment as notice to debtor

When a mortgage or deed of trust is executed as security for money due or to become due, on a promissory note, bond, or other instrument, designated in the mortgage or deed of trust, the record of the assignment of the mortgage or of the assignment of the beneficial interest under the deed of trust, is not of itself notice to the debtor, his heirs, or personal representatives, so as to invalidate any payment made by them, or any of them, to the person holding such note, bond, or other instrument. **Leg.H.** Enacted 1872. Amended Code Amdts 1873–74 ch 612 §259; Stats 1931 ch 80 §2.

§2936. Mortgage passes by assignment of debt

The assignment of a debt secured by mortgage carries with it the security. **Leg.H.** Enacted 1872.

§2937. Transfer of servicing of indebtedness on single family residential real property; Notice; Insurance policy information; Payments made prior to notice

(a) The Legislature hereby finds and declares that borrowers or subsequent obligors have the right to know when a person holding a promissory note, bond, or other instrument transfers servicing of the indebtedness secured by a mortgage or deed of trust on real property containing one to four residential units located in this state. The Legislature also finds that notification to the borrower or subsequent obligor of the transfer may protect the borrower or subsequent obligor from fraudulent business practices and may ensure timely payments.

It is the intent of the Legislature in enacting this section to mandate that a borrower or subsequent obligor be given written notice when a person transfers the servicing of the indebtedness on notes, bonds, or other instruments secured by a mortgage or deed of trust on real property containing one to four residential units and located in this state.

(b) Any person transferring the servicing of indebtedness as provided in subdivision (a) to a different servicing agent and any person assuming from another responsibility for servicing the instrument evidencing indebtedness, shall give written notice to the borrower or subsequent obligor before the borrower or subsequent obligor becomes obligated to make payments to a new servicing agent.

(c) In the event a notice of default has been recorded or a judicial foreclosure proceeding has been commenced, the person transferring the servicing of the indebtedness and the person assuming from another the duty of servicing the indebtedness shall give written notice to the trustee or attorney named in the notice of default or judicial foreclosure of the transfer. A notice of default, notice of sale, or judicial foreclosure shall not be invalidated solely because the servicing agent is changed during the foreclosure process.

(d) Any person transferring the servicing of indebtedness as provided in subdivision (a) to a different servicing agent shall provide to the new servicing agent all existing insurance policy information that the person is responsible for maintaining, including, but not limited to, flood and hazard insurance policy information.

(e) The notices required by subdivision (b) shall be sent by first-class mail, postage prepaid, to the borrower's or subsequent obligor's address designated for loan payment billings, or if escrow is pending, as provided in the escrow, and shall contain each of the following:

(1) The name and address of the person to which the transfer of the servicing of the indebtedness is made.

(2) The date the transfer was or will be completed.

(3) The address where all payments pursuant to the transfer are to be made.

(f) Any person assuming from another responsibility for servicing the instrument evidencing indebtedness shall include in the notice required by subdivision (b) a statement of the due date of the next payment.

(g) The borrower or subsequent obligor shall not be liable to the holder of the note, bond, or other instrument or to any servicing agent for payments made to the previous servicing agent or for late charges if these payments were made prior to the borrower or subsequent obligor receiving written notice of the transfer as provided by subdivision (e) and the payments were otherwise on time.

(h) For purposes of this section, the term servicing agent shall not include a trustee exercising a power of sale pursuant to a deed of trust.
Leg.H. Added Stats 1988 ch 1190 §1. Amended Stats 1989 ch 96 §1, effective July 7, 1989; Stats 2002 ch 70 §1 (SB 1370).

Prior Law: Former §2937, was enacted 1872, and repealed by Code Amdts 1873-74 ch 612 §260.

§2937.7. Effect of service of process to trustee

In any action affecting the interest of any trustor or beneficiary under a deed of trust or mortgage, service of process to the trustee does not constitute service to the trustor or beneficiary and does not impose any obligation on the trustee to notify the trustor or beneficiary of the action.
Leg.H. Added Stats 1988 ch 530 §1.

1988 Note: It is the intent of the Legislature in enacting this act that the changes made by this act shall not create an inference regarding the status or application of the law prior to the effective date of these changes. Stats 1988 ch 530 §3.

§2938. Written assignment of interest to create security interest; Demand to pay rent to party other than landlord

(a) A written assignment of an interest in leases, rents, issues, or profits of real property made in connection with an obligation secured by real property, irrespective of whether the assignment is denoted as absolute, absolute conditioned upon default, additional security for an obligation, or otherwise, shall, upon execution and delivery by the assignor, be effective to create a present security interest in existing and future leases, rents, issues, or profits of that real property. As used in this section, "leases, rents, issues, and profits of real property" includes the cash proceeds thereof. "Cash proceeds" means cash, checks, deposit accounts, and the like.

(b) An assignment of an interest in leases, rents, issues, or profits of real property may be recorded in the records of the county recorder in the county in which the underlying real property is located in the same manner as any other conveyance of an interest in real property, whether the assignment is in a separate document or part of a mortgage or deed of trust, and when so duly recorded in accordance with the methods, procedures, and requirements for recordation of conveyances of other interests in real property, (1) the assignment shall be deemed to give constructive notice of the content of the assignment with the same force and effect as any other duly recorded conveyance of an interest in real property and (2) the interest granted by the assignment shall be deemed fully perfected as of the time of recordation with the same force and effect as any other duly recorded conveyance of an interest in real property, notwithstanding a provision of the assignment or a provision of law that would otherwise preclude or defer enforcement of the rights granted the assignee under the assignment until the occurrence of a subsequent event, including, but not limited to, a subsequent default of the assignor, or the assignee's obtaining possession of the real property or the appointment of a receiver.

(c) Upon default of the assignor under the obligation secured by the assignment of leases, rents, issues, and profits, the assignee shall be entitled to enforce the assignment in accordance with this section. On and after the date the assignee takes one or more of the enforcement steps described in this subdivision, the assignee shall be entitled to collect and receive all rents, issues, and profits that have accrued but remain unpaid and uncollected by the assignor or its agent or for the assignor's benefit on that date, and all rents, issues, and profits that accrue on or after the date. The assignment shall be enforced by one or more of the following:

(1) The appointment of a receiver.

(2) Obtaining possession of the rents, issues, or profits.

(3) Delivery to any one or more of the tenants of a written demand for turnover of rents, issues, and profits in the form specified in subdivision (k), a copy of which demand shall also be delivered to the assignor; and a copy of which shall be mailed to all other assignees of record of the leases, rents, issues, and profits of the real property at the address for notices provided in the assignment or, if none, to the address to which the recorded assignment was to be mailed after recording.

(4) Delivery to the assignor of a written demand for the rents, issues, or profits, a copy of which shall be mailed to all other assignees of record of the leases, rents, issues, and profits of the real property at the address for notices provided in the assignment or, if none, to the address to which the recorded assignment was to be mailed after recording.

Moneys received by the assignee pursuant to this subdivision, net of amounts paid pursuant to subdivision (g), if any, shall be applied by the assignee to the debt or otherwise in accordance with the assignment or the promissory note, deed of trust, or other instrument evidencing the obligation, provided, however, that neither the application nor the failure to so apply the rents, issues, or profits shall result in a loss of any lien or security interest that the assignee may have in the underlying real property or any other collateral, render the obligation unenforceable, constitute a violation of Section 726 of the Code of Civil Procedure, or otherwise limit a right available to the assignee with respect to its security.

(d) If an assignee elects to take the action provided for under paragraph (3) of subdivision (c), the demand provided for therein shall be signed under penalty of perjury by the assignee or an authorized agent of the assignee and shall be effective as against the tenant when actually received by the tenant at the address for notices provided under the lease or other contractual agreement under which the tenant occupies the property or, if no address for notices is so provided, at the property. Upon receipt of this demand, the tenant shall be obligated to pay to the assignee all rents, issues, and profits that are past due and payable on the date of receipt of the demand, and all rents, issues, and profits coming due under the lease following the date of receipt of the demand, unless either of the following occurs:

(1) The tenant has previously received a demand that is valid on its face from another assignee of the leases, issues, rents, and profits sent by the other assignee in accordance with this subdivision and subdivision (c).

(2) The tenant, in good faith and in a manner that is not inconsistent with the lease, has previously paid, or within 10 days following receipt of the demand notice pays, the rent to the assignor.

Payment of rent to an assignee following a demand under an assignment of leases, rents, issues, and profits shall satisfy the tenant's obligation to pay the amounts under the lease. If a tenant pays rent to the assignor after receipt of a demand other than under the circumstances described in this subdivision, the tenant shall not be discharged of the obligation to pay rent to the assignee, unless the tenant occupies the property for residential purposes. The obligation of a tenant to pay rent pursuant to this subdivision and subdivision (c) shall continue until receipt by the tenant of a written notice from a court directing the tenant to pay the rent in a different manner or receipt by the tenant of a written notice from the assignee from whom the demand was received canceling the demand, whichever occurs first. This subdivision does not affect the entitlement to rents, issues, or profits as between assignees as set forth in subdivision (h).

(e) An enforcement action of the type authorized by subdivision (c), and a collection, distribution, or application of rents, issues, or profits by the assignee following an enforcement action of the type authorized by subdivision (c), shall not do any of the following:

(1) Make the assignee a mortgagee in possession of the property, except if the assignee obtains actual possession of the real property, or an agent of the assignor.

(2) Constitute an action, render the obligation unenforceable, violate Section 726 of the Code of Civil Procedure, or, other than with respect to marshaling requirements, otherwise limit any rights available to the assignee with respect to its security.

(3) Be deemed to create a bar to a deficiency judgment pursuant to a provision of law governing or relating to deficiency judgments following the enforcement of any encumbrance, lien, or security interest, notwithstanding that the action, collection, distribution, or application may reduce the indebtedness secured by the assignment or by a deed of trust or other security instrument.

The application of rents, issues, or profits to the secured obligation shall satisfy the secured obligation to the extent of those rents, issues, or profits, and, notwithstanding any provisions of the assignment or other loan documents to the contrary, shall be credited against any amounts necessary to cure any monetary default for purposes of reinstatement under Section 2924c.

(f) If cash proceeds of rents, issues, or profits to which the assignee is entitled following enforcement as set forth in subdivision (c) are received by the assignor or its agent for collection or by another person who has collected such rents, issues, or profits for the assignor's benefit, or for the benefit of a subsequent assignee under the circumstances described in subdivision (h), following the taking by the assignee of either of the enforcement actions authorized in paragraph (3) or (4) of subdivision (c), and the assignee has not authorized the assignor's disposition of the cash proceeds in a writing signed by the assignee, the rights to the cash proceeds and to the recovery of the cash proceeds shall be determined by the following:

(1) The assignee shall be entitled to an immediate turnover of the cash proceeds received by the assignor or its agent for collection or any other person who has collected the rents, issues, or profits for the assignor's benefit, or for the benefit of a subsequent assignee under the circumstances described in subdivision (h), and the assignor or other described party in possession of those cash proceeds shall turn over the full amount of cash proceeds to the assignee, less any amount representing payment of expenses authorized by the assignee in writing. The assignee shall have a right to bring an action for recovery of the cash proceeds, and to recover the cash proceeds, without the necessity of bringing an action to foreclose a security interest that it may have in the real property. This action shall not violate Section 726 of the Code of Civil Procedure or otherwise limit a right available to the assignee with respect to its security.

(2) As between an assignee with an interest in cash proceeds perfected in the manner set forth in subdivision (b) and enforced in accordance with paragraph (3) or (4) of subdivision (c) and another person claiming an interest in the cash proceeds, other than the assignor or its agent for collection or one collecting rents, issues, and profits for the benefit of the assignor, and subject to subdivision (h), the assignee shall have a continuously perfected security interest in the cash proceeds to the extent that the cash proceeds are identifiable. For purposes hereof, cash proceeds are identifiable if they are either (A) segregated or (B) if commingled with other funds of the assignor or its agent or one acting on its behalf, can be traced using the lowest intermediate balance principle, unless the assignor or other party claiming an interest in proceeds shows that some other method of tracing would better serve the interests of justice and equity under the circumstances of the case. The provisions of this paragraph are subject to any generally applicable law with respect to payments made in the operation of the assignor's business.

(g)(1) If the assignee enforces the assignment under subdivision (c) by means other than the appointment of a receiver and receives rents, issues, or profits pursuant to this enforcement, the assignor or another assignee of the affected real property may make written demand upon the assignee to pay the reasonable costs of protecting and preserving the property, including payment of taxes and insurance and compliance with building and housing codes, if any.

(2) On and after the date of receipt of the demand, the assignee shall pay for the reasonable costs of protecting and preserving the real property to the extent of any rents, issues, or profits actually received by the assignee, provided, however, that no such acts by the assignee shall cause the assignee to become a mortgagee in possession and the assignee's duties under this subdivision, upon receipt of a demand from the assignor or any other assignee of the leases, rents, issues, and profits pursuant to paragraph (1), shall not be construed to require the assignee to operate or manage the property, which obligation shall remain that of the assignor.

(3) The obligation of the assignee hereunder shall continue until the earlier of (A) the date on which the assignee obtains the appointment of a receiver for the real property pursuant to application to a court of competent jurisdiction, or (B) the date on which the assignee ceases to enforce the assignment.

(4) This subdivision does not supersede or diminish the right of the assignee to the appointment of a receiver.

(h) The lien priorities, rights, and interests among creditors concerning rents, issues, or profits collected before the enforcement by the assignee shall be governed by subdivisions (a) and (b). Without limiting the generality of the foregoing, if an assignee who has recorded its interest in leases, rents, issues, and profits prior to the recordation of that interest by a subsequent assignee seeks to enforce its interest in those rents, issues, or profits in accordance with this section after any enforcement action has been taken by a subsequent assignee, the prior assignee shall be entitled only to the rents, issues, and profits that are accrued and unpaid as of the date of its enforcement action and unpaid rents, issues, and profits accruing thereafter. The prior assignee shall have no right to rents, issues, or profits paid prior to the date of the enforcement action, whether in the hands of the assignor or any subsequent assignee. Upon receipt of notice that the prior assignee has enforced its interest in the rents, issues, and profits, the subsequent assignee shall immediately send a notice to any tenant to whom it has given notice under subdivision (c). The notice shall inform the tenant that the subsequent assignee cancels its demand that the tenant pay rent to the subsequent assignee.

(i)(1) This section shall apply to contracts entered into on or after January 1, 1997.

(2) Sections 2938 and 2938.1, as these sections were in effect prior to January 1, 1997, shall govern contracts entered into prior to January 1, 1997, and shall govern actions and proceedings initiated on the basis of these contracts.

(j) "Real property," as used in this section, means real property or any estate or interest therein.

(k) The demand required by paragraph (3) of subdivision (c) shall be in the following form:

DEMAND TO PAY RENT TO
PARTY OTHER THAN LANDLORD
(SECTION 2938 OF THE CIVIL CODE)

Tenant: [Name of Tenant]
Property Occupied by Tenant: [Address]
Landlord: [Name of Landlord]
Secured Party: [Name of Secured Party]
Address: [Address for Payment of Rent to Secured Party and for Further Information]:
The secured party named above is the assignee of leases, rents, issues, and profits under [name of document] dated _____ , and recorded at [recording information] in the official records of _____ County, California. You may request a copy of the assignment from the secured party at _____ (address).
THIS NOTICE AFFECTS YOUR LEASE OR RENTAL AGREEMENT RIGHTS AND OBLIGATIONS. YOU ARE THEREFORE ADVISED TO CONSULT AN ATTORNEY CONCERNING THOSE RIGHTS AND OBLIGATIONS IF YOU HAVE ANY QUESTIONS REGARDING YOUR RIGHTS AND OBLIGATIONS UNDER THIS NOTICE.
IN ACCORDANCE WITH SUBDIVISION (C) OF SECTION 2938 OF THE CIVIL CODE, YOU ARE HEREBY DIRECTED TO PAY TO THE SECURED PARTY, _____ (NAME OF SECURED PARTY) AT _____ (ADDRESS), ALL RENTS UNDER YOUR LEASE OR OTHER RENTAL AGREEMENT WITH THE LANDLORD OR PREDECESSOR IN INTEREST OF LANDLORD, FOR THE OCCUPANCY OF THE PROPERTY AT _____ (ADDRESS OF RENTAL PREMISES) WHICH ARE PAST DUE AND PAYABLE ON THE DATE YOU RECEIVE THIS DEMAND, AND ALL RENTS COMING DUE UNDER THE LEASE OR OTHER RENTAL AGREEMENT FOLLOWING THE DATE YOU RECEIVE THIS DEMAND UNLESS YOU HAVE ALREADY PAID THIS RENT TO THE LANDLORD IN GOOD FAITH AND IN A MANNER NOT INCONSISTENT WITH THE AGREEMENT BETWEEN YOU AND THE LANDLORD. IN THIS CASE, THIS DEMAND NOTICE SHALL REQUIRE YOU TO PAY TO THE SECURED PARTY, _____ (NAME OF THE SECURED PARTY), ALL RENTS THAT COME DUE FOLLOWING THE DATE OF THE PAYMENT TO THE LANDLORD.
IF YOU PAY THE RENT TO THE UNDERSIGNED SECURED PARTY, _____ (NAME OF SECURED PARTY), IN ACCORDANCE WITH THIS NOTICE, YOU DO NOT HAVE TO PAY THE RENT TO THE LANDLORD. YOU WILL NOT BE SUBJECT TO DAMAGES OR OBLIGATED TO PAY RENT TO THE SECURED PARTY IF YOU HAVE PREVIOUSLY RECEIVED A DEMAND OF THIS TYPE FROM A DIFFERENT SECURED PARTY.
[For other than residential tenants] IF YOU PAY RENT TO THE LANDLORD THAT BY THE TERMS OF THIS DEMAND YOU ARE REQUIRED TO PAY TO THE SECURED PARTY, YOU MAY BE SUBJECT TO DAMAGES INCURRED BY THE SECURED PARTY BY REASON OF YOUR FAILURE TO COMPLY WITH THIS DEMAND, AND YOU MAY NOT BE DISCHARGED FROM YOUR

OBLIGATION TO PAY THAT RENT TO THE SECURED PARTY. YOU WILL NOT BE SUBJECT TO THOSE DAMAGES OR OBLIGATED TO PAY THAT RENT TO THE SECURED PARTY IF YOU HAVE PREVIOUSLY RECEIVED A DEMAND OF THIS TYPE FROM A DIFFERENT ASSIGNEE.

Your obligation to pay rent under this demand shall continue until you receive either (1) a written notice from a court directing you to pay the rent in a manner provided therein, or (2) a written notice from the secured party named above canceling this demand.

The undersigned hereby certifies, under penalty of perjury, that the undersigned is an authorized officer or agent of the secured party and that the secured party is the assignee, or the current successor to the assignee, under an assignment of leases, rents, issues, or profits executed by the landlord, or a predecessor in interest, that is being enforced pursuant to and in accordance with Section 2938 of the Civil Code.

Executed at _____, California, this ____ day of ____, ____.

    [Secured Party]
    Name: _____
    Title: _____

Leg.H. Added Stats 1996 ch 49 §2 (SB 947). Amended Stats 1997 ch 8 §1 (SB 23), effective April 15, 1997; Stats 2008 ch 179 §33 (SB 1498), effective January 1, 2009.

Prior Law: Former §2938, similar to the present section, was added Stats 1991 ch 501 §1 and repealed Stats 1996 ch 49 §1.

Former §2938, relating to how mortgage was discharged, was enacted 1872 and repealed Stats 1955 ch 247 §3.

§2938.1. [Section repealed 1996]

Leg.H. Added Stats 1992 ch 453 §1 (SB 1323). Repealed Stats 1996 ch 49 §3 (SB 947). See CC §2938.

§2939. Discharge of recorded mortgage

A recorded mortgage must be discharged by a certificate signed by the mortgagee, his personal representatives or assigns, acknowledged or proved and certified as prescribed by the chapter on "recording transfers," stating that the mortgage has been paid, satisfied, or discharged. Reference shall be made in said certificate to the book and page where the mortgage is recorded. **Leg.H.** Enacted 1872. Amended Stats 1945 ch 1074 §1; Stats 1957 ch 297 §1, ch 1865 §12.

§2939½. [Section renumbered 1979]

Leg.H. Added Stats 1895 ch 22 §1. Amended Stats 1913 ch 128 §1. Amended and renumbered to CC §2939.5 by Stats 1979 ch 730 §10, operative January 1, 1981.

§2939.5. Satisfaction by foreign executors

Foreign executors, administrators and guardians may satisfy mortgages upon the records of any county in this state, upon producing and recording in the office of the county recorder of the county in which such mortgage is recorded, a duly certified and authenticated copy of their letters testamentary, or of administration or of guardianship, and which certificate or authentication shall also recite that said letters have not been revoked. For the purposes of this section, "guardian" includes a foreign conservator, committee, or comparable fiduciary. **Leg.H.** Added Stats 1895 ch 22 §1, as CC §2939½. Amended Stats 1913 ch 128 §1. Amended and renumbered by Stats 1979 ch 730 §10, operative January 1, 1981.

§2940. Recording of certificate of discharge

A certificate of the discharge of a mortgage, and the proof or acknowledgment thereof, must be recorded in the office of the county recorder in which the mortgage is recorded. **Leg.H.** Enacted 1872. Amended Stats 1945 ch 1074 §3; Stats 1957 ch 1865 §13.

§2941. Certificate of discharge; Request for full reconveyance; Damages for violations; Fee for services connected with reconveyance; "Original" as including optically imaged reproduction

(a) Within 30 days after any mortgage has been satisfied, the mortgagee or the assignee of the mortgagee shall execute a certificate of the discharge thereof, as provided in Section 2939, and shall record or cause to be recorded in the office of the county recorder in which the mortgage is recorded. The mortgagee shall then deliver, upon the written request of the mortgagor or the mortgagor's heirs, successors, or assignees, as the case may be, the original note and mortgage to the person making the request.

(b)(1) Within 30 calendar days after the obligation secured by any deed of trust has been satisfied, the beneficiary or the assignee of the beneficiary shall execute and deliver to the trustee the original note, deed of trust, request for a full reconveyance, and other documents as may be necessary to reconvey, or cause to be reconveyed, the deed of trust.

(A) The trustee shall execute the full reconveyance and shall record or cause it to be recorded in the office of the county recorder in which the deed of trust is recorded within 21 calendar days after receipt by the trustee of the original note, deed of trust, request for a full reconveyance, the fee that may be charged pursuant to subdivision (e), recorder's fees, and other documents as may be necessary to reconvey, or cause to be reconveyed, the deed of trust.

(B) The trustee shall deliver a copy of the reconveyance to the beneficiary, its successor in interest, or its servicing agent, if known. The reconveyance instrument shall specify one of the following options for delivery of the instrument, the addresses of which the recorder has no duty to validate:

(i) The trustor or successor in interest, and that person's last known address, as the person to whom the recorder will deliver the recorded instrument pursuant to Section 27321 of the Government Code.

(ii) That the recorder shall deliver the recorded instrument to the trustee's address. If the trustee's address is specified for delivery, the trustee shall mail the recorded instrument to the trustor or the successor in interest to the last known address for that party.

(C) Following execution and recordation of the full reconveyance, upon receipt of a written request by the trustor or the trustor's heirs, successors, or assignees, the trustee shall then deliver, or caused to be delivered, the original note and deed of trust to the person making that request.

(D) If the note or deed of trust, or any copy of the note or deed of trust, is electronic, upon satisfaction of an obligation secured by a deed of trust, any electronic original, or electronic copy which has not been previously marked solely for use as a copy, of the note and deed of trust, shall be altered to indicate that the obligation is paid in full.

(2) If the trustee has failed to execute and record, or cause to be recorded, the full reconveyance within 60 calendar days of satisfaction of the obligation, the beneficiary, upon receipt of a written request by the trustor or trustor's heirs, successor in interest, agent, or assignee, shall execute and acknowledge a document pursuant to Section 2934a substituting itself or another as trustee and issue a full reconveyance.

(3) If a full reconveyance has not been executed and recorded pursuant to either paragraph (1) or paragraph (2) within 75 calendar days of satisfaction of the obligation, then a title insurance company may prepare and record a release of the obligation. However, at least 10 days prior to the issuance and recording of a full release pursuant to this paragraph, the title insurance company shall mail by first-class mail with postage prepaid, the intention to release the obligation to the trustee, trustor, and beneficiary of record, or their successor in interest of record, at the last known address.

(A) The release shall set forth:

(i) The name of the beneficiary.

(ii) The name of the trustor.

(iii) The recording reference to the deed of trust.

(iv) A recital that the obligation secured by the deed of trust has been paid in full.

(v) The date and amount of payment.

(B) The release issued pursuant to this subdivision shall be entitled to recordation and, when recorded, shall be deemed to be the equivalent of a reconveyance of a deed of trust.

(4) Where an obligation secured by a deed of trust was paid in full prior to July 1, 1989, and no reconveyance has been issued and recorded by October 1, 1989, then a release of obligation as provided for in paragraph (3) may be issued.

(5) Paragraphs (2) and (3) do not excuse the beneficiary or the trustee from compliance with paragraph (1). Paragraph (3) does not excuse the beneficiary from compliance with paragraph (2).

(6) In addition to any other remedy provided by law, a title insurance company preparing or recording the release of the obligation shall be liable to any party for damages, including attorney's fees, which any

person may sustain by reason of the issuance and recording of the release, pursuant to paragraphs (3) and (4).

(7) A beneficiary may, at its discretion, in accordance with the requirements and procedures of Section 2934a, substitute the title company conducting the escrow through which the obligation is satisfied for the trustee of record, in which case the title company assumes the obligation of a trustee under this subdivision, and may collect the fee authorized by subdivision (e).

(8) In lieu of delivering the original note and deed of trust to the trustee within 30 days of loan satisfaction, as required by paragraph (1) of subdivision (b), a beneficiary who executes and delivers to the trustee a request for a full reconveyance within 30 days of loan satisfaction may, within 120 days of loan satisfaction, deliver the original note and deed of trust to either the trustee or trustor. If the note and deed of trust are delivered as provided in this paragraph, upon satisfaction of the note and deed of trust, the note and deed of trust shall be altered to indicate that the obligation is paid in full. Nothing in this paragraph alters the requirements and obligations set forth in paragraphs (2) and (3).

(c) For the purposes of this section, the phrases "cause to be recorded" and "cause it to be recorded" include, but are not limited to, sending by certified mail with the United States Postal Service or by an independent courier service using its tracking service that provides documentation of receipt and delivery, including the signature of the recipient, the full reconveyance or certificate of discharge in a recordable form, together with payment for all required fees, in an envelope addressed to the county recorder's office of the county in which the deed of trust or mortgage is recorded. Within two business days from the day of receipt, if received in recordable form together with all required fees, the county recorder shall stamp and record the full reconveyance or certificate of discharge. Compliance with this subdivision shall entitle the trustee to the benefit of the presumption found in Section 641 of the Evidence Code.

(d) The violation of this section shall make the violator liable to the person affected by the violation for all damages which that person may sustain by reason of the violation, and shall require that the violator forfeit to that person the sum of five hundred dollars ($500).

(e)(1) The trustee, beneficiary, or mortgagee may charge a reasonable fee to the trustor or mortgagor, or the owner of the land, as the case may be, for all services involved in the preparation, execution, and recordation of the full reconveyance, including, but not limited to, document preparation and forwarding services rendered to effect the full reconveyance, and, in addition, may collect official fees. This fee may be made payable no earlier than the opening of a bona fide escrow or no more than 60 days prior to the full satisfaction of the obligation secured by the deed of trust or mortgage.

(2) If the fee charged pursuant to this subdivision does not exceed forty-five dollars ($45), the fee is conclusively presumed to be reasonable.

(3) The fee described in paragraph (1) may not be charged unless demand for the fee was included in the payoff demand statement described in Section 2943.

(f) For purposes of this section, "original" may include an optically imaged reproduction when the following requirements are met:

(1) The trustee receiving the request for reconveyance and executing the reconveyance as provided in subdivision (b) is an affiliate or subsidiary of the beneficiary or an affiliate or subsidiary of the assignee of the beneficiary, respectively.

(2) The optical image storage media used to store the document shall be nonerasable write once, read many (WORM) optical image media that does not allow changes to the stored document.

(3) The optical image reproduction shall be made consistent with the minimum standards of quality approved by either the National Institute of Standards and Technology or the Association for Information and Image Management.

(4) Written authentication identifying the optical image reproduction as an unaltered copy of the note, deed of trust, or mortgage shall be stamped or printed on the optical image reproduction.

(g) No fee or charge may be imposed on the trustor in connection with, or relating to, any act described in this section except as expressly authorized by this section.

(h) The amendments to this section enacted at the 1999–2000 Regular Session shall apply only to a mortgage or an obligation secured by a deed of trust that is satisfied on or after January 1, 2001.

(i)(1) In any action filed before January 1, 2002, that is dismissed as a result of the amendments to this section enacted at the 2001–02 Regular Session, the plaintiff shall not be required to pay the defendant's costs.

(2) Any claimant, including a claimant in a class action lawsuit, whose claim is dismissed or barred as a result of the amendments to this section enacted at the 2001–02 Regular Session, may, within 6 months of the dismissal or barring of the action or claim, file or refile a claim for actual damages occurring before January 1, 2002, that were proximately caused by a time lapse between loan satisfaction and the completion of the beneficiary's obligations as required under paragraph (1) of subdivision (b). In any action brought under this section, the defendant may be found liable for actual damages, but may not be found liable for any civil penalty authorized by Section 2941.

(j) Notwithstanding any other penalties, if a beneficiary collects a fee for reconveyance and thereafter has knowledge, or should have knowledge, that no reconveyance has been recorded, the beneficiary shall cause to be recorded the reconveyance, or in the event a release of obligation is earlier and timely recorded, the beneficiary shall refund to the trustor the fee charged to perform the reconveyance. Evidence of knowledge includes, but is not limited to, notice of a release of obligation pursuant to paragraph (3) of subdivision (b). **Leg.H.** Enacted 1872. Amended Code Amdts 1873–74 ch 612 §261; Code Amdts 1880 ch 81 §1; Stats 1946 1st Ex Sess ch 58 §1, effective February 25, 1946; Stats 1947 ch 1411 §1; Stats 1974 ch 267 §1; Stats 1978 ch 509 §1; Stats 1988 ch 1006 §1, operative July 1, 1989; Stats 1991 ch 1155 §2 (AB 2146); Stats 1993 ch 754 §3 (SB 313), effective October 2, 1993; Stats 1994 ch 374 §1 (AB 3397); Stats 1996 ch 230 §1 (AB 372); Stats 1997 ch 74 §7 (SB 665); Stats 2000 ch 1013 §1 (AB 996); Stats 2001 ch 560 §1 (AB 1090); Stats 2002 ch 809 §2 (SB 1504); Stats 2003 ch 62 §20 (SB 600).

2001 Note: The Legislature finds and declares all of the following:

(a) That, prior to this act, Section 2941, read as a whole, required that within 60 calendar days of satisfaction of an obligation secured by a deed of trust, the trustee was to execute and record or cause to be recorded, or alternatively, deliver to escrow, a full reconveyance pursuant to paragraph (2) of subdivision (c), and that the beneficiary was to deliver to the trustee such documents as were necessary for the trustee to perform within this time frame.

(b) That delivery of a full reconveyance within 60 calendar days of satisfaction of an obligation to an escrow that had closed was not a violation of Section 2941 if, by such delivery, the reconveyance was actually recorded by the former escrow holder as a voluntary accommodation to the trustee.

(c) That, in order for the trustee to act, as required by subparagraph (A) of paragraph (1) of subdivision (b) of Section 2941, within 21 calendar days of receipt of the necessary documents from the beneficiary, and meet its obligation under paragraph (2) of subdivision (b) to execute and record, or cause to be recorded, the deed of reconveyance within 60 calendar days of satisfaction of the obligation, the time allowed for the beneficiary to perform its obligations under paragraph (1) of subdivision (b) was 39 calendar days.

(d) That, Section 2941, as it existed prior to this act, was violated if either the beneficiary failed to deliver to the trustee, within 39 calendar days of satisfaction of the obligation, the documents necessary to reconvey the deed of trust by the trustee, or the trustee failed to record or cause to be recorded a full reconveyance, pursuant to paragraph (1) of subdivision (b), or, alternatively, deliver to escrow a full reconveyance pursuant to paragraph (2) of subdivision (c), within 21 calendar days of receipt of the necessary documents from the beneficiary.

(e) That the trustee satisfied its obligation to cause a reconveyance to be recorded where it delivered to a closed escrow a full reconveyance within 60 calendar days of satisfaction of an obligation if, by that delivery, the reconveyance was actually recorded by the former escrowholder as a voluntary accommodation to the trustee.

(f) That this act is intended to specifically abrogate the decision in *Bartold v. Glendale Federal Bank* (2000) 81 Cal.App.4th 816, to the extent that it is contrary to this clarification of existing law.

(g) That subdivision (j) of Section 2941, added by this act, does not represent a change in current law, but is declarative of existing law. Stats 2001 ch 560 §3.

§2941.1. Reconveyance fee where no payoff demand statement issued

Notwithstanding any other provision of law, if no payoff demand statement is issued pursuant to Section 2943, nothing in Section 2941 shall be construed to prohibit the charging of a reconveyance fee. **Leg.H.** Added Stats 2001 ch 438 §6 (SB 958), effective October 2, 2001, operative January 1, 2002.

§2941.5. Criminal penalties

Every person who willfully violates Section 2941 is guilty of a misdemeanor punishable by fine of not less than fifty dollars ($50) nor more than four hundred dollars ($400), or by imprisonment in the county jail for not to exceed six months, or by both such fine and imprisonment.

For purposes of this section, "willfully" means simply a purpose or willingness to commit the act, or make the omission referred to. It does not require an intent to violate the law, to injure another, or to acquire any advantage. **Leg.H.** Added Stats 1946 1st Ex Sess ch 58 §2, effective February 25, 1946. Amended Stats 1983 ch 1092 §67, effective September 27, 1983, operative January 1, 1984; Stats 1988 ch 1006 §2, operative July 1, 1989.

§2941.7. Discharge when mortgagee or beneficiary cannot be located or refuses to execute

Whenever the obligation secured by a mortgage or deed of trust has been fully satisfied and the present mortgagee or beneficiary of record cannot be located after diligent search, or refuses to execute and deliver a proper certificate of discharge or request for reconveyance, or whenever a specified balance, including principal and interest, remains due and the mortgagor or trustor or the mortgagor's or trustor's successor in interest cannot, after diligent search, locate the then mortgagee or beneficiary of record, the lien of any mortgage or deed of trust shall be released when the mortgagor or trustor or the mortgagor's or trustor's successor in interest records or causes to be recorded, in the office of the county recorder of the county in which the encumbered property is located, a corporate bond accompanied by a declaration, as specified in subdivision (b), and with respect to a deed of trust, a reconveyance as hereinafter provided.

(a) The bond shall be acceptable to the trustee and shall be issued by a corporation lawfully authorized to issue surety bonds in the State of California in a sum equal to the greater of either (1) two times the amount of the original obligation secured by the mortgage or deed of trust and any additional principal amounts, including advances, shown in any recorded amendment thereto, or (2) one-half of the total amount computed pursuant to (1) and any accrued interest on such amount, and shall be conditioned for payment of any sum which the mortgagee or beneficiary may recover in an action on the obligation secured by the mortgage or deed of trust, with costs of suit and reasonable attorneys' fees. The obligees under the bond shall be the mortgagee or mortgagee's successor in interest or the trustee who executes a reconveyance under this section and the beneficiary or beneficiary's successor in interest.

The bond recorded by the mortgagor or trustor or mortgagor's or trustor's successor in interest shall contain the following information describing the mortgage or deed of trust:

(1) Recording date and instrument number or book and page number of the recorded instrument.

(2) Names of original mortgagor and mortgagee or trustor and beneficiary.

(3) Amount shown as original principal sum secured thereby.

(4) The recording information and new principal amount shown in any recorded amendment thereto.

(b) The declaration accompanying the corporate bond recorded by the mortgagor or trustor or the mortgagor's or trustor's successor in interest shall state:

(1) That it is recorded pursuant to this section.

(2) The name of the original mortgagor or trustor and mortgagee or beneficiary.

(3) The name and address of the person making the declaration.

(4) That either the obligation secured by the mortgage or deed of trust has been fully satisfied and the present mortgagee or beneficiary of record cannot be located after diligent search, or refuses to execute and deliver a proper certificate of discharge or request for reconveyance as required under Section 2941; or that a specified balance, including principal and interest, remains due and the mortgagor or trustor or mortgagor's or trustor's successor in interest cannot, after diligent search, locate the then mortgagee or beneficiary.

(5) That the declarant has mailed by certified mail, return receipt requested, to the last address of the person to whom payments under the mortgage or deed of trust were made and to the last mortgagee or beneficiary of record at the address for such mortgagee or beneficiary shown on the instrument creating, assigning, or conveying the interest, a notice of recording a declaration and bond under this section and informing the recipient of the name and address of the mortgagor or trustee, if any, and of the right to record a written objection with respect to the release of the lien of the mortgage or, with respect to a deed of trust, notify the trustee in writing of any objection to the reconveyance of the deed of trust. The declaration shall state the date any notices were mailed pursuant to this section and the names and addresses of all persons to whom mailed.

The declaration provided for in this section shall be signed by the mortgagor or trustor under penalty of perjury.

(c) With respect to a deed of trust, after the expiration of 30 days following the recording of the corporate bond and accompanying declaration provided in subdivisions (a) and (b), and delivery to the trustee of the usual reconveyance fees plus costs and a demand for reconveyance under this section, the trustee shall execute and record, or otherwise deliver as provided in Section 2941, a reconveyance in the same form as if the beneficiary had delivered to the trustee a proper request for reconveyance, provided that the trustee has not received a written objection to the reconveyance from the beneficiary of record. No trustee shall have any liability to any person by reason of its execution of a reconveyance in reliance upon a trustor's or trustor's successor's in interest substantial compliance with this section. The sole remedy of any person damaged by reason of the reconveyance shall be against the trustor, the affiant, or the bond. With respect to a mortgage, a mortgage shall be satisfied of record when 30 days have expired following recordation of the corporate bond and accompanying declaration, provided no objection to satisfaction has been recorded by the mortgagee within that period. A bona fide purchaser or encumbrancer for value shall take the interest conveyed free of such mortgage, provided there has been compliance with subdivisions (a) and (b) and the deed to the purchaser recites that no objections by the mortgagee have been recorded.

Upon recording of a reconveyance under this section, or, in the case of a mortgage the expiration of 30 days following recordation of the corporate bond and accompanying declaration without objection thereto having been recorded, interest shall no longer accrue as to any balance remaining due to the extent the balance due has been alleged in the declaration recorded under subdivision (b).

The sum of any specified balance, including principal and interest, which remains due and which is remitted to any issuer of a corporate bond in conjunction with the issuance of a bond pursuant to this section shall, if unclaimed, escheat to the state after three years pursuant to the Unclaimed Property Law. From the date of escheat the issuer of the bond shall be relieved of any liability to pay to the beneficiary or his or her heirs or other successors in interest the escheated funds and the sole remedy shall be a claim for property paid or delivered to the Controller pursuant to the Unclaimed Property Law.

(d) The term "diligent search," as used in this section, shall mean all of the following:

(1) The mailing of notices as provided in paragraph (5) of subdivision (b), and to any other address that the declarant has used to correspond with or contact the mortgagee or beneficiary.

(2) A check of the telephone directory in the city where the mortgagee or beneficiary maintained the mortgagee's or beneficiary's last known address or place of business.

(3) In the event the mortgagee or beneficiary or the mortgagee's or beneficiary's successor in interest is a corporation, a check of the records of the California Secretary of State and the secretary of state in the state of incorporation, if known.

(4) In the event the mortgagee or beneficiary is a state or national bank or a state or federal savings and loan association, an inquiry of the regulatory authority of such bank or savings and loan association.

(e) This section shall not be deemed to create an exclusive procedure for the issuance of reconveyances and the issuance of bonds and declarations to release the lien of a mortgage and shall not affect any other procedures, whether or not such procedures are set forth in statute, for the issuance of reconveyances and the issuance of bonds and declarations to release the lien of a mortgage.

(f) For purposes of this section, the trustor or trustor's successor in interest may substitute the present trustee of record without conferring any duties upon the trustee other than those that are incidental to the execution of a reconveyance pursuant to this section if all of the following requirements are met:

(1) The present trustee of record and the present mortgagee or beneficiary of record cannot be located after diligent search.

(2) The declaration filed pursuant to subdivision (b) shall state in addition that it is filed pursuant to this subdivision, and shall, in lieu of the

provisions of paragraph (4) of subdivision (b), state that the obligation secured by the mortgage or deed of trust has been fully satisfied and the present trustee of record and present mortgagee or beneficiary of record cannot be located after diligent search.

(3) The substitute trustee is a title insurance company that agrees to accept the substitution. This subdivision shall not impose a duty upon a title insurance company to accept the substitution.

(4) The corporate bond required in subdivision (a) is for a period of five or more years. **Leg.H.** Added Stats 1980 ch 529 §1. Amended Stats 1995 ch 244 §1 (SB 784); Stats 1996 ch 762 §2 (SB 2014).

§2941.9. Holders of more than fifty percent

(a) The purpose of this section is to establish a process through which all of the beneficiaries under a trust deed may agree to be governed by beneficiaries holding more than 50 percent of the record beneficial interest of a series of notes secured by the same real property or of undivided interests in a note secured by real property equivalent to a series transaction, exclusive of any notes or interests of a licensed real estate broker that is the issuer or servicer of the notes or interests or any affiliate of that licensed real estate broker.

(b) All holders of notes secured by the same real property or a series of undivided interests in notes secured by real property equivalent to a series transaction may agree in writing to be governed by the desires of the holders of more than 50 percent of the record beneficial interest of those notes or interests, exclusive of any notes or interests of a licensed real estate broker that is the issuer or servicer of the notes or interests of any affiliate of the licensed real estate broker, with respect to actions to be taken on behalf of all holders in the event of default or foreclosure for matters that require direction or approval of the holders, including designation of the broker, servicing agent, or other person acting on their behalf, and the sale, encumbrance, or lease of real property owned by the holders resulting from foreclosure or receipt of a deed in lieu of foreclosure.

(c) A description of the agreement authorized in subdivision (b) of this section shall be disclosed pursuant to Section 10232.5 of the Business and Professions Code and shall be included in a recorded document such as the deed of trust or the assignment of interests.

(d) Any action taken pursuant to the authority granted in this section is not effective unless all the parties agreeing to the action sign, under penalty of perjury, a separate written document entitled "Majority Action Affidavit" stating the following:

(1) The action has been authorized pursuant to this section.

(2) None of the undersigned is a licensed real estate broker or an affiliate of the broker that is the issuer or servicer of the obligation secured by the deed of trust.

(3) The undersigned together hold more than 50 percent of the record beneficial interest of a series of notes secured by the same real property or of undivided interests in a note secured by real property equivalent to a series transaction.

(4) Notice of the action was sent by certified mail, postage prepaid, with return receipt requested, to each holder of an interest in the obligation secured by the deed of trust who has not joined in the execution of the substitution or this document.

This document shall be recorded in the office of the county recorder of each county in which the real property described in the deed of trust is located. Once the document in this subdivision is recorded, it shall constitute conclusive evidence of compliance with the requirements of this subdivision in favor of trustees acting pursuant to this section, substituted trustees acting pursuant to Section 2934a, subsequent assignees of the obligation secured by the deed of trust, and subsequent bona fide purchasers or encumbrancers for value of the real property described therein.

(e) For purposes of this section, "affiliate of the licensed real estate broker" includes any person as defined in Section 25013 of the Corporations Code who is controlled by, or is under common control with, or who controls, a licensed real estate broker. "Control" means the possession, direct or indirect, of the power to direct or cause the direction of management and policies. **Leg.H.** Added Stats 1996 ch 839 §3 (SB 1638).

§2942. Provisions of this chapter do not affect bottomry or respondentia

Contracts of bottomry or respondentia, although in the nature of mortgages, are not affected by any of the provisions of this chapter. **Leg.H.** Enacted 1872.

§2943. Beneficiary's obligation to furnish beneficiary statement or payoff demand statement; Liability for noncompliance

(a) As used in this section:

(1) "Beneficiary" means a mortgagee or beneficiary of a mortgage or deed of trust, or his or her assignees.

(2) "Beneficiary statement" means a written statement showing:

(A) The amount of the unpaid balance of the obligation secured by the mortgage or deed of trust and the interest rate, together with the total amounts, if any, of all overdue installments of either principal or interest, or both.

(B) The amounts of periodic payments, if any.

(C) The date on which the obligation is due in whole or in part.

(D) The date to which real estate taxes and special assessments have been paid to the extent the information is known to the beneficiary.

(E) The amount of hazard insurance in effect and the term and premium of that insurance to the extent the information is known to the beneficiary.

(F) The amount in an account, if any, maintained for the accumulation of funds with which to pay taxes and insurance premiums.

(G) The nature and, if known, the amount of any additional charges, costs, or expenses paid or incurred by the beneficiary which have become a lien on the real property involved.

(H) Whether the obligation secured by the mortgage or deed of trust can or may be transferred to a new borrower.

(3) "Delivery" means depositing or causing to be deposited in the United States mail an envelope with postage prepaid, containing a copy of the document to be delivered, addressed to the person whose name and address is set forth in the demand therefor. The document may also be transmitted by facsimile machine to the person whose name and address is set forth in the demand therefor.

(4) "Entitled person" means the trustor or mortgagor of, or his or her successor in interest in, the mortgaged or trust property or any part thereof, any beneficiary under a deed of trust, any person having a subordinate lien or encumbrance of record thereon, the escrowholder licensed as an agent pursuant to Division 6 (commencing with Section 17000) of the Financial Code, or the party exempt by virtue of Section 17006 of the Financial Code who is acting as the escrowholder.

(5) "Payoff demand statement" means a written statement, prepared in response to a written demand made by an entitled person or authorized agent, setting forth the amounts required as of the date of preparation by the beneficiary, to fully satisfy all obligations secured by the loan that is the subject of the payoff demand statement. The written statement shall include information reasonably necessary to calculate the payoff amount on a per diem basis for the period of time, not to exceed 30 days, during which the per diem amount is not changed by the terms of the note.

(b)(1) A beneficiary, or his or her authorized agent, shall, within 21 days of the receipt of a written demand by an entitled person or his or her authorized agent, prepare and deliver to the person demanding it a true, correct, and complete copy of the note or other evidence of indebtedness with any modification thereto, and a beneficiary statement.

(2) A request pursuant to this subdivision may be made by an entitled person or his or her authorized agent at any time before, or within two months after, the recording of a notice of default under a mortgage or deed of trust, or may otherwise be made more than 30 days prior to the entry of the decree of foreclosure.

(c) A beneficiary, or his or her authorized agent, shall, on the written demand of an entitled person, or his or her authorized agent, prepare and deliver a payoff demand statement to the person demanding it within 21 days of the receipt of the demand. However, if the loan is subject to a recorded notice of default or a filed complaint commencing a judicial foreclosure, the beneficiary shall have no obligation to prepare and deliver this statement as prescribed unless the written demand is received prior to the first publication of a notice of sale or the notice of the first date of sale established by a court.

(d)(1) A beneficiary statement or payoff demand statement may be relied upon by the entitled person or his or her authorized agent in accordance with its terms, including with respect to the payoff demand statement reliance for the purpose of establishing the amount necessary to pay the obligation in full. If the beneficiary notifies the entitled person or his or her authorized agent of any amendment to the statement, then the amended statement may be relied upon by the entitled person or his or her authorized agent as provided in this subdivision.

(2) If notification of any amendment to the statement is not given in writing, then a written amendment to the statement shall be delivered to the entitled person or his or her authorized agent no later than the next business day after notification.

(3) Upon the dates specified in subparagraphs (A) and (B) any sums that were due and for any reason not included in the statement or amended statement shall continue to be recoverable by the beneficiary as an unsecured obligation of the obligor pursuant to the terms of the note and existing provisions of law.

(A) If the transaction is voluntary, the entitled party or his or her authorized agent may rely upon the statement or amended statement upon the earlier of (i) the close of escrow, (ii) transfer of title, or (iii) recordation of a lien.

(B) If the loan is subject to a recorded notice of default or a filed complaint commencing a judicial foreclosure, the entitled party or his or her authorized agent may rely upon the statement or amended statement upon the acceptance of the last and highest bid at a trustee's sale or a court supervised sale.

(e) The following provisions apply to a demand for either a beneficiary statement or a payoff demand statement:

(1) If an entitled person or his or her authorized agent requests a statement pursuant to this section and does not specify a beneficiary statement or a payoff demand statement the beneficiary shall treat the request as a request for a payoff demand statement.

(2) If the entitled person or the entitled person's authorized agent includes in the written demand a specific request for a copy of the deed of trust or mortgage, it shall be furnished with the written statement at no additional charge.

(3) The beneficiary may, before delivering a statement, require reasonable proof that the person making the demand is, in fact, an entitled person or an authorized agent of an entitled person, in which event the beneficiary shall not be subject to the penalties of this section until 21 days after receipt of the proof herein provided for. A statement in writing signed by the entitled person appointing an authorized agent when delivered personally to the beneficiary or delivered by registered return receipt mail shall constitute reasonable proof as to the identity of an agent. Similar delivery of a policy of title insurance, preliminary report issued by a title company, original or photographic copy of a grant deed or certified copy of letters testamentary, guardianship, or conservatorship shall constitute reasonable proof as to the identity of a successor in interest, provided the person demanding a statement is named as successor in interest in the document.

(4) If a beneficiary for a period of 21 days after receipt of the written demand willfully fails to prepare and deliver the statement, he or she is liable to the entitled person for all damages which he or she may sustain by reason of the refusal and, whether or not actual damages are sustained, he or she shall forfeit to the entitled person the sum of three hundred dollars ($300). Each failure to prepare and deliver the statement, occurring at a time when, pursuant to this section, the beneficiary is required to prepare and deliver the statement, creates a separate cause of action, but a judgment awarding an entitled person a forfeiture, or damages and forfeiture, for any failure to prepare and deliver a statement bars recovery of damages and forfeiture for any other failure to prepare and deliver a statement, with respect to the same obligation, in compliance with a demand therefor made within six months before or after the demand as to which the award was made. For the purposes of this subdivision, "willfully" means an intentional failure to comply with the requirements of this section without just cause or excuse.

(5) If the beneficiary has more than one branch, office, or other place of business, then the demand shall be made to the branch or office address set forth in the payment billing notice or payment book, and the statement, unless it specifies otherwise, shall be deemed to apply only to the unpaid balance of the single obligation named in the request and secured by the mortgage or deed of trust which is payable at the branch or office whose address appears on the aforesaid billing notice or payment book.

(6) The beneficiary may make a charge not to exceed thirty dollars ($30) for furnishing each required statement. The provisions of this paragraph shall not apply to mortgages or deeds of trust insured by the Federal Housing Administrator or guaranteed by the Administrator of Veterans Affairs.

(f) The preparation and delivery of a beneficiary statement or a payoff demand statement pursuant to this section shall not change a date of sale established pursuant to Section 2924g.

(g) This section shall become operative on January 1, 2014. **Leg.H.** Added Stats 2009 ch 43 §6 (SB 306), effective January 1, 2010, operative January 1, 2014.

Prior Law: Former §2943, similar to the present section, was added Stats 1961 ch 817 §1, amended Stats 1963 ch 733 §1; Stats 1968 ch 966 §1; Stats 1970 ch 27 §1, effective March 23, 1970; Stats 1982 ch 626 §1, ch 1203 §2, effective September 22, 1982, operative January 1, 1983; Stats 1988 ch 966 §1; Stats 1994 ch 374 §2 (AB 3397); Stats 2000 ch 636 §8 (AB 2284); Stats 2001 ch 560 §2 (AB 1090); Stats 2009 ch 43 §5 (SB 306), effective January 1, 2010, repealed January 1, 2014.

Former CC §2943 was added in 1961 and repealed operative January 1, 2014, by its own provisions. Stats 2009 ch 43 (SB 306) §5

§2943.1. Borrower's instruction to suspend and close equity line of credit

(a) For purposes of this section, the following definitions apply:

(1) "Beneficiary" has the same meaning as defined in Section 2943.

(2) "Borrower's Instruction to Suspend and Close Equity Line of Credit" means the instruction described in subdivision (c), signed by the borrower or borrowers under an equity line of credit.

(3) "Entitled person" has the same meaning as defined in Section 2943.

(4) "Equity line of credit" means a revolving line of credit used for consumer purposes, which is secured by a mortgage or deed of trust encumbering residential real property consisting of one to four dwelling units, at least one of which is occupied by the borrower.

(5) "Payoff demand statement" has the same meaning as defined in Section 2943.

(6) "Suspend" means to prohibit the borrower from drawing on, increasing, or incurring any additional principal debt on the equity line of credit.

(b) Notwithstanding paragraph (5) of subdivision (a) of Section 2943, a payoff demand statement issued by a beneficiary in connection with an equity line of credit shall include an email address, fax number, or mailing address designated by the beneficiary for delivery of the Borrower's Instruction to Suspend and Close Equity Line of Credit by the entitled person.

(c) Upon receipt from an entitled person of a Borrower's Instruction to Suspend and Close Equity Line of Credit, that has been prepared and presented to the borrower by the entitled person and signed by a borrower, a beneficiary shall suspend the equity line of credit for a minimum of 30 days. A Borrower's Instruction to Suspend and Close Equity Line of Credit shall be effective if made substantially in the following form and signed by the borrower:

"Borrower's Instruction to Suspend and Close Equity Line of Credit

Lender: [Name of Lender]
Borrower(s): [Name of Borrower(s)]
Account Number of the Equity Line of Credit: [Account Number]
Encumbered Property Address: [Property Address]
Escrow or Settlement Agent: [Name of Agent]:

In connection with a sale or refinance of the above-referenced property, my Escrow or Settlement Agent has requested a payoff demand statement for the above-described equity line of credit. I understand my ability to use this equity line of credit has been suspended for at least 30 days to accommodate this pending transaction. I understand that I cannot use any credit cards, debit cards, or checks associated with this equity line of credit while it is suspended and all amounts will be due and payable upon close of escrow. I also understand that when payment is made in accordance with the payoff demand statement, my equity line of credit will be closed. If any amounts remain due after the payment is made, I understand I will remain personally liable for those amounts even if the equity line of credit has been closed and the property released.

This is my written authorization and instruction that you are to close my equity line of credit and cause the secured lien against this property to be released when you are in receipt of both this instruction and payment in accordance with your payoff demand statement.

_____   _____
(Date)   (Signature of Each Borrower)"

(d) When a beneficiary is in receipt of both a Borrower's Instruction to Suspend and Close Equity Line of Credit and payment in accordance with the payoff demand statement as set forth in Section 2943, the beneficiary shall do all of the following:

(1) Close the equity line of credit.

(2) Release or reconvey the property securing the equity line of credit, as provided by this chapter.

(e) The beneficiary may conclusively rely on the Borrower's Instruction to Suspend and Close Equity Line of Credit provided by the entitled person as coming from the borrower.

(f) This section shall become operative on July 1, 2015. **Leg.H.** Added Stats 2014 ch 206 §1 (AB 1770), effective January 1, 2015, operative July 1, 2015, repealed July 1, 2019. Amended Stats 2018 ch 90 §1 (SB 1139), effective January 1, 2019.

§2944. Application of chapter to matters governed by Commercial Code

None of the provisions of this chapter applies to any transaction or security interest governed by the Commercial Code, except to the extent made applicable by reason of an election made by the secured party pursuant to subparagraph (B) of paragraph (1) of subdivision (a) of Section 9604 of the Commercial Code. **Leg.H.** Added Stats 1963 ch 819 §15, effective January 1, 1965. Amended Stats 1992 ch 1095 §3 (AB 2734); Stats 1999 ch 991 §7 (SB 45), operative July 1, 2001.

§2944.5. Refusal to accept policy issued by admitted insurer for continuous period without fixed expiration date

No lender, mortgagee, or any third party having an interest in real or personal property shall refuse to accept a policy issued by an admitted insurer solely because the policy is issued for a continuous period without a fixed expiration date even though the policy premium is due and payable every six months, provided the lender, mortgagee, or third party is entitled to receive (a) notice of renewal from the insurer within 15 days of receipt of payment on the policy by the insured or (b) notice of cancellation or nonrenewal under the terms and conditions set forth in Sections 678 and 2074.8 of the Insurance Code, whichever is applicable. **Leg.H.** Added Stats 1993 ch 522 §1 (AB 421).

§2944.6. Notice provided to borrower; Translation; Fine; Applicability

(a) Notwithstanding any other provision of law, any person who negotiates, attempts to negotiate, arranges, attempts to arrange, or otherwise offers to perform a mortgage loan modification or other form of mortgage loan forbearance for a fee or other compensation paid by the borrower, shall provide the following to the borrower, as a separate statement, in not less than 14-point bold type, prior to entering into any fee agreement with the borrower:

It is not necessary to pay a third party to arrange for a loan modification or other form of forbearance from your mortgage lender or servicer. You may call your lender directly to ask for a change in your loan terms. Nonprofit housing counseling agencies also offer these and other forms of borrower assistance free of charge. A list of nonprofit housing counseling agencies approved by the United States Department of Housing and Urban Development (HUD) is available from your local HUD office or by visiting www.hud.gov.

(b) If loan modification or other mortgage loan forbearance services are offered or negotiated in one of the languages set forth in Section 1632, a translated copy of the statement in subdivision (a) shall be provided to the borrower in that foreign language.

(c) A violation of this section by a natural person is a public offense punishable by a fine not exceeding ten thousand dollars ($10,000), by imprisonment in the county jail for a term not to exceed one year, or by both that fine and imprisonment, or if by a business entity, the violation is punishable by a fine not exceeding fifty thousand dollars ($50,000). These penalties are cumulative to any other remedies or penalties provided by law.

(d) This section does not apply to a person, or an agent acting on that person's behalf, offering loan modification or other loan forbearance services for a loan owned or serviced by that person.

(e) This section shall apply only to mortgages and deeds of trust secured by residential real property containing four or fewer dwelling units. **Leg.H.** Added Stats 2009 ch 630 §9 (SB 94), effective October 11, 2009.

§2944.7. Unlawful activities in conjunction with mortgage loan modification; Penalties; Civil action; Permissible activities; Applicability

(a) Notwithstanding any other law, it shall be unlawful for any person who negotiates, attempts to negotiate, arranges, attempts to arrange, or otherwise offers to perform a mortgage loan modification or other form of mortgage loan forbearance for a fee or other compensation paid by the borrower, to do any of the following:

(1) Claim, demand, charge, collect, or receive any compensation until after the person has fully performed each and every service the person contracted to perform or represented that he or she would perform.

(2) Take any wage assignment, any lien of any type on real or personal property, or other security to secure the payment of compensation.

(3) Take any power of attorney from the borrower for any purpose.

(b) A violation of this section by a natural person is punishable by a fine not exceeding ten thousand dollars ($10,000), by imprisonment in the county jail for a term not to exceed one year, or by both that fine and imprisonment, or if by a business entity, the violation is punishable by a fine not exceeding fifty thousand dollars ($50,000). These penalties are cumulative to any other remedies or penalties provided by law.

(c) In addition to the penalties and remedies provided by Chapter 5 (commencing with Section 17200) of Part 2 of Division 7 of the Business and Professions Code, a person who violates this section shall be liable for a civil penalty not to exceed twenty thousand dollars ($20,000) for each violation, which shall be assessed and recovered in a civil action brought in the name of the people of the State of California by the Attorney General, by any district attorney, by any county counsel authorized by agreement with the district attorney in actions involving a violation of a county ordinance, by any city attorney of a city having a population in excess of 750,000, by any city attorney of any city and county, or, with the consent of the district attorney, by a city prosecutor in any city having a full-time city prosecutor, in any court of competent jurisdiction pursuant to Chapter 5 (commencing with Section 17200) of Part 2 of Division 7 of the Business and Professions Code.

(d) Nothing in this section precludes a person, or an agent acting on that person's behalf, who offers loan modification or other loan forbearance services for a loan owned or serviced by that person, from doing any of the following:

(1) Collecting principal, interest, or other charges under the terms of a loan, before the loan is modified, including charges to establish a new payment schedule for a nondelinquent loan, after the borrower reduces the unpaid principal balance of that loan for the express purpose of lowering the monthly payment due under the terms of the loan.

(2) Collecting principal, interest, or other charges under the terms of a loan, after the loan is modified.

(3) Accepting payment from a federal agency in connection with the federal Making Home Affordable Plan or other federal plan intended to help borrowers refinance or modify their loans or otherwise avoid foreclosures.

(e) This section shall apply only to mortgages and deeds of trust secured by residential real property containing four or fewer dwelling units. **Leg.H.** Added Stats 2009 ch 630 §10 (SB 94), effective October 11, 2009, repealed January 1, 2013. Amended Stats 2012 ch 563 §4 (SB 980), effective January 1, 2013, ch 569 §3 (AB 1950), effective January 1, 2013; Stats 2014 ch 457 §1 (AB 1730), effective January 1, 2015.

§2944.8. Unlawful activities in conjunction with mortgage loan modification where victim is senior citizen or disabled

(a) In addition to any liability for a civil penalty pursuant to Section 2944.7, if a person violates Section 2944.7 with respect to a victim who is a senior citizen or a disabled person, the violator may be liable for a civil penalty not to exceed two thousand five hundred dollars ($2,500) for each violation, which may be assessed and recovered in a civil action.

(b) As used in this section, the following terms have the following meanings:

(1) "Disabled person" means a person who has a physical or mental disability, as defined in Sections 12926 and 12926.1 of the Government Code.

(2) "Senior citizen" means a person who is 65 years of age or older.

(c) In determining whether to impose a civil penalty pursuant to subdivision (a) and the amount thereof, the court shall consider, in addition to any other appropriate factors, the extent to which one or more of the following factors are present:

(1) Whether the defendant knew or should have known that his or her conduct was directed to one or more senior citizens or disabled persons.

(2) Whether the defendant's conduct caused one or more senior citizens or disabled persons to suffer any of the following: loss or encumbrance of a primary residence, principal employment, or source of income, substantial loss of property set aside for retirement, or for personal or family care and maintenance, or substantial loss of payments received under a pension or retirement plan or a government benefits program, or assets essential to the health or welfare of the senior citizen or disabled person.

(3) Whether one or more senior citizens or disabled persons are substantially more vulnerable than other members of the public to the defendant's conduct because of age, poor health or infirmity, impaired understanding, restricted mobility, or disability, and actually suffered substantial physical, emotional, or economic damage resulting from the defendant's conduct.

(d) A court of competent jurisdiction hearing an action pursuant to this section may make orders and judgments as necessary to restore to a senior citizen or disabled person money or property, real or personal, that may have been acquired by means of a violation of Section 2944.7. **Leg.H.** Added Stats 2014 ch 457 §2 (AB 1730), effective January 1, 2015.

§2944.10. Unlawful activities in conjunction with mortgage loan modification; Time limitation

Any action to enforce any cause of action pursuant to Section 2944.7 or 2944.8 shall be commenced within four years after the cause of action accrued. No cause of action barred under existing law on the effective date of this section shall be revived by its enactment. **Leg.H.** Added Stats 2014 ch 457 §3 (AB 1730), effective January 1, 2015.

ARTICLE 1.5
Mortgage Foreclosure Consultants

Legislative findings and declarations; Intent and purposes of article; Liberal construction. §2945.

Definitions. §2945.1.

Owner's right of cancellation; Notice. §2945.2.

Form and contents of contract; Notice of cancellation; Right to cancel pending compliance. §2945.3.

Violations. §2945.4.

Foreclosure consultant, requirements; Foreclosure Consultant Regulation Fund created; Denial or revocation of certificate of registration; Penalties for violation. §2945.45.

Waiver. §2945.5.

Owner's right of action; Damages; Limitations period. §2945.6.

Punishment. §2945.7.

Effect of unconstitutional provision. §2945.8.

Liability of foreclosure consultant for damages resulting from statements made by representative. §2945.9.

Voidness of contract provision attempting to limit liability. §2945.10.

Statements required of representatives. §2945.11.

§2945. Legislative findings and declarations; Intent and purposes of article; Liberal construction

(a) The Legislature finds and declares that homeowners whose residences are in foreclosure are subject to fraud, deception, harassment, and unfair dealing by foreclosure consultants from the time a Notice of Default is recorded pursuant to Section 2924 until the time surplus funds from any foreclosure sale are distributed to the homeowner or his or her successor. Foreclosure consultants represent that they can assist homeowners who have defaulted on obligations secured by their residences. These foreclosure consultants, however, often charge high fees, the payment of which is often secured by a deed of trust on the residence to be saved, and perform no service or essentially a worthless service. Homeowners, relying on the foreclosure consultants' promises of help, take no other action, are diverted from lawful businesses which could render beneficial services, and often lose their homes, sometimes to the foreclosure consultants who purchase homes at a fraction of their value before the sale. Vulnerable homeowners are increasingly relying on the services of foreclosure consultants who advise the homeowner that the foreclosure consultant can obtain the remaining funds from the foreclosure sale if the homeowner executes an assignment of the surplus, a deed, or a power of attorney in favor of the foreclosure consultant. This results in the homeowner paying an exorbitant fee for a service when the homeowner could have obtained the remaining funds from the trustee's sale from the trustee directly for minimal cost if the homeowner had consulted legal counsel or had sufficient time to receive notices from the trustee pursuant to Section 2924j regarding how and where to make a claim for excess proceeds.

(b) The Legislature further finds and declares that foreclosure consultants have a significant impact on the economy of this state and on the welfare of its citizens.

(c) The intent and purposes of this article are the following:

(1) To require that foreclosure consultant service agreements be expressed in writing; to safeguard the public against deceit and financial hardship; to permit rescission of foreclosure consultation contracts; to prohibit representations that tend to mislead; and to encourage fair dealing in the rendition of foreclosure services.

(2) The provisions of this article shall be liberally construed to effectuate this intent and to achieve these purposes. **Leg.H.** Added Stats 1979 ch 1029 §2. Amended Stats 1980 ch 676 §51; Stats 2004 ch 177 §6 (SB 1277).

§2945.1. Definitions

The following definitions apply to this chapter:

(a) "Foreclosure consultant" means any person who makes any solicitation, representation, or offer to any owner to perform for compensation or who, for compensation, performs any service which the person in any manner represents will in any manner do any of the following:

(1) Stop or postpone the foreclosure sale.

(2) Obtain any forbearance from any beneficiary or mortgagee.

(3) Assist the owner to exercise the right of reinstatement provided in Section 2924c.

(4) Obtain any extension of the period within which the owner may reinstate his or her obligation.

(5) Obtain any waiver of an acceleration clause contained in any promissory note or contract secured by a deed of trust or mortgage on a residence in foreclosure or contained that deed of trust or mortgage.

(6) Assist the owner to obtain a loan or advance of funds.

(7) Avoid or ameliorate the impairment of the owner's credit resulting from the recording of a notice of default or the conduct of a foreclosure sale.

(8) Save the owner's residence from foreclosure.

(9) Assist the owner in obtaining from the beneficiary, mortgagee, trustee under a power of sale, or counsel for the beneficiary, mortgagee, or trustee, the remaining proceeds from the foreclosure sale of the owner's residence.

(b) A foreclosure consultant does not include any of the following:

(1) A person licensed to practice law in this state when the person renders service in the course of his or her practice as an attorney at law.

(2) A person licensed under Division 3 (commencing with Section 12000) of the Financial Code when the person is acting as a prorater as defined therein.

(3) A person licensed under Part 1 (commencing with Section 10000) of Division 4 of the Business and Professions Code when the person is acting under the authority of that license, as described in Section 10131 or 10131.1 of the Business and Professions Code.

(4) A person licensed under Chapter 1 (commencing with Section 5000) of Division 3 of the Business and Professions Code when the person is acting in any capacity for which the person is licensed under those provisions.

(5) A person or his or her authorized agent acting under the express authority or written approval of the Department of Housing and Urban Development or other department or agency of the United States or this state to provide services.

(6) A person who holds or is owed an obligation secured by a lien on any residence in foreclosure when the person performs services in connection with this obligation or lien.

(7) Any person licensed to make loans pursuant to Division 9 (commencing with Section 22000) of the Financial Code when the person is acting under the authority of that license.

(8) Any person or entity doing business under any law of this state, or of the United States relating to banks, trust companies, savings and loan associations, industrial loan companies, pension trusts, credit unions, insurance companies, or any person or entity authorized under the laws of this state to conduct a title or escrow business, or a mortgagee which is a United States Department of Housing and Urban Development approved

mortgagee and any subsidiary or affiliate of the above, and any agent or employee of the above while engaged in the business of these persons or entities.

(9) A person licensed as a residential mortgage lender or servicer pursuant to Division 20 (commencing with Section 50000) of the Financial Code, when acting under the authority of that license.

(c) Notwithstanding subdivision (b), any person who provides services pursuant to paragraph (9) of subdivision (a) is a foreclosure consultant unless he or she is the owner's attorney.

(d) "Person" means any individual, partnership, corporation, limited liability company, association or other group, however organized.

(e) "Service" means and includes, but is not limited to, any of the following:

(1) Debt, budget, or financial counseling of any type.

(2) Receiving money for the purpose of distributing it to creditors in payment or partial payment of any obligation secured by a lien on a residence in foreclosure.

(3) Contacting creditors on behalf of an owner of a residence in foreclosure.

(4) Arranging or attempting to arrange for an extension of the period within which the owner of a residence in foreclosure may cure his or her default and reinstate his or her obligation pursuant to Section 2924c.

(5) Arranging or attempting to arrange for any delay or postponement of the time of sale of the residence in foreclosure.

(6) Advising the filing of any document or assisting in any manner in the preparation of any document for filing with any bankruptcy court.

(7) Giving any advice, explanation, or instruction to an owner of a residence in foreclosure which in any manner relates to the cure of a default in or the reinstatement of an obligation secured by a lien on the residence in foreclosure, the full satisfaction of that obligation, or the postponement or avoidance of a sale of a residence in foreclosure pursuant to a power of sale contained in any deed of trust.

(8) Arranging or attempting to arrange for the payment by the beneficiary, mortgagee, trustee under a power of sale, or counsel for the beneficiary, mortgagee, or trustee, of the remaining proceeds to which the owner is entitled from a foreclosure sale of the owner's residence in foreclosure. Arranging or attempting to arrange for the payment shall include any arrangement where the owner transfers or assigns the right to the remaining proceeds of a foreclosure sale to the foreclosure consultant or any person designated by the foreclosure consultant, whether that transfer is effected by agreement, assignment, deed, power of attorney, or assignment of claim.

(9) Arranging or attempting to arrange an audit of any obligation secured by a lien on a residence in foreclosure.

(f) "Residence in foreclosure" means a residence in foreclosure as defined in Section 1695.1.

(g) "Owner" means a property owner as defined in Section 1695.1.

(h) "Contract" means any agreement, or any term thereof, between a foreclosure consultant and an owner for the rendition of any service as defined in subdivision (e). **Leg.H.** Added Stats 1979 ch 1029 §2. Amended Stats 1980 ch 108 §3, effective May 20, 1980, ch 423 §15, effective July 11, 1980, ch 706 §2; Stats 1981 ch 724 §4; Stats 1982 ch 1082 §3; Stats 1986 ch 248 §17; Stats 1994 ch 1010 §49 (SB 2053); Stats 1995 ch 564 §4 (SB 946); Stats 2004 ch 177 §7 (SB 1277); Stats 2009 ch 630 §11 (SB 94), effective October 11, 2009; Stats 2010 ch 596 §1 (AB 2325), effective January 1, 2011.

§2945.2. Owner's right of cancellation; Notice

(a) In addition to any other right under law to rescind a contract, an owner has the right to cancel such a contract until midnight of the fifth business day, as defined in subdivision (e) of Section 1689.5, after the day on which the owner signs a contract that complies with Section 2945.3.

(b) Cancellation occurs when the owner gives written notice of cancellation to the foreclosure consultant by mail at the address specified in the contract, or by facsimile or electronic mail at the number or address identified in the contract.

(c) Notice of cancellation, if given by mail, is effective when deposited in the mail properly addressed with postage prepaid. If given by facsimile or electronic mail, notice of cancellation is effective when successfully transmitted.

(d) Notice of cancellation given by the owner need not take the particular form as provided with the contract and, however expressed, is effective if it indicates the intention of the owner not to be bound by the contract. **Leg.H.** Added Stats 1979 ch 1029 §2. Amended Stats 2008 ch 278 §2 (AB 180), effective January 1, 2009, operative July 1, 2009.

§2945.3. Form and contents of contract; Notice of cancellation; Right to cancel pending compliance

(a) Every contract shall be in writing and shall fully disclose the exact nature of the foreclosure consultant's services and the total amount and terms of compensation.

(b) The following notice, printed in at least 14-point boldface type and completed with the name of the foreclosure consultant, shall be printed immediately above the statement required by subdivision (d):

"NOTICE REQUIRED BY CALIFORNIA LAW

_____ or anyone working for him or her CAN-
(Name)
NOT:
(1) Take any money from you or ask you for money
until _____ has completely finished doing everything he or
         (Name)
she said he or she would do; and (2) Ask you to sign or have you sign any lien, deed of trust, or deed."

(c) The contract shall be written in the same language as principally used by the foreclosure consultant to describe his or her services or to negotiate the contract. In addition, the foreclosure consultant shall provide the owner, before the owner signs the contract, with a copy of a completed contract written in any other language used in any communication between the foreclosure consultant and the owner and in any language described in subdivision (b) of Section 1632 and requested by the owner. If English is the language principally used by the foreclosure consultant to describe the foreclosure consultant's services or to negotiate the contract, the foreclosure consultant shall notify the owner orally and in writing before the owner signs the contract that the owner has the right to ask for a completed copy of the contract in a language described in subdivision (b) of Section 1632.

(d) The contract shall be dated and signed by the owner and shall contain in immediate proximity to the space reserved for the owner's signature a conspicuous statement in a size equal to at least 10-point boldface type, as follows: "You, the owner, may cancel this transaction at any time prior to midnight of the fifth business day after the date of this transaction. See the attached notice of cancellation form for an explanation of this right."

(e) The contract shall contain on the first page, in a type size no smaller than that generally used in the body of the document, each of the following:

(1) The name, mailing address, electronic mail address, and facsimile number of the foreclosure consultant to which the notice of cancellation is to be mailed.

(2) The date the owner signed the contract.

(f) The contract shall be accompanied by a completed form in duplicate, captioned "notice of cancellation," which shall be attached to the contract, shall be easily detachable, and shall contain in type of at least 10-point the following statement written in the same language as used in the contract:

"NOTICE OF CANCELLATION

_____
(Enter date of transaction) (Date)

You may cancel this transaction, without any penalty or obligation, within five business days from the above date.
To cancel this transaction, mail or deliver a signed and dated copy of this cancellation notice, or any other written notice, or send a telegram,
to _____
         (Name of foreclosure consultant)
at _____
(Address of foreclosure consultant's place of business)
You may also cancel by sending a facsimile (fax) of a signed and dated copy of this cancellation notice, or any other written notice, to the following number:

_____
(Facsimile telephone number of foreclosure consultant's place of business)

You may also cancel by sending an e-mail canceling this transaction to the following e-mail address:

_____
(E-mail address of foreclosure consultant's business)
I hereby cancel this transaction _____.
(Date)
_____,"
(Owner's signature)

(g) The foreclosure consultant shall provide the owner with a copy of the contract and the attached notice of cancellation.

(h) Until the foreclosure consultant has complied with this section, the owner may cancel the contract. **Leg.H.** Added Stats 1979 ch 1029 §2. Amended Stats 1980 ch 423 §16, effective July 11, 1980; Stats 1997 ch 50 §4 (AB 669); Stats 2004 ch 177 §8 (SB 1277) (ch 177 prevails), ch 183 §39 (AB 3082); Stats 2006 ch 538 §54 (SB 1852), effective January 1, 2007; Stats 2008 ch 278 §3 (AB 180), effective January 1, 2009, operative July 1, 2009.

§2945.4. Violations

It shall be a violation for a foreclosure consultant to:

(a) Claim, demand, charge, collect, or receive any compensation until after the foreclosure consultant has fully performed each and every service the foreclosure consultant contracted to perform or represented that he or she would perform.

(b) Claim, demand, charge, collect, or receive any fee, interest, or any other compensation for any reason which exceeds 10 percent per annum of the amount of any loan which the foreclosure consultant may make to the owner.

(c) Take any wage assignment, any lien of any type on real or personal property, or other security to secure the payment of compensation. That security shall be void and unenforceable.

(d) Receive any consideration from any third party in connection with services rendered to an owner unless that consideration is fully disclosed to the owner.

(e) Acquire any interest in a residence in foreclosure from an owner with whom the foreclosure consultant has contracted. Any interest acquired in violation of this subdivision shall be voidable, provided that nothing herein shall affect or defeat the title of a bona fide purchaser or encumbrancer for value and without notice of a violation of this article. Knowledge that the property was "residential real property in foreclosure," does not constitute notice of a violation of this article. This subdivision may not be deemed to abrogate any duty of inquiry which exists as to rights or interests of persons in possession of residential real property in foreclosure.

(f) Take any power of attorney from an owner for any purpose.

(g) Induce or attempt to induce any owner to enter into a contract which does not comply in all respects with Sections 2945.2 and 2945.3.

(h) Enter into an agreement at any time to assist the owner in arranging, or arrange for the owner, the release of surplus funds after the trustee's sale is conducted, whether the agreement involves direct payment, assignment, deed, power of attorney, assignment of claim from an owner to the foreclosure consultant or any person designated by the foreclosure consultant, or any other compensation. **Leg.H.** Added Stats 1979 ch 1029 §2. Amended Stats 1980 ch 423 §17, effective July 11, 1980; Stats 2004 ch 177 §9 (SB 1277); Stats 2008 ch 278 §4 (AB 180), effective January 1, 2009, operative July 1, 2009.

§2945.45. Foreclosure consultant, requirements; Foreclosure Consultant Regulation Fund created; Denial or revocation of certificate of registration; Penalties for violation

(a) Except as provided in subdivision (b) of Section 2945.1, a person shall not take any action specified in subdivision (a) of Section 2945.1 unless the person satisfies the following requirements:

(1) The person registers with, and is issued and maintains a certificate of registration from, the Department of Justice in accordance with the following requirements:

(A) The person shall submit a completed registration form, along with applicable fees, to the department. The registration form shall include the name, address, and telephone number of the foreclosure consultant, all of the names, addresses, telephone numbers, Internet Web sites, and e-mail addresses used or proposed to be used in connection with acting as a foreclosure consultant, a statement that the person has not been convicted of, or pled nolo contendere to, any crime involving fraud, misrepresentation, dishonesty, or a violation of this article, a statement that the person has not been liable under any civil judgment for fraud, misrepresentation, or violations of this article or of Section 17200 or 17500 of the Business and Professions Code, and any additional information required by the department.

(B) The registration form shall be accompanied by a copy of all print or electronic advertising and other promotional material, and scripts of all telephonic or broadcast advertising and other statements used or proposed to be used in connection with acting as a foreclosure consultant.

(C) The registration form shall be accompanied by a copy of the bond required pursuant to paragraph (2).

(D) The person shall file an update of any material change in the information required by subparagraphs (A) and (B) with the department.

(E) The person shall pay any fee set by the department to defray reasonable costs incurred in connection with the department's responsibilities under this article.

(2) The person obtains and maintains in force a surety bond in the amount of one hundred thousand dollars ($100,000). The bond shall be executed by a corporate surety admitted to do business in this state. The bond shall be made in favor of the State of California for the benefit of homeowners for damages caused by the foreclosure consultant's violation of this article or any other provision of law. A copy of the bond shall be filed with the Secretary of State, with a copy provided to the department pursuant to subparagraph (C) of paragraph (1).

(b) The Foreclosure Consultant Regulation Fund is hereby created in the State Treasury for the deposit of fees submitted to the Department of Justice pursuant to subparagraph (A) of paragraph (1) of subdivision (a) for registration as a foreclosure consultant. Moneys in the fund shall be available, upon appropriation by the Legislature, for the costs of the department incurred in connection with the administration of the registration program.

(c) The Department of Justice may refuse to issue, or may revoke, a certificate of registration because of any misstatement in the registration form, because the foreclosure consultant has been held liable for the violation of any law described in subparagraph (A) of paragraph (1) of subdivision (a), because the foreclosure consultant has failed to maintain the bond required under paragraph (2) of subdivision (a), or because of any violation of this chapter.

(d) A person who violates subdivision (a) shall be punished, for each violation, by a fine of not less than one thousand dollars ($1,000) and not more than twenty-five thousand dollars ($25,000), by imprisonment in the county jail for not more than one year, or by both that fine and imprisonment. The imposition of a penalty pursuant to this subdivision shall not be affected by the availability of any other relief, remedy, or penalty provided by law, and shall not affect the availability of any such relief, remedy, or penalty. **Leg.H.** Added Stats 2008 ch 278 §5 (AB 180), effective January 1, 2009, operative July 1, 2009.

§2945.5. Waiver

Any waiver by an owner of the provisions of this article shall be deemed void and unenforceable as contrary to public policy. Any attempt by a foreclosure consultant to induce an owner to waive his rights shall be deemed a violation of this article. **Leg.H.** Added Stats 1979 ch 1029 §2. Amended Stats 1980 ch 676 §53.

§2945.6. Owner's right of action; Damages; Limitations period

(a) An owner may bring an action against a foreclosure consultant for any violation of this chapter. Judgment shall be entered for actual damages, reasonable attorneys' fees and costs, and appropriate equitable relief. The court also may, in its discretion, award exemplary damages and shall award exemplary damages equivalent to at least three times the compensation received by the foreclosure consultant in violation of subdivision (a), (b), or (d) of Section 2945.4, and three times the owner's actual damages for any violation of subdivision (c), (e), or (g) of Section 2945.4, in addition to any other award of actual or exemplary damages.

(b) The rights and remedies provided in subdivision (a) are cumulative to, and not a limitation of, any other rights and remedies provided by law. Any action brought pursuant to this section shall be commenced within four years from the date of the alleged violation. **Leg.H.** Added Stats 1979 ch 1029 §2. Amended Stats 1980 ch 676 (ch 423 prevails), ch 423 §18, effective July 11, 1980; Stats 1997 ch 50 §5 (AB 669).

§2945.7. Punishment

Any person who commits any violation described in Section 2945.4 shall be punished by a fine of not more than ten thousand dollars ($10,000), by imprisonment in the county jail for not more than one year, or pursuant to subdivision (h) of Section 1170 of the Penal Code, or by both that fine and imprisonment for each violation. These penalties are cumulative to any other remedies or penalties provided by law. **Leg.H.** Added Stats 1979 ch 1029 §2. Amended Stats 1980 ch 423 §19, effective July 11, 1980; Stats 1985 ch 270 §2; Stats 2011 ch 15 §35 (AB 109), effective April 4, 2011, operative October 1, 2011.

2011 Notes: This act is titled and may be cited as the 2011 Realignment Legislation addressing public safety. Stats 2011 ch 15 (AB 109) §1.

This act will become operative no earlier than October 1, 2011, and only upon creation of a community corrections grant program to assist in implementing this act and upon an appropriation to fund the grant program. Stats 2011 ch 15 (AB 109) §636; Stats 2011 ch 39 (AB 117) §68.

The Community Corrections Grant Program referred to in Stats 2011 ch 15 (AB 109) §636, as amended by Stats 2011 ch 39 (AB 117) §68, was created by Stats 2011 ch 40 (AB 118) §3, operative October 1, 2011.

§2945.8. Effect of unconstitutional provision

If any provision of this article or the application thereof to any person or circumstance is held to be unconstitutional, the remainder of the article and the application of such provision to other persons and circumstances shall not be affected thereby. **Leg.H.** Added Stats 1979 ch 1029 §2.

§2945.9. Liability of foreclosure consultant for damages resulting from statements made by representative

(a) A foreclosure consultant is liable for all damages resulting from any statement made or act committed by the foreclosure consultant's representative in any manner connected with the foreclosure consultant's (1) performance, offer to perform, or contract to perform any of the services described in subdivision (a) of Section 2945.1, (2) receipt of any consideration or property from or on behalf of an owner, or (3) performance of any act prohibited by this article.

(b) "Representative" for the purposes of this section means a person who in any manner solicits, induces, or causes (1) any owner to contract with a foreclosure consultant, (2) any owner to pay any consideration or transfer title to the residence in foreclosure to the foreclosure consultant, or (3) any member of the owner's family or household to induce or cause any owner to pay any consideration or transfer title to the residence in foreclosure to the foreclosure consultant. **Leg.H.** Added Stats 1990 ch 1537 §4 (SB 2641). Amended Stats 2006 ch 538 §55 (SB 1852), effective January 1, 2007.

§2945.10. Voidness of contract provision attempting to limit liability

(a) Any provision in a contract which attempts or purports to limit the liability of the foreclosure consultant under Section 2945.9 shall be void and shall at the option of the owner render the contract void. The foreclosure consultant shall be liable to the owner for all damages proximately caused by that provision. Any provision in a contract which attempts or purports to require arbitration of any dispute arising under this chapter shall be void at the option of the owner only upon grounds as exist for the revocation of any contract.

(b) This section shall apply to any contract entered into on or after January 1, 1991. **Leg.H.** Added Stats 1990 ch 1537 §5 (SB 2641).

§2945.11. Statements required of representatives

(a) Any representative, as defined in subdivision (b) of Section 2945.9, deemed to be the agent or employee or both the agent and the employee of the foreclosure consultant shall be required to provide both of the following:

(1) Written proof to the owner that the representative has a valid current California Real Estate Sales License and that the representative is bonded by an admitted surety insurer in an amount equal to at least twice the fair market value of the real property that is the subject of the contract.

(2) A statement in writing, under penalty of perjury, that the representative has a valid current California Real Estate Sales License, that the representative is bonded by an admitted surety insurer in an amount equal to at least twice the value of the real property that is the subject of the contract and has complied with paragraph (1). The written statement required by this paragraph shall be provided to all parties to the contract prior to the transfer of any interest in the real property that is the subject of the contract.

(b) The failure to comply with subdivision (a) shall, at the option of the owner, render the contract void and the foreclosure consultant shall be liable to the owner for all damages proximately caused by the failure to comply. **Leg.H.** Added Stats 1990 ch 1537 §6 (SB 2641). Amended Stats 1996 ch 124 §8 (AB 3470).

ARTICLE 2
Mortgage of Real Property

What real property may be mortgaged. §2947.
Form of mortgage. §2948.
Accrual of interest on obligation secured by mortgage or deed of trust on property with one to four residential dwellings; Disclosure requirements; Applicability. §2948.5.
Junior encumbrance on single-family, owner-occupied dwelling as basis for default or acceleration of primary encumbrance. §2949.
Defeasance, to affect grant absolute on its face, must be recorded. §2950.
Assumption of mortgage loan by remaining borrower. §2951.
Recording of fictitious mortgage or deed of trust; Effect. §2952.
Validity of waiver by borrower of statutory rights; Liens not affected by section. §2953.
"Real property security instrument"; "Subordination clause"; "Subordination agreement". §2953.1.
Notices required in real property security agreement containing subordination clause. §2953.2.
Notices required in subordination agreement. §2953.3.
Voidability of subordination clause or agreement where required notices not given; Recording of notice of election; Waiver. §2953.4.
Loans and subordinating loans to which Sections 2953.1–2953.4 inapplicable. §2953.5.
Restriction on establishment of impound or trust accounts for payment of taxes, insurance, and related charges; Accounting. §2954.
Maximum required deposits in impound accounts; Prohibited payments from accounts. §2954.1.
Annual statement by mortgagee. §2954.2.
Late payment charges on real estate loans encumbering single-family owner-occupied dwellings. §2954.4.
Notice as prerequisite to assessment of charges for default, delinquency, or late payment. §2954.5.
Notice of right to cancel mortgage insurance. §2954.6.
Refund of unused premium. §2954.65.
Right to terminate future payments; Conditions; Exceptions; Compliance. §2954.7.
Interest on impound account. §2954.8.
Prepayment; Permissible charges. §2954.9.
Prohibition against prepayment penalty upon acceleration of maturity date of loan secured by certain residential property. §2954.10.
Prepayment charge for installment loan secured by lien on residential property; Disclosure; Rescission rights. §2954.11.
No private mortgage insurance or mortgage guaranty insurance under specified conditions. §2954.12.
Investment of money held in impound account. §2955.
Disclosures regarding earthquake insurance requirements. §2955.1.
Hazard insurance coverage. §2955.5.

§2947. What real property may be mortgaged

Any interest in real property which is capable of being transferred may be mortgaged. **Leg.H.** Enacted 1872.

§2948. Form of mortgage

A mortgage of real property may be made in substantially the following form:

This mortgage, made the ____ day of _____, in the year ____, by A B, of _____, mortgagor, to C D, of _____, mortgagee, witnesseth:

That the mortgagor mortgages to the mortgagee [here describe the property], as security for the payment to him of _____ dollars, on [or before] the ____ day of _____, in the year ____, with interest thereon [or as security for the payment of an obligation, describing it, etc.] A. B. **Leg.H.** Enacted 1872.

§2948.5. Accrual of interest on obligation secured by mortgage or deed of trust on property with one to four residential dwellings; Disclosure requirements; Applicability

(a) A borrower shall not be required to pay interest on a principal obligation under a promissory note secured by a mortgage or deed of trust on real property improved with between one to four residential dwelling units for any period that meets any of the following requirements:

(1) Is more than one day prior to the date that the loan proceeds are disbursed from escrow.

(2) In the event of no escrow, if a request for recording is made in connection with the disbursement, is more than one day prior to the date the loan proceeds are disbursed to the borrower, to a third party on behalf of the borrower, or to the lender to satisfy an existing obligation of the borrower.

(3) In all other circumstances where there is no escrow and no request for recording, is prior to the date funds are disbursed to the borrower, to a third party on behalf of the borrower, or to the lender to satisfy an existing obligation of the borrower.

(b) Interest may commence to accrue on the business day immediately preceding the day of disbursement, for obligations described in paragraphs (1) and (2) of subdivision (a) if both of the following occur:

(1) The borrower affirmatively requests, and the lender agrees, that the disbursement will occur on Monday, or a day immediately following a bank holiday.

(2) The following information is disclosed to the borrower in writing: (A) the amount of additional per diem interest charged to facilitate disbursement on Monday or the day following a holiday, as the case may be, and (B) that it may be possible to avoid the additional per diem interest charge by disbursing the loan proceeds on a day immediately following a business day. This disclosure shall be provided to the borrower and acknowledged by the borrower by signing a copy of the disclosure document prior to placing funds in escrow.

(c) This section does not apply to a loan that is subject to subdivision (c) of Section 10242 of the Business and Professions Code. **Leg.H.** Added Stats 1985 ch 1393 §1. Amended Stats 1990 ch 872 §1 (AB 4267); Stats 2001 ch 302 §1 (SB 364); Stats 2003 ch 554 §1 (AB 313).

§2949. Junior encumbrance on single-family, owner-occupied dwelling as basis for default or acceleration of primary encumbrance

(a) No mortgage or deed of trust on real property containing only a single-family, owner-occupied dwelling may be declared in default, nor may the maturity date of the indebtedness secured thereby be accelerated, solely by reason of the owner further encumbering the real property or any portion thereof, with a junior mortgage or junior deed of trust.

(b) As used in this section, "single-family, owner-occupied dwelling" means a dwelling which will be owned and occupied by a signatory to the mortgage or deed of trust secured by such dwelling within 90 days of the execution of such mortgage or deed of trust. **Leg.H.** Added by Stats 1972 ch 698 §1.

Prior Law: Former §2949, relating to what must be recorded as a mortgage, was enacted 1872 and repealed by Code Amdts 1873–74 ch 612 §262.

§2950. Defeasance, to affect grant absolute on its face, must be recorded

When a grant of real property purports to be an absolute conveyance, but is intended to be defeasible on the performance of certain conditions, such grant is not defeated or affected as against any person other than the grantee or his or her heirs or devisees, or persons having actual notice, unless an instrument of defeasance, duly executed and acknowledged, shall have been recorded in the office of the county recorder of the county where the property is situated. **Leg.H.** Enacted 1872. Amended Stats 2013 ch 76 §19 (AB 383), effective January 1, 2014.

§ 2951. Assumption of mortgage loan by remaining borrower

(a) A conventional home mortgage loan originated on or after January 1, 2027, and secured by owner-occupied residential real property containing four or fewer dwelling units with multiple borrowers shall include provisions to allow for any of the existing borrowers to purchase the property interest of another borrower on the loan by assuming the seller's portion of the mortgage in connection with a decree of dissolution of marriage, a legal separation agreement, or an incidental property settlement if the assuming borrower qualifies for the underlying loan, as determined by the lender.

(b) For purposes of this section:

(1) "Conventional home mortgage loan" means a mortgage loan that is not insured or guaranteed by the federal government.

(2) "Owner-occupied" means that the property is the principal residence of the borrowers and is security for a loan made for personal, family, or household purposes. **Leg.H.** Added Stats 2024 ch 431 §1 (AB 3100), effective January 1, 2025.

Prior Law Former CC §2951, relating to similar subject matter, was enacted 1872, and repealed Code Amdts 1873–74 ch 612 §262.

§2952. Recording of fictitious mortgage or deed of trust; Effect

Mortgages and deeds of trust of real property may be acknowledged or proved, certified and recorded, in like manner and with like effect, as grants thereof; provided, however, that a mortgage or deed of trust of real property may be recorded and constructive notice of the same and the contents thereof given in the following manner:

Any person may record in the office of the county recorder of any county fictitious mortgages and deeds of trust of real property. Those fictitious mortgages and deeds of trust need not be acknowledged, or proved or certified to be recorded or entitled to record. Those mortgages and deeds of trust shall have noted upon the face thereof that they are fictitious. The county recorder shall index and record fictitious mortgages and deeds of trust in the same manner as other mortgages and deeds of trust are recorded, and shall note on all indices and records of the same that they are fictitious. Thereafter, any of the provisions of any recorded fictitious mortgage or deed of trust may be included for any and all purposes in any mortgage or deed of trust by reference therein to any of those provisions, without setting the same forth in full; provided, the fictitious mortgage or deed of trust is of record in the county in which the mortgage or deed of trust adopting or including by reference any of the provisions thereof is recorded. The reference shall contain a statement, as to each county in which the mortgage or deed of trust containing such a reference is recorded, of the date the fictitious mortgage or deed of trust was recorded, the county recorder's office wherein it is recorded, and the book or volume and the first page of the records in the recorder's office wherein and at which the fictitious mortgage or deed of trust was recorded, and a statement by paragraph numbers or any other method that will definitely identify the same, of the specific provisions of the fictitious mortgage or deed of trust that are being so adopted and included therein. The recording of any mortgage or deed of trust which has included therein any of those provisions by reference as aforesaid shall operate as constructive notice of the whole thereof including the terms, as a part of the written contents of the mortgage or deed of trust, of those provisions so included by reference as though the same were written in full therein. The parties bound or to be bound by provisions so adopted and included by reference shall be bound thereby in the same manner and with like effect for all purposes as though those provisions had been and were set forth in full in any mortgage or deed of trust.

The amendment to this section enacted by the 1957 Regular Session of the Legislature does not constitute a change in, but is declaratory of, the preexisting law. **Leg.H.** Enacted 1872. Amended Stats Code Amdts 1873–74 ch 612 §263; Stats 1947 ch 1497 §5; Stats 1949 ch 443 §1; Stats 1957 ch 1220 §1; Stats 1969 ch 287 §1, operative July 1, 1970; Stats 2000 ch 924 §1 (AB 2935).

§2953. Validity of waiver by borrower of statutory rights; Liens not affected by section

Any express agreement made or entered into by a borrower at the time of or in connection with the making of or renewing of any loan secured by a deed of trust, mortgage or other instrument creating a lien on real property, whereby the borrower agrees to waive the rights, or privileges conferred upon the borrower by Sections 2924, 2924b, or 2924c of the Civil Code or by Sections 580a or 726 of the Code of Civil Procedure, shall be void and of no effect. The provisions of this section shall not apply to any deed of trust, mortgage, or other liens given to secure the payment of bonds or other evidences of indebtedness authorized or permitted to be issued by the Commissioner of Financial Protection and Innovation, or made by a public utility subject to the provisions of the Public Utilities Act. **Leg.H.** Added Stats 1937 ch 564 §1. Amended Stats 1939 ch 585 §1; Stats 1941 ch 599 §1; Stats 2019 ch 143 §17 (SB 251), effective January 1, 2020; Stats 2022 ch 452 §36 (SB 1498), effective January 1, 2023.

§2953.1. "Real property security instrument"; "Subordination clause"; "Subordination agreement"

As used in this section:

(a) "Real property security instrument" shall include any mortgage or trust deed or land contract in or on real property.

(b) "Subordination clause" shall mean a clause in a real property security instrument whereby the holder of the security interest under such instrument agrees that upon the occurrence of conditions or circumstances specified therein his security interest will become subordinate to or he will execute an agreement subordinating his interest to the lien of another real property security instrument which would otherwise be of lower priority than his lien or security interest.

(c) "Subordination agreement" shall mean a separate agreement or instrument whereby the holder of the security interest under a real property security instrument agrees that (1) his existing security interest is subordinate to, or (2) upon the occurrence of conditions or circumstances specified in such separate agreement his security interest will become subordinate to, or (3) he will execute an agreement subordinating his interest to, the lien of another real property security instrument which would otherwise be of lower priority than his lien or security interest. **Leg.H.** Added Stats 1963 ch 1861 §1, operative January 2, 1964.

§2953.2. Notices required in real property security agreement containing subordination clause

Every real property security instrument which contains or has attached a subordination clause shall contain:

(a) At the top of the real property security instrument there shall appear in at least 10-point bold type, or, if typewritten, in capital letters and underlined, the word "Subordinated" followed by a description of the type of security instrument.

(b) A notice in at least eight-point bold type, or, if typewritten, in capital letters, shall appear immediately below the legend required by subdivision (a) of this section reading as follows: "Notice: This (insert description of real property security instrument) contains a subordination clause which may result in your security interest in the property becoming subject to and of lower priority than the lien of some other or later security instrument."

(c) If the terms of the subordination clause allow the obligor on the debt secured by the real property security instrument to obtain a loan, secured by another real property security instrument covering all or any part of the same parcel of real property, the proceeds of which may be used for any purpose or purposes other than defraying the costs for improvement of the land covered by the real property security instrument containing the subordination clause, a notice in at least eight-point bold type, or, if typewritten, in capital letters shall appear directly above the space reserved for the signature of the person whose security interest is to be subordinated, reading as follows: "Notice: This (insert description of real property security instrument) contains a subordination clause which allows the person obligated on your real property security instrument to obtain a loan a portion of which may be expended for other purposes than improvement of the land." **Leg.H.** Added Stats 1963 ch 1861 §2, operative January 2, 1964.

§2953.3. Notices required in subordination agreement

Every subordination agreement shall contain:

(a) At the top of the subordination agreement there shall appear in at least 10-point bold type, or, if typewritten, in capital letters and underlined, the words "Subordination Agreement."

(b) A notice in at least eight-point bold type, or, if typewritten, in capital letters, shall appear immediately below the legend required by subdivision (a) of this section reading as follows:

"Notice: This subordination agreement ("may result" or "results" as appropriate) in your security interest in the property becoming subject to and of lower priority than the lien of some other or later security instrument."

(c) If the terms of the subordination agreement provide that the obligor on the debt secured by the real property security instrument may either obtain a loan, or obtain an agreement from the holder of the real property security which will allow him to obtain a loan, the proceeds of which may be used for any purpose or purposes other than defraying the actual contract costs for improvement of the land, covered by the real property security instrument which is, or is to become subordinated, a notice in at least eight-point bold type or, if typewritten, in capital letters, shall appear directly above the space reserved for the signature of the person whose security interest is to be subordinated, reading as follows: "Notice: This subordination agreement contains a provision which ("allows" or "may allow" as appropriate) the person obligated on your real property security to obtain a loan a portion of which may be expended for other purposes than improvement of the land." **Leg.H.** Added Stats 1963 ch 1861 §3, operative January 2, 1964.

§2953.4. Voidability of subordination clause or agreement where required notices not given; Recording of notice of election; Waiver

(a) Any subordination clause and any subordination agreement which is executed after the effective date of this act and which does not substantially comply with the provisions of Section 2953.2 or Section 2953.3 shall be voidable upon the election of the person whose security interest is to be subordinated or his successor-in-interest exercised within two years of the date on which the instrument to which his security interest is subordinated is executed; provided that such power of avoidance shall not be exercisable by any person having actual knowledge of the existence and terms of the subordination clause or agreement.

(b) The person whose security interest was to be subordinated or his successor-in-interest shall exercise his election to void the subordination clause or subordination agreement provided by subdivision (a) of this section by recording a notice stating that the provisions of Civil Code Section 2953.2 or Civil Code Section 2953.3 have not been complied with, and that he is the holder of the security instrument which is or was to become subordinated and that he elects to avoid the effect of the subordination clause or subordination agreement.

(c) The provisions of this section may be waived by the subsequent execution and recordation by the holder of the security interest which is or may become subordinated, of a statement that he knows of the existence of the subordination clause or agreement and of its terms and that he waives the provisions of this section and the requirements of Sections 2953.1, 2953.2, and 2953.3. **Leg.H.** Added Stats 1963 ch 1861 §4, operative January 2, 1964.

§2953.5. Loans and subordinating loans to which Sections 2953.1–2953.4 inapplicable

(a) Sections 2953.1 through 2953.4 shall not apply to any subordination clause or subordination agreement which expressly states that the subordinating loan shall exceed twenty-five thousand dollars ($25,000).

(b) Sections 2953.1 through 2953.4 shall not apply to any subordination clause or subordination agreement which is executed in connection with a loan which exceeds twenty-five thousand dollars ($25,000). **Leg.H.** Added Stats 1963 ch 1861 §5, operative January 2, 1964.

§2954. Restriction on establishment of impound or trust accounts for payment of taxes, insurance, and related charges; Accounting

(a)(1) No impound, trust, or other type of account for payment of taxes on the property, insurance premiums, or other purposes relating to the property shall be required as a condition of a real property sale contract or a loan secured by a deed of trust or mortgage on real property containing only a single-family, owner-occupied dwelling, except: (A) where required by a state or federal regulatory authority, (B) where a loan is made, guaranteed, or insured by a state or federal governmental lending or insuring agency, (C) upon a failure of the purchaser or borrower to pay two consecutive tax installments on the property prior to the delinquency date for such payments, (D) where the original principal amount of such a loan is (i) 90 percent or more of the sale price, if the property involved is sold, or is (ii) 90 percent or more of the appraised value of the property securing the loan, (E) whenever the combined principal amount of all loans secured by the real property exceeds 80 percent of the appraised value of the property securing the loans, (F) where a loan is made in compliance with the requirements for higher priced mortgage loans established in Regulation Z, whether or not the loan is a higher priced mortgage loan, or (G) where a loan is refinanced or modified in connection with a lender's homeownership preservation program or a lender's participation in such a program sponsored by a federal, state, or local government authority or a nonprofit organization. Nothing contained in this section shall preclude establishment of such an account on terms mutually agreeable to the parties to the loan, if, prior to the execution of the loan or sale agreement, the seller or lender has furnished to the purchaser or borrower a statement in writing, which may be set forth in the loan application, to the effect that the establishment of such an account shall not be required as a condition to the execution of the loan or sale agreement, and further, stating whether or not interest will be paid on the funds in such an account.

An impound, trust, or other type of account for the payment of taxes, insurance premiums, or other purposes relating to property established in violation of this subdivision is voidable, at the option of the purchaser or borrower, at any time, but shall not otherwise affect the validity of the loan or sale.

(2) For the purposes of this subdivision, "Regulation Z" means any rule, regulation, or interpretation promulgated by the Board of Governors of the Federal Reserve System and any interpretation or approval issued by an official or employee duly authorized by the board to issue interpretations or approvals dealing with, respectively, consumer leasing or consumer lending, pursuant to the federal Truth in Lending Act, as amended (15 U.S.C. Sec. 1601 et seq.).

(b) Every mortgagee of real property, beneficiary under a deed of trust on real property, or vendor on a real property sale contract upon the written request of the mortgagor, trustor, or vendee shall furnish to the mortgagor, trustor, or vendee for each calendar year within 60 days after the end of the year an itemized accounting of moneys received for interest and principal repayment and received and held in or disbursed from an impound or trust account, if any, for payment of taxes on the property, insurance premiums, or other purposes relating to the property subject to the mortgage, deed of trust, or real property sale contract. The mortgagor, trustor, or vendee shall be entitled to receive one such accounting for each calendar year without charge and shall be entitled to additional similar accountings for one or more months upon written request and on payment in advance of fees as follows:

(1) Fifty cents ($0.50) per statement when requested in advance on a monthly basis for one or more years.

(2) One dollar ($1) per statement when requested for only one month.

(3) Five dollars ($5) if requested for a single cumulative statement giving all the information described above back to the last statement rendered.

If the mortgagee, beneficiary or vendor transmits to the mortgagor, trustor or vendee a monthly statement or passbook showing moneys received for interest and principal repayment and received and held in and disbursed from an impound or trust account, if any, the mortgagee, beneficiary or vendor shall be deemed to have complied with this section.

No increase in the monthly rate of payment of a mortgagor, trustor or vendee on a real property sale contract for impound or trust accounts shall be effective until after the mortgagee, beneficiary or vendor has furnished the mortgagor, trustor or vendee with an itemized accounting of the moneys presently held by it in the accounts, and a statement of the new monthly rate of payment, and an explanation of the factors necessitating the increase.

The provisions of this section shall be in addition to the obligations of the parties as stated by Section 2943 of this code.

Every person who willfully or repeatedly violates this subdivision shall be subject to punishment by a fine of not less than fifty dollars ($50) nor more than two hundred dollars ($200).

(c) As used in this section, "single-family, owner-occupied dwelling" means a dwelling that will be owned and occupied by a signatory to the mortgage or deed of trust secured by that dwelling within 90 days of the execution of the mortgage or deed of trust. **Leg.H.** Added Stats 1961 ch 1452 §1. Amended Stats 1963 ch 1543 §1; Stats 1971 ch 117 §1; Stats 1973 ch 975 §1; Stats 1974 ch 389 §1; Stats 1982 ch 1196 §1; Stats 1983 ch 1092 §68, effective September 27, 1983, operative January 1, 1984; Stats 2009 ch 57 §1 (SB 633), effective January 1, 2010; Stats 2010 ch 328 §30 (SB 1330), effective January 1, 2011.

Prior Law: There was another section of this number, relating to maximum charge for statement regarding obligation secured by mortgage or deed of trust, which was added by Stats 1961 ch 1561 §1 p 3382 and repealed by Stats 1963 ch 733 §2 p 1748.

§2954.1. Maximum required deposits in impound accounts; Prohibited payments from accounts

No lender or person who purchases obligations secured by real property, or any agent of such lender or person, who maintains an impound, trust, or other type of account for the payment of taxes and assessments on real property, insurance premiums, or other purposes relating to such property shall do any of the following:

(a) Require the borrower or vendee to deposit in such account in any month an amount in excess of that which would be permitted in connection with a federally related mortgage loan pursuant to Section 10 of the Real Estate Settlement Procedures Act of 1974 (12 U.S.C. 2609), as amended.

(b) Require the sums maintained in such account to exceed at any time the amount or amounts reasonably necessary to pay such obligations as they become due. Any sum held in excess of the reasonable amount shall be refunded within 30 days unless the parties mutually agree to the contrary. Such an agreement may be rescinded at any time by any party.

(c) Make payments from the account in a manner so as to cause any policy of insurance to be canceled or so as to cause property taxes or other similar payments to become delinquent.

Nothing contained herein shall prohibit requiring additional amounts to be paid into an impound account in order to recover any deficiency which may exist in the account.

Any person harmed by a violation of this section shall be entitled to sue to recover his or her damages or for injunctive relief; but such violation shall not otherwise affect the validity of the loan or sale.

This section applies to all such accounts maintained after the effective date of this act. **Leg.H.** Added Stats 1979 ch 257 §1, effective July 11, 1979. Amended Stats 1983 ch 74 §1.

§2954.2. Annual statement by mortgagee

(a) Every mortgagee of record of real property containing only a one- to four-family residence, when the mortgage is given to secure payment of the balance of the purchase price of the property or to refinance such a mortgage, shall furnish to the mortgagor within 60 days after the end of each calendar year a written statement showing the amount of moneys received for interest and principal repayment, late charges, moneys received and held in or disbursed from an impound account, if any, for the payment of taxes on the property, insurance premiums, bond assessments, or other purposes relating to the property, and interest credited to the account, if any. The written statement required to be furnished by this section shall be deemed furnished if the mortgagee of record transmits to the mortgagor of record cumulative statements or receipts which, for each calendar year, provide in one of the statements or receipts the information required by this section. The mortgagor, trustor or vendee shall be entitled to receive one such statement for each calendar year without charge and without request. Such statement shall include a notification in 10-point type that additional accountings can be requested by the mortgagor, trustor, or vendee, pursuant to Section 2954.

(b) For the purposes of this section:

(1) "Mortgagee" includes a beneficiary under a deed of trust, a vendor under a real property sale contract, and an organization which services a mortgage or deed of trust by receiving and disbursing payments for the mortgagee or beneficiary.

(2) "Mortgage" includes a first or second mortgage, a first or second deed of trust, and a real property sale contract.

(3) "Impound account" includes a trust or other type of account established for the purposes described in subdivision (a).

(c) The requirements of this section shall be in addition to the requirements of Section 2954.

(d) This section shall become operative on December 31, 1978, and apply to moneys received by a mortgagee on and after January 1, 1978. **Leg.H.** Added Stats 1976 ch 774 §1, operative December 31, 1978.

§2954.4. Late payment charges on real estate loans encumbering single-family owner-occupied dwellings

(a) A charge that may be imposed for late payment of an installment due on a loan secured by a mortgage or a deed of trust on real property containing only a single-family, owner-occupied dwelling, shall not exceed either (1) the equivalent of 6 percent of the installment due that is applicable to payment of principal and interest on the loan, or (2) five dollars ($5), whichever is greater. A charge may not be imposed more than once for the late payment of the same installment. However, the imposition of a late charge on any late payment does not eliminate or supersede late charges imposed on prior late payments. A payment is not a "late payment" for the purposes of this section until at least 10 days following the due date of the installment.

(b) A late charge may not be imposed on any installment which is paid or tendered in full on or before its due date, or within 10 days thereafter, even though an earlier installment or installments, or any late charge thereon, may not have been paid in full when due. For the purposes of determining whether late charges may be imposed, any payment tendered by the borrower shall be applied by the lender to the most recent installment due.

(c) A late payment charge described in subdivision (a) is valid if it satisfies the requirements of this section and Section 2954.5.

(d) Nothing in this section shall be construed to alter in any way the duty of the borrower to pay any installment then due or to alter the rights of the lender to enforce the payment of the installments.

(e) This section is not applicable to loans made by a credit union subject to Division 5 (commencing with Section 14000) of the Financial Code, by an industrial loan company subject to Division 7 (commencing with Section 18000) of the Financial Code, or by a finance lender subject to Division 9 (commencing with Section 22000) of the Financial Code, and is not applicable to loans made or negotiated by a real estate broker subject to Article 7 (commencing with Section 10240) of Chapter 3 of Part 1 of Division 4 of the Business and Professions Code.

(f) As used in this section, "single-family, owner-occupied dwelling" means a dwelling that will be owned and occupied by a signatory to the mortgage or deed of trust secured by the dwelling within 90 days of the execution of the mortgage or deed of trust.

(g) This section applies to loans executed on and after January 1, 1976. **Leg.H.** Added Stats 1975 ch 736 §1. Amended Stats 1984 ch 890 §2; Stats 2001 ch 159 §35 (SB 662).

§2954.5. Notice as prerequisite to assessment of charges for default, delinquency, or late payment

(a) Before the first default, delinquency, or late payment charge may be assessed by any lender on a delinquent payment of a loan, other than a loan made pursuant to Division 9 (commencing with Section 22000) of the Financial Code, secured by real property, and before the borrower becomes obligated to pay this charge, the borrower shall either (1) be notified in writing and given at least 10 days from mailing of the notice in which to cure the delinquency, or (2) be informed, by a billing or notice sent for each payment due on the loan, of the date after which this charge will be assessed.

The notice provided in either paragraph (1) or (2) shall contain the amount of the charge or the method by which it is calculated.

(b) If a subsequent payment becomes delinquent the borrower shall be notified in writing, before the late charge is to be imposed, that the charge will be imposed if payment is not received, or the borrower shall be notified at least semiannually of the total amount of late charges imposed during the period covered by the notice.

(c) Notice provided by this section shall be sent to the address specified by the borrower, or, if no address is specified, to the borrower's address as shown in the lender's records.

(d) In case of multiple borrowers obligated on the same loan, a notice mailed to one shall be deemed to comply with this section.

(e) The failure of the lender to comply with the requirements of this section does not excuse or defer the borrower's performance of any obligation incurred in the loan transaction, other than his or her obligation to pay a late payment charge, nor does it impair or defer the right of the lender to enforce any other obligation including the costs and expenses incurred in any enforcement authorized by law.

(f) The provisions of this section as added by Chapter 1430 of the Statutes of 1970 shall only affect loans made on and after January 1, 1971.

The amendments to this section made at the 1975–76 Regular Session of the Legislature shall only apply to loans executed on and after January 1, 1976. **Leg.H.** Added Stats 1970 ch 1430 §1. Amended Stats 1971 ch 813 §1, effective September 29, 1971; Stats 1975 ch 736 §2; Stats 1984 ch 890 §3; Stats 2001 ch 159 §36 (SB 662).

§2954.6. Notice of right to cancel mortgage insurance

(a) If private mortgage insurance or mortgage guaranty insurance, as defined in subdivision (a) of Section 12640.02 of the Insurance Code, is required as a condition of a loan secured by a deed of trust or mortgage on real property, the lender or person making or arranging the loan shall notify the borrower whether or not the borrower has the right to cancel the insurance. If the borrower has the right to cancel, then the lender or person making or arranging the loan shall notify the borrower in writing of the following:

(1) Any identifying loan or insurance information necessary to permit the borrower to communicate with the insurer or the lender concerning the insurance.

(2) The conditions that are required to be satisfied before the private mortgage insurance or mortgage guaranty insurance may be subject to cancellation, which shall include, but is not limited to, both of the following:

(A) If the condition is a minimum ratio between the remaining principal balance of the loan and the original or current value of the property, that ratio shall be stated.

(B) Information concerning whether or not an appraisal may be necessary.

(3) The procedure the borrower is required to follow to cancel the private mortgage insurance or mortgage guaranty insurance.

(b) The notice required in subdivision (a) shall be given to the borrower no later than 30 days after the close of escrow. The notice shall be set forth in at least 10-point bold type.

(c) With respect to any loan specified in subdivision (a) for which private mortgage insurance or mortgage guaranty insurance is still maintained, the lender or person making, arranging, or servicing the loan shall provide the borrower with a notice containing the same information as specified in subdivision (a) or a clear and conspicuous written statement indicating that (1) the borrower may be able to cancel the private mortgage insurance or mortgage guaranty insurance based upon various factors, including appreciation of the value of the property derived from a current appraisal performed by an appraiser selected by the lender or servicer, and paid for by the borrower, and (2) the borrower may contact the lender or person making, arranging, or servicing the loan at a designated address and telephone number to determine whether the borrower has a right of cancellation and, if so, the conditions and procedure to effect cancellation. The notice or statement required by this subdivision shall be provided in or with each written statement required by Section 2954.2.

(d) The notice required under this section shall be provided without cost to the borrower.

(e) Any person harmed by a violation of this section may obtain injunctive relief and may recover treble damages and reasonable attorney's fees and costs.

(f) This section shall not apply to any mortgage funded with bond proceeds issued under an indenture requiring mortgage insurance for the life of the loan nor to any insurance issued pursuant to Part 4 (commencing with Section 51600) of Division 31 of the Health and Safety Code, or loans insured by the Federal Housing Administration or Veterans Administration. **Leg.H.** Added Stats 1988 ch 569 §1. Amended Stats 1990 ch 1099 §1 (AB 3746); Stats 2001 ch 137 §1 (SB 270), operative July 1, 2002.

§2954.65. Refund of unused premium

Within 30 days after notice of cancellation from the insured, a private mortgage insurer or mortgage guaranty insurer shall, if the policy is cancellable, refund the remaining portion of the unused premium to the person or persons designated by the insured. **Leg.H.** Added Stats 1990 ch 1099 §2 (AB 3746).

§2954.7. Right to terminate future payments; Conditions; Exceptions; Compliance

Except when a statute, regulation, rule, or written guideline promulgated by an institutional third party applicable to notes or evidence of indebtedness secured by a deed of trust or mortgage purchased in whole or in part by an institutional third party specifically prohibits cancellation during the term of the indebtedness, if a borrower so requests and the conditions established by paragraphs (1) to (5), inclusive, of subdivision (a) are met, a borrower may terminate future payments for private mortgage insurance, or mortgage guaranty insurance as defined in subdivision (a) of Section 12640.02 of the Insurance Code, issued as a condition to the extension of credit in the form of a loan evidenced by a note or other evidence of indebtedness that is secured by a deed of trust or mortgage on the subject real property.

(a) The following conditions shall be satisfied in order for a borrower to be entitled to terminate payments for private mortgage insurance or mortgage guaranty insurance:

(1) The request to terminate future payments for private mortgage insurance or mortgage guaranty insurance shall be in writing.

(2) The origination date of the note or evidence of indebtedness shall be at least two years prior to the date of the request.

(3) The note or evidence of indebtedness shall be for personal, family, household, or purchase money purposes, secured by a deed of trust or mortgage on owner-occupied, one- to four-unit, residential real property.

(4) The unpaid principal balance owed on the secured obligation that is the subject of the private mortgage insurance or mortgage guaranty

insurance shall not be more than 75 percent, unless the borrower and lender or servicer of the loan agree in writing upon a higher loan-to-value ratio, of either of the following:

(A) The sale price of the property at the origination date of the note or evidence of indebtedness, provided that the current fair market value of the property is equal to or greater than the original appraised value used at the origination date.

(B) The current fair market value of the property as determined by an appraisal, the cost of which shall be paid for by the borrower. The appraisal shall be ordered and the appraiser shall be selected by the lender or servicer of the loan.

(5) The borrower's monthly installments of principal, interest, and escrow obligations on the encumbrance or encumbrances secured by the real property shall be current at the time the request is made and those installments shall not have been more than 30 days past due over the 24-month period immediately preceding the request, provided further, that no notice of default has been recorded against the security real property pursuant to Section 2924, as a result of a nonmonetary default by the borrower (trustor) during the 24-month period immediately preceding the request.

(b) This section does not apply to any of the following:

(1) A note or evidence of indebtedness secured by a deed of trust or mortgage, or mortgage insurance, executed under the authority of Part 3 (commencing with Section 50900) or Part 4 (commencing with Section 51600) of Division 31 of the Health and Safety Code.

(2) Any note or evidence of indebtedness secured by a deed of trust or mortgage that is funded in whole or in part pursuant to authority granted by statute, regulation, or rule that, as a condition of that funding, prohibits or limits termination of payments for private mortgage insurance or mortgage guaranty insurance during the term of the indebtedness.

(3) Notes or evidence of indebtedness that require private mortgage insurance and were executed prior to January 1, 1991.

(c) If the note secured by the deed of trust or mortgage will be or has been sold in whole or in part to an institutional third party, adherence to the institutional third party's standards for termination of future payments for private mortgage insurance or mortgage guaranty insurance shall be deemed in compliance with the requirements of this section.

(d) For the purposes of this section, "institutional third party" means the Federal National Mortgage Association, the Federal Home Loan Mortgage Corporation, the Government National Mortgage Association, and other substantially similar institutions, whether public or private, provided the institutions establish and adhere to rules applicable to the right of cancellation of private mortgage insurance or mortgage guaranty insurance, which are the same or substantially the same as those utilized by the above-named institutions. **Leg.H.** Added Stats 1990 ch 1098 §1 (AB 3610), Amended Stats 1994 ch 356 §1 (AB 2481); Stats 2006 ch 538 §56 (SB 1852), effective January 1, 2007.

1994 Note: Civil Code 2954.7, as amended by 1994 ch 356, shall not apply to notes or evidence of indebtedness that require private mortgage insurance and were executed prior to March 1, 1995. Stats 1994 ch 356 §2.

§2954.8. Interest on impound account

(a) Every financial institution that makes loans upon the security of real property containing only a one- to four-family residence and located in this state or purchases obligations secured by such property and that receives money in advance for payment of taxes and assessments on the property, for insurance, or for other purposes relating to the property, shall pay interest on the amount so held to the borrower. The interest on such amounts shall be at the rate of at least 2 percent simple interest per annum. Such interest shall be credited to the borrower's account annually or upon termination of such account, whichever is earlier.

(b) No financial institution subject to the provisions of this section shall impose any fee or charge in connection with the maintenance or disbursement of money received in advance for the payment of taxes and assessments on real property securing loans made by such financial institution, or for the payment of insurance, or for other purposes relating to such real property, that will result in an interest rate of less than 2 percent per annum being paid on the moneys so received.

(c) For the purposes of this section, "financial institution" means a bank, savings and loan association or credit union chartered under the laws of this state or the United States, or any other person or organization making loans upon the security of real property containing only a one- to four-family residence.

(d) The provisions of this section do not apply to any of the following:

(1) Loans executed prior to the effective date of this section.

(2) Moneys which are required by a state or federal regulatory authority to be placed by a financial institution other than a bank in a non-interest-bearing demand trust fund account of a bank.

The amendment of this section made by the 1979–80 Regular Session of the Legislature shall only apply to loans executed on or after January 1, 1980. **Leg.H.** Added Stats 1976 ch 25 §1. Amended Stats 1979 ch 803 §1.

§2954.9. Prepayment; Permissible charges

(a)(1) Except as otherwise provided by statute, where the original principal obligation is a loan for residential property of four units or less, the borrower under any note or evidence of indebtedness secured by a deed of trust or mortgage or any other lien on real property shall be entitled to prepay the whole or any part of the balance due, together with accrued interest, at any time.

(2) Nothing in this subdivision shall prevent a borrower from obligating himself, by an agreement in writing, to pay a prepayment charge.

(3) This subdivision does not apply during any calendar year to a bona fide loan secured by a deed of trust or mortgage given back during such calendar year to the seller by the purchaser on account of the purchase price if the seller does not take back four or more such deeds of trust or mortgages during such calendar year. Nothing in this subdivision shall be construed to prohibit a borrower from making a prepayment by an agreement in writing with the lender.

(b) Except as otherwise provided in Section 10242.6 of the Business and Professions Code, the principal and accrued interest on any loan secured by a mortgage or deed of trust on owner–occupied residential real property containing only four units or less may be prepaid in whole or in part at any time but only a prepayment made within five years of the date of execution of such mortgage or deed of trust may be subject to a prepayment charge and then solely as herein set forth. An amount not exceeding 20 percent of the original principal amount may be prepaid in any 12–month period without penalty. A prepayment charge may be imposed on any amount prepaid in any 12–month period in excess of 20 percent of the original principal amount of the loan which charge shall not exceed an amount equal to the payment of six months' advance interest on the amount prepaid in excess of 20 percent of the original principal amount.

(c) Notwithstanding subdivisions (a) and (b), there shall be no prepayment penalty charged to a borrower under a loan subject to this section if the residential structure securing the loan has been damaged to such an extent by a natural disaster for which a state of emergency is declared by the Governor, pursuant to Chapter 7 (commencing with Section 8550) of Division 1 of Title 2 of the Government Code, that the residential structure cannot be occupied and the prepayment is causally related thereto. **Leg.H.** Added Stats 1974 ch 1059 §1. Amended Stats 1975 ch 763 §2; Stats 1977 ch 579 §32; Stats 1979 ch 391 §1; Stats 1990 ch 663 §2 (AB 3660).

§2954.10. Prohibition against prepayment penalty upon acceleration of maturity date of loan secured by certain residential property

An obligee which accelerates the maturity date of the principal and accrued interest, pursuant to contract, on any loan secured by a mortgage or deed of trust on real property or an estate for years therein, upon the conveyance of any right, title, or interest in that property, may not claim, exact, or collect any charge, fee, or penalty for any prepayment resulting from that acceleration.

The provisions of this section shall not apply to a loan other than a loan secured by residential real property or any interest therein containing four units or less, in which the obligor has expressly waived, in writing, the right to repay in whole or part without penalty, or has expressly agreed, in writing, to the payment of a penalty for prepayment upon acceleration. For any loan executed on or after January 1, 1984, this waiver or agreement shall be separately signed or initialed by the obligor and its enforcement shall be supported by evidence of a course of conduct by the obligee of individual weight to the consideration in that transaction for the waiver or agreement. **Leg.H.** Added Stats 1983 ch 1115 §1. Amended Stats 1989 ch 698 §11.

§2954.11. Prepayment charge for installment loan secured by lien on residential property; Disclosure; Rescission rights

(a) As used in this section:

(1) "Open-end credit plan" has the meaning set forth in Regulation Z of the Federal Reserve System (12 C.F.R. 226.2(a) (20)).

(2) "Installment loan" means any loan specified in subdivision (h) extended under an installment loan feature.

(3) "Installment loan feature" means a feature of an open-end credit plan which provides for a separate subaccount of the open-end credit plan pursuant to which the principal of, and interest on, the loan associated with that subaccount are to be repaid in substantially equal installments over a specified period without regard to the amount outstanding under any other feature of the open-end credit plan or the payment schedule with respect to the other feature.

(b)(1) Except as otherwise provided by statute, the borrower under any installment loan shall be entitled to prepay the whole or any part of the installment loan, together with any accrued interest, at any time.

(2) With respect to any installment loan, nothing in this section shall preclude a borrower from becoming obligated, by an agreement in writing, to pay a prepayment charge; but only a prepayment made within five years of the date the installment loan is made may be subject to a prepayment charge and then solely as herein set forth. An amount not exceeding 20 percent of the original principal amount of the installment loan may be prepaid in any one 12-month period without incurring a prepayment charge. A prepayment charge may be imposed on any amount prepaid in any 12-month period in excess of 20 percent of the original principal amount of the installment loan, which charge shall not exceed an amount equal to the payment of six months' advance interest on the amount prepaid in excess of 20 percent of the original principal amount of the installment loan.

(c) For purposes of subdivision (b):

(1) If the deed of trust or mortgage secures repayment of more than one installment loan, each of the installment loans shall be deemed to have been separately made on the date that the proceeds of the installment loan are advanced.

(2) If the outstanding balance of a loan advanced pursuant to an open-end credit plan thereafter becomes subject to an installment loan feature of the credit plan, the loan shall be deemed to have been made when the loan becomes subject to the installment loan feature, whether the feature was available at the borrower's option under original terms of the open-end credit plan or the feature thereafter became available upon modification of the original terms of the open-end credit plan.

(d) Notwithstanding subdivision (b), no prepayment charge may be imposed with respect to an installment loan subject to this section if any of the following apply:

(1) The residential structure securing the installment loan has been damaged to such an extent by a natural disaster for which a state of emergency is declared by the Governor, pursuant to Chapter 7 (commencing with Section 8550) of Division 1 of Title 2 of the Government Code, that the residential structure cannot be occupied and the prepayment is causally related thereto.

(2) The prepayment is made in conjunction with a bona fide sale of the real property securing the installment loan.

(3) The lender does not comply with subdivision (e).

(4) The term of the installment loan is for not more than five years and the original principal amount of the installment loan is less than five thousand dollars ($5,000).

(e)(1) The lender receiving a borrower's obligation to pay a prepayment charge authorized by subdivision (b) shall furnish the borrower with a written disclosure describing the existence of the prepayment charge obligation, the conditions under which the prepayment charge shall be payable, and the method by which the amount of the prepayment charge shall be determined. If subdivision (f) provides the borrower with a right to rescind the installment loan and the related obligation to pay a prepayment charge, the disclosure required by this subdivision shall also inform the borrower of this right to rescind, how and when to exercise the right, and where to mail or deliver a notice of rescission.

(2) The amount of, or the method for determining the amount of, the prepayment charge for an installment loan shall be set forth in the agreement governing the open–end credit plan.

(f)(1) The disclosure required by paragraph (1) of subdivision (e) shall be furnished when or up to 30 days before the borrower signs the agreement or other documents required by the lender for the installment loan, or no earlier than 30 days before nor later than 10 days following the making of the installment loan, if made without the borrower having to sign an agreement or other documentation, such as may be the case if the installment loan may be made on the basis of telephone or other discussions between the lender and the borrower not taking place in person. If the installment loan is made before the borrower has been furnished with the disclosure required by paragraph (1) of subdivision (e), the borrower shall have the right to rescind the installment loan and the related obligation to pay a prepayment charge by personally delivering or mailing notice to that effect to the lender, by first-class mail with postage prepaid, at the lender's location stated in its disclosure concerning the right to rescind within 10 days following the furnishing of the disclosure.

(2) If the disclosure required by paragraph (1) of subdivision (e) is included in the agreement or other document signed by the borrower for the installment loan, the disclosure shall be deemed given at that time. In other cases, the disclosure shall be deemed furnished when personally delivered to the borrower or three days after it is mailed to the borrower, first-class mail with postage prepaid, at the address to which billing statements for the open-end credit plan are being sent.

(3) The disclosure required by paragraph (1) of subdivision (e) may be separately furnished or may be included in the agreement or other document for the installment loan, provided that a copy of the disclosure that the borrower may retain is furnished to the borrower.

(4) If there is more than one borrower with respect to the open-end credit plan, a disclosure to any one of them pursuant to subdivision (e) shall satisfy the requirements of that subdivision with respect to all of them.

(g) If after an installment loan is made the lender receives the borrower's timely notice of the rescission of the installment loan in accordance with subdivision (f), the balance of the installment loan shall be transferred to the open-end subaccount of the open-end credit plan and the borrower shall be obligated to repay the amount under the same terms and conditions, and subject to the same fees and other charges, as would be applicable had the loan initially been extended pursuant to the open-end credit plan or had the installment loan never been made.

(h) This section applies to any installment loan secured by a deed of trust or mortgage or any other lien on residential property of four units or less and Section 2954.9 does not apply to such installment loans. This section shall not apply to any loan that is subject to Section 10242.6 of the Business and Professions Code. **Leg.H.** Added Stats 1996 ch 32 §1 (SB 1106).

§2954.12. No private mortgage insurance or mortgage guaranty insurance under specified conditions

(a) Notwithstanding Section 2954.7, and except when a statute, regulation, rule, or written guideline promulgated by an institutional third party applicable to notes or evidence of indebtedness secured by a deed of trust or mortgage purchased in whole or in part by an institutional third party specifically prohibits cancellation during the term of the indebtedness, the lender or servicer of a loan evidenced by a note or other evidence of indebtedness that is secured by a deed of trust or mortgage on the subject property may not charge or collect future payments from a borrower for private mortgage insurance or mortgage guaranty insurance as defined in subdivision (a) of Section 12640.02 of the Insurance Code, if all of the following conditions are satisfied:

(1) The loan is for personal, family, household, or purchase money purposes, the subject property is owner-occupied, one-to-four unit residential real property, and the outstanding principal balance of the note or evidence of indebtedness secured by the senior deed of trust or mortgage on the subject property is equal to or less than 75 percent of the lesser of (A) if the loan was made for purchase of the property, the sales price of the property under such purchase; or (B) the appraised value of the property, as determined by the appraisal conducted in connection with the making of the loan.

(2) The borrower's scheduled payment of monthly installments of principal, interest, and escrow obligations is current at the time the right to cancellation of mortgage insurance accrues.

(3) During the 12 months prior to the date upon which the right to cancellation accrues, the borrower has not been assessed more than one late penalty for any scheduled payment and has not made any scheduled payment more than 30 days late.

(4) The loan evidenced by a note or evidence of indebtedness was made or executed on or after January 1, 1998.

(5) No notice of default has been recorded against the real property pursuant to Section 2924, as a result of a nonmonetary default on the

extension of credit by the borrower during the last 12 months prior to the accrual of the borrower's right to cancellation.

(b) This section does not apply to any of the following:

(1) A note or evidence of indebtedness secured by a deed of trust or mortgage, or mortgage insurance, executed under the authority of Part 3 (commencing with Section 50900) or Part 4 (commencing with Section 51600) of Division 31 of the Health and Safety Code.

(2) Any note or evidence of indebtedness secured by a deed of trust or mortgage that is funded in whole or in part pursuant to authority granted by statute, regulation, or rule that, as a condition of that funding, prohibits or limits termination of payments for private mortgage insurance or mortgage guaranty insurance during the term of the indebtedness.

(c) If the note secured by the deed of trust or mortgage will be or has been sold in whole or in part to an institutional third party, adherence to the institutional third party's standards for termination of future payments for private mortgage insurance or mortgage guaranty insurance shall be deemed in compliance with the requirements of this section.

(d) For the purposes of this section, "institutional third party" means the Federal National Mortgage Association, the Federal Home Loan Mortgage Corporation, the Government National Mortgage Association and other substantially similar institutions, whether public or private, provided the institutions establish and adhere to rules applicable to the right of cancellation of private mortgage insurance or mortgage guaranty insurance, which are the same or substantially the same as those utilized by the above-named institutions. **Leg.H.** Added Stats 1997 ch 62 §1 (AB 1160).

§2955. Investment of money held in impound account

(a) Money held by a mortgagee or a beneficiary of a deed of trust on real property in this state, or held by a vendor on a contract of sale of real property in this state, in an impound account for the payment of taxes and assessments or insurance premiums or other purposes on or relating to the property, shall be retained in this state and, if invested, shall be invested only with residents of this state in the case of individuals, or with partnerships, corporations, or other persons, or the branches or subsidiaries thereof, which are engaged in business within this state.

(b) Notwithstanding subdivision (a), a mortgagee or beneficiary of a deed of trust, secured by a first lien on real property, may deposit money held for the payment of taxes and assessments or insurance premiums or other purposes in an impound account in an out-of-state depository institution insured by the Federal Deposit Insurance Corporation if the mortgagee or beneficiary is any one of the following:

(1) The Federal National Mortgage Association, the Government National Mortgage Association, the Federal Home Loan Mortgage Corporation, the Federal Housing Administration, or the Veteran's Administration.

(2) A bank or subsidiary thereof, bank holding company or subsidiary thereof, trust company, savings bank or savings and loan association or subsidiary thereof, savings bank or savings association holding company or subsidiary thereof, credit union, industrial bank or industrial loan company, commercial finance lender, personal property broker, consumer finance lender, or insurer doing business under the authority of and in accordance with the laws of this state, any other state, or of the United States relating to banks, trust companies, savings banks or savings associations, credit unions, industrial banks or industrial loan companies, commercial finance lenders, personal property brokers, consumer finance lenders, or insurers, as evidenced by a license, certificate, or charter issued by the United States or a state, district, territory, or commonwealth of the United States.

(3) Trustees of a pension, profit-sharing, or welfare fund, if the pension, profit-sharing, or welfare fund has a net worth of not less than fifteen million dollars ($15,000,000).

(4) A corporation with outstanding securities registered under Section 12 of the Securities Exchange Act of 1934, or a wholly owned subsidiary of that corporation.

(5) A syndication or other combination of any of the entities specified in paragraphs (1) to (4), inclusive, that is organized to purchase the promissory note.

(6) The California Housing Finance Agency or a local housing finance agency organized under the Health and Safety Code.

(7) A licensed real estate broker selling all or part of the loan, note, or contract to a lender or purchaser described in paragraphs (1) to (6), inclusive, of this subdivision.

(8) A licensed residential mortgage lender or servicer when acting under the authority of that license.

(c) A mortgagee or beneficiary of a deed of trust who deposits funds held in trust in an out-of-state depository institution in accordance with subdivision (b) shall make available, in this state, the books, records, and files pertaining to those trust accounts to the appropriate state regulatory department or agency, or pay the reasonable expenses for travel and lodging incurred by the regulatory department or agency in order to conduct an examination at an out-of-state location.

(d) The Attorney General may bring an action on behalf of the people of California to enjoin a violation of subdivision (a) or subdivision (b). **Leg.H.** Added Stats 1970 ch 1212 §1. Amended Stats 1992 ch 1055 §3; Stats 1995 ch 564 §5 (SB 946).

Prior Law: Former §2955, relating to what personal property may be mortgaged, was enacted 1872, amended Code Amdts 1975–76 ch 600 §1, Code Amdts 1877–78 ch 595 §1, Stats 1887 ch 8 §1, Stats 1893 ch 75 §1, Stats 1895 ch 60 §1, Stats 1897 ch 91 §1, Stats 1903 ch 70 §1, Stats 1905 ch 40 §1, Stats 1907 ch 482 §1, Stats 1909 ch 39 §1, Stats 1935 ch 817 §1, and repealed Stats 1963 ch 819 §2, effective January 1, 1965.

There was another section of this number, similar to this section, which was added Stats 1992 ch 1055 §4, operative January 1, 1996, amended Stats 1994 ch 994 §5, operative January 1, 1996, Stats 1995 ch 91 §18, operative January 1, 1996 (ch 564 prevails), and repealed Stats 1995 ch 564 §6.

§2955.1. Disclosures regarding earthquake insurance requirements

(a) Any lender originating a loan secured by the borrower's separate interest in a condominium project, as defined in Section 4125 or 6542, which requires earthquake insurance or imposes a fee or any other condition in lieu thereof pursuant to an underwriting requirement imposed by an institutional third-party purchaser shall disclose all of the following to the potential borrower:

(1) That the lender or the institutional third party in question requires earthquake insurance or imposes a fee or any other condition in lieu thereof pursuant to an underwriting requirement imposed by an institutional third-party purchaser.

(2) That not all lenders or institutional third parties require earthquake insurance or impose a fee or any other condition in lieu thereof pursuant to an underwriting requirement imposed by an institutional third-party purchaser.

(3) Earthquake insurance may be required on the entire condominium project.

(4) That lenders or institutional third parties may also require that a condominium project maintain, or demonstrate an ability to maintain, financial reserves in the amount of the earthquake insurance deductible.

(b) For the purposes of this section, "institutional third party" means the Federal Home Loan Mortgage Corporation, the Federal National Mortgage Association, the Government National Mortgage Association, and other substantially similar institutions, whether public or private.

(c) The disclosure required by this section shall be made in writing by the lender as soon as reasonably practicable. **Leg.H.** Added Stats 1995 ch 925 §1 (SB 1326), effective October 16, 1995. Amended Stats 2012 ch 181 §41 (AB 806), effective January 1, 2013, operative January 1, 2014; Stats 2013 ch 605 §18 (SB 752), effective January 1, 2014.

§2955.5. Hazard insurance coverage

(a) No lender shall require a borrower, as a condition of receiving or maintaining a loan secured by real property, to provide hazard insurance coverage against risks to the improvements on that real property in an amount exceeding the replacement value of the improvements on the property.

(b) A lender shall disclose to a borrower, in writing, the contents of subdivision (a), as soon as practicable, but before execution of any note or security documents.

(c) Any person harmed by a violation of this section shall be entitled to obtain injunctive relief and may recover damages and reasonable attorney's fees and costs.

(d) A violation of this section does not affect the validity of the loan, note secured by a deed of trust, mortgage, or deed of trust.

(e) For purposes of this section:

(1) "Hazard insurance coverage" means insurance against losses caused by perils which are commonly covered in policies described as a "Homeowner's Policy," "General Property Form," "Guaranteed Replacement Cost Insurance," "Special Building Form," "Standard Fire," "Stan-

dard Fire with Extended Coverage," "Standard Fire with Special Form Endorsement," or comparable insurance coverage to protect the real property against loss or damage from fire and other perils covered within the scope of a standard extended coverage endorsement.

(2) "Improvements" means buildings or structures attached to the real property. **Leg.H.** Added Stats 1987 ch 715 §1. Amended Stats 1988 ch 276 §1, effective July 6, 1988; Stats 1999 ch 412 §1 (AB 1454), operative July 1, 2000.

1988 Note: This act is applicable to contracts entered into on or after January 1, 1988. Stats 1988 ch 276 §2.

ARTICLE 3
Disclosures on Purchase Money Liens on Residential Property

Disclosures required on sales of small residential properties in which extension of credit from vendor is arranged. §2956.
Definitions. §2957.
When disclosure not required. §2958.
Time for making disclosure; Signature; Delivery. §2959.
Effect of subsequent inaccuracy; Approximation of unavailable information. §2960.
Good faith requirement. §2961.
Amendment. §2962.
Particular disclosures required. §2963.
Other obligations and disclosures required by law. §2964.
Failure to comply; Violations; Liability. §2965.
Transaction including balloon payment note; Notice required; Failure to comply. §2966.
Limitations on actions. §2967.

§2956. Disclosures required on sales of small residential properties in which extension of credit from vendor is arranged

In a transaction for the purchase of a dwelling for not more than four families in which there is an arranger of credit, which purchase includes an extension of credit by the vendor, a written disclosure with respect to that credit transaction shall be made, as required by this article:

(a) To the purchaser, by the arranger of credit and the vendor (with respect to information within the knowledge of the vendor).

(b) To the vendor, by the arranger of credit and the purchaser (with respect to information within the knowledge of the purchaser).

If there is more than one arranger of credit and one of those arrangers has obtained the offer by the purchaser to purchase the property, that arranger shall make the disclosure, unless the parties designate another person in writing. **Leg.H.** Added Stats 1982 ch 968 §1, operative July 1, 1983.

Prior Law: Former §2956, relating to mortgage of personal property, was enacted 1872, amended State 1935 ch 817 §2, Stats 1947 ch 1081 §1, and repealed Stats 1963 ch 819 §2, effective January 1, 1965.

§2957. Definitions

The following definitions shall apply for the purposes of this article:

(a) "Arranger of credit" means:

(1) A person, other than a party to the credit transaction (except as provided in paragraph (2)), who is involved in developing or negotiating credit terms, participates in the completion of the credit documents, and directly or indirectly receives compensation for arrangement of the credit or from any transaction or transfer of the real property which is facilitated by that extension of credit. As used in this paragraph, "arranger of credit" does not apply to an attorney who is representing one of the parties to the credit transaction.

(2) A party to the transaction who is either a real estate licensee, licensed under provisions of Part 1 (commencing with Section 10000) of Division 4 of the Business and Professions Code, or is an attorney licensed under Chapter 4 (commencing with Section 6000) of Division 3 of the Business and Professions Code if neither party to the transaction is represented by an agent who is a real estate licensee. In any transaction in which disclosure is required solely by the provisions of this paragraph, the obligations of this article shall apply only to a real estate licensee or attorney who is a party to the transaction, and not to any other party.

(3) An arranger of credit does not include a person acting in the capacity as an escrow in the transaction.

(4) Persons described in paragraph (2) who are acting in the capacity as an escrowholder in the transaction shall nevertheless be deemed arrangers of credit where such persons act on behalf of a party to the transaction or an agent of such party in the development or negotiation of credit terms. Neither the completion of credit documents in accordance with instructions of a party or his or her agent nor the furnishing of information regarding credit terms to a party or his or her agent shall be considered to be the development or negotiation of credit terms.

(b) "Balloon payment note" means a note which provides for a final payment as originally scheduled which is more than twice the amount of any of the immediately preceding six regularly scheduled payments or which contains a call provision; provided, however, that if the call provision is not exercised by the holder of the note, the existence of the unexercised call provision shall not cause the note to be deemed to be a balloon payment note.

(c) "Call provision" means a note contract term that provides the holder of the note with the right to call the note due and payable either after a specified period has elapsed following closing or after a specified date.

(d) "Credit" means the right granted by a vendor to a purchaser to purchase property and to defer payment therefore.

The credit involved must be subject to a finance charge or payable by written agreement in more than four installments, whether providing for payment of principal and interest, or interest only, not including a downpayment.

(e) "Credit documents" are those documents which contain the binding credit terms, and include a note or a contract of sale if the contract spells out terms upon which a vendor agrees to provide financing for a purchaser.

(f) "Purchase" includes acquisition of equitable title by a real property sales contract as defined in Section 2985, or lease with an option to purchase, where the facts demonstrate intent to transfer equitable title.

(g) "Security documents" include a mortgage, deed of trust, real property sales contract as defined in Section 2985, or lease with an option to purchase, where the facts demonstrate an intent to transfer equitable title.

(h) "All inclusive trust deed" is an instrument which secures indebtedness owed by the trustor to the beneficiary, which indebtedness includes a debt or debts owed by that beneficiary to the beneficiary of another security document secured by the same property which is senior in priority. **Leg.H.** Added Stats 1982 ch 968 §1, operative July 1, 1983. Amended Stats 1983 ch 1217 §3; Stats 1986 ch 1360 §2.

Prior Law: Former §2957, similar to present UCC §9501, was enacted 1872, amended Stats 1935 ch 817 §3, Stats 1937 ch 227 §1, Stats 1941 ch 470 §1, Stats 1945 ch 93 §1, ch 226 §1, Stats 1st Ex Sess 1946 ch 58 §3, effective February 25, 1946, Stats 1947 ch 117 §1, Stats 1955 ch 1603 §1, and repealed Stats 1963 ch 819 §2, effective January 1, 1965.

§2958. When disclosure not required

A disclosure is not required under this article, to a purchaser when that purchaser is entitled to receive, a disclosure pursuant to the Federal Truth-In-Lending Act (15 U.S. Code 1604, as amended), the Real Estate Settlement Procedures Act (12 U.S. Code 2601, as amended), or Section 10240 of the Business and Professions Code; or to a vendor if the vendor is entitled to receive, a disclosure pursuant to Sections 10232.4 and 10232.5 of the Business and Professions Code, or disclosure pursuant to a qualification under Section 25110 of the Corporations Code or disclosure pursuant to regulations of the Department of Corporations granting an exemption from Section 25110 of the Corporations Code. **Leg.H.** Added Stats 1982 ch 968 §1, operative July 1, 1983.

Prior Law: Former §2958, relating to mortgage of personal property, was enacted 1872 and repealed 1963 ch 819 §2, effective January 1, 1965.

§2958a. [Section repealed 1965]

Leg.H. Added Stats 1941 ch 235 §1. Repealed Stats 1963 ch 819 §2, effective January 1, 1965. The repealed section related to mortgage of personal property.

§2959. Time for making disclosure; Signature; Delivery

The disclosures required by this article shall be made as soon as practicable, but before execution of any note or security documents. If any disclosure is made after the execution of credit documents by the purchaser, such documents shall be contingent on the purchaser's approval of the disclosures prior to execution of the security documents. The disclosure statement shall be receipted for by the purchaser and the vendor. The disclosure shall be signed by the arranger of credit and a copy shall be delivered respectively to the purchaser and the vendor and the arranger shall retain a true copy of the executed statements for three years.

The provisions of this section do not apply to the disclosures required by Section 2966. **Leg.H.** Added Stats 1982 ch 968 §1, operative July 1, 1983.

Prior Law: Former §2959, relating to mortgage of personal property, was enacted 1872, amended Stats 1907 ch 468 §1, Stats 1923 ch 72 §1, and repealed Stats 1935 ch 817 §13.

§2959a. [Section repealed 1965]

Leg.H. Added Stats 1935 ch 817 §4. Repealed Stats 1963 ch 819 §2, effective January 1, 1965. The repealed section related to mortgage of personal property.

§2960. Effect of subsequent inaccuracy; Approximation of unavailable information

If information disclosed in accordance with this article is subsequently rendered inaccurate as a result of any act, occurrence, or agreement between the parties to the transaction subsequent to the delivery of the required disclosures, the inaccuracy resulting therefrom shall not constitute a violation of this article. If, at the time disclosure is to be made, an item of information required to be disclosed is unknown or not available to the vendor, purchaser, or arranger of credit, and the arranger of credit has made a reasonable effort to ascertain it, the disclosure may employ an approximation of the information, provided the approximation is clearly identified as such, is reasonable, is based on the best information available to the arranger, and is not used for the purpose of circumventing or evading the provisions of this article. **Leg.H.** Added Stats 1982 ch 968 §1, operative July 1, 1983.

Prior Law: Former §2960, relating to mortgage of personal property, was enacted 1872 and repealed 1963 ch 819 §2, effective January 1, 1965.

§2961. Good faith requirement

Every disclosure required by this article and every act which is to be performed in making that disclosure shall be made in good faith. For the purposes of this article, "good faith" means honesty in fact in the conduct of the transaction. **Leg.H.** Added Stats 1982 ch 968 §1, operative July 1, 1983.

Prior Law: Former §2961, relating to mortgage of personal property, was enacted 1872 and repealed 1963 ch 819 §2, effective January 1, 1965.

§2962. Amendment

Any disclosure made pursuant to this article may be amended in writing by the person making the disclosure, provided that any amendment shall be subject to the provisions of Section 2959. **Leg.H.** Added Stats 1982 ch 968 §1, operative July 1, 1983.

Prior Law: Former §2962, relating to mortgage of personal property, was enacted 1872, amended Stats 1955 ch 1603 §2, and repealed Stats 1963 ch 819 §2, effective January 1, 1965.

§2963. Particular disclosures required

The disclosures required to both purchaser and vendor by this article are:

(a) An identification of the note or other credit documents or security documents and of the property which is the security for the transaction.

(b) A description of the terms of the promissory note or other credit documents or a copy of the note or other credit documents.

(c) Insofar as available, the principal terms and conditions of each recorded encumbrance which constitutes a lien upon the property which is or will be senior to the financing being arranged, including the original balance, the current balance, the periodic payment, any balloon payment, the interest rate (and any provisions with respect to variations in the interest rate), the maturity date, and whether or not there is any current default in payment on that encumbrance.

(d) A warning that, if refinancing would be required as a result of lack of full amortization under the terms of any existing or proposed loans, such refinancing might be difficult or impossible in the conventional mortgage marketplace.

(e) If negative amortization is possible as a result of any variable or adjustable rate financing being arranged, a clear disclosure of this fact and an explanation of its potential effect.

(f) In the event that the financing involves an all inclusive trust deed, the disclosure shall indicate whether the credit or security documents specify who is liable for payment or responsible for defense in the case of an attempted acceleration by a lender or other obligee under a prior encumbrance, and whether or not the credit or security documents specify the responsibilities and rights of the parties in the event of a loan prepayment respecting a prior encumbrance which may result in a requirement for refinancing, a prepayment penalty, or a prepayment discount and, if such specification occurs, a recital of the provisions which apply.

(g) If the financing being arranged or any of the financing represented by a prior encumbrance could result in a balloon payment, or in a right in the lender or other obligee under such financing to require a prepayment of the principal balance at or after a stipulated date, or upon the occurrence of a stipulated event, a disclosure of the date and amount of any balloon payment or the amount which would be due upon the exercise of such right by the lender or obligee, and a statement that there is no assurance that new financing or loan extension will be available at the time of such occurrence.

(h) If the financing being arranged involves an all inclusive trust deed or real property sales contract, a disclosure of the party to whom payments will be made and who will be responsible for remitting these funds to payees under prior encumbrances and vendors under this transaction and a warning that, if that person is not a neutral third party, the parties may wish to agree to have a neutral third party designated for these purposes.

(i) A disclosure on the identity, occupation, employment, income, and credit data about the prospective purchaser, as represented to the arranger by the prospective purchaser; or, specifically, that no representation as to the credit-worthiness of the specific prospective purchaser is made by the arranger. A warning should also be expressed that Section 580b of the Code of Civil Procedure may limit any recovery by the vendor to the net proceeds of the sale of the security property in the event of foreclosure.

(j) A statement that loss payee clauses have been added to property insurance protecting the vendor, or that instructions have been or will be directed to the escrowholder, if any, in the transaction or the appropriate insurance carriers for addition of such loss payee clauses, or a statement that, if such provisions have not been made, that the vendor should consider protecting himself or herself by securing such clauses.

(k) A statement that a request for notice of default under Section 2924b has been recorded, or that, if it has not been recorded, the vendor should consider recording a request for notice of default.

(*l*) That a policy of title insurance has been obtained or will be obtained and be furnished to the vendor and purchaser, insuring the respective interests of the vendor and purchaser, or that the vendor and purchaser individually should consider obtaining a policy of title insurance.

(m) That a tax service has been arranged to report to the vendor whether property taxes have been paid on the property, and who will be responsible for the continued retention and compensation of tax service; or that the vendor should otherwise assure for himself or herself that the taxes on the property have been paid.

(n) A disclosure whether the security documents on the financing being arranged have been or will be recorded pursuant to Section 27280 of the Government Code, or a statement that the security of the vendor may be subject to intervening liens or judgments which may occur after the note is executed and before any resort to security occurs if the security documents are not recorded.

(o) If the purchaser is to receive any cash from the proceeds of the transaction, a statement of that fact, the amount, the source of the funds, and the purpose of the disbursement as represented by the purchaser.

(p) A statement that a request for notice of delinquency under Section 2924e has been made, or that, if it has not been made, the vendor should consider making a request for a notice of delinquency. **Leg.H.** Added Stats 1982 ch 968 §1, operative July 1, 1983. Amended Stats 1983 ch 1217 §4; Stats 1984 ch 1331 §4, operative July 1, 1985; Stats 1990 ch 788 §2 (SB 2042).

Prior Law: Former §2963, relating to mortgage of personal property, was enacted 1872, amended Stats 1935 ch 817 §5, Stats 1961 ch 484 §1, and repealed Stats 1963 ch 819 §2, effective January 1, 1965.

§2964. Other obligations and disclosures required by law

The specification of items for disclosure in this article does not limit or abridge any obligation for disclosure created by any other provision of law or which may exist in order to avoid fraud, misrepresentation, or deceit in the transaction. **Leg.H.** Added Stats 1982 ch 968 §1, operative July 1, 1983.

Prior Law: Former §2964, relating to mortgage of personal property, was enacted 1872 and repealed Stats 1963 ch 819 §2, effective January 1, 1965.

§2965. Failure to comply; Violations; Liability

The validity of any credit document or of any security document subject to the provisions of this article shall not be invalidated solely because of the failure of any person to comply with this article. However, any person who willfully violates any provision of this article shall be liable in the amount of actual damages suffered by the vendor or purchaser as the proximate result of the violation.

No person may be held liable in any action under this article if it is shown by a preponderance of the evidence that the violation was not intentional and resulted from a bona fide error notwithstanding the maintenance of procedures reasonably adopted to avoid any such error. **Leg.H.** Added Stats 1982 ch 968 §1, operative July 1, 1983.

Prior Law: Former §2965, relating to mortgage of personal property, was enacted 1872, amended Stats 1909 ch 53 §1, Stats 1923 ch 72 §2, Stats 1935 ch 817 §6, Stats 1955 ch 1603 §3, Stats 1957 ch 297 §2, and repealed Stats 1963 ch 819 §2, effective January 1, 1965.

§2966. Transaction including balloon payment note; Notice required; Failure to comply

(a) In a transaction regulated by this article, which includes a balloon payment note when the term for repayment is for a period in excess of one year, the holder of the note shall, not less than 90 nor more than 150 days before the balloon payment is due, deliver or mail by first-class mail, with a certificate of mailing obtained from the United States Postal Service, to the trustor, or his or her successor in interest, at the last known address of such person a written notice, to include:

(1) A statement of the name and address of the person to whom the balloon payment is required to be paid.

(2) The date on or before which the balloon payment was or is required to be paid.

(3) The amount of the balloon payment, or if its exact amount is unknown a good faith estimate of the amount thereof, including unpaid principal, interest, and any other charges (assuming payment in full of all scheduled installments coming due between the date of the notice and the date when the balloon payment is due).

(4) A description of the trustor's right, if any, to refinance the balloon payment, including a summary of the actual terms of the refinancing or an estimate or approximation thereof, to the extent known.

If the due date of the balloon payment of a note subject to this subdivision is extended prior to the time notice is otherwise required under this subdivision, this notice requirement shall apply only to the due date as extended (or as subsequently extended).

(b) Failure to provide notice as required by subdivision (a) does not extinguish any obligation of payment by the trustor, except that the due date for any balloon payment shall be the date specified in the note, or 90 days from the date the delivery or mailing of the notice, or the date specified in the notice, whichever date is later. If the operation of this section acts to extend the term of any such note, interest shall continue to accrue for the extended term at the contract rate and payments shall continue to be due at any periodic interval and on any scheduled payment schedule specified in the note and shall be credited to principal or interest under terms of the note. Default in any extended periodic payment shall be considered a default under terms of the note or security instrument.

(c) Any failure to comply with the provisions of this section shall not affect the validity of a sale in favor of a bona fide purchaser or the rights of an encumbrancer for value and without notice.

(d) Every note subject to the provisions of this section shall include the following statement:

"This note is subject to Section 2966 of the Civil Code, which provides that the holder of this note shall give written notice to the trustor, or his successor in interest, of prescribed information at least 90 and not more than 150 days before any balloon payment is due."

Failure to include this notice shall not invalidate the note.

(e) The provisions of this section shall apply to any note executed on or after July 1, 1983. **Leg.H.** Added Stats 1982 ch 968 §1, operative July 1, 1983. Amended Stats 1986 ch 1360 §3.

Prior Law: Former §2966, relating to mortgage of personal property, was enacted 1872, amended Stats 1923 ch 72 §3, Stats 1935 ch 817 §7, and repealed Stats 1963 ch 817 §2, effective January 1, 1965.

§2967. Limitations on actions

Any action arising under this article may be brought within two years from the date on which the liability arises, except that where any material disclosure under this article has been materially and willfully misrepresented, the action may be brought within two years of discovery of the misrepresentation. **Leg.H.** Added Stats 1982 ch 968 §1, operative July 1, 1983.

Prior Law: Former §2967, relating to mortgage of personal property, was enacted 1872 and repealed Stats 1963 ch 819 §2, effective January 1, 1965.

§§2968–2978. [Sections repealed 1965]

Leg.H. Enacted 1872. Amended Code Amdts 1877–78 ch 602 §1; Stats 1905 ch 460 §1; Stats 1921 ch 87 §§1, 2; Stats 1927 ch 475 §1; Stats 1935 ch 817 §§8–12; Stats 1937 582 §1; Stats 1941 ch 235 §2; Stats 1945 ch 750 §1; Stats 1947 ch 722 §1; Ch 723 §1; Stats 1959 ch 528 §2. Repealed Stats 1963 ch 819 §2, effective January 1, 1965. The repealed sections related to mortgage of personal property.

Prior Law: Former §2975, relating to mortgage of personal property to secure future advances, was added Stats 1935 ch 817 §9 and repealed Stats 1959 ch 528 §1.

ARTICLE 4
State of Emergency

Mortgage servicer securing property in proclaimed state of emergency. § 2968.

§ 2968. Mortgage servicer securing property in proclaimed state of emergency

(a) For purposes of this article, the following definitions apply:

(1) "Mortgage servicer" has the same meaning as defined in subdivision (a) of Section 2920.5.

(2) "Property" means residential real property that is improved by four or fewer residential dwelling units, affixed mobilehomes, and manufactured homes.

(3) "State of emergency" and "local emergency" have the same meanings as defined in subdivisions (b) and (c), respectively, of Section 8558 of the Government Code.

(b) A transferor mortgage servicer servicing a mortgage secured by property within the geographic limits of a proclaimed state of emergency or local emergency shall deliver to a transferee mortgage servicer any material written records between the borrower and the mortgage servicer relating to the borrower's election to use insurance proceeds to repair or replace property damaged by a disaster for which the state of emergency or local emergency was proclaimed.

(c) A transferee mortgage servicer pursuant to subdivision (b) shall not dishonor a previous written agreement to repair property made prior to the transfer between the transferor mortgage servicer and the borrower and approved by the owner of the promissory note.

(d) This article shall not be interpreted to prohibit a mortgage servicer from delivering to a transferee mortgage servicer any material written records relating to a borrower's election to use insurance proceeds to repair or replace damaged property that was not caused by a disaster for which a state of emergency or local emergency was proclaimed. **Leg.H.** Added Stats 2023 ch 873 §1 (SB 455), effective January 1, 2024.

CHAPTER 2A
HOME EQUITY LOAN DISCLOSURE ACT

"Home equity loan". §2970.
Disclosure by creditor. §2971.

§2970. "Home equity loan"

For purposes of this chapter "home equity loan" means any open end consumer credit plan in which a consensual security interest is created or retained against the consumer's dwelling. **Leg.H.** Added Stats 1988 ch 1315 §1.

Prior Law: Former § 2970, enacted 1872, amended Stats 1921 ch 87 § 2, relating to application of proceeds of sale, was repealed by Stats 1947 ch 723 § 1, effective September 19, 1947.

§2971. Disclosure by creditor

(a) At the time that a customer makes an initial application to a creditor for a home equity loan in person, or within three business days if the customer applies by mail or telephone, the creditor shall provide the applicant with a disclosure in either of the following forms:

(1) The statement: "This home equity loan that you are applying for will be secured by your home and your failure to repay the loan for any reason could cause you to lose your home!"

(2) A statement to the effect that a home equity loan is secured by a lien against the home of the consumer and in the event of any default the consumer risks the loss of the home.

(b) The disclosure required in subdivision (a) shall be made by either of the following means:

(1) A separate and specific document attached to or accompanying the application.

(2) A clear and conspicuous statement on the application.

(c) If a creditor is required by federal statute or regulation to make a substantially similar disclosure to that required by subdivision (a), and the creditor complies with that federal statute or regulation, the creditor shall be deemed to have complied with the requirements of this chapter. **Leg.H.** Added Stats 1988 ch 1315 §1.

Prior Law: Former § 2971, enacted 1872, amended by Stats 1941 ch 235 § 2, relating to sections not applicable to mortgages of certain ships and aircraft, was repealed by Stats 1963 ch 819 § 2, effective January 1, 1965.

1961 Note: This act will be known as the Rees-Levering Motor Vehicle Sales and Finance Act. Stats 1961 ch 1626 §7.

§2980. [Section repealed 1965]

Leg.H. Added Stats 1927 ch 796 §1. Amended Stats 1931 ch 767 §1; Stats 1933 ch 295 §1; Stats 1935 ch 819 §1; Stats 1941 ch 724 §1; Stats 1951 ch 412 §1; Stats 1953 ch 1885 §1. Repealed Stats 1963 ch 819 §16, effective January 1, 1965. The repealed section related to recordation of conditional sales contract of mining equipment.

§2980.5. [Section repealed 1984]

Leg.H. Added Stats 1951 ch 412 §2. Amended Stats 1953 ch 1783 §1; Stats 1963 ch 819 §17, effective January 1, 1965. Repealed Stats 1984 ch 859 §1. The repealed section related to contracts for leasing of livestock or other animate chattels or agreements for bailments of feeding of dairy cattle.

CHAPTER 2B
AUTOMOBILE SALES FINANCE ACT

Definitions. §2981.
Bailment or leasing contract establishing maximum liability of bailee or lessee. §2981.5.
Calculation of finance charge on contracts after January 1, 1983. §2981.7.
Finance charges determined by more than one basis. §2981.8.
Requisites of conditional sale contract. §2981.9.
Disclosures required in a conditional sale contract. §2982.
Inducing contract by offering rebate or discount on condition that buyer sells or assists in sale of same or related goods. §2982.1.
Elements of written disclosure prior to execution of conditional sales contract; Buyer's signature required on written disclosure. §2982.2.
Extension of due date or deferral of payment of installment. §2982.3.
Exclusion of loan between purchaser and supervised financial organization; Assistance in obtaining loan. §2982.5.
Refund of payment; Recovery of value of vehicle left as down payment. §2982.7.
Cost of insurance. §2982.8.
Rescission of purchase order where buyer unable to obtain financing. §2982.9.
Acceptance of payment or credit in consideration of assignment of conditional sales contract limited. §2982.10.
Disclosures required for conditional sale contract that includes charge for electric vehicle charging station. §2982.11.
Offer, sale, or provision of guaranteed asset protection waiver in connection with conditional sale contract. § 2982.12.
Unenforceable contract; Recovery by buyer. §2983.
Penalties for certain violations. §2983.1.
Notice of intent to dispose of repossessed or surrendered motor vehicle; Accounting regarding disposition. §2983.2.
Acceleration of maturity or repossession of vehicle; Reinstatement of contract. §2983.3.
Notice of delinquency to cosigner. §2983.35.
Obligations of buy-here-pay-here dealer; Violation as misdemeanor. §2983.37.
Award of attorney's fees and costs to prevailing party. §2983.4.
Equities and defenses affecting assignee. § 2983.5.
Violation declared misdemeanor. §2983.6.
Prohibited contractual provisions. §2983.7.
Prohibition of deficiency judgment after sale of mobilehome or sale or other disposition of motor vehicle. §2983.8.
Correction of contract provisions in violation of chapter. §2984.
Statement in satisfaction of requirements of Vehicle Code. §2984.1.
Title to or lien on property. §2984.2.
Acknowledgment; Presumptions. §2984.3.
Jurisdiction and venue; Plaintiff's affidavit. §2984.4.
Seller to maintain certain documents for specified length of time. §2984.5.
Subsequent assignment to skip trace, locate or repossess a vehicle; Notice requirements. §2984.6.

§2981. Definitions

As used in this chapter, unless the context otherwise requires:

(a) "Conditional sale contract" means:

(1) A contract for the sale of a motor vehicle between a buyer and a seller, with or without accessories, under which possession is delivered to the buyer and either of the following:

(A) The title vests in the buyer thereafter only upon the payment of all or a part of the price, or the performance of any other condition.

(B) A lien on the property is to vest in the seller as security for the payment of part or all of the price, or for the performance of any other condition.

(2) A contract for the bailment of a motor vehicle between a buyer and a seller, with or without accessories, by which the bailee or lessee agrees to pay as compensation for use a sum substantially equivalent to or in excess of the aggregate value of the vehicle and its accessories, if any, at the time the contract is executed, and by which it is agreed that the bailee or lessee will become, or for no other or for a nominal consideration has the option of becoming, the owner of the vehicle upon full compliance with the terms of the contract.

(b) "Seller" means a person engaged in the business of selling or leasing motor vehicles under conditional sale contracts.

(c) "Buyer" means the person who buys or hires a motor vehicle under a conditional sale contract.

(d) "Person" includes an individual, company, firm, association, partnership, trust, corporation, limited liability company, or other legal entity.

(e) "Holder" means the person entitled to enforce the conditional sale contract against the buyer at the time.

(f) "Cash price" means the amount for which the seller would sell and transfer to the buyer unqualified title to the motor vehicle described in the conditional sale contract, if the property were sold for cash at the seller's place of business on the date the contract is executed, and shall include taxes to the extent imposed on the cash sale and the cash price of accessories or services related to the sale, including, but not limited to, delivery, installation, alterations, modifications, improvements, document preparation fees, a service contract, a vehicle contract cancellation option agreement, and payment of a prior credit or lease balance remaining on property being traded in.

(g) "Downpayment" means a payment that the buyer pays or agrees to pay to the seller in cash or property value or money's worth at or prior to delivery by the seller to the buyer of the motor vehicle described in the conditional sale contract. The term shall also include the amount of any portion of the downpayment the payment of which is deferred until not later than the due date of the second otherwise scheduled payment, if the amount of the deferred downpayment is not subject to a finance charge. The term does not include any administrative finance charge charged, received, or collected by the seller as provided in this chapter.

(h) "Amount financed" means the amount required to be disclosed pursuant to paragraph (8) of subdivision (a) of Section 2982.

(i) "Unpaid balance" means the difference between subdivisions (f) and (g), plus all insurance premiums (except for credit life or disability insurance when the amount thereof is included in the finance charge), which are included in the contract balance, and the total amount paid or to be paid as follows:

(1) To a public officer in connection with the transaction.

(2) For license, certificate of title, and registration fees imposed by law, and the amount of the state fee for issuance of a certificate of compliance or certificate of waiver pursuant to Section 9889.56 of the Business and Professions Code.

(j) "Finance charge" has the meaning set forth for that term in Section 226.4 of Regulation Z. The term shall not include delinquency charges or collection costs and fees as provided by subdivision (k) of Section 2982, extension or deferral agreement charges as provided by Section 2982.3, or amounts for insurance, repairs to or preservation of the motor vehicle, or preservation of the security interest therein advanced by the holder under the terms of the contract.

(k) "Total of payments" means the amount required to be disclosed pursuant to subdivision (h) of Section 226.18 of Regulation Z. The term includes any portion of the downpayment that is deferred until not later than the second otherwise scheduled payment and that is not subject to a finance charge. The term shall not include amounts for which the buyer may later become obligated under the terms of the contract in connection with insurance, repairs to or preservation of the motor vehicle, preservation of the security interest therein, or otherwise.

(l) "Motor vehicle" means a vehicle required to be registered under the Vehicle Code that is bought for use primarily for personal or family purposes, and does not mean any vehicle that is bought for use primarily for business or commercial purposes or a mobilehome, as defined in Section 18008 of the Health and Safety Code that is sold on or after July 1, 1981. "Motor vehicle" does not include any trailer that is sold in conjunction with a vessel and that comes within the definition of "goods" under Section 1802.1.

(m) "Purchase order" means a sales order, car reservation, statement of transaction, or any other such instrument used in the conditional sale of a motor vehicle pending execution of a conditional sale contract. The purchase order shall conform to the disclosure requirements of subdivision (a) of Section 2982 and Section 2984.1, and subdivision (m) of Section 2982 shall apply.

(n) "Regulation Z" means a rule, regulation, or interpretation promulgated by the Board of Governors of the Federal Reserve System ("Board") under the federal Truth in Lending Act, as amended (15 U.S.C. Sec. 1601, et seq.), and an interpretation or approval issued by an official or employee of the Federal Reserve System duly authorized by the board under the Truth in Lending Act, as amended, to issue the interpretations or approvals.

(o) "Simple-interest basis" means the determination of a finance charge, other than an administrative finance charge, by applying a constant rate to the unpaid balance as it changes from time to time either:

(1) Calculated on the basis of a 365-day year and actual days elapsed (although the seller may, but need not, adjust its calculations to account for leap years); reference in this chapter to the "365-day basis" shall mean this method of determining the finance charge, or

(2) For contracts entered into prior to January 1, 1988, calculated on the basis of a 360-day year consisting of 12 months of 30 days each and on the assumption that all payments will be received by the seller on their respective due dates; reference in this chapter to the "360-day basis" shall mean this method of determining the finance charge.

(p) "Precomputed basis" means the determination of a finance charge by multiplying the original unpaid balance of the contract by a rate and multiplying that product by the number of payment periods elapsing between the date of the contract and the date of the last scheduled payment.

(q) "Service contract" means "vehicle service contract" as defined in subdivision (c) of Section 12800 of the Insurance Code.

(r) "Surface protection product" means the following products installed by the seller after the motor vehicle is sold:

(1) Undercoating.
(2) Rustproofing.
(3) Chemical or film paint sealant or protectant.
(4) Chemical sealant or stain inhibitor for carpet and fabric.

(s) "Theft deterrent device" means the following devices installed by the seller after the motor vehicle is sold:

(1) A vehicle alarm system.
(2) A window etch product.
(3) A body part marking product.
(4) A steering lock.
(5) A pedal or ignition lock.
(6) A fuel or ignition kill switch.

(t) "Guaranteed asset protection waiver" means an optional contractual obligation under which a seller agrees, for additional consideration, to cancel or waive all or part of amounts due on the buyer's conditional sale contract subject to this chapter in the event of a total loss or unrecovered theft of the motor vehicle specified in the conditional sale contract. **Leg.H.** Added Stats 1961 ch 1626 §4, effective January 1, 1962. Amended Stats 1968 ch 1338 §1; Stats 1970 ch 1003 §1; Stats 1973 ch 696 §1; Stats 1976 ch 1285 §1; Stats 1979 ch 805 §18; Stats 1980 ch 1149 §7, ch 1380 §19, effective October 1, 1980; Stats 1981 ch 134 §1, effective and operative July 1, 1981, ch 1075 §12, operative October 1, 1982; Stats 1985 ch 1186 §2; Stats 1994 ch 1010 §50 (SB 2053); Stats 1999 ch 212 §1 (SB 1092); Stats 2005 ch 128 §2 (AB 68), effective January 1, 2006, operative July 1, 2006; Stats 2022 ch 283 §1 (AB 2311), effective January 1, 2023.

2005 Note: (a) This act shall be known and may be cited as the "Car Buyer's Bill of Rights."

(b) It is the intent of the Legislature to place limits and restrictions on motor vehicle dealers licensed pursuant to Article 1 (commencing with Section 11700) of Chapter 4 of Division 5 of the Vehicle Code. Nothing in this act is intended to change or limit the rights or defenses available under current law to an assignee who obtains a conditional sale contract for value without notice of any claim or defense against him or her by any other person. Stats 2005 ch 128 (AB 68) §1.

Prior Law: Former §2981, similar in part to the present section, was added Stats 1945 ch 1030 §1, amended Stats 1959 ch 1466 §1, and repealed Stats 1961 ch 1626 §1, effective January 1, 1962.

§2981.5. Bailment or leasing contract establishing maximum liability of bailee or lessee

A contract for the bailment or leasing of a motor vehicle, with or without accessories, which establishes the maximum for which a bailee or lessee could be held liable at the end of the lease or bailment period, or upon an earlier termination, by reference to the value of the vehicle at such time, is not a contract by which the bailee or lessee will become or for no other or for a nominal consideration has the option of becoming the owner of the vehicle, for the purposes of paragraph (2) of subdivision (a) of Section 2981 or any other provision of this chapter. **Leg.H.** Added Stats 1973 ch 696 §2.

§2981.7. Calculation of finance charge on contracts after January 1, 1983

All contracts entered into between a buyer and a seller on or after January 1, 1983, shall provide for the calculation of the finance charge contemplated by item (A) of paragraph (1) of subdivision (j) of Section 2982 on the simple-interest basis, if the date on which the final installment is due, according to the original terms of the contract, is more than 62 months after the date of the contract. **Leg.H.** Added Stats 1979 ch 805 §19. Amended Stats 1983 ch 142 §3.

§2981.8. Finance charges determined by more than one basis

No contract shall provide for a finance charge which is determined in part by the precomputed basis and in part by the simple-interest basis except for any finance charge permitted by subdivisions (a) and (c) of Section 2982.8. **Leg.H.** Added Stats 1979 ch 805 §19.5. Amended Stats 1980 ch 1380 §20, effective October 1, 1980.

§2981.9. Requisites of conditional sale contract

Every conditional sale contract subject to this chapter shall be in writing and, if printed, shall be printed in type no smaller than 6-point, and shall contain in a single document all of the agreements of the buyer and seller with respect to the total cost and the terms of payment for the motor vehicle, including any promissory notes or any other evidences of indebtedness. The conditional sale contract or a purchase order shall be signed by the buyer or his or her authorized representative and by the seller or its authorized representative. An exact copy of the contract or purchase order shall be furnished to the buyer by the seller at the time the buyer and the seller have signed it. No motor vehicle shall be delivered pursuant to a contract subject to this chapter until the seller delivers to the buyer a fully executed copy of the conditional sale contract or purchase order and any vehicle purchase proposal and any credit statement which the seller has required or requested the buyer to sign and which he or she has signed during the contract negotiations. The seller shall not obtain the signature of the buyer to a contract when it contains blank spaces to be filled in after it has been signed. **Leg.H.** Added Stats 1981 ch 1075 §13, operative October 1, 1982.

§2982. Disclosures required in a conditional sale contract

A conditional sale contract subject to this chapter shall contain the disclosures required by Regulation Z, whether or not Regulation Z applies to the transaction. In addition, to the extent applicable, the contract shall contain the other disclosures and notices required by, and shall satisfy the requirements and limitations of, this section. The disclosures required by subdivision (a) may be itemized or subtotaled to a greater extent than as required by that subdivision and shall be made together and in the sequence set forth in that subdivision. All other disclosures and notices may appear in the contract in any location or sequence and may be combined or interspersed with other provisions of the contract.

(a) The contract shall contain the following disclosures, as applicable, which shall be labeled "itemization of the amount financed":

(1)(A) The cash price, exclusive of document processing charges, charges to electronically register or transfer the vehicle, taxes imposed on the sale, pollution control certification fees, prior credit or lease balance on property being traded in, the amount charged for a service contract, the amount charged for a theft deterrent system, the amount charged for a surface protection product, the amount charged for an optional debt cancellation agreement or guaranteed asset protection waiver, and the amount charged for a contract cancellation option agreement.

(B) The charge to be retained by the seller for document processing authorized pursuant to Section 4456.5 of the Vehicle Code.

(C) The fee charged by the seller for certifying that the motor vehicle complies with applicable pollution control requirements.

(D) A charge for a theft deterrent device.

(E) A charge for a surface protection product.

(F) The total amount charged by the seller for an electric vehicle charging station, which may include only the charges for the electric vehicle charging station device, any materials and wiring, and any installation services. The total amount shall be labeled "EV Charging Station."

(G) Taxes imposed on the sale.

(H) The charge to electronically register or transfer the vehicle authorized pursuant to Section 4456.5 of the Vehicle Code.

(I) The amount charged for a service contract.

(J) The prior credit or lease balance remaining on property being traded in, as required by paragraph (6). The disclosure required by this subparagraph shall be labeled "prior credit or lease balance (see downpayment and trade-in calculation)."

(K) Any charge for an optional debt cancellation agreement or guaranteed asset protection waiver.

(L) Any charge for a used vehicle contract cancellation option agreement.

(M) The total cash price, which is the sum of subparagraphs (A) to (L), inclusive.

(N) The disclosures described in subparagraphs (D), (E), and (L) are not required on contracts involving the sale of a motorcycle, as defined in Section 400 of the Vehicle Code, or on contracts involving the sale of an off-highway motor vehicle that is subject to identification under Section 38010 of the Vehicle Code, and the amounts of those charges, if any, are not required to be reflected in the total price under subparagraph (M).

(2) Amounts paid to public officials for the following:

(A) Vehicle license fees.

(B) Registration, transfer, and titling fees.

(C) California tire fees imposed pursuant to Section 42885 of the Public Resources Code.

(3) The aggregate amount of premiums agreed, upon execution of the contract, to be paid for policies of insurance included in the contract, excluding the amount of any insurance premium included in the finance charge.

(4) The amount of the state fee for issuance of a certificate of compliance, noncompliance, exemption, or waiver pursuant to any applicable pollution control statute.

(5) A subtotal representing the sum of the amounts described in paragraphs (1) to (4), inclusive.

(6) The amount of the buyer's downpayment itemized to show the following:

(A) The agreed value of the property being traded in.

(B) The prior credit or lease balance, if any, owing on the property being traded in.

(C) The net agreed value of the property being traded in, which is the difference between the amounts disclosed in subparagraphs (A) and (B). If the prior credit or lease balance of the property being traded in exceeds the agreed value of the property, a negative number shall be stated.

(D) The amount of any portion of the downpayment to be deferred until not later than the due date of the second regularly scheduled installment under the contract and that is not subject to a finance charge.

(E) The amount of any manufacturer's rebate applied or to be applied to the downpayment.

(F) The remaining amount paid or to be paid by the buyer as a downpayment.

(G) The total downpayment. If the sum of subparagraphs (C) to (F), inclusive, is zero or more, that sum shall be stated as the total downpayment, and no amount shall be stated as the prior credit or lease balance under subparagraph (I) of paragraph (1). If the sum of subparagraphs (C) to (F), inclusive, is less than zero, then that sum, expressed as a positive number, shall be stated as the prior credit or lease balance under subparagraph (I) of paragraph (1), and zero shall be stated as the total downpayment. The disclosure required by this subparagraph shall be labeled "total downpayment" and shall contain a descriptor indicating that if the total downpayment is a negative number, a zero shall be disclosed as the total downpayment and a reference made that the remainder shall be included in the disclosure required pursuant to subparagraph (I) of paragraph (1).

(7) The amount of any administrative finance charge, labeled "prepaid finance charge."

(8) The difference between the amount described in paragraph (5) and the sum of the amounts described in paragraphs (6) and (7), labeled "amount financed."

(b) No particular terminology is required to disclose the items set forth in subdivision (a) except as expressly provided in that subdivision.

(c) If payment of all or a portion of the downpayment is to be deferred, the deferred payment shall be reflected in the payment schedule disclosed pursuant to Regulation Z.

(d) If the downpayment includes property being traded in, the contract shall contain a brief description of that property.

(e) The contract shall contain the names and addresses of all persons to whom the notice required pursuant to Section 2983.2 and permitted pursuant to Sections 2983.5 and 2984 is to be sent.

(f)(1) If the contract includes a finance charge determined on the precomputed basis, the contract shall identify the method of computing the unearned portion of the finance charge in the event of prepayment in full of the buyer's obligation and contain a statement of the amount or method of computation of any charge that may be deducted from the amount of any unearned finance charge in computing the amount that will be credited to the obligation or refunded to the buyer. The method of computing the unearned portion of the finance charge shall be sufficiently identified with a reference to the actuarial method if the computation will be under that method. The method of computing the unearned portion of the finance charge shall be sufficiently identified with a reference to the Rule of 78's, the sum of the digits, or the sum of the periodic time balances method in all other cases, and those references shall be deemed to be equivalent for disclosure purposes.

(2) If the contract includes a finance charge that is determined on the simple-interest basis but provides for a minimum finance charge in the event of prepayment in full, the contract shall contain a statement of that fact and the amount of the minimum finance charge or its method of calculation.

(g)(1) If the contract includes a finance charge that is determined on the precomputed basis and provides that the unearned portion of the finance charge to be refunded upon full prepayment of the contract is to be determined by a method other than actuarial, the contract shall contain a notice, in at least 10-point boldface type if the contract is printed, reading as follows: "Notice to buyer:(1) Do not sign this agreement before you read it or if it contains any blank spaces to be filled in.(2) You are entitled to a completely filled-in copy of this agreement.(3) You can prepay the full amount due under this agreement at any time and obtain a partial refund of the finance charge if it is $1 or more. Because of the way the amount of this refund will be figured, the time when you prepay could increase the ultimate cost of credit under this agreement.(4) If you default in the performance of your obligations under this agreement, the vehicle may be repossessed and you may be subject to suit and liability for the unpaid indebtedness evidenced by this agreement."

(2) If the contract includes a finance charge that is determined on the precomputed basis and provides for the actuarial method for computing the unearned portion of the finance charge upon prepayment in full, the contract shall contain a notice, in at least 10-point boldface type if the contract is printed, reading as follows: "Notice to buyer:(1) Do not sign this agreement before you read it or if it contains any blank spaces to be filled in.(2) You are entitled to a completely filled-in copy of this agreement.(3) You can prepay the full amount due under this agreement at

any time and obtain a partial refund of the finance charge if it is $1 or more. (4) If you default in the performance of your obligations under this agreement, the vehicle may be repossessed and you may be subject to suit and liability for the unpaid indebtedness evidenced by this agreement."

(3) If the contract includes a finance charge that is determined on the simple-interest basis, the contract shall contain a notice, in at least 10-point boldface type if the contract is printed, reading as follows: "Notice to buyer: (1) Do not sign this agreement before you read it or if it contains any blank spaces to be filled in. (2) You are entitled to a completely filled-in copy of this agreement. (3) You can prepay the full amount due under this agreement at any time. (4) If you default in the performance of your obligations under this agreement, the vehicle may be repossessed and you may be subject to suit and liability for the unpaid indebtedness evidenced by this agreement."

(h) The contract shall contain a notice in at least 8-point boldface type, acknowledged by the buyer, that reads as follows:

If you have a complaint concerning this sale, you should try to resolve it with the seller.

Complaints concerning unfair or deceptive practices or methods by the seller may be referred to the city attorney, the district attorney, or an investigator for the Department of Motor Vehicles, or any combination thereof.

After this contract is signed, the seller may not change the financing or payment terms unless you agree in writing to the change. You do not have to agree to any change, and it is an unfair or deceptive practice for the seller to make a unilateral change.

_____
Buyer's Signature"

(i)(1) The contract shall contain an itemization of any insurance included as part of the amount financed disclosed pursuant to paragraph (3) of subdivision (a) and of any insurance included as part of the finance charge. The itemization shall identify the type of insurance coverage and the premium charged therefor, and, if the insurance expires before the date of the last scheduled installment included in the repayment schedule, the term of the insurance shall be stated.

(2) If any charge for insurance, other than for credit life or disability, is included in the contract balance and disbursement of any part thereof is to be made more than one year after the date of the conditional sale contract, any finance charge on the amount to be disbursed after one year shall be computed from the month the disbursement is to be made to the due date of the last installment under the conditional sale contract.

(j)(1) Except for contracts in which the finance charge or a portion of the finance charge is determined by the simple-interest basis and the amount financed disclosed pursuant to paragraph (8) of subdivision (a) is more than two thousand five hundred dollars ($2,500), the dollar amount of the disclosed finance charge may not exceed the greater of:

(A)(i) One and one-half percent on so much of the unpaid balance as does not exceed two hundred twenty-five dollars ($225), 1⅙ percent on so much of the unpaid balance in excess of two hundred twenty-five dollars ($225) as does not exceed nine hundred dollars ($900) and five-sixths of 1 percent on so much of the unpaid balance in excess of nine hundred dollars ($900) as does not exceed two thousand five hundred dollars ($2,500).

(ii) One percent of the entire unpaid balance; multiplied in either case by the number of months (computed on the basis of a full month for any fractional month period in excess of 15 days) elapsing between the date of the contract and the due date of the last installment.

(B) If the finance charge is determined by the precomputed basis, twenty-five dollars ($25).

(C) If the finance charge or a portion thereof is determined by the simple-interest basis:

(i) Twenty-five dollars ($25) if the unpaid balance does not exceed one thousand dollars ($1,000).

(ii) Fifty dollars ($50) if the unpaid balance exceeds one thousand dollars ($1,000) but does not exceed two thousand dollars ($2,000).

(iii) Seventy-five dollars ($75) if the unpaid balance exceeds two thousand dollars ($2,000).

(2) The holder of the contract shall not charge, collect, or receive a finance charge that exceeds the disclosed finance charge, except to the extent (A) caused by the holder's receipt of one or more payments under a contract that provides for determination of the finance charge or a portion thereof on the 365-day basis at a time or times other than as originally scheduled whether or not the parties enter into an agreement pursuant to Section 2982.3, (B) permitted by paragraph (2), (3), or (4) of subdivision (c) of Section 226.17 of Regulation Z, or (C) permitted by subdivisions (a) and (c) of Section 2982.8.

(3) If the finance charge or a portion thereof is determined by the simple-interest basis and the amount of the unpaid balance exceeds five thousand dollars ($5,000), the holder of the contract may, in lieu of its right to a minimum finance charge under subparagraph (C) of paragraph (1), charge, receive, or collect on the date of the contract an administrative finance charge not to exceed seventy-five dollars ($75), provided that the sum of the administrative finance charge and the portion of the finance charge determined by the simple-interest basis shall not exceed the maximum total finance charge permitted by subparagraph (A) of paragraph (1). Any administrative finance charge that is charged, received, or collected by a holder shall be deemed a finance charge earned on the date of the contract.

(4) If a contract provides for unequal or irregular payments, or payments on other than a monthly basis, the maximum finance charge shall be at the effective rate provided for in paragraph (1), having due regard for the schedule of installments.

(k) The contract may provide that for each installment in default for a period of not less than 10 days the buyer shall pay a delinquency charge in an amount not to exceed in the aggregate 5 percent of the delinquent installment, which amount may be collected only once on any installment regardless of the period during which it remains in default. Payments timely received by the seller under an extension or deferral agreement may not be subject to a delinquency charge unless the charge is permitted by Section 2982.3. The contract may provide for reasonable collection costs and fees in the event of delinquency.

(*l*) Notwithstanding any provision of a contract to the contrary, the buyer may pay at any time before maturity the entire indebtedness evidenced by the contract without penalty. In the event of prepayment in full:

(1) If the finance charge was determined on the precomputed basis, the amount required to prepay the contract shall be the outstanding contract balance as of that date, provided, however, that the buyer shall be entitled to a refund credit in the amount of the unearned portion of the finance charge, except as provided in paragraphs (3) and (4). The amount of the unearned portion of the finance charge shall be at least as great a proportion of the finance charge, including any additional finance charge imposed pursuant to Section 2982.8 or other additional charge imposed because the contract has been extended, deferred, or refinanced, as the sum of the periodic monthly time balances payable more than 15 days after the date of prepayment bears to the sum of all the periodic monthly time balances under the schedule of installments in the contract or, if the contract has been extended, deferred, or refinanced, as so extended, deferred, or refinanced. If the amount of the refund credit is less than one dollar ($1), no refund credit need be made by the holder. Any refund credit may be made in cash or credited to the outstanding obligations of the buyer under the contract.

(2) If the finance charge or a portion of the finance charge was determined on the simple-interest basis, the amount required to prepay the contract shall be the outstanding contract balance as of that date, including any earned finance charges that are unpaid as of that date and, if applicable, the amount provided in paragraph (3), and provided further that in cases where a finance charge is determined on the 360-day basis, the payments received under the contract shall be assumed to have been received on their respective due dates regardless of the actual dates on which the payments were received.

(3) If the minimum finance charge provided by subparagraph (B) or subparagraph (C) of paragraph (1) of subdivision (j), if either is applicable, is greater than the earned finance charge as of the date of prepayment, the holder shall be additionally entitled to the difference.

(4) This subdivision shall not impair the right of the seller or the seller's assignee to receive delinquency charges on delinquent installments and reasonable costs and fees as provided in subdivision (k) or extension or deferral agreement charges as provided in Section 2982.3.

(5) Notwithstanding any provision of a contract to the contrary, if the indebtedness created by any contract is satisfied prior to its maturity through surrender of the motor vehicle, repossession of the motor vehicle, redemption of the motor vehicle after repossession, or any judgment, the outstanding obligation of the buyer shall be determined as provided in

paragraph (1) or (2), except that the buyer's outstanding obligation shall be computed by the holder as of the date the holder recovers the value of the motor vehicle through disposition thereof or judgment is entered or, if the holder elects to keep the motor vehicle in satisfaction of the buyer's indebtedness, as of the date the holder takes possession of the motor vehicle.

(m) Notwithstanding any other provision of this chapter to the contrary, any information required to be disclosed in a conditional sale contract under this chapter may be disclosed in any manner, method, or terminology required or permitted under Regulation Z, as in effect at the time that disclosure is made, except that permitted by paragraph (2) of subdivision (c) of Section 226.18 of Regulation Z, if all of the requirements and limitations set forth in subdivision (a) are satisfied. This chapter does not prohibit the disclosure in that contract of additional information required or permitted under Regulation Z, as in effect at the time that disclosure is made.

(n) If the seller imposes a charge for document processing or to electronically register or transfer the vehicle, the contract shall contain a disclosure that the charge is not a governmental fee.

(o) A seller shall not impose an application fee for a transaction governed by this chapter.

(p) The seller or holder may charge and collect a fee not to exceed fifteen dollars ($15) for the return by a depository institution of a dishonored check, negotiated order of withdrawal, or share draft issued in connection with the contract if the contract so provides or if the contract contains a generalized statement that the buyer may be liable for collection costs incurred in connection with the contract.

(q) The contract shall disclose on its face, by printing the word "new" or "used" within a box outlined in red, that is not smaller than one-half inch high and one-half inch wide, whether the vehicle is sold as a new vehicle, as defined in Section 430 of the Vehicle Code, or as a used vehicle, as defined in Section 665 of the Vehicle Code.

(r) The contract shall contain a notice with a heading in at least 12-point bold type and the text in at least 10-point bold type, circumscribed by a line, immediately above the contract signature line, that reads as follows:

THERE IS NO COOLING-OFF PERIOD UNLESS YOU OBTAIN A CONTRACT CANCELLATION OPTION

California law does not provide for a "cooling-off" or other cancellation period for vehicle sales. Therefore, you cannot later cancel this contract simply because you change your mind, decide the vehicle costs too much, or wish you had acquired a different vehicle. After you sign below, you may only cancel this contract with the agreement of the seller or for legal cause, such as fraud.

However, California law does require a seller to offer a two-day contract cancellation option on used vehicles with a purchase price of less than forty thousand dollars ($40,000), subject to certain statutory conditions. This contract cancellation option requirement does not apply to the sale of a recreational vehicle, a motorcycle, or an off-highway motor vehicle subject to identification under California law. See the vehicle contract cancellation option agreement for details.

Leg.H. Added Stats 2012 ch 675 §2 (AB 2502), effective September 27, 2012, operative July 1, 2013. Amended Stats 2022 ch 283 §2 (AB 2311), effective January 1, 2023; Stats 2023 ch 478 §7 (AB 1756), effective January 1, 2024.

Prior Law: Former Civ C §2982, similar to present section, was added Stats 1979 ch 805 §20.5, operative January 1, 1981, ch 1028 §2, effective September 26, 1979, operative January 1, 1981, ch 1160 §1.6, operative January 1, 1981. Amended Stats 1980 ch 1149 §8, ch 1380 §22, effective October 1, 1980, operative July 1, 1981; Stats 1981 ch 107 §6, effective June 29, 1981, ch 134 §4, effective July 1, 1981, ch 243 §6, effective July 21, 1981, operative April 1, 1982, ch 1075 §14, operative October 1, 1982; Stats 1984 ch 710 §1, ch 1114 §3; Stats 1985 ch 33 §1, effective May 7, 1985; Stats 1987 ch 448 §1; Stats 1988 ch 1092 §1; Stats 1990 ch 189 §1 (AB 2618), effective June 29, 1990, operative January 1, 1991; Stats 1991 ch 1054 §1 (SB 245); Stats 1992 ch 1092 §1 (AB 3482); Stats 1993 ch 101 §3 (SB 329), ch 1092 §2 (AB 431), operative July 1, 1994; Stats 1994 ch 146 §14 (AB 3601) (ch 704 prevails), ch 704 §1 (SB 1699); Stats 1996 ch 665 §1 (SB 1576); Stats 1997 ch 891 §1 (SB 1325); Stats 1999 ch 212 §2 (SB 1092); Stats 2001 ch 287 §1 (SB 281); Stats 2003 ch 37 §1 (AB 964); Stats 2004 ch 183 §40 (AB 3082). Amended Stats 2005 ch 128 §3 (AB 68), effective January 1, 2006, operative July 1, 2006; Stats 2006 ch 567 §3 (AB 2303), effective January 1, 2007; Stats 2011 ch 329 §3 (AB 1215), effective January 1, 2012, inoperative July 1, 2012, repealed January 1, 2013; Stats 2012 ch 675 §1 (AB 2502), effective September 27, 2012, inoperative July 1, 2013, and repealed January 1, 2014.

Former Civ C §2982, similar to the present section, was added Stats 1961 ch 1626 §4, effective January 1, 1962, amended Stats 1963 ch 1319 §1, Stats 1969 ch 255 §2, ch 1189 §1, Stats 1970 ch 1003 §2, Stats 1971 ch 595 §1, Stats 1975 ch 645 §1, effective September 10, 1975, Stats 1976 ch 1286 §4, Stats 1978 ch 632 §1, Stats 1979 ch 805 §20, ch 1028 §1, effective September 26, 1979, operative January 1, 1980, ch 1160 §1.5, Stats 1980 ch 1380 §21, effective October 1, 1980, Stats 1981 ch 107 §5, effective June 429, 1981, ch 134 §3, effective and operative July 1, 1981, ch 243 §5, effective July 21, 1981, Stats 1982 ch 129 §11, effective March 24, 1982 and, repealed, effective October 1, 1982, by its own terms.

Original Civ C §2982, similar to the present section, was added Stats 1945 ch 1030 §2, amended Stats 1949 ch 1594 §1, Stats 1951 ch 342 §2, Stats 1957 ch 613 §1, Stats 1959 ch 1466 §2, Stats 1961 ch 243 §1, and repealed Stats 1961 ch 1626 §2, effective January 1, 1962.

Former Sections: Former CC §2982 was added in 2011 and became inoperative July 1, 2013, and repealed operative January 1, 2014, by its own provisions. Stats 2012 ch 675 (AB 2502) §3.

Former CC §2982 was added in 1979 and became inoperative July 1, 2012, and repealed operative January 1, 2013, by its own provisions. Stats 2011 ch 329 (AB 1215) §3.

§2982.05. [Section repealed 1990]

Leg.H. Added Stats 1989 ch 1141 sec 1, operative July 1, 1990. Repealed Stats 1990 ch 189 §2 (AB 2618), effective June 29, 1990. The repealed section related to notice to buyer.

§2982.1. Inducing contract by offering rebate or discount on condition that buyer sells or assists in sale of same or related goods

It shall be unlawful for any seller to induce or attempt to induce any person to enter into a contract subject to this chapter by offering a rebate, discount, commission, or other consideration, contingent upon the happening of a future event, on the condition that the buyer either sells, or gives information or assistance for the purpose of leading to a sale by the seller of, the same or related goods. **Leg.H.** Added Stats 1968 ch 452 §3 p 1074.

§2982.2. Elements of written disclosure prior to execution of conditional sales contract; Buyer's signature required on written disclosure

(a) Prior to the execution of a conditional sale contract, the seller shall provide to a buyer, and obtain the buyer's signature on, a written disclosure that sets forth the following information:

(1)(A) A description and the price of each item sold if the contract includes a charge for the item.

(B) Subparagraph (A) applies to each item in the following categories:

(i) A service contract.

(ii) An insurance product.

(iii) A debt cancellation agreement or guaranteed asset protection waiver agreement.

(iv) A theft deterrent device.

(v) A surface protection product.

(vi) A vehicle contract cancellation option agreement.

(2) The sum of all of the charges disclosed under subdivision (a), labeled "total."

(3) The amount that would be calculated under the contract as the regular installment payment if charges for the items disclosed pursuant to subdivision (a) are not included in the contract. The amount disclosed pursuant to this subdivision shall be labeled "Installment Payment EXCLUDING Listed Items."

(4) The amount that would be calculated under the contract as the regular installment payment if charges for the items disclosed under subdivision (a) are included in the contract. The amount disclosed pursuant to this subdivision shall be labeled "Installment Payment INCLUDING Listed Items."

(b) The disclosures required under this section shall be in at least 10-point type and shall be contained in a document that is separate from the conditional sale contract and a purchase order.

(c) This section does not apply to the sale of a motorcycle, as defined in Section 400 of the Vehicle Code, or an off-highway vehicle subject to identification under Section 38010 of the Vehicle Code. **Leg.H.** Added Stats 2005 ch 128 §4 (AB 68), effective January 1, 2006, operative July 1, 2006. Amended Stats 2006 ch 567 §3.5 (AB 2303), effective January 1, 2007; Stats 2022 ch 283 §3 (AB 2311), effective January 1, 2023.

Prior Law: Former CC 2982.2, similar to present section, was added Stats 1994 ch 28 §1, effective March 30, 1994, amended Stats 1994 ch 85 §1, effective May 20, 1994; Stats 1994 ch 1220 §2, effective September 30, 1994 and repealed Stats 1999 ch 212 §3.

2005 Note: (a) This act shall be known and may be cited as the "Car Buyer's Bill of Rights."

(b) It is the intent of the Legislature to place limits and restrictions on motor vehicle dealers licensed pursuant to Article 1 (commencing with Section 11700) of Chapter 4 of Division 5 of the Vehicle Code. Nothing in this act is intended to change or limit the rights or defenses available under current law to an assignee who obtains a conditional sale contract for value without notice of any claim or defense against him or her by any other person. Stats 2005 ch 128 (AB 68) §1.

Former Sections: Former CC §2982.2 was added in 1994 and repealed Stats 1999 ch 212.

§2982.3. Extension of due date or deferral of payment of installment

(a) The holder of a conditional sale contract may, upon agreement with the buyer, extend the scheduled due date or defer the scheduled payment of all or of any part of any installment or installments payable thereunder. No charge shall be made for any such extension or deferment unless the agreement for such extension or deferment is in writing and signed by the parties thereto. However, the seller or holder may, as an adjunct to or to assist in efforts to collect one or more delinquent installments on the contract, advise one or more obligors on the contract, either in writing or orally, that the due date for one or more installments under the contract shall be extended, with no charge being made for such extension other than any applicable late charge provided for in the contract.

(b) Where the contract includes a finance charge determined on the precomputed basis, the holder may charge and contract for the payment of an extension or deferral agreement charge by the buyer and collect and receive the same, but such charge may not exceed an amount equal to 1 percent per month simple interest on the amount of the installment or installments, or part thereof, extended or deferred for the period of extension or deferral. Such period shall not exceed the period from the date when such extended or deferred installment or installments, or part thereof, would have been payable in the absence of such extension or deferral to the date when such installment or installments, or part thereof, are made payable under the agreement of extension or deferment; except that a minimum charge of one dollar ($1) for the period of extension or deferral may be made in any case where the extension or deferral agreement charge, when computed at such rate, amounts to less than one dollar ($1).

(c) Where the contract includes a finance charge determined on the simple-interest basis, the holder may charge and contract for the payment of an extension or deferral agreement charge by the buyer and collect and receive the same, but the charge for the extension or deferral agreement may not exceed the lesser of twenty-five dollars ($25) or 10 percent of the then outstanding principal balance of the contract. Such charge shall be in addition to any finance charges which accrue because such extended or deferred payments are received at a time other than as originally scheduled. **Leg.H.** Added Stats 1980 ch 1380 §23, effective October 1, 1980. Amended Stats 1981 ch 1075 §15, operative October 1, 1982; Stats 1987 ch 448 §2.

§2982.5. Exclusion of loan between purchaser and supervised financial organization; Assistance in obtaining loan

(a) This chapter may not be deemed to affect a loan, or the security therefor, between a purchaser of a motor vehicle and a supervised financial organization, other than the seller of the motor vehicle, all or a portion of which loan is used in connection with the purchase of a motor vehicle. As used in this chapter, "supervised financial organization" means a person organized, chartered, or holding a license or authorization certificate under a law of this state or the United States to make loans and subject to supervision by an official or agency of this state or the United States.

(b) This chapter may not be deemed to prohibit the seller's assisting the buyer in obtaining a loan upon any security from any third party to be used as a part or all of the downpayment or any other payment on a conditional sale contract or purchase order; provided that the conditional sale contract sets forth on its face the amount of the loan, the finance charge, the total thereof, the number of installments scheduled to repay the loan and the amount of each installment, that the buyer may be required to pledge security for the loan, which security shall be mutually agreed to by the buyer and the lender and notice to the buyer in at least 8-point type that he or she is obligated for the installment payments on both the conditional sale contract and the loan. The seller may not provide any security or other guarantee of payment on the loan, nor shall the seller receive any commission or other remuneration for assisting the buyer to obtain the loan. If the buyer obligates himself or herself to purchase, or receives possession of, the motor vehicle prior to securing the loan, and if the buyer upon appropriate application for the loan is unable to secure the loan, on the conditions stated in the conditional sale contract, the conditional sale contract or purchase order shall be deemed rescinded and all consideration thereupon shall be returned by the respective parties without demand.

(c) The proceeds of any loan payable to the seller after the date of the contract but prior to the due date of the second payment otherwise scheduled thereunder may not be subject to a finance charge and the amount thereof shall be disclosed pursuant to subparagraph (D) of paragraph (6) of subdivision (a) of Section 2982.

(d) This chapter may not be deemed to prohibit the seller's assisting the buyer in obtaining a loan from any third party to be used to pay for the full purchase price, or any part thereof, of a motor vehicle, if each of the following provisions applies:

(1) The loan may be upon any security, but except as provided in paragraph (2), the loan may not be secured in whole or in part by a lien on real property. Any lien on real property taken in violation of this section shall be void and unenforceable.

(2) A lien on real property may be taken to secure a loan of seven thousand five hundred dollars ($7,500) or more used to pay the full purchase price, or any part thereof, of a recreational vehicle, as defined in Section 18010 of the Health and Safety Code, which is not less than 20 feet in length.

(3) The provisions of Sections 2983.2, 2983.3, and 2984.4 shall apply to the loan, but may not authorize the lender or the lender's successor in interest to charge for any costs, fees, or expenses or to obtain any other benefit which the lender is prohibited from charging or obtaining under any regulatory law applicable to the lender. Notwithstanding this paragraph, the provisions of Sections 2983.2 and 2983.3 may not apply to a loan made by a lender licensed under Division 9 (commencing with Section 22000) or Division 10 (commencing with Section 24000) of the Financial Code.

(4) The lender or the lender's successor in interest shall be subject to all claims and defenses which the buyer could assert against the seller, but liability may not exceed the amount of the loan.

(5) If the buyer becomes obligated to purchase, or receives possession of, the motor vehicle prior to obtaining the loan, the agreement between the buyer and the seller shall set forth on its face the amount of the loan, the finance charge, the total thereof, the number of installments scheduled to repay the loan and the amount of each installment, that the buyer may be required to pledge security for the loan, which security must be mutually agreed to by the buyer and the lender, and notice to the buyer in at least 8-point type that the buyer is obligated for the installment payments on the loan and for any payments which may be due on the agreement between the buyer and the seller. The seller may not provide any security or other guarantee of payment on the loan, and the seller may not receive any commission or other remuneration for assisting the buyer to obtain the loan. If the buyer upon proper application for the loan is unable to obtain the loan, on the condition stated in the agreement between the buyer and the seller, the agreement shall be deemed rescinded and all consideration thereupon shall be returned by the respective parties without demand.

(6) Any waiver by the buyer of the provisions of this section shall be void and unenforceable.

This subdivision does not apply to state or federally chartered banks and savings and loan associations and may not be construed to affect existing law regarding a seller's assisting a buyer to obtain a loan from a bank or savings and loan association or any loan obtained by the buyer from those lenders. **Leg.H.** Added Stats 1968 ch 979 §1. Amended Stats 1970 ch 1003 §3; 1979 ch 805 §21; Stats 1981 ch 1075 §16, operative October 1, 1982; Stats 1983 ch 405 §1; Stats 1985 ch 226 §1; Stats 2003 ch 37 §2 (AB 964).

Prior Law: Former §2982.5, relating to statement of notice of change of address of buyer or registered owner in a conditional sales contract, was added Stats 1959 ch 1874 §1 p 4435 and repealed Stats 1961 ch 1626 §3 p 3534, effective January 1, 1962.

§2982.7. Refund of payment; Recovery of value of vehicle left as down payment

(a) Any payment made by a buyer to a seller pending execution of a conditional sale contract shall be refunded to the buyer in the event the conditional sale contract is not executed.

(b) In the event of breach by the seller of a conditional sale contract or purchase order where the buyer leaves his motor vehicle with the seller as downpayment and such motor vehicle is not returned by the seller to the buyer for whatever reason, the buyer may recover from the seller either the fair market value of the motor vehicle left as a downpayment or its value as stated in the contract or purchase order, whichever is greater. The recovery shall be tendered to the buyer within five business days after the breach.

(c) The remedies of the buyer provided for in subdivision (b) are nonexclusive and cumulative and shall not preclude the buyer from pursuing any other remedy which he may have under any other provision of law. **Leg.H.** Added Stats 1968 ch 1338 §2. Amended Stats 1970 ch 1003 §4; Stats 1976 ch 1285 §4.

§2982.8. Cost of insurance

(a) If a buyer is obligated under the terms of the conditional sale contract to maintain insurance on the vehicle and subsequent to the execution of the contract the buyer either fails to maintain or requests the holder to procure the insurance, any amounts advanced by the holder to procure the insurance may be the subject of finance charges from the date of advance as provided in subdivision (e).

(b) These amounts shall be secured as provided in the contract and permitted by Section 2984.2 if the holder notifies the buyer in writing of his or her option to repay those amounts in any one of the following ways:

(1) Full payment within 10 days from the date of giving or mailing the notice.

(2) Full amortization during the term of the insurance.

(3) If offered by the holder, full amortization after the term of the conditional sale contract, to be payable in installments which do not exceed the average payment allocable to a monthly period under the contract.

(4) If offered by the holder, a combination of the methods described in paragraphs (2) and (3), so that there is some amortization during the term of the insurance, with the remainder of the amortization being accomplished after the term of the conditional sale contract, to be payable in installments which do not exceed the average payment allocable to a monthly period under the original terms of the contract.

(5) If offered by the holder, any other amortization plan.

If the buyer neither pays in full the amounts advanced nor notifies the holder in writing of his or her choice regarding amortization options before the expiration of 10 days from the date of giving or mailing the notice by the holder, the holder may amortize the amounts advanced on a secured basis pursuant to paragraph (2) or, if offered by the holder as an option to the buyer, paragraph (3) or (4).

(c) The written notification described in subdivision (b) shall also set forth the amounts advanced by the holder and, with respect to each amortization plan the amount of the additional finance charge, the sum of the amounts advanced and the additional finance charge, the number of installments required, the amount of each installment and the date for payment of the installments.

In addition, the notice shall contain a statement in contrasting red print in at least 8-point bold type, which reads as follows:

"WARNING-IT IS YOUR RESPONSIBILITY UNDER CALIFORNIA LAW TO OBTAIN LIABILITY INSURANCE OR BE SUBJECT TO PENALTIES FOR VIOLATING SECTION 16020 OF THE VEHICLE CODE, WHICH MAY INCLUDE LOSS OF LICENSE OR A FINE. THE INSURANCE ACQUIRED BY THE LIENHOLDER DOES NOT PROVIDE LIABILITY COVERAGE AND DOES NOT SATISFY YOUR RESPONSIBILITY UNDER CALIFORNIA LAW."

(d) If subsequent to the execution of the contract the holder advances amounts for repairs to or preservation of the motor vehicle or preservation of the holder's security interest therein and such advances are occasioned by the buyer's default under the contract, such advances may be the subject of finance charges from the date of advance as provided in subdivision (e) and shall be secured as provided in the contract and permitted by Section 2984.2.

(e) The maximum rate of finance charge which may be imposed on amounts advanced by the holder subsequent to the execution of the contract for insurance, repairs to or preservation of the motor vehicle, or preservation of the holder's security interest therein, shall not exceed the annual percentage rate disclosed pursuant to Section 2982. **Leg.H.** Added Stats 1976 ch 1265 §2. Amended Stats 1977 ch 777 §1, effective September 13, 1977; Stats 1978 ch 1057 §1; Stats 1979 ch 805 §22; Stats 1980 ch 1149 §9, ch 1380 §24, effective October 1, 1980; Stats 1981 ch 134 §5, effective and operative July 1, 1981, ch 1075 §17, operative October 1, 1982; Stats 1983 ch 33 §1; Stats 1985 ch 1292 §1; Stats 1986 ch 412 §1; Stats 1987 ch 448 §3; Stats 1988 ch 1092 §2.

§2982.9. Rescission of purchase order where buyer unable to obtain financing

In the event a buyer obligates himself to purchase, or receive possession of, a motor vehicle pursuant to a contract or purchase order, and the seller knows that the buyer intends to obtain financing from a third party without the assistance of the seller, and the buyer is unable to obtain such financing, the contract or purchase order shall be deemed rescinded and all consideration thereupon shall be returned by the respective parties without demand. **Leg.H.** Added Stats 1976 ch 1285 §4.5.

§2982.10. Acceptance of payment or credit in consideration of assignment of conditional sales contract limited

(a) In consideration of the assignment of a conditional sale contract, the seller shall not receive or accept from the assignee any payment or credit based upon any amount collected or received, or to be collected or received, under the contract as a finance charge except to the extent the payment or credit does not exceed the amount that would be calculated in accordance with Regulation Z, whether or not Regulation Z applies to the contract, as the contract's finance charge using, for the purposes of the calculation, an annual percentage rate equal to 2.5 percent for a contract having an original scheduled term of 60 monthly payments or less or 2 percent for a contract having an original scheduled term of more than 60 monthly payments.

(b) Subdivision (a) does not apply in the following circumstances:

(1) An assignment that is with full recourse or under other terms requiring the seller to bear the entire risk of financial performance of the buyer.

(2) An assignment that is more than six months following the date of the conditional sale contract.

(3) Isolated instances resulting from bona fide errors that would otherwise constitute a violation of subdivision (a) if the seller maintains reasonable procedures to guard against any errors and promptly, upon notice of the error, remits to the assignee any consideration received in excess of that permitted by subdivision (a).

(4) The assignment of a conditional sale contract involving the sale of a motorcycle, as defined in Section 400 of the Vehicle Code.

(5) The assignment of a conditional sale contract involving the sale of an off-highway motor vehicle that is subject to identification under Section 38010 of the Vehicle Code. **Leg.H.** Added Stats 2005 ch 128 §5 (AB 68), effective January 1, 2006, operative July 1, 2006.

2005 Note: (a) This act shall be known and may be cited as the "Car Buyer's Bill of Rights."

(b) It is the intent of the Legislature to place limits and restrictions on motor vehicle dealers licensed pursuant to Article 1 (commencing with Section 11700) of Chapter 4 of Division 5 of the Vehicle Code. Nothing in this act is intended to change or limit the rights or defenses available under current law to an assignee who obtains a conditional sale contract for value without notice of any claim or defense against him or her by any other person. Stats 2005 ch 128 (AB 68) §1.

§2982.11. Disclosures required for conditional sale contract that includes charge for electric vehicle charging station

(a) Prior to the execution of a conditional sale contract that includes a charge for an electric vehicle charging station, the seller shall provide the buyer with, and obtain the buyer's signature on, a written disclosure that includes a description and price of each of the following:

(1) The electric vehicle charging station device.

(2) Any materials and wiring.

(3) Any installation services included in the total charge.

(b) The disclosures required under this section shall be in at least 12-point type and shall be contained in a document that is separate from the conditional sale contract or purchase order.

(c) This section shall become operative July 1, 2013. **Leg.H.** Added Stats 2012 ch 675 §3 (AB 2502), effective September 27, 2012, operative July 1, 2013.

§2982.12. Offer, sale, or provision of guaranteed asset protection waiver in connection with conditional sale contract

(a)(1) A guaranteed asset protection waiver may be offered, sold, or provided to a buyer, or administered, in connection with a conditional sale contract subject to this chapter only in compliance with this chapter and paragraph (2) of subdivision (h) of Section 1758.992 of the Insurance Code.

(2) A guaranteed asset protection waiver, which may be titled as an addendum, forms part of the conditional sale contract and remains a part of the conditional sale contract upon the assignment, sale, or transfer of that conditional sale contract.

(3) Neither the extension of credit, the term of credit, nor the terms of a conditional sale contract may be conditioned upon the purchase of a guaranteed asset protection waiver.

(4)(A) The terms and conditions of the guaranteed asset protection waiver, including those terms required by subdivision (b), shall appear on a document separate from the conditional sale contract and a buyer or potential buyer shall separately sign the document setting forth the guaranteed asset protection waiver's terms and conditions in addition to the conditional sale contract.

(B) The separate document displaying the guaranteed asset protection waiver's terms and conditions shall do the following:

(i) Conspicuously state that the guaranteed asset protection waiver is an optional addition to the conditional sale contract, and that the holder of the conditional sale contract is the contracting party to the guaranteed asset protection waiver, and state the name and mailing address of the seller. If the conditional sale contract is assigned, written notice of the assignment of both the conditional sale contract and guaranteed asset protection waiver, and the assignee's name and mailing address, shall be provided to the buyer in person or by mail, or by a means of notice that the buyer previously agreed to with the seller or holder in connection with the conditional sale contract within 30 days of the assignment.

(ii) Conspicuously disclose the name and mailing address of any administrator known as of the date of the sale. In this section, "administrator" means any person, other than an insurer, that performs administrative or operational functions in connection with the guaranteed asset protection waiver. An administrator is deemed to be an agent of the contemporaneous holder with respect to performance of the holder's obligations under the guaranteed asset protection waiver and this section.

(iii) Contain a notice with a heading in at least 12-point bold type and the text in at least 10-point bold type, circumscribed by a line, immediately above the contract signature line, that reads as follows:

STOP AND READ:

YOU CANNOT BE REQUIRED TO BUY A GAP WAIVER OR ANY OTHER OPTIONAL ADD-ON PRODUCTS OR SERVICES. IT IS OPTIONAL.

NO ONE CAN MAKE YOU BUY A GAP WAIVER OR ANY OTHER OPTIONAL ADD-ON PRODUCTS OR SERVICES TO GET FINANCING, TO GET CERTAIN FINANCING TERMS, OR TO GET CERTAIN TERMS FOR THE SALE OF A VEHICLE.

IT IS UNLAWFUL TO REQUIRE OR ATTEMPT TO REQUIRE THE PURCHASE OF THIS GAP WAIVER OR ANY OTHER OPTIONAL ADD-ON PRODUCTS OR SERVICES.

(5) A person that sells a guaranteed asset protection waiver subject to this chapter shall not do either of the following:

(A) Charge more for the guaranteed asset protection waiver than 4 percent of the amount the buyer finances under a conditional sale contract.

(B) Sell a guaranteed asset protection waiver if one of the following applies:

(i) The amount financed through the conditional sale contract exceeds a maximum dollar amount covered by the guaranteed asset protection waiver.

(ii) The conditional sale contract's loan-to-value ratio at the contracting date exceeds the maximum loan-to-value ratio covered by the guaranteed asset protection waiver, unless the terms of the guaranteed asset protection waiver conspicuously disclose the maximum loan-to-value ratio limitation, including the method by which the limitation is applied, and the buyer is informed in a writing, acknowledged by the buyer, that the amount financed in the buyer's conditional sale contract exceeds the waiver's maximum loan-to-value limitation and therefore the waiver will not cover the total amount owed on the conditional sale contract. As used in this subclause, "loan-to-value ratio" means the total amount financed through a conditional sale contract as a percentage of the manufacturer suggested retail price for a new motor vehicle or the average retail value for a used motor vehicle, as determined by a nationally recognized pricing guide, as defined in paragraph (2) of subdivision (c) of Section 11950 of the Vehicle Code.

(iii) The amount financed through a conditional sale contract is less than 70 percent of the manufacturer suggested retail price for a new motor vehicle or the average retail value for a used motor vehicle, as determined by a nationally recognized pricing guide, as defined in paragraph (2) of subdivision (c) of Section 11950 of the Vehicle Code.

(6) Notwithstanding any provision in any conditional sale contract for the sale of a motor vehicle to the contrary, when communicating in writing an itemized contract balance to the buyer, including a payoff letter, payoff quote, or any written notice required under subdivision (a) of Section 2983.2 of this code or subdivision (b) of Section 22328 of the Financial Code, the holder of a conditional sale contract that includes a guaranteed asset protection waiver shall do either of the following:

(A) Individually identify as a credit or refund available to the buyer the unearned portion of all guaranteed asset protection waiver charges paid by the buyer as of the date of the communication on a pro rata basis.

(B) Conspicuously state that a buyer who purchased a guaranteed asset protection waiver is generally entitled to a refund of the unearned portion of the guaranteed asset protection waiver charges on a pro rata basis upon early termination of their conditional sale contract or cancellation of the guaranteed asset protection waiver, and that the buyer should contact the administrator identified in the buyer's guaranteed asset protection waiver, or any other appropriate person designated by the holder, for identification of the amount of such a refund available to the buyer at that time.

(b)(1) A guaranteed asset protection waiver terminates no later than the earliest of the following events:

(A) Cancellation of the guaranteed asset protection waiver by the buyer, as provided by paragraph (4).

(B) Payment in full by the buyer of the conditional sale contract.

(C) Expiration of any redemption and reinstatement periods after a repossession or surrender of the motor vehicle specified in the conditional sale contract pursuant to subdivision (a) of Section 2983.2.

(D) Upon total loss or unrecovered theft of the motor vehicle specified in the conditional sale contract, after the holder has applied all applicable benefits required under the guaranteed asset protection waiver.

(E) Upon any other event that occurs earlier than the events listed in subparagraphs (A) to (D), inclusive, as specified in the guaranteed asset protection waiver.

(2) Subject to paragraph (3), upon termination of a guaranteed asset protection waiver, the buyer is entitled to a refund as follows:

(A) If the termination occurs within 30 days after the date the buyer purchased the guaranteed asset protection waiver, the buyer is entitled to a full refund of the guaranteed asset protection waiver charges plus all finance charges attributable to the guaranteed asset protection waiver.

(B)(i) If the termination occurs later than 30 days after the date the buyer purchased the guaranteed asset protection waiver, the buyer is entitled to a refund of the unearned guaranteed asset protection waiver charges, which shall be calculated on a pro rata basis.

(ii) For the purposes of this subparagraph, "calculating a refund on a pro rata basis" shall require multiplying the total dollar amount of guaranteed asset protection waiver charges by the quotient of the number of calendar days from the termination date to the conditional sale contract's original full term date, including the termination date as a full calendar day, divided by the total number of calendar days in the conditional sale contract's original term.

(iii) Notwithstanding clause (ii), if the original full term of the conditional sale contract exceeded the original full term of the guaranteed asset protection waiver as of the date the buyer purchased the guaranteed asset protection waiver, "calculating a refund on a pro rata basis" shall require multiplying the total dollar amount of guaranteed asset protection waiver charges by the quotient of the number of calendar days from the termination date to the guaranteed asset protection waiver's original full term date, including the termination date as a full calendar day, divided by the total number of calendar days in the guaranteed asset protection waiver's original term.

(C) No refund is required upon termination if there has been a total loss or unrecovered theft of the motor vehicle specified in the conditional sale contract and the buyer has or will receive the benefit of the guaranteed asset protection waiver.

(3) Within 60 business days from the termination of a guaranteed asset protection waiver, the holder shall tender the refund required under paragraph (2) or shall cause to be made the refund under paragraph (2) by instructing in writing the administrator or any other appropriate party to make the refund.

(A) A refund owed under this section may be applied by the holder as a reduction of the amount owed under the conditional sale contract unless the conditional sale contract has been paid in full.

(B) Refunds owed under this section are not exclusive and shall be in addition to any other refunds provided for in this chapter.

(4) A guaranteed asset protection waiver may be canceled by the buyer at any time without penalty.

(5) A cancellation fee, termination fee, or similar fee shall not be assessed in connection with the termination of a guaranteed asset protection waiver.

(6) In addition to the requirements of Section 2984.5, the holder shall maintain records identifying any refund made and tendered under paragraphs (2) and (3) of this subdivision, including those refunds the holder instructed the administrator or other appropriate party to make, and provide electronic access to those records, in response to any subpoena or other administratively or judicially enforceable request, until four years after the date the refund was tendered.

(c) **Any waiver of a provision of this section is contrary to public policy and is void and unenforceable. Leg.H.** Added Stats 2022 ch 283 §4 (AB 2311), effective January 1, 2023. Amended Stats 2023 ch 478 §8 (AB 1756), effective January 1, 2024; Stats 2024 ch 853 §16 (AB 3281), effective January 1, 2025.

§2983. Unenforceable contract; Recovery by buyer

(a) Except as provided in subdivision (b), if the seller, except as the result of an accidental or bona fide error in computation, violates any provision of Section 2981.9, or of subdivision (a), (j), or (k) of Section 2982, the conditional sale contract shall not be enforceable, except by a bona fide purchaser, assignee, or pledgee for value, or until after the violation is corrected as provided in Section 2984, and, if the violation is not corrected, the buyer may recover from the seller the total amount paid, pursuant to the terms of the contract, by the buyer to the seller or his or her assignee. The amount recoverable for property traded in as all or part of the downpayment shall be equal to the agreed cash value of the property as the value appears on the conditional sale contract or the fair market value of the property as of the time the contract is made, whichever is greater.

(b) A conditional sale contract executed or entered into on or after January 1, 2012, shall not be made unenforceable solely because of a violation by the seller of paragraph (2) or (5) of subdivision (a) of Section 2982. In addition to any other remedies that may be available, the buyer is entitled to any actual damages sustained as a result of a violation of those provisions. Nothing in this subdivision affects any legal rights, claims, or remedies otherwise available under law. **Leg.H.** Added Stats 1961 ch 1626 §4, effective January 1, 1962. Amended Stats 1967 ch 815 §1; Stats 1979 ch 805 §23; Stats 1981 ch 1075 §18, operative October 1, 1982; Stats 2011 ch 526 §2 (AB 238), effective October 7, 2011; Stats 2012 ch 162 §11 (SB 1171), effective January 1, 2013.

2011 Note: The Legislature finds and declares as follows:

(a) The Rees-Levering Motor Vehicle Sales and Finance Act (Chapter 2b (commencing with Section 2981) of Title 14 of Part 4 of Division 3 of the Civil Code) sets forth a statutory scheme to regulate the retail sale and financing of motor vehicles. The act contains detailed disclosure requirements intended to protect the consuming public and includes provisions that render a conditional sale contract unenforceable if any of those disclosure requirements are violated, regardless of the nature of the disclosure violation or any consumer harm.

(b) It is the intent of the Legislature in enacting this act to limit the contract unenforceability remedies of the Rees-Levering Motor Vehicle Sales and Finance Act for certain disclosure violations that involve fees paid by a vehicle purchaser to the state. It is not the intent of the Legislature in enacting this act to relieve a seller from making full and accurate contract disclosures, or to limit other consumer remedies for any disclosure violation. Stats 2011 ch 526 (AB 238) §1.

§2983.1. Penalties for certain violations

(a) If the seller or holder of a conditional sale contract, except as the result of an accidental or bona fide error of computation, violates any provision of subdivision (l) of Section 2982, the buyer may recover from the person three times the amount of any finance charge paid to that person.

(b) If a holder of a conditional sale contract that includes a guaranteed asset protection waiver, except as the result of an accidental or bona fide error of computation, violates any provision of subdivision (b) of Section 2982.12, the buyer may recover from the holder three times the amount of any guaranteed asset protection charges paid.

(c) Except as provided in subdivision (f), if a holder acquires a conditional sale contract without actual knowledge of the violation by the seller of Section 2981.9, or of subdivision (a), (j), or (k) of Section 2982, the contract shall be valid and enforceable by the holder except the buyer is excused from payment of the unpaid finance charge, unless the violation is corrected as provided in Section 2984.

(d) Except as provided in subdivision (f), if a holder acquires a conditional sale contract with knowledge of a violation of Section 2981.9, or of subdivision (a), (j), or (k) of Section 2982, the conditional sale contract shall not be enforceable except by a bona fide purchaser, assignee, or pledgee for value, or unless the violation is corrected as provided in Section 2984, and, if the violation is not corrected, the buyer may recover the amounts specified in Section 2983 from the person to whom payment was made.

(e) When a conditional sale contract is not enforceable under Section 2983 or this section, the buyer may elect to retain the motor vehicle and continue the contract in force, or may, with reasonable diligence, elect to rescind the contract and return the motor vehicle. The value of the motor vehicle returned shall be credited as restitution by the buyer without any decrease that results from the passage of time in the cash price of the motor vehicle as the price appears on the conditional sale contract.

(f) A conditional sale contract executed or entered into on or after January 1, 2012, shall not be made unenforceable, and the buyer shall not be excused from payment of any finance charge, solely because of a violation by the seller of paragraph (2) or (5) of subdivision (a) of Section 2982. In addition to any other remedies that may be available, the buyer is entitled to any actual damages sustained as a result of a violation of those provisions. Nothing in this subdivision affects any legal rights, claims, or remedies otherwise available under law. **Leg.H.** Added Stats 1961 ch 1626 §4 p 3538, effective January 1, 1962. Amended Stats 1979 ch 805 §24; Stats 1981 ch 1075 §19, operative October 1, 1982; Stats 2011 ch 526 §3 (AB 238), effective October 7, 2011; Stats 2022 ch 283 §5 (AB 2311), effective January 1, 2023.

2011 Note: The Legislature finds and declares as follows:

(a) The Rees-Levering Motor Vehicle Sales and Finance Act (Chapter 2b (commencing with Section 2981) of Title 14 of Part 4 of Division 3 of the Civil Code) sets forth a statutory scheme to regulate the retail sale and financing of motor vehicles. The act contains detailed disclosure requirements intended to protect the consuming public and includes provisions that render a conditional sale contract unenforceable if any of those disclosure requirements are violated, regardless of the nature of the disclosure violation or any consumer harm.

(b) It is the intent of the Legislature in enacting this act to limit the contract unenforceability remedies of the Rees-Levering Motor Vehicle Sales and Finance Act for certain disclosure violations that involve fees paid by a vehicle purchaser to the state. It is not the intent of the Legislature in enacting this act to relieve a seller from making full and accurate contract disclosures, or to limit other consumer remedies for any disclosure violation. Stats 2011 ch 526 (AB 238) §1.

§2983.2. Notice of intent to dispose of repossessed or surrendered motor vehicle; Accounting regarding disposition

(a) Except where the motor vehicle has been seized as described in paragraph (6) of subdivision (b) of Section 2983.3, any provision in any conditional sale contract for the sale of a motor vehicle to the contrary notwithstanding, at least 15 days' written notice of intent to dispose of a repossessed or surrendered motor vehicle shall be given to all persons liable on the contract. The notice shall be personally served or shall be sent by certified mail, return receipt requested, or first-class mail, postage prepaid, directed to the last known address of the persons liable on the contract. If those persons are married to each other, and, according to the most recent records of the seller or holder of the contract, reside at the same address, one notice addressed to both persons at that address is sufficient. Except as otherwise provided in Section 2983.8, those persons shall be liable for any deficiency after disposition of the repossessed or surrendered motor vehicle only if the notice prescribed by this section is given within 60 days of repossession or surrender and does all of the following:

(1) Sets forth that those persons shall have a right to redeem the motor vehicle by paying in full the indebtedness evidenced by the contract until the expiration of 15 days from the date of giving or mailing the notice and provides an itemization of the contract balance and of any delinquency, collection or repossession costs and fees and sets forth the computation or estimate of the amount of any credit for unearned finance charges or canceled insurance as of the date of the notice.

(2) States either that there is a conditional right to reinstate the contract until the expiration of 15 days from the date of giving or mailing the notice and all the conditions precedent thereto or that there is no right of reinstatement and provides a statement of reasons therefor.

(3) States that, upon written request, the seller or holder shall extend for an additional 10 days the redemption period or, if entitled to the conditional right of reinstatement, both the redemption and reinstatement periods. The seller or holder shall provide the proper form for applying for the extensions with the substance of the form being limited to the extension request, spaces for the requesting party to sign and date the form, and instructions that it must be personally served or sent by certified or registered mail, return receipt requested, to a person or office and address designated by the seller or holder and received before the expiration of the initial redemption and reinstatement periods.

(4) Discloses the place at which the motor vehicle will be returned to those persons upon redemption or reinstatement.

(5) Designates the name and address of the person or office to whom payment shall be made.

(6) States the seller's or holder's intent to dispose of the motor vehicle upon the expiration of 15 days from the date of giving or mailing the notice, or if by mail and either the place of deposit in the mail or the place of address is outside of this state, the period shall be 20 days instead of 15 days, and further, that upon written request to extend the redemption period and any applicable reinstatement period for 10 days, the seller or holder shall without further notice extend the period accordingly.

(7) Informs those persons that upon written request, the seller or holder will furnish a written accounting regarding the disposition of the motor vehicle as provided for in subdivision (b). The seller or holder shall advise them that this request must be personally served or sent first-class mail, postage prepaid, or certified mail, return receipt requested, to a person or office and address designated by the seller or holder.

(8) Includes notice, in at least 10-point bold type if the notice is printed, reading as follows: "NOTICE. YOU MAY BE SUBJECT TO SUIT AND LIABILITY IF THE AMOUNT OBTAINED UPON DISPOSITION OF THE VEHICLE IS INSUFFICIENT TO PAY THE CONTRACT BALANCE AND ANY OTHER AMOUNTS DUE."

(9) Informs those persons that upon the disposition of the motor vehicle, they will be liable for the deficiency balance plus interest at the contract rate, or at the legal rate of interest pursuant to Section 3289 if there is no contract rate of interest, from the date of disposition of the motor vehicle to the date of entry of judgment.

The notice prescribed by this section shall not affect the discretion of the court to strike out an unconscionable interest rate in the contract for which the notice is required, nor affect the court in its determination of whether the rate is unconscionable.

(b) Unless automatically provided to the buyer within 45 days after the disposition of the motor vehicle, the seller or holder shall provide to any person liable on the contract within 45 days after their written request, if the request is made within one year after the disposition, a written accounting regarding the disposition. The accounting shall itemize:

(1) The gross proceeds of the disposition.

(2) The reasonable and necessary expenses incurred for retaking, holding, preparing for and conducting the sale and to the extent provided for in the agreement and not prohibited by law, reasonable attorney fees and legal expenses incurred by the seller or holder in retaking the motor vehicle from any person not a party to the contract.

(3) The satisfaction of indebtedness secured by any subordinate lien or encumbrance on the motor vehicle if written notification of demand therefor is received before distribution of the proceeds is completed. If requested by the seller or holder, the holder of a subordinate lien or encumbrance must seasonably furnish reasonable proof of its interest, and unless it does so, the seller or holder need not comply with its demand.

(c) In all sales which result in a surplus, the seller or holder shall furnish an accounting as provided in subdivision (b) whether or not requested by the buyer. Any surplus shall be returned to the buyer within 45 days after the sale is conducted.

(d) This section does not apply to a loan made by a lender licensed under Division 9 (commencing with Section 22000) of the Financial Code. **Leg.H.** Added Stats 1977 ch 777 §3, effective September 13, 1977, operative January 1, 1978. Amended Stats 1985 ch 226 §2; Stats 1987 ch 448 §4; Stats 1988 ch 1092 §3; Stats 1996 ch 124 §9 (AB 3470) (ch 313 prevails), ch 313 §1 (SB 1639); Stats 2019 ch 497 §28 (AB 991), effective January 1, 2020.

Prior Law: Former §2983.2, similar to the present section, was added Stats 1961 ch 1626 §4, effective January 1, 1962, amended Stats 1965 ch 804 §1, operative March 15, 1966, Stats 1967 ch 1144 §1, Stats 1976 ch 1265 §3, Stats 1977 ch 777 §2, effective September 13, 1977, and repealed, effective January 1, 1978, by its own terms.

§2983.3. Acceleration of maturity or repossession of vehicle; Reinstatement of contract

(a)(1) In the absence of default in the performance of any of the buyer's obligations under the contract, the seller or holder may not accelerate the maturity of any part or all of the amount due thereunder or repossess the motor vehicle.

(2) Neither the act of filing a petition commencing a case for bankruptcy under Title 11 of the United States Code by the buyer or other individual liable on the contract nor the status of either of those persons as a debtor in bankruptcy constitutes a default in the performance of any of the buyer's obligations under the contract, and neither may be used as a basis for accelerating the maturity of any part or all of the amount due under the contract or for repossessing the motor vehicle. A provision of a contract that states that the act of filing a petition commencing a case for bankruptcy under Title 11 of the United States Code by the buyer or other individual liable on the contract or the status of either of those persons as a debtor in bankruptcy is a default is void and unenforceable.

(b) If after default by the buyer, the seller or holder repossesses or voluntarily accepts surrender of the motor vehicle, any person liable on the contract shall have a right to reinstate the contract and the seller or holder shall not accelerate the maturity of any part or all of the contract prior to expiration of the right to reinstate, unless the seller or holder reasonably and in good faith determines that any of the following has occurred:

(1) The buyer or any other person liable on the contract by omission or commission intentionally provided false or misleading information of material importance on the buyer's or other person's credit application.

(2) The buyer, any other person liable on the contract, or any permissive user in possession of the motor vehicle, in order to avoid repossession has concealed the motor vehicle or removed it from the state.

(3) The buyer, any other person liable on the contract, or any permissive user in possession of the motor vehicle, has committed or threatens to commit acts of destruction, or has failed to take care of the motor vehicle in a reasonable manner, so that the motor vehicle has become substantially impaired in value, or the buyer, any other person liable on the contract, or any nonoccasional permissive user in possession of the motor vehicle has failed to take care of the motor vehicle in a reasonable manner, so that the motor vehicle may become substantially impaired in value.

(4) The buyer or any other person liable on the contract has committed, attempted to commit, or threatened to commit criminal acts of violence or bodily harm against an agent, employee, or officer of the seller or holder in connection with the seller's or holder's repossession of or attempt to repossess the motor vehicle.

(5) The buyer has knowingly used the motor vehicle, or has knowingly permitted it to be used, in connection with the commission of a criminal offense, other than an infraction, as a consequence of which the motor vehicle has been seized by a federal, state, or local agency or authority pursuant to federal, state, or local law.

(6) The motor vehicle has been seized by a federal, state, or local public agency or authority pursuant to (A) Section 1324 of Title 8 of the United States Code or Part 274 of Title 8 of the Code of Federal

Regulations, (B) Section 881 of Title 21 of the United States Code or Part 9 of Title 28 of the Code of Federal Regulations, or (C) other federal, state, or local law, including regulations, and, pursuant to that other law, the seizing authority, as a precondition to the return of the motor vehicle to the seller or holder, prohibits the return of the motor vehicle to the buyer or other person liable on the contract or any third person claiming the motor vehicle by or through them or otherwise effects or requires the termination of the property rights in the motor vehicle of the buyer or other person liable on the contract or claimants by or through them.

(c) Exercise of the right to reinstate the contract shall be limited to once in any 12-month period and twice during the term of the contract.

(d) The provisions of this subdivision cover the method by which a contract shall be reinstated with respect to curing events of default which were a ground for repossession or occurred subsequent to repossession:

(1) When the default is the result of the buyer's failure to make any payment due under the contract, the buyer or any other person liable on the contract shall make the defaulted payments and pay any applicable delinquency charges.

(2) When the default is the result of the buyer's failure to keep and maintain the motor vehicle free from all encumbrances and liens of every kind, the buyer or any other person liable on the contract shall either satisfy all encumbrances and liens or, in the event the seller or holder satisfies the encumbrances and liens, the buyer or any other person liable on the contract shall reimburse the seller or holder for all reasonable costs and expenses incurred therefor.

(3) When the default is the result of the buyer's failure to keep and maintain insurance on the motor vehicle, the buyer or any other person liable on the contract shall either obtain the insurance or, in the event the seller or holder has obtained the insurance, the buyer or any other person liable on the contract shall reimburse the seller or holder for premiums paid and all reasonable costs and expenses, including, but not limited to, any finance charge in connection with the premiums permitted by Section 2982.8, incurred therefor.

(4) When the default is the result of the buyer's failure to perform any other obligation under the contract, unless the seller or holder has made a good faith determination that the default is so substantial as to be incurable, the buyer or any other person liable on the contract shall either cure the default or, if the seller or holder has performed the obligation, reimburse the seller or holder for all reasonable costs and expenses incurred in connection therewith.

(5) Additionally, the buyer or any other person liable on the contract shall, in all cases, reimburse the seller or holder for all reasonable and necessary collection and repossession costs and fees actually paid by the seller or holder, including attorney's fees and legal expenses expended in retaking and holding the vehicle.

(e) If the seller or holder denies the right to reinstatement under subdivision (b) or paragraph (4) of subdivision (d), the seller or holder shall have the burden of proof that the denial was justified in that it was reasonable and made in good faith. If the seller or holder fails to sustain the burden of proof, the seller or holder shall not be entitled to a deficiency, but it shall not be presumed that the buyer is entitled to damages by reason of the failure of the seller or holder to sustain the burden of proof.

(f) This section does not apply to a loan made by a lender licensed under Division 9 (commencing with Section 22000) of the Financial Code. **Leg.H.** Added Stats 1961 ch 1626 §4 p 3539, effective January 1, 1962. Amended Stats 1976 ch 1265 §4; Stats 1985 ch 226 §3; Stats 1986 ch 1236 §1; Stats 1987 ch 448 §5; Stats 2019 ch 497 §29 (AB 991), effective January 1, 2020; Stats 2021 ch 401 §2 (AB 1578), effective January 1, 2022; Stats 2022 ch 716 §1 (SB 1099), effective January 1, 2023.

§2983.35. Notice of delinquency to cosigner

(a) If a creditor has requested a cosigner as a condition of granting credit to any person for the purpose of acquisition of a motor vehicle, the creditor or holder shall give the cosigner a written notice of delinquency prior to the repossession of the motor vehicle if the motor vehicle is to be repossessed pursuant to the motor vehicle credit agreement. The written notice of delinquency shall be personally served or shall be sent by certified mail, return receipt requested, or first-class mail, postage prepaid, directed to the last known address of the cosigner. If the last known address of the buyer and the cosigner are the same, a single written notice of delinquency given to both the borrower and cosigner prior to repossession satisfies the cosigner notice requirement of this section.

(b) A creditor or holder who fails to comply with this section may not recover any costs associated with the repossession of the vehicle from the cosigner.

(c) This section applies to any motor vehicle credit agreement, notwithstanding Section 2982.5.

(d) The following definitions govern the construction of this section.

(1) "Cosigner" means a buyer who executes a motor vehicle credit agreement but does not in fact receive possession of the motor vehicle that is the subject of the agreement.

(2) "Creditor" means a seller or lender described in paragraph (4).

(3) "Holder" means any other person who is entitled to enforce the motor vehicle credit agreement.

(4) "Motor vehicle credit agreement" means any conditional sales contract as defined in Section 2981 and any contract or agreement in which a lender gives value to enable a purchaser to acquire a motor vehicle and in which the lender obtains a security interest in the motor vehicle. **Leg.H.** Added Stats 1996 ch 313 §2 (SB 1639).

§2983.37. Obligations of buy-here-pay-here dealer; Violation as misdemeanor

(a) After a sale of a vehicle under this chapter, a buy-here-pay-here dealer, as defined in Section 241 of the Vehicle Code, shall not do any of the following:

(1) Utilize electronic tracking technology to obtain or record the location of the vehicle, unless the buyer is expressly made aware of the existence and use of the tracking technology by the buy-here-pay-here dealer, the buyer's written consent is obtained, and either subparagraph (A) or (B), or both, apply:

(A) The electronic tracking technology is used solely to verify and maintain the operational status of the tracking technology, to repossess the vehicle, or to locate the vehicle to service the loan or keep the loan current.

(B) The electronic tracking technology is used solely for any optional service to the buyer and both of the following conditions are met:

(i) The agreement to utilize electronic tracking technology for the optional service is separate from the purchase and sale agreement, is not a condition of the purchase or sale agreement for the vehicle, and is executed after the completion of the purchase or sale agreement for the vehicle.

(ii) The buyer is permitted to cancel the optional service at any point in the future without affecting the sale of the vehicle, and is informed of his or her ability to do so.

(2) Disable the vehicle by using starter interrupt technology, unless the buy-here-pay-here dealer complies with all of the following provisions:

(A) Notifies the buyer in writing at the time of the sale that the vehicle is equipped with starter interrupt technology, which the buy-here-pay-here dealer can use to shut down the vehicle remotely.

(B) The written disclosure provided to the buyer at the time of sale informs the buyer that a warning will be provided five days before the use of the starter interrupt technology for all weekly payment term contracts and 10 days before the use of starter interrupt technology on all other contracts, and a final warning will be provided no less than 48 hours before the use of the starter interrupt technology to shut down the vehicle remotely and discloses the manner and method in which that warning will occur. The dealer shall offer the buyer a choice of warning methods, including warning from the device, telephone call, email, or text message, if available, provided that the warning method does not violate applicable state or federal law.

(C) The written disclosure provided to the buyer at the time of sale informs the buyer that in the event of an emergency, the buyer will be provided with the ability to start a dealer-disabled vehicle for no less than 24 hours after the vehicle's initial disablement.

(b) A buy-here-pay-here dealer shall not require the buyer to make payments to the seller in person. For purposes of this subdivision, "payments" does not include the downpayment. If the buyer tenders timely payment of a deferred downpayment, the dealer shall not repossess the vehicle or impose any other charge or penalty on the grounds that the payment was not made in person.

(c) Each violation of this section is a misdemeanor punishable by a fine not exceeding two thousand dollars ($2,000). **Leg.H.** Added Stats 2012 ch

740 §3 (AB 1447), effective January 1, 2013. Amended Stats 2015 ch 179 §1 (AB 265), effective January 1, 2016.

§2983.4. Award of attorney's fees and costs to prevailing party

Reasonable attorney's fees and costs shall be awarded to the prevailing party in any action on a contract or purchase order subject to the provisions of this chapter regardless of whether the action is instituted by the seller, holder or buyer. Where the defendant alleges in his answer that he tendered to the plaintiff the full amount to which he was entitled, and thereupon deposits in court, for the plaintiff, the amount so tendered, and the allegation is found to be true, then the defendant is deemed to be a prevailing party within the meaning of this section. **Leg.H.** Added Stats 1961 ch 1626 §4 p 3539, effective January 1, 1962. Amended Stats 1976 ch 1285 §5.

§2983.5. Equities and defenses affecting assignee

(a) An assignee of the seller's right is subject to all equities and defenses of the buyer against the seller, notwithstanding an agreement to the contrary, but the assignee's liability may not exceed the amount of the debt owing to the assignee at the time of the assignment.

(b) The assignee shall have recourse against the seller to the extent of any liability incurred by the assignee pursuant to this section regardless of whether the assignment was with or without recourse. **Leg.H.** Added Stats 1961 ch 1626 §4, effective January 1, 1962. Amended Stats 1965 ch 327 §1; Stats 1971 ch 999 §2; Stats 1975 ch 66 §2.

§2983.6. Violation declared misdemeanor

Any person who shall willfully violate any provision of this chapter shall be guilty of a misdemeanor. **Leg.H.** Added Stats 1968 ch 1338 §3 p 2558.

§2983.7. Prohibited contractual provisions

No conditional sale contract shall contain any provision by which:

(a) The buyer agrees not to assert against the seller a claim or defense arising out of the sale or agrees not to assert against an assignee such a claim or defense.

(b) A power of attorney is given to confess judgment in this state, or an assignment of wages is given; provided, that nothing herein contained shall prohibit the giving of an assignment of wages contained in a separate instrument pursuant to Section 300 of the Labor Code.

(c) The buyer waives any right of action against the seller or holder of the contract or other person acting on his behalf, for any illegal act committed in the collection of payments under the contract or in the repossession of the motor vehicle.

(d) The buyer executes a power of attorney appointing the seller or holder of the contract, or other person acting on his behalf, as the buyer's agent in the collection of payments under the contract or in the repossession of the motor vehicle.

(e) The buyer relieves the seller from liability for any legal remedies which the buyer may have against the seller under the contract or any separate instrument executed in connection therewith.

(f) The seller or holder of the contract is given the right to commence action on a contract under the provisions of this chapter in a county other than the county in which the contract was in fact signed by the buyer, the county in which the buyer resides at the commencement of the action, the county in which the buyer resided at the time the contract was entered into, or in the county in which the motor vehicle purchased pursuant to such contract is permanently garaged. **Leg.H.** Added Stats 1968 ch 1288 §1 p 2428.

§2983.8. Prohibition of deficiency judgment after sale of mobilehome or sale or other disposition of motor vehicle

Notwithstanding Section 2983.2 or any other provision of law, no deficiency judgment shall lie in any event in any of the following instances:

(a) After any sale of any mobilehome for which a permit is required pursuant to Section 35780 or 35790 of the Vehicle Code for failure of the purchaser to complete his or her conditional sale contract given to the seller to secure payment of the balance of the purchase price of such mobilehome. The provisions of this subdivision shall not apply in the event there is substantial damage to the mobilehome other than wear and tear from normal usage. This subdivision shall apply only to contracts entered into on or after the effective date of the act that enacted this subdivision and before July 1, 1981.

(b) After any sale or other disposition of a motor vehicle unless the court has determined that the sale or other disposition was in conformity with the provisions of this chapter and the relevant provisions of Division 9 (commencing with Section 9101) of the Commercial Code, including Sections 9610, 9611, 9612, 9613, 9614, 9615, and 9626. The determination may be made upon an affidavit unless the court requires a hearing in the particular case. **Leg.H.** Added Stats 1972 ch 1001 §3. Amended Stats 1980 ch 1149 §10; Stats 1984 ch 1376 §1; Stats 1999 ch 991 §8 (SB 45), operative July 1, 2001.

§2984. Correction of contract provisions in violation of chapter

Any failure to comply with any provision of this chapter (commencing with Section 2981) may be corrected by the holder, provided, however, that a willful violation may not be corrected unless it is a violation appearing on the face of the contract and is corrected within 30 days of the execution of the contract or within 20 days of its sale, assignment or pledge, whichever is later, provided that the 20-day period shall commence with the initial sale, assignment or pledge of the contract, and provided that any other violation appearing on the face of the contract may be corrected only within such time periods. A correction which will increase the amount of the contract balance or the amount of any installment as such amounts appear on the conditional sale contract shall not be effective unless the buyer concurs in writing to the correction. If notified in writing by the buyer of such a failure to comply with any provision of this chapter, the correction shall be made within 10 days of notice. Where any provision of a conditional sale contract fails to comply with any provision of this chapter, the correction shall be made by mailing or delivering a corrected copy of the contract to the buyer. Any amount improperly collected by the holder from the buyer shall be credited against the indebtedness evidenced by the contract or returned to the buyer. A violation corrected as provided in this section shall not be the basis of any recovery by the buyer or affect the enforceability of the contract by the holder and shall not be deemed to be a substantive change in the agreement of the parties. **Leg.H.** Added Stats 1961 ch 1626 §4, effective January 1, 1962. Amended Stats 1963 ch 838 §1.

§2984.1. Statement in satisfaction of requirements of Vehicle Code

Every conditional sale contract shall contain a statement in contrasting red print in at least 8-point bold type which shall satisfy the requirements of Section 5604 of the Vehicle Code and be signed or initialed by the buyer, as follows:

THE MINIMUM PUBLIC LIABILITY INSURANCE LIMITS PROVIDED IN LAW MUST BE MET BY EVERY PERSON WHO PURCHASES A VEHICLE. IF YOU ARE UNSURE WHETHER OR NOT YOUR CURRENT INSURANCE POLICY WILL COVER YOUR NEWLY ACQUIRED VEHICLE IN THE EVENT OF AN ACCIDENT, YOU SHOULD CONTACT YOUR INSURANCE AGENT.
WARNING:
YOUR PRESENT POLICY MAY NOT COVER COLLISION DAMAGE OR MAY NOT PROVIDE FOR FULL REPLACEMENT COSTS FOR THE VEHICLE BEING PURCHASED. IF YOU DO NOT HAVE FULL COVERAGE, SUPPLEMENTAL COVERAGE FOR COLLISION DAMAGE MAY BE AVAILABLE TO YOU THROUGH YOUR INSURANCE AGENT OR THROUGH THE SELLING DEALER. HOWEVER, UNLESS OTHERWISE SPECIFIED, THE COVERAGE YOU OBTAIN THROUGH THE DEALER PROTECTS ONLY THE DEALER, USUALLY UP TO THE AMOUNT OF THE UNPAID BALANCE REMAINING AFTER THE VEHICLE HAS BEEN REPOSSESSED AND SOLD. FOR ADVICE ON FULL COVERAGE THAT WILL PROTECT YOU IN THE EVENT OF LOSS OR DAMAGE TO YOUR VEHICLE, YOU SHOULD CONTACT YOUR INSURANCE AGENT.
THE BUYER SHALL SIGN TO ACKNOWLEDGE THAT HE/SHE UNDERSTANDS THESE PUBLIC LIABILITY TERMS AND CONDITIONS.
s/s _____.

No person shall print for use as a sales contract form, any form which does not comply with this section. **Leg.H.** Added Stats 1961 ch 1626 §4, effective January 1, 1962. Amended Stats 1965 ch 666 §1; Stats 1974 ch 577 §1; Stats 1988 ch 177 §1.

§2984.2. Title to or lien on property

(a) No conditional sale contract, and no agreement between a seller and a buyer made in connection with a conditional sale contract, may provide for the inclusion of title to or a lien upon any property other than the following:

(1) The motor vehicle which is the subject matter of the sale, including any replacement of that motor vehicle, or accessories, accessions, or replacement of those accessories or accessions, or proceeds thereof.

(2) The proceeds of any insurance policies covering the motor vehicle which are required by the seller or the returned premiums of any such policies if the premiums for such policies are included in the amount financed.

(3) The proceeds of any credit insurance policies which the buyer purchases in connection with the motor vehicle conditional sale contract or the returned premiums of any such policies if the premiums for such policies are included in the amount financed.

(4) The proceeds and returned price of any service contract if the cost of such contract is included in the amount financed.

(b) Subdivision (a) shall not apply to any agreement which meets the requirements of subdivision (b) of Section 2982.5 and otherwise complies with this chapter, nor, with respect to a mobilehome sold prior to July 1, 1981, to any agreement whereby a security interest is taken in real property on which the mobilehome is installed on a foundation system pursuant to Section 18551 of the Health and Safety Code.

(c) A provision in violation of this section shall be void. **Leg.H.** Added Stats 1980 ch 1380 §26, effective October 1, 1980. Amended Stats 1981 ch 134 §6, effective and operative July 1, 1981, ch 1075 §20, operative October 1, 1982; Stats 1987 ch 1043 §1.

Prior Law: Former §2984.2, similar to the present section, was added Stats 1961 ch 1626 §4, effective January 1, 1962, amended Stats 1967 ch 800 §1, Stats 1969 ch 254 §1, Stats 1971 ch 689 §1, Stats 1980 ch 1149 §11, and repealed Stats 1980 ch 1380 §25, effective October 1, 1980.

§2984.3. Acknowledgment; Presumptions

Any acknowledgment by the buyer of delivery of a copy of a conditional sale contract or purchase order and any vehicle purchase proposal and any credit statement that the seller has required or requested the buyer to sign, and that he or she has signed, during the contract negotiations, shall be printed or written in size equal to at least 10-point boldface type and, if contained in the contract, shall appear directly above the space reserved for the buyer's signature or adjacent to any other notices required by law to be placed immediately above the signature space. The buyer's written acknowledgment, conforming to the requirements of this section, of delivery of a completely filled-in copy of the contract, and a copy of the other documents shall be a rebuttable presumption of delivery in any action or proceeding by or against a third party without knowledge to the contrary when he or she acquired his or her interest in the contract. If the third party furnishes the buyer a copy of the documents, or a notice containing the disclosures identified in subdivision (a) of Section 2982, and stating that the buyer shall notify the third party in writing within 30 days if a copy of the documents was not furnished, and that notification is not given, it shall be conclusively presumed in favor of the third party that copies of the documents were furnished as required by this chapter. **Leg.H.** Added Stats 1985 ch 1626 §4, effective January 1, 1962. Amended Stats 1970 ch 1003 §5; Stats 1979 ch 805 §25; Stats 1980 ch 1149 §12; Stats 1993 ch 1092 §3 (AB 431), operative July 1, 1994; Stats 1994 ch 146 §15 (AB 3601).

§2984.4. Jurisdiction and venue; Plaintiff's affidavit

(a) An action on a contract or purchase order under this chapter shall be tried in the superior court in the county where the contract or purchase order was in fact signed by the buyer, where the buyer resided at the time the contract or purchase order was entered into, where the buyer resides at the commencement of the action, or where the motor vehicle purchased pursuant to the contract or purchase order is permanently garaged.

In any action involving multiple claims, or causes of action, venue shall lie in those courts if there is at least one claim or cause of action arising from a contract subject to this chapter.

(b) In the superior court designated as the proper court in subdivision (a), the proper court location for trial of an action under this chapter is the location where the court tries that type of action that is nearest or most accessible to where the contract, conditional sale contract, or purchase order was in fact signed by the buyer, where the buyer resided at the time the contract, conditional sale contract, or purchase order was entered into, where the buyer resides at the commencement of the action, or where the motor vehicle purchased pursuant to the contract is permanently garaged.

Otherwise, any location of the superior court designated as the proper superior court in subdivision (a) is the proper court location for the trial of the action. The court may specify by local rule the nearest or most accessible court location where the court tries that type of case.

(c) In any action subject to this section, concurrently with the filing of the complaint, the plaintiff shall file an affidavit stating facts showing that the action has been commenced in a superior court and court location described in this section as a proper place for the trial of the action. Those facts may be stated in a verified complaint and shall not be stated on information or belief. When that affidavit is filed with the complaint, a copy shall be served with the summons. If a plaintiff fails to file the affidavit or state facts in a verified complaint required by this section, no further proceedings may occur, but the court shall, upon its own motion or upon motion of any party, dismiss the action without prejudice. The court may, on terms that are just, permit the affidavit to be filed subsequent to the filing of the complaint and a copy of the affidavit shall be served on the defendant. The time to answer or otherwise plead shall date from that service. **Leg.H.** Added Stats 1969 ch 724 §1. Amended Stats 1970 ch 725 §2; Stats 1971 ch 1529 §2; Stats 1974 ch 1516 §3, operative January 1, 1977; Stats 1976 ch 1285 §6; Stats 1998 ch 931 §17 (SB 2139), effective September 28, 1998; Stats 2002 ch 806 §2 (AB 3027).

§2984.5. Seller to maintain certain documents for specified length of time

(a) A seller shall maintain the following documents for at least seven years or the length of the conditional sales contract, whichever is longer:

(1) A copy of each buyer's conditional sales contract.

(2) Any documents relied upon by the seller to determine a buyer's creditworthiness, including, but not limited to, any consumer credit report, as defined in Section 1785.3, or any other document containing a buyer's credit score, as defined in Section 1785.15.1.

(3) If the conditional sales contract is sold, assigned, or otherwise transferred, a copy of the terms of that sale, assignment, or transfer.

(b) A seller that unlawfully fails to comply with a court order to produce the documents described in subdivision (a) shall be liable in an action brought by the Attorney General for a civil penalty of five thousand dollars ($5,000) per violation. The penalties provided by this section are in addition to all rights and remedies that are otherwise available under law. **Leg.H.** Added Stats 2003 ch 59 §1 (SB 508).

§2984.6. Subsequent assignment to skip trace, locate or repossess a vehicle; Notice requirements

A holder of a conditional sales contract, purchase order, or security interest, or the agent of a holder, who has received a notice pursuant to Section 7507.6 of the Business and Professions Code, shall not make a subsequent assignment to skip trace, locate, or repossess the vehicle without simultaneously, and in the same manner by which the assignment is given, advising the assignee of the assignment of the information contained in the notice. As used in this section, "assignment" has the same meaning set forth in Section 7500.1 of the Business and Professions Code. **Leg.H.** Added Stats 2007 ch 192 §4 (SB 659), effective September 7, 2007.

CHAPTER 2C
REAL PROPERTY SALES CONTRACTS

Real property sales contract. §2985.
Transfer of real property sales contract and real property. §2985.1.
Prohibition against vendor placing encumbrance on unrecorded real property without consent. §2985.2.
Misappropriation of installment payment under real property sales contract. §2985.3.
Payments to seller for insurance and taxes held in trust. §2985.4.
Required statements to be contained in real property sales contract. §2985.5.
Statement indicating real property division and compliance with Subdivision Map Act. §2985.51.
Right to prepay balance of contract for sale of subdivided land. §2985.6.

§2985. Real property sales contract

(a) A real property sales contract is an agreement in which one party agrees to convey title to real property to another party upon the satisfaction of specified conditions set forth in the contract and that does not require conveyance of title within one year from the date of formation of the contract.

(b) For purposes of this chapter only, a real property sales contract does not include a contract for purchase of an attached residential condominium unit entered into pursuant to a conditional public report issued by the Bureau of Real Estate pursuant to Section 11018.12 of the Business and Professions Code. **Leg.H.** Added Stats 1961 ch 886 §30. Amended Stats 1963 ch 560 §6; Stats 2006 ch 51 §1 (SB 504), effective June 30, 2006; Stats 2013 ch 352 §53 (AB 1317), effective September 26, 2013, operative July 1, 2013.

§2985.1. Transfer of real property sales contract and real property

A real property sales contract may not be transferred by the fee owner of the real property unless accompanied by a transfer of the real property which is the subject of the contract, and real property may not be transferred by the fee owner thereof unless accompanied by an assignment of the contract.

Nothing herein shall be deemed to prohibit the assignment or pledge of a real property sales contract, as security or for the purpose of effecting collection thereon, to the holder of a first lien on the real property which is the subject of the contract without a transfer of the real property or the transfer of a fee title in trust without the concurrent assignment of the sales contract. **Leg.H.** Added Stats 1961 ch 886 §30, effective June 27, 1961. Amended Stats 1963 ch 71 §1.

§2985.2. Prohibition against vendor placing encumbrance on unrecorded real property without consent

Any person, or the assignee of such person, who sells a parcel of land under a sales contract which is not recorded and who thereafter causes an encumbrance or encumbrances not consented to in writing by the parties upon such property in an amount which, together with existing encumbrances thereon exceeds the amount then due under the contract, or under which the aggregate amount of any periodic payments exceeds the periodic payments due on the contract, excluding any pro rata amount for insurance and taxes, shall be guilty of a public offense punishable by a fine not exceeding ten thousand dollars ($10,000), or by imprisonment pursuant to subdivision (h) of Section 1170 of the Penal Code, or in a county jail not exceeding one year, or by both that fine and imprisonment. **Leg.H.** Added Stats 1963 ch 560 §3 p 1441. Amended Stats 1976 ch 1139 §7, operative July 1, 1977; Stats 1983 ch 1092 §69, effective September 27, 1983, operative January 1, 1984; Stats 2011 ch 15 §36 (AB 109), effective April 4, 2011, operative October 1, 2011.

2011 Notes: This act is titled and may be cited as the 2011 Realignment Legislation addressing public safety. Stats. 2011 ch. 15 (AB 109) §1.

This act will become operative no earlier than October 1, 2011, and only upon creation of a community corrections grant program to assist in implementing this act and upon an appropriation to fund the grant program. Stats. 2011 ch. 15 (AB 109) §636; Stats. 2011 ch. 39 (AB 117) §68.

The Community Corrections Grant Program referred to in Stats. 2011 ch. 15 (AB 109) §636, as amended by Stats. 2011 ch. 39 (AB 117) §68, was created by Stats. 2011 ch. 40 (AB 118) §3, operative October 1, 2011.

§2985.3. Misappropriation of installment payment under real property sales contract

Every seller of improved or unimproved real property under a real property sales contract, or his assignee, who knowingly receives an installment payment from the buyer under a real property sales contract at a time when there is then due any payment by the seller, or his assignee, on an obligation secured by an encumbrance on the property subject to the real property sales contract, and who appropriates such payment received from the buyer to a use other than payment of the amount then due on the seller's or assignee's obligation, except to the extent the payment received from the buyer exceeds the amount due from the seller or assignee, is guilty of a public offense punishable by a fine not exceeding ten thousand dollars ($10,000), or by imprisonment pursuant to subdivision (h) of Section 1170 of the Penal Code, or in a county jail not exceeding one year, or by both that fine and imprisonment. **Leg.H.** Added Stats 1963 ch 560 §4 p 1442. Amended Stats 1976 ch 1139 §8, operative July 1, 1977; Stats 1983 ch 1092 §70, effective September 27, 1983, operative January 1, 1984; Stats 2011 ch 15 §37 (AB 109), effective April 4, 2011, operative October 1, 2011.

2011 Notes: This act is titled and may be cited as the 2011 Realignment Legislation addressing public safety. Stats. 2011 ch. 15 (AB 109) §1.

This act will become operative no earlier than October 1, 2011, and only upon creation of a community corrections grant program to assist in implementing this act and upon an appropriation to fund the grant program. Stats. 2011 ch. 15 (AB 109) §636; Stats. 2011 ch. 39 (AB 117) §68.

The Community Corrections Grant Program referred to in Stats. 2011 ch. 15 (AB 109) §636, as amended by Stats. 2011 ch. 39 (AB 117) §68, was created by Stats. 2011 ch. 40 (AB 118) §3, operative October 1, 2011.

§2985.4. Payments to seller for insurance and taxes held in trust

Every seller of improved or unimproved real property under a real property sales contract who receives pro rata payments for insurance and taxes shall hold these amounts in trust for the purpose designated. These amounts shall not be disbursed for any other purpose without the consent of the payor and any person or corporation holding an encumbrance on the property.

This section shall not apply to a state-or federal-supervised assignee of a seller who as agent for the seller receives and disburses payments. **Leg.H.** Added Stats 1963 ch 560 §5.

§2985.5. Required statements to be contained in real property sales contract

Every real property sales contract entered into after January 1, 1966, shall contain a statement of:

(a) The number of years required to complete payment in accordance with the terms of the contract.

(b) The basis upon which the tax estimate is made. **Leg.H.** Added Stats 1965 ch 1214 §1 p 3034.

§2985.51. Statement indicating real property division and compliance with Subdivision Map Act

(a) Every real property sales contract entered into on and after January 1, 1978, where the real property that is the subject of such contract resulted from a division of real property occurring on or after January 1, 1978, shall contain or have attached thereto a statement indicating the fact that the division creating the parcel or parcels to be conveyed:

(1) Was made in compliance with the provisions of the Subdivision Map Act, Division 2 (commencing with Section 66410) of Title 7 of the Government Code and local ordinances adopted pursuant thereto, and in such event the statement shall expressly refer to the location, in the records of the county recorder for the county in which the real property is located, of a previously recorded certificate of compliance or conditional certificate of compliance issued pursuant to Section 66499.35 of the Government Code with respect to the real property being sold, or the statement shall describe the real property to be conveyed as an entire lot or parcel by referencing the recorded final or parcel map creating the parcel or parcels to be conveyed and such description shall constitute a certificate of compliance as set forth in subdivision (d) of Section 66499.35 of the Government Code. Provided, however, where reference is made to a recorded parcel map and the approval of such map was conditioned upon the construction of specified offsite and onsite improvements as a precondition to the issuance of a permit or grant of approval for the development of such parcel and the construction of the improvements has not been completed as of the date of execution of the real property sales contract, then the statement shall expressly set forth all such required offsite and onsite improvements; or

(2) Was exempt from the provisions of the Subdivision Map Act and local ordinances adopted pursuant thereto, and in such event the statement shall expressly set forth the basis for such exemption; or

(3) Was the subject of a waiver of the provisions of the Subdivision Map Act and local ordinances adopted pursuant thereto, and in such event the contract shall have attached thereto a copy of the document issued by the local agency granting the waiver. Provided, however, where the granting of the waiver was conditioned upon the construction of specified offsite and onsite improvements as a precondition to the issuance of a permit or grant of approval for the development of the parcel and the construction of the improvements has not been completed as of the date of execution of the real property sales contract, then such statement shall expressly set forth all such required offsite and onsite improvements; or

(4) Was not subject to the provisions of the Subdivision Map Act and local ordinances adopted pursuant thereto, and in such event the statement shall expressly set forth the basis for the nonapplicability of the Subdivision Map Act to the division.

(b) Every real property sales contract entered into after January 1, 1978, where the real property that is the subject of such contract resulted from a division of real property occurring prior to January 1, 1978, shall:

(1) Contain or have attached thereto a signed statement by the vendor that the parcel or parcels which are the subject of the contract have been

created in compliance with, or a waiver has been granted with respect to, the provisions of the Subdivision Map Act, Division 2 (commencing with Section 66410) of Title 7 of The Government Code and local ordinances adopted pursuant thereto, or any prior law regulating the division of land, or, were exempt from or not otherwise subject to any such law at the time of their creation. Provided, however, where the division creating the parcel or parcels being conveyed was by means of a parcel map, or in the event that a waiver of the provisions of the Subdivision Map Act has been granted, and the approval of the parcel map or the granting of the waiver was conditioned upon the construction of specified offsite and onsite improvements as a precondition to the issuance of a permit or grant of approval for the development of such parcel and the construction of the improvements has not been completed as of the date of execution of the real property sales contract, then such contract shall expressly set forth all such required offsite and onsite improvements.

(2) In lieu of the above, the vendor may include in the real property sales contract a description of the real property being conveyed as an entire lot or parcel by referencing the recorded final or parcel map creating the parcel or parcels being conveyed and such description shall constitute a certificate of compliance as set forth in subdivision (d) of Section 66499.35 of the Government Code. Provided, however, where reference is made to a recorded parcel map, or in the event that a waiver of the provisions of the Subdivision Map Act has been granted, and the approval of the parcel map or the granting of the waiver was conditioned upon the construction of specified offsite and onsite improvements as a precondition to the issuance of a permit or grant of approval for the development of such parcel and the construction of the improvements has not been completed as of the date of execution of the real property sales contract, then such contract shall expressly set forth all such required offsite and onsite improvements.

(3) Notwithstanding paragraphs (1) and (2), in the event that the parcel or parcels which are the subject of the real property sales contract were not created in compliance with the provisions of the Subdivision Map Act, Division 2 (commencing with Section 66410) of Title 7 of the Government Code and local ordinances adopted pursuant thereto, or any other prior law regulating the division of land, and were not exempt from, or were otherwise subject to any such law at the time of their creation, the real property sales contract shall contain a statement signed by the vendor and vendee acknowledging such fact. In addition, the vendor shall attach to the real property sales contract a conditional certificate of compliance issued pursuant to Section 66499.35 of the Government Code.

(c) In the event that the parcel or parcels which are the subject of the real property sales contract are found not to have been created in compliance with, or a waiver has not been granted with respect to, the provisions of the Subdivision Map Act, Division 2 (commencing with Section 66410) of Title 7 of the Government Code, or any other prior law regulating the division of land nor to be exempt from, or otherwise subject to such laws and the vendee has reasonably relied upon the statement of such compliance or exemption made by the vendor, or in the event that the vendor has failed to provide the conditional certificate of compliance as required by paragraph (3) of subdivision (b), and the vendor knew or should have known of the fact of such noncompliance, or lack of exemption, or the failure to provide the conditional certificate of compliance, the vendee, or his successor in interest, shall be entitled to: (1) recover from the vendor or his assigns the amount of all costs incurred by the vendee or his successor in interest in complying with all conditions imposed pursuant to Section 66499.35 of the Government Code; or, (2) the real property sales contract, at the sole option of the vendee, or his successor in interest, shall be voidable and in such event the vendee or his successor in interest shall be entitled to damages from the vendor or his assigns. For purposes of this section, damages shall mean all amounts paid under the real estate sales contract with interest thereon at the rate of 9 percent per annum, and in addition thereto a civil penalty in the amount of five hundred dollars ($500) plus attorney's fees and costs. Any action to enforce the rights of a vendee or his successor in interest shall be commenced within one year of the date of discovery of the failure to comply with the provisions of this section.

(d) Any vendor who willfully violates the provisions of subdivision (a) of this section by knowingly providing a vendee with a false statement of compliance with, exemption from, waiver of, or nonapplicability of, the provisions of the Subdivision Map Act, with respect to the real property that is the subject of the real property sales contract, shall be guilty of a misdemeanor punishable by a fine of not to exceed one thousand dollars ($1,000), or imprisonment for not to exceed six months, or both such fine and imprisonment.

(e) For purposes of this section a real property sales contract is an agreement wherein one party agrees to convey title to unimproved real property to another party upon the satisfaction of specified conditions set forth in the contract and which does not require conveyance of title within one year from the date of formation of the contract. Unimproved real property means real property. upon which no permanent structure intended for human occupancy or commercial use is located.

(f) The provisions of this section shall not apply to a real property sales contract which, by its terms, requires either a good faith downpayment and a single payment of the balance of the purchase price or a single payment of the purchase price upon completion of the contract, and the provisions of such contract do not require periodic payment of principal or interest. **Leg.H.** Added Stats 1977 ch 1228 §1.

§2985.6. Right to prepay balance of contract for sale of subdivided land

(a) A buyer shall be entitled to prepay all or any part of the balance due on any real property sales contract with respect to the sale of land which has been subdivided into a residential lot or lots which contain a dwelling for not more than four families entered into on or after January 1, 1969; provided, however, that the seller, by an agreement in writing with the buyer, may prohibit prepayment for up to a 12-month period following the sale.

(b) Any waiver by the buyer of the provisions of this section shall be deemed contrary to public policy and shall be unenforceable and void; provided, however, that any such waiver shall in no way affect the validity of the remainder of the contract. **Leg.H.** Added Stats 1968 ch 437 §1. Amended Stats 1969 ch 399 §1; Stats 1978 ch 565 §1.

CHAPTER 2D
VEHICLE LEASING ACT

Definitions. §2985.7.
Disclosures for lease contracts. § 2985.71.
Required provisions in lease contracts. §2985.8.
Required information exceptions. §2985.9.
Lease contract; Prohibited provisions. §2986.3.
Acknowledgment by lessee. §2986.4.
Lease of used vehicle; Refund of excess fees. §2986.5.
Lien on other property. §2986.6.
Rights of assignee of lessor. §2986.10.
Unlawful rebates, discounts, and commissions. §2986.12.
Refund of prepayment. §2986.13.
Lessee's liability on termination of lease contract. §2987.
Lessee to bear risk of vehicle's depreciation. §2988.
Liability of lessor. §2988.5.
Rescission of contract. §2988.7.
Attorney's fees and costs. §2988.9.
Effect of federal civil action. §2989.
Sale of leased vehicle. §2989.2.
Duties of lessor. §2989.4.
Production of lessor's records. §2989.5.
Rules and regulations. §2989.6.
Knowing and wilful violations. §2989.8.
Application of chapter. §2990.
Spanish translation. §2991.
Specified print form. §2992.
Subsequent assignment to skip trace, locate or repossess a vehicle; Notice requirements. §2993.

§2985.7. Definitions

(a) "Motor vehicle" means any vehicle required to be registered under the Vehicle Code. Motor vehicle does not include any trailer which is sold in conjunction with a vessel.

(b) "Lessor" includes "bailor" and is a person who is engaged in the business of leasing, offering to lease or arranging the lease of a motor vehicle under a lease contract.

For the purpose of this subdivision, "person" means an individual, partnership, corporation, limited liability company, estate, trust, cooperative, association or any other legal entity.

(c) "Lessee" includes "bailee" and is a natural person who leases, offers to lease or is offered the lease of a motor vehicle under a lease contract.

(d) "Lease contract" means any contract for or in contemplation of the lease or bailment for the use of a motor vehicle, and the purchase of services incidental thereto, by a natural person for a term exceeding four months, primarily for personal, family or household purposes, whether or not it is agreed that the lessee bear the risk of the motor vehicle's depreciation. Lease contract does not include a lease for agricultural, business or commercial purposes, or to a government or governmental agency or instrumentality.

(e) "Regulation M" means any rule, regulation, or interpretation promulgated by the Board of Governors of the Federal Reserve System under the federal Consumer Leasing Act (15 U.S.C. Secs. 1667–1667e), and any interpretation or approval issued by an official or employee of the Federal Reserve System duly authorized by the board to issue such interpretations or approvals.

(f) "Constant yield method" means the following:

(1) In the case of a periodic payment lease, the method of determining the rent charge portion of each base payment in which the rent charge for each computational period is earned in advance by multiplying the constant rate implicit in the lease contract times the balance subject to rent charge as it declines during the scheduled lease term. At any time during the scheduled term of a periodic payment lease, the balance subject to rent charge is the difference between the adjusted capitalized cost and the sum of (A) all depreciation and other amortized amounts accrued during the preceding computational periods and (B) the first base periodic payment.

(2) In the case of a single payment lease, the method of determining the periodic earning of rent charges in which the rent charge for each computational period is earned in advance by multiplying the constant rate implicit in the lease contract times the balance subject to rent charge as it increases during the scheduled lease term. At any time during the scheduled term of a single payment lease, the balance subject to rent charge is determined by subtracting from the residual value the total rent charge scheduled to be earned over the term of the lease contract and adding to the difference all rent charges accrued during the preceding computational periods.

(3) Periodic rent charge calculations are based on the assumption that the lessor will receive the lease payments on their exact due dates and that the lease does not end before its scheduled termination date. **Leg.H.** Added Stats 1976 ch 1284 §2, operative March 23, 1977. Amended Stats 1984 ch 1114 §4; Stats 1994 ch 1010 §51 (SB 2053); Stats 1997 ch 800 §3 (SB 1291).

Prior Law: Former §2985.7, similar to the present section, was added Stats 1969 ch 1208 §1, and repealed Stats 1976 ch 1284 §2, operative March 23, 1977.

§ 2985.71. Disclosures for lease contracts

(a) Any solicitation to enter into a lease contract that includes any of the following items shall contain the disclosures described in subdivision (b):

(1) The amount of any payment.

(2) A statement of any capitalized cost reduction or other payment required prior to or at consummation or by delivery, if delivery occurs after consummation.

(3) A statement that no capitalized cost reduction or other payment is required prior to or at consummation or by delivery, if delivery occurs after consummation.

(b) A solicitation to enter into a lease contract that includes any item listed in subdivision (a) shall also clearly and conspicuously state all of the following items:

(1) All of the disclosures prescribed by Regulation M set forth in the manner required or permitted by Regulation M, whether or not Regulation M applies to the transaction.

(2) The mileage limit after which mileage charges may accrue and the charge per mile for mileage in excess of the stated mileage limit.

(3) The statement "Plus tax and license" or a substantially similar statement, if amounts due for use tax, license fees, and registration fees are not included in the payments.

(c) No solicitation to aid, promote, or assist directly or indirectly any lease contract may state that a specific lease of any motor vehicle at specific amounts or terms is available unless the lessor usually and customarily leases or will lease that motor vehicle at those amounts or terms.

(d) A failure to comply with the provisions of this section shall not affect the validity of the leasing contract. No owner or employee of any entity, other than the lessor, that serves as a medium in which a lease solicitation appears or through which a lease solicitation is disseminated, shall be liable under this section.

(e) A lessor is not in violation of paragraph (29) of subdivision (a) of Section 1770 because it excludes from the advertised, displayed, or offered lease payment a fee or charge in accordance with paragraph (3) of subdivision (b).

(f) This section shall become operative on July 1, 2024. **Leg.H.** Added Stats 2023 ch 400 §6 (SB 478), effective January 1, 2024, operative July 1, 2024.

§2985.8. Required provisions in lease contracts

(a) A lease contract shall be in writing, and the print portion of the contract shall be printed in at least 8-point type and shall contain in a single document all of the agreements of the lessor and lessee with respect to the obligations of each party.

(b) At the top of the lease contract, a title that contains the words "LEASE CONTRACT" or "LEASE AGREEMENT" shall appear in at least 12-point boldface type.

(c) A lease contract shall disclose all of the following:

(1) All of the information prescribed by Regulation M set forth in the manner required or permitted by Regulation M, whether or not Regulation M applies to the transaction.

(2) A separate statement labeled "Itemization of Gross Capitalized Cost" that shall appear immediately following or directly adjacent to the disclosures required to be segregated by Regulation M. The Itemization of Gross Capitalized Cost shall include all of the following and shall be circumscribed by a line:

(A) The agreed-upon value of the vehicle as equipped at the time of signing the lease.

(B) The agreed-upon value and a description of each accessory and item of optional equipment the lessor agrees to add to the vehicle after signing the lease.

(C) The premium for each policy of insurance.

(D) The amount charged for each service contract.

(E) Any charge for an optional debt cancellation agreement.

(F) Any outstanding prior credit or lease balance.

(G) An itemization by type and agreed-upon value of each good or service included in the gross capitalized cost other than those items included in the disclosures required in subparagraphs (A) to (F), inclusive.

(3) The vehicle identification number of the leased vehicle.

(4) A brief description of each vehicle or other property being traded in and the agreed-upon value of the vehicle or property if the amount due at the time of signing the lease or upon delivery is paid in whole or in part with a net trade-in allowance or the "Itemization of Gross Capitalized Cost" includes any portion of the outstanding prior credit or lease balance from the trade-in property.

(5) The charge, if any, to be retained by the lessor for document processing authorized pursuant to Section 4456.5 of the Vehicle Code, which may not be represented as a governmental fee.

(6) The charge, if any, to electronically register or transfer the vehicle authorized pursuant to Section 4456.5 of the Vehicle Code, which shall not be represented as a governmental fee.

(d) A lease contract shall contain, in at least 8-point boldface type, above the space provided for the lessee's signature and circumscribed by a line, the following notice: "(1) Do not sign this lease before you read it or if it contains any blank spaces to be filled in; (2) You are entitled to a completely filled in copy of this lease; (3) Warning—Unless a charge is included in this lease for public liability or property damage insurance, payment for that coverage is not provided by this lease."

(e) A lease contract shall contain, in at least 8-point boldface type, on the first page of the contract and circumscribed by a line, the following notice.

"THERE IS NO COOLING-OFF PERIOD

California law does not provide for a "cooling off" or other cancellation period for vehicle leases. Therefore, you cannot later cancel this lease simply because you change your mind, decided the vehicle costs too much, or wish you had acquired a different vehicle. You may cancel this lease only with the agreement of the lessor or for legal cause, such as fraud."

(f) A lease contract shall contain, in at least 8-point boldface type, the following notice: "You have the right to return the vehicle, and receive a refund of any payments made if the credit application is not approved, unless nonapproval results from an incomplete application or from incorrect information provided by you."

(g) The lease contract shall be signed by the lessor and lessee, or their authorized representatives, and an exact copy of the fully executed lease contract shall be provided to the lessee at the time of signing.

(h) A motor vehicle shall not be delivered under a lease contract subject to this chapter until the lessor provides to the lessee a fully executed copy of the lease contract.

(i) The lessor shall not obtain the signature of the lessee to a contract when it contains blank spaces to be filled in after it has been signed.

(j) If the lease contract contains a provision that holds the lessee liable for the difference between (1) the adjusted capitalized cost disclosed in the lease contract reduced by the amounts described in subparagraph (A) of paragraph (5) of subdivision (b) of Section 2987 and (2) the settlement proceeds of the lessee's required insurance and deductible in the event of theft or damage to the vehicle that results in a total loss, the lease contract shall contain the following notice in at least 8-point boldface type on the first page of the contract:

"GAP LIABILITY NOTICE

In the event of theft or damage to the vehicle that results in a total loss, there may be a GAP between the amount due upon early termination and the proceeds of your insurance settlement and deductible. THIS LEASE PROVIDES THAT YOU ARE LIABLE FOR THE GAP AMOUNT. Optional coverage for the GAP amount may be offered for an additional price."

(k) This section shall become operative on July 1, 2012. **Leg.H.** Added Stats 2011 ch 329 §6 (AB 1215), effective January 1, 2012, operative July 1, 2012.

Prior Law: Former §2985.8, relating to leasing contract requirements, was added Stats 1969 ch 1208 §1 and repealed Stats 1976 ch 1284 §2, operative March 23, 1977.

Former Sections: Former CC §2985.8 was added in 1997, and became inoperative July 1, 2012, and repealed operative January 1, 2013, by its own provisions. Stats 2011 ch 329 (AB 1215) §5.

Former CC §2985.8 was added in 1976 and repealed Stats 1997 ch 800 §6, operative March 1, 1998.

§2985.81. [Section repealed 1977]

Leg.H. Added Stats 1973 ch 696 §3. Amended Stats 1974 ch 895 §1, ch 1110 §2. Repealed Stats 1976 ch 1284 §1, operative March 23, 1977. See CC §2986.6.

§2985.9. Required information exceptions

The following documents and agreements are not required to be contained in a lease contract:

(a) An "express warranty," as that term is defined in paragraph (1) of subdivision (a) of Section 1791.2, whether it relates to the sale or lease of a consumer good.

(b) Titling and transfer documents utilized to register, title, or transfer ownership of vehicles described in the lease contract with government registration authorities.

(c) Insurance policies, service contracts, and optional debt cancellation agreements.

(d) Documents that memorialize the sale or lease of goods or services, relating to the leased vehicle, between the provider of those goods or services and lessee that are included in the gross capitalized cost of the lease and separately itemized in the "Itemization of Gross Capitalized Cost." **Leg.H.** Added Stats 2001 ch 287 §3 (SB 281).

2001 Note: The amendments and provisions contained in this act shall apply prospectively only and to motor vehicle sale or lease contracts entered into on and after January 1, 2002. No court may construe or imply any legislative intent or policy with respect to the provisions of this act in any legal proceeding involving a motor vehicle lease contract entered into prior to January 1, 2002. Stats 2001 ch 287 §5.

§§2985.91–2985.93. [Sections repealed 1977]

Leg.H. Added Stats 1969 ch 1208 §1. Repealed Stats 1976 ch 1284 §1, operative March 23, 1977. See CC §§2988.5, 2988.7, 2990.

§2986. [Section repealed 1965]

Leg.H. Enacted Stats 1872. Repealed Stats 1963 ch 819 §2, effective January 1, 1965. The repealed section related to pledges.

§2986.2. [Section repealed 1997]

Leg.H. Added Stats 1976 ch 1284 §2, operative March 23, 1977. Amended Stats 1993 ch 1092 §4 (AB 431), operative July 1, 1994; Stats 1994 ch 146 §16 (AB 3601). Repealed Stats 1997 ch 800 §8 (SB 1291). The repealed section related to warnings in lease contracts.

§2986.3. Lease contract; Prohibited provisions

No lease contract shall contain any provision by which:

(a) A power of attorney is given to confess judgment in this state, or an assignment of wages is given; provided that nothing herein contained shall prohibit the giving of an assignment of wages contained in a separate instrument pursuant to Section 300 of the Labor Code.

(b) The lessee waives any right of action against the lessor or holder of the contract or other person acting on his or her behalf for any illegal act committed in the collection of payments under the contract or in the repossession of the motor vehicle.

(c) The lessee relieves the lessor from liability for any legal remedies which the lessee may have against the lessor under the contract or any separate instruments executed in connection therewith.

(d) The lessor or holder of the contract is given the right to commence action on a contract under the provisions of this chapter in a county other than the county in which the contract was in fact signed by the lessee, the county in which the lessee resides at the commencement of the action, the county in which the lessee resided at the time the contract was entered into or in the county in which the motor vehicle leased pursuant to such contract is permanently garaged. **Leg.H.** Added Stats 1976 ch 1284 §2, operative March 23, 1977. Amended Stats 1997 ch 800 §9 (SB 1291).

§2986.4. Acknowledgment by lessee

Any acknowledgment by the lessee of delivery of a copy of a lease contract or purchase order and any vehicle lease proposal and any credit statement which the lessor has required or requested the lessee to sign, and which the lessee has signed, during the contract negotiations, shall be printed or written in size equal to at least 10-point bold type and, if contained in the contract, shall appear directly above the space reserved for the lessee's signature. The lessee's written acknowledgment, conforming to the requirements of this section, of delivery of a completely filled in copy of the contract, and a copy of such other documents shall be a rebuttable presumption of delivery in any action or proceeding by or against a third party without knowledge to the contrary when he or she acquired his or her interest in the contract. If such third party furnishes the lessee a copy of such documents, or a notice containing items set forth in subdivision (c) of Section 2985.8, and stating that the lessee shall notify such third party in writing within 30 days if he or she was not furnished a copy of such documents, and no such notification is given, it shall be conclusively presumed in favor of such a third party that copies of the documents were furnished as required by this chapter. **Leg.H.** Added Stats 1976 ch 1284 §2, operative March 23, 1977. Amended Stats 1997 ch 800 §10 (SB 1291).

§2986.5. Lease of used vehicle; Refund of excess fees

(a) No person shall lease a used motor vehicle for operation on California highways if such vehicle does not meet all of the equipment requirements of Division 12 (commencing with Section 24000) of the Vehicle Code. This subdivision does not apply to an extension or a subsequent lease of the same motor vehicle to the same lessee.

(b) If a lessee of a vehicle pays to the lessor an amount for the licensing or transfer of title of the vehicle which amount is in excess of the actual fees due for such licensing or transfer, or which amount is in excess of the amount which has been paid, prior to the sale, by the lessor to the state in order to avoid penalties that would have accrued because of late payment of such fees, the lessor shall return such excess amount to the lessee, whether or not such lessee requests the return of the excess amount. **Leg.H.** Added Stats 1976 ch 1284 §2, operative March 23, 1977.

§2986.6. Lien on other property

No agreement in connection with a lease contract which provides for the inclusion of title to or a lien upon any personal or real property, other than the motor vehicle which is the subject matter of the lease contract, or accessories therefor, or special and auxiliary equipment used in connection therewith, as security for the payment of the contract obligations, shall be enforceable. This section does not apply to a security deposit, advance payment of rent or other cash prepayment. **Leg.H.** Added Stats 1976 ch 1284 §2, operative March 23, 1977.

§2986.10. Rights of assignee of lessor

(a) An assignee of the lessor's rights is subject to all equities and defenses of the lessee against the lessor, notwithstanding an agreement to the contrary, but the assignee's liability may not exceed the amount of the obligation owing to the assignee at the time of the assignment.

(b) The assignee shall have recourse against the lessor to the extent of any liability incurred by the assignee pursuant to this section regardless of whether the assignment was with or without recourse. **Leg.H.** Added Stats 1976 ch 1284 §2, operative March 23, 1977.

§2986.12. Unlawful rebates, discounts, and commissions

It shall be unlawful for any lessor to induce or attempt to induce any person to enter into a contract subject to this chapter by offering a rebate, discount, commission or other consideration, on the condition that the lessee gives information or assistance for the purpose of enabling a lessor to either lease or sell a motor vehicle to another. **Leg.H.** Added Stats 1976 ch 1284 §2, operative March 23, 1977.

§2986.13. Refund of prepayment

(a) Any payment made by a lessee to a lessor pending the execution of a lease contract shall be refunded to the lessee in the event the lease contract is not executed.

(b) In the event of breach by the lessor of a lease contract where the lessee leaves his or her motor vehicle with the lessor as a trade-in downpayment and the motor vehicle is not returned by the lessor to the lessee for whatever reason, the lessee may recover from the lessor either the fair market value of the motor vehicle left as a downpayment or its value as stated in the lease contract, whichever is greater. The recovery shall be tendered to the lessee within five business days after the breach.

(c) The remedies of the buyer provided for in subdivision (b) are nonexclusive and cumulative and shall not preclude the lessee from pursuing any other remedy which he or she may have under any other provision of law. **Leg.H.** Added Stats 1976 ch 1284 §2, operative March 23, 1977. Amended Stats 1997 ch 800 §11 (SB 1291).

§2987. Lessee's liability on termination of lease contract

(a) A lessee has the right to terminate a lease contract at any time prior to the scheduled expiration date specified in the lease contract. Except as provided in subdivision (f), all of the following subdivisions of this section apply in the event of an early termination.

(b) The lessee's liability shall not exceed the sum of the following:

(1) All unpaid periodic lease payments that have accrued up to the date of termination.

(2) All other amounts due and unpaid by the lessee under the lease contract, other than excess wear and mileage charges and unpaid periodic lease payments.

(3) Any charges, however denominated, that the lessor or holder of the lease contract may assess in connection with termination not to exceed in the aggregate the amount of a reasonable disposition fee, if any, disclosed in the lease contract and assessed upon termination of the lease contract.

(4) In the event of the lessee's default, reasonable fees paid by the lessor or holder for reconditioning of the leased vehicle and reasonable and necessary fees paid by the lessor or holder, if any, in connection with the repossession and storage of the leased vehicle.

(5) The difference, if any, between the adjusted capitalized cost disclosed in the lease contract and the sum of (A) all depreciation and other amortized amounts accrued through the date of early termination, calculated in accordance with the constant yield or other generally accepted actuarial method, and (B) the realized value of the vehicle as provided in subdivision (c).

(c) Subject to subdivision (d), the realized value of the vehicle used to calculate the lessee's liability under paragraph (5) of subdivision (b) shall be (1) if the lessee maintains insurance on the leased vehicle as required in the lease contract and the vehicle is a total loss as a result of theft or damage, the amount of any applicable insurance deductible owed by the lessee and the proceeds of the settlement of the insurance claim, unless a higher amount is agreed to by the holder of the lease contract, (2) if the lessee elects to have an appraisal conducted as provided in Regulation M, the value determined on appraisal, (3) if the holder of the lease contract or lessor elects to retain ownership of the vehicle for use or to lease to a subsequent lessee, the wholesale value of the vehicle as specified in the current edition of a recognized used vehicle value guide customarily used by California motor vehicle dealers to value vehicles in this state, including, but not limited to, the Kelley Blue Book Auto Market Report and the N.A.D.A. Official Used Car Guide, or (4) under all other circumstances, the higher of (A) the price paid for the vehicle upon disposition, or (B) any other amount established by the lessor or the lease contract.

(d)(1) The lessor or holder of the lease contract shall act in good faith and in a commercially reasonable manner in connection with the disposition of the vehicle.

(2) In addition to the requirements of paragraph (1), any disposition of the vehicle shall be preceded by a notice complying with both of the following:

(A) The notice shall be in writing and given by the holder of the contract to each lessee and guarantor at least 10 days in advance of any disposition or the date by which the value of the vehicle will be determined pursuant to paragraph (3) of subdivision (c). The notice shall be personally served or shall be sent by certified mail, return receipt requested, or first-class mail, postage prepaid, directed to the last known address of each lessee and guarantor. One notice is sufficient if those persons are married to each other and the most recent records of the holder of the lease contract indicate that they reside at the same address. The last known address of each lessee and guarantor shall be presumed to be the address stated in the lease contract or guaranty for each lessee and guarantor unless the lessee or guarantor notifies the holder of the lease contract of a change of address.

(B) The notice shall set forth (i) the time and place of any public sale, the time on or after which a private sale or other intended disposition is to be made, or the date by which the value of the vehicle will be determined pursuant to paragraph (3) of subdivision (c), (ii) an itemization of all amounts claimed under paragraphs (1) to (4), inclusive, of subdivision (b), (iii) the amount of the difference between the adjusted capitalized cost and the sum of all depreciation and other amortized amounts paid through the date of early termination as provided in paragraph (5) of subdivision (b), (iv) the total of these amounts identified as the "Gross Early Termination Amount," and (v) one of the following statements, whichever is applicable:

[To be inserted when the realized value will be determined pursuant to paragraph (3) of subdivision (c)]

"The amount you owe for early termination will be no more than the difference between the Gross Early Termination Amount stated above and (1) the appraised value of the vehicle or (2) if there is no appraisal, the wholesale value specified in a recognized used vehicle value guide.

You have the right to get a professional appraisal to establish the value of the vehicle for the purpose of figuring how much you owe on the lease. If you want an appraisal, you will have to arrange for it to be completed at least three days before the scheduled valuation date. The appraiser has to be an independent person acceptable to the holder of the lease. You will have to pay for the appraiser. The appraised value will be considered final and binding on you and the holder of the lease."

[To be inserted in all other circumstances]

"The amount you owe for early termination will be no more than the difference between the Gross Early Termination Amount stated above and (1) the appraised value of the vehicle or (2) if there is no appraisal, either the price received for the vehicle upon disposition or a greater amount established by the lessor or the lease contract.

You have the right to get a professional appraisal to establish the value of the vehicle for the purpose of figuring how much you owe on the lease. If you want an appraisal, you will have to arrange for it to be completed at least three days before the scheduled sale date of the vehicle. The appraiser has to be an independent person acceptable to the holder of the lease. You will have to pay for the appraiser. The appraised value will be considered final and binding on you and the holder of the lease."

(3) The lessee shall have no liability under subdivision (b) if the lessor or holder of the lease contract does not comply with this subdivision. This paragraph does not apply under all the following conditions:

(A) Noncompliance was the result of a bona fide error in stating an amount required to be disclosed pursuant to clause (ii), (iii), or (iv) of subparagraph (B) of paragraph (2).

(B) The holder of the lease gives the lessee written notice of the error within 30 days after discovering the error and before (i) an action is filed to recover the amount claimed to be owed or (ii) written notice of the error is received by the holder of the lease from the lessee.

(C) The lessee is liable for the lesser of the originally claimed amount or the correct amount.

(D) The holder of the lease refunds any amount collected in excess of the amount described in subparagraph (C) within 10 days after notice of the error is given. "Bona fide error," as used in this paragraph, means an error that was not intentional and occurred notwithstanding the maintenance of procedures reasonably adapted to avoid that error. Examples of a bona fide error include clerical errors, calculation errors, errors due to unintentionally improper computer programming or data entry, and printing errors, but does not include an error of legal judgment with respect to a lessor's or lease contractholder's obligations under this section.

(4) This subdivision does not apply when the lessee maintains insurance on the leased vehicle as required in the lease contract and the vehicle is declared a total loss by the insurer as a result of theft or damage.

(e) The lessor or holder of the lease contract shall credit any security deposit or advance rental payment held by the lessor or holder of the lease contract against the lessee's liability under the lease contract as limited by this section. The portion of a security deposit or advance rental payment, if any, remaining after the lessee's liability under the lease contract as limited by this section has been satisfied shall be returned to the lessee within 30 days of the satisfaction of the obligation.

(f) Subdivisions (b) to (d), inclusive, do not apply if, prior to the scheduled expiration date specified in the lease contract, the lessee terminates the lease and purchases the vehicle or trades in the vehicle in connection with the purchase or lease of another vehicle. In such an event, the selling price of the leased vehicle, exclusive of taxes and other charges incidental to the sale, shall not exceed the sum of the following and shall relieve the lessee of any further liability under the lease contract:

(1) All unpaid periodic lease payments that have accrued up to the date of termination.

(2) All other amounts due and unpaid by the lessee under the lease contract, other than excess wear and mileage charges and unpaid periodic lease payments.

(3) Any charges, however denominated, that the lessor or holder of the lease contract may assess in connection with termination of the lease contract and the acquisition of the vehicle, not to exceed in the aggregate the amount of a reasonable purchase option fee, if any, disclosed in the lease contract and assessed upon the scheduled termination of the lease contract.

(4) The adjusted capitalized cost disclosed in the lease contract less all depreciation and other amortized amounts accrued through the date of early termination, calculated in accordance with the constant yield or other generally accepted actuarial method.

(g) If the lessee terminates a lease contract, voluntarily returns possession of the vehicle to the lessor, and timely pays all sums required under the lease contract as limited by this section, the lessor or holder shall not provide any adverse information concerning the early termination to any consumer credit reporting agency.

(h) The Rule of 78 shall not be used to calculate accrued rent charges.

(i) This section shall only apply to lease contracts entered into on and after January 1, 1998. **Leg.H.** Added Stats 1997 ch 800 §12 (SB 1291).

Prior Law: Former §2987, relating to pledges, was enacted Stats 1872 and repealed Stats 1963 ch 819 §2, effective January 1, 1965. Historical derivation: Field's Draft NY CC §1648.

§2988. Lessee to bear risk of vehicle's depreciation

(a) The Legislature finds that it is necessary to provide some protection for consumers who enter into lease contracts in which the lessee will bear the risk of the motor vehicle's depreciation. This section is intended to provide relief to the consumer when an ostensibly inexpensive lease contract establishes an excessively low level of periodic payment which results, conversely, in an excessively high liability being imposed on the lessee at the expiration of the lease term because the lessor has failed to act in good faith in either estimating a residual value of the motor vehicle or establishing a level of periodic payment which bears no reasonable relation to the motor vehicle's reasonably expected depreciation during the lease term. Therefore, the lessor will have the obligation to act in good faith and to come forward with competent evidence showing that the estimated residual value was so determined given the circumstances existing at the inception of the lease contract.

(b) Where the lessee is to bear the risk of the motor vehicle's depreciation and the lessee's liability on expiration of a consumer lease is based on the estimated residual value of the motor vehicle such estimated residual value shall be a reasonable approximation of the anticipated actual fair market value of the motor vehicle on lease expiration. There shall be a rebuttable presumption that the estimated residual value is unreasonable to the extent that the estimated residual value exceeds the actual residual value by more than three times the average payment allocable to a monthly period under the lease. The presumption stated in the preceding sentence shall not apply to the extent the excess of estimated over actual residual value is due to physical damage to the motor vehicle beyond reasonable wear and use, or to excessive use, and the lease may set standards for such wear and use if such standards are not unreasonable.

(c) For the purposes of this chapter, "fair market value" means the value the motor vehicle would have when sold in a commercially reasonable manner in the customary market for such motor vehicle. **Leg.H.** Added Stats 1976 ch 1284 §2, operative March 23, 1977.

Prior Law: Former §2988, relating to pledge, was enacted Stats 1872, amended Stats 1935 ch 716 §2, and repealed Stats 1963 ch 819 §2, effective January 1, 1965.

§2988.5. Liability of lessor

(a) Except as otherwise provided by this section, any lessor who fails to comply with any requirement imposed under Section 2985.8 or 2988 for which no specific relief is provided with respect to any person shall be liable to such person in an amount equal to the sum of:

(1) Any actual damages sustained by such person as a result of the failure.

(2) In the case of an individual action, 25 percent of the total amount of monthly payments under the lease except that liability under this subparagraph shall not be less than one hundred dollars ($100) nor greater than one thousand dollars ($1,000); or in the case of a class action, such amount as the court may allow, except that as to each member of the class no minimum recovery shall be applicable, and the total recovery in such action shall not be more than the lesser of five hundred thousand dollars ($500,000) or 1 percent of the net worth of the lessor.

(3) The costs of the action, together with a reasonable attorney's fee as determined by the court.

(b) In determining the amount of award in any class action, the court shall consider, among other relevant factors, the amount of any actual damages sustained, the frequency and persistence of failure of compliance by the lessor, the resources of the lessor, the number of persons adversely affected, and the extent to which the lessor's failure of compliance was intentional.

(c) A lessor shall not be liable under this section if within 15 days after discovery of an error, and prior to the institution of an action under this section or the receipt of written notice of the error, the lessor notifies the person concerned of the error and makes whatever adjustments in the appropriate account are necessary to insure that the person will not be required to pay any amount in excess of the amount that should correctly have been disclosed.

(d) A lessor may not be held liable in any action brought under this section for a violation of this chapter if the lessor shows by a preponderance of evidence that the violation was not intentional and resulted from a bona fide error notwithstanding the maintenance of procedures reasonably adopted to avoid any such error.

(e) Except as otherwise specifically provided in this chapter, any civil action for a violation of this chapter which may be brought against the original lessor in any lease transaction may be maintained against any subsequent assignee of the original lessor where the violation from which the alleged liability arose is apparent on the face of the instrument assigned unless the assignment is involuntary.

(f) A person may not take any action to offset any amount for which a lessor is potentially liable to such person under paragraph (2) of subdivision (a) against any amount owing to such lessor by such person, unless the amount of the lessor's liability to such person has been determined by judgment of a court of competent jurisdiction in an action to which such person was a party.

(g) No provision of this section imposing any liability shall apply to any act done or omitted in good faith conformity with any rule, regulation or interpretation of federal law, notwithstanding that after such act or omission has occurred, such rule, regulation or interpretation is amended, rescinded or determined by judicial or other authority to be invalid for any reason.

(h) The multiple failure to disclose any information required under this chapter to be disclosed in connection with a single lease transaction shall entitle the person to a single recovery under this section, but continued failure to disclose after a recovery has been granted shall give rise to rights to additional recoveries.

(i) Actions alleging a failure to disclose or otherwise comply with the requirements of this chapter shall be brought within one year of the termination of the lease contract. **Leg.H.** Added Stats 1976 ch 1284 §2, operative March 23, 1977.

§2988.7. Rescission of contract

If the lessor fails to comply with Section 2985.8, as an alternative to an action under Section 2988.5, the lessee may rescind the contract if the failure to comply was willful, or if correction will increase the amount of the contract balance, unless the lessor waives the collection of the increased amount. **Leg.H.** Added Stats 1976 ch 1284 §2, operative March 23, 1977.

§2988.9. Attorney's fees and costs

Reasonable attorney's fees and costs shall be awarded to the prevailing party in any action on a lease contract subject to the provisions of this chapter regardless of whether the action is instituted by the lessor, assignee, or lessee. Where the defendant alleges in his or her answer that he or she tendered to the plaintiff the full amount to which he or she was entitled, and thereupon deposits in court, for the plaintiff, the amount so tendered, and the allegation is found to be true, then the defendant is deemed to be the prevailing party within the meaning of this section. **Leg.H.** Added Stats 1976 ch 1284 §2, operative March 23, 1977. Amended Stats 2004 ch 183 §42 (AB 3082).

§2989. Effect of federal civil action

No civil action shall be filed against a lessor under the authority of this chapter if a federal civil action has previously been filed based on facts that give rise to a similar cause of action under this chapter. **Leg.H.** Added Stats 1976 ch 1284 §2, operative March 23, 1977.

Prior Law: Former §2989, relating to pledge, was enacted Stats 1872 and repealed Stats 1963 ch 819 §2, effective January 1, 1965.

§2989.2. Sale of leased vehicle

Where the lessee is to bear the risk of the motor vehicle's depreciation upon the scheduled expiration of the lease contract, the following applies:

(a) When disposing of a vehicle or obtaining cash bids for the purpose of setting the fair market value of a vehicle, the lessor shall act in a commercially reasonable manner in the customary market for such vehicle.

(b) Any provision in a lease contract to the contrary notwithstanding, at least 10 days written notice of intent to sell such motor vehicle shall be given by the holder of the contract to each lessee and guarantor, unless the lessor and lessee have agreed in writing to the amount of the lessee's liability under the lease contract after the lessee returns the motor vehicle to the lessor, or the lessee has satisfied the lease contract obligations by payment to the lessor. The notice shall be personally served or shall be sent by certified mail, return receipt requested, directed to the address of the lessee shown on the contract, unless the lessee has notified the holder in writing of a different address. The notice shall set forth separately any charges or sums due and state that the lessee will be liable for the difference between the amount of liability imposed on the lessee at the expiration of the lease term and the actual cash value of the motor vehicle when it is sold. The notice shall also state that the lessee has the right to submit a cash bid for the purchase of the vehicle. **Leg.H.** Added Stats 1976 ch 1284 §2, operative March 23, 1977. Amended Stats 1997 ch 800 §13 (SB 1291).

§2989.4. Duties of lessor

(a) A lessor shall not:

(1) Fail to register the leased vehicle pursuant to the lease contract.

(2) Advertise any specific vehicle in the inventory of the lessor for lease without identifying such vehicle by either its vehicle identification number or license number.

(3) Refuse to lease a vehicle to any creditworthy person at the advertised total price, exclusive of sales tax, vehicle registration fees and finance charges.

(b) Notwithstanding Section 2988.5, a lessor shall not suffer civil liability for a violation of this section. **Leg.H.** Added Stats 1976 ch 1284 §2, operative March 23, 1977.

§2989.5. Production of lessor's records

(a) Except as provided in subdivision (c), a lessor shall make available to investigators of the Department of Motor Vehicles, upon presentation of an affidavit that the department has a consumer complaint within its jurisdiction, the records relevant to the transaction complained of. If the affidavit states that the department has reasonable cause to believe there is a pattern of conduct or common scheme in similar transactions, the records relevant to all such similar transactions shall be made available.

(b) Except as provided in subdivision (c), on petition of the department alleging the receipt of a consumer complaint within its jurisdiction and alleging that the lessor refuses to make available his records as required, the court shall order the lessor to make available such records or show cause why such records should not be produced. The department shall be awarded reasonable attorney's fees and costs if it prevails in such action.

(c)(1) In the case of a financial institution, or a subsidiary or affiliated corporation of such institution, the Director of Motor Vehicles shall report in writing an apparent violation, or failure to comply with this chapter, evidenced by a consumer complaint, to the agency or department of the state or federal government responsible for supervising the leasing activities of such institution.

(2) Within 20 days, such agency or department shall advise the director of the action taken with respect to such report.

(3) If such agency or department fails to so advise the director, the director may commence an action to compel the agency or department to cause the production of the records relevant to the consumer complaint. **Leg.H.** Added Stats 1976 ch 1284 §2, operative March 23, 1977.

§2989.6. Rules and regulations

The Director of Motor Vehicles may adopt and enforce rules and regulations as may be necessary to carry out or implement the provisions of this chapter.

Rules and regulations shall be adopted, amended or repealed in accordance with Chapter 4.5 (commencing with Section 11370) of Part 1 of Division 3 of Title 2 of the Government Code. **Leg.H.** Added Stats 1976 ch 1284 §2, operative March 23, 1977.

§2989.8. Knowing and wilful violations

Any person who shall knowingly and willfully violate any provisions of this chapter shall be guilty of a misdemeanor. **Leg.H.** Added Stats 1976 ch 1284 §2, operative March 23, 1977.

§2990. Application of chapter

This chapter shall not apply to any transaction which is regulated by Chapter 2b (commencing with Section 2981) of this title. **Leg.H.** Added Stats 1976 ch 1284 §2, operative March 23, 1977.

Prior Law: Former §2990, relating to pledge, was enacted Stats 1872 and repealed Stats 1963 ch 819 §2, effective January 1, 1965.

§2991. Spanish translation

Any prospective assignee that provides a lessor under a lease contract with any preprinted form for use as a lease contract shall, upon the request of a lessor, provide the lessor with a Spanish language translation of the preprinted form. **Leg.H.** Added Stats 1999 ch 235 §1 (AB 713), operative January 1, 2001.

Prior Law: Former §2991, relating to pledges, was enacted Stats 1872 and repealed Stats 1963 ch 819 §2, effective January 1, 1965.

§2992. Specified print form

A prospective assignee that provides a lessor under a lease contract with a preprinted form for use as a lease contract shall design the form in such a manner so as to provide on its face sufficient space for the lessor to include all disclosures and itemizations required pursuant to Section 2985.8 and shall also contain on its face a separate blank space no smaller than seven and one-half square inches for the lessor and lessee to memorialize trade-in, turn-in, and other individualized agreements. **Leg.H.** Added Stats 2001 ch 287 §4 (SB 281).

Prior Law: Former §2992, relating to pledges, was enacted Stats 1872 and repealed Stats 1963 ch 819 §2, effective January 1, 1965.

2001 Note: The amendments and provisions contained in this act shall apply prospectively only and to motor vehicle sale or lease contracts entered into on and after January 1, 2002. No court may construe or imply any legislative intent or policy with respect to the provisions of this act in any legal proceeding involving a motor vehicle lease contract entered into prior to January 1, 2002. Stats 2001 ch 287 §5.

§2993. Subsequent assignment to skip trace, locate or repossess a vehicle; Notice requirements

A holder of a lease contract, or the agent of a holder, who has received a notice pursuant to Section 7507.6 of the Business and Professions Code, shall not make a subsequent assignment to skip trace, locate, or repossess the vehicle without simultaneously, and in the same manner by which the assignment is given, advising the assignee of the assignment of the information contained in the notice. As used in this section, "assignment" has the same meaning set forth in Section 7500.1 of the Business and Professions Code. **Leg.H.** Added Stats 2007 ch 192 §5 (SB 659), effective September 7, 2007.

Prior Law: Former CC §2993, relating to pledges, was added Stats 1872, and repealed Stats 1963 ch 819 §2, effective January 1, 1965.

§2994. [Section repealed 1965]

Leg.H. Enacted Stats 1872. Repealed Stats 1963 ch 819 §2, effective January 1, 1965. The repealed section related to pledges.

CHAPTER 2E
CONTROLLED ESCROWS

Real estate developer; Conflict of interests. §2995.

§2995. Real estate developer; Conflict of interests

No real estate developer shall require as a condition precedent to the transfer of real property containing a single family residential dwelling that escrow services effectuating such transfer shall be provided by an escrow entity in which the real estate developer has a financial interest.

A real estate developer who violates the provisions of this section shall be liable to the purchaser of the real property in the amount of three times the amount charged for the escrow services, but in no event less than two hundred fifty dollars ($250), plus reasonable attorney's fees and costs.

For purposes of this section "financial interest" means ownership or control of 5 percent or more of an escrow entity.

For purposes of this section "real estate developer" means a person or entity having an ownership interest in real property which is improved by such person or entity with single family residential dwellings which are offered for sale to the public.

For purposes of this section "escrow entity" includes a person, firm or corporation.

Any waiver of the prohibition contained in this section shall be against public policy and void. **Leg.H.** Added Stats 1978 ch 552 §1, effective August 25, 1978.

Prior Law: Former §2995, relating to pledge, was enacted Stats 1872 and repealed Stats 1963 ch 819 §2, effective January 1, 1965.

CHAPTER 3
PLEDGE [REPEALED]

§§2996–3011. [Sections repealed 1965]

Leg.H. Enacted Stats 1872, amended Code Amdts 1873–74 ch 612 §§264, 266, Stats 1895 ch 18 §1, Stats 1909 ch 636 §1, repealed Stats 1963 ch 819 §2, effective January 1, 1965. The repealed sections related to pledges.

CHAPTER 3A
TRUST RECEIPTS [REPEALED]

§§3012–3016.16. [Sections repealed 1965]

Leg.H. Added Stats 1935 ch 716 §1. Amended Stats 1939 ch 1022, Stats 1940 1st Ex Sess ch 48, Stats 1946 1st Ex Sess ch 130, Stats 1953 ch 483, Stats 1955 ch 292, Stats 1961 ch 549. Repealed Stats 1963 ch 819 §2, effective January 1, 1965.

CHAPTER 3B
ASSIGNMENT OF ACCOUNTS RECEIVABLE [REPEALED]

§§3017–3029. [Sections repealed 1965]

Leg.H. Added Stats 1943 ch 766 §1. Amended Stats 1945 ch 295; Stats 1951 ch 1280; Stats 1953 ch 1242; Stats 1955 ch 940; Stats 1957 ch 954, effective June 8, 1957, chs 1074, 1745. Repealed Stats 1963 ch 819 §2, effective January 1, 1965.

Prior Law: Former §§3017–3029, similar to present H & N C §§450–462, were enacted Stats 1872 and repealed Stats 1937 ch 368 (H & N C §10001) p 1002.

CHAPTER 3C
INVENTORY LIENS [REPEALED]

§§3030–3043. [Sections repealed 1965]

Leg.H. Added Stats 1957 ch 1745 §1, operative January 1, 1958. Amended Stats 1959 ch 1914 §1. Repealed Stats 1963 ch 819 §2, effective January 1, 1965.

Prior Law: Former §§3036–3040, similar to present H & N C §§470–474, were enacted Stats 1872 and repealed Stats 1937 ch 368 (H & N C §10001) p 1002.

CHAPTER 3.5
HEALTH CARE LIENS

Maximum amounts; Exemptions; Rights; Use in civil action or proceeding. §3040.

§3040. Maximum amounts; Exemptions; Rights; Use in civil action or proceeding

(a) No lien asserted by a licensee of the Department of Managed Care or the Department of Insurance, and no lien of a medical group or an independent practice association, to the extent that it asserts or enforces a lien, for the recovery of money paid or payable to or on behalf of an enrollee or insured for health care services provided under a health care service plan contract or a disability insurance policy, when the right of the licensee, medical group, or independent practice association to assert that lien is granted in a plan contract subject to the Knox-Keene Health Care Service Plan Act of 1975 (Chapter 2.2 (commencing with Section 1340) of Division 2 of the Health and Safety Code) or a disability insurance policy subject to the Insurance Code, may exceed the sum of the reasonable costs actually paid by the licensee, medical group, or independent practice association to perfect the lien and one of the following:

(1) For health care services not provided on a capitated basis, the amount actually paid by the licensee, medical group, or independent practice association pursuant to that contract or policy to any treating medical provider.

(2) For health care services provided on a capitated basis, the amount equal to 80 percent of the usual and customary charge for the same services by medical providers that provide health care services on a noncapitated basis in the geographic region in which the services were rendered.

(b) If an enrollee or insured received health care services on a capitated basis and on a noncapitated basis, and the licensee, medical group, or independent practice association that provided the health care services on the capitated basis paid for the health care services the enrollee received on the noncapitated basis, then a lien that is subject to subdivision (a) may not exceed the sum of the reasonable costs actually paid to perfect the lien, and the amounts determined pursuant to both paragraphs (1) and (2) of subdivision (a).

(c) If the enrollee or insured engaged an attorney, then the lien subject to subdivision (a) may not exceed the lesser of the following amounts:

(1) The maximum amount determined pursuant to subdivision (a) or (b), whichever is applicable.

(2) One-third of the moneys due to the enrollee or insured under any final judgment, compromise, or settlement agreement.

(d) If the enrollee or insured did not engage an attorney, then the lien subject to subdivision (a) may not exceed the lesser of the following amounts:

(1) The maximum amount determined pursuant to subdivision (a) or (b), whichever is applicable.

(2) One-half of the moneys due to the enrollee or insured under any final judgment, compromise, or settlement agreement.

(e) Where a final judgment includes a special finding by a judge, jury, or arbitrator, that the enrollee or insured was partially at fault, the lien subject to subdivision (a) or (b) shall be reduced by the same comparative fault percentage by which the enrollee or insured's recovery was reduced.

(f) A lien subject to subdivision (a) or (b) is subject to pro rata reduction, commensurate with the enrollee's or insured's reasonable attorney's fees and costs, in accordance with the common fund doctrine.

(g) This section is not applicable to any of the following:

(1) A lien made against a workers' compensation claim.

(2) A lien for Medi-Cal benefits pursuant to Article 3.5 (commencing with Section 14124.70) of Chapter 7 of Part 3 of Division 9 of the Welfare and Institutions Code.

(3) A lien for hospital services pursuant to Chapter 4 (commencing with Section 3045.1).

(h) This section does not create any lien right that does not exist at law, and does not make a lien that arises out of an employee benefit plan or fund enforceable if preempted by federal law.

(i) The provisions of this section may not be admitted into evidence nor given in any instruction in any civil action or proceeding between an enrollee or insured and a third party. **Leg.H.** Added Stats 2000 ch 848 §1 (SB 1471).

CHAPTER 4
HOSPITAL LIENS

Claim of lien for emergency medical care and services. §3045.1.
Application of lien. §3045.2.
Notice of lien. §3045.3.
Liability for amount of lien claimed in notice. §3045.4.
Enforcement of lien. §3045.5.
Application of chapter. §3045.6.

§3045.1. Claim of lien for emergency medical care and services

Every person, partnership, association, corporation, public entity, or other institution or body maintaining a hospital licensed under the laws of this state which furnishes emergency and ongoing medical or other services to any person injured by reason of an accident or negligent or other wrongful act not covered by Division 4 (commencing with Section 3201) or Division 4.5 (commencing with Section 6100) of the Labor Code, shall, if the person has a claim against another for damages on account of his or her injuries, have a lien upon the damages recovered, or to be recovered, by the person, or by his or her heirs or personal representative in case of his or her death to the extent of the amount of the reasonable and necessary charges of the hospital and any hospital affiliated health facility, as defined in Section 1250 of the Health and Safety Code, in which services are provided for the treatment, care, and maintenance of the person in the hospital or health facility affiliated with the hospital resulting from that accident or negligent or other wrongful act. **Leg.H.** Added Stats 1961 ch 2080 §1 p 4340. Amended Stats 1992 ch 302 §1 (AB 2733).

§3045.2. Application of lien

The lien shall apply whether the damages are recovered, or are to be recovered, by judgment, settlement, or compromise. **Leg.H.** Added Stats 1961 ch 2080 §1 p 4340.

§3045.3. Notice of lien

A lien shall not be effective, however, unless a written notice containing the name and address of the injured person, the date of the accident, the name and location of the hospital, the amount claimed as reasonable and necessary charges, and the name of each person, firm, or corporation known to the hospital and alleged to be liable to the injured person for the injuries received, is delivered or is mailed by registered mail, return receipt requested, postage prepaid, to each person, firm, or corporation known to the hospital and alleged to be liable to the injured person for the injuries sustained prior to the payment of any moneys to the injured person, his attorney, or legal representative as compensation for the injuries.

The hospital shall, also, deliver or mail by registered mail, return receipt requested, postage prepaid, a copy of the notice to any insurance carrier known to the hospital which has insured the person, firm, or corporation alleged to be liable to the injured person against the liability. The person, firm, or corporation alleged to be liable to the injured person shall, upon request of the hospital, disclose to the hospital the name of the insurance carrier which has insured it against the liability. **Leg.H.** Added Stats 1961 ch 2080 §1 p 4340. Amended Stats 1992 ch 302 §2 (AB 2733).

§3045.4. Liability for amount of lien claimed in notice

Any person, firm, or corporation, including, but not limited to, an insurance carrier, making any payment to the injured person, or to his or her attorney, heirs, or legal representative, for the injuries he or she sustained, after the receipt of the notice as provided by Section 3045.3, without paying to the association, corporation, public entity, or other institution or body maintaining the hospital the amount of its lien claimed in the notice, or so much thereof as can be satisfied out of 50 percent of the moneys due under any final judgment, compromise, or settlement agreement after paying any prior liens shall be liable to the person, partnership, association, corporation, public entity, or other institution or body maintaining the hospital for the amount of its lien claimed in the notice which the hospital was entitled to receive as payment for the medical care and services rendered to the injured person. **Leg.H.** Added Stats 1961 ch 2080 §1 p 4341. Amended Stats 1992 ch 302 §3 (AB 2733).

§3045.5. Enforcement of lien

The person, partnership, association, corporation or other institution or body maintaining the hospital may, at any time within one year after the date of the payment to the injured person, or to his heirs, attorney, or legal representative, enforce its lien by filing an action at law against the person, firm, or corporation making the payment and to whom such notice was given as herein provided. **Leg.H.** Added Stats 1961 ch 2080 §1 p 4341.

§3045.6. Application of chapter

The provisions of this chapter shall not apply to any claim or cause of action against a common carrier subject to the jurisdiction of the Public Utilities Commission or the Interstate Commerce Commission. **Leg.H.** Added Stats 1961 ch 2080 §1 p 4341.

CHAPTER 5
RESPONDENTIA [REPEALED]

CHAPTER 6
OTHER LIENS

Lien of seller of real property. §3046.
When transfer of contract waives lien. §3047.
Extent of seller's lien. §3048.
Purchaser's lien on real property. §3050.
Personal property lien for services, manufacture, or repair. §3051.
Notice of lien in excess of specified amount. §3051a.
Carrier's lien on freight in its possession. §3051.5.
Incorrect certification of weights and description; Exclusion. §3051.6.
Sale of property by lienholder. §3052.
Jeweler's lien; Notice and sale. §3052a.
Alternative lien-sale procedure. §3052b.
Registered service dealers' disposal of serviced products of nominal value. §3052.5.
Lien of factor. §3053.
Banker's lien. §3054.
Mechanics lien. §3059.
Mining liens. §3060.
Lien on barley-crusher or threshing machine. §3061.
Agricultural laborer's lien. §3061.5.
Enforcement of agricultural laborer's lien. §3061.6.
Lien for service of stallion, jack, or bull. §3062.
Recording of verified claim as to animal breeder's lien. §3063.
Action to enforce animal breeder's lien. §3064.
Effect of false advertising as to animal's pedigree. §3064.1.
Logger's lien. §3065.
Duration of logger's lien; Joinder of claimants. §3065a.
Cessation of work defined. §3065b.
Lien of faller, bucker, or millhand for wages owed by contractor. §3065c.
Sale of garment or clothing to pay charges for cleaning or alterations. §3066.

§3046. Lien of seller of real property

One who sells real property has a vendor's lien thereon, independent of possession, for so much of the price as remains unpaid and unsecured otherwise than by the personal obligation of the buyer. **Leg.H.** Enacted Stats 1872.

§3047. When transfer of contract waives lien

Where a buyer of real property gives to the seller a written contract for payment of all or part of the price, an absolute transfer of such contract by the seller waives his lien to the extent of the sum payable under the contract, but a transfer of such contract in trust to pay debts, and return the surplus, is not a waiver of the lien. **Leg.H.** Enacted Stats 1872.

§3048. Extent of seller's lien

The liens defined in sections three thousand and forty-six and three thousand and fifty are valid against everyone claiming under the debtor, except a purchaser or incumbrancer in good faith and for value. **Leg.H.** Enacted Stats 1872.

§3049. [Section repealed 1931]

Leg.H. Enacted Stats 1872. Repealed Stats 1931 ch 1070 §2 p 2258.

§3050. Purchaser's lien on real property

One who pays to the owner any part of the price of real property, under an agreement for the sale thereof, has a special lien upon the property, independent of possession, for such part of the amount paid as he may be entitled to recover back, in case of a failure of consideration. **Leg.H.** Enacted Stats 1872.

§3051. Personal property lien for services, manufacture, or repair

Every person who, while lawfully in possession of an article of personal property, renders any service to the owner thereof, by labor or skill, employed for the protection, improvement, safekeeping, or carriage thereof, has a special lien thereon, dependent on possession, for the compensation, if any, which is due to him from the owner for such service; a person who makes, alters, or repairs any article of personal property, at the request of the owner, or legal possessor of the property, has a lien on the same for his reasonable charges for the balance due for such work done and materials furnished, and may retain possession of the same until the charges are paid; and foundry proprietors and persons conducting a foundry business, have a lien, dependent on possession, upon all patterns in their hands belonging to a customer, for the balance due them from such customers for foundry work; and plastic fabricators and persons conducting a plastic fabricating business, have a lien, dependent on possession, upon all patterns and molds in their hands belonging to a customer, for the balance due them from such customer for plastic fabrication work; and laundry proprietors and persons conducting a laundry business, and drycleaning establishment proprietors and persons conducting a drycleaning establishment, have a general lien, dependent on possession, upon all personal property in their hands belonging to a customer, for the balance due them from such customer for laundry work, and for the balance due them from such customers for drycleaning work, but nothing in this section shall be construed to confer a lien in favor of a wholesale drycleaner on materials received from a drycleaning establishment proprietor or a person conducting a drycleaning establishment; and veterinary proprietors and veterinary surgeons shall have a lien dependent on possession, for their compensation in caring for, boarding, feeding, and medical treatment of animals.

This section shall have no application to any vessel, as defined in Section 21 of the Harbors and Navigation Code, to any vehicle, as defined in Section 670 of the Vehicle Code, which is subject to registration pursuant to that code, to any manufactured home, as defined in Section 18007 of the Health and Safety Code, to any mobilehome, as defined in Section 18008 of the Health and Safety Code, or to any commercial coach, as defined in Section 18001.8 of the Health and Safety Code, whether or not the manufactured home, mobilehome, or commercial coach is subject to registration under the Health and Safety Code. **Leg.H.** Enacted Stats 1872. Amended Code Amdts 1877–78 ch 451; Stats 1901 ch 108 §1; Stats 1907 ch 66 §1; Stats 1911 ch 435 §1; Stats 1929 ch 868 §1; Stats 1935 ch 381 §1; Stats 1945 ch 861 §1; Stats 1949 ch 1436 §4; Stats 1970 ch 1341 §1; Stats 1976 ch 839 §1; Stats 1978 ch 1005 §1; Stats 1979 ch 600 §1; Stats 1981 ch 202 §1; Stats 1983 ch 1124 §6.

§3051a. Notice of lien in excess of specified amount

That portion of any lien, as provided for in the next preceding section, in excess of three hundred dollars ($300) for any work, services, or care, or in excess of two hundred dollars ($200) for any safekeeping, rendered or performed at the request of any person other than the holder of the legal title, shall be invalid, unless prior to commencing any such work, service, care, or safekeeping, the person claiming such lien shall give actual notice in writing either by personal service or by registered letter addressed to the holder of the legal title to such property, if known. **Leg.H.** Added Stats 1923 ch 338 §1. Amended Stats 1931 ch 1048 §1; Stats 1949 ch 1436 §5; Stats 1959 ch 197 §1; Stats 1968 ch 830 §1; Stats 1978 ch 1005 §2.

§3051.5. Carrier's lien on freight in its possession

(a) A carrier has a lien on freight in its possession for the total amount owed the carrier by the shipper for freightage, charges for services and advances due on freight previously delivered upon the promise of the shipper to pay freightage, charges and advances, as provided in this section.

(b) The lien provided by this section shall not arise:

(1) Unless the carrier has notified the shipper, in writing, that failure to pay billed charges may result in a lien on future shipments, including the cost of storage and appropriate security for the subsequent shipment held pursuant to this section.

(2) As to any freight which consists of perishable goods.

(c) Except as otherwise provided in this section, the notice and sale provisions of Section 3052 shall apply to the sale of property subject to a lien provided by this section.

(d) No sale of property subject to a lien provided by this section may take place for at least 35 days from the date that possession of the property is delivered to the carrier but the notice period set forth in Section 3052 may run concurrently with the 35-day period provided by this subdivision. In addition to the notices required by Section 3052, the lienholder, at least 10 days prior to any sale of the property, shall notify the shipper and the consignee of the property, and each secured party having a perfected security interest in the property, of the date, time and place of the intended sale. This notice shall include the names of both the shipper and the consignee and shall describe the property to be sold.

(e) Any perfected security interest in the property is prior to the lien provided by this section. No sale of the property may be concluded if the amount bid at the sale is not at least equal to the total amount of all outstanding obligations secured by a perfected security interest in the property. If the minimum bid required for the sale of property pursuant to this subdivision is not received, the lienholder shall promptly release the property to the legal owner upon payment of the current amount for freightage, charges for services and advances due for shipment of that property, not including amounts due on freight previously delivered.

The proceeds of the sale shall be applied as follows:

(1) First, to secured parties having a perfected security interest, in the amounts to which they are respectively entitled.

(2) Second, to the discharge of the lien provided by this section and the costs of storage, appropriate security, and of the sale.

(3) The remainder, if any, to the legal owner of the property.

In the event of any violation by the lienholder of any provision of this subdivision the lienholder shall be liable to any secured party for all damages sustained by the secured party as a result thereof plus all expenses reasonably and necessarily incurred in the enforcement of the secured party's rights, including reasonable attorney's fees and costs of suit.

(f) The shipper shall be liable to the consignee for any damage which results from the failure of the property to reach the consignee as scheduled due to the carrier's proper exercise of its lien rights pursuant to this section. The measure of damages shall be determined as set forth in Section 2713 of the Commercial Code. **Leg.H.** Added Stats 1984 ch 1375 §1.

§3051.6. Incorrect certification of weights and description; Exclusion

(a) Except as provided in subdivision (b), a carrier has a lien on freight in its possession for the total amount owed to the carrier by the owner or beneficial owner of the cargo being shipped for the aggregate amount of any fines, penalties, costs, expenses, or interest incurred by the carrier resulting from the inclusion of false or erroneous information as to gross cargo weight in a written or electronic certification provided by the owner, beneficial owner, or person responsible for making the certification pursuant to Section 508 of Title 49 of the United States Code.

(b) This section does not apply to any of the following freight:

(1) Perishable goods.

(2) Freight shipped by a means involving other than intermodal transportation, as that term is defined by Section 508 of Title 49 of the United States Code.

(3) Freight shipped by loaded containers or trailers having a gross projected cargo weight, including packing material and pallets, of less than 10,000 pounds.

(c) Any sale to foreclose a lien specified in this section shall be conducted in accordance with Section 3052, except that (1) the lien sale shall not take place for at least 35 days from the date that possession of the property is delivered to the carrier, but the notice period specified in Section 3052 may run concurrently with this 35-day period and (2), in addition to the notices required by Section 3052, at least 10 days prior to the sale of the property the lienholder shall notify the shipper and consignee of the property of the date, time, and place of the intended sale. This notice shall contain the names of the shipper and consignee and shall generally describe the property to be sold. **Leg.H.** Added Stats 1993 ch 757 §2 (SB 619).

§3052. Sale of property by lienholder

If the person entitled to the lien provided in Section 3051 is not paid the amount due, and for which such lien is given, within 10 days after the same shall have become due, then such lienholder may proceed to sell such property, or so much thereof as may be necessary to satisfy such lien and costs of sale at public auction, and by giving at least 10 days' but not more than twenty 20 days' previous notice of such sale by advertising in some newspaper published in the county in which such property is situated; or if there be no newspaper printed in such county, then by posting notice of sale in three of the most public places in the town and at the place where such property is to be sold, for 10 days previous to the date of the sale; provided, however, that within 20 days after such sale, the legal owner may redeem any such property so sold to satisfy such lien upon the payment of the amount thereof, all costs and expenses of such sale, together with interest on such sum at the rate of 12 percent per annum from the due date thereof or the date when the same were advanced until the repayment. The proceeds of the sale must be applied to the discharge of the lien and the cost of keeping and selling the property; the remainder, if any, must be paid over to the legal owner thereof. **Leg.H.** Enacted Stats 1872. Amended Stats 1907 ch 66 §2; Stats 1927 ch 368 §1; Stats 1949 ch 1436 §6; Stats 1959 ch 781 §1; Stats 1974 ch 1262 §1, effective September 23, 1974, operative November 1, 1974; Stats 1977 ch 579 §34; Stats 1978 ch 1005 §3.

§3052a. Jeweler's lien; Notice and sale

Every person, firm, or corporation, engaged in performing work upon any watch, clock or jewelry, for a price, shall have a lien upon the watch, clock, or jewelry for the amount of any account that may be due for the work done thereon. The lien shall also include the value or agreed price, if any, of all materials furnished by the lienholder in connection with the work. If any account for work done or materials furnished shall remain unpaid for one year after completing the work, the lienholder may, upon 30 days notice in writing to the owner, specifying the amount due, and informing him that the payment of the amount due within 30 days will entitle him to redeem the property, sell any such article or articles at public or bona fide private sale to satisfy the account. The proceeds of the sale, after paying the expenses thereof, shall first be applied to liquidate the indebtedness secured by the lien and the balance, if any, shall be paid over to the owner.

The notice may be served by registered mail with return receipt demanded, directed to the owner's last known address, or, if the owner or his address be unknown, it may be posted in two public places in the town or city where the property is located. Nothing herein contained shall be construed as preventing the lienholder from waiving the lien herein provided for suing upon the amount if he elects to do so. **Leg.H.** Added Stats 1937 ch 279 §1 p 614.

§3052b. Alternative lien-sale procedure

(a) The procedure in this section shall be an alternative to the lien-sale procedure provided in Section 3052, but applies only to liens under Section 3051 for charges not exceeding one hundred fifty dollars ($150), exclusive of additional charges and interest authorized by this section. As a condition precedent to using the procedure specified in this section, the lienholder shall have done all of the following:

(1) Provided the property owner with an accurate written summary of the lien provisions of this section.

(2) Obtained the property owner's address and telephone number, together with a written declaration signed by the property owner stating that the property owner has read and understands the summary provided pursuant to paragraph (1), at the time of entering into the transaction from which the lien arose.

(3) Posted, at the time of the transaction from which the lien arose, a notice which fully and fairly informs the public of the substance of this section. The notice shall be posted in a location clearly visible to the public in the lienholder's business premises.

(b) Any lienholder proceeding under this section shall notify the owner of the property subject to the lien upon completion of the work for which the lien is claimed. This notice shall be by first–class mail.

(c) If a property owner who has actually received notice pursuant to subdivision (b) fails to pay the charges for which the lien is claimed for 30 days following receipt of the notice, the lienholder may thereafter charge two dollars ($2) per day for storing the property subject to the lien and these charges shall also be secured by the lien.

(d) Not less than 30 days following the notice specified in subdivision (b), the lienholder shall notify the property owner by first-class mail that the property will be sold to satisfy the lien, unless the charges are paid within 30 days following the mailing of the notice.

(e) If the lienholder has complied with the notice requirements of subdivisions (b) and (d), not less than 30 days have elapsed since the mailing of the notice required by subdivision (d), and the property owner has not fully paid the original charges for which the lien is claimed plus any additional charges authorized by subdivision (c), the lienholder may sell the property subject to the lien at a public or bona fide private sale to satisfy the sum of those obligations, all costs and expenses of the sale, and interest at the rate of 12 percent per annum from 30 days following receipt of the notice specified in subdivision (b) or the date the same were advanced until repayment.

(f) However, the owner of the property sold pursuant to subdivision (e) may redeem the property sold to satisfy the lien, within 20 days following the sale, upon payment of all charges, costs and expenses, and interest specified in subdivision (e).

(g) The proceeds of the sale shall first be applied to the discharge of the lien, the costs of sale, and interest specified in subdivision (e). The remainder, if any, shall be paid to the former owner of the property so sold. **Leg.H.** Added Stats 1991 ch 606 §1 (AB 1939).

§3052.5. Registered service dealers' disposal of serviced products of nominal value

(a) Sections 3052 and 3052b shall not apply to any service dealer registered with the Bureau of Repair Services pursuant to Chapter 20 (commencing with Section 9800) of Division 3 of the Business and Professions Code if the dealer reasonably believes that the serviced product is of nominal value. For purposes of this section, nominal value shall be ascertained as follows: the product is not readily salable for more than the legitimate charges against it, and either the original retail value of the product was under two hundred dollars ($200) and the product is over three years old, or the original retail value is over two hundred dollars ($200) and the product is over six years old.

Service dealers may use any available materials or information, including, but not limited to, industry publications, code dates, sales records, or receipts to assist in determining value and age of the serviced product.

(b) A service dealer may select one of the following alternative methods for the disposal of unclaimed serviced products determined to have a value as specified in subdivision (a):

(1) The service dealer may provide the owner of the product with the following written notice to be mailed following completion of work on the serviced product:

DATE BROUGHT IN _____
DATE MAILED _____
DATE PRODUCT TO BE SOLD IF NOT CLAIMED _____

NOTICE: YOUR PRODUCT HAS BEEN DETERMINED BY THIS SERVICE DEALER TO BE ONE WHICH WAS EITHER ORIGINALLY SOLD FOR LESS THAN $200 AND IS NOW OVER THREE YEARS OLD OR ONE WHICH WAS ORIGINALLY SOLD FOR MORE THAN $200 AND WHICH IS NOW OVER SIX YEARS OLD AND THE CHARGES FOR SERVICING YOUR PRODUCT WILL EXCEED ITS CURRENT VALUE. UNDER CALIFORNIA CIVIL CODE SECTION 3052.5(a) IF YOU OR YOUR AGENT FAIL TO CLAIM YOUR PRODUCT WITHIN 90 DAYS AFTER THE DEALER MAILS A COPY OF THIS NOTICE TO YOU IT MAY BE SOLD OR OTHERWISE DISPOSED OF BY HIM OR HER.

The notice shall be sent by certified mail, return receipt requested. A serviced product may be disposed of 90 days after the date of deliverance evidenced by the signature in the returned receipt.

(2) The service dealer may publish public notice of the intended sale in a newspaper of general circulation. The notice shall contain a description of the serviced product, the name of the serviced product owner, and the time by which and place where the product may be redeemed. The notice shall be published for a minimum of five times. A serviced product may be disposed of 90 days after the last date of publication.

(3) A service dealer may, upon receipt of any product to be serviced by him or her, provide the owner of the product with the following notice, written in at least 10-point boldface type:

DATE BROUGHT IN _____
DATE MAILED _____
DATE PRODUCT TO BE SOLD IF NOT CLAIMED _____

NOTICE: YOUR PRODUCT HAS BEEN DETERMINED BY THIS SERVICE DEALER TO BE ONE WHICH WAS EITHER ORIGINALLY

SOLD FOR LESS THAN $200 AND IS NOW OVER THREE YEARS OLD OR ONE WHICH WAS ORIGINALLY SOLD FOR MORE THAN $200 AND WHICH IS NOW OVER SIX YEARS OLD AND THE CHARGES FOR SERVICING YOUR PRODUCT WILL EXCEED ITS CURRENT VALUE. UNDER CALIFORNIA CIVIL CODE SECTION 3052.5(a) IF YOU OR YOUR AGENT FAIL TO CLAIM YOUR PRODUCT WITHIN 90 DAYS AFTER THE DEALER MAILS A COPY OF THIS NOTICE TO YOU IT MAY BE SOLD OR OTHERWISE DISPOSED OF BY HIM OR HER.

PRINT YOUR NAME AND MAILING ADDRESS WHERE NOTICE MAY BE SENT TO YOU IN THE SPACE PROVIDED BELOW AND SIGN WHERE INDICATED TO SHOW THAT YOU HAVE READ THIS NOTICE.

_____
(Print Name)

_____
(Street Address)

_____
(City, State and ZIP Code)

IF YOU DO NOT AGREE WITH THE ABOVE DETERMINED VALUE OF YOUR ITEM, DO NOT SIGN THIS DOCUMENT.

Signature: _____
(Owner or Agent)

This notice shall be signed, addressed, and dated by the owner, with a copy to be retained by both the owner and the service dealer. At the completion of service, the service dealer shall by first-class mail, mail a completed copy of the notice to the owner of the serviced product at the address given on the notice form. A serviced product may be disposed of 90 days after the date of mailing.

(c) For purposes of this section, an owner is the person or agent who authorizes the original service or repair, or delivers the product to the service dealer. **Leg.H.** Added Stats 1977 ch 988 §1. Amended Stats 1991 ch 606 §2 (AB 1939); Stats 2006 ch 538 §57 (SB 1852), effective January 1, 2007.

§3053. Lien of factor

A factor has a general lien, dependent on possession, for all that is due to him as such, upon all articles of commercial value that are intrusted to him by the same principal. **Leg.H.** Enacted Stats 1872.

§3054. Banker's lien

(a) A banker, or a savings and loan association, has a general lien, dependent on possession, upon all property in their hands belonging to a customer, for the balance due to the banker or savings and loan association from the customer in the course of the business.

(b) The exercise of this lien with respect to deposit accounts shall be subject to the limitations and procedures set forth in Section 1411 or 6660 of the Financial Code. **Leg.H.** Enacted Stats 1872. Amended Stats 1975 ch 948 §1; Stats 1980 ch 1288 §1; Stats 1987 ch 56 §21; Stats 2019 ch 497 §30 (AB 991), effective January 1, 2020.

§§3055, 3056. [Sections repealed 1937]

Leg.H. Enacted Stats 1872. Repealed Stats 1937 ch 368 (H & N C §10001) p 1002. See H & N C §§492, 493.

§3057. [Section repealed 1983]

Leg.H. Enacted Stats 1872. Repealed Stats 1982 ch 497 §11, operative July 1, 1983.

§3058. [Section repealed 1983]

Leg.H. Enacted Stats 1872. Repealed Stats 1982 ch 497 §12, operative July 1, 1983.

§3059. Mechanics lien

The liens of mechanics, for materials and services upon real property, are regulated by Chapter 4 (commencing with Section 8400) of Title 2 of Part 6 of Division 4. **Leg.H.** Enacted Stats 1872. Amended Stats 1975 ch 678 §4; Stats 2010 ch 697 §13 (SB 189), effective January 1, 2011, operative July 1, 2012.

§3060. Mining liens

(a) As used in this section, "mine" means a mining claim or real property worked on as a mine including, but not limited to, any quarry or pit, from which rock, gravel, sand, or any other mineral-containing property is extracted by any mining, or surface mining, operation.

(b) Any person who performs labor in a mine, either in its development or in working on it by the subtractive process, or furnishes materials to be used or consumed in it, has a lien upon the mine and the works owned and used by the owners for milling or reducing the ores from the mine, for the value of the work or labor done or materials furnished by each, whether done or furnished at the instance of the owner of the mine, or the owner's agent, and every contractor, subcontractor, superintendent, or other person having charge of any mining or work or labor performed in and about the mine, either as lessee or under a working bond or contract thereon, shall be held to be the agent of the owner for the purposes of this section. The liens provided for by this section shall be enforced in the same manner as those provided for by Part 6 (commencing with Section 8000) of Division 4.

(c) This section shall become operative on July 1, 2012. **Leg.H.** Added Stats 1951 ch 1159 §2. Amended Stats 1969 ch 1362 §1; Stats 2010 ch 697 §14 (SB 189), effective January 1, 2011, operative July 1, 2012; Stats 2012 ch 263 §2 (AB 2654), effective September 7, 2012, operative July 1, 2012.

Prior Law: Former §3060, similar to present H & N C §490, was enacted Stats 1872 and repealed Stats 1937 ch 368 (H & N C §10001) p 1002.

There was another section of this number that was added Stats 1951 ch 1159 §2, was amended Stats 1969 ch 1362 §1, Stats 2012 ch 263 §1, effective September 7, 2012, inoperative July 1, 2012, repealed January 1, 2013.

2012 Note: It is the intent of the Legislature, in amending the definition of "mine" in Section 3060 of the Civil Code, to supersede the holding of the Fourth District Court of Appeal in *Sukut Const., Inc. v. Rimrock CA LLC* (2011) 199 Cal.App.4th 817. Stats 2012 ch 263 (AB 2654) §3.

Former Sections: Former CC §3060 was added in 1951, became inoperative July 1, 2012, and repealed operative January 1, 2013, by its own provisions. Stats 2012 ch 263 (AB 2654) §1, effective September 7, 2012.

§3061. Lien on barley-crusher or threshing machine

Every person performing work or labor in, with, about, or upon any barley-crusher, threshing-machine or engine, horse-power, wagon, or other appliance thereof, while engaged in crushing or threshing, has a lien thereon to the extent of the value of his services. Such lien extends for ten days after any such person ceases such work or labor; provided, within that time, an action is brought to recover the amount of the claim. If judgment is given in favor of the plaintiff in any such action, and it is further found that he is entitled to a lien under the provisions of this section, property subject thereto, or so much thereof as may be necessary, may be sold to satisfy such judgment; but if several judgment have been recovered against the same property for the enforcement of such liens, the proceeds of the sale must be divided pro rata among the judgment creditors. **Leg.H.** Added Stats 1905 ch 461 §1.

§3061.5. Agricultural laborer's lien

(a) Except as provided in subdivision (d), any person who as an employee shall, by his or her own labor, do or perform any work harvesting or transporting harvested crops or farm products as defined in Section 55403 of the Food and Agricultural Code which are owned and grown or produced by a limited partnership as defined in Section 15501 of the Corporations Code, has a lien upon any and all of the severed crops or severed farm products or proceeds from their sale for the value of the labor done up to a maximum of earnings for two weeks. The liens attach whether the work was done at the instance of the owner who is the grower or producer of severed crops or severed farm products or of any other person acting by or under the owner's authority, directly or indirectly, as contractor or otherwise; and every contractor, subcontractor, or other person having charge of the harvesting or transporting of the severed crops or severed farm products shall be held to be the agent of the owner for the purposes of this section.

(b) The liens provided for in this section attach from the date of the commencement of the work or labor, and are preferred liens, prior in dignity to all other liens, claims, or encumbrances. Except as provided in subdivisions (a) and (c) they shall not be limited as to amount by any contract price agreed upon between the owner who is the grower or producer of the severed crops or severed farm products and any contractor, but the several liens shall not in any case exceed in amount the reasonable value of the labor done, nor the price agreed upon for the labor between the claimant and his or her employer. In no event, where the claimant was employed by a contractor, or subcontractor, shall the lien extend to any labor not contemplated by, covered by, or reasonably necessary to the execution of, the original contract between the contractor and the owner who is the grower or producer of severed crops or severed farm products and of which contract, or modification thereof, the claimant had actual notice before the performance of the labor.

(c) The maximum liability of severed crops, severed farm products or the proceeds from their sale subject to liens under this section is limited to the lesser of actual proved claims or 25 percent of the fair market value of the severed crops, severed farm products, or 25 percent of the proceeds after their sale.

(d) No person has a lien if the owner who is the grower or producer of the severed crops, severed farm products, or their proceeds, who otherwise would be subject to a lien pursuant to subdivision (a), either gives directly, or requires a person or entity hired or used to furnish labor in connection with harvesting or transporting the severed crops, to give to the Labor Commissioner prior to the harvest and for 45 days after its completion, a bond executed by an admitted surety insurer in an amount and form acceptable to the Labor Commissioner, which is conditioned upon the payment of all wages found to be due and unpaid in connection with such operations under any provision of this code.

(e) A buyer in the ordinary course of business, as defined in paragraph (9) of subdivision (b) of Section 1201 of the Commercial Code, shall take free of any security interest created by this section, notwithstanding the fact that the lien is perfected and the buyer knows of its existence. **Leg.H.** Added Stats 1976 ch 1059 §1, operative July 1, 1977. Amended Stats 1982 ch 517 §76; Stats 2006 ch 254 §3 (SB 1481), effective January 1, 2007.

§3061.6. Enforcement of agricultural laborer's lien

(a) The lien created by Section 3061.5 shall continue in force for a period of 45 days from the time the person claiming such lien shall have ceased to do or perform the work for which such lien is claimed, and such lien shall cease at the expiration of the 45 days unless the claimant, his or her assignee or successor in interest, files a claim with the Labor Commissioner or brings suit to foreclose the lien in which case the lien continues in force until the claim filed with the Labor Commissioner or the lien foreclosure suit is finally determined and closed. If a claim is filed with the Labor Commissioner, the Labor Commissioner shall act upon and finally determine such claim within 180 days after filing. In case such proceedings are not prosecuted to trial within two years after the commencement thereof, the court may in its discretion dismiss the same for want of prosecution.

(b) Upon filing a claim with the Labor Commissioner, the Labor Commissioner, if the owner who is the grower or producer has failed to satisfy the conditions of subdivision (d) of Section 3061.5, shall determine whether or not such owner of the severed crops, severed farm products, or their proceeds is capable financially of satisfying such claim. For purposes of this determination, it shall be proper for the Labor Commissioner after investigation to take into account the potential liability faced by such owner of such severed crops, severed farm products, or their proceeds. If the Labor Commissioner determines that a lien is necessary to protect the interest of claimants, the Labor Commissioner shall file such lien on the crop, the severed farm product, or their proceeds and notify, in writing, the owner and notify, in writing, all persons who have filed financing statements on the crop, the farm product, or their proceeds pursuant to the provisions of the Commercial Code.

(c) The plaintiff in any such lien foreclosure suit, at the time of issuing the summons or at any time afterwards, may have the severed crops or severed farm products or proceeds from their sale upon which such lien subsists attached, as provided in this code and Title 6.5 (commencing with Section 488.010) of Part 2 of the Code of Civil Procedure, upon delivering to the clerk an affidavit, by or on behalf of the plaintiff, showing that: (1) the plaintiff, or his assignor or predecessor in interest, performed labor in harvesting or transporting the severed crops or severed farm products or both; (2) that such labor has not been paid for; (3) that the sum for which the attachment is asked does not exceed the lesser of the reasonable value of the services rendered or if earnings, does not exceed the lesser of two weeks unpaid earnings or reasonable value of actual services rendered, or 25 percent of the fair market value of the severed crop or severed farm product; and (4) that the attachment is not sought and the action is not brought to hinder, delay or defraud any creditor or creditors of any defendant.

(d) Any number of persons claiming liens under this section and Section 3061.5 may join in the same action and when separate actions are commenced, the court may consolidate them. If after sale of the property subject to the liens provided for in this section and Section 3061.5, under the judgment or decree of foreclosure of such lien or liens, there is a deficiency of proceeds, the proceeds shall be divided pro rata among the lien claimants whose liens are established, regardless of the order in which the liens were created or the order in which the suits to foreclose same were commenced. Judgment for the deficiency may be docketed against the party personally liable therefor and his sureties.

(e) Nothing contained in this section or Section 3061.5 shall be construed to impair or affect the right of any person to whom any debt may be due for work done, to maintain a personal action to recover such debt against the person liable therefor, or his sureties, either in connection with the lien suit or in a separate action. The person bringing such personal action may take out a separate attachment therefor, notwithstanding his or her lien, and in his or her affidavit or procure an attachment need not state that his or her demand is not secured by a lien, and the judgment, if any, obtained by the plaintiff in such personal action shall not be construed to impair or merge any lien held by the plaintiff under this section or Section 3061.5; provided that any money collected on the judgment shall be credited on the amount of such lien in any action brought to enforce the same, in accordance with the provisions of this section.

(f) If the lien has attached to perishable goods, the lienholder may, during the period for which the lien is in effect and prior to the filing of a foreclosure suit, obtain a court order for the sale of such perishable goods pursuant to the provisions of Section 488.530 of the Code of Civil Procedure; provided, however, that in the event that such perishable crop is subject in whole or in part to a valid marketing agreement which is in force between the owner who is the grower or producer and an agricultural marketing cooperative organized under the Food and Agricultural Code or similar laws of other states, the agricultural marketing cooperative may purchase or otherwise take possession or custody of such crop or portion thereof according to the terms of the marketing agreement. Any moneys due and payable to such owner who is the grower or producer in return for such crop shall be paid by the agricultural marketing cooperative to the court. **Leg.H.** Added Stats 1976 ch 1059 §2, operative July 1, 1977.

§3062. Lien for service of stallion, jack, or bull

Every owner or person having in charge any stallion, jack, or bull, used for propagating purposes, has a lien for the agreed price of its service upon any mare or cow and upon the offspring of such service, unless some willfully false representation concerning the breeding or pedigree of such stallion, jack, or bull has been made or published by the owner or person in charge thereof, or by some other person, at the request or instigation of such owner or person in charge. **Leg.H.** Added Stats 1905 ch 461 §2 p 618.

§3063. Recording of verified claim as to animal breeder's lien

Every claimant of a lien provided for in the preceding section must, within 90 days after the service on account of which the lien is claimed, record in the office of the county recorder of the county where the mare or cow subject thereto is kept, a verified claim containing a particular description of the mare or cow, the date and place of service, the name of the owner or reputed owner of such mare or cow, a description by name, or otherwise, of the stallion, jack, or bull performing the service, the name of the owner or person in charge thereof, and the amount of the lien claimed. Such claim, so recorded, is notice to subsequent purchasers and encumbrancers of such mare or cow and of the offspring of such service for one year after such recording. **Leg.H.** Added Stats 1905 ch 461 §3. Amended Stats 1957 ch 815 §1.

§3064. Action to enforce animal breeder's lien

An action to enforce any lien created under Section 3062 may be brought in any county wherein any of the property subject thereto may be found, and the plaintiff is entitled to the remedies provided in Section 3065 upon complying with such section, which is hereby made applicable to the proceedings in such action. **Leg.H.** Added Stats 1905 ch 461 §4. Amended Stats 1968 ch 48 §4.

§3064.1. Effect of false advertising as to animal's pedigree

Every person who wilfully advertises any cattle, horse, sheep, swine, or other domestic animal for purposes of copulation or profit as having a pedigree other than the true pedigree of such animal shall forfeit all right by law to collect pay for the services of such animal. **Leg.H.** Added Stats 1955 ch 60 §1 p 501.

§3065. Logger's lien

Any person who shall, by his own labor, or by using his livestock, machinery or appliances, or both, do or perform any work or render any service in connection with felling, preparing or transporting any logs, or in manufacturing lumber or other timber products from such logs, including the production of tanbark, shall have a lien upon any and all of such logs and upon any and all of the lumber and other timber products manufactured therefrom, whether said work was done or service was rendered on the logs themselves, or any of them, or in manufacturing the lumber or other timber products from them, for the value of such labor done and for the value of the use of such livestock, machinery and appliances, or both, whether said work was done or service was rendered at the instance of the owner of such logs or timber products manufactured therefrom, or of any other person acting by his authority or under him, directly or indirectly, as contractor or otherwise; and every contractor, subcontractor or other person having charge of the felling, preparing or transporting of the said logs or of their manufacture into timber products shall be held to be the agent of the said owner for the purposes of this section.

The liens provided for in this section shall attach from the date of the commencement of such work or labor, or the date of the commencement of the use of such livestock, machinery or appliances, as the case may be, and shall be preferred liens, prior in dignity to all other liens, claims or encumbrances, except the landowner's claim for a reasonable stumpage in cases where the landowner himself is not the direct employer or contractor, as the case may be. They shall not be limited as to amount by any contract price agreed upon between the owner of said logs or timber products manufactured therefrom and any contractor, except as hereinafter provided, but said several liens shall not in any case exceed in amount the reasonable value of the labor done, or the reasonable value of the use of the livestock, machinery or appliances for which the lien is claimed, nor the price agreed upon for the same between the claimant and the person by whom he was employed or with whom the agreement to use livestock, machinery or appliances was made, nor in any case, where the claimant was employed by a contractor, or subcontractor, shall the lien extend to any labor or the use of any livestock, machinery or appliances not embraced within, contemplated by, covered by, or reasonably necessary to the execution of, the original contract between the contractor and the owner of such logs or timber products manufactured therefrom, or any modification thereof made by or with the consent of such owner, and of which said contract, or modification thereof, the claimant shall have had actual notice before the performance of such labor or the use of such livestock, machinery or appliances.

The recording of such original contract, or modification thereof, in the office of the county recorder of the county in which the timberland on which the work is to be done is situated or in which the logs are to be manufactured into timber products, as the case may be, before the commencement of the work, shall be equivalent to the giving of such actual notice by the owner to all persons performing work or using livestock, machinery or appliances thereunder. In case said original contract shall, before the work is commenced, be so recorded, together with a bond of the contractor with good and sufficient sureties in an amount not less than fifty (50) percent of the contract price named in said contract, which bond shall in addition to any conditions for the performance of the contract, be also conditioned for the payment in full of the claims of all persons performing labor, or using livestock, machinery or appliances, in the execution of such contract and shall also by its terms be made to inure to the benefit of any and all persons who perform labor or use livestock, machinery or appliances in the execution of the work to be done under the contract so as to give such persons, and their assigns or successors in interest, a right of action to recover upon said bond in any suit brought to enforce the liens provided for in this section, or in a separate suit brought on said bond, then the court must, where it would be equitable so to do, restrict the recovery under such liens to an aggregate amount equal to the amount found to be due from the owner of the said logs or timber products manufactured therefrom to the contractor, and render judgment against the contractor and his sureties on said bond for any deficiency or difference there may remain between said amount so found to be due to the claimants for such labor and for the use of such livestock, machinery and appliances. It is the intent and purpose of this section to limit the owner's liability, in all cases, to the measure of the contract price where he shall have filed or cause to be filed, in good faith, with his original contract a valid bond with good and sufficient sureties in the amount and upon the conditions herein provided. It shall be lawful for the owner of such logs and timber products to protect himself against any failure of the contractor to perform his contract and make full payment for all work done thereunder by exacting such bond or other security as he may deem satisfactory. **Leg.H.** Added Stats 1905 ch 461 §5. Amended Stats 1927 ch 505 §1; Stats 1973 ch 665 §2.

§3065a. Duration of logger's lien; Joinder of claimants

The lien created by the last preceding section shall continue in force for a period of 30 days from the time the person claiming such lien shall have ceased to do or perform the work or render the service for which said lien is claimed, while such logs, lumber or other manufactured timber products are in the county in which such labor was performed or service rendered, and said lien shall cease at the expiration of the said 30 days unless the claimant thereof, or his assignee or successor in interest, brings suit to foreclose the same, in which case the lien continues in force until the said lien foreclosure suit is finally determined and closed, and in case such proceeding be not prosecuted to trial within two years after the commencement thereof, the court may in its discretion dismiss the same for want of prosecution. If any part of the property on which the lien existed is removed from the said county, the lien continues on the balance remaining in the county to the full extent of the claim.

The plaintiff in any such lien foreclosure suit may have the logs, lumber and other manufactured timber products upon which such lien subsists attached, as provided in this code and the Code of Civil Procedure.

Any number of persons claiming liens under this and the next preceding section may join in the same action and when separate actions are commenced, the court may consolidate them. Whenever upon the sale of the property subject to the liens provided for in this and the next preceding section, under the judgment or decree of foreclosure of such lien or liens, there is a deficiency of proceeds, the proceeds shall be divided pro rata among the lien claimants whose liens are established, regardless of the order in which the liens were created or the order in which the suits to foreclose same were commenced, and judgment for the deficiency may be docketed against the party personally liable therefor and his sureties, in like manner and with like effect as in actions for the foreclosure of mortgages.

Nothing contained in this or the next preceding section shall be construed to impair or affect the right of any person to whom any debt may be due for work done, or for the use of livestock, machinery or appliances, to maintain a personal action to recover said debt against the person liable therefor, or his sureties, either in connection with the lien suit or in a separate action, and the person bringing such personal action may take out a separate attachment therefor, notwithstanding his lien or the amount of his debt, and in his affidavit to procure an attachment he shall state that the attachment is made pursuant to this section, and the judgment, if any, obtained by the plaintiff in such personal action shall not be construed to impair or merge any lien held by said plaintiff under this or the next preceding section; provided, only, that any money collected on said judgment shall be credited on the amount of such lien in any action brought to enforce the same, in accordance with the provisions of this section. **Leg.H.** Added Stats 1927 ch 505 §2. Amended Stats 1974 ch 1516 §4, operative January 1, 1977.

§3065b. Cessation of work defined

As used in the next preceding section the words "the time the person claiming such lien shall have ceased to do or perform the work or render the service for which said lien is claimed" shall be construed to mean the final date work was done or services were rendered on any of the logs, lumber or other manufactured timber products on which the lien is claimed, so as to give the lien claimant, or his assignee or successor in interest, a full thirty days after final cessation of labor to bring suit to foreclose his lien on any or all of the logs, lumber or other manufactured timber products in question. **Leg.H.** Added Stats 1929 ch 157 §1 p 301.

§3065c. Lien of faller, bucker, or millhand for wages owed by contractor

Whenever any faller, bucker, or millhand has a lien pursuant to Section 3065 and has not been paid for his labor by the contractor employing him, and money is owing to such contractor by a mill operator, any such faller, bucker, or millhand, or several of them acting jointly, may file with the

Labor Commissioner an affidavit stating the amount of wages unpaid to him or them and describing the labor for which wages are owed and the period in which such labor was performed. If the Labor Commissioner finds the affidavit in order, he shall send to such mill operator a stop notice directing such mill operator to withhold funds in the amount of the unpaid wages from the contractor. The mill operator shall withhold such funds pursuant to the stop notice for 15 days from the date of service of the notice, subject to garnishment within that period by the faller, bucker, or millhand or any assignee thereof. **Leg.H.** Added Stats 1957 ch 338 §1.

§3066. Sale of garment or clothing to pay charges for cleaning or alterations

(a) Any garment, clothing, wearing apparel or household goods remaining in the possession of a person, firm, partnership or corporation, on which cleaning, pressing, glazing or washing has been done or upon which alterations or repairs have been made, or on which materials or supplies have been used or furnished, for a period of 90 days or more after the completion of such work may be sold to pay the reasonable or agreed charges and the costs of notifying the owner or owners. Provided, however, that the person, firm, partnership, or corporation to whom such charges are payable and owing shall first notify the owner or owners of the time and place of such sale. Provided further, that property that is to be placed in storage after any of the services or labors mentioned herein, shall not be affected by the provisions of this section.

(b) All garments, clothing, wearing apparel or household goods placed in storage, or on which any of the services or labors mentioned in the preceding section of this act have been performed and then placed in storage by agreement and remaining in the possession of a person, firm, partnership or corporation without the reasonable or agreed charges having been paid for a period of 12 months, may be sold to pay said charges. Provided that the person, firm, partnership or corporation to whom the charges are payable, shall first notify the owner or owners thereof of the time and place of sale. Provided, however, that the persons, firms, partnerships, or corporations operating as warehouses or warehousemen shall not be affected by this section.

(c) The posting or mailing of a registered letter, with a return address marked thereon, addressed to the owner or owners, at their address given at the time of delivery of the article or articles to a person, firm, partnership or corporation to render any of the services or labors set out in this act, stating the time and place of sale, shall constitute notice. Said notice shall be posted or mailed at least 30 days before the date of sale. The cost of posting or mailing said letter shall be added to the charges.

Where the address of an owner is unknown, a posting of notice, for a period of 30 days, at a prominent place in the receiving office of the person, firm, partnership or corporation required to give the notice is sufficient.

(d) The person, firm, partnership or corporation to whom the charges are payable, shall, from the proceeds of the sale, deduct the charges due plus the costs of notifying the owner and shall hold the overplus, if any, subject to the order of the owner and shall immediately thereafter mail to the owner thereof at his address, if known, a notice of the sale, the amount of the overplus, if any, due him, and at any time within 12 months, upon demand by the owner, pay to the owner said sums or overplus in his hands.

(e) All persons, firms, partnerships or corporations taking advantage of this act must keep posted in a prominent place in their receiving office or offices at all times one notice which shall read as follows:

"All articles cleaned, pressed, glazed, laundered, washed, altered or repaired and not called for in 90 days shall be sold to pay charges." "All articles stored by agreement and charges not having been paid for 12 months will be sold to pay charges." **Leg.H.** Added Stats 1945 ch 910 §1 p 1695. Amended Stats 1955 ch 665 §1.

CHAPTER 6.5
LIENS ON VEHICLES

Definitions. §3067.
Forms. §3067.1.
Limitations of chapter. §3067.2.
Labor and material liens on vehicles. §3068.
Towing and storage liens. §3068.1.
Tow truck operator's lien. §3068.2.
Assignment of lien. §3069.
Revival of lost liens; Misdemeanor violations; Forfeiture of claims. §3070.

Lien sales. §3071.
Release of owner's interest in vehicle. §3071.5.
Notice of sale. §3072.
Disposal of proceeds of vehicle lien sale. §3073.
Recovery of costs. §3074.

§3067. Definitions

Words used in this chapter which are defined in Division 1 of the Vehicle Code shall have the same meaning as in the Vehicle Code. **Leg.H.** Added Stats 1959 ch 3 §3 p 1791.

§3067.1. Forms

All forms required pursuant to the provisions of this chapter shall be prescribed by the Department of Motor Vehicles. The language used in the notices and declarations shall be simple and nontechnical. **Leg.H.** Added Stats 1980 ch 1111 §1.

§3067.2. Limitations of chapter

This chapter shall not apply to any manufactured home, as defined in Section 18007 of the Health and Safety Code, to any mobilehome, as defined in Section 18008 of the Health and Safety Code, or to any commercial coach, as defined in Section 18001.8 of the Health and Safety Code, whether or not the manufactured home, mobilehome, or commercial coach is subject to registration under the Health and Safety Code. **Leg.H.** Added Stats 1983 ch 1124 §7.

§3068. Labor and material liens on vehicles

(a) Every person has a lien dependent upon possession for the compensation to which the person is legally entitled for making repairs or performing labor upon, and furnishing supplies or materials for, and for the storage, repair, or safekeeping of, and for the rental of parking space for, any vehicle of a type subject to registration under the Vehicle Code, subject to the limitations set forth in this chapter. The lien shall be deemed to arise at the time a written statement of charges for completed work or services is presented to the registered owner or 15 days after the work or services are completed, whichever occurs first. Upon completion of the work or services, the lienholder shall not dismantle, disengage, remove, or strip from the vehicle the parts used to complete the work or services.

(b)(1) Any lien under this section that arises because work or services have been performed on a vehicle with the consent of the registered owner shall be extinguished and no lien sale shall be conducted unless either of the following occurs:

(A) The lienholder applies for an authorization to conduct a lien sale within 30 days after the lien has arisen.

(B) An action in court is filed within 30 days after the lien has arisen.

(2) A person whose lien for work or services on a vehicle has been extinguished shall turn over possession of the vehicle, at the place where the work or services were performed, to the legal owner or the lessor upon demand of the legal owner or lessor, and upon tender by the legal owner or lessor, by cashier's check or in cash, of only the amount for storage, safekeeping, or parking space rental for the vehicle to which the person is entitled by subdivision (c).

(3) Any lien under this section that arises because work or services have been performed on a vehicle with the consent of the registered owner shall be extinguished, and no lien sale shall be conducted, if the lienholder, after written demand made by either personal service or certified mail with return receipt requested by the legal owner or the lessor to inspect the vehicle, fails to permit that inspection by the legal owner or lessor, or his or her agent, within a period of time not sooner than 24 hours nor later than 72 hours after the receipt of that written demand, during the normal business hours of the lienholder.

(4) Any lien under this section that arises because work or services have been performed on a vehicle with the consent of the registered owner shall be extinguished, and no lien sale shall be conducted, if the lienholder, after written demand made by either personal service or certified mail with return receipt requested by the legal owner or the lessor to receive a written copy of the work order or invoice reflecting the services or repairs performed on the vehicle and the authorization from the registered owner requesting the lienholder to perform the services or repairs, fails to provide that copy to the legal owner or lessor, or his or her agent, within 10 days after the receipt of that written demand.

(c) The lienholder shall not charge the legal owner or lessor any amount for release of the vehicle in excess of the amounts authorized by this subdivision.

(1) That portion of the lien in excess of one thousand five hundred dollars ($1,500) for any work or services, or that amount, subject to the limitations contained in Section 10652.5 of the Vehicle Code, in excess of one thousand twenty-five dollars ($1,025) for any storage, safekeeping, or rental of parking space or, if an application for an authorization to conduct a lien sale has been filed pursuant to Section 3071 within 30 days after the commencement of the storage or safekeeping, in excess of one thousand two hundred fifty dollars ($1,250) for any storage or safekeeping, rendered or performed at the request of any person other than the legal owner or lessor, is invalid, unless prior to commencing any work, services, storage, safekeeping, or rental of parking space, the person claiming the lien gives actual notice in writing either by personal service or by registered letter addressed to the legal owner named in the registration certificate, and the written consent of that legal owner is obtained before any work, services, storage, safekeeping, or rental of parking space are performed.

(2) Subject to the limitations contained in Section 10652.5 of the Vehicle Code, if any portion of a lien includes charges for the care, storage, or safekeeping of, or for the rental of parking space for, a vehicle for a period in excess of 60 days, the portion of the lien that accrued after the expiration of that period is invalid unless Sections 10650 and 10652 of the Vehicle Code have been complied with by the holder of the lien.

(3) The charge for the care, storage, or safekeeping of a vehicle which may be charged to the legal owner or lessor shall not exceed that for one day of storage if, 24 hours or less after the vehicle is placed in storage, a request is made for the release of the vehicle. If the request is made more than 24 hours after the vehicle is placed in storage, charges may be imposed on a full, calendar-day basis for each day, or part thereof, that the vehicle is in storage.

(d) In any action brought by or on behalf of the legal owner or lessor to recover a vehicle alleged to be wrongfully withheld by the person claiming a lien pursuant to this section, the prevailing party shall be entitled to reasonable attorney's fees and costs, not to exceed one thousand seven hundred fifty dollars ($1,750). **Leg.H.** Added Stats 1959 ch 3 §3. Amended Stats 1959 ch 197 §2; Stats 1965 ch 1135 §1; Stats 1968 ch 830 §2; Stats 1974 ch 1262 §2, effective September 23, 1974, operative November 1, 1974; Stats 1978 ch 1005 §4; Stats 1980 ch 1111 §2; Stats 1983 ch 764 §1; Stats 1988 ch 1092 §4; Stats 1991 ch 727 §1 (AB 1882); Stats 1994 ch 799 §1 (AB 3164); Stats 2007 ch 121 §1 (AB 1575), effective January 1, 2008.

§3068.1. Towing and storage liens

(a)(1) Every person has a lien dependent upon possession for the compensation to which the person is legally entitled for towing, storage, or labor associated with recovery or load salvage of any vehicle subject to registration that has been authorized to be removed by a public agency, a private property owner pursuant to Section 22658 of the Vehicle Code, or a lessee, operator, or registered owner of the vehicle. The lien is deemed to arise on the date of possession of the vehicle. Possession is deemed to arise when the vehicle is removed and is in transit, or when vehicle recovery operations or load salvage operations have begun. A person seeking to enforce a lien for the storage and safekeeping of a vehicle shall impose no charge exceeding that for one day of storage if, 24 hours or less after the vehicle is placed in storage, the vehicle is released. If the release is made more than 24 hours after the vehicle is placed in storage, charges may be imposed on a full-calendar-day basis for each day, or part thereof, that the vehicle is in storage. If a request to release the vehicle is made and the appropriate fees are tendered and documentation establishing that the person requesting release is entitled to possession of the vehicle, or is the owner's insurance representative, is presented within the initial 24 hours of storage, and the storage facility fails to comply with the request to release the vehicle or is not open for business during normal business hours, then only one day's charge may be required to be paid until after the first business day. A "business day" is any day in which the lienholder is open for business to the public for at least eight hours. If the request is made more than 24 hours after the vehicle is placed in storage, charges may be imposed on a full-calendar-day basis for each day, or part thereof, that the vehicle is in storage.

(2) "Documentation" that would entitle a person to possession of the vehicle includes, but is not limited to, a certificate of ownership, vehicle registration, information in the possession of the lienholder including ownership information obtained from the Department of Motor Vehicles or a facially valid registration found within the vehicle, or a notarized letter or statement from the legal or registered owner providing authorization to release to a particular person with a government-issued photographic identification card. Documentation that establishes that a person is the owner's insurance representative includes, but is not limited to, a faxed letter or other letter from the owner's insurance company. A lienholder is not responsible for determining the authenticity of documentation specifically described in this subdivision that establishes either a person's entitlement to possession or that a person is the owner's insurance representative.

(b) If the vehicle has been determined to have a value not exceeding four thousand dollars ($4,000), the lien shall be satisfied pursuant to Section 3072. Lien sale proceedings pursuant to Section 3072 shall commence within 15 days of the date the lien arises. No storage shall accrue beyond the 15-day period unless lien sale proceedings pursuant to Section 3072 have commenced. The storage lien may be for a period not exceeding 60 days if a completed notice of a pending lien sale form has been filed pursuant to Section 3072 within 15 days after the lien arises. Notwithstanding this 60-day limitation, the storage lien may be for a period not exceeding 120 days if any one of the following occurs:

(1) A Declaration of Opposition form is filed with the department pursuant to Section 3072.

(2) The vehicle has an out-of-state registration.

(3) The vehicle identification number was altered or removed.

(4) A person who has an interest in the vehicle becomes known to the lienholder after the lienholder has complied with subdivision (b) of Section 3072.

(c) If the vehicle has been determined to have a value exceeding four thousand dollars ($4,000) pursuant to Section 22670 of the Vehicle Code, the lien shall be satisfied pursuant to Section 3071. The storage lien may be for a period not exceeding 120 days if an application for an authorization to conduct a lien sale has been filed pursuant to Section 3071.

(d)(1) Any lien under this section shall be extinguished, and a lien sale shall not be conducted, if any one of the following occurs:

(A) The lienholder, after written demand to inspect the vehicle made by either personal service or certified mail with return receipt requested by the legal owner or the lessor, fails to permit the inspection by the legal owner or lessor, or his or her agent, within a period of time of at least 24 hours, but not to exceed 72 hours, after the receipt of that written demand, during the normal business hours of the lienholder. The legal owner or lessor shall comply with inspection and vehicle release policies of the impounding public agency.

(B) The amount claimed for storage exceeds the posted rates.

(2) "Agent" includes, but is not limited to, any person designated to inspect the vehicle by the request of the legal owner or lessor, in writing or by telephone, to the lienholder. A lienholder is not responsible for determining the authenticity of documentation establishing a person's agency for the purposes of inspection of a vehicle.

(e) A lienholder shall not be liable for any claim or dispute directly arising out of the reliance on documentation specifically described in paragraph (2) of subdivision (a) for purposes of releasing a vehicle. **Leg.H.** Added Stats 1980 ch 1111 §3. Amended Stats 1984 ch 73 §1; Stats 1987 ch 1091 §1; Stats 1989 ch 457 §1; Stats 1991 ch 727 §2 (AB 1882), ch 1004 §1 (SB 887); Stats 1992 ch 1220 §1 (AB 3424); Stats 1994 ch 799 §2 (AB 3164) Stats 1995 ch 404 §1 (SB 240); Stats 1996 ch 267 §1 (SB 223); Stats 1998 ch 203 §1 (SB 1650); Stats 2010 ch 566 §1 (AB 519), effective January 1, 2011.

§3068.2. Tow truck operator's lien

(a) A tow truck operator who has a lien on a vehicle pursuant to Section 3068.1 has a deficiency claim against the registered owner of the vehicle if the vehicle is not leased or leased with a driver for an amount equal to the towing and storage charges, not to exceed 120 days of storage, and the lien sale processing fee pursuant to Section 3074, less the amount received from the sale of the vehicle.

(b) A tow truck operator who has a lien on a vehicle pursuant to Section 3068.1 has a deficiency claim against the lessee of the vehicle if the vehicle is leased without a driver for an amount equal to the towing and storage charge, not to exceed 120 days of storage, and the lien sale processing fee described in Section 3074, less the amount received from the sale of the vehicle.

(c) Storage costs incurred after the sale shall not be included in calculating the amount received from the sale of the vehicle.

(d) A registered owner who has sold or transferred the owner's vehicle prior to the vehicle's removal and who was not responsible for creating the circumstances leading to the removal of the vehicle is not liable for any deficiency under this section if that registered owner has fulfilled the requirements of Section 5602 of the Vehicle Code. The person identified as the transferee in the notice submitted to the Department of Motor Vehicles shall be liable for the amount of any deficiency only if that person received notice of the transfer and is responsible for the event leading to abandonment of the vehicle or requested the removal.

(e) Except as provided in Section 22524.5 of the Vehicle Code, if the transferee is an insurer and the transferor is its insured or the transferor's agent or representative, the insurer shall not be liable for any deficiency, unless the insurer agrees at the time of the transfer, to assume liability for the deficiency. **Leg.H.** Added Stats 1994 ch 1220 §2.5 (AB 3132), effective September 30, 1994. Amended Stats 2020 ch 50 §1 (AB 2319), effective January 1, 2021.

§3069. Assignment of lien

Any lien provided for in this chapter for labor or materials, or for storage or safekeeping of a vehicle when abandoned on private property may be assigned by written instrument accompanied by delivery of possession of the vehicle, subject to the lien, and the assignee may exercise the rights of a lienholder as provided in this chapter. Any lienholder assigning a lien as authorized herein shall at the time of assigning the lien give written notice either by personal delivery or by registered or certified mail, to the registered and legal owner of the assignment, including the name and address of the person to whom the lien is assigned. **Leg.H.** Added Stats 1959 ch 3 §3. Amended Stats 1969 ch 125 §1.

§3070. Revival of lost liens; Misdemeanor violations; Forfeiture of claims

(a) Whenever the possessory lien upon any vehicle is lost through trick, fraud, or device, the repossession of the vehicle by the lienholder revives the possessory lien but any lien so revived is subordinate to any right, title, or interest of any person under any sale, transfer, encumbrance, lien, or other interest acquired or secured in good faith and for value between the time of the loss of possession and the time of repossession.

(b) It is a misdemeanor for any person to obtain possession of any vehicle or any part thereof subject to a lien pursuant to this chapter by trick, fraud, or device.

(c) It is a misdemeanor for any person claiming a lien on a vehicle to knowingly violate this chapter.

(d)(1) Any person who improperly causes a vehicle to be towed or removed in order to create or acquire a lienhold interest enforceable under this chapter, or who violates subdivision (c), shall forfeit all claims for towing, removal, or storage, and shall be liable to the owner or lessee of the vehicle for the cost of removal, transportation, and storage, damages resulting from the towing, removal, transportation, or storage of the vehicle, attorneys' fees, and court costs.

(2) For purposes of this subdivision, "improperly causes a vehicle to be towed or removed" includes, but is not limited to, engaging in any of the following acts, the consequence of which is the towing or removal of a vehicle:

(A) Failure to comply with Section 10650, 10652.5, or 10655 of the Vehicle Code.

(B) Misrepresentation of information described in subdivision (b) of Section 10650 of the Vehicle Code.

(C) Failure to comply with Section 22658 of the Vehicle Code.

(D) Failure, when obtaining authorization for the removal of a vehicle from a vehicle owner or operator where a law enforcement officer is not present at the scene of an accident, to present a form for signature that plainly identifies all applicable towing and storage fees and charges by type and amount, and identifies the name and address of the storage facility unless a different storage facility is specified by the vehicle owner or operator, and to furnish a copy of the signed form to the owner or operator.

(E) Failure by the owner or operator of a facility used for the storage of towed vehicles to display, in plain view at all cashiers' stations, a sign not less than 17 by 22 inches in size with lettering not less than one inch in height, disclosing all storage fees and charges in force, including the maximum daily storage rate.

(F) Undertaking repairs or service on a vehicle which is being stored at a facility used for the storage of towed vehicles without first providing a written estimate to, and obtaining the express written consent of, the owner of the vehicle.

(G) The promise to pay or the payment of money or other valuable consideration by any owner or operator of a towing service to the owner or operator of the premises from which the vehicle is towed or removed, for the privilege of towing or removing the vehicle. **Leg.H.** Added Stats 1980 ch 1111 §5. Amended Stats 1991 ch 1004 §2 (SB 887); Stats 1993 ch 479 §1 (AB 1113); Stats 1994 ch 799 §3 (AB 3164).

Prior Law: Former §3070, similar to the present section, was added Stats 1959 ch 3 §3 and repealed Stats 1980 ch 1111 §4.

§3071. Lien sales

(a) A lienholder shall apply to the department for the issuance of an authorization to conduct a lien sale pursuant to this section for any vehicle with a value determined to be over four thousand dollars ($4,000). A filing fee shall be charged by the department and may be recovered by the lienholder if a lien sale is conducted or if the vehicle is redeemed. The application shall be executed under penalty of perjury and shall include all of the following information:

(1) A description of the vehicle, including make, year model, identification number, license number, and state of registration. For motorcycles, the engine number also shall be included. If the vehicle identification number is not available, the department shall request an inspection of the vehicle by a peace officer, licensed vehicle verifier, or departmental employee before accepting the application.

(2) The names and addresses of the registered and legal owners of the vehicle, if ascertainable from the registration certificates within the vehicle, and the name and address of any person whom the lienholder knows, or reasonably should know, claims an interest in the vehicle.

(3) A statement of the amount of the lien and the facts that give rise to the lien.

(b) Upon receipt of an application made pursuant to subdivision (a), the department shall do all of the following:

(1) Notify the vehicle registry agency of a foreign state of the pending lien sale, if the vehicle bears indicia of registration in that state.

(2) By certified mail, send a notice, a copy of the application, and a return envelope preaddressed to the department to the registered and legal owners at their addresses of record with the department, and to any other person whose name and address is listed in the application.

(c) The notice required pursuant to subdivision (b) shall include all of the following statements and information:

(1) An application has been made with the department for authorization to conduct a lien sale.

(2) The person has a right to a hearing in court.

(3) If a hearing in court is desired, a Declaration of Opposition form, signed under penalty of perjury, shall be signed and returned to the department within 10 days of the date that the notice required pursuant to subdivision (b) was mailed.

(4) If the Declaration of Opposition form is signed and returned to the department, the lienholder shall be allowed to sell the vehicle only if he or she obtains a court judgment, if he or she obtains a subsequent release from the declarant or if the declarant, cannot be served as described in subdivision (e).

(5) If a court action is filed, the declarant shall be notified of the lawsuit at the address shown on the Declaration of Opposition form and may appear to contest the claim.

(6) The person may be liable for court costs if a judgment is entered in favor of the lienholder.

(d) If the department receives the Declaration of Opposition form in the time specified, the department shall notify the lienholder within 16 days of the receipt of the form that a lien sale shall not be conducted unless the lienholder files an action in court within 30 days of the department's notice under this subdivision. A lien sale of the vehicle shall not be conducted unless judgment is subsequently entered in favor of the lienholder or the declarant subsequently releases his or her interest in the vehicle. If a money judgment is entered in favor of the lienholder and the judgment is not paid within five days after becoming final, then the judgment may be enforced by lien sale proceedings conducted pursuant to subdivision (f).

(e) Service on the declarant in person or by certified mail with return receipt requested, signed by the declarant or an authorized agent of the declarant at the address shown on the Declaration of Opposition form, shall be effective for the serving of process. If the lienholder has served the declarant by certified mail at the address shown on the Declaration of Opposition form and the mail has been returned unclaimed, or if the lienholder has attempted to effect service on the declarant in person with a marshal, sheriff, or licensed process server and the marshal, sheriff, or licensed process server has been unable to effect service on the declarant, the lienholder may proceed with the judicial proceeding or proceed with the lien sale without a judicial proceeding. The lienholder shall notify the department of the inability to effect service on the declarant and shall provide the department with a copy of the documents with which service on the declarant was attempted. Upon receipt of the notification of unsuccessful service, the department shall send authorization of the sale to the lienholder and send notification of the authorization to the declarant.

(f) Upon receipt of authorization to conduct the lien sale from the department, the lienholder shall immediately do all of the following:

(1) At least five days, but not more than 20 days, prior to the lien sale, not counting the day of the sale, give notice of the sale by advertising once in a newspaper of general circulation published in the county in which the vehicle is located. If there is no newspaper published in the county, notice shall be given by posting a Notice of Sale form in three of the most public places in the town in which the vehicle is located and at the place where the vehicle is to be sold for 10 consecutive days prior to and including the day of the sale.

(2) Send a Notice of Pending Lien Sale form 20 days prior to the sale but not counting the day of sale, by certified mail with return receipt requested, to each of the following:

(A) The registered and legal owners of the vehicle, if registered in this state.

(B) All persons known to have an interest in the vehicle.

(C) The department.

(g) All notices required by this section, including the notice forms prescribed by the department, shall specify the make, year model, vehicle identification number, license number, and state of registration, if available, and the specific date, exact time, and place of sale. For motorcycles, the engine number shall also be included.

(h) Following the sale of a vehicle, the person who conducts the sale shall do both of the following:

(1) Remove and destroy the vehicle's license plates.

(2) Within five days of the sale, submit a completed "Notice of Release of Liability" form to the Department of Motor Vehicles.

(i) The Department of Motor Vehicles shall retain all submitted forms described in paragraph (2) of subdivision (h) for two years.

(j) No lien sale shall be undertaken pursuant to this section unless the vehicle has been available for inspection at a location easily accessible to the public for at least one hour before the sale and is at the place of sale at the time and date specified on the notice of sale. Sealed bids shall not be accepted. The lienholder shall conduct the sale in a commercially reasonable manner.

(k) Within 10 days after the sale of any vehicle pursuant to this section, the legal or registered owner may redeem the vehicle upon the payment of the amount of the sale, all costs and expenses of the sale, together with interest on the sum at the rate of 12 percent per annum from the due date thereof or the date when that sum was advanced until the repayment. If the vehicle is not redeemed, all lien sale documents required by the department shall then be completed and delivered to the buyer.

(*l*) Any lien sale pursuant to this section shall be void if the lienholder does not comply with this chapter. Any lien for fees or storage charges for parking and storage of a motor vehicle shall be subject to Section 10652.5 of the Vehicle Code. **Leg.H.** Added Stats 1980 ch 1111 §7. Amended Stats 1984 ch 73 §2, operative until January 1, 1988; Stats 1987 ch 1091 §2; Stats 1990 ch 1284 §1 (AB 3049); Stats 1992 ch 1220 §2 (AB 3424); Stats 1994 ch 799 §4 (AB 3164); Stats 1998 ch 203 §2 (SB 1650); Stats 1999 ch 376 §1 (AB 327); Stats 2001 ch 127 §1 (SB 46), effective July 30, 2001.

Prior Law: Former §3071, similar to the present section, was added Stats 1959 ch 3 §3, amended Stats 1974 ch 1262 §3, effective September 23, 1974, Stats 1975 ch 1036 §1, effective September 24, 1975, Stats 1978 ch 1005 §5, and repealed Stats 1980 ch 1111 §6.

§3071.3. [Section repealed 1980]

Leg.H. Added Stats 1975 ch 1036 §2, effective September 24, 1975. Amended Stats 1978 ch 1005 §6. Repealed Stats 1980 ch 1111 §8. See CC §3072.

§3071.5. Release of owner's interest in vehicle

(a) A registered or legal owner of a vehicle in the possession of a person holding a lien under this chapter may release any interest in the vehicle after the lien has arisen. The release shall be dated when signed and a copy shall be given at the time the release is signed to the person releasing the interest.

(b) The release shall be in at least 12-point type and shall contain all of the following information in simple, nontechnical language:

(1) A description of the vehicle, including the year and make, the engine or vehicle identification number, and the license number, if available.

(2) The names and addresses of the registered and legal owners of record with the Department of Motor Vehicles, if available.

(3) A statement of the amount of the lien and the facts concerning the claim which gives rise to the lien.

(4) A statement that the person releasing the interest understands that (i) he has a legal right to a hearing in court prior to any sale of the vehicle to satisfy the lien and (ii) he is giving up the right to appear to contest the claim of the lienholder.

(5) A statement that (i) the person releasing the interest gives up any interest he may have in the vehicle and (ii) he is giving the lienholder permission to sell the vehicle.

(c) The release required by this section shall not be filed with the department in connection with any transfer of interest in a vehicle. **Leg.H.** Added Stats 1974 ch 1262 §4, effective September 23, 1974, operative November 1, 1974. Amended Stats 1978 ch 1005 §7.

§3072. Notice of sale

(a) For vehicles with a value determined to be four thousand dollars ($4,000) or less, the lienholder shall apply to the department for the names and addresses of the registered and legal owners of record. The request shall include a description of the vehicle, including make, year, model, identification number, license number, and state of registration. If the vehicle identification number is not available, the Department of Motor Vehicles shall request an inspection of the vehicle by a peace officer, licensed vehicle verifier, or departmental employee before releasing the names and addresses of the registered and legal owners and interested parties.

(b) The lienholder shall, immediately upon receipt of the names and addresses, send, by certified mail with return receipt requested or by United States Postal Service Certificate of Mailing, a completed Notice of Pending Lien Sale form, a blank Declaration of Opposition form, and a return envelope preaddressed to the department, to the registered owner and legal owner at their addresses of record with the department, and to any other person known to have an interest in the vehicle. The lienholder shall additionally send a copy of the completed Notice of Pending Lien Sale form to the department by certified mail on the same day that the other notices are mailed pursuant to this subdivision.

(c) All notices to persons having an interest in the vehicle shall be signed under penalty of perjury and shall include all of the following information and statements:

(1) A description of the vehicle, including make, year model, identification number, license number, and state of registration. For motorcycles, the engine number shall also be included.

(2) The specific date, exact time, and place of sale, which shall be set not less than 31 days, but not more than 41 days, from the date of mailing.

(3) The names and addresses of the registered and legal owners of the vehicle and any other person known to have an interest in the vehicle.

(4) All of the following statements:

(A) The amount of the lien and the facts concerning the claim which gives rise to the lien.

(B) The person has a right to a hearing in court.

(C) If a court hearing is desired, a Declaration of Opposition form, signed under penalty of perjury, shall be signed and returned to the department within 10 days of the date the Notice of Pending Lien Sale form was mailed.

(D) If the Declaration of Opposition form is signed and returned, the lienholder shall be allowed to sell the vehicle only if he or she obtains a court judgment or if he or she obtains a subsequent release from the declarant or if the declarant cannot be served as described in subdivision (e).

(E) If a court action is filed, the declarant shall be notified of the lawsuit at the address shown on the Declaration of Opposition form and may appear to contest the claim.

(F) The person may be liable for court costs if a judgment is entered in favor of the lienholder.

(d) If the department receives the completed Declaration of Opposition form within the time specified, the department shall notify the lienholder within 16 days that a lien sale shall not be conducted unless the lienholder files an action in court within 30 days of the notice and judgment is subsequently entered in favor of the lienholder or the declarant subsequently releases his or her interest in the vehicle. If a money judgment is entered in favor of the lienholder and the judgment is not paid within five days after becoming final, then the judgment may be enforced by lien sale proceedings conducted pursuant to subdivision (f).

(e) Service on the declarant in person or by certified mail with return receipt requested, signed by the declarant or an authorized agent of the declarant at the address shown on the Declaration of Opposition form, shall be effective for the serving of process. If the lienholder has served the declarant by certified mail at the address shown on the Declaration of Opposition form and the mail has been returned unclaimed, or if the lienholder has attempted to effect service on the declarant in person with a marshal, sheriff, or licensed process server and the marshal, sheriff, or licensed process server has been unable to effect service on the declarant, the lienholder may proceed with the judicial proceeding or proceed with the lien sale without a judicial proceeding. The lienholder shall notify the Department of Motor Vehicles of the inability to effect service on the declarant and shall provide the Department of Motor Vehicles with a copy of the documents with which service on the declarant was attempted. Upon receipt of the notification of unsuccessful service, the Department of Motor Vehicles shall send authorization of the sale to the lienholder and shall send notification of the authorization to the declarant.

(f) At least 10 consecutive days prior to and including the day of the sale, the lienholder shall post a Notice of Pending Lien Sale form in a conspicuous place on the premises of the business office of the lienholder and if the pending lien sale is scheduled to occur at a place other than the premises of the business office of the lienholder, at the site of the forthcoming sale. The Notice of Pending Lien Sale form shall state the specific date and exact time of the sale and description of the vehicle, including the make, year model, identification number, license number, and state of registration. For motorcycles, the engine number shall also be included. The notice of sale shall remain posted until the sale is completed.

(g) Following the sale of a vehicle, the person who conducts the sale shall do both of the following:

(1) Remove and destroy the vehicle's license plates.

(2) Within five days of the sale, submit a completed "Notice of Release of Liability" form with the Department of Motor Vehicles.

(h) The Department of Motor Vehicles shall retain all submitted forms described in paragraph (2) of subdivision (g) for two years.

(i) No lien sale shall be undertaken pursuant to this section unless the vehicle has been available for inspection at a location easily accessible to the public at least one hour before the sale and is at the place of sale at the time and date specified on the notice of sale. Sealed bids shall not be accepted. The lienholder shall conduct the sale in a commercially reasonable manner. All lien sale documents required by the department shall be completed and delivered to the buyer immediately following the sale.

(j) Any lien sale pursuant to this section shall be void if the lienholder does not comply with this chapter. Any lien for fees or storage charges for parking and storage of a motor vehicle shall be subject to Section 10652.5 of the Vehicle Code. **Leg.H.** Added Stats 1980 ch 1111 §10. Amended Stats 1984 ch 73 §3, operative until January 1, 1988; Stats 1987 ch 1091 §3; Stats 1990 ch 1284 §2 (AB 3049); Stats 1992 ch 1220 §3 (AB 3424); Stats 1994 ch 799 §5 (AB 3164); Stats 1998 ch 203 §3 (SB 1650); Stats 1999 ch 376 §2 (AB 327); Stats 2001 ch 127 §2 (SB 46), effective July 30, 2001.

Prior Law: Former §3072, similar to the present section, was added Stats 1959 ch 3 §3, amended Stats 1967 ch 1085 §1, Stats 1974 ch 1262 §5, effective September 23, 1974, operative November 1, 1974, Stats 1978 ch 1005 §8, and repealed Stats 1980 ch 1111 §9.

§3072.2. [Section repealed 1980]

Leg.H. Added Stats 1978 ch 1005 §9. Repealed Stats 1980 ch 1111 §11. See CC §3073.

§3073. Disposal of proceeds of vehicle lien sale

The proceeds of a vehicle lien sale under this article shall be disposed of as follows:

(a) The amount necessary to discharge the lien and the cost of processing the vehicle shall be paid to the lienholder. The cost of processing shall not exceed seventy dollars ($70) for each vehicle valued at four thousand dollars ($4,000) or less, or one hundred dollars ($100) for each vehicle valued over four thousand dollars ($4,000).

(b) The balance, if any, shall be forwarded to the Department of Motor Vehicles within 15 days of any sale conducted pursuant to Section 3071 or within five days of any sale conducted pursuant to Section 3072 and deposited in the Motor Vehicle Account in the State Transportation Fund, unless federal law requires these funds to be disposed in a different manner.

(c) Any person claiming an interest in the vehicle may file a claim with the Department of Motor Vehicles for any portion of the funds from the lien sale that were forwarded to the department pursuant to subdivision (b). Upon a determination of the Department of Motor Vehicles that the claimant is entitled to an amount from the balance deposited with the department, the department shall pay that amount determined by the department, which amount shall not exceed the amount forwarded to the department pursuant to subdivision (b) in connection with the sale of the vehicle in which the claimant claims an interest. The department shall not honor any claim unless the claim has been filed within three years of the date the funds were deposited in the Motor Vehicle Account. **Leg.H.** Added Stats 1980 ch 1111 §13. Amended Stats 1988 ch 511 §1; Stats 1990 ch 1284 §3 (AB 3049); Stats 1992 ch 1220 §4 (AB 3424); Stats 1994 ch 799 §6 (AB 3164); Stats 1998 ch 203 §4 (SB 1650).

Prior Law: Former §3073, relating to sale of abandoned vehicles by lienholder, was added Stats 1959 ch 3 §3, amended Stats 1965 ch 1135 §2, Stats 1967 ch 1085 §2, Stats 1969 ch 125 §2, Stats 1975 ch 1063 §3, effective September 24, 1975, Stats 1978 ch 1005 §10, and repealed Stats 1980 ch 1111 §12.

§3074. Recovery of costs

The lienholder may charge a fee for lien sale preparations not to exceed seventy dollars ($70) in the case of a vehicle having a value determined to be four thousand dollars ($4,000) or less and not to exceed one hundred dollars ($100) in the case of a vehicle having a value determined to be greater than four thousand dollars ($4,000), from any person who redeems the vehicle prior to disposal or is paid through a lien sale pursuant to this chapter. These charges may commence and become part of the possessory lien when the lienholder requests the names and addresses of all persons having an interest in the vehicle from the Department of Motor Vehicles. Not more than 50 percent of the allowable fee may be charged until the lien sale notifications are mailed to all interested parties and the lienholder or registration service agent has possession of the required lien processing documents. This charge shall not be made in the case of any vehicle redeemed prior to 72 hours from the initial storage. **Leg.H.** Added Stats 1995 ch 404 §3 (SB 240). Amended Stats 1996 ch 676 §1 (SB 1111); Stats 1998 ch 203 §5 (SB 1650).

Prior Law: Former §3074, similar to the present section, was added Stats 1980 ch 1111 §15, amended Stats 1988 ch 511 §2, Stats 1990 ch 1284 §4, Stats 1992 ch 1220 §5, and repealed Stats 1995 ch 404 §2.

Former §3074, similar to present CC §3071, was added Stats 1959 ch 3 §3, amended Stats 1978 ch 1005 §11, and repealed Stats 1980 ch 1111 §14.

§3075. [Section repealed 1983]

Leg.H. Added Stats 1980 ch 1111 §17. Repealed Stats 1983 ch 1124 §8. The repealed section related to mobilehomes.

Prior Law: Former §3075, similar to present §3070, was added Stats 1959 ch 3 §3 and repealed Stats 1980 ch 1111 §16.

§§3076, 3077. [Sections repealed 1965]

Leg.H. Enacted Stats 1872. Repealed Stats 1963 ch 819 §§18, 19 p 2001, effective January 1, 1965. See UCC §2702.

§§3078, 3079. [Sections repealed 1931]

Leg.H. Enacted Stats 1872 and repealed Stats 1931 ch 1070 §2 p 2258. The repealed sections related to stoppage in transit.

CHAPTER 6.7
LIVESTOCK SERVICE LIEN

Definitions. §3080.
General lien. §3080.01.

Rights of lienholder. §3080.02.
Application for order authorizing sale of livestock. §3080.03.
Notice of application and hearing. §3080.04.
Notice of opposition. §3080.05.
Showing required to authorize sale. §3080.06.
Denial of application. §3080.07.
Court findings; Effect. §3080.08.
Application for order for substitution of undertaking. §3080.09.
Order directing release of livestock; Conditions. §3080.10.
Undertaking substituted for livestock; Amount. §3080.11.
Showing great or irreparable injury. §3080.15.
Manner of sale; Application of proceeds; Accounting. §3080.16.
Notice of sale. §3080.17.
Public sale. §3080.18.
Effect of sale. §3080.19.
Release of livestock; Contents. §3080.20.
Retention of livestock in satisfaction of claim; Written proposal. §3080.21.
Assignment. §3080.22.

§3080. Definitions

As used in this chapter, the following definitions shall apply:

(a) "Livestock" means any cattle, sheep, swine, goat, or horse, mule, or other equine.

(b) "Livestock servicer" means any individual, corporation, partnership, joint venture, cooperative, association or any other organization or entity which provides livestock services.

(c) "Livestock services" means any and all grazing, feeding, boarding, general care, which includes animal health services, obtained or provided by the livestock servicer, or his employee, transportation or other services rendered by a person to livestock for the owner of livestock, or for any person acting by or under the owner's authority. **Leg.H.** Added Stats 1979 ch 600 §2.

Prior Law: Former §3080, relating to stoppage in transit, was enacted Stats 1872 and repealed Stats 1931 ch 1070 §2.

§3080.01. General lien

A livestock servicer shall have a general lien upon the livestock in its possession to secure the performance of all obligations of the owner of the livestock to the livestock servicer for both of the following:

(a) The provision of livestock services to the livestock in possession of the livestock servicer.

(b) The provision of livestock services to other livestock for which livestock services were provided in connection with or as part of the same livestock service transaction, if such livestock services were provided within the immediately preceding 12 months prior to the date upon which the lien arose. The lien shall have priority over all other liens upon and security interests in the livestock, shall arise as the charges for livestock services become due, and shall be dependent upon possession. The lien shall secure the owner's contractual obligations to the lienholder for the provision of livestock services, the lienholder's reasonable charges for the provision of livestock services after the lien has arisen as set forth in Section 3080.02, and the lienholder's costs of lien enforcement, including attorney's fees. **Leg.H.** Added Stats 1979 ch 600 §2.

§3080.02. Rights of lienholder

In addition to any other rights and remedies provided by law, a lienholder may:

(a) Retain possession of the livestock and charge the owner for the reasonable value of providing livestock services to the livestock until the owner's obligations secured by the lien have been satisfied.

(b) Proceed to sell all or any portion of the livestock pursuant to Section 3080.16 if:

(1) A judicial order authorizing sale has been entered pursuant to Section 3080.06;

(2) A judgment authorizing sale has been entered in favor of the lienholder on the claim which gives rise to the lien; or

(3) The owner of the livestock has released, after the lien has arisen, its interest in the livestock in the form prescribed by Section 3080.20.

(c) A lienholder may commence a legal action on its claim against the owner of the livestock or any other person indebted to the lienholder for services to the livestock and reduce the claim to judgment. When the lienholder has reduced the claim to judgment, any lien or levy or other form of enforcement which may be made upon the livestock by virtue of any execution based upon the judgment shall relate back to the attachment of and have the same priority as the livestock service lien. The lienholder may purchase at a judicial sale held pursuant to the execution on the judgment and thereafter hold the livestock free of any liens upon or security interests in the livestock. **Leg.H.** Added Stats 1979 ch 600 §2.

§3080.03. Application for order authorizing sale of livestock

Upon the filing of the complaint, or at any time thereafter prior to judgment, the lienholder may apply to the court in which the action was commenced for an order authorizing sale of livestock.

(a) The application shall include all of the following:

(1) A statement showing that the sale is sought pursuant to this chapter to enforce a livestock service lien;

(2) A statement of the amount the lienholder seeks to recover from the defendant and the date that amount became due;

(3) A statement setting forth the reasons why a sale should be held prior to judgment;

(4) A description of the livestock to be sold and an estimate of the fair market value thereof; and

(5) A statement of the manner in which the lienholder intends to sell the livestock. The statement shall include, but not be limited to, whether the sale will be public or private, the amount of proceeds expected from the sale, and, why the sale, if authorized, would conform to the standard of commercial reasonableness set forth in Section 3080.16.

(b) The application shall be supported by an affidavit or affidavits showing that on the facts presented therein the lienholder would be entitled to a judgment on the claim upon which the action is brought.

(c) A hearing shall be held in the court in which the lienholder has brought the action before an order authorizing sale is issued under this chapter. Except as provided in Section 3080.15, or as ordered by the court upon good cause shown, the defendant shall be served with a copy of all of the following at least 10 days prior to the date set for hearing:

(1) A summons and complaint;

(2) A notice of application and hearing; and

(3) An application and all affidavits filed in support thereof. **Leg.H.** Added Stats 1979 ch 600 §2.

§3080.04. Notice of application and hearing

The notice of application and hearing shall inform the defendant of all of the following:

(a) The date, time and place of the hearing on the application;

(b) That the order will issue if the court finds, after hearing, that the lienholder has established the probable validity of the claim and has satisfied the other requirements set forth in this chapter;

(c) The hearing is not held for the purpose of determining the actual validity of the claim which determination will be made in other proceedings in the action and will not be affected by the findings made at the hearing on the application for the order;

(d) If the order authorizing sale is issued, the lienholder may proceed to sell the livestock in the manner set forth in the order, and the sale proceeds will be deposited with the court pending judgment on the lienholder's claim;

(e) If the defendant desires to oppose the issuance of the order, the defendant must file with the court and serve on the lienholder a notice of opposition and supporting affidavit as required by Section 3080.05 no later than three days prior to the date set for hearing;

(f) At the hearing, the court may deny the lienholder's application if the defendant files an undertaking as set forth in Section 3080.11; and

(g) The notice shall contain the following statement: "You may seek the advice of an attorney as to any matters concerning the lienholder's complaint and application. If an attorney is to assist you, he or she should be consulted promptly. You or your attorney or both of you may be present at the hearing." **Leg.H.** Added Stats 1979 ch 600 §2.

§3080.05. Notice of opposition

(a) If a defendant desires to oppose the issuance of an order authorizing sale the defendant shall file and serve upon the lienholder a notice of opposition no later than three days prior to the date set for hearing. The notice shall:

(1) State the grounds upon which the defendant opposes the order;

(2) Be accompanied by an affidavit or affidavits supporting any factual issues raised;

(3) State whether the defendant is prepared to file an undertaking as provided in Section 3080.11; and

(4) If the defendant is prepared to file an undertaking, include an estimate of the amount of such undertaking as set forth in Section 3080.09 and the defendant's basis for the estimate.

(b) Except when the lienholder has made an ex parte application for an order as set forth in Section 3080.15, or for good cause shown, a defendant shall not be permitted to oppose the issuance of an order if it has failed to file a notice of opposition within the time prescribed. **Leg.H.** Added Stats 1979 ch 600 §2.

§3080.06. Showing required to authorize sale

(a) At the hearing, the court shall consider the showing made by the parties and shall issue an order authorizing the sale of the livestock if it finds all of the following:

(1) The claim upon which the lienholder's action is based is a claim giving rise to a lien upon which an order authorizing sale may be issued under this chapter;

(2) The lienholder has established the probable validity of the claim upon which the action is based;

(3) The lienholder has established the probable validity of the lien sought to be enforced by sale;

(4) The sale is necessary to prevent a possible decline in the value or condition of the livestock or that the sale should be held in the interest of equity;

(5) The sale is not sought for a purpose other than the recovery on the claim upon which the lien is based; and

(6) The sale, if conducted in the manner set forth in the application, would be conducted in a commercially reasonable manner.

(b) The order authorizing sale shall:

(1) Identify the livestock for which sale is authorized;

(2) Specify the manner of sale including the date, time, place, necessary publication or other notice; and

(3) Except as may be ordered pursuant to subdivision (c), direct the lienholder to deposit the proceeds of sale with the clerk of the court pending final judgment in the action.

(c) The court may in its discretion do either of the following:

(1) Authorize the lienholder to deduct and retain funds from the sale proceeds in an amount sufficient to compensate the lienholder for services provided to the livestock from the date that the lien arose until the date of sale.

(2) Determine the amount of sale proceeds reasonably necessary to satisfy the indebtedness secured by the livestock service lien and order any portion or all of the remaining sale proceeds distributed and applied as set forth in paragraph (3) of subdivision (c) of Section 3080.16.

The balance of sale proceeds, if any, remaining after any deductions authorized in this section shall be deposited with the clerk of the court pursuant to this section. **Leg.H.** Added Stats 1979 ch 600 §2.

§3080.07. Denial of application

(a) After hearing, the court may issue an order denying the lienholder's application if it finds that:

(1) A sale is not necessary prior to judgment; and

(2) The defendant has filed an undertaking pursuant to Section 3080.11.

(b) If the defendant has filed an undertaking pursuant to Section 3080.11, the order shall direct the lienholder to assemble and make the livestock available to defendant, or to defendant's agent, at a specified date, time and place. **Leg.H.** Added Stats 1979 ch 600 §2.

§3080.08. Court findings; Effect

(a) The court's findings at the hearing shall be made upon the basis of the pleadings and other papers in the record. Upon cause shown, the court may receive and consider additional oral or documentary evidence or points and authorities at the hearing, or it may continue the hearing to allow the production of such additional evidence or points and authorities.

(b) The court's findings at the hearing shall have no effect on the determination of any issues in the action other than issues relevant to the proceedings authorized by this chapter, nor shall they affect the rights of the defendant in any other action arising out of the same claim. The court's determinations at the hearing shall neither be admissible as evidence nor referred to at the trial of any such action.

(c) Neither the failure of the defendant to oppose the issuance of an order authorizing sale, nor the defendant's failure to rebut any evidence produced by the lienholder at the hearing held for the issuance of such order, shall constitute a waiver of any defense to the lienholder's claim in the action or in any other action or have any effect on the right of the defendant to produce or exclude evidence at the trial of such action. **Leg.H.** Added Stats 1979 ch 600 §2.

§3080.09. Application for order for substitution of undertaking

(a) At any time after the lienholder has filed a complaint and claimed a lien under this chapter, or at any time after the owner of the livestock has commenced an action to recover possession of the livestock, the owner of the livestock may apply to the court in which the action was brought for an order for substitution of an undertaking which meets the requirements of Section 3080.11 for the livestock held by the lienholder.

(b) The application for such order shall be executed under oath and, unless included within a notice of opposition to sale as set forth in Section 3080.05, or except for good cause shown, shall be made upon noticed motion. Unless the parties otherwise agree, a hearing shall be held on the motion not less than five nor more than 10 days after service of notice of motion. The application shall contain all of the following:

(1) A description of the livestock to be recovered;

(2) An estimate and the basis for the estimate of the fair market value of the livestock;

(3) A statement identifying and describing the sureties for the undertaking. **Leg.H.** Added Stats 1979 ch 600 §2.

§3080.10. Order directing release of livestock; Conditions

After hearing, the court may enter an order directing the lienholder to release all or a portion of the livestock to the owner, or to the owner's agent. The order shall be conditioned upon the filing by the owner of an undertaking as set forth in Section 3080.11, and shall include all of the following:

(1) The amount of the undertaking required.

(2) The basis for the court's finding as to the fair market value of the livestock.

(3) A statement that the lienholder has the right to object to the undertaking pursuant to Section 995.910 of the Code of Civil Procedure.

(4) A description of the livestock to be substituted.

(5) A statement of the date, time, place and manner in which the lienholder is to turn over the livestock to the owner. **Leg.H.** Added Stats 1979 ch 600 §2. Amended Stats 1982 ch 517 §77.

§3080.11. Undertaking substituted for livestock; Amount

The undertaking to be substituted for livestock shall be by the owner to pay to the lienholder an amount equal to the sum of (1) the fair market value of the livestock sought to be recovered, and (2) the costs to be incurred by the lienholder in order to assemble and turn over the livestock. **Leg.H.** Added Stats 1979 ch 600 §2. Amended Stats 1982 ch 517 §78.

§3080.12. [Section repealed 1982]

Leg.H. Added Stats 1979 ch 600 §2. Repealed Stats 1982 ch 517 §79. The repealed section related to grounds on which the lienholder may object to the undertaking.

§3080.13. [Section repealed 1982]

Leg.H. Added Stats 1979 ch 600 §2. Repealed Stats 1982 ch 517 §80. The repealed section related to the hearing and determination on the sufficiency of the undertaking.

§3080.14. [Section repealed 1982]

Leg.H. Added Stats 1979 ch 600 §2. Repealed Stats 1982 ch 517 §81. The repealed section related to liability on an undertaking.

§3080.15. Showing great or irreparable injury

(a) Except as otherwise provided by statute, or upon noticed hearing as provided in this chapter, no order authorizing sale or order for substitution of undertaking for livestock may issue unless it appears from facts shown by affidavit that great or irreparable injury would result to the party seeking the order if the issuance of the order were delayed until the matter could be heard upon noticed hearing.

(b) In addition to a specific statement of the facts showing great or irreparable injury, any application made under this section for either an order authorizing sale or an order substituting undertaking for livestock shall include the substantive requirements of an application made under Section 3080.03 or Section 3080.09, respectively.

(c) The court shall examine the ex parte application, supporting affidavits and other papers on record and may issue the order sought if it finds all of the following:

(1) The party seeking the order is entitled to the order under the substantive provisions of this chapter;

(2) The party seeking the order will suffer great and irreparable injury if the order is not issued; and

(3) If the ex parte application is made for an order authorizing sale, the court determines that the condition of the livestock will greatly deteriorate or the value of the livestock will greatly depreciate before an order authorizing sale could be obtained pursuant to noticed hearing.

(d) An order issued under this section shall contain such provisions as the court determines to be in the interests of justice and equity to the parties, taking into account the effects on all parties under the circumstances of the particular case. If an order authorizing sale issues under this section, the court may authorize the lienholder to take any action necessary to preserve the value of the livestock so long as the court has determined that such action would be commercially reasonable under the circumstances.

(e) Upon ex parte application of any party affected by an order issued under this section or, if the court so orders, after a noticed hearing, the court may modify or vacate the order if it determines that such action would be proper under the circumstances. **Leg.H.** Added Stats 1979 ch 600 §2.

§3080.16. Manner of sale; Application of proceeds; Accounting

(a) Except as otherwise specified by the order authorizing sale or as agreed to by the parties after the lien has arisen, a sale of livestock under this chapter may be held in bulk or in parcels, at wholesale or retail, and at any time and place and on any terms, provided the lienholder acts in good faith and in a commercially reasonable manner. The livestock may be sold in its existing condition or following any commercially reasonable preparation or processing. The fact that a better price could have been obtained by a sale at a different time or in a different manner from that selected by the lienholder is not of itself sufficient to establish that the sale was not made in a commercially reasonable manner. If the lienholder either sells the livestock in the usual manner in any recognized market therefor or sells at the price current in such market at the time of the sale or, if it has otherwise sold in conformity with reasonable commercial sales practices for the type of livestock sold, it has sold in a commercially reasonable manner.

(b) Except as otherwise specified by order of the court, or as agreed to by all interested parties after the lien has arisen, the proceeds of sale shall be deposited with the clerk of the court in an interest-bearing account to abide the judgment in the action.

(c) Except as otherwise specified in the judgment in the action, the proceeds of sale shall be applied in the following order:

(1) For reasonable expenses incurred by the lienholder in enforcing the lien, including, but not limited to, the charges for livestock services from the date the lien arose to the date of sale; the costs of transporting and preparing the livestock for sale and of conducting the sale; and, the reasonable attorneys' fees and legal costs and expenses incurred by the lienholder;

(2) For satisfaction of the contractual indebtedness secured by the lien; and

(3) For satisfaction of indebtedness secured by any subordinate lien or security interest in the livestock if written notification or demand therefor is received by the court or the lienholder before the proceeds have been distributed. If requested by the lienholder, the holder of a subordinate lien or security interest must seasonably furnish reasonable proof to the court of its subordinate interest before the lienholder need comply with the demand.

(d) The lienholder must account to the owner of the livestock for any surplus and, unless otherwise provided in the judgment in the action, the owner shall be liable for any deficiency. **Leg.H.** Added Stats 1979 ch 600 §2.

§3080.17. Notice of sale

Except as otherwise agreed or specified by order of court, notice of sale shall be given as follows:

(a) A notice in writing of the date, time and place of sale shall be delivered personally or be deposited in the United States mail, postage prepaid, addressed to the owner of the livestock, at his last known address, and to any other person claiming a lien upon or security interest in the livestock, who had on file with the California Secretary of State on the date the lien arose a financing statement covering the livestock for which livestock services secured by the lien were provided at least five days before the date fixed for any public sale or before the day on or after which any private sale or other disposition is to be made.

(b) Notice of the time and place of a public sale shall also be given at least five days before the date of sale by publication once in a newspaper of general circulation published in the county in which the sale is to be held. If there is no such newspaper, notice shall be given by posting, for five days prior to sale, a notice of sale where the sale is to be conducted. **Leg.H.** Added Stats 1979 ch 600 §2.

§3080.18. Public sale

(a) Any sale of which notice is delivered or mailed and published as provided in this chapter and which is held as provided in this chapter is a public sale.

(b) Any public sale may be postponed from time to time by public announcement at the time and place last scheduled for sale.

(c) The lienholder may purchase the livestock at a public sale. **Leg.H.** Added Stats 1979 ch 600 §2.

§3080.19. Effect of sale

(a) A sale of livestock held pursuant to this chapter shall:

(1) Transfer to a purchaser for value all of the owner's rights in the livestock; and

(2) Discharge the lien under which the sale is made and any lien or security interest subordinate thereto.

(b) The purchaser shall take free of all such subordinate rights and interests even though the lienholder fails to comply with the requirements of this chapter or of any judicial proceeding if:

(1) In the case of a public sale, the purchaser has no knowledge of any defects in the sale and does not buy in collusion with the lienholder, other bidders or the person conducting the sale; or

(2) In any other case, the purchaser acts in good faith. **Leg.H.** Added Stats 1979 ch 600 §2.

§3080.20. Release of livestock; Contents

(a) The owner of livestock or any other person claiming an interest in livestock may release its interest in the livestock at any time after the lien has arisen. The release shall be in writing and dated when signed. A copy of the release shall be given to the person releasing the interest at the time the release is signed.

(b) The release shall contain all of the following information in simple, nontechnical language:

(1) A description of the livestock covered by the release and the releasing party's interest in the livestock;

(2) A statement of the amount of the lien to which the livestock is subject;

(3) A statement that the releasing party has a legal right to a hearing in court prior to any sale of the livestock to satisfy the lien;

(4) A statement by the releasing party that it is giving the lienholder permission to sell the livestock;

(5) A statement of the extent to which the releasing party gives up any interest it may have in the livestock or in the sale proceeds of the livestock; and,

(6) To the extent that the release is not given in full satisfaction of the lienholder's claim or claims against the releasing party, a statement by the releasing party that it is aware that the lienholder may still have a claim against it after the release has been executed. **Leg.H.** Added Stats 1979 ch 600 §2.

§3080.21. Retention of livestock in satisfaction of claim; Written proposal

At any time after a lien has arisen, the lienholder may propose to retain any portion or all of the livestock in satisfaction of any portion or all of the claim against the owner or other person indebted to the lienholder for livestock services. The proposal shall be made in writing to the owner and written notice thereof shall be given to any person entitled to receive notice under subdivision (a) of Section 3080.17. If, within 21 days after the notice was sent, the lienholder receives objection in writing from a person entitled to receive notification, the lienholder must proceed to sell the livestock and account for the proceeds pursuant to this chapter. In the absence of such written objection, the lienholder may retain the livestock, or so much thereof as proposed, in satisfaction of all or a portion of the claim against the owner and other person indebted to the lienholder for livestock services, upon the owner's and such other person's execution of a release conforming to Section 3080.20. **Leg.H.** Added Stats 1979 ch 600 §2.

§3080.22. Assignment

Any lien provided for in this chapter may be assigned by written instrument accompanied by delivery of possession of the livestock, subject to the lien, and the assignee may exercise the rights of a lienholder as provided in this chapter. Any lienholder assigning a lien as authorized herein shall at the time of assigning the lien give written notice of the assignment either by personal delivery or by registered or certified mail, to the legal owner and any other person entitled to receive notice under subdivision (a) of Section 3080.17, including the name and address of the person to whom the lien has been assigned. **Leg.H.** Added Stats 1979 ch 600 §2.

CHAPTER 7
STOPPAGE IN TRANSIT

Safe deposit boxes; Disposal of unclaimed contents. §3081.

§3081. Safe deposit boxes; Disposal of unclaimed contents

Any corporation engaged in the business of renting to the public safe deposit boxes may dispose of the unclaimed contents of the safe deposit boxes in the manner set forth in Sections 1660 to 1679, inclusive, of the Financial Code. **Leg.H.** Added Stats 1943 ch 846 §19. Amended Stats 1968 ch 48 §5.

CHAPTER 8
DESIGN PROFESSIONALS' LIENS [REPEALED]

§3081.1. [Section repealed 2012]

Leg.H. Added Stats 1990 ch 1615 §1 (AB 1789). Repealed Stats 2010 ch 697 §15 (SB 189), effective January 1, 2011, operative July 1, 2012. The repealed section related to "design professional". See CC §§8014, 8300.

Prior Law: Former CC §3081.1, relating to statement of person negotiating a loan secured by real estate property, was added Stats 1955 ch 1791 §1, effective October 1, 1955 and repealed Stats 1961 ch 886 §29, effective June 17, 1961.

§3081.2. [Section repealed 2012]

Leg.H. Added Stats 1990 ch 1615 §1 (AB 1789). Repealed Stats 2010 ch 697 §15 (SB 189), effective January 1, 2011, operative July 1, 2012. The repealed section related to design professional's lien fee for services. See CC §8302.

Prior Law: Former CC §3081.2, relating to contents of loan statement, was added Stats 1955 ch 1791 §1, effective October 1, 1955 amended Stats 1957 ch 1988 §1 and repealed Stats 1961 ch 886 §29, effective June 17, 1961.

§3081.3. [Section repealed 2012]

Leg.H. Added Stats 1990 ch 1615 §1 (AB 1789). Repealed Stats 2010 ch 697 §15 (SB 189), effective January 1, 2011, operative July 1, 2012. The repealed section related to conditions for entitlement to lien. See CC §8304.

Prior Law: Former CC §3081.3, relating to maximum costs to be paid on a note, was added Stats 1955 ch 1791 §1, effective October 1, 1955 amended Stats 1957 ch 1423 §1 and repealed Stats 1961 ch 886 §29, effective June 17, 1961.

§3081.4. [Section repealed 2012]

Leg.H. Added Stats 1990 ch 1615 §1 (AB 1789). Repealed Stats 2010 ch 697 §15 (SB 189), effective January 1, 2011, operative July 1, 2012. The repealed section related to the creation and expiration of a lien. See CC §8306.

Prior Law: Former CC §3081.4, relating to liability of borrower for costs, was added Stats 1955 ch 1791 §1, effective October 1, 1955 and repealed Stats 1961 ch 886 §29, effective June 17, 1961.

§3081.5. [Section repealed 2012]

Leg.H. Added Stats 1990 ch 1615 §1 (AB 1789). Repealed Stats 2010 ch 697 §15 (SB 189), effective January 1, 2011, operative July 1, 2012. The repealed section related to the enforcement of a lien. See CC §8308.

Prior Law: Former CC §3081.5, relating to installment payments on loans, was added Stats 1955 ch 1791 §1, effective October 1, 1955 amended Stats 1957 ch 178 §1 and repealed Stats 1961 ch 886 §29, effective June 17, 1961.

§3081.6. [Section repealed 2012]

Leg.H. Added Stats 1990 ch 1615 §1 (AB 1789). Repealed Stats 2010 ch 697 §15 (SB 189), effective January 1, 2011, operative July 1, 2012. The repealed section related to effect of ability to obtain a mechanic's lien. See CC §8310.

Prior Law: Former CC §3081.6, relating to foreclosure of security, was added Stats 1955 ch 1791 §1, effective October 1, 1955 and repealed Stats 1961 ch 886 §29, effective June 17, 1961.

§3081.7. [Section repealed 2012]

Leg.H. Added Stats 1990 ch 1615 §1 (AB 1789). Repealed Stats 2010 ch 697 §15 (SB 189), effective January 1, 2011, operative July 1, 2012. The repealed section related to the time for recording notice of a lien. See CC §8312.

Prior Law: Former CC §3081.7, relating to exceptions to application of former chapter, was added Stats 1955 ch 1791 §1, amended Stats 1957 ch 1349 §1 and repealed Stats 1961 ch 886 §29, effective June 17, 1961.

§3081.8. [Section repealed 2012]

Leg.H. Added Stats 1990 ch 1615 §1 (AB 1789). Repealed Stats 2010 ch 697 §15 (SB 189), effective January 1, 2011, operative July 1, 2012. The repealed section related to the effect on the ability to pursue other remedies. See CC §8314.

Prior Law: Former CC §3081.8, relating to exceptions to application of former chapter, was added Stats 1955 ch 1791 §1, effective October 1, 1955 and repealed Stats 1961 ch 886 §29, effective June 17, 1961.

§3081.9. [Section repealed 2012]

Leg.H. Added Stats 1990 ch 1615 §1 (AB 1789). Repealed Stats 2010 ch 697 §15 (SB 189), effective January 1, 2011, operative July 1, 2012. The repealed section related to the priority of a lien. See CC §8316.

Prior Law: Former CC §3081.9, relating to damages, was added Stats 1955 ch 1791 §1, effective October 1, 1955 and repealed Stats 1961 ch 886 §29, effective June 17, 1961.

§3081.10. [Section repealed 2012]

Leg.H. Added Stats 1990 ch 1615 §1 (AB 1789). Repealed Stats 2010 ch 697 §15 (SB 189), effective January 1, 2011, operative July 1, 2012. The repealed section related to application to single-family owner occupied residence. See CC §8318.

§§3081.92–3081.93. [Sections repealed 1961]

Leg.H. Added or amended Stats 1955 ch 1791, effective October 1, 1955, Stats 1957 chs 178, 1349, 1423, 1424, 1988, Stats 1959 ch 1942 §2, Stats 1960 1st Ex Sess ch 77, effective May 4, 1960, ch 78, effective May 4, 1960, operative May 15, 1960, Stats 1961 ch 123, effective April 12, 1961, and repealed Stats 1961 ch 886 §29, effective June 27, 1961. See B & P C §§10240 et seq.

TITLE 15
INTERNET NEUTRALITY

Definitions. §3100.
Unlawful actions for fixed Internet service providers. §3101.
Unlawful for fixed Internet service providers to offer or provide services other than broadband; Conditions. §3102.
Obligation of fixed or mobile service providers; Emergency communications. §3103.
Waiver of provisions. §3104.

§3100. Definitions

For purposes of this title, the following definitions apply:

(a) "Application-agnostic" means not differentiating on the basis of source, destination, Internet content, application, service, or device, or class of Internet content, application, service, or device.

(b) "Broadband Internet access service" means a mass-market retail service by wire or radio provided to customers in California that provides the capability to transmit data to, and receive data from, all or substantially all Internet endpoints, including, but not limited to, any capabilities that are incidental to and enable the operation of the communications service, but excluding dial-up Internet access service. "Broadband Internet access service" also encompasses any service provided to customers in California that provides a functional equivalent of that service or that is used to evade the protections set forth in this title.

(c) "Class of Internet content, application, service, or device" means Internet content, or a group of Internet applications, services, or devices, sharing a common characteristic, including, but not limited to, sharing the same source or destination, belonging to the same type of content, application, service, or device, using the same application- or transport-layer protocol, or having similar technical characteristics, including, but not limited to, the size, sequencing, or timing of packets, or sensitivity to delay.

(d) "Content, applications, or services" means all Internet traffic transmitted to or from end users of a broadband Internet access service, including, but not limited to, traffic that may not fit clearly into any of these categories.

(e) "Edge provider" means any individual or entity that provides any content, application, or service over the Internet, and any individual or entity that provides a device used for accessing any content, application, or service over the Internet.

(f) "End user" means any individual or entity that uses a broadband Internet access service.

(g) "Enterprise service offering" means an offering to larger organizations through customized or individually negotiated arrangements or special access services.

(h) "Fixed broadband Internet access service" means a broadband Internet access service that serves end users primarily at fixed endpoints using stationary equipment. Fixed broadband Internet access service includes, but is not limited to, fixed wireless services including, but not limited to, fixed unlicensed wireless services, and fixed satellite services.

(i) "Fixed Internet service provider" means a business that provides fixed broadband Internet access service to an individual, corporation, government, or other customer in California.

(j) "Impairing or degrading lawful Internet traffic on the basis of Internet content, application, or service, or use of a nonharmful device" means impairing or degrading any of the following: (1) particular content, applications, or services; (2) particular classes of content, applications, or services; (3) lawful Internet traffic to particular nonharmful devices; or (4) lawful Internet traffic to particular classes of nonharmful devices. The term includes, without limitation, differentiating, positively or negatively, between any of the following: (1) particular content, applications, or services; (2) particular classes of content, applications, or services; (3) lawful Internet traffic to particular nonharmful devices; or (4) lawful Internet traffic to particular classes of nonharmful devices.

(k) "Internet service provider" means a business that provides broadband Internet access service to an individual, corporation, government, or other customer in California.

(*l*) "ISP traffic exchange" means the exchange of Internet traffic destined for, or originating from, an Internet service provider's end users between the Internet service provider's network and another individual or entity, including, but not limited to, an edge provider, content delivery network, or other network operator.

(m) "ISP traffic exchange agreement" means an agreement between an Internet service provider and another individual or entity, including, but not limited to, an edge provider, content delivery network, or other network operator, to exchange Internet traffic destined for, or originating from, an Internet service provider's end users between the Internet service provider's network and the other individual or entity.

(n) "Mass market" service means a service marketed and sold on a standardized basis to residential customers, small businesses, and other customers, including, but not limited to, schools, institutions of higher learning, and libraries. "Mass market" services also include broadband Internet access services purchased with support of the E-rate and Rural Health Care programs and similar programs at the federal and state level, regardless of whether they are customized or individually negotiated, as well as any broadband Internet access service offered using networks supported by the Connect America Fund or similar programs at the federal and state level. "Mass market" service does not include enterprise service offerings.

(o) "Mobile broadband Internet access service" means a broadband Internet access service that serves end users primarily using mobile stations. Mobile broadband Internet access service includes, but is not limited to, broadband Internet access services that use smartphones or mobile-network-enabled tablets as the primary endpoints for connection to the Internet, as well as mobile satellite broadband services.

(p) "Mobile Internet service provider" means a business that provides mobile broadband Internet access service to an individual, corporation, government, or other customer in California.

(q) "Mobile station" means a radio communication station capable of being moved and which ordinarily does move.

(r) "Paid prioritization" means the management of an Internet service provider's network to directly or indirectly favor some traffic over other traffic, including, but not limited to, through the use of techniques such as traffic shaping, prioritization, resource reservation, or other forms of preferential traffic management, either (1) in exchange for consideration, monetary or otherwise, from a third party, or (2) to benefit an affiliated entity.

(s) "Reasonable network management" means a network management practice that is reasonable. A network management practice is a practice that has a primarily technical network management justification, but does not include other business practices. A network management practice is reasonable if it is primarily used for, and tailored to, achieving a legitimate network management purpose, taking into account the particular network architecture and technology of the broadband Internet access service, and is as application-agnostic as possible.

(t) "Zero-rating" means exempting some Internet traffic from a customer's data usage allowance. **Leg.H.** Added Stats 2018 ch 976 §2 (SB 822), effective January 1, 2019.

Prior Law Former CC §3100, relating to public work, similar to present CC §8038, was added Stats 1969 ch 1362 §2, operative January 1, 1971, and repealed Stats 2010 ch 697 §16 (SB 189), effective January 1, 2011, operative July 1, 2012.

Former CC §3100, similar to present UCC §3402, was added Stats 1917 ch 751 §1 and repealed Stats 1963 ch 819 §2, effective January 1, 1965.

Former CC §3100, relating to place of payment, was enacted Stats 1872, amended Code Amdts 1873–74 ch 612 §267, and repealed Stats 1917 ch 751 §1.

2018 Note: This act shall be known, and may be cited, as the California Internet Consumer Protection and Net Neutrality Act of 2018. Stats 2018 ch 976 §1(b).

§3101. Unlawful actions for fixed Internet service providers

(a) It shall be unlawful for a fixed Internet service provider, insofar as the provider is engaged in providing fixed broadband Internet access service, to engage in any of the following activities:

(1) Blocking lawful content, applications, services, or nonharmful devices, subject to reasonable network management.

(2) Impairing or degrading lawful Internet traffic on the basis of Internet content, application, or service, or use of a nonharmful device, subject to reasonable network management.

(3) Requiring consideration, monetary or otherwise, from an edge provider, including, but not limited to, in exchange for any of the following:

(A) Delivering Internet traffic to, and carrying Internet traffic from, the Internet service provider's end users.

(B) Avoiding having the edge provider's content, application, service, or nonharmful device blocked from reaching the Internet service provider's end users.

(C) Avoiding having the edge provider's content, application, service, or nonharmful device impaired or degraded.

(4) Engaging in paid prioritization.

(5) Engaging in zero-rating in exchange for consideration, monetary or otherwise, from a third party.

(6) Zero-rating some Internet content, applications, services, or devices in a category of Internet content, applications, services, or devices, but not the entire category.

(7)(A) Unreasonably interfering with, or unreasonably disadvantaging, either an end user's ability to select, access, and use broadband Internet access service or the lawful Internet content, applications, services, or devices of the end user's choice, or an edge provider's ability to make lawful content, applications, services, or devices available to end users. Reasonable network management shall not be a violation of this paragraph.

(B) Zero-rating Internet traffic in application-agnostic ways shall not be a violation of subparagraph (A) provided that no consideration, monetary or otherwise, is provided by any third party in exchange for the Internet service provider's decision whether to zero-rate traffic.

(8) Failing to publicly disclose accurate information regarding the network management practices, performance, and commercial terms of its broadband Internet access services sufficient for consumers to make informed choices regarding use of those services and for content, application, service, and device providers to develop, market, and maintain Internet offerings.

(9) Engaging in practices, including, but not limited to, agreements, with respect to, related to, or in connection with, ISP traffic exchange that have the purpose or effect of evading the prohibitions contained in this section and Section 3102. Nothing in this paragraph shall be construed to prohibit Internet service providers from entering into ISP traffic exchange agreements that do not evade the prohibitions contained in this section and Section 3102.

(b) It shall be unlawful for a mobile Internet service provider, insofar as the provider is engaged in providing mobile broadband Internet access service, to engage in any of the activities described in paragraphs (1), (2), (3), (4), (5), (6), (7), (8), and (9) of subdivision (a). **Leg.H.** Added Stats 2018 ch 976 §2 (SB 822), effective January 1, 2019.

Prior Law Former CC §3101, defining "site," similar to present CC §8040, was added Stats 1969 ch 1362 §2, operative January 1, 1971, and repealed Stats 2010 ch 697 §16 (SB 189), effective January 1, 2011, operative July 1, 2012.

Former CC §3101, similar to present UCC §3402, was added Stats 1917 ch 751 §1 and repealed Stats 1963 ch 819 §2, effective January 1, 1965.

Former CC §3101, relating to instruments payable to a person or his order, was enacted Stats 1872 and repealed Stats 1917 ch 751 §1.

2018 Note: For citation of act, see the 2018 Note following CC §3100.

§3102. Unlawful for fixed Internet service providers to offer or provide services other than broadband; Conditions

(a) It shall be unlawful for a fixed Internet service provider to offer or provide services other than broadband Internet access service that are delivered over the same last-mile connection as the broadband Internet access service, if those services satisfy either of the following conditions:

(1) They have the purpose or effect of evading the prohibitions in Section 3101.

(2) They negatively affect the performance of broadband Internet access service.

(b) It shall be unlawful for a mobile Internet service provider to offer or provide services other than broadband Internet access service that are delivered over the same last-mile connection as the broadband Internet access service, if those services satisfy either of the conditions specified in paragraphs (1) and (2) of subdivision (a).

(c) Nothing in this section shall be construed to prohibit a fixed or mobile Internet service provider from offering or providing services other than broadband Internet access service that are delivered over the same last-mile connection as the broadband Internet access service and do not violate this section. **Leg.H.** Added Stats 2018 ch 976 §2 (SB 822), effective January 1, 2019.

Prior Law Former CC §3102, defining "site improvement," similar to present CC §8042, was added Stats 1969 ch 1362 §2, operative January 1, 1971, and repealed Stats 2010 ch 697 §16 (SB 189), effective January 1, 2011, operative July 1, 2012.

Former CC §3102, similar to present UCC §3402, was added Stats 1917 ch 751 §1 and repealed Stats 1963 ch 819 §2, effective January 1, 1965.

Former CC §3102, relating to unindorsed note, was enacted Stats 1872 and repealed Stats 1917 ch 751 §1.

2018 Note: For citation of act, see the 2018 Note following CC §3100.

§3103. Obligation of fixed or mobile service providers; Emergency communications

(a) Nothing in this title supersedes any obligation or authorization a fixed or mobile Internet service provider may have to address the needs of emergency communications or law enforcement, public safety, or national security authorities, consistent with or as permitted by applicable law, or limits the provider's ability to do so.

(b) Nothing in this title prohibits reasonable efforts by a fixed or mobile Internet service provider to address copyright infringement or other unlawful activity. **Leg.H.** Added Stats 2018 ch 976 §2 (SB 822), effective January 1, 2019.

Prior Law Former CC §3103, relating to stop notice, similar to present CC §§8044, 8502, 8506, 9352, 9354, was added Stats 1969 ch 1362 §2, operative January 1, 1971, amended Stats 1980 ch 676 §55, Stats 1988 ch 1627 §1, and repealed Stats 2010 ch 697 §16 (SB 189), effective January 1, 2011, operative July 1, 2012.

Former CC §3103, similar to present UCC §3202, was added Stats 1917 ch 751 §1 and repealed Stats 1963 ch 819 §2, effective January 1, 1965.

Former CC §3103, relating to fictitious payee, was enacted Stats 1872 and repealed Stats 1917 ch 751 §1.

2018 Note: For citation of act, see the 2018 Note following CC §3100.

§3104. Waiver of provisions

Notwithstanding Section 3268 or any other law, any waiver of the provisions of this title is contrary to public policy and shall be unenforceable and void. **Leg.H.** Added Stats 2018 ch 976 §2 (SB 822), effective January 1, 2019.

Prior Law Former CC §3104, defining "subcontractor," similar to present CC §8046, was added Stats 1969 ch 1362 §2, operative January 1, 1971, and repealed Stats 2010 ch 697 §16 (SB 189), effective January 1, 2011, operative July 1, 2012.

Former CC §3104, similar to present UCC §§3403, 8202, 8205, 8311, was added Stats 1917 ch 751 §1 and repealed Stats 1963 ch 819 §2, effective January 1, 1965.

Former CC §3104, relating to presumption of consideration, was enacted Stats 1872 and repealed Stats 1917 ch 751 §1.

2018 Note: For citation of act, see the 2018 Note following CC §3100.

TITLE 15.2
ARTIFICIAL INTELLIGENCE TRAINING DATA TRANSPARENCY

Definitions. § 3110.
Artificial intelligence system or service. § 3111.

§ 3110. Definitions

For purposes of this title, the following definitions shall apply:

(a) "Artificial intelligence" means an engineered or machine-based system that varies in its level of autonomy and that can, for explicit or implicit objectives, infer from the input it receives how to generate outputs that can influence physical or virtual environments.

(b) "Developer" means a person, partnership, state or local government agency, or corporation that designs, codes, produces, or substantially modifies an artificial intelligence system or service for use by members of the public. For purposes of this subdivision, "members of the public" does not include an affiliate as defined in subparagraph (A) of paragraph (1) of subdivision (c) of Section 1799.1a, or a hospital's medical staff member.

(c) "Generative artificial intelligence" means artificial intelligence that can generate derived synthetic content, such as text, images, video, and audio, that emulates the structure and characteristics of the artificial intelligence's training data.

(d) "Substantially modifies" or "substantial modification" means a new version, new release, or other update to a generative artificial intelligence system or service that materially changes its functionality or performance, including the results of retraining or fine tuning.

(e) "Synthetic data generation" means a process in which seed data are used to create artificial data that have some of the statistical characteristics of the seed data.

(f) "Train a generative artificial intelligence system or service" includes testing, validating, or fine tuning by the developer of the artificial intelligence system or service. **Leg.H.** Added Stats 2024 ch 817 §1 (AB 2013), effective January 1, 2025.

§ 3111. Artificial intelligence system or service

On or before January 1, 2026, and before each time thereafter that a generative artificial intelligence system or service, or a substantial modification to a generative artificial intelligence system or service, released on or after January 1, 2022, is made publicly available to Californians for use, regardless of whether the terms of that use include compensation, the developer of the system or service shall post on the developer's internet website documentation regarding the data used by the developer to train the generative artificial intelligence system or service, including, but not be limited to, all of the following:

(a) A high-level summary of the datasets used in the development of the generative artificial intelligence system or service, including, but not limited to:

(1) The sources or owners of the datasets.

(2) A description of how the datasets further the intended purpose of the artificial intelligence system or service.

(3) The number of data points included in the datasets, which may be in general ranges, and with estimated figures for dynamic datasets.

(4) A description of the types of data points within the datasets. For purposes of this paragraph, the following definitions apply:

(A) As applied to datasets that include labels, "types of data points" means the types of labels used.

(B) As applied to datasets without labeling, "types of data points" refers to the general characteristics.

(5) Whether the datasets include any data protected by copyright, trademark, or patent, or whether the datasets are entirely in the public domain.

(6) Whether the datasets were purchased or licensed by the developer.

(7) Whether the datasets include personal information, as defined in subdivision (v) of Section 1798.140.

(8) Whether the datasets include aggregate consumer information, as defined in subdivision (b) of Section 1798.140.

(9) Whether there was any cleaning, processing, or other modification to the datasets by the developer, including the intended purpose of those efforts in relation to the artificial intelligence system or service.

(10) The time period during which the data in the datasets were collected, including a notice if the data collection is ongoing.

(11) The dates the datasets were first used during the development of the artificial intelligence system or service.

(12) Whether the generative artificial intelligence system or service used or continuously uses synthetic data generation in its development. A developer may include a description of the functional need or desired purpose of the synthetic data in relation to the intended purpose of the system or service.

(b) A developer shall not be required to post documentation regarding the data used to train a generative artificial intelligence system or service for any of the following:

(1) A generative artificial intelligence system or service whose sole purpose is to help ensure security and integrity. For purposes of this paragraph, "security and integrity" has the same meaning as defined in subdivision (ac) of Section 1798.140, except as applied to any developer or user and not limited to businesses, as defined in subdivision (d) of that section.

(2) A generative artificial intelligence system or service whose sole purpose is the operation of aircraft in the national airspace.

(3) A generative artificial intelligence system or service developed for national security, military, or defense purposes that is made available only to a federal entity. **Leg.H.** Added Stats 2024 ch 817 §1 (AB 2013), effective January 1, 2025.

TITLE 15.5
DIGITAL EQUITY BILL OF RIGHTS

Citation of title. § 3120.
Legislative findings. § 3121.
Principle of the state to ensure digital equity. § 3122.
No obligation of state to enforce. § 3123.

§ 3120. Citation of title

This title shall be known, and may be cited, as the Digital Equity Bill of Rights. **Leg.H.** Added Stats 2023 ch 436 §1 (AB 414), effective January 1, 2024.

§ 3121. Legislative findings

The Legislature finds and declares that digital equity, in which all individuals and communities have the information technology capacity needed for full participation in society, democracy, and the economy, is necessary for civic and cultural participation, employment, lifelong learning, and to access essential services. The Legislature further finds and declares that digital equity requires deployment and adoption of information technologies enabled by access to high-speed internet infrastructure, including wireline and wireless technologies. **Leg.H.** Added Stats 2023 ch 436 §1 (AB 414), effective January 1, 2024.

§ 3122. Principle of the state to ensure digital equity

(a) It is the principle of the state, to ensure digital equity for all its residents, that residents shall have access to all of the following:

(1) Broadband that is sufficient and reliable, with internet speeds that are sufficient to meet the growing demand and reliance on access to education, government, public safety, economic prosperity, and health care through high-speed internet access. Determining minimum speeds for high-speed internet infrastructure should be performance based to support online educational opportunities, telehealth, and remote working by a majority of households online simultaneously with an increasing need for symmetrical network speeds.

(2) Broadband that is ubiquitous by ensuring that sufficient and reliable broadband access is available throughout the state, from the most rural areas, including tribal lands, to the most populated urban areas, including all low-income neighborhoods. Public broadband investments should be prioritized to connect entire communities and address digital redlining in historically unserved and underserved communities.

(3) Broadband that is affordable by ensuring that internet service plans are affordable for all residents of the state, regardless of their geographic location or household income.

(4) Broadband that provides educational opportunities and supports digital skills proficiency by providing residents of the state with access to opportunities to develop the skills needed to thrive in a digital world.

(5) Broadband that ensures public safety and maintains the peace of mind of the residents of the state that comes with knowing they have reliable access to emergency response services and emergency alert systems in the event of emergencies or catastrophic disasters.

(6) Broadband that improves quality of life by advancing economic status with access to educational opportunities, new job opportunities, and health care.

(7) Broadband that supports economic prosperity by ensuring that all workers, employers, businesses, entrepreneurs, startups, and enterprises, regardless of size, and including agriculture, have high-speed internet access that optimizes the value of their contributions to the economy to ensure global competitiveness.

(8) Broadband that attracts capital investment because ubiquitous high-speed internet infrastructure is essential to ensuring that the state continues to attract its fair share of global capital investment to support and enhance economic prosperity.

(9) Broadband that supports innovation and research by ensuring that high-speed internet infrastructure connects all research institutions to sustain world-class research and innovation that drives economic productivity.

(10) Broadband that empowers and enables participation in the democratic process so that all residents of the state are connected to the internet with sufficient speeds to participate in government, online educational opportunities, and telehealth for quality of life and public safety.

(b) It is the policy of the state that, to the extent technically feasible, broadband internet subscribers benefit from equal access to broadband internet service within the service area of a broadband provider.

(c) For purposes of this title, the following definitions apply:

(1) "Equal access" means the equal opportunity to subscribe to an offered service that provides comparable speeds, capacities, latency, and other quality-of-service metrics in a given geographical area, for comparable terms and conditions.

(2) "Broadband" means "Broadband Internet access service" as defined in subdivision (b) of Section 3100. **Leg.H.** Added Stats 2023 ch 436 §1 (AB 414), effective January 1, 2024.

§ 3123. No obligation of state to enforce

(a) This title does not create a private right of action against the state to enforce this title.

(b) This title does not create an obligation of the state to enforce the principle or policy established by this title. **Leg.H.** Added Stats 2023 ch 436 §1 (AB 414), effective January 1, 2024.

TITLE 16
GENERAL PROVISIONS

Parties may waive provisions of code. §3268.

§3268. Parties may waive provisions of code

Except where it is otherwise declared, the provisions of the foregoing titles of this part, in respect to the rights and obligations of parties to contracts, are subordinate to the intention of the parties, when ascertained in the manner prescribed by the chapter on the interpretation of contracts; and the benefit thereof may be waived by any party entitled thereto, unless such waiver would be against public policy. **Leg.H.** Enacted Stats 1872. Amended Stats 1963 ch 819 §20, effective January 1, 1965.

TITLE 17
YEAR 2000 INFORMATION DISCLOSURES

Definitions. §3269.
Immunity from liability for tort damages relating to disclosures about Year 2000 Problem or potential solutions. §3270.
Liability for disclosures that are materially false or misleading and are knowingly made or made with gross negligence. §3271.

§3269. Definitions

For purposes of this title, the following definitions apply:

(a) "Year 2000 Problem" means any expected or actual computing, physical, enterprise, or distribution system complications that may occur in any computer system, computer program, software application, embedded systems, embedded chip calculations, or other computing application as a result of the year change from 1999 to 2000. These complications are often associated with the common programming practice of using a two-digit field to represent a year, resulting in erroneous date calculations, an ambiguous interpretation of the term "00," the failure to recognize the year 2000 as a leap year, the use of algorithms that use the year "99" or "00" as a flag for another function, or the use of applications, software, or hardware that are date sensitive.

(b) "Information" means any assessment, projection, estimate, planning document, objective, timetable, test plan, test date, or test result related to the implementation or verification of Year 2000 Problem processing capabilities of a computer system, computer program, software application, embedded systems, embedded chip calculations, or other computing application and intended to solve a Year 2000 Problem.

(c) "Disclosure" and "discloses" mean any dissemination or provision of information without any expectation or right to remuneration or fee therefor.

(d) "Person" means any individual, corporation, partnership, business entity, joint venture, association, the State of California or any of its subdivisions, or any other organization, or any combination thereof. **Leg.H.** Added Stats 1998 ch 860 §3 (SB 1173), effective September 25, 1998. Amended Stats 1999 ch 83 §23 (SB 966).

§3270. Immunity from liability for tort damages relating to disclosures about Year 2000 Problem or potential solutions

(a) Notwithstanding any other law, any person that discloses information regarding the Year 2000 Problem or any potential solutions to the problem, including, but not limited to, those persons described in subdivision (b), shall not be liable for damages in any tort action brought against that person regarding the Year 2000 Problem for any injury caused by, arising out of, or relating to, the use of the information disclosed, except as provided in Section 3271.

(b) This section shall apply to any person that, when making the disclosures described in subdivision (a), specifically disclaims the universal applicability of the potential solutions disclosed, and expresses a unique experience with any Year 2000 information.

(c) This section does not apply to prospective solutions sold or exchanged for profit or provided for profit by a person or entity holding itself out as a provider of Year 2000 solutions. **Leg.H.** Added Stats 1998 ch 860 §3 (SB 1173), effective September 25, 1998.

§3271. Liability for disclosures that are materially false or misleading and are knowingly made or made with gross negligence

(a) Section 3270 shall not apply if the claimant in an action described in that section establishes that the Year 2000 Problem information disclosure was all of the following:

(1) Material.

(2) False, inaccurate, or misleading.

(3) Either (A) made with the knowledge that the statement was false, inaccurate, or misleading, (B) if the information disclosed was a republication of or otherwise a repetition of information from another person, made without a disclosure that the information was based on information supplied by another person or made with the knowledge that the statement was false, inaccurate, or misleading, or (C) made with gross negligence in the determination of the truth or accuracy of the disclosure or in the determination of whether the disclosure was misleading.

(b) Nothing in this title shall be deemed to affect any other remedy available at law, including, but not limited to, temporary or permanent injunctive relief, against a public or private entity or individual with respect to Year 2000 Problem information disclosures. **Leg.H.** Added Stats 1998 ch 860 §3 (SB 1173), effective September 25, 1998.

§3272. [Section repealed 2016]

Leg.H. Added Stats 1999 ch 698 §2 (AB 1476), inoperative July 1, 2001, by the terms of CC §3272.9. Repealed Stats 2015 ch 303 §32 (AB 731), effective January 1, 2016. The repealed section related to legislative intent to define legal standards relating to the Year 2000 Problem and conformity of state law to federal law.

§3272.1. [Section repealed 2016]

Leg.H. Added Stats 1999 ch 698 §2 (AB 1476), inoperative July 1, 2001, by the terms of CC §3272.9. Repealed Stats 2015 ch 303 §32 (AB 731), effective January 1, 2016. The repealed section related to definitions for the title.

§3272.2. [Section repealed 2016]

Leg.H. Added Stats 1999 ch 698 §2 (AB 1476), inoperative July 1, 2001, by the terms of CC §3272.9. Repealed Stats 2015 ch 303 §32 (AB 731), effective January 1, 2016. The repealed section related to construction of state statutes regarding damages or liability of defendants in Year 2000 Problem actions.

§3272.3. [Section repealed 2016]

Leg.H. Added Stats 1999 ch 698 §2 (AB 1476), inoperative July 1, 2001, by the terms of CC §3272.9. Repealed Stats 2015 ch 303 §32 (AB 731), effective January 1, 2016. The repealed section related to prohibition against civil fines for violations of rules or noncriminal statutes by a small business as a result of a Year 2000 Problem.

§3272.4. [Section repealed 2016]

Leg.H. Added Stats 1999 ch 698 §2 (AB 1476), inoperative July 1, 2001, by the terms of CC §3272.9. Repealed Stats 2015 ch 303 §32 (AB 731), effective January 1, 2016. The repealed section related to title not creating a new cause of action or expanding liability.

§3272.7. [Section repealed 2016]

Leg.H. Added Stats 1999 ch 698 §2 (AB 1476), inoperative July 1, 2001, by the terms of CC §3272.9. Repealed Stats 2015 ch 303 §32 (AB 731), effective January 1, 2016. The repealed section related to nothing in title superseding any provision of Civil or Government codes, or abrogating any existing rights or remedies applicable to public entities.

§3272.9. [Section repealed 2016]

Leg.H. Added Stats 1999 ch 698 §2 (AB 1476), inoperative July 1, 2001, by its own provisions. Repealed Stats 2015 ch 303 §32 (AB 731), effective January 1, 2016. The repealed section related to the operative term of the title.

TITLE 18
PROVIDERS OF HEALTH AND SAFETY LABOR OR SERVICES

Display of public agency logo or identifying mark; Disclosure requirements; Penalties. §3273.

§3273. Display of public agency logo or identifying mark; Disclosure requirements; Penalties

(a) It is unlawful for a person, firm, corporation, or association that is a nongovernmental entity and contracts to perform public health and safety labor or services for a public agency to display on a vehicle a logo of the public agency that reasonably could be interpreted or construed as implying that the labor or services are being provided by employees of the public agency, unless the vehicle conspicuously displays a statement indicating that the contractor is the service provider, contractor, or other appropriate descriptor, such as "SERVICE PROVIDED BY:" or "CONTRACTED BY:", immediately followed by all of the following:

(1) The logo and the name of the person, firm, corporation, or association that is the nongovernmental entity providing the public health and safety labor or services for the public agency.

(2) The state, or if outside of the United States, the country where the nongovernmental entity's controlling person, firm, corporation, or association is legally incorporated, organized, or formed.

(b) It is unlawful for a person or an employee of a person, firm, corporation, or association that is a nongovernmental entity and contracts to perform public health and safety labor or services for a public agency to wear a uniform bearing a logo of the public agency that reasonably could be interpreted or construed as implying that the labor or services are being provided by employees of the public agency, unless the uniform conspicuously displays the logo and the name of the person, firm, corporation, or association that is the nongovernmental entity providing the labor or services for the public agency.

(c) The disclosures required pursuant to subdivisions (a) and (b) shall apply to all labor or services provided pursuant to a contract entered into on or after January 1, 2015.

(d)(1) It is unlawful for a public agency to require, through a contract with a person, firm, corporation, or association that is a nongovernmental entity providing public health and safety labor or services, a person or employee of the nongovernmental entity to wear a badge containing the logo of the public agency.

(2) It is unlawful for a person, firm, corporation, or association that is a nongovernmental entity contracting to perform public health and safety labor or services for a public agency to require a person or its employee to wear a badge containing the logo of the public agency.

(e) For the purposes of subdivision (b), an identifying mark affixed to a uniform as required by state or federal law, and a local agency regulating the activity of the person, firm, corporation, or association shall not be construed as implying that the labor or services are being provided by employees of the public agency.

(f) If a vehicle or uniform displays more than one logo referring to the public agency, then the required disclosure shall be placed near the largest logo referring to the public agency.

(g) The disclosure requirements in subdivisions (a) and (b) of this section shall not apply to uniforms or vehicles if the person, firm, corporation, or association that is the nongovernmental entity is providing the labor or services for a public agency under Article 3.3 (commencing with Section 2430) of Chapter 2 of Division 2 of the Vehicle Code.

(h) The disclosure requirements in subdivisions (a) and (b) shall not apply to a public agency vehicle utilized by the nongovernmental entity during a declared state or federal disaster, mass-casualty incident, or other incident that requires the use of state or federal resources when the public agency requires the use of the public agency vehicle.

(i)(1) Violations of this section shall be subject to the remedies provided in the Consumers Legal Remedies Act (Title 1.5 (commencing with Section 1750)).

(2) The duties, rights, and remedies provided in this section are in addition to any other duties, rights, and remedies provided by state law.

(j) For the purposes of this section, the following terms have the following meanings:

(1) "Conspicuously displays" means to display a disclosure on the exterior of a vehicle or uniform in the same location as the logo of the public agency, placed prominently as compared with other words, statements, or designs displayed in connection with the logo of the public agency. With respect to a uniform, "in the same location" includes, but is not limited to, a location on the opposing shoulder, pocket, or similar opposing location relative to the location of the logo of the public agency.

(2) "Logo" means a symbol, graphic, seal, emblem, insignia, trade name, brand name, or picture identifying a person, firm, corporation, association, or public agency. "Logo" shall not mean the name of a public agency used alone.

(3) "Public agency" means a state entity, a city, county, city and county, special district, or other political subdivision of the state.

(4) "Public health and safety labor or services" means fire protection services, rescue services, prehospital emergency medical services, hazardous material emergency response services, and ambulance services. **Leg.H.** Added Stats 2014 ch 832 §1 (SB 556), effective January 1, 2015. Amended Stats 2015 ch 25 §1 (SB 84), effective June 24, 2015.

TITLE 19
COVID-19 SMALL LANDLORD AND HOMEOWNER RELIEF ACT

Chapter 1. Title and Definitions.
Chapter 2. Mortgages.

CHAPTER 1
TITLE AND DEFINITIONS

Citation of title. § 3273.01.
Definitions. § 3273.1.
Applicability of title. § 3273.2.

§ 3273.01. Citation of title

This title is known, and may be cited, as the "COVID-19 Small Landlord and Homeowner Relief Act of 2020." **Leg.H.** Added Stats 2020 ch 37 §13 (AB 3088), effective August 31, 2020.

§ 3273.1. Definitions

For purposes of this title:

(a)(1) "Borrower" means any of the following:

(A) A natural person who is a mortgagor or trustor or a confirmed successor in interest, as defined in Section 1024.31 of Title 12 of the Code of Federal Regulations.

(B) An entity other than a natural person only if the secured property contains no more than four dwelling units and is currently occupied by one or more residential tenants.

(2) "Borrower" shall not include an individual who has surrendered the secured property as evidenced by either a letter confirming the surrender or delivery of the keys to the property to the mortgagee, trustee, beneficiary, or authorized agent.

(3) Unless the property securing the mortgage contains one or more deed-restricted affordable housing units or one or more affordable housing units subject to a regulatory restriction limiting rental rates that is contained in an agreement with a government agency, the following mortgagors shall not be considered a "borrower":

(A) A real estate investment trust, as defined in Section 856 of the Internal Revenue Code.

(B) A corporation.

(C) A limited liability company in which at least one member is a corporation.

(4) "Borrower" shall also mean a person who holds a power of attorney for a borrower described in paragraph (1).

(b) "Effective time period" means the time period between the operational date of this title and December 1, 2021.

(c)(1) "Mortgage servicer" or "lienholder" means a person or entity who directly services a loan or who is responsible for interacting with the borrower, managing the loan account on a daily basis, including collecting and crediting periodic loan payments, managing any escrow account, or enforcing the note and security instrument, either as the current owner of the promissory note or as the current owner's authorized agent.

(2) "Mortgage servicer" or "lienholder" also means a subservicing agent to a master servicer by contract.

(3) "Mortgage servicer" shall not include a trustee, or a trustee's authorized agent, acting under a power of sale pursuant to a deed of trust. **Leg.H.** Added Stats 2020 ch 37 §13 (AB 3088), effective August 31, 2020. Amended Stats 2021 ch 2 §8 (SB 91), effective January 29, 2021; Stats 2021 ch 27 §6 (AB 832), effective June 28, 2021.

§ 3273.2. Applicability of title

(a) The provisions of this title apply to a mortgage or deed of trust that is secured by residential property containing no more than four dwelling units, including individual units of condominiums or cooperatives, and that was outstanding as of the enactment date of this title.

(b) The provisions of this title shall apply to a depository institution chartered under federal or state law, a person covered by the licensing requirements of Division 9 (commencing with Section 22000) or Division 20 (commencing with Section 50000) of the Financial Code, or a person licensed pursuant to Part 1 (commencing with Section 10000) of Division 4 of the Business and Professions Code. **Leg.H.** Added Stats 2020 ch 37 §13 (AB 3088), effective August 31, 2020.

CHAPTER 2
MORTGAGES

Written notice of denial of forbearance request. § 3273.10.
Compliance with federal guidance. § 3273.11.
Communication on forbearance and postforbearance options in borrower's preferred language. § 3273.12.
Postforbearance loss mitigation option. § 3273.14.
Violations. § 3273.15.
Waivers void. § 3273.16.

§ 3273.10. Written notice of denial of forbearance request

(a) If a mortgage servicer denies a forbearance request made during the effective time period, the mortgage servicer shall provide written notice to the borrower that sets forth the specific reason or reasons that forbearance was not provided, if both of the following conditions are met:

(1) The borrower was current on payment as of February 1, 2020.

(2) The borrower is experiencing a financial hardship that prevents the borrower from making timely payments on the mortgage obligation due, directly or indirectly, to the COVID-19 emergency.

(b) If the written notice in subdivision (a) cites any defect in the borrower's request, including an incomplete application or missing information, that is curable, the mortgage servicer shall do all of the following:

(1) Specifically identify any curable defect in the written notice.

(2) Provide 21 days from the mailing date of the written notice for the borrower to cure any identified defect.

(3) Accept receipt of the borrower's revised request for forbearance before the aforementioned 21-day period lapses.

(4) Respond to the borrower's revised request within five business days of receipt of the revised request.

(c) If a mortgage servicer denies a forbearance [1] **request made during the effective time period, the** declaration required by subdivision (b) of Section 2923.5 shall include the written notice together with a statement as to whether forbearance was or was not subsequently provided.

(d) A mortgage servicer, mortgagee, or beneficiary of the deed of trust, or an authorized agent thereof, who, with respect to a borrower of a federally backed mortgage, complies with the relevant provisions regarding forbearance in Section 4022 of the federal Coronavirus Aid, Relief, and Economic Security Act (the CARES Act) (Public Law 116-136), including any amendments or revisions to those provisions, shall be deemed to be in compliance with this section. A mortgage servicer of a nonfederally backed mortgage that provides forbearance that is consistent with the requirements of the CARES Act for federally backed mortgages shall be deemed to be in compliance with this section. **Leg.H.** Added Stats 2020 ch 37 §13 (AB 3088), effective August 31, 2020. Amended Stats 2024 ch 142 §6 (AB 295), effective July 18, 2024.

§ 3273.10. 2024 Deletes. [1] request the

§ 3273.11. Compliance with federal guidance

(a) A mortgage servicer shall comply with applicable federal guidance regarding borrower options following a COVID-19 related forbearance.

(b) Any mortgage servicer, mortgagee, or beneficiary of the deed of trust, or authorized agent thereof, who, with respect to a borrower of a federally backed loan, complies with the guidance to mortgagees regarding borrower options following a COVID-19-related forbearance provided by the Federal National Mortgage Association (Fannie Mae), the Federal Home Loan Mortgage Corporation (Freddie Mac), the Federal Housing Administration of the United States Department of Housing and Urban Development, the United States Department of Veterans Affairs, or the Rural Development division of the United States Department of Agriculture, including any amendments, updates, or revisions to that guidance, shall be deemed to be in compliance with this section.

(c) With respect to a nonfederally backed loan, any mortgage servicer, mortgagee, or beneficiary of the deed of trust, or authorized agent thereof, who, regarding borrower options following a COVID-19 related forbearance, reviews a customer for a solution that is consistent with the guidance to servicers, mortgagees, or beneficiaries provided by Fannie Mae, Freddie Mac, the Federal Housing Administration of the Department of Housing and Urban Development, the Department of Veterans Affairs, or the Rural Development division of the Department of Agriculture, including any amendments, updates or revisions to such guidance, shall be deemed to be in compliance with this section. **Leg.H.** Added Stats 2020 ch 37 §13 (AB 3088), effective August 31, 2020.

§ 3273.12. Communication on forbearance and postforbearance options in borrower's preferred language

It is the intent of the Legislature that a mortgage servicer offer a borrower a postforbearance loss mitigation option that is consistent with the mortgage servicer's contractual or other authority. **Leg.H.** Added Stats 2020 ch 37 §13 (AB 3088), effective August 31, 2020.

§ 3273.14. Postforbearance loss mitigation option

A mortgage servicer shall communicate about forbearance and postforbearance options described in this article in the borrower's preferred language when the mortgage servicer regularly communicates with any borrower in that language. **Leg.H.** Added Stats 2020 ch 37 §13 (AB 3088), effective August 31, 2020.

§ 3273.15. Violations

(a) A borrower who is harmed by a material violation of this title may bring an action to obtain injunctive relief, damages, restitution, and any other remedy to redress the violation.

(b) A court may award a prevailing borrower reasonable attorney's fees and costs in any action based on any violation of this title in which injunctive relief against a sale, including a temporary restraining order, is granted. A court may award a prevailing borrower reasonable attorney's fees and costs in an action for a violation of this article in which relief is granted but injunctive relief against a sale is not granted.

(c) The rights, remedies, and procedures provided to borrowers by this section are in addition to and independent of any other rights, remedies, or procedures under any other law. This section shall not be construed to alter, limit, or negate any other rights, remedies, or procedures provided to borrowers by law. **Leg.H.** Added Stats 2020 ch 37 §13 (AB 3088), effective August 31, 2020.

§ 3273.16. Waivers void

Any waiver by a borrower of the provisions of this article is contrary to public policy and shall be void. **Leg.H.** Added Stats 2020 ch 37 §13 (AB 3088), effective August 31, 2020.

TITLE 20
FIREARM INDUSTRY RESPONSIBILITY ACT

Definitions. § 3273.50.
Firearm industry standard of conduct. § 3273.51.
Violations of standard of conduct; Civil actions. § 3273.52.
Construction of title. § 3273.54.
Operation of title. § 3273.55.

§ 3273.50. Definitions

As used in this title, the following definitions apply:

(a) "Ammunition" has the same meaning as provided in subdivision (b) of Section 16150 of the Penal Code.

(b) "Firearm" has the same meaning as provided in subdivisions (a) and (b) of Section 16520 of the Penal Code.

(c) "Firearm accessory" means an attachment or device designed or adapted to be inserted into, affixed onto, or used in conjunction with a firearm that is designed, intended, or functions to alter or enhance the firing capabilities of a firearm, the lethality of the firearm, or a shooter's ability to hold and use a firearm.

(d) "Firearm-related product" means a firearm, ammunition, a firearm precursor part, a firearm component, firearm manufacturing machine, and a firearm accessory that meets any of the following conditions:

(1) The item is sold, made, or distributed in California.

(2) The item is intended to be sold or distributed in California.

(3) The item is or was possessed in California and it was reasonably foreseeable that the item would be possessed in California.

(e) "Firearm precursor part" has the same meaning as provided in Section 16531 of the Penal Code.

(f) "Firearm industry member" shall mean a person, firm, corporation, company, partnership, society, joint stock company, or any other entity or association engaged in the manufacture, distribution, importation, marketing, wholesale sale, or retail sale of firearm-related products.

(g) "Firearm manufacturing machine" means a three-dimensional printer, as defined in Section 29185 of the Penal Code, or CNC milling machine that, as described in that section, is marketed or sold as, or reasonably designed or intended to be used to manufacture or produce a firearm.

(h) "Reasonable controls" means reasonable procedures, acts, or practices that are designed, implemented, and enforced to do the following:

(1) Prevent the sale or distribution of a firearm-related product to a straw purchaser, a firearm trafficker, a person prohibited from possessing a firearm under state or federal law, or a person who the firearm industry member has reasonable cause to believe is at substantial risk of using a firearm-related product to harm themselves or another or of possessing or using a firearm-related product unlawfully.

(2) Prevent the loss or theft of a firearm-related product from the firearm industry member.

(3) Ensure that the firearm industry member complies with all provisions of California and federal law and does not otherwise promote the unlawful manufacture, sale, possession, marketing, or use of a firearm-related product. **Leg.H.** Added Stats 2022 ch 98 §3 (AB 1594), effective January 1, 2023, operative July 1, 2023. Amended Stats 2023 ch 131 §16

(AB 1754), effective January 1, 2024; Stats 2023 ch 243 §1 (AB 1089), effective January 1, 2024 (ch 243 prevails).

§ 3273.51. Firearm industry standard of conduct

(a) A firearm industry member shall comply with the firearm industry standard of conduct. It shall be a violation of the firearm industry standard of conduct for a firearm industry member to fail to comply with any requirement of this section.

(b) A firearm industry member shall do both of the following:

(1) Establish, implement, and enforce reasonable controls.

(2) Take reasonable precautions to ensure that the firearm industry member does not sell, distribute, or provide a firearm-related product to a downstream distributor or retailer of firearm-related products who fails to establish, implement, and enforce reasonable controls.

(c) A firearm industry member shall not manufacture, market, import, offer for wholesale sale, or offer for retail sale a firearm-related product that is abnormally dangerous and likely to create an unreasonable risk of harm to public health and safety in California. For the purposes of this subdivision, the following shall apply:

(1) A firearm-related product shall not be considered abnormally dangerous and likely to create an unreasonable risk of harm to public health and safety based on a firearm's inherent capacity to cause injury or lethal harm.

(2) There shall be a presumption that a firearm-related product is abnormally dangerous and likely to create an unreasonable risk of harm to public health and safety if any of the following is true:

(A) The firearm-related product's features render the product most suitable for assaultive purposes instead of lawful self-defense, hunting, or other legitimate sport and recreational activities.

(B) The firearm-related product is designed, sold, or marketed in a manner that foreseeably promotes conversion of legal firearm-related products into illegal firearm-related products.

(C) The firearm-related product is designed, sold, or marketed in a manner that is targeted at minors or other individuals who are legally prohibited from accessing firearms.

(d) A firearm industry member shall not engage in any conduct related to the sale or marketing of firearm-related products that is in violation of the following sections:

(1) Paragraph (1), (2), (3), (4), (5), (6), (7), (8), or (9) of subdivision (a) of Section 1770.

(2) Section 17200 of the Business and Professions Code.

(3) Section 17500 of the Business and Professions Code.

(4) Section 17508 of the Business and Professions Code. **Leg.H.** Added Stats 2022 ch 98 §3 (AB 1594), effective January 1, 2023, operative July 1, 2023.

§ 3273.52. Violations of standard of conduct; Civil actions

(a) An act or omission by a firearm industry member in violation of the firearm industry standard of conduct set forth in Section 3273.51 shall be actionable under this section.

(b) A person who has suffered harm in California because of a firearm industry member's conduct described by subdivision (a) may bring an action in a court of competent jurisdiction.

(c)(1) The Attorney General may bring a civil action in a court of competent jurisdiction in the name of the people of the State of California to enforce this title and remedy harm caused by a violation of this title.

(2) A city attorney may bring a civil action in a court of competent jurisdiction in the name of the people of that city to enforce this title and remedy harm caused by a violation of this title.

(3) A county counsel may bring a civil action in a court of competent jurisdiction in the name of the people of that county to enforce this title and remedy harm caused by a violation of this title.

(d) If a court determines that a firearm industry member engaged in conduct described by subdivision (a), the court may award any or all of the following:

(1) Injunctive relief sufficient to prevent the firearm industry member and any other defendant from further violating the law.

(2) Damages.

(3) Attorney's fees and costs.

(4) Any other appropriate relief necessary to enforce this title and remedy the harm caused by the conduct.

(e)(1) In an action alleging that a firearm industry member failed to establish, implement, and enforce reasonable controls in violation of paragraph (1) of subdivision (b) of Section 3273.51, there shall be a rebuttable presumption that the firearm industry member failed to implement reasonable controls if both of the following conditions are satisfied:

(A) The firearm industry member's action or failure to act created a reasonably foreseeable risk that the harm alleged by the claimant would occur.

(B) The firearm industry member could have established, implemented, and enforced reasonable controls to prevent or substantially mitigate the risk that the harm would occur.

(2) If the rebuttable presumption described by paragraph (1) is established, the firearm industry member has the burden of proving by a preponderance of the evidence that the firearm industry member established, implemented, and enforced reasonable controls.

(f) An intervening act by a third party, including, but not limited to, criminal misuse of a firearm-related product, shall not preclude a firearm industry member from liability under this section. **Leg.H.** Added Stats 2022 ch 98 §3 (AB 1594), effective January 1, 2023, operative July 1, 2023.

§ 3273.54. Construction of title

(a) This title shall not be construed or implied to limit or impair in any way the right of a person or entity to pursue a legal action under any other authority.

(b) This title shall not be construed or implied to limit or impair in any way an obligation or requirement placed on a firearm industry member by any other authority.

(c) This title shall be construed and applied in a manner that is consistent with the requirements of the California and the United States Constitutions. **Leg.H.** Added Stats 2022 ch 98 §3 (AB 1594), effective January 1, 2023, operative July 1, 2023.

§ 3273.55. Operation of title

This title shall become operative on July 1, 2023. **Leg.H.** Added Stats 2022 ch 98 §3 (AB 1594), effective January 1, 2023, operative July 1, 2023.

TITLE 21
FIREARM MANUFACTURING

Definitions. § 3273.60.
Civil action; Strict liability, Penalties. § 3273.61.
CNC milling machine or three-dimensional printers; Rebuttable presumption of violation; Action for injuries. § 3273.62.

§ 3273.60. Definitions

As used in this title, the following definitions apply:

(a) "Digital firearm manufacturing code" means any digital instructions in the form of computer-aided design files or other code or instructions stored and displayed in electronic format as a digital model that may be used to program a CNC milling machine, a three-dimensional printer, or a similar machine, to manufacture or produce a firearm, including a completed frame or receiver or a firearm precursor part.

(b) "Federally licensed firearms manufacturer" means a person, firm, corporation, or other entity that holds a valid license to manufacture firearms issued pursuant to Chapter 44 (commencing with Section 921) of Part I of Title 18 of the United States Code and regulations issued pursuant thereto.

(c) "Firearm" has the same meaning as in subdivisions (a) and (b) of Section 16520 of the Penal Code.

(d) "Three-dimensional printer" means a computer-aided manufacturing device capable of producing a three-dimensional object from a three-dimensional digital model through an additive manufacturing process that involves the layering of two-dimensional cross sections formed of a resin or similar material that are fused together to form a three-dimensional object. **Leg.H.** Added Stats 2023 ch 243 §2 (AB 1089), effective January 1, 2024.

§ 3273.61. Civil action; Strict liability, Penalties

(a) A civil action may be brought against a person who knowingly does either of the following:

(1) Distributes or causes to be distributed, by any means including the internet, any digital firearm manufacturing code to any other person in this state who is not a federally licensed firearms manufacturer, member of the Armed Forces of the United States or the National Guard, while on duty

and acting within the scope and course of employment, or any law enforcement agency or forensic laboratory.

(2) Commits an act that violates Section 29185 of the Penal Code, regardless of whether the act results in a conviction.

(b)(1) A person who commits an act described in subdivision (a) shall be strictly liable for any personal injury or property damage inflicted by the use of a firearm that is manufactured or produced using the digital firearm manufacturing code that they distributed or caused to be distributed, or that is manufactured by means of a computer numerical control (CNC) milling machine, a three-dimensional printer, or a similar machine.

(2) This subdivision does not apply to any injury or property damage sustained by a person who commits an unlawful act described in subdivision (a).

(c) The Attorney General, county counsel, or city attorney may bring an action in any court of competent jurisdiction to establish that a person has violated this section and may seek a civil penalty not to exceed twenty-five thousand dollars ($25,000) for each violation, as well as injunctive relief sufficient to prevent the person and any other defendant from further violating the law.

(d) A prevailing plaintiff shall be entitled to recover reasonable attorney's fees and costs.

(e) The remedies provided by this section are cumulative and shall not be construed as restricting any other rights, causes of action, claims, or defenses available under any other law. **Leg.H.** Added Stats 2023 ch 243 §2 (AB 1089), effective January 1, 2024.

§ 3273.62. CNC milling machine or three-dimensional printers; Rebuttable presumption of violation; Action for injuries

(a) A person shall not sell, offer to sell, transfer, advertise, or market a CNC milling machine or three-dimensional printer in a manner that knowingly or recklessly causes another person in this state to engage in conduct prohibited by Section 29185 of the Penal Code, or in a manner that otherwise knowingly or recklessly aids, abets, promotes, or facilitates conduct prohibited by that section.

(b) There shall be a rebuttable presumption that a person is engaged in conduct in violation of subdivision (a) if both of the following are true:

(1) The person offers to sell, advertises, or markets a CNC milling machine or three-dimensional printer in a manner that, under the totality of the circumstances, is targeted at purchasers seeking to manufacture firearms or that otherwise affirmatively promotes the machine or printer's utility in manufacturing firearms, regardless of whether the machine or printer is otherwise described or classified as having any other capabilities.

(2) The person sells or transfers the CNC milling machine or three-dimensional printer described in paragraph (1) without verifying that a purchaser or transferee in this state is a federally licensed firearms manufacturer or not otherwise prohibited from purchasing or using the machine or printer to manufacture firearms under Section 29185 of the Penal Code.

(c) A person who has suffered harm because of conduct in violation of this section, including conduct in violation of Section 29185 of the Penal Code that was precipitated by a violation of this section, may bring an action in a court of competent jurisdiction to seek appropriate relief, which may include injunctive relief sufficient to prevent the person and any other defendant from further violating the law, compensatory or statutory damages, punitive damages, reasonable attorney's fees and costs, and any other appropriate relief necessary to enforce this title and remedy the harm caused by the violation.

(d) In the name of the people of the State of California, the Attorney General, county counsel, or city attorney may bring an action in any court of competent jurisdiction to establish that a person has violated this section, or Section 29185 of the Penal Code, and seek a civil penalty not to exceed twenty-five thousand dollars ($25,000) for each violation, as well as injunctive relief sufficient to prevent the person and any other defendant from further violating the law. **Leg.H.** Added Stats 2023 ch 243 §2 (AB 1089), effective January 1, 2024.

TITLE 22
CHILD SEXUAL ABUSE MATERIAL HOSTED ON A SOCIAL MEDIA PLATFORM

Definitions. § 3273.65.
Social media platform duties. § 3273.66.
Liability for failures to comply. § 3273.67.
Waiver. § 3273.68.
Provisions. § 3273.69.

§ 3273.65. Definitions

As used in this title:

(a) "Child pornography" has the same meaning as defined in Section 2256 of Title 18 of the United States Code, as amended from time to time.

(b) "Child sexual abuse material" means either of the following:

(1) Child pornography.

(2) Obscene matter that depicts a minor personally engaging in, or personally simulating, sexual conduct.

(c) "Identifiable minor" has the same meaning as defined in Section 2256 of Title 18 of the United States Code, as amended from time to time.

(d) "Minor" has the same meaning as defined in Section 2256 of Title 18 of the United States Code, as amended from time to time.

(e) "Obscene matter" has the same meaning as defined in Section 311 of the Penal Code.

(f) "Reporting user" means a natural person who reports material to a social media platform using the means provided by the social media platform pursuant to Section 3273.61.

(g)(1) "Social media company" has, except as provided in paragraph (2), the same meaning as defined in Section 22675 of the Business and Professions Code.

(2) "Social media company" does not include a nonprofit organization exempt from federal income tax pursuant to Section 501(c)(3) of the Internal Revenue Code.

(h)(1) "Social media platform" has, except as provided in paragraph (2), the same meaning as defined in Section 22675 of the Business and Professions Code.

(2) "Social media platform" does not include either of the following:

(A) A stand-alone direct messaging service that provides end-to-end encrypted communication or the portion of a multiservice platform that uses end-to-end encrypted communication.

(B) An internet-based service or application owned or operated by a nonprofit organization exempt from federal income tax pursuant to Section 501(c)(3) of the Internal Revenue Code. **Leg.H.** Added Stats 2023 ch 579 §2 (AB 1394), effective January 1, 2024, operative January 1, 2025.

§ 3273.66. Social media platform duties

A social media platform shall do all of the following:

(a) Provide, in a mechanism that is reasonably accessible to users, a means for a user who is a California resident to report material to the social media platform that the user reasonably believes meets all of the following criteria:

(1) The reported material is child sexual abuse material.

(2) The reporting user is an identifiable minor depicted in the reported material.

(3) The reported material is displayed, stored, or hosted on the social media platform.

(b) Collect information reasonably sufficient to enable the social media platform to contact, pursuant to subdivision (c), a reporting user.

(c) A social media platform shall contact a reporting user in writing by a method, including, but not limited to, a telephone number for purposes of sending text messages, or an email address, that meets both of the following criteria:

(1) The method is chosen by the reporting user.

(2) The method is not a method that is within the control of the social media company that owns or operates the social media platform.

(d)(1) Permanently block the instance of reported material from being viewable on the social media platform if the reported material meets all of the following criteria:

(A) There is a reasonable basis to believe that the reported material is child sexual abuse material.

(B) The reported material is displayed, stored, or hosted on the social media platform.

(C)(i) The report contains basic identifying information, such as an account identifier, sufficient to permit the social media platform to locate the reported material.

(ii) A social media platform shall not require a report to contain a specific piece of information for purposes of this subparagraph.

(2) A social media platform shall make reasonable efforts to remove and block other instances of the same reported material blocked pursuant to this subdivision from being viewable on the social media platform.

(e) Provide written confirmation to a reporting user that the social media platform received that person's report that meets all of the following criteria:

(1) The written confirmation is provided to the reporting user within 36 hours of when the material was first reported.

(2) The written confirmation is provided using the information collected from the reporting user under subdivision (b).

(3) The written confirmation informs the reporting user of the schedule of regular written updates that the social media platform is required to make under subdivision (f).

(f)(1) Provide a written update to the reporting user as to the status of the social media platform's handling of the reported material using the information collected from the reporting user under subdivision (b).

(2) The written update required by this subdivision shall be provided seven days after the date on which the written confirmation required under subdivision (e) was provided and every seven days thereafter until the final written determination required by subdivision (g) is provided.

(g) Issue a final written determination to the reporting user, using the information collected from the reporting user under subdivision (b), stating one of the following:

(1) The reported material has been determined to be child sexual abuse material that was displayed, stored, or hosted on the social media platform and has been blocked on the social media platform.

(2) The reported material has been determined not to be child sexual abuse material.

(3) The reported material has been determined not to be displayed, stored, or hosted on the social media platform.

(h)(1) Except as provided in paragraph (2), comply with subdivisions (c) to (g), inclusive, no later than 30 days after the date on which material was first reported pursuant to this section.

(2)(A) If the social media platform cannot comply with subdivisions (c) to (g), inclusive, due to circumstances beyond the reasonable control of the social media platform, the social media platform shall comply with subdivisions (c) to (g), inclusive, no later than 60 days after the date on which material was first reported pursuant to this section.

(B) If this paragraph applies, the social media platform shall promptly provide written notice of the delay, no later than 48 hours from the time the social media platform knew the delay was likely to occur, to the reporting user using the information collected from the reporting user under subdivision (b). **Leg.H.** Added Stats 2023 ch 579 §2 (AB 1394), effective January 1, 2024, operative January 1, 2025.

§ 3273.67. Liability for failures to comply

(a) A social media company that fails to comply with the requirements of this title shall be liable to a reporting user for all of the following:

(1) Any actual damages sustained by the reporting user as a result of the violation.

(2)(A)(i) Subject to clauses (ii) and (iii), statutory damages of no more than two hundred fifty thousand dollars ($250,000) per violation.

(ii) If a social media platform has permanently blocked the instance of the reported material pursuant to subdivision (d) of Section 3273.66 before a complaint is filed for a violation of this title, the maximum statutory damages awarded pursuant to clause (i) shall be one hundred twenty-five thousand dollars ($125,000) per violation.

(iii) If a social media platform meets all of the following requirements, the maximum statutory damages awarded pursuant to clause (i) for a violation of subdivisions (d) to (g), inclusive, of Section 3273.66 shall be seventy-five thousand dollars ($75,000) per violation:

(I) The social media platform registers with, and participates in, the National Center for Missing and Exploited Children's Take It Down service or its successor.

(II) The social media platform receives updated hash values for identified child sexual abuse material from the National Center for Missing and Exploited Children's Take It Down service, or its successor, at least once every 36 hours.

(III) Within 36 hours of receiving updated hash values for identified child sexual abuse material from the National Center for Missing and Exploited Children's Take it Down service, or its successor, pursuant to subclause (II), the social media platform removes child sexual abuse material identified by hash values from the social media platform.

(IV) The social media platform reports identified child sexual abuse material to the National Center for Missing and Exploited Children's CyberTipline, as required by Section 2258A of Title 18 of the United States Code.

(V) The social media platform provides to a reporting user both of the following when a user reports child sexual abuse material to the platform directly:

(ia) Written confirmation to the reporting user that the social media platform received that person's report within 36 hours after the child sexual abuse material was reported.

(ib) A final written determination to the reporting user within 30 days after the date on which the material was first reported.

(B) In determining the amount of statutory damages pursuant to this paragraph, a court shall consider the willfulness and severity of the violation and whether the social media platform has previously violated this title.

(3) Costs of the action, together with reasonable attorney's fees, as determined by the court.

(4) Any other relief that the court deems proper.

(b) The failure of a social media platform to comply with subdivisions (c) to (g), inclusive, of Section 3273.66 within 60 days after the date on which material was first reported pursuant to Section 3273.66 shall establish a rebuttable presumption that the reporting user is entitled to statutory damages under this section.

(c) This title shall not be construed to limit or impair in any way a cause of action under paragraph (1) of Section 1710. **Leg.H.** Added Stats 2023 ch 579 §2 (AB 1394), effective January 1, 2024, operative January 1, 2025.

§ 3273.68. Waiver

A waiver of the provisions of this title is contrary to public policy and is void and unenforceable. **Leg.H.** Added Stats 2023 ch 579 §2 (AB 1394), effective January 1, 2024, operative January 1, 2025.

§ 3273.69. Provisions

The provisions of this title are severable. If any provision of this title or its application is held invalid, that invalidity shall not affect other provisions or applications that can be given effect without the invalid provision or application. **Leg.H.** Added Stats 2023 ch 579 §2 (AB 1394), effective January 1, 2024, operative January 1, 2025.

DIVISION 4
GENERAL PROVISIONS

Part 1. Relief.
Part 2. Special Relations of Debtor and Creditor.
Part 3. Nuisance.
Part 4. Maxims Of Jurisprudence.
Part 5. Common Interest Developments.
Part 5.3. Commercial and Industrial Common Interest Developments.
Part 5.5. Automatic Checkout System.
Part 6. Works of Improvement.
Part 8. Automatic Checkout System.

PART 1
RELIEF

Title 1. Relief in General.
Title 2. Compensatory Relief.
Title 3. Specific and Preventive Relief.
Title 4. Uniform Single Publication Act.
Title 5. Uniform Trade Secrets Act.
Title 6. Interference With Access to Health Care.
Title 7. Duty of Health Care Service Plans and Managed Care Entities.

TITLE 1
RELIEF IN GENERAL

Species of relief. §3274.
Relief in case of forfeiture. §3275.

§3274. Species of relief

As a general rule, compensation is the relief or remedy provided by the law of this state for the violation of private rights, and the means of securing their observance; and specific and preventive relief may be given in no other cases than those specified in this part of the Civil Code. **Leg.H.** Enacted Stats 1872.

§3275. Relief in case of forfeiture

Whenever, by the terms of an obligation, a party thereto incurs a forfeiture, or a loss in the nature of a forfeiture, by reason of his failure to comply with its provisions, he may be relieved therefrom, upon making full compensation to the other party, except in case of a grossly negligent, willful, or fraudulent breach of duty. **Leg.H.** Enacted Stats 1872.

TITLE 2
COMPENSATORY RELIEF

Chapter 1. Damages in General.
Chapter 2. Measure of Damages.

CHAPTER 1
DAMAGES IN GENERAL

Article 1. General Principles.
Article 2. Interest as Damages.
Article 3. Exemplary Damages.

ARTICLE 1
General Principles

Authorization for compensation. §3281.
Detriment defined. §3282.
Subsequent or probable detriment. §3283.

§3281. Authorization for compensation

Every person who suffers detriment from the unlawful act or omission of another, may recover from the person in fault a compensation therefor in money, which is called damages. **Leg.H.** Enacted Stats 1872.

§3282. Detriment defined

Detriment is a loss or harm suffered in person or property. **Leg.H.** Enacted Stats 1872.

§3283. Subsequent or probable detriment

Damages may be awarded, in a judicial proceeding, for detriment resulting after the commencement thereof, or certain to result in the future. **Leg.H.** Enacted Stats 1872.

ARTICLE 2
Interest as Damages

Authorization; Recovery of interest; Calculation of interest. §3287.
In actions other than contract. §3288.
Limit of rate by contract. §3289.
Rate of contracted finance charge. §3289.5.
Waiver. §3290.
Personal injury actions. §3291.

§3287. Authorization; Recovery of interest; Calculation of interest

(a) A person who is entitled to recover damages certain, or capable of being made certain by calculation, and the right to recover which is vested in the person upon a particular day, is entitled also to recover interest thereon from that day, except when the debtor is prevented by law, or by the act of the creditor from paying the debt. This section is applicable to recovery of damages and interest from any debtor, including the state or any county, city, city and county, municipal corporation, public district, public agency, or any political subdivision of the state.

(b) Every person who is entitled under any judgment to receive damages based upon a cause of action in contract where the claim was unliquidated, may also recover interest thereon from a date prior to the entry of judgment as the court may, in its discretion, fix, but in no event earlier than the date the action was filed.

(c) Unless another statute provides a different interest rate, in a tax or fee claim against a public entity that results in a judgment against the public entity, interest shall accrue at a rate equal to the weekly average one year constant maturity United States Treasury yield, but shall not exceed 7 percent per annum. That rate shall control until the judgment becomes enforceable under Section 965.5 or 970.1 of the Government Code, at which time interest shall accrue at an annual rate equal to the weekly average one year constant maturity United States Treasury yield at the time of the judgment plus 2 percent, but shall not exceed 7 percent per annum. **Leg.H.** Enacted Stats 1872. Amended Stats 1955 ch 1477 §1; Stats 1959 ch 1735 §1; Stats 1967 ch 1230 §1; Stats 2013 ch 424 §1 (AB 748), effective January 1, 2014.

§3288. In actions other than contract

In an action for the breach of an obligation not arising from contract, and in every case of oppression, fraud, or malice, interest may be given, in the discretion of the jury. **Leg.H.** Enacted Stats 1872.

§3289. Limit of rate by contract

(a) Any legal rate of interest stipulated by a contract remains chargeable after a breach thereof, as before, until the contract is superseded by a verdict or other new obligation.

(b) If a contract entered into after January 1, 1986, does not stipulate a legal rate of interest, the obligation shall bear interest at a rate of 10 percent per annum after a breach.

For the purposes of this subdivision, the term contract shall not include a note secured by a deed of trust on real property. **Leg.H.** Enacted Stats 1872. Amended Stats 1985 ch 663 §1; Stats 1986 ch 176 §1, effective June 23, 1986.

§3289.5. Rate of contracted finance charge

For purposes of Section 3289, the rate of the contracted finance charge shall be the legal rate of interest stipulated by a retail installment contract subject to Chapter 1 (commencing with Section 1801) of Title 2 of Part 4 of Division 3. **Leg.H.** Added Stats 1985 ch 224 §1.

§3290. Waiver

Accepting payment of the whole principal, as such, waives all claim to interest. **Leg.H.** Enacted Stats 1872.

§3291. Personal injury actions

In any action brought to recover damages for personal injury sustained by any person resulting from or occasioned by the tort of any other person, corporation, association, or partnership, whether by negligence or by willful intent of the other person, corporation, association, or partnership, and whether the injury was fatal or otherwise, it is lawful for the plaintiff in the complaint to claim interest on the damages alleged as provided in this section.

If the plaintiff makes an offer pursuant to Section 998 of the Code of Civil Procedure which the defendant does not accept prior to trial or within 30 days, whichever occurs first, and the plaintiff obtains a more favorable judgment, the judgment shall bear interest at the legal rate of 10 percent per annum calculated from the date of the plaintiff's first offer pursuant to Section 998 of the Code of Civil Procedure which is exceeded by the judgment, and interest shall accrue until the satisfaction of judgment.

This section shall not apply to a public entity, or to a public employee for an act or omission within the scope of employment, and neither the public entity nor the public employee shall be liable, directly or indirectly, to any person for any interest imposed by this section. **Leg.H.** Added Stats 1982 ch 150 §1.

ARTICLE 3
Exemplary Damages

When permitted. §3294.
Protection of evidence of financial condition. §3295.
Judgment for punitive damages. §3296.

§3294. When permitted

(a) In an action for the breach of an obligation not arising from contract, where it is proven by clear and convincing evidence that the defendant has been guilty of oppression, fraud, or malice, the plaintiff, in addition to the actual damages, may recover damages for the sake of example and by way of punishing the defendant.

(b) An employer shall not be liable for damages pursuant to subdivision (a), based upon acts of an employee of the employer, unless the employer had advance knowledge of the unfitness of the employee and employed him or her with a conscious disregard of the rights or safety of others or authorized or ratified the wrongful conduct for which the damages are awarded or was personally guilty of oppression, fraud, or malice. With respect to a corporate employer, the advance knowledge and conscious disregard, authorization, ratification or act of oppression, fraud, or malice must be on the part of an officer, director, or managing agent of the corporation.

(c) As used in this section, the following definitions shall apply:

(1) "Malice" means conduct which is intended by the defendant to cause injury to the plaintiff or despicable conduct which is carried on by the defendant with a willful and conscious disregard of the rights or safety of others.

(2) "Oppression" means despicable conduct that subjects a person to cruel and unjust hardship in conscious disregard of that person's rights.

(3) "Fraud" means an intentional misrepresentation, deceit, or concealment of a material fact known to the defendant with the intention on the part of the defendant of thereby depriving a person of property or legal rights or otherwise causing injury.

(d) Damages may be recovered pursuant to this section in an action pursuant to Chapter 4 (commencing with Section 377.10) of Title 3 of Part 2 of the Code of Civil Procedure based upon a death which resulted from a homicide for which the defendant has been convicted of a felony, whether or not the decedent died instantly or survived the fatal injury for some period of time. The procedures for joinder and consolidation contained in Section 377.62 of the Code of Civil Procedure shall apply to prevent multiple recoveries of punitive or exemplary damages based upon the same wrongful act.

(e) The amendments to this section made by Chapter 1498 of the Statutes of 1987 apply to all actions in which the initial trial has not commenced prior to January 1, 1988. **Leg.H.** Enacted Stats 1872. Amended Stats 1905 ch 463 §1; Stats 1980 ch 1242 §1; Stats 1982 ch 174 §1; Stats 1983 ch 408 §1; Stats 1987 ch 1498 §5; Stats 1988 ch 160 §17; Stats 1992 ch 178 §5 (SB 1496).

§3294.5. [Section repealed 2006]

Leg.H. Added Stats 2004 ch 227 §8.5 (SB 1102), effective August 16, 2004, repealed July 1, 2006, by its own provisions. The repealed section related to creation of Public Benefit Trust Fund.

§3295. Protection of evidence of financial condition

(a) The court may, for good cause, grant any defendant a protective order requiring the plaintiff to produce evidence of a prima facie case of liability for damages pursuant to Section 3294, prior to the introduction of evidence of:

(1) The profits the defendant has gained by virtue of the wrongful course of conduct of the nature and type shown by the evidence.

(2) The financial condition of the defendant.

(b) Nothing in this section shall prohibit the introduction of prima facie evidence to establish a case for damages pursuant to Section 3294.

(c) No pretrial discovery by the plaintiff shall be permitted with respect to the evidence referred to in paragraphs (1) and (2) of subdivision (a) unless the court enters an order permitting such discovery pursuant to this subdivision. However, the plaintiff may subpoena documents or witnesses to be available at the trial for the purpose of establishing the profits or financial condition referred to in subdivision (a), and the defendant may be required to identify documents in the defendant's possession which are relevant and admissible for that purpose and the witnesses employed by or related to the defendant who would be most competent to testify to those facts. Upon motion by the plaintiff supported by appropriate affidavits and after a hearing, if the court deems a hearing to be necessary, the court may at any time enter an order permitting the discovery otherwise prohibited by this subdivision if the court finds, on the basis of the supporting and opposing affidavits presented, that the plaintiff has established that there is a substantial probability that the plaintiff will prevail on the claim pursuant to Section 3294. Such order shall not be considered to be a determination on the merits of the claim or any defense thereto and shall not be given in evidence or referred to at the trial.

(d) The court shall, on application of any defendant, preclude the admission of evidence of that defendant's profits or financial condition until after the trier of fact returns a verdict for plaintiff awarding actual damages and finds that a defendant is guilty of malice, oppression, or fraud in accordance with Section 3294. Evidence of profit and financial condition shall be admissible only as to the defendant or defendants found to be liable to the plaintiff and to be guilty of malice, oppression, or fraud. Evidence of profit and financial condition shall be presented to the same trier of fact that found for the plaintiff and found one or more defendants guilty of malice, oppression, or fraud.

(e) No claim for exemplary damages shall state an amount or amounts.

(f) The amendments to this section made by Senate Bill No. 241 of the 1987–88 Regular Session apply to all actions in which the initial trial has not commenced prior to January 1, 1988. **Leg.H.** Added Stats 1979 ch 778 §1. Amended Stats 1980 ch 1242 §2; Stats 1987 ch 1498 §6.

§3296. Judgment for punitive damages

(a) Whenever a judgment for punitive damages is entered against an insurer or health care service plan licensed pursuant to Chapter 2.2 (commencing with Section 1340) of Division 2 of the Health and Safety Code, the plaintiff in the action shall, within 10 days of entry of judgment, provide all of the following to the Commissioner of the Department of Insurance or the Director of the Department of Managed Health Care, whichever commissioner has regulatory jurisdiction over the insurer or health care service plan:

(1) A copy of the judgment.

(2) A brief recitation of the facts of the case.

(3) Copies of relevant pleadings, as determined by the plaintiff.

(b) The willful failure to comply with this section may, at the discretion of the trial court, result in the imposition of sanctions against the plaintiff or his or her attorney.

(c) This section shall apply to all judgments entered on or after January 1, 1995.

(d) "Insurer," for purposes of this section, means any person or entity transacting any of the classes of insurance described in Chapter 1 (commencing with Section 100) of Part 1 of Division 1 of the Insurance Code. **Leg.H.** Added Stats 1994 ch 1061 §1 (AB 3570). Amended Stats 1999 ch 525 §7 (AB 78); Stats 2000 ch 857 §5 (AB 2903).

CHAPTER 2
MEASURE OF DAMAGES

Article 1. Damages for Breach of Contract.
Article 2. Damages for Wrongs.
Article 3. Penal Damages.
Article 4. General Provisions.

ARTICLE 1
Damages for Breach of Contract

Measure of damages for breach of contract. §3300.
Requirement of certainty. §3301.
Contract to pay money. §3302.
Covenants of seizin, right to convey, warranty, and quiet enjoyment. §3304.
Covenant against encumbrances. §3305.
Agreement to convey real property. §3306.
Contract to deliver quitclaim deed. §3306a.
Agreement to buy real property. §3307.
Agreement as to damages upon breach of lease. §3308.
Carrier's obligation to receive goods. §3315.
Carrier's obligation to deliver goods. §3316.
Carrier's delay. §3317.
Warranty of authority. §3318.
Contract for private works improvements; Late payment penalty in lieu of interest. §3319.
Contract for public works improvements; Progress payment; Penalty for withheld or late payment. §3320.
Contract for public works improvements; Payment from prime design professional to subconsultant; Penalty for withheld or late payment. §3321.
Payment of transportation charges by construction trucking services broker. §3322.

§3300. Measure of damages for breach of contract

Section Thirty-three Hundred. For the breach of an obligation arising from contract, the measure of damages, except where otherwise expressly provided by this Code, is the amount which will compensate the party aggrieved for all the detriment proximately caused thereby, or which, in the ordinary course of things, would be likely to result therefrom. **Leg.H.** Enacted Stats 1872. Amended Code Amdts 1873–74 ch 612 §276 p 266.

§3301. Requirement of certainty

No damages can be recovered for a breach of contract which are not clearly ascertainable in both their nature and origin. **Leg.H.** Enacted Stats 1872.

§3302. Contract to pay money

The detriment caused by the breach of an obligation to pay money only, is deemed to be the amount due by the terms of the obligation, with interest thereon. **Leg.H.** Enacted Stats 1872.

§3303. [Section repealed 1968]

Leg.H. Enacted Stats 1872. Repealed Stats 1968 ch 113 §1.

§3304. Covenants of seizin, right to convey, warranty, and quiet enjoyment

The detriment caused by the breach of a covenant of "seizin," of "right to convey," of "warranty," or of "quiet enjoyment," in a grant of an estate in real property, is deemed to be:

1. The price paid to the grantor; or, if the breach is partial only, such proportion of the price as the value of the property affected by the breach bore at the time of the grant to the value of the whole property;
2. Interest thereon for the time during which the grantee derived no benefit from the property, not exceeding five years;
3. Any expenses properly incurred by the covenantee in defending his possession. **Leg.H.** Enacted Stats 1872.

§3305. Covenant against encumbrances

The detriment caused by the breach of a covenant against incumbrances in a grant of an estate in real property is deemed to be the amount which has been actually expended by the covenantee in extinguishing either the principal or interest thereof, not exceeding in the former case a proportion of the price paid to the grantor equivalent to the relative value at the time of the grant of the property affected by the breach, as compared with the whole, or, in the latter case, interest on a like amount. **Leg.H.** Enacted Stats 1872.

§3306. Agreement to convey real property

The detriment caused by the breach of an agreement to convey an estate in real property, is deemed to be the price paid, and the expenses properly incurred in examining the title and preparing the necessary papers, the difference between the price agreed to be paid and the value of the estate agreed to be conveyed at the time of the breach, the expenses properly incurred in preparing to enter upon the land, consequential damages according to proof, and interest. **Leg.H.** Enacted Stats 1872. Amended Stats 1983 ch 262 §1.

§3306a. Contract to deliver quitclaim deed

The minimum detriment caused by the breach of an agreement to execute and deliver a quitclaim deed to real property is deemed to be the expenses incurred by the promisee in quieting title to such property, and the expenses incidental to the entry upon such property. Such expenses which shall include reasonable attorneys' fees shall be fixed by the court in the quiet title action. **Leg.H.** Added Stats 1935 ch 661 §1.

§3307. Agreement to buy real property

The detriment caused by the breach of an agreement to purchase an estate in real property is deemed to be the excess, if any, of the amount which would have been due to the seller under the contract over the value of the property to him or her, consequential damages according to proof, and interest. **Leg.H.** Enacted Stats 1872. Amended Stats 1983 ch 262 §2.

§3308. Agreement as to damages upon breach of lease

The parties to any lease of real or personal property may agree therein that if the lease shall be terminated by the lessor by reason of any breach thereof by the lessee, the lessor shall thereupon be entitled to recover from the lessee the worth at the time of the termination, of the excess, if any, of the amount of rent and charges equivalent to rent reserved in the lease for the balance of the stated term or any shorter period of time over the then reasonable rental value of the property for the same period.

The rights of the lessor under the agreement shall be cumulative to all other rights or remedies now or hereafter given to the lessor by law or by the terms of the lease; provided, however, that the election of the lessor to exercise the remedy hereinabove permitted shall be binding upon him or her and exclude recourse thereafter to any other remedy for rental or charges equivalent to rental or damages for breach of the covenant to pay the rent or charges accruing subsequent to the time of the termination. The parties to the lease may further agree therein that unless the remedy provided by this section is exercised by the lessor within a specified time the right thereto shall be barred.

This section does not apply to a lease of real property unless (a) the lease was executed before July 1, 1971, or (b) the terms of the lease were fixed by a lease, option, or other agreement executed before July 1, 1971.

This section does not apply to leases subject to Division 10 (commencing with Section 10101) of the Commercial Code. **Leg.H.** Added Stats 1937 ch 504 §1, operative July 1, 1971. Amended Stats 1970 ch 89 §11, operative July 1, 1971; Stats 1988 ch 1368 §2, operative January 1, 1990.

Prior Law: Former CC §3308, relating to damages for the breach of an agreement to sell personal property, was enacted Stats. 1872 and repealed Stats 1931 ch 1070 §2. Historical derivation: Field's Draft NY CC §1848.

§§3309–3314. [Sections repealed 1931]

Leg.H. Enacted Stats 1872. Repealed Stats 1931 ch 1070 §2. See UCC §§1103, 1201, 1206, 2106, 2201 et seq.

§3315. Carrier's obligation to receive goods

The detriment caused by the breach of a carrier's obligation to accept freight, messages, or passengers, is deemed to be the difference between the amount which he had a right to charge for the carriage and the amount which it would be necessary to pay for the same service when it ought to be performed. **Leg.H.** Enacted Stats 1872.

§3316. Carrier's obligation to deliver goods

The detriment caused by the breach of a carrier's obligation to deliver freight, where he has not converted it to his own use, is deemed to be the value thereof at the place and on the day at which it should have been delivered, deducting the freightage to which he would have been entitled if he had completed the delivery. **Leg.H.** Enacted Stats 1872.

§3317. Carrier's delay

The detriment caused by a carrier's delay in the delivery of freight, is deemed to be the depreciation in the intrinsic value of the freight during the delay, and also the depreciation, if any, in the market value thereof, otherwise than by reason of a depreciation in its intrinsic value, at the place where it ought to have been delivered, and between the day at which it ought to have been delivered, and the day of its actual delivery. **Leg.H.** Enacted Stats 1872.

§3318. Warranty of authority

The detriment caused by the breach of a warranty of an agent's authority, is deemed to be the amount which could have been recovered and collected from his principal if the warranty had been complied with, and the reasonable expenses of legal proceedings taken, in good faith, to enforce the act of the agent against his principal. **Leg.H.** Enacted Stats 1872.

§3319. Contract for private works improvements; Late payment penalty in lieu of interest

(a) In each written contract for private works of improvement entered into on or after January 1, 1996, the contracting party and the design professional may agree to contractual provisions that include a late payment penalty, in lieu of any interest otherwise due. The terms of the late payment penalty shall be specifically set forth in the written contract.

(b) The penalty authorized pursuant to subdivision (a) shall be separate from, and in addition to, the design professionals liens provided by Chapter 3 (commencing with Section 8300) of Title 2 of Part 6 of Division 4, mechanics liens provided by Chapter 4 (commencing with Section 8400) of Title 2 of Part 6 of Division 4, and stop payment notices provided by Chapter 5 (commencing with Section 8500) of Title 2 of Part 6 of Division 4.

(c) None of the rights or obligations created or permitted by this section between design professionals and contracting parties shall apply to construction loan funds held by a lender pursuant to a construction loan agreement.

(d) For purposes of this section, the following definitions apply:

(1) "Contracting party" means any person or entity entering into a written contract with a design professional for professional design services for a private work of improvement.

(2) "Design professional" means a person licensed as an architect pursuant to Chapter 3 (commencing with Section 5500) of Division 3 of the Business and Professions Code, registered as a professional engineer pursuant to Chapter 7 (commencing with Section 6700) of Division 3 of the Business and Professions Code, or licensed as a land surveyor pursuant to Chapter 15 (commencing with Section 8700) of Division 3 of the Business and Professions Code. **Leg.H.** Added Stats 1995 ch 429 §1 (SB 1286). Amended Stats 1996 ch 124 §10 (AB 3470); Stats 2010 ch 697 §17 (SB 189), effective January 1, 2011, operative July 1, 2012.

Prior Law: Former CC §3319 was enacted Stats 1872 and repealed Stats 1939 ch 128 §4.

Former Sections: Former CC §3319 was added in 1872 and repealed Stats 1939 ch 128.

§3320. Contract for public works improvements; Progress payment; Penalty for withheld or late payment

(a) In each contract for public works of improvement, entered into on or after January 1, 1996, the public agency shall pay to the prime design professional any progress payment within 30 days of receipt of a written demand for payment in accordance with the contract, and the final retention payment within 45 days of receipt of a written demand for payment in accordance with the contract. If the public agency disputes in good faith any portion of the amount due, it may withhold from the payment an amount not to exceed 150 percent of the disputed amount. The disputed amount withheld is not subject to any penalty authorized by this section.

(b) If any amount is wrongfully withheld or is not timely paid in violation of this section, the prime design professional shall be entitled to a penalty of 1 ½ percent for the improperly withheld amount, in lieu of any interest otherwise due, per month for every month that payment is not made. In any action for the collection of amounts withheld in violation of this section, the prevailing party is entitled to his or her reasonable attorney's fees and costs.

(c) The penalty described in subdivision (b) is separate from, and in addition to, the design professionals liens provided by Chapter 3 (commencing with Section 8300) of Title 2 of Part 6 of Division 4, mechanics liens provided by Chapter 4 (commencing with Section 8400) of Title 2 of Part 6 of Division 4, and stop payment notices on public works provided by Chapter 4 (commencing with Section 9350) of Title 3 of Part 6 of Division 4.

(d) This section does not apply to state agency contracts subject to Section 927.6 of the Government Code.

(e) None of the rights or obligations created by this section between prime design professionals and public agencies apply to construction loan funds held by a lender pursuant to a construction loan agreement.

(f) For purposes of this section:

(1) "Public agency" means the state, any county, any city, any city and county, any district, any public authority, any public agency, any municipal corporation, or other political subdivision or political corporation of the state.

(2) "Design professional" means a person licensed as an architect pursuant to Chapter 3 (commencing with Section 5500) of Division 3 of the Business and Professions Code, registered as a professional engineer pursuant to Chapter 7 (commencing with Section 6700) of Division 3 of the Business and Professions Code, or licensed as a land surveyor pursuant to Chapter 15 (commencing with Section 8700) of Division 3 of the Business and Professions Code.

(3) "Prime design professional" means a design professional with a written contract directly with the public agency. **Leg.H.** Added Stats 1995 ch 429 §2 (SB 1286). Amended Stats 1996 ch 124 §11 (AB 3470); Stats 2000 ch 776 §1 (AB 2890), effective September 27, 2000; Stats 2010 ch 697 §18 (SB 189), effective January 1, 2011, operative July 1, 2012.

Prior Law: Former CC §3320, similar to UCC §4402, was added Stats 1917 ch 503 §1 and repealed Stats 1963 ch 819 §21, effective January 1, 1965.

Former Sections: Former CC §3320 was added in 1917 and repealed Stats 1963 ch 819.

§3321. Contract for public works improvements; Payment from prime design professional to subconsultant; Penalty for withheld or late payment

(a) In each contract for public works of improvement, a prime design professional shall pay to each subconsultant design professional the amount due him or her from the payment received, not later than 15 days after receipt of each progress payment or final retention payment. If the prime design professional disputes in good faith any portion of the amount due, he or she may withhold from the payment an amount not to exceed 150 percent of the disputed amount. The disputed amount withheld shall not be subject to any penalty authorized by this section.

(b) If any amount is wrongfully withheld or is not timely paid in violation of this section, the subconsultant design professional shall be entitled to a penalty of 1 ½ percent of the improperly withheld amount, in lieu of any interest otherwise due, per month, for each month that payment is not made. In any action for the collection of amounts withheld in violation of this section, the prevailing party shall be entitled to his or her reasonable attorney's fees and costs.

(c) The penalty described in subdivision (b) shall be separate from, and in addition to, the design professionals liens provided by Chapter 3 (commencing with Section 8300) of Title 2 of Part 6 of Division 4, mechanics liens provided by Chapter 4 (commencing with Section 8400) of Title 2 of Part 6 of Division 4, and stop payment notices on public works provided by Chapter 4 (commencing with Section 9350) of Title 3 of Part 6 of Division 4.

(d) None of the rights or obligations created by this section between prime design professionals and subconsultant design professionals shall apply to construction loan funds held by a lender pursuant to a construction loan agreement.

(e) For purposes of this section:

(1) "Public agency" means the state, any county, any city, any city and county, any district, any public authority, any public agency, any municipal corporation, or other political subdivision or political corporation of the state.

(2) "Design professional" means a person licensed as an architect pursuant to Chapter 3 (commencing with Section 5500) of Division 3 of the Business and Professions Code, registered as a professional engineer pursuant to Chapter 7 (commencing with Section 6700) of Division 3 of the Business and Professions Code, or licensed as a land surveyor pursuant to Chapter 15 (commencing with Section 8700) of Division 3 of the Business and Professions Code.

(3) "Prime design professional" means a design professional having a written contract directly with the public agency.

(4) "Subconsultant design professional" means a design professional having a written contract with a prime design professional. **Leg.H.** Added Stats 1995 ch 429 §3 (SB 1286). Amended Stats 1996 ch 124 §12 (AB 3470); Stats 2010 ch 697 §19 (SB 189), effective January 1, 2011, operative July 1, 2012.

§3322. Payment of transportation charges by construction trucking services broker

(a)(1) A broker of construction trucking services shall pay all transportation charges submitted by a motor carrier of property in dump truck equipment by the 25th day following the last day of the calendar month in which the transportation was performed, if the charges, including all necessary documentation, are submitted by the fifth day following the last day of the calendar month in which the transportation was performed. If there is a good faith dispute over a portion of the charges claimed, the broker may withhold payment of an amount not to exceed 150 percent of the estimated cost of the disputed amount.

(2) A broker who violates paragraph (1) shall pay to the motor carrier of property in dump truck equipment a penalty of 2 percent per month on the improperly withheld amount.

(3) In an action for the collection of moneys not paid in accordance with paragraph (1), the prevailing party shall be entitled to his or her attorney's fees and costs.

(b) For purposes of subdivision (a), the following definitions apply:

(1) A "broker of construction trucking services" means any person, excluding a licensed contractor, that, as a principal or agent, arranges for transportation services to be provided by an independent contractor motor carrier of property in dump truck equipment and who is responsible for paying the transportation charges of the motor carrier.

(2) A "motor carrier of property in dump truck equipment" means a motor carrier of property permitted by the Department of Motor Vehicles that hauls any type of construction commodity or material in dump truck equipment.

(c) Subdivision (a) only applies if a motor carrier of property is in compliance with Division 14.85 (commencing with Section 36000) of the Vehicle Code at the time the dump truck transportation work is performed. **Leg.H.** Added Stats 2004 ch 518 §1 (AB 2201).

ARTICLE 2
Damages for Wrongs

Measure of damages. §3333.
Collateral benefits in medical malpractice actions. §3333.1.
Noneconomic losses in medical malpractice actions. §3333.2.
Award of damages following felony conviction. §3333.3.
Recovery of non-economic losses arising out of motor vehicle accident. §3333.4.
Absolute liability for damages caused by discharge of crude oil from public utility pipeline; Exceptions; Costs; Cleanup responsibilities; Certification by Fire Marshal. §3333.5.
Recovery of damages from employer in motor vehicle. §3333.7.
Immunity for prescribed burn. § 3333.8.
Wrongful occupation. §3334.
Willful holding over. §3335.
Conversion. §3336.
Liability of junk dealer or recycler for wrongful possession of fire hydrants or fire department connections. §3336.5.
Conversion benefitting owner. §3337.
Damages of lienor. §3338.
Legislative findings and declarations regarding employment protections available regardless of immigration status. §3339.
Minor child's immigration status. §3339,5.
Immigration or citizenship status of any person is irrelevant to any issue of liability or remedy. §3339.10.
Injuries to animals. §3340.
Infliction by pet of injury upon farm or ranch animal. §3341.
Liability of owner of dog for damages suffered by dog bite; Bites by dogs in military or police work. §3342.
Duty to remove danger presented from dog bites; Enforcement. §3342.5.
Fraudulent property sales. §3343.
Unlawful motor vehicle subleasing. §3343.5.
Rescission action for fraudulent inducement to join nonprofit cooperative of independent retailers. §3343.7.
Unauthorized commercial use of name, voice, signature, photograph or likeness. §3344.
Rights of deceased personality. §3344.1.
Civil cause of action for publication of deceptive campaign advertisement containing unauthorized signature. §3344.5.
Cause of action for candidate whose election or defeat advocated with false or fraudulent representations. §3344.6.

§3333. Measure of damages

For the breach of an obligation not arising from contract, the measure of damages, except where otherwise expressly provided by this Code, is the amount which will compensate for all the detriment proximately caused thereby, whether it could have been anticipated or not. **Leg.H.** Enacted Stats 1872.

§3333.1. Collateral benefits in medical malpractice actions

(a) In the event the defendant so elects, in an action for personal injury against a health care provider based upon professional negligence, he may introduce evidence of any amount payable as a benefit to the plaintiff as a result of the personal injury pursuant to the United States Social Security Act, any state or federal income disability or worker's compensation act, any health, sickness or income-disability insurance, accident insurance that provides health benefits or income-disability coverage, and any contract or agreement of any group, organization, partnership, or corporation to provide, pay for, or reimburse the cost of medical, hospital, dental, or other health care services. Where the defendant elects to introduce such evidence, the plaintiff may introduce evidence of any amount which the plaintiff has paid or contributed to secure his right to any insurance benefits concerning which the defendant has introduced evidence.

(b) No source of collateral benefits introduced pursuant to subdivision (a) shall recover any amount against the plaintiff nor shall it be subrogated to the rights of the plaintiff against a defendant.

(c) For the purposes of this section:

(1) "Health care provider" means any person licensed or certified pursuant to Division 2 (commencing with Section 500) of the Business and Professions Code, or licensed pursuant to the Osteopathic Initiative Act, or the Chiropractic Initiative Act, or licensed pursuant to Chapter 2.5 (commencing with Section 1440) of Division 2 of the Health and Safety Code; and any clinic, health dispensary, or health facility, licensed pursuant to Division 2 (commencing with Section 1200) of the Health and Safety Code. "Health care provider" includes the legal representatives of a health care provider;

(2) "Professional negligence" means a negligent act or omission to act by a health care provider in the rendering of professional services, which act or omission is the proximate cause of a personal injury or wrongful death, provided that such services are within the scope of services for which the provider is licensed and which are not within any restriction imposed by the licensing agency or licensed hospital. **Leg.H.** Added Stats 1975 2nd Ex Sess ch 1 §24.5. Amended Stats 1975 2nd Ex Sess ch 2 §1.19, effective December 12, 1975; Stats 1976 ch 1079 §4.

§3333.2. Noneconomic losses in medical malpractice actions

(a) In any action for injury against a health care provider or health care institution based on professional negligence, the injured plaintiff shall be entitled to recover noneconomic losses to compensate for pain, suffering, inconvenience, physical impairment, disfigurement and other nonpecuniary damage, subject to the limitations in this section.

(b) In any action for injury that does not involve wrongful death against one or more health care providers or health care institutions based on professional negligence, the following limitations shall apply:

(1) Civil liability for damages for noneconomic losses against one or more health care providers, collectively, shall not exceed three hundred fifty thousand dollars ($350,000), regardless of the number of health care providers, which does not include any unaffiliated health care providers that are responsible for noneconomic losses pursuant to paragraph (3).

(2) Civil liability for damages for noneconomic losses against one or more health care institutions, collectively, shall not exceed three hundred fifty thousand dollars ($350,000), regardless of the number of health care institutions, which does not include any unaffiliated health care institutions that are responsible for noneconomic losses pursuant to paragraph (3).

(3) Civil liability for damages for noneconomic losses against one or more health care providers or health care institutions that are unaffiliated with a defendant described in paragraph (1) or (2) based on acts of professional negligence separate and independent from the acts of professional negligence of a defendant described in paragraph (1) or (2) and that occurred at, or in relation to medical transport to, a health care institution unaffiliated with a health care institution described in paragraph (2), collectively, shall not exceed three hundred fifty thousand dollars ($350,000), regardless of the number of defendants described in this paragraph, which does not include any unaffiliated health care providers or unaffiliated health care institutions that are responsible for noneconomic losses pursuant to paragraph (1) or (2).

(c) In any action for wrongful death against one or more health care providers or health care institutions based on professional negligence, the following limitations shall apply:

(1) Civil liability for damages for noneconomic losses against one or more health care providers, collectively, shall not exceed five hundred thousand dollars ($500,000), regardless of the number of health care

providers, which does not include any unaffiliated health care providers that are responsible for noneconomic losses pursuant to paragraph (3).

(2) Civil liability for damages for noneconomic losses against one or more health care institutions, collectively, shall not exceed five hundred thousand dollars ($500,000), regardless of the number of health care institutions, which does not include any unaffiliated health care institutions that are responsible for noneconomic losses pursuant to paragraph (3).

(3) Civil liability for damages for noneconomic losses against one or more health care providers or health care institutions that are unaffiliated with a defendant described in paragraph (1) or (2) based on acts of professional negligence separate and independent from the acts of professional negligence of a defendant described in paragraph (1) or (2) that occurred at, or in relation to medical transport to, a health care institution unaffiliated with a health care institution described in paragraph (2), collectively, shall not exceed five hundred thousand dollars ($500,000), regardless of the number of defendants described in this paragraph, which does not include any unaffiliated health care providers or unaffiliated health care institutions that are responsible for noneconomic losses pursuant to paragraph (1) or (2).

(d) No health care provider defendant shall be liable for damages for noneconomic losses in more than one of the categories set forth in this section, regardless of the application or combined application thereof.

(e) No health care institution defendant shall be liable for damages for noneconomic losses in more than one of the categories set forth in this section, regardless of the application or combined application thereof.

(f) The applicable dollar amounts set forth in this section apply regardless of the number of defendant health care providers or health care institutions against whom the claim is asserted or the number of separate causes of actions on which the claim is based. For a claim subject to subdivision (b), the applicable dollar amounts set forth in subdivisions (b), (g), and (h) provide three separate limits of liability that may apply. For a claim subject to subdivision (c), the applicable dollar amounts set forth in subdivisions (c), (g), and (h) provide three separate limits of liability that may apply.

(g) This section shall be deemed effective as of, and shall apply to all cases filed or arbitrations demanded on or after, January 1, 2023. Thereafter, the dollar amounts set forth in subdivision (b) shall increase by forty thousand dollars ($40,000) each January 1st for 10 years up to seven hundred fifty thousand dollars ($750,000), and the dollar amounts set forth in subdivision (c) shall increase each January 1st by fifty thousand dollars ($50,000) for 10 years up to one million dollars ($1,000,000). The dollar amount in effect at the time of judgment, arbitration award, or settlement shall apply to an action, subject to subdivision (h).

(h) The applicable amounts for noneconomic damages for personal injury of $750,000, and for wrongful death of $1,000,000, as set forth in subdivision (g), shall be adjusted for inflation on January 1 of each year by 2 percent beginning on January 1, 2034.

(i) In no action shall the amount of damages for noneconomic losses exceed the applicable dollar amounts set forth in subdivisions (b), (c), (g), or (h).

(j) For the purposes of this section:

(1) "Health care provider" means any person licensed or certified pursuant to Division 2 (commencing with Section 500) of the Business and Professions Code, or licensed pursuant to the Osteopathic Initiative Act, or the Chiropractic Initiative Act, or licensed pursuant to Chapter 2.5 (commencing with Section 1440) of Division 2 of the Health and Safety Code; and any clinic, health dispensary, or health facility, licensed pursuant to Chapter 1 (commencing with Section 1200) or Chapter 1.3 (commencing with Section 1248) of Division 2 of the Health and Safety Code, and does not include health care institutions that are defined in paragraph (2). "Health care provider" includes the legal representatives of a health care provider and the health care provider's employer, professional corporation, partnership, or other form of legally recognized professional practice organization.

(2) "Health care institution" means one or more health care facilities licensed pursuant to Chapter 2 (commencing with Section 1250) of Division 2 of the Health and Safety Code owned or operated by the same entity or its affiliates and includes all persons and entities for which vicarious liability theories, including, but not limited to, the doctrines of respondeat superior, actual agency, and ostensible agency, may apply.

(3) "Unaffiliated" means a specified health care provider, health care institution, or other entity not covered by the definition of affiliated, or affiliated with, as defined in Section 150 of the Corporations Code, or that is not employed by, performing under a contract with, an owner of, or in a joint venture with another specified entity, health care institution, health care provider, organized medical group, professional corporation, or partnership, or that is otherwise not in the same health system with that health care provider, health care institution, or other entity. Whether a health care provider, health care institution, or other entity is unaffiliated is determined at the time of the professional negligence.

(4) "Professional negligence" means a negligent act or omission to act by a health care provider in the rendering of professional services, which act or omission is the proximate cause of a personal injury or wrongful death, provided that such services are within the scope of services for which the provider is licensed and which are not within any restriction imposed by the licensing agency or licensed hospital. **Leg.H.** Added Stats 1975 2nd Ex Sess ch 1 §24.6. Amended Stats 1975 2nd Ex Sess ch 2 §1.191, effective December 12, 1975; Stats 2022 ch 17 §3 (AB 35), effective January 1, 2023.

§3333.3. Award of damages following felony conviction

In any action for damages based on negligence, a person may not recover any damages if the plaintiff's injuries were in any way proximately caused by the plaintiff's commission of any felony, or immediate flight therefrom, and the plaintiff has been duly convicted of that felony. **Leg.H.** Addition adopted by voters, Prop 213 §3, effective November 6, 1996.

1996 Note: This act shall apply to all actions in which the initial trial has not commenced prior to January 1, 1997. Prop. 213 §4, November 5, 1996, General Election.

§3333.4. Recovery of non-economic losses arising out of motor vehicle accident

(a) Except as provided in subdivision (c), in any action to recover damages arising out of the operation or use of a motor vehicle, a person shall not recover non-economic losses to compensate for pain, suffering, inconvenience, physical impairment, disfigurement, and other nonpecuniary damages if any of the following applies:

(1) The injured person was at the time of the accident operating the vehicle in violation of Section 23152 or 23153 of the Vehicle Code, and was convicted of that offense.

(2) The injured person was the owner of a vehicle involved in the accident and the vehicle was not insured as required by the financial responsibility laws of this state.

(3) The injured person was the operator of a vehicle involved in the accident and the operator can not establish his or her financial responsibility as required by the financial responsibility laws of this state.

(b) Except as provided in subdivision (c), an insurer shall not be liable, directly or indirectly, under a policy of liability or uninsured motorist insurance to indemnify for non-economic losses of a person injured as described in subdivision (a).

(c) In the event a person described in paragraph (2) of subdivision (a) was injured by a motorist who at the time of the accident was operating his or her vehicle in violation of Section 23152 or 23153 of the Vehicle Code, and was convicted of that offense, the injured person shall not be barred from recovering non–economic losses to compensate for pain, suffering, inconvenience, physical impairment, disfigurement, and other nonpecuniary damages. **Leg.H.** Addition adopted by voters, Prop 213 §3, effective November 6, 1996.

1996 Note: This act shall apply to all actions in which the initial trial has not commenced prior to January 1, 1997. Prop. 213 §4, November 5, 1996, General Election.

Prior Law: There was another section of this number which was added Stats 1995 ch 979 §2 and amended and renumbered CC §3333.5 by Stats 1998 ch 485 §40.

§3333.5. Absolute liability for damages caused by discharge of crude oil from public utility pipeline; Exceptions; Costs; Cleanup responsibilities; Certification by Fire Marshal

(a) Each pipeline corporation that qualifies as a public utility within Section 216 of the Public Utilities Code that transports any crude oil or fraction thereof in a public utility oil pipeline system that meets the requirements of subdivision (h) shall be absolutely liable without regard to fault for any damages incurred by any injured party that arise out of, or are caused by, the discharge or leaking of crude oil or fraction thereof from the public utility pipeline.

(b) A pipeline corporation is not liable to an injured party under this section for any of the following:

(1) Damages, other than costs of removal incurred by the state or a local government caused solely by an act of war, hostilities, civil war, or insurrection or by an unanticipated grave natural disaster or other act of God of an exceptional, inevitable, and irresistible character, other than an earthquake, which damages could not have been prevented or avoided by the exercise of due care or foresight.

(2) Damages in the proportion caused by the negligence, intentional malfeasance, or criminal act of the landowner, or an agent, employee, or contractor of the landowner, upon whose property the pipeline system is located.

(3) Except as provided by paragraph (2), damages caused solely by the negligence or intentional malfeasance of the injured person.

(4) Except as provided by paragraph (2), damages caused solely by the criminal act of a third party other than the pipeline corporation or an agent or employee of the pipeline corporation.

(5) Natural seepage from sources other than the public utility oil pipeline.

(6) Damages that arise out of, or are caused by, a discharge that is authorized by a state or federal permit.

(c) Damages for which a pipeline corporation is liable under this section are the following:

(1) All costs of response, containment, cleanup, removal, and treatment, including, but not limited to, monitoring and administration costs.

(2) Injury to, or economic losses resulting from destruction of or injury to, real or personal property.

(3) Injury to, destruction of, or loss of, natural resources, including, but not limited to, the reasonable cost of rehabilitating wildlife, habitat, and other resources and the reasonable cost of assessing that injury, destruction, or loss, in any action brought by the state, a county, city, or district.

(4) Loss of taxes, royalties, rents, use, or profit shares caused by the injury, destruction, loss, or impairment of use of real property, personal property, or natural resources.

(5) Loss of use and enjoyment of natural resources and other public resources or facilities in any action brought by the state, county, city, or district.

(d) The court may award reasonable costs of the suit, attorneys' fees, and the cost of any necessary expert witnesses to any prevailing plaintiff. The court may award reasonable costs of the suit, attorneys' fees, and the cost of any necessary expert witnesses to any prevailing defendant if the court finds that the plaintiff commenced or prosecuted the suit under this section in bad faith or solely for purposes of harassing the defendant.

(e)(1) A pipeline corporation shall immediately clean up all crude oil, or any fraction thereof, that leaks or is discharged from a pipeline subject to this section. Additionally, the pipeline corporation shall abate immediately, or as soon as practical, the effects of the leak or discharge and take all other necessary remedial action.

(2) A pipeline corporation may recover the costs of the activities specified in this section for which it is not at fault by means of any otherwise available cause of action, including, but not limited to, indemnification or subrogation.

(f) This section shall not apply to claims, or causes of action, for damages for personal injury or wrongful death.

(g) This section shall not prohibit any party from bringing any action for damages under any other provision or principle of law, including but not limited to, common law. However, damages shall not be awarded pursuant to this section to an injured party to the extent the same party is or has been awarded damages for the same injury under any other provision or principle of law.

(h) This section shall only apply to all of the following:

(1) The pipeline system proposed to be constructed by Pacific Pipeline System, Inc., identified in Public Utilities Commission Application No. 91-10-013, for which the maximum requirement of one hundred million dollars ($100,000,000) set forth in paragraph (1) of subdivision (j) shall apply.

(2) Any other public utility pipeline system for which construction is completed on or after January 1, 1996, other than a pipeline system the entire length of which is subject to the Lempert-Keene-Seastrand Oil Spill Prevention and Response Act, (Division 7.8 (commencing with Section 8750) of the Public Resources Code). If part, but not all, of a pipeline system is subject to the Lempert-Keene-Seastrand Oil Spill Prevention and Response Act, any evidence of financial responsibility that satisfies that act, and that meets the conditions of this section, shall be credited toward the requirements of this section.

(3) Any major relocation of three miles or greater of a portion of a pipeline system along substantially new alignments accomplished through the exercise of eminent domain. This section shall not apply to the portions of the pipeline not relocated.

(i) This section shall not apply to the following:

(1) A pipeline system in existence prior to January 1, 1996, that is converted to a public utility prior or subsequent to January 1, 1996.

(2) A public utility pipeline system not otherwise subject to this section, that is the object of repair, replacement or maintenance, unless that activity constitutes relocation as described in paragraph (3) of subdivision (h).

(j)(1) No pipeline system subject to this section shall be permitted to operate unless the State Fire Marshal certifies that the pipeline corporation demonstrates sufficient financial responsibility to respond to the liability imposed by this section. The minimum financial responsibility required by the State Fire Marshal shall be seven hundred fifty dollars ($750) times the maximum capacity of the pipeline in the number of barrels per day up to a maximum of one hundred million dollars ($100,000,000) per pipeline system, or a maximum of two hundred million dollars ($200,000,000) per multiple pipeline systems.

(2) For the purposes of this section, financial responsibility shall be demonstrated by evidence that is substantially equivalent to that required by regulations issued under Section 8670.37.54 of the Government Code, including insurance, surety bond, letter of credit, guaranty, qualification as a self-insurer, or combination thereof or any other evidence of financial responsibility. The State Fire Marshal shall require the documentation evidencing financial responsibility to be placed on file with that office, and shall administer the documentation in a manner substantially equivalent to that provided by regulations issued under Section 8670.37.54 of the Government Code. Financial responsibility shall be available for payment of claims for damages described in subdivision (c) of any party, including, but not limited to, the State of California, local governments, special districts, and private parties, that obtains a final judgment therefor against the pipeline corporation.

(k) The State Fire Marshal shall require evidence of financial responsibility to fund postclosure cleanup costs. The evidence of financial responsibility shall be 15 percent of the amount of financial responsibility required under subdivision (j) and shall be maintained by the pipeline corporation for four years from the date the pipeline is fully idled pursuant to a closure plan approved by the State Fire Marshal.

(l) "Fraction" of crude oil means a group of compounds collected by fractional distillation that condenses within the same temperature band, or a material that consists primarily of that group of compounds or of a mixture of those groups of compounds.

(m)(1) Notwithstanding Section 228 of the Public Utilities Code, for purposes of this section, "pipeline corporation" means every corporation or person directly operating, managing or owning any pipeline system that qualifies as a public utility within Section 216 of the Public Utilities Code and for compensation within this state.

(2) For purposes of this section, "owning" refers to the legal entity owning the pipeline system itself and does not include legal entities having an ownership interest, in whole or in part, in the entity owning the pipeline system or multiple pipeline systems.

(3) "Pipeline system" means a collective assemblage of intrastate line pipe, valves, and other appurtenances connected to line pipe, pumping units, fabricated assemblies associated with pumping units, metering and delivery station, and fabricated assemblies constructed for the same purpose at substantially the same time that form a facility through which crude oil or a fraction thereof moves in transportation. **Leg.H.** Added Stats 1995 ch 979 §2 (AB 1868), as CC §3333.4. Amended and renumbered by Stats 1998 ch 485 §40 (AB 2803).

§3333.7. Recovery of damages from employer in motor vehicle

(a) Notwithstanding any other provision of law, any person who suffers injury that is proximately caused by the driver of a commercial motor vehicle shall be entitled to recover treble damages from the driver's employer where it is shown both that the driver of a commercial motor vehicle was under the influence of alcohol or a controlled substance at the time that the injury was caused and that the driver's employer willfully failed at the time of the injury to comply with any of the requirements of federal law described in subdivision (a) of Section 34520 of the Vehicle Code in regard to the involved driver.

(b) For the purposes of subdivision (a), "willfully failed" has the same meaning as "willful failure" as defined in paragraph (3) of subdivision (c) of Section 34623 of the Vehicle Code.

(c) For purposes of subdivision (a), an "employer" is a person or entity who employs the driver or who contracts with an owner-operator, who meets the requirements set forth in subdivision (b) of Section 34624 of the Vehicle Code, to provide transportation services, and who is required to engage in mandatory substance abuse testing pursuant to subdivision (a) of Section 34520 of the Vehicle Code. This subdivision shall not be construed to change the definition of "employer," "employee," or "independent contractor" for any purpose.

(d) Nothing in this section is intended to preclude or affect existing rights. **Leg.H.** Added Stats 2001 ch 298 §1 (SB 871).

§ 3333.8. Immunity for prescribed burn

(a) The Legislature finds and declares that in order to meet fuel management goals, the state must rely on private entities to engage in prescribed burning for public benefit.

(b) Notwithstanding Sections 13009 and 13009.1 of the Health and Safety Code, no person shall be liable for any fire suppression or other costs otherwise recoverable pursuant to Section 13009 or 13009.1 of the Health and Safety Code resulting from a prescribed **fire or cultural** burn if all of the following conditions are met:

(1) The purpose of the burn is for wildland fire hazard reduction, ecological maintenance and restoration, cultural burning, silviculture, or agriculture.

(2) A [1] **burn boss, as defined in paragraph (1) of subdivision (a) of Section 4500** of the Public Resources Code**, has** reviewed and approved a written prescription for the burn that includes adequate risk mitigation measures.

(3) The burn is conducted in compliance with the written prescription.

(4) The burn is authorized pursuant to Chapter 6 (commencing with Section 4411) or Chapter 7 (commencing with Section 4461) of Part 2 of Division 4 of the Public Resources Code.

(5) The burner has a landowner's written permission or the approval of the governing body of a **California** Native American [2] **tribe** to burn.

(6) The burn is conducted in compliance with any air quality permit required pursuant to Article 3 (commencing with Section 41850) of Chapter 3 of Part 4 of Division 26 of the Health and Safety Code.

[3] **(c)** Cultural burns conducted by a cultural fire practitioner are exempt from paragraphs (2) and (3) **of subdivision (b)**.

[4] **(d)** This section shall not be construed to grant immunity from fire suppression or other costs otherwise recoverable pursuant to Section 13009 or 13009.1 of the Health and Safety Code to any person whose conduct constitutes gross negligence.

[5] **(e)** Nothing in this section affects the ability of a private or public entity plaintiff to bring a civil action against any defendant.

[6] **(f)** "Cultural burn" **or "cultural burning"** means the intentional application of fire to land by **a California** Native American [7] **tribe, a tribal organization, or a cultural fire** [8] **practitioner** to achieve cultural goals or objectives, including [9] **for sustenance**, ceremonial activities, biodiversity, or other benefits.

[10] **(g)** "Cultural fire practitioner" means a person [11] **recognized by a California** Native American tribe or tribal organization with **substantial** experience in burning to meet cultural goals or objectives, including [12] **for sustenance**, ceremonial activities, biodiversity, or other benefits. **Leg.H.** Added Stats 2021 ch 600 §1 (SB 332), effective January 1, 2022. Amended Stats 2024 ch 666 §1 (SB 310), effective January 1, 2025.

§ 3333.8. 2024 Deletes. [1] person certified as a burn boss pursuant to [2] Tribe [3] (7) [4] (c) [5] (d) [6] (e) [7] tribes, tribal organizations, or [8] practitioners [9] subsistence [10] (f) [11] associated with a [12] subsistence

§3334. Wrongful occupation

(a) The detriment caused by the wrongful occupation of real property, in cases not embraced in Section 3335 of this code, the Eminent Domain Law (Title 7 (commencing with Section 1230.010) of Part 3 of the Code of Civil Procedure), or Section 1174 of the Code of Civil Procedure, is deemed to include the value of the use of the property for the time of that wrongful occupation, not exceeding five years next preceding the commencement of the action or proceeding to enforce the right to damages, the reasonable cost of repair or restoration of the property to its original condition, and the costs, if any, of recovering the possession.

(b)(1) Except as provided in paragraph (2), for purposes of subdivision (a), the value of the use of the property shall be the greater of the reasonable rental value of that property or the benefits obtained by the person wrongfully occupying the property by reason of that wrongful occupation.

(2) If a wrongful occupation of real property subject to this section is the result of a mistake of fact of the wrongful occupier, the value of the use of the property, for purposes of subdivision (a), shall be the reasonable rental value of the property. **Leg.H.** Enacted Stats 1872. Amended Stats 1979 ch 373 §47; Stats 1992 ch 469 §1 (AB 2663).

§3335. Willful holding over

For willfully holding over real property, by a person who entered upon the same, as guardian or trustee for an infant, or by right of an estate terminable with any life or lives, after the termination of the trust or particular estate, without the consent of the party immediately entitled after such termination, the measure of damages is the value of the profits received during such holding over. **Leg.H.** Enacted Stats 1872.

§3336. Conversion

The detriment caused by the wrongful conversion of personal property is presumed to be:

First—The value of the property at the time of the conversion, with the interest from that time, or, an amount sufficient to indemnify the party injured for the loss which is the natural, reasonable and proximate result of the wrongful act complained of and which a proper degree of prudence on his part would not have averted; and

Second—A fair compensation for the time and money properly expended in pursuit of the property. **Leg.H.** Enacted Stats 1872. Amended Code Amdts 1873–74 ch 612 §277 p 266; Code Amdts 1877–78 ch 20 §1 p 90; Stats 1931 ch 633 §1 p 1358.

§3336.5. Liability of junk dealer or recycler for wrongful possession of fire hydrants or fire department connections

(a)(1) Any junk dealer or recycler who possesses a fire hydrant, fire department connection, including, but not limited to, brass fittings and parts, manhole cover or lid or part of that cover or lid, or backflow device or connection to that device or part of that device without a written certification from the agency or utility owning or previously owning the material shall be liable to the agency or utility for the wrongful possession of that material as provided in subdivision (b).

(2) A written certification under this subdivision shall be on the agency's or utility's letterhead and shall certify both that the agency or utility has sold the material described or is offering the material for sale, salvage, or recycling, and that the person possessing the certification or identified in the certification is authorized to negotiate the sale of that material.

(b) Except as provided in subdivision (c), a junk dealer or recycler in violation of this section shall be liable to the agency or utility owning or previously owning the prohibited material as described in subdivision (a) for the actual damages incurred by the agency or utility, including the value of the material, the cost of replacing the material, labor costs, and the costs of repairing any damage caused by the removal of the material. The court shall also award exemplary damages of three times the actual damages incurred by the agency or utility, unless the court decides that extenuating circumstances do not justify awarding these exemplary damages.

(c)(1) A junk dealer or recycler who unknowingly takes possession of one or more of the materials described in subdivision (a) as part of a load of otherwise nonprohibited materials without the written certification described in subdivision (a) shall notify the appropriate law enforcement agency by the end of the next business day upon discovery of the prohibited materials. Written confirmation of that notice shall relieve the junk dealer or recycler of liability to the agency or utility for the possession of those materials.

(2) The following definitions shall apply for purposes of this subdivision:

(A) "Appropriate law enforcement agency" means, in the case of any material described in subdivision (a) that is located within the territorial limits of an incorporated city, the police chief of the city or his or her designee, or, in the case of any material described in subdivision (a) that is located outside the territorial limits of an incorporated city, the sheriff of the county or his or her designee.

(B) "Written confirmation" means any confirmation received from the law enforcement agency as electronic mail, facsimile, or other written correspondence, including, but not limited to, a letter delivered in person or by certified mail.

(d) Nothing in this section is intended to create a basis for liability on the part of the junk dealers and recyclers to third parties for damages or injuries related to or arising from the theft of the materials described in this section. **Leg.H.** Added Stats 2012 ch 393 §2 (SB 1045), effective January 1, 2013.

§3337. Conversion benefitting owner

The presumption declared by the last section cannot be repelled, in favor of one whose possession was wrongful from the beginning, by his subsequent application of the property to the benefit of the owner, without his consent. **Leg.H.** Enacted Stats 1872.

§3338. Damages of lienor

One having a mere lien on personal property, cannot recover greater damages for its conversion, from one having a right thereto superior to his, after his lien is discharged, than the amount secured by the lien, and the compensation allowed by Section 3336 for loss of time and expenses. **Leg.H.** Enacted Stats 1872.

§3339. Legislative findings and declarations regarding employment protections available regardless of immigration status

The Legislature finds and declares the following:

(a) All protections, rights, and remedies available under state law, except any reinstatement remedy prohibited by federal law, are available to all individuals regardless of immigration status who have applied for employment, or who are or who have been employed, in this state.

(b) For purposes of enforcing state labor, employment, civil rights, consumer protection, and housing laws, a person's immigration status is irrelevant to the issue of liability, and in proceedings or discovery undertaken to enforce those state laws no inquiry shall be permitted into a person's immigration status unless the person seeking to make this inquiry has shown by clear and convincing evidence that this inquiry is necessary in order to comply with federal immigration law.

(c) The provisions of this section are declaratory of existing law.

(d) The provisions of this section are severable. If any provision of this section or its application is held invalid, that invalidity shall not affect other provisions or applications that can be given effect without the invalid provision or application.

(e) Any waiver of a provision of this section is contrary to public policy and is void and unenforceable. Leg.H. Added Stats 2002 ch 1071 §1 (SB 1818). Amended Stats 2017 ch 160 §1 (AB 1690), effective January 1, 2018; Stats 2024 ch 853 §17 (AB 3281), effective January 1, 2025.

Prior Law: Former CC §3339, relating to seduction, was enacted Stats 1872 and repealed Stats 1994 ch 270 §1. Historical Derivation: Field's Draft NY CC §1866.

Former Sections: Former CC §3339 was added in 1872 and repealed Stats 1994 ch 270.

§3339.5. Minor child's immigration status

(a) The immigration status of a minor child seeking recovery under any applicable law is irrelevant to the issues of liability or remedy, except for employment-related prospective injunctive relief that would directly violate federal law.

(b) Discovery or other inquiry in a civil action or proceeding relating to a minor child's immigration status shall not be permitted except where the minor child's claims place the minor child's immigration status directly in contention or the person seeking to make this inquiry has shown by clear and convincing evidence that the inquiry is necessary in order to comply with federal immigration law.

(c) The provisions of this section are declaratory of existing law.

(d) The express application of this act to minors is not intended to imply that adults are not likewise protected by existing law in the same circumstances. **Leg.H.** Added Stats 2015 ch 151 §1 (AB 560), effective January 1, 2016.

§3339.10. Immigration or citizenship status of any person is irrelevant to any issue of liability or remedy

(a) The immigration or citizenship status of any person is irrelevant to any issue of liability or remedy under Chapter 2 (commencing with Section 1940) of Title 5 of Part 4 of Division 3, Chapter 2 (commencing with Section 789) of Title 2 of Part 2 of Division 2 of this code, or under Chapter 4 (commencing with Section 1159) of Title 3 of Part 3 of the Code of Civil Procedure, or in any civil action involving a tenant's housing rights.

(b)(1) In proceedings or discovery undertaken in a civil action to enforce Chapter 2 (commencing with Section 1940) of Title 5 of Part 4 of Division 3, Chapter 2 (commencing with Section 789) of Title 2 of Part 2 of Division 2 of this code, or under Chapter 4 (commencing with Section 1159) of Title 3 of Part 3 of the Code of Civil Procedure, or in any civil action involving a tenant's housing rights, no inquiry shall be permitted into a person's immigration or citizenship status, except as follows:

(A) The tenant's claims or defenses raised place the person's immigration or citizenship status directly in contention.

(B) The person seeking to make this inquiry demonstrates by clear and convincing evidence that this inquiry is necessary in order to comply with federal immigration law.

(2) The assertion of an affirmative defense to an unlawful detainer action under Section 1161.4 of the Code of Civil Procedure does not constitute cause under this subdivision for discovery or other inquiry into that person's immigration or citizenship status. **Leg.H.** Added Stats 2017 ch 489 §7 (AB 291), effective January 1, 2018.

§3340. Injuries to animals

For wrongful injuries to animals being subjects of property, committed willfully or by gross negligence, in disregard of humanity, exemplary damages may be given. **Leg.H.** Enacted Stats 1872.

§3341. Infliction by pet of injury upon farm or ranch animal

The owner, possessor, or harborer of any dog or other animal, that shall, on the premises of any person other than the owner, possessor, or harborer of such dog or other animal, kill, worry, or wound any bovine animal, swine, horse, mule, burro, sheep, angora goat, or cashmere goat, or poultry, shall be liable to the owner of the same for the damages and costs of suit, to be recovered in any court of competent jurisdiction:

1. In the prosecution of actions under the provisions of this chapter, it shall not be necessary for the plaintiff to show that the owner, possessor, or harborer of such dog or other animal, had knowledge of the fact that such dog or other animal would kill, wound or worry bovine animals, swine, horses, mules, burros, sheep, goats, or poultry.

2. Any person on finding any dog or dogs, or other animal, not on the premises of the owner or possessor of such dog or dogs, or other animal, worrying, wounding, or killing any bovine animals, swine, horses, mules, burros, sheep, angora or cashmere goats, may, at the time of finding such dog or dogs, or other animal, kill the same, and the owner or owners thereof shall sustain no action for damages against any person so killing such dog or dogs, or other animal.

Nothing in this section shall render an owner, possessor, or harborer of a dog liable for the accidental or unavoidable killing or injury of any bovine animal, swine, horse, mule, burro, sheep, angora goat, cashmere goat, or poultry which occurs in connection with or as an incident to the driving or herding the same from the premises of the owner, possessor, or harborer of the dog, whether such killing or injury occurs upon such premises or off of such premises. **Leg.H.** Added Stats 1883 ch 55 §1 p 283. Amended Stats 1903 ch 51 §1 p 54; Stats 1945 ch 1327 §1 p 2500.

§3342. Liability of owner of dog for damages suffered by dog bite; Bites by dogs in military or police work

(a) The owner of any dog is liable for the damages suffered by any person who is bitten by the dog while in a public place or lawfully in a private place, including the property of the owner of the dog, regardless of the former viciousness of the dog or the owner's knowledge of such viciousness. A person is lawfully upon the private property of such owner within the meaning of this section when he is on such property in the performance of any duty imposed upon him by the laws of this state or by the laws or postal regulations of the United States, or when he is on such property upon the invitation, express or implied, of the owner.

(b) Nothing in this section shall authorize the bringing of an action pursuant to subdivision (a) against any governmental agency using a dog in military or police work if the bite or bites occurred while the dog was defending itself from an annoying, harassing, or provoking act, or assisting an employee of the agency in any of the following:

(1) In the apprehension or holding of a suspect where the employee has a reasonable suspicion of the suspect's involvement in criminal activity.

(2) In the investigation of a crime or possible crime.

(3) In the execution of a warrant.

(4) In the defense of a peace officer or another person.

(c) Subdivision (b) shall not apply in any case where the victim of the bite or bites was not a party to, nor a participant in, nor suspected to be a party to or a participant in, the act or acts that prompted the use of the dog in the military or police work.

(d) Subdivision (b) shall apply only where a governmental agency using a dog in military or police work has adopted a written policy on the necessary and appropriate use of a dog for the police or military work enumerated in subdivision (b). **Leg.H.** Added Stats 1953 ch 37 §6 p 675. Amended Stats 1988 ch 298 §1.

Prior Law: Former CC §3342, incorporated in Gov C §§820.4, 820.6, was added Stats 1933 ch 248 §1 p 779, amended Stats 1933 ch 1053 §1 p 2708, and repealed Stats 1943 ch 134 (Gov C §500003) p 1010.

1988 Note: It is the intent of the Legislature to provide only a limited immunity from the strict liability imposed by Section 3342 of the Civil Code. Any other cause of action predicated on common law theories of negligence, intentional tort, and other theories is unaffected by this act. Stats 1988 ch 298 §2.

Former Sections: Former CC §3342 was added in 1933 and repealed Stats 1943 ch 134.

§3342.5. Duty to remove danger presented from dog bites; Enforcement

(a) The owner of any dog that has bitten a human being shall have the duty to take such reasonable steps as are necessary to remove any danger presented to other persons from bites by the animal.

(b) Whenever a dog has bitten a human being on at least two separate occasions, any person, the district attorney, or city attorney may bring an action against the owner of the animal to determine whether conditions of the treatment or confinement of the dog or other circumstances existing at the time of the bites have been changed so as to remove the danger to other persons presented by the animal. This action shall be brought in the county where a bite occurred. The court, after hearing, may make any order it deems appropriate to prevent the recurrence of such an incident, including, but not limited to, the removal of the animal from the area or its destruction if necessary.

(c) Whenever a dog trained to fight, attack, or kill has bitten a human being, causing substantial physical injury, any person, including the district attorney, or city attorney may bring an action against the owner of the animal to determine whether conditions of the treatment or confinement of the dog or other circumstances existing at the time of the bites have been changed so as to remove the danger to other persons presented by the animal. This action shall be brought in the county where a bite occurred. The court, after hearing, may make any order it deems appropriate to prevent the recurrence of such an incident, including, but not limited to, the removal of the animal from the area or its destruction if necessary.

(d) Nothing in this section shall authorize the bringing of an action pursuant to subdivision (b) based on a bite or bites inflicted upon a trespasser, or by a dog used in military or police work if the bite or bites occurred while the dog was actually performing in that capacity.

(e) Nothing in this section shall be construed to prevent legislation in the field of dog control by any city, county, or city and county.

(f) Nothing in this section shall be construed to affect the liability of the owner of a dog under Section 3342 or any other provision of the law.

(g) A proceeding under this section is a limited civil case. **Leg.H.** Added Stats 1968 ch 1274 §1. Amended Stats 1976 ch 470 §1; Stats 1984 ch 655 §1, effective August 16, 1984; Stats 1998 ch 931 §18 (SB 2139), effective September 28, 1998.

§3343. Fraudulent property sales

(a) One defrauded in the purchase, sale or exchange of property is entitled to recover the difference between the actual value of that with which the defrauded person parted and the actual value of that which he received, together with any additional damage arising from the particular transaction, including any of the following:

(1) Amounts actually and reasonably expended in reliance upon the fraud.

(2) An amount which would compensate the defrauded party for loss of use and enjoyment of the property to the extent that any such loss was proximately caused by the fraud.

(3) Where the defrauded party has been induced by reason of the fraud to sell or otherwise part with the property in question, an amount which will compensate him for profits or other gains which might reasonably have been earned by use of the property had he retained it.

(4) Where the defrauded party has been induced by reason of the fraud to purchase or otherwise acquire the property in question, an amount which will compensate him for any loss of profits or other gains which were reasonably anticipated and would have been earned by him from the use or sale of the property had it possessed the characteristics fraudulently attributed to it by the party committing the fraud, provided that lost profits from the use or sale of the property shall be recoverable only if and only to the extent that all of the following apply:

(i) The defrauded party acquired the property for the purpose of using or reselling it for a profit.

(ii) The defrauded party reasonably relied on the fraud in entering into the transaction and in anticipating profits from the subsequent use or sale of the property.

(iii) Any loss of profits for which damages are sought under this paragraph have been proximately caused by the fraud and the defrauded party's reliance on it.

(b) Nothing in this section shall do either of the following:

(1) Permit the defrauded person to recover any amount measured by the difference between the value of property as represented and the actual value thereof.

(2) Deny to any person having a cause of action for fraud or deceit any legal or equitable remedies to which such person may be entitled. **Leg.H.** Added Stats 1935 ch 536 §1 p 1612. Amended Stats 1971 ch 943 §1.

§3343.5. Unlawful motor vehicle subleasing

(a) Any one or more of the following who suffers any damage proximately resulting from one or more acts of unlawful motor vehicle subleasing, as described in Chapter 12.7 (commencing with Section 570) of Title 13 of Part 1 of the Penal Code, may bring an action against the person who has engaged in those acts:

(1) A seller or other secured party under a conditional sale contract or a security agreement.

(2) A lender under a direct loan agreement.

(3) A lessor under a lease contract.

(4) A buyer under a conditional sale contract.

(5) A purchaser under a direct loan agreement, an agreement which provides for a security interest, or an agreement which is equivalent to these types of agreements.

(6) A lessee under a lease contract.

(7) An actual or purported transferee or assignee of any right or interest of a buyer, a purchaser, or a lessee.

(b) The court in an action under subdivision (a) may award actual damages; equitable relief, including, but not limited to, an injunction and restitution of money and property; punitive damages; reasonable attorney's fees and costs; and any other relief which the court deems proper.

(c) As used in this section, the following terms have the following meanings:

(1) "Buyer" has the meaning set forth in subdivision (c) of Section 2981.

(2) "Conditional sale contract" has the meaning set forth in subdivision (a) of Section 2981. Notwithstanding subdivision (k) of Section 2981, "conditional sale contract" includes any contract for the sale or bailment of a motor vehicle between a buyer and a seller primarily for business or commercial purposes.

(3) "Direct loan agreement" means an agreement between a lender and a purchaser whereby the lender has advanced funds pursuant to a loan secured by the motor vehicle which the purchaser has purchased.

(4) "Lease contract" means a lease contract between a lessor and lessee as this term and these parties are defined in Section 2985.7. Notwithstanding subdivision (d) of Section 2985.7, "lease contract" includes a lease for business or commercial purposes.

(5) "Motor vehicle" means any vehicle required to be registered under the Vehicle Code.

(6) "Person" means an individual, company, firm, association, partnership, trust, corporation, limited liability company, or other legal entity.

(7) "Purchaser" has the meaning set forth in paragraph (30) of subdivision (b) of Section 1201 of the Commercial Code.

(8) "Security agreement" and "secured party" have the meanings set forth, respectively, in paragraphs (74) and (73) of subdivision (a) of Section 9102 of the Commercial Code. "Security interest" has the meaning set forth in paragraph (35) of subdivision (b) of Section 1201 of the Commercial Code.

(9) "Seller" has the meaning set forth in subdivision (b) of Section 2981, and includes the present holder of the conditional sale contract.

(d) The rights and remedies provided in this section are in addition to any other rights and remedies provided by law. **Leg.H.** Added Stats 1987 ch 1072 §1. Amended Stats 1994 ch 1010 §52 (SB 2053); Stats 1999 ch 991 §8.5 (SB 45), operative July 1, 2001; Stats 2006 ch 254 §4 (SB 1481), effective January 1, 2007; Stats 2013 ch 531 §1 (AB 502), effective January 1, 2014, operative July 1, 2014.

§3343.7. Rescission action for fraudulent inducement to join nonprofit cooperative of independent retailers

An action may be brought against any nonprofit organization operated on a cooperative basis by and for independent retailers which wholesales goods and services primarily to its member retailers as described in paragraph (3) of subdivision (d) of Section 20001 of the Business and Professions Code or subdivision (c) of Section 31005 of the Corporations Code, for rescission of a membership contract entered into, or for any damages sustained, as a consequence of being fraudulently induced to join the organization. For purposes of this section, "fraudulently induced" means the misrepresentation of a material fact, or the omission of a material fact, including the failure of the organization to disclose all information required under subparagraph (H) of paragraph (3) of subdivision (d) of Section 20001 of the Business and Professions Code or paragraph (8) of subdivision (c) of Section 31005 of the Corporations Code, unless the defendant proves that the plaintiff knew the facts concerning the untruth or omission or that the defendant exercised reasonable care and did not know (or if the defendant had exercised reasonable care would not have known) of the untruth or omission. **Leg.H.** Added Stats 1989 ch 1380 §2.

§3344. Unauthorized commercial use of name, voice, signature, photograph or likeness

(a) Any person who knowingly uses another's name, voice, signature, photograph, or likeness, in any manner, on or in products, merchandise, or goods, or for purposes of advertising or selling, or soliciting purchases of, products, merchandise, goods or services, without such person's prior consent, or, in the case of a minor, the prior consent of his parent or legal guardian, shall be liable for any damages sustained by the person or persons injured as a result thereof. In addition, in any action brought under this section, the person who violated the section shall be liable to the injured party or parties in an amount equal to the greater of seven hundred fifty dollars ($750) or the actual damages suffered by him or her as a result of the unauthorized use, and any profits from the unauthorized use that are attributable to the use and are not taken into account in computing the actual damages. In establishing such profits, the injured party or parties are required to present proof only of the gross revenue attributable to such use, and the person who violated this section is required to prove his or her deductible expenses. Punitive damages may also be awarded to the injured party or parties. The prevailing party in any action under this section shall also be entitled to attorney's fees and costs.

(b) As used in this section, "photograph" means any photograph or photographic reproduction, still or moving, or any videotape or live television transmission, of any person, such that the person is readily identifiable.

(1) A person shall be deemed to be readily identifiable from a photograph when one who views the photograph with the naked eye can reasonably determine that the person depicted in the photograph is the same person who is complaining of its unauthorized use.

(2) If the photograph includes more than one person so identifiable, then the person or persons complaining of the use shall be represented as individuals rather than solely as members of a definable group represented in the photograph. A definable group includes, but is not limited to, the following examples: a crowd at any sporting event, a crowd in any street or public building, the audience at any theatrical or stage production, a glee club, or a baseball team.

(3) A person or persons shall be considered to be represented as members of a definable group if they are represented in the photograph solely as a result of being present at the time the photograph was taken and have not been singled out as individuals in any manner.

(c) Where a photograph or likeness of an employee of the person using the photograph or likeness appearing in the advertisement or other publication prepared by or in behalf of the user is only incidental, and not essential, to the purpose of the publication in which it appears, there shall arise a rebuttable presumption affecting the burden of producing evidence that the failure to obtain the consent of the employee was not a knowing use of the employee's photograph or likeness.

(d) For purposes of this section, a use of a name, voice, signature, photograph, or likeness in connection with any news, public affairs, or sports broadcast or account, or any political campaign, shall not constitute a use for which consent is required under subdivision (a).

(e) The use of a name, voice, signature, photograph, or likeness in a commercial medium shall not constitute a use for which consent is required under subdivision (a) solely because the material containing such use is commercially sponsored or contains paid advertising. Rather it shall be a question of fact whether or not the use of the person's name, voice, signature, photograph, or likeness was so directly connected with the commercial sponsorship or with the paid advertising as to constitute a use for which consent is required under subdivision (a).

(f) Nothing in this section shall apply to the owners or employees of any medium used for advertising, including, but not limited to, newspapers, magazines, radio and television networks and stations, cable television systems, billboards, and transit ads, by whom any advertisement or solicitation in violation of this section is published or disseminated, unless it is established that such owners or employees had knowledge of the unauthorized use of the person's name, voice, signature, photograph, or likeness as prohibited by this section.

(g) The remedies provided for in this section are cumulative and shall be in addition to any others provided for by law. **Leg.H.** Added Stats 1971 ch 1595 §1. Amended Stats 1984 ch 1704 §2.

Prior Law: Former CC §3344, similar in part to present CCP §1161, was enacted Stats 1872 and repealed Stats 1961 ch 792 §2 p 2045.

Former Sections: Former CC §3344 was added in 1872 and repealed Stats 1961 ch 782.

§3344.1. Rights of deceased personality

(a)(1)(A) [1] **Subject to subparagraph (B), a** person who uses a deceased personality's name, voice, signature, photograph, or likeness, in any manner, on or in products, merchandise, or goods, or for purposes of advertising or selling, or soliciting purchases of, products, merchandise, goods, or services, without prior consent from the person or persons specified in subdivision (c), shall be liable for any damages sustained by the person or persons injured as a result thereof. In addition, in any action brought under this section, the person who violated the section shall be liable to the injured party or parties in an amount equal to the greater of seven hundred fifty dollars ($750) or the actual damages suffered by the injured party or parties, as a result of the unauthorized use, and any profits from the unauthorized use that are attributable to the use and are not taken into account in computing the actual damages. In establishing these profits, the injured party or parties shall be required to present proof only of the gross revenue attributable to the use, and the person who violated the section [2] **shall prove the person's** deductible expenses. Punitive damages may also be awarded to the injured party or parties. The prevailing party or parties in any action under this section shall also be entitled to attorney's fees and costs.

[3] **(B)(i)** [4] **Except as provided in clause (ii)**, a play, book, magazine, newspaper, musical composition, audiovisual work, radio or television program, single and original work of art, work of political or newsworthy value, or an advertisement or commercial announcement for any of these works, shall not be considered a product, article of merchandise, good, or service if it is fictional or nonfictional entertainment, or a dramatic, literary, or musical work.

[5] **(ii)** If a work [6] **described in clause (i)** includes within it a use in connection with a product, article of merchandise, good, or service, this use shall not be exempt under this [7] **subparagraph**, notwithstanding the

unprotected use's inclusion in a work otherwise exempt under this [8] **subparagraph**, if the claimant proves that this use is so directly connected with a product, article of merchandise, good, or service as to constitute an act of advertising, selling, or soliciting purchases of that product, article of merchandise, good, or service by the deceased personality without prior consent from the person or persons specified in subdivision (c).

(2)(A)(i) **Notwithstanding paragraph (1) and subject to clause (ii), a person who produces, distributes, or makes available the digital replica of a deceased personality's voice or likeness in an expressive audiovisual work or sound recording without prior consent from a person specified in subdivision (c) shall be liable to any injured party in an amount equal to the greater of ten thousand dollars ($10,000) or the actual damages suffered by a person controlling the rights to the deceased personality's likeness.**

(ii) For purposes of this section, a digital replica may be used without consent if the use of the digital replica meets any of the following criteria:

(I) The use is in connection with any news, public affairs, or sports broadcast or account.

(II) The use is for purposes of comment, criticism, scholarship, satire, or parody.

(III) The use is a representation of the individual as the individual's self in a documentary or in a historical or biographical manner, including some degree of fictionalization, unless the use is intended to create, and does create, the false impression that the work is an authentic recording in which the individual participated.

(IV) The use is fleeting or incidental.

(V) The use is in an advertisement or commercial announcement for a work described in subclauses (I) to (IV), inclusive.

(B) For purposes of this paragraph:

(i) "Audiovisual work" means a work that consists of a series of related images that are intrinsically intended to be shown by the use of machines or devices, including projectors, viewers, or electronic equipment, together with accompanying sounds, if any, regardless of the nature of the material objects, including films or tapes, in which the works are embodied.

(ii)(I) "Digital replica" means a computer-generated, highly realistic electronic representation that is readily identifiable as the voice or visual likeness of an individual that is embodied in a sound recording, image, audiovisual work, or transmission in which the actual individual either did not actually perform or appear, or the actual individual did perform or appear, but the fundamental character of the performance or appearance has been materially altered.

(II) "Digital replica" does not include the electronic reproduction, use of a sample of one sound recording or audiovisual work into another, remixing, mastering, or digital remastering of a sound recording or audiovisual work authorized by the copyrightholder.

(b) The rights recognized under this section are property rights, freely transferable or descendible, in whole or in part, by contract or by means of any trust or any other testamentary instrument, executed before or after January 1, 1985. The rights recognized under this section shall be deemed to have existed at the time of death of any deceased personality who died prior to January 1, 1985, and, except as provided in subdivision (o), shall vest in the persons entitled to these property rights under the testamentary instrument of the deceased personality effective as of the date of [9] **their** death. In the absence of an express transfer in a testamentary instrument of the deceased personality's rights in [10] **the deceased personality's** name, voice, signature, photograph, or likeness, a provision in the testamentary instrument that provides for the disposition of the residue of the deceased personality's assets shall be effective to transfer the rights recognized under this section in accordance with the terms of that provision. The rights established by this section shall also be freely transferable or descendible by contract, trust, or any other testamentary instrument by any subsequent owner of the deceased personality's rights as recognized by this section. Nothing in this section shall be construed to render invalid or unenforceable any contract entered into by a deceased personality during [11] **the deceased personality's** lifetime by which the deceased personality assigned the rights, in whole or in part, to use [12] **the deceased personality's** name, voice, signature, photograph, or likeness, regardless of whether the contract was entered into before or after January 1, 1985.

(c) The consent required by this section shall be exercisable by the person or persons to whom the right of consent, or portion thereof, has been transferred in accordance with subdivision (b), or if no transfer has occurred, then by the person or persons to whom the right of consent, or portion thereof, has passed in accordance with subdivision (d).

(d) Subject to subdivisions (b) and (c), after the death of any person, the rights under this section shall belong to the following person or persons and may be exercised, on behalf of and for the benefit of all of those persons, by those persons who, in the aggregate, are entitled to more than a one-half interest in the rights:

(1) The entire interest in those rights belongs to the surviving spouse of the deceased personality unless there are any surviving children or grandchildren of the deceased personality, in which case one-half of the entire interest in those rights belongs to the surviving spouse.

(2) The entire interest in those rights belongs to the surviving children of the deceased personality and to the surviving children of any dead child of the deceased personality unless the deceased personality has a surviving spouse, in which case the ownership of a one-half interest in rights is divided among the surviving children and grandchildren.

(3) If there is no surviving spouse, and no surviving children or grandchildren, then the entire interest in those rights belongs to the surviving parent or parents of the deceased personality.

(4) The rights of the deceased personality's children and grandchildren are in all cases divided among them and exercisable in the manner provided in Section 240 of the Probate Code according to the number of the deceased personality's children represented. The share of the children of a dead child of a deceased personality can be exercised only by the action of a majority of them.

(e) If any deceased personality does not transfer [13] **the deceased personality's** rights under this section by contract, or by means of a trust or testamentary instrument, and there are no surviving persons as described in subdivision (d), then the rights set forth in subdivision (a) shall terminate.

(f)(1) A successor in interest to the rights of a deceased personality under this section or a licensee thereof shall not recover damages for a use prohibited by this section that occurs before the successor in interest or licensee registers a claim of the rights under paragraph (2).

(2) Any person claiming to be a successor in interest to the rights of a deceased personality under this section or a licensee thereof may register that claim with the Secretary of State on a form prescribed by the Secretary of State and upon payment of a fee as set forth in subdivision (d) of Section 12195 of the Government Code. The form shall be verified and shall include the name and date of death of the deceased personality, the name and address of the claimant, the basis of the claim, and the rights claimed.

(3) Upon receipt and after filing of any document under this section, the Secretary of State shall post the document along with the entire registry of persons claiming to be a successor in interest to the rights of a deceased personality or a registered licensee under this section upon the Secretary of State's [14] **internet website**. The Secretary of State may microfilm or reproduce by other techniques any of the filings or documents and destroy the original filing or document. The microfilm or other reproduction of any document under this section shall be admissible in any court of law. The microfilm or other reproduction of any document may be destroyed by the Secretary of State 70 years after the death of the personality named therein.

(4) Claims registered under this subdivision shall be public records.

(g) An action shall not be brought under this section by reason of any use of a deceased personality's name, voice, signature, photograph, or likeness occurring after the expiration of 70 years after the death of the deceased personality.

(h) As used in this section, "deceased personality" means any natural person whose name, voice, signature, photograph, or likeness has commercial value at the time of [15] **that person's** death, or because of [16] **that person's** death, whether or not during the lifetime of that natural person the person used [17] **the person's** name, voice, signature, photograph, or likeness on or in products, merchandise, or goods, or for purposes of advertising or selling, or solicitation of purchase of, products, merchandise, goods, or services. A "deceased personality" shall include, without limitation, any such natural person who has died within 70 years prior to January 1, 1985.

(i) As used in this section, "photograph" means any photograph or photographic reproduction, still or moving, or any videotape or live television transmission, of any person, such that the deceased personality is readily identifiable. A deceased personality shall be deemed to be readily identifiable from a photograph if one who views the photograph with the naked eye can reasonably determine who the person depicted in the photograph is.

(j) For purposes of this section, the use of a name, voice, signature, photograph, or likeness in connection with any news, public affairs, or sports broadcast or account, or any political campaign, shall not constitute a use for which consent is required under subdivision (a).

(k) The use of a name, voice, signature, photograph, or likeness in a commercial medium shall not constitute a use for which consent is required under subdivision (a) solely because the material containing the use is commercially sponsored or contains paid advertising. Rather, it shall be a question of fact whether or not the use of the deceased personality's name, voice, signature, photograph, or likeness was so directly connected with the commercial sponsorship or with the paid advertising as to constitute a use for which consent is required under subdivision (a).

(*l*) Nothing in this section shall apply to the owners or employees of any medium used for advertising, including, but not limited to, newspapers, magazines, radio and television networks and stations, cable television systems, billboards, and transit advertisements, by whom any advertisement or solicitation in violation of this section is published or disseminated, unless it is established that the owners or employees had knowledge of the unauthorized use of the deceased personality's name, voice, photograph, or likeness as prohibited by this section.

(m) The remedies provided for in this section are cumulative and shall be in addition to any others provided for by law.

(n) In the case of an individual who performs music as a profession, an action to enforce this section may be brought by that individual and by any person or entity that has entered into a contract for the individual's exclusive personal services as a recording artist or an exclusive license to distribute sound recordings that capture the individual's audio performances.

[18] (o) This section shall apply to the adjudication of liability and the imposition of any damages or other remedies in cases in which the liability, damages, and other remedies arise from acts occurring directly in this state. For purposes of this section, acts giving rise to liability shall be limited to the use, on or in products, merchandise, goods, or services, or the advertising or selling, or soliciting purchases of, products, merchandise, goods, or services prohibited by this section.

[19] (p) Notwithstanding any provision of this section to the contrary, if an action was taken prior to May 1, 2007, to exercise rights recognized under this section relating to a deceased personality who died prior to January 1, 1985, by a person described in subdivision (d), other than a person who was disinherited by the deceased personality in a testamentary instrument, and the exercise of those rights was not challenged successfully in a court action by a person described in subdivision (b), that exercise shall not be affected by subdivision (b). In that case, the rights that would otherwise vest in one or more persons described in subdivision (b) shall vest solely in the person or persons described in subdivision (d), other than a person disinherited by the deceased personality in a testamentary instrument, for all future purposes.

[20] **(q)** The rights recognized by this section are expressly made retroactive, including to those deceased personalities who died [21] **prior to** January 1, 1985. **Leg.H.** Added Stats 1984 ch 1704 §1, as CC §990. Amended Stats 1988 ch 113 §2, effective May 25, 1988, operative July 1, 1988. Amended and renumbered by Stats 1999 ch 998 §1 (SB 209), ch 1000 §9.5 (SB 284). Amended Stats 2007 ch 439 §1 (SB 771), effective January 1, 2008; Stats 2009 ch 88 §15 (AB 176), effective January 1, 2010; Stats 2010 ch 20 §1 (AB 585), effective January 1, 2011; Stats 2011 ch 296 §35 (AB 1023), effective January 1, 2012; Stats 2024 ch 258 §2 (AB 1836), effective January 1, 2025.

§3344.1. 2024 Deletes. [1] Any [2] is required to prove his or her [3] (2) [4] For purposes of this subdivision [5] (3) [6] that is protected under paragraph (2) [7] subdivision [8] subdivision [9] his or her [10] his or her [11] his or her [12] his or her [13] his or her [14] Internet Web site [15] his or her [16] his or her [17] his or her [18] (n) [19] (o) [20] (p) [21] before

2007 Note: It is the intent of the Legislature to abrogate the summary judgment orders entered in *The Milton H. Greene Archives, Inc. v. CMG Worldwide, Inc.*, United States District Court, Central District of California, Case No. CV 05-2200 MMM (MCx), filed May 14, 2007, and in *Shaw Family Archives Ltd. v. CMG Worldwide, Inc.*, United States District Court, Southern District of New York, Case No. 05 Civ. 3939 (CM), dated May 2, 2007. Stats 2007 ch 439 (SB 771) §2.

§3344.5. Civil cause of action for publication of deceptive campaign advertisement containing unauthorized signature

(a) Any person whose signature is used in violation of, and any candidate for elective office whose election or defeat is expressly advocated in any campaign advertisement that violates, subdivision (b) of Section 115.1 of the Penal Code, shall have a civil cause of action against any person committing the violation.

(b) If a mass mailing or other printed matter that violates subdivision (b) of Section 115.1 of the Penal Code expressly advocates the election or defeat of more than one candidate only a person whose signature is used and the candidate or candidates to whom the unauthorized signature directly relates shall have a civil cause of action pursuant to this section.

(c) Any person bringing a cause of action pursuant to this section may recover damages in an amount of two times the cost of the communication, but not to exceed fifty thousand dollars ($50,000), with regard to which the unauthorized signature was used.

(d) As used in this section, "signature" means either of the following:

(1) A handwritten or mechanical signature, or a copy thereof.

(2) Any representation of a person's name, including, but not limited to, a printed or typewritten representation, that serves the same purpose as a handwritten or mechanical signature. **Leg.H.** Added Stats 1990 ch 1590 §1 (SB 1865), effective September 30, 1990. Amended Stats 1993 ch 334 §1 (AB 1117).

§3344.6. Cause of action for candidate whose election or defeat advocated with false or fraudulent representations

(a) Any candidate for elective office whose election or defeat is expressly advocated in any campaign advertisement which violates subdivision (a) of Section 115.2 of the Penal Code shall have a civil cause of action against any person committing the violation.

(b) If a mass mailing or other printed matter which violates subdivision (a) of Section 115.2 of the Penal Code expressly advocates the election or defeat of more than one candidate, only the candidate or candidates to whom the misstatement or misrepresentation directly relates shall have a civil cause of action pursuant to this section.

(c) Any person bringing a cause of action pursuant to this section may recover damages in an amount of two times the cost of the communication, but not to exceed fifty thousand dollars ($50,000). **Leg.H.** Added Stats 1991 ch 1051 §1 (SB 209).

ARTICLE 3
Penal Damages

Acts against senior citizens, disabled persons or veterans. §3345.
Commercial sexual exploitation of minor or nonminor dependent. §3345.1.
Injuries to timber or while trespassing in reliance on boundary lines. §3346.

§3345. Acts against senior citizens, disabled persons or veterans

(a) This section shall apply only in actions brought by, on behalf of, or for the benefit of those individuals specified in paragraphs (1) to (3), inclusive, to redress unfair or deceptive acts or practices or unfair methods of competition.

(1) Senior citizens, as defined in subdivision (f) of Section 1761.

(2) Disabled persons, as defined in subdivision (g) of Section 1761.

(3) Veterans, as defined in Section 18540.4 of the Government Code.

(b) Whenever a trier of fact is authorized by a statute to impose either a fine, or a civil penalty or other penalty, or any other remedy the purpose or effect of which is to punish or deter, and the amount of the fine, penalty, or other remedy is subject to the trier of fact's discretion, the trier of fact shall consider the factors set forth in paragraphs (1) to (3), inclusive, in addition to other appropriate factors, in determining the amount of fine, civil penalty or other penalty, or other remedy to impose. Whenever the trier of fact makes an affirmative finding in regard to one or more of the factors set forth in paragraphs (1) to (3), inclusive, it may impose a fine, civil penalty or other penalty, or other remedy in an amount up to three times greater than authorized by the statute, or, where the statute does not authorize a specific amount, up to three times greater than the amount the trier of fact would impose in the absence of that affirmative finding.

(1) Whether the defendant knew or should have known that their conduct was directed to one or more senior citizens, disabled persons, or veterans.

(2) Whether the defendant's conduct caused one or more senior citizens, disabled persons, or veterans to suffer: loss or encumbrance of a primary residence, principal employment, or source of income; substantial loss of property set aside for retirement, or for personal or family care and maintenance; or substantial loss of payments received under a pension or retirement plan or a government benefits program, or assets essential to the health or welfare of the senior citizen, disabled person, or veteran.

(3) Whether one or more senior citizens, disabled persons, or veterans are substantially more vulnerable than other members of the public to the defendant's conduct because of age, poor health or infirmity, impaired understanding, restricted mobility, or disability, and actually suffered substantial physical, emotional, or economic damage resulting from the defendant's conduct. **Leg.H.** Added Stats 1988 ch 823 §4. Amended Stats 2022 ch 78 §1 (AB 1730), effective January 1, 2023.

Prior Law: Former CC §3345, similar to present CCP §1161, was enacted Stats 1872, amended Stats 1953 ch 813 §1, and repealed Stats 1961 ch 782 §3.

Former Sections: Former CC §3345 was added in 1872 and repealed Stats 1961 ch 782.

§3345.1. Commercial sexual exploitation of minor or nonminor dependent

(a) This section shall apply only in a civil action brought by, or on behalf of, or for the benefit of, a person who is a minor or nonminor dependent and is a victim of commercial sexual exploitation committed by a person who is over 18 years of age or facilitated, aided, or abetted by a social media platform in violation of subdivision (g). For purposes of this section, the age of the victim, the status of the victim as a minor or nonminor dependent, and the age of the defendant is determined at the time of the defendant's act of commercial sexual exploitation of the victim.

(b) In a civil action brought by, on behalf of, or for the benefit of a minor, or nonminor dependent, against a person who engaged in any act of commercial sexual exploitation of a minor or nonminor dependent, whenever a trier of fact is authorized by a statute, other than subdivision (c), to impose either a fine, or a civil penalty or other penalty, or any other remedy the purpose or effect of which is to punish or deter, and the amount of the fine, penalty, or other remedy is subject to the trier of fact's discretion, the trier of fact shall consider all of the following factors, in addition to other appropriate factors, in determining the amount of fine, civil penalty, or other penalty, or other remedy to impose. If the trier of fact makes an affirmative finding in regard to one or more of the following factors, it may impose a fine, civil penalty, or other penalty, or other remedy in an amount up to three times greater than authorized by the statute, or, if the statute does not authorize a specific amount, up to three times greater than the amount the trier of fact would impose in the absence of that affirmative finding:

(1) Whether the defendant's conduct was directed to more than one minor or nonminor dependent.

(2) Whether one or more minors or nonminor dependents suffered substantial physical, emotional, or economic damage resulting from the defendant's conduct.

(3) Whether the defendant knew or reasonably should have known that the victim was a minor or nonminor dependent. It shall not be a defense to imposition of fines, penalties, or other remedies pursuant to this paragraph that the defendant was unaware of the victim's age or status as a nonminor dependent at the time of the act.

(c) If the trier of fact is not authorized by statute to impose a civil penalty in an action described in subdivision (b), the court may award a civil penalty not exceeding fifty thousand dollars ($50,000), and not less than ten thousand dollars ($10,000), for each act of commercial sexual exploitation committed by the defendant upon making an affirmative finding in regard to one or more of the factors set forth in paragraphs (1) to (3), inclusive, of subdivision (b). This penalty may be imposed in addition to any other remedy available in law or in equity.

(d) Any penalty imposed pursuant to this section shall be paid to the victim of the act of sexual exploitation.

(e) It shall not be a defense to the imposition of fines or penalties pursuant to this section that the victim consented to the act of commercial sexual exploitation.

(f) If the victim is under 18 years of age, the court, in its discretion, may order that any penalty imposed pursuant to this section be held in trust for the victim and used exclusively for the benefit and well-being of the victim. When the victim reaches 18 years of age or is emancipated, the trust shall expire and any unspent remainder shall be the sole property of the victim.

(g)(1) A social media platform shall not knowingly facilitate, aid, or abet commercial sexual exploitation.

(2) For a violation of this subdivision, a court shall award statutory damages not exceeding four million dollars ($4,000,000) and not less than one million dollars ($1,000,000) for each act of commercial sexual exploitation facilitated, aided, or abetted by the social media platform.

(3) A social media platform shall not be deemed to be in violation of this subdivision if it demonstrates all of the following:

(A) The social media platform instituted and maintained a program of at least biannual audits of its designs, algorithms, practices, affordances, and features to detect designs, algorithms, practices, affordances, or features that have the potential to cause or contribute to violations of this subdivision.

(B) The social media platform took action, within 30 days of the completion of an audit described in subparagraph (A), designed to mitigate or eliminate the reasonably foreseeable risk that a design, algorithm, practice, affordance, or feature violates, or contributes to a violation of, this subdivision.

(C) The social media platform provided to each member of the social media platform's board of directors a true and correct copy of each audit within 90 days of the audit being completed accompanied by a description of any action taken pursuant to subparagraph (B).

(4) Without in any way limiting the application of the term "knowingly" under paragraph (1), for purposes of this subdivision, a social media platform shall be deemed to have knowledge under paragraph (1) if all of the following are true:

(A) Material was reported to a social media platform using the mechanism required under subdivision (a) of Section 3273.66 for four consecutive months.

(B) The criteria set forth in paragraphs (1) to (3), inclusive, subdivision (a) of Section 3273.66 are established with respect to that reported material.

(C) The reported material was first displayed, stored, or hosted on the platform after January 1, 2025.

(5) As used in this subdivision, "facilitate, aid, or abet" means to deploy a system, design, feature, or affordance that is a substantial factor in causing minor users to be victims of commercial sexual exploitation.

(h) As used in this section:

(1) "Commercial sexual exploitation" means an act committed for the purpose of obtaining property, money, or anything else of value in exchange for, or as a result of, a sexual act of a minor or nonminor dependent, including, but not limited to, an act that would constitute a violation of any of the following:

(A) Sex trafficking of a minor in violation of subdivision (c) of Section 236.1 of the Penal Code.

(B) Pimping of a minor in violation of Section 266h of the Penal Code.

(C) Pandering of a minor in violation of subdivision (b) of Section 266i of the Penal Code.

(D) Procurement of a child under 16 years of age for lewd and lascivious acts in violation of Section 266j of the Penal Code.

(E) Solicitation of a child for a purpose that is either in violation of subparagraph (A) or pursuant to paragraph (3) of subdivision (b) of Section 647 of the Penal Code.

(F) An act of sexual exploitation described in subdivision (c) or (d) of Section 11165.1 of the Penal Code.

(2) "Nonminor dependent" has the same meaning as in subdivision (v) of Section 11400 of the Welfare and Institutions Code.

(3)(A) "Social media platform" has, except as provided in subparagraph (B), the same meaning as defined in Section 22675 of the Business and Professions Code.

(B) "Social media platform" does not include either of the following:

(i) A stand-alone direct messaging service that provides end-to-end encrypted communication or the portion of a multiservice platform that uses end-to-end encrypted communication.

(ii) An internet-based service or application owned or operated by a nonprofit organization exempt from federal income tax pursuant to Section 501(c)(3) of the Internal Revenue Code.

(i) A waiver of the provisions of this section is contrary to public policy and is void and unenforceable. **Leg.H.** Added Stats 2018 ch 166 §1 (AB 2105), effective January 1, 2019. Amended Stats 2023 ch 579 §3 (AB 1394), effective January 1, 2024, operative January 1, 2025.

§3346. Injuries to timber or while trespassing in reliance on boundary lines

(a) For wrongful injuries to timber, trees, or underwood upon the land of another, or removal thereof, the measure of damages is three times such sum as would compensate for the actual detriment, except that where the trespass was casual or involuntary, or that the defendant in any action brought under this section had probable cause to believe that the land on which the trespass was committed was his own or the land of the person in whose service or by whose direction the act was done, the measure of damages shall be twice the sum as would compensate for the actual detriment, and excepting further that where the wood was taken by the authority of highway officers for the purpose of repairing a public highway or bridge upon the land or adjoining it, in which case judgment shall only be given in a sum equal to the actual detriment.

(b) The measure of damages to be assessed against a defendant for any trespass committed while acting in reliance upon a survey of boundary lines which improperly fixes the location of a boundary line, shall be the actual detriment incurred if both of the following conditions exist:

(1) The trespass was committed by a defendant who either himself procured, or whose principal, lessor, or immediate predecessor in title procured the survey to be made; and

(2) The survey was made by a person licensed under the laws of this State to practice land surveying.

(c) Any action for the damages specified by subdivisions (a) and (b) of this section must be commenced within five years from the date of the trespass. **Leg.H.** Added Stats 1957 ch 2346 §2.

Prior Law: Former CC §3346, similar to the present section, was enacted Stats 1872 and repealed Stats 1957 ch 2346 §1.

Former Sections: Former CC §3346 was added in 1872 and repealed Stats 1957 ch 2346.

§3346a. [Section repealed 1931]

Leg.H. Added Stats 1905 ch 464 §1. Repealed Stats 1931 ch 790 §6, Stats 1939 ch 759 §2. The repealed section related to damages for negligence in setting or failing to control fires. See H & S C §13008.

§3347. [Section repealed 1995]

Leg.H. Enacted Stats 1872. Amended Stats 1976 ch 1171 §5. Repealed Stats 1994 ch 270 §2 (AB 3326). The repealed section related to injuries inflicted in duel.

§3348. [Section repealed 1995]

Leg.H. Enacted Stats 1872. Repealed Stats 1994 ch 270 §3 (AB 3326). The repealed section related to debts of slain or disabled dueler.

ARTICLE 4
General Provisions

Value, how estimated in favor of seller. §3353.
Value, how estimated in favor of buyer. §3354.
Property of peculiar value. §3355.
Value of written instrument. §3356.
Damages allowed in this chapter, exclusive of others. §3357.
Limitation of damages. §3358.
Damages to be reasonable. §3359.
Nominal damages. §3360.
Damages for lost earnings or impaired earning capacity; No reduction based on race, ethnicity, or gender. §3361.

§3353. Value, how estimated in favor of seller

In estimating damages, the value of property to a seller thereof is deemed to be the price which he could have obtained therefor in the market nearest to the place at which it should have been accepted by the buyer, and at such time after the breach of the contract as would have sufficed, with reasonable diligence, for the seller to effect a resale. **Leg.H.** Enacted Stats 1872.

§3354. Value, how estimated in favor of buyer

In estimating damages, except as provided by Sections 3355 and 3356, the value of property, to a buyer or owner thereof, deprived of its possession, is deemed to be the price at which he might have bought an equivalent thing in the market nearest to the place where the property ought to have been put into his possession, and at such time after the breach of duty upon which his right to damages is founded as would suffice, with reasonable diligence, for him to make such a purchase. **Leg.H.** Enacted Stats 1872.

§3355. Property of peculiar value

Where certain property has a peculiar value to a person recovering damages for deprivation thereof, or injury thereto, that may be deemed to be its value against one who had notice thereof before incurring a liability to damages in respect thereof, or against a willful wrongdoer. **Leg.H.** Enacted Stats 1872.

§3356. Value of written instrument

For the purpose of estimating damages, the value of an instrument in writing is presumed to be equal to that of the property to which it entitles its owner. **Leg.H.** Enacted Stats 1872. Amended Code Amdts 1873–74 ch 612 §278 p 266.

§3357. Damages allowed in this chapter, exclusive of others

The damages prescribed by this chapter are exclusive of exemplary damages and interest, except where those are expressly mentioned. **Leg.H.** Enacted Stats 1872.

§3358. Limitation of damages

Except as expressly provided by statute, no person can recover a greater amount in damages for the breach of an obligation, than he could have gained by the full performance thereof on both sides. **Leg.H.** Enacted Stats 1872. Amended Stats 1977 ch 198 §9, operative July 1, 1978.

§3359. Damages to be reasonable

Damages must, in all cases, be reasonable, and where an obligation of any kind appears to create a right to unconscionable and grossly oppressive damages, contrary to substantial justice, no more than reasonable damages can be recovered. **Leg.H.** Enacted Stats 1872.

§3360. Nominal damages

When a breach of duty has caused no appreciable detriment to the party affected, he may yet recover nominal damages. **Leg.H.** Enacted Stats 1872.

§3361. Damages for lost earnings or impaired earning capacity; No reduction based on race, ethnicity, or gender

Estimations, measures, or calculations of past, present, or future damages for lost earnings or impaired earning capacity resulting from personal injury or wrongful death shall not be reduced based on race, ethnicity, or gender. **Leg.H.** Added Stats 2019 ch 136 §2 (SB 41), effective January 1, 2020.

2019 Note: The Legislature finds and declares the following:

(a) The principals of equal protection and due process are fundamental to our democracy and the concept of civil liberty.

(b) California has been a pioneer in civil rights, leading the way in prohibiting discrimination on the basis of race, ethnicity, gender, and other protected categories.

(c) However, in tort actions around the state and country, race, ethnicity, and gender are routinely used in calculating damage awards that are meant to provide restitution to victims. For example, since women in America earn lower wages, on average, than men, the damages awarded to women are substantially lower than those received by men.

(d) Nearly one-half of economists surveyed by the National Association of Forensic Economics said they consider race, and 92 percent consider gender, when projecting earning potential for an injured person, including children. Future lost earning potential is a significant component of the damages awarded in tort actions.

(e) To determine projected lost earning potential, court experts typically rely on the Bureau of Labor Statistics' Current Population Survey. The results are a reflection of gender pay gaps and workforce discrimination, and they fail to account for possible progress or individual achievement.

(f) The consequence of this bias to use averages that represent generations of discriminatory practices is to perpetuate systemic inequalities. These practices disproportionately injure women and minority individuals by depriving them of fair compensation.

(g) Using race and gender-based tables can, by some estimates, under-value women and minorities by hundreds of thousands of dollars, including children who have not yet had the opportunity to work or identify career options. Specifically, these practices greatly disadvantage children of color, who are more likely to be impacted by environmental hazards created by the industrial facilities and factories located in low-income communities.

(h) Any generalized reduction of civil damages using statistical tables alone, based on a plaintiff's membership in a protected class identified in Section 51 of the Civil Code, is counter to the public policy of the State of California.

(i) This act shall not be construed to explicitly permit the generalized reduction of damages for lost earnings or impaired earnings capacity based on protected classifications not identified in the Bureau of Labor Statistics' Current Population Survey unless otherwise permitted by existing law. Stats 2019 ch 136 §1 (SB 41).

TITLE 3
SPECIFIC AND PREVENTIVE RELIEF

Chapter 1. General Principles.
Chapter 1.5. Investment Advisers.
Chapter 2. Specific Relief.
Chapter 3. Preventive Relief.

CHAPTER 1
GENERAL PRINCIPLES

Specific relief, etc., when allowed. §3366.
Specific relief, how given. §3367.
Preventive relief, how given. §3368.
Relief not granted to enforce penalty, forfeiture or penal law; Exceptions. §3369.

§3366. Specific relief, etc., when allowed

Specific or preventive relief may be given as provided by the laws of this state. **Leg.H.** Enacted Stats 1872. Amended Stats 1905 ch 465 §1 p 622.

§3367. Specific relief, how given

Specific relief is given:
1. By taking possession of a thing, and delivering it to a claimant;
2. By compelling a party himself to do that which ought to be done; or,
3. By declaring and determining the rights of parties, otherwise than by an award of damages. **Leg.H.** Enacted Stats 1872.

§3368. Preventive relief, how given

Preventive relief is given by prohibiting a party from doing that which ought not to be done. **Leg.H.** Enacted Stats 1872.

§3369. Relief not granted to enforce penalty, forfeiture or penal law; Exceptions

Neither specific nor preventive relief can be granted to enforce a penalty or forfeiture in any case, nor to enforce a penal law, except in a case of nuisance or as otherwise provided by law. **Leg.H.** Enacted Stats 1872. Amended Stats 1933 ch 953 §1 p 2482; Stats 1963 ch 1606 §1 p 3184; Stats 1972 ch 1084 §1; Stats 1974 ch 746 §1; Stats 1976 ch 1005 §1; Stats 1977 ch 299 §2.

§3370. [Section repealed 1976]

Leg.H. Added Stats 1949 ch 652 §1. Repealed Stats 1976 ch 837 §1. The repealed section related to acts constituting unfair competition. See B & P C §17200.

§3370.1. [Section repealed 1977]

Leg.H. Added Stats 1972 ch 1084 §2. Amended Stats 1974 ch 746 §2. Repealed Stats 1977 ch 299 §3. The repealed section related to the penalty for a violation of the chapter which contained the section. See B & P C §17206.

§3370.2. [Section repealed 1977]

Leg.H. Added Stats 1976 ch 1006 §1. Repealed Stats 1977 ch 299 §4. The repealed section related to the penalty for violation of an injunction prohibiting unfair competition. See B & P C §17207.

CHAPTER 1.5
INVESTMENT ADVISERS

Liability; Burden of proof. §3372.

§3372. Liability; Burden of proof

(a) Any person engaged in the business of advising others for compensation as to the advisability of purchasing, holding or selling property for investment and who represents himself or herself to be an expert with respect to investment decisions in such property, or any class of such property, shall be liable to any person to whom such advisory services are furnished for compensation and who is damaged by reason of such person's reliance upon such services, for the amount of such compensation and for such damages, unless the person rendering such services proves that such services were performed with the due care and skill reasonably to be expected of a person who is such an expert.

(b) For the purposes of this section, the following apply:

(1) A person represents that such person is an "expert" within the meaning of this section if such person represents that he or she is a "financial planner," "financial adviser," "financial counselor," "financial consultant" or an "investment adviser," "investment counselor" or "investment consultant" or that such person renders "financial planning services," "financial advisory services," "financial counseling services," "financial consulting services" or "investment advisory services," "investment counseling services" or "investment consulting services" or makes substantially equivalent representations with respect to such person's business or qualifications.

(2) "Person" includes an individual, corporation, partnership, limited liability company, joint venture, an association, joint stock company, a trust or unincorporated association.

(c) The following persons are not liable under the provisions of this section:

(1) Any person, when engaged in the purchase or sale of tangible personal property for his or her own account, and the agents and employees of such persons.

(2) Any person, and the agents and employees of such person, licensed under, exempted from licensing under, or not subject to licensing under by reason of an express exclusion from a definition contained in, the Commodity Exchange Act, the Investment Advisers Act of 1940, the California Commodity Law, the Corporate Securities Law of 1968, the Insurance Code, the Real Estate Law, or any state or federal law for the licensing and regulation of banks or savings and loan associations. **Leg.H.** Added Stats 1978 ch 1380 §1. Amended Stats 1986 ch 698 §1; Stats 1994 ch 1010 §53 (SB 2053).

CHAPTER 2
SPECIFIC RELIEF

Article 1. Possession of Real Property.
Article 2. Possession of Personal Property.
Article 3. Specific Performance of Obligations.
Article 4. Revision of Contracts.
Article 5. Rescission of Contracts.
Article 6. Cancellation of Instruments.

ARTICLE 1
Possession of Real Property

Judgment for possession or title. §3375.

§3375. Judgment for possession or title

A person entitled to specific real property, by reason either of a perfected title, or of a claim to title which ought to be perfected, may recover the same in the manner prescribed by the Code of Civil Procedure, either by a judgment for its possession, to be executed by the sheriff, or by a judgment requiring the other party to perfect the title, and to deliver possession of the property. **Leg.H.** Enacted Stats 1872.

ARTICLE 2
Possession of Personal Property

Judgment for delivery. §3379.
Specific delivery. §3380.

§3379. Judgment for delivery

A person entitled to the immediate possession of specific personal property may recover the same in the manner provided by the Code of Civil Procedure. **Leg.H.** Enacted Stats 1872.

§3380. Specific delivery

Any person having the possession or control of a particular article of personal property, of which he is not the owner, may be compelled specifically to deliver it to the person entitled to its immediate possession. **Leg.H.** Enacted Stats 1872. Amended Code Amdts 1873–74 ch 612 §279 p 266.

ARTICLE 3
Specific Performance of Obligations

Specific performance. §3384.
Mutuality not required. §3386.
Breach of real property transfer agreement; Presumption of inadequacy of pecuniary compensation. §3387.
Contract signed by one party only, may be enforced by other. §3388.
Liquidation of damages not a bar to specific performance. §3389.
Obligations which cannot be specifically enforced. §3390.
What parties cannot be compelled to perform. §3391.

What parties cannot have specific performance in their favor. §3392.
Agreement to sell property by one who has no title. §3394.
Relief against parties claiming under person bound to perform. §3395.

§3384. Specific performance

Except as otherwise provided in this article, the specific performance of an obligation may be compelled. **Leg.H.** Enacted Stats 1872. Amended Code Amdts 1873–74 ch 612 §280 p 266.

§3385. [Section repealed 1873–74]

Leg.H. Enacted Stats 1872. Repealed Code Amdts 1873–74 ch 612 §281.

§3386. Mutuality not required

Notwithstanding that the agreed counterperformance is not or would not have been specifically enforceable, specific performance may be compelled if:

(a) Specific performance would otherwise be an appropriate remedy; and

(b) The agreed counterperformance has been substantially performed or its concurrent or future performance is assured or, if the court deems necessary, can be secured to the satisfaction of the court. **Leg.H.** Enacted Stats 1872. Amended Stats 1969 ch 156 §1 p 410.

§3387. Breach of real property transfer agreement; Presumption of inadequacy of pecuniary compensation

It is to be presumed that the breach of an agreement to transfer real property cannot be adequately relieved by pecuniary compensation. In the case of a single-family dwelling which the party seeking performance intends to occupy, this presumption is conclusive. In all other cases, this presumption is a presumption affecting the burden of proof. **Leg.H.** Enacted Stats 1872. Amended Stats 1931 ch 1070 §11 p 2261; Stats 1984 ch 937 §1.

§3388. Contract signed by one party only, may be enforced by other

A party who has signed a written contract may be compelled specifically to perform it, though the other party has not signed it, if the latter has performed, or offers to perform it on his part, and the case is otherwise proper for enforcing specific performance. **Leg.H.** Enacted Stats 1872.

§3389. Liquidation of damages not a bar to specific performance

A contract otherwise proper to be specifically enforced, may be thus enforced, though a penalty is imposed, or the damages are liquidated for its breach, and the party in default is willing to pay the same. **Leg.H.** Enacted Stats 1872.

§3390. Obligations which cannot be specifically enforced

The following obligations cannot be specifically enforced:

(a) An obligation to render personal service.

(b) An obligation to employ another in personal service.

(c) An agreement to perform an act which the party has not power lawfully to perform when required to do so.

(d) An agreement to procure the act or consent of the spouse of the contracting party, or of any other third person.

(e) An agreement, the terms of which are not sufficiently certain to make the precise act which is to be done clearly ascertainable. **Leg.H.** Enacted Stats 1872. Amended Stats 1961 ch 461 §5 p 1551; Stats 2016 ch 50 §12 (SB 1005), effective January 1, 2017.

2016 Note: For legislative intent, see the 2016 Note following §14.

§3391. What parties cannot be compelled to perform

Specific performance cannot be enforced against a party to a contract in any of the following cases:

1. If he has not received an adequate consideration for the contract;

2. If it is not, as to him, just and reasonable;

3. If his assent was obtained by the misrepresentation, concealment, circumvention, or unfair practices of any party to whom performance would become due under the contract, or by any promise of such party which has not been substantially fulfilled; or,

4. If his assent was given under the influence of mistake, misapprehension, or surprise, except that where the contract provides for compensation in case of mistake, a mistake within the scope of such provision may be compensated for, and the contract specifically enforced in other respects, if proper to be so enforced. **Leg.H.** Enacted Stats 1872.

§3392. What parties cannot have specific performance in their favor

Specific performance cannot be enforced in favor of a party who has not fully and fairly performed all the conditions precedent on his part to the obligation of the other party, except where his failure to perform is only partial, and either entirely immaterial, or capable of being fully compensated, in which case specific performance may be compelled, upon full compensation being made for the default. **Leg.H.** Enacted Stats 1872.

§3393. [Section repealed 1873–74]

Leg.H. Enacted Stats 1872. Repealed Code Amdts 1873–74 ch 612 §281.

§3394. Agreement to sell property by one who has no title

An agreement for the sale of property cannot be specifically enforced in favor of a seller who cannot give to the buyer a title free from reasonable doubt. **Leg.H.** Enacted Stats 1872.

§3395. Relief against parties claiming under person bound to perform

Whenever an obligation in respect to real property would be specifically enforced against a particular person, it may be in like manner enforced against any other person claiming under him by a title created subsequently to the obligation, except a purchaser or incumbrancer in good faith and for value, and except, also, that any such person may exonerate himself by conveying all his estate to the person entitled to enforce the obligation. **Leg.H.** Enacted Stats 1872.

§3397. [Section repealed 1933]

Leg.H. Added Stats 1925 ch 154 §1. Repealed Stats 1933 ch 25 (Ag C §1301). The repealed section related to specific enforcement of agreements to deliver certain products. See Fd & Ag C §54263.

ARTICLE 4
Revision of Contracts

When contract may be revised. §3399.
Presumption as to intent of parties. §3400.
Principles of revision. §3401.
Enforcement of revised contract. §3402.

§3399. When contract may be revised

When, through fraud or a mutual mistake of the parties, or a mistake of one party, which the other at the time knew or suspected, a written contract does not truly express the intention of the parties, it may be revised on the application of a party aggrieved, so as to express that intention, so far as it can be done without prejudice to rights acquired by third persons, in good faith and for value. **Leg.H.** Enacted Stats 1872.

§3400. Presumption as to intent of parties

For the purpose of revising a contract, it must be presumed that all the parties thereto intended to make an equitable and conscientious agreement. **Leg.H.** Enacted Stats 1872.

§3401. Principles of revision

In revising a written instrument, the court may inquire what the instrument was intended to mean, and what were intended to be its legal consequences, and is not confined to the inquiry what the language of the instrument was intended to be. **Leg.H.** Enacted Stats 1872.

§3402. Enforcement of revised contract

A contract may be first revised and then specifically enforced. **Leg.H.** Enacted Stats 1872.

ARTICLE 5
Rescission of Contracts

§§3406–3408. [Sections repealed 1961]

Leg.H. Enacted Stats 1872. Amended Stats 1953 ch 588 §1. Repealed Stats 1961 ch 589 §5. See CC §§1688 et seq.

ARTICLE 6
Cancellation of Instruments

When cancellation may be ordered. §3412.
Instrument obviously void. §3413.
Cancellation in part. §3414.
Reissuance of lost private documents or instruments. §3415.

§3412. When cancellation may be ordered

A written instrument, in respect to which there is a reasonable apprehension that if left outstanding it may cause serious injury to a person against whom it is void or voidable, may, upon his application, be so adjudged, and ordered to be delivered up or canceled. **Leg.H.** Enacted Stats 1872.

§3413. Instrument obviously void

An instrument, the invalidity of which is apparent upon its face, or upon the face of another instrument which is necessary to the use of the former in evidence, is not to be deemed capable of causing injury, within the provisions of the last section. **Leg.H.** Enacted Stats 1872.

§3414. Cancellation in part

Where an instrument is evidence of different rights or obligations, it may be canceled in part, and allowed to stand for the residue. **Leg.H.** Enacted Stats 1872.

§3415. Reissuance of lost private documents or instruments

(a) An action may be maintained by any person interested in any private document or instrument in writing, which has been lost or destroyed, to prove or establish the document or instrument or to compel the issuance, execution, and acknowledgment of a duplicate of the document or instrument.

(b) If the document or instrument is a negotiable instrument, the court shall compel the owner of the negotiable instrument to give an indemnity bond to the person reissuing, reexecuting, or reacknowledging the same, against loss, damage, expense, or other liability that may be suffered by the person by reason of the issuance of the duplicate instrument or by the original instrument still remaining outstanding. **Leg.H.** Added Stats 1906 Ex Sess ch 64 §1. Amended Stats 1947 ch 313 §1; Stats 1982 ch 517 §85; Stats 2006 ch 538 §59 (SB 1852), effective January 1, 2007.

CHAPTER 3
PREVENTIVE RELIEF

Preventive relief, how granted. §3420.
Provisional injunctions. §3421.
Injunction, when allowed. §3422.
When injunction may not be granted. §3423.
Modification or dissolution of final injunction; Service of process. §3424.

§3420. Preventive relief, how granted

Preventive relief is granted by injunction, provisional or final. **Leg.H.** Enacted Stats 1872.

§3421. Provisional injunctions

Provisional injunctions are regulated by the Code of Civil Procedure. **Leg.H.** Enacted Stats 1872.

§3422. Injunction, when allowed

Except where otherwise provided by this title, a final injunction may be granted to prevent the breach of an obligation existing in favor of the applicant:

1. Where pecuniary compensation would not afford adequate relief;
2. Where it would be extremely difficult to ascertain the amount of compensation which would afford adequate relief;
3. Where the restraint is necessary to prevent a multiplicity of judicial proceedings; or,
4. Where the obligation arises from a trust. **Leg.H.** Enacted Stats 1872.

§3423. When injunction may not be granted

An injunction may not be granted:

(a) To stay a judicial proceeding pending at the commencement of the action in which the injunction is demanded, unless this restraint is necessary to prevent a multiplicity of proceedings.

(b) To stay proceedings in a court of the United States.

(c) To stay proceedings in another state upon a judgment of a court of that state.

(d) To prevent the execution of a public statute, by officers of the law, for the public benefit.

(e) To prevent the breach of a contract the performance of which would not be specifically enforced, other than a contract in writing for the rendition of personal services from one to another where the promised service is of a special, unique, unusual, extraordinary, or intellectual character, which gives it peculiar value, the loss of which cannot be reasonably or adequately compensated in damages in an action at law, and where the compensation for the personal services is as follows:

(1) As to contracts entered into on or before December 31, 1993, the minimum compensation provided in the contract for the personal services shall be at the rate of six thousand dollars ($6,000) per annum.

(2) As to contracts entered into on or after January 1, 1994, the criteria of subparagraph (A) or (B), as follows, are satisfied:

(A) The compensation is as follows:

(i) The minimum compensation provided in the contract shall be at the rate of nine thousand dollars ($9,000) per annum for the first year of the contract, twelve thousand dollars ($12,000) per annum for the second year of the contract, and fifteen thousand dollars ($15,000) per annum for the third to seventh years, inclusive, of the contract.

(ii) In addition, after the third year of the contract, there shall actually have been paid for the services through and including the contract year during which the injunctive relief is sought, over and above the minimum contractual compensation specified in clause (i), the amount of fifteen thousand dollars ($15,000) per annum during the fourth and fifth years of the contract, and thirty thousand dollars ($30,000) per annum during the sixth and seventh years of the contract. As a condition to petitioning for an injunction, amounts payable under this clause may be paid at any time prior to seeking injunctive relief.

(B) The aggregate compensation actually received for the services provided under a contract that does not meet the criteria of subparagraph (A), is at least 10 times the applicable aggregate minimum amount specified in clauses (i) and (ii) of subparagraph (A) through and including the contract year during which the injunctive relief is sought. As a condition to petitioning for an injunction, amounts payable under this subparagraph may be paid at any time prior to seeking injunctive relief.

(3) Compensation paid in any contract year in excess of the minimums specified in subparagraphs (A) and (B) of paragraph (2) shall apply to reduce the compensation otherwise required to be paid under those provisions in any subsequent contract years.

However, an injunction may be granted to prevent the breach of a contract entered into between any nonprofit cooperative corporation or association and a member or stockholder thereof in respect to any provision regarding the sale or delivery to the corporation or association of the products produced or acquired by the member or stockholder.

(f) To prevent the exercise of a public or private office, in a lawful manner, by the person in possession.

(g) To prevent a legislative act by a municipal corporation. **Leg.H.** Enacted Stats 1872. Amended Code Amdts 1873–74 ch 612 §282; Stats 1919 ch 226 §1; Stats 1925 ch 409 §1; Stats 1992 ch 177 §1 (SB 1459); Stats 1993 ch 5 §1 (SB 32), effective April 3, 1993, ch 836 §1 (SB 487).

§3424. Modification or dissolution of final injunction; Service of process

(a) Upon notice and motion, the court may modify or dissolve a final injunction upon a showing that there has been a material change in the facts upon which the injunction was granted, that the law upon which the injunction was granted has changed, or that the ends of justice would be served by the modification or dissolution of the injunction.

(b) Service of this motion to modify or dissolve a final injunction shall be made upon the nonmoving party by one of the following methods:

(1) If the party has not appeared in the action, the motion shall be served in the same manner as a summons pursuant to Article 3 (commencing with Section 415.10) of Chapter 4 of Title 5 of Part 2 of the Code of Civil Procedure.

(2) If the party has appeared in the action, the motion shall be served either upon the party or his or her attorney, or upon the party if he or she has appeared without an attorney, either in the same manner as a summons pursuant to Article 3 (commencing with Section 415.10) of Chapter 4 of Title 5 of the Code of Civil Procedure or in the manner provided by Chapter 5 (commencing with Section 1010) of Title 14 of Part 2 of the Code of Civil Procedure.

(c) This section does not apply to a final injunction issued pursuant to the Family Code. **Leg.H.** Added Stats 1995 ch 796 §1.5 (SB 45).

TITLE 4
UNIFORM SINGLE PUBLICATION ACT

Citation. §3425.1.
Interpretation. §3425.2.
Single cause of action; Damages. §3425.3.
Effect of judgment. §3425.4.

Retroactivity. §3425.5.

§3425.1. Citation
This title may be cited as the Uniform Single Publication Act. **Leg.H.** Added Stats 1955 ch 867 §1 p 1481.

§3425.2. Interpretation
This act shall be so interpreted as to effectuate its purpose to make uniform the law of those states or jurisdictions which enact it. **Leg.H.** Added Stats 1955 ch 867 §1 p 1481.

§3425.3. Single cause of action; Damages
No person shall have more than one cause of action for damages for libel or slander or invasion of privacy or any other tort founded upon any single publication or exhibition or utterance, such as any one issue of a newspaper or book or magazine or any one presentation to an audience or any one broadcast over radio or television or any one exhibition of a motion picture. Recovery in any action shall include all damages for any such tort suffered by the plaintiff in all jurisdictions. **Leg.H.** Added Stats 1955 ch 867 §1 p 1481.

§3425.4. Effect of judgment
A judgment in any jurisdiction for or against the plaintiff upon the substantive merits of any action for damages founded upon a single publication or exhibition or utterance as described in Section 3425.3 shall bar any other action for damages by the same plaintiff against the same defendant founded upon the same publication or exhibition or utterance. **Leg.H.** Added Stats 1955 ch 867 §1 p 1481.

§3425.5. Retroactivity
This title shall not be retroactive as to causes of action existing on its effective date. **Leg.H.** Added Stats 1955 ch 867 §1 p 1481.

TITLE 5
UNIFORM TRADE SECRETS ACT

Citation of title. §3426.
Definitions. §3426.1.
Injunction against actual or threatened misappropriation. §3426.2.
Damages. §3426.3.
Attorney fees and costs. §3426.4.
Methods for preserving secrecy of trade secret. §3426.5.
Limitation period; Accrual of cause of action. §3426.6.
Effect of title on other statutes or remedies. §3426.7.
Statutory Construction. §3426.8.
Severability. §3426.9.
Application of title to acts occurring prior to statutory date; Continuing acts. §3426.10.
Applicability of official proceedings privilege to disclosure of trade secret information. §3426.11.

§3426. Citation of title
This title may be cited as the Uniform Trade Secrets Act. **Leg.H.** Added Stats 1984 ch 1724 §1.

§3426.1. Definitions
As used in this title, unless the context requires otherwise:
(a) "Improper means" includes theft, bribery, misrepresentation, breach or inducement of a breach of a duty to maintain secrecy, or espionage through electronic or other means. Reverse engineering or independent derivation alone shall not be considered improper means.
(b) "Misappropriation" means:
(1) Acquisition of a trade secret of another by a person who knows or has reason to know that the trade secret was acquired by improper means; or
(2) Disclosure or use of a trade secret of another without express or implied consent by a person who:
(A) Used improper means to acquire knowledge of the trade secret; or
(B) At the time of disclosure or use, knew or had reason to know that his or her knowledge of the trade secret was:
(i) Derived from or through a person who had utilized improper means to acquire it;
(ii) Acquired under circumstances giving rise to a duty to maintain its secrecy or limit its use; or
(iii) Derived from or through a person who owed a duty to the person seeking relief to maintain its secrecy or limit its use; or
(C) Before a material change of his or her position, knew or had reason to know that it was a trade secret and that knowledge of it had been acquired by accident or mistake.
(c) "Person" means a natural person, corporation, business trust, estate, trust, partnership, limited liability company, association, joint venture, government, governmental subdivision or agency, or any other legal or commercial entity.
(d) "Trade secret" means information, including a formula, pattern, compilation, program, device, method, technique, or process, that:
(1) Derives independent economic value, actual or potential, from not being generally known to the public or to other persons who can obtain economic value from its disclosure or use; and
(2) Is the subject of efforts that are reasonable under the circumstances to maintain its secrecy. **Leg.H.** Added Stats 1984 ch 1724 §1. Amended Stats 1994 ch 1010 §54 (SB 2053).

§3426.2. Injunction against actual or threatened misappropriation
(a) Actual or threatened misappropriation may be enjoined. Upon application to the court, an injunction shall be terminated when the trade secret has ceased to exist, but the injunction may be continued for an additional period of time in order to eliminate commercial advantage that otherwise would be derived from the misappropriation.
(b) If the court determines that it would be unreasonable to prohibit future use, an injunction may condition future use upon payment of a reasonable royalty for no longer than the period of time the use could have been prohibited.
(c) In appropriate circumstances, affirmative acts to protect a trade secret may be compelled by court order. **Leg.H.** Added Stats 1984 ch 1724 §1.

§3426.3. Damages
(a) A complainant may recover damages for the actual loss caused by misappropriation. A complainant also may recover for the unjust enrichment caused by misappropriation that is not taken into account in computing damages for actual loss.
(b) If neither damages nor unjust enrichment caused by misappropriation are provable, the court may order payment of a reasonable royalty for no longer than the period of time the use could have been prohibited.
(c) If willful and malicious misappropriation exists, the court may award exemplary damages in an amount not exceeding twice any award made under subdivision (a) or (b). **Leg.H.** Added Stats 1984 ch 1724 §1.

§3426.4. Attorney fees and costs
If a claim of misappropriation is made in bad faith, a motion to terminate an injunction is made or resisted in bad faith, or willful and malicious misappropriation exists, the court may award reasonable attorney's fees and costs to the prevailing party. Recoverable costs hereunder shall include a reasonable sum to cover the services of expert witnesses, who are not regular employees of any party, actually incurred and reasonably necessary in either, or both, preparation for trial or arbitration, or during trial or arbitration, of the case by the prevailing party. **Leg.H.** Added Stats 1984 ch 1724 §1. Amended Stats 2006 ch 62 §1 (SB 1636), effective January 1, 2007.

§3426.5. Methods for preserving secrecy of trade secret
In an action under this title, a court shall preserve the secrecy of an alleged trade secret by reasonable means, which may include granting protective orders in connection with discovery proceedings, holding in-camera hearings, sealing the records of the action, and ordering any person involved in the litigation not to disclose an alleged trade secret without prior court approval. **Leg.H.** Added Stats 1984 ch 1724 §1.

§3426.6. Limitation period; Accrual of cause of action
An action for misappropriation must be brought within three years after the misappropriation is discovered or by the exercise of reasonable diligence should have been discovered. For the purposes of this section, a continuing misappropriation constitutes a single claim. **Leg.H.** Added Stats 1984 ch 1724 §1.

§3426.7. Effect of title on other statutes or remedies
(a) Except as otherwise expressly provided, this title does not supersede any statute relating to misappropriation of a trade secret, or any statute otherwise regulating trade secrets.
(b) This title does not affect (1) contractual remedies, whether or not based upon misappropriation of a trade secret, (2) other civil remedies that are not based upon misappropriation of a trade secret, or (3) criminal remedies, whether or not based upon misappropriation of a trade secret.

(c) This title does not affect the disclosure of a record by a state or local agency under the California Public Records Act (Division 10 (commencing with Section 7920.000) of Title 1 of the Government Code). Any determination as to whether the disclosure of a record under the California Public Records Act constitutes a misappropriation of a trade secret and the rights and remedies with respect thereto shall be made pursuant to the law in effect before the operative date of this title. **Leg.H.** Added Stats 1984 ch 1724 §1. Amended Stats 2021 ch 615 §52 (AB 474), effective January 1, 2022.

§3426.8. Statutory Construction
This title shall be applied and construed to effectuate its general purpose to make uniform the law with respect to the subject of this title among states enacting it. **Leg.H.** Added Stats 1984 ch 1724 §1.

§3426.9. Severability
If any provision of this title or its application to any person or circumstances is held invalid, the invalidity does not affect other provisions or applications of the title which can be given effect without the invalid provision or application, and to this end the provisions of this title are severable. **Leg.H.** Added Stats 1984 ch 1724 §1.

§3426.10. Application of title to acts occurring prior to statutory date; Continuing acts
This title does not apply to misappropriation occurring prior to January 1, 1985. If a continuing misappropriation otherwise covered by this title began before January 1, 1985, this title does not apply to the part of the misappropriation occurring before that date. This title does apply to the part of the misappropriation occurring on or after that date unless the appropriation was not a misappropriation under the law in effect before the operative date of this title. **Leg.H.** Added Stats 1984 ch 1724 §1.

§3426.11. Applicability of official proceedings privilege to disclosure of trade secret information
Notwithstanding subdivision (b) of Section 47, in any legislative or judicial proceeding, or in any other official proceeding authorized by law, or in the initiation or course of any other proceeding authorized by law and reviewable pursuant to Chapter 2 (commencing with Section 1084) of Title 1 of Part 3 of the Code of Civil Procedure, the voluntary, intentional disclosure of trade secret information, unauthorized by its owner, to a competitor or potential competitor of the owner of the trade secret information or the agent or representative of such a competitor or potential competitor is not privileged and is not a privileged communication for purposes of Part 2 (commencing with Section 43) of Division 1.

This section does not in any manner limit, restrict, impair, or otherwise modify either the application of the other subdivisions of Section 47 to the conduct to which this section applies or the court's authority to control, order, or permit access to evidence in any case before it.

Nothing in this section shall be construed to limit, restrict, or otherwise impair, the capacity of persons employed by public entities to report improper government activity, as defined in Section 10542 of the Government Code, or the capacity of private persons to report improper activities of a private business. **Leg.H.** Added Stats 1992 ch 165 §1 (AB 1445).

TITLE 6
INTERFERENCE WITH ACCESS TO HEALTH CARE

Definitions. §3427.
Tort of commercial blockade. §3427.1.
Action for civil damages. §3427.2.
Protection of individual privacy and prevention of harassment. §3427.3.
Construction of title. §3427.4.

§3427. Definitions
As used in this title:

(a) "Aggrieved" means and refers to any of the following persons or entities:

(1) A person physically present at a health care facility when a commercial blockade occurs whose access is obstructed or impeded.

(2) A person physically present at a health care facility when a commercial blockade occurs whose health care is disrupted.

(3) A health care facility where a commercial blockade occurs, its employees, contractors, or volunteers.

(4) The owner of a health care facility where a commercial blockade occurs or of the building or property upon which the health care facility is located.

(b) "Commercial blockade" means acts constituting the tort of commercial blockade, as defined in Section 3427.1.

(c) "Disrupting the normal functioning of a health care facility" means intentionally rendering or attempting to render a health care facility temporarily or permanently unavailable or unusable by a licensed health practitioner, the facility's staff, or patients. "Disrupting the normal functioning of a health care facility" does not include acts of the owner of the facility, an agent acting on behalf of the owner, or officers or employees of a governmental entity acting to protect the public health or safety.

(d) "Health care facility" means a facility that provides health care services directly to patients, including, but not limited to, a hospital, clinic, licensed health practitioner's office, health maintenance organization, diagnostic or treatment center, neuropsychiatric or mental health facility, hospice, or nursing home. **Leg.H.** Added Stats 1994 ch 1193 §1 (AB 600).

§3427.1. Tort of commercial blockade
It is unlawful, and constitutes the tort of commercial blockade for a person, alone or in concert with others, to intentionally prevent an individual from entering or exiting a health care facility by physically obstructing the individual's passage or by disrupting the normal functioning of a health care facility. **Leg.H.** Added Stats 1994 ch 1193 §1 (AB 600).

§3427.2. Action for civil damages
A person or health care facility aggrieved by the actions prohibited by this title may seek civil damages from those who committed the prohibited acts and those acting in concert with them. **Leg.H.** Added Stats 1994 ch 1193 §1 (AB 600). Amended Stats 1995 ch 91 §19 (SB 975).

§3427.3. Protection of individual privacy and prevention of harassment
The court having jurisdiction over a civil proceeding under this title shall take all steps reasonably necessary to safeguard the individual privacy and prevent harassment of a health care patient, licensed health practitioner, or employee, client, or customer of a health care facility who is a party or witness in the proceeding, including granting protective orders. Health care patients, licensed health practitioners, and employees, clients, and customers of the health care facility may use pseudonyms to protect their privacy. **Leg.H.** Added Stats 1994 ch 1193 §1 (AB 600).

§3427.4. Construction of title
This title shall not be construed to impair any constitutionally protected activity or any activities protected by the labor laws of this state or the United States of America. **Leg.H.** Added Stats 1994 ch 1193 §1 (AB 600).

TITLE 7
DUTY OF HEALTH CARE SERVICE PLANS AND MANAGED CARE ENTITIES

Duty to provide medically necessary health care service; Liability for failure to exercise ordinary care; Waiver; Exceptions; Severability. §3428.

§3428. Duty to provide medically necessary health care service; Liability for failure to exercise ordinary care; Waiver; Exceptions; Severability
(a) For services rendered on or after January 1, 2001, a health care service plan or managed care entity, as described in subdivision (f) of Section 1345 of the Health and Safety Code, shall have a duty of ordinary care to arrange for the provision of medically necessary health care service to its subscribers and enrollees, where the health care service is a benefit provided under the plan, and shall be liable for any and all harm legally caused by its failure to exercise that ordinary care when both of the following apply:

(1) The failure to exercise ordinary care resulted in the denial, delay, or modification of the health care service recommended for, or furnished to, a subscriber or enrollee.

(2) The subscriber or enrollee suffered substantial harm.

(b) For purposes of this section: (1) substantial harm means loss of life, loss or significant impairment of limb or bodily function, significant disfigurement, severe and chronic physical pain, or significant financial loss; (2) health care services need not be recommended or furnished by an in-plan provider, but may be recommended or furnished by any health care provider practicing within the scope of his or her practice; and (3) health care services shall be recommended or furnished at any time prior to the inception of the action, and the recommendation need not be made prior to the occurrence of substantial harm.

(c) Health care service plans and managed care entities are not health care providers under any provision of law, including, but not limited to, Section 6146 of the Business and Professions Code, Sections 3333.1 or 3333.2 of this code, or Sections 340.5, 364, 425.13, 667.7, or 1295 of the Code of Civil Procedure.

(d) A health care service plan or managed care entity shall not seek indemnity, whether contractual or equitable, from a provider for liability imposed under subdivision (a). Any provision to the contrary in a contract with providers is void and unenforceable.

(e) This section shall not create any liability on the part of an employer or an employer group purchasing organization that purchases coverage or assumes risk on behalf of its employees or on behalf of self-funded employee benefit plans.

(f) Any waiver by a subscriber or enrollee of the provisions of this section is contrary to public policy and shall be unenforceable and void.

(g) This section does not create any new or additional liability on the part of a health care service plan or managed care entity for harm caused that is attributable to the medical negligence of a treating physician or other treating health care provider.

(h) This section does not abrogate or limit any other theory of liability otherwise available at law.

(i) This section shall not apply in instances where subscribers or enrollees receive treatment by prayer, consistent with the provisions of subdivision (a) of Section 1270 of the Health and Safety Code, in lieu of medical treatment.

(j) Damages recoverable for a violation of this section include, but are not limited to, those set forth in Section 3333.

(k)(1) A person may not maintain a cause of action pursuant to this section against any entity required to comply with any independent medical review system or independent review system required by law unless the person or his or her representative has exhausted the procedures provided by the applicable independent review system.

(2) Compliance with paragraph (1) is not required in a case where either of the following applies:

(A) Substantial harm, as defined in subdivision (b), has occurred prior to the completion of the applicable review.

(B) Substantial harm, as defined, in subdivision (b), will imminently occur prior to the completion of the applicable review.

(3) This subdivision shall become operative only if Senate Bill 189 and Assembly Bill 55 of the 1999–2000 Regular Session are also enacted and enforceable.

(*l*) If any provision of this section or the application thereof to any person or circumstance is held to be unconstitutional or otherwise invalid or unenforceable, the remainder of the section and the application of those provisions to other persons or circumstances shall not be affected thereby.

Leg.H. Added Stats 1999 ch 536 §3 (SB 21).

1999 Note: Subsection (k)(3) expresses the condition for subdivision (k) becoming operative. Senate Bill 189 was enacted as Chapter 542; Assembly Bill 55 was enacted as Chapter 533. Both bills relate to independent medical reviews.

PART 2
SPECIAL RELATIONS OF DEBTOR AND CREDITOR

Title 1. General Principles.
Title 2. Void and Voidable Transfers and Undertakings.

TITLE 1
GENERAL PRINCIPLES

Who is a debtor. §3429.
Who is a creditor. §3430.
Validity of debtor's contracts. §3431.
Payments in preference. §3432.
Relative rights of different creditors. §3433.
Lender's liability to third parties. §3434.

§3429. Who is a debtor

A debtor, within the meaning of this title, is one who, by reason of an existing obligation, is or may become liable to pay money to another, whether such liability is certain or contingent. **Leg.H.** Enacted Stats 1872.

§3430. Who is a creditor

A creditor, within the meaning of this title, is one in whose favor an obligation exists, by reason of which he is, or may become, entitled to the payment of money. **Leg.H.** Enacted Stats 1872.

§3431. Validity of debtor's contracts

In the absence of fraud, every contract of a debtor is valid against all his creditors, existing or subsequent, who have not acquired a lien on the property affected by such contract. **Leg.H.** Enacted Stats 1872.

§3432. Payments in preference

A debtor may pay one creditor in preference to another, or may give to one creditor security for the payment of his demand in preference to another. **Leg.H.** Enacted Stats 1872.

§3433. Relative rights of different creditors

Where a creditor is entitled to resort to each of several funds for the satisfaction of his claim, and another person has an interest in, or is entitled as a creditor to resort to some, but not all of them, the latter may require the former to seek satisfaction from those funds to which the latter has no such claim, so far as it can be done without impairing the right of the former to complete satisfaction, and without doing injustice to third persons. **Leg.H.** Enacted Stats 1872.

§3434. Lender's liability to third parties

A lender who makes a loan of money, the proceeds of which are used or may be used by the borrower to finance the design, manufacture, construction, repair, modification or improvement of real or personal property for sale or lease to others, shall not be held liable to third persons for any loss or damage occasioned by any defect in the real or personal property so designed, manufactured, constructed, repaired, modified or improved or for any loss or damage resulting from the failure of the borrower to use due care in the design, manufacture, construction, repair, modification or improvement of such real or personal property, unless such loss or damage is a result of an act of the lender outside the scope of the activities of a lender of money or unless the lender has been a party to misrepresentations with respect to such real or personal property. **Leg.H.** Added Stats 1969 ch 1584 §1 p 3221.

TITLE 2
VOID AND VOIDABLE TRANSFERS AND UNDERTAKINGS

Chapter 1. Uniform Voidable Transactions Act.
Chapter 2. Conveyance of Personal Property Without Delivery.
Chapter 3. Undertaking in Voidable Transfer Action.

CHAPTER 1
UNIFORM VOIDABLE TRANSACTIONS ACT

Citation of chapter. §3439.
Definitions. §3439.01.
Insolvency. §3439.02.
Value for transfer or obligation. §3439.03.
Transfer with intent to defraud or transfer not given in exchange for value: Determining actual intent. §3439.04.
Transfer resulting in debtor's insolvency. §3439.05.
When transfer made or obligation incurred. §3439.06.
Creditor's remedies. §3439.07.
Transfers that are not voidable; Judgment for creditor; Remedies of good faith transferee. §3439.08.
Time within which action must be brought. §3439.09.
Determination of debtor's location. §3439.10.
[Section renumbered 2016]. §3439.11.
Principles of law and equity; Applicability. §3439.12.
Application and construction of chapter. §3439.13.
Applicability and construction of chapter. §3439.14.

§3439. Citation of chapter

This chapter may be cited as the Uniform Voidable Transactions Act. **Leg.H.** Added Stats 1986 ch 383 §2. Amended Stats 2015 ch 44 §3 (SB 161), effective January 1, 2016.

Prior Law: Former CC §3439, similar to the present section, was added Stats 1939 ch 329 §2, amended Stats 1982 ch 517 §87, and repealed Stats 1986 ch 383 §1.

Former CC §3439, relating to transfers, etc., with intent to defraud creditors, was enacted Stats 1872 and repealed Stats 1939 ch 329 §1.

§3439.01. Definitions

As used in this chapter the following definitions are applicable:

(a) "Asset" means property of a debtor, but the term does not include the following:

(1) Property to the extent it is encumbered by a valid lien.

(2) Property to the extent it is generally exempt under nonbankruptcy law.

(3) An interest in property held in tenancy by the entireties to the extent it is not subject to process by a creditor holding a claim against only one tenant.

(b) "Claim," except as used in "claim for relief," means a right to payment, whether or not the right is reduced to judgment, liquidated, unliquidated, fixed, contingent, matured, unmatured, disputed, undisputed, legal, equitable, secured, or unsecured.

(c) "Creditor" means a person that has a claim, and includes an assignee of a general assignment for the benefit of creditors, as defined in Section 493.010 of the Code of Civil Procedure, of a debtor.

(d) "Debt" means liability on a claim.

(e) "Debtor" means a person that is liable on a claim.

(f) "Electronic" means relating to technology having electrical, digital, magnetic, wireless, optical, electromagnetic, or similar capabilities.

(g) "Lien" means a charge against or an interest in property to secure payment of a debt or performance of an obligation, and includes a security interest created by agreement, a judicial lien obtained by legal or equitable process or proceedings, a common-law lien, or a statutory lien.

(h) "Organization" means a person other than an individual.

(i) "Person" means an individual, partnership, corporation, limited liability company, association, government or governmental subdivision, instrumentality or agency, business trust, estate, trust, business or nonprofit entity, or other legal entity.

(j) "Property" means anything that may be the subject of ownership.

(k) "Record" means information that is inscribed on a tangible medium or that is stored in an electronic or other medium and is retrievable in perceivable form.

(*l*) "Sign" means, with present intent to authenticate or adopt a record, to either (1) execute or adopt a tangible symbol, or (2) attach to or logically associate with the record an electronic symbol, sound, or process.

(m) "Transfer" means every mode, direct or indirect, absolute or conditional, voluntary or involuntary, of disposing of or parting with an asset or an interest in an asset, and includes payment of money, release, lease, license, and creation of a lien or other encumbrance.

(n) "Valid lien" means a lien that is effective against the holder of a judicial lien subsequently obtained by legal or equitable process or proceedings. **Leg.H.** Added Stats 1986 ch 383 §2. Amended Stats 1994 ch 1010 §55 (SB 2053); Stats 2015 ch 44 §4 (SB 161), effective January 1, 2016.

Prior Law: Former CC §3439.01, similar to the present section, was added Stats 1939 ch 329 §3, and repealed Stats 1986 ch 383 §1.

§3439.02. Insolvency

(a) A debtor is insolvent if, at a fair valuation, the sum of the debtor's debts is greater than the sum of the debtor's assets.

(b) A debtor that is generally not paying the debtor's debts as they become due other than as a result of a bona fide dispute is presumed to be insolvent. The presumption imposes on the party against which the presumption is directed the burden of proving that the nonexistence of insolvency is more probable than its existence.

(c) Assets under this section do not include property that has been transferred, concealed, or removed with intent to hinder, delay, or defraud creditors or that has been transferred in a manner making the transfer voidable under this chapter.

(d) Debts under this section do not include an obligation to the extent it is secured by a valid lien on property of the debtor not included as an asset. **Leg.H.** Added Stats 1986 ch 383 §2. Amended Stats 2015 ch 44 §5 (SB 161), effective January 1, 2016.

Prior Law: Former CC § 3439.02, similar to the present section, was added Stats 1939 ch 329 §4 and repealed Stats 1986 ch 383 §1.

§3439.03. Value for transfer or obligation

Value is given for a transfer or an obligation if, in exchange for the transfer or obligation, property is transferred or an antecedent debt is secured or satisfied, but value does not include an unperformed promise made otherwise than in the ordinary course of the promisor's business to furnish support to the debtor or another person. **Leg.H.** Added Stats 1986 ch 383 §2.

Prior Law: Former CC §3439.03, similar to the present section, was added Stats 1939 ch 329 §5 and repealed Stats 1986 ch 383 §1.

§3439.04. Transfer with intent to defraud or transfer not given in exchange for value: Determining actual intent

(a) A transfer made or obligation incurred by a debtor is voidable as to a creditor, whether the creditor's claim arose before or after the transfer was made or the obligation was incurred, if the debtor made the transfer or incurred the obligation as follows:

(1) With actual intent to hinder, delay, or defraud any creditor of the debtor.

(2) Without receiving a reasonably equivalent value in exchange for the transfer or obligation, and the debtor either:

(A) Was engaged or was about to engage in a business or a transaction for which the remaining assets of the debtor were unreasonably small in relation to the business or transaction.

(B) Intended to incur, or believed or reasonably should have believed that the debtor would incur, debts beyond the debtor's ability to pay as they became due.

(b) In determining actual intent under paragraph (1) of subdivision (a), consideration may be given, among other factors, to any or all of the following:

(1) Whether the transfer or obligation was to an insider.

(2) Whether the debtor retained possession or control of the property transferred after the transfer.

(3) Whether the transfer or obligation was disclosed or concealed.

(4) Whether before the transfer was made or obligation was incurred, the debtor had been sued or threatened with suit.

(5) Whether the transfer was of substantially all the debtor's assets.

(6) Whether the debtor absconded.

(7) Whether the debtor removed or concealed assets.

(8) Whether the value of the consideration received by the debtor was reasonably equivalent to the value of the asset transferred or the amount of the obligation incurred.

(9) Whether the debtor was insolvent or became insolvent shortly after the transfer was made or the obligation was incurred.

(10) Whether the transfer occurred shortly before or shortly after a substantial debt was incurred.

(11) Whether the debtor transferred the essential assets of the business to a lienor that transferred the assets to an insider of the debtor.

(c) A creditor making a claim for relief under subdivision (a) has the burden of proving the elements of the claim for relief by a preponderance of the evidence. **Leg.H.** Added Stats 1986 ch 383 §2. Amended Stats 2004 ch 50 §1 (SB 1408); Stats 2015 ch 44 §6 (SB 161), effective January 1, 2016.

Prior Law: Former CC §3439.04, similar to present CC §3439.05, was added Stats 1939 ch 329 §6 and repealed Stats 1986 ch 383 §1.

§3439.05. Transfer resulting in debtor's insolvency

(a) A transfer made or obligation incurred by a debtor is voidable as to a creditor whose claim arose before the transfer was made or the obligation was incurred if the debtor made the transfer or incurred the obligation without receiving a reasonably equivalent value in exchange for the transfer or obligation and the debtor was insolvent at that time or the debtor became insolvent as a result of the transfer or obligation.

(b) A creditor making a claim for relief under subdivision (a) has the burden of proving the elements of the claim for relief by a preponderance of the evidence. **Leg.H.** Added Stats 1986 ch 383 §2. Amended Stats 2015 ch 44 §7 (SB 161), effective January 1, 2016.

Prior Law: Former CC §3439.05, similar to present CC §3439.04, was added Stats 1939 ch 329 §7 and repealed Stats 1986 ch 383 §1.

§3439.06. When transfer made or obligation incurred

For the purposes of this chapter:

(a) A transfer is made:

(1) With respect to an asset that is real property other than a fixture, but including the interest of a seller or purchaser under a contract for the sale of the asset, when the transfer is so far perfected that a good faith purchaser of the asset from the debtor against which applicable law permits the transfer to be perfected cannot acquire an interest in the asset that is superior to the interest of the transferee; and

(2) With respect to an asset that is not real property or that is a fixture, when the transfer is so far perfected that a creditor on a simple contract cannot acquire a judicial lien otherwise than under this chapter that is superior to the interest of the transferee.

(b) If applicable law permits the transfer to be perfected as provided in subdivision (a) and the transfer is not so perfected before the commencement of an action for relief under this chapter, the transfer is deemed made immediately before the commencement of the action.

(c) If applicable law does not permit the transfer to be perfected as provided in subdivision (a), the transfer is made when it becomes effective between the debtor and the transferee.

(d) A transfer is not made until the debtor has acquired rights in the asset transferred.

(e) An obligation is incurred:

(1) If oral, when it becomes effective between the parties; or

(2) If evidenced by a record, when the record signed by the obligor is delivered to or for the benefit of the obligee. **Leg.H.** Added Stats 1986 ch 383 §2. Amended Stats 2015 ch 44 §8 (SB 161), effective January 1, 2016.

Prior Law: Former CC §3439.06, similar to present CC §3439.04, was added Stats 1939 ch 329 §8 and repealed Stats 1986 ch 383 §1.

§3439.07. Creditor's remedies

(a) In an action for relief against a transfer or obligation under this chapter, a creditor, subject to the limitations in Section 3439.08, may obtain:

(1) Avoidance of the transfer or obligation to the extent necessary to satisfy the creditor's claim.

(2) An attachment or other provisional remedy against the asset transferred or other property of the transferee in accordance with the procedures described in Title 6.5 (commencing with Section 481.010) of Part 2 of the Code of Civil Procedure, or as may otherwise be available under applicable law.

(3) Subject to applicable principles of equity and in accordance with applicable rules of civil procedure, the following:

(A) An injunction against further disposition by the debtor or a transferee, or both, of the asset transferred or other property of the transferee.

(B) Appointment of a receiver to take charge of the asset transferred or other property of the transferee.

(C) Any other relief the circumstances may require.

(b) If a creditor has commenced an action on a claim against the debtor, the creditor may attach the asset transferred or other property of the transferee if the remedy of attachment is available in the action under applicable law and the property is subject to attachment in the hands of the transferee under applicable law.

(c) If a creditor has obtained a judgment on a claim against the debtor, the creditor may levy execution on the asset transferred or its proceeds.

(d) A creditor who is an assignee of a general assignment for the benefit of creditors, as defined in Section 493.010 of the Code of Civil Procedure, may exercise any and all of the rights and remedies specified in this section if they are available to any one or more creditors of the assignor who are beneficiaries of the assignment, and, in that event (1) only to the extent the rights or remedies are so available and (2) only for the benefit of those creditors whose rights are asserted by the assignee. **Leg.H.** Added Stats 1986 ch 383 §2. Amended Stats 2015 ch 44 §9 (SB 161), effective January 1, 2016.

Prior Law: Former CC § 3439.07, similar to present CC §3439.04, was added Stats 1939 ch 329 §9 and repealed Stats 1986 ch 383 §1.

§3439.08. Transfers that are not voidable; Judgment for creditor; Remedies of good faith transferee

(a) A transfer or obligation is not voidable under paragraph (1) of subdivision (a) of Section 3439.04, against a person that took in good faith and for a reasonably equivalent value given the debtor or against any subsequent transferee or obligee.

(b) To the extent a transfer is avoidable in an action by a creditor under paragraph (1) of subdivision (a) of Section 3439.07, the following rules apply:

(1) Except as otherwise provided in this section, the creditor may recover judgment for the value of the asset transferred, as adjusted under subdivision (c), or the amount necessary to satisfy the creditor's claim, whichever is less. The judgment may be entered against the following:

(A) The first transferee of the asset or the person for whose benefit the transfer was made.

(B) An immediate or mediate transferee of the first transferee, other than either of the following:

(i) A good faith transferee that took for value.

(ii) An immediate or mediate good faith transferee of a person described in clause (i).

(2) Recovery pursuant to paragraph (1) of subdivision (a), or subdivision (b), or subdivision (c) of Section 3439.07 of or from the asset transferred or its proceeds, or other property of the transferee, as applicable, by levy or otherwise, is available only against a person described in subparagraph (A) or (B) of paragraph (1).

(c) If the judgment under subdivision (b) is based upon the value of the asset transferred, the judgment shall be for an amount equal to the value of the asset at the time of the transfer, subject to adjustment as the equities may require.

(d) Notwithstanding voidability of a transfer or an obligation under this chapter, a good faith transferee or obligee is entitled, to the extent of the value given the debtor for the transfer or obligation, to the following:

(1) A lien on or a right to retain an interest in the asset transferred.

(2) Enforcement of an obligation incurred.

(3) A reduction in the amount of the liability on the judgment.

(e) A transfer is not voidable under paragraph (2) of subdivision (a) of Section 3439.04 or Section 3439.05 if the transfer results from either of the following:

(1) Termination of a lease upon default by the debtor when the termination is pursuant to the lease and applicable law.

(2) Enforcement of a lien in a noncollusive manner and in compliance with applicable law, including Division 9 (commencing with Section 9101) of the Commercial Code, other than a retention of collateral under Sections 9620 and 9621 of the Commercial Code and other than a voluntary transfer of the collateral by the debtor to the lienor in satisfaction of all or part of the secured obligation.

(f) The following rules determine the burden of proving matters referred to in this section:

(1) A party that seeks to invoke subdivision (a), (d), or (e) has the burden of proving the applicability of that subdivision.

(2) Except as otherwise provided in paragraph (3) or (4), the creditor has the burden of proving each applicable element of subdivision (b) or (c).

(3) The transferee has the burden of proving the applicability to the transferee of subparagraph (B) of paragraph (1) of subdivision (b).

(4) A party that seeks adjustment under subdivision (c) has the burden of proving the adjustment.

(g) The standard of proof required to establish matters referred to in this section is preponderance of the evidence. **Leg.H.** Added Stats 1986 ch 383 §1, effective June 8, 1987. Amended Stats 1999 ch 991 §9 (SB 45), operative July 1, 2001; Stats 2005 ch 34 §1 (AB 248), effective July 7, 2005; Stats 2015 ch 44 §10 (SB 161), effective January 1, 2016.

§3439.09. Time within which action must be brought

A cause of action with respect to a transfer or obligation under this chapter is extinguished unless action is brought pursuant to subdivision (a) of Section 3439.07 or levy made as provided in subdivision (b) or (c) of Section 3439.07:

(a) Under paragraph (1) of subdivision (a) of Section 3439.04, not later than four years after the transfer was made or the obligation was incurred or, if later, not later than one year after the transfer or obligation was or could reasonably have been discovered by the claimant.

(b) Under paragraph (2) of subdivision (a) of Section 3439.04 or Section 3439.05, not later than four years after the transfer was made or the obligation was incurred.

(c) Notwithstanding any other provision of law, a cause of action under this chapter with respect to a transfer or obligation is extinguished if no action is brought or levy made within seven years after the transfer was made or the obligation was incurred. **Leg.H.** Added Stats 1986 ch 383 §2. Amended Stats 2005 ch 34 §2 (AB 248), effective July 7, 2005; Stats 2015 ch 44 §11 (SB 161), effective January 1, 2016.

Prior Law: Former CC §3439.09, similar to present CC §3439.07, was added Stats 1939 ch 329 §11 and repealed Stats 1986 ch 383 §1.

§3439.10. Determination of debtor's location

(a) In this section, the following rules determine a debtor's location:

(1) A debtor who is an individual is located at the individual's principal residence.

(2) A debtor that is an organization and has only one place of business is located at its place of business.

(3) A debtor that is an organization and has more than one place of business is located at its chief executive office.

(b) A claim in the nature of a claim under this chapter is governed by the local law of the jurisdiction in which the debtor is located when the transfer is made or the obligation is incurred. **Leg.H.** Added Stats 2015 ch 44 §13 (SB 161), effective January 1, 2016.

Prior Law: Former CC §3439.10 was added Stats 1986 ch 383 §2 and amended and renumbered CC §3439.12 by Stats 2015 ch 44 §12, effective January 1, 2016.

Former CC § 3439.10, similar to present CC §3439.07, was added Stats 1939 ch 329 §12 and repealed Stats 1986 ch 383 §1.

§3439.11. [Section renumbered 2016]

Leg.H. Added Stats 1986 ch 383 §2. Amended and renumbered to CC §3439.13 by Stats 2015 ch 44 §14 (SB 161), effective January 1, 2016.

Prior Law: Former CC §3439.11, similar to present CC §3439.12, was added Stats 1939 ch 329 §13 and repealed Stats 1986 ch 383 §1.

§3439.12. Principles of law and equity; Applicability

Unless displaced by the provisions of this chapter, the principles of law and equity, including the law merchant and the law relating to principal and agent, estoppel, laches, fraud, misrepresentation, duress, coercion, mistake, insolvency, or other validating or invalidating cause, supplement its provisions. **Leg.H.** Added Stats 1986 ch 383 §2, as CC §3439.10. Amended and renumbered by Stats 2015 ch 44 §12 (SB 161), effective January 1, 2016.

Former Sections Former CC §3439.12 was added Stats 1987 ch 40 §2, effective June 8, 1987, and amended and renumbered CC §3439.14 by Stats 2015 ch 44 §15, effective January 1, 2016.

Former CC §3439.12, similar to present CC §3439.13, was added Stats 1939 ch 329 §14 and repealed Stats 1986 ch 383 §1.

§3439.13. Application and construction of chapter

This chapter shall be applied and construed to effectuate its general purpose to make uniform the law with respect to the subject of this chapter among states enacting it. **Leg.H.** Added Stats 1986 ch 383 §2, as CC §3439.11. Amended and renumbered by Stats 2015 ch 44 §14 (SB 161), effective January 1, 2016.

§3439.14. Applicability and construction of chapter

(a) The changes to this chapter made by the act adding this subdivision apply only to a right of action that accrued, transfer made, or obligation incurred, on or after the effective date of that act.

(b) This chapter, and the other changes in the law made by Chapter 383 of the Statutes of 1986, apply only to transfers made or obligations incurred before the effective date of the act that added subdivision (a) and on or after January 1, 1987. As to transfers made or obligations incurred prior to January 1, 1987, the law in effect at the time the transfer was made or the obligation was incurred shall apply.

(c) Section 3439.06 shall determine the date that a transfer was made or obligation incurred.

(d) The provisions of this chapter, insofar as they are substantially the same as the provisions of this chapter in effect on December 31, 2015, shall be construed as restatements and continuations, and not as new enactments. **Leg.H.** Added Stats 1987 ch 40 §2, effective June 8, 1987, as CC §3439.12. Amended and renumbered by Stats 2015 ch 44 §15 (SB 161), effective January 1, 2016.

CHAPTER 2
CONVEYANCE OF PERSONAL PROPERTY WITHOUT DELIVERY

Transfer without delivery void as to transferor's creditors. §3440.
Application of chapter. §3440.1.
Conditions under which transfer without delivery is not void as against creditor. §3440.2.
Specified transfers void as against buyer in ordinary course of business. §3440.3.
Rights of buyer for value in good faith. §3440.4.
Rights of secured party. §3440.5.
Time within which to bring action or make levy. §3440.6.
Commercial Code provisions. §3440.9.
[Sections renumbered 1985]. §3441–3443.

§3440. Transfer without delivery void as to transferor's creditors

(a) Except as otherwise provided in this chapter, every transfer of personal property made by a person having at the time the possession of the property, and not accompanied by an immediate delivery followed by an actual and continued change of possession of the property, is void as against the transferor's creditors (secured or unsecured) at the time of the transfer and those who become creditors while the transferor remains in possession and the successors in interest of those creditors, and as against buyers from the transferor for value in good faith subsequent to the transfer.

(b) As used in this chapter, "creditor" means a person who has a claim, as defined in Section 3439.01, and includes an assignee of a general assignment for the benefit of creditors, as defined in Section 493.010 of the Code of Civil Procedure, of a debtor. "Creditor" also includes any person to whom the transferor's estate devolves in trust for the benefit of persons other than the transferor. Any such assignee or trustee may exercise any and all the rights and remedies specified in this chapter, if they are available to any one or more creditors of the assignor or transferor who are beneficiaries of the assignment or trust, and, in that event (1) only to the extent the rights or remedies are so available and (2) only for the benefit of those creditors whose rights are asserted by the assignee or trustee. **Leg.H.** Added Stats 1951 ch 1687 §2. Amended Stats 1953 ch 1775 §1; Stats 1959 ch 1794 §1, ch 1795 §2; Stats 1963 ch 819 §22; Stats 1967 ch 799 §1; Stats 1982 ch 517 §89; Stats 1985 ch 1368 §1; Stats 1987 ch 40 §3, effective June 8, 1987.

Prior Law: Former CC §3440, relating to transfers presumed fraudulent, was enacted Stats 1872, amended Stats 1895 ch 42, Stats 1903 ch 100 § 1, Stats 1917 ch 171 § 1, Stats 1923 ch 91 § 1, Stats 1925 ch 389 § 1, Stats 1951 ch 1676 §5, operative January 1, 1952, and repealed Stats 1951 ch 1687 §1.

Former Sections: Former CC §3440 was added in 1872 and repealed Stats 1951 ch 1687.

§3440.1. Application of chapter

This chapter does not apply to any of the following:

(a) Things in action.

(b) Ships or cargoes if either are at sea or in a foreign port.

(c) The sale of accounts, chattel paper, payment intangibles, or promissory notes governed by the Uniform Commercial Code, security interests, and contracts of bottomry or respondentia.

(d) Wines or brandies in the wineries, distilleries, or wine cellars of the makers or owners of the wines or brandies, or other persons having possession, care, and control of the wines or brandies, and the pipes, casks, and tanks in which the wines or brandies are contained, if the transfers are made in writing and executed and acknowledged, and if the transfers are recorded in the book of official records in the office of the county recorder of the county in which the wines, brandies, pipes, casks, and tanks are situated.

(e) A transfer or assignment made for the benefit of creditors generally or by an assignee acting under an assignment for the benefit of creditors generally.

(f) Property exempt from enforcement of a money judgment.

(g) Standing timber.

(h) Subject to the limitations in Section 3440.3, a transfer of personal property if all of the following conditions are satisfied:

(1) Before the date of the intended transfer, the transferor or the transferee files a financing statement, with respect to the property transferred, authorized in an authenticated record by the transferor. The financing statement shall be filed in the office of the Secretary of State in accordance with Chapter 5 (commencing with Section 9501) of Division 9 of the Commercial Code, but may use the terms "transferor" in lieu of "debtor" and "transferee" in lieu of "secured party." The provisions of Chapter 5 (commencing with Section 9501) of Division 9 of the Commercial Code shall apply as appropriate to the financing statement.

(2) The transferor or the transferee publishes a notice of the intended transfer one time in a newspaper of general circulation published in the public notice district in which the personal property is located, if there is one, and if there is none in the public notice district, then in a newspaper of general circulation in the county in which the personal property is located. The publication shall be completed not less than 10 days before the date the transfer occurs. The notice shall contain the name and address of the transferor and transferee and a general statement of the character of the personal property intended to be transferred, and shall indicate the place where the personal property is located and a date on or after which the transfer is to be made.

(i) Personal property not located within this state at the time of the transfer or attachment of the lien if the provisions of this subdivision are not used for the purpose of evading this chapter.

(j) A transfer of property that (1) is subject to a statute or treaty of the United States or a statute of this state that provides for the registration of transfers of title or issuance of certificates of title and (2) is so far perfected under that statute or treaty that a bona fide purchaser cannot acquire an interest in the property transferred that is superior to the interest of the transferee.

(k) A transfer of personal property in connection with a transaction in which the property is immediately thereafter leased by the transferor from the transferee provided the transferee purchased the property for value and in good faith pursuant to subdivision (c) of Section 10308 of the Commercial Code.

(*l*) Water supply property, as defined in Section 849 of the Public Utilities Code.

(m) A transfer of property by any governmental entity.

(n) For the purposes of this section, publication of notice in a public notice district is governed by Chapter 1.1 (commencing with Section 6080) of Division 7 of Title 1 of the Government Code. **Leg.H.** Added Stats 1982 ch 517 §90 as §3441. Amended and renumbered Stats 1985 ch 1368 §6. Amended Stats 1988 ch 1368 §3, operative January 1, 1990; Stats 1994 ch 668 §3 (SB 1405); Stats 1996 ch 854 §3 (AB 1890), effective September 24, 1996; Stats 1999 ch 991 §10 (SB 45), operative July 1, 2001; Stats 2004 ch 46 §3 (SB 772), effective June 7, 2004; Stats 2005 ch 43 §1 (AB 238), effective January 1, 2006; Stats 2012 ch 60 §1 (AB 2667), effective January 1, 2013; Stats 2014 ch 482 §3 (SB 936), effective January 1, 2015; Stats 2016 ch 703 §4 (AB 2881), effective January 1, 2017.

Prior Law: Former CC §3440.1, similar to present UCC §6106.4, was added Stats 1967 ch 737 §1 and repealed Stats 1978 ch 490 §1.

Former CC §3440.1. similar in part to UCC §§6103, 6107, was added Stats 1951 ch 1687 §3, amended Stats 1953 ch 1775 § 2, Stats 1957 ch 453 § 1, Stats 1961 ch 1363 §1, and repealed Stats 1963 ch 819 §23, effective January 1, 1965.

2014 Note: For legislative findings and declarations, see the 2014 Note following CC §955.1.

Former Sections: Former CC §3440.1 was added in 1967 and repealed Stats 1978 ch 490.

Former CC §3440.1 was added in 1951 and repealed Stats 1963 ch 819.

§3440.2. Conditions under which transfer without delivery is not void as against creditor

Subject to Section 3440.3, a transfer of personal property shall not be void under Section 3440 as against a creditor of the transferor or as against a buyer from the transferor, if the creditor's or buyer's claim or right against the transferor arises after the date all of the requirements of subdivision (h) of Section 3440.1 have been met, other than the requirement that filing of the financing statement and publication of the notice referred to therein be completed prior to the transfer. **Leg.H.** Added Stats 1985 ch 1368 §2.

§3440.3. Specified transfers void as against buyer in ordinary course of business

A transfer of personal property, as to which the conditions set forth in subdivision (h) of Section 3440.1, Section 3440.2, or subdivision (b) of Section 3440.5 are satisfied, shall, nevertheless, be void under Section 3440 as against a person who has purchased the personal property from the transferor and who is a "buyer in the ordinary course of business," as defined in paragraph (9) of subdivision (b) of Section 1201 of the Commercial Code. **Leg.H.** Added Stats 1985 ch 1368 §3. Amended Stats 2006 ch 254 §5 (SB 1481), effective January 1, 2007.

§3440.4. Rights of buyer for value in good faith

This chapter does not affect the rights of a buyer for value in good faith who purchases the transferred personal property from the transferee or from a successor in interest of the transferee, provided the transferor is no longer in possession of the personal property at the time of the purchase by that buyer. **Leg.H.** Added Stats 1985 ch 1368 §4.

§3440.5. Rights of secured party

(a) This chapter does not affect the rights of a secured party who, for value and in good faith, acquires a security interest in the transferred personal property from the transferee, or from the transferee's successor in interest, if the transferor is no longer in possession of the personal property at the time the security interest attaches.

(b) Additionally, except as provided in Section 3440.3, this chapter does not affect the rights of a secured party who acquires a security interest from the transferee, or from the transferee's successor in interest, in the personal property, if all of the following conditions are satisfied:

(1) On or before the date the security agreement is executed, the intended debtor or secured party files a financing statement with respect to the property transferred, signed by the intended debtor. The financing statement shall be filed in the office of the Secretary of State in accordance with Chapter 5 (commencing with Section 9501) of Division 9 of the Commercial Code, but shall use the terms "transferor" in lieu of "debtor," "transferee" in lieu of "secured party," and "secured party" in lieu of "assignee of secured party." The provisions of Chapter 5 (commencing with Section 9501) of Division 9 of the Commercial Code shall apply as appropriate to the financing statement. For the purpose of indexing, and in any certification of search, the Secretary of State may refer to any financing statement filed pursuant to this paragraph as a financing statement under the Commercial Code and may describe the transferor as a debtor and the transferee as a secured party.

(2) The intended debtor or secured party publishes a notice of the transfer one time in a newspaper of general circulation published in the public notice district in which the personal property is located, if there is one, and if there is none in the public notice district, then in a newspaper of general circulation in the county in which the personal property is located. The publication shall be completed not less than 10 days before the date of execution by the intended debtor of the intended security agreement. The notice shall contain the names and addresses of the transferor and transferee and of the intended debtor and secured party, a general statement of the character of the personal property transferred and intended to be subject to the security interest, the location of the personal property, and the date on or after which the security agreement is to be executed by the intended debtor.

(c) Compliance with paragraph (1) of subdivision (b) shall not perfect the security interest of the secured party. Perfection of that security interest shall be governed by Division 9 (commencing with Section 9101) of the Commercial Code.

(d) For the purposes of this section, publication of notice in a public notice district is governed by Chapter 1.1 (commencing with Section 6080) of Division 7 of Title 1 of the Government Code. **Leg.H.** Added Stats 1982 ch 517 §91 as CC §3442. Amended and renumbered to CC §3440.5 by Stats 1985 ch 1368 §9. Amended Stats 1999 ch 991 §11 (SB 45), operative July 1, 2001; Stats 2000 ch 1003 §2 (SB 2002), operative July 1, 2001; Stats 2016 ch 703 §5 (AB 2881), effective January 1, 2017.

Former Sections: Former CC §3440.5 was added in 1939 and repealed Stats 1963 ch 819.

Prior Law: Former CC § 3440.5, was added Stats 1982 ch 517 §91 as §3442, amended and renumbered Stats 1985 ch 1368 §9, and repealed, effective July 1, 2001, by its own terms.

Former CC § 3440.5, similar to present UCC §6103(7), was added Stats 1939 ch 1036 §1, amended Stats 1941 ch 1142 § 1, Stats 1951 ch 1687 §4, and repealed Stats 1963 ch 819 §24, effective January 1, 1965.

§3440.6. Time within which to bring action or make levy

No action shall be brought or levy made under this chapter more than one year after the earliest of the following dates:

(a) The date the person bringing the action or making the levy should have discovered the transfer in the exercise of reasonable diligence.

(b) The date the person bringing the action or making the levy obtained actual knowledge of the transfer.

(c) The date the delivery of, and actual and continued change of possession of, the property transferred occurred.

(d) If the financing statement filed pursuant to subdivision (h) of Section 3440.1 has not lapsed, the date the filing and publication requirements of subdivision (h) of Section 3440.1 were met, other than the requirement that the filing of the financing statement and publication of the notice referred to therein be completed prior to the transfer. **Leg.H.** Added Stats 1985 ch 1368 §5.

§3440.9. Commercial Code provisions

Subdivision (2) of Section 2402 and subdivision (a) of Section 10308 of the Commercial Code are not restricted by the provisions of this chapter. **Leg.H.** Added Stats 1982 ch 517 §92 as §3443. Renumbered Stats 1985 ch 1368 §10. Amended Stats 1988 ch 1368 §4, operative January 1, 1990; Stats 1994 ch 668 §4 (SB 1405).

§§3441–3443. [Sections renumbered 1985]

Leg.H. Added Stats 1982 ch 517 §§90–92. Amended and renumbered to CC §§3440.1, 3440.5, 3440.9 by Stats 1985 ch 1368 §§6, 9, 10.

Prior Law: Former CC §3441, relating to judicial ascertainment of creditor's right, was enacted Stats 1872 and repealed Stats 1939 ch 329 §1.

Former CC §3442, relating to determination of question of fraud, was enacted Stats 1872, amended Stats 1895 ch 145 §1, and repealed Stats 1939 ch 329 §1.

CHAPTER 3
UNDERTAKING IN VOIDABLE TRANSFER ACTION

Definitions. §3445.
Effect of undertaking. §3446.
Condition of undertaking. §3447.
Amount of undertaking. §3448.
Effect of service on creditor. §3449.

§3445. Definitions

As used in this chapter:

(a) "Transfer" means "transfer" as defined in Section 3439.01.

(b) "Creditor" means "creditor" as defined in Section 3439.01.

(c) "Transferee" means the person to whom property was transferred or an obligation was incurred, or the successors or assigns of the person. **Leg.H.** Added Stats 1982 ch 517 §93. Amended Stats 1986 ch 383 §4.

§3446. Effect of undertaking

(a) In an action by a creditor for relief against a transfer or obligation under Chapter 1 (commencing with Section 3439) of Title 2 of Part 2 of Division 4 on the ground that the transfer or obligation is voidable as to the creditor, the transferee may give an undertaking as provided in this chapter.

(b) If an undertaking is given as provided in this chapter, the transferee may sell, encumber, transfer, convey, mortgage, pledge, or otherwise dispose of the property or obligation, or a part thereof, and the purchaser, encumbrancer, transferee, mortgagee, grantee, or pledgee of the property or obligation takes, owns, holds, and possesses the property or obligation unaffected by the action and any judgment that is rendered in the action. **Leg.H.** Added Stats 1982 ch 517 §93. Amended Stats 1986 ch 383 §5; Stats 2015 ch 44 §17 (SB 161), effective January 1, 2016.

§3447. Condition of undertaking

The undertaking shall be conditioned that, if it is determined in the action that the transfer or obligation was voidable as to the creditor, the transferee will pay to the creditor the lesser of the following amounts:

(a) The value of the property or obligation as estimated in the undertaking.

(b) The amount determined in the action to be due and owing to the creditor by the person who transferred the property or incurred the obligation. **Leg.H.** Added Stats 1982 ch 517 §93. Amended Stats 1986 ch 383 §6; Stats 2015 ch 44 §18 (SB 161), effective January 1, 2016.

§3448. Amount of undertaking

The undertaking shall be in the lesser of the following amounts:
(a) Double the value of the property or obligation.
(b) Double the amount of the creditor's claim in the action. **Leg.H.** Added Stats 1982 ch 517 §93.

Prior Law: Former CC §3448, relating to effect and construction of Title 3, was added by Stats 1959 ch 1284 §1 p 3435 and repealed by Stats 1980 ch 135 §3.

§3449. Effect of service on creditor

The undertaking becomes effective 10 days after service of the undertaking on the creditor. **Leg.H.** Added Stats 1982 ch 517 §93.

Prior Law: Former CC §3449, relating to execution of assignment by debtor, was enacted Stats 1872, amended Stats 1889 ch 79 §1 p 80, Stats 1895 ch 94 §1 p 82, and repealed Stats 1980 ch 135 §3.

TITLE 3
ASSIGNMENTS FOR THE BENEFIT OF CREDITORS [REPEALED]

§§3450–3473. [Sections repealed 1980]

Leg.H. Enacted Stats 1872. Amended Code Amdts 1873–74 ch 612; Code Amdts 1877–78 ch 93; Stats 1883 ch 4; Stats 1889 ch 79; Stats 1905 ch 466; Stats 1957 ch 815; Stats 1973 ch 665. Repealed Stats 1980 ch 135 §3. The repealed sections related to assignments for the benefit of creditors.

PART 3
NUISANCE

Title 1. General Principles.
Title 2. Public Nuisances.
Title 3. Private Nuisances.
Title 4. Motion Pictures.

TITLE 1
GENERAL PRINCIPLES

What constitutes a nuisance. §3479.
Public nuisance. §3480.
Private nuisance. §3481.
What is not deemed a nuisance. §3482.
Sport shooting ranges; Exemption. §3482.1.
Commercial agricultural activities. §3482.5.
Commercial agricultural processing activities. §3482.6.
Use of property to conduct dogfighting or cockfighting; Public nuisance. §3482.8.
Successive owners. §3483.
Abatement does not preclude action. §3484.
Action for unlawful detainer for controlled substance purpose on real property; Procedures required prior to filing action; Costs and attorney's fees; Possible orders [Operative date contingent]. §3486.

§3479. What constitutes a nuisance

Anything which is injurious to health, including, but not limited to, the illegal sale of controlled substances, or is indecent or offensive to the senses, or an obstruction to the free use of property, so as to interfere with the comfortable enjoyment of life or property, or unlawfully obstructs the free passage or use, in the customary manner, of any navigable lake, or river, bay, stream, canal, or basin, or any public park, square, street, or highway, is a nuisance. **Leg.H.** Enacted Stats 1872. Amended Code Amdts 1873–74 ch 612 §284; Stats 1996 ch 658 §1 (AB 2970).

§3480. Public nuisance

A public nuisance is one which affects at the same time an entire community or neighborhood, or any considerable number of persons, although the extent of the annoyance or damage inflicted upon individuals may be unequal. **Leg.H.** Enacted Stats 1872. Amended Code Amdts 1873–74 ch 612 §285 p 268.

§3481. Private nuisance

Every nuisance not included in the definition of the last section is private. **Leg.H.** Enacted Stats 1872.

§3482. What is not deemed a nuisance

Nothing which is done or maintained under the express authority of a statute can be deemed a nuisance. **Leg.H.** Enacted Stats 1872.

§3482.1. Sport shooting ranges; Exemption

(a) As used in this section:

(1) "Person" means an individual, proprietorship, partnership, corporation, club, or other legal entity.

(2) "Sport shooting range" or "range" means an area designed and operated for the use of rifles, shotguns, pistols, silhouettes, skeet, trap, black powder, or any other similar sport or law enforcement training purpose.

(3) "Indoor shooting range" means a totally enclosed facility designed to offer a totally controlled shooting environment that includes impenetrable walls, floor and ceiling, adequate ventilation and lighting systems, and acoustical treatment for sound attenuation suitable for the range's approved use.

(4) "Nighttime" means between the hours of 10 p.m. and 7 a.m.

(b)(1) Except as provided in subdivision (f), a person who operates or uses a sport shooting range in this state shall not be subject to civil liability or criminal prosecution in any matter relating to noise or noise pollution resulting from the operation or use of the range if the range is in compliance with any noise control laws or ordinances that applied to the range and its operation at the time construction or operation of the range was approved by a local public entity having jurisdiction in the matter, or if there were no such laws or ordinances that applied to the range and its operation at that time.

(2) Except as provided in subdivision (f), a person who operates or uses a sport shooting range or law enforcement training range is not subject to an action for nuisance, and a court shall not enjoin the use or operation of a range, on the basis of noise or noise pollution if the range is in compliance with any noise control laws or ordinances that applied to the range and its operation at the time construction or operation of the range was approved by a local public entity having jurisdiction in the matter, or if there were no such laws or ordinances that applied to the range and its operation at that time.

(3) Rules or regulations adopted by any state department or agency for limiting levels of noise in terms of decibel level which may occur in the outdoor atmosphere shall not apply to a sport shooting range exempted from liability under this section.

(c) A person who acquires title to or who owns real property adversely affected by the use of property with a permanently located and improved sport shooting range may not maintain a nuisance action with respect to noise or noise pollution against the person who owns the range to restrain, enjoin, or impede the use of the range where there has been no substantial change in the nature or use of the range. This section does not prohibit actions for negligence or recklessness in the operation of the range or by a person using the range.

(d) A sport shooting range that is in operation and not in violation of existing law at the time of the enactment of an ordinance described in subdivision (b) shall be permitted to continue in operation even if the operation of the sport shooting range at a later date does not conform to a new ordinance or an amendment to an existing ordinance if there has been no substantial change in the nature or use of the range. Nothing in this section shall be construed to limit the authority of a local agency to enforce any term of a conditional use permit.

(e) Except as otherwise provided in this section, this section does not prohibit a local public entity having jurisdiction in the matter from regulating the location and construction of a sport shooting range after the effective date of this section.

(f) This section does not prohibit a local public entity having jurisdiction in the matter from requiring that noise levels at the nearest residential property line to a range not exceed the level of normal city street noise which shall not be more than 60 decibels for nighttime shooting. The subdivision does not abrogate any existing local standards for nighttime shooting. The operator of a sport shooting range shall not unreasonably refuse to use trees, shrubs, or barriers, when appropriate, to mitigate the noise generated by nighttime shooting. For the purpose of this section, a reasonable effort to mitigate is an action that can be accomplished in a manner and at a cost that does not impose an unreasonable financial burden upon the operator of the range.

(g) This section does not apply to indoor shooting ranges.

(h) This section does not apply to a range in existence prior to January 1, 1998, that is operated for law enforcement training purposes by a county of the sixth class if the range is located without the boundaries of that county and within the boundaries of another county. This subdivision shall become operative on July 1, 1999. **Leg.H.** Added Stats 1997 ch 880 §1 (SB 517). Amended Stats 1998 ch 141 §1 (SB 1620), effective July 13, 1998.

§3482.5. Commercial agricultural activities

(a)(1) No agricultural activity, operation, or facility, or appurtenances thereof, conducted or maintained for commercial purposes, and in a manner consistent with proper and accepted customs and standards, as established and followed by similar agricultural operations in the same locality, shall be or become a nuisance, private or public, due to any changed condition in or about the locality, after it has been in operation for more than three years if it was not a nuisance at the time it began.

(2) No activity of a district agricultural association that is operated in compliance with Division 3 (commencing with Section 3001) of the Food and Agricultural Code, shall be or become a private or public nuisance due to any changed condition in or about the locality, after it has been in operation for more than three years if it was not a nuisance at the time it began. This paragraph shall not apply to any activities of the 52nd District Agricultural Association that are conducted on the grounds of the California Exposition and State Fair, nor to any public nuisance action brought by a city, county, or city and county alleging that the activities,

operations, or conditions of a district agricultural association have substantially changed after more than three years from the time that the activities, operations, or conditions began.

(b) Paragraph (1) of subdivision (a) shall not apply if the agricultural activity, operation, or facility, or appurtenances thereof obstruct the free passage or use, in the customary manner, of any navigable lake, river, bay, stream, canal, or basin, or any public park, square, street, or highway.

(c) Paragraph (1) of subdivision (a) shall not invalidate any provision contained in the Health and Safety Code, Fish and Game Code, Food and Agricultural Code, or Division 7 (commencing with Section 13000) of the Water Code, if the agricultural activity, operation, or facility, or appurtenances thereof constitute a nuisance, public or private, as specifically defined or described in any of those provisions.

(d) This section shall prevail over any contrary provision of any ordinance or regulation of any city, county, city and county, or other political subdivision of the state. However, nothing in this section shall preclude a city, county, city and county, or other political subdivision of this state, acting within its constitutional or statutory authority and not in conflict with other provisions of state law, from adopting an ordinance that allows notification to a prospective homeowner that the dwelling is in close proximity to an agricultural activity, operation, facility, or appurtenances thereof and is subject to the provisions of this section consistent with Section 1102.6a.

(e) For purposes of this section, the term "agricultural activity, operation, or facility, or appurtenances thereof" shall include, but not be limited to, the cultivation and tillage of the soil, dairying, the production, cultivation, growing, and harvesting of any agricultural commodity including timber, viticulture, apiculture, or horticulture, the raising of livestock, fur bearing animals, fish, or poultry, and any practices performed by a farmer or on a farm as incident to or in conjunction with those farming operations, including preparation for market, delivery to storage or to market, or delivery to carriers for transportation to market. **Leg.H.** Added Stats 1981 ch 545 §1. Amended Stats 1991 ch 828 §1 (SB 1093); Stats 1992 ch 97 §1 (AB 1190).

§3482.6. Commercial agricultural processing activities

(a) No agricultural processing activity, operation, facility, or appurtenances thereof, conducted or maintained for commercial purposes, and in a manner consistent with proper and accepted customs and standards, shall be or become a nuisance, private or public, due to any changed condition in or about the locality, after it has been in continuous operation for more than three years if it was not a nuisance at the time it began.

(b) If an agricultural processing activity, operation, facility, or appurtenances thereof substantially increases its activities or operations after January 1, 1993, then a public or private nuisance action may be brought with respect to those increases in activities or operations that have a significant effect on the environment. For increases in activities or operations that have been in effect more than three years, there is a rebuttable presumption affecting the burden of producing evidence that the increase was not substantial.

(c) This section does not supersede any other provision of law, except other provisions of this part, if the agricultural processing activity, operation, facility, or appurtenances thereof, constitute a nuisance, public or private, as specifically defined or described in the provision.

(d) This section prevails over any contrary provision of any ordinance or regulation of any city, county, city and county, or other political subdivision of the state, except regulations adopted pursuant to Section 41700 of the Health and Safety Code as applied to agricultural processing activities, operations, facilities, or appurtenances thereof that are surrounded by housing or commercial development on January 1, 1993. However, nothing in this section precludes a city, county, city and county, or other political subdivision of this state, acting within its constitutional or statutory authority and not in conflict with other provisions of state law, from adopting an ordinance that allows notification to a prospective homeowner that the dwelling is in close proximity to an agricultural processing activity, operation, facility, or appurtenances thereof and is subject to provisions of this section consistent with Section 1102.6a.

(e) For the purposes of this section, the following definitions apply:

(1) "Agricultural processing activity, operation, facility, or appurtenances thereof" includes, but is not limited to rendering plants licensed pursuant to Section 19300 of the Food and Agricultural Code and collection centers licensed pursuant to Section 19300.5 of the Food and Agricultural Code, the canning or freezing of agricultural products, the processing of dairy products, the production and bottling of beer and wine, the processing of meat and egg products, the drying of fruits and grains, the packing and cooling of fruits and vegetables, and the storage or warehousing of any agricultural products, and includes processing for wholesale or retail markets of agricultural products.

(2) "Continuous operation" means at least 30 days of agricultural processing operations per year.

(3) "Proper and accepted customs and standards" means the compliance with all applicable state and federal statutes and regulations governing the operation of the agricultural processing activity, operation, facility, or appurtenances thereof with respect to the condition or effect alleged to be a nuisance.

(f) This section does not apply to any litigation pending or cause of action accruing prior to January 1, 1993. **Leg.H.** Added Stats 1992 ch 97 §2 (AB 1190). Amended Stats 1993 ch 99 §1 (AB 258); Stats 1994 ch 146 §17 (AB 3601); Stats 1999 ch 329 §1 (SB 1274).

Prior Law: Former CC §3482.6, relating to actions against airports, was added Stats 1982 ch 1027 §1.5 and repealed January 1, 1985, by its own terms.

Former Sections: Former CC §3482.6, relating to actions against airports, was added Stats 1982 ch 1027 §1.5 and repealed operative January 1, 1985, by its own provisions. Stats 1982 ch 1027.

§3482.7. [Section repealed 1985]

Leg.H. Added Stats 1982 ch 1027 §1.6. Repealed January 1, 1985, by its own provisions. The repealed section related to airport as nuisance.

§3482.8. Use of property to conduct dogfighting or cockfighting; Public nuisance

Any building or property used for the purpose of willfully conducting dogfighting in violation of Section 597.5 of the Penal Code or cockfighting in violation of subdivision (b) of Section 597b of the Penal Code is a public nuisance. **Leg.H.** Added Stats 2011 ch 128 §1 (SB 426), effective January 1, 2012.

§3483. Successive owners

Every successive owner of property who neglects to abate a continuing nuisance upon, or in the use of, such property, created by the former owner, is liable therefor in the same manner as the one who first created it. **Leg.H.** Enacted Stats 1872.

§3484. Abatement does not preclude action

The abatement of a nuisance does not prejudice the right of any person to recover damages for its past existence. **Leg.H.** Enacted Stats 1872.

§3485. Illegal conduct involving an unlawful weapons or ammunition on real property; Procedures required prior to filing action to abate; Applicability; Report [Repealed]

Leg.H. Added Stats 2014 ch 339 §1 (AB 2310), effective September 15, 2014, repealed January 1, 2019. Amended Stats 2018 ch 880 §1 (AB 2930), effective January 1, 2019, repealed January 1, 2024.

Prior Law: Former CC §3485, similar to the present section, was added Stats 2007 ch 456 §1, amended Stats 2009 ch 244 §1, Stats 2010 ch 178 §19, and repealed January 1, 2014, by its own terms.

§3486. Action for unlawful detainer for controlled substance purpose on real property; Procedures required prior to filing action; Costs and attorney's fees; Possible orders [Operative date contingent]

(a) To abate the nuisance caused by illegal conduct involving a controlled substance purpose on real property, the city prosecutor or city attorney may file, in the name of the people, an action for unlawful detainer against any person who is in violation of the nuisance or illegal purpose provisions of subdivision 4 of Section 1161 of the Code of Civil Procedure, with respect to that controlled substance purpose. In filing this action, which shall be based upon an arrest report by a law enforcement agency, reporting an offense committed on the property and documented by the observations of a police officer, the city prosecutor or city attorney shall use the procedures set forth in Chapter 4 (commencing with Section 1159) of Title 3 of Part 3 of the Code of Civil Procedure, except that in cases filed under this section, the following also shall apply:

(1)(A) Prior to filing an action pursuant to this section, the city prosecutor or city attorney shall give 30 calendar days' written notice to the owner, requiring the owner to file an action for the removal of the person who is in violation of the nuisance or illegal purpose provisions of subdivision 4 of Section 1161 of the Code of Civil Procedure with respect to a controlled substance purpose.

(B) This notice shall include sufficient documentation establishing a violation of the nuisance or illegal purpose provisions of subdivision 4 of Section 1161 of the Code of Civil Procedure and an advisement to the owner of the assignment provision contained in subparagraph (D). The notice shall be served upon the owner and the tenant in accordance with subdivision (e).

(C) The notice to the tenant shall, in at least 14-point bold type, meet the following requirements:

(i) The notice shall contain the following language:

"(Date)

(Name of tenant)
(Address of tenant)

Re: Civil Code Section 3486

Dear (name of tenant):

This letter is to inform you that an eviction action may soon be filed in court against you for suspected drug activity. According to state law, Civil Code Section 3486 provides for eviction of persons engaging in such conduct, as described below.

(Name of police department) records indicate that you, (name of arrestee), were arrested on (date) for violations of (list violations) on (address of property).

A letter has been sent to the property owner(s) advising of your arrest and the requirements of state law, as well as the landlord's option to assign the unlawful detainer action to the (name of city attorney or prosecutor's office).

A list of legal assistance providers is provided below. Please note, this list is not exclusive and is provided for your information only; the (name of city attorney or prosecutor's office) does not endorse or recommend any of the listed agencies.

Sincerely,

(Name of deputy city attorney or city prosecutor)
Deputy City (Attorney or Prosecutor)

Notice to Tenant: This notice is not a notice of eviction. You should call (name of the city attorney or prosecutor pursuing the action) at (telephone number) or a legal assistance provider to stop the eviction action if any of the following is applicable:

(1) You are not the person named in this notice.
(2) The person named in the notice does not live with you.
(3) The person named in the notice has permanently moved.
(4) You do not know the person named in the notice.
(5) You want to request that only the person involved in the nuisance be evicted, allowing the other residents to stay.
(6) You have any other legal defense or legal reason to stop the eviction action.

A list of legal assistance providers is attached to this notice. Some provide free legal assistance if you are eligible."

(ii) The notice shall be provided to the tenant in English and, as translated, in all of the languages identified in subdivision (a) of Section 1632 of the Civil Code.

(D) The owner shall, within 30 calendar days of the mailing of the written notice, either provide the city prosecutor or city attorney with all relevant information pertaining to the unlawful detainer case, or provide a written explanation setting forth any safety-related reasons for noncompliance, and an assignment to the city prosecutor or city attorney of the right to bring an unlawful detainer action against the tenant.

(E) The assignment shall be on a form provided by the city prosecutor or city attorney and may contain a provision for costs of investigation, discovery, and reasonable attorney's fees, in an amount not to exceed six hundred dollars ($600). An owner shall only be required to pay the costs or fees upon acceptance of the assignment and the filing of the action for unlawful detainer by the city prosecutor or city attorney.

(F) If the city prosecutor or city attorney accepts the assignment of the right of the owner to bring the unlawful detainer action, the owner shall retain all other rights and duties, including the handling of the tenant's personal property, following issuance of the writ of possession and its delivery to and execution by the appropriate agency.

(2) Upon the failure of the owner to file an action pursuant to this section, or to respond to the city prosecutor or city attorney as provided in paragraph (1), or having filed an action, if the owner fails to prosecute it diligently and in good faith, the city prosecutor or city attorney may file and prosecute the action, and join the owner as a defendant in the action. This action shall have precedence over any similar proceeding thereafter brought by the owner, or to one previously brought by the owner and not prosecuted diligently and in good faith. Service of the summons and complaint upon the defendant owner shall be in accordance with Sections 415.10, 415.20, 415.30, 415.40, and 415.50 of the Code of Civil Procedure.

(3) If a jury or court finds the defendant tenant guilty of unlawful detainer in a case filed pursuant to paragraph (2), the city prosecutor or city attorney may be awarded costs, including the costs of investigation and discovery and reasonable attorney's fees. These costs shall be assessed against the defendant owner, to whom notice was directed pursuant to paragraph (1), and once an abstract of judgment is recorded, it shall constitute a lien on the subject real property.

(4) This section does not prevent a local governing body from adopting and enforcing laws, consistent with this article, relating to drug abatement. If local laws duplicate or supplement this section, this section shall be construed as providing alternative remedies and not preempting the field.

(5) This section does not prevent a tenant from receiving relief against a forfeiture of a lease pursuant to Section 1179 of the Code of Civil Procedure.

(b) In any proceeding brought under this section, the court may, upon a showing of good cause, issue a partial eviction ordering the removal of any person, including, but not limited to, members of the tenant's household if the court finds that the person has engaged in the activities described in subdivision (a). Persons removed pursuant to this section may be permanently barred from returning to or reentering any portion of the entire premises. The court may further order as an express condition of the tenancy that the remaining tenants shall not give permission to or invite any person who has been removed pursuant to this subdivision to return to or reenter any portion of the entire premises.

(c) For the purposes of this section, "controlled substance purpose" means the manufacture, cultivation, importation into the state, transportation, possession, possession for sale, sale, furnishing, administering, or giving away, or providing a place to use or fortification of a place involving, cocaine, phencyclidine, heroin, methamphetamine, or any other controlled substance, in a violation of subdivision (a) of Section 11350, Section 11351, 11351.5, 11352, or 11359, subdivision (a) of Section 11360, or Section 11366, 11366.6, 11377, 11378, 11378.5, 11379, 11379.5, 11379.6, or 11383 of the Health and Safety Code.

(d) Notwithstanding subdivision (b) of Section 68097.2 of the Government Code, a public entity may waive all or part of the costs incurred in furnishing the testimony of a peace officer in an unlawful detainer action brought pursuant to this section.

(e) The notice and documentation described in paragraph (1) of subdivision (a) shall be given in writing and may be given either by personal delivery or by deposit in the United States mail in a sealed envelope, postage prepaid, addressed to the owner at the address known to the public entity giving the notice, or as shown on the last equalized assessment roll, if not known. Separate notice of not less than 30 calendar days and documentation shall be provided to the tenant in accordance with this subdivision. Service by mail shall be deemed to be completed at the time of deposit in the United States mail. Proof of giving the notice may be made by a declaration signed under penalty of perjury by any employee of the public entity which shows service in conformity with this section.

(f) In an unlawful detainer action filed pursuant to this section, the court shall make one of the following orders:

(1) If the grounds for an eviction have not been established pursuant to this section, the court shall dismiss, without prejudice, the unlawful detainer action.

(2) If the grounds for an eviction have been established pursuant to this section, the court shall do either of the following:

(A) Order that the tenant and all occupants be immediately evicted from the property.

(B) Dismiss the unlawful detainer action with or without prejudice or stay execution of an eviction order for a reasonable length of time if the tenant establishes by clear and convincing evidence that the immediate eviction would pose an extreme hardship to the tenant and that this hardship outweighs the health, safety, or welfare of the neighbors or surrounding community. However, the court shall not find an extreme hardship solely on the basis of an economic hardship or the financial inability of the tenant to pay for and secure other housing or lodging accommodations.

(3) If the grounds for a partial eviction have been established pursuant to subdivision (b), the court shall order that those persons be immediately removed and barred from the property, but the court shall not order the tenancy be terminated.

(g) This section applies only in the County of Los Angeles to a court having jurisdiction over unlawful detainer cases involving real property situated in the City of Los Angeles.

(h) This section shall become operative on January 1, 2014, only if the City of Los Angeles has regularly reported to the California Research Bureau as required by this section as it read during the period from January 1, 2010, to January 1, 2014, inclusive. For purposes of this section, the City of Los Angeles shall be deemed to have complied with this reporting requirement if the 2013 report to the Legislature by the California Research Bureau indicates that the City of Los Angeles has regularly reported to the bureau. **Leg.H.** Added Stats 2009 ch 244 §3 (AB 530), effective January 1, 2010, operative date contingent. Amended Stats 2014 ch 341 §1 (AB 2485), effective September 15, 2014; Stats 2015 ch 303 §33 (AB 731), effective January 1, 2016.

Prior Law: Former CC §3486, similar to the present section, was added Stats 2009 ch 244 §2 and repealed January 1, 2014, by its own terms.

Former Sections: Former CC §3486, similar to the present section, was added Stats 2009 ch 244 §2 and repealed operative January 1, 2014, by its own terms.

§3486.5. Pilot program for unlawful detainer actions for controlled substance purpose on real property in County of Sacramento and City of Oakland; Provision of information to California Research Bureau [Repealed]

Leg.H. Added Stats 2014 ch 341 §2 (AB 2485), effective September 15, 2014, repealed January 1, 2019. Amended Stats 2018 ch 880 §2 (AB 2930), effective January 1, 2019, repealed January 1, 2024.

TITLE 2
PUBLIC NUISANCES

Effect of lapse of time. §3490.
Remedies. §3491.
Pleading procedure. §3492.
Private actions. §3493.
Publications. §3494.
Participation in lead paint abatement program; Liability. §3494.5.
Abatement procedure. §3495.
Award of costs and fees to prevailing party. §3496.

§3490. Effect of lapse of time

No lapse of time can legalize a public nuisance, amounting to an actual obstruction of public right. **Leg.H.** Enacted Stats 1872.

§3491. Remedies

The remedies against a public nuisance are:
1. Indictment or information;
2. A civil action; or,
3. Abatement. **Leg.H.** Enacted Stats 1872. Amended Code Amdts 1880 ch 11 §1 p 1.

§3492. Pleading procedure

The remedy by indictment or information is regulated by the Penal Code. **Leg.H.** Enacted Stats 1872. Amended Code Amdts 1880 ch 11 §2 p 1.

§3493. Private actions

A private person may maintain an action for a public nuisance, if it is specially injurious to himself, but not otherwise. **Leg.H.** Enacted Stats 1872.

§3494. Publications

A public nuisance may be abated by any public body or officer authorized thereto by law. **Leg.H.** Enacted Stats 1872.

§3494.5. Participation in lead paint abatement program; Liability

(a)(1) A property owner who voluntarily participates in a lead paint abatement program, and all public entities, shall be immune from liability in any lawsuit where a responsible party seeks to recover any cost associated with a lead paint abatement program from a property owner or public entity.

(2) For purposes of this subdivision, participation in a lead paint abatement program may be as limited as submission of an application to a lead paint abatement program or as extensive as completion of all activities conducted pursuant to a lead paint abatement program.

(b)(1) A property owner's participation in a lead paint abatement program shall not be evidence that the participating property is any of the following:

(A) A nuisance.

(B) Substandard under Section 17920.3 of the Health and Safety Code or is in violation of Section 17920.10 of the Health and Safety Code, to the extent that those sections apply to lead-based paint or other substandard conditions controlled utilizing program funds.

(C) Untenantable under Section 1941.1 of the Civil Code, as that section applies to lead-based paint or other conditions controlled utilizing program funds.

(2) For the purposes of this subdivision, "participation in a lead paint abatement program" means that a property has been voluntarily enrolled in a lead paint abatement program, qualifies for inspection and services, is deemed to contain actionable lead-based paint, and has been satisfactorily abated, is in the process of being satisfactorily abated, or is awaiting abatement under the lead paint abatement program.

(c) For the purposes of this section:

(1) "Lead paint abatement program" means a program that satisfies both of the following:

(A) The program is created to abate lead-based paint.

(B) The program is created as a result of a judgment or settlement in any public nuisance or similar litigation.

(2) "Property owner" means the property owner as well as all agents or employees thereof acting within the course and scope of their agency or employment.

(3) "Public entities" includes the state, the Regents of the University of California, the Trustees of the California State University, a county, city, district, public authority, public agency, and any other political subdivision or public corporation in the state, including any employees or agents thereof acting within the course and scope of their employment or agency.

(4) "Responsible party" means a private party legally responsible for the inspection costs, abatement costs, or any other costs associated with a lead paint abatement program.

(d) This section shall not alter existing obligations on homeowners to maintain their property under applicable law or otherwise limit a tenant's legal remedies for addressing the presence of lead paint on a dwelling. **Leg.H.** Added Stats 2019 ch 171 §1 (AB 206), effective January 1, 2020.

§3495. Abatement procedure

Any person may abate a public nuisance which is specially injurious to him by removing, or, if necessary, destroying the thing which constitutes the same, without committing a breach of the peace, or doing unnecessary injury. **Leg.H.** Enacted Stats 1872.

§3496. Award of costs and fees to prevailing party

In any of the following described cases, the court may award costs, including the costs of investigation and discovery, and reasonable attorney's fees, which are not compensated for pursuant to some other provision of law, to the prevailing party:

(a) In any case in which a governmental agency seeks to enjoin the sale, distribution, or public exhibition, for commercial consideration, of obscene matter, as defined in Section 311 of the Penal Code.

(b) In any case in which a governmental agency seeks to enjoin the use of a building or place for the purpose of illegal gambling, lewdness, assignation, human trafficking, or prostitution; or any case in which a governmental agency seeks to enjoin acts of illegal gambling, lewdness, assignation, human trafficking, or prostitution in or upon a building or place, as authorized in Article 2 (commencing with Section 11225) of Chapter 3 of Title 1 of Part 4 of the Penal Code.

(c) In any case in which a governmental agency seeks to enjoin the use of a building or place, or seeks to enjoin in or upon any building or place the unlawful sale, manufacture, service, storage, or keeping or giving away of any controlled substance, as authorized in Article 3 (commencing with Section 11570) of Chapter 10 of Division 10 of the Health and Safety Code.

(d) In any case in which a governmental agency seeks to enjoin the unlawful sale, service, storage, or keeping or giving away of alcoholic liquor, as authorized in Article 1 (commencing with Section 11200) of Chapter 3 of Title 1 of Part 4 of the Penal Code. **Leg.H.** Added Stats 1982 ch 1267 §1. Amended Stats 1983 ch 1178 §1; Stats 1987 ch 1076 §1; Stats 2012 ch 254 §1 (AB 2212), effective January 1, 2013.

TITLE 3
PRIVATE NUISANCES

Remedies. §3501.
Abatement. §3502.
Notice. §3503.

§3501. Remedies

The remedies against a private nuisance are:
1. A civil action; or,
2. Abatement. **Leg.H.** Enacted Stats 1872.

§3502. Abatement

A person injured by a private nuisance may abate it by removing, or, if necessary, destroying the thing which constitutes the nuisance, without committing a breach of the peace, or doing unnecessary injury. **Leg.H.** Enacted Stats 1872.

§3503. Notice

Where a private nuisance results from a mere omission of the wrong-doer, and cannot be abated without entering upon his land, reasonable notice must be given to him before entering to abate it. **Leg.H.** Enacted Stats 1872.

TITLE 4
MOTION PICTURES

Definitions. §3504.
Exhibition of intentional killing. §3505.
Actions. §3506.
Trial; Injunction; Appeal. §3507.
Evidence and proof of nuisance. §3507.1.
Precedence of actions. §3507.2.
Penalty for violation of injunction. §3507.3.
Parties liable. §3507.4.
Exceptions. §3508.
Willful misstatement by producer. §3508.1.
Severability of provisions. §3508.2.

§3504. Definitions

As used in this title:

(a) "Animal" means any amphibian, bird, mammal or reptile. It does not include any fish or insect.

(b) "Motion picture" means any motion picture, regardless of length or content, which is exhibited in a motion picture theater to paying customers, or is exhibited on television to paying customers or under the sponsorship of a paying advertiser. It shall not include motion pictures made for scientific, research, or educational purposes, or motion pictures exhibited as home movies, or amateur films, which are shown free or at cost to friends, neighbors or civic groups.

(c) "Person" means individuals, corporations, associations, partnerships, limited liability companies, trustees, lessees, agents and assignees. **Leg.H.** Added Stats 1978 ch 1152 §1. Amended Stats 1994 ch 1010 §56 (SB 2053).

§3505. Exhibition of intentional killing

(a) The exhibition of any motion picture, if any intentional killing of, or cruelty to, a human being or an animal is shown in the motion picture and such intentional killing of, or cruelty to, a human being or an animal actually occurred in the production of the motion picture for the purpose of such production, is a nuisance, which shall be enjoined, abated, and prevented.

(b) As used in this section, "killing" and "cruelty" mean conduct which both (1) results in the death or the infliction of any physical injury or wound, including, but not limited to, any temporary or permanent physical harm resulting from the administration of any drug or chemical, and (2) is patently offensive to the average person, applying contemporary statewide community standards. It does not include conduct committed against a human being to which the human being has given his or her consent. In determining whether conduct is patently offensive, the trier of fact may consider any or all of the following: (i) the degree or extent of the physical injury inflicted, (ii) the manner in which the injury is inflicted, (iii) the extent to which the injuring or wounding or acts resulting therein are depicted on the screen, (iv) the number of instances of infliction of injury, wound or harm occurring in the making of the motion picture, and (v) whether such conduct is lawful or unlawful under any provision of law other than this title.

(c) For the purposes of this section, it shall not be a requirement that the entire motion picture and all of the conduct resulting therein be taken into account in determining whether a nuisance exists, and to this end, the Legislature finds and declares that any specific conduct which intentionally results in the killing of, or cruelty to, an animal or a human being in the making of a motion picture is unnecessary and is a nuisance, and that if a motion picture cannot be completed in the absence of such conduct, it is, therefore, a nuisance in its entirety. **Leg.H.** Added Stats 1978 ch 1152 §1.

§3506. Actions

Whenever there is reasonable cause to believe that a nuisance as defined in this title is kept, maintained or is in existence in any county, the district attorney or the Attorney General, in the name of the people of the State of California, shall, on a proper showing, commence an action in equity to abate and prevent the nuisance and to perpetually enjoin the person conducting or maintaining it, and the owner, lessee or agent of the building, or place, in or upon which the nuisance exists, from maintaining or permitting it. As used herein, a proper showing to commence an action under this title must be based upon evidence independent of the motion picture itself that intentional killing of, or cruelty to, a human being or an animal actually occurred in the production of the motion picture for the purpose of such production. **Leg.H.** Added Stats 1978 ch 1152 §1.

§3507. Trial; Injunction; Appeal

Whenever an action is initiated under this title to abate an alleged nuisance, an adversary trial on the merits shall be held pursuant to Section 3507.2. If the court finds that the exhibition of the particular motion picture constitutes a nuisance, it shall issue a permanent injunction to abate and prevent the continuance or recurrence of such nuisance. No temporary restraining order or preliminary injunction shall be granted in such an action. An appeal may be taken from an order issuing a permanent injunction, and any injunction issued pursuant to this title by the trial court may be stayed by such court pending the outcome of such appeal. No appeal may be taken from a ruling by the trial court denying an injunction requested under this title. **Leg.H.** Added Stats 1978 ch 1152 §1.

§3507.1. Evidence and proof of nuisance

In actions brought under this title, the motion picture shall be admissible into evidence. The burden of proof that the exhibition of the particular motion picture constitutes a nuisance shall be met by the district attorney or Attorney General only when clear and convincing evidence, independent of the motion picture itself, is provided that the acts alleged actually occurred in the production of the motion picture. **Leg.H.** Added Stats 1978 ch 1152 §1.

§3507.2. Precedence of actions

Actions brought under this title shall be brought as promptly as possible. Such actions shall have precedence over all actions, excepting criminal proceedings and election contests. It is also the intent of the Legislature that actions commenced under this title be adjudicated in the most speedy and expeditious manner. **Leg.H.** Added Stats 1978 ch 1152 §1.

§3507.3. Penalty for violation of injunction

Any violation or disobedience of an injunction or order expressly provided for by this title is punishable as a contempt of court by a fine of not less than two hundred dollars ($200) nor more than one thousand dollars ($1,000). **Leg.H.** Added Stats 1978 ch 1152 §1.

§3507.4. Parties liable

The distributor who furnished a motion picture to a person who is made a defendant in an action under this title, and the producer of a motion picture which is the subject of this title shall be jointly and severally liable, upon proof and after an opportunity to appear and interpose any appropriate defenses, to such person and the exhibitor for damages, including loss of profits, attorney's fees, and other costs of defending such action. Such distributor and such producer shall actively assist in such defense to the extent that such person possesses information necessary to such defense concerning the production of the motion picture which is not otherwise available to the defendant. The exhibitor shall not be liable upon any portion of any contract made on or after January 1, 1979, which requires the exhibition or advertisement of a motion picture subject to this title on or after the date of the filing of any action under this title, if the motion picture by final decision of a court is determined to be a nuisance under this title. **Leg.H.** Added Stats 1978 ch 1152 §1.

§3508. Exceptions

(a) This title shall not apply to any of the following:

(1) The exhibition of any motion picture, such as a newsreel or documentary, involving acts of killing or cruelty which were not intentionally committed for the purpose of producing the motion picture.

(2) Any motion picture made, in whole or in part, prior to January 1, 1979.

(3) Any motion picture all or part of which has been edited or remade so that any previous conduct which constituted a nuisance under this title no longer appears.

(4) The taking of any animal as permitted by any provision of the Fish and Game Code or pursuant thereto in accordance with regulations adopted by the Fish and Game Commission unless the time, place, or manner of such taking violates any provision of law except this title. This title shall apply to any other animal whether or not the time, place, or manner of the taking is prohibited by any laws other than this title; however, this title shall not apply to the taking of any animal authorized by law in any other jurisdiction unless the time, place or manner of such taking is prohibited by law or regulation.

(5) A motion picture which includes scenes of killing or cruelty to animals if the acts constituting the killing or cruelty were authorized by the laws governing such acts in the jurisdiction where the scenes were filmed.

(6) Any motion picture which bears within its contents a statement from the producer of the motion picture that all scenes depicting animals were filmed without the intentional killing of, or cruelty to an animal or that any killing or cruelty to an animal was authorized by the laws of the jurisdiction where the scenes were filmed or that the film is otherwise exempt under this title.

(7) Any motion picture if the exhibitor thereof has a written signed statement, or a copy thereof, from the producer of the motion picture that all scenes depicting animals were filmed without the intentional killing of, or cruelty to an animal or that any killing or cruelty to an animal was authorized by the laws of the jurisdiction where the scenes were filmed or that the film is otherwise exempt under this title.

(b) This title shall not apply in any case in which it would conflict with federal supremacy in the field of television broadcasting. **Leg.H.** Added Stats 1978 ch 1152 §1.

§3508.1. Willful misstatement by producer

Any producer who willfully misstates or causes to be misstated any fact contained in a statement under paragraph (6) or (7) of Section 3508 is guilty of a misdemeanor. **Leg.H.** Added Stats 1978 ch 1152 §1.

§3508.2. Severability of provisions

If any provision of this title or the application thereof to any person or circumstances is held invalid, such invalidity shall not affect other provisions or applications of this title which can be given effect without the invalid provision or application, and to this end the provisions of this title are severable. **Leg.H.** Added Stats 1978 ch 1152 §1.

PART 4
MAXIMS OF JURISPRUDENCE

Purpose of maxims. §3509.
Cessation of rule. §3510.
Equal application of rule. §3511.
Change of purpose. §3512.
Waiver of legal right. §3513.
Restriction on use of rights. §3514.
Consent as defense. §3515.
Acquiescence in error. §3516.
Clean hands. §3517.
Fraudulent dispossession. §3518.
Failure to forbid act. §3519.
Responsibility for third-party act. §3520.
Benefit and burden. §3521.
Scope of express grant. §3522.
Remedies. §3523.
Parties equally in right or in wrong. §3524.
Earlier right as preferred. §3525.
Responsibility in absence of control. §3526.
Laches. §3527.
Substance over form. §3528.
Acts regarded as having been done. §3529.
Presumption as to nonexistence of fact. §3530.
Impossibilities. §3531.
Idle acts. §3532.
Trifles. §3533.
Qualification of expression. §3534.
Contemporaneous exposition. §3535.
Greater as containing the lesser. §3536.
Superfluity. §3537.
Certainty. §3538.
Effect of time on void acts. §3539.
Relationship between incident and principal. §3540.
Preferred interpretations. §3541.
Reasonable interpretation. §3542.
Innocent party's negligence. §3543.
Private transactions. §3545.
Ordinary course of events. §3546.
Continuation of things. §3547.
Legal obedience. §3548.

§3509. Purpose of maxims
The maxims of jurisprudence hereinafter set forth are intended not to qualify any of the foregoing provisions of this code, but to aid in their just application. **Leg.H.** Enacted Stats 1872. Amended Stats 2013 ch 76 §20 (AB 383), effective January 1, 2014.

§3510. Cessation of rule
When the reason of a rule ceases, so should the rule itself. **Leg.H.** Enacted Stats 1872.

§3511. Equal application of rule
Where the reason is the same, the rule should be the same. **Leg.H.** Enacted Stats 1872.

§3512. Change of purpose
One [1] **shall** not change [2] **their** purpose to the injury of another. **Leg.H.** Enacted Stats 1872. Amended Stats 2024 ch 812 §1 (AB 1899), effective January 1, 2025.

§3512. 2024 Deletes. [1] must [2] his

§3513. Waiver of legal right
Any one may waive the advantage of a law intended solely for [1] **their** benefit. But a law established for a public reason cannot be contravened by a private agreement. **Leg.H.** Enacted Stats 1872. Amended Stats 2024 ch 812 §2 (AB 1899), effective January 1, 2025.

§3513. 2024 Deletes. [1] his

§3514. Restriction on use of rights
One must so use his own rights as not to infringe upon the rights of another. **Leg.H.** Enacted Stats 1872.

§3515. Consent as defense
[1] **A person** who consents to an act is not wronged by it. **Leg.H.** Enacted Stats 1872. Amended Stats 2024 ch 812 §3 (AB 1899), effective January 1, 2025.

§3515. 2024 Deletes. [1] He

§3516. Acquiescence in error
Acquiescence in error takes away the right of objecting to it. **Leg.H.** Enacted Stats 1872.

§3517. Clean hands
No one can take advantage of [1] **their** own wrong. **Leg.H.** Enacted Stats 1872. Amended Stats 2024 ch 812 §4 (AB 1899), effective January 1, 2025.

§3517. 2024 Deletes. [1] his

§3518. Fraudulent dispossession
[1] **A person** who has fraudulently dispossessed [2] **themselves** of a thing may be treated as if [3] **they** still had possession. **Leg.H.** Enacted Stats 1872. Amended Stats 2024 ch 812 §5 (AB 1899), effective January 1, 2025.

§3518. 2024 Deletes. [1] He [2] himself [3] he

§3519. Failure to forbid act
[1] **A person** who can and does not forbid that which is done on [2] **their** behalf, is deemed to have bidden it. **Leg.H.** Enacted Stats 1872. Amended Stats 2024 ch 812 §6 (AB 1899), effective January 1, 2025.

§3519. 2024 Deletes. [1] He [2] his

§3520. Responsibility for third-party act
No one should suffer by the act of another. **Leg.H.** Enacted Stats 1872.

§3521. Benefit and burden
[1] **A person** who takes the benefit must bear the burden. **Leg.H.** Enacted Stats 1872. Amended Stats 2024 ch 812 §7 (AB 1899), effective January 1, 2025.

§3521. 2024 Deletes. [1] He

§3522. Scope of express grant
One who grants a thing is presumed to grant also whatever is essential to its use. **Leg.H.** Enacted Stats 1872.

§3523. Remedies
For every wrong there is a remedy. **Leg.H.** Enacted Stats 1872.

§3524. Parties equally in right or in wrong
Between those who are equally in the right, or equally in the wrong, the law does not interpose. **Leg.H.** Enacted Stats 1872.

§3525. Earlier right as preferred
Between rights otherwise equal, the earliest is preferred. **Leg.H.** Enacted Stats 1872.

§3526. Responsibility in absence of control
No [1] **person** is responsible for that which no [2] **person** can control. **Leg.H.** Enacted Stats 1872. Amended Stats 2024 ch 812 §8 (AB 1899), effective January 1, 2025.

§3526. 2024 Deletes. [1] man [2] man

§3527. Laches
The law helps the vigilant, before those who sleep on their rights. **Leg.H.** Enacted Stats 1872.

§3528. Substance over form
The law respects form less than substance. **Leg.H.** Enacted Stats 1872.

§3529. Acts regarded as having been done
That which ought to have been done is to be regarded as done, in favor of [1] **a person** to whom, and against [2] **a person** from whom, performance is due. **Leg.H.** Enacted Stats 1872. Amended Stats 2024 ch 812 §9 (AB 1899), effective January 1, 2025.

§3529. 2024 Deletes. [1] him [2] him

§3530. Presumption as to nonexistence of fact
That which does not appear to exist is to be regarded as if it did not exist. **Leg.H.** Enacted Stats 1872.

§3531. Impossibilities
The law never requires impossibilities. **Leg.H.** Enacted Stats 1872.

§3532. Idle acts
The law neither does nor requires idle acts. **Leg.H.** Enacted Stats 1872.

§3533. Trifles
The law disregards trifles. **Leg.H.** Enacted Stats 1872.

§3534. Qualification of expression
Particular expressions qualify those which are general. **Leg.H.** Enacted Stats 1872.

§3535. Contemporaneous exposition
Contemporaneous exposition is in general the best. **Leg.H.** Enacted Stats 1872.

§3536. Greater as containing the lesser
The greater contains the less. **Leg.H.** Enacted Stats 1872.

§3537. Superfluity
Superfluity does not vitiate. **Leg.H.** Enacted Stats 1872.

§3538. Certainty
That is certain which can be made certain. **Leg.H.** Enacted Stats 1872.

§3539. Effect of time on void acts
Time does not confirm a void act. **Leg.H.** Enacted Stats 1872.

§3540. Relationship between incident and principal
The incident follows the principal, and not the principal the incident. **Leg.H.** Enacted Stats 1872.

§3541. Preferred interpretations
An interpretation which gives effect is preferred to one which makes void. **Leg.H.** Enacted Stats 1872.

§3542. Reasonable interpretation
Interpretation must be reasonable. **Leg.H.** Enacted Stats 1872.

§3543. Innocent party's negligence
Where one of two innocent persons must suffer by the act of a third, [1] **the person**, by whose negligence it happened, must be the sufferer. **Leg.H.** Enacted Stats 1872. Amended Stats 2024 ch 812 §10 (AB 1899), effective January 1, 2025.

§3543. 2024 Deletes. [1] he

§3545. Private transactions
Private transactions are fair and regular. **Leg.H.** Added Stats 1965 ch 299 §11 p 1357, operative January 1, 1967.

§3546. Ordinary course of events
Things happen according to the ordinary course of nature and the ordinary habits of life. **Leg.H.** Added Stats 1965 ch 299 §12 p 1357, operative January 1, 1967.

§3547. Continuation of things
A thing continues to exist as long as is usual with things of that nature. **Leg.H.** Added Stats 1965 ch 299 §13 p 1357, operative January 1, 1967.

§3548. Legal obedience
The law has been obeyed. **Leg.H.** Added Stats 1965 ch 299 §14 p 1357, operative January 1, 1967.

PART 5
COMMON INTEREST DEVELOPMENTS

Chapter 1. General Provisions.
Chapter 2. Application of Act.
Chapter 3. Governing Documents.
Chapter 4. Ownership and Transfer of Interests.
Chapter 5. Property Use and Maintenance.
Chapter 6. Association Governance.
Chapter 7. Finances.
Chapter 8. Assessments and Assessment Collection.
Chapter 9. Insurance and Liability.
Chapter 10. Dispute Resolution and Enforcement.
Chapter 11. Construction Defect Litigation.

CHAPTER 1
GENERAL PROVISIONS

Article 1. Preliminary Provisions.
Article 2. Definitions.

ARTICLE 1
Preliminary Provisions

Short title. §4000.
Effect of headings. §4005.
Application of act. §4010.
Construction of zoning ordinance. §4020.
Delivered to an association. §4035.
Individual notice. § 4040.
Annual notice to association. §4041.
General notice. §4045.
Time and proof of delivery. §4050.
Electronic delivery; Requirements. §4055.
Approved by majority of all members. §4065.
Approved by majority of quorum of members. §4070.

§4000. Short title

This part shall be known and may be cited as the Davis-Stirling Common Interest Development Act. In a provision of this part, the part may be referred to as the act. **Leg.H.** Added Stats 2012 ch 180 §2 (AB 805), effective January 1, 2013, operative January 1, 2014.

Prior Law: Former CC §4000, relating to statutory citation, was added Stats 1969 ch 1608 §8, operative January 1, 1970, and repealed Stats 1992 ch 162 §3 (AB 2650), operative January 1, 1994.

§4005. Effect of headings

Division, part, title, chapter, article, and section headings do not in any manner affect the scope, meaning, or intent of this act. **Leg.H.** Added Stats 2012 ch 180 §2 (AB 805), effective January 1, 2013, operative January 1, 2014. Amended Stats 2013 ch 183 §7 (SB 745), effective January 1, 2014.

§4010. Application of act

Nothing in the act that added this part shall be construed to invalidate a document prepared or action taken before January 1, 2014, if the document or action was proper under the law governing common interest developments at the time that the document was prepared or the action was taken. For the purposes of this section, "document" does not include a governing document. **Leg.H.** Added Stats 2012 ch 180 §2 (AB 805), effective January 1, 2013, operative January 1, 2014.

§4020. Construction of zoning ordinance

Unless a contrary intent is clearly expressed, a local zoning ordinance is construed to treat like structures, lots, parcels, areas, or spaces in like manner regardless of the form of the common interest development. **Leg.H.** Added Stats 2012 ch 180 §2 (AB 805), effective January 1, 2013, operative January 1, 2014.

§4035. Delivered to an association

(a) If a provision of this act requires that a document be delivered to an association, the document shall be delivered to the person designated in the annual policy statement, prepared pursuant to Section 5310, to receive documents on behalf of the association. If no person has been designated to receive documents, the document shall be delivered to the president or secretary of the association.

(b) A document delivered pursuant to this section may be delivered by any of the following methods:

(1) By email, facsimile, or other electronic means, if the association has assented to that method of delivery.

(2) By personal delivery, if the association has assented to that method of delivery. If the association accepts a document by personal delivery it shall provide a written receipt acknowledging delivery of the document.

(3) By first-class mail, postage prepaid, registered or certified mail, express mail, or overnight delivery by an express service center. **Leg.H.** Added Stats 2012 ch 180 §2 (AB 805), effective January 1, 2013, operative January 1, 2014. Amended Stats 2013 ch 183 §8 (SB 745), effective January 1, 2014.

§ 4040. Individual notice

(a)(1) If a provision of this act requires an association to deliver a document by "individual delivery" or "individual notice," the association shall deliver that document in accordance with the preferred delivery method specified by the member pursuant to Section 4041.

(2) If the member has not provided a valid delivery method pursuant to Section 4041, the association shall deliver the document by first-class mail, registered or certified mail, express mail, or overnight delivery by an express service carrier addressed to the recipient at the address last shown on the books of the association.

(b) Upon receipt of a request by a member identifying a secondary email or mailing address for delivery of notices, pursuant to Section 5260, the association shall deliver an additional copy of both of the following to the secondary address identified in that request:

(1) The documents to be delivered to the member pursuant to Article 7 (commencing with Section 5300) of Chapter 6.

(2) The documents to be delivered to the member pursuant to Article 2 (commencing with Section 5650) of Chapter 8 and Section 5710.

(c) For the purposes of this section, an unrecorded provision of the governing documents providing for a particular method of delivery does not constitute agreement by a member to that method of delivery.

(d) This section shall become operative on January 1, 2023. **Leg.H.** Added Stats 2021 ch 640 §2 (SB 392), effective January 1, 2022, operative January 1, 2023.

Prior Law Former CC §4040, similar to the present section, was added Stats 2012 ch 180 §2 (AB 805), effective January 1, 2013, operative January 1,2014, amended Stats 2018 ch 836 §1 (SB 261), effective January 1, 2019 and Stats 2021 ch 640 §1 (SB 392), effective January 1, 2022, and was repealed by its own terms January 1, 2023.

§4041. Annual notice to association

(a) A member shall, on an annual basis, provide written notice to the association of all of the following:

(1) The member's preferred delivery method for receiving notices from the association, which shall include the option of receiving notices at one or both of the following:

(A) A mailing address.

(B) A valid email address.

(2) An alternate or secondary delivery method for receiving notices from the association, which shall include the option to receive notices at one or both of the following:

(A) A mailing address.

(B) A valid email address.

(3) The name, mailing address, and, if available, valid email address of the owner's legal representative, if any, including any person with power of attorney or other person who can be contacted in the event of the member's extended absence from the separate interest.

(4) Whether the separate interest is owner-occupied, is rented out, if the parcel is developed but vacant, or if the parcel is undeveloped land.

(b)(1) The association shall solicit the annual notices described in subdivision (a) of each owner and, at least 30 days before making its own required disclosure under Sections 5300 and 5310, shall enter the data into its books and records.

(2) The association shall include in the solicitation required by paragraph (1) both of the following:

(A) Notification that the member does not have to provide an email address to the association.

(B) A simple method for the member to inform the association in writing that the member wishes to change their preferred delivery method for receiving notices from the association.

(c) If a member fails to provide the notices set forth in subdivision (a), the last mailing address provided in writing by the member or, if none, the property address shall be deemed to be the address to which notices are to be delivered.

(d)(1) To the extent that interests regulated in Chapter 2 (commencing with Section 11210) of Part 2 of Division 4 of the Business and Professions Code are part of a mixed-use project where those interests comprise a portion of a common interest development, the association, as defined in Section 4080, shall be deemed compliant with this section if, at least once annually, it obtains from the time-share plan association a copy of the list described in subdivision (e) of Section 11273 of the Business and Professions Code, and enters the data into its books and records.

(2) Notwithstanding subdivision (e) of Section 11273 of the Business and Professions Code, the time-share plan association shall provide the list required by paragraph (1) to the association at least annually for this purpose.

(e) For the purposes of this section, a valid email address is one that, after a notice is sent, does not result in a bounce or other error notification indicating failure of the message. If the association delivers a notice to a member's email address and finds that the email address provided is no longer valid, the association shall resend the notice to a mailing or email address identified by the member pursuant to Section 4040. **Leg.H.** Added Stats 2016 ch 780 §1 (SB 918), effective January 1, 2017. Amended Stats 2017 ch 278 §1 (AB 1412), effective January 1, 2018; Stats 2018 ch 91 §1 (SB 1173), effective January 1, 2019; Stats 2021 ch 640 §3 (SB 392), effective January 1, 2022; Stats 2022 ch 632 §1 (SB 1252), effective January 1, 2023.

§4045. General notice

(a) If a provision of this act requires "general delivery" or "general notice," the document shall be provided by one or more of the following methods:

(1) Any method provided for delivery of an individual notice pursuant to Section 4040.

(2) Inclusion in a billing statement, newsletter, or other document that is delivered by one of the methods provided in this section.

(3) Posting the printed document in a prominent location that is accessible to all members, if the location has been designated for the posting of general notices by the association in the annual policy statement prepared pursuant to Section 5310.

(4) If the association broadcasts television programming for the purpose of distributing information on association business to its members, by inclusion in the programming.

(5) If the association maintains an internet website for the purpose of distributing information on association business to its members, by posting the notice on the association's internet website in a prominent location that is accessible to all members if designated as a location for posting general notices in the annual policy statement prepared pursuant to Section 5310.

(b) Notwithstanding subdivision (a), if a member requests to receive general notices by individual delivery, all general notices to that member, given under this section, shall be delivered pursuant to Section 4040. The option provided in this subdivision shall be described in the annual policy statement prepared pursuant to Section 5310. **Leg.H.** Added Stats 2012 ch 180 §2 (AB 805), effective January 1, 2013, operative January 1, 2014. Amended Stats 2021 ch 640 §4 (SB 392), effective January 1, 2022.

§4050. Time and proof of delivery

(a) This section governs the delivery of a document pursuant to this act.

(b) If a document is delivered by mail, delivery is deemed to be complete on deposit into the United States mail.

(c) If a document is delivered by electronic means, delivery is complete at the time of transmission. **Leg.H.** Added Stats 2012 ch 180 §2 (AB 805), effective January 1, 2013, operative January 1, 2014.

§4055. Electronic delivery; Requirements

If the association or a member receives information by electronic delivery pursuant to Section 4040, and a provision of this act requires that the information be in writing, that requirement is satisfied if the information is provided in an electronic record capable of retention by the recipient at the time of receipt. An electronic record is not capable of retention by the recipient if the sender or its information processing system inhibits the ability of the recipient to print or store the electronic record. **Leg.H.** Added Stats 2012 ch 180 §2 (AB 805), effective January 1, 2013, operative January 1, 2014. Amended Stats 2021 ch 640 §5 (SB 392), effective January 1, 2022.

§4065. Approved by majority of all members

If a provision of this act requires that an action be approved by a majority of all members, the action shall be approved or ratified by an affirmative vote of a majority of the votes entitled to be cast. **Leg.H.** Added Stats 2012 ch 180 §2 (AB 805), effective January 1, 2013, operative January 1, 2014.

§4070. Approved by majority of quorum of members

If a provision of this act requires that an action be approved by a majority of a quorum of the members, the action shall be approved or ratified by an affirmative vote of a majority of the votes represented and voting in a duly held election in which a quorum is represented, which affirmative votes also constitute a majority of the required quorum. **Leg.H.** Added Stats 2012 ch 180 §2 (AB 805), effective January 1, 2013, operative January 1, 2014. Amended Stats 2013 ch 183 §9 (SB 745), effective January 1, 2014.

ARTICLE 2
Definitions

Application of definitions. §4075.
"Annual budget report". §4076.
"Annual policy statement". §4078.
"Association". §4080.
"Board". §4085.
"Board meeting". §4090.
"Common area". §4095.
"Common interest development". §4100.
"Community apartment project". §4105.
"Community service organization or similar entity". §4110.
"Condominium plan". §4120.
"Condominium project". §4125.
"Declarant". §4130.
"Declaration". §4135.
"Director". §4140.
"Exclusive use common area". §4145.
"General notice". §4148.
"Governing documents". §4150.
"Individual notice". §4153.
"Item of business". §4155.
"Managing agent". §4158.
"Member". §4160.
"Person". §4170.
"Planned development". §4175.
"Reserve accounts". §4177.
"Reserve account requirements". §4178.
"Separate interest". §4185.
"Stock cooperative". §4190.

§4075. Application of definitions

The definitions in this article govern the construction of this act. **Leg.H.** Added Stats 2012 ch 180 §2 (AB 805), effective January 1, 2013, operative January 1, 2014.

§4076. "Annual budget report"

"Annual budget report" means the report described in Section 5300. **Leg.H.** Added Stats 2012 ch 180 §2 (AB 805), effective January 1, 2013, operative January 1, 2014.

§4078. "Annual policy statement"

"Annual policy statement" means the statement described in Section 5310. **Leg.H.** Added Stats 2012 ch 180 §2 (AB 805), effective January 1, 2013, operative January 1, 2014.

§4080. "Association"

"Association" means a nonprofit corporation or unincorporated association created for the purpose of managing a common interest development. **Leg.H.** Added Stats 2012 ch 180 §2 (AB 805), effective January 1, 2013, operative January 1, 2014.

§4085. "Board"

"Board" means the board of directors of the association. **Leg.H.** Added Stats 2012 ch 180 §2 (AB 805), effective January 1, 2013, operative January 1, 2014.

§4090. "Board meeting"

"Board meeting" means either of the following:

(a) A congregation, at the same time and place, of a sufficient number of directors to establish a quorum of the board, to hear, discuss, or deliberate upon any item of business that is within the authority of the board.

(b) A teleconference, where a sufficient number of directors to establish a quorum of the board, in different locations, are connected by electronic means, through audio or video, or both. A teleconference meeting shall be conducted in a manner that protects the rights of members of the association and otherwise complies with the requirements of this act. Except for a meeting that will be held solely in executive session or conducted under Section 4926 or 5450, the notice of the teleconference meeting shall identify at least one physical location so that members of the association may attend, and at least one director or a person designated by the board shall be present at that location. Participation by directors in a teleconference meeting constitutes presence at that meeting as long as all directors participating are able to hear one another, as well as members of the association speaking on matters before the board. **Leg.H.** Added Stats 2012 ch 180 §2 (AB 805), effective January 1, 2013, operative January 1, 2014. Amended Stats 2013 ch 183 §10 (SB 745), effective January 1, 2014; Stats 2021 ch 276 §1 (SB 391), effective September 23, 2021; Stats 2023 ch 203 §2 (AB 648), effective January 1, 2024.

§4095. "Common area"

(a) "Common area" means the entire common interest development except the separate interests therein. The estate in the common area may be a fee, a life estate, an estate for years, or any combination of the foregoing.

(b) Notwithstanding subdivision (a), in a planned development described in subdivision (b) of Section 4175, the common area may consist of mutual or reciprocal easement rights appurtenant to the separate interests. **Leg.H.** Added Stats 2012 ch 180 §2 (AB 805), effective January 1, 2013, operative January 1, 2014.

§4100. "Common interest development"

"Common interest development" means any of the following:

(a) A community apartment project.
(b) A condominium project.
(c) A planned development.
(d) A stock cooperative. **Leg.H.** Added Stats 2012 ch 180 §2 (AB 805), effective January 1, 2013, operative January 1, 2014.

Prior Law: Former CC §4100, similar to present Fam C §30, was added Stats 1969 ch 1608 §8, operative January 1, 1970, amended Stats 1977 ch 339 §1, repealed Stats 1992 ch 162 §3 (AB 2650), operative January 1, 1994, amended Stats 1992 ch 318 §1 (AB 1101) (ch 318 prevails), and repealed Stats 1993 ch 219 §29 (AB 1500).

§4101. [Section repealed 1994.]

Leg.H. Added Stats 1969 ch 1608 §8, operative January 1, 1970. Amended Stats 1970 ch 474 §1; Stats 1971 ch 1748 §26; Stats 1977 ch 339 §2; Stats 1978 ch 374 §1; Stats 1979 ch 621 §2. Repealed Stats 1992 ch 162 §3 (AB 2650), operative January 1, 1994. See Fam C §§301, 302, 304.

§4102. [Section repealed 1994.]

Leg.H. Added Stats 1969 ch 1608 §8, operative January 1, 1970. Repealed Stats 1992 ch 162 §3 (AB 2650), operative January 1, 1994. See Fam C §303.

§4103. [Section repealed 1994.]

Leg.H. Added Stats 1969 ch 1608 §8, operative January 1, 1970. Repealed Stats 1992 ch 162 §3 (AB 2650), operative January 1, 1994. See Fam C §305.

§4104. [Section repealed 1994.]

Leg.H. Added Stats 1969 ch 1608 §8, operative January 1, 1970. Repealed Stats 1992 ch 162 §3 (AB 2650), operative January 1, 1994. See Fam C §308.

§4105. "Community apartment project"

"Community apartment project" means a development in which an undivided interest in land is coupled with the right of exclusive occupancy of any apartment located thereon. **Leg.H.** Added Stats 2012 ch 180 §2 (AB 805), effective January 1, 2013, operative January 1, 2014.

§4110. "Community service organization or similar entity"

(a) "Community service organization or similar entity" means a nonprofit entity, other than an association, that is organized to provide services to residents of the common interest development or to the public in addition to the residents, to the extent community common area or facilities are available to the public.

(b) "Community service organization or similar entity" does not include an entity that has been organized solely to raise moneys and contribute to other nonprofit organizations that are qualified as tax exempt under Section 501(c)(3) of the Internal Revenue Code and that provide housing or housing assistance. **Leg.H.** Added Stats 2012 ch 180 §2 (AB 805), effective January 1, 2013, operative January 1, 2014.

§4120. "Condominium plan"

"Condominium plan" means a plan described in Section 4285. **Leg.H.** Added Stats 2012 ch 180 §2 (AB 805), effective January 1, 2013, operative January 1, 2014.

§4125. "Condominium project"

(a) A "condominium project" means a real property development consisting of condominiums.

(b) A condominium consists of an undivided interest in common in a portion of real property coupled with a separate interest in space called a unit, the boundaries of which are described on a recorded final map, parcel map, or condominium plan in sufficient detail to locate all boundaries thereof. The area within these boundaries may be filled with air, earth, water, or fixtures, or any combination thereof, and need not be physically attached to land except by easements for access and, if necessary, support. The description of the unit may refer to (1) boundaries described in the recorded final map, parcel map, or condominium plan, (2) physical boundaries, either in existence, or to be constructed, such as walls, floors, and ceilings of a structure or any portion thereof, (3) an entire structure containing one or more units, or (4) any combination thereof.

(c) The portion or portions of the real property held in undivided interest may be all of the real property, except for the separate interests, or may include a particular three-dimensional portion thereof, the boundaries of which are described on a recorded final map, parcel map, or condominium plan. The area within these boundaries may be filled with air, earth, water, or fixtures, or any combination thereof, and need not be physically attached to land except by easements for access and, if necessary, support.

(d) An individual condominium within a condominium project may include, in addition, a separate interest in other portions of the real property. **Leg.H.** Added Stats 2012 ch 180 §2 (AB 805), effective January 1, 2013, operative January 1, 2014.

§4130. "Declarant"

"Declarant" means the person or group of persons designated in the declaration as declarant, or if no declarant is designated, the person or group of persons who sign the original declaration or who succeed to special rights, preferences, or privileges designated in the declaration as belonging to the signator of the original declaration. **Leg.H.** Added Stats 2012 ch 180 §2 (AB 805), effective January 1, 2013, operative January 1, 2014.

§4135. "Declaration"

"Declaration" means the document, however denominated, that contains the information required by Sections 4250 and 4255. **Leg.H.** Added Stats 2012 ch 180 §2 (AB 805), effective January 1, 2013, operative January 1, 2014.

§4140. "Director"

"Director" means a natural person who serves on the board. **Leg.H.** Added Stats 2012 ch 180 §2 (AB 805), effective January 1, 2013, operative January 1, 2014.

§4145. "Exclusive use common area"

(a) "Exclusive use common area" means a portion of the common area designated by the declaration for the exclusive use of one or more, but fewer than all, of the owners of the separate interests and which is or will be appurtenant to the separate interest or interests.

(b) Unless the declaration otherwise provides, any shutters, awnings, window boxes, doorsteps, stoops, porches, balconies, patios, exterior doors, doorframes, and hardware incident thereto, screens and windows or other fixtures designed to serve a single separate interest, but located outside the boundaries of the separate interest, are exclusive use common area allocated exclusively to that separate interest.

(c) Notwithstanding the provisions of the declaration, internal and external telephone wiring designed to serve a single separate interest, but located outside the boundaries of the separate interest, is exclusive use common area allocated exclusively to that separate interest. **Leg.H.** Added Stats 2012 ch 180 §2 (AB 805), effective January 1, 2013, operative January 1, 2014.

§4148. "General notice"

"General notice" means the delivery of a document pursuant to Section 4045. **Leg.H.** Added Stats 2012 ch 180 §2 (AB 805), effective January 1, 2013, operative January 1, 2014.

§4150. "Governing documents"

"Governing documents" means the declaration and any other documents, such as bylaws, operating rules, articles of incorporation, or articles of association, which govern the operation of the common interest development or association. **Leg.H.** Added Stats 2012 ch 180 §2 (AB 805), effective January 1, 2013, operative January 1, 2014.

§4153. "Individual notice"

"Individual notice" means the delivery of a document pursuant to Section 4040. **Leg.H.** Added Stats 2012 ch 180 §2 (AB 805), effective January 1, 2013, operative January 1, 2014.

§4155. "Item of business"

"Item of business" means any action within the authority of the board, except those actions that the board has validly delegated to any other person or persons, managing agent, officer of the association, or committee of the board comprising less than a quorum of the board. **Leg.H.** Added Stats 2012 ch 180 §2 (AB 805), effective January 1, 2013, operative January 1, 2014.

§4158. "Managing agent"

(a) A "managing agent" is a person who, for compensation or in expectation of compensation, exercises control over the assets of a common interest development.

(b) A "managing agent" does not include any of the following:

(1) A regulated financial institution operating within the normal course of its regulated business practice.

(2) An attorney at law acting within the scope of the attorney's license. **Leg.H.** Added Stats 2012 ch 180 §2 (AB 805), effective January 1, 2013, operative January 1, 2014.

§4160. "Member"

"Member" means an owner of a separate interest. **Leg.H.** Added Stats 2012 ch 180 §2 (AB 805), effective January 1, 2013, operative January 1, 2014.

§4170. "Person"

"Person" means a natural person, corporation, government or governmental subdivision or agency, business trust, estate, trust, partnership, limited liability company, association, or other entity. **Leg.H.** Added Stats 2012 ch 180 §2 (AB 805), effective January 1, 2013, operative January 1, 2014.

§4175. "Planned development"

"Planned development" means a real property development other than a community apartment project, a condominium project, or a stock cooperative, having either or both of the following features:

(a) Common area that is owned either by an association or in common by the owners of the separate interests who possess appurtenant rights to the beneficial use and enjoyment of the common area.

(b) Common area and an association that maintains the common area with the power to levy assessments that may become a lien upon the separate interests in accordance with Article 2 (commencing with Section 5650) of Chapter 8. **Leg.H.** Added Stats 2012 ch 180 §2 (AB 805), effective January 1, 2013, operative January 1, 2014.

§4177. "Reserve accounts"

"Reserve accounts" means both of the following:

(a) Moneys that the board has identified for use to defray the future repair or replacement of, or additions to, those major components that the association is obligated to maintain.

(b) The funds received, and not yet expended or disposed of, from either a compensatory damage award or settlement to an association from any person for injuries to property, real or personal, arising from any construction or design defects. These funds shall be separately itemized from funds described in subdivision (a). **Leg.H.** Added Stats 2012 ch 180 §2 (AB 805), effective January 1, 2013, operative January 1, 2014.

§4178. "Reserve account requirements"

"Reserve account requirements" means the estimated funds that the board has determined are required to be available at a specified point in time to repair, replace, or restore those major components that the association is obligated to maintain. **Leg.H.** Added Stats 2012 ch 180 §2 (AB 805), effective January 1, 2013, operative January 1, 2014.

§4185. "Separate interest"

(a) "Separate interest" has the following meanings:

(1) In a community apartment project, "separate interest" means the exclusive right to occupy an apartment, as specified in Section 4105.

(2) In a condominium project, "separate interest" means a separately owned unit, as specified in Section 4125.

(3) In a planned development, "separate interest" means a separately owned lot, parcel, area, or space.

(4) In a stock cooperative, "separate interest" means the exclusive right to occupy a portion of the real property, as specified in Section 4190.

(b) Unless the declaration or condominium plan, if any exists, otherwise provides, if walls, floors, or ceilings are designated as boundaries of a separate interest, the interior surfaces of the perimeter walls, floors, ceilings, windows, doors, and outlets located within the separate interest are part of the separate interest and any other portions of the walls, floors, or ceilings are part of the common area.

(c) The estate in a separate interest may be a fee, a life estate, an estate for years, or any combination of the foregoing. **Leg.H.** Added Stats 2012 ch 180 §2 (AB 805), effective January 1, 2013, operative January 1, 2014.

§4190. "Stock cooperative"

(a) "Stock cooperative" means a development in which a corporation is formed or availed of, primarily for the purpose of holding title to, either in fee simple or for a term of years, improved real property, and all or substantially all of the shareholders of the corporation receive a right of exclusive occupancy in a portion of the real property, title to which is held by the corporation. The owners' interest in the corporation, whether evidenced by a share of stock, a certificate of membership, or otherwise, shall be deemed to be an interest in a common interest development and a real estate development for purposes of subdivision (f) of Section 25100 of the Corporations Code.

(b) A "stock cooperative" includes a limited equity housing cooperative which is a stock cooperative that meets the criteria of Section 817. **Leg.H.** Added Stats 2012 ch 180 §2 (AB 805), effective January 1, 2013, operative January 1, 2014.

CHAPTER 2
APPLICATION OF ACT

Application of act. §4200.
Exemption of development without common area. §4201.
Commercial and industrial developments. §4202.

§4200. Application of act

This act applies and a common interest development is created whenever a separate interest coupled with an interest in the common area or membership in the association is, or has been, conveyed, provided all of the following are recorded:

(a) A declaration.

(b) A condominium plan, if any exists.

(c) A final map or parcel map, if Division 2 (commencing with Section 66410) of Title 7 of the Government Code requires the recording of either a final map or parcel map for the common interest development. **Leg.H.** Added Stats 2012 ch 180 §2 (AB 805), effective January 1, 2013, operative January 1, 2014.

Prior Law: Former CC §4200, similar to Fam C §306, was added Stats 1969 ch 1608 §8, operative January 1, 1970, repealed Stats 1992 ch 162 §3 (AB 2650), operative January 1, 1994, amended Stats 1992 ch 318 §2 (AB 1101) (ch 318 prevails), and repealed Stats 1993 ch 219 §30 (AB 1500).

§4201. Exemption of development without common area

Nothing in this act may be construed to apply to a real property development that does not contain common area. This section is declaratory of existing law. **Leg.H.** Added Stats 2012 ch 180 §2 (AB 805), effective January 1, 2013, operative January 1, 2014.

Prior Law: Former CC §4201, similar to Fam C §§350–35, was added Stats 1969 ch 1608 §8, operative January 1, 1970, amended Stats 1971 ch 1748 §27, Stats 1980 ch 676 §57, Stats 1986 ch 1460 §1, Stats 1988 ch 228 §1, and repealed Stats 1992 ch 162 §3 (AB 2650), operative January 1, 1994.

§4201.5. [Section repealed 1994.]
Leg.H. Added Stats 1976 ch 1380 §1. Amended Stats 1980 ch 676 §58; Stats 1986 ch 1460 §2. Repealed Stats 1992 ch 162 §3 (AB 2650), operative January 1, 1994. See Fam C §358.

§4202. Commercial and industrial developments
This part does not apply to a commercial or industrial common interest development, as defined in Section 6531. **Leg.H.** Added Stats 2012 ch 180 §2 (AB 805), effective January 1, 2013, operative January 1, 2014. Amended Stats 2013 ch 605 §19 (SB 752), effective January 1, 2014.

Prior Law: Former CC §4202, similar to Fam C §359, was added Stats 1969 ch 1608 §8, operative January 1, 1970, repealed Stats 1992 ch 162 §3 (AB 2650), operative January 1, 1994, amended Stats 1992 ch 318 §3 (AB 1101) (ch 318 prevails), and repealed Stats 1993 ch 219 §31 (AB 1500).

§4203. [Section repealed 1994.]
Leg.H. Added Stats 1969 ch 1608 §8, operative January 1, 1970. Amended Stats 1979 ch 139 §2. Repealed Stats 1992 ch 162 §3 (AB 2650), operative January 1, 1994. Amended Stats 1992 ch 318 §4 (AB 1101) (ch 318 prevails). Repealed Stats 1993 ch 219 §32 (AB 1500). See Fam C §360.

§4204. [Section repealed 1994.]
Leg.H. Added Stats 1969 ch 1608 §8, operative January 1, 1970. Repealed Stats 1992 ch 162 §3 (AB 2650), operative January 1, 1994. Amended Stats 1992 ch 318 §5 (AB 1101) (ch 318 prevails). Repealed Stats 1993 ch 219 §33 (AB 1500). See Fam C §§356, 357.

CHAPTER 3
GOVERNING DOCUMENTS

Article 1. General Provisions.
Article 2. Declaration.
Article 3. Articles of Incorporation.
Article 4. Condominium Plan.
Article 5. Operating Rules.

ARTICLE 1
General Provisions

Document authority. §4205.
Record notice of agent to receive payments. §4210.
Liberal construction of instruments. §4215.
Boundaries of units. §4220.
Deletion of unlawful restrictive covenants. §4225.
Deletion of declarant provisions in governing documents. §4230.
Correction of statutory cross-reference. §4235.

§4205. Document authority
(a) To the extent of any conflict between the governing documents and the law, the law shall prevail.

(b) To the extent of any conflict between the articles of incorporation and the declaration, the declaration shall prevail.

(c) To the extent of any conflict between the bylaws and the articles of incorporation or declaration, the articles of incorporation or declaration shall prevail.

(d) To the extent of any conflict between the operating rules and the bylaws, articles of incorporation, or declaration, the bylaws, articles of incorporation, or declaration shall prevail. **Leg.H.** Added Stats 2012 ch 180 §2 (AB 805), effective January 1, 2013, operative January 1, 2014. Amended Stats 2013 ch 183 §11 (SB 745), effective January 1, 2014.

Prior Law: Former CC §4205, similar to Fam C §400, as added Stats 1969 ch 1608 §8, operative January 1, 1970, amended Stats 1971 ch 642 §1, ch 671 §1, ch 1748 §28, Stats 1973 ch 979 §5, Stats 1977 ch 10 §1, effective March 21, 1977, Stats 1984 ch 250 §1, Stats 1985 ch 5 §1, effective February 19, 1985, ch 586 §1, and repealed Stats 1992 ch 162 §3 (AB 2650), operative January 1, 1994.

§4205.1. [Section repealed 1994.]
Leg.H. Added Stats 1973 ch 979 §2. Amended Stats 1976 ch 383 §1; Stats 1982 ch 1543 §1; Stats 1984 ch 250 §2. Repealed Stats 1992 ch 162 §3 (AB 2650), operative January 1, 1994. See Fam C §401.

§4205.5. [Section repealed 1994.]
Leg.H. Added Stats 1973 ch 804 §1. Repealed Stats 1992 ch 162 §3 (AB 2650), operative January 1, 1994. See Fam C §402.

§4206. [Section repealed 1994.]
Leg.H. Added Stats 1969 ch 1608 §8, operative January 1, 1970. Repealed Stats 1992 ch 162 §3 (AB 2650), operative January 1, 1994. Amended Stats 1992 ch 318 §6 (AB 1101) (ch 318 prevails). Repealed Stats 1993 ch 219 §34 (AB 1500). See Fam C §420.

§4206.5. [Section repealed 1994.]
Leg.H. Added Stats 1970 ch 789 §2, operative November 3, 1970. Repealed Stats 1992 ch 162 §3 (AB 2650), operative January 1, 1994. See Fam C §420.

§4207. [Section repealed 1994.]
Leg.H. Added Stats 1969 ch 1608 §8, operative January 1, 1970. Repealed Stats 1992 ch 162 §3 (AB 2650), operative January 1, 1994. See Fam C §421.

§4208. [Section repealed 1994.]
Leg.H. Added Stats 1969 ch 1608 §8, operative January 1, 1970. Amended Stats 1988 ch 228 §2. Repealed Stats 1992 ch 162 §3 (AB 2650), operative January 1, 1994. Amended Stats 1992 ch 318 §7 (AB 1101) (ch 318 prevails). Repealed Stats 1993 ch 219 §35 (AB 1500). See Fam C §§422, 423.

§4209. [Section repealed 1994.]
Leg.H. Added Stats 1969 ch 1608 §8, operative January 1, 1970. Repealed Stats 1992 ch 162 §3 (AB 2650), operative January 1, 1994. See Fam C §424.

§4210. Record notice of agent to receive payments
In order to facilitate the collection of regular assessments, special assessments, transfer fees as authorized by Sections 4530, 4575, and 4580, and similar charges, the board is authorized to record a statement or amended statement identifying relevant information for the association. This statement may include any or all of the following information:

(a) The name of the association as shown in the declaration or the current name of the association, if different.

(b) The name and address of a managing agent or treasurer of the association or other individual or entity authorized to receive assessments and fees imposed by the association.

(c) A daytime telephone number of the authorized party identified in subdivision (b) if a telephone number is available.

(d) A list of separate interests subject to assessment by the association, showing the assessor's parcel number or legal description, or both, of the separate interests.

(e) The recording information identifying the declaration governing the association.

(f) If an amended statement is being recorded, the recording information identifying the prior statement or statements which the amendment is superseding. **Leg.H.** Added Stats 2012 ch 180 §2 (AB 805), effective January 1, 2013, operative January 1, 2014.

Prior Law: Former CC §4210, similar to Fam C §425, was added Stats 1969 ch 1608 §8, operative January 1, 1970, amended Stats 1988 ch 228 §3, repealed Stats 1992 ch 162 §3 (AB 2650), operative January 1, 1994, amended Stats 1992 ch 318 §8 (AB 1101) (ch 318 prevails), and repealed Stats 1993 ch 219 §36 (AB 1500).

§4211. [Section repealed 1989.]
Leg.H. Added Stats 1969 ch 1608 §8, operative January 1, 1970. Repealed Stats 1988 ch 228 §4. The repealed section related to acknowledgment and recordation of declarations of marriage.

§4212. [Section repealed 1994.]
Leg.H. Added Stats 1969 ch 1608 §8, operative January 1, 1970. Amended Stats 1972 ch 579 §14. Repealed Stats 1992 ch 162 §3 (AB 2650), operative January 1, 1994. See Fam C §309.

§4213. [Section repealed 1994.]
Leg.H. Added Stats 1969 ch 1608 §8, operative January 1, 1970. Amended Stats 1971 ch 1244 §1; Stats 1973 ch 142 §11, effective June 30, 1973, operative July 1, 1973; Stats 1977 ch 585 §1; Stats 1980 ch 676 §59; Stats 1981 ch 872 §1; Stats 1982 ch 125 §1, effective March 19, 1982, ch 449 §1; Stats 1983 ch 476 §1; Stats 1984 ch 149 §1; Stats 1985

ch 586 §2; Stats 1986 ch 1460 §3. Repealed Stats 1992 ch 162 §3 (AB 2650), operative January 1, 1994. Amended Stats 1992 ch 318 §9 (AB 1101) (ch 318 prevails). Repealed Stats 1993 ch 219 §37 (AB 1500). See Fam C §§500, 501, 503–511, 530–536.

§4213.1. [Section repealed 1994.]

Leg.H. Added Stats 1981 ch 872 §2. Amended Stats 1985 ch 586 §3. Repealed Stats 1992 ch 162 §3 (AB 2650), operative January 1, 1994. See Fam C §§502.

§4213.2. [Section repealed 1994.]

Leg.H. Added Stats 1982 ch 125 §2, effective March 18, 1982. Repealed Stats 1992 ch 162 §3 (AB 2650), operative January 1, 1994. See Fam C §511.

§4214. [Section repealed 1994.]

Leg.H. Added Stats 1969 ch 1608 §8, operative January 1, 1970. Repealed Stats 1992 ch 162 §3 (AB 2650), operative January 1, 1994. The repealed section related to validity of marriage performed without license.

§4215. Liberal construction of instruments

Any deed, declaration, or condominium plan for a common interest development shall be liberally construed to facilitate the operation of the common interest development, and its provisions shall be presumed to be independent and severable. Nothing in Article 3 (commencing with Section 715) of Chapter 2 of Title 2 of Part 1 of Division 2 shall operate to invalidate any provisions of the governing documents. **Leg.H.** Added Stats 2012 ch 180 §2 (AB 805), effective January 1, 2013, operative January 1, 2014.

Prior Law: Former CC §4215, similar to Fam C §307, was added Stats 1969 ch 1608 §8, operative January 1, 1970, amended Stats 1985 ch 586 §4, and repealed Stats 1988 ch 228 §5.

§4216. [Section repealed 1994.]

Leg.H. Added Stats 1988 ch 228 §6. Repealed Stats 1992 ch 162 §3 (AB 2650), operative January 1, 1994. Amended Stats 1992 ch 318 §10 (AB 1101) (ch 318 prevails). Repealed Stats 1993 ch 219 §38 (AB 1500). See Fam C §307.

§4220. Boundaries of units

In interpreting deeds and condominium plans, the existing physical boundaries of a unit in a condominium project, when the boundaries of the unit are contained within a building, or of a unit reconstructed in substantial accordance with the original plans thereof, shall be conclusively presumed to be its boundaries rather than the metes and bounds expressed in the deed or condominium plan, if any exists, regardless of settling or lateral movement of the building and regardless of minor variance between boundaries shown on the plan or in the deed and those of the building. **Leg.H.** Added Stats 2012 ch 180 §2 (AB 805), effective January 1, 2013, operative January 1, 2014.

§4225. Deletion of unlawful restrictive covenants

(a) No declaration or other governing document shall include a restrictive covenant in violation of Section 12955 of the Government Code.

(b) Notwithstanding any other provision of law or provision of the governing documents, the board, without approval of the members, shall amend any declaration or other governing document that includes a restrictive covenant prohibited by this section to delete the restrictive covenant, and shall restate the declaration or other governing document without the restrictive covenant but with no other change to the declaration or governing document.

(c) If the declaration is amended under this section, the board shall record the restated declaration in each county in which the common interest development is located. If the articles of incorporation are amended under this section, the board shall file a certificate of amendment with the Secretary of State pursuant to Section 7814 of the Corporations Code.

(d) If after providing written notice to an association, pursuant to Section 4035, requesting that the association delete a restrictive covenant that violates subdivision (a), and the association fails to delete the restrictive covenant within 30 days of receiving the notice, the Civil Rights Department, a city or county in which a common interest development is located, or any person may bring an action against the association for injunctive relief to enforce subdivision (a). The court may award attorney's fees to the prevailing party. **Leg.H.** Added Stats 2012 ch 180 §2 (AB 805), effective January 1, 2013, operative January 1, 2014. Amended Stats 2022 ch 48 §7 (SB 189), effective June 30, 2022.

§4230. Deletion of declarant provisions in governing documents

(a) Notwithstanding any provision of the governing documents to the contrary, the board may, after the developer has completed construction of the development, has terminated construction activities, and has terminated marketing activities for the sale, lease, or other disposition of separate interests within the development, adopt an amendment deleting from any of the governing documents any provision which is unequivocally designed and intended, or which by its nature can only have been designed or intended, to facilitate the developer in completing the construction or marketing of the development. However, provisions of the governing documents relative to a particular construction or marketing phase of the development may not be deleted under the authorization of this subdivision until that construction or marketing phase has been completed.

(b) The provisions which may be deleted by action of the board shall be limited to those which provide for access by the developer over or across the common area for the purposes of (1) completion of construction of the development, and (2) the erection, construction, or maintenance of structures or other facilities designed to facilitate the completion of construction or marketing of separate interests.

(c) At least 30 days prior to taking action pursuant to subdivision (a), the board shall deliver to all members, by individual delivery, pursuant to Section 4040, (1) a copy of all amendments to the governing documents proposed to be adopted under subdivision (a), and (2) a notice of the time, date, and place the board will consider adoption of the amendments. The board may consider adoption of amendments to the governing documents pursuant to subdivision (a) only at a meeting that is open to all members, who shall be given opportunity to make comments thereon. All deliberations of the board on any action proposed under subdivision (a) shall only be conducted in an open meeting.

(d) The board may not amend the governing documents pursuant to this section without the approval of a majority of a quorum of the members, pursuant to Section 4070. For the purposes of this section, "quorum" means more than 50 percent of the members who own no more than two separate interests in the development. **Leg.H.** Added Stats 2012 ch 180 §2 (AB 805), effective January 1, 2013, operative January 1, 2014.

§4235. Correction of statutory cross-reference

(a) Notwithstanding any other provision of law or provision of the governing documents, if the governing documents include a reference to a provision of the Davis-Stirling Common Interest Development Act that was repealed and continued in a new provision by the act that added this section, the board may amend the governing documents, solely to correct the cross-reference, by adopting a board resolution that shows the correction. Member approval is not required in order to adopt a resolution pursuant to this section.

(b) A declaration that is corrected under this section may be restated in corrected form and recorded, provided that a copy of the board resolution authorizing the corrections is recorded along with the restated declaration. **Leg.H.** Added Stats 2012 ch 180 §2 (AB 805), effective January 1, 2013, operative January 1, 2014.

ARTICLE 2
Declaration

Contents of declaration. §4250.
Special disclosures. §4255.
Amendment authorized. §4260.
Amendment to extend term of declaration authorized. §4265.
Amendment procedure. §4270.
Judicial authorization of amendment. §4275.

§4250. Contents of declaration

(a) A declaration, recorded on or after January 1, 1986, shall contain a legal description of the common interest development, and a statement that the common interest development is a community apartment project, condominium project, planned development, stock cooperative, or combination thereof. The declaration shall additionally set forth the name of the association and the restrictions on the use or enjoyment of any portion of the common interest development that are intended to be enforceable equitable servitudes.

(b) The declaration may contain any other matters the declarant or the members consider appropriate. **Leg.H.** Added Stats 2012 ch 180 §2 (AB 805), effective January 1, 2013, operative January 1, 2014.

§4255. Special disclosures

(a) If a common interest development is located within an airport influence area, a declaration, recorded after January 1, 2004, shall contain the following statement:

"NOTICE OF AIRPORT IN VICINITY

This property is presently located in the vicinity of an airport, within what is known as an airport influence area. For that reason, the property may be subject to some of the annoyances or inconveniences associated with proximity to airport operations (for example: noise, vibration, or odors). Individual sensitivities to those annoyances can vary from person to person. You may wish to consider what airport annoyances, if any, are associated with the property before you complete your purchase and determine whether they are acceptable to you."

(b) For purposes of this section, an "airport influence area," also known as an "airport referral area," is the area in which current or future airport-related noise, overflight, safety, or airspace protection factors may significantly affect land uses or necessitate restrictions on those uses as determined by an airport land use commission.

(c) If a common interest development is within the San Francisco Bay Conservation and Development Commission jurisdiction, as described in Section 66610 of the Government Code, a declaration recorded on or after January 1, 2006, shall contain the following notice:

"NOTICE OF SAN FRANCISCO BAY CONSERVATION AND DEVELOPMENT COMMISSION JURISDICTION

This property is located within the jurisdiction of the San Francisco Bay Conservation and Development Commission. Use and development of property within the commission's jurisdiction may be subject to special regulations, restrictions, and permit requirements. You may wish to investigate and determine whether they are acceptable to you and your intended use of the property before you complete your transaction."

(d) The statement in a declaration acknowledging that a property is located in an airport influence area or within the jurisdiction of the San Francisco Bay Conservation and Development Commission does not constitute a title defect, lien, or encumbrance. **Leg.H.** Added Stats 2012 ch 180 §2 (AB 805), effective January 1, 2013, operative January 1, 2014.

§4260. Amendment authorized

Except to the extent that a declaration provides by its express terms that it is not amendable, in whole or in part, a declaration that fails to include provisions permitting its amendment at all times during its existence may be amended at any time. **Leg.H.** Added Stats 2012 ch 180 §2 (AB 805), effective January 1, 2013, operative January 1, 2014.

§4265. Amendment to extend term of declaration authorized

(a) The Legislature finds that there are common interest developments that have been created with deed restrictions that do not provide a means for the members to extend the term of the declaration. The Legislature further finds that covenants and restrictions contained in the declaration, are an appropriate method for protecting the common plan of developments and to provide for a mechanism for financial support for the upkeep of common area including, but not limited to, roofs, roads, heating systems, and recreational facilities. If declarations terminate prematurely, common interest developments may deteriorate and the housing supply of affordable units could be impacted adversely. The Legislature further finds and declares that it is in the public interest to provide a vehicle for extending the term of the declaration if the extension is approved by a majority of all members, pursuant to Section 4065.

(b) A declaration that specifies a termination date, but that contains no provision for extension of the termination date, may be extended, before its termination date, by the approval of members pursuant to Section 4270.

(c) No single extension of the terms of the declaration made pursuant to this section shall exceed the initial term of the declaration or 20 years, whichever is less. However, more than one extension may occur pursuant to this section. **Leg.H.** Added Stats 2012 ch 180 §2 (AB 805), effective January 1, 2013, operative January 1, 2014.

§4270. Amendment procedure

(a) A declaration may be amended pursuant to the declaration or this act. Except where an alternative process for approving, certifying, or recording an amendment is provided in Section 4225, 4230, 4235, or 4275, an amendment is effective after all of the following requirements have been met:

(1) The amendment has been approved by the percentage of members required by the declaration and any other person whose approval is required by the declaration.

(2) That fact has been certified in a writing executed and acknowledged by the officer designated in the declaration or by the association for that purpose, or if no one is designated, by the president of the association.

(3) The amendment has been recorded in each county in which a portion of the common interest development is located.

(b) If the declaration does not specify the percentage of members who must approve an amendment of the declaration, an amendment may be approved by a majority of all members, pursuant to Section 4065. **Leg.H.** Added Stats 2012 ch 180 §2 (AB 805), effective January 1, 2013, operative January 1, 2014. Amended Stats 2016 ch 714 §6 (SB 944), effective January 1, 2017.

§4275. Judicial authorization of amendment

(a) If in order to amend a declaration, the declaration requires members having more than 50 percent of the votes in the association, in a single class voting structure, or members having more than 50 percent of the votes in more than one class in a voting structure with more than one class, to vote in favor of the amendment, the association, or any member, may petition the superior court of the county in which the common interest development is located for an order reducing the percentage of the affirmative votes necessary for such an amendment. The petition shall describe the effort that has been made to solicit approval of the association members in the manner provided in the declaration, the number of affirmative and negative votes actually received, the number or percentage of affirmative votes required to effect the amendment in accordance with the existing declaration, and other matters the petitioner considers relevant to the court's determination. The petition shall also contain, as exhibits thereto, copies of all of the following:

(1) The governing documents.

(2) A complete text of the amendment.

(3) Copies of any notice and solicitation materials utilized in the solicitation of member approvals.

(4) A short explanation of the reason for the amendment.

(5) Any other documentation relevant to the court's determination.

(b) Upon filing the petition, the court shall set the matter for hearing and issue an ex parte order setting forth the manner in which notice shall be given.

(c) The court may, but shall not be required to, grant the petition if it finds all of the following:

(1) The petitioner has given not less than 15 days written notice of the court hearing to all members of the association, to any mortgagee of a mortgage or beneficiary of a deed of trust who is entitled to notice under the terms of the declaration, and to the city, county, or city and county in which the common interest development is located that is entitled to notice under the terms of the declaration.

(2) Balloting on the proposed amendment was conducted in accordance with the governing documents, this act, and any other applicable law.

(3) A reasonably diligent effort was made to permit all eligible members to vote on the proposed amendment.

(4) Members having more than 50 percent of the votes, in a single class voting structure, voted in favor of the amendment. In a voting structure with more than one class, where the declaration requires a majority of more than one class to vote in favor of the amendment, members having more than 50 percent of the votes of each class required by the declaration to vote in favor of the amendment voted in favor of the amendment.

(5) The amendment is reasonable.

(6) Granting the petition is not improper for any reason stated in subdivision (e).

(d) If the court makes the findings required by subdivision (c), any order issued pursuant to this section may confirm the amendment as being validly approved on the basis of the affirmative votes actually received during the balloting period or the order may dispense with any requirement relating to quorums or to the number or percentage of votes needed for approval of the amendment that would otherwise exist under the governing documents.

(e) Subdivisions (a) to (d), inclusive, notwithstanding, the court shall not be empowered by this section to approve any amendment to the declaration that:

(1) Would change provisions in the declaration requiring the approval of members having more than 50 percent of the votes in more than one class to vote in favor of an amendment, unless members having more than 50 percent of the votes in each affected class approved the amendment.

(2) Would eliminate any special rights, preferences, or privileges designated in the declaration as belonging to the declarant, without the consent of the declarant.

(3) Would impair the security interest of a mortgagee of a mortgage or the beneficiary of a deed of trust without the approval of the percentage of the mortgagees and beneficiaries specified in the declaration, if the declaration requires the approval of a specified percentage of the mortgagees and beneficiaries.

(f) An amendment is not effective pursuant to this section until the court order and amendment have been recorded in every county in which a portion of the common interest development is located. The amendment may be acknowledged by, and the court order and amendment may be recorded by, any person designated in the declaration or by the association for that purpose, or if no one is designated for that purpose, by the president of the association. Upon recordation of the amendment and court order, the declaration, as amended in accordance with this section, shall have the same force and effect as if the amendment were adopted in compliance with every requirement imposed by the governing documents.

(g) Within a reasonable time after the amendment is recorded the association shall deliver to each member, by individual delivery, pursuant to Section 4040, a copy of the amendment, together with a statement that the amendment has been recorded. **Leg.H.** Added Stats 2012 ch 180 §2 (AB 805), effective January 1, 2013, operative January 1, 2014.

ARTICLE 3
Articles of Incorporation

Content of articles. §4280.

§4280. Content of articles

(a) The articles of incorporation of an association filed with the Secretary of State shall include a statement, which shall be in addition to the statement of purposes of the corporation, that does all of the following:

(1) Identifies the corporation as an association formed to manage a common interest development under the Davis-Stirling Common Interest Development Act.

(2) States the business or corporate office of the association, if any, and, if the office is not on the site of the common interest development, states the front street and nearest cross street for the physical location of the common interest development.

(3) States the name and address of the association's managing agent, if any.

(b) The statement filed by an incorporated association with the Secretary of State pursuant to Section 8210 of the Corporations Code shall also contain a statement identifying the corporation as an association formed to manage a common interest development under the Davis-Stirling Common Interest Development Act.

(c) Documents filed prior to January 1, 2014, in compliance with former Section 1363.5, as it read on January 1, 2013, are deemed to be in compliance with this section. **Leg.H.** Added Stats 2012 ch 180 §2 (AB 805), effective January 1, 2013, operative January 1, 2014. Amended Stats 2013 ch 605 §20 (SB 752), effective January 1, 2014.

ARTICLE 4
Condominium Plan

"Condominium plan", §4285.
Recordation of condominium plan. §4290.
Amendment or revocation of condominium plan. §4295.

§4285. "Condominium plan"

A condominium plan shall contain all of the following:

(a) A description or survey map of a condominium project, which shall refer to or show monumentation on the ground.

(b) A three-dimensional description of a condominium project, one or more dimensions of which may extend for an indefinite distance upwards or downwards, in sufficient detail to identify the common area and each separate interest.

(c) A certificate consenting to the recordation of the condominium plan pursuant to this act that is signed and acknowledged as provided in Section 4290. **Leg.H.** Added Stats 2012 ch 180 §2 (AB 805), effective January 1, 2013, operative January 1, 2014.

§4290. Recordation of condominium plan

(a) The certificate consenting to the recordation of a condominium plan that is required by subdivision (c) of Section 4285 shall be signed and acknowledged by all of the following persons:

(1) The record owner of fee title to that property included in the condominium project.

(2) In the case of a condominium project that will terminate upon the termination of an estate for years, by all lessors and lessees of the estate for years.

(3) In the case of a condominium project subject to a life estate, by all life tenants and remainder interests.

(4) The trustee or the beneficiary of each recorded deed of trust, and the mortgagee of each recorded mortgage encumbering the property.

(b) Owners of mineral rights, easements, rights-of-way, and other nonpossessory interests do not need to sign the certificate.

(c) In the event a conversion to condominiums of a community apartment project or stock cooperative has been approved by the required number of owners, trustees, beneficiaries, and mortgagees pursuant to Section 66452.10 of the Government Code, the certificate need only be signed by those owners, trustees, beneficiaries, and mortgagees approving the conversion. **Leg.H.** Added Stats 2012 ch 180 §2 (AB 805), effective January 1, 2013, operative January 1, 2014. Amended Stats 2013 ch 183 §12 (SB 745), effective January 1, 2014.

§4295. Amendment or revocation of condominium plan

A condominium plan may be amended or revoked by a recorded instrument that is acknowledged and signed by all the persons who, at the time of amendment or revocation, are persons whose signatures are required under Section 4290. **Leg.H.** Added Stats 2012 ch 180 §2 (AB 805), effective January 1, 2013, operative January 1, 2014.

§4300. [Section repealed 1994.]

Leg.H. Added Stats 1973 ch 130 §2, effective June 30, 1973. Amended Stats 1978 ch 429 §29, effective July 17, 1978, operative July 1, 1978; Stats 1987 ch 911 §1; Stats 1988 ch 1581 §1. Repealed Stats 1992 ch 162 §3 (AB 2650), operative January 1, 1994. The repealed section related to premarital medical examinations.

Prior Law: Former CC §4300, relating to premarital medical examinations, was added Stats 1969 ch 1608 §8, operative January 1, 1970, amended Stats 1972 ch 714 §1, and repealed Stats 1973 ch 130 §1, effective June 30, 1973.

§4301. [Section repealed 1994.]

Leg.H. Added Stats 1969 ch 1608 §8, operative January 1, 1970. Repealed Stats 1992 ch 162 §3 (AB 2650), operative January 1, 1994. The repealed section related to laboratory statement.

§4302. [Section repealed 1980.]

Leg.H. Added Stats 1969 ch 1608 §8, operative January 1, 1970. Amended Stats 1972 ch 714 §2; Stats 1973 ch 142 §12, effective June 30, 1973, operative July 1, 1973. Repealed Stats 1980 ch 1191 §2, effective September 29, 1980. The repealed section related to "the certificate form" for physician's examination required for issuance of a marriage license.

§4303. [Section repealed 1994.]

Leg.H. Added Stats 1969 ch 1608 §8, operative January 1, 1970. Amended Stats 1974 ch 725 §1. Repealed Stats 1992 ch 162 §3 (AB 2650), operative January 1, 1994. The repealed section related to certificate forms from other states and armed forces.

§4304. [Section repealed 1994.]

Leg.H. Added Stats 1969 ch 1608 §8, operative January 1, 1970. Amended Stats 1978 ch 429 §31, effective July 17, 1978, operative July 1, 1978. Repealed Stats 1992 ch 162 §3 (AB 2650), operative January 1, 1994. The repealed section related to definition.

§4305. [Section repealed 1994.]

Leg.H. Added Stats 1969 ch 1608 §8, operative January 1, 1970. Amended Stats 1978 ch 429 §32, effective July 17, 1978, operative July 1, 1978. Repealed Stats 1992 ch 162 §3 (AB 2650), operative January 1,

1994. The repealed section related to submission of laboratory reports or records.

§4306. [Section repealed 1994.]

Leg.H. Added Stats 1969 ch 1608 §8, operative January 1, 1970. Amended Stats 1978 ch 429 §33, effective July 17, 1978, operative July 1, 1978. Repealed Stats 1992 ch 162 §3 (AB 2650), operative January 1, 1994. The repealed section related to court waiver of examination and text requirements.

§4307. [Section repealed 1994.]

Leg.H. Added Stats 1969 ch 1608 §8, operative January 1, 1970. Repealed Stats 1992 ch 162 §3 (AB 2650), operative January 1, 1994. The repealed section related to filing, preservation ad distribution of certificate of forms and court orders.

§4308. [Section repealed 1994.]

Leg.H. Added Stats 1969 ch 1608 §8, operative January 1, 1970. Repealed Stats 1992 ch 162 §3 (AB 2650), operative January 1, 1994. The repealed section related to published acts and criminal penalty.

§4309. [Section repealed 1994.]

Leg.H. Added Stats 1969 ch 1608 §8, operative January 1, 1970. Repealed Stats 1992 ch 162 §3 (AB 2650), operative January 1, 1994. The repealed section related to confidential documents and criminal penalty for unlawful disclosure.

ARTICLE 5
Operating Rules

"Operating rule"; "Rule change". §4340.
Requirements for validity and enforceability. §4350.
Application of rulemaking procedures. §4355.
Approval of rule change by board. §4360.
Reversal of rule change by members. §4365.
Applicability of article to changes commenced before and after January 1, 2004. §4370.

§4340. "Operating rule"; "Rule change"

For the purposes of this article:

(a) "Operating rule" means a regulation adopted by the board that applies generally to the management and operation of the common interest development or the conduct of the business and affairs of the association.

(b) "Rule change" means the adoption, amendment, or repeal of an operating rule by the board. **Leg.H.** Added Stats 2012 ch 180 §2 (AB 805), effective January 1, 2013, operative January 1, 2014.

§4350. Requirements for validity and enforceability

An operating rule is valid and enforceable only if all of the following requirements are satisfied:

(a) The rule is in writing.

(b) The rule is within the authority of the board conferred by law or by the declaration, articles of incorporation or association, or bylaws of the association.

(c) The rule is not in conflict with governing law and the declaration, articles of incorporation or association, or bylaws of the association.

(d) The rule is adopted, amended, or repealed in good faith and in substantial compliance with the requirements of this article.

(e) The rule is reasonable. **Leg.H.** Added Stats 2012 ch 180 §2 (AB 805), effective January 1, 2013, operative January 1, 2014. Amended Stats 2013 ch 183 §13 (SB 745), effective January 1, 2014.

Prior Law: Former CC §4350, similar to Fam C §310, was added Stats 1970 ch 311 §1, effective July 6, 1970, and repealed Stats 1992 ch 162 §3 (AB 2650), operative January 1, 1994.

§4350.5. [Section repealed 1994.]

Leg.H. Added Stats 1989 ch 1105 §1. Repealed Stats 1992 ch 162 §3 (AB 2650), operative January 1, 1994. See Fam C §11.

§4351. [Section repealed 1994.]

Leg.H. Added Stats 1970 ch 311 §1, effective July 6, 1970. Amended Stats 1977 ch 860 §1; Stats 1983 ch 1159 §1, operative July 1, 1984; Stats 1985 ch 419 §1. Repealed Stats 1992 ch 162 §3 (AB 2650), operative January 1, 1994. See Fam C §§2010, 2060.

§4351.5. [Section repealed 1994.]

Leg.H. Added Stats 1982 ch 1071 §1. Amended Stats 1983 ch 1277 §1; Stats 1988 ch 1550 §1. Repealed Stats 1992 ch 162 §3 (AB 2650), operative January 1, 1994. See Fam C §§3101, 3103, 3161, 3164, 3171, 3176–3180, 3182, 3183, 3185, 3186.

§4351.6. [Section repealed 1994.]

Leg.H. Added Stats 1990 ch 994 §1 (SB 2812). Repealed Stats 1992 ch 162 §3 (AB 2650), operative January 1, 1994. The repealed section related to legislative intent regarding support person.

§4352. [Section repealed 1994.]

Leg.H. Added Stats 1980 ch 1188 §1. Amended Stats 1983 ch 842 §8, ch 1159 §2, operative July 1, 1984; Stats 1984 ch 397 §1, effective July 11, 1984. Repealed Stats 1992 ch 162 §3 (AB 2650), operative January 1, 1994. See Fam C §2024.

§4353. [Section repealed 1994.]

Leg.H. Added Stats 1989 ch 1105 §2. Amended Stats 1990 ch 1493 §3 (AB 3974). Repealed Stats 1992 ch 162 §3 (AB 2650), operative January 1, 1994. See Fam C §2556.

§4355. Application of rulemaking procedures

(a) Sections 4360 and 4365 only apply to an operating rule that relates to one or more of the following subjects:

(1) Use of the common area or of an exclusive use common area.

(2) Use of a separate interest, including any aesthetic or architectural standards that govern alteration of a separate interest.

(3) Member discipline, including any schedule of monetary penalties for violation of the governing documents and any procedure for the imposition of penalties.

(4) Any standards for delinquent assessment payment plans.

(5) Any procedures adopted by the association for resolution of disputes.

(6) Any procedures for reviewing and approving or disapproving a proposed physical change to a member's separate interest or to the common area.

(7) Procedures for elections.

(b) Sections 4360 and 4365 do not apply to the following actions by the board:

(1) A decision regarding maintenance of the common area.

(2) A decision on a specific matter that is not intended to apply generally.

(3) A decision setting the amount of a regular or special assessment.

(4) A rule change that is required by law, if the board has no discretion as to the substantive effect of the rule change.

(5) Issuance of a document that merely repeats existing law or the governing documents. **Leg.H.** Added Stats 2012 ch 180 §2 (AB 805), effective January 1, 2013, operative January 1, 2014.

Prior Law: Former CC §4355, similar to Fam C §2020, was added Stats 1970 ch 311 §1, effective July 6, 1970, and repealed Stats 1992 ch 162 §3 (AB 2650), operative January 1, 1994.

§4355.6. [Section repealed 1994.]

Leg.H. Added Stats 1988 ch 159 §1. Repealed Stats 1992 ch 162 §3 (AB 2650), operative January 1, 1994. See Fam C §213.

§4356. [Section repealed 1994.]

Leg.H. Added Stats 1984 ch 156 §1. Repealed Stats 1992 ch 162 §3 (AB 2650), operative January 1, 1994. See Fam C §2012.

Prior Law: Former CC §4356, relating to conciliation court questionnaire in dissolution proceedings, was added Stats 1970 ch 311 §1, effective July 6, 1970, amended Stats 1970 ch 1575 §1, and repealed Stats 1974 ch 437 §1.

§4357. [Section repealed 1994.]

Leg.H. Added Stats 1970 ch 311 §1, effective July 6, 1970. Amended Stats 1972 ch 738 §1; Stats 1986 ch 366 §1. Repealed Stats 1992 ch 162 §3 (AB 2650), operative January 1, 1994. See Fam C §§3600–3604.

§4357.5. [Section repealed 1994.]

Leg.H. Added Stats 1985 ch 1069 §1. Amended Stats 1987 ch 57 §1. Repealed Stats 1992 ch 162 §3 (AB 2650), operative January 1, 1994. See Fam C §§95, 3620–3634 (ch 848 prevails). Amended Stats 1992 ch 848 §1 (SB 1614), effective September 22, 1992. Repealed Stats 1993 ch 219 §39 (AB 1500). See Fam C §§95, 3620 3634.

§4358. [Section repealed 1994.]

Leg.H. Added Stats 1970 ch 311 §1, effective July 6, 1970. Repealed Stats 1992 ch 162 §3 (AB 2650), operative January 1, 1994. See Fam C §2023.

§4358.5. [Section repealed 1994.]

Leg.H. Added Stats 1986 ch 1217 §1. Repealed Stats 1992 ch 162 §3 (AB 2650), operative January 1, 1994. The repealed section related to consignments of reimbursement under plans.

§4359. [Section repealed 1994.]

Leg.H. Added Stats 1970 ch 311 §1, effective July 6, 1970. Amended Stats 1975 ch 497 §1; Stats 1979 ch 795 §1, operative July 1, 1980; Stats 1980 ch 1158 §1; Stats 1983 ch 234 §1; Stats 1984 ch 402 §1; Stats 1988 ch 271 §1; Stats 1990 ch 935 §1 (AB 3593). Repealed Stats 1992 ch 162 §3 (AB 2650), operative January 1, 1994. Amended Stats 1992 ch 1136 §1 (SB 1541) (ch 1136 prevails). Repealed Stats 1993 ch 219 §39.5 (AB 1500). See Fam C §§2045, 6224, 6226, 6302, 6305, 6320–6324, 6380–6383, 6388.

§4360. Approval of rule change by board

(a) The board shall provide general notice pursuant to Section 4045 of a proposed rule change at least 28 days before making the rule change. The notice shall include the text of the proposed rule change and a description of the purpose and effect of the proposed rule change. Notice is not required under this subdivision if the board determines that an immediate rule change is necessary to address an imminent threat to public health or safety or imminent risk of substantial economic loss to the association.

(b) A decision on a proposed rule change shall be made at a board meeting, after consideration of any comments made by association members.

(c) As soon as possible after making a rule change, but not more than 15 days after making the rule change, the board shall deliver general notice pursuant to Section 4045 of the rule change. If the rule change was an emergency rule change made under subdivision (d), the notice shall include the text of the rule change, a description of the purpose and effect of the rule change, and the date that the rule change expires.

(d) If the board determines that an immediate rule change is required to address an imminent threat to public health or safety, or an imminent risk of substantial economic loss to the association, it may make an emergency rule change, and no notice is required, as specified in subdivision (a). An emergency rule change is effective for 120 days, unless the rule change provides for a shorter effective period. A rule change made under this subdivision may not be readopted under this subdivision. **Leg.H.** Added Stats 2012 ch 180 §2 (AB 805), effective January 1, 2013, operative January 1, 2014. Amended Stats 2018 ch 836 §2 (SB 261), effective January 1, 2019.

Prior Law: Former CC §4360, similar to Fam C §214, was added Stats 1970 ch 311 §1, effective July 6, 1970, and repealed Stats 1992 ch 162 §3 (AB 2650), operative January 1, 1994.

§4361. [Section repealed 1994.]

Leg.H. Added Stats 1970 ch 311 §1, effective July 6, 1970. Repealed Stats 1992 ch 162 §3 (AB 2650), operative January 1, 1994. See Fam C §2022.

§4362. [Section repealed 1994.]

Leg.H. Added Stats 1970 ch 311 §1, effective July 6, 1970. Amended Stats 1974 ch 1235 §1; Stats 1975 ch 1070 §1. Repealed Stats 1992 ch 162 §3 (AB 2650), operative January 1, 1994. See CCP §1279.6, Fam C §§2080–2082.

§4363. [Section repealed 1994.]

Leg.H. Added Stats 1970 ch 1211 §1. Amended Stats 1977 ch 860 §2. Repealed Stats 1992 ch 162 §3 (AB 2650), operative January 1, 1994. See Fam C §2021.

§4363.1. [Section repealed 1994.]

Leg.H. Added Stats 1977 ch 860 §3. Amended Stats 1978 ch 687 §1. Repealed Stats 1992 ch 162 §3 (AB 2650), operative January 1, 1994. See Fam C §§2060–2065.

§4363.2. [Section repealed 1994.]

Leg.H. Added Stats 1977 ch 860 §4. Amended Stats 1978 ch 687 §2; Stats 1983 ch 302 §3. Repealed Stats 1992 ch 162 §3 (AB 2650), operative January 1, 1994. See Fam C §§2063, 2070–2074.

§4363.3. [Section repealed 1994.]

Leg.H. Added Stats 1977 ch 860 §5. Amended Stats 1978 ch 687 §3. Repealed Stats 1992 ch 162 §3 (AB 2650), operative January 1, 1994. See Fam C §80.

§4364. [Section repealed 1994.]

Leg.H. Added Stats 1978 ch 435 §1. Repealed Stats 1992 ch 162 §3 (AB 2650), operative January 1, 1994. See Fam C §2330.5.

§4365. Reversal of rule change by members

(a) Members of an association owning 5 percent or more of the separate interests may call a special vote of the members to reverse a rule change.

(b) A special vote of the members may be called by delivering a written request to the association. Not less than 35 days nor more than 90 days after receipt of a proper request, the association shall hold a vote of the members on whether to reverse the rule change, pursuant to Article 4 (commencing with Section 5100) of Chapter 6. The written request may not be delivered more than 30 days after the association gives general notice of the rule change, pursuant to Section 4045.

(c) For the purposes of Section 5225 of this code and Section 8330 of the Corporations Code, collection of signatures to call a special vote under this section is a purpose reasonably related to the interests of the members of the association. A member request to copy or inspect the membership list solely for that purpose may not be denied on the grounds that the purpose is not reasonably related to the member's interests as a member.

(d) The rule change may be reversed by the affirmative vote of a majority of a quorum of the members, pursuant to Section 4070, or if the declaration or bylaws require a greater percentage, by the affirmative vote of the percentage required.

(e) Unless otherwise provided in the declaration or bylaws, for the purposes of this section, a member may cast one vote per separate interest owned.

(f) A rule change reversed under this section may not be readopted for one year after the date of the vote reversing the rule change. Nothing in this section precludes the board from adopting a different rule on the same subject as the rule change that has been reversed.

(g) As soon as possible after the close of voting, but not more than 15 days after the close of voting, the board shall provide general notice pursuant to Section 4045 of the results of the member vote.

(h) This section does not apply to an emergency rule change made under subdivision (d) of Section 4360. **Leg.H.** Added Stats 2012 ch 180 §2 (AB 805), effective January 1, 2013, operative January 1, 2014.

Prior Law: Former CC §4365, similar to Fam C §2025, was added Stats 1988 ch 678 §1 and repealed Stats 1992 ch 162 §3 (AB 2650), operative January 1, 1994.

§4366. [Section repealed 1994.]

Leg.H. Added Stats 1990 ch 1493 §4 (AB 3974). Repealed Stats 1992 ch 162 §3 (AB 2650), operative January 1, 1994. See Fam C §§2050–2053.

§4370. Applicability of article to changes commenced before and after January 1, 2004

(a) This article applies to a rule change commenced on or after January 1, 2004.

(b) Nothing in this article affects the validity of a rule change commenced before January 1, 2004.

(c) For the purposes of this section, a rule change is commenced when the board takes its first official action leading to adoption of the rule change. **Leg.H.** Added Stats 2012 ch 180 §2 (AB 805), effective January 1, 2013, operative January 1, 2014.

Prior Law: Former CC §4370, similar to Fam C §§270, 273, 2030, 2031, 3557, was added Stats 1970 ch 311 §1, effective July 6, 1970, amended Stats 1979 ch 1030 §2, Stats 1981 ch 715 §1, Stats 1984 ch 359 §1, Stats 1991 ch 110 §4 (SB 101), ch 500 §1 (SB 324), and repealed Stats 1992 ch 162 §3 (AB 2650), operative January 1, 1994.

§4370.5. [Section repealed 1994.]

Leg.H. Added Stats 1985 ch 362 §1. Amended Stats 1989 ch 1105 §3; Stats 1990 ch 893 §1 (AB 2686). Repealed Stats 1992 ch 162 §3 (AB 2650), operative January 1, 1994. Amended Stats 1992 ch 356 §1 (AB 3399) (ch 356 prevails). Repealed Stats 1993 ch 219 §40 (AB 1500). See Fam C §2032.

§4370.6. [Section repealed 1994.]

Leg.H. Added Stats 1990 ch 893 §2 (AB 2686). Repealed Stats 1992 ch 162 §3 (AB 2650), operative January 1, 1994. See Fam C §§271, 274.

§4371. [Section repealed 1994.]

Leg.H. Added Stats 1970 ch 311 §1, effective July 6, 1970. Repealed Stats 1992 ch 162 §3 (AB 2650), operative January 1, 1994. See Fam C §272.

§4372. [Section repealed 1994.]

Leg.H. Added Stats 1992 ch 356 §2 (AB 3399). Repealed Stats 1993 ch 219 §41 (AB 1500). See Fam C §2033.

§4373. [Section repealed 1994.]

Leg.H. Added Stats 1992 ch 356 §3 (AB 3399). Repealed Stats 1993 ch 219 §42 (AB 1500). See Fam C §2034.

§4380. [Section repealed 1994.]

Leg.H. Added Stats 1970 ch 311 §1, effective July 6, 1970. Amended Stats 1974 ch 1516 §6, operative January 1, 1977. Repealed Stats 1992 ch 162 §3 (AB 2650), operative January 1, 1994. See Fam C §290.

§4381. [Section repealed 1994.]

Leg.H. Added Stats 1971 ch 867 §1. Repealed Stats 1992 ch 162 §3 (AB 2650), operative January 1, 1994. See Fam C §2026.

§4382. [Section repealed 1994.]

Leg.H. Added Stats 1980 ch 237 §1. Repealed Stats 1992 ch 162 §3 (AB 2650), operative January 1, 1994. See Fam C §3556.

§4383. [Section repealed 1994.]

Leg.H. Added Stats 1982 ch 497 §15, operative July 1, 1983. Amended Stats 1985 ch 285 §1, ch 362 §2; Stats 1987 ch 960 §1. Repealed Stats 1992 ch 162 §3 (AB 2650), operative January 1, 1994. See Fam C §§5100, 5103, 5104.

§4384. [Section repealed 1994.]

Leg.H. Added Stats 1982 ch 497 §16, operative July 1, 1983. Amended Stats 1987 ch 960 §2. Repealed Stats 1992 ch 162 §3 (AB 2650), operative January 1, 1994. See Fam C §291.

§4384.5. [Section repealed 1994]

Leg.H. Added Stats 1992 ch 718 §3 (AB 568). Repealed Stats 1993 ch 219 §43 (AB 1500). Amended Stats 1993 ch 876 §1 (SB 1068), effective October 6, 1993, operative until January 1, 1994. Repealed operative January 1, 1994, by its own provisions. See CCP §683.130, Fam C §4502.

Prior Law: Former CC §4384.5, was added Stats 1986 ch 1046 §1, repealed Stats 1992 ch 162 §3 (AB 2650), operative January 1, 1994 (ch 718 prevails), and repealed Stats 1992 ch 718 §2 (AB 568). See CCP §683.130, Fam C §4502.

§4385. [Section repealed 1994.]

Leg.H. Added Stats 1982 ch 497 §16.5, operative July 1, 1983. Repealed Stats 1992 ch 162 §3 (AB 2650), operative January 1, 1994. See Fam C §4500.

§4390. [Section repealed 1994.]

Leg.H. Added Stats 1989 ch 1359 §1, operative July 1, 1990. Amended Stats 1990 ch 411 §1 (AB 3973), effective July 24, 1990, operative July 24, 1990; Stats 1991 ch 110 §5 (SB 101). Repealed Stats 1992 ch 162 §3 (AB 2650), operative January 1, 1994. Amended Stats 1992 ch 848 §2 (SB 1614), effective September 22, 1992 (ch 848 prevails). Repealed Stats 1993 ch 219 §44 (AB 1500). See Fam C §§150, 5200, 5202, 5204, 5206, 5210, 5212, 5214, 5216, 5220.

§4390.1. [Section repealed 1994.]

Leg.H. Added Stats 1989 ch 1359 §1, operative July 1, 1990. Repealed Stats 1992 ch 162 §3 (AB 2650), operative January 1, 1994. See Fam C §5244.

§4390.2. [Section repealed 1994.]

Leg.H. Added Stats 1989 ch 1359 §1, operative July 1, 1990. Repealed Stats 1992 ch 162 §3 (AB 2650), operative January 1, 1994. See Fam C §5239.

§4390.3. [Section repealed 1994.]

Leg.H. Added Stats 1989 ch 1359 §1, operative July 1, 1990. Amended Stats 1990 ch 411 §2 (AB 3973), effective July 24, 1990, operative July 24, 1990; Stats 1991 ch 110 §6 (SB 101), ch 1091 §16 (AB 1487) (ch 110 prevails). Repealed Stats 1992 ch 162 §3 (AB 2650), operative January 1, 1994. Amended Stats 1992 ch 848 §3 (SB 1614), effective September 22, 1992 (ch 848 prevails). Repealed Stats 1993 ch 219 §45 (AB 1500). Amended Stats 1993 ch 876 §2 (SB 1068), effective October 6, 1993, operative until January 1, 1994. Repealed January 1, 1994, by its own provisions. See Fam C §§5208, 5230, 5231, 5260.

§4390.4. [Section repealed 1994.]

Leg.H. Added Stats 1989 ch 1359 §1, operative July 1, 1990. Repealed Stats 1992 ch 162 §3 (AB 2650), operative January 1, 1994. See Fam C §5261.

§4390.5. [Section repealed 1994.]

Leg.H. Added Stats 1989 ch 1359 §1, operative July 1, 1990. Amended Stats 1991 ch 110 §7 (SB 101). Repealed Stats 1992 ch 162 §3 (AB 2650), operative January 1, 1994. See Fam C §§5208, 5250–5253.

§4390.6. [Section repealed 1994.]

Leg.H. Added Stats 1989 ch 1359 §1, operative July 1, 1990. Repealed Stats 1992 ch 162 §3 (AB 2650), operative January 1, 1994. See Fam C §5280.

§4390.7. [Section repealed 1994.]

Leg.H. Added Stats 1989 ch 1359 §1, operative July 1, 1990. Repealed Stats 1992 ch 162 §3 (AB 2650), operative January 1, 1994. See Fam C §§5231, 5281, 5282.

§4390.8. [Section repealed 1994.]

Leg.H. Added Stats 1989 ch 1359 §1, operative July 1, 1990. Repealed Stats 1992 ch 162 §3 (AB 2650), operative January 1, 1994. See Fam C §§5232–5234.

§4390.9. [Section repealed 1994.]

Leg.H. Added Stats 1989 ch 1359 §1, operative July 1, 1990. Amended Stats 1990 ch 411 §3 (AB 3973), effective July 24, 1990, operative July 24, 1990. Repealed Stats 1992 ch 162 §3 (AB 2650), operative January 1, 1994. See Fam C §§5270, 5272.

§4390.10. [Section repealed 1994.]

Leg.H. Added Stats 1989 ch 1359 §1, operative July 1, 1990. Repealed Stats 1992 ch 162 §3 (AB 2650), operative January 1, 1994. Amended Stats 1993 ch 876 §3 (SB 1068), effective October 6, 1993, operative until January 1, 1994. Repealed January 1, 1994, by its own provisions. See Fam C §§5235, 5241, 5242.

§4390.11. [Section repealed 1994.]

Leg.H. Added Stats 1989 ch 1359 §1, operative July 1, 1990. Repealed Stats 1992 ch 162 §3 (AB 2650), operative January 1, 1994. See Fam C §5271.

§4390.12. [Section repealed 1994.]

Leg.H. Added Stats 1989 ch 1359 §1, operative July 1, 1990. Amended Stats 1991 ch 110 §8 (SB 101). Repealed Stats 1992 ch 162 §3 (AB 2650), operative January 1, 1994. See Fam C §§5238, 5243.

§4390.13. [Section repealed 1994.]

Leg.H. Added Stats 1989 ch 1359 §1, operative July 1, 1990. Repealed Stats 1992 ch 162 §3 (AB 2650), operative January 1, 1994. See Fam C §5237.

§4390.14. [Section repealed 1994.]

Leg.H. Added Stats 1989 ch 1359 §1, operative July 1, 1990. Amended Stats 1990 ch 411 §4 (AB 3973), effective July 24, 1990, operative July 24, 1990. Repealed Stats 1992 ch 162 §3 (AB 2650), operative January 1, 1994. Amended Stats 1993 ch 876 §4 (SB 1068), effective October 6, 1993, operative until January 1, 1994. Repealed January 1, 1994, by its own provisions. See Fam C §5240.

§4390.15. [Section repealed 1994.]

Leg.H. Added Stats 1989 ch 1359 §1, operative July 1, 1990. Repealed Stats 1992 ch 162 §3 (AB 2650), operative January 1, 1994. See Fam C §5295.

§4390.16. [Section repealed 1994.]

Leg.H. Added Stats 1989 ch 1359 §1, operative July 1, 1990. Amended Stats 1991 ch 110 §9 (SB 101), ch 542 §4 (SB 1161). Repealed Stats 1992 ch 162 §3 (AB 2650), operative January 1, 1994. See Fam C §5236.

§4390.17. [Section repealed 1994.]

Leg.H. Added Stats 1989 ch 1359 §1, operative July 1, 1990. Repealed Stats 1992 ch 162 §3 (AB 2650), operative January 1, 1994. See Fam C §5290.

§4390.18. [Section repealed 1994.]

Leg.H. Added Stats 1989 ch 1359 §1, operative July 1, 1990. Repealed Stats 1992 ch 162 §3 (AB 2650), operative January 1, 1994. See Fam C §3555.

§4390.19. [Section repealed 1994.]

Leg.H. Added Stats 1989 ch 1359 §1, operative July 1, 1990. Repealed Stats 1992 ch 162 §3 (AB 2650), operative January 1, 1994. See Fam C §5245.

§4395. [Section repealed 1994.]

Leg.H. Added Stats 1992 ch 1157 §1 (SB 1680). Repealed Stats 1993 ch 219 §46 (AB 1500). See Fam C §3830.

§4400. [Section repealed 1994.]

Leg.H. Added Stats 1969 ch 1608 §8, operative January 1, 1970. Repealed Stats 1992 ch 162 §3 (AB 2650), operative January 1, 1994. See Fam C §2200.

§4401. [Section repealed 1994.]

Leg.H. Added Stats 1969 ch 1608 §8, operative January 1, 1970. Repealed Stats 1992 ch 162 §3 (AB 2650), operative January 1, 1994. See Fam C §2201.

§4425. [Section repealed 1994.]

Leg.H. Added Stats 1969 ch 1608 §8, operative January 1, 1970. Amended Stats 1969 ch 1609 §6, operative January 1, 1970. Repealed Stats 1992 ch 162 §3 (AB 2650), operative January 1, 1994. See Fam C §2210.

§4426. [Section repealed 1994.]

Leg.H. Added Stats 1969 ch 1608 §8, operative January 1, 1970. Amended Stats 1979 ch 730 §11, operative January 1, 1981. Repealed Stats 1992 ch 162 §3 (AB 2650), operative January 1, 1994. See Fam C §2211.

§4429. [Section repealed 1994.]

Leg.H. Added Stats 1969 ch 1609 §7, operative January 1, 1970. Repealed Stats 1992 ch 162 §3 (AB 2650), operative January 1, 1994. See Fam C §2212.

§4450. [Section repealed 1994.]

Leg.H. Added Stats 1969 ch 1608 §8, operative January 1, 1970. Amended Stats 1969 ch 1609 §8, operative January 1, 1970. Repealed Stats 1992 ch 162 §3 (AB 2650), operative January 1, 1994. See Fam C §2250.

§4451. [Section repealed 1994.]

Leg.H. Added Stats 1969 ch 1608 §8, operative January 1, 1970. Repealed Stats 1992 ch 162 §3 (AB 2650), operative January 1, 1994. See Fam C §2212.

§4452. [Section repealed 1994.]

Leg.H. Added Stats 1969 ch 1608 §8, operative January 1, 1970. Amended Stats 1970 ch 962 §2; Stats 1984 ch 1671 §2. Repealed Stats 1992 ch 162 §3 (AB 2650), operative January 1, 1994. See Fam C §§2251, 2252.

§4453. [Section repealed 1975.]

Leg.H. Added Stats 1969 ch 1608 §8, operative January 1, 1970. Repealed Stats 1975 ch 1244 §10. See Fam C §§7600 et seq.

§4454. [Section repealed 1994.]

Leg.H. Added Stats 1969 ch 1608 §8, operative January 1, 1970. Amended Stats 1969 ch 1609 §9, operative January 1, 1970. Repealed Stats 1992 ch 162 §3 (AB 2650), operative January 1, 1994. See Fam C §2253.

§4455. [Section repealed 1994.]

Leg.H. Added Stats 1969 ch 1608 §8, operative January 1, 1970. Amended Stats 1970 ch 1545 §1. Repealed Stats 1992 ch 162 §3 (AB 2650), operative January 1, 1994. See Fam C §2254.

§4456. [Section repealed 1994.]

Leg.H. Added Stats 1969 ch 1608 §8, operative January 1, 1970. Amended States 1975 ch 678 §5. Repealed Stats 1992 ch 162 §3 (AB 2650), operative January 1, 1994. See Fam C §2255.

§4457. [Section repealed 1994.]

Leg.H. Added Stats 1969 ch 1608 §8, operative January 1, 1970. Amended Stats 1974 ch 1235 §2; Stats 1975 ch 1070 §2. Repealed Stats 1992 ch 162 §3 (AB 2650), operative January 1, 1994. See CCP §1279.6, Fam C §§2080–2082.

§4458. [Section repealed 1994.]

Leg.H. Added Stats 1979 ch 795 §2, operative July 1, 1980. Amended Stats 1980 ch 1158 §2; Stats 1987 ch 391 §1. Repealed Stats 1992 ch 162 §3 (AB 2650), operative January 1, 1994. See Fam C §§6360, 6361, 6380, 6388.

CHAPTER 4
OWNERSHIP AND TRANSFER OF INTERESTS

Article 1. Ownership Rights and Interests.
Article 2. Transfer Disclosure.
Article 3. Transfer Fee.
Article 4. Restrictions on Transfer.
Article 5. Transfer of Separate Interest.

ARTICLE 1
Ownership Rights and Interests

Ownership of common area. §4500.
Appurtenant rights and easements. §4505.
Access to separate interest property. §4510.
Permitted activities. §4515.

§4500. Ownership of common area

Unless the declaration otherwise provides, in a condominium project, or in a planned development in which the common area is owned by the owners of the separate interests, the common area is owned as tenants in common, in equal shares, one for each separate interest. **Leg.H.** Added Stats 2012 ch 180 §2 (AB 805), effective January 1, 2013, operative January 1, 2014.

Prior Law: Former CC §4500, similar to CC §4350, was added Stats 1969 ch 1608 §8, operative January 1, 1970, amended Stats 1969 ch 1609 §10, operative January 2, 1970, and repealed Stats 1970 ch 311 §2, effective July 6, 1970.

§4501. [Section repealed 1994.]

Leg.H. Added Stats 1969 ch 1608 §8, operative January 1, 1970. Repealed Stats 1992 ch 162 §3 (AB 2650), operative January 1, 1994. See Fam C §2300.

§4502. [Section repealed 1970.]

Leg.H. Added Stats 1969 ch 1608 §8, operative January 1, 1970. Amended Stats 1969 ch 1609 §11, operative January 1, 1970. Repealed Stats 1970 ch 311 §3, effective July 6, 1970. See Fam C §§2010, 2060.

§4503. [Section repealed 1994.]

Leg.H. Added Stats 1969 ch 1608 §8, operative January 1, 1970. Amended Stats 1969 ch 1609 §12, operative January 1, 1970. Repealed Stats 1992 ch 162 §3 (AB 2650), operative January 1, 1994. See Fam C §§2330, 2331.

§4504. [Section repealed 1970.]

Leg.H. Added Stats 1969 ch 1608 §8, operative January 1, 1970. Amended Stats 1969 ch 1609 §13, operative January 1, 1970. Repealed Stats 1970 ch 311 §5, effective July 6, 1970. See Fam C §2020.

§4505. Appurtenant rights and easements

Unless the declaration otherwise provides:

(a) In a community apartment project and condominium project, and in those planned developments with common area owned in common by the owners of the separate interests, there are appurtenant to each separate interest nonexclusive rights of ingress, egress, and support, if necessary, through the common area. The common area is subject to these rights.

(b) In a stock cooperative, and in a planned development with common area owned by the association, there is an easement for ingress, egress, and support, if necessary, appurtenant to each separate interest. The common area is subject to these easements. **Leg.H.** Added Stats 2012 ch 180 §2 (AB 805), effective January 1, 2013, operative January 1, 2014.

Prior Law: Former CC §4505, similar to Fam C §2020, was added Stats 1969 ch 1608 §8, operative January 1, 1970, amended Stats 1969 ch 1609 §13, operative January 1, 1970, and repealed Stats 1970 ch 311 §5, effective July 6, 1970.

§4506. [Section repealed 1994.]

Leg.H. Added Stats 1969 ch 1608 §8, operative January 1, 1970. Repealed Stats 1992 ch 162 §3 (AB 2650), operative January 1, 1994. See Fam C §2310.

§4507. [Section repealed 1994.]

Leg.H. Added Stats 1969 ch 1608 §8, operative January 1, 1970. Repealed Stats 1992 ch 162 §3 (AB 2650), operative January 1, 1994. See Fam C §2311.

§4508. [Section repealed 1994.]

Leg.H. Added Stats 1969 ch 1608 §8, operative January 1, 1970. Amended Stats 1974 ch 437 §2. Repealed Stats 1992 ch 162 §3 (AB 2650), operative January 1, 1994. See Fam C §§2333, 2334, 2345, 2347.

§4509. [Section repealed 1994.]

Leg.H. Added Stats 1969 ch 1608 §8, operative January 1, 1970. Amended Stats 1969 ch 1609 §14, operative January 1, 1970; Stats 1975 ch 35 §1. Repealed Stats 1992 ch 162 §3 (AB 2650), operative January 1, 1994. See Fam C §2335.

§4510. Access to separate interest property

Except as otherwise provided in law, an order of the court, or an order pursuant to a final and binding arbitration decision, an association may not deny a member or occupant physical access to the member's or occupant's separate interest, either by restricting access through the common area to the separate interest, or by restricting access solely to the separate interest. **Leg.H.** Added Stats 2012 ch 180 §2 (AB 805), effective January 1, 2013, operative January 1, 2014.

Prior Law: Former CC §4510, similar to Fam C §§2312, 2313, 2332, was added Stats 1969 ch 1608 §8, operative January 1, 1970, amended Stats 1979 ch 730 §12, operative January 1, 1981, and repealed Stats 1992 ch 162 §3 (AB 2650), operative January 1, 1994.

§4511. [Section repealed 1994.]

Leg.H. Added Stats 1969 ch 1608 §8, operative January 1, 1970. Amended Stats 1969 ch 1609 §15, operative January 1, 1970; Stats 1980 ch 367 §1; Stats 1986 ch 143 §1. Repealed Stats 1992 ch 162 §3 (AB 2650), operative January 1, 1994. See Fam C §2336.

§4512. [Section repealed 1994.]

Leg.H. Added Stats 1969 ch 1608 §8, operative January 1, 1970. Amended Stats 1983 ch 302 §4, ch 1159 §3.5, operative July 1, 1984. Repealed Stats 1992 ch 162 §3 (AB 2650), operative January 1, 1994. See Fam C §2338.

§4513. [Section repealed 1994.]

Leg.H. Added Stats 1969 ch 1608 §8, operative January 1, 1970. Amended Stats 1983 ch 1159 §4, operative July 1, 1984; Stats 1985 ch 106 §10 (ch 96 prevails), ch 96 §1; Stats 1989 ch 1266 §1. Repealed Stats 1992 ch 162 §3 (AB 2650), operative January 1, 1994. See Fam C §2346.

§4514. [Section repealed 1994.]

Leg.H. Added Stats 1969 ch 1608 §8, operative January 1, 1970. Amended Stats 1969 ch 1609 §16, operative January 1, 1970; Stats 1978 ch 508 §1; Stats 1979 ch 164 §1; Stats 1983 ch 1159 §5, operative July 1, 1984; Stats 1984 ch 397 §2, effective July 11, 1984. Repealed Stats 1992 ch 162 §3 (AB 2650), operative January 1, 1994. See Fam C §§2339–2344.

§4515. Permitted activities

(a) It is the intent of the Legislature to ensure that members and residents of common interest developments have the ability to exercise their rights under law to peacefully assemble and freely communicate with one another and with others with respect to common interest development living or for social, political, or educational purposes.

(b) The governing documents, including bylaws and operating rules, shall not prohibit a member or resident of a common interest development from doing any of the following:

(1) Peacefully assembling or meeting with members, residents, and their invitees or guests during reasonable hours and in a reasonable manner for purposes relating to common interest development living, association elections, legislation, election to public office, or the initiative, referendum, or recall processes.

(2) Inviting public officials, candidates for public office, or representatives of homeowner organizations to meet with members, residents, and their invitees or guests and speak on matters of public interest.

(3) Using the common area, including the community or recreation hall or clubhouse, or, with the consent of the member, the area of a separate interest, for an assembly or meeting described in paragraph (1) or (2) when that facility or separate interest is not otherwise in use.

(4) Canvassing and petitioning the members, the association board, and residents for the activities described in paragraphs (1) and (2) at reasonable hours and in a reasonable manner.

(5) Distributing or circulating, without prior permission, information about common interest development living, association elections, legislation, election to public office, or the initiative, referendum, or recall processes, or other issues of concern to members and residents at reasonable hours and in a reasonable manner.

(6)(A) Using social media or other online resources to discuss any of the following, even if the content is critical of the association or its governance:

(i) Development living.

(ii) Association elections.

(iii) Legislation.

(iv) Election to public office.

(v) The initiative, referendum, or recall processes.

(vi) Any other issues of concern to members and residents.

(B) This paragraph does not require an association to provide social media or other online resources to members.

(C) This paragraph does not require an association to allow members to post content on the association's internet website.

(c) A member or resident of a common interest development shall not be required to pay a fee, make a deposit, obtain liability insurance, or pay the premium or deductible on the association's insurance policy, in order to use a common area for the activities described in paragraphs (1), (2), and (3) of subdivision (b).

(d) A member or resident of a common interest development who is prevented by the association or its agents from engaging in any of the activities described in this section may bring a civil or small claims court action to enjoin the enforcement of a governing document, including a bylaw and operating rule, that violates this section. The court may assess a civil penalty of not more than five hundred dollars ($500) for each violation.

(e) An association shall not retaliate against a member or a resident for exercising any of the rights contained in this section. **Leg.H.** Added Stats 2017 ch 236 §1 (SB 407), effective January 1, 2018. Amended Stats 2022 ch 858 §2 (AB 1410), effective January 1, 2023.

Prior Law: Former CC §4515, similar to present Fam C §2337, was added Stats 1988 ch 890 §1 and repealed Stats 1992 ch 162 §3 (AB 2650), effective January 1, 1993, operative January 1, 1994.

§4516. [Section repealed 1994.]

Leg.H. Added Stats 1979 ch 795 §3, operative July 1, 1980. Amended Stats 1988 ch 271 §2. Repealed Stats 1992 ch 162 §3 (AB 2650), operative January 1, 1994. See Fam C §§6361, 6380, 6388.

Prior Law: Former CC §4516, similar to present §4357, was added Stats 1969 ch 1608 §8, operative January 1, 1970, and repealed Stats 1970 ch 311 §6, effective July 6, 1970.

§§4517–4526. [Sections repealed 1970.]

Leg.H. Added Stats 1969 ch 1608 §8, operative January 1, 1970. Amended Stats 1969 ch 1609 §§17–19, operative January 1, 1970. Repealed Stats 1970 ch 311 §§7–12, effective July 6, 1970. See CC §§4358–4371.

ARTICLE 2
Transfer Disclosure

Disclosure to prospective purchaser. §4525.
Document disclosure summary form. §4528.
Documents to be provided by association; Fee for providing requested documents. §4530.

Related requirements. §4535.
Enforcement of article. §4540.
Validity of title unaffected. §4545.

§4525. Disclosure to prospective purchaser

(a) The owner of a separate interest shall provide the following documents to a prospective purchaser of the separate interest, as soon as practicable before the transfer of title or the execution of a real property sales contract, as defined in Section 2985:

(1) A copy of all governing documents. If the association is not incorporated, this shall include a statement in writing from an authorized representative of the association that the association is not incorporated.

(2) If there is a restriction in the governing documents limiting the occupancy, residency, or use of a separate interest on the basis of age in a manner different from that provided in Section 51.3, a statement that the restriction is only enforceable to the extent permitted by Section 51.3 and a statement specifying the applicable provisions of Section 51.3.

(3) A copy of the most recent documents distributed pursuant to Article 7 (commencing with Section 5300) of Chapter 6.

(4) A true statement in writing obtained from an authorized representative of the association as to the amount of the association's current regular and special assessments and fees, any assessments levied upon the owner's interest in the common interest development that are unpaid on the date of the statement, and any monetary fines or penalties levied upon the owner's interest and unpaid on the date of the statement. The statement obtained from an authorized representative shall also include true information on late charges, interest, and costs of collection which, as of the date of the statement, are or may be made a lien upon the owner's interest in a common interest development pursuant to Article 2 (commencing with Section 5650) of Chapter 8.

(5) A copy or a summary of any notice previously sent to the owner pursuant to Section 5855 that sets forth any alleged violation of the governing documents that remains unresolved at the time of the request. The notice shall not be deemed a waiver of the association's right to enforce the governing documents against the owner or the prospective purchaser of the separate interest with respect to any violation. This paragraph shall not be construed to require an association to inspect an owner's separate interest.

(6) A copy of the initial list of defects provided to each member pursuant to Section 6000, unless the association and the builder subsequently enter into a settlement agreement or otherwise resolve the matter and the association complies with Section 6100. Disclosure of the initial list of defects pursuant to this paragraph does not waive any privilege attached to the document. The initial list of defects shall also include a statement that a final determination as to whether the list of defects is accurate and complete has not been made.

(7) A copy of the latest information provided for in Section 6100.

(8) Any change in the association's current regular and special assessments and fees which have been approved by the board, but have not become due and payable as of the date disclosure is provided pursuant to this subdivision.

(9) If there is a provision in the governing documents that prohibits the rental or leasing of any of the separate interests in the common interest development to a renter, lessee, or tenant, a statement describing the prohibition.

(10) If requested by the prospective purchaser, a copy of the minutes of board meetings, excluding meetings held in executive session, conducted over the previous 12 months, that were approved by the board.

(b) This section does not apply to an owner that is subject to Section 11018.6 of the Business and Professions Code. **Leg.H.** Added Stats 2012 ch 180 §2 (AB 805), effective January 1, 2013, operative January 1, 2014. Amended Stats 2013 ch 183 §14 (SB 745), effective January 1, 2014.

§4528. Document disclosure summary form

The form for billing disclosures required by Section 4530 shall be in at least 10-point type and substantially the following form:

CHARGES FOR DOCUMENTS PROVIDED AS REQUIRED BY SECTION 4525*

The seller may, in accordance with Section 4530 of the Civil Code, provide to the prospective purchaser, at no cost, current copies of any documents specified by Section 4525 that are in the possession of the seller.

A seller may request to purchase some or all of these documents, but shall not be required to purchase ALL of the documents listed on this form.

Property Address
Owner of Property
Owner's Mailing Address (If known or different from property address.)
Provider of the Section 4525 Items:
Print Name _____ Position or Title _____ Association or Agent
Date Form Completed

Check or Complete Applicable Column or Columns Below

Document	Civil Code Section Included	Fee for Document	Not Available (N/A), Not Applicable (N/App), or Directly Provided by Seller and confirmed in writing by Seller as a current document (DP)
Articles of Incorporation or statement that not incorporated	Section 4525(a)(1)		
CC&Rs	Section 4525(a)(1)		
Bylaws	Section 4525(a)(1)		
Operating Rules	Section 4525(a)(1)		
Age restrictions, if any	Section 4525(a)(2)		
Rental restrictions, if any	Section 4525(a)(9)		
Annual budget report or summary, including reserve study	Sections 5300 and 4525(a)(3)		
Assessment and reserve funding disclosure summary	Sections 5300 and 4525(a)(4)		
Financial statement review	Sections 5305 and 4525(a)(3)		
Assessment enforcement policy	Sections 5310 and 4525(a)(4)		
Insurance summary	Sections 5300 and 4525(a)(3)		
Regular assessment	Section 4525(a)(4)		
Special assessment	Section 4525(a)(4)		
Emergency assessment	Section 4525(a)(4)		
Other unpaid obligations of seller	Sections 5675 and 4525(a)(4)		
Approved changes to assessments	Sections 5300 and 4525(a)(4), (8)		
Settlement notice regarding common area defects	Sections 4525(a)(6), (7), and 6100		
Preliminary list of defects	Sections 4525(a)(6), 6000, and 6100		
Notice(s) of violation	Sections 5855 and 4525(a)(5)		
Required statement of fees	Section 4525		
Minutes of regular board meetings conducted over	Section 4525(a)(10)		

Document	Civil Code Section Included	Fee for Document	Not Available (N/A), Not Applicable (N/App), or Directly Provided by Seller and confirmed in writing by Seller as a current document (DP)
the previous 12 months, if requested			
Total fees for these documents:			

* The information provided by this form may not include all fees that may be imposed before the close of escrow. Additional fees that are not related to the requirements of Section 4525 shall be charged separately. **Leg.H.** Added Stats 2012 ch 180 §2 (AB 805), effective January 1, 2013, operative January 1, 2014. Amended Stats 2013 ch 183 §15 (SB 745), effective January 1, 2014; Stats 2014 ch 185 §1 (AB 2430), effective January 1, 2015; Stats 2017 ch 127 §2 (AB 690), effective January 1, 2018.

§4530. Documents to be provided by association; Fee for providing requested documents

(a)(1) Upon written request, the association shall, within 10 days of the mailing or delivery of the request, provide the owner of a separate interest, or any other recipient authorized by the owner, with a copy of all of the requested documents specified in Section 4525.

(2) The documents required to be made available pursuant to this section may be maintained in electronic form, and may be posted on the association's Internet Web site. Requesting parties shall have the option of receiving the documents by electronic transmission if the association maintains the documents in electronic form.

(3) Delivery of the documents required by this section shall not be withheld for any reason nor subject to any condition except the payment of the fee authorized pursuant to subdivision (b).

(b)(1) The association may collect a reasonable fee from the seller based upon the association's actual cost for the procurement, preparation, reproduction, and delivery of the documents requested pursuant to this section. An additional fee shall not be charged for the electronic delivery in lieu of a hard copy delivery of the documents requested.

(2) Upon receipt of a written request, the association shall provide, on the form described in Section 4528, a written or electronic estimate of the fees that will be assessed for providing the requested documents prior to processing the request in paragraph (1) of subdivision (a).

(3)(A) A cancellation fee for documents specified in subdivision (a) shall not be collected if either of the following applies:

(i) The request was canceled in writing by the same party that placed the order and work had not yet been performed on the order.

(ii) The request was canceled in writing and any work that had been performed on the order was compensated.

(B) The association shall refund all fees collected pursuant to paragraph (1) if the request was canceled in writing and work had not yet been performed on the order.

(C) If the request was canceled in writing, the association shall refund the share of fees collected pursuant to paragraph (1) that represents the portion of the work not performed on the order.

(4) Fees for any documents required by this section shall be distinguished from, separately stated, and separately billed from, all other fees, fines, or assessments billed as part of the transfer or sales transaction.

(5) Any documents not expressly required by Section 4525 to be provided to a prospective purchaser by the seller shall not be included in the document disclosure required by this section. Bundling of documents required to be provided pursuant to this section with other documents relating to the transaction is prohibited.

(6) A seller shall provide to the prospective purchaser, at no cost, current copies of any documents specified by Section 4525 that are in the possession of the seller.

(7) The fee for each document provided to the seller for the purpose of transmission to the prospective purchaser shall be individually itemized in the statement required to be provided by the seller to the prospective purchaser.

(8) It is the responsibility of the seller to compensate the association, person, or entity that provides the documents required to be provided by Section 4525 to the prospective purchaser.

(c) An association may contract with any person or entity to facilitate compliance with this section on behalf of the association.

(d) The association shall also provide a recipient authorized by the owner of a separate interest with a copy of the completed form specified in Section 4528 at the time the required documents are delivered. A seller may request to purchase some or all of these documents, but shall not be required to purchase all of the documents listed on the form specified in Section 4528. **Leg.H.** Added Stats 2012 ch 180 §2 (AB 805), effective January 1, 2013, operative January 1, 2014. Amended Stats 2013 ch 183 §16 (SB 745), effective January 1, 2014; Stats 2014 ch 185 §2 (AB 2430), effective January 1, 2015; Stats 2017 ch 127 §3 (AB 690), effective January 1, 2018.

Prior Law: Former CC §4530, similar to Fam C §§2320, 2321, was added Stats 1969 ch 1608 §8, operative January 1, 1970, amended Stats 1980 ch 234 §1, and repealed Stats 1992 ch 162 §3 (AB 2650), operative January 1, 1994.

§4531. [Section repealed 1994.]

Leg.H. Added Stats 1969 ch 1608 §8, operative January 1, 1970. Amended Stats 1977 ch 332 §1. Repealed Stats 1992 ch 162 §3 (AB 2650), operative January 1, 1994. See Fam C §2322.

§4535. Related requirements

In addition to the requirements of this article, an owner transferring title to a separate interest shall comply with applicable requirements of Sections 1133 and 1134. **Leg.H.** Added Stats 2012 ch 180 §2 (AB 805), effective January 1, 2013, operative January 1, 2014.

§4540. Enforcement of article

Any person who willfully violates this article is liable to the purchaser of a separate interest that is subject to this section for actual damages occasioned thereby and, in addition, shall pay a civil penalty in an amount not to exceed five hundred dollars ($500). In an action to enforce this liability, the prevailing party shall be awarded reasonable attorney's fees. **Leg.H.** Added Stats 2012 ch 180 §2 (AB 805), effective January 1, 2013, operative January 1, 2014.

Prior Law: Former CC §4540, similar to Fam C §290, was added Stats 1969 ch 1608 §8, operative January 1, 1970, and repealed Stats 1970 ch 311 §14, effective July 6, 1970.

§4545. Validity of title unaffected

Nothing in this article affects the validity of title to real property transferred in violation of this article. **Leg.H.** Added Stats 2012 ch 180 §2 (AB 805), effective January 1, 2013, operative January 1, 2014.

§4550. [Section repealed 1994.]

Leg.H. Added Stats 1978 ch 508 §2. Amended Stats 1978 ch 1323 §1; Stats 1980 ch 627 §1; Stats 1981 ch 123 §1; Stats 1983 ch 302 §5; Stats 1990 ch 1493 §5 (AB 3974). Repealed Stats 1992 ch 162 §3 (AB 2650), operative January 1, 1994. See Fam C §2400.

§4551. [Section repealed 1994.]

Leg.H. Added Stats 1978 ch 508 §2. Repealed Stats 1992 ch 162 §3 (AB 2650), operative January 1, 1994. See Fam C §2401.

§4552. [Section repealed 1994.]

Leg.H. Added Stats 1978 ch 508 §2. Repealed Stats 1992 ch 162 §3 (AB 2650), operative January 1, 1994. See Fam C §2402.

§4553. [Section repealed 1994.]

Leg.H. Added Stats 1978 ch 508 §2. Repealed Stats 1992 ch 162 §3 (AB 2650), operative January 1, 1994. See Fam C §2403.

§4554. [Section repealed 1994.]

Leg.H. Added Stats 1978 ch 508 §2. Amended Stats 1983 ch 302 §6. Repealed Stats 1992 ch 162 §3 (AB 2650), operative January 1, 1994. See Fam C §2404.

§4555. [Section repealed 1994.]

Leg.H. Added Stats 1978 ch 508 §2. Amended Stats 1980 ch 627 §2, ch 1341 §3; Stats 1981 ch 714 §55. Repealed Stats 1992 ch 162 §3 (AB 2650), operative January 1, 1994. See Fam C §2405.

§4556. [Section repealed 1994.]

Leg.H. Added Stats 1978 ch 508 §2. Repealed Stats 1992 ch 162 §3 (AB 2650), operative January 1, 1994. See Fam C §2406.

ARTICLE 3
Transfer Fee

Transfer fee. §4575.
Exemption from transfer fee limitations. §4580.

§4575. Transfer fee

Except as provided in Section 4580, neither an association nor a community service organization or similar entity may impose or collect any assessment, penalty, or fee in connection with a transfer of title or any other interest except for the following:

(a) An amount not to exceed the association's actual costs to change its records.

(b) An amount authorized by Section 4530. **Leg.H.** Added Stats 2012 ch 180 §2 (AB 805), effective January 1, 2013, operative January 1, 2014.

§4580. Exemption from transfer fee limitations

The prohibition in Section 4575 does not apply to a community service organization or similar entity, or to a nonprofit entity that provides services to a common interest development under a declaration of trust, of either of the following types:

(a) An organization or entity that satisfies both of the following conditions:

(1) It was established before February 20, 2003.

(2) It exists and operates, in whole or in part, to fund or perform environmental mitigation or to restore or maintain wetlands or native habitat, as required by the state or local government as an express written condition of development.

(b) An organization or entity that satisfies all of the following conditions:

(1) It is not an organization or entity described by subdivision (a).

(2) It was established and received a transfer fee before January 1, 2004.

(3) On and after January 1, 2006, it offers a purchaser the following payment options for the fee or charge it collects at time of transfer:

(A) Paying the fee or charge at the time of transfer.

(B) Paying the fee or charge pursuant to an installment payment plan for a period of not less than seven years. If the purchaser elects to pay the fee or charge in installment payments, the organization or entity may also collect additional amounts that do not exceed the actual costs for billing and financing on the amount owed. If the purchaser sells the separate interest before the end of the installment payment plan period, the purchaser shall pay the remaining balance before the transfer. **Leg.H.** Added Stats 2012 ch 180 §2 (AB 805), effective January 1, 2013, operative January 1, 2014.

ARTICLE 4
Restrictions on Transfer

Grant of exclusive use. §4600.
Civil action to enforce Section 4600. §4605.
Partition of condominium project. §4610.
Lien for work performed in common interest development. §4615.

§4600. Grant of exclusive use

(a) Unless the governing documents specify a different percentage, the affirmative vote of members owning at least 67 percent of the separate interests in the common interest development shall be required before the board may grant exclusive use of any portion of the common area to a member.

(b) Subdivision (a) does not apply to the following actions:

(1) A reconveyance of all or any portion of that common area to the subdivider to enable the continuation of development that is in substantial conformance with a detailed plan of phased development submitted to the Real Estate Commissioner with the application for a public report.

(2) Any grant of exclusive use that is in substantial conformance with a detailed plan of phased development submitted to the Real Estate Commissioner with the application for a public report or in accordance with the governing documents approved by the Real Estate Commissioner.

(3) Any grant of exclusive use that is for any of the following reasons:

(A) To eliminate or correct engineering errors in documents recorded with the county recorder or on file with a public agency or utility company.

(B) To eliminate or correct encroachments due to errors in construction of any improvements.

(C) To permit changes in the plan of development submitted to the Real Estate Commissioner in circumstances where the changes are the result of topography, obstruction, hardship, aesthetic considerations, or environmental conditions.

(D) To fulfill the requirement of a public agency.

(E) To transfer the burden of management and maintenance of any common area that is generally inaccessible and not of general use to the membership at large of the association.

(F) To accommodate a disability.

(G) To assign a parking space, storage unit, or other amenity, that is designated in the declaration for assignment, but is not assigned by the declaration to a specific separate interest.

(H) To install and use an electric vehicle charging station in an owner's garage or a designated parking space that meets the requirements of Section 4745, where the installation or use of the charging station requires reasonable access through, or across, the common area for utility lines or meters.

(I) To install and use an electric vehicle charging station through a license granted by an association under Section 4745.

(J) To install and use a solar energy system on the common area roof of a residence that meets the requirements of Sections 714, 714.1, and, if applicable, Section 4746.

(K) To comply with governing law.

(c) Any measure placed before the members requesting that the board grant exclusive use of any portion of the common area shall specify whether the association will receive any monetary consideration for the grant and whether the association or the transferee will be responsible for providing any insurance coverage for exclusive use of the common area. **Leg.H.** Added Stats 2012 ch 180 §2 (AB 805), effective January 1, 2013, operative January 1, 2014. Amended Stats 2017 ch 818 §2 (AB 634), effective January 1, 2018.

Prior Law: Former CC §4600, similar to Fam C §§3020, 3022, 3040–3043, was added Stats 1969 ch 1608 §8, operative January 1, 1970, amended Stats 1970 ch 1545 §2, Stats 1972 ch 1007 §1, Stats 1979 ch 204 §1, ch 730 §13, operative January 1, 1981, ch 915 §3, Stats 1984 ch 1679 §1, Stats 1988 ch 1442 §2, Stats 1990 ch 610 §1 (AB 2700), and repealed Stats 1992 ch 162 §3 (AB 2650), operative January 1, 1994.

§4600.1. [Section repealed 1994.]

Leg.H. Added Stats 1976 ch 1399 §2. Amended Stats 1984 ch 109 §1; Stats 1989 ch 1265 §1; Stats 1990 ch 610 §2 (AB 2700). Repealed Stats 1992 ch 162 §3 (AB 2650), operative January 1, 1994. See Fam C §3060–3064.

§4600.2. [Section repealed 1994.]

Leg.H. Added Stats 1979 ch 1030 §3. Amended Stats 1984 ch 1605 §2, operative July 1, 1985. Repealed Stats 1992 ch 162 §3 (AB 2650), operative January 1, 1994. See Fam C §3029.

§4600.5. [Section repealed 1994.]

Leg.H. Added Stats 1979 ch 915 §2. Amended Stats 1983 ch 304 §1; Stats 1984 ch 1679 §2; Stats 1988 ch 1550 §2. Repealed Stats 1992 ch 162 §3 (AB 2650), operative January 1, 1994. See Fam C §§3002–3004, 3006, 3007, 3024, 3025, 3080–3089.

Prior Law: There was another section of this number, similar to the repealed section, which was added Stats 1979 ch 204 §2 and repealed Stats 1981 ch 714 §56.

§4600.6. [Section repealed 1994.]

Leg.H. Added Stats 1980 ch 863 §1. Repealed Stats 1992 ch 162 §3 (AB 2650), operative January 1, 1994. See Fam C §3023.

§4601. [Section repealed 1994.]

Leg.H. Added Stats 1969 ch 1608 §8, operative January 1, 1970. Amended Stats 1988 ch 1550 §3. Repealed Stats 1992 ch 162 §3 (AB 2650), operative January 1, 1994. See Fam C §3100.

§4601.5. [Section repealed 1994.]

Leg.H. Added Stats 1982 ch 359 §1. Amended Stats 1988 ch 1550 §4; Stats 1991 ch 321 §1 (AB 370). Repealed Stats 1992 ch 162 §3 (AB 2650), operative January 1, 1994. See Fam C §3100.

§4602. [Section repealed 1994.]

Leg.H. Added Stats 1969 ch 1608 §8, operative January 1, 1970. Amended Stats 1969 ch 1609 §20, operative January 1, 1970; Stats 1977 ch 772 §1; Stats 1978 ch 949 §1; Stats 1982 ch 292 §1; Stats 1985 ch 361 §1, effective July 30, 1985; Stats 1991 ch 410 §1 (AB 162). Repealed Stats 1992 ch 162 §3 (AB 2650), operative January 1, 1994. Amended Stats 1992 ch 427 §13 (AB 3355) (ch 162 prevails). Repealed Stats 1993 ch 219 §46.5 (AB 1500). See Fam C §§3111–3114.

§4603. [Section repealed 1994.]

Leg.H. Added Stats 1969 ch 1608 §8, operative January 1, 1970. Repealed Stats 1992 ch 162 §3 (AB 2650), operative January 1, 1994. See Fam C §3120.

§4604. [Section repealed 1994.]

Leg.H. Added Stats 1976 ch 1399 §3. Amended Stats 1983 ch 990 §1; Stats 1989 ch 1428 §1. Repealed Stats 1992 ch 162 §3 (AB 2650), operative January 1, 1994. See Fam C §§3130–3133.

§4604.5. [Section repealed 1994.]

Leg.H. Added Stats 1987 ch 954 §1. Repealed Stats 1992 ch 162 §3 (AB 2650), operative January 1, 1994. See Fam C §3140.

§4605. Civil action to enforce Section 4600

(a) A member of an association may bring a civil action for declaratory or equitable relief for a violation of Section 4600 by the association, including, but not limited to, injunctive relief, restitution, or a combination thereof, within one year of the date the cause of action accrues.

(b) A member who prevails in a civil action to enforce the member's rights pursuant to Section 4600 shall be entitled to reasonable attorney's fees and court costs, and the court may impose a civil penalty of up to five hundred dollars ($500) for each violation, except that each identical violation shall be subject to only one penalty if the violation affects each member equally. A prevailing association shall not recover any costs, unless the court finds the action to be frivolous, unreasonable, or without foundation. **Leg.H.** Added Stats 2012 ch 180 §2 (AB 805), effective January 1, 2013, operative January 1, 2014.

Prior Law: Former CC §4605, similar to Fam C §3134, was added Stats 1976 ch 1399 §4 and repealed Stats 1992 ch 162 §3 (AB 2650), operative January 1, 1994.

§4606. [Section repealed 1994.]

Leg.H. Added Stats 1976 ch 588 §1. Amended Stats 1985 ch 361 §2, effective July 30, 1985; Stats 1988 ch 153 §1; Stats 1989 ch 636 §1; Stats 1990 ch 754 §1 (AB 2708). Repealed Stats 1992 ch 162 §3 (AB 2650), operative January 1, 1994. See Fam C §§3150–3153.

§4607. [Section repealed 1994]

Leg.H. Added Stats 1980 ch 48 §5, effective March 27, 1980, operative January 1, 1981. Amended Stats 1983 ch 990 §2; Stats 1985 ch 361 §3, effective July 30, 1985; Stats 1987 ch 1086 §1; Stats 1988 ch 1377 §1, ch 1550 §6; Stats 1990 ch 348 §1 (SB 1897); Stats 1991 ch 410 §2 (AB 162). Repealed Stats 1992 ch 162 §3 (AB 2650), operative January 1, 1994. See Fam C §§3160, 3161, 3163, 3164, 3170, 3172, 3173, 3175, 3177–3184, 3186.

§4607.1. [Section repealed 1994.]

Leg.H. Added Stats 1988 ch 1550 §7. Amended Stats 1989 ch 1265 §2. Repealed Stats 1992 ch 162 §3 (AB 2650), operative January 1, 1994. See Fam C §3162.

§4607.2. [Section repealed 1994.]

Leg.H. Added Stats 1988 ch 1377 §2. Amended Stats 1990 ch 994 §2 (SB 2812); Stats 1991 ch 410 §3 (AB 162). Repealed Stats 1992 ch 162 §3 (AB 2650), operative January 1, 1994. See Fam C §3181.

§4608. [Section repealed 1994.]

Leg.H. Added Stats 1982 ch 359 §2. Amended Stats 1984 ch 1679 §3; Stats 1990 ch 610 §3 (AB 2700). Repealed Stats 1992 ch 162 §3 (AB 2650), operative January 1, 1994. See Fam C §3011.

§4608.1. [Section repealed 1994.]

Leg.H. Added Stats 1989 ch 636 §2. Amended Stats 1991 ch 410 §4 (AB 162). Repealed Stats 1992 ch 162 §3 (AB 2650), operative January 1, 1994. See Fam C §§3190–3192.

§4609. [Section repealed 1994.]

Leg.H. Added Stats 1985 ch 1068 §1, effective September 27, 1985. Repealed Stats 1992 ch 162 §3 (AB 2650), operative January 1, 1994. See Fam C §3026.

§4610. Partition of condominium project

(a) Except as provided in this section, the common area in a condominium project shall remain undivided, and there shall be no judicial partition thereof. Nothing in this section shall be deemed to prohibit partition of a cotenancy in a condominium.

(b) The owner of a separate interest in a condominium project may maintain a partition action as to the entire project as if the owners of all of the separate interests in the project were tenants in common in the entire project in the same proportion as their interests in the common area. The court shall order partition under this subdivision only by sale of the entire condominium project and only upon a showing of one of the following:

(1) More than three years before the filing of the action, the condominium project was damaged or destroyed, so that a material part was rendered unfit for its prior use, and the condominium project has not been rebuilt or repaired substantially to its state prior to the damage or destruction.

(2) Three-fourths or more of the project is destroyed or substantially damaged and owners of separate interests holding in the aggregate more than a 50-percent interest in the common area oppose repair or restoration of the project.

(3) The project has been in existence more than 50 years, is obsolete and uneconomic, and owners of separate interests holding in the aggregate more than a 50-percent interest in the common area oppose repair or restoration of the project.

(4) Any conditions in the declaration for sale under the circumstances described in this subdivision have been met. **Leg.H.** Added Stats 2012 ch 180 §2 (AB 805), effective January 1, 2013, operative January 1, 2014.

Prior Law: Former CC §4610, similar to Fam C §3030, was added Stats 1988 ch 1128 §1 and repealed Stats 1992 ch 162 §3 (AB 2650), operative January 1, 1994.

§4611. [Section repealed 1994.]

Leg.H. Added Stats 1990 ch 297 §1 (AB 3546). Repealed Stats 1992 ch 162 §3 (AB 2650), operative January 1, 1994. See Fam C §3027.

§4612. [Section repealed 1994.]

Leg.H. Added Stats 1992 ch 1136 §2 (SB 1541). Repealed Stats 1993 ch 219 §46.7 (AB 1500). See Fam C §3031.

§4615. Lien for work performed in common interest development

(a) In a common interest development, no labor performed or services or materials furnished with the consent of, or at the request of, an owner in the common interest development or the owners' agent or contractor shall be the basis for the filing of a lien against any other property of another owner in the common interest development unless that other owner has expressly consented to or requested the performance of the labor or furnishing of the materials or services. However, express consent is deemed to have been given by the owner of any separate interest in the case of emergency repairs thereto.

(b) Labor performed or services or materials furnished for the common area, if duly authorized by the association, are deemed to be performed or furnished with the express consent of each separate interest owner.

(c) The owner of any separate interest may remove that owner's separate interest from a lien against two or more separate interests or any part thereof by doing either of the following:

(1) Pay to the holder of the lien the fraction of the total sum secured by the lien that is attributable to the owner's separate interest.

(2) Record a lien release bond, pursuant to Section 8424, in an amount equal to 125 percent of the sum secured by the lien that is attributable to the owner's separate interest. **Leg.H.** Added Stats 2012 ch 180 §2 (AB 805), effective January 1, 2013, operative January 1, 2014. Amended Stats 2017 ch 44 §1 (AB 534), effective January 1, 2018; Stats 2018 ch 92 §38 (SB 1289), effective January 1, 2019.

ARTICLE 5
Transfer of Separate Interest

Notice of claim of lien. §4620.
Community apartment project. §4625.

Condominium project. §4630.
Planned development. §4635.
Stock cooperative. §4640.
Transfer of exclusive use common area. §4645.
Severability of interests. §4650.

§4620. Notice of claim of lien

If the association is served with a claim of lien pursuant to Part 6 (commencing with Section 8000) for a work of improvement on a common area, the association shall, within 60 days of service, give individual notice to the members, pursuant to Section 4040. **Leg.H.** Added Stats 2017 ch 44 §2 (AB 534), effective January 1, 2018.

§4625. Community apartment project

In a community apartment project, any conveyance, judicial sale, or other voluntary or involuntary transfer of the separate interest includes the undivided interest in the community apartment project. Any conveyance, judicial sale, or other voluntary or involuntary transfer of the owner's entire estate also includes the owner's membership interest in the association. **Leg.H.** Added Stats 2012 ch 180 §2 (AB 805), effective January 1, 2013, operative January 1, 2014.

§4630. Condominium project

In a condominium project the common area is not subject to partition, except as provided in Section 4610. Any conveyance, judicial sale, or other voluntary or involuntary transfer of the separate interest includes the undivided interest in the common area. Any conveyance, judicial sale, or other voluntary or involuntary transfer of the owner's entire estate also includes the owner's membership interest in the association. **Leg.H.** Added Stats 2012 ch 180 §2 (AB 805), effective January 1, 2013, operative January 1, 2014.

§4635. Planned development

In a planned development, any conveyance, judicial sale, or other voluntary or involuntary transfer of the separate interest includes the undivided interest in the common area, if any exists. Any conveyance, judicial sale, or other voluntary or involuntary transfer of the owner's entire estate also includes the owner's membership interest in the association. **Leg.H.** Added Stats 2012 ch 180 §2 (AB 805), effective January 1, 2013, operative January 1, 2014.

§4640. Stock cooperative

In a stock cooperative, any conveyance, judicial sale, or other voluntary or involuntary transfer of the separate interest includes the ownership interest in the corporation, however evidenced. Any conveyance, judicial sale, or other voluntary or involuntary transfer of the owner's entire estate also includes the owner's membership interest in the association. **Leg.H.** Added Stats 2012 ch 180 §2 (AB 805), effective January 1, 2013, operative January 1, 2014.

§4645. Transfer of exclusive use common area

Nothing in this article prohibits the transfer of exclusive use areas, independent of any other interest in a common interest subdivision, if authorization to separately transfer exclusive use areas is expressly stated in the declaration and the transfer occurs in accordance with the terms of the declaration. **Leg.H.** Added Stats 2012 ch 180 §2 (AB 805), effective January 1, 2013, operative January 1, 2014.

§4650. Severability of interests

Any restrictions upon the severability of the component interests in real property which are contained in the declaration shall not be deemed conditions repugnant to the interest created within the meaning of Section 711. However, these restrictions shall not extend beyond the period in which the right to partition a project is suspended under Section 4610. **Leg.H.** Added Stats 2012 ch 180 §2 (AB 805), effective January 1, 2013, operative January 1, 2014.

CHAPTER 5
PROPERTY USE AND MAINTENANCE

Article 1. Protected Uses.
Article 2. Modification of Separate Interest.
Article 3. Maintenance.

ARTICLE 1
Protected Uses

Application of article. §4700.
Display of United States flag. §4705.
Restriction on religious items displayed on entry of member's separate interest; Temporary removal. §4706.
Noncommercial sign. §4710.
Pets. §4715.
Roofing materials. §4720.
Television antenna or satellite dish. §4725.
Marketing restriction. §4730.
Low water-using plants; Landscaping rules; Fine or assessment. §4735.
Pressure washing of separate interest and appurtenant common area during declared drought emergency. §4736.
Owner of a separate interest in a common interest development. § 4739.
Rental restriction. §4740.
Prohibited restrictions on separate interest rental. § 4741.
Electric vehicle charging station. §4745.
EV-dedicated TOU meters; Restrictions unenforceable. §4745.1.
Installation of solar energy system on multifamily common area roof. §4746.
Restrictions on housing development projects using authorized floor area ratio standards void and unenforceable. § 4747.
Personal agriculture; Homeowner may not be unreasonably prohibited or restricted from engaging in; Applicability. §4750.
Validity and enforceability of governing document that prohibits or restricts use of clothesline or drying rack in backyard [Renumbered]. §4750.10.
Accessory dwelling unit or junior accessory dwelling unit; Void and unenforceable covenant, restriction, or condition; Applicability. §4751.
Validity and enforceability of governing document that prohibits or restricts use of clothesline or drying rack in backyard. §4753.

§4700. Application of article

This article includes provisions that limit the authority of an association or the governing documents to regulate the use of a member's separate interest. Nothing in this article is intended to affect the application of any other provision that limits the authority of an association to regulate the use of a member's separate interest, including, but not limited to, the following provisions:

(a) Sections 712 and 713, relating to the display of signs.

(b) Sections 714 and 714.1, relating to solar energy systems.

(c) Section 714.5, relating to structures that are constructed offsite and moved to the property in sections or modules.

(d) Sections 782, 782.5, and 6150 of this code and Section 12956.1 of the Government Code, relating to racial restrictions.

(e) Section 12927 of the Government Code, relating to the modification of property to accommodate a disability.

(f) Section 1597.40 of the Health and Safety Code, relating to the operation of a family day care home. **Leg.H.** Added Stats 2012 ch 180 §2 (AB 805), effective January 1, 2013, operative January 1, 2014.

Prior Law: Former CC §4700, was added Stats 1990 ch 1493 §7 (AB 3974), operative January 1, 1993, and repealed Stats 1992 ch 162 §3 (AB 2650), operative January 1, 1994. See Fam C §§270, 3028, 3651– 3653, 4001, 4007, 4009, 4011–4013. Amended Stats 1993 ch 876 §5 (SB 1068), effective October 6, 1993, operative until January 1, 1994, and repealed January 1, 1994, by its own terms. See Fam C §§270, 3028, 3651– 3653, 4001, 4007, 4009, 4011– 4013.

§4700.1. [Section repealed 1994.]

Leg.H. Added Stats 1983 ch 1036 §1, operative July 1, 1984. Amended Stats 1987 ch 57 §2. Repealed Stats 1992 ch 162 §3 (AB 2650), operative January 1, 1994. See Fam C §§3680, 3680.5, 3690–3694, 4010.

§4700.2. [Section repealed 1994.]

Leg.H. Added Stats 1985 ch 1358 §2. Amended Stats 1989 ch 1359 §2. Repealed Stats 1992 ch 162 §3 (AB 2650), operative January 1, 1994. See Fam C §§3660, 3662–3668.

§4700.3. [Section repealed 1994.]

Leg.H. Added Stats 1983 ch 1036 §2, operative July 1, 1984. Repealed Stats 1992 ch 162 §3 (AB 2650), operative January 1, 1994. The repealed section related to consideration of age in cease factor in modification of child support order.

§4700.5. [Section repealed 1994.]

Leg.H. Added Stats 1983 ch 1304 §5, operative July 1, 1984. Repealed Stats 1992 ch 162 §3 (AB 2650), operative January 1, 1994. See Fam C §4004.

§4700.7. [Section repealed 1994.]

Leg.H. Added Stats 1983 ch 1304 §6, operative July 1, 1984. Amended Stats 1985 ch 303 §1; Stats 1986 ch 707 §1. Repealed Stats 1992 ch 162 §3 (AB 2650), operative January 1, 1994. See Fam C §3552.

§4700.9. [Section repealed 1994.]

Leg.H. Added Stats 1983 ch 1304 §7, operative July 1, 1984. Amended Stats 1985 ch 419 §3. Repealed Stats 1992 ch 162 §3 (AB 2650), operative January 1, 1994. See Fam C §§3587, 4500.

§4700.10. [Section repealed 1994.]

Leg.H. Added Stats 1988 ch 729 §1. Amended Stats 1990 ch 1493 §8 (AB 3974). Repealed Stats 1992 ch 162 §3 (AB 2650), operative January 1, 1994. See Fam C §§3800–3804, 3806–3810.

§4700.11. [Section repealed 1994]

Leg.H. Added Stats 1991 ch 110 §10 (SB 101). Amended Stats 1992 ch 50 §2 (AB 1394), effective May 11, 1992. Repealed Stats 1992 ch 162 §3 (AB 2650), operative January 1, 1994 (ch 50 prevails). Repealed Stats 1993 ch 219 §47 (AB 1500). See Fam C §§4720–4733.

§4701. [Section repealed 1991.]

Leg.H. Added Stats 1983 ch 853 §2, operative January 1, 1987. Amended Stats 1984 ch 432 §2, operative January 1, 1987, ch 1463 §1.5, effective September 26, 1984, operative January 1, 1987; Stats 1985 ch 404 §2, ch 1061 §2, effective September 26, 1985, operative January 1, 1987, ch 1069 §3.4, operative January 1, 1987; Stats 1986 ch 1408 §1, ch 1409 §2, operative January 1, 1987; Stats 1989 ch 639 §1, ch 1359 §3.5, operative until July 1, 1990. Repealed January 1, 1991, by its own provisions. The repealed section related to wage assignment for child support.

Prior Law: Former CC §4701, relating to wage assignment for child support, was added Stats 1969 ch 1608 §8, operative January 1, 1970, amended Stats 1969 ch 1609 §21, operative January 1, 1970, Stats 1972 ch 802 § 1, Stats 1974 ch 514 § 1, Stats 1975 ch 509 § 1, Stats 1980 ch 173 §1, effective June 13, 1980, ch 1341 § 5, Stats 1982 ch 497 §17, operative July 1, 1983, Stats 1983 ch 853 §1, operative until January 1, 1987, Stats 1984 ch 432 §1, operative until January 1, 1987, ch 1463 §1, effective September 26, 1984, operative until January 1, 1987, Stats 1985 ch 404 §1, ch 1061 §1, effective September 27, 1985, operative until January 1, 1987, ch 1069 §3.2, operative until January 1, 1987, and repealed January 1, 1987, by its own terms.

§4701.1. [Section repealed 1994.]

Leg.H. Added Stats 1987 ch 1389 §1. Amended Stats 1990 ch 1493 §8.5 (AB 3974). Repealed Stats 1992 ch 162 §3 (AB 2650), operative January 1, 1994. See Fam C §§4600, 4602–4604, 4610–4617, 4620, 4630–4632, 4640, 4641.

§4701.2. [Section repealed 1994.]

Leg.H. Added Stats 1988 ch 231 §1, operative July 1, 1989. Repealed Stats 1992 ch 162 §3 (AB 2650), operative January 1, 1994. The repealed section related to court ordered payment of support by deductions from salary or wages.

§4702. [Section repealed 1994]

Leg.H. Added Stats 1969 ch 1608 §8, operative January 1, 1970. Amended Stats 1971 ch 1675 §1; Stats 1972 ch 1167 §2; Stats 1974 ch 514 §2; Stats 1979 ch 1030 §4; Stats 1985 ch 404 §3. Repealed Stats 1992 ch 162 §3 (AB 2650), operative January 1, 1994. See Fam C §§4200–4203 (ch 848 prevails). Amended Stats 1992 ch 848 §4 (SB 1614), effective September 22, 1992. Repealed Stats 1993 ch 219 §48 (AB 1500). See Fam C §§4200–4203.

§4703. [Section repealed 1994.]

Leg.H. Added Stats 1969 ch 1608 §8, operative January 1, 1970. Repealed Stats 1992 ch 162 §3 (AB 2650), operative January 1, 1994. See Fam C §4000.

§4704. [Section repealed 1994.]

Leg.H. Added Stats 1974 ch 81 §1. Repealed Stats 1992 ch 162 §3 (AB 2650), operative January 1, 1994. The repealed section related to modification of orders for support of child based on prior age of majority.

§4704.5. [Section repealed 1994.]

Leg.H. Added Stats 1988 ch 153 §2. Repealed Stats 1992 ch 162 §3 (AB 2650), operative January 1, 1994. See Fam C §§3901, 4000.

§4705. Display of United States flag

(a) Except as required for the protection of the public health or safety, no governing document shall limit or prohibit, or be construed to limit or prohibit, the display of the flag of the United States by a member on or in the member's separate interest or within the member's exclusive use common area.

(b) For purposes of this section, "display of the flag of the United States" means a flag of the United States made of fabric, cloth, or paper displayed from a staff or pole or in a window, and does not mean a depiction or emblem of the flag of the United States made of lights, paint, roofing, siding, paving materials, flora, or balloons, or any other similar building, landscaping, or decorative component.

(c) In any action to enforce this section, the prevailing party shall be awarded reasonable attorney's fees and costs. **Leg.H.** Added Stats 2012 ch 180 §2 (AB 805), effective January 1, 2013, operative January 1, 2014.

Prior Law: Former CC §4705, added Stats 1979 ch 69 §1, and repealed Stats 1992 ch 162 §3 (AB 2650), operative January 1, 1994. See Fam C §4504.

§4706. Restriction on religious items displayed on entry of member's separate interest; Temporary removal

(a) Except as restricted in Section 1940.5, no governing document shall limit or prohibit the display of one or more religious items on the entry door or entry door frame of the member's separate interest.

(b) If an association is performing maintenance, repair, or replacement of an entry door or door frame that serves a member's separate interest, the member may be required to remove a religious item during the time the work is being performed. After completion of the association's work, the member may again display or affix the religious item. The association shall provide individual notice to the member regarding the temporary removal of the religious item. **Leg.H.** Added Stats 2019 ch 154 §2 (SB 652), effective January 1, 2020.

Former Sections: Former CC §4706, relating to health insurance coverage as factor, was added Stats 1981 ch 927 §1. Repealed Stats 1992 ch 162 §3 (AB 2650), operative January 1, 1994. Repealed Stats ch 876 §6 (SB 1068), effective October 6, 1993. See Fam C §4006.

Prior Law: Former CC §4706, relating to health insurance coverage as factor, was added Stats 1981 ch 927 §1, amended Stats 1984 ch 379 §1, repealed Stats 1992 ch 162 §3 (AB 2650), operative January 1, 1994, and repealed Stats 1993 ch 876 §6 (SB 1068), effective October 6, 1993.

§4707. [Section repealed 1994.]

Leg.H. Added Stats 1982 ch 550 §1. Repealed Stats 1992 ch 162 §3 (AB 2650), operative January 1, 1994. See Fam C §4003.

§4708. [Section repealed 1994.]

Leg.H. Added Stats 1985 ch 373 §1. Repealed Stats 1992 ch 162 §3 (AB 2650), operative January 1, 1994. See Fam C §4503.

§4709. [Section repealed 1994.]

Leg.H. Added Stats 1988 ch 900 §2. Repealed Stats 1992 ch 162 §3 (AB 2650), operative January 1, 1994. See Fam C §4505.

§4710. Noncommercial sign

(a) The governing documents may not prohibit posting or displaying of noncommercial signs, posters, flags, or banners on or in a member's separate interest, except as required for the protection of public health or safety or if the posting or display would violate a local, state, or federal law.

(b) For purposes of this section, a noncommercial sign, poster, flag, or banner may be made of paper, cardboard, cloth, plastic, or fabric, and may be posted or displayed from the yard, window, door, balcony, or outside wall of the separate interest, but may not be made of lights, roofing, siding, paving materials, flora, or balloons, or any other similar building, landscaping, or decorative component, or include the painting of architectural surfaces.

(c) An association may prohibit noncommercial signs and posters that are more than nine square feet in size and noncommercial flags or banners that are more than 15 square feet in size. **Leg.H.** Added Stats 2012 ch 180 §2 (AB 805), effective January 1, 2013, operative January 1, 2014.

Prior Law: Former CC §4710, added Stats 1991 ch 1141 §3 (SB 1068), and repealed Stats 1992 ch 162 §3 (AB 2650), operative January 1, 1994. See Fam C §§4550, 4551, 4554, 4560–4563, 4565–4567, 4570–4573.

§4715. Pets

(a) No governing documents shall prohibit the owner of a separate interest within a common interest development from keeping at least one pet within the common interest development, subject to reasonable rules and regulations of the association. This section may not be construed to affect any other rights provided by law to an owner of a separate interest to keep a pet within the development.

(b) For purposes of this section, "pet" means any domesticated bird, cat, dog, aquatic animal kept within an aquarium, or other animal as agreed to between the association and the homeowner.

(c) If the association implements a rule or regulation restricting the number of pets an owner may keep, the new rule or regulation shall not apply to prohibit an owner from continuing to keep any pet that the owner currently keeps in the owner's separate interest if the pet otherwise conforms with the previous rules or regulations relating to pets.

(d) For the purposes of this section, "governing documents" shall include, but are not limited to, the conditions, covenants, and restrictions of the common interest development, and the bylaws, rules, and regulations of the association.

(e) This section shall become operative on January 1, 2001, and shall only apply to governing documents entered into, amended, or otherwise modified on or after that date. **Leg.H.** Added Stats 2012 ch 180 §2 (AB 805), effective January 1, 2013, operative January 1, 2014.

§4720. Roofing materials

(a) No association may require a homeowner to install or repair a roof in a manner that is in violation of Section 13132.7 of the Health and Safety Code.

(b) Governing documents of a common interest development located within a very high fire severity zone, as designated by the Director of Forestry and Fire Protection pursuant to Article 9 (commencing with Section 4201) of Chapter 1 of Part 2 of Division 4 of the Public Resources Code or by a local agency pursuant to Chapter 6.8 (commencing with Section 51175) of Part 1 of Division 1 of Title 5 of the Government Code, shall allow for at least one type of fire retardant roof covering material that meets the requirements of Section 13132.7 of the Health and Safety Code. **Leg.H.** Added Stats 2012 ch 180 §2 (AB 805), effective January 1, 2013, operative January 1, 2014.

Prior Law: Former CC §4720, added Stats 1992 ch 46 §5 (SB 370), effective May 11, 1992, operative July 1, 1992, and repealed Stats 1992 ch 162 §3 (AB 2650), operative January 1, 1994 (ch 848 prevails). Amended Stats 1992 ch 848 §5 (SB 1614), effective September 22, 1992. Repealed Stats 1993 ch 219 §49 (AB 1500). See Fam C §§4050–4054.

Former CC §4720, was added Stats 1990 ch 1493 §10 (AB 3974), operative March 1, 1991, operative until January 1, 1993, and repealed Stats 1992 ch 46 §3 (SB 370), effective May 11, 1992, operative July 1, 1992. See Fam C §§4050–4054.

Former CC §4720, was added Stats 1984 ch 1605 §4, operative July 1, 1985, amended Stats 1990 ch 1493 §9 (AB 3974), operative term contingent, and repealed, operative March 1, 1991, by its own terms. See Fam C §§4050–4054.

There was another section of this number, similar to the repealed section, which was added Stats 1990 ch 1493 §11 (AB 3974), to become operative January 1, 1993, and repealed Stats 1992 ch 46 §4 (SB 370), effective May 11, 1992, operative July 1, 1992.

§4720.1. [Section repealed 1992.]

Leg.H. Added Stats 1990 ch 1493 §12 (AB 3974). Repealed Stats 1991 ch 110 §11 (SB 101), operative July 1, 1992. See Fam C §§4050–4054.

Prior Law: There was another section of this number which was added Stats 1991 ch 110 §12 (SB 101), to become operative July 1, 1992, operative until January 1, 1994, repealed Stats 1992 ch 46 §6 (SB 370), effective May 11, 1992, operative July 1, 1992 (ch 46 prevails), and repealed Stats 1992 ch 162 §3 (AB 2650), operative January 1, 1994. See Fam C §§4050–4052, 4066, 4067.

§4720.2. [Section repealed 1992.]

Leg.H. Added Stats 1991 ch 110 §13 (SB 101). Amended Stats 1991 ch 542 §4.5 (SB 1161). Repealed Stats 1992 ch 46 §7 (SB 370), effective May 11, 1992, operative July 1, 1992 (ch 46 prevails), Stats 1992 ch 162 §3 (AB 2650), operative January 1, 1994. See Fam C §§4055–4069.

§4721. [Section repealed 1994.]

Leg.H. Added Stats 1992 ch 46 §9 (SB 370), effective May 11, 1992, operative July 1, 1992. Repealed Stats 1992 ch 162 §3 (AB 2650), operative January 1, 1994 (ch 848 prevails). Amended Stats 1992 ch 848 §6 (SB 1614), effective September 22, 1992. Repealed Stats 1993 ch 219 §50 (AB 1500). See Fam C §§4055–4069.

Prior Law: Former CC §4721, was added Stats 1984 ch 1605 §4, operative July 1, 1985, amended Stats 1985 ch 379 §2, effective July 30, 1985, Stats 1987 ch 964 §1, Stats 1988 ch 153 §3, Stats 1990 ch 1493 §13 (AB 3974), and repealed March 1, 1991, by its own terms. See Fam C §§4055–4069.

There was another section of this number, similar to the repealed section, which was added Stats 1990 ch 1493 §14, to become operative January 1, 1993, and repealed Stats 1992 ch 46 §8, effective May 11, 1992, operative July 1, 1992.

§4722. [Section repealed 1994.]

Leg.H. Added Stats 1992 ch 46 §11 (SB 370), effective May 11, 1992, operative July 1, 1992. Repealed Stats 1992 ch 162 §3 (AB 2650), operative January 1, 1994 (ch 848 prevails). Amended Stats 1992 ch 848 §7 (SB 1614), effective August 22, 1992. Repealed Stats 1993 ch 219 §51 (AB 1500). See Fam C §§4070–4073.

Prior Law: Former CC §4722, similar to present Fam C §§4055–4069, was added Stats 1984 ch 1605 §4, operative July 1, 1985, amended Stats 1985 ch 379 §3, effective July 30, 1985, Stats 1990 ch 1493 §15 (AB 3974), and repealed March 1, 1991, by its own terms.

There was another section of this number, relating to standards for determination of ability to pay minimum mandatory child support, which was added Stats 1990 ch 1493 §16, to become operative January 1, 1993, and repealed Stats 1992 ch 46 §10, effective May 11, 1992, operative July 1, 1992.

§4722.5. [Section repealed 1994.]

Leg.H. Added Stats 1993 ch 69 §1 (SB 35), effective June 30, 1993. Repealed Stats 1994 ch 146 §18 (AB 3601), ch 1269 §1 (AB 2208). The repealed section related to effect of aid to families with dependent children payments to parent on determination of hardship.

§4723. [Section repealed 1991.]

Leg.H. Added Stats 1984 ch 1605 §4, operative July 1, 1985. Amended Stats 1985 ch 379 §4, effective July 30, 1985; Stats 1990 ch 1493 §17 (AB 3974). Repealed March 1, 1991, by its own provisions. See Fam C §§4050–4069.

Prior Law: There was another section of this number, relating to expenses intended to be covered by mandatory minimum child support award, which was added Stats 1990 ch 1493 §18, to become operative January 1, 1993, and repealed Stats 1992 ch 46 §12, effective May 11, 1992, operative July 1, 1992, ch 162 §3, operative January 1, 1994 (ch 46 prevails).

§4724. [Section repealed 1991.]

Leg.H. Added Stats 1984 ch 1605 §4, operative July 1, 1985. Amended Stats 1990 ch 1493 §19 (AB 3974). Repealed March 1, 1991, by its own provisions. See Fam C §4050–4069.

Prior Law: There was another section of this number, relating to setting of higher level of child support by court, which was added Stats 1990 ch 1493 §20, to become operative January 1, 1993, and repealed Stats 1992 ch 46 §13, effective May 11, 1992, operative July 1, 1992, ch 162 §3, operative January 1, 1994 (ch 46 prevails).

§4725. Television antenna or satellite dish

(a) Any covenant, condition, or restriction contained in any deed, contract, security instrument, or other instrument affecting the transfer or sale of, or any interest in, a common interest development that effectively prohibits or restricts the installation or use of a video or television antenna, including a satellite dish, or that effectively prohibits or restricts the attachment of that antenna to a structure within that development where the antenna is not visible from any street or common area, except as otherwise prohibited or restricted by law, is void and unenforceable as to its application to the installation or use of a video or television antenna that has a diameter or diagonal measurement of 36 inches or less.

(b) This section shall not apply to any covenant, condition, or restriction, as described in subdivision (a), that imposes reasonable restrictions on the installation or use of a video or television antenna, including a satellite dish, that has a diameter or diagonal measurement of 36 inches or less. For purposes of this section, "reasonable restrictions" means those restrictions that do not significantly increase the cost of the video or television antenna system, including all related equipment, or significantly decrease its efficiency or performance and include all of the following:

(1) Requirements for application and notice to the association prior to the installation.

(2) Requirement of a member to obtain the approval of the association for the installation of a video or television antenna that has a diameter or diagonal measurement of 36 inches or less on a separate interest owned by another.

(3) Provision for the maintenance, repair, or replacement of roofs or other building components.

(4) Requirements for installers of a video or television antenna to indemnify or reimburse the association or its members for loss or damage caused by the installation, maintenance, or use of a video or television antenna that has a diameter or diagonal measurement of 36 inches or less.

(c) Whenever approval is required for the installation or use of a video or television antenna, including a satellite dish, the application for approval shall be processed by the appropriate approving entity for the common interest development in the same manner as an application for approval of an architectural modification to the property, and the issuance of a decision on the application shall not be willfully delayed.

(d) In any action to enforce compliance with this section, the prevailing party shall be awarded reasonable attorney's fees. **Leg.H.** Added Stats 2012 ch 180 §2 (AB 805), effective January 1, 2013, operative January 1, 2014.

Prior Law: Former CC §4725, was added Stats 1984 ch 1605 §4, operative July 1, 1985, amended Stats 1987 ch 964 §2, Stats 1988 ch 1295 §1, Stats 1990 ch 1493 §21, and repealed March 1, 1991, by its own terms. See Fam C §§4070– 4073.

There was another section of this number, relating to income deductions for parent experiencing extreme financial hardship, which was added Stats 1990 ch 1493 §22, to become operative January 1, 1993, and repealed Stats 1992 ch 46 §14, effective May 11, 1992, operative July 1, 1992, ch 162 §3, operative January 1, 1994 (ch 46 prevails).

§4726. [Section repealed 1994.]

Leg.H. Added Stats 1984 ch 1605 §4, operative July 1, 1985. Amended Stats 1986 ch 1317 §2; Stats 1987 ch 948 §2; Stats 1989 ch 804 §1, ch 1359 §4.5. Repealed Stats 1992 ch 162 §3 (AB 2650), operative January 1, 1994. Stats 1993 ch 876 §7 (SB 1068), effective October 6, 1993, operative until January 1, 1994. Repealed January 1, 1994, by its own provisions. See Fam C §§3750–3753.

§4726.1. [Section repealed 1994.]

Leg.H. Added Stats 1988 1395 §1. Amended Stats 1989 ch 1359 §5; Stats 1990 ch 1313 §1 (SB 2718). Repealed Stats 1992 ch 162 §3 (AB 2650), operative January 1, 1994. See Fam C §§3760–3772.

§4727. [Section repealed 1991.]

Leg.H. Added Stats 1984 ch 1605 §4, operative July 1, 1985. Amended Stats 1990 ch 1493 §23 (AB 3974). Repealed March 1, 1991, by its own provisions. See Fam C §§4050–4069.

Prior Law: There was another section of this number, relating to consideration of shared physical custody expenses in determining of pro rata share of award, which was added Stats 1990 ch 1493 §23.5, to become operative January 1, 1993, and repealed Stats 1992 ch 46 §15, effective May 11, 1992, operative July 1, 1992, ch 162 §3, operative January 1, 1994 (ch 46 prevails).

§4728. [Section repealed 1991.]

Leg.H. Added Stats 1984 ch 1605 §4, operative July 1, 1985. Amended Stats 1990 ch 1493 §24 (AB 3974). Repealed March 1, 1991, by its own provisions. See Fam C §§4050–4069.

Prior Law: There was another section of this number, relating to stipulated agreements for child support award, which was added Stats 1990 ch 1493 §25, to become operative January 1, 1993, and repealed Stats 1992 ch 46 §16, effective May 11, 1992, operative July 1, 1992, ch 162 §3, operative January 1, 1994 (ch 46 prevails).

§4728.5. [Section repealed 1991.]

Leg.H. Added Stats 1985 ch 379 §5, effective July 30, 1985. Amended Stats 1990 ch 1493 §26 (AB 3974). Repealed March 1, 1991, by its own provisions. The repealed section related to rental value of house as payment.

Prior Law: There was another section of this number, similar to the repealed section, which was added Stats 1990 ch 1493 §27, to become operative January 1, 1993, and repealed Stats 1992 ch 46 §17, effective May 11, 1992, operative July 1, 1992, ch 162 §3, operative January 1, 1994 (ch 46 prevails).

§4729. [Section repealed 1992.]

Leg.H. Added Stats 1984 ch 1605 §4, operative July 1, 1985. Repealed Stats 1992 ch 46 §18 (SB 370), effective May 11, 1992, operative July 1, 1992, ch 162 §3 (AB 2650), operative January 1, 1994 (ch 46 prevails). See Fam C §§4050–4069.

§4730. Marketing restriction

(a) Any provision of a governing document that arbitrarily or unreasonably restricts an owner's ability to market the owner's interest in a common interest development is void.

(b) No association may adopt, enforce, or otherwise impose any governing document that does either of the following:

(1) Imposes an assessment or fee in connection with the marketing of an owner's interest in an amount that exceeds the association's actual or direct costs. That assessment or fee shall be deemed to violate the limitation set forth in subdivision (b) of Section 5600.

(2) Establishes an exclusive relationship with a real estate broker through which the sale or marketing of interests in the development is required to occur. The limitation set forth in this paragraph does not apply to the sale or marketing of separate interests owned by the association or to the sale or marketing of common area by the association.

(c) For purposes of this section, "market" and "marketing" mean listing, advertising, or obtaining or providing access to show the owner's interest in the development.

(d) This section does not apply to rules or regulations made pursuant to Section 712 or 713 regarding real estate signs. **Leg.H.** Added Stats 2012 ch 180 §2 (AB 805), effective January 1, 2013, operative January 1, 2014.

Prior Law: Former CC §4730, was added Stats 1984 ch 1605 §4, operative July 1, 1985, and repealed Stats 1992 ch 46 §19 (SB 370), effective May 11, 1992, operative July 1, 1992, ch 162 §3 (AB 2650), operative January 1, 1994 (ch 46 prevails). See Fam C §§4050–4069.

§4731. [Section repealed 1994.]

Leg.H. Added Stats 1984 ch 1605 §4, operative July 1, 1985. Repealed Stats 1992 ch 162 §3 (AB 2650), operative January 1, 1994. See Fam C §4074.

§4732. [Section repealed 1994.]

Leg.H. Added Stats 1984 ch 1605 §4, operative July 1, 1985. Repealed Stats 1992 ch 162 §3 (AB 2650), operative January 1, 1994. See Fam C §4075.

§4735. Low water-using plants; Landscaping rules; Fine or assessment

(a) Notwithstanding any other law, a provision of the governing documents or architectural or landscaping guidelines or policies shall be void and unenforceable if it does any of the following:

(1) Prohibits, or includes conditions that have the effect of prohibiting, the use of low water-using plants as a group or as a replacement of existing turf.

(2) Prohibits, or includes conditions that have the effect of prohibiting, the use of artificial turf or any other synthetic surface that resembles grass.

(3) Has the effect of prohibiting or restricting compliance with either of the following:

(A) A water-efficient landscape ordinance adopted or in effect pursuant to subdivision (c) of Section 65595 of the Government Code.

(B) Any regulation or restriction on the use of water adopted pursuant to Section 353 or 375 of the Water Code.

(b) This section shall not prohibit an association from applying landscaping rules established in the governing documents, to the extent the rules fully conform with subdivision (a).

(c) Notwithstanding any other provision of this part, except as provided in subdivision (d), an association shall not impose a fine or assessment against an owner of a separate interest for reducing or eliminating the watering of vegetation or lawns during any period for which either of the following have occurred:

(1) The Governor has declared a state of emergency due to drought pursuant to subdivision (b) of Section 8558 of the Government Code.

(2) A local government has declared a local emergency due to drought pursuant to subdivision (c) of Section 8558 of the Government Code.

(d) Subdivision (c) shall not apply to an owner of a separate interest that, prior to the imposition of a fine or assessment described in subdivision (c), receives recycled water, as defined in Section 13050 of the Water Code, from a retail water supplier, as defined in Section 13575 of the Water Code, and fails to use that recycled water for landscaping irrigation.

(e) An owner of a separate interest upon which water-efficient landscaping measures have been installed in response to a declaration of a state of emergency described in subdivision (c) shall not be required to reverse or remove the water-efficient landscaping measures upon the conclusion of the state of emergency. **Leg.H.** Added Stats 2012 ch 180 §2 (AB 805), effective January 1, 2013, operative January 1, 2014. Amended Stats 2014 ch 164 §1 (AB 2100), effective July 21, 2014, ch 421 §1 (AB

2104), effective January 1, 2015, ch 434 §1 (SB 992), effective September 18, 2014, ch 434 §1.5 (SB 992), effective September 18, 2014, operative January 1, 2015; Stats 2015 ch 266 §2 (AB 349), effective September 4, 2015, ch 780 §2.5 (AB 786), effective October 11, 2015.

§4736. Pressure washing of separate interest and appurtenant common area during declared drought emergency

(a) A provision of the governing documents shall be void and unenforceable if it requires pressure washing the exterior of a separate interest and any exclusive use common area appurtenant to the separate interest during a state or local government declared drought emergency.

(b) For purposes of this section, "pressure washing" means the use of a high-pressure sprayer or hose and potable water to remove loose paint, mold, grime, dust, mud, and dirt from surfaces and objects, including buildings, vehicles, and concrete surfaces. **Leg.H.** Added Stats 2014 ch 434 §2 (SB 992), effective September 18, 2014.

§ 4739. Owner of a separate interest in a common interest development

(a) Notwithstanding Section 4740, an owner of a separate interest in a common interest development shall not be subject to a provision in a governing document, or amendments thereto, that prohibits the rental or leasing of a portion of the owner-occupied separate interest in that common interest development to a renter, lessee, or tenant for a period of more than 30 days.

(b) Nothing in this section shall permit an owner of a separate interest or a resident renting or leasing a portion of the owner-occupied separate interest to violate any provision of the association governing documents that govern conduct in the separate interest or common areas, or that govern membership rights or privileges, including, but not limited to, parking restrictions and guest access to common facilities. **Leg.H.** Added Stats 2022 ch 858 §3 (AB 1410), effective January 1, 2023.

§4740. Rental restriction

(a) An owner of a separate interest in a common interest development shall not be subject to a provision in a governing document or an amendment to a governing document that prohibits the rental or leasing of any of the separate interests in that common interest development to a renter, lessee, or tenant unless that governing document, or amendment thereto, was effective prior to the date the owner acquired title to their separate interest.

(b) For purposes of this section, the right to rent or lease the separate interest of an owner shall not be deemed to have terminated if the transfer by the owner of all or part of the separate interest meets at least one of the following conditions:

(1) Pursuant to Section 62 or 480.3 of the Revenue and Taxation Code, the transfer is exempt, for purposes of reassessment by the county tax assessor.

(2) Pursuant to subdivision (b) of, solely with respect to probate transfers, or subdivision (e), (f), or (g) of, Section 1102.2, the transfer is exempt from the requirements to prepare and deliver a Real Estate Transfer Disclosure Statement, as set forth in Section 1102.6.

(c) Prior to renting or leasing their separate interest as provided by this section, an owner shall provide the association verification of the date the owner acquired title to the separate interest and the name and contact information of the prospective tenant or lessee or the prospective tenant's or lessee's representative.

(d) Nothing in this section shall be deemed to revise, alter, or otherwise affect the voting process by which a common interest development adopts or amends its governing documents. **Leg.H.** Added Stats 2012 ch 180 §2 (AB 805), effective January 1, 2013, operative January 1, 2014. Amended Stats 2020 ch 198 §1 (AB 3182), effective January 1, 2021.

§ 4741. Prohibited restrictions on separate interest rental

(a) An owner of a separate interest in a common interest development shall not be subject to a provision in a governing document or an amendment to a governing document that prohibits, has the effect of prohibiting, or unreasonably restricts the rental or leasing of any of the separate interests, accessory dwelling units, or junior accessory dwelling units in that common interest development to a renter, lessee, or tenant.

(b) A common interest development shall not adopt or enforce a provision in a governing document or amendment to a governing document that restricts the rental or lease of separate interests within a common interest to less than 25 percent of the separate interests. Nothing in this subdivision prohibits a common interest development from adopting or enforcing a provision authorizing a higher percentage of separate interests to be rented or leased.

(c) This section does not prohibit a common interest development from adopting and enforcing a provision in a governing document that prohibits transient or short-term rental of a separate property interest for a period of 30 days or less.

(d) For purposes of this section, an accessory dwelling unit or junior accessory dwelling unit shall not be construed as a separate interest.

(e) For purposes of this section, a separate interest shall not be counted as occupied by a renter if the separate interest, or the accessory dwelling unit or junior accessory dwelling unit of the separate interest, is occupied by the owner.

(f) A common interest development shall comply with the prohibition on rental restrictions specified in this section on and after January 1, 2021, regardless of whether the common interest development has revised their governing documents to comply with this section. Notwithstanding any other provision of law or provision of the governing documents, the board, without approval of the members, shall amend any declaration or other governing document no later than July 1, 2022, that includes a restrictive covenant prohibited by this section by either deleting or restating the restrictive covenant to be compliant with this section, and shall restate the declaration or other governing document without the restrictive covenant but with no other change to the declaration or governing document. A board shall provide general notice pursuant to Section 4045 of the amendment at least 28 days before approving the amendment. The notice shall include the text of the amendment and a description of the purpose and effect of the amendment. The decision on the amendment shall be made at a board meeting, after consideration of any comments made by association members.

(g) A common interest development that willfully violates this section shall be liable to the applicant or other party for actual damages, and shall pay a civil penalty to the applicant or other party in an amount not to exceed one thousand dollars ($1,000).

(h) In accordance with Section 4740, this section does not change the right of an owner of a separate interest who acquired title to their separate interest before the effective date of this section to rent or lease their property. **Leg.H.** Added Stats 2020 ch 198 §2 (AB 3182), effective January 1, 2021. Amended Stats 2021 ch 360 §6 (AB 1584), effective January 1, 2022.

§4745. Electric vehicle charging station

(a) Any covenant, restriction, or condition contained in any deed, contract, security instrument, or other instrument affecting the transfer or sale of any interest in a common interest development, and any provision of a governing document, as defined in Section 4150, that either effectively prohibits or unreasonably restricts the installation or use of an electric vehicle charging station within an owner's unit or in a designated parking space, including, but not limited to, a deeded parking space, a parking space in an owner's exclusive use common area, or a parking space that is specifically designated for use by a particular owner, or is in conflict with this section is void and unenforceable.

(b)(1) This section does not apply to provisions that impose reasonable restrictions on electric vehicle charging stations. However, it is the policy of the state to promote, encourage, and remove obstacles to the use of electric vehicle charging stations.

(2) For purposes of this section, "reasonable restrictions" are restrictions that do not significantly increase the cost of the station or significantly decrease its efficiency or specified performance.

(c) An electric vehicle charging station shall meet applicable health and safety standards and requirements imposed by state and local authorities, and all other applicable zoning, land use, or other ordinances, or land use permits.

(d) For purposes of this section, "electric vehicle charging station" means a station that is designed in compliance with the California Building Standards Code and delivers electricity from a source outside an electric vehicle into one or more electric vehicles. An electric vehicle charging station may include several charge points simultaneously connecting several electric vehicles to the station and any related equipment needed to facilitate charging plug-in electric vehicles.

(e) If approval is required for the installation or use of an electric vehicle charging station, the application for approval shall be processed and approved by the association in the same manner as an application for approval of an architectural modification to the property, and shall not be willfully avoided or delayed. The approval or denial of an application shall be in writing. If an application is not denied in writing within 60 days from the date of receipt of the application, the application shall be deemed approved, unless that delay is the result of a reasonable request for additional information.

(f) If the electric vehicle charging station is to be placed in a common area or an exclusive use common area, as designated in the common interest development's declaration, the following provisions apply:

(1) The owner first shall obtain approval from the association to install the electric vehicle charging station and the association shall approve the installation if the owner agrees in writing to do all of the following:

(A) Comply with the association's architectural standards for the installation of the charging station.

(B) Engage a licensed contractor to install the charging station.

(C) Within 14 days of approval, provide a certificate of insurance that names the association as an additional insured under the owner's insurance policy in the amount set forth in paragraph (3).

(D) Pay for both the costs associated with the installation of and the electricity usage associated with the charging station.

(2) The owner and each successive owner of the charging station shall be responsible for all of the following:

(A) Costs for damage to the charging station, common area, exclusive use common area, or separate interests resulting from the installation, maintenance, repair, removal, or replacement of the charging station.

(B) Costs for the maintenance, repair, and replacement of the charging station until it has been removed and for the restoration of the common area after removal.

(C) The cost of electricity associated with the charging station.

(D) Disclosing to prospective buyers the existence of any charging station of the owner and the related responsibilities of the owner under this section.

(3) The owner of the charging station, whether located within a separate unit or within the common area or exclusive use common area, shall, at all times, maintain a liability coverage policy. The owner that submitted the application to install the charging station shall provide the association with the corresponding certificate of insurance within 14 days of approval of the application. That owner and each successor owner shall provide the association with the certificate of insurance annually thereafter.

(4) A homeowner shall not be required to maintain a homeowner liability coverage policy for an existing National Electrical Manufacturers Association standard alternating current power plug.

(g) Except as provided in subdivision (h), installation of an electric vehicle charging station for the exclusive use of an owner in a common area, that is not an exclusive use common area, shall be authorized by the association only if installation in the owner's designated parking space is impossible or unreasonably expensive. In such cases, the association shall enter into a license agreement with the owner for the use of the space in a common area, and the owner shall comply with all of the requirements in subdivision (f).

(h) The association or owners may install an electric vehicle charging station in the common area for the use of all members of the association and, in that case, the association shall develop appropriate terms of use for the charging station.

(i) An association may create a new parking space where one did not previously exist to facilitate the installation of an electric vehicle charging station.

(j) An association that willfully violates this section shall be liable to the applicant or other party for actual damages, and shall pay a civil penalty to the applicant or other party in an amount not to exceed one thousand dollars ($1,000).

(k) In any action by a homeowner requesting to have an electric vehicle charging station installed and seeking to enforce compliance with this section, the prevailing plaintiff shall be awarded reasonable attorney's fees. **Leg.H.** Added Stats 2012 ch 180 §2 (AB 805), effective January 1, 2013, operative January 1, 2014. Amended Stats 2018 ch 376 §1 (SB 1016), effective January 1, 2019.

§4745.1. EV-dedicated TOU meters; Restrictions unenforceable

(a) Any covenant, restriction, or condition contained in any deed, contract, security instrument, or other instrument affecting the transfer or sale of any interest in a common interest development, and any provision of a governing document, as defined in Section 4150, that either effectively prohibits or unreasonably restricts the installation or use of an EV-dedicated TOU meter or is in conflict with this section is void and unenforceable.

(b)(1) This section does not apply to provisions that impose reasonable restrictions on the installation of an EV-dedicated TOU meter. However, it is the policy of the state to promote, encourage, and remove obstacles to the effective installation of EV-dedicated TOU meters.

(2) For purposes of this section, "reasonable restrictions" are restrictions based upon space, aesthetics, structural integrity, and equal access to these services for all homeowners, but an association shall attempt to find a reasonable way to accommodate the installation request, unless the association would need to incur an expense.

(c) An EV-dedicated TOU meter shall meet applicable health and safety standards and requirements imposed by state and local authorities, and all other applicable zoning, land use, or other ordinances, or land use permits.

(d) For purposes of this section, an "EV-dedicated TOU meter" means an electric meter supplied and installed by an electric utility, that is separate from, and in addition to, any other electric meter and is devoted exclusively to the charging of electric vehicles, and that tracks the time of use (TOU) when charging occurs. An "EV-dedicated TOU meter" includes any wiring or conduit necessary to connect the electric meter to an electric vehicle charging station, as defined in Section 4745, regardless of whether it is supplied or installed by an electric utility.

(e) If approval is required for the installation or use of an EV-dedicated TOU meter, the application for approval shall be processed and approved by the association in the same manner as an application for approval of an architectural modification to the property, and shall not be willfully avoided or delayed. The approval or denial of an application shall be in writing. If an application is not denied in writing within 60 days from the date of receipt of the application, the application shall be deemed approved, unless that delay is the result of a reasonable request for additional information.

(f) If the EV-dedicated TOU meter is to be placed in a common area or an exclusive use common area, as designated in the common interest development's declaration, the following provisions apply:

(1) The owner first shall obtain approval from the association to install the EV-dedicated TOU meter and the association shall approve the installation if the owner agrees in writing to do both of the following:

(A) Comply with the association's architectural standards for the installation of the EV-dedicated TOU meter.

(B) Engage the relevant electric utility to install the EV-dedicated TOU meter and, if necessary, a licensed contractor to install wiring or conduit necessary to connect the electric meter to an EV charging station.

(2) The owner and each successive owner of an EV-dedicated TOU meter shall be responsible for all of the following:

(A) Costs for damage to the EV-dedicated TOU meter, common area, exclusive use common area, or separate interests resulting from the installation, maintenance, repair, removal, or replacement of the EV-dedicated TOU meter.

(B) Costs for the maintenance, repair, and replacement of the EV-dedicated TOU meter until it has been removed and for the restoration of the common area after removal.

(C) Disclosing to prospective buyers the existence of any EV-dedicated TOU meter of the owner and the related responsibilities of the owner under this section.

(g) The association or owners may install an EV-dedicated TOU meter in the common area for the use of all members of the association and, in that case, the association shall develop appropriate terms of use for the EV-dedicated TOU meter.

(h) An association that willfully violates this section shall be liable to the applicant or other party for actual damages, and shall pay a civil penalty to the applicant or other party in an amount not to exceed one thousand dollars ($1,000).

(i) In any action by a homeowner requesting to have an EV-dedicated TOU meter installed and seeking to enforce compliance with this section, the prevailing plaintiff shall be awarded reasonable attorney's fees. **Leg.H.** Added Stats 2018 ch 376 §2 (SB 1016), effective January 1, 2019.

§4746. Installation of solar energy system on multifamily common area roof

(a) When reviewing a request to install a solar energy system on a multifamily common area roof shared by more than one homeowner pursuant to Sections 714 and 714.1, an association shall require both of the following:

(1) An applicant to notify each owner of a unit in the building on which the installation will be located of the application to install a solar energy system.

(2) The owner and each successive owner to maintain a homeowner liability coverage policy at all times and provide the association with the corresponding certificate of insurance within 14 days of approval of the application and annually thereafter.

(b) When reviewing a request to install a solar energy system on a multifamily common area roof shared by more than one homeowner pursuant to Sections 714 and 714.1, an association may impose additional reasonable provisions that:

(1)(A) Require the applicant to submit a solar site survey showing the placement of the solar energy system prepared by a licensed contractor or the contractor's registered salesperson knowledgeable in the installation of solar energy systems to determine usable solar roof area. This survey or the costs to determine useable space shall not be deemed as part of the cost of the system as used in Section 714.

(B) The solar site survey shall also include a determination of an equitable allocation of the usable solar roof area among all owners sharing the same roof, garage, or carport.

(2) Require the owner and each successive owner of the solar energy system to be responsible for all of the following:

(A) Costs for damage to the common area, exclusive use common area, or separate interests resulting from the installation, maintenance, repair, removal, or replacement of the solar energy system.

(B) Costs for the maintenance, repair, and replacement of solar energy system until it has been removed and for the restoration of the common area, exclusive use common area, or separate interests after removal.

(C) Disclosing to prospective buyers the existence of any solar energy system of the owner and the related responsibilities of the owner under this section.

(c) For purposes of this section:

(1) "Association" has the same meaning as defined in Section 4080 or 6528.

(2) "Common area" has the same meaning as defined in Section 4095 or 6532.

(3) "Separate interest" has the same meaning as defined in Section 4185 or 6564.

(d) This section imposes additional requirements for any proposed installation of a solar energy system on a multifamily common area roof shared by more than one homeowner.

(e) This section does not diminish the authority of an association to impose reasonable provisions pursuant to Section 714.1. **Leg.H.** Added Stats 2017 ch 818 §3 (AB 634), effective January 1, 2018.

§ 4747. Restrictions on housing development projects using authorized floor area ratio standards void and unenforceable

(a) Any covenant, restriction, or condition contained in any deed, contract, security instrument, or other instrument affecting the transfer or sale of any interest in a planned development, and any provision of a governing document, is void and unenforceable if it effectively prohibits or unreasonably restricts an eligible housing development project from using the floor area ratio standards authorized under Section 65913.11 of the Government Code.

(b) This section does not apply to provisions that impose reasonable restrictions on an eligible housing development that do not make the implementation of the floor area standards authorized in Section 65913.11 of the Government Code infeasible.

(c) For purposes of this section:

(1) "Eligible housing development project" means a housing development project that meets the requirements of subdivision (b) of Section 65913.11 of the Government Code.

(2) "Reasonable restrictions" means restrictions that do not unreasonably increase the cost to construct, effectively prohibit the construction of, or extinguish the ability to otherwise construct an eligible housing development project using the floor area ratio standards in a manner authorized by Section 65913.11 of the Government Code.

(d) The Legislature finds and declares that the provision of adequate housing, in light of the severe shortage of housing at all income levels in this state, is a matter of statewide concern and that this section serves a significant and legitimate public purpose by eliminating potential restrictions that could inhibit the production of adequate housing. **Leg.H.** Added Stats 2021 ch 363 §1 (SB 478), effective January 1, 2022.

§4750. Personal agriculture; Homeowner may not be unreasonably prohibited or restricted from engaging in; Applicability

(a) For the purposes of this section, "personal agriculture" has the same definition as in Section 1940.10.

(b) Any provision of a governing document, as defined in Section 4150, shall be void and unenforceable if it effectively prohibits or unreasonably restricts the use of a homeowner's backyard for personal agriculture.

(c)(1) This section does not apply to provisions that impose reasonable restrictions on the use of a homeowner's yard for personal agriculture.

(2) For purposes of this section, "reasonable restrictions" are restrictions that do not significantly increase the cost of engaging in personal agriculture or significantly decrease its efficiency.

(d) This section applies only to yards that are designated for the exclusive use of the homeowner.

(e) This section shall not prohibit a homeowners' association from applying rules and regulations requiring that dead plant material and weeds, with the exception of straw, mulch, compost, and other organic materials intended to encourage vegetation and retention of moisture in the soil, are regularly cleared from the backyard. **Leg.H.** Added Stats 2014 ch 584 §3 (AB 2561), effective January 1, 2015.

Prior Law: Former CC §4750, relating to child support delinquency reporting, was added Stats 1984 ch 1702 §1 and repealed Stats 1992 ch 162 §3, operative January 1, 1994. See Fam C §4700.

2014 Note: The Legislature finds and declares all of the following:

(a) California industrial agriculture is at risk due to water shortages, soil degradation, pollution, environmental, and structural threats to the San Francisco Bay Delta, and the rising cost of oil. Providing Californians with the capacity to feed themselves and their communities would drastically improve local food security and mediate the risks of water, soil, environmental, or fuel-related crises.

(b) Although California is the "bread basket" of the United States and has regions of climate and land ideal for agriculture, a significant amount of California's food is grown hundreds or thousands of miles from where it is consumed. This results in high transportation costs, energy consumption, and lost economic opportunity for our state. Even food grown in the heart of California's farming region is expensive to disperse to the rest of the state due to rising fuel costs.

(c) California is no exception to rising obesity and obesity-related diseases in the United States. Two-thirds of American adults and nearly one-third of American children are obese or overweight, putting them at risk for developing chronic diseases, including diabetes, heart disease, or cancer. In California, one in every nine children, one in three teens, and over one-half of adults are already overweight or obese. This epidemic affects virtually all Californians. Many of these health conditions are preventable and curable through lifestyle choices that include consumption of healthy fresh foods.

(d) One of every $10 dollars spent on health care in the United States goes toward treating diabetes and its complications. Facilitating opportunities for California residents to grow and consume fresh, healthy foods will promote lifestyles and diets that benefit individuals and communities, as well as being a more effective use of public moneys.

(e) Many homeowners' associations have rules prohibiting homeowners from growing food in their yards or from selling food grown on the property.

(f) Forty percent of Californians live in residences that they do not own, and may, as a result of lease restrictions or disapproval by the landlord, face limitations on their ability to grow food on the land where they reside.

(g) According to a 2011 United States Census Bureau report, California has the highest poverty rate in the United States. Giving California residents the right to grow food where they live will help reduce food costs and the overall burden of poverty for low-income Californians.

(h) Lawncare is resource intensive, at no nutritional gain. Lawns are the largest irrigated crop in the United States. In the urban areas in the United States, 30 to 60 percent of residential water is used for watering lawns. In arid and semiarid regions, this figure can reach up to 75 percent. Annually, 67 million pounds (33,500 tons) of synthetic pesticides are used on lawns in the United States. Furthermore, lawnmowers use 580 million gallons of gasoline yearly. These resources could be allocated to more productive activities, including growing food, thus increasing access to healthy options for low-income individuals.

(i) Gardens and agriculture on public lands help communities increase their access to fresh fruits and vegetables, enhance urban landscapes, motivate healthier eating, and connect neighborhoods.

(j) It is the policy of the state to promote and remove obstacles to increased community access to fresh fruit and vegetables and encourage the practice of homeowners growing food in their private yard space for personal use or for donation to others.

(k) These findings are all matters of statewide concern. The Legislature recently identified the importance of small-scale, neighborhood-based food enterprises throughout California in achieving common, statewide economic, health, and environmental goals. The Legislature acted upon this by enacting Chapter 415 of the Statutes of 2012 governing cottage food operations and the Urban Agriculture Incentive Zones Act (Chapter 406 of the Statutes of 2013). Legalizing the growing of produce throughout California will enhance the positive impacts of such previous legislation. Stats 2014 ch 484 (AB 2561) §1.

§4750.10. Validity and enforceability of governing document that prohibits or restricts use of clothesline or drying rack in backyard [Renumbered]

Leg.H. Added Stats 2015 ch 602 §2 (AB 1448), effective January 1, 2016. Amended and renumbered to CC §4753 by Stats 2016 ch 714 §7 (SB 944), effective January 1, 2017.

§4751. Accessory dwelling unit or junior accessory dwelling unit; Void and unenforceable covenant, restriction, or condition; Applicability

(a) Any covenant, restriction, or condition contained in any deed, contract, security instrument, or other instrument affecting the transfer or sale of any interest in a planned development, and any provision of a governing document, that either effectively prohibits or unreasonably restricts the construction or use of an accessory dwelling unit or junior accessory dwelling unit on a lot zoned for single-family residential use that meets the requirements of [1] **Article 2 (commencing with Section 66314) or Article 3 (commencing with Section 66333) of Chapter 13 of Division 1 of Title 7** of the Government Code, is void and unenforceable.

(b) This section does not apply to provisions that impose reasonable restrictions on accessory dwelling units or junior accessory dwelling units. For purposes of this subdivision, "reasonable restrictions" means restrictions that do not unreasonably increase the cost to construct, effectively prohibit the construction of, or extinguish the ability to otherwise construct, an accessory dwelling unit or junior accessory dwelling unit consistent with the provisions of [2] **Article 2 (commencing with Section 66314) or Article 3 (commencing with Section 66333) of Chapter 13 of Division 1 of Title 7** of the Government Code. **Leg.H.** Added Stats 2019 ch 178 §2 (AB 670), effective January 1, 2020. Amended Stats 2024 ch 7 §2 (SB 477), effective March 25, 2024.

§4751. 2024 Deletes. [1] Section 65852.2 or 65852.22 [2] Section 65852.2 or 65852.22

2019 Note: It is the intent of the Legislature in enacting this act to encourage the construction of affordable accessory dwelling units and junior accessory dwelling units that are owner-occupied and that are used for rentals of terms longer than 30 days. Stats 2019 ch 178 §1 (AB 670).

§4752. [Section repealed 1994.]

Leg.H. Added Stats 1988 ch 900 §4. Repealed Stats 1992 ch 162 §3 (AB 2650), operative January 1, 1994. See Fam C §4701.

§4753. Validity and enforceability of governing document that prohibits or restricts use of clothesline or drying rack in backyard

(a) For the purposes of this section, "clothesline" includes a cord, rope, or wire from which laundered items may be hung to dry or air. A balcony, railing, awning, or other part of a structure or building shall not qualify as a clothesline.

(b) For the purposes of this section, "drying rack" means an apparatus from which laundered items may be hung to dry or air. A balcony, railing, awning, or other part of a structure or building shall not qualify as a drying rack.

(c) Any provision of a governing document, as defined in Section 4150, shall be void and unenforceable if it effectively prohibits or unreasonably restricts an owner's ability to use a clothesline or drying rack in the owner's backyard.

(d)(1) This section does not apply to provisions that impose reasonable restrictions on an owner's backyard for the use of a clothesline or drying rack.

(2) For purposes of this section, "reasonable restrictions" are restrictions that do not significantly increase the cost of using a clothesline or drying rack.

(3) This section applies only to backyards that are designated for the exclusive use of the owner.

(e) Nothing in this section shall prohibit an association from establishing and enforcing reasonable rules governing clotheslines or drying racks. **Leg.H.** Added Stats 2015 ch 602 §2 (AB 1448), effective January 1, 2016. Renumbered from Cal Civ Code §4750.10 by Stats 2016 ch 714 §7 (SB 944), effective January 1, 2017.

ARTICLE 2
Modification of Separate Interest

Improvements to separate interest. §4760.
Architectural review and decision making. §4765.

§4760. Improvements to separate interest

(a) Subject to the governing documents and applicable law, a member may do the following:

(1) Make any improvement or alteration within the boundaries of the member's separate interest that does not impair the structural integrity or mechanical systems or lessen the support of any portions of the common interest development.

(2) Modify the member's separate interest, at the member's expense, to facilitate access for persons who are blind, visually handicapped, deaf, or physically disabled, or to alter conditions which could be hazardous to these persons. These modifications may also include modifications of the route from the public way to the door of the separate interest for the purposes of this paragraph if the separate interest is on the ground floor or already accessible by an existing ramp or elevator. The right granted by this paragraph is subject to the following conditions:

(A) The modifications shall be consistent with applicable building code requirements.

(B) The modifications shall be consistent with the intent of otherwise applicable provisions of the governing documents pertaining to safety or aesthetics.

(C) Modifications external to the dwelling shall not prevent reasonable passage by other residents, and shall be removed by the member when the separate interest is no longer occupied by persons requiring those modifications who are blind, visually handicapped, deaf, or physically disabled.

(D) Any member who intends to modify a separate interest pursuant to this paragraph shall submit plans and specifications to the association for review to determine whether the modifications will comply with the provisions of this paragraph. The association shall not deny approval of the proposed modifications under this paragraph without good cause.

(b) Any change in the exterior appearance of a separate interest shall be in accordance with the governing documents and applicable provisions of law. **Leg.H.** Added Stats 2012 ch 180 §2 (AB 805), effective January 1, 2013, operative January 1, 2014.

Prior Law: Former CC §4760, was added Stats 1992 ch 411 §2 (SB 1817), effective August 1, 1992, and repealed Stats 1993 ch 219 §52 (AB 1500). See Fam C §20000.

Former CC §4760, was added Stats 1991 ch 1131 §1 and repealed Stats 1992 ch 162 §3, operative January 1, 1994 (ch 411 prevails), ch 411 §1, effective August 1, 1992. See Fam C §20000.

§4761. [Section repealed 1994.]

Leg.H. Added Stats 1992 ch 411 §2 (SB 1817), effective August 1, 1992. Repealed Stats 1993 ch 219 §52 (AB 1500). See Fam C §20001.

Prior Law: Former CC §4761, similar to Fam C §20030, was added Stats 1991 ch 1131 §1 and repealed Stats 1992 ch 162 §3 (AB 2650), operative January 1, 1994 (ch 411 prevails), ch 411 §1, effective August 1, 1992.

§4762. [Section repealed 1994.]

Leg.H. Added Stats 1992 ch 411 §2 (SB 1817), effective August 1, 1992. Repealed Stats 1993 ch 219 §52 (AB 1500). See Fam C §20002.

Prior Law: Former CC §4762, similar to Fam C §20030, was added Stats 1991 ch 1131 §1 and repealed Stats 1992 ch 162 §3, operative January 1, 1994 (ch 411 prevails), ch 411 §1, effective August 1, 1992.

§4763. [Section repealed 1994.]

Leg.H. Added Stats 1992 ch 411 §2 (SB 1817), effective August 1, 1992. Repealed Stats 1993 ch 219 §52 (AB 1500). See Fam C §20010.

Prior Law: Former CC §4763, similar to Fam C §20002, was added Stats 1991 ch 1131 §1 and repealed Stats 1992 ch 162 §3, operative January 1, 1994 (ch 411 prevails), ch 411 §1, effective August 1, 1992.

§4764. [Section repealed 1994.]

Leg.H. Added Stats 1992 ch 411 §2 (SB 1817), effective August 1, 1992. Repealed Stats 1993 ch 219 §52 (AB 1500). See Fam C §§20011, 20023.

Prior Law: Former CC §4764, similar to Fam C §§20013, 20037, was added Stats 1991 ch 1131 §1 and repealed Stats 1992 ch 162 §3, operative January 1, 1994 (ch 411 prevails), ch 411 §1, effective August 1, 1992.

§4765. Architectural review and decision making

(a) This section applies if the governing documents require association approval before a member may make a physical change to the member's separate interest or to the common area. In reviewing and approving or disapproving a proposed change, the association shall satisfy the following requirements:

(1) The association shall provide a fair, reasonable, and expeditious procedure for making its decision. The procedure shall be included in the association's governing documents. The procedure shall provide for prompt deadlines. The procedure shall state the maximum time for response to an application or a request for reconsideration by the board.

(2) A decision on a proposed change shall be made in good faith and may not be unreasonable, arbitrary, or capricious.

(3) Notwithstanding a contrary provision of the governing documents, a decision on a proposed change may not violate any governing provision of law, including, but not limited to, the Fair Employment and Housing Act (Part 2.8 (commencing with Section 12900) of Division 3 of Title 2 of the Government Code), or a building code or other applicable law governing land use or public safety.

(4) A decision on a proposed change shall be in writing. If a proposed change is disapproved, the written decision shall include both an explanation of why the proposed change is disapproved and a description of the procedure for reconsideration of the decision by the board.

(5) If a proposed change is disapproved, the applicant is entitled to reconsideration by the board, at an open meeting of the board. This paragraph does not require reconsideration of a decision that is made by the board or a body that has the same membership as the board, at a meeting that satisfies the requirements of Article 2 (commencing with Section 4900) of Chapter 6. Reconsideration by the board does not constitute dispute resolution within the meaning of Section 5905.

(b) Nothing in this section authorizes a physical change to the common area in a manner that is inconsistent with an association's governing documents, unless the change is required by law.

(c) An association shall annually provide its members with notice of any requirements for association approval of physical changes to property. The notice shall describe the types of changes that require association approval and shall include a copy of the procedure used to review and approve or disapprove a proposed change. **Leg.H.** Added Stats 2012 ch 180 §2 (AB 805), effective January 1, 2013, operative January 1, 2014.

Prior Law: Former CC §4765, was added Stats 1992 ch 411 §2 (SB 1817), effective August 1, 1992, and repealed Stats 1993 ch 219 §52 (AB 1500). See Fam C §20012.

Former CC §4765, similar to Fam C §20011, was added Stats 1991 ch 1131 §1 and repealed Stats 1992 ch 162 §3, operative January 1, 1994 (ch 411 prevails), ch 411 §1, effective August 1, 1992.

§4766. [Section repealed 1994.]

Leg.H. Added Stats 1992 ch 411 §2 (SB 1817), effective August 1, 1992. Repealed Stats 1993 ch 219 §52 (AB 1500). See Fam C §20013.

Prior Law: Former CC §4766, relating to participation in proceedings by parties or by appointment, and representation by attorney, was added Stats 1991 ch 1131 §1 and repealed Stats 1992 ch 162 §3, operative January 1, 1994 (ch 411 prevails), ch 411 §1, effective August 1, 1992.

§4767. [Section repealed 1994.]

Leg.H. Added Stats 1992 ch 411 §2 (SB 1817), effective August 1, 1992. Repealed Stats 1993 ch 219 §52 (AB 1500). See Fam C §20014.

Prior Law: Former CC §4767, relating to child support advisors, was added Stats 1991 ch 1131 §1 and repealed Stats 1992 ch 162 §3, operative January 1, 1994 (ch 411 prevails), ch 411 §1, effective August 1, 1992.

§4768. [Section repealed 1994.]

Leg.H. Added Stats 1992 ch 411 §2 (SB 1817), effective August 1, 1992. Repealed Stats 1993 ch 219 §52 (AB 1500). See Fam C §20015.

Prior Law: Former CC §4768, similar to Fam C §§20018, 20035, was added Stats 1991 ch 1131 §1 and repealed Stats 1992 ch 162 §3, operative January 1, 1994 (ch 411 prevails), ch 411 §1, effective August 1, 1992.

§4769. [Section repealed 1994.]

Leg.H. Added Stats 1992 ch 411 §2 (SB 1817), effective August 1, 1992. Repealed Stats 1993 ch 219 §52 (AB 1500). See Fam C §20016.

Prior Law: Former CC §4769, similar to Fam C §20040, was added Stats 1991 ch 1131 §1 and repealed Stats 1992 ch 162 §3, operative January 1, 1994 (ch 411 prevails), ch 411 §1, effective August 1, 1992.

§4770. [Section repealed 1994.]

Leg.H. Added Stats 1992 ch 411 §2 (SB 1817), effective August 1, 1992. Repealed Stats 1993 ch 219 §52 (AB 1500). See Fam C §20017.

Prior Law: Former CC §4770, relating to requirements for motions for temporary child support or other temporary orders, was added Stats 1991 ch 1131 §1 and repealed Stats 1992 ch 162 §3, operative January 1, 1994 (ch 411 prevails), ch 411 §1, effective August 1, 1992.

§4771. [Section repealed 1994.]

Leg.H. Added Stats 1992 ch 411 §2 (SB 1817), effective August 1, 1992. Repealed Stats 1993 ch 219 §52 (AB 1500). See Fam C §20018.

Prior Law: Former CC §4771, similar to Fam C §§20020–20022, 20032, was added Stats 1991 ch 1131 §1 and repealed Stats 1992 ch 162 §3, operative January 1, 1994 (ch 411 prevails), ch 411 §1, effective August 1, 1992.

§4772. [Section repealed 1994.]

Leg.H. Added Stats 1992 ch 411 §2 (SB 1817), effective August 1, 1992. Repealed Stats 1993 ch 219 §52 (AB 1500). See Fam C §20019.

Prior Law: Former CC §4770, similar to Fam C §20019, was added Stats 1991 ch 1131 §1 and repealed Stats 1992 ch 162 §3, operative January 1, 1994 (ch 411 prevails), ch 411 §1, effective August 1, 1992.

§4773. [Section repealed 1994.]

Leg.H. Added Stats 1992 ch 411 §2 (SB 1817), effective August 1, 1992. Repealed Stats 1993 ch 219 §52 (AB 1500). See Fam C §20020.

§4774. [Section repealed 1994.]

Leg.H. Added Stats 1992 ch 411 §2 (SB 1817), effective August 1, 1992. Repealed Stats 1993 ch 219 §52 (AB 1500). See Fam C §20021.

ARTICLE 3
Maintenance

Maintenance and repair responsibility. §4775.
Notice of pesticide application to separate interest or common area without licensed pest control operator. §4777.
Wood-destroying pests or organisms. §4780.
Temporary removal of occupant to perform treatment of wood-destroying pests. §4785.
Exclusive use communication wiring. §4790.

§4775. Maintenance and repair responsibility

(a)(1) Except as provided in paragraph [1] **(4)**, unless otherwise provided in the declaration of a common interest development, the association is responsible for repairing, replacing, and maintaining the common area.

(2)(A) Unless otherwise provided in the declaration of a common interest development, or unless the utility service that failed is required to be maintained, repaired, or replaced by a public, private, or other utility service provider, the association is responsible for repairs and replacements necessary to restore interrupted gas, heat, water, or electrical services that begin in the common area even if the matter extends into a separate interest or the exclusive use common area appurtenant to a separate interest.

(B) This paragraph does not change any legal duty or obligation of a utility company or local government to repair or replace components pertaining to gas, heat, water, or electrical services.

[2] **(3)** Unless otherwise provided in the declaration of a common interest development, the owner of each separate interest is responsible for repairing, replacing, and maintaining that separate interest.

[3] **(4)** Unless otherwise provided in the declaration of a common interest development, the owner of each separate interest is responsible for maintaining the exclusive use common area appurtenant to that separate interest and the association is responsible for repairing and replacing the exclusive use common area.

(b)(1) An association's board shall commence the process to make the repairs necessary to restore gas, heat, water, or electrical services, as required by this section, within 14 days of the interruption of services.

(2) If there are insufficient reserve funds available to cover the costs of repairs or replacements, as required by this section, an association may obtain competitive financing from a financial institution, in compliance with Section 5735, to pay for the costs of the repairs or replacements described in paragraph (1) without requiring a vote of the members and levy an emergency assessment to allow for the repayment of the loan. However, before obtaining that financing, the board shall pass a resolution containing written findings regarding the nature of the association's expenses and how the association's reserves do not cover the necessary costs. The resolution shall be distributed to the members with the notice of the emergency assessment and with notices otherwise required by law or governing documents pursuant to the board's action, if any.

(3) Notwithstanding any other section of law or the association's governing documents, if an association's board is unable to meet a quorum within 14 days, pursuant to this section, then at the next duly noticed board meeting following the 14th day, the requirements for a quorum shall be reduced so that the total number of directors at that board meeting shall constitute a quorum. This reduced quorum shall only apply for the vote to commence the process specified in paragraph (1). The notice shall contain a provision indicating the use of a reduced quorum.

(4) Notwithstanding the requirements of Section 4910, if directors of an association are required to vote to initiate any repairs or replacements pursuant to this subdivision, voting may be performed by electronic means, including, but not limited to, email. All records of the vote shall be deemed association records and subject to the inspection and retention rules specified in Section 5210.

[4] **(c)** The costs of temporary relocation during the repair [5], **replacement, or** maintenance of the areas within the responsibility of the association shall be borne by the owner of the separate interest affected.

(d) Nothing in this section shall be construed to result in the personal liability of a director of an association.

[6] **(e)** This section shall [7] **not apply if the association is in an area affected by one or more of the following conditions, and such condition or conditions materially affect the association's ability to perform its responsibilities pursuant to this section:**

(1) A state of disaster or emergency declared by the federal government.

(2) A state of emergency proclaimed by the Governor pursuant to Section 8625 of the Government Code.

(3) A local emergency proclaimed by a local governing body or official under Section 8630 of the Government Code. Leg.H. Added Stats 2014 ch 405 §2 (AB 968), effective January 1, 2015, operative January 1, 2017. Amended Stats 2024 ch 288 §1 (SB 900), effective January 1, 2025.

§4775. 2024 Deletes. [1] (3) [2] (2) [3] (3) [4] (b) [5] and [6] (c) [7] become operative on January 1, 2017.

Prior Law: Former CC §4775, was added Stats 1992 ch 411 §2 (SB 1817), effective August 1, 1992, and repealed Stats 1993 ch 219 §52 (AB 1500). See Fam C §20022.

Former CC §4775, similar to the present section, was added Stats 2012 ch 180 §2 (AB 805), effective January 1, 2013, operative January 1, 2014, amended Stats 2014 ch 405 §1 (AB 968), effective January 1, 2015, and repealed January 1, 2017, by its own terms.

Former Sections: Former CC §4775, similar to the present section, was added Stats 2012 ch 180 §2 (AB 805), operative January 1, 2014, and repealed operative January 1, 2017, by its own terms.

Former CC §4775, was added Stats 1992 ch 411 §2 (SB 1817), effective August 1, 1992, and repealed Stats 1993 ch 219 §52 (AB 1500). See Fam C §20022.

§4776. [Section repealed 1994.]

Leg.H. Added Stats 1992 ch 411 §2 (SB 1817), effective August 1, 1992. Repealed Stats 1993 ch 219 §52 (AB 1500). See Fam C §20023.

§4777. Notice of pesticide application to separate interest or common area without licensed pest control operator

(a) For the purposes of this section:

(1) "Adjacent separate interest" means a separate interest that is directly beside, above, or below a particular separate interest or the common area.

(2) "Authorized agent" means an individual, organization, or other entity that has entered into an agreement with the association to act on the association's behalf.

(3) "Broadcast application" means spreading pesticide over an area greater than two square feet.

(4) "Electronic delivery" means delivery of a document by electronic means to the electronic address at, or through which, an owner of a separate interest has authorized electronic delivery.

(5) "Licensed pest control operator" means anyone licensed by the state to apply pesticides.

(6) "Pest" means a living organism that causes damage to property or economic loss, or transmits or produces diseases.

(7) "Pesticide" means any substance, or mixture of substances, that is intended to be used for controlling, destroying, repelling, or mitigating any pest or organism, excluding antimicrobial pesticides as defined by the Federal Insecticide, Fungicide, and Rodenticide Act (7 U.S.C. Sec. 136(mm)).

(b)(1) An association or its authorized agent that applies any pesticide to a separate interest or to the common area without a licensed pest control operator shall provide the owner and, if applicable, the tenant of an affected separate interest and, if making broadcast applications, or using total release foggers or aerosol sprays, the owner and, if applicable, the tenant in an adjacent separate interest that could reasonably be impacted by the pesticide use with written notice that contains the following statements and information using words with common and everyday meaning:

(A) The pest or pests to be controlled.

(B) The name and brand of the pesticide product proposed to be used.

(C) "State law requires that you be given the following information: CAUTION - PESTICIDES ARE TOXIC CHEMICALS. The California Department of Pesticide Regulation and the United States Environmental Protection Agency allow the unlicensed use of certain pesticides based on existing scientific evidence that there are no appreciable risks if proper use conditions are followed or that the risks are outweighed by the benefits. The degree of risk depends upon the degree of exposure, so exposure should be minimized.

If within 24 hours following application of a pesticide, a person experiences symptoms similar to common seasonal illness comparable to influenza, the person should contact a physician, appropriate licensed health care provider, or the California Poison Control System (1-800-222-1222).

For further information, contact any of the following: for Health Questions - the County Health Department (telephone number) and for Regulatory Information - the Department of Pesticide Regulation (916-324-4100)."

(D) The approximate date, time, and frequency with which the pesticide will be applied.

(E) The following notification:

"The approximate date, time, and frequency of this pesticide application is subject to change."

(2) At least 48 hours prior to application of the pesticide to a separate interest, the association or its authorized agent shall provide individual notice to the owner and, if applicable, the tenant of the separate interest and notice to an owner and, if applicable, the tenant occupying any adjacent separate interest that is required to be notified pursuant to paragraph (1).

(3)(A) At least 48 hours prior to application of the pesticide to a common area, the association or its authorized agent shall, if practicable, post the written notice described in paragraph (1) in a conspicuous place in or around the common area in which the pesticide is to be applied. Otherwise, if not practicable, the association or its authorized agent shall provide individual notice to the owner and, if applicable, the tenant of the separate interest that is adjacent to the common area.

(B) If the pest poses an immediate threat to health and safety, thereby making compliance with notification prior to the pesticide application unreasonable, the association or its authorized agent shall post the written notice as soon as practicable, but not later than one hour after the pesticide is applied.

(4) Notice to tenants of separate interests shall be provided, in at least one of the following ways:

(A) First-class mail.

(B) Personal delivery to a tenant 18 years of age or older.

(C) Electronic delivery, if an electronic mailing address has been provided by the tenant.

(5)(A) Upon receipt of written notification, the owner of the separate interest or the tenant may agree in writing or, if notification was delivered electronically, the tenant may agree through electronic delivery, to allow the association or authorized agent to apply a pesticide immediately or at an agreed upon time.

(B)(i) Prior to receipt of written notification, the association or authorized agent may agree orally to an immediate pesticide application if the owner or, if applicable, the tenant requests that the pesticide be applied before the 48-hour notice of the pesticide product proposed to be used.

(ii) With respect to an owner or, if applicable, a tenant entering into an oral agreement for immediate pesticide application, the association or authorized agent, no later than the time of pesticide application, shall leave the written notice specified in paragraph (1) in a conspicuous place in the separate interest or at the entrance of the separate interest in a manner in which a reasonable person would discover the notice.

(iii) If any owner or, if applicable, any tenant of a separate interest or an owner or, if applicable, a tenant of an adjacent separate interest is also required to be notified pursuant to this subparagraph, the association or authorized agent shall provide that person with this notice as soon as practicable after the oral agreement is made authorizing immediate pesticide application, but in no case later than commencement of application of the pesticide.

(6) A copy of a written notice provided pursuant to paragraph (1) shall be attached to the minutes of the board meeting immediately subsequent the application of the pesticide. **Leg.H.** Added Stats 2016 ch 330 §2 (AB 2362), effective January 1, 2017. Amended Stats 2017 ch 561 §19 (AB 1516), effective January 1, 2018.

Prior Law: Former CC §4777, relating to costs of Family Law Evaluator and booklet in San Mateo County and solicitation of computers, printers, software, and other equipment donations from existing hardware and software providers, was added Stats 1992 ch 411 §2 (SB 1817), effective August 1, 1992, amended Stats 1993 ch 158 §1 (AB 392), effective July 20, 1993, repealed July 1, 1994, and repealed Stats 1993 ch 219 §52 (AB 1500), effective January 1, 1994.

2016 Note: The Legislature finds and declares the following:

(a) Existing law, Section 1940.8.5 of the Civil Code, requires a landlord or his or her agent who applies pesticide in certain ways to a dwelling unit or common area without a licensed pest control operator to provide to tenants of potentially affected units written notification that includes the pest to be targeted, the pesticide to be used, the frequency of its use, and a health and safety statement prior to the pesticide application.

(b) It is the intent of this bill, therefore, that when pesticides are about to be applied to the separate interests or to the common areas of a common interest development either by the homeowner association or by one of its agents rather than by a licensed pest control operator, that the owners and, if applicable, tenants of the separate interests and the owners and, if applicable, tenants of adjacent separate units that could reasonably be impacted by the pesticide be provided with substantially the same written notification that they would have received under existing law had the pesticides been applied by a licensed pest control operator. Stats. 2016 ch. 330 (AB 2362) §1.

§4778. [Section repealed 1994.]

Leg.H. Added Stats 1992 ch 411 §2 (SB 1817), effective August 1, 1992. Repealed Stats 1993 ch 219 §52 (AB 1500). The repealed section related to the study and report of the San Mateo County Pilot Project.

§4778.5. [Section repealed 1994.]

Leg.H. Added Stats 1992 ch 411 §2 (SB 1817), effective August 1, 1992. Repealed Stats 1993 ch 219 §52 (AB 1500). See Fam C §20026.

§4779. [Section repealed 1994.]

Leg.H. Added Stats 1992 ch 411 §2 (SB 1817), effective August 1, 1992. Repealed Stats 1993 ch 219 §52 (AB 1500). See Fam C §20030.

§4780. Wood-destroying pests or organisms

(a) In a community apartment project, condominium project, or stock cooperative, unless otherwise provided in the declaration, the association is responsible for the repair and maintenance of the common area occasioned by the presence of wood-destroying pests or organisms.

(b) In a planned development, unless a different maintenance scheme is provided in the declaration, each owner of a separate interest is responsible for the repair and maintenance of that separate interest as may be occasioned by the presence of wood-destroying pests or organisms. Upon approval of the majority of all members of the association, pursuant to Section 4065, that responsibility may be delegated to the association, which shall be entitled to recover the cost thereof as a special assessment.

Leg.H. Added Stats 2012 ch 180 §2 (AB 805), effective January 1, 2013, operative January 1, 2014.

Prior Law: Former CC §4780, was added Stats 1992 ch 411 §2 (SB 1817), effective August 1, 1992, and repealed Stats 1993 ch 219 §52 (AB 1500). See Fam C §20002.

§4781. [Section repealed 1994.]

Leg.H. Added Stats 1992 ch 411 §2 (SB 1817), effective August 1, 1992. Repealed Stats 1993 ch 219 §52 (AB 1500). See Fam C §20031.

§4782. [Section repealed 1994.]

Leg.H. Added Stats 1992 ch 411 §2 (SB 1817), effective August 1, 1992. Repealed Stats 1993 ch 219 §52 (AB 1500). See Fam C §20032.

§4783. [Section repealed 1994.]

Leg.H. Added Stats 1992 ch 411 §2 (SB 1817), effective August 1, 1992. Repealed Stats 1993 ch 219 §52 (AB 1500). See Fam C §20033.

§4784. [Section repealed 1994.]

Leg.H. Added Stats 1992 ch 411 §2 (SB 1817), effective August 1, 1992. Repealed Stats 1993 ch 219 §52 (AB 1500). See Fam C §20034.

§4785. Temporary removal of occupant to perform treatment of wood-destroying pests

(a) The association may cause the temporary, summary removal of any occupant of a common interest development for such periods and at such times as may be necessary for prompt, effective treatment of wood-destroying pests or organisms.

(b) The association shall give notice of the need to temporarily vacate a separate interest to the occupants and to the owners, not less than 15 days nor more than 30 days prior to the date of the temporary relocation. The notice shall state the reason for the temporary relocation, the date and time of the beginning of treatment, the anticipated date and time of termination of treatment, and that the occupants will be responsible for their own accommodations during the temporary relocation.

(c) Notice by the association shall be deemed complete upon either:

(1) Personal delivery of a copy of the notice to the occupants, and if an occupant is not the owner, individual delivery pursuant to Section 4040, of a copy of the notice to the owner.

(2) Individual delivery pursuant to Section 4040 to the occupant at the address of the separate interest, and if the occupant is not the owner, individual delivery pursuant to Section 4040, of a copy of the notice to the owner.

(d) For purposes of this section, "occupant" means an owner, resident, guest, invitee, tenant, lessee, sublessee, or other person in possession of the separate interest. **Leg.H.** Added Stats 2012 ch 180 §2 (AB 805), effective January 1, 2013, operative January 1, 2014.

Prior Law: Former CC §4785, was added Stats 1992 ch 411 §2 (SB 1817), effective August 1, 1992, and repealed Stats 1993 ch 219 §52 (AB 1500). See Fam C §20035.

§4786. [Section repealed 1994.]

Leg.H. Added Stats 1992 ch 411 §2 (SB 1817), effective August 1, 1992. Repealed Stats 1993 ch 219 §52 (AB 1500). See Fam C §20036.

§4787. [Section repealed 1994.]

Leg.H. Added Stats 1992 ch 411 §2 (SB 1817), effective August 1, 1992. Repealed Stats 1993 ch 219 §52 (AB 1500). See Fam C §20037.

§4788. [Section repealed 1994.]

Leg.H. Added Stats 1992 ch 411 §2 (SB 1817), effective August 1, 1992. Repealed Stats 1993 ch 219 §52 (AB 1500). See Fam C §20038.

§4789. [Section repealed 1994.]

Leg.H. Added Stats 1992 ch 411 §2 (SB 1817), effective August 1, 1992. Amended Stats 1993 ch 158 §2 (AB 392), effective July 20, 1993, operative until July 1, 1994. Repealed Stats 1993 ch 219 §52 (AB 1500). See Fam C §20039.

§4790. Exclusive use communication wiring

Notwithstanding the provisions of the declaration, a member is entitled to reasonable access to the common area for the purpose of maintaining the internal and external telephone wiring made part of the exclusive use common area of the member's separate interest pursuant to subdivision (c) of Section 4145. The access shall be subject to the consent of the association, whose approval shall not be unreasonably withheld, and which may include the association's approval of telephone wiring upon the exterior of the common area, and other conditions as the association determines reasonable. **Leg.H.** Added Stats 2012 ch 180 §2 (AB 805), effective January 1, 2013, operative January 1, 2014.

Prior Law: Former CC §4790, was added Stats 1992 ch 411 §2 (SB 1817), effective August 1, 1992, and repealed Stats 1993 ch 219 §52 (AB 1500). See Fam C §20040.

§4791. [Section repealed 1994.]

Leg.H. Added Stats 1992 ch 411 §2 (SB 1817), effective August 1, 1992. Repealed Stats 1993 ch 219 §52 (AB 1500). See Fam C §20041.

§4792. [Section repealed 1994.]

Leg.H. Added Stats 1992 ch 411 §2 (SB 1817), effective August 1, 1992. Repealed Stats 1993 ch 219 §52 (AB 1500). The repealed section related to the study and report of the Santa Clara County Pilot Project.

§4793. [Section repealed 1994.]

Leg.H. Added Stats 1992 ch 411 §2 (SB 1817), effective August 1, 1992. Repealed Stats 1993 ch 219 §52 (AB 1500). See Fam C §20043.

CHAPTER 6
ASSOCIATION GOVERNANCE

Article 1. Association Existence and Powers.
Article 2. Board Meeting.
Article 3. Member Meeting.
Article 4. Member Election.
Article 5. Record Inspection.
Article 6. Recordkeeping.
Article 7. Annual Reports.
Article 8. Conflict of Interest.
Article 9. Managing Agent.
Article 10. Government Assistance.
Article 11. Emergency powers and procedures.

ARTICLE 1
Association Existence and Powers

Association [Repealed July 2, 2026]. §4800.
Association powers. §4805.
Joint neighborhood association. §4820.

§4800. Association [Repealed July 2, 2026]

A common interest development shall be managed by an association that may be incorporated or unincorporated. The association may be referred to as an owners' association or a community association. **Leg.H.** Added Stats 2012 ch 180 §2 (AB 805), effective January 1, 2013, operative January 1, 2014.

Prior Law: Former CC §4800, similar to Fam C §§63, 780, 2550–2553, 2600–2604, 2620–2627, was added Stats 1969 ch 1608 §8, operative January 1, 1970, amended Stats 1970 ch 962 §3.5, ch 1575 §3, Stats 1976 ch 762 §1, Stats 1978 ch 1323 §2, Stats 1979 ch 638 §1, Stats 1982 ch 497 §18, operative July 1, 1983, Stats 1983 ch 1159 §7, operative July 1, 1984, Stats 1984 ch 29 §1, ch 1661 §1, ch 1671 §23, Stats 1986 ch 215 §1, and repealed Stats 1992 ch 162 §3 (AB 2650), operative January 1, 1994.

§4800.1. [Section repealed 1994.]

Leg.H. Added Stats 1983 ch 342 §1. Amended Stats 1986 ch 539 §1. Repealed Stats 1992 ch 162 §3 (AB 2650), operative January 1, 1994. See Fam C §§2580, 2581.

§4800.2. [Section repealed 1994.]

Leg.H. Added Stats 1983 ch 342 §2. Repealed Stats 1992 ch 162 §3 (AB 2650), operative January 1, 1994. See Fam C §2640.

§4800.3. [Section repealed 1994.]

Leg.H. Added Stats 1984 ch 1661 §2. Repealed Stats 1992 ch 162 §3 (AB 2650), operative January 1, 1994. See Fam C §2641.

§4800.4. [Section repealed 1994.]

Leg.H. Added Stats 1985 ch 362 §3. Repealed Stats 1992 ch 162 §3 (AB 2650), operative January 1, 1994. See Fam C §2650.

§4800.5. [Section repealed 1994.]

Leg.H. Added Stats 1970 ch 312 §2. Repealed Stats 1992 ch 162 §3 (AB 2650), operative January 1, 1994. See Fam C §2660.

§4800.6. [Section repealed 1994]

Leg.H. Added Stats 1981 ch 715 §3. Amended Stats 1983 ch 1159 §8, operative July 1, 1984; Stats 1984 ch 397 §3, effective July 11, 1984; Stats 1992 ch 159 §1 (AB 3630). Repealed Stats 1992 ch 162 §3 (AB 2650), January 1, 1994 (ch 159 prevails). Repealed Stats 1993 ch 219 §53 (AB 1500). See Fam C §2024.

Prior Law: Former CC §4800.6, similar to the repealed section, was added Stats 1980 ch 329 §1 and repealed Stats 1981 ch 715 §2.

§4800.7. [Section repealed 1988.]

Leg.H. Added Stats 1984 ch 463 §1. Amended Stats 1985 ch 419 §4. Repealed Stats 1988 ch 729 §2. See Fam C §§3800–3804, 3806–3810.

§4800.8. [Section repealed 1994.]

Leg.H. Added Stats 1986 ch 686 §1. Amended Stats 1988 ch 542 §1, effective August 23, 1988. Repealed Stats 1992 ch 162 §3 (AB 2650), operative January 1, 1994. See Fam C §2610 (chs 176, 431 prevail). Amended Stats 1992 ch 176 §1 (SB 1129), effective July 11, 1992, ch 431 §1 (SB 2018). Repealed Stats 1993 ch 219 §54 (AB 1500). See Fam C §2610.

§4800.9. [Section repealed 1994.]

Leg.H. Added Stats 1983 ch 320 §1. Amended Stats 1988 ch 153 §4; Stats 1989 ch 1266 §2. Repealed Stats 1992 ch 162 §3 (AB 2650), January 1, 1994. See Fam C §2554.

§4800.10. [Section repealed 1994.]

Leg.H. Added Stats 1992 ch 37 §1 (AB 1437). Amended Stats 1992 ch 356 §4 (AB 3399). Repealed Stats 1993 ch 219 §55 (AB 1500). Amended Stats 1993 ch 1101 §1 (AB 1469), effective October 10, 1993, operative until January 1, 1994. Repealed January 1, 1994, by its own provisions. See Fam C §§2100–2113.

§4800.11. [Section repealed 1994.]

Leg.H. Added Stats 1992 ch 36 §1 (AB 1396). Amended Stats 1992 ch 356 §5 (AB 3399). Repealed Stats 1993 ch 219 §56 (AB 1500). Amended Stats 1993 ch 1101 §2 (AB 1469), effective October 10, 1993, operative until January 1, 1994. Repealed January 1, 1994, by its own provisions. See Fam C §§2120–2129.

§4801. [Section repealed 1994.]

Leg.H. Added Stats 1969 ch 1608 §8, operative January 1, 1970. Amended Stats 1970 ch 1545 §3, ch 1575 §4; Stats 1971 ch 1210 §6, ch 1675 §3; Stats 1976 ch 130 §5; Stats 1979 ch 912 §1; Stats 1980 ch 676 §60; Stats 1981 ch 514 §1; Stats 1983 ch 302 §7; Stats 1984 ch 19 §1, 1661 §3; Stats 1985 ch 1358 §3; Stats 1986 ch 1096 §1; Stats 1987 ch 1086 §2; Stats 1988 ch 407 §1; Stats 1991 ch 1207 §1 (SB 863). Repealed Stats 1992 ch 162 §3 (AB 2650), January 1, 1994. See Fam C §§3651, 3653, 3654, 4320, 4330–4337, 4339. Amended Stats 1992 ch 427 §15 (AB 3355) (ch 162 prevails). Repealed Stats 1993 ch 219 §57 (AB 1500). See Fam C §§3651, 3653, 3654, 4320, 4330–4337, 4339.

§4801.1. [Section repealed 1994.]

Leg.H. Added Stats 1985 ch 1358 §4. Amended Stats 1989 ch 1359 §6. Repealed Stats 1992 ch 162 §3 (AB 2650), January 1, 1994. See Fam C §§3660, 3662–3668.

§4801.4. [Section repealed 1994.]

Leg.H. Added Stats 1984 ch 1573 §1. Amended Stats 1985 ch 362 §4. Repealed Stats 1992 ch 162 §3 (AB 2650), January 1, 1994. See Fam C §4360.

§4801.5. [Section repealed 1994.]

Leg.H. Added Stats 1974 ch 1338 §1. Amended Stats 1976 ch 380 §1; Stats 1983 ch 302 §8. Repealed Stats 1992 ch 162 §3 (AB 2650), January 1, 1994. See Fam C §4323.

§4801.6. [Section repealed 1991.]

Leg.H. Added Stats 1985 ch 404 §10, operative January 1, 1987. Amended Stats 1988 ch 153 §5, ch 969 §1; Stats 1989 ch 1359 §7, operative until July 1, 1990. Repealed January 1, 1991, by its own provisions. The repealed section related to wage assignment for spousal support.

Prior Law: Former CC §4801.6, relating to wage assignment for spousal support, was added Stats 1980 ch 866 §1, amended Stats 1982 ch 497 §19, operative July 1, 1983, Stats 1985 ch 404 §4, ch 1069 §4.2, and repealed January 1, 1987, by its own terms.

§4801.7. [Section repealed 1994.]

Leg.H. Added Stats 1980 ch 866 §2. Amended Stats 1981 ch 822 §1; Stats 1985 ch 404 §6. Repealed Stats 1992 ch 162 §3 (AB 2650), operative January 1, 1994. See Fam C §§4350–4352.

§4801.9. [Section repealed 1994.]

Leg.H. Added Stats 1987 ch 1086 §3. Repealed Stats 1992 ch 162 §3 (AB 2650), operative January 1, 1994. See Fam C §§3680–3685, 3690–3693.

§4802. [Section repealed 1994.]

Leg.H. Added Stats 1969 ch 1608 §8, operative January 1, 1970. Repealed Stats 1992 ch 162 §3 (AB 2650), operative January 1, 1994. See Fam C §§1620, 3580.

§4803. [Section repealed 1994.]

Leg.H. Added Stats 1969 ch 1608 §8, operative January 1, 1970. Amended Stats 1970 ch 312 §3. Repealed Stats 1992 ch 162 §3 (AB 2650), operative January 1, 1994. See Fam C §125.

§4804. [Section repealed 1994.]

Leg.H. Added Stats 1969 ch 1608 §8, operative January 1, 1970. Repealed Stats 1992 ch 162 §3 (AB 2650), operative January 1, 1994. See Fam C §§2502, 3515.

§4805. Association powers

(a) Unless the governing documents provide otherwise, and regardless of whether the association is incorporated or unincorporated, the association may exercise the powers granted to a nonprofit mutual benefit corporation, as enumerated in Section 7140 of the Corporations Code, except that an unincorporated association may not adopt or use a corporate seal or issue membership certificates in accordance with Section 7313 of the Corporations Code.

(b) The association, whether incorporated or unincorporated, may exercise the powers granted to an association in this act. **Leg.H.** Added Stats 2012 ch 180 §2 (AB 805), effective January 1, 2013, operative January 1, 2014.

Prior Law: Former CC §4805, similar to Fam C §4338, was added Stats 1969 ch 1608 §8, operative January 1, 1970, amended Stats 1974 ch 1329 §1, and repealed Stats 1992 ch 162 §3 (AB 2650), operative January 1, 1994.

§4806. [Section repealed 1994.]

Leg.H. Added Stats 1969 ch 1608 §8, operative January 1, 1970. Amended Stats 1970 ch 988 §1. Repealed Stats 1992 ch 162 §3 (AB 2650), operative January 1, 1994. See Fam C §§4321, 4322.

§4807. [Section repealed 1994.]

Leg.H. Added Stats 1969 ch 1608 §8, operative January 1, 1970. Repealed Stats 1992 ch 162 §3 (AB 2650), operative January 1, 1994. See Fam C §4008.

§4808. [Section repealed 1970.]

Leg.H. Added Stats 1969 ch 1608 §8, operative January 1, 1970. Repealed Stats 1970 ch 962 §5. The repealed section related to assignment of homestead.

§4809. [Section repealed 1994.]

Leg.H. Added Stats 1969 ch 1608 §8, operative January 1, 1970. Amended Stats 1983 ch 1159 §9, operative July 1, 1984. Repealed Stats 1992 ch 162 §3 (AB 2650), operative January 1, 1994. See Fam C §215.

§4810. [Section repealed 1994.]

Leg.H. Added Stats 1969 ch 1608 §8, operative January 1, 1970. Amended Stats 1982 ch 497 §20, operative July 1, 1983. Repealed Stats 1992 ch 162 §3 (AB 2650), operative January 1, 1994. See Fam C §2555.

§4811. [Section repealed 1994.]

Leg.H. Added Stats 1969 ch 1608 §8, operative January 1, 1970. Amended Stats 1970 ch 1545 §4; Stats 1981 ch 715 §4; Stats 1983 ch 1304 §8, operative July 1, 1984. Repealed Stats 1992 ch 162 §3 (AB 2650), operative January 1, 1994. See Fam C §§92, 3585, 3586, 3590, 3591, 3593, 3651, 4501.

§4812. [Section repealed 1994.]

Leg.H. Added Stats 1969 ch 1608 §8, operative January 1, 1970. Amended Stats 1977 ch 332 §2. Repealed Stats 1992 ch 162 §3 (AB 2650), operative January 1, 1994. See Fam C §3592.

§4813. [Section repealed 1994.]

Leg.H. Added Stats 1970 ch 1545 §5. Repealed Stats 1992 ch 162 §3 (AB 2650), operative January 1, 1994. See Fam C §2011.

§4820. Joint neighborhood association

Whenever two or more associations have consolidated any of their functions under a joint neighborhood association or similar organization, members of each participating association shall be (a) entitled to attend all meetings of the joint association other than executive sessions, (b) given reasonable opportunity for participation in those meetings, and (c) entitled to the same access to the joint association's records as they are to the participating association's records. **Leg.H.** Added Stats 2012 ch 180 §2 (AB 805), effective January 1, 2013, operative January 1, 2014.

ARTICLE 2
Board Meeting

Common Interest Development Open Meeting Act. §4900.
Board action outside of meeting prohibited. §4910.
Notice of board meeting. §4920.
Emergency board meeting. §4923.
Board meeting open. §4925.
Board or member meeting by teleconference. § 4926.
Limitation on meeting content. §4930.
Executive session. §4935.
Minutes. §4950.
Civil action to enforce article. §4955.

§4900. Common Interest Development Open Meeting Act

This article shall be known and may be cited as the Common Interest Development Open Meeting Act. **Leg.H.** Added Stats 2012 ch 180 §2 (AB 805), effective January 1, 2013, operative January 1, 2014.

§4910. Board action outside of meeting prohibited

(a) The board shall not take action on any item of business outside of a board meeting.

(b)(1) Notwithstanding Section 7211 of the Corporations Code, the board shall not conduct a meeting via a series of electronic transmissions, including, but not limited to, electronic mail, except as specified in paragraph (2).

(2) Electronic transmissions may be used as a method of conducting an emergency board meeting if all directors, individually or collectively, consent in writing to that action, and if the written consent or consents are filed with the minutes of the board meeting. These written consents may be transmitted electronically. **Leg.H.** Added Stats 2012 ch 180 §2 (AB 805), effective January 1, 2013, operative January 1, 2014.

§4920. Notice of board meeting

(a) Except as provided in subdivision (b), the association shall give notice of the time and place of a board meeting at least four days before the meeting.

(b)(1) If a board meeting is an emergency meeting held pursuant to Section 4923, the association is not required to give notice of the time and place of the meeting.

(2) If a nonemergency board meeting is held solely in executive session, the association shall give notice of the time and place of the meeting at least two days prior to the meeting.

(3) If the association's governing documents require a longer period of notice than is required by this section, the association shall comply with the period stated in its governing documents. For the purposes of this paragraph, a governing document provision does not apply to a notice of an emergency meeting or a meeting held solely in executive session unless it specifically states that it applies to those types of meetings.

(c) Notice of a board meeting shall be given by general delivery pursuant to Section 4045.

(d) Notice of a board meeting shall contain the agenda for the meeting. **Leg.H.** Added Stats 2012 ch 180 §2 (AB 805), effective January 1, 2013, operative January 1, 2014. Amended Stats 2013 ch 183 §17 (SB 745), effective January 1, 2014.

§4923. Emergency board meeting

An emergency board meeting may be called by the president of the association, or by any two directors other than the president, if there are circumstances that could not have been reasonably foreseen which require immediate attention and possible action by the board, and which of necessity make it impracticable to provide notice as required by Section 4920. **Leg.H.** Added Stats 2012 ch 180 §2 (AB 805), effective January 1, 2013, operative January 1, 2014.

§4925. Board meeting open

(a) Any member may attend board meetings, except when the board adjourns to, or meets solely in, executive session. As specified in subdivision (b) of Section 4090, a member of the association shall be entitled to attend a teleconference meeting or the portion of a teleconference meeting that is open to members, and that meeting or portion of the meeting shall be audible to the members in a location specified in the notice of the meeting.

(b) The board shall permit any member to speak at any meeting of the association or the board, except for meetings of the board held in executive session. A reasonable time limit for all members of the association to speak to the board or before a meeting of the association shall be established by the board. **Leg.H.** Added Stats 2012 ch 180 §2 (AB 805), effective January 1, 2013, operative January 1, 2014.

§ 4926. Board or member meeting by teleconference

(a) Notwithstanding any other law or the association's governing documents, a board meeting or meeting of the members may be conducted entirely by teleconference, without any physical location being held open for the attendance of any director or member, if all of the following conditions are satisfied:

(1) The notice for each meeting conducted under this section includes, in addition to other required content for meeting notices, all of the following:

(A) Clear technical instructions on how to participate by teleconference.

(B) The telephone number and electronic mail address of a person who can provide technical assistance with the teleconference process, both before and during the meeting.

(C) A reminder that a member may request individual delivery of meeting notices, with instructions on how to do so.

(2) Every director and member has the same ability to participate in the meeting that would exist if the meeting were held in person.

(3) Any vote of the directors shall be conducted by a roll call vote.

(4) Any person who is entitled to participate in the meeting shall be given the option of participating by telephone.

(b) Subdivision (a) does not apply to a meeting at which ballots are counted and tabulated pursuant to Section 5120. **Leg.H.** Added Stats 2023 ch 203 §3 (AB 648), effective January 1, 2024.

§4930. Limitation on meeting content

(a) Except as described in subdivisions (b) to (e), inclusive, the board may not discuss or take action on any item at a nonemergency meeting unless the item was placed on the agenda included in the notice that was distributed pursuant to subdivision (a) of Section 4920. This subdivision does not prohibit a member or resident who is not a director from speaking on issues not on the agenda.

(b) Notwithstanding subdivision (a), a director, a managing agent or other agent of the board, or a member of the staff of the board, may do any of the following:

(1) Briefly respond to statements made or questions posed by a person speaking at a meeting as described in subdivision (b) of Section 4925.

(2) Ask a question for clarification, make a brief announcement, or make a brief report on the person's own activities, whether in response to questions posed by a member or based upon the person's own initiative.

(c) Notwithstanding subdivision (a), the board or a director, subject to rules or procedures of the board, may do any of the following:

(1) Provide a reference to, or provide other resources for factual information to, its managing agent or other agents or staff.

(2) Request its managing agent or other agents or staff to report back to the board at a subsequent meeting concerning any matter, or take action to direct its managing agent or other agents or staff to place a matter of business on a future agenda.

(3) Direct its managing agent or other agents or staff to perform administrative tasks that are necessary to carry out this section.

(d) Notwithstanding subdivision (a), the board may take action on any item of business not appearing on the agenda distributed pursuant to subdivision (a) of Section 4920 under any of the following conditions:

(1) Upon a determination made by a majority of the board present at the meeting that an emergency situation exists. An emergency situation exists if there are circumstances that could not have been reasonably foreseen by the board, that require immediate attention and possible action by the board, and that, of necessity, make it impracticable to provide notice.

(2) Upon a determination made by the board by a vote of two-thirds of the directors present at the meeting, or, if less than two-thirds of total membership of the board is present at the meeting, by a unanimous vote of the directors present, that there is a need to take immediate action and that the need for action came to the attention of the board after the agenda was distributed pursuant to subdivision (a) of Section 4920.

(3) The item appeared on an agenda that was distributed pursuant to subdivision (a) of Section 4920 for a prior meeting of the board that occurred not more than 30 calendar days before the date that action is taken on the item and, at the prior meeting, action on the item was continued to the meeting at which the action is taken.

(e) Before discussing any item pursuant to subdivision (d), the board shall openly identify the item to the members in attendance at the meeting. **Leg.H.** Added Stats 2012 ch 180 §2 (AB 805), effective January 1, 2013, operative January 1, 2014.

§4935. Executive session

(a) The board may adjourn to, or meet solely in, executive session to consider litigation, matters relating to the formation of contracts with third parties, member discipline, personnel matters, or to meet with a member, upon the member's request, regarding the member's payment of assessments, as specified in Section 5665.

(b) The board shall adjourn to, or meet solely in, executive session to discuss member discipline, if requested by the member who is the subject of the discussion. That member shall be entitled to attend the executive session.

(c) The board shall adjourn to, or meet solely in, executive session to discuss a payment plan pursuant to Section 5665.

(d) The board shall adjourn to, or meet solely in, executive session to decide whether to foreclose on a lien pursuant to subdivision (b) of Section 5705.

(e) Any matter discussed in executive session shall be generally noted in the minutes of the immediately following meeting that is open to the entire membership. **Leg.H.** Added Stats 2012 ch 180 §2 (AB 805), effective January 1, 2013, operative January 1, 2014.

§4950. Minutes

(a) The minutes, minutes proposed for adoption that are marked to indicate draft status, or a summary of the minutes, of any board meeting, other than an executive session, shall be available to members within 30 days of the meeting. The minutes, proposed minutes, or summary minutes shall be distributed to any member upon request and upon reimbursement of the association's costs for making that distribution.

(b) The annual policy statement, prepared pursuant to Section 5310, shall inform the members of their right to obtain copies of board meeting minutes and of how and where to do so. **Leg.H.** Added Stats 2012 ch 180 §2 (AB 805), effective January 1, 2013, operative January 1, 2014.

§4955. Civil action to enforce article

(a) A member of an association may bring a civil action for declaratory or equitable relief for a violation of this article by the association, including, but not limited to, injunctive relief, restitution, or a combination thereof, within one year of the date the cause of action accrues.

(b) A member who prevails in a civil action to enforce the member's rights pursuant to this article shall be entitled to reasonable attorney's fees and court costs, and the court may impose a civil penalty of up to five hundred dollars ($500) for each violation, except that each identical violation shall be subject to only one penalty if the violation affects each member equally. A prevailing association shall not recover any costs, unless the court finds the action to be frivolous, unreasonable, or without foundation. **Leg.H.** Added Stats 2012 ch 180 §2 (AB 805), effective January 1, 2013, operative January 1, 2014.

ARTICLE 3
Member Meeting

Member meeting. §5000.

§5000. Member meeting

(a) Meetings of the membership of the association shall be conducted in accordance with a recognized system of parliamentary procedure or any parliamentary procedures the association may adopt.

(b) The board shall permit any member to speak at any meeting of the membership of the association. A reasonable time limit for all members to speak at a meeting of the association shall be established by the board. **Leg.H.** Added Stats 2012 ch 180 §2 (AB 805), effective January 1, 2013, operative January 1, 2014.

Prior Law: Former CC §5000, similar to Fam C §2090, was added Stats 1969 ch 1608 §8, operative January 1, 1970, and repealed Stats 1992 ch 162 §3 (AB 2650), operative January 1, 1994.

§5001. [Section repealed 1994.]
Leg.H. Added Stats 1969 ch 1608 §8, operative January 1, 1970. Repealed Stats 1992 ch 162 §3 (AB 2650) January 1, 1994. See Fam C §2091.

§5002. [Section repealed 1994.]
Leg.H. Added Stats 1969 ch 1608 §8, operative January 1, 1970. Repealed Stats 1992 ch 162 §3 (AB 2650) January 1, 1994. See Fam C §2092.

§5003. [Section repealed 1994.]
Leg.H. Added Stats 1969 ch 1608 §8, operative January 1, 1970. Repealed Stats 1992 ch 162 §3 (AB 2650) January 1, 1994. See Fam C §3.

§5004. [Section repealed 1994.]
Leg.H. Added Stats 1969 ch 1608 §8, operative January 1, 1970. Repealed Stats 1992 ch 162 §3 (AB 2650), operative January 1, 1994. See Fam C §2093.

ARTICLE 4
Member Election

Application of article. §5100.
Election by acclamation. § 5103.
Election rules. § 5105.
Inspector of elections. §5110.
Voting procedure. §5115.
Counting ballots. §5120.
Retention of ballots; Signed voter envelopes, voter lists, proxies, and candidate registration lists. §5125.
Proxies. §5130.
Campaign-related information. §5135.
Judicial enforcement. §5145.

§5100. Application of article
(a)(1) Notwithstanding any other law or provision of the governing documents, elections regarding assessments legally requiring a vote, election and removal of directors, amendments to the governing documents, or the grant of exclusive use of common area pursuant to Section 4600 shall be held by secret ballot in accordance with the procedures set forth in this article.

(2) An association shall hold an election for a seat on the board of directors in accordance with the procedures set forth in this article at the expiration of the corresponding director's term and at least once every four years.

(b) This article also governs an election on any topic that is expressly identified in the operating rules as being governed by this article.

(c) The provisions of this article apply to both incorporated and unincorporated associations, notwithstanding any contrary provision of the governing documents.

(d) The procedures set forth in this article shall apply to votes cast directly by the membership, but do not apply to votes cast by delegates or other elected representatives.

(e) In the event of a conflict between this article and the provisions of the Nonprofit Mutual Benefit Corporation Law (Part 3 (commencing with Section 7110) of Division 2 of Title 1 of the Corporations Code) relating to elections, the provisions of this article shall prevail.

(f) Directors shall not be required to be elected pursuant to this article if the governing documents provide that one member from each separate interest is a director. **Leg.H.** Added Stats 2012 ch 180 §2 (AB 805), effective January 1, 2013, operative January 1, 2014. Amended Stats 2014 ch 661 §4 (AB 569), effective January 1, 2015; Stats 2019 ch 848 §1 (SB 323), effective January 1, 2020; Stats 2019 ch 858 §1.1 (SB 754), effective January 1, 2020 (ch 858 prevails); Stats 2021 ch 517 §1 (AB 502), effective January 1, 2022.

Former Sections: Former CC §5100, similar to Fam C §720, was added Stats 1969 ch 1608 §8, operative January 1, 1970, and repealed Stats 1992 ch 162 §3 (AB 2650), operative January 1, 1994.

§5101. [Section repealed 1973.]
Leg.H. Added Stats 1969 ch 1608 §8. Amended Stats 1972 ch 1071 §1. Repealed Stats 1973 ch 987 §2, operative January 1, 1975 The repealed section related to husband as head of household.

§5102. [Section repealed 1994.]
Leg.H. Added Stats 1969 ch 1608 §8, operative January 1, 1970. Amended Stats 1969 ch 1609 §22, operative January 1, 1970; Stats 1973 ch 987 §3, operative January 1, 1975; Stats 1979 ch 795 §4, operative July 1, 1980; Stats 1982 ch 497 §21, operative July 1, 1983; Stats 1983 ch 192 §1, ch 234 §2.5. Repealed Stats 1992 ch 162 §3 (AB 2650), operative January 1, 1994. See Fam C §§752–754, 6321, 6340.

§5103. Election by acclamation
Notwithstanding the secret balloting requirement in Section 5100, or any contrary provision in the governing documents, when, as of the deadline for submitting nominations provided for in subdivision (a) of Section 5115, the number of qualified candidates is not more than the number of vacancies to be elected, as determined by the inspector or inspectors of the elections, the association may, but is not required to, consider the qualified candidates elected by acclamation if all of the following conditions have been met:

(a) The association has held a regular election for the directors in the last three years. The three-year time period shall be calculated from the date ballots were due in the last full election to the start of voting for the proposed election.

(b) The association provided individual notice of the election and the procedure for nominating candidates as follows:

(1) Initial notice at least 90 days before the deadline for submitting nominations provided for in subdivision (a) of Section 5115. The initial notice shall include all of the following:

(A) The number of board positions that will be filled at the election.

(B) The deadline for submitting nominations.

(C) The manner in which nominations can be submitted.

(D) A statement informing members that if, at the close of the time period for making nominations, there are the same number or fewer qualified candidates as there are board positions to be filled, then the board of directors may, after voting to do so, seat the qualified candidates by acclamation without balloting.

(2) A reminder notice between 7 and 30 days before the deadline for submitting nominations provided for in subdivision (a) of Section 5115. The reminder notice shall include all of the following:

(A) The number of board positions that will be filled at the election.

(B) The deadline for submitting nominations.

(C) The manner in which nominations can be submitted.

(D) A list of the names of all of the qualified candidates to fill the board positions as of the date of the reminder notice.

(E) A statement reminding members that if, at the close of the time period for making nominations, there are the same number or fewer qualified candidates as there are board positions to be filled, then the board of directors may, after voting to do so, seat the qualified candidates by acclamation without balloting. This statement is not required if, at the time the reminder notice will be delivered, the number of qualified candidates already exceeds the number of board positions to be filled.

(c)(1) The association provides, within seven business days of receiving a nomination, a written or electronic communication acknowledging the nomination to the member who submitted the nomination.

(2) The association provides, within seven business days of receiving a nomination, a written or electronic communication to the nominee, indicating either of the following:

(A) The nominee is a qualified candidate for the board of directors.

(B) The nominee is not a qualified candidate for the board of directors, the basis for the disqualification, and the procedure, which shall comply with Article 2 (commencing with Section 5900) of Chapter 10, by which the nominee may appeal the disqualification.

(3) The association may combine the written or electronic communication described in paragraphs (1) and (2) into a single written or electronic communication if the nominee and the nominator are the same person.

(d)(1) The association permits all candidates to run if nominated, except for nominees disqualified for running as allowed or required pursuant to subdivisions (b) to (e), inclusive, of Section 5105.

(2) If an association disqualifies a nominee pursuant to this subdivision, an association in its election rules shall also require a director to comply with the same requirements.

(e) The association board votes to consider the qualified candidates elected by acclamation at a meeting pursuant to Article 2 (commencing with Section 4900) for which the agenda item reflects the name of each qualified candidate that will be seated by acclamation if the item is approved. **Leg.H.** Added Stats 2021 ch 517 §2.5 (AB 502), effective January 1, 2022. Amended Stats 2023 ch 770 §3 (AB 1764), effective January 1, 2024.

Prior Law: Former Civ C §5103, relating to transactions involving marital property, was added Stats 1969 ch 1608 §8, operative January 1, 1970, Amended Stats 1984 ch 892 §2, Stats 1986 ch 820 §13, operative July 1, 1987, Stats 1991 ch 1026 §2 (SB 716), and repealed Stats 1992 ch 162 §3 (AB 2650), operative January 1, 1994. See Fam C §721.

§5104. [Section repealed 1994.]

Leg.H. Added Stats 1969 ch 1608 §8, operative January 1, 1970. Repealed Stats 1992 ch 162 §3 (AB 2650), operative January 1, 1994. See Fam C §750.

§5105. Election rules

(a) An association shall adopt operating rules in accordance with the procedures prescribed by Article 5 (commencing with Section 4340) of Chapter 3, that do all of the following:

(1) Ensure that if any candidate or member advocating a point of view is provided access to association media, newsletters, or internet websites during a campaign, for purposes that are reasonably related to that election, equal access shall be provided to all candidates and members advocating a point of view, including those not endorsed by the board, for purposes that are reasonably related to the election. The association shall not edit or redact any content from these communications, but may include a statement specifying that the candidate or member, and not the association, is responsible for that content.

(2) Ensure access to the common area meeting space, if any exists, during a campaign, at no cost, to all candidates, including those who are not incumbents, and to all members advocating a point of view, including those not endorsed by the board, for purposes reasonably related to the election.

(3) Specify the qualifications for candidates for the board and any other elected position, subject to subdivision (b), and procedures for the nomination of candidates, consistent with the governing documents. A nomination or election procedure shall not be deemed reasonable if it disallows any member from nominating themself for election to the board.

(4) Specify the voting power of each membership, the authenticity, validity, and effect of proxies, and the voting period for elections, including the times at which polls will open and close, consistent with the governing documents.

(5) Specify a method of selecting one or three independent third parties as inspector or inspectors of elections utilizing one of the following methods:

(A) Appointment of the inspector or inspectors by the board.

(B) Election of the inspector or inspectors by the members of the association.

(C) Any other method for selecting the inspector or inspectors.

(6) Allow the inspector or inspectors to appoint and oversee additional persons to verify signatures and to count and tabulate votes as the inspector or inspectors deem appropriate, provided that the persons are independent third parties who meet the requirements in subdivision (b) of Section 5110.

(7) Require retention of, as association election materials, both a candidate registration list and a voter list. The candidate list shall include [1] **names and addresses** of individuals nominated as a candidate for election to the board of directors. The voter list shall include **the** name, voting power, and either the physical address of the voter's separate interest, the parcel number, or both. The mailing address for the ballot shall be listed on the voter list if it differs from the physical address of the voter's separate interest or if only the parcel number is used. The association shall permit members to verify the accuracy of their individual information on both lists at least 30 days before the ballots are distributed. The association or member shall report any errors or omissions to either list to the inspector or inspectors who shall make the corrections within two business days.

(b) An association shall disqualify a person from a nomination as a candidate for not being a member of the association at the time of the nomination. An association shall disqualify a nominee if that person has served the maximum number of terms or sequential terms allowed by the association. A director who ceases to be a member shall be disqualified from continuing to serve as a director.

(1) This subdivision does not restrict a developer from making a nomination of a nonmember candidate consistent with the voting power of the developer as set forth in the regulations of the Department of Real Estate and the association's governing documents.

(2) If title to a separate interest parcel is held by a legal entity that is not a natural person, the governing authority of that legal entity shall have the power to appoint a natural person to be a member for purposes of this article.

(c) Through its bylaws or election operating rules adopted pursuant to subdivision (a) [2] only, an association may disqualify a person from nomination as a candidate pursuant to any of the following:

(1) Subject to paragraph (2) of subdivision (d), an association may require a nominee for a board seat, and a director during their board tenure, to be current in the payment of regular and special assessments, which are consumer debts subject to validation. If an association requires a nominee to be current in the payment of regular and special assessments, it shall also require a director to be current in the payment of regular and special assessments.

(2) An association may disqualify a person from nomination as a candidate if the person, if elected, would be serving on the board at the same time as another person who holds a joint ownership interest in the same separate interest parcel as the person and the other person is either properly nominated for the current election or an incumbent director.

(3) An association may disqualify a nominee if that person has been a member of the association for less than one year.

(4) An association may disqualify a nominee if that person discloses, or if the association is aware or becomes aware of, a past criminal conviction that would, if the person was elected, either prevent the association from purchasing the insurance required by Section 5806 or terminate the association's existing insurance coverage required by Section 5806 as to that person should the person be elected.

(d) An association may disqualify a person from nomination for nonpayment of regular and special assessments, but may not disqualify a nominee for nonpayment of fines, fines renamed as assessments, collection charges, late charges, or costs levied by a third party. The person shall not be disqualified for failure to be current in payment of regular and special assessments if either of the following circumstances is true:

(1) The person has paid the regular or special assessment under protest pursuant to Section 5658.

(2) The person has entered into and is in compliance with a payment plan pursuant to Section 5665.

(e) An association shall not disqualify a person from nomination if the person has not been provided the opportunity to engage in internal dispute resolution pursuant to Article 2 (commencing with Section 5900) of Chapter 10.

(f) If an association disqualifies a nominee pursuant to this section, an association in its election rules shall also require a director to comply with the same requirements.

(g) [3] **Except as provided in subdivision (i), notwithstanding** any other law, the rules adopted pursuant to this section may provide for the nomination of candidates from the floor of membership meetings or nomination by any other manner. Those rules may permit write-in candidates for ballots.

(h) Notwithstanding any other law, the rules adopted pursuant to this section shall do all of the following:

(1) Prohibit the denial of a ballot to a member for any reason other than not being a member at the time when ballots are distributed.

(2) Prohibit the denial of a ballot to a person with general power of attorney for a member.

(3) Require the ballot of a person with general power of attorney for a member to be counted if returned in a timely manner.

(4) Require the inspector or inspectors of elections to deliver, or cause to be delivered, at least 30 days before an election, to each member both of the following documents:

(A) The ballot or ballots.

(B) A copy of the election operating rules. Delivery of the election operating rules may be accomplished by [4] **any** of the following methods:

(i) Posting the election operating rules to an internet website and including the corresponding internet website address on the ballot together with the phrase, in at least 12-point [5] **type**: "The rules governing this election may be found here:"

(ii) Individual delivery.

(iii) Election operating rules adopted pursuant to this section shall not be amended less than 90 days prior to an election.

(i) Notwithstanding an association's governing documents, the association may adopt an election operating rule that allows an association to utilize an inspector or inspectors of elections, as specified in Section 5110, to conduct an election by electronic secret ballot, except for an election regarding regular or special assessments, as provided for in Chapter 8 (commencing with Section 5600).

(1) An election operating rule adopted pursuant to this subdivision shall include, but not be limited to, all of the following purposes:

(A) Permitting a member to change their preferred method of voting from electronic secret ballot to written ballot or written ballot to electronic secret ballot no later than 90 days before an election.

(B) Requiring an electronic secret ballot and a written ballot to contain the same list of items being voted on.

(C)(i) For an election operating rule where a member is permitted to opt out of voting by electronic secret ballot to vote by written ballot, requiring the association to mail a written ballot only to a member who has opted out of voting by electronic secret ballot or for whom the association does not have an email address required to vote by electronic secret ballot.

(ii) For an election operating rule where a member who is permitted to opt into voting by electronic secret ballot, requiring the association to send an electronic secret ballot only to a member who has opted into voting by electronic secret ballot.

(D) Requiring the association to maintain a voting list identifying which members will vote by electronic secret ballot and which members will vote by written ballot, and include information on the procedures to either opt out of or opt into voting by electronic secret ballot, as applicable, in the annual statement prepared pursuant to Section 5310.

(E) Requiring a member who votes by electronic secret ballot to provide a valid email address to the association.

(F) Prohibiting nomination of candidates from the floor of membership meetings, notwithstanding subdivision (g).

(2) An electronic secret ballot may be accompanied by or contained in an electronic individual notice in accordance with paragraph (2) of subdivision (a) of Section 4040.

(3)(A) The association shall deliver individual notice of the electronic secret ballot to each member 30 days before the election and shall contain instructions on both of the following:

(i) How to obtain access to that internet-based voting system.

(ii) How to vote by electronic secret ballot.

(B) Delivery of the individual notice described in subparagraph (A) may be accomplished by electronic submission to an address, location, or system designated by the member.

(4) For an election operating rule where members are permitted to opt out of voting by electronic secret ballot to vote by written ballot, the association shall provide individual notice, delivered pursuant to Section 4040, at least 30 days before the deadline to opt out of voting by electronic secret ballot, of all of the following:

(A) The member's current voting method.

(B) If the member's voting method is by electronic secret ballot and the association has an email address for the member, the email address of the member that will be used for voting by electronic secret ballot.

(C) An explanation that the member is required to opt out of voting by electronic secret ballot if the member elects to vote by written secret ballot.

(D) An explanation of how a member may opt out of voting by electronic secret ballot.

(E) The deadline by which the member is required to opt out of voting by electronic secret ballot if the member elects to exercise that right.

(5) A vote made by electronic secret ballot is effective when it is electronically transmitted to an address, location, or system designated by an inspector or inspectors of elections.

(6) A vote made by electronic secret ballot shall not be revoked.

(7) If the association does not have a member's email address required to vote by electronic secret ballot by the time at which ballots are to be distributed, the association shall send the member a written secret ballot.

(8) For purposes of determining a quorum, a member voting electronically pursuant to this subdivision shall be counted as a member in attendance at the meeting. Once the quorum is established, a substantive vote of the members shall not be taken on any issue other than the issues specifically identified in the electronic vote.

(9) As used in this subdivision, "electronic secret ballot" means a ballot conducted by an electronic voting system that ensures the secrecy and integrity of a ballot pursuant to the requirements of this article. **Leg.H.** Added Stats 2012 ch 180 §2 (AB 805), effective January 1, 2013, operative January 1, 2014. Amended Stats 2019 ch 848 §2 (SB 323), effective January 1, 2020; Stats 2021 ch 642 §2 (SB 432), effective January 1, 2022; Stats 2023 ch 770 §4 (AB 1764), effective January 1, 2024; Stats 2024 ch 383 §1 (AB 2159), effective January 1, 2025.

§5105. 2024 Deletes. [1] name and address [2] of Section 5105 [3] Notwithstanding [4] either [5] font

Former Sections: Former CC §5105, similar to Fam C §751, was added Stats 1969 ch 1608 §8, operative January 1, 1970, amended Stats 1973 ch 987 §4, operative January 1, 1975, and repealed Stats 1992 ch 162 §3 (AB 2650), operative January 1, 1994.

§5106. [Section repealed 1994.]

Leg.H. Added Stats 1969 ch 1608 §8, operative January 1, 1970. Amended Stats 1976 ch 1164 §1. Repealed Stats 1992 ch 162 §3 (AB 2650), operative January 1, 1994. See Fam C §755.

§5107. [Section repealed 1994.]

Leg.H. Added Stats 1969 ch 1608 §8, operative January 1, 1970. Repealed Stats 1992 ch 162 §3 (AB 2650), operative January 1, 1994. See Fam C §770.

§5108. [Section repealed 1994.]

Leg.H. Added Stats 1969 ch 1608 §8, operative January 1, 1970. Repealed Stats 1992 ch 162 §3 (AB 2650), operative January 1, 1994. See Fam C §770.

§5109. [Section repealed 1979.]

Leg.H. Added Stats 1969 ch 1608 §8, operative January 1, 1970. Repealed stats 1979 ch 638 §2. See Fam C §781.

§5110. Inspector of elections

(a) The association shall select an independent third party or parties as an inspector of elections. The number of inspectors of elections shall be one or three.

(b) For the purposes of this section, an independent third party includes, but is not limited to, a volunteer poll worker with the county registrar of voters, a licensee of the California Board of Accountancy, or a notary public. An independent third party may be a member, but may not be a director or a candidate for director or be related to a director or to a candidate for director. An independent third party may not be a person, business entity, or subdivision of a business entity who is currently employed or under contract to the association for any compensable services other than serving as an inspector of elections.

(c) The inspector or inspectors of elections shall do all of the following:

(1) Determine the number of memberships entitled to vote and the voting power of each.

(2) Determine the authenticity, validity, and effect of proxies, if any.

(3) Receive ballots.

(4) Ensure compliance with all of the following, if the inspector or inspectors of elections conducts an election by electronic secret ballot pursuant to Section 5105:

(A) Each member voting by electronic secret ballot shall be provided with all of the following:

(i) A method to authenticate the member's identity to the internet-based voting system.

(ii) A method to transmit an electronic secret ballot to the internet-based voting system that ensures the secrecy and integrity of each ballot.

(iii) A method to confirm, at least 30 days before the voting deadline, that the member's electronic device can successfully communicate with the internet-based voting system.

(B) Any internet-based voting system that is utilized shall have the ability to accomplish all of the following:

(i) Authenticate the member's identity.

(ii) Authenticate the validity of each electronic secret ballot to ensure that the electronic secret ballot is not altered in transit.

(iii) Transmit a receipt from the internet-based voting system to each member who casts an electronic secret ballot.

(iv) Permanently separate any authenticating or identifying information from the electronic secret ballot, rendering it impossible to connect an election ballot to a specific member.

(v) Store and keep electronic secret ballots accessible to elections officials or their authorized representatives for recount, inspection, and review purposes.

[1] **(5)** Hear and determine all challenges and questions in any way arising out of or in connection with the right to vote.

[2] **(6)** Count and tabulate all votes.

[3] **(7)** Determine when the polls shall close, consistent with the governing documents.

[4] **(8)** Determine the tabulated results of the election.

[5] **(9)** Perform any acts as may be proper to conduct the election with fairness to all members in accordance with this article, the Corporations Code, and all applicable rules of the association regarding the conduct of the election that are not in conflict with this article.

(d) An inspector **or inspectors** of elections shall perform all duties impartially, in good faith, to the best of the inspector [6] **or inspectors of elections'** ability, as expeditiously as is practical, and in a manner that protects the interest of all members of the association. If there are three inspectors of elections, the decision or act of a majority shall be effective in all respects as the decision or act of all. Any report made by the inspector or inspectors of elections is prima facie evidence of the facts stated in the report. **Leg.H.** Added Stats 2012 ch 180 §2 (AB 805), effective January 1, 2013, operative January 1, 2014. Amended Stats 2019 ch 848 §3 (SB 323), effective January 1, 2020; Stats 2024 ch 383 §2 (AB 2159), effective January 1, 2025.

§5110. 2024 Deletes. [1] (4) [2] (5) [3] (6) [4] (7) [5] (8) [6] of election's

Former Sections: Former CC §5110, similar to Fam C §§700, 760, 803, was added Stats 1969 ch 1608 §8, operative January 1, 1970, amended Stats 1970 ch 517 §1, Stats 1973 ch 987 §5, operative January 1, 1975, Stats 1977 ch 332 §3, Stats 1979 ch 373 §48, Stats 1983 ch 342 §3, Stats 1987 ch 128 §1, effective July 6, 1987, operative July 1, 1987, and repealed Stats 1992 ch 162 §§3 (AB 2650), operative January 1, 1994.

§5110.150. [Section repealed 1994.]

Leg.H. Added Stats 1986 ch 820 §14, operative July 1, 1987. Repealed Stats 1992 ch 162 §3 (AB 2650), operative January 1, 1994. See Fam C §761.

§5110.710. [Section repealed 1994.]

Leg.H. Added Stats 1984 ch 1733 §1. Repealed Stats 1992 ch 162 §3 (AB 2650), operative January 1, 1994. See Fam C §850.

§5110.720. [Section repealed 1994.]

Leg.H. Added Stats 1984 ch 1733 §2. Repealed Stats 1992 ch 162 §3 (AB 2650), operative January 1, 1994. See Fam C §851.

§5110.730. [Section repealed 1994.]

Leg.H. Added Stats 1984 ch 1733 §3. Repealed Stats 1992 ch 162 §3 (AB 2650), operative January 1, 1994. See Fam C §852.

§5110.740. [Section repealed 1994.]

Leg.H. Added Stats 1984 ch 1733 §4. Amended Stats 1992 ch 51 §1 (AB 1719). Repealed Stats 1992 ch 162 §3 (AB 2650), operative January 1, 1994 (ch 51 prevails). Repealed Stats 1993 ch 219 §58 (AB 1500). See Fam C §853.

§5111. [Section repealed 1994.]

Leg.H. Added Stats 1969 ch 1608 §8, operative January 1, 1970. Repealed Stats 1992 ch 162 §3 (AB 2650), operative January 1, 1994. See Fam C §802.

§5112. [Section repealed 1994.]

Leg.H. Added Stats 1969 ch 1608 §8, operative January 1, 1970. Repealed Stats 1992 ch 162 §3 (AB 2650), operative January 1, 1994. See Fam C §783.

§5113. [Section repealed 1994.]

Leg.H. Added Stats 1969 ch 1608 §8, operative January 1, 1970. Repealed Stats 1992 ch 162 §3 (AB 2650), operative January 1, 1994. See Fam C §782.

§5113.5. [Section repealed 1987.]

Leg.H. Added Stats 1969 ch 1608 §8, operative January 1, 1970. Amended Stats 1970 ch 517 §2; Stats 1973 ch 987 §6, operative January 1, 1975. Repealed Stats 1986 ch 820 §15, operative July 1, 1987. The repealed section related to character of property transferred to trust.

§5114. [Section repealed 1994.]

Leg.H. Added Stats 1969 ch 1608 §8, operative January 1, 1970. Repealed Stats 1992 ch 162 §3 (AB 2650), operative January 1, 1994. The repealed section related to separate property inventory.

§5115. Voting procedure

(a) An association shall provide general notice of the procedure and deadline for submitting a nomination at least 30 days before any deadline for submitting a nomination. Individual notice shall be delivered pursuant to Section 4040 if individual notice is requested by a member. This subdivision shall only apply to elections of directors and to recall elections.

(b) For elections of directors and for recall elections, an association shall provide general notice of all of the following at least 30 days before the ballots are distributed:

(1) The date and time by which, and the physical address where, ballots are to be returned by mail or handed to the inspector or inspectors of elections.

(2) **If the association allows for voting in an election by electronic secret ballot as provided for in Section 5105, the date and time by which electronic secret ballots are to be transmitted to the internet-based voting system and preliminary instructions on how to vote by electronic secret ballot upon commencement of the voting period.**

(3) The date, time, and location of the meeting at which a quorum will be determined, if the association's governing documents require a quorum, and at which ballots will be counted.

[1] **(4)** The list of all candidates' names that will appear on the ballot.

[2] **(5)** Individual notice of the above paragraphs shall be delivered pursuant to Section 4040 if individual notice is requested by a member.

[3] **(6)(A)** If the association's governing documents require a quorum for **an** election of directors, a statement that the [4] **association** may call a [5] **reconvened meeting to be held** at least 20 days after a scheduled election if the required quorum is not reached, at which time the quorum of the membership to elect directors will be 20 percent of the association's members, voting in person, by proxy, or by secret ballot.

(B) This paragraph shall not apply if the governing documents of the association provide for a quorum lower than 20 percent.

(c) Ballots and two preaddressed envelopes with instructions on how to return ballots shall be mailed by first-class mail or delivered by the association to every member not less than 30 days prior to the deadline for voting, **unless an association conducts an election by electronic secret ballot as provided for in Section 5105, in which case only members who will vote by written secret ballot pursuant to Section 5105 shall be mailed or delivered the ballots and envelopes**. In order to preserve confidentiality, a voter may not be identified by name, address, or lot, parcel, or unit number on the ballot. The association shall use as a model those procedures used by California counties for ensuring confidentiality of vote by mail ballots, including [6] **both** of the following:

(1) The ballot itself is not signed by the voter, but is inserted into an envelope that is sealed. This envelope is inserted into a second envelope that is sealed. In the upper left-hand corner of the second envelope, the voter shall sign the voter's name, indicate the voter's name, and indicate the address or separate interest identifier that entitles the voter to vote.

(2) The second envelope is addressed to the inspector or inspectors of elections, who will be tallying the votes. The envelope may be mailed or delivered by hand to a location specified by the inspector or inspectors of elections. The member may request a receipt for delivery.

(d)(1) A quorum shall be required only if so stated in the governing documents or other provisions of law. If a quorum is required by the governing documents, each ballot received by the inspector **or inspectors** of elections shall be treated as a member present at a meeting for purposes of establishing a quorum.

(2) For an election of directors of [7] **an association**, and in the absence of meeting quorum as required by the association's governing documents or Section 7512 of the Corporations Code, unless a lower quorum **for a reconvened meeting** is authorized by the association's governing documents, the association may adjourn the [8] **meeting** to a date at least 20 days after the adjourned [9] **meeting**, at which time the quorum required for purposes of a [10] **reconvened** meeting to elect directors shall be 20 percent of the association's **members,** voting [11] in person, by proxy, or by secret [12] **ballot**.

(3) No less than 15 days prior to [13] **the date of the reconvened meeting described in** paragraph (2), the association shall provide general notice of the [14] **reconvened** meeting, which shall include:

(A) The date, time, and location of the meeting.

(B) The list of all candidates.

(C) **Unless the association's governing documents provide for a lower quorum,** a statement that 20 percent of the [15] **association's members, voting in person, by proxy,** or secret ballot will satisfy the quorum requirements for the election of directors **at that reconvened meeting** and that the ballots will be counted if a quorum is reached, if the association's governing documents require a quorum.

(e) An association shall allow for cumulative voting using the secret ballot procedures provided in this section, if cumulative voting is provided for in the governing documents.

(f) **Notwithstanding any contrary provision in the governing documents,** except for the meeting to count the votes required in subdivision (a) of Section 5120, an election may be conducted entirely by mail [16], **electronic secret ballot, or a combination of mail and electronic secret ballot, pursuant to Section 5105**.

(g)(1) **Except as provided in paragraph (2),** in an election to approve an amendment of the governing documents, the text of the proposed amendment shall be delivered to the members with the ballot.

(2) **Notwithstanding paragraph (1), if an association conducts an election to approve an amendment of governing documents by electronic secret ballot, the association may deliver, by electronic means, the text of the proposed amendment to those members who vote by electronic secret ballot, pursuant to Section 5105. The association shall also deliver a written copy of the text of the proposed amendment to those members upon request and without charge. If a member votes by written secret ballot, pursuant to Section 5105, the association shall deliver a written copy of the text of the proposed amendment to the member with the ballot. Leg.H.** Added Stats 2012 ch 180 §2 (AB 805), effective January 1, 2013, operative January 1, 2014. Amended Stats 2019 ch 848 §4 (SB 323), effective January 1, 2020; Stats 2021 ch 642 §3 (SB 432), effective January 1, 2022; Stats 2023 ch 303 §1 (AB 1458), effective January 1, 2024; Stats 2024 ch 383 §3 (AB 2159), effective January 1, 2025; Stats 2024 ch 401 §1.5 (AB 2460), effective January 1, 2025 (ch 401 prevails).

§5115. 2024 Deletes. [1] (3) [2] (4) [3] (5) [4] board of directors [5] subsequent meeting [6] all [7] a corporation that is a common interest development [8] proceeding [9] proceeding [10] membership [11] members present [12] written ballot received [13] an election authorized pursuant to [14] membership [15] association present or voting by proxy [16] unless otherwise specified in the governing documents

Former Sections: Former CC §5115, relating to separate property inventory as evidence of title, was added Stats 1969 ch 1608 §8, operative January 1, 1970, and repealed Stats 1992 ch 162 §3 (AB 2650), operative January 1, 1994. Historical Derivation: (a) Former CC §166, as enacted 1872, amended Code Amdts 1873–74 ch 612 §37, Stats 1935 ch 102 §2. (b) Stats 1850 ch 103 §5.

§5116. [Section repealed 1984.]

Leg.H. Added Stats 1969 ch 1608 §8, operative January 1, 1970. Amended Stats 1973 ch 987 §§6.8, 7, ch 999 §§2, 3, operative January 1, 1975; Stats 1974 ch 1206 §2. Repealed Stats 1984 ch 1671 §7. See Fam C §910.

§5117. [Section repealed 1974].

Leg.H. Added Stats 1969 ch 1608 §8, operative January 1, 1970. Amended Stats 1973 ch 987 §8, operative January 1, 1975. Repealed Stats 1974 ch 1206 §3. The repealed section related to liability of wife's earnings and community property personal injury damages for debts of husband and for necessities.

§5118. [Section repealed 1994].

Leg.H. Added Stats 1969 ch 1608 §8, operative January 1, 1970. Amended Stats 1971 ch 1699 §1. Repealed Stats 1992 ch 162 §3 (AB 2650), operative January 1, 1994. See Fam C §771.

§5119. [Section repealed 1994].

Leg.H. Added Stats 1969 ch 1608 §8, operative January 1, 1970. Amended Stats 1971 ch 1699 §2. Repealed Stats 1992 ch 162 §3 (AB 2650), operative January 1, 1994. See Fam C §772.

§5120. Counting ballots

(a) All votes shall be counted and tabulated by the inspector or inspectors of elections, or the designee of the inspector **or inspectors** of elections, in public at a properly noticed open meeting of the board or members. Any candidate or other member of the association may witness the counting and tabulation of the votes. [1] **A** person, including a member of the association or an employee of the management company, shall **not** open or otherwise review any ballot [2] **before** the time and place at which the ballots are counted and tabulated. The inspector **or inspectors** of elections, or the designee of the inspector **or inspectors** of elections, may verify the member's information and signature on the outer envelope prior to the meeting at which ballots are tabulated. Once a secret ballot is received by the inspector **or inspectors** of elections, it shall be irrevocable.

(b) The tabulated results of the election shall be promptly reported to the board and shall be recorded in the minutes of the next meeting of the board and shall be available for review by members of the association. Within 15 days of the election, the board shall give general notice pursuant to Section 4045 of the tabulated results of the election.

(c) **A person, including a member of the association or an employee of the management company, shall not open or otherwise review any tally sheet of votes cast by electronic secret ballots before the time and place at which the ballots are counted and tabulated. Leg.H.** Added Stats 2012 ch 180 §2 (AB 805), effective January 1, 2013, operative January 1, 2014. Amended Stats 2024 ch 383 §4 (AB 2159), effective January 1, 2025.

§5120. 2024 Deletes. [1] No [2] prior to

Former Sections: Former CC §5120, similar to Fam C §§910, 911, was added Stats 1969 ch 1608 §8, operative January 1, 1970, amended Stats 1973 ch 987 §9, operative January 1, 1975, Stats 1984 ch 249 §1, and repealed Stats 1984 ch 1671 §8.

§5120.010. [Section repealed 1994.]

Leg.H. Added Stats 1984 ch 1671 §9. Repealed Stats 1992 ch 162 §3 (AB 2650) January 1, 1994. See Fam C §900.

§5120.020. [Section repealed 1994.]

Leg.H. Added Stats 1984 ch 1671 §9. Repealed Stats 1992 ch 162 §3 (AB 2650), operative January 1, 1994. See Fam C §§63, 760.

§5120.030. [Section repealed 1994.]

Leg.H. Added Stats 1984 ch 1671 §9. Repealed Stats 1992 ch 162 §3 (AB 2650), operative January 1, 1994. See Fam C §902.

§5120.040. [Section repealed 1994.]

Leg.H. Added Stats 1984 ch 1671 §9. Repealed Stats 1992 ch 162 §3 (AB 2650), operative January 1, 1994. See Fam C §903.

§5120.110. [Section repealed 1994].

Leg.H. Added Stats 1984 ch 1671 §21. Amended Stats 1989 ch 1266 §3. Repealed Stats 1992 ch 162 §3 (AB 2650), operative January 1, 1994. See Fam C §§910, 911.

§5120.120. [Section repealed 1994].

Leg.H. Added Stats 1984 ch 1671 §9. Repealed Stats 1992 ch 162 §3 (AB 2650), operative January 1, 1994. See Fam C §912.

§5120.130. [Section repealed 1994.]

Leg.H. Added Stats 1984 ch 1671 §9. Repealed Stats 1992 ch 162 §3 (AB 2650), operative January 1, 1994. See Fam C §913.

§5120.140. [Section repealed 1994.]

Leg.H. Added Stats 1984 ch 1671 §9. Repealed Stats 1992 ch 162 §3 (AB 2650), operative January 1, 1994. See Fam C §914.

§5120.150. [Section repealed 1994.]

Leg.H. Added Stats 1984 ch 1671 §22. Repealed Stats 1992 ch 162 §3 (AB 2650), operative January 1, 1994. See Fam C §915.

§5120.160. [Section repealed 1994.]

Leg.H. Added Stats 1984 ch 1671 §9. Repealed Stats 1992 ch 162 §3 (AB 2650), operative January 1, 1994. See Fam C §916.

§5120.210. [Section repealed 1994.]

Leg.H. Added Stats 1984 ch 1671 §9. Repealed Stats 1992 ch 162 §3 (AB 2650), operative January 1, 1994. See Fam C §920.

§5120.310. [Section repealed 1994.]

Leg.H. Added Stats 1984 ch 1671 §9. Repealed Stats 1992 ch 162 §3 (AB 2650), operative January 1, 1994. See Fam C §§930, 931.

§5120.320. [Section repealed 1994.]

Leg.H. Added Stats 1984 ch 1671 §9. Repealed Stats 1992 ch 162 §3 (AB 2650), operative January 1, 1994. See Fam C §930.

§5120.330. [Section repealed 1994]

Leg.H. Added Stats 1984 ch 1671 §9. Repealed Stats 1992 ch 162 §3 (AB 2650), operative January 1, 1994. See Fam C §931.

§5121. [Section repealed 1984.]

Leg.H. Added Stats 1969 ch 1608 §8, operative January 1, 1970. Amended Stats 1973 ch 987 §2, operative January 1, 1975; Stats 1982 ch 497 §22, operative July 1, 1983. Repealed Stats 1984 ch 1671 §10. See Fam C §§913, 914, 916.

§5122. [Section repealed 1994.]

Leg.H. Added Stats 1969 ch 1608 §8, operative January 1, 1970. Amended Stats 1973 ch 987 §11, operative January 1, 1975; Stats 1984 ch 1671 §1. Repealed Stats 1992 ch 162 §3 (AB 2650), operative January 1, 1994. See Fam C §1000.

§5123. [Section repealed 1984.]

Leg.H. Added Stats 1969 ch 1608 §8, operative January 1, 1970. Amended Stats 1973 ch 987 §12, operative January 1, 1975. Repealed Stats 1984 ch 1671 §12. The repealed section related to liability of separate property for obligations secured by community property.

§5124. [Section repealed 1986.]

Leg.H. Added Stats 1983 ch 775 §1. Repealed operative January 1, 1986, by its own provisions. The repealed section related to modification of final property settlements to include military retirement benefits.

Former Sections: Former CC §5124, relating to wife's rights and obligations concerning community personal property in marriage, was added Stats 1969 ch 1608 §8, operative January 1, 1970, and repealed Stats 1973 ch 987 §13, operative January 1, 1975.

§5125. Retention of ballots; Signed voter envelopes, voter lists, proxies, and candidate registration lists

The sealed ballots, signed voter envelopes, voter list, proxies, [1] **candidate registration list, and tally sheet of votes cast by electronic secret ballot** shall at all times be in the custody of the inspector or inspectors of elections or at a location designated by the inspector or inspectors until after the tabulation of the vote, and until the time allowed by Section 5145 for challenging the election has expired, at which time custody shall be transferred to the association. If there is a recount or other challenge to the election process, the inspector or inspectors of elections shall, upon written request, make the ballots **and the tally sheet of votes cast by electronic secret ballot** available for inspection and review by an association member or the member's authorized representative. Any recount shall be conducted in a manner that preserves the confidentiality of the vote. **Leg.H.** Added Stats 2012 ch 180 §2 (AB 805), effective January 1, 2013, operative January 1, 2014. Amended Stats 2019 ch 848 §5 (SB 323), effective January 1, 2020; Stats 2024 ch 383 §5 (AB 2159), effective January 1, 2025.

§5125. 2024 Deletes. [1] and

Former Sections: Former CC §5125, similar to Fam C §1100, was added Stats 1969 ch 1608 §8, operative January 1, 1970, amended Stats 1969 ch 1609 §24, operative January 1, 1970, Stats 1973 ch 987 §14, operative January 1, 1975, Stats 1974 ch 1206 §4, Stats 1977 ch 692 §1, Stats 1982 ch 497 §23, operative July 1, 1983, Stats 1982 ch 497 §23, operative July 1, 1983, Stats 1986 ch 1091 §1, operative July 1, 1987, Stats 1987 ch 128 §2, effective July 6, 1987, operative July 1, 1987, Stats 1991 ch 1026 §3 (SB 716), and repealed Stats 1992 ch 162 §3 (AB 2650), operative January 1, 1994.

§5125.1. [Section repealed 1994.]

Leg.H. Added Stats 1986 ch 1091 §2, operative July 1, 1987. Amended Stats 1991 ch 1026 §4 (SB 716). Repealed Stats 1992 ch 162 §3 (AB 2650), operative January 1, 1994. See Fam C §1101.

§5126. [Section repealed 1994.]

Leg.H. Added Stats 1969 ch 1608 §8, operative January 1, 1970. Amended Stats 1970 ch 1575 §5; Stats 1972 ch 905 §1; Stats 1979 ch 683 §3; Stats 1983 ch 1159 §10, operative July 1, 1984. Repealed Stats 1992 ch 162 §3 (AB 2650), operative January 1, 1994. See Fam C §781.

§5127. [Section repealed 1994.]

Leg.H. Added Stats 1969 ch 1608 §8, operative January 1, 1970. Amended Stats 1969 ch 1609 §25, operative January 1, 1970; Stats 1973 ch 987 §15, operative January 1, 1975; Stats 1974 ch 1206 §5; Stats 1987 ch 128 §3, effective July 6, 1987, operative July 1, 1987. Repealed Stats 1992 ch 162 §3 (AB 2650), operative January 1, 1994 (ch 356 prevails). Amended Stats 1992 ch 356 §6 (AB 3399). Repealed Stats 1993 ch 219 §59 (AB 1500). See Fam C §1102.

§5127.5. [Section repealed 1984.]

Leg.H. Added Stats 1971 ch 578 §8.6, effective August 13, 1971, operative October 1, 1971. Repealed Stats 1984 ch 1671 §14. The repealed section related to wife's right to use community property for support for children.

§5127.6. [Section repealed 1984.]

Leg.H. Added Stats 1979 ch 1171 §2. Repealed Stats 1984 ch 1671 §15. The repealed section related to community obligation to child of one spouse.

§5128. [Section repealed 1994.]

Leg.H. Added Stats 1969 ch 1608 §8, operative January 1, 1970. Amended Stats 1979 ch 730 §14, operative January 1, 1981. Repealed Stats 1992 ch 162 §3 (AB 2650), operative January 1, 1994. See Fam C §1103.

§5129. [Section repealed 1985.]

Leg.H. Added Stats 1969 ch 1608 §8, operative January 1, 1970. Repealed Stats 1983 ch 842 §9, operative January 1, 1985. The repealed section related to tenancy by courtesy, and estate in dower.

§5130. Proxies

(a) For purposes of this article, the following definitions shall apply:

(1) "Proxy" means a written authorization signed by a member or the authorized representative of the member that gives another member or members the power to vote on behalf of that member.

(2) "Signed" means the placing of the member's name on the proxy (whether by manual signature, typewriting, telegraphic transmission, or otherwise) by the member or authorized representative of the member.

(b) Proxies shall not be construed or used in lieu of a ballot. An association may use proxies if permitted or required by the bylaws of the association and if those proxies meet the requirements of this article, other laws, and the governing documents, but the association shall not be required to prepare or distribute proxies pursuant to this article.

(c) Any instruction given in a proxy issued for an election that directs the manner in which the proxyholder is to cast the vote shall be set forth on a separate page of the proxy that can be detached and given to the proxyholder to retain. The proxyholder shall cast the member's vote by secret ballot. The proxy may be revoked by the member prior to the receipt of the ballot by the inspector of elections as described in Section 7613 of the Corporations Code. **Leg.H.** Added Stats 2012 ch 180 §2 (AB 805), effective January 1, 2013, operative January 1, 2014.

Former Sections: Former CC §5130, relating to husband's liability to third persons supplying necessary articles for support of wife, was added Stats 1969 ch 1608 §8, operative January 1, 1970, repealed Stats 1974 ch 1206 §6. Historical Derivation: (a) Former CC §174, as enacted 1872, amended Code Amdts 1873–74 ch 612 §39. (b) Field's Draft NY CC §84.

§5131. [Section repealed 1994.]
Leg.H. Added Stats 1969 ch 1608 §8, operative January 1, 1970. Amended Stats 1973 ch 987 §16, operative January 1, 1975. Repealed Stats 1992 ch 162 §3 (AB 2650), operative January 1, 1994. See Fam C §4302.

§5132. [Section repealed 1994.]
Leg.H. Added Stats 1969 ch 1608 §8, operative January 1, 1970. Amended Stats 1973 ch 987 §17, operative January 1, 1975; Stats 1984 ch 1671 §17. Repealed Stats 1992 ch 162 §3 (AB 2650), operative January 1, 1994. See Fam C §4301.

§5133. [Section repealed 1985.]
Leg.H. Added Stats 1969 ch 1608 §8, operative January 1, 1970. Repealed Stats 1985 1315 §2. See Fam C §1500.

§5134. [Section repealed 1985.]
Leg.H. Added Stats 1969 ch 1608 §8, operative January 1, 1970. Repealed Stats 1985 ch 1315 §2. See Fam C §1611.

§5135. Campaign-related information
(a) Association funds shall not be used for campaign purposes in connection with any association board election. Funds of the association shall not be used for campaign purposes in connection with any other association election except to the extent necessary to comply with duties of the association imposed by law.

(b) For the purposes of this section, "campaign purposes" includes, but is not limited to, the following:

(1) Expressly advocating the election or defeat of any candidate that is on the association election ballot.

(2) Including the photograph or prominently featuring the name of any candidate on a communication from the association or its board, excepting the ballot, ballot materials, or a communication that is legally required, within 30 days of an election. This is not a campaign purpose if the communication is one for which subdivision (a) of Section 5105 requires that equal access be provided to another candidate or advocate. **Leg.H.** Added Stats 2012 ch 180 §2 (AB 805), effective January 1, 2013, operative January 1, 2014.

Former Sections: Former CC §5135, similar to Fam C §1502, was added Stats 1969 ch 1608 §8, operative January 1, 1970, and repealed Stats 1985 ch 1315 §2.

§5135.5. [Section repealed 1985.]
Leg.H. Added Stats 1983 ch 842 §10, operative January 1, 1985. Repealed Stats 1985 ch 1315 §2. The repealed section related to marriage settlements affecting rights of surviving spouse.

§5136. [Section repealed 1985.]
Leg.H. Added Stats 1969 ch 1608 §8, operative January 1, 1970. Repealed Stats 1985 ch 1315 §2. See Fam C §1502.

§5137. [Section repealed 1985.]
Leg.H. Added Stats 1969 ch 1608 §8, operative January 1, 1970. Repealed Stats 1985 ch 1315 §2. See Fam C §1501.

§5138. [Section repealed 1994.]
Leg.H. Added Stats 1969 ch 1608 §8, operative January 1, 1970. Amended Stats 1969 ch 1609 §26, operative January 1, 1970. Repealed Stats 1992 ch 162 §3 (AB 2650), operative January 1, 1994. See Fam C §295.

§5145. Judicial enforcement
(a) A member of an association may bring a civil action for declaratory or equitable relief for a violation of this article by the association, including, but not limited to, injunctive relief, restitution, or a combination thereof, within one year of the date that the inspector or inspectors of elections notifies the board and membership of the election results or the cause of action accrues, whichever is later. If a member establishes, by a preponderance of the evidence, that the election procedures of this article, or the adoption of and adherence to rules provided by Article 5 (commencing with Section 4340) of Chapter 3, were not followed, a court shall void any results of the election unless the association establishes, by a preponderance of the evidence, that the association's noncompliance with this article or the election operating rules did not affect the results of the election. The findings of the court shall be stated in writing as part of the record.

(b) A member who prevails in a civil action to enforce the member's rights pursuant to this article shall be entitled to reasonable attorney's fees and court costs, and the court may impose a civil penalty of up to five hundred dollars ($500) for each violation, except that each identical violation shall be subject to only one penalty if the violation affects each member of the association equally. A prevailing association shall not recover any costs, unless the court finds the action to be frivolous, unreasonable, or without foundation. If a member prevails in a civil action brought in small claims court, the member shall be awarded court costs and reasonable attorney's fees incurred for consulting an attorney in connection with this civil action.

(c) A cause of action under subdivision (a) may be brought in either the superior court or, if the amount of the demand does not exceed the jurisdictional amount of the small claims court, in small claims court. **Leg.H.** Added Stats 2012 ch 180 §2 (AB 805), effective January 1, 2013, operative January 1, 2014. Amended Stats 2019 ch 848 §6 (SB 323), effective January 1, 2020.

§5150. [Section repealed 1994.]
Leg.H. Added Stats 1973 ch 693 §1. Repealed Stats 1992 ch 162 §3 (AB 2650), operative January 1, 1994. See Fam C §§3, 3401.

§5151. [Section repealed 1994.]
Leg.H. Added Stats 1973 ch 693 §1. Repealed Stats 1992 ch 162 §3 (AB 2650), operative January 1, 1994. See Fam C §3402.

§5152. [Section repealed 1994.]
Leg.H. Added Stats 1973 ch 693 §1. Repealed Stats 1992 ch 162 §3 (AB 2650), operative January 1, 1994. See Fam C §3403 (ch 392 prevails). Amended Stats 1992 ch 392 §1 (SB 804); Stats 1993 ch 219 §60 (AB 1500). See Fam C §3403.

§5153. [Section repealed 1994.]
Leg.H. Added Stats 1973 ch 693 §1. Repealed Stats 1992 ch 162 §3 (AB 2650), operative January 1, 1994. See Fam C §3404.

§5154. [Section repealed 1994.]
Leg.H. Added Stats 1973 ch 693 §1. Repealed Stats 1992 ch 162 §3 (AB 2650), operative January 1, 1994. See Fam C §3405.

§5155. [Section repealed 1994.]
Leg.H. Added Stats 1973 ch 693 §1. Amended Stats 1980 ch 676 §61. Repealed Stats 1992 ch 162 §3 (AB 2650), operative January 1, 1994. See Fam C §3406.

§5156. [Section repealed 1994.]
Leg.H. Added Stats 1973 ch 693 §1. Amended Stats 1980 ch 676 §62. Repealed Stats 1992 ch 162 §3 (AB 2650), operative January 1, 1994. See Fam C §3407.

§5157. [Section repealed 1994.]
Leg.H. Added Stats 1973 ch 693 §1. Amended Stats 1976 ch 1399 §5. Repealed Stats 1992 ch 162 §3 (AB 2650), operative January 1, 1994. See Fam C §3408 (ch 392 prevails). Amended Stats 1992 ch 392 §2 (SB 804); Stats 1993 ch 219 §61 (AB 1500). See Fam C §3408.

§5158. [Section repealed 1994.]
Leg.H. Added Stats 1973 ch 693 §1. Repealed Stats 1992 ch 162 §3 (AB 2650), operative January 1, 1994. See Fam C §3409 (ch 392 prevails). Amended Stats 1992 ch 392 §3 (SB 804); Stats 1993 ch 219 §62 (AB 1500). See Fam C §3409.

§5159. [Section repealed 1994.]
Leg.H. Added Stats 1973 ch 693 §1. Repealed Stats 1992 ch 162 §3 (AB 2650), operative January 1, 1994. See Fam C §3410.

§5160. [Section repealed 1994].
Leg.H. Added Stats 1973 ch 693 §1. Amended Stats 1976 ch 1399 §6. Repealed Stats 1992 ch 162 §3 (AB 2650), operative January 1, 1994. See Fam C §3411.

§5161. [Section repealed 1994].
Leg.H. Added Stats 1973 ch 693 §1. Repealed Stats 1992 ch 162 §3 (AB 2650), operative January 1, 1994. See Fam C §3412.

§5162. [Section repealed 1994].

Leg.H. Added Stats 1973 ch 693 §1. Repealed Stats 1992 ch 162 §3 (AB 2650), operative January 1, 1994. See Fam C §3443.

§5163. [Section repealed 1994].

Leg.H. Added Stats 1973 ch 693 §1. Repealed Stats 1992 ch 162 §3 (AB 2650), operative January 1, 1994. See Fam C §3423.

§5163.5. [Section repealed 1994].

Leg.H. Added Stats 1987 ch 954 §2. Repealed Stats 1992 ch 162 §3 (AB 2650), operative January 1, 1994. The repealed section related to clerk to determine whether child was missing person.

§5164. [Section repealed 1994].

Leg.H. Added Stats 1973 ch 693 §1. Repealed Stats 1992 ch 162 §3 (AB 2650), operative January 1, 1994. See Fam C §3445.

§5165. [Section repealed 1994].

Leg.H. Added Stats 1973 ch 693 §1. Amended Stats 1990 ch 1493 §28 (AB 3974). Repealed Stats 1992 ch 162 §3 (AB 2650), operative January 1, 1994. See Fam C §3417.

§5166. [Section repealed 1994].

Leg.H. Added Stats 1973 ch 693 §1. Repealed Stats 1992 ch 162 §3 (AB 2650), operative January 1, 1994. The repealed section related to clerk's obligation to forward certified copy custody decree.

§5167. [Section repealed 1994].

Leg.H. Added Stats 1973 ch 693 §2. Repealed Stats 1992 ch 162 §3 (AB 2650), operative January 1, 1994. See Fam C §3419.

§5168. [Section repealed 1994].

Leg.H. Added Stats 1973 ch 693 §1. Repealed Stats 1992 ch 162 §3 (AB 2650), operative January 1, 1994. See Fam C §3420.

§5169. [Section repealed 1994].

Leg.H. Added Stats 1973 ch 693 §1. Amended Stats 1976 ch 1399 §7. Repealed Stats 1992 ch 162 §3 (AB 2650), operative January 1, 1994. See Fam C §3421.

§5170. [Section repealed 1994].

Leg.H. Added Stats 1973 ch 693 §1. Repealed Stats 1992 ch 162 §3 (AB 2650), operative January 1, 1994. See Fam C §3422.

§5171. [Section repealed 1994].

Leg.H. Added Stats 1973 ch 693 §1. Repealed Stats 1992 ch 162 §3 (AB 2650), operative January 1, 1994. See Fam C §3423.

§5172. [Section repealed 1994].

Leg.H. Added Stats 1973 ch 693 §1. Repealed Stats 1992 ch 162 §3 (AB 2650), operative January 1, 1994. See Fam C §3424.

§5173. [Section repealed 1994].

Leg.H. Added Stats 1973 ch 693 §1. Repealed Stats 1992 ch 162 §3 (AB 2650), operative January 1, 1994. See Fam C §3425.

§5174. [Section repealed 1994].

Leg.H. Added Stats 1973 ch 693 §1. Repealed Stats 1992 ch 162 §3 (AB 2650), operative January 1, 1994. See Fam C §3400.

§5180. [Section repealed 1994].

Leg.H. Added Stats 1984 ch 893 §1, effective September 6, 1984, operative January 1, 1985. Repealed Stats 1992 ch 162 §3 (AB 2650), operative January 1, 1994. The repealed section related to legislative findings.

§5181. [Section repealed 1994].

Leg.H. Added Stats 1984 ch 893 §1, effective September 6, 1984, operative January 1, 1985. Amended Stats 1988 ch 1550 §9. Repealed Stats 1992 ch 162 §3 (AB 2650), operative January 1, 1994. See Fam C §1850.

§5182. [Section repealed 1994].

Leg.H. Added Stats 1984 ch 893 §1, effective September 6, 1984, operative January 1, 1985. Repealed Stats 1992 ch 162 §3 (AB 2650), operative January 1, 1994. See Fam C §1851.

§5183. [Section repealed 1994].

Leg.H. Added Stats 1984 ch 893 §1, effective September 6, 1984, operative January 1, 1985. Amended Stats 1985 ch 851 §1. Repealed Stats 1992 ch 162 §3 (AB 2650), operative January 1, 1994. See Fam C §1852.

ARTICLE 5
Record Inspection

Definitions. §5200.
Document. §5205.
Time periods. §5210.
Withholding and redaction. §5215.
Safe at Home participants. §5216.
Membership list opt out. §5220.
Membership list request. §5225.
Restriction on use of records. §5230.
Enforcement. §5235.
Application of article. §5240.

§5200. Definitions

For the purposes of this article, the following definitions shall apply:

(a) "Association records" means all of the following:

(1) Any financial document required to be provided to a member in Article 7 (commencing with Section 5300) or in Sections 5565 and 5810.

(2) Any financial document or statement required to be provided in Article 2 (commencing with Section 4525) of Chapter 4.

(3) Interim financial statements, periodic or as compiled, containing any of the following:

(A) Balance sheet.

(B) Income and expense statement.

(C) Budget comparison.

(D) General ledger. A "general ledger" is a report that shows all transactions that occurred in an association account over a specified period of time.

The records described in this paragraph shall be prepared in accordance with an accrual or modified accrual basis of accounting.

(4) Executed contracts not otherwise privileged under law.

(5) Written board approval of vendor or contractor proposals or invoices.

(6) State and federal tax returns.

(7) Reserve account balances and records of payments made from reserve accounts.

(8) Agendas and minutes of meetings of the members, the board, and any committees appointed by the board pursuant to Section 7212 of the Corporations Code; excluding, however, minutes and other information from executive sessions of the board as described in Article 2 (commencing with Section 4900).

(9) Membership lists, including name, property address, mailing address, email address, as collected by the association in accordance with Section 4041 where applicable, but not including information for members who have opted out pursuant to Section 5220.

(10) Check registers.

(11) The governing documents.

(12) An accounting prepared pursuant to subdivision (b) of Section 5520.

(13) An "enhanced association record" as defined in subdivision (b).

(14) "Association election materials" as defined in subdivision (c).

(b) "Enhanced association records" means invoices, receipts, and canceled checks for payments made by the association, purchase orders approved by the association, bank account statements for bank accounts in which assessments are deposited or withdrawn, credit card statements for credit cards issued in the name of the association, statements for services rendered, and reimbursement requests submitted to the association.

(c) "Association election materials" means returned ballots, signed voter envelopes, the voter list of names, parcel numbers, and voters to whom ballots were to be sent, proxies, [1] the candidate registration list, **and the tally sheet of votes cast by electronic secret ballot**. Signed voter envelopes may be inspected but may not be copied. An association shall maintain association election materials for one year after the date of the election. **Leg.H.** Added Stats 2012 ch 180 §2 (AB 805), effective January 1, 2013, operative January 1, 2014. Amended Stats 2019 ch 848 §7 (SB 323), effective January 1, 2020; Stats 2021 ch 640 §6 (SB 392), effective January 1, 2022; Stats 2021 ch 642 §4 (SB 432), effective January 1, 2022 (ch 642 prevails); Stats 2024 ch 383 §6 (AB 2159), effective January 1, 2025.

§5200. 2024 Deletes. [1] and

Prior Law: Former CC §5200, similar to Fam C §1500, was added Stats 1985 ch 1315 §3, and repealed Stats 1992 ch 162 §3 (AB 2650), operative January 1, 1994.

§5201. [Section repealed 1994.]

Leg.H. Added Stats 1985 ch 1315 §3. Repealed Stats 1992 ch 162 §3 (AB 2650), operative January 1, 1994. See Fam C §1501.

§5202. [Section repealed 1994.]

Leg.H. Added Stats 1985 ch 1315 §3. Repealed Stats 1992 ch 162 §3 (AB 2650), operative January 1, 1994. See Fam C §1502.

§5203. [Section repealed 1994.]

Leg.H. Added Stats 1985 ch 1315 §3. Repealed Stats 1992 ch 162 §3 (AB 2650), operative January 1, 1994. See Fam C §1503.

§5205. Document

(a) The association shall make available association records for the time periods and within the timeframes provided in Section 5210 for inspection and copying by a member of the association, or the member's designated representative.

(b) A member of the association may designate another person to inspect and copy the specified association records on the member's behalf. The member shall make this designation in writing.

(c) The association shall make the specified association records available for inspection and copying in the association's business office within the common interest development.

(d) If the association does not have a business office within the development, the association shall make the specified association records available for inspection and copying at a place agreed to by the requesting member and the association.

(e) If the association and the requesting member cannot agree upon a place for inspection and copying pursuant to subdivision (d) or if the requesting member submits a written request directly to the association for copies of specifically identified records, the association may satisfy the requirement to make the association records available for inspection and copying by delivering copies of the specifically identified records to the member by individual delivery pursuant to Section 4040 within the timeframes set forth in subdivision (b) of Section 5210.

(f) The association may bill the requesting member for the direct and actual cost of copying and mailing requested documents. The association shall inform the member of the amount of the copying and mailing costs, and the member shall agree to pay those costs, before copying and sending the requested documents.

(g) In addition to the direct and actual costs of copying and mailing, the association may bill the requesting member an amount not in excess of ten dollars ($10) per hour, and not to exceed two hundred dollars ($200) total per written request, for the time actually and reasonably involved in redacting an enhanced association record. If the enhanced association record includes a reimbursement request, the person submitting the reimbursement request shall be solely responsible for removing all personal identification information from the request. The association shall inform the member of the estimated costs, and the member shall agree to pay those costs, before retrieving the requested documents.

(h) Requesting parties shall have the option of receiving specifically identified records by electronic transmission or machine-readable storage media as long as those records can be transmitted in a redacted format that does not allow the records to be altered. The cost of duplication shall be limited to the direct cost of producing the copy of a record in that electronic format. The association may deliver specifically identified records by electronic transmission or machine-readable storage media as long as those records can be transmitted in a redacted format that prevents the records from being altered. **Leg.H.** Added Stats 2012 ch 180 §2 (AB 805), effective January 1, 2013, operative January 1, 2014.

§5210. Time periods

(a) Association records are subject to member inspection for the following time periods:

(1) For the current fiscal year and for each of the previous two fiscal years.

(2) Notwithstanding paragraph (1), minutes of member and board meetings are subject to inspection permanently. If a committee has decisionmaking authority, minutes of the meetings of that committee shall be made available commencing January 1, 2007, and shall thereafter be permanently subject to inspection.

(b) When a member properly requests access to association records, access to the requested records shall be granted within the following time periods:

(1) Association records prepared during the current fiscal year, within 10 business days following the association's receipt of the request.

(2) Association records prepared during the previous two fiscal years, within 30 calendar days following the association's receipt of the request.

(3) Any record or statement available pursuant to Article 2 (commencing with Section 4525) of Chapter 4, Article 7 (commencing with Section 5300), Section 5565, or Section 5810, within the timeframe specified therein.

(4) Minutes of member and board meetings, within the timeframe specified in subdivision (a) of Section 4950.

(5) Minutes of meetings of committees with decisionmaking authority for meetings commencing on or after January 1, 2007, within 15 calendar days following approval.

(6) Membership list, within the timeframe specified in Section 8330 of the Corporations Code.

(c) There shall be no liability pursuant to this article for an association that fails to retain records for the periods specified in subdivision (a) that were created prior to January 1, 2006. **Leg.H.** Added Stats 2012 ch 180 §2 (AB 805), effective January 1, 2013, operative January 1, 2014.

§5215. Withholding and redaction

(a) Except as provided in subdivision (b), the association may withhold or redact information from the association records if any of the following are true:

(1) The release of the information is reasonably likely to lead to identity theft. For the purposes of this section, "identity theft" means the unauthorized use of another person's personal identifying information to obtain credit, goods, services, money, or property. Examples of information that may be withheld or redacted pursuant to this paragraph include bank account numbers of members or vendors, social security or tax identification numbers, and check, stock, and credit card numbers.

(2) The release of the information is reasonably likely to lead to fraud in connection with the association.

(3) The information is privileged under law. Examples include documents subject to attorney-client privilege or relating to litigation in which the association is or may become involved, and confidential settlement agreements.

(4) The release of the information is reasonably likely to compromise the privacy of an individual member of the association.

(5) The information contains any of the following:

(A) Records of goods or services provided a la carte to individual members of the association for which the association received monetary consideration other than assessments.

(B) Records of disciplinary actions, collection activities, or payment plans of members other than the member requesting the records.

(C) Any person's personal identification information, including, without limitation, social security number, tax identification number, driver's license number, credit card account numbers, bank account number, and bank routing number.

(D) Minutes and other information from executive sessions of the board as described in Article 2 (commencing with Section 4900), except for executed contracts not otherwise privileged. Privileged contracts shall not include contracts for maintenance, management, or legal services.

(E) Personnel records other than the payroll records required to be provided under subdivision (b).

(F) Interior architectural plans, including security features, for individual homes.

(b) Except as provided by the attorney-client privilege, the association may not withhold or redact information concerning the compensation paid to employees, vendors, or contractors. Compensation information for individual employees shall be set forth by job classification or title, not by the employee's name, social security number, or other personal information.

(c) No association, officer, director, employee, agent, or volunteer of an association shall be liable for damages to a member of the association or any third party as the result of identity theft or other breach of privacy because of the failure to withhold or redact that member's information under this section unless the failure to withhold or redact the information was intentional, willful, or negligent.

(d) If requested by the requesting member, an association that denies or redacts records shall provide a written explanation specifying the legal basis for withholding or redacting the requested records. **Leg.H.** Added Stats 2012 ch 180 §2 (AB 805), effective January 1, 2013, operative January 1, 2014.

§ 5216. Safe at Home participants

(a) Notwithstanding any other law, upon request of a member of an association who is an active participant in the Safe at Home program, the association shall do both of the following:

(1) Accept and use the address designated by the Secretary of State as the Safe at Home participant's substitute address under the Safe at Home program for all association communications.

(2) Withhold or redact information that would reveal the name, community property address, or email address of the Safe at Home participant from both of the following:

(A) All resident community membership lists, including mailbox bank listings, resident directories, electronic keypads, unit property numbers, and internet web portal accounts.

(B) Any membership list that will be shared with other members of the association.

(b) An association shall keep member participation in the Safe at Home program confidential.

(c) For purposes of this section:

(1) "Community property address" means the address of the member's property within the community governed by the association.

(2) "Safe at Home participant" means a person certified as a program participant in the Safe at Home program.

(3) "Safe at Home program" means the address confidentiality program established pursuant to Chapter 3.1 (commencing with Section 6205) of Division 7 of Title 1 of the Government Code. **Leg.H.** Added Stats 2021 ch 151 §2 (AB 611), effective January 1, 2022.

§5220. Membership list opt out

A member of the association may opt out of the sharing of that member's name, property address, email address, and mailing address by notifying the association in writing that the member prefers to be contacted via the alternative process described in subdivision (c) of Section 8330 of the Corporations Code. This opt-out shall remain in effect until changed by the member. **Leg.H.** Added Stats 2012 ch 180 §2 (AB 805), effective January 1, 2013, operative January 1, 2014. Amended Stats 2021 ch 640 §7 (SB 392), effective January 1, 2022.

§5225. Membership list request

A member requesting the membership list shall state the purpose for which the list is requested which purpose shall be reasonably related to the requester's interest as a member. If the association reasonably believes that the information in the list will be used for another purpose, it may deny the member access to the list. If the request is denied, in any subsequent action brought by the member under Section 5235, the association shall have the burden to prove that the member would have allowed use of the information for purposes unrelated to the member's interest as a member. **Leg.H.** Added Stats 2012 ch 180 §2 (AB 805), effective January 1, 2013, operative January 1, 2014.

§5230. Restriction on use of records

(a) The association records, and any information from them, may not be sold, used for a commercial purpose, or used for any other purpose not reasonably related to a member's interest as a member. An association may bring an action against any person who violates this article for injunctive relief and for actual damages to the association caused by the violation.

(b) This article may not be construed to limit the right of an association to damages for misuse of information obtained from the association records pursuant to this article or to limit the right of an association to injunctive relief to stop the misuse of this information.

(c)(1) An association or its managing agent shall not do either of the following:

(A) Sell a member's personal information for any purpose without the consent of the member.

(B) Transmit a member's personal information to a third party without the consent of the member unless required to do so by law, including, but not limited to, Article 5 (commencing with Section 5200).

(2) A member may bring an action against an association that violates this subdivision for injunctive relief and actual damages caused by the violation. A member shall be entitled to recover reasonable costs and expenses, including reasonable attorney's fees, in a successful action to enforce the member's rights under this subdivision.

(d) An association shall be entitled to recover reasonable costs and expenses, including reasonable attorney's fees, in a successful action to enforce its rights under this article. **Leg.H.** Added Stats 2012 ch 180 §2 (AB 805), effective January 1, 2013, operative January 1, 2014. Amended Stats 2021 ch 640 §8 (SB 392), effective January 1, 2022.

§5235. Enforcement

(a) A member may bring an action to enforce that member's right to inspect and copy the association records. If a court finds that the association unreasonably withheld access to the association records, the court shall award the member reasonable costs and expenses, including reasonable attorney's fees, and may assess a civil penalty of up to five hundred dollars ($500) for the denial of each separate written request.

(b) A cause of action under this section may be brought in small claims court if the amount of the demand does not exceed the jurisdiction of that court.

(c) A prevailing association may recover any costs if the court finds the action to be frivolous, unreasonable, or without foundation. **Leg.H.** Added Stats 2012 ch 180 §2 (AB 805), effective January 1, 2013, operative January 1, 2014.

§5240. Application of article

(a) As applied to an association and its members, the provisions of this article are intended to supersede the provisions of Sections 8330 and 8333 of the Corporations Code to the extent those sections are inconsistent.

(b) Except as provided in subdivision (a), members of the association shall have access to association records, including accounting books and records and membership lists, in accordance with Article 3 (commencing with Section 8330) of Chapter 13 of Part 3 of Division 2 of Title 1 of the Corporations Code.

(c) This article applies to any community service organization or similar entity that is related to the association, and to any nonprofit entity that provides services to a common interest development under a declaration of trust. This article shall operate to give a member of the organization or entity a right to inspect and copy the records of that organization or entity equivalent to that granted to association members by this article.

(d) This article shall not apply to any common interest development in which separate interests are being offered for sale by a subdivider under the authority of a public report issued by the Bureau of Real Estate so long as the subdivider or all subdividers offering those separate interests for sale, or any employees of those subdividers or any other person who receives direct or indirect compensation from any of those subdividers, comprise a majority of the directors. Notwithstanding the foregoing, this article shall apply to that common interest development no later than 10 years after the close of escrow for the first sale of a separate interest to a member of the general public pursuant to the public report issued for the first phase of the development. **Leg.H.** Added Stats 2012 ch 180 §2 (AB 805), effective January 1, 2013, operative January 1, 2014. Amended Stats 2013 ch 352 §54 (AB 1317), effective September 26, 2013, operative January 1, 2014.

ARTICLE 6
Recordkeeping

Mailing-related requests. §5260.

§5260. Mailing-related requests

To be effective, any of the following requests shall be delivered in writing to the association, pursuant to Section 4035:

(a) A request to change the member's information in the association membership list.

(b) A request to add or remove a second email or mailing address for delivery of individual notices to the member, pursuant to Section 4040.

(c) A request for individual delivery of general notices to the member, pursuant to subdivision (b) of Section 4045, or a request to cancel a prior request for individual delivery of general notices.

(d) A request to opt out of the membership list pursuant to Section 5220, or a request to cancel a prior request to opt out of the membership list.

(e) A request to receive a full copy of a specified annual budget report or annual policy statement pursuant to Section 5320.

(f) A request to receive all reports in full, pursuant to subdivision (b) of Section 5320, or a request to cancel a prior request to receive all reports in full.

(g) **A request to opt out of or opt into electronically voting by electronic secret ballot, pursuant to Section 5105. Leg.H.** Added Stats 2012 ch 180 §2 (AB 805), effective January 1, 2013, operative January 1, 2014. Amended Stats 2021 ch 640 §9 (SB 392), effective January 1, 2022; Stats 2024 ch 383 §7 (AB 2159), effective January 1, 2025.

ARTICLE 7
Annual Reports

Annual budget report. §5300.
Review of financial statement. §5305.
Annual policy statement. §5310.
Notice of availability. §5320.

§5300. Annual budget report

(a) Notwithstanding a contrary provision in the governing documents, an association shall distribute an annual budget report 30 to 90 days before the end of its fiscal year.

(b) Unless the governing documents impose more stringent standards, the annual budget report shall include all of the following information:

(1) A pro forma operating budget, showing the estimated revenue and expenses on an accrual basis.

(2) A summary of the association's reserves, prepared pursuant to Section 5565.

(3) A summary of the reserve funding plan adopted by the board, as specified in paragraph (5) of subdivision (b) of Section 5550. The summary shall include notice to members that the full reserve study plan is available upon request, and the association shall provide the full reserve plan to any member upon request.

(4) A statement as to whether the board has determined to defer or not undertake repairs or replacement of any major component with a remaining life of 30 years or less, including a justification for the deferral or decision not to undertake the repairs or replacement.

(5) A statement as to whether the board, consistent with the reserve funding plan adopted pursuant to Section 5560, has determined or anticipates that the levy of one or more special assessments will be required to repair, replace, or restore any major component or to provide adequate reserves therefor. If so, the statement shall also set out the estimated amount, commencement date, and duration of the assessment.

(6) A statement as to the mechanism or mechanisms by which the board will fund reserves to repair or replace major components, including assessments, borrowing, use of other assets, deferral of selected replacements or repairs, or alternative mechanisms.

(7) A general statement addressing the procedures used for the calculation and establishment of those reserves to defray the future repair, replacement, or additions to those major components that the association is obligated to maintain. The statement shall include, but need not be limited to, reserve calculations made using the formula described in paragraph (4) of subdivision (b) of Section 5570, and may not assume a rate of return on cash reserves in excess of 2 percent above the discount rate published by the Federal Reserve Bank of San Francisco at the time the calculation was made.

(8) A statement as to whether the association has any outstanding loans with an original term of more than one year, including the payee, interest rate, amount outstanding, annual payment, and when the loan is scheduled to be retired.

(9) A summary of the association's property, general liability, earthquake, flood, and fidelity insurance policies. For each policy, the summary shall include the name of the insurer, the type of insurance, the policy limit, and the amount of the deductible, if any. To the extent that any of the required information is specified in the insurance policy declaration page, the association may meet its obligation to disclose that information by making copies of that page and distributing it with the annual budget report. The summary distributed pursuant to this paragraph shall contain, in at least 10-point boldface type, the following statement:

This summary of the association's policies of insurance provides only certain information, as required by Section 5300 of the Civil Code, and should not be considered a substitute for the complete policy terms and conditions contained in the actual policies of insurance. Any association member may, upon request and provision of reasonable notice, review the association's insurance policies and, upon request and payment of reasonable duplication charges, obtain copies of those policies. Although the association maintains the policies of insurance specified in this summary, the association's policies of insurance may not cover your property, including personal property or real property improvements to or around your dwelling, or personal injuries or other losses that occur within or around your dwelling. Even if a loss is covered, you may nevertheless be responsible for paying all or a portion of any deductible that applies. Association members should consult with their individual insurance broker or agent for appropriate additional coverage.

(10) When the common interest development is a condominium project, a statement describing the status of the common interest development as a Federal Housing Administration (FHA)-approved condominium project pursuant to FHA guidelines, including whether the common interest development is an FHA-approved condominium project. The statement shall be in at least 10-point font on a separate piece of paper and in the following form:

Certification by the Federal Housing Administration may provide benefits to members of an association, including an improvement in an owner's ability to refinance a mortgage or obtain secondary financing and an increase in the pool of potential buyers of the separate interest.

This common interest development [is/is not (circle one)] a condominium project. The association of this common interest development [is/is not (circle one)] certified by the Federal Housing Administration.

(11) When the common interest development is a condominium project, a statement describing the status of the common interest development as a federal Department of Veterans Affairs (VA)-approved condominium project pursuant to VA guidelines, including whether the common interest development is a VA-approved condominium project. The statement shall be in at least 10-point font on a separate piece of paper and in the following form:

Certification by the federal Department of Veterans Affairs may provide benefits to members of an association, including an improvement in an owner's ability to refinance a mortgage or obtain secondary financing and an increase in the pool of potential buyers of the separate interest.

This common interest development [is/is not (circle one)] a condominium project. The association of this common interest development [is/is not (circle one)] certified by the federal Department of Veterans Affairs.

(12) A copy of the completed "Charges For Documents Provided" disclosure identified in Section 4528. For purposes of this section, "completed" means that the "Fee for Document" section of the form individually identifies the costs associated with providing each document listed on the form.

(c) The annual budget report shall be made available to the members pursuant to Section 5320.

(d) The summary of the association's reserves disclosed pursuant to paragraph (2) of subdivision (b) shall not be admissible in evidence to show improper financial management of an association, provided that other relevant and competent evidence of the financial condition of the association is not made inadmissible by this provision.

(e) The Assessment and Reserve Funding Disclosure Summary form, prepared pursuant to Section 5570, shall accompany each annual budget report or summary of the annual budget report that is delivered pursuant to this article. **Leg.H.** Added Stats 2015 ch 184 §2 (AB 596), effective January 1, 2016, operative July 1, 2016. Amended Stats 2017 ch 127 §4 (AB 690), effective January 1, 2018.

Former Sections: Former CC §5300, similar to the present section, was added Stats 2012 ch 180 §2 (AB 805), operative January 1, 2014, became inoperative July 1, 2016, and repealed operative January 1, 2017, by its own terms.

Former CC §5300, similar to present Fam C §1600, was added Stats 1985 ch 1315 §3, and repealed Stats 1992 ch 162 §3 (AB 2650), operative January 1, 1994.

Prior Law: Former CC §5300, similar to present Fam C §1600, was added Stats 1985 ch 1315 §3, and repealed Stats 1992 ch 162 §3 (AB 2650), operative January 1, 1994.

Former CC §5300, similar to the present section, was added Stats 2012 ch 180 §2 (AB 805), effective January 1, 2013, operative January 1, 2014, amended Stats 2015 ch 184 §1 (AB 596), effective January 1, 2016, inoperative July 1, 2016, and repealed January 1, 2017, by its own terms.

§5301. [Section repealed 1994.]

Leg.H. Added Stats 1985 ch 1315 §3. Repealed Stats 1992 ch 162 §3 (AB 2650), operative January 1, 1994. See Fam C §3.

§5302. [Section repealed 1994.]
Leg.H. Added Stats 1985 ch 1315 §3. Repealed Stats 1992 ch 162 §3 (AB 2650), operative January 1, 1994. See Fam C §1601.

§5305. Review of financial statement
Unless the governing documents impose more stringent standards, a review of the financial statement of the association shall be prepared in accordance with generally accepted accounting principles by a licensee of the California Board of Accountancy for any fiscal year in which the gross income to the association exceeds seventy-five thousand dollars ($75,000). A copy of the review of the financial statement shall be distributed to the members within 120 days after the close of each fiscal year, by individual delivery pursuant to Section 4040. **Leg.H.** Added Stats 2012 ch 180 §2 (AB 805), effective January 1, 2013, operative January 1, 2014.

§5310. Annual policy statement
(a) Within 30 to 90 days before the end of its fiscal year, the board shall distribute an annual policy statement that provides the members with information about association policies. The annual policy statement shall include all of the following information:

(1) The name and address of the person designated to receive official communications to the association, pursuant to Section 4035.

(2) A statement explaining that a member may submit a request to have notices sent to up to two different specified addresses, pursuant to Section 4040.

(3) The location, if any, designated for posting of a general notice, pursuant to subdivision (a) of Section 4045.

(4) Notice of a member's option to receive general notices by individual delivery, pursuant to subdivision (b) of Section 4045.

(5) Notice of a member's right to receive copies of meeting minutes, pursuant to subdivision (b) of Section 4950.

(6) The statement of assessment collection policies required by Section 5730.

(7) A statement describing the association's policies and practices in enforcing lien rights or other legal remedies for default in the payment of assessments.

(8) A statement describing the association's discipline policy, if any, including any schedule of penalties for violations of the governing documents pursuant to Section 5850.

(9) A summary of dispute resolution procedures, pursuant to Sections 5920 and 5965.

(10) A summary of any requirements for association approval of a physical change to property, pursuant to Section 4765.

(11) The mailing address for overnight payment of assessments, pursuant to Section 5655.

(12) Any other information that is required by law or the governing documents or that the board determines to be appropriate for inclusion.

(b) The annual policy statement shall be made available to the members pursuant to Section 5320. **Leg.H.** Added Stats 2012 ch 180 §2 (AB 805), effective January 1, 2013, operative January 1, 2014. Amended Stats 2021 ch 640 §10 (SB 392), effective January 1, 2022.

Prior Law: Former CC §5310, relating to definition of premarital agreement and property, was added Stats 1985 ch 1315 §3, and repealed Stats 1992 ch 162 §3 (AB 2650), operative January 1, 1994.

§5311. [Section repealed 1994]
Leg.H. Added Stats 1985 ch 1315 §3. Repealed Stats 1992 ch 162 §3 (AB 2650), operative January 1, 1994. See Fam C §1611.

§5312. [Section repealed 1994]
Leg.H. Added Stats 1985 ch 1315 §3. Repealed Stats 1992 ch 162 §3 (AB 2650), operative January 1, 1994. See Fam C §1612.

§5313. [Section repealed 1994]
Leg.H. Added Stats 1985 ch 1315 §3. Repealed Stats 1992 ch 162 §3 (AB 2650), operative January 1, 1994. See Fam C §1613.

§5314. [Section repealed 1994]
Leg.H. Added Stats 1985 ch 1315 §3. Repealed Stats 1992 ch 162 §3 (AB 2650), operative January 1, 1994. See Fam C §1614.

§5315. [Section repealed 1994]
Leg.H. Added Stats 1985 ch 1315 §3. Repealed Stats 1992 ch 162 §3 (AB 2650), operative January 1, 1994. See Fam C §1615.

§5316. [Section repealed 1994]
Leg.H. Added Stats 1985 ch 1315 §3. Repealed Stats 1992 ch 162 §3 (AB 2650), operative January 1, 1994. See Fam C §1616.

§5317. [Section repealed 1994]
Leg.H. Added Stats 1985 ch 1315 §3. Repealed Stats 1992 ch 162 §3 (AB 2650), operative January 1, 1994. See Fam C §1617.

§5320. Notice of availability
(a) When a report is prepared pursuant to Section 5300 or 5310, the association shall deliver one of the following documents to all members by individual delivery pursuant to Section 4040:

(1) The full report.

(2) A summary of the report that includes, on the first page, a general description of the content of the report and instructions, printed in at least 10-point boldface type, regarding how to request a complete copy of the report at no cost to the member.

(b) Notwithstanding subdivision (a), if a member has requested to receive all reports in full, the association shall deliver the full report to that member, rather than a summary of the report. **Leg.H.** Added Stats 2012 ch 180 §2 (AB 805), effective January 1, 2013, operative January 1, 2014. Amended Stats 2021 ch 640 §11 (SB 392), effective January 1, 2022.

ARTICLE 8
Conflict of Interest

Interested director. §5350.

§5350. Interested director
(a) Notwithstanding any other law, and regardless of whether an association is incorporated or unincorporated, the provisions of Sections 7233 and 7234 of the Corporations Code shall apply to any contract or other transaction authorized, approved, or ratified by the board or a committee of the board.

(b) A director or member of a committee shall not vote on any of the following matters:

(1) Discipline of the director or committee member.

(2) An assessment against the director or committee member for damage to the common area or facilities.

(3) A request, by the director or committee member, for a payment plan for overdue assessments.

(4) A decision whether to foreclose on a lien on the separate interest of the director or committee member.

(5) Review of a proposed physical change to the separate interest of the director or committee member.

(6) A grant of exclusive use common area to the director or committee member.

(c) Nothing in this section limits any other provision of law or the governing documents that govern a decision in which a director may have an interest. **Leg.H.** Added Stats 2012 ch 180 §2 (AB 805), effective January 1, 2013, operative January 1, 2014.

ARTICLE 9
Managing Agent

Prospective managing agent disclosure. §5375.
Conflict of interest disclosure. §5375.5.
Facilitation of disclosure delivery. §5376.
Trust fund account. §5380.
Managing agent. §5385.

§5375. Prospective managing agent disclosure
A prospective managing agent of a common interest development shall provide a written statement to the board as soon as practicable, but in no event more than 90 days, before entering into a management agreement which shall contain all of the following information concerning the managing agent:

(a) The names and business addresses of the owners or general partners of the managing agent. If the managing agent is a corporation, the written statement shall include the names and business addresses of the directors and officers and shareholders holding greater than 10 percent of the shares of the corporation.

(b) Whether or not any relevant licenses such as architectural design, construction, engineering, real estate, or accounting have been issued by this state and are currently held by the persons specified in subdivision (a). If a license is currently held by any of those persons, the statement shall contain the following information:

(1) What license is held.

(2) The dates the license is valid.

(3) The name of the licensee appearing on that license.

(c) Whether or not any relevant professional certifications or designations such as architectural design, construction, engineering, real property management, or accounting are currently held by any of the persons specified in subdivision (a), including, but not limited to, a professional common interest development manager. If any certification or designation is held, the statement shall include the following information:

(1) What the certification or designation is and what entity issued it.

(2) The dates the certification or designation is valid.

(3) The names in which the certification or designation is held.

(d) Disclose any business or company in which the common interest development manager or common interest development management firm has any ownership interests, profit-sharing arrangements, or other monetary incentives provided to the management firm or managing agent.

(e) Whether or not the common interest development manager or common interest development management firm receives a referral fee or other monetary benefit from a third-party provider distributing documents pursuant to Sections 4528 and 4530. **Leg.H.** Added Stats 2012 ch 180 §2 (AB 805), effective January 1, 2013, operative January 1, 2014. Amended Stats 2017 ch 127 §5 (AB 690), effective January 1, 2018.

§5375.5. Conflict of interest disclosure

A common interest development manager or common interest development management firm shall disclose, in writing, any potential conflict of interest when presenting a bid for service to an association's board of directors. "Conflict of interest," for purposes of this section, means:

(a) Any referral fee or other monetary benefit that could be derived from a business or company providing products or services to the association.

(b) Any ownership interests or profit-sharing arrangements with service providers recommended to, or used by, the association. **Leg.H.** Added Stats 2017 ch 127 §6 (AB 690), effective January 1, 2018.

§5376. Facilitation of disclosure delivery

The common interest development manager, common interest development management firm, or its contracted third-party agent shall facilitate the delivery of disclosures required pursuant to paragraph (1) of subdivision (a), paragraph (2) of subdivision (b), and subdivision (d), of Section 4530 if the common interest development manager, or common interest development management firm, is contractually responsible for delivering those documents. **Leg.H.** Added Stats 2017 ch 127 §7 (AB 690), effective January 1, 2018.

§5380. Trust fund account

(a) A managing agent of a common interest development who accepts or receives funds belonging to the association shall deposit those funds that are not placed into an escrow account with a bank, savings association, or credit union or into an account under the control of the association, into a trust fund account maintained by the managing agent in a bank, savings association, or credit union in this state. All funds deposited by the managing agent in the trust fund account shall be kept in this state in a financial institution, as defined in Section 31041 of the Financial Code, which is insured by the federal government, or is a guaranty corporation subject to Section 14858 of the Financial Code, and shall be maintained there until disbursed in accordance with written instructions from the association entitled to the funds.

(b) At the written request of the board, the funds the managing agent accepts or receives on behalf of the association shall be deposited into an account in a bank, savings association, or credit union in this state that is insured by the Federal Deposit Insurance Corporation, National Credit Union Administration Insurance Fund, or a guaranty corporation subject to Section 14858 of the Financial Code, provided all of the following requirements are met:

(1) The account is in the name of the managing agent as trustee for the association or in the name of the association.

(2) All of the funds in the account are covered by insurance provided by an agency of the federal government or a guaranty corporation subject to Section 14858 of the Financial Code. Those funds may only be deposited in accounts that protect the principal. In no event may those funds be invested in stocks or high-risk investment options.

(3) The funds in the account are kept separate, distinct, and apart from the funds belonging to the managing agent or to any other person for whom the managing agent holds funds in trust.

(4) The managing agent discloses to the board the nature of the account, how interest will be calculated and paid, whether service charges will be paid to the depository and by whom, and any notice requirements or penalties for withdrawal of funds from the account.

(5) No interest earned on funds in the account shall inure directly or indirectly to the benefit of the managing agent or the managing agent's employees.

(6) Transfers of funds out of the association's reserve or operating accounts shall not be authorized without prior written approval from the board of the association unless the amount of the transfer is less than the following:

(A) The lesser of five thousand dollars ($5,000) or 5 percent of the estimated income in the annual operating budget, for associations with 50 or less separate interests.

(B) The lesser of ten thousand dollars ($10,000) or 5 percent of estimated income in the annual operating budget, for associations with 51 or more separate interests.

(c) The managing agent shall maintain a separate record of the receipt and disposition of all funds described in this section, including any interest earned on the funds.

(d) The managing agent shall not commingle the funds of the association with the managing agent's own money or with the money of others that the managing agent receives or accepts.

(e) The prevailing party in an action to enforce this section shall be entitled to recover reasonable legal fees and court costs.

(f) As used in this section, "completed payment" means funds received that clearly identify the account to which the funds are to be credited. **Leg.H.** Added Stats 2012 ch 180 §2 (AB 805), effective January 1, 2013, operative January 1, 2014. Amended Stats 2018 ch 396 §2 (AB 2912), effective January 1, 2019; Stats 2021 ch 270 §1 (AB 1101), effective January 1, 2022.

§5385. Managing agent

For the purposes of this article, "managing agent" does not include a full-time employee of the association. **Leg.H.** Added Stats 2012 ch 180 §2 (AB 805), effective January 1, 2013, operative January 1, 2014.

ARTICLE 10
Government Assistance

Director training course. §5400.
State registry. §5405.

§5400. Director training course

To the extent existing funds are available, the Department of Consumer Affairs and the Bureau of Real Estate shall develop an online education course for the board regarding the role, duties, laws, and responsibilities of directors and prospective directors, and the nonjudicial foreclosure process. **Leg.H.** Added Stats 2012 ch 180 §2 (AB 805), effective January 1, 2013, operative January 1, 2014. Amended Stats 2013 ch 352 §55 (AB 1317), effective September 26, 2013, operative January 1, 2014.

§5405. State registry

(a) To assist with the identification of common interest developments, each association, whether incorporated or unincorporated, shall submit to the Secretary of State, on a form and for a fee not to exceed thirty dollars ($30) that the Secretary of State shall prescribe, the following information concerning the association and the development that it manages:

(1) A statement that the association is formed to manage a common interest development under the Davis-Stirling Common Interest Development Act.

(2) The name of the association.

(3) The street address of the business or corporate office of the association, if any.

(4) The street address of the association's onsite office, if different from the street address of the business or corporate office, or if there is no onsite office, the street address of the responsible officer or managing agent of the association.

(5) The name, address, and either the daytime telephone number or email address of the president of the association, other than the address, telephone number, or email address of the association's onsite office or managing agent.

(6) The name, street address, and daytime telephone number of the association's managing agent, if any.

(7) The county, and, if in an incorporated area, the city in which the development is physically located. If the boundaries of the development are physically located in more than one county, each of the counties in which it is located.

(8) If the development is in an unincorporated area, the city closest in proximity to the development.

(9) The front street and nearest cross street of the physical location of the development.

(10) The type of common interest development managed by the association.

(11) The number of separate interests in the development.

(b) The association shall submit the information required by this section as follows:

(1) By incorporated associations, within 90 days after the filing of its original articles of incorporation, and thereafter at the time the association files its statement of principal business activity with the Secretary of State pursuant to Section 8210 of the Corporations Code.

(2) By unincorporated associations, in July 2003, and in that same month biennially thereafter. Upon changing its status to that of a corporation, the association shall comply with the filing deadlines in paragraph (1).

(c) The association shall notify the Secretary of State of any change in the street address of the association's onsite office or of the responsible officer or managing agent of the association in the form and for a fee prescribed by the Secretary of State, within 60 days of the change.

(d) The penalty for an incorporated association's noncompliance with the initial or biennial filing requirements of this section shall be suspension of the association's rights, privileges, and powers as a corporation and monetary penalties, to the same extent and in the same manner as suspension and monetary penalties imposed pursuant to Section 8810 of the Corporations Code.

(e) The statement required by this section may be filed, notwithstanding suspension of the corporate powers, rights, and privileges under this section or under provisions of the Revenue and Taxation Code. Upon the filing of a statement under this section by a corporation that has suffered suspension under this section, the Secretary of State shall certify that fact to the Franchise Tax Board and the corporation may thereupon be relieved from suspension, unless the corporation is held in suspension by the Franchise Tax Board by reason of Section 23301, 23301.5, or 23775 of the Revenue and Taxation Code.

(f) The Secretary of State shall make the information submitted pursuant to paragraph (5) of subdivision (a) available only for governmental purposes and only to Members of the Legislature and the Business, Consumer Services, and Housing Agency, upon written request. All other information submitted pursuant to this section shall be subject to public inspection pursuant to the California Public Records Act (Division 10 (commencing with Section 7920.000) of Title 1 of the Government Code). The information submitted pursuant to this section shall be made available for governmental or public inspection.

(g) Whenever any form is filed pursuant to this section, it supersedes any previously filed form.

(h) The Secretary of State may destroy or otherwise dispose of any form filed pursuant to this section after it has been superseded by the filing of a new form. **Leg.H.** Added Stats 2012 ch 180 §2 (AB 805), effective January 1, 2013, operative January 1, 2014. Amended Stats 2013 ch 353 §12 (SB 820), effective September 26, 2013, operative January 1, 2014; Stats 2021 ch 615 §53 (AB 474), effective January 1, 2022.

ARTICLE 11
Emergency powers and procedures

Applicability; Emergency procedures. § 5450.

§ 5450. Applicability; Emergency procedures

(a) This section only applies to a common interest development if gathering in person is unsafe or impossible because the common interest development is in an area affected by one or more of the following conditions:

(1) A state of disaster or emergency declared by the federal government.

(2) A state of emergency proclaimed by the Governor under Section 8625 of the Government Code.

(3) A local emergency proclaimed by a local governing body or official under Section 8630 of the Government Code.

(b) Notwithstanding any other law or the association's governing documents, and except as provided in subdivision (d), a board meeting or meeting of the members may be conducted entirely by teleconference, without any physical location being held open for the attendance of any director or member, if all of the following conditions are satisfied:

(1) Notice of the first meeting that is conducted under this section for a particular disaster or emergency affecting the association is delivered to members by individual delivery.

(2) The notice for each meeting conducted under this section includes, in addition to other required content for meeting notices, all of the following:

(A) Clear technical instructions on how to participate by teleconference.

(B) The telephone number and electronic mail address of a person who can provide technical assistance with the teleconference process, both before and during the meeting.

(C) A reminder that a member may request individual delivery of meeting notices, with instructions on how to do so.

(3) Every director and member has the same ability to participate in the meeting that would exist if the meeting were held in person.

(4) Any vote of the directors shall be conducted by a roll call vote.

(5) Any person who is entitled to participate in the meeting shall be given the option of participating by telephone.

(c) If, as a result of the disaster or emergency, mail delivery or retrieval is not possible at any association onsite address and the address on file with the association for that member is the same association onsite address, then the association shall send the notice of the first meeting referenced in paragraph (1) of subdivision (b) to any email address provided to the association by that member, in writing, pursuant to paragraph (2) of subdivision (a) of Section 4040 or subdivision (b) of Section 4041.

(d) Subdivision (b) does not apply to a meeting at which ballots are counted and tabulated pursuant to Section 5120, unless both of the following conditions are met:

(1) The meeting at which ballots are to be counted and tabulated is conducted by video conference.

(2) The camera is placed in a location such that members can witness the inspector of elections counting and tabulating the votes.

(e) The remedies available pursuant to Section 4955 shall also be available to address violations of this section. **Leg.H.** Added Stats 2021 ch 276 §2 (SB 391), effective September 23, 2021.

CHAPTER 7
FINANCES

Article 1. Accounting.
Article 2. Use of Reserve Funds.
Article 3. Reserve Planning.

ARTICLE 1
Accounting

Board review. §5500.
Satisfaction of review requirements. §5501.
Transfers requiring board approval. §5502.

§5500. Board review

Unless the governing documents impose more stringent standards, the board shall do all of the following:

(a) Review, on a monthly basis, a current reconciliation of the association's operating accounts.

(b) Review, on a monthly basis, a current reconciliation of the association's reserve accounts.

(c) Review, on a monthly basis, the current year's actual operating revenues and expenses compared to the current year's budget.

(d) Review, on a monthly basis, the latest account statements prepared by the financial institutions where the association has its operating and reserve accounts.

(e) Review, on a monthly basis, an income and expense statement for the association's operating and reserve accounts.

(f) Review, on a monthly basis, the check register, monthly general ledger, and delinquent assessment receivable reports. **Leg.H.** Added Stats 2012 ch 180 §2 (AB 805), effective January 1, 2013, operative January 1, 2014. Amended Stats 2018 ch 396 §3 (AB 2912), effective January 1, 2019.

§5501. Satisfaction of review requirements

The review requirements of Section 5500 may be met when every individual member of the board, or a subcommittee of the board consisting of the treasurer and at least one other board member, reviews the documents and statements described in Section 5500 independent of a board meeting, so long as the review is ratified at the board meeting subsequent to the review and that ratification is reflected in the minutes of that meeting. **Leg.H.** Added Stats 2018 ch 396 §4 (AB 2912), effective January 1, 2019.

§5502. Transfers requiring board approval

(a) Notwithstanding any other law, transfers shall not be authorized from the association's reserve or operating accounts without prior written approval from the board of the association unless the amount of the transfer is less than the following:

(1) The lesser of five thousand dollars ($5,000) or 5 percent of the estimated income in the annual operating budget, for associations with 50 or less separate interests.

(2) The lesser of ten thousand dollars ($10,000) or 5 percent of the estimated income in the annual operating budget, for associations with 51 or more separate interests.

(b) This section applies in addition to any other applicable requirements of this part. **Leg.H.** Added Stats 2018 ch 396 §5 (AB 2912), effective January 1, 2019. Amended Stats 2019 ch 497 §31 (AB 991), effective January 1, 2020; Stats 2021 ch 270 §2 (AB 1101), effective January 1, 2022.

ARTICLE 2
Use of Reserve Funds

Use of reserve funds. §5510.
Temporary transfer of reserve funds. §5515.
Use of reserve funds for litigation. §5520.

§5510. Use of reserve funds

(a) The signatures of at least two persons, who shall be directors, or one officer who is not a director and one who is a director, shall be required for the withdrawal of moneys from the association's reserve accounts.

(b) The board shall not expend funds designated as reserve funds for any purpose other than the repair, restoration, replacement, or maintenance of, or litigation involving the repair, restoration, replacement, or maintenance of, major components that the association is obligated to repair, restore, replace, or maintain and for which the reserve fund was established. **Leg.H.** Added Stats 2012 ch 180 §2 (AB 805), effective January 1, 2013, operative January 1, 2014.

§5515. Temporary transfer of reserve funds

(a) Notwithstanding Section 5510, the board may authorize the temporary transfer of moneys from a reserve fund to the association's general operating fund to meet short-term cashflow requirements or other expenses, if the board has provided notice of the intent to consider the transfer in a board meeting notice provided pursuant to Section 4920.

(b) The notice shall include the reasons the transfer is needed, some of the options for repayment, and whether a special assessment may be considered.

(c) If the board authorizes the transfer, the board shall issue a written finding, recorded in the board's minutes, explaining the reasons that the transfer is needed, and describing when and how the moneys will be repaid to the reserve fund.

(d) The transferred funds shall be restored to the reserve fund within one year of the date of the initial transfer, except that the board may, after giving the same notice required for considering a transfer, and, upon making a finding supported by documentation that a temporary delay would be in the best interests of the common interest development, temporarily delay the restoration.

(e) The board shall exercise prudent fiscal management in maintaining the integrity of the reserve account, and shall, if necessary, levy a special assessment to recover the full amount of the expended funds within the time limits required by this section. This special assessment is subject to the limitation imposed by Section 5605. The board may, at its discretion, extend the date the payment on the special assessment is due. Any extension shall not prevent the board from pursuing any legal remedy to enforce the collection of an unpaid special assessment. **Leg.H.** Added Stats 2012 ch 180 §2 (AB 805), effective January 1, 2013, operative January 1, 2014.

§5520. Use of reserve funds for litigation

(a) When the decision is made to use reserve funds or to temporarily transfer moneys from the reserve fund to pay for litigation pursuant to subdivision (b) of Section 5510, the association shall provide general notice pursuant to Section 4045 of that decision, and of the availability of an accounting of those expenses.

(b) Unless the governing documents impose more stringent standards, the association shall make an accounting of expenses related to the litigation on at least a quarterly basis. The accounting shall be made available for inspection by members of the association at the association's office. **Leg.H.** Added Stats 2012 ch 180 §2 (AB 805), effective January 1, 2013, operative January 1, 2014.

ARTICLE 3
Reserve Planning

Visual inspection of major components and reserve study. §5550.
Visual inspection of exterior elevated elements; Written report. §5551.
Reserve funding plan. §5560.
Summary of association reserves. §5565.
Assessment and reserve funding disclosure summary. §5570.
Community service organization report. §5580.

§5550. Visual inspection of major components and reserve study

(a) At least once every three years, the board shall cause to be conducted a reasonably competent and diligent visual inspection of the accessible areas of the major components that the association is obligated to repair, replace, restore, or maintain as part of a study of the reserve account requirements of the common interest development, if the current replacement value of the major components is equal to or greater than one-half of the gross budget of the association, excluding the association's reserve account for that period. The board shall review this study, or cause it to be reviewed, annually and shall consider and implement necessary adjustments to the board's analysis of the reserve account requirements as a result of that review.

(b) The study required by this section shall at a minimum include:

(1) Identification of the major components that the association is obligated to repair, replace, restore, or maintain that, as of the date of the study, have a remaining useful life of less than 30 years.

(2) Identification of the probable remaining useful life of the components identified in paragraph (1) as of the date of the study.

(3) An estimate of the cost of repair, replacement, restoration, or maintenance of the components identified in paragraph (1).

(4) An estimate of the total annual contribution necessary to defray the cost to repair, replace, restore, or maintain the components identified in paragraph (1) during and at the end of their useful life, after subtracting total reserve funds as of the date of the study.

(5) A reserve funding plan that indicates how the association plans to fund the contribution identified in paragraph (4) to meet the association's obligation for the repair and replacement of all major components with an expected remaining life of 30 years or less, not including those components that the board has determined will not be replaced or repaired.

(c) For purposes of this section, "major components" includes gas, water, and electrical service to the extent that the association is responsible for repair or replacement of those lines pursuant to Section 4775. Leg.H. Added Stats 2012 ch 180 §2 (AB 805), effective January 1, 2013, operative January 1, 2014. Amended Stats 2024 ch 288 §2 (SB 900), effective January 1, 2025.

§5551. Visual inspection of exterior elevated elements; Written report

(a) For purposes of this section, the following definitions apply:

(1) "Associated waterproofing systems" include flashings, membranes, coatings, and sealants that protect the load-bearing components of exterior elevated elements from exposure to water.

(2) "Exterior elevated elements" mean the load-bearing components together with their associated waterproofing system.

(3) "Load-bearing components" means those components that extend beyond the exterior walls of the building to deliver structural loads to the building from decks, balconies, stairways, walkways, and their railings, that have a walking surface elevated more than six feet above ground level, that are designed for human occupancy or use, and that are supported in whole or in substantial part by wood or wood-based products.

(4) "Statistically significant sample" means a sufficient number of units inspected to provide 95 percent confidence that the results from the sample are reflective of the whole, with a margin of error of no greater than plus or minus 5 percent.

(5) "Visual inspection" means inspection through the least intrusive method necessary to inspect load-bearing components, including visual observation only or visual observation in conjunction with, for example, the use of moisture meters, borescopes, or infrared technology.

(b)(1) At least once every nine years, the board of an association of a condominium project shall cause a reasonably competent and diligent visual inspection to be conducted by a licensed structural **or civil** engineer or architect of a random and statistically significant sample of exterior elevated elements for which the association has maintenance or repair responsibility.

(2) The inspection shall determine whether the exterior elevated elements are in a generally safe condition and performing in accordance with applicable standards.

(c) Prior to conducting the first visual inspection, the inspector shall generate a random list of the locations of each type of exterior elevated element. The list shall include all exterior elevated elements for which the association has maintenance or repair responsibility. The list shall be provided to the association for future use.

(d) The inspector shall perform the visual inspections in accordance with the random list generated pursuant to subdivision (c). If during the visual inspection the inspector observes building conditions indicating that unintended water or water vapor has passed into the associated waterproofing system, thereby creating the potential for damage to the load-bearing components, then the inspector may conduct a further inspection. The inspector shall exercise their best professional judgment in determining the necessity, scope, and breadth of any further inspection.

(e) Based upon the inspector's visual inspections, further inspection, and construction and materials expertise, the inspector shall issue a written report containing the following information:

(1) The identification of the building components comprising the load-bearing components and associated waterproofing system.

(2) The current physical condition of the load-bearing components and associated waterproofing system, including whether the condition presents an immediate threat to the health and safety of the residents.

(3) The expected future performance and remaining useful life of the load-bearing components and associated waterproofing system.

(4) Recommendations for any necessary repair or replacement of the load-bearing components and associated waterproofing system.

(f) The report issued pursuant to subdivision (e) shall be stamped or signed by the inspector, presented to the board, and incorporated into the study required by Section 5550.

(g)(1) If, after inspection of any exterior elevated element, the inspector advises that the exterior elevated element poses an immediate threat to the safety of the occupants, the inspector shall provide a copy of the inspection report to the association immediately upon completion of the report, and to the local code enforcement agency within 15 days of completion of the report. Upon receiving the report, the association shall take preventive measures immediately, including preventing occupant access to the exterior elevated element until repairs have been inspected and approved by the local enforcement agency.

(2) Local enforcement agencies shall have the ability to recover enforcement costs associated with the requirements of this section from the association.

(h) Each subsequent visual inspection conducted under this section shall commence with the next exterior elevated element identified on the random list and shall proceed in order through the list.

(i) The first inspection shall be completed by January 1, 2025, and then every nine years thereafter in coordination with the reserve study inspection pursuant to Section 5550. All written reports shall be maintained for two inspection cycles as records of the association.

(j)(1) The association shall be responsible for complying with the requirements of this section.

(2) The continued and ongoing maintenance and repair of the load-bearing components and associated waterproofing systems in a safe, functional, and sanitary condition shall be the responsibility of the association as required by the association's governing documents.

(k) The inspection of buildings for which a building permit application has been submitted on or after January 1, 2020, shall occur no later than six years following the issuance of a certificate of occupancy. The inspection shall otherwise comply with the provisions of this section.

(*l*) This section shall only apply to buildings containing three or more multifamily dwelling units.

(m) The association board may enact rules or bylaws imposing requirements greater than those imposed by this section.

(n) A local government or local enforcement agency may enact an ordinance or other rule imposing requirements greater than those imposed by this section. **Leg.H.** Added Stats 2019 ch 207 §1 (SB 326), effective January 1, 2020. Amended Stats 2024 ch 100 §1 (AB 2114), effective July 15, 2024.

§5560. Reserve funding plan

(a) The reserve funding plan required by Section 5550 shall include a schedule of the date and amount of any change in regular or special assessments that would be needed to sufficiently fund the reserve funding plan.

(b) The plan shall be adopted by the board at an open meeting before the membership of the association as described in Article 2 (commencing with Section 4900) of Chapter 6.

(c) If the board determines that an assessment increase is necessary to fund the reserve funding plan, any increase shall be approved in a separate action of the board that is consistent with the procedure described in Section 5605. **Leg.H.** Added Stats 2012 ch 180 §2 (AB 805), effective January 1, 2013, operative January 1, 2014.

§5565. Summary of association reserves

The summary of the association's reserves required by paragraph (2) of subdivision (b) of Section 5300 shall be based on the most recent review or study conducted pursuant to Section 5550, shall be based only on assets held in cash or cash equivalents, shall be printed in boldface type, and shall include all of the following:

(a) The current estimated replacement cost, estimated remaining life, and estimated useful life of each major component.

(b) As of the end of the fiscal year for which the study is prepared:

(1) The current estimate of the amount of cash reserves necessary to repair, replace, restore, or maintain the major components.

(2) The current amount of accumulated cash reserves actually set aside to repair, replace, restore, or maintain major components.

(3) If applicable, the amount of funds received from either a compensatory damage award or settlement to an association from any person for injuries to property, real or personal, arising out of any construction or design defects, and the expenditure or disposition of funds, including the amounts expended for the direct and indirect costs of repair of construction or design defects. These amounts shall be reported at the end of the fiscal year for which the study is prepared as separate line items under cash reserves pursuant to paragraph (2). Instead of complying with the requirements set forth in this paragraph, an association that is obligated to issue a review of its financial statement pursuant to Section 5305 may include in the review a statement containing all of the information required by this paragraph.

(c) The percentage that the amount determined for purposes of paragraph (2) of subdivision (b) equals the amount determined for purposes of paragraph (1) of subdivision (b).

(d) The current deficiency in reserve funding expressed on a per unit basis. The figure shall be calculated by subtracting the amount determined for purposes of paragraph (2) of subdivision (b) from the amount determined for purposes of paragraph (1) of subdivision (b) and then dividing the result by the number of separate interests within the association, except that if assessments vary by the size or type of ownership interest, then the association shall calculate the current deficiency in a manner that reflects the variation. **Leg.H.** Added Stats

2012 ch 180 §2 (AB 805), effective January 1, 2013, operative January 1, 2014.

§5570. Assessment and reserve funding disclosure summary

(a) The disclosures required by this article with regard to an association or a property shall be summarized on the following form:

Assessment and Reserve Funding Disclosure Summary For the Fiscal Year Ending _____

(1) The regular assessment per ownership interest is $_____ per _____.
Note: If assessments vary by the size or type of ownership interest, the assessment applicable to this ownership interest may be found on page _____ of the attached summary.

(2) Additional regular or special assessments that have already been scheduled to be imposed or charged, regardless of the purpose, if they have been approved by the board and/or members:

Date assessment will be due:	Amount per ownership interest per month or year (If assessments are variable, see note immediately below):	Purpose of the assessment:
	Total:	

Note: If assessments vary by the size or type of ownership interest, the assessment applicable to this ownership interest may be found on page _____ of the attached report.

(3) Based upon the most recent reserve study and other information available to the board of directors, will currently projected reserve account balances be sufficient at the end of each year to meet the association's obligation for repair and/or replacement of major components during the next 30 years?
Yes _____ No _____

(4) If the answer to (3) is no, what additional assessments or other contributions to reserves would be necessary to ensure that sufficient reserve funds will be available each year during the next 30 years that have not yet been approved by the board or the members?

Approximate date assessment will be due:	Amount per ownership interest per month or year:
Total:	

(5) All major components are included in the reserve study and are included in its calculations.

(6) Based on the method of calculation in paragraph (4) of subdivision (b) of Section 5570, the estimated amount required in the reserve fund at the end of the current fiscal year is $_____, based in whole or in part on the last reserve study or update prepared by _____ as of _____ (month), ____ (year). The projected reserve fund cash balance at the end of the current fiscal year is $_____, resulting in reserves being _____ percent funded at this date.
If an alternate, but generally accepted, method of calculation is also used, the required reserve amount is $_____. (See attached explanation)

(7) Based on the method of calculation in paragraph (4) of subdivision (b) of Section 5570 of the Civil Code, the estimated amount required in the reserve fund at the end of each of the next five budget years is $_____, and the projected reserve fund cash balance in each of those years, taking into account only assessments already approved and other known revenues, is $_____, leaving the reserve at _____ percent funded. If the reserve funding plan approved by the association is implemented, the projected reserve fund cash balance in each of those years will be $_____, leaving the reserve at _____ percent funded.
Note: The financial representations set forth in this summary are based on the best estimates of the preparer at that time. The estimates are subject to change. At the time this summary was prepared, the assumed long-term before-tax interest rate earned on reserve funds was _____ percent per year, and the assumed long-term inflation rate to be applied to major component repair and replacement costs was _____ percent per year.

(b) For the purposes of preparing a summary pursuant to this section:
(1) "Estimated remaining useful life" means the time reasonably calculated to remain before a major component will require replacement.
(2) "Major component" has the meaning used in Section 5550. Components with an estimated remaining useful life of more than 30 years may be included in a study as a capital asset or disregarded from the reserve calculation, so long as the decision is revealed in the reserve study report and reported in the Assessment and Reserve Funding Disclosure Summary.
(3) The form set out in subdivision (a) shall accompany each annual budget report or summary thereof that is delivered pursuant to Section 5300. The form may be supplemented or modified to clarify the information delivered, so long as the minimum information set out in subdivision (a) is provided.
(4) For the purpose of the report and summary, the amount of reserves needed to be accumulated for a component at a given time shall be computed as the current cost of replacement or repair multiplied by the number of years the component has been in service divided by the useful life of the component. This shall not be construed to require the board to fund reserves in accordance with this calculation. **Leg.H.** Added Stats 2012 ch 180 §2 (AB 805), effective January 1, 2013, operative January 1, 2014. Amended Stats 2015 ch 349 §1 (AB 1516), effective January 1, 2016; Stats 2016 §8 (SB 944), effective January 1, 2017.

§5580. Community service organization report

(a) Unless the governing documents impose more stringent standards, any community service organization whose funding from the association or its members exceeds 10 percent of the organization's annual budget shall prepare and distribute to the association a report that meets the requirements of Section 5012 of the Corporations Code, and that describes in detail administrative costs and identifies the payees of those costs in a manner consistent with the provisions of Article 5 (commencing with Section 5200) of Chapter 6.

(b) If the community service organization does not comply with the standards, the report shall disclose the noncompliance in detail. If a community service organization is responsible for the maintenance of major components for which an association would otherwise be responsible, the community service organization shall supply to the association the information regarding those components that the association would use to complete disclosures and reserve reports required under this article and Section 5300. An association may rely upon information received from a community service organization, and shall provide access to the information pursuant to the provisions of Article 5 (commencing with Section 5200) of Chapter 6. **Leg.H.** Added Stats 2012 ch 180 §2 (AB 805), effective January 1, 2013, operative January 1, 2014.

CHAPTER 8
ASSESSMENTS AND ASSESSMENT COLLECTION

Article 1. Establishment and Imposition of Assessments.
Article 2. Assessment Payment and Delinquency.
Article 3. Assessment Collection.

ARTICLE 1
Establishment and Imposition of Assessments

Levy of assessment. §5600.
Assessment approval requirements. §5605.
Emergency exception to assessment approval requirements. §5610.
Notice of assessment increase. §5615.
Exemption from execution. §5620.
Property tax value as basis for assessments. §5625.

§5600. Levy of assessment

(a) Except as provided in Section 5605, the association shall levy regular and special assessments sufficient to perform its obligations under the governing documents and this act.

(b) An association shall not impose or collect an assessment or fee that exceeds the amount necessary to defray the costs for which it is levied. **Leg.H.** Added Stats 2012 ch 180 §2 (AB 805), effective January 1, 2013, operative January 1, 2014.

§5605. Assessment approval requirements

(a) Annual increases in regular assessments for any fiscal year shall not be imposed unless the board has complied with paragraphs (1), (2), (4),

(5), (6), (7), and (8) of subdivision (b) of Section 5300 with respect to that fiscal year, or has obtained the approval of a majority of a quorum of members, pursuant to Section 4070, at a member meeting or election.

(b) Notwithstanding more restrictive limitations placed on the board by the governing documents, the board may not impose a regular assessment that is more than 20 percent greater than the regular assessment for the association's preceding fiscal year or impose special assessments which in the aggregate exceed 5 percent of the budgeted gross expenses of the association for that fiscal year without the approval of a majority of a quorum of members, pursuant to Section 4070, at a member meeting or election.

(c)(1)(A) For an association that records its original declaration on or after January 1, 2025, notwithstanding more restrictive limitations placed on the board by the governing documents, except as provided in paragraph (3), the board shall not impose a regular assessment against an owner of a deed-restricted affordable housing unit that is more than 5 percent plus the percentage change in the cost of living, not to exceed 10 percent greater than the preceding regular assessment.

(B) For purposes of this paragraph, "percentage change in the cost of living" means the percentage change from April 1 of the prior year to April 1 of the current year in the regional Consumer Price Index for the region where the residential real property is located, as published by the United States Bureau of Labor Statistics. If a regional index is not available, the California Consumer Price Index for All Urban Consumers for all items, as determined by the Department of Industrial Relations, shall apply.

(2) For an association that records its original declaration on or after January 1, 2025, notwithstanding any other law, except as provided in paragraph (3), the board may impose an assessment against an owner of a deed-restricted affordable housing unit that is lower than the assessment imposed against other owners according to the proportional ownership of total subdivision interests subject to assessments.

(3) This subdivision does not apply to any of the following:

(A) A development where the percentage of the units, exclusive of a manager's unit or units, that are deed-restricted affordable housing units exceeds the percentage required by an applicable zoning ordinance in effect at the time the development received final approval.

(B) A development that is located within a city, county, or city and county that does not have an applicable zoning ordinance requiring a percentage of deed-restricted affordable housing units and meet either of the following conditions:

(i) The percentage of the units, exclusive of a manager's unit or units, that are deed-restricted affordable housing exceeds 10 percent of the total number of units in the development at the time the development received final approval.

(ii) If the development met the requirements described in subparagraph (B) of paragraph (1) of subdivision (b) of Section 65912.122 of the Government Code and was approved pursuant to Section 65912.124 of the Government Code, the percentage of the units, exclusive of a manager's unit or units, that are deed-restricted affordable housing exceeds 15 percent of the total number of units in the development at the time the development received final approval.

(C) A development of 20 units or fewer.

(d) For the purposes of this section, all of the following definitions apply:

(1) "Affordable housing unit" means a unit occupied by, or available at affordable housing cost to, lower income and moderate-income households, as defined by Sections 50079.5 and 50052.5, respectively, of the Health and Safety Code.

(2) "Final approval" has the same meaning as defined in clause (ii) of subparagraph (D) of paragraph (2) of subdivision (o) of Section 65589.5 of the Government Code.

(3) "Quorum" means more than 50 percent of the members. **Leg.H.** Added Stats 2012 ch 180 §2 (AB 805), effective January 1, 2013, operative January 1, 2014. Amended Stats 2023 ch 745 §1 (AB 572), effective January 1, 2024.

§5610. Emergency exception to assessment approval requirements

Section 5605 does not limit assessment increases necessary for emergency situations. For purposes of this section, an emergency situation is any one of the following:

(a) An extraordinary expense required by an order of a court.

(b) An extraordinary expense necessary to [1] **operate, repair** or maintain the common interest development or any part of it for which the association is responsible where a threat to personal [2] **health or safety or another hazardous condition or circumstance** on the property is discovered.

(c) An extraordinary expense necessary to repair or maintain the common interest development or any part of it for which the association is responsible that could not have been reasonably foreseen by the board in preparing and distributing the annual budget report under Section 5300. However, [3] **before** the imposition or collection of an assessment under this subdivision, the board shall pass a resolution containing written findings as to the necessity of the extraordinary expense involved and why the expense was not or could not have been reasonably foreseen in the budgeting process, and the resolution shall be distributed to the members with the notice of assessment. **Leg.H.** Added Stats 2012 ch 180 §2 (AB 805), effective January 1, 2013, operative January 1, 2014. Amended Stats 2024 ch 288 §3 (SB 900), effective January 1, 2025.

§5610. **2024 Deletes.** [1] repair [2] safety [3] prior to

§5615. Notice of assessment increase

The association shall provide individual notice pursuant to Section 4040 to the members of any increase in the regular or special assessments of the association, not less than 30 nor more than 60 days prior to the increased assessment becoming due. **Leg.H.** Added Stats 2012 ch 180 §2 (AB 805), effective January 1, 2013, operative January 1, 2014.

§5620. Exemption from execution

(a) Regular assessments imposed or collected to perform the obligations of an association under the governing documents or this act shall be exempt from execution by a judgment creditor of the association only to the extent necessary for the association to perform essential services, such as paying for utilities and insurance. In determining the appropriateness of an exemption, a court shall ensure that only essential services are protected under this subdivision.

(b) This exemption shall not apply to any consensual pledges, liens, or encumbrances that have been approved by a majority of a quorum of members, pursuant to Section 4070, at a member meeting or election, or to any state tax lien, or to any lien for labor or materials supplied to the common area. **Leg.H.** Added Stats 2012 ch 180 §2 (AB 805), effective January 1, 2013, operative January 1, 2014.

§5625. Property tax value as basis for assessments

(a) Except as provided in subdivision (b), notwithstanding any provision of this act or the governing documents to the contrary, an association shall not levy assessments on separate interests within the common interest development based on the taxable value of the separate interests unless the association, on or before December 31, 2009, in accordance with its governing documents, levied assessments on those separate interests based on their taxable value, as determined by the tax assessor of the county in which the separate interests are located.

(b) An association that is responsible for paying taxes on the separate interests within the common interest development may levy that portion of assessments on separate interests that is related to the payment of taxes based on the taxable value of the separate interest, as determined by the tax assessor. **Leg.H.** Added Stats 2012 ch 180 §2 (AB 805), effective January 1, 2013, operative January 1, 2014.

ARTICLE 2
Assessment Payment and Delinquency

Assessment debt and delinquency. §5650.
Payments. §5655.
Payment under protest. §5658.
Notice prior to recording a lien. §5660.
Payment plan. §5665.
Dispute resolution. §5670.
Decision to record a lien. §5673.
Notice of delinquent assessment. §5675.
Lien priority. §5680.
Lien release. §5685.
Procedural noncompliance. §5690.

§5650. Assessment debt and delinquency

(a) A regular or special assessment and any late charges, reasonable fees and costs of collection, reasonable attorney's fees, if any, and interest, if any, as determined in accordance with subdivision (b), shall be a debt of the owner of the separate interest at the time the assessment or other sums are levied.

(b) Regular and special assessments levied pursuant to the governing documents are delinquent 15 days after they become due, unless the declaration provides a longer time period, in which case the longer time period shall apply. If an assessment is delinquent, the association may recover all of the following:

(1) Reasonable costs incurred in collecting the delinquent assessment, including reasonable attorney's fees.

(2) A late charge not exceeding 10 percent of the delinquent assessment or ten dollars ($10), whichever is greater, unless the declaration specifies a late charge in a smaller amount, in which case any late charge imposed shall not exceed the amount specified in the declaration.

(3) Interest on all sums imposed in accordance with this section, including the delinquent assessments, reasonable fees and costs of collection, and reasonable attorney's fees, at an annual interest rate not to exceed 12 percent, commencing 30 days after the assessment becomes due, unless the declaration specifies the recovery of interest at a rate of a lesser amount, in which case the lesser rate of interest shall apply.

(c) Associations are hereby exempted from interest-rate limitations imposed by Article XV of the California Constitution, subject to the limitations of this section. **Leg.H.** Added Stats 2012 ch 180 §2 (AB 805), effective January 1, 2013, operative January 1, 2014.

§5655. Payments

(a) Any payments made by the owner of a separate interest toward a debt described in subdivision (a) of Section 5650 shall first be applied to the assessments owed, and, only after the assessments owed are paid in full shall the payments be applied to the fees and costs of collection, attorney's fees, late charges, or interest.

(b) When an owner makes a payment, the owner may request a receipt and the association shall provide it. The receipt shall indicate the date of payment and the person who received it.

(c) The association shall provide a mailing address for overnight payment of assessments. The address shall be provided in the annual policy statement. **Leg.H.** Added Stats 2012 ch 180 §2 (AB 805), effective January 1, 2013, operative January 1, 2014.

§5658. Payment under protest

(a) If a dispute exists between the owner of a separate interest and the association regarding any disputed charge or sum levied by the association, including, but not limited to, an assessment, fine, penalty, late fee, collection cost, or monetary penalty imposed as a disciplinary measure, and the amount in dispute does not exceed the jurisdictional limits of the small claims court stated in Sections 116.220 and 116.221 of the Code of Civil Procedure, the owner of the separate interest may, in addition to pursuing dispute resolution pursuant to Article 3 (commencing with Section 5925) of Chapter 10, pay under protest the disputed amount and all other amounts levied, including any fees and reasonable costs of collection, reasonable attorney's fees, late charges, and interest, if any, pursuant to subdivision (b) of Section 5650, and commence an action in small claims court pursuant to Chapter 5.5 (commencing with Section 116.110) of Title 1 of the Code of Civil Procedure.

(b) Nothing in this section shall impede an association's ability to collect delinquent assessments as provided in this article or Article 3 (commencing with Section 5700). **Leg.H.** Added Stats 2012 ch 180 §2 (AB 805), effective January 1, 2013, operative January 1, 2014.

§5660. Notice prior to recording a lien

At least 30 days prior to recording a lien upon the separate interest of the owner of record to collect a debt that is past due under Section 5650, the association shall notify the owner of record in writing by certified mail of the following:

(a) A general description of the collection and lien enforcement procedures of the association and the method of calculation of the amount, a statement that the owner of the separate interest has the right to inspect the association records pursuant to Section 5205, and the following statement in 14-point boldface type, if printed, or in capital letters, if typed:

"IMPORTANT NOTICE: IF YOUR SEPARATE INTEREST IS PLACED IN FORECLOSURE BECAUSE YOU ARE BEHIND IN YOUR ASSESSMENTS, IT MAY BE SOLD WITHOUT COURT ACTION."

(b) An itemized statement of the charges owed by the owner, including items on the statement which indicate the amount of any delinquent assessments, the fees and reasonable costs of collection, reasonable attorney's fees, any late charges, and interest, if any.

(c) A statement that the owner shall not be liable to pay the charges, interest, and costs of collection, if it is determined the assessment was paid on time to the association.

(d) The right to request a meeting with the board as provided in Section 5665.

(e) The right to dispute the assessment debt by submitting a written request for dispute resolution to the association pursuant to the association's "meet and confer" program required in Article 2 (commencing with Section 5900) of Chapter 10.

(f) The right to request alternative dispute resolution with a neutral third party pursuant to Article 3 (commencing with Section 5925) of Chapter 10 before the association may initiate foreclosure against the owner's separate interest, except that binding arbitration shall not be available if the association intends to initiate a judicial foreclosure. **Leg.H.** Added Stats 2012 ch 180 §2 (AB 805), effective January 1, 2013, operative January 1, 2014.

§5665. Payment plan

(a) An owner, other than an owner of any interest that is described in Section 11212 of the Business and Professions Code that is not otherwise exempt from this section pursuant to subdivision (a) of Section 11211.7 of the Business and Professions Code, may submit a written request to meet with the board to discuss a payment plan for the debt noticed pursuant to Section 5660. The association shall provide the owners the standards for payment plans, if any exists.

(b) The board shall meet with the owner in executive session within 45 days of the postmark of the request, if the request is mailed within 15 days of the date of the postmark of the notice, unless there is no regularly scheduled board meeting within that period, in which case the board may designate a committee of one or more directors to meet with the owner.

(c) Payment plans may incorporate any assessments that accrue during the payment plan period. Additional late fees shall not accrue during the payment plan period if the owner is in compliance with the terms of the payment plan.

(d) Payment plans shall not impede an association's ability to record a lien on the owner's separate interest to secure payment of delinquent assessments.

(e) In the event of a default on any payment plan, the association may resume its efforts to collect the delinquent assessments from the time prior to entering into the payment plan. **Leg.H.** Added Stats 2012 ch 180 §2 (AB 805), effective January 1, 2013, operative January 1, 2014.

§5670. Dispute resolution

Prior to recording a lien for delinquent assessments, an association shall offer the owner and, if so requested by the owner, participate in dispute resolution pursuant to the association's "meet and confer" program required in Article 2 (commencing with Section 5900) of Chapter 10. **Leg.H.** Added Stats 2012 ch 180 §2 (AB 805), effective January 1, 2013, operative January 1, 2014.

§5673. Decision to record a lien

For liens recorded on or after January 1, 2006, the decision to record a lien for delinquent assessments shall be made only by the board and may not be delegated to an agent of the association. The board shall approve the decision by a majority vote of the directors in an open meeting. The board shall record the vote in the minutes of that meeting. **Leg.H.** Added Stats 2012 ch 180 §2 (AB 805), effective January 1, 2013, operative January 1, 2014.

§5675. Notice of delinquent assessment

(a) The amount of the assessment, plus any costs of collection, late charges, and interest assessed in accordance with subdivision (b) of Section 5650, shall be a lien on the owner's separate interest in the common interest development from and after the time the association causes to be recorded with the county recorder of the county in which the separate interest is located, a notice of delinquent assessment, which shall state the amount of the assessment and other sums imposed in accordance with subdivision (b) of Section 5650, a legal description of the owner's separate interest in the common interest development against which the assessment and other sums are levied, and the name of the record owner of the separate interest in the common interest development against which the lien is imposed.

(b) The itemized statement of the charges owed by the owner described in subdivision (b) of Section 5660 shall be recorded together with the notice of delinquent assessment.

(c) In order for the lien to be enforced by nonjudicial foreclosure as provided in Sections 5700 to 5710, inclusive, the notice of delinquent assessment shall state the name and address of the trustee authorized by the association to enforce the lien by sale.

(d) The notice of delinquent assessment shall be signed by the person designated in the declaration or by the association for that purpose, or if no one is designated, by the president of the association.

(e) A copy of the recorded notice of delinquent assessment shall be mailed by certified mail to every person whose name is shown as an owner of the separate interest in the association's records, and the notice shall be mailed no later than 10 calendar days after recordation. **Leg.H.** Added Stats 2012 ch 180 §2 (AB 805), effective January 1, 2013, operative January 1, 2014.

§5680. Lien priority

A lien created pursuant to Section 5675 shall be prior to all other liens recorded subsequent to the notice of delinquent assessment, except that the declaration may provide for the subordination thereof to any other liens and encumbrances. **Leg.H.** Added Stats 2012 ch 180 §2 (AB 805), effective January 1, 2013, operative January 1, 2014.

§5685. Lien release

(a) Within 21 days of the payment of the sums specified in the notice of delinquent assessment, the association shall record or cause to be recorded in the office of the county recorder in which the notice of delinquent assessment is recorded a lien release or notice of rescission and provide the owner of the separate interest a copy of the lien release or notice that the delinquent assessment has been satisfied.

(b) If it is determined that a lien previously recorded against the separate interest was recorded in error, the party who recorded the lien shall, within 21 calendar days, record or cause to be recorded in the office of the county recorder in which the notice of delinquent assessment is recorded a lien release or notice of rescission and provide the owner of the separate interest with a declaration that the lien filing or recording was in error and a copy of the lien release or notice of rescission.

(c) If it is determined that an association has recorded a lien for a delinquent assessment in error, the association shall promptly reverse all late charges, fees, interest, attorney's fees, costs of collection, costs imposed for the notice prescribed in Section 5660, and costs of recordation and release of the lien authorized under subdivision (b) of Section 5720, and pay all costs related to any related dispute resolution or alternative dispute resolution. **Leg.H.** Added Stats 2012 ch 180 §2 (AB 805), effective January 1, 2013, operative January 1, 2014.

§5690. Procedural noncompliance

An association that fails to comply with the procedures set forth in this article shall, prior to recording a lien, recommence the required notice process. Any costs associated with recommencing the notice process shall be borne by the association and not by the owner of a separate interest. **Leg.H.** Added Stats 2012 ch 180 §2 (AB 805), effective January 1, 2013, operative January 1, 2014.

ARTICLE 3
Assessment Collection

Collection generally. §5700.
Decision to foreclose. §5705.
Foreclosure. §5710.
Right of redemption after trustee sale. §5715.
Limitation on foreclosure. §5720.
Limitations on authority to foreclose liens for monetary penalties and damage to the common area. §5725.
Statement of collection procedure. §5730.
Assignment or pledge. §5735.
Application of article. §5740.

§5700. Collection generally

(a) Except as otherwise provided in this article, after the expiration of 30 days following the recording of a lien created pursuant to Section 5675, the lien may be enforced in any manner permitted by law, including sale by the court, sale by the trustee designated in the notice of delinquent assessment, or sale by a trustee substituted pursuant to Section 2934a.

(b) Nothing in Article 2 (commencing with Section 5650) or in subdivision (a) of Section 726 of the Code of Civil Procedure prohibits actions against the owner of a separate interest to recover sums for which a lien is created pursuant to Article 2 (commencing with Section 5650) or prohibits an association from taking a deed in lieu of foreclosure. **Leg.H.** Added Stats 2012 ch 180 §2 (AB 805), effective January 1, 2013, operative January 1, 2014.

§5705. Decision to foreclose

(a) Notwithstanding any law or any provisions of the governing documents to the contrary, this section shall apply to debts for assessments that arise on and after January 1, 2006.

(b) Prior to initiating a foreclosure on an owner's separate interest, the association shall offer the owner and, if so requested by the owner, participate in dispute resolution pursuant to the association's "meet and confer" program required in Article 2 (commencing with Section 5900) of Chapter 10 or alternative dispute resolution as set forth in Article 3 (commencing with Section 5925) of Chapter 10. The decision to pursue dispute resolution or a particular type of alternative dispute resolution shall be the choice of the owner, except that binding arbitration shall not be available if the association intends to initiate a judicial foreclosure.

(c) The decision to initiate foreclosure of a lien for delinquent assessments that has been validly recorded shall be made only by the board and may not be delegated to an agent of the association. The board shall approve the decision by a majority vote of the directors in an executive session. The board shall record the vote in the minutes of the next meeting of the board open to all members. The board shall maintain the confidentiality of the owner or owners of the separate interest by identifying the matter in the minutes by the parcel number of the property, rather than the name of the owner or owners. A board vote to approve foreclosure of a lien shall take place at least 30 days prior to any public sale.

(d) The board shall provide notice by personal service in accordance with the manner of service of summons in Article 3 (commencing with Section 415.10) of Chapter 4 of Title 5 of Part 2 of the Code of Civil Procedure to an owner of a separate interest who occupies the separate interest or to the owner's legal representative, if the board votes to foreclose upon the separate interest. The board shall provide written notice to an owner of a separate interest who does not occupy the separate interest by first-class mail, postage prepaid, at the most current address shown on the books of the association. In the absence of written notification by the owner to the association, the address of the owner's separate interest may be treated as the owner's mailing address. **Leg.H.** Added Stats 2012 ch 180 §2 (AB 805), effective January 1, 2013, operative January 1, 2014.

§5710. Foreclosure

(a) Any sale by the trustee shall be conducted in accordance with Sections 2924, 2924b, and 2924c applicable to the exercise of powers of sale in mortgages and deeds of trust.

(b) In addition to the requirements of Section 2924, the association shall serve a notice of default on the person named as the owner of the separate interest in the association's records or, if that person has designated a legal representative pursuant to this subdivision, on that legal representative. Service shall be in accordance with the manner of service of summons in Article 3 (commencing with Section 415.10) of Chapter 4 of Title 5 of Part 2 of the Code of Civil Procedure. An owner may designate a legal representative in a writing that is mailed to the association in a manner that indicates that the association has received it.

(c) The fees of a trustee may not exceed the amounts prescribed in Sections 2924c and 2924d, plus the cost of service for either of the following:

(1) The notice of default pursuant to subdivision (b).

(2) The decision of the board to foreclose upon the separate interest of an owner as described in subdivision (d) of Section 5705. **Leg.H.** Added Stats 2012 ch 180 §2 (AB 805), effective January 1, 2013, operative January 1, 2014.

§5715. Right of redemption after trustee sale

(a) Notwithstanding any law or any provisions of the governing documents to the contrary, this section shall apply to debts for assessments that arise on and after January 1, 2006.

(b) A nonjudicial foreclosure by an association to collect upon a debt for delinquent assessments shall be subject to a right of redemption. The redemption period within which the separate interest may be redeemed from a foreclosure sale under this paragraph ends 90 days after the sale. In addition to the requirements of Section 2924f, a notice of sale in connection with an association's foreclosure of a separate interest in a common interest development shall include a statement that the property is being sold subject to the right of redemption created in this section. **Leg.H.** Added Stats 2012 ch 180 §2 (AB 805), effective January 1, 2013, operative January 1, 2014.

§5720. Limitation on foreclosure

(a) Notwithstanding any law or any provisions of the governing documents to the contrary, this section shall apply to debts for assessments that arise on and after January 1, 2006.

(b) An association that seeks to collect delinquent regular or special assessments of an amount less than one thousand eight hundred dollars ($1,800), not including any accelerated assessments, late charges, fees and costs of collection, attorney's fees, or interest, may not collect that debt through judicial or nonjudicial foreclosure, but may attempt to collect or secure that debt in any of the following ways:

(1) By a civil action in small claims court, pursuant to Chapter 5.5 (commencing with Section 116.110) of Title 1 of Part 1 of the Code of Civil Procedure. An association that chooses to proceed by an action in small claims court, and prevails, may enforce the judgment as permitted under Article 8 (commencing with Section 116.810) of Chapter 5.5 of Title 1 of Part 1 of the Code of Civil Procedure. The amount that may be recovered in small claims court to collect upon a debt for delinquent assessments may not exceed the jurisdictional limits of the small claims court and shall be the sum of the following:

(A) The amount owed as of the date of filing the complaint in the small claims court proceeding.

(B) In the discretion of the court, an additional amount to that described in subparagraph (A) equal to the amount owed for the period from the date the complaint is filed until satisfaction of the judgment, which total amount may include accruing unpaid assessments and any reasonable late charges, fees and costs of collection, attorney's fees, and interest, up to the jurisdictional limits of the small claims court.

(2) By recording a lien on the owner's separate interest upon which the association may not foreclose until the amount of the delinquent assessments secured by the lien, exclusive of any accelerated assessments, late charges, fees and costs of collection, attorney's fees, or interest, equals or exceeds one thousand eight hundred dollars ($1,800) or the assessments secured by the lien are more than 12 months delinquent. An association that chooses to record a lien under these provisions, prior to recording the lien, shall offer the owner and, if so requested by the owner, participate in dispute resolution as set forth in Article 2 (commencing with Section 5900) of Chapter 10.

(3) Any other manner provided by law, except for judicial or nonjudicial foreclosure.

(c) The limitation on foreclosure of assessment liens for amounts under the stated minimum in this section does not apply to any of the following:

(1) Assessments secured by a lien that are more than 12 months delinquent.

(2) Assessments owed by owners of separate interests in time-share estates, as defined in subdivision (x) of Section 11212 of the Business and Professions Code.

(3) Assessments owed by the developer. **Leg.H.** Added Stats 2012 ch 180 §2 (AB 805), effective January 1, 2013, operative January 1, 2014.

§5725. Limitations on authority to foreclose liens for monetary penalties and damage to the common area

(a) A monetary charge imposed by the association as a means of reimbursing the association for costs incurred by the association in the repair of damage to common area and facilities caused by a member or the member's guest or tenant may become a lien against the member's separate interest enforceable by the sale of the interest under Sections 2924, 2924b, and 2924c, provided the authority to impose a lien is set forth in the governing documents. It is the intent of the Legislature not to contravene Section 2792.26 of Title 10 of the California Code of Regulations, as that section appeared on January 1, 1996, for associations of subdivisions that are being sold under authority of a subdivision public report, pursuant to Part 2 (commencing with Section 11000) of Division 4 of the Business and Professions Code.

(b) A monetary penalty imposed by the association as a disciplinary measure for failure of a member to comply with the governing documents, except for the late payments, may not be characterized nor treated in the governing documents as an assessment that may become a lien against the member's separate interest enforceable by the sale of the interest under Sections 2924, 2924b, and 2924c. **Leg.H.** Added Stats 2012 ch 180 §2 (AB 805), effective January 1, 2013, operative January 1, 2014.

§5730. Statement of collection procedure

(a) The annual policy statement, prepared pursuant to Section 5310, shall include the following notice, in at least 12-point type:

"NOTICE ASSESSMENTS AND FORECLOSURE

This notice outlines some of the rights and responsibilities of owners of property in common interest developments and the associations that manage them. Please refer to the sections of the Civil Code indicated for further information. A portion of the information in this notice applies only to liens recorded on or after January 1, 2003. You may wish to consult a lawyer if you dispute an assessment.

ASSESSMENTS AND FORECLOSURE

Assessments become delinquent 15 days after they are due, unless the governing documents provide for a longer time. The failure to pay association assessments may result in the loss of an owner's property through foreclosure. Foreclosure may occur either as a result of a court action, known as judicial foreclosure, or without court action, often referred to as nonjudicial foreclosure. For liens recorded on and after January 1, 2006, an association may not use judicial or nonjudicial foreclosure to enforce that lien if the amount of the delinquent assessments or dues, exclusive of any accelerated assessments, late charges, fees, attorney's fees, interest, and costs of collection, is less than one thousand eight hundred dollars ($1,800). For delinquent assessments or dues in excess of one thousand eight hundred dollars ($1,800) or more than 12 months delinquent, an association may use judicial or nonjudicial foreclosure subject to the conditions set forth in Article 3 (commencing with Section 5700) of Chapter 8 of Part 5 of Division 4 of the Civil Code. When using judicial or nonjudicial foreclosure, the association records a lien on the owner's property. The owner's property may be sold to satisfy the lien if the amounts secured by the lien are not paid. (Sections 5700 through 5720 of the Civil Code, inclusive)

In a judicial or nonjudicial foreclosure, the association may recover assessments, reasonable costs of collection, reasonable attorney's fees, late charges, and interest. The association may not use nonjudicial foreclosure to collect fines or penalties, except for costs to repair common area damaged by a member or a member's guests, if the governing documents provide for this. (Section 5725 of the Civil Code)

The association must comply with the requirements of Article 2 (commencing with Section 5650) of Chapter 8 of Part 5 of Division 4 of the Civil Code when collecting delinquent assessments. If the association fails to follow these requirements, it may not record a lien on the owner's property until it has satisfied those requirements. Any additional costs that result from satisfying the requirements are the responsibility of the association. (Section 5675 of the Civil Code)

At least 30 days prior to recording a lien on an owner's separate interest, the association must provide the owner of record with certain documents by certified mail, including a description of its collection and lien enforcement procedures and the method of calculating the amount. It must also provide an itemized statement of the charges owed by the owner. An owner has a right to review the association's records to verify the debt. (Section 5660 of the Civil Code)

If a lien is recorded against an owner's property in error, the person who recorded the lien is required to record a lien release within 21 days, and to provide an owner certain documents in this regard. (Section 5685 of the Civil Code)

The collection practices of the association may be governed by state and federal laws regarding fair debt collection. Penalties can be imposed for debt collection practices that violate these laws.

PAYMENTS

When an owner makes a payment, the owner may request a receipt, and the association is required to provide it. On the receipt, the association must indicate the date of payment and the person who received it. The association must inform owners of a mailing address for overnight payments. (Section 5655 of the Civil Code)

An owner may, but is not obligated to, pay under protest any disputed charge or sum levied by the association, including, but not limited to, an assessment, fine, penalty, late fee, collection cost, or monetary penalty imposed as a disciplinary measure, and by so doing, specifically reserve the right to contest the disputed charge or sum in court or otherwise.

An owner may dispute an assessment debt by submitting a written request for dispute resolution to the association as set forth in Article 2 (commencing with Section 5900) of Chapter 10 of Part 5 of Division 4 of the Civil Code. In addition, an association may not initiate a foreclosure without participating in alternative dispute resolution with a neutral third party as set forth in Article 3 (commencing with Section 5925) of Chapter 10 of Part 5 of Division 4 of the Civil Code, if so requested by the owner. Binding arbitration shall not be available if the association intends to initiate a judicial foreclosure.

An owner is not liable for charges, interest, and costs of collection, if it is established that the assessment was paid properly on time. (Section 5685 of the Civil Code)

MEETINGS AND PAYMENT PLANS

An owner of a separate interest that is not a time-share interest may request the association to consider a payment plan to satisfy a delinquent assessment. The association must inform owners of the standards for payment plans, if any exists. (Section 5665 of the Civil Code)

The board must meet with an owner who makes a proper written request for a meeting to discuss a payment plan when the owner has received a notice of a delinquent assessment. These payment plans must conform with the payment plan standards of the association, if they exist. (Section 5665 of the Civil Code)"

(b) An association distributing the notice required by this section to an owner of an interest that is described in Section 11212 of the Business and Professions Code that is not otherwise exempt from this section pursuant to subdivision (a) of Section 11211.7 of the Business and Professions Code may delete from the notice described in subdivision (a) the portion regarding meetings and payment plans. **Leg.H.** Added Stats 2012 ch 180 §2 (AB 805), effective January 1, 2013, operative January 1, 2014.

§5735. Assignment or pledge

(a) An association may not voluntarily assign or pledge the association's right to collect payments or assessments, or to enforce or foreclose a lien to a third party, except when the assignment or pledge is made to a financial institution or lender chartered or licensed under federal or state law, when acting within the scope of that charter or license, as security for a loan obtained by the association.

(b) Nothing in subdivision (a) restricts the right or ability of an association to assign any unpaid obligations of a former member to a third party for purposes of collection. **Leg.H.** Added Stats 2012 ch 180 §2 (AB 805), effective January 1, 2013, operative January 1, 2014.

§5740. Application of article

(a) Except as otherwise provided, this article applies to a lien created on or after January 1, 2003.

(b) A lien created before January 1, 2003, is governed by the law in existence at the time the lien was created. **Leg.H.** Added Stats 2012 ch 180 §2 (AB 805), effective January 1, 2013, operative January 1, 2014.

CHAPTER 9
INSURANCE AND LIABILITY

Limitation on liability of volunteer officer or director; Applicability. §5800.
Limitation of member liability. §5805.
Fidelity bond coverage requirements. §5806.
Notice of change in coverage. §5810.

§5800. Limitation on liability of volunteer officer or director; Applicability

(a) A volunteer officer or volunteer director described in subdivision (e) of an association that manages a common interest development that is residential or mixed use shall not be personally liable in excess of the coverage of insurance specified in paragraph (4) to any person who suffers injury, including, but not limited to, bodily injury, emotional distress, wrongful death, or property damage or loss as a result of the tortious act or omission of the volunteer officer or volunteer director if all of the following criteria are met:

(1) The act or omission was performed within the scope of the officer's or director's association duties.

(2) The act or omission was performed in good faith.

(3) The act or omission was not willful, wanton, or grossly negligent.

(4) The association maintained and had in effect at the time the act or omission occurred and at the time a claim is made one or more policies of insurance that shall include coverage for (A) general liability of the association and (B) individual liability of officers and directors of the association for negligent acts or omissions in that capacity; provided that both types of coverage are in the following minimum amounts:

(A) At least five hundred thousand dollars ($500,000) if the common interest development consists of 100 or fewer separate interests.

(B) At least one million dollars ($1,000,000) if the common interest development consists of more than 100 separate interests.

(b) The payment of actual expenses incurred by a director or officer in the execution of the duties of that position does not affect the director's or officer's status as a volunteer within the meaning of this section.

(c) An officer or director who at the time of the act or omission was a declarant, or who received either direct or indirect compensation as an employee from the declarant, or from a financial institution that purchased a separate interest at a judicial or nonjudicial foreclosure of a mortgage or deed of trust on real property, is not a volunteer for the purposes of this section.

(d) Nothing in this section shall be construed to limit the liability of the association for its negligent act or omission or for any negligent act or omission of an officer or director of the association.

(e) This section shall only apply to a volunteer officer or director who is a tenant of a residential separate interest in the common interest development or is an owner of no more than two separate interests and whose ownership in the common interest development consists exclusively of residential separate interests.

(f)(1) For purposes of paragraph (1) of subdivision (a), the scope of the officer's or director's association duties shall include, but shall not be limited to, both of the following decisions:

(A) Whether to conduct an investigation of the common interest development for latent deficiencies prior to the expiration of the applicable statute of limitations.

(B) Whether to commence a civil action against the builder for defects in design or construction.

(2) It is the intent of the Legislature that this section clarify the scope of association duties to which the protections against personal liability in this section apply. It is not the intent of the Legislature that these clarifications be construed to expand, or limit, the fiduciary duties owed by the directors or officers. **Leg.H.** Added Stats 2012 ch 180 §2 (AB 805), effective January 1, 2013, operative January 1, 2014. Amended Stats 2017 ch 278 §2 (AB 1412), effective January 1, 2018.

§5805. Limitation of member liability

(a) It is the intent of the Legislature to offer civil liability protection to owners of the separate interests in a common interest development that have common area owned in tenancy-in-common if the association carries a certain level of prescribed insurance that covers a cause of action in tort.

(b) Any cause of action in tort against any owner of a separate interest arising solely by reason of an ownership interest as a tenant-in-common in the common area of a common interest development shall be brought only against the association and not against the individual owners of the separate interests, if both of the insurance requirements in paragraphs (1) and (2) are met:

(1) The association maintained and has in effect for this cause of action, one or more policies of insurance that include coverage for general liability of the association.

(2) The coverage described in paragraph (1) is in the following minimum amounts:

(A) At least two million dollars ($2,000,000) if the common interest development consists of 100 or fewer separate interests.

(B) At least three million dollars ($3,000,000) if the common interest development consists of more than 100 separate interests. **Leg.H.** Added Stats 2012 ch 180 §2 (AB 805), effective January 1, 2013, operative January 1, 2014.

§5806. Fidelity bond coverage requirements

Unless the governing documents require greater coverage amounts, the association shall maintain crime insurance, employee dishonesty coverage, fidelity bond coverage, or their equivalent, for its directors, officers, and employees in an amount that is equal to or more than the combined amount of the reserves of the association and total assessments for three months. The coverage maintained by the association shall also include protection in an equal amount against computer fraud and funds transfer fraud. If the association uses a managing agent or management company, the association's crime insurance, employee dishonesty coverage, fidelity bond coverage, or their equivalent, shall additionally include coverage for, or otherwise be endorsed to provide coverage for, dishonest acts by that person or entity and its employees. Self-insurance does not meet the requirements of this section. **Leg.H.** Added Stats 2018 ch 396 §6 (AB 2912), effective January 1, 2019. Amended Stats 2021 ch 270 §3 (AB 1101), effective January 1, 2022.

§5810. Notice of change in coverage

The association shall, as soon as reasonably practicable, provide individual notice pursuant to Section 4040 to all members if any of the policies described in the annual budget report pursuant to Section 5300 have lapsed, been canceled, and are not immediately renewed, restored, or replaced, or if there is a significant change, such as a reduction in coverage or limits or an increase in the deductible, as to any of those policies. If the association receives any notice of nonrenewal of a policy described in the annual budget report pursuant to Section 5300, the association shall immediately notify its members if replacement coverage will not be in effect by the date the existing coverage will lapse. **Leg.H.** Added Stats 2012 ch 180 §2 (AB 805), effective January 1, 2013, operative January 1, 2014.

CHAPTER 10
DISPUTE RESOLUTION AND ENFORCEMENT

Article 1. Discipline and Cost Reimbursement.
Article 2. Internal Dispute Resolution.
Article 3. Alternative Dispute Resolution Prerequisite to Civil Action.
Article 4. Civil Action.

ARTICLE 1
Discipline and Cost Reimbursement

Schedule of monetary penalties. §5850.
Hearing. §5855.
No effect on authority of board. §5865.
Pursuit of enforcement actions. § 5875.

§5850. Schedule of monetary penalties

(a) If an association adopts or has adopted a policy imposing any monetary penalty, including any fee, on any association member for a violation of the governing documents, including any monetary penalty relating to the activities of a guest or tenant of the member, the board shall adopt and distribute to each member, in the annual policy statement prepared pursuant to Section 5310, a schedule of the monetary penalties that may be assessed for those violations, which shall be in accordance with authorization for member discipline contained in the governing documents.

(b) Any new or revised monetary penalty that is adopted after complying with subdivision (a) may be included in a supplement that is delivered to the members individually, pursuant to Section 4040.

(c) A monetary penalty for a violation of the governing documents shall not exceed the monetary penalty stated in the schedule of monetary penalties or supplement that is in effect at the time of the violation.

(d) An association shall provide a copy of the most recently distributed schedule of monetary penalties, along with any applicable supplements to that schedule, to any member upon request. **Leg.H.** Added Stats 2012 ch 180 §2 (AB 805), effective January 1, 2013, operative January 1, 2014.

§5855. Hearing

(a) When the board is to meet to consider or impose discipline upon a member, or to impose a monetary charge as a means of reimbursing the association for costs incurred by the association in the repair of damage to common area and facilities caused by a member or the member's guest or tenant, the board shall notify the member in writing, by either personal delivery or individual delivery pursuant to Section 4040, at least 10 days prior to the meeting.

(b) The notification shall contain, at a minimum, the date, time, and place of the meeting, the nature of the alleged violation for which a member may be disciplined or the nature of the damage to the common area and facilities for which a monetary charge may be imposed, and a statement that the member has a right to attend and may address the board at the meeting. The board shall meet in executive session if requested by the member.

(c) If the board imposes discipline on a member or imposes a monetary charge on the member for damage to the common area and facilities, the board shall provide the member a written notification of the decision, by either personal delivery or individual delivery pursuant to Section 4040, within 15 days following the action.

(d) A disciplinary action or the imposition of a monetary charge for damage to the common area shall not be effective against a member unless the board fulfills the requirements of this section. **Leg.H.** Added Stats 2012 ch 180 §2 (AB 805), effective January 1, 2013, operative January 1, 2014.

§5865. No effect on authority of board

Nothing in Section 5850 or 5855 shall be construed to create, expand, or reduce the authority of the board to impose monetary penalties on a member for a violation of the governing documents. **Leg.H.** Added Stats 2012 ch 180 §2 (AB 805), effective January 1, 2013, operative January 1, 2014.

§ 5875. Pursuit of enforcement actions

An association shall not pursue any enforcement actions for a violation of the governing documents, except those actions relating to the homeowner's nonpayment of assessments, during a declared state or local emergency if the nature of the emergency giving rise to the declaration makes it unsafe or impossible for the homeowner to either prevent or fix the violation. **Leg.H.** Added Stats 2022 ch 858 §4 (AB 1410), effective January 1, 2023.

ARTICLE 2
Internal Dispute Resolution

Application of article. §5900.
Fair, reasonable, and expeditious dispute resolution procedure required. §5905.
Minimum requirements of association procedure. §5910.
Internal dispute resolution as condition precedent to civil action. §5910.1.
Default meet and confer procedure. §5915.
Notice in policy statement. §5920.

§5900. Application of article

(a) This article applies to a dispute between an association and a member involving their rights, duties, or liabilities under this act, under the Nonprofit Mutual Benefit Corporation Law (Part 3 (commencing with Section 7110) of Division 2 of Title 1 of the Corporations Code), or under the governing documents of the common interest development or association.

(b) This article supplements, and does not replace, Article 3 (commencing with Section 5925), relating to alternative dispute resolution as a prerequisite to an enforcement action. **Leg.H.** Added Stats 2012 ch 180 §2 (AB 805), effective January 1, 2013, operative January 1, 2014.

§5905. Fair, reasonable, and expeditious dispute resolution procedure required

(a) An association shall provide a fair, reasonable, and expeditious procedure for resolving a dispute within the scope of this article.

(b) In developing a procedure pursuant to this article, an association shall make maximum, reasonable use of available local dispute resolution programs involving a neutral third party, including low-cost mediation programs such as those listed on the Internet Web sites of the Department of Consumer Affairs and the United States Department of Housing and Urban Development.

(c) If an association does not provide a fair, reasonable, and expeditious procedure for resolving a dispute within the scope of this article, the procedure provided in Section 5915 applies and satisfies the requirement of subdivision (a). **Leg.H.** Added Stats 2012 ch 180 §2 (AB 805), effective January 1, 2013, operative January 1, 2014.

§5910. Minimum requirements of association procedure

A fair, reasonable, and expeditious dispute resolution procedure shall, at a minimum, satisfy all of the following requirements:

(a) The procedure may be invoked by either party to the dispute. A request invoking the procedure shall be in writing.

(b) The procedure shall provide for prompt deadlines. The procedure shall state the maximum time for the association to act on a request invoking the procedure.

(c) If the procedure is invoked by a member, the association shall participate in the procedure.

(d) If the procedure is invoked by the association, the member may elect not to participate in the procedure. If the member participates but the dispute is resolved other than by agreement of the member, the member shall have a right of appeal to the board.

(e) A written resolution, signed by both parties, of a dispute pursuant to the procedure that is not in conflict with the law or the governing documents binds the association and is judicially enforceable. A written agreement, signed by both parties, reached pursuant to the procedure that is not in conflict with the law or the governing documents binds the parties and is judicially enforceable.

(f) The procedure shall provide a means by which the member and the association may explain their positions. The member and association may be assisted by an attorney or another person in explaining their positions at their own cost.

(g) A member of the association shall not be charged a fee to participate in the process. **Leg.H.** Added Stats 2012 ch 180 §2 (AB 805), effective January 1, 2013, operative January 1, 2014. Amended Stats 2014 ch 411 §1 (AB 1738), effective January 1, 2015; Stats 2015 ch 303 §34 (AB 731), effective January 1, 2016.

§5910.1. Internal dispute resolution as condition precedent to civil action

An association may not file a civil action regarding a dispute in which the member has requested dispute resolution unless the association has complied with Section 5910 by engaging in good faith in the internal dispute resolution procedures after a member invokes those procedures. **Leg.H.** Added Stats 2019 ch 848 §8 (SB 323), effective January 1, 2020.

§5915. Default meet and confer procedure

(a) This section applies to an association that does not otherwise provide a fair, reasonable, and expeditious dispute resolution procedure. The procedure provided in this section is fair, reasonable, and expeditious within the meaning of this article.

(b) Either party to a dispute within the scope of this article may invoke the following procedure:

(1) The party may request the other party to meet and confer in an effort to resolve the dispute. The request shall be in writing.

(2) A member of an association may refuse a request to meet and confer. The association shall not refuse a request to meet and confer.

(3) The board shall designate a director to meet and confer.

(4) The parties shall meet promptly at a mutually convenient time and place, explain their positions to each other, and confer in good faith in an effort to resolve the dispute. The parties may be assisted by an attorney or another person at their own cost when conferring.

(5) A resolution of the dispute agreed to by the parties shall be memorialized in writing and signed by the parties, including the board designee on behalf of the association.

(c) A written agreement reached under this section binds the parties and is judicially enforceable if it is signed by both parties and both of the following conditions are satisfied:

(1) The agreement is not in conflict with law or the governing documents of the common interest development or association.

(2) The agreement is either consistent with the authority granted by the board to its designee or the agreement is ratified by the board.

(d) A member shall not be charged a fee to participate in the process. **Leg.H.** Added Stats 2012 ch 180 §2 (AB 805), effective January 1, 2014. Amended Stats 2014 ch 411 §2 (AB 1738), effective January 1, 2015; Stats 2015 ch 303 §35 (AB 731), effective January 1, 2016.

§5920. Notice in policy statement

The annual policy statement prepared pursuant to Section 5310 shall include a description of the internal dispute resolution process provided pursuant to this article. **Leg.H.** Added Stats 2012 ch 180 §2 (AB 805), effective January 1, 2013, operative January 1, 2014.

ARTICLE 3
Alternative Dispute Resolution Prerequisite to Civil Action

Definitions. §5925.
ADR prerequisite to enforcement action. §5930.
Request for resolution. §5935.
ADR process. §5940.
Tolling of statute of limitations. §5945.
Certification of efforts to resolve dispute. §5950.
Stay of litigation for dispute resolution. §5955.
Attorney's fees. §5960.
Notice in annual policy statement. §5965.

§5925. Definitions

As used in this article:

(a) "Alternative dispute resolution" means mediation, arbitration, conciliation, or other nonjudicial procedure that involves a neutral party in the decisionmaking process. The form of alternative dispute resolution chosen pursuant to this article may be binding or nonbinding, with the voluntary consent of the parties.

(b) "Enforcement action" means a civil action or proceeding, other than a cross-complaint, for any of the following purposes:

(1) Enforcement of this act.

(2) Enforcement of the Nonprofit Mutual Benefit Corporation Law (Part 3 (commencing with Section 7110) of Division 2 of Title 1 of the Corporations Code).

(3) Enforcement of the governing documents. **Leg.H.** Added Stats 2012 ch 180 §2 (AB 805), effective January 1, 2013, operative January 1, 2014.

§5930. ADR prerequisite to enforcement action

(a) An association or a member may not file an enforcement action in the superior court unless the parties have endeavored to submit their dispute to alternative dispute resolution pursuant to this article.

(b) This section applies only to an enforcement action that is solely for declaratory, injunctive, or writ relief, or for that relief in conjunction with a claim for monetary damages not in excess of the jurisdictional limits stated in Sections 116.220 and 116.221 of the Code of Civil Procedure.

(c) This section does not apply to a small claims action.

(d) Except as otherwise provided by law, this section does not apply to an assessment dispute. **Leg.H.** Added Stats 2012 ch 180 §2 (AB 805), effective January 1, 2013, operative January 1, 2014.

§5935. Request for resolution

(a) Any party to a dispute may initiate the process required by Section 5930 by serving on all other parties to the dispute a Request for Resolution. The Request for Resolution shall include all of the following:

(1) A brief description of the dispute between the parties.

(2) A request for alternative dispute resolution.

(3) A notice that the party receiving the Request for Resolution is required to respond within 30 days of receipt or the request will be deemed rejected.

(4) If the party on whom the request is served is the member, a copy of this article.

(b) Service of the Request for Resolution shall be by personal delivery, first-class mail, express mail, facsimile transmission, or other means reasonably calculated to provide the party on whom the request is served actual notice of the request.

(c) A party on whom a Request for Resolution is served has 30 days following service to accept or reject the request. If a party does not accept the request within that period, the request is deemed rejected by the party. **Leg.H.** Added Stats 2012 ch 180 §2 (AB 805), effective January 1, 2013, operative January 1, 2014.

§5940. ADR process

(a) If the party on whom a Request for Resolution is served accepts the request, the parties shall complete the alternative dispute resolution within 90 days after the party initiating the request receives the acceptance, unless this period is extended by written stipulation signed by both parties.

(b) Chapter 2 (commencing with Section 1115) of Division 9 of the Evidence Code applies to any form of alternative dispute resolution initiated by a Request for Resolution under this article, other than arbitration.

(c) The costs of the alternative dispute resolution shall be borne by the parties. **Leg.H.** Added Stats 2012 ch 180 §2 (AB 805), effective January 1, 2013, operative January 1, 2014.

§5945. Tolling of statute of limitations

If a Request for Resolution is served before the end of the applicable time limitation for commencing an enforcement action, the time limitation is tolled during the following periods:

(a) The period provided in Section 5935 for response to a Request for Resolution.

(b) If the Request for Resolution is accepted, the period provided by Section 5940 for completion of alternative dispute resolution, including any extension of time stipulated to by the parties pursuant to Section 5940. **Leg.H.** Added Stats 2012 ch 180 §2 (AB 805), effective January 1, 2013, operative January 1, 2014.

§5950. Certification of efforts to resolve dispute

(a) At the time of commencement of an enforcement action, the party commencing the action shall file with the initial pleading a certificate stating that one or more of the following conditions are satisfied:

(1) Alternative dispute resolution has been completed in compliance with this article.

(2) One of the other parties to the dispute did not accept the terms offered for alternative dispute resolution.

(3) Preliminary or temporary injunctive relief is necessary.

(b) Failure to file a certificate pursuant to subdivision (a) is grounds for a demurrer or a motion to strike unless the court finds that dismissal of the action for failure to comply with this article would result in substantial prejudice to one of the parties. **Leg.H.** Added Stats 2012 ch 180 §2 (AB 805), effective January 1, 2013, operative January 1, 2014.

§5955. Stay of litigation for dispute resolution

(a) After an enforcement action is commenced, on written stipulation of the parties, the matter may be referred to alternative dispute resolution. The referred action is stayed. During the stay, the action is not subject to the rules implementing subdivision (c) of Section 68603 of the Government Code.

(b) The costs of the alternative dispute resolution shall be borne by the parties. **Leg.H.** Added Stats 2012 ch 180 §2 (AB 805), effective January 1, 2013, operative January 1, 2014.

§5960. Attorney's fees

In an enforcement action in which attorney's fees and costs may be awarded, the court, in determining the amount of the award, may consider whether a party's refusal to participate in alternative dispute resolution before commencement of the action was reasonable. **Leg.H.** Added Stats 2012 ch 180 §2 (AB 805), effective January 1, 2013, operative January 1, 2014.

§5965. Notice in annual policy statement

(a) An association shall annually provide its members a summary of the provisions of this article that specifically references this article. The summary shall include the following language:

"Failure of a member of the association to comply with the alternative dispute resolution requirements of Section 5930 of the Civil Code may result in the loss of the member's right to sue the association or another member of the association regarding enforcement of the governing documents or the applicable law."

(b) The summary shall be included in the annual policy statement prepared pursuant to Section 5310. **Leg.H.** Added Stats 2012 ch 180 §2 (AB 805), effective January 1, 2013, operative January 1, 2014.

ARTICLE 4
Civil Action

Enforcement of governing documents. §5975.
Standing. §5980.
Comparative fault. §5985.
Legal proceedings against declarant, developer, or builder; Limitations in governing documents; Effect of statute of limitations. §5986.

§5975. Enforcement of governing documents

(a) The covenants and restrictions in the declaration shall be enforceable equitable servitudes, unless unreasonable, and shall inure to the benefit of and bind all owners of separate interests in the development. Unless the declaration states otherwise, these servitudes may be enforced by any owner of a separate interest or by the association, or by both.

(b) A governing document other than the declaration may be enforced by the association against an owner of a separate interest or by an owner of a separate interest against the association.

(c) In an action to enforce the governing documents, the prevailing party shall be awarded reasonable attorney's fees and costs. **Leg.H.** Added Stats 2012 ch 180 §2 (AB 805), effective January 1, 2013, operative January 1, 2014.

§5980. Standing

An association has standing to institute, defend, settle, or intervene in litigation, arbitration, mediation, or administrative proceedings in its own name as the real party in interest and without joining with it the members, in matters pertaining to the following:

(a) Enforcement of the governing documents.

(b) Damage to the common area.

(c) Damage to a separate interest that the association is obligated to maintain or repair.

(d) Damage to a separate interest that arises out of, or is integrally related to, damage to the common area or a separate interest that the association is obligated to maintain or repair. **Leg.H.** Added Stats 2012 ch 180 §2 (AB 805), effective January 1, 2013, operative January 1, 2014.

§5985. Comparative fault

(a) In an action maintained by an association pursuant to subdivision (b), (c), or (d) of Section 5980, the amount of damages recovered by the association shall be reduced by the amount of damages allocated to the association or its managing agents in direct proportion to their percentage of fault based upon principles of comparative fault. The comparative fault of the association or its managing agents may be raised by way of defense, but shall not be the basis for a cross-action or separate action against the association or its managing agents for contribution or implied indemnity, where the only damage was sustained by the association or its members. It is the intent of the Legislature in enacting this subdivision to require that comparative fault be pleaded as an affirmative defense, rather than a separate cause of action, where the only damage was sustained by the association or its members.

(b) In an action involving damages described in subdivision (b), (c), or (d) of Section 5980, the defendant or cross-defendant may allege and prove the comparative fault of the association or its managing agents as a setoff to the liability of the defendant or cross-defendant even if the association is not a party to the litigation or is no longer a party whether by reason of settlement, dismissal, or otherwise.

(c) Subdivisions (a) and (b) apply to actions commenced on or after January 1, 1993.

(d) Nothing in this section affects a person's liability under Section 1431, or the liability of the association or its managing agent for an act or omission that causes damages to another. **Leg.H.** Added Stats 2012 ch 180 §2 (AB 805), effective January 1, 2013, operative January 1, 2014.

§5986. Legal proceedings against declarant, developer, or builder; Limitations in governing documents; Effect of statute of limitations

(a) Subject to compliance with Section 6150, which requires the board to provide notice of a meeting with the members to discuss, among other things, problems that may lead to the filing of a civil action, before the board files a civil action against a declarant or other developer, or within 30 days after it files the action, if the association has reason to believe that the applicable statute of limitations will expire, and notwithstanding any provision to the contrary in the governing documents, the board shall have the authority to commence and pursue a claim, civil action, arbitration, prelitigation process pursuant to Section 6000 or Title 7 (commencing with Section 895) of Part 2 of Division 2, or other legal proceeding against a declarant, developer, or builder of a common interest development. If the board includes members appointed by, or affiliated with, the declarant, developer, or builder, the decision and authority to commence and pursue legal proceedings shall be vested solely in the nonaffiliated board members.

(b) The governing documents shall not impose any preconditions or limitations on the board's authority to commence and pursue any claim, civil action, arbitration, prelitigation process pursuant to Section 6000 or Title 7 (commencing with Section 895) of Part 2 of Division 2, or other legal proceeding against a declarant, developer, or builder of a common interest development. Any limitation or precondition, including, but not limited to, requiring a membership vote as a prerequisite to, or otherwise providing the declarant, developer, or builder with veto authority over, the board's commencement and pursuit of a claim, civil action, arbitration, prelitigation process, or legal proceeding against the declarant, developer, or builder, or any incidental decision of the board, including, but not limited to, retaining legal counsel or incurring costs or expenses, is unenforceable, null, and void. The failure to comply with those limitations or preconditions, if only, shall not be asserted as a defense to any claim or action described in this section.

(c) Notwithstanding subdivision (a) or (b), any provision in the governing documents imposing limitations or preconditions on the board's authority to commence and pursue claims shall be valid and enforceable if the provision is adopted solely by the nondeclarant affiliated members of the association and the provision is adopted in accordance with the requirements necessary to amend the governing documents of the association.

(d) This section applies to all governing documents, whether recorded before or after the effective date of this section, and applies retroactively to claims initiated before the effective date of this section, except if those claims have been resolved through an executed settlement, a final arbitration decision, or a final judicial decision on the merits.

(e) Nothing in this section extends any applicable statute of limitation or repose to file or initiate any claim, civil action, arbitration, prelitigation process, or other legal proceeding. Nothing in this section shall affect any other obligations of an association contained in Title 7 (commencing with Section 895) of Part 2 of Division 2, or any other provision in the covenants, conditions, and restrictions of the association related to arbitration or other alternative dispute resolution procedures. **Leg.H.** Added Stats 2019 ch 207 §2 (SB 326), effective January 1, 2020.

CHAPTER 11
CONSTRUCTION DEFECT LITIGATION

Notice of resolution. §6100.
Notice of civil action. §6150.

§6100. Notice of resolution

(a) As soon as is reasonably practicable after the association and the builder have entered into a settlement agreement or the matter has otherwise been resolved regarding alleged defects in the common areas, alleged defects in the separate interests that the association is obligated to maintain or repair, or alleged defects in the separate interests that arise out of, or are integrally related to, defects in the common areas or separate interests that the association is obligated to maintain or repair, where the defects giving rise to the dispute have not been corrected, the association shall, in writing, inform only the members of the association whose names appear on the records of the association that the matter has been resolved, by settlement agreement or other means, and disclose all of the following:

(1) A general description of the defects that the association reasonably believes, as of the date of the disclosure, will be corrected or replaced.

(2) A good faith estimate, as of the date of the disclosure, of when the association believes that the defects identified in paragraph (1) will be corrected or replaced. The association may state that the estimate may be modified.

(3) The status of the claims for defects in the design or construction of the common interest development that were not identified in paragraph (1) whether expressed in a preliminary list of defects sent to each member of the association or otherwise claimed and disclosed to the members of the association.

(b) Nothing in this section shall preclude an association from amending the disclosures required pursuant to subdivision (a), and any amendments shall supersede any prior conflicting information disclosed to the members of the association and shall retain any privilege attached to the original disclosures.

(c) Disclosure of the information required pursuant to subdivision (a) or authorized by subdivision (b) shall not waive any privilege attached to the information.

(d) For the purposes of the disclosures required pursuant to this section, the term "defects" shall be defined to include any damage resulting from defects. **Leg.H.** Added Stats 2012 ch 180 §2 (AB 805), effective January 1, 2013, operative January 1, 2014.

§6150. Notice of civil action

(a) Not later than 30 days before filing of any civil action by the association against the declarant or other developer of a common interest development for alleged damage to the common areas, alleged damage to the separate interests that the association is obligated to maintain or repair, or alleged damage to the separate interests that arises out of, or is integrally related to, damage to the common areas or separate interests that the association is obligated to maintain or repair, the board shall provide a written notice to each member of the association who appears on the records of the association when the notice is provided. This notice shall specify all of the following:

(1) That a meeting will take place to discuss problems that may lead to the filing of a civil action, in addition to the potential impacts thereof to the association and its members, including any financial impacts.

(2) The options, including civil actions, that are available to address the problems.

(3) The time and place of the meeting.

(b) Notwithstanding subdivision (a), if the association has reason to believe that the applicable statute of limitations will expire before the association files the civil action, the association may give the notice, as described above, within 30 days after the filing of the action. **Leg.H.** Added Stats 2012 ch 180 §2 (AB 805), effective January 1, 2013, operative January 1, 2014. Amended Stats 2019 ch 207 §3 (SB 326), effective January 1, 2020.

PART 5.3
COMMERCIAL AND INDUSTRIAL COMMON INTEREST DEVELOPMENTS

Chapter 1. General Provisions.
Chapter 2. Application of Act.
Chapter 3. Governing Documents.
Chapter 4. Ownership and Transfer of Interests.
Chapter 5. Property Use and Maintenance.
Chapter 6. Association Governance.
Chapter 7. Assessments and Assessment Collection.
Chapter 8. Insurance and Liability.
Chapter 9. Dispute Resolution and Enforcement.
Chapter 10. Construction Defect Litigation.

CHAPTER 1
GENERAL PROVISIONS

Article 1. Preliminary Provisions.
Article 2. Definitions.

ARTICLE 1
Preliminary Provisions

Name of act. §6500.
Hierarchy titles are not law. §6502.
Act not applicable to pre-January 1, 2014 documents. §6505.
Local zoning to treat like structures alike. §6510.
Delivery of documents to an association. §6512.
Individual delivery; Individual notice. §6514.
Delivery by mail; Electronic delivery. §6518.
Electronic delivery "in writing". §6520.
Majority vote. §6522.
Majority of a quorum. §6524.

§6500. Name of act

This part shall be known, and may be cited, as the Commercial and Industrial Common Interest Development Act. In a provision of this part, the part may be referred to as the act. **Leg.H.** Added Stats 2013 ch 605 §21 (SB 752), effective January 1, 2014.

§6502. Hierarchy titles are not law

Division, part, title, chapter, article, and section headings do not in any manner affect the scope, meaning, or intent of this act. **Leg.H.** Added Stats 2013 ch 605 §21 (SB 752), effective January 1, 2014.

§6505. Act not applicable to pre-January 1, 2014 documents

Nothing in the act that added this part shall be construed to invalidate a document prepared or action taken before January 1, 2014, if the document or action was proper under the law governing common interest developments at the time that the document was prepared or the action was taken. For the purposes of this section, "document" does not include a governing document. **Leg.H.** Added Stats 2013 ch 605 §21 (SB 752), effective January 1, 2014.

§6510. Local zoning to treat like structures alike

Unless a contrary intent is clearly expressed, a local zoning ordinance is construed to treat like structures, lots, parcels, areas, or spaces in like manner regardless of the form of the common interest development. **Leg.H.** Added Stats 2013 ch 605 §21 (SB 752), effective January 1, 2014.

§6512. Delivery of documents to an association

(a) If a provision of this act requires that a document be delivered to an association, the document shall be delivered to the person designated to receive documents on behalf of the association, in a written notice delivered by the association to members by individual delivery. If notice of this designation has not been given, the document shall be delivered to the president or secretary of the association.

(b) A document delivered pursuant to this section may be delivered by any of the following methods:

(1) First-class mail, postage prepaid, registered or certified mail, express mail, or overnight delivery by an express service carrier.

(2) By email, facsimile, or other electronic means, if the association has assented to that method of delivery.

(3) By personal delivery, if the association has assented to that method of delivery. If the association accepts a document by personal delivery it shall provide a written receipt acknowledging delivery of the document. **Leg.H.** Added Stats 2013 ch 605 §21 (SB 752), effective January 1, 2014.

§6514. Individual delivery; Individual notice

(a) If a provision of this act requires that an association deliver a document by "individual delivery" or "individual notice," the document shall be delivered by one of the following methods:

(1) First-class mail, postage prepaid, registered or certified mail, express mail, or overnight delivery by an express service carrier. The document shall be addressed to the recipient at the address last shown on the books of the association.

(2) Email, facsimile, or other electronic means, if the recipient has consented, in writing, to that method of delivery. The consent may be revoked, in writing, by the recipient.

(b) For the purposes of this section, an unrecorded provision of the governing documents providing for a particular method of delivery does not constitute agreement by a member to that method of delivery. **Leg.H.** Added Stats 2013 ch 605 §21 (SB 752), effective January 1, 2014.

§6518. Delivery by mail; Electronic delivery

(a) This section governs the delivery of a document pursuant to this act.

(b) If a document is delivered by mail, delivery is deemed to be complete on deposit into the United States mail.

(c) If a document is delivered by electronic means, delivery is complete at the time of transmission. **Leg.H.** Added Stats 2013 ch 605 §21 (SB 752), effective January 1, 2014.

§6520. Electronic delivery "in writing"

If the association or a member has consented to receive information by electronic delivery, and a provision of this act requires that the information be in writing, that requirement is satisfied if the information is provided in an electronic record capable of retention by the recipient at the time of receipt. An electronic record is not capable of retention by the recipient if the sender or its information processing system inhibits the ability of the recipient to print or store the electronic record. **Leg.H.** Added Stats 2013 ch 605 §21 (SB 752), effective January 1, 2014.

§6522. Majority vote

If a provision of this act requires that an action be approved by a majority of all members, the action shall be approved or ratified by an affirmative vote of a majority of the votes entitled to be cast. **Leg.H.** Added Stats 2013 ch 605 §21 (SB 752), effective January 1, 2014.

§6524. Majority of a quorum

If a provision of this act requires that an action be approved by a majority of a quorum of the members, the action shall be approved or ratified by an affirmative vote of a majority of the votes represented and voting in a duly held election in which a quorum is represented, which affirmative votes also constitute a majority of the required quorum. **Leg.H.** Added Stats 2013 ch 605 §21 (SB 752), effective January 1, 2014.

ARTICLE 2
Definitions

Definitions govern construction of act. §6526.
Association. §6528.
Board. §6530.
Commercial or industrial common interest development. §6531.
Common area. §6532.
Common interest development. §6534.
Condominium plan. §6540.
Condominium project. §6542.
Declarant. §6544.
Declaration. §6546.
Director. §6548.
Exclusive use common area. §6550.
Governing documents. §6552.
Individual notice. §6553.
Member. §6554.
Person. §6560.

Planned development. §6562.
Separate interest. §6564.
Stock cooperative. §6566.

§6526. Definitions govern construction of act
The definitions in this article govern the construction of this act. **Leg.H.** Added Stats 2013 ch 605 §21 (SB 752), effective January 1, 2014.

§6528. Association
"Association" means a nonprofit corporation or unincorporated association created for the purpose of managing a common interest development. **Leg.H.** Added Stats 2013 ch 605 §21 (SB 752), effective January 1, 2014.

§6530. Board
"Board" means the board of directors of the association. **Leg.H.** Added Stats 2013 ch 605 §21 (SB 752), effective January 1, 2014.

§6531. Commercial or industrial common interest development
A "commercial or industrial common interest development" means a common interest development that is limited to industrial or commercial uses by law or by a declaration of covenants, conditions, and restrictions that has been recorded in the official records of each county in which the common interest development is located. For the purposes of this section, "commercial use" includes, but is not limited to, the operation of a business that provides facilities for the overnight stay of its customers, employees, or agents. **Leg.H.** Added Stats 2013 ch 605 §21 (SB 752), effective January 1, 2014.

§6532. Common area
(a) "Common area" means the entire common interest development except the separate interests therein. The estate in the common area may be a fee, a life estate, an estate for years, or any combination of the foregoing.

(b) Notwithstanding subdivision (a), in a planned development described in subdivision (b) of Section 6562, the common area may consist of mutual or reciprocal easement rights appurtenant to the separate interests. **Leg.H.** Added Stats 2013 ch 605 §21 (SB 752), effective January 1, 2014.

§6534. Common interest development
"Common interest development" means any of the following:
(a) A condominium project.
(b) A planned development.
(c) A stock cooperative. **Leg.H.** Added Stats 2013 ch 605 §21 (SB 752), effective January 1, 2014.

§6540. Condominium plan
"Condominium plan" means a plan described in Section 6624. **Leg.H.** Added Stats 2013 ch 605 §21 (SB 752), effective January 1, 2014.

§6542. Condominium project
(a) A "condominium project" means a real property development consisting of condominiums.

(b) A condominium consists of an undivided interest in common in a portion of real property coupled with a separate interest in space called a unit, the boundaries of which are described on a recorded final map, parcel map, or condominium plan in sufficient detail to locate all boundaries thereof. The area within these boundaries may be filled with air, earth, water, or fixtures, or any combination thereof, and need not be physically attached to land except by easements for access and, if necessary, support. The description of the unit may refer to (1) boundaries described in the recorded final map, parcel map, or condominium plan, (2) physical boundaries, either in existence, or to be constructed, such as walls, floors, and ceilings of a structure or any portion thereof, (3) an entire structure containing one or more units, or (4) any combination thereof.

(c) The portion or portions of the real property held in undivided interest may be all of the real property, except for the separate interests, or may include a particular three-dimensional portion thereof, the boundaries of which are described on a recorded final map, parcel map, or condominium plan. The area within these boundaries may be filled with air, earth, water, or fixtures, or any combination thereof, and need not be physically attached to land except by easements for access and, if necessary, support.

(d) An individual condominium within a condominium project may include, in addition, a separate interest in other portions of the real property. **Leg.H.** Added Stats 2013 ch 605 §21 (SB 752), effective January 1, 2014.

§6544. Declarant
"Declarant" means the person or group of persons designated in the declaration as declarant, or if no declarant is designated, the person or group of persons who sign the original declaration or who succeed to special rights, preferences, or privileges designated in the declaration as belonging to the signator of the original declaration. **Leg.H.** Added Stats 2013 ch 605 §21 (SB 752), effective January 1, 2014.

§6546. Declaration
"Declaration" means the document, however denominated, that contains the information required by Section 6614. **Leg.H.** Added Stats 2013 ch 605 §21 (SB 752), effective January 1, 2014.

§6548. Director
"Director" means a natural person who serves on the board. **Leg.H.** Added Stats 2013 ch 605 §21 (SB 752), effective January 1, 2014.

§6550. Exclusive use common area
(a) "Exclusive use common area" means a portion of the common area designated by the declaration for the exclusive use of one or more, but fewer than all, of the owners of the separate interests and which is or will be appurtenant to the separate interest or interests.

(b) Unless the declaration otherwise provides, any shutters, awnings, window boxes, doorsteps, stoops, porches, balconies, patios, exterior doors, doorframes, and hardware incident thereto, screens and windows or other fixtures designed to serve a single separate interest, but located outside the boundaries of the separate interest, are exclusive use common area allocated exclusively to that separate interest.

(c) Notwithstanding the provisions of the declaration, internal and external telephone wiring designed to serve a single separate interest, but located outside the boundaries of the separate interest, is exclusive use common area allocated exclusively to that separate interest. **Leg.H.** Added Stats 2013 ch 605 §21 (SB 752), effective January 1, 2014.

§6552. Governing documents
"Governing documents" means the declaration and any other documents, such as bylaws, operating rules, articles of incorporation, or articles of association, which govern the operation of the common interest development or association. **Leg.H.** Added Stats 2013 ch 605 §21 (SB 752), effective January 1, 2014.

§6553. Individual notice
"Individual notice" means the delivery of a document pursuant to Section 6514. **Leg.H.** Added Stats 2013 ch 605 §21 (SB 752), effective January 1, 2014.

§6554. Member
"Member" means an owner of a separate interest. **Leg.H.** Added Stats 2013 ch 605 §21 (SB 752), effective January 1, 2014.

§6560. Person
"Person" means a natural person, corporation, government or governmental subdivision or agency, business trust, estate, trust, partnership, limited liability company, association, or other entity. **Leg.H.** Added Stats 2013 ch 605 §21 (SB 752), effective January 1, 2014.

§6562. Planned development
"Planned development" means a real property development other than a condominium project, or a stock cooperative, having either or both of the following features:

(a) Common area that is owned either by an association or in common by the owners of the separate interests who possess appurtenant rights to the beneficial use and enjoyment of the common area.

(b) Common area and an association that maintains the common area with the power to levy assessments that may become a lien upon the separate interests in accordance with Article 2 (commencing with Section 6808) of Chapter 7. **Leg.H.** Added Stats 2013 ch 605 §21 (SB 752), effective January 1, 2014.

§6564. Separate interest
(a) "Separate interest" has the following meanings:

(1) In a condominium project, "separate interest" means a separately owned unit, as specified in Section 6542.

(2) In a planned development, "separate interest" means a separately owned lot, parcel, area, or space.

(3) In a stock cooperative, "separate interest" means the exclusive right to occupy a portion of the real property, as specified in Section 6566.

(b) Unless the declaration or condominium plan, if any exists, otherwise provides, if walls, floors, or ceilings are designated as boundaries of a separate interest, the interior surfaces of the perimeter walls, floors, ceilings, windows, doors, and outlets located within the separate interest are part of the separate interest and any other portions of the walls, floors, or ceilings are part of the common area.

(c) The estate in a separate interest may be a fee, a life estate, an estate for years, or any combination of the foregoing. **Leg.H.** Added Stats 2013 ch 605 §21 (SB 752), effective January 1, 2014.

§6566. Stock cooperative

"Stock cooperative" means a development in which a corporation is formed or availed of, primarily for the purpose of holding title to, either in fee simple or for a term of years, improved real property, and all or substantially all of the shareholders of the corporation receive a right of exclusive occupancy in a portion of the real property, title to which is held by the corporation. The owners' interest in the corporation, whether evidenced by a share of stock, a certificate of membership, or otherwise, shall be deemed to be an interest in a common interest development and a real estate development for purposes of subdivision (f) of Section 25100 of the Corporations Code. **Leg.H.** Added Stats 2013 ch 605 §21 (SB 752), effective January 1, 2014.

CHAPTER 2
APPLICATION OF ACT

Creation of common interest development. §6580.
Act applicable only to commercial or industrial common interest development. §6582.

§6580. Creation of common interest development

Subject to Section 6582, this act applies and a common interest development is created whenever a separate interest coupled with an interest in the common area or membership in the association is, or has been, conveyed, provided all of the following are recorded:

(a) A declaration.

(b) A condominium plan, if any exists.

(c) A final map or parcel map, if Division 2 (commencing with Section 66410) of Title 7 of the Government Code requires the recording of either a final map or parcel map for the common interest development. **Leg.H.** Added Stats 2013 ch 605 §21 (SB 752), effective January 1, 2014.

§6582. Act applicable only to commercial or industrial common interest development

(a) This act applies only to a commercial or industrial common interest development.

(b) Nothing in this act may be construed to apply to a real property development that does not contain common area. This subdivision is declaratory of existing law. **Leg.H.** Added Stats 2013 ch 605 §21 (SB 752), effective January 1, 2014.

CHAPTER 3
GOVERNING DOCUMENTS

Article 1. General Provisions.
Article 2. Declaration.
Article 3. Articles of Incorporation.
Article 4. Condominium Plan.
Article 5. Operating Rules.

ARTICLE 1
General Provisions

Conflicts between various laws and documents. §6600.
Liberal construction. §6602.
Actual physical boundaries control. §6604.
Restrictive covenants. §6606.
Deletion of terms regarding developer. §6608.
Reference in documents to Davis-Stirling Act. §6610.

§6600. Conflicts between various laws and documents

(a) To the extent of any conflict between the governing documents and the law, the law shall prevail.

(b) To the extent of any conflict between the articles of incorporation and the declaration, the declaration shall prevail.

(c) To the extent of any conflict between the bylaws and the articles of incorporation or declaration, the articles of incorporation or declaration shall prevail.

(d) To the extent of any conflict between the operating rules and the bylaws, articles of incorporation, or declaration, the bylaws, articles of incorporation, or declaration shall prevail. **Leg.H.** Added Stats 2013 ch 605 §21 (SB 752), effective January 1, 2014.

§6602. Liberal construction

Any deed, declaration, or condominium plan for a common interest development shall be liberally construed to facilitate the operation of the common interest development, and its provisions shall be presumed to be independent and severable. Nothing in Article 3 (commencing with Section 715) of Chapter 2 of Title 2 of Part 1 of Division 2 shall operate to invalidate any provisions of the governing documents. **Leg.H.** Added Stats 2013 ch 605 §21 (SB 752), effective January 1, 2014.

§6604. Actual physical boundaries control

In interpreting deeds and condominium plans, the existing physical boundaries of a unit in a condominium project, when the boundaries of the unit are contained within a building, or of a unit reconstructed in substantial accordance with the original plans thereof, shall be conclusively presumed to be its boundaries rather than the metes and bounds expressed in the deed or condominium plan, if any exists, regardless of settling or lateral movement of the building and regardless of minor variance between boundaries shown on the plan or in the deed and those of the building. **Leg.H.** Added Stats 2013 ch 605 §21 (SB 752), effective January 1, 2014.

§6606. Restrictive covenants

(a) No declaration or other governing document shall include a restrictive covenant in violation of Section 12955 of the Government Code.

(b) Notwithstanding any other provision of law or provision of the governing documents, the board, without approval of the members, shall amend any declaration or other governing document that includes a restrictive covenant prohibited by this section to delete the restrictive covenant, and shall restate the declaration or other governing document without the restrictive covenant but with no other change to the declaration or governing document.

(c) If the declaration is amended under this section, the board shall record the restated declaration in each county in which the common interest development is located. If the articles of incorporation are amended under this section, the board shall file a certificate of amendment with the Secretary of State pursuant to Section 7814 of the Corporations Code.

(d) If after providing written notice to an association, pursuant to Section 6512, requesting that the association delete a restrictive covenant that violates subdivision (a), and the association fails to delete the restrictive covenant within 30 days of receiving the notice, Civil Rights Department, a city or county in which a common interest development is located, or any person may bring an action against the association for injunctive relief to enforce subdivision (a). The court may award attorney's fees to the prevailing party. **Leg.H.** Added Stats 2013 ch 605 §21 (SB 752), effective January 1, 2014. Amended Stats 2022 ch 48 §8 (SB 189), effective June 30, 2022.

§6608. Deletion of terms regarding developer

(a) Notwithstanding any provision of the governing documents to the contrary, the board may, after the developer has completed construction of the development, has terminated construction activities, and has terminated marketing activities for the sale, lease, or other disposition of separate interests within the development, adopt an amendment deleting from any of the governing documents any provision which is unequivocally designed and intended, or which by its nature can only have been designed or intended, to facilitate the developer in completing the construction or marketing of the development. However, provisions of the governing documents relative to a particular construction or marketing phase of the development may not be deleted under the authorization of this subdivision until that construction or marketing phase has been completed.

(b) The provisions which may be deleted by action of the board shall be limited to those which provide for access by the developer over or across the common area for the purposes of (1) completion of construction of the development, and (2) the erection, construction, or maintenance of structures or other facilities designed to facilitate the completion of construction or marketing of separate interests.

(c) At least 30 days prior to taking action pursuant to subdivision (a), the board shall deliver to all members, by individual delivery pursuant to Section 6514, (1) a copy of all amendments to the governing documents proposed to be adopted under subdivision (a), and (2) a notice of the time, date, and place the board will consider adoption of the amendments.

The board may consider adoption of amendments to the governing documents pursuant to subdivision (a) only at a meeting that is open to all members, who shall be given opportunity to make comments thereon. All deliberations of the board on any action proposed under subdivision (a) shall only be conducted in an open meeting.

(d) The board may not amend the governing documents pursuant to this section without the approval of a majority of a quorum of the members, pursuant to Section 6524. For the purposes of this section, "quorum" means more than 50 percent of the members who own no more than two separate interests in the development. **Leg.H.** Added Stats 2013 ch 605 §21 (SB 752), effective January 1, 2014.

§6610. Reference in documents to Davis-Stirling Act

(a) Notwithstanding any other law or provision of the governing documents, if the governing documents include a reference to a provision of the Davis-Stirling Common Interest Development Act that was continued in a new provision by the act that added this section, the board may amend the governing documents, solely to correct the cross-reference, by adopting a board resolution that shows the correction. Member approval is not required in order to adopt a resolution pursuant to this section.

(b) A declaration that is corrected under this section may be restated in corrected form and recorded, provided that a copy of the board resolution authorizing the corrections is recorded along with the restated declaration. **Leg.H.** Added Stats 2013 ch 605 §21 (SB 752), effective January 1, 2014.

ARTICLE 2
Declaration

Contents. §6614.
Declarations are amendable. §6616.
Extension of termination date. §6618.
Amendments. §6620.

§6614. Contents

(a) A declaration, recorded on or after January 1, 1986, shall contain a legal description of the common interest development, and a statement that the common interest development is a condominium project, planned development, stock cooperative, or combination thereof. The declaration shall additionally set forth the name of the association and the restrictions on the use or enjoyment of any portion of the common interest development that are intended to be enforceable equitable servitudes.

(b) The declaration may contain any other matters the declarant or the members consider appropriate. **Leg.H.** Added Stats 2013 ch 605 §21 (SB 752), effective January 1, 2014.

§6616. Declarations are amendable

Except to the extent that a declaration provides by its express terms that it is not amendable, in whole or in part, a declaration that fails to include provisions permitting its amendment at all times during its existence may be amended at any time. **Leg.H.** Added Stats 2013 ch 605 §21 (SB 752), effective January 1, 2014.

§6618. Extension of termination date

(a) The Legislature finds that there are common interest developments that have been created with deed restrictions that do not provide a means for the members to extend the term of the declaration. The Legislature further finds that covenants and restrictions, contained in the declaration, are an appropriate method for protecting the common plan of developments and to provide for a mechanism for financial support for the upkeep of common area including, but not limited to, roofs, roads, heating systems, and recreational facilities. If declarations terminate prematurely, common interest developments may deteriorate and the supply of affordable units could be impacted adversely. The Legislature further finds and declares that it is in the public interest to provide a vehicle for extending the term of the declaration if the extension is approved by a majority of all members, pursuant to Section 6522.

(b) A declaration that specifies a termination date, but that contains no provision for extension of the termination date, may be extended, before its termination date, by the approval of members pursuant to Section 6620.

(c) No single extension of the terms of the declaration made pursuant to this section shall exceed the initial term of the declaration or 20 years, whichever is less. However, more than one extension may occur pursuant to this section. **Leg.H.** Added Stats 2013 ch 605 §21 (SB 752), effective January 1, 2014.

§6620. Amendments

(a) A declaration may be amended pursuant to the declaration or this act. An amendment is effective after all of the following requirements have been met:

(1) The proposed amendment has been delivered by individual notice to all members not less than 15 days and not more than 60 days prior to any approval being solicited.

(2) The amendment has been approved by the percentage of members required by the declaration and any other person whose approval is required by the declaration.

(3) That fact has been certified in a writing executed and acknowledged by the officer designated in the declaration or by the association for that purpose, or if no one is designated, by the president of the association.

(4) The amendment has been recorded in each county in which a portion of the common interest development is located.

(b) If the declaration does not specify the percentage of members who must approve an amendment of the declaration, an amendment may be approved by a majority of all members, pursuant to Section 6522. **Leg.H.** Added Stats 2013 ch 605 §21 (SB 752), effective January 1, 2014.

ARTICLE 3
Articles of Incorporation

Articles of incorporation; Contents; Compliance. §6622.

§6622. Articles of incorporation; Contents; Compliance

(a) The articles of incorporation of an association filed with the Secretary of State shall include a statement, which shall be in addition to the statement of purposes of the corporation, that does all of the following:

(1) Identifies the corporation as an association formed to manage a common interest development under the Commercial and Industrial Common Interest Development Act.

(2) States the business or corporate office of the association, if any, and, if the office is not on the site of the common interest development, states the front street and nearest cross street for the physical location of the common interest development.

(3) States the name and address of the association's managing agent, if any.

(b) The statement filed by an incorporated association with the Secretary of State pursuant to Section 8210 of the Corporations Code shall also contain a statement identifying the corporation as an association formed to manage a common interest development under the Commercial and Industrial Common Interest Development Act.

(c) Documents filed prior to January 1, 2014, in compliance with former Section 1363.5, as it read on January 1, 2013, are deemed to be in compliance with this section. **Leg.H.** Added Stats 2013 ch 605 §21 (SB 752), effective January 1, 2014.

ARTICLE 4
Condominium Plan

Contents. §6624.
Signatories. §6626.
Amendment; Revocation. §6628.

§6624. Contents

A condominium plan shall contain all of the following:

(a) A description or survey map of a condominium project, which shall refer to or show monumentation on the ground.

(b) A three-dimensional description of a condominium project, one or more dimensions of which may extend for an indefinite distance upwards or downwards, in sufficient detail to identify the common area and each separate interest.

(c) A certificate consenting to the recordation of the condominium plan pursuant to this act that is signed and acknowledged as provided in Section 6626. **Leg.H.** Added Stats 2013 ch 605 §21 (SB 752), effective January 1, 2014.

§6626. Signatories

(a) The certificate consenting to the recordation of a condominium plan that is required by subdivision (c) of Section 6624 shall be signed and acknowledged by all of the following persons:

(1) The record owner of fee title to that property included in the condominium project.

(2) In the case of a condominium project that will terminate upon the termination of an estate for years, by all lessors and lessees of the estate for years.

(3) In the case of a condominium project subject to a life estate, by all life tenants and remainder interests.

(4) The trustee or the beneficiary of each recorded deed of trust, and the mortgagee of each recorded mortgage encumbering the property.

(b) Owners of mineral rights, easements, rights-of-way, and other nonpossessory interests do not need to sign the certificate.

(c) In the event a conversion to condominiums of a stock cooperative has been approved by the required number of owners, trustees, beneficiaries, and mortgagees pursuant to Section 66452.10 of the Government Code, the certificate need only be signed by those owners, trustees, beneficiaries, and mortgagees approving the conversion. **Leg.H.** Added Stats 2013 ch 605 §21 (SB 752), effective January 1, 2014.

§6628. Amendment; Revocation

A condominium plan may be amended or revoked by a recorded instrument that is acknowledged and signed by all the persons who, at the time of amendment or revocation, are persons whose signatures are required under Section 6626. **Leg.H.** Added Stats 2013 ch 605 §21 (SB 752), effective January 1, 2014.

ARTICLE 5
Operating Rules

"Operating rule". §6630.
Requirements. §6632.

§6630. "Operating rule"

For the purposes of this article, "operating rule" means a regulation adopted by the board that applies generally to the management and operation of the common interest development or the conduct of the business and affairs of the association. **Leg.H.** Added Stats 2013 ch 605 §21 (SB 752), effective January 1, 2014.

§6632. Requirements

An operating rule is valid and enforceable only if all of the following requirements are satisfied:

(a) The rule is in writing.

(b) The rule is within the authority of the board conferred by law or by the declaration, articles of incorporation or association, or bylaws of the association.

(c) The rule is not in conflict with governing law and the declaration, articles of incorporation or association, or bylaws of the association.

(d) The rule is reasonable, and is adopted, amended, or repealed in good faith. **Leg.H.** Added Stats 2013 ch 605 §21 (SB 752), effective January 1, 2014.

CHAPTER 4
OWNERSHIP AND TRANSFER OF INTERESTS

Article 1. Ownership Rights and Interests.
Article 2. Restrictions on Transfers.
Article 3. Transfer of Separate Interest.

ARTICLE 1
Ownership Rights and Interests

Common area; Tenants in common. §6650.
Right of ingress, egress, and support. §6652.
No denial of access to member's separate interest. §6654.

§6650. Common area; Tenants in common

Unless the declaration otherwise provides, in a condominium project, or in a planned development in which the common area is owned by the owners of the separate interests, the common area is owned as tenants in common, in equal shares, one for each separate interest. **Leg.H.** Added Stats 2013 ch 605 §21 (SB 752), effective January 1, 2014.

§6652. Right of ingress, egress, and support

Unless the declaration otherwise provides:

(a) In a condominium project, and in those planned developments with common area owned in common by the owners of the separate interests, there are appurtenant to each separate interest nonexclusive rights of ingress, egress, and support, if necessary, through the common area. The common area is subject to these rights.

(b) In a stock cooperative, and in a planned development with common area owned by the association, there is an easement for ingress, egress, and support, if necessary, appurtenant to each separate interest. The common area is subject to these easements. **Leg.H.** Added Stats 2013 ch 605 §21 (SB 752), effective January 1, 2014.

§6654. No denial of access to member's separate interest

Except as otherwise provided in law, an order of the court, or an order pursuant to a final and binding arbitration decision, an association may not deny a member or occupant physical access to the member's or occupant's separate interest, either by restricting access through the common area to the separate interest, or by restricting access solely to the separate interest. **Leg.H.** Added Stats 2013 ch 605 §21 (SB 752), effective January 1, 2014.

ARTICLE 2
Restrictions on Transfers

No partition of common areas; Partition actions. §6656.
Lien for work performed or materials furnished in common interest development. §6658.
Notice of claim of lien. §6660.

§6656. No partition of common areas; Partition actions

(a) Except as provided in this section, the common area in a condominium project shall remain undivided, and there shall be no judicial partition thereof. Nothing in this section shall be deemed to prohibit partition of a cotenancy in a condominium.

(b) The owner of a separate interest in a condominium project may maintain a partition action as to the entire project as if the owners of all of the separate interests in the project were tenants in common in the entire project in the same proportion as their interests in the common area. The court shall order partition under this subdivision only by sale of the entire condominium project and only upon a showing of one of the following:

(1) More than three years before the filing of the action, the condominium project was damaged or destroyed, so that a material part was rendered unfit for its prior use, and the condominium project has not been rebuilt or repaired substantially to its state prior to the damage or destruction.

(2) Three-fourths or more of the project is destroyed or substantially damaged and owners of separate interests holding in the aggregate more than a 50-percent interest in the common area oppose repair or restoration of the project.

(3) The project has been in existence more than 50 years, is obsolete and uneconomic, and owners of separate interests holding in the aggregate more than a 50-percent interest in the common area oppose repair or restoration of the project.

(4) Any conditions in the declaration for sale under the circumstances described in this subdivision have been met. **Leg.H.** Added Stats 2013 ch 605 §21 (SB 752), effective January 1, 2014.

§6658. Lien for work performed or materials furnished in common interest development

(a) In a common interest development, no labor performed or services or materials furnished with the consent of, or at the request of, an owner in the common interest development or the owners' agent or contractor shall be the basis for the filing of a lien against any other property of any other owner in the common interest development unless that other owner has expressly consented to or requested the performance of the labor or furnishing of the materials or services. However, express consent shall be deemed to have been given by the owner of any separate interest in the case of emergency repairs thereto.

(b) Labor performed or services or materials furnished for the common area, if duly authorized by the association, shall be deemed to be performed or furnished with the express consent of each separate interest owner.

(c) The owner of any separate interest may remove that owner's separate interest from a lien against two or more separate interests or any part thereof by doing either of the following:

(1) Pay to the holder of the lien the fraction of the total sum secured by the lien that is attributable to the owner's separate interest.

(2) Record a lien release bond, pursuant to Section 8424, in an amount equal to 125 percent of the sum secured by the lien that is attributable to the owner's separate interest. **Leg.H.** Added Stats 2013 ch 605 §21 (SB

752), effective January 1, 2014. Amended Stats 2017 ch 44 §3 (AB 534), effective January 1, 2018.

§6660. Notice of claim of lien

If the association is served with a claim of lien pursuant to Part 6 (commencing with Section 8000) for a work of improvement on a common area, the association shall, within 60 days of service, give individual notice to the members, pursuant to Section 6514. **Leg.H.** Added Stats 2017 ch 44 §4 (AB 534), effective January 1, 2018.

ARTICLE 3
Transfer of Separate Interest

Condominium sale includes common areas. §6662.
Planned development sale includes common areas. §6664.
Stock cooperative sale includes common areas. §6666.
Transfer of exclusive use areas. §6668.
Restrictions on the severability of component interests. §6670.

§6662. Condominium sale includes common areas

In a condominium project the common area is not subject to partition, except as provided in Section 6656. Any conveyance, judicial sale, or other voluntary or involuntary transfer of the separate interest includes the undivided interest in the common area. Any conveyance, judicial sale, or other voluntary or involuntary transfer of the owner's entire estate also includes the owner's membership interest in the association. **Leg.H.** Added Stats 2013 ch 605 §21 (SB 752), effective January 1, 2014.

§6664. Planned development sale includes common areas

In a planned development, any conveyance, judicial sale, or other voluntary or involuntary transfer of the separate interest includes the undivided interest in the common area, if any exists. Any conveyance, judicial sale, or other voluntary or involuntary transfer of the owner's entire estate also includes the owner's membership interest in the association. **Leg.H.** Added Stats 2013 ch 605 §21 (SB 752), effective January 1, 2014.

§6666. Stock cooperative sale includes common areas

In a stock cooperative, any conveyance, judicial sale, or other voluntary or involuntary transfer of the separate interest includes the ownership interest in the corporation, however evidenced. Any conveyance, judicial sale, or other voluntary or involuntary transfer of the owner's entire estate also includes the owner's membership interest in the association. **Leg.H.** Added Stats 2013 ch 605 §21 (SB 752), effective January 1, 2014.

§6668. Transfer of exclusive use areas

Nothing in this article prohibits the transfer of exclusive use areas, independent of any other interest in a common interest subdivision, if authorization to separately transfer exclusive use areas is expressly stated in the declaration and the transfer occurs in accordance with the terms of the declaration. **Leg.H.** Added Stats 2013 ch 605 §21 (SB 752), effective January 1, 2014.

§6670. Restrictions on the severability of component interests

Any restrictions upon the severability of the component interests in real property which are contained in the declaration shall not be deemed conditions repugnant to the interest created within the meaning of Section 711. However, these restrictions shall not extend beyond the period in which the right to partition a project is suspended under Section 6656. **Leg.H.** Added Stats 2013 ch 605 §21 (SB 752), effective January 1, 2014.

CHAPTER 5
PROPERTY USE AND MAINTENANCE

Article 1. Protected Uses.
Article 2. Modification of Separate Interest.
Article 3. Maintenance.

ARTICLE 1
Protected Uses

Regulation of separate interest. §6700.
Display of American flag. §6702.
Display of noncommercial signage. §6704.
Pets. §6706.
Antenna; Satellite dish. §6708.
Marketing of individual interest. §6710.
Water-efficient landscaping. §6712.
Electric vehicle charging station. §6713.

§6700. Regulation of separate interest

This article includes provisions that limit the authority of an association or the governing documents to regulate the use of a member's separate interest. Nothing in this article is intended to affect the application of any other provision that limits the authority of an association to regulate the use of a member's separate interest, including, but not limited to, the following provisions:

(a) Sections 712 and 713, relating to the display of signs.

(b) Sections 714 and 714.1, relating to solar energy systems.

(c) Section 714.5, relating to structures that are constructed offsite and moved to the property in sections or modules.

(d) Sections 782, 782.5, and 6150 of this code and Section 12956.1 of the Government Code, relating to racial restrictions. **Leg.H.** Added Stats 2013 ch 605 §21 (SB 752), effective January 1, 2014.

§6702. Display of American flag

(a) Except as required for the protection of the public health or safety, no governing document shall limit or prohibit, or be construed to limit or prohibit, the display of the flag of the United States by a member on or in the member's separate interest or within the member's exclusive use common area.

(b) For purposes of this section, "display of the flag of the United States" means a flag of the United States made of fabric, cloth, or paper displayed from a staff or pole or in a window, and does not mean a depiction or emblem of the flag of the United States made of lights, paint, roofing, siding, paving materials, flora, or balloons, or any other similar building, landscaping, or decorative component.

(c) In any action to enforce this section, the prevailing party shall be awarded reasonable attorney's fees and costs. **Leg.H.** Added Stats 2013 ch 605 §21 (SB 752), effective January 1, 2014.

§6704. Display of noncommercial signage

(a) The governing documents may not prohibit posting or displaying of noncommercial signs, posters, flags, or banners on or in a member's separate interest, except as required for the protection of public health or safety or if the posting or display would violate a local, state, or federal law.

(b) For purposes of this section, a noncommercial sign, poster, flag, or banner may be made of paper, cardboard, cloth, plastic, or fabric, and may be posted or displayed from the yard, window, door, balcony, or outside wall of the separate interest, but may not be made of lights, roofing, siding, paving materials, flora, or balloons, or any other similar building, landscaping, or decorative component, or include the painting of architectural surfaces.

(c) An association may prohibit noncommercial signs and posters that are more than nine square feet in size and noncommercial flags or banners that are more than 15 square feet in size. **Leg.H.** Added Stats 2013 ch 605 §21 (SB 752), effective January 1, 2014.

§6706. Pets

Notwithstanding Section 4202, Section 4715 applies to an owner of a separate interest in a common interest development who kept a pet in that common interest development before January 1, 2014. **Leg.H.** Added Stats 2013 ch 605 §21 (SB 752), effective January 1, 2014.

§6708. Antenna; Satellite dish

(a) Any covenant, condition, or restriction contained in any deed, contract, security instrument, or other instrument affecting the transfer or sale of, or any interest in, a common interest development that effectively prohibits or restricts the installation or use of a video or television antenna, including a satellite dish, or that effectively prohibits or restricts the attachment of that antenna to a structure within that development where the antenna is not visible from any street or common area, except as otherwise prohibited or restricted by law, is void and unenforceable as to its application to the installation or use of a video or television antenna that has a diameter or diagonal measurement of 36 inches or less.

(b) This section shall not apply to any covenant, condition, or restriction, as described in subdivision (a), that imposes reasonable restrictions on the installation or use of a video or television antenna, including a satellite dish, that has a diameter or diagonal measurement of 36 inches or less. For purposes of this section, "reasonable restrictions" means those restrictions that do not significantly increase the cost of the video or television antenna system, including all related equipment, or significantly decrease its efficiency or performance and include all of the following:

(1) Requirements for application and notice to the association prior to the installation.

(2) Requirement of a member to obtain the approval of the association for the installation of a video or television antenna that has a diameter or diagonal measurement of 36 inches or less on a separate interest owned by another.

(3) Provision for the maintenance, repair, or replacement of roofs or other building components.

(4) Requirements for installers of a video or television antenna to indemnify or reimburse the association or its members for loss or damage caused by the installation, maintenance, or use of a video or television antenna that has a diameter or diagonal measurement of 36 inches or less.

(c) Whenever approval is required for the installation or use of a video or television antenna, including a satellite dish, the application for approval shall be processed by the appropriate approving entity for the common interest development in the same manner as an application for approval of an architectural modification to the property, and the issuance of a decision on the application shall not be willfully delayed.

(d) In any action to enforce compliance with this section, the prevailing party shall be awarded reasonable attorney's fees. **Leg.H.** Added Stats 2013 ch 605 §21 (SB 752), effective January 1, 2014.

§6710. Marketing of individual interest

(a) Any provision of a governing document that arbitrarily or unreasonably restricts an owner's ability to market the owner's interest in a common interest development is void.

(b) No association may adopt, enforce, or otherwise impose any governing document that does either of the following:

(1) Imposes an assessment or fee in connection with the marketing of an owner's interest in an amount that exceeds the association's actual or direct costs.

(2) Establishes an exclusive relationship with a real estate broker through which the sale or marketing of interests in the development is required to occur. The limitation set forth in this paragraph does not apply to the sale or marketing of separate interests owned by the association or to the sale or marketing of common area by the association.

(c) For purposes of this section, "market" and "marketing" mean listing, advertising, or obtaining access to show the owner's interest in the development.

(d) This section does not apply to rules or regulations made pursuant to Section 712 or 713 regarding real estate signs. **Leg.H.** Added Stats 2013 ch 605 §21 (SB 752), effective January 1, 2014.

§6712. Water-efficient landscaping

(a) Notwithstanding any other law, a provision of the governing documents shall be void and unenforceable if it does any of the following:

(1) Prohibits, or includes conditions that have the effect of prohibiting, the use of low water-using plants as a group.

(2) Has the effect of prohibiting or restricting compliance with either of the following:

(A) A water-efficient landscape ordinance adopted or in effect pursuant to subdivision (c) of Section 65595 of the Government Code.

(B) Any regulation or restriction on the use of water adopted pursuant to Section 353 or 375 of the Water Code.

(b) This section shall not prohibit an association from applying landscaping rules established in the governing documents, to the extent the rules fully conform with the requirements of subdivision (a). **Leg.H.** Added Stats 2013 ch 605 §21 (SB 752), effective January 1, 2014.

§6713. Electric vehicle charging station

(a) Any covenant, restriction, or condition contained in any deed, contract, security instrument, or other instrument affecting the transfer or sale of any interest in a common interest development, and any provision of a governing document, as defined in Section 6552, that either effectively prohibits or unreasonably restricts the installation or use of an electric vehicle charging station in an owner's designated parking space, including, but not limited to, a deeded parking space, a parking space in an owner's exclusive use common area, or a parking space that is specifically designated for use by a particular owner, or is in conflict with the provisions of this section is void and unenforceable.

(b)(1) This section does not apply to provisions that impose reasonable restrictions on electric vehicle charging stations. However, it is the policy of the state to promote, encourage, and remove obstacles to the use of electric vehicle charging stations.

(2) For purposes of this section, "reasonable restrictions" are restrictions that do not significantly increase the cost of the station or significantly decrease its efficiency or specified performance.

(c) An electric vehicle charging station shall meet applicable health and safety standards and requirements imposed by state and local authorities, and all other applicable zoning, land use or other ordinances, or land use permits.

(d) For purposes of this section, "electric vehicle charging station" means a station that is designed in compliance with the California Building Standards Code and delivers electricity from a source outside an electric vehicle into one or more electric vehicles. An electric vehicle charging station may include several charge points simultaneously connecting several electric vehicles to the station and any related equipment needed to facilitate charging plug-in electric vehicles.

(e) If approval is required for the installation or use of an electric vehicle charging station, the application for approval shall be processed and approved by the association in the same manner as an application for approval of an architectural modification to the property, and shall not be willfully avoided or delayed. The approval or denial of an application shall be in writing. If an application is not denied in writing within 60 days from the date of receipt of the application, the application shall be deemed approved, unless that delay is the result of a reasonable request for additional information.

(f) If the electric vehicle charging station is to be placed in a common area or an exclusive use common area, as designated in the common interest development's declaration, the following provisions apply:

(1) The owner first shall obtain approval from the association to install the electric vehicle charging station and the association shall approve the installation if the owner agrees in writing to do all of the following:

(A) Comply with the association's architectural standards for the installation of the charging station.

(B) Engage a licensed contractor to install the charging station.

(C) Within 14 days of approval, provide a certificate of insurance that names the association as an additional insured under the owner's insurance policy in the amount set forth in paragraph (3).

(D) Pay for the electricity usage associated with the charging station.

(2) The owner and each successive owner of the charging station shall be responsible for all of the following:

(A) Costs for damage to the charging station, common area, exclusive use common area, or separate interests resulting from the installation, maintenance, repair, removal, or replacement of the charging station.

(B) Costs for the maintenance, repair, and replacement of the charging station until it has been removed and for the restoration of the common area after removal.

(C) The cost of electricity associated with the charging station.

(D) Disclosing to prospective buyers the existence of any charging station of the owner and the related responsibilities of the owner under this section.

(3) The owner and each successive owner of the charging station, at all times, shall maintain a liability coverage policy in the amount of one million dollars ($1,000,000), and shall name the association as a named additional insured under the policy with a right to notice of cancellation.

(4) An owner shall not be required to maintain a liability coverage policy for an existing National Electrical Manufacturers Association standard alternating current power plug.

(g) Except as provided in subdivision (h), installation of an electric vehicle charging station for the exclusive use of an owner in a common area, that is not an exclusive use common area, shall be authorized by the association only if installation in the owner's designated parking space is impossible or unreasonably expensive. In such cases, the association shall enter into a license agreement with the owner for the use of the space in a common area, and the owner shall comply with all of the requirements in subdivision (f).

(h) The association or owners may install an electric vehicle charging station in the common area for the use of all members of the association and, in that case, the association shall develop appropriate terms of use for the charging station.

(i) An association may create a new parking space where one did not previously exist to facilitate the installation of an electric vehicle charging station.

ARTICLE 2
Assessment Payment and Delinquency

Assessment collection costs. §6808.
Payment of assessments. §6810.
Pre-lien notice to owner. §6812.
Lien; Contents. §6814.
Order of Liens. §6816.
Release of Lien. §6818.
Association failure to comply with lien procedures. §6819.

§6808. Assessment collection costs

A regular or special assessment and any late charges, reasonable fees and costs of collection, reasonable attorney's fees, if any, and interest, if any, shall be a debt of the owner of the separate interest at the time the assessment or other sums are levied. **Leg.H.** Added Stats 2013 ch 605 §21 (SB 752), effective January 1, 2014.

§6810. Payment of assessments

(a) When an owner of a separate interest makes a payment toward an assessment, the owner may request a receipt and the association shall provide it. The receipt shall indicate the date of payment and the person who received it.

(b) The association shall provide a mailing address for overnight payment of assessments.

(c) An owner shall not be liable for any charges, interest, or costs of collection for an assessment payment that is asserted to be delinquent, if it is determined the assessment was paid on time to the association. **Leg.H.** Added Stats 2013 ch 605 §21 (SB 752), effective January 1, 2014.

§6812. Pre-lien notice to owner

At least 30 days prior to recording a lien upon the separate interest of the owner of record to collect a debt that is past due under Section 6808, the association shall notify the owner of record in writing by certified mail of the following:

(a) A general description of the collection and lien enforcement procedures of the association and the method of calculation of the amount, a statement that the owner of the separate interest has the right to inspect the association records pursuant to Section 8333 of the Corporations Code, and the following statement in 14-point boldface type, if printed, or in capital letters, if typed:

"IMPORTANT NOTICE: IF YOUR SEPARATE INTEREST IS PLACED IN FORECLOSURE BECAUSE YOU ARE BEHIND IN YOUR ASSESSMENTS, IT MAY BE SOLD WITHOUT COURT ACTION."

(b) An itemized statement of the charges owed by the owner, including items on the statement which indicate the amount of any delinquent assessments, the fees and reasonable costs of collection, reasonable attorney's fees, any late charges, and interest, if any.

(c) A statement that the owner shall not be liable to pay the charges, interest, and costs of collection, if it is determined the assessment was paid on time to the association. **Leg.H.** Added Stats 2013 ch 605 §21 (SB 752), effective January 1, 2014.

§6814. Lien; Contents

(a) The amount of the assessment, plus any costs of collection, late charges, and interest assessed in accordance with Section 6808, shall be a lien on the owner's separate interest in the common interest development from and after the time the association causes to be recorded with the county recorder of the county in which the separate interest is located, a notice of delinquent assessment, which shall state the amount of the assessment and other sums imposed in accordance with Section 6808, a legal description of the owner's separate interest in the common interest development against which the assessment and other sums are levied, and the name of the record owner of the separate interest in the common interest development against which the lien is imposed.

(b) The itemized statement of the charges owed by the owner described in subdivision (b) of Section 6812 shall be recorded together with the notice of delinquent assessment.

(c) In order for the lien to be enforced by nonjudicial foreclosure as provided in Sections 6820 and 6822, the notice of delinquent assessment shall state the name and address of the trustee authorized by the association to enforce the lien by sale.

(d) The notice of delinquent assessment shall be signed by the person designated in the declaration or by the association for that purpose, or if no one is designated, by the president of the association.

(e) A copy of the recorded notice of delinquent assessment shall be mailed by certified mail to every person whose name is shown as an owner of the separate interest in the association's records, and the notice shall be mailed no later than 10 calendar days after recordation. **Leg.H.** Added Stats 2013 ch 605 §21 (SB 752), effective January 1, 2014.

§6816. Order of Liens

A lien created pursuant to Section 6814 shall be prior to all other liens recorded subsequent to the notice of delinquent assessment, except that the declaration may provide for the subordination thereof to any other liens and encumbrances. **Leg.H.** Added Stats 2013 ch 605 §21 (SB 752), effective January 1, 2014.

§6818. Release of Lien

(a) Within 21 days of the payment of the sums specified in the notice of delinquent assessment, the association shall record or cause to be recorded in the office of the county recorder in which the notice of delinquent assessment is recorded a lien release or notice of rescission and provide the owner of the separate interest a copy of the lien release or notice that the delinquent assessment has been satisfied.

(b) If it is determined that a lien previously recorded against the separate interest was recorded in error, the party who recorded the lien shall, within 21 calendar days, record or cause to be recorded in the office of the county recorder in which the notice of delinquent assessment is recorded a lien release or notice of rescission and provide the owner of the separate interest with a declaration that the lien filing or recording was in error and a copy of the lien release or notice of rescission. **Leg.H.** Added Stats 2013 ch 605 §21 (SB 752), effective January 1, 2014.

§6819. Association failure to comply with lien procedures

An association that fails to comply with the procedures set forth in this section shall, prior to recording a lien, recommence the required notice process. Any costs associated with recommencing the notice process shall be borne by the association and not by the owner of a separate interest. **Leg.H.** Added Stats 2013 ch 605 §21 (SB 752), effective January 1, 2014.

ARTICLE 3
Assessment Collection

Enforcement of lien; Sale. §6820.
Sale; Notice; Fees. §6822.
Lien for damages to common areas; No lien for fines for failure to comply with governing documents. §6824.
Assignment of right to collect payments. §6826.
Applicability date of article. §6828.

§6820. Enforcement of lien; Sale

(a) Except as otherwise provided in this article, after the expiration of 30 days following the recording of a lien created pursuant to Section 6814, the lien may be enforced in any manner permitted by law, including sale by the court, sale by the trustee designated in the notice of delinquent assessment, or sale by a trustee substituted pursuant to Section 2934a.

(b) Nothing in Article 2 (commencing with Section 6808) or in subdivision (a) of Section 726 of the Code of Civil Procedure prohibits actions against the owner of a separate interest to recover sums for which a lien is created pursuant to Article 2 (commencing with Section 6808) or prohibits an association from taking a deed in lieu of foreclosure. **Leg.H.** Added Stats 2013 ch 605 §21 (SB 752), effective January 1, 2014.

§6822. Sale; Notice; Fees

(a) Any sale by the trustee shall be conducted in accordance with Sections 2924, 2924b, and 2924c applicable to the exercise of powers of sale in mortgages and deeds of trust.

(b) In addition to the requirements of Section 2924, the association shall serve a notice of default on the person named as the owner of the separate interest in the association's records or, if that person has designated a legal representative pursuant to this subdivision, on that legal representative. Service shall be in accordance with the manner of service of summons in Article 3 (commencing with Section 415.10) of Chapter 4 of Title 5 of Part 2 of the Code of Civil Procedure. An owner may designate a legal representative in a writing that is mailed to the association in a manner that indicates that the association has received it.

(c) The fees of a trustee may not exceed the amounts prescribed in Sections 2924c and 2924d, plus the cost of service for the notice of default pursuant to subdivision (b). **Leg.H.** Added Stats 2013 ch 605 §21 (SB 752), effective January 1, 2014.

§6824. Lien for damages to common areas; No lien for fines for failure to comply with governing documents

(a) A monetary charge imposed by the association as a means of reimbursing the association for costs incurred by the association in the repair of damage to common areas and facilities caused by a member or the member's guest or tenant may become a lien against the member's separate interest enforceable by the sale of the interest under Sections 2924, 2924b, and 2924c, provided the authority to impose a lien is set forth in the governing documents.

(b) A monetary penalty imposed by the association as a disciplinary measure for failure of a member to comply with the governing documents, except for the late payments, may not be characterized nor treated in the governing documents as an assessment that may become a lien against the member's separate interest enforceable by the sale of the interest under Sections 2924, 2924b, and 2924c. **Leg.H.** Added Stats 2013 ch 605 §21 (SB 752), effective January 1, 2014.

§6826. Assignment of right to collect payments

(a) An association may not voluntarily assign or pledge the association's right to collect payments or assessments, or to enforce or foreclose a lien to a third party, except when the assignment or pledge is made to a financial institution or lender chartered or licensed under federal or state law, when acting within the scope of that charter or license, as security for a loan obtained by the association.

(b) Nothing in subdivision (a) restricts the right or ability of an association to assign any unpaid obligations of a former member to a third party for purposes of collection. **Leg.H.** Added Stats 2013 ch 605 §21 (SB 752), effective January 1, 2014.

§6828. Applicability date of article

(a) Except as otherwise provided, this article applies to a lien created on or after January 1, 2014.

(b) A lien created before January 1, 2014, is governed by the law in existence at the time the lien was created. **Leg.H.** Added Stats 2013 ch 605 §21 (SB 752), effective January 1, 2014.

CHAPTER 8
INSURANCE AND LIABILITY

Insurance on common areas. §6840.

§6840. Insurance on common areas

(a) It is the intent of the Legislature to offer civil liability protection to owners of the separate interests in a common interest development that have common area owned in tenancy in common if the association carries a certain level of prescribed insurance that covers a cause of action in tort.

(b) Any cause of action in tort against any owner of a separate interest arising solely by reason of an ownership interest as a tenant in common in the common area of a common interest development shall be brought only against the association and not against the individual owners of the separate interests, if both of the insurance requirements in paragraphs (1) and (2) are met:

(1) The association maintained and has in effect for this cause of action, one or more policies of insurance that include coverage for general liability of the association.

(2) The coverage described in paragraph (1) is in the following minimum amounts:

(A) At least two million dollars ($2,000,000) if the common interest development consists of 100 or fewer separate interests.

(B) At least three million dollars ($3,000,000) if the common interest development consists of more than 100 separate interests. **Leg.H.** Added Stats 2013 ch 605 §21 (SB 752), effective January 1, 2014.

CHAPTER 9
DISPUTE RESOLUTION AND ENFORCEMENT

Article 1. Disciplinary Action.
Article 2. Civil Actions.

ARTICLE 1
Disciplinary Action

Monetary penalty for violation of governing documents. §6850.
Act does not restrict monetary penalties for violation of governing documents. §6854.

§6850. Monetary penalty for violation of governing documents

(a) If an association adopts or has adopted a policy imposing any monetary penalty, including any fee, on any association member for a violation of the governing documents, including any monetary penalty relating to the activities of a guest or tenant of the member, the board shall adopt and distribute to each member, by individual notice, a schedule of the monetary penalties that may be assessed for those violations, which shall be in accordance with authorization for member discipline contained in the governing documents.

(b) Any new or revised monetary penalty that is adopted after complying with subdivision (a) may be included in a supplement that is delivered to the members individually, pursuant to Section 6553.

(c) A monetary penalty for a violation of the governing documents shall not exceed the monetary penalty stated in the schedule of monetary penalties or supplement that is in effect at the time of the violation.

(d) An association shall provide a copy of the most recently distributed schedule of monetary penalties, along with any applicable supplements to that schedule, to any member on request. **Leg.H.** Added Stats 2013 ch 605 §21 (SB 752), effective January 1, 2014.

§6854. Act does not restrict monetary penalties for violation of governing documents

Nothing in Section 6850 shall be construed to create, expand, or reduce the authority of the board to impose monetary penalties on a member for a violation of the governing documents. **Leg.H.** Added Stats 2013 ch 605 §21 (SB 752), effective January 1, 2014.

ARTICLE 2
Civil Actions

Declaration enforceable by association and owners. §6856.
Standing of association. §6858.
Damages; Comparative fault. §6860.

§6856. Declaration enforceable by association and owners

(a) The covenants and restrictions in the declaration shall be enforceable equitable servitudes, unless unreasonable, and shall inure to the benefit of and bind all owners of separate interests in the development. Unless the declaration states otherwise, these servitudes may be enforced by any owner of a separate interest or by the association, or by both.

(b) A governing document other than the declaration may be enforced by the association against an owner of a separate interest or by an owner of a separate interest against the association. **Leg.H.** Added Stats 2013 ch 605 §21 (SB 752), effective January 1, 2014.

§6858. Standing of association

An association has standing to institute, defend, settle, or intervene in litigation, arbitration, mediation, or administrative proceedings in its own name as the real party in interest and without joining with it, the members, in matters pertaining to the following:

(a) Enforcement of the governing documents.

(b) Damage to the common area.

(c) Damage to a separate interest that the association is obligated to maintain or repair.

(d) Damage to a separate interest that arises out of, or is integrally related to, damage to the common area or a separate interest that the association is obligated to maintain or repair. **Leg.H.** Added Stats 2013 ch 605 §21 (SB 752), effective January 1, 2014.

§6860. Damages; Comparative fault

(a) In an action maintained by an association pursuant to subdivision (b), (c), or (d) of Section 6858, the amount of damages recovered by the association shall be reduced by the amount of damages allocated to the association or its managing agents in direct proportion to their percentage of fault based upon principles of comparative fault. The comparative fault of the association or its managing agents may be raised by way of defense, but shall not be the basis for a cross-action or separate action against the association or its managing agents for contribution or implied indemnity, where the only damage was sustained by the association or its members. It is the intent of the Legislature in enacting this subdivision to require that comparative fault be pleaded as an affirmative defense, rather than a separate cause of action, where the only damage was sustained by the association or its members.

(b) In an action involving damages described in subdivision (b), (c), or (d) of Section 6858, the defendant or cross-defendant may allege and prove the comparative fault of the association or its managing agents as a setoff to the liability of the defendant or cross-defendant even if the association is not a party to the litigation or is no longer a party whether by reason of settlement, dismissal, or otherwise.

(c) Subdivisions (a) and (b) apply to actions commenced on or after January 1, 1993.

(d) Nothing in this section affects a person's liability under Section 1431, or the liability of the association or its managing agent for an act or omission that causes damages to another. **Leg.H.** Added Stats 2013 ch 605 §21 (SB 752), effective January 1, 2014.

CHAPTER 10
CONSTRUCTION DEFECT LITIGATION

Settlement agreement; Notice. §6874.
Meeting of association members prior to filing civil action. §6876.

§6870. Requirements for association to file complaint [Repealed]

Leg.H. Added Stats 2013 ch 605 §21 (SB 752), effective January 1, 2014, inoperative July 1, 2017. Repealed operative January 1, 2018, by its own provisions. The repealed section related to requirements for association to file complaint for damages against builder, developer, or general contractor for defects in design or construction of a common interest development.

§6874. Settlement agreement; Notice

(a) As soon as is reasonably practicable after the association and the builder have entered into a settlement agreement or the matter has otherwise been resolved regarding alleged defects in the common areas, alleged defects in the separate interests that the association is obligated to maintain or repair, or alleged defects in the separate interests that arise out of, or are integrally related to, defects in the common areas or separate interests that the association is obligated to maintain or repair, where the defects giving rise to the dispute have not been corrected, the association shall, in writing, inform only the members of the association whose names appear on the records of the association that the matter has been resolved, by settlement agreement or other means, and disclose all of the following:

(1) A general description of the defects that the association reasonably believes, as of the date of the disclosure, will be corrected or replaced.

(2) A good faith estimate, as of the date of the disclosure, of when the association believes that the defects identified in paragraph (1) will be corrected or replaced. The association may state that the estimate may be modified.

(3) The status of the claims for defects in the design or construction of the common interest development that were not identified in paragraph (1) whether expressed in a preliminary list of defects sent to each member of the association or otherwise claimed and disclosed to the members of the association.

(b) Nothing in this section shall preclude an association from amending the disclosures required pursuant to subdivision (a), and any amendments shall supersede any prior conflicting information disclosed to the members of the association and shall retain any privilege attached to the original disclosures.

(c) Disclosure of the information required pursuant to subdivision (a) or authorized by subdivision (b) shall not waive any privilege attached to the information.

(d) For the purposes of the disclosures required pursuant to this section, the term "defects" shall be defined to include any damage resulting from defects. **Leg.H.** Added Stats 2013 ch 605 §21 (SB 752), effective January 1, 2014.

§6876. Meeting of association members prior to filing civil action

(a) Not later than 30 days prior to the filing of any civil action by the association against the declarant or other developer of a common interest development for alleged damage to the common areas, alleged damage to the separate interests that the association is obligated to maintain or repair, or alleged damage to the separate interests that arises out of, or is integrally related to, damage to the common areas or separate interests that the association is obligated to maintain or repair, the board shall provide a written notice to each member of the association who appears on the records of the association when the notice is provided. This notice shall specify all of the following:

(1) That a meeting will take place to discuss problems that may lead to the filing of a civil action.

(2) The options, including civil actions, that are available to address the problems.

(3) The time and place of this meeting.

(b) Notwithstanding subdivision (a), if the association has reason to believe that the applicable statute of limitations will expire before the association files the civil action, the association may give the notice, as described above, within 30 days after the filing of the action. **Leg.H.** Added Stats 2013 ch 605 §21 (SB 752), effective January 1, 2014.

PART 5.5
AUTOMATIC CHECKOUT SYSTEM

Requirement of readable prices on packages; Exemptions. §7100.
Penalty; Intent to violate. §7101.
Liability for losses and expenses incurred by individuals. §7102.
Unintentional error excepted. §7103.
Exclusive remedies. §7104.
Citation of part. §7105.
Preemption of field. §7106.

§7100. Requirement of readable prices on packages; Exemptions

(a) Every retail grocery store or grocery department within a general retail merchandise store which uses a point-of-sale system shall cause to have a clearly readable price indicated on 85 percent of the total number of packaged consumer commodities offered for sale which are not exempt pursuant to subdivision (b).

The management of any such retail grocery store or grocery department shall determine the number of consumer commodities normally offered for sale on a daily basis, shall determine the consumer commodities to be exempted pursuant to this subdivision, and shall maintain a list of those consumer commodities exempt pursuant to this subdivision. The list shall be made available to a designated representative of the appropriate local union, the members of which are responsible for item pricing, in those stores or departments that have collective bargaining agreements, seven days prior to an item or items being exempted pursuant to this subdivision. In addition, the list shall be available and posted in a prominent place in the store seven days prior to an item or items being exempted pursuant to this subdivision.

(b) The provisions of this section shall not apply to any of the following:

(1) Any consumer commodity which was not generally item-priced on January 1, 1977, as determined by the Department of Food and Agriculture pursuant to subdivision (c) of Section 12604.5 of the Business and Professions Code, as in effect July 8, 1977.

(2) Any unpackaged fresh food produce, or to consumer commodities which are under three cubic inches in size, weigh less than three ounces, and are priced under forty cents ($0.40).

(3) Any consumer commodity offered as a sale item or as a special.

(4) Any business which has as its only regular employees the owner thereof, or the parent, spouse, or child of such owner, or, in addition thereto, not more than two other regular employees.

(5) Identical items within a multi-item package.

(6) Items sold through a vending machine.

(c) For the purposes of this section:

(1) "Point-of-sale system" means any computer or electronic system used by a retail establishment such as, but not limited to, Universal Product Code scanners, price lookup codes, or an electronic price lookup system as a means for determining the price of the item being purchased by a consumer.

(2) "Consumer commodity" includes:

(A) Food, including all material whether solid, liquid, or mixed, and whether simple or compound, which is used or intended for consumption by human beings or domestic animals normally kept as household pets, and all substances or ingredients added to any such material for any purpose. This definition shall not apply to individual packages of cigarettes or individual cigars.

(B) Napkins, facial tissues, toilet tissues, foil wrapping, plastic wrapping, paper toweling, and disposable plates and cups.

(C) Detergents, soaps, and other cleaning agents.

(D) Pharmaceuticals, including nonprescription drugs, bandages, female hygiene products, and toiletries.

(3) "Grocery department" means an area within a general retail merchandise store which is engaged primarily in the retail sale of packaged food, rather than food prepared for immediate consumption on or off the premises.

(4) "Grocery store" means a store engaged primarily in the retail sale of packaged food, rather than food prepared for consumption on the premises.

(5) "Sale item or special" means any consumer commodity offered in good faith for a period of 14 days or less, on sale at a price below the normal price that item is usually sold for in that store. The Department of Food and Agriculture shall determine the normal length of a sale held for consumer commodities generally item priced on January 1, 1977, in stores regulated pursuant to this chapter, and that period shall be used for the purposes of this subdivision. The department's determination as to the normal length of a sale shall be binding for the purposes of this section, but each such determination shall not exceed seven days. **Leg.H.** Added Stats 1981 ch 224 §2. Amended Stats 2006 ch 566 §6 (AB 2285), effective January 1, 2007.

§7101. Penalty; Intent to violate

(a) The intentional violation of Section 7100 is punishable by a civil penalty of not less than twenty-five dollars ($25) nor more than five hundred dollars ($500).

(b) Failure to have a clearly readable price indicated on 12 units of the same item required to be item-priced of the same commodity shall constitute a presumption of intent to violate Section 7100.

(c) Every additional 12 units of the same item required to be item-priced that fail to have a price indicated on them shall constitute a presumption of intent to violate Section 7100.

(d) Each day that a violation continues shall also constitute a separate violation after notification thereof to the manager or assistant manager of the retail grocery store or the grocery department of the general retail merchandise store and shall constitute a presumption of intent to violate Section 7100.

(e) Notwithstanding any other provision of law, any person may bring an action to enjoin a violation of Section 7100. **Leg.H.** Added Stats 1981 ch 224 §2.

§7102. Liability for losses and expenses incurred by individuals

Any person, firm, corporation, or association who violates Sections 7100 and 7101 shall be liable to any person injured for any losses and expenses thereby incurred, and for the sum of fifty dollars ($50) in addition thereto. The remedy set forth herein is applicable only to actions brought in the name of, and on behalf of, a single plaintiff and shall not be applicable in multiple plaintiff or class actions. **Leg.H.** Added Stats 1981 ch 224 §2.

§7103. Unintentional error excepted

Improper pricing on the shelf or on the item due to unintentional error shall not constitute a violation of this division. **Leg.H.** Added Stats 1981 ch 224 §2.

§7104. Exclusive remedies

The remedies set forth in Sections 7101 and 7102 are the exclusive remedies available to any person, state or local agency or law enforcement official. **Leg.H.** Added Stats 1981 ch 224 §2.

§7105. Citation of part

This part shall be known and may be cited as the Rosenthal-Roberti Item Pricing Act. **Leg.H.** Added Stats 1981 ch 224 §2.

§7106. Preemption of field

It is the intention of the Legislature that this part shall occupy the field with regard to item pricing and shall preempt all local ordinances, rules, or regulations concerning item pricing. **Leg.H.** Added Stats 1981 ch 224 §2.

PART 6
WORKS OF IMPROVEMENT

Title 1. Works of Improvement Generally.
Title 2. Private Works of Improvement.
Title 3. Public Work of Improvement.

TITLE 1
WORKS OF IMPROVEMENT GENERALLY

Chapter 1. General Provisions.
Chapter 2. Notice.
Chapter 3. Waiver and Release.
Chapter 4. Bonds.

CHAPTER 1
GENERAL PROVISIONS

Article 1. Definitions.
Article 2. Miscellaneous Provisions.

ARTICLE 1
Definitions

Definitions as governing construction of part. §8000.
"Admitted surety insurer". §8002.
"Claimant". §8004.
"Construction lender". §8006.
"Contract". §8008.
"Contract price". §8010.
"Contractor". §8012.
"Design professional". §8014.
"Direct contract". §8016.
"Direct contractor". §8018.
"Funds". §8020.
"Labor, service, equipment, or material". §8022.
"Laborer"; Standing to enforce rights or claims of laborer; Public policy. §8024.
"Lien". §8026.
"Material supplier". §8028.
"Payment bond". §8030.
"Person". §8032.
"Preliminary notice". §8034.
"Public entity". §8036.
"Public works contract". §8038.
"Site". §8040.
"Site improvement". §8042.
"Stop payment notice"; "Bonded stop payment notice"; "Stop notice". §8044.
"Subcontractor". §8046.
"Work". §8048.
"Work of improvement". §8050.

§8000. Definitions as governing construction of part

Unless the provision or context otherwise requires, the definitions in this article govern the construction of this part. **Leg.H.** Added Stats 2010 ch 697 §20 (SB 189), effective January 1, 2011, operative July 1, 2012.

Prior Law: Former CC §3082, relating to UCC §§3102, 3104, was added Stats 1917 ch 751 §1 p 1532 and repealed Stats 1963 ch 819 §2 p 1997, effective January 1, 1965.

§8002. "Admitted surety insurer"

"Admitted surety insurer" has the meaning provided in Section 995.120 of the Code of Civil Procedure. **Leg.H.** Added Stats 2010 ch 697 §20 (SB 189), effective January 1, 2011, operative July 1, 2012.

§8004. "Claimant"

"Claimant" means a person that has a right under this part to record a claim of lien, give a stop payment notice, or assert a claim against a payment bond, or do any combination of the foregoing. **Leg.H.** Added Stats 2010 ch 697 §20 (SB 189), effective January 1, 2011, operative July 1, 2012.

Prior Law: Former CC §3085, similar to UCC §3109, was added Stats 1917 ch 751 §1 p 1533 and repealed Stats 1963 ch 819 §2 p 1997, effective January 1, 1965.

§8006. "Construction lender"

"Construction lender" means either of the following:

(a) A mortgagee or beneficiary under a deed of trust lending funds with which the cost of all or part of a work of improvement is to be paid, or the assignee or successor in interest of the mortgagee or beneficiary.

(b) An escrow holder or other person holding funds provided by an owner, lender, or another person as a fund for with which the cost of all or part of a work of improvement is to be paid. **Leg.H.** Added Stats 2010 ch 697 §20 (SB 189), effective January 1, 2011, operative July 1, 2012.

Prior Law: Former CC §3087, similar to UCC §§1201, 3106, 3107, 3112–3114, was added Stats 1917 ch 751 §1 p 1534 and repealed Stats 1963 ch 819 §2 p 1997, effective January 1, 1965.

Former CC §3087, relating to negotiability of instrument was enacted Stats 1872 and repealed Stats 1917 ch 751 §1 p 1531.

§8008. "Contract"

"Contract" means an agreement that provides for all or part of a work of improvement. **Leg.H.** Added Stats 2010 ch 697 §20 (SB 189), effective January 1, 2011, operative July 1, 2012.

Prior Law: Former CC §3088, similar to UCC §§3108, 3502, was added Stats 1917 ch 751 §1 p 1534 and repealed Stats 1963 ch 819 §2 p 1997, effective January 1, 1965.

Former CC §3088, relating to unconditional payment of money was enacted Stats 1872, amended Stats 1905 ch 97 §1 p 96, Stats 1915 ch 78 §1 p 99, and repealed Stats 1917 ch 751 §1 p 1531.

§8010. "Contract price"

"Contract price" means the price agreed to in a direct contract for a work of improvement. **Leg.H.** Added Stats 2010 ch 697 §20 (SB 189), effective January 1, 2011, operative July 1, 2012.

§8012. "Contractor"

"Contractor" includes a direct contractor, subcontractor, or both. This section does not apply to Sections 8018 and 8046. **Leg.H.** Added Stats 2010 ch 697 §20 (SB 189), effective January 1, 2011, operative July 1, 2012.

§8014. "Design professional"

"Design professional" means a person licensed as an architect pursuant to Chapter 3 (commencing with Section 5500) of Division 3 of the Business and Professions Code, licensed as a landscape architect pursuant to Chapter 3.5 (commencing with Section 5615) of Division 3 of the Business and Professions Code, registered as a professional engineer pursuant to Chapter 7 (commencing with Section 6700) of Division 3 of the Business and Professions Code, or licensed as a land surveyor pursuant to Chapter 15 (commencing with Section 8700) of Division 3 of the Business and Professions Code. **Leg.H.** Added Stats 2010 ch 697 §20 (SB 189), effective January 1, 2011, operative July 1, 2012.

Prior Law: Former CC §3081.1, relating to statement of person negotiating a loan secured by real estate property, was added Stats 1955 ch 1791 §1, effective October 1, 1955 and repealed Stats 1961 ch 886 §29, effective June 17, 1961.

§8016. "Direct contract"

"Direct contract" means a contract between an owner and a direct contractor that provides for all or part of a work of improvement. **Leg.H.** Added Stats 2010 ch 697 §20 (SB 189), effective January 1, 2011, operative July 1, 2012.

Prior Law: Former CC §3088, similar to UCC §§3108, 3502, was added Stats 1917 ch 751 §1 p 1534 and repealed Stats 1963 ch 819 §2 p 1997, effective January 1, 1965.

Former CC §3088, relating to unconditional payment of money was enacted Stats 1872, amended Stats 1905 ch 97 §1 p 96, Stats 1915 ch 78 §1 p 99, and repealed Stats 1917 ch 751 §1 p 1531.

§8018. "Direct contractor"

"Direct contractor" means a contractor that has a direct contractual relationship with an owner. A reference in another statute to a "prime contractor" in connection with the provisions in this part means a "direct contractor." **Leg.H.** Added Stats 2010 ch 697 §20 (SB 189), effective January 1, 2011, operative July 1, 2012.

Prior Law: Former CC §3095, similar to UCC §§3115, 3407, 8206, was added Stats 1917 ch 751 §1 p 1535 and repealed Stats 1963 ch 819 §2 p 1997, effective January 1, 1965.

Former CC §3095, relating to classes of negotiable instruments, was enacted Stats 1872 and repealed Stats 1917 ch 751 §1 p 1531.

§8020. "Funds"

For the purposes of Title 3 (commencing with Section 9000), "funds" means warrant, check, money, or bonds (if bonds are to be issued in payment of the public works contract). **Leg.H.** Added Stats 2010 ch 697 §20 (SB 189), effective January 1, 2011, operative July 1, 2012.

§8022. "Labor, service, equipment, or material"

"Labor, service, equipment, or material" includes, but is not limited to, labor, skills, services, material, supplies, equipment, appliances, power, and surveying, provided for a work of improvement. **Leg.H.** Added Stats 2010 ch 697 §20 (SB 189), effective January 1, 2011, operative July 1, 2012.

§8024. "Laborer"; Standing to enforce rights or claims of laborer; Public policy

(a) "Laborer" means a person who, acting as an employee, performs labor upon, or bestows skill or other necessary services on, a work of improvement.

(b) "Laborer" includes a person or entity to which a portion of a laborer's compensation for a work of improvement, including, but not limited to, employer payments described in Section 1773.1 of the Labor Code and implementing regulations, is paid by agreement with that laborer or the collective bargaining agent of that laborer.

(c) A person or entity described in subdivision (b) that has standing under applicable law to maintain a direct legal action, in its own name or as an assignee, to collect any portion of compensation owed for a laborer for a work of improvement, shall have standing to enforce any rights or claims of the laborer under this part, to the extent of the compensation agreed to be paid to the person or entity for labor on that improvement. This subdivision is intended to give effect to the longstanding public policy of this state to protect the entire compensation of a laborer on a work of improvement, regardless of the form in which that compensation is to be paid. **Leg.H.** Added Stats 2010 ch 697 §20 (SB 189), effective January 1, 2011, operative July 1, 2012.

Prior Law: Former CC §3089, similar to UCC §3110, was added Stats 1917 ch 751 §1 p 1534 and repealed Stats 1963 ch 819 §2 p 1997, effective January 1, 1965.

Former CC §3089, relating to payee, was enacted Stats 1872 and repealed Stats 1917 ch 751 §1 p 1531.

Former CC §3111, similar to UCC §§3202, 8304, was added Stats 1917 ch 751 §1 p 1538 and repealed Stats 1963 ch 819 §2 p 1997, effective January 1, 1965.

Former CC §3111, relating to kinds of indorsement, was enacted Stats 1872 and repealed Stats 1917 ch 751 §1 p 1531.

§8026. "Lien"

"Lien" means a lien under Title 2 (commencing with Section 8160) and includes a lien of a design professional under Section 8302, a lien for a work of improvement under Section 8400, and a lien for a site improvement under Section 8402. **Leg.H.** Added Stats 2010 ch 697 §20 (SB 189), effective January 1, 2011, operative July 1, 2012.

§8028. "Material supplier"

"Material supplier" means a person that provides material or supplies to be used or consumed in a work of improvement. **Leg.H.** Added Stats 2010 ch 697 §20 (SB 189), effective January 1, 2011, operative July 1, 2012.

Prior Law: Former CC §3090, similar to present UCC §§3111, 3204, 3405, was added Stats 1917 ch 751 §1 p 1534, amended Stats 1945 ch 658 §1 p 1315, and repealed Stats 1963 ch 819 §2 p 1997, effective January 1, 1965.

Former CC §3090, providing that instrument may be in alternative, was enacted Stats 1872 and repealed Stats 1917 ch 751 §1 p 1531.

§8030. "Payment bond"

(a) For the purposes of Title 2 (commencing with Section 8160), "payment bond" means a bond given under Section 8600.

(b) For the purposes of Title 3 (commencing with Section 9000), "payment bond" means a bond required by Section 9550. **Leg.H.** Added Stats 2010 ch 697 §20 (SB 189), effective January 1, 2011, operative July 1, 2012.

§8032. "Person"

"Person" means an individual, corporation, public entity, business trust, estate, trust, partnership, limited liability company, association, or other entity. **Leg.H.** Added Stats 2010 ch 697 §20 (SB 189), effective January 1, 2011, operative July 1, 2012.

§8034. "Preliminary notice"

(a) For the purposes of Title 2 (commencing with Section 8160), "preliminary notice" means the notice provided for in Chapter 2 (commencing with Section 8200) of Title 2.

(b) For the purposes of Title 3 (commencing with Section 9000), "preliminary notice" means the notice provided for in Chapter 3 (commencing with Section 9300) of Title 3. **Leg.H.** Added Stats 2010 ch 697 §20 (SB 189), effective January 1, 2011, operative July 1, 2012.

Prior Law: Former CC §3097, similar to UCC §§3305, 3306, 8202, was added Stats 1917 ch 751 §1 and repealed Stats 1963 ch 819 §2, effective January 1, 1965.

Former CC §3098, similar to UCC §§3109, 3114, 3118, 3402, was added Stats 1917 ch 751 §1 p 1536 and repealed Stats 1963 ch 819 §2 p 1997, effective January 1, 1965.

§8036. "Public entity"

"Public entity" means the state, Regents of the University of California, a county, city, district, public authority, public agency, and any other political subdivision or public corporation in the state. **Leg.H.** Added Stats 2010 ch 697 §20 (SB 189), effective January 1, 2011, operative July 1, 2012.

Prior Law: Former CC §3099, similar to UCC §3401, was added Stats 1917 ch 751 §1 p 1536 and repealed Stats 1963 ch 819 §2 p 1997, effective January 1, 1965.

Former CC §3099, relating to time and place of payment, was enacted Stats 1872 and repealed Stats 1917 ch 751 §1 p 1531.

§8038. "Public works contract"

"Public works contract" has the meaning provided in Section 1101 of the Public Contract Code. **Leg.H.** Added Stats 2010 ch 697 §20 (SB 189), effective January 1, 2011, operative July 1, 2012.

Prior Law: Former CC §3100, similar to UCC §3403, was added Stats 1917 ch 751 §1 p 1536 and repealed Stats 1963 ch 819 §2 p 1997, effective January 1, 1965.

Former CC §3100, relating to place of payment, was enacted Stats 1872, amended Code Amdts 1873–74 ch 612 §267 p 262, and repealed Stats 1917 ch 751 §1 p 1531.

§8040. "Site"

"Site" means the real property on which a work of improvement is situated or planned. **Leg.H.** Added Stats 2010 ch 697 §20 (SB 189), effective January 1, 2011, operative July 1, 2012.

Prior Law: Former CC §3101, similar to UCC §3103, was added Stats 1917 ch 751 §1 p 1536 and repealed Stats 1963 ch 819 §2 p 1997, effective January 1, 1965.

Former CC §3101, relating to instruments payable to a person or his order, was enacted Stats 1872 and repealed Stats 1917 ch 751 §1 p 1531.

§8042. "Site improvement"

"Site improvement" means any of the following work on real property:

(a) Demolition or removal of improvements, trees, or other vegetation.

(b) Drilling test holes.

(c) Grading, filling, or otherwise improving the real property or a street, highway, or sidewalk in front of or adjoining the real property.

(d) Construction or installation of sewers or other public utilities.

(e) Construction of areas, vaults, cellars, or rooms under sidewalks.

(f) Any other work or improvements in preparation of the site for a work of improvement. **Leg.H.** Added Stats 2010 ch 697 §20 (SB 189), effective January 1, 2011, operative July 1, 2012.

Prior Law: Former CC §3102, similar to UCC §3403, was added Stats 1917 ch 751 §1 p 1536 and repealed Stats 1963 ch 819 §2 p 1997, effective January 1, 1965.

Former CC §3102, relating to unindorsed note, was enacted Stats 1872 and repealed Stats 1917 ch 751 §1 p 1531.

§8044. "Stop payment notice"; "Bonded stop payment notice"; "Stop notice"

(a)(1) For the purposes of Title 2 (commencing with Section 8160), "stop payment notice" means the notice given by a claimant under Chapter 5 (commencing with Section 8500) of Title 2.

(2) A stop payment notice given under Title 2 (commencing with Section 8160) may be bonded or unbonded. A "bonded stop payment notice" is a notice given with a bond under Section 8532. An "unbonded stop payment notice" is a notice not given with a bond under Section 8532.

(3) Except to the extent Title 2 (commencing with Section 8160) distinguishes between a bonded and an unbonded stop payment notice, a reference in that title to a stop payment notice includes both a bonded and an unbonded notice.

(b) For the purposes of Title 3 (commencing with Section 9000), "stop payment notice" means the notice given by a claimant under Chapter 4 (commencing with Section 9350) of Title 3.

(c) A reference in another statute to a "stop notice" in connection with the remedies provided in this part means a stop payment notice. **Leg.H.** Added Stats 2010 ch 697 §20 (SB 189), effective January 1, 2011, operative July 1, 2012.

Prior Law: Former CC §3103, similar to UCC §3207, was added Stats 1917 ch 751 §1 p 1536 and repealed Stats 1963 ch 819 §2 p 1997, effective January 1, 1965.

Former CC §3103, relating to fictitious payee, was enacted Stats 1872 and repealed Stats 1917 ch 751 §1 p 1531.

§8046. "Subcontractor"

"Subcontractor" means a contractor that does not have a direct contractual relationship with an owner. The term includes a contractor that has a contractual relationship with a direct contractor or with another subcontractor. **Leg.H.** Added Stats 2010 ch 697 §20 (SB 189), effective January 1, 2011, operative July 1, 2012.

Prior Law: Former CC §3104, similar to UCC §§3404, 8202, 8205, 8311, was added Stats 1917 ch 751 §1 p 1536 and repealed Stats 1963 ch 819 §2 p 1997, effective January 1, 1965.

Former CC §3104, relating to presumption of consideration, was enacted Stats 1872 and repealed Stats 1917 ch 751 §1 p 1531.

§8048. "Work"

"Work" means labor, service, equipment, or material provided to a work of improvement. **Leg.H.** Added Stats 2010 ch 697 §20 (SB 189), effective January 1, 2011, operative July 1, 2012.

§8050. "Work of improvement"

(a) "Work of improvement" includes, but is not limited to:

(1) Construction, alteration, repair, demolition, or removal, in whole or in part, of, or addition to, a building, wharf, bridge, ditch, flume, aqueduct, well, tunnel, fence, machinery, railroad, or road.

(2) Seeding, sodding, or planting of real property for landscaping purposes.

(3) Filling, leveling, or grading of real property.

(b) Except as otherwise provided in this part, "work of improvement" means the entire structure or scheme of improvement as a whole, and includes site improvement. **Leg.H.** Added Stats 2010 ch 697 §20 (SB 189), effective January 1, 2011, operative July 1, 2012.

Prior Law: Former CC §3106, similar to UCC §§1201(44), 3303, 3408, was added Stats 1917 ch 751 §1 p 1537 and repealed Stats 1963 ch 819 §2 p 1997, effective January 1, 1965.

ARTICLE 2
Miscellaneous Provisions

Operative date; Effectiveness of notice on work of improvement; Provisions construed as restatements and continuations. §8052.
Applicability of part. §8054.
Applicable Code of Civil Procedure provisions. §8056.
"Day". §8058.
Filing documents with county recorder; Duties of county recorder. §8060.
Construction of acts of owner; Exoneration of surety on performance or payment bond. §8062.
Acts on behalf of co-owner; Requirements. §8064.
Acts within scope of agent's authority. §8066.

§8052. Operative date; Effectiveness of notice on work of improvement; Provisions construed as restatements and continuations

(a) This part is operative on July 1, 2012.

(b) Notwithstanding subdivision (a), the effectiveness of a notice given or other action taken on a work of improvement before July 1, 2012, is governed by the applicable law in effect before July 1, 2012, and not by this part.

(c) A provision of this part, insofar as it is substantially the same as a previously existing provision relating to the same subject matter, shall be construed as a restatement and continuation thereof and not as a new enactment. **Leg.H.** Added Stats 2010 ch 697 §20 (SB 189), effective January 1, 2011, operative July 1, 2012.

§8054. Applicability of part

(a) This part does not apply to a transaction governed by the Oil and Gas Lien Act (Chapter 2.5 (commencing with Section 1203.50) of Title 4 of Part 3 of the Code of Civil Procedure).

(b) This part does not apply to or change improvement security under the Subdivision Map Act (Division 2 (commencing with Section 66410) of Title 7 of the Government Code).

(c) This part does not apply to a transaction governed by Sections 20457 to 20464, inclusive, of the Public Contract Code. **Leg.H.** Added Stats 2010 ch 697 §20 (SB 189), effective January 1, 2011, operative July 1, 2012.

Prior Law: Former CC §3266, similar to UCC §§1201, 3102, 3410 and former UCC §8313, was added Stats 1917 ch 751 §1 p 1559 and repealed Stats 1963 ch 819 §2 p 1997, effective January 1, 1965.

§8056. Applicable Code of Civil Procedure provisions

Except as otherwise provided in this part, Part 2 (commencing with Section 307) of the Code of Civil Procedure provides the rules of practice in proceedings under this part. **Leg.H.** Added Stats 2010 ch 697 §20 (SB 189), effective January 1, 2011, operative July 1, 2012.

Prior Law: Former CC §3259, similar to former UCC §3801, was added Stats 1917 ch 751 §1 p 1558 and repealed Stats 1963 ch 819 §2 p 1997, effective January 1, 1965. Historical Derivation: (a) Former CCP §1201.1, as added Stats 1951 ch 1159 §1 p 2957. (b) Former CCP §1198, as enacted 1872. (c) Former CCP §1199, as enacted Stats 1872, amended Stats 1945 ch 40 §6 p 357.

§8058. "Day"

For purposes of this part, "day" means a calendar day. **Leg.H.** Added Stats 2010 ch 697 §20 (SB 189), effective January 1, 2011, operative July 1, 2012.

§8060. Filing documents with county recorder; Duties of county recorder

(a) If this part provides for filing a contract, plan, or other paper with the county recorder, the provision is satisfied by filing the paper in the office of the county recorder of the county in which the work of improvement or part of it is situated.

(b) If this part provides for recording a notice, claim of lien, release of lien, payment bond, or other paper, the provision is satisfied by filing the paper for record in the office of the county recorder of the county in which the work of improvement or part of it is situated.

(c) The county recorder shall number, index, and preserve a contract, plan, or other paper presented for filing under this part, and shall number, index, and transcribe into the official records, in the same manner as a conveyance of real property, a notice, claim of lien, payment bond, or other paper recorded under this part.

(d) The county recorder shall charge and collect the fees provided in Article 5 (commencing with Section 27360) of Chapter 6 of Part 3 of Division 2 of Title 3 of the Government Code for performing duties under this section. **Leg.H.** Added Stats 2010 ch 697 §20 (SB 189), effective January 1, 2011, operative July 1, 2012.

Prior Law: Former CC §3258, similar to UCC §3603, was added Stats 1917 ch 751 §1 p 1558 and repealed Stats 1963 ch 819 §2 p 1997, effective January 1, 1965. Historical Derivation: (a) Former CCP §1203.1, as added Stats 1951 ch 1159 §1 p 2957. (b) Former CCP §1189, as enacted 1872.

§8062. Construction of acts of owner; Exoneration of surety on performance or payment bond

No act of an owner in good faith and in compliance with a provision of this part shall be construed to prevent a direct contractor's performance of the contract, or exonerate a surety on a performance or payment bond. **Leg.H.** Added Stats 2010 ch 697 §20 (SB 189), effective January 1, 2011, operative July 1, 2012.

Prior Law: Former CC §3263, similar to former UCC §3801, was added Stats 1917 ch 751 §1 p 1558 and repealed Stats 1963 ch 819 §2 p 1997, effective January 1, 1965. Historical Derivation: (a) Former CCP §1186.1, as added Stats 1951 ch 1159 §1 p 2944. (b) Former CCP §1193, as enacted 1872, amended by Code Amdts 1873–74 ch 586 §4 p 411, Stats 1911 ch 681 §7 p 1318.

§8064. Acts on behalf of co-owner; Requirements

An owner may give a notice or execute or file a document under this part on behalf of a co-owner if the owner acts on the co-owner's behalf and includes in the notice or document the name and address of the co-owner on whose behalf the owner acts. **Leg.H.** Added Stats 2010 ch 697 §20 (SB 189), effective January 1, 2011, operative July 1, 2012.

§8066. Acts within scope of agent's authority

An act that may be done by or to a person under this part may be done by or to the person's agent to the extent the act is within the scope of the agent's authority. **Leg.H.** Added Stats 2010 ch 697 §20 (SB 189), effective January 1, 2011, operative July 1, 2012.

CHAPTER 2
NOTICE

Form of notice; "Writings". §8100.
Contents of notice; Sufficiency. §8102.

Failure to pay full compensation to laborer; Notice required; Contents; Grounds for disciplinary action. §8104.
Manner of giving notice. §8106.
Person to be notified at person's residence, place of business, or specified addresses. §8108.
Registered or certified mail, express mail, or overnight delivery by express service carrier. §8110.
Posting of notice. §8114.
When notice is complete and deemed to have been given at specified times. §8116.
Proof that notice was given; Proof of notice declaration; Contents. §8118.
Delivery of notices and claims for work on common area within common interest development. §8119.

§8100. Form of notice; "Writings"

Notice under this part shall be in writing. Writing includes printing and typewriting. **Leg.H.** Added Stats 2010 ch 697 §20 (SB 189), effective January 1, 2011, operative July 1, 2012.

§8102. Contents of notice; Sufficiency

(a) Notice under this part shall, in addition to any other information required by statute for that type of notice, include all of the following information to the extent known to the person giving the notice:

(1) The name and address of the owner or reputed owner.

(2) The name and address of the direct contractor.

(3) The name and address of the construction lender, if any.

(4) A description of the site sufficient for identification, including the street address of the site, if any. If a sufficient legal description of the site is given, the effectiveness of the notice is not affected by the fact that the street address is erroneous or is omitted.

(5) The name, address, and relationship to the parties of the person giving the notice.

(6) If the person giving the notice is a claimant:

(A) A general statement of the work provided.

(B) The name of the person to or for whom the work is provided.

(C) A statement or estimate of the claimant's demand, if any, after deducting all just credits and offsets.

(b) Notice is not invalid by reason of any variance from the requirements of this section if the notice is sufficient to substantially inform the person given notice of the information required by this section and other information required in the notice. **Leg.H.** Added Stats 2010 ch 697 §20 (SB 189), effective January 1, 2011, operative July 1, 2012.

Prior Law: Former CC §3097, similar to UCC §§3305, 3306, 8202, was added Stats 1917 ch 751 §1 and repealed Stats 1963 ch 819 §2, effective January 1, 1965.

§8104. Failure to pay full compensation to laborer; Notice required; Contents; Grounds for disciplinary action

(a) A direct contractor or subcontractor on a work of improvement governed by this part that employs a laborer and fails to pay the full compensation due the laborer, including any employer payments described in Section 1773.1 of the Labor Code and implementing regulations, shall not later than the date the compensation became delinquent, give the laborer, the laborer's bargaining representative, if any, the construction lender or reputed construction lender, if any, and the owner or reputed owner, notice that includes all of the following information, in addition to the information required by Section 8102:

(1) The name and address of the laborer, and of any person or entity described in subdivision (b) of Section 8024 to which employer payments are due.

(2) The total number of straight time and overtime hours worked by the laborer on each job.

(3) The amount then past due and owing.

(b) Failure to give the notice required by subdivision (a) constitutes grounds for disciplinary action under the Contractors' State License Law, Chapter 9 (commencing with Section 7000) of Division 3 of the Business and Professions Code. **Leg.H.** Added Stats 2010 ch 697 §20 (SB 189), effective January 1, 2011, operative July 1, 2012.

Prior Law: Former CC §3097, similar to UCC §§3305, 3306, 8202, was added Stats 1917 ch 751 §1 and repealed Stats 1963 ch 819 §2, effective January 1, 1965.

§8106. Manner of giving notice

Except as otherwise provided by statute, notice under this part shall be given by any of the following means:

(a) Personal delivery.

(b) Mail in the manner provided in Section 8110.

(c) Leaving the notice and mailing a copy in the manner provided in Section 415.20 of the Code of Civil Procedure for service of summons and complaint in a civil action. **Leg.H.** Added Stats 2010 ch 697 §20 (SB 189), effective January 1, 2011, operative July 1, 2012.

§8108. Person to be notified at person's residence, place of business, or specified addresses

Except as otherwise provided by this part, notice under this part shall be given to the person to be notified at the person's residence, the person's place of business, or at any of the following addresses:

(a) If the person to be notified is an owner other than a public entity, the owner's address shown on the direct contract, the building permit, or a construction trust deed.

(b) If the person to be notified is a public entity, the office of the public entity or another address specified by the public entity in the contract or elsewhere for service of notices, papers, and other documents.

(c) If the person to be notified is a construction lender, the construction lender's address shown on the construction loan agreement or construction trust deed.

(d) If the person to be notified is a direct contractor or a subcontractor, the contractor's address shown on the building permit, on the contractor's contract, or on the records of the Contractors' State License Board.

(e) If the person to be notified is a claimant, the claimant's address shown on the claimant's contract, preliminary notice, claim of lien, stop payment notice, or claim against a payment bond, or on the records of the Contractors' State License Board.

(f) If the person to be notified is a surety on a bond, the surety's address shown on the bond for service of notices, papers, and other documents, or on the records of the Department of Insurance. **Leg.H.** Added Stats 2010 ch 697 §20 (SB 189), effective January 1, 2011, operative July 1, 2012.

§8110. Registered or certified mail, express mail, or overnight delivery by express service carrier

Except as otherwise provided by this part, notice by mail under this part shall be given by registered or certified mail, express mail, or overnight delivery by an express service carrier. **Leg.H.** Added Stats 2010 ch 697 §20 (SB 189), effective January 1, 2011, operative July 1, 2012.

§8114. Posting of notice

A notice required by this part to be posted shall be displayed in a conspicuous location at the site. **Leg.H.** Added Stats 2010 ch 697 §20 (SB 189), effective January 1, 2011, operative July 1, 2012.

§8116. When notice is complete and deemed to have been given at specified times

Notice under this part is complete and deemed to have been given at the following times:

(a) If given by personal delivery, when delivered.

(b) If given by mail, when deposited in the mail or with an express service carrier in the manner provided in Section 1013 of the Code of Civil Procedure.

(c) If given by leaving the notice and mailing a copy in the manner provided in Section 415.20 of the Code of Civil Procedure for service of summons in a civil action, five days after mailing.

(d) If given by posting, when displayed.

(e) If given by recording, when recorded in the office of the county recorder. **Leg.H.** Added Stats 2010 ch 697 §20 (SB 189), effective January 1, 2011, operative July 1, 2012.

Prior Law: Former CC §3097, similar to UCC §§3305, 3306, 8202, was added Stats 1917 ch 751 §1 and repealed Stats 1963 ch 819 §2, effective January 1, 1965.

§8118. Proof that notice was given; Proof of notice declaration; Contents

(a) Proof that notice was given to a person in the manner required by this part shall be made by a proof of notice declaration that states all of the following:

(1) The type or description of the notice given.

(2) The date, place, and manner of notice, and facts showing that notice was given in the manner required by statute.

(3) The name and address of the person to which notice was given, and, if appropriate, the title or capacity in which the person was given notice.

(b) If the notice is given by mail, the declaration shall be accompanied by one of the following:

(1) Documentation provided by the United States Postal Service showing that payment was made to mail the notice using registered or certified mail, or express mail.

(2) Documentation provided by an express service carrier showing that payment was made to send the notice using an overnight delivery service.

(3) A return receipt, delivery confirmation, signature confirmation, tracking record, or other proof of delivery or attempted delivery provided by the United States Postal Service, or a photocopy of the record of delivery and receipt maintained by the United States Postal Service, showing the date of delivery and to whom delivered, or in the event of nondelivery, by the returned envelope itself.

(4) A tracking record or other documentation provided by an express service carrier showing delivery or attempted delivery of the notice. **Leg.H.** Added Stats 2010 ch 697 §20 (SB 189), effective January 1, 2011, operative July 1, 2012.

§8119. Delivery of notices and claims for work on common area within common interest development

(a) With respect to a work of improvement on a common area within a common interest development: (1) The association is deemed to be an agent of the owners of separate interests in the common interest development for all notices and claims required by this part. (2) If any provision of this part requires the delivery or service of a notice or claim to or on the owner of common area property, the notice or claim may be delivered to or served on the association.

(b) For the purposes of this section, the terms "association," "common area," "common interest development," and "separate interest" have the meanings provided in Article 2 (commencing with Section 4075) of Chapter 1 of Part 5 and Article 2 (commencing with Section 6526) of Chapter 1 of Part 5.3. **Leg.H.** Added Stats 2017 ch 44 §5 (AB 534), effective January 1, 2018.

CHAPTER 3
WAIVER AND RELEASE

Applicability of chapter. §8120.
Affecting claimant's rights; Exception. §8122.
Effect of claimant's waiver and release on payment bond from lien or claim; Conditions. §8124.
Validity and enforceability of oral or written statement. §8126.
Reduction or release of stop payment notice; Writing; Effect. §8128.
Enforceability of accord and satisfaction or agreement and settlement; Effect of article. §8130.
Conditional waiver and release in exchange for progress payment; Form. §8132.
Unconditional waiver and release in exchange for progress payment; Form. §8134.
Conditional waiver and release in exchange for final payment; Form. §8136.
Unconditional waiver and release in exchange for final payment; Form. §8138.

§8120. Applicability of chapter

The provisions of this chapter apply to a work of improvement governed by this part. **Leg.H.** Added Stats 2010 ch 697 §20 (SB 189), effective January 1, 2011, operative July 1, 2012.

§8122. Affecting claimant's rights; Exception

An owner, direct contractor, or subcontractor may not, by contract or otherwise, waive, affect, or impair any other claimant's rights under this part, whether with or without notice, and any term of a contract that purports to do so is void and unenforceable unless and until the claimant executes and delivers a waiver and release under this article. **Leg.H.** Added Stats 2010 ch 697 §20 (SB 189), effective January 1, 2011, operative July 1, 2012.

Prior Law: Former CC §3262, similar to former UCC §3801, was added Stats 1917 ch 751 §1 and repealed Stats 1963 ch 819 §2, effective January 1, 1965.

Former CC §3262, relating to title acquired by indorsee, was enacted Stats 1872 and repealed Code Amdts 1873–74 ch 612 §275. Historical Derivation: (a) Former CCP §1187.1, as added Stats 1951 ch 1159 §1. (b) Former CCP §1201, as added Stats 1885 ch 152 §7.

§8124. Effect of claimant's waiver and release on payment bond from lien or claim; Conditions

A claimant's waiver and release does not release the owner, construction lender, or surety on a payment bond from a lien or claim unless both of the following conditions are satisfied:

(a) The waiver and release is in substantially the form provided in this article and is signed by the claimant.

(b) If the release is a conditional release, there is evidence of payment to the claimant. Evidence of payment may be either of the following:

(1) The claimant's endorsement on a single or joint payee check that has been paid by the financial institution on which it was drawn.

(2) Written acknowledgment of payment by the claimant. **Leg.H.** Added Stats 2010 ch 697 §20 (SB 189), effective January 1, 2011, operative July 1, 2012.

§8126. Validity and enforceability of oral or written statement

An oral or written statement purporting to waive, release, impair or otherwise adversely affect a lien or claim is void and unenforceable and does not create an estoppel or impairment of the lien or claim unless either of the following conditions is satisfied:

(a) The statement is pursuant to a waiver and release under this article.

(b) The claimant has actually received payment in full for the claim. **Leg.H.** Added Stats 2010 ch 697 §20 (SB 189), effective January 1, 2011, operative July 1, 2012.

§8128. Reduction or release of stop payment notice; Writing; Effect

(a) A claimant may reduce the amount of, or release in its entirety, a stop payment notice. The reduction or release shall be in writing and may be given in a form other than a waiver and release form provided in this article.

(b) The writing shall identify whether it is a reduction of the amount of the stop payment notice, or a release of the notice in its entirety. If the writing is a reduction, it shall state the amount of the reduction, and the amount to remain withheld after the reduction.

(c) A claimant's reduction or release of a stop payment notice has the following effect:

(1) The reduction or release releases the claimant's right to enforce payment of the claim stated in the notice to the extent of the reduction or release.

(2) The reduction or release releases the person given the notice from the obligation to withhold funds pursuant to the notice to the extent of the reduction or release.

(3) The reduction or release does not preclude the claimant from giving a subsequent stop payment notice that is timely and proper.

(4) The reduction or release does not release any right of the claimant other than the right to enforce payment of the claim stated in the stop payment notice to the extent of the reduction or release. **Leg.H.** Added Stats 2010 ch 697 §20 (SB 189), effective January 1, 2011, operative July 1, 2012.

§8130. Enforceability of accord and satisfaction or agreement and settlement; Effect of article

This article does not affect the enforceability of either an accord and satisfaction concerning a good faith dispute or an agreement made in settlement of an action pending in court if the accord and satisfaction or agreement and settlement make specific reference to the lien or claim. **Leg.H.** Added Stats 2010 ch 697 §20 (SB 189), effective January 1, 2011, operative July 1, 2012.

§8132. Conditional waiver and release in exchange for progress payment; Form

If a claimant is required to execute a waiver and release in exchange for, or in order to induce payment of, a progress payment and the claimant is not, in fact, paid in exchange for the waiver and release or a single payee check or joint payee check is given in exchange for the waiver and release, the waiver and release shall be null, void, and unenforceable unless it is in substantially the following form:

CONDITIONAL WAIVER AND RELEASE ON PROGRESS PAYMENT

NOTICE: THIS DOCUMENT WAIVES THE CLAIMANT'S LIEN, STOP PAYMENT NOTICE, AND PAYMENT BOND RIGHTS EFFECTIVE ON RECEIPT OF PAYMENT. A PERSON SHOULD NOT RELY ON THIS DOCUMENT UNLESS SATISFIED THAT THE CLAIMANT HAS RECEIVED PAYMENT.

Identifying Information

Name of Claimant:_____
Name of Customer:_____
Job Location:_____
Owner:_____
Through Date:_____

Conditional Waiver and Release

This document waives and releases lien, stop payment notice, and payment bond rights the claimant has for labor and service provided, and equipment and material delivered, to the customer on this job through the Through Date of this document. Rights based upon labor or service provided, or equipment or material delivered, pursuant to a written change order that has been fully executed by the parties prior to the date that this document is signed by the claimant, are waived and released by this document, unless listed as an Exception below. This document is effective only on the claimant's receipt of payment from the financial institution on which the following check is drawn:

Maker of Check:_____
Amount of Check: $_____
Check Payable to:_____

Exceptions

This document does not affect any of the following:

(1) Retentions.

(2) Extras for which the claimant has not received payment.

(3) The following progress payments for which the claimant has previously given a conditional waiver and release but has not received payment:

Date(s) of waiver and release: _____
Amount(s) of unpaid progress payment(s): $_____

(4) Contract rights, including (A) a right based on rescission, abandonment, or breach of contract, and (B) the right to recover compensation for work not compensated by the payment.

Signature

Claimant's Signature:_____
Claimant's Title:_____
Date of Signature:_____

Leg.H. Added Stats 2010 ch 697 §20 (SB 189), effective January 1, 2011, operative July 1, 2012.

§8134. Unconditional waiver and release in exchange for progress payment; Form

If the claimant is required to execute a waiver and release in exchange for, or in order to induce payment of, a progress payment and the claimant asserts in the waiver that the claimant has, in fact, been paid the progress payment, the waiver and release shall be null, void, and unenforceable unless it is in substantially the following form, with the text of the "Notice to Claimant" in at least as large a type as the largest type otherwise in the form:

UNCONDITIONAL WAIVER AND RELEASE ON PROGRESS PAYMENT

NOTICE TO CLAIMANT: THIS DOCUMENT WAIVES AND RELEASES LIEN, STOP PAYMENT NOTICE, AND PAYMENT BOND RIGHTS UNCONDITIONALLY AND STATES THAT YOU HAVE BEEN PAID FOR GIVING UP THOSE RIGHTS. THIS DOCUMENT IS ENFORCEABLE AGAINST YOU IF YOU SIGN IT, EVEN IF YOU HAVE NOT BEEN PAID. IF YOU HAVE NOT BEEN PAID, USE A CONDITIONAL WAIVER AND RELEASE FORM.

Identifying Information

Name of Claimant:_____
Name of Customer:_____
Job Location:_____
Owner:_____
Through Date:_____

Unconditional Waiver and Release

This document waives and releases lien, stop payment notice, and payment bond rights the claimant has for labor and service provided, and equipment and material delivered, to the customer on this job through the Through Date of this document. Rights based upon labor or service provided, or equipment or material delivered, pursuant to a written change order that has been fully executed by the parties prior to the date that this document is signed by the claimant, are waived and released by this document, unless listed as an Exception below. The claimant has received the following progress payment:

$_____

Exceptions

This document does not affect any of the following:

(1) Retentions.

(2) Extras for which the claimant has not received payment.

(3) Contract rights, including (A) a right based on rescission, abandonment, or breach of contract, and (B) the right to recover compensation for work not compensated by the payment.

Signature

Claimant's Signature:_____
Claimant's Title:_____
Date of Signature:_____

Leg.H. Added Stats 2010 ch 697 §20 (SB 189), effective January 1, 2011, operative July 1, 2012.

§8136. Conditional waiver and release in exchange for final payment; Form

If the claimant is required to execute a waiver and release in exchange for, or in order to induce payment of, a final payment and the claimant is not, in fact, paid in exchange for the waiver and release or a single payee check or joint payee check is given in exchange for the waiver and release, the waiver and release shall be null, void, and unenforceable unless it is in substantially the following form:

CONDITIONAL WAIVER AND RELEASE ON FINAL PAYMENT

NOTICE: THIS DOCUMENT WAIVES THE CLAIMANT'S LIEN, STOP PAYMENT NOTICE, AND PAYMENT BOND RIGHTS EFFECTIVE ON RECEIPT OF PAYMENT. A PERSON SHOULD NOT RELY ON THIS DOCUMENT UNLESS SATISFIED THAT THE CLAIMANT HAS RECEIVED PAYMENT.

Identifying Information

Name of Claimant:_____
Name of Customer:_____
Job Location:_____
Owner:_____

Conditional Waiver and Release

This document waives and releases lien, stop payment notice, and payment bond rights the claimant has for labor and service provided, and equipment and material delivered, to the customer on this job. Rights based upon labor or service provided, or equipment or material delivered, pursuant to a written change order that has been fully executed by the parties prior to the date that this document is signed by the claimant, are waived and released by this document, unless listed as an Exception below. This document is effective only on the claimant's receipt of payment from the financial institution on which the following check is drawn:

Maker of Check:_____
Amount of Check: $_____
Check Payable to:_____

Exceptions

This document does not affect any of the following:

Disputed claims for extras in the amount of: $_____

Signature

Claimant's Signature:_____
Claimant's Title:_____
Date of Signature:_____

Leg.H. Added Stats 2010 ch 697 §20 (SB 189), effective January 1, 2011, operative July 1, 2012.

§8138. Unconditional waiver and release in exchange for final payment; Form

If the claimant is required to execute a waiver and release in exchange for, or in order to induce payment of, a final payment and the claimant asserts in the waiver that the claimant has, in fact, been paid the final payment, the waiver and release shall be null, void, and unenforceable unless it is in substantially the following form, with the text of the "Notice to Claimant" in at least as large a type as the largest type otherwise in the form:

UNCONDITIONAL WAIVER AND RELEASE ON FINAL PAYMENT

NOTICE TO CLAIMANT: THIS DOCUMENT WAIVES AND RELEASES LIEN, STOP PAYMENT NOTICE, AND PAYMENT BOND RIGHTS UNCONDITIONALLY AND STATES THAT YOU HAVE BEEN PAID FOR GIVING UP THOSE RIGHTS. THIS DOCUMENT IS ENFORCEABLE AGAINST YOU IF YOU SIGN IT, EVEN IF YOU

HAVE NOT BEEN PAID. IF YOU HAVE NOT BEEN PAID, USE A CONDITIONAL WAIVER AND RELEASE FORM.

Identifying Information
Name of Claimant:_____
Name of Customer:_____
Job Location:_____
Owner:_____

Unconditional Waiver and Release

This document waives and releases lien, stop payment notice, and payment bond rights the claimant has for all labor and service provided, and equipment and material delivered, to the customer on this job. Rights based upon labor or service provided, or equipment or material delivered, pursuant to a written change order that has been fully executed by the parties prior to the date that this document is signed by the claimant, are waived and released by this document, unless listed as an Exception below. The claimant has been paid in full.

Exceptions

This document does not affect the following:
Disputed claims for extras in the amount of: $_____

Signature
Claimant's Signature:_____
Claimant's Title:_____
Date of Signature:_____

Leg.H. Added Stats 2010 ch 697 §20 (SB 189), effective January 1, 2011, operative July 1, 2012.

CHAPTER 4
BONDS

Law governing bond. §8150.
Release of surety from liability. §8152.
Construction of bonds; Effect of breach of contract, Conditions of recovery. §8154.

§8150. Law governing bond

The Bond and Undertaking Law (Chapter 2 (commencing with Section 995.010) of Title 14 of Part 2 of the Code of Civil Procedure) applies to a bond given under this part, except to the extent this part prescribes a different rule or is inconsistent. **Leg.H.** Added Stats 2010 ch 697 §20 (SB 189), effective January 1, 2011, operative July 1, 2012.

§8152. Release of surety from liability

None of the following releases a surety from liability on a bond given under this part:

(a) A change, alteration, or modification to a contract, plan, specification, or agreement for a work of improvement or for work provided for a work of improvement.

(b) A change or modification to the terms of payment or an extension of the time for payment for a work of improvement.

(c) A rescission or attempted rescission of a contract, agreement, or bond.

(d) A condition precedent or subsequent in the bond purporting to limit the right of recovery of a claimant otherwise entitled to recover pursuant to a contract, agreement, or bond.

(e) In the case of a bond given for the benefit of claimants, the fraud of a person other than the claimant seeking to recover on the bond. **Leg.H.** Added Stats 2010 ch 697 §20 (SB 189), effective January 1, 2011, operative July 1, 2012.

Prior Law: Former CC §3225, similar to UCC §§3501–3503, was added Stats 1917 ch 751 §1 p 1553 and repealed Stats 1963 ch 819 §2 p 1997, effective January 1, 1965.

Former CC §3225, relating to necessity of protest, was enacted Stats 1872 and repealed Stats 1917 ch 751 §1 p 1531. Historical Derivation: (a) Former CCP §1200.1, as added Stats 1951 ch 1159 §1 p 2955, amended Stats 1955 ch 1750 §1 p 3235, Stats 1961 ch 804 §5 p 2077, Stats 1969 ch 1611 §26 p 3396. (b) Former CCP §1183, as enacted 1872, amended by Code Amdts 1873–74 ch 586 §1 p 409, Code Amdts 1880 ch 67 §1 p 63, Stats 1885 ch 152 §1 p 143, Stats 1887 ch 137 §1 p 152, Stats 1899 ch 35 §1 p 34, Stats 1903 ch 76 §1 p 84, Stats 1911 ch 681 §1 p 1313, Stats 1929 ch 869 §1 p 1924.

§8154. Construction of bonds; Effect of breach of contract, Conditions of recovery

(a) A bond given under this part shall be construed most strongly against the surety and in favor of all persons for whose benefit the bond is given.

(b) A surety is not released from liability to those for whose benefit the bond has been given by reason of a breach of the direct contract or on the part of any obligee named in the bond.

(c) Except as otherwise provided by statute, the sole conditions of recovery on the bond are that the claimant is a person described in Article 1 (commencing with Section 8400) of Chapter 4 of Title 2, or in Section 9100, and has not been paid the full amount of the claim. **Leg.H.** Added Stats 2010 ch 697 §20 (SB 189), effective January 1, 2011, operative July 1, 2012.

Prior Law: Former CC §3226, similar to UCC §§3501–3503, was added Stats 1917 ch 751 §1 p 1554 and repealed Stats 1963 ch 819 §2 p 1997, effective January 1, 1965.

Former CC §3226, relating to by whom protest made, was enacted Stats 1872 and repealed Stats 1917 ch 751 §1 p 1531. Historical Derivation: (a) Former CCP §1200.1, as added Stats 1951 ch 1159 §1 p 2955, amended Stats 1955 ch 1750 §1 p 3235, Stats 1961 ch 804 §5 p 2077, Stats 1969 ch 1611 §26 p 3396. (b) Former CCP §1183, as enacted 1872, amended by Code Amdts 1873–74 ch 586 §1 p 409, Code Amdts 1880 ch 67 §1 p 63, Stats 1885 ch 152 §1 p 143, Stats 1887 ch 137 §1 p 152, Stats 1899 ch 35 §1 p 34, Stats 1903 ch 76 §1 p 84, Stats 1911 ch 681 §1 p 1313, Stats 1929 ch 869 §1 p 1924.

TITLE 2
PRIVATE WORKS OF IMPROVEMENT

Chapter 1. General Provisions.
Chapter 2. Preliminary Notice.
Chapter 3. Design Professionals Lien.
Chapter 4. Mechanics Lien.
Chapter 5. Stop Payment Notice.
Chapter 6. Payment Bond.
Chapter 7. Security for Large Project.
Chapter 8. Prompt Payment.

CHAPTER 1
GENERAL PROVISIONS

Article 1. Application of Title.
Article 2. Construction Documents.
Article 3. Completion.

ARTICLE 1
Application of Title

Applicability of title. §8160.

§8160. Applicability of title

This title applies to a work of improvement that is not governed by Title 3 (commencing with Section 9000) of this part. **Leg.H.** Added Stats 2010 ch 697 §20 (SB 189), effective January 1, 2011, operative July 1, 2012.

Prior Law: Former CC §3109, similar to UCC §§3306, 3408, 3415, 8202, was added Stats 1917 ch 751 §1 p 1537 and repealed Stats 1963 ch 819 §2 p 1997, effective January 1, 1965.

Former CC §3156, similar to UCC §3503, was added Stats 1917 ch 751 §1 p 1544 and repealed Stats 1963 ch 819 §2 p 1997, effective January 1, 1965.

Former CC §3156, relating to when presentment and notice excused, was enacted Stats 1872 and repealed Stats 1917 ch 751 §1 p 1531.

ARTICLE 2
Construction Documents

Written direct contract; Required information. §8170.
Application form for building permit. §8172.
Specified instruments to bear designation "Construction Trust Deed"; Information required; Duties of county recorder. §8174.

§8170. Written direct contract; Required information

(a) A written direct contract shall provide a space for the owner to enter the following information:

(1) The owner's name, address, and place of business, if any.

(2) The name and address of the construction lender, if any. This paragraph does not apply to a home improvement contract or swimming pool contract subject to Article 10 (commencing with Section 7150) of Chapter 9 of Division 3 of the Business and Professions Code.

(b) A written contract entered into between a direct contractor and subcontractor, or between subcontractors, shall provide a space for the name and address of the owner, direct contractor, and construction lender, if any. **Leg.H.** Added Stats 2010 ch 697 §20 (SB 189), effective January 1, 2011, operative July 1, 2012.

Prior Law: Former CC §3097, similar to UCC §§3305, 3306, 8202, was added Stats 1917 ch 751 §1 and repealed Stats 1963 ch 819 §2, effective January 1, 1965.

§8172. Application form for building permit

(a) A public entity that issues building permits shall, in its application form for a building permit, provide space and a designation for the applicant to enter the name, branch designation, if any, and address of the construction lender and shall keep the information on file open for public inspection during the regular business hours of the public entity.

(b) If there is no known construction lender, the applicant shall note that fact in the designated space.

(c) Failure of the applicant to indicate the name and address of the construction lender on the application does not relieve a person required to give the construction lender preliminary notice from that duty. **Leg.H.** Added Stats 2010 ch 697 §20 (SB 189), effective January 1, 2011, operative July 1, 2012.

Prior Law: Former CC §3097, similar to UCC §§3305, 3306, 8202, was added Stats 1917 ch 751 §1 and repealed Stats 1963 ch 819 §2, effective January 1, 1965.

§8174. Specified instruments to bear designation "Construction Trust Deed"; Information required; Duties of county recorder

(a) A mortgage, deed of trust, or other instrument securing a loan, any of the proceeds of which may be used for a work of improvement, shall bear the designation "Construction Trust Deed" prominently on its face and shall state all of the following:

(1) The name and address of the construction lender.

(2) The name and address of the owner of the real property described in the instrument.

(3) A legal description of the real property that secures the loan and, if known, the street address of the property.

(b) Failure to comply with subdivision (a) does not affect the validity of the mortgage, deed of trust, or other instrument.

(c) Failure to comply with subdivision (a) does not relieve a person required to give preliminary notice from that duty.

(d) The county recorder of the county in which the instrument is recorded shall indicate in the general index of the official records of the county that the instrument secures a construction loan. **Leg.H.** Added Stats 2010 ch 697 §20 (SB 189), effective January 1, 2011, operative July 1, 2012.

Prior Law: Former CC §3097, similar to UCC §§3305, 3306, 8202, was added Stats 1917 ch 751 §1 and repealed Stats 1963 ch 819 §2, effective January 1, 1965.

ARTICLE 3
Completion

Completion of work of improvement. §8180.
Notice of completion; Recordation; Contents. §8182.
Acceptance of notice of completion. §8184.
When work of improvement is made pursuant to two or more direct contracts. §8186.
Recordation of notice of cessation; Form of notice. §8188.
Persons entitled to copy of notice of completion or cessation; Responsibilities of owner; Applicability. §8190.

§8180. Completion of work of improvement

(a) For the purpose of this title, completion of a work of improvement occurs upon the occurrence of any of the following events:

(1) Actual completion of the work of improvement.

(2) Occupation or use by the owner accompanied by cessation of labor.

(3) Cessation of labor for a continuous period of 60 days.

(4) Recordation of a notice of cessation after cessation of labor for a continuous period of 30 days.

(b) Notwithstanding subdivision (a), if a work of improvement is subject to acceptance by a public entity, completion occurs on acceptance. **Leg.H.** Added Stats 2010 ch 697 §20 (SB 189), effective January 1, 2011, operative July 1, 2012.

Prior Law: Former CC §3086, similar to UCC §§3104, 3112, was added Stats 1917 ch 751 §1 p 1533 and repealed Stats 1963 ch 819 §2 p 1997, effective January 1, 1965.

Former CC §3086, relating to non-negotiable instruments, was enacted Stats 1872 and repealed Stats 1917 ch 751 §1 p 1531.

§8182. Notice of completion; Recordation; Contents

(a) An owner may record a notice of completion on or within 15 days after the date of completion of a work of improvement.

(b) The notice of completion shall be signed and verified by the owner.

(c) The notice shall comply with the requirements of Chapter 2 (commencing with Section 8100) of Title 1, and shall also include all of the following information:

(1) If the notice is given only of completion of a contract for a particular portion of the work of improvement as provided in Section 8186, the name of the direct contractor under that contract and a general statement of the work provided pursuant to the contract.

(2) If signed by the owner's successor in interest, the name and address of the successor's transferor.

(3) The nature of the interest or estate of the owner.

(4) The date of completion. An erroneous statement of the date of completion does not affect the effectiveness of the notice if the true date of completion is 15 days or less before the date of recordation of the notice.

(d) A notice of completion that does not comply with the provisions of this section is not effective.

(e) For the purpose of this section, "owner" means the owner who causes a building, improvement, or structure to be constructed, altered, or repaired, or that person's successor in interest at the date a notice of completion is recorded, whether the interest or estate of the owner be in fee, as vendee under a contract of purchase, as lessee, or other interest or estate less than the fee. Where the interest or estate is held by two or more persons as joint tenants or tenants in common, any one or more of the cotenants may be deemed to be the "owner" within the meaning of this section. **Leg.H.** Added Stats 2010 ch 697 §20 (SB 189), effective January 1, 2011, operative July 1, 2012.

Prior Law: Former CC §3093, similar to UCC §3114, was added Stats 1917 ch 751 §1 p 1535 and repealed Stats 1963 ch 819 §2 p 1997, effective January 1, 1965.

Former CC §3093, relating to contents of negotiable instrument, was enacted Stats 1872 and repealed Stats 1917 ch 751 §1 p 1531.

§8184. Acceptance of notice of completion

A notice of completion in otherwise proper form, verified and containing the information required by this title, shall be accepted by the recorder for recording and is deemed duly recorded without acknowledgment. **Leg.H.** Added Stats 2010 ch 697 §20 (SB 189), effective January 1, 2011, operative July 1, 2012.

Prior Law: Former CC §3093, similar to UCC §3114, was added Stats 1917 ch 751 §1 p 1535 and repealed Stats 1963 ch 819 §2 p 1997, effective January 1, 1965.

Former CC §3093, relating to contents of negotiable instrument, was enacted Stats 1872 and repealed Stats 1917 ch 751 §1 p 1531.

§8186. When work of improvement is made pursuant to two or more direct contracts

If a work of improvement is made pursuant to two or more direct contracts, each covering a portion of the work of improvement:

(a) The owner may record a notice of completion of a direct contract for a portion of the work of improvement. On recordation of the notice of completion, for the purpose of Sections 8412 and 8414, a direct contractor is deemed to have completed the contract for which the notice of completion is recorded and a claimant other than a direct contractor is deemed to have ceased providing work.

(b) If the owner does not record a notice of completion under this section, the period for recording a claim of lien is that provided in Sections 8412 and 8414. **Leg.H.** Added Stats 2010 ch 697 §20 (SB 189), effective January 1, 2011, operative July 1, 2012.

Prior Law: Former CC § 3117, similar to UCC §§3204–3206, 8107, 8304, was added Stats 1917 ch 751 §1 p 1538 and repealed Stats 1963 ch 819 §2 p 1997, effective January 1, 1965.

Former CC §3117, relating to liability of indorser to payee, was enacted Stats 1872 and repealed Stats 1917 ch 751 §1 p 1531.

§8188. Recordation of notice of cessation; Form of notice

(a) An owner may record a notice of cessation if there has been a continuous cessation of labor on a work of improvement for at least 30 days prior to the recordation that continues through the date of the recordation.

(b) The notice shall be signed and verified by the owner.

(c) The notice shall comply with the requirements of Chapter 2 (commencing with Section 8100) of Title 1, and shall also include all of the following information:

(1) The date on or about which labor ceased.

(2) A statement that the cessation has continued until the recordation of the notice.

(d) For the purpose of this section, "owner" means the owner who causes a building, improvement, or structure to be constructed, altered, or repaired, or that person's successor in interest at the date a notice of cessation is recorded, whether the interest or estate of the owner be in fee, as vendee under a contract of purchase, as lessee, or other interest or estate less than the fee. Where the interest or estate is held by two or more persons as joint tenants or tenants in common, any one or more of the cotenants may be deemed to be the "owner" within the meaning of this section. **Leg.H.** Added Stats 2010 ch 697 §20 (SB 189), effective January 1, 2011, operative July 1, 2012.

Prior Law: Former CC §3092, similar to UCC §3114, was added Stats 1917 ch 751 §1 p 1534, amended Stats 1921 ch 194 §2 p 213, and repealed Stats 1963 ch 819 §2 p 1997, effective January 1, 1965.

Former CC §3092, relating to pledge, etc., was enacted Stats 1872 and repealed Stats 1917 ch 751 §1 p 1531.

§8190. Persons entitled to copy of notice of completion or cessation; Responsibilities of owner; Applicability

(a) An owner that records a notice of completion or cessation shall, within 10 days of the date the notice of completion or cessation is filed for record, give a copy of the notice to all of the following persons:

(1) A direct contractor.

(2) A claimant that has given the owner preliminary notice.

(b) The copy of the notice shall be given in compliance with the requirements of Chapter 2 (commencing with Section 8100) of Title 1.

(c) If the owner fails to give notice to a person as required by subdivision (a), the notice is ineffective to shorten the time within which that person may record a claim of lien under Sections 8412 and 8414. The ineffectiveness of the notice is the sole liability of the owner for failure to give notice to a person under subdivision (a).

(d) For the purpose of this section, "owner" means a person who has an interest in real property, or the person's successor in interest on the date a notice of completion or notice of cessation is recorded, who causes a building, improvement, or structure, to be constructed, altered, or repaired on the property. If the property is owned by two or more persons as joint tenants or tenants in common, any one or more of the cotenants may be deemed to be the "owner" within the meaning of this section. However, this section does not apply to any of the following owners:

(1) A person that occupies the real property as a personal residence, if the dwelling contains four or fewer residential units.

(2) A person that has a security interest in the property.

(3) A person that obtains an interest in the property pursuant to a transfer described in subdivision (b), (c), or (d) of Section 1102.2. **Leg.H.** Added Stats 2010 ch 697 §20 (SB 189), effective January 1, 2011, operative July 1, 2012.

CHAPTER 2
PRELIMINARY NOTICE

Notice prior to recording lien claim, giving stop payment notice, or asserting claim against payment bond; Persons entitled to notice; Compliance with specified provisions. §8200.

Preliminary notice to comply with requirements of Section 8102; Contents; Statement. §8202.

Time for preliminary notice. §8204.

Total number of preliminary notices. §8206.

Contractor to provide specified information to person seeking to give preliminary notice. §8208.

When one or more construction loans are obtained after commencement of work of improvement; Notice by owner. §8210.

Validity and enforceability of waiver by owner of statutory rights. §8212.

Filing preliminary notice with county recorder; Duties of county recorder; Purpose of notice; Effect of filing. §8214.

When work of improvement contract provides for specified payment to subcontractor; Failure to comply with notice; Grounds for disciplinary action. §8216.

§8200. Notice prior to recording lien claim, giving stop payment notice, or asserting claim against payment bond; Persons entitled to notice; Compliance with specified provisions

(a) Except as otherwise provided by statute, before recording a lien claim, giving a stop payment notice, or asserting a claim against a payment bond, a claimant shall give preliminary notice to the following persons:

(1) The owner or reputed owner.

(2) The direct contractor or reputed direct contractor to which the claimant provides work, either directly or through one or more subcontractors.

(3) The construction lender or reputed construction lender, if any.

(b) The notice shall comply with the requirements of Chapter 2 (commencing with Section 8100) of Title 1.

(c) Compliance with this section is a necessary prerequisite to the validity of a lien claim or stop payment notice under this title.

(d) Compliance with this section or with Section 8612 is a necessary prerequisite to the validity of a claim against a payment bond under this title.

(e) Notwithstanding the foregoing subdivisions:

(1) A laborer is not required to give preliminary notice.

(2) A claimant with a direct contractual relationship with an owner or reputed owner is required to give preliminary notice only to the construction lender or reputed construction lender, if any. **Leg.H.** Added Stats 2010 ch 697 §20 (SB 189), effective January 1, 2011, operative July 1, 2012.

Prior Law: Former CC §3097, similar to UCC §§3305, 3306, 8202, was added Stats 1917 ch 751 §1 and repealed Stats 1963 ch 819 §2, effective January 1, 1965.

§8202. Preliminary notice to comply with requirements of Section 8102; Contents; Statement

(a) The preliminary notice shall comply with the requirements of Section 8102, and shall also include:

(1) A general description of the work to be provided.

(2) An estimate of the total price of the work provided and to be provided.

(3) The following statement in boldface type:

NOTICE TO PROPERTY OWNER

EVEN THOUGH YOU HAVE PAID YOUR CONTRACTOR IN FULL, if the person or firm that has given you this notice is not paid in full for labor, service, equipment, or material provided or to be provided to your construction project, a lien may be placed on your property. Foreclosure of the lien may lead to loss of all or part of your property. You may wish to protect yourself against this by (1) requiring your contractor to provide a signed release by the person or firm that has given you this notice before making payment to your contractor, or (2) any other method that is appropriate under the circumstances.

This notice is required by law to be served by the undersigned as a statement of your legal rights. This notice is not intended to reflect upon the financial condition of the contractor or the person employed by you on the construction project.

If you record a notice of cessation or completion of your construction project, you must within 10 days after recording, send a copy of the notice of completion to your contractor and the person or firm that has given you this notice. The notice must be sent by registered or certified mail. Failure to send the notice will extend the deadline to record a claim of lien. You are not required to send the notice if you are a residential homeowner of a dwelling containing four or fewer units.

(b) If preliminary notice is given by a subcontractor that has not paid all compensation due to a laborer, the notice shall include the name and address of the laborer and any person or entity described in subdivision (b) of Section 8024 to which payments are due.

(c) If an invoice for material or certified payroll contains the information required by this section and Section 8102, a copy of the invoice or payroll, given in compliance with the requirements of Chapter 2 (commencing with Section 8100) of Title 1, is sufficient. **Leg.H.** Added Stats 2010 ch 697 §20 (SB 189), effective January 1, 2011, operative July 1, 2012.

Prior Law: Former CC §3097, similar to UCC §§3305, 3306, 8202, was added Stats 1917 ch 751 §1 and repealed Stats 1963 ch 819 §2, effective January 1, 1965.

§8204. Time for preliminary notice

(a) A preliminary notice shall be given not later than 20 days after the claimant has first furnished work on the work of improvement. If work has been provided by a claimant who did not give a preliminary notice, that claimant shall not be precluded from giving a preliminary notice at any time thereafter. The claimant shall, however, be entitled to record a lien, give a stop payment notice, and assert a claim against a payment bond only for work performed within 20 days prior to the service of the preliminary notice, and at any time thereafter.

(b) A design professional who has furnished services for the design of the work of improvement and who gives a preliminary notice not later than 20 days after the work of improvement has commenced shall be deemed to have complied with Section 8200 with respect to the design services furnished, or to be furnished. **Leg.H.** Added Stats 2010 ch 697 §20 (SB 189), effective January 1, 2011, operative July 1, 2012.

Prior Law: Former CC §3097, similar to UCC §§3305, 3306, 8202, was added Stats 1917 ch 751 §1 and repealed Stats 1963 ch 819 §2, effective January 1, 1965.

§8206. Total number of preliminary notices

(a) Except as provided in subdivision (b), a claimant need give only one preliminary notice to each person to which notice must be given under this chapter with respect to all work provided by the claimant for a work of improvement.

(b) If a claimant provides work pursuant to contracts with more than one subcontractor, the claimant shall give a separate preliminary notice with respect to work provided pursuant to each contract.

(c) A preliminary notice that contains a general description of work provided by the claimant through the date of the notice also covers work provided by the claimant after the date of the notice whether or not they are within the scope of the general description contained in the notice. **Leg.H.** Added Stats 2010 ch 697 §20 (SB 189), effective January 1, 2011, operative July 1, 2012.

Prior Law: Former CC §3097, similar to UCC §§3305, 3306, 8202, was added Stats 1917 ch 751 §1 and repealed Stats 1963 ch 819 §2, effective January 1, 1965.

§8208. Contractor to provide specified information to person seeking to give preliminary notice

A direct contractor shall make available to any person seeking to give preliminary notice the following information:

(a) The name and address of the owner.

(b) The name and address of the construction lender, if any. **Leg.H.** Added Stats 2010 ch 697 §20 (SB 189), effective January 1, 2011, operative July 1, 2012.

Prior Law: Former CC §3097, similar to UCC §§3305, 3306, 8202, was added Stats 1917 ch 751 §1 and repealed Stats 1963 ch 819 §2, effective January 1, 1965.

§8210. When one or more construction loans are obtained after commencement of work of improvement; Notice by owner

If one or more construction loans are obtained after commencement of a work of improvement, the owner shall give notice of the name and address of the construction lender or lenders to each person that has given the owner preliminary notice. **Leg.H.** Added Stats 2010 ch 697 §20 (SB 189), effective January 1, 2011, operative July 1, 2012.

Prior Law: Former CC §3097, similar to UCC §§3305, 3306, 8202, was added Stats 1917 ch 751 §1 and repealed Stats 1963 ch 819 §2, effective January 1, 1965.

§8212. Validity and enforceability of waiver by owner of statutory rights

An agreement made or entered into by an owner whereby the owner agrees to waive the rights conferred on the owner by this chapter is void and unenforceable. **Leg.H.** Added Stats 2010 ch 697 §20 (SB 189), effective January 1, 2011, operative July 1, 2012.

Prior Law: Former CC §3097, similar to UCC §§3305, 3306, 8202, was added Stats 1917 ch 751 §1 and repealed Stats 1963 ch 819 §2, effective January 1, 1965.

§8214. Filing preliminary notice with county recorder; Duties of county recorder; Purpose of notice; Effect of filing

(a) Each person who has served a preliminary notice may file the preliminary notice with the county recorder. A preliminary notice filed pursuant to this section shall comply with the requirements of Section 8102.

(b) Upon the acceptance for recording of a notice of completion or notice of cessation the county recorder shall mail to those persons who have filed a preliminary notice, notification that a notice of completion or notice of cessation has been recorded on the property, and shall affix the date that the notice of completion or notice of cessation was recorded with the county recorder. The notification given by the county recorder under this section is not governed by the requirements of Chapter 2 (commencing with Section 8100) of Title 1.

(c) The failure of the county recorder to mail the notification to the person who filed a preliminary notice, or the failure of those persons to receive the notification or to receive complete notification, shall not affect the period within which a claim of lien is required to be recorded. However, the county recorder shall make a good faith effort to mail notification to those persons who have filed the preliminary notice under this section and to do so within five days after the recording of a notice of completion or notice of cessation.

(d) The county recorder may cause to be destroyed all documents filed pursuant to this section, two years after the date of filing.

(e) The preliminary notice that a person may file pursuant to this section is for the limited purpose of facilitating the mailing of notice by the county recorder of recorded notices of completion and notices of cessation. The notice that is filed is not a recordable document and shall not be entered into those official records of the county which by law impart constructive notice. Notwithstanding any other provision of law, the index maintained by the recorder of filed preliminary notices shall be separate and distinct from those indexes maintained by the county recorder of those official records of the county which by law impart constructive notice. The filing of a preliminary notice with the county recorder does not give rise to any actual or constructive notice with respect to any party of the existence or contents of a filed preliminary notice nor to any duty of inquiry on the part of any party as to the existence or contents of that notice. **Leg.H.** Added Stats 2010 ch 697 §20 (SB 189), effective January 1, 2011, operative July 1, 2012.

Prior Law: Former CC §3097, similar to UCC §§3305, 3306, 8202, was added Stats 1917 ch 751 §1 and repealed Stats 1963 ch 819 §2, effective January 1, 1965.

§8216. When work of improvement contract provides for specified payment to subcontractor; Failure to comply with notice; Grounds for disciplinary action

If the contract of any subcontractor on a particular work of improvement provides for payment to the subcontractor of more than four hundred dollars ($400), the failure of that subcontractor, licensed under the Contractors' State License Law (Chapter 9 (commencing with Section 7000) of Division 3 of the Business and Professions Code), to give the notice provided for in this chapter, constitutes grounds for disciplinary action under the Contractors' State License Law. **Leg.H.** Added Stats 2010 ch 697 §20 (SB 189), effective January 1, 2011, operative July 1, 2012.

Prior Law: Former CC §3097, similar to UCC §§3305, 3306, 8202, was added Stats 1917 ch 751 §1 and repealed Stats 1963 ch 819 §2, effective January 1, 1965.

CHAPTER 3
DESIGN PROFESSIONALS LIEN

"Design professional". §8300.
Lien. §8302.
Entitlement to lien; Conditions. §8304.
Effect of recordation of claim of lien; Expiration; Satisfaction. §8306.
Applicability of specified provisions of part to liens created under Chapter 3. §8308.
Ability of design professional to obtain lien for work of improvement. §8310.
Recordation of claim of lien by design professional. §8312.
Ability of design professional to pursue other remedies. §8314.
Priorities of lien. §8316.
Work of improvement relating to single-family, owner-occupied residence for specified construction cost; Lien prohibited. §8318.
Authorization to convert recorded design professional lien to mechanics lien if certain requirements are met. §8319.

§8300. "Design professional"

For purposes of this chapter, a "design professional" is a person described in Section 8014 who provides services pursuant to a written contract with a landowner for the design, engineering, or planning of a work of improvement. **Leg.H.** Added Stats 2010 ch 697 §20 (SB 189), effective January 1, 2011, operative July 1, 2012.

§8302. Lien

(a) A design professional has, from the date of recordation of a claim of lien under this chapter, a lien on the site notwithstanding the absence of commencement of the planned work of improvement, if the landowner who contracted for the design professional's services is also the owner of the site at the time of recordation of the claim of lien.

(b) The lien of the design professional is for the amount of the design professional's fee for services provided under the contract or the reasonable value of those services, whichever is less. The amount of the lien is reduced by the amount of any deposit or prior payment under the contract.

(c) A design professional may not record a claim of lien, and a lien may not be created, under this chapter unless a building permit or other governmental approval in furtherance of the work of improvement has been obtained in connection with or utilizing the services provided by the design professional. **Leg.H.** Added Stats 2010 ch 697 §20 (SB 189), effective January 1, 2011, operative July 1, 2012.

Prior Law: Former CC §3081.2, relating to contents of loan statement, was added Stats 1955 ch 1791 §1, effective October 1, 1955 amended Stats 1957 ch 1988 §1 and repealed Stats 1961 ch 886 §29, effective June 17, 1961.

§8304. Entitlement to lien; Conditions

A design professional is not entitled to a lien under this chapter unless all of the following conditions are satisfied:

(a) The work of improvement for which the design professional provided services has not commenced.

(b) The landowner defaults in a payment required under the contract or refuses to pay the demand of the design professional made under the contract.

(c) Not less than 10 days before recording a claim of lien, the design professional gives the landowner notice making a demand for payment, and stating that a default has occurred under the contract and the amount of the default.

(d) The design professional records a claim of lien. The claim of lien shall include all of the following information:

(1) The name of the design professional.

(2) The amount of the claim.

(3) The current owner of record of the site.

(4) A legal description of the site.

(5) Identification of the building permit or other governmental approval for the work of improvement. **Leg.H.** Added Stats 2010 ch 697 §20 (SB 189), effective January 1, 2011, operative July 1, 2012.

Prior Law: Former CC §3081.3, relating to maximum costs to be paid on a note, was added Stats 1955 ch 1791 §1, effective October 1, 1955 amended Stats 1957 ch 1423 §1 and repealed Stats 1961 ch 886 §29, effective June 17, 1961.

§8306. Effect of recordation of claim of lien; Expiration; Satisfaction

(a) On recordation of the claim of lien, a lien is created in favor of the named design professional.

(b) The lien automatically expires and is null and void and of no further force or effect on the occurrence of either of the following events:

(1) The commencement of the work of improvement for which the design professional provided services.

(2) The expiration of 90 days after recording the claim of lien, unless the design professional commences an action to enforce the lien within that time.

(c) If the landowner partially or fully satisfies the lien, the design professional shall execute and record a document that evidences a partial or full satisfaction and release of the lien, as applicable. **Leg.H.** Added Stats 2010 ch 697 §20 (SB 189), effective January 1, 2011, operative July 1, 2012.

Prior Law: Former CC §3081.4, relating to liability of borrower for costs, was added Stats 1955 ch 1791 §1, effective October 1, 1955 and repealed Stats 1961 ch 886 §29, effective June 17, 1961.

§8308. Applicability of specified provisions of part to liens created under Chapter 3

(a) Except as provided in subdivision (b), no provision of this part applies to a lien created under this chapter.

(b) The following provisions of this part apply to a lien created under this chapter:

(1) This chapter.

(2) Article 1 (commencing with Section 8000) of Chapter 1 of Title 1.

(3) Section 8424.

(4) Article 6 (commencing with Section 8460) of Chapter 4.

(5) Article 7 (commencing with Section 8480) of Chapter 4.

(6) Article 8 (commencing with Section 8490) of Chapter 4. **Leg.H.** Added Stats 2010 ch 697 §20 (SB 189), effective January 1, 2011, operative July 1, 2012.

Prior Law: Former CC §3081.5, relating to installment payments on loans, was added Stats 1955 ch 1791 §1, effective October 1, 1955 amended Stats 1957 ch 178 §1 and repealed Stats 1961 ch 886 §29, effective June 17, 1961.

§8310. Ability of design professional to obtain lien for work of improvement

This chapter does not affect the ability of a design professional to obtain a lien for a work of improvement under Section 8400. **Leg.H.** Added Stats 2010 ch 697 §20 (SB 189), effective January 1, 2011, operative July 1, 2012.

Prior Law: Former CC §3081.6, relating to foreclosure of security, was added Stats 1955 ch 1791 §1, effective October 1, 1955 and repealed Stats 1961 ch 886 §29, effective June 17, 1961.

§8312. Recordation of claim of lien by design professional

A design professional shall record a claim of lien under this chapter no later than 90 days after the design professional knows or has reason to know that the work of improvement will not be commenced. **Leg.H.** Added Stats 2010 ch 697 §20 (SB 189), effective January 1, 2011, operative July 1, 2012.

Prior Law: Former CC §3081.7, relating to exceptions to application of former chapter, was added Stats 1955 ch 1791 §1, amended Stats 1957 ch 1349 §1 and repealed Stats 1961 ch 886 §29, effective June 17, 1961.

§8314. Ability of design professional to pursue other remedies

The creation of a lien under this chapter does not affect the ability of the design professional to pursue other remedies. **Leg.H.** Added Stats 2010 ch 697 §20 (SB 189), effective January 1, 2011, operative July 1, 2012.

Prior Law: Former CC §3081.8, relating to exceptions to application of former chapter, was added Stats 1955 ch 1791 §1, effective October 1, 1955 and repealed Stats 1961 ch 886 §29, effective June 17, 1961.

§8316. Priorities of lien

(a) No lien created under this chapter affects or takes priority over the interest of record of a purchaser, lessee, or encumbrancer, if the interest of the purchaser, lessee, or encumbrancer in the real property was duly recorded before recordation of the claim of lien.

(b) No lien created under this chapter affects or takes priority over an encumbrance of a construction lender that funds the loan for the work of improvement for which the design professional provided services. **Leg.H.** Added Stats 2010 ch 697 §20 (SB 189), effective January 1, 2011, operative July 1, 2012.

Prior Law: Former CC §3081.9, relating to damages, was added Stats 1955 ch 1791 §1, effective October 1, 1955 and repealed Stats 1961 ch 886 §29, effective June 17, 1961.

§8318. Work of improvement relating to single-family, owner-occupied residence for specified construction cost; Lien prohibited

A design professional may not obtain a lien under this chapter for services provided for a work of improvement relating to a single-family, owner-occupied residence for which the expected construction cost is less than one hundred thousand dollars ($100,000). **Leg.H.** Added Stats 2010 ch 697 §20 (SB 189), effective January 1, 2011, operative July 1, 2012.

§8319. Authorization to convert recorded design professional lien to mechanics lien if certain requirements are met

(a) A design professional may convert a recorded design professional lien to a mechanics lien if all of the following requirements are met:

(1) The design professional lien expires pursuant to paragraph (1) of subdivision (b) of Section 8306.

(2) The design professional lien remains fully or partially unpaid.

(3) Within 30 days of the expiration of the design professional lien pursuant to paragraph (1) of subdivision (b) of Section 8306, the design professional records a mechanics lien for the amount of the unpaid design professional lien.

(4) The recorded mechanics lien states that it is a converted design professional lien but shall be recorded and enforced as a mechanics lien, except the design professional need not provide a preliminary notice to enforce this mechanics lien. This mechanics lien shall be effective as of the date of recordation of this mechanics lien and shall be given priority pursuant to the provisions of Section 8450.

(b) This section shall not apply if a design professional lien expires pursuant to paragraph (2) of subdivision (b) of Section 8306. **Leg.H.** Added Stats 2011 ch 127 §1 (SB 424), effective January 1, 2012, operative July 1, 2012.

CHAPTER 4
MECHANICS LIEN

Article 1. Who is Entitled to Lien.
Article 2. Conditions to Enforcing a Lien.

Article 3. Amount of Lien.
Article 4. Property Subject to Lien.
Article 5. Priorities.
Article 6. Enforcement of Lien.
Article 7. Release Order.
Article 8. Removal of Claim of Lien from Record.

ARTICLE 1
Who is Entitled to Lien

Persons entitled to lien right. §8400.
Person providing work for site improvement. §8402.
When work is authorized for work of improvement or for site improvement; Circumstances. §8404.

§8400. Persons entitled to lien right

A person that provides work authorized for a work of improvement, including, but not limited to, the following persons, has a lien right under this chapter:

(a) Direct contractor.
(b) Subcontractor.
(c) Material supplier.
(d) Equipment lessor.
(e) Laborer.
(f) Design professional. **Leg.H.** Added Stats 2010 ch 697 §20 (SB 189), effective January 1, 2011, operative July 1, 2012.

Prior Law: Former CC §3110, similar to UCC §§3415, 8201, was added Stats 1917 ch 751 §1 p 1537 and repealed Stats 1963 ch 819 §2 p 1997, effective January 1, 1965.

Former CC§3110, relating to signature on separate paper, was enacted Stats 1872 and repealed Stats 1917 ch 751 §1 p 1531.

§8402. Person providing work for site improvement

A person that provides work authorized for a site improvement has a lien right under this chapter. **Leg.H.** Added Stats 2010 ch 697 §20 (SB 189), effective January 1, 2011, operative July 1, 2012.

Prior Law: Former CC §3112, similar to present UCC §§3202, 8107, 8304, was added Stats 1917 ch 751 §1 and repealed Stats 1963 ch 819 §2, effective January 1, 1965.

Former CC §3112, relating to general indorsement, was enacted Stats 1872 and repealed Stats 1917 ch 751 §1 p 1531.

§8404. When work is authorized for work of improvement or for site improvement; Circumstances

Work is authorized for a work of improvement or for a site improvement in any of the following circumstances:

(a) It is provided at the request of or agreed to by the owner.
(b) It is provided or authorized by a direct contractor, subcontractor, architect, project manager, or other person having charge of all or part of the work of improvement or site improvement. **Leg.H.** Added Stats 2010 ch 697 §20 (SB 189), effective January 1, 2011, operative July 1, 2012.

Prior Law: Former CC§3110, similar to UCC §§3415, 8201, was added Stats 1917 ch 751 §1 p 1537 and repealed Stats 1963 ch 819 §2 p 1997, effective January 1, 1965.

Former CC §3110, relating to signature on separate paper, was enacted Stats 1872 and repealed Stats 1917 ch 751 §1 p 1531.

Former CC §3112, similar to present UCC §§3202, 8107, 8304, was added Stats 1917 ch 751 §1 and repealed Stats 1963 ch 819 §2, effective January 1, 1965.

Former CC §3112, relating to general indorsement, was enacted Stats 1872 and repealed Stats 1917 ch 751 §1 p 1531.

ARTICLE 2
Conditions to Enforcing a Lien

Preliminary notice required. §8410.
Recordation of claim of lien by direct contractor; Times. §8412.
Recordation of claim of lien by claimant; Times. §8414.
Claim of mechanics lien; Form; Contents; Service; Failure to serve. §8416.
Effect of erroneous information. §8422.
Dispute as to correctness or validity of claims; Bond; Notice; Time of commencing action. §8424.

§8410. Preliminary notice required

A claimant may enforce a lien only if the claimant has given preliminary notice to the extent required by Chapter 2 (commencing with Section 8200) and made proof of notice. **Leg.H.** Added Stats 2010 ch 697 §20 (SB 189), effective January 1, 2011, operative July 1, 2012.

Prior Law: Former CC §3114, similar to UCC §§3204, 8107, 8304, was added Stats 1917 ch 751 §1 p 1538 and repealed Stats 1963 ch 819 §2 p 1997, effective January 1, 1965.

Former CC §3114, relating to general indorsement, was enacted Stats 1872 and repealed Stats 1917 ch 751 §1 p 1531.

§8412. Recordation of claim of lien by direct contractor; Times

A direct contractor may not enforce a lien unless the contractor records a claim of lien after the contractor completes the direct contract, and before the earlier of the following times:

(a) Ninety days after completion of the work of improvement.
(b) Sixty days after the owner records a notice of completion or cessation. **Leg.H.** Added Stats 2010 ch 697 §20 (SB 189), effective January 1, 2011, operative July 1, 2012.

Prior Law: Former CC §3115, similar to UCC §§3204, 8107, 8304, was added Stats 1917 ch 751 §1 p 1538 and repealed Stats 1963 ch 819 §2 p 1997, effective January 1, 1965.

Former CC §3115, relating to destruction of negotiability, was enacted Stats 1872 and repealed Stats 1917 ch 751 §1 p 1531.

§8414. Recordation of claim of lien by claimant; Times

A claimant other than a direct contractor may not enforce a lien unless the claimant records a claim of lien within the following times:

(a) After the claimant ceases to provide work.
(b) Before the earlier of the following times:
(1) Ninety days after completion of the work of improvement.
(2) Thirty days after the owner records a notice of completion or cessation. **Leg.H.** Added Stats 2010 ch 697 §20 (SB 189), effective January 1, 2011, operative July 1, 2012.

Prior Law: Former CC §3116, similar to UCC §§3204, 8107, 8304, was added Stats 1917 ch 751 §1 p 1538 and repealed Stats 1963 ch 819 §2 p 1997, effective January 1, 1965.

Former CC §3116, relating to implied warranty of indorser, was enacted Stats 1872, amended Code Amdts 1873–74 ch 612 §268 p 263, and repealed Stats 1917 ch 751 §1 p 1531.

§8416. Claim of mechanics lien; Form; Contents; Service; Failure to serve

(a) A claim of mechanics lien shall be a written statement, signed and verified by the claimant, containing all of the following:

(1) A statement of the claimant's demand after deducting all just credits and offsets.
(2) The name of the owner or reputed owner, if known.
(3) A general statement of the kind of work furnished by the claimant.
(4) The name of the person by whom the claimant was employed or to whom the claimant furnished work.
(5) A description of the site sufficient for identification.
(6) The claimant's address.
(7) A proof of service affidavit completed and signed by the person serving a copy of the claim of mechanics lien pursuant to subdivision (c). The affidavit shall show the date, place, and manner of service, and facts showing that the service was made in accordance with this section. The affidavit shall show the name and address of the owner or reputed owner upon whom the copy of the claim of mechanics lien was served pursuant to paragraphs (1) or (2) of subdivision (c), and the title or capacity in which the person or entity was served.
(8) The following statement, printed in at least 10-point boldface type. The letters of the last sentence shall be printed in uppercase type, excepting the Internet Web site address of the Contractors' State License Board, which shall be printed in lowercase type:

"NOTICE OF MECHANICS LIEN
ATTENTION!

Upon the recording of the enclosed MECHANICS LIEN with the county recorder's office of the county where the property is located, your property is subject to the filing of a legal action seeking a court-ordered foreclosure sale of the real property on which the lien has been recorded. That legal action must be filed with the court no later than 90 days after the date the mechanics lien is recorded.

The party identified in the enclosed mechanics lien may have provided labor or materials for improvements to your property and may not have been paid for these items. You are receiving this notice because it is a required step in filing a mechanics lien foreclosure action against your property. The foreclosure action will seek a sale of your property in order to pay for unpaid labor, materials, or improvements provided to your property. This may affect your ability to borrow against, refinance, or sell the property until the mechanics lien is released.

BECAUSE THE LIEN AFFECTS YOUR PROPERTY, YOU MAY WISH TO SPEAK WITH YOUR CONTRACTOR IMMEDIATELY, OR CONTACT AN ATTORNEY, OR FOR MORE INFORMATION ON MECHANICS LIENS GO TO THE CONTRACTORS' STATE LICENSE BOARD WEB SITE AT www.cslb.ca.gov."

(b) A claim of mechanics lien in otherwise proper form, verified and containing the information required in subdivision (a), shall be accepted by the recorder for recording and shall be deemed duly recorded without acknowledgment.

(c) A copy of the claim of mechanics lien, which includes the Notice of Mechanics Lien required by paragraph (8) of subdivision (a), shall be served on the owner or reputed owner. Service shall be made as follows:

(1) For an owner or reputed owner to be notified who resides in or outside this state, by registered mail, certified mail, or first-class mail, evidenced by a certificate of mailing, postage prepaid, addressed to the owner or reputed owner at the owner's or reputed owner's residence or place of business address or at the address shown by the building permit on file with the authority issuing a building permit for the work, or as otherwise provided in Section 8174.

(2) If the owner or reputed owner cannot be served by this method, then the copy of the claim of mechanics lien may be given by registered mail, certified mail, or first-class mail, evidenced by a certificate of mailing, postage prepaid, addressed to the construction lender or to the original contractor.

(d) Service of the copy of the claim of mechanics lien by registered mail, certified mail, or first-class mail, evidenced by a certificate of mailing, postage prepaid, is complete at the time of the deposit of that first-class, certified, or registered mail.

(e) Failure to serve the copy of the claim of mechanics lien as prescribed by this section, including the Notice of Mechanics Lien required by paragraph (8) of subdivision (a), shall cause the claim of mechanics lien to be unenforceable as a matter of law. **Leg.H.** Added Stats 2010 ch 697 §20 (SB 189), effective January 1, 2011, operative July 1, 2012. Amended Stats 2011 ch 673 §2 (AB 456), effective January 1, 2012.

Prior Law: Former CC §3084, related to "claim of lien" or "mechanics lien"; recordation; and service of mechanics lien, was added Stats 1969 ch 1362 §2, operative January 1, 1971, amended Stats 1981 ch 321 §1 and repealed January 1, 2011, by its own terms.

Former CC §3084, similar to UCC §3105, was added Stats 1917 ch 751 §1 p 1533 and repealed Stats 1963 ch 819 §2 p 1997, effective January 1, 1965.

§8422. Effect of erroneous information

(a) Except as provided in subdivisions (b) and (c), erroneous information contained in a claim of lien relating to the claimant's demand, credits and offsets deducted, the work provided, or the description of the site, does not invalidate the claim of lien.

(b) Erroneous information contained in a claim of lien relating to the claimant's demand, credits and offsets deducted, or the work provided, invalidates the claim of lien if the court determines either of the following:

(1) The claim of lien was made with intent to defraud.

(2) An innocent third party, without notice, actual or constructive, became the bona fide owner of the property after recordation of the claim of lien, and the claim of lien was so deficient that it did not put the party on further inquiry in any manner.

(c) Any person who shall willfully include in a claim of lien labor, services, equipment, or materials not furnished for the property described in the claim, shall thereby forfeit the person's lien. **Leg.H.** Added Stats 2010 ch 697 §20 (SB 189), effective January 1, 2011, operative July 1, 2012. Amended Stats 2011 ch 44 §5 (SB 190), effective January 1, 2012, operative July 1, 2012.

Prior Law: Former CC §3118, similar to UCC §§3206, 8105, 8107, 8304, was added Stats 1917 ch 751 §1 p 1539 and repealed Stats 1963 ch 819 §2 p 1997, effective January 1, 1965.

Former CC §3118, relating to indorsement without recourse, was enacted Stats 1872 and repealed Stats 1917 ch 751 §1 p 1531. Historical Derivation: (a) Former CC §3118, as added Stats 1969 ch 1362 §2, operative January 1, 1971. (b) Former CCP §1193.1, as added Stats 1951 ch 1376 §2, amended Stats 1955 ch 1511 § 1, Stats 1959 ch 1549 —x § 1, Stats 1963 ch 1081 §1. (c) Former CCP §1187, as enacted Stats 1872, amended Code Amdts 1873–74 ch 586 §2 p 410, Stats 1887 ch 137 §3 p 154, Stats 1897 ch 141 p 202, Stats 1911 ch 681 §4 p 1316, Stats 1919 ch 146 §1 p 190, Stats 1929 ch 870 §1 p 1928, Stats 1939 ch 1068 §1 p 2994, Stats 1947 ch 28 §1 p 510, Stats 1949 ch 632 §1 p 1129. (d) Former CCP §1202, as added Stats 1885 ch 152 §7 p 146, amended Stats 1911 ch 681 §11 p 1319.

Former CC §3261, similar to former UCC §3801, was added Stats 1917 ch 751 §1 p 1558 and repealed Stats 1963 ch 819 §2 p 1997, effective January 1, 1965.

Former CC §3261, providing bank note negotiable after payment, was enacted Stats 1872 and repealed Stats 1917 ch 751 §1 p 1531. Historical Derivation: (a) Former CCP §1196.1, as added Stats 1951 ch 1159 §1 p 2952. (b) Former CCP §1203, as added Stats 1893 ch 171 §1 p 202, amended Stats 1911 ch 681 §12 p 1319.

§8424. Dispute as to correctness or validity of claims; Bond; Notice; Time of commencing action

(a) An owner of real property or an owner of any interest in real property subject to a recorded claim of lien, or a direct contractor or subcontractor affected by the claim of lien, that disputes the correctness or validity of the claim may obtain release of the real property from the claim of lien by recording a lien release bond. The principal on the bond may be the owner of the property, the direct contractor, or the subcontractor.

(b) The bond shall be conditioned on payment of any judgment and costs the claimant recovers on the lien. The bond shall be in an amount equal to 125 percent of the amount of the claim of lien or 125 percent of the amount allocated in the claim of lien to the real property to be released. The bond shall be executed by an admitted surety insurer.

(c) The bond may be recorded either before or after commencement of an action to enforce the lien. On recordation of the bond, the real property is released from the claim of lien and from any action to enforce the lien.

(d) A person that obtains and records a lien release bond shall give notice to the claimant. The notice shall comply with the requirements of Chapter 2 (commencing with Section 8100) of Title 1 and shall include a copy of the bond. Failure to give the notice required by this section does not affect the validity of the bond, but the statute of limitations for an action on the bond is tolled until notice is given. The claimant shall commence an action on the bond within six months after notice is given. **Leg.H.** Added Stats 2010 ch 697 §20 (SB 189), effective January 1, 2011, operative July 1, 2012.

Prior Law: Former CC §3143, similar to UCC §§3413, 3418, 8201, 8202, was added Stats 1917 ch 751 §1 p 1542 and repealed Stats 1963 ch 819 §2 p 1997, effective January 1, 1965.

Former CC §3143, relating to form of notice (based on Field's Draft was enacted Stats 1872 and repealed Stats 1917 ch 751 §1 p 1531.

ARTICLE 3
Amount of Lien

Amount of lien. §8430.
When work is not included in direct contract or modification of contract; Constructive notice of provisions of contract or modification. §8432.
Enforcement of lien by direct contractor or subcontractor; Amount. §8434.

§8430. Amount of lien

(a) The lien is a direct lien for the lesser of the following amounts:

(1) The reasonable value of the work provided by the claimant.

(2) The price agreed to by the claimant and the person that contracted for the work.

(b) The lien is not limited in amount by the contract price for the work of improvement except as provided in Section 8600.

(c) This section does not preclude the claimant from including in a claim of lien work performed based on a written modification of the contract, or as a result of rescission, abandonment, or breach of the contract. If there is a rescission, abandonment, or breach of the contract, the amount of the lien may not exceed the reasonable value of the work provided by the claimant. **Leg.H.** Added Stats 2010 ch 697 §20 (SB 189), effective January 1, 2011, operative July 1, 2012.

Prior Law: Former CC §3110, similar to UCC §§3415, 8201, was added Stats 1917 ch 751 §1 p 1537 and repealed Stats 1963 ch 819 §2 p 1997, effective January 1, 1965.

Former CC §3110, relating to signature on separate paper, was enacted Stats 1872 and repealed Stats 1917 ch 751 §1 p 1531.

Former CC §3123, similar to present UCC §3117, was added Stats 1917 ch 751 §1 and repealed Stats 1963 ch 819 §2, effective January 1, 1965.

Former CC §3123, relating to indorsee in due course, was enacted Stats 1872 and repealed Stats 1917 ch 751 §1.

§8432. When work is not included in direct contract or modification of contract; Constructive notice of provisions of contract or modification

(a) A lien does not extend to work, whether or not the work is authorized by a direct contractor or subcontractor, if the work is not included in a direct contract or a modification of that contract, and the claimant had actual knowledge or constructive notice of the provisions of that contract or modification before providing the work.

(b) The filing of a contract or modification of that contract with the county recorder, before the commencement of a work of improvement, is constructive notice of the provisions of the contract or modification to a person providing work on that work of improvement. **Leg.H.** Added Stats 2010 ch 697 §20 (SB 189), effective January 1, 2011, operative July 1, 2012.

Prior Law: Former CC §3124, similar to present UCC §3203, was added Stats 1917 ch 751 §1 p 1539 and repealed Stats 1963 ch 819 §2 p 1997, effective January 1, 1965.

Former CC §3124, relating to rights of indorsee in due course, was enacted Stats 1872 and repealed Stats 1917 ch 751 §1 p 1531.

§8434. Enforcement of lien by direct contractor or subcontractor; Amount

A direct contractor or a subcontractor may enforce a lien only for the amount due pursuant to that contractor's contract after deducting all lien claims of other claimants for work provided and embraced within that contract. **Leg.H.** Added Stats 2010 ch 697 §20 (SB 189), effective January 1, 2011, operative July 1, 2012.

Prior Law: Former CC §3140, similar to UCC §§3207, 3306, 3307, 8302, was added Stats 1917 ch 751 §1 p 1541 and repealed Stats 1963 ch 819 §2 p 1997, effective January 1, 1965.

ARTICLE 4
Property Subject to Lien

Attachment of lien. §8440.
Specified interests in real property subject to lien. §8442.
Notice of nonresponsibility; Contents. §8444.
Recordation of one claim of lien on two or more works of improvement; Conditions. §8446.
When work of improvement consists of construction of two or more separate residential units. §8448.

§8440. Attachment of lien

Subject to Section 8442, a lien attaches to the work of improvement and to the real property on which the work of improvement is situated, including as much space about the work of improvement as is required for the convenient use and occupation of the work of improvement. **Leg.H.** Added Stats 2010 ch 697 §20 (SB 189), effective January 1, 2011, operative July 1, 2012.

Prior Law: Former CC §3112, similar to present UCC §§3202, 8107, 8304, was added Stats 1917 ch 751 §1 and repealed Stats 1963 ch 819 §2, effective January 1, 1965.

Former CC §3112, relating to general indorsement, was enacted Stats 1872 and repealed Stats 1917 ch 751 §1 p 1531.

Former CC §3128, similar to UCC §3206, was added Stats 1917 ch 751 §1 p 1539 and repealed Stats 1963 ch 819 §2 p 1997, effective January 1, 1965.

§8442. Specified interests in real property subject to lien

The following interests in real property to which a lien attaches are subject to the lien:

(a) The interest of a person that contracted for the work of improvement.

(b) The interest of a person that did not contract for the work of improvement, if work for which the lien is claimed was provided with the knowledge of that person, unless that person gives notice of nonresponsibility under Section 8444. **Leg.H.** Added Stats 2010 ch 697 §20 (SB 189), effective January 1, 2011, operative July 1, 2012.

Prior Law: Former CC §3128, similar to UCC §3206, was added Stats 1917 ch 751 §1 p 1539 and repealed Stats 1963 ch 819 §2 p 1997, effective January 1, 1965.

Former CC §3129, similar to UCC §§3207, 3605, was added Stats 1917 ch 751 §1 p 1540 and repealed Stats 1963 ch 819 §2 p 1997, effective January 1, 1965.

§8444. Notice of nonresponsibility; Contents

(a) An owner of real property or a person claiming an interest in real property on which a work of improvement is situated that did not contract for the work of improvement may give notice of nonresponsibility.

(b) A notice of nonresponsibility shall be signed and verified by the owner.

(c) The notice shall comply with the requirements of Chapter 2 (commencing with Section 8100) of Title 1.

(d) The notice shall also include all of the following information:

(1) The nature of the owner's title or interest.

(2) The name of a purchaser under contract, if any, or lessee, if known.

(3) A statement that the person giving the notice is not responsible for claims arising from the work of improvement.

(e) A notice of nonresponsibility is not effective unless, within 10 days after the person giving notice has knowledge of the work of improvement, the person both posts and records the notice. **Leg.H.** Added Stats 2010 ch 697 §20 (SB 189), effective January 1, 2011, operative July 1, 2012.

Prior Law: Former CC §3094, similar to UCC §3115, was added Stats 1917 ch 751 §1 p 1535, amended Stats 1921 ch 194 §3 p 214, and repealed Stats 1963 ch 819 §2 p 1997, effective January 1, 1965.

Original CC §3094, relating to date, was enacted Stats 1872 and repealed Stats 1917 ch 751 §1 p 1531.

§8446. Recordation of one claim of lien on two or more works of improvement; Conditions

A claimant may record one claim of lien on two or more works of improvement, subject to the following conditions:

(a) The works of improvement have or are reputed to have the same owner, or the work was contracted for by the same person for the works of improvement whether or not they have the same owner.

(b) The claimant in the claim of lien designates the amount due for each work of improvement. If the claimant contracted for a lump sum payment for work provided for the works of improvement and the contract does not segregate the amount due for each work of improvement separately, the claimant may estimate an equitable distribution of the amount due for each work of improvement based on the proportionate amount of work provided for each. If the claimant does not designate the amount due for each work of improvement, the lien is subordinate to other liens.

(c) If there is a single structure on real property of different owners, the claimant need not segregate the proportion of work provided for the portion of the structure situated on real property of each owner. In the lien enforcement action the court may, if it determines it equitable to do so, designate an equitable distribution of the lien among the real property of the owners.

(d) The lien does not extend beyond the amount designated as against other creditors having liens, by judgment, mortgage, or otherwise, on either the works of improvement or the real property on which the works of improvement are situated. **Leg.H.** Added Stats 2010 ch 697 §20 (SB 189), effective January 1, 2011, operative July 1, 2012.

Prior Law: Former CC §3130, similar to UCC §§3201, 8304, was added Stats 1917 ch 751 §1 p 1540 and repealed Stats 1963 ch 819 §2 p 1997, effective January 1, 1965.

Former CC §3130, relating to effect of want of demand on principal debtor, was enacted Stats 1872 and repealed Stats 1917 ch 751 §1 p 1531.

§8448. When work of improvement consists of construction of two or more separate residential units

(a) As used in this section, "separate residential unit" means one residential structure, including a residential structure containing multiple condominium units, together with any common area, garage, or other appurtenant improvements.

(b) If a work of improvement consists of the construction of two or more separate residential units:

(1) Each unit is deemed a separate work of improvement, and completion of each unit is determined separately for purposes of the time for recording a claim of lien on that unit. This paragraph does not affect any lien right under Section 8402 or 8446.

(2) Material provided for the work of improvement is deemed to be provided for use or consumption in each separate residential unit in which the material is actually used or consumed; but if the claimant is unable to segregate the amounts used or consumed in separate residential units, the claimant has the right to all the benefits of Section 8446. **Leg.H.** Added Stats 2010 ch 697 §20 (SB 189), effective January 1, 2011, operative July 1, 2012.

Prior Law: Former CC §3131, similar to UCC §3207, was added Stats 1917 ch 751 §1 p 1540 and repealed Stats 1963 ch 819 §2 p 1997, effective January 1, 1965.

Former CC §3131, relating to presentment, was enacted Stats 1872, amended Code Amdts 1873–74 ch 612 §270 p 263, Stats 1905 ch 462 §1 p 620, and repealed Stats 1917 ch 751 §1 p 1531.

ARTICLE 5
Priorities

Priority over specified encumbrances on work of improvement or property; Exception. §8450.

Priority of mortgage or deed of trust, otherwise subordinate to lien under Section 8450 over certain liens for work provided after recordation of payment bond; Requirements. §8452.
When site improvement is deemed separate work of improvement. §8454.
Priority of optional advance of funds used for construction costs. §8456.
Priority of lien provided for in Section 8402 over specified encumbrances; Exception. §8458.

§8450. Priority over specified encumbrances on work of improvement or property; Exception

(a) A lien under this chapter, other than a lien provided for in Section 8402, has priority over a lien, mortgage, deed of trust, or other encumbrance on the work of improvement or the real property on which the work of improvement is situated, that (1) attaches after commencement of the work of improvement or (2) was unrecorded at the commencement of the work of improvement and of which the claimant had no notice.

(b) Subdivision (a) is subject to the exception provided for in Section 8452. **Leg.H.** Added Stats 2010 ch 697 §20 (SB 189), effective January 1, 2011, operative July 1, 2012.

Prior Law: Former CC §3134, similar to UCC §§3304, 8105, 8203, was added Stats 1917 ch 751 §1 p 1540 and repealed Stats 1963 ch 819 §2 p 1997, effective January 1, 1965.

Original §3134, relating to apparent maturity of bill, was enacted Stats 1872 and repealed Stats 1917 ch 751 §1 p 1531.

§8452. Priority of mortgage or deed of trust, otherwise subordinate to lien under Section 8450 over certain liens for work provided after recordation of payment bond; Requirements

A mortgage or deed of trust, otherwise subordinate to a lien under Section 8450, has priority over a lien for work provided after recordation of a payment bond that satisfies all of the following requirements:

(a) The bond refers to the mortgage or deed of trust.

(b) The bond is in an amount not less than 75 percent of the principal amount of the mortgage or deed of trust. **Leg.H.** Added Stats 2010 ch 697 §20 (SB 189), effective January 1, 2011, operative July 1, 2012.

Prior Law: Former CC §3138, similar to UCC §§3305, 8202, 8302, was added Stats 1917 ch 751 §1 p 1541 and repealed Stats 1963 ch 819 §2 p 1997, effective January 1, 1965.

§8454. When site improvement is deemed separate work of improvement

If a site improvement is provided for in a direct contract separate from the direct contract for the remainder of the work of improvement, the site improvement is deemed a separate work of improvement and commencement of the site improvement is not commencement of the remainder of the work of improvement. **Leg.H.** Added Stats 2010 ch 697 §20 (SB 189), effective January 1, 2011, operative July 1, 2012.

Prior Law: Former CC §3135, similar to UCC §3303, was added Stats 1917 ch 751 §1 p 1540 and repealed Stats 1963 ch 819 §2 p 1997, effective January 1, 1965.

Former CC §3135, relating to apparent maturity of note, was enacted Stats 1872 and repealed Stats 1917 ch 751 §1 p 1531.

§8456. Priority of optional advance of funds used for construction costs

(a) This section applies to a construction loan secured by a mortgage or deed of trust that has priority over a lien under this chapter.

(b) An optional advance of funds by the construction lender that is used for construction costs has the same priority as a mandatory advance of funds by the construction lender, provided that the total of all advances does not exceed the amount of the original construction loan. **Leg.H.** Added Stats 2010 ch 697 §20 (SB 189), effective January 1, 2011, operative July 1, 2012.

Prior Law: Former CC §3136, similar to UCC §3304, was added Stats 1917 ch 751 §1 p 1541 and repealed Stats 1963 ch 819 §2 p 1997, effective January 1, 1965.

Former CC §3136, relating to apparent maturity of note, was enacted Stats 1872 and repealed Stats 1917 ch 751 §1 p 1531.

§8458. Priority of lien provided for in Section 8402 over specified encumbrances; Exception

(a) Except as provided in subdivision (b), a lien provided for in Section 8402 has priority over:

(1) A mortgage, deed of trust, or other encumbrance that attaches after commencement of the site improvement.

(2) A mortgage, deed of trust, or other encumbrance that was unrecorded at the commencement of the site improvement and of which the claimant had no notice.

(3) A mortgage, deed of trust, or other encumbrance that was recorded before commencement of the site improvement, if given for the sole or primary purpose of financing the site improvement. This subdivision does not apply if the loan proceeds are, in good faith, placed in the control of the lender pursuant to a binding agreement with the borrower to the effect that (A) the proceeds are to be applied to the payment of claimants and (B) no portion of the proceeds will be paid to the borrower in the absence of satisfactory evidence that all claims have been paid or that the time for recording a claim of lien has expired and no claim of lien has been recorded.

(b) A mortgage or deed of trust, otherwise subordinate under subdivision (a), has priority over a lien provided for in Section 8402 if a payment bond in an amount not less than 50 percent of the principal amount of the mortgage or deed of trust is recorded before completion of the work of improvement. **Leg.H.** Added Stats 2010 ch 697 §20 (SB 189), effective January 1, 2011, operative July 1, 2012.

Prior Law: Former CC §3137, similar to present UCC §§1201(25), 3304, 8105, 8202, was added Stats 1917 ch 751 §1 and repealed Stats 1963 ch 819 §2, effective January 1, 1965.

Former CC §3137, relating to surrender of instrument as condition of payment, was enacted Stats 1872 and repealed Stats 1917 ch 751 §1 p 1531.

Former CC §3139, similar to UCC §§3201, 3207, 3306, 8302, was added Stats 1917 ch 751 §1 p 1541 and repealed Stats 1963 ch 819 §2 p 1997, effective January 1, 1965.

ARTICLE 6
Enforcement of Lien

Time for commencement of action. §8460.
Recordation of notice of pendency of action with county recorder; Constructive notice. §8461.
Dismissal of action for want of prosecution. §8462.
Amount paid to verify and record claim of lien; Costs. §8464.
Deficiency of proceeds from sale of property on judgment for enforcement of lien; Deficiency judgment. §8466.
Effect of chapter on rights of claimant; Credits on amount of lien. §8468.
Actions to enforce lien for work provided to contractor; Judgment. §8470.

§8460. Time for commencement of action

(a) The claimant shall commence an action to enforce a lien within 90 days after recordation of the claim of lien. If the claimant does not commence an action to enforce the lien within that time, the claim of lien expires and is unenforceable.

(b) Subdivision (a) does not apply if the claimant and owner agree to extend credit, and notice of the fact and terms of the extension of credit is recorded (1) within 90 days after recordation of the claim of lien or (2) more than 90 days after recordation of the claim of lien but before a purchaser or encumbrancer for value and in good faith acquires rights in the property. In that event the claimant shall commence an action to enforce the lien within 90 days after the expiration of the credit, but in no case later than one year after completion of the work of improvement. If the claimant does not commence an action to enforce the lien within that time, the claim of lien expires and is unenforceable. **Leg.H.** Added Stats 2010 ch 697 §20 (SB 189), effective January 1, 2011, operative July 1, 2012.

Prior Law: Former CC §3144, similar to UCC §3402, was added Stats 1917 ch 751 §1 and repealed Stats 1963 ch 819 §2, effective January 1, 1965.

Former CC §3144, relating to method of giving notice, was enacted Stats 1872 and repealed Stats 1917 ch 751 §1.

Former CC §3145, similar to UCC §§3415, 8304, was added Stats 1917 ch 751 §1 p 1542 and repealed Stats 1963 ch 819 §2 p 1997, effective January 1, 1965.

Former CC §3145, relating to notice after indorser's death, was enacted Stats 1872 and repealed Stats 1917 ch 751 §1 p 1531.

§8461. Recordation of notice of pendency of action with county recorder; Constructive notice

After commencement of an action to enforce a lien, the plaintiff shall record in the office of the county recorder of the county, or of the several counties in which the property is situated, a notice of the pendency of the action, as provided in Title 4.5 (commencing with Section 405) of Part 2 of the Code of Civil Procedure, on or before 20 days after the commencement of the action. Only from the time of recording that notice shall a purchaser or encumbrancer of the property affected thereby be deemed to have constructive notice of the pendency of the action, and in that event only of its pendency against parties designated by their real names. **Leg.H.** Added Stats 2010 ch 697 §20 (SB 189), effective January 1, 2011, operative July 1, 2012.

Prior Law: Former CC §3146, similar to UCC §§3417, 8108, 8304, was added Stats 1917 ch 751 §1 p 1542 and repealed Stats 1963 ch 819 §2 p 1997, effective January 1, 1965.

Former CC §3146, relating to notice in ignorance of death, was enacted Stats 1872 and repealed Stats 1917 ch 751 §1 p 1531.

§8462. Dismissal of action for want of prosecution

Notwithstanding Section 583.420 of the Code of Civil Procedure, if an action to enforce a lien is not brought to trial within two years after commencement of the action, the court may in its discretion dismiss the action for want of prosecution. **Leg.H.** Added Stats 2010 ch 697 §20 (SB 189), effective January 1, 2011, operative July 1, 2012.

Prior Law: Former CC §3147, similar to UCC §§3414, 8108, 8304, was added Stats 1917 ch 751 §1 p 1542 and repealed Stats 1963 ch 819 §2 p 1997, effective January 1, 1965.

Former CC §3147, relating to when notice to be given, was enacted Stats 1872 and repealed Stats 1917 ch 751 §1 p 1531.

§8464. Amount paid to verify and record claim of lien; Costs

In addition to any other costs allowed by law, the court in an action to enforce a lien shall allow as costs to each claimant whose lien is established the amount paid to verify and record the claim of lien, whether the claimant is a plaintiff or defendant. **Leg.H.** Added Stats 2010 ch 697 §20 (SB 189), effective January 1, 2011, operative July 1, 2012.

Prior Law: Former CC §3150, similar to UCC §§3417, 8108, 8304, was added Stats 1917 ch 751 §1 p 1543 and repealed Stats 1963 ch 819 §2 p 1997, effective January 1, 1965.

Former CC §3150, relating to additional time for notice, was enacted Stats 1872 and repealed Stats 1917 ch 751 §1 p 1531.

§8466. Deficiency of proceeds from sale of property on judgment for enforcement of lien; Deficiency judgment

If there is a deficiency of proceeds from the sale of property on a judgment for enforcement of a lien, a deficiency judgment may be entered against a party personally liable for the deficiency in the same manner and with the same effect as in an action to foreclose a mortgage. **Leg.H.** Added Stats 2010 ch 697 §20 (SB 189), effective January 1, 2011, operative July 1, 2012.

Prior Law: Former CC §3151, similar to UCC §§3501, 3502, 3604, was added Stats 1917 ch 751 §1 p 1543 and repealed Stats 1963 ch 819 §2 p 1997, effective January 1, 1965.

Former CC §3151, relating to effect of notice of dishonor, was enacted Stats 1872 and repealed Stats 1917 ch 751 §1 p 1531.

§8468. Effect of chapter on rights of claimant; Credits on amount of lien

(a) This chapter does not affect any of the following rights of a claimant:

(1) The right to maintain a personal action to recover a debt against the person liable, either in a separate action or in an action to enforce a lien.

(2) The right to a writ of attachment. In an application for a writ of attachment, the claimant shall refer to this section. The claimant's recording of a claim of lien does not affect the right to a writ of attachment.

(3) The right to enforce a judgment.

(b) A judgment obtained by the claimant in a personal action described in subdivision (a) does not impair or merge the claim of lien, but any amount collected on the judgment shall be credited on the amount of the lien. **Leg.H.** Added Stats 2010 ch 697 §20 (SB 189), effective January 1, 2011, operative July 1, 2012.

Prior Law: Former CC §3152, similar to UCC §3503, was added Stats 1917 ch 751 §1 p 1543 and repealed Stats 1963 ch 819 §2 p 1997, effective January 1, 1965.

§8470. Actions to enforce lien for work provided to contractor; Judgment

In an action to enforce a lien for work provided to a contractor:

(a) The contractor shall defend the action at the contractor's own expense. During the pendency of the action the owner may withhold from the direct contractor the amount of the lien claim.

(b) If the judgment in the action is against the owner or the owner's property, the owner may deduct the amount of the judgment and costs from any amount owed to the direct contractor. If the amount of the judgment and costs exceeds the amount owed to the direct contractor, or if the owner has settled with the direct contractor in full, the owner may recover from the direct contractor, or the sureties on a bond given by the direct contractor for faithful performance of the direct contract, the amount of the judgment and costs that exceed the contract price and for which the direct contractor was originally liable. **Leg.H.** Added Stats 2010 ch 697 §20 (SB 189), effective January 1, 2011, operative July 1, 2012.

Prior Law: Former CC §3153, similar to UCC §§3503, 3504, was added Stats 1917 ch 751 §1 p 1544 and repealed Stats 1963 ch 819 §2 p 1997, effective January 1, 1965.

ARTICLE 7
Release Order

Rights of owner of property or owner of any interest in property; Other cause of actions or claims; Petition for release; Applicability of Code of Civil Procedure. §8480.
Petition the court for release order; Time; Notice. §8482.
Petition for release order; Allegations. §8484.
Hearing; Continuation; Terms; Service of copy of petition and notice of hearing. §8486.
Burden of proof; Judgment; Attorney's fees. §8488.

§8480. Rights of owner of property or owner of any interest in property; Other cause of actions or claims; Petition for release; Applicability of Code of Civil Procedure

(a) The owner of property or the owner of any interest in property subject to a claim of lien may petition the court for an order to release the property from the claim of lien if the claimant has not commenced an action to enforce the lien within the time provided in Section 8460.

(b) This article does not bar any other cause of action or claim for relief by the owner of the property. A release order does not bar any other cause of action or claim for relief by the claimant, other than an action to enforce the claim of lien that is the subject of the release order.

(c) A petition for a release order under this article may be joined with a pending action to enforce the claim of lien that is the subject of the petition. No other action or claim for relief may be joined with a petition under this article.

(d) Notwithstanding Section 8056, Chapter 2.5 (commencing with Section 1141.10) of Title 3 of Part 3 of the Code of Civil Procedure does not apply to a proceeding under this article. **Leg.H.** Added Stats 2010 ch 697 §20 (SB 189), effective January 1, 2011, operative July 1, 2012.

Prior Law: Former CC §3154, similar to UCC §3501, was enacted Stats 1872 and repealed Stats 1963 ch 819 §2, effective January 1, 1965.

§8482. Petition the court for release order; Time; Notice

An owner of property may not petition the court for a release order under this article unless at least 10 days before filing the petition the owner gives the claimant notice demanding that the claimant execute and record a release of the claim of lien. The notice shall comply with the requirements of Chapter 2 (commencing with Section 8100) of Title 1, and shall state the grounds for the demand. **Leg.H.** Added Stats 2010 ch 697 §20 (SB 189), effective January 1, 2011, operative July 1, 2012.

§8484. Petition for release order; Allegations

A petition for a release order shall be verified and shall allege all of the following:

(a) The date of recordation of the claim of lien. A certified copy of the claim of lien shall be attached to the petition.

(b) The county in which the claim of lien is recorded.

(c) The book and page or series number of the place in the official records where the claim of lien is recorded.

(d) The legal description of the property subject to the claim of lien.

(e) Whether an extension of credit has been granted under Section 8460, if so to what date, and that the time for commencement of an action to enforce the lien has expired.

(f) That the owner has given the claimant notice under Section 8482 demanding that the claimant execute and record a release of the lien and that the claimant is unable or unwilling to do so or cannot with reasonable diligence be found.

(g) Whether an action to enforce the lien is pending.

(h) Whether the owner of the property or interest in the property has filed for relief in bankruptcy or there is another restraint that prevents the claimant from commencing an action to enforce the lien. **Leg.H.** Added Stats 2010 ch 697 §20 (SB 189), effective January 1, 2011, operative July 1, 2012.

Prior Law: Former CC §3154, similar to UCC §3501, was enacted Stats 1872 and repealed Stats 1963 ch 819 §2, effective January 1, 1965.

§8486. Hearing; Continuation; Terms; Service of copy of petition and notice of hearing

(a) On the filing of a petition for a release order, the clerk shall set a hearing date. The date shall be not more than 30 days after the filing of the petition. The court may continue the hearing only on a showing of good cause, but in any event the court shall rule and make any necessary orders on the petition not later than 60 days after the filing of the petition.

(b) The petitioner shall serve a copy of the petition and a notice of hearing on the claimant at least 15 days before the hearing. Service shall be made in the same manner as service of summons, or by certified or registered mail, postage prepaid, return receipt requested, addressed to the claimant as provided in Section 8108.

(c) Notwithstanding Section 8116, when service is made by mail, service is complete on the fifth day following deposit of the petition and notice in the mail. **Leg.H.** Added Stats 2010 ch 697 §20 (SB 189), effective January 1, 2011, operative July 1, 2012.

Prior Law: Former CC §3154, similar to UCC §3501, was enacted Stats 1872 and repealed Stats 1963 ch 819 §2, effective January 1, 1965.

§8488. Burden of proof; Judgment; Attorney's fees

(a) At the hearing both (1) the petition and (2) the issue of compliance with the service and date for hearing requirements of this article are deemed controverted by the claimant. The petitioner has the initial burden of producing evidence on those matters. The petitioner has the burden of proof as to the issue of compliance with the service and date for hearing requirements of this article. The claimant has the burden of proof as to the validity of the lien.

(b) If judgment is in favor of the petitioner, the court shall order the property released from the claim of lien.

(c) The prevailing party is entitled to reasonable attorney's fees. **Leg.H.** Added Stats 2010 ch 697 §20 (SB 189), effective January 1, 2011, operative July 1, 2012.

Prior Law: Former CC §3154, similar to UCC §3501, was enacted Stats 1872 and repealed Stats 1963 ch 819 §2, effective January 1, 1965.

ARTICLE 8
Removal of Claim of Lien from Record

Court order or judgment; Contents; Applicability. §8490.
When claim of lien does not constitute actual or constructive notice of claim. §8494.

§8490. Court order or judgment; Contents; Applicability

(a) A court order dismissing a cause of action to enforce a lien or releasing property from a claim of lien, or a judgment that no lien exists, shall include all of the following information:

(1) The date of recordation of the claim of lien.
(2) The county in which the claim of lien is recorded.
(3) The book and page or series number of the place in the official records where the claim of lien is recorded.
(4) The legal description of the property.

(b) A court order or judgment under this section is equivalent to cancellation of the claim of lien and its removal from the record.

(c) A court order or judgment under this section is a recordable instrument. On recordation of a certified copy of the court order or judgment, the property described in the order or judgment is released from the claim of lien.

(d) This section does not apply to a court order dismissing an action to enforce a lien that is expressly stated to be without prejudice. **Leg.H.** Added Stats 2010 ch 697 §20 (SB 189), effective January 1, 2011, operative July 1, 2012.

Prior Law: Former CC §3148, similar to UCC §§3414, 8108, 8304, was added Stats 1917 ch 751 §1 p 1543 and repealed Stats 1963 ch 819 §2 p 1997, effective January 1, 1965.

Former CC §3148, relating to notice of dishonor, was enacted Stats 1872 and repealed Stats 1917 ch 751 §1 p 1531.

Former CC §3154, similar to UCC §3501, was enacted Stats 1872 and repealed Stats 1963 ch 819 §2, effective January 1, 1965.

§8494. When claim of lien does not constitute actual or constructive notice of claim

If a claim of lien expires and is unenforceable under Section 8460, or if a court order or judgment is recorded under Section 8490, the claim of lien does not constitute actual or constructive notice of any of the matters contained, claimed, alleged, or contended in the claim of lien, or create a duty of inquiry in any person thereafter dealing with the affected property. **Leg.H.** Added Stats 2010 ch 697 §20 (SB 189), effective January 1, 2011, operative July 1, 2012.

CHAPTER 5
STOP PAYMENT NOTICE

Article 1. General Provisions.
Article 2. Stop Payment Notice to Owner.
Article 3. Stop Payment Notice to Construction Lender.
Article 4. Priorities.
Article 5. Enforcement of Claim Stated in Stop Payment Notice.

ARTICLE 1
General Provisions

Rights with respect to funds for payment of construction. §8500.
Stop payment notice; Form; Contents; Amount. §8502.
False stop payment notice or information; Forfeiture of rights to participate in distribution of funds. §8504.
Stop payment notice to owner or construction lender holding construction funds. §8506.
Validity of stop payment notice; Conditions. §8508.
Release bond; Amount. §8510.

§8500. Rights with respect to funds for payment of construction

The rights of all persons furnishing work for any work of improvement, with respect to any fund for payment of construction costs, are governed exclusively by this chapter, and no person may assert any legal or equitable right with respect to the fund, other than a right created by a written contract between that person and the person holding the fund, except pursuant to the provisions of this chapter. **Leg.H.** Added Stats 2010 ch 697 §20 (SB 189), effective January 1, 2011, operative July 1, 2012.

Prior Law: Former CC §3264, similar to former UCC §3801, was added Stats 1917 ch 751 §1 p 1558 and repealed Stats 1963 ch 819 §2 p 1997, effective January 1, 1965. Historical Derivation: (a) Former CCP §1190.1, as added Stats 1951 ch 1159 §1 p 2946, amended Stats 1951 ch 1382 §1 p 3304, Stats 1957 ch 1833 §1 p 3230, Stats 1961 ch 72 §5 p 1047, ch 804 §4 p 2072, Stats 1963 ch 298 §2 p 1066, Stats 1967 ch 789 §1 p 2177. (b) Former CCP §1184, as enacted Stats 1872, amended Stats 1885 ch 152 §2 p 144, Stats 1887 ch 137 §2 p 153, Stats 1911 ch 681 §2 p 1315, Stats 1919 ch 277 §1 p 452, Stats 1921 ch 144 §1 p 144, Stats 1931 ch 830 §1 p 1713. (c) Former CCP §1184b, as added Stats 1919 ch 277 §2 p 453. (d) Former CCP §1184c, as added Stats 1919 ch 277 §2 p 454. (e) Former CCP §1202, as added Stats 1885 ch 152 §8 p 146, amended Stats 1911 ch 681 §11 p 1319.

§8502. Stop payment notice; Form; Contents; Amount

(a) A stop payment notice shall comply with the requirements of Chapter 2 (commencing with Section 8100) of Title 1, and shall be signed and verified by the claimant.

(b) The notice shall include a general description of work to be provided, and an estimate of the total amount in value of the work to be provided.

(c) The amount claimed in the notice may include only the amount due the claimant for work provided through the date of the notice. **Leg.H.** Added Stats 2010 ch 697 §20 (SB 189), effective January 1, 2011, operative July 1, 2012.

Prior Law: Former CC §3103, similar to UCC §3207, was added Stats 1917 ch 751 §1 p 1536 and repealed Stats 1963 ch 819 §2 p 1997, effective January 1, 1965.

Former CC §3103, relating to fictitious payee, was enacted Stats 1872 and repealed Stats 1917 ch 751 §1 p 1531.

§8504. False stop payment notice or information; Forfeiture of rights to participate in distribution of funds

A claimant that willfully gives a false stop payment notice or that willfully includes in the notice a demand to withhold for work that has not been provided forfeits all right to participate in the distribution of the funds withheld and all right to a lien under Chapter 4 (commencing with Section 8400). **Leg.H.** Added Stats 2010 ch 697 §20 (SB 189), effective January 1, 2011, operative July 1, 2012.

§8506. Stop payment notice to owner or construction lender holding construction funds

(a) A stop payment notice to an owner shall be given to the owner or to the owner's architect, if any.

(b) A stop payment notice to a construction lender holding construction funds shall not be effective unless given to the manager or other responsible officer or person at the office or branch of the lender administering or holding the construction funds.

(c) A stop payment notice shall comply with the requirements of Chapter 2 (commencing with Section 8100) of Title 1. **Leg.H.** Added Stats 2010 ch 697 §20 (SB 189), effective January 1, 2011, operative July 1, 2012.

Prior Law: Former CC §3083, similar to UCC §3106, was added Stats 1917 ch 751 §1 p 1533 and repealed Stats 1963 ch 819 §2 p 1997, effective January 1, 1965.

Former CC §3103, similar to UCC §3207, was added Stats 1917 ch 751 §1 p 1536 and repealed Stats 1963 ch 819 §2 p 1997, effective January 1, 1965.

Former CC §3103, relating to fictitious payee, was enacted Stats 1872 and repealed Stats 1917 ch 751 §1 p 1531.

§8508. Validity of stop payment notice; Conditions

A stop payment notice is not valid unless both of the following conditions are satisfied:

(a) The claimant gave preliminary notice to the extent required by Chapter 2 (commencing with Section 8200).

(b) The claimant gave the stop payment notice before expiration of the time within which a claim of lien must be recorded under Chapter 4 (commencing with Section 8400). **Leg.H.** Added Stats 2010 ch 697 §20 (SB 189), effective January 1, 2011, operative July 1, 2012.

Prior Law: Former CC §§3159, 3160, similar to UCC §3504, was added Stats 1917 ch 751 §1 and repealed Stats 1963 ch 819 §2, effective January 1, 1965.

Former CC §3159, relating to waiver of presentment and notice, was enacted Stats 1872 and repealed Stats 1917 ch 751 §1.

Former CC §3160, relating to waiver of protest, was enacted Stats 1872 and repealed Stats 1917 ch 751 §1.

§8510. Release bond; Amount

(a) A person may obtain release of funds withheld pursuant to a stop payment notice by giving the person withholding the funds a release bond.

(b) A release bond shall be given by an admitted surety insurer and shall be conditioned for payment of any amount not exceeding the penal obligation of the bond that the claimant recovers on the claim, together with costs of suit awarded in the action. The bond shall be in an amount equal to 125 percent of the amount claimed in the stop payment notice.

(c) On receipt of a release bond, the person withholding funds pursuant to the stop payment notice shall release them. **Leg.H.** Added Stats 2010 ch 697 §20 (SB 189), effective January 1, 2011, operative July 1, 2012.

Prior Law: Former CC §3171, similar to present UCC §3503, was added Stats 1917 ch 751 §1 and repealed Stats 1963 ch 819 §2, effective January 1, 1965.

Former CC §3171, relating to bill of exchange, was enacted Stats 1872 and repealed Stats 1917 ch 751 §1.

ARTICLE 2
Stop Payment Notice to Owner

Person entitled to give stop payment notice; Failure to give bonded or unbonded stop payment notice. §8520.
Withholding of amount due to direct contractor or funds. §8522.

§8520. Person entitled to give stop payment notice; Failure to give bonded or unbonded stop payment notice

(a) A person that has a lien right under Chapter 4 (commencing with Section 8400), other than a direct contractor, may give the owner a stop payment notice.

(b) The owner may give notice, in compliance with the requirements of Chapter 2 (commencing with Section 8100) of Title 1, demanding that a person that has a lien right under Chapter 4 (commencing with Section 8400) give the owner a stop payment notice. If the person fails to give the owner a bonded or unbonded stop payment notice, the person forfeits the right to a lien under Chapter 4 (commencing with Section 8400). **Leg.H.** Added Stats 2010 ch 697 §20 (SB 189), effective January 1, 2011, operative July 1, 2012.

Prior Law: Former CC §3158, similar to UCC §3504, was added Stats 1917 ch 751 §1 p 1544 and repealed Stats 1963 ch 819 §2 p 1997, effective January 1, 1965.

Former CC §3158, relating to excuse of delay, was enacted Stats 1872 and repealed Stats 1917 ch 751 §1 p 1531.

§8522. Withholding of amount due to direct contractor or funds

(a) Except as provided in subdivision (b), on receipt of a stop payment notice an owner shall withhold from the direct contractor or from any person acting under authority of a direct contractor a sufficient amount due or to become due to the direct contractor to pay the claim stated in the notice.

(b) The owner may, but is not required to, withhold funds if the owner has previously recorded a payment bond under Section 8600. If the owner does not withhold funds, the owner shall, within 30 days after receipt of the stop payment notice, give notice to the claimant that a payment bond has been recorded and provide the claimant a copy of the bond. The notice shall comply with the requirements of Chapter 2 (commencing with Section 8100) of Title 1. **Leg.H.** Added Stats 2010 ch 697 §20 (SB 189), effective January 1, 2011, operative July 1, 2012.

Prior Law: Former CC §3161, similar to UCC §3504, was added Stats 1917 ch 751 §1 p 1544 and repealed Stats 1963 ch 819 §2 p 1997, effective January 1, 1965.

ARTICLE 3
Stop Payment Notice to Construction Lender

Person entitled to give stop payment notice. §8530.
Stop payment notice by claimant; Bond. §8532.
Objection to sufficiency of sureties on bond; Notice; Term; Substitution of bond. §8534.
Withholdings of funds to pay claim; Election. §8536.
Written request for notice of election regarding withholding funds to pay claim; Form; Liability for failure to include copy of bond with notice. §8538.

§8530. Person entitled to give stop payment notice

A person that has a lien right under Chapter 4 (commencing with Section 8400) may give a construction lender a stop payment notice. **Leg.H.** Added Stats 2010 ch 697 §20 (SB 189), effective January 1, 2011, operative July 1, 2012.

§8532. Stop payment notice by claimant; Bond

A claimant may give a construction lender a stop payment notice accompanied by a bond in an amount equal to 125 percent of the amount of the claim. The bond shall be conditioned that if the defendant recovers judgment in an action to enforce payment of the claim stated in the stop payment notice or to enforce a claim of lien recorded by the claimant, the claimant will pay all costs that are awarded the owner, direct contractor, or construction lender, and all damages to the owner, direct contractor, or construction lender that result from the stop payment notice or recordation of the claim of lien, not exceeding the amount of the bond. **Leg.H.** Added Stats 2010 ch 697 §20 (SB 189), effective January 1, 2011, operative July 1, 2012.

§8534. Objection to sufficiency of sureties on bond; Notice; Term; Substitution of bond

(a) A construction lender that objects to the sufficiency of sureties on the bond given with a bonded stop payment notice shall give notice to the claimant of the objection, within 20 days after the bonded stop payment notice is given. The notice shall comply with the requirements of Chapter 2 (commencing with Section 8100) of Title 1.

(b) The claimant may within 10 days after notice of the objection is given substitute for the initial bond a bond executed by an admitted surety insurer. If the claimant does not substitute a bond executed by an admitted surety insurer, the construction lender may disregard the bonded stop payment notice and release all funds withheld in response to that notice. **Leg.H.** Added Stats 2010 ch 697 §20 (SB 189), effective January 1, 2011, operative July 1, 2012.

Prior Law: Former CC §3163, similar to UCC §3504, was added Stats 1917 ch 751 §1 p 1545 and repealed Stats 1963 ch 819 §2 p 1997, effective January 1, 1965.

§8536. Withholdings of funds to pay claim; Election

(a) Except as provided in subdivision (b), on receipt of a stop payment notice a construction lender shall withhold from the borrower or other person to whom the lender or the owner is obligated to make payments or advancement out of the construction fund sufficient funds to pay the claim stated in the notice.

(b) The construction lender may, at its option, elect not to withhold funds in any of the following circumstances:

(1) The stop payment notice is unbonded.

(2) The stop payment notice is given by a claimant other than a direct contractor, and a payment bond is recorded before the lender is given any stop payment notice. **Leg.H.** Added Stats 2010 ch 697 §20 (SB 189), effective January 1, 2011, operative July 1, 2012.

Prior Law: Former CC §3162, similar to UCC §3504, was added Stats 1917 ch 751 §1 p 1545 and repealed Stats 1963 ch 819 §2 p 1997, effective January 1, 1965.

§8538. Written request for notice of election regarding withholding funds to pay claim; Form; Liability for failure to include copy of bond with notice

(a) The claimant may make a written request for notice of an election by the construction lender under Section 8536 not to withhold funds. The request shall be made at the time the claimant gives the construction lender the stop payment notice and shall be accompanied by a preaddressed, stamped envelope.

(b) If the construction lender elects not to withhold funds under Section 8536, the lender shall, within 30 days after making the election, give notice of that fact to a claimant who has requested notice of the election under subdivision (a). The notice shall comply with the requirements of Chapter 2 (commencing with Section 8100) of Title 1. If the basis of the election is the recordation of a payment bond under Section 8600, the construction lender shall include a copy of the bond with the notice.

(c) A construction lender is not liable for failure to include a copy of the bond with the notice under this section if all of the following conditions are satisfied:

(1) The failure was not intentional and resulted from a bona fide error.

(2) The lender maintains reasonable procedures to avoid an error of that type.

(3) The lender corrected the error not later than 20 days after the date the lender discovered the violation. **Leg.H.** Added Stats 2010 ch 697 §20 (SB 189), effective January 1, 2011, operative July 1, 2012.

Prior Law: Former CC §3162, similar to UCC §3504, was added Stats 1917 ch 751 §1 p 1545 and repealed Stats 1963 ch 819 §2 p 1997, effective January 1, 1965.

ARTICLE 4
Priorities

Distribution of funds; Pro rata distribution. §8540.
Withholding of funds pursuant to stop payment notice; Recovery of net amount due to direct contractor or subcontractor after deducting specified funds. §8542.
Rights of claimant who gives a construction lender stop payment notice. §8544.

§8540. Distribution of funds; Pro rata distribution

(a) Funds withheld pursuant to a stop payment notice shall be distributed in the following order of priority:

(1) First, to pay claims of persons that have given a bonded stop payment notice. If funds are insufficient to pay the claims of those persons in full, the funds shall be distributed pro rata among the claimants in the ratio that the claim of each bears to the aggregate of all claims for which a bonded stop payment notice is given.

(2) Second, to pay claims of persons that have given an unbonded stop payment notice. If funds are insufficient to pay the claims of those persons in full, the funds shall be distributed among the claimants in the ratio that the claim of each bears to the aggregate of all claims for which an unbonded stop payment notice is given.

(b) Pro rata distribution under this section shall be made among the persons entitled to share in the distribution without regard to the order in which the person has given a stop payment notice or commenced an enforcement action. **Leg.H.** Added Stats 2010 ch 697 §20 (SB 189), effective January 1, 2011, operative July 1, 2012.

Prior Law: Former CC §3167, similar to UCC §3503, was added Stats 1917 ch 751 §1 p 1545 and repealed Stats 1963 ch 819 §2 p 1997, effective January 1, 1965.

§8542. Withholding of funds pursuant to stop payment notice; Recovery of net amount due to direct contractor or subcontractor after deducting specified funds

Notwithstanding Section 8540:

(a) If funds are withheld pursuant to a stop payment notice given to a construction lender by a direct contractor or subcontractor, the direct contractor or subcontractor may recover only the net amount due the direct contractor or subcontractor after deducting any funds that are withheld by the construction lender pursuant to the claims of subcontractors and material suppliers that have given a stop payment notice for work done on behalf of the direct contractor or subcontractor.

(b) In no event is the construction lender required to withhold, pursuant to a stop payment notice, more than the net amount provided in subdivision (a). Notwithstanding any other provision of this chapter, a construction lender is not liable for failure to withhold more than that net amount on receipt of a stop payment notice. **Leg.H.** Added Stats 2010 ch 697 §20 (SB 189), effective January 1, 2011, operative July 1, 2012.

Prior Law: Former CC §3162, similar to UCC §3504, was added Stats 1917 ch 751 §1 p 1545 and repealed Stats 1963 ch 819 §2 p 1997, effective January 1, 1965.

§8544. Rights of claimant who gives a construction lender stop payment notice

The rights of a claimant who gives a construction lender a stop payment notice are not affected by an assignment of construction loan funds made by the owner or direct contractor, and the stop payment notice has priority over the assignment, whether the assignment is made before or after the stop payment notice is given. **Leg.H.** Added Stats 2010 ch 697 §20 (SB 189), effective January 1, 2011, operative July 1, 2012.

Prior Law: Former CC §3166, similar to UCC §3503, was added Stats 1917 ch 751 §1 p 1545, amended Stats 1921 ch 194 §6 p 214, Stats 1939 ch 414 §2 p 1749, Stats 1941 ch 234 §1 p 1301, Stats 1955 ch 198 §2 p 671, ch 599 §2 p 1902, and repealed Stats 1963 ch 819 §1 p 1997, effective January 1, 1965.

ARTICLE 5
Enforcement of Claim Stated in Stop Payment Notice

Commencement of action; Term; Notice. §8550.
When more than one claimant has given stop payment notice. §8552.
Dismissal for want of prosecution. §8554.
Effect of dismissal. §8556.
Attorney's fee, costs and damages; Prevailing party; Limitations. §8558.
Inclusion of interest in amount awarded on claim. §8560.

§8550. Commencement of action; Term; Notice

(a) A claimant shall commence an action to enforce payment of the claim stated in a stop payment notice at any time after 10 days from the date the claimant gives the stop payment notice.

(b) A claimant shall commence an action to enforce payment of the claim stated in a stop payment notice not later than 90 days after expiration of the time within which a stop payment notice must be given.

(c) An action under this section may not be brought to trial or judgment entered before expiration of the time provided in subdivision (b).

(d) If a claimant does not commence an action to enforce payment of the claim stated in a stop payment notice within the time prescribed in subdivision (b), the notice ceases to be effective and the person withholding funds pursuant to the notice shall release them.

(e) Within five days after commencement of an action to enforce payment of the claim stated in a stop payment notice, the claimant shall give notice of commencement of the action to the persons to whom the stop payment notice was given. The notice shall comply with the requirements of Chapter 2 (commencing with Section 8100) of Title 1. **Leg.H.** Added Stats 2010 ch 697 §20 (SB 189), effective January 1, 2011, operative July 1, 2012.

Prior Law: Former CC §3172, similar to UCC §3503, was added Stats 1917 ch 751 §1 p 1546, amended Stats 1921 ch 194 §7 p 214, and repealed Stats 1963 ch 819 §2 p 1997, effective January 1, 1965.

Former CC §3172, relating to drawee, was enacted in 1872 and repealed Stats 1917 ch 751 §1 p 1531.

§8552. When more than one claimant has given stop payment notice

If more than one claimant has given a stop payment notice:

(a) Any number of claimants may join in the same enforcement action.

(b) If claimants commence separate actions, the court first acquiring jurisdiction may order the actions consolidated.

(c) On motion of the owner or construction lender the court shall require all claimants to be impleaded in one action, to the end that the rights of all parties may be adjudicated in the action. **Leg.H.** Added Stats 2010 ch 697 §20 (SB 189), effective January 1, 2011, operative July 1, 2012.

Prior Law: Former CC §3175, similar to UCC §3503, was added Stats 1917 ch 751 §1 p 1546 and repealed Stats 1963 ch 819 §2 p 1997, effective January 1, 1965.

Former CC §3175, relating to presentment of part of set, was enacted Stats 1872 and repealed Stats 1917 ch 751 §1 p 1531.

§8554. Dismissal for want of prosecution

Notwithstanding Section 583.420 of the Code of Civil Procedure, if an action to enforce payment of the claim stated in a stop payment notice is not brought to trial within two years after commencement of the action, the court may in its discretion dismiss the action for want of prosecution. **Leg.H.** Added Stats 2010 ch 697 §20 (SB 189), effective January 1, 2011, operative July 1, 2012.

Prior Law: Former CC §3173, similar to UCC §3503, was added Stats 1917 ch 751 §1 p 1546 and repealed Stats 1963 ch 819 §2 p 1997, effective January 1, 1965.

Former CC §3173, relating to bill in parts of a set, was enacted Stats 1872 and repealed Stats 1917 ch 751 §1 p 1531.

§8556. Effect of dismissal

A stop payment notice ceases to be effective, and a person withholding funds pursuant to the notice shall release them, in either of the following circumstances:

(a) An action to enforce payment of the claim stated in the stop payment notice is dismissed, unless expressly stated to be without prejudice.

(b) Judgment in an action to enforce payment of the claim stated in the stop payment notice is against the claimant. **Leg.H.** Added Stats 2010 ch 697 §20 (SB 189), effective January 1, 2011, operative July 1, 2012.

Prior Law: Former CC §3174, similar to UCC §3503, was added Stats 1917 ch 751 §1 p 1546 and repealed Stats 1963 ch 819 §2 p 1997, effective January 1, 1965.

Former CC §3174, relating to when bill must be in a set, was enacted Stats 1872 and repealed Stats 1917 ch 751 §1 p 1531.

§8558. Attorney's fee, costs and damages; Prevailing party; Limitations

(a) In an action to enforce payment of the claim stated in a bonded stop payment notice, the prevailing party is entitled to a reasonable attorney's fee in addition to costs and damages.

(b) The court, on notice and motion by a party, shall determine who is the prevailing party or that there is no prevailing party for the purpose of this section, regardless of whether the action proceeds to final judgment. The prevailing party is the party that recovers greater relief in the action, subject to the following limitations:

(1) If the action is voluntarily dismissed or dismissed pursuant to a settlement, there is no prevailing party.

(2) If the defendant tenders to the claimant the full amount to which the claimant is entitled, and deposits in court for the claimant the amount so tendered, and alleges those facts in the answer and the allegation is determined to be true, the defendant is deemed to be the prevailing party. **Leg.H.** Added Stats 2010 ch 697 §20 (SB 189), effective January 1, 2011, operative July 1, 2012.

Prior Law: Former CC §3176, relating to when bills are payable, was enacted Stats 1872, amended Code Amdts 1873–74 ch 612 §272 p 264, Stats 1905 ch 462 §2 p 620, and repealed Stats 1917 ch 751 §1 p 1531.

Former CC §3176, similar to UCC §3503, was added Stats 1917 ch 751 §1 p 1547 and repealed Stats 1963 ch 819 §2 p 1997, effective January 1, 1965.

§8560. Inclusion of interest in amount awarded on claim

If the claimant is the prevailing party in an action to enforce payment of the claim stated in a bonded stop payment notice, any amount awarded on the claim shall include interest at the legal rate calculated from the date the stop payment notice is given. **Leg.H.** Added Stats 2010 ch 697 §20 (SB 189), effective January 1, 2011, operative July 1, 2012.

CHAPTER 6
PAYMENT BOND

Authority of court to restrict lien enforcement under specified conditions; Deficiencies. §8600.
Bond or other security as protection allowed. §8602.
Objection by lending institution to validity of payment bond to finance work of improvement. §8604.
Payment bond conditioned for payment in full of all claims and inures to benefit of all claimants. §8606.
Requirement to have provided work in order to recover on direct contractor's payment bond. §8608.
Validity of provision in payment bond attempting to shorten period for commencement of action on bond. §8609.
Action to enforce liability on bond where title recorded before completion of work of improvement. §8610.
Requirements for enforcing claim against payment bond. §8612.
Notice compliance. §8614.

§8600. Authority of court to restrict lien enforcement under specified conditions; Deficiencies

(a) This section applies if, before the commencement of work, the owner in good faith files a direct contract with the county recorder, and records a payment bond of the direct contractor in an amount not less than 50 percent of the price stated in the direct contract.

(b) If the conditions of subdivision (a) are satisfied, the court shall, where equitable to do so, restrict lien enforcement under this title to the aggregate amount due from the owner to the direct contractor and shall enter judgment against the direct contractor and surety on the bond for any deficiency that remains between the amount due to the direct contractor and the whole amount due to claimants. **Leg.H.** Added Stats 2010 ch 697 §20 (SB 189), effective January 1, 2011, operative July 1, 2012.

Prior Law: Former CC §3235, similar to UCC §3505, was added Stats 1917 ch 751 §1 p 1555, amended Stats 1939 ch 856 §1 p 2433, and repealed Stats 1963 ch 819 §2 p 1997, effective January 1, 1965.

Former CC §3235, relating to rate of damages, was enacted Stats 1872, amended Stats 1905 ch 462 §4 p 621, and repealed Stats 1917 ch 751 §1 p 1531. Historical Derivation: (a) Former CCP §1185.1, as added Stats 1951 ch 1159 §1 p 2943, amended Stats 1961 ch 804 §1 p 2068. (b) Former CCP §1183, as enacted 1872, amended Code Amdts 1873-74 ch 586 §1 p 409, Code Amdts 1880 ch 67 §1 p 63, Stats 1885 ch 152 §1 p 143, Stats 1887 ch 137 §1 p 152, Stats 1899 ch 35 §1 p 34, Stats 1903 ch 76 §1 p 84, Stats 1911 ch 681 §1 p 1313, Stats 1929 ch 869 §1 p 1924.

Former CC §3236, similar to UCC §3505, was added Stats 1917 ch 751 §1 p 1555 and repealed Stats 1963 ch 819 §2 p 1997, effective January 1, 1965.

Former CC §3236, relating to interest on amount of protested bill, was enacted Stats 1872 and repealed Stats 1917 ch 751 §1 p 1531. Historical Derivation: (a) Former CCP §1185.1, as added Stats 1951 ch 1159 §1 p 2943, amended Stats 1961 ch 804 §1 p 2068. (b) Former CCP §1183, as enacted 1872, amended Code Amdts 1873–74 ch 586 §1 p 409, Code Amdts 1880 ch 67 §1 p 63, Stats 1885 ch 152 §1 p 143, Stats 1887 ch 137 §1 p 152, Stats 1899 ch 35 §1 p 34, Stats 1903 ch 76 §1 p 84, Stats 1911 ch 681 §1 p 1313, Stats 1929 ch 869 §1 p 1924.

§8602. Bond or other security as protection allowed

Section 8600 does not preclude an owner from requiring a performance bond, payment bond, or other security as protection against a direct contractor's failure to perform the direct contract or to make full payment for all work provided pursuant to the contract. **Leg.H.** Added Stats 2010 ch 697 §20 (SB 189), effective January 1, 2011, operative July 1, 2012.

§8604. Objection by lending institution to validity of payment bond to finance work of improvement

(a) If a lending institution requires that a payment bond be given as a condition of lending money to finance a work of improvement, and accepts in writing as sufficient a bond given in fulfillment of the requirement, the lending institution may not thereafter object to the borrower as to the validity of the bond or refuse to make the loan based on an objection to the bond if the bond is given by an admitted surety insurer.

(b) For purposes of this section, a "lending institution" includes a commercial bank, savings and loan institution, credit union, or other organization or person engaged in the business of financing loans. **Leg.H.** Added Stats 2010 ch 697 §20 (SB 189), effective January 1, 2011, operative July 1, 2012.

Prior Law: Former CC §3237, similar to present UCC §2501, was added Stats 1917 ch 751 §1 and repealed Stats 1963 ch 819 §2, effective January 1, 1965.

Former CC §3237, relating to estimated damages, was enacted Stats 1872 and repealed Stats 1917 ch 751 §1.

§8606. Payment bond conditioned for payment in full of all claims and inures to benefit of all claimants

(a) A payment bond under this title shall be conditioned for the payment in full of the claims of all claimants and shall by its terms inure to the benefit of all claimants so as to give a claimant a right of action to enforce the liability on the bond. The bond shall be given by an admitted surety insurer.

(b) An owner, direct contractor, or subcontractor may be the principal on the bond.

(c) A claimant may enforce the liability on the bond in an action to enforce a lien under this part or in a separate action on the bond. **Leg.H.** Added Stats 2010 ch 697 §20 (SB 189), effective January 1, 2011, operative July 1, 2012.

Prior Law: Former CC §3096, similar to UCC §§3115, 3305, 3407, was added Stats 1917 ch 751 §1 p 1535 and repealed Stats 1963 ch 819 §2 p 1997, effective January 1, 1965.

§8608. Requirement to have provided work in order to recover on direct contractor's payment bond

(a) This title does not give a claimant a right to recover on a direct contractor's payment bond given under this chapter unless the claimant provided work to the direct contractor either directly or through one or more subcontractors, pursuant to a direct contract.

(b) Nothing in this section affects the stop payment notice right of, and relative priorities among, design professionals and holders of secured interests in the real property. **Leg.H.** Added Stats 2010 ch 697 §20 (SB 189), effective January 1, 2011, operative July 1, 2012.

§8609. Validity of provision in payment bond attempting to shorten period for commencement of action on bond

Any provision in a payment bond attempting by contract to shorten the period prescribed in Section 337 of the Code of Civil Procedure for the commencement of an action on the bond shall not be valid under either of the following circumstances:

(a) If the provision attempts to limit the time for commencement of an action on the bond to a shorter period than six months from the completion of any work of improvement.

(b) As applied to any action brought by a claimant, unless the bond is recorded before the work of improvement is commenced. **Leg.H.** Added Stats 2010 ch 697 §20 (SB 189), effective January 1, 2011, operative July 1, 2012.

Prior Law: Former CC §3239, similar to UCC §§3501, 3505, was added Stats 1917 ch 751 §1 p 1555 and repealed Stats 1963 ch 819 §2 p 1997, effective January 1, 1965. Historical Derivation: (a) Former CCP §1200.1, as added Stats 1951 ch 1159 §1 p 2955, amended Stats 1955 ch 1750 §1 p 3235, Stats 1961 ch 804 §5 p 2077, Stats 1969 ch 1611 §26 p 3396. (b) Former CCP §1183, as enacted 1872, amended by Code Amdts 1873–74 ch 586 §1 p 409, Code Amdts 1880 ch 67 §1 p 63, Stats 1885 ch 152 §1 p 143, Stats 1887 ch 137 §1 p 152, Stats 1899 ch 35 §1 p 34, Stats 1903 ch 76 §1 p 84, Stats 1911 ch 681 §1 p 1313, Stats 1929 ch 869 §1 p 1924.

§8610. Action to enforce liability on bond where title recorded before completion of work of improvement

Notwithstanding Section 8609, if a payment bond under this title is recorded before completion of a work of improvement, an action to enforce the liability on the bond may not be commenced later than six months after completion of the work of improvement. **Leg.H.** Added Stats 2010 ch 697 §20 (SB 189), effective January 1, 2011, operative July 1, 2012.

Prior Law: Former CC §3240, similar to present CC §3227, was added Stats 1969 ch 1362 §2, operative January 1, 1971, and repealed Stats 1994 ch 974 §5 (AB 3357).

Former CC §3240, similar to UCC §3504, was added Stats 1917 ch 751 §1 and repealed Stats 1963 ch 819 §2, effective January 1, 1965.

§8612. Requirements for enforcing claim against payment bond

(a) In order to enforce a claim against a payment bond under this title, a claimant shall give the preliminary notice provided in Chapter 2 (commencing with Section 8200).

(b) If preliminary notice was not given as provided in Chapter 2 (commencing with Section 8200), a claimant may enforce a claim by giving written notice to the surety and the bond principal within 15 days after recordation of a notice of completion. If no notice of completion has been recorded, the time for giving written notice to the surety and the bond principal is extended to 75 days after completion of the work of improvement.

(c) Commencing July 1, 2012, and except as provided in subdivision (b), if the preliminary notice was required to be given by a person who has no direct contractual relationship with the contractor, and who has not given notice as provided in Chapter 2 (commencing with Section 8200), that person may enforce a claim by giving written notice to the surety and the bond principal, as provided in Section 8614, within 15 days after recordation of a notice of completion. If no notice of completion has been recorded, the time for giving written notice to the surety and the bond principal is extended to 75 days after completion of the work of improvement.

(d) Subdivision (c) shall not apply in either of the following circumstances:

(1) All progress payments, except for those disputed in good faith, have been made to a subcontractor who has a direct contractual relationship with the general contractor to whom the claimant has provided materials or services.

(2) The subcontractor who has a direct contractual relationship with the general contractor to whom the claimant has provided materials or services has been terminated from the project pursuant to the contract, and all progress payments, except those disputed in good faith, have been made as of the termination date.

(e) Pursuant to Section 8200, this section shall not apply to a laborer, as defined under Section 8024.

(f) This section shall become operative on July 1, 2012. **Leg.H.** Added Stats 2010 ch 697 §20 (SB 189), effective January 1, 2011, operative July 1, 2012. Amended Stats 2011 ch 700 §3 (SB 293), effective January 1, 2012, operative July 1, 2012.

Prior Law: Former CC §3242, similar to UCC §3505, was added Stats 1917 ch 751 §1 and repealed Stats 1963 ch 819 §2, effective January 1, 1965.

Former CC §3242, relating to promissory notes, was enacted Stats 1872 and repealed Stats 1917 ch 751 §1.

§8614. Notice compliance

Notice to the principal and surety under Section 8612 shall comply with the requirements of Chapter 2 (commencing with Section 8100) of Title 1. **Leg.H.** Added Stats 2010 ch 697 §20 (SB 189), effective January 1, 2011, operative July 1, 2012.

Prior Law: Former CC §3227, similar to CCP §995.610, was added Stats 1969 ch 1362 §2, operative January 1, 1971, and repealed Stats 1982 ch 517 §82.

Former CC §3227, similar to UCC §3501, was added Stats 1917 ch 751 §1, amended Stats 1921 ch 194 §9, Stats 1939 ch 414 §39, and repealed Stats 1963 ch 819 §2, effective January 1, 1965.

Former CC §3227, relating to protest, was enacted Stats 1872 and repealed Stats 1917 ch 751 §1. Historical Derivation: (a) Former CC §3240, as added Stats 1969 ch 1362 §2. (b) Former CC §3253, as added Stats 1994 ch 974 §9. (c) Former CCP §1183, as enacted 1872, amended Code Amdts 1873–74 ch 586 §1, Code Amdts 1880 ch 67 § 1, Stats 1885 ch 152 § 1, Stats 1887 ch 137 § 1, Stats 1899 ch 35 § 1, Stats 1903 ch 76 § 1, Stats 1911 ch 681 § 1, Stats 1929 ch 869 §1. (d) Former CCP §1200.1, as added Stats 1951 ch 1159 §1, amended Stats 1955 ch 1750 § 1, Stats 1961 ch 804 § 5, Stats 1969 ch 1611 §26.

CHAPTER 7
SECURITY FOR LARGE PROJECT

Article 1. Application of Chapter.
Article 2. Security Requirement.
Article 3. Form of Security.

ARTICLE 1
Application of Chapter

Applicability of chapter upon satisfaction of conditions. §8700.
Applicability of chapter to works of improvement. §8702.
Applicability of chapter to owners. §8704.

§8700. Applicability of chapter upon satisfaction of conditions

(a) This chapter applies if any of the following conditions is satisfied:

(1) The owner of the fee interest in property contracts for a work of improvement on the property with a contract price greater than five million dollars ($5,000,000).

(2) The owner of a less than fee interest in property, including a leasehold interest, contracts for a work of improvement on the property with a contract price greater than one million dollars ($1,000,000).

(b) For the purpose of this section:

(1) The owner of the fee interest in property is not deemed to be the owner of a less than fee interest by reason of a mortgage, deed of trust, ground lease, or other lien or encumbrance or right of occupancy that encumbers the fee interest.

(2) A lessee of real property is deemed to be the owner of a fee interest in the real property if all of the following conditions are satisfied:

(A) The initial term of the lease is at least 35 years.

(B) The lease covers one or more lawful parcels under the Subdivision Map Act, Division 2 (commencing with Section 66410) of Title 7 of the Government Code, and any applicable local ordinance adopted under that act, in their entirety, including, but not limited to, a parcel approved pursuant to a certificate of compliance proceeding. **Leg.H.** Added Stats 2010 ch 697 §20 (SB 189), effective January 1, 2011, operative July 1, 2012.

§8702. Applicability of chapter to works of improvement

This chapter does not apply to any of the following works of improvement:

(a) A single-family residence, including a single-family residence located within a subdivision, and any associated fixed work that requires the services of a general engineering contractor as defined in Section 7056 of the Business and Professions Code. As used in this subdivision, "single-family residence" means a real property improvement used or intended to be used as a dwelling unit for one family.

(b) A housing development eligible for a density bonus under Section 65915 of the Government Code. **Leg.H.** Added Stats 2010 ch 697 §20 (SB 189), effective January 1, 2011, operative July 1, 2012.

§8704. Applicability of chapter to owners

This chapter does not apply to any of the following owners:

(a) A qualified publicly traded company or a wholly owned subsidiary of a qualified publicly traded company, if the obligations of the subsidiary pursuant to the contract for the work of improvement are guaranteed by the parent. As used in this subdivision, "qualified publicly traded company" means a company having a class of equity securities listed for trading on the New York Stock Exchange, the American Stock Exchange, or the NASDAQ stock market, and the nonsubordinated debt securities of which are rated as "investment grade" by either Fitch ICBA, Inc., Moody's Investor Services, Inc., Standard & Poor's Ratings Services, or a similar statistical rating organization that is nationally recognized for rating the creditworthiness of a publicly traded company. If at any time before final payment of all amounts due pursuant to the contract the nonsubordinated debt securities of the qualified publicly traded company are downgraded to below "investment grade" by any of those rating organizations, the owner is no longer exempt from this chapter.

(b) A qualified private company or a wholly owned subsidiary of a qualified private company, if the obligations of the subsidiary pursuant to the contract for the work of improvement are guaranteed by the parent. As used in this subdivision, "qualified private company" means a company that has no equity securities listed for trading on the New York Stock Exchange, the American Stock Exchange, or the NASDAQ stock market, and that has a net worth determined in accordance with generally accepted accounting principles in excess of fifty million dollars ($50,000,000). If at any time before final payment of all amounts due pursuant to the contract the net worth of the qualified private company is reduced below that level, the owner is no longer exempt from this chapter. **Leg.H.** Added Stats 2010 ch 697 §20 (SB 189), effective January 1, 2011, operative July 1, 2012.

ARTICLE 2
Security Requirement

Owner security requirements. §8710.
Notice demanding security. §8712.
Waiver of provisions proscribed. §8714.
Effect of chapter on statutes. §8716.

§8710. Owner security requirements

An owner described in subdivision (a) of Section 8700 shall provide the direct contractor all of the following:

(a) Security for the owner's payment obligation pursuant to the contract. The security shall be used only if the owner defaults on the payment obligation to the direct contractor. This subdivision does not apply to an owner that is the majority owner of the direct contractor.

(b) A copy, certified by the county recorder, of any recorded mortgage or deed of trust that secures the construction loan of a lending institution for the work of improvement, disclosing the amount of the loan. **Leg.H.** Added Stats 2010 ch 697 §20 (SB 189), effective January 1, 2011, operative July 1, 2012.

§8712. Notice demanding security

If an owner fails to provide or maintain the security required by this chapter, the direct contractor may give the owner notice demanding security. The notice shall comply with the requirements of Chapter 2 (commencing with Section 8100) of Title 1. If the owner does not provide or maintain the security within 10 days after notice demanding security is given, the direct contractor may suspend work until the owner provides or maintains the security. **Leg.H.** Added Stats 2010 ch 697 §20 (SB 189), effective January 1, 2011, operative July 1, 2012.

§8714. Waiver of provisions proscribed

It is against public policy to waive the provisions of this chapter by contract. **Leg.H.** Added Stats 2010 ch 697 §20 (SB 189), effective January 1, 2011, operative July 1, 2012.

§8716. Effect of chapter on statutes

This chapter does not affect any statute providing for mechanics liens, stop payment notices, bond remedies, or prompt payment rights of a subcontractor, including the direct contractor's payment responsibilities under Section 7108.5 of the Business and Professions Code. **Leg.H.** Added Stats 2010 ch 697 §20 (SB 189), effective January 1, 2011, operative July 1, 2012.

ARTICLE 3
Form of Security

Approved forms of security. §8720.
Requirements for bond. §8722.
Requirements for irrevocable letter of credit. §8724.
Requirements for escrow account. §8726.
Deposit to or disbursement from construction security escrow account. §8728.
Security amount. §8730.

§8720. Approved forms of security

An owner shall provide security by any of the following means:

(a) A bond that satisfies Section 8722.
(b) An irrevocable letter of credit that satisfies Section 8724.
(c) An escrow account that satisfies Section 8726. **Leg.H.** Added Stats 2010 ch 697 §20 (SB 189), effective January 1, 2011, operative July 1, 2012.

§8722. Requirements for bond

A bond under this chapter shall satisfy all of the following requirements:

(a) The bond shall be executed by an admitted surety insurer that is either listed in the Department of the Treasury's Listing of Approved Sureties (Department Circular 570) or that has an A.M. Best rating of A or better and has an underwriting limitation, under Section 12090 of the Insurance Code, greater than the amount of the bond.

(b) The bond shall be in an amount not less than 15 percent of the contract price for the work of improvement or, if the work of improvement is to be substantially completed within six months after the commencement of work, not less than 25 percent of the contract price.

(c) The bond shall be conditioned for payment on default by the owner of any undisputed amount pursuant to the contract that is due and payable for more than 30 days. **Leg.H.** Added Stats 2010 ch 697 §20 (SB 189), effective January 1, 2011, operative July 1, 2012.

§8724. Requirements for irrevocable letter of credit

An irrevocable letter of credit under this chapter shall satisfy all of the following requirements:

(a) The letter of credit shall be issued by a financial institution, as defined in Section 5107 of the Financial Code, inuring to the benefit of the direct contractor.

(b) The letter of credit shall be in an amount not less than 15 percent of the contract price for the work of improvement or, if the work of improvement is to be substantially completed within six months after the commencement of work, not less than 25 percent of the contract price.

(c) The maturity date and other terms of the letter of credit shall be determined by agreement between the owner, the direct contractor, and the financial institution, except that the owner shall maintain the letter of credit in effect until the owner has satisfied its payment obligation to the direct contractor. **Leg.H.** Added Stats 2010 ch 697 §20 (SB 189), effective January 1, 2011, operative July 1, 2012.

§8726. Requirements for escrow account

An escrow account under this chapter shall satisfy all of the following requirements:

(a) The account shall be designated as a "construction security escrow account."

(b) The account shall be located in this state and maintained with an escrow agent licensed under the Escrow Law, Division 6 (commencing with Section 17000) of the Financial Code, or with any person exempt from the Escrow Law under paragraph (1) or (3) of subdivision (a) of Section 17006 of the Financial Code.

(c) The owner shall deposit funds in the account in the amount provided in Section 8728. This chapter does not require a construction lender to agree to deposit proceeds of a construction loan in the account.

(d) The owner shall grant the direct contractor a perfected, first priority security interest in the account and in all funds deposited by the owner in the account and in their proceeds, established to the reasonable satisfaction of the direct contractor, which may be by a written opinion of legal counsel for the owner.

(e) The funds on deposit in the account shall be the sole property of the owner, subject to the security interest of the direct contractor. The owner and the direct contractor shall instruct the escrow holder to hold the funds on deposit in the account for the purpose of perfecting the direct contractor's security interest in the account and to disburse those funds only on joint authorization of the owner and the direct contractor, or pursuant to a court order that is binding on both of them. **Leg.H.** Added Stats 2010 ch 697 §20 (SB 189), effective January 1, 2011, operative July 1, 2012.

§8728. Deposit to or disbursement from construction security escrow account

The following provisions govern a deposit to or disbursement from a construction security escrow account under this chapter:

(a) Before the commencement of work the owner shall make an initial deposit to the account in an amount not less than 15 percent of the contract price for the work of improvement or, if the work of improvement is to be substantially completed within six months after the commencement of work, not less than 25 percent of the contract price.

(b) If the contract provides for a retention to be withheld from a periodic payment to the direct contractor, the owner shall deposit to the account the amount withheld as retention at the time the owner makes the corresponding payment to the direct contractor from which the retention is withheld.

(c) The amount required to be maintained on deposit shall not exceed the total amount remaining to be paid to the direct contractor pursuant to the contract or as adjusted by agreement between the owner and the direct contractor. If the amount on deposit equals or exceeds the total amount remaining to be paid to the direct contractor, the owner and the direct contractor shall authorize disbursement to the direct contractor for progress payments then due the direct contractor, but a party is not obligated to authorize disbursement that would cause the amount remaining on deposit following the disbursement to be less than the total amount remaining to be paid to the direct contractor.

(d) The owner and the direct contractor shall authorize the disbursement to the owner of any funds remaining on deposit after the direct contractor has been paid all amounts due pursuant to the contract. The owner and the direct contractor shall authorize the disbursement of funds on deposit pursuant to a court order that is binding on both of them. The owner and the direct contractor may agree in the contract to additional conditions for the disbursement of funds on deposit, except that the conditions may not cause the amount remaining on deposit to be less than the amount required under this section. **Leg.H.** Added Stats 2010 ch 697 §20 (SB 189), effective January 1, 2011, operative July 1, 2012.

§8730. Security amount

If the contract price for a work of improvement is not a fixed price, the amount of security provided under this chapter shall be the guaranteed maximum price or, if there is no guaranteed maximum price, the owner's and direct contractor's good faith estimate of the reasonable value of the work to be provided pursuant to the contract. **Leg.H.** Added Stats 2010 ch 697 §20 (SB 189), effective January 1, 2011, operative July 1, 2012.

CHAPTER 8
PROMPT PAYMENT

Article 1. Progress Payment.
Article 2. Retention Payment.
Article 3. Stop Work Notice.

ARTICLE 1
Progress Payment

Payment due direct contractor. §8800.
Payment due subcontractor in contract between public utility and direct contractor. §8802.

§8800. Payment due direct contractor

(a) Except as otherwise agreed in writing by the owner and direct contractor, the owner shall pay the direct contractor, within 30 days after notice demanding payment pursuant to the contract is given, any progress payment due as to which there is no good faith dispute between them. The notice given shall comply with the requirements of Chapter 2 (commencing with Section 8100) of Title 1.

(b) If there is a good faith dispute between the owner and direct contractor as to a progress payment due, the owner may withhold from the progress payment an amount not in excess of 150 percent of the disputed amount.

(c) An owner that violates this section is liable to the direct contractor for a penalty of 2 percent per month on the amount wrongfully withheld, in place of any interest otherwise due. In an action for collection of the amount wrongfully withheld, the prevailing party is entitled to costs and a reasonable attorney's fee.

(d) This section does not supersede any requirement of Article 2 (commencing with Section 8810) relating to the withholding of a retention. **Leg.H.** Added Stats 2010 ch 697 §20 (SB 189), effective January 1, 2011, operative July 1, 2012.

§8802. Payment due subcontractor in contract between public utility and direct contractor

(a) This section applies to a contract between a public utility and a direct contractor for all or part of a work of improvement.

(b) Unless the direct contractor and a subcontractor otherwise agree in writing, within 21 days after receipt of a progress payment from the public utility the direct contractor shall pay the subcontractor the amount allowed the direct contractor on account of the work performed by the subcontractor to the extent of the subcontractor's interest in the work. If there is a good faith dispute over all or part of the amount due on a progress payment from the direct contractor to a subcontractor, the direct contractor may withhold an amount not in excess of 150 percent of the disputed amount.

(c) A direct contractor that violates this section is liable to the subcontractor for a penalty of 2 percent of the disputed amount due per month for every month that payment is not made. In an action for collection of the amount wrongfully withheld, the prevailing party is entitled to costs and a reasonable attorney's fee.

(d) This section does not limit or impair a contractual, administrative, or judicial remedy otherwise available to a contractor or subcontractor in a dispute involving late payment or nonpayment by the contractor or deficient performance or nonperformance by the subcontractor. **Leg.H.** Added Stats 2010 ch 697 §20 (SB 189), effective January 1, 2011, operative July 1, 2012.

ARTICLE 2
Retention Payment

Scope of article. §8810.
Payment of retention by owner. §8812.
Payment of withheld retention by direct contractor. §8814.
Notice of acceptance or rejection of disputed work. §8816.
Result of failure to make retention payment. §8818.
Waiver of provisions proscribed. §8820.
Applicability. §8822.

§8810. Scope of article

This article governs a retention payment withheld by an owner from a direct contractor or by a direct contractor from a subcontractor. **Leg.H.** Added Stats 2010 ch 697 §20 (SB 189), effective January 1, 2011, operative July 1, 2012.

Prior Law: Former CC §3260, relating to exemption from attachment, etc., of materials furnished for work of improvement or for mining claims, was added Stats 1969 ch 1362 §2, operative January 1, 1971, and repealed Stats 1970 ch 1523 §1.5.

Former CC §3260, relating to right of holders where different parts are negotiated, was added Stats 1917 ch 751 §1 and repealed Stats 1963 ch 819 §2, effective January 1, 1965. Historical Derivation: (a) Former CCP §1202.1, as added Stats 1951 ch 1159 §1. (b) Former CCP §1196, as enacted 1872, amended Code Amdts 1873–74 ch 586 §7.

§8812. Payment of retention by owner

(a) If an owner withholds a retention from a direct contractor, the owner shall, within 45 days after completion of the work of improvement, pay the retention to the contractor.

(b) If part of a work of improvement ultimately will become the property of a public entity, the owner may condition payment of a retention allocable to that part on acceptance of the part by the public entity.

(c) If there is a good faith dispute between the owner and direct contractor as to a retention payment due, the owner may withhold from final payment an amount not in excess of 150 percent of the disputed amount. **Leg.H.** Added Stats 2010 ch 697 §20 (SB 189), effective January 1, 2011, operative July 1, 2012.

§8814. Payment of withheld retention by direct contractor

(a) If a direct contractor has withheld a retention from one or more subcontractors, the direct contractor shall, within 10 days after receiving all or part of a retention payment, pay to each subcontractor from whom retention has been withheld that subcontractor's share of the payment.

(b) If a retention received by the direct contractor is specifically designated for a particular subcontractor, the direct contractor shall pay the retention payment to the designated subcontractor, if consistent with the terms of the subcontract.

(c) If a good faith dispute exists between the direct contractor and a subcontractor, the direct contractor may withhold from the retention to the subcontractor an amount not in excess of 150 percent of the estimated value of the disputed amount. **Leg.H.** Added Stats 2010 ch 697 §20 (SB 189), effective January 1, 2011, operative July 1, 2012.

§8816. Notice of acceptance or rejection of disputed work

(a) If the direct contractor gives the owner, or a subcontractor gives the direct contractor, notice that work in dispute has been completed in accordance with the contract, the owner or direct contractor shall within 10 days give notice advising the notifying party of the acceptance or rejection of the disputed work. Both notices shall comply with the requirements of Chapter 2 (commencing with Section 8100) of Title 1.

(b) Within 10 days after acceptance of disputed work, the owner or direct contractor shall pay the portion of the retention relating to the disputed work. **Leg.H.** Added Stats 2010 ch 697 §20 (SB 189), effective January 1, 2011, operative July 1, 2012.

§8818. Result of failure to make retention payment

If an owner or direct contractor does not make a retention payment within the time required by this article:

(a) The owner or direct contractor is liable to the person to which payment is owed for a penalty of 2 percent per month on the amount wrongfully withheld, in place of any interest otherwise due.

(b) In an action for collection of the amount wrongfully withheld, the prevailing party is entitled to costs and reasonable attorney's fees. **Leg.H.** Added Stats 2010 ch 697 §20 (SB 189), effective January 1, 2011, operative July 1, 2012.

§8820. Waiver of provisions proscribed

It is against public policy to waive the provisions of this article by contract. **Leg.H.** Added Stats 2010 ch 697 §20 (SB 189), effective January 1, 2011, operative July 1, 2012.

§8822. Applicability

This article does not apply to a retention payment withheld by a lender pursuant to a construction loan agreement. **Leg.H.** Added Stats 2010 ch 697 §20 (SB 189), effective January 1, 2011, operative July 1, 2012.

ARTICLE 3
Stop Work Notice

"Stop work notice" defined. §8830.
When stop work notice may be given. §8832.
Additional notice required. §8834.
Copy of notice to construction lender. §8836.
Liability. §8838.
Resolution or cancellation; Notice. §8840.
Additional right. §8842.
Judicial proceeding authorized. §8844.
Waiver of provisions proscribed. §8846.
Application of article. §8848.

§8830. "Stop work notice" defined

"Stop work notice" means notice given under this article by a direct contractor to an owner that the contractor will stop work if the amount owed the contractor is not paid within 10 days after notice is given. **Leg.H.** Added Stats 2010 ch 697 §20 (SB 189), effective January 1, 2011, operative July 1, 2012.

§8832. When stop work notice may be given

If a direct contractor is not paid the amount due pursuant to a written contract within 35 days after the date payment is due under the contract, and there is no dispute as to the satisfactory performance of the contractor, the contractor may give the owner a stop work notice. The notice shall comply with the requirements of Chapter 2 (commencing with Section 8100) of Title 1. **Leg.H.** Added Stats 2010 ch 697 §20 (SB 189), effective January 1, 2011, operative July 1, 2012.

§8834. Additional notice required

A direct contractor that gives an owner a stop work notice shall give the following additional notice:

(a) At least five days before giving the stop work notice, the contractor shall post notice of intent to give a stop work notice. The notice shall comply with the requirements of Chapter 2 (commencing with Section 8100) of Title 1. In addition to posting the notice pursuant to Section 8114, the notice shall also be posted at the main office of the site, if one exists.

(b) At the same time the contractor gives the stop work notice, the contractor shall give a copy of the stop work notice to all subcontractors with whom the contractor has a direct contractual relationship on the work of improvement. **Leg.H.** Added Stats 2010 ch 697 §20 (SB 189), effective January 1, 2011, operative July 1, 2012.

§8836. Copy of notice to construction lender

Within five days after receipt of a stop work notice from a direct contractor, the owner shall give a copy of the notice to the construction lender, if any. The copy of the notice shall be given in compliance with the requirements of Chapter 2 (commencing with Section 8100) of Title 1. **Leg.H.** Added Stats 2010 ch 697 §20 (SB 189), effective January 1, 2011, operative July 1, 2012.

§8838. Liability

(a) The direct contractor or the direct contractor's surety, or a subcontractor or a subcontractor's surety, is not liable for delay or damage that the owner or a contractor of a subcontractor may suffer as a result of the direct contractor giving a stop work notice and subsequently stopping work for nonpayment, if the notice and posting requirements of this article are satisfied.

(b) A direct contractor's or original subcontractor's liability to a subcontractor or material supplier after the direct contractor stops work under this article is limited to the amount the subcontractor or material supplier could otherwise recover under this title for work provided up to the date the subcontractor or material supplier ceases work, subject to the following exceptions:

(1) The direct contractor's or original subcontractor's liability continues for work provided up to and including the 10-day notice period and not beyond.

(2) This subdivision does not limit liability for custom work, including materials that have been fabricated, manufactured, or ordered to specifications that are unique to the job. **Leg.H.** Added Stats 2010 ch 697 §20 (SB 189), effective January 1, 2011, operative July 1, 2012.

§8840. Resolution or cancellation; Notice

On resolution of the claim in the stop work notice or the direct contractor's cancellation of the stop work notice, the contractor shall post, and give subcontractors with whom the contractor has a direct contractual relationship on the work of improvement, notice of the resolution or cancellation. The notice shall comply with the requirements of Chapter 2 (commencing with Section 8100) of Title 1. In addition to posting the notice pursuant to Section 8114, the notice shall also be posted at the main office of the site, if one exists. **Leg.H.** Added Stats 2010 ch 697 §20 (SB 189), effective January 1, 2011, operative July 1, 2012.

§8842. Additional right

A direct contractor's right to stop work under this article is in addition to other rights the direct contractor may have under the law. **Leg.H.** Added Stats 2010 ch 697 §20 (SB 189), effective January 1, 2011, operative July 1, 2012.

§8844. Judicial proceeding authorized

(a) If payment of the amount claimed is not made within 10 days after a stop work notice is given, the direct contractor, the direct contractor's surety, or an owner may in an expedited proceeding in the superior court in the county in which the private work of improvement is located, seek a judicial determination of liability for the amount due.

(b) The expedited proceeding shall be set for hearing or trial at the earliest possible date in order that it shall be quickly heard and determined, and shall take precedence over all other cases except older matter of the same character and other matters to which special precedence has been given. **Leg.H.** Added Stats 2010 ch 697 §20 (SB 189), effective January 1, 2011, operative July 1, 2012.

§8846. Waiver of provisions proscribed

It is against public policy to waive the provisions of this article by contract. **Leg.H.** Added Stats 2010 ch 697 §20 (SB 189), effective January 1, 2011, operative July 1, 2012.

§8848. Application of article

(a) This article applies to a contract entered into on or after January 1, 1999.

(b) This article does not apply to a retention withheld by a lender pursuant to a construction loan agreement. **Leg.H.** Added Stats 2010 ch 697 §20 (SB 189), effective January 1, 2011, operative July 1, 2012.

TITLE 3
PUBLIC WORK OF IMPROVEMENT

Chapter 1. General Provisions.
Chapter 2. Completion.
Chapter 3. Preliminary Notice.
Chapter 4. Stop Payment Notice.
Chapter 5. Payment Bond.

CHAPTER 1
GENERAL PROVISIONS

Article 1. Application of Title.
Article 2. Claimants.

ARTICLE 1
Application of Title

Applicability. §9000.

§9000. Applicability

This title applies to a work of improvement contracted for by a public entity. **Leg.H.** Added Stats 2010 ch 697 §20 (SB 189), effective January 1, 2011, operative July 1, 2012.

Prior Law: Former CC §3179, similar to UCC §3503, was added Stats 1917 ch 751 §1 p 1547 and repealed Stats 1963 ch 819 §2 p 1997, effective January 1, 1965.

ARTICLE 2
Claimants

Persons entitled to give stop payment notice. §9100.

§9100. Persons entitled to give stop payment notice

(a) Except as provided in subdivision (b), any of the following persons that have not been paid in full may give a stop payment notice to the public entity or assert a claim against a payment bond:

(1) A person that provides work for a public works contract, if the work is authorized by a direct contractor, subcontractor, architect, project manager, or other person having charge of all or part of the public works contract.

(2) A laborer.

(3) A person described in Section 4107.7 of the Public Contract Code.

(b) A direct contractor may not give a stop payment notice or assert a claim against a payment bond under this title. **Leg.H.** Added Stats 2010 ch 697 §20 (SB 189), effective January 1, 2011, operative July 1, 2012.

Prior Law: Former CC §3110, similar to UCC §§3415, 8201, was added Stats 1917 ch 751 §1 p 1537 and repealed Stats 1963 ch 819 §2 p 1997, effective January 1, 1965.

Former CC§3110, relating to signature on separate paper, was enacted Stats 1872 and repealed Stats 1917 ch 751 §1 p 1531.

Former CC §3112, similar to present UCC §§3202, 8107, 8304, was added Stats 1917 ch 751 §1 and repealed Stats 1963 ch 819 §2, effective January 1, 1965.

Former CC §3112, relating to general indorsement, was enacted Stats 1872 and repealed Stats 1917 ch 751 §1 p 1531.

Former CC §3181, similar to UCC §3503, was added Stats 1917 ch 751 §1 p 1547 and repealed Stats 1963 ch 819 §2 p 1997, effective January 1, 1965.

Former CC §3181, relating to days of grace, was enacted Stats 1872 and repealed Stats 1917 ch 751 §1 p 1531.

CHAPTER 2
COMPLETION

When completion occurs. §9200.
Notice of cessation. §9202.
Requirements for notice of completion. §9204.
Recording notice of completion. §9208.

§9200. When completion occurs

For the purpose of this title, completion of a work of improvement occurs at the earliest of the following times:

(a) Acceptance of the work of improvement by the public entity.

(b) Cessation of labor on the work of improvement for a continuous period of 60 days. This subdivision does not apply to a contract awarded under the State Contract Act, Part 2 (commencing with Section 10100) of Division 2 of the Public Contract Code. **Leg.H.** Added Stats 2010 ch 697 §20 (SB 189), effective January 1, 2011, operative July 1, 2012.

Prior Law: Former CC §3086, similar to UCC §§3104, 3112, was added Stats 1917 ch 751 §1 p 1533 and repealed Stats 1963 ch 819 §2 p 1997, effective January 1, 1965.

Former CC §3086, relating to non–negotiable instruments, was enacted Stats 1872 and repealed Stats 1917 ch 751 §1 p 1531.

§9202. Notice of cessation

(a) A public entity may record a notice of cessation if there has been a continuous cessation of labor for at least 30 days prior to the recordation that continues through the date of the recordation.

(b) The notice shall be signed and verified by the public entity or its agent.

(c) The notice shall comply with the requirements of Chapter 2 (commencing with Section 8100) of Title 1, and shall also include all of the following information:

(1) The date on or about which the labor ceased.

(2) A statement that the cessation has continued until the recordation of the notice. **Leg.H.** Added Stats 2010 ch 697 §20 (SB 189), effective January 1, 2011, operative July 1, 2012.

Prior Law: Former CC §3092, similar to UCC §3114, was added Stats 1917 ch 751 §1 p 1534, amended Stats 1921 ch 194 §2 p 213, and repealed Stats 1963 ch 819 §2 p 1997, effective January 1, 1965.

Former §3092, relating to pledge, etc., was enacted Stats 1872 and repealed Stats 1917 ch 751 §1 p 1531.

§9204. Requirements for notice of completion

(a) A public entity may record a notice of completion on or within 15 days after the date of completion of a work of improvement.

(b) The notice shall be signed and verified by the public entity or its agent.

(c) The notice shall comply with the requirements of Chapter 2 (commencing with Section 8100) of Title 1, and shall also include the date of completion. An erroneous statement of the date of completion does not affect the effectiveness of the notice if the true date of completion is 15 days or less before the date of recordation of the notice. **Leg.H.** Added Stats 2010 ch 697 §20 (SB 189), effective January 1, 2011, operative July 1, 2012.

Prior Law: Former CC §3093, similar to UCC §3114, was added Stats 1917 ch 751 §1 p 1535 and repealed Stats 1963 ch 819 §2 p 1997, effective January 1, 1965.

Former §3093, relating to contents of negotiable instrument, was enacted Stats 1872 and repealed Stats 1917 ch 751 §1 p 1531.

§9208. Recording notice of completion

A notice of completion in otherwise proper form, verified and containing the information required by this title shall be accepted by the recorder for recording and is deemed duly recorded without acknowledgment. **Leg.H.** Added Stats 2010 ch 697 §20 (SB 189), effective January 1, 2011, operative July 1, 2012.

Prior Law: Former CC §3093, similar to UCC §3114, was added Stats 1917 ch 751 §1 p 1535 and repealed Stats 1963 ch 819 §2 p 1997, effective January 1, 1965.

Former CC §3093, relating to contents of negotiable instrument, was enacted Stats 1872 and repealed Stats 1917 ch 751 §1 p 1531.

CHAPTER 3
PRELIMINARY NOTICE

Persons entitled to receive preliminary notice. §9300.
Preliminary notice requirements. §9302.
Components of preliminary notice. §9303.
When stop payment notice may be given. §9304.
Subcontractor's duty to give notice. §9306.

§9300. Persons entitled to receive preliminary notice

(a) Except as otherwise provided by statute, before giving a stop payment notice or asserting a claim against a payment bond, a claimant shall give preliminary notice to the following persons:

(1) The public entity.

(2) The direct contractor to which the claimant provides work.

(b) Notwithstanding subdivision (a):

(1) A laborer is not required to give preliminary notice.

(2) A claimant that has a direct contractual relationship with a direct contractor is not required to give preliminary notice.

(c) Compliance with this section is a necessary prerequisite to the validity of a stop payment notice under this title.

(d) Compliance with this section or with Section 9562 is a necessary prerequisite to the validity of a claim against a payment bond under this title. **Leg.H.** Added Stats 2010 ch 697 §20 (SB 189), effective January 1, 2011, operative July 1, 2012.

Prior Law: Former CC §3098, similar to UCC §§3109, 3114, 3118, 3402, was added Stats 1917 ch 751 §1 p 1536 and repealed Stats 1963 ch 819 §2 p 1997, effective January 1, 1965.

§9302. Preliminary notice requirements

(a) Except as provided in subdivision (b), preliminary notice shall be given in compliance with the requirements of Chapter 2 (commencing with Section 8100) of Title 1.

(b) If the public works contract is for work constructed by the Department of Public Works or the Department of General Services of the state, preliminary notice to the public entity shall be given to the disbursing officer of the department constructing the work. **Leg.H.** Added Stats 2010 ch 697 §20 (SB 189), effective January 1, 2011, operative July 1, 2012.

Prior Law: Former CC §3098, similar to UCC §§3109, 3114, 3118, 3402, was added Stats 1917 ch 751 §1 p 1536 and repealed Stats 1963 ch 819 §2 p 1997, effective January 1, 1965.

§9303. Components of preliminary notice

The preliminary notice shall comply with the requirements of Section 8102, and shall also include:

(a) A general description of the work to be provided.

(b) An estimate of the total price of the work provided and to be provided. **Leg.H.** Added Stats 2010 ch 697 §20 (SB 189), effective January 1, 2011, operative July 1, 2012.

Prior Law: Former CC §3098, similar to UCC §§3109, 3114, 3118, 3402, was added Stats 1917 ch 751 §1 p 1536 and repealed Stats 1963 ch 819 §2 p 1997, effective January 1, 1965.

§9304. When stop payment notice may be given

A claimant may give a stop payment notice or assert a claim against a payment bond only for work provided within 20 days before giving preliminary notice and at any time thereafter. **Leg.H.** Added Stats 2010 ch 697 §20 (SB 189), effective January 1, 2011, operative July 1, 2012.

Prior Law: Former CC §3098, similar to UCC §§3109, 3114, 3118, 3402, was added Stats 1917 ch 751 §1 p 1536 and repealed Stats 1963 ch 819 §2 p 1997, effective January 1, 1965.

§9306. Subcontractor's duty to give notice

If the contract of any subcontractor on a particular work of improvement provides for payment to the subcontractor of more than four hundred dollars ($400), the failure of that subcontractor, licensed under the Contractors' State License Law (Chapter 9 (commencing with Section 7000) of Division 3 of the Business and Professions Code), to give the notice provided for in this chapter, constitutes grounds for disciplinary action under the Contractors' State License Law. **Leg.H.** Added Stats 2010 ch 697 §20 (SB 189), effective January 1, 2011, operative July 1, 2012.

Prior Law: Former CC §3098, similar to UCC §§3109, 3114, 3118, 3402, was added Stats 1917 ch 751 §1 p 1536 and repealed Stats 1963 ch 819 §2 p 1997, effective January 1, 1965.

CHAPTER 4
STOP PAYMENT NOTICE

Article 1. General Provisions.
Article 2. Summary Proceeding for Release of Funds.
Article 3. Distribution of Funds Withheld.
Article 4. Enforcement of Payment of Claim Stated in Stop Payment Notice.

ARTICLE 1
General Provisions

Chapter controls. §9350.
Signature and verification; General description of work and estimate of total amount. §9352.
Requirements for giving stop payment notice. §9354.
Effectiveness of stop payment notice. §9356.
Withholding of funds to pay claims. §9358.
Payments not prohibited by chapter. §9360.
Notice of time within which action to enforce payment of claim must be commenced. §9362.

Release bond. §9364.

§9350. Chapter controls

The rights of all persons furnishing work pursuant to a public works contract, with respect to any fund for payment of construction costs, are governed exclusively by this chapter, and no person may assert any legal or equitable right with respect to that fund, other than a right created by direct written contract between the person and the person holding the fund, except pursuant to the provisions of this chapter. **Leg.H.** Added Stats 2010 ch 697 §20 (SB 189), effective January 1, 2011, operative July 1, 2012.

§9352. Signature and verification; General description of work and estimate of total amount

(a) A stop payment notice shall comply with the requirements of Chapter 2 (commencing with Section 8100) of Title 1, and shall be signed and verified by the claimant.

(b) The notice shall include a general description of work to be provided, and an estimate of the total amount in value of the work to be provided.

(c) The amount claimed in the notice may include only the amount due the claimant for work provided through the date of the notice. **Leg.H.** Added Stats 2010 ch 697 §20 (SB 189), effective January 1, 2011, operative July 1, 2012.

Prior Law: Former CC §3103, similar to UCC §3207, was added Stats 1917 ch 751 §1 p 1536 and repealed Stats 1963 ch 819 §2 p 1997, effective January 1, 1965.
Former CC §3103, relating to fictitious payee, was enacted Stats 1872 and repealed Stats 1917 ch 751 §1 p 1531.

§9354. Requirements for giving stop payment notice

(a) Except as provided in subdivision (b), a stop payment notice shall be given in compliance with the requirements of Chapter 2 (commencing with Section 8100) of Title 1.

(b) A stop payment notice shall be given to the public entity by giving the notice to the following person:

(1) In the case of a public works contract of the state, the director of the department that awarded the contract.

(2) In the case of a public works contract of a public entity other than the state, the office of the controller, auditor, or other public disbursing officer whose duty it is to make payment pursuant to the contract, or the commissioners, managers, trustees, officers, board of supervisors, board of trustees, common council, or other body by which the contract was awarded. **Leg.H.** Added Stats 2010 ch 697 §20 (SB 189), effective January 1, 2011, operative July 1, 2012.

Prior Law: Former CC §3103, similar to UCC §3207, was added Stats 1917 ch 751 §1 p 1536 and repealed Stats 1963 ch 819 §2 p 1997, effective January 1, 1965.
Former CC §3103, relating to fictitious payee, was enacted Stats 1872 and repealed Stats 1917 ch 751 §1 p 1531.

§9356. Effectiveness of stop payment notice

A stop payment notice is not effective unless given before the expiration of whichever of the following time periods is applicable:

(a) If a notice of completion, acceptance, or cessation is recorded, 30 days after that recordation.

(b) If a notice of completion, acceptance, or cessation is not recorded, 90 days after cessation or completion. **Leg.H.** Added Stats 2010 ch 697 §20 (SB 189), effective January 1, 2011, operative July 1, 2012.

Prior Law: Former CC §3184, similar to UCC §3503, was added Stats 1917 ch 751 §1 p 1547 and repealed Stats 1963 ch 819 §2 p 1997, effective January 1, 1965.

§9358. Withholding of funds to pay claims

(a) The public entity shall, on receipt of a stop payment notice, withhold from the direct contractor sufficient funds due or to become due to the direct contractor to pay the claim stated in the stop payment notice and to provide for the public entity's reasonable cost of any litigation pursuant to the stop payment notice.

(b) The public entity may satisfy its duty under this section by refusing to release funds held in escrow under Section 10263 or 22300 of the Public Contract Code. **Leg.H.** Added Stats 2010 ch 697 §20 (SB 189), effective January 1, 2011, operative July 1, 2012.

Prior Law: Former CC §3186, similar to UCC §3503, was added Stats 1917 ch 751 §1, and repealed Stats 1963 ch 819 §2, effective January 1, 1965.
Former CC §3186, relating to presentment, was enacted Stats 1872, amended Code Amdts 1873–74 ch 612 §273, and repealed Stats 1917 ch 751 §1.

§9360. Payments not prohibited by chapter

(a) This chapter does not prohibit payment of funds to a direct contractor or a direct contractor's assignee if a stop payment notice is not received before the disbursing officer actually surrenders possession of the funds.

(b) This chapter does not prohibit payment of any amount due to a direct contractor or a direct contractor's assignee in excess of the amount necessary to pay the total amount of all claims stated in stop payment notices received by the public entity at the time of payment plus any interest and court costs that might reasonably be anticipated in connection with the claims. **Leg.H.** Added Stats 2010 ch 697 §20 (SB 189), effective January 1, 2011, operative July 1, 2012.

Prior Law: Former CC §3187, similar to UCC §3503, was added Stats 1917 ch 751 §1 p 1548 and repealed Stats 1963 ch 819 §2 p 1997, effective January 1, 1965.

Former CC §3187, relating to presentment to joint drawees, was enacted Stats 1872 and repealed Stats 1917 ch 751 §1 p 1531.

§9362. Notice of time within which action to enforce payment of claim must be commenced

(a) Not later than 10 days after each of the following events, the public entity shall give notice to a claimant that has given a stop payment notice of the time within which an action to enforce payment of the claim stated in the stop payment notice must be commenced:

(1) Completion of a public works contract, whether by acceptance or cessation.

(2) Recordation of a notice of cessation or completion.

(b) The notice shall comply with the requirements of Chapter 2 (commencing with Section 8100) of Title 1.

(c) A public entity need not give notice under this section unless the claimant has paid the public entity ten dollars ($10) at the time of giving the stop payment notice. **Leg.H.** Added Stats 2010 ch 697 §20 (SB 189), effective January 1, 2011, operative July 1, 2012.

Prior Law: Former CC §3185, similar to UCC §3503, was added Stats 1917 ch 751 §1 p 1547 and repealed Stats 1963 ch 819 §2 p 1997, effective January 1, 1965.

Former CC §3185, relating to time to present bill, was enacted Stats 1872 and repealed Stats 1917 ch 751 §1 p 1531.

§9364. Release bond

(a) A public entity may, in its discretion, permit the direct contractor to give the public entity a release bond. The bond shall be executed by an admitted surety insurer, in an amount equal to 125 percent of the claim stated in the stop payment notice, conditioned for the payment of any amount the claimant recovers in an action on the claim, together with court costs if the claimant prevails.

(b) On receipt of a release bond, the public entity shall not withhold funds from the direct contractor pursuant to the stop payment notice.

(c) The surety on a release bond is jointly and severally liable to the claimant with the sureties on any payment bond given under Chapter 5 (commencing with Section 9550). **Leg.H.** Added Stats 2010 ch 697 §20 (SB 189), effective January 1, 2011, operative July 1, 2012.

Prior Law: Former CC §3196, similar to UCC §3504, was added Stats 1917 ch 751 §1 p 1549 and repealed Stats 1963 ch 819 §2 p 1997, effective January 1, 1965.

Former CC §3196, relating to acceptance by separate instrument, was enacted Stats 1872 and repealed Stats 1917 ch 751 §1 p 1531.

ARTICLE 2
Summary Proceeding for Release of Funds

Grounds for obtaining release of funds under summary proceeding. §9400.
Service of affidavit on public entity. §9402.
Service of affidavit on claimant. §9404.
Counteraffidavit. §9406.
Motion for determination of rights. §9408.
Pleadings; Burden of proof. §9410.
Findings and evidence. §9412.
Determination in summary proceeding not res judicata. §9414.

§9400. Grounds for obtaining release of funds under summary proceeding

A direct contractor may obtain release of funds withheld pursuant to a stop payment notice under the summary proceeding provided in this article on any of the following grounds:

(a) The claim on which the notice is based is not a type for which a stop payment notice is authorized under this chapter.

(b) The claimant is not a person authorized under Section 9100 to give a stop payment notice.

(c) The amount of the claim stated in the stop payment notice is excessive.

(d) There is no basis for the claim stated in the stop payment notice. **Leg.H.** Added Stats 2010 ch 697 §20 (SB 189), effective January 1, 2011, operative July 1, 2012.

Prior Law: Former CC §3197, similar to UCC §3504, was added Stats 1917 ch 751 §1 p 1549 and repealed Stats 1963 ch 819 §2 p 1997, effective January 1, 1965.

Former CC §3197, relating to promise to accept, was enacted Stats 1872, amended Stats 1905 ch 462 §3 p 621, and repealed Stats 1917 ch 751 §1 p 1531.

§9402. Service of affidavit on public entity

The direct contractor shall serve on the public entity an affidavit, together with a copy of the affidavit, in compliance with the requirements of Chapter 2 (commencing with Section 8100) of Title 1, that includes all of the following information:

(a) An allegation of the grounds for release of the funds and a statement of the facts supporting the allegation.

(b) A demand for the release of all or the portion of the funds that are alleged to be withheld improperly or in an excessive amount.

(c) A statement of the address of the contractor within the state for the purpose of permitting service by mail on the contractor of any notice or document. **Leg.H.** Added Stats 2010 ch 697 §20 (SB 189), effective January 1, 2011, operative July 1, 2012.

Prior Law: Former CC §3198, relating to effect of omission to give notice of nonacceptance, was added Stats 1917 ch 751 §1 p 1549 and repealed Stats 1963 ch 819 §2 p 1997, effective January 1, 1965.

Former CC §3198, relating to cancellation of acceptance, was enacted Stats 1872 and repealed Stats 1917 ch 751 §1 p 1531.

§9404. Service of affidavit on claimant

The public entity shall serve on the claimant a copy of the direct contractor's affidavit, together with a notice stating that the public entity will release the funds withheld, or the portion of the funds demanded, unless the claimant serves on the public entity a counteraffidavit on or before the time stated in the notice. The time stated in the notice shall be not less than 10 days nor more than 20 days after service on the claimant of the copy of the affidavit. The notice shall comply with the requirements of Chapter 2 (commencing with Section 8100) of Title 1. **Leg.H.** Added Stats 2010 ch 697 §20 (SB 189), effective January 1, 2011, operative July 1, 2012.

Prior Law: Former CC §3199, similar to UCC §3501, was added Stats 1917 ch 751 §1 p 1549 and repealed Stats 1963 ch 819 §2 p 1997, effective January 1, 1965.

Former CC §3199, relating to what admitted by acceptance, was enacted Stats 1872, amended Code Amdts 1873–74 ch 612 §274 p 265, and repealed Stats 1917 ch 751 §1 p 1531.

§9406. Counteraffidavit

(a) A claimant that contests the direct contractor's affidavit shall serve on the public entity a counteraffidavit alleging the details of the claim and describing the specific basis on which the claimant contests or rebuts the allegations of the contractor's affidavit. The counteraffidavit shall be served within the time stated in the public entity's notice, together with proof of service of a copy of the counteraffidavit on the direct contractor. The service of the counteraffidavit on the public entity and the copy of the affidavit on the direct contractor shall comply with the requirements of Chapter 2 (commencing with Section 8100) of Title 1.

(b) If no counteraffidavit with proof of service is served on the public entity within the time stated in the public entity's notice, the public entity shall immediately release the funds, or the portion of the funds demanded by the affidavit, without further notice to the claimant, and the public entity is not liable in any manner for their release.

(c) The public entity is not responsible for the validity of an affidavit or counteraffidavit under this article. **Leg.H.** Added Stats 2010 ch 697 §20 (SB 189), effective January 1, 2011, operative July 1, 2012.

Prior Law: Former CC §3200, similar to UCC §§1107, 3601, 3603, 3605, was added Stats 1917 ch 751 §1 p 1549 and repealed Stats 1963 ch 819 §2 p 1997, effective January 1, 1965.

§9408. Motion for determination of rights

(a) If a counteraffidavit, together with proof of service, is served under Section 9406, either the direct contractor or the claimant may commence an action for a declaration of the rights of the parties.

(b) After commencement of the action, either the direct contractor or the claimant may move the court for a determination of rights under the affidavit and counteraffidavit. The party making the motion shall give not less than five days' notice of the hearing to the public entity and to the other party.

(c) The notice of hearing shall comply with the requirements of Chapter 2 (commencing with Section 8100) of Title 1. Notwithstanding Section 8116, when notice of the hearing is made by mail, the notice is complete on the fifth day following deposit of the notice in the mail.

(d) The court shall hear the motion within 15 days after the date of the motion, unless the court continues the hearing for good cause. **Leg.H.** Added Stats 2010 ch 697 §20 (SB 189), effective January 1, 2011, operative July 1, 2012.

Prior Law: Former CC §3201, similar to UCC §§1107, 3601, 3604–3605, was added Stats 1917 ch 751 §1 p 1549 and repealed Stats 1963 ch 819 §2 p 1997, effected January 1, 1965.

§9410. Pleadings; Burden of proof

(a) The affidavit and counteraffidavit shall be filed with the court by the public entity and shall constitute the pleadings, subject to the power of the court to permit an amendment in the interest of justice. The affidavit of the direct contractor shall be deemed controverted by the counteraffidavit of the claimant, and both shall be received in evidence.

(b) At the hearing, the direct contractor has the burden of proof. **Leg.H.** Added Stats 2010 ch 697 §20 (SB 189), effective January 1, 2011, operative July 1, 2012.

Prior Law: Former CC §3202, similar to UCC §§3207, 3601, 3603, was added Stats 1917 ch 751 §1 p 1550 and repealed Stats 1963 ch 819 §2 p 1997, effective January 1, 1965.

§9412. Findings and evidence

(a) No findings are required in a summary proceeding under this article.

(b) If at the hearing no evidence other than the affidavit and counteraffidavit is offered, the court may, if satisfied that sufficient facts are shown, make a determination on the basis of the affidavit and counteraffidavit. If the court is not satisfied that sufficient facts are shown, the court shall order the hearing continued for production of other evidence, oral or documentary, or the filing of other affidavits and counteraffidavits.

(c) At the conclusion of the hearing, the court shall make an order determining whether the demand for release is allowed. The court's order is determinative of the right of the claimant to have funds further withheld by the public entity.

(d) The direct contractor shall serve a copy of the court's order on the public entity in compliance with the requirements of Chapter 2 (commencing with Section 8100) of Title 1. **Leg.H.** Added Stats 2010 ch 697 §20 (SB 189), effective January 1, 2011, operative July 1, 2012.

Prior Law: Former CC §3203, similar to UCC §§1107, 3605, was added Stats 1917 ch 751 §1 p 1550 and repealed Stats 1963 ch 819 §2 p 1997, effective January 1, 1965.

Former CC §3203, relating to when bill may be accepted or paid for honor, was enacted Stats 1872 and repealed Stats 1917 ch 751 §1 p 1531.

§9414. Determination in summary proceeding not res judicata

A determination in a summary proceeding under this article is not res judicata with respect to a right of action by the claimant against either the principal or surety on a payment bond or with respect to a right of action against a party personally liable to the claimant. **Leg.H.** Added Stats 2010 ch 697 §20 (SB 189), effective January 1, 2011, operative July 1, 2012.

Prior Law: Former CC §3205, similar to UCC §§3407, 8206, was added Stats 1917 ch 751 §1 p 1550 and repealed Stats 1963 ch 819 §2 p 1997, effective January 1, 1965.

Former CC §3205, relating to acceptance for honor, was enacted Stats 1872 and repealed Stats 1917 ch 751 §1 p 1531.

ARTICLE 3
Distribution of Funds Withheld

Distribution in case of insufficient funds. §9450.
Claimant's right to recover not impaired. §9452.
Willful false stop payment notice. §9454.
Priority. §9456.

§9450. Distribution in case of insufficient funds

If funds withheld pursuant to a stop payment notice are insufficient to pay in full the claims of all persons who have given a stop payment notice, the funds shall be distributed among the claimants in the ratio that the claim of each bears to the aggregate of all claims for which a stop payment notice is given, without regard to the order in which the notices were given or enforcement actions were commenced. **Leg.H.** Added Stats 2010 ch 697 §20 (SB 189), effective January 1, 2011, operative July 1, 2012.

Prior Law: Former CC §3190, similar to UCC §3504, was added Stats 1917 ch 751 §1 p 1548 and repealed Stats 1963 ch 819 §2 p 1997, effective January 1, 1965.

§9452. Claimant's right to recover not impaired

Nothing in this chapter impairs the right of a claimant to recover from the direct contractor or the contractor's sureties in an action on a payment bond under Chapter 5 (commencing with Section 9550) any deficit that remains unpaid after the distribution under Section 9450. **Leg.H.** Added Stats 2010 ch 697 §20 (SB 189), effective January 1, 2011, operative July 1, 2012.

Prior Law: Former CC §3191, relating to whom affected by waiver, was added Stats 1917 ch 751 §1 p 1548 and repealed Stats 1963 ch 819 §2 p 1997, effective January 1, 1965.

§9454. Willful false stop payment notice

A person that willfully gives a false stop payment notice to the public entity or that willfully includes in the notice work not provided for the public works contract for which the stop payment notice is given forfeits all right to participate in the distribution under Section 9450. **Leg.H.** Added Stats 2010 ch 697 §20 (SB 189), effective January 1, 2011, operative July 1, 2012.

Prior Law: Former CC §3192, similar to UCC §3504, was added Stats 1917 ch 751 §1 p 1548 and repealed Stats 1963 ch 819 §2 p 1997, effective January 1, 1965.

§9456. Priority

(a) A stop payment notice takes priority over an assignment by a direct contractor of any amount due or to become due pursuant to a public works contract, including contract changes, whether made before or after the giving of a stop payment notice, and the assignment has no effect on the rights of the claimant.

(b) Any garnishment of an amount due or to become due pursuant to a public works contract by a creditor of a direct contractor under Article 8 (commencing with Section 708.710) of Chapter 6 of Division 2 of Title 9 of Part 2 of the Code of Civil Procedure and any statutory lien on that amount is subordinate to the rights of a claimant. **Leg.H.** Added Stats 2010 ch 697 §20 (SB 189), effective January 1, 2011, operative July 1, 2012.

Prior Law: Former CC §3193, similar to UCC §3504, was added Stats 1917 ch 751 §1 p 1548 and repealed Stats 1963 ch 819 §2 p 1997, effective January 1, 1965.

Former CC §3193, relating to acceptance, was enacted Stats 1872 and repealed Stats 1917 ch 751 §1 p 1531.

ARTICLE 4
Enforcement of Payment of Claim Stated in Stop Payment Notice

Requirements to enforce payment of claim in stop payment notice. §9500.
Commencement of action to enforce payment of claim. §9502.
Notice of commencement of action. §9504.
Multiple claimants. §9506.
Dismissal of action for want of prosecution. §9508.
Cessation of stop payment notice. §9510.

§9500. Requirements to enforce payment of claim in stop payment notice

(a) A claimant may not enforce payment of the claim stated in a stop payment notice unless the claimant has complied with all of the following conditions:

(1) The claimant has given preliminary notice to the extent required by Chapter 3 (commencing with Section 9300).

(2) The claimant has given the stop payment notice within the time provided in Section 9356.

(b) The claim filing procedures of Part 3 (commencing with Section 900) of Division 3.6 of Title 1 of the Government Code do not apply to an action under this article. **Leg.H.** Added Stats 2010 ch 697 §20 (SB 189), effective January 1, 2011, operative July 1, 2012.

Prior Law: Former CC §3183, similar to UCC §3503, was added Stats 1917 ch 751 §1 p 1547 and repealed Stats 1963 ch 819 §2 p 1997, effective January 1, 1965.

Former CC §3265, similar to UCC §3104, was added Stats 1917 ch 751 §1 p 1559, amended Stats 1923 ch 98 §1 p 193, and repealed Stats 1963 ch 819 §2 p 1997, effective January 1, 1965.

§9502. Commencement of action to enforce payment of claim

(a) The claimant shall commence an action against the public entity and the direct contractor to enforce payment of the claim stated in a stop payment notice at any time after 10 days from the date the claimant gives the stop payment notice.

(b) The claimant shall commence an action against the public entity and the direct contractor to enforce payment of the claim stated in a stop payment notice not later than 90 days after expiration of the time within which a stop payment notice must be given.

(c) An action under this section may not be brought to trial or judgment entered before expiration of the time provided in subdivision (b).

(d) If a claimant does not commence an action to enforce payment of the claim stated in a stop payment notice within the time provided in subdivision (b), the notice ceases to be effective and the public entity shall release funds withheld pursuant to the notice. **Leg.H.** Added Stats 2010 ch 697 §20 (SB 189), effective January 1, 2011, operative July 1, 2012.

Prior Law: Former CC §3210, similar to UCC §3501, was added Stats 1917 ch 751 §1 p 1551, amended Stats 1947 ch 295 §1 p 859, and repealed Stats 1963 ch 819 §2 p 1997, effective January 1, 1965.

§9504. Notice of commencement of action

Within five days after commencement of an action to enforce payment of the claim stated in a stop payment notice, the claimant shall give notice of commencement of the action to the public entity in the same manner that a stop payment notice is given. **Leg.H.** Added Stats 2010 ch 697 §20 (SB 189), effective January 1, 2011, operative July 1, 2012.

Prior Law: Former CC §3211, similar to UCC §3504, was added Stats 1917 ch 751 §1 p 1551 and repealed Stats 1963 ch 819 §2 p 1997, effective January 1, 1965.

Former CC §3211, relating to presentment when bill not accepted where made, was enacted Stats 1872 and repealed Stats 1917 ch 751 §1 p 1531.

§9506. Multiple claimants

If more than one claimant has given a stop payment notice:

(a) Any number of claimants may join in the same enforcement action.

(b) If claimants commence separate actions, the court that first acquires jurisdiction may order the actions consolidated.

(c) On request of the public entity, the court shall require that all claimants be impleaded in one action and shall adjudicate the rights of all parties in the action. **Leg.H.** Added Stats 2010 ch 697 §20 (SB 189), effective January 1, 2011, operative July 1, 2012.

Prior Law: Former CC §3214, similar to UCC §3410, was added Stats 1917 ch 751 §1 p 1552 and repealed Stats 1963 ch 819 §2 p 1997, effective January 1, 1965.

Former CC §3214, relating to effect of delay, was enacted Stats 1872 and repealed Stats 1917 ch 751 §1 p 1531.

§9508. Dismissal of action for want of prosecution

Notwithstanding Section 583.420 of the Code of Civil Procedure, if an action to enforce payment of the claim stated in a stop payment notice is not brought to trial within two years after commencement of the action, the court may in its discretion dismiss the action for want of prosecution. **Leg.H.** Added Stats 2010 ch 697 §20 (SB 189), effective January 1, 2011, operative July 1, 2012.

Prior Law: Former CC §3212, similar to UCC §4503, was added Stats 1917 ch 751 §1 p 1551 and repealed Stats 1963 ch 819 §2 p 1997, effective January 1, 1965.

Former CC §3212, relating to presentment of bill payable at particular place, was enacted Stats 1872 and repealed Stats 1917 ch 751 §1 p 1531.

§9510. Cessation of stop payment notice

A stop payment notice ceases to be effective, and the public entity shall release funds withheld, in either of the following circumstances:

(a) An action to enforce payment of the claim stated in the stop payment notice is dismissed, unless expressly stated to be without prejudice.

(b) Judgment in an action to enforce payment of the claim stated in the stop payment notice is against the claimant. **Leg.H.** Added Stats 2010 ch 697 §20 (SB 189), effective January 1, 2011, operative July 1, 2012.

Prior Law: Former CC §3213, similar to UCC §3410, was added Stats 1917 ch 751 §1 p 1552 and repealed Stats 1963 ch 819 §2 p 1997, effective January 1, 1965.

Former CC §3213, relating to effect of delay in presentment, was enacted Stats 1872 and repealed Stats 1917 ch 751 §1 p 1531.

CHAPTER 5
PAYMENT BOND

Payment bond required. §9550.
Result of failure to give and approve payment bond. §9552.
Requirements of payment bond. §9554.
When an action to enforce liability on bond may be commenced. §9558.
Preliminary notice; Written notice of completion. §9560.
Notice requirements. §9562.
Actions that may be maintained. §9564.
Right to recover on payment bond. §9566.

§9550. Payment bond required

(a) A direct contractor that is awarded a public works contract involving an expenditure in excess of twenty-five thousand dollars ($25,000) shall, before commencement of work, give a payment bond to and approved by the officer or public entity by whom the contract was awarded.

(b) A public entity shall state in its call for bids that a payment bond is required for a public works contract involving an expenditure in excess of twenty-five thousand dollars ($25,000).

(c) A payment bond given and approved under this section will permit performance of and provide coverage for work pursuant to a public works contract that supplements the contract for which the bond is given, if the requirement of a new bond is waived by the public entity.

(d) For the purpose of this section, a design professional is not deemed a direct contractor and is not required to give a payment bond.

(e) This section does not apply to a public works contract with a "state entity" as defined in subdivision (d) of Section 7103 of the Public Contract Code. **Leg.H.** Added Stats 2010 ch 697 §20 (SB 189), effective January 1, 2011, operative July 1, 2012.

Prior Law: Former CC §3247, similar to UCC §3410, was added Stats 1917 ch 751 §1 p 1556 and repealed Stats 1963 ch 819 §2 p 1997, effective January 1, 1965.

Former CC §3247, relating to sections applicable to notes, was enacted Stats 1872 and repealed Stats 1917 ch 751 §1 p 1531. Historical Derivation: Former Gov C §§4200, 4201, as enacted Stats 1943, amended Stats 1947 ch 406 § 1, Stats 1955 ch 1103 § 1, Stats 1963 ch 1632 §1.

§9552. Result of failure to give and approve payment bond

If a payment bond is not given and approved as required by Section 9550:

(a) Neither the public entity awarding the public works contract nor any officer of the public entity shall audit, allow, or pay a claim of the direct contractor pursuant to the contract.

(b) A claimant shall receive payment of a claim pursuant to a stop payment notice in the manner provided by Chapter 4 (commencing with Section 9350). **Leg.H.** Added Stats 2010 ch 697 §20 (SB 189), effective January 1, 2011, operative July 1, 2012.

Prior Law: Former CC §3251, relating to conditions to allowance of claim and manner of payment, was added Stats 1969 ch 1362 §2 p 2752, operative January 1, 1971, amended Stats 1972 ch 227 §1 (amendment expired on September 3, 1972), Stats 1974 ch 147 §1, effective April 4, 1974 and repealed October 2, 1974, by its own terms.

Former CC §3251, similar to UCC §3410, was added Stats 1917 ch 751 §1 p 1557 and repealed Stats 1963 ch 819 §2 p 1997, effective January 1, 1965. Historical Derivation: (a) Former CC §3251, as added Stats 1969 ch 1362 §2 p 2752, amended Stats 1972 ch 227 § 1, Stats 1974 ch 147 §1. (b) Former Gov C §4208, as enacted Stats 1943, amended Stats 1957 ch 66 §3.

§9554. Requirements of payment bond

(a) A payment bond shall be in an amount not less than 100 percent of the total amount payable pursuant to the public works contract. The bond shall be in the form of a bond and not a deposit in lieu of a bond. The bond shall be executed by an admitted surety insurer.

(b) The payment bond shall provide that if the direct contractor or a subcontractor fails to pay any of the following, the surety will pay the obligation and, if an action is brought to enforce the liability on the bond, a reasonable attorney's fee, to be fixed by the court:

(1) A person authorized under Section 9100 to assert a claim against a payment bond.

(2) Amounts due under the Unemployment Insurance Code with respect to work or labor performed pursuant to the public works contract.

(3) Amounts required to be deducted, withheld, and paid over to the Employment Development Department from the wages of employees of the contractor and subcontractors under Section 13020 of the Unemployment Insurance Code with respect to the work and labor.

(c) The payment bond shall be conditioned for the payment in full of the claims of all claimants and by its terms inure to the benefit of any person authorized under Section 9100 to assert a claim against a payment bond so as to give a right of action to that person or that person's assigns in an action to enforce the liability on the bond.

(d) The direct contractor may require that a subcontractor give a bond to indemnify the direct contractor for any loss sustained by the direct contractor because of any default of the subcontractor under this section. **Leg.H.** Added Stats 2010 ch 697 §20 (SB 189), effective January 1, 2011, operative July 1, 2012.

Prior Law: Former CC §3096, similar to UCC §§3115, 3305, 3407, was added Stats 1917 ch 751 §1 p 1535 and repealed Stats 1963 ch 819 §2 p 1997, effective January 1, 1965.

Former CC §3248, similar to present UCC §3410, was added Stats 1917 ch 751 §1 and repealed Stats 1963 ch 819 §2, effective January 1, 1965.

Former CC §3248, relating to delay in presentment of promissory note, was enacted Stats 1872 and repealed Stats 1917 ch 751 §1. Historical Derivation: Former Gov C §§4202–4205, as enacted Stats 1943, amended Stats 1947 ch 1093 §1, Stats 1953 ch 599 §1, Stats 1961 ch 1873 §1.

§9558. When an action to enforce liability on bond may be commenced

A claimant may commence an action to enforce the liability on the bond at any time after the claimant ceases to provide work, but not later than six months after the period in which a stop payment notice may be given under Section 9356. **Leg.H.** Added Stats 2010 ch 697 §20 (SB 189), effective January 1, 2011, operative July 1, 2012.

Prior Law: Former CC §3249, similar to UCC §3410, was added Stats 1917 ch 751 §1 p 1557, amended Stats 1921 ch 194 §10 p 215, and repealed Stats 1963 ch 819 §2 p 1997, effective January 1, 1965. Historical Derivation: Former Gov C §4206, as enacted Stats 1943, amended Stats 1957 ch 66 §2.

§9560. Preliminary notice; Written notice of completion

(a) In order to enforce a claim against a payment bond, a claimant shall give the preliminary notice provided in Chapter 3 (commencing with Section 9300).

(b) If preliminary notice was not given as provided in Chapter 3 (commencing with Section 9300), a claimant may enforce a claim by giving written notice to the surety and the bond principal within 15 days after recordation of a notice of completion. If no notice of completion has been recorded, the time for giving written notice to the surety and the bond principal is extended to 75 days after completion of the work of improvement.

(c) Commencing July 1, 2012, and except as provided in subdivision (b), if the preliminary notice was required to be given by a person who has no direct contractual relationship with the contractor, and who has not given notice as provided in Chapter 3 (commencing with Section 9300), that person may enforce a claim by giving written notice to the surety and the bond principal, as provided in Section 9562, within 15 days after recordation of a notice of completion. If no notice of completion has been recorded, the time for giving written notice to the surety and the bond principal is extended to 75 days after completion of the work of improvement.

(d) Subdivision (c) shall not apply in either of the following circumstances:

(1) All progress payments, except for those disputed in good faith, have been made to a subcontractor who has a direct contractual relationship with the general contractor to whom the claimant has provided materials or services.

(2) The subcontractor who has a direct contractual relationship with the general contractor to whom the claimant has provided materials or services has been terminated from the project pursuant to the contract, and all progress payments, except those disputed in good faith, have been made as of the termination date.

(e) Pursuant to Section 9300, this section shall not apply to a laborer, as defined under Section 8024.

(f) This section shall become operative on July 1, 2012. **Leg.H.** Added Stats 2010 ch 697 §20.1 (SB 189), effective January 1, 2011, operative July 1, 2012. Amended Stats 2011 ch 700 §4 (SB 293), effective January 1, 2012, operative July 1, 2012.

Prior Law: Former CC §3252, similar to UCC §3603, was added Stats 1917 ch 751 §1 p 1557 and repealed Stats 1963 ch 819 §2 p 1997, effective January 1, 1965. Historical Derivation: Former Gov C §4209, as added Stats 1959 ch 1594 §1.

§9562. Notice requirements

Notice to the principal and surety under Section 9560 shall comply with the requirements of Chapter 2 (commencing with Section 8100) of Title 1. **Leg.H.** Added Stats 2010 ch 697 §20 (SB 189), effective January 1, 2011, operative July 1, 2012.

§9564. Actions that may be maintained

(a) A claimant may maintain an action to enforce the liability of a surety on a payment bond whether or not the claimant has given the public entity a stop payment notice.

(b) A claimant may maintain an action to enforce the liability on the bond separately from and without commencement of an action against the public entity by whom the contract was awarded or against any officer of the public entity.

(c) In an action to enforce the liability on the bond, the court shall award the prevailing party a reasonable attorney's fee. **Leg.H.** Added Stats 2010 ch 697 §20 (SB 189), effective January 1, 2011, operative July 1, 2012.

Prior Law: Former CC §3250, similar to UCC §3410, was added Stats 1917 ch 751 §1 p 1557, amended Stats 1921 ch 194 §11 p 215, and repealed Stats 1963 ch 819 §2 p 1997, effective January 1, 1965. Historical Derivation: Former Gov C §4207, as enacted Stats 1943, amended Stats 1970 ch 479 §2.

§9566. Right to recover on payment bond

(a) A claimant does not have a right to recover on a payment bond unless the claimant provided work to the direct contractor either directly or through one or more subcontractors pursuant to a public works contract.

(b) Nothing in this section affects the stop payment notice rights of, and relative priorities among, design professionals. **Leg.H.** Added Stats 2010 ch 697 §20 (SB 189), effective January 1, 2011, operative July 1, 2012.

PART 7
UNIFORM PARENTAGE ACT [REPEALED]

§7000. [Section repealed 1994.]

Leg.H. Added Stats 1975 ch 1244 §11. Repealed Stats 1992 ch 162 §4 (AB 2650), operative January 1, 1994. See Fam C §7600.

§7001. [Section repealed 1994.]

Leg.H. Added Stats 1975 ch 1244 §11. Repealed Stats 1992 ch 162 §4 (AB 2650), operative January 1, 1994. See Fam C §7601.

§7002. [Section repealed 1994.]

Leg.H. Added Stats 1975 ch 1244 §11. Repealed Stats 1992 ch 162 §4 (AB 2650), operative January 1, 1994. See Fam C §7602.

§7003. [Section repealed 1994.]

Leg.H. Added Stats 1975 ch 1244 §11. Repealed Stats 1992 ch 162 §4 (AB 2650), operative January 1, 1994. See Fam C §7610.

§7004. [Section repealed 1993.]

Leg.H. Added Stats 1975 ch 1244 §11. Amended Stats 1987 ch 192 §1. Repealed Stats 1992 ch 162 §4 (AB 2650), operative January 1, 1994. See Fam C §§7611, 7612 (ch 849 prevails). Amended Stats 1992 ch 559 §1 (AB 1296); Stats 1992 ch 849 §1.5 (SB 1959). Repealed Stats 1993 ch 219 §63 (AB 1500). See Fam C §§7611, 7611.5, 7612.

§7004.5. [Section repealed 1994.]

Leg.H. Added Stats 1990 ch 543 §1 (SB 2015). Amended Stats 1991 ch 321 §2 (AB 370). Repealed Stats 1992 ch 162 §4 (AB 2650), operative January 1, 1994. See Fam C §7604.

§7005. [Section repealed 1994.]

Leg.H. Added Stats 1975 ch 1244 §11. Amended Stats 1978 ch 429 §34, effective July 17, 1978, operative July 1, 1978; Stats 1979 ch 889 §1, effective September 22, 1979. Repealed Stats 1992 ch 162 §4 (AB 2650), operative January 1, 1994. See Fam C §7613.

§7006. [Section repealed 1994.]

Leg.H. Added Stats 1975 ch 1244 §11. Amended Stats 1978 ch 429 §35, effective July 17, 1978, operative July 1, 1978; Stats 1979 ch 752 §1; Stats 1986 ch 1370 §1, ch 1408 §3; Stats 1987 ch 114 §1. Repealed Stats 1992 ch 162 §4 (AB 2650), operative January 1, 1994. See Fam C §§7630–7634.

§7007. [Section repealed 1994.]

Leg.H. Added Stats 1975 ch 1244 §11. Amended Stats 1989 ch 1105 §4. Repealed Stats 1992 ch 162 §4 (AB 2650), operative January 1, 1994. See Fam C §§200, 7620, 7638.

§7008. [Section repealed 1994.]

Leg.H. Added Stats 1975 ch 1244 §11. Amended Stats 1977 ch 207 §1; Stats 1978 ch 380 §13. Repealed Stats 1992 ch 162 §4 (AB 2650), operative January 1, 1994. See Fam C §7635.

§7009. [Section repealed 1993.]

Leg.H. Added Stats 1992 ch 1136 §3 (SB 1541). Repealed Stats 1993 ch 219 §63.1 (AB 1500). See Fam C §3031.

§7010. [Section repealed 1994.]

Leg.H. Added Stats 1990 ch 1493 §30 (AB 3974), operative January 1, 1993. Repealed Stats 1992 ch 162 §4 (AB 2650), operative January 1, 1994. See Fam C §§7636, 7637, 7639.

Prior Law: Former §7010, similar to the repealed section, was added Stats 1975 ch 1244 §11, amended Stats 1988 ch 1577 §4, Stats 1990 ch 1493 §29 (AB 3974), operative until January 1, 1993, and repealed January 1, 1993, by its own terms.

§7011. [Section repealed 1994.]

Leg.H. Added Stats 1975 ch 1244 §11. Repealed Stats 1992 ch 162 §4 (AB 2650), operative January 1, 1994. See Fam C §7640.

§7012. [Section repealed 1994.]

Leg.H. Added Stats 1975 ch 1244 §11. Amended Stats 1988 ch 1128 §2. Repealed Stats 1992 ch 162 §4 (AB 2650), operative January 1, 1994. See Fam C §7641.

§7013. [Section repealed 1994.]

Leg.H. Added Stats 1975 ch 1244 §11. Amended Stats 1976 ch 404 §2; Stats 1990 ch 1363 §8 (AB 3532), operative July 1, 1991. Repealed Stats 1992 ch 162 §4 (AB 2650), operative January 1, 1994. See Fam C §7642.

§7014. [Section repealed 1994.]

Leg.H. Added Stats 1975 ch 1244 §11. Amended Stats 1983 ch 438 §1. Repealed Stats 1992 ch 162 §4 (AB 2650), operative January 1, 1994. See Fam C §7643.

§7015. [Section repealed 1994.]

Leg.H. Added Stats 1975 ch 1244 §11. Repealed Stats 1992 ch 162 §4 (AB 2650), operative January 1, 1994. See Fam C §7650.

§7016. [Section repealed 1994.]

Leg.H. Added Stats 1975 ch 1244 §11. Repealed Stats 1992 ch 162 §4 (AB 2650), operative January 1, 1994. See Fam C §7614.

§7017. [Section repealed 1994.]

Leg.H. Added Stats 1975 ch 1244 §11. Amended Stats 1977 ch 207 §2; Stats 1978 ch 429 §36, effective July 17, 1978, operative July 1, 1978, ch 1045 §1; Stats 1979 ch 752 §2; Stats 1986 ch 1370 §2; Stats 1990 ch 1363 §9 (AB 3532), operative July 1, 1991. Repealed Stats 1992 ch 162 §4 (AB 2650), operative January 1, 1994. See Fam C §§7660–7666, 7669.

§7017.1. [Section repealed 1994.]

Leg.H. Added Stats 1976 ch 404 §3. Repealed Stats 1992 ch 162 §4 (AB 2650), operative January 1, 1994. See Fam C §7670.

§7017.2. [Section repealed 1994.]

Leg.H. Added Stats 1987 ch 114 §2. Repealed Stats 1992 ch 162 §4 (AB 2650), operative January 1, 1994. See Fam C §§7667, 7668.

§7017.6. [Section repealed 1994.]

Leg.H. Added Stats 1987 ch 954 §3. Repealed Stats 1992 ch 162 §4 (AB 2650), operative January 1, 1994. See Fam C §7603.

§7018. [Section repealed 1994.]

Leg.H. Added Stats 1975 ch 1244 §11. Repealed Stats 1992 ch 162 §4 (AB 2650), operative January 1, 1994. See Fam C §13.

§7020. [Section repealed 1993]

Leg.H. Added Stats 1979 ch 795 §5, operative July 1, 1980. Amended Stats 1980 ch 1158 §3; Stats 1982 ch 439 §1; Stats 1983 ch 234 §3; Stats 1984 ch 439 §1; Stats 1988 ch 271 §3; Stats 1990 ch 935 §2 (AB 3593). Repealed Stats 1992 ch 162 §4 (AB 2650), operative January 1, 1994 (ch 1136 prevails); Amended Stats 1992 ch 1136 §4 (SB 1541). Repealed Stats 1993 ch 219 §63.2 (AB 1500). See Fam C §§242, 243, 6224, 6302, 6305, 6320–6323, 6340, 6342, 6345, 6380, 6382, 6383, 6388.

§7021. [Section repealed 1994.]

Leg.H. Added Stats 1979 ch 795 §6, operative July 1, 1980. Amended Stats 1980 ch 1158 §4; Stats 1988 ch 271 §4. Repealed Stats 1992 ch 162 §4 (AB 2650), operative January 1, 1994. See Fam C §§6360, 6361, 6380, 6388.

PART 8
AUTOMATIC CHECKOUT SYSTEM

The STANDARD
CODE OF CIVIL PROCEDURE

of the

STATE OF CALIFORNIA

2025 EDITION

The Original Code of Civil Procedure
Adopted March 11, 1872—Effective January 1, 1873
With All Subsequent Legislative Enactments

Table Showing 2024 Changes in the Code of Civil Procedure

Effective January 1, 2025, unless otherwise noted at end of section.

Section	Effect	Chapter	Section	Effect	Chapter
35	Amended	261, 262	871.24	Added	938
129	Amended	654	871.25	Added	938
155	Amended	955	871.26	Added	938
205	Added	812	871.27	Added	938
214	Amended	967	871.28	Added	938
242	Added	204	998	Amended	444
338	Amended	257	1010.6	Amended	151
338.2	Added	257	Ch. 11		
367.8	Amended	51	w/1062.30)	Added	403
367.75	Amended	51, 965	1062.30–1062.34	Added	403
367.76	Amended	51	1062.30	Added	403
397.5	Added	853	1062.30	Added	403
367.75	Amended	853	1062.30	Added	403
425.16	Amended	444	1062.30	Added	403
437c	Amended	99	1062.30	Added	403
488.610	Amended	222	1161	Amended	287
527.6	Amended	652	1161.2	Amended	711
527.9	Amended & Added	544	1167	Amended	512
527.11	Added	544	1170	Amended	512
527.12	Added	478	1281.9	Amended	986
527.85	Amended & Added	947	1281.93	Added	986
529	Amended	557	1282.6	Amended	986
529.2	Amended	285	1283.05	Amended	986
659	Amended	853	1283.1	Repealed	986
684.115	Amended	222	1245.270	Amended	72
683.130	Amended	514	1297.12	Amended	90
685.070	Amended	514	1297.20	Added	90
701.030	Amended	222	1297.72	Amended	90
703.150	Amended	80	1297.73	Added	90
703.510	Amended	514	Art. 3		
703.570	Amended	514	w/1297.90)	Added	90
703.580	Amedned	514	1297.90–1297.92	Added	90
703.610	Amended	514	1297.91	Added	90
704.115	Amended	514	1297.92	Amended	90
704.220	Amended	514	1297.171	Amended	90
704.235	Added	1010	1297.172	Amended	90
704.730	Amended	80	1297.173	Added	90
706.021	Amended	514	1297.174	Added	90
706.022	Amended	514	1297.175	Added	90
706.103	Amended	514	1297.176	Added	90
706.105	Amended	514	1297.177	Added	90
Ch. 12 (comm. w/871.20)			1297.178	Added	90
w/871.20)	Added	938	1297.179	Added	90
871.20–871.28	Added	938	1297.180	Added	90
871.20	Added	938	1298	Amended	516
871.21	Added	938	2015	Amended	227
871.22	Added	938			
871.23	Added	938			

CONTENTS

	Sections
Title of Act	1
Preliminary Provisions	2 – 34

PART 1. OF COURTS OF JUSTICE
Title 1. Organization and Jurisdiction	35 – 155
Title 2. Judicial Officers	165 – 187
Title 3. Persons Specially Invested With Powers of a Judicial Nature	190 – 261b
Title 4. Ministerial Officers of Courts of Justice	262 – 274a
Title 5. Persons Specially Invested With Ministerial Powers Relating to Courts of Justice	283 – 286

PART 2. OF CIVIL ACTIONS
Title 1. Of the Form of Civil Actions	307 – 309
Title 2. Of the Time of Commencing Civil Actions	312 – 366.3
Title 3. Of the Parties to Civil Actions	367 – 389.5
Title 3A. Vexatious Litigants	391 – 391.8
Title 4. Of the Place of Trial, Reclassification, and Coordination of Civil Actions	392 – 404.9
Title 4.5. Recording Notice of Certain Actions	405 – 405.61
Title 5. Jurisdiction and Service of Process	410.10 – 418.11
Title 6. Of the Pleadings in Civil Actions	420 – 476
Title 6.5. Attachment	481.010 – 493.060
Title 7. Other Provisional Remedies in Civil Actions	501 – 574
Title 7a. Pretrial Conferences	575 – 576
Title 8. Of the Trial and Judgment in Civil Actions	577 – 674
Title 8.5. Uniform Foreign-Money Claims Act	676 – 676.16
Title 9. Enforcement of Judgments	680.010 – 724.260
Title 10. Actions in Particular Cases	725a – 871.28
Title 10.5. Partition of Real and Personal Property	872.010 – 874.323
Title 11. Contribution Among Joint Judgment Debtors	875 – 883
Title 13. Appeals in Civil Actions	901 – 936.1
Title 14. Of Miscellaneous Provisions	989 – 1062.34

PART 3. OF SPECIAL PROCEEDINGS OF A CIVIL NATURE
Preliminary Provisions	1063 – 1064
Title 1. Of Writs of Review, Mandate, and Prohibition	1067 – 1110b
Title 3. Of Summary Proceedings	1132 – 1179.07
Title 4. Of the Enforcement of Liens	1180 – 1208.70
Title 5. Of Contempts	1209 – 1222
Title 7. Eminent Domain Law	1230.010 – 1273.050
Title 8. Change of Names	1275 – 1279.6
Title 9. Arbitration	1280 – 1294.4
Title 9.1. Arbitration of Medical Malpractice	1295
Title 9.2. Public Construction Contract Arbitration	1296
Title 9.3. Arbitration and Conciliation of International Commercial Disputes	1297.11 – 1297.432
Title 9.4. Real Estate Contract Arbitration	1298 – 1298.8
Title 9.5. Arbitration of Firefighter and Law Enforcement Officer Labor Disputes	1299 – 1299.9
Title 10. Unclaimed Property	1300 – 1615
Title 11. Money Judgments of Other Jurisdictions	1710.10 – 1741
Title 11.6. Civil Action Mediation	1775 – 1775.15
Title 11b. Recovery of Preferences in an Assignment for the Benefit of Creditors [Renumbered.]	
Title 11.7. Recovery of Preferences and Exempt Property in an Assignment for the Benefit of Creditors	1800 – 1802
Title 12. Tribal Injunctions	1811

v

Title 13.	Inspection Warrants	1822.50 – 1822.60

PART 4. MISCELLANEOUS PROVISIONS

Title 1.	Of the General Principles of Evidence	1855 – 1866
Title 2.	Of the Kinds and Degrees of Evidence	1878 – 1974
Title 3.	Of the Production of Evidence	1985 – 2015.6
Title 4.	Civil Discovery Act	2016.010 – 2036.050
Title 5.	Of the Rights and Duties of Witnesses	2064 – 2065
Title 6.	Of Evidence in Particular Cases, and Miscellaneous and General Provisions	2074 – 2094
Title 7.	Uniform Federal Lien Registration Act	2100 – 2107

CODE OF CIVIL PROCEDURE

An act to establish a Code of Civil Procedure

TITLE OF ACT

§1. Citation of act

This act shall be known as the Code of Civil Procedure, and is divided into four parts, as follows:
1. Of Courts of Justice.
2. Of Civil Actions.
3. Of Special Proceedings of a Civil Nature.
4. Miscellaneous Provisions. **Leg.H.** Enacted 1872. Amended Stats 1965 ch 299 §15, operative January 1, 1967.

PRELIMINARY PROVISIONS

When this code takes effect. §2.
Not retroactive. §3.
Rule of construction of this code. §4.
Provisions similar to existing laws, how construed. §5.
Tenure of officers preserved. §6.
Construction of repeal as to certain offices. §7.
Actions, etc., not affected by this code. §8.
Limitations shall continue to run. §9.
Holidays. §10.
Notice by certified mail as compliance with requirement of notice by registered mail. §11.
Computation of time, first and last days. §12.
Computation of time where last day for performance of act is holiday. §12a.
Public office closed for whole of day to be considered as holiday. §12b.
Computation of last day to perform act before hearing date. §12c.
Certain acts not to be done on holidays. §13.
Performance of acts on special holidays. §13a.
Performance of acts on Saturdays. §13b.
"Seal" defined. §14.
Joint authority; Majority exercise. §15.
Words and phrases; Construction. §16.
Definitions. §17.
Statutes, etc., inconsistent with code repealed. §18.
This act, how cited, enumerated, etc. §19.
Judicial remedies defined. §20.
Division of judicial remedies into classes. §21.
Action defined. §22.
Special proceeding defined. §23.
Division of actions. §24.
Civil actions arise out of obligations or injuries. §25.
Obligation defined. §26.
Division of injuries. §27.
Injuries to property. §28.
Injuries to the person. §29.
Civil actions. §30.
Criminal actions. §31.
Civil and criminal remedies not merged. §32.
"Jurisdictional classification". §32.5.
Civil resolution of offense against property. §33.
Electronic signature by court or judicial officer. §34.

§2. When this code takes effect

This code takes effect at twelve o'clock noon, on the first day of January, eighteen hundred and seventy-three. **Leg.H.** Enacted 1872.

§3. Not retroactive

No part of it is retroactive, unless expressly so declared. **Leg.H.** Enacted 1872.

§4. Rule of construction of this code

The rule of the common law, that statutes in derogation thereof are to be strictly construed, has no application to this code. The code establishes the law of this state respecting the subjects to which it relates, and its provisions and all proceedings under it are to be liberally construed, with a view to effect its objects and to promote justice. **Leg.H.** Enacted 1872.

§5. Provisions similar to existing laws, how construed

The provisions of this code, so far as they are substantially the same as existing statutes must be construed as continuations thereof, and not as new enactments. **Leg.H.** Enacted 1872.

§6. Tenure of officers preserved

All persons who at the time this code takes effect hold office under any of the acts repealed, continue to hold the same according to the tenure thereof, except those offices which are not continued by one of the codes adopted at this session of the legislature. **Leg.H.** Enacted 1872.

§7. Construction of repeal as to certain offices

When any office is abolished by the repeal of any act, and such act is not in substance reenacted or continued in either of the codes, such office ceases at the time the codes take effect. **Leg.H.** Enacted 1872.

§8. Actions, etc., not affected by this code

No action or proceeding commenced before this code takes effect, and no right accrued, is affected by its provisions, but the proceedings therein must conform to the requirements of this code as far as applicable. **Leg.H.** Enacted 1872.

§9. Limitations shall continue to run

When a limitation or period of time prescribed in any existing statute for acquiring a right or barring a remedy, or for any other purpose, has begun to run before this code goes into effect, and the same or any limitation is prescribed in this code, the time that has already run shall be deemed part of the time prescribed as such limitation by this code. **Leg.H.** Enacted 1872. Amended Code Amdts 1873–74 ch 383 §1; Stats 2017 ch 561 §20 (AB 1516), effective January 1, 2018.

§10. Holidays

Holidays within the meaning of this code are every Sunday and any other days that are specified or provided for as judicial holidays in Section 135. **Leg.H.** Enacted 1872. Amended Code Amdts 1880 ch 51 §1; Stats 1889 ch 43 §1; Stats 1893 ch 159 §1; Stats 1897 ch 19 §1; Stats 1907 ch 287 §1; Stats 1907 1st Ex Sess ch 7 §1; Stats 1909 ch 29 §1; Stats 1911 ch 597 §1; Stats 1925 ch 93 §1; Stats 1957 ch 43 §1; Stats 1982 ch 838 §1, effective September 10, 1982; Stats 1994 ch 1011 §1 (SB 1373); Stats 2001 ch 542 §1 (SB 1112).

§11. Notice by certified mail as compliance with requirement of notice by registered mail

Wherever any notice or other communication is required by this code to be mailed by registered mail by or to any person or corporation, the mailing of such notice or other communication by certified mail shall be deemed to be a sufficient compliance with the requirements of law. **Leg.H.** Added Stats 1959 ch 426 §2.

Prior Law: Former CCP §11, similar to present section, was added by Stats 1959 ch 400 §2 and repealed by Stats 1961 ch 72 §1.

Former CCP §11, similar to present Gov C §6701, was enacted 1872, amended Code Amdts 1873–74 ch 383 §2 p 280, Stats 1909 ch 29 §2 p 22, and repealed Stats 1925 ch 93 §2 p 225.

§12. Computation of time, first and last days

The time in which any act provided by law is to be done is computed by excluding the first day, and including the last, unless the last day is a holiday, and then it is also excluded. **Leg.H.** Enacted 1872.

§12a. Computation of time where last day for performance of act is holiday

(a) If the last day for the performance of any act provided or required by law to be performed within a specified period of time is a holiday, then that period is hereby extended to and including the next day that is not a holiday. For purposes of this section, "holiday" means all day on Saturdays, all holidays specified in Section 135 and, to the extent provided in Section 12b, all days that by terms of Section 12b are required to be considered as holidays.

(b) This section applies to Sections 659, 659a, and 921, and to all other provisions of law providing or requiring an act to be performed on a particular day or within a specified period of time, whether expressed in this or any other code or statute, ordinance, rule, or regulation. **Leg.H.** Added Stats 1933 ch 29 §1. Amended Stats 1951 ch 492 §2; Stats 1955 ch 59 §1; Stats 1961 ch 1370 §1; Stats 1982 ch 838 §2, effective

September 10, 1982; Stats 1994 ch 1011 §2 (SB 1373); Stats 2001 ch 542 §2 (SB 1112); Stats 2007 ch 263 §3 (AB 310), effective January 1, 2008.

§12b. Public office closed for whole of day to be considered as holiday

If any city, county, state, or public office, other than a branch office, is closed for the whole of any day, insofar as the business of that office is concerned, that day shall be considered as a holiday for the purposes of computing time under Sections 12 and 12a. **Leg.H.** Added Stats 1951 ch 655 §25.

§12c. Computation of last day to perform act before hearing date

(a) Where any law requires an act to be performed no later than a specified number of days before a hearing date, the last day to perform that act shall be determined by counting backward from the hearing date, excluding the day of the hearing as provided by Section 12.

(b) Any additional days added to the specified number of days because of a particular method of service shall be computed by counting backward from the day determined in accordance with subdivision (a). **Leg.H.** Added Stats 2010 ch 41 §1 (AB 2119), effective January 1, 2011.

§13. Certain acts not to be done on holidays

Whenever any act of a secular nature, other than a work of necessity or mercy, is appointed by law or contract to be performed upon a particular day, which days falls upon a holiday, such act may be performed upon the next business day with the same effect as if it had been performed upon the day appointed. **Leg.H.** Enacted 1872.

§13a. Performance of acts on special holidays

Any act required by law to be performed on a particular day or within a specified period of time may be performed (but is not hereby required to be performed) on a special holiday as that term is used in Section 6705 of the Government Code, with like effect as if performed on a day which is not a holiday. **Leg.H.** Added Stats 1933 ch 29 §2. Amended Stats 1959 ch 594 §1.

§13b. Performance of acts on Saturdays

Any act required by law to be performed on a particular day or within a specified period may be performed (but is not hereby required to be performed) on a Saturday, with like effect as if performed on a day which is not a holiday. **Leg.H.** Added Stats 1961 ch 1370 §2.

§14. "Seal" defined

When the seal of a court, public officer, or person is required by law to be affixed to any paper, the word "seal" includes an impression of such seal upon the paper alone as well as upon wax or a wafer affixed thereto. **Leg.H.** Enacted 1872.

§15. Joint authority; Majority exercise

Words giving a joint authority to three or more public officers or other persons are construed as giving such authority to a majority of them, unless it is otherwise expressed in the act giving the authority. **Leg.H.** Enacted 1872.

§16. Words and phrases; Construction

Words and phrases are construed according to the context and the approved usage of the language; but technical words and phrases, and such others as have acquired a peculiar and appropriate meaning in law, or are defined in the succeeding section, are to be construed according to such peculiar and appropriate meaning or definition. **Leg.H.** Enacted 1872.

§17. Definitions

(a) Words used in this code in the present tense include the future as well as the present. Words used in the masculine gender include the feminine and neuter. The singular number includes the plural and the plural number includes the singular.

(b) As used in this code, the following words have the following meanings, unless otherwise apparent from the context:

(1) "Affinity" signifies the connection existing in consequence of marriage, between each of the married persons and the blood relatives of the other when applied to the marriage relation.

(2) "County" includes "city and county."

(3) "Electronic signature" means an electronic sound, symbol, or process attached to or logically associated with an electronic record and executed or adopted by a person with the intent to sign the electronic record.

(4) "Month" means a calendar month, unless otherwise expressed.

(5) "Oath" includes an affirmation or declaration.

(A) "Depose" includes any written statement made under oath or affirmation.

(B) "Testify" includes any mode of oral statement made under oath or affirmation.

(6) "Person" includes a corporation as well as a natural person.

(7) "Process" signifies a writ or summons issued in the course of a judicial proceeding.

(8) "Property" includes both personal and real property.

(A) "Personal property" includes money, goods, chattels, things in action, and evidences of debt.

(B) "Real property" is coextensive with lands, tenements, and hereditaments.

(9) "Section" refers to a section of this code, unless some other code or statute is expressly mentioned.

(10) "Sheriff" includes marshal.

(11) "Signature" or "subscription" includes a mark of a person's name, if the person cannot write, with his or her name being written near it by a person who writes his or her own name as a witness. In order that a mark may be acknowledged or serve as the signature to any sworn statement, it shall be witnessed by two persons who shall subscribe their own names as witnesses thereto.

(12) "Spouse" includes "registered domestic partner," as required by Section 297.5 of the Family Code.

(13) "State" includes the District of Columbia and the territories when applied to the different parts of the United States, and the words "United States" may include the district and territories.

(14) "Will" includes codicil.

(15) "Writ" means an order or precept in writing, issued in the name of the people, or of a court or judicial officer.

(16) "Writing" includes printing and typewriting. **Leg.H.** Enacted 1872. Amended Code Amdts 1873–74 ch 383 §3; Stats 1903 ch 123 §1; Stats 1933 ch 742 §1; Stats 1951 ch 1737 §1; Stats 1996 ch 872 §5 (AB 3472); Stats 2002 ch 784 §21 (SB 1316); Stats 2003 ch 62 §21 (SB 600); Stats 2015 ch 32 §1 (AB 432), effective January 1, 2016; Stats 2016 ch 50 §13 (SB 1005), effective January 1, 2017.

2016 Note: It is the intent of the Legislature that the changes made by this act have only technical and nonsubstantive effect. Hence, no change made by this act shall create any new right, duty, or other obligation that did not exist immediately preceding the effective date of this act, or result in the limitation or termination of any right, duty, or other obligation that existed immediately preceding the effective date of this act. Stats 2016 ch 50 (SB 1005) §125.

§18. Statutes, etc., inconsistent with code repealed

No statute, law, or rule is continued in force because it is consistent with the provisions of this code on the same subject; but in all cases provided for by this code, all statutes, laws, and rules heretofore in force in this state, whether consistent or not with the provisions of this code, unless expressly continued in force by it, are repealed and abrogated. This repeal or abrogation does not revive any former law heretofore repealed, nor does it affect any right already existing or accrued, or any action or proceeding already taken, except as in this code provided; nor does it affect any private statute not expressly repealed. **Leg.H.** Enacted 1872.

§19. This act, how cited, enumerated, etc.

This act, whenever cited, enumerated, referred to, or amended, may be designated simply as "The Code of Civil Procedure," adding, when necessary, the number of the section. **Leg.H.** Enacted 1872.

§20. Judicial remedies defined

Judicial remedies are such as are administered by the courts of justice, or by judicial officers empowered for that purpose by the constitution and statutes of this state. **Leg.H.** Enacted 1872.

§21. Division of judicial remedies into classes

These remedies are divided into two classes:

1. Actions; and,
2. Special proceedings. **Leg.H.** Enacted 1872.

§22. Action defined

An action is an ordinary proceeding in a court of justice by which one party prosecutes another for the declaration, enforcement, or protection of a right, the redress or prevention of a wrong, or the punishment of a public offense. **Leg.H.** Enacted 1872. Amended Stats 1933 ch 742 §2.

§23. Special proceeding defined
Every other remedy is a special proceeding. **Leg.H.** Enacted 1872.

§24. Division of actions
Actions are of two kinds:
1. Civil; and,
2. Criminal. **Leg.H.** Enacted 1872.

§25. Civil actions arise out of obligations or injuries
A civil action arises out of:
1. An obligation;
2. An injury. **Leg.H.** Enacted 1872.

§26. Obligation defined
An obligation is a legal duty, by which one person is bound to do or not to do a certain thing, and arises from either of the following:
(a) Contract.
(b) Operation of law. **Leg.H.** Enacted 1872. Amended Code Amdts 1873–74 ch 383 §4; Stats 2017 ch 561 §21 (AB 1516), effective January 1, 2018.

§27. Division of injuries
An injury is of two kinds:
1. To the person; and,
2. To property. **Leg.H.** Enacted 1872.

§28. Injuries to property
An injury to property consists in depriving its owner of the benefit of it, which is done by taking, withholding, deteriorating, or destroying it. **Leg.H.** Enacted 1872.

§29. Injuries to the person
Every other injury is an injury to the person. **Leg.H.** Enacted 1872.

§30. Civil actions
A civil action is prosecuted by one party against another for the declaration, enforcement or protection of a right, or the redress or prevention of a wrong. **Leg.H.** Enacted 1872. Amended Stats 1933 ch 742 §3.

§31. Criminal actions
The Penal Code defines and provides for the prosecution of a criminal action. **Leg.H.** Enacted 1872.

§32. Civil and criminal remedies not merged
When the violation of a right admits of both a civil and criminal remedy the right to prosecute the one is not merged in the other. **Leg.H.** Enacted 1872.

§32.5. "Jurisdictional classification"
The "jurisdictional classification" of a case means its classification as a limited civil case or an unlimited civil case. **Leg.H.** Added Stats 1998 ch 931 §19 (SB 2139), effective September 28, 1998. Amended Stats 2002 ch 784 §22 (SB 1316).

§33. Civil resolution of offense against property
A prosecuting attorney, in his or her discretion, may assist in the civil resolution of a violation of an offense described in Title 13 (commencing with Section 450) of Part 1 of the Penal Code in lieu of filing a criminal complaint. **Leg.H.** Added Stats 1982 ch 1518 §1.

Prior Law: Former CCP §33, similar to present Const Art VI §1, was enacted 1872, repealed and reenacted Code Amdts 1880 ch 35 §1, amended Stats 1933 ch 743 §1, and repealed Stats 1953 ch 206 §7.

§34. Electronic signature by court or judicial officer
An electronic signature, as defined in Section 17, by a court or judicial officer shall be as effective as an original signature. **Leg.H.** Added Stats 2015 ch 32 §2 (AB 432), effective January 1, 2016.

Former Sections: Former CCP §34, relating to the application of the Code of Civil Procedure to all courts, was enacted 1872, repealed and re-enacted Code Amdts 1880 ch 35 §1, amended Stats 1933 ch 743 §2, and repealed Stats 2002 ch 784 §23, effective January 1, 2003.

Prior Law: Former CCP §34, relating to the application of the Code of Civil Procedure to all courts, was enacted 1872, repealed and re-enacted Code Amdts 1880 ch 35 §1, amended Stats 1933 ch 743 §2, and repealed Stats 2002 ch 784 §23, effective January 1, 2003. Historical derivation: (a) former CCP §831c, as added Stats 1925 ch 436 §1, amended Stats 1927 ch 727 §1, Stats 1929 ch 494 §1; (b) former CCP §831d, as added Stats 1925 ch 436 §1, amended Stats 1927 ch 727 §1, Stats 1929 ch 494 §2, Stats 1931 ch 835 §1; (c) former CCP §831e, as added Stats 1925 ch 436 §1, amended Stats 1927 ch 727 §1; (d) former CCP §831h, as added Stats 1929 ch 470 §1; (e) former CCP §831j, as added Stats 1931 ch 77 §1; (f) former CCP §839, as enacted 1872, amended Code Amdts 1875-76 ch 182 §1; (g) former CCP §§869, 889, as enacted 1872; (h) former CCP §905, as enacted 1872, amended Stats 1907 ch 478 §14, Stats 1921 ch 128 §2, Stats 1929 ch 321 §1; (i) former CCP §925, as enacted 1872.

PART 1
OF COURTS OF JUSTICE

Title 1. Organization and Jurisdiction.
Title 2. Judicial Officers.
Title 3. Persons Specially Invested With Powers of a Judicial Nature.
Title 4. Ministerial Officers of Courts of Justice.
Title 5. Persons Specially Invested With Ministerial Powers Relating to Courts of Justice.

TITLE 1
ORGANIZATION AND JURISDICTION

Chapter 1. Courts of Justice in General.
Chapter 3. Supreme Court.
Chapter 4. Superior Courts.
Chapter 5.1. Limited Civil Cases.
Chapter 5.5. Small Claims Court.
Chapter 6. General Provisions Respecting Courts of Justice.
Chapter 7. Special Immigrant Juvenile Findings.
Chapter 8. Of Justices' Courts [Renumbered].
Chapter 9. Of Police Courts [Renumbered].
Chapter 10. General Provisions Respecting Courts of Justice [Renumbered].

CHAPTER 1
COURTS OF JUSTICE IN GENERAL

Precedence on calendar of proceedings involving elections [Repealed January 1, 2027]. §35.
Precedence on calendar of proceedings involving elections [Operative January 1, 2027]. §35.
Motion for preference; Time of trial; Continuance. §36.
Affidavit in support of motion for preference. §36.5.
Preference in action for injuries caused during commission of felony. §37.
Meaning of statutory reference to judicial district. §38.

§35. Precedence on calendar of proceedings involving elections [Repealed January 1, 2027]

(a) Proceedings in cases involving the registration or denial of registration of voters, the certification or denial of certification of candidates, the certification or denial of certification of ballot measures, election contests, actions under Section **20010 or** 20012 of the Elections Code, actions under Chapter 7 (commencing with Section 20510) of Division 20 of the Elections Code, and actions under Chapter 2 (commencing with Section 21100) of Division 21 of the Elections Code shall be placed on the calendar in the order of their date of filing and shall be given precedence.

(b) This section shall [1] **remain in effect only until January 1, 2027, and as of that date is repealed, unless a later enacted statute, that is enacted before January 1, 2027, deletes or extends that date.** Leg.H. Added Stats 1971 ch 980 §1. Amended Stats 2019 ch 493 §1 (AB 730), effective January 1, 2020, repealed January 1, 2023; Stats 2022 ch 745 §1 (AB 972), effective January 1, 2023, repealed January 1, 2027; Stats 2023 ch 343 §1 (AB 764), effective January 1, 2024, repealed January 1, 2027; Stats 2024 ch 261 §1 (AB 2655), effective January 1, 2025, repealed January 1, 2027; Stats 2024 ch 262 §1 (AB 2839), effective September 17, 2024, repealed January 1, 2027; Stats 2024 ch 262 §1.5 (AB 2839), effective September 17, 2024, repealed January 1, 2027.

§35. 2024 Deletes. [1] become operative January 1, 2027

Prior Law: Former CCP §35 was enacted 1872 and amended and renumbered §36 by Code Amdts 1880 ch 35 §1 p 22.

§35. Precedence on calendar of proceedings involving elections [Operative January 1, 2027]

(a) Proceedings in cases involving the registration or denial of registration of voters, the certification or denial of certification of candidates, the certification or denial of certification of ballot measures, election contests, **actions under Chapter 7 (commencing with Section 20510) of Division 20 of the Elections Code**, and actions under Chapter 2 (commencing with Section 21100) of Division 21 of the Elections Code shall be placed on the calendar in the order of their date of filing and shall be given precedence.

(b) This section shall become operative January 1, 2027. **Leg.H.** Added Stats 2019 ch 493 §2 (AB 730), effective January 1, 2020, operative January 1, 2023. Amended Stats 2022 ch 745 §2 (AB 972), effective January 1, 2023, operative January 1, 2027; Stats 2023 ch 343 §2 (AB 764), effective January 1, 2024, operative January 1, 2027; Stats 2024 ch 261 §2 (AB 2655), effective January 1, 2025, operative January 1, 2027; Stats 2024 ch 262 §2 (AB 2839), effective September 17, 2024; Stats 2024 ch 262 §2.5 (AB 2839), effective September 17, 2024, operative January 1, 2027.

§36. Motion for preference; Time of trial; Continuance

(a) A party to a civil action who is over 70 years of age may petition the court for a preference, which the court shall grant if the court makes both of the following findings:

(1) The party has a substantial interest in the action as a whole.

(2) The health of the party is such that a preference is necessary to prevent prejudicing the party's interest in the litigation.

(b) A civil action to recover damages for wrongful death or personal injury shall be entitled to preference upon the motion of any party to the action who is under 14 years of age unless the court finds that the party does not have a substantial interest in the case as a whole. A civil action subject to subdivision (a) shall be given preference over a case subject to this subdivision.

(c) Unless the court otherwise orders:

(1) A party may file and serve a motion for preference supported by a declaration of the moving party that all essential parties have been served with process or have appeared.

(2) At any time during the pendency of the action, a party who reaches 70 years of age may file and serve a motion for preference.

(d) In its discretion, the court may also grant a motion for preference that is accompanied by clear and convincing medical documentation that concludes that one of the parties suffers from an illness or condition raising substantial medical doubt of survival of that party beyond six months, and that satisfies the court that the interests of justice will be served by granting the preference.

(e) Notwithstanding any other provision of law, the court may in its discretion grant a motion for preference that is supported by a showing that satisfies the court that the interests of justice will be served by granting this preference.

(f) Upon the granting of such a motion for preference, the court shall set the matter for trial not more than 120 days from that date and there shall be no continuance beyond 120 days from the granting of the motion for preference except for physical disability of a party or a party's attorney, or upon a showing of good cause stated in the record. Any continuance shall be for no more than 15 days and no more than one continuance for physical disability may be granted to any party.

(g) Upon the granting of a motion for preference pursuant to subdivision (b), a party in an action based upon a health provider's alleged professional negligence, as defined in Section 364, shall receive a trial date not sooner than six months and not later than nine months from the date that the motion is granted. **Leg.H.** Added Stats 1979 ch 151 §2. Amended Stats 1981 ch 215 §1; Stats 1988 ch 1237 §1; Stats 1989 ch 913 §1; Stats 1990 ch 428 §1 (AB 3811); Stats 2008 ch 218 §1 (AB 1949), effective January 1, 2009.

Prior Law: Former CCP §36, similar to present Gov C §3020.5, was enacted 1872 as §35, amended and renumbered §36 Code Amdts 1880 ch 35 §1, amended Stats 1933 ch 743 §3, and repealed Stats 1953 ch 206 §§4, 7.

§36.5. Affidavit in support of motion for preference

An affidavit submitted in support of a motion for preference under subdivision (a) of Section 36 may be signed by the attorney for the party seeking preference based upon information and belief as to the medical diagnosis and prognosis of any party. The affidavit is not admissible for any purpose other than a motion for preference under subdivision (a) of Section 36. **Leg.H.** Added Stats 1990 ch 1232 §1 (AB 3820).

§37. Preference in action for injuries caused during commission of felony

(a) A civil action shall be entitled to preference, if the action is one in which the plaintiff is seeking damages which were alleged to have been caused by the defendant during the commission of a felony offense for which the defendant has been criminally convicted.

(b) The court shall endeavor to try the action within 120 days of the grant of preference. **Leg.H.** Added Stats 1982 ch 514 §1. Amended Stats 1983 ch 938 §1, effective September 20, 1983.

Prior Law: Former CCP §37 was enacted 1872 as §36, amended and renumbered §37 Code Amdts 1880 ch 35 §1, and repealed Stats 1933 ch 743 §61.

§38. Meaning of statutory reference to judicial district

Unless the provision or context otherwise requires, a reference in a statute to a judicial district means:

(a) As it relates to a court of appeal, the court of appeal district.

(b) As it relates to a superior court, the county. **Leg.H.** Added Stats 1998 ch 931 §20 (SB 2139), effective September 28, 1998. Amended Stats 2018 ch 92 §39 (SB 1289), effective January 1, 2019.

Prior Law: Former CCP §38, similar to present Const Art IV §18, was enacted as CCP §37, amended and renumbered by Code Amdts 1880 ch 35 §1, and repealed Stats 1933 ch 743 §61.

CHAPTER 2
COURT OF IMPEACHMENT [REPEALED]
CHAPTER 2.5
THE JUDICIAL COUNCIL [REPEALED]

§39. [Section repealed 1953]

Leg.H. Added Stats 1951 ch 655 §3. Repealed Stats 1953 ch 206 §7. See Gov C §68500.

Prior Law: Former CCP §39 was enacted 1872 as §38, amended and renumbered Code Amdts 1880 ch 35 §1, and repealed Stats 1933 ch 743 §61.

§§39.1–39.6. [Sections repealed 1953]

Leg.H. Added Stats 1951 ch 655 §3. Repealed Stats 1953 ch 206 §7. See Gov C §§68501–68503, 68504–68506.

CHAPTER 3
SUPREME COURT

Transaction of business. §41.
Adjournments as recesses. §42.
Powers of appellate court; Determination of law questions; Remittal of judgment. §43.
Preference for probate, election, and certain defamation cases. §44.
Precedence to be given to appeals from judgments freeing minors from parental custody and control; Extensions of time. §45.
[Section renumbered 1967]. §48.
[Section renumbered 1967]. §53.
[Section renumbered 1967]. §57.
[Repealed]. §61.1–61.3.
[Section renumbered 1967]. §61.4.

§40. [Section repealed 1953]

Leg.H. Enacted 1872. Repealed and re-enacted Code Amdts 1880 ch 35 §1. Amended Stats 1933 ch 743 §4. Repealed Stats 1953 ch 206 §7. The repealed section related to the organization and jurisdiction of the supreme court and courts of appeal.

§41. Transaction of business

The Supreme Court and the courts of appeal may transact business at any time. **Leg.H.** Added Stats 1951 ch 655 §8 as §61.4. Amended Stats 1953 ch 206 §2. Amended and renumbered Stats 1967 ch 17 §7.

Prior Law: Former CCP §41, similar to Gov C §§68200, 68201, was added by Stats 1951 ch 655 §4, amended by Stats 1951 ch 1435 §1, and repealed by Stats 1953 ch 206 §7.

Former CCP §41, relating to computation of years of office, was enacted 1872, repealed and reenacted by Code Amdts 1880 ch 35 §1, and repealed by Stats 1933 ch 743 §61 p 1835. See Const Art VI §3.

§42. Adjournments as recesses

Adjournments from day to day, or from time to time, are to be construed as recesses in the sessions, and shall not prevent the Supreme Court or the courts of appeal from sitting at any time. **Leg.H.** Added Code Amdts 1880 ch 35 §1 as §48. Amended and renumbered Stats 1967 ch 17 §4.

Prior Law: Former CCP §42, relating to vacancies, was added Code Amdts 1880 ch 35 §1 and repealed Stats 1933 ch 743 §61.

Former CCP §42 was enacted 1872 and repealed and re-enacted as §50 by Code Amdts 1880 ch 35 §1.

§43. Powers of appellate court; Determination of law questions; Remittal of judgment

The Supreme Court, and the courts of appeal, may affirm, reverse, or modify any judgment or order appealed from, and may direct the proper judgment or order to be entered, or direct a new trial or further proceedings to be had. In giving its decision, if a new trial be granted, the court shall pass upon and determine all the questions of law involved in the case, presented upon such appeal, and necessary to the final determination of the case. Its judgment in appealed cases shall be remitted to the court from which the appeal was taken. **Leg.H.** Enacted 1872 as §45. Repealed and re-enacted as §53 Code Amdts 1880 ch 35 §1. Amended Stats 1933 ch 743 §6. Amended and renumbered Stats 1967 ch 17 §5.

Prior Law: Former CCP §43, similar to Const Art VI §2, was added by Code Amdts 1880 ch 35 §1 and repealed by Stats 1933 ch 743 §61.

Former CCP §43 was enacted 1872, amended by Code Amdts 1873–74 ch 383 §5, and repealed and re-enacted as §51 by Code Amdts 1880 ch 35 §1.

§44. Preference for probate, election, and certain defamation cases

Appeals in probate proceedings, in contested election cases, and in actions for libel or slander by a person who holds any elective public office or a candidate for any such office alleged to have occurred during the course of an election campaign shall be given preference in hearing in the courts of appeal, and in the Supreme Court when transferred thereto. All these cases shall be placed on the calendar in the order of their date of issue, next after cases in which the people of the state are parties. **Leg.H.** Added Stats 1887 ch 73 §1 as §57. Amended Stats 1903 ch 62 §1; Stats 1933 ch 743 §7. Amended and renumbered Stats 1967 ch 17 §6. Amended Stats 1982 ch 1642 §1, operative June 5, 1984.

Prior Law: Former CCP §44, similar to Cal Const Art VI §2, was added by Code Amdts 1880 ch 35 §1 and repealed by Stats 1933 ch 743 §61.

Former CCP §44 was enacted 1872 and repealed and re-enacted as §52 by Code Amdts 1880 ch 35 §1.

§45. Precedence to be given to appeals from judgments freeing minors from parental custody and control; Extensions of time

An appeal from a judgment freeing a minor who is a dependent child of the juvenile court from parental custody and control, or denying a recommendation to free a minor from parental custody or control, shall have precedence over all cases in the court to which an appeal in the matter is taken. In order to enable the child to be available for adoption as soon as possible and to minimize the anxiety to all parties, the appellate court shall grant an extension of time to a court reporter or to counsel only upon an exceptional showing of good cause. **Leg.H.** Added Stats 1988 ch 805 §2, operative January 1, 1993. Amended Stats 1997 ch 510 §1 (AB 329).

Prior Law: Former CCP §45, similar to the present section, was added Stats 1984 ch 605 §2, amended Stats 1988 ch 805 §1, operative until January 1, 1993, and repealed January 1, 1993, by its own terms.

Former CCP §45 was added Code Amdts 1880 ch 35 §1 and repealed Stats 1933 ch 743 §61.

Former CCP §45 was enacted 1872 and repealed and reenacted Code Amdts 1880 ch 35 §1 pp 21, 25, as §53.

§46. [Section repealed 1933]

Leg.H. Added Code Amdts 1880 ch 35 §1. Repealed Stats 1933 ch 743 §61. See Cal Const Art VI §2.

Prior Law: Former CCP §46 was enacted 1872 and repealed and re-enacted as Code Amdts 1880 ch 35 §1 pp 21, 25, as §54.

§47. [Section repealed 1953]

Leg.H. Enacted 1872 as §50. Amended Code Amdts 1873–74 ch 675 §1; Code Amdts 1877–78 ch 142 §2. Repealed and re-enacted as §47 by Code Amdts 1880 ch 35 §1. Amended Stats 1933 ch 743 §5; Stats 1945 ch 40 §1. Repealed Stats 1953 ch 206 §7. See Gov C §§68801–68803.

Prior Law: Former CCP §47, relating to number of justices necessary to pronounce judgment, was enacted 1872 and omitted by Code Amdts 1880 ch 35 §1 p 21, in amending Part I.

§48. [Section renumbered 1967]

Leg.H. Added Code Amdts 1880 ch 35 §1. Amended and renumbered as CCP §42 by Stats 1967 ch 17 §4.

Prior Law: Former CCP §48, similar to Gov C §§68801–68803, was enacted 1872 and incorporated in §47 by Code Amdts 1880 ch 35 §1 p 24.

§49. [Section repealed 1933]

Leg.H. Added Code Amdts 1880 ch 35 §1. Repealed Stats 1933 ch 743 §61. See CCP §43.

Prior Law: Former CCP §49, relating to terms of court, was enacted 1872, amended by Code Amdts 1877–78 ch 142 §1 p 22, and incorporated in §47 by Code Amdts 1880 ch 35 §1 p 24.

§50. [Section repealed 1933]

Leg.H. Enacted 1872 as §42. Repealed and re-enacted Code Amdts ch 35 §1 as §50. Repealed Stats 1933 ch 743 §61. See Cal Const Art VII §§10, 11.

Prior Law: Former CCP §50 was enacted 1872, amended by Code Amdts 1873–74 ch 675 §1 p 395, Code Amdts 1877–78 ch 142 §2 p 22, and repealed and re-enacted as §47 by Code Amdts 1880 ch 35 §1 pp 21, 24.

§51. [Section repealed 1933]

Leg.H. Enacted 1872 as §43. Amended Code Amdts 1873–74 ch 383 §5. Repealed and re-enacted Code Amdts 1880 ch 35 §1 as §51. Repealed Stats 1933 ch 743 §61. See Cal Const Art VII §§10, 11.

§52. [Section repealed 1933]

Leg.H. Enacted 1872 as §44. Repealed and re-enacted Code Amdts 1880 ch 35 §1 as §52. Amended Stats 1919 ch 58 §1. Repealed Stats 1933 ch 743 §61. See Cal Const Art VII §§10, 11.

§52a. [Section repealed 1933]

Leg.H. Added Stats 1919 ch 57 §1. Repealed Stats 1933 ch 743 §61. See Cal Const Art VII §§10, 11.

§53. [Section renumbered 1967]

Leg.H. Enacted 1872 as §45. Repealed and re-enacted Code Amdts 1880 ch 35 §1 as §53. Amended Stats 1933 ch 743 §6; Amended and renumbered as CCP §43 by Stats 1967 ch 17 §5.

§54. [Section repealed 1933]

Leg.H. Enacted 1872 as §46. Repealed and re-enacted Code Amdts 1880 ch 35 §1 as §54. Repealed Stats 1933 ch 743 §61. See Const Art VI §§2, 10–12, 14.

Prior Law: Former CCP §54, relating to judicial districts, was enacted 1872 and omitted by Code Amdts 1880 ch 35 §1 in amending Part I.

§§55, 56. [Sections repealed 1933]

Leg.H. Amended Code Amdts 1880 ch 35 §1. Repealed Stats 1933 ch 743 §61. See Cal R of Court 25.

Prior Law: Former CCP §55, relating to court in each district, was enacted 1872 and omitted Code Amdts 1880 ch 35 §1 in amending Part I.

Former CCP §56, relating to election and terms of judges, was enacted 1872 and omitted Code Amdts 1880 ch 35 §1 in amending Part I.

§57. [Section renumbered 1967]

Leg.H. Added Stats 1887 ch 73 §1. Amended Stats 1903 ch 62 §1; Stats 1933 ch 743 §7. Amended and renumbered as CCP §44 by Stats 1967 ch 17 §6.

Prior Law: Former CCP §57, relating to jurisdiction of district courts, was enacted 1872 and omitted by Code Amdts 1880 ch 35 §1 in amending Part I.

§§58–58.5. [Sections repealed 1953]

Leg.H. Added Stats 1951 ch 655 §5. Repealed Stats 1953 ch 206 §7. See Gov C §§68806, 68807, 68843, 68846, 68847.

Prior Law: Former CCP §58, relating to terms of court in first district, was enacted 1872, amended by Code Amdts 1873–74 ch 65 §1, ch 348 §1, Code Amdts 1875–76 ch 19 §1, and omitted by Code Amdts 1880 ch 35 §1 in amending Part I.

§58.6. [Section repealed 1953]

Leg.H. Added Stats 1951 ch 655 §5. Amended Stats 1951 ch 1328 §2. Repealed Stats 1953 ch 206 §7. The repealed section related to the annual salary of the Clerk of the Supreme Court and ex officio secretary of the Judicial Council.

§§58.7, 58.8. [Sections repealed 1953]

Leg.H. Added Stats 1951 ch 655 §5. Repealed Stats 1953 ch 206 §7. The repealed sections related to the clerk's bond and office hours.

§§59, 59.1. [Sections repealed 1953]

Leg.H. Added Stats 1951 ch 655 §6. Amended Stats 1951 ch 1330 §2. Repealed Stats 1953 ch 206 §7. See Gov C §§68900, 68901.

Prior Law: Former CCP §59, relating to terms of court in second district, was enacted 1872, amended by Code Amdts 1875–76 ch 228 §1, and omitted by Code Amdts 1880 ch 35 §1 in amending Part I.

§§59.2–60.4. [Sections repealed 1953]

Leg.H. Added Stats 1951 ch 655 §§6, 7. Repealed Stats 1953 ch 206 §7. See Gov C §§68900–68903.

Prior Law: Former CCP §60, relating to terms of court in third district, was enacted 1872, amended by Code Amdts 1877–78 ch 668 §1, and omitted by Code Amdts 1880 ch 35 §1 in amending Part I.

§61. [Section repealed 1953]

Leg.H. Added Stats 1951 ch 655 §8. Amended Stats 1951 ch 1435 §2. Repealed Stats 1953 ch 206 §7. See Gov C §68201.

Prior Law: Former CCP §61, relating to terms of court in fourth district, was enacted 1872 and omitted by Code Amdts 1880 ch 35 §1 p 21 in amending Part I.

§§61.1–61.3. [Sections repealed 1953]

Leg.H. Added Stats 1951 ch 655 §8. Repealed Stats 1953 ch 206 §7. See Gov C §§69102, 69103.

§61.4. [Section renumbered 1967]

Leg.H. Added Stats 1951 ch 655 §8. Amended Stats 1953 ch 206 §2. Renumbered CCP §41 by Stats 1967 ch 17 §7.

§§61.5–62.1. [Sections repealed 1953]

Leg.H. Added Stats 1951 ch 655 §8. Repealed Stats 1953 ch 206 §7. See Gov C §§69105, 69141, 69143.

Prior Law: Former CCP §62, relating to terms of court in fifth district, was enacted 1872 and omitted by Code Amdts 1880 ch 35 §1 in amending Part I.

§63. [Section omitted 1880]

Leg.H. Enacted 1872. Omitted Code Amdts 1880 ch 35 §1.

§64. [Section omitted 1880]

Leg.H. Enacted 1872. Amended Code Amdts 1875–76 ch 382 §1. Omitted Code Amdts 1880 ch 35 §1.

CHAPTER 4
SUPERIOR COURTS

Process throughout state. §71.
Disposition of property of savings and loan associations; Place of hearings. §73c.
Hearing in another county; Expenses. §73d.
Juvenile hall not located in county seat; Sessions in judicial district where juvenile hall located. §73e.
Adjournments. §74.
Submission of noncontested matter. §75.
Appellate division; Term; Expenses; Jurisdiction; Powers; Rules. §77.

§65. [Section repealed 1953]

Leg.H. Added Code Amdts 1880 ch 35 §1. Amended Stats 1933 ch 743 §8. Repealed Stats 1953 ch 206 §7. See Cal Const Art VI §§4, 16 and Gov C §69741.5.

Prior Law: Former CCP §65, relating to eighth district, was enacted 1872 and omitted by Code Amdts 1880 ch 35 §1 in amending Part I.

§65.1. [Section repealed 1953]

Leg.H. Added Stats 1951 ch 655 §10. Repealed Stats 1953 ch 206 §7. See Cal Const Art VI §§4, 16 and Gov C §69741.5.

§65.2. [Section repealed 1959]

Leg.H. Added Stats 1951 ch 655 §10. Amended Stats 1957 ch 43 §2. Repealed Stats 1959 ch 501 §3. See Pen C §914.1.

§66. [Section repealed 1953]

Leg.H. Added Code Amdts 1880 ch 35 §1. Amended Stats 1933 ch 743 §9; Stats 1951 ch 1061 §1. Repealed Stats 1953 ch 206 §7. See Gov C §69603.

Prior Law: Former CCP §66, relating to ninth district, was enacted 1872 and omitted by Code Amdts 1880 ch 35 §1 in amending Part I.

§66a. [Section repealed 1953]

Leg.H. Added Stats 1943 ch 268 §1. Repealed Stats 1953 ch 206 §7. See Gov C §69602.

Prior Law: Former CCP §66l was added by Stats 1945 ch 415 §1, renumbered §66a-1 by Stats 1949 ch 1563 §1, and repealed by Stats 1953 ch 206 §7.

§66a-1. [Section repealed 1953]

Leg.H. Added Stats 1945 ch 415 §1 as §66a. Amended and renumbered Stats 1949 ch 1563 §1. Repealed Stats 1953 ch 206 §7. See Gov C §69595.

§66b. [Section repealed 1953]

Leg.H. Added Stats 1931 ch 646 §1. Repealed Stats 1953 ch 206 §7. See Gov C §69589.

§66c. [Section repealed 1953]

Leg.H. Added Stats 1945 ch 76 §1. Amended Stats 1951 ch 1120 §1. Repealed Stats 1953 ch 206 §7. See Gov C §69582.

§66d. [Section repealed 1953]

Leg.H. Added Stats 1947 ch 64 §1. Repealed Stats 1953 ch 206 §7. See Gov C §69580.

Prior Law: Former CCP §66d, similar to Gov C §69606, was added Stats 1946 1st Ex Sess ch 26 §1 and repealed Stats 1953 ch 206 §7.

§66e. [Section repealed 1953]

Leg.H. Added Stats 1947 ch 63 §1. Amended Stats 1949 ch 1565 §1. Repealed Stats 1953 ch 206 §7. See Gov C §69600.

§66f. [Section repealed 1953]

Leg.H. Added Stats 1949 ch 1567 §1. Repealed Stats 1953 ch 206 §7. See Gov C §69599.

§66g. [Section repealed 1953]

Leg.H. Added Stats 1947 ch 1022 §1. Repealed Stats 1953 ch 206 §7. See Gov C §69591.

§66h. [Section repealed 1953]

Leg.H. Added Stats 1947 ch 138 §1. Repealed Stats 1953 ch 206 §7. See Gov C §69605.

§§66i, 66j. [Sections repealed 1953]

Leg.H. Added Stats 1947 ch 156 §1. Repealed Stats 1953 ch 206 §7. See Gov C §69598.

§66k. [Section repealed 1953]

Leg.H. Added Stats 1949 ch 1560 §1. Repealed Stats 1953 ch 206 §7. See Gov C §69588.

§66l. [Section repealed 1953]

Leg.H. Added Stats 1949 ch 1564 §1. Repealed Stats 1953 ch 206 §7. See Gov C §69592.

§66m. [Section repealed 1953]

Leg.H. Added Stats 1949 ch 1556 §1. Repealed Stats 1953 ch 206 §7. See Gov C §69594.

§66n. [Section repealed 1953]

Leg.H. Added Stats 1949 ch 1559 §1. Repealed Stats 1953 ch 206 §7. See Gov C §69593.

§66p. [Section repealed 1953]

Leg.H. Added Stats 1949 ch 1558 §1. Repealed Stats 1953 ch 206 §7. See Gov C §69583.

§66q. [Section repealed 1953]

Leg.H. Added Stats 1949 ch 1557 §1. Repealed Stats 1953 ch 206 §7. See Gov C §69581.

§66r. [Section repealed 1953]

Leg.H. Added Stats 1949 ch 1562 §1. Repealed Stats 1953 ch 206 §7. See Gov C §69590.

§66s. [Section repealed 1953]

Leg.H. Added Stats 1949 ch 1561 §1. Repealed Stats 1953 ch 206 §7. See Gov C §69584.

§66t. [Section repealed 1953]

Leg.H. Added Stats 1949 ch 1569 §1. Repealed Stats 1953 ch 206 §7. See Gov C §69604.

§66u. [Section repealed 1953]

Leg.H. Added Stats 1951 ch 1395 §1. Repealed Stats 1953 ch 206 §7. See Gov C §69601.

§67. [Section repealed 1953]

Leg.H. Added Code Amdts 1880 ch 35 §1. Amended Stats 1913 ch 47 §1; Stats 1939 ch 930 §1; Stats 1947 ch 1274 §1; Stats 1949 ch 1566 §1. Repealed Stats 1953 ch 206 §7. See Gov C §§69596.

§67a. [Section repealed 1953]

Leg.H. Added Stats 1909 ch 21 §1. Amended Stats 1913 ch 190 §1; Stats 1917 ch 161 §1; Stats 1921 ch 692; Stats 1923 ch 433 §1; Stats 1927 ch 416 §1; Stats 1931 ch 488 §1; Stats 1947 ch 896 §1; Stats 1949 ch 1568 §1. Repealed Stats 1953 ch 206 §7. See Gov C §69586.

§67b. [Section repealed 1953]

Leg.H. Added Stats 1909 ch 670 §1. Amended Stats 1933 ch 743 §9a. Repealed Stats 1953 ch 206 §7. The repealed sections related to extra sessions.

§§68–70. [Sections repealed 1933]

Leg.H. Added Code Amdts 1880 ch 35 §1. Repealed Stats 1933 ch 743 §61. See Const Art VI §8.

Prior Law: Former CCP §68, relating to eleventh district, was enacted 1872, amended by Code Amdts 1875–76 ch 145 §1, and omitted by Code Amdts 1880 ch 35 §1 in amending Part I.

Former CCP §69, relating to twelfth district, was enacted 1872 and omitted by Code Amdts 1880 ch 35 §1 in amending Part I.

Former CCP §70, relating to thirteenth district, was enacted 1872, amended by Code Amdts 1873–74 ch 2 §1, and omitted by Code Amdts 1880 ch 35 §1, in amending Part I.

§71. Process throughout state

The process of superior courts shall extend throughout the state. **Leg.H.** Added Stats 1967 ch 17 §8.

Prior Law: Former CCP §71, relating to superior courts by judges of other counties, was added by Code Amdts 1880 ch 35 §1 and repealed by Stats 1933 ch 743 §61.

Former CCP §71, relating to fourteenth district, was enacted 1872 and omitted by Code Amdts 1880 ch 35 §1 in amending Part I.

§72. [Section repealed 1933]

Leg.H. Added Code Amdts 1880 ch 35 §1. Repealed Stats 1933 ch 743 §61. See Cal Const Art VI §§10, 11.

Prior Law: Former CCP §72, relating to fifteenth district, was enacted 1872 and omitted Code Amdts 1880 ch 35 §1 in amending Part I.

§73. [Section repealed 1953]

Leg.H. Added Code Amdts 1880 ch 35 §1. Amended Stats 1923 ch 42 §1; Stats 1925 ch 85 §1; Stats 1931 ch 182 §1, ch 706 §1; Stats 1933 ch 743 §10; Stats 1935 ch 271 §1. Repealed Stats 1953 ch 206 §7. The repealed section related to sessions of the superior court.

§73a. [Section repealed 1953]

Leg.H. Added Stats 1933 ch 186 §1. Amended Stats 1935 ch 242 §1; Stats 1939 ch 716 §1. Repealed Stats 1953 ch 206 §7. The repealed section related to expenses when court was held at other than the county seat.

§73b. [Section repealed 1953]

Leg.H. Added Stats 1933 ch 392 §1. Amended Stats 1941 ch 1247 §1; Stats 1947 ch 681 §1. Repealed Stats 1953 ch 206 §7. The repealed section related to sessions of the superior court.

§73c. Disposition of property of savings and loan associations; Place of hearings

Notwithstanding anything to the contrary contained in any other law of this state, the judges of the superior court of the county in which is located the principal office in this state of any savings and loan association of whose business, property and assets possession shall have been taken by the Commissioner of Financial Institutions, may, in their discretion, whenever those judges deem it necessary or advisable, hold hearings relating to the sale, exchange or other disposition of any parcel of real property or any item of personal property of the association, regardless of the location of the property, at the county seat of any county in this state or at the places in the county in which the principal office in this state of the association is located at which sessions of the superior court are held. **Leg.H.** Added Stats 1945 ch 3 §1, effective January 22, 1945. Amended Stats 2003 ch 149 §1 (SB 79).

§73d. Hearing in another county; Expenses

Whenever, under Section 73c, it becomes necessary for a judge, clerk, deputy clerk, court reporter or bailiff of or sitting in the superior court of the county in this state in which is located the principal office of any savings and loan association whose business, property and assets are in the possession of the Commissioner of Financial Institutions, to travel to another county, there temporarily to attend hearings relating to the sale, exchange or other disposition of real or personal property of the association, each judge, clerk, deputy clerk, court reporter or bailiff shall be allowed the necessary expenses in going to, returning from and attending upon the business of the court. The expenses shall, upon order of the court, be a charge against the funds of the association and paid out of those funds by the Commissioner of Financial Institutions. **Leg.H.** Added Stats 1945 ch 3 §2, effective January 22, 1945. Amended Stats 2003 ch 149 §2 (SB 79).

§73e. Juvenile hall not located in county seat; Sessions in judicial district where juvenile hall located

Notwithstanding any other provisions of law, in each county wherein the juvenile hall is not located at the county seat of the county, a majority of the judges of the superior court in and for such county may by an order filed with the clerk of the court direct that a session or sessions of the superior court, while sitting for the purpose of hearing and determining cases and proceedings arising under Chapter 2 of Part 1 of Division 2 or Chapter 2 of Part 1 of Division 6 or Chapter 4 of Part 4 of Division 6 of the Welfare and Institutions Code, may be held or continued in any place in the county in which the juvenile hall is located and thereafter such session or sessions of the court may be held or continued in the location designated in such order. In a county having two superior court judges the presiding judge may make the order. **Leg.H.** Added Stats 1947 ch 1346 §1. Amended Stats 1951 ch 1737 §2, operative January 1, 1952; Stats 1955 ch 966 §1; Stats 2002 ch 784 §24 (SB 1316).

§73f. [Section repealed 1953]

Leg.H. Added Stats 1949 ch 1285 §1. Repealed Stats 1953 ch 206 §7. The repealed section related to court sessions not at the county seat.

§74. Adjournments

Adjournments from day to day, or from time to time, are to be construed as recesses in the sessions, and shall not prevent the court from sitting at any time. **Leg.H.** Added Code Amdts 1880 ch 35 §1.

Prior Law: Former CCP §74, relating to seventeenth district, was enacted 1872 and omitted Code Amdts 1880 ch 35 §1 in amending Part I.

§75. Submission of noncontested matter

The superior court in any county may by rule provide that, whenever all judges are absent from the county, any noncontested matter in which no evidence is required, or which may be submitted upon affidavits, shall be deemed submitted upon the filing with the clerk of a statement of submission by the party or the party's attorney or upon the date set for the hearing. **Leg.H.** Added Stats 1953 ch 1111 §1. Amended Stats 1959 ch 744 §1; Stats 2002 ch 784 §25 (SB 1316).

Prior Law: Former CCP §75, relating to jurisdiction of two kinds, was added Code Amdts 1880 ch 35 §1 and repealed Stats 1933 ch 743 §61.

§76. [Section repealed 1933]

Leg.H. Added Code Amdts 1880 ch 35 §1. Amended Stats 1929 ch 465 §1. Repealed Stats 1933 ch 743 §61. See Cal Const Art VI §§10, 11.

Prior Law: Former CCP §76, relating to duration of terms, was enacted 1872, amended Code Amdts 1873–74 ch 383 §6, and omitted Code Amdts 1880 ch 35 §1 in amending Part I.

§77. Appellate division; Term; Expenses; Jurisdiction; Powers; Rules

(a) In every county there is an appellate division of the superior court consisting of three judges or, when the Chief Justice finds it necessary, four judges.

The Chief Justice shall assign judges to the appellate division for specified terms pursuant to rules, not inconsistent with statute, adopted by the Judicial Council to promote the independence and quality of each appellate division. Each judge assigned to the appellate division of a superior court shall be a judge of that court, a judge of the superior court of another county, or a judge retired from the superior court or a court of higher jurisdiction in this state.

The Chief Justice shall designate one of the judges of each appellate division as the presiding judge of the division.

(b) In each appellate division, no more than three judges shall participate in a hearing or decision. The presiding judge of the division shall designate the three judges who shall participate.

(c) In addition to their other duties, the judges designated as members of the appellate division of the superior court shall serve for the period specified in the order of designation. Whenever a judge is designated to serve in the appellate division of the superior court of a county other than the county in which that judge was elected or appointed as a superior court judge, or if the judge is retired, in a county other than the county in which the judge resides, the judge shall receive expenses for travel, board, and lodging. If the judge is out of the judge's county overnight or longer, by reason of the designation, that judge shall be paid a per diem allowance in lieu of expenses for board and lodging in the same amounts as are payable for those purposes to justices of the Supreme Court under the rules of the Department of General Services. In addition, a retired judge shall receive for the time so served, amounts equal to that which the judge would have received if the judge had been assigned to the superior court of the county.

(d) The concurrence of two judges of the appellate division of the superior court shall be necessary to render the decision in every case in, and to transact any other business except business that may be done at chambers by the presiding judge of, the division. A judgment of the appellate division in an appeal shall contain a brief statement of the reasons for the judgment. A judgment stating only "affirmed" or "reversed" is insufficient. The presiding judge shall convene the appellate division when necessary. The presiding judge shall also supervise its business and transact any business that may be done at chambers.

(e) The appellate division of the superior court has jurisdiction on appeal in all cases in which an appeal may be taken to the superior court or the appellate division of the superior court as provided by law, except where the appeal is a retrial in the superior court.

(f) The powers of each appellate division shall be the same as are now or may hereafter be provided by law or rule of the Judicial Council relating to appeals to the appellate division of the superior courts.

(g) The Judicial Council shall promulgate rules, not inconsistent with law, to promote the independence of, and govern the practice and procedure and the disposition of the business of, the appellate division.

(h) Notwithstanding subdivisions (b) and (d), appeals from convictions of traffic infractions may be heard and decided by one judge of the appellate division of the superior court. **Leg.H.** Added Stats 1955 ch 527 §1. Amended Stats 1961 ch 937 §1; Stats 1976 ch 1288 §1; Stats 1984 ch 704 §1; Stats 1998 ch 931 §21 (SB 2139), effective September 28, 1998, ch 932 §11.5 (AB 1094); Stats 1999 ch 344 §2 (SB 210), effective September 7, 1999, ch 853 §1.5 (SB 832); Stats 2002 ch 784 §26 (SB 1316); Stats 2006 ch 538 §60 (SB 1852), effective January 1, 2007; Stats 2014 ch 58 §1 (AB 1932), effective January 1, 2015; Stats 2016 ch 31 §10 (SB 836), effective June 27, 2016; Stats 2018 ch 92 §40 (SB 1289), effective January 1, 2019.

Prior Law: Former CCP §77, relating to appellate jurisdiction, was added Code Amdts 1880 ch 35 §1, amended Stats 1929 ch 465 §2, and repealed Stats 1933 ch 743 §61.

Former CCP §77, relating to adjournment of the court, was enacted 1872 and omitted by Code Amdts 1880 ch 35 §1 in amending Part I.

§77a. [Section repealed 1953]

Leg.H. Added Stats 1929 ch 475 §1. Amended Stats 1949 ch 1516 §1, effective November 7, 1950, operative January 1, 1952. Repealed Stats 1953 ch 206 §7. See CCP §77.

§77b. [Section repealed 1955]

Leg.H. Added Stats 1929 ch 475 §2. Amended Stats 1951 ch 1737 §3, operative January 1, 1952. Repealed Stats 1955 ch 527 §2. See CCP §77.

§§78, 78.1 [Sections repealed 1953]

Leg.H. Added Stats 1951 ch 655 §11. Repealed Stats 1953 ch 206 §7. See Gov C §§69841–69844, 69845, 69846.

> **Prior Law:** Former CCP §78, relating to process, was added Code Amdts 1880 ch 35 §1 and repealed Stats 1933 ch 743 §61.
>
> Former CCP §78, providing that judgments and orders may be entered in vacation, was enacted 1872 and omitted by Code Amdts 1880 ch 35 §1 in amending Part I.

§79. [Section repealed 1953]

Leg.H. Added Stats 1951 ch 655 §12. Amended Stats 1951 ch 1410 §2. Repealed Stats 1953 ch 206 §7. See Gov C §68202.

> **Prior Law:** Former CCP §79, relating to transfer of books, etc., was added Code Amdts 1880 ch 35 §1 and repealed Stats 1933 ch 743 §61.

§79.1. [Section repealed 1953]

Leg.H. Added Stats 1951 ch 655 §12. Amended Stats 1951 ch 1433 §3. Repealed Stats 1953 ch 206 §7. See Gov C §68202.

§§79.2, 79.3. [Sections repealed 1953]

Leg.H. Added Stats 1951 ch 655 §12. Repealed Stats 1953 ch 206 §7. See Gov C §68202.

§79.4. [Section repealed 1953]

Leg.H. Added Stats 1951 ch 655 §12. Amended Stats 1951 ch 1691 §1. Repealed Stats 1953 ch 206 §7. See Gov C §68202.

§§79.5, 79.6. [Sections repealed 1953]

Leg.H. Added Stats 1951 ch 655 §12. Repealed Stats 1953 ch 206 §7. See Gov C §68202.

§79.7. [Section repealed 1953]

Leg.H. Added Stats 1951 ch 655 §12. Amended Stats 1951 ch 1732 §2. Repealed Stats 1953 ch 206 §7. See Gov C §68202.

§§79.8–79.14. [Sections repealed 1953]

Leg.H. Added Stats 1951 ch 655 §12. Repealed Stats 1953 ch 206 §7. See Gov C §68202.

§79.15. [Section repealed 1953]

Leg.H. Added Stats 1951 ch 655 §12. Amended Stats 1951 ch 1507 §2. Repealed Stats 1953 ch 206 §57. See Gov C §68202.

§79.16. [Section repealed 1953]

Leg.H. Added Stats 1951 ch 655 §12. Repealed Stats 1953 ch 2 §7. See Gov C §68202.

§79.17. [Section repealed 1953]

Leg.H. Added Stats 1951 ch 655 §12. Amended Stats 1951 ch 1720 §2. Repealed Stats 1953 ch 206 §7. See Gov C §68202.

§79.18. [Section repealed 1953]

Leg.H. Added Stats 1951 ch 655 §12. Repealed Stats 1953 ch 206 §7. See Gov C §68202.

§79.19. [Section repealed 1953]

Leg.H. Added Stats 1951 ch 655 §12. Amended Stats 1951 ch 1431 §1. Repealed Stats 1953 ch 206 §7. See Gov C §68202.

§79.20. [Section repealed 1953]

Leg.H. Added Stats 1951 ch 655 §12. Amended Stats 1951 ch 4295 §1. Repealed Stats 1953 ch 206 §7. See Gov C §68202.

§79.21. [Section repealed 1953]

Leg.H. Added Stats 1951 ch 655 §12. Amended Stats 1951 ch 1513 §2. Repealed Stats 1953 ch 206 §7. See Gov C §68202.

§79.22. [Section repealed 1953]

Leg.H. Added Stats 1951 ch 655 §12. Repealed Stats 1953 ch 206 §7. See Gov C §68202.

§79.23. [Section repealed 1953]

Leg.H. Added Stats 1951 ch 655 §12. Amended Stats 1951 ch 1654 §2. Repealed Stats 1953 ch 206 §7. See Gov C §68202.

§79.24. [Section repealed 1953]

Leg.H. Added Stats 1951 ch 655 §12. Amended Stats 1951 ch 1415 §5. Repealed Stats 1953 ch 206 §7. See Gov C §68202.

§§79.25–79.27. [Sections repealed 1953]

Leg.H. Added Stats 1951 ch 655 §12. Repealed Stats 1953 ch 206 §7. See Gov C §68202.

§79.28. [Section repealed 1953]

Leg.H. Added Stats 1951 ch 655 §12. Amended Stats 1951 ch 1221 §2. Repealed Stats 1953 ch 206 §7. See Gov C §68202.

§§79.29, 79.30. [Sections repealed 1953]

Leg.H. Added Stats 1951 ch 655 §12. Repealed Stats 1953 ch 206 §7. See Gov C §68202.

§79.31. [Section repealed 1953]

Leg.H. Added Stats 1951 ch 655 §12. Amended Stats 1951 ch 1429 §2. Repealed Stats 1953 ch 206 §7. See Gov C §68202.

§79.32. [Section repealed 1953]

Leg.H. Added Stats 1951 ch 655 §12. Repealed Stats 1953 ch 206 §7. See Gov C §68202.

§79.33. [Section repealed 1953]

Leg.H. Added Stats 1951 ch 655 §12. Amended Stats 1951 ch 1520 §1. Repealed Stats 1953 ch 206 §7. See Gov C §68202.

§79.34. [Section repealed 1953]

Leg.H. Added Stats 1951 ch 655 §12. Amended Stats 1951 ch 1508 §2. Repealed Stats 1953 ch 206 §7. See Gov C §68202.

§79.35. [Section repealed 1953]

Leg.H. Added Stats 1951 ch 655 §12. Repealed Stats 1953 ch 206 §7. See Gov C §68202.

§79.36. [Section repealed 1953]

Leg.H. Added Stats 1951 ch 655 §12. Amended Stats 1951 ch 1432 §1. Repealed Stats 1953 ch 206 §7. See Gov C §68202.

§79.37. [Section repealed 1953]

Leg.H. Added Stats 1951 ch 655 §12. Amended Stats 1951 ch 1431 §2. Repealed Stats 1953 ch 206 §7. See Gov C §68202.

§79.38. [Section repealed 1953]

Leg.H. Added Stats 1951 ch 55 §12. Amended Stats 1951 ch 1433 §4. Repealed Stats 1953 ch 206 §7. See Gov C §68202.

§79.39. [Section repealed 1953]

Leg.H. Added Stats 1951 ch 655 §12. Amended Stats 1951 ch 1421 §2. Repealed Stats 1953 ch 206 §7. See Gov C §68202.

§79.40. [Section repealed 1953]

Leg.H. Added Stats 1951 ch 655 §12. Repealed Stats 1953 ch 206 §7. See Gov C §68202.

§79.41. [Section repealed 1953]

Leg.H. Added Stats 1951 ch 655 §12. Amended Stats 1951 ch 1418 §2. Repealed Stats 1953 ch 206 §7. See Gov C §68202.

§79.42. [Section repealed 1953]

Leg.H. Added Stats 1951 ch 655 §12. Amended Stats 1951 ch 1432 §2. Repealed Stats 1953 ch 206 §7. See Gov C §68202.

§79.43. [Section repealed 1953]

Leg.H. Added Stats 1951 ch 655 §12. Repealed Stats 1953 ch 206 §7. See Gov C §68202.

§79.44. [Section repealed 1953]

Leg.H. Added Stats 1951 ch 655 §12. Amended Stats 1951 ch 1430 §2. Repealed Stats 1953 ch 206 §7. See Gov C §68202.

§79.45. [Section repealed 1953]

Leg.H. Added Stats 1951 ch 655 §12. Amended Stats 1951 ch 1427 §1. Repealed Stats 1953 ch 206 §7. See Gov C §68202.

§§79.46, 79.47. [Sections repealed 1953]

Leg.H. Added Stats 1951 ch 655 §12. Repealed Stats 1953 ch 206 §7. See Gov C §68202.

§79.48. [Section repealed 1953]

Leg.H. Added Stats 1951 ch 655 §12. Amended Stats 1951 ch 1422 §2. Repealed Stats 1953 ch 206 §7. See Gov C §68202.

§79.49. [Section repealed 1953]

Leg.H. Added Stats 1951 ch 655 §12. Repealed Stats 1953 ch 206 §7. See Gov C §68202.

§79.50. [Section repealed 1953]

Leg.H. Added Stats 1951 ch 655 §12. Amended Stats 1951 ch 1434 §3. Repealed Stats 1953 ch 206 §7. See Gov C §68202.

§79.51. [Section repealed 1953]

Leg.H. Added Stats 1951 ch 655 §12. Amended Stats 1951 ch 1691 §2. Repealed Stats 1953 ch 206 §7. See Gov C §68202.

§79.52. [Section repealed 1953]

Leg.H. Added Stats 1951 ch 655 §12. Repealed Stats 1953 ch 206 §7. See Gov C §68202.

§79.53. [Section repealed 1953]

Leg.H. Added Stats 1951 ch 655 §12. Amended Stats 1951 ch 1428 §1. Repealed Stats 1953 ch 206 §7. See Gov C §68202.

§§79.54, 79.55. [Sections repealed 1953]

Leg.H. Added Stats 1951 ch 655 §12. Repealed Stats 1953 ch 206 §7. See Gov C §68202.

§79.56. [Section repealed 1953]

Leg.H. Added Stats 1951 ch 655 §12. Amended Stats 1951 ch 1471 §2. Repealed Stats 1953 ch 206 §7. See Gov C §68202.

§79.57. [Section repealed 1953]

Leg.H. Added Stats 1951 ch 655 §12. Repealed Stats 1953 ch 206 §7. See Gov C §68202.

§79.58. [Section repealed 1953]

Leg.H. Added Stats 1951 ch 655 §12. Amended Stats 1951 ch 1691 §3. Repealed Stats 1953 ch 206 §7. See Gov C §68202.

CHAPTER 5
MUNICIPAL COURTS [REPEALED]

§81. [Section repealed 2003]

Leg.H. Added Stats 1955 ch 59 §2. Repealed Stats 2002 ch 784 §27 (SB 1316). The repealed section related to the effect of chapter and article headings.

Prior Law: Former CCP §81, relating to classification of justices' courts, was added Stats 1933 ch 743 §12, amended Stats 1933 ch 946 §1, Stats 1939 ch 236 §1, Stats 1941 ch 778 §1, and repealed Stats 1949 ch 1286 §4, effective November 7, 1950, operative January 1, 1952.

§82. [Section repealed 2003]

Leg.H. Added Stats 1933 ch 743 §12. Amended Stats 1951 ch 1737 §5, operative January 1, 1952; Stats 1998 ch 931 §24 (SB 2139), effective September 28, 1998. Repealed Stats 2002 ch 784 §27 (SB 1316). The repealed section related to the effect of establishment of municipal court upon jurisdiction of superior court.

Prior Law: Former CCP §82, providing for a court in each county, was enacted 1872 and omitted Code Amdts 1880 ch 35 §1 in amending Part I.

§83. [Section repealed 1998]

Leg.H. Added Stats 1933 ch 743 §12. Amended Stats 1951 ch 1737 §6, operative January 1, 1952; Stats 1976 ch 1288 §2; Stats 1977 ch 1051 §2; Stats 1976 ch 1288 §2, operative January 1, 1983. Repealed Stats 1998 ch 931 §25 (SB 2139), effective September 28, 1998. The repealed section related to concurrent jurisdiction of justice and municipal courts.

Prior Law: Former CCP §83, relating to election and terms of judges, was enacted Stats 1872 and omitted Code Amdts 1880 ch 35 §1 in amending Part I.

§84. [Section repealed 2003]

Leg.H. Added Stats 1933 ch 743 §12. Amended Stats 1951 ch 1737 §7, operative January 1, 1952; Stats 1998 ch 931 §26 (SB 2139), effective September 28, 1998. Repealed Stats 2002 ch 784 §27 (SB 1316). The repealed section extended the process of municipal courts throughout state.

Prior Law: Former CCP §84, relating to jurisdiction of two kinds, was enacted Stats 1872 and omitted Code Amdts 1880 ch 35 §1 in amending Part I.

CHAPTER 5.1
LIMITED CIVIL CASES

Article 1. Jurisdiction in Limited Civil Cases.
Article 2. Economic Litigation for Limited Civil Cases.

ARTICLE 1
Jurisdiction in Limited Civil Cases

Conditions for treatment as limited civil case. §85.
Specific cases and proceedings that are limited civil cases. §86.
Action under Long-Term Care, Health, Safety and Security Act as limited civil case. §86.1.
Bringing limited civil case in small claims division; Conflict in applicable statutes or rules. §87.
"Unlimited civil case". §88.
Establishment of requisite conditions. §89.

§85. Conditions for treatment as limited civil case

Notwithstanding any law, including, but not limited to, a law that classified an action or special proceeding as a limited civil case, an action or special proceeding shall be treated as a limited civil case only if all of the following conditions are satisfied:

(a) The amount in controversy does not exceed thirty-five thousand dollars ($35,000). As used in this section, "amount in controversy" means the amount of the demand, or the recovery sought, or the value of the property, or the amount of the lien, that is in controversy in the action, exclusive of attorneys' fees, interest, and costs.

(b) The relief sought is a type that may be granted in a limited civil case.

(c) The relief sought, whether in the complaint, a cross-complaint, or otherwise, is exclusively of a type described in one or more laws that classify an action or special proceeding as a limited civil case or that provide that an action or special proceeding is within the original jurisdiction of the superior court, including, but not limited to, the following provisions:

(1) Section 798.61 or 798.88 of the Civil Code.
(2) Section 1719 of the Civil Code.
(3) Section 3342.5 of the Civil Code.
(4) Section 86.
(5) Section 86.1.
(6) Section 1710.20.
(7) Section 7581 of the Food and Agricultural Code.
(8) Section 12647 of the Food and Agricultural Code.
(9) Section 27601 of the Food and Agricultural Code.
(10) Section 31503 of the Food and Agricultural Code.
(11) Section 31621 of the Food and Agricultural Code.
(12) Section 52514 of the Food and Agricultural Code.
(13) Section 53564 of the Food and Agricultural Code.
(14) Section 53069.4 of the Government Code.
(15) Section 53075.6 of the Government Code.
(16) Section 53075.61 of the Government Code.
(17) Section 5411.5 of the Public Utilities Code.
(18) Section 9872.1 of the Vehicle Code.
(19) Section 10751 of the Vehicle Code.
(20) Section 14607.6 of the Vehicle Code.
(21) Section 40230 of the Vehicle Code.
(22) Section 40256 of the Vehicle Code. **Leg.H.** Added Stats 1998 ch 931 §28 (SB 2139), effective September 28, 1998. Amended Stats 2012 ch 99 §3 (AB 2272), effective January 1, 2013, repealed January 1, 2016; Stats 2015 ch 176 §3 (SB 244); Stats 2023 ch 861 §2 (SB 71), effective January 1, 2024.

Former Sections: Former CCP §85, similar to the present section, was added Stats 2012 ch 99 §4, effective January 1, 2013, operative January 1, 2016, and repealed Stats 2015 ch 176 §4, effective January 1, 2016.

Former CCP §85, similar to present CCP §582.5, was added Stats 1976 ch 1288 §4, amended Stats 1977 ch 71 §1, Stats 1982 ch 497 §24, operative July 1, 1983, and repealed Stats 1998 ch 931 §27, effective September 28, 1998.

Former CCP §85, relating to payment of money judgments in municipal or justice courts, was added Stats 1974 ch 1415 §1 and repealed Stats 1976 ch 1288 §3.

Former CCP §85, relating to establishment of municipal courts, was added Stats 1933 ch 743 §13, amended Stats 1951 ch 1737 §8, operative January 1, 1952, and repealed Stats 1953 ch 206 §7.

Former CCP §85, relating to justices' courts and justices, was added Code Amdts 1880 ch 35 §1, amended Stats 1915 ch 731 §1, and repealed Stats 1933 ch 743 §12.

Former CCP §85, relating to original jurisdiction of county courts, was enacted Stats 1872, amended Code Amdts 1873–74 ch 383 §7, and omitted Code Amdts 1880 ch 35 §1 in amending Part I.

Prior Law: Former CCP §85, similar to the present section, was added Stats 2012 ch 99 §4, effective January 1, 2013, operative January 1, 2016, and repealed Stats 2015 ch 176 §4, effective January 1, 2016.

Former CCP §85, similar to present CCP §582.5, was added Stats 1976 ch 1288 §4, amended Stats 1977 ch 71 §1, Stats 1982 ch 497 §24, operative July 1, 1983, and repealed Stats 1998 ch 931 §27, effective September 28, 1998.

Former CCP §85, relating to payment of money judgments in municipal or justice courts, was added Stats 1974 ch 1415 §1 and repealed Stats 1976 ch 1288 §3.

Former CCP §85, relating to establishment of municipal courts, was added Stats 1933 ch 743 §13, amended Stats 1951 ch 1737 §8, operative January 1, 1952, and repealed Stats 1953 ch 206 §7.

Former CCP §85, relating to justices' courts and justices, was added Code Amdts 1880 ch 35 §1, amended Stats 1915 ch 731 §1, and repealed Stats 1933 ch 743 §12.

Former CCP §85, relating to original jurisdiction of county courts, was enacted Stats 1872, amended Code Amdts 1873–74 ch 383 §7, and omitted Code Amdts 1880 ch 35 §1 in amending Part I.

§85.1. [Section repealed 2003]

Leg.H. Added Stats 1998 ch 931 §28 (SB 2139), effective September 28, 1998. Repealed Stats 2002 ch 784 §28 (SB 1316). The repealed section gave municipal courts original jurisdiction.

§86. Specific cases and proceedings that are limited civil cases

(a) The following civil cases and proceedings are limited civil cases:

(1) A case at law if the demand, exclusive of interest, or the value of the property in controversy amounts to thirty-five thousand dollars ($35,000) or less. This paragraph does not apply to a case that involves the legality of any tax, impost, assessment, toll, or municipal fine, except an action to enforce payment of delinquent unsecured personal property taxes if the legality of the tax is not contested by the defendant.

(2) An action for dissolution of partnership if the total assets of the partnership do not exceed thirty-five thousand dollars ($35,000) or an action of interpleader if the amount of money or the value of the property involved does not exceed thirty-five thousand dollars ($35,000).

(3) An action to cancel or rescind a contract if the relief is sought in connection with an action to recover money not exceeding thirty-five thousand dollars ($35,000) or property of a value not exceeding thirty-five thousand dollars ($35,000), paid or delivered under, or in consideration of, the contract; an action to revise a contract where the relief is sought in an action upon the contract if the action otherwise is a limited civil case.

(4) A proceeding in forcible entry or forcible or unlawful detainer if the whole amount of damages claimed is thirty-five thousand dollars ($35,000) or less.

(5) An action to enforce and foreclose a lien on personal property if the amount of the lien is thirty-five thousand dollars ($35,000) or less.

(6) An action to enforce and foreclose, or a petition to release, a lien arising under Chapter 4 (commencing with Section 8400) of Title 2 of Part 6 of Division 4 of the Civil Code, or to enforce and foreclose an assessment lien on a common interest development as defined in Section 4100 or 6534 of the Civil Code, if the amount of the liens is thirty-five thousand dollars ($35,000) or less. However, if an action to enforce the lien affects property that is also affected by a similar pending action that is not a limited civil case, or if the total amount of liens sought to be foreclosed against the same property aggregates an amount in excess of thirty-five thousand dollars ($35,000), the action is not a limited civil case.

(7) An action for declaratory relief if brought pursuant to either of the following:

(A) By way of cross-complaint as to a right of indemnity with respect to the relief demanded in the complaint or a cross-complaint in an action or proceeding that is otherwise a limited civil case.

(B) To conduct a trial after a nonbinding fee arbitration between an attorney and client, pursuant to Article 13 (commencing with Section 6200) of Chapter 4 of Division 3 of the Business and Professions Code, if the amount in controversy is thirty-five thousand dollars ($35,000) or less.

(8) An action to issue a temporary restraining order or preliminary injunction; to take an account, if necessary to preserve the property or rights of any party to a limited civil case; to make any order or perform any act, pursuant to Title 9 (commencing with Section 680.010) of Part 2 (enforcement of judgments) in a limited civil case; to appoint a receiver pursuant to Section 564 in a limited civil case; or to determine title to personal property seized in a limited civil case.

(9) An action under Article 3 (commencing with Section 708.210) of Chapter 6 of Division 2 of Title 9 of Part 2 for the recovery of an interest in personal property or to enforce the liability of the debtor of a judgment debtor if the interest claimed adversely is of a value not exceeding thirty-five thousand dollars ($35,000) or the debt denied does not exceed thirty-five thousand dollars ($35,000).

(10) An arbitration-related petition filed pursuant to either of the following:

(A) Article 2 (commencing with Section 1292) of Chapter 5 of Title 9 of Part 3, except for uninsured motorist arbitration proceedings in accordance with Section 11580.2 of the Insurance Code, if the petition is filed before the arbitration award becomes final and the matter to be resolved by arbitration is a limited civil case under paragraphs (1) to (9), inclusive, of subdivision (a) or if the petition is filed after the arbitration award becomes final and the amount of the award and all other rulings, pronouncements, and decisions made in the award are within paragraphs (1) to (9), inclusive, of subdivision (a).

(B) To confirm, correct, or vacate a fee arbitration award between an attorney and client that is binding or has become binding, pursuant to Article 13 (commencing with Section 6200) of Chapter 4 of Division 3 of the Business and Professions Code, if the arbitration award is thirty-five thousand dollars ($35,000) or less.

(b) The following cases in equity are limited civil cases:

(1) A case to try title to personal property when the amount involved is not more than thirty-five thousand dollars ($35,000).

(2) A case when equity is pleaded as a defensive matter in any case that is otherwise a limited civil case.

(3) A case to vacate a judgment or order of the court obtained in a limited civil case through extrinsic fraud, mistake, inadvertence, or excusable neglect. **Leg.H.** Added Stats 1976 ch 1288 §5. Amended Stats 1978 ch 146 §1, operative July 1, 1979; Stats 1979 ch 958 §1; Stats 1981 ch 714 §57; Stats 1982 ch 466 §14 (ch 497 prevails), ch 497 §25, operative July 1, 1983; Stats 1984 ch 538 §1, ch 1719 §1.1; Stats 1985 ch 879 §1, ch 1383 §1; Stats 1986 ch 88 §1, effective May 13, 1986, ch 953 §1; Stats 1987 ch 104 §1; Stats 1988 ch 463 §1; Stats 1993 ch 1261 §1 (SB 401), ch 1262 §4.5 (AB 1272); Stats 1997 ch 527 §2 (SB 150); Stats 1998 ch 931 §29 (SB 2139), effective September 28, 1998; Stats 2001 ch 44 §1 (SB 562); Stats 2012 ch 181 §42 (AB 806), effective January 1, 2013, operative January 1, 2014; Stats 2013 ch 605 §22 (SB 752), effective January 1, 2014; Stats 2023 ch 861 §3 (SB 71), effective January 1, 2024.

Prior Law: Former CCP §86, relating to records, was added Stats 1933 ch 743 §13, amended Stats 1947 ch 1217 §1, and repealed Stats 1953 ch 206 §7.

Former CCP §86, relating to justices' clerk, was added Code Amdts 1880 ch 35 §1, amended Stats 1915 ch 53 §1, Stats 1917 ch 88 §1, Stats 1919 ch 600 §1, Stats 1929 ch 551 §1, and repealed Stats 1933 ch 743 §12.

Former CCP §86, relating to appellate jurisdiction of county courts, was enacted 1872 and omitted by Code Amdts 1880 ch 35 §1.

§86a. [Section repealed 1953]

Leg.H. Added Stats 1945 ch 719 §1. Amended Stats 1947 ch 1217 §2. Repealed Stats 1953 ch 206 §7. The repealed section related to destruction of old records.

§86.1. Action under Long-Term Care, Health, Safety and Security Act as limited civil case

An action brought pursuant to the Long-Term Care, Health, Safety, and Security Act of 1973 (Chapter 2.4 (commencing with Section 1417) of Division 2 of the Health and Safety Code) is a limited civil case if civil penalties are not sought or amount to thirty-five thousand dollars ($35,000) or less. **Leg.H.** Added Stats 1985 ch 11 §1, effective March 6,

1985. Amended Stats 1990 ch 1133 §1 (AB 3536), ch 1134 §1 (SB 1967); Stats 1998 ch 931 §30 (SB 2139), effective September 28, 1998; Stats 2002 ch 784 §29 (SB 1316); Stats 2023 ch 861 §4 (SB 71), effective January 1, 2024.

§87. Bringing limited civil case in small claims division; Conflict in applicable statutes or rules

(a) A limited civil case may be brought in the small claims division if the case is within the jurisdiction of the small claims division as otherwise provided by statute. Where a statute or rule applicable to a small claims case conflicts with a statute or rule applicable to a limited civil case, the statute or rule applicable to a small claims case governs the small claims case and the statute or rule applicable to a limited civil case does not.

(b) Nothing in this section affects the jurisdiction of the small claims division as otherwise provided by statute. **Leg.H.** Added Stats 1999 ch 344 §3 (SB 210), effective September 7, 1999.

Prior Law: Former CCP §87, relating to appearance by corporation as party in justice or municipal court, was added Stats 1976 ch 1288 §6 and repealed Stats 1998 ch 931 §31, effective September 28, 1998, ch 932 §12. Historical Derivation: Former CCP §90, as added Stats 1975 ch 633 §1.

Former CCP §87, relating to the clerk of the municipal court, was added Stats 1933 ch 743 §13 and repealed Stats 1953 ch 206 §7.

Former CCP §87, relating to sheriff and deputies, was added Code Amdts 1880 ch 35 §1 and repealed Stats 1933 ch 743 §12.

Former CCP §87, relating to presumptions in favor of judgments, was enacted 1872 and omitted by Code Amdts 1880 ch 35 §1 in amending Part I.

§88. "Unlimited civil case"

A civil action or proceeding other than a limited civil case may be referred to as an unlimited civil case. **Leg.H.** Added Stats 1999 ch 344 §4 (SB 210), effective September 7, 1999.

Prior Law: Former CCP §88, relating to powers of justice court clerks, was added Stats 1976 ch 1288 §7 and repealed Stats 1998 ch 931 §32, effective September 28, 1998. Historical Derivation: (a) Former CCP §103a, as added Stats 1915 ch 565 §1, amended Stats 1933 ch 743 §15, Stats 1951 ch 867 §1. (b) Former CCP §102, as added Stats 1911 ch 264 §4, amended Stats 1913 ch 678 §1.

Former CCP §88, relating to powers and duties of marshal of municipal court, was added Stats 1933 ch 743 §13 and repealed Stats 1953 ch 206 §7.

Former CCP §88, relating to terms of the county court for their respective counties, was enacted 1872, amended by Code Amdts 1877–78 ch 250 §2, and omitted by Code Amdts 1880 ch 35 §1 in amending Part I.

§89. Establishment of requisite conditions

(a) The existence of a statute relating to the authority of the court in a limited civil case does not, by itself, imply that the same authority does or does not exist in an unlimited civil case.

(b) The existence of a statute relating to the authority of the court in an unlimited civil case does not, by itself, imply that the same authority does or does not exist in a limited civil case. **Leg.H.** Added Stats 2001 ch 44 §2 (SB 562).

Former Sections: Former CCP §89, relating to blanks in papers and process, as added Stats 1976 ch 1288 §8, was repealed Stats 1998 ch 931 §33.

Prior Law: Former CCP §89, relating to blanks in papers and process, as added Stats 1976 ch 1288 §8, was repealed Stats 1998 ch 931 §33.

ARTICLE 2
Economic Litigation for Limited Civil Cases

Applicability of laws relating to civil actions. §90.
Application of article; Exceptions. §91.
Pleadings; Answers; Demurrers; Motions. §92.
Case questionnaire; Form; Order compelling response; Sanctions. §93.
Discovery. §94.
Additional discovery. §95.
Request for disclosure of witnesses and evidence; Service; Response. §96.
Witnesses and evidence impermissible when not included in statement; Exceptions. §97.
Use of prepared testimony in lieu of direct testimony; Conditions. §98.
Judgment or final order conclusive; Collateral estoppel. §99.
Appeal. §100.

§90. Applicability of laws relating to civil actions

Except where changed by the provisions of this article, all provisions of law applicable to civil actions generally apply to actions subject to this article. **Leg.H.** Added Stats 1982 ch 1581 §1. Amended Stats 2003 ch 149 §3 (SB 79).

Prior Law: Former CCP §90, similar to present CCP §87, was added Stats 1975 ch 633 §1 and repealed Stats 1976 ch 1288 §3.

§91. Application of article; Exceptions

(a) Except as otherwise provided in this section, the provisions of this article apply to every limited civil case.

(b) The provisions of this article do not apply to any action under Chapter 5.5 (commencing with Section 116.110) or any proceeding under Chapter 4 (commencing with Section 1159) of Title 3 of Part 3.

(c) Any action may, upon noticed motion, be withdrawn from the provisions of this article, upon a showing that it is impractical to prosecute or defend the action within the limitations of these provisions. **Leg.H.** Added Stats 1982 ch 1581 §1. Amended Stats 1983 ch 102 §1, effective June 16, 1983; Stats 1985 ch 1383 §2; Stats 1998 ch 931 §37 (SB 2139), effective September 28, 1998.

Prior Law: Former CCP §91 was added Code Amdts 1880 ch 35 §1 and repealed Stats 1933 ch 743 §12.

§92. Pleadings; Answers; Demurrers; Motions

(a) The pleadings allowed are complaints, answers, cross-complaints, answers to cross-complaints and general demurrers.

(b) The answer need not be verified, even if the complaint or cross-complaint is verified.

(c) Special demurrers are not allowed.

(d) Motions to strike are allowed only on the ground that the damages or relief sought are not supported by the allegations of the complaint.

(e) Except as limited by this section, all other motions are permitted. **Leg.H.** Added Stats 1982 ch 1581 §1. Amended Stats 1983 ch 102 §2, effective June 16, 1983.

Prior Law: Former CCP §92, as added Code Amdts 1880 ch 35 and repealed Stats 1933 ch 743 §12.

§93. Case questionnaire; Form; Order compelling response; Sanctions

(a) The plaintiff has the option to serve case questionnaires with the complaint, using forms approved by the Judicial Council. The questionnaires served shall include a completed copy of the plaintiff's completed case questionnaire, and a blank copy of the defendant's case questionnaire.

(b) Any defendant upon whom a case questionnaire is served shall serve a completed defendant's case questionnaire upon the requesting plaintiff with the answer.

(c) The case questionnaire shall be designed to elicit fundamental information about each party's case, including names and addresses of all witnesses with knowledge of any relevant facts, a list of all documents relevant to the case, a statement of the nature and amount of damages, and information covering insurance coverages, injuries and treating physicians. The Judicial Council shall design and develop forms for case questionnaires.

(d) Approved forms shall be made available by the clerk of the court.

(e) If a party on whom a case questionnaire has been served under subdivision (a) or (b) fails to serve a timely or a complete response to that questionnaire, the party serving the questionnaire may move for an order compelling a response or a further response and for a monetary sanction under Chapter 7 (commencing with Section 2023.010) of Title 4 of Part 4. If a party then fails to obey an order compelling a response or a further response, the court may make those orders that are just, including the imposition of an issue sanction, an evidence sanction, or a terminating sanction under Chapter 7 (commencing with Section 2023.010) of Title 4 of Part 4. In lieu of or in addition to that sanction, the court may impose a monetary sanction under Chapter 7 (commencing with Section 2023.010) of Title 4 of Part 4. **Leg.H.** Added Stats 1982 ch 1581 §1. Amended Stats 1987 ch 86 §1, effective and operative July 1, 1987; Stats 2004 ch 182 §5 (AB 3081), operative July 1, 2005.

§94. Discovery

Discovery is permitted only to the extent provided by this section and Section 95. This discovery shall comply with the notice and format requirements of the particular method of discovery, as provided in Title 4 (commencing with Section 2016.010) of Part 4. As to each adverse party, a party may use the following forms of discovery:

(a) Any combination of 35 of the following:

(1) Interrogatories (with no subparts) under Chapter 13 (commencing with Section 2030.010) of Title 4 of Part 4.

(2) Demands to produce documents or things under Chapter 14 (commencing with Section 2031.010) of Title 4 of Part 4.

(3) Requests for admission (with no subparts) under Chapter 16 (commencing with Section 2033.010) of Title 4 of Part 4.

(b) One oral or written deposition under Chapter 9 (commencing with Section 2025.010), Chapter 10 (commencing with Section 2026.010), or Chapter 11 (commencing with Section 2028.010) of Title 4 of Part 4. For purposes of this subdivision, a deposition of an organization shall be treated as a single deposition even though more than one person may be designated or required to testify pursuant to Section 2025.230.

(c) Any party may serve on any person a deposition subpoena duces tecum requiring the person served to mail copies of documents, books, or records to the party's counsel at a specified address, along with an affidavit complying with Section 1561 of the Evidence Code.

The party who issued the deposition subpoena shall mail a copy of the response to any other party who tenders the reasonable cost of copying it.

(d) Physical and mental examinations under Chapter 15 (commencing with Section 2032.010) of Title 4 of Part 4.

(e) The identity of expert witnesses under Chapter 18 (commencing with Section 2034.010) of Title 4 of Part 4. **Leg.H.** Added Stats 1982 ch 1581 §1. Amended Stats 1987 ch 86 §1.3, effective and operative July 1, 1987; Stats 2004 ch 182 §6 (AB 3081), operative July 1, 2005; Stats 2005 ch 294 §2 (AB 333), operative January 1, 2006; Stats 2006 ch 538 §61 (SB 1852), effective January 1, 2007.

Prior Law: Former CCP §94, as added Code Amdts 1880 ch 35 §1 and repealed Stats 1933 ch 743 §12.

Former CCP §94, enacted 1872 and omitted Code Amdts Stats 1880 ch 35 in amending Part I.

§95. Additional discovery

(a) The court may, on noticed motion and subject to such terms and conditions as are just, authorize a party to conduct additional discovery, but only upon a showing that the moving party will be unable to prosecute or defend the action effectively without the additional discovery. In making a determination under this section, the court shall take into account whether the moving party has used all applicable discovery in good faith, and whether the party has attempted to secure the additional discovery by stipulation or by means other than formal discovery.

(b) The parties may stipulate to additional discovery. **Leg.H.** Added Stats 1982 ch 1581 §1.

Prior Law: Former CCP §95, as added Code Amdts 1880 ch 35 §1 and repealed Stats 1933 ch 743 §12.

Former CCP §95, enacted 1872 and omitted Code Amdts 1880 ch 35 §1 in amending Part I.

§96. Request for disclosure of witnesses and evidence; Service; Response

(a) Any party may serve on any other party a request in substantially the following form:

TO: _____,
attorney for _____:

You are requested to serve on the undersigned, within 20 days, a statement of: the names and addresses of witnesses (OTHER THAN A PARTY WHO IS AN INDIVIDUAL) you intend to call at trial; a description of physical evidence you intend to offer; and a description and copies of documentary evidence you intend to offer or, if the documents are not available to you, a description of them. Witnesses and evidence that will be used only for impeachment need not be included. YOU WILL NOT BE PERMITTED TO CALL ANY WITNESS, OR INTRODUCE ANY EVIDENCE, NOT INCLUDED IN THE STATEMENT SERVED IN RESPONSE TO THIS REQUEST, EXCEPT AS OTHERWISE PROVIDED BY LAW.

(b) The request shall be served no more than 45 days or less than 30 days prior to the date first set for trial, unless otherwise ordered.

(c) A statement responding to the request shall be served within 20 days from the service of the request.

(d) No additional, amended or late statement is permitted except by written stipulation or unless ordered for good cause on noticed motion.

(e) No request or statement served under this section shall be filed, unless otherwise ordered.

(f) The clerk shall furnish forms for requests under this rule.

(g) The time for performing acts required under this section shall be computed as provided by law, including Section 1013. **Leg.H.** Added Stats 1982 ch 1581 §1.

Prior Law: Former CCP §96, as added Code Amdts 1880 ch 35 §1 and repealed Stats 1933 ch 743 §1.

Former CCP §96, enacted 1872 and omitted Code Amdts Stats 1880 ch 35 §in amending Part I.

§97. Witnesses and evidence impermissible when not included in statement; Exceptions

(a) Except as provided in this section, upon objection of a party who served a request in compliance with Section 96, no party required to serve a responding statement may call a witness or introduce evidence, except for purposes of impeachment, against the objecting party unless the witness or evidence was included in the statement served.

(b) The exceptions to subdivision (a) are:

(1) A person who, in his or her individual capacity, is a party to the litigation and who calls himself or herself as a witness.

(2) An adverse party.

(3) Witnesses and evidence used solely for purposes of impeachment.

(4) Documents obtained by discovery authorized by this chapter.

(5) The court may, upon such terms as may be just (including, but not limited to, continuing the trial for a reasonable period of time and awarding costs and litigation expenses), permit a party to call a witness or introduce evidence which is required to be, but is not included in such party's statement so long as the court finds that such party has made a good faith effort to comply with subdivision (c) of Section 96 or that the failure to comply was the result of his or her mistake, inadvertence, surprise or excusable neglect as provided in Section 473.

(c) Nothing in this article limits the introduction of evidence in any hearing pursuant to Section 585. **Leg.H.** Added Stats 1982 ch 1581 §1. Amended Stats 1983 ch 102 §3, effective June 16, 1983.

Prior Law: Former CCP §97, as added Code Amdts 1880 ch 35 §1, amended Stats 1905 ch 14 §1, Stats 1915 ch 731 §2, Stats 1927 ch 26 §1, and repealed Stats 1933 ch 743 §12.

Former CCP §97, relating to jurisdiction of probate court, was enacted 1872, amended Code Amdts 1873–74 ch 383 §8 p 282, and omitted Code Amdts 1880 ch 35 §1 p 21 in amending Part I.

§98. Use of prepared testimony in lieu of direct testimony; Conditions

A party may, in lieu of presenting direct testimony, offer the prepared testimony of relevant witnesses in the form of affidavits or declarations under penalty of perjury. The prepared testimony may include, but need not be limited to, the opinions of expert witnesses, and testimony which authenticates documentary evidence. To the extent the contents of the prepared testimony would have been admissible were the witness to testify orally thereto, the prepared testimony shall be received as evidence in the case, provided that either of the following applies:

(a) A copy has been served on the party against whom it is offered at least 30 days prior to the trial, together with a current address of the affiant that is within 150 miles of the place of trial, and the affiant is available for service of process at that place for a reasonable period of time, during the 20 days immediately prior to trial.

(b) The statement is in the form of all or part of a deposition in the case, and the party against whom it is offered had an opportunity to participate in the deposition.

The court shall determine whether the affidavit or declaration shall be read into the record in lieu of oral testimony or admitted as a documentary exhibit. **Leg.H.** Added Stats 1982 ch 1581 §1. Amended Stats 1983 ch 102 §4, effective June 16, 1983; Stats 2023 ch 131 §17 (AB 1754), effective January 1, 2024.

Prior Law: Former CCP §98, relating to qualifications of judge, was added Stats 1951 ch 655 §13 and repealed Stats 1953 ch 206 §7.

Former CCP §98, relating to successors of justices, was added Code Amdts 1880 ch 35 §1 and repealed Stats 1933 ch 743 §12.

Former CCP §98, relating to presumptions in favor of judgments, was enacted 1872 and omitted by Code Amdts 1880 ch 35 §1 in amending Part I.

§98.1. [Section repealed 1953]

Leg.H. Added Stats 1951 ch 655 §13. Repealed Stats 1953 ch 206 §7. The repealed section related to qualifications for a justice of the peace.

§§98.2–98.6. [Sections repealed 1953]

Leg.H. Added Stats 1951 ch 655 §13. Repealed Stats 1953 ch 206 §7. The repealed sections related to fee statements and receipts.

§98.7. [Section repealed 1953]

Leg.H. Added Stats 1951 ch 655 §13. Repealed Stats 1953 ch 206 §7. The repealed section related to fees.

§99. Judgment or final order conclusive; Collateral estoppel

A judgment or final order, in respect to the matter directly adjudged, is conclusive between the parties and their successors in interest but does not operate as collateral estoppel of a party or a successor in interest to a party in other litigation with a person who was not a party or a successor in interest to a party to the action in which the judgment or order is rendered. **Leg.H.** Added Stats 1982 ch 1581 §1.

Prior Law: Former CCP §99, was added Stats 1911 ch 264 §1, amended Stats 1915 ch 120 §1, Stats 1923 ch 470 §1, and repealed Stats 1951 ch 867 §15, operative January 1, 1952.

Former CCP §99, relating to terms of the probate court in the respective counties, was enacted 1872, amended by Code Amdts 1877–78 ch 250 §3, and omitted by Code Amdts 1880 ch 35 §1 in amending Part I.

§100. Appeal

Any party shall have the right to appeal any judgment or final order consistent with the law governing appeals. **Leg.H.** Added Stats 1982 ch 1581 §1.

Prior Law: Former CCP §100, was added Stats 1911 ch 264 §2, amended Stats 1913 ch 676 §1, and repealed Stats 1951 ch 867 §15, operative January 1, 1952.

Former CCP §100, relating to terms of probate court, was enacted 1872, and omitted by Code Amdts 1880 ch 35 §1 in amending Part I.

CHAPTER 5.5
SMALL CLAIMS COURT

Article 1. General Provisions.
Article 2. Small Claims Court.
Article 3. Actions.
Article 4. Parties.
Article 5. Hearing.
Article 6. Judgment.
Article 7. Motion to Vacate, Appeal, and Related Matters.
Article 8. Satisfaction and Enforcement of Judgment.
Article 9. Administration.

ARTICLE 1
General Provisions

Citation of chapter. §116.110.
Legislative findings and declarations. §116.120.
Definitions. §116.130.
Provisions not applicable in small claims actions. §116.140.

§116.110. Citation of chapter

This chapter shall be known and may be cited as "The Small Claims Act." **Leg.H.** Added Stats 1990 ch 1305 §3 (SB 2627).

§116.120. Legislative findings and declarations

The Legislature hereby finds and declares as follows:

(a) Individual minor civil disputes are of special importance to the parties and of significant social and economic consequence collectively.

(b) In order to resolve minor civil disputes expeditiously, inexpensively, and fairly, it is essential to provide a judicial forum accessible to all parties directly involved in resolving these disputes.

(c) The small claims divisions have been established to provide a forum to resolve minor civil disputes, and for that reason constitute a fundamental element in the administration of justice and the protection of the rights and property of individuals.

(d) The small claims divisions, the provisions of this chapter, and the rules of the Judicial Council regarding small claims actions shall operate to ensure that the convenience of parties and witnesses who are individuals shall prevail, to the extent possible, over the convenience of any other parties or witnesses. **Leg.H.** Added Stats 1990 ch 1305 §3 (SB 2627). Amended Stats 1998 ch 931 §37 (SB 2139), effective September 28, 1998.

§116.130. Definitions

In this chapter, unless the context indicates otherwise:

(a) "Plaintiff" means the party who has filed a small claims action. The term includes a defendant who has filed a claim against a plaintiff.

(b) "Defendant" means the party against whom the plaintiff has filed a small claims action. The term includes a plaintiff against whom a defendant has filed a claim.

(c) "Judgment creditor" means the party, whether plaintiff or defendant, in whose favor a money judgment has been rendered.

(d) "Judgment debtor" means the party, whether plaintiff or defendant, against whom a money judgment has been rendered.

(e) "Person" means an individual, corporation, partnership, limited liability partnership, limited liability company, firm, association, or other entity.

(f) "Individual" means a natural person.

(g) "Party" means a plaintiff or defendant.

(h) "Motion" means a party's written request to the court for an order or other action. The term includes an informal written request to the court, such as a letter.

(i) "Declaration" means a written statement signed by an individual which includes the date and place of signing, and a statement under penalty of perjury under the laws of this state that its contents are true and correct.

(j) "Good cause" means circumstances sufficient to justify the requested order or other action, as determined by the judge.

(k) "Mail" means first-class mail with postage fully prepaid, unless stated otherwise. **Leg.H.** Added Stats 1990 ch 1305 §3 (SB 2627). Amended Stats 1991 ch 915 §1 (SB 771); Stats 1994 ch 1010 §57 (SB 2053); Stats 2003 ch 449 §4 (AB 1712).

§116.140. Provisions not applicable in small claims actions

The following do not apply in small claims actions:

(a) Subdivision (a) of Section 1013 and subdivision (b) of Section 1005, on the extension of the time for taking action when notice is given by mail.

(b) Title 6.5 (commencing with Section 481.010) of Part 2, on the issuance of prejudgment attachments. **Leg.H.** Added Stats 1991 ch 915 §2 (SB 771).

ARTICLE 2
Small Claims Court

Small claims division. §116.210.
Jurisdiction. §116.220.
Additional jurisdiction. §116.221.
Action to enforce payment of debt. §116.222.
COVID-19 rental debt; Small claims court jurisdiction; Commencement of action; Reduction in damages [Repealed October 1, 2025]. § 116.223.
Certain choice of forum clauses void and unenforceable. §116.225.
Fees for filing and service by mail. §116.230.
Filing of more than two small claims actions. §116.231.
Fee for each defendant to whom copy of claim is mailed. §116.232.
Case heard by temporary judge. §116.240.
Sessions; Night or Saturday sessions; Proceeding by mediator or referee. §116.250.
Individual assistance for small claims litigants. §116.260.
Law clerks. §116.270.

§116.210. Small claims division

In each superior court there shall be a small claims division. The small claims division may be known as the small claims court. **Leg.H.** Added Stats 1990 ch 1305 §3 (SB 2627). Amended Stats 1998 ch 931 §38 (SB 2139), effective September 28, 1998; Stats 2002 ch 784 §30 (SB 1316).

§116.220. Jurisdiction

(a) The small claims court has jurisdiction in the following actions:

(1) Except as provided in subdivisions (c), (e), and (f), for recovery of money, if the amount of the demand does not exceed six thousand two hundred fifty dollars ($6,250).

(2) Except as provided in subdivisions (c), (e), and (f), to enforce payment of delinquent unsecured personal property taxes in an amount not to exceed six thousand two hundred fifty dollars ($6,250), if the legality of the tax is not contested by the defendant.

(3) To issue the writ of possession authorized by Sections 1861.5 and 1861.10 of the Civil Code if the amount of the demand does not exceed six thousand two hundred fifty dollars ($6,250).

(4) To confirm, correct, or vacate a fee arbitration award not exceeding six thousand two hundred fifty dollars ($6,250) between an attorney and client that is binding or has become binding, or to conduct a hearing de novo between an attorney and client after nonbinding arbitration of a fee dispute involving no more than six thousand two hundred fifty dollars ($6,250) in controversy, pursuant to Article 13 (commencing with Section 6200) of Chapter 4 of Division 3 of the Business and Professions Code.

(5) For an injunction or other equitable relief only when a statute expressly authorizes a small claims court to award that relief.

(b) In any action seeking relief authorized by paragraphs (1) to (4), inclusive, of subdivision (a), the court may grant equitable relief in the form of rescission, restitution, reformation, and specific performance, in lieu of, or in addition to, money damages. The court may issue a conditional judgment. The court shall retain jurisdiction until full payment and performance of any judgment or order.

(c) Notwithstanding subdivision (a), the small claims court has jurisdiction over a defendant guarantor as follows:

(1) For any action brought by a natural person against the Registrar of the Contractors State License Board as the defendant guarantor, the small claims jurisdictional limit stated in Section 116.221 shall apply.

(2) For any action against a defendant guarantor that does not charge a fee for its guarantor or surety services, if the amount of the demand does not exceed three thousand one hundred twenty-five dollars ($3,125).

(3) For any action brought by a natural person against a defendant guarantor that charges a fee for its guarantor or surety services, if the amount of the demand does not exceed eight thousand one hundred twenty-five dollars ($8,125).

(4) For any action brought by an entity other than a natural person against a defendant guarantor that charges a fee for its guarantor or surety services or against the Registrar of the Contractors State License Board as the defendant guarantor, if the amount of the demand does not exceed five thousand dollars ($5,000).

(d) In any case in which the lack of jurisdiction is due solely to an excess in the amount of the demand, the excess may be waived, but any waiver is not operative until judgment.

(e) Notwithstanding subdivision (a), in any action filed by a plaintiff incarcerated in a Department of Corrections and Rehabilitation facility, the small claims court has jurisdiction over a defendant only if the plaintiff has alleged in the complaint that the plaintiff has exhausted the plaintiff's administrative remedies against that department, including compliance with Sections 905.2 and 905.4 of the Government Code. The final administrative adjudication or determination of the plaintiff's administrative claim by the department may be attached to the complaint at the time of filing in lieu of that allegation.

(f) In any action governed by subdivision (e), if the plaintiff fails to provide proof of compliance with the requirements of subdivision (e) at the time of trial, the judicial officer shall, at the plaintiff's discretion, either dismiss the action or continue the action to give the plaintiff an opportunity to provide that proof.

(g) For purposes of this section, "department" includes an employee of a department against whom a claim has been filed under this chapter arising out of an employee's duties as an employee of that department. **Leg.H.** Added Stats 1990 ch 1305 §3 (SB 2627). Amended Stats 1990 ch 1683 §3 (AB 3916); Stats 1991 ch 133 §1 (AB 1827), ch 915 §3 (SB 771); Stats 1992 ch 8 §1 (AB 1551), effective February 19, 1992, ch 142 §2 (SB 1376); Stats 1993 ch 1262 §5 (AB 1272), ch 1264 §95 (SB 574); Stats 1994 ch 479 §10 (AB 3219); Stats 1995 ch 366 §1 (AB 725); Stats 1998 ch 240 §2 (AB 771); Stats 1999 ch 982 §6 (AB 1678); Stats 2006 ch 150 §1 (AB 2455), effective January 1, 2007; Stats 2008 ch 157 §4 (SB 1432), effective January 1, 2009; Stats 2009 ch 468 §1 (AB 712), effective January 1, 2010; Stats 2023 ch 861 §5 (SB 71), effective January 1, 2024.

2009 Note: Nothing in this act is intended to expand, or to encourage the expansion of, the jurisdiction of the small claims court. Stats 2009 ch 468 (AB 712) §2.

§116.221. Additional jurisdiction

In addition to the jurisdiction conferred by Section 116.220, the small claims court has jurisdiction in an action brought by a natural person, if the amount of the demand does not exceed twelve thousand five hundred dollars ($12,500), except as otherwise prohibited by subdivision (c) of Section 116.220 or subdivision (a) of Section 116.231. **Leg.H.** Added Stats 2005 ch 600 §2 (SB 422), effective January 1, 2006. Amended Stats 2011 ch 64 §1 (SB 221), effective January 1, 2012; Stats 2018 ch 92 §41 (SB 1289), effective January 1, 2019; Stats 2023 ch 861 §6 (SB 71), effective January 1, 2024.

Former Sections: Former CCP §116.221, similar to the present section, was added Stats 2005 ch 618 §2 and repealed Stats 2011 ch 64 §2.

Prior Law: Former CCP §116.221, similar to the present section, was added Stats 2005 ch 618 §2 and repealed Stats 2011 ch 64 §2.

§116.222. Action to enforce payment of debt

If the action is to enforce the payment of a debt, the statement of calculation of liability shall separately state the original debt, each payment credited to the debt, each fee and charge added to the debt, each payment credited against those fees and charges, all other debits or charges to the account, and an explanation of the nature of those fees, charges, debits, and all other credits to the debt, by source and amount. **Leg.H.** Added Stats 2005 ch 618 §3 (AB 1459), effective January 1, 2006.

Former Sections: Former CCP §116.222, similar to the present section, was added Stats 2005 ch 600 §3, effective January 1, 2006, and repealed Stats 2015 ch 303 §36, effective January 1, 2016.

Prior Law: Former CCP §116.222, similar to the present section, was added Stats 2005 ch 600 §3, effective January 1, 2006, and repealed Stats 2015 ch 303 §36, effective January 1, 2016.

§ 116.223. COVID-19 rental debt; Small claims court jurisdiction; Commencement of action; Reduction in damages [Repealed October 1, 2025]

(a) The Legislature hereby finds and declares as follows:

(1) There is anticipated to be an unprecedented number of claims arising out of nonpayment of residential rent that occurred between March 1, 2020, and September 30, 2021, related to the COVID-19 pandemic.

(2) These disputes are of special importance to the parties and of significant social and economic consequence collectively as the people of the State of California grapple with the health, economic, and social impacts of the COVID-19 pandemic.

(3) It is essential that the parties have access to a judicial forum to resolve these disputes expeditiously, inexpensively, and fairly.

(4) It is the intent of the Legislature that landlords of residential real property and their tenants have the option to litigate disputes regarding rent which is unpaid for the time period between March 1, 2020, and September 30, 2021, in the small claims court. It is the intent of the Legislature that the jurisdictional limits of the small claims court not apply to these disputes over COVID-19 rental debt.

(b)(1) Notwithstanding paragraph (1) of subdivision (a) Section 116.220, Section 116.221, or any other law, the small claims court has jurisdiction in any action for recovery of COVID-19 rental debt, as defined in Section 1179.02, and any defenses thereto, regardless of the amount demanded.

(2) In an action described in paragraph (1), the court shall reduce the damages awarded for any amount of COVID-19 rental debt sought by payments made to the landlord to satisfy the COVID-19 rental debt, including payments by the tenant, rental assistance programs, or another third party pursuant to paragraph (3) of subdivision (a) of Section 1947.3 of the Civil Code.

(3) An action to recover COVID-19 rental debt, as defined in Section 1179.02, brought pursuant to this subdivision shall not be commenced before November 1, 2021.

(c) Any claim for recovery of COVID-19 rental debt, as defined in Section 1179.02, shall not be subject to Section 116.231, notwithstanding the fact that a landlord of residential rental property may have brought two or more small claims actions in which the amount demanded exceeded two thousand five hundred dollars ($2,500) in any calendar year.

(d) This section shall remain in effect until October 1, 2025, and as of that date is repealed. **Leg.H.** Added Stats 2020 ch 37 §14 (AB 3088), effective August 31, 2020, repealed February 1, 2025. Amended Stats 2021 ch 2 §9 (SB 91), effective January 29, 2021, repealed July 1, 2025; Stats 2021 ch 27 §7 (AB 832), effective June 28, 2021, repealed October 1, 2025.

§116.224. [Section repealed 2015]

Leg.H. Added Stats 2011 ch 64 §3 (SB 221), effective January 1, 2012. Repealed January 1, 2015, by its own terms. The repealed section related to small claims court jurisdiction in action brought by a person for damages not exceeding a specified amount for bodily injuries resulting from an automobile accident.

§116.225. Certain choice of forum clauses void and unenforceable

An agreement entered into or renewed on or after January 1, 2003, establishing a forum outside of California for an action arising from an offer or provision of goods, services, property, or extensions of credit primarily for personal, family, or household purposes that is otherwise within the jurisdiction of a small claims court of this state is contrary to public policy and is void and unenforceable. **Leg.H.** Added Stats 2002 ch 247 §1 (AB 2949).

§116.230. Fees for filing and service by mail

(a) In a small claims case, the clerk of the court shall charge and collect only those fees authorized under this chapter.

(b) If the party filing a claim has filed 12 or fewer small claims in the state within the previous 12 months, the filing fee is the following:

(1) Thirty dollars ($30) if the amount of the demand is one thousand five hundred dollars ($1,500) or less.

(2) Fifty dollars ($50) if the amount of the demand is more than one thousand five hundred dollars ($1,500) but less than or equal to five thousand dollars ($5,000).

(3) Seventy-five dollars ($75) if the amount of the demand is more than five thousand dollars ($5,000).

(c) If the party has filed more than 12 other small claims in the state within the previous 12 months, the filing fee is one hundred dollars ($100).

(d)(1) If, after having filed a claim and paid the required fee under paragraph (1) of subdivision (b), a party files an amended claim or amendment to a claim that raises the amount of the demand so that the filing fee under paragraph (2) of subdivision (b) would be charged, the filing fee for the amended claim or amendment is twenty dollars ($20).

(2) If, after having filed a claim and paid the required fee under paragraph (2) of subdivision (b), a party files an amended claim or amendment to a claim that raises the amount of the demand so that the filing fee under paragraph (3) of subdivision (b) would be charged, the filing fee for the amended claim or amendment is twenty-five dollars ($25).

(3) If, after having filed a claim and paid the required fee under paragraph (1) of subdivision (b), a party files an amended claim or amendment to a claim that raises the amount of the demand so that the filing fee under paragraph (3) of subdivision (b) would be charged, the filing fee for the amended claim or amendment is forty-five dollars ($45).

(4) The additional fees paid under this subdivision are due upon filing. The court shall not reimburse a party if the party's claim is amended to demand a lower amount that falls within the range for a filing fee lower than that originally paid.

(e) Each party filing a claim shall file a declaration with the claim stating whether that party has filed more than 12 other small claims in the state within the last 12 months

(f) The clerk of the court shall deposit fees collected under this section into a bank account established for this purpose by the Administrative Office of the Courts and maintained under rules adopted by or trial court financial policies and procedures authorized by the Judicial council under subdivision (a) of Section 77206 of the Government Code. The deposits shall be made as required under Section 68085.1 of the Government Code and trial court financial policies and procedures authorized by the Judicial Council.

(g)(1) The Administrative Office of the Courts shall distribute six dollars ($6) of each thirty-dollar ($30) fee, eight dollars ($8) of each fifty-dollar ($50) fee, ten dollars ($10) of each seventy-five-dollar ($75) fee, and fourteen dollars ($14) of each one hundred-dollar ($100) fee collected under subdivision (b) or (c) to a special account in the county in which the court is located to be used for the small claims advisory services described in Section 116.940, or, if the small claims advisory services are administered by the court, to the court. The Administrative Office of the Courts shall also distribute two dollars ($2) of each seventy-five-dollar ($75) fee collected under subdivision (b) to the law library fund in the county in which the court is located.

(2) From the fees collected under subdivision (d), the Administrative Office of the Courts shall distribute two dollars ($2) to the law library fund in the county in which the court is located, and three dollars ($3) to the small claims advisory services described in Section 116.940, or, if the small claims advisory services are administered by the court, to the court.

(3) Records of these moneys shall be available from the Administrative Office of the Courts for inspection by the public on request.

(4) Nothing in this section precludes the court or county from contracting with a third party to provide small claims advisory services as described in Section 116.940.

(h) The remainder of the fees collected under subdivisions (b), (c) and (d) shall be transmitted monthly to the Controller for deposit in the Trial Court Trust Fund.

(i) All money distributed under this section to be used for small claims advisory services shall be used only for providing those services as described in Section 116.940. Nothing in this section shall preclude the county or the court from procuring other funding to comply with the requirements of Section 116.940. **Leg.H.** Added Stats 2005 ch 75 §19 (AB 145), effective July 19, 2005, operative January 1, 2006. Amended Stats 2005 ch 706 §3 (AB 1742); Stats 2007 ch 738 §3 (AB 1248), effective January 1, 2008.

Former Sections: Former CCP §116.230, was added Stats 1990 ch 1305 §3 and repealed Stats 2005 ch 75 §16, effective July 19, 2005, operative January 1, 2006.

Prior Law: Former CCP §116.230, was added Stats 1990 ch 1305 §3, amended Stats 1991 ch 915 §4, Stats 1992 ch 696 §4, effective September 14, 1992, Stats 1997 ch 850 §4, Stats 2003 ch 159 §1, effective August 2, 2003, operative August 17, 2003, inoperative July 1, 2006, and repealed Stats 2005 ch 75 §16, effective July 19, 2005, operative January 1, 2006.

§116.231. Filing of more than two small claims actions

(a) Except as provided in subdivision (d), no person may file more than two small claims actions in which the amount demanded exceeds two thousand five hundred dollars ($2,500), anywhere in the state in any calendar year.

(b) Except as provided in subdivision (d), if the amount demanded in any small claims action exceeds two thousand five hundred dollars ($2,500), the party making the demand shall file a declaration under penalty of perjury attesting to the fact that not more than two small claims actions in which the amount of the demand exceeded two thousand five hundred dollars ($2,500) have been filed by that party in this state within the calendar year.

(c) The Legislature finds and declares that the pilot project conducted under the authority of Chapter 1196 of the Statutes of 1991 demonstrated the efficacy of the removal of the limitation on the number of actions public entities may file in the small claims courts on claims exceeding two thousand five hundred dollars ($2,500).

(d) The limitation on the number of filings exceeding two thousand five hundred dollars ($2,500) does not apply to filings where the claim does not exceed five thousand dollars ($5,000) that are filed by a city, county, city and county, school district, county office of education, community college district, local district, or any other local public entity. If any small claims action is filed by a city, county, city and county, school district, county office of education, community college district, local district, or any other local public entity pursuant to this section, and the defendant informs the court either in advance of the hearing by written notice or at the time of the hearing, that he or she is represented in the action by legal counsel, the action shall be transferred out of the small claims division. A city, county, city and county, school district, county office of education, community college district, local district, or any other local public entity may not file a claim within the small claims division if the amount of the demand exceeds five thousand dollars ($5,000). **Leg.H.** Added Stats 1990 ch 1683 §4 (AB 3916). Amended Stats 1991 ch 915 §5 (SB 771), ch 1196 §4 (AB 1755); Stats 1994 ch 971 §1 (AB 2937); Stats 1998 ch 931 §39 (SB 2139), effective September 28, 1998.

§116.232. Fee for each defendant to whom copy of claim is mailed

A fee of fifteen dollars ($15) shall be charged and collected from the plaintiff for each defendant to whom the court clerk mails a copy of the claim under Section 116.340. This fee shall be distributed to the court in which it was collected. **Leg.H.** Added Stats 2005 ch 75 §20 (AB 145), effective July 19, 2005, operative January 1, 2006. Amended Stats 2013 ch 31 §1 (SB 75), effective June 27, 2013.

Former Sections: Former CCP §116.232, relating to pilot projects in the counties of San Francisco and Stanislaus, was added Stats 1991 ch 1196 §5 and repealed operative January 1, 1995, by its own provisions.

Prior Law: Former CCP §116.232, relating to pilot projects in the counties of San Francisco and Stanislaus, was added Stats 1991 ch 1196 §5, amended Stats 1993 ch 589 §24, and repealed January 1, 1995, by its own terms.

§116.240. Case heard by temporary judge

(a) With the consent of the parties who appear at the hearing, the court may order a case to be heard by a temporary judge who is a member of the State Bar, and who has been sworn and empowered to act until final determination of the case.

(b) Prior to serving as a temporary judge in small claims court, on and after July 1, 2006, and at least every three years thereafter, each temporary judge shall take the course of study offered by the courts on ethics and substantive law under rules adopted by the Judicial Council. The course shall include, but not be limited to, state and federal consumer laws, landlord-tenant law along with any applicable county specific rent deposit law, the state and federal Fair Debt Collection Practices Acts, the federal Truth in Lending Act, the federal Fair Credit Billing Act, the federal Electronic Fund Transfer Act, tort law, and contract law, including defenses to contracts and defenses to debts. On substantive law, the courts may receive assistance from the Department of Consumer Affairs, to the extent that the department is fiscally able to provide that assistance. **Leg.H.** Added Stats 1990 ch 1305 §3 (SB 2627). Amended Stats 2005 ch 600 §4 (SB 422), ch 618 §4 (AB 1459).

§116.250. Sessions; Night or Saturday sessions; Proceeding by mediator or referee

(a) Sessions of the small claims court may be scheduled at any time and on any day, including Saturdays, but excluding other judicial holidays.

(b) Each small claims division of a superior court with seven or more judicial officers shall conduct at least one night session or Saturday session each month for the purpose of hearing small claims cases other than small claims appeals. The term "session" includes, but is not limited to, a proceeding conducted by a member of the State Bar acting as a mediator or referee. **Leg.H.** Added Stats 1990 ch 1305 §3 (SB 2627). Amended Stats 1998 ch 931 §40 (SB 2139), effective September 28, 1998; Stats 2002 ch 784 §31 (SB 1316); Stats 2003 ch 149 §4 (SB 79).

§116.260. Individual assistance for small claims litigants

In each county, individual assistance shall be made available to advise small claims litigants and potential litigants without charge as provided in Section 116.940 and by rules adopted by the Judicial Council. **Leg.H.** Added Stats 1990 ch 1305 §3 (SB 2627).

§116.270. Law clerks

Any small claims division may use law clerks to assist the judge with legal research of small claims cases. **Leg.H.** Added Stats 1990 ch 1305 §3 (SB 2627).

ARTICLE 3
Actions

Pleadings necessary to initiate action; Pretrial discovery not permitted. §116.310.
Commencement of action. §116.320.
Procedure once claim is filed. §116.330.
Service on defendant. §116.340.
Counterclaim. §116.360.
Venue. §116.370.
[Section renumbered 1992]. §116.380.
Transfer of action when defendant's claim exceeds jurisdictional limit. §116.390.

§116.310. Pleadings necessary to initiate action; Pretrial discovery not permitted

(a) No formal pleading, other than the claim described in Section 116.320 or 116.360, is necessary to initiate a small claims action.

(b) The pretrial discovery procedures described in Section 2019.010 are not permitted in small claims actions. **Leg.H.** Added Stats 1990 ch 1305 §3 (SB 2627). Amended Stats 1991 ch 915 §6 (SB 771); Stats 2003 ch 149 §5 (SB 79); Stats 2004 ch 182 §7 (AB 3081), operative July 1, 2005.

§116.320. Commencement of action

(a) A plaintiff may commence an action in the small claims court by filing a claim under oath with the clerk of the small claims court in person, by mail, by facsimile transmission if authorized pursuant to Section 1010.5, or by electronic means as authorized by Section 1010.6.

(b) The claim form shall be a simple nontechnical form approved or adopted by the Judicial Council. The claim form shall set forth a place for (1) the name and address of the defendant, if known; (2) the amount and the basis of the claim; (3) that the plaintiff, where possible, has demanded payment and, in applicable cases, possession of the property; (4) that the defendant has failed or refused to pay, and, where applicable, has refused to surrender the property; and (5) that the plaintiff understands that the judgment on his or her claim will be conclusive and without a right of appeal.

(c) The form or accompanying instructions shall include information that the plaintiff (1) may not be represented by an attorney, (2) has no right of appeal, and (3) may ask the court to waive fees for filing and serving the claim on the ground that the plaintiff is unable to pay them, using the forms approved by the Judicial Council for that purpose. **Leg.H.** Added Stats 1990 ch 1305 §3 (SB 2627). Amended Stats 1991 ch 915 §7 (SB 771); Stats 2007 ch 738 §4 (AB 1248), effective January 1, 2008.

§116.330. Procedure once claim is filed

(a) When a claim is filed, the clerk shall schedule the case for hearing and shall issue an order directing the parties to appear at the time set for the hearing with witnesses and documents to prove their claim or defense. The case shall be scheduled for hearing no earlier than 20 days but not more than 70 days from the date of the order.

(b) In lieu of the method of setting the case for hearing described in subdivision (a), at the time a claim is filed the clerk may do all of the following:

(1) Cause a copy of the claim to be mailed to the defendant by any form of mail providing for a return receipt.

(2) On receipt of proof that the claim was served as provided in paragraph (1), issue an order scheduling the case for hearing in accordance with subdivision (a) and directing the parties to appear at the time set for the hearing with witnesses and documents to prove their claim or defense.

(3) Cause a copy of the order setting the case for hearing and directing the parties to appear, to be served upon the parties by any form of mail providing for a return receipt. **Leg.H.** Added Stats 1990 ch 1305 §3 (SB 2627). Amended Stats 2005 ch 706 §4 (AB 1742), effective January 1, 2006.

§116.340. Service on defendant

(a) Service of the claim and order on the defendant may be made by any one of the following methods:

(1) The clerk may cause a copy of the claim and order to be mailed to the defendant by any form of mail providing for a return receipt.

(2) The plaintiff may cause a copy of the claim and order to be delivered to the defendant in person.

(3) The plaintiff may cause service of a copy of the claim and order to be made by substituted service as provided in subdivision (a) or (b) of Section 415.20 without the need to attempt personal service on the defendant. For these purposes, substituted service as provided in subdivision (b) of Section 415.20 may be made at the office of the sheriff or marshal who shall deliver a copy of the claim and order to any person authorized by the defendant to receive service, as provided in Section 416.90, who is at least 18 years of age, and thereafter mailing a copy of the claim and order to the defendant's usual mailing address.

(4) The clerk may cause a copy of the claim to be mailed, the order to be issued, and a copy of the order to be mailed as provided in subdivision (b) of Section 116.330.

(b) Service of the claim and order on the defendant shall be completed at least 15 days before the hearing date if the defendant resides within the county in which the action is filed, or at least 20 days before the hearing date if the defendant resides outside the county in which the action is filed.

(c) Proof of service of the claim and order shall be filed with the small claims court at least five days before the hearing.

(d) Service by the methods described in subdivision (a) shall be deemed complete on the date that the defendant signs the mail return receipt, on the date of the personal service, as provided in Section 415.20, or as established by other competent evidence, whichever applies to the method of service used.

(e) Service shall be made within this state, except as provided in subdivisions (f) and (g).

(f) The owner of record of real property in California who resides in another state and who has no lawfully designated agent in California for service of process may be served by any of the methods described in this section if the claim relates to that property.

(g) A nonresident owner or operator of a motor vehicle involved in an accident within this state may be served pursuant to the provisions on constructive service in Sections 17450 to 17461, inclusive, of the Vehicle Code without regard to whether the defendant was a nonresident at the time of the accident or when the claim was filed. Service shall be made by serving both the Director of the California Department of Motor Vehicles and the defendant, and may be made by any of the methods authorized by this chapter or by registered mail as authorized by Section 17454 or 17455 of the Vehicle Code.

(h) If an action is filed against a principal and his or her guaranty or surety pursuant to a guarantor or suretyship agreement, a reasonable attempt shall be made to complete service on the principal. If service is not completed on the principal, the action shall be transferred to the court of appropriate jurisdiction. **Leg.H.** Added Stats 1990 ch 1305 §3 (SB 2627). Amended Stats 1991 ch 915 §8 (SB 771); Stats 1995 ch 576 §1 (AB 1225); Stats 1996 ch 1159 §1 (AB 3471); Stats 2002 ch 806 §3 (AB 3027); Stats 2005 ch 706 §5 (AB 1742), effective January 1, 2006.

§116.350. [Section repealed 1992]
Leg.H. Added Stats 1990 ch 1305 §3 (SB 2627). Repealed Stats 1991 ch 915 §9 (SB 771). The repealed section related to postponement ordered by court.

§116.360. Counterclaim
(a) The defendant may file a claim against the plaintiff in the same action in an amount not to exceed the jurisdictional limits stated in Sections 116.220, 116.221, and 116.231. The claim need not relate to the same subject or event as the plaintiff's claim.

(b) The defendant's claim shall be filed and served in the manner provided for filing and serving a claim of the plaintiff under Sections 116.330 and 116.340.

(c) The defendant shall cause a copy of the claim and order to be served on the plaintiff at least five days before the hearing date, unless the defendant was served 10 days or less before the hearing date, in which event the defendant shall cause a copy of the defendant's claim and order to be served on the plaintiff at least one day before the hearing date. **Leg.H.** Added Stats 1990 ch 1305 §3 (SB 2627) as §116.380. Amended and renumbered by Stats 1991 ch 915 §11; Amended Stats 1996 ch 1159 §2 (AB 3471); Stats 2006 ch 167 §4 (AB 2618), effective January 1, 2007.

Prior Law: Former CCP §116.360, relating to postponement ordered by court, was added Stats 1990 ch 1305 §3 (SB 2627) and repealed Stats 1991 ch 915 §10.

§116.370. Venue
(a) Venue and court location requirements in small claims actions shall be the same as in other civil actions. The court may prescribe by local rule the proper court locations for small claims actions.

(b) A defendant may challenge venue or court location by writing to the court and mailing a copy of the challenge to each of the other parties to the action, without personally appearing at the hearing.

(c) In all cases, including those in which the defendant does not either challenge venue or court location or appear at the hearing, the court shall inquire into the facts sufficiently to determine whether venue and court location are proper, and shall make its determination accordingly.

(1) If the court determines that the action was not commenced in the proper venue, the court, on its own motion, shall dismiss the action without prejudice, unless all defendants are present and agree that the action may be heard. If the court determines that the action was not commenced in the proper court location, the court may transfer the action to a proper location pursuant to local rule.

(2) If the court determines that the action was commenced in the proper venue and court location, the court may hear the case if all parties are present. If the defendant challenged venue or court location and all parties are not present, the court shall postpone the hearing for at least 15 days and shall notify all parties by mail of the court's decision and the new hearing date, time, and place. **Leg.H.** Added Stats 1990 ch 1305 §3 (SB 2627). Amended Stats 1991 ch 133 §2 (AB 1827), ch 915 §10.5 (SB 771); Stats 1992 ch 201 §1 (AB 3653); Stats 1996 ch 1159 §3 (AB 3471); Stats 2002 ch 806 §4 (AB 3027).

§116.380. [Section renumbered 1992]
Leg.H. Added Stats 1990 ch 1305 §3 (SB 2627). Renumbered CCP §116.360 by Stats 1991 ch 915 §11 (SB 771).

§116.390. Transfer of action when defendant's claim exceeds jurisdictional limit
(a) If a defendant has a claim against a plaintiff that exceeds the jurisdictional limits stated in Sections 116.220, 116.221, and 116.231, and the claim relates to the contract, transaction, matter, or event which is the subject of the plaintiff's claim, the defendant may commence an action against the plaintiff in a court of competent jurisdiction and request the small claims court to transfer the small claims action to that court.

(b) The defendant may make the request by filing with the small claims court in which the plaintiff commenced the action, at or before the time set for the hearing of that action, a declaration stating the facts concerning the defendant's action against the plaintiff with a true copy of the complaint so filed by the defendant against the plaintiff. The defendant shall cause a copy of the declaration and complaint to be personally delivered to the plaintiff at or before the time set for the hearing of the small claims action.

(c) In ruling on a motion to transfer, the small claims court may do any of the following: (1) render judgment on the small claims case prior to the transfer; (2) not render judgment and transfer the small claims case; (3) refuse to transfer the small claims case on the grounds that the ends of justice would not be served. If the small claims action is transferred prior to judgment, both actions shall be tried together in the transferee court.

(d) When the small claims court orders the action transferred, it shall transmit all files and papers to the transferee court.

(e) The plaintiff in the small claims action shall not be required to pay to the clerk of the transferee court any transmittal, appearance, or filing fee unless the plaintiff appears in the transferee court, in which event the plaintiff shall be required to pay the filing fee and any other fee required of a defendant in the transferee court. However, if the transferee court rules against the plaintiff in the action filed in that court, the court may award to the defendant in that action the costs incurred as a consequence of the transfer, including attorney's fees and filing fees. **Leg.H.** Added Stats 1990 ch 1305 §3 (SB 2627). Amended Stats 1991 ch 915 §11.5 (SB 771); Stats 1996 ch 1159 §4 (AB 3471); Stats 2005 ch 75 §21 (AB 145), effective July 19, 2005, operative January 1, 2006; Stats 2006 ch 167 §5 (AB 2618), effective January 1, 2007.

ARTICLE 4
Parties

Who may be party; Appearance by guardian ad litem. §116.410.
Filing of claim by assignee prohibited. §116.420.
Fictitious business names. §116.430.

§116.410. Who may be party; Appearance by guardian ad litem
(a) Any person who is at least 18 years of age, or legally emancipated, and mentally competent may be a party to a small claims action.

(b) A minor or incompetent person may appear by a guardian ad litem appointed by a judge of the court in which the action is filed. **Leg.H.** Added Stats 1990 ch 1305 §3 (SB 2627). Amended Stats 2004 ch 171 §1 (AB 3078).

§116.420. Filing of claim by assignee prohibited
(a) No claim shall be filed or maintained in small claims court by the assignee of the claim.

(b) This section does not prevent the filing or defense of an action in the small claims court by (1) a trustee in bankruptcy in the exercise of the trustee's duties as trustee, or (2) by the holder of a security agreement, retail installment contract, or lien contract subject to the Unruh Act (Chapter 1 (commencing with Section 1801) of Title 2 of Part 4 of Division 3 of the Civil Code) or the Automobile Sales Finance Act (Chapter 2b (commencing with Section 2981) of Title 14 of Part 4 of Division 3 of the Civil Code), purchased by the holder for the holder's portfolio of investments, provided that the holder is not an assignee for the purpose of collection.

(c) This section does not prevent the filing in small claims court by a local government which is self-insured for purposes of workers' compensation and is seeking subrogation pursuant to Section 3852 of the Labor Code. **Leg.H.** Added Stats 1990 ch 1305 §3 (SB 2627). Amended Stats 1994 ch 231 §1 (SB 1771).

§116.430. Fictitious business names
(a) If the plaintiff operates or does business under a fictitious business name and the claim relates to that business, the claim shall be accompanied by the filing of a declaration stating that the plaintiff has complied with the fictitious business name laws by executing, filing, and publishing a fictitious business name statement as required.

(b) A small claims action filed by a person who has not complied with the applicable fictitious business name laws by executing, filing, and publishing a fictitious business name statement as required shall be dismissed without prejudice.

(c) For purposes of this section, "fictitious business name" means the term as defined in Section 17900 of the Business and Professions Code, and "fictitious business name statement" means the statement described in Section 17913 of the Business and Professions Code. **Leg.H.** Added Stats 1990 ch 1305 §3 (SB 2627). Amended Stats 1991 ch 915 §12 (SB 771).

ARTICLE 5
Hearing

Hearing and disposition of action. §116.510.

Presentation of evidence at hearing. §116.520.
Attorney participation. §116.530.
Assistance to party by insurer or other expert. §116.531.
Participation by individuals other than plaintiff and defendant. §116.540.
Participation in small claims actions by Department of Corrections and Department of Youth Authority. §116.541.
Amendment of claim to correct name of defendant. §116.560.
Postponement of hearing. §116.570.

§116.510. Hearing and disposition of action

The hearing and disposition of the small claims action shall be informal, the object being to dispense justice promptly, fairly, and inexpensively. **Leg.H.** Added Stats 1990 ch 1305 §3 (SB 2627). Amended Stats 1991 ch 915 §13 (SB 771).

§116.520. Presentation of evidence at hearing

(a) The parties have the right to offer evidence by witnesses at the hearing or, with the permission of the court, at another time.

(b) If the defendant fails to appear, the court shall still require the plaintiff to present evidence to prove his or her claim.

(c) The court may consult witnesses informally and otherwise investigate the controversy with or without notice to the parties. **Leg.H.** Added Stats 1990 ch 1305 §3 (SB 2627).

§116.530. Attorney participation

(a) Except as permitted by this section, no attorney may take part in the conduct or defense of a small claims action.

(b) Subdivision (a) does not apply if the attorney is appearing to maintain or defend an action in any of the following capacities:

(1) By or against himself or herself.

(2) By or against a partnership in which he or she is a general partner and in which all the partners are attorneys.

(3) By or against a professional corporation of which he or she is an officer or director and of which all other officers and directors are attorneys.

(c) Nothing in this section shall prevent an attorney from doing any of the following:

(1) Providing advice to a party to a small claims action, either before or after the commencement of the action.

(2) Testifying to facts of which he or she has personal knowledge and about which he or she is competent to testify.

(3) Representing a party in an appeal to the superior court.

(4) Representing a party in connection with the enforcement of a judgment. **Leg.H.** Added Stats 1990 ch 1305 §3 (SB 2627). Amended Stats 1991 ch 915 §14 (SB 771); Stats 2003 ch 449 §5 (AB 1712).

§116.531. Assistance to party by insurer or other expert

Nothing in this article shall prevent a representative of an insurer or other expert in the matter before the small claims court from rendering assistance to a party in the litigation except during the conduct of the hearing, either before or after the commencement of the action, unless otherwise prohibited by law; nor shall anything in this article prevent those individuals from testifying to facts of which they have personal knowledge and about which they are competent to testify. **Leg.H.** Added Stats 1990 ch 1683 §5 (AB 3916).

§116.540. Participation by individuals other than plaintiff and defendant

(a) Except as permitted by this section, no individual other than the plaintiff and the defendant may take part in the conduct or defense of a small claims action.

(b) Except as additionally provided in subdivision (i), a corporation may appear and participate in a small claims action only through a regular employee, or a duly appointed or elected officer or director, who is employed, appointed, or elected for purposes other than solely representing the corporation in small claims court.

(c) A party who is not a corporation or a natural person may appear and participate in a small claims action only through a regular employee, or a duly appointed or elected officer or director, or in the case of a partnership, a partner, engaged for purposes other than solely representing the party in small claims court.

(d) If a party is an individual doing business as a sole proprietorship, the party may appear and participate in a small claims action by a representative and without personally appearing if both of the following conditions are met:

(1) The claim can be proved or disputed by evidence of an account that constitutes a business record as defined in Section 1271 of the Evidence Code, and there is no other issue of fact in the case.

(2) The representative is a regular employee of the party for purposes other than solely representing the party in small claims actions and is qualified to testify to the identity and mode of preparation of the business record.

(e) A plaintiff who is a service member is not required to personally appear, and may submit declarations to serve as evidence supporting their claim, appear via video appearance, or allow another individual to appear and participate on their behalf, if the service member is assigned to a location more than 100 miles from the court where the action is proceeding, or is otherwise unable to personally appear due to the performance of military duty, the representative is serving without compensation, other than compensation from the United States or the State of California, and, except as to representatives who are employed by the United States or the State of California, the representative has appeared in small claims actions on behalf of others no more than four times during the calendar year. The defendant may file a claim in the same action in an amount not to exceed the jurisdictional limits stated in Sections 116.220, 116.221, and 116.231.

(f) A party incarcerated in a county jail, a Department of Corrections and Rehabilitation facility, or a Division of Juvenile Facilities facility is not required to personally appear, and may submit declarations to serve as evidence supporting their claim, or may authorize another individual to appear and participate on their behalf if that individual is serving without compensation and has appeared in small claims actions on behalf of others no more than four times during the calendar year.

(g) A defendant who is a nonresident owner of real property may defend against a claim relating to that property without personally appearing by (1) submitting written declarations to serve as evidence supporting their defense, (2) allowing another individual to appear and participate on their behalf if that individual is serving without compensation and has appeared in small claims actions on behalf of others no more than four times during the calendar year, or (3) taking the action described in both (1) and (2).

(h) A party who is an owner of rental real property may appear and participate in a small claims action through a property agent under contract with the owner to manage the rental of that property, if (1) the owner has retained the property agent principally to manage the rental of that property and not principally to represent the owner in small claims court, and (2) the claim relates to the rental property.

(i) A party that is an association created to manage a common interest development, as defined in Section 4100 or in Sections 6528 and 6534 of the Civil Code, may appear and participate in a small claims action through an agent, a management company representative, or bookkeeper who appears on behalf of that association.

(j) At the hearing of a small claims action, the court shall require any individual who is appearing as a representative of a party under subdivisions (b) to (i), inclusive, to file a declaration stating (1) that the individual is authorized to appear for the party, and (2) the basis for that authorization. If the representative is appearing under subdivision (b), (c), (d), (h), or (i), the declaration also shall state that the individual is not employed solely to represent the party in small claims court. If the representative is appearing under subdivision (e), (f), or (g), the declaration also shall state that the representative is serving without compensation, and has appeared in small claims actions on behalf of others no more than four times during the calendar year.

(k) A spouse who sues or who is sued with their spouse may appear and participate on behalf of their spouse if (1) the claim is a joint claim, (2) the represented spouse has given their consent, and (3) the court determines that the interests of justice would be served.

(*l*) If the court determines that a party cannot properly present their claim or defense and needs assistance, the court may in its discretion allow another individual to assist that party.

(m) Nothing in this section shall operate or be construed to authorize an attorney to participate in a small claims action except as expressly provided in Section 116.530. **Leg.H.** Added Stats 1990 ch 1305 §3 (SB 2627). Amended Stats 1991 ch 915 §15 (SB 771); Stats 1992 ch 201 §2 (AB 3653); Stats 1996 ch 693 §1 (AB 2567); Stats 2005 ch 452 §7 (SB 137), effective January 1, 2006; Stats 2006 ch 167 §6 (AB 2618), effective January 1, 2007; Stats 2012 ch 181 §43 (AB 806), effective January 1,

2013, operative January 1, 2014; Stats 2013 ch 605 §23 (SB 752), effective January 1, 2014; Stats 2016 ch 50 §14 (SB 1005), effective January 1, 2017; Stats 2022 ch 620 §3 (SB 1311), effective January 1, 2023.

2016 Note: For legislative intent, see the 2016 Note following CCP §17.

§116.541. Participation in small claims actions by Department of Corrections and Department of Youth Authority

(a) Notwithstanding Section 116.540 or any other provision of law, the Department of Corrections or the Department of the Youth Authority may appear and participate in a small claims action through a regular employee, who is employed or appointed for purposes other than solely representing that department in small claims court.

(b) Where the Department of Corrections or the Department of the Youth Authority is named as a defendant in small claims court, the representative of the department is not required to personally appear to challenge the plaintiff's compliance with the pleading requirements and may submit pleadings or declarations to assert that challenge.

(c) At the hearing of a small claims action, the court shall require any individual who is appearing as a representative of the Department of Corrections or the Department of the Youth Authority under subdivision (a) to file a declaration stating (1) that the individual is authorized to appear for the party, (2) the basis for that authorization, and (3) that the individual is not employed solely to represent the party in small claims court.

(d) Nothing in this section shall operate or be construed to authorize an attorney to participate in a small claims action except as expressly provided in Section 116.530.

(e) For purposes of this section, all references to the Department of Corrections or the Department of the Youth Authority include an employee thereof, against whom a claim has been filed under this chapter arising out of his or her duties as an employee of that department. **Leg.H.** Added Stats 1995 ch 366 §2 (AB 725).

§116.550. List of interpreters; Postponement when interpreter not available [Repealed]

Leg.H. Added Stats 1990 ch 1305 §3 (SB 2627). Amended Stats 1991 ch 915 §16 (SB 771); Stats 1993 ch 1191 §2 (SB 236). Repealed Stats 2018 ch 852 §1 (SB 1155), effective January 1, 2019.

§116.560. Amendment of claim to correct name of defendant

(a) Whenever a claim that is filed against a person operating or doing business under a fictitious business name relates to the defendant's business, the court shall inquire at the time of the hearing into the defendant's correct legal name and the name or names under which the defendant does business. If the correct legal name of the defendant, or the name actually used by the defendant, is other than the name stated on the claim, the court shall amend the claim to state the correct legal name of the defendant, and the name or names actually used by the defendant.

(b) The plaintiff may request the court at any time, whether before or after judgment, to amend the plaintiff's claim or judgment to include both the correct legal name and the name or names actually used by the defendant. Upon a showing of good cause, the court shall amend the claim or judgment to state the correct legal name of the defendant, and the name or names actually used by the defendant.

(c) For purposes of this section, "fictitious business name" means the term as defined in Section 17900 of the Business and Professions Code. **Leg.H.** Added Stats 1991 ch 915 §17 (SB 771).

§116.570. Postponement of hearing

(a) Any party may submit a written request to postpone a hearing date for good cause.

(1) The written request may be made either by letter or on a form adopted or approved by the Judicial Council.

(2) The request shall be filed at least 10 days before the hearing date, unless the court determines that the requesting party has good cause to file the request at a later date.

(3) On the date of making the written request, the requesting party shall mail or personally deliver a copy to each of the other parties to the action.

(4)(A) If the court finds that the interests of justice would be served by postponing the hearing, the court shall postpone the hearing, and shall notify all parties by mail of the new hearing date, time, and place.

(B) On one occasion, upon the written request of a defendant guarantor, the court shall postpone the hearing for at least 30 days, and the court shall take this action without a hearing. This subparagraph does not limit the discretion of the court to grant additional postponements under subparagraph (A).

(5) The court shall provide a prompt response by mail to any person making a written request for postponement of a hearing date under this subdivision.

(b) If service of the claim and order upon the defendant is not completed within the number of days before the hearing date required by subdivision (b) of Section 116.340, and the defendant has not personally appeared and has not requested a postponement, the court shall postpone the hearing for at least 15 days. If a postponement is ordered under this subdivision, the clerk shall promptly notify all parties by mail of the new hearing date, time, and place.

(c) This section does not limit the inherent power of the court to order postponements of hearings in appropriate circumstances.

(d) A fee of ten dollars ($10) shall be charged and collected for the filing of a request for postponement and rescheduling of a hearing date after timely service pursuant to subdivision (b) of Section 116.340 has been made upon the defendant. **Leg.H.** Added Stats 1991 ch 915 §18 (SB 771). Amended Stats 1992 ch 696 §5 (AB 1344), effective September 14, 1992; Stats 1994 ch 587 §2 (AB 3600); Stats 1996 ch 1159 §5 (AB 3471); Stats 1998 ch 240 §3 (AB 771); Stats 2002 ch 806 §5 (AB 3027).

ARTICLE 6
Judgment

Judgments. §116.610.
Payment by judgment debtor; Terms and conditions of payment. §116.620.
Amendment of party name on judgment. §116.630.

§116.610. Judgments

(a) The small claims court shall give judgment for damages, or equitable relief, or both damages and equitable relief, within the jurisdictional limits stated in Sections 116.220, 116.221, and 116.231, and may make any orders as to time of payment or otherwise as the court deems just and equitable for the resolution of the dispute.

(b) The court may, at its discretion or on request of any party, continue the matter to a later date in order to permit and encourage the parties to attempt resolution by informal or alternative means.

(c) The judgment shall include a determination whether the judgment resulted from a motor vehicle accident on a California highway caused by the defendant's operation of a motor vehicle, or by the operation by some other individual, of a motor vehicle registered in the defendant's name.

(d) If the defendant has filed a claim against the plaintiff, or if the judgment is against two or more defendants, the judgment, and the statement of decision if one is rendered, shall specify the basis for and the character and amount of the liability of each of the parties, including, in the case of multiple judgment debtors, whether the liability of each is joint or several.

(e) If specific property is referred to in the judgment, whether it be personal or real, tangible or intangible, the property shall be identified with sufficient detail to permit efficient implementation or enforcement of the judgment.

(f) In an action against several defendants, the court may, in its discretion, render judgment against one or more of them, leaving the action to proceed against the others, whenever a several judgment is proper.

(g)(1) The prevailing party is entitled to the costs of the action, including the costs of serving the order for the appearance of the defendant.

(2) Notwithstanding paragraph (1) of this subdivision and subdivision (b) of Section 1032, the amount of the small claims court fee paid by a party pursuant to subdivision (c) of Section 116.230 that exceeds the amount that would have been paid if the party had paid the fee pursuant to subdivision (b) of Section 116.230 shall not be recoverable as costs.

(h) When the court renders judgment, the clerk shall promptly deliver or mail notice of entry of the judgment to the parties, and shall execute a certificate of personal delivery or mailing and place it in the file.

(i) The notice of entry of judgment shall be on a form approved or adopted by the Judicial Council. **Leg.H.** Added Stats 1990 ch 1305 §3 (SB 2627). Amended Stats 1991 ch 133 §3 (AB 1827), ch 915 §19 (SB 771); Stats 1992 ch 8 §2 (AB 1551), effective February 19, 1992, ch 142 §3 (SB

1376); Stats 1996 ch 1159 §6 (AB 3471); Stats 2005 ch 600 §5 (SB 422); ch 618 §5 (AB 1459) effective January 1, 2006; Stats 2006 ch 167 §7 (AB 2618), effective January 1, 2007.

§116.620. Payment by judgment debtor; Terms and conditions of payment

(a) The judgment debtor shall pay the amount of the judgment either immediately or at the time and upon the terms and conditions, including payment by installments, which the court may order.

(b) The court may at any time, for good cause, upon motion by a party and notice by the clerk to all affected parties at their last known address, amend the terms and conditions for payment of the judgment to provide for payment by installment. The determination shall be made without regard to the nature of the underlying debt and without regard to whether the moving party appeared before entry of the judgment.

(c) In determining the terms and conditions of payment, the court may consider any factors which would be relevant to a claim of exemption under Chapter 4 (commencing with Section 703.010) of Division 2 of Title 9 of Part 2. **Leg.H.** Added Stats 1990 ch 1305 §3 (SB 2627).

§116.630. Amendment of party name on judgment

The court may, at any time after judgment, for good cause, upon motion by a party and notice by the clerk to all affected parties at their last known address, amend the name of any party to include both the correct legal name and the actually used name or names of that party. **Leg.H.** Added Stats 1990 ch 1305 §3 (SB 2627).

ARTICLE 7
Motion to Vacate, Appeal, and Related Matters

Right to appeal; Motion to vacate. §116.710.
Motion to vacate; Procedure. §116.720.
Correction of errors. §116.725.
Defendant's right to file motion to vacate; Procedure. §116.730.
Defendant's motion to vacate; Grounds. §116.740.
Fee for filing of motion to vacate. §116.745.
Notice of appeal. §116.750.
Appeal filing fees. §116.760.
Appeal procedure. §116.770.
Judgment of superior court. §116.780.
Award of attorney's fees, lost earnings, and expenses. §116.790.
Dismissal of appeal. §116.795.
Writs of review, mandate, or prohibition relating to small claims division. §116.798.

§116.710. Right to appeal; Motion to vacate

(a) The plaintiff in a small claims action shall have no right to appeal the judgment on the plaintiffs claim, but a plaintiff who did not appear at the hearing may file a motion to vacate the judgment in accordance with Section 116.720.

(b) The defendant with respect to the plaintiffs claim, and a plaintiff with respect to a claim of the defendant, may appeal the judgment to the superior court in the county in which the action was heard.

(c) With respect to the plaintiff's claim, the insurer of the defendant may appeal the judgment to the superior court in the county in which the matter was heard if the judgment exceeds two thousand five hundred dollars ($2,500) and the insurer stipulates that its policy with the defendant covers the matter to which the judgment applies.

(d) A defendant who did not appear at the hearing has no right to appeal the judgment, but may file a motion to vacate the judgment in accordance with Section 116.730 or 116.740 and also may appeal the denial of that motion. **Leg.H.** Added Stats 1990 ch 1305 §3 (SB 2627). Amended Stats 1990 ch 1683 §6 (AB 3916).

§116.720. Motion to vacate; Procedure

(a) A plaintiff who did not appear at the hearing in the small claims court may file a motion to vacate the judgment with the clerk of the small claims court. The motion shall be filed within 30 days after the clerk has mailed notice of entry of the judgment to the parties.

(b) The clerk shall schedule the hearing on the motion to vacate for a date no earlier than 10 days after the clerk has mailed written notice of the date, time, and place of the hearing to the parties.

(c) Upon a showing of good cause, the small claims court may grant the motion. If the defendant is not present, the court shall hear the motion in the defendant's absence.

(d) If the motion is granted, and if all parties are present and agree, the court may hear the case without rescheduling it. If the defendant is not present, the judge or clerk shall reschedule the case and give notice in accordance with Section 116.330. **Leg.H.** Added Stats 1990 ch 1305 §3 (SB 2627). Amended Stats 1991 ch 915 §20 (SB 771).

§116.725. Correction of errors

(a) A motion to correct a clerical error in a judgment or to set aside and vacate a judgment on the ground of an incorrect or erroneous legal basis for the decision may be made as follows:

(1) By the court on its own motion at any time.

(2) By a party within 30 days after the clerk mails notice of entry of judgment to the parties.

(b) Each party may file only one motion to correct a clerical error or to set aside and vacate the judgment on the ground of an incorrect or erroneous legal basis for the decision. **Leg.H.** Added Stats 2005 ch 706 §7 (AB 1742).

Former Sections: Former CCP §116.725, similar to the present section, added Stats 1992 ch 201 §3 and repealed Stats 2005 ch 706 §6.

Prior Law: Former CCP §116.725, similar to the present section, added Stats 1992 ch 201 §3 and was repealed Stats 2005 ch 706 §6.

§116.730. Defendant's right to file motion to vacate; Procedure

(a) A defendant who did not appear at the hearing in the small claims court may file a motion to vacate the judgment with the clerk of the small claims court. The motion shall be filed within 30 days after the clerk has mailed notice of entry of the judgment to the parties.

(b) The defendant shall appear at any hearing on the motion, or submit written justification for not appearing together with a declaration in support of the motion.

(c) Upon a showing of good cause, the court may grant the motion to vacate the judgment. If the plaintiff is not present, the court shall hear the motion in the plaintiff's absence.

(d) If the motion is granted, and if all parties are present and agree, the court may hear the case without rescheduling it. If the plaintiff is not present, the judge or clerk shall reschedule the case and give notice in accordance with Section 116.330.

(e) If the motion is denied, the defendant may appeal to the superior court only on the denial of the motion to vacate the judgment. The defendant shall file the notice of appeal with the clerk of the small claims court within 10 days after the small claims court has mailed or delivered notice of the court's denial of the motion to vacate the judgment.

(f) If the superior court determines that the defendant's motion to vacate the judgment should have been granted, the superior court may hear the claims of all parties without rescheduling the matter, provided that all parties are present and the defendant has previously complied with this article, or may order the case transferred to the small claims court for a hearing. **Leg.H.** Added Stats 1990 ch 1305 §3 (SB 2627). Amended Stats 1991 ch 915 §21 (SB 771).

§116.740. Defendant's motion to vacate; Grounds

(a) If the defendant was not properly served as required by Section 116.330 or 116.340 and did not appear at the hearing in the small claims court, the defendant may file a motion to vacate the judgment with the clerk of the small claims court. The motion shall be accompanied by a supporting declaration, and shall be filed within 180 days after the defendant discovers or should have discovered that judgment was entered against the defendant.

(b) The court may order that the enforcement of the judgment shall be suspended pending a hearing and determination of the motion to vacate the judgment.

(c) Upon a showing of good cause, the court may grant the motion to vacate the judgment. If the plaintiff is not present, the court shall hear the motion in the plaintiff's absence.

(d) Subdivisions (d), (e), and (f) of Section 116.730 apply to any motion to vacate a judgment. **Leg.H.** Added Stats 1990 ch 1305 §3 (SB 2627). Amended Stats 1991 ch 915 §22 (SB 771).

§116.745. Fee for filing of motion to vacate

The clerk shall collect a fee of twenty dollars ($20) for the filing of a motion to vacate. **Leg.H.** Added Stats 1995 ch 576 §1.5 (AB 1225). Amended Stats 2005 ch 75 §22 (AB 145), effective July 19, 2005, operative January 1, 2006.

§116.750. Notice of appeal

(a) An appeal from a judgment in a small claims action is taken by filing a notice of appeal with the clerk of the small claims court.

(b) A notice of appeal shall be filed not later than 30 days after the clerk has delivered or mailed notice of entry of the judgment to the parties. A notice of appeal filed after the 30-day period is ineffective for any purpose.

(c) The time for filing a notice of appeal is not extended by the filing of a request to correct a mistake or by virtue of any subsequent proceedings on that request, except that a new period for filing notice of appeal shall begin on the delivery or mailing of notice of entry of any modified judgment. **Leg.H.** Added Stats 1990 ch 1305 §3 (SB 2627). Amended Stats 1991 ch 915 §23 (SB 771).

§116.760. Appeal filing fees

(a) The appealing party shall pay a fee of seventy-five dollars ($75) for filing a notice of appeal.

(b) A party who does not appeal shall not be charged any fee for filing any document relating to the appeal.

(c) The fee shall be distributed as follows:

(1) To the county law library fund, as provided in Section 6320 of the Business and Professions Code, the amount specified in Section 6321 and 6322.1 of the Business and Professions Code.

(2) To the Trial Court Trust Fund, the remainder of the fee. **Leg.H.** Added Stats 1990 ch 1305 §3 (SB 2627). Amended Stats 1991 ch 915 §24 (SB 771); Stats 1998 ch 931 §41 (SB 2139), effective September 28, 1998; Stats 2000 ch 447 §1 (SB 1533); Stats 2005 ch 75 §23 (AB 145), effective July 19, 2005, operative January 1, 2006.

§116.770. Appeal procedure

(a) The appeal to the superior court shall consist of a new hearing before a judicial officer other than the judicial officer who heard the action in the small claims division.

(b) The hearing on an appeal to the superior court shall be conducted informally. The pretrial discovery procedures described in Section 2019.010 are not permitted, no party has a right to a trial by jury, and no tentative decision or statement of decision is required.

(c) Article 5 (commencing with Section 116.510) on hearings in the small claims court applies in hearings on appeal in the superior court, except that attorneys may participate.

(d) The scope of the hearing shall include the claims of all parties who were parties to the small claims action at the time the notice of appeal was filed. The hearing shall include the claim of a defendant that was heard in the small claims court.

(e) The clerk of the superior court shall schedule the hearing for the earliest available time and shall mail written notice of the hearing to the parties at least 14 days prior to the time set for the hearing.

(f) The Judicial Council may prescribe by rule the practice and procedure on appeal and the time and manner in which the record on appeal shall be prepared and filed. **Leg.H.** Added Stats 1990 ch 1305 §3 (SB 2627). Amended Stats 1991 ch 133 §4 (AB 1827), ch 915 §25 (SB 771); Stats 1992 ch 8 §3 (AB 1551), effective February 19, 1992; Stats 1998 ch 931 §42 (SB 2139), effective September 28, 1998; Stats 2004 ch 182 §8 (AB 3081), operative July 1, 2005.

§116.780. Judgment of superior court

(a) The judgment of the superior court after a hearing on appeal is final and not appealable.

(b) Article 6 (commencing with Section 116.610) on judgments of the small claims court applies to judgments of the superior court after a hearing on appeal, except as provided in subdivision (c).

(c) For good cause and where necessary to achieve substantial justice between the parties, the superior court may award a party to an appeal reimbursement of (1) attorney's fees actually and reasonably incurred in connection with the appeal, not exceeding one hundred fifty dollars ($150), and (2) actual loss of earnings and expenses of transportation and lodging actually and reasonably incurred in connection with the appeal, not exceeding one hundred fifty dollars ($150). **Leg.H.** Added Stats 1990 ch 1305 §3 (SB 2627). Amended Stats 1991 ch 915 §26 (SB 771); Stats 1994 ch 587 §3 (AB 3600); Stats 2005 ch 706 §8 (AB 1742), effective January 1, 2006; Stats 2011 ch 308 §1 (SB 647), effective January 1, 2012.

§116.790. Award of attorney's fees, lost earnings, and expenses

If the superior court finds that the appeal was without substantial merit and not based on good faith, but was intended to harass or delay the other party, or to encourage the other party to abandon the claim, the court may award the other party (a) attorney's fees actually and reasonably incurred in connection with the appeal, not exceeding one thousand dollars ($1,000), and (b) any actual loss of earnings and any expenses of transportation and lodging actually and reasonably incurred in connection with the appeal, not exceeding one thousand dollars ($1,000), following a hearing on the matter. **Leg.H.** Added Stats 1990 ch 1305 §3 (SB 2627). Amended Stats 1990 ch 1683 §7 (AB 3916); Stats 1991 ch 915 §27 (SB 771).

§116.795. Dismissal of appeal

(a) The superior court may dismiss the appeal if the appealing party does not appear at the hearing or if the appeal is not heard within one year from the date of filing the notice of appeal with the clerk of the small claims court.

(b) Upon dismissal of an appeal by the superior court, the small claims court shall thereafter have the same jurisdiction as if no appeal had been filed. **Leg.H.** Added Stats 1990 ch 1305 §3 (SB 2627).

§116.798. Writs of review, mandate, or prohibition relating to small claims division

(a)(1) A petition that seeks a writ of review, a writ of mandate, or a writ of prohibition relating to an act of the small claims division, other than a postjudgment enforcement order, may be heard by a judge who is assigned to the appellate division of the superior court.

(2) A petition described by paragraph (1) may also be heard by the court of appeal or by the Supreme Court.

(3) Where a judge described in paragraph (1) grants a writ directed to the small claims division, the small claims division is an inferior tribunal for purposes of Title 1 (commencing with Section 1067) of Part 3.

(4) The fee for filing a writ petition in the superior court under paragraph (1) is the same as the fee for filing a notice of appeal under Section 116.760.

(5) The Judicial Council shall promulgate procedural rules for a writ proceeding under paragraph (1).

(6) An appeal shall not be taken from a judgment granting or denying a petition under paragraph (1) for issuance of a writ. An appellate court may, in its discretion, upon petition for extraordinary writ, review the judgment.

(b) A petition that seeks a writ of review, a writ of mandate, or a writ of prohibition relating to an act of a superior court in a small claims appeal may be heard by the court of appeal or by the Supreme Court.

(c) A petition that seeks a writ of review, a writ of mandate, or a writ of prohibition relating to a postjudgment enforcement order of the small claims division may be heard by the appellate division of the superior court, by the court of appeal, or by the Supreme Court. **Leg.H.** Added Stats 2012 ch 470 §3 (AB 1529), effective January 1, 2013.

ARTICLE 8
Satisfaction and Enforcement of Judgment

Enforcement of judgment. §116.810.
Enforcement of small claims judgment; Fees and costs. §116.820.
Form regarding nature and location of assets of judgment debtor. §116.830.
Satisfaction of judgment. §116.840.
Full or partial payment of judgment. §116.850.
Judgment debtor's request to make payment. §116.860.
Suspension of driver's license for failure to pay judgment arising out of motor vehicle accident. §116.870.
Notice requesting suspension of driver's license for failure to satisfy certain judgments; Attempt to notify judgment debtor; Termination of proceedings. §116.880.

§116.810. Enforcement of judgment

(a) Enforcement of the judgment of a small claims court, including the issuance or recording of any abstract of the judgment, is automatically suspended, without the filing of a bond by the defendant, until the expiration of the time for appeal.

(b) If an appeal is filed as provided in Article 7 (commencing with Section 116.710), enforcement of the judgment of the small claims court is suspended unless (1) the appeal is dismissed by the superior court pursuant to Section 116.795, or (2) the superior court determines that the small claims court properly denied the defendant's motion to vacate filed under Section 116.730 or 116.740. In either of those events, the judgment of the small claims court may be enforced.

(c) The scope of the suspension of enforcement under this section and, unless otherwise ordered, of any suspension of enforcement ordered by the court, shall include any enforcement procedure described in Title 9 (commencing with Section 680.010) of Part 2 and in Sections 674 and 1174. **Leg.H.** Added Stats 1990 ch 1305 §3 (SB 2627). Amended Stats 1991 ch 915 §28 (SB 771).

§116.820. Enforcement of small claims judgment; Fees and costs

(a) The judgment of a small claims court, or the judgment of the superior court after a hearing on appeal, may be enforced by the small claims court as provided in Title 9 (commencing with Section 680.010) of Part 2 and in Sections 674 and 1174 on the enforcement of judgments of other courts.

(b) The clerk of the court shall charge and collect all fees associated with the enforcement of judgments under Title 9 (commencing with Section 680.010) of Part 2. The clerk shall immediately deposit all the fees collected under this section into a bank account established for this purpose by the Administrative Office of the Courts. The money shall be remitted to the State Treasury under rules adopted by, or trial court financial policies and procedures authorized by, the Judicial Council under subdivision (a) of Section 77206 of the Government Code. The Controller shall distribute the fees to the Trial Court Trust Fund as provided in Section 68085.1 of the Government Code.

(c) The prevailing party in any action subject to this chapter is entitled to the costs of enforcing the judgment and accrued interest. **Leg.H.** Added Stats 1990 ch 1305 §3 (SB 2627); Amended Stats 1991 ch 915 §29 (SB 771); Stats 1993 ch 158 §3 (AB 392), effective July 20, 1993; Stats 1994 ch 926 §2 (AB 2533); Stats 1995 ch 576 §2 (AB 1225); Stats 1996 ch 1159 §7 (AB 3471); Stats 2003 ch 159 §3 (AB 1759), effective August 2, 2003; Stats 2005 ch 75 §24 (AB 145), effective July 19, 2005, operative January 1, 2006; Stats 2009 ch 596 §1 (SB 556), effective January 1, 2010; Stats 2011 ch 308 §2 (SB 647), effective January 1, 2012.

§116.830. Form regarding nature and location of assets of judgment debtor

(a) At the time judgment is rendered, or notice of entry of the judgment is mailed to the parties, the clerk shall deliver or mail to the judgment debtor a form containing questions regarding the nature and location of any assets of the judgment debtor.

(b) Within 30 days after the clerk has mailed notice of entry of the judgment, unless the judgment has been satisfied, the judgment debtor shall complete the form, and cause it to be delivered to the judgment creditor.

(c) In the event a motion is made to vacate the judgment or a notice of appeal is filed, a judgment debtor shall complete and deliver the form within 30 days after the clerk has delivered or mailed notice of denial of the motion to vacate, or notice of dismissal of or entry of judgment on the appeal, whichever is applicable.

(d) In case of the judgment debtor's willful failure to comply with subdivision (b) or (c), the judgment creditor may request the court to apply the sanctions, including arrest and attorney's fees, as provided in Section 708.170, on contempt of court.

(e) The Judicial Council shall approve or adopt the form to be used for the purpose of this section. **Leg.H.** Added Stats 1990 ch 1305 §3 (SB 2627). Amended Stats 1991 ch 915 §30 (SB 771).

§116.840. Satisfaction of judgment

(a) At the option of the judgment debtor, payment of the judgment may be made either (1) to the judgment creditor in accordance with Section 116.850, or (2) to the court in which the judgment was entered in accordance with Section 116.860.

(b) The small claims court may order entry of satisfaction of judgment in accordance with subdivisions (c) and (d) of Section 116.850, or subdivision (b) of Section 116.860. **Leg.H.** Added Stats 1990 ch 1305 §3 (SB 2627).

§116.850. Full or partial payment of judgment

(a) If full payment of the judgment is made to the judgment creditor or to the judgment creditor's assignee of record, then immediately upon receipt of payment, the judgment creditor or assignee shall file with the clerk of the court an acknowledgment of satisfaction of the judgment.

(b) Any judgment creditor or assignee of record who, after receiving full payment of the judgment and written demand by the judgment debtor, fails without good cause to execute and file an acknowledgment of satisfaction of the judgment with the clerk of the court in which the judgment is entered within 14 days after receiving the request, is liable to the judgment debtor or the judgment debtor's grantees or heirs for all damages sustained by reason of the failure and, in addition, the sum of fifty dollars ($50).

(c) The clerk of the court shall enter a satisfaction of judgment at the request of the judgment debtor if the judgment debtor either (1) establishes a rebuttable presumption of full payment under subdivision (d), or (2) establishes a rebuttable presumption of partial payment under subdivision (d) and complies with Subdivision (c) of Section 116.860.

(d) A rebuttable presumption of full or partial payment of the judgment, whichever is applicable, is created if the judgment debtor files both of the following with the clerk of the court in which the judgment was entered:

(1) Either a canceled check or money order for the full or partial amount of the judgment written by the judgment debtor after judgment and made payable to and endorsed by the judgment creditor, or a cash receipt for the full or partial amount of the judgment written by the judgment debtor after judgment and signed by the judgment creditor.

(2) A declaration stating that (A) the judgment debtor has made full or partial payment of the judgment including accrued interest and costs; (B) the judgment creditor has been requested to file an acknowledgment of satisfaction of the judgment and refuses to do so, or refuses to accept subsequent payments, or the present address of the judgment creditor is unknown; and (C) the documents identified in and accompanying the declaration constitute evidence of the judgment creditor's receipt of full or partial payment. **Leg.H.** Added Stats 1990 ch 1305 §3 (SB 2627). Amended Stats 1991 ch 915 §31 (SB 771).

§116.860. Judgment debtor's request to make payment

(a) A judgment debtor who desires to make payment to the court in which the judgment was entered may file a request to make payment, which shall be made on a form approved or adopted by the Judicial Council.

(b) Upon the filing of the request to make payment and the payment to the clerk of the court of the amount of the judgment and any accrued interest and costs after judgment, plus any required fee authorized by this section, the clerk shall enter satisfaction of the judgment and shall remit payment to the judgment creditor as provided in this section.

(c) If partial payment of the judgment has been made to the judgment creditor, and the judgment debtor files the declaration and evidence of partial payment described in subdivision (d) of Section 116.850, the clerk shall enter satisfaction of the judgment upon receipt by the clerk of the balance owing on the judgment, including any accrued interest and costs after judgment, and the fee required by this section.

(d) If payment is made by means other than money order, certified or cashier's check, or cash, entry of satisfaction of the judgment shall be delayed for 30 days.

(e) The clerk shall notify the judgment creditor, at his or her last known address, that the judgment debtor has satisfied the judgment by making payment to the court. The notification shall explain the procedures which the judgment creditor has to follow to receive payment.

(f) For purposes of this section, "costs after judgment" consist of only those costs itemized in a memorandum of costs filed by the judgment creditor or otherwise authorized by the court.

(g) Payments that remain unclaimed for three years shall go to the superior court pursuant to Section 68084.1 of the Government Code.

(h) A fee of twenty dollars ($20) shall be paid by the judgment debtor for the costs of administering this section. **Leg.H.** Added Stats 1990 ch 1305 §3 (SB 2627). Amended Stats 1991 ch 915 §32 (SB 771); Stats 2005 ch 75 §25 (AB 145), effective July 19, 2005, operative January 1, 2006.

§116.870. Suspension of driver's license for failure to pay judgment arising out of motor vehicle accident

(a) Sections 16250 to 16381, inclusive, of the Vehicle Code, regarding the suspension of the judgment debtor's privilege to operate a motor vehicle for failing to satisfy a judgment, apply if the judgment (1) was for damage to property in excess of one thousand dollars ($1,000) or for bodily injury to, or death of, a person in any amount, and (2) resulted from the operation of a motor vehicle upon a California highway by the defendant, or by any other person for whose conduct the defendant was liable, unless the liability resulted from the defendant's signing the application of a minor for a driver's license.

(b) This section shall become operative on January 1, 2017. **Leg.H.** Added Stats 2015 ch 451 §2 (SB 491), effective January 1, 2016, operative January 1, 2017.

Former Sections: Former CCP §116.870 was enacted 1990 and repealed operative January 1, 2017, by its own provisions. 2015 ch 451 (SB 491) §1.

§116.880. Notice requesting suspension of driver's license for failure to satisfy certain judgments; Attempt to notify judgment debtor; Termination of proceedings

(a) If the judgment (1) was for one thousand dollars ($1,000) or less, (2) resulted from a motor vehicle accident occurring on a California highway caused by the defendant's operation of a motor vehicle, and (3) has remained unsatisfied for more than 90 days after the judgment became final, the judgment creditor may file with the Department of Motor Vehicles a notice requesting a suspension of the judgment debtor's privilege to operate a motor vehicle.

(b) The notice shall state that the judgment has not been satisfied, and shall be accompanied by (1) a fee set by the department, (2) the judgment of the court determining that the judgment resulted from a motor vehicle accident occurring on a California highway caused by the judgment debtor's operation of a motor vehicle, and (3) a declaration that the judgment has not been satisfied. The fee shall be used by the department to finance the costs of administering this section and shall not exceed the department's actual costs.

(c) Upon receipt of a notice, the department shall attempt to notify the judgment debtor by telephone, if possible, otherwise by certified mail, that the judgment debtor's privilege to operate a motor vehicle will be suspended for a period of 90 days, beginning 20 days after receipt of notice by the department from the judgment creditor, unless satisfactory proof, as provided in subdivision (e), is provided to the department before that date.

(d) At the time the notice is filed, the department shall give the judgment creditor a copy of the notice that indicates the filing fee paid by the judgment creditor, and includes a space to be signed by the judgment creditor acknowledging payment of the judgment by the judgment debtor. The judgment creditor shall mail or deliver a signed copy of the acknowledgment to the judgment debtor once the judgment is satisfied.

(e) The department shall terminate the suspension, or the suspension proceedings, upon the occurrence of one or more of the following:

(1) Receipt of proof that the judgment has been satisfied, either (A) by a copy of the notice required by this section signed by the judgment creditor acknowledging satisfaction of the judgment, or (B) by a declaration of the judgment debtor stating that the judgment has been satisfied.

(2) Receipt of proof that the judgment debtor is complying with a court-ordered payment schedule.

(3) Proof that the judgment debtor had insurance covering the accident sufficient to satisfy the judgment.

(4) A deposit with the department of the amount of the unsatisfied judgment, if the judgment debtor presents proof, satisfactory to the department, of inability to locate the judgment creditor.

(5) At the end of 90 days.

(f) If the suspension has been terminated under subdivision (e), the action is final and shall not be reinstituted. If the suspension is terminated, Section 14904 of the Vehicle Code shall apply. Money deposited with the department under this section shall be handled in the same manner as money deposited under paragraph (4) of subdivision (a) of Section 16377 of the Vehicle Code.

(g) A public agency is not liable for an injury caused by the suspension, termination of suspension, or the failure to suspend a person's privilege to operate a motor vehicle as authorized by this section.

(h) This section shall become operative on January 1, 2017. **Leg.H.** Added Stats 2015 ch 451 §4 (SB 491), effective January 1, 2016, operative January 1, 2017.

Former Sections: Former CCP §116.880 was enacted 1990 and repealed operative January 1, 2017, by its own provisions. 2015 ch 451 (SB 491) §3.

ARTICLE 9
Administration

Rules and forms. §116.920.
Manual describing small claims court law and procedure. §116.930.
Advisory services. §116.940.
Advisory committee to study small claims practice and procedure [Operation contingent]. §116.950.

§116.910. [Section repealed 2006]

Leg.H. Added Stats 1990 ch 1305 §3 (SB 2627). Amended Stats 1991 ch 915 §34 (SB 771); Stats 1996 ch 1159 §8 (AB 3471). Repealed Stats 2005 ch 75 §26 (AB 145), effective July 19, 2005, operative January 1, 2006. The repealed section related to fees and charges in special account and the use of money deposited in the account.

§116.920. Rules and forms

(a) The Judicial Council shall provide by rule for the practice and procedure and for the forms and their use in small claims actions. The rules and forms so adopted shall be consistent with this chapter.

(b) The Judicial Council, in consultation with the Department of Consumer Affairs, shall adopt rules to ensure that litigants receive adequate notice of the availability of assistance from small claims advisors, to prescribe other qualifications and the conduct of advisors, to prescribe training standards for advisors and for temporary judges hearing small claims matters, to prescribe, where appropriate, uniform rules and procedures regarding small claims actions and judgments, and to address other matters that are deemed necessary and appropriate. **Leg.H.** Added Stats 1990 ch 1305 §3 (SB 2627). Amended Stats 1991 ch 915 §35 (SB 771).

§116.930. Manual describing small claims court law and procedure

(a) Each small claims division shall provide in each courtroom in which small claims actions are heard a current copy of a publication describing small claims court law and the procedures that are applicable in the small claims courts, including the law and procedures that apply to the enforcement of judgments. The Small Claims Court and Consumer Law California Judge's Bench Book developed by the California Center for Judicial Education and Research is illustrative of a publication that satisfies the requirement of this subdivision.

(b) Each small claims division may formulate and distribute to litigants and the public a manual on small claims court rules and procedures. The manual shall explain how to complete the necessary forms, how to determine the proper court in which small claims actions may be filed, how to present and defend against claims, how to appeal, how to enforce a judgment, how to protect property that is exempt from execution, and such other matters that the court deems necessary or desirable.

(c) If the Department of Consumer Affairs determines there are sufficient private or public funds available in addition to the funds available within the department's current budget, the department, in cooperation with the Judicial Council, shall prepare a manual or information booklet on small claims court rules and procedures. The department shall distribute copies to the general public and to each small claims division.

(d) If funding is available, the Judicial Council, in cooperation with the Department of Consumer Affairs, shall prepare and distribute to each judge who sits in a small claims court a bench book describing all state and federal consumer protection laws reasonably likely to apply in small claims actions. **Leg.H.** Added Stats 1990 ch 1305 §3 (SB 2627).

§116.940. Advisory services

(a) Except as otherwise provided in this section or in rules adopted by the Judicial Council, which are consistent with the requirements of this section, the characteristics of the small claims advisory service required by Section 116.260 shall be determined by each county, or by the superior court in a county where the small claims advisory service is administered by the court, in accordance with local needs and conditions.

(b) Each advisory service shall provide the following services:

(1) Individual personal advisory services, in person or by telephone, and by any other means reasonably calculated to provide timely and appropriate assistance. The topics covered by individual personal advisory services shall include, but not be limited to, preparation of small claims court filings, procedures, including procedures related to the conduct of the hearing, and information on the collection of small claims court judgments.

(2) Recorded telephone messages may be used to supplement the individual personal advisory services, but shall not be the sole means of providing advice available in the county.

(3) Adjacent counties, superior courts in adjacent counties, or any combination thereof, may provide advisory services jointly.

(c) In a county in which the number of small claims actions filed annually is 1,000 or less as averaged over the immediately preceding two fiscal years, the county or the superior court may elect to exempt itself from the requirements set forth in subdivision (b). If the small claims advisory service is administered by the county, this exemption shall be formally noticed through the adoption of a resolution by the board of supervisors. If the small claims advisory service is administered by the superior court, this exemption shall be formally noticed through adoption of a local rule. If a county or court so exempts itself, the county or court shall nevertheless provide the following minimum advisory services in accordance with rules adopted by the Judicial Council:

(1) Recorded telephone messages providing general information relating to small claims actions filed in the county shall be provided during regular business hours.

(2) Small claims information booklets shall be provided in the court clerk's office of each superior court, appropriate county offices, and in any other location that is convenient to prospective small claims litigants in the county.

(d) The advisory service shall operate in conjunction and cooperation with the small claims division, and shall be administered so as to avoid the existence or appearance of a conflict of interest between the individuals providing the advisory services and any party to a particular small claims action or any judicial officer deciding small claims actions.

(e) Advisers may be volunteers, and shall be members of the State Bar, law students, paralegals, or persons experienced in resolving minor disputes, and shall be familiar with small claims court rules and procedures. Advisers may not appear in court as an advocate for any party.

(f) Advisers, including independent contractors, other employees, and volunteers, have the immunity conferred by Section 818.9 of the Government Code with respect to advice provided as a public service on behalf of a court or county to small claims litigants and potential litigants under this chapter.

(g) This section does not preclude a court or county from contracting with a third party to provide small claims advisory services as described in this section. **Leg.H.** Added Stats 1990 ch 1305 §3 (SB 2627). Amended Stats 1998 ch 931 §43 (SB 2139), effective September 28, 1998; Stats 2002 ch 806 §6 (AB 3027); Stats 2005 ch 600 §6 (SB 422), ch 618 §6 (AB 1459); Stats 2012 ch 470 §4 (AB 1529), effective January 1, 2013; Stats 2013 ch 76 §21 (AB 383), effective January 1, 2014.

§116.950. Advisory committee to study small claims practice and procedure [Operation contingent]

(a) This section shall become operative only if the Department of Consumer Affairs determines that sufficient private or public funds are available in addition to the funds available in the department's current budget to cover the costs of implementing this section.

(b) There shall be established an advisory committee, constituted as set forth in this section, to study small claims practice and procedure, with particular attention given to the improvement of procedures for the enforcement of judgments.

(c) The members of the advisory committee shall serve without compensation, but shall be reimbursed for expenses actually and necessarily incurred by them in the performance of their duties.

(d) The advisory committee shall be composed as follows:

(1) The Attorney General or a representative.

(2) Two consumer representatives from consumer groups or agencies, appointed by the Secretary of the State and Consumer Services Agency.

(3) One representative appointed by the Speaker of the Assembly and one representative appointed by the President pro Tempore of the Senate.

(4) Two representatives appointed by the Board of Governors of the State Bar.

(5) Two representatives of the business community, appointed by the Secretary of Technology, Trade, and Commerce.

(6) Six judicial officers who have extensive experience presiding in small claims court, appointed by the Judicial Council. Judicial officers appointed under this subdivision may include judicial officers of the superior court, judges of the appellate courts, retired judicial officers, and temporary judges.

(7) One representative appointed by the Governor.

(8) Two clerks of the court appointed by the Judicial Council.

(e) Staff assistance to the advisory committee shall be provided by the Department of Consumer Affairs, with the assistance of the Judicial Council, as needed. **Leg.H.** Added Stats 1990 ch 1305 §3 (SB 2627), operation contingent. Amended Stats 1993 ch 1153 §1 (AB 1732), effective October 10, 1993; Stats 1998 ch 931 §44 (SB 2139), effective September 28, 1998; Stats 1999 ch 344 §5 (SB 210), effective September 7, 1999; Stats 2001 ch 745 §8 (SB 1191), effective October 12, 2001; Stats 2002 ch 664 §46 (AB 3034), ch 784 §32 (SB 1316).

§117. [Section repealed 1991]

Leg.H. Added Stats 1976 ch 1289 §2. Amended Stats 1978 ch 163 §1; Stats 1981 ch 958 §4; Stats 1982 ch 497 §26, operative July 1, 1983. Repealed Stats 1990 ch 1305 §2 (SB 2627). See CCP §§116.510, 116.520.

Prior Law: Former CCP §117, relating to jurisdiction, Venue, and small claims court, was added Stats 1933 ch 743 §30, amended Stats 1943 ch 186 §1, Stats 1949 ch 451 §1, Stats 1951 ch 1737 §11, operative January 1, 1952, Stats 1955 ch 168 §1, ch 1927 §1, Stats 1956 1st Ex Sess ch 24 §1, Stats 1957 ch 201 §1, Stats 1961 ch 2022 §1, Stats 1967 ch 195 §1, Stats 1968 ch 503 §3, Stats 1971 ch 572 §1; Stats 1972 ch 1119 §1, and repealed Stats 1976 ch 1289 §1. See §§116.2, 116.6.

Former CCP §117 was enacted 1872, amended by Code Amdts 1873–74 ch 383 §9, Code Amdts 1875–76 ch 199 §1, and repealed and reenacted as §115 by Code Amdts 1880 ch 35 §1.

§117a. [Section repealed 1977]

Leg.H. Added Stats 1933 ch 743 §30 p 1818. Amended Stats 1951 ch 1737 §12 p 4084, operative January 1, 1952; Stats 1972 ch 527 §1. Repealed Stats 1976 ch 1289 §1. See CCP §§116.320 et seq.

§117b. [Section repealed 1977]

Leg.H. Added Stats 1933 ch 743 §30. Amended Stats 1941 ch 810 §1; Stats 1943 ch 95 §1; Stats 1951 ch 1737 §13, operative January 1, 1952; Stats 1955 ch 1927 §2; Stats 1972 ch 527 §2; Stats 1975 ch 1228 §1. Repealed Stats 1976 ch 1289 §1. See CCP §§116.320 et seq.

§117c. [Section repealed 1977]

Leg.H. Added Stats 1933 ch 743 §30. Amended Stats 1941 ch 877 §1; Stats 1951 ch 1737 §14, operative January 1, 1952; Stats 1955 ch 1401 §1; Stats 1972 ch 527 §3; Stats 1974 ch 247 §1. Repealed Stats 1976 ch 1289 §1. See CCP §§116.320 et seq.

§117d. [Section repealed 1977]

Leg.H. Added Stats 1933 ch 743 §30. Amended Stats 1935 ch 303 §1, ch 800 §1; Stats 1943 ch 185 §1; Stats 1951 ch 1737 §15, operative January 1, 1952; Stats 1953 ch 1611 §1; Stats 1955 ch 509 §1; Stats 1965 ch 1596 §1; Stats 1972 ch 527 §4. Repealed Stats 1976 ch 1289 §1. See CCP §§116.320 et seq.

§117e. [Section repealed 1977]

Leg.H. Added Stats 1933 ch 743 §30 p 1819. Amended Stats 1951 ch 1737 §16 p 4086, operative January 1, 1952. Repealed Stats 1976 ch 1289 §1. The repealed section related to court records.

§117f. [Section repealed 1977]

Leg.H. Added Stats 1933 ch 743 §30 p 1820. Amended Stats 1969 ch 4091 §1. Repealed Stats 1976 ch 1289 §1. See CCP §116.420.

§117g. [Section repealed 1977]

Leg.H. Added Stats 1933 ch 743 §30. Amended Stats 1951 ch 1488 §1; Stats 1955 ch 885 §1; Stats 1965 ch 299 §16, operative January 1, 1967; Stats 1969 ch 491 §2; Stats 1970 ch 722 §1; Stats 1974 ch 120 §1; Stats 1975 ch 1228 §2. Repealed Stats 1976 ch 1289 §1. See CCP §116.530.

§117h. [Section repealed 1977]

Leg.H. Added Stats 1933 ch 743 §30. Amended Stats 1933 ch 895 §1; Stats 1951 ch 1737 §17; Stats 1971 ch 244 §2, operative July 1, 1972; Stats 1972 ch 527 §5. Repealed Stats 1976 ch 1289 §1. See CCP §§116.310, 116.360, 116.510, 116.520.

§117ha. [Section repealed 1977]

Leg.H. Added Stats 1933 ch 896 §1. Amended Stats 1951 ch 1737 §18, operative January 1, 1952; Stats 1955 ch 605 §1, ch 1927 §3; Stats 1975 ch 266 §1. Repealed Stats 1976 ch 1289 §1. See CCP §§116.810, 116.820.

§117i. [Section repealed 1977]

Leg.H. Added Stats 1933 ch 743 §30 p 1820. Amended Stats 1951 ch 1737 §19 p 4087, operative January 1, 1952. Repealed Stats 1976 ch 1289 §1. See CCP §§116.840, 116.850.

§117j. [Section repealed 1977]

Leg.H. Added Stats 1933 ch 743 §30. Amended Stats 1951 ch 1143 §1, ch 1737 §20, operative January 1, 1952; Stats 1955 ch 566 §1; Stats 1959 ch 341 §1, ch 1982 §1; Stats 1963 ch 871 §1, operative July 1, 1964; Stats 1975 ch 266 §2, ch 990 §2. Repealed Stats 1976 ch 1289 §1. See CCP §§116.730, 116.740, 116.770.

§117jj. [Section repealed 1964]

Leg.H. Added Stats 1959 ch 342 §1. Repealed Stats 1963 ch 371 §12, operative July 1, 1964. The repealed section related to dismissal of appeal.

§117k. [Section repealed 1964]

Leg.H. Added Stats 1933 ch 743 §30. Repealed Stats 1963 ch 871 §13, operative July 1, 1964. The repealed section related to the form for an appeal.

§117l. [Section repealed 1976]

Leg.H. Added Stats 1933 ch 743 §30. Amended Stats 1951 ch 1737 §21, operative January 1, 1952; Stats 1961 ch 693 §1, operative January 2, 1963; Stats 1963 ch 871 §2, operative July 1, 1964. Repealed Stats 1975 ch 266 §3. The repealed section related to bond on appeal, notice of filing of appeal and undertaking, exception to sureties, and justification.

§117ll. [Section repealed 1976]

Leg.H. Added Stats 1941 ch 331 §1. Amended Stats 1953 ch 1726 §1. Repealed Stats 1975 ch 266 §4. The repealed section related to deposit in lieu of bond.

§117m. [Section repealed 1977]

Leg.H. Added Stats 1933 ch 743 §30. Amended Stats 1951 ch 1443 §1; Stats 1955 ch 606 §1; Stats 1966 1st Ex Sess ch 120 §2. Repealed Stats 1976 ch 1289 §1. The repealed section related to abstract of judgment.

§117n. [Section repealed 1964]

Leg.H. Added Stats 1959 ch 183 §1. Repealed Stats 1963 ch 871 §14, operative July 1, 1964. The repealed section related to time and place of trial and to notice.

§117o. [Section repealed 1977]

Leg.H. Added Stats 1933 ch 743 §30 p 1822. Amended Stats 1951 ch 1737 §22, operative January 1, 1952. Repealed Stats 1976 ch 1289 §1. The repealed section related to the duty of supervisors to furnish forms.

§117p. [Section repealed 1977]

Leg.H. Added Stats 1933 ch 743 §30. Amended Stats 1939 ch 303 §2; Stats 1943 ch 903 §1; Stats 1949 ch 129 §1; Stats 1951 ch 1737 §23, operative January 1, 1952; Stats 1953 ch 1300 §1; Stats 1959 ch 106 §1, ch 1353 §1; Stats 1966 1st Ex Sess ch 120 §3; Stats 1967 ch 729 §1; Stats 1972 ch 527 §6. Repealed Stats 1976 ch 1289 §1. See CCP §116.550.

§117q. [Section repealed 1977]

Leg.H. Added Stats 1933 ch 743 §30. Amended Stats 1935 ch 800 §2. Repealed Stats 1976 ch 1289 §1. The repealed section related to costs.

§117r. [Section repealed 1977]

Leg.H. Added Stats 1933 ch 916 §1. Amended Stats 1949 ch 451 §2; Stats 1951 ch 178 §1; Stats 1959 ch 1146 §1; Stats 1971 ch 244 §3, operative July 1, 1972. Repealed Stats 1976 ch 1289 §1. See CCP §§116.310, 116.380.

§117.1. [Section repealed 1991]

Leg.H. Added Stats 1976 ch 1289 §2. Amended Stats 1981 ch 958 §5. Repealed Stats 1990 ch 1305 §2 (SB 2627). The repealed section related to claims forms and fee waivers.

§117.3. [Section repealed 1991]

Leg.H. Added Stats 1976 ch 1289 §2. Amended Stats 1977 ch 46 §3, effective May 14, 1977. Repealed Stats 1990 ch 1305 §2 (SB 2627). The repealed section related to appearance date.

§117.4. [Section repealed 1991]

Leg.H. Added Stats 1976 ch 1289 §2. Amended Stats 1977 ch 46 §4, effective May 14, 1977; Stats 1982 ch 1350 §1. Repealed Stats 1990 ch 1305 §2 (SB 2627). See CCP §116.530.

§117.40. [Section repealed 1991]

Leg.H. Added Stats 1985 ch 216 §1. Repealed Stats 1990 ch 1305 §2 (SB 2627). See CCP §116.540.

§117.41. [Section repealed 1991]

Leg.H. Added Stats 1978 ch 35 §2, effective March 12, 1978. Amended Stats 1985 ch 1515 §2; Stats 1988 ch 1321 §1. Repealed Stats 1990 ch 1305 §2 (SB 2627). See CCP §116.420.

§117.42. [Section repealed 1991]

Leg.H. Added Stats 1988 ch 443 §2. Repealed Stats 1990 ch 1305 §2 (SB 2627). See CCP §116.420.

§117.5. [Section repealed 1991]

Leg.H. Added Stats 1976 ch 1289 §2. Amended Stats 1981 ch 313 §1. Repealed Stats 1990 ch 1305 §2 (SB 2627). See CCP §116.420.

§117.6. [Section repealed 1991]

Leg.H. Added Stats 1981 ch 958 §6. Repealed Stats 1990 ch 1305 §2 (SB 2627). The repealed section related to service or principal.

Prior Law: Former CCP §117.6, relating to limit on number of claims, was added by Stats 1976 ch 1289 §2 and repealed by Stats 1978 ch 35 §1, effective March 12, 1978.

§117.7. [Section repealed 1991]

Leg.H. Added Stats 1976 ch 1289 §2. Amended Stats 1982 ch 497 §27, operative July 1, 1983. Repealed Stats 1990 ch 1305 §2 (SB 2627). See CCP §§116.810, 116.820.

§117.8. [Section repealed 1991]

Leg.H. Added Stats 1976 ch 1289 §2. Amended Stats 1978 ch 35 §3, effective March 12, 1978, ch 1137 §1; Stats 1984 ch 296 §1; Stats 1989 ch 1416 §6. Repealed Stats 1990 ch 1305 §2 (SB 2627). See CCP §§116.730, 116.740.

§117.9. [Section repealed 1991]

Leg.H. Added Stats 1976 ch 1289 §2. Amended Stats 1980 ch 1018 §1, Stats 1981 ch 86 §1, Stats 1982 ch 497 §28, operative July 1, 1983, Stats 1984 ch 1225; Stats 1982 ch 497 §28, operative January 1, 1988; Stats 1989 ch 1028 §1, effective September 29, 1989. Repealed Stats 1990 ch 1305 §2 (SB 2627). See CCP §§116.840, 116.850.

§117.10. [Section repealed 1991]

Leg.H. Added Stats 1976 ch 1289 §2. Amended Stats 1989 ch 1416 §7. Repealed Stats 1990 ch 1305 §2 (SB 2627). See CCP §116.770.

§117.12. [Section repealed 1991]

Leg.H. Added Stats 1976 ch 1289 §2 as §118.1. Renumbered Stats 1978 ch 723 §5. Amended Stats 1982 ch 605 §2; Stats 1983 ch 219 §1. Repealed Stats 1990 ch 1305 §2 (SB 2627). See CCP §§116.780, 116.790.

§117.14. [Section repealed 1991]

Leg.H. Added Stats 1976 ch 1289 §2 as §118.6. Amended and renumbered Stats 1978 ch 723 §6; Amended Stats 1980 ch 1372 §1; Stats 1981 ch 958 §7; Stats 1984 ch 481 §1, ch 1288 §1; Stats 1989 ch 15 §1, effective May 10, 1989, ch 1450 §2. Repealed Stats 1990 ch 1305 §2 (SB 2627). See CCP §116.230.

§117.16. [Section repealed 1991]

Leg.H. Added Stats 1976 ch 1289 §2 as §118.7. Renumbered Stats 1978 ch 723 §7. Repealed Stats 1990 ch 1305 §2 (SB 2627). See CCP §116.550.

§117.18. [Section repealed 1991]

Leg.H. Added Stats 1978 ch 723 §4. Amended Stats 1981 ch 958 §8; Stats 1989 ch 1450 §3. Repealed Stats 1990 ch 1305 §2 (SB 2627). See CCP §§116.260, 116.940.

§117.19. [Section repealed 1991]

Leg.H. Added Stats 1980 ch 1018 §2. Amended Stats 1982 ch 497 §29, operative July 1, 1983. Repealed Stats 1990 ch 1305 §2 (SB 2627). See CCP §116.430.

§117.20. [Section repealed 1991]

Leg.H. Added Stats 1981 ch 958 §9. Repealed Stats 1990 ch 1305 §2 (SB 2627). See CCP §116.270.

Prior Law: There was another section of this number which was added by Stats 1980 ch 1018 §3 and repealed effective June 1, 1983, by the terms of Stats 1980 ch 1018 §4.

§117.22. [Section repealed 1991]

Leg.H. Added Stats 1982 ch 605 §3. Repealed Stats 1990 ch 1305 §2 (SB 2627). The repealed section related to advisory committee.

§117.24. [Section repealed 1991]

Leg.H. Added Stats 1988 ch 395 §1, effective August 11, 1988. Repealed Stats 1990 ch 1305 §2 (SB 2627). See CCP §§116.870, 116.880.

Prior Law: Former CCP §117.24, relating to unsatisfied motor vehicle accident small claims judgments and notice to Department of Motor Vehicles, was added Stats 1984 ch 1225 §2, operative July 1, 1985 and repealed effective January 1, 1988, by its own terms.

CHAPTER 5A
SMALL CLAIMS COURTS [REPEALED]

§116.1. [Section repealed 1991]

Leg.H. Added Stats 1981 ch 958 §1. Repealed Stats 1990 ch 1305 §2 (SB 2627). See CCP §116.120.

§116.2. [Section repealed 1991]

Leg.H. Added Stats 1976 ch 1289 §2. Amended Stats 1979 ch 964 §1; Stats 1981 ch 957 §1, ch 958 §2; Stats 1988 ch 481 §1. Repealed Stats 1990 ch 1305 §2 (SB 2627). See CCP §116.220.

§116.3. [Section repealed 1991]

Leg.H. Added Stats 1978 ch 723 §2. Repealed Stats 1990 ch 1305 §2 (SB 2627). The repealed section related to equitable relief in lieu of or in addition to damages.

§116.4. [Section repealed 1991]

Leg.H. Added Stats 1976 ch 1289 §2. Amended Stats 1977 ch 46 §1, effective May 14, 1977, ch 889 §2; Stats 1988 ch 443 §1; Stats 1989 ch 1153 §1. Repealed Stats 1990 ch 1305 §2 (SB 2627). See CCP §§116.320, 116.330, 116.340, 116.360.

§116.41. [Section repealed 1991]

Leg.H. Added Stats 1989 ch 1153 §2. Repealed Stats 1990 ch 1305 §2 (SB 2627). The repealed section related to a written request for continuance of a hearing date.

§116.5. [Section repealed 1991]

Leg.H. Added Stats 1981 ch 65 §1. Repealed Stats 1990 ch 1305 §2 (SB 2627). The repealed section related to extension of appearance date.

§116.6. [Section repealed 1991]

Leg.H. Added Stats 1976 ch 1289 §2. Amended Stats 1977 ch 46 §2, effective May 14, 1977; Stats 1989 ch 1450 §1.5. Repealed Stats 1990 ch 1305 §2 (SB 2627). See CCP §116.370.

§116.7. [Section repealed 1991]

Leg.H. Added Stats 1976 ch 1289 §2. Amended Stats 1981 ch 958 §3; Stats 1986 ch 1398 §1, operative January 1, 1989. Repealed Stats 1990 ch 1305 §2 (SB 2627). See CCP §116.250.

§116.8. [Section repealed 1991]

Leg.H. Added Stats 1976 ch 1289 §2. Amended Stats 1978 ch 723 §3; Stats 1980 ch 536 §1. Repealed Stats 1990 ch 1305 §2 (SB 2627). See CCP §§116.310, 116.360.

CHAPTER 5-B
SMALL CLAIMS COURT EXPERIMENTAL PROJECT [REPEALED]

§118. [Section repealed 1980]

Leg.H. Added Stats 1976 ch 1287 §1, operative July 1, 1977. Amended Stats 1978 ch 723 §8. Repealed June 30, 1980, by the terms of Stats 1976 ch 1287 §2, as amended Stats 1978 ch 723 §15. The repealed section related to legislative intent.

Prior Law: Former CCP §118 was enacted 1872 and omitted by Code Amdts 1880 ch 35 §1 in amending Part I.

§119. [Section repealed 1980]

Leg.H. Added Stats 1976 ch 1287 §1, operative July 1, 1977. Repealed June 30, 1980, by the terms of Stats 1976 ch 1287 §2, as amended Stats 1978 ch 723 §15. The repealed section related to membership.

Prior Law: Former CCP §119 was added by Code Amdts 1873–74 ch 383 §10 and omitted by Code Amdts 1880 ch 35 §1 in amending Part I.

§§119.1–119.3. [Sections repealed 1980]

Leg.H. Added Stats 1976 ch 1287 §1, operative July 1, 1977. Repealed June 30, 1980, by the terms of Stats 1976 ch 1287 §2, as amended Stats 1978 ch 723 §15. The repealed sections related to the advisory committee.

§119.4. [Section repealed 1980]

Leg.H. Added Stats 1976 ch 1287 §1, operative July 1, 1977. Amended Stats 1978 ch 723 §9. Repealed June 30, 1980, by the terms of Stats 1976 ch 1287 §2, as amended Stats 1978 ch 723 §15. The repealed section related to the advisory committee as assisting in evaluating data.

§119.6. [Section repealed 1980]

Leg.H. Added Stats 1976 ch 1287 §1, operative July 1, 1977, as §120. Amended and renumbered Stats 1978 ch 723 §11; Repealed June 30, 1980, by the terms of Stats 1976 ch 1287 §2, as amended Stats 1978 ch 723 §15. Stats 1981 ch 714 §58. The repealed section related to the small claims divisions as being experimental districts.

§119.9. [Section repealed 1980]

Leg.H. Added Stats 1978 ch 723 §10. Repealed June 30, 1980, by the terms of Stats 1976 ch 1287 §2, as amended Stats 1978 ch 723 §15. Stats 1981 ch 714 §59. The repealed section related to the specification of certain municipal court districts in which the experiment would take place.

§120. [Section renumbered 1979]

Leg.H. Added Stats 1976 ch 1287 §1, operative July 1, 1977. Amended and renumbered Stats 1978 ch 723 §11 as CCP §119.6.

§120.1. [Section repealed 1980]

Leg.H. Added Stats 1976 ch 1287 §1, operative July 1, 1977. Amended Stats 1978 ch 723 §12; Stats 1979 ch 968 §1, effective September 22, 1979; Repealed June 30, 1980, by the terms of Stats 1976 ch 1287 §2, as amended Stats 1978 ch 723 §15. Stats 1981 ch 714 §60. The repealed section related to implementation of the chapter in stages.

§§120.2, 120.3. [Sections repealed 1980]

Leg.H. Added Stats 1976 ch 1287 §1, operative July 1, 1977. Repealed June 30, 1980, by the terms of Stats 1976 ch 1287 §2, as amended Stats 1978 ch 723 §15. The repealed sections related to administration of the project.

§120.4. [Section repealed 1980]

Leg.H. Added Stats 1977 ch 889 §3. Repealed June 30, 1980, by the terms of Stats 1976 ch 1287 §2, as amended Stats 1978 ch 723 §15. Stats 1981 ch 714 §60. The repealed section related to attaches and employees.

§121. [Section repealed 1980]

Leg.H. Added Stats 1976 ch 1287 §1, operative July 1, 1977. Repealed June 30, 1980, by the terms of Stats 1976 ch 1287 §2, as amended Stats 1978 ch 723 §15. The repealed section related to procedures, data collection, and evaluation.

Prior Law: Former CCP §121 was added Stats 1933 ch 743 §31 and repealed Stats 1951 ch 1737 §24, operative January 1, 1952.

Former CCP §121 was enacted 1872 and repealed Stats 1933 ch 743 §31.

§§121.1–121.8. [Sections repealed 1980]

Leg.H. Added Stats 1976 ch 1287 §1, operative July 1, 1977. Repealed June 30, 1980, by the terms of Stats 1976 ch 1287 §2, as amended Stats 1978 ch 723 §15. The repealed sections related to procedures in experimental districts.

§122. [Section repealed 1980]

Leg.H. Added Stats 1976 ch 1287 §1, operative July 1, 1977. Repealed June 30, 1980, by the terms of Stats 1976 ch 1287 §2, as amended Stats 1978 ch 723 §15. The repealed section related to additional entries in project data.

Prior Law: Former CCP §122 was added Stats 1933 ch 743 §31 and repealed Stats 1951 ch 1737 §24, operative January 1, 1952.

§§122.1, 122.2. [Sections repealed 1980]

Leg.H. Added Stats 1976 ch 1287 §1, operative July 1, 1977. Repealed June 30, 1980, by the terms of Stats 1976 ch 1287 §2, as amended Stats

1978 ch 723 §15. The repealed section related to additional entries in project data.

§§122a–122e. [Sections repealed 1952]

Leg.H. Added Stats 1933 ch 743 §31. Repealed Stats 1951 ch 1737 §24, operative January 1, 1952. The repealed sections related to procedures in police courts.

§§123–123.5. [Sections repealed 1980]

Leg.H. Added Stats 1978 ch 723 §14. Repealed June 30, 1980, by the terms of Stats 1976 ch 1287 §2, as amended Stats 1978 ch 723 §15. Stats 1981 ch 714 §§63–66. The repealed sections related to the monetary jurisdiction experiment in small claims divisions.

§123.7. [Section repealed 1980]

Leg.H. Added Stats 1978 ch 723 §14. Amended Stats 1979 ch 15 §1, effective April 2, 1979; Repealed June 30, 1980, by the terms of Stats 1976 ch 1287 §2, as amended Stats 1978 ch 723 §15. Stats 1981 ch 714 §67. The repealed section related to the charge of an additional fee for filing a claim under oath in the commencement of an action.

CHAPTER 6
GENERAL PROVISIONS RESPECTING COURTS OF JUSTICE

Article 1. Open Court Access.
Article 2. Incidental Powers and Duties of Court.
Article 3. Judicial Holidays.
Article 4. Proceedings in Case of Absence of Judge.
Article 6. Seals of Courts.

ARTICLE 1
Open Court Access

Public sittings; Exclusion from physical access due to availability of remote access not permitted. §124.

§124. Public sittings; Exclusion from physical access due to availability of remote access not permitted

(a) Except as provided in Section 214 of the Family Code or any other law, the sittings of every court shall be public.

(b)(1) The court shall not exclude the public from physical access because remote access is available, unless it is necessary to restrict or limit physical access to protect the health or safety of the public or court personnel.

(2) When a courthouse is physically closed, to the extent permitted by law, the court shall provide, at a minimum, a public audio stream or telephonic means by which to listen to the proceedings. This paragraph does not apply to proceedings pursuant to Section 214 of the Family Code or other law that authorizes or requires a proceeding to be closed.

(3) For purposes of this subdivision, "remote access" shall include, but is not limited to, an audio stream that is available on an internet website or telephonic means to listen to a court proceeding. **Leg.H.** Enacted 1872. Repealed and re-enacted Code Amdts 1880 ch 35 §1. Amended Stats 1971 ch 762 §2; Stats 1990 ch 1363 §10 (AB 3532), operative July 1, 1991; Stats 1992 ch 163 §12 (AB 2641), operative January 1, 1994; Stats 2021 ch 526 §3 (AB 716), effective January 1, 2022.

§125. [Section repealed 1970]

Leg.H. Enacted 1872. Amended Code Amdts 1873–74 ch 383 §11. Repealed and re-enacted Code Amdts 1880 ch 35 §1. Amended Stats 1939 ch 129 §1; Stats 1965 ch 299 §17, operative January 1, 1967. Repealed Stats 1969 ch 1608 §9, operative January 1, 1970. The repealed section related to private sittings and sequestration of witnesses in certain cases.

ARTICLE 2
Incidental Powers and Duties of Court

Powers respecting conduct of proceedings; Contempt. §128.
Expenses for frivolous action, bad faith or delay; Punitive damages. §128.5.
Signing of pleadings and motion papers by attorney; Signature as of specified conditions; Sanctions. §128.7.
Restrictions on dissemination of coroner photographs and recordings. §129.
Sealing of autopsy report and evidence relating to examination of deceased child victim; Exceptions; Opposition; Removal. §130.

§128. Powers respecting conduct of proceedings; Contempt

(a) Every court shall have the power to do all of the following:

(1) To preserve and enforce order in its immediate presence.

(2) To enforce order in the proceedings before it, or before a person or persons empowered to conduct a judicial investigation under its authority.

(3) To provide for the orderly conduct of proceedings before it, or its officers.

(4) To compel obedience to its judgments, orders, and process, and to the orders of a judge out of court, in an action or proceeding pending therein.

(5) To control in furtherance of justice, the conduct of its ministerial officers, and of all other persons in any manner connected with a judicial proceeding before it, in every matter pertaining thereto.

(6) To compel the attendance of persons to testify in an action or proceeding pending therein, in the cases and manner provided in this code.

(7) To administer oaths in an action or proceeding pending therein, and in all other cases where it may be necessary in the exercise of its powers and duties.

(8) To amend and control its process and orders so as to make them conform to law and justice. An appellate court shall not reverse or vacate a duly entered judgment upon an agreement or stipulation of the parties unless the court finds both of the following:

(A) There is no reasonable possibility that the interests of nonparties or the public will be adversely affected by the reversal.

(B) The reasons of the parties for requesting reversal outweigh the erosion of public trust that may result from the nullification of a judgment and the risk that the availability of stipulated reversal will reduce the incentive for pretrial settlement.

(b) Notwithstanding Section 1211 or any other law, if an order of contempt is made affecting an attorney, his or her agent, investigator, or any person acting under the attorney's direction, in the preparation and conduct of any action or proceeding, the execution of any sentence shall be stayed pending the filing within three judicial days of a petition for extraordinary relief testing the lawfulness of the court's order, the violation of which is the basis of the contempt except for the conduct as may be proscribed by subdivision (b) of Section 6068 of the Business and Professions Code, relating to an attorney's duty to maintain respect due to the courts and judicial officers.

(c) Notwithstanding Section 1211 or any other law, if an order of contempt is made affecting a public safety employee acting within the scope of employment for reason of the employee's failure to comply with a duly issued subpoena or subpoena duces tecum, the execution of any sentence shall be stayed pending the filing within three judicial days of a petition for extraordinary relief testing the lawfulness of the court's order, a violation of which is the basis for the contempt.

As used in this subdivision, "public safety employee" includes any peace officer, firefighter, paramedic, or any other employee of a public law enforcement agency whose duty is either to maintain official records or to analyze or present evidence for investigative or prosecutorial purposes.

(d) Notwithstanding Section 1211 or any other law, if an order of contempt is made affecting the victim of a sexual assault, where the contempt consists of refusing to testify concerning that sexual assault, the execution of any sentence shall be stayed pending the filing within three judicial days of a petition for extraordinary relief testing the lawfulness of the court's order, a violation of which is the basis for the contempt.

As used in this subdivision, "sexual assault" means any act made punishable by Section 261, 262, 264.1, 285, 286, 287, 288, or 289 of, or former Section 288a of, the Penal Code.

(e) Notwithstanding Section 1211 or any other law, if an order of contempt is made affecting the victim of domestic violence, where the contempt consists of refusing to testify concerning that domestic violence, the execution of any sentence shall be stayed pending the filing within three judicial days of a petition for extraordinary relief testing the lawfulness of the court's order, a violation of which is the basis for the contempt.

As used in this subdivision, the term "domestic violence" means "domestic violence" as defined in Section 6211 of the Family Code.

(f) Notwithstanding Section 1211 or any other provision of law, no order of contempt shall be made affecting a county government or any member of its governing body acting pursuant to its constitutional or statutory authority unless the court finds, based on a review of evidence presented at a hearing conducted for this purpose, that either of the following conditions exist:

(1) That the county has the resources necessary to comply with the order of the court.

(2) That the county has the authority, without recourse to voter approval or without incurring additional indebtedness, to generate the additional resources necessary to comply with the order of the court, that compliance with the order of the court will not expose the county, any member of its governing body, or any other county officer to liability for failure to perform other constitutional or statutory duties, and that compliance with the order of the court will not deprive the county of resources necessary for its reasonable support and maintenance. **Leg.H.** Added Stats 1987 ch 3 §2, effective March 11, 1987, operative March 11, 1989. Amended Stats 1991 ch 866 §1 (AB 363); Stats 1992 ch 163 §13 (AB 2641), operative January 1, 1994, ch 697 §2 (SB 1559) (ch 697 prevails); Stats 1993 ch 219 §63.3 (AB 1500); Stats 1999 ch 508 §1 (AB 1676); Stats 2018 ch 423 §7 (SB 1494), effective January 1, 2019.

Prior Law: Former CCP §128, similar to the present section, was enacted 1872, repealed and reenacted Code Amdts 1880 ch 35 §1, amended Stats 1987 ch 3 §1, effective March 11, 1987, and repealed Stats 1987 ch 3 §3, effective March 11, 1987, operative March 11, 1989.

§128.5. Expenses for frivolous action, bad faith or delay; Punitive damages

(a) A trial court may order a party, the party's attorney, or both, to pay the reasonable expenses, including attorney's fees, incurred by another party as a result of actions or tactics, made in bad faith, that are frivolous or solely intended to cause unnecessary delay. This section also applies to judicial arbitration proceedings under Chapter 2.5 (commencing with Section 1141.10) of Title 3 of Part 3.

(b) For purposes of this section:

(1) "Actions or tactics" include, but are not limited to, the making or opposing of motions or the filing and service of a complaint, cross-complaint, answer, or other responsive pleading. The mere filing of a complaint without service thereof on an opposing party does not constitute "actions or tactics" for purposes of this section.

(2) "Frivolous" means totally and completely without merit or for the sole purpose of harassing an opposing party.

(c) Expenses pursuant to this section shall not be imposed except on notice contained in a party's moving or responding papers or, on the court's own motion, after notice and opportunity to be heard. An order imposing expenses shall be in writing and shall recite in detail the action or tactic or circumstances justifying the order.

(d) In addition to any award pursuant to this section for an action or tactic described in subdivision (a), the court may assess punitive damages against the plaintiff on a determination by the court that the plaintiff's action was an action maintained by a person convicted of a felony against the person's victim, or the victim's heirs, relatives, estate, or personal representative, for injuries arising from the acts for which the person was convicted of a felony, and that the plaintiff is guilty of fraud, oppression, or malice in maintaining the action.

(e) This section shall not apply to disclosures and discovery requests, responses, objections, and motions.

(f) Sanctions ordered pursuant to this section shall be ordered pursuant to the following conditions and procedures:

(1) If, after notice and a reasonable opportunity to respond, the court issues an order pursuant to subdivision (a), the court may, subject to the conditions stated below, impose an appropriate sanction upon the party, the party's attorneys, or both, for an action or tactic described in subdivision (a). In determining what sanctions, if any, should be ordered, the court shall consider whether a party seeking sanctions has exercised due diligence.

(A) A motion for sanctions under this section shall be made separately from other motions or requests and shall describe the specific alleged action or tactic, made in bad faith, that is frivolous or solely intended to cause unnecessary delay.

(B) If the alleged action or tactic is the making or opposing of a written motion or the filing and service of a complaint, cross-complaint, answer, or other responsive pleading that can be withdrawn or appropriately corrected, a notice of motion shall be served as provided in Section 1010, but shall not be filed with or presented to the court, unless 21 days after service of the motion or any other period as the court may prescribe, the challenged action or tactic is not withdrawn or appropriately corrected.

(C) If warranted, the court may award to the party prevailing on the motion the reasonable expenses and attorney's fees incurred in presenting or opposing the motion. Absent exceptional circumstances, a law firm shall be held jointly responsible for violations committed by its partners, associates, and employees.

(D) If the alleged action or tactic is the making or opposing of a written motion or the filing and service of a complaint, cross-complaint, answer, or other responsive pleading that can be withdrawn or appropriately corrected, the court on its own motion may enter an order describing the specific action or tactic, made in bad faith, that is frivolous or solely intended to cause unnecessary delay, and direct an attorney, law firm, or party to show cause why it has made an action or tactic as defined in subdivision (b), unless, within 21 days of service of the order to show cause, the challenged action or tactic is withdrawn or appropriately corrected.

(2) An order for sanctions pursuant to this section shall be limited to what is sufficient to deter repetition of the action or tactic or comparable action or tactic by others similarly situated. Subject to the limitations in subparagraphs (A) and (B), the sanction may consist of, or include, directives of a nonmonetary nature, an order to pay a penalty into court, or, if imposed on motion and warranted for effective deterrence, an order directing payment to the movant of some or all of the reasonable attorney's fees and other expenses incurred as a direct result of the action or tactic described in subdivision (a).

(A) Monetary sanctions may not be awarded against a represented party for a violation of presenting a claim, defense, and other legal contentions that are warranted by existing law or by a nonfrivolous argument for the extension, modification, or reversal of existing law or the establishment of new law.

(B) Monetary sanctions may not be awarded on the court's motion unless the court issues its order to show cause before a voluntary dismissal or settlement of the claims made by or against the party that is, or whose attorneys are, to be sanctioned.

(g) A motion for sanctions brought by a party or a party's attorney primarily for an improper purpose, such as to harass or to cause unnecessary delay or needless increase in the cost of litigation, shall itself be subject to a motion for sanctions. It is the intent of the Legislature that courts shall vigorously use its sanction authority to deter the improper actions or tactics or comparable actions or tactics of others similarly situated.

(h) The liability imposed by this section is in addition to any other liability imposed by law for acts or omissions within the purview of this section.

(i) This section applies to actions or tactics that were part of a civil case filed on or after January 1, 2015. **Leg.H.** Added Stats 1981 ch 762 §1. Amended Stats 1984 ch 355 §1 Stats 1985 ch 296 §1; Stats 1990 ch 887 §1 (SB 2766); Stats 1994 ch 1062 §1 (AB 3594); Stats 2014 ch 425 §1 (AB 2494), effective January 1, 2015, repealed January 1, 2018; Stats 2017 ch 169 §1 (AB 984), effective August 7, 2017.

1990 Note: It is the intent of the Legislature, in adding the new subdivision (d) to Section 128.5 of the Code of Civil Procedure, and in giving judges the capacity to assess punitive damages against a plaintiff, as set out in subdivision (d), that the court will screen these cases carefully in order to ensure that the suit was not filed for a vexatious, fraudulent, malicious, or oppressive purpose. Stats 1990 ch 887 §2.

Former Sections: Former CCP §128.5 was enacted 2014 and repealed 2017 ch 169 (AB 984) §2, effective August 7, 2017.

Prior Law: Former Cal CCP §128.5, similar to the present section, was added Stats 2014 ch 425 §2 (AB 2494), effective January 1, 2015, operative January 1, 2018, and repealed Stats 2016 ch 169 § 2 (AB 984), effective August 7, 2017.

§128.6. [Section repealed 2011]

Leg.H. Added Stats 1994 ch 1062 §2 (AB 3594), operative January 1, 1999. Amended Stats 1998 ch 121 §1 (SB 1511), operative January 1, 2003. Repealed Stats 2010 ch 328 §31 (SB 1330), effective January 1, 2011. The repealed section related to payment of expenses for frivolous action, bad faith, or delay, and punitive damages.

§128.7. Signing of pleadings and motion papers by attorney; Signature as of specified conditions; Sanctions

(a) Every pleading, petition, written notice of motion, or other similar paper shall be signed by at least one attorney of record in the attorney's individual name, or, if the party is not represented by an attorney, shall be signed by the party. Each paper shall state the signer's address and telephone number, if any. Except when otherwise provided by law, pleadings need not be verified or accompanied by affidavit. An unsigned paper shall be stricken unless omission of the signature is corrected promptly after being called to the attention of the attorney or party.

(b) By presenting to the court, whether by signing, filing, submitting, or later advocating, a pleading, petition, written notice of motion, or other similar paper, an attorney or unrepresented party is certifying that to the best of the person's knowledge, information, and belief, formed after an inquiry reasonable under the circumstances, all of the following conditions are met:

(1) It is not being presented primarily for an improper purpose, such as to harass or to cause unnecessary delay or needless increase in the cost of litigation.

(2) The claims, defenses, and other legal contentions therein are warranted by existing law or by a nonfrivolous argument for the extension, modification, or reversal of existing law or the establishment of new law.

(3) The allegations and other factual contentions have evidentiary support or, if specifically so identified, are likely to have evidentiary support after a reasonable opportunity for further investigation or discovery.

(4) The denials of factual contentions are warranted on the evidence or, if specifically so identified, are reasonably based on a lack of information or belief.

(c) If, after notice and a reasonable opportunity to respond, the court determines that subdivision (b) has been violated, the court may, subject to the conditions stated below, impose an appropriate sanction upon the attorneys, law firms, or parties that have violated subdivision (b) or are responsible for the violation. In determining what sanctions, if any, should be ordered, the court shall consider whether a party seeking sanctions has exercised due diligence.

(1) A motion for sanctions under this section shall be made separately from other motions or requests and shall describe the specific conduct alleged to violate subdivision (b). Notice of motion shall be served as provided in Section 1010, but shall not be filed with or presented to the court unless, within 21 days after service of the motion, or any other period as the court may prescribe, the challenged paper, claim, defense, contention, allegation, or denial is not withdrawn or appropriately corrected. If warranted, the court may award to the party prevailing on the motion the reasonable expenses and attorney's fees incurred in presenting or opposing the motion. Absent exceptional circumstances, a law firm shall be held jointly responsible for violations committed by its partners, associates, and employees.

(2) On its own motion, the court may enter an order describing the specific conduct that appears to violate subdivision (b) and directing an attorney, law firm, or party to show cause why it has not violated subdivision (b), unless, within 21 days of service of the order to show cause, the challenged paper, claim, defense, contention, allegation, or denial is withdrawn or appropriately corrected.

(d) A sanction imposed for violation of subdivision (b) shall be limited to what is sufficient to deter repetition of this conduct or comparable conduct by others similarly situated. Subject to the limitations in paragraphs (1) and (2), the sanction may consist of, or include, directives of a nonmonetary nature, an order to pay a penalty into court, or, if imposed on motion and warranted for effective deterrence, an order directing payment to the movant of some or all of the reasonable attorney's fees and other expenses incurred as a direct result of the violation.

(1) Monetary sanctions may not be awarded against a represented party for a violation of paragraph (2) of subdivision (b).

(2) Monetary sanctions may not be awarded on the court's motion unless the court issues its order to show cause before a voluntary dismissal or settlement of the claims made by or against the party that is, or whose attorneys are, to be sanctioned.

(e) When imposing sanctions, the court shall describe the conduct determined to constitute a violation of this section and explain the basis for the sanction imposed.

(f) In addition to any award pursuant to this section for conduct described in subdivision (b), the court may assess punitive damages against the plaintiff upon a determination by the court that the plaintiff's action was an action maintained by a person convicted of a felony against the person's victim, or the victim's heirs, relatives, estate, or personal representative, for injuries arising from the acts for which the person was convicted of a felony, and that the plaintiff is guilty of fraud, oppression, or malice in maintaining the action.

(g) This section shall not apply to disclosures and discovery requests, responses, objections, and motions.

(h) A motion for sanctions brought by a party or a party's attorney primarily for an improper purpose, such as to harass or to cause unnecessary delay or needless increase in the cost of litigation, shall itself be subject to a motion for sanctions. It is the intent of the Legislature that courts shall vigorously use its sanctions authority to deter that improper conduct or comparable conduct by others similarly situated.

(i) This section shall apply to a complaint or petition filed on or after January 1, 1995, and any other pleading, written notice of motion, or other similar paper filed in that matter. **Leg.H.** Added Stats 1994 ch 1062 §3 (AB 3594), operative until January 1, 1999. Amended Stats 1998 ch 121 §2 (SB 1511), operative until January 1, 2003; Stats 2002 ch 491 §1 (SB 2009); Stats 2005 ch 706 §9 (AB 1742), effective January 1, 2006.

§129. Restrictions on dissemination of coroner photographs and recordings

(a) Notwithstanding any other law, a copy, reproduction, or facsimile of any kind of a photograph, negative, or print, including instant photographs and video recordings, of the body, or any portion of the body, of a deceased person, taken by or for the coroner at the scene of death or in the course of a post mortem examination or autopsy, shall not be made or disseminated except as follows:

(1) For use in a criminal action or proceeding in this state that relates to the death of that person.

(2) As a court of this state permits, by order after good cause has been shown and after written notification of the request for the court order has been served, at least five days before the order is made, upon the district attorney of the county in which the post mortem examination or autopsy has been made or caused to be made.

(3) For use or potential use in a civil action or proceeding in this state that relates to the death of that person, if either of the following applies:

(A) The coroner receives written authorization from a legal heir [1], **representative, or family member** of that person. **The written authorization may be provided** before the action is filed or while the action is pending. To verify the identity of the legal heir [2], **representative, or family member**, all of the following shall be provided to the coroner:

(i) A declaration under penalty of perjury that the individual is a legal heir [3], **representative, or family member** of the deceased person.

(ii) A valid form of identification.

(iii) A certified death certificate.

(B) A subpoena is issued by a party who is a legal heir or representative of the deceased person in a pending civil action.

(b) This section shall not apply to the making or dissemination of a copy, reproduction, or facsimile for use in the field of forensic pathology, in medical or scientific education or research, or by a coroner or any law enforcement agency in the United States for investigative purposes, including identification and identification confirmation.

(c) This section shall apply to a copy, reproduction, or facsimile, and to a photograph, negative, or print, regardless of when it was made.

(d) A coroner is not personally liable for monetary damages in a civil action for any act or omission in compliance with this section.

(e) For the purposes of this section, "family member" means a parent, sibling, or child of the deceased. Leg.H. Added Stats 1968 1st Ex Sess ch 6 §1, effective September 25, 1968. Amended Stats 1985 ch 304 §1; Stats 2009 ch 88 §16 (AB 176), effective January 1, 2010; Stats 2013 ch 53 §1 (AB 957), effective January 1, 2014; Stats 2016 ch 467 §1 (AB 2427), effective January 1, 2017; Stats 2024 ch 654 §2 (SB 989), effective January 1, 2025.

§129. 2024 Deletes. [1] or representative [2] or representative [3] or representative

Prior Law: Former CCP §129, similar to Gov C §§68070, 68071, was enacted 1872, repealed and reenacted by Code Amdts 1880 ch 35 §1, amended by Stats 1913 ch 85 §1, Stats 1933 ch 743 §32, Stats 1949 ch 1471 §1, and repealed by Stats 1953 ch 206 §7.

§130. Sealing of autopsy report and evidence relating to examination of deceased child victim; Exceptions; Opposition; Removal

(a) Subject to the provisions of this section, when a child who is under 18 years of age is killed as a result of a criminal act and a person has been convicted and sentenced for the commission of that criminal act, or a person has been found to have committed that offense by the juvenile court and adjudged a ward of the juvenile court, upon the request of a qualifying family member of the deceased child, the autopsy report and evidence associated with the examination of the victim in the possession of a public agency, as defined in Section 7920.525 of the Government Code, shall be sealed and not disclosed, except that an autopsy report and evidence associated with the examination of the victim that has been sealed pursuant to this section may be disclosed, as follows:

(1) To law enforcement, prosecutorial agencies and experts hired by those agencies, public social service agencies, child death review teams, or the hospital that treated the child immediately prior to death, to be used solely for investigative, prosecutorial, or review purposes, and may not be disseminated further.

(2) To the defendant and the defense team in the course of criminal proceedings or related habeas proceedings, to be used solely for investigative, criminal defense, and review purposes, including review for the purpose of initiating any criminal proceeding or related habeas proceeding, and may not be disseminated further. The "defense team" includes, but is not limited to, all of the following: attorneys, investigators, experts, paralegals, support staff, interns, students, and state and privately funded legal assistance projects hired or consulted for the purposes of investigation, defense, appeal, or writ of habeas corpus on behalf of the person accused of killing the deceased child victim.

(3) To civil litigants in a cause of action related to the victim's death with a court order upon a showing of good cause and proper notice under Section 129, to be used solely to pursue the cause of action, and may not be disseminated further.

(b) Nothing in this section shall prohibit the use of autopsy reports and evidence in relation to court proceedings.

(c) Nothing in this section shall abrogate the rights of victims, their authorized representatives, or insurance carriers to request the release of information pursuant to Article 1 (commencing with Section 7923.600) of Chapter 1 of Part 5 of Division 10 of Title 1 of the Government Code. However, if a seal has been requested, an insurance carrier receiving items pursuant to a request under that article is prohibited from disclosing the requested items except as necessary in the normal course of business. An insurance carrier shall not, under any circumstances, disclose to the general public items received pursuant to Article 1 (commencing with Section 7923.600) of Chapter 1 of Part 5 of Division 10 of Title 1 of the Government Code.

(d) This section may not be invoked by a qualifying family member who has been charged with or convicted of any act in furtherance of the victim's death. Upon the filing of those charges against a qualifying family member, any seal maintained at the request of that qualifying family member under this section shall be removed.

(e) A coroner or medical examiner shall not be liable for damages in a civil action for any reasonable act or omission taken in good faith in compliance with this section.

(f) If sealing of the autopsy report has been requested by a qualifying family member and another qualifying family member opposes sealing, the opposing party may request a hearing in the superior court in the county with jurisdiction over the crime leading to the child's death for a determination of whether the sealing should be maintained. The opposing party shall notify all other qualifying family members, the medical examiner's office that conducted the autopsy, and the district attorney's office with jurisdiction over the crime at least 10 court days in advance of the hearing. At the hearing, the court shall consider the interests of all qualifying family members, the protection of the memory of the deceased child, any evidence that the qualifying family member requesting the seal was involved in the crime that resulted in the death of the child, the public interest in scrutiny of the autopsy report or the performance of the medical examiner, any impact that unsealing would have on pending investigations or pending litigation, and any other relevant factors. Official information in the possession of a public agency necessary to the determination of the hearing shall be received in camera upon a proper showing. In its discretion, the court may, to the extent allowable by law and with good cause shown, restrict the dissemination of an autopsy report or evidence associated with the examination of a victim. This section shall not apply if a public agency has independently determined that the autopsy report may not be disclosed pursuant to Article 1 (commencing with Section 7923.600) of Chapter 1 of Part 5 of Division 10 of Title 1 of the Government Code because it is an investigative file. In that instance, nothing in this section shall preclude the application of Part 5 (commencing with Section 7923.000) of Division 10 of Title 1 of the Government Code.

(g) If a seal has been maintained pursuant to this section, a qualifying family member, or a biological or adoptive aunt, uncle, sibling, first cousin, child, or grandparent of the deceased child may request that the seal be removed. The request to remove the seal shall be adjudicated pursuant to subdivision (f), with the party requesting the removal of the seal being the opposing party.

(h) Nothing in this section shall limit the public access to information contained in the death certificate including: name, age, gender, race, date, time and location of death, the name of a physician reporting a death in a hospital, the name of the certifying pathologist, date of certification, burial information, and cause of death.

(i) When a medical examiner declines a request to provide a copy of an autopsy report that has been sealed pursuant to this section, the examiner shall cite this section as the reason for declining to provide a copy of the report.

(j) For purposes of this section:

(1) A "child who is under 18 years of age" does not include any child who comes within either of the following descriptions:

(A) The child was a dependent child of the juvenile court pursuant to Section 300 of the Welfare and Institutions Code at the time of the child's death, or, pursuant to subdivision (b) of Section 10850.4 of the Welfare and Institutions Code, abuse or neglect is determined to have led to the child's death.

(B) The child was residing in a state or county juvenile facility, or a private facility under contract with the state or county for the placement of juveniles, as a ward of the juvenile court pursuant to Section 602 of the Welfare and Institutions Code at the time of the child's death.

(2) "Evidence associated with the examination of a victim" means any object, writing, diagram, recording, computer file, photograph, video, DVD, CD, film, digital device, or other item that was collected during, or serves to document, the autopsy of a deceased child.

(3) "Qualifying family member" means the biological or adoptive parent, spouse, or legal guardian.

(k) Nothing in this section shall limit the discovery provisions set forth in Chapter 10 (commencing with Section 1054) of Title 6 of the Penal Code.

(*l*) Nothing in this section shall be construed to limit the authority of the court to seal records or restrict the dissemination of an autopsy report or evidence associated with the examination of a victim under case law, other statutory law, or the rules of court.

(m) The provisions of this section are severable. If any provision of this section or its application is held invalid, that invalidity shall not affect other provisions or applications that can be given effect without the invalid provision or application. **Leg.H.** Added Stats 2010 ch 302 §3 (SB 5), effective September 27, 2010. Amended Stats 2021 ch 615 §55 (AB 474), effective January 1, 2022.

Prior Law: Former CCP §130, relating to effective date of court rules, was added Stats 1872; repealed and reenacted Code Amdts 1880 ch 35 §1 pp 21, 39; amended Stats 1907 ch 356 §1 p 680; Stats 1949 ch 1514 §1 p 2697; and repealed Stats 1953 ch 206 §7 p 1341.

2010 Note: This act shall be known and may be cited as the Deceased Child Victims' Protection and Privacy Act. Stats 2010 ch 302 (SB 5) §1.

§131. [Section repealed 1961]

Leg.H. Added Stats 1903 ch 35 §1. Amended Stats 1903 ch 579 §1; Stats 1931 ch 758 §1; Stats 1939 ch 1093 §1. Repealed Stats 1961 ch 1616 §7. The repealed section related to the probation committee.

§131.1. [Section repealed 1961]

Leg.H. Added Stats 1939 ch 1093 §2. Repealed Stats 1961 ch 1616 §8. The repealed section related to the examination of societies and others.

§131.2. [Section repealed 1963]

Leg.H. Added Stats 1939 ch 1093 §3. Amended Stats 1961 ch 1616 §9. Repealed Stats 1963 ch 1147 §1. The repealed section related to probation officers.

§131.3. [Section repealed 2002]

Leg.H. Added Stats 1939 ch 1093 §4. Amended Stats 1951 ch 1737 §26, operative January 1, 1952; Stats 1961 ch 2043 §1. Repealed Stats 2001 ch

473 §1 (SB 485). The repealed section related to duties of probation officers.

§131.4. [Section repealed 2002]

Leg.H. Added Stats 1939 ch 1093 §5 p 3024. Amended Stats 2000 ch 135 §14 (AB 2539). Repealed Stats 2001 ch 473 §2 (SB 485). The repealed section related to performance of duty by deputy.

§131.5. [Section repealed 2002]

Leg.H. Added Stats 1969 ch 522 §1. Repealed Stats 2001 ch 473 §3 (SB 485). The repealed section related to availability of probation report before pronouncing judgment.

Prior Law: Former CCP §131.5, relating to intent of preceding sections, was added Stats 1939 ch 1093 §6, amended Stats 1941 ch 491 §1, Stats 1961 ch 1616 §10, and repealed Stats 1963 ch 1147 §2.

§131.6. [Section repealed 2002]

Leg.H. Added Stats 1939 ch 1093 §7. Repealed Stats 2001 ch 473 §4 (SB 485). The repealed section related to expenses of probation officers and deputies.

§131.7. [Section repealed 2002]

Leg.H. Added Stats 1979 ch 1174 §1. Amended Stats 1981 ch 1142 §1. Repealed Stats 2001 ch 473 §5 (SB 485). The repealed section related to financial resources.

ARTICLE 3
Judicial Holidays

Days on which court may be held and judicial business transacted. §133.
Transaction of judicial business on judicial holidays. §134.
Designation of judicial holidays. §135.
Appointed or adjourned date falling on judicial holiday. §136.

§133. Days on which court may be held and judicial business transacted

Courts of justice may be held and judicial business transacted on any day, except as provided in this article. **Leg.H.** Added Stats 1985 ch 1450 §2, operative January 1, 1989.

Prior Law: Former CCP §133, similar to the present section, was enacted 1872, repealed and reenacted Code Amdts 1880 ch 35 §1, and repealed Stats 1985 ch 1450 §1, operative January 1, 1989.

§134. Transaction of judicial business on judicial holidays

(a) Except as provided in subdivision (c), the courts shall be closed for the transaction of judicial business on judicial holidays for all but the following purposes:

(1) To give, upon their request, instructions to a jury when deliberating on their verdict.

(2) To receive a verdict or discharge a jury.

(3) For the conduct of arraignments and the exercise of the powers of a magistrate in a criminal action, or in a proceeding of a criminal nature.

(4) For the conduct of Saturday small claims court sessions pursuant to the Small Claims Act set forth in Chapter 5.5 (commencing with Section 116.110).

(b) Injunctions and writs of prohibition may be issued and served on any day.

(c) In any superior court, one or more departments of the court may remain open and in session for the transaction of any business that may come before the department in the exercise of the civil or criminal jurisdiction of the court, or both, on a judicial holiday or at any hours of the day or night, or both, as the judges of the court prescribe.

(d) The fact that a court is open on a judicial holiday shall not make that day a nonholiday for purposes of computing the time required for the conduct of any proceeding nor for the performance of any act. Any paper lodged with the court at a time when the court is open pursuant to subdivision (c), shall be filed by the court on the next day that is not a judicial holiday, if the document meets appropriate criteria for filing. **Leg.H.** Added Stats 1985 ch 1450 §2, operative January 1, 1989. Amended Stats 1986 ch 1398 §2, operative January 1, 1989; Stats 1990 ch 1305 §4 (SB 2627); Stats 1992 ch 460 §2 (SB 1805); Stats 1998 ch 931 §45 (SB 2139), effective September 28, 1998; Stats 2002 ch 784 §33 (SB 1316).

Prior Law: Former CCP §134, similar to the present section, was enacted 1872, repealed and reenacted Code Amdts 1880 ch 35 §1, amended Stats 1889 ch 43 §1, Stats 1893 ch 159 §2, Stats 1897 ch 19 §2, Stats 1907 ch 358 §1, Stats 1931 ch 973 §1, Stats 1933 ch 743 §34, Stats 1951 ch 1737 §27, operative January 1, 1952, Stats 1957 ch 43 §3, Stats 1963 ch 1922 §1, Stats 1967 ch 17 §9, Stats 1977 ch 1257 §5, effective October 3, 1977, Stats 1982 ch 838 §3, effective September 10, 1982, and repealed Stats 1985 ch 1450 §1, operative January 1, 1989.

§135. Designation of judicial holidays

Every full day designated as a holiday by Section 6700 of the Government Code, including that Thursday of November declared by the President to be Thanksgiving Day, is a judicial holiday, except the date corresponding with the second new moon following the winter solstice, or the third new moon following the winter solstice should an intercalary month intervene, known as "Lunar New Year," April 24, known as "Genocide Remembrance Day," September 9, known as "Admission Day," the second Monday in October, known as "Columbus Day," and any other day appointed by the President, but not by the Governor, for a public fast, thanksgiving, or holiday. If a judicial holiday falls on a Saturday or a Sunday, the Judicial Council may designate an alternative day for observance of the holiday. Every Saturday and the day after Thanksgiving Day are judicial holidays. Officers and employees of the courts shall observe only the judicial holidays established pursuant to this section. **Leg.H.** Added Stats 1985 ch 1450 §2, operative January 1, 1989. Amended Stats 1986 ch 1398 §3, operative January 1, 1989; Stats 1992 ch 460 §3 (SB 1805); Stats 1994 ch 1011 §3 (SB 1373); Stats 2001 ch 542 §3 (SB 1112); Stats 2015 ch 26 §2 (SB 85), effective June 24, 2015; Stats 2021 ch 283 §1 (AB 855), effective January 1, 2022; Stats 2022 ch 761 §2 (AB 1801), effective January 1, 2023; Stats 2022 ch 792 §1.5 (AB 2596), effective January 1, 2023 (ch 792 prevails).

Prior Law: Former CCP §135, relating to transaction of business on "special holidays" and election days, was enacted 1872, repealed and reenacted by Code Amdts 1880 ch 35 §1, amended Stats 1907 ch 358 §2, Stats 1st Sess 1907 ch 9 §1, Stats 1933 ch 743 §35, Stats 1957 ch 43 §4, Stats 1963 ch 1922 §2, Stats 1982 ch 838 §4, effective September 10, 1982, and repealed Stats 1985 ch 1450 §1, operative January 1, 1989.

§136. Appointed or adjourned date falling on judicial holiday

If a day appointed for the holding or sitting of a court, or to which it is adjourned, falls on a judicial holiday, it shall be deemed appointed for or adjourned to the next day. **Leg.H.** Added Stats 1985 ch 1450 §2, operative January 1, 1989.

ARTICLE 4
Proceedings in Case of Absence of Judge

Adjournment on absence of judge. §139.

§139. Adjournment on absence of judge

If no judge attends on the day appointed for the holding or sitting of a court, or on the day to which it may have been adjourned, within one hour after the time appointed, the sheriff, marshal, or clerk shall adjourn the same until the next day, at 10 o'clock a.m., and if no judge attend on that day, before noon, the sheriff, marshal, or clerk shall adjourn the same until the following day at the same hour; and so on, from day to day unless the judge, by written order, directs it to be adjourned to some day certain, fixed in said order, in which case it shall be so adjourned. **Leg.H.** Enacted 1872. Repealed and re-enacted by Code Amdts 1880 ch 35 §1. Amended Stats 1907 ch 357 §1, Stats 1933 ch 743 §36, Stats 1951 ch 737 §28, operative January 1, 1952; Stats 1996 ch 872 §6 (AB 3472).

§140. [Section repealed 1907]

Leg.H. Enacted 1872. Repealed and re-enacted Code Amdts 1880 ch 35 §1. Repealed Stats 1907 ch 357 §2. See CCP §139.

ARTICLE 5
Provisions Respecting Places of Holding Courts [Repealed]

§§142–144. [Sections repealed 1953]

Leg.H. Enacted 1872. Repealed Stats 1953 ch 206 §7. See Gov C §§68073, 68100, 68115, 69742, 69744.

ARTICLE 6
Seals of Courts

Documents under seal. §153.

§147. [Section repealed 1953]

Leg.H. Enacted 1872. Repealed and re-enacted by Code Amdts 1880 ch 35 §1. Amended Stats 1933 ch 743 §38; Stats 1937 ch 161 §1; Stats 1951 ch 1737 §30, operative January 1, 1952. Repealed Stats 1953 ch 206 §7. See Gov C §68074.

§§148, 149. [Sections repealed 1953]

Leg.H. Enacted 1872. Repealed and re-enacted Code Amdts 1880 ch 35 §1. Repealed Stats 1953 ch 206 §7. See Gov C §§68075, 68076.

§149a. [Section repealed 1953]

Leg.H. Added Stats 1925 ch 443 §1. Amended Stats 1951 ch 1737 §31, operative January 1, 1952. Repealed Stats 1953 ch 206 §7. The repealed section related to seals of municipal courts.

§150. [Section repealed 1953]

Leg.H. Added Code Amdts 1880 ch 35 §1. Amended Stats 1933 ch 743 §39; Stats 1937 ch 161 §2; Stats 1951 ch 1737 §32, operative January 1, 1952. Repealed Stats 1953 ch 206 §7. The repealed section related to seals of justice courts.

Prior Law: Former CCP §150, providing when private seal to be used, was enacted 1872 and omitted by Code Amdts 1880 ch 35 §1 p 21 in amending Part I.

§151. [Section repealed 1953]

Leg.H. Added Code Amdts 1880 ch 35 §1. Amended Stats 1933 ch 743 §40; Stats 1951 ch 1737 §33, operative January 1, 1952. Repealed Stats 1953 ch 206 §7. See Gov C §68079.

Prior Law: Former CCP §151 enacted was 1872 and repealed and reenacted as §152 by Code Amdts 1880 ch 35 §1 pp 21, 40.

§152. [Section repealed 1953]

Leg.H. Enacted 1872 as §151. Repealed and re-enacted as §152 Code Amdts 1880 ch 35 §1. Amended Stats 1933 ch 743 §42; Stats 1951 ch 1737 §34, operative January 1, 1952. Repealed Stats 1953 ch 206 §7. See Gov C §68080.

Prior Law: Former CCP §152 was enacted 1872, amended by Code Amdts 1873–74 ch 383 §12 p 284, and repealed and reenacted as §153 by Code Amdts 1880 ch 35 §1 pp 21, 40.

§153. Documents under seal

Except as otherwise expressly provided by law, the seal of a court need not be affixed to any proceeding therein, or to any document, except to the following:

(a) A writ.

(b) A summons.

(c) A warrant of arrest. **Leg.H.** Enacted 1872 as §152. Amended Code Amdts 1873–74 ch 383 §12. Repealed and re-enacted as §153 Code Amdts 1880 ch 35 §1. Amended Stats 1933 ch 743 §42; Stats 1951 ch 1737 §35, operative January 1, 1952; Stats 1965 ch 299 §18, operative January 1, 1967; Stats 1979 ch 730 §15, operative January 1, 1981; Stats 1988 ch 1199 §2, operative July 1, 1989.

CHAPTER 7
SPECIAL IMMIGRANT JUVENILE FINDINGS

Jurisdiction of superior court to make judicial determinations regarding custody and care of children within federal Immigration and Nationality Act; Order of special immigrant juvenile status. § 155.

§ 155. Jurisdiction of superior court to make judicial determinations regarding custody and care of children within federal Immigration and Nationality Act; Order of special immigrant juvenile status

(a)(1) A superior court has jurisdiction under California law to make judicial determinations regarding the dependency or custody, or both, and care of children within the meaning of the federal Immigration and Nationality Act (8 U.S.C. Sec. 1101 et seq. and 8 C.F.R. Sec. 204.11), which includes, but is not limited to, the juvenile, probate, and family court divisions of the superior court. These courts have jurisdiction to make the judicial determinations necessary to enable a child to petition the United States Citizenship and Immigration Services for classification as a special immigrant juvenile pursuant to Section 1101(a)(27)(J) of Title 8 of the United States Code.

(2) The judicial determinations set forth in paragraph (1) of subdivision (b) may be made for a child up to 21 years of age at any point in a proceeding regardless of the division of the superior court or type of proceeding if the prerequisites of that subdivision are met. A nunc pro tunc entry is permissible and shall not require proof of any clerical or other error, as long as the determinations could have been made as of the nunc pro tunc date.

(b)(1) If an order is requested from the superior court making the necessary determinations regarding special immigrant juvenile status pursuant to Section 1101(a)(27)(J) of Title 8 of the United States Code, and there is evidence to support those determinations, which may consist solely of, but is not limited to, a declaration by the child who is the subject of the petition, the court shall issue the order, which shall include all of the following determinations, each of which shall be supported by reference to the relevant provisions of California law:

(A) The child was either of the following:

(i) Declared a dependent of the court.

(ii) Legally committed to, or placed under the custody of, a state agency or department, or an individual or entity appointed by the court. The court shall indicate the date on which the dependency, commitment, or custody was ordered and the factual basis for making the order.

(B) That reunification of the child with one or both of the child's parents was determined not to be viable because of abuse, neglect, abandonment, or a similar basis pursuant to California law. The court shall indicate the date on which reunification was determined not to be viable, and the factual basis for making the determination.

(C) That it is not in the best interest of the child to be returned to the child's, or the child's parent's, previous country of nationality or country of last habitual residence. The court shall indicate the factual basis for making the determination.

(2) The superior court may make additional determinations pursuant to this section that are supported by evidence only if requested by a party. The asserted, purported, or perceived motivation of the child seeking classification as a special immigrant juvenile shall not be admissible in making the findings under this section. The court shall not include nor reference the asserted, purported, or perceived motivation of the child seeking classification as a special immigrant juvenile in the court's findings under this section.

(3) If a court grants an order that includes the determinations described in paragraph (1), and the person who requested the determinations has submitted a request for expedited processing accompanied by a properly conformed proposed order, the court shall provide the person who requested the determinations with a certified copy of the order within three court days of the date of the hearing at which the determinations were made, or the date the proposed order was submitted, whichever is later.

(c) In any judicial proceedings in response to a request that the superior court make the determinations necessary to support a petition for classification as a special immigrant juvenile, information regarding the child's immigration status that is not otherwise protected by state confidentiality laws shall remain confidential and shall be available for inspection only by the court, the child who is the subject of the proceeding, the parties, the attorneys for the parties, the child's counsel, and the child's guardian.

(d) In any judicial proceedings in response to a request that the superior court make the findings necessary to support a petition for classification as a special immigrant juvenile, records of the proceedings that are not otherwise protected by state confidentiality laws may be sealed using the procedure set forth in California Rules of Court 2.550 and 2.551.

(e) This section shall be operative on January 1, 2025. **Leg.H.** Added Stats 2023 ch 851 §2 (AB 1650), effective January 1, 2024, operative January 1, 2025. Amended Stats 2024 ch 955 §1 (AB 2224), effective January 1, 2025, operative January 1, 2025.

Prior Law Former CCP §155, similar to the present section was added Stats 2014 ch 685 §1 (SB 873), effective September 27, 2014, amended Stats 2016 ch 25 §1 (AB 1603), effective June 27, 2016, Stats 2023 ch 851 §1 (AB 1650), effective January 1, 2024, and repealed January 1, 2025, by its own provision.

CHAPTER 8
OF JUSTICES' COURTS [RENUMBERED]

CHAPTER 9
OF POLICE COURTS [RENUMBERED]

CHAPTER 10
GENERAL PROVISIONS RESPECTING COURTS OF JUSTICE [RENUMBERED]

TITLE 2
JUDICIAL OFFICERS

Chapter 2. Powers of Judges at Chambers.
Chapter 3. Disqualifications of Judges.
Chapter 4. Incidental Powers and Duties of Judicial Officers.
Chapter 5. Miscellaneous Provisions Respecting Courts of Justice.

CHAPTER 1
JUDICIAL OFFICERS IN GENERAL
[REPEALED]

§156. [Section repealed 1953]

Leg.H. Enacted 1872. Repealed and re-enacted Code Amdts 1880 ch 35 §1. Amended Stats 1933 ch 743 §43. Repealed Stats 1953 ch 206 §7. The repealed section related to qualifications for Supreme Court justices.

§§157, 158. [Sections repealed 1953]

Leg.H. Enacted 1872. Repealed and re-enacted Code Amdts 1880 ch 35 §1. Amended Stats 1931 ch 1000 §1; Stats 1933 ch 743 §44. Repealed Stats 1953 ch 206 §7. See Gov C §69502.

§159. [Section repealed 1952]

Leg.H. Added Code Amdts 1880 ch 35 §1. Amended Stats 1933 ch 743 §45; Stats 1941 ch 1157 §1. Repealed Stats 1949 ch 1513 §1, effective November 7, 1950, operative January 1, 1952. See Gov C §71140.

Prior Law: Former CCP §159, construing residence in San Francisco, was enacted 1872 and omitted by Code Amdts 1880 ch 35 §1 in amending Part I.

§159a. [Section repealed 1952]

Leg.H. Added Stats 1933 ch 743 §46. Repealed Stats 1949 ch 1513 §2, effective November 7, 1950, operative January 1, 1952. The repealed section related to qualifications for justices of the justice of the peace courts.

§160. [Section repealed 1923]

Leg.H. Enacted 1872. Amended Code Amdts 1875–76 ch 165 §1. Repealed and re-enacted Code Amdts 1880 ch 35 §1. Amended Stats 1887 ch 129 §1. Repealed by Stats 1923 ch 743 §61. The repealed section related to appointment of a superior court judge to hold court in another county.

§161. [Section repealed 1933]

Leg.H. Added Code Amdts 1880 ch 35 §1. Repealed Stats 1933 ch 743 §61. See Const Art VI §17.

Prior Law: Former CCP §161, providing that county and probate judges could hold court in another county, was enacted 1872, amended by Code Amdts 1873–74 ch 383 p 284, and omitted by Code Amdts 1880 ch 35 §1 p 21 in amending Part I.

§162. [Section repealed 1873]

Leg.H. Enacted 1872. Repealed Code Amdts 1873–74 ch 383 §14. The repealed section related to the designation of a probate judge to hold court in another county.

CHAPTER 2
POWERS OF JUDGES AT CHAMBERS

Justices of Supreme Court; Justices of courts of appeal. §165.
Judges of superior courts. §166.
Request for interlocutory order that appellate resolution of controlling question of law would advance litigation. §166.1.
Judge's performance of clerk's act. §167.

§165. Justices of Supreme Court; Justices of courts of appeal

The justices of the Supreme Court and of the courts of appeal, or any of them, may, at chambers, grant all orders and writs which are usually granted in the first instance upon an ex parte application, except writs of mandamus, certiorari, and prohibition; and may, in their discretion, hear application to discharge such orders and writs. **Leg.H.** Enacted 1872. Repealed and re-enacted Code Amdts 1880 ch 35 §1. Amended Stats 1935 ch 74 §3; Stats 1967 ch 17 §10.

§166. Judges of superior courts

(a) The judges of the superior courts may, in chambers:

(1) Grant all orders and writs that are usually granted in the first instance upon an ex parte application, and hear and dispose of those orders and writs, appoint referees, require and receive inventories and accounts to be filed, order notice of settlement of supplemental accounts, suspend the powers of personal representatives, guardians, or conservators in the cases allowed by law, appoint special administrators, grant letters of temporary guardianship or conservatorship, approve or reject claims, and direct the issuance from the court of all writs and process necessary in the exercise of their powers in matters of probate.

(2) Hear and determine all motions made pursuant to Section 657 or 663.

(3) Hear and determine all uncontested actions, proceedings, demurrers, motions, petitions, applications, and other matters pending before the court other than actions for dissolution of marriage, for legal separation, or for a judgment of nullity of the marriage, and except also applications for confirmation of sale of real property in probate proceedings.

(4) Hear and determine motions to tax costs of enforcing a judgment.

(5) Approve bonds and undertakings.

(b) A judge may, out of court, anywhere in the state, exercise all the powers and perform all the functions and duties conferred upon a judge as contradistinguished from the court, or that a judge may exercise or perform in chambers. **Leg.H.** Enacted 1872. Repealed and re-enacted Code Amdts 1880 ch 35 §1. Amended Stats 1929 ch 487 §1; Stats 1933 ch 743 §47; Stats 1951 ch 1737 §36, operative January 1, 1952; Stats 1979 ch 730 §16, operative January 1, 1981; Stats 1982 ch 517 §94 (ch 497 prevails), ch 497 §30, operative July 1, 1983; Stats 1983 ch 18 §6, effective April 21, 1983; Stats 1988 ch 1199 §3, operative July 1, 1989; Stats 1998 ch 931 §46 (SB 2139), effective September 28, 1998; Stats 2002 ch 784 §34 (SB 1316).

§166.1. Request for interlocutory order that appellate resolution of controlling question of law would advance litigation

Upon the written request of any party or his or her counsel, or at the judge's discretion, a judge may indicate in any interlocutory order a belief that there is a controlling question of law as to which there are substantial grounds for difference of opinion, appellate resolution of which may materially advance the conclusion of the litigation. Neither the denial of a request for, nor the objection of another party or counsel to, such a commentary in the interlocutory order, may be grounds for a writ or appeal. **Leg.H.** Added Stats 2002 ch 708 §1 (AB 2865).

§167. Judge's performance of clerk's act

Any act required or permitted to be performed by the clerk of a court may be performed by a judge thereof. **Leg.H.** Added Stats 1969 ch 1610 §1, operative July 1, 1970. Amended Stats 1989 ch 1417 §1.

Prior Law: Former CCP §167, relating to the powers of the judge of the superior court, was added by Stats 1929 ch 491 §1 and repealed by Stats 1922 ch 742 §61.

Former CCP §167, relating to the powers of probate judges at chambers, was enacted 1872 and omitted by Code Amdts 1880 ch 35 §1 p in amending Part I.

CHAPTER 3
DISQUALIFICATIONS OF JUDGES

Duty to decide proceeding. §170.
Grounds for disqualification. §170.1.
Grounds not allowed for disqualification. §170.2.
Procedure. §170.3.
Permissible actions by disqualified judge. §170.4.
Definitions. §170.5.
Motion to disqualify. §170.6.
Effect of motion to disqualify on superior court appellate division judge. §170.7.
No judge of court qualified to hear cause; Judge assigned by Chairman of Judicial Council. §170.8.
Restrictions on gifts and honoraria to judges. §170.9.
[Section renumbered 1880]. §173.

§170. Duty to decide proceeding

A judge has a duty to decide any proceeding in which he or she is not disqualified. **Leg.H.** Added Stats 1984 ch 1555 §2.

Prior Law: Former CCP §170, similar to present CCP §170.1, was enacted 1872, repealed and reenacted Code Amdts 1880 ch 35 §1, amended Stats 1893 ch 189 §1, Stats 1897 ch 190 §1, Stats 1905 ch 370 §1, Stats 1915 ch 362 §1, Stats 1921 ch 153 §1, Stats 1925 ch 15 §1, Stats 1927 ch 744 §1, Stats 1929 ch 556 §1, Stats 1933 ch 743 §48, Stats 1937 ch 136 §1, Stats 1939 ch 1047 §1, Stats 1941 ch 70 §1, Stats 1951 ch 1737 §37, operative January 1, 1952, Stats 1957 ch 1545 §1, Stats 1959 ch 744 §2, Stats 1965 ch 1260 §1, Stats 1969 ch 446 §1, Stats 1971 ch 807 §1, Stats 1975 ch 1240 §2, operative July 1, 1976, Stats 1977 ch 1257 §6, effective October 3, 1977, Stats 1979 ch 730 §17, operative January 1, 1981, Stats 1981 ch 255 §1, Stats 1982 ch 1644 §1, Stats 1984 ch 193 §9, and repealed Stats 1984 ch 1555 §1.

§170a. [Section repealed 1985]

Leg.H. Added Stats 1919 ch 278 §1. Amended Stats 1951 ch 1737 §38, operative January 1, 1952. Repealed Stats 1984 ch 1555 §3. See CCP §170.1.

§170b. [Section repealed 1933]

Leg.H. Added Stats 1931 ch 1069. Repealed Stats 1933 ch 743 §61. The repealed section related to the prohibition against judges of inferior courts sitting in a court of higher jurisdiction.

§170.1. Grounds for disqualification

(a) A judge shall be disqualified if any one or more of the following are true:

(1)(A) The judge has personal knowledge of disputed evidentiary facts concerning the proceeding.

(B) A judge shall be deemed to have personal knowledge within the meaning of this paragraph if the judge, or the spouse of the judge, or a person within the third degree of relationship to either of them, or the spouse of such a person is to the judge's knowledge likely to be a material witness in the proceeding.

(2)(A) The judge served as a lawyer in the proceeding, or in any other proceeding involving the same issues he or she served as a lawyer for a party in the present proceeding or gave advice to a party in the present proceeding upon a matter involved in the action or proceeding.

(B) A judge shall be deemed to have served as a lawyer in the proceeding if within the past two years:

(i) A party to the proceeding, or an officer, director, or trustee of a party, was a client of the judge when the judge was in the private practice of law or a client of a lawyer with whom the judge was associated in the private practice of law.

(ii) A lawyer in the proceeding was associated in the private practice of law with the judge.

(C) A judge who served as a lawyer for, or officer of, a public agency that is a party to the proceeding shall be deemed to have served as a lawyer in the proceeding if he or she personally advised or in any way represented the public agency concerning the factual or legal issues in the proceeding.

(3)(A) The judge has a financial interest in the subject matter in a proceeding or in a party to the proceeding.

(B) A judge shall be deemed to have a financial interest within the meaning of this paragraph if:

(i) A spouse or minor child living in the household has a financial interest.

(ii) The judge or the spouse of the judge is a fiduciary who has a financial interest.

(C) A judge has a duty to make reasonable efforts to inform himself or herself about his or her personal and fiduciary interests and those of his or her spouse and the personal financial interests of children living in the household.

(4) The judge, or the spouse of the judge, or a person within the third degree of relationship to either of them, or the spouse of such a person is a party to the proceeding or an officer, director, or trustee of a party.

(5) A lawyer or a spouse of a lawyer in the proceeding is the spouse, former spouse, child, sibling, or parent of the judge or the judge's spouse or if such a person is associated in the private practice of law with a lawyer in the proceeding.

(6)(A) For any reason:

(i) The judge believes his or her recusal would further the interests of justice.

(ii) The judge believes there is a substantial doubt as to his or her capacity to be impartial.

(iii) A person aware of the facts might reasonably entertain a doubt that the judge would be able to be impartial.

(B) Bias or prejudice toward a lawyer in the proceeding may be grounds for disqualification.

(7) By reason of permanent or temporary physical impairment, the judge is unable to properly perceive the evidence or is unable to properly conduct the proceeding.

(8)(A) The judge has a current arrangement concerning prospective employment or other compensated service as a dispute resolution neutral or is participating in, or, within the last two years has participated in, discussions regarding prospective employment or service as a dispute resolution neutral, or has been engaged in that employment or service, and any of the following applies:

(i) The arrangement is, or the prior employment or discussion was, with a party to the proceeding.

(ii) The matter before the judge includes issues relating to the enforcement of either an agreement to submit a dispute to an alternative dispute resolution process or an award or other final decision by a dispute resolution neutral.

(iii) The judge directs the parties to participate in an alternative dispute resolution process in which the dispute resolution neutral will be an individual or entity with whom the judge has the arrangement, has previously been employed or served, or is discussing or has discussed the employment or service.

(iv) The judge will select a dispute resolution neutral or entity to conduct an alternative dispute resolution process in the matter before the judge, and among those available for selection is an individual or entity with whom the judge has the arrangement, with whom the judge has previously been employed or served, or with whom the judge is discussing or has discussed the employment or service.

(B) For the purposes of this paragraph, all of the following apply:

(i) "Participating in discussions" or "has participated in discussion" means that the judge solicited or otherwise indicated an interest in accepting or negotiating possible employment or service as an alternative dispute resolution neutral, or responded to an unsolicited statement regarding, or an offer of, that employment or service by expressing an interest in that employment or service, making an inquiry regarding the employment or service, or encouraging the person making the statement or offer to provide additional information about that possible employment or service. If a judge's response to an unsolicited statement regarding, a question about, or offer of, prospective employment or other compensated service as a dispute resolution neutral is limited to responding negatively, declining the offer, or declining to discuss that employment or service, that response does not constitute participating in discussions.

(ii) "Party" includes the parent, subsidiary, or other legal affiliate of any entity that is a party and is involved in the transaction, contract, or facts that gave rise to the issues subject to the proceeding.

(iii) "Dispute resolution neutral" means an arbitrator, mediator, temporary judge appointed under Section 21 of Article VI of the California Constitution, referee appointed under Section 638 or 639, special master, neutral evaluator, settlement officer, or settlement facilitator.

(9)(A) The judge has received a contribution in excess of one thousand five hundred dollars ($1500) from a party or lawyer in the proceeding, and either of the following applies:

(i) The contribution was received in support of the judge's last election, if the last election was within the last six years.

(ii) The contribution was received in anticipation of an upcoming election.

(B) Notwithstanding subparagraph (A), the judge shall be disqualified based on a contribution of a lesser amount if subparagraph (A) of paragraph (6) applies.

(C) The judge shall disclose any contribution from a party or lawyer in a matter that is before the court that is required to be reported under subdivision (f) of Section 84211 of the Government Code, even if the amount would not require disqualification under this paragraph. The manner of disclosure shall be the same as that provided in Canon 3E of the Code of Judicial Ethics.

(D) Notwithstanding paragraph (1) of subdivision (b) of Section 170.3, the disqualification required under this paragraph may be waived by the party that did not make the contribution unless there are other circumstances that would prohibit a waiver pursuant to paragraph (2) of subdivision (b) of Section 170.3.

(b) A judge before whom a proceeding was tried or heard shall be disqualified from participating in any appellate review of that proceeding.

(c) At the request of a party or on its own motion an appellate court shall consider whether in the interests of justice it should direct that further proceedings be heard before a trial judge other than the judge whose judgment or order was reviewed by the appellate court. **Leg.H.** Added Stats 1984 ch 1555 §5. Amended Stats 2002 ch 1094 §1 (AB 2504); Stats 2005 ch 332 §1 (AB 1322), effective September 22, 2005; Stats 2010 ch 686 §1 (AB 2487), effective January 1, 2011.

Prior Law: Former CCP §170.1, relating to degree of spousal affinity, was added Stats 1945 ch 960 §1 and repealed Stats 1984 ch 1555 §4.

2005 Note: It is the intent of the Legislature in enacting this act to construe and clarify the meaning and effect of existing law and to reject the interpretation given to the law in *Hartford Casualty Ins. Co. v. Superior Court of Los Angeles* (2004) 125 Cal.App.4th 250.Stats 2005 ch 332 (AB 1322) §2.

§170.2. Grounds not allowed for disqualification

It shall not be grounds for disqualification that the judge:

(a) Is or is not a member of a racial, ethnic, religious, sexual or similar group and the proceeding involves the rights of such a group.

(b) Has in any capacity expressed a view on a legal or factual issue presented in the proceeding, except as provided in paragraph (2) of subdivision (a) of, or subdivision (b) or (c) of, Section 170.1.

(c) Has as a lawyer or public official participated in the drafting of laws or in the effort to pass or defeat laws, the meaning, effect or application of which is in issue in the proceeding unless the judge believes that his or her prior involvement was so well known as to raise a reasonable doubt in the public mind as to his or her capacity to be impartial. **Leg.H.** Added Stats 1984 ch 1555 §6.

§170.3. Procedure

(a)(1) If a judge determines himself or herself to be disqualified, the judge shall notify the presiding judge of the court of his or her recusal and shall not further participate in the proceeding, except as provided in Section 170.4, unless his or her disqualification is waived by the parties as provided in subdivision (b).

(2) If the judge disqualifying himself or herself is the only judge or the presiding judge of the court, the notification shall be sent to the person having authority to assign another judge to replace the disqualified judge.

(b)(1) A judge who determines himself or herself to be disqualified after disclosing the basis for his or her disqualification on the record may ask the parties and their attorneys whether they wish to waive the disqualification, except where the basis for disqualification is as provided in paragraph (2). A waiver of disqualification shall recite the basis for the disqualification, and is effective only when signed by all parties and their attorneys and filed in the record.

(2) There shall be no waiver of disqualification if the basis therefor is either of the following:

(A) The judge has a personal bias or prejudice concerning a party.

(B) The judge served as an attorney in the matter in controversy, or the judge has been a material witness concerning that matter.

(3) The judge shall not seek to induce a waiver and shall avoid any effort to discover which lawyers or parties favored or opposed a waiver of disqualification.

(4) If grounds for disqualification are first learned of or arise after the judge has made one or more rulings in a proceeding, but before the judge has completed judicial action in a proceeding, the judge shall, unless the disqualification be waived, disqualify himself or herself, but in the absence of good cause the rulings he or she has made up to that time shall not be set aside by the judge who replaces the disqualified judge.

(c)(1) If a judge who should disqualify himself or herself refuses or fails to do so, any party may file with the clerk a written verified statement objecting to the hearing or trial before the judge and setting forth the facts constituting the grounds for disqualification of the judge. The statement shall be presented at the earliest practicable opportunity after discovery of the facts constituting the ground for disqualification. Copies of the statement shall be served on each party or his or her attorney who has appeared and shall be personally served on the judge alleged to be disqualified, or on his or her clerk, provided that the judge is present in the courthouse or in chambers.

(2) Without conceding his or her disqualification, a judge whose impartiality has been challenged by the filing of a written statement may request any other judge agreed upon by the parties to sit and act in his or her place.

(3) Within 10 days after the filing or service, whichever is later, the judge may file a consent to disqualification in which case the judge shall notify the presiding judge or the person authorized to appoint a replacement of his or her recusal as provided in subdivision (a), or the judge may file a written verified answer admitting or denying any or all of the allegations contained in the party's statement and setting forth any additional facts material or relevant to the question of disqualification. The clerk shall forthwith transmit a copy of the judge's answer to each party or his or her attorney who has appeared in the action.

(4) A judge who fails to file a consent or answer within the time allowed shall be deemed to have consented to his or her disqualification and the clerk shall notify the presiding judge or person authorized to appoint a replacement of the recusal as provided in subdivision (a).

(5) A judge who refuses to recuse himself or herself shall not pass upon his or her own disqualification or upon the sufficiency in law, fact, or otherwise, of the statement of disqualification filed by a party. In that case, the question of disqualification shall be heard and determined by another judge agreed upon by all the parties who have appeared or, in the event they are unable to agree within five days of notification of the judge's answer, by a judge selected by the chairperson of the Judicial Council, or if the chairperson is unable to act, the vice chairperson. The clerk shall notify the executive officer of the Judicial Council of the need for a selection. The selection shall be made as expeditiously as possible. No challenge pursuant to this subdivision or Section 170.6 may be made against the judge selected to decide the question of disqualification.

(6) The judge deciding the question of disqualification may decide the question on the basis of the statement of disqualification and answer and any written arguments as the judge requests, or the judge may set the matter for hearing as promptly as practicable. If a hearing is ordered, the judge shall permit the parties and the judge alleged to be disqualified to argue the question of disqualification and shall for good cause shown hear evidence on any disputed issue of fact. If the judge deciding the question of disqualification determines that the judge is disqualified, the judge hearing the question shall notify the presiding judge or the person having authority to appoint a replacement of the disqualified judge as provided in subdivision (a).

(d) The determination of the question of the disqualification of a judge is not an appealable order and may be reviewed only by a writ of mandate from the appropriate court of appeal sought only by the parties to the proceeding. The petition for the writ shall be filed and served within 10 days after service of written notice of entry of the court's order determining the question of disqualification. If the notice of entry is served by mail, that time shall be extended as provided in subdivision (a) of Section 1013. **Leg.H.** Added Stats 1984 ch 1555 §7. Amended Stats 1990 ch 910 §1 (SB 2316); Stats 2006 ch 567 §4 (AB 2303), effective January 1, 2007.

§170.4. Permissible actions by disqualified judge

(a) A disqualified judge, notwithstanding his or her disqualification may do any of the following:

(1) Take any action or issue any order necessary to maintain the jurisdiction of the court pending the assignment of a judge not disqualified.

(2) Request any other judge agreed upon by the parties to sit and act in his or her place.

(3) Hear and determine purely default matters.

(4) Issue an order for possession prior to judgment in eminent domain proceedings.

(5) Set proceedings for trial or hearing.

(6) Conduct settlement conferences.

(b) Notwithstanding paragraph (5) of subdivision (c) of Section 170.3, if a statement of disqualification is untimely filed or if on its face it discloses no legal grounds for disqualification, the trial judge against whom it was filed may order it stricken.

(c)(1) If a statement of disqualification is filed after a trial or hearing has commenced by the start of voir dire, by the swearing of the first witness or by the submission of a motion for decision, the judge whose impartiality has been questioned may order the trial or hearing to continue, notwithstanding the filing of the statement of disqualification. The issue of disqualification shall be referred to another judge for decision as provided in subdivision (a) of Section 170.3, and if it is determined that the judge is disqualified, all orders and rulings of the judge found to be disqualified made after the filing of the statement shall be vacated.

(2) For the purposes of this subdivision, if (A) a proceeding is filed in a single judge court or has been assigned to a single judge for comprehensive disposition, and (B) the proceeding has been set for trial or hearing 30 or more days in advance before a judge whose name was known at the time, the trial or hearing shall be deemed to have commenced 10 days prior to the date scheduled for trial or hearing as to any grounds for disqualification known before that time.

(3) A party may file no more than one statement of disqualification against a judge unless facts suggesting new grounds for disqualification are first learned of or arise after the first statement of disqualification was filed. Repetitive statements of disqualification not alleging facts suggesting new grounds for disqualification shall be stricken by the judge against whom they are filed.

(d) Except as provided in this section, a disqualified judge shall have no power to act in any proceeding after his or her disqualification or after the filing of a statement of disqualification until the question of his or her disqualification has been determined. **Leg.H.** Added Stats 1984 ch 1555 §8.

§170.5. Definitions

For the purposes of Sections 170 to 170.5, inclusive, the following definitions apply:

(a) "Judge" means judges of the superior courts, and court commissioners and referees.

(b) "Financial interest" means ownership of more than a 1 percent legal or equitable interest in a party, or a legal or equitable interest in a party of a fair market value in excess of one thousand five hundred dollars ($1,500), or a relationship as director, advisor or other active participant in the affairs of a party, except as follows:

(1) Ownership in a mutual or common investment fund that holds securities is not a "financial interest" in those securities unless the judge participates in the management of the fund.

(2) An office in an educational, religious, charitable, fraternal, or civic organization is not a "financial interest" in securities held by the organization.

(3) The proprietary interest of a policyholder in a mutual insurance company, or a depositor in a mutual savings association, or a similar proprietary interest, is a "financial interest" in the organization only if the outcome of the proceeding could substantially affect the value of the interest.

(c) "Officer of a public agency" does not include a Member of the Legislature or a state or local agency official acting in a legislative capacity.

(d) The third degree of relationship shall be calculated according to the civil law system.

(e) "Private practice of law" includes a fee for service, retainer, or salaried representation of private clients or public agencies, but excludes lawyers as full-time employees of public agencies or lawyers working exclusively for legal aid offices, public defender offices, or similar nonprofit entities whose clientele is by law restricted to the indigent.

(f) "Proceeding" means the action, case, cause, motion, or special proceeding to be tried or heard by the judge.

(g) "Fiduciary" includes any executor, trustee, guardian, or administrator. **Leg.H.** Added Stats 1984 ch 1555 §9. Amended Stats 1998 ch 931 §47 (SB 2139), effective September 28, 1998; Stats 2002 ch 784 §35 (SB 1316).

Prior Law: Former CCP §170.5 was added Stats 1937 ch 507 §1 and repealed Stats 1959 ch 1099 §1.

§170.6. Motion to disqualify

(a)(1) A judge, court commissioner, or referee of a superior court of the State of California shall not try a civil or criminal action or special proceeding of any kind or character nor hear any matter therein that involves a contested issue of law or fact when it is established as provided in this section that the judge or court commissioner is prejudiced against a party or attorney or the interest of a party or attorney appearing in the action or proceeding.

(2) A party to, or an attorney appearing in, an action or proceeding may establish this prejudice by an oral or written motion without prior notice supported by affidavit or declaration under penalty of perjury, or an oral statement under oath, that the judge, court commissioner, or referee before whom the action or proceeding is pending, or to whom it is assigned, is prejudiced against a party or attorney, or the interest of the party or attorney, so that the party or attorney cannot, or believes that he or she cannot, have a fair and impartial trial or hearing before the judge, court commissioner, or referee. If the judge, other than a judge assigned to the case for all purposes, court commissioner, or referee assigned to, or who is scheduled to try, the cause or hear the matter is known at least 10 days before the date set for trial or hearing, the motion shall be made at least 5 days before that date. If directed to the trial of a cause with a master calendar, the motion shall be made to the judge supervising the master calendar not later than the time the cause is assigned for trial. If directed to the trial of a criminal cause that has been assigned to a judge for all purposes, the motion shall be made to the assigned judge or to the presiding judge by a party within 10 days after notice of the all purpose assignment, or if the party has not yet appeared in the action, then within 10 days after the appearance. If directed to the trial of a civil cause that has been assigned to a judge for all purposes, the motion shall be made to the assigned judge or to the presiding judge by a party within 15 days after notice of the all purpose assignment, or if the party has not yet appeared in the action, then within 15 days after the appearance. If the court in which the action is pending is authorized to have no more than one judge, and the motion claims that the duly elected or appointed judge of that court is prejudiced, the motion shall be made before the expiration of 30 days from the date of the first appearance in the action of the party who is making the motion or whose attorney is making the motion. In no event shall a judge, court commissioner, or referee entertain the motion if it is made after the drawing of the name of the first juror, or if there is no jury, after the making of an opening statement by counsel for plaintiff, or if there is no opening statement by counsel for plaintiff, then after swearing in the first witness or the giving of any evidence or after trial of the cause has otherwise commenced. If the motion is directed to a hearing, other than the trial of a cause, the motion shall be made not later than the commencement of the hearing. In the case of trials or hearings not specifically provided for in this paragraph, the procedure specified herein shall be followed as nearly as possible. The fact that a judge, court commissioner, or referee has presided at, or acted in connection with, a pretrial conference or other hearing, proceeding, or motion prior to trial, and not involving a determination of contested fact issues relating to the merits, shall not preclude the later making of the motion provided for in this paragraph at the time and in the manner herein provided.

A motion under this paragraph may be made following reversal on appeal of a trial court's decision, or following reversal on appeal of a trial court's final judgment, if the trial judge in the prior proceeding is assigned to conduct a new trial on the matter. Notwithstanding paragraph (4), the party who filed the appeal that resulted in the reversal of a final judgment of a trial court may make a motion under this section regardless of whether that party or side has previously done so. The motion shall be made within 60 days after the party or the party's attorney has been notified of the assignment.

(3) A party to a civil action making that motion under this section shall serve notice on all parties no later than five days after making the motion.

(4) If the motion is duly presented, and the affidavit or declaration under penalty of perjury is duly filed or an oral statement under oath is duly made, thereupon and without any further act or proof, the judge supervising the master calendar, if any, shall assign some other judge, court commissioner, or referee to try the cause or hear the matter. In other cases, the trial of the cause or the hearing of the matter shall be assigned or transferred to another judge, court commissioner, or referee of the court in which the trial or matter is pending or, if there is no other judge, court commissioner, or referee of the court in which the trial or matter is pending, the Chair of the Judicial Council shall assign some other judge, court commissioner, or referee to try the cause or hear the matter as promptly as possible. Except as provided in this section, no party or attorney shall be permitted to make more than one such motion in any one action or special proceeding pursuant to this section. In actions or special proceedings where there may be more than one plaintiff or similar party or more than one defendant or similar party appearing in the action or special proceeding, only one motion for each side may be made in any one action or special proceeding.

(5) Unless required for the convenience of the court or unless good cause is shown, a continuance of the trial or hearing shall not be granted by reason of the making of a motion under this section. If a continuance

is granted, the cause or matter shall be continued from day to day or for other limited periods upon the trial or other calendar and shall be reassigned or transferred for trial or hearing as promptly as possible.

(6) Any affidavit filed pursuant to this section shall be in substantially the following form:

(Here set forth court and cause)

PEREMPTORY CHALLENGE

State of California,
County of _____ } ss.

_____, being duly sworn, deposes and says: That he or she is a party (or attorney for a party) to the within action (or special proceeding). That _____ the judge, court commissioner, or referee before whom the trial of the (or a hearing in the) action (or special proceeding) is pending (or to whom it is assigned) is prejudiced against the party (or his or her attorney) or the interest of the party (or his or her attorney) so that affiant cannot or believes that he or she cannot have a fair and impartial trial or hearing before the judge, court commissioner, or referee.

Subscribed and sworn to before me this ____ day of _____, 20____.

(Clerk or notary public or other
officer administering oath)

(7) Any oral statement under oath or declaration under penalty of perjury made pursuant to this section shall include substantially the same contents as the affidavit above.

(b) Nothing in this section shall affect or limit Section 170 or Title 4 (commencing with Section 392) of Part 2, and this section shall be construed as cumulative thereto.

(c) If any provision of this section or the application to any person or circumstance is held invalid, that invalidity shall not affect other provisions or applications of the section that can be given effect without the invalid provision or application and, to this end, the provisions of this section are declared to be severable. **Leg.H.** Added Stats 1957 ch 1055 §1. Amended Stats 1959 ch 640 §1; Stats 1961 ch 526 §1; Stats 1965 ch 1442 §1; Stats 1967 ch 1602 §2; Stats 1976 ch 1071 §1; Stats 1981 ch 192 §1; Stats 1982 ch 1644 §2; Stats 1985 ch 715 §1; Stats 1989 ch 537 §1; Stats 1998 ch 167 §1 (AB 1199); Stats 2002 ch 784 §36 (SB 1316); Stats 2003 ch 62 §22 (SB 600); Stats 2010 ch 131 §1 (AB 1894), effective January 1, 2011.

§170.65. [Section repealed 2001]

Leg.H. Added Stats 1995 ch 349 §1, operative until January 1, 2001, as CCP §107.65. Renumbered by Stats 1996 ch 124 §13. Repealed January 1, 2001, by its own terms. The repealed section related to stipulation by prosecuting attorney and defendant that retired judge not hear and try criminal cause.

§170.7. Effect of motion to disqualify on superior court appellate division judge

Section 170.6 does not apply to a judge designated or assigned to serve on the appellate division of a superior court in the judge's capacity as a judge of that division. **Leg.H.** Added Stats 1963 ch 872 §1. Amended Stats 1998 ch 931 §48 (SB 2139), effective September 28, 1998.

§170.8. No judge of court qualified to hear cause; Judge assigned by Chairman of Judicial Council

When there is no judge of a court qualified to hear an action or proceeding, the clerk shall forthwith notify the Chairman of the Judicial Council of that fact. The judge assigned by the Chairman of the Judicial Council shall hear the action or proceeding at the time fixed therefor or, if no time has been fixed or good cause appears for changing the time theretofore fixed, the judge shall fix a time for hearing in accordance with law and rules and hear the action or proceeding at the time so fixed. **Leg.H.** Added Stats 1963 ch 872 §2. Amended Stats 1989 ch 1417 §2.

§170.9. Restrictions on gifts and honoraria to judges

(a) A judge shall not accept gifts from a single source in a calendar year with a total value of more than two hundred fifty dollars ($250). This section shall not be construed to authorize the receipt of gifts that would otherwise be prohibited by the Code of Judicial Ethics adopted by the California Supreme Court or any other law.

(b) This section shall not prohibit or limit the following:

(1) Payments, advances, or reimbursements for travel and related lodging and subsistence permitted by subdivision (e).

(2) Wedding gifts and gifts exchanged between individuals on birthdays, holidays, and other similar occasions, if the gifts exchanged are not substantially disproportionate in value.

(3) A gift, bequest, favor, or loan from a person whose preexisting relationship with a judge would prevent the judge from hearing a case involving that person, under the Code of Judicial Ethics adopted by the California Supreme Court.

(c) For purposes of this section, "judge" includes all of the following:

(1) Judges of the superior courts.

(2) Justices of the courts of appeal and the Supreme Court.

(3) Subordinate judicial officers, as defined in Section 71601 of the Government Code.

(d) The gift limitation amounts in this section shall be adjusted biennially by the Commission on Judicial Performance to reflect changes in the Consumer Price Index, rounded to the nearest ten dollars ($10).

(e) Payments, advances, or reimbursements for travel, including actual transportation and related lodging and subsistence that is reasonably related to a judicial or governmental purpose, or to an issue of state, national, or international public policy, are not prohibited or limited by this section if any of the following apply:

(1) The travel is in connection with a speech, practice demonstration, or group or panel discussion given or participated in by the judge, the lodging and subsistence expenses are limited to the day immediately preceding, the day of, and the day immediately following the speech, demonstration, or discussion, and the travel is within the United States.

(2) The travel is provided by a government, a governmental agency or authority, a foreign government, a foreign bar association, an international service organization, a bona fide public or private educational institution, as defined in Section 203 of the Revenue and Taxation Code, or a nonprofit charitable or religious organization that is exempt from taxation under Section 501(c)(3) of the Internal Revenue Code, or by a person domiciled outside the United States who substantially satisfies the requirements for tax-exempt status under Section 501(c)(3) of the Internal Revenue Code.

For purposes of this section, "foreign bar association" means an association of attorneys located outside the United States (A) that performs functions substantially equivalent to those performed by state or local bar associations in this state and (B) that permits membership by attorneys in that country representing various legal specialties and does not limit membership to attorneys generally representing one side or another in litigation. "International service organization" means a bona fide international service organization of which the judge is a member. A judge who accepts travel payments from an international service organization pursuant to this subdivision shall not preside over or participate in decisions affecting that organization, its state or local chapters, or its local members.

(3) The travel is provided by a state or local bar association or judges professional association in connection with testimony before a governmental body or attendance at any professional function hosted by the bar association or judges professional association, the lodging and subsistence expenses are limited to the day immediately preceding, the day of, and the day immediately following the professional function.

(f) Payments, advances, and reimbursements for travel not described in subdivision (e) are subject to the limit in subdivision (a).

(g) No judge shall accept any honorarium.

(h) "Honorarium" means a payment made in consideration for any speech given, article published, or attendance at a public or private conference, convention, meeting, social event, meal, or like gathering.

(i) "Honorarium" does not include earned income for personal services that are customarily provided in connection with the practice of a bona fide business, trade, or profession, such as teaching or writing for a publisher, and does not include fees or other things of value received pursuant to Section 94.5 of the Penal Code for performance of a marriage.

For purposes of this section, "teaching" shall include presentations to impart educational information to lawyers in events qualifying for credit under mandatory continuing legal education, to students in bona fide educational institutions, and to associations or groups of judges.

(j) Subdivisions (a) and (e) shall apply to all payments, advances, and reimbursements for travel and related lodging and subsistence.

(k) This section does not apply to any honorarium that is not used and, within 30 days after receipt, is either returned to the donor or delivered to the Controller for deposit in the General Fund without being claimed as a deduction from income for tax purposes.

(*l*) "Gift" means a payment to the extent that consideration of equal or greater value is not received and includes a rebate or discount in the price of anything of value unless the rebate or discount is made in the regular course of business to members of the public without regard to official status. A person, other than a defendant in a criminal action, who claims that a payment is not a gift by reason of receipt of consideration has the burden of proving that the consideration received is of equal or greater value. However, the term "gift" does not include any of the following:

(1) Informational material such as books, reports, pamphlets, calendars, periodicals, cassettes and discs, or free or reduced-price admission, tuition, or registration, for informational conferences or seminars. No payment for travel or reimbursement for any expenses shall be deemed "informational material."

(2) Gifts that are not used and, within 30 days after receipt, are returned to the donor or delivered to a charitable organization without being claimed as a charitable contribution for tax purposes.

(3) Gifts from a judge's spouse, child, parent, grandparent, grandchild, brother, sister, parent-in-law, brother-in-law, sister-in-law, nephew, niece, aunt, uncle, or first cousin or the spouse of any such person. However, a gift from any of those persons shall be considered a gift if the donor is acting as an agent or intermediary for a person not covered by this paragraph.

(4) Campaign contributions required to be reported under Chapter 4 (commencing with Section 84100) of Title 9 of the Government Code.

(5) Any devise or inheritance.

(6) Personalized plaques and trophies with an individual value of less than two hundred fifty dollars ($250).

(7) Admission to events hosted by state or local bar associations or judges professional associations, and provision of related food and beverages at those events, when attendance does not require "travel," as described in paragraph (3) of subdivision (e).

(m) The Commission on Judicial Performance shall enforce the prohibitions of this section with regard to judges of the superior courts and justices of the courts of appeal and the Supreme Court. With regard to subordinate judicial officers, consistent with Section 18.1 of Article VI of the California Constitution, the court employing the subordinate judicial officer shall exercise initial jurisdiction to enforce the prohibitions of this section, and the Commission on Judicial Performance shall exercise discretionary jurisdiction with respect to the enforcement of the prohibitions of this section. **Leg.H.** Added Stats 1994 ch 1238 §1 (AB 3638). Amended Stats 1995 ch 378 §1 (SB 353); Stats 1996 ch 557 §1 (SB 1589); Stats 2002 ch 784 §37 (SB 1316); Stats 2010 ch 206 §1 (AB 2116), effective January 1, 2011; Stats 2011 ch 296 §36 (AB 1023), effective January 1, 2012.

§171. [Section repealed 1953]

Leg.H. Enacted 1872 as §§171, 172. Repealed and re-enacted Code Amdts 1880 ch 35 §1. Amended Stats 1881 ch 70 §1; Stats 1951 ch 1737 §39, operative January 1, 1952. Repealed by Stats 1953 ch 206 §7. See Gov C §68082.

§172. [Section repealed 1953]

Leg.H. Enacted 1872 as §173. Repealed and re-enacted as §172 Code Amdts 1880 ch 35 §1. Amended Stats 1947 ch 1069 §1; Stats 1951 ch 1737 §40, operative January 1, 1952. Repealed by Stats 1953 ch 206 §7. The repealed section related to a restriction on judicial officers from having a partner acting as an attorney in a state court.

Prior Law: Former §172 was enacted 1872 and repealed and Incorporated in §171 by Code Amdts 1880 ch 35 §1.

§173. [Section renumbered 1880]

Leg.H. Enacted 1872. Repealed and re-enacted as §172 Code Amdts 1880 ch 35 §1. The repealed section related to a restriction on judicial officers from having a partner acting as an attorney in a state court.

CHAPTER 4
INCIDENTAL POWERS AND DUTIES OF JUDICIAL OFFICERS

Conduct of proceedings. §177.
Imposition of sanctions for violations of lawful orders. §177.5.
Punishment for contempt. §178.
Taking affidavits and depositions and certification of acknowledgments. §179.

§176. [Section repealed 1933]

Leg.H. Enacted 1872. Repealed and re-enacted 1872; Repealed and re-enacted Code Amdts 1880 ch 35 §1. Repealed Stats 1933 ch 743 §61. See CCP §166.

§177. Conduct of proceedings

A judicial officer shall have power:

(a) To preserve and enforce order in the officer's immediate presence, and in proceedings before the officer, when the officer is engaged in the performance of official duty.

(b) To compel obedience to the officer's lawful orders as provided in this code.

(c) To compel the attendance of persons to testify in a proceeding before the officer, in the cases and manner provided in this code.

(d) To administer oaths to persons in a proceeding pending before the officer, and in all other cases where it may be necessary in the exercise of the officer's powers and duties.

(e) To prohibit activities that threaten access to state courthouses and court proceedings, and to prohibit interruption of judicial administration, including protecting the privilege from civil arrest at courthouses and court proceedings. **Leg.H.** Enacted 1872. Repealed and re-enacted Code Amdts 1880 ch 35 §1. Amended Stats 2019 ch 787 §3 (AB 668), effective January 1, 2020.

§177.5. Imposition of sanctions for violations of lawful orders

A judicial officer shall have the power to impose reasonable money sanctions, not to exceed fifteen hundred dollars ($1,500), notwithstanding any other provision of law, payable to the court, for any violation of a lawful court order by a person, done without good cause or substantial justification. This power shall not apply to advocacy of counsel before the court. For the purposes of this section, the term "person" includes a witness, a party, a party's attorney, or both.

Sanctions pursuant to this section shall not be imposed except on notice contained in a party's moving or responding papers; or on the court's own motion, after notice and opportunity to be heard. An order imposing sanctions shall be in writing and shall recite in detail the conduct or circumstances justifying the order. **Leg.H.** Added Stats 1982 ch 1564 §1. Amended Stats 2005 ch 75 §27 (AB 145), effective July 19, 2005, operative January 1, 2006.

§178. Punishment for contempt

For the effectual exercise of the powers conferred by the last section, a judicial officer may punish for contempt in the cases provided in this code. **Leg.H.** Enacted 1872. Repealed and re-enacted Code Amdts 1880 ch 35 §1.

§179. Taking affidavits and depositions and certification of acknowledgments

Each of the justices of the Supreme Court and of any court of appeal and the judges of the superior courts, shall have power in any part of the state to take and certify:

(a) The proof and acknowledgment of a conveyance of real property, or of any other written instrument.

(b) The acknowledgment of satisfaction of a judgment of any court.

(c) An affidavit or deposition to be used in this state. **Leg.H.** Enacted 1872. Repealed and re-enacted Code Amdts 1880 ch 35 §1. Amended Stats 1933 ch 743 §49; Stats 1953 ch 457 §4; Stats 1967 ch 17 §11; Stats 1998 ch 931 §49 (SB 2139), effective September 28, 1998; Stats 2002 ch 784 §38 (SB 1316); Stats 2003 ch 62 §23 (SB 600).

CHAPTER 5
MISCELLANEOUS PROVISIONS RESPECTING COURTS OF JUSTICE

Chapter heading not deemed to affect its provisions. §182.
Vacancy not to affect proceedings. §184.

Proceedings to be in English language. §185.
Abbreviations and figures. §186.
Means to carry jurisdiction into effect. §187.

§182. Chapter heading not deemed to affect its provisions

The heading to this chapter shall not be deemed to govern or limit the scope or meaning of this chapter. **Leg.H.** Added Stats 1955 ch 59 §4.

Prior Law: Present CCP §182, incorporated in present CCP §1008, was enacted 1872, repealed and re-enacted by Code Amdts 1880 ch 35 §1, and repealed by Stats 1933 ch 743 §61.

§183. [Section repealed 1933]

Leg.H. Enacted 1872. Repealed and re-enacted Code Amdts 1880 ch 35 §1. Repealed Stats 1933 ch 743 §61. See CCP §1008.

§184. Vacancy not to affect proceedings

No proceeding in any court of justice, in an action or special proceeding pending therein, shall be affected by a vacancy in the office of all or any of the judges or justices thereof. **Leg.H.** Enacted 1872. Repealed and re-enacted Code Amdts 1880 ch 35 §1. Amended Stats 1933 ch 743 §51.

§185. Proceedings to be in English language

(a) Every written proceeding in a court of justice in this state shall be in the English language, and judicial proceedings shall be conducted, preserved, and published in no other. Nothing in this section shall prohibit a court from providing an unofficial translation of a court order issued pursuant to Section 527.6 or 527.8 of the Code of Civil Procedure, or Part 1 (commencing with Section 6200) of Division 10 of the Family Code, or Section 136.2 of the Penal Code, in a language other than English.

(b) The Judicial Council shall, by July 1, 2001, make available to all courts, translations of domestic violence protective order forms in languages other than English, as the Judicial Council deems appropriate, for protective orders issued pursuant to Section 527.6 or 527.8 of the Code of Civil Procedure, or Part 1 (commencing with Section 6200) of Division 10 of the Family Code, or Section 136.2 of the Penal Code. **Leg.H.** Enacted 1872. Repealed and re-enacted Code Amdts 1880 ch 35 §1. Amended Stats 1999 ch 662 §1 (SB 218).

§186. Abbreviations and figures

Such abbreviations as are in common use may be used, and numbers may be expressed by figures or numerals in the customary manner. **Leg.H.** Enacted 1872; Repealed and re-enacted Code Amdts 1880 ch 35 §1.

§187. Means to carry jurisdiction into effect

When jurisdiction is, by the Constitution or this Code, or by any other statute, conferred on a Court or judicial officer, all the means necessary to carry it into effect are also given; and in the exercise of this jurisdiction, if the course of proceeding be not specifically pointed out by this Code or the statute, any suitable process or mode of proceeding may be adopted which may appear most conformable to the spirit of this Code. **Leg.H.** Enacted 1872; Repealed and re-enacted Code Amdts 1880 ch 35 §1.

§188. [Section repealed 1953]

Leg.H. Added Stats 1915 ch 564 §1. Amended Stats 1933 ch 743 §52; Stats 1951 ch 1737 §41, operative January 1, 1952. Repealed Stats 1953 ch 206 §7. See Gov C §68084.

§189. [Section repealed 1953]

Leg.H. Added Stats 1931 ch 644 §1. Amended Stats 1933 ch 743 §53; Stats 1943 ch 867 §1; Stats 1949 ch 1401 §1; Stats 1951 ch 44 §1. Repealed Stats 1953 ch 206 §7. The repealed section related to the authority and procedure for the destruction of records.

§189.5. [Section repealed 1953]

Leg.H. Added Stats 1943 ch 121 §1. Repealed Stats 1953 ch 206 §7. See Gov C §68089.

§189.7. [Section repealed 1953]

Leg.H. Added Stats 1951 ch 1138 §1. Repealed Stats 1953 ch 206 §7, See Gov C §68152.

TITLE 3
PERSONS SPECIALLY INVESTED WITH POWERS OF A JUDICIAL NATURE

Chapter 1. Trial Jury Selection and Management Act.
Chapter 2. Court Commissioners.

CHAPTER 1
TRIAL JURY SELECTION AND MANAGEMENT ACT

Citation of chapter. §190.
Declaration of state policy. §191.
Application of chapter. §192.
Different kinds of juries. §193.
Definitions. §194.
Jury commissioner; Appointment; Powers and duties. §195.
Jury commissioner or court inquiries. §196.
Random selection of jurors; Appropriate source lists. §197.
Master and qualified juror lists. §198.
Sessions of superior court in cities other than county seat. §198.5.
Separate trial jury panel. §201.
Mechanical, electric, or electronic equipment. §202.
Persons not qualified to be jurors. §203.
Exemption from service. §204.
[Section renumbered 1981]. §204a.
[Section renumbered 1981]. §204c.
[Section renumbered 1981]. §204e.
Questionnaires to prospective jurors [Repealed January 1, 2026]. §205.
Juror questionnaires; Judicial Council standard for gender identity and expression [Operative January 1, 2026]. § 205.
Right of jurors not to discuss deliberations or verdict; Petition for access to personal juror information. §206.
Maintenance of records of selection and service of jurors. §207.
Prospective jurors; Estimate of number; Summons. §208.
Enforcement of summons; Punishment; Monetary sanctions. §209.
Contents of summons. §210.
Standardized jury summons. §210.5.
Summoning jurors to complete panel. §211.
One-hour telephone notice. §213.
Juror orientation. §214.
Juror fees and expenses; Use of public transit service. § 215.
Deliberations rooms. §216.
Criminal cases; Provision of food and lodging. §217.
Hearing excuses. §218.
Selection of jury panels. §219.
Adoption of rules to give certain peace officers scheduling accommodations. §219.5.
Number of trial jury. §220.
Selection for voir dire. §222.
Voir dire in civil cases; "Improper question". §222.5.
Voir dire in criminal jury trial. §223.
Juror with specified physical disabilities; "Service provider". §224.
Challenges. §225.
Challenge to individual juror. §226.
Challenges for cause. §227.
Challenges for general disqualification. §228.
Challenges for implied bias. §229.
Challenges tried by court. §230.
Peremptory challenges. §231.
Assumption of bias. §231.5.
Prohibition to use of peremptory challenge based on specified criteria [Repealed January 1, 2026]. § 231.7.
Prohibition to use of peremptory challenge based on specified criteria [Operative January 1, 2026]. § 231.7.
Perjury admonishment; Acknowledgment and agreement. §232.
Discharge of juror before verdict returned. §233.
Alternate jurors. §234.
Provision of prospective jurors; Juries of inquest. §235.
Jury of inquest; Purpose. §236.
Names of qualified jurors made available to public; Petition for access to records; Notice; Hearing; Violations. §237.
Pilot program to study whether increases in juror compensation and mileage reimbursement rates increase juror diversity and participation [Repealed January 1, 2027]. § 241.
Mental health awareness information provided to jurors. § 242.

§190. Citation of chapter

This chapter shall be known and may be cited as the Trial Jury Selection and Management Act. **Leg.H.** Added Stats 1988 ch 1245 §2.

Prior Law: Former CCP §190, similar to present CCP §194, was enacted 1872, repealed and reenacted Code Amdts 1880 ch 35 §1, amended Stats 1917 ch 692 §1, Stats 1980 ch 81 §1, and repealed Stats 1988 ch 1245 §1.

§191. Declaration of state policy

The Legislature recognizes that trial by jury is a cherished constitutional right, and that jury service is an obligation of citizenship.

It is the policy of the State of California that all persons selected for jury service shall be selected at random from the population of the area served by the court; that all qualified persons have an equal opportunity, in accordance with this chapter, to be considered for jury service in the state and an obligation to serve as jurors when summoned for that purpose; and that it is the responsibility of jury commissioners to manage all jury systems in an efficient, equitable, and cost-effective manner, in accordance with this chapter. **Leg.H.** Added Stats 1988 ch 1245 §2.

Prior Law: Former CCP §191, similar to present CCP §193, was enacted 1872, repealed and reenacted Code Amdts 1880 ch 35 §1, and repealed Stats 1988 ch 1245 §1.

§192. Application of chapter

This chapter applies to the selection of jurors, and the formation of trial juries, for both civil and criminal cases, in all trial courts of the state. **Leg.H.** Added Stats 1988 ch 1245 §2.

Prior Law: Former CCP §192, similar to present CCP §193, was enacted 1872, amended Code Amdts 1875–76 ch 514 §1, repealed and reenacted Code Amdts 1880 ch 35 §1, amended Stats 1917 ch 692 §2, Stats 1959 ch 501 §4, and repealed Stats 1988 ch 1245 §1.

§193. Different kinds of juries

Juries are of three kinds:

(a) Grand juries established pursuant to Title 4 (commencing with Section 888) of Part 2 of the Penal Code.

(b) Trial juries.

(c) Juries of inquest. **Leg.H.** Added Stats 1988 ch 1245 §2.

Prior Law: Former CCP §193, similar to present CCP §194, was enacted 1872, repealed and reenacted Code Amdts 1880 ch 35 §1, amended Stats 1917 ch 692 §3, and repealed Stats 1988 ch 1245 §1.

§193.2. [Section repealed 1989]

Leg.H. Added Stats 1980 ch 81 §3. Repealed Stats 1988 ch 1245 §1. See CCP §194.

§194. Definitions

The following definitions govern the construction of this chapter:

(a) "County" means any county or any coterminous city and county.

(b) "Court" means a superior court of this state, and includes, when the context requires, any judge of the court.

(c) "Deferred jurors" are those prospective jurors whose request to reschedule their service to a more convenient time is granted by the jury commissioner.

(d) "Excused jurors" are those prospective jurors who are excused from service by the jury commissioner for valid reasons based on statute, state or local court rules, and policies.

(e) "Juror pool" means the group of prospective qualified jurors appearing for assignment to trial jury panels.

(f) "Jury of inquest" is a body of persons summoned from the citizens before the sheriff, coroner, or other ministerial officers, to inquire of particular facts.

(g) "Master list" means a list of names randomly selected from the source lists.

(h) "Potential juror" means any person whose name appears on a source list.

(i) "Prospective juror" means a juror whose name appears on the master list.

(j) "Qualified juror" means a person who meets the statutory qualifications for jury service.

(k) "Qualified juror list" means a list of qualified jurors.

(*l*) "Random" means that which occurs by mere chance indicating an unplanned sequence of selection where each juror's name has substantially equal probability of being selected.

(m) "Source list" means a list used as a source of potential jurors.

(n) "Summons list" means a list of prospective or qualified jurors who are summoned to appear or to be available for jury service.

(o) "Trial jurors" are those jurors sworn to try and determine by verdict a question of fact.

(p) "Trial jury" means a body of persons selected from the citizens of the area served by the court and sworn to try and determine by verdict a question of fact.

(q) "Trial jury panel" means a group of prospective jurors assigned to a courtroom for the purpose of voir dire. **Leg.H.** Added Stats 1988 ch 1245 §2. Amended Stats 1998 ch 931 §50 (SB 2139), effective September 28, 1998; Stats 2002 ch 784 §39 (SB 1316).

Prior Law: Former CCP §194, similar to present CCP §220, was enacted 1872, repealed and reenacted Code Amdts 1880 ch 35 §1, amended Stats 1917 ch 692 §4, Stats 1981 ch 884 §1, and repealed Stats 1988 ch 1245 §1.

§194.5. [Section repealed 1989]

Leg.H. Added Stats 1981 ch 884 §2. Amended Stats 1986 ch 1337 §1. Repealed Stats 1988 ch 1245 §1. The repealed section related to Los Angeles County juries.

§195. Jury commissioner; Appointment; Powers and duties

(a) In each county, there shall be one jury commissioner who shall be appointed by, and serve at the pleasure of, a majority of the judges of the superior court. In any county where there is a superior court administrator or executive officer, that person shall serve as ex officio jury commissioner. In any court jurisdiction where any person other than a court administrator or clerk/administrator is serving as jury commissioner on the effective date of this section, that person shall continue to so serve at the pleasure of a majority of the judges of the appointing court.

(b) Any jury commissioner may, whenever the business of court requires, appoint deputy jury commissioners. Salaries and benefits of those deputies shall be fixed in the same manner as salaries and benefits of other court employees.

(c) The jury commissioner shall be primarily responsible for managing the jury system under the general supervision of the court in conformance with the purpose and scope of this act. He or she shall have authority to establish policies and procedures necessary to fulfill this responsibility. **Leg.H.** Added Stats 1988 ch 1245 §2. Amended Stats 1998 ch 931 §51 (SB 2139), effective September 28, 1998; Stats 2002 ch 784 §40 (SB 1316).

Prior Law: Former CCP §195, similar to present CCP §236, was enacted 1872, repealed and reenacted Code Amdts 1880 ch 35 §1, amended Stats 1917 ch 692 §5, Stats 1980 ch 81 §4, and repealed Stats 1988 ch 1245 §1.

§196. Jury commissioner or court inquiries

(a) The jury commissioner or the court shall inquire as to the qualifications of persons on the master list or source list who are or may be summoned for jury service. The commissioner or the court may require any person to answer, under oath, orally or in written form, all questions as may be addressed to that person, regarding the person's qualifications and ability to serve as a prospective trial juror. The commissioner and his or her assistants shall have power to administer oaths and shall be allowed actual traveling expenses incurred in the performance of their duties.

(b) Response to the jury commissioner or the court concerning an inquiry or summons may be made by any person having knowledge that the prospective juror is unable to respond to such inquiry or summons.

(c) Any person who fails to respond to jury commissioner or court inquiry as instructed, may be summoned to appear before the jury commissioner or the court to answer the inquiry, or may be deemed to be qualified for jury service in the absence of a response to the inquiry. Any information thus acquired by the court or jury commissioner shall be noted in jury commissioner or court records. **Leg.H.** Added Stats 1988 ch 1245 §2. Amended Stats 2003 ch 149 §6 (SB 79).

Prior Law: Former CCP §196, similar to present CCP §215, was added Stats 1951 ch 655 §17, amended Stats 1951 ch 1693 §2, Stats 1957 ch 43 §5, ch 1406 §3, Stats 1959 ch 501 §5, Stats 1980 ch 81 §5, Stats 1984 ch 1640 §1, Stats 1987 ch 134 §1, effective July 7, 1987, and repealed Stats 1988 ch 1245 §1.

§196.1. [Section repealed 1989]

Leg.H. Added Stats 1951 ch 655 §17. Amended Stats 1959 ch 594 §4; Stats 1980 ch 81 §6. Repealed Stats 1988 ch 1245 §1. The repealed section related to source of payment of jury fees.

§197. Random selection of jurors; Appropriate source lists

(a) All persons selected for jury service shall be selected at random, from a source or sources inclusive of a representative cross section of the population of the area served by the court. Sources may include, in addition to other lists, customer mailing lists, telephone directories, or utility company lists.

(b)(1) The list of registered voters and the Department of Motor Vehicles' list of licensed drivers and identification cardholders resident within the area served by the court, are appropriate source lists for selection of jurors. Until January 1, 2022, only these two source lists, when substantially purged of duplicate names, shall be considered inclusive of a representative cross section of the population, within the meaning of subdivision (a).

(2) The list of resident state tax filers is an appropriate source list for selection of jurors. Beginning on January 1, 2022, the list of resident state tax filers, the list of registered voters, and the Department of Motor Vehicles' list of licensed drivers and identification cardholders resident within the area served by the court, when substantially purged of duplicate names, shall be considered inclusive of a representative cross section of the population, within the meaning of subdivision (a).

(c) The Department of Motor Vehicles shall furnish the jury commissioner of each county with the current list of the names, addresses, and other identifying information of persons residing in the county who are age 18 years or older and who are holders of a current driver's license or identification card issued pursuant to Article 3 (commencing with Section 12800) of, or Article 5 (commencing with Section 13000) of, Chapter 1 of Division 6 of the Vehicle Code. The conditions under which these lists shall be compiled semiannually shall be determined by the director, consistent with any rules which may be adopted by the Judicial Council. This service shall be provided by the Department of Motor Vehicles pursuant to Section 1812 of the Vehicle Code. The jury commissioner shall not disclose the information furnished by the Department of Motor Vehicles pursuant to this section to any person, organization, or agency.

(d)(1) The Franchise Tax Board shall annually furnish the jury commissioner of each county with a list of resident state tax filers for their county in consultation with the Judicial Council.

(2) The list of resident state tax filers shall be submitted to the jury commissioner of each county by November 1, 2021, and each November 1 thereafter.

(3)(A) For purposes of this section, "list of resident state tax filers" means a list that includes the name, date of birth, principal residence address, and county of principal residence, of persons who are 18 years of age or older and have filed a California resident income tax return for the preceding taxable year.

(B) For purposes of this paragraph, "county of principal residence" means the county in which the taxpayer has their principal residence on the date that the taxpayer filed their California resident income tax return.

(C) For the purposes of this paragraph, "principal residence" is used in the same manner it is used in Section 121 of the Internal Revenue Code. **Leg.H.** Added Stats 1988 ch 1245 §2. Amended Stats 2020 ch 230 §1 (SB 592), effective January 1, 2021.

Prior Law: Former CCP §197, similar to present CCP §191, was added Stats 1980 ch 81 §7 and repealed Stats 1988 ch 1245 §1.

§197.1. [Section repealed 1989]

Leg.H. Added Stats 1980 ch 81 §8. Repealed Stats 1988 ch 1245 §1. See CCP §204.

§198. Master and qualified juror lists

(a) Random selection shall be utilized in creating master and qualified juror lists, commencing with selection from source lists, and continuing through selection of prospective jurors for voir dire.

(b) The jury commissioner shall, at least once in each 12-month period, randomly select names of prospective trial jurors from the source list or lists, to create a master list.

(c) The master jury list shall be used by the jury commissioner, as provided by statute and state and local court rules, for the purpose of (1) mailing juror questionnaires and subsequent creation of a qualified juror list, and (2) summoning prospective jurors to respond or appear for qualification and service. **Leg.H.** Added Stats 1988 ch 1245 §2.

Prior Law: Former CCP §198, similar to present CCP §203, was enacted 1872, amended Code Amdts 1875–76 ch 306 §1, repealed and reenacted Code Amdts 1880 ch 35§1, amended Stats 1915 ch 497 §1, Stats 1971 ch 1690§1, ch 1798 §29, Stats 1975 ch 172 §1, Stats 1977 ch 597 §1, Stats 1978 ch 301 §1, Stats 1980 ch 1227 §1, Stats 1986 ch 1171 §1, and repealed Stats 1988 ch 1245 §1.

§198.5. Sessions of superior court in cities other than county seat

If sessions of the superior court are held in a location other than the county seat, the names for master jury lists and qualified jury lists to serve in a session may be selected from the area in which the session is held, pursuant to a local superior court rule that divides the county in a manner that provides all qualified persons in the county an equal opportunity to be considered for jury service. Nothing in this section precludes the court, in its discretion, from ordering a countywide venire in the interest of justice. **Leg.H.** Added Stats 1988 ch 1245 §2. Amended Stats 1998 ch 931 §52 (SB 2139), effective September 28, 1998; Stats 2002 ch 784 §41 (SB 1316), operative January 1, 2004; Stats 2003 ch 449 §6 (AB 1712).

§199. [Section repealed 2004]

Leg.H. Added Stats 1988 ch 1245 §2. Repealed Stats 2002 ch 784 §42 (SB 1316), operative January 1, 2004. The repealed section related to jury trial venires in El Dorado County.

Prior Law: Former CCP §199, similar to present CCP §203, was enacted 1872, repealed and reenacted Code Amdts 1880 ch 35 §1, amended Stats 1905 ch 73 §1, Stats 1909 ch 645 §1, Stats 1927 ch 341 §1, Stats 1953 ch 1292 §1, Stats 1959 ch 501 §7, Stats 1975 ch 593 §1, and repealed Stats 1988 ch 1245 §1.

§199.2. [Section repealed 2004]

Leg.H. Added Stats 1991 ch 720 §1 (AB 1621). Amended Stats 1995 ch 954 §1 (AB 737). Repealed Stats 2002 ch 784 §43 (SB 1316), operative January 1, 2004. The repealed section related to inclusion of jurors from Tahoe Judicial District in trial court venires in Placer County.

§199.3. [Section repealed 2004]

Leg.H. Added Stats 1997 ch 571 §1.2 (AB 1088). Repealed Stats 2002 ch 784 §44 (SB 1316), operative January 1, 2004. The repealed section related to trial jury venires in Nevada County.

Prior Law: Former CCP §199.3, relating to superior court jury venires in Nevada County, was added Stats 1992 ch 245 §1 and repealed Stats 1997 ch 571 §1.

§199.5. [Section repealed 2004]

Leg.H. Added Stats 1988 ch 1245 §2. Repealed Stats 2002 ch 784 §45 (SB 1316), operative January 1, 2004. The repealed section related to jury trial venires in Santa Barbara County.

§200. [Section repealed 2003]

Leg.H. Added Stats 1988 ch 1245 §2. Amended Stats 1998 ch 931 §53 (SB 2139), effective September 28, 1998, ch 932 §13.5 (AB 1094). Repealed Stats 2002 ch 784 §46 (SB 1316). The repealed section related to the use of the same jury panel by superior and municipal courts.

Prior Law: Former CCP §200, similar to present CCP §204, was added Stats 1975 ch 593 §3 and repealed Stats 1988 ch 1245 §1.

Former CCP §200, similar to present CCP §204, was enacted 1872, amended Code Amdts 1873–74 ch 383 §10, Code Amdts 1875–76 ch 514 §2, repealed and reenacted Code Amdts 1880 ch 35 §1, amended Stats 1897 ch 125 §1, Stats 1905 ch 73 §2, Stats 1907 ch 480 §1, Stats 1915 ch 647 §1, Stats 1919 ch 192 §1, Stats 1927 ch 341 §2, Stats 1931 ch 1179 §1, Stats 1935 ch 583 §1, Stats 1941 ch 800 §1, Stats 1957 ch 1868 §1, Stats 1959 ch 1406 §1, Stats 1961 ch 215 §35, Stats 1965 ch 30 §1, Stats 1967 ch 935 §1, Stats 1968 ch 47 §1, Stats 1970 ch 57 §1, Stats 1972 ch 390 §1, ch 617 §1, ch 1028 §1.7, ch 1337 §1, and repealed Stats 1975 ch 593 §2.

§201. Separate trial jury panel

In any superior court, a separate trial jury panel may be drawn, summoned, and impaneled for each judge, or any one panel may be drawn, summoned, and impaneled by any one of the judges, for use in the trial of cases before any of the judges, as occasion may require. In those courts, when a panel of jurors is in attendance for service before one or more of the judges, whether impaneled for common use or not, the whole or any number of the jurors from such panel may be required to attend and serve in the trial of cases, or to complete a panel, or jury, before any other of the judges. **Leg.H.** Added Stats 1988 ch 1245 §2. Amended Stats 2002 ch 784 §47 (SB 1316).

Prior Law: Former CCP §201, relating to considerations governing excuse of juror, was enacted 1872, repealed and reenacted Code Amdts 1880 ch 35 §1, amended Stats 1917 ch 692 §6, and repealed Stats 1975 ch 593 §4.

§201a. [Section repealed 1989]

Leg.H. Added Stats 1959 ch 759 §1. Amended Stats 1961 ch 1099 §1; Stats 1975 ch 593 §5; Stats 1978 ch 718 §2. Repealed Stats 1988 ch 1245 §1. The repealed section related to adoption of procedural rules for granting excuses from jury service.

§202. Mechanical, electric, or electronic equipment

Mechanical, electric, or electronic equipment, which in the opinion of the jury commissioner is satisfactory therefor, may be used in the performance of any function specified by this chapter for the selection and drawing of jurors. **Leg.H.** Added Stats 1988 ch 1245 §2.

Prior Law: Former CCP §202, relating to affidavit of claim to exemption, was added Code Amdts 1873–74 ch 383 §17, repealed and reenacted Code Amdts 1880 ch 35 §1, amended Stats 1972 ch 1028 §2, and repealed Stats 1975 ch 593 §6.

§202.5. [Section repealed 1989]

Leg.H. Added Stats 1977 ch 748 §1. Amended Stats 1982 ch 178 §1; Stats 1985 ch 79 §1. Repealed Stats 1988 ch 1245 §1. The repealed section related to exemption of peace officer and judge from service.

§202.7. [Section repealed 1989]

Leg.H. Added Stats 1983 ch 1186 §1. Repealed Stats 1988 ch 1245 §1. The repealed section related to exemption of armed services member not domiciled in state.

§203. Persons not qualified to be jurors

(a) All persons are eligible and qualified to be prospective trial jurors, except the following:

(1) Persons who are not citizens of the United States.

(2) Persons who are less than 18 years of age.

(3) Persons who are not domiciliaries of the State of California, as determined pursuant to Article 2 (commencing with Section 2020) of Chapter 1 of Division 2 of the Elections Code.

(4) Persons who are not residents of the jurisdiction wherein they are summoned to serve.

(5) Persons who have been convicted of malfeasance in office and whose civil rights have not been restored.

(6) Persons who are not possessed of sufficient knowledge of the English language, provided that no person shall be deemed incompetent solely because of the loss of sight or hearing in any degree or other disability which impedes the person's ability to communicate or which impairs or interferes with the person's mobility.

(7) Persons who are serving as grand or trial jurors in any court of this state.

(8) Persons who are the subject of conservatorship.

(9) Persons while they are incarcerated in any prison or jail.

(10) Persons who have been convicted of a felony and are currently on parole, postrelease community supervision, felony probation, or mandated supervision for the conviction of a felony.

(11) Persons who are currently required to register as a sex offender pursuant to Section 290 of the Penal Code based on a felony conviction.

(b) No person shall be excluded from eligibility for jury service in the State of California, for any reason other than those reasons provided by this section.

(c) The provisions of this section are severable. If any provision of this section or its application is held invalid, that invalidity shall not affect other provisions or applications that can be given effect without the invalid provision or application. **Leg.H.** Added Stats 1988 ch 1245 §2. Amended Stats 1994 ch 923 §1 (SB 1546); Stats 2019 ch 591 §1 (SB 310), effective January 1, 2020.

Prior Law Former CCP §203, similar to present CCP §197, was added Stats 1933 ch 743 §54, amended Stats 1939 ch 697 §1, Stats 1951 ch 1495 §1, operative January 1, 1952, Stats 1980 ch 81 §9, and repealed Stats 1988 ch 1245 §1.

§203.1. [Section repealed 1989]

Leg.H. Added Stats 1965 ch 1695 §3. Amended Stats 1967 ch 834 §1; Stats 1968 ch 740 §1, effective July 25, 1968. Repealed Stats 1988 ch

1245 §1. The repealed section related to use by municipal court district of same jury panel as that summoned for use in superior court.

§203.2. [Section repealed 1989]
Leg.H. Added Stats 1968 ch 740 §2, effective July 5, 1968. Repealed Stats 1988 ch 1245 §1. The repealed section related to applicability in Alameda County of former CCP §203.1, allowing use by municipal court district of the same jury panel as that summoned for use in superior court.

§203.3. [Section repealed 1989]
Leg.H. Added Stats 1974 ch 806 §1. Repealed Stats 1988 ch 1245 §1. The repealed section related to use of same jury panel in counties of the first class.

§204. Exemption from service
(a) No eligible person shall be exempt from service as a trial juror by reason of occupation, economic status, or any characteristic listed or defined in Section 11135 of the Government Code, or for any other reason. No person shall be excused from service as a trial juror except as specified in subdivision (b).

(b) An eligible person may be excused from jury service only for undue hardship, upon themselves or upon the public, as defined by the Judicial Council. **Leg.H.** Added Stats 1988 ch 1245 §2. Amended Stats 2000 ch 43 §2 (AB 2418); Stats 2007 ch 568 §15 (AB 14).

Prior Law: Former CCP §204, relating to jury lists, was enacted 1872, amended Code Amdts 1873–74 ch 383 §18, Code Amdts 1875–76 ch 514 §3, repealed and reenacted by Code Amdts 1880 ch 35 §1, amended Stats 1881 ch 60 §1, Stats 1893 ch 213 §1, Stats 1917 ch 692 §7, Stats 1923 ch 195 §1, Stats 1929 ch 295 §1, Stats 1931 ch 1129 §1, Stats 1937 ch 552 §1, Stats 1951 ch 1495 §2, operative January 1, 1952, Stats 1953 ch 793 §1, Stats 1959 ch 501 §8, Stats 1959 ch 501 §8, Stats 1963 ch 1412 §2, Stats 1961 ch 1721 §1, Stats 1963 ch 195 §2, Stats 1974 ch 806 §2, Stats 1978 ch 718 §3, and repealed Stats 1980 ch 81 §10.

2007 Notes: The Legislature finds and declares as follows:

(a) Even prior to passage of the Unruh Civil Rights Act, California law afforded broad protection against arbitrary discrimination by business establishments. The Unruh Civil Rights Act was enacted to provide broader, more effective protection against arbitrary discrimination. California's interest in preventing that discrimination is longstanding and compelling.

(b) In keeping with that history and the legislative history of the Unruh Civil Rights Act, California courts have interpreted the categories enumerated in the act to be illustrative rather than restrictive. It is the intent of the Legislature that these enumerated bases shall continue to be construed as illustrative rather than restrictive, and, consistent with the Unruh Civil Rights Act, that the civil rights provisions of this act that reference Section 51 of the Civil Code also be interpreted to be illustrative rather than restrictive. Stats 2007 ch 568 (AB 14) §1.

This act shall be known and may be cited as the Civil Rights Act of 2007. Stats 2007 ch 568 (AB 14) §1.5.

2000 Note: It is the intent of the Legislature to codify the decision in *People v. Garcia* (2000) 77 Cal.App.4th 1269. Stats 2000 ch 43 §1(b).

§204a. [Section renumbered 1981]
Leg.H. Added Stats 1917 ch 665 §1. Amended Stats 1943 ch 149 §1; Stats 1947 ch 157 §1; Stats 1949 ch 1425 §1; Stats 1951 ch 523 §1, ch 936 §1; Stats 1953 ch 1330 §1; Stats 1955 ch 260 §1; Stats 1961 ch 1721 §1; Stats 1963 ch 195 §2; Amended and renumbered CCP §204.1 by Stats 1980 ch 81 §11.

§204b. [Section repealed 1981]
Leg.H. Added Stats 1917 ch 665 §1. Amended Stats 1959 ch 501 §13; Stats 1961 ch 1099 §2; Stats 1978 ch 718 §4. Repealed Stats 1980 ch 81 §12. The repealed section related to the commissioner's furnishing to judges a list of qualified jurors. See Pen C §903.1.

§204c. [Section renumbered 1981]
Leg.H. Added Stats 1917 ch 665 §1. Amended Stats 1941 ch 975 §1; Stats 1943 ch 1039 §1; Stats 1959 ch 501 §14; Stats 1975 ch 657 §1; Amended and renumbered CCP §204.3 by Stats 1980 ch 81 §13.

§204d. [Section repealed 1981]
Leg.H. Added Stats 1917 ch 665 §1. Amended Stats 1959 ch 501 §15; Stats 1961 ch 1099 §3; Stats 1975 ch 657 §2. Repealed Stats 1980 ch 81 §14. The repealed section related to the selection of jurors from the commissioner's list. See Pen C §§903.3, 903.4.

§204e. [Section renumbered 1981]
Leg.H. Added Stats 1975 ch 657 §3. Amended and renumbered CCP §204.7 by Stats 1980 ch 81 §16, operative July 1, 1981.

Prior Law: Former CCP §204e, relating to secretary of superior judges as jury commissioner, was added Stats 1917 ch 665 §1, amended Stats 1921 ch 817 §1, Stats 1927 ch 682 §1, Stats 1929 ch 848 §1, Stats 1931 ch 1075 §1, Stats 1941 ch 975 §2, Stats 1943 ch 59 §1, Stats 1945 ch 535 §1, Stats 1947 ch 827 §1, Stats 1949 ch 987 §1, Stats 1951 ch 1360 §1, and repealed Stats 1953 ch 206 §7.

§204f. [Section repealed 1951]
Leg.H. Added Stats 1945 ch 1246 §1. Amended Stats 1949 ch 1412 §1. Repealed Stats 1951 ch 1316 §2.

§204g. [Section repealed 1953]
Leg.H. Added Stats 1951 ch 1316 §1. Repealed Stats 1953 ch 206 §7. The repealed section related to secretaries of superior courts in certain counties.

§204h. [Section repealed 1953]
Leg.H. Added Stats 1947 ch 950 §1. Amended Stats 1949 ch 1131 §1; Stats 1951 ch 1195 §1. Repealed Stats 1953 ch 206 §7. The repealed section related to performance of duties of jury commissioner by the secretary of the judges of the superior court.

§204.1. [Section repealed 1989]
Leg.H. Added Stats 1917 ch 665 §1 as CCP §204a. Amended Stats 1943 ch 149 §1; Stats 1947 ch 157 §1; Stats 1949 ch 1425 §1; Stats 1951 ch 523 §1, ch 936 §1; Stats 1953 ch 1330 §1; Stats 1955 ch 260 §1; Stats 1961 ch 1721 §1; Stats 1963 ch 195 §2. Amended and renumbered by Stats 1980 ch 81 §11. Repealed Stats 1988 ch 1245 §1. The repealed section related to appointment of jury commissioner in county where court administrator did not perform duties of jury commissioner, and salaries and duties of commissioner and deputies.

§204.3. [Section repealed 1989]
Leg.H. Added Stats 1917 ch 665 §1 as CCP §204c. Amended Stats 1941 ch 975 §1; Stats 1943 ch 1039 §1; Stats 1959 ch 501 §14; Stats 1975 ch 657 §1. Amended and renumbered Stats 1980 ch 81 §13. Amended Stats 1984 ch 589 §1. Repealed Stats 1988 ch 1245 §1. See CCP §§196, 205, 207.

§204.4. [Section repealed 1989]
Leg.H. Added Stats 1984 ch 589 §2. Repealed Stats 1988 ch 1245 §1. See CCP §205.

§204.5. [Section repealed 1989]
Leg.H. Added Stats 1980 ch 81 §14. Repealed Stats 1988 ch 1245 §1. See CCP §198.

§204.7. [Section repealed 1989]
Leg.H. Added Stats 1975 ch 657 §3 as CCP §204e. Amended and renumbered Stats 1980 ch 81 §16, operative July 1, 1981; Amended Stats 1983 ch 425 §1. Repealed Stats 1988 ch 1245 §1. See CCP §197.

§205. Questionnaires to prospective jurors [Repealed January 1, 2026]
(a) If a jury commissioner requires a person to complete a questionnaire, the questionnaire shall ask only questions related to juror identification, qualification, and ability to serve as a prospective juror.

(b) Except as ordered by the court, the questionnaire referred to in subdivision (a) shall be used solely for qualifying prospective jurors, and for management of the jury system, and not for assisting in the courtroom voir dire process of selecting trial jurors for specific cases.

(c) The court may require a prospective juror to complete such additional questionnaires as may be deemed relevant and necessary for assisting in the voir dire process or to ascertain whether a fair cross section of the population is represented as required by law, if such procedures are established by local court rule.

(d) The trial judge may direct a prospective juror to complete additional questionnaires as proposed by counsel in a particular case to assist the voir dire process.

(e) **This section shall remain in effect only until January 1, 2026, and as of that date is repealed. Leg.H.** Added Stats 1988 ch 1245 §2. Amended Stats 2024 ch 812 §11 (AB 1899), effective January 1, 2025, repealed January 1, 2026.

Prior Law: Former CCP §205, similar to present CCP §198, was enacted 1872, repealed and reenacted Code Amdts 1880 ch 35 §1, amended Stats 1881 ch 60 §2, Stats 1893 ch 213 §2, Stats 1915 ch 496 §1, Stats 1959 ch 501 §9, Stats 1972 ch

1028 §3, Stats 1975 ch 657 §4, Stats 1977 ch 591 §2, Stats 1978 ch 301 §2, Stats 1980 ch 81 §17, ch 1227 §2, Stats 1986 ch 1171 §2, and repealed Stats 1988 ch 1245 §1.

§ 205. Juror questionnaires; Judicial Council standard for gender identity and expression [Operative January 1, 2026]

(a) If a jury commissioner requires a person to complete a questionnaire, the questionnaire shall ask only questions related to juror identification, qualification, and ability to serve as a prospective juror.

(b) Except as ordered by the court, the questionnaire referred to in subdivision (a) shall be used solely for qualifying prospective jurors, and for management of the jury system, and not for assisting in the courtroom voir dire process of selecting trial jurors for specific cases.

(c) The court may require a prospective juror to complete such additional questionnaires as may be deemed relevant and necessary for assisting in the voir dire process or to ascertain whether a fair cross section of the population is represented as required by law, if such procedures are established by local court rule.

(d) The trial judge may direct a prospective juror to complete additional questionnaires as proposed by counsel in a particular case to assist the voir dire process.

(e) The Judicial Council shall adopt a standard of judicial administration to ensure that juror identification and any juror questionnaire is inclusive, including allowing a juror the ability to express their gender identity or gender expression, if applicable.

(f) This section shall become operative on January 1, 2026. **Leg.H.** Added Stats 2024 ch 812 §12 (AB 1899), effective January 1, 2025, operative January 1, 2026.

§206. Right of jurors not to discuss deliberations or verdict; Petition for access to personal juror information

(a) Prior to discharging the jury from the case, the judge in a criminal action shall inform the jurors that they have an absolute right to discuss or not to discuss the deliberation or verdict with anyone. The judge shall also inform the jurors of the provisions set forth in subdivisions (b), (d), and (e).

(b) Following the discharge of the jury in a criminal case, the defendant, or his or her attorney or representative, or the prosecutor, or his or her representative, may discuss the jury deliberation or verdict with a member of the jury, provided that the juror consents to the discussion and that the discussion takes place at a reasonable time and place.

(c) If a discussion of the jury deliberation or verdict with a member of the jury pursuant to subdivision (b) occurs at any time more than 24 hours after the verdict, prior to discussing the jury deliberation or verdict with a member of a jury pursuant to subdivision (b), the defendant or his or her attorney or representative, or the prosecutor or his or her representative, shall inform the juror of the identity of the case, the party in that case which the person represents, the subject of the interview, the absolute right of the juror to discuss or not discuss the deliberations or verdict in the case with the person, and the juror's right to review and have a copy of any declaration filed with the court.

(d) Any unreasonable contact with a juror by the defendant, or his or her attorney or representative, or by the prosecutor, or his or her representative, without the juror's consent shall be immediately reported to the trial judge.

(e) Any violation of this section shall be considered a violation of a lawful court order and shall be subject to reasonable monetary sanctions in accordance with Section 177.5 of the Code of Civil Procedure.

(f) Nothing in the section shall prohibit a peace officer from investigating an allegation of criminal conduct.

(g) Pursuant to Section 237, a defendant or defendant's counsel may, following the recording of a jury's verdict in a criminal proceeding, petition the court for access to personal juror identifying information within the court's records necessary for the defendant to communicate with jurors for the purpose of developing a motion for new trial or any other lawful purpose. This information consists of jurors' names, addresses, and telephone numbers. The court shall consider all requests for personal juror identifying information pursuant to Section 237. **Leg.H.** Added Stats 1988 ch 1245 §2. Amended Stats 1992 ch 971 §2 (SB 1299); Stats 1993 ch 632 §1 (AB 1915); Stats 1995 ch 964 §2 (SB 508); Stats 1996 ch 636 §1 (SB 2123), effective September 19, 1996; Stats 2000 ch 242 §1 (AB 2567).

Prior Law: Former CCP §206, similar to present CCP §198, was enacted 1872, amended Code Amdts 1875–76 ch 514 §4, repealed and reenacted Code Amdts 1880 ch 35 §1, amended Stats 1881 ch 60 §3, Stats 1923 ch 195 §2, Stats 1951 ch 1495 §3, Stats 1959 ch 501 §10, Stats 1963 ch 1412 §1, Stats 1974 ch 806 §3, Stats 1980 ch 81 §18, and repealed Stats 1988 ch 1245 §1.

§206a. [Section repealed 1989]

Leg.H. Added Stats 1953 ch 1691 §1. Amended Stats 1965 ch 470 §1; Stats 1980 ch 81 §19. Repealed Stats 1988 ch 1245 §1. See CCP §198.5.

§206b. [Section repealed 1989]

Leg.H. Added Stats 1967 ch 930 §1. Amended Stats 1972 ch 554 §1. Repealed Stats 1988 ch 1245 §1. The repealed section related to drawing jury venires in 16th class counties.

§206c. [Section repealed 1989]

Leg.H. Added Stats 1977 ch 229 §1, effective July 7, 1977. Repealed Stats 1988 ch 1245 §1. The repealed section related to trial jury venires for the superior court in El Dorado County.

§207. Maintenance of records of selection and service of jurors

(a) The jury commissioner shall maintain records regarding selection, qualification, and assignment of prospective jurors.

(b) The jury commissioner shall maintain records providing a clear audit trail regarding a juror's attendance, jury fees, and mileage.

(c) All records and papers maintained or compiled by the jury commissioner in connection with the selection or service of a juror may be kept on an electronic or microfilm medium and such records shall be preserved for at least three years after the list used in their selection is prepared, or for any longer period ordered by the court or the jury commissioner. **Leg.H.** Added Stats 1988 ch 1245 §2.

Prior Law: Former CCP §207, relating to prohibition against selecting persons to serve as jurors in courts of record who actually served as jurors during the preceding year, was enacted 1872 and repealed Code Amdts 1875–76 ch 514 §5.

§208. Prospective jurors; Estimate of number; Summons

The jury commissioner shall estimate the number of prospective jurors that may be required to serve the needs of the court, and shall summon prospective jurors for service. Prospective jurors shall be summoned by mailing a summons by first-class mail or by personal service or, in urgency situations, as elsewhere provided by law. The summons, when served by mail, shall be mailed at least 10 days prior to the date of required appearance. Once a prospective juror has been summoned, the date, time, or place of appearance may be modified or further specified by the jury commissioner, by means of written, telegraphic, telephonic, or direct oral communication with the prospective juror. **Leg.H.** Added Stats 1988 ch 1245 §2. Amended Stats 2003 ch 149 §7 (SB 79).

Prior Law: Former CCP §208, relating to certified list to be filed with clerk of superior court or jury commissioner, was enacted 1872, repealed and reenacted Code Amdts 1880 ch 35 §1, amended Stats 1881 ch 60 §4, Stats 1893 ch 213 §3, Stats 1961 ch 728 §1, and repealed Stats 1980 ch 81 §20.

§209. Enforcement of summons; Punishment; Monetary sanctions

(a) Any prospective trial juror who has been summoned for service, and who fails to attend as directed or to respond to the court or jury commissioner and to be excused from attendance, may be attached and compelled to attend. Following an order to show cause hearing, the court may find the prospective juror in contempt of court, punishable by fine, incarceration, or both, as otherwise provided by law.

(b) In lieu of imposing sanctions for contempt as set forth in subdivision (a), the court may impose reasonable monetary sanctions, as provided in this subdivision, on a prospective juror who has not been excused pursuant to Section 204 after first providing the prospective juror with notice and an opportunity to be heard. If a juror fails to respond to the initial summons the court may issue a second summons indicating that the person failed to appear in response to a previous summons and ordering the person to appear for jury duty. The second summons may be issued no earlier than 90 days after the initial failure to appear. Upon the failure of the juror to appear in response to the second summons, the court may issue a failure to appear notice informing the person that failure to respond may result in the imposition of money sanctions. If the prospective juror does not attend the court within the time period as directed by the failure to appear notice, the court shall issue an order to show cause. Payment of monetary sanctions imposed pursuant to this subdivision does not relieve the person of his or her obligation to perform jury duty.

(c)(1) The court may give notice of its intent to impose sanctions by either of the following means:

(A) Verbally to a prospective juror appearing in person in open court.

(B) The issuance on its own motion of an order to show cause requiring the prospective juror to demonstrate reasons for not imposing sanctions. The court may serve the order to show cause by certified or first-class mail.

(2) The monetary sanctions imposed pursuant to subdivision (b) may not exceed two hundred fifty dollars ($250) for the first violation, seven hundred fifty dollars ($750) for the second violation, and one thousand five hundred dollars ($1,500) for the third and any subsequent violation. Monetary sanctions may not be imposed on a prospective juror more than once during a single juror pool cycle. The prospective juror may be excused from paying sanctions pursuant to subdivision (b) of Section 204 or in the interests of justice. The full amount of any sanction paid shall be deposited in a bank account established for this purpose by the Administrative Office of the Courts and transmitted from that account monthly to the Controller for deposit in the Trial Court Trust Fund, as provided in Section 68085.1 of the Government Code. It is the intent of the Legislature that the funds derived from the monetary sanctions authorized in this section be allocated, to the extent feasible, to the family courts and the civil courts. The Judicial Council shall, by rule, provide for a procedure by which a prospective juror against whom a sanction has been imposed by default may move to set aside the default. **Leg.H.** Added Stats 1988 ch 1245 §2. Amended Stats 2003 ch 359 §1 (AB 1180); Stats 2005 ch 75 §28 (AB 145), effective July 19, 2005, operative January 1, 2006, repealed January 1, 2007; Stats 2006 ch 567 §5 (AB 2303), effective January 1, 2007, repealed January 1, 2010; Stats 2009 ch 44 §1 (SB 319), effective January 1, 2010.

Former Sections: Former CCP §209, relating to enforcement of summons and punishment for prospective juror who fails to attend or respond to court, was added Stats 2003 ch 359 §2, operative January 1, 2007, and repealed Stats 2010 ch 328 §32.

Former CCP §209, relating to duty of clerk or jury commissioner to deposit names for drawing, was enacted 1872 and repealed Stats 1980 ch 81 §21.

Prior Law: Former CCP §209, relating to enforcement of summons and punishment for prospective juror who fails to attend or respond to court, was added Stats 2003 ch 359 §2, operative January 1, 2007, amended Stats 2006 ch 567 §6, effective January 1, 2007, operative January 1, 2010, and repealed Stats 2010 ch 328 §32, effective January 1, 2011.

Former CCP §209, relating to duty of clerk or jury commissioner to deposit names for drawing, was enacted 1872, amended Code Amdts 1875–76 ch 514 §6, repealed and reenacted Code Amdts 1880 ch 35 §1, amended Stats 1881 ch 60 §5, Stats 1959 ch 501 §11, Stats 1961 ch 728 §2, and repealed Stats 1980 ch 81 §21.

§210. Contents of summons

The summons shall contain the date, time, and place of appearance required of the prospective juror or, alternatively, instructions as to the procedure for calling the jury commissioner for telephonic instructions for appearance as well as such additional juror information as deemed appropriate by the jury commissioner. **Leg.H.** Added Stats 1988 ch 1245 §2.

Prior Law: Former CCP§210, relating to regular jurors serving for one year, was enacted 1872, repealed and reenacted Code Amdts 1880 ch 35 §1, amended Stats 1978 ch 718 §5, and repealed Stats 1980 ch 81 §21.5.

§210.5. Standardized jury summons

The Judicial Council shall adopt a standardized jury summons for use, with appropriate modifications, around the state, that is understandable and has consumer appeal. The standardized jury summons shall include a specific reference to the rules for breast-feeding mothers. The use of the standardized jury summons shall be voluntary, unless otherwise prescribed by the rules of court. **Leg.H.** Added Stats 2000 ch 266 §2 (AB 1814).

2000 Note: The Judicial Council shall adopt a rule of court to specifically allow the mother of a breast-fed child to postpone jury duty for a period of up to one year, providing that all steps should be taken to eliminate the need for the mother to physically appear in court to make this request, and providing that at the end of the one-year period, jury duty may be further postponed upon written request by the mother of a breast-fed child. Stats 2000 ch 266 §1.

§211. Summoning jurors to complete panel

When a court has no prospective jurors remaining available for voir dire from panels furnished by, or available from, the jury commissioner, and finds that not proceeding with voir dire will place a party's right to a trial by jury in jeopardy, the court may direct the sheriff or marshal to summon, serve, and immediately attach the person of a sufficient number of citizens having the qualifications of jurors, to complete the panel. **Leg.H.** Added Stats 1988 ch 1245 §2. Amended Stats 1996 ch 872 §7 (AB 3472).

Prior Law: Former CCP §211, relating to drawing of jurors names from jury box and the placing of undrawn names on the following year's list, was added Code Amdts 1875–76 ch 514 §7, repealed and reenacted Code Amdts 1880 ch 35 §1, amended Stats 1881 ch 60 §6, Stats 1959 ch 501 §12, and repealed Stats 1980 ch 81 §22.

§213. One-hour telephone notice

Unless excused by reason of undue hardship, all or any portion of the summoned prospective jurors shall be available on one-hour notice by telephone to appear for service, when the jury commissioner determines that it will efficiently serve the operational requirements of the court.

Jurors available on one-hour telephone notice shall receive credit for each day of such availability towards their jury service obligation, but they shall not be paid unless they are actually required to make an appearance. **Leg.H.** Added Stats 1988 ch 1245 §2.

§214. Juror orientation

The jury commissioner shall provide orientation for new jurors, which shall include necessary basic information concerning jury service. The jury commissioner shall notify each juror of [1] **paragraph (1) of subdivision (a) of Section 12945.8 of the Government** Code. **Leg.H.** Added Stats 1988 ch 1245 §2. Amended Stats 1989 ch 1416 §8; Stats 2024 ch 967 §1 (AB 2499), effective January 1, 2025.

§214. 2024 Deletes. [1] the provisions of Section 230 of the Labor

Prior Law: Former CCP §214, relating to order of judge or judges for drawing of jury, was enacted 1872, amended Code Amdts 1873–74 ch 383 §19, Code Amdts 1875–76 ch 514 §8, repealed and reenacted Code Amdts 1880 ch 35 §1, and repealed Stats 1988 ch 1245 §1.

§ 215. Juror fees and expenses; Use of public transit service

(a) Except as provided in subdivision (b), on and after July 1, 2000, the fee for jurors in the superior court, in civil and criminal cases, is fifteen dollars ($15) a day for each day's attendance as a juror after the first day.

(b) A juror who is employed by a federal, state, or local government entity, or by any other public entity as defined in Section 481.200, and who receives regular compensation and benefits while performing jury service, shall not be paid the fee described in subdivision (a).

(c) All jurors in the superior court, in civil and criminal cases, shall be reimbursed for mileage at the rate of thirty-four cents ($0.34) per mile for each mile actually traveled in attending and returning from court as a juror after the first day.

(d) All jurors and prospective jurors who have been summoned shall be provided with access to existing public transit services at no cost utilizing one of the following options:

(1) Courts may partner with public transit operators in their county to create new programs or continue existing public transit programs that provide no-cost service for jurors and prospective jurors who have been summoned.

(2) A method of reimbursement determined by the court up to a daily maximum of twelve dollars ($12).

(e) Subdivision (d) does not apply to a court in an area where a public transit operator does not provide existing service that is reasonably available to the court facility.

(f) In determining whether transit service is reasonably available to the court facility, the court shall consider factors that include, but are not limited to, all of the following:

(1) Proximity of transit service to the court location.

(2) Hours of operation of transit service in the vicinity of the court location.

(3) Frequency of operation of transit service in the vicinity of the court location.

(4) Availability of transit access to all areas of the court's jurisdiction from which a potential juror may reside.

(g) Prior to determining that transit service is not reasonably available to the court facility, the court shall contact the public transit operator to inquire whether new transit options may be implemented near the court. **Leg.H.** Added Stats 1988 ch 1245 §2. Amended Stats 1998 ch 931 §54

(SB 2139), effective September 28, 1998; Stats 2000 ch 127 §1 (AB 2866), effective July 10, 2000; Stats 2002 ch 144 §1 (AB 2925) (ch 144 prevails), ch 784 §48 (SB 1316); Stats 2004 ch 227 §9 (SB 1102), effective August 16, 2004; Stats 2022 ch 326 §2 (AB 1981), effective January 1, 2023.

Prior Law: Former CCP §215, relating to drawing of jurors by clerk or attaché, was added Code Amdts 1880 ch 35 §1, amended Stats 1881 ch 60 §7, Stats 1961 ch 728 §3, and repealed Stats 1980 ch 81 §23.

Former CCP §215, requiring clerk to notify county judge and sheriff of time of drawing, was enacted 1872 and repealed Code Amdts 1880 ch 35 §1.

§216. Deliberations rooms

(a) At each court facility where jury cases are heard, the court shall provide a deliberation room or rooms for use of jurors when they have retired for deliberation. The deliberation rooms shall be designed to minimize unwarranted intrusions by other persons in the court facility, shall have suitable furnishings, equipment, and supplies, and shall also have restroom accommodations for male and female jurors.

(b) Unless authorized by the jury commissioner, jury assembly facilities shall be restricted to use by jurors and jury commissioner staff. **Leg.H.** Added Stats 1988 ch 1245 §2. Amended Stats 1996 ch 872 §8 (AB 3472); Stats 2020 ch 210 §1 (AB 1984), effective January 1, 2021.

Prior Law: Former CCP §216 was enacted 1872 and repealed Code Amdts 1880 ch 35 §1.

§217. Criminal cases; Provision of food and lodging

In criminal cases only, while the jury is kept together, either during the progress of the trial or after their retirement for deliberation, the court may direct the sheriff or marshal to provide the jury with suitable and sufficient food and lodging, or other reasonable necessities. The expenses incurred under this section shall be charged against the Trial Court Operations Fund of the county in which the court is held. All those expenses shall be paid on the order of the court. **Leg.H.** Added Stats 1988 ch 1245 §2. Amended Stats 1996 ch 872 §9 (AB 3472); Stats 1998 ch 931 §55 (SB 2139), effective September 28, 1998; Stats 2002 ch 784 §49 (SB 1316).

Prior Law: Former CCP §217 was enacted 1872, amended Code Amdts 1873–74 ch 383 §21, and repealed Code Amdts 1880 ch 35 §1.

§218. Hearing excuses

The jury commissioner shall hear the excuses of jurors summoned, in accordance with the standards prescribed by the Judicial Council. It shall be left to the discretion of the jury commissioner to accept an excuse under subdivision (b) of Section 204 without a personal appearance. All excuses shall be in writing setting forth the basis of the request and shall be signed by the juror. **Leg.H.** Added Stats 1988 ch 1245 §2.

Prior Law: Former CCP §218 was enacted 1872 and repealed Code Amdts 1880 ch 35 §1.

§219. Selection of jury panels

(a) Except as provided in subdivision (b), the jury commissioner shall randomly select jurors for jury panels to be sent to courtrooms for voir dire.

(b)(1) Notwithstanding subdivision (a), no peace officer, as defined in Section 830.1, subdivision (a) of Section 830.2, and subdivision (a) of Section 830.33, of the Penal Code, shall be selected for voir dire in civil or criminal matters.

(2) Notwithstanding subdivision (a), no peace officer, as defined in subdivisions (b) and (c) of Section 830.2 of the Penal Code, shall be selected for voir dire in criminal matters. **Leg.H.** Added Stats 1988 ch 1245 §2. Amended Stats 1992 ch 324 §1 (AB 2577); Stats 1994 ch 742 §2 (SB 2066); Stats 1998 ch 606 §1 (SB 1880); Stats 2001 ch 55 §1 (SB 303).

Prior Law: Former CCP §219, relating to conduct of drawing, was enacted 1872, repealed and reenacted Code Amdts 1880 ch 35 §1, amended Stats 1881 ch 60 §8, Stats 1961 ch 728 §4, and repealed Stats 1980 ch 81 §24.

§219.5. Adoption of rules to give certain peace officers scheduling accommodations

The Judicial Council shall adopt a rule of court, on or before January 1, 2005, requiring the trial courts to establish procedures for jury service that gives peace officers, as defined by Section 830.5 of the Penal Code, scheduling accommodations when necessary. **Leg.H.** Added Stats 2003 ch 353 §1 (AB 513).

§220. Number of trial jury

A trial jury shall consist of 12 persons, except that in civil actions and cases of misdemeanor, it may consist of 12 or any number less than 12, upon which the parties may agree. **Leg.H.** Added Stats 1988 ch 1245 §2.

Prior Law: Former CCP §220, relating to the preservation of ballots drawn, was enacted 1872, amended Code Amdts 1875–76 ch 514 §9, repealed and reenacted Code Amdts 1880 ch 35 §1, amended Stats 1961 ch 728 §5, and repealed Stats 1980 ch 81 §25.

§221. [Section repealed 2002]

Leg.H. Added Stats 1988 ch 1245 §2. Repealed Stats 2001 ch 115 §1 (SB 153). The repealed section related to 8-person jury in Los Angeles County.

Prior Law: Former CCP §221 was enacted 1872 and repealed Code Amdts 1880 ch 35 §1.

§222. Selection for voir dire

(a) Except as provided in subdivision (b), when an action is called for trial by jury, the clerk shall randomly select the names of the jurors for voir dire, until the jury is selected or the panel is exhausted.

(b) When the jury commissioner has provided the court with a listing of the trial jury panel in random order, the court shall seat prospective jurors for voir dire in the order provided by the panel list. **Leg.H.** Added Stats 1988 ch 1245 §2. Amended Stats 2007 ch 263 §4 (AB 310), effective January 1, 2008.

§222.5. Voir dire in civil cases; "Improper question"

(a) To select a fair and impartial jury in a civil jury trial, the trial judge shall conduct an initial examination of prospective jurors. At the final status conference or at the first practical opportunity prior to voir dire, whichever comes first, the trial judge shall consider and discuss with counsel the form and subject matter of voir dire questions. Before voir dire by the trial judge, the parties may submit questions to the trial judge. The trial judge may include additional questions requested by the parties as the trial judge deems proper.

(b)(1) Upon completion of the trial judge's initial examination, counsel for each party shall have the right to examine, by oral and direct questioning, any of the prospective jurors in order to enable counsel to intelligently exercise both peremptory challenges and challenges for cause. The scope of the examination conducted by counsel shall be within reasonable limits prescribed by the trial judge in the judge's sound discretion subject to the provisions of this chapter. During any examination conducted by counsel for the parties, the trial judge shall permit liberal and probing examination calculated to discover bias or prejudice with regard to the circumstances of the particular case before the court. The fact that a topic has been included in the trial judge's examination shall not preclude appropriate followup questioning in the same area by counsel. The trial judge shall permit counsel to conduct voir dire examination without requiring prior submission of the questions unless a particular counsel engages in improper questioning.

(2) The trial judge shall not impose specific unreasonable or arbitrary time limits or establish an inflexible time limit policy for voir dire.

(3) For purposes of this section, an "improper question" is any question that, as its dominant purpose, attempts to precondition the prospective jurors to a particular result, indoctrinate the jury, or question the prospective jurors concerning the pleadings or the applicable law.

(c) (1) In exercising the judge's sound discretion, the trial judge shall give due consideration to all of the following:

(A) The amount of time requested by trial counsel.
(B) Any unique or complex elements, legal or factual, in the case.
(C) Length of the trial.
(D) Number of parties.
(E) Number of witnesses.
(F) Whether the case is designated as a complex or long cause.

(2) As voir dire proceeds, the judge shall permit supplemental time for questioning based on any of the following:

(A) Individual responses or conduct of jurors that may evince attitudes inconsistent with suitability to serve as a fair and impartial juror in the particular case.
(B) Composition of the jury panel.
(C) An unusual number of for cause challenges.

(d) Upon the request of a party, the trial judge shall allow a brief opening statement by counsel for each party prior to the commencement of the oral questioning phase of the voir dire process.

(e) In civil cases, the trial judge may, upon stipulation by counsel for all the parties appearing in the action, permit counsel to examine the prospective jurors outside a judge's presence.

(f) A trial judge shall not arbitrarily or unreasonably refuse to submit reasonable written questionnaires, the contents of which are determined by the court in its sound discretion, when requested by counsel. If a questionnaire is utilized, the parties shall be given reasonable time to evaluate the responses to the questionnaires before oral questioning commences.

(g) To help facilitate the jury selection process, at the earliest practical time, the judge in a civil trial shall provide the parties with both the alphabetical list and the list of prospective jurors in the order in which they will be called. **Leg.H.** Added Stats 1990 ch 1232 §1.5 (AB 3820). Amended Stats 2011 ch 409 §1 (AB 1403), effective January 1, 2012; Stats 2017 ch 337 §1 (SB 658), effective January 1, 2018.

§223. Voir dire in criminal jury trial

(a) To select a fair and impartial jury in a criminal jury trial, the trial judge shall conduct an initial examination of prospective jurors. At the first practical opportunity prior to voir dire, the trial judge shall consider the form and subject matter of voir dire questions. Before voir dire by the trial judge, the parties may submit questions to the trial judge. The trial judge may include additional questions requested by the parties as the trial judge deems proper.

(b)(1) Upon completion of the trial judge's initial examination, counsel for each party shall have the right to examine, by oral and direct questioning, any of the prospective jurors. The scope of the examination conducted by counsel shall be within reasonable limits prescribed by the trial judge in the judge's sound discretion subject to the provisions of this chapter. During any examination conducted by counsel for the parties, the trial judge shall permit liberal and probing examination calculated to discover bias or prejudice with regard to the circumstances of the particular case or the parties before the court. The fact that a topic has been included in the trial judge's examination shall not preclude appropriate followup questioning in the same area by counsel. The trial judge should permit counsel to conduct voir dire examination without requiring prior submission of the questions unless a particular counsel engages in improper questioning.

(2) The trial judge shall not impose specific unreasonable or arbitrary time limits or establish an inflexible time limit policy for voir dire. As voir dire proceeds, the trial judge shall permit supplemental time for questioning based on individual responses or conduct of jurors that may evince attitudes inconsistent with suitability to serve as a fair and impartial juror in the particular case.

(3) For purposes of this section, an "improper question" is any question that, as its dominant purpose, attempts to precondition the prospective jurors to a particular result or indoctrinate the jury.

(c) In exercising the judge's sound discretion, the trial judge shall consider all of the following:

(1) The amount of time requested by trial counsel.
(2) Any unique or complex legal or factual elements in the case.
(3) The length of the trial.
(4) The number of parties.
(5) The number of witnesses.

(d) Voir dire of any prospective jurors shall, where practicable, take place in the presence of the other jurors in all criminal cases, including death penalty cases. Examination of prospective jurors shall be conducted only in aid of the exercise of challenges for cause.

(e) The trial judge shall, in his or her sound discretion, consider reasonable written questionnaires when requested by counsel. If a questionnaire is utilized, the parties shall be given reasonable time to evaluate the responses to the questionnaires before oral questioning commences.

(f) To help facilitate the jury selection process, at the earliest practical time, the trial judge in a criminal trial shall provide the parties with the list of prospective jurors in the order in which they will be called.

(g) The trial judge's exercise of discretion in the manner in which voir dire is conducted, including any limitation on the time that will be allowed for direct questioning of prospective jurors by counsel and any determination that a question is not in aid of the exercise of challenges for cause, is not cause for a conviction to be reversed, unless the exercise of that discretion results in a miscarriage of justice, as specified in Section 13 of Article VI of the California Constitution. **Leg.H.** Added Stats 2017 ch 302 §2 (AB 1541), effective January 1, 2018.

Former Sections: Former CCP §223 was enacted by Initiative (Prop. 115 §7) at the June 5, 1990, Primary Election, operative June 6, 1990, and repealed 2017 ch 302 (AB 1541) §1.

Prior Law: Former CCP §223, similar to the present section, was adopted by voters, Prop. 115 §7, effective June 6, 1990, amended Stats 2000 ch 192 §1 (AB 2406), effective January 1, 2001, and repealed Stats 2017 ch 302 §1 (AB 1541), effective January 1, 2018.

Former CCP §223, similar to the present section, was added Stats 1988 ch 1245 §2 and repealed by voters, Prop 115 §6, effective June 6, 1990.

§223.5. [Section repealed 1990]

Leg.H. Added Stats 1988 ch 1245 §2. Repeal adopted by voters, Prop 115 §7.5, effective June 6, 1990. The repealed section related to voir dire in criminal cases in Fresno and Santa Cruz counties.

§224. Juror with specified physical disabilities; "Service provider"

(a) If a party does not cause the removal by challenge of an individual juror who is deaf, hard of hearing, blind, visually impaired, or speech impaired and who requires auxiliary services to facilitate communication, the party shall stipulate to the presence of a service provider in the jury room during jury deliberations, and prepare and deliver to the court proposed jury instructions to the service provider.

(b) As used in this section, "service provider" includes, but is not limited to, a person who is a sign language interpreter, oral interpreter, deaf-blind interpreter, reader, or speech interpreter. If auxiliary services are required during the course of jury deliberations, the court shall instruct the jury and the service provider that the service provider for the juror with a disability is not to participate in the jury's deliberations in any manner except to facilitate communication between the juror with a disability and other jurors.

(c) The court shall appoint a service provider whose services are needed by a juror with a disability to facilitate communication or participation. A sign language interpreter, oral interpreter, or deaf-blind interpreter appointed pursuant to this section shall be a qualified interpreter, as defined in subdivision (f) of Section 754 of the Evidence Code. Service providers appointed by the court under this subdivision shall be compensated in the same manner as provided in subdivision (i) of Section 754 of the Evidence Code. **Leg.H.** Added Stats 1988 ch 1245 §2. Amended Stats 1992 ch 913 §9 (AB 1077); Stats 1993 ch 1214 §3 (AB 551); Stats 2016 ch 94 §3 (AB 1709), effective January 1, 2017.

§225. Challenges

A challenge is an objection made to the trial jurors that may be taken by any party to the action, and is of the following classes and types:

(a) A challenge to the trial jury panel for cause.

(1) A challenge to the panel may only be taken before a trial jury is sworn. The challenge shall be reduced to writing, and shall plainly and distinctly state the facts constituting the ground of challenge.

(2) Reasonable notice of the challenge to the jury panel shall be given to all parties and to the jury commissioner, by service of a copy thereof.

(3) The jury commissioner shall be permitted the services of legal counsel in connection with challenges to the jury panel.

(b) A challenge to a prospective juror by either:

(1) A challenge for cause, for one of the following reasons:

(A) General disqualification—that the juror is disqualified from serving in the action on trial.

(B) Implied bias—as, when the existence of the facts as ascertained, in judgment of law disqualifies the juror.

(C) Actual bias—the existence of a state of mind on the part of the juror in reference to the case, or to any of the parties, which will prevent the juror from acting with entire impartiality, and without prejudice to the substantial rights of any party.

(2) A peremptory challenge to a prospective juror. **Leg.H.** Added Stats 1988 ch 1245 §2.

Prior Law: Former CCP §225, similar to present CCP §208, was enacted 1872, repealed and reenacted Code Amdts 1880 ch 35 §1, amended Stats 1915 ch 552 §1, Stats 1933 ch 743 §55, Stats 1955 ch 1401 §2, Stats 1959 ch 759 §2, Stats 1961 ch 1102 §1, Stats 1967 ch 82 §1, and repealed Stats 1988 ch 1245 §1.

§226. Challenge to individual juror

(a) A challenge to an individual juror may only be made before the jury is sworn.

(b) A challenge to an individual juror may be taken orally or may be made in writing, but no reason need be given for a peremptory challenge, and the court shall exclude any juror challenged peremptorily.

(c) All challenges for cause shall be exercised before any peremptory challenges may be exercised.

(d) All challenges to an individual juror, except a peremptory challenge, shall be taken, first by the defendants, and then by the people or plaintiffs. **Leg.H.** Added Stats 1988 ch 1245 §2.

Prior Law: Former CCP §226, similar to present CCP §211, was enacted 1872, amended Code Amdts 1873–74 ch 383 §22, repealed and reenacted Code Amdts 1880 ch 35 §1, amended Stats 1917 ch 692 §8, Stats 1933 ch 743 §56, Stats 1951 ch 1495 §4, operative January 1, 1952, and repealed Stats 1988 ch 1245 §1.

§227. Challenges for cause

The challenges of either party for cause need not all be taken at once, but they may be taken separately, in the following order, including in each challenge all the causes of challenge belonging to the same class and type:
 (a) To the panel.
 (b) To an individual juror, for a general disqualification.
 (c) To an individual juror, for an implied bias.
 (d) To an individual juror, for an actual bias. **Leg.H.** Added Stats 1988 ch 1245 §2.

Prior Law: Former CCP §227, similar to present CCP §211, was enacted 1872, amended Code Amdts 1873–74 ch 383 §23, repealed and reenacted Code Amdts 1880 ch 35 §1, amended Stats 1933 ch 743 §57, Stats 1951 ch 1495 §5, operative January 1, 1952, and repealed Stats 1988 ch 1245 §1.

§228. Challenges for general disqualification

Challenges for general disqualification may be taken on one or both of the following grounds, and for no other:
 (a) A want of any of the qualifications prescribed by this code to render a person competent as a juror.
 (b) The existence of any incapacity which satisfies the court that the challenged person is incapable of performing the duties of a juror in the particular action without prejudice to the substantial rights of the challenging party. **Leg.H.** Added Stats 1988 ch 1245 §2. Amended Stats 2002 ch 1008 §1 (AB 3028).

Prior Law: Former CCP §228, relating to compensation of elisor, was added Code Amdts 1875–76 ch 514 §10, repealed and reenacted Code Amdts 1880 ch 35 §1, amended Stats 1933 ch 743 §58, and repealed Stats 1988 ch 1245 §1.

§229. Challenges for implied bias

A challenge for implied bias may be taken for one or more of the following causes, and for no other:
 (a) Consanguinity or affinity within the fourth degree to any party, to an officer of a corporation which is a party, or to any alleged witness or victim in the case at bar.
 (b) Standing in the relation of, or being the parent, spouse, or child of one who stands in the relation of, guardian and ward, conservator and conservatee, master and servant, employer and clerk, landlord and tenant, principal and agent, or debtor and creditor, to either party or to an officer of a corporation which is a party, or being a member of the family of either party; or a partner in business with either party; or surety on any bond or obligation for either party, or being the holder of bonds or shares of capital stock of a corporation which is a party; or having stood within one year previous to the filing of the complaint in the action in the relation of attorney and client with either party or with the attorney for either party. A depositor of a bank or a holder of a savings account in a savings and loan association shall not be deemed a creditor of that bank or savings and loan association for the purpose of this paragraph solely by reason of his or her being a depositor or account holder.
 (c) Having served as a trial or grand juror or on a jury of inquest in a civil or criminal action or been a witness on a previous or pending trial between the same parties, or involving the same specific offense or cause of action; or having served as a trial or grand juror or on a jury within one year previously in any criminal or civil action or proceeding in which either party was the plaintiff or defendant or in a criminal action where either party was the defendant.
 (d) Interest on the part of the juror in the event of the action, or in the main question involved in the action, except his or her interest as a member or citizen or taxpayer of a county, city and county, incorporated city or town, or other political subdivision of a county, or municipal water district.
 (e) Having an unqualified opinion or belief as to the merits of the action founded on knowledge of its material facts or of some of them.
 (f) The existence of a state of mind in the juror evincing enmity against, or bias towards, either party.
 (g) That the juror is party to an action pending in the court for which he or she is drawn and which action is set for trial before the panel of which the juror is a member.
 (h) If the offense charged is punishable with death, the entertaining of such conscientious opinions as would preclude the juror finding the defendant guilty; in which case the juror may neither be permitted nor compelled to serve. **Leg.H.** Added Stats 1988 ch 1245 §2.

§230. Challenges tried by court

Challenges for cause shall be tried by the court. The juror challenged and any other person may be examined as a witness in the trial of the challenge, and shall truthfully answer all questions propounded to them. **Leg.H.** Added Stats 1988 ch 1245 §2.

Prior Law: Former CCP §230, relating to jurors for justice courts, was enacted 1872, repealed and reenacted Code Amdts 1880 ch 35 §1, amended Stats 1907 ch 355 §1, Stats 1951 ch 1495 §6, operative January 1, 1952, and repealed Stats 1980 ch 81 §26.

§231. Peremptory challenges

(a) In criminal cases, if the offense charged is punishable with death, or with imprisonment in the state prison for life, the defendant is entitled to 20 and the people to 20 peremptory challenges. Except as provided in subdivision (b), in a trial for any other offense, the defendant is entitled to 10 and the state to 10 peremptory challenges. When two or more defendants are jointly tried, their challenges shall be exercised jointly, but each defendant shall also be entitled to five additional challenges which may be exercised separately, and the people shall also be entitled to additional challenges equal to the number of all the additional separate challenges allowed the defendants.

(b) If the offense charged is punishable with a maximum term of imprisonment of 90 days or less, the defendant is entitled to six and the state to six peremptory challenges. When two or more defendants are jointly tried, their challenges shall be exercised jointly, but each defendant shall also be entitled to four additional challenges which may be exercised separately, and the state shall also be entitled to additional challenges equal to the number of all the additional separate challenges allowed the defendants.

(c) In civil cases, each party shall be entitled to six peremptory challenges. If there are more than two parties, the court shall, for the purpose of allotting peremptory challenges, divide the parties into two or more sides according to their respective interests in the issues. Each side shall be entitled to eight peremptory challenges. If there are several parties on a side, the court shall divide the challenges among them as nearly equally as possible. If there are more than two sides, the court shall grant such additional peremptory challenges to a side as the interests of justice may require, provided that the peremptory challenges of one side shall not exceed the aggregate number of peremptory challenges of all other sides. If any party on a side does not use his or her full share of peremptory challenges, the unused challenges may be used by the other party or parties on the same side.

(d) Peremptory challenges shall be taken or passed by the sides alternately, commencing with the plaintiff or people, and each party shall be entitled to have the panel full before exercising any peremptory challenge. When each side passes consecutively, the jury shall then be sworn, unless the court, for good cause, shall otherwise order. The number of peremptory challenges remaining with a side shall not be diminished by any passing of a peremptory challenge.

(e) If all the parties on both sides pass consecutively, the jury shall then be sworn, unless the court, for good cause, shall otherwise order. The number of peremptory challenges remaining with a side shall not be diminished by any passing of a peremptory challenge.

(f) This section shall become operative on January 1, 2021. **Leg.H.** Added Stats 2016 ch 33 §3 (SB 843), effective June 27, 2016, operative January 1, 2021.

Prior Law: Former CCP §231, relating to the summoning of jurors in courts not of record, was enacted 1872, repealed and reenacted Code Amdts 1880 ch 35 §1, amended Stats 1923 ch 117 §1, Stats 1927 ch 656 §1, Stats 1933 ch 743 §59, Stats 1941 ch 1024 §1, Stats 1943 ch 512 §1, Stats 1951 ch 1495 §7, operative January 1, 1952, Stats 1965 ch 861 §1, Stats 1967 ch 82 §2, and repealed Stats 1980 ch 81 §26. Former CCP §231, similar to the present section, was added Stats 1988 ch 1245 §2, amended Stats 1989 ch 1416 §9, Stats 2016 ch 33 §1 (SB 843), effective June 27, 2016, and repealed January 1, 2017, by its own terms.

§231.5. Assumption of bias

A party shall not use a peremptory challenge to remove a prospective juror on the basis of an assumption that the prospective juror is biased merely because of a characteristic listed or defined in Section 11135 of the

Government Code, or similar grounds. **Leg.H.** Added Stats 2000 ch 43 §3 (AB 2418). Amended Stats 2015 ch 115 §1 (AB 87), effective January 1, 2016.

Prior Law: Former CCP §231.5, relating to use of superior court jury list by justice court, was added Stats 1975 ch 395 §1 and repealed Stats 1980 ch 81 §26.

2000 Note: It is the intent of the Legislature to codify the decision in *People v. Garcia* (2000) 77 Cal.App.4th 1269. Stats 2000 ch 43 §1(b).

§ 231.7. Prohibition to use of peremptory challenge based on specified criteria [Repealed January 1, 2026]

(a) A party shall not use a peremptory challenge to remove a prospective juror on the basis of the prospective juror's race, ethnicity, gender, gender identity, sexual orientation, national origin, or religious affiliation, or the perceived membership of the prospective juror in any of those groups.

(b) A party, or the trial court on its own motion, may object to the improper use of a peremptory challenge under subdivision (a). After the objection is made, any further discussion shall be conducted outside the presence of the panel. The objection shall be made before the jury is impaneled, unless information becomes known that could not have reasonably been known before the jury was impaneled.

(c) Notwithstanding Section 226, upon objection to the exercise of a peremptory challenge pursuant to this section, the party exercising the peremptory challenge shall state the reasons the peremptory challenge has been exercised.

(d)(1) The court shall evaluate the reasons given to justify the peremptory challenge in light of the totality of the circumstances. The court shall consider only the reasons actually given and shall not speculate on, or assume the existence of, other possible justifications for the use of the peremptory challenge. If the court determines there is a substantial likelihood that an objectively reasonable person would view race, ethnicity, gender, gender identity, sexual orientation, national origin, or religious affiliation, or perceived membership in any of those groups, as a factor in the use of the peremptory challenge, then the objection shall be sustained. The court need not find purposeful discrimination to sustain the objection. The court shall explain the reasons for its ruling on the record. A motion brought under this section shall also be deemed a sufficient presentation of claims asserting the discriminatory exclusion of jurors in violation of the United States and California Constitutions.

(2)(A) For purposes of this section, an objectively reasonable person is aware that unconscious bias, in addition to purposeful discrimination, have resulted in the unfair exclusion of potential jurors in the State of California.

(B) For purposes of this section, a "substantial likelihood" means more than a mere possibility but less than a standard of more likely than not.

(C) For purposes of this section, "unconscious bias" includes implicit and institutional biases.

(3) In making its determination, the circumstances the court may consider include, but are not limited to, any of the following:

(A) Whether any of the following circumstances exist:

(i) The objecting party is a member of the same perceived cognizable group as the challenged juror.

(ii) The alleged victim is not a member of that perceived cognizable group.

(iii) Witnesses or the parties are not members of that perceived cognizable group.

(B) Whether race, ethnicity, gender, gender identity, sexual orientation, national origin, or religious affiliation, or perceived membership in any of those groups, bear on the facts of the case to be tried.

(C) The number and types of questions posed to the prospective juror, including, but not limited to, any of the following:

(i) Consideration of whether the party exercising the peremptory challenge failed to question the prospective juror about the concerns later stated by the party as the reason for the peremptory challenge pursuant to subdivision (c).

(ii) Whether the party exercising the peremptory challenge engaged in cursory questioning of the challenged potential juror.

(iii) Whether the party exercising the peremptory challenge asked different questions of the potential juror against whom the peremptory challenge was used in contrast to questions asked of other jurors from different perceived cognizable groups about the same topic or whether the party phrased those questions differently.

(D) Whether other prospective jurors, who are not members of the same cognizable group as the challenged prospective juror, provided similar, but not necessarily identical, answers but were not the subject of a peremptory challenge by that party.

(E) Whether a reason might be disproportionately associated with a race, ethnicity, gender, gender identity, sexual orientation, national origin, or religious affiliation, or perceived membership in any of those groups.

(F) Whether the reason given by the party exercising the peremptory challenge was contrary to or unsupported by the record.

(G) Whether the counsel or counsel's office exercising the challenge has used peremptory challenges disproportionately against a given race, ethnicity, gender, gender identity, sexual orientation, national origin, or religious affiliation, or perceived membership in any of those groups, in the present case or in past cases, including whether the counsel or counsel's office who made the challenge has a history of prior violations under Batson v. Kentucky (1986) 476 U.S. 79, People v. Wheeler (1978) 22 Cal.3d 258, Section 231.5, or this section.

(e) A peremptory challenge for any of the following reasons is presumed to be invalid unless the party exercising the peremptory challenge can show by clear and convincing evidence that an objectively reasonable person would view the rationale as unrelated to a prospective juror's race, ethnicity, gender, gender identity, sexual orientation, national origin, or religious affiliation, or perceived membership in any of those groups, and that the reasons articulated bear on the prospective juror's ability to be fair and impartial in the case:

(1) Expressing a distrust of or having a negative experience with law enforcement or the criminal legal system.

(2) Expressing a belief that law enforcement officers engage in racial profiling or that criminal laws have been enforced in a discriminatory manner.

(3) Having a close relationship with people who have been stopped, arrested, or convicted of a crime.

(4) A prospective juror's neighborhood.

(5) Having a child outside of marriage.

(6) Receiving state benefits.

(7) Not being a native English speaker.

(8) The ability to speak another language.

(9) Dress, attire, or personal appearance.

(10) Employment in a field that is disproportionately occupied by members listed in subdivision (a) or that serves a population disproportionately comprised of members of a group or groups listed in subdivision (a).

(11) Lack of employment or underemployment of the prospective juror or prospective juror's family member.

(12) A prospective juror's apparent friendliness with another prospective juror of the same group as listed in subdivision (a).

(13) Any justification that is similarly applicable to a questioned prospective juror or jurors, who are not members of the same cognizable group as the challenged prospective juror, but were not the subject of a peremptory challenge by that party. The unchallenged prospective juror or jurors need not share any other characteristics with the challenged prospective juror for peremptory challenge relying on this justification to be considered presumptively invalid.

(f) For purposes of subdivision (e), the term "clear and convincing" refers to the degree of certainty the factfinder must have in determining whether the reasons given for the exercise of a peremptory challenge are unrelated to the prospective juror's cognizable group membership, bearing in mind conscious and unconscious bias. To determine that a presumption of invalidity has been overcome, the factfinder shall determine that it is highly probable that the reasons given for the exercise of a peremptory challenge are unrelated to conscious or unconscious bias and are instead specific to the juror and bear on that juror's ability to be fair and impartial in the case.

(g)(1) The following reasons for peremptory challenges have historically been associated with improper discrimination in jury selection:

(A) The prospective juror was inattentive, or staring or failing to make eye contact.

(B) The prospective juror exhibited either a lack of rapport or problematic attitude, body language, or demeanor.

(C) The prospective juror provided unintelligent or confused answers.

(2) The reasons set forth in paragraph (1) are presumptively invalid unless the trial court is able to confirm that the asserted behavior occurred,

based on the court's own observations or the observations of counsel for the objecting party. Even with that confirmation, the counsel offering the reason shall explain why the asserted demeanor, behavior, or manner in which the prospective juror answered questions matters to the case to be tried.

(h) Upon a court granting an objection to the improper exercise of a peremptory challenge, the court shall do one or more of the following:

(1) Quash the jury venire and start jury selection anew. This remedy shall be provided if requested by the objecting party.

(2) If the motion is granted after the jury has been impaneled, declare a mistrial and select a new jury if requested by the defendant.

(3) Seat the challenged juror.

(4) Provide the objecting party additional challenges.

(5) Provide another remedy as the court deems appropriate.

(i) This section applies in all jury trials in which jury selection begins on or after January 1, 2022.

(j) The denial of an objection made under this section shall be reviewed by the appellate court de novo, with the trial court's express factual findings reviewed for substantial evidence. The appellate court shall not impute to the trial court any findings, including findings of a prospective juror's demeanor, that the trial court did not expressly state on the record. The reviewing court shall consider only reasons actually given under subdivision (c) and shall not speculate as to or consider reasons that were not given to explain either the party's use of the peremptory challenge or the party's failure to challenge similarly situated jurors who are not members of the same cognizable group as the challenged juror, regardless of whether the moving party made a comparative analysis argument in the trial court. Should the appellate court determine that the objection was erroneously denied, that error shall be deemed prejudicial, the judgment shall be reversed, and the case remanded for a new trial.

(k) This section shall not apply to civil cases.

(*l*) It is the intent of the Legislature that enactment of this section shall not, in purpose or effect, lower the standard for judging challenges for cause or expand use of challenges for cause.

(m) The provisions of this section are severable. If any provision of this section or its application is held invalid, that invalidity shall not affect other provisions or applications that can be given effect without the invalid provision or application.

(n) This section shall remain in effect only until January 1, 2026, and as of that date is repealed. **Leg.H.** Added Stats 2020 ch 318 §2 (AB 3070), effective January 1, 2021, repealed January 1, 2026.

§ 231.7. Prohibition to use of peremptory challenge based on specified criteria [Operative January 1, 2026]

(a) A party shall not use a peremptory challenge to remove a prospective juror on the basis of the prospective juror's race, ethnicity, gender, gender identity, sexual orientation, national origin, or religious affiliation, or the perceived membership of the prospective juror in any of those groups.

(b) A party, or the trial court on its own motion, may object to the improper use of a peremptory challenge under subdivision (a). After the objection is made, any further discussion shall be conducted outside the presence of the panel. The objection shall be made before the jury is impaneled, unless information becomes known that could not have reasonably been known before the jury was impaneled.

(c) Notwithstanding Section 226, upon objection to the exercise of a peremptory challenge pursuant to this section, the party exercising the peremptory challenge shall state the reasons the peremptory challenge has been exercised.

(d)(1) The court shall evaluate the reasons given to justify the peremptory challenge in light of the totality of the circumstances. The court shall consider only the reasons actually given and shall not speculate on, or assume the existence of, other possible justifications for the use of the peremptory challenge. If the court determines there is a substantial likelihood that an objectively reasonable person would view race, ethnicity, gender, gender identity, sexual orientation, national origin, or religious affiliation, or perceived membership in any of those groups, as a factor in the use of the peremptory challenge, then the objection shall be sustained. The court need not find purposeful discrimination to sustain the objection. The court shall explain the reasons for its ruling on the record. A motion brought under this section shall also be deemed a sufficient presentation of claims asserting the discriminatory exclusion of jurors in violation of the United States and California Constitutions.

(2)(A) For purposes of this section, an objectively reasonable person is aware that unconscious bias, in addition to purposeful discrimination, have resulted in the unfair exclusion of potential jurors in the State of California.

(B) For purposes of this section, a "substantial likelihood" means more than a mere possibility but less than a standard of more likely than not.

(C) For purposes of this section, "unconscious bias" includes implicit and institutional biases.

(3) In making its determination, the circumstances the court may consider include, but are not limited to, any of the following:

(A) Whether any of the following circumstances exist:

(i) The objecting party is a member of the same perceived cognizable group as the challenged juror.

(ii) The alleged victim is not a member of that perceived cognizable group.

(iii) Witnesses or the parties are not members of that perceived cognizable group.

(B) Whether race, ethnicity, gender, gender identity, sexual orientation, national origin, or religious affiliation, or perceived membership in any of those groups, bear on the facts of the case to be tried.

(C) The number and types of questions posed to the prospective juror, including, but not limited to, any the following:

(i) Consideration of whether the party exercising the peremptory challenge failed to question the prospective juror about the concerns later stated by the party as the reason for the peremptory challenge pursuant to subdivision (c).

(ii) Whether the party exercising the peremptory challenge engaged in cursory questioning of the challenged potential juror.

(iii) Whether the party exercising the peremptory challenge asked different questions of the potential juror against whom the peremptory challenge was used in contrast to questions asked of other jurors from different perceived cognizable groups about the same topic or whether the party phrased those questions differently.

(D) Whether other prospective jurors, who are not members of the same cognizable group as the challenged prospective juror, provided similar, but not necessarily identical, answers but were not the subject of a peremptory challenge by that party.

(E) Whether a reason might be disproportionately associated with a race, ethnicity, gender, gender identity, sexual orientation, national origin, or religious affiliation, or perceived membership in any of those groups.

(F) Whether the reason given by the party exercising the peremptory challenge was contrary to or unsupported by the record.

(G) Whether the counsel or counsel's office exercising the challenge has used peremptory challenges disproportionately against a given race, ethnicity, gender, gender identity, sexual orientation, national origin, or religious affiliation, or perceived membership in any of those groups, in the present case or in past cases, including whether the counsel or counsel's office who made the challenge has a history of prior violations under Batson v. Kentucky (1986) 476 U.S. 79, People v. Wheeler (1978) 22 Cal.3d 258, Section 231.5, or this section.

(e) A peremptory challenge for any of the following reasons is presumed to be invalid unless the party exercising the peremptory challenge can show by clear and convincing evidence that an objectively reasonable person would view the rationale as unrelated to a prospective juror's race, ethnicity, gender, gender identity, sexual orientation, national origin, or religious affiliation, or perceived membership in any of those groups, and that the reasons articulated bear on the prospective juror's ability to be fair and impartial in the case:

(1) Expressing a distrust of or having a negative experience with law enforcement or the criminal legal system.

(2) Expressing a belief that law enforcement officers engage in racial profiling or that criminal laws have been enforced in a discriminatory manner.

(3) Having a close relationship with people who have been stopped, arrested, or convicted of a crime.

(4) A prospective juror's neighborhood.

(5) Having a child outside of marriage.

(6) Receiving state benefits.

(7) Not being a native English speaker.

(8) The ability to speak another language.

(9) Dress, attire, or personal appearance.

(10) Employment in a field that is disproportionately occupied by members listed in subdivision (a) or that serves a population disproportionately comprised of members of a group or groups listed in subdivision (a).

(11) Lack of employment or underemployment of the prospective juror or prospective juror's family member.

(12) A prospective juror's apparent friendliness with another prospective juror of the same group as listed in subdivision (a).

(13) Any justification that is similarly applicable to a questioned prospective juror or jurors, who are not members of the same cognizable group as the challenged prospective juror, but were not the subject of a peremptory challenge by that party. The unchallenged prospective juror or jurors need not share any other characteristics with the challenged prospective juror for peremptory challenge relying on this justification to be considered presumptively invalid.

(f) For purposes of subdivision (e), the term "clear and convincing" refers to the degree of certainty the factfinder must have in determining whether the reasons given for the exercise of a peremptory challenge are unrelated to the prospective juror's cognizable group membership, bearing in mind conscious and unconscious bias. To determine that a presumption of invalidity has been overcome, the factfinder shall determine that it is highly probable that the reasons given for the exercise of a peremptory challenge are unrelated to conscious or unconscious bias and are instead specific to the juror and bear on that juror's ability to be fair and impartial in the case.

(g)(1) The following reasons for peremptory challenges have historically been associated with improper discrimination in jury selection:

(A) The prospective juror was inattentive, or staring or failing to make eye contact.

(B) The prospective juror exhibited either a lack of rapport or problematic attitude, body language, or demeanor.

(C) The prospective juror provided unintelligent or confused answers.

(2) The reasons set forth in paragraph (1) are presumptively invalid unless the trial court is able to confirm that the asserted behavior occurred, based on the court's own observations or the observations of counsel for the objecting party. Even with that confirmation, the counsel offering the reason shall explain why the asserted demeanor, behavior, or manner in which the prospective juror answered questions matters to the case to be tried.

(h) Upon a court granting an objection to the improper exercise of a peremptory challenge, the court shall do one or more of the following:

(1) Quash the jury venire and start jury selection anew. This remedy shall be provided if requested by the objecting party.

(2) If the motion is granted after the jury has been impaneled, declare a mistrial and select a new jury if requested by the defendant.

(3) Seat the challenged juror.

(4) Provide the objecting party additional challenges.

(5) Provide another remedy as the court deems appropriate.

(i) This section applies in all jury trials in which jury selection begins on or after January 1, 2022.

(j) The denial of an objection made under this section shall be reviewed by the appellate court de novo, with the trial court's express factual findings reviewed for substantial evidence. The appellate court shall not impute to the trial court any findings, including findings of a prospective juror's demeanor, that the trial court did not expressly state on the record. The reviewing court shall consider only reasons actually given under subdivision (c) and shall not speculate as to or consider reasons that were not given to explain either the party's use of the peremptory challenge or the party's failure to challenge similarly situated jurors who are not members of the same cognizable group as the challenged juror, regardless of whether the moving party made a comparative analysis argument in the trial court. Should the appellate court determine that the objection was erroneously denied, that error shall be deemed prejudicial, the judgment shall be reversed, and the case remanded for a new trial.

(k) It is the intent of the Legislature that enactment of this section shall not, in purpose or effect, lower the standard for judging challenges for cause or expand use of challenges for cause.

(*l*) The provisions of this section are severable. If any provision of this section or its application is held invalid, that invalidity shall not affect other provisions or applications that can be given effect without the invalid provision or application.

(m) This section shall become operative January 1, 2026. **Leg.H.** Added Stats 2020 ch 318 §3 (AB 3070), effective January 1, 2021, operative January 1, 2026.

§232. Perjury admonishment; Acknowledgment and agreement

(a) Prior to the examination of prospective trial jurors in the panel assigned for voir dire, the following perjury acknowledgement and agreement shall be obtained from the panel, which shall be acknowledged by the prospective jurors with the statement "I do":

"Do you, and each of you, understand and agree that you will accurately and truthfully answer, under penalty of perjury, all questions propounded to you concerning your qualifications and competency to serve as a trial juror in the matter pending before this court; and that failure to do so may subject you to criminal prosecution."

(b) As soon as the selection of the trial jury is completed, the following acknowledgment and agreement shall be obtained from the trial jurors, which shall be acknowledged by the statement "I do":

"Do you and each of you understand and agree that you will well and truly try the cause now pending before this court, and a true verdict render according only to the evidence presented to you and to the instructions of the court." **Leg.H.** Added Stats 1988 ch 1245 §2. Amended Stats 1989 ch 1416 §10.

Prior Law: Former CCP §232, relating to return by officer summoning jurors for courts not of record, was enacted 1872, repealed and reenacted Code Amdts 1880 ch 35 §1, amended Stats 1923 ch 116 §1, and repealed Stats 1980 ch 81 §26.

§233. Discharge of juror before verdict returned

If, before the jury has returned its verdict to the court, a juror becomes sick or, upon other good cause shown to the court, is found to be unable to perform his or her duty, the court may order the juror to be discharged. If any alternate jurors have been selected as provided by law, one of them shall then be designated by the court to take the place of the juror so discharged. If after all alternate jurors have been made regular jurors or if there is no alternate juror, a juror becomes sick or otherwise unable to perform the juror's duty and has been discharged by the court as provided in this section, the jury shall be discharged and a new jury then or afterwards impaneled, and the cause may again be tried. Alternatively, with the consent of all parties, the trial may proceed with only the remaining jurors, or another juror may be sworn and the trial begin anew. **Leg.H.** Added Stats 1988 ch 1245 §2.

Prior Law: Former CCP §233, relating to jury fees in justice courts, was added Stats 1949 ch 1406 §1, amended Stats 1951 ch 1495 §8, operative January 1, 1952, Stats 1957 ch 1406 §4, Stats 1969 ch 350 §1, and repealed Stats 1980 ch 81 §26.

§234. Alternate jurors

Whenever, in the opinion of a judge of a superior court about to try a civil or criminal action or proceeding, the trial is likely to be a protracted one, or upon stipulation of the parties, the court may cause an entry to that effect to be made in the minutes of the court and thereupon, immediately after the jury is impaneled and sworn, the court may direct the calling of one or more additional jurors, in its discretion, to be known as "alternate jurors."

These alternate jurors shall be drawn from the same source, and in the same manner, and have the same qualifications, as the jurors already sworn, and shall be subject to the same examination and challenges. However, each side, or each defendant, as provided in Section 231, shall be entitled to as many peremptory challenges to the alternate jurors as there are alternate jurors called.

The alternate jurors shall be seated so as to have equal power and facilities for seeing and hearing the proceedings in the case, and shall take the same oath as the jurors already selected, and shall, unless excused by the court, attend at all times upon the trial of the cause in company with the other jurors, but shall not participate in deliberation unless ordered by the court, and for a failure to do so are liable to be punished for contempt.

They shall obey the orders of and be bound by the admonition of the court, upon each adjournment of the court; but if the regular jurors are ordered to be kept in the custody of the sheriff or marshal during the trial of the cause, the alternate jurors shall also be kept in confinement with the other jurors; and upon final submission of the case to the jury, the alternate jurors shall be kept in the custody of the sheriff or marshal who shall not suffer any communication to be made to them except by order of the court, and shall not be discharged until the original jurors are discharged, except as provided in this section.

If at any time, whether before or after the final submission of the case to the jury, a juror dies or becomes ill, or upon other good cause shown to the court is found to be unable to perform his or her duty, or if a juror requests a discharge and good cause appears therefor, the court may order the juror to be discharged and draw the name of an alternate, who shall then take his or her place in the jury box, and be subject to the same rules and regulations as though he or she had been selected as one of the original jurors.

All laws relative to fees, expenses, and mileage or transportation of jurors shall be applicable to alternate jurors, except that in civil cases the sums for fees and mileage or transportation need not be deposited until the judge directs alternate jurors to be impaneled. **Leg.H.** Added Stats 1988 ch 1245 §2. Amended Stats 1996 ch 872 §10 (AB 3472); Stats 1998 ch 931 §56 (SB 2139), effective September 28, 1998; Stats 2002 ch 784 §50 (SB 1316); Stats 2010 ch 328 §33 (SB 1330), effective January 1, 2011.

§235. Provision of prospective jurors; Juries of inquest

At the request of the sheriff, coroner, or other ministerial officer, the jury commissioner shall provide such prospective jurors as may be required to form a jury of inquest. Prospective jurors so provided shall be selected, obligated, and compensated in the same manner as other jurors selected under the provisions of this chapter. **Leg.H.** Added Stats 1988 ch 1245 §2.

Prior Law: Former CCP §235, similar to present CCP §208, was enacted 1872, repealed and reenacted Code Amdts 1880 ch 35 §1, amended Stats 1945 ch 815 §1, and repealed Stats 1947 ch 424 §3 (Gov C §500037).

§236. Jury of inquest; Purpose

When six or more prospective jurors of inquest attend, they shall be sworn by the coroner to inquire who the person was, and when, where, and by what means the person came to his or her death, to inquire into the circumstances attending the death, and to render a true verdict thereon, according to the evidence offered them or arising from the inspection of the body. **Leg.H.** Added Stats 1988 ch 1245 §2.

§237. Names of qualified jurors made available to public; Petition for access to records; Notice; Hearing; Violations

(a)(1) The names of qualified jurors drawn from the qualified juror list for the superior court shall be made available to the public upon request unless the court determines that a compelling interest, as defined in subdivision (b), requires that this information should be kept confidential or its use limited in whole or in part.

(2) Upon the recording of a jury's verdict in a criminal jury proceeding, the court's record of personal juror identifying information of trial jurors, as defined in Section 194, consisting of names, addresses, and telephone numbers, shall be sealed until further order of the court as provided by this section.

(3) For purposes of this section, "sealed" or "sealing" means extracting or otherwise removing the personal juror identifying information from the court record.

(4) This subdivision applies only to cases in which a jury verdict was returned on or after January 1, 1996.

(b) Any person may petition the court for access to these records. The petition shall be supported by a declaration that includes facts sufficient to establish good cause for the release of the juror's personal identifying information. The court shall set the matter for hearing if the petition and supporting declaration establish a prima facie showing of good cause for the release of the personal juror identifying information, but shall not set the matter for hearing if there is a showing on the record of facts that establish a compelling interest against disclosure. A compelling interest includes, but is not limited to, protecting jurors from threats or danger of physical harm. If the court does not set the matter for hearing, the court shall by minute order set forth the reasons and make express findings either of a lack of a prima facie showing of good cause or the presence of a compelling interest against disclosure.

(c) If a hearing is set pursuant to subdivision (b), the petitioner shall provide notice of the petition and the time and place of the hearing at least 20 days prior to the date of the hearing to the parties in the criminal action. The court shall provide notice to each affected former juror by personal service or by first-class mail, addressed to the last known address of the former juror as shown in the records of the court. In a capital case, the petitioner shall also serve notice on the Attorney General. Any affected former juror may appear in person, in writing, by telephone, or by counsel to protest the granting of the petition. A former juror who wishes to appear at the hearing to oppose the unsealing of the personal juror identifying information may request the court to close the hearing in order to protect the former juror's anonymity.

(d) After the hearing, the records shall be made available as requested in the petition, unless a former juror's protest to the granting of the petition is sustained. The court shall sustain the protest of the former juror if, in the discretion of the court, the petitioner fails to show good cause, the record establishes the presence of a compelling interest against disclosure as defined in subdivision (b), or the juror is unwilling to be contacted by the petitioner. The court shall set forth reasons and make express findings to support the granting or denying of the petition to disclose. The court may require the person to whom disclosure is made, or his or her agent or employee, to agree not to divulge jurors' identities or identifying information to others; the court may otherwise limit disclosure in any manner it deems appropriate.

(e) Any court employee who has legal access to personal juror identifying information sealed under subdivision (a), who discloses the information, knowing it to be a violation of this section or a court order issued under this section, is guilty of a misdemeanor.

(f) Any person who intentionally solicits another to unlawfully access or disclose personal juror identifying information contained in records sealed under subdivision (a), knowing that the records have been sealed, or who, knowing that the information was unlawfully secured, intentionally discloses it to another person is guilty of a misdemeanor. **Leg.H.** Added Stats 1992 ch 971 §3 (SB 1299). Amended Stats 1993 ch 632 §2 (AB 1915); Stats 1995 ch 964 §3 (SB 508); Stats 1996 ch 636 §2 (SB 2123), effective September 19, 1996.

§238. [Section repealed 1989]

Leg.H. Enacted 1872. Repealed and re-enacted Code Amdts 1880 ch 35 §1. Amended Stats 1959 ch 501 §16; Stats 1983 ch 425 §2 (ch 425 prevails), ch 1092 §71, effective September 27, 1983, operative January 1, 1984. Repealed Stats 1988 ch 1245 §1. See CCP §209.

§239. [Section repealed 2001]

Leg.H. Added Stats 1997 ch 509 §1 (AB 127). Repealed July 1, 2001, by its own terms. The repealed section related to the jury selection pilot program.

Prior Law: Former CCP §239, similar to present CCP §213, was added Stats 1978 ch 718 §7, amended Stats 1984 ch 65 §1, Stats 1987 ch 134 §2, effective July 7, 1987, and repealed Stats 1988 ch 1245 §1.

§240. [Section repealed 1989]

Leg.H. Added Stats 1978 ch 718 §8. Repealed Stats 1988 ch 1245 §1. The repealed section related to notice to juror that discharge by employer for service prohibited.

§ 240. San Francisco low-income juror pilot program [Repealed]

Leg.H. Added Stats 2021 ch 717 §2 (AB 1452), effective January 1, 2022, repealed January 1, 2025.

Prior Law: Former CCP §240, relating to the discharge of jurors, was added by Stats 1978 ch 718 §8, and repealed January 1, 1989, by Stats 1988 ch 1245 §1.

§241. [Section repealed 1959]

Leg.H. Enacted 1872. Repealed and re-enacted Code Amdts 1880 ch 35 §1. Amended Stats 1881 ch 60 §9; Stats 1905 ch 137 §1. Repealed Stats 1959 ch 501 §3. See Pen C §§904–906.

§ 241. Pilot program to study whether increases in juror compensation and mileage reimbursement rates increase juror diversity and participation [Repealed January 1, 2027]

(a) The Judicial Council shall sponsor a pilot program for two fiscal years to study whether increases in juror compensation and mileage reimbursement rates increase juror diversity and participation. The Judicial Council shall select at least six trial courts, in counties with regional and geographic diversity, including the County of Alameda, to participate in the pilot program.

(b) As part of the pilot program, the participating pilot courts shall collect demographic information, as reported by jurors.

(c) No later than September 1, 2026, the Judicial Council shall provide a report to the Legislature pursuant to Section 9795 of the Government Code describing the findings of the pilot program and providing information for promoting juror diversity.

(d) The Judicial Council may enlist the services of a consultant to conduct the study.

(e) This section shall remain in effect only until January 1, 2027, and as of that date is repealed. **Leg.H.** Added Stats 2022 ch 326 §3 (AB 1981), effective January 1, 2023, repealed January 1, 2027.

Prior Law Former CCP §241 was enacted 1872; repealed and re-enacted Code Amdts 1880 ch 35 §1; amended Stats 1881 ch 60 §9, Stats 1905 ch 137 §1; and repealed Stats 1959 ch 501 §3. See Pen C §§904-906.

§242. Mental health awareness information provided to jurors

(a) Following the receipt of a verdict and before discharging the jury in a criminal action or proceeding alleging a violent felony, the court shall provide written information to the trial jurors about mental health awareness, including information about stress relief and symptoms that may be experienced following exposure to trauma.

(b) Following the receipt of a verdict in a criminal action or proceeding alleging a violent felony, the court shall distribute, in a manner determined by the court, information to the alternate jurors who have been discharged from their duty about mental health awareness, including information about stress relief and symptoms that may be experienced following exposure to trauma.

(c) At the conclusion of a criminal action or proceeding alleging a violent felony in which evidence was presented, but a verdict was not rendered by the jury, the court shall provide written information about mental health awareness, including information about stress relief and symptoms that may be experienced following exposure to trauma, before discharging the jury and alternate jurors. The information shall only be provided after the jurors and alternate jurors are no longer responsible for rendering a verdict in the trial.

(d) The court may share this information with jurors and alternate jurors following the conclusion of a criminal action or proceeding alleging an offense that is not a violent felony.

(e) The Judicial Council shall develop the written educational information that the court shall print and distribute pursuant to this section. The information shall include, but shall not be limited to, the signs and symptoms of distress, healthy coping mechanisms, and how to seek help for exposure to trauma if needed.

(f) For the purposes of this section, "violent felony" has the same definition as in subdivision (c) of Section 667.5 of the Penal Code. **Leg.H.** Added Stats 2024 ch 204 §1 (AB 2985), effective January 1, 2025.

Prior Law Former CCP § 242 was enacted 1872, amended Code Amdts 1875–76 ch 514 §11, repealed and re-enacted Code Amdts 1880 ch 35 §1 and repealed Stats 1959 ch 501 §3

§242a. [Section repealed 1961]

Leg.H. Added Stats 1959 ch 714 §1. Repealed Stats 1961 ch 72 §2. See Pen C §908.1.

§243. [Section repealed 1959]

Leg.H. Enacted 1872. Repealed and re-enacted Code Amdts 1880 ch 35 §1. Repealed Stats 1959 ch 501 §3. See Pen C §§904–906.

§246. [Section repealed 1989]

Leg.H. Enacted 1872. Repealed and re-enacted Code Amdts 1880 ch 35 §1. Amended Stats 1917 ch 692 §9; Stats 1980 ch 81 §28. Repealed Stats 1988 ch 1245 §1. See CCP §218.

§247. [Section repealed 1989]

Leg.H. Enacted 1872. Repealed and re-enacted Code Amdts 1880 ch 35 §1. Repealed Stats 1988 ch 1245 §1. The repealed section related to manner of impaneling as prescribed elsewhere.

§248. [Section repealed 1989]

Leg.H. Added Stats 1907 ch 355 §2. Amended Stats 1933 ch 743 §60; Stats 1951 ch 1495 §9, operative January 1, 1952; Stats 1955 ch 1186 §1. Repealed Stats 1988 ch 1245 §1. See CCP §201.

§250. [Section repealed 1981]

Leg.H. Enacted 1872. Repealed and re-enacted Code Amdts 1880 ch 35 §1. Amended Stats 1951 ch 1495 §10, operative January 1, 1952. Repealed Stats 1980 ch 81 §29. The repealed section related to proceedings in forming jury.

§251. [Section repealed 1981]

Leg.H. Enacted 1872. Repealed and re-enacted Code Amdts 1880 ch 35 §1. Repealed Stats 1980 ch 81 §29. The repealed section related to manner of impaneling.

§254. [Section repealed 1989]

Leg.H. Enacted 1872. Repealed and re-enacted Code Amdts 1880 ch 35 §1. Repealed Stats 1988 ch 1245 §1. The repealed section related to manner of impaneling described elsewhere.

§255. [Section repealed 1989]

Leg.H. Added Stats 1959 ch 828 §1. Repealed Stats 1988 ch 1245 §1. See CCP §202.

CHAPTER 2
COURT COMMISSIONERS

Powers and duties. §259.
[Section renumbered 1951]. §261b.

§258. [Section repealed 1953]

Leg.H. Enacted 1872. Repealed and re-enacted Code Amdts 1880 ch 35 §1. Amended Stats 1929 ch 874 §1; Stats 1931 ch 875 §2. Repealed Stats 1953 ch 206 §7. The repealed section related to appointment of court commissioners.

§259. Powers and duties

Subject to the supervision of the court, every court commissioner shall have power to do all of the following:

(a) Hear and determine ex parte motions for orders and alternative writs and writs of habeas corpus in the superior court for which the court commissioner is appointed.

(b) Take proof and make and report findings thereon as to any matter of fact upon which information is required by the court. Any party to any contested proceeding may except to the report and the subsequent order of the court made thereon within five days after written notice of the court's action. A copy of the exceptions shall be filed and served upon opposing party or counsel within the five days. The party may argue any exceptions before the court on giving notice of motion for that purpose within 10 days from entry thereof. After a hearing before the court on the exceptions, the court may sustain, or set aside, or modify its order.

(c) Take and approve any bonds and undertakings in actions or proceedings, and determine objections to the bonds and undertakings.

(d) Act as temporary judge when otherwise qualified so to act and when appointed for that purpose, on stipulation of the parties litigant. While acting as temporary judge the commissioner shall receive no compensation therefor other than compensation as commissioner.

(e) Hear and report findings and conclusions to the court for approval, rejection, or change, all preliminary matters including motions or petitions for the custody and support of children, the allowance of temporary spousal support, costs and attorneys' fees, and issues of fact in contempt proceedings in proceedings for support, dissolution of marriage, nullity of marriage, or legal separation.

(f) Hear actions to establish paternity and to establish or enforce child and spousal support pursuant to subdivision (a) of Section 4251 of the Family Code.

(g) Hear, report on, and determine all uncontested actions and proceedings subject to the requirements of subdivision (d). **Leg.H.** Enacted 1872. Amended Code Amdts 1877–78 ch 154 §1. Repealed and re-enacted Code Amdts 1880 ch 35 §1. Amended Stats 1980 ch 229 §1; Stats 1982 ch 517 §95; Stats 1989 ch 1105 §5; Stats 1990 ch 411 §5 (AB 3973), effective July 24, 1990; Stats 1992 ch 163 §14 (AB 2641), operative January 1, 1994; Stats 1994 ch 1266 §1; Stats 1996 ch 957 §1 (AB 1058); Stats 2004 ch 49 §1 (SB 1225).

§259a. [Section repealed 1981]

Leg.H. Added Stats 1929 ch 874 §2. Amended Stats 1949 ch 469 §1, effective May 27, 1949. Repealed Stats 1980 ch 229 §2. The repealed section related to additional powers in counties with population over 900,000.

§260. [Section repealed 1953]

Leg.H. Added Stats 1951 ch 1105 §1. Repealed Stats 1953 ch 206 §7. The repealed section related to court commissioners' salary.

§261. [Section repealed 1953]

Leg.H. Added Stats 1929 ch 746 §1. Amended Stats 1931 ch 875 §3; Stats 1933 ch 734 §1; Stats 1939 ch 69 §1; Stats 1943 ch 183 §1; Stats 1945 ch 536 §1; Stats 1947 ch 716 §1; Stats 1949 ch 1251 §1; Stats 1951 ch 1466 §1. Repealed Stats 1953 ch 206 §7. The repealed section related to the appointment of Los Angeles Superior Court Commissioners.

§261.5. [Section repealed 1953]

Leg.H. Added Stats 1947 ch 901 §1. Amended Stats 1949 ch 1330 §1; Stats 1951 ch 1133 §1. Repealed Stats 1953 ch 206 §7. The repealed section related to appointment of Los Angeles Superior Court employees.

§261a. [Section repealed 1953]

Leg.H. Added Stats 1929 ch 748 §2. Amended Stats 1931 ch 875 §1; Stats 1941 ch 975 §3; Stats 1943 ch 60 §1; Stats 1945 ch 536 §2; Stats 1947 ch 900 §1; Stats 1949 ch 1129 §1; Stats 1951 ch 1134 §1. Repealed Stats 1953 ch 206 §7. The repealed section related to appointment of Los Angeles Superior Court employees.

§261a.5. [Section repealed 1953]

Leg.H. Added Stats 1943 ch 1031 §1 as CCP §261b. Amended Stats 1945 ch 717 §1, ch 965 §1; Stats 1947 ch 544 §1. Renumbered and amended Stats 1951 ch 40 §1. Amended Stats 1951 ch 1601 §1. Repealed Stats 1953 ch 206 §7. See Gov C §§70041, 70043, 70044, 70051, 70052, 70060–70062.

§261a.7. [Section repealed 1953]

Leg.H. Added Stats 1951 ch 1497 §1. Repealed Stats 1953 ch 206 §7. See Gov C §§70041, 70043, 70044, 70046, 70051, 70052, 70060–70062.

§261a.8. [Section repealed 1953]

Leg.H. Added Stats 1951 ch 1763 §1. Repealed Stats 1953 ch 206 §7. See Gov C §§70041, 70043, 70044, 70048, 70051–70053, 70057, 70060–70062.

§261b. [Section renumbered 1951]

Leg.H. Added Stats 1943 ch 1031 §1. Amended Stats 1945 ch 717 §1, ch 965 §1; Stats 1947 ch 544 §1. Amended and renumbered CCP §261a.5 by Stats 1951 ch 40 §1.

Prior Law: Former CCP §261b was added Stats 1943 ch 1039 §2 and amended and renumbered CCP §261bb by Stats 1951 ch 1105 §2.

§261bb. [Section repealed 1953]

Leg.H. Added Stats 1943 ch 1039 §2 as CCP §261b. Renumbered and amended Stats 1951 ch 1105 §2. Repealed Stats 1953 ch 206 §7. The repealed section related to court commissioners' or referees' expenses.

§261c. [Section repealed 1953]

Leg.H. Added Stats 1947 ch 181 §1. Repealed Stats 1953 ch 206 §7.

§261d. [Section repealed 1953]

Leg.H. Added Stats 1949 ch 1117 §2. Repealed Stats 1953 ch 206 §7. See Gov C §§70041–70045, 70051–70052, 70060, 70062.

§261e. [Section repealed 1953]

Leg.H. Added Stats 1947 ch 882 §1. Amended Stats 1949 ch 988 §1; Stats 1951 ch 1360 §2. Repealed Stats 1953 ch 206 §7. See Gov C §§69900, 69901.

§261f. [Section repealed 1953]

Leg.H. Added Stats 1947 ch 882 §2. Repealed Stats 1953 ch 206 §7. See Gov C §69897.

§261g. [Section repealed 1953]

Leg.H. Added Stats 1949 ch 1104 §1. Amended Stats 1951 ch 844 §2. Repealed Stats 1953 ch 206 §7. See Gov C §69991.

§261h. [Section repealed 1953]

Leg.H. Added Stats 1951 ch 1601 §2. Repealed Stats 1953 ch 206 §7. The repealed section related to phonographic reporters' salary in county or city and county having population of 750,000 inhabitants or over.

§261j. [Section repealed 1953]

Leg.H. Added Stats 1951 ch 1301 §1. Repealed Stats 1953 ch 206 §7. See Gov C §§70041–70044, 70047, 70051, 70052, 70060, 70062.

TITLE 4
MINISTERIAL OFFICERS OF COURTS OF JUSTICE

Chapter 1. Of Ministerial Officers Generally.
Chapter 2. Levying Officer Electronic Transactions Act.
Chapter 3. Phonographic Reporters.

CHAPTER 1
OF MINISTERIAL OFFICERS GENERALLY

Liability of sheriff regarding execution of process. §262.
Execution of process and orders regular on face. §262.1.
Duty to exhibit process upon request or at office; Exception. §262.2.
Execution of unexecuted process by sheriff's successor. §262.3.
Execution of deeds and conveyances to purchasers of real estate at execution sale; Validity when executed by other than sheriff who made the sale. §262.4.
Service of paper other than process, upon sheriff. §262.5.
Execution of process and orders by coroner. §262.6.
Service of process and orders in action against sheriff. §262.7.
Execution of process and orders by elisor. §262.8.
Manner of execution and return of process by elisor. §262.9.
Compensation of coroner and elisor; Payment. §262.10.
Execution of process and orders affecting real estate after creation of new county. §262.11.

§262. Liability of sheriff regarding execution of process

The direction or authority of a party or his or her attorney to a sheriff, in respect to the execution of process or return thereof, or to any related act or omission, is not available to discharge or excuse the sheriff from a liability for neglect or misconduct, unless it is contained in written instructions by the attorney of the party, including the signature and name of the attorney of the party, or by the party, if he or she has no attorney. Subject to subdivision (c) of Section 263, the instructions may be transmitted electronically pursuant to Chapter 2 (commencing with Section 263). **Leg.H.** Added Stats 1951 ch 655 §14. Amended Stats 2010 ch 680 §1 (AB 2394), effective January 1, 2011.

Prior Law: Former CCP §262, similar to present Gov C §69902, was added Stats 1947 ch 1278 §1 and repealed Stats 1953 ch 206 §7.
Former CCP §262, relating to election powers and duties, was enacted 1872, repealed and reenacted Code Amdts 1880 ch 35 §1, and repealed Stats 1945 ch 111 §11 (Gov C §500023).

§262.1. Execution of process and orders regular on face

A sheriff or other ministerial officer is justified in the execution of, and shall execute, all process and orders regular on their face and issued by competent authority, whatever may be the defect in the proceedings upon which they were issued. **Leg.H.** Added Stats 1951 ch 655 §14.

§262.2. Duty to exhibit process upon request or at office; Exception

Except as otherwise provided, the officer executing process shall, so long as he or she retains the original process, show it to any interested person, upon request. The officer shall show the process, with all papers, or electronic copies of all papers, attached, at his or her office whenever the office is open for business. **Leg.H.** Added Stats 1951 ch 655 §14. Amended Stats 1955 ch 1197 §1; Stats 2010 ch 680 §2 (AB 2394), effective January 1, 2011.

§262.3. Execution of unexecuted process by sheriff's successor

When any process remains with the sheriff unexecuted, in whole or in part, at the time of his death, resignation of office, or at the expiration of his term of office, such process shall be executed by his successor or successors in office. **Leg.H.** Added Stats 1951 ch 655 §14.

§262.4. Execution of deeds and conveyances to purchasers of real estate at execution sale; Validity when executed by other than sheriff who made the sale

If the sheriff sells real estate, under and by virtue of an execution or order of court, the sheriff, or his or her successors in office, shall execute and deliver to the purchaser or purchasers all deeds and conveyances required by law and necessary for the purpose, and those deeds and conveyances shall be valid in law as if they had been executed by the sheriff who made the sale. The deeds and conveyances may be recorded electronically pursuant to Chapter 2 (commencing with Section 263) if they comply with the Electronic Recording Delivery Act of 2004 (Article 6 (commencing with Section 27390) of Chapter 6 of Part 3 of Division 2 of Title 3 of the Government Code). **Leg.H.** Added Stats 1951 ch 655 §14. Amended Stats 2010 ch 680 §3 (AB 2394), effective January 1, 2011.

§262.5. Service of paper other than process, upon sheriff

Service of a paper, other than process, upon the sheriff may be made by delivering it to him or to one of his deputies, or to a person in charge of the office during office hours, or, if no such person is there, by leaving it in a conspicuous place in the office. **Leg.H.** Added Stats 1951 ch 655 §14.

§262.6. Execution of process and orders by coroner

When the sheriff is a party to an action or proceeding, the process and orders therein, which it would otherwise be the duty of the sheriff to execute, shall be executed by the coroner of the county. **Leg.H.** Added Stats 1951 ch 655 §14.

§262.7. Service of process and orders in action against sheriff

If an action is begun against a sheriff, all process and orders may be served by any person in the manner provided in this code. **Leg.H.** Added Stats 1951 ch 655 §14. Amended Stats 2014 ch 470 §1 (AB 2256), effective January 1, 2015.

§262.8. Execution of process and orders by elisor

Process or orders in an action or proceeding may be executed by a person residing in the county, designated by the court, or the judge thereof, and denominated an elisor, in the following cases:
(a) When the sheriff and coroner are both parties.
(b) When either of these officers is a party, and the process is against the other.
(c) When either of these officers is a party, and there is a vacancy in the office of the other, or where it appears, by affidavit, to the satisfaction of the court in which the proceeding is pending, or the judge thereof, that both of these officers are disqualified, or by reason of any bias, prejudice, or other cause would not act promptly or impartially. **Leg.H.** Added Stats 1951 ch 655 §14.

§262.9. Manner of execution and return of process by elisor

When process is delivered to an elisor, he shall execute and return it in the same manner as the sheriff is required to execute similar process. **Leg.H.** Added Stats 1959 ch 655 §14.

§262.10. Compensation of coroner and elisor; Payment

Whenever process is executed, or any act performed by a coroner or elisor, he shall receive a reasonable compensation, to be fixed by the court, to be paid by the plaintiff in case of the summoning of jurors to complete the panel, and by the person or party requiring the service in all other cases in private action. If rendered at the instance of the people, it shall be audited and paid as a county charge. **Leg.H.** Added Stats 1951 ch 655 §14.

§262.11. Execution of process and orders affecting real estate after creation of new county

In all cases where new counties have been or may hereafter be created, and executions, orders of sale upon foreclosures of mortgages, or other process affecting specific real estate have been or may hereafter be adjudged by the final judgment or decree of a court of competent jurisdiction, to be executed by the sheriff of the county in which such real estate was originally situated, such process may be executed by the sheriff of the new county in which such real estate is found to be situated, with the like effect as if he were the sheriff of the county designated in the judgment, decree, or order of sale to execute the same. **Leg.H.** Added Stats 1955 ch 59 §5.

CHAPTER 2
LEVYING OFFICER ELECTRONIC TRANSACTIONS ACT

Citation of chapter; Findings and declarations; Construction. §263.
Definitions. §263.1.
Levying officer's information processing system; Filing day in case of technical problem. §263.2.

Procedure for facsimile transmission. §263.3.
Electronic record as substitute for paper record; Requirements; Procedure. §263.4.
Writ of execution; Retention of original or electronic copy; Accounting. §263.6.
Exclusion or redaction of identifiers. §263.7.

§263. Citation of chapter; Findings and declarations; Construction

(a) This chapter may be cited as the Levying Officer Electronic Transactions Act.

(b) The Legislature finds and declares that modern technologies offer alternatives to paper-based systems and provide the means to create, store, retrieve, and transmit records and documents in electronic form resulting in increased efficiency, taxpayer savings, and improved public access to levying officers. It is the intent of the Legislature in enacting this act to accommodate current and future technologies based on industry standards.

(c) Nothing in this chapter shall be construed to require a court or levying officer to comply with any of its provisions unless the court and the levying officer have (1) jointly determined that both the court and the sheriff's department have the resources and the technological capacity to do so, and (2) have mutually agreed to electronically act upon documents as provided in this chapter. **Leg.H.** Added Stats 2010 ch 680 §4 (AB 2394), effective January 1, 2011.

Prior Law: Former CCP §263, relating to child custody investigation and similar to present Fam C §§ 3111–3113, 3115, 3116, was added Stats 1951 ch 1360 §3 and repealed Stats 1992 ch 163 §15, operative January 1, 1994.

§263.1. Definitions

As used in this chapter, the following terms have the following definitions:

(a) "Electronic mail" or "e-mail" means an electronic message that is sent to an e-mail address and transmitted between two or more telecommunications devices, computers, or electronic devices capable of receiving electronic messages through a local, regional, or global computer network, whether or not the message is converted to hard copy format after receipt, viewed upon transmission, or stored for later retrieval.

(b) "Electronic record" means a document or record created, generated, sent, communicated, received, or stored by electronic means.

(c) "Electronic signature" means an electronic sound, symbol, or process attached to, or logically associated with, an electronic record and executed or adopted by a person with the intent to sign the electronic record.

(d) "Fax" is an abbreviation for "facsimile" and refers, as indicated by the context, to a facsimile transmission or to a document so transmitted.

(e) "Fax machine" means a machine that can send and receive a facsimile transmission using industry standards and includes a fax modem connected to a computer.

(f) "Fax transmission" means the electronic transmission and reconstruction of a document that prints a duplicate of the original document at the receiving end. "Fax transmission" includes, but is not limited to, the use of a facsimile machine or the process of integrating an electronic fax software application to automate the sending and receiving of a faxed document as an electronic record, in portable data format, by e-mail or similar electronic means.

(g) "Information processing system" means an electronic system for creating, generating, sending, receiving, storing, displaying, retrieving, or processing information, but does not include a fax machine.

(h) "Instructions" and "levying officer instructions" mean a written request to a levying officer to serve process, perform a levy, execute an arrest warrant, or perform some other act.

(i) "Legal entity" means the legal form of an artificial person and includes a corporation, defunct corporation, unincorporated association, partnership, public agency, limited liability company, joint stock company or association, and limited liability partnership.

(j) "Levying officer" means the sheriff or marshal acting as a ministerial officer pursuant to Section 26608 of the Government Code.

(k) "Record" means information that is inscribed on a tangible medium, or that is stored in an electronic or other medium and is retrievable in perceivable form.

(*l*) "Transmission record" means the electronic record or document printed by the sending fax machine, stating the telephone number of the receiving fax machine, the number of pages sent, the transmission time and date, and an indication of any errors in transmission. **Leg.H.** Added Stats 2010 ch 680 §4 (AB 2394), effective January 1, 2011.

§263.2. Levying officer's information processing system; Filing day in case of technical problem

(a) A levying officer may utilize an information processing system to create, generate, send, receive, store, display, retrieve, or process information, electronic records, and documents when based on industry standards and only to the extent that the levying officer has the resources and technological capacity to do so.

(b) If a technical problem with the levying officer's system prevents the levying officer from receiving an electronic transmission during regular business hours on a particular court day, and the electronic sender demonstrates an attempt to electronically transmit the document on that day, the levying officer shall deem the document or record as filed on that day. **Leg.H.** Added Stats 2010 ch 680 §4 (AB 2394), effective January 1, 2011.

§263.3. Procedure for facsimile transmission

Whenever the fax transmission of a document or record to a levying officer is authorized pursuant to this chapter, all of the following shall apply:

(a) A levying officer may act upon an electronic record or document transmitted by a facsimile machine in the same manner as the paper record or document upon which the electronic record or document is based.

(b) A facsimile cover sheet shall accompany the faxed record or document and include all of the following information:

(1) The name of the sender.

(2) The fax number of the sender.

(3) The name of the levying officer.

(4) The fax number of the levying officer.

(5) A description of the record or document, including its name, if any, and the number of pages.

(6) A statement directing the recipient of the faxed document or record to fax to the sender a confirmation, if true, that the fax was properly received.

(c) A person authorized to fax a record or document to the levying officer pursuant to this chapter shall do all of the following:

(1) Retain the paper version of the record or document.

(2) Print or otherwise retain a transmission record of the fax transmission.

(3) Deliver the paper version of the record, document, or transmission record to the levying officer within five days after a request to do so has been mailed to the sender by the levying officer.

(d) The levying officer shall retain the facsimile cover sheet together with the faxed record or document.

(e) The levying officer may electronically copy and store the printed cover sheet, record, or document as an electronic record. **Leg.H.** Added Stats 2010 ch 680 §4 (AB 2394), effective January 1, 2011.

§263.4. Electronic record as substitute for paper record; Requirements; Procedure

(a) A levying officer may create, store, print, or transmit an electronic record in the place of, and in the same manner as, the paper record or document upon which the electronic record is based.

(b) An electronic record transmitted to a levying officer shall be accompanied by all of the following information:

(1) The name of the sender.

(2) The electronic address of the sender.

(3) The name of the levying officer.

(4) The electronic address or fax number of the levying officer.

(c) The person transmitting the electronic record shall do both of the following:

(1) Retain the paper version of the record or document.

(2) Deliver the paper version of the record or document to the levying officer within five days after a request to do so has been mailed to the sender by the levying officer.

(d) For the purpose of this section, "transmission" of an electronic record includes sending the electronic record included in, or in conjunction with, an electronic mail message, as defined in Section 263.1. **Leg.H.** Added Stats 2010 ch 680 §4 (AB 2394), effective January 1, 2011.

§263.6. Writ of execution; Retention of original or electronic copy; Accounting

(a) In lieu of returning to court the paper version of an original writ of execution, the levying officer may retain the original writ or an electronic copy of the original writ and file only a return of the levying officer's actions.

(b) If the original writ is not returned to court as provided in subdivision (a), the levying officer shall retain, for not less than two years after the levying officer's return is filed with court, each of the following, as applicable:

(1) The original paper writ or digital image of the writ.
(2) The memorandum of garnishee.
(3) The employer's return.
(4) An inventory of the levied property.

(c) A creditor seeking the issuance of a writ directed to another county may direct the levying officer to file an accounting of the levying officer's actions with the court.

(1) The filing of the accounting described in this subdivision does not constitute a return of the writ.

(2) The accounting shall indicate that the levying officer is in possession of an active writ. **Leg.H.** Added Stats 2010 ch 680 §4 (AB 2394), effective January 1, 2011.

§263.7. Exclusion or redaction of identifiers

(a) A levying officer shall exclude or redact the following identifiers from any record or document made available to the public:

(1) Social security number.
(2) Financial account number.

(b) If an identifier is redacted, only the last four digits of the number may be used.

(c) A levying officer also shall exclude or redact the identifiers listed in subdivision (a) from any writ return filed with the court.

(d) The term "public" does not include the creditor, debtor, garnishee, or third-party claimant. **Leg.H.** Added Stats 2010 ch 680 §4 (AB 2394), effective January 1, 2011.

§264. [Section repealed 1993]

Leg.H. Added Stats 1963 ch 1617 §1. Amended Stats 1977 ch 1257 §7, effective October 3, 1977. Repealed Stats 1992 ch 770 §1. The repealed section related to adoption of rules by judges of superior, municipal, and justice courts requiring examination or other suitable means to assure that interpreters used in such courts perform competently.

§§265, 266. [Sections repealed 1927]

Leg.H. Enacted 1872. Repealed and re-enacted Code Amdts 1880 ch 35 §1. Repealed Stats 1927 ch 565 §6. See Gov C §68806.

CHAPTER 3
PHONOGRAPHIC REPORTERS

Reporters for superior courts; Duties. §269.
Electronic transcripts; Provision of full text-searchable PDF copy if paper transcript delivered; Compliance with format requirements. §271.
Reports prima facie evidence; Use of rough draft transcripts. §273.
Matters to be transcribed in superior court. §274a.

§268. [Section repealed 1953]

Leg.H. Added Stats 1951 ch 655 §15. Repealed Stats 1953 ch 206 §7.

Prior Law: Former CCP §268, relating to phonographic reporters for supreme court, was added Code Amdts 1880 ch 35 §1 and repealed Stats 1927 ch 565 §6.

§269. Reporters for superior courts; Duties

(a) An official reporter or official reporter pro tempore of the superior court shall take down in shorthand all testimony, objections made, rulings of the court, exceptions taken, arraignments, pleas, sentences, arguments of the attorneys to the jury, and statements and remarks made and oral instructions given by the judge or other judicial officer, in the following cases:

(1) In a civil case, on the order of the court or at the request of a party.
(2) In a felony case, on the order of the court or at the request of the prosecution, the defendant, or the attorney for the defendant.
(3) In a misdemeanor or infraction case, on the order of the court.

(b) If a transcript is ordered by the court or requested by a party, or if a nonparty requests a transcript that the nonparty is entitled to receive, regardless of whether the nonparty was permitted to attend the proceeding to be transcribed, the official reporter or official reporter pro tempore shall, within a reasonable time after the trial of the case that the court designates, write the transcripts out, or the specific portions thereof as may be requested, in plain and legible longhand, or by typewriter, or other printing machine, and certify that the transcripts were correctly reported and transcribed, and when directed by the court, file the transcripts with the clerk of the court.

(c) If a defendant is convicted of a felony, after a trial on the merits, the record on appeal shall be prepared immediately after the verdict or finding of guilt is announced unless the court determines that it is likely that no appeal from the decision will be made. The court's determination of a likelihood of appeal shall be based upon standards and rules adopted by the Judicial Council. **Leg.H.** Enacted 1872. Amended Code Amdts 1873–74 ch 383 §24. Repealed and re-enacted Code Amdts 1880 ch 35 §1. Amended Stats 1903 ch 200 §1; Stats 1953 ch 206 §3; Stats 1990 ch 636 §1 (AB 2865); Stats 1993 ch 1016 §1 (AB 1929); Stats 1998 ch 931 §57 (SB 2139), effective September 28, 1998; Stats 2002 ch 71 §1 (SB 1371).

2002 Note: Nothing is this act is intended to change the extent to which official reporter services or electronic reporting may be used in the courts. Stats 2002 ch 71 (SB 1371) §8.

§269a. [Section repealed 1953]

Leg.H. Added Stats 1947 ch 153 §1. Repealed Stats 1953 ch 206 §7. See Gov C §69955.

§269b. [Section repealed 1953]

Leg.H. Added Stats 1951 ch 844 §1. Repealed Stats 1953 ch 206 §7. See Gov C §§70100, 70101, 70104.

§270. [Section repealed 2002]

Leg.H. Added Stats 1986 ch 373 §1. Amended Stats 1989 ch 678 §1. Repealed Stats 2001 ch 115 §2 (SB 153). The repealed section related to demonstration project to assess use of audio and video recording of proceedings.

Prior Law: Former CCP §270, similar to present Gov C §§69942–69944, was added Code Amdts 1873–74 ch 591 §3 as CCP §272, repealed and reenacted as CCP §270 by Code Amdts 1880 ch 35 §1, amended Stats 1909 ch 708 §1, and repealed Stats 1953 ch 206 §7.

Former CCP §270 was enacted 1872, amended Code Amdts 1873–74 ch 591 §1, and repealed and reenacted as CCP §273 by Code Amdts 1880 ch 35 §1.

§271. Electronic transcripts; Provision of full text-searchable PDF copy if paper transcript delivered; Compliance with format requirements

(a) An official reporter or official reporter pro tempore shall deliver a transcript in electronic form, in compliance with the California Rules of Court, to any court, party, or person entitled to the transcript, unless any of the following apply:

(1) The party or person entitled to the transcript requests the reporter's transcript in paper form.

(2) Prior to January 1, 2023, the court lacks the technical ability to use or store a transcript in electronic form pursuant to this section and provides advance notice of this fact to the official reporter or official reporter pro tempore.

(3) Prior to January 1, 2023, the official reporter or official reporter pro tempore lacks the technical ability to deliver a transcript in electronic form pursuant to this section and provides advance notice of this fact to the court, party, or person entitled to the transcript.

(b) If a paper transcript is delivered in lieu of an electronic transcript described in subdivision (a), within 120 days of the official reporter or official reporter pro tempore filing or delivering the paper transcript, the official reporter or official reporter pro tempore shall provide, upon request, a copy of the original transcript in full text-searchable portable document format (PDF) if the proceedings were produced with computer-aided transcription equipment. The copy of the original transcript in full text-searchable PDF format shall not be deemed to be an original transcript.

(c) Nothing in this section changes any requirement set forth in Section 69950 or 69954 of the Government Code, regardless of whether a transcript is delivered in electronic or paper form.

(d) Except as provided in subdivision (b), an electronic transcript delivered in accordance with this section shall be deemed to be an original transcript for all purposes, including any obligation of an attorney to maintain or deliver a file to a client.

(e) An electronic transcript shall comply with any format requirement imposed pursuant to subdivision (a). However, an official reporter or official reporter pro tempore shall not be required to use a specific vendor, technology, or software to comply with this section, unless the official reporter or official reporter pro tempore agrees with the court, party, or person entitled to the transcript to use a specific vendor, technology, or software. Absent that agreement, an official reporter or official reporter pro tempore may select the vendor, technology, and software to comply with this section and the California Rules of Court. In adopting transcript format requirements for the California Rules of Court, consideration shall be given on a technology-neutral basis to the availability of relevant vendors of transcript products, technologies, and software.

(f) After January 1, 2023, if new or updated rule of court format requirements for electronic transcripts necessitate a significant change in equipment or software owned by official reporters or official reporters pro tempore, the official reporters and official reporters pro tempore shall be given no less than one year to comply with the format requirements. If the change is necessary to address a security issue, then a reasonable time shall be given to comply with the new format requirements. **Leg.H.** Added Stats 2017 ch 532 §2 (AB 1450), effective January 1, 2018.

Former Sections: Former CCP §271, relating to delivery of transcripts in computer-readable form, was added Stats 2002 ch 71 §2 (SB 1371) and repealed Stats 2017 ch 532 §1 (AB 1450).

Former CCP §271 was enacted 1872, amended Code Amdts 1873–74 ch 591 §2, and repealed and re-enacted as CCP §274 by Code Amdts 1880 ch 35 §1.

Former CCP §271 was added Code Amdts 1873–74 ch 591 §4, as CCP §273, repealed and re-enacted by Code Amdts 1880 ch 35 §1, and repealed Stats 1953 ch 206 §7.

Prior Law: Former CCP §271, relating to delivery of transcripts in computer-readable form, was added Stats 2002 ch 71 §2 (SB 1371), effective January 1, 2003, and repealed Stats 2017 ch 532 §1 (AB 1450), effective January 1, 2018.

Former CCP §271 was enacted 1872, amended Code Amdts 1873-74 ch 591 §2, and repealed and reenacted as CCP §274 by Code Amdts 1880 ch 35 §1.

Former CCP §271 was added Code Amdts 1873-74 ch 591 §4, as CCP §273, repealed and reenacted by Code Amdts 1880 ch 35 §1, and repealed Stats 1953 ch 206 §7.

§272. [Section repealed 1953]

Leg.H. Added Code Amdts 1873–74 ch 591 §5 as CCP §274. Repealed and re-enacted as CCP §272 by Code Amdts 1880 ch 35 §1. Repealed Stats 1953 ch 206 §7. See Gov C §69946.

Prior Law: Former CCP §272 was added Code Amdts 1873–74 ch 591 §3 and repealed and reenacted as CCP §270 by Code Amdts 1880 ch 35 §1.

§273. Reports prima facie evidence; Use of rough draft transcripts

(a) The report of the official reporter, or official reporter pro tempore, of any court, duly appointed and sworn, when transcribed and certified as being a correct transcript of the testimony and proceedings in the case, is prima facie evidence of that testimony and proceedings.

(b) The report of the official reporter, or official reporter pro tempore, of any court, duly appointed and sworn, when prepared as a rough draft transcript, shall not be certified and cannot be used, cited, distributed, or transcribed as the official certified transcript of the proceedings. A rough draft transcript shall not be cited or used in any way or at any time to rebut or contradict the official certified transcript of the proceedings as provided by the official reporter or official reporter pro tempore. The production of a rough draft transcript shall not be required.

(c) This section shall become operative on January 1, 2022. **Leg.H.** Added Stats 2009 ch 87 §2 (AB 170), effective January 1, 2010, operative January 1, 2017. Amended Stats 2016 ch 703 §7 (AB 2881), effective January 1, 2017, operative January 1, 2022.

Prior Law: Former CCP §273, similar to the present section, was added Stats 1872 as CCP §270, amended Code Amdts 1873-74 ch 591 §1, repealed and reenacted as §273 by Code Amdts 1880 ch 35 §1, amended Stats 1903 ch 200 §2; Stats 1997 ch183 §1 (AB 1372), amended Stats 2009 ch 87 §1 (AB170), effective January 1, 2010, repealed January 1 2017, amended Stats 2016 ch 703 §6 (AB 2881), effective January 1, 2017, and repealed January 1, 2022, by its own terms.

§274. [Section repealed 1953]

Leg.H. Enacted 1872 as CCP §271. Amended Code Amdts 1873–74 ch 591 §2. Repealed and re-enacted as CCP §274 by Code Amdts 1880 ch 35 §1. Amended Stats 1885 ch 167 §1; Stats 1903 ch 200 §3; Stats 1929 ch 722 §1; Stats 1933 ch 740 §1; Stats 1945 ch 471 §1; Stats 1947 ch 220 §1; Stats 1951 ch 1653 §2. Repealed Stats 1953 ch 206 §7. See Gov C §§69947–69953.

§274a. Matters to be transcribed in superior court

Any judge of the superior court may have any opinion given or rendered by the judge in the trial of a felony case or an unlimited civil case, pending in that court, or any necessary order, petition, citation, commitment or judgment in any probate proceeding, proceeding concerning new or additional bonds of county officials or juvenile court proceeding, or the testimony or judgment relating to the custody or support of minor children in any proceeding in which the custody or support of minor children is involved, taken down in shorthand and transcribed together with such copies as the court may deem necessary by the official reporter or an official reporter pro tempore of the court. **Leg.H.** Added Stats 1907 ch 22 §1. Amended Stats 1911 ch 308 §1; Stats 1929 ch 720 §1; Stats 1933 ch 740 §2; Stats 1947 ch 152 §1; Stats 1963 ch 298 §1; Stats 1998 ch 931 §58 (SB 2139), effective September 28, 1998; Stats 2002 ch 784 §51 (SB 1316).

§274b. [Section repealed 1929]

Leg.H. Added Stats 1909 ch 708 §2. Repealed Stats 1929 ch 721 §1.

§274c. [Section repealed 2003]

Leg.H. Added Stats 1927 ch 448 §1. Amended Stats 1929 ch 468 §1; Stats 1933 ch 743 §60a; Stats 1951 ch 1737 §42, operative January 1, 1952; Stats 1953 ch 206 §6; Stats 1955 ch 1424 §1; Stats 1977 ch 1257 §8, effective October 3, 1977; Stats 1998 ch 931 §59 (SB 2139), effective September 28, 1998. Repealed Stats 2002 ch 71 §3 (SB 1371). See CCP §269.

§274d. [Section repealed 1953]

Leg.H. Added Stats 1935 ch 165 §1. Repealed Stats 1953 ch 206 §7. The repealed section related to phonographic reporters for the criminal division of the San Francisco Municipal Court.

§274e. [Section repealed 1953]

Leg.H. Added Stats 1949 ch 862 §1. Repealed Stats 1953 ch 206 §7. The repealed section related to phonographic reporter fees.

TITLE 5
PERSONS SPECIALLY INVESTED WITH MINISTERIAL POWERS RELATING TO COURTS OF JUSTICE

Chapter 1. Attorneys and Counselors at Law.

CHAPTER 1
ATTORNEYS AND COUNSELORS AT LAW

Authority. §283.
Change of attorney. §284.
Notice of change. §285.
Withdrawal of attorney in domestic relations actions. §285.1.
Withdrawal from representation by legal service attorney based on lack of agency funding. §285.2.
Tolling of time limits upon withdrawal of legal service agency attorney. §285.3.
Appointment of counsel upon withdrawal of legal service agency attorney; Recovery of attorneys' fees and costs. §285.4.
Death or removal of attorney. §286.

§275. [Section repealed 1931]
Leg.H. Enacted 1872. Amended Code Amdts 1877–78 ch 600 §1. Repealed and re-enacted Code Amdts 1880 ch 35 §1. Amended Stats 1921 ch 358 §1; Stats 1923 ch 104 §1. Repealed Stats 1931 ch 861 §2. See B & P C §§6060 et seq.

§276. [Section repealed 1931]
Leg.H. Enacted 1872. Amended Code Amdts 1873–74 ch 306 §1, ch 383 §25. Repealed and re-enacted Code Amdts 1880 ch 35 §1. Amended Stats 1895 ch 58 §1; Stats 1905 ch 8 §1; Stats 1917 ch 593 §1; Stats 1919 ch 347 §1. Repealed Stats 1931 ch 861 §2. See B & P C §§6060 et seq.

§276a. [Section repealed 1931]
Leg.H. Added Stats 1919 ch 347 §2. Amended Stats 1921 ch 346 §1. Repealed Stats 1931 ch 861 §2. See B & P C §6046.

§277. [Section repealed 1931]
Leg.H. Enacted 1872. Repealed and re-enacted Code Amdts 1880 ch 35 §1. Amended Stats 1905 ch 8 §2; Stats 1919 ch 347 §3. Repealed Stats 1931 ch 861 §2. See B & P C §6064.

§278. [Section repealed 1939]
Leg.H. Enacted 1872. Repealed and re-enacted Code Amdts 1880 ch 35 §1. Repealed Stats 1939 ch 34 §2 (B & P C §30013). See B & P C §6067.

§279. [Section repealed 1931]
Leg.H. Enacted 1872. Amended Code Amdts 1877–78 Ch 600 §2. Repealed and re-enacted Code Amdts 1880 ch 35 §1. Amended Stats 1905 ch 8 §3; Stats 1919 ch 347 §4; Stats 1921 ch 360 §1; Stats 1923 ch 104 §2. Repealed Stats 1931 ch 861 §2. See B & P C §6062.

§280. [Section repealed 1931]
Leg.H. Enacted 1872. Repealed and re-enacted Code Amdts 1880 ch 35 §1. Amended Stats 1905 ch 8 §4. Repealed Stats 1931 ch 861 §2.

§280a. [Section repealed 1917]
Leg.H. Added Stats 1905 ch 8 §5. Repealed Stats 1917 ch 587 §1.

§280b. [Section repealed 1917]
Leg.H. Added Stats 1907 ch 438 §1. Amended Stats 1909 ch 327 §1; Stats 1913 ch 82 §1; Stats 1915 ch 407 §1. Repealed Stats 1917 ch 585 §1.

§281. [Section repealed 1939]
Leg.H. Enacted 1872. Repealed and re-enacted Code Amdts 1880 ch 35 §1. Repealed Stats 1939 ch 34 §2 (B & P C §30013). See B & P C §6127.

§282. [Section repealed 1939]
Leg.H. Enacted in 1872. Repealed and re-enacted Code Amdts 1880 ch 35 §1. 1. Repealed Stats 1939 ch 34 §2 (B & P C §30013). See B & PC §6068.

§283. Authority
An attorney and counselor shall have authority:
1. To bind his client in any of the steps of an action or proceeding by his agreement filed with the clerk, or entered upon the minutes of the court, and not otherwise;
2. To receive money claimed by his client in an action or proceeding during the pendency thereof, or after judgment, unless a revocation of his authority is filed, and upon the payment thereof, and not otherwise, to discharge the claim or acknowledge satisfaction of the judgment. **Leg.H.** Enacted 1872. Repealed and re-enacted Code Amdts 1880 ch 35 §1.

§284. Change of attorney
The attorney in an action or special proceeding may be changed at any time before or after judgment of final determination, as follows:
1. Upon the consent of both client and attorney, filed with the clerk, or entered upon the minutes;
2. Upon the order of the court, upon the application of either client or attorney, after notice from one to the other. **Leg.H.** Enacted 1872. Amended Code Amdts 1873–74 ch 383 §26. Repealed and re-enacted Code Amdts 1880 ch 35 §1. Amended Stats 1935 ch 560 §1; Stats 1967 ch 161 §1.

§285. Notice of change
When an attorney is changed, as provided in the last section, written notice of the change and of the substitution of a new attorney, or of the appearance of the party in person, must be given to the adverse party. Until then he must recognize the former attorney. **Leg.H.** Enacted 1872. Repealed and re-enacted Code Amdts 1880 ch 35 §1.

§285.1. Withdrawal of attorney in domestic relations actions
An attorney of record for any party in any civil action or proceeding for dissolution of marriage, legal separation, or for a declaration of void or voidable marriage, or for the support, maintenance or custody of minor children may withdraw at any time subsequent to the time when any judgment in such action or proceeding, other than an interlocutory judgment, becomes final, and prior to service upon him of pleadings or motion papers in any proceeding then pending in said cause, by filing a notice of withdrawal. Such notice shall state (a) date of entry of final decree or judgment, (b) the last known address of such party, (c) that such attorney withdraws as attorney for such party. A copy of such notice shall be mailed to such party at his last known address and shall be served upon the adverse party. **Leg.H.** Added Stats 1963 ch 1333 §1. Amended Stats 1969 ch 1608 §10, operative January 1, 1970.

§285.2. Withdrawal from representation by legal service attorney based on lack of agency funding
If a reduction in public funding for legal service materially impairs a legal service agency attorney's ability to represent an indigent client, the court, on its own motion or on the motion of either the client or attorney, shall permit the withdrawal of such attorney upon a showing that all of the following apply:
(a) There are not adequate public funds to continue the effective representation of the indigent client.
(b) A good faith effort was made to find alternate representation for such client.
(c) All reasonable steps to reduce the legal prejudice to the client have been taken.
A showing of indigency of the client, in and of itself, will not be deemed sufficient cause to deny the application for withdrawal. **Leg.H.** Added Stats 1983 ch 279 §1.

§285.3. Tolling of time limits upon withdrawal of legal service agency attorney
The court, upon the granting of a motion for withdrawal pursuant to Section 285.2, may toll the running of any statute of limitations, filing requirement, statute providing for mandatory dismissal, notice of appeal, or discovery requirement, for a period not to exceed 90 days, on the court's own motion or on motion of any party or attorney, when the court finds that tolling is required to avoid legal prejudice caused by the withdrawal of the legal service agency attorney. **Leg.H.** Added Stats 1983 ch 279 §2.

§285.4. Appointment of counsel upon withdrawal of legal service agency attorney; Recovery of attorneys' fees and costs

The court, upon the granting of a motion for withdrawal pursuant to Section 285.2, may appoint any member of the bar or any law firm or professional law corporation to represent the indigent client without compensation, upon a showing of good cause. Nothing herein shall preclude the appointed attorney from recovering any attorneys' fees and costs to which the client may be entitled by law. In determining the existence of good cause, the court may consider, but is not limited to, the following factors:

(a) The probable merit of the client's claim.
(b) The client's financial ability to pay for legal services.
(c) The availability of alternative legal representation.
(d) The need for legal representation to avoid irreparable legal prejudice to the indigent client.
(e) The ability of appointed counsel to effectively represent the indigent client.
(f) Present and recent pro bono work of the appointed attorney, law firm or private law corporation.
(g) The ability of the indigent client to represent himself.
(h) The workload of the appointed attorney. **Leg.H.** Added Stats 1983 ch 279 §3.

§286. Death or removal of attorney

When an attorney dies, or is removed or suspended, or ceases to act as such, a party to an action, for whom he was acting as attorney, must, before any further proceedings are had against him, be required by the adverse party, by written notice, to appoint another attorney, or to appear in person. **Leg.H.** Enacted 1872. Repealed and re-enacted Code Amdts 1880 ch 35 §1.

§287. [Section repealed 1939]

Leg.H. Enacted 1872. Amended Code Amdts 1873–74 ch 383 §27. Repealed and re-enacted Code Amdts 1880 ch 35 §1. Amended Stats 1911 ch 422 §1. Repealed Stats 1939 ch 34 §2 (B & P C §30013). See B & P C §§6100, 6101, 6103–6106.

§§288, 289. [Sections repealed 1939]

Leg.H. Enacted 1872. Repealed and re-enacted Code Amdts 1880 ch 35 §1. Amended Stats 1921 ch 107 §§1, 2. Repealed Stats 1939 ch 34 §2 (B & P C §30013). See B & P C §§6101, 6102, 6107.

§290. [Section repealed 1939]

Leg.H. Enacted 1872. Repealed and re-enacted Code Amdts 1880 ch 35 §1. Repealed Stats 1939 ch 34 §2 (B & P C §30013). See B & P C §6108.

§291. [Section repealed 1939]

Leg.H. Enacted 1872. Repealed and re-enacted Code Amdts 1880 ch 35 §1. Amended Stats 1921 ch 107 §3. Repealed Stats 1939 ch 34 §2 (B & P C §30013). See B & P C §6108.

§292. [Section repealed 1939]

Leg.H. Enacted 1872. Repealed and re-enacted Code Amdts 1880 ch 35 §1. Amended Stats 1911 ch 491 §1. Repealed Stats 1939 ch 34 §2 (B & P C §30013). See B & P C §§6109, 6110.

§§293–295. [Sections repealed 1939]

Leg.H. Enacted 1872. Repealed and re-enacted Code Amdts 1880 ch 35 §1. Repealed Stats 1939 ch 34 §2 (B & P C §30013). See B & P C §§6111, 6112.

§296. [Section repealed 1939]

Leg.H. Enacted 1872. Amended Code Amdts 1873–74 ch 383 §28. Repealed and re-enacted Code Amdts 1880 ch 35 §1. Repealed Stats 1939 ch 34 §2 (B & P C §30013). See B & P C §6113.

§§297, 298. [Sections repealed 1939]

Leg.H. Enacted 1872. Repealed and re-enacted Code Amdts 1880 ch 35 §1. Repealed Stats 1939 ch 34 §2 (B & P C §30013). See B & P C §§6114, 6115.

§299. [Section repealed 1939]

Leg.H. Enacted 1872. Amended Code Amdts 1873–74 ch 383 §29. Repealed and re-enacted Code Amdts 1880 ch 35 §1. Amended Stats 1919 ch 98 §1; Stats 1921 ch 107 §4. Repealed Stats 1939 ch 34 §2 (B & P C §30013). See B & P C §§6102, 6116, 6117.

§300. [Section repealed 1939]

Leg.H. Added Stats 1921 ch 107 §5. Amended Stats 1923 ch 361 §1. Repealed Stats 1939 ch 34 §2 (B & P C §30013). See B & P C §6130.

§301. [Section repealed 1939]

Leg.H. Added Stats 1923 ch 104 §3. Repealed Stats 1939 ch 34 §2 (B & P C §30013).

CHAPTER 2
OTHER PERSONS INVESTED WITH SUCH POWERS [REPEALED]

§304. [Section repealed 1983]

Leg.H. Added Stats 1951 ch 655 §16. Amended Stats 1979 ch 730 §18, operative July 1, 1981. Repealed Stats 1982 ch 517 §96. See CCP §995.810.

Prior Law: Former CCP §304, relating to bonds of receivers, executors, administrators, and guardians, was enacted 1872, repealed and reenacted Code Amdts 1880 ch 35 §1, and repealed Stats 1933 ch 743 §61.

§304.1. [Section repealed 1983]

Leg.H. Added Stats 1951 ch 655 §16. Repealed Stats 1982 ch 517 §96. See CCP §§995.820, 995.850.

§304.2. [Section repealed 1983]

Leg.H. Added Stats 1951 ch 655 §16. Repealed Stats 1982 ch 517 §96. See CCP §§996.510, 996.520, 996.530.

§§304.3, 304.4. [Sections repealed 1953]

Leg.H. Added Stats 1951 ch 655 §16. Repealed Stats 1953 ch 206 §7. The repealed sections related to court costs and fees.

PART 2
OF CIVIL ACTIONS

Title 1. Of the Form of Civil Actions.
Title 2. Of the Time of Commencing Civil Actions.
Title 3. Of the Parties to Civil Actions.
Title 3A. Vexatious Litigants.
Title 4. Of the Place of Trial, Reclassification, and Coordination of Civil Actions.
Title 4.5. Recording Notice of Certain Actions.
Title 5. Jurisdiction and Service of Process.
Title 6. Of the Pleadings in Civil Actions.
Title 6.5. Attachment.
Title 7. Other Provisional Remedies in Civil Actions.
Title 7a. Pretrial Conferences.
Title 8. Of the Trial and Judgment in Civil Actions.
Title 8.5. Uniform Foreign-Money Claims Act.
Title 9. Enforcement of Judgments.
Title 10. Actions in Particular Cases.
Title 10.5. Partition of Real and Personal Property.
Title 11. Contribution Among Joint Judgment Debtors.
Title 13. Appeals in Civil Actions.
Title 14. Of Miscellaneous Provisions.

TITLE 1
OF THE FORM OF CIVIL ACTIONS

One form of civil action only. §307.
Parties to actions, how designated. §308.
Special issues not made by pleadings, how tried. §309.

§307. One form of civil action only

There is in this state but one form of civil actions for the enforcement or protection of private rights and the redress or prevention of private wrongs. **Leg.H.** Enacted 1872.

§308. Parties to actions, how designated

In such action the party complaining is known as the plaintiff, and the adverse party as the defendant. **Leg.H.** Enacted 1872.

§309. Special issues not made by pleadings, how tried

A question of fact not put in issue by the pleadings may be tried by a jury, upon an order for the trial, stating distinctly and plainly the question of fact to be tried; and such order is the only authority necessary for a trial. **Leg.H.** Enacted 1872.

TITLE 2
OF THE TIME OF COMMENCING CIVIL ACTIONS

Chapter 1. The Time of Commencing Actions in General.
Chapter 2. The Time of Commencing Actions for the Recovery of Real Property.
Chapter 3. The Time of Commencing Actions Other Than for the Recovery of Real Property.
Chapter 4. General Provisions as to the Time of Commencing Actions.
Chapter 5. The Commencement of Actions Based Upon Professional Negligence.
Chapter 6. Time of Commencement of Action After Person's Death.

CHAPTER 1
THE TIME OF COMMENCING ACTIONS IN GENERAL

Commencement of civil actions. §312.
General procedure for presentation of claims against the State. §313.

§312. Commencement of civil actions

Civil actions, without exception, can only be commenced within the periods prescribed in this title, after the cause of action shall have accrued, unless where, in special cases, a different limitation is prescribed by statute. **Leg.H.** Enacted 1872. Amended Stats 1897 ch 21 §1.

§313. General procedure for presentation of claims against the State

The general procedure for the presentation of claims as a prerequisite to commencement of actions for money or damages against the State of California, counties, cities, cities and counties, districts, local authorities, and other political subdivisions of the State, and against the officers, employees, and servants thereof, is prescribed by Division 3.6 (commencing with Section 810) of Title 1 of the Government Code. **Leg.H.** Added Stats 1959 ch 1724 §3. Amended Stats 1963 ch 1715 §9.

CHAPTER 2
THE TIME OF COMMENCING ACTIONS FOR THE RECOVERY OF REAL PROPERTY

When the people will not sue. §315.
When action cannot be brought by grantee from the state. §316.
When actions by the people or their grantees are to be brought within five years. §317.
Seizin within five years, when necessary in action for real property. §318.
Such seisin, when necessary in action or defense arising out of title to or rents of real property. §319.
Entry on real estate. §320.
Possession, when presumed; Occupation deemed under legal title, unless adverse. §321.
Occupation under written instrument or judgment, when deemed adverse. §322.
What constitutes adverse possession under written instrument or judgment. §323.
Premises actually occupied under claim of title deemed to be held adversely. §324.
What constitutes adverse possession under claim of unwritten title. §325.
Relation of landlord and tenant, as affecting adverse possession. §326.
Right of possession not affected by descent cast. §327.
Certain disabilities excluded from time to commence actions. §328.
Time to bring action for prisoners. §328.5.
Foreclosure of street improvement liens; Cessation of lien; Marking payment. §329.
Contesting validity of assessment; Time for perfecting appeal. §329.5.
Time for sale under public improvement assessment lien. §330.

§315. When the people will not sue

The people of this state will not sue any person for or in respect to any real property, or the issues or profits thereof, by reason of the right or title of the people to the same, unless:

1. Such right or title shall have accrued within ten years before any action or other proceeding for the same is commenced; or,
2. The people, or those from whom they claim, shall have received the rents and profits of such real property, or some part thereof, within the space of ten years. **Leg.H.** Enacted 1872.

§316. When action cannot be brought by grantee from the state

No action can be brought for or in respect to real property by any person claiming under letters patent or grants from this state, unless the same might have been commenced by the people as herein specified, in case such patent had not been issued or grant made. **Leg.H.** Enacted 1872.

§317. When actions by the people or their grantees are to be brought within five years

When letters or grants of real property issued or made by the people of this state, are declared void by the determination of a competent court, an action for the recovery of the property so conveyed may be brought, either by the people of the state, or by any subsequent patentee or grantee of the property, his heirs or assigns, within five years after such determination, but not after that period. **Leg.H.** Enacted 1872. Amended Code Amdts 1873–74 ch 383 §30.

§318. Seizin within five years, when necessary in action for real property

No action for the recovery of real property, or for the recovery of the possession thereof, can be maintained, unless it appear that the plaintiff, his ancestor, predecessor, or grantor, was seized or possessed of the property in question, within five years before the commencement of the action. **Leg.H.** Enacted 1872.

§319. Such seisin, when necessary in action or defense arising out of title to or rents of real property

No cause of action, or defense to an action, arising out of the title to real property, or to rents or profits out of the same, can be effectual, unless it appear that the person prosecuting the action, or making the defense, or under whose title the action is prosecuted, or the defense is made, or the ancestor, predecessor, or grantor of such person was seised or possessed of the premises in question within five years before the commencement of the act in respect to which such action is prosecuted or defense made. **Leg.H.** Enacted 1872.

§320. Entry on real estate

No entry upon real estate is deemed sufficient or valid as a claim, unless an action be commenced thereupon within one year after making such entry, and within five years from the time when the right to make it descended or accrued. **Leg.H.** Enacted 1872.

§321. Possession, when presumed; Occupation deemed under legal title, unless adverse

In every action for the recovery of real property, or the possession thereof, the person establishing a legal title to the property is presumed to have been possessed thereof within the time required by law, and the occupation of the property by any other person is deemed to have been under and in subordination to the legal title, unless it appear that the property has been held and possessed adversely to such legal title, for five years before the commencement of the action. **Leg.H.** Enacted 1872.

§322. Occupation under written instrument or judgment, when deemed adverse

When it appears that the occupant, or those under whom he claims, entered into the possession of the property under claim of title, exclusive of other right, founding such claim upon a written instrument, as being a conveyance of the property in question, or upon the decree or judgment of a competent court, and that there has been a continued occupation and possession of the property included in such instrument, decree, or judgment, or of some part of the property, under such claim, for five years, the property so included is deemed to have been held adversely, except that when it consists of a tract divided into lots, the possession of one lot is not deemed a possession of any other lot of the same tract. **Leg.H.** Enacted 1872.

§323. What constitutes adverse possession under written instrument or judgment

For the purpose of constituting an adverse possession by any person claiming a title, founded upon a written instrument, or a judgment or decree, land is deemed to have been possessed and occupied in the following cases:

1. Where it has been usually cultivated or improved;
2. Where it has been protected by a substantial inclosure;

3. Where, although not inclosed, it has been used for the supply of fuel, or of fencing-timber for the purposes of husbandry, or for pasturage, or for the ordinary use of the occupant;

4. Where a known farm or single lot has been partly improved, the portion of such farm or lot that may have been left not cleared, or not inclosed according to the usual course and custom of the adjoining country, shall be deemed to have been occupied for the same length of time as the part improved and cultivated. **Leg.H.** Enacted 1872.

§324. Premises actually occupied under claim of title deemed to be held adversely

Where it appears that there has been an actual continued occupation of land, under a claim of title, exclusive of any other right, but not founded upon a written instrument, judgment, or decree, the land so actually occupied, and no other, is deemed to have been held adversely. **Leg.H.** Enacted 1872.

§325. What constitutes adverse possession under claim of unwritten title

(a) For the purpose of constituting an adverse possession by a person claiming title, not founded upon a written instrument, judgment, or decree, land is deemed to have been possessed and occupied in the following cases only:

(1) Where it has been protected by a substantial enclosure.

(2) Where it has been usually cultivated or improved.

(b) In no case shall adverse possession be considered established under the provision of any section of this code, unless it shall be shown that the land has been occupied and claimed for the period of five years continuously, and the party or persons, their predecessors and grantors, have timely paid all state, county, or municipal taxes that have been levied and assessed upon the land for the period of five years during which the land has been occupied and claimed. Payment of those taxes by the party or persons, their predecessors and grantors shall be established by certified records of the county tax collector. **Leg.H.** Enacted 1872. Amended Stats 1877–78 ch 590 §1; Stats 2010 ch 55 §1 (AB 1684), effective January 1, 2011.

§326. Relation of landlord and tenant, as affecting adverse possession

When the relation of landlord and tenant has existed between any persons, the possession of the tenant is deemed the possession of the landlord until the expiration of five years from the termination of the tenancy, or, where there has been no written lease, until the expiration of five years from the time of the last payment of rent, notwithstanding that such tenant may have acquired another title, or may have claimed to hold adversely to his landlord. But such presumptions cannot be made after the periods herein limited. **Leg.H.** Enacted 1872.

§327. Right of possession not affected by descent cast

The right of a person to the possession of real property is not impaired or affected by a descent cast in consequence of the death of a person in possession of such property. **Leg.H.** Enacted 1872.

§328. Certain disabilities excluded from time to commence actions

If a person entitled to commence an action for the recovery of real property, or for the recovery of the possession thereof, or to make an entry or defense founded on the title to real property, or to rents or services out of the property, is, at the time title first descends or accrues, either under the age of majority or lacking legal capacity to make decisions, the time, not exceeding 20 years, during which the disability continues is not deemed a portion of the time in this chapter limited for the commencement of the action, or the making of the entry or defense, but the action may be commenced, or entry or defense made, within the period of five years after the disability shall cease, or after the death of the person entitled, who shall die under the disability. The action shall not be commenced, or entry or defense made, after that period. **Leg.H.** Enacted 1872. Amended Stats 1903 ch 160 §1; Stats 1994 ch 1083 §2 (SB 1445); Stats 2014 ch 144 §3 (AB 1847), effective January 1, 2015.

§328.5. Time to bring action for prisoners

If a person entitled to commence an action for the recovery of real property, or for the recovery of the possession thereof, or to make any entry or defense founded on the title to real property, or to rents or services out of the property, is, at the time the title first descends or accrues, imprisoned on a criminal charge, or in execution upon conviction of a criminal offense, for a term less than life, the time, not exceeding two years, during which imprisonment continues is not deemed any portion of the time in this chapter limited for the commencement of the action, or the making of the entry or defense, but the action may be commenced, or entry or defense made, within the period of five years after the imprisonment ceases, or after the death of the person entitled, who dies while imprisoned; but the action shall not be commenced, or entry or defense made, after that period. **Leg.H.** Added Stats 1994 ch 1083 §3 (SB 1445).

§329. Foreclosure of street improvement liens; Cessation of lien; Marking payment

The time within which an action for the foreclosure of a lien securing an assessment against real property for street improvements, the proceedings for which are prescribed by legislation of any political unit other than the state, may be commenced, shall be two years from and after the date on which the assessment, or any bond secured thereby, or the last installment of the assessment or bond, shall be due, or, as to existing rights of action not heretofore barred, one year after the effective date hereof, whichever time is later. After that time, if the lien has not been otherwise removed, the lien ceases to exist and the assessment is conclusively presumed to be paid. The official having charge of the records of the assessment shall mark it "Conclusively presumed paid," if, at the expiration of the time within which such action might be brought he has received no written notice of the pendency of the action. **Leg.H.** Added Stats 1933 ch 883 §1. Amended Stats 1945 ch 362 §1; Stats 1981 ch 714 §68.

§329.5. Contesting validity of assessment; Time for perfecting appeal

The validity of an assessment or supplemental assessment against real property for public improvements, the proceedings for which are prescribed by the legislature body of any chartered city, shall not be contested in any action or proceeding unless the action or proceeding is commenced within 30 days after the assessment is levied, or such longer period as the legislative body may provide. Any appeal from a final judgment in such an action or proceeding shall be perfected within 30 days after the entry of judgment. **Leg.H.** Added Stats 1959 ch 1007 §1.

§330. Time for sale under public improvement assessment lien

In all cases in which there is now vested or there shall hereafter be vested in a treasurer, street superintendent, or other public official the power to sell at public auction, after demand upon him by the holder of any public improvement bond, any lot or parcel of land upon which exists or which shall hereafter exist a lien to secure the payment of a public improvement assessment represented by said bond, and the act or law establishing such power fails to prescribe the time within which such official may act, said official may sell at any time prior to the expiration of four years after the due date of said bond or of the last installment thereof or of the last principal coupon attached thereto, or prior to January 1, 1947, whichever is later, but not thereafter. This section is not intended to extend, enlarge or revive any power of sale which has heretofore been lost by reason of lapse of time or otherwise. **Leg.H.** Added Stats 1945 ch 360 §1 p 821.

CHAPTER 3
THE TIME OF COMMENCING ACTIONS OTHER THAN FOR THE RECOVERY OF REAL PROPERTY

Periods of limitation prescribed. §335.
Assault; Battery; Personal injury; Wrongful death. §335.1.
Mesne profits; Violation of restriction on use of real property. §336.
Corporate bonds, notes, etc., and underlying mortgages, trust deeds, etc.; Six years. §336a.
Written obligation; Four years. §337.
"Book account". § 337a.
Patent deficiency in real property improvement design, survey, construction, etc., and resulting injury to property or person; Four years. §337.1.
Action for latent deficiency in construction or survey of real property or injury arising out of such deficiency; Ten years. §337.15.
Lessee's breach of written lease; Four years. §337.2.
Bonds or coupons issued by political subdivisions of State; Judgments or decrees; Ten years. §337.5.

Bonds and coupons against which statute of limitations ran on or after August 27, 1937, when action brought on or before June 30, 1959. §337.6.
Statutory liability; Injury to real property; Taking or injuring goods or chattels; Fraud or mistake; Bonds of public officials and notaries; Slander of title; False advertising; Pollution violations; Challenge to tax levy; Personal rights violations. §338.
Action for civil penalties or punitive damages related to hazardous substances; Five years. §338.1.
Person with legal standing to action. § 338.2.
Two Years: Oral obligations; Certificate, abstract, or guaranty of title; Title insurance; Liability of sheriff or coroner; Rescission of oral contract. §339.
Lessee's breach of unwritten lease; Two years. §339.5.
Statutory penalties or forfeitures; Libel; Slander; False imprisonment; Seduction of person under age of consent; Payment by bank of forged check; Injury or death of animal; Damages in making property seizure; Good faith improvements. §340.
Damages suffered as a result of childhood sexual assault; Certificates of merit. §340.1.
Action for recovery of damages suffered as a result of childhood sexual assault that occurred before January 1, 2024; Time for commencement of action. § 340.11.
Action for damages resulting from domestic violence. §340.15.
Action for damages resulting from sexual assault; Revival of claims; Declaration by attorney of good faith belief that claim valued to be more than $250,000. §340.16.
Exposure to asbestos; Injury or illness; "Disability"; Wrongful death. §340.2.
Time for commencement of damage action based on commission of felony offense. §340.3.
Action for damages against person for childhood sexual abuse following certain dismissed criminal actions; Application of section. §340.35.
Statute of limitations for action by minor for personal injuries sustained before or during birth. §340.4.
Professional negligence of health care provider; Tolling of time limitation. §340.5.
Action against attorney for wrongful act or omission, other than fraud. §340.6.
Dalkon Shield Claimants' Trust. §340.7.
Injury, illness, or death based on exposure to hazardous material or toxic substance; Time for commencement; Media reports as notice. §340.8.
Insurance claim for damages arising out of Northridge earthquake of 1994; Revival of cause of action. §340.9.
"Terrorist victim". §340.10.
Property seized by tax collector; Stock sold for delinquent assessment; Action respecting dissolved corporation; Six months. §341.
Personal property left in establishment; Ninety days. §341a.
Local agency challenging state funding. §341.5.
Claim against public entity. §342.
Relief for which no period previously provided; Four years. §343.
Where cause of action accrues on mutual account. §344.
Actions by or for benefit of State or county; Four years. §345.
Mortgage redemption; Preclusion by adverse possession. §346.
Redemption if there are several mortgagors or claimants. §347.
No limitation of action for deposit of money or property; Exception. §348.
No limitation for action upon any bonds or coupons issued by the State. §348.5.
Trespass or conversion involving oil or gas wells; One hundred eighty days. § 349.05.
Trespass or conversion involving oil or gas wells; One hundred eighty days [Renumbered]. §349¾.
Contesting formation or territorial changes of cities or districts; Six months. §349.1.
Contesting bond proceedings of public entities; Six months. §349.2.
Confirmation and validation of actions and proceedings of local public entities. §349.4.

§335. Periods of limitation prescribed

The periods prescribed for the commencement of actions other than for the recovery of real property, are as follows: **Leg.H.** Enacted 1872.

§335.1. Assault; Battery; Personal injury; Wrongful death

Within two years: An action for assault, battery, or injury to, or for the death of, an individual caused by the wrongful act or neglect of another. **Leg.H.** Added Stats 2002 ch 448 §2 (SB 688).

§336. Mesne profits; Violation of restriction on use of real property

Within five years:
(a) An action for mesne profits of real property.
(b) An action for violation of a restriction, as defined in Section 784 of the Civil Code. The period prescribed in this subdivision runs from the time the person seeking to enforce the restriction discovered or, through the exercise of reasonable diligence, should have discovered the violation. A failure to commence an action for violation of a restriction within the period prescribed in this subdivision does not waive the right to commence an action for any other violation of the restriction and does not, in itself, create an implication that the restriction is abandoned, obsolete, or otherwise unenforceable. This subdivision shall not bar commencement of an action for violation of a restriction before January 1, 2001, and until January 1, 2001, any other applicable statutory or common law limitation shall continue to apply to that action. **Leg.H.** Enacted 1872. Amended Code Amdts 1873–74 ch 383 §31; Stats 1953 ch 1153 §1; Stats 1998 ch 14 §3 (AB 707).

§336a. Corporate bonds, notes, etc., and underlying mortgages, trust deeds, etc.; Six years

Within six years:
(a) An action upon any bonds, notes, or debentures issued by any corporation or pursuant to permit of the Commissioner of Financial Protection and Innovation, or upon any coupons issued with the bonds, notes, or debentures, if those bonds, notes, or debentures shall have been issued to or held by the public.
(b) An action upon any mortgage, trust deed, or other agreement pursuant to which the bonds, notes, or debentures were issued. This section does not apply to bonds or other evidences of indebtedness of a public district or corporation. **Leg.H.** Added Stats 1935 ch 614 §1. Amended Stats 2019 ch 143 §18 (SB 251), effective January 1, 2020; Stats 2020 ch 370 §33 (SB 1371), effective January 1, 2021; Stats 2022 ch 452 §37 (SB 1498), effective January 1, 2023.

§337. Written obligation; Four years

Within four years:
(a) An action upon any contract, obligation or liability founded upon an instrument in writing, except as provided in Section 336a; provided, that the time within which any action for a money judgment for the balance due upon an obligation for the payment of which a deed of trust or mortgage with power of sale upon real property or any interest therein was given as security, following the exercise of the power of sale in such deed of trust or mortgage, may be brought shall not extend beyond three months after the time of sale under such deed of trust or mortgage.
(b) An action to recover (1) upon a book account whether consisting of one or more entries; (2) upon an account stated based upon an account in writing, but the acknowledgment of the account stated need not be in writing; (3) a balance due upon a mutual, open and current account, the items of which are in writing; provided, however, that if an account stated is based upon an account of one item, the time shall begin to run from the date of the item, and if an account stated is based upon an account of more than one item, the time shall begin to run from the date of the last item.
(c) An action based upon the rescission of a contract in writing. The time begins to run from the date upon which the facts that entitle the aggrieved party to rescind occurred. Where the ground for rescission is fraud or mistake, the time shall not begin to run until the discovery by the aggrieved party of the facts constituting the fraud or mistake. Where the ground for rescission is misrepresentation under Section 359 of the Insurance Code, the time shall not begin to run until the representation becomes false.
(d) When the period in which an action must be commenced under this section has run, a person shall not bring suit or initiate an arbitration or other legal proceeding to collect the debt. The period in which an action may be commenced under this section shall only be extended pursuant to Section 360. **Leg.H.** Enacted 1872. Amended Code Amdts 1873–74 ch 383 §32; Stats 1906 Ex Sess ch 1 §1; Stats 1907 ch 323 §1; Stats 1917 ch 203 §1; Stats 1933 ch 790 §1; Stats 1935 ch 614 §2; Stats 1947 ch 809 §1; Stats 1961 ch 589 §6; Stats 2018 ch 247 §2 (AB 1526), effective January 1, 2019.

§337a. "Book account"

(a) The term "book account" means a detailed statement which constitutes the principal record of one or more transactions between a debtor and a creditor arising out of a contract or some fiduciary relation, and shows the debits and credits in connection therewith, and against whom and in favor of whom entries are made, is entered in the regular course of business as conducted by such creditor or fiduciary, and is kept in a reasonably permanent form and manner and is (1) in a bound book, or (2) on a sheet or sheets fastened in a book or to backing but detachable therefrom, or (3) on a card or cards of a permanent character, or is kept in any other reasonably permanent form and manner. A "book account" does not include consumer debt.

(b) For purposes of this section, "consumer debt" means any obligation or alleged obligation, incurred on or after July 1, 2024, of a consumer to pay money arising out of a transaction in which the money, property, insurance, or services that are the subject of the transaction are primarily for personal, family, or household purposes and where the obligation to pay appears on the face of a note or in a written contract. **Leg.H.** Added Stats 1959 ch 1010 §1. Amended Stats 2023 ch 688 §1 (AB 1414), effective January 1, 2024.

§337.1. Patent deficiency in real property improvement design, survey, construction, etc., and resulting injury to property or person; Four years

(a) Except as otherwise provided in this section, no action shall be brought to recover damages from any person performing or furnishing the design, specifications, surveying, planning, supervision or observation of construction or construction of an improvement to real property more than four years after the substantial completion of such improvement for any of the following:

(1) Any patent deficiency in the design, specifications, surveying, planning, supervision or observation of construction or construction of an improvement to, or survey of, real property;

(2) Injury to property, real or personal, arising out of any such patent deficiency; or

(3) Injury to the person or for wrongful death arising out of any such patent deficiency.

(b) If, by reason of such patent deficiency, an injury to property or the person or an injury causing wrongful death occurs during the fourth year after such substantial completion, an action in tort to recover damages for such an injury or wrongful death may be brought within one year after the date on which such injury occurred, irrespective of the date of death, but in no event may such an action be brought more than five years after the substantial completion of construction of such improvement.

(c) Nothing in this section shall be construed as extending the period prescribed by the laws of this state for the bringing of any action.

(d) The limitation prescribed by this section shall not be asserted by way of defense by any person in actual possession or the control, as owner, tenant or otherwise, of such an improvement at the time any deficiency in such an improvement constitutes the proximate cause of the injury or death for which it is proposed to bring an action.

(e) As used in this section, "patent deficiency" means a deficiency which is apparent by reasonable inspection.

(f) Subdivisions (a) and (b) shall not apply to any owner-occupied single-unit residence. **Leg.H.** Added Stats 1967 ch 1326 §1.

§337.15. Action for latent deficiency in construction or survey of real property or injury arising out of such deficiency; Ten years

(a) No action may be brought to recover damages from any person, or the surety of a person, who develops real property or performs or furnishes the design, specifications, surveying, planning, supervision, testing, or observation of construction or construction of an improvement to real property more than 10 years after the substantial completion of the development or improvement for any of the following:

(1) Any latent deficiency in the design, specification, surveying, planning, supervision, or observation of construction or construction of an improvement to, or survey of, real property.

(2) Injury to property, real or personal, arising out of any such latent deficiency.

(b) As used in this section, "latent deficiency" means a deficiency which is not apparent by reasonable inspection.

(c) As used in this section, "action" includes an action for indemnity brought against a person arising out of that person's performance or furnishing of services or materials referred to in this section, except that a cross-complaint for indemnity may be filed pursuant to subdivision (b) of Section 428.10 in an action which has been brought within the time period set forth in subdivision (a) of this section.

(d) Nothing in this section shall be construed as extending the period prescribed by the laws of this state for bringing any action.

(e) The limitation prescribed by this section shall not be asserted by way of defense by any person in actual possession or the control, as owner, tenant or otherwise, of such an improvement, at the time any deficiency in the improvement constitutes the proximate cause for which it is proposed to bring an action.

(f) This section shall not apply to actions based on willful misconduct or fraudulent concealment.

(g) The 10-year period specified in subdivision (a) shall commence upon substantial completion of the improvement, but not later than the date of one of the following, whichever first occurs:

(1) The date of final inspection by the applicable public agency.

(2) The date of recordation of a valid notice of completion.

(3) The date of use or occupation of the improvement.

(4) One year after termination or cessation of work on the improvement.

The date of substantial completion shall relate specifically to the performance or furnishing design, specifications, surveying, planning, supervision, testing, observation of construction or construction services by each profession or trade rendering services to the improvement. **Leg.H.** Added Stats 1971 ch 1569 §1. Amended Stats 1979 ch 571 §1; Stats 1980 ch 676 §63; Stats 1981 ch 88 §1.

§337.2. Lessee's breach of written lease; Four years

Where a lease of real property is in writing, no action shall be brought under Section 1951.2 of the Civil Code more than four years after the breach of the lease and abandonment of the property, or more than four years after the termination of the right of the lessee to possession of the property, whichever is the earlier time. **Leg.H.** Added Stats 1970 ch 89 §12, operative July 1, 1971.

§337.5. Bonds or coupons issued by political subdivisions of State; Judgments or decrees; Ten years

Within 10 years:

An action upon any bonds or coupons issued by the State of California.

(a) An action upon any general obligation bonds or coupons, not secured in whole or in part by a lien on real property, issued by any county, city and county, municipal corporation, district (including school districts), or other political subdivision of the State of California.

(b) An action upon a judgment or decree of any court of the United States or of any state within the United States. **Leg.H.** Added Stats 1939 ch 724 §1. Amended Stats 1947 ch 626 §1; Stats 1953 ch 1153 §2; Stats 2010 ch 719 §7 (SB 856), effective October 19, 2010.

§337.6. Bonds and coupons against which statute of limitations ran on or after August 27, 1937, when action brought on or before June 30, 1959

Notwithstanding the provisions of Section 337.5 of this code actions may be brought on bonds or coupons as set forth in subsection 2 of said section, against which the statute of limitations ran on or after August 27, 1937; provided, such actions are brought on or before June 30, 1959. Upon presentation for payment they shall be registered and payment shall not be made thereon until the next fiscal year following presentation unless available funds are sufficient to first pay obligations which are due or will become due from the same fund during the fiscal year of presentation and during the next succeeding six months. Interest shall not be paid on bonds or coupons registered for the purpose of this section. **Leg.H.** Added Stats 1949 ch 1282 §1. Amended Stats 1957 ch 719 §1.

§338. Statutory liability; Injury to real property; Taking or injuring goods or chattels; Fraud or mistake; Bonds of public officials and notaries; Slander of title; False advertising; Pollution violations; Challenge to tax levy; Personal rights violations

Within three years:

(a) An action upon a liability created by statute, other than a penalty or forfeiture.

(b) An action for trespass upon or injury to real property.

(c)(1) An action for taking, detaining, or injuring goods or chattels, including an action for the specific recovery of personal property.

(2) The cause of action in the case of theft, as described in Section 484 of the Penal Code, of an article of historical, interpretive, scientific, or artistic significance is not deemed to have accrued until the discovery of the whereabouts of the article by the aggrieved party, the aggrieved party's agent, or the law enforcement agency that originally investigated the theft.

(3)(A) Notwithstanding paragraphs (1) and (2), an action for the specific recovery of a work of fine art brought against a museum, gallery, auctioneer, or dealer, in the case of an unlawful taking or theft, as described in Section 484 of the Penal Code, of a work of fine art, including a taking or theft by means of fraud or duress, shall be commenced within six years of the actual discovery by the claimant or the claimant's agent, of both of the following:

(i) The identity and the whereabouts of the work of fine art. In the case where there is a possibility of misidentification of the object of fine art in question, the identity can be satisfied by the identification of facts sufficient to determine that the work of fine art is likely to be the work of fine art that was unlawfully taken or stolen.

(ii) Information or facts that are sufficient to indicate that the claimant has a claim for a possessory interest in the work of fine art that was unlawfully taken or stolen.

(B) This paragraph shall apply to all pending and future actions commenced on or before December 31, 2017, including an action dismissed based on the expiration of statutes of limitations in effect prior to the date of enactment of this statute if the judgment in that action is not yet final or if the time for filing an appeal from a decision on that action has not expired, provided that the action concerns a work of fine art that was taken within 100 years prior to the date of enactment of this statute.

(C) For purposes of this paragraph:

(i) "Actual discovery," notwithstanding Section 19 of the Civil Code, does not include constructive knowledge imputed by law.

(ii) "Auctioneer" means an individual who is engaged in, or who by advertising or otherwise holds the individual out as being available to engage in, the calling for, the recognition of, and the acceptance of, offers for the purchase of goods at an auction as defined in subdivision (b) of Section 1812.601 of the Civil Code.

(iii) "Dealer" means a person who holds a valid seller's permit and who is actively and principally engaged in, or conducting the business of, selling works of fine art.

(iv) "Duress" means a threat of force, violence, danger, or retribution against an owner of the work of fine art in question, or the owner's family member, sufficient to coerce a reasonable person of ordinary susceptibilities to perform an act that otherwise would not have been performed or to acquiesce to an act to which the person would otherwise not have acquiesced.

(v) "Fine art" has the same meaning as defined in paragraph (1) of subdivision (d) of Section 982 of the Civil Code.

(vi) "Museum or gallery" shall include any public or private organization or foundation operating as a museum or gallery.

(4) Section 361 shall not apply to an action brought pursuant to paragraph (3).

(5) A party in an action to which paragraph (3) applies may raise all equitable and legal affirmative defenses and doctrines, including, without limitation, laches and unclean hands.

(6) Notwithstanding any other law or prior judicial decision, in any action brought by a California resident, or by an heir, trustee, assignee, or representative of the estate of a California resident, involving claims relating to title, ownership, or recovery of personal property as described in paragraph (2) or (3), or in the Holocaust Expropriated Art Recovery Act of 2016 (HEAR) (Pub. L. No. 114-308), including claims for money damages, California substantive law shall apply. This paragraph shall apply to all actions pending on the date this paragraph becomes operative or that are commenced thereafter, including any action in which the judgment is not yet final or the time for filing any appeal, including a petition for a writ of certiorari in the United States Supreme Court, has not expired, or, if filed, has not been decided.

(d) An action for relief on the ground of fraud or mistake. The cause of action in that case is not deemed to have accrued until the discovery, by the aggrieved party, of the facts constituting the fraud or mistake.

(e) An action upon a bond of a public official except any cause of action based on fraud or embezzlement is not deemed to have accrued until the discovery, by the aggrieved party or the aggrieved party's agent, of the facts constituting the cause of action upon the bond.

(f)(1) An action against a notary public on the notary public's bond or in the notary public's official capacity except that a cause of action based on malfeasance or misfeasance is not deemed to have accrued until discovery, by the aggrieved party or the aggrieved party's agent, of the facts constituting the cause of action.

(2) Notwithstanding paragraph (1), an action based on malfeasance or misfeasance shall be commenced within one year from discovery, by the aggrieved party or the aggrieved party's agent, of the facts constituting the cause of action or within three years from the performance of the notarial act giving rise to the action, whichever is later.

(3) Notwithstanding paragraph (1), an action against a notary public on the notary public's bond or in the notary public's official capacity shall be commenced within six years.

(g) An action for slander of title to real property.

(h) An action commenced under Section 17536 of the Business and Professions Code. The cause of action in that case shall not be deemed to have accrued until the discovery by the aggrieved party, the Attorney General, the district attorney, the county counsel, the city prosecutor, or the city attorney of the facts constituting grounds for commencing the action.

(i) An action commenced under the Porter-Cologne Water Quality Control Act (Division 7 (commencing with Section 13000) of the Water Code). The cause of action in that case shall not be deemed to have accrued until the discovery by the State Water Resources Control Board or a regional water quality control board of the facts constituting grounds for commencing actions under their jurisdiction.

(j) An action to recover for physical damage to private property under Section 19 of Article I of the California Constitution.

(k) An action commenced under Division 26 (commencing with Section 39000) of the Health and Safety Code. These causes of action shall not be deemed to have accrued until the discovery by the State Air Resources Board or by a district, as defined in Section 39025 of the Health and Safety Code, of the facts constituting grounds for commencing the action under its jurisdiction.

(l) An action commenced under Section 1602, 1615, or 5650.1 of the Fish and Game Code. These causes of action shall not be deemed to have accrued until discovery by the agency bringing the action of the facts constituting the grounds for commencing the action.

(m) An action challenging the validity of the levy upon a parcel of a special tax levied by a local agency on a per parcel basis.

(n) An action commencing under Section 51.7 of the Civil Code.

(o) An action commenced under Section 4601.1 of the Public Resources Code, if the underlying violation is of Section 4571, 4581, or 4621 of the Public Resources Code, or of Section 1103.1 of Title 14 of the California Code of Regulations, and the underlying violation is related to the conversion of timberland to nonforestry-related agricultural uses. These causes of action shall not be deemed to have accrued until discovery by the Department of Forestry and Fire Protection.

(p) An action for civil penalties commenced under Section 26038 of the Business and Professions Code. **Leg.H.** Enacted 1872. Amended Stats 1921 ch 183 §1; Stats 1933 ch 306 §1; Stats 1935 ch 581 §1; Stats 1943 ch 1025 §1; Stats 1949 ch 1540 §1; Stats 1957 ch 649 §1; Stats 1972 ch 823 §2; Stats 1981 ch 247 §1, effective July 21, 1981, ch 494 §2; Stats 1982 ch 340 §1; Stats 1987 ch 1200 §1, ch 1201 §1; Stats 1988 ch 1186 §1; Stats 1989 ch 467 §1; Stats 1990 ch 669 §1 (AB 4049); Stats 1995 ch 238 §1 (AB 1174); Stats 1998 ch 342 §1 (AB 1933); Stats 2005 ch 123 §2 (AB 378), ch 383 §1.5 (SB 1110); Stats 2006 ch 538 §62 (SB 1852), effective January 1, 2007; Stats 2010 ch 691 §2 (AB 2765), effective January 1, 2011; Stats 2015 ch 683 §1 (SB 798), effective January 1, 2016; Stats 2018 ch 796 §1 (SB 1453), effective January 1, 2019; Stats 2021 ch 264 §1 (AB 287), effective January 1, 2022; Stats 2024 ch 257 §2 (AB 2867), effective September 16, 2024.

§338.1. Action for civil penalties or punitive damages related to hazardous substances; Five years

An action for civil penalties or punitive damages authorized under Chapter 6.5 (commencing with Section 25100), Chapter 6.67 (commencing with Section 25270), Chapter 6.7 (commencing with Section 25280), or Chapter 6.95 (commencing with Section 25500) of Division 20 of, or Part 2 (commencing with Section 78000) of Division 45 of, the Health and Safety Code, or Chapter 1 (commencing with Section 3000) of Division 3 of the Public Resources Code, shall be commenced within five years after the discovery by the agency bringing the action of the facts constituting the grounds for commencing the action. **Leg.H.** Added Stats 1988 ch 1186 §2. Amended Stats 2009 ch 429 §1 (AB 305), effective January 1, 2010; Stats 2018 ch 141 §1 (AB 1980), effective January 1, 2019; Stats 2022 ch 258 §7 (AB 2327), effective January 1, 2023, operative January 1, 2024; Stats 2023 ch 337 §1 (AB 631), effective January 1, 2024.

§338.2. Person with legal standing to action

(a) A California resident, or an heir, trustee, assignee, or representative of the estate of a California resident, may bring an action for damages, other financial recovery, title, recovery, or ownership, of artwork or other personal property that was taken or otherwise lost as a result of political persecution.

(b) Notwithstanding any other law, actions brought pursuant to this section shall be commenced within six years of the actual discovery by the claimant or the claimant's agent, of both of the following:

(1) The identity and the whereabouts of the artwork or other personal property. Where there is a possibility of misidentification of the object in question, the identity can be satisfied by the identification of facts sufficient to determine that the artwork or other personal property is likely to be the artwork or other personal property that was unlawfully taken or stolen.

(2) Information or facts that are sufficient to indicate that the claimant has a claim for a possessory interest in the artwork or other personal property that was unlawfully taken or stolen.

(c) If a claimant had actual knowledge of the facts described in subdivision (b) prior to the enactment of this section, any action brought pursuant to this section shall be commenced within of six years of actual discovery or two years from the enactment of this section, whichever is later.

(d) For purposes of this section the following definitions shall apply:
(1) "Artwork or other personal property" means any of the following:
(A) Pictures, paintings, and drawings.
(B) Statuary art and sculpture.
(C) Engravings, prints lithographs, and other works of graphic art.
(D) Applied art and original artistic assemblages and montages.
(E) Books, archives, musical instruments, musical objects, and manuscripts, including musical manuscripts and sheets, and sound, photographic, and cinematographic archives and mediums.
(F) Sacred and ceremonial objects.
(G) Objects of cultural significance.
(2) "Political persecution" means persecution of a specific group of individuals based on their membership in a protected class under the state's Unruh Civil Rights Act (Section 51 of the Civil Code).

(e) Notwithstanding any other provision of law or prior judicial decision, in any action brought pursuant to this section or in the Holocaust Expropriated Art Recovery Act of 2016 (HEAR) (Pub. L. No. 114-308), California substantive law shall apply.

(f) In an action brought pursuant to this section, where an item specified in subdivision (d) is taken or lost as a result of political persecution, clear title is not conveyed to any subsequent purchaser or owner. Defenses that the defendant acquired the title in good faith, by acquisitive prescription, or by adverse possession, and the defense of laches do not apply to cases brought under this section.

(g) An action may be brought by a claimant who, prior to the enactment of this section, brought a claim to recover personal property that was stolen or lost due to political persecution, and the case was dismissed by a court based on any of the defenses listed in subdivision (f), or based on any procedural basis such as standing, personal jurisdiction, or subject matter jurisdiction. Any such actions shall be commenced within two years of the effective date of this section or the entry of a final judgment and the termination of all appeals, including any petition for a writ of certiorari, whichever is later.

(h) A prevailing plaintiff shall be entitled to reasonable attorney's costs and fees. **Leg.H.** Added Stats 2024 ch 257 §3 (AB 2867), effective September 16, 2024.

§339. Two Years; Oral obligations; Certificate, abstract, or guaranty of title; Title insurance; Liability of sheriff or coroner; Rescission of oral contract

Within two years:

1. An action upon a contract, obligation or liability not founded upon an instrument of writing, except as provided in Section 2725 of the Commercial Code or subdivision 2 of Section 337 of this code; or an action founded upon a contract, obligation or liability, evidenced by a certificate, or abstract or guaranty of title of real property, or by a policy of title insurance; provided, that the cause of action upon a contract, obligation or liability evidenced by a certificate, or abstract or guaranty of title of real property or policy of title insurance shall not be deemed to have accrued until the discovery of the loss or damage suffered by the aggrieved party thereunder.

2. An action against a sheriff or coroner upon a liability incurred by the doing of an act in an official capacity and in virtue of office, or by the omission of an official duty including the nonpayment of money collected in the enforcement of a judgment.

3. An action based upon the rescission of a contract not in writing. The time begins to run from the date upon which the facts that entitle the aggrieved party to rescind occurred. Where the ground for rescission is fraud or mistake, the time does not begin to run until the discovery by the aggrieved party of the facts constituting the fraud or mistake. **Leg.H.** Enacted 1872. Amended Code Amdts 1873–74 ch 383 §33; Stats 1905 ch 258 §1; Stats 1906 1st Ex Sess ch 1 §2; Stats 1907 ch 323 §2; Stats 1913 ch 187 §1; Stats 1917 ch 203 §2; Stats 1961 ch 589 §7; Stats 1980 ch 1307 §1; Stats 1982 ch 497 §31, operative July 1, 1983; Stats 1996 ch 872 §11 (AB 3472).

§339.5. Lessee's breach of unwritten lease; Two years

Where a lease of real property is not in writing, no action shall be brought under Section 1951.2 of the Civil Code more than two years after the breach of the lease and abandonment of the property, or more than two years after the termination of the right of the lessee to possession of the property, whichever is the earlier time. **Leg.H.** Added Stats 1970 ch 89 §13, operative July 1, 1971.

§340. Statutory penalties or forfeitures; Libel; Slander; False imprisonment; Seduction of person under age of consent; Payment by bank of forged check; Injury or death of animal; Damages in making property seizure; Good faith improvements

Within one year:

(a) An action upon a statute for a penalty or forfeiture, if the action is given to an individual, or to an individual and the state, except if the statute imposing it prescribes a different limitation.

(b) An action upon a statute for a forfeiture or penalty to the people of this state.

(c) An action for libel, slander, false imprisonment, seduction of a person below the age of legal consent, or by a depositor against a bank for the payment of a forged or raised check, or a check that bears a forged or unauthorized endorsement, or against any person who boards or feeds an animal or fowl or who engages in the practice of veterinary medicine as defined in Section 4826 of the Business and Professions Code, for that person's neglect resulting in injury or death to an animal or fowl in the course of boarding or feeding the animal or fowl or in the course of the practice of veterinary medicine on that animal or fowl.

(d) An action against an officer to recover damages for the seizure of any property for a statutory forfeiture to the state, or for the detention of, or injury to property so seized, or for damages done to any person in making that seizure.

(e) An action by a good faith improver for relief under Chapter 10 (commencing with Section 871.1) of Title 10 of Part 2. The time begins to run from the date upon which the good faith improver discovers that the good faith improver is not the owner of the land upon which the improvements have been made. **Leg.H.** Enacted 1872. Amended Code Amdts 1873–74 ch 383 §34; Code Amdts 1875–76 ch 29 §1; Stats 1905 ch 258 §2; Stats 1929 ch 518 §1; Stats 1939 ch 1103 §1; Stats 1949 ch 863 §1; Stats 1953 ch 1382 §1; Stats 1963 ch 1681 §2; Stats 1968 ch 150 §1; Stats 1973 ch 20 §1; Stats 1982 ch 517 §97; Stats 2002 ch 448 §3 (SB 688).

§340.1. Damages suffered as a result of childhood sexual assault; Certificates of merit

(a) There is no time limit for the commencement of any of the following actions for recovery of damages suffered as a result of childhood sexual assault:

(1) An action against any person for committing an act of childhood sexual assault.

(2) An action for liability against any person or entity who owed a duty of care to the plaintiff, if a wrongful or negligent act by that person or entity was a legal cause of the childhood sexual assault that resulted in the injury to the plaintiff.

(3) An action for liability against any person or entity if an intentional act by that person or entity was a legal cause of the childhood sexual assault that resulted in the injury to the plaintiff.

(b)(1) In an action described in subdivision (a), a person who is sexually assaulted and proves it was as the result of a cover up may recover up to treble damages against a defendant who is found to have covered up the sexual assault of a minor, unless prohibited by another law.

(2) For purposes of this subdivision, a "cover up" is a concerted effort to hide evidence relating to childhood sexual assault.

(c) "Childhood sexual assault" as used in this section includes any act committed against the plaintiff that occurred when the plaintiff was under the age of 18 years and that would have been proscribed by Section 266j of the Penal Code; Section 285 of the Penal Code; paragraph (1) or (2) of subdivision (b), or of subdivision (c), of Section 286 of the Penal Code; subdivision (a) or (b) of Section 288 of the Penal Code; paragraph (1) or (2) of subdivision (b), or of subdivision (c), of Section 287 or of former Section 288a of the Penal Code; subdivision (h), (i), or (j) of Section 289 of the Penal Code; any sexual conduct as defined in paragraph (1) of subdivision (d) of Section 311.4 of the Penal Code; Section 647.6 of the Penal Code; or any prior laws of this state of similar effect at the time the act was committed. This subdivision does not limit the availability of causes of action permitted under subdivision (a), including causes of action against persons or entities other than the alleged perpetrator of the abuse.

(d) This section shall not be construed to alter the otherwise applicable burden of proof, as defined in Section 115 of the Evidence Code, that a plaintiff has in a civil action subject to this section.

(e) Every plaintiff 40 years of age or older at the time the action is filed shall file certificates of merit as specified in subdivision (f).

(f) Certificates of merit setting forth the facts that support the declaration shall be executed by the attorney for the plaintiff and by a licensed mental health practitioner selected by the plaintiff declaring, respectively, as follows:

(1) That the attorney has reviewed the facts of the case, consulted with at least one mental health practitioner who the attorney reasonably believes is knowledgeable of the relevant facts and issues involved in the particular action, and concluded on the basis of that review and consultation that there is reasonable and meritorious cause for the filing of the action.

(2) That the mental health practitioner consulted is licensed to practice and practices in this state and is not a party to the action, that the practitioner is not treating and has not treated the plaintiff, and that the practitioner has interviewed the plaintiff and is knowledgeable of the relevant facts and issues involved in the particular action, and has concluded, on the basis of the practitioner's knowledge of the facts and issues, that in the practitioner's professional opinion there is a reasonable basis to believe that the plaintiff had been subject to childhood sexual abuse.

(g) If certificates are required pursuant to subdivision (e), the attorney for the plaintiff shall execute a separate certificate of merit for each defendant named in the complaint.

(h) In any action subject to subdivision (e), a defendant shall not be served, and the duty to serve a defendant with process does not attach, until the court has reviewed the certificates of merit filed pursuant to subdivision (f) with respect to that defendant, and has found, in camera, based solely on those certificates of merit, that there is reasonable and meritorious cause for the filing of the action against that defendant. At that time, the duty to serve that defendant with process shall attach.

(i) A violation of this section may constitute unprofessional conduct and may be the grounds for discipline against the attorney.

(j) The failure to file certificates in accordance with this section shall be grounds for a demurrer pursuant to Section 430.10 or a motion to strike pursuant to Section 435.

(k) In any action subject to subdivision (e), a defendant shall be named by "Doe" designation in any pleadings or papers filed in the action until there has been a showing of corroborative fact as to the charging allegations against that defendant.

(*l*) At any time after the action is filed, the plaintiff may apply to the court for permission to amend the complaint to substitute the name of the defendant or defendants for the fictitious designation, as follows:

(1) The application shall be accompanied by a certificate of corroborative fact executed by the attorney for the plaintiff. The certificate shall declare that the attorney has discovered one or more facts corroborative of one or more of the charging allegations against a defendant or defendants, and shall set forth in clear and concise terms the nature and substance of the corroborative fact. If the corroborative fact is evidenced by the statement of a witness or the contents of a document, the certificate shall declare that the attorney has personal knowledge of the statement of the witness or of the contents of the document, and the identity and location of the witness or document shall be included in the certificate. For purposes of this section, a fact is corroborative of an allegation if it confirms or supports the allegation. The opinion of any mental health practitioner concerning the plaintiff shall not constitute a corroborative fact for purposes of this section.

(2) If the application to name a defendant is made before that defendant's appearance in the action, neither the application nor the certificate of corroborative fact by the attorney shall be served on the defendant or defendants, nor on any other party or their counsel of record.

(3) If the application to name a defendant is made after that defendant's appearance in the action, the application shall be served on all parties and proof of service provided to the court, but the certificate of corroborative fact by the attorney shall not be served on any party or their counsel of record.

(m) The court shall review the application and the certificate of corroborative fact in camera and, based solely on the certificate and any reasonable inferences to be drawn from the certificate, shall, if one or more facts corroborative of one or more of the charging allegations against a defendant has been shown, order that the complaint may be amended to substitute the name of the defendant or defendants.

(n) The court shall keep under seal and confidential from the public and all parties to the litigation, other than the plaintiff, any and all certificates of corroborative fact filed pursuant to subdivision (*l*).

(o) Upon the favorable conclusion of the litigation with respect to any defendant for whom a certificate of merit was filed or for whom a certificate of merit should have been filed pursuant to this section, the court may, upon the motion of a party or upon the court's own motion, verify compliance with this section by requiring the attorney for the plaintiff who was required by subdivision (f) to execute the certificate to reveal the name, address, and telephone number of the person or persons consulted with pursuant to subdivision (f) that were relied upon by the attorney in preparation of the certificate of merit. The name, address, and telephone number shall be disclosed to the trial judge in camera and in the absence of the moving party. If the court finds there has been a failure to comply with this section, the court may order a party, a party's attorney, or both, to pay any reasonable expenses, including attorney's fees, incurred by the defendant for whom a certificate of merit should have been filed.

(p) This section applies to any claim in which the childhood sexual assault occurred on and after January 1, 2024. Notwithstanding any other law, a claim for damages based on conduct described in paragraphs (1) through (3), inclusive, of subdivision (a), in which the childhood sexual assault occurred on or before December 31, 2023 may only be commenced pursuant to the applicable statute of limitations set forth in existing law as it read on December 31, 2023.

(q) Notwithstanding any other law, including Chapter 1 of Part 3 of Division 3.6 of Title 1 of the Government Code (commencing with Section 900) and Chapter 2 of Part 3 of Division 3.6 of Title 1 of the Government Code (commencing with Section 910), a claim for damages described in paragraphs (1) through (3), inclusive, of subdivision (a), is not required to be presented to any government entity prior to the commencement of an action. **Leg.H.** Added Stats 1986 ch 914 §1. Amended Stats 1990 ch 1578 §1 (SB 108); Stats 1994 ch 288 §1 (AB 2846); Stats 1998 ch 1032 §1 (AB 1651); Stats 1999 ch 120 §1 (SB 674); Stats 2002 ch 149 §1 (SB 1779); Stats 2018 ch 423 §8 (SB 1494), effective January 1, 2019; Stats 2019 ch 861 §1 (AB 218), effective January 1, 2020; Stats 2022 ch 444 §1 (AB 2959), effective January 1, 2023; Stats 2023 ch 655 §1 (AB 452), effective January 1, 2024.

§ 340.11. Action for recovery of damages suffered as a result of childhood sexual assault that occurred before January 1, 2024; Time for commencement of action

(a)(1) Notwithstanding Section 340.1, in an action for recovery of damages suffered as a result of childhood sexual assault that occurred before January 1, 2024, the time for commencement of the action shall be within 22 years of the date the plaintiff attains the age of majority or within five years of the date the plaintiff discovers or reasonably should have discovered that psychological injury or illness occurring after the age of majority was caused by the sexual assault, whichever period expires later, for any of the following actions:

(A) An action against any person for committing an act of childhood sexual assault.

(B) An action for liability against any person or entity who owed a duty of care to the plaintiff, if a wrongful or negligent act by that person or entity was a legal cause of the childhood sexual assault that resulted in the injury to the plaintiff.

(C) An action for liability against any person or entity if an intentional act by that person or entity was a legal cause of the childhood sexual assault that resulted in the injury to the plaintiff.

(2) Notwithstanding paragraph (1) or Section 340.1, in an action for recovery of damages suffered as a result of childhood sexual assault that occurred before January 1, 2024, involving an act that would have been proscribed by Sections 311.1 or 311.2 of the Penal Code, the time for commencement of the action shall be within 22 years of the date the plaintiff attains the age of majority or within 10 years of the date the plaintiff discovers or reasonably should have discovered, after the age of majority, the existence of obscene matter, for any of the actions identified in subparagraphs (A) to (C), inclusive, of paragraph (1).

(b)(1) In an action described in subdivision (a), a person who is sexually assaulted and proves it was as the result of a cover up may recover up to treble damages against a defendant who is found to have covered up the sexual assault of a minor, unless prohibited by another law.

(2) For purposes of this subdivision, a "cover up" is a concerted effort to hide evidence relating to childhood sexual assault.

(c) An action described in subparagraph (B) or (C) of paragraph (1) of subdivision (a) shall not be commenced on or after the plaintiff's 40th birthday unless the person or entity knew or had reason to know, or was otherwise on notice, of any misconduct that creates a risk of childhood sexual assault by an employee, volunteer, representative, or agent, or the person or entity failed to take reasonable steps or to implement reasonable safeguards to avoid acts of childhood sexual assault. For purposes of this subdivision, providing or requiring counseling is not sufficient, in and of itself, to constitute a reasonable step or reasonable safeguard. Nothing in this subdivision shall be construed to constitute a substantive change in negligence law.

(d) "Childhood sexual assault" as used in this section includes any act committed against the plaintiff that occurred when the plaintiff was under the age of 18 years and that would have been proscribed by Section 266j of the Penal Code; Section 285 of the Penal Code; paragraph (1) or (2) of subdivision (b), or of subdivision (c), of Section 286 of the Penal Code; subdivision (a) or (b) of Section 288 of the Penal Code; paragraph (1) or (2) of subdivision (b), or of subdivision (c), of Section 287 or of former Section 288a of the Penal Code; subdivision (h), (i), or (j) of Section 289 of the Penal Code; subdivision (a) of Section 311.1 of the Penal Code; subdivisions (b) to (d), inclusive, of Section 311.2 of the Penal Code; any sexual conduct as defined in paragraph (1) of subdivision (d) of Section 311.4 of the Penal Code; Section 647.6 of the Penal Code; or any prior laws of this state of similar effect at the time the act was committed. This subdivision does not limit the availability of causes of action permitted under subdivision (a), including causes of action against persons or entities other than the alleged perpetrator of the abuse.

(e) This section shall not be construed to alter the otherwise applicable burden of proof, as defined in Section 115 of the Evidence Code, that a plaintiff has in a civil action subject to this section.

(f) Every plaintiff 40 years of age or older at the time the action is filed shall file certificates of merit as specified in subdivision (g).

(g) Certificates of merit shall be executed by the attorney for the plaintiff and by a licensed mental health practitioner selected by the plaintiff declaring, respectively, as follows:

(1) That the attorney has reviewed the facts of the case, consulted with at least one mental health practitioner who the attorney reasonably believes is knowledgeable of the relevant facts and issues involved in the particular action, and concluded on the basis of that review and consultation that there is reasonable and meritorious cause for the filing of the action.

(2) That the mental health practitioner consulted is licensed to practice and practices in this state and is not a party to the action, that the practitioner is not treating and has not treated the plaintiff, and that the practitioner has interviewed the plaintiff and is knowledgeable of the relevant facts and issues involved in the particular action, and has concluded, on the basis of the practitioner's knowledge of the facts and issues, that in the practitioner's professional opinion there is a reasonable basis to believe that the plaintiff had been subject to childhood sexual abuse.

(3) That the attorney was unable to obtain the consultation required by paragraph (1) because a statute of limitations would impair the action and that the certificates required by paragraphs (1) and (2) could not be obtained before the impairment of the action. If a certificate is executed pursuant to this paragraph, the certificates required by paragraphs (1) and (2) shall be filed within 60 days after filing the complaint.

(h) If certificates are required pursuant to subdivision (f), the attorney for the plaintiff shall execute a separate certificate of merit for each defendant named in the complaint.

(i) In any action subject to subdivision (f), a defendant shall not be served, and the duty to serve a defendant with process does not attach, until the court has reviewed the certificates of merit filed pursuant to subdivision (g) with respect to that defendant, and has found, in camera, based solely on those certificates of merit, that there is reasonable and meritorious cause for the filing of the action against that defendant. At that time, the duty to serve that defendant with process shall attach.

(j) A violation of this section may constitute unprofessional conduct and may be the grounds for discipline against the attorney.

(k) The failure to file certificates in accordance with this section shall be grounds for a demurrer pursuant to Section 430.10 or a motion to strike pursuant to Section 435.

(l) In any action subject to subdivision (f), a defendant shall be named by "Doe" designation in any pleadings or papers filed in the action until there has been a showing of corroborative fact as to the charging allegations against that defendant.

(m) At any time after the action is filed, the plaintiff may apply to the court for permission to amend the complaint to substitute the name of the defendant or defendants for the fictitious designation, as follows:

(1) The application shall be accompanied by a certificate of corroborative fact executed by the attorney for the plaintiff. The certificate shall declare that the attorney has discovered one or more facts corroborative of one or more of the charging allegations against a defendant or defendants, and shall set forth in clear and concise terms the nature and substance of the corroborative fact. If the corroborative fact is evidenced by the statement of a witness or the contents of a document, the certificate shall declare that the attorney has personal knowledge of the statement of the witness or of the contents of the document, and the identity and location of the witness or document shall be included in the certificate. For purposes of this section, a fact is corroborative of an allegation if it confirms or supports the allegation. The opinion of any mental health practitioner concerning the plaintiff shall not constitute a corroborative fact for purposes of this section.

(2) If the application to name a defendant is made before that defendant's appearance in the action, neither the application nor the certificate of corroborative fact by the attorney shall be served on the defendant or defendants, nor on any other party or their counsel of record.

(3) If the application to name a defendant is made after that defendant's appearance in the action, the application shall be served on all parties and proof of service provided to the court, but the certificate of corroborative fact by the attorney shall not be served on any party or their counsel of record.

(n) The court shall review the application and the certificate of corroborative fact in camera and, based solely on the certificate and any reasonable inferences to be drawn from the certificate, shall, if one or more facts corroborative of one or more of the charging allegations against a defendant has been shown, order that the complaint may be amended to substitute the name of the defendant or defendants.

(o) The court shall keep under seal and confidential from the public and all parties to the litigation, other than the plaintiff, any and all certificates of corroborative fact filed pursuant to subdivision (m).

(p) Upon the favorable conclusion of the litigation with respect to any defendant for whom a certificate of merit was filed or for whom a certificate of merit should have been filed pursuant to this section, the court may, upon the motion of a party or upon the court's own motion, verify compliance with this section by requiring the attorney for the plaintiff who was required by subdivision (g) to execute the certificate to reveal the name, address, and telephone number of the person or persons consulted with pursuant to subdivision (g) that were relied upon by the attorney in preparation of the certificate of merit. The name, address, and telephone number shall be disclosed to the trial judge in camera and in the absence of the moving party. If the court finds there has been a failure to comply with this section, the court may order a party, a party's attorney, or both, to pay any reasonable expenses, including attorney's fees, incurred by the defendant for whom a certificate of merit should have been filed.

(q) Notwithstanding any other law, a claim for damages described in subparagraphs (A) to (C), inclusive, of paragraph (1) of subdivision (a) that has not been litigated to finality and that would otherwise be barred as of January 1, 2020, because the applicable statute of limitations, claim presentation deadline, or any other time limit had expired, is revived, and these claims may be commenced within three years of January 1, 2020. A plaintiff shall have the later of the three-year time period under this subdivision or the time period under subdivision (a) as amended by the act that added this subdivision.

(r) The changes made to the time period under subdivision (a) of Section 340.1 by Chapter 861 of the Statutes of 2019 apply to and revive any action commenced on or after the date of enactment of that act, and to any action filed before the date of enactment, and still pending on that date, including any action or causes of action that would have been barred by the laws in effect before the date of enactment.

(s) Notwithstanding any other law, including Chapter 1 of Part 3 of Division 3.6 of Title 1 of the Government Code (commencing with Section 900) and Chapter 2 of Part 3 of Division 3.6 of Title 1 of the Government Code (commencing with Section 910), a claim for damages described in paragraphs (1) to (3), inclusive, of subdivision (a), is not required to be presented to any government entity prior to the commencement of an action. **Leg.H.** Added Stats 2023 ch 877 §1 (SB 558), effective January 1, 2024.

§340.15. Action for damages resulting from domestic violence

(a) In any civil action for recovery of damages suffered as a result of domestic violence, the time for commencement of the action shall be the later of the following:

(1) Within three years from the date of the last act of domestic violence by the defendant against the plaintiff.

(2) Within three years from the date the plaintiff discovers or reasonably should have discovered that an injury or illness resulted from an act of domestic violence by the defendant against the plaintiff.

(b) As used in this section, "domestic violence" has the same meaning as defined in Section 6211 of the Family Code. **Leg.H.** Added Stats 1995 ch 602 §1 (SB 924). Amended Stats 1998 ch 123 §1 (SB 1939).

§340.16. Action for damages resulting from sexual assault; Revival of claims; Declaration by attorney of good faith belief that claim valued to be more than $250,000

(a) In any civil action for recovery of damages suffered as a result of sexual assault, where the assault occurred on or after the plaintiff's 18th birthday, the time for commencement of the action shall be the later of the following:

(1) Within 10 years from the date of the last act, attempted act, or assault with the intent to commit an act, of sexual assault against the plaintiff.

(2) Within three years from the date the plaintiff discovers or reasonably should have discovered that an injury or illness resulted from an act, attempted act, or assault with the intent to commit an act, of sexual assault against the plaintiff.

(b)(1) As used in this section, "sexual assault" means any of the crimes described in Section 243.4, 261, 264.1, 286, 287, or 289, or former Sections 262 and 288a, of the Penal Code, assault with the intent to commit any of those crimes, or an attempt to commit any of those crimes.

(2) For the purpose of this section, it is not necessary that a criminal prosecution or other proceeding have been brought as a result of the sexual assault or, if a criminal prosecution or other proceeding was brought, that the prosecution or proceeding resulted in a conviction or adjudication. This subdivision does not limit the availability of causes of action permitted under subdivision (a), including causes of action against persons or entities other than the alleged person who committed the crime.

(3) This section applies to any action described in subdivision (a) that is based upon conduct that occurred on or after January 1, 2009, and is commenced on or after January 1, 2019, that would have been barred solely because the applicable statute of limitations has or had expired. Such claims are hereby revived and may be commenced until December 31, 2026. This subdivision does not revive any of the following claims:

(A) A claim that has been litigated to finality in a court of competent jurisdiction before January 1, 2023.

(B) A claim that has been compromised by a written settlement agreement between the parties entered into before January 1, 2023.

(c)(1) Notwithstanding any other law, any claim seeking to recover more than two hundred fifty thousand dollars ($250,000) in damages arising out of a sexual assault or other inappropriate contact, communication, or activity of a sexual nature by a physician occurring at a student health center between January 1, 1988, and January 1, 2017, that would otherwise be barred before January 1, 2020, solely because the applicable statute of limitations has or had expired, is hereby revived and, a cause of action may proceed if already pending in court on October 2, 2019, or, if not filed by that date, may be commenced between January 1, 2020, and December 31, 2020.

(2) This subdivision does not revive any of the following claims:

(A) A claim that has been litigated to finality in a court of competent jurisdiction before January 1, 2020.

(B) A claim that has been compromised by a written settlement agreement between the parties entered into before January 1, 2020.

(C) A claim brought against a public entity.

(3) An attorney representing a claimant seeking to recover under this subdivision shall file a declaration with the court under penalty of perjury stating that the attorney has reviewed the facts of the case and consulted with a mental health practitioner, and that the attorney has concluded on the basis of this review and consultation that it is the attorney's good faith belief that the claim value is more than two hundred fifty thousand dollars ($250,000). The declaration shall be filed upon filing the complaint, or for those claims already pending, by December 1, 2019.

(d)(1) Notwithstanding any other law, any claim seeking to recover damages arising out of a sexual assault or other inappropriate contact, communication, or activity of a sexual nature by a physician while employed by a medical clinic owned and operated by the University of California, Los Angeles, or a physician who held active privileges at a hospital owned and operated by the University of California, Los Angeles, at the time that the sexual assault or other inappropriate contact, communication, or activity of a sexual nature occurred, between January 1, 1983, and January 1, 2019, that would otherwise be barred before January 1, 2021, solely because the applicable statute of limitations has or had expired, is hereby revived, and a cause of action may proceed if already pending in court on January 1, 2021, or, if not filed by that date, may be commenced between January 1, 2021, and December 31, 2021.

(2) This subdivision does not revive either of the following claims:

(A) A claim that has been litigated to finality in a court of competent jurisdiction before January 1, 2021.

(B) A claim that has been compromised by a written settlement agreement between the parties entered into before January 1, 2021.

(e)(1) Notwithstanding any other law, any claim seeking to recover damages suffered as a result of a sexual assault that occurred on or after the plaintiff's 18th birthday that would otherwise be barred before January 1, 2023, solely because the applicable statute of limitations has or had expired, is hereby revived, and a cause of action may proceed if already pending in court on January 1, 2023, or, if not filed by that date, may be commenced between January 1, 2023, and December 31, 2023.

(2) This subdivision revives claims brought by a plaintiff who alleges all of the following:

(A) The plaintiff was sexually assaulted.

(B) One or more entities are legally responsible for damages arising out of the sexual assault.

(C) The entity or entities, including, but not limited to, their officers, directors, representatives, employees, or agents, engaged in a cover up or attempted a cover up of a previous instance or allegations of sexual assault by an alleged perpetrator of such abuse.

(3) Failure to allege a cover up as required by subparagraph (C) of paragraph (2) as to one entity does not affect revival of the plaintiff's claim or claims against any other entity.

(4) For purposes of this subdivision:

(A) "Cover up" means a concerted effort to hide evidence relating to a sexual assault that incentivizes individuals to remain silent or prevents information relating to a sexual assault from becoming public or being disclosed to the plaintiff, including, but not limited to, the use of nondisclosure agreements or confidentiality agreements.

(B) "Entity" means a sole proprietorship, partnership, limited liability company, corporation, association, or other legal entity.

(C) "Legally responsible" means that the entity or entities are liable under any theory of liability established by statute or common law, including, but not limited to, negligence, intentional torts, and vicarious liability.

(5) This subdivision revives any related claims, including, but not limited to, wrongful termination and sexual harassment, arising out of the sexual assault that is the basis for a claim pursuant to this subdivision.

(6) This subdivision does not revive either of the following claims:

(A) A claim that has been litigated to finality in a court of competent jurisdiction before January 1, 2023.

(B) A claim that has been compromised by a written settlement agreement between the parties entered into before January 1, 2023.

(7) This subdivision shall not be construed to alter the otherwise applicable burden of proof, as defined in Section 115 of the Evidence Code, that a plaintiff has in a civil action subject to this section.

(8) Nothing in this subdivision precludes a plaintiff from bringing an action for sexual assault pursuant to subdivisions (a) and (b). **Leg.H.** Added Stats 2018 ch 939 §1 (AB 1619), effective January 1, 2019. Amended Stats 2019 ch 462 §1 (AB 1510), effective October 2, 2019; Stats 2020 ch 246 §1 (AB 3092), effective January 1, 2021; Stats 2022 ch 442 §3 (AB 2777), effective January 1, 2023.

§340.2. Exposure to asbestos; Injury or illness; "Disability"; Wrongful death

(a) In any civil action for injury or illness based upon exposure to asbestos, the time for the commencement of the action shall be the later of the following:

(1) Within one year after the date the plaintiff first suffered disability.

(2) Within one year after the date the plaintiff either knew, or through the exercise of reasonable diligence should have known, that such disability was caused or contributed to by such exposure.

(b) "Disability" as used in subdivision (a) means the loss of time from work as a result of such exposure which precludes the performance of the employee's regular occupation.

(c) In an action for the wrongful death of any plaintiff's decedent, based upon exposure to asbestos, the time for commencement of an action shall be the later of the following:

(1) Within one year from the date of the death of the plaintiff's decedent.

(2) Within one year from the date the plaintiff first knew, or through the exercise of reasonable diligence should have known, that the death was caused or contributed to by such exposure. **Leg.H.** Added Stats 1979 ch 513 §1.

§340.3. Time for commencement of damage action based on commission of felony offense

(a) Unless a longer period is prescribed for a specific action, in any action for damages against a defendant based upon the defendant's commission of a felony offense for which the defendant has been convicted, the time for commencement of the action shall be within one year after judgment is pronounced.

(b)(1) Notwithstanding subdivision (a), an action for damages against a defendant based upon the defendant's commission of a felony offense for which the defendant has been convicted may be commenced within 10 years of the date on which the defendant is discharged from parole if the conviction was for any offense specified in paragraph (1), except voluntary manslaughter, (2), (3), (4), (5), (6), (7), (9), (16), (17), (20), (22), (25), (34), or (35) of subdivision (c) of Section 1192.7 of the Penal Code.

(2) No civil action may be commenced pursuant to paragraph (1) if any of the following applies:

(A) The defendant has received either a certificate of rehabilitation as provided in Chapter 3.5 (commencing with Section 4852.01) of Title 6 of Part 3 of the Penal Code or a pardon as provided in Chapter 1 (commencing with Section 4800) or Chapter 3 (commencing with Section 4850) of Title 6 of Part 3 of the Penal Code.

(B) Following a conviction for murder or attempted murder, the defendant has been paroled based in whole or in part upon evidence presented to the Board of Prison Terms that the defendant committed the crime because he or she was the victim of intimate partner battering.

(C) The defendant was convicted of murder or attempted murder in the second degree in a trial at which substantial evidence was presented that the person committed the crime because he or she was a victim of intimate partner battering.

(D) The defendant was unlawfully imprisoned or restrained but has been released from prison after successfully prosecuting a writ of habeas corpus pursuant to Chapter 1 (commencing with Section 1473) of Title 12 of Part 2 of the Penal Code.

(c) If the sentence or judgment is stayed, the time for the commencement of the action shall be tolled until the stay is lifted. For purposes of this section, a judgment is not stayed if the judgment is appealed or the defendant is placed on probation.

(d)(1) Subdivision (b) shall apply to any action commenced before, on, or after the effective date of this section, including any action otherwise barred by a limitation of time in effect prior to the effective date of this section, thereby reviving those causes of action that had lapsed or expired under the law in effect prior to the effective date of this section.

(2) Paragraph (1) does not apply to either of the following:

(A) Any claim that has been litigated to finality on the merits in any court of competent jurisdiction prior to January 1, 2003. For purposes of this section, termination of a prior action on the basis of the statute of limitations does not constitute a claim that has been litigated to finality on the merits.

(B) Any written, compromised settlement agreement that has been entered into between a plaintiff and a defendant if the plaintiff was represented by an attorney who was admitted to practice law in this state at the time of the settlement, and the plaintiff signed the agreement.

(e) Any restitution paid by the defendant to the victim shall be credited against any judgment, award, or settlement obtained pursuant to this section. Any judgment, award, or settlement obtained pursuant to an action under this section shall be subject to the provisions of Section 13963 of the Government Code. **Leg.H.** Added Stats 1983 ch 938 §2, effective September 20, 1983. Amended Stats 2002 ch 633 §1 (SB 1887), effective September 18, 2002; Stats 2005 ch 215 §1 (AB 220), effective January 1, 2006; Stats 2015 ch 465 §1 (AB 538), effective January 1, 2016.

§340.35. Action for damages against person for childhood sexual abuse following certain dismissed criminal actions; Application of section

(a) This section shall apply if both of the following conditions are met:

(1) A complaint, information, or indictment was filed in a criminal case initiated pursuant to subdivision (f), (g), or (h) of Section 803 of the Penal Code.

(2) The case was dismissed or overturned pursuant to the United States Supreme Court's decision in Stogner v. California (2003) 156 L.Ed.2d 544.

(b) Unless a longer period is prescribed for a specific action, any action for damages against an individual for committing an act of childhood sexual abuse shall be commenced before January 1, 2006.

(c) This section shall apply to any action commenced before, on, or after the effective date of this section, including any action otherwise barred by a limitation of time in effect prior to the effective date of this section, thereby reviving those causes of action that had lapsed or expired under the law in effect prior to the effective date of this section.

(d) This section shall not apply to any of the following:

(1) Any claim against a person or entity other than the individual against whom a complaint, information, or indictment was filed as described in paragraph (1) of subdivision (a).

(2) Any claim that has been litigated to finality on the merits in any court of competent jurisdiction prior to the effective date of this section. For purposes of this section, termination of a prior action on the basis of the statute of limitations does not constitute a claim that has been "litigated to finality on the merits."

(3) Any written, compromised settlement agreement that has been entered into between a plaintiff and a defendant, if the plaintiff was represented by an attorney who was admitted to practice law in this state at the time of the settlement, and the plaintiff signed the agreement.

(e) Any restitution paid by the defendant to the victim shall be credited against any judgment, award, or settlement obtained pursuant to this section. Any judgment, award, or settlement obtained pursuant to an action under this section shall be subject to Section 13966.01 of the Government Code. **Leg.H.** Added Stats 2004 ch 741 §1 (SB 1678).

§340.4. Statute of limitations for action by minor for personal injuries sustained before or during birth

An action by or on behalf of a minor for personal injuries sustained before or in the course of his or her birth must be commenced within six years after the date of birth, and the time the minor is under any disability mentioned in Section 352 shall not be excluded in computing the time limited for the commencement of the action. **Leg.H.** Added Stats 1992 ch 163 §16 (AB 2641), operative January 1, 1994.

§340.5. Professional negligence of health care provider; Tolling of time limitation

In an action for injury or death against a health care provider based upon such person's alleged professional negligence, the time for the commencement of action shall be three years after the date of injury or one year after the plaintiff discovers, or through the use of reasonable diligence should have discovered, the injury, whichever occurs first. In no event shall the time for commencement of legal action exceed three years unless tolled for any of the following: (1) upon proof of fraud, (2) intentional concealment, or (3) the presence of a foreign body, which has no therapeutic or diagnostic purpose or effect, in the person of the injured person. Actions by a minor shall be commenced within three years from the date of the alleged wrongful act except that actions by a minor under the full age of six years shall be commenced within three years or prior to his eighth birthday whichever provides a longer period. Such time limitation shall be tolled for minors for any period during which parent or guardian and defendant's insurer or health care provider have committed fraud or collusion in the failure to bring an action on behalf of the injured minor for professional negligence.

For the purposes of this section:

(1) "Health care provider" means any person licensed or certified pursuant to Division 2 (commencing with Section 500) of the Business and Professions Code, or licensed pursuant to the Osteopathic Initiative Act, or the Chiropractic Initiative Act, or licensed pursuant to Chapter 2.5 (commencing with Section 1440) of Division 2 of the Health and Safety Code; and any clinic, health dispensary, or health facility, licensed pursuant to Division 2 (commencing with Section 1200) of the Health and Safety Code. "Health care provider" includes the legal representatives of a health care provider;

(2) "Professional negligence" means a negligent act or omission to act by a health care provider in the rendering of professional services, which act or omission is the proximate cause of a personal injury or wrongful death, provided that such services are within the scope of services for which the provider is licensed and which are not within any restriction imposed by the licensing agency or licensed hospital. **Leg.H.** Added Stats 1970 ch 360 §1. Amended Stats 1975 2nd Ex Sess ch 1 §25, ch 2 §1.192, effective September 24, 1975, operative December 12, 1975.

1990 Note: The Court of Appeal, Second District, held in *Torres v. County of Los Angeles* (209 Cal. App. 3d 325, 257 Cal. Rptr. 211 (1989)) that CCP §340.5 is unconstitutional as a denial of equal protection to the extent that it provides different accrual dates for minors and adults in medical malpractice actions.

§340.6. Action against attorney for wrongful act or omission, other than fraud

(a) An action against an attorney for a wrongful act or omission, other than for actual fraud, arising in the performance of professional services shall be commenced within one year after the plaintiff discovers, or through the use of reasonable diligence should have discovered, the facts constituting the wrongful act or omission, or four years from the date of the wrongful act or omission, whichever occurs first. If the plaintiff is required to establish the plaintiff's factual innocence for an underlying criminal charge as an element of the plaintiff's claim, the action shall be commenced within two years after the plaintiff achieves postconviction exoneration in the form of a final judicial disposition of the criminal case. Except for a claim for which the plaintiff is required to establish the plaintiff's factual innocence, the time for commencement of legal action shall not exceed four years except that the period shall be tolled during the time that any of the following exist:

(1) The plaintiff has not sustained actual injury.

(2) The attorney continues to represent the plaintiff regarding the specific subject matter in which the alleged wrongful act or omission occurred.

(3) The attorney willfully conceals the facts constituting the wrongful act or omission when those facts are known to the attorney, except that this subdivision shall toll only the four-year limitation.

(4) The plaintiff is under a legal or physical disability that restricts the plaintiff's ability to commence legal action.

(5) A dispute between the lawyer and client concerning fees, costs, or both is pending resolution under Article 13 (commencing with Section 6200) of Chapter 4 of Division 3 of the Business and Professions Code. As used in this paragraph, "pending" means from the date a request for arbitration is filed until 30 days after receipt of notice of the award of the arbitrators, or receipt of notice that the arbitration is otherwise terminated, whichever occurs first.

(b) In an action based upon an instrument in writing, the effective date of which depends upon some act or event of the future, the period of limitations provided for by this section shall commence to run upon the occurrence of that act or event. **Leg.H.** Added Stats 1977 ch 863 §1. Amended Stats 2009 ch 432 §2 (AB 316), effective January 1, 2010; Stats 2019 ch 13 §2 (AB 692), effective January 1, 2020.

§340.7. Dalkon Shield Claimants' Trust

(a) Notwithstanding Section 335.1, a civil action brought by, or on behalf of, a Dalkon Shield victim against the Dalkon Shield Claimants' Trust, shall be brought in accordance with the procedures established by A.H. Robins Company, Inc. Plan of Reorganization, and shall be brought within 15 years of the date on which the victim's injury occurred, except that the statute shall be tolled from August 21, 1985, the date on which the A.H. Robins Company filed for Chapter 11 Reorganization in Richmond, Virginia.

(b) This section applies regardless of when the action or claim shall have accrued or been filed and regardless of whether it might have lapsed or otherwise be barred by time under California law. However, this section shall only apply to victims who, prior to January 1, 1990, filed a civil action, a timely claim, or a claim that is declared to be timely under the sixth Amended and Restated Disclosure Statement filed pursuant to Section 1125 of the Federal Bankruptcy Code in re: A.H. Robins Company, Inc., dated March 28, 1988, U.S. Bankruptcy Court, Eastern District of Virginia (case number 85-01307-R). **Leg.H.** Added Stats 1994 ch 107 §1 (AB 2855). Amended Stats 2007 ch 130 §35 (AB 299), effective January 1, 2008; Stats 2008 ch 179 §34 (SB 1498), effective January 1, 2009.

§340.8. Injury, illness, or death based on exposure to hazardous material or toxic substance; Time for commencement; Media reports as notice

(a) In any civil action for injury or illness based upon exposure to a hazardous material or toxic substance, the time for commencement of the action shall be no later than either two years from the date of injury, or two years after the plaintiff becomes aware of, or reasonably should have become aware of, (1) an injury, (2) the physical cause of the injury, and (3) sufficient facts to put a reasonable person on inquiry notice that the injury was caused or contributed to by the wrongful act of another, whichever occurs later.

(b) In an action for the wrongful death of any plaintiff's decedent, based upon exposure to a hazardous material or toxic substance, the time for commencement of an action shall be no later than either (1) two years from the date of the death of the plaintiff's decedent, or (2) two years from the first date on which the plaintiff is aware of, or reasonably should have become aware of, the physical cause of the death and sufficient facts to put a reasonable person on inquiry notice that the death was caused or contributed to by the wrongful act of another, whichever occurs later.

(c) For purposes of this section:

(1) A "civil action for injury or illness based upon exposure to a hazardous material or toxic substance" does not include an action subject to Section 340.2 or 340.5.

(2) Media reports regarding the hazardous material or toxic substance contamination do not, in and of themselves, constitute sufficient facts to put a reasonable person on inquiry notice that the injury or death was caused or contributed to by the wrongful act of another.

(d) Nothing in this section shall be construed to limit, abrogate, or change the law in effect on the effective date of this section with respect to actions not based upon exposure to a hazardous material or toxic substance. **Leg.H.** Added Stats 2003 ch 873 §1 (SB 331).

2003 Note: It is the intent of the legislature to codify the rulings in *Jolly v. Eli Lilly & Co.* (1988) 44 Cal.3d 1103, *Norgart v. Upjohn Co.* (1999) 21 Cal.4th 383, and *Clark v. Baxter HealthCare Corp.* (2000) 83 Cal.App.4th 1048, in subdivisions (a) and (b) of Section 340.8 of the Code of Civil Procedure, as set forth in this measure, and to disapprove the ruling *McKelvey v. Boeing North American, Inc.* (1999) 74 Cal.App.4th 151, to the extent the ruling in *McKelvey* is inconsistent with paragraph (2) of subdivision (c) of Section 340.8 of the Code of Civil Procedure, as set forth in this measure. Stats 2003 ch 873 (SB 331) §2.

§340.9. Insurance claim for damages arising out of Northridge earthquake of 1994; Revival of cause of action

(a) Notwithstanding any other provision of law or contract, any insurance claim for damages arising out of the Northridge earthquake of 1994 which is barred as of the effective date of this section solely because the applicable statute of limitations has or had expired is hereby revived and a cause of action thereon may be commenced provided that the action is commenced within one year of the effective date of this section. This subdivision shall only apply to cases in which an insured contacted an insurer or an insurer's representative prior to January 1, 2000, regarding potential Northridge earthquake damage.

(b) Any action pursuant to this section commenced prior to, or within one year from, the effective date of this section shall not be barred based upon this limitations period.

(c) Nothing in this section shall be construed to alter the applicable limitations period of an action that is not time barred as of the effective date of this section.

(d) This section shall not apply to either of the following:

(1) Any claim that has been litigated to finality in any court of competent jurisdiction prior to the effective date of this section.

(2) Any written compromised settlement agreement which has been made between an insurer and its insured where the insured was represented by counsel admitted to the practice of law in California at the time of the settlement, and who signed the agreement. **Leg.H.** Added Stats 2000 ch 1090 §1 (SB 1899).

§340.10. "Terrorist victim"

(a) For purposes of this section, "terrorist victim" means any individual who died or was injured as a consequence of the terrorist-related aircraft crashes of September 11, 2001, including persons who were present at the World Trade Center in New York City, New York, the Pentagon in Arlington, Virginia, or at the site of the crash at Shanksville, Pennsylvania, or in the immediate aftermath of the terrorist-related aircraft crashes of September 11, 2001, including members of the flight crew and passengers on American Airlines Flight 11, American Airlines Flight 77, United Airlines Flight 175, and United Airlines Flight 93, and who suffered physical harm or death as a result of any of the crashes, as defined in Section 40101 of Title 49 of the United States Code and the related, applicable regulations, other than an individual identified by the Attorney General of the United States as a participant or conspirator in the terrorist-related aircraft crashes, or a representative or heir of such an individual.

(b) The statute of limitations for injury or death set forth in Section 335.1 shall apply to any action brought for injury to, or for the death of, any terrorist victim described in subdivision (a) and caused by the wrongful act or neglect of another, regardless of whether that action lapsed or was otherwise barred by time under California law predating the passage of this section and Section 335.1. **Leg.H.** Added Stats 2002 ch 448 §4 (SB 688).

§341. Property seized by tax collector; Stock sold for delinquent assessment; Action respecting dissolved corporation; Six months

Within six months:

An action against an officer, or officer de facto:

1. To recover any goods, wares, merchandise, or other property, seized by any such officer in his official capacity as tax collector, or to recover the price or value of any goods, wares, merchandise, or other personal property so seized, or for damages for the seizure, detention, sale of, or injury to any goods, wares, merchandise, or other personal property seized, or for damages done to any person or property in making any such seizure.

2. To recover stock sold for a delinquent assessment, as provided in section three hundred forty-seven [three hundred and thirty-nine] of the Civil Code.

3. To set aside or invalidate any action taken or performed by a majority of the trustees of any corporation heretofore or hereafter dissolved by operation of law, including the revivor of any such corporation. **Leg.H.** Enacted 1872. Amended Code Amdts 1873–74 ch 383 §35; Stats 1917 ch 217 §1.

§341a. Personal property left in establishment; Ninety days

All civil actions for the recovery or conversion of personal property, wearing apparel, trunks, valises or baggage alleged to have been left at a hotel, hospital, rest home, sanitarium, boarding house, lodging house, furnished apartment house, or furnished bungalow court, shall be begun within 90 days from and after the date of the departure of the owner of said personal property, wearing apparel, trunks, valises or baggage from said hotel, hospital, rest home, sanitarium, boarding house, lodging house, furnished apartment house, or furnished bungalow court. **Leg.H.** Added Stats 1921 ch 152 §1. Amended Stats 1927 ch 826 §1; Stats 1943 ch 405 §1.

§341.5. Local agency challenging state funding

Notwithstanding any other provision of law, any action or proceeding in which a county, city, city and county, school district, special district, or any other local agency is a plaintiff or petitioner, that is brought against the State of California challenging the constitutionality of any statute relating to state funding for counties, cities, cities and counties, school districts, special districts, or other local agencies, shall be commenced within 90 days of the effective date of the statute at issue in the action. For purposes of this section, "State of California" means the State of California itself, or any of its agencies, departments, commissions, boards, or public officials. **Leg.H.** Added Stats 1994 ch 155 §1 (AB 860), effective July 9, 1994. Amended Stats 1994 ch 156 §1 (SB 2127), effective July 9, 1994.

Prior Law: Former CCP §341.5, relating to statute of limitation, was added Stats 1939 ch 129 §4, amended Stats 1939 ch 1103 §2, and repealed Stats 1975 ch 1241 §1.

§342. Claim against public entity

An action against a public entity upon a cause of action for which a claim is required to be presented in accordance with Chapter 1 (commencing with Section 900) and Chapter 2 (commencing with Section 910) of Part 3 of Division 3.6 of Title 1 of the Government Code must be commenced within the time provided in Section 945.6 of the Government Code. **Leg.H.** Added Stats 1963 ch 1715 §4.

Prior Law: Former CCP §342, relating to when actions on claims against county must be commenced, was enacted 1872 and repealed by Stats 1959 ch 1724 §2.

§343. Relief for which no period previously provided; Four years

An action for relief not hereinbefore provided for must be commenced within four years after the cause of action shall have accrued. **Leg.H.** Enacted 1872.

§344. Where cause of action accrues on mutual account

In an action brought to recover a balance due upon a mutual, open, and current account, where there have been reciprocal demands between the parties, the cause of action is deemed to have accrued from the time of the last item proved in the account on either side. **Leg.H.** Enacted 1872.

§345. Actions by or for benefit of State or county; Four years

The limitations prescribed in this chapter apply to actions brought in the name of the state or county or for the benefit of the state or county, in the same manner as to actions by private parties. Accounts for the support of patients at state or county hospitals are book accounts as defined in Section 337a, and actions on them may be commenced at any time within four years after the last date of service or the last date of payment. **Leg.H.** Enacted 1872. Amended Stats 1905 ch 381 §1; Stats 1921 ch 475 §1; Stats 1943 ch 177 §1; Stats 1984 ch 797 §1.

§346. Mortgage redemption; Preclusion by adverse possession

An action to redeem a mortgage of real property, with or without an account of rents and profits, may be brought by the mortgagor or those claiming under him, against the mortgagee in possession, or those claiming under him, unless he or they have continuously maintained an adverse possession of the mortgaged premises for five years after breach of some condition of the mortgage. **Leg.H.** Enacted 1872.

§347. Redemption if there are several mortgagors or claimants

If there is more than one such mortgagor, or more than one person claiming under a mortgagor, some of whom are not entitled to maintain such an action under the provisions of this chapter, any one of them who is entitled to maintain such an action may redeem therein a divided or undivided part of the mortgaged premises, according as his interests may appear and have an accounting, for a part of the rents and profits proportionate to his interest in the mortgaged premises, on payment of a part of the mortgage-money, bearing the same proportion to the whole of such money as the value of his divided or undivided interest in the premises bears to the whole of such premises. **Leg.H.** Enacted 1872.

§348. No limitation of action for deposit of money or property; Exception

To actions brought to recover money or other property deposited with any bank, banker, trust company, building and loan association, or savings and loan society or evidenced by a certificate issued by an industrial loan company or credit union there is no limitation.

This section shall not apply to banks, bankers, trust companies, building and loan associations, industrial loan companies, credit unions, and savings and loan societies which have become insolvent and are in process of liquidation and in such cases the statute of limitations shall be deemed to have commenced to run from the beginning of the process of liquidation; provided, however, nothing herein contained shall be construed so as to relieve any stockholder of any banking corporation or trust company from stockholders' liability as shall at any time, be provided by law. **Leg.H.** Added Code Amdts 1873–74 ch 383 §36. Amended Stats 1915 ch 411 §1; Stats 1917 ch 756 §1; Stats 1955 ch 208 §1.

§348.5. No limitation for action upon any bonds or coupons issued by the State

An action upon any bonds or coupons issued by the State of California shall have no limitation. **Leg.H.** Added Stats 2010 ch 719 §8 (SB 856), effective October 19, 2010.

§349. [Section repealed 2011]

Leg.H. Added Stats 1901 ch 39 §1. Repealed Stats 2010 ch 328 §33.5 (SB 1330), effective January 1, 2011. The repealed section related to contesting local improvement assessment.

§ 349.05. Trespass or conversion involving oil or gas wells; One hundred eighty days

Within one hundred eighty days:

(a) An action to enjoin, abate, or for damages on account of, an underground trespass, use or occupancy, by means of a well drilled for oil or gas or both from a surface location on land other than real property in which the aggrieved party has some right, title or interest or in respect to which the aggrieved party has some right, title or interest.

(b) An action for conversion or for the taking or removing of oil, gas or other liquid, or fluids by means of any such well.

When any of said acts is by means of a new well the actual drilling of which is commenced after this section becomes effective, and such act was knowingly committed with actual intent to commit such act, the cause of action in such case shall not be deemed to have accrued until the discovery, by the aggrieved party, of the act or acts complained of; but in all other cases, and as to wells heretofore or hereafter drilled, the cause of action shall be deemed to have accrued ten days after the time when the well which is the subject of the cause of action was first placed on production.

Notwithstanding the continuing character of any such act, there shall be but one cause of action for any such act, and the cause of action shall accrue as aforesaid.

In all cases where oil or gas has been heretofore or is hereafter extracted from any existing or subsequently drilled well in this state, by a person without right but asserting a claim of right in good faith or acting under an honest mistake of law or fact, the measure of damages, if there be any right of recovery under existing law, shall be the value of the oil or gas at the time of extraction, without interest, after deducting all costs of development, operation and production, which costs shall include taxes and interest on all expenditures from the date thereof.

This section applies to causes of action existing when this section becomes effective. The time for commencement of existing causes of action which would be barred by this section within the first one hundred eighty days after this section becomes effective, shall be the said first one hundred eighty days.

Whenever the term "oil" is used in this section it shall be taken to include "petroleum," and the term "gas" shall mean natural gas coming from the earth.

The limitations prescribed by this section do not apply to rights of action or actions to be brought in the name of or for the benefit of the people of this State, or of any county, city and county, city or other political subdivision of this State. **Leg.H.** Added Stats 1935 ch 852 §1. Amended and renumbered from Cal Code Civ Proc §349¾ by Stats 2020 ch 370 §34 (SB 1371), effective January 1, 2021.

§349½. [Section repealed 2011]

Leg.H. Added Stats 1923 ch 34 §1. Amended Stats 1957 ch 636 §1. Repealed Stats 2010 ch 699 (SB 894), §1.3, effective January 1, 2011. The repealed section related to contesting municipal annexation or consolidation.

§349¾. Trespass or conversion involving oil or gas wells; One hundred eighty days [Renumbered]

Leg.H. Added Stats 1935 ch 852 §1. Amended and renumbered to Cal Code Civ Proc §349.05 by Stats 2020 §34 (SB 1371), effective January 1, 2021.

§349.1. Contesting formation or territorial changes of cities or districts; Six months

The validity of any acts or proceedings taken under color of law for the formation, organization, incorporation, dissolution, consolidation, change of organization or reorganization of, or for any change in the territorial boundaries of, any city, county, city and county, special district, public corporation or other public entity, or improvement district within any of the foregoing, shall not be contested in any action unless such action shall have been brought within six months from the date of completion of said acts or proceedings. Unless an action is commenced within said period all said acts or proceedings shall be held valid and in every respect legal and incontestable.

This section shall not amend or repeal any existing statute prescribing a shorter period of limitation than that specified herein. **Leg.H.** Added Stats 1957 ch 1344 §1. Amended Stats 1959 ch 1995 §1; Stats 1965 ch 2044 §3.5.

§349.2. Contesting bond proceedings of public entities; Six months

Where any acts or proceedings are taken under color of law by or on behalf of any city, county, city and county, special district, public corporation or other public entity for the authorization, sale or issuance of bonds:

(1) The validity of any such acts or proceedings for the authorization of bonds shall not be contested in any action unless such action shall have been brought within six months from the date of election authorizing said bonds, in cases where said bonds are required by law to be authorized at an election, or within six months from the date of adoption of a resolution or ordinance authorizing such bonds, in cases where bonds are not required by law to be authorized at an election;

(2) The validity of any such acts or proceedings for the sale of bonds (including all acts or proceedings taken prior thereto and providing for the issuance of such bonds) shall not be contested in any action unless such action shall have been brought within six months from the date of sale of said bonds;

(3) The validity of any such acts or proceedings for the issuance and delivery of, or payment for, bonds shall not be contested in any action unless such action shall have been brought within six months from the date of issuance and delivery of, or payment for, said bonds.

Unless an action is commenced within the applicable time hereinabove specified, said acts or proceedings for the authorization, sale or issuance of bonds shall be held valid and in every respect legal and incontestable.

This section shall not amend or repeal any existing statute prescribing a shorter period of limitation than that specified herein.

As used in this section, the term "bonds" means all instruments evidencing indebtedness incurred or to be incurred for any public purpose, all instruments evidencing the borrowing of money in anticipation of taxes, revenues or other income of a public body, all instruments payable from revenues or special funds, and all instruments funding or refunding any thereof or any indebtedness, but shall not include any special assessment bonds, special assessment refunding bond, or bonds or other instruments issued to represent special assessments which are, directly or indirectly, secured by or payable from specific assessments levied against lands benefited, including bonds or other instruments issued under or pursuant to any statute, charter or ordinance providing for the improvement of streets, the opening and widening of streets, the provision for off-street parking, or the refunding of any of the same. **Leg.H.** Added Stats 1957 ch 1345 §1.

§349.3. [Section repealed 1977]

Leg.H. Added Stats 1963 ch 1152 §1, effective July 8, 1963. Repealed Stats 1977 ch 7 §1, effective March 4, 1977.

§349.4. Confirmation and validation of actions and proceedings of local public entities

All acts and proceedings heretofore or hereafter taken under color of law for the formation, organization or incorporation of, or for any change in the territorial boundaries of, any city, county, city and county, special district, public corporation or other public entity, or improvement district, annexed area or zone within any of the foregoing, and for the authorization, issuance, sale, or exchange of bonds of the entity or the territory thereof may be confirmed, validated, and declared legally effective in the manner provided in this section.

The legislative body of the entity may instruct its clerk or secretary to mail a notice to all owners of property within the entity, within the improvement district or zone, or within the annexed area, as the case may be, as their names and addresses appear on the last equalized county assessment roll, or as known to the clerk or secretary. Such notice shall include the name of the entity, the date the entity or the zone or improvement district therein was ordered formed or its territory changed by annexation or otherwise, as the case may be, the amount of bonds authorized, if any, and a statement that commencing with the date of mailing of said notice there shall be a 60-calendar-day period during which period any property owner may file an action contesting the validity of the formation of the entity, or of such improvement district or zone, or of such change of boundaries by annexation or otherwise, as the case may be, or the validity of the bond authorization, if any. The clerk or secretary shall make and file with the legislative body of the entity a certificate of mailing of the notices. The legislative body of the entity may order the clerk or secretary to include in such notice such other additional information that it deems pertinent.

If no action is filed during such 60-day period, the formation of the entity or of such improvement district or zone, or the change of boundaries by annexation or otherwise, as the case may be, and the bond authorization, if any, are valid and uncontestable. **Leg.H.** Added Stats 1977 ch 7 §2, effective March 4, 1977.

Prior Law: Former CCP §349.4, similar to the present section, was added Stats 1969 ch 356 §2, effective July 3, 1969, and repealed Stats 1976 ch 1281 §1.

Former CCP §349.4, relating to confirmation, validation, etc. of acts and proceedings to change boundaries of cities, etc., was added by Stats 1963 ch 1152 §3, effective July 8, 1963, and repealed by Stats 1969 ch 356 §1, effective July 3, 1969.

CHAPTER 4
GENERAL PROVISIONS AS TO THE TIME OF COMMENCING ACTIONS

When an action is commenced. §350.
Exception, where defendant is out of the state. §351.
Persons under disabilities. §352.
Time to bring action for prisoners. §352.1.
Tolling while person liable is under order of restitution. §352.5.
Extension when court assumes jurisdiction over practice of attorney. §353.1.
Time of continuance of state-of-war disability not part of limitation period. §354.
Action to recover Holocaust-era artwork. §354.3.
Claim by Armenian Genocide victim, or by heir or beneficiary; Action to be filed on or before December 31, 2016. §354.4.
Armenian genocide victims. §354.45.
Extension of limitations period for Holocaust victim's claim under insurance policy issued during specified period. §354.5.
Compensation for slave and forced labor. §354.6.
Legal action by bracero or heir or beneficiary of bracero; Time limitation. §354.7.
Actions for assault, battery, or wrongful death when conduct also constitutes torture, war crime, attempted extrajudicial killing, or crimes against humanity; Attorney's fees and litigation costs. §354.8.

Provision where judgment has been reversed. §355.
Provision where action is stayed by injunction. §356.
Disability must exist when right of action accrued. §357.
When two or more disabilities exist, etc. §358.
This title not applicable to actions against directors, etc.; Limitations in such cases prescribed. §359.
Expiration of statute of limitations with respect to obligations of principal as bar to action under surety bond. §359.5.
Acknowledgment or promise. §360.
Waivers. §360.5.
Limitation laws of other states, effect of. §361.
Existing causes of action not affected. §362.
Word "action" construed, how. §363.

§350. When an action is commenced

An action is commenced, within the meaning of this title, when the complaint is filed. **Leg.H.** Enacted 1872.

§351. Exception, where defendant is out of the state

If, when the cause of action accrues against a person, he is out of the State, the action may be commenced within the term herein limited, after his return to the State, and if, after the cause of action accrues, he departs from the State, the time of his absence is not part of the time limited for the commencement of the action. **Leg.H.** Enacted 1872.

1990 Note: The United States Court of Appeals, Ninth Circuit, held in *Abramson v Brownstein* (897 F2d 389 (9th Cir. [N.D. Cal.] 1990)) that CCP §351 is unconstitutional under the Commerce Clause because it places an unreasonable burden on interstate commerce to choose between being present in California throughout the limitations period of forfeiting the limitations defense.

§352. Persons under disabilities

(a) If a person entitled to bring an action, mentioned in Chapter 3 (commencing with Section 335) is, at the time the cause of action accrued either under the age of majority or lacking the legal capacity to make decisions, the time of the disability is not part of the time limited for the commencement of the action.

(b) This section shall not apply to an action against a public entity or public employee upon a cause of action for which a claim is required to be presented in accordance with Chapter 1 (commencing with Section 900) or Chapter 2 (commencing with Section 910) of Part 3, or Chapter 3 (commencing with Section 950) of Part 4, of Division 3.6 of Title 1 of the Government Code. This subdivision shall not apply to any claim presented to a public entity prior to January 1, 1971. **Leg.H.** Enacted 1872. Amended Stats 1959 ch 192 §1; Stats 1970 ch 104 §1, operative January 1, 1971; Stats 1975 ch 1241 §1.5; Stats 1986 ch 1161 §1; Stats 1994 ch 1083 §4 (SB 1445); Stats 2014 ch 144 §4 (AB 1847), effective January 1, 2015.

§352.1. Time to bring action for prisoners

(a) If a person entitled to bring an action, mentioned in Chapter 3 (commencing with Section 335), is, at the time the cause of action accrued, imprisoned on a criminal charge, or in execution under the sentence of a criminal court for a term less than for life, the time of that disability is not a part of the time limited for the commencement of the action, not to exceed two years.

(b) This section does not apply to an action against a public entity or public employee upon a cause of action for which a claim is required to be presented in accordance with Chapter 1 (commencing with Section 900) or Chapter 2 (commencing with Section 910) of Part 3, or Chapter 3 (commencing with Section 950) of Part 4, of Division 3.6 of Title 1 of the Government Code. This subdivision shall not apply to any claim presented to a public entity prior to January 1, 1971.

(c) This section does not apply to an action, other than an action to recover damages or that portion of an action that is for the recovery of damages, relating to the conditions of confinement, including an action brought by that person pursuant to Section 1983 of Title 42 of the United States Code. **Leg.H.** Added Stats 1994 ch 1083 §5 (SB 1445).

§352.5. Tolling while person liable is under order of restitution

If, after a cause of action accrues against a person, that person comes under an order for restitution as a condition of probation with respect to the specific act or omission giving rise to such person's liability, the time during which the order is in effect is not a part of the time limited for the commencement of such an action based upon the act or omission. **Leg.H.** Added Stats 1976 ch 282 §1.

§353. [Section repealed 1993]

Leg.H. Enacted 1872. Amended Stats 1971 ch 1226 §1, ch 1638 §1; Stats 1987 ch 923 §1, operative July 1, 1988; Stats 1988 ch 1199 §4, operative July 1, 1989; Stats 1990 ch 140 §1. Repealed Stats 1992 ch 178 §6. See CCP §§366.1, 366.2, 377.30, 377.40.

§353.1. Extension when court assumes jurisdiction over practice of attorney

If a person entitled to bring an action or other proceeding, which action or other proceeding has not been filed or otherwise instituted, is represented by an attorney over whose practice a court of this state has assumed jurisdiction pursuant to Section 6180 or Section 6190 of the Business and Professions Code, and the application for the court to assume jurisdiction is filed prior to the expiration of the applicable statute of limitation or claim statute, the person shall have six months from the date of entry of the order assuming jurisdiction within which to file or otherwise institute the matter, if the applicable statute of limitation otherwise would have expired. **Leg.H.** Added Stats 1983 ch 254 §3.

§353.5. [Section repealed 1991.]

Leg.H. Added Stats 1974 ch 752 §1. Amended Stats 1975 ch 173 §1, effective June 30, 1975; Stats 1983 ch 842 §11, operative January 1, 1985; Stats 1986 ch 783 §1, operative July 1, 1987. Repealed Stats 1990 ch 140 §2 (SB 1855). The repealed section related to death of person against whom action may be brought.

§354. Time of continuance of state-of-war disability not part of limitation period

When a person is, by reason of the existence of a state of war, under a disability to commence an action, the time of the continuance of such disability is not part of the period limited for the commencement of the action whether such cause of action shall have accrued prior to or during the period of such disability. **Leg.H.** Enacted 1872. Amended Stats 1943 ch 151 §1.

§354.3. Action to recover Holocaust-era artwork

(a) The following definitions govern the construction of this section:

(1) "Entity" means any museum or gallery that displays, exhibits, or sells any article of historical, interpretive, scientific, or artistic significance.

(2) "Holocaust-era artwork" means any article of artistic significance taken as a result of Nazi persecution during the period of 1929 to 1945, inclusive.

(b) Notwithstanding any other provision of law, any owner, or heir or beneficiary of an owner, of Holocaust-era artwork, may bring an action to recover Holocaust-era artwork from any entity described in paragraph (1) of subdivision (a). Subject to Section 410.10, that action may be brought in a superior court of this state, which court shall have jurisdiction over that action until its completion or resolution. Section 361 does not apply to this section.

(c) Any action brought under this section shall not be dismissed for failure to comply with the applicable statute of limitation, if the action is commenced on or before December 31, 2010. **Leg.H.** Added Stats 2002 ch 332 §2 (AB 1758).

§354.4. Claim by Armenian Genocide victim, or by heir or beneficiary; Action to be filed on or before December 31, 2016

(a) The following definitions govern the construction of this section:

(1) "Armenian Genocide victim" means any person of Armenian or other ancestry living in the Ottoman Empire during the period of 1915 to 1923, inclusive, who died, was deported, or escaped to avoid persecution during that period.

(2) "Insurer" means an insurance provider doing business in the state, or whose contacts in the state satisfy the constitutional requirements for jurisdiction, that sold life, property, liability, health, annuities, dowry, educational, casualty, or any other insurance covering persons or property to persons in Europe or Asia at any time between 1875 and 1923.

(b) Notwithstanding any other provision of law, any Armenian Genocide victim, or heir or beneficiary of an Armenian Genocide victim, who resides in this state and has a claim arising out of an insurance policy or policies purchased or in effect in Europe or Asia between 1875 and 1923 from an insurer described in paragraph (2) of subdivision (a), may bring a legal action or may continue a pending legal action to recover on that claim in any court of competent jurisdiction in this state, which court shall be deemed the proper forum for that action until its completion or resolution.

(c) Any action, including any pending action brought by an Armenian Genocide victim or the heir or beneficiary of an Armenian Genocide victim, whether a resident or nonresident of this state, seeking benefits under the insurance policies issued or in effect between 1875 and 1923 shall not be dismissed for failure to comply with the applicable statute of limitation, provided the action is filed on or before December 31, 2016.

(d) The provisions of this section are severable. If any provision of this section or its application is held invalid, that invalidity shall not affect other provisions or applications that can be given effect without the invalid provision or application. **Leg.H.** Added Stats 2000 ch 543 §2 (SB 1915), effective September 20, 2000. Amended Stats 2011 ch 70 §1 (AB 173), effective July 8, 2011.

§354.45. Armenian genocide victims

(a) For purposes of this section, the following terms have the following meanings:

(1) "Armenian Genocide victim" means any person of Armenian or other ancestry living in the Ottoman Empire during the period of 1890 to 1923, inclusive, who died, was injured in person or property, was deported, or escaped to avoid persecution during that period.

(2) "Bank" means any banking or financial institution, including any institution that issued bonds, that conducted business in Ottoman Turkey at any time during the period of 1890 to 1923, inclusive.

(3) "Deposited assets" means any and all cash, securities, bonds, gold, jewels or jewelry, or any other tangible or intangible items of personal property, or any documents indicating ownership or possessory interests in real, personal, or intangible property, that were deposited with and held by a bank.

(4) "Looted assets" means any and all personal, commercial, real, and intangible property, including cash, securities, gold, jewelry, businesses, artwork, equipment, and intellectual property, that was taken from the ownership or control of an individual, organization, or entity, by theft, forced transfer, or exploitation, during the period of 1890 to 1923, inclusive, by any person, organization, or entity acting on behalf of, or in furtherance of the acts of, the Turkish Government, that were received by and deposited with a bank.

(b) Notwithstanding any other law, any Armenian Genocide victim, or heir or beneficiary of an Armenian Genocide victim, who resides in this state and has a claim arising out of a failure of a bank to pay or turn over deposited assets, or to turn over looted assets, may bring an action or may continue a pending action, to recover on that claim in any court of competent jurisdiction in this state, which court shall be deemed the proper forum for that action until its completion or resolution.

(c) Any action, including any pending action brought by an Armenian Genocide victim, or the heir or beneficiary of an Armenian Genocide victim, who resides in this state, seeking payment for, or the return of, deposited assets, or the return of looted assets, shall not be dismissed for failure to comply with the applicable statute of limitation, if the action is filed on or before December 31, 2016.

(d) The provisions of this section are severable. If any provision of this section or its application is held invalid, that invalidity shall not affect other provisions or applications that can be given effect without the invalid provision or application. **Leg.H.** Added Stats 2006 ch 443 §2 (SB 1524), effective January 1, 2007.

§354.5. Extension of limitations period for Holocaust victim's claim under insurance policy issued during specified period

(a) The following definitions govern the construction of this section:

(1) "Holocaust victim" means any person who was persecuted during the period of 1929 to 1945, inclusive, by Nazi Germany, its allies, or sympathizers.

(2) "Related company" means any parent, subsidiary, reinsurer, successor in interest, managing general agent, or affiliate company of the insurer.

(3) "Insurer" means an insurance provider doing business in the state, or whose contacts in the state satisfy the constitutional requirements for jurisdiction, that sold life, property, liability, health, annuities, dowry, educational, casualty, or any other insurance covering persons or property to persons in Europe at any time before 1945, directly or through a related

company, whether the sale of the insurance occurred before or after the insurer and the related company became related.

(b) Notwithstanding any other provision of law, any Holocaust victim, or heir or beneficiary of a Holocaust victim, who resides in this state and has a claim arising out of an insurance policy or policies purchased or in effect in Europe before 1945 from an insurer described in paragraph (3) of subdivision (a), may bring a legal action to recover on that claim in any superior court of the state for the county in which the plaintiff or one of the plaintiffs resides, which court shall be vested with jurisdiction over that action until its completion or resolution.

(c) Any action brought by a Holocaust victim or the heir or beneficiary of a Holocaust victim, whether a resident or nonresident of this state, seeking proceeds of the insurance policies issued or in effect before 1945 shall not be dismissed for failure to comply with the applicable statute of limitation, provided the action is commenced on or before December 31, 2010. **Leg.H.** Added Stats 1998 ch 43 §2 (AB 1334), effective May 22, 1998. Amended Stats 1999 ch 827 §1 (AB 600), effective October 10, 1999.

§354.6. Compensation for slave and forced labor

(a) As used in this section:

(1) "Second World War slave labor victim" means any person taken from a concentration camp or ghetto or diverted from transportation to a concentration camp or from a ghetto to perform labor without pay for any period of time between 1929 and 1945, by the Nazi regime, its allies and sympathizers, or enterprises transacting business in any of the areas occupied by or under control of the Nazi regime or its allies and sympathizers.

(2) "Second World War forced labor victim" means any person who was a member of the civilian population conquered by the Nazi regime, its allies or sympathizers, or prisoner-of-war of the Nazi regime, its allies or sympathizers, forced to perform labor without pay for any period of time between 1929 and 1945, by the Nazi regime, its allies and sympathizers, or enterprises transacting business in any of the areas occupied by or under control of the Nazi regime or its allies and sympathizers.

(3) "Compensation" means the present value of wages and benefits that individuals should have been paid and damages for injuries sustained in connection with the labor performed. Present value shall be calculated on the basis of the market value of the services at the time they were performed, plus interest from the time the services were performed, compounded annually to date of full payment without diminution for wartime or postwar currency devaluation.

(b) Any Second World War slave labor victim, or heir of a Second World War slave labor victim, Second World War forced labor victim, or heir of a Second World War forced labor victim, may bring an action to recover compensation for labor performed as a Second World War slave labor victim or Second World War forced labor victim from any entity or successor in interest thereof, for whom that labor was performed, either directly or through a subsidiary or affiliate. That action may be brought in a superior court of this state, which court shall have jurisdiction over that action until its completion or resolution.

(c) Any action brought under this section shall not be dismissed for failure to comply with the applicable statute of limitation, if the action is commenced on or before December 31, 2010. **Leg.H.** Added Stats 1999 ch 216 §4 (SB 1245), effective July 28, 1999.

1999 Note: To the extent that the statute of limitations applicable to claims for compensation is extended by this act, that extension of the limitations period is intended to be applied retroactively, irrespective of whether the claims were otherwise barred by any applicable statute of limitations under any other provision of law prior to the enactment of this acts. Stats 1999 ch 216 §1(d).

§354.7. Legal action by bracero or heir or beneficiary of bracero; Time limitation

(a) The following definitions govern the construction of this section:

(1) "Bracero" means any person who participated in the labor importation program known as the Bracero program between January 1, 1942, and January 1, 1950, pursuant to agreements between the United States and Mexico.

(2) "Savings fund" means funds withheld from the wages of braceros as savings to be paid to braceros upon their return to Mexico.

(b) Notwithstanding any other provision of law, any bracero, or heir or beneficiary of a bracero, who has a claim arising out of a failure to pay or turn over savings fund amounts may bring a legal action or may continue a pending legal action to recover on that claim in any court of competent jurisdiction in this state, which court shall be deemed a proper forum for that action until its completion or resolution.

(c) Notwithstanding any other provision of law, any action brought by a bracero, or heir or beneficiary of a bracero, arising out of a failure to pay or turn over savings fund amounts shall not be dismissed for failure to comply with the otherwise applicable statute of limitations, provided the action is filed on or before December 31, 2005.

(d) The provisions of this section are severable. If any provision of this section or its application is held invalid, that invalidity shall not affect other provisions or applications that can be given effect without the invalid provision or application. **Leg.H.** Added Stats 2002 ch 1070 §2 (AB 2913), effective September 29, 2002.

§354.8. Actions for assault, battery, or wrongful death when conduct also constitutes torture, war crime, attempted extrajudicial killing, or crimes against humanity; Attorney's fees and litigation costs

(a) Notwithstanding any other law, including, but not limited to Section 335.1, the following actions shall be commenced within 10 years:

(1) An action for assault, battery, or both, where the conduct constituting the assault or battery would also constitute any of the following:

(A) An act of torture, as described in Section 206 of the Penal Code.

(B) An act of genocide, as described in Section 1091(a) of Title 18 of the United States Code.

(C) A war crime, as defined in Section 2441 of Title 18 of the United States Code.

(D) An attempted extrajudicial killing, as defined in Section 3(a) of Public Law 102-256.

(E)(i) Crimes against humanity.

(ii) For purposes of this paragraph, "crimes against humanity" means any of the following acts as part of a widespread or systematic attack directed against a civil population, with knowledge of the attack:

(I) Murder.

(II) Extermination.

(III) Enslavement.

(IV) Forcible transfer of population.

(V) Arbitrary detention.

(VI) Rape, sexual slavery, enforced prostitution, forced pregnancy, enforced sterilization, or any other form of sexual violence of comparable gravity.

(VII) Persecution on political, race, national, ethnic, cultural, religious, or gender grounds.

(VIII) Enforced disappearance of persons.

(IX) Other inhuman acts of similar character intentionally causing great suffering, serious bodily injury, or serious mental injury.

(2) An action for wrongful death, where the death arises out of conduct constituting any of the acts described in paragraph (1), or where the death would constitute an extrajudicial killing, as defined in Section 3(a) of Public Law 102-256.

(3) An action for the taking of property in violation of international law, in which either of the following apply:

(A) That property, or any property exchanged for such property, is present in the United States in connection with a commercial activity carried on in the United States by a foreign state.

(B) That property, or any property exchanged for such property, is owned or operated by an agency or instrumentality of a foreign state and that agency or instrumentality is engaged in a commercial activity in the United States.

(4) An action seeking benefits under an insurance policy where the insurance claim arises out of any of the conduct described in paragraphs (1) to (3), inclusive.

(b) An action brought under this section shall not be dismissed for failure to comply with any previously applicable statute of limitations.

(c) Section 361 shall not apply to an action brought pursuant to this section if all or part of the unlawful act or acts out of which the action arises occurred in this state.

(d) A prevailing plaintiff may be awarded reasonable attorney's fees and litigation costs including, but not limited to, expert witness fees and expenses as part of the costs.

(e) This section shall apply to all actions commenced concerning an act described in paragraphs (1) to (4), inclusive, of subdivision (a), that occurs on or after January 1, 2016.

(f) The provisions of this section are severable. If any provision of this section or its application is held invalid, that invalidity shall not affect other provisions or applications that can be given effect without the invalid provision or application. **Leg.H.** Added Stats 2015 ch 474 §2 (AB 15), effective January 1, 2016.

§355. Provision where judgment has been reversed

If an action is commenced within the time prescribed therefor, and a judgment therein for the plaintiff be reversed on appeal other than on the merits, a new action may be commenced within one year after the reversal. **Leg.H.** Enacted 1872. Amended Stats 1992 ch 178 §7 (SB 1496).

§356. Provision where action is stayed by injunction

When the commencement of an action is stayed by injunction or statutory prohibition, the time of the continuance of the injunction or prohibition is not part of the time limited for the commencement of the action. **Leg.H.** Enacted 1872.

§357. Disability must exist when right of action accrued

No person can avail himself of a disability, unless it existed when his right of action accrued. **Leg.H.** Enacted 1872.

§358. When two or more disabilities exist, etc.

When two or more disabilities coexist at the time the right of action accrues, the limitation does not attach until they are removed. **Leg.H.** Enacted 1872.

§359. This title not applicable to actions against directors, etc.; Limitations in such cases prescribed

This title does not affect actions against directors, shareholders, or members of a corporation, to recover a penalty or forfeiture imposed, or to enforce a liability created by law; but such actions must be brought within three years after the discovery by the aggrieved party of the facts upon which the penalty or forfeiture attached, or the liability was created. **Leg.H.** Enacted 1872. Amended Stats 1978 ch 1305 §1, operative January 1, 1980.

§359.5. Expiration of statute of limitations with respect to obligations of principal as bar to action under surety bond

If the obligations under a surety bond are conditioned upon performance of the principal, the expiration of the statute of limitations with respect to the obligations of the principal, other than the obligations of the principal under the bond, shall also bar an action against the principal or surety under the bond, unless the terms of the bond provide otherwise. **Leg.H.** Added Stats 1982 ch 106 §1.

§360. Acknowledgment or promise

No acknowledgment or promise is sufficient evidence of a new or continuing contract, by which to take the case out of the operation of this title, unless the same is contained in some writing, signed by the party to be charged thereby, provided that any payment on account of principal or interest due on a promissory note made by the party to be charged shall be deemed a sufficient acknowledgment or promise of a continuing contract to stop, from time to time as any such payment is made, the running of the time within which an action may be commenced upon the principal sum or upon any installment of principal or interest due on such note, and to start the running of a new period of time, but no such payment of itself shall revive a cause of action once barred. **Leg.H.** Enacted 1872. Amended Stats 1947 ch 1108 §1; Stats 1955 ch 417 §1.

§360.5. Waivers

No waiver shall bar a defense to any action that the action was not commenced within the time limited by this title unless the waiver is in writing and signed by the person obligated. No waiver executed prior to the expiration of the time limited for the commencement of the action by this title shall be effective for a period exceeding four years from the date of expiration of the time limited for commencement of the action by this title and no waiver executed after the expiration of such time shall be effective for a period exceeding four years from the date thereof, but any such waiver may be renewed for a further period of not exceeding four years from the expiration of the immediately preceding waiver. Such waivers may be made successively. The provisions of this section shall not be applicable to any acknowledgment, promise or any form of waiver which is in writing and signed by the person obligated and given to any county to secure repayment of indigent aid or the repayment of moneys fraudulently or illegally obtained from the county. **Leg.H.** Added Stats 1951 ch 1106 §1. Amended Stats 1953 ch 655 §1.

§361. Limitation laws of other states, effect of

When a cause of action has arisen in another state, or in a foreign country, and by the laws thereof an action thereon cannot there be maintained against a person by reason of the lapse of time, an action thereon shall not be maintained against him in this state, except in favor of one who has been a citizen of this state, and who has held the cause of action from the time it accrued. **Leg.H.** Enacted 1872.

§362. Existing causes of action not affected

This title does not extend to actions already commenced, nor to cases where the time prescribed in any existing statute for acquiring a right or barring a remedy has fully run, but the laws now in force are applicable to such actions and cases, and are repealed subject to the provisions of this section. **Leg.H.** Enacted 1872.

§363. Word "action" construed, how

The word "action" as used in this title is to be construed, whenever it is necessary so to do, as including a special proceeding of a civil nature. **Leg.H.** Enacted 1872.

CHAPTER 5
THE COMMENCEMENT OF ACTIONS BASED UPON PROFESSIONAL NEGLIGENCE

Notice required as condition precedent to bringing action. §364.
Failure to comply. §365.

§364. Notice required as condition precedent to bringing action

(a) No action based upon the health care provider's professional negligence may be commenced unless the defendant has been given at least 90 days' prior notice of the intention to commence the action.

(b) No particular form of notice is required, but it shall notify the defendant of the legal basis of the claim and the type of loss sustained, including with specificity the nature of the injuries suffered.

(c) The notice may be served in the manner prescribed in Chapter 5 (commencing with Section 1010) of Title 14 of Part 2.

(d) If the notice is served within 90 days of the expiration of the applicable statute of limitations, the time for the commencement of the action shall be extended 90 days from the service of the notice.

(e) The provisions of this section shall not be applicable with respect to any defendant whose name is unknown to the plaintiff at the time of filing the complaint and who is identified therein by a fictitious name, as provided in Section 474.

(f) For the purposes of this section:

(1) "Health care provider" means any person licensed or certified pursuant to Division 2 (commencing with Section 500) of the Business and Professions Code, or licensed pursuant to the Osteopathic Initiative Act, or the Chiropractic Initiative Act, or licensed pursuant to Chapter 2.5 (commencing with Section 1440) of Division 2 of the Health and Safety Code; and any clinic, health dispensary, or health facility, licensed pursuant to Division 2 (commencing with Section 1200) of the Health and Safety Code. "Health care provider" includes the legal representatives of a health care provider;

(2) "Professional negligence" means negligent act or omission to act by a health care provider in the rendering of professional services, which act or omission is the proximate cause of a personal injury or wrongful death, provided that such services are within the scope of services for which the provider is licensed and which are not within any restriction imposed by the licensing agency or licensed hospital. **Leg.H.** Added Stats 1975 2nd Ex Sess ch 1 §25.5. Amended Stats 1975 2nd Ex Sess ch 2 §1.193, effective September 24, 1975, operative December 12, 1975.

§364.1. [Section repealed 2006]

Leg.H. Added Stats 1993 ch 1267 §49 (SB 916). Repealed Stats 2005 ch 674 §20 (SB 231), effective January 1, 2006. The repealed section related to transmittal of notice to Medical Board or Board of Podiatric Medicine.

§365. Failure to comply

Failure to comply with this chapter shall not invalidate any proceedings of any court of this state, nor shall it affect the jurisdiction of the court to render a judgment therein. However, failure to comply with such provisions by any attorney at law shall be grounds for professional discipline and the State Bar of California shall investigate and take appropriate action in any such cases brought to its attention. **Leg.H.** Added Stats 1975 2nd Ex Sess ch 1 §25.5.

CHAPTER 6
TIME OF COMMENCEMENT OF ACTION AFTER PERSON'S DEATH

Death of person entitled to bring action before expiration of limitations period. §366.1.

Death of person against whom action may be brought before expiration of limitations period. §366.2.

Statute of limitation on promise of decedent. §366.3.

§366.1. Death of person entitled to bring action before expiration of limitations period

If a person entitled to bring an action dies before the expiration of the applicable limitations period, and the cause of action survives, an action may be commenced before the expiration of the later of the following times:

(a) Six months after the person's death.

(b) The limitations period that would have been applicable if the person had not died. **Leg.H.** Added Stats 1992 ch 178 §8 (SB 1496).

§366.2. Death of person against whom action may be brought before expiration of limitations period

(a) If a person against whom an action may be brought on a liability of the person, whether arising in contract, tort, or otherwise, and whether accrued or not accrued, dies before the expiration of the applicable limitations period, and the cause of action survives, an action may be commenced within one year after the date of death, and the limitations period that would have been applicable does not apply.

(b) The limitations period provided in this section for commencement of an action shall not be tolled or extended for any reason except as provided in any of the following, where applicable:

(1) Sections 12, 12a, and 12b of this code.

(2) Part 4 (commencing with Section 9000) of Division 7 of the Probate Code (creditor claims in administration of estates of decedents).

(3) Part 8 (commencing with Section 19000) of Division 9 of the Probate Code (payment of claims, debts, and expenses from revocable trust of deceased settlor).

(4) Former Part 3 (commencing with Section 21300) of Division 11 of the Probate Code (no contest clauses), as that part read prior to its repeal by Chapter 174 of the Statutes of 2008.

(c) This section applies to actions brought on liabilities of persons dying on or after January 1, 1993. **Leg.H.** Added Stats 1992 ch 178 §8 (SB 1496). Amended Stats 1993 ch 151 §2 (AB 1704), effective July 16, 1993; Stats 1994 ch 40 §1 (AB 797), effective April 19, 1994, operative January 1, 1995; Stats 1996 ch 862 §1 (AB 2751); Stats 1998 ch 581 §1 (AB 2801); Stats 2006 ch 221 §1 (AB 2864), effective January 1, 2007; Stats 2009 ch 348 §2 (SB 308), effective January 1, 2010.

§366.3. Statute of limitation on promise of decedent

(a) If a person has a claim that arises from a promise or agreement with a decedent to distribution from an estate or trust or under another instrument, whether the promise or agreement was made orally or in writing, an action to enforce the claim to distribution may be commenced within one year after the date of death, and the limitations period that would have been applicable does not apply.

(b) The limitations period provided in this section for commencement of an action shall not be tolled or extended for any reason except as provided in Sections 12, 12a, and 12b of this code, and former Part 3 (commencing with Section 21300) of Division 11 of the Probate Code, as that part read prior to its repeal by Chapter 174 of the Statutes of 2008.

(c) This section applies to actions brought on claims concerning persons dying on or after the effective date of this section. **Leg.H.** Added Stats 2000 ch 17 §1 (AB 1491). Amended Stats 2006 ch 221 §2 (AB 2864), effective January 1, 2007; Stats 2009 ch 348 §3 (SB 308), effective January 1, 2010.

TITLE 3
OF THE PARTIES TO CIVIL ACTIONS

Chapter 1. General Provisions.
Chapter 2. Married Person.
Chapter 3. Disability of Party.
Chapter 4. Effect of Death.
Chapter 5. Permissive Joinder.
Chapter 6. Interpleader.
Chapter 7. Intervention.
Chapter 8. Compulsory Joinder.

CHAPTER 1
GENERAL PROVISIONS

Real party in interest requirement. §367.
Confidentiality requirements for protected party in civil proceeding. §367.3.
Remote appearance permitted [Repealed January 1, 2027]. § 367.75.
Definitions [Repealed January 1, 2027]. § 367.76.
Report on use of remote technology in civil actions by trial courts [Repealed January 1, 2027]. § 367.8.
Remote court proceeding. § 367.10.
Assignment of thing in action not to prejudice defense. §368.
Effect of transfer of interest. §368.5.
Persons who may sue without joining persons for whose benefit action is prosecuted. §369.
Partnerships and associations. §369.5.

§367. Real party in interest requirement

Every action must be prosecuted in the name of the real party in interest, except as otherwise provided by statute. **Leg.H.** Enacted 1872. Amended Code Amdts 1880 ch 68 §1; Stats 1976 ch 595 §1; Stats 1992 ch 178 §10 (SB 1496).

§367.3. Confidentiality requirements for protected party in civil proceeding

(a) For purposes of this section, the following definitions apply:

(1) "Identifying characteristics" means the name or any part thereof, address or any part thereof, city or unincorporated area of residence, age, marital status, relationship to other parties, and race or ethnic background, telephone number, email address, social media profiles, online identifiers, contact information, or any other information, including images of the protected person, from which the protected person's identity can be discerned.

(2) "Online identifiers" means any personally identifying information or signifiers that would tie an individual to a particular electronic service, device, or internet application, website, or platform account, including, access names, access codes, account names, aliases, avatars, credentials, gamer tags, display names, handles, login names, member names, online identities, pseudonyms, screen names, user accounts, user identifications, usernames, Uniform Resource Locators (URLs), domain names, Internet Protocol (IP) addresses, and media access control (MAC) addresses.

(3) "Protected person" means a person who is an active participant in the address confidentiality program created pursuant to Chapter 3.1 (commencing with Section 6205) of Division 7 of Title 1 of the Government Code.

(b)(1) A protected person who is a party in a civil proceeding may proceed using a pseudonym, either John Doe, Jane Doe, or Doe, for the true name of the protected person and may exclude or redact from all pleadings and documents filed in the action other identifying characteristics of the protected person. A protected person who proceeds using a pseudonym as provided in this section shall file with the court and serve upon all other parties to the proceeding a confidential information form for this purpose that includes the protected person's name and other identifying characteristics being excluded or redacted. The court shall keep the confidential information form confidential.

(2) In cases where a protected person proceeds using a pseudonym under this section, the following provisions shall apply, subject to sanction for an intentional violation:

(A) Except as provided in subparagraph (B), all parties and their agents and attorneys shall use the pseudonym in all pleadings, discovery requests or discovery motion documents, and other documents filed or served in the action, and at hearings, trial, and other court proceedings that are open to the public.

(B) A party seeking discovery in which the true name of the protected person and identifying information must be divulged for the purposes of fair and reasonable discovery, may use the true name of the protected person and identifying information for purposes of that discovery. The discovery request and all information collected through the discovery process shall not be made public and, if filed in court, shall be subject to subparagraph (C).

(C)(i) A party filing a pleading, discovery document, or other document in the action shall exclude or redact any identifying characteristics of the protected person from the pleading, discovery document, or other document, except for a confidential information form filed pursuant to this subdivision.

(ii) A party excluding or redacting identifying characteristics shall file with the court and serve upon all other parties a confidential information form that includes the protected person's name and other identifying characteristics being excluded or redacted. The court shall keep the confidential information form confidential.

(D) Following final disposition of the proceedings a party in possession of any pleading, discovery document, or other document containing confidential information of the protected person obtained in the course of the action shall treat the documents as a nonpublic consumer record in accordance with Section 1798.81 of the Civil Code, subject to penalty for violations of that section.

(E) If the protected person is a minor dependent or minor ward of the state, the minor's parent, guardian, or attorney shall inform the minor's social worker or probation officer of the minor's participation in the action. The social worker or probation officer shall keep this information confidential.

(3) The responsibility to exclude or redact identifying characteristics of the protected person from documents filed with the court rests solely with the parties and their attorneys. This section does not require the court to review pleadings or other papers for compliance.

(4) The court, on motion of the protected person, may order a record or part of a record to be filed under seal in accordance with Rules 2.550 and 2.551 of the California Rules of Court, as those rules may be amended.

(c) In an action filed under this section, the plaintiff shall state in the caption of the complaint "ACTION BASED ON CODE OF CIVIL PROCEDURE SECTION 367.3."

(d) This section does not alter or negate any rights, obligations, or immunities of an interactive service provider under Section 230 of Title 47 of the United States Code. This section does not limit or preclude a plaintiff from securing or recovering any other available remedy.

(e) The Judicial Council shall coordinate with the Secretary of State to adopt or revise as appropriate rules and forms to implement this section, on or before January 1, 2021.

(f) The provisions of this section are severable. If any provision of this section or its application is held invalid, that invalidity shall not affect other provisions or applications that can be given effect without the invalid provision or application. **Leg.H.** Added Stats 2019 ch 439 §1 (AB 800), effective January 1, 2020.

§367.5. Telephonic appearances; Exceptions; Adoption of rules [Repealed]

Leg.H. Added Stats 2007 ch 268 §1 (AB 500), effective January 1, 2008. Repealed Stats 2022 ch 979 §1 (SB 233), effective January 1, 2023.

§367.6. Fees to be paid for telephone appearances; Waiver of fees; Conditions [Repealed]

Leg.H. Added Stats 2010 ch 720 §3 (SB 857), effective October 19, 2010, inoperative July 1, 2013, repealed January 1, 2014. Amended Stats 2012 ch 41 §1 (SB 1021), effective June 27, 2012. Repealed Stats 2022 ch 979 §2 (SB 233), effective January 1, 2023.

Prior Law: Former CCP §367.6, similar to the present section, was added Stats 2010 ch 720 §4 (SB 857), effective October 19, 2010, to become operative July 1, 2013, and repealed Stats 2012 ch 41 §2, effective June 27, 2012.

§ 367.75. Remote appearance permitted [Repealed January 1, 2027]

(a)(1) Except as provided in subdivisions (b) and (d), in civil cases, when a party has provided notice to the court and all other parties that it intends to appear remotely, a party may appear remotely and the court may conduct conferences, hearings, and proceedings, in whole or in part, through the use of remote technology.

(2) This section does not apply to any of the following type of proceedings:

(A) Any proceeding in matters identified in paragraph (1) of subdivision (a) of Section 367.76.

(B) A juvenile justice proceeding covered by Section 679.5 of the Welfare and Institutions Code.

(b) Except as otherwise provided by law, the court may require a party or witness to appear in person at a conference, hearing, or proceeding described in subdivision (a), or under subdivisions (e) and (h), if any of the following conditions are present:

(1) The court with jurisdiction over the case does not have the technology necessary to conduct the conference, hearing, or proceeding remotely.

(2) Although the court has the requisite technology, the quality of the technology or audibility at a conference, hearing, or proceeding prevents the effective management or resolution of the conference, hearing, or proceeding.

(3) The court determines on a hearing-by-hearing basis that an in-person appearance would materially assist in the determination of the conference, hearing, or proceeding or in the effective management or resolution of the particular case.

(4) The quality of the technology or audibility at a conference, hearing, or proceeding inhibits the court reporter's ability to accurately prepare a transcript of the conference, hearing, or proceeding.

(5) The quality of the technology or audibility at a conference, hearing, or proceeding prevents an attorney from being able to provide effective representation to the attorney's client.

(6) The quality of the technology or audibility at a conference, hearing, or proceeding inhibits a court interpreter's ability to provide language access to a court user or authorized individual.

(c) Notwithstanding paragraph (3) of subdivision (b), an expert witness may appear remotely absent good cause to compel in-person testimony.

(d)(1) Except as otherwise provided by law and subject to the limitations of subdivision (b), upon its own motion or the motion of any party, the court may conduct a trial or evidentiary hearing, in whole or in part, through the use of remote technology, absent a showing by the opposing party as to why a remote appearance or testimony should not be allowed.

(2)(A) Except as provided in Section 269 of the Code of Civil Procedure and Section 69957 of the Government Code, if the court conducts a trial, in whole or in part, through the use of remote technology, the official reporter or official reporter pro tempore shall be physically present in the courtroom.

(B) If the court conducts a trial, in whole or in part, through the use of remote technology, upon request, the court interpreter shall be physically present in the courtroom.

(e)(1) Before the court with jurisdiction over the case may proceed with a remote conference, hearing, proceeding, or trial, the court shall have a process for a party, witness, official reporter, official reporter pro tempore, court interpreter, or other court personnel to alert the judicial officer of technology or audibility issues that arise during the conference, hearing, proceeding, or trial.

(2) The court shall require that a remote appearance by a party or witness have the necessary privacy and security appropriate for the conference, hearing, proceeding, or trial.

(3) The court shall inform all parties, particularly parties without legal representation, about the potential technological or audibility issues that could arise when using remote technology, which may require a delay of or halt the conference, hearing, proceeding, or trial. The court shall make information available to self-represented parties regarding the options for appearing in person and through the use of remote technology.

(f) The court shall not require a party to appear through the use of remote technology. If the court permits an appearance through remote technology, the court must ensure that technology in the courtroom enables all parties, whether appearing remotely or in person, to fully participate in the conference, hearing, or proceeding.

(g) A self-represented party may appear remotely in a conference, hearing, or proceeding conducted through the use of remote technology only if they agree to do so.

(h) Any juvenile dependency proceeding may be conducted in whole or in part through the use of remote technology subject to the following:

(1) Any person authorized to be present may request to appear remotely.

(2)(A) Any party to the proceeding may request that the court compel the physical presence of a witness or party. A witness, including a party providing testimony, may appear through remote technology only with the consent of all parties, **except as provided in subparagraph (B),** and if the witness has access to the appropriate technology.

(B) A parent, child, nonminor dependent, or Indian tribe as defined in Section 224.1 of the Welfare and Institutions Code, may utilize remote technology for the appearance of an expert witness without the consent of all parties.

(3) A court shall not require a party to appear through the use of remote technology.

(4) The confidentiality requirements that apply to an in-person juvenile dependency proceeding shall apply to a juvenile dependency proceeding conducted through the use of remote technology.

(i)(1) Notwithstanding Section 8613.5 of the Family Code, in an adoption proceeding under Division 13 (commencing with Section 8500) of the Family Code, the court may conduct an adoption finalization hearing, in whole or in part, through the use of remote technology, without the court finding that it is impossible or impracticable for either prospective adoptive parent to make the appearance in person.

(2) A court shall not require a party to appear through the use of remote technology.

(3) The confidentiality and privacy requirements that apply to an in-person adoption finalization hearing, including, but not limited to, the requirements in Section 8611 of the Family Code, apply to an adoption finalization hearing conducted through the use of remote technology.

(j) For purposes of this section, a party includes a nonparty subject to Chapter 6 of Title 4 of Part 4 (commencing with Section 2020.010).

(k) Subject to the limitations in subdivision (b), this section is not intended to prohibit the use of appearances through the use of remote technology when stipulated by attorneys for represented parties.

(*l*) Consistent with its constitutional rulemaking authority, the Judicial Council shall adopt rules to implement the policies and provisions in this section to promote statewide consistency, including, but not limited to, the following procedures:

(1) A deadline by which a party must notify the court and the other parties of their request to appear remotely.

(2) Procedures and standards for a judicial officer to determine when a conference, hearing, or proceeding may be conducted through the use of remote technology. The procedures and standards shall require that a judicial officer give consideration to the limited access to technology or transportation that a party or witness might have.

(m) This section shall remain in effect only until January 1, 2027, and as of that date is repealed. **Leg.H.** Added Stats 2021 ch 214 §5 (SB 241), effective January 1, 2022, repealed July 1, 2023. Amended Stats 2023 ch 34 §3 (SB 133), effective June 30, 2023, repealed January 1, 2026; Stats 2024 ch 51 §2 (AB 170), effective July 2, 2024, repealed January 1, 2027; Stats 2024 ch 965 §1 (AB 2484), effective January 1, 2025, repealed January 1, 2027.

§ 367.76. Definitions [Repealed January 1, 2027]

(a)(1) This section applies to proceedings in the following matters:

(A) Judicial commitments under Part 2 (commencing with Section 6250) of Division 6 of the Welfare and Institutions Code, except for delinquency proceedings.

(B) Involuntary treatment and conservatorships of gravely disabled persons under Chapter 1 (commencing with Section 5000), Chapter 2 (commencing with Section 5150), and Chapter 3 (commencing with Section 5350) of Part 1 of Division 5 of the Welfare and Institutions Code, including Murphy conservatorships.

(C) Contempt proceedings under Title 5 (commencing with Section 1209) of Part 3 of this code.

(D) Mentally disordered offender proceedings under Article 4 (commencing with Section 2960) of Chapter 7 of Title 1 of Part 3 of the Penal Code.

(E) Commitment proceedings under Section 1026, et seq. of the Penal Code.

(F) Competency proceedings under Chapter 6 (commencing with Section 1367) of Title 10 of Part 2 of the Penal Code.

(G) Placement and revocation proceedings pursuant to Section 1600 et seq. of the Penal Code.

(H) Involuntary medication and treatment hearings for individuals committed or awaiting admission to a State Department of State Hospitals facility as described in Section 4100 of the Welfare and Institutions Code.

(2) This section does not apply to proceedings in matters brought pursuant to Sections 601 and 602 of the Welfare and Institutions Code.

(b) For the purposes of this section, the following definitions apply:

(1) "Person" means the person subject to any proceeding in matters described in paragraph (1) of subdivision (a).

(2) "Proceeding" or "proceedings" includes, but is not limited to, all hearings, conferences, and trials in matters described in paragraph (1) of subdivision (a).

(3) "Remote technology" means technology that provides for the two-way transmission of video and audio signals except that audio signals alone may be permitted where specifically authorized by law. Remote technology shall include, but not be limited to, a computer, tablet, telephone, cellular telephone, or other electronic or communications device. Notwithstanding the foregoing and subject to subdivision (h), the person subject to the proceeding, in consultation with counsel if represented, may, at their request, participate through audio-only technology.

(c) Proceedings in matters arising under subdivision (a) may be conducted through the use of remote technology subject to the following:

(1) A person has the right to be physically present for all proceedings and shall not be required to appear through the use of remote technology.

(2) A person may waive their right to be physically present and may elect to appear remotely.

(3) Except as provided in subdivisions (d), (e), and (h), a party, counsel for a party, or witness may appear through the use of remote technology.

(4) The confidentiality requirements that apply to inperson proceedings shall apply with equal force and effect when conducted through the use of remote technology.

(d) If the person is physically present in court the following shall apply:

(1) Absent exceptional circumstances and except as provided in paragraphs (3) and (4), counsel for the person, counsel for the other party or parties, the other party or parties, and the judicial officer shall be physically present in the courtroom.

(2) Except as provided in paragraphs (3) and (4) and paragraph (3) of subdivision (b) of Section 1370 of the Penal Code, absent a waiver by the person or a finding of good cause by the court, any witness the other party or parties calls shall be physically present in the courtroom. In determining whether good cause exists to excuse the physical presence of a witness, the court shall consider the distance the witness must travel, the nature of the testimony, and the nature of the proceeding.

(3) Notwithstanding paragraphs (1) and (2), counsel and witnesses for the State Department of Developmental Services shall not be required to be physically present in the courtroom absent a finding of good cause by the court.

(4) Notwithstanding paragraphs (1) and (2), counsel and witnesses for the State Department of State Hospitals shall not be required to be physically present in the courtroom in any nonjury trial matters or proceedings described in paragraph (1) of subdivision (a) absent a finding of good cause by the court.

(e) Notwithstanding any other law, unless good cause exists, a court shall not compel the physical presence of the person who is a patient in a State Department of State Hospitals or State Department of Developmental Services facility or other inpatient or outpatient treatment facility absent consent of the person in consultation with counsel. In determining whether good cause exists to compel the physical presence of a patient, the court shall consider the nature of the hearing and whether requiring the physical presence of the patient would interfere with the person's program of treatment or be detrimental to their mental or physical health.

(f)(1) Until July 1, 2024, when the court conducts proceedings that will be reported by an official reporter or official reporter pro tempore, the reporter shall be physically present in the same room as the judicial officer except where the court finds that, as the result of unusual circumstances, this requirement would place extreme or undue hardship on the court or the litigants. For purposes of this paragraph, "unusual circumstances" means a work stoppage, a circumstance described in subdivision (a) of Section 68115 of the Government Code, an unforeseen emergency, court proceedings conducted in a remote court location to which a judicial officer is not regularly assigned to sit, or when a judicial officer has to travel to a location outside of a courthouse to conduct the proceeding.

(2) Beginning July 1, 2024, when the court conducts proceedings that will be reported by an official reporter or official reporter pro tempore, the reporter shall be physically present in the same room as the judicial officer if the court cannot provide the technology standards described in subdivision (o).

(g) If the court conducts a trial, in whole or in part, through the use of remote technology, upon request, the court interpreter shall be physically present in the courtroom.

(h)(1) If any of the following conditions are present and cannot be resolved, the court shall not permit any party, counsel, or witness to appear or participate in proceedings through the use of remote technology, and shall continue any proceeding being conducted with the use of remote technology:

(A) The court does not have the technology necessary to conduct the proceeding remotely.

(B) Although the court has the requisite technology, the quality of the technology or audibility at a proceeding prevents the effective management or resolution of the proceeding.

(C) The quality of the technology or audibility at a proceeding inhibits the court reporter's ability to accurately prepare and certify a transcript of the proceeding.

(D) The court reporter is unable to capture the verbatim record and certify a transcript of any proceeding that is conducted remotely, in whole or in part, to the same extent and in the same manner as if it were not conducted remotely.

(E) The quality of the technology or audibility at a proceeding inhibits the ability of the person to understand or participate in the proceeding.

(F) The quality of the technology or audibility at a proceeding inhibits counsel from being able to provide effective representation to the person.

(G) The court does not have the technology necessary for secure, confidential communication between counsel and the person.

(H) The quality of the technology or audibility at a proceeding inhibits a court interpreter's ability to provide language access, including to communicate and interpret directly with the person and the court during the proceedings.

(2) Except as provided in subdivision (e) or otherwise provided by law, the court may require a party or witness to appear in person at a proceeding if the court determines on a hearing-by-hearing basis that an inperson appearance would materially assist in the determination of the proceeding or resolution of the case. The court's determination shall be based on the individual case before the court and shall be entered into the minutes or otherwise made on the record. In making its determination, the court shall consider the request of the person, the nature of the proceedings, and whether requiring the physical presence of the person would disrupt the person's program of treatment or be detrimental to their mental or physical health.

(3) The court shall not continue proceedings beyond statutory time limits pursuant to this section absent a waiver by the person in consultation with counsel.

(i) Subject to the limitations in subdivision (h), this section is not intended to prohibit the use of appearances through the use of remote technology when stipulated by attorneys for represented parties.

(j) Before the court may conduct proceedings through the use of remote technology, the court shall have a process for a party, witness, official reporter, official reporter pro tempore, court interpreter, or other court personnel to alert the judicial officer of technology or audibility issues that arise during the proceedings.

(k) The court shall inform all parties, particularly parties without legal representation, about the potential technological or audibility issues that could arise when using remote technology, which may require a delay of or halt the proceedings. The court shall make information available to self-represented parties regarding the options for appearing in person and through the use of remote technology.

(*l*) A self-represented party may appear remotely in a proceeding conducted through the use of remote technology only if they agree to do so.

(m) For purposes of this section, a party includes a nonparty subject to Chapter 6 (commencing with Section 2020.010) of Title 4 of Part 4.

(n) Consistent with its constitutional rulemaking authority, the Judicial Council shall adopt such other rules and standards as are necessary to implement the policies and provisions of this section and the intent of the Legislature.

(o) By April 1, 2024, the Judicial Council shall adopt, and trial courts shall implement by July 1, 2024, minimum standards for the courtroom technology necessary to permit remote participation in proceedings subject to this section. Those standards shall include, but not be limited to, hard-wired or other reliable high-speed internet connections in the courtroom for the judicial officer and court reporter, and monitors, dedicated cameras, speakers, and microphones so the judicial officer, court reporter, and court interpreter can appropriately see and hear remote participants, as well as to ensure that remote participants can appropriately see and hear the judicial officer and other courtroom participants.

(p) Consistent with federal and California labor law, a trial court shall not retaliate or threaten to retaliate against an official reporter or an official reporter pro tempore who notifies the judicial officer that technology or audibility issues are impeding the creation of the verbatim record of a proceeding that includes participation through remote technology. This subdivision shall only apply to an official reporter and an official reporter pro tempore when they meet the definition of "trial court employee" under subdivision (*l*) of Section 71601 of the Government Code.

(q) This section shall remain in effect only until January 1, [1] **2027**, and as of that date is repealed. **Leg.H.** Added Stats 2023 ch 34 §4 (SB 133), effective June 30, 2023, repealed January 1, 2026. Amended Stats 2024 ch 51 §3 (AB 170), effective July 2, 2024, repealed January 1, 2027.

§ 367.76. 2024 Deletes. [1] 2026

§ 367.8. Report on use of remote technology in civil actions by trial courts [Repealed January 1, 2027]

(a) Each superior court shall report to the Judicial Council on or before October 1, 2023, and annually thereafter, and the Judicial Council shall report to the Legislature on or before December 31, 2023, and annually thereafter, to assess the impact of technology issues or problems affecting remote proceedings, as included under Sections 367.75 and 367.76 of this code, and Section 679.5 of the Welfare and Institutions Code, and all purchases and leases of technology or equipment to facilitate remote conferences, hearings, or proceedings. The report by each superior court and the Judicial Council shall specify all of the following for each annual reporting period:

(1) The number of proceedings conducted with the use of remote technology.

(2) Any superior court in which technology issues or problems occurred.

(3) The superior courts in which remote technology was used.

(4) The types of trial court conferences, hearings, or proceedings in which remote technology was used.

(5) The cost of purchasing, leasing, or upgrading remote technology.

(6) The type of technology and equipment purchased or leased.

(7) Any other information necessary to evaluate the use of remote proceedings by the courts.

(b) Each superior court shall report to the Judicial Council on or before October 1, 2025, and annually thereafter, and the Judicial Council shall report to the Legislature on or before December 31, 2025, and annually thereafter, the information identified in subdivision (a) to assess the impact of technology issues or problems affecting criminal remote proceedings, as included under Sections 977, 977.3, and 1043.5 of the Penal Code.

(c)(1) By October 1, 2025, and annually thereafter, the court executive officer of each superior court shall certify to the Judicial Council, in a form and manner determined by the Judicial Council, that each courtroom of the superior court in which the court is conducting a remote proceeding meets the minimum standards for courtroom technology required pursuant to subdivision (o) of Section 367.76 of this code, subdivision (j) of Section 977 of the Penal Code, or subdivision (n) of Section 679.5 of the Welfare and Institutions Code.

(2) By December 31, 2025, and annually thereafter, the Judicial Council shall report the information identified in paragraph (1) to the Legislature.

[1] **(d)** A report to be submitted to the Legislature pursuant to this section shall be submitted in compliance with Section 9795 of the Government Code.

(e) This section shall remain in effect only until January 1, 2027, and as of that date is repealed. Leg.H. Added Stats 2023 ch 34 §5 (SB 133), effective June 30, 2023. Amended Stats 2024 ch 51 §4 (AB 170), effective July 2, 2024, repealed January 1, 2027.

§ 367.8. 2024 Deletes. [1] (b)

Prior Law Former Code Civ Proc §367.8 similar to the present section, was added Stats 2021 ch 257 §4 (AB 177), effective September 23, 2021, repealed July 1, 2023.

§ 367.9. Working group for statewide framework for remote civil court proceedings that address equal and fair access to justice; Submission of recommendations [Repealed]

Leg.H. Added Stats 2021 ch 257 §5 (AB 177), effective September 23, 2021, repealed July 1, 2023.

§367.10. Remote court proceeding

Consistent with its constitutional rulemaking authority, the Judicial Council shall adopt rules that include standards for when a judicial officer, in limited situations and in the interest of justice, may preside over a remote court proceeding from a location other than a courtroom. **Leg.H.** Added Stats 2023 ch 34 §6 (SB 133), effective June 30, 2023.

Prior Law Former CCP §367.9, similar to present section, was added Stats 2021 ch 257 §5 (AB 177), effective September 23, 2021, repealed July 1, 2023.

§368. Assignment of thing in action not to prejudice defense

In the case of an assignment of a thing in action, the action by the assignee is without prejudice to any set-off, or other defense existing at the time of, or before, notice of the assignment; but this section does not apply to a negotiable promissory note or bill of exchange, transferred in good faith, and upon good consideration, before maturity. **Leg.H.** Enacted 1872.

§368.5. Effect of transfer of interest

An action or proceeding does not abate by the transfer of an interest in the action or proceeding or by any other transfer of an interest. The action or proceeding may be continued in the name of the original party, or the court may allow the person to whom the transfer is made to be substituted in the action or proceeding. **Leg.H.** Added Stats 1992 ch 178 §11 (SB 1496).

§369. Persons who may sue without joining persons for whose benefit action is prosecuted

(a) The following persons may sue without joining as parties the persons for whose benefit the action is prosecuted:

(1) A personal representative, as defined in subdivision (a) of Section 58 of the Probate Code.

(2) A trustee of an express trust.

(3) Except for a person upon whom a power of sale has been conferred pursuant to a deed of trust or mortgage, a person with whom, or in whose name, a contract is made for the benefit of another.

(4) Any other person expressly authorized by statute.

(b) Notwithstanding subdivision (a), a trustee upon whom a power of sale has been conferred pursuant to a deed of trust or mortgage may sue to exercise the trustee's powers and duties pursuant to Chapter 2 (commencing with Section 2920) of Title 14 of Part 4 of Division 3 of the Civil Code. **Leg.H.** Enacted 1872. Amended Stats 1988 ch 530 §2; Stats 1992 ch 178 §12 (SB 1496).

§369.5. Partnerships and associations

(a) A partnership or other unincorporated association, whether organized for profit or not, may sue and be sued in the name it has assumed or by which it is known.

(b) A member of the partnership or other unincorporated association may be joined as a party in an action against the unincorporated association. If service of process is made on the member as an individual, whether or not the member is also served as a person upon whom service is made on behalf of the unincorporated association, a judgment against the member based on the member's personal liability may be obtained in the action, whether the liability is joint, joint and several, or several. **Leg.H.** Added Stats 1992 ch 178 §13 (SB 1496).

CHAPTER 2
MARRIED PERSON

Married person as parties. §370.
Spouse may defend. §371.

§370. Married person as parties

A married person may be sued without his or her spouse being joined as a party, and may sue without his or her spouse being joined as a party in all actions. **Leg.H.** Enacted 1872. Amended Code Amdts 1873–74 ch 383 §37; Stats 1913 ch 130 §1; Stats 1921 ch 110 §1; Stats 1975 ch 1241 §2.

§371. Spouse may defend

If spouses are sued together, each may defend for his or her own right, but if one spouse neglects to defend, the other spouse may defend for that spouse's right also. **Leg.H.** Enacted 1872. Amended Stats 1975 ch 1241 §3; Stats 2016 ch 50 §15 (SB 1005), effective January 1, 2017.

2016 Note: For legislative intent, see the 2016 Note following CCP §17.

CHAPTER 3
DISABILITY OF PARTY

Minors and persons lacking legal capacity to make decisions; Manner of appearing; Appointment of guardian ad litem; Handling of moneys recovered. §372.
Appointment of guardian ad litem under pseudonym. §372.5.
Manner of appointment of guardian ad litem. §373.
Appointment of guardian ad litem where unascertained persons of designated class are interested in property. §373.5.
Minor accompanied by guardian to appear without counsel. §374.
Court where matters are heard. §374.5.
Disability of party. §375.
Action by parents of child for injuries. §376.

§372. Minors and persons lacking legal capacity to make decisions; Manner of appearing; Appointment of guardian ad litem; Handling of moneys recovered

(a)(1) When a minor, a person who lacks legal capacity to make decisions, or a person for whom a conservator has been appointed is a party, that person shall appear either by a guardian or conservator of the estate or by a guardian ad litem appointed by the court in which the action or proceeding is pending, or by a judge thereof, in each case.

(2)(A) A guardian ad litem may be appointed in any case when it is deemed by the court in which the action or proceeding is prosecuted, or by a judge thereof, expedient to appoint a guardian ad litem to represent the minor, person who lacks legal capacity to make decisions, or person for whom a conservator has been appointed, notwithstanding that the person may have a guardian or conservator of the estate and may have appeared by the guardian or conservator of the estate.

(B) If application is made for appointment of a guardian ad litem for a person described in paragraph (1), and that person has a guardian or conservator of the estate, the application may be granted only if all of the following occur:

(i) The applicant gives notice and a copy of the application to the guardian or conservator of the estate upon filing the application.

(ii) The application discloses the existence of a guardian or conservator of the estate.

(iii) The application sets forth the reasons why the guardian or conservator of the estate is inadequate to represent the interests of the proposed ward in the action.

(C) The guardian or conservator of the estate shall have five court days from receiving notice of the application to file any opposition to the application.

(3) The guardian or conservator of the estate or guardian ad litem so appearing for any minor, person who lacks legal capacity to make decisions, or person for whom a conservator has been appointed shall have power, with the approval of the court in which the action or proceeding is pending, to compromise the same, to agree to the order or judgment to be entered therein for or against the ward or conservatee, and to satisfy any judgment or order in favor of the ward or conservatee or release or discharge any claim of the ward or conservatee pursuant to that compromise. Money or other property to be paid or delivered pursuant to the order or judgment for the benefit of a minor, person lacking legal capacity to make decisions, or person for whom a conservator has been appointed shall be paid and delivered as provided in Chapter 4 (commencing with Section 3600) of Part 8 of Division 4 of the Probate Code.

(4) Where reference is made in this chapter to "a person who lacks legal capacity to make decisions," the reference shall be deemed to include all of the following:

(A) A person who lacks capacity to understand the nature or consequences of the action or proceeding.

(B) A person who lacks capacity to assist the person's attorney in the preparation of the case.

(C) A person for whom a conservator may be appointed pursuant to Section 1801 of the Probate Code.

(5) Nothing in this section, or in any other provision of this code, the Civil Code, the Family Code, or the Probate Code is intended by the Legislature to prohibit a minor from exercising an intelligent and knowing waiver of the minor's constitutional rights in a proceeding under the Juvenile Court Law (Chapter 2 (commencing with Section 200) of Part 1 of Division 2 of the Welfare and Institutions Code).

(b)(1) Notwithstanding subdivision (a), a minor 12 years of age or older may appear in court without a guardian, counsel, or guardian ad litem, for the purpose of requesting or opposing a request for any of the following:

(A) An injunction or temporary restraining order or both to prohibit harassment pursuant to Section 527.6.

(B) An injunction or temporary restraining order or both against violence or a credible threat of violence in the workplace pursuant to Section 527.8.

(C) A protective order pursuant to Division 10 (commencing with Section 6200) of the Family Code.

(D) A protective order pursuant to Sections 7710 and 7720 of the Family Code.

The court may, either upon motion or in its own discretion, and after considering reasonable objections by the minor to the appointment of specific individuals, appoint a guardian ad litem to assist the minor in obtaining or opposing the order, provided that the appointment of the guardian ad litem does not delay the issuance or denial of the order being sought. In making the determination concerning the appointment of a particular guardian ad litem, the court shall consider whether the minor and the guardian have divergent interests.

(2) For purposes of this subdivision only, upon the issuance of an order pursuant to paragraph (1), if the minor initially appeared in court seeking an order without a guardian or guardian ad litem, and if the minor is residing with a parent or guardian, the court shall send a copy of the order to at least one parent or guardian designated by the minor, unless, in the discretion of the court, notification of a parent or guardian would be contrary to the best interest of the minor. The court is not required to send the order to more than one parent or guardian.

(c)(1) Notwithstanding subdivision (a), a minor may appear in court without a guardian ad litem in the following proceedings if the minor is a parent of the child who is the subject of the proceedings:

(A) Family court proceedings pursuant to Part 3 (commencing with Section 7600) of Division 12 of the Family Code.

(B) Dependency proceedings pursuant to Chapter 2 (commencing with Section 200) of Part 1 of Division 2 of the Welfare and Institutions Code.

(C) Guardianship proceedings for a minor child pursuant to Part 2 (commencing with Section 1500) of Division 4 of the Probate Code.

(D) Any other proceedings concerning child custody, visitation, or support.

(2) If the court finds that the minor parent is unable to understand the nature of the proceedings or to assist counsel in preparing the case, the court shall, upon its own motion or upon a motion by the minor parent or the minor parent's counsel, appoint a guardian ad litem.

(d) Before a court appoints a guardian ad litem pursuant to this chapter, a proposed guardian ad litem shall disclose both of the following to the court and all parties to the action or proceeding:

(1) Any known actual or potential conflicts of interest that would or might arise from the appointment.

(2) Any familial or affiliate relationship the proposed guardian ad litem has with any of the parties.

(e) If a guardian ad litem becomes aware that a potential conflict of interest has become an actual conflict of interest or that a new potential or actual conflict of interest exists, the guardian ad litem shall promptly disclose the conflict of interest to the court. **Leg.H.** Enacted 1872. Amended Code Amdts 1873–74 ch 383 §38; Code Amdts 1880 ch 68 §2; Stats 1913 ch 202 §1; Stats 1933 ch 744 §1; Stats 1939 ch 313 §1; Stats 1951 ch 1737 §43, operative January 1, 1952; Stats 1953 ch 1315 §1; Stats 1961 ch 721 §1; Stats 1963 ch 127 §4; Stats 1967 ch 1259 §1; Stats 1979 ch 730 §19, operative January 1, 1981; Stats 1994 ch 1269 §2 (AB 2208); Stats 1996 ch 727 §2 (AB 2155); Stats 1998 ch 706 §1 (SB 326), effective September 22, 1998; Stats 2008 ch 181 §1 (SB 1612), effective January 1,

2009; Stats 2014 ch 144 §5 (AB 1847), effective January 1, 2015; Stats 2022 ch 843 §1 (SB 1279), effective January 1, 2023.

§372.5. Appointment of guardian ad litem under pseudonym

(a) The court may appoint a guardian ad litem under a pseudonym pursuant to the requirements of this section.

(b) A person who applies for appointment as a guardian ad litem under a pseudonym shall, at the same time that the application is filed, file an ex parte request for leave to appear under a pseudonym. The ex parte request shall allege facts and circumstances establishing the guardian ad litem's overriding interest in preserving his or her anonymity.

(c) To permit an applicant for appointment as a guardian ad litem to appear under pseudonym, the court shall make each of the following findings:

(1) That the applicant has an overriding interest in preserving anonymity that supports permitting the applicant to appear under a pseudonym.

(2) That there is a substantial probability that the applicant's interest in preserving anonymity will be prejudiced if the applicant is not permitted to appear under a pseudonym.

(3) That permitting the applicant to appear under a pseudonym is narrowly tailored to serve the applicant's interest in preserving anonymity without unduly prejudicing the public's right of access or the ability of the other parties to prosecute, defend, or resolve the action.

(4) That there are no less restrictive means of protecting the applicant's interest in preserving his or her anonymity.

(d)(1) The court may make any further orders necessary to preserve the applicant's anonymity or to allow the other parties or financial institutions to know the applicant's identity to the extent necessary to prosecute, defend, or resolve the action.

(2) In addition to any other orders, the court may require a guardian ad litem who is permitted to appear under a pseudonym and is not represented by counsel to designate a mailing or electronic address for service of process and to consent to accept service of process under the pseudonym at that address for purposes of the action.

(e)(1) If a guardian ad litem is permitted to appear under a pseudonym, all court decisions, orders, petitions, and any documents filed with the court shall be written in a manner that protects the name and personal identifying information of the guardian ad litem from public disclosure, except to the extent the information is necessary for the parties to prosecute, defend, or resolve the action.

(2) For purposes of this subdivision, "personal identifying information" includes the guardian ad litem's name or any part thereof, his or her address or any part thereof, and the city or unincorporated area of the guardian ad litem's residence.

(f) The responsibility for excluding the name and personal identifying information of the guardian ad litem from documents filed with the court rests solely with the parties and their attorneys. This section does not require the court to review pleadings or other papers for compliance with this subdivision.

(g) After granting permission for a guardian ad litem to appear under a pseudonym pursuant to this section, the court shall retain discretion to reconsider its decision.

(h) This section does not affect the right of a plaintiff or petitioner to pursue litigation under a pseudonym in appropriate circumstances. **Leg.H.** Added Stats 2018 ch 817 §1 (AB 2185), effective January 1, 2019.

§373. Manner of appointment of guardian ad litem

When a guardian ad litem is appointed, he or she shall be appointed as follows:

(a) If the minor is the plaintiff the appointment must be made before the summons is issued, upon the application of the minor, if the minor is 14 years of age or older, or, if under that age, upon the application of a relative or friend of the minor.

(b) If the minor is the defendant, upon the application of the minor, if the minor is 14 years of age or older, and the minor applies within 10 days after the service of the summons, or, if under that age or if the minor neglects to apply, then upon the application of a relative or friend of the minor, or of any other party to the action, or by the court on its own motion.

(c) If the person lacking legal competence to make decisions is a party to an action or proceeding, upon the application of a relative or friend of the person lacking legal competence to make decisions, or of any other party to the action or proceeding, or by the court on its own motion. **Leg.H.** Enacted 1872. Amended Code Amdts 1880 ch 68 §3; Stats 1933 ch 744 §2; Stats 1971 ch 755 §1; Stats 1980 ch 676 §64; Stats 2014 ch 144 §6 (AB 1847), effective January 1, 2015.

§373.5. Appointment of guardian ad litem where unascertained persons of designated class are interested in property

If under the terms of a written instrument, or otherwise, a person or persons of a designated class who are not ascertained or who are not in being, or a person or persons who are unknown, may be or may become legally or equitably interested in any property, real or personal, the court in which any action, petition or proceeding of any kind relative to or affecting the property is pending, may, upon the representation of any party thereto, or of any person interested, appoint a suitable person to appear and act therein as guardian ad litem of the person or persons not ascertained, not in being, or who are unknown; and the judgment, order or decree in the proceedings, made after the appointment, shall be conclusive upon all persons for whom the guardian ad litem was appointed.

The guardian ad litem shall have power, with the approval of the court in which the action, petition or proceeding is pending, to compromise the same, to agree to the order or judgment to be entered therein for or against the persons for whom the guardian ad litem was appointed, and to satisfy any judgment or order in favor of the persons, or release, or discharge any claim of the persons pursuant to the compromise. The court shall have the same power with respect to the money or other property to be paid or delivered under such order or judgment as is provided in Section 372 of this code.

The reasonable expenses of the guardian ad litem, including compensation and counsel fees, shall be determined by the court and paid as it may order, either out of the property or by plaintiff or petitioner. If the expenses are to be paid by the plaintiff or petitioner, execution therefor may issue in the name of the guardian ad litem. **Leg.H.** Added Stats 1949 ch 511 §1. Amended Stats 1957 ch 976 §1; Stats 1961 ch 435 §1.

§374. Minor accompanied by guardian to appear without counsel

(a) A minor under 12 years of age, accompanied by a duly appointed and acting guardian ad litem, shall be permitted to appear in court without counsel for the limited purpose of requesting or opposing a request for (1) an injunction or temporary restraining order or both to prohibit harassment pursuant to Section 527.6, (2) an injunction or temporary restraining order or both against violence or a credible threat of violence in the workplace pursuant to Section 527.8, (3) a protective order pursuant to Division 10 (commencing with Section 6200) of the Family Code, or (4) a protective order pursuant to Sections 7710 and 7720 of the Family Code.

(b) In making the determination concerning appointment of a particular guardian ad litem for purposes of this section, the court shall consider whether the minor and the guardian have divergent interests.

(c) The Judicial Council shall adopt forms by July 1, 1999, to implement this section. The forms shall be designed to facilitate the appointment of the guardian ad litem for purposes of this section. **Leg.H.** Added Stats 1998 ch 706 §2 (SB 326), effective September 22, 1998.

Prior Law: Former CCP §374 was added Stats 1985 ch 874 §18, amended Stats 1986 ch 9 §6, effective February 25, 1986, repealed Stats 1992 ch 178 §16, amended Stats 1992 ch 1283 §1, and renumbered CCP §383 by Stats 1993 ch 151 §3, effective July 16, 1993.

Former CCP §374, similar to §383, was added Stats 1976 ch 595 §2, amended Stats 1979 ch 168 §1, Stats 1985 ch 233 §1, and repealed Stats 1985 ch 874 §17.

Former CCP §374 was enacted 1872 and repealed Stats 1967 ch 1231 §1.

§374.5. Court where matters are heard

A proceeding initiated by or brought against a minor for any of the injunctions or orders described in paragraph (1) of subdivision (b) of Section 372 or subdivision (a) of Section 374 shall be heard in the court assigned to hear those matters; except that, if the minor bringing the action or against whom the action is brought has previously been adjudged a dependent child or a ward of the juvenile court, the matter shall be heard in the juvenile court having jurisdiction over the minor. **Leg.H.** Added Stats 1998 ch 706 §3 (SB 326), effective September 22, 1998.

§375. Disability of party

An action or proceeding does not abate by the disability of a party. The court, on motion, shall allow the action or proceeding to be continued by or against the party's representative. **Leg.H.** Added Stats 1992 ch 178 §17 (SB 1496).

Prior Law: Former CCP §375 was enacted 1872 and repealed Stats 1967 ch 1231 §2.

§376. Action by parents of child for injuries

(a) The parents of a legitimate unmarried minor child, acting jointly, may maintain an action for injury to the child caused by the wrongful act or neglect of another. If either parent fails on demand to join as plaintiff in the action or is dead or cannot be found, then the other parent may maintain the action. The parent, if living, who does not join as plaintiff shall be joined as a defendant and, before trial or hearing of any question of fact, shall be served with summons either in the manner provided by law for the service of a summons in a civil action or by sending a copy of the summons and complaint by registered mail with proper postage prepaid addressed to that parent's last known address with request for a return receipt. If service is made by registered mail, the production of a return receipt purporting to be signed by the addressee creates a rebuttable presumption that the summons and complaint have been duly served. The presumption established by this section is a presumption affecting the burden of producing evidence. The respective rights of the parents to any award shall be determined by the court.

(b) A parent may maintain an action for such an injury to his or her illegitimate unmarried minor child if a guardian has not been appointed. Where a parent who does not have care, custody, or control of the child brings the action, the parent who has care, custody, or control of the child shall be served with the summons either in the manner provided by law for the serving of a summons in a civil action or by sending a copy of the summons and complaint by registered mail, with proper postage prepaid, addressed to the last known address of that parent, with request for a return receipt. If service is made by registered mail, the production of a return receipt purporting to be signed by the addressee creates a rebuttable presumption that the summons and complaint have been duly served. The presumption established by this section is a presumption affecting the burden of producing evidence. The respective rights of the parents to any award shall be determined by the court.

(c) The father of an illegitimate child who maintains an action under this section shall have acknowledged in writing prior to the child's injury, in the presence of a competent witness, that he is the father of the child, or, prior to the child's injury, have been judicially determined to be the father of the child.

(d) A parent of an illegitimate child who does not maintain an action under this section may be joined as a party thereto.

(e) A guardian may maintain an action for such an injury to his or her ward.

(f) An action under this section may be maintained against the person causing the injury. If any other person is responsible for the wrongful act or neglect, the action may also be maintained against the other person. The death of the child or ward does not abate the parents' or guardian's cause of action for the child's injury as to damages accruing before the child's death.

(g) In an action under this section, damages may be awarded that, under all of the circumstances of the case, may be just, except that:

(1) In an action maintained after the death of the child, the damages recoverable are as provided in Section 377.34.

(2) Where the person causing the injury is deceased, the damages recoverable in an action against the decedent's personal representative are as provided in Section 377.42.

(h) If an action arising out of the same wrongful act or neglect may be maintained pursuant to Section 377.60 for wrongful death of a child described in this section, the action authorized by this section may be consolidated therewith for trial as provided in Section 1048. **Leg.H.** Enacted 1872. Amended Code Amdts 1873–74 ch 383 §39; Stats 1939 ch 425 §1; Stats 1949 ch 1380 §3; Stats 1961 ch 657 §4; Stats 1969 ch 1611 §4; Stats 1975 ch 1241 §4; Stats 1992 ch 178 §18 (SB 1496).

§377. [Section repealed 1993]

Leg.H. Enacted 1872. Amended Code Amdts 1873–74 ch 383 §40; Stats 1935 ch 108 §1; Stats 1949 ch 1380 §4; Stats 1961 ch 567 §5; Stats 1968 ch 766 §1; Stats 1975 ch 334 §1, ch 1241 §5.5; Stats 1977 ch 792 §1; Stats 1983 ch 842 §12, operative January 1, 1985. Repealed Stats 1992 ch 178 §19 (SB 1496). See CCP §§377.20, 377.40, 377.60, 377.61, 377.62.

CHAPTER 4
EFFECT OF DEATH

Article 1. Definitions.
Article 2. Survival and Continuation.
Article 3. Decedent's Cause of Action.
Article 4. Cause of Action Against Decedent.
Article 5. Insured Claims.
Article 6. Wrongful Death.

ARTICLE 1
Definitions

"Beneficiary of the decedent's estate". §377.10.
"Decedent's successor in interest". §377.11.

§377.10. "Beneficiary of the decedent's estate"

For the purposes of this chapter, "beneficiary of the decedent's estate" means:

(a) If the decedent died leaving a will, the sole beneficiary or all of the beneficiaries who succeed to a cause of action, or to a particular item of property that is the subject of a cause of action, under the decedent's will.

(b) If the decedent died without leaving a will, the sole person or all of the persons who succeed to a cause of action, or to a particular item of property that is the subject of a cause of action, under Sections 6401 and 6402 of the Probate Code or, if the law of a sister state or foreign nation governs succession to the cause of action or particular item of property, under the law of the sister state or foreign nation. **Leg.H.** Added Stats 1992 ch 178 §20 (SB 1496).

§377.11. "Decedent's successor in interest"

For the purposes of this chapter, "decedent's successor in interest" means the beneficiary of the decedent's estate or other successor in interest who succeeds to a cause of action or to a particular item of the property that is the subject of a cause of action. **Leg.H.** Added Stats 1992 ch 178 §20 (SB 1496).

ARTICLE 2
Survival and Continuation

Survival of cause of action for or against decedent. §377.20.
Abatement. §377.21.
Assignability. §377.22.

§377.20. Survival of cause of action for or against decedent

(a) Except as otherwise provided by statute, a cause of action for or against a person is not lost by reason of the person's death, but survives subject to the applicable limitations period.

(b) This section applies even though a loss or damage occurs simultaneously with or after the death of a person who would have been liable if the person's death had not preceded or occurred simultaneously with the loss or damage. **Leg.H.** Added Stats 1992 ch 178 §20 (SB 1496).

§377.21. Abatement

A pending action or proceeding does not abate by the death of a party if the cause of action survives. **Leg.H.** Added Stats 1992 ch 178 §20 (SB 1496).

§377.22. Assignability

Nothing in this chapter shall be construed as affecting the assignability of causes of action. **Leg.H.** Added Stats 1992 ch 178 §20 (SB 1496).

ARTICLE 3
Decedent's Cause of Action

Who may commence action. §377.30.
Who may continue pending action. §377.31.
Affidavit or declaration by person commencing or continuing action as decedent's successor in interest. §377.32.
Court orders to ensure proper administration of justice. §377.33.
Damages recoverable; Restricted damages for pain, suffering, or disfigurement. §377.34.
Actions to which article applies. §377.35.

§377.30. Who may commence action

A cause of action that survives the death of the person entitled to commence an action or proceeding passes to the decedent's successor in interest, subject to Chapter 1 (commencing with Section 7000) of Part 1 of Division 7 of the Probate Code, and an action may be commenced by the decedent's personal representative or, if none, by the decedent's successor in interest. **Leg.H.** Added Stats 1992 ch 178 §20 (SB 1496).

§377.31. Who may continue pending action

On motion after the death of a person who commenced an action or proceeding, the court shall allow a pending action or proceeding that does not abate to be continued by the decedent's personal representative or, if none, by the decedent's successor in interest. **Leg.H.** Added Stats 1992 ch 178 §20 (SB 1496).

§377.32. Affidavit or declaration by person commencing or continuing action as decedent's successor in interest

(a) The person who seeks to commence an action or proceeding or to continue a pending action or proceeding as the decedent's successor in interest under this article, shall execute and file an affidavit or a declaration under penalty of perjury under the laws of this state stating all of the following:

(1) The decedent's name.

(2) The date and place of the decedent's death.

(3) "No proceeding is now pending in California for administration of the decedent's estate."

(4) If the decedent's estate was administered, a copy of the final order showing the distribution of the decedent's cause of action to the successor in interest.

(5) Either of the following, as appropriate, with facts in support thereof:

(A) "The affiant or declarant is the decedent's successor in interest (as defined in Section 377.11 of the California Code of Civil Procedure) and succeeds to the decedent's interest in the action or proceeding."

(B) "The affiant or declarant is authorized to act on behalf of the decedent's successor in interest (as defined in Section 377.11 of the California Code of Civil Procedure) with respect to the decedent's interest in the action or proceeding."

(6) "No other person has a superior right to commence the action or proceeding or to be substituted for the decedent in the pending action or proceeding."

(7) "The affiant or declarant affirms or declares under penalty of perjury under the laws of the State of California that the foregoing is true and correct."

(b) Where more than one person executes the affidavit or declaration under this section, the statements required by subdivision (a) shall be modified as appropriate to reflect that fact.

(c) A certified copy of the decedent's death certificate shall be attached to the affidavit or declaration. **Leg.H.** Added Stats 1992 ch 178 §20 (SB 1496).

§377.33. Court orders to ensure proper administration of justice

The court in which all action is commenced or continued under this article may make any order concerning parties that is appropriate to ensure proper administration of justice in the case, including appointment of the decedent's successor in interest as a special administrator or guardian ad litem. **Leg.H.** Added Stats 1992 ch 178 §20 (SB 1496).

§377.34. Damages recoverable; Restricted damages for pain, suffering, or disfigurement

(a) In an action or proceeding by a decedent's personal representative or successor in interest on the decedent's cause of action, the damages recoverable are limited to the loss or damage that the decedent sustained or incurred before death, including any penalties or punitive or exemplary damages that the decedent would have been entitled to recover had the decedent lived, and do not include damages for pain, suffering, or disfigurement.

(b) Notwithstanding subdivision (a), in an action or proceeding by a decedent's personal representative or successor in interest on the decedent's cause of action, the damages recoverable may include damages for pain, suffering, or disfigurement if the action or proceeding was granted a preference pursuant to Section 36 before January 1, 2022, or was filed on or after January 1, 2022, and before January 1, 2026.

(c) A plaintiff who recovers damages pursuant to subdivision (b) between January 1, 2022, and January 1, 2025, inclusive, shall, within 60 days after obtaining a judgment, consent judgment, or court-approved settlement agreement entitling the plaintiff to the damages, submit to the Judicial Council a copy of the judgment, consent judgment, or court-approved settlement agreement, along with a cover sheet detailing all of the following information:

(1) The date the action was filed.

(2) The date of the final disposition of the action.

(3) The amount and type of damages awarded, including economic damages and damages for pain, suffering, or disfigurement.

(d)(1) On or before January 1, 2025, the Judicial Council shall transmit to the Legislature a report detailing the information received pursuant to subdivision (c) for all judgments, consent judgments, or court-approved settlement agreements rendered from January 1, 2022, to July 31, 2024, inclusive, in which damages were recovered pursuant to subdivision (b). The report shall comply with Section 9795 of the Government Code.

(2) This subdivision shall become inoperative on January 1, 2029, pursuant to Section 10231.5 of the Government Code.

(e) Nothing in this section alters Section 3333.2 of the Civil Code.

(f) Nothing in this section affects claims brought pursuant to Chapter 11 (commencing with Section 15600) of Part 3 of Division 9 of the Welfare and Institutions Code. **Leg.H.** Added Stats 1992 ch 178 §20 (SB 1496). Amended Stats 2021 ch 448 §1 (SB 447), effective January 1, 2022; Stats 2023 ch 131 §18 (AB 1754), effective January 1, 2024.

§377.35. Actions to which article applies

On or after January 1, 1993, this article applies to the commencement of an action or proceeding the decedent was entitled to commence, and to the continuation of an action or proceeding commenced by the decedent, regardless of whether the decedent died before, on, or after January 1, 1993. **Leg.H.** Added Stats 1992 ch 178 §20 (SB 1496).

ARTICLE 4
Cause of Action Against Decedent

Persons against whom cause of action may be asserted. §377.40.
Continuation of pending action against decedent. §377.41.
Damages recoverable. §377.42.
Actions to which article applies. §377.43.

§377.40. Persons against whom cause of action may be asserted

Subject to Part 4 (commencing with Section 9000) of Division 7 of the Probate Code governing creditor claims, a cause of action against a decedent that survives may be asserted against the decedent's personal representative or, to the extent provided by statute, against the decedent's successor in interest. **Leg.H.** Added Stats 1992 ch 178 §20 (SB 1496).

§377.41. Continuation of pending action against decedent

On motion, the court shall allow a pending action or proceeding against the decedent that does not abate to be continued against the decedent's personal representative or, to the extent provided by statute, against the decedent's successor in interest, except that the court may not permit an action or proceeding to be continued against the personal representative unless proof of compliance with Part 4 (commencing with Section 9000) of Division 7 of the Probate Code governing creditor claims is first made. **Leg.H.** Added Stats 1992 ch 178 §20 (SB 1496).

§377.42. Damages recoverable

In an action or proceeding against a decedent's personal representative or, to the extent provided by statute, against the decedent's successor in interest, on a cause of action against the decedent, all damages are recoverable that might have been recovered against the decedent had the decedent lived except damages recoverable under Section 3294 of the Civil Code or other punitive or exemplary damages. **Leg.H.** Added Stats 1992 ch 178 §20 (SB 1496).

§377.43. Actions to which article applies

This article applies to the commencement on or after January 1, 1993, of an action or proceeding against the decedent's personal representative or successor in interest, or to the making of a motion on or after January 1, 1993, to continue a pending action or proceeding against the decedent's personal representative or successor in interest, regardless of whether the decedent died before, on, or after January 1, 1993. **Leg.H.** Added Stats 1992 ch 178 §20 (SB 1496).

ARTICLE 5
Insured Claims

Liability for which decedent was protected by insurance. §377.50.

§377.50. Liability for which decedent was protected by insurance

An action to establish the decedent's liability for which the decedent was protected by insurance may be commenced or continued against the decedent's estate as provided in Chapter 1 (commencing with Section 550) of Part 13 of Division 2 of the Probate Code. **Leg.H.** Added Stats 1992 ch 178 §20 (SB 1496).

ARTICLE 6
Wrongful Death

Persons who may assert cause of action. §377.60.
Damages recoverable. §377.61.
Joinder or consolidation of survival action. §377.62.

§377.60. Persons who may assert cause of action

A cause of action for the death of a person caused by the wrongful act or neglect of another may be asserted by any of the following persons or by the decedent's personal representative on their behalf:

(a) The decedent's surviving spouse, domestic partner, children, and issue of deceased children, or, if there is no surviving issue of the decedent, the persons, including the surviving spouse or domestic partner, who would be entitled to the property of the decedent by intestate succession. If the parents of the decedent would be entitled to bring an action under this subdivision, and the parents are deceased, then the legal guardians of the decedent, if any, may bring an action under this subdivision as if they were the decedent's parents.

(b)(1) Whether or not qualified under subdivision (a), if they were dependent on the decedent, the putative spouse, children of the putative spouse, stepchildren, parents, or the legal guardians of the decedent if the parents are deceased.

(2) As used in this subdivision, "putative spouse" means the surviving spouse of a void or voidable marriage who is found by the court to have believed in good faith that the marriage to the decedent was valid.

(c) A minor, whether or not qualified under subdivision (a) or (b), if, at the time of the decedent's death, the minor resided for the previous 180 days in the decedent's household and was dependent on the decedent for one-half or more of the minor's support.

(d) This section applies to any cause of action arising on or after January 1, 1993.

(e) The addition of this section by Chapter 178 of the Statutes of 1992 was not intended to adversely affect the standing of any party having standing under prior law, and the standing of parties governed by that version of this section as added by Chapter 178 of the Statutes of 1992 shall be the same as specified herein as amended by Chapter 563 of the Statutes of 1996.

(f)(1) For the purpose of this section, "domestic partner" means a person who, at the time of the decedent's death, was the domestic partner of the decedent in a registered domestic partnership established in accordance with subdivision (b) of Section 297 of the Family Code.

(2) Notwithstanding paragraph (1), for a death occurring prior to January 1, 2002, a person may maintain a cause of action pursuant to this section as a domestic partner of the decedent by establishing the factors listed in paragraphs (1) to (6), inclusive, of subdivision (b) of Section 297 of the Family Code, as it read pursuant to Section 3 of Chapter 893 of the Statutes of 2001, prior to its becoming inoperative on January 1, 2005.

(3) The amendments made to this subdivision during the 2003–04 Regular Session of the Legislature are not intended to revive any cause of action that has been fully and finally adjudicated by the courts, or that has been settled, or as to which the applicable limitations period has run. **Leg.H.** Added Stats 1992 ch 178 §20 (SB 1496). Amended Stats 1996 ch 563 §1 (SB 392); Stats 1997 ch 13 §1 (SB 449), effective May 23, 1997; Stats 2001 ch 893 §2 (AB 25); Stats 2004 ch 947 §1 (AB 2580); Stats 2020 ch 51 §1 (AB 2445), effective September 9, 2020.

§377.61. Damages recoverable

In an action under this article, damages may be awarded that, under all the circumstances of the case, may be just, but may not include damages recoverable under Section 377.34. The court shall determine the respective rights in an award of the persons entitled to assert the cause of action. **Leg.H.** Added Stats 1992 ch 178 §20 (SB 1496).

§377.62. Joinder or consolidation of survival action

(a) An action under Section 377.30 may be joined with an action under Section 377.60 arising out of the same wrongful act or neglect.

(b) An action under Section 377.60 and an action under Section 377.31 arising out of the same wrongful act or neglect may be consolidated for trial as provided in Section 1048. **Leg.H.** Added Stats 1992 ch 178 §20 (SB 1496).

CHAPTER 5
PERMISSIVE JOINDER

Joinder as plaintiffs. §378.
Joinder as defendants. §379.
Order for separate trials. §379.5.
Party who cannot be joined as plaintiff being made defendant; Defense by parties on behalf of others having common interest. §382.
Distribution of settlement in class action; Attorney connection or relationship with nonparty recipient. §382.4.
Legislative intent; Determination of total amount payable to all class members prior to entry of judgment; Exemption for class action brought against public entity. §384.
Judgment in a class action; Distribution of money; Transmission of copy to the Judicial Council. §384.5.

§378. Joinder as plaintiffs

(a) All persons may join in one action as plaintiffs if:

(1) They assert any right to relief jointly, severally, or in the alternative, in respect of or arising out of the same transaction, occurrence, or series of transactions or occurrences and if any question of law or fact common to all these persons will arise in the action; or

(2) They have a claim, right, or interest adverse to the defendant in the property or controversy which is the subject of the action.

(b) It is not necessary that each plaintiff be interested as to every cause of action or as to all relief prayed for. Judgment may be given for one or more of the plaintiffs according to their respective right to relief. **Leg.H.** Enacted 1872. Amended Stats 1927 ch 386 §1; Stats 1971 ch 244 §4, operative July 1, 1972.

§379. Joinder as defendants

(a) All persons may be joined in one action as defendants if there is asserted against them:

(1) Any right to relief jointly, severally, or in the alternative, in respect of or arising out of the same transaction, occurrence, or series of transactions or occurrences and if any question of law or fact common to all these persons will arise in the action; or

(2) A claim, right, or interest adverse to them in the property or controversy which is the subject of the action.

(b) It is not necessary that each defendant be interested as to every cause of action or as to all relief prayed for. Judgment may be given against one or more defendants according to their respective liabilities.

(c) Where the plaintiff is in doubt as to the person from whom he or she is entitled to redress, he or she may join two or more defendants, with the intent that the question as to which, if any, of the defendants is liable, and to what extent, may be determined between the parties. **Leg.H.** Enacted 1872. Amended Stats 1971 ch 244 §5, operative July 1, 1972, ch 950 §1, operative July 1, 1972; Stats 1975 ch 1241 §6.

§379.5. Order for separate trials

When parties have been joined under Section 378 or 379, the court may make such orders as may appear just to prevent any party from being embarrassed, delayed, or put to undue expense, and may order separate trials or make such other order as the interests of justice may require. **Leg.H.** Added Stats 1971 ch 244 §9, operative July 1, 1972.

§§379a–379c. [Sections repealed 1972]

Leg.H. Added Stats 1927 ch 259 §1. Repealed Stats 1971 ch 244 §§6–8, operative July 1, 1972. See CCP §§379, 379.5.

§380. [Section repealed 1972]

Leg.H. Enacted 1872. Amended Code Amdts 1873–74 ch 383 §41. Repealed Stats 1971 ch 244 §10, operative July 1, 1972.

§381. [Section repealed 1972]

Leg.H. Enacted 1872. Amended Code Amdts 1873–74 ch 383 §42. Repealed Stats 1971 ch 244 §11, operative July 1, 1972.

§382. Party who cannot be joined as plaintiff being made defendant; Defense by parties on behalf of others having common interest

If the consent of any one who should have been joined as plaintiff cannot be obtained, he may be made a defendant, the reason thereof being stated in the complaint; and when the question is one of a common or general interest, of many persons, or when the parties are numerous, and it is impracticable to bring them all before the court, one or more may sue or defend for the benefit of all. **Leg.H.** Enacted 1872. Amended Stats 1971 ch 244 §12, operative July 1, 1972.

§382.4. Distribution of settlement in class action; Attorney connection or relationship with nonparty recipient

If a proposed settlement in a class action established pursuant to Section 382, including a consent judgment, decree, or settlement agreement, provides for the distribution of money or any other thing of value to a person or entity that is not a party to the action, an attorney for a party to the action shall, in connection with the hearing for preliminary approval pursuant to subdivision (c) of Rule 3.769 of the California Rules of Court, notify the court if the attorney has a connection to or a relationship with a nonparty recipient of the distribution that could reasonably create the appearance of impropriety as between the selection of the recipient of the money or thing of value and the interests of the class. **Leg.H.** Added Stats 2018 ch 45 §1 (SB 847), effective June 27, 2018.

§383. [Section repealed 2005]

Leg.H. Added Stats 1985 ch 874 §18 as §374. Amended Stats 1986 ch 9 §6, effective February 25, 1986. Repealed Stats 1992 ch 178 §16 (SB 1496). Amended Stats 1992 ch 1283 §1 (AB 3708). Renumbered by Stats 1993 ch 151 §3 (AB 1704), effective July 16, 1993. Repealed Stats 2004 ch 754 §7 (AB 1836). The repealed section related to management associations of common interest developments. See now CC §§1368.3, 1368.4.

Prior Law: Former CCP §383, relating to persons severally liable as sureties joining as plaintiffs in actions affecting the obligation, was enacted 1872, amended Stats 1897 ch 23 §1, Stats 1903 ch 181 §1, and repealed Stats 1971 ch 244 §13, operative July 1, 1972.

Former CCP §383 was added Stats 1993 ch 863 §2 and amended and renumbered §384 by Stats 1994 ch 146 §19(ch 237 prevails), ch 127 §1, effective July 15, 1994.

§384. Legislative intent; Determination of total amount payable to all class members prior to entry of judgment; Exemption for class action brought against public entity

(a) It is the policy of the State of California to ensure that the unpaid cash residue and unclaimed or abandoned funds in class action litigation are distributed, to the fullest extent possible, in a manner designed either to further the purposes of the underlying class action or causes of action, or to promote justice for all Californians. The Legislature finds that the use of funds for these purposes is in the public interest, is a proper use of the funds, and is consistent with essential public and governmental purposes.

(b) Except as provided in subdivision (c), before the entry of a judgment in a class action established pursuant to Section 382 that provides for the payment of money to members of the class, the court shall determine the total amount that will be payable to all class members if all class members are paid the amount to which they are entitled pursuant to the judgment. The court shall also set a date when the parties shall report to the court the total amount that was actually paid to the class members. After the report is received, the court shall amend the judgment to direct the defendant to pay the sum of the unpaid residue or unclaimed or abandoned class member funds, plus any interest that has accrued thereon, to nonprofit organizations or foundations to support projects that will benefit the class or similarly situated persons, or that promote the law consistent with the objectives and purposes of the underlying cause of action, to child advocacy programs, or to nonprofit organizations providing civil legal services to the indigent. The court shall ensure that the distribution of any unpaid residue or unclaimed or abandoned class member funds derived from multistate or national cases brought under California law shall provide substantial or commensurate benefit to California consumers. For purposes of this subdivision, "judgment" includes a consent judgment, decree, or settlement agreement that has been approved by the court.

(c) This section shall not apply to any class action brought against any public entity, as defined in Section 811.2 of the Government Code, or against any public employee, as defined in Section 811.4 of the Government Code. However, this section shall not be construed to abrogate any equitable cy pres remedy that may be available in any class action with regard to all or part of the cash residue or unclaimed or abandoned class member funds. **Leg.H.** Added Stats 1993 ch 863 §2 (SB 536) as §383. Amended and renumbered by Stats 1994 ch 146 §19 (AB 3601) (ch 237 prevails), ch 237 §1 (SB 2105), effective July 15, 1994. Amended Stats 2001 ch 96 §2 (SB 1218); Stats 2017 ch 17 §4 (AB 103), effective June 27, 2017; Stats 2018 ch 45 §2 (SB 847), effective June 27, 2018; Stats 2018 ch 776 §6 (AB 3250), effective January 1, 2019.

Prior Law: Former CCP §384 was enacted 1872 and repealed Stats 1971 ch 244 §14, operative July 1, 1972.

§384.5. Judgment in a class action; Distribution of money; Transmission of copy to the Judicial Council

If a judgment in a class action established pursuant to Section 382, including a consent judgment, decree, or settlement agreement that has been approved by a court, provides for a distribution of money or any other thing of value to a person or entity that is not a party to the action, the court shall transmit a copy of the order, judgment, or decree to the Judicial Council. The order, judgment, or decree shall contain, at a minimum, the information necessary for the California Research Bureau to complete the report required by Section 68520 of the Government Code. **Leg.H.** Added Stats 2018 ch 45 §3 (SB 847), effective June 27, 2018.

§385. [Section repealed 1993]

Leg.H. Enacted 1872. Amended Code Amdts 1873–74 ch 383 §43; Stats 1971 ch 1226 §2, ch 1638 §2; Stats 1986 ch 783 §1.5, operative July 1, 1987; Stats 1988 ch 1199 §5, operative July 1, 1989. Repealed Stats 1992 ch 178 §22 (SB 1496). See CCP §§368.5, 375, 377.21, 377.31, 377.41.

CHAPTER 6
INTERPLEADER

Interpleader. §386.
Investment of deposit, and allocation of interest. §386.1.
Discharge of defendant who is stakeholder. §386.5.
Allowance of costs and attorney fees by party following procedure set forth in Section 386 or 386.5. §386.6.

§386. Interpleader

(a) A defendant, against whom an action is pending upon a contract, or for specific personal property, may, at any time before answer, upon affidavit that a person not a party to the action makes against him, and without any collusion with him, a demand upon such contract, or for such property, upon notice to such person and the adverse party, apply to the court for an order to substitute such person in his place, and discharge him from liability to either party, on his depositing in court the amount claimed on the contract, or delivering the property or its value to such person as the court may direct; and the court may, in its discretion, make the order; or such defendant may file a verified cross-complaint in interpleader, admitting that he has no interest in such amount or such property claimed, or in a portion of such amount or such property and alleging that all or such portion of the amount or property is demanded by parties to such action or cross-action and apply to the court upon notice to such parties for an order to deliver such property or portion thereof or its value to such person as the court shall direct. And whenever conflicting claims are or may be made upon a person for or relating to personal property, or the performance of an obligation, or any portion thereof, such person may bring an action against the conflicting claimants to compel them to interplead and litigate their several claims. The order of substitution may be made and the action of interpleader may be maintained, and the applicant or interpleading party be discharged from liability to all or any of the conflicting claimants, although their titles or claims have not a common origin, or are not identical but are adverse to and independent of one another.

(b) Any person, firm, corporation, association or other entity against whom double or multiple claims are made, or may be made, by two or more persons which are such that they may give rise to double or multiple liability, may bring an action against the claimants to compel them to interplead and litigate their several claims.

When the person, firm, corporation, association or other entity against whom such claims are made, or may be made, is a defendant in an action brought upon one or more of such claims, it may either file a verified cross-complaint in interpleader, admitting that it has no interest in the money or property claimed, or in only a portion thereof, and alleging that all or such portion is demanded by parties to such action, and apply to the court upon notice to such parties for an order to deliver such money or property or such portion thereof to such person as the court shall direct; or may bring a separate action against the claimants to compel them to interplead and litigate their several claims. The action of interpleader may be maintained although the claims have not a common origin, are not identical but are adverse to and independent of one another, or the claims are unliquidated and no liability on the part of the party bringing the action or filing the cross-complaint has arisen. The applicant or interpleading party may deny liability in whole or in part to any or all of the claimants. The applicant or interpleading party may join as a defendant in such action any other party against whom claims are made by one or more of the claimants or such other party may interplead by cross-complaint; provided, however, that such claims arise out of the same transaction or occurrence.

(c) Any amount which a plaintiff or cross-complainant admits to be payable may be deposited by him with the clerk of the court at the time of the filing of the complaint or cross-complaint in interpleader without first obtaining an order of the court therefor. Any interest on amounts deposited and any right to damages for detention of property so delivered, or its value, shall cease to accrue after the date of such deposit or delivery.

(d) A defendant named in a complaint to compel conflicting claimants to interplead and litigate their claims, or a defendant named in a cross-complaint in interpleader, may, in lieu of or in addition to any other pleading, file an answer to the complaint or cross-complaint which shall be served upon all other parties to the action and which shall contain allegations of fact as to his ownership of or other interest in the amount or property and any affirmative defenses and the relief requested. The allegations in such answer shall be deemed denied by all other parties to the action, unless otherwise admitted in the pleadings.

(e) Except in cases where by the law a right to a jury trial is now given, conflicting claims to funds or property or the value thereof so deposited or delivered shall be deemed issues triable by the court, and such issues may be first tried. In the event the amount deposited shall be less than the amount claimed to be due by one or more of the conflicting claimants thereto, or in the event the property or the value thereof delivered is less than all of the property or the value thereof claimed by one or more of such conflicting claimants, any issues of fact involved in determining whether there is a deficiency in such deposit or delivery shall be tried by the court or a jury as provided in Title 8 (commencing with Section 577) of Part 2 of this code.

(f) After any such complaint or cross-complaint in interpleader has been filed, the court in which it is filed may enter its order restraining all parties to the action from instituting or further prosecuting any other proceeding in any court in this state affecting the rights and obligations as between the parties to the interpleader until further order of the court. **Leg.H.** Enacted 1872. Amended Stats 1881 ch 23 §1; Stats 1951 ch 1142 §1; Stats 1970 ch 563 §1; Stats 1975 ch 670 §1.

§386.1. Investment of deposit, and allocation of interest

Where a deposit has been made pursuant to Section 386, the court shall, upon the application of any party to the action, order such deposit to be invested in an insured interest-bearing account. Interest on such amount shall be allocated to the parties in the same proportion as the original funds are allocated. **Leg.H.** Added Stats 1972 ch 553 §1. Amended Stats 1979 ch 173 §1.

§386.5. Discharge of defendant who is stakeholder

Where the only relief sought against one of the defendants is the payment of a stated amount of money alleged to be wrongfully withheld, such defendant may, upon affidavit that he is a mere stakeholder with no interest in the amount or any portion thereof and that conflicting demands have been made upon him for the amount by parties to the action, upon notice to such parties, apply to the court for an order discharging him from liability and dismissing him from the action on his depositing with the clerk of the court the amount in dispute and the court may, in its discretion, make such order. **Leg.H.** Added Stats 1953 ch 328 §1.

§386.6. Allowance of costs and attorney fees by party following procedure set forth in Section 386 or 386.5

(a) A party to an action who follows the procedure set forth in Section 386 or 386.5 may insert in his motion, petition, complaint, or cross complaint a request for allowance of his costs and reasonable attorney fees incurred in such action. In ordering the discharge of such party, the court may, in its discretion, award such party his costs and reasonable attorney fees from the amount in dispute which has been deposited with the court. At the time of final judgment in the action the court may make such further provision for assumption of such costs and attorney fees by one or more of the adverse claimants as may appear proper.

(b) A party shall not be denied the attorney fees authorized by subdivision (a) for the reason that he is himself an attorney, appeared in pro se, and performed his own legal services. **Leg.H.** Added Stats 1955 ch 951 §1. Amended Stats 1974 ch 273 §1.

CHAPTER 7
INTERVENTION

Intervention. §387.
Service on Attorney General in action based on pollution or adverse environmental effects affecting public generally. §388.

§387. Intervention

(a) For purposes of this section:
(1) "Defendant" includes a cross-defendant.
(2) "Plaintiff" includes a cross-complainant.
(b) An intervention takes place when a nonparty, deemed an intervenor, becomes a party to an action or proceeding between other persons by doing any of the following:
(1) Joining a plaintiff in claiming what is sought by the complaint.
(2) Uniting with a defendant in resisting the claims of a plaintiff.
(3) Demanding anything adverse to both a plaintiff and a defendant.
(c) A nonparty shall petition the court for leave to intervene by noticed motion or ex parte application. The petition shall include a copy of the proposed complaint in intervention or answer in intervention and set forth the grounds upon which intervention rests.
(d)(1) The court shall, upon timely application, permit a nonparty to intervene in the action or proceeding if either of the following conditions is satisfied:
(A) A provision of law confers an unconditional right to intervene.
(B) The person seeking intervention claims an interest relating to the property or transaction that is the subject of the action and that person is so situated that the disposition of the action may impair or impede that person's ability to protect that interest, unless that person's interest is adequately represented by one or more of the existing parties.
(2) The court may, upon timely application, permit a nonparty to intervene in the action or proceeding if the person has an interest in the matter in litigation, or in the success of either of the parties, or an interest against both.
(e) If leave to intervene is granted by the court, the intervenor shall do both of the following:
(1) Separately file the complaint in intervention, answer in intervention, or both.
(2) Serve a copy of the order, or notice of the court's decision or order, granting leave to intervene and the pleadings in intervention as follows:
(A) A party to the action or proceeding who has not yet appeared shall be served in the same manner for service of summons pursuant to Article 3 (commencing with Section 415.10) of Chapter 4 of Title 5 of Part 2.
(B) A party who has appeared in the action or proceeding, whether represented by an attorney or not represented by an attorney, shall be served in the same manner for service of summons pursuant to Article 3 (commencing with Section 415.10) of Chapter 4 of Title 5 of Part 2, or in the manner provided by Chapter 5 (commencing with Section 1010) of Title 14 of Part 2.
(f) Within 30 days after service of a complaint in intervention or answer in intervention, a party may move, demur, or otherwise plead to the complaint in intervention or answer in intervention in the same manner as to an original complaint or answer. **Leg.H.** Enacted 1872. Amended Code Amdts 1873–74 ch 383 §44; Stats 1907 ch 371 §1; Stats 1969 ch 1611 §5, operative July 1, 1970; Stats 1970 ch 484 §1; Stats 1977 ch 450 §1; Stats 2017 ch 131 §1 (AB 1693), effective January 1, 2018.

§388. Service on Attorney General in action based on pollution or adverse environmental effects affecting public generally

In an action brought by a party for relief of any nature other than solely for money damages where a pleading alleges facts or issues concerning alleged pollution or adverse environmental effects which could affect the public generally, the party filing the pleading shall furnish a copy to the Attorney General of the State of California. The copy shall be furnished by the party filing the pleading within 10 days after filing. **Leg.H.** Added Stats 1992 ch 178 §26 (SB 1496).

Prior Law: Former CCP §388, similar to present CCP §369.5, was enacted 1872, amended Stats 1907 ch 371 §2, Stats 1967 ch 1324 §1, and repealed Stats 1992 ch 178 §25 (SB 1496).

CHAPTER 8
COMPULSORY JOINDER

Indispensable or conditionally necessary parties; Order to bring in party, and dismissal on failure to comply; Separate trials. §389.

Recovery of property or determination of conflicting claims; Right of party to be brought in. §389.5.

§389. Indispensable or conditionally necessary parties; Order to bring in party, and dismissal on failure to comply; Separate trials

(a) A person who is subject to service of process and whose joinder will not deprive the court of jurisdiction over the subject matter of the action shall be joined as a party in the action if (1) in his absence complete relief cannot be accorded among those already parties or (2) he claims an interest relating to the subject of the action and is so situated that the disposition of the action in his absence may (i) as a practical matter impair or impede his ability to protect that interest or (ii) leave any of the persons already parties subject to a substantial risk of incurring double, multiple, or otherwise inconsistent obligations by reason of his claimed interest. If he has not been so joined, the court shall order that he be made a party.

(b) If a person as described in paragraph (1) or (2) of subdivision (a) cannot be made a party, the court shall determine whether in equity and good conscience the action should proceed among the parties before it, or should be dismissed without prejudice, the absent person being thus regarded as indispensable. The factors to be considered by the court include: (1) to what extent a judgment rendered in the person's absence might be prejudicial to him or those already parties; (2) the extent to which, by protective provisions in the judgment, by the shaping of relief, or other measures, the prejudice can be lessened or avoided; (3) whether a judgment rendered in the person's absence will be adequate; (4) whether the plaintiff or cross-complainant will have an adequate remedy if the action is dismissed for nonjoinder.

(c) A complaint or cross-complaint shall state the names, if known to the pleader, of any persons as described in paragraph (1) or (2) of subdivision (a) who are not joined, and the reasons why they are not joined.

(d) Nothing in this section affects the law applicable to class actions.

Leg.H. Enacted 1872. Amended Stats 1897 ch 12 §1; Stats 1907 ch 371 §3; Stats 1957 ch 1498 §2; Stats 1971 ch 244 §15, operative July 1, 1972.

§389.5. Recovery of property or determination of conflicting claims; Right of party to be brought in

When, in an action for the recovery of real or personal property, or to determine conflicting claims thereto, a person not a party to the action but having an interest in the subject thereof makes application to the court to be made a party, it may order him to be brought in by the proper amendment. **Leg.H.** Added Stats 1957 ch 1498 §3.

§389.6. [Section repealed 1993]

Leg.H. Added Stats 1971 ch 1518 §1. Repealed Stats 1992 ch 178 §28 (SB 1496). See CCP §388.

§390. [Section repealed 1993]

Leg.H. Added Stats 1885 ch 111 §1. Repealed Stats 1992 ch 178 §29 (SB 1496). The repealed section related to actions against fire departments.

TITLE 3A
VEXATIOUS LITIGANTS

Definitions. §391.
Motion for order requiring plaintiff to post security; Motion for order dismissing the litigation; Grounds; Time of filing. §391.1.
Hearing procedure. §391.2.
Finding; Amount of security; Dismissal. §391.3.
Dismissal on failure to post security. §391.4.
Motion as stay of proceedings; Time for pleading to complaint. §391.6.
Vexatious litigant; Prefiling order prohibiting filing of new litigation. §391.7.
Application to vacate prefiling order and removing vexatious litigant's name from Judicial Council's list of vexatious litigants; Effect of denial. §391.8.

§391. Definitions

As used in this title, the following terms have the following meanings:

(a) "Litigation" means any civil action or proceeding, commenced, maintained or pending in any state or federal court.

(b) "Vexatious litigant" means a person who does any of the following:

(1) In the immediately preceding seven-year period has commenced, prosecuted, or maintained in propria persona at least five litigations other than in a small claims court that have been (i) finally determined adversely to the person or (ii) unjustifiably permitted to remain pending at least two years without having been brought to trial or hearing.

(2) After a litigation has been finally determined against the person, repeatedly relitigates or attempts to relitigate, in propria persona, either (i) the validity of the determination against the same defendant or defendants as to whom the litigation was finally determined or (ii) the cause of action, claim, controversy, or any of the issues of fact or law, determined or concluded by the final determination against the same defendant or defendants as to whom the litigation was finally determined.

(3) In any litigation while acting in propria persona, repeatedly files unmeritorious motions, pleadings, or other papers, conducts unnecessary discovery, or engages in other tactics that are frivolous or solely intended to cause unnecessary delay.

(4) Has previously been declared to be a vexatious litigant by any state or federal court of record in any action or proceeding based upon the same or substantially similar facts, transaction, or occurrence.

(5) After being restrained pursuant to a restraining order issued after a hearing pursuant to Chapter 1 (commencing with Section 6300) of Part 4 of Division 10 of the Family Code, and while the restraining order is still in place, they commenced, prosecuted, or maintained one or more litigations against a person protected by the restraining order in this or any other court or jurisdiction that are determined to be meritless and caused the person protected by the order to be harassed or intimidated.

(c) "Security" means an undertaking to assure payment, to the party for whose benefit the undertaking is required to be furnished, of the party's reasonable expenses, including attorney's fees and not limited to taxable costs, incurred in or in connection with a litigation instituted, caused to be instituted, or maintained or caused to be maintained by a vexatious litigant.

(d) "Plaintiff" means the person who commences, institutes or maintains a litigation or causes it to be commenced, instituted or maintained, including an attorney at law acting in propria persona.

(e) "Defendant" means a person (including corporation, association, partnership and firm or governmental entity) against whom a litigation is brought or maintained or sought to be brought or maintained. **Leg.H.** Added Stats 1963 ch 1471 §1. Amended Stats 1982 ch 517 §98; Stats 1990 ch 621 §1 (SB 2675); Stats 1994 ch 587 §3.5 (AB 3600); Stats 2022 ch 84 §1 (AB 2391), effective January 1, 2023.

§391.1. Motion for order requiring plaintiff to post security; Motion for order dismissing the litigation; Grounds; Time of filing

(a) In any litigation pending in any court of this state, at any time until final judgment is entered, a defendant may move the court, upon notice and hearing, for an order requiring the plaintiff to furnish security or for an order dismissing the litigation pursuant to subdivision (b) of Section 391.3. The motion for an order requiring the plaintiff to furnish security shall be based upon the ground, and supported by a showing, that the plaintiff is a vexatious litigant and that there is not a reasonable probability that they will prevail in the litigation against the moving defendant.

(b) A motion pursuant to subdivision (a) on the grounds that plaintiff is a vexatious litigant pursuant to paragraph (5) of subdivision (b) of Section 391 may be brought only by a person protected by the restraining order. A person filing a motion as described in this subdivision shall not be required to pay a filing fee. **Leg.H.** Added Stats 1963 ch 1471 §1. Amended Stats 1975 ch 381 §1; Stats 1990 ch 621 §2 (SB 2675); Stats 2012 ch 417 §1 (AB 2274), effective January 1, 2013; Stats 2022 ch 84 §2 (AB 2391), effective January 1, 2023.

§391.2. Hearing procedure

At the hearing upon the motion the court shall consider any evidence, written or oral, by witnesses or affidavit, as may be material to the ground of the motion. Except for an order dismissing the litigation pursuant to subdivision (b) of Section 391.3, no determination made by the court in determining or ruling upon the motion shall be or be deemed to be a determination of any issue in the litigation or of the merits thereof. **Leg.H.** Added Stats 1963 ch 1471 §1. Amended Stats 2012 ch 417 §2 (AB 2274), effective January 1, 2013.

§391.3. Finding; Amount of security; Dismissal

(a) Except as provided in subdivision (b), if, after hearing the evidence upon the motion, the court determines that the plaintiff is a vexatious litigant and that there is no reasonable probability that the plaintiff will prevail in the litigation against the moving defendant, the court shall order the plaintiff to furnish, for the benefit of the moving defendant, security in such amount and within such time as the court shall fix.

(b) If, after hearing evidence on the motion, the court determines that the litigation has no merit and has been filed for the purposes of harassment or delay, the court shall order the litigation dismissed. This subdivision shall only apply to litigation filed in a court of this state by a vexatious litigant subject to a prefiling order pursuant to Section 391.7 who was represented by counsel at the time the litigation was filed and who became in propria persona after the withdrawal of his or her attorney.

(c) A defendant may make a motion for relief in the alternative under either subdivision (a) or (b) and shall combine all grounds for relief in one motion. **Leg.H.** Added Stats 1963 ch 1471 §1. Amended Stats 1982 ch 517 §99; Stats 2012 ch 417 §3 (AB 2274), effective January 1, 2013.

§391.4. Dismissal on failure to post security

When security that has been ordered furnished is not furnished as ordered, the litigation shall be dismissed as to the defendant for whose benefit it was ordered furnished. **Leg.H.** Added Stats 1963 ch 1471 §1.

§391.5. [Section repealed 1983]

Leg.H. Added Stats 1963 ch 1471 §1. Repealed Stats 1982 ch 517 §100. See CCP §996.460.

§391.6. Motion as stay of proceedings; Time for pleading to complaint

Except as provided in subdivision (b) of Section 391.3, when a motion pursuant to Section 391.1 is filed prior to trial the litigation is stayed, and the moving defendant need not plead, until 10 days after the motion shall have been denied, or if granted, until 10 days after the required security has been furnished and the moving defendant given written notice thereof. When a motion pursuant to Section 391.1 is made at any time thereafter, the litigation shall be stayed for such period after the denial of the motion or the furnishing of the required security as the court shall determine. **Leg.H.** Added Stats 1963 ch 1471 §1. Amended Stats 1975 ch 381 §2; Stats 2012 ch 417 §4 (AB 2274), effective January 1, 2013.

§391.7. Vexatious litigant; Prefiling order prohibiting filing of new litigation

(a) In addition to any other relief provided in this title, the court may, on its own motion or the motion of any party, enter a prefiling order which prohibits a vexatious litigant from filing any new litigation in the courts of this state in propria persona without first obtaining leave of the presiding justice or presiding judge of the court where the litigation is proposed to be filed. Disobedience of the order by a vexatious litigant may be punished as a contempt of court.

(b) The presiding justice or presiding judge shall permit the filing of that litigation only if it appears that the litigation has merit and has not been filed for the purposes of harassment or delay. The presiding justice or presiding judge may condition the filing of the litigation upon the furnishing of security for the benefit of the defendants as provided in Section 391.3.

(c) The clerk may not file any litigation presented by a vexatious litigant subject to a prefiling order unless the vexatious litigant first obtains an order from the presiding justice or presiding judge permitting the filing. If the clerk mistakenly files the litigation without the order, any party may file with the clerk and serve, or the presiding justice or presiding judge may direct the clerk to file and serve, on the plaintiff and other parties a notice stating that the plaintiff is a vexatious litigant subject to a prefiling order as set forth in subdivision (a). The filing of the notice shall automatically stay the litigation. The litigation shall be automatically dismissed unless the plaintiff within 10 days of the filing of that notice obtains an order from the presiding justice or presiding judge permitting the filing of the litigation as set forth in subdivision (b). If the presiding justice or presiding judge issues an order permitting the filing, the stay of the litigation shall remain in effect, and the defendants need not plead, until 10 days after the defendants are served with a copy of the order.

(d) For purposes of this section, "litigation" includes any petition, application, or motion other than a discovery motion, in a proceeding under the Family Code or Probate Code, for any order.

(e) The presiding justice or presiding judge of a court may designate a justice or judge of the same court to act on his or her behalf in exercising the authority and responsibilities provided under subdivisions (a) to (c), inclusive.

(f) The clerk of the court shall provide the Judicial Council a copy of any prefiling orders issued pursuant to subdivision (a). The Judicial Council shall maintain a record of vexatious litigants subject to those prefiling orders and shall annually disseminate a list of those persons to the clerks of the courts of this state. **Leg.H.** Added Stats 1990 ch 621 §3 (SB 2675). Amended Stats 2002 ch 1118 §1 (AB 1938); Stats 2011 ch 49 §1 (SB 731), effective January 1, 2012.

§391.8. Application to vacate prefiling order and removing vexatious litigant's name from Judicial Council's list of vexatious litigants; Effect of denial

(a) A vexatious litigant subject to a prefiling order under Section 391.7 may file an application to vacate the prefiling order and remove his or her name from the Judicial Council's list of vexatious litigants subject to prefiling orders. The application shall be filed in the court that entered the prefiling order, either in the action in which the prefiling order was entered or in conjunction with a request to the presiding justice or presiding judge to file new litigation under Section 391.7. The application shall be made before the justice or judge who entered the order, if that justice or judge is available. If that justice or judge who entered the order is not available, the application shall be made before the presiding justice or presiding judge, or his or her designee.

(b) A vexatious litigant whose application under subdivision (a) was denied shall not be permitted to file another application on or before 12 months has elapsed after the date of the denial of the previous application.

(c) A court may vacate a prefiling order and order removal of a vexatious litigant's name from the Judicial Council's list of vexatious litigants subject to prefiling orders upon a showing of a material change in the facts upon which the order was granted and that the ends of justice would be served by vacating the order. **Leg.H.** Added Stats 2011 ch 49 §2 (SB 731), effective January 1, 2012.

TITLE 4
OF THE PLACE OF TRIAL, RECLASSIFICATION, AND COORDINATION OF CIVIL ACTIONS

Chapter 1. Place of Trial.
Chapter 2. Reclassification of Civil Actions and Proceedings.
Chapter 3. Coordination.

CHAPTER 1
PLACE OF TRIAL

Venue of actions involving real property. §392.
Venue of actions for penalty or forfeiture, and actions against officers. §393.
Venue of actions by or against county, city, or local agency. §394.
County in which defendants reside; Personal injury; Family law matters; Contract to perform obligation in county; Contract involving goods for personal or family use. §395.
Venue of action against defendant sued in official or representative capacity. §395.1.
Venue of action against association. §395.2.
Venue of action on obligation of corporation or association. §395.5.
Filing of appeal or petition in wrong state court not grounds for dismissal; Transfer from superior court to court of appeal or Supreme Court having jurisdiction. §396.
Filing of affidavit of jurisdiction by plaintiff; Motion to transfer. §396a.
Procedure to transfer; Authority of court. §396b.
Cases in which venue may be changed. §397.
Transfer of proceedings under Family Law Act. §397.5.
Court to which action should be transferred. §398.
Transmittal of records or transcript to transferee court; Payment of costs and fees; Recovery or offset; Notice of transmittal; Jurisdiction of transferee court. §399.
Writ of mandate requiring trial of case in proper court. §400.
Actions commenced or removed to county with office of attorney general. §401.
Superior court to decide location of filing and hearing; Transfer. §402.
Transfers. §403.

§392. Venue of actions involving real property

(a) Subject to the power of the court to transfer actions and proceedings as provided in this title, the superior court in the county where the real property that is the subject of the action, or some part thereof, is situated, is the proper court for the trial of the following actions:

(1) For the recovery of real property, or of an estate or interest therein, or for the determination in any form, of that right or interest, and for injuries to real property.

(2) For the foreclosure of all liens and mortgages on real property.

(b) In the court designated as the proper court in subdivision (a), the proper court location for trial of a proceeding for an unlawful detainer, as defined in Section 1161, is the location where the court tries that type of proceeding that is nearest or most accessible to where the real property that is the subject of the action, or some part thereof, is situated. Otherwise any location of the superior court designated as the proper court in subdivision (a) is a proper court location for the trial. The court may specify by local rule the nearest or most accessible court location where the court tries that type of case. **Leg.H.** Enacted 1872. Amended Code Admts 1875–76 ch 117 §1; Stats 1889 ch 242 §1; Stats 1907 ch 369 §1; Stats 1933 ch 744 §3; Stats 1951 ch 869 §1, operative January 1, 1952; Stats 1976 ch 73 §3; Stats 1998 ch 931 §60 (SB 2139), effective September 28, 1998; Stats 2002 ch 806 §7 (AB 3027).

§393. Venue of actions for penalty or forfeiture, and actions against officers

Subject to the power of the court to transfer actions and proceedings as provided in this title, the county in which the cause, or some part of the cause, arose, is the proper county for the trial of the following actions:

(a) For the recovery of a penalty or forfeiture imposed by statute, except, that when it is imposed for an offense committed on a lake, river, or other stream of water, situated in two or more counties, the action may be tried in any county bordering on the lake, river, or stream, and opposite to the place where the offense was committed.

(b) Against a public officer or person especially appointed to execute the duties of a public officer, for an act done by the officer or person in virtue of the office, or against a person who, by the officer's command or in the officer's aid, does anything touching the duties of the officer. **Leg.H.** Enacted 1872. Amended Stats 1933 ch 744 §4; Stats 1951 ch 869 §2; Stats 1998 ch 931 §61 (SB 2139), effective September 28, 1998; Stats 2003 ch 449 §7 (AB 1712).

§394. Venue of actions by or against county, city, or local agency

(a) An action or proceeding against a county, or city and county, a city, or local agency, may be tried in the county, or city and county, or the county in which the city or local agency is situated, unless the action or proceeding is brought by a county, or city and county, a city, or local agency, in which case it may be tried in any county, or city and county, not a party thereto and in which the city or local agency is not situated. Except for actions initiated by the local child support agency pursuant to Section 17400, 17402, 17404, or 17416 of the Family Code, any action or proceeding brought by a county, city and county, city, or local agency within a certain county, or city and county, against a resident of another county, city and county, or city, or a corporation doing business in the latter, shall be, on motion of either party, transferred for trial to a county, or city and county, other than the plaintiff, if the plaintiff is a county, or city and county, and other than that in which the plaintiff is situated, if the plaintiff is a city, or a local agency, and other than that in which the defendant resides, or is doing business, or is situated. Whenever an action or proceeding is brought against a county, city and county, city, or local agency, in any county, or city and county, other than the defendant, if the defendant is a county, or city and county, or, if the defendant is a city, or local agency, other than that in which the defendant is situated, the action or proceeding must be, on motion of that defendant, transferred for trial to a county, or city and county, other than that in which the plaintiff, or any of the plaintiffs, resides, or is doing business, or is situated, and other than the plaintiff county, or city and county, or county in which that plaintiff city or local agency is situated, and other than the defendant county, or city and county, or county in which the defendant city or local agency is situated; provided, however, that any action or proceeding against the city, county, city and county, or local agency for injury occurring within the city, county, or city and county, or within the county in which the local agency is situated, to person or property or person and property caused by the negligence or alleged negligence of the city, county, city and county, local agency, or its agents or employees, shall be tried in that county, or city and county, or if a city is a defendant, in the city or in the county in which the city is situated, or if a local agency is a defendant, in the county in which the local agency is situated. In that action or proceeding, the parties thereto may, by stipulation in writing, or made in open court, and entered in the minutes, agree upon any county, or city and county, for the place of trial thereof. When the action or proceeding is one in which a jury is not of right, or in case a jury is waived, then in lieu of transferring the cause, the court in the original county may request the chairperson of the Judicial Council to assign a disinterested judge from a neutral county to hear that cause and all proceedings in connection therewith. When the action or proceeding is transferred to another county for trial, a witness required to respond to a subpoena for a hearing within the original county shall be compelled to attend hearings in the county to which the cause is transferred. If the demand for transfer is made by one party and the opposing party does not consent thereto, the additional costs of the nonconsenting party occasioned by the transfer of the cause, including living and traveling expenses of the nonconsenting party and material witnesses, found by the court to be material, and called by the nonconsenting party, not to exceed five dollars ($5) per day each in excess of witness fees and mileage otherwise allowed by law, shall be assessed by the court hearing the cause against the party requesting the transfer. To the extent of that excess, those costs shall be awarded to the nonconsenting party regardless of the outcome of the trial. This section shall apply to actions or proceedings now pending or hereafter brought.

(b) For the purposes of this section, "local agency" shall mean any governmental district, board, or agency, or any other local governmental body or corporation, but shall not include the State of California or any of its agencies, departments, commissions, or boards. **Leg.H.** Enacted 1872. Amended Stats 1881 ch 30 §1, ch 61 §1; Stats 1907 ch 369 §2; Stats 1915 ch 434 §1; Stats 1921 ch 382 §1; Stats 1929 ch 112 §1; Stats 1931 ch 942 §1; Stats 1933 ch 744 §5; Stats 1970 ch 604 §1; Stats 1971 ch 957 §1; Stats 1994 ch 1269 §2.2 (AB 2208); Stats 2002 ch 784 §52 (SB 1316), ch 927 §1 (AB 3032) (ch 927 prevails).

§395. County in which defendants reside; Personal injury; Family law matters; Contract to perform obligation in county; Contract involving goods for personal or family use

(a) Except as otherwise provided by law and subject to the power of the court to transfer actions or proceedings as provided in this title, the superior court in the county where the defendants or some of them reside at the commencement of the action is the proper court for the trial of the action. If the action is for injury to person or personal property or for death from wrongful act or negligence, the superior court in either the county where the injury occurs or the injury causing death occurs or the county where the defendants, or some of them reside at the commencement of the action, is a proper court for the trial of the action. In a proceeding for dissolution of marriage, the superior court in the county where either the petitioner or respondent has been a resident for three months next preceding the commencement of the proceeding is the proper court for the trial of the proceeding. In a proceeding for nullity of marriage or legal separation of the parties, the superior court in the county where either the petitioner or the respondent resides at the commencement of the proceeding is the proper court for the trial of the proceeding. In a proceeding to enforce an obligation of support under Section 3900 of the Family Code, the superior court in the county where the child resides is the proper court for the trial of the action. In a proceeding to establish and enforce a foreign judgment or court order for the support of a minor child, the superior court in the county where the child resides is the proper court for the trial of the action. Subject to subdivision (b), if a defendant has contracted to perform an obligation in a particular county, the superior court in the county where the obligation is to be performed, where the contract in fact was entered into, or where the defendant or any defendant resides at the commencement of the action is a proper court for the trial of an action founded on that obligation, and the county where the obligation is incurred is the county where it is to be performed, unless there is a special contract in writing to the contrary. If none of the defendants reside in the state or if they reside in the state and the county where they reside is unknown to the plaintiff, the action may be tried in the superior court in any county that the plaintiff may designate in his or her complaint, and, if the defendant is about to depart from the state, the action may be tried in the superior court in any county where either of the parties reside or service is made. If any person is improperly joined as a defendant or has been made a defendant solely for the purpose of having the action tried in the superior court in the county where he or she resides, his or her residence shall not be considered in determining the proper place for the trial of the action.

(b) Subject to the power of the court to transfer actions or proceedings as provided in this title, in an action arising from an offer or provision of goods, services, loans or extensions of credit intended primarily for personal, family or household use, other than an obligation described in Section 1812.10 or Section 2984.4 of the Civil Code, or an action arising from a transaction consummated as a proximate result of either an unsolicited telephone call made by a seller engaged in the business of consummating transactions of that kind or a telephone call or electronic transmission made by the buyer or lessee in response to a solicitation by the seller, the superior court in the county where the buyer or lessee in fact signed the contract, where the buyer or lessee resided at the time the contract was entered into, or where the buyer or lessee resides at the commencement of the action is the proper court for the trial of the action. In the superior court designated in this subdivision as the proper court, the proper court location for trial of a case is the location where the court tries that type of case that is nearest or most accessible to where the buyer or lessee resides, where the buyer or lessee in fact signed the contract, where the buyer or lessee resided at the time the contract was entered into, or where the buyer or lessee resides at the commencement of the action. Otherwise, any location of the superior court designated as the proper court in this subdivision is a proper court location for the trial. The court may specify by local rule the nearest or most accessible court location where the court tries that type of case.

(c) Any provision of an obligation described in subdivision (b) waiving that subdivision is void and unenforceable. **Leg.H.** Enacted 1872.

Amended Stats 1907 ch 369 §3; Stats 1911 ch 421 §1; Stats 1933 ch 744 §6; Stats 1939 ch 981 §1; Stats 1951 ch 869 §3, operative January 1, 1952; Stats 1955 ch 832 §1; Stats 1969 ch 1608 §11, operative January 1, 1970; Stats 1970 ch 75 §1; Stats 1971 ch 1640 §1; Stats 1972 ch 1117 §1, ch 1118 §3, ch 1119 §3; Stats 1976 ch 610 §1; Stats 1991 ch 228 §3 (AB 1889); Stats 1992 ch 163 §17 (AB 2641), operative January 1, 1994; Stats 1994 ch 1269 §2.4 (AB 2208); Stats 1998 ch 473 §1 (AB 2134), ch 931 §62 (SB 2139), effective September 28, 1998, operative until January 1, 1999, §62.5 (SB 2139), effective September 28, 1998, operative January 1, 1999; Stats 2002 ch 806 §8 (AB 3027).

§395.1. Venue of action against defendant sued in official or representative capacity

Except as otherwise provided in Section 17005 of the Probate Code pertaining to trustees, when a defendant is sued in an official or representative capacity as executor, administrator, guardian, conservator, or trustee on a claim for the payment of money or for the recovery of personal property, the county which has jurisdiction of the estate which the defendant represents shall be the proper county for the trial of the action. **Leg.H.** Added Stats 1943 ch 1043 §1. Amended Stats 1979 ch 730 §20, operative January 1, 1981; Stats 1986 ch 820 §16, effective September 15, 1986, operative July 1, 1987.

§395.2. Venue of action against association

If an unincorporated association has filed a statement with the Secretary of State pursuant to statute, designating its principal office in this state, the proper county for the trial of an action against the unincorporated association is the same as it would be if the unincorporated association were a corporation and, for the purpose of determining the proper county, the principal place of business of the unincorporated association shall be deemed to be the principal office in this state listed in the statement. **Leg.H.** Added Stats 1967 ch 1324 §2. Amended Stats 2004 ch 178 §2 (SB 1746).

§395.5. Venue of action on obligation of corporation or association

A corporation or association may be sued in the county where the contract is made or is to be performed, or where the obligation or liability arises, or the breach occurs; or in the county where the principal place of business of such corporation is situated, subject to the power of the court to change the place of trial as in other cases. **Leg.H.** Added by Stats 1972 ch 118 §1, effective June 5, 1972, operative June 6, 1972.

§395.9. [Section repealed 1999]

Leg.H. Added Stats 1998 ch 931 §63 (SB 2139), effective September 28, 1998. Repealed Stats 1999 ch 344 §8 (SB 210), effective September 7, 1999. See CCP §§403.010, 403.040, 403.050, 403.070.

§396. Filing of appeal or petition in wrong state court not grounds for dismissal; Transfer from superior court to court of appeal or Supreme Court having jurisdiction

(a) No appeal or petition filed in the superior court shall be dismissed solely because the appeal or petition was not filed in the proper state court.

(b) If the superior court lacks jurisdiction of an appeal or petition, and a court of appeal or the Supreme Court would have jurisdiction, the appeal or petition shall be transferred to the court having jurisdiction upon terms as to costs or otherwise as may be just, and proceeded with as if regularly filed in the court having jurisdiction. **Leg.H.** Added Stats 2008 ch 56 §2 (SB 1182), effective January 1, 2009.

Former Sections: Former CCP §396, relating to transfer of case from court lacking jurisdiction, was added Stats 1933 ch 744 §7 and repealed Stats 2008 ch 56 §1 (SB 1182).

Prior Law: Former CCP §396, relating to transfer of case from court lacking jurisdiction, was added Stats 1933 ch 744 §7, amended Stats 1935 ch 722 §1, Stats 1941 ch 454 §1, Stats 1951 ch 869 §4, Stats 1959 ch 1487 §1, Stats 1971 ch 244 §16, Stats 1974 ch 1369 §1, Stats 1998 ch 931 §64 (SB 2139), effective September 28, 1998, Stats 2002 ch 784 §53 (SB 1316), ch 806 §9 (AB 3027) (ch 806 prevails), and repealed Stats 2008 ch 56 §1 (SB 1182), effective January 1, 2009.

§396a. Filing of affidavit of jurisdiction by plaintiff; Motion to transfer

In a case that is subject to Sections 1812.10 and 2984.4 of the Civil Code, or subdivision (b) of Section 395 of the Code of Civil Procedure, or in an action or proceeding for an unlawful detainer as defined in Section 1161 of the Code of Civil Procedure:

(a) The plaintiff shall state facts in the complaint, verified by the plaintiff's oath, or the oath of the plaintiff's attorney, or in an affidavit of the plaintiff or of the plaintiff's attorney filed with the complaint, showing that the action has been commenced in the proper superior court and the proper court location for the trial of the action or proceeding, and showing that the action is subject to the provisions of Sections 1812.10 and 2984.4 of the Civil Code or subdivision (b) of Section 395 of the Code of Civil Procedure, or is an action for an unlawful detainer. When the affidavit is filed with the complaint, a copy thereof shall be served with the summons. Except as provided in this section, if the complaint or affidavit is not filed pursuant to this subdivision, no further proceedings may occur in the action or proceeding, except to dismiss the action or proceeding without prejudice. However, the court may, on terms that are just, permit the affidavit to be filed after the filing of the complaint, and a copy of the affidavit shall be served on the defendant and the time to answer or otherwise plead shall date from that service.

(b) If it appears from the complaint or affidavit, or otherwise, that the superior court or court location where the action or proceeding is commenced is not the proper court or court location for the trial, the court where the action or proceeding is commenced, or a judge thereof, shall, whenever that fact appears, transfer it to the proper court or court location, on its own motion, or on motion of the defendant, unless the defendant consents in writing, or in open court (consent in open court being entered in the minutes of the court), to the keeping of the action or proceeding in the court or court location where commenced. If that consent is given, the action or proceeding may continue in the court or court location where commenced. Notwithstanding Section 1801.1 and subdivision (f) of Section 2983.7 of the Civil Code, that consent may be given by a defendant who is represented by counsel at the time the consent is given, and if an action or proceeding is subject to subdivision (b) of Section 395 or is for an unlawful detainer, that consent may only be given by a defendant who is represented by counsel at the time the consent is given.

(c) In any case where the transfer of the action or proceeding is ordered under subdivision (a) or (b), if summons is served prior to the filing of the action or proceeding in the superior court or court location to which it is transferred, as to any defendant, so served, who has not appeared in the action or proceeding, the time to answer or otherwise plead shall date from service upon that defendant of written notice of the filing.

(d) If it appears from the complaint or affidavit of the plaintiff that the superior court and court location where the action or proceeding is commenced are a proper court and court location for the trial thereof, all proper proceedings may be had, and the action or proceeding may be tried in that court at that location.

(e) A motion for a transfer of the action or proceeding to a different superior court may be made as in other cases, within the time, upon the grounds, and in the manner provided in this title, and if upon that motion it appears that the action or proceeding is not pending in the proper court, or should for other cause be transferred, the action or proceeding shall be ordered transferred as provided in this title.

If any action or proceeding is ordered transferred to another court as provided in this section, proceedings shall be had, and the costs and fees shall be paid, as provided in Sections 398 and 399.

(f) If a motion is made for transfer of an action or proceeding to a different court location within the same superior court as provided in this section, proceedings shall be had as provided by local rules of the superior court. **Leg.H.** Added Stats 1933 ch 744 §8. Amended Stats 1935 ch 722 §2; Stats 1937 ch 97 §1; Stats 1949 ch 1286 §3, effective November 7, 1950, operative January 1, 1952; Stats 1951 ch 869 §5, operative January 1, 1952; Stats 1970 ch 725 §3; Stats 1976 ch 1288 §11; Stats 1982 ch 38 §1; Stats 1998 ch 931 §65 (SB 2139), effective September 28, 1998; Stats 2002 ch 806 §10 (AB 3027); Stats 2007 ch 263 §5 (AB 310), effective January 1, 2008.

§396b. Procedure to transfer; Authority of court

(a) Except as otherwise provided in Section 396a, if an action or proceeding is commenced in a court having jurisdiction of the subject matter thereof, other than the court designated as the proper court for the trial thereof, under this title, the action may, notwithstanding, be tried in the court where commenced, unless the defendant, at the time he or she answers, demurs, or moves to strike, or, at his or her option, without answering, demurring, or moving to strike and within the time otherwise allowed to respond to the complaint, files with the clerk, a notice of motion for an order transferring the action or proceeding to the proper court, together with proof of service, upon the adverse party, of a copy of those papers. Upon the hearing of the motion the court shall, if it appears that the action or proceeding was not commenced in the proper court, order the action or proceeding transferred to the proper court.

(b) In its discretion, the court may order the payment to the prevailing party of reasonable expenses and attorney's fees incurred in making or resisting the motion to transfer whether or not that party is otherwise entitled to recover his or her costs of action. In determining whether that order for expenses and fees shall be made, the court shall take into consideration (1) whether an offer to stipulate to change of venue was reasonably made and rejected, and (2) whether the motion or selection of venue was made in good faith given the facts and law the party making the motion or selecting the venue knew or should have known. As between the party and his or her attorney, those expenses and fees shall be the personal liability of the attorney not chargeable to the party. Sanctions shall not be imposed pursuant to this subdivision except on notice contained in a party's papers, or on the court's own noticed motion, and after opportunity to be heard.

(c) The court in a proceeding for dissolution of marriage or legal separation or under the Uniform Parentage Act (Part 3 (commencing with Section 7600) of Division 12 of the Family Code) may, prior to the determination of the motion to transfer, consider and determine motions for allowance of temporary spousal support, support of children, and counsel fees and costs, and motions to determine custody of and visitation with children, and may make all necessary and proper orders in connection therewith.

(d) In any case, if an answer is filed, the court may consider opposition to the motion to transfer, if any, and may retain the action in the county where commenced if it appears that the convenience of the witnesses or the ends of justice will thereby be promoted.

(e) If the motion to transfer is denied, the court shall allow the defendant time to move to strike, demur, or otherwise plead if the defendant has not previously filed a response. **Leg.H.** Added Stats 1933 ch 744 §8a. Amended Stats 1939 ch 149 §1; Stats 1951 ch 869 §6, operative January 1, 1952; Stats 1969 ch 345 §1, ch 1608 §12, ch 1609 §28, operative January 1, 1970; Stats 1974 ch 1369 §2; Stats 1981 ch 122 §1; Stats 1982 ch 704 §1; Stats 1983 ch 1167 §1; Stats 1989 ch 1416 §11, ch 1417 §3.5; Stats 1992 ch 163 §18 (AB 2641), operative January 1, 1994; Stats 2005 ch 706 §10 (AB 1742), effective January 1, 2006.

§397. Cases in which venue may be changed

The court may, on motion, change the place of trial in the following cases:

(a) When the court designated in the complaint is not the proper court.

(b) When there is reason to believe that an impartial trial cannot be had therein.

(c) When the convenience of witnesses and the ends of justice would be promoted by the change.

(d) When from any cause there is no judge of the court qualified to act.

(e) When a proceeding for dissolution of marriage has been filed in the county in which the petitioner has been a resident for three months next preceding the commencement of the proceeding, and the respondent at the time of the commencement of the proceeding is a resident of another county in this state, to the county of the respondent's residence when the ends of justice would be promoted by the change. If a motion to change the place of trial is made pursuant to this paragraph, the court may, prior to the determination of such motion, consider and determine motions for allowance of temporary spousal support, support of children, temporary restraining orders, attorneys' fees, and costs, and make all necessary and proper orders in connection therewith. **Leg.H.** Enacted 1872. Amended Stats 1907 ch 369 §5; Stats 1933 ch 744 §9; Stats 1955 ch 832 §2; Stats 1969 ch 1608 §13, operative January 1, 1970; Stats 1992 ch 163 §19 (AB 2641), operative January 1, 1994.

§397.5. Transfer of proceedings under Family Law Act

In any proceeding [1] under the Family Code [2] where it appears that both petitioner and respondent have moved from the county rendering the order, the court may, when the ends of justice and the convenience of the parties would be promoted by the change, order that the proceedings be transferred to the county of residence of either party. **In any proceeding in which there is a concurrent action or proceeding under Division 17 (commencing with Section 17000) of the Family Code involving the local child support agency, the court may transfer venue under this** section for any action or proceeding not subject to Division 17 (commencing with Section 17000) of the Family Code, but shall redirect any motion pursuant to this section to the court of competent jurisdiction under Section 4251 of the Family Code for change of venue in those actions and proceedings subject to Division 17 (commencing with Section 17000) of the Family Code. The decision on any motion redirected pursuant to the preceding sentence shall apply only to the action or proceeding under Division 17 (commencing with Section 17000) of the Family Code and shall be at the sole discretion of the court of competent jurisdiction hearing the action or proceeding pursuant to Section 4251 of the Family Code. **Leg.H.** Added Stats 1971 ch 1210 §7. Amended Stats 1980 ch 234 §2; Stats 1994 ch 1269 §2.6 (AB 2208); Stats 2024 ch 853 §18 (AB 3281), effective January 1, 2025.

§397.5. 2024 Deletes. [1] for dissolution or nullity of marriage or legal separation of the parties [2].

§398. Court to which action should be transferred

(a) If a court orders the transfer of an action or proceeding for a cause specified in subdivisions (b), (c), and (d) of Section 397, the action or proceeding shall be transferred to a court having jurisdiction of the subject matter of the action upon agreement of the parties by stipulation in writing, or in open court and entered in the minutes or docket. If the parties do not so agree, the action or proceeding shall be transferred to the nearest or most accessible court where the like objection or cause for making the order does not exist.

(b) If an action or proceeding is commenced in a court other than one designated as a proper court for the trial thereof by the provisions of this title, and the same is ordered transferred for that reason, the action or proceeding shall be transferred to a proper court upon agreement of the parties by stipulation in writing, or in open court and entered in the minutes or docket. If the parties do not so agree, the action or proceeding shall be transferred to a proper court in the county in which the action or proceeding was commenced which the defendant may designate or, if there is no proper court in that county, to a proper court, in a proper county, designated by the defendant. If the defendant does not designate the court as herein provided, or if the court orders the transfer of an action on its own motion as provided in this title, the action or proceeding shall be transferred to the proper court as determined by the court in which the action or proceeding is pending.

(c) The designation of the court by the defendant as provided for in subdivision (b), may be made in the notice of motion for change of venue or in open court and entered in the minutes or docket at the time the order for transfer is made. **Leg.H.** Enacted 1872. Amended Stats 1881 ch 30 §2; Stats 1897 ch 124 §1; Stats 1925 ch 438 §1; Stats 1927 ch 744 §2; Stats 1933 ch 744 §10; 2015 ch 303 §39 (AB 731), effective January 1, 2016.

§399. Transmittal of records or transcript to transferee court; Payment of costs and fees; Recovery or offset; Notice of transmittal; Jurisdiction of transferee court

(a) If an order is made transferring an action or proceeding under any provision of this title, the clerk shall, after expiration of the time within which a petition for writ of mandate could have been filed pursuant to Section 400, or if a writ petition is filed after judgment denying the writ becomes final, and upon payment of the costs and fees, transmit the pleadings and papers of the action or proceeding, or, if the pleadings are oral, a transcript of the pleadings, to the clerk of the court to which the action or proceeding is transferred. If the transfer is sought on any ground specified in subdivision (b), (c), (d), or (e) of Section 397 **or in Section 397.5**, the costs and fees of the transfer, and of filing the papers in the court to which the transfer is ordered, shall be paid at the time the notice of motion is filed by the party making the motion for the transfer. If the transfer is sought solely, or is ordered, because the action or proceeding was commenced in a court other than that designated as proper by this title, those costs and fees, including any expenses and attorney's fees awarded to the defendant pursuant to Section 396b, shall be paid by the plaintiff before the transfer is made. If the defendant has paid those costs and fees at the time of filing a notice of motion, those costs and fees shall be repaid to the defendant, upon the making of the transfer order. If those costs and fees have not been paid by the plaintiff within five days after service of notice of the transfer order, any other party interested in the action or proceeding, whether named in the complaint as a party or not, may pay those costs and fees, and the clerk shall transmit the papers and pleadings of the action or proceeding as if those costs and fees had been originally paid by the plaintiff, and those costs and fees shall be a proper item of costs of the party paying them, recoverable by that party if that party prevails in the action. Otherwise, those costs and fees shall be offset against and deducted from the amount, if any, awarded to the plaintiff if the plaintiff prevails against that party in the action. The cause of action shall not be further prosecuted in any court until those costs and fees are paid. If those costs and fees are not paid within 30 days after service of notice of the transfer order, if a copy of a petition for writ of mandate pursuant to Section 400 is filed in the trial court, or if an appeal is taken pursuant to Section 904.2, then, within 30 days after notice of finality of the order of transfer, the court on a duly noticed motion by any party may dismiss the action without prejudice to the cause on the condition that no other action on the cause may be commenced in another court before satisfaction of the court's order for costs and fees. If a petition for writ of mandate or appeal does not result in a stay of proceedings, the time for payment of those costs and fees shall be 60 days after service of the notice of the order.

(b) At the time of transmittal of the papers and pleadings, the clerk shall mail notice to all parties who have appeared in the action or special proceeding, stating the date on which the transmittal occurred. Promptly upon receipt of the papers and pleadings, the clerk of the court to which the action or proceeding is transferred shall mail notice to all parties who have appeared in the action or special proceeding, stating the date of the filing of the case and number assigned to the case in the court.

(c) The court to which an action or proceeding is transferred under this title shall have and exercise over the action or proceeding the like jurisdiction as if it had been originally commenced in that court, all prior proceedings being saved, and the court may require amendment of the pleadings, the filing and service of amended, additional, or supplemental pleadings, and the giving of notice, as may be necessary for the proper presentation and determination of the action or proceeding in the court.

(d) Notwithstanding subdivision (c), the court transferring jurisdiction of a family law action or proceeding pursuant to Section **397, 397.5, or** 398 shall, if another court has not assumed jurisdiction over the action or proceeding, retain jurisdiction to make orders designed to prevent:

(1) Immediate danger or irreparable harm to a party or to the children involved in the matter.

(2) Immediate loss or damage to property subject to disposition in the matter.

(e) By January 1, 2019, the Judicial Council shall, by rule of court, establish:

(1) The timeframe for a court to transfer jurisdiction over a family law action or proceeding.

(2) The timeframe for a court to assume jurisdiction over a family law action or proceeding. **Leg.H.** Enacted 1872. Amended Stats 1909 ch 723 §1; Stats 1933 ch 744 §11; Stats 1935 ch 722 §3; Stats 1951 ch 869 §7, operative January 1, 1952; Stats 1955 ch 832 §3; Stats 1959 ch 1487 §2; Stats 1961 ch 1059 §1; Stats 1969 ch 345 §2; Stats 1974 ch 1369 §3; Stats 1989 ch 1417 §4; Stats 2007 ch 43 §4 (SB 649), effective January 1, 2008; Stats 2017 ch 316 §1 (AB 712), effective January 1, 2018; Stats 2024 ch 853 §19 (AB 3281), effective January 1, 2025.

§399.5. [Section repealed 1999]

Leg.H. Added Stats 1998 ch 931 §66 (SB 2139), effective September 28, 1998. Repealed Stats 1999 ch 344 §9 (SB 210), effective September 7, 1999. See CCP §§403.020, 403.060, 403.070.

§400. Writ of mandate requiring trial of case in proper court

When an order is made by the superior court granting or denying a motion to change the place of trial, the party aggrieved by the order may, within 20 days after service of a written notice of the order, petition the court of appeal for the district in which the court granting or denying the motion is situated for a writ of mandate requiring trial of the case in the proper court. The superior court may, for good cause, and prior to the expiration of the initial 20-day period, extend the time for one additional period not to exceed 10 days. The petitioner shall file a copy of the petition in the trial court immediately after the petition is filed in the court of appeal. The court of appeal may stay all proceedings in the case, pending judgment on the petition becoming final. The clerk of the court of appeal shall file with the clerk of the trial court, a copy of any final order or final judgment immediately after the order or judgment becomes final. **Leg.H.** Added Stats 1961 ch 1059 §3. Amended Stats 1963 ch 461 §1;

Stats 1967 ch 17 §12; Stats 1984 ch 145 §1; Stats 1989 ch 1416 §12; Stats 1998 ch 931 §67 (SB 2139), effective September 28, 1998; Stats 1999 ch 344 §10 (SB 210), effective September 7, 1999.

Prior Law: Former CCP §400, relating to transfer of judgment in actions affecting real property, was enacted 1872, amended by Stats 1933 ch 744 §12, and repealed by Stats 1957 ch 2388 §1.

§401. Actions commenced or removed to county with office of attorney general

(1) Whenever it is provided by any law of this State that an action or proceeding against the State or a department, institution, board, commission, bureau, officer or other agency thereof shall or may be commenced in, tried in, or removed to the County of Sacramento, the same may be commenced and tried in any city or city and county of this State in which the Attorney General has an office.

(2) Whenever it is provided by any law of this State that the State or a department, institution, board, commission, bureau, officer or other agency thereof shall or may commence an action or proceeding in the County of Sacramento, the same, on motion of the defendants or some of them, shall be removed for trial to the county or city and county in which the Attorney General has an office nearest to the county in which the defendants or some of them reside or have their principal office in this State. **Leg.H.** Added Stats 1947 ch 306 §1.

§402. Superior court to decide location of filing and hearing; Transfer

(a) Except as otherwise provided by law:

(1) A superior court may specify by local rule the locations where certain types of actions or proceedings are to be filed.

(2) A superior court may specify by local rule the locations where certain types of actions or proceedings are to be heard or tried.

(3) A superior court may not dismiss a case, and the clerk may not reject a case for filing, because it is filed, or a person seeks to file it, in a court location other than the location specified by local rule. However, the court may transfer the case on its own motion to the proper court location.

(b) A superior court may transfer an action or proceeding filed in one location to another location of the superior court. This section does not affect the authority of the presiding judge to apportion the business of the court as provided by the California Rules of Court. **Leg.H.** Added Stats 2002 ch 806 §12 (AB 3027).

Former Sections: Former CCP §402, relating to transfer to contiguous municipal court district in same county, was added Stats 1963 ch 966 §1 and repealed Stats 2002 ch 784 §54, ch 806 §11.

Prior Law: Former CCP §402, relating to transfer to contiguous municipal court district in same county, was added Stats 1963 ch 966 §1, amended Stats 1965 ch 1695 §4, ch 1696 §2; Stats 1977 ch 1257 §9, Stats 1998 ch 931 §68, and repealed Stats 2002 ch 784 §54, ch 806 §11 (806 prevails).

§402.5. [Section repealed 2003]

Leg.H. Added Stats 1998 ch 931 §69 (SB 2139), effective September 28, 1998. Repealed Stats 2002 ch 806 §13 (AB 3027). The repealed section related to transfer of cases by superior court to another location in same county.

§403. Transfers

A judge may, on motion, transfer an action or actions from another court to that judge's court for coordination with an action involving a common question of fact or law within the meaning of Section 404. The motion shall be supported by a declaration stating facts showing that the actions meet the standards specified in Section 404.1, are not complex as defined by the Judicial Council and that the moving party has made a good faith effort to obtain agreement to the transfer from all parties to each action. Notice of the motion shall be served on all parties to each action and on each court in which an action is pending. Any party to that action may file papers opposing the motion within the time permitted by rule of the Judicial Council. The court to which a case is transferred may order the cases consolidated for trial pursuant to Section 1048 without any further motion or hearing.

The Judicial Council may adopt rules to implement this section, including rules prescribing procedures for preventing duplicative or conflicting transfer orders issued by different courts. **Leg.H.** Added Stats 1996 ch 713 §1 (SB 1726), effective September 23, 1996. Amended Stats 2000 ch 688 §2 (AB 1669); Stats 2002 ch 784 §55 (SB 1316).

Prior Law: Former CCP §403, similar to present CCP §402, was added Stats 1965 ch 1694 §1 and repealed Stats 1979 ch 212 §1.

CHAPTER 2
RECLASSIFICATION OF CIVIL ACTIONS AND PROCEEDINGS

Affect on law governing amended pleadings. §403.010.
Amendment to pleading that changes jurisdictional classification; Clerk's duty to reclassify case. §403.020.
Filing of cross-complaint that renders case ineligible to proceed as limited civil case; Clerk's duty to reclassify the case. §403.030.
Plaintiff's motion for reclassification within time allowed for amending initial pleading; Defendant's motion following time allowed response; Remitting of excess in amount of demand. §403.040.
Stipulation by parties to reclassification; Fee; Clerk's duty to reclassify the case. §403.050.
Reclassify fees; Nonpayment of fees; Reclassification from unlimited civil case to limited civil case. §403.060.
Time of commencement of reclassified action; Effect of reclassification on court's authority. §403.070.
Petition for writ of mandate requiring proper classification of action or proceeding. §403.080.
Rules of procedure. §403.090.

§403.010. Affect on law governing amended pleadings

Nothing in this chapter expands or limits the law on whether a plaintiff, cross-complainant, or petitioner may file an amended complaint or other amended initial pleading. Nothing in this chapter expands or limits the law on whether, and to what extent, an amendment relates back to the date of filing the original complaint or other initial pleading. **Leg.H.** Added Stats 1999 ch 344 §11 (SB 210), effective September 7, 1999. Amended Stats 2002 ch 784 §56 (SB 1316).

§403.020. Amendment to pleading that changes jurisdictional classification; Clerk's duty to reclassify case

(a) If a plaintiff, cross-complainant, or petitioner files an amended complaint or other amended initial pleading that changes the jurisdictional classification from limited to unlimited, the party at the time of filing the pleading shall pay the reclassification fee provided in Section 403.060, and the clerk shall promptly reclassify the case. If the amendment changes the jurisdictional classification from unlimited to limited, no reclassification fee is required, and the clerk shall promptly reclassify the case.

(b) For purposes of this chapter, an amendment to an initial pleading shall be treated in the same manner as an amended initial pleading. **Leg.H.** Added Stats 1999 ch 344 §11 (SB 210), effective September 7, 1999. Amended Stats 2001 ch 159 §38 (SB 662); Ch 824 §2 (AB 1700).

§403.030. Filing of cross-complaint that renders case ineligible to proceed as limited civil case; Clerk's duty to reclassify the case

If a party in a limited civil case files a cross-complaint that causes the action or proceeding to exceed the maximum amount in controversy for a limited civil case or otherwise fail to satisfy the requirements for a limited civil case as prescribed by Section 85, the caption of the cross-complaint shall state that the action or proceeding is a limited civil case to be reclassified by cross-complaint, or words to that effect. The party at the time of filing the cross-complaint shall pay the reclassification fees provided in Section 403.060, and the clerk shall promptly reclassify the case. **Leg.H.** Added Stats 1999 ch 344 §11 (SB 210), effective September 7, 1999. Amended Stats 2001 ch 824 §3 (AB 1700).

§403.040. Plaintiff's motion for reclassification within time allowed for amending initial pleading; Defendant's motion following time allowed response; Remitting of excess in amount of demand

(a) The plaintiff, cross-complainant, or petitioner may file a motion for reclassification within the time allowed for that party to amend the initial pleading. The defendant or cross-defendant may file a motion for reclassification within the time allowed for that party to respond to the initial pleading. The court, on its own motion, may reclassify a case at any time. A motion for reclassification does not extend the moving party's time to amend or answer or otherwise respond. The court shall grant the motion and enter an order for reclassification, regardless of any fault or lack of fault, if the case has been classified in an incorrect jurisdictional classification.

(b) If a party files a motion for reclassification after the time for that party to amend that party's initial pleading or to respond to a complaint, cross-complaint, or other initial pleading, the court shall grant the motion and enter an order for reclassification only if both of the following conditions are satisfied:

(1) The case is incorrectly classified.

(2) The moving party shows good cause for not seeking reclassification earlier.

(c) If the court grants a motion for reclassification, the payment of the reclassification fee shall be determined, unless the court orders otherwise, as follows:

(1) If a case is reclassified as an unlimited civil case, the party whose pleading causes the action or proceeding to exceed the maximum amount in controversy for a limited civil case or otherwise fails to satisfy the requirements of a limited civil case under Section 85 shall pay the reclassification fee provided in Section 403.060.

(2) If a case is reclassified as a limited civil case, no reclassification fee is required.

(d) If the court grants an order for reclassification of an action or proceeding pursuant to this section, the reclassification shall proceed as follows:

(1) If the required reclassification fee is paid pursuant to Section 403.060 or no reclassification fee is required, the clerk shall promptly reclassify the case.

(2) An action that has been reclassified pursuant to this section shall not be further prosecuted in any court until the required reclassification fee is paid. If the required reclassification fee has not been paid within five days after service of notice of the order for reclassification, any party interested in the case, regardless of whether that party is named in the complaint, may pay the fee, and the clerk shall promptly reclassify the case as if the fee had been paid as provided in Section 403.060. The fee shall then be a proper item of costs of the party paying it, recoverable if that party prevails in the action or proceeding. Otherwise, the fee shall be offset against and deducted from the amount, if any, awarded to the party responsible for the fee, if that party prevails in the action or proceeding.

(3) If the fee is not paid within 30 days after service of notice of an order of reclassification, the court on its own motion or the motion of any party may order the case to proceed as a limited civil case, dismiss the action or cross-action without prejudice on the condition that no other action or proceeding on the same matters may be commenced in any other court until the reclassification fee is paid, or take such other action as the court may deem appropriate.

(e) Nothing in this section shall be construed to require the superior court to reclassify an action or proceeding because the judgment to be rendered, as determined at the trial or hearing, is one that might have been rendered in a limited civil case.

(f) In any case where the misclassification is due solely to an excess in the amount of the demand, the excess may be remitted and the action may continue as a limited civil case. **Leg.H.** Added Stats 1999 ch 344 §11 (SB 210), effective September 7, 1999. Amended Stats 2001 ch 824 §4 (AB 1700).

§403.050. Stipulation by parties to reclassification; Fee; Clerk's duty to reclassify the case

(a) The parties to the action or proceeding may stipulate to reclassification of the case within the time allowed to respond to the initial pleading.

(b) If the stipulation for reclassification changes the jurisdictional classification of the case from limited to unlimited, the reclassification fee provided in Section 403.060 shall be paid at the time the stipulation is filed.

(c) Upon filing of the stipulation and, if required under subdivision (b), the payment of the reclassification fee provided in Section 403.060, the clerk shall promptly reclassify the case. **Leg.H.** Added Stats 2001 ch 824 §6 (AB 1700).

Former Sections: Former CCP §403.050, similar to present section, as added Stats 1999 ch 344 §11, effective September 7, 1999, was repealed Stats 2001 ch 824 §5.

Prior Law: Former CCP §403.050, similar to present section, as added Stats 1999 ch 344 §11, effective September 7, 1999, was repealed Stats 2001 ch 824 §5.

§403.060. Reclassify fees; Nonpayment of fees; Reclassification from unlimited civil case to limited civil case

(a) For reclassification of a case from a limited civil case to an unlimited civil case, a fee shall be charged as provided in Section 70619 of the Government Code. This reclassification fee shall be in addition to any other fee due for that appearance or filing in a limited civil case. No additional amounts shall be charged for appearance or filing fees paid prior to reclassification. After reclassification, the fees ordinarily charged in an unlimited case shall be charged.

(b) If a reclassification fee is required and is not paid at the time an amended complaint or other initial pleading, a cross-complaint, or a stipulation for reclassification is filed under Section 403.020, 403.030, or 403.050, the clerk shall not reclassify the case and the case shall remain and proceed as a limited civil case.

(c) No fee shall be charged for reclassification of a case from an unlimited civil case to a limited civil case. The fees ordinarily required for filing or appearing in a limited civil case shall be charged at the time of filing a pleading that reclassifies the case. Parties are not entitled to a refund of the difference between any fees previously paid for appearance or filing in an unlimited civil case and the fees due in a limited civil case. After reclassification, the fees ordinarily charged in a limited civil case shall be charged. **Leg.H.** Added Stats 2001 ch 824 §8 (AB 1700). Amended Stats 2005 ch 75 §29 (AB 145), effective July 19, 2005, operative January 1, 2006.

Former Sections: Former CCP §403.060, similar to present section, as added Stats 1999 ch 344 §11, effective September 7, 1999, was repealed Stats 2001 ch 824 §7.

Prior Law: Former CCP §403.060, similar to present section, as added Stats 1999 ch 344 §11, effective September 7, 1999, was repealed Stats 2001 ch 824 §7.

§403.070. Time of commencement of reclassified action; Effect of reclassification on court's authority

(a) An action or proceeding that is reclassified shall be deemed to have been commenced at the time the complaint or petition was initially filed, not at the time of reclassification.

(b) The court shall have and exercise over the reclassified action or proceeding the same authority as if the action or proceeding had been originally commenced as reclassified, all prior proceedings being saved. The court may allow or require whatever amendment of the pleadings, filing and service of amended, additional, or supplemental pleadings, or giving of notice, or other appropriate action, as may be necessary for the proper presentation and determination of the action or proceeding as reclassified. **Leg.H.** Added Stats 1999 ch 344 §11 (SB 210), effective September 7, 1999.

§403.080. Petition for writ of mandate requiring proper classification of action or proceeding

When an order is made by the superior court granting or denying a motion to reclassify an action or proceeding pursuant to Section 403.040, the party aggrieved by the order may, within 20 days after service of a written notice of the order, petition the court of appeal for the district in which the court granting or denying the motion is situated for a writ of mandate requiring proper classification of the action or proceeding pursuant to Section 403.040. The superior court may, for good cause, and prior to the expiration of the initial 20-day period, extend the time for one additional period not to exceed 10 days. The petitioner shall file a copy of the petition in the superior court immediately after the petition is filed in the court of appeal. The court of appeal may stay all proceedings in the case, pending judgment on the petition becoming final. The clerk of the court of appeal shall file with the clerk of the superior court, a copy of any final order or final judgment immediately after the order or judgment becomes final. **Leg.H.** Added Stats 1999 ch 344 §11 (SB 210), effective September 7, 1999.

§403.090. Rules of procedure

The Judicial Council may prescribe rules, not inconsistent with statute, governing the procedure for reclassification of civil actions and proceedings. **Leg.H.** Added Stats 1999 ch 344 §11 (SB 210), effective September 7, 1999.

CHAPTER 3
COORDINATION

Coordination of actions pending in different courts. §404.
Specified conditions for coordination of civil actions. §404.1.
Selection of reviewing court. §404.2.
Assignment of judge. §404.3.
Order for coordinating particular action, on motion or judge's initiative. §404.4.
Stay pending determination. §404.5.

Mandamus petition. §404.6.
Judicial Council rule. §404.7.
State's payment of expenses. §404.8.
Delegation. §404.9.

§404. Coordination of actions pending in different courts

When civil actions sharing a common question of fact or law are pending in different courts, a petition for coordination may be submitted to the Chairperson of the Judicial Council, by the presiding judge of any such court, or by any party to one of the actions after obtaining permission from the presiding judge, or by all of the parties plaintiff or defendant in any such action. A petition for coordination, or a motion for permission to submit a petition, shall be supported by a declaration stating facts showing that the actions are complex, as defined by the Judicial Council and that the actions meet the standards specified in Section 404.1. On receipt of a petition for coordination, the Chairperson of the Judicial Council may assign a judge to determine whether the actions are complex, and if so, whether coordination of the actions is appropriate, or the Chairperson of the Judicial Council may authorize the presiding judge of a court to assign the matter to judicial officers of the court to make the determination in the same manner as assignments are made in other civil cases. **Leg.H.** Added Stats 1972 ch 1162 §2, operative January 1, 1974. Amended Stats 1982 ch 250 §1; Stats 1996 ch 713 §3 (SB 1726), effective September 23, 1996; Stats 2000 ch 688 §3 (AB 1669); Stats 2002 ch 784 §57 (SB 1316).

§404.1. Specified conditions for coordination of civil actions

Coordination of civil actions sharing a common question of fact or law is appropriate if one judge hearing all of the actions for all purposes in a selected site or sites will promote the ends of justice taking into account whether the common question of fact or law is predominating and significant to the litigation; the convenience of parties, witnesses, and counsel; the relative development of the actions and the work product of counsel; the efficient utilization of judicial facilities and manpower; the calendar of the courts; the disadvantages of duplicative and inconsistent rulings, orders, or judgments; and, the likelihood of settlement of the actions without further litigation should coordination be denied. **Leg.H.** Added by Stats 1972 ch 1162 §2, operative January 1, 1974.

§404.2. Selection of reviewing court

A judge assigned pursuant to Section 404 who determines that coordination is appropriate shall select the reviewing court having appellate jurisdiction if the actions to be coordinated are within the jurisdiction of more than one reviewing court. The assigned judge shall select the reviewing court which will promote the ends of justice as determined under the standards specified in Section 404.1. **Leg.H.** Added by Stats 1972 ch 1162 §2, operative January 1, 1974. Amended Stats 1996 ch 713 §4 (SB 1726), effective September 23, 1996.

§404.3. Assignment of judge

A judge assigned pursuant to Section 404 who determines that coordination is appropriate shall order the actions coordinated, report that fact to the Chairperson of the Judicial Council, and the Chairperson of the Judicial Council shall either assign a judge to hear and determine the actions in the site or sites the assigned judge finds appropriate or authorize the presiding judge of a court to assign the matter to judicial officers of the court in the same manner as assignments are made in other civil cases. **Leg.H.** Added Stats 1972 ch 1162 §2, operative January 1, 1974. Amended Stats 1980 ch 318 §1; Stats 1996 ch 713 §5 (SB 1726), effective September 23, 1996; Stats 2002 ch 784 §58 (SB 1316).

§404.4. Order for coordinating particular action, on motion or judge's initiative

The presiding judge of any court in which there is pending an action sharing a common question of fact or law with actions coordinated pursuant to Section 404, on the court's own motion or the motion of any party supported by an affidavit stating facts showing that the action meets the standards specified in Section 404.1, or all the parties plaintiff or defendant in any such action, supported by an affidavit stating facts showing that the action meets the standards specified in Section 404.1, may request the judge assigned to hear the coordinated actions for an order coordinating the action. Coordination of the action shall be determined under the standards specified in Section 404.1. **Leg.H.** Added by Stats 1972 ch 1162 §2, operative January 1, 1974. Amended Stats 1996 ch 713 §6 (SB 1726), effective September 23, 1996.

§404.5. Stay pending determination

Pending any determination of whether coordination is appropriate, the judge making that determination may stay any action being considered for, or affecting an action being considered for, coordination. **Leg.H.** Added by Stats 1972 ch 1162 §2, operative January 1, 1974.

§404.6. Mandamus petition

Within 20 days after service upon him or her of a written notice of entry of an order of the court under this chapter, any party may petition the appropriate reviewing court for a writ of mandate to require the court to make such order as the reviewing court finds appropriate. The superior court may, for good cause, and prior to the expiration of the initial 20-day period, extend the time for one additional period not to exceed 10 days. **Leg.H.** Added Stats 1972 ch 1162 §2, operative January 1, 1974. Amended Stats 1989 ch 1416 §13.

§404.7. Judicial Council rule

Notwithstanding any other provision of law, the Judicial Council shall provide by rule the practice and procedure for coordination of civil actions in convenient courts, including provision for giving notice and presenting evidence. **Leg.H.** Added by Stats 1972 ch 1162 §2, operative January 1, 1974.

§404.8. State's payment of expenses

Expenses of the assigned judge, other necessary judicial officers and employees, and facilities for cases coordinated under Section 404 shall be paid or reimbursed by the state from funds appropriated to the Judicial Council. **Leg.H.** Added by Stats 1972 ch 1162 §2, operative January 1, 1974. Amended Stats 1996 ch 713 §7 (SB 1726), effective September 23, 1996.

§404.9. Delegation

Any duties of the presiding judge specified in this chapter may be delegated by the presiding judge to another judge of the court. **Leg.H.** Added Stats 1996 ch 713 §8 (SB 1726), effective September 23, 1996. Amended Stats 2002 ch 784 §59 (SB 1316).

TITLE 4.5
RECORDING NOTICE OF CERTAIN ACTIONS

Chapter 1. Definitions and General Provisions.
Chapter 2. Recordation Service and Filing.
Chapter 3. Expungement and Other Relief.
Chapter 4. Withdrawal.
Chapter 5. Effect of Withdrawal or Expungement of Notice.

CHAPTER 1
DEFINITIONS AND GENERAL PROVISIONS

Governing definitions. §405.
"Claimant". §405.1.
"Notice of pendency of action"; "Notice". §405.2.
"Probable validity". §405.3.
"Real property claim". §405.4.
Application of title to federal actions. §405.5.
Action in eminent domain. §405.6.
Action to declare building uninhabitable. §405.7.
Other relief. §405.8.

§405. Governing definitions
The definitions in this chapter govern the construction of this title. **Leg.H.** Added Stats 1992 ch 883 §2 (AB 3620).

Prior Law: Former CCP §405, similar to present CCP §411.10, was enacted Stats 1872, amended Code Amdts 1873–74 ch 383 §45, and repealed Stats 1969 ch 1610 §4, operative July 1, 1970.

§405.1. "Claimant"
"Claimant" means a party to an action who asserts a real property claim and records a notice of the pendency of the action. **Leg.H.** Added Stats 1992 ch 883 §2 (AB 3620).

§405.2. "Notice of pendency of action"; "Notice"
"Notice of pendency of action" or "notice" means a notice of the pendency of an action in which a real property claim is alleged. **Leg.H.** Added Stats 1992 ch 883 §2 (AB 3620).

§405.3. "Probable validity"
"Probable validity," with respect to a real property claim, means that it is more likely than not that the claimant will obtain a judgment against the defendant on the claim. **Leg.H.** Added Stats 1992 ch 883 §2 (AB 3620).

§405.4. "Real property claim"
"Real property claim" means the cause or causes of action in a pleading which would, if meritorious, affect (a) title to, or the right to possession of, specific real property or (b) the use of an easement identified in the pleading, other than an easement obtained pursuant to statute by any regulated public utility. **Leg.H.** Added Stats 1992 ch 883 §2 (AB 3620).

§405.5. Application of title to federal actions
This title applies to an action pending in any United States District Court in the same manner that it applies to an action pending in the courts of this state. **Leg.H.** Added Stats 1992 ch 883 §2 (AB 3620).

Prior Law: Former CCP §405.5, similar to CCP §411.20, was added Stats 1955 ch 1446 §1 and repealed Stats 1969 ch 1610 §5, operative July 1, 1970.

§405.6. Action in eminent domain
In an action by a public agency in eminent domain pursuant to Title 7 (commencing with Section 1230.010) of Part 3, the issuance, service, and recordation of a notice of pendency of action shall be governed by Section 1250.150 and shall not be subject to Chapter 2 (commencing with Section 405.20). **Leg.H.** Added Stats 1992 ch 883 §2 (AB 3620).

§405.7. Action to declare building uninhabitable
Whenever an action is commenced to declare a building uninhabitable, the plaintiff public agency, at the time of filing the complaint, shall record in the office of the recorder of the county in which the building is situated, a notice of the pendency of the action, containing the names of the parties and a description of the real property upon which the building affected by the action is situated. **Leg.H.** Added Stats 1992 ch 883 §2 (AB 3620).

Prior Law: Former CCP §405.7 was added Stats 1967 ch 393 §1 and amended and renumbered CCP §1029.5 by Stats 1969 ch 1610 §6, operative July 1, 1970.

§405.8. Other relief
Nothing in this title precludes any party from seeking an attachment, injunction, or other relief in connection with a real property claim or the expungement of a notice of pending action. **Leg.H.** Added Stats 1992 ch 883 §2 (AB 3620).

Prior Law: Former CCP §405.8 was added Stats 1969 ch 608 §1 and renumbered CCP §1029.6 by Stats 1970 ch 910 §1.

CHAPTER 2
RECORDATION SERVICE AND FILING

Recording. §405.20.
Signature; Approval by judge. §405.21.
Service; Filing with court in which action pending. §405.22.
Effect of failure to properly serve. §405.23.
Notice imparted from time of recording; Rights and interest of claimant. §405.24.

§405.20. Recording
A party to an action who asserts a real property claim may record a notice of pendency of action in which that real property claim is alleged. The notice may be recorded in the office of the recorder of each county in which all or part of the real property is situated. The notice shall contain the names of all parties to the action and a description of the property affected by the action. **Leg.H.** Added Stats 1992 ch 883 §2 (AB 3620). Amended Stats 2004 ch 227 §10 (SB 1102), effective August 16, 2004.

§405.21. Signature; Approval by judge
An attorney of record in an action may sign a notice of pendency of action. Alternatively, a judge of the court in which an action that includes a real property claim is pending may, upon request of a party thereto, approve a notice of pendency of action. A notice of pendency of action shall not be recorded unless (a) it has been signed by the attorney of record, (b) it is signed by a party acting in propria persona and approved by a judge as provided in this section, or (c) the action is subject to Section 405.6. **Leg.H.** Added Stats 1992 ch 883 §2 (AB 3620). Amended Stats 1994 ch 146 §20 (AB 3601).

§405.22. Service; Filing with court in which action pending
Except in actions subject to Section 405.6, the claimant shall, prior to recordation of the notice, cause a copy of the notice to be mailed, by registered or certified mail, return receipt requested, to all known addresses of the parties to whom the real property claim is adverse and to all owners of record of the real property affected by the real property claim as shown by the latest county assessment roll. If there is no known address for service on an adverse party or owner, then as to that party or owner a declaration under penalty of perjury to that effect may be recorded instead of the proof of service required above, and the service on that party or owner shall not be required. Immediately following recordation, a copy of the notice shall also be filed with the court in which the action is pending. Service shall also be made immediately and in the same manner upon each adverse party later joined in the action. **Leg.H.** Added Stats 1992 ch 883 §2 (AB 3620). Amended Stats 1996 ch 1159 §9 (AB 3471); Stats 2004 ch 227 §11 (SB 1102), effective August 16, 2004.

§405.23. Effect of failure to properly serve
Any notice of pendency of action shall be void and invalid as to any adverse party or owner of record unless the requirements of Section 405.22 are met for that party or owner and a proof of service in the form and content specified in Section 1013a has been recorded with the notice of pendency of action. **Leg.H.** Added Stats 1992 ch 883 §2 (AB 3620).

§405.24. Notice imparted from time of recording; Rights and interest of claimant
From the time of recording the notice of pendency of action, a purchaser, encumbrancer, or other transferee of the real property described in the notice shall be deemed to have constructive notice of the pendency of the noticed action as it relates to the real property and only of its pendency against parties not fictitiously named. The rights and interest of the claimant in the property, as ultimately determined in the pending noticed action, shall relate back to the date of the recording of the notice. **Leg.H.** Added Stats 1992 ch 883 §2 (AB 3620).

CHAPTER 3
EXPUNGEMENT AND OTHER RELIEF

Application for expungement. §405.30.
Underlying action not containing real property claim. §405.31.

Claimant's failure to establish probable validity of claim. §405.32.
Undertaking. §405.33.
Undertaking as condition of maintaining notice independent of motion to expunge. §405.34.
When order expunging effective. §405.35.
Recording another notice after expungement. §405.36.
Exoneration or modification of undertaking. §405.37.
Attorney's fees and costs. §405.38.
Judicial review. §405.39.

§405.30. Application for expungement

At any time after notice of pendency of action has been recorded, any party, or any nonparty with an interest in the real property affected thereby, may apply to the court in which the action is pending to expunge the notice. However, a person who is not a party to the action shall obtain leave to intervene from the court at or before the time the party brings the motion to expunge the notice. Evidence or declarations may be filed with the motion to expunge the notice. The court may permit evidence to be received in the form of oral testimony, and may make any orders it deems just to provide for discovery by any party affected by a motion to expunge the notice. The claimant shall have the burden of proof under Sections 405.31 and 405.32. **Leg.H.** Added Stats 1992 ch 883 §2 (AB 3620).

§405.31. Underlying action not containing real property claim

In proceedings under this chapter, the court shall order the notice expunged if the court finds that the pleading on which the notice is based does not contain a real property claim. The court shall not order an undertaking to be given as a condition of expunging the notice where the court finds the pleading does not contain a real property claim. **Leg.H.** Added Stats 1992 ch 883 §2 (AB 3620).

§405.32. Claimant's failure to establish probable validity of claim

In proceedings under this chapter, the court shall order that the notice be expunged if the court finds that the claimant has not established by a preponderance of the evidence the probable validity of the real property claim. The court shall not order an undertaking to be given as a condition of expunging the notice if the court finds the claimant has not established the probable validity of the real property claim. **Leg.H.** Added Stats 1992 ch 883 §2 (AB 3620).

§405.33. Undertaking

In proceedings under this chapter, the court shall order that the notice be expunged if the court finds that the real property claim has probable validity, but adequate relief can be secured to the claimant by the giving of an undertaking. The expungement order shall be conditioned upon the giving of the undertaking of such nature and in such amount as will indemnify the claimant for all damages proximately resulting from the expungement which the claimant may incur if the claimant prevails upon the real property claim. In its order conditionally expunging the notice, the court shall set a return date for the moving party to show fulfillment of the condition, and if the moving party fails to show fulfillment of the condition on the return day, the court shall deny the motion to expunge without further notice or hearing. Recovery may be had on the undertaking pursuant to Section 996.440.

For purposes only of determining under this section whether the giving of an undertaking will secure adequate relief to the claimant, the presumption of Section 3387 of the Civil Code that real property is unique shall not apply, except in the case of real property improved with a single-family dwelling which the claimant intends to occupy. **Leg.H.** Added Stats 1992 ch 883 §2 (AB 3620).

§405.34. Undertaking as condition of maintaining notice independent of motion to expunge

Subject to the provisions of Sections 405.31 and 405.32, at any time after a notice of pendency of action has been recorded, and regardless of whether a motion to expunge has been filed, the court may, upon motion by any person with an interest in the property, require the claimant to give the moving party an undertaking as a condition of maintaining the notice in the record title. However, a person who is not a party to the action shall obtain leave to intervene from the court at or before the time the person moves to require an undertaking. The court may permit evidence to be received in the form of oral testimony and may make any orders it deems just to provide for discovery by any affected party. An undertaking required pursuant to this section shall be of such nature and in such amount as the court may determine to be just. In its order requiring an undertaking, the court shall set a return date for the claimant to show compliance and if the claimant fails to show compliance on the return date, the court shall order the notice of pendency of action expunged without further notice or hearing.

Recovery on an undertaking required pursuant to this section may be had in an amount not to exceed the undertaking, pursuant to Section 996.440, upon a showing (a) that the claimant did not prevail on the real property claim and (b) that the person seeking recovery suffered damages as a result of the maintenance of the notice. In assessing these damages, the court shall not consider the claimant's intent or the presence or absence of probable cause. **Leg.H.** Added Stats 1992 ch 883 §2 (AB 3620).

§405.35. When order expunging effective

No order expunging a notice of pendency of action shall be effective, nor shall it be recorded in the office of any county recorder, until the time within which a petition for writ of mandate may be filed pursuant to Section 405.39 has expired. No order expunging a notice of pendency of action shall be effective, nor shall it be recorded in the office of any county recorder, after a petition for writ of mandate has been timely filed pursuant to Section 405.39, until the proceeding commenced by the petition is finally adjudicated. This section imposes no duty on the county recorder to determine whether the requirements of this section or of any order expunging a notice of pendency of action have been met. **Leg.H.** Added Stats 1992 ch 883 §2 (AB 3620).

§405.36. Recording another notice after expungement

Once a notice of pending action has been expunged, the claimant may not record another notice of pending action as to the affected property without leave of the court in which the action is pending. **Leg.H.** Added Stats 1992 ch 883 §2 (AB 3620).

§405.37. Exoneration or modification of undertaking

After notice and hearing, for good cause and upon such terms as are just, the court may exonerate or modify any undertaking required by an order issued pursuant to Section 405.33 or 405.34 or pursuant to a stipulation made in lieu of such an order. An order of the court under this section may be made conditional upon the giving of a new undertaking under Section 405.33 or 405.34. **Leg.H.** Added Stats 1992 ch 883 §2 (AB 3620).

§405.38. Attorney's fees and costs

The court shall direct that the party prevailing on any motion under this chapter be awarded the reasonable attorney's fees and costs of making or opposing the motion unless the court finds that the other party acted with substantial justification or that other circumstances make the imposition of attorney's fees and costs unjust. **Leg.H.** Added Stats 1992 ch 883 §2 (AB 3620).

§405.39. Judicial review

No order or other action of the court under this chapter shall be appealable. Any party aggrieved by an order made on a motion under this chapter may petition the proper reviewing court to review the order by writ of mandate. The petition for writ of mandate shall be filed and served within 20 days of service of written notice of the order by the court or any party. The court which issued the order may, within the initial 20-day period, extend the initial 20-day period for one additional period not to exceed 10 days. A copy of the petition for writ of mandate shall be delivered to the clerk of the court which issued the order with a request that it be placed in the court file. **Leg.H.** Added Stats 1992 ch 883 §2 (AB 3620).

CHAPTER 4
WITHDRAWAL

Notice of withdrawal. §405.50.

§405.50. Notice of withdrawal

At any time after notice of pendency of an action has been recorded pursuant to this title or other law, the notice may be withdrawn by recording in the office of the recorder in which the notice of pendency was recorded a notice of withdrawal executed by the party who recorded the notice of pendency of action or by the party's successor in interest. The notice of withdrawal shall be acknowledged. **Leg.H.** Added Stats 1992 ch 883 §2 (AB 3620).

CHAPTER 5
EFFECT OF WITHDRAWAL OR EXPUNGEMENT OF NOTICE

Notice imparted upon withdrawal or expungement. §405.60.
Presumption regarding knowledge of one acquiring rights in property after withdrawal or expungement. §405.61.

§405.60. Notice imparted upon withdrawal or expungement

Upon the withdrawal of a notice of pendency of action pursuant to Section 405.50 or upon recordation of a certified copy of an order expunging a notice of pendency of action pursuant to this title, neither the notice nor any information derived from it, prior to the recording of a certified copy of the judgment or decree issued in the action, shall constitute actual or constructive notice of any of the matters contained, claimed, alleged, or contended therein, or of any of the matters related to the action, or create a duty of inquiry in any person thereafter dealing with the affected property. **Leg.H.** Added Stats 1992 ch 883 §2 (AB 3620).

§405.61. Presumption regarding knowledge of one acquiring rights in property after withdrawal or expungement

Upon the withdrawal of a notice of pendency of action pursuant to Section 405.50 or upon recordation of a certified copy of an order expunging a notice of pendency of action pursuant to this title, no person except a nonfictitious party to the action at the time of recording of the notice of withdrawal or order, who thereafter becomes, by conveyance recorded prior to the recording of a certified copy of the judgment or decree issued in the action, a purchaser, transferee, mortgagee, or other encumbrancer for a valuable consideration of any interest in the real property subject to the action, shall be deemed to have actual knowledge of the action or any of the matters contained, claimed, or alleged therein, or of any of the matters related to the action, irrespective of whether that person possessed actual knowledge of the action or matter and irrespective of when or how the knowledge was obtained.

It is the intent of the Legislature that this section shall provide for the absolute and complete free transferability of real property after the expungement or withdrawal of a notice of pendency of action. **Leg.H.** Added Stats 1992 ch 883 §2 (AB 3620).

§406. [Section repealed 1970]

Leg.H. Enacted Stats 1872. Amended Code Amdts 1873–74 ch 383 §46; Stats 1933 ch 744 §14; Stats 1951 ch 1737 §44, operative January 1, 1952; Stats 1963 ch 498 §1. Repealed Stats 1969 ch 1610 §7, operative July 1, 1970. See CCP §§167, 412.10; Gov C §§69846.5, 71280.4.

§407. [Section repealed 1970]

Leg.H. Enacted Stats 1872. Amended Code Amdts 1880 ch 32 §1; Stats 1897 ch 58 §1; Stats 1933 ch 744 §15; Stats 1945 ch 1363 §2; Stats 1951 ch 1737 §45, operative January 1, 1952; Stats 1967 ch 567 §1; Stats 1968 ch 121 §1. Repealed Stats 1969 ch 1610 §8, operative July 1, 1970. See CCP §§167, 412.20.

§408. [Section repealed 1970]

Leg.H. Enacted Stats 1872. Amended Code Amdts 1875–76 ch 85 §1; Stats 1887 ch 37 §1; Stats 1921 ch 149 §1; Stats 1933 ch 744 §16; Stats 1951 ch 1737 §46, operative January 1, 1952; Stats 1963 ch 498 §2. Repealed Stats 1969 ch 1610 §9, operative July 1, 1970. See CCP §417.30.

§409. [Section repealed 1993]

Leg.H. Enacted Stats 1872. Amended Code Amdts 1873–74 ch 383 §47; Stats 1959 ch 382 §1; Stats 1980 ch 163 §1; Stats 1981 ch 889 §1; Stats 1983 ch 78 §1; Stats 1984 ch 572 §1, ch 760 §1; Stats 1985 ch 154 §2; Stats 1986 ch 540 §1. Repealed Stats 1992 ch 883 §1 (AB 3620). The repealed section related to notice of pendency of action.

§409.1. [Section repealed 1993]

Leg.H. Added Stats 1968 ch 815 §1. Amended Stats 1976 ch 27 §1; Stats 1990 ch 1491 §4 (AB 3765); Stats 1991 ch 112 §1 (SB 979). Repealed Stats 1992 ch 883 §1 (AB 3620). See CCP §405.30.

§409.2. [Section repealed 1993]

Leg.H. Added Stats 1968 ch 815 §2. Amended Stats 1976 ch 27 §2; Stats 1991 ch 112 §2 (SB 979). Repealed Stats 1992 ch 883 §1 (AB 3620). See CCP §405.33.

§409.3. [Section repealed 1993]

Leg.H. Added Stats 1968 ch 815 §3. Amended Stats 1976 ch 27 §3. Repealed Stats 1992 ch 883 §1 (AB 3620). See CCP §405.38.

§409.4. [Section repealed 1993]

Leg.H. Added Stats 1968 ch 815 §4. Amended Stats 1986 ch 603 §2; Stats 1989 ch 1416 §14. Repealed Stats 1992 ch 883 §1 (AB 3620). See CCP §405.39.

§409.5. [Section repealed 1993]

Leg.H. Added Stats 1968 ch 815 §5. Amended Stats 1982 ch 151 §1. Repealed Stats 1992 ch 883 §1 (AB 3620). See CCP §405.35.

§409.55. [Section repealed 1993]

Leg.H. Added Stats 1980 ch 307 §1. Amended Stats 1982 ch 560 §1. Repealed Stats 1992 ch 883 §1 (AB 3620). See CCP §§405.50, 405.60.

§409.6. [Section repealed 1993]

Leg.H. Added Stats 1968 ch 815 §6. Amended Stats 1974 ch 839 §1; Stats 1980 ch 307 §2. Repealed Stats 1992 ch 883 §1 (AB 3620). The repealed section related to liability of person recording notice of pendency of action for damages.

§409.7. [Section repealed 1993]

Leg.H. Added Stats 1974 ch 839 §2. Amended Stats 1975 ch 201 §1. Repealed Stats 1992 ch 883 §1 (AB 3620). See CCP §§405.24, 405.7.

§409.8. [Section repealed 1993]

Leg.H. Added Stats 1982 ch 560 §2. Repealed Stats 1992 ch 883 §1 (AB 3620). See CCP §405.61.

§409.9. [Section repealed 1993]

Leg.H. Added Stats 1989 ch 815 §1. Repealed Stats 1992 ch 883 §1 (AB 3620). The repealed section related to notice of pendency of action to prospective transferees.

§410. [Section repealed 1970]

Leg.H. Enacted 1872. Amended Code Amdts 1873–74 ch 383 §48; Stats 1893 ch 174 §1; Stats 1933 ch 744 §17; Stats 1945 ch 1329 §1; Stats 1951 ch 1737 §47, operative January 1, 1952; Stats 1957 ch 497 §1; Stats 1959 ch 792 §1, operative January 1, 1960; Stats 1967 ch 1324 §3. Repealed Stats 1969 ch 1610 §10, operative July 1, 1970. See CCP §§412.30, 413.10 et seq.

§410.1. [Section repealed 1970]

Leg.H. Added Stats 1953 ch 52 §1. Repealed Stats 1969 ch 1610 §11, operative July 1, 1970. See CCP §1033.5.

TITLE 5
JURISDICTION AND SERVICE OF PROCESS

Chapter 1. Jurisdiction and Forum.
Chapter 2. Commencing Civil Actions.
Chapter 3. Summons.
Chapter 4. Service of Summons.
Chapter 5. Objection to Jurisdiction.

CHAPTER 1
JURISDICTION AND FORUM

Article 1. Jurisdiction.
Article 2. Forum.
Article 3. Jurisdiction in Action.

ARTICLE 1
Jurisdiction

Jurisdiction exercisable. §410.10.

§410.10. Jurisdiction exercisable

A court of this state may exercise jurisdiction on any basis not inconsistent with the Constitution of this state or of the United States. **Leg.H.** Added Stats 1969 ch 1610 §3, operative July 1, 1970.

ARTICLE 2
Forum

Stay or dismissal of action; Finding. §410.30.
Action arising out of contract providing for application of California law. §410.40.
Void and unenforceable contract provisions between contractor and subcontractor. §410.42.

§410.30. Stay or dismissal of action; Finding

(a) When a court upon motion of a party or its own motion finds that in the interest of substantial justice an action should be heard in a forum outside this state, the court shall stay or dismiss the action in whole or in part on any conditions that may be just.

(b) The provisions of Section 418.10 do not apply to a motion to stay or dismiss the action by a defendant who has made a general appearance. **Leg.H.** Added Stats 1969 ch 1610 §3, operative July 1, 1970. Amended Stats 1972 ch 601 §1, operative January 1, 1992; Stats 1986 ch 968 §4, effective September 22, 1986.

§410.40. Action arising out of contract providing for application of California law

Any person may maintain an action or proceeding in a court of this state against a foreign corporation or nonresident person where the action or proceeding arises out of or relates to any contract, agreement, or undertaking for which a choice of California law has been made in whole or in part by the parties thereto and which (a) is a contract, agreement, or undertaking, contingent or otherwise, relating to a transaction involving in the aggregate not less than one million dollars ($1,000,000), and (b) contains a provision or provisions under which the foreign corporation or nonresident agrees to submit to the jurisdiction of the courts of this state.

This section applies to contracts, agreements, and undertakings entered into before, on, or after its effective date; it shall be fully retroactive. Contracts, agreements, and undertakings selecting California law entered into before the effective date of this section shall be valid, enforceable, and effective as if this section had been in effect on the date they were entered into; and actions and proceedings commencing in a court of this state before the effective date of this section may be maintained as if this section were in effect on the date they were commenced. **Leg.H.** Added Stats 1992 ch 615 §5 (SB 1804).

Prior Law: Former CCP §410.40, relating to action arising out of contract providing for application of California law, was added Stats 1986 ch 968 §5, effective September 22, 1986, and repealed, January 1, 1992, by its own terms.

§410.42. Void and unenforceable contract provisions between contractor and subcontractor

(a) The following provisions of a contract between the contractor and a subcontractor with principal offices in this state, for the construction of a public or private work of improvement in this state, shall be void and unenforceable:

(1) A provision which purports to require any dispute between the parties to be litigated, arbitrated, or otherwise determined outside this state.

(2) A provision which purports to preclude a party from commencing such a proceeding or obtaining a judgment or other resolution in this state or the courts of this state.

(b) For purposes of this section, "construction" means any work or services performed on, or materials provided for, a work of improvement, as defined in Section 8050 of the Civil Code, and for which a lien may be claimed pursuant to Section 8400 of the Civil Code (whether or not a lien is in fact claimed) or for which such a lien could be claimed but for Section 8160 of the Civil Code.

For purposes of this section, "construction" means any work or services performed on, or materials provided for, a work of improvement, as defined in Section 3106 of the Civil Code, and for which a lien may be claimed pursuant to Section 3110 of the Civil Code (whether or not a lien is in fact claimed) or for which such a lien could be claimed but for Section 3109. **Leg.H.** Added Stats 1991 ch 582 §1 (AB 1051). Amended Stats 2010 ch 697 §22 (SB 189), effective January 1, 2011, operative July 1, 2012.

ARTICLE 3
Jurisdiction in Action

Jurisdiction over party; Service of summons, and general appearance; Continuance of jurisdiction over parties and subject matter. §410.50.
Pending action against corporation that has forfeited its charter, or right to do business, or that has dissolved; Jurisdiction over corporation's trustees, stockholders, or members. §410.60.
Action against persons liable on contract; Jurisdiction against defendants served. §410.70.

§410.50. Jurisdiction over party; Service of summons, and general appearance; Continuance of jurisdiction over parties and subject matter

(a) Except as otherwise provided by statute, the court in which an action is pending has jurisdiction over a party from the time summons is served on him as provided by Chapter 4 (commencing with Section 413.10). A general appearance by a party is equivalent to personal service of summons on such party.

(b) Jurisdiction of the court over the parties and the subject matter of an action continues throughout subsequent proceedings in the action. **Leg.H.** Added Stats 1969 ch 1610 §3, operative July 1, 1970.

§410.60. Pending action against corporation that has forfeited its charter, or right to do business, or that has dissolved; Jurisdiction over corporation's trustees, stockholders, or members

In an action against a corporation which has forfeited its charter or right to do business, or has dissolved, the court in which the action is pending has jurisdiction over all the trustees of such corporation and of its stockholders or members from the time summons is served on one of the trustees as provided by Chapter 4 (commencing with Section 413.10). **Leg.H.** Added Stats 1969 ch 1610 §3, operative July 1, 1970.

§410.70. Action against persons liable on contract; Jurisdiction against defendants served

In an action against two or more persons who are jointly, jointly and severally, or severally liable on a contract, the court in which the action is pending has jurisdiction to proceed against such of the defendants as are served as if they were the only defendants. **Leg.H.** Added Stats 1969 ch 1610 §3, operative July 1, 1970.

§411. [Section repealed 1970]

Leg.H. Enacted 1872. Amended Code Amdts 1873–74 ch 383 §49; Stats 1915 ch 566 §1; Stats 1919 ch 41 §1; Stats 1921 ch 108 §1; Stats 1931 ch 863 §1; Stats 1941 ch 1230 §2; Stats 1943 ch 159 §2; Stats 1945 ch 1377 §1; Stats 1947 ch 1090 §1; Stats 1955 ch 1519 §2; Stats 1957 ch 826 §1; Stats 1961 ch 638 §1; Stats 1965 ch 1659 §1; Stats 1967 ch 1324 §4; Stats 1968 ch 132 §2; effective May 16, 1968, operative November 13, 1968. Repealed Stats 1969 ch 1610 §12, operative July 1, 1970. See CCP §§413.10, 415.10–415.40, 416.10–416.90.

CHAPTER 2
COMMENCING CIVIL ACTIONS

Commencement of action. §411.10.
Check accompanying filing; Return without payment; Underpayment; Notice; Void or suspended filing. §411.20.
Attorney sanctioning; Nonpayment of fees to electronic filing service provider. §411.20.5.
Check accompanying filing; Underpayment; Notice; Void or suspended filing. §411.21.
Filing of certificate in actions for professional negligence against architects, engineers and land surveyors. §411.35.

§411.10. Commencement of action

A civil action is commenced by filing a complaint with the court. **Leg.H.** Added Stats 1969 ch 1610 §3, operative July 1, 1970.

§411.20. Check accompanying filing; Return without payment; Underpayment; Notice; Void or suspended filing

(a) If the clerk accepts for filing a complaint or other first paper, or any subsequent filing, and payment is made by check which is later returned without payment, the clerk shall, by mail, notify the party who tendered the check that (1) the check has been returned without payment, (2) the administrative charge specified in subdivision (g) has been imposed to reimburse the court for the costs of processing the returned check and providing the notice specified in this subdivision, and (3) the party has 20 days from the date of mailing of the notice within which to pay the filing fee and the administrative charge, except as provided in subdivision (e). The notice also shall state that the administrative charge and the filing fee shall be paid in cash, by certified check, or by other means specified by the court, but not by traveler's check or personal check. If the person who tendered the check is not a party to the action or proposed action, but only is acting on behalf of a party, the clerk shall notify not only the person who tendered the check, but also the party or that party's attorney if the party is represented. The clerk's certificate as to the mailing of notice pursuant to this section establishes a rebuttable presumption that the fees were not paid. This presumption is a presumption affecting the burden of producing evidence.

(b) The clerk shall void the filing if the party who tendered a returned check or on whose behalf a returned check was tendered has not paid the full amount of the fee and the administrative charge by a means specified in subdivision (a) within 20 days of the date on which the notice required by subdivision (a) was mailed. Any filing voided by this section can be disposed of immediately after the 20 days have elapsed without preserving a copy in the court records, notwithstanding Section 68152 of the Government Code.

(c) If an adverse party files a response to a complaint, paper or filing referred to in subdivision (a), together with a filing fee, and the original filing is voided pursuant to subdivision (b), the responsive filing is not required and shall be voided. The court shall, by mail, provide notice to the parties or their attorneys that the initial paper and the response have been voided. The responding party's filing fee shall be refunded upon request, provided that the request for a refund is made within 20 days from the date on which the notice was mailed. Upon receipt of the request, the court shall refund the responding party's filing fee without imposing any administrative charge. A refund under this subdivision is available if the adverse party has filed only a responsive pleading, but not if the party has also filed a cross-complaint or other first paper seeking affirmative relief for which there is a filing fee.

(d) If an adverse party, or a person acting on behalf of the adverse party, tenders a check for a required filing fee that is later returned without payment, the procedures in subdivisions (a) and (b) shall apply.

(e) If any trial or other hearing is scheduled to be heard prior to the expiration of the 20-day period provided for in subdivision (a), the fee shall be paid prior to the trial or hearing. Failure of the party to pay the fee prior to the trial or hearing date shall cause the court to void the filing and proceed as if it had not been filed.

(f) If the clerk performs a service or issues any document for which a fee is required and payment is made by check which is later returned without payment, the court may order further proceedings suspended as to the party for whom the check was tendered. If the court so orders, the clerk shall, by mail, notify the party who tendered the check that proceedings have been suspended until the receipt of payment of the required fee and the administrative charge specified in subdivision (g), by cash, cashier's check, or other means specified by the court, but not by personal check or traveler's check. If the person who tendered the check is not a party to the action or proposed action, but only is acting on behalf of a party, the clerk shall notify not only the person who tendered the check, but also the party or that party's attorney if the party is represented. The clerk's certificate as to the mailing of notice pursuant to this section establishes a rebuttable presumption that the fees were not paid. This presumption is a presumption affecting the burden of producing evidence.

(g) The clerk shall impose an administrative charge for providing notice that a check submitted for a filing fee has been returned without payment and for all related administrative, clerical, and other costs incurred under this section. The administrative charge shall, in each instance, be either twenty-five dollars ($25) or a reasonable amount that does not exceed the actual cost incurred by the court, as determined by the court. The notices provided by the court under subdivisions (a) and (f) shall state the specific amount of the administrative charge that shall be paid to the court. Each administrative charge collected shall be distributed to the court that incurred the charge as described in Section 68085.1 of the Government Code. **Leg.H.** Added Stats 1982 ch 1543 §3. Amended Stats 1994 ch 587 §3.7 (AB 3600); Stats 2004 ch 171 §2 (AB 3078); Stats 2005 ch 75 §30 (AB 145), effective July 19, 2005, operative January 1, 2006.

Prior Law: Former CCP §411.20, similar to the present section, was added Stats 1969 ch 1610 §3, operative July 1, 1970, amended Stats 1970 ch 480 §7, and repealed Stats 1982 ch 1543 §2.

§411.20.5. Attorney sanctioning; Nonpayment of fees to electronic filing service provider

If an electronic filing is made to the clerk by an electronic filing service provider acting as the agent of the court for purposes of collecting and remitting filing fees, and fees owed to the electronic filing service provider remain unpaid for a period of five days after notice to the attorney of record, and the filing was made by the attorney of record and not a self-represented party, the electronic filing service provider may notify the clerk that fees remain unpaid despite notice to the attorney of record. The clerk may then notify the attorney of record that the attorney of record may be sanctioned by the court for nonpayment of fees. The court may sanction the attorney of record if the fees to the electronic filing service provider remain unsatisfied 20 days after notice by the clerk. **Leg.H.** Added Stats 2018 ch 248 §1 (AB 1531), effective January 1, 2019.

§411.21. Check accompanying filing; Underpayment; Notice; Void or suspended filing

(a) If a complaint or other first paper is accompanied by payment by check in an amount less than the required fee, the clerk shall accept the paper for filing, but shall not issue a summons until the court receives full payment of the required fee. The clerk shall, by mail, notify the party tendering the check that (1) the check was made out for an amount less than the required filing fee, (2) the administrative charge specified in subdivision (g) has been imposed to reimburse the court for the costs of processing the partial payment and providing the notice specified in this subdivision, and (3) the party has 20 days from the date of mailing of the notice within which to pay the remainder of the required fee and the administrative charge, except as provided in subdivision (f). If the person who tendered the check is not a party to the action or proposed action, but only is acting on behalf of a party, the clerk shall notify not only the person who tendered the check, and also the party or that party's attorney, if the party is represented. The clerk's certificate as to the mailing of notice pursuant to this section establishes a rebuttable presumption that the fees were not paid. This presumption is a presumption affecting the burden of producing evidence. This subdivision does not apply to an unlawful detainer action.

(b) The clerk shall void the filing if the party who tendered a check in an amount less than the required filing fee or on whose behalf a check in an amount less than the required filing fee was tendered has not paid the full amount of the fee and the administrative charge by a means specified in subdivision (a) within 20 days of the date on which the notice required by subdivision (a) was mailed. Any filing voided by this section may be disposed of immediately after the 20 days have elapsed without preserving a copy in the court records notwithstanding Section 68152 of the Government Code.

(c) If a check for less than the required fee was tendered, the remainder of the required fee and the administrative charge were not paid within the period specified in subdivision (a), and a refund of the partial payment has not been requested in a writing mailed or presented by the party or person who tendered the check within 20 days from the date on which the remainder of the required fee was due, the partial payment shall be remitted to the State Treasurer to be deposited in the Trial Court Trust Fund, except for the amount of the administrative charge described in subdivision (g), that shall be deducted from the partial payment and shall be distributed as described in subdivision (g) to the court which incurred the charge. If the party or person who tendered the check for partial payment requests a refund of the partial payment, in writing, within the time specified in this subdivision, the clerk shall refund the amount of the partial payment less the amount of the administrative charge imposed by that court. All partial payments that the court received before January 1, 2006, and that remain on deposit for filings that the clerk voided pursuant to this section, once three years have passed from the date that the filing was voided, shall be remitted to the State Treasurer for deposit into the Trial Court Trust Fund.

(d) If an adverse party files a response to a complaint or other first paper referred to in subdivision (a), together with a filing fee, and the original filing is voided pursuant to subdivision (b), the responsive filing is not required and shall be voided. The court shall, by mail, provide notice to the parties that the initial paper and the response have been voided. The responding party's filing fee shall be refunded upon request, provided that the request for a refund is made in writing within 20 days from the date on which the notice was mailed. Upon receipt of the request, the court shall reimburse the responding party's filing fee without imposing any administrative charge. A refund under this subdivision is available if the adverse party has filed only a responsive pleading, but not if the party has also filed a cross-complaint or other first paper seeking affirmative relief for which there is a filing fee.

(e) If an adverse party, or a person acting on behalf of the adverse party, tenders a check for a required filing fee in an amount less than the required fee, the procedures in subdivisions (a), (b), and (c) shall apply.

(f) If any trial or other hearing is scheduled to be heard prior to the expiration of the 20-day period provided for in subdivision (a), the fee shall be paid prior to the trial or hearing. Failure of the party to pay the fee prior to the trial or hearing date shall cause the court to void the filing and proceed as if it had not been filed.

(g) The clerk shall impose an administrative charge for providing notice that a check submitted for a filing fee is in an amount less than the required fee and for all related administrative, clerical, and other costs incurred under this section. The administrative charge shall, in each instance, be either twenty-five dollars ($25) or a reasonable amount that does not exceed the actual cost incurred by the court, as determined by the court. The notices provided by the court under subdivision (a) shall state the specific amount of the administrative charge that shall be paid to the court. Each administrative charge collected shall be distributed to the court that incurred the charge as described in Section 68085.1 of the Government Code. When a partial payment is to be remitted to the State Treasurer under subdivision (c), the court shall notify the Administrative Office of the Courts of the amount of (1) the partial payment collected, and (2) the administrative charge to be deducted from the payment and to be distributed to the court. **Leg.H.** Added Stats 2005 ch 75 §31 (AB 145), effective July 19, 2005, operative January 1, 2006. Amended Stats 2007 ch 738 §5 (AB 1248), effective January 1, 2008.

§411.30. [Section repealed 1989]

Leg.H. Added Stats 1978 ch 1165 §1. Amended Stats 1979 ch 988 §1; Stats 1982 ch 1040 §2; Stats 1983 ch 429 §1; Stats 1984 ch 1705 §1; Stats 1986 ch 247 §1. Repealed operative January 1, 1989, by its own terms.

§411.35. Filing of certificate in actions for professional negligence against architects, engineers and land surveyors

(a) In every action, including a cross-complaint for damages or indemnity, arising out of the professional negligence of a person holding a valid architect's certificate issued pursuant to Chapter 3 (commencing with Section 5500) of Division 3 of the Business and Professions Code, or of a person holding a valid registration as a professional engineer issued pursuant to Chapter 7 (commencing with Section 6700) of Division 3 of the Business and Professions Code, or a person holding a valid land surveyor's license issued pursuant to Chapter 15 (commencing with Section 8700) of Division 3 of the Business and Professions Code on or before the date of service of the complaint or cross-complaint on any defendant or cross-defendant, the attorney for the plaintiff or cross-complainant shall file and serve the certificate specified by subdivision (b).

(b) A certificate shall be executed by the attorney for the plaintiff or cross-complainant declaring one of the following:

(1) That the attorney has reviewed the facts of the case, that the attorney has consulted with and received an opinion from at least one architect, professional engineer, or land surveyor who is licensed to practice and practices in this state or any other state, or who teaches at an accredited college or university and is licensed to practice in this state or any other state, in the same discipline as the defendant or cross-defendant and who the attorney reasonably believes is knowledgeable in the relevant issues involved in the particular action, and that the attorney has concluded on the basis of this review and consultation that there is reasonable and meritorious cause for the filing of this action. The person consulted may not be a party to the litigation. The person consulted shall render his or her opinion that the named defendant or cross-defendant was negligent or was not negligent in the performance of the applicable professional services.

(2) That the attorney was unable to obtain the consultation required by paragraph (1) because a statute of limitations would impair the action and that the certificate required by paragraph (1) could not be obtained before the impairment of the action. If a certificate is executed pursuant to this paragraph, the certificate required by paragraph (1) shall be filed within 60 days after filing the complaint.

(3) That the attorney was unable to obtain the consultation required by paragraph (1) because the attorney had made three separate good faith attempts with three separate architects, professional engineers, or land surveyors to obtain this consultation and none of those contacted would agree to the consultation.

(c) Where a certificate is required pursuant to this section, only one certificate shall be filed, notwithstanding that multiple defendants have been named in the complaint or may be named at a later time.

(d) Where the attorney intends to rely solely on the doctrine of "res ipsa loquitur," as defined in Section 646 of the Evidence Code, or exclusively on a failure to inform of the consequences of a procedure, or both, this section shall be inapplicable. The attorney shall certify upon filing of the complaint that the attorney is solely relying on the doctrines of "res ipsa loquitur" or failure to inform of the consequences of a procedure or both, and for that reason is not filing a certificate required by this section.

(e) For purposes of this section, and subject to Section 912 of the Evidence Code, an attorney who submits a certificate as required by paragraph (1) or (2) of subdivision (b) has a privilege to refuse to disclose the identity of the architect, professional engineer, or land surveyor consulted and the contents of the consultation. The privilege shall also be held by the architect, professional engineer, or land surveyor so consulted. If, however, the attorney makes a claim under paragraph (3) of subdivision (b) that he or she was unable to obtain the required consultation with the architect, professional engineer, or land surveyor, the court may require the attorney to divulge the names of architects, professional engineers, or land surveyors refusing the consultation.

(f) A violation of this section may constitute unprofessional conduct and be grounds for discipline against the attorney, except that the failure to file the certificate required by paragraph (1) of subdivision (b), within 60 days after filing the complaint and certificate provided for by paragraph (2) of subdivision (b), shall not be grounds for discipline against the attorney.

(g) The failure to file a certificate in accordance with this section shall be grounds for a demurrer pursuant to Section 430.10 or a motion to strike pursuant to Section 435.

(h) Upon the favorable conclusion of the litigation with respect to any party for whom a certificate of merit was filed or for whom a certificate of merit should have been filed pursuant to this section, the trial court may, upon the motion of a party or upon the court's own motion, verify compliance with this section, by requiring the attorney for the plaintiff or cross-complainant who was required by subdivision (b) to execute the certificate to reveal the name, address, and telephone number of the person or persons consulted with pursuant to subdivision (b) that were relied upon by the attorney in preparation of the certificate of merit. The name, address, and telephone number shall be disclosed to the trial judge in an in-camera proceeding at which the moving party shall not be present. If the trial judge finds there has been a failure to comply with this section, the court may order a party, a party's attorney, or both, to pay any reasonable expenses, including attorney's fees, incurred by another party as a result of the failure to comply with this section.

(i) For purposes of this section, "action" includes a complaint or cross-complaint for equitable indemnity arising out of the rendition of professional services whether or not the complaint or cross-complaint specifically asserts or utilizes the terms "professional negligence" or "negligence." **Leg.H.** Added Stats 1979 ch 973 §1. Amended Stats 1983 ch 414 §1; Stats 1986 ch 1231 §1; Stats 1988 ch 1070 §1, operative until January 1, 1992; Stats 1990 ch 204 §1 (SB 2089); Stats 1991 ch 272 §1 (SB 527); Stats 1995 ch 241 §1 (SB 934); Stats 1999 ch 176 §1 (AB 540).

§411.36. [Section repealed 1997]

Leg.H. Added Stats 1992 ch 1278 §1 (AB 3412), operative until January 1, 1997. Amended Stats 1993 ch 151 §4 (AB 1704), effective July 16, 1993. Repealed operative January 1, 1997, by its own terms. The repealed section related to certificate to be filed in occupational negligence action by common interest development association against contractor.

§412. [Section repealed 1970]

Leg.H. Enacted 1872. Amended Code Amdts 1880 ch 32 §2; Stats 1893 ch 202 §1; Stats 1905 ch 142 §1; Stats 1913 ch 64 §1, ch 693 §1; Stats 1919 ch 201 §1; Stats 1933 ch 744 §19; Stats 1949 ch 42 §1, ch 1124 §1; Stats 1951 ch 1737 §48, operative January 1, 1952; Stats 1968 ch 132 §3, effective May 16, 1968, operative November 13, 1968. Repealed Stats 1969 ch 1610 §13, operative July 1, 1970. See CCP §§415.50.

CHAPTER 3
SUMMONS

Issuance. §412.10.
Directing, signing, and sealing; Contents; Approved form. §412.20.
Notice in action against corporation or unincorporated association; Prerequisite to default. §412.30.

§412.10. Issuance

After payment of all applicable fees, the plaintiff may have the clerk issue one or more summons for any defendant. The clerk shall keep each original summons in the court records and provide a copy of each summons issued to the plaintiff who requested issuance of the summons. **Leg.H.** Added Stats 1969 ch 1610 §3, operative July 1, 1970. Amended Stats 2005 ch 300 §2 (AB 496), effective January 1, 2006.

§412.20. Directing, signing, and sealing; Contents; Approved form

(a) Except as otherwise required by statute, a summons shall be directed to the defendant, signed by the clerk and issued under the seal of the court in which the action is pending, and it shall contain:

(1) The title of the court in which the action is pending.

(2) The names of the parties to the action.

(3) A direction that the defendant file with the court a written pleading in response to the complaint within 30 days after summons is served on him or her.

(4) A notice that, unless the defendant so responds, his or her default will be entered upon application by the plaintiff, and the plaintiff may apply to the court for the relief demanded in the complaint, which could result in garnishment of wages, taking of money or property, or other relief.

(5) The following statement in boldface type: "You may seek the advice of an attorney in any matter connected with the complaint or this summons. Such attorney should be consulted promptly so that your pleading may be filed or entered within the time required by this summons."

(6) The following introductory legend at the top of the summons above all other matter, in boldface type, in English and Spanish:

"Notice! You have been sued. The court may decide against you without your being heard unless you respond within 30 days. Read information below."

(b) Each county may, by ordinance, require that the legend contained in paragraph (6) of subdivision (a) be set forth in every summons issued out of the courts of that county in any additional foreign language, if the legend in the additional foreign language is set forth in the summons in the same manner as required in that paragraph.

(c) A summons in a form approved by the Judicial Council is deemed to comply with this section. **Leg.H.** Added Stats 1969 ch 1610 §3, operative July 1, 1970. Amended Stats 1974 ch 363 §1; Stats 1989 ch 79 §1, effective June 30, 1989, ch 1105 §6.

§412.21. [Section repealed 1994]

Leg.H. Added Stats 1989 ch 1105 §7. Amended Stats 1990 ch 935 §3 (AB 3593). Repealed Stats 1992 ch 163 §20 (AB 2641), operative January 1, 1994. See Fam C §§232–235, 2040, 7700.

§412.30. Notice in action against corporation or unincorporated association; Prerequisite to default

In an action against a corporation or an unincorporated association (including a partnership), the copy of the summons that is served shall contain a notice stating in substance: "To the person served: You are hereby served in the within action (or special proceeding) on behalf of (here state the name of the corporation or the unincorporated association) as a person upon whom a copy of the summons and of the complaint may be delivered to effect service on said party under the provisions of (here state appropriate provisions of Chapter 4 (commencing with Section 413.10) of the Code of Civil Procedure)." If service is also made on such person as an individual, the notice shall also indicate that service is being made on such person as an individual as well as on behalf of the corporation or the unincorporated association.

If such notice does not appear on the copy of the summons served, no default may be taken against such corporation or unincorporated association or against such person individually, as the case may be. **Leg.H.** Added Stats 1969 ch 1610 §3, operative July 1, 1970.

§413. [Section repealed 1970]

Leg.H. Enacted 1872. Amended Code Amdts 1873–74 ch 383 §50; Stats 1931 ch 884 §1; Stats 1933 ch 744 §20; Stats 1937 ch 548 §1; Stats 1947 ch 248 §1; Stats 1949 ch 456 §1; Stats 1951 ch 43 §1; Stats 1957 ch 1669 §1. Repealed Stats 1969 ch 1610 §14, operative July 1, 1970. See CCP §415.50.

CHAPTER 4
SERVICE OF SUMMONS

Article 1. General.
Article 2. Persons Who May Serve Summons.
Article 3. Manner of Service of Summons.
Article 4. Persons Upon Whom Summons May Be Served.
Article 5. Proof of Service.

ARTICLE 1
General

Application of chapter; Service outside state or country. §413.10.
Extension of time on service by mail. §413.20.
Direction of manner of service by court in which action is pending. §413.30.
Relation to Business and Professions Code. §413.40.

§413.10. Application of chapter; Service outside state or country

Except as otherwise provided by statute, a summons shall be served on a person:

(a) Within this state, as provided in this chapter.

(b) Outside this state but within the United States, as provided in this chapter or as prescribed by the law of the place where the person is served.

(c) Outside the United States, as provided in this chapter or as directed by the court in which the action is pending, or, if the court before or after service finds that the service is reasonably calculated to give actual notice, as prescribed by the law of the place where the person is served or as directed by the foreign authority in response to a letter rogatory. These rules are subject to the provisions of the Convention on the "Service Abroad of Judicial and Extrajudicial Documents" in Civil or Commercial Matters (Hague Serviee Convention). **Leg.H.** Added Stats 1969 ch 1610 §3, operative July 1, 1970. Amended Stats 1984 ch 191 §1.

§413.20. Extension of time on service by mail

If a summons is served by mail pursuant to this chapter, the provisions of Section 1013 that extend the time for exercising a right or doing an act shall not extend any time specified in this title. **Leg.H.** Added Stats 1969 ch 1610 §3, operative July 1, 1970.

§413.30. Direction of manner of service by court in which action is pending

Where no provision is made in this chapter or other law for the service of summons, the court in which the action is pending may direct that summons be served in a manner which is reasonably calculated to give actual notice to the party to be served and that proof of such service be made as prescribed by the court. **Leg.H.** Added Stats 1969 ch 1610 §3, operative July 1, 1970.

§413.40. Relation to Business and Professions Code

Any service of summons which complies with the provisions of this chapter shall not be rendered invalid or ineffective because it was made by a person in violation of Chapter 16 (commencing with Section 22350) of Division 8 of the Business and Professions Code. **Leg.H.** Added Stats 1971 ch 1661 §2, operative July 1, 1972.

§414. [Section repealed 1970]

Leg.H. Enacted 1872. Repealed Stats 1969 ch 1610 §15, operative July 1, 1970. See CCP §410.70.

ARTICLE 2
Persons Who May Serve Summons

Person permitted to serve. §414.10.

§414.10. Person permitted to serve

A summons may be served by any person who is at least 18 years of age and not a party to the action. **Leg.H.** Added Stats 1969 ch 1610 §3, operative July 1, 1970.

§415. [Section repealed 1970]

Leg.H. Enacted 1872. Amended Stats 1933 ch 744 §21. Repealed Stats 1969 ch 1610 §16, operative July 1, 1970. See CCP §§417.10, 417.20.

ARTICLE 3
Manner of Service of Summons

Personal delivery; Completion of service. §415.10.
Leaving and mailing copies; Where and with whom; When service deemed complete. §415.20.
Access to gated community or covered multifamily dwelling to serve process or subpoena. §415.21.
Service by mail; Articles mailed; Form of notice; When service complete; Liability for expense on failure to return acknowledgment; Approved form. §415.30.
Service outside state; Completion of service. §415.40.
Posting summons in action for unlawful detainer. §415.45.
Prejudgment claim of right to possession; Procedure for service; Form; Effect of service upon occupant. §415.46.
Alternative method of service on lessee giving lessor notice of intent not to abandon leased real property. §415.47.
Service by publication; Prerequisite affidavit; Order for publication in named newspaper; When service complete; Service other than by publication. §415.50.
Service on "business organization, form unknown" by leaving and mailing copy; Where and with whom; When service is complete; Inapplicability to corporation with registered agent. §415.95.

§415.10. Personal delivery; Completion of service

A summons may be served by personal delivery of a copy of the summons and of the complaint to the person to be served. Service of a summons in this manner is deemed complete at the time of such delivery.

The date upon which personal delivery is made shall be entered on or affixed to the face of the copy of the summons at the time of its delivery. However, service of a summons without such date shall be valid and effective. **Leg.H.** Added Stats 1969 ch 1610 §3, operative July 1, 1970. Amended Stats 1976 ch 789 §1.

§415.20. Leaving and mailing copies; Where and with whom; When service deemed complete

(a) In lieu of personal delivery of a copy of the summons and complaint to the person to be served as specified in Section 416.10, 416.20, 416.30, 416.40, or 416.50, a summons may be served by leaving a copy of the summons and complaint during usual office hours in his or her office or, if no physical address is known, at his or her usual mailing address, other than a United States Postal Service post office box, with the person who is apparently in charge thereof, and by thereafter mailing a copy of the summons and complaint by first-class mail, postage prepaid to the person to be served at the place where a copy of the summons and complaint were left. When service is effected by leaving a copy of the summons and complaint at a mailing address, it shall be left with a person at least 18 years of age, who shall be informed of the contents thereof. Service of a summons in this manner is deemed complete on the 10th day after the mailing.

(b) If a copy of the summons and complaint cannot with reasonable diligence be personally delivered to the person to be served, as specified in Section 416.60, 416.70, 416.80, or 416.90, a summons may be served by leaving a copy of the summons and complaint at the person's dwelling house, usual place of abode, usual place of business, or usual mailing address other than a United States Postal Service post office box, in the presence of a competent member of the household or a person apparently in charge of his or her office, place of business, or usual mailing address other than a United States Postal Service post office box, at least 18 years of age, who shall be informed of the contents thereof, and by thereafter mailing a copy of the summons and of the complaint by first-class mail, postage prepaid to the person to be served at the place where a copy of the summons and complaint were left. Service of a summons in this manner is deemed complete on the 10th day after the mailing.

(c) Notwithstanding subdivision (b), if the only address reasonably known for the person to be served is a private mailbox obtained through a commercial mail receiving agency, service of process may be effected on the first delivery attempt by leaving a copy of the summons and complaint with the commercial mail receiving agency in the manner described in subdivision (d) of Section 17538.5 of the Business and Professions Code. **Leg.H.** Added Stats 1969 ch 1610 §3, operative July 1, 1970. Amended Stats 1989 ch 1416 §15; Stats 2003 ch 128 §1 (AB 418); Stats 2017 ch 129 §1 (AB 1093), effective January 1, 2018.

§415.21. Access to gated community or covered multifamily dwelling to serve process or subpoena

(a) Notwithstanding any other law, any person shall be granted access to a gated community or a covered multifamily dwelling for a reasonable period of time for the sole purpose of performing lawful service of process or service of a subpoena upon displaying a current driver's license or other identification, and one of the following:

(1) A badge or other confirmation that the individual is acting in the individual's capacity as a representative of a county sheriff or marshal, or as an investigator employed by an office of the Attorney General, a county counsel, a city attorney, a district attorney, or a public defender.

(2) Evidence of current registration as a process server pursuant to Chapter 16 (commencing with Section 22350) of Division 8 of the Business and Professions Code or of licensure as a private investigator pursuant to Chapter 11.3 (commencing with Section 7512) of Division 3 of the Business and Professions Code.

(b) This section shall only apply to a gated community or a covered multifamily dwelling that is staffed at the time service of process is attempted by a guard or other security personnel assigned to control access to the community or dwelling.

(c) For purposes of this section, "covered multifamily dwelling" means either of the following:

(1) An apartment building, including a timeshare apartment building not considered a place of public accommodation or transient lodging, with three or more dwelling units.

(2) A condominium, including a timeshare condominium not considered a place of public accommodation or transient lodging, with four or more dwelling units. **Leg.H.** Added Stats 1994 ch 691 §1 (AB 3307). Amended Stats 2005 ch 706 §11 (AB 1742), effective January 1, 2006; Stats 2012 ch 113 §1 (AB 1720), effective January 1, 2013; Stats 2014 ch 470 §2 (AB 2256), effective January 1, 2015; Stats 2016 ch 88 §1 (SB 1431), effective January 1, 2017; Stats 2019 ch 12 §1 (AB 622), effective January 1, 2020.

2012 Note: In enacting Section 1 of Stats 2012 ch 113 (AB 1720), which amends Section 415.21 of the Code of Civil Procedure, it is not the intent of the Legislature to abrogate or modify the holding of the court in *Bein v. Brechtel-Jochim Group, Inc.* (1992) 6 Cal.App.4th 1387, relating to service upon a guard in a gated community. Stats 2012 ch 113 (AB 1720) §2.

1994 Note: In enacting §415.21, it is not the intent of the Legislature to abrogate or modify the holding of the court in *Bein v. Brechtel-Jochim Group, Inc.* (1992) 6 Cal. App. 4th 1387, relating to service upon a guard in a gated community.

§415.30. Service by mail; Articles mailed; Form of notice; When service complete; Liability for expense on failure to return acknowledgment; Approved form

(a) A summons may be served by mail as provided in this section. A copy of the summons and of the complaint shall be mailed (by first-class mail or airmail, postage prepaid) to the person to be served, together with two copies of the notice and acknowledgment provided for in subdivision (b) and a return envelope, postage prepaid, addressed to the sender.

(b) The notice specified in subdivision (a) shall be in substantially the following form:

(Title of court and cause, with action number, to be inserted by the sender prior to mailing)

NOTICE

To: (Here state the name of the person to be served.)

This summons is served pursuant to Section 415.30 of the California Code of Civil Procedure. Failure to complete this form and return it to the sender within 20 days may subject you (or the party on whose behalf you are being served) to liability for the payment of any expenses incurred in serving a summons upon you in any other manner permitted by law. If you are served on behalf of a corporation, unincorporated association (including a partnership), or other entity, this form must be signed in the name of such entity by you or by a person authorized to receive service of process on behalf of such entity. In all other cases, this form must be signed by you personally or by a person authorized by you to acknowledge receipt of summons. Section 415.30 provides that this summons is deemed served on the date of execution of an acknowledgment of receipt of summons.

_____
Signature of sender

ACKNOWLEDGMENT OF RECEIPT OF SUMMONS

This acknowledges receipt on (insert date) of a copy of the summons and of the complaint at (insert address).

Date: _____
(Date this acknowledgment is executed)

_____
Signature of person acknowledging receipt, with title if acknowledgment is made on behalf of another person

(c) Service of a summons pursuant to this section is deemed complete on the date a written acknowledgment of receipt of summons is executed, if such acknowledgment thereafter is returned to the sender.

(d) If the person to whom a copy of the summons and of the complaint are mailed pursuant to this section fails to complete and return the acknowledgment form set forth in subdivision (b) within 20 days from the date of such mailing, the party to whom the summons was mailed shall be liable for reasonable expenses thereafter incurred in serving or attempting to serve the party by another method permitted by this chapter, and, except for good cause shown, the court in which the action is pending, upon motion, with or without notice, shall award the party such expenses whether or not he is otherwise entitled to recover his costs in the action.

(e) A notice or acknowledgment of receipt in form approved by the Judicial Council is deemed to comply with this section. **Leg.H.** Added Stats 1969 ch 1610 §3, operative July 1, 1970.

§415.40. Service outside state; Completion of service

A summons may be served on a person outside this state in any manner provided by this article or by sending a copy of the summons and of the complaint to the person to be served by first-class mail, postage prepaid, requiring a return receipt. Service of a summons by this form of mail is deemed complete on the 10th day after such mailing. **Leg.H.** Added Stats 1969 ch 1610 §3, operative July 1, 1970. Amended Stats 1982 ch 249 §1.

§415.45. Posting summons in action for unlawful detainer

(a) A summons in an action for unlawful detainer of real property may be served by posting if upon affidavit it appears to the satisfaction of the court in which the action is pending that the party to be served cannot with reasonable diligence be served in any manner specified in this article other than publication and that:

(1) A cause of action exists against the party upon whom service is to be made or he is a necessary or proper party to the action; or

(2) The party to be served has or claims an interest in real property in this state that is subject to the jurisdiction of the court or the relief demanded in the action consists wholly or in part in excluding such party from any interest in such property.

(b) The court shall order the summons to be posted on the premises in a manner most likely to give actual notice to the party to be served and direct that a copy of the summons and of the complaint be forthwith mailed by certified mail to such party at his last known address.

(c) Service of summons in this manner is deemed complete on the 10th day after posting and mailing.

(d) Notwithstanding an order for posting of the summons, a summons may be served in any other manner authorized by this article, except publication, in which event such service shall supersede any posted summons. **Leg.H.** Added Stats 1972 ch 719 §1. Amended Stats 1978 ch 625 §1.

§415.46. Prejudgment claim of right to possession; Procedure for service; Form; Effect of service upon occupant

(a) In addition to the service of a summons and complaint in an action for unlawful detainer upon a tenant and subtenant, if any, as prescribed by this article, a prejudgment claim of right to possession may also be served on any person who appears to be or who may claim to have occupied the premises at the time of the filing of the action. Service upon occupants shall be made pursuant to subdivision (c) by serving a copy of a prejudgment claim of right to possession, as specified in subdivision (f), attached to a copy of the summons and complaint at the same time service is made upon the tenant and subtenant, if any.

(b) Service of the prejudgment claim of right to possession in this manner shall be effected by a marshal, sheriff, or registered process server.

(c)(1) When serving the summons and complaint upon a tenant and subtenant, if any, the marshal, sheriff, or registered process server shall make a reasonably diligent effort to ascertain whether there are other adult occupants of the premises who are not named in the summons and complaint by inquiring of the person or persons who are being personally served, or any person of suitable age and discretion who appears to reside upon the premises, whether there are other occupants of the premises.

(2) If the identity of such an occupant is disclosed to the officer or process server and the occupant is present at the premises, the officer or process server shall serve that occupant with a copy of the prejudgment claim of right to possession attached to a copy of the summons and complaint. If personal service cannot be made upon that occupant at that time, service may be effected by leaving a copy of a prejudgment claim of right to possession attached to a copy of the summons and complaint addressed to that occupant with a person of suitable age and discretion at the premises, affixing the same so that it is not readily removable in a conspicuous place on the premises in a manner most likely to give actual notice to that occupant, and sending the same addressed to that occupant by first-class mail.

(3) In addition to the service on an identified occupant, or if no occupant is disclosed to the officer or process server, or if substituted service is made upon the tenant and subtenant, if any, the officer or process server shall serve a prejudgment claim of right to possession for all other persons who may claim to occupy the premises at the time of the filing of the action by leaving a copy of a prejudgment claim of right to possession attached to a copy of the summons and complaint at the premises at the same time service is made upon the tenant and subtenant, if any, affixing the same so that it is not readily removable in a conspicuous place on the premises so that it is likely to give actual notice to an occupant, and sending the same addressed to "all occupants in care of the named tenant" to the premises by first-class mail.

(4) The person serving process shall state the date of service on the prejudgment claim of right to possession form. However, the absence of the date of service on the prejudgment claim of right to possession does not invalidate the claim.

(d) Proof of service under this section shall be filed with the court and shall include a statement that service was made pursuant to this section. Service on occupants in accordance with this section shall not alter or affect service upon the tenant or subtenant, if any.

(e)(1) If an owner or his or her agent has directed and obtained service of a prejudgment claim of right to possession in accordance with this section, no occupant of the premises, whether or not that occupant is named in the judgment for possession, may object to the enforcement of that judgment as prescribed in Section 1174.3.

(2) In any action for unlawful detainer resulting from a foreclosure sale of a rental housing unit pursuant to Section 1161a, paragraph (1) shall not limit the right of any tenant or subtenant of the property to file a prejudgment claim of right of possession pursuant to subdivision (a) of Section 1174.25 at any time before judgment, or to object to enforcement of a judgment for possession as prescribed in Section 1174.3, regardless

of whether the tenant or subtenant was served with a prejudgment claim of right to possession.

(f) The prejudgment claim of right to possession shall be made on the following form:

NOTICE

EVERYONE WHO LIVES IN THIS RENTAL UNIT MAY BE EVICTED BY COURT ORDER. READ THIS FORM IF YOU LIVE HERE AND YOUR NAME IS NOT ON THE ATTACHED SUMMONS AND COMPLAINT.

(1) If you live here and you do not complete and submit this form, you may be evicted without further hearing by the court along with the persons named in the summons and complaint.

(2) You must file this form within 10 days of the date of service listed in the box on the right hand side of this form.

- **Exception:** If you are a tenant being evicted after your landlord lost the property to foreclosure, the 10-day deadline does not apply to you and you may file this form at any time before judgment is entered.

(3) If you file this form, your claim will be determined in the eviction action against the persons named in the complaint.

(4) If you do not file this form, you may be evicted without further hearing.

(5) If you are a tenant being evicted due to foreclosure, you have additional rights and should seek legal advice immediately.

CLAIMANT OR CLAIMANT'S ATTORNEY (Name and Address):	TELEPHONE NO.	FOR COURT USE ONLY
ATTORNEY FOR (Name):		

NAME OF COURT:
STREET ADDRESS:
MAILING ADDRESS:
CITY AND ZIP CODE:
BRANCH NAME:

PLAINTIFF:
DEFENDANT:

PREJUDGMENT CLAIM OF RIGHT TO POSSESSION

CASE NUMBER:

DATE OF SERVICE:
(Date that form is served or delivered, posted and mailed by the officer or process server)

Complete this form only if ALL of these statements are true:
1. You are NOT named in the accompanying Summons and Complaint.
2. You occupied the subject premises on or before the date the unlawful detainer (eviction) complaint was filed. (The date is in the accompanying Summons and Complaint.)
3. You still occupy the subject premises.

I DECLARE THE FOLLOWING UNDER PENALTY OF PERJURY:
1. My name is (specify):
2. I reside at (street address, unit no., city and ZIP code):
3. The address of "the premises" subject to this claim is (address):
4. On (insert date): _____, the landlord or the landlord's authorized agent filed a complaint to recover possession of the premises. (This date is in the accompanying Summons and Complaint.)
5. I occupied the premises on the date the complaint was filed (the date in item 4). I have continued to occupy the premises ever since.
6. I was at least 18 years of age on the date the complaint was filed (the date in item 4).
7. I claim a right to possession of the premises because I occupied the premises on the date the complaint was filed (the date in item 4).
8. I was not named in the Summons and Complaint.
9. I understand that if I make this claim of possession, I will be added as a defendant to the unlawful detainer (eviction) action.
10. (Filing fee) I understand that I must go to the court and pay a filing fee of $_____ or file with the court "Application for Waiver of Court Fees and Costs." I understand that if I don't pay the filing fee or file the form for waiver of court fees, I will not be entitled to make a claim of right to possession.
11. If my landlord lost this property to foreclosure, I understand that I can file this form at any time before judgment is entered, and that I have additional rights and should seek legal advice.
12. I understand that I will have five days (excluding court holidays) to file a response to the Summons and Complaint after I file this Prejudgment Claim of Right to Possession form.

> **NOTICE:** If you fail to file this claim, you may be evicted without further hearing.

11. Rental agreement. I have (check all that apply to you):
    a. ☐ an oral or written rental agreement with the landlord.
    b. ☐ an oral or written rental agreement with a person other than the landlord.
    c. ☐ an oral or written rental agreement with the former owner who lost the property to foreclosure.
    d. ☐ other (explain):

I declare under penalty of perjury under the laws of the State of California that the foregoing is true and correct.

> **WARNING:** Perjury is a felony punishable by imprisonment in the state prison.

Date:

....................................▶ _____
(TYPE OR PRINT NAME)   (SIGNATURE OF CLAIMANT)

> **NOTICE:** If you file this claim to possession, the unlawful detainer action against you will be determined at trial. At trial, you may be found liable for rent, costs, and, in some cases, treble damages.

NOTICE TO OCCUPANTS

YOU MUST ACT AT ONCE IF ALL THE FOLLOWING ARE TRUE:

(1) You are not named in the accompanying Summons and Complaint.

(2) You occupied the premises on or before the date the unlawful detainer (eviction) complaint was filed.

(3) You still occupy the premises.

You can complete and SUBMIT THIS CLAIM FORM within 10 days from the date of service (on the form) at the court where the unlawful detainer (eviction) complaint was filed. If you are a tenant and your landlord lost the property you occupy through foreclosure, this 10-day deadline does not apply to you. You may file this form at any time before judgment is entered. You should seek legal advice immediately.

If you do not complete and submit this form (and pay a filing fee or file a fee waiver form if you cannot pay the fee), YOU WILL BE EVICTED.

After this form is properly filed, you will be added as a defendant in the unlawful detainer (eviction) action and your right to occupy the premises will be decided by the court. If you do not file this claim, you may be evicted without a hearing.

Leg.H. Added Stats 1990 ch 1535 §1 (SB 2508). Amended Stats 1991 ch 57 §1 (SB 323), effective June 14, 1991; Stats 2012 ch 562 §2 (AB 2610), effective January 1, 2013; Stats 2014 ch 913 §7 (AB 2747), effective January 1, 2015.

2014 Note: It is the intent of the Legislature in amending Sections 415.46, 1174.25, and 1174.3 of the Code of Civil Procedure to appropriately update statutory language and statutory forms to properly reflect the changes to law enacted by Assembly Bill 2610, Chapter 562 of the Statutes of 2012. Stats 2014 ch 913 (AB 2747) §1.

§415.47. Alternative method of service on lessee giving lessor notice of intent not to abandon leased real property

(a) Where the lessee has given the lessor written notice of the lessee's intent not to abandon leased real property as provided in Section 1951.3 of the Civil Code, the summons in an action for unlawful detainer of the real property may be served on the lessee by certified mail, postage prepaid, addressed to the lessee at the address stated in the lessee's notice of intent not to abandon if such summons is deposited in the mail within 60 days from the date the lessee's notice of intent not to abandon is received by the lessor. Service in this manner is deemed completed on the 10th day after such mailing.

(b) Where the lessee has given the lessor written notice of the lessee's intent not to abandon leased real property as provided in Section 1951.3 of the Civil Code, but failed to include in such notice an address at which the lessee may be served by certified mail in any action for unlawful detainer of the real property, the summons in an action for unlawful detainer of the real property may be served on the lessee by certified mail, postage prepaid, addressed to the lessee at (1) the same address or addresses to which the lessor's notice of belief of abandonment was addressed if that notice was given by mail or (2) the address of the real property if the lessor's notice of belief of abandonment was personally served on the lessee. Service may not be made pursuant to this subdivision unless the summons is deposited in the mail within 60 days from the date the lessee's notice of intent not to abandon is received by the lessor. Service in the manner authorized by this subdivision is deemed completed on the 10th day after such mailing.

(c) This section provides an alternative method of service on the lessee and does not preclude service in any other manner authorized by this chapter. **Leg.H.** Added Stats 1974 ch 332 §2.

§415.50. Service by publication; Prerequisite affidavit; Order for publication in named newspaper; When service complete; Service other than by publication

(a) A summons may be served by publication if upon affidavit it appears to the satisfaction of the court in which the action is pending that the party to be served cannot with reasonable diligence be served in another manner specified in this article and that either:

(1) A cause of action exists against the party upon whom service is to be made or he or she is a necessary or proper party to the action.

(2) The party to be served has or claims an interest in real or personal property in this state that is subject to the jurisdiction of the court or the relief demanded in the action consists wholly or in part in excluding the party from any interest in the property.

(b) The court shall order the summons to be published in a named newspaper, published in this state, that is most likely to give actual notice to the party to be served. If the party to be served resides or is located out of this state, the court may also order the summons to be published in a named newspaper outside this state that is most likely to give actual notice to that party. The order shall direct that a copy of the summons, the complaint, and the order for publication be forthwith mailed to the party if his or her address is ascertained before expiration of the time prescribed for publication of the summons. Except as otherwise provided by statute, the publication shall be made as provided by Section 6064 of the Government Code unless the court, in its discretion, orders publication for a longer period.

(c) Service of a summons in this manner is deemed complete as provided in Section 6064 of the Government Code.

(d) Notwithstanding an order for publication of the summons, a summons may be served in another manner authorized by this chapter, in which event the service shall supersede any published summons.

(e) As a condition of establishing that the party to be served cannot with reasonable diligence be served in another manner specified in this article, the court may not require that a search be conducted of public databases where access by a registered process server to residential addresses is prohibited by law or by published policy of the agency providing the database, including, but not limited to, voter registration rolls and records of the Department of Motor Vehicles. **Leg.H.** Added Stats 1969 ch 1610 §3, operative July 1, 1970. Amended Stats 1972 ch 601 §2; Stats 1984 ch 352 §1; Stats 2002 ch 197 §2 (AB 2493); Stats 2003 ch 449 §8 (AB 1712).

§415.95. Service on "business organization, form unknown" by leaving and mailing copy; Where and with whom; When service is complete; Inapplicability to corporation with registered agent

(a) A summons may be served on a business organization, form unknown, by leaving a copy of the summons and complaint during usual office hours with the person who is apparently in charge of the office of that business organization, and by thereafter mailing a copy of the summons and complaint by first-class mail, postage prepaid, to the person to be served at the place where a copy of the summons and complaint was left. Service of a summons in this manner is deemed complete on the 10th day after the mailing.

(b) Service of a summons pursuant to this section is not valid for a corporation with a registered agent for service of process listed with the Secretary of State. **Leg.H.** Added Stats 2003 ch 128 §2 (AB 418).

§416. [Section repealed 1970]

Leg.H. Enacted 1872. Amended Code Amdts 1873–74 ch 383 §51; Stats 1919 ch 44 §1; Stats 1921 ch 113 §1. Stats 1933 ch 744 §22; Repealed Stats 1969 ch 1610 §17, operative July 1, 1970. See CCP §§410.10, 410.50, 410.60, Corp C §2011.

§416.1. [Section repealed 1970]

Leg.H. Added Stats 1955 ch 1452 §1. Amended Stats 1963 ch 878 §1. Repealed Stats 1969 ch 1610 §18, operative July 1, 1970. The repealed section related to notice of a motion to quash service of a summons.

§§416.2, 416.3. [Sections repealed 1970]

Leg.H. Added Stats 1955 ch 1452 §§2, 3. Repealed Stats 1969 ch 1610 §§19, 20, operative July 1, 1970. See CCP §418.10.

ARTICLE 4
Persons Upon Whom Summons May Be Served

Service on corporation. §416.10.
Service on corporation that has forfeited its charter or right to do business, or that has dissolved. §416.20.
Service on joint stock company or association. §416.30.
Service on unincorporated association, general or limited partnership. §416.40.
Service on public entity. §416.50.
Service on minor. §416.60.
Service on person (other than minor) for whom fiduciary appointed. §416.70.
Service on candidate for election for public office. §416.80.
Service on other persons. §416.90.

§416.10. Service on corporation

A summons may be served on a corporation by delivering a copy of the summons and the complaint by any of the following methods:

(a) To the person designated as agent for service of process as provided by any provision in Section 202, 1502, 2105, or 2107 of the Corporations Code (or Sections 3301 to 3303, inclusive, or Sections 6500 to 6504, inclusive, of the Corporations Code, as in effect on December 31, 1976, with respect to corporations to which they remain applicable).

(b) To the president, chief executive officer, or other head of the corporation, a vice president, a secretary or assistant secretary, a treasurer or assistant treasurer, a controller or chief financial officer, a general manager, or a person authorized by the corporation to receive service of process.

(c) If the corporation is a bank, to a cashier or assistant cashier or to a person specified in subdivision (a) or (b).

(d) If authorized by any provision in Section 1701, 1702, 2110, or 2111 of the Corporations Code (or Sections 3301 to 3303, inclusive, or Sections 6500 to 6504, inclusive, of the Corporations Code, as in effect on December 31, 1976, with respect to corporations to which they remain applicable), as provided by that provision. **Leg.H.** Added Stats 1969 ch 1610 §3, operative July 1, 1970. Amended Stats 1975 ch 682 §3, effective January 1, 1977; Stats 1976 ch 641 §1.1; Stats 2006 ch 567 §7 (AB 2303), effective January 1, 2007.

§416.20. Service on corporation that has forfeited its charter or right to do business, or that has dissolved

A summons may be served on a corporation that has forfeited its charter or right to do business, or has dissolved, by delivering a copy of the summons and of the complaint:

(a) To a person who is a trustee of the corporation and of its stockholders or members; or

(b) When authorized by any provision in Sections 2011 or 2114 of the Corporations Code (or Sections 3301 to 3303, inclusive, or Sections 6500 to 6504, inclusive, of the Corporations Code as in effect on December 31, 1976, with respect to corporations to which they remain applicable), as provided by such provision. **Leg.H.** Added Stats 1969 ch 1610 §3, operative July 1, 1970. Amended Stats 1970 ch 585 §1; Stats 1975 ch 682 §4, effective January 1, 1977; Stats 1977 ch 235 §1.1.

§416.30. Service on joint stock company or association

A summons may be served on a joint stock company or association by delivering a copy of the summons and of the complaint as provided by Section 416.10 or 416.20. **Leg.H.** Added Stats 1969 ch 1610 §3, operative July 1, 1970.

§416.40. Service on unincorporated association, general or limited partnership

A summons may be served on an unincorporated association (including a partnership) by delivering a copy of the summons and of the complaint:

(a) If the association is a general or limited partnership, to the person designated as agent for service of process in a statement filed with the Secretary of State or to a general partner or the general manager of the partnership;

(b) If the association is not a general or limited partnership, to the person designated as agent for service of process in a statement filed with the Secretary of State or to the president or other head of the association, a vice president, a secretary or assistant secretary, a treasurer or assistant treasurer, a general manager, or a person authorized by the association to receive service of process;

(c) When authorized by Section 18220 of the Corporations Code, as provided by that section. **Leg.H.** Added Stats 1969 ch 1610 §3, operative July 1, 1970. Amended Stats 2004 ch 178 §3 (SB 1746).

§416.50. Service on public entity

(a) A summons may be served on a public entity by delivering a copy of the summons and of the complaint to the clerk, secretary, president, presiding officer, or other head of its governing body.

(b) As used in this section, "public entity" includes the state and any office, department, division, bureau, board, commission, or agency of the state, the Regents of the University of California, a county, city, district, public authority, public agency, and any other political subdivision or public corporation in this state. **Leg.H.** Added Stats 1969 ch 1610 §3, operative July 1, 1970.

§416.60. Service on minor

A summons may be served on a minor by delivering a copy of the summons and of the complaint to his parent, guardian, conservator, or similar fiduciary, or, if no such person can be found with reasonable diligence, to any person having the care or control of such minor or with whom he resides or by whom he is employed, and to the minor if he is at least 12 years of age. **Leg.H.** Added Stats 1969 ch 1610 §3, operative July 1, 1970. Amended Stats 1972 ch 579 §14.5.

§416.70. Service on person (other than minor) for whom fiduciary appointed

A summons may be served on a person (other than a minor) for whom a guardian, conservator, or similar fiduciary has been appointed by delivering a copy of the summons and of the complaint to his guardian, conservator, or similar fiduciary and to such person, but, for good cause shown, the court in which the action is pending may dispense with delivery to such person. **Leg.H.** Added Stats 1969 ch 1610 §3, operative July 1, 1970. Amended Stats 1972 ch 579 §15.

§416.80. Service on candidate for election for public office

When authorized by Section 12 of the Elections Code, a summons may be served as provided by that section. **Leg.H.** Added Stats 1969 ch 1610 §3, operative July 1, 1970. Amended Stats 1976 ch 1438 §24.1; Stats 1994 ch 923 §2 (SB 1546); Stats 2009 ch 140 §38 (AB 1164), effective January 1, 2010.

§416.90. Service on other persons

A summons may be served on a person not otherwise specified in this article by delivering a copy of the summons and of the complaint to such person or to a person authorized by him to receive service of process. **Leg.H.** Added Stats 1969 ch 1610 §3, operative July 1, 1970.

§417. [Section repealed 1970]

Leg.H. Added Stats 1951 ch 935 §1. Amended Stats 1957 ch 1674 §1. Repealed Stats 1969 ch 1610 §21, operative July 1, 1970. See CCP §§410.10, 410.50.

ARTICLE 5
Proof of Service

Proof of service on person in state. §417.10.
Proof of service on person outside state. §417.20.
Return of summons with proof of service; Affidavit when summons lost after service but before return. §417.30.
Statement of county registration. §417.40.

§417.10. Proof of service on person in state

Proof that a summons was served on a person within this state shall be made:

(a) If served under Section 415.10, 415.20, or 415.30, by the affidavit of the person making the service showing the time, place, and manner of service and facts showing that the service was made in accordance with this chapter. The affidavit shall recite or in other manner show the name of the person to whom a copy of the summons and of the complaint were delivered, and, if appropriate, his or her title or the capacity in which he or she is served, and that the notice required by Section 412.30 appeared on the copy of the summons served, if in fact it did appear.

If service is made by mail pursuant to Section 415.30, proof of service shall include the acknowledgment of receipt of summons in the form provided by that section or other written acknowledgment of receipt of summons satisfactory to the court.

(b) If served by publication pursuant to Section 415.50, by the affidavit of the publisher or printer, or his or her foreperson or principal clerk, showing the time and place of publication, and an affidavit showing the time and place a copy of the summons and of the complaint were mailed to the party to be served, if in fact mailed.

(c) If served pursuant to another law of this state, in the manner prescribed by that law or, if no manner is prescribed, in the manner prescribed by this section for proof of a similar manner of service.

(d) By the written admission of the party.

(e) If served by posting pursuant to Section 415.45, by the affidavit of the person who posted the premises, showing the time and place of posting, and an affidavit showing the time and place copies of the summons and of the complaint were mailed to the party to be served, if in fact mailed.

(f) All proof of personal service shall be made on a form adopted by the Judicial Council. **Leg.H.** Added Stats 1969 ch 1610 §3, operative July 1, 1970. Amended Stats 1972 ch 719 §2; Stats 1980 ch 676 §65; Stats 1986 ch 953 §2, operative July 1, 1987; Stats 2006 ch 538 §63 (SB 1852), effective January 1, 2007.

§417.20. Proof of service on person outside state

Proof that a summons was served on a person outside this state shall be made:

(a) If served in a manner specified in a statute of this state, as prescribed by Section 417.10, and if service is made by mail pursuant to Section 415.40, proof of service shall include evidence satisfactory to the court establishing actual delivery to the person to be served, by a signed return receipt or other evidence;

(b) In the manner prescribed by the court order pursuant to which the service is made;

(c) Subject to any additional requirements that may be imposed by the court in which the action is pending, in the manner prescribed by the law of the place where the person is served for proof of service in an action in its courts of general jurisdiction; or

(d) By the written admission of the party.

(e) If served by posting pursuant to Section 415.45, by the affidavit of the person who posted the premises, showing the time and place of posting, and an affidavit showing the time and place copies of the summons and of the complaint were mailed to the party to be served, if in fact mailed. **Leg.H.** Added Stats 1969 ch 1610 §3, operative July 1, 1970. Amended Stats 1972 ch 719 §3.

§417.30. Return of summons with proof of service; Affidavit when summons lost after service but before return

After a summons has been served on a person, proof of service of the summons as provided in Section 417.10 or 417.20 shall be filed, unless the defendant has previously made a general appearance. **Leg.H.** Added Stats 1969 ch 1610 §3, operative July 1, 1970. Amended Stats 1971 ch 1366 §1; Stats 2005 ch 300 §3 (AB 496), effective January 1, 2006.

§417.40. Statement of county registration

Any proof of service which is signed by a person registered under Chapter 16 (commencing with Section 22350) of Division 8 of the Business and Professions Code or his employee or independent contractor shall indicate the county in which he is registered and the number assigned to him pursuant to Section 22355 of the Business and Professions Code. **Leg.H.** Added Stats 1971 ch 1661 §3, operative July 1, 1972.

CHAPTER 5
OBJECTION TO JURISDICTION

Notice of motion to quash service or to stay or dismiss action; Petition for writ of mandate, and responsive pleading; Default and general appearance. §418.10.
Appearance in certain ex parte matters not considered general appearance. §418.11.

§418.10. Notice of motion to quash service or to stay or dismiss action; Petition for writ of mandate, and responsive pleading; Default and general appearance

(a) A defendant, on or before the last day of his or her time to plead or within any further time that the court may for good cause allow, may serve and file a notice of motion for one or more of the following purposes:

(1) To quash service of summons on the ground of lack of jurisdiction of the court over him or her.

(2) To stay or dismiss the action on the ground of inconvenient forum.

(3) To dismiss the action pursuant to the applicable provisions of Chapter 1.5 (commencing with Section 583.110) of Title 8.

(b) The notice shall designate, as the time for making the motion, a date not more than 30 days after filing of the notice. The notice shall be served in the same manner, and at the same times, prescribed by subdivision (b) of Section 1005. The service and filing of the notice shall extend the defendant's time to plead until 15 days after service upon him or her of a written notice of entry of an order denying his or her motion, except that for good cause shown the court may extend the defendant's time to plead for an additional period not exceeding 20 days.

(c) If the motion is denied by the trial court, the defendant, within 10 days after service upon him or her of a written notice of entry of an order of the court denying his or her motion, or within any further time not exceeding 20 days that the trial court may for good cause allow, and before pleading, may petition an appropriate reviewing court for a writ of mandate to require the trial court to enter its order quashing the service of summons or staying or dismissing the action. The defendant shall file or enter his or her responsive pleading in the trial court within the time prescribed by subdivision (b) unless, on or before the last day of the defendant's time to plead, he or she serves upon the adverse party and files with the trial court a notice that he or she has petitioned for a writ of mandate. The service and filing of the notice shall extend the defendant's time to plead until 10 days after service upon him or her of a written notice of the final judgment in the mandate proceeding. The time to plead may for good cause shown be extended by the trial court for an additional period not exceeding 20 days.

(d) No default may be entered against the defendant before expiration of his or her time to plead, and no motion under this section, or under Section 473 or 473.5 when joined with a motion under this section, or application to the court or stipulation of the parties for an extension of the time to plead, shall be deemed a general appearance by the defendant.

(e) A defendant or cross-defendant may make a motion under this section and simultaneously answer, demur, or move to strike the complaint or cross-complaint.

(1) Notwithstanding Section 1014, no act by a party who makes a motion under this section, including filing an answer, demurrer, or motion to strike constitutes an appearance, unless the court denies the motion made under this section. If the court denies the motion made under this section, the defendant or cross-defendant is not deemed to have generally appeared until entry of the order denying the motion.

(2) If the motion made under this section is denied and the defendant or cross-defendant petitions for a writ of mandate pursuant to subdivision (c), the defendant or cross-defendant is not deemed to have generally appeared until the proceedings on the writ petition have finally concluded.

(3) Failure to make a motion under this section at the time of filing a demurrer or motion to strike constitutes a waiver of the issues of lack of personal jurisdiction, inadequacy of process, inadequacy of service of process, inconvenient forum, and delay in prosecution. **Leg.H.** Added Stats 1969 ch 1610 §3, operative July 1, 1970. Amended Stats 1989 ch 693 §1; Stats 1993 ch 456 §1 (AB 58); Stats 2002 ch 69 §1 (SB 1325).

2002 Note: It is the intent of the Legislature in enacting this act to conform California practice with respect to challenging personal jurisdiction to the practice under Rule 12(b) of the Federal Rules of Civil Procedure. State 2002 ch 69 (SB 1325) §2.

§418.11. Appearance in certain ex parte matters not considered general appearance

An appearance at a hearing at which ex parte relief is sought, or an appearance at a hearing for which an ex parte application for a provisional remedy is made, is not a general appearance and does not constitute a waiver of the right to make a motion under Section 418.10. **Leg.H.** Added Stats 1987 ch 62 §1.

TITLE 6
OF THE PLEADINGS IN CIVIL ACTIONS

Chapter 1. The Pleadings in General.
Chapter 2. Pleadings Demanding Relief.
Chapter 3. Objections to Pleadings; Denials and Defenses.
Chapter 4. Motion to Strike.
Chapter 5. Summary Judgments and Motions for Judgment on the Pleadings.
Chapter 6. Verification of Pleadings.
Chapter 7. General Rules of Pleading.
Chapter 8. Variance—Mistakes in Pleadings and Amendments.

CHAPTER 1
THE PLEADINGS IN GENERAL

Definition of pleadings. §420.
This code prescribes the form and rules of pleadings. §421.
Pleadings allowed. §422.10.
Caption. §422.30.
Names of parties in complaint's title of action. §422.40.

§420. Definition of pleadings

The pleadings are the formal allegations by the parties of their respective claims and defenses, for the judgment of the court. **Leg.H.** Enacted 1872.

§421. This code prescribes the form and rules of pleadings

The forms of pleading in civil actions, and the rules by which the sufficiency of the pleadings is to be determined, are those prescribed in this code. **Leg.H.** Enacted 1872.

§422. [Section repealed 1972]

Leg.H. Enacted 1872. Amended Stats 1907 ch 372 §1; Stats 1933 ch 744 §23; Stats 1951 ch 1737 §49, operative January 1, 1952. Repealed Stats 1971 ch 244 §17, operative July 1, 1972. See CCP §§422.10, 422.20.

§422.10. Pleadings allowed

The pleadings allowed in civil actions are complaints, demurrers, answers, and cross-complaints. **Leg.H.** Added Stats 1971 ch 244 §18, operative July 1, 1972.

§422.20. [Section repealed 1998]

Leg.H. Added Stats 1977 ch 1257 §11, effective October 3, 1977. Repealed Stats 1998 ch 931 §70 (SB 2139), effective September 28, 1998. The repealed section related to pleadings in justice courts.

Prior Law: Former CCP §422.20, similar to the present section, was added Stats 1971 ch 244 §19, operative July 1, 1972, and repealed Stats 1977 ch 1257 §10, effective October 3, 1977.

§422.30. Caption

(a) Every pleading shall contain a caption setting forth:
(1) The name of the court and county in which the action is brought.
(2) The title of the action.
(b) In a limited civil case, the caption shall state that the case is a limited civil case, and the clerk shall classify the case accordingly. **Leg.H.** Added Stats 1971 ch 244 §20, operative July 1, 1972. Amended Stats 1998 ch 931 §71 (SB 2139), effective September 28, 1998; Stats 1999 ch 344 §13 (SB 210), effective September 7, 1999; Stats 2002 ch 784 §60 (SB 1316).

§422.40. Names of parties in complaint's title of action

In the complaint, the title of the action shall include the names of all the parties; but, except as otherwise provided by statute or rule of the Judicial Council, in other pleadings it is sufficient to state the name of the first party on each side with an appropriate indication of other parties. **Leg.H.** Added Stats 1971 ch 244 §21, operative July 1, 1972.

§425. [Section repealed 1972]

Leg.H. Enacted 1872. Repealed Stats 1971 ch 244 §22, operative July 1, 1972. See CCP §411.10.

CHAPTER 2
PLEADINGS DEMANDING RELIEF

Article 1. General Provisions.
Article 2. Compulsory Cross-Complaints.
Article 3. Permissive Joinder of Causes of Action.
Article 4. Cross-Complaints.
Article 5. Contents of Documents in Particular Actions or Proceedings.

ARTICLE 1
General Provisions

Contents of complaint or cross-complaint. §425.10.
Damages statement. §425.11.
Preservation of right to seek punitive damages on default judgment; Service of statement on defendant. §425.115.
Approved forms for pleading. §425.12.
Claim for punitive damages against health care provider. §425.13.
Claim for punitive damages against religious corporation. §425.14.
Procedure for filing cause of action against officer or director of nonprofit corporation serving without compensation. §425.15.
Legislative findings; Special motion to strike action arising from "act in furtherance of person's right of petition or free speech under United States or California Constitution in connection with a public issue". §425.16.
Legislative findings as to abuse of Section 425.16; Inapplicability of Section 425.16 to certain actions; Appeal provisions not applicable. §425.17.
"SLAPPback"; Special motion to strike. §425.18.
Civil actions challenging priority housing development projects; Special motion to strike. § 425.19.
"Common count"; "Consumer debt". § 425.30.
Requirement of complaint alleging construction-related accessibility claim. §425.50.
"High-frequency litigant". §425.55.

§425.10. Contents of complaint or cross-complaint

(a) A complaint or cross-complaint shall contain both of the following:
(1) A statement of the facts constituting the cause of action, in ordinary and concise language.
(2) A demand for judgment for the relief to which the pleader claims to be entitled. If the recovery of money or damages is demanded, the amount demanded shall be stated.
(b) Notwithstanding subdivision (a), where an action is brought to recover actual or punitive damages for personal injury or wrongful death, the amount demanded shall not be stated, but the complaint shall comply with Section 422.30 and, in a limited civil case, with subdivision (b) of Section 70613 of the Government Code. **Leg.H.** Added Stats 1971 ch 244 §23, operative July 1, 1972. Amended Stats 1974 ch 1481 §1; Stats 1979 ch 778 §2; Stats 1998 ch 931 §72 (SB 2139), effective September 28, 1998; Stats 2001 ch 812 §1 (AB 223); Stats 2005 ch 75 §32 (AB 145), effective July 19, 2005, operative January 1, 2006.

§425.11. Damages statement

(a) As used in this section:
(1) "Complaint" includes a cross-complaint.
(2) "Plaintiff" includes a cross-complainant.
(3) "Defendant" includes a cross-defendant.
(b) When a complaint is filed in an action to recover damages for personal injury or wrongful death, the defendant may at any time request a statement setting forth the nature and amount of damages being sought. The request shall be served upon the plaintiff, who shall serve a responsive statement as to the damages within 15 days. In the event that a response is not served, the defendant, on notice to the plaintiff, may petition the court in which the action is pending to order the plaintiff to serve a responsive statement.
(c) If no request is made for the statement referred to in subdivision (b), the plaintiff shall serve the statement on the defendant before a default may be taken.
(d) The statement referred to in subdivision (b) shall be served in the following manner:
(1) If a party has not appeared in the action, the statement shall be served in the same manner as a summons.
(2) If a party has appeared in the action, the statement shall be served upon the party's attorney, or upon the party if the party has appeared without an attorney, in the manner provided for service of a summons or in the manner provided by Chapter 5 (commencing with Section 1010) of Title 14 of Part 2.

(e) The statement referred to in subdivision (b) may be combined with the statement described in Section 425.115. **Leg.H.** Added Stats 1974 ch 1481 §2. Amended Stats 1993 ch 456 §2 (AB 58); Stats 1995 ch 796 §2 (SB 45); Stats 1998 ch 931 §73 (SB 2139), effective September 28, 1998; Stats 2001 ch 812 §2 (AB 223); Stats 2006 ch 538 §63.5 (SB 1852), effective January 1, 2007.

§425.115. Preservation of right to seek punitive damages on default judgment; Service of statement on defendant

(a) As used in this section:

(1) "Complaint" includes a cross-complaint.

(2) "Plaintiff" includes a cross-complainant.

(3) "Defendant" includes a cross-defendant.

(b) The plaintiff preserves the right to seek punitive damages pursuant to Section 3294 of the Civil Code on a default judgment by serving upon the defendant the following statement, or its substantial equivalent:

NOTICE TO _____ (Insert name of defendant or cross-defendant):

_____ (Insert name of plaintiff or cross-complainant) reserves the right to seek $_____ (Insert dollar amount) in punitive damages when _____ (Insert name of plaintiff or cross-complainant) seeks a judgment in the suit filed against you.

_____
(Insert name of attorney or   (Date)
party appearing in propria persona)

(c) If the plaintiff seeks punitive damages pursuant to Section 3294 of the Civil Code, and if the defendant appears in the action, the plaintiff shall not be limited to the amount set forth in the statement served on the defendant pursuant to this section.

(d) A plaintiff who serves a statement on the defendant pursuant to this section shall be deemed to have complied with Sections 425.10 and 580 of this code and Section 3295 of the Civil Code.

(e) The plaintiff may serve a statement upon the defendant pursuant to this section, and may serve the statement as part of the statement required by Section 425.11.

(f) The plaintiff shall serve the statement upon the defendant pursuant to this section before a default may be taken, if the motion for default judgment includes a request for punitive damages.

(g) The statement referred to in subdivision (b) shall be served by one of the following methods:

(1) If the party has not appeared in the action, the statement shall be served in the same manner as a summons pursuant to Article 3 (commencing with Section 415.10) of Chapter 4 of Title 5 of Part 2 of the Code of Civil Procedure.

(2) If the party has appeared in the action, the statement shall be served upon his or her attorney, or upon the party if he or she has appeared without an attorney, either in the same manner as a summons pursuant to Article 3 (commencing with Section 415.10) of Chapter 4 or in the manner provided by Chapter 5 (commencing with Section 1010) of Title 14. **Leg.H.** Added Stats 1995 ch 796 §3 (SB 45). Amended Stats 2005 ch 706 §12 (AB 1742), effective January 1, 2006.

§425.12. Approved forms for pleading

(a) The Judicial Council shall develop and approve official forms for use in trial courts of this state for any complaint, cross-complaint, or answer in any action based upon personal injury, property damage, wrongful death, unlawful detainer, breach of contract or fraud.

(b) The Judicial Council shall develop and approve an official form for use as a statement of damages pursuant to Sections 425.11 and 425.115.

(c) In developing the forms required by this section, the Judicial Council shall consult with a representative advisory committee which shall include, but not be limited to, representatives of the plaintiff's bar, the defense bar, the public interest bar, court administrators and the public. The forms shall be drafted in nontechnical language and shall be made available through the office of the clerk of the appropriate trial court. **Leg.H.** Added Stats 1979 ch 843 §1. Amended Stats 1982 ch 272 §1; Stats 1984 ch 354 §1; Stats 1995 ch 796 §4 (SB 45).

§425.13. Claim for punitive damages against health care provider

(a) In any action for damages arising out of the professional negligence of a health care provider, no claim for punitive damages shall be included in a complaint or other pleading unless the court enters an order allowing an amended pleading that includes a claim for punitive damages to be filed. The court may allow the filing of an amended pleading claiming punitive damages on a motion by the party seeking the amended pleading and on the basis of the supporting and opposing affidavits presented that the plaintiff has established that there is a substantial probability that the plaintiff will prevail on the claim pursuant to Section 3294 of the Civil Code. The court shall not grant a motion allowing the filing of an amended pleading that includes a claim for punitive damages if the motion for such an order is not filed within two years after the complaint or initial pleading is filed or not less than nine months before the date the matter is first set for trial, whichever is earlier.

(b) For the purposes of this section, "health care provider" means any person licensed or certified pursuant to Division 2 (commencing with Section 500) of the Business and Professions Code, or licensed pursuant to the Osteopathic Initiative Act, or the Chiropractic Initiative Act, or licensed pursuant to Chapter 2.5 (commencing with Section 1440) of Division 2 of the Health and Safety Code; and any clinic, health dispensary, or health facility, licensed pursuant to Division 2 (commencing with Section 1200) of the Health and Safety Code. "Health care provider" includes the legal representatives of a health care provider. **Leg.H.** Added Stats 1987 ch 1498 §7. Amended Stats 1988 ch 1204 §1, ch 1205 §1.

§425.14. Claim for punitive damages against religious corporation

No claim for punitive or exemplary damages against a religious corporation or religious corporation sole shall be included in a complaint or other pleading unless the court enters an order allowing an amended pleading that includes a claim for punitive or exemplary damages to be filed. The court may allow the filing of an amended pleading claiming punitive or exemplary damages on a motion by the party seeking the amended pleading and upon a finding, on the basis of the supporting and opposing affidavits presented, that the plaintiff has established evidence which substantiates that plaintiff will meet the clear and convincing standard of proof under Section 3294 of the Civil Code.

Nothing in this section is intended to affect the plaintiff's right to discover evidence on the issue of punitive or exemplary damages. **Leg.H.** Added Stats 1988 ch 1410 §1.

§425.15. Procedure for filing cause of action against officer or director of nonprofit corporation serving without compensation

(a) No cause of action against a person serving without compensation as a director or officer of a nonprofit corporation described in this section, on account of any negligent act or omission by that person within the scope of that person's duties as a director acting in the capacity of a board member, or as an officer acting in the capacity of, and within the scope of the duties of, an officer, shall be included in a complaint or other pleading unless the court enters an order allowing the pleading that includes that claim to be filed after the court determines that the party seeking to file the pleading has established evidence that substantiates the claim. The court may allow the filing of a pleading that includes that claim following the filing of a verified petition therefor accompanied by the proposed pleading and supporting affidavits stating the facts upon which the liability is based. The court shall order service of the petition upon the party against whom the action is proposed to be filed and permit that party to submit opposing affidavits prior to making its determination. The filing of the petition, proposed pleading, and accompanying affidavits shall toll the running of any applicable statute of limitations until the final determination of the matter, which ruling, if favorable to the petitioning party, shall permit the proposed pleading to be filed.

(b) Nothing in this section shall affect the right of the plaintiff to discover evidence on the issue of damages.

(c) Nothing in this section shall be construed to affect any action against a nonprofit corporation for any negligent action or omission of a volunteer director or officer occurring within the scope of the person's duties.

(d) For the purposes of this section, "compensation" means remuneration whether by way of salary, fee, or other consideration for services rendered. However, the payment of per diem, mileage, or other reimbursement expenses to a director or officer shall not constitute compensation.

(e)(1) This section applies only to officers and directors of nonprofit corporations that are subject to Part 2 (commencing with Section 5110), Part 3 (commencing with Section 7110), or Part 4 (commencing with Section 9110) of Division 2 of Title 1 of the Corporations Code that are organized to provide charitable, educational, scientific, social, or other forms of public service and that are exempt from federal income taxation under Section 501(c)(1), except any credit union, or Section 501(c)(4), 501(c)(5), 501(c)(7),or 501(c)(19) of the Internal Revenue Code.

(2) This section does not apply to any corporation that unlawfully restricts membership, services, or benefits conferred on the basis of political affiliation, age, or any characteristic listed or defined in subdivision (b) or (e) of Section 51 of the Civil Code. **Leg.H.** Added Stats 1992 ch 726 §1 (SB 1264). Amended Stats 2007 ch 568 §16 (AB 14), effective January 1, 2008.

2007 Notes: The Legislature finds and declares as follows:

(a) Even prior to passage of the Unruh Civil Rights Act, California law afforded broad protection against arbitrary discrimination by business establishments. The Unruh Civil Rights Act was enacted to provide broader, more effective protection against arbitrary discrimination. California's interest in preventing that discrimination is longstanding and compelling.

(b) In keeping with that history and the legislative history of the Unruh Civil Rights Act, California courts have interpreted the categories enumerated in the act to be illustrative rather than restrictive. It is the intent of the Legislature that these enumerated bases shall continue to be construed as illustrative rather than restrictive, and, consistent with the Unruh Civil Rights Act, that the civil rights provisions of this act that reference Section 51 of the Civil Code also be interpreted to be illustrative rather than restrictive. Stats 2007 ch 568 (AB 14) §1.

This act shall be known and may be cited as the Civil Rights Act of 2007. Stats 2007 ch 568 (AB 14) §1.5.

Prior Law: Former CCP §425.15, relating to cause of action for negligence against uncompensated director or office of nonprofit corporation, was added Stats 1988 ch 1204 §2, amended Stats 1988 ch 1205 §2, operative until January 1, 1992, Stats 1989 ch 864 §1, Stats 1990 ch 107 §1, operative until January 1, 1992, and repealed January 1, 1992, by its own terms.

§425.16. Legislative findings; Special motion to strike action arising from "act in furtherance of person's right of petition or free speech under United States or California Constitution in connection with a public issue"

(a) The Legislature finds and declares that there has been a disturbing increase in lawsuits brought primarily to chill the valid exercise of the constitutional rights of freedom of speech and petition for the redress of grievances. The Legislature finds and declares that it is in the public interest to encourage continued participation in matters of public significance, and that this participation should not be chilled through abuse of the judicial process. To this end, this section shall be construed broadly.

(b)(1) A cause of action against a person arising from any act of that person in furtherance of the person's right of petition or free speech under the United States Constitution or the California Constitution in connection with a public issue shall be subject to a special motion to strike, unless the court determines that the plaintiff has established that there is a probability that the plaintiff will prevail on the claim.

(2) In making its determination, the court shall consider the pleadings, and supporting and opposing affidavits stating the facts upon which the liability or defense is based.

(3) If the court determines that the plaintiff has established a probability that the plaintiff will prevail on the claim, neither that determination nor the fact of that determination shall be admissible in evidence at any later stage of the case, or in any subsequent action, and no burden of proof or degree of proof otherwise applicable shall be affected by that determination in any later stage of the case or in any subsequent proceeding.

(c)(1) Except as provided in paragraph (2), in any action subject to subdivision (b), a prevailing defendant on a special motion to strike shall be entitled to recover that defendant's attorney's fees and costs. If the court finds that a special motion to strike is frivolous or is solely intended to cause unnecessary delay, the court shall award costs and reasonable attorney's fees to a plaintiff prevailing on the motion, pursuant to Section 128.5.

(2) A defendant who prevails on a special motion to strike in an action subject to paragraph (1) shall not be entitled to attorney's fees and costs if that cause of action is brought pursuant to Section 11130, 11130.3, 54960, or 54960.1 of the Government Code, or pursuant to Chapter 2 (commencing with Section 7923.100) of Part 4 of Division 10 of Title 1 of the Government Code. Nothing in this paragraph shall be construed to prevent a prevailing defendant from recovering attorney's fees and costs pursuant to Section 7923.115, 11130.5, or 54960.5 of the Government Code.

(d) This section shall not apply to any enforcement action brought in the name of the people of the State of California by the Attorney General, **Insurance Commissioner,** district attorney, or city attorney, acting as a public prosecutor.

(e) As used in this section, "act in furtherance of a person's right of petition or free speech under the United States or California Constitution in connection with a public issue" includes: (1) any written or oral statement or writing made before a legislative, executive, or judicial proceeding, or any other official proceeding authorized by law, (2) any written or oral statement or writing made in connection with an issue under consideration or review by a legislative, executive, or judicial body, or any other official proceeding authorized by law, (3) any written or oral statement or writing made in a place open to the public or a public forum in connection with an issue of public interest, or (4) any other conduct in furtherance of the exercise of the constitutional right of petition or the constitutional right of free speech in connection with a public issue or an issue of public interest.

(f) The special motion may be filed within 60 days of the service of the complaint or, in the court's discretion, at any later time upon terms it deems proper. The motion shall be scheduled by the clerk of the court for a hearing not more than 30 days after the service of the motion unless the docket conditions of the court require a later hearing.

(g) All discovery proceedings in the action shall be stayed upon the filing of a notice of motion made pursuant to this section. The stay of discovery shall remain in effect until notice of entry of the order ruling on the motion. The court, on noticed motion and for good cause shown, may order that specified discovery be conducted notwithstanding this subdivision.

(h) For purposes of this section, "complaint" includes "cross-complaint" and "petition," "plaintiff" includes "cross-complainant" and "petitioner," and "defendant" includes "cross-defendant" and "respondent."

(i) An order granting or denying a special motion to strike shall be appealable under Section 904.1.

(j)(1) Any party who files a special motion to strike pursuant to this section, and any party who files an opposition to a special motion to strike, shall, promptly upon so filing, transmit to the Judicial Council, by email or facsimile, a copy of the endorsed, filed caption page of the motion or opposition, a copy of any related notice of appeal or petition for a writ, and a conformed copy of any order issued pursuant to this section, including any order granting or denying a special motion to strike, discovery, or fees.

(2) The Judicial Council shall maintain a public record of information transmitted pursuant to this subdivision for at least three years, and may store the information on microfilm or other appropriate electronic media. **Leg.H.** Added Stats 1992 ch 726 §2 (SB 1264). Amended Stats 1993 ch 1239 §1 (SB 9); Stats 1997 ch 271 §1 (SB 1296); Stats 1999 ch 960 §1 (AB 1675), effective October 10, 1999; Stats 2005 ch 535 §1 (AB 1158), effective October 5, 2005; Stats 2009 ch 65 §1 (SB 786), effective January 1, 2010; Stats 2010 ch 328 §34 (SB 1330), effective January 1, 2011; Stats 2014 ch 71 §17 (SB 1304), effective January 1, 2015; Stats 2021 ch 615 §56 (AB 474), effective January 1, 2022; Stats 2024 ch 444 §1 (SB 577), effective January 1, 2025.

2005 Note: It is the intent of the Legislature, in amending subdivision (f) of Section 425.16 of the Code of Civil Procedure, to overrule the decisions in *Decker v. U.D. Registry, Inc.* (2003) 105 Cal.App.4th 1382, 1387-1390, and *Fair Political Practices Commission v. American Civil Rights Coalition, Inc.* (2004) 121 Cal.App.4th 1171, 1174–1178. Stats 2005 ch 535 (AB 1158) §3.

§425.17. Legislative findings as to abuse of Section 425.16; Inapplicability of Section 425.16 to certain actions; Appeal provisions not applicable

(a) The Legislature finds and declares that there has been a disturbing abuse of Section 425.16, the California Anti-SLAPP Law, which has undermined the exercise of the constitutional rights of freedom of speech and petition for the redress of grievances, contrary to the purpose and intent of Section 425.16. The Legislature finds and declares that it is in the public interest to encourage continued participation in matters of public significance, and that this participation should not be chilled through abuse of the judicial process or Section 425.16.

(b) Section 425.16 does not apply to any action brought solely in the public interest or on behalf of the general public if all of the following conditions exist:

(1) The plaintiff does not seek any relief greater than or different from the relief sought for the general public or a class of which the plaintiff is a member. A claim for attorney's fees, costs, or penalties does not constitute greater or different relief for purposes of this subdivision.

(2) The action, if successful, would enforce an important right affecting the public interest, and would confer a significant benefit, whether pecuniary or nonpecuniary, on the general public or a large class of persons.

(3) Private enforcement is necessary and places a disproportionate financial burden on the plaintiff in relation to the plaintiff's stake in the matter.

(c) Section 425.16 does not apply to any cause of action brought against a person primarily engaged in the business of selling or leasing goods or services, including, but not limited to, insurance, securities, or financial instruments, arising from any statement or conduct by that person if both of the following conditions exist:

(1) The statement or conduct consists of representations of fact about that person's or a business competitor's business operations, goods, or services, that is made for the purpose of obtaining approval for, promoting, or securing sales or leases of, or commercial transactions in, the person's goods or services, or the statement or conduct was made in the course of delivering the person's goods or services.

(2) The intended audience is an actual or potential buyer or customer, or a person likely to repeat the statement to, or otherwise influence, an actual or potential buyer or customer, or the statement or conduct arose out of or within the context of a regulatory approval process, proceeding, or investigation, except where the statement or conduct was made by a telephone corporation in the course of a proceeding before the California Public Utilities Commission and is the subject of a lawsuit brought by a competitor, notwithstanding that the conduct or statement concerns an important public issue.

(d) Subdivisions (b) and (c) do not apply to any of the following:

(1) Any person enumerated in subdivision (b) of Section 2 of Article I of the California Constitution or Section 1070 of the Evidence Code, or any person engaged in the dissemination of ideas or expression in any book or academic journal, while engaged in the gathering, receiving, or processing of information for communication to the public.

(2) Any action against any person or entity based upon the creation, dissemination, exhibition, advertisement, or other similar promotion of any dramatic, literary, musical, political, or artistic work, including, but not limited to, a motion picture or television program, or an article published in a newspaper or magazine of general circulation.

(3) Any nonprofit organization that receives more than 50 percent of its annual revenues from federal, state, or local government grants, awards, programs, or reimbursements for services rendered.

(e) If any trial court denies a special motion to strike on the grounds that the action or cause of action is exempt pursuant to this section, the appeal provisions in subdivision (i) of Section 425.16 and paragraph (13) of subdivision (a) of Section 904.1 do not apply to that action or cause of action. **Leg.H.** Amended Stats 2011 ch 296 §36.5 (AB 1023), effective January 1, 2012.

§425.18. "SLAPPback"; Special motion to strike

(a) The Legislature finds and declares that a SLAPPback is distinguishable in character and origin from the ordinary malicious prosecution action. The Legislature further finds and declares that a SLAPPback cause of action should be treated differently, as provided in this section, from an ordinary malicious prosecution action because a SLAPPback is consistent with the Legislature's intent to protect the valid exercise of the constitutional rights of free speech and petition by its deterrent effect on SLAPP (strategic lawsuit against public participation) litigation and by its restoration of public confidence in participatory democracy.

(b) For purposes of this section, the following terms have the following meanings:

(1) "SLAPPback" means any cause of action for malicious prosecution or abuse of process arising from the filing or maintenance of a prior cause of action that has been dismissed pursuant to a special motion to strike under Section 425.16.

(2) "Special motion to strike" means a motion made pursuant to Section 425.16.

(c) The provisions of subdivisions (c), (f), (g), and (i) of Section 425.16, and paragraph (13) of subdivision (a) of Section 904.1, shall not apply to a special motion to strike a SLAPPback.

(d)(1) A special motion to strike a SLAPPback shall be filed within any one of the following periods of time, as follows:

(A) Within 120 days of the service of the complaint.

(B) At the court's discretion, within six months of the service of the complaint.

(C) At the court's discretion, at any later time in extraordinary cases due to no fault of the defendant and upon written findings of the court stating the extraordinary case and circumstance.

(2) The motion shall be scheduled by the clerk of the court for a hearing not more than 30 days after the service of the motion unless the docket conditions of the court require a later hearing.

(e) A party opposing a special motion to strike a SLAPPback may file an ex parte application for a continuance to obtain necessary discovery. If it appears that facts essential to justify opposition to that motion may exist, but cannot then be presented, the court shall grant a reasonable continuance to permit the party to obtain affidavits or conduct discovery or may make any other order as may be just.

(f) If the court finds that a special motion to strike a SLAPPback is frivolous or solely intended to cause unnecessary delay, the court shall award costs and reasonable attorney's fees to a plaintiff prevailing on the motion, pursuant to Section 128.5.

(g) Upon entry of an order denying a special motion to strike a SLAPPback claim, or granting the special motion to strike as to some but less than all causes of action alleged in a complaint containing a SLAPPback claim, an aggrieved party may, within 20 days after service of a written notice of the entry of the order, petition an appropriate reviewing court for a peremptory writ.

(h) A special motion to strike may not be filed against a SLAPPback by a party whose filing or maintenance of the prior cause of action from which the SLAPPback arises was illegal as a matter of law.

(i) This section does not apply to a SLAPPback filed by a public entity. **Leg.H.** Added Stats 2005 ch 535 §2 (AB 1158), effective October 5, 2005.

§ 425.19. Civil actions challenging priority housing development projects; Special motion to strike

(a) The Legislature finds and declares all of the following:

(1) The lack of affordable housing is a critical problem that threatens the economic, environmental, and social quality of life in California.

(2) It is in the public interest to encourage priority housing development projects in which 100 percent of the units, exclusive of any manager's unit or units, are reserved for lower income households, as defined in Section 50079.5 of the Health and Safety Code, and ensure such developments are not unnecessarily delayed or caused to fail through abuse of the judicial process. To this end, this section shall be construed broadly.

(b)(1)(A) In all civil actions brought by any plaintiff to challenge the approval or permitting of a priority housing development project, including, but not limited to, actions brought pursuant to Section 21167 of the Public Resources Code, a defendant may bring a special motion to strike the whole or any part of a pleading. The court shall deny the motion to strike if it determines that the plaintiff has established that there is a probability that the plaintiff will prevail on the claim.

(B) The court shall make its determination on the special motion to strike based on the pleadings, and supporting and opposing affidavits stating the facts upon which the liability or defense is based. Affidavits submitted with the pleadings may include a request for judicial notice of facts and documents relevant to the court's determination.

(C)(i) If the court is unable to determine whether the plaintiff has established a probability that the plaintiff will prevail on the claim without reviewing the administrative record in an action where the administrative record is required, the court shall make its determination on the special motion to strike based on the documents specified in subparagraph (B) and the administrative record, once prepared.

(ii) If the court determines that an administrative record is required for its decision, the moving party may, notwithstanding the 60-day filing requirement pursuant to paragraph (4) and without appealing an order denying a special motion to strike pursuant to paragraph (7), file the special motion to strike within 60 days of the service of the administrative record or, in the court's discretion, at any later time it deems proper.

(D) If the court determines that the plaintiff has established a probability that the plaintiff will prevail on the claim, neither that determination nor the fact of that determination shall be admissible in evidence at any later stage of the case, or in any subsequent action, and no burden of proof or degree of proof otherwise applicable shall be affected by that determination in any later stage of the case or in any subsequent proceeding.

(2) In any action subject to paragraph (1), a prevailing defendant on a special motion to strike shall be entitled to recover that defendant's attorney's fees and costs. If the court finds that a special motion to strike is frivolous or is solely intended to cause unnecessary delay, the court shall award costs and reasonable attorney's fees to a plaintiff prevailing on the motion, pursuant to Section 128.5.

(3) This subdivision does not apply to any enforcement action brought in the name of the people of the State of California by the Attorney General, district attorney, or city attorney, acting as a public prosecutor.

(4) The special motion may be filed within 60 days of the service of the complaint or, in the court's discretion, at any later time upon terms it deems proper. The motion shall be scheduled by the clerk of the court for a hearing not more than 30 days after the service of the motion unless the docket conditions of the court require a later hearing.

(5) All discovery proceedings in the action shall be stayed upon the filing of a notice of motion made pursuant to this section. The stay of discovery shall remain in effect until notice of entry of the order ruling on the motion. The court, on noticed motion and for good cause shown, may order that specified discovery be conducted notwithstanding this subdivision.

(6) For purposes of this section, "complaint" includes "cross-complaint" and "petition," "plaintiff" includes "cross-complainant" and "petitioner," and "defendant" includes "cross-defendant" and "respondent."

(7) An order granting or denying a special motion to strike is appealable under Section 904.1.

(c) "Priority housing development" means a development in which 100 percent of the units, exclusive of any manager's unit or units, will be reserved for lower income households, as defined in Section 50079.5 of the Health and Safety Code, for at least 55 years. **Leg.H.** Added Stats 2023 ch 779 §1 (SB 439), effective January 1, 2024.

§425.20. [Section repealed 1974]

Leg.H. Added Stats 1971 ch 244 §23, operative July 1, 1972. Repealed Stats 1973 ch 828 §1. The repealed section related to separate statement of causes of action.

§425.30. "Common count"; "Consumer debt"

(a) In an action for collection of consumer debt, common counts may not be used. For purposes of this section, a "common count" includes, but is not limited to, a claim for recovery of any of the following:

(1) An open book account for money due.

(2) An account stated in writing by and between plaintiff and defendant in which it was agreed that defendant was indebted to plaintiff.

(3) Money had and received by defendant for the use and benefit of plaintiff.

(4) Work, labor, services, and materials rendered at the special instance and request of defendant and for which defendant promised to pay plaintiff.

(5) Goods, wares, and merchandise sold and delivered to defendant and for which defendant promised to pay plaintiff.

(6) Money lent by plaintiff to defendant at defendant's request.

(7) Money paid out, laid out, and expended to or for defendant at defendant's special instance and request.

(b) For purposes of this section, "consumer debt" means any obligation or alleged obligation, incurred on or after July 1, 2024, of a consumer to pay money arising out of a transaction in which the money, property, insurance, or services that are the subject of the transaction are primarily for personal, family, or household purposes and where the obligation to pay appears on the face of a note or in a written contract.

(c) In an action under this section for the collection of consumer debt brought by a debt buyer, as defined in Section 1788.50 of the Civil Code, the debt buyer shall also comply with Section 1788.58 of the Civil Code and the remaining provisions of Title 1.6C.5 (commencing with Section 1788.50) of Part 4 of Division 3 of the Civil Code. **Leg.H.** Added Stats 2023 ch 688 §2 (AB 1414), effective January 1, 2024.

§425.50. Requirement of complaint alleging construction-related accessibility claim

(a) An allegation of a construction-related accessibility claim in a complaint, as defined in subdivision (a) of Section 55.52 of the Civil Code, shall state facts sufficient to allow a reasonable person to identify the basis of the violation or violations supporting the claim, including all of the following:

(1) A plain language explanation of the specific access barrier or barriers the individual encountered, or by which the individual alleges he or she was deterred, with sufficient information about the location of the alleged barrier to enable a reasonable person to identify the access barrier.

(2) The way in which the barrier denied the individual full and equal use or access, or in which it deterred the individual, on each particular occasion.

(3) The date or dates of each particular occasion on which the claimant encountered the specific access barrier, or on which he or she was deterred.

(4)(A) Except in complaints that allege physical injury or damage to property, a complaint filed by or on behalf of a high-frequency litigant shall also state all of the following:

(i) Whether the complaint is filed by, or on behalf of, a high-frequency litigant.

(ii) In the case of a high-frequency litigant who is a plaintiff, the number of complaints alleging a construction-related accessibility claim that the high-frequency litigant has filed during the 12 months prior to filing the complaint.

(iii) In the case of a high-frequency litigant who is a plaintiff, the reason the individual was in the geographic area of the defendant's business.

(iv) In the case of a high-frequency litigant who is a plaintiff, the reason why the individual desired to access the defendant's business, including the specific commercial, business, personal, social, leisure, recreational, or other purpose.

(B) As used in this section "high-frequency litigant" has the same meaning as set forth in subdivision (b) of Section 425.55.

(b)(1) A complaint alleging a construction-related accessibility claim, as those terms are defined in subdivision (a) of Section 55.3 of the Civil Code, shall be verified by the plaintiff. A complaint filed without verification shall be subject to a motion to strike.

(2) A complaint alleging a construction-related accessibility claim filed by, or on behalf of, a high-frequency litigant shall state in the caption "ACTION SUBJECT TO THE SUPPLEMENTAL FEE IN GOVERNMENT CODE SECTION 70616.5."

(c) A complaint alleging a construction-related accessibility claim shall be signed by at least one attorney of record in the attorney's individual name, or, if the party is not represented by an attorney, shall be signed by the party. By signing the complaint, the attorney or unrepresented party is certifying that, to the best of the person's knowledge, information, and belief, formed after an inquiry reasonable under the circumstances, all of the following conditions are met:

(1) It is not being presented primarily for an improper purpose, such as to harass or to cause unnecessary delay or needless increase in the cost of litigation.

(2) The claims, defenses, and other legal contentions therein are warranted by existing law or by a nonfrivolous argument for the extension, modification, or reversal of existing law or the establishment of new law.

(3) The allegations and other factual contentions have evidentiary support or, if specifically so identified, are likely to have evidentiary support after a reasonable opportunity for further investigation or discovery.

(4) The denials of factual contentions are warranted on the evidence or, if specifically so identified, are reasonably based on a lack of information or belief.

(d) A court may, after notice and a reasonable opportunity to respond, determine whether subdivision (c) has been violated and, if so, impose sanctions as provided in Section 128.7 for violations of subdivision (b) of Section 128.7.

(e) Nothing in this section shall limit the right of a plaintiff to amend a complaint under Section 472, or with leave of the court under Section 473. However, an amended pleading alleging a construction-related accessibility claim shall be pled as required by subdivision (a).

(f) The determination whether an attorney is a high-frequency litigant shall be made solely on the basis of the verified complaint and any other publicly available documents. Notwithstanding any other law, no party to the proceeding may conduct discovery with respect to whether an attorney is a high-frequency litigant.

(g) This section shall become operative on January 1, 2013. **Leg.H.** Added Stats 2012 ch 383 §13 (SB 1186), effective September 19, 2012, operative January 1, 2013. Amended Stats 2013 ch 76 §22 (AB 383), effective January 1, 2014; Stats 2015 ch 755 §5 (AB 1521), effective October 10, 2015.

2012 Note: The Legislature finds and declares that a very small number of plaintiffs' attorneys have been abusing the right of petition under Sections 52 and 54.3 of the Civil Code by issuing a demand for money to a California business owner that demands the owner pay a quick settlement of the attorney's alleged claim under those laws or else incur greater liability and legal costs if a lawsuit is filed. These demands for money allege one or more, but frequently multiple, claims for asserted violations of a construction-related accessibility standard and often demand a quick money settlement based on the alleged multiple claims without seeking and obtaining actual repair or correction of the alleged violations on the site. These "pay me now or pay me more" demands are used to scare businesses into paying quick settlements that only financially enrich the attorney and claimant and do not promote accessibility either for the claimant or the disability community as a whole. These practices, often involving a series of demand for money letters sent to numerous businesses, do not promote compliance with the accessibility requirements and erode public support for and confidence in our laws. Therefore, the Legislature finds and declares that it is necessary and appropriate to enact Sections 55.31 and 55.32 of the Civil Code, and Section 425.50 of the Code of Civil Procedure to protect the public's confidence and support of the right to petition under Sections 52 and 54.3 of the Civil Code. Stats 2012 ch 383 (SB 1186) §24.

§425.55. "High-frequency litigant"

(a) The Legislature finds and declares all of the following:

(1) Protection of the civil rights of persons with disabilities is of the utmost importance to this state, and private enforcement is the essential means of achieving that goal, as the law has been designed.

(2) According to information from the California Commission on Disability Access, more than one-half, or 54 percent, of all construction-related accessibility complaints filed between 2012 and 2014 were filed by two law firms. Forty-six percent of all complaints were filed by a total of 14 parties. Therefore, a very small number of plaintiffs have filed a disproportionately large number of the construction-related accessibility claims in the state, from 70 to 300 lawsuits each year. Moreover, these lawsuits are frequently filed against small businesses on the basis of boilerplate complaints, apparently seeking quick cash settlements rather than correction of the accessibility violation. This practice unfairly taints the reputation of other innocent disabled consumers who are merely trying to go about their daily lives accessing public accommodations as they are entitled to have full and equal access under the state's Unruh Civil Rights Act (Section 51 of the Civil Code) and the federal Americans with Disability Act of 1990 (Public Law 101-336).

(3) Therefore, given these special and unique circumstances, the provisions of this section are warranted for this limited group of plaintiffs.

(b) For the purposes of this article, "high-frequency litigant" means a person, except as specified in paragraph (3), who utilizes court resources in actions arising from alleged construction-related access violations at such a high level that it is appropriate that additional safeguards apply so as to ensure that the claims are warranted. A "high-frequency litigant" means one or more of the following:

(1) A plaintiff who has filed 10 or more complaints alleging a construction-related accessibility violation within the 12-month period immediately preceding the filing of the current complaint alleging a construction-related accessibility violation.

(2) An attorney who has represented as attorney of record 10 or more high-frequency litigant plaintiffs in actions that were resolved within the 12-month period immediately preceding the filing of the current complaint alleging a construction-related accessibility violation, excluding all of the following actions:

(A) An action in which an early evaluation conference was held pursuant to Section 55.54 of the Civil Code.

(B) An action in which judgment was entered in favor of the plaintiff.

(C) An action in which the construction-related accessibility violations alleged in the complaint were remedied in whole or in part, or a favorable result was achieved, after the plaintiff filed a complaint or provided a demand letter, as defined in Section 55.3 of the Civil Code.

(3) This section does not apply to an attorney employed or retained by a qualified legal services project or a qualified support center, as defined in Section 6213 of the Business and Professions Code, when acting within the scope of employment to represent a client in asserting a construction-related accessibility claim, or the client in such a case. **Leg.H.** Added Stats 2015 ch 755 §6 (AB 1521), effective October 10, 2015.

§426. [Section repealed 1972]

Leg.H. Enacted 1872. Amended Stats 1933 ch 744 §24; Stats 1947 ch 481 §1; Stats 1951 ch 1737 §50, operative January 1, 1952. Repealed Stats 1971 ch 244 §22, operative July 1, 1972. See CCP §§422.20–422.40, 425.10, 429.30.

§426a. [Section repealed 1972]

Leg.H. Added Stats 1913 ch 150 §1. Amended Stats 1965 ch 1893 §3, operative January 1, 1966; Stats 1969 ch 1608 §14, operative January 1, 1970. Repealed Stats 1971 ch 244 §22, operative July 1, 1972. The repealed section related to furnishing information to the State Registrar of Vital Statistics on filing a petition for dissolution of marriage.

§426b. [Section repealed 1970]

Leg.H. Added Stats 1939 ch 333 §1. Amended Stats 1961 ch 1062 §1. Repealed Stats 1969 ch 1608 §15, operative January 1, 1970. The repealed section related to pleading requirements in a petition for dissolution of marriage.

§426c. [Section repealed 1972]

Leg.H. Added Stats 1966 1st Ex Sess ch 107 §1. Amended Stats 1968 ch 938 §1; Stats 1969 ch 1608 §16, operative January 1, 1970. Repealed Stats 1971 ch 244 §22, operative July 1, 1972. The repealed section related to pleading requirements in a petition for dissolution of marriage.

ARTICLE 2
Compulsory Cross-Complaints

Definitions. §426.10.
Assertion of related causes of action; Preclusion against subsequent assertion in another action. §426.30.
Applicability of article. §426.40.
Application for leave to amend or file cross-complaint. §426.50.
Actions to which article applies. §426.60.
Eminent domain proceedings. §426.70.

§426.10. Definitions

As used in this article:

(a) "Complaint" means a complaint or cross-complaint.

(b) "Plaintiff" means a person who files a complaint or cross-complaint.

(c) "Related cause of action" means a cause of action which arises out of the same transaction, occurrence, or series of transactions or occurrences as the cause of action which the plaintiff alleges in his complaint. **Leg.H.** Added Stats 1971 ch 244 §23, operative July 1, 1972.

§426.30. Assertion of related causes of action; Preclusion against subsequent assertion in another action

(a) Except as otherwise provided by statute, if a party against whom a complaint has been filed and served fails to allege in a cross-complaint any related cause of action which (at the time of serving his answer to the complaint) he has against the plaintiff, such party may not thereafter in any other action assert against the plaintiff the related cause of action not pleaded.

(b) This section does not apply if either of the following are established:

(1) The court in which the action is pending does not have jurisdiction to render a personal judgment against the person who failed to plead the related cause of action.

(2) The person who failed to plead the related cause of action did not file an answer to the complaint against him. **Leg.H.** Added Stats 1971 ch 244 §23, operative July 1, 1972.

§426.40. Applicability of article

This article does not apply if any of the following are established:

(a) The cause of action not pleaded requires for its adjudication the presence of additional parties over whom the court cannot acquire jurisdiction.

(b) Both the court in which the action is pending and any other court to which the action is transferrable pursuant to Section 396 are prohibited by the federal or state constitution or by a statute from entertaining the cause of action not pleaded.

(c) At the time the action was commenced, the cause of action not pleaded was the subject of another pending action. **Leg.H.** Added Stats 1971 ch 244 §23, operative July 1, 1972.

§426.50. Application for leave to amend or file cross-complaint

A party who fails to plead a cause of action subject to the requirements of this article, whether through oversight, inadvertence, mistake, neglect, or other cause, may apply to the court for leave to amend his pleading, or to file a cross-complaint, to assert such cause at any time during the course of the action. The court, after notice to the adverse party, shall grant, upon such terms as may be just to the parties, leave to amend the pleading, or to file the cross-complaint, to assert such cause if the party who failed to plead the cause acted in good faith. This subdivision shall be liberally construed to avoid forfeiture of causes of action. **Leg.H.** Added Stats 1971 ch 244 §23, operative July 1, 1972.

§426.60. Actions to which article applies

(a) This article applies only to civil actions and does not apply to special proceedings.

(b) This article does not apply to actions in the small claims court.

(c) This article does not apply where the only relief sought is a declaration of the rights and duties of the respective parties in an action for declaratory relief under Chapter 8 (commencing with Section 1060) of Title 14 of this part. **Leg.H.** Added Stats 1971 ch 244 §23, operative July 1, 1972.

§426.70. Eminent domain proceedings

(a) Notwithstanding subdivision (a) of Section 426.60, this article applies to eminent domain proceedings.

(b) The related cause of action may be asserted by cross-complaint in an eminent domain proceeding whether or not the party asserting such cause of action has presented a claim in compliance with Part 3 (commencing with Section 900) of Division 3.6 of Title 1 of the Government Code to the plaintiff in the original eminent domain proceeding. **Leg.H.** Added Stats 1975 ch 1240 §3, operative July 1, 1976.

§426.80. [Section repealed 1988]

Leg.H. Added Stats 1987 ch 1200 §2. Repealed Stats 1987 ch 1201 §1. The repealed section related to comparative indemnity of public entity in inverse condemnation proceedings.

§427. [Section repealed 1972]

Leg.H. Enacted 1872. Amended Stats 1907 ch 372 §2; Stats 1913 ch 135 §1; Stats 1915 ch 28 §1; Stats 1931 ch 224 §1; Stats 1961 ch 589 §8. Repealed Stats 1971 ch 244 §22, operative July 1, 1972. See CCP §427.10.

ARTICLE 3
Permissive Joinder of Causes of Action

Plaintiff's right to unite causes of action; Joinder in cross-complaint. §427.10.

§427.10. Plaintiff's right to unite causes of action; Joinder in cross-complaint

(a) A plaintiff who in a complaint, alone or with coplaintiffs, alleges a cause of action against one or more defendants may unite with such cause any other causes which he has either alone or with any coplaintiffs against any of such defendants.

(b) Causes of action may be joined in a cross-complaint in accordance with Sections 428.10 and 428.30. **Leg.H.** Added Stats 1971 ch 244 §23, operative July 1, 1972.

ARTICLE 4
Cross-Complaints

Causes of action assertable in cross-complaint. §428.10.
Permitted joinder of person as cross-complaint or cross-defendant. §428.20.
Permitted joinder of causes of action. §428.30.
Separate document. §428.40.
Time for filing cross-complaint; Leave of court to file cross-complaint. §428.50.
Service of cross-complaint. §428.60.
Special answer of "third-party defendant" alleging defenses of "third-party plaintiff"; Service. §428.70.
Abolition of counterclaim; Assertion of cause of action by cross-complaint. §428.80.

§428.10. Causes of action assertable in cross-complaint

A party against whom a cause of action has been asserted in a complaint or cross-complaint may file a cross-complaint setting forth either or both of the following:

(a) Any cause of action he has against any of the parties who filed the complaint or cross-complaint against him. Nothing in this subdivision authorizes the filing of a cross-complaint against the plaintiff in an action commenced under Title 7 (commencing with Section 1230.010) of Part 3.

(b) Any cause of action he has against a person alleged to be liable thereon, whether or not such person is already a party to the action, if the cause of action asserted in his cross-complaint (1) arises out of the same transaction, occurrence, or series of transactions or occurrences as the cause brought against him or (2) asserts a claim, right, or interest in the property or controversy which is the subject of the cause brought against him. **Leg.H.** Added Stats 1971 ch 244 §23, operative July 1, 1972. Amended Stats 1975 ch 1240 §4, operative July 1, 1976.

§428.20. Permitted joinder of person as cross-complaint or cross-defendant

When a person files a cross-complaint as authorized by Section 428.10, he may join any person as a cross-complainant or cross-defendant, whether or not such person is already a party to the action, if, had the cross-complaint been filed as an independent action, the joinder of that party would have been permitted by the statutes governing joinder of parties. **Leg.H.** Added Stats 1971 ch 244 §23, operative July 1, 1972.

§428.30. Permitted joinder of causes of action

Where a person files a cross-complaint as authorized by Section 428.10, he may unite with the cause of action asserted in the cross-complaint any other causes of action he has against any of the cross-defendants, other than the plaintiff in an eminent domain proceeding, whether or not such cross-defendant is already a party to the action. **Leg.H.** Added Stats 1971 ch 244 §23, operative July 1, 1972.

§428.40. Separate document

The cross-complaint shall be a separate document. **Leg.H.** Added Stats 1971 ch 244 §23, operative July 1, 1972.

§428.50. Time for filing cross-complaint; Leave of court to file cross-complaint

(a) A party shall file a cross-complaint against any of the parties who filed the complaint or cross-complaint against him or her before or at the same time as the answer to the complaint or cross-complaint.

(b) Any other cross-complaint may be filed at any time before the court has set a date for trial.

(c) A party shall obtain leave of court to file any cross-complaint except one filed within the time specified in subdivision (a) or (b). Leave may be granted in the interest of justice at any time during the course of the action. **Leg.H.** Added Stats 1971 ch 244 §23, operative July 1, 1972. Amended Stats 1983 ch 176 §1.

§428.60. Service of cross-complaint

A cross-complaint shall be served on each of the parties in an action in the following manner:

(1) If a party has not appeared in the action, a summons upon the cross-complaint shall be issued and served upon him in the same manner as upon commencement of an original action.

(2) If a party has appeared in the action, the cross-complaint shall be served upon his attorney, or upon the party if he has appeared without an attorney, in the manner provided for service of summons or in the manner provided by Chapter 5 (commencing with Section 1010) of Title 14 of Part 2 of this code. **Leg.H.** Added Stats 1971 ch 244 §23, operative July 1, 1972. Amended Stats 1974 ch 429 §1.

§428.70. Special answer of "third-party defendant" alleging defenses of "third-party plaintiff"; Service

(a) As used in this section:

(1) "Third-party plaintiff" means a person against whom a cause of action has been asserted in a complaint or cross-complaint, who claims the right to recover all or part of any amounts for which he may be held liable on such cause of action from a third person, and who files a cross-complaint stating such claim as a cause of action against the third person.

(2) "Third-party defendant" means the person who is alleged in a cross-complaint filed by a third-party plaintiff to be liable to the

third-party plaintiff if the third-party plaintiff is held liable on the claim against him.

(b) In addition to the other rights and duties a third-party defendant has under this article, he may, at the time he files his answer to the cross-complaint, file as a separate document a special answer alleging against the person who asserted the cause of action against the third-party plaintiff any defenses which the third-party plaintiff has to such cause of action. The special answer shall be served on the third-party plaintiff and on the person who asserted the cause of action against the third-party plaintiff. **Leg.H.** Added Stats 1971 ch 244 §23, operative July 1, 1972.

§428.80. Abolition of counterclaim; Assertion of cause of action by cross-complaint

The counterclaim is abolished. Any cause of action that formerly was asserted by a counterclaim shall be asserted by a cross-complaint. Where any statute refers to asserting a cause of action as a counterclaim, such cause shall be asserted as a cross-complaint. The erroneous designation of a pleading as a counterclaim shall not affect its validity, but such pleading shall be deemed to be a cross-complaint. **Leg.H.** Added Stats 1971 ch 244 §23, operative July 1, 1972.

ARTICLE 5
Contents of Documents in Particular Actions or Proceedings

Actions for infringements of rights in literary, artistic, or intellectual production. §429.30.

§429.10. [Section repealed 1994]

Leg.H. Added Stats 1971 ch 244 §23, operative July 1, 1972. Repealed Stats 1992 ch 163 §21 (AB 2641), operative January 1, 1994. See Fam C §2330.

§429.20. [Section repealed 1978]

Leg.H. Added Stats 1971 ch 244 §23, operative July 1, 1972. Repealed Stats 1977 ch 676 §1. The repealed section related to furnishing information for State Registrar of Vital Statistics on filing petition for dissolution of marriage, legal separation, or declaration of void or voidable marriage.

§429.30. Actions for infringements of rights in literary, artistic, or intellectual production

(a) As used in this section:

(1) "Complaint" includes a cross-complaint.

(2) "Plaintiff" includes the person filing a cross-complaint.

(b) If the complaint contains a demand for relief on account of the alleged infringement of the plaintiff's rights in and to a literary, artistic, or intellectual production, there shall be attached to the complaint a copy of the production as to which the infringement is claimed and a copy of the alleged infringing production. If, by reason of bulk or the nature of the production, it is not practicable to attach a copy to the complaint, that fact and the reasons why it is impracticable to attach a copy of the production to the complaint shall be alleged; and the court, in connection with any demurrer, motion, or other proceedings in the cause in which a knowledge of the contents of such production may be necessary or desirable, shall make such order for a view of the production not attached as will suit the convenience of the court to the end that the contents of such production may be deemed to be a part of the complaint to the same extent and with the same force as though such production had been capable of being and had been attached to the complaint. The attachment of any such production in accordance with the provisions of this section shall not be deemed a making public of the production within the meaning of Section 983 of the Civil Code. **Leg.H.** Added Stats 1971 ch 244 §23, operative July 1, 1972.

§429.40. [Section repealed 1994]

Leg.H. Added Stats 1971 ch 244 §23, operative July 1, 1972. Repealed Stats 1992 ch 163 §22 (AB 2641), operative January 1, 1994. The repealed section related to application of the title to the Family Law Act.

§430. [Section repealed 1972]

Leg.H. Enacted 1872. Amended Stats 1907 ch 372 §3; Stats 1939 ch 446 §1; Stats 1967 ch 512 §1; Stats 1968 ch 307 §1; Stats 1970 ch 258 §1. Repealed Stats 1971 ch 244 §25, operative July 1, 1972. See CCP §§430.10, 430.30, and 430.40.

CHAPTER 3
OBJECTIONS TO PLEADINGS; DENIALS AND DEFENSES

Article 1. Objections to Pleadings.
Article 2. Denials and Defenses.
Article 3. Time to Respond to Cross-Complaint.

ARTICLE 1
Objections to Pleadings

Demurrer or defense to complaint or cross-complaint. §430.10.
Demurrer to answer. §430.20.
Objection by demurrer or by answer. §430.30.
Time periods within which demurrers permitted. §430.40.
Conference between parties before demurrer is filed. §430.41.
Extent to which demurrer may be taken. §430.50.
Specification of grounds of demurrer. §430.60.
Specification of matters subject to judicial notice. §430.70.
Waiver of objection by failure to object. §430.80.
Civil action improperly moved to federal court; Time to file response on remand. §430.90.

§430.10. Demurrer or defense to complaint or cross-complaint

The party against whom a complaint or cross-complaint has been filed may object, by demurrer or answer as provided in Section 430.30, to the pleading on any one or more of the following grounds:

(a) The court has no jurisdiction of the subject of the cause of action alleged in the pleading.

(b) The person who filed the pleading does not have the legal capacity to sue.

(c) There is another action pending between the same parties on the same cause of action.

(d) There is a defect or misjoinder of parties.

(e) The pleading does not state facts sufficient to constitute a cause of action.

(f) The pleading is uncertain. As used in this subdivision, "uncertain" includes ambiguous and unintelligible.

(g) In an action founded upon a contract, it cannot be ascertained from the pleading whether the contract is written, is oral, or is implied by conduct.

(h) No certificate was filed as required by Section 411.35. **Leg.H.** Added Stats 1971 ch 244 §29, operative July 1, 1972. Amended Stats 1973 ch 828 §2; Stats 1979 ch 973 §2, ch 988 §2; Stats 1980 ch 163 §2, ch 500 §1; Stats 1990 ch 216 §8; Stats 1993 ch 456 §3 (AB 58); Stats 2020 ch 370 §35 (SB 1371), effective January 1, 2021.

§430.20. Demurrer to answer

A party against whom an answer has been filed may object, by demurrer as provided in Section 430.30, to the answer upon any one or more of the following grounds:

(a) The answer does not state facts sufficient to constitute a defense.

(b) The answer is uncertain. As used in this subdivision, "uncertain" includes ambiguous and unintelligible.

(c) Where the answer pleads a contract, it cannot be ascertained from the answer whether the contract is written or oral. **Leg.H.** Added Stats 1971 ch 244 §29, operative July 1, 1972.

§430.30. Objection by demurrer or by answer

(a) When any ground for objection to a complaint, cross-complaint, or answer appears on the face thereof, or from any matter of which the court is required to or may take judicial notice, the objection on that ground may be taken by a demurrer to the pleading.

(b) When any ground for objection to a complaint or cross-complaint does not appear on the face of the pleading, the objection may be taken by answer.

(c) A party objecting to a complaint or cross-complaint may demur and answer at the same time. **Leg.H.** Added Stats 1971 ch 244 §29, operative July 1, 1972.

§430.40. Time periods within which demurrers permitted

(a) A person against whom a complaint or cross-complaint has been filed may, within 30 days after service of the complaint or cross-complaint, demur to the complaint or cross-complaint.

(b) A party who has filed a complaint or cross-complaint may, within 10 days after service of the answer to his pleading, demur to the answer. **Leg.H.** Added Stats 1971 ch 244 §29, operative July 1, 1972.

§430.41. Conference between parties before demurrer is filed

(a) Before filing a demurrer pursuant to this chapter, the demurring party shall meet and confer in person, by telephone, or by video conference with the party who filed the pleading that is subject to demurrer for the purpose of determining whether an agreement can be reached that would resolve the objections to be raised in the demurrer. If an amended complaint, cross-complaint, or answer is filed, the responding party shall meet and confer again with the party who filed the amended pleading before filing a demurrer to the amended pleading.

(1) As part of the meet and confer process, the demurring party shall identify all of the specific causes of action that it believes are subject to demurrer and identify with legal support the basis of the deficiencies. The party who filed the complaint, cross-complaint, or answer shall provide legal support for its position that the pleading is legally sufficient or, in the alternative, how the complaint, cross-complaint, or answer could be amended to cure any legal insufficiency.

(2) The parties shall meet and confer at least 5 days before the date the responsive pleading is due. If the parties are not able to meet and confer at least 5 days before the date the responsive pleading is due, the demurring party shall be granted an automatic 30-day extension of time within which to file a responsive pleading, by filing and serving, on or before the date on which a demurrer would be due, a declaration stating under penalty of perjury that a good faith attempt to meet and confer was made and explaining the reasons why the parties could not meet and confer. The 30-day extension shall commence from the date the responsive pleading was previously due, and the demurring party shall not be subject to default during the period of the extension. Any further extensions shall be obtained by court order upon a showing of good cause.

(3) The demurring party shall file and serve with the demurrer a declaration stating either of the following:

(A) The means by which the demurring party met and conferred with the party who filed the pleading subject to demurrer, and that the parties did not reach an agreement resolving the objections raised in the demurrer.

(B) That the party who filed the pleading subject to demurrer failed to respond to the meet and confer request of the demurring party or otherwise failed to meet and confer in good faith.

(4) A determination by the court that the meet and confer process was insufficient shall not be grounds to overrule or sustain a demurrer.

(b) A party demurring to a pleading that has been amended after a demurrer to an earlier version of the pleading was sustained shall not demur to any portion of the amended complaint, cross-complaint, or answer on grounds that could have been raised by demurrer to the earlier version of the complaint, cross-complaint, or answer.

(c) If a court sustains a demurrer to one or more causes of action and grants leave to amend, the court may order a conference of the parties before an amended complaint or cross-complaint or a demurrer to an amended complaint or cross-complaint, may be filed. If a conference is held, the court shall not preclude a party from filing a demurrer and the time to file a demurrer shall not begin until after the conference has concluded. This section does not prohibit the court from ordering a conference on its own motion at any time or prevent a party from requesting that the court order a conference to be held.

(d) This section does not apply to the following civil actions:

(1) An action in which a party not represented by counsel is incarcerated in a local, state, or federal correctional institution.

(2) A proceeding in forcible entry, forcible detainer, or unlawful detainer.

(e)(1) In response to a demurrer and prior to the case being at issue, a complaint or cross-complaint shall not be amended more than three times, absent an offer to the trial court as to such additional facts to be pleaded that there is a reasonable possibility the defect can be cured to state a cause of action. The three-amendment limit shall not include an amendment made without leave of the court pursuant to Section 472, provided the amendment is made before a demurrer to the original complaint or cross-complaint is filed.

(2) Nothing in this section affects the rights of a party to amend its pleading or respond to an amended pleading after the case is at issue.

(f) Nothing in this section affects appellate review or the rights of a party pursuant to Section 430.80.

(g) If a demurrer is overruled as to a cause of action and that cause of action is not further amended, the demurring party preserves its right to appeal after final judgment without filing a further demurrer. **Leg.H.** Added Stats 2015 ch 418 §1 (SB 383), effective January 1, 2016, repealed January 1, 2021. Amended Stats 2020 ch 36 §15 (AB 3364), effective January 1, 2021; Stats 2023 ch 478 §9 (AB 1756), effective January 1, 2024.

§430.50. Extent to which demurrer may be taken

(a) A demurrer to a complaint or cross-complaint may be taken to the whole complaint or cross-complaint or to any of the causes of action stated therein.

(b) A demurrer to an answer may be taken to the whole answer or to any one or more of the several defenses set up in the answer. **Leg.H.** Added Stats 1971 ch 244 §29, operative July 1, 1972.

§430.60. Specification of grounds of demurrer

A demurrer shall distinctly specify the grounds upon which any of the objections to the complaint, cross-complaint, or answer are taken. Unless it does so, it may be disregarded. **Leg.H.** Added Stats 1971 ch 244 §29, operative July 1, 1972.

§430.70. Specification of matters subject to judicial notice

When the ground of demurrer is based on a matter of which the court may take judicial notice pursuant to Section 452 or 453 of the Evidence Code, such matter shall be specified in the demurrer, or in the supporting points and authorities for the purpose of invoking such notice, except as the court may otherwise permit. **Leg.H.** Added Stats 1971 ch 244 §29, operative July 1, 1972.

§430.80. Waiver of objection by failure to object

(a) If the party against whom a complaint or cross-complaint has been filed fails to object to the pleading, either by demurrer or answer, that party is deemed to have waived the objection unless it is an objection that the court has no jurisdiction of the subject of the cause of action alleged in the pleading or an objection that the pleading does not state facts sufficient to constitute a cause of action.

(b) If the party against whom an answer has been filed fails to demur thereto, that party is deemed to have waived the objection unless it is an objection that the answer does not state facts sufficient to constitute a defense. **Leg.H.** Added Stats 1971 ch 244 §29, operative July 1, 1972. Amended Stats 1983 ch 1167 §2.

§430.90. Civil action improperly moved to federal court; Time to file response on remand

(a) Where the defendant has removed a civil action to federal court without filing a response in the original court and the case is later remanded for improper removal, the time to respond shall be as follows:

(1) If the defendant has not generally appeared in either the original or federal court, then 30 days from the day the original court receives the case on remand to move to dismiss the action pursuant to Section 583.250 or to move to quash service of summons or to stay or dismiss the action pursuant to Section 418.10, if the court has not ruled on a similar motion filed by the defendant prior to the removal of the action to federal court.

(2) If the defendant has not filed an answer in the original court, then 30 days from the day the original court receives the case on remand to do any of the following:

(A) Answer the complaint.

(B) Demur or move to strike all or a portion of the complaint if: (i) an answer was not filed in the federal court, and (ii) a demurrer or motion to strike raising the same or similar issues was not filed and ruled upon by the original court prior to the removal of the action to federal court or was not filed and ruled upon in federal court prior to the remand. If the demurrer or motion to strike is denied by the court, the defendant shall have 30 days to answer the complaint unless an answer was filed with the demurrer or motion to strike.

(b) For the purposes of this section, time shall be calculated from the date of the original court's receipt of the order of remand. **Leg.H.** Added Stats 1995 ch 796 §5 (SB 45).

§431. [Section repealed 1972]

Leg.H. Enacted 1872. Amended Stats 1907 ch 372 §3. Repealed Stats 1971 ch 244 §26, operative July 1, 1972. See CCP §§430.30, 430.50, and 430.60.

§431.5. [Section repealed 1972]

Leg.H. Added Stats 1968 ch 307 §2. Repealed Stats 1971 ch 244 §27, operative July 1, 1972. See CCP §430.70.

ARTICLE 2
Denials and Defenses

Material and immaterial allegations. §431.10.
Taking uncontroverted allegations as true; Taking new matter as controverted. §431.20.
Answer to complaint; Affirmative relief; Denials; Defenses. §431.30.
Option to file denial and statement of new matter where demand less than specified sum; Cross-complaint requirements. §431.40.
Answer in action on insurance contract. §431.50.
Defense of payment as to cross-demands for money; Statute of limitations. §431.70.

§431.10. Material and immaterial allegations

(a) A material allegation in a pleading is one essential to the claim or defense and which could not be stricken from the pleading without leaving it insufficient as to that claim or defense.

(b) An immaterial allegation in a pleading is any of the following:

(1) An allegation that is not essential to the statement of a claim or defense.

(2) An allegation that is neither pertinent to nor supported by an otherwise sufficient claim or defense.

(3) A demand for judgment requesting relief not supported by the allegations of the complaint or cross-complaint.

(c) An "immaterial allegation" means "irrelevant matter" as that term is used in Section 436. **Leg.H.** Added Stats 1971 ch 244 §29, operative July 1, 1972. Amended Stats 1982 ch 704 §2; Stats 1983 ch 1167 §3; Stats 1986 ch 540 §2.

§431.20. Taking uncontroverted allegations as true; Taking new matter as controverted

(a) Every material allegation of the complaint or cross-complaint, not controverted by the answer, shall, for the purposes of the action, be taken as true.

(b) The statement of any new matter in the answer, in avoidance or constituting a defense, shall, on the trial, be deemed controverted by the opposite party. **Leg.H.** Added Stats 1971 ch 244 §29, operative July 1, 1972.

§431.30. Answer to complaint; Affirmative relief; Denials; Defenses

(a) As used in this section:

(1) "Complaint" includes a cross-complaint.

(2) "Defendant" includes a person filing an answer to a cross-complaint.

(b) The answer to a complaint shall contain:

(1) The general or specific denial of the material allegations of the complaint controverted by the defendant.

(2) A statement of any new matter constituting a defense.

(c) Affirmative relief may not be claimed in the answer.

(d) If the complaint is subject to Article 2 (commencing with Section 90) of Chapter 5.1 of Title 1 of Part 1 or is not verified, a general denial is sufficient but only puts in issue the material allegations of the complaint. If the complaint is verified, unless the complaint is subject to Article 2 (commencing with Section 90) of Chapter 5.1 of Title 1 of Part 1, the denial of the allegations shall be made positively or according to the information and belief of the defendant. However, if the cause of action is a claim assigned to a third party for collection and the complaint is verified, the denial of the allegations shall be made positively or according to the information and belief of the defendant, even if the complaint is subject to Article 2 (commencing with Section 90) of Chapter 5.1 of Title 1 of Part 1.

(e) If the defendant has no information or belief upon the subject sufficient to enable him or her to answer an allegation of the complaint, he or she may so state in his or her answer and place his or her denial on that ground.

(f) The denials of the allegations controverted may be stated by reference to specific paragraphs or parts of the complaint; or by express admission of certain allegations of the complaint with a general denial of all of the allegations not so admitted; or by denial of certain allegations upon information and belief, or for lack of sufficient information or belief, with a general denial of all allegations not so denied or expressly admitted.

(g) The defenses shall be separately stated, and the several defenses shall refer to the causes of action which they are intended to answer, in a manner by which they may be intelligibly distinguished. **Leg.H.** Added Stats 1971 ch 244 §29, operative July 1, 1972. Amended Stats 1979 ch 212 §2; Stats 1985 ch 621 §1; Stats 1986 ch 281 §1; Stats 2003 ch 149 §8 (SB 79).

§431.40. Option to file denial and statement of new matter where demand less than specified sum; Cross-complaint requirements

(a) Any provision of law to the contrary notwithstanding, in any action in which the demand, exclusive of interest, or the value of the property in controversy does not exceed one thousand dollars ($1000), the defendant at his option, in lieu of demurrer or other answer, may file a general written denial and a brief statement of any new matter constituting a defense.

(b) Nothing in this section excuses the defendant from complying with the provisions of law applicable to a cross-complaint, and any cross-complaint of the defendant shall be subject to the requirements applicable in any other action.

(c) The general written denial described in subdivision (a) shall be on a blank available at the place of filing and shall be in a form prescribed by the Judicial Council. This form need not be verified. **Leg.H.** Added Stats 1971 ch 244 §29, operative July 1, 1972. Amended Stats 1972 ch 562 §1; Stats 1976 ch 1389 §1; Stats 1977 ch 93 §1.

§431.50. Answer in action on insurance contract

In an action to recover upon a contract of insurance wherein the defendant claims exemption from liability upon the ground that, although the proximate cause of the loss was a peril insured against, the loss was remotely caused by or would not have occurred but for a peril excepted in the contract of insurance, the defendant shall in his answer set forth and specify the peril which was the proximate cause of the loss, in what manner the peril excepted contributed to the loss or itself caused the peril insured against, and if he claims that the peril excepted caused the peril insured against, he shall in his answer set forth and specify upon what premises or at what place the peril excepted caused the peril insured against. **Leg.H.** Added Stats 1971 ch 244 §29, operative July 1, 1972.

§431.60. [Section repealed 1983]

Leg.H. Added Stats 1971 ch 244 §29, operative July 1, 1972. Repealed Stats 1982 ch 517 §101. The repealed section related to the answer in an action to recover possession of personal property.

§431.70. Defense of payment as to cross-demands for money; Statute of limitations

Where cross-demands for money have existed between persons at any point in time when neither demand was barred by the statute of limitations, and an action is thereafter commenced by one such person, the other person may assert in the answer the defense of payment in that the two demands are compensated so far as they equal each other, notwithstanding that an independent action asserting the person's claim would at the time of filing the answer be barred by the statute of limitations. If the cross-demand would otherwise be barred by the statute of limitations, the relief accorded under this section shall not exceed the value of the relief granted to the other party. The defense provided by this section is not available if the cross-demand is barred for failure to assert it in a prior action under Section 426.30. Neither person can be deprived of the benefits of this section by the assignment or death of the other. For the purposes of this section, a money judgment is a "demand for money" and, as applied to a money judgment, the demand is barred by the statute of limitations when enforcement of the judgment is barred under Chapter 3 (commencing with Section 683.010) of Division 1 of Title 9. **Leg.H.** Added Stats 1971 ch 244 §29, operative July 1, 1972. Amended Stats 1982 ch 497 §32, operative July 1, 1983.

§432. [Section repealed 1972]

Leg.H. Enacted 1872. Amended Code Amdts 1880 ch 14 §1. Repealed Stats 1971 ch 244 §28, operative July 1, 1972. See CCP §471.5.

ARTICLE 3
Time to Respond to Cross-Complaint

Time to respond after service. §432.10.

§432.10. Time to respond after service

A party served with a cross-complaint may within 30 days after service move, demur, or otherwise plead to the cross-complaint in the same manner as to an original complaint. **Leg.H.** Added Stats 1971 ch 244 §29, operative July 1, 1972.

§433. [Section repealed 1972]

Leg.H. Enacted 1872. Amended Stats 1957 ch 1442 §1; Stats 1965 ch 299 §19, operative January 1, 1967; Stats 1968 ch 307 §3. Repealed Stats 1971 ch 244 §30, operative July 1, 1972. See CCP §430.30.

§434. [Section repealed 1972]

Leg.H. Enacted 1872. Repealed Stats 1971 ch 244 §31, operative July 1, 1972. See CCP §430.80.

CHAPTER 4
MOTION TO STRIKE

Notice of motion to strike complaint or pleading; Extension of time to answer. §435.
Meet and confer process prior to filing motion to strike; Amended pleading; Declaration; Exceptions; Appeal. §435.5.
Improper matter or nonconforming pleading; Discretion of court. §436.
Grounds for motion. §437.

§435. Notice of motion to strike complaint or pleading; Extension of time to answer

(a) As used in this section:

(1) The term "complaint" includes a cross-complaint.

(2) The term "pleading" means a demurrer, answer, complaint, or cross-complaint.

(b)(1) Any party, within the time allowed to respond to a pleading may serve and file a notice of motion to strike the whole or any part thereof, but this time limitation shall not apply to motions specified in subdivision (e).

(2) A notice of motion to strike the answer or the complaint, or a portion thereof, shall specify a hearing date set in accordance with Section 1005.

(3) A notice of motion to strike a demurrer, or a portion thereof, shall set the hearing thereon concurrently with the hearing on the demurrer.

(c) If a party serves and files a notice of motion to strike without demurring to the complaint, the time to answer is extended and no default may be entered against that defendant, except as provided in Sections 585 and 586.

(d) The filing of a notice of motion to strike an answer or complaint, or portion thereof, shall not extend the time within which to demur.

(e) A motion to strike, as specified in this section, may be made as part of a motion pursuant to subparagraph (A) of paragraph (1) of subdivision (i) of Section 438. **Leg.H.** Added Stats 1955 ch 1452 §3a. Amended Stats 1971 ch 244 §33, operative July 1, 1972; Stats 1982 ch 704 §3; Stats 1993 ch 456 §3.5 (AB 58).

§435.5. Meet and confer process prior to filing motion to strike; Amended pleading; Declaration; Exceptions; Appeal

(a) Before filing a motion to strike pursuant to this chapter, the moving party shall meet and confer in person, by telephone, or by video conference with the party who filed the pleading that is subject to the motion to strike for the purpose of determining if an agreement can be reached that resolves the objections to be raised in the motion to strike. If an amended pleading is filed, the responding party shall meet and confer again with the party who filed the amended pleading before filing a motion to strike the amended pleading.

(1) As part of the meet and confer process, the moving party shall identify all of the specific allegations that it believes are subject to being stricken and identify with legal support the basis of the deficiencies. The party who filed the pleading shall provide legal support for its position that the pleading is legally sufficient, or, in the alternative, how the pleading could be amended to cure any legal insufficiency.

(2) The parties shall meet and confer at least 5 days before the date a motion to strike must be filed. If the parties are unable to meet and confer at least 5 days before the date the motion to strike must be filed, the moving party shall be granted an automatic 30-day extension of time within which to file a motion to strike, by filing and serving, on or before the date a motion to strike must be filed, a declaration stating under penalty of perjury that a good faith attempt to meet and confer was made and explaining the reasons why the parties could not meet and confer. The 30-day extension shall commence from the date the motion to strike was previously due, and the moving party shall not be subject to default during the period of the extension. Any further extensions shall be obtained by court order upon a showing of good cause.

(3) The moving party shall file and serve with the motion to strike a declaration stating either of the following:

(A) The means by which the moving party met and conferred with the party who filed the pleading subject to the motion to strike, and that the parties did not reach an agreement resolving the objections raised by the motion to strike.

(B) That the party who filed the pleading subject to the motion to strike failed to respond to the meet and confer request of the moving party or otherwise failed to meet and confer in good faith.

(4) A determination by the court that the meet and confer process was insufficient shall not be grounds to grant or deny the motion to strike.

(b) A party moving to strike a pleading that has been amended after a motion to strike an earlier version of the pleading was granted shall not move to strike any portion of the pleadings on grounds that could have been raised by a motion to strike as to the earlier version of the pleading.

(c)(1) If a court grants a motion to strike and grants leave to amend, the court may order a conference of the parties before an amended pleading, or a motion to strike an amended pleading, may be filed. If the conference is held, the court shall not preclude a party from filing a motion to strike and the time to file a motion to strike shall not begin until after the conference has concluded.

(2) This section does not prohibit the court from ordering a conference on its own motion at any time or prevent a party from requesting that the court order that a conference be held.

(d) This section does not apply to any of the following:

(1) An action in which a party not represented by counsel is incarcerated in a local, state, or federal correctional institution.

(2) A proceeding in forcible entry, forcible detainer, or unlawful detainer.

(3) A special motion brought pursuant to Section 425.16.

(4) A motion brought less than 30 days before trial.

(e)(1) In response to a motion to strike and before the case is at issue, a pleading shall not be amended more than three times, absent an offer to the trial court of additional facts to be pleaded that, if pleaded, would result in a reasonable possibility that the defect can be cured. The three-amendment limit does not include an amendment made without leave of the court pursuant to Section 472, if the amendment is made before a motion to strike as to the original pleading is filed.

(2) This section does not affect the rights of a party to amend its pleading or respond to an amended pleading after the case is at issue.

(f) This section does not affect appellate review or the rights of a party pursuant to Section 430.80.

(g) If a motion to strike is denied and the pleading is not further amended, the moving party preserves its right to appeal after final judgment without filing a further motion to strike. **Leg.H.** Added Stats 2017 ch 273 §1 (AB 644), effective January 1, 2018, repealed January 1, 2021. Amended Stats 2020 ch 36 §16 (AB 3364), effective January 1, 2021; Stats 2023 ch 478 §10 (AB 1756), effective January 1, 2024.

§436. Improper matter or nonconforming pleading; Discretion of court

The court may, upon a motion made pursuant to Section 435, or at any time in its discretion, and upon terms it deems proper:

(a) Strike out any irrelevant, false, or improper matter inserted in any pleading.

(b) Strike out all or any part of any pleading not drawn or filed in conformity with the laws of this state, a court rule, or an order of the court. **Leg.H.** Added Stats 1982 ch 704 §3.5. Amended Stats 1983 ch 1167 §4.

§437. Grounds for motion

(a) The grounds for a motion to strike shall appear on the face of the challenged pleading or from any matter of which the court is required to take judicial notice.

(b) Where the motion to strike is based on matter of which the court may take judicial notice pursuant to Section 452 or 453 of the Evidence Code, such matter shall be specified in the notice of motion, or in the supporting points and authorities, except as the court may otherwise permit. **Leg.H.** Added Stats 1982 ch 704 §4.

Prior Law: Former CCP §437, similar to present CCP §431.30, was enacted 1872, amended Code Amdts 1873–74 ch 383 §52, Stats 1927 ch 317 §1, Sats 1933 ch 744 §25, Stats 1951 ch 1737 §51, operative January 1, 1952, and repealed Stats 1971 ch 244 §35, operative July 1, 1972.

§437a. [Section repealed 1972]

Leg.H. Added Stats 1907 ch 447 §1. Repealed Stats 1971 ch 244 §36, operative July 1, 1972. See CCP §431.50.

§437b. [Section repealed 1972]

Leg.H. Added Stats 1933 ch 744 §26. Amended Stats 1951 ch 1737 §52, operative January 1, 1952. Repealed Stats 1971 ch 244 §37, operative July 1, 1972. See CCP §431.40.

CHAPTER 5
SUMMARY JUDGMENTS AND MOTIONS FOR JUDGMENT ON THE PLEADINGS

Summary judgment. §437c.
Judgment on the pleadings. §438.
Meet and confer process prior to filing motion for judgment on the pleadings; Amended pleading; Declaration; Exceptions; Appeal. §439.

§437c. Summary judgment

(a)(1) A party may move for summary judgment in an action or proceeding if it is contended that the action has no merit or that there is no defense to the action or proceeding. The motion may be made at any time after 60 days have elapsed since the general appearance in the action or proceeding of each party against whom the motion is directed or at any earlier time after the general appearance that the court, with or without notice and upon good cause shown, may direct.

(2) Notice of the motion and supporting papers shall be served on all other parties to the action at least [1] **81** days before the time appointed for hearing. If the notice is served by mail, the required [2] **81-day** period of notice shall be increased by 5 days if the place of address is within the State of California, 10 days if the place of address is outside the State of California but within the United States, and 20 days if the place of address is outside the United States. If the notice is served by facsimile transmission, express mail, or another method of delivery providing for overnight delivery, the required [3] **81-day** period of notice shall be increased by two court days.

(3) The motion shall be heard no later than 30 days before the date of trial, unless the court for good cause orders otherwise. The filing of the motion shall not extend the time within which a party must otherwise file a responsive pleading.

(4) A party shall not bring more than one motion for summary judgment against an adverse party to the action or proceeding. This limitation does not apply to motions for summary adjudication.

(5) Notwithstanding any other provision of this section, on motion or application of any party and a showing of good cause, the court may grant leave for the moving party to bring an additional motion for summary judgment. The moving party shall serve the notice and supporting papers for any such additional motion in accordance with paragraph (2) of subdivision (a).

(b)(1) The motion shall be supported by affidavits, declarations, admissions, answers to interrogatories, depositions, and matters of which judicial notice shall or may be taken. The supporting papers shall include a separate statement setting forth plainly and concisely all material facts that the moving party contends are undisputed. Each of the material facts stated shall be followed by a reference to the supporting evidence. The failure to comply with this requirement of a separate statement may in the court's discretion constitute a sufficient ground for denying the motion.

(2) An opposition to the motion shall be served and filed not less than [4] **20** days preceding the noticed or continued date of hearing, unless the court for good cause orders otherwise. The opposition, where appropriate, shall consist of affidavits, declarations, admissions, answers to interrogatories, depositions, and matters of which judicial notice shall or may be taken.

(3) The opposition papers shall include a separate statement that responds to each of the material facts contended by the moving party to be undisputed, indicating if the opposing party agrees or disagrees that those facts are undisputed. The statement also shall set forth plainly and concisely any other material facts the opposing party contends are disputed. Each material fact contended by the opposing party to be disputed shall be followed by a reference to the supporting evidence. Failure to comply with this requirement of a separate statement may constitute a sufficient ground, in the court's discretion, for granting the motion.

(4) A reply to the opposition shall be served and filed by the moving party not less than [5] **11** days preceding the noticed or continued date of hearing, unless the court for good cause orders otherwise. **The reply shall not include any new evidentiary matter, additional material facts, or separate statement submitted with the reply and not presented in the moving papers or opposing papers.**

(5) Evidentiary objections not made at the hearing shall be deemed waived.

(6) Except for subdivision (c) of Section 1005 relating to the method of service of opposition and reply papers, Sections 1005 and 1013, extending the time within which a right may be exercised or an act may be done, do not apply to this section.

(7) An incorporation by reference of a matter in the court's file shall set forth with specificity the exact matter to which reference is being made and shall not incorporate the entire file.

(c) The motion for summary judgment shall be granted if all the papers submitted show that there is no triable issue as to any material fact and that the moving party is entitled to a judgment as a matter of law. In determining if the papers show that there is no triable issue as to any material fact, the court shall consider all of the evidence set forth in the papers, except the evidence to which objections have been made and sustained by the court, and all inferences reasonably deducible from the evidence, except summary judgment shall not be granted by the court based on inferences reasonably deducible from the evidence if contradicted by other inferences or evidence that raise a triable issue as to any material fact.

(d) Supporting and opposing affidavits or declarations shall be made by a person on personal knowledge, shall set forth admissible evidence, and shall show affirmatively that the affiant is competent to testify to the matters stated in the affidavits or declarations. An objection based on the failure to comply with the requirements of this subdivision, if not made at the hearing, shall be deemed waived.

(e) If a party is otherwise entitled to summary judgment pursuant to this section, summary judgment shall not be denied on grounds of credibility or for want of cross-examination of witnesses furnishing affidavits or declarations in support of the summary judgment, except that summary judgment may be denied in the discretion of the court if the only proof of a material fact offered in support of the summary judgment is an affidavit or declaration made by an individual who was the sole witness to that fact; or if a material fact is an individual's state of mind, or lack thereof, and that fact is sought to be established solely by the individual's affirmation thereof.

(f)(1) A party may move for summary adjudication as to one or more causes of action within an action, one or more affirmative defenses, one or more claims for damages, or one or more issues of duty, if the party contends that the cause of action has no merit, that there is no affirmative defense to the cause of action, that there is no merit to an affirmative defense as to any cause of action, that there is no merit to a claim for damages, as specified in Section 3294 of the Civil Code, or that one or more defendants either owed or did not owe a duty to the plaintiff or plaintiffs. A motion for summary adjudication shall be granted only if it completely disposes of a cause of action, an affirmative defense, a claim for damages, or an issue of duty.

(2) A motion for summary adjudication may be made by itself or as an alternative to a motion for summary judgment and shall proceed in all procedural respects as a motion for summary judgment. A party shall not move for summary judgment based on issues asserted in a prior motion for summary adjudication and denied by the court unless that party establishes, to the satisfaction of the court, newly discovered facts or circumstances or a change of law supporting the issues reasserted in the summary judgment motion.

(g) Upon the denial of a motion for summary judgment on the ground that there is a triable issue as to one or more material facts, the court shall, by written or oral order, specify one or more material facts raised by the motion that the court has determined there exists a triable controversy. This determination shall specifically refer to the evidence proffered in support of and in opposition to the motion that indicates that a triable controversy exists. Upon the grant of a motion for summary judgment on the ground that there is no triable issue of material fact, the court shall, by written or oral order, specify the reasons for its determination. The order shall specifically refer to the evidence proffered in support of and, if applicable, in opposition to the motion that indicates no triable issue exists. The court shall also state its reasons for any other determination. The court shall record its determination by court reporter or written order.

(h) If it appears from the affidavits submitted in opposition to a motion for summary judgment or summary adjudication, or both, that facts essential to justify opposition may exist but cannot, for reasons stated, be presented, the court shall deny the motion, order a continuance to permit affidavits to be obtained or discovery to be had, or make any other order as may be just. The application to continue the motion to obtain necessary discovery may also be made by ex parte motion at any time on or before the date the opposition response to the motion is due.

(i) If, after granting a continuance to allow specified additional discovery, the court determines that the party seeking summary judgment has unreasonably failed to allow the discovery to be conducted, the court shall grant a continuance to permit the discovery to go forward or deny the motion for summary judgment or summary adjudication. This section does not affect or limit the ability of a party to compel discovery under the Civil Discovery Act (Title 4 (commencing with Section 2016.010) of Part 4).

(j) If the court determines at any time that an affidavit was presented in bad faith or solely for the purpose of delay, the court shall order the party who presented the affidavit to pay the other party the amount of the reasonable expenses the filing of the affidavit caused the other party to incur. Sanctions shall not be imposed pursuant to this subdivision except on notice contained in a party's papers or on the court's own noticed motion, and after an opportunity to be heard.

(k) Unless a separate judgment may properly be awarded in the action, a final judgment shall not be entered on a motion for summary judgment before the termination of the action, but the final judgment shall, in addition to any matters determined in the action, award judgment as established by the summary proceeding provided for in this section.

[6] (l) In an action arising out of an injury to the person or to property, if a motion for summary judgment is granted on the basis that the defendant was without fault, no other defendant during trial, over plaintiff's objection, may attempt to attribute fault to, or comment on, the absence or involvement of the defendant who was granted the motion.

(m)(1) A summary judgment entered under this section is an appealable judgment as in other cases. Upon entry of an order pursuant to this section, except the entry of summary judgment, a party may, within 20 days after service upon [7] **the party** of a written notice of entry of the order, petition an appropriate reviewing court for a peremptory writ. If the notice is served by mail, the initial period within which to file the petition shall be increased by five days if the place of address is within the State of California, 10 days if the place of address is outside the State of California but within the United States, and 20 days if the place of address is outside the United States. If the notice is served by facsimile transmission, express mail, or another method of delivery providing for overnight delivery, the initial period within which to file the petition shall be increased by two court days. The superior court may, for good cause, and before the expiration of the initial period, extend the time for one additional period not to exceed 10 days.

(2) Before a reviewing court affirms an order granting summary judgment or summary adjudication on a ground not relied upon by the trial court, the reviewing court shall afford the parties an opportunity to present their views on the issue by submitting supplemental briefs. The supplemental briefs may include an argument that additional evidence relating to that ground exists, but the party has not had an adequate opportunity to present the evidence or to conduct discovery on the issue. The court may reverse or remand based upon the supplemental briefs to allow the parties to present additional evidence or to conduct discovery on the issue. If the court fails to allow supplemental briefs, a rehearing shall be ordered upon timely petition of a party.

(n)(1) If a motion for summary adjudication is granted, at the trial of the action, the cause or causes of action within the action, affirmative defense or defenses, claim for damages, or issue or issues of duty as to the motion that has been granted shall be deemed to be established and the action shall proceed as to the cause or causes of action, affirmative defense or defenses, claim for damages, or issue or issues of duty remaining.

(2) In the trial of the action, the fact that a motion for summary adjudication is granted as to one or more causes of action, affirmative defenses, claims for damages, or issues of duty within the action shall not bar any cause of action, affirmative defense, claim for damages, or issue of duty as to which summary adjudication was either not sought or denied.

(3) In the trial of an action, neither a party, a witness, nor the court shall comment to a jury upon the grant or denial of a motion for summary adjudication.

(o) A cause of action has no merit if either of the following exists:

(1) One or more of the elements of the cause of action cannot be separately established, even if that element is separately pleaded.

(2) A defendant establishes an affirmative defense to that cause of action.

(p) For purposes of motions for summary judgment and summary adjudication:

(1) A plaintiff or cross-complainant has met [8] **that party's** burden of showing that there is no defense to a cause of action if that party has proved each element of the cause of action entitling the party to judgment on the cause of action. Once the plaintiff or cross-complainant has met that burden, the burden shifts to the defendant or cross-defendant to show that a triable issue of one or more material facts exists as to the cause of action or a defense thereto. The defendant or cross-defendant shall not rely upon the allegations or denials of its pleadings to show that a triable issue of material fact exists but, instead, shall set forth the specific facts showing that a triable issue of material fact exists as to the cause of action or a defense thereto.

(2) A defendant or cross-defendant has met [9] **that party's** burden of showing that a cause of action has no merit if the party has shown that one or more elements of the cause of action, even if not separately pleaded, cannot be established, or that there is a complete defense to the cause of action. Once the defendant or cross-defendant has met that burden, the burden shifts to the plaintiff or cross-complainant to show that a triable issue of one or more material facts exists as to the cause of action or a defense thereto. The plaintiff or cross-complainant shall not rely upon the allegations or denials of its pleadings to show that a triable issue of material fact exists but, instead, shall set forth the specific facts showing that a triable issue of material fact exists as to the cause of action or a defense thereto.

(q) In granting or denying a motion for summary judgment or summary adjudication, the court need rule only on those objections to evidence that it deems material to its disposition of the motion. Objections to evidence that are not ruled on for purposes of the motion shall be preserved for appellate review.

(r) This section does not extend the period for trial provided by Section 1170.5.

(s) Subdivisions (a) and (b) do not apply to actions brought pursuant to Chapter 4 (commencing with Section 1159) of Title 3 of Part 3.

(t) Notwithstanding subdivision (f), a party may move for summary adjudication of a legal issue or a claim for damages other than punitive damages that does not completely dispose of a cause of action, affirmative defense, or issue of duty pursuant to this subdivision.

(1)(A) Before filing a motion pursuant to this subdivision, the parties whose claims or defenses are put at issue by the motion shall submit to the court both of the following:

(i) A joint stipulation stating the issue or issues to be adjudicated.

(ii) A declaration from each stipulating party that the motion will further the interest of judicial economy by decreasing trial time or significantly increasing the likelihood of settlement.

(B) The joint stipulation shall be served on any party to the civil action who is not also a party to the motion.

(2) Within 15 days of receipt of the stipulation and declarations, unless the court has good cause for extending the time, the court shall notify the stipulating parties if the motion may be filed. In making this determination, the court may consider objections by a nonstipulating party made within 10 days of the submission of the stipulation and declarations.

(3) If the court elects not to allow the filing of the motion, the stipulating parties may request, and upon request the court shall conduct, an informal conference with the stipulating parties to permit further evaluation of the proposed stipulation. The stipulating parties shall not file additional papers in support of the motion.

(4)(A) A motion for summary adjudication made pursuant to this subdivision shall contain a statement in the notice of motion that reads substantially similar to the following: This motion is made pursuant to subdivision (t) of Section 437c of the Code of Civil Procedure. The parties to this motion stipulate that the court shall hear this motion and that the resolution of this motion will further the interest of judicial economy by decreasing trial time or significantly increasing the likelihood of settlement.

(B) The notice of motion shall be signed by counsel for all parties, and by those parties in propria persona, to the motion.

(5) A motion filed pursuant to this subdivision may be made by itself or as an alternative to a motion for summary judgment and shall proceed in all procedural respects as a motion for summary judgment.

(u) For purposes of this section, a change in law does not include a later enacted statute without retroactive application. **Leg.H.** Added Stats 2011 ch 419 §4 (SB 384), effective January 1, 2012, operative January 1, 2015. Amended Stats 2015 ch 161 §1 (SB 470), effective January 1, 2016, ch 345 §1.5 (AB 1141), effective January 1, 2016; Stats 2016 ch 86 §22 (SB 1171), effective January 1, 2017; Stats 2024 ch 99 §1 (AB 2049), effective January 1, 2025.

§437c. 2024 Deletes. [1] 75 [2] 75-day [3] 75-day [4] 14 [5] five [6] ( ) [7] him or her [8] his or her [9] his or her

Former Sections: Former CCP §437c, similar to the present section, was added Stats 1973 ch 366 §2 and repealed operative January 1, 2015, by its own terms. Former CCP §437c, similar to the present section, was added Stats 1933 ch 744 §27 and repealed Stats 1973 ch 366 §1.

Prior Law: Former CCP §437c, similar to the present section, was added Stats 1973 ch 366 §2, amended Stats 1976 ch 675 §1, Stats 1978 ch 949 §2, Stats 1980 ch 57 §1, Stats 1982 ch 1510 §1, Stats 1983 ch 490 §1, Stats 1984 ch 171 §1, Stats 1986 ch 540 §3, Stats 1989 ch 1416 §16, Stats 1990 ch 1561 §2, Stats 1992 ch 339 §1, ch 1348 §1, Stats 1993 ch 276 §1, Stats 1994 ch 493 §1, Stats 2002 ch 448 §5, Stats 2003 ch 62 §24, Stats 2004 ch 182 §9, Stats 2011 ch 419 §3, and repealed January 1, 2015, by its own terms.

Former CCP §437c, similar to the present section, was added Stats 1933 ch 744 §27, amended Stats 1937 ch 533 §1, Stats 1939 ch 331 §1, Stats 1951 ch 1737 §53, operative January 1, 1952, Stats 1953 ch 908 §1, Stats 1957 ch 1457 §1, Stats 1965 ch 162 §1, ch 1877 §1, Stats 1971 ch 244 §39, operative July 1, 1972, and repealed Stats 1973 ch 366 §1.

§437d. [Section repealed 1972]

Leg.H. Added Stats 1933 ch 744 §28. Repealed Stats 1971 ch 244 §40, operative July 1, 1972. The repealed section related to answer of officer or sureties in an action to recover possession of personal property when the affidavit did not truly state the value of the property.

§438. Judgment on the pleadings

(a) As used in this section:

(1) "Complaint" includes a cross-complaint.

(2) "Plaintiff" includes a cross-complainant.

(3) "Defendant" includes a cross-defendant.

(b)(1) A party may move for judgment on the pleadings.

(2) The court may upon its own motion grant a motion for judgment on the pleadings.

(c)(1) The motion provided for in this section may only be made on one of the following grounds:

(A) If the moving party is a plaintiff, that the complaint states facts sufficient to constitute a cause or causes of action against the defendant and the answer does not state facts sufficient to constitute a defense to the complaint.

(B) If the moving party is a defendant, that either of the following conditions exist:

(i) The court has no jurisdiction of the subject of the cause of action alleged in the complaint.

(ii) The complaint does not state facts sufficient to constitute a cause of action against that defendant.

(2) The motion provided for in this section may be made as to either of the following:

(A) The entire complaint or cross-complaint or as to any of the causes of action stated therein.

(B) The entire answer or one or more of the affirmative defenses set forth in the answer.

(3) If the court on its own motion grants the motion for judgment on the pleadings, it shall be on one of the following bases:

(A) If the motion is granted in favor of the plaintiff, it shall be based on the grounds that the complaint states facts sufficient to constitute a cause or causes of action against the defendant and the answer does not state facts sufficient to constitute a defense to the complaint.

(B) If the motion is granted in favor of the defendant, that either of the following conditions exist:

(i) The court has no jurisdiction of the subject of the cause of action alleged in the complaint.

(ii) The complaint does not state facts sufficient to constitute a cause of action against that defendant.

(d) The grounds for motion provided for in this section shall appear on the face of the challenged pleading or from any matter of which the court is required to take judicial notice. Where the motion is based on a matter of which the court may take judicial notice pursuant to Section 452 or 453 of the Evidence Code, the matter shall be specified in the notice of motion, or in the supporting points and authorities, except as the court may otherwise permit.

(e) No motion may be made pursuant to this section if a pretrial conference order has been entered pursuant to Section 575, or within 30 days of the date the action is initially set for trial, whichever is later, unless the court otherwise permits.

(f) The motion provided for in this section may be made only after one of the following conditions has occurred:

(1) If the moving party is a plaintiff, and the defendant has already filed his or her answer to the complaint and the time for the plaintiff to demur to the answer has expired.

(2) If the moving party is a defendant, and the defendant has already filed his or her answer to the complaint and the time for the defendant to demur to the complaint has expired.

(g) The motion provided for in this section may be made even though either of the following conditions exist:

(1) The moving party has already demurred to the complaint or answer, as the case may be, on the same grounds as is the basis for the motion provided for in this section and the demurrer has been overruled, provided that there has been a material change in applicable case law or statute since the ruling on the demurrer.

(2) The moving party did not demur to the complaint or answer, as the case may be, on the same grounds as is the basis for the motion provided for in this section.

(h)(1) The motion provided for in this section may be granted with or without leave to file an amended complaint or answer, as the case may be.

(2) Where a motion is granted pursuant to this section with leave to file an amended complaint or answer, as the case may be, then the court shall grant 30 days to the party against whom the motion was granted to file an amended complaint or answer, as the case may be.

(3) If the motion is granted with respect to the entire complaint or answer without leave to file an amended complaint or answer, as the case may be, then judgment shall be entered forthwith in accordance with the motion granting judgment to the moving party.

(4) If the motion is granted with leave to file an amended complaint or answer, as the case may be, then the following procedures shall be followed:

(A) If an amended complaint is filed after the time to file an amended complaint has expired, then the court may strike the complaint pursuant to Section 436 and enter judgment in favor of that defendant against that plaintiff or a plaintiff.

(B) If an amended answer is filed after the time to file an amended answer has expired, then the court may strike the answer pursuant to Section 436 and proceed to enter judgment in favor of that plaintiff and against that defendant or a defendant.

(C) Except where subparagraphs (A) and (B) apply, if the motion is granted with respect to the entire complaint or answer with leave to file an amended complaint or answer, as the case may be, but an amended complaint or answer is not filed, then after the time to file an amended complaint or answer, as the case may be, has expired, judgment shall be entered forthwith in favor of the moving party.

(i)(1) Where a motion for judgment on the pleadings is granted with leave to amend, the court shall not enter a judgment in favor of a party until the following proceedings are had:

(A) If an amended pleading is filed and the moving party contends that pleading is filed after the time to file an amended pleading has expired or that the pleading is in violation of the court's prior ruling on the motion, then that party shall move to strike the pleading and enter judgment in its favor.

(B) If no amended pleading is filed, then the party shall move for entry of judgment in its favor.

(2) All motions made pursuant to this subdivision shall be made pursuant to Section 1010.

(3) At the hearing on the motion provided for in this subdivision, the court shall determine whether to enter judgment in favor of a particular party. **Leg.H.** Added Stats 1993 ch 456 §5 (AB 58). Amended Stats 1994 ch 493 §2, effective September 11, 1994.

Prior Law: Former CCP §438, similar to present CCP §428.10, was enacted 1872, amended Stats 1927 ch 813 §1, and repealed Stats 1971 ch 244 §41, operative July 1, 1972.

§439. Meet and confer process prior to filing motion for judgment on the pleadings; Amended pleading; Declaration; Exceptions; Appeal

(a) Before filing a motion for judgment on the pleadings pursuant to this chapter, the moving party shall meet and confer in person, by telephone, or by video conference with the party who filed the pleading that is subject to the motion for judgment on the pleadings for the purpose of determining if an agreement can be reached that resolves the claims to be raised in the motion for judgment on the pleadings. If an amended pleading is filed, the responding party shall meet and confer again with the party who filed the amended pleading before filing a motion for judgment on the pleadings against the amended pleading.

(1) As part of the meet and confer process, the moving party shall identify all of the specific allegations that it believes are subject to judgment and identify with legal support the basis of the claims. The party who filed the pleading shall provide legal support for its position that the pleading is not subject to judgment, or, in the alternative, how the pleading could be amended to cure any claims it is subject to judgment.

(2) The parties shall meet and confer at least 5 days before the date a motion for judgment on the pleadings is filed. If the parties are unable to meet and confer by that time, the moving party shall be granted an automatic 30-day extension of time within which to file a motion for judgment on the pleadings, by filing and serving, on or before the date a motion for judgment on the pleadings must be filed, a declaration stating under penalty of perjury that a good faith attempt to meet and confer was made and explaining the reasons why the parties could not meet and confer. The 30-day extension shall commence from the date the motion for judgment on the pleadings was previously filed, and the moving party shall not be subject to default during the period of the extension. Any further extensions shall be obtained by court order upon a showing of good cause.

(3) The moving party shall file and serve with the motion for judgment on the pleadings a declaration stating either of the following:

(A) The means by which the moving party met and conferred with the party who filed the pleading subject to the motion for judgment on the pleadings, and that the parties did not reach an agreement resolving the claims raised by the motion for judgment on the pleadings.

(B) That the party who filed the pleading subject to the motion for judgment on the pleadings failed to respond to the meet and confer request of the moving party or otherwise failed to meet and confer in good faith.

(4) A determination by the court that the meet and confer process was insufficient shall not be grounds to grant or deny the motion for judgment on the pleadings.

(b) A party moving for judgment on a pleading that has been amended after a motion for judgment on the pleadings on an earlier version of the pleading was granted shall not move for judgment on any portion of the pleadings on grounds that could have been raised by a motion for judgment on the pleadings as to the earlier version of the pleading.

(c)(1) If a court grants a motion for judgment on the pleadings and grants leave to amend, the court may order a conference of the parties before an amended pleading, or a motion for judgment on an amended pleading, may be filed. If the conference is held, the court shall not preclude a party from filing a motion for judgment on the pleadings and the time to file a motion for judgment on the pleadings shall not begin until after the conference has concluded.

(2) This section does not prohibit the court from ordering a conference on its own motion at any time or prevent a party from requesting that the court order that a conference be held.

(d) This section does not apply to any of the following:

(1) An action in which a party not represented by counsel is incarcerated in a local, state, or federal correctional institution.

(2) A proceeding in forcible entry, forcible detainer, or unlawful detainer.

(3) A special motion brought pursuant to Section 425.16.

(4) A motion brought less than 30 days before trial.

(e)(1) In response to a motion for judgment on the pleadings and before the case is at issue, a pleading shall not be amended more than three times, absent an offer to the trial court of additional facts to be pleaded that, if pleaded, would result in a reasonable possibility that the defect can be cured. The three-amendment limit does not include an amendment made without leave of the court pursuant to Section 472, if the amendment is made before a motion for judgments on the pleadings as to the original pleading is filed.

(2) This section does not affect the rights of a party to amend its pleading or respond to an amended pleading after the case is at issue.

(f) This section does not affect appellate review or the rights of a party pursuant to Section 430.80.

(g) If a motion for judgment on the pleadings is denied and the pleading is not further amended, the moving party preserves its right to appeal after final judgment without filing a further motion for judgment on the pleadings. **Leg.H.** Added Stats 2017 ch 273 §2 (AB 644), effective January 1, 2018, repealed January 1, 2021. Amended Stats 2020 ch 36 §17 (AB 3364), effective January 1, 2021; Stats 2023 ch 478 §11 (AB 1756), effective January 1, 2024.

Prior Law: Former CCP §439, similar to present CCP §§426.10, 426.30–426.60, was enacted 1872, amended Stats 1907 ch 372 §5, Stats 1939 ch 533 §1, Stats 1941 ch 454 §2, and repealed Stats 1971 ch 244 §42, operative July 1, 1972.

§440. [Section repealed 1972]

Leg.H. Enacted 1872. Amended Code Amdts 1873–74 ch 383 §53. Repealed Stats 1971 ch 244 §43, operative July 1, 1972. See CCP §431.70.

§441. [Section repealed 1972]

Leg.H. Enacted 1872. Repealed Stats 1971 ch 244 §44, operative July 1, 1972. See CCP §§430.30, 431.30.

§442. [Section repealed 1972]

Leg.H. Added Code Amdts 1873–74 ch 383 §54. Amended Stats 1907 ch 372 §6; Stats 1909 ch 629 §1; Stats 1915 ch 141 §1; Stats 1923 ch 376 §1; Stats 1955 ch 1452 §4; Stats 1957 ch 1498 §1; Stats 1970 ch 484 §2. Repealed Stats 1971 ch 244 §45, operative July 1, 1972. See Article 4 (commencing with CCP §428.10) and CCP §§430.40, 432.10, 435.

§443. [Section repealed 1972]

Leg.H. Enacted 1872. Amended Code Amdts 1873–74 ch 383 §55; Stats 1907 ch 372 §7. Repealed Stats 1971 ch 244 §46, operative July 1, 1972. See CCP §§430.40, 430.50.

§444. [Section repealed 1972]

Leg.H. Enacted 1872. Amended Stats 1907 ch 372 §8; Stats 1943 ch 209 §1; Stats 1967 ch 512 §2. Repealed Stats 1971 ch 244 §46, operative July 1, 1972. See CCP §§430.20, 430.30.

CHAPTER 6
VERIFICATION OF PLEADINGS

Subscription and verification of pleadings. §446.

§446. Subscription and verification of pleadings

(a) Every pleading shall be subscribed by the party or his or her attorney. When the state, any county thereof, city, school district, district, public agency, or public corporation, or any officer of the state, or of any county thereof, city, school district, district, public agency, or public corporation, in his or her official capacity, is plaintiff, the answer shall be verified, unless an admission of the truth of the complaint might subject the party to a criminal prosecution, or, unless a county thereof, city, school district, district, public agency, or public corporation, or an officer of the state, or of any county, city, school district, district, public agency, or public corporation, in his or her official capacity, is defendant. When the complaint is verified, the answer shall be verified. In all cases of a verification of a pleading, the affidavit of the party shall state that the same is true of his own knowledge, except as to the matters which are therein stated on his or her information or belief, and as to those matters that he or she believes it to be true; and where a pleading is verified, it shall be by the affidavit of a party, unless the parties are absent from the county where the attorney has his or her office, or from some cause unable to verify it, or the facts are within the knowledge of his or her attorney or other person verifying the same. When the pleading is verified by the attorney, or any other person except one of the parties, he or she shall set forth in the affidavit the reasons why it is not made by one of the parties.

When a corporation is a party, the verification may be made by any officer thereof. When the state, any county thereof, city, school district, district, public agency, or public corporation, or an officer of the state, or of any county thereof, city, school district, district, public agency, or public corporation, in his or her official capacity is plaintiff, the complaint need not be verified; and if the state, any county thereof, city, school district, district, public agency, or public corporation, or an officer of such state, county, city, school district, district, public agency, or public corporation, in his or her official capacity is defendant, its or his or her answer need not be verified.

When the verification is made by the attorney for the reason that the parties are absent from the county where he or she has his or her office, or from some other cause are unable to verify it, or when the verification is made on behalf of a corporation or public agency by any officer thereof, the attorney's or officer's affidavit shall state that he or she has read the pleading and that he or she is informed and believes the matters therein to be true and on that ground alleges that the matters stated therein are true. However, in those cases the pleadings shall not otherwise be considered as an affidavit or declaration establishing the facts therein alleged.

A person verifying a pleading need not swear to the truth or his or her belief in the truth of the matters stated therein but may, instead, assert the truth or his or her belief in the truth of those matters "under penalty of perjury."

(b) This section shall become operative on January 1, 1999, unless a statute that becomes effective on or before this date extends or deletes the repeal date of Section 446, as amended by Assembly Bill 3594 of the 1993–94 Regular Session. **Leg.H.** Added Stats 1994 ch 1062 §5 (AB 3594), operative January 1, 1999.

Prior Law: Former CCP §446, similar to the present section, was enacted 1872, amended Stats 1907 ch 372 §9, Stats 1933 ch 744 §29, Stats 1939 ch 712 §1, Stats 1945 ch 505 §1, Stats 1951 ch 1737 §54, operative January 1, 1952, Stats 1955 ch 873 §1, Stats 1963 ch 732 §1, Stats 1967 ch 1242 §1, Stats 1977 ch 1257 §12, effective October 3, 1977, Stats 1981 ch 714 §69, Stats 1994 ch 1062 §4, and repealed January 1, 1999, by its own terms.

§447. [Section repealed 1995]
Leg.H. Added Stats 1993 ch 982 §7 (SB 645). Repealed Stats 1994 ch 1062 §6 (AB 3594). See CCP §128.7.

Prior Law: Former CCP §447, similar to present CCP §128.7, was added Stats 1987 ch 1003 §1, amended Stats 1988 ch 10 §1, effective February 17, 1988, Stats 1990 ch 584 §1, and repealed January 1, 1993, by its own terms.

Former CCP §447, relating to genuineness and execution of instrument attached or annexed to complaint, was enacted 1872, amended Stats 1929 ch 489 §1, Stats 1933 ch 987 §1, and repealed Stats 1965 ch 105 §1.

§448. [Section repealed 1965]
Leg.H. Enacted 1872. Amended Code Amdts 1873–74 ch 383 §56; Stats 1929 ch 489 §2; Stats 1933 ch 987 §2. Repealed Stats 1965 ch 105 §2. The repealed section related to the deemed admission of genuineness and due execution of a written instrument contained or annexed to an answer.

§449. [Section repealed 1965]
Leg.H. Enacted 1872. Amended Code Amdts 1880 ch 96 §1. Repealed Stats 1965 ch 105 §3.

CHAPTER 7
GENERAL RULES OF PLEADING

Pleadings to be liberally construed. §452.
Pleading of accounts. §454.
Description of real property in pleading. §455.
Pleading court judgments. §456.
Conditions precedent, how to be pleaded. §457.
Statute of limitations, how pleaded. §458.
Private statutes, how pleaded. §459.
Libel and slander, how stated in complaint; Not necessary to allege or prove special damages. §460.
Ex parte order for time to respond in action for defamation; Time in absence of order; Precedence; Continuance. §460.5.
Time to respond in action by candidate; Precedence over other actions. §460.7.
Defendant's allegation of both truth of defamatory matter and mitigating circumstances. §461.
Supplemental complaint and answer. §464.
Subsequent pleadings. §465.

§452. Pleadings to be liberally construed
In the construction of a pleading, for the purpose of determining its effect, its allegations must be liberally construed, with a view to substantial justice between the parties. **Leg.H.** Enacted 1872.

§453. [Section repealed 1983]
Leg.H. Enacted 1872. Repealed Stats 1982 ch 704 §5. See CCP §436.

§454. Pleading of accounts
It is not necessary for a party to set forth in a pleading the items of an account therein alleged, but he must deliver to the adverse party, within ten days after a demand thereof in writing, a copy of the account, or be precluded from giving evidence thereof. The court or judge thereof may order a further account when the one delivered is too general, or is defective in any particular.

If the pleading is verified the account must be verified by the affidavit of the party to the effect that he believes it to be true; or if the facts are within the personal knowledge of the agent or attorney for the party, or the party is not within the county where the attorney has his office or from some cause unable to make the affidavit, by the affidavit of the agent or attorney. **Leg.H.** Enacted 1872. Amended Code Amdts 1880 ch 14 §2; Stats 1939 ch 63 §1.

§455. Description of real property in pleading
In an action for the recovery of real property, it must be described in the complaint with such certainty as to enable an officer, upon execution, to identify it. **Leg.H.** Enacted 1872.

§456. Pleading court judgments
In pleading a judgment or other determination of a court, officer, or board, it is not necessary to state the facts conferring jurisdiction, but such judgment or determination may be stated to have been duly given or made and to have become final. If such allegation be controverted, the party pleading must establish on the trial the facts conferring jurisdiction and creating finality. **Leg.H.** Enacted 1872. Amended Stats 1957 ch 1365 §1.

§457. Conditions precedent, how to be pleaded
In pleading the performance of conditions precedent in a contract, it is not necessary to state the facts showing such performance, but it may be stated generally that the party duly performed all the conditions on his part, and if such allegation be controverted, the party pleading must establish, on the trial, the facts showing such performance. **Leg.H.** Enacted 1872.

§458. Statute of limitations, how pleaded
In pleading the statute of limitations it is not necessary to state the facts showing the defense, but it may be stated generally that the cause of action is barred by the provisions of section ____ (giving the number of the section and subdivision thereof, if it is so divided, relied upon) of the Code of Civil Procedure; and if such allegation be controverted, the party pleading must establish, on the trial, the facts showing that the cause of action is so barred. **Leg.H.** Enacted 1872.

§459. Private statutes, how pleaded
In pleading a private statute, or an ordinance of a county or municipal corporation, or a right derived therefrom, it is sufficient to refer to such statute or ordinance by its title and the day of its passage. In pleading the performance of conditions precedent under a statute or an ordinance of a county or municipal corporation, or of a right derived therefrom, it is not necessary to state the facts showing such performance, but it may be stated generally that the party duly performed all the conditions on his part required thereby: if such allegations be controverted the party pleading must establish on the trial the facts showing such performance. **Leg.H.** Enacted 1872. Amended Stats 1907 ch 372 §10.

§460. Libel and slander, how stated in complaint; Not necessary to allege or prove special damages
In an action for libel or slander it is not necessary to state in the complaint any extrinsic facts for the purpose of showing the application to the plaintiff of the defamatory matter out of which the cause of action arose; but it is sufficient to state, generally, that the same was published or spoken concerning the plaintiff; and if such allegation be controverted, the plaintiff must establish on the trial that it was so published or spoken. **Leg.H.** Enacted 1872.

§460.5. Ex parte order for time to respond in action for defamation; Time in absence of order; Precedence; Continuance
(a) In any action for libel or slander, for good cause shown upon ex

parte written application, the court may order that the time to respond to the complaint is 20 days after the service of summons on the defendant. The application shall be supported by an affidavit stating facts showing, among other things, that the alleged defamatory matter has been continuously published and that there is a reasonable likelihood that the publication will continue. The order shall direct the clerk to endorse the summons to show that the time to respond has been shortened pursuant to this section. A copy of the application, affidavit, and order shall be served with the summons.

(b) In any such action, unless otherwise ordered by the court for good cause shown, the time allowed the defendant to respond to the complaint or amend the answer under Section 586 shall not exceed 10 days.

(c) The court shall give any such action precedence over all other civil actions, except actions to which special precedence is given by law, in the matter of setting the case for hearing or trial, and in hearing the case, to the end that all such actions shall be quickly heard and determined. Except for good cause shown, the court shall not grant a continuance in excess of 10 days without the consent of the adverse party.

(d) For purposes of this section, "continuously published" means three or more publications within 15 days. **Leg.H.** Added Stats 1972 ch 594 §1.

§460.7. Time to respond in action by candidate; Precedence over other actions

(a) In any action by a candidate or former candidate for elective public office against a holder of elective public office or an opposing candidate for libel or slander that is alleged to have occurred during the course of an election campaign, the court shall order that the time to respond to the complaint is 20 days after the service of summons on the defendant. The order shall direct the clerk to endorse the summons to show that the time to respond has been shortened pursuant to this section. A copy of the affidavit and order shall be served with the summons.

(b) In any action described in subdivision (a), unless otherwise ordered by the court for good cause shown, the time allowed the defendant to respond to the complaint or amend the answer under Section 586 shall not exceed 10 days.

(c) The court shall give any action described in subdivision (a) precedence over all other civil actions, except actions to which special precedence is given by law, in the matter of the setting of the case of hearing or trial, and in hearing the case, to the end that all actions described in subdivision (a) shall be quickly heard and determined. Except for good cause shown, the court shall not grant a continuance in excess of 10 days without the consent of the adverse party. **Leg.H.** Added Stats 1978 ch 1642 §2, operative June 5, 1984. Amended Stats 2006 ch 538 §64 (SB 1852), effective January 1, 2007.

§461. Defendant's allegation of both truth of defamatory matter and mitigating circumstances

In any action within Section 460 or 460.5, the defendant may, in his answer, allege both the truth of the matter charged as defamatory, and any mitigating circumstances, to reduce the amount of damages. Whether he proves the justification or not, he may give in evidence the mitigating circumstances. **Leg.H.** Enacted 1872. Amended Stats 1972 ch 594 §2.

§462. [Section repealed 1972]

Leg.H. Enacted 1872. Repealed Stats 1971 ch 244 §47, operative July 1, 1972. See CCP §431.20.

§463. [Section repealed 1972]

Leg.H. Enacted 1872. Repealed Stats 1971 ch 244 §48, operative July 1, 1972. See CCP §431.10.

§464. Supplemental complaint and answer

(a) The plaintiff and defendant, respectively, may be allowed, on motion, to make a supplemental complaint or answer, alleging facts material to the case occurring after the former complaint or answer.

(b) The plaintiff and defendant, or petitioner and respondent, may, in any action in which the support of children is an issue, file a supplemental complaint seeking a judgment or order of paternity or support for a child of the mother and father of the child whose paternity and support are already in issue before the court. A supplemental complaint for paternity or child support may be filed without leave of court either before or after final judgment in the underlying action.

(c) Upon the filing of a supplemental complaint, the court clerk shall issue an amended or supplemental summons pursuant to Section 412.10. Service of the supplemental summons and complaint shall be made in the manner provided for the initial service of a summons by this code. **Leg.H.** Enacted 1872. Amended Stats 1994 ch 1269 §2.8 (AB 2208).

§465. Subsequent pleadings

Except with leave of the court, all pleadings subsequent to the complaint, together with proof of service unless a summons need be issued, shall be filed with the clerk or judge, and copies thereof served upon the adverse party or his or her attorney. **Leg.H.** Enacted 1872. Amended Code Amdts 1873–74 ch 383 §57; Stats 1933 ch 744 §30; Stats 1951 ch 1737 §55, operative January 1, 1952; Stats 1979 ch 212 §3; Stats 1986 ch 953 §3.

CHAPTER 8
VARIANCE—MISTAKES IN PLEADINGS AND AMENDMENTS

Materiality of variance; Order to amend. §469.
Immaterial variance. §470.
Unproved allegation not deemed variance. §471.
Proceedings on amended complaint or cross-complaint. §471.5.
Amendment of pleading as of course; Special motion exception. §472.
Effect of answer filed at same time as demurrer; Proceedings when demurrer overruled or sustained, motion to strike is granted or denied, motion to dismiss is denied. §472a.
Time for pleading after ruling on demurrer. §472b.
Question on appeal after order sustaining demurrer without leave to amend; Orders deemed open on appeal when amended pleading filed after court's order. §472c.
Statement of grounds for sustaining demurrer; Waiver. §472d.
Amendment of pleadings. §473.
Relief from judgment or proceeding where court has assumed jurisdiction over practice of attorney. §473.1.
Relief from judgment where summons does not result in actual notice. §473.5.
Fictitious names. §474.
Effect of errors or defects. §475.
[Section renumbered 1933]. §476.

§469. Materiality of variance; Order to amend

Variance between the allegation in a pleading and the proof shall not be deemed material, unless it has actually misled the adverse party to his or her prejudice in maintaining his or her action or defense upon the merits. If it appears that a party has been so misled, the court may order the pleading to be amended, upon such terms as may be just. **Leg.H.** Enacted 1872. Amended Code Amdts 1873–74 ch 383 §58; Stats 2017 ch 561 §22 (AB 1516), effective January 1, 2018.

§470. Immaterial variance

Where the variance is not material, as provided in Section 469 the court may direct the fact to be found according to the evidence, or may order an immediate amendment, without costs. **Leg.H.** Enacted 1872. Amended Stats 1986 ch 540 §4.

§471. Unproved allegation not deemed variance

Where, however, the allegation of the claim or defense to which the proof is directed, is unproved, not in some particular or particulars only, but in its general scope and meaning, it is not to be deemed a case of variance, within the meaning of Sections 469 and 470, but a failure of proof. **Leg.H.** Enacted 1872. Amended Stats 1986 ch 540 §5.

§471.5. Proceedings on amended complaint or cross-complaint

(a) If the complaint is amended, a copy of the amendments shall be filed, or the court may, in its discretion, require the complaint as amended to be filed, and a copy of the amendments or amended complaint must be served upon the defendants affected thereby. The defendant shall answer the amendments, or the complaint as amended, within 30 days after service thereof, or such other time as the court may direct, and judgment by default may be entered upon failure to answer, as in other cases. For the purposes of this subdivision, "complaint" includes a cross-complaint, and "defendant" includes a person against whom a cross-complaint is filed.

(b) If the answer is amended, the adverse party has 10 days after service thereof, or such other time as the court may direct, in which to demur to the amended answer. **Leg.H.** Added Stats 1972 ch 73 §2, effective May 15, 1972, operative July 1, 1972.

Prior Law: Former CCP §471.5, similar to the present section, was added Stats 1971 ch 244 §49, operative July 1, 1972, and repealed Stats 1972 ch 73 §1, effective May 15, 1972, operative July 1, 1972.

§472. Amendment of pleading as of course; Special motion exception

(a) A party may amend its pleading once without leave of the court at any time before the answer, demurrer, or motion to strike is filed, or after a demurrer or motion to strike is filed but before the demurrer or motion to strike is heard if the amended pleading is filed and served no later than the date for filing an opposition to the demurrer or motion to strike. A party may amend the pleading after the date for filing an opposition to the demurrer or motion to strike, upon stipulation by the parties. The time for responding to an amended pleading shall be computed from the date of service of the amended pleading.

(b) This section shall not apply to a special motion brought pursuant to Section 425.16. **Leg.H.** Enacted 1872. Amended Code Amdts 1873–74 ch 383 §59; Stats 1933 ch 744 §31; Stats 1951 ch 1737 §56, operative January 1, 1952; Stats 1972 ch 73 §3, effective May 15, 1972, operative July 1, 1972; Stats 1977 ch 1257 §13, effective October 3, 1977; Stats 1983 ch 142 §4; Stats 2015 ch 418 §2 (SB 383), effective January 1, 2016, repealed January 1, 2021; Stats 2017 ch 273 §3 (AB 644), effective January 1, 2018, repealed January 1, 2021; Stats 2020 ch 36 §19 (AB 3364), effective January 1, 2021.

Prior Law: Former CCP §472, relating to amendment of pleading as of course, was added Stats 2015 ch 418 §3 (SB 383), effective January 1, 2016, operative January 1, 2021 and repealed by Stats 2020 ch 36 §18 (AB 3364) effective January 1, 2021.

§472a. Effect of answer filed at same time as demurrer; Proceedings when demurrer overruled or sustained, motion to strike is granted or denied, motion to dismiss is denied

(a) A demurrer is not waived by an answer filed at the same time.

(b) Except as otherwise provided by rule adopted by the Judicial Council, if a demurrer to a complaint or to a cross-complaint is overruled and there is no answer filed, the court shall allow an answer to be filed upon such terms as may be just. If a demurrer to the answer is overruled, the action shall proceed as if no demurrer had been interposed, and the facts alleged in the answer shall be considered as denied to the extent mentioned in Section 431.20.

(c) Subject to the limitations imposed by subdivision (e) of Section 430.41, if a demurrer is sustained, the court may grant leave to amend the pleading upon any terms as may be just and shall fix the time within which the amendment or amended pleading shall be filed. If a demurrer is stricken pursuant to Section 436 and there is no answer filed, the court shall allow an answer to be filed on terms that are just.

(d) If a motion to strike is granted pursuant to Section 436, the court may order that an amendment or amended pleading be filed upon terms it deems proper. If a motion to strike a complaint or cross-complaint, or portion thereof, is denied, the court shall allow the party filing the motion to strike to file an answer.

(e) If a motion to dismiss an action pursuant to Article 2 (commencing with Section 583.210) of Chapter 1.5 of Title 8 is denied, the court shall allow a pleading to be filed. **Leg.H.** Added Stats 1933 ch 744 §32. Amended Stats 1951 ch 1737 §57, operative January 1, 1952; Stats 1971 ch 1475 §1; Stats 1982 ch 704 §6; Stats 1983 ch 142 §5, ch 1167 §5; Stats 1984 ch 572 §2; Stats 1989 ch 1416 §17; Stats 1993 ch 456 §6 (AB 58); Stats 2015 ch 418 §4 (SB 383), effective January 1, 2016, repealed January 1, 2021; Stats 2020 ch 36 §20 (AB 3364), effective January 1, 2021.

Prior Law: Former CCP §472a, relating to the effect of answer filed at same time as demurrer, proceedings when demurrer overruled or sustained, and motions to strike or dismiss, was added Stats 2015 ch 418 §5 (SB 383) effective January 1, 2016, operative January 1, 2021, amended Stats 2016 ch 86 §23 (SB 1171), effective January 1, 2017, operative January 1, 2021, and repealed by Stats 2020 ch 36 §21 (AB 3364) effective January 1, 2021.

§472b. Time for pleading after ruling on demurrer

When a demurrer to any pleading is sustained or overruled, and time to amend or answer is given, the time so given runs from the service of notice of the decision or order, unless the notice is waived in open court, and the waiver entered in the minutes. When an order sustaining a demurrer without leave to amend is reversed or otherwise remanded by any order issued by a reviewing court, any amended complaint shall be filed within 30 days after the clerk of the reviewing court mails notice of the issuance of the remittitur. **Leg.H.** Added Code Amdts 1873–74 ch 383 §61 as CCP §476. Amended and renumbered by Stats 1933 ch 744 §33; Amended Stats 1994 ch 41 §1 (AB 911) (ch 41 prevails), ch 146 §24 (AB 3601); Stats 2001 ch 44 §3 (SB 562).

§472c. Question on appeal after order sustaining demurrer without leave to amend; Orders deemed open on appeal when amended pleading filed after court's order

(a) When any court makes an order sustaining a demurrer without leave to amend the question as to whether or not such court abused its discretion in making such an order is open on appeal even though no request to amend such pleading was made.

(b) The following orders shall be deemed open on appeal where an amended pleading is filed after the court's order:

(1) An order sustaining a demurrer to a cause of action within a complaint or cross-complaint where the order did not sustain the demurrer as to the entire complaint or cross-complaint.

(2) An order sustaining a demurrer to an affirmative defense within an answer where the order sustaining the demurrer did not sustain the demurrer as to the entire answer.

(3) An order granting a motion to strike a portion of a pleading where the order granting the motion to strike did not strike the entire pleading.

(c) As used in this section, "open on appeal" means that a party aggrieved by an order listed in subdivision (b) may claim the order as error in an appeal from the final judgment in the action. **Leg.H.** Added Stats 1939 ch 714 §1. Amended Stats 1993 ch 456 §7 (AB 58).

§472d. Statement of grounds for sustaining demurrer; Waiver

Whenever a demurrer in any action or proceeding is sustained, the court shall include in its decision or order a statement of the specific ground or grounds upon which the decision or order is based which may be by reference to appropriate pages and paragraphs of the demurrer.

The party against whom a demurrer has been sustained may waive these requirements. **Leg.H.** Added Stats 1961 ch 727 §1.

§473. Amendment of pleadings

(a)(1) The court may, in furtherance of justice, and on any terms as may be proper, allow a party to amend any pleading or proceeding by adding or striking out the name of any party, or by correcting a mistake in the name of a party, or a mistake in any other respect; and may, upon like terms, enlarge the time for answer or demurrer. The court may likewise, in its discretion, after notice to the adverse party, allow, upon any terms as may be just, an amendment to any pleading or proceeding in other particulars; and may upon like terms allow an answer to be made after the time limited by this code.

(2) When it appears to the satisfaction of the court that the amendment renders it necessary, the court may postpone the trial, and may, when the postponement will by the amendment be rendered necessary, require, as a condition to the amendment, the payment to the adverse party of any costs as may be just.

(b) The court may, upon any terms as may be just, relieve a party or his or her legal representative from a judgment, dismissal, order, or other proceeding taken against him or her through his or her mistake, inadvertence, surprise, or excusable neglect. Application for this relief shall be accompanied by a copy of the answer or other pleading proposed to be filed therein, otherwise the application shall not be granted, and shall be made within a reasonable time, in no case exceeding six months, after the judgment, dismissal, order, or proceeding was taken. However, in the case of a judgment, dismissal, order, or other proceeding determining the ownership or right to possession of real or personal property, without extending the six-month period, when a notice in writing is personally served within the State of California both upon the party against whom the judgment, dismissal, order, or other proceeding has been taken, and upon his or her attorney of record, if any, notifying that party and his or her attorney of record, if any, that the order, judgment, dismissal, or other proceeding was taken against him or her and that any rights the party has to apply for relief under the provisions of Section 473 of the Code of Civil Procedure shall expire 90 days after service of the notice, then the application shall be made within 90 days after service of the notice upon the defaulting party or his or her attorney of record, if any, whichever service shall be later. No affidavit or declaration of merits shall be required of the moving party. Notwithstanding any other requirements of this section, the court shall, whenever an application for relief is made no more than six months after entry of judgment, is in proper form, and is accompanied by an attorney's sworn affidavit attesting to his or her mistake, inadvertence, surprise, or neglect, vacate any (1) resulting default entered by the clerk against his or her client, and which will result in entry of a default judgment, or (2) resulting default judgment or dismissal entered against his or her client, unless the court finds that the default or dismissal was not in fact caused by the attorney's mistake, inadvertence, surprise, or neglect. The court shall, whenever relief is granted based on an attorney's affidavit of fault, direct the attorney to pay reasonable compensatory legal fees and costs to opposing counsel or parties. However, this section shall not lengthen the time within which an action shall be brought to trial pursuant to Section 583.310.

(c)(1) Whenever the court grants relief from a default, default judgment, or dismissal based on any of the provisions of this section, the court may do any of the following:

(A) Impose a penalty of no greater than one thousand dollars ($1,000) upon an offending attorney or party.

(B) Direct that an offending attorney pay an amount no greater than one thousand dollars ($1,000) to the State Bar Client Security Fund.

(C) Grant other relief as is appropriate.

(2) However, where the court grants relief from a default or default judgment pursuant to this section based upon the affidavit of the defaulting party's attorney attesting to the attorney's mistake, inadvertence, surprise, or neglect, the relief shall not be made conditional upon the attorney's payment of compensatory legal fees or costs or monetary penalties imposed by the court or upon compliance with other sanctions ordered by the court.

(d) The court may, upon motion of the injured party, or its own motion, correct clerical mistakes in its judgment or orders as entered, so as to conform to the judgment or order directed, and may, on motion of either party after notice to the other party, set aside any void judgment or order. **Leg.H.** Enacted 1872. Amended Code Amdts 1873–74 ch 383 §60; Code Amdts 1880 ch 14 §3; Stats 1917 ch 159 §1; Stats 1933 ch 744 §34; Stats 1961 ch 722 §1; Stats 1981 ch 122 §2; Stats 1988 ch 1131 §1; Stats 1991 ch 1003 §1 (SB 882); Stats 1992 ch 427 §16 (AB 3355), ch 876 §4 (AB 3296) (ch 876 prevails); Stats 1996 ch 60 §1 (SB 52).

§473a. [Section repealed 1970]

Leg.H. Added Stats 1933 ch 744 §35. Amended Stats 1961 ch 722 §2. Repealed Stats 1969 ch 1610 §22, operative July 1, 1970. See CCP §167.

§473.1. Relief from judgment or proceeding where court has assumed jurisdiction over practice of attorney

The court may, upon such terms as may be just, relieve a party from a judgment, order, or other proceeding taken against him or her, including dismissal of an action pursuant to Section 581 or Chapter 1.5 (commencing with Section 583.110) of Title 8, where a court of this state has assumed jurisdiction, pursuant to Section 6180 or 6190 of the Business and Professions Code, over the law practice of the attorney for the party and the judgment, order or other proceeding was taken against the party after the application for the court to assume jurisdiction over the practice was filed. Application for this relief shall be made within a reasonable period of time, in no case exceeding six months, after the court takes jurisdiction over the practice. However, in the case of a judgment, order, or other proceeding determining the ownership or right to possession of real or personal property, without extending the six-month period, when a notice in writing is personally served within the state both upon the party against whom the judgment, order, or other proceeding has been taken, and upon the attorney appointed pursuant to Section 6180.5 of the Business and Professions Code to act under the court's direction, notifying the party and the appointed attorney that the order, judgment, or other proceeding was taken against him or her and that any rights the party has to apply for relief under the provisions of the section shall expire 90 days after service of notice, then application for relief must be made within 90 days after service of the notice upon the defaulting party or the attorney appointed to act under the court's direction pursuant to Section 6180.5 of the Business and Professions Code, whichever service is later. No affidavit or declaration of merits shall be required of the moving party. **Leg.H.** Added Stats 1983 ch 254 §4. Amended Stats 1993 ch 589 §25 (AB 2211).

§473.5. Relief from judgment where summons does not result in actual notice

(a) When service of a summons has not resulted in actual notice to a party in time to defend the action and a default or default judgment has been entered against him or her in the action, he or she may serve and file a notice of motion to set aside the default or default judgment and for leave to defend the action. The notice of motion shall be served and filed within a reasonable time, but in no event exceeding the earlier of: (i) two years after entry of a default judgment against him or her; or (ii) 180 days after service on him or her of a written notice that the default or default judgment has been entered.

(b) A notice of motion to set aside a default or default judgment and for leave to defend the action shall designate as the time for making the motion a date prescribed by subdivision (b) of Section 1005, and it shall be accompanied by an affidavit showing under oath that the party's lack of actual notice in time to defend the action was not caused by his or her avoidance of service or inexcusable neglect. The party shall serve and file with the notice a copy of the answer, motion, or other pleading proposed to be filed in the action.

(c) Upon a finding by the court that the motion was made within the period permitted by subdivision (a) and that his or her lack of actual notice in time to defend the action was not caused by his or her avoidance of service or inexcusable neglect, it may set aside the default or default judgment on whatever terms as may be just and allow the party to defend the action. **Leg.H.** Added Stats 1969 ch 1610 §23, operative July 1, 1970. Amended Stats 1990 ch 1491 §5 (AB 3765).

§474. Fictitious names

When the plaintiff is ignorant of the name of a defendant, he must state that fact in the complaint, or the affidavit if the action is commenced by affidavit, and such defendant may be designated in any pleading or proceeding by any name, and when his true name is discovered, the pleading or proceeding must be amended accordingly; provided, that no default or default judgment shall be entered against a defendant so designated, unless it appears that the copy of the summons or other process, or, if there be no summons or process, the copy of the first pleading or notice served upon such defendant bore on the face thereof a notice stating in substance: "To the person served: You are hereby served in the within action (or proceedings) as (or on behalf of) the person sued under the fictitious name of (designating it)." The certificate or affidavit of service must state the fictitious name under which such defendant was served and the fact that notice of identity was given by endorsement upon the document served as required by this section. The foregoing requirements for entry of a default or default judgment shall be applicable only as to fictitious names designated pursuant to this section and not in the event the plaintiff has sued the defendant by an erroneous name and shall not be applicable to entry of a default or default judgment based upon service, in the manner otherwise provided by law, of an amended pleading, process or notice designating defendant by his true name. **Leg.H.** Enacted 1872. Amended Stats 1953 ch 1244 §1; Stats 1955 ch 886 §1.

§475. Effect of errors or defects

The court must, in every stage of an action, disregard any error, improper ruling, instruction, or defect, in the pleadings or proceedings which, in the opinion of said court, does not affect the substantial rights of the parties. No judgment, decision, or decree shall be reversed or affected by reason of any error, ruling, instruction, or defect, unless it shall appear from the record that such error, ruling, instruction, or defect was prejudicial, and also that by reason of such error, ruling, instruction, or defect, the said party complaining or appealing sustained and suffered substantial injury, and that a different result would have been probable if such error, ruling, instruction, or defect had not occurred or existed. There shall be no presumption that error is prejudicial, or that injury was done if error is shown. **Leg.H.** Enacted 1872. Amended Stats 1897 ch 47 §1.

§476. [Section renumbered 1933]

Leg.H. Added Code Amdts 1873–74 ch 383 §61. Amended and renumbered CCP §472b by Stats 1933 ch 744 §33.

§477. [Section repealed 1977]

Leg.H. Added Stats 1973 ch 20 §4. Repealed Stats 1974 ch 1516 §8, operative January 1, 1977. The repealed section related to provisional remedies not available in justice court.

Prior Law: Former CCP §477, similar to the repealed section, was added Stats 1933 ch 744 §36, amended Stats 1951 ch 1737 §58, operative January 1, 1952, and repealed Stats 1973 ch 20 §2.

§478. [Section repealed 1977]

Leg.H. Added Stats 1973 ch 20 §4. Repealed Stats 1974 ch 1516 §8, operative January 1, 1977. The repealed section related to no person to be arrested except as prescribed by this code.

Prior Law: Former CCP §478, relating to no person to be arrested except as prescribed by this code, was enacted 1872 and repealed Stats 1973 ch 20 §3.

§479. [Section repealed 1974]

Leg.H. Enacted 1872. Amended Code Amdts 1873–74 ch 383 §62. Repealed Stats 1973 ch 20 §3. The repealed section related to cases in which defendant may be arrested.

§480. [Section repealed 1974]

Leg.H. Enacted 1872. Amended Code Amdts 1880 ch 15 §1; Stats 1933 ch 744 §37; Stats 1951 ch 1737 §59, operative January 1, 1952. Repealed Stats 1973 ch 20 §3. The repealed section related to order for arrest.

§481. [Section repealed 1974]

Leg.H. Enacted 1872. Amended Code Amdts 1873–74 ch 383 §63; Stats 1933 ch 744 §38; Stats 1951 ch 1737 §60, operative January 1, 1952. Repealed Stats 1973 ch 20 §3. The repealed section related to when order may be made, affidavit, requisites and filing.

TITLE 6.5
ATTACHMENT

Chapter 1. Words and Phrases Defined.
Chapter 2. General Provisions.
Chapter 3. Actions in Which Attachment Authorized.
Chapter 4. Noticed Hearing Procedure for Obtaining Writ of Attachment.
Chapter 5. Ex Parte Hearing Procedure for Obtaining Writ of Attachment.
Chapter 6. Temporary Protective Order.
Chapter 7. Property Subject to Attachment.
Chapter 8. Levy Procedures; Lien of Attachment; Management and Disposition of Attached Property.
Chapter 9. Undertakings.
Chapter 10. Liability for Wrongful Attachment.
Chapter 11. Attaching Plaintiff's Miscellaneous Remedies.
Chapter 12. Nonresident Attachment.
Chapter 13. Effect of Bankruptcy Proceedings and General Assignments for The Benefit of Creditors.

CHAPTER 1
WORDS AND PHRASES DEFINED

Application of definitions. §481.010.
"Account debtor". §481.020.
"Account receivable". §481.030.
"Chattel paper". §481.040.
"Costs". §481.055.
"Complaint". §481.060.
"Defendant". §481.070.
"Deposit account". §481.080.
"Document of title". §481.090.
"Equipment". §481.100.
"Farm products". §481.110.
"Financial institution". §481.113.
"General intangibles". §481.115.
"Instrument". §481.117.
"Inventory". §481.120.
"Levying officer". §481.140.
"Person". §481.170.
"Personal property". §481.175.
"Plaintiff". §481.180.
"Probable validity". §481.190.
"Property". §481.195.
"Public entity". §481.200.
"Real property". §481.203.
"Registered process server". §481.205.
"Secured party". §481.207.
"Security". §481.210.
"Security agreement". §481.220.
"Security interest". §481.223.
"Tangible personal property". §481.225.

§481.010. Application of definitions
Unless the provision or context otherwise requires, the definitions in this chapter govern the construction of this title. **Leg.H.** Added Stats 1974 ch 1516 §9, operative January 1, 1977.

§481.020. "Account debtor"
"Account debtor" means "account debtor" as defined in paragraph (3) of subdivision (a) of Section 9102 of the Commercial Code. **Leg.H.** Added Stats 1974 ch 1516 §9, operative January 1, 1977. Amended Stats 1982 ch 1198 §1, operative July 1, 1983; Stats 1999 ch 991 §11.5 (SB 45), operative July 1, 2001.

§481.030. "Account receivable"
"Account receivable" means "account" as defined in paragraph (2) of subdivision (a) of Section 9102 of the Commercial Code. **Leg.H.** Added Stats 1974 ch 1516 §9, operative January 1, 1977. Amended Stats 1982 ch 1198 §2, operative July 1, 1983; Stats 1999 ch 991 §12 (SB 45), operative July 1, 2001.

§481.040. "Chattel paper"
"Chattel paper" means "chattel paper" as defined in paragraph (11) of subdivision (a) of Section 9102 of the Commercial Code. **Leg.H.** Added Stats 1974 ch 1516 §9, operative January 1, 1977. Amended Stats 1982 ch 1198 §3, operative July 1, 1983; Stats 1999 ch 991 §12.1 (SB 45), operative July 1, 2001.

§481.050. [Section repealed 1983]
Leg.H. Added Stats 1974 ch 1516 §9, operative January 1, 1977. Amended Stats 1976 ch 437 §1; Stats 1978 ch 273 §1. Repealed Stats 1982 ch 1198 §4, operative July 1, 1983. The repealed section defined "chose in action.".

§481.055. "Costs"
"Costs" means costs and disbursements, including, but not limited to, statutory fees, charges, commissions, and expenses. **Leg.H.** Added Stats 1982 ch 1198 §5, operative July 1, 1983.

§481.060. "Complaint"
"Complaint" includes a cross-complaint. **Leg.H.** Added Stats 1974 ch 1516 §9, operative January 1, 1977.

§481.070. "Defendant"
"Defendant" includes a cross-defendant. **Leg.H.** Added Stats 1974 ch 1516 §9, operative January 1, 1977.

§481.080. "Deposit account"
"Deposit account" means "deposit account" as defined in paragraph (29) of subdivision (a) of Section 9102 of the Commercial Code. **Leg.H.** Added Stats 1974 ch 1516 §9, operative January 1, 1977. Amended Stats 1982 ch 1198 §6, operative July 1, 1983; Stats 1999 ch 991 §12.2 (SB 45), operative July 1, 2001.

§481.090. "Document of title"
"Document of title" means "document" as defined in paragraph (30) of subdivision (a) of Section 9102 of the Commercial Code. A document of title is negotiable if it is negotiable within the meaning of Section 7104 of the Commercial Code. **Leg.H.** Added Stats 1974 ch 1516 §9, operative January 1, 1977. Amended Stats 1982 ch 1198 §7, operative July 1, 1983; Stats 1999 ch 991 §12.3 (SB 45), operative July 1, 2001.

§481.100. "Equipment"
"Equipment" means tangible personal property in the possession of the defendant and used or bought for use primarily in the defendant's trade, business, or profession if it is not included in the definitions of inventory or farm products. **Leg.H.** Added Stats 1974 ch 1516 §9, operative January 1, 1977.

§481.110. "Farm products"
"Farm products" means crops or livestock or supplies used or produced in farming operations or products of crops or livestock in their unmanufactured states (such as ginned cotton, wool clip, maple syrup, milk, and eggs), while in the possession of a defendant engaged in raising, fattening, grazing, or other farming operations. If tangible personal property is a farm product, it is neither equipment nor inventory. **Leg.H.** Added Stats 1974 ch 1516 §9, operative January 1, 1977. Amended Stats 1982 ch 1198 §8, operative July 1, 1983.

§481.113. "Financial institution"
"Financial institution" means a state or national bank, state or federal savings and loan association or credit union, or like organization, and includes a corporation engaged in a safe deposit business. **Leg.H.** Added Stats 1982 ch 1198 §9, operative July 1, 1983.

§481.115. "General intangibles"
"General intangibles" means "general intangibles," as defined in paragraph (42) of subdivision (a) of Section 9102 of the Commercial Code, consisting of rights to payment. **Leg.H.** Added Stats 1982 ch 1198 §10, operative July 1, 1983. Amended Stats 1999 ch 991 §13 (SB 45), operative July 1, 2001.

§481.117. "Instrument"
"Instrument" means "instrument" as defined in paragraph (47) of subdivision (a) of Section 9102 of the Commercial Code. **Leg.H.** Added Stats 1982 ch 1198 §11, operative July 1, 1983. Amended Stats 1999 ch 991 §13.1 (SB 45), operative July 1, 2001.

§481.120. "Inventory"
"Inventory" means tangible personal property in the possession of a defendant that (a) is held by the defendant for sale or lease or to be

furnished under contracts of service or (b) is raw materials, work in process, or materials used or consumed in his trade, business, or profession. Inventory of a person is not to be classified as his equipment. **Leg.H.** Added Stats 1974 ch 1516 §9, operative January 1, 1977.

§481.140. "Levying officer"
"Levying officer" means the sheriff or marshal who is directed to execute a writ or order issued under this title. **Leg.H.** Added Stats 1974 ch 1516 §9, operative January 1, 1977. Amended Stats 1996 ch 872 §12 (AB 3472).

§§481.150, 481.160. [Sections repealed 1983]
Leg.H. Added Stats 1974 ch 1516 §9, operative January 1, 1977. Repealed Stats 1982 ch 1198 §§12, 13, operative July 1, 1983. The repealed sections defined "motor vehicle" and "negotiable instrument.".

§481.170. "Person"
"Person" includes a natural person, a corporation, a partnership or other unincorporated association, a limited liability company, and a public entity. **Leg.H.** Added Stats 1974 ch 1516 §9, operative January 1, 1977. Amended Stats 1982 ch 1198 §14, operative July 1, 1983; Stats 1994 ch 1010 §58 (SB 2053).

§481.175. "Personal property"
"Personal property" includes both tangible and intangible personal property. **Leg.H.** Added Stats 1982 ch 1198 §15, operative July 1, 1983.

§481.180. "Plaintiff"
"Plaintiff" means a person who files a complaint or cross-complaint. **Leg.H.** Added Stats 1974 ch 1516 §9, operative January 1, 1977.

§481.190. "Probable validity"
A claim has "probable validity" where it is more likely than not that the plaintiff will obtain a judgment against the defendant on that claim. **Leg.H.** Added Stats 1974 ch 1516 §9, operative January 1, 1977.

§481.195. "Property"
"Property" includes real and personal property and any interest therein. **Leg.H.** Added Stats 1982 ch 1198 §16, operative July 1, 1983.

§481.200. "Public entity"
"Public entity" includes the state, the Regents of the University of California, a county, a city, district, public authority, public agency, and any other political subdivision or public corporation in the state. **Leg.H.** Added Stats 1974 ch 1516 §9, operative January 1, 1977.

§481.203. "Real property"
"Real property" includes any right in real property, including, but not limited to, a leasehold interest in real property. **Leg.H.** Added Stats 1982 ch 1198 §17, operative July 1, 1983.

§481.205. "Registered process server"
"Registered process server" means a person registered as a process server pursuant to Chapter 16 (commencing with Section 22350) of Division 8 of the Business and Professions Code. **Leg.H.** Added Stats 1982 ch 1198 §18, operative July 1, 1983.

§481.207. "Secured party"
"Secured party" means "secured party" as defined in paragraph (73) of subdivision (a) of Section 9102 of the Commercial Code. **Leg.H.** Added Stats 1982 ch 1198 §19, operative July 1, 1983. Amended Stats 1999 ch 991 §13.2 (SB 45), operative July 1, 2001; Stats 2013 ch 531 §2 (AB 502), effective January 1, 2014, operative July 1, 2014.

§481.210. "Security"
"Security" means a "security" as defined by Section 8102 of the Commercial Code. **Leg.H.** Added Stats 1974 ch 1516 §9, operative January 1, 1977.

§481.220. "Security agreement"
"Security agreement" means a "security agreement" as defined by paragraph (74) of subdivision (a) of Section 9102 of the Commercial Code. **Leg.H.** Added Stats 1974 ch 1516 §9, operative January 1, 1977. Amended Stats 1999 ch 991 §13.3 (SB 45), operative July 1, 2001; Stats 2013 ch 531 §3 (AB 502), effective January 1, 2014, operative July 1, 2014.

§481.223. "Security interest"
"Security interest" means "security interest" as defined in Section 1201 of the Commercial Code. **Leg.H.** Added Stats 1982 ch 1198 §20, operative July 1, 1983.

§481.225. "Tangible personal property"
"Tangible personal property" includes chattel paper, documents of title, instruments, securities, and money. **Leg.H.** Added Stats 1982 ch 1198 §21, operative July 1, 1983.

§481.230. [Section repealed 1983]
Leg.H. Added Stats 1974 ch 1516 §9, operative January 1, 1977. Repealed Stats 1982 ch 1198 §22, operative July 1, 1983. The repealed section defined "vessel".

§482. [Section repealed 1974]
Leg.H. Enacted 1872. Amended Code Amdts 1873–74 ch 383 §64; Stats 1933 ch 744 §39; Stats 1951 ch 1737 §61, operative January 1, 1952. Repealed Stats 1973 ch 20 §3. The repealed section related to undertaking.

CHAPTER 2
GENERAL PROVISIONS

Short title. §482.010.
Injunctive relief not precluded. §482.020.
Rules for practice and procedure; Forms. §482.030.
General requirements for affidavits. §482.040.
Secrecy prior to return of service; Request; Exception. §482.050.
Subordinate judicial duties; Exceptions. §482.060.
Method of service. §482.070.
Order directing transfer of property or documents by defendant. §482.080.
Issuance of multiple and duplicate writs. §482.090.
Post-levy exemption claims based on change in circumstances. §482.100.
Attachment may include amount for costs and attorney's fees. §482.110.
Determination of order of levy; order restricting attachment. §482.120.

§482.010. Short title
This title shall be known and may be cited as "The Attachment Law." **Leg.H.** Added Stats 1974 ch 1516 §9, operative January 1, 1977.

§482.020. Injunctive relief not precluded
Nothing in this title precludes the granting of relief pursuant to Chapter 3 (commencing with Section 525) of Title 7. **Leg.H.** Added Stats 1974 ch 1516 §9, operative January 1, 1977.

§482.030. Rules for practice and procedure; Forms
(a) The Judicial Council may provide by rule for the practice and procedure in proceedings under this title.

(b) The Judicial Council shall prescribe the form of the applications, notices, orders, and other documents required by this title. **Leg.H.** Added Stats 1974 ch 1516 §9, operative January 1, 1977.

§482.040. General requirements for affidavits
The facts stated in each affidavit filed pursuant to this title shall be set forth with particularity. Except where matters are specifically permitted by this title to be shown by information and belief, each affidavit shall show affirmatively that the affiant, if sworn as a witness, can testify competently to the facts stated therein. As to matters shown by information and belief, the affidavit shall state the facts on which the affiant's belief is based, showing the nature of his information and the reliability of his informant. The affiant may be any person, whether or not a party to the action, who has knowledge of the facts. A verified complaint that satisfies the requirements of this section may be used in lieu of or in addition to an affidavit. **Leg.H.** Added Stats 1974 ch 1516 §9, operative January 1, 1977.

§482.050. Secrecy prior to return of service; Request; Exception
(a) If the plaintiff so requests in writing at the time he files his complaint, the clerk of the court with whom the complaint is filed shall not make available to the public the records and documents in such action before either (1) 30 days after the filing of the complaint or (2) the filing pursuant to this title of the return of service of the notice of hearing and any temporary protective order, or of the writ of attachment if issued without notice, whichever event occurs first.

(b) Notwithstanding subdivision (a), the clerk of the court shall make the entire file in the action available for inspection at any time to any party named in the complaint or to his attorney.

(c) The request by plaintiff that the fact of filing of a complaint or application for relief not be made public may take the form of a notation to that effect, made by rubber stamp or other suitable means, at the top of the first page of the complaint filed with the clerk. **Leg.H.** Added Stats 1974 ch 1516 §9, operative January 1, 1977.

§482.060. Subordinate judicial duties; Exceptions

(a) Except as otherwise provided in subdivision (b), the judicial duties to be performed under this title are subordinate judicial duties within the meaning of Section 22 of Article VI of the California Constitution and may be performed by appointed officers such as court commissioners.

(b) The judicial duties to be performed in the determination of the following matters are not subordinate judicial duties:

(1) A contested claim of exemption.

(2) A contested motion for determination of the liability and damages for wrongful attachment.

(3) A contested third-party claim.

(4) A contested proceeding to enforce a third person's liability.

(c) Nothing in subdivision (b) limits the power of a court to appoint a temporary judge pursuant to Section 21 of Article VI of the California Constitution. **Leg.H.** Added Stats 1978 ch 151 §1. Amended Stats 1982 ch 1198 §23, operative July 1, 1983.

§482.070. Method of service

(a)(1) Except as otherwise provided in this title, legal process required or permitted to be served under this title may be served personally or by mail.

(2) For purposes of this title, the term "legal process" shall refer to each and all of the writs, notices, orders, or other papers required or permitted to be served pursuant to this title.

(b) Except as otherwise provided in this section, service of legal process under this title is governed by Article 1 (commencing with Section 684.010) and Article 2 (commencing with Section 684.110) of Chapter 4 of Division 1 of Title 9, including the provisions of Section 684.120 extending time when service is made by mail.

(c) For the purpose of subdivision (b), in Article 1 (commencing with Section 684.010) and Article 2 (commencing with Section 684.110) of Chapter 4 of Division 1 of Title 9:

(1) References to the "judgment debtor" shall be deemed references to the defendant.

(2) References to the "judgment creditor" shall be deemed references to the plaintiff.

(3) References to a "writ" shall be deemed references to a writ of attachment.

(4) References to a "notice of levy" shall be deemed references to a notice of attachment.

(d) If the defendant has not appeared in the action and legal process is required to be personally served on the defendant under this title, service shall be made in the same manner as a summons is served under Chapter 4 (commencing with Section 413.10) of Title 5.

(e) Except for service of a subpoena or other process to require the attendance of the defendant or service of a paper to bring the defendant into contempt, if the defendant has an attorney of record in the action, service shall be made on the attorney rather than on the defendant.

(f) Proof of service under this title is governed by Article 3 (commencing with Section 684.210) of Chapter 4 of Division 1 of Title 9. **Leg.H.** Added Stats 1974 ch 1516 §9, operative January 1, 1977. Amended Stats 1982 ch 1198 §24, operative July 1, 1983; Stats 2012 ch 484 §1 (AB 2364), effective January 1, 2013.

§482.080. Order directing transfer of property or documents by defendant

(a) If a writ of attachment is issued, the court may also issue an order directing the defendant to transfer to the levying officer either or both of the following:

(1) Possession of the property to be attached if the property is sought to be attached by taking it into custody.

(2) Possession of documentary evidence of title to property of or a debt owed to the defendant that is sought to be attached. An order pursuant to this paragraph may be served when the property or debt is levied upon or thereafter.

(b) The order shall be personally served on the defendant and shall contain a notice to the defendant that failure to comply with the order may subject the defendant to arrest and punishment for contempt of court. **Leg.H.** Added Stats 1974 ch 1516 §9, operative January 1, 1977. Amended Stats 1976 ch 437 §2; Stats 1982 ch 1198 §25, operative July 1, 1983.

§482.090. Issuance of multiple and duplicate writs

(a) Several writs in the same form may be issued simultaneously or from time to time upon the same undertaking, whether or not any writ previously issued has been returned.

(b) After the return of the writ of attachment, or upon the filing by the plaintiff of an affidavit setting forth the loss of the writ of attachment, the clerk, upon demand of the plaintiff at any time before judgment, may issue an alias writ which shall be in the same form as the original without requirement of a new undertaking.

(c) The date of issuance of a writ of attachment shall be deemed to be the date the writ is first issued. **Leg.H.** Added Stats 1974 ch 1516 §9, operative January 1, 1977.

§482.100. Post-levy exemption claims based on change in circumstances

(a) The defendant may claim an exemption provided in Section 487.020 for property levied upon pursuant to a writ issued under this title if the right to the exemption is the result of a change in circumstances occurring after (1) the denial of a claim of exemption for the property earlier in the action or (2) the expiration of the time for claiming the exemption earlier in the action.

(b) A claim of exemption under this section shall follow the procedure provided in Article 2 (commencing with Section 703.510) of Chapter 4 of Division 2 of Title 9 except that, subject to subdivision (a), the defendant may claim the exemption at any time. For this purpose, references in Article 2 (commencing with Section 703.510) of Chapter 4 of Division 2 of Title 9 to the "judgment debtor" shall be deemed references to the defendant, and references to the "judgment creditor" shall be deemed references to the plaintiff.

(c) The exemption provided by subdivision (b) of Section 487.020 may be claimed at the defendant's option either pursuant to subdivision (b) of this section or by following the procedure provided in this subdivision. The claim shall be made by filing with the court and serving on the plaintiff a notice of motion. Service on the plaintiff shall be made not less than three days prior to the date set for the hearing. The hearing shall be held not more than five days after the filing of the notice of motion unless, for good cause shown, the court orders otherwise. The notice of motion shall state the relief requested and shall be accompanied by an affidavit supporting any factual issues raised and points and authorities supporting any legal issues raised. At the hearing on the motion, the defendant has the burden of showing that the property is exempt pursuant to subdivision (b) of Section 487.020. Upon this showing and the showing required by subdivision (a), the court shall order the release of the property. **Leg.H.** Added Stats 1976 ch 437 §3. Amended Stats 1982 ch 1198 §26, operative July 1, 1983.

§482.110. Attachment may include amount for costs and attorney's fees

(a) The plaintiff's application for a right to attach order and a writ of attachment pursuant to this title may include an estimate of the costs and allowable attorney's fees.

(b) In the discretion of the court, the amount to be secured by the attachment may include an estimated amount for costs and allowable attorney's fees. **Leg.H.** Added Stats 1976 ch 437 §4.

§482.120. Determination of order of levy; order restricting attachment

If the court determines at the hearing on issuance of a writ of attachment under this title that the value of the defendant's interest in the property described in the plaintiff's application clearly exceeds the amount necessary to satisfy the amount to be secured by the attachment, the court may direct the order of levy on the property described in the writ or restrict the amount of the property to be levied upon. **Leg.H.** Added Stats 1976 ch 437 §5.

§483. [Section repealed 1974]

Leg.H. Enacted 1872. Amended Stats 1933 ch 744 §40; Stats 1951 ch 1737 §62, operative January 1, 1952; Stats 1969 ch 690 §1. Repealed Stats 1973 ch 20 §3. The repealed section related to order and arrest.

CHAPTER 3
ACTIONS IN WHICH ATTACHMENT AUTHORIZED

Rights and duties of secured party. §483.010.
Remedy not action to recover debt for foreclosure. §483.012.

Benefits awarded to veterans for service-connected disabilities; Exemptions. §483.013.
Amount to be secured by attachment. §483.015.
Amount secured by attachment in unlawful detainer proceeding. §483.020.

§483.010. Rights and duties of secured party

(a) Except as otherwise provided by statute, an attachment may be issued only in an action on a claim or claims for money, each of which is based upon a contract, express or implied, where the total amount of the claim or claims is a fixed or readily ascertainable amount not less than five hundred dollars ($500) exclusive of costs, interest, and attorney's fees.

(b) An attachment may not be issued on a claim which is secured by any interest in real property arising from agreement, statute, or other rule of law (including any mortgage or deed of trust of realty and any statutory, common law, or equitable lien on real property, but excluding any security interest in fixtures subject to Division 9 (commencing with Section 9101) of the Commercial Code). However, an attachment may be issued where the claim was originally so secured but, without any act of the plaintiff or the person to whom the security was given, the security has become valueless or has decreased in value to less than the amount then owing on the claim, in which event the amount to be secured by the attachment shall not exceed the lesser of the amount of the decrease or the difference between the value of the security and the amount then owing on the claim.

(c) If the action is against a defendant who is a natural person, an attachment may be issued only on a claim which arises out of the conduct by the defendant of a trade, business, or profession. An attachment may not be issued on a claim against a defendant who is a natural person if the claim is based on the sale or lease of property, a license to use property, the furnishing of services, or the loan of money where the property sold or leased, or licensed for use, the services furnished, or the money loaned was used by the defendant primarily for personal, family, or household purposes.

(d) An attachment may be issued pursuant to this section whether or not other forms of relief are demanded. **Leg.H.** Added Stats 1974 ch 1516 §9, operative January 1, 1977. Amended Stats 1976 ch 437 §6, Stats 1982 ch 1198 §27, operative July 1, 1983; Stats 1990 ch 943 §1 (SB 2170), operative until January 1, 1996; Stats 1993 ch 589 §26 (AB 2211), operative until January 1, 1996; Stats 1995 ch 591 §1 (AB 1689), operative until January 1, 1998; Stats 1997 ch 222 §1 (AB 1258).

Former Sections: Former CCP §483.010, similar to the present section, was added Stats 1990 ch 943 §1.5, operative January 1, 1996, and repealed Stats 1997 ch 222 §2.

Prior Law: Former CCP §483.010, similar to the present section, was added Stats 1990 ch 943 §1.5, operative January 1, 1996, amended Stats 1995 ch 591 §2, operative January 1, 1998, and repealed Stats 1997 ch 222 §2.

§483.012. Remedy not action to recover debt for foreclosure

Subject to the restrictions of Sections 580b and 580d, in an action to foreclose a mortgage or deed of trust on real property or an estate for years therein, pursuit of any remedy provided by this title shall not constitute an action for the recovery of a debt for purposes of subdivision (a) of Section 726 or a failure to comply with any other statutory or judicial requirement to proceed first against security. **Leg.H.** Added Stats 1997 ch 222 §3 (AB 1258).

§483.013. Benefits awarded to veterans for service-connected disabilities; Exemptions

Notwithstanding Section 483.010, federal disability benefits awarded to veterans for service-connected disabilities pursuant to Chapter 11 of Title 38 of the United States Code shall be exempt from the claim of creditors, and shall not be liable to attachment, levy, or seizure by or under any legal or equitable process whatsoever, as provided by federal law. This section does not apply to that portion of service-connected disability benefits that are subject to child and spousal support enforcement under Section 659(h)(1)(A)(ii)(V) of Title 42 of the United States Code. **Leg.H.** Added Stats 2009 ch 162 §2 (SB 285), effective January 1, 2010.

2009 Note: It is the intent of the Legislature to enact legislation to conform to existing federal law, which provides that payments or benefits due to a veteran for a service-connected disability shall be exempt from creditor claims, and shall not be liable to attachment, levy, or seizure by or under any legal or equitable process. Stats 2009 ch 162 (SB 285) §1.

§483.015. Amount to be secured by attachment

(a) Subject to subdivision (b) and to Section 483.020, the amount to be secured by an attachment is the sum of the following:

(1) The amount of the defendant's indebtedness claimed by the plaintiff.

(2) Any additional amount included by the court under Section 482.110.

(b) The amount described in subdivision (a) shall be reduced by the sum of the following:

(1) The amount of any money judgment in favor of the defendant and against the plaintiff that remains unsatisfied and is enforceable.

(2) The amount of any indebtedness of the plaintiff that the defendant has claimed in a cross-complaint filed in the action if the defendant's claim is one upon which an attachment could be issued.

(3) The amount of any claim of the defendant asserted as a defense in the answer pursuant to Section 431.70 if the defendant's claim is one upon which an attachment could be issued had an action been brought on the claim when it was not barred by the statute of limitations.

(4) The value of any security interest in the property of the defendant held by the plaintiff to secure the defendant's indebtedness claimed by the plaintiff, together with the amount by which the value of the security interest has decreased due to the act of the plaintiff or a prior holder of the security interest. **Leg.H.** Added Stats 1982 ch 1198 §28, operative July 1, 1983. Amended Stats 1983 ch 155 §1, effective June 30, 1983, operative July 1, 1983; Stats 1990 ch 943 §2 (SB 2170), operative until January 1, 1996; Stats 1993 ch 589 §27 (AB 2211), operative until January 1, 1996; Stats 1995 ch 591 §3 (AB 1689), operative until January 1, 1998; Stats 1997 ch 222 §4 (AB 1258).

Former Sections: Former CCP §483.015, similar to the present section, was added Stats 1990 ch 943 §2.5, operative January 1, 1998, and repealed Stats 1997 ch 222 §5.

Prior Law: Former CCP §483.015, similar to the present section, was added Stats 1990 ch 943 §2.5, operative January 1, 1998, amended Stats 1995 ch 591 §4, operative January 1, 1998, and repealed Stats 1997 ch 222 §5.

§483.020. Amount secured by attachment in unlawful detainer proceeding

(a) Subject to subdivisions (d) and (e), the amount to be secured by the attachment in an unlawful detainer proceeding is the sum of the following:

(1) The amount of the rent due and unpaid as of the date of filing the complaint in the unlawful detainer proceeding.

(2) Any additional amount included by the court under subdivision (c).

(3) Any additional amount included by the court under Section 482.110.

(b) In an unlawful detainer proceeding, the plaintiff's application for a right to attach order and a writ of attachment pursuant to this title may include (in addition to the rent due and unpaid as of the date of the filing of the complaint and any additional estimated amount authorized by Section 482.110) an amount equal to the rent for the period from the date the complaint is filed until the estimated date of judgment or such earlier estimated date as possession has been or is likely to be delivered to the plaintiff, such amount to be computed at the rate provided in the lease.

(c) The amount to be secured by the attachment in the unlawful detainer proceeding may, in the discretion of the court, include an additional amount equal to the amount of rent for the period from the date the complaint is filed until the estimated date of judgment or such earlier estimated date as possession has been or is likely to be delivered to the plaintiff, such amount to be computed at the rate provided in the lease.

(d) Except as provided in subdivision (e), the amount to be secured by the attachment as otherwise determined under this section shall be reduced by the amounts described in subdivision (b) of Section 483.015.

(e) Where the plaintiff has received a payment or holds a deposit to secure (1) the payment of rent and the performance of other obligations under the lease or (2) only the performance of other obligations under the lease, the amount of the payment or deposit shall not be subtracted in determining the amount to be secured by the attachment. **Leg.H.** Added Stats 1978 ch 273 §2. Amended Stats 1982 ch 1198 §29, operative July 1, 1983; Stats 1997 ch 222 §6 (AB 1258).

§484. [Section repealed 1974]

Leg.H. Enacted 1872. Amended Stats 1933 ch 744 §41; Stats 1969 ch 690 §2. Repealed Stats 1973 ch 20 §3. The repealed section related to copy of order served on arrest.

CHAPTER 4
NOTICED HEARING PROCEDURE FOR OBTAINING WRIT OF ATTACHMENT

Article 1. Right to Attach Order; Issuance of Writ of Attachment.

Article 2. Noticed Hearing Procedure for Obtaining Additional Writs.
Article 3. Ex Parte Procedure for Obtaining Additional Writs.

ARTICLE 1
Right to Attach Order; Issuance of Writ of Attachment

Application for order and writ. §484.010.
Contents of application. §484.020.
Supporting affidavit. §484.030.
Notice to defendant. §484.040.
Contents of notice of application and hearing. §484.050.
Notice of opposition and supporting affidavit. §484.060.
Claim of exemption and supporting affidavit; Notice of opposition. §484.070.
Readiness for hearing; Continuance. §484.080.
Hearing; Issuance of order and writ. §484.090.
Effect of court's determinations. §484.100.
Defendant's defense of action on claim not affected. §484.110.

§484.010. Application for order and writ

Upon the filing of the complaint or at any time thereafter, the plaintiff may apply pursuant to this article for a right to attach order and a writ of attachment by filing an application for the order and writ with the court in which the action is brought. **Leg.H.** Added Stats 1974 ch 1516 §9, operative January 1, 1977.

§484.020. Contents of application

The application shall be executed under oath and shall include all of the following:

(a) A statement showing that the attachment is sought to secure the recovery on a claim upon which an attachment may be issued.

(b) A statement of the amount to be secured by the attachment.

(c) A statement that the attachment is not sought for a purpose other than the recovery on the claim upon which the attachment is based.

(d) A statement that the applicant has no information or belief that the claim is discharged in a proceeding under Title 11 of the United States Code (Bankruptcy) or that the prosecution of the action is stayed in a proceeding under Title 11 of the United States Code (Bankruptcy).

(e) A description of the property to be attached under the writ of attachment and a statement that the plaintiff is informed and believes that such property is subject to attachment. Where the defendant is a corporation, a reference to "all corporate property which is subject to attachment pursuant to subdivision (a) of Code of Civil Procedure Section 487.010" satisfies the requirements of this subdivision. Where the defendant is a partnership or other unincorporated association, a reference to "all property of the partnership or other unincorporated association which is subject to attachment pursuant to subdivision (b) of Code of Civil Procedure Section 487.010" satisfies the requirements of this subdivision. Where the defendant is a natural person, the description of the property shall be reasonably adequate to permit the defendant to identify the specific property sought to be attached. **Leg.H.** Added Stats 1974 ch 1516 §9, operative January 1, 1977. Amended Stats 1982 ch 1198 §30, operative July 1, 1983.

§484.030. Supporting affidavit

The application shall be supported by an affidavit showing that the plaintiff on the facts presented would be entitled to a judgment on the claim upon which the attachment is based. **Leg.H.** Added Stats 1974 ch 1516 §9, operative January 1, 1977.

§484.040. Notice to defendant

No order or writ shall be issued under this article except after a hearing. At the times prescribed by subdivision (b) of Section 1005, the defendant shall be served with all of the following:

(a) A copy of the summons and complaint.

(b) A notice of application and hearing.

(c) A copy of the application and of any affidavit in support of the application. **Leg.H.** Added Stats 1974 ch 1516 §9, operative January 1, 1977. Amended Stats 1989 ch 693 §2.

§484.050. Contents of notice of application and hearing

The notice of application and hearing shall inform the defendant of all of the following:

(a) A hearing will be held at a place and at a time, to be specified in the notice, on plaintiff's application for a right to attach order and a writ of attachment.

(b) The order will be issued if the court finds that the plaintiff's claim is probably valid and the other requirements for issuing the order are established. The hearing is not for the purpose of determining whether the claim is actually valid. The determination of the actual validity of the claim will be made in subsequent proceedings in the action and will not be affected by the decisions at the hearing on the application for the order.

(c) The amount to be secured by the attachment is determined pursuant to Sections 482.110, 483.010, 483.015, and 483.020, which statutes shall be summarized in the notice.

(d) If the right to attach order is issued, a writ of attachment will be issued to attach the property described in the plaintiff's application unless the court determines that such property is exempt from attachment or that its value clearly exceeds the amount necessary to satisfy the amount to be secured by the attachment. However, additional writs of attachment may be issued to attach other nonexempt property of the defendant on the basis of the right to attach order.

(e) If the defendant desires to oppose the issuance of the order, the defendant shall file with the court and serve on the plaintiff a notice of opposition and supporting affidavit as required by Section 484.060 not later than five court days prior to the date set for hearing.

(f) If the defendant claims that the personal property described in the application, or a portion thereof, is exempt from attachment, the defendant shall include that claim in the notice of opposition filed and served pursuant to Section 484.060 or file and serve a separate claim of exemption with respect to the property as provided in Section 484.070. If the defendant does not do so, the claim of exemption will be barred in the absence of a showing of a change in circumstances occurring after the expiration of the time for claiming exemptions.

(g) The defendant may obtain a determination at the hearing whether real or personal property not described in the application or real property described in the application is exempt from attachment by including the claim in the notice of opposition filed and served pursuant to Section 484.060 or by filing and serving a separate claim of exemption with respect to the property as provided in Section 484.070, but the failure to so claim that the property is exempt from attachment will not preclude the defendant from making a claim of exemption with respect to the property at a later time.

(h) Either the defendant or the defendant's attorney or both of them may be present at the hearing.

(i) The notice shall contain the following statement: "You may seek the advice of an attorney as to any matter connected with the plaintiff's application. The attorney should be consulted promptly so that the attorney may assist you before the time set for hearing." **Leg.H.** Added Stats 1974 ch 1516 §9, operative January 1, 1977. Amended Stats 1976 ch 437 §7; Stats 1982 ch 1198 §31, operative July 1, 1983; Stats 1983 ch 155 §2, effective June 30, 1983, operative July 1, 1983; Stats 1994 ch 587 §4 (AB 3600); Stats 1997 ch 222 §7 (AB 1258).

§484.060. Notice of opposition and supporting affidavit

(a) If the defendant desires to oppose the issuance of the right to attach order sought by plaintiff or objects to the amount sought to be secured by the attachment, the defendant shall file and serve upon the plaintiff no later than five court days prior to the date set for the hearing a notice of opposition. The notice shall state the grounds on which the defendant opposes the issuance of the order or objects to the amount sought to be secured by the attachment and shall be accompanied by an affidavit supporting any factual issues raised and points and authorities supporting any legal issues raised. If the defendant fails to file a notice of opposition within the time prescribed, the defendant shall not be permitted to oppose the issuance of the order.

(b) If a defendant filing a notice of opposition desires to make any claim of exemption as provided in Section 484.070, the defendant may include that claim in the notice of opposition filed pursuant to this section.

(c) The plaintiff may file and serve upon the opposing party a reply two court days prior to the date set for the hearing. **Leg.H.** Added Stats 1974 ch 1516 §9, operative January 1, 1977. Amended Stats 1983 ch 155 §3, effective June 30, 1983, operative July 1, 1983; Stats 1990 ch 1491 §6 (AB 3765).

§484.070. Claim of exemption and supporting affidavit; Notice of opposition

(a) If the defendant claims that the personal property described in the plaintiff's application, or a portion of such property, is exempt from attachment, the defendant shall claim the exemption as provided in this section. If the defendant fails to make the claim or makes the claim but fails to prove that the personal property is exempt, the defendant may not later claim the exemption except as provided in Section 482.100.

(b) If the defendant desires to claim at the hearing that real or personal property not described in the plaintiff's application or real property described in the plaintiff's application is exempt from attachment, in whole or in part, the defendant shall claim the exemption as provided in this section. Failure to make the claim does not preclude the defendant from later claiming the exemption. If the claim is made as provided in this section but the defendant fails to prove that the property is exempt from attachment, the defendant may not later claim that the property, or a portion thereof, is exempt except as provided in Section 482.100.

(c) The claim of exemption shall:

(1) Describe the property claimed to be exempt.

(2) Specify the statute section supporting the claim.

(d) The claim of exemption shall be accompanied by an affidavit supporting any factual issues raised by the claim and points and authorities supporting any legal issues raised.

(e) The claim of exemption, together with any supporting affidavit and points and authorities, shall be filed and served on the plaintiff not less than five court days before the date set for the hearing.

(f) If the plaintiff desires to oppose the claim of exemption, the plaintiff shall file and serve on the defendant, not less than two days before the date set for the hearing, a notice of opposition to the claim of exemption, accompanied by an affidavit supporting any factual issues raised and points and authorities supporting any legal issues raised. If the plaintiff does not file and serve a notice of opposition as provided in this subdivision, no writ of attachment shall be issued as to the property claimed to be exempt. If all of the property described in the plaintiff's application is claimed to be exempt and the plaintiff does not file and serve a notice of opposition as provided in this subdivision, no hearing shall be held and no right to attach order or writ of attachment shall be issued and any temporary protective order issued pursuant to Chapter 6 (commencing with Section 486.010) immediately expires.

(g) If the plaintiff files and serves a notice of opposition to the claim as provided in this section, the defendant has the burden of proving that the property is exempt from attachment. **Leg.H.** Added Stats 1974 ch 1516 §9, operative January 1, 1977. Amended Stats 1976 ch 437 §8; Stats 1982 ch 1198 §32, operative July 1, 1983; Stats 1998 ch 932 §14 (AB 1094).

§484.080. Readiness for hearing; Continuance

(a) At the time set for the hearing, the plaintiff shall be ready to proceed. If the plaintiff is not ready, or if he has failed to comply with Section 484.040, the court may either deny the application for the order or, for good cause shown, grant the plaintiff a continuance for a reasonable period. If such a continuance is granted, the effective period of any protective order issued pursuant to Chapter 6 (commencing with Section 486.010) may be extended by the court for a period ending not more than 10 days after the new hearing date if the plaintiff shows a continuing need for such protective order.

(b) The court may, in its discretion and for good cause shown, grant the defendant a continuance for a reasonable period to enable him to oppose the issuance of the right to attach order. If such a continuance is granted, the court shall extend the effective period of any protective order issued pursuant to Chapter 6 (commencing with Section 486.010) for a period ending not more than 10 days after the new hearing date unless the defendant shows pursuant to Section 486.100 that the protective order should be modified or vacated. **Leg.H.** Added Stats 1974 ch 1516 §9, operative January 1, 1977.

§484.090. Hearing; Issuance of order and writ

(a) At the hearing, the court shall consider the showing made by the parties appearing and shall issue a right to attach order, which shall state the amount to be secured by the attachment determined by the court in accordance with Section 483.015 or 483.020, if it finds all of the following:

(1) The claim upon which the attachment is based is one upon which an attachment may be issued.

(2) The plaintiff has established the probable validity of the claim upon which the attachment is based.

(3) The attachment is not sought for a purpose other than the recovery on the claim upon which the attachment is based.

(4) The amount to be secured by the attachment is greater than zero.

(b) If, in addition to the findings required by subdivision (a), the court finds that the defendant has failed to prove that all the property sought to be attached is exempt from attachment, it shall order a writ of attachment to be issued upon the filing of an undertaking as provided by Sections 489.210 and 489.220.

(c) If the court determines that property of the defendant is exempt from attachment, in whole or in part, the right to attach order shall describe the exempt property and prohibit attachment of the property.

(d) The court's determinations shall be made upon the basis of the pleadings and other papers in the record; but, upon good cause shown, the court may receive and consider at the hearing additional evidence, oral or documentary, and additional points and authorities, or it may continue the hearing for the production of the additional evidence or points and authorities. **Leg.H.** Added Stats 1974 ch 1516 §9, operative January 1, 1977. Amended Stats 1976 ch 437 §9; Stats 1982 ch 1198 §33, operative July 1, 1983; Stats 1997 ch 222 §8 (AB 1258).

§484.100. Effect of court's determinations

The court's determinations under this chapter shall have no effect on the determination of any issues in the action other than issues relevant to proceedings under this chapter nor shall they affect the rights of the plaintiff or defendant in any other action arising out of the same claim of the plaintiff or defendant. The court's determinations under this chapter shall not be given in evidence nor referred to at the trial of any such action. **Leg.H.** Added Stats 1974 ch 1516 §9, operative January 1, 1977. Amended Stats 1982 ch 1198 §34, operative July 1, 1983.

§484.110. Defendant's defense of action on claim not affected

(a) Neither the failure of the defendant to oppose the issuance of a right to attach order under this chapter nor the defendant's failure to rebut any evidence produced by the plaintiff in connection with proceedings under this chapter shall constitute a waiver of any defense to the plaintiff's claim in the action or any other action or have any effect on the right of the defendant to produce or exclude evidence at the trial of any such action.

(b) Neither the failure of the plaintiff to oppose the issuance of an order reducing the amount to be secured by the attachment under this chapter nor the plaintiff's failure to rebut any evidence produced by the defendant in connection with proceedings under this chapter shall constitute a waiver of any defense to the defendant's claim in the action or any other action or have any effect on the right of the plaintiff to produce or exclude evidence at the trial of any such action. **Leg.H.** Added Stats 1974 ch 1516 §9, operative January 1, 1977. Amended Stats 1982 ch 1198 §35, operative July 1, 1983.

ARTICLE 2
Noticed Hearing Procedure for Obtaining Additional Writs

Application. §484.310.
Contents of application. §484.320.
Notice to defendant. §484.330.
Contents of notice of application and hearing. §484.340.
Claim of exemption and supporting affidavit. §484.350.
Plaintiff's notice of opposition. §484.360.
Hearing; issuance of writ. §484.370.

§484.310. Application

At any time after a right to attach order has been issued under Article 1 (commencing with Section 484.010) or after the court has found pursuant to Section 485.240 that the plaintiff is entitled to a right to attach order, the plaintiff may apply for a writ of attachment under this article by filing an application with the court in which the action is brought. **Leg.H.** Added Stats 1974 ch 1516 §9, operative January 1, 1977.

§484.320. Contents of application

The application shall be executed under oath and shall include all of the following:

(a) A statement that the plaintiff has been issued a right to attach order under Article 1 (commencing with Section 484.010) or that the court has found pursuant to Section 485.240 that the plaintiff is entitled to a right to attach order.

(b) A statement of the amount to be secured by the attachment.

(c) A description of the property to be attached under the writ of attachment and a statement that the plaintiff is informed and believes that the property is subject to attachment. The description shall satisfy the requirements of Section 484.020.

(d) A statement that the applicant has no information or belief that the claim is discharged in a proceeding under Title 11 of the United States Code (Bankruptcy) or that the prosecution of the action is stayed in a proceeding under Title 11 of the United States Code (Bankruptcy). **Leg.H.** Added Stats 1974 ch 1516 §9, operative January 1, 1977. Amended Stats 1982 ch 1198 §36, operative July 1, 1983.

§484.330. Notice to defendant

No writ of attachment shall be issued under this article except after a hearing. At least 15 days prior to the hearing, the defendant shall be served with both of the following:

(a) A notice of application and hearing.

(b) A copy of the application. **Leg.H.** Added Stats 1974 ch 1516 §9, operative January 1, 1977. Amended Stats 1991 ch 1090 §2 (AB 1484).

§484.340. Contents of notice of application and hearing

The notice of application and hearing shall inform the defendant of all of the following:

(a) The plaintiff has applied for a writ of attachment to attach the property described in the application.

(b) A hearing will be held at a place and at a time, to be specified in the notice, to determine whether the plaintiff is entitled to the writ.

(c) A writ of attachment will be issued to attach the property described in the plaintiff's application unless the court determines that the property is exempt from attachment or that its value clearly exceeds the amount necessary to satisfy the amount to be secured by the attachment.

(d) If the defendant claims that the property described in the application, or a portion thereof, is exempt from attachment, the defendant may file with the court and serve on the plaintiff a claim of exemption with respect to the property as provided in Section 484.350 not later than five days prior to the date set for hearing. If the defendant fails to make such a claim with respect to personal property, the defendant may not later claim the exemption in the absence of a showing of a change in circumstances occurring after the expiration of the time for claiming exemptions.

(e) Either the defendant or the defendant's attorney or both of them may be present at the hearing.

(f) The notice shall contain the following statement: "You may seek the advice of an attorney as to any matter connected with the plaintiff's application. The attorney should be consulted promptly so that the attorney may assist you before the time set for hearing." **Leg.H.** Added Stats 1974 ch 1516 §9, operative January 1, 1977. Amended Stats 1976 ch 437 §10; Stats 1982 ch 1198 §37, operative July 1, 1983.

§484.350. Claim of exemption and supporting affidavit

(a) If the defendant claims that the property described in the plaintiff's application, or a portion of such property, is exempt from attachment, the defendant may claim the exemption as provided in this section. If the defendant fails to make a claim with respect to personal property, or makes a claim with respect to real or personal property but fails to prove that the property is exempt, the defendant may not later claim the exemption except as provided in Section 482.100.

(b) The claim of exemption shall:

(1) Describe the property claimed to be exempt.

(2) Specify the statute section supporting the claim.

(c) The claim of exemption shall be accompanied by an affidavit supporting any factual issues raised by the claim and points and authorities supporting any legal issues raised.

(d) The claim of exemption, together with any supporting affidavit and points and authorities, shall be filed and served on the plaintiff not less than five court days before the date set for the hearing. **Leg.H.** Added Stats 1974 ch 1516 §9, operative January 1, 1977. Amended Stats 1976 ch 437 §11; Stats 1982 ch 1198 §38, operative July 1, 1983; Stats 1998 ch 932 §15 (AB 1094).

§484.360. Plaintiff's notice of opposition

(a) If the defendant files and serves a claim of exemption and the plaintiff desires to oppose the claim, he shall file and serve on the defendant, not less than two days before the date set for the hearing, a notice of opposition to the claim of exemption, accompanied by an affidavit supporting any factual issues raised and points and authorities supporting any legal issues raised.

(b) If the defendant files and serves a claim of exemption and supporting affidavit as provided in Section 484.350 and the plaintiff does not file and serve a notice of opposition as provided in this section, no writ of attachment shall be issued as to the property claimed to be exempt. If all of the property described in the plaintiff's application is claimed to be exempt and the plaintiff does not file and serve a notice of opposition as provided in this section, no hearing shall be held and no writ of attachment shall be issued.

(c) If the plaintiff files and serves a notice of opposition to the claim as provided in this section, the defendant has the burden of proving that the property is exempt from attachment. **Leg.H.** Added Stats 1974 ch 1516 §9, operative January 1, 1977.

§484.370. Hearing; issuance of writ

The hearing shall be conducted in the manner prescribed in Section 484.090 and the court shall order a writ of attachment to be issued upon the filing of an undertaking as provided by Sections 489.210 and 489.220, if it finds both of the following:

(a) A right to attach order has been issued in the action pursuant to Article 1 (commencing with Section 484.010) or the court has found pursuant to Section 485.240 that the plaintiff is entitled to a right to attach order.

(b) The defendant has failed to prove that the property sought to be attached, or the portion thereof to be described in the writ, is exempt from attachment. **Leg.H.** Added Stats 1974 ch 1516 §9, operative January 1, 1977. Amended Stats 1976 ch 437 §12.

ARTICLE 3
Ex Parte Procedure for Obtaining Additional Writs

Application and supporting affidavit. §484.510.
Ex parte hearing; issuance of writ. §484.520.
Defendant's right to claim exemption; Time. §484.530.

§484.510. Application and supporting affidavit

(a) At any time after a right to attach order has been issued under Article 1 (commencing with Section 484.010) or after the court has found pursuant to Section 485.240 that the plaintiff is entitled to a right to attach order, the plaintiff may apply for a writ of attachment under this article by filing an application which meets the requirements of Section 484.320 with the court in which the action is brought.

(b) The application shall be accompanied by an affidavit showing that the property sought to be attached is not exempt from attachment. Such affidavit may be based on the affiant's information and belief. **Leg.H.** Added Stats 1974 ch 1516 §9, operative January 1, 1977.

§484.520. Ex parte hearing; issuance of writ

The court shall examine the application and supporting affidavit and shall order a writ of attachment to be issued upon the filing of an undertaking as provided by Sections 489.210 and 489.220, if it finds both of the following:

(a) A right to attach order has been issued in the action pursuant to Article 1 (commencing with Section 484.010) or the court has found pursuant to Section 485.240 that the plaintiff is entitled to a right to attach order.

(b) The affidavit accompanying the application shows that the property sought to be attached, or the portion thereof to be described in the writ, is not exempt from attachment. **Leg.H.** Added Stats 1974 ch 1516 §9, operative January 1, 1977. Amended Stats 1976 ch 437 §13.

§484.530. Defendant's right to claim exemption; Time

(a) The defendant may claim an exemption as to real or personal property levied upon pursuant to a writ issued under this article by following the procedure set forth in Article 2 (commencing with Section 703.510) of Chapter 4 of Division 2 of Title 9, except that the defendant shall claim the exemption as to personal property not later than 30 days after the levying officer serves the defendant with the notice of attachment describing such property. For this purpose, references in Article 2 (commencing with Section 703.510) of Chapter 4 of Division 2 of Title 9 to the "judgment debtor" shall be deemed references to the defendant, and references to the "judgment creditor" shall be deemed references to the plaintiff.

(b) The defendant may claim the exemption provided by subdivision (b) of Section 487.020 within the time provided by subdivision (a) of this section either (1) by following the procedure set forth in Article 2 (commencing with Section 703.510) of Chapter 4 of Division 2 of Title 9 or (2) by following the procedure set forth in subdivision (c) of Section 482.100 except that the requirement of showing changed circumstances under subdivision (a) of Section 482.100 does not apply.

(c) Notwithstanding subdivisions (a) and (b), a claim of exemption shall be denied if the claim has been denied earlier in the action and there is no change in circumstances affecting the claim. **Leg.H.** Added Stats 1974 ch 1516 §9, operative January 1, 1977. Amended Stats 1976 ch 437 §14; Stats 1982 ch 1198 §39, operative July 1, 1983.

§485. [Section repealed 1974]

Leg.H. Enacted 1872. Amended Stats 1933 ch 744 §42. Repealed Stats 1973 ch 20 §3. The repealed section related to arrest of defendant.

CHAPTER 5
EX PARTE HEARING PROCEDURE FOR OBTAINING WRIT OF ATTACHMENT

Article 1. Great or Irreparable Injury Requirement.
Article 2. Order Determining Right to Attach; Issuance of Writ of Attachment.
Article 3. Procedure for Obtaining Additional Writs.
Article 4. Claim of Exemption.

ARTICLE 1
Great or Irreparable Injury Requirement

Prerequisite of great or irreparable injury. §485.010.

§485.010. Prerequisite of great or irreparable injury

(a) Except as otherwise provided by statute, no right to attach order or writ of attachment may be issued pursuant to this chapter unless it appears from facts shown by affidavit that great or irreparable injury would result to the plaintiff if issuance of the order were delayed until the matter could be heard on notice.

(b) The requirement of subdivision (a) is satisfied if any of the following are shown:

(1) Under the circumstances of the case, it may be inferred that there is a danger that the property sought to be attached would be concealed, substantially impaired in value, or otherwise made unavailable to levy if issuance of the order were delayed until the matter could be heard on notice.

(2) Under the circumstances of the case, it may be inferred that the defendant has failed to pay the debt underlying the requested attachment and the defendant is insolvent in the sense that the defendant is generally not paying his or her debts as those debts become due, unless the debts are subject to a bona fide dispute. Plaintiff's affidavit filed in support of the ex parte attachment shall state, in addition to the requirements of Section 485.530, the known undisputed debts of the defendant, that the debts are not subject to bona fide dispute, and the basis for plaintiff's determination that the defendant's debts are undisputed.

(3) A bulk sales notice has been recorded and published pursuant to Division 6 (commencing with Section 6101) of the Commercial Code with respect to a bulk transfer by the defendant.

(4) An escrow has been opened pursuant to the provisions of Section 24074 of the Business and Professions Code with respect to the sale by the defendant of a liquor license.

(5) Any other circumstance showing that great or irreparable injury would result to the plaintiff if issuance of the order were delayed until the matter could be heard on notice.

(c) Upon a writ being issued solely on a showing under paragraph (2) of subdivision (b), if the defendant requests the court to review the issuance of the writ, the court shall conduct a hearing within five court days after the plaintiff is served with notice of the defendant's request. A writ issued solely on a showing under paragraph (3) of subdivision (b) shall be limited to the property covered by the bulk sales notice or the proceeds of the sale of such property. In addition to any other service required by this title, such writ shall be served by the levying officer on the transferee or auctioneer identified by the bulk sales notice not more than five days after the levy of such writ. A writ issued solely on a showing under paragraph (4) of subdivision (b) shall be limited to the plaintiff's pro rata share of the proceeds of the sale in escrow. **Leg.H.** Added Stats 1974 ch 1516 §9, operative January 1, 1977. Amended Stats 1976 ch 437 §14.5; Stats 1988 ch 727 §1.

ARTICLE 2
Order Determining Right to Attach; Issuance of Writ of Attachment

Application for order and writ; Supporting affidavit. §485.210.
Issuance of order and writ. §485.220.
Discovery related to property in which defendant has interest. §485.230.
Setting aside right to attach order and quashing writ; Notice and hearing. §485.240.

§485.210. Application for order and writ; Supporting affidavit

(a) Upon the filing of the complaint or at any time thereafter, the plaintiff may apply pursuant to this article for a right to attach order and a writ of attachment by filing an application for the order and writ with the court in which the action is brought.

(b) The application shall satisfy the requirements of Section 484.020 and, in addition, shall include a statement showing that the requirement of Section 485.010 is satisfied.

(c) The application shall be supported by an affidavit showing all of the following:

(1) The plaintiff on the facts presented would be entitled to a judgment on the claim upon which the attachment is based.

(2) The plaintiff would suffer great or irreparable injury (within the meaning of Section 485.010) if issuance of the order were delayed until the matter could be heard on notice.

(3) The property sought to be attached is not exempt from attachment.

(d) An affidavit in support of the showing required by paragraph (3) of subdivision (c) may be based on the affiant's information and belief. **Leg.H.** Added Stats 1974 ch 1516 §9, operative January 1, 1977.

§485.220. Issuance of order and writ

(a) The court shall examine the application and supporting affidavit and, except as provided in Section 486.030, shall issue a right to attach order, which shall state the amount to be secured by the attachment, and order a writ of attachment to be issued upon the filing of an undertaking as provided by Sections 489.210 and 489.220, if it finds all of the following:

(1) The claim upon which the attachment is based is one upon which an attachment may be issued.

(2) The plaintiff has established the probable validity of the claim upon which the attachment is based.

(3) The attachment is not sought for a purpose other than the recovery upon the claim upon which the attachment is based.

(4) The affidavit accompanying the application shows that the property sought to be attached, or the portion thereof to be specified in the writ, is not exempt from attachment.

(5) The plaintiff will suffer great or irreparable injury (within the meaning of Section 485.010) if issuance of the order is delayed until the matter can be heard on notice.

(6) The amount to be secured by the attachment is greater than zero.

(b) If the court finds that the application and the supporting affidavit do not satisfy the requirements of Section 485.010, it shall so state and deny the order. If denial is solely on the ground that Section 485.010 is not satisfied, the court shall so state and such denial does not preclude the plaintiff from applying for a right to attach order and writ of attachment under Chapter 4 (commencing with Section 484.010) with the same affidavits and supporting papers. **Leg.H.** Added Stats 1974 ch 1516 §9, operative January 1, 1977. Amended Stats 1976 ch 437 §15; Stats 1997 ch 222 §9 (AB 1258).

§485.230. Discovery related to property in which defendant has interest

Where a right to attach order has been issued by the court, a plaintiff may discover, through any means provided for by, and subject to the protections included in, Title 4 (commencing with Section 2016.010) of Part 4, the identity, location, and value of property in which the defendant has an interest. **Leg.H.** Added Stats 1992 ch 1348 §2 (AB 2616). Amended Stats 2004 ch 182 §10 (AB 3081), operative July 1, 2005.

Prior Law: Former CCP §485.230, similar to present CCP §485.610, was added Stats 1974 ch 1516 §9, operative January 1, 1977, and repealed Stats 1976 ch 437 §16.

§485.240. Setting aside right to attach order and quashing writ; Notice and hearing

(a) Any defendant whose property has been attached pursuant to a writ issued under this chapter may apply for an order (1) that the right to attach order be set aside, the writ of attachment quashed, and any property levied upon pursuant to the writ be released, or (2) that the amount to be secured by the attachment be reduced as provided in Section 483.015. Such application shall be made by filing with the court and serving on the plaintiff a notice of motion.

(b) The notice of motion shall state the grounds on which the motion is based and shall be accompanied by an affidavit supporting any factual issues raised and points and authorities supporting any legal issues raised. It shall not be grounds to set aside an order that the plaintiff would not have suffered great or irreparable injury (within the meaning of Section 485.010) if issuance of the order had been delayed until the matter could have been heard on notice.

(c) At the hearing on the motion, the court shall determine whether the plaintiff is entitled to the right to attach order or whether the amount to be secured by the attachment should be reduced. If the court finds that the plaintiff is not entitled to the right to attach order, it shall order the right to attach order set aside, the writ of attachment quashed, and any property levied on pursuant to the writ released. If the court finds that the plaintiff is entitled to the right to attach order, thereafter the plaintiff may apply for additional writs pursuant to Article 2 (commencing with Section 484.310) or Article 3 (commencing with Section 484.510) of Chapter 4.

(d) The court's determinations shall be made upon the basis of the pleadings and other papers in the record; but, upon good cause shown, the court may receive and consider at the hearing additional evidence, oral or documentary, and additional points and authorities, or it may continue the hearing for the production of such additional evidence or points and authorities.

(e) The hearing provided for in this section shall take precedence over all other civil matters on the calendar of that day except older matters of the same character. **Leg.H.** Added Stats 1974 ch 1516 §9, operative January 1, 1977. Amended Stats 1983 ch 155 §4, effective June 30, 1983, operative July 1, 1983.

ARTICLE 3
Procedure for Obtaining Additional Writs

Application. §485.510.
Contents of application. §485.520.
Supporting affidavit. §485.530.
Issuance of writ. §485.540.

§485.510. Application

At any time after a right to attach order and writ of attachment have been issued under Article 2 (commencing with Section 485.210), the plaintiff may apply for an additional writ of attachment under this article by filing an application with the court in which the action is brought. **Leg.H.** Added Stats 1974 ch 1516 §9, operative January 1, 1977.

§485.520. Contents of application

The application shall be executed under oath and shall include all of the following:

(a) A statement that the plaintiff has been issued a right to attach order and writ of attachment pursuant to Article 2 (commencing with Section 485.210) in the action.

(b) A statement of the amount to be secured by the attachment under the right to attach order.

(c) A description of the property to be attached under the writ of attachment and a statement that the plaintiff is informed and believes that the property is not exempt from attachment. The description shall satisfy the requirements of Section 484.020.

(d) A statement showing that the requirement of Section 485.010 has been satisfied. **Leg.H.** Added Stats 1974 ch 1516 §9, operative January 1, 1977. Amended Stats 1982 ch 1198 §41, operative July 1, 1983.

§485.530. Supporting affidavit

(a) The application shall be supported by an affidavit showing both of the following:

(1) The plaintiff would suffer great or irreparable injury (within the meaning of Section 485.010) if the issuance of the writ of attachment were delayed until the matter could be heard on notice.

(2) The property sought to be attached is not exempt from attachment.

(b) The affidavit in support of the showing required by paragraph (2) of subdivision (a) may be based on the affiant's information and belief. **Leg.H.** Added Stats 1974 ch 1516 §9, operative January 1, 1977. Amended Stats 1976 ch 437 §17.

§485.540. Issuance of writ

The court shall examine the application and supporting affidavit and shall order a writ of attachment to be issued upon the filing of an undertaking as provided by Sections 489.210 and 489.220, if it finds all of the following:

(a) A right to attach order has been issued in the action pursuant to Article 2 (commencing with Section 485.210).

(b) The affidavit accompanying the application shows that the property sought to be attached, or the portion thereof to be specified in the writ, is not exempt from attachment.

(c) The plaintiff will suffer great or irreparable injury (within the meaning of Section 485.010) if issuance of the writ of attachment is delayed until the matter can be heard on notice. **Leg.H.** Added Stats 1974 ch 1516 §9, operative January 1, 1977. Amended Stats 1976 ch 437 §18.

ARTICLE 4
Claim of Exemption

Claim of exemption. §485.610.

§485.610. Claim of exemption

(a) The defendant may claim an exemption as to real or personal property levied upon pursuant to a writ of attachment issued under this chapter by following the procedure set forth in Article 2 (commencing with Section 703.510) of Chapter 4 of Division 2 of Title 9, except that the defendant shall claim the exemption as to personal property not later than 30 days after the levying officer serves the defendant with the notice of attachment describing such property and may claim an exemption for real property within the time provided in Section 487.030. For this purpose, references in Article 2 (commencing with Section 703.510) of Chapter 4 of Division 2 of Title 9 to the "judgment debtor" shall be deemed references to the defendant, and references to the "judgment creditor" shall be deemed references to the plaintiff.

(b) The defendant may claim the exemption provided by subdivision (b) of Section 487.020 within the time provided by subdivision (a) of this section either (1) by following the procedure set forth in Article 2 (commencing with Section 703.510) of Chapter 4 of Division 2 of Title 9 or (2) by following the procedure set forth in subdivision (c) of Section 482.100 except that the requirement of showing changed circumstances under subdivision (a) of Section 482.100 does not apply. **Leg.H.** Added Stats 1976 ch 437 §19. Amended Stats 1982 ch 1198 §42, operative July 1, 1983; Stats 1984 ch 538 §2.

§486. [Section repealed 1974]

Leg.H. Enacted 1872. Amended Stats 1969 ch 690 §3. Repealed Stats 1973 ch 20 §3. The repealed section related to defendant to be discharged on bail or deposit.

CHAPTER 6
TEMPORARY PROTECTIVE ORDER

Application; supporting affidavit. §486.010.
Ex parte hearing; Issuance of order. §486.020.
Issuance of temporary protective order in lieu of writ of attachment. §486.030.
Contents of temporary protective order generally. §486.040.
Effect on transfers in the ordinary course of business. §486.050.
Effect on deposit accounts. §486.060.
Persons bound by temporary protective order. §486.070.
Service on defendant. §486.080.
Expiration of order. §486.090.
Modification or vacation of order on defendant's application. §486.100.
Lien. §486.110.

§486.010. Application; supporting affidavit

(a) At the time of applying for a right to attach order under Chapter 4 (commencing with Section 484.010), the plaintiff may apply pursuant to this chapter for a temporary protective order by filing an application for the order with the court in which the action is brought.

(b) The application shall state what relief is requested and shall be supported by an affidavit, which may be based on information and belief, showing that the plaintiff would suffer great or irreparable injury (within the meaning of Section 485.010) if the temporary protective order were not issued. **Leg.H.** Added Stats 1974 ch 1516 §9, operative January 1, 1977.

§486.020. Ex parte hearing; Issuance of order

The court shall examine the application, supporting affidavit, and other papers on record and shall issue a temporary protective order, which shall state the amount sought to be secured by the attachment under the application for the right to attach order, upon the filing of an undertaking as provided by Sections 489.210 and 489.220, if it finds all of the following:

(a) The claim upon which the application for attachment is based is one upon which an attachment may be issued.

(b) The plaintiff has established the probable validity of the claim upon which the application for the attachment is based.

(c) The order is not sought for a purpose other than the recovery upon the claim upon which the application for the attachment is based.

(d) The plaintiff will suffer great or irreparable injury (within the meaning of Section 485.010) if the temporary protective order is not issued. **Leg.H.** Added Stats 1974 ch 1516 §9, operative January 1, 1977. Amended Stats 1976 ch 437 §19.5; Stats 1982 ch 1198 §42.5, operative July 1, 1983.

§486.030. Issuance of temporary protective order in lieu of writ of attachment

(a) In any case where the plaintiff has applied for a right to attach order and writ of attachment under Chapter 5 (commencing with Section 485.010), the court may in its discretion deny the application for the order and writ and issue instead a temporary protective order under this chapter if it determines that the requirements of Section 485.220 are satisfied but that the issuance of the temporary protective order instead of the right to attach order and writ would be in the interest of justice and equity to the parties, taking into account the effect on the defendant of issuing a writ of attachment ex parte, the effect on the plaintiff of issuing the temporary protective order instead of the writ, and other factors that bear on equity and justice under the circumstances of the particular case.

(b) If the court issues a temporary protective order under this section, the plaintiff's application for a right to attach order and writ shall be treated as an application for a right to attach order and writ under Article 1 (commencing with Section 484.010) of Chapter 4 and the plaintiff shall comply with the requirements of service provided in Section 484.040. **Leg.H.** Added Stats 1974 ch 1516 §9, operative January 1, 1977.

§486.040. Contents of temporary protective order generally

The temporary protective order issued under this chapter shall contain such provisions as the court determines would be in the interest of justice and equity to the parties, taking into account the effects on both the defendant and the plaintiff under the circumstances of the particular case. **Leg.H.** Added Stats 1974 ch 1516 §9, operative January 1, 1977.

§486.050. Effect on transfers in the ordinary course of business

(a) Except as otherwise provided in Section 486.040, the temporary protective order may prohibit a transfer by the defendant of any of the defendant's property in this state subject to the levy of the writ of attachment. The temporary protective order shall describe the property in a manner adequate to permit the defendant to identify the property subject to the temporary protective order.

(b) Notwithstanding subdivision (a), if the property is farm products held for sale or is inventory, the temporary protective order shall not prohibit the defendant from transferring the property in the ordinary course of business, but the temporary protective order may impose appropriate restrictions on the disposition of the proceeds from that type of transfer. **Leg.H.** Added Stats 1974 ch 1516 §9, operative January 1, 1977. Amended Stats 1976 ch 437 §20; Stats 2008 ch 179 §35 (SB 1498), effective January 1, 2009.

§486.060. Effect on deposit accounts

(a) Notwithstanding any terms of the temporary protective order, the defendant may issue any number of checks against any of the defendant's accounts in a financial institution in this state to the extent permitted by this section.

(b) The defendant may issue any number of checks in any amount for the following purposes:

(1) Payment of any payroll expense (including fringe benefits and taxes and premiums for workers' compensation and unemployment insurance) falling due in the ordinary course of business prior to the levy of a writ of attachment.

(2) Payment for goods thereafter delivered to the defendant C.O.D. for use in the defendant's trade, business, or profession.

(3) Payment of taxes if payment is necessary to avoid penalties which will accrue if there is any further delay in payment.

(4) Payment of reasonable legal fees and reasonable costs and expenses required for the representation of the defendant in the action.

(c) In addition to the checks permitted to be issued by subdivision (b), the defendant may issue any number of checks for any purpose so long as the total amount of the checks does not exceed the greater of the following:

(1) The amount by which the total amount on deposit exceeds the sum of the amount sought to be secured by the attachment and the amounts permitted to be paid pursuant to subdivision (b).

(2) One thousand dollars ($1,000). **Leg.H.** Added Stats 1974 ch 1516 §9, operative January 1, 1977. Amended Stats 1976 ch 437 §21; Stats 1982 ch 1198 §43, operative July 1, 1983.

§486.070. Persons bound by temporary protective order

Except as otherwise provided by Section 486.110, a temporary protective order issued under this chapter binds only the defendant, whether or not any other person knows of or is served with a copy of the temporary protective order. **Leg.H.** Added Stats 1974 ch 1516 §9, operative January 1, 1977. Amended Stats 1976 ch 437 §22.

§486.080. Service on defendant

The temporary protective order shall be personally served on the defendant together with the documents referred to in Section 484.040. **Leg.H.** Added Stats 1974 ch 1516 §9, operative January 1, 1977. Amended Stats 1982 ch 1198 §44, operative July 1, 1983.

§486.090. Expiration of order

Except as otherwise provided in this title, the temporary protective order shall expire at the earliest of the following times:

(a) Forty days after the issuance of the order or, if an earlier date is prescribed by the court in the order, on such earlier date.

(b) As to specific property described in the order, when a levy of attachment upon that property is made by the plaintiff. **Leg.H.** Added Stats 1974 ch 1516 §9, operative January 1, 1977. Amended Stats 1976 ch 437 §23.

§486.100. Modification or vacation of order on defendant's application

Upon ex parte application of the defendant or, if the court so orders, after a noticed hearing, the court may modify or vacate the temporary protective order if it determines that such action would be in the interest of justice and equity to the parties, taking into account the effect on the defendant of the continuance of the original order, the effect on the plaintiff of modifying or vacating the order, and any other factors. **Leg.H.** Added Stats 1974 ch 1516 §9, operative January 1, 1977.

§486.110. Lien

(a) The service upon the defendant of a temporary protective order pursuant to Section 486.080 creates a lien upon any property, or the proceeds thereof, which is described in the order, is owned by the defendant at the time of such service, and is subject to attachment pursuant to this title. The lien continues on property subject to the lien, notwithstanding the transfer or encumbrance of the property subject to the lien, unless the person receiving the property, whether real or personal, is a person listed in Section 697.740.

(b) The lien terminates upon the date of expiration of the temporary protective order except with respect to property levied upon while the temporary protective order is in effect under a writ of attachment issued upon application of the plaintiff. **Leg.H.** Added Stats 1974 ch 1516 §9, operative January 1, 1977. Amended Stats 1982 ch 1198 §45, operative July 1, 1983; Stats 1984 ch 538 §2.5.

§487. [Section repealed 1974]

Leg.H. Enacted 1872. Repealed Stats 1973 ch 20 §3. The repealed section related to the manner in which defendant may give bail.

CHAPTER 7
PROPERTY SUBJECT TO ATTACHMENT

Property subject to attachment. §487.010.
Property exempt from attachment. §487.020.
Homestead. §487.025.
Claim of exemption as to real property. §487.030.

§487.010. Property subject to attachment

The following property of the defendant is subject to attachment:

(a) Where the defendant is a corporation, all corporate property for which a method of levy is provided by Article 2 (commencing with Section 488.300) of Chapter 8.

(b) Where the defendant is a partnership or other unincorporated association, all partnership or association property for which a method of levy is provided by Article 2 (commencing with Section 488.300) of Chapter 8.

(c) Where the defendant is a natural person, all of the following property:

(1) Interests in real property except leasehold estates with unexpired terms of less than one year.

(2) Accounts receivable, chattel paper, and general intangibles arising out of the conduct by the defendant of a trade, business, or profession, except any such individual claim with a principal balance of less than one hundred fifty dollars ($150).

(3) Equipment.

(4) Farm products.

(5) Inventory.

(6) Final money judgments arising out of the conduct by the defendant of a trade, business, or profession.

(7) Money on the premises where a trade, business, or profession is conducted by the defendant and, except for the first one thousand dollars ($1,000), money located elsewhere than on such premises and deposit accounts, but, if the defendant has more than one deposit account or has at least one deposit account and money located elsewhere than on the premises where a trade, business, or profession is conducted by the defendant, the court, upon application of the plaintiff, may order that the writ of attachment be levied so that an aggregate amount of one thousand dollars ($1,000) in the form of such money and in such accounts remains free of levy.

(8) Negotiable documents of title.

(9) Instruments.

(10) Securities.

(11) Minerals or the like (including oil and gas) to be extracted.

(d) In the case of a defendant described in subdivision (c), community property of a type described in subdivision (c) is subject to attachment if the community property would be subject to enforcement of the judgment obtained in the action in which the attachment is sought. Unless the provision or context otherwise requires, if community property that is subject to attachment is sought to be attached:

(1) Any provision of this title that applies to the property of the defendant or to obligations owed to the defendant also applies to the community property interest of the spouse of the defendant and to obligations owed to either spouse that are community property.

(2) Any provision of this title that applies to property in the possession or under the control of the defendant also applies to community property in the possession or under the control of the spouse of the defendant. **Leg.H.** Added Stats 1974 ch 1516 §9, operative January 1, 1977. Amended Stats 1976 ch 437 §24; Stats 1982 ch 1198 §46, operative July 1, 1983.

§487.020. Property exempt from attachment

Except as provided in paragraph (2) of subdivision (a) of Section 3439.07 of the Civil Code, the following property is exempt from attachment:

(a) All property exempt from enforcement of a money judgment.

(b) Property which is necessary for the support of a defendant who is a natural person or the family of such defendant supported in whole or in part by the defendant.

(c) "Earnings" as defined by Section 706.011.

(d) All property not subject to attachment pursuant to Section 487.010. **Leg.H.** Added Stats 1974 ch 1516 §9, operative January 1, 1977. Amended Stats 1976 ch 437 §25; Stats 1982 ch 1198 §47, operative July 1, 1983; Stats 1986 ch 383 §7.

§487.025. Homestead

(a) The recording of a homestead declaration (as defined in Section 704.910) does not limit or affect the right of a plaintiff to attach the declared homestead described in the homestead declaration, whether the homestead declaration is recorded before or after the declared homestead is attached.

(b) An attachment lien attaches to a homestead (as defined in Section 704.710) in the amount of any surplus over the total of the following:

(1) All liens and encumbrances on the homestead at the time the attachment lien is created.

(2) The homestead exemption set forth in Section 704.730.

(c) Nothing in subdivision (a) or (b) limits the right of the defendant to an exemption under subdivision (b) of Section 487.020.

(d) Notwithstanding subdivision (b), a homestead (as defined in Section 704.710) is exempt from sale to the extent provided in Section 704.800 when it is sought to be sold to enforce the judgment obtained in the action in which the attachment was obtained. **Leg.H.** Added Stats 1982 ch 1198 §47.5, operative July 1, 1983.

§487.030. Claim of exemption as to real property

(a) At any time prior to the entry of judgment in the action, the defendant may claim any exemption provided by subdivision (a) of Section 487.020 with respect to real property by following the procedure set forth in Article 2 (commencing with Section 703.510) of Chapter 4 of Division 2 of Title 9. A claim of exemption under this subdivision shall be denied if the claim has been denied earlier in the action.

(b) At any time prior to the entry of judgment in the action, the defendant may claim the exemption provided by subdivision (b) of Section 487.020 with respect to real property either (1) by following the procedure set forth in Article 2 (commencing with Section 703.510) of Chapter 4 of Division 2 of Title 9 or (2) by following the procedure set forth in subdivision (c) of Section 482.100 except that the requirement of showing changed circumstances under subdivision (a) of Section 482.100 does not apply. A claim of exemption under this subdivision shall be denied if the claim has been denied earlier in the action and there is no change in circumstances affecting the claim.

(c) For the purposes of this section, references in Article 2 (commencing with Section 703.510) of Chapter 4 of Division 2 of Title 9 to the "judgment debtor" shall be deemed references to the defendant, and references to the "judgment creditor" shall be deemed references to the plaintiff.

(d) Nothing in this section limits the right to claim after the entry of judgment a homestead exemption for real property under Article 4 (commencing with Section 704.710) of Chapter 4 of Division 2 of Title 9 unless prior to entry of judgment the defendant has claimed the exemption provided by subdivision (a) of Section 487.020 with respect to such property and the claim has been denied. **Leg.H.** Added Stats 1982 ch 1198 §48, operative July 1, 1983.

§488. [Section repealed 1974]

Leg.H. Enacted 1872. Amended Stats 1933 ch 744 §43. Repealed Stats 1973 ch 20 §3. The repealed section related to surrender of defendant.

CHAPTER 8
LEVY PROCEDURES; LIEN OF ATTACHMENT; MANAGEMENT AND DISPOSITION OF ATTACHED PROPERTY

Article 1. General Provisions.
Article 2. Methods of Levy.
Article 3. Lien of Attachment.
Article 4. Duties and Liabilities of Third Persons After Levy.
Article 5. Management and Disposition of Attached Property.

ARTICLE 1
General Provisions

Contents of writ of attachment. §488.010.
Delivery and execution of writ. §488.020.
Instructions to levying officer. §488.030.
Instructions to include name and address of persons to be served. §488.040.
Deposit of levying officer's costs. §488.050.
Notice of attachment. §488.060.
Service of copy of original notice of attachment on defendant or other party. §488.065.
Attachment of property in private place. §488.070.
Levy of attachment by registered process server. §488.080.
Manner of custody. §488.090.
Levying officer's lien. §488.100.
Third-party claims. §488.110.
Effect of failure to give notice of attachment. §488.120.
Return of writ. §488.130.

Liability of levying officer. §488.140.

§488.010. Contents of writ of attachment
The writ of attachment shall include the following information:
(a) The date of issuance of the writ.
(b) The title of the court that issued the writ and the cause and number of the action.
(c) The name and address of the plaintiff and the name and last known address of the defendant.
(d) The amount to be secured by the attachment.
(e) A description of the property to be levied upon to satisfy the attachment. **Leg.H.** Added Stats 1982 ch 1198 §50, operative July 1, 1983.

Prior Law: Former CCP §488.010, similar to the present section and present CCP §§488.030, 488.040, 488.060, 488.315, 488.325, 700.015, 700.020, was added Stats 1974 ch 1516 §9, operative January 1, 1977, amended Stats 1976 ch 437 §26, and repealed Stats 1982 ch 1198 §49, operative July 1, 1983.

§488.020. Delivery and execution of writ
(a) A writ of attachment shall be directed to a levying officer in the county in which property of the defendant described in the writ may be located and to any registered process server.
(b) Upon the receipt of written instructions from the plaintiff's attorney of record or, if the plaintiff has no attorney of record, from the plaintiff, the levying officer to whom the writ is directed and delivered shall levy the writ without delay in the manner provided in this chapter on the property described in the writ or so much thereof as is clearly sufficient to satisfy the amount to be secured by the attachment. The levying officer is not liable for a determination made in good faith under this subdivision.
(c) If a copy of the summons and complaint has not previously been served on the defendant, the instructions to the levying officer shall instruct the levying officer to make the service at the same time the levying officer serves the defendant with a copy of the writ of attachment. **Leg.H.** Added Stats 1982 ch 1198 §50, operative July 1, 1983.

Prior Law: Former CCP §488.020, similar to present CCP §488.060, was added Stats 1974 ch 1516 §9, operative January 1, 1977 and repealed Stats 1982 ch 1198 §49, operative July 1, 1983.

§488.030. Instructions to levying officer
(a) The plaintiff shall give the levying officer instructions in writing. The instructions shall be signed by the plaintiff's attorney of record or, if the plaintiff does not have an attorney of record, by the plaintiff. The instructions shall contain the information needed or requested by the levying officer to comply with the provisions of this title, including but not limited to:
(1) An adequate description of any property to be levied upon.
(2) A statement whether the property is a dwelling.
(3) If the property is a dwelling, whether it is real or personal property.
(b) Subject to subdivision (c), the levying officer shall act in accordance with the written instructions to the extent the actions are taken in conformance with the provisions of this title.
(c) Except to the extent the levying officer has actual knowledge that the information is incorrect, the levying officer may rely on any information contained in the written instructions. **Leg.H.** Added Stats 1982 ch 1198 §50, operative July 1, 1983.

Prior Law: Former CCP §488.030, similar to present CCP §488.020, was added Stats 1974 ch 1516 §9, operative January 1, 1977, amended Stats 1976 ch 437 §27, and repealed Stats 1982 ch 1198 §49, operative July 1, 1983.

§488.040. Instructions to include name and address of persons to be served
(a) If the levying officer is required by any provision of this title to serve any writ, order, notice, or other paper on any person, the plaintiff shall include in the instructions to the levying officer the correct name and address of the person. The plaintiff shall use reasonable diligence to ascertain the correct name and address of the person.
(b) Unless the levying officer has actual knowledge that the name or address included in the instructions is incorrect, the levying officer shall rely on the instructions in serving the writ, order, notice, or other paper on the person. **Leg.H.** Added Stats 1982 ch 1198 §50, operative July 1, 1983.

Prior Law: Former CCP §488.040, similar to present CCP §§482.070, 684.110, was added Stats 1974 ch 1516 §9, operative January 1, 1977 and repealed Stats 1982 ch 1198 §49, operative July 1, 1983.

§488.045. [Section repealed 1983]
Leg.H. Added Stats 1974 ch 1516 §9, operative January 1, 1977. Repealed Stats 1982 ch 1198 §49, operative July 1, 1983. See CCP §488.090.

§488.050. Deposit of levying officer's costs
(a) Except as otherwise provided by law:
(1) As a prerequisite to the performance by the levying officer of a duty under this title, the plaintiff shall deposit a sum of money with the levying officer sufficient to pay the costs of performing the duty.
(2) As a prerequisite to the taking of property into custody by the levying officer under this chapter, whether by keeper or otherwise, the plaintiff shall deposit with the levying officer a sum of money sufficient to pay the costs of taking the property and keeping it safely for a period not to exceed 15 days. If continuation of the custody of the property is required, the levying officer shall, from time to time, demand orally or in writing that the plaintiff deposit additional amounts to cover estimated costs for periods not to exceed 30 days each. A written demand may be mailed or delivered to the plaintiff. The plaintiff has not less than three business days after receipt of the demand within which to comply with the demand. If the amount demanded is not paid within the time specified in the oral or written demand, the levying officer shall release the property.
(b) The levying officer is not liable for failure to take or hold property unless the plaintiff has complied with the provisions of this section. **Leg.H.** Added Stats 1982 ch 1198 §50, operative July 1, 1983.

Prior Law: Former CCP §488.050, similar to present section, was added Stats 1974 ch 1516 §9, operative January 1, 1977 and repealed Stats 1982 ch 1198 §49, operative July 1, 1983.

§488.060. Notice of attachment
The notice of attachment shall inform the person notified of all of the following:
(a) The capacity in which the person is notified.
(b) The specific property which is sought to be attached.
(c) The person's rights under the attachment, including the right to make a third-party claim pursuant to Division 4 (commencing with Section 720.010) of Title 9.
(d) The person's duties under the attachment. **Leg.H.** Added Stats 1982 ch 1198 §50, operative July 1, 1983.

Prior Law: Former CCP §488.060, similar to the present CCP §§488.050, 488.140, was added Stats 1974 ch 1516 §9, operative January 1, 1977 and repealed Stats 1982 ch 1198 §49, operative July 1, 1983.

§488.065. Service of copy of original notice of attachment on defendant or other party
A copy of the original notice of attachment which has been served upon a third party holding the property sought to be attached, if served upon the defendant or any other party, shall suffice as the notice of attachment to that person. **Leg.H.** Added Stats 1984 ch 759 §1.

§488.070. Attachment of property in private place
If a writ of attachment has been issued and personal property sought to be attached under the writ is located in a private place of the defendant:
(a) The levying officer shall comply with the provisions of Section 699.030.
(b) The plaintiff may obtain the relief provided under Section 699.030 in the manner and subject to the requirements of that section. **Leg.H.** Added Stats 1982 ch 1198 §50, operative July 1, 1983.

Prior Law: Former CCP §488.070, similar to present CCP §488.130, was added Stats 1974 ch 1516 §9, operative January 1, 1977 and repealed Stats 1982 ch 1198 §49, operative July 1, 1983.

§488.080. Levy of attachment by registered process server
(a) A registered process server may levy under a writ of attachment on the following types of property:
(1) Real property, pursuant to Section 488.315.
(2) Growing crops, timber to be cut, or minerals or the like, including oil and gas, to be extracted or accounts receivable resulting from the sale thereof at the wellhead or minehead, pursuant to Section 488.325.
(3) Personal property in the custody of a levying officer, pursuant to Section 488.355.
(4) Equipment of a going business, pursuant to Section 488.375.
(5) Motor vehicles, vessels, mobilehomes, or commercial coaches used as equipment of a going business, pursuant to Section 488.385.
(6) Farm products or inventory of a going business, pursuant to Section 488.405.

(7) Personal property used as a dwelling, pursuant to subdivision (a) of Section 700.080.

(8) Deposit accounts, pursuant to Section 488.455.

(9) Property in a safe-deposit box, pursuant to Section 488.460.

(10) Accounts receivable or general intangibles, pursuant to Section 488.470.

(11) Final money judgments, pursuant to Section 488.480.

(12) Interest of a defendant in personal property in the estate of a decedent, pursuant to Section 488.485.

(b) Before levying under the writ of attachment, the registered process server shall cause to be deposited with the levying officer a copy of the writ and the fee, as provided by Section 26721 of the Government Code.

(c) If a registered process server levies on property pursuant to subdivision (a), the registered process server shall do both of the following:

(1) Comply with the applicable levy, posting, and service provisions of Article 2 (commencing with Section 488.300).

(2) Request any third person served to give a garnishee's memorandum to the levying officer in compliance with Section 488.610 on a form provided by the registered process server.

(d) Within five court days after levy under this section, all of the following shall be filed with the levying officer:

(1) The writ of attachment.

(2) A proof of service by the registered process server stating the manner of levy performed.

(3) Proof of service of the copy of the writ and notice of attachment on other persons, as required by Article 2 (commencing with Section 488.300).

(4) Instructions in writing, as required by the provisions of Section 488.030.

(e) If the fee provided by Section 26721 of the Government Code has been paid, the levying officer shall perform all other duties under the writ as if the levying officer had levied under the writ and shall return the writ to the court. If the registered process server does not comply with subdivisions (b) and (d), the levy is ineffective and the levying officer is not required to perform any duties under the writ and may issue a release for any property sought to be attached. The levying officer is not liable for actions taken in conformance with the provisions of this title in reliance on information provided to the levying officer under subdivision (d), except to the extent that the levying officer has actual knowledge that the information is incorrect. Nothing in this subdivision limits any liability the plaintiff or registered process server may have if the levying officer acts on the basis of incorrect information provided under subdivision (d).

(f) The fee for services of a registered process server under this section is a recoverable cost pursuant to Section 1033.5. **Leg.H.** Added Stats 1982 ch 1198 §50.5, operative July 1, 1983. Amended Stats 1983 ch 155 §5, effective June 30, 1983, operative July 1, 1983; Stats 1984 ch 538 §3, ch 759 §2.5; Stats 1987 ch 1080 §2; Stats 2007 ch 15 §1 (AB 859), effective January 1, 2008; Stats 2016 ch 102 §1 (AB 2211), effective January 1, 2017.

Prior Law: Former CCP §488.080, similar to present CCP §§488.130, 488.610, was added Stats 1974 ch 1516 §9, operative January 1, 1977, amended Stats 1976 ch 437 §28, and repealed Stats 1982 ch 1198 §49, operative July 1, 1983.

§488.090. Manner of custody

Except as otherwise provided by statute, where the method of levy upon property requires that property be taken into custody or where the levying officer is otherwise directed to take property into custody, the levying officer may do so by any of the following methods:

(a) Removing the property to a place of safekeeping.

(b) Installing a keeper.

(c) Otherwise obtaining possession or control of the property. **Leg.H.** Added Stats 1982 ch 1198 §50, operative July 1, 1983.

Prior Law: Former CCP §488.090, similar to present CCP §488.110, was added Stats 1974 ch 1516 §9, operative January 1, 1977, and repealed Stats 1982 ch 1198 §49, operative July 1, 1983.

§488.100. Levying officer's lien

The levying officer has a special lien, dependent upon possession, on personal property levied upon in the amount of the levying officer's costs for which an advance has not been made. **Leg.H.** Added Stats 1982 ch 1198 §50, operative July 1, 1983.

§488.110. Third-party claims

A third person shall claim an interest in property attached in the manner provided for third-party claims under Division 4 (commencing with Section 720.010) of Title 9. **Leg.H.** Added Stats 1982 ch 1198 §50, operative July 1, 1983.

§488.120. Effect of failure to give notice of attachment

In any case where property has been levied upon and, pursuant to a levy, a copy of the writ of attachment and a notice of attachment are required by statute to be posted or to be served on or mailed to the defendant or other person, failure to post, serve, or mail the copy of the writ and the notice does not affect the attachment lien created by the levy. **Leg.H.** Added Stats 1982 ch 1198 §50, operative July 1, 1983.

§488.130. Return of writ

(a) The levying officer to whom the writ of attachment is delivered shall return the writ to the court from which the writ issued, together with a report of the levying officer's actions. The return shall be made promptly in accordance with the plaintiff's instructions given to the levying officer but in no event later than 60 days after the levying officer receives the writ.

(b) The levying officer shall make a full inventory of property attached and return the inventory with the writ. **Leg.H.** Added Stats 1982 ch 1198 §50, operative July 1, 1983.

§488.140. Liability of levying officer

(a) The levying officer or registered process server is not liable for actions taken in conformance with the provisions of this title, including actions taken in conformance with the provisions of this title in reliance on information contained in the written instructions of the plaintiff except to the extent the levying officer or registered process server has actual knowledge that the information is incorrect. Nothing in this subdivision limits any liability the plaintiff may have if the levying officer or registered process server acts on the basis of incorrect information given in the written instructions.

(b) Unless the levying officer is negligent in the care or handling of the property, the levying officer is not liable to either the plaintiff or the defendant for loss by fire, theft, injury, or damage of any kind to personal property while (1) in the possession of the levying officer either in a warehouse or other storage place or in the custody of a keeper or (2) in transit to or from a warehouse or other storage place. **Leg.H.** Added Stats 1982 ch 1198 §50, operative July 1, 1983. Amended Stats 1983 ch 155 §5.5, effective June 30, 1983, operative July 1, 1983.

ARTICLE 2
Methods of Levy

Incorporated terms. §488.300.
Service of writ and notice of attachment on defendant. §488.305.
Real property. §488.315.
Growing crops, timber to be cut, minerals to be extracted. §488.325.
Tangible personal property in possession of defendant. §488.335.
Tangible personal property in possession of third person. §488.345.
Personal property in custody of levying officer. §488.355.
Bailed goods not covered by negotiable document of title. §488.365.
Equipment of going business. §488.375.
Vehicle, vessel, mobilehome or commercial coach that is equipment of going business; Form; Notice; Fee; Certificate; Effect of property becoming a fixture. §488.385.
Keeper for farm products, inventory, and cash proceeds of going business. §488.395.
Alternative method of attaching farm products or inventory of going business; Filing with Secretary of State. §488.405.
Personal property used as dwelling. §488.415.
Vehicle, vessel, mobilehome, or commercial coach for which certificate of ownership issued. §488.425.
Chattel paper. §488.435.
Instruments. §488.440.
Negotiable documents of title. §488.445.
Securities. §488.450.
Deposit accounts. §488.455.
Safe-deposit boxes; Notice, fee and costs; Opportunity for removal; Liability. §488.460.
Deposit accounts and safe-deposit boxes not exclusively in name of defendant. §488.465.
Accounts receivable and general intangibles. §488.470.
Property that is subject of pending action or proceeding. §488.475.
Final money judgments. §488.480.

Interests in personal property of estate of decedent. §488.485.

§488.300. Incorporated terms

If the method of levy under a writ of execution is incorporated by this article, for the purposes of this article references in Article 4 (commencing with Section 700.010) of Chapter 3 of Division 2 of Title 9 to:

(a) "Judgment creditor" shall be deemed references to the plaintiff.

(b) "Judgment debtor" shall be deemed references to the defendant.

(c) "Notice of levy" shall be deemed references to a notice of attachment.

(d) "Writ" shall be deemed references to a writ of attachment. **Leg.H.** Added Stats 1982 ch 1198 §50, operative July 1, 1983.

§488.305. Service of writ and notice of attachment on defendant

At the time of levy pursuant to this article or promptly thereafter, the levying officer shall serve a copy of the writ of attachment and a notice of attachment on the defendant. **Leg.H.** Added Stats 1982 ch 1198 §50, operative July 1, 1983.

§488.310. [Section repealed 1983]

Leg.H. Added Stats 1974 ch 1516 §9, operative January 1, 1977. Amended Stats 1976 ch 437 §29. Repealed Stats 1982 ch 1198 §49, operative July 1, 1983. See CCP §§488.120, 488.305, 488.315, 700.015.

§488.315. Real property

To attach real property, the levying officer shall comply with Section 700.015 and the recorder shall index the copy of the writ of attachment and a notice of attachment as provided in that section. **Leg.H.** Added Stats 1982 ch 1198 §50, operative July 1, 1983.

§488.320. [Section repealed 1983]

Leg.H. Added Stats 1974 ch 1516 §9, operative January 1, 1977. Repealed Stats 1982 ch 1198 §49, operative July 1, 1983. See CCP §§488.120, 488.305, 488.335.

§488.325. Growing crops, timber to be cut, minerals to be extracted

To attach (1) growing crops, (2) timber to be cut, or (3) minerals or the like (including oil and gas) to be extracted or accounts receivable resulting from the sale thereof at the wellhead or minehead, the levying officer shall comply with Section 700.020 and the recorder shall index the copy of the writ of attachment and a notice of attachment as provided in that section. **Leg.H.** Added Stats 1982 ch 1198 §50, operative July 1, 1983.

§488.330. [Section repealed 1983]

Leg.H. Added Stats 1974 ch 1516 §9, operative January 1, 1977. Repealed Stats 1982 ch 1198 §49, operative July 1, 1983. See CCP §§488.120, 488.305, 488.345, 488.365, 488.600, 700.040, 701.010.

§488.335. Tangible personal property in possession of defendant

Unless another method of attachment is provided by this article, to attach tangible personal property in the possession or under the control of the defendant, the levying officer shall take the property into custody. **Leg.H.** Added Stats 1982 ch 1198 §50, operative July 1, 1983.

§488.340. [Section repealed 1983]

Leg.H. Added Stats 1974 ch 1516 §9, operative January 1, 1977. Repealed Stats 1982 ch 1198 §49, operative July 1, 1983. See CCP §§488.120, 488.305, 488.375.

§488.345. Tangible personal property in possession of third person

Unless another method of attachment is provided by this article, to attach tangible personal property in the possession or under the control of a third person, the levying officer shall comply with Section 700.040. **Leg.H.** Added Stats 1982 ch 1198 §50, operative July 1, 1983.

§488.350. [Section repealed 1983]

Leg.H. Added Stats 1974 ch 1516 §9, operative January 1, 1977. Amended Stats 1976 ch 437 §30. Repealed Stats 1982 ch 1198 §49, operative July 1, 1983. See CCP §§488.120, 488.305, 488.385, 488.425, 488.500, 700.090.

§488.355. Personal property in custody of levying officer

(a) To attach personal property in the custody of a levying officer, the plaintiff or levying officer shall comply with subdivision (a) of Section 700.050.

(b) The levying officer having custody of the property shall comply with the writs in the order they are received and is not subject to the provisions of Article 4 (commencing with Section 488.600). **Leg.H.** Added Stats 1982 ch 1198 §50, operative July 1, 1983.

§488.360. [Section repealed 1983]

Leg.H. Added Stats 1974 ch 1516 §9, operative January 1, 1977. Amended Stats 1976 ch 437 §31. Repealed Stats 1982 ch 1198 §49, operative July 1, 1983. See CCP §§488.120, 488.305, 488.325, 488.395, 488.405, 488.500.

§488.365. Bailed goods not covered by negotiable document of title

To attach goods in the possession of a bailee (as defined in Section 7102 of the Commercial Code) other than one who has issued a negotiable document of title therefor, the levying officer shall comply with Section 700.060. **Leg.H.** Added Stats 1982 ch 1198 §50, operative July 1, 1983.

§488.370. [Section repealed 1983]

Leg.H. Added Stats 1974 ch 1516 §9, operative January 1, 1977. Repealed Stats 1982 ch 1198 §49, operative July 1, 1983. See CCP §§488.120, 488.305, 488.470.

§488.375. Equipment of going business

(a) Except as provided by Section 488.385, to attach equipment of a going business in the possession or under the control of the defendant, the levying officer shall file with the office of the Secretary of State a notice of attachment, in the form prescribed by the Secretary of State, which shall contain all of the following:

(1) The name and mailing address of the plaintiff.

(2) The name and last known mailing address of the defendant.

(3) The title of the court where the action is pending and the cause and number of the action.

(4) A description of the specific property attached.

(5) A statement that the plaintiff has acquired an attachment lien on the specified property of the defendant.

(b) Upon presentation of a notice of attachment under this section for filing, and tender of the filing fee to the office of the Secretary of State, the notice of attachment shall be filed, marked, and indexed in the same manner as a financing statement. The fee for filing in the office of the Secretary of State is the same as the fee for filing a financing statement in the standard form.

(c) Upon the request of any person, the Secretary of State shall issue a certificate showing whether there is on file in that office on the date and hour stated therein any notice of attachment filed against the equipment of a particular person named in the request. If a notice of attachment is on file, the certificate shall state the date and hour of filing of each such notice and any notice affecting any such notice of attachment and the name and address of the plaintiff. Upon request, the Secretary of State shall furnish a copy of any notice of attachment or notice affecting a notice of attachment. The certificate shall be issued as part of a combined certificate pursuant to Section 9528 of the Commercial Code, and the fee for the certificate and copies shall be in accordance with that section.

(d) The fee for filing, indexing, and furnishing filing data for a notice of extension of attachment is the same as the fee for a continuation statement under Section 9525 of the Commercial Code. The fee for filing, indexing, and furnishing filing data for a notice of release of attachment is the same as the fee for a statement of release under Section 9525 of the Commercial Code.

(e) If property subject to an attachment lien under this section becomes a fixture (as defined in paragraph (41) of subdivision (a) of Section 9102 of the Commercial Code), the attachment lien under this section is extinguished. **Leg.H.** Added Stats 1982 ch 1198 §50, operative July 1, 1983. Amended Stats 1983 ch 155 §6, effective June 30, 1983, operative July 1, 1983; Stats 1988 ch 393 §7; Stats 1999 ch 991 §13.4 (SB 45), operative July 1, 2001; Stats 2021 ch 124 §7 (AB 938), effective January 1, 2022.

§488.380. [Section repealed 1983]

Leg.H. Added Stats 1974 ch 1516 §9, operative January 1, 1977. Repealed Stats 1982 ch 1198 §49, operative July 1, 1983. See CCP §§488.120, 488.435, 700.100.

§488.385. Vehicle, vessel, mobilehome or commercial coach that is equipment of going business; Form; Notice; Fee; Certificate; Effect of property becoming a fixture

(a) To attach a vehicle or vessel for which a certificate of ownership has been issued by the Department of Motor Vehicles, or a mobilehome or commercial coach for which a certificate of title has been issued by the Department of Housing and Community Development, which is equipment of a going business in the possession or under the control of the defendant, the levying officer shall file with the appropriate department a notice of attachment, in the form prescribed by the appropriate department, which shall contain all of the following:

(1) The name and mailing address of the plaintiff.

(2) The name and last known mailing address of the defendant.

(3) The title of the court where the action is pending and the cause and number of the action.

(4) A description of the specific property attached.

(5) A statement that the plaintiff has acquired an attachment lien on the specific property of the defendant.

(b) Upon presentation of a notice of attachment, notice of extension, or notice of release under this section for filing and tender of the filing fee to the appropriate department, the notice shall be filed and indexed. The fee for filing and indexing the notice is fifteen dollars ($15).

(c) Upon the request of any person, the department shall issue its certificate showing whether there is on file in that department on the date and hour stated therein any notice of attachment filed against the property of a particular person named in the request. If a notice of attachment is on file, the certificate shall state the date and hour of filing of each such notice of attachment and any notice affecting any such notice of attachment and the name and address of the plaintiff. The fee for the certificate issued pursuant to this subdivision is fifteen dollars ($15). Upon request, the department shall furnish a copy of any notice of attachment or notice affecting a notice of attachment for a fee of one dollar ($1) per page.

(d) If property subject to an attachment lien under this section becomes a fixture (as defined in paragraph (41) of subdivision (a) of Section 9102 of the Commercial Code), the attachment lien under this section is extinguished. **Leg.H.** Added Stats 1982 ch 1198 §50, operative July 1, 1983. Amended Stats 1983 ch 155 §7, effective June 30, 1983, operative July 1, 1983; Stats 1999 ch 991 §13.5 (SB 45), operative July 1, 2001; Stats 2003 ch 719 §1 (SB 1055).

§488.390. [Section repealed 1983]

Leg.H. Added Stats 1974 ch 1516 §9, operative January 1, 1977. Repealed Stats 1982 ch 1198 §49, operative July 1, 1983. See CCP §§488.120, 488.305, 488.455.

§488.395. Keeper for farm products, inventory, and cash proceeds of going business

Except as specified in subdivision (e) and as provided by Sections 488.325 and 488.405:

(a) To attach farm products or inventory of a going business in the possession or under the control of the defendant, the levying officer shall place a keeper in charge of the property for the period prescribed by subdivisions (b) and (c). During the keeper period, the business may continue to operate in the ordinary course of business provided that all sales are final and are for cash or its equivalent. For the purpose of this subdivision, a check is the equivalent of cash. The levying officer is not liable for accepting payment in the form of a cash equivalent. The keeper shall take custody of the proceeds from all sales unless otherwise directed by the plaintiff.

(b) Subject to subdivision (c), the period during which the business may continue to operate under the keeper is:

(1) Ten days, if the defendant is a natural person and the writ of attachment has been issued ex parte pursuant to Article 3 (commencing with Section 484.510) of Chapter 4 or pursuant to Chapter 5 (commencing with Section 485.010).

(2) Two days, in cases not described in paragraph (1).

(c) Unless some other disposition is agreed upon by the plaintiff and the defendant, the levying officer shall take the farm products or inventory into exclusive custody at the earlier of the following times:

(1) At any time the defendant objects to placement of a keeper in charge of the business.

(2) At the conclusion of the applicable period prescribed by subdivision (b).

(d) A defendant described in paragraph (1) of subdivision (b) may claim an exemption pursuant to subdivision (b) of Section 487.020 by following the procedure set forth in subdivision (c) of Section 482.100 except that the requirement of showing changed circumstances under subdivision (a) of Section 482.100 does not apply. Upon a showing that the property is exempt pursuant to subdivision (b) of Section 487.020, the court shall order the release of the exempt property and may make such further order as the court deems appropriate to protect against frustration of the collection of the plaintiff's claim. The order may permit the plaintiff to attach farm products or inventory of the going business and proceeds or after-acquired property, or both, by filing pursuant to Section 488.405 and may provide reasonable restrictions on the disposition of the property previously attached.

(e) This section does not apply to the placement of a keeper in a business for the purpose of attaching tangible personal property consisting solely of money or equivalent proceeds of sales, which shall be conducted in the same manner as provided in Section 700.070. **Leg.H.** Added Stats 1982 ch 1198 §50, operative July 1, 1983. Amended Stats 1996 ch 1159 §10 (AB 3471).

§488.400. [Section repealed 1983]

Leg.H. Added Stats 1974 ch 1516 §9, operative January 1, 1977. Repealed Stats 1982 ch 1198 §49, operative July 1, 1983. See CCP §§488.120, 488.305, 488.335, 488.345, 488.440, 488.445, 700.110, 701.060.

§488.405. Alternative method of attaching farm products or inventory of going business; Filing with Secretary of State

(a) This section provides an alternative method of attaching farm products or inventory of a going business in the possession or under the control of the defendant, but this section does not apply to property described in Section 488.325. This section applies if the plaintiff instructs the levying officer to attach the farm products or inventory under this section.

(b) To attach under this section farm products or inventory of a going business in the possession or under the control of the defendant, the levying officer shall file a notice of attachment with the Secretary of State.

(c) Except as provided in subdivisions (d) and (e), the filing of the notice of attachment gives the plaintiff an attachment lien on all of the following:

(1) The farm products or inventory described in the notice.

(2) Identifiable cash proceeds (as that term is used in Section 9315 of the Commercial Code).

(3) If permitted by the writ of attachment or court order, after-acquired property.

(d) The attachment lien created by the filing of the notice of attachment under this section does not extend to either of the following:

(1) A vehicle or vessel required to be registered with the Department of Motor Vehicles or a mobilehome or commercial coach required to be registered pursuant to the Health and Safety Code.

(2) The inventory of a retail merchant held for sale except to the extent that the inventory of the retail merchant consists of durable goods having a unit retail value of at least five hundred dollars ($500). For the purposes of this paragraph, "retail merchant" does not include (A) a person whose sales for resale exceeded 75 percent in dollar volume of the person's total sales of all goods during the 12 months preceding the filing of the notice of attachment or (B) a cooperative association organized pursuant to Chapter 1 (commencing with Section 54001) of Division 20 of the Food and Agricultural Code (agricultural cooperative associations) or Part 3 (commencing with Section 13200) of Division 3 of Title 1 of the Corporations Code (Fish Marketing Act).

(e) If property subject to an attachment lien under this section becomes a fixture (as defined in paragraph (41) of subdivision (a) of Section 9102 of the Commercial Code), the attachment lien under this section is extinguished.

(f) The notice of attachment shall be in the form prescribed by the Secretary of State and shall contain all of the following:

(1) The name and mailing address of the plaintiff.

(2) The name and last known mailing address of the defendant.

(3) The title of the court where the action is pending and the cause and number of the action.

(4) A description of the farm products and inventory attached.

(5) A statement that the plaintiff has acquired an attachment lien on the described property and on identifiable cash proceeds (as that term is used in Section 9315 of the Commercial Code) and, if permitted by the writ of attachment or court order, on after-acquired property.

(g) Upon presentation of a notice of attachment under this section for filing and tender of the filing fee to the office of the Secretary of State, the notice of attachment shall be filed, marked, and indexed in the same manner as a financing statement. The fee for filing in the office of the Secretary of State is the same as the fee for filing a financing statement in the standard form.

(h) Upon the request of any person, the Secretary of State shall issue a certificate showing whether there is on file in that office on the date and hour stated therein any notice of attachment filed against the farm products or inventory of a particular person named in the request. If a notice of attachment is on file, the certificate shall state the date and hour of filing of each such notice of attachment and any notice affecting any such notice of attachment and the name and address of the plaintiff. Upon request, the Secretary of State shall furnish a copy of any notice of attachment or notice affecting a notice of attachment. The certificate shall be issued as part of a combined certificate pursuant to Section 9528 of the Commercial Code, and the fee for the certificate and copies shall be in accordance with that section.

(i) The fee for filing, indexing, and furnishing filing data for a notice of extension of attachment is the same as the fee for a continuation statement under Section 9525 of the Commercial Code. The fee for filing, indexing, and furnishing filing data for a notice of release of attachment is the same as the fee for a statement of release under Section 9525 of the Commercial Code. **Leg.H.** Added Stats 1982 ch 1198 §50, operative July 1, 1983. Amended Stats 1988 ch 393 §8; Stats 1999 ch 991 §14 (SB 45), operative July 1, 2001; Stats 2021 ch 124 §8 (AB 938), effective January 1, 2022.

§488.410. [Section repealed 1983]

Leg.H. Added Stats 1974 ch 1516 §9, operative January 1, 1977. Repealed Stats 1982 ch 1198 §49, operative July 1, 1983. See CCP §§488.120, 488.305, 488.450.

§488.415. Personal property used as dwelling

To attach personal property used as a dwelling, the levying officer shall comply with Section 700.080. **Leg.H.** Added Stats 1982 ch 1198 §50, operative July 1, 1983.

§488.420. [Section repealed 1983]

Leg.H. Added Stats 1974 ch 1516 §9, operative January 1, 1977. Repealed Stats 1982 ch 1198 §49, operative July 1, 1983. See CCP §§488.120, 488.305, 488.480.

§488.425. Vehicle, vessel, mobilehome, or commercial coach for which certificate of ownership issued

If a vehicle or vessel is attached and a certificate of ownership has been issued by the Department of Motor Vehicles for the vehicle or vessel and the certificate of ownership is still in effect, or if a mobilehome or commercial coach is attached and a certificate of title has been issued by the Department of Housing and Community Development for the mobilehome or commercial coach and the certificate of title is still in effect, the levying officer shall comply with Section 700.090. **Leg.H.** Added Stats 1982 ch 1198 §50, operative July 1, 1983.

§488.430. [Section repealed 1983]

Leg.H. Added Stats 1974 ch 1516 §9, operative January 1, 1977. Repealed Stats 1982 ch 1198 §49, operative July 1, 1983. See CCP §§488.120, 488.305, 488.485.

§488.435. Chattel paper

(a) To attach chattel paper, the levying officer shall comply with Section 700.100.

(b) In addition to any other rights created by a levy on chattel paper, the levy creates a lien on the defendant's rights in specific goods subject to the chattel paper. **Leg.H.** Added Stats 1982 ch 1198 §50, operative July 1, 1983.

§488.440. Instruments

To attach an instrument, the levying officer shall comply with Section 700.110. **Leg.H.** Added Stats 1982 ch 1198 §50, operative July 1, 1983.

§488.445. Negotiable documents of title

To attach a negotiable document of title, the levying officer shall comply with Section 700.120. **Leg.H.** Added Stats 1982 ch 1198 §50, operative July 1, 1983.

§488.450. Securities

To attach a security, the levying officer shall comply with Section 8112 of the Commercial Code. The legal process referred to in Section 8112 of the Commercial Code means the legal process required by the state in which the chief executive office of the issuer of the security is located and, where that state is California, means personal service by the levying officer of a copy of the writ of attachment and notice of attachment on the person who is to be served. **Leg.H.** Added Stats 1982 ch 1198 §50, operative July 1, 1983. Amended Stats 1984 ch 927 §1; Stats 1985 ch 41 §1; Stats 1996 ch 497 §1.5 (SB 1591), operative January 1, 1997.

§488.455. Deposit accounts

(a) Subject to Sections 488.465 and 684.115, to attach a deposit account, the levying officer shall personally serve a copy of the writ of attachment and a notice of attachment on the financial institution with which the deposit account is maintained.

(b) The attachment lien that arises upon service of a writ of attachment and notice of attachment reaches only amounts in a deposit account at the time of service on the financial institution, including the amount of any deposit not yet finally collected, unless the deposit is returned unpaid to the financial institution.

(c) The levying officer shall serve a copy of the writ of attachment and a notice of attachment on any third person in whose name any deposit account described therein stands. That service shall be made personally or by mail as follows:

(1) At the time of levy or promptly thereafter, if the party seeking the levy informs the levying officer of that person and his, her, or its residence or business address.

(2) Promptly following the levying officer's receipt of a garnishee's memorandum if service was not accomplished pursuant to paragraph (1), if the garnishee's memorandum identifies that person and his, her, or its residence or business address.

(d) The financial institution shall not honor a withdrawal request or a check or other order for the payment of money from the deposit account if presentation of that withdrawal request or item to the financial institution occurs during the time the attachment lien is in effect unless, following that withdrawal or payment, sufficient funds are available to cover the levy. For these purposes, a withdrawal from the deposit account to cover the financial institution's standard fee or charge for processing the levy shall not be considered a payment of money from the account in violation of this subdivision.

(e) During the time the attachment lien is in effect, the financial institution is not liable to any person for any of the following:

(1) Performance of the duties of a garnishee under the levy.

(2) Nonpayment of a check or other order for the payment or transfer of money drawn or presented against the deposit account if the nonpayment is pursuant to the requirements of subdivision (d).

(3) Refusal to pay a withdrawal from the deposit account if the refusal is pursuant to the requirements of subdivision (d).

(f) For the purposes of this section, none of the following is a third person in whose name the deposit account stands:

(1) A person who is only a person named as the beneficiary of a Totten trust account.

(2) A person who is only a payee designated in a pay-on-death provision in an account pursuant to Section 18318.5 of the Financial Code or Section 5140 of the Probate Code, or other similar provision.

(3) A person who is only acting in a representative or custodial capacity with respect to benefits paid or payable by the United States government. Rather, accounts maintained by the representative or custodian shall be deemed to stand in that beneficiary's name, and the amounts therein shall be covered by a levy against that beneficiary.

(g) For purposes of this section, final payment of a deposit shall be deemed to have occurred in accordance with Section 4215 or 11210 of the Commercial Code or with automated clearinghouse or Federal Reserve System rule, regulation, operating circular, or similar governing document, as applicable to the deposit. If, for any reason, a deposit is returned by the financial institution upon which it is drawn, that deposit shall not be deemed finally collected for purposes of this subdivision regardless of any later payment by the financial institution upon which the deposit is drawn.

(h) When a deposit account has been attached, as an alternative to paying the amount of the deposit account that is attached to the levying officer as required by Section 488.600, the financial institution may continue to hold the deposit account until the deposit account is levied upon after judgment in the action or is earlier released, the deposit account to be held in one of the following manners:

(1) If the entire deposit account is attached, the financial institution may hold the deposit account on the terms applicable before the attachment, subject to the requirements of subdivision (d).

(2) If less than the entire deposit account is attached:

(A) With the consent of the defendant, and any third person in whose name the deposit account stands, the financial institution may hold in the deposit account on the same terms an amount larger than the attached amount as necessary to avoid a penalty or a reduction of the rate of interest.

(B) If the defendant, and any third person in whose name the deposit account stands, do not consent as provided in subparagraph (A), the financial institution may hold the attached amount on the same terms affecting the deposit account before the attachment, subject to the requirements of subdivision (d).

(3) The financial institution may hold the attached deposit account in any other manner agreed upon by the plaintiff, the defendant, and any third person in whose name the deposit account stands.

(i) Subdivision (h) does not prevent a financial institution that is holding an attached deposit account as provided in subdivision (h) from paying the attached amount to the levying officer before the time the financial institution otherwise is required to pay the amount under subdivision (h). **Leg.H.** Added Stats 1982 ch 1198 §50, operative July 1, 1983. Amended Stats 1983 ch 155 §8, effective June 30, 1983, operative July 1, 1983; Stats 1984 ch 538 §4; Stats 2002 ch 664 §47 (AB 3034); Stats 2003 ch 110 §1 (AB 690); Stats 2012 ch 484 §2 (AB 2364), effective January 1, 2013.

§488.460. Safe-deposit boxes; Notice, fee and costs; Opportunity for removal; Liability

(a) Subject to Sections 488.465 and 684.115, to attach property in a safe-deposit box, the levying officer shall personally serve a copy of the writ of attachment and a notice of attachment on the financial institution with which the safe-deposit box is maintained.

(b) At the time of levy or promptly thereafter, the levying officer shall serve a copy of the writ of attachment and a notice of attachment on any third person in whose name the safe-deposit box stands.

(c) During the time the attachment lien is in effect, the financial institution may not permit the removal of any of the contents of the safe-deposit box except as directed by the levying officer.

(d) Upon receipt of a garnishee's memorandum from the financial institution, as required by Section 488.610, indicating a safe-deposit box is under levy, the levying officer shall promptly mail a written notice to the judgment creditor demanding an additional fee as required by Section 26723 of the Government Code, plus the costs to open the safe-deposit box and seize and store the contents. The levying officer shall release the levy on the safe-deposit box if the plaintiff does not pay the required fee, plus costs, within three business days plus the extended time period specified in subdivision (a) of Section 1013 for service by mail by the levying officer.

(e) The levying officer may first give the person in whose name the safe-deposit box stands an opportunity to open the safe-deposit box to permit the removal pursuant to the attachment of the attached property. The financial institution may refuse to permit the forcible opening of the safe-deposit box to permit the removal of the attached property unless the plaintiff or levying officer pays in advance the cost of forcibly opening the safe-deposit box and of repairing any damage caused thereby.

(f) During the time the attachment lien is in effect, the financial institution is not liable to any person for any of the following:

(1) Performance of the duties of a garnishee under the attachment.

(2) Refusal to permit access to the safe-deposit box by the person in whose name it stands.

(3) Removal of any of the contents of the safe-deposit box pursuant to the attachment.

(g) If the levying officer removes any property from the safe-deposit box to satisfy the levy, but allows other property to remain in the safe-deposit box, the attachment lien is released automatically with respect to any property that remains in the safe-deposit box. **Leg.H.** Added Stats 1982 ch 1198 §50, operative July 1, 1983. Amended Stats 1984 ch 538 §5; Stats 2003 ch 888 §1 (AB 394); Stats 2012 ch 484 §3 (AB 2364), effective January 1, 2013.

§488.465. Deposit accounts and safe-deposit boxes not exclusively in name of defendant

(a) Except as provided in subdivision (b), a deposit account or safe-deposit box standing in the name of a person other than the defendant, either alone or together with other third persons, is not subject to levy under Section 488.455 or 488.460 unless the levy is authorized by court order. The levying officer shall serve a copy of the court order on the third person at the time the copy of the writ of attachment and the notice of attachment are served on the third person.

(b) A court order is not required as a prerequisite to levy on a deposit account or safe-deposit box standing in the name of any of the following:

(1) The defendant, whether alone or together with third persons.

(2) The defendant's spouse, whether alone or together with other third persons. An affidavit showing that the person in whose name the account stands is the defendant's spouse shall be delivered to the financial institution at the time of levy.

(3) A fictitious business name if an unexpired fictitious business name statement filed pursuant to Chapter 5 (commencing with Section 17900) of Part 3 of Division 7 of the Business and Professions Code lists as the persons doing business under the fictitious business name either (A) the defendant or (B) the defendant's spouse or (C) the defendant and the defendant's spouse, but does not list any other person. A copy of a fictitious business name statement, certified as provided in Section 17926 of the Business and Professions Code, that satisfies these requirements shall be delivered to the financial institution at the time of levy and, if a person other than the defendant is listed in the statement, an affidavit showing that the other person is the defendant's spouse shall also be delivered to the financial institution at the time of levy.

(c) In any case where a deposit account in the name of a person other than the defendant, whether alone or together with the defendant, is levied upon, the financial institution shall not pay to the levying officer the amount levied upon until being notified to do so by the levying officer. The levying officer may not require the financial institution to pay the amount levied upon until the expiration of 15 days after service of notice of attachment on the third person. **Leg.H.** Added Stats 1984 ch 538 §6.3.

Prior Law: Former CCP §488.465, similar to the present section, was added Stats 1982 ch 1198 §50, operative July 1, 1983, amended Stats 1983 ch 18 §7, effective April 21, 1983, operative July 1, 1983, ch 155 §8.2, effective June 30, 1983, operative July 1, 1983, and repealed Stats 1984 ch 538 §6.

§488.470. Accounts receivable and general intangibles

(a) Unless another method of attachment is provided by this article, to attach an account receivable or general intangible, the levying officer shall personally serve a copy of the writ of attachment and a notice of attachment on the account debtor.

(b) If an attachment is made under subdivision (a) and payments on the account receivable or general intangible are made to a person other than the defendant (whether pursuant to a security agreement, assignment for collection, or otherwise), the levying officer shall, if so instructed by the plaintiff, personally serve a copy of the writ of attachment and a notice of attachment on such third person. Service of the copy of the writ and notice of attachment on the third person is an attachment of any amounts owed to the defendant by the third person. **Leg.H.** Added Stats 1982 ch 1198 §50, operative July 1, 1983.

§488.475. Property that is subject of pending action or proceeding

(a) The following property may be attached pursuant to this article notwithstanding that the property levied upon is the subject of a pending action or special proceeding:

(1) Real property.

(2) Growing crops, timber to be cut, or minerals or the like (including oil and gas) to be extracted or accounts receivable resulting from the sale thereof at the wellhead or minehead.

(3) Tangible personal property in the possession or under the control of the defendant or in the custody of a levying officer.

(4) The interest of a defendant in personal property in the estate of a decedent, whether the interest arises by testate or intestate succession.

(b) Except as provided in subdivision (a), attachment of property that is the subject of an action or special proceeding pending at the time of the attachment is not effective.

(c) If attachment is attempted but is ineffective under subdivision (b) and the levying officer has requested a garnishee's memorandum under Section 488.610 in connection with the ineffective attachment, the garnishee's memorandum shall include the following information in addition to that required by Section 488.610:

(1) A statement that the attachment of the property is not effective because the property is the subject of a pending action or special proceeding.

(2) The title of the court and the cause and number of the pending action or proceeding.

(d) For the purpose of this section, an action or proceeding is pending from the time the action or proceeding is commenced until judgment has been entered and the time for appeal has expired or, if an appeal is filed, until the appeal has been finally determined.

(e) Nothing in this section affects or limits the right of the plaintiff to obtain a lien pursuant to Article 3 (commencing with Section 491.410) of Chapter 11. **Leg.H.** Added Stats 1982 ch 1198 §50, operative July 1, 1983.

§488.480. Final money judgments

(a) As used in this section, "final money judgment" means a money judgment after the time for appeal from the judgment has expired or, if an appeal is filed, after the appeal has been finally determined.

(b) To attach a final money judgment, the levying officer shall file a copy of the writ of attachment and a notice of attachment with the clerk of the court that entered the final money judgment. The court clerk shall endorse upon the judgment a statement of the existence of the attachment lien and the time it was created. If an abstract of the judgment is issued, it shall include a statement of the attachment lien in favor of the plaintiff.

(c) At the time of levy or promptly thereafter, the levying officer shall serve a copy of the writ of attachment and a notice of attachment on the judgment debtor obligated to pay the final money judgment attached. **Leg.H.** Added Stats 1982 ch 1198 §50, operative July 1, 1983. Amended Stats 1984 ch 538 §6.5.

§488.485. Interests in personal property of estate of decedent

(a) To attach the interest of the defendant in personal property in the estate of a decedent, whether the interest arises by testate or intestate succession, the levying officer shall personally serve a copy of the writ of attachment and a notice of attachment on the personal representative of the decedent. The attachment does not impair the powers of the representative over the property for the purposes of administration.

(b) The personal representative shall report the attachment to the court in which the estate is being administered when any petition for distribution is filed. If a decree orders distribution to the defendant, the court making the decree shall order the attached property to be deliverd to the levying officer. The property may not be delivered to the levying officer until the decree distributing the propety has become final. To the extent the property delivered to the levying officer is not necessary to satisfy the attachment, it shall be released to the defendant.

(c) Promptly after the property is delivered to the levying officer pursuant to subdivision (b), the levying officer shall serve a notice describing the property on the defendant. Notwithstanding Sections 484.070, 484.350, 484.530, and 485.610, a claim of exemption for the property described in the notice may be made within 10 days after the notice was served on the defendant. **Leg.H.** Added Stats 1982 ch 1198 §50, operative July 1, 1983.

ARTICLE 3
Lien of Attachment

Creation and duration of lien; Effect of transfer or attachment; Effect of lien on specified kinds of property; Priorities. §488.500.
Duration; Extension. §488.510.

§488.500. Creation and duration of lien; Effect of transfer or attachment; Effect of lien on specified kinds of property; Priorities

(a) A levy on property under a writ of attachment creates an attachment lien on the property from the time of levy until the expiration of the time provided by Section 488.510.

(b) Except as provided in subdivisions (c) and (d), if property subject to an attachment lien is transferred or encumbered, the property transferred or encumbered remains subject to the lien after the transfer or encumbrance to the same extent that the property would remain subject to an execution lien pursuant to Sections 697.720 to 697.750, inclusive.

(c) Except as otherwise provided in this title, if equipment is attached pursuant to Section 488.375 or farm products or inventory is attached pursuant to Section 488.405, the attachment lien on the property covered by the attachment lien has the same force and effect as a judgment lien on personal property created at the same time would have pursuant to Sections 697.590 to 697.620, inclusive.

(d) If equipment consisting of a vehicle, vessel, mobilehome, or commercial coach is attached pursuant to Section 488.385, the attachment lien on the specified property does not affect the rights of a person who is a bona fide purchaser or encumbrancer and obtains possession of both the property and its certificate of ownership issued by the Department of Motor Vehicles or its certificate of title or registration card issued by the Department of Housing and Community Development. If the levying officer obtains possession of the certificate of ownership or certificate of title or registration card, the attachment lien has the priority of the lien of a lien creditor under Sections 9317 and 9323 of the Commercial Code as of the time possession is obtained by the levying officer. If the levying officer does not obtain possession of the certificate of ownership or certificate of title or registration card, the attachment lien has the same force and effect as an unperfected security interest that attached at the same time as the notice of attachment was filed.

(e) If an attachment lien is created on property that is subject to the lien of a temporary protective order or a lien under Article 1 (commencing with Section 491.110) of Chapter 11, the priority of the attachment lien relates back to the date the earlier lien was created. Nothing in this subdivision affects priorities or rights of third persons established while the lien of the temporary protective order or the lien under Article 1 (commencing with Section 491.110) of Chapter 11 was in effect as determined under the law governing the effect of such lien. **Leg.H.** Added Stats 1982 ch 1198 §50, operative July 1, 1983. Amended Stats 1999 ch 991 §15 (SB 45), operative July 1, 2001.

Prior Law: Former CCP §488.500, similar to the present section and former CCP §488.360, (see now CCP §§488.120 et seq.), was added Stats 1974 ch 1516 §9, operative January 1, 1977, amended Stats 1976 ch 437 §33, and repealed Stats 1982 ch 1198 §49, operative July 1, 1983.

§488.510. Duration; Extension

(a) Unless sooner released or discharged, any attachment shall cease to be of any force or effect, and the property levied upon shall be released from the operation of the attachment, at the expiration of three years from the date of issuance of the writ of attachment under which the levy was made.

(b) Notwithstanding subdivision (a), upon motion of the plaintiff, made not less than 10 or more than 60 days before the expiration of the three-year period and upon notice of not less than five days to the defendant whose property is attached, the court in which the action is pending may, by order filed prior to the expiration of the period and for good cause, extend the time of the attachment for a period not exceeding one year from the date on which the attachment would otherwise expire.

(c) The levying officer shall serve notice of the order upon any person holding property pursuant to an attachment and shall record or file the notice in any office where the writ and notice of attachment are recorded or filed prior to the expiration of the period described in subdivision (a) or any extension thereof. Where the attached property is real property, the plaintiff or the plaintiff's attorney, instead of the levying officer, may record the required notice.

(d) Any attachment may be extended from time to time in the manner prescribed in this section, but the maximum period of the attachment, including the extensions, shall not exceed eight years from the date of issuance of the writ of attachment under which the levy of attachment was made.

(e) The death of the defendant whose property is attached does not terminate the attachment. **Leg.H.** Added Stats 1982 ch 1198 §50, operative July 1, 1983.

Prior Law: Former CCP §488.510, similar to the present section, was added Stats 1974 ch 1516 §9, operative January 1, 1977, amended Stats 1980 ch 124 §1, and repealed Stats 1982 ch 1198 §49, operative July 1, 1983.

§488.520. [Section repealed 1983]

Leg.H. Added Stats 1974 ch 1516 §9, operative January 1, 1977. Repealed Stats 1982 ch 1198 §49, operative July 1, 1983. See CCP §488.710.

§488.530. [Section repealed 1983]

Leg.H. Added Stats 1974 ch 1516 §9. Amended Stats 1976 ch 437 §34. Repealed Stats 1982 ch 1198 §49, operative July 1, 1983. See CCP §488.700.

§488.540. [Section repealed 1983]

Leg.H. Added Stats 1974 ch 1516 §9, operative January 1, 1977. Repealed Stats 1982 ch 1198 §49, operative July 1, 1983. See CCP §§488.600, 701.010.

§488.550. [Section repealed 1983]

Leg.H. Added Stats 1974 ch 1516 §9, operative January 1, 1977. Repealed Stats 1982 ch 1198 §49, operative July 1, 1983. See CCP §§488.600, 491.310, 491.320, 491.330, 701.010, 701.020.

§488.555. [Section repealed 1983]

Leg.H. Added Stats 1976 ch 437 §35. Repealed Stats 1982 ch 1198 §49, operative July 1, 1983. See CCP §488.720.

§488.560. [Section repealed 1983]

Leg.H. Added Stats 1974 ch 1516 §9, operative January 1, 1977. Amended Stats 1976 ch 437 §36. Repealed Stats 1982 ch 1198 §49, operative July 1, 1983. See CCP §488.730.

§488.570. [Section repealed 1983]

Leg.H. Added Stats 1974 ch 1516 §9, operative January 1, 1977. Repealed Stats 1982 ch 1198 §49, operative July 1, 1983. See CCP §488.740.

ARTICLE 4
Duties and Liabilities of Third Persons After Levy

Definitions. §488.600.
Garnishee's memorandum. §488.610.
Liability of person giving garnishee's memorandum. §488.620.

§488.600. Definitions

(a) Sections 701.010, 701.020, 701.040, 701.050, 701.060, and 701.070 prescribe duties and liabilities of a third person under a levy made under this title.

(b) For the purposes of this section, references in Sections 701.010, 701.020, 701.040, 701.050, and 701.060 to:

(1) "Amount required to satisfy the judgment" shall be deemed references to the amount required to satisfy the amount to be secured by the attachment.

(2) "Execution lien" or "lien" shall be deemed references to the attachment lien.

(3) "Judgment creditor" shall be deemed references to the plaintiff.

(4) "Judgment debtor" shall be deemed references to the defendant.

(5) "Levy" shall be deemed references to levy of attachment.

(6) "Notice of levy" shall be deemed references to notice of attachment.

(7) "Release" of property shall be deemed references to release of property pursuant to this title.

(8) "Satisfaction or discharge of the judgment" shall be deemed references to the satisfaction or termination of the attachment.

(9) "Writ" or "writ of execution" shall be deemed references to a writ of attachment.

(c) For the purposes of this section, references in Section 701.070 to:

(1) "Levy" shall be deemed references to levy of attachment.

(2) "Notice of the levy" shall be deemed references to notice of attachment. **Leg.H.** Added Stats 1982 ch 1198 §50, operative July 1, 1983. Amended Stats 1984 ch 538 §6.7; Stats 2012 ch 484 §4 (AB 2364), effective January 1, 2013.

§488.610. Garnishee's memorandum

(a) At the time of service of a copy of the writ of attachment and a notice of attachment on a third person, the levying officer shall request the third person to give the levying officer a garnishee's memorandum containing the information required by this section. Within 10 days after the request is made, the third person shall mail or deliver the garnishee's memorandum to the levying officer whether or not the levy is effective.

(b) The garnishee's memorandum shall be executed under oath and shall contain the following information:

(1) A description of any property of the defendant sought to be attached that is not delivered to the levying officer and the reason for not delivering the property.

(2) A statement of the amount and terms of any obligation to the defendant sought to be attached that is due and payable and is not paid to the levying officer and the reason for not paying the obligation.

(3) A statement of the amount and terms of any obligation to the defendant sought to be attached that is not due and payable at the time of levy.

(4) A description of claims and rights of other persons to the attached property or obligation that are known to the third person and the names and addresses of those other persons.

(5) A statement that the garnishee holds neither any property nor any obligations in favor of the judgment debtor.

(c) If a garnishee's memorandum is received from the third person, the levying officer shall promptly mail or deliver a copy of the memorandum to the plaintiff and attach the original to the writ when it is returned to the court. If a garnishee's memorandum is not received from the third person, the levying officer shall so state in the return.

(d) Except as provided in subdivisions (e) and (f), if a third person does not give the levying officer a garnishee's memorandum within the time provided in subdivision (a) or does not provide complete information, the third person may, in the court's discretion, be required to pay the costs and reasonable attorney's fees incurred in any proceedings to obtain the information required in the garnishee's memorandum.

(e) Notwithstanding subdivision (a), where a deposit account or property in a safe-deposit box is attached, the financial institution need not give a garnishee's memorandum to the levying officer if the financial institution fully complies with the levy and, if a garnishee's memorandum is required, the garnishee's memorandum need provide information with respect only to property which is carried on the records available at the office or branch where the levy is made, unless the levy has been served at a central location designated by a financial institution in accordance with Section 684.115, in which case the garnishee's memorandum shall apply to all offices and branches of the financial institution except to the extent acceptance of the levy at that central location is limited pursuant to paragraph (3) of subdivision [1] (b) of Section 684.115.

(f) Notwithstanding subdivision (a), the third person need not give a garnishee's memorandum to the levying officer if both of the following conditions are satisfied:

(1) The third person has delivered to the levying officer all of the property sought to be attached.

(2) The third person has paid to the levying officer the amount due at the time of levy on any obligation to the defendant that was attached and there is no additional amount that thereafter will become payable on the obligation levied upon. **Leg.H.** Added Stats 1982 ch 1198 §50, operative July 1, 1983. Amended Stats 2012 ch 484 §5 (AB 2364), effective January 1, 2013; Stats 2024 ch 222 §1 (AB 2067), effective January 1, 2025.

§488.610. 2024 Deletes. [1] (a)

§488.620. Liability of person giving garnishee's memorandum

A third person who gives a garnishee's memorandum pursuant to this title is not liable to any person for the disclosure in the garnishee's memorandum of any information contained in the garnishee's memorandum. **Leg.H.** Added Stats 1983 ch 155 §8.3, effective June 30, 1983, operative July 1, 1983.

ARTICLE 5
Management and Disposition of Attached Property

Sale of or appointment of receiver for attached property. §488.700.
Endorsement and collection of certain instruments by levying officer. §488.710.
Release of property in excess of that needed to satisfy amount secured. §488.720.
Release of attached property. §488.730.
Release on judgment for defendant. §488.740.

§488.700. Sale of or appointment of receiver for attached property

(a) If property has been or is sought to be attached, the court may appoint a receiver or order the levying officer to take any action the court orders that is necessary to preserve the value of the property, including but not limited to selling the property, if the court determines that the property is perishable or will greatly deteriorate or greatly depreciate in value or that for some other reason the interests of the parties will be best served by the order. An order may be made under this subdivision upon application of the plaintiff, the defendant, or a person who has filed a third-party claim pursuant to Division 4 (commencing with Section 720.010) of Title 9. The application shall be made on noticed motion if the court so directs or a court rule so requires. Otherwise, the application may be made ex parte.

(b) If the levying officer determines that property is extremely perishable or will greatly deteriorate or greatly depreciate in value before a court order pursuant to subdivision (a) could be obtained, the levying officer may take any action necessary to preserve the value of the property or may sell the property. The levying officer is not liable for a determination made in good faith under this subdivision.

(c) Except as otherwise provided by order of the court, a sale of the property pursuant to this section shall be made in the manner provided by Article 6 (commencing with Section 701.510) of Chapter 3 of Division 2 of Title 9 and the proceeds shall be deposited in the court to abide the judgment in the action. Notwithstanding subdivisions (b) and (d) of Section 701.530, notice of sale shall be posted and served at a reasonable time before sale, considering the character and condition of the property.

(d) If a receiver is appointed, the court shall fix the daily fee of the receiver and may order the plaintiff to pay the fees and expenses of the receiver in advance or may direct that the whole or any part of the fees and expenses be paid from the proceeds of any sale of the property. Except as otherwise provided in this section, the provisions of Chapter 5 (commencing with Section 564) and Chapter 5a (commencing with Section 571) of Title 7 govern the appointment, qualifications, powers, rights, and duties of a receiver appointed under this section. **Leg.H.** Added Stats 1982 ch 1198 §50, operative July 1, 1983.

§488.710. Endorsement and collection of certain instruments by levying officer

(a) As used in this section, "instrument" means a check, draft, money order, or other order for the withdrawal of money from a financial institution, the United States, any state, or any public entity within any state.

(b) If an instrument is payable to the defendant on demand and comes into the possession of a levying officer pursuant to this title, the levying officer shall promptly endorse and present the instrument for payment.

(c) The levying officer shall endorse the instrument by writing on the instrument (1) the name of the defendant, (2) the name and official title of the levying officer, and (3) the title of the court and the cause in which the writ was issued. The endorsement is as valid as if the instrument were endorsed by the defendant. No financial institution or public entity on which the instrument is drawn is liable to any person for payment of the instrument to the levying officer rather than to the defendant by reason of the endorsement. No levying officer is liable by reason of endorsing, presenting, and obtaining payment of the instrument. The funds or credit resulting from the payment of the instrument shall be held by the levying officer subject to the lien of attachment.

(d) If it appears from the face of the instrument that it has been tendered to the defendant in satisfaction of a claim or demand and that endorsement of the instrument is considered a release and satisfaction by the defendant of the claim or demand, the levying officer shall not endorse the instrument unless the defendant has first endorsed it to the levying officer. If the defendant does not endorse the instrument to the levying officer, the levying officer shall hold the instrument for 30 days and is not liable to the defendant or to any other person for delay in presenting it for payment. At the end of the 30-day holding period, the levying officer shall return the instrument to the maker. **Leg.H.** Added Stats 1982 ch 1198 §50, operative July 1, 1983.

§488.720. Release of property in excess of that needed to satisfy amount secured

(a) The defendant may apply by noticed motion to the court in which the action is pending or in which the judgment in the action was entered for an order releasing the attachment of property to the extent that the value of the defendant's interest in the property clearly exceeds the amount necessary to satisfy the amount to be secured by the attachment.

(b) The notice of motion shall state the grounds on which the motion is based and shall be accompanied by an affidavit supporting any factual issues raised and points and authorities supporting any legal issues raised.

(c) At the hearing on the motion, the court shall determine the value of the defendant's interest in the property and order the release of the attachment of the property to the extent that the value of the defendant's interest in the property attached clearly exceeds the amount necessary to satisfy the amount to be secured by the attachment. After entry of judgment in the action in which the property was attached, the court shall also take into consideration in determining whether the attachment is clearly excessive the value of any property not attached in the action that (1) has been levied upon pursuant to a writ of execution issued to satisfy the judgment in the action or (2) otherwise has been sought to be applied to the satisfaction of the judgment in the action.

(d) The court's determinations shall be made upon the basis of the pleadings and other papers in the record; but, upon good cause shown, the court may receive and consider at the hearing additional evidence, oral or documentary, and additional points and authorities, or it may continue the hearing for the production of the additional evidence or points and authorities. **Leg.H.** Added Stats 1982 ch 1198 §50, operative July 1, 1983.

§488.730. Release of attached property

(a) The levying officer shall release attached property when the levying officer receives a written direction to release the property from the plaintiff's attorney of record or, if the plaintiff does not have an attorney of record, from the plaintiff or when the levying officer receives a certified copy of a court order for release or when otherwise required to release the property. The release extinguishes any attachment lien in favor of the plaintiff on the property released.

(b) If the property to be released has been taken into custody under the levy, it shall be released to the person from whom it was taken unless otherwise ordered by the court. If the person does not claim the property to be released, the levying officer shall retain custody of the property and shall serve on the person a notice of where possession of the property may be obtained. If the person does not claim the property within 30 days after the notice is served, the levying officer shall sell the property (other than cash which does not have a value exceeding its face value) in the manner provided by Article 6 (commencing with Section 701.510) of Chapter 3 of Division 2 of Title 9. The levying officer shall deposit the proceeds of sale and cash, after first deducting the levying officer's costs, with the county treasurer of the county where the property is located payable to the order of the person. If the amount deposited is not claimed by the person or the legal representative of the person within five years after the deposit is made, by making application to the treasurer or other official designated by the county, it shall be paid into the general fund of the county.

(c) If the property to be released has not been taken into custody under the levy, the levying officer shall release the attachment by issuing a written notice of release and serving it on the person who was served with a copy of the writ and a notice of attachment to create the lien.

(d) If the property to be released was levied upon by recording or filing a copy of the writ and a notice of attachment, the levying officer shall record or file a written notice of release in the same office. If the notice of attachment had been filed with the Secretary of State, any release shall have the effect prescribed in Section 697.650.

(e) The levying officer is not liable for releasing an attachment in accordance with this section and no other person is liable for acting in conformity with the release. **Leg.H.** Added Stats 1982 ch 1198 §50, operative July 1, 1983. Amended Stats 1983 ch 155 §9, effective June 30, 1983, operative July 1, 1983; Stats 1989 ch 445 §1.

§488.740. Release on judgment for defendant

If the defendant recovers judgment against the plaintiff and no timely motion for vacation of judgment or for judgment notwithstanding the verdict or for a new trial is filed and served and is pending and no appeal is perfected and undertaking executed and filed as provided in Section 921, any undertaking received from the defendant in the action, all the proceeds of sales and money collected by the levying officer, and all the property attached remaining in the levying officer's hands shall be delivered to the person from whom it was collected or taken, unless otherwise ordered by the court; and the court shall order the discharge of any attachment made in the action and the release of any property held thereunder. **Leg.H.** Added Stats 1982 ch 1198 §50, operative July 1, 1983.

§489. [Section repealed 1974]

Leg.H. Enacted 1872. Amended Stats 1933 ch 744 §44. Repealed Stats 1973 ch 20 §3. The repealed section related to when bail are liable.

CHAPTER 9
UNDERTAKINGS

Article 1. General Provisions.
Article 2. Undertakings to Obtain Writ of Attachment or Protective Order.
Article 3. Undertaking to Obtain Release of Attachment or Protective Order.
Article 4. Undertaking on Appeal.

ARTICLE 1
General Provisions

Application of Bond and Undertaking Law. §489.010.
Filing and approval of undertaking. §489.060.
Failure to increase undertaking. §489.130.

§489.010. Application of Bond and Undertaking Law

The Bond and Undertaking Law (Chapter 2 (commencing with Section 995.010) of Title 14) applies to a bond given pursuant to this title, except to the extent this title prescribes a different rule or is inconsistent. **Leg.H.** Added Stats 1985 ch 41 §2.

Prior Law: Former CCP §489.010, relating to application of bond and undertaking chapter, was added Stats 1974 ch 1516 §9, operative January 1, 1977 and repealed Stats 1982 ch 517 §102.

§§489.020–489.050 [Sections repealed 1983]

Leg.H. Added Stats 1974 ch 1516 §9, operative January 1, 1977. Repealed Stats 1982 ch 517 §§103–106.

§489.060. Filing and approval of undertaking

(a) Except as provided in subdivision (b), all undertakings given pursuant to this title shall be presented to a proper court for approval and upon approval shall be filed with the court in which the action is pending.

(b) If the surety on the undertaking is an admitted surety insurer, the undertaking is not required to be approved by the court. **Leg.H.** Added Stats 1974 ch 1516 §9, operative January 1, 1977. Amended Stats 1976 ch 437 §36.5; Stats 1982 ch 517 §107.

§§489.070–489.120. [Sections repealed 1983]

Leg.H. Added Stats 1974 ch 1516 §9, operative January 1, 1977. Repealed Stats 1982 ch 517 §§108–113.

§489.130. Failure to increase undertaking

Where the court orders the amount of the undertaking increased pursuant to Section 489.220 or 489.410, the plaintiff's failure to increase the amount of the undertaking is not a wrongful attachment within the meaning of Section 490.010. **Leg.H.** Added Stats 1976 ch 437 §37.

ARTICLE 2
Undertakings to Obtain Writ of Attachment or Protective Order

Undertaking required. §489.210.
Amount of undertaking. §489.220.
Notice to defendant. §489.230.

§489.210. Undertaking required

Before issuance of a writ of attachment, a temporary protective order, or an order under subdivision (b) of Section 491.415, the plaintiff shall file an undertaking to pay the defendant any amount the defendant may recover for any wrongful attachment by the plaintiff in the action. **Leg.H.** Added Stats 1974 ch 1516 §9, operative January 1, 1977. Amended Stats 1976 ch 437 §37.5; Stats 1984 ch 538 §7.

§489.220. Amount of undertaking

(a) Except as provided in subdivision (b), the amount of an undertaking filed pursuant to this article shall be ten thousand dollars ($10,000).

(b) If, upon objection to the undertaking, the court determines that the probable recovery for wrongful attachment exceeds the amount of the undertaking, it shall order the amount of the undertaking increased to the amount it determines to be the probable recovery for wrongful attachment if it is ultimately determined that the attachment was wrongful. **Leg.H.** Added Stats 1974 ch 1516 §9, operative January 1, 1977. Amended Stats 1976 ch 437 §38; Stats 1977 ch 1257 §14, effective October 3, 1977; Stats 1998 ch 931 §74 (SB 2139), effective September 28, 1998; Stats 2001 ch 812 §3 (AB 223).

§489.230. Notice to defendant

(a) The notice of attachment shall include a statement, in a form adopted by the Judicial Council, advising the defendant that the undertaking has been filed and informing the defendant of the right to object to the undertaking.

(b) The form for the temporary protective order shall include a statement comparable to the one required by subdivision (a). **Leg.H.** Added Stats 1974 ch 1516 §9, operative January 1, 1977. Amended Stats 1976 ch 437 §39; Stats 1982 ch 517 §114.

§489.240. [Section repealed 1983]

Leg.H. Added Stats 1974 ch 1516 §9, operative January 1, 1977. Amended Stats 1978 ch 273 §3. Repealed Stats 1982 ch 1198 §51, operative July 1, 1983. See CCP §488.465.

ARTICLE 3
Undertaking to Obtain Release of Attachment or Protective Order

Undertaking for release of attachment. §489.310.
Application to terminate temporary protective order. §489.320.

§489.310. Undertaking for release of attachment

(a) Whenever a writ is issued, a defendant who has appeared in the action may apply by noticed motion to the court in which the action is pending for an order permitting the defendant to substitute an undertaking for any of his property in the state which has been or is subject to being attached.

(b) In a case (1) where the defendant applies for an order to release a portion of property which has been attached or (2) where the defendant applies for an order preventing the attachment of property and the amount of the undertaking to be given is less than the amount to be secured by the attachment, the application shall include a statement, executed under oath, describing the property to be so released or so protected from attachment.

(c) The defendant shall file an undertaking to pay the plaintiff the value of the property released not exceeding the amount of any judgment which may be recovered by the plaintiff in the action against the defendant. The amount of the undertaking filed pursuant to this section shall be equal to the lesser of (1) the value of the property attached or prevented from being attached or (2) the amount specified by the writ to be secured by the attachment. The court shall issue such order upon the condition that a sufficient undertaking be filed.

(d) Where an action is against more than one defendant, any defendant may make such application. The filing of an undertaking by such defendant shall not subject him to any demand against any other defendant; however, the levying officer shall not be prevented thereby from attaching, or be obliged to release from attachment, any property of any other defendant. Where all the defendants do not join in the application, the application shall include a statement, executed under oath, describing the character of the defendant's title to the property and the manner in which the defendant acquired such title and stating whether any other defendant who has not joined in the application has an interest in the property. Where two or more defendants have an interest in the same property, a joint application and undertaking shall be filed to secure the release of such property. **Leg.H.** Added Stats 1974 ch 1516 §9, operative January 1, 1977. Amended Stats 1976 ch 437 §40.

§489.320. Application to terminate temporary protective order

(a) A defendant who has been served with a temporary protective order and who has appeared in the action may apply by noticed motion to the court in which the action is pending for an order terminating the temporary protective order with respect to that defendant.

(b) The defendant shall file an undertaking to pay the plaintiff the amount of any judgment recovered by the plaintiff in the action against the defendant. The amount of the undertaking filed pursuant to this section shall be equal to the amount sought to be secured by the attachment. The court shall issue the order terminating the temporary protective order with respect to the defendant upon the condition that a sufficient undertaking be filed. **Leg.H.** Added Stats 1974 ch 1516 §9, operative January 1, 1977. Amended Stats 1976 ch 437 §41; Stats 1982 ch 1198 §52, operative July 1, 1983.

ARTICLE 4
Undertaking on Appeal

Postjudgment continuance of attachment. §489.410.
Release from attachment. §489.420.

§489.410. Postjudgment continuance of attachment

(a) At any time after entry of judgment in favor of the defendant and before perfection of an appeal under Section 921, upon motion of the defendant, the trial court may order an increase in the amount of the original undertaking on attachment in such amount, if any, as is justified by the detriment reasonably to be anticipated by continuing the attachment. Unless such undertaking is filed within 10 days after such order, the attachment shall be set aside and the property released therefrom.

(b) If an order increasing the undertaking is made, the amount of the undertaking on appeal required by Section 921 shall be the same as the amount fixed by the trial court in such order.

(c) Neither the pendency nor granting of a motion timely filed and served by the plaintiff for vacation of judgment or for judgment notwithstanding the verdict or for new trial shall continue an attachment in force unless an undertaking is given by the plaintiff to pay all costs and damages sustained by continuing the attachment. The undertaking may be included in the undertaking specified in Section 921. If not so included, the same procedure shall apply as in case of an undertaking pursuant to Section 921. **Leg.H.** Added Stats 1974 ch 1516 §9, operative January 1, 1977.

§489.420. Release from attachment

If a defendant appeals and the enforcement of the judgment against the defendant is stayed by the filing of a sufficient undertaking on appeal as provided by this code, all property of the defendant which has been attached in the action shall be released from the attachment upon the failure of the respondent to object to the undertaking within the time prescribed by statute or, if an objection is made, upon a determination that the undertaking is sufficient. **Leg.H.** Added Stats 1974 ch 1516 §9, operative January 1, 1977. Amended Stats 1982 ch 517 §115.

§490. [Section repealed 1974]

Leg.H. Enacted 1872. Repealed Stats 1973 ch 20 §3. The repealed section related to the procedure for action against bail.

CHAPTER 10
LIABILITY FOR WRONGFUL ATTACHMENT

Wrongful attachment. §490.010.
Liability for wrongful attachment. §490.020.
Setoff of wrongful attachment recovery. §490.040.
Common law remedies not limited. §490.060.

§490.010. Wrongful attachment

A wrongful attachment consists of any of the following:

(a) The levy under a writ of attachment or the service of a temporary protective order in an action in which attachment is not authorized, except that it is not a wrongful attachment if both of the following are established:

(1) The levy was not authorized solely because of the prohibition of subdivision (c) of Section 483.010.

(2) The person who sold or leased, or licensed for use, the property, furnished the services, or loaned the money reasonably believed that it would not be used primarily for personal, family, or household purposes.

(b) The levy under a writ of attachment or the service of a temporary protective order in an action in which the plaintiff does not recover judgment.

(c) The levy under writ of attachment obtained pursuant to Article 3 (commencing with Section 484.510) of Chapter 4 or Chapter 5 (commencing with Section 485.010) on property exempt from attachment except where the plaintiff shows that the plaintiff reasonably believed that the property attached was not exempt from attachment. **Leg.H.** Added Stats 1974 ch 1516 §9, operative January 1, 1977. Amended Stats 1976 ch 437 §42; Stats 1982 ch 1198 §53, operative July 1, 1983.

§490.020. Liability for wrongful attachment

(a) The liability of a plaintiff for causing a wrongful attachment under Section 490.010 includes both of the following:

(1) All damages proximately caused to the defendant by the wrongful attachment.

(2) All costs and expenses, including attorney's fees, reasonably expended in defeating the attachment.

(b) The liability of a plaintiff for wrongful attachment pursuant to Section 490.010 is limited by the amount of the undertaking. **Leg.H.** Added Stats 1974 ch 1516 §9, operative January 1, 1977. Amended Stats 1982 ch 1198 §54, operative July 1, 1983.

§490.030. [Section repealed 1983]

Leg.H. Added Stats 1974 ch 1516 §9, operative January 1, 1977. Repealed Stats 1982 ch 517 §116. See CCP §§996.440, 996.460, 996.470.

§490.040. Setoff of wrongful attachment recovery

The amount of any recovery for wrongful attachment shall be offset insofar as possible against any unsatisfied amounts owed to the plaintiff by the defendant on the judgment in the action for which wrongful attachment damages are awarded. **Leg.H.** Added Stats 1974 ch 1516 §9, operative January 1, 1977.

§490.050. [Section repealed 1983]

Leg.H. Added Stats 1974 ch 1516 §9, operative January 1, 1977. Repealed Stats 1982 ch 1198 §55, operative July 1, 1983. The repealed section related to liability for wrongful attachment.

§490.060. Common law remedies not limited

Nothing in this chapter limits the right to recover for damages caused by an attachment or protective order on any common law theory of recovery. **Leg.H.** Added Stats 1974 ch 1516 §9, operative January 1, 1977.

§491. [Section repealed 1974]

Leg.H. Enacted 1872. Repealed Stats 1973 ch 20 §3. The repealed section related to exoneration of bail.

§§491.010–491.040. [Sections repealed 1983]

Leg.H. Added Stats 1974 ch 1516 §9, operative January 1, 1977. Amended Stats 1976 ch 437 §43, Stats 1980 ch 1372 §2. Repealed Stats 1982 ch 1198 §56, operative July 1, 1983.

CHAPTER 11
ATTACHING PLAINTIFF'S MISCELLANEOUS REMEDIES

Article 1.   Examination of Third Person.
Article 2.   Creditor's Suit.
Article 3.   Lien in Pending Action or Proceeding.

ARTICLE 1
Examination of Third Person

Application and order for examination of third person. §491.110.
Witnesses. §491.120.
Powers and qualifications of referee. §491.130.
Appearance for examination by representatives of organizations. §491.140.
Proper court for examination. §491.150.
Failure to appear for examination; Penalty for unjustified arrest. §491.160.
Determination of third person's adverse claim. §491.170.
Protective orders. §491.180.
Order in examination proceeding. §491.190.
Effect of lien in examination proceeding. §491.200.

§491.110. Application and order for examination of third person

(a) Upon ex parte application by the plaintiff and proof by the plaintiff by affidavit or otherwise to the satisfaction of the proper court that the plaintiff has a right to attach order and that a third person has possession or control of property in which the defendant has an interest or is indebted to the defendant in an amount exceeding two hundred fifty dollars ($250), the court shall make an order directing the third person to appear before the court, or before a referee appointed by the court, at a time and place specified in the order, to answer concerning the property or debt. The affidavit in support of the plaintiff's application may be based on the affiant's information and belief.

(b) Not less than 10 days prior to the date set for the examination, a copy of the order shall be:

(1) Served personally on the third person.

(2) Served personally or by mail on the defendant.

(c) If the property or the debt is described in the affidavit or application for an order under subdivision (a) in a manner reasonably adequate to permit it to be identified, service of the order on the third person creates a lien on the defendant's interest in the property in the third person's possession or control or on the debt owed by the third person to the defendant. The lien continues for a period of one year from the date of the order unless extended or sooner terminated by the court.

(d) The order shall contain the following statement in 14-point boldface type if printed or in capital letters if typed: "NOTICE TO PERSON SERVED. If you fail to appear at the time and place specified in this order, you may be subject to arrest and punishment for contempt of court and the court may make an order requiring you to pay the reasonable attorney's fees incurred by the plaintiff in this proceeding."

(e) The order is not effective unless, at the time it is served on the third person, the person serving the order tenders to the third person fees for the mileage necessary to be traveled from the third person's residence to the place of examination. The fees shall be in the same amount generally provided for witnesses when legally required to attend civil proceedings in the court where the examination proceeding is to be conducted. **Leg.H.** Added Stats 1982 ch 1198 §57, operative July 1, 1983.

§491.120. Witnesses

In any proceeding for the examination of a third person under this article, witnesses, including the defendant, may be required to appear and testify before the court or referee in the same manner as upon the trial of an issue. **Leg.H.** Added Stats 1982 ch 1198 §57, operative July 1, 1983.

§491.130. Powers and qualifications of referee

(a) The examination proceedings authorized by this article may be conducted by a referee appointed by the court. The referee may issue, modify, or vacate an order authorized by Section 491.190, may make a protective order authorized by Section 491.180, and may issue a warrant authorized by Section 491.160, and has the same power as the court to grant adjournments, to preserve order, and to subpoena witnesses to attend the examination, but only the court that ordered the reference has power to do any of the following:

(1) Punish for contempt for disobeying an order of the referee.

(2) Make an award of attorney's fees pursuant to Section 491.160.

(3) Determine a third-party claim under Section 491.170.

(b) Only a member of the State Bar of California is eligible for appointment as a referee pursuant to this article.

(c) Nothing in subdivision (a) limits the power of a court to appoint a temporary judge pursuant to Section 21 of Article VI of the California Constitution. **Leg.H.** Added Stats 1982 ch 1198 §57, operative July 1, 1983.

§491.140. Appearance for examination by representatives of organizations

(a) If a corporation, partnership, association, trust, or other organization is served with an order to appear for an examination, it shall designate to appear and be examined one or more officers, directors, managing agents, or other persons who are familiar with its property and debts.

(b) If the order to appear for an examination requires the appearance of a specified individual, the specified individual shall appear for the examination and may be accompanied by one or more officers, directors, managing agents, or other persons familiar with the property and debts of the corporation, partnership, association, trust, or other organization.

(c) If the order to appear for the examination does not require the appearance of a specified individual, the order shall advise the corporation, partnership, association, trust, or other organization of its duty to make a designation under subdivision (a).

(d) A corporation, partnership, association, trust, or other organization, whether or not a party, may appear at an examination through any authorized officer, director, or employee, whether or not the person is an attorney. **Leg.H.** Added Stats 1982 ch 1198 §57, operative July 1, 1983. Amended Stats 1984 ch 538 §7.5.

§491.150. Proper court for examination

(a) Except as otherwise provided in this section, the proper court for examination of a person under this article is the court that issued the writ of attachment.

(b) A person sought to be examined may not be required to attend an examination before a court located outside the county in which the person resides or has a place of business unless the distance from the person's place of residence or place of business to the place of examination is less than 150 miles.

(c) If a person sought to be examined does not reside or have a place of business in the county where the court that issued the writ is located, the superior court in the county where the person resides or has a place of business is a proper court for examination of the person.

(d) If the plaintiff seeks an examination of a person before a court other than the court that issued the writ, the plaintiff shall file an application that shall include all of the following:

(1) A certified copy of the complaint in the pending action.

(2) An affidavit in support of the application stating the place of residence or place of business of the person sought to be examined.

(3) Any necessary affidavit or showing for the examination as required by Section 491.110.

(4) The filing fee for a motion as provided in subdivision (a) of Section 70617 of the Government Code. **Leg.H.** Added Stats 1982 ch 1198 §57, operative July 1, 1983. Amended Stats 2005 ch 75 §33 (AB 145), effective July 19, 2005, operative January 01, 2006.

§491.160. Failure to appear for examination; Penalty for unjustified arrest

(a) If an order requiring a person to appear for an examination was served by a sheriff, marshal, a person specially appointed by the court in the order, or a registered process server, and the person fails to appear:

(1) The court may do either of the following:

(A) Pursuant to a warrant, have the person brought before the court to answer for the failure to appear and may punish the person for contempt.

(B) Issue a warrant for the arrest of the person who failed to appear as required by the court order, pursuant to Section 1993.

(2) If the person's failure to appear is without good cause, the plaintiff shall be awarded reasonable attorney's fees incurred in the examination proceeding.

(b) A person who willfully makes an improper service of an order for an examination which subsequently results in the arrest pursuant to subdivision (a) of the person who fails to appear is guilty of a misdemeanor. **Leg.H.** Added Stats 1982 ch 1198 §57, operative July 1, 1983. Amended Stats 1996 ch 872 §13 (AB 3472); Stats 2006 ch 277 §1 (AB 2369), effective January 1, 2007.

§491.170. Determination of third person's adverse claim

(a) Subject to subdivision (b), if a third person examined pursuant to this article claims an interest in the property adverse to the defendant or denies the debt, the court may, if the plaintiff so requests, determine the interests in the property or the existence of the debt. Such a determination is conclusive as to the plaintiff, the defendant, and the third person, but an appeal may be taken from the determination in the manner provided for appeals from the court in which the proceeding takes place. The court may grant a continuance for a reasonable time for discovery proceedings, the production of evidence, or other preparation for the hearing.

(b) The court may not make the determination provided in subdivision (a) if the third person's claim is made in good faith and any of the following conditions is satisfied:

(1) The court would not be a proper court for the trial of an independent civil action (including a creditor's suit) for the determination of the interests in the property or the existence of the debt, and the third person objects to the determination of the matter under subdivision (a).

(2) At the time an order for examination pursuant to this article is served on the third person a civil action (including a creditor's suit) is pending with respect to the interests in the property or the existence of the debt.

(3) The court determines that the interests in the property or the existence of the debt should be determined in a creditor's suit.

(c) Upon application of the plaintiff made ex parte, the court may make an order forbidding transfer of the property to the defendant or payment of the debt to the defendant until the interests in the property or the existence of the debt is determined pursuant to subdivision (a) or until a creditor's suit may be commenced and an order obtained pursuant to Section 491.340. An undertaking may be required in the discretion of the court. The court may modify or vacate the order at any time with or without a hearing on such terms as are just.

(d) Upon application of the plaintiff upon noticed motion, the court, if it determines that the defendant probably owns an interest in the property or that the debt probably is owed to the defendant, may make an order forbidding the transfer or other disposition of the property to any person or forbidding payment of the debt until the interests in the property or the existence of the debt is determined pursuant to subdivision (a) or until a creditor's suit may be commenced and an order obtained pursuant to

Section 491.340. The court shall require the plaintiff to furnish an undertaking as provided in Section 529. The court may modify or vacate the order at any time after notice and hearing on such terms as are just. **Leg.H.** Added Stats 1982 ch 1198 §57, operative July 1, 1983.

§491.180. Protective orders

In any proceeding under this article, the court may, on motion of the person to be examined or on its own motion, make such protective orders as justice may require. **Leg.H.** Added Stats 1982 ch 1198 §57, operative July 1, 1983.

§491.190. Order in examination proceeding

(a) Except as provided in subdivision (b), at the conclusion of a proceeding pursuant to this article:

(1) The court may order the defendant's interest in the property in the possession or under the control of the third person or a debt owed by the third person to the defendant to be attached in the manner and under the conditions provided by this title or to be delivered or paid to the levying officer if the levying officer has a writ of attachment permitting the attachment of the property or debt. After the property or debt has been attached, the order may be enforced as provided in Section 491.360. The order creates a lien on the property or debt. The lien continues for a period of one year from the date of the order unless the court extends or reduces the period of the existence of the lien.

(2) If the property or debt has previously been attached, the court may make an order determining the third person's liability, and the order may be enforced as provided in Section 491.360.

(b) If a third person examined pursuant to this article claims an interest in the property adverse to the defendant or denies the debt and the court does not determine the matter as provided in subdivision (a) of Section 491.170, the court may not make an order under subdivision (a) of this section, but may make an order pursuant to subdivision (c) or (d) of Section 491.170 forbidding transfer or payment to the extent authorized by that section. **Leg.H.** Added Stats 1982 ch 1198 §57, operative July 1, 1983.

§491.200. Effect of lien in examination proceeding

A lien created under this article continues on property subject to the lien notwithstanding the transfer or encumbrance of the property subject to the lien unless the transfer or encumbrance is made to a person listed in Section 697.740. **Leg.H.** Added Stats 1982 ch 1198 §57, operative July 1, 1983.

ARTICLE 2
Creditor's Suit

Authority to bring action. §491.310.
Joinder of defendant. §491.320.
Time for bringing action. §491.330.
Order forbidding transfer of property or payment of debt. §491.340.
No right to jury trial. §491.350.
Judgment in creditor's suit. §491.360.
Costs. §491.370.

§491.310. Authority to bring action

If a third person has possession or control of property in which the defendant has an interest or is indebted to the defendant and the property or debt has been subjected to an attachment lien, the plaintiff may bring an action against the third person to enforce the third person's liability under this title. **Leg.H.** Added Stats 1982 ch 1198 §57, operative July 1, 1983.

§491.320. Joinder of defendant

The defendant shall be joined in an action brought pursuant to this article but is not an indispensable party. The residence of the defendant may not be considered in the determination of proper venue unless otherwise provided by contract between the defendant and the third person. **Leg.H.** Added Stats 1982 ch 1198 §57, operative July 1, 1983.

§491.330. Time for bringing action

(a) Except as provided in subdivision (b), an action shall be commenced pursuant to this article before the expiration of the later of the following times:

(1) The time when the defendant may bring an action against the third person concerning the property or debt.

(2) One year after creation of an attachment lien on the property or debt pursuant to this title if the lien is created at the time when the defendant may bring an action against the third person concerning the property or debt.

(b) An action may not be commenced pursuant to this article if the attachment lien is not in effect.

(c) If an action is commenced pursuant to this article within the time permitted in this section, the action may be prosecuted to judgment so long as the attachment lien or a lien of the plaintiff on the same property pursuant to Title 9 (commencing with Section 680.010) is in effect. **Leg.H.** Added Stats 1982 ch 1198 §57, operative July 1, 1983.

§491.340. Order forbidding transfer of property or payment of debt

The plaintiff may apply to the court in which an action under this article is pending for either or both of the following:

(a) An order restraining the third person from transferring the attached property to the defendant or from paying the attached debt to the defendant. The order shall be made on noticed motion if the court so directs or a court rule so requires. Otherwise, the order may be made on ex parte application. The order shall remain in effect until judgment is entered in the action or until such earlier time as the court may provide in the order. An undertaking may be required in the discretion of the court. The court may modify or vacate the order at any time with or without a hearing on such terms as are just.

(b) A temporary restraining order or a preliminary injunction or both, restraining the third person from transferring to any person or otherwise disposing of the attached property, pursuant to Chapter 3 (commencing with Section 525) of Title 7, and the court may make, dissolve, and modify such orders as provided therein. **Leg.H.** Added Stats 1982 ch 1198 §57, operative July 1, 1983.

§491.350. No right to jury trial

There is no right to a jury trial in an action under this article. **Leg.H.** Added Stats 1982 ch 1198 §57, operative July 1, 1983.

§491.360. Judgment in creditor's suit

If the plaintiff establishes the liability of the third person, the court shall render judgment accordingly. The judgment may be enforced in the same manner as it could be enforced if it had been obtained by the defendant against the third party; but, prior to entry of judgment in favor of the plaintiff against the defendant, any money or property obtained in enforcing the judgment against the third party shall be paid or delivered into court to abide the judgment in the action of the plaintiff against the defendant or shall be held by a levying officer, or otherwise held, as ordered by the court. **Leg.H.** Added Stats 1982 ch 1198 §57, operative July 1, 1983.

§491.370. Costs

Costs incurred by or taxed against the plaintiff in an action under this article may not be recovered from the defendant. **Leg.H.** Added Stats 1982 ch 1198 §57, operative July 1, 1983.

ARTICLE 3
Lien in Pending Action or Proceeding

Plaintiff's lien in pending action or proceeding. §491.410.
Property subject to attachment; Application for order permitting creation of lien; Claim of exemption by defendant. §491.415.
Contents of notice of lien. §491.420.
Intervention; Plaintiff deemed a party for certain purposes. §491.430.
Enforcement, compromise, dismissal, settlement, satisfaction. §491.440.
Endorsement of lien on judgment and abstract. §491.450.
Orders in action or special proceeding to enforce lien. §491.460.
Application for exemption; Determination. §491.470.

§491.410. Plaintiff's lien in pending action or proceeding

(a) If the defendant is a party to a pending action or special proceeding, the plaintiff may obtain a lien under this article, to the extent required to secure the amount to be secured by the attachment, on both of the following:

(1) Any cause of action of the defendant for money or property that is the subject of the other action or proceeding, if the money or property would be subject to attachment if the defendant prevails in the action or proceedings.

(2) The rights of the defendant to money or property under any judgment subsequently procured in the other action or proceeding, if the money or property would be subject to attachment.

(b) To obtain a lien under this article, the plaintiff shall file all of the following in the other pending action or special proceeding:

(1) A notice of lien.

(2) A copy of the right to attach order.

(3) A copy of an order permitting creation of a lien under this article made by the court that issued the right to attach order.

(c) At the time of the filing under subdivision (b) or promptly thereafter, the plaintiff shall serve on all parties who, prior thereto, have made an appearance in the other action or special proceeding a copy of the notice of lien and a statement of the date when the notice of lien was filed in the other action or special proceeding. Failure to serve all parties as required by this subdivision does not affect the lien created by the filing under subdivision (b), but the rights of a party are not affected by the lien until the party has notice of the lien.

(d) For the purpose of this article, an action or special proceeding is pending until the time for appeal from the judgment has expired or, if an appeal is filed, until the appeal has been finally determined. **Leg.H.** Added Stats 1982 ch 1198 §57, operative July 1, 1983. Amended Stats 1984 ch 538 §8.

§491.415. Property subject to attachment; Application for order permitting creation of lien; Claim of exemption by defendant

(a) For the purpose of applying for a right to attach order, the defendant's cause of action that is the subject of the pending action or proceeding and the defendant's rights to money or property under a judgment procured in the action or proceeding shall be treated as property subject to attachment.

(b) At the time the plaintiff applies for a right to attach order, the plaintiff may apply for an order permitting creation of a lien under this article. If the plaintiff has already obtained a right to attach order, an application for an order permitting creation of a lien under this article may be applied for in the same manner as a writ of attachment. As a prerequisite to obtaining an order under this subdivision, the plaintiff shall file an undertaking as provided by Sections 489.210 and 489.220.

(c) The defendant may, but is not required to, claim an exemption in a proceeding initiated by the plaintiff for an order permitting creation of a lien under this article. An exemption may be claimed if the money or property sought by the defendant would be exempt from attachment should the defendant prevail in the other action or proceeding. The exemption shall be claimed and determined pursuant to this subdivision in the same manner as an exemption is claimed and determined upon application for a writ of attachment. **Leg.H.** Added Stats 1984 ch 538 §9.

§491.420. Contents of notice of lien

The notice of lien under Section 491.410 shall contain all of the following:

(a) A statement that a lien has been created under this article and the title of the court and the cause and number of the pending action or proceeding in which the notice of lien is filed.

(b) The name and last known address of the defendant.

(c) The name and address of the plaintiff.

(d) The title of the court where the plaintiff's action against the defendant is pending and the cause and number of the action.

(e) The amount required to secure the amount to be secured by the attachment at the time the notice of lien is filed in the action or proceeding.

(f) A statement that the lien attaches to any cause of action of the defendant that is the subject of such action or proceeding and to the defendant's rights to money or property under any judgment subsequently procured in the action or proceeding.

(g) A statement that no compromise, dismissal, settlement, or satisfaction of the pending action or proceeding or any of the defendant's rights to money or property under any judgment procured therein may be entered into by or on behalf of the defendant, and that the defendant may not enforce the defendant's rights to money or property under any judgment procured in the pending action or proceeding by a writ or otherwise, unless one of the following requirements is satisfied:

(1) The prior approval by order of the court in which the action or proceeding is pending has been obtained.

(2) The written consent of the plaintiff has been obtained or the plaintiff has released the lien. **Leg.H.** Added Stats 1982 ch 1198 §57, operative July 1, 1983.

§491.430. Intervention; Plaintiff deemed a party for certain purposes

(a) The court in which the action or special proceeding subject to the lien under this article is pending may permit the plaintiff who has obtained the lien to intervene in the action or proceeding pursuant to Section 387.

(b) For the purposes of subdivision (a) of Section 491.460 and Section 491.470, a plaintiff shall be deemed to be a party to the action or special proceeding even though the plaintiff has not become a party to the action or proceeding under subdivision (a). **Leg.H.** Added Stats 1982 ch 1198 §57, operative July 1, 1983. Amended Stats 1984 ch 538 §10.

§491.440. Enforcement, compromise, dismissal, settlement, satisfaction

(a) Except as provided in subdivision (c) of Section 491.410, unless the lien is released, the judgment recovered in the action or special proceeding in favor of the defendant may not be enforced by a writ or otherwise, and no compromise, dismissal, settlement, or satisfaction of the pending action or special proceeding or the judgment procured therein may be entered into by or on behalf of the defendant, without the written consent of the plaintiff or authorization by order of the court obtained under subdivision (b).

(b) Upon application by the defendant, the court in which the action or special proceeding subject to the lien under this article is pending or the judgment procured therein is entered may, in its discretion, after a hearing, make an order described in subdivision (a) that may include such terms and conditions as the court deems necessary. The application for an order under this subdivision shall be made on noticed motion. The notice of motion shall be served on the plaintiff. **Leg.H.** Added Stats 1982 ch 1198 §57, operative July 1, 1983.

§491.450. Endorsement of lien on judgment and abstract

(a) If a lien is created pursuant to this article, the court clerk shall endorse upon the judgment recovered in the action or special proceeding a statement of the existence of the lien and the time it was created.

(b) Any abstract issued upon the judgment shall include a statement of the lien in favor of the plaintiff. **Leg.H.** Added Stats 1982 ch 1198 §57, operative July 1, 1983.

§491.460. Orders in action or special proceeding to enforce lien

(a) If the defendant is entitled to money or property under the judgment in the action or special proceeding and a lien created under this article exists, upon application of any party to the action or special proceeding, the court may order that the defendant's rights to money or property under the judgment be attached or otherwise applied to the satisfaction of the lien created under this article as ordered by the court. Application for an order under this section shall be on noticed motion. The notice of motion shall be served on all other parties.

(b) If the judgment determines that the defendant has an interest in property, the court may order the party having custody or control of the property not to transfer the property until it can be attached or otherwise applied to the satisfaction of the lien created under this article.

(c) If the court determines that a party (other than the defendant) having notice of the lien created under this article has transferred property that was subject to the lien, or has paid an amount to the defendant that was subject to the lien, the court shall render judgment against the party in an amount equal to the lesser of the following:

(1) The value of the defendant's interest in the property or the amount paid to the defendant.

(2) The amount of the plaintiff's lien created under this article.

(d) A judgment or order under this section may be enforced in the same manner as it could be enforced if it had been obtained by the defendant against the third party; but, prior to entry of judgment in favor of the plaintiff against the defendant, any money or property obtained in enforcing the judgment or order against the third party shall be paid or delivered into court to abide the judgment in the action of the plaintiff against the defendant or shall be held by a levying officer, or otherwise held, as ordered by the court. **Leg.H.** Added Stats 1982 ch 1198 §57, operative July 1, 1983.

§491.470. Application for exemption; Determination

(a) If a lien is created under this article, the defendant may claim that all or any portion of the money or property that the defendant may recover in the action or special proceeding is exempt from attachment. The claim shall be made by application on noticed motion to the court in which the action or special proceeding is pending, filed, and served on the plaintiff not later than 30 days after the defendant has notice of the creation of lien. The defendant shall execute an affidavit in support of the application that includes the matters set forth in subdivision (c) of Section 484.070. No notice of opposition to the claim of exemption is required. The failure of the defendant to make a claim of exemption under this section constitutes a waiver of the exemption.

(b) The court may determine the exemption claim at any time prior to the entry of judgment in the action or special proceeding or may consolidate the exemption hearing with the hearing on a motion pursuant to Section 491.460.

(c) If the defendant establishes to the satisfaction of the court that the money or property that the defendant may recover in the action or special proceeding is all or partially exempt from attachment, the court shall order the termination of the lien created under this article on the exempt portion of the money or property. **Leg.H.** Added Stats 1984 ch 538 §11.

§492. [Section repealed 1974]

Leg.H. Enacted 1872. Amended Stats 1933 ch 744 §45; Stats 1951 ch 1737 §63, operative January 1, 1952. Repealed Stats 1973 ch 20 §3. The repealed section related to return of order and exception to bail.

CHAPTER 12
NONRESIDENT ATTACHMENT

Attachment in action against nonresident. §492.010.
Application for order and writ; supporting affidavit. §492.020.
Issuance of order and writ. §492.030.
Property subject to attachment. §492.040.
Setting aside right to attach order and quashing writ. §492.050.
Application for additional writ. §492.060.
Application for additional writ. §492.070.
Issuance of additional writ. §492.090.

§492.010. Attachment in action against nonresident

Notwithstanding subdivision (a) of Section 483.010, an attachment may be issued in any action for the recovery of money brought against any of the following:

(a) A natural person who does not reside in this state.

(b) A foreign corporation not qualified to do business in this state under the provisions of Chapter 21 (commencing with Section 2100) of Division 1 of Title 1 of the Corporations Code.

(c) A foreign partnership which has not filed a designation pursuant to Section 15800 of the Corporations Code. **Leg.H.** Added Stats 1974 ch 1516 §9, operative January 1, 1977. Amended Stats 1975 ch 682 §5, effective January 1, 1977; Stats 1982 ch 1198 §58, operative July 1, 1983; Stats 2021 ch 124 §9 (AB 938), effective January 1, 2022.

§492.020. Application for order and writ; supporting affidavit

(a) Upon the filing of the complaint or at any time thereafter, the plaintiff may apply pursuant to this chapter for a right to attach order and a writ of attachment by filing an application for the order and writ with the court in which the action is brought.

(b) The application shall satisfy the requirements of Section 484.020 and shall be supported by an affidavit showing all of the following:

(1) The action is one described in Section 492.010 and is brought against a defendant described in Section 492.010.

(2) The plaintiff on the facts presented would be entitled to a judgment on the claim upon which the attachment is based.

(3) The property sought to be attached is subject to attachment pursuant to Section 492.040.

(c) The affidavit in support of the showing required by paragraph (3) of subdivision (b) may be based on the affiant's information and belief. **Leg.H.** Added Stats 1974 ch 1516 §9, operative January 1, 1977.

§492.030. Issuance of order and writ

(a) The court shall examine the application and supporting affidavit and shall issue a right to attach order, which shall state the amount to be secured by the attachment, and order a writ of attachment to be issued upon the filing of an undertaking as provided by Sections 489.210 and 489.220, if it finds all of the following:

(1) The claim upon which the attachment is based is one upon which an attachment may be issued.

(2) The plaintiff has established the probable validity of the claim upon which the attachment is based.

(3) The defendant is one described in Section 492.010.

(4) The attachment is not sought for a purpose other than the recovery on the claim upon which the attachment is based.

(5) The affidavit accompanying the application shows that the property sought to be attached, or the portion thereof to be specified in the writ, is subject to attachment pursuant to Section 492.040.

(6) The amount to be secured by the attachment is greater than zero.

(b) If the court finds that the application and supporting affidavit do not satisfy the requirements of this chapter, it shall so state and deny the order. If denial is solely on the ground that the defendant is not one described in Section 492.010, the judicial officer shall so state and such denial does not preclude the plaintiff from applying for a right to attach order and writ of attachment under Chapter 4 (commencing with Section 484.010) with the same affidavits and supporting papers. **Leg.H.** Added Stats 1974 ch 1516 §9, operative January 1, 1977. Amended Stats 1976 ch 437 §44; Stats 1997 ch 222 §10 (AB 1258).

§492.040. Property subject to attachment

Notwithstanding Sections 487.010 and 487.020, a writ of attachment issued under this chapter may be levied upon any property of a defendant for which a method of levy is provided by Article 2 (commencing with Section 488.300) of Chapter 8. However, after the defendant has filed a general appearance in the action, only nonexempt property of the defendant may be levied upon and property previously levied upon which is exempt under Section 487.020 shall be released upon order of the court. **Leg.H.** Added Stats 1974 ch 1516 §9, operative January 1, 1977. Amended Stats 1982 ch 1198 §59, operative July 1, 1983.

§492.050. Setting aside right to attach order and quashing writ

(a) Any defendant whose property has been attached pursuant to a writ issued under this chapter may apply for an order that the right to attach order be set aside, the writ of attachment quashed, and any property levied upon pursuant to the writ released. Such application shall be made by filing with the court and serving on the plaintiff a notice of motion.

(b) The notice of motion shall state the grounds on which the motion is based and shall be accompanied by an affidavit supporting any factual issues raised and points and authorities supporting any legal issues raised.

(c) If the defendant has filed a general appearance in the action, the right to attach order shall be set aside unless the plaintiff shows that his right to attach is authorized by a provision other than Section 492.010.

(d) At the hearing on the motion, the court shall determine whether the plaintiff is entitled to a right to attach order. If the court finds that the plaintiff is not entitled to a right to attach order, it shall order the right to attach order set aside, the writ of attachment quashed, and any property levied upon pursuant to the writ released. If the court finds that the plaintiff is entitled to a right to attach order, the attachment shall continue in effect except as provided in Section 492.040 and, thereafter, the plaintiff may apply for additional writs pursuant to Article 2 (commencing with Section 484.310) or Article 3 (commencing with Section 484.510) of Chapter 4.

(e) The court's determination shall be made upon the basis of the pleadings and other papers in the record; but, upon good cause shown, the court may receive and consider at the hearing additional evidence, oral or documentary, and additional points and authorities, or it may continue the hearing for the production of such additional evidence or points and authorities.

(f) The hearing provided for in this section shall take precedence over all other civil matters on the calendar of that day except older matters of the same character. **Leg.H.** Added Stats 1974 ch 1516 §9, operative January 1, 1977.

§492.060. Application for additional writ

At any time after a right to attach order and writ of attachment have been issued under this chapter and before the hearing provided by Section 492.050, the plaintiff may apply for an additional writ of attachment under this chapter as provided in Sections 492.060 to 492.090, inclusive. The application shall be filed with the court in which the action is brought. **Leg.H.** Added Stats 1974 ch 1516 §9, operative January 1, 1977.

§492.070. Application for additional writ

The application shall be executed under oath and shall include all of the following:

(a) A statement that the plaintiff has been issued a right to attach order and writ of attachment pursuant to Section 492.030.

(b) A statement of the amount to be secured by the attachment.

(c) A description of the property to be attached under the writ of attachment and a statement that the plaintiff is informed and believes that such property is subject to attachment pursuant to Section 492.040. The description shall satisfy the requirements of Section 484.020. **Leg.H.** Added Stats 1974 ch 1516 §9, operative January 1, 1977. Amended Stats 1982 ch 1198 §60, operative July 1, 1983.

§492.090. Issuance of additional writ

The court shall examine the application and supporting affidavit and shall order a writ of attachment to be issued upon the filing of an undertaking as provided by Sections 489.210 and 489.220, if it finds both of the following:

(a) A right to attach order has been issued in the action pursuant to Section 492.030.

(b) The affidavit accompanying the application shows that the property sought to be attached, or the portion thereof to be specified in the writ, is subject to attachment pursuant to Section 492.040. **Leg.H.** Added Stats 1974 ch 1516 §9, operative January 1, 1977. Amended Stats 1976 ch 437 §45.

§493. [Section repealed 1974]

Leg.H. Enacted 1872. Amended Code Amdts 1880 ch 15 §2; Stats 1933 ch 744 §46; Stats 1951 ch 1737 §64, operative January 1, 1952. Repealed Stats 1973 ch 20 §3. The repealed section related to justification of bail.

CHAPTER 13
EFFECT OF BANKRUPTCY PROCEEDINGS AND GENERAL ASSIGNMENTS FOR THE BENEFIT OF CREDITORS

"General assignment for the benefit of creditors". §493.010.
General assignment for the benefit of creditors not precluded. §493.020.
Termination of lien of temporary protective order or attachment. §493.030.
Release of attached property. §493.040.
Reinstatement of lien. §493.050.
Assignee subrogated to rights of plaintiff. §493.060.

§493.010. "General assignment for the benefit of creditors"

As used in this chapter, "general assignment for the benefit of creditors" means an assignment which satisfies all of the following requirements:

(a) The assignment is an assignment of all the defendant's assets that are transferable and not exempt from enforcement of a money judgment.

(b) The assignment is for the benefit of all the defendant's creditors.

(c) The assignment does not itself create a preference of one creditor or class of creditors over any other creditor or class of creditors, but the assignment may recognize the existence of preferences to which creditors are otherwise entitled. **Leg.H.** Added Stats 1977 ch 499 §1. Amended Stats 1982 ch 1198 §61, operative July 1, 1983.

§493.020. General assignment for the benefit of creditors not precluded

Notwithstanding any other provision of this title, the defendant may make a general assignment for the benefit of creditors. **Leg.H.** Added Stats 1977 ch 499 §1.

§493.030. Termination of lien of temporary protective order or attachment

(a) The making of a general assignment for the benefit of creditors terminates a lien of a temporary protective order or of attachment if the lien was created within 90 days prior to the making of the general assignment.

(b) The filing of a petition commencing a voluntary or involuntary case under Title 11 of the United States Code (Bankruptcy) terminates a lien of a temporary protective order or of attachment if the lien was created within 90 days prior to the filing of the petition.

(c) Subdivisions (a) and (b) do not apply unless all liens of attachment on the defendant's property in other states that were created within 90 days prior to the making of a general assignment for the benefit of creditors or the filing of a petition commencing a case under Title 11 of the United States Code (Bankruptcy) have terminated. **Leg.H.** Added Stats 1977 ch 499 §1. Amended Stats 1979 ch 177 §1, effective June 29, 1979, operative October 1, 1979.

§493.040. Release of attached property

(a) Where a lien of attachment terminates pursuant to Section 493.030, the assignee under a general assignment for the benefit of creditors or, in the case of a bankruptcy, the trustee, interim trustee, or the debtor in possession if there is no trustee or interim trustee, may secure the release of the attached property by filing with the levying officer a request for release of attachment stating the grounds for release and describing the property to be released, executed under oath, together with a copy thereof.

(b) In the case of an assignee, the request shall include two copies of the general assignment for the benefit of creditors.

(c) In the case of a trustee, interim trustee, or debtor in possession, the request shall include a certified copy of the petition in bankruptcy, together with a copy thereof.

(d) If immediate release of the attachment is sought, the request shall be accompanied by an undertaking to pay the plaintiff any damages resulting from an improper release of the attachment, in the amount to be secured by the attachment, executed by an admitted surety insurer.

(e) Within five days after the filing of the request for release of attachment, the levying officer shall mail to the plaintiff:

(1) A copy of the request for release of the attachment, including the copy of the document filed pursuant to subdivision (b) or (c).

(2) If an undertaking has not been given, a notice that the attachment will be released pursuant to the request for release of attachment unless otherwise ordered by a court within 10 days after the date of mailing the notice.

(3) If an undertaking has been given, a notice that the attachment has been released.

(f) Unless otherwise ordered by a court, if an undertaking has not been given, the levying officer shall release the attachment pursuant to the request for release of attachment after the expiration of 10 days from the date of mailing the papers referred to in subdivision (e) to the plaintiff. If an undertaking has been given, the levying officer shall immediately release the attachment pursuant to the request for release of attachment.

(g) Where the attached property has been taken into custody, it shall be released to the person making the request for release of attachment or some other person designated in the request. Where the attached property has not been taken into custody, it shall be released as provided in subdivision (c) or (d) of Section 488.730.

(h) The levying officer is not liable for releasing an attachment in accordance with this section nor is any other person liable for acting in conformity with the release. **Leg.H.** Added Stats 1977 ch 499 §1. Amended Stats 1979 ch 177 §2, effective June 29, 1979, operative October 1, 1979; Stats 1982 ch 517 §117 (ch 1198 prevails), ch 1198 §62.5, operative July 1, 1983.

§493.050. Reinstatement of lien

(a) The lien of a temporary protective order or of attachment, which has terminated pursuant to Section 493.030, is reinstated with the same effect as if it had not been terminated in the following cases:

(1) Where the termination is the result of the making of a general assignment for the benefit of creditors and the general assignment for the benefit of creditors is set aside otherwise than by the filing of a petition commencing a case under Title 11 of the United States Code (Bankruptcy).

(2) Where the termination is the result of the filing of a petition commencing a case under Title 11 of the United States Code (Bankruptcy) and the petition is dismissed.

(3) Where the termination is the result of the filing of a petition commencing a case under Title 11 of the United States Code (Bankruptcy) and the trustee abandons property which had been subject to the lien of the temporary protective order or of attachment.

(b) The period from the making of a general assignment for the benefit of creditors until reinstatement of the lien of the temporary protective order or of attachment is not counted in determining the duration of the temporary protective order or the lien of attachment. **Leg.H.** Added Stats 1977 ch 499 §1. Amended Stats 1979 ch 177 §3, effective June 29, 1979, operative October 1, 1979.

§493.060. Assignee subrogated to rights of plaintiff

(a) Upon the making of a general assignment for the benefit of creditors that terminates a lien under this chapter, the assignee is subrogated to the rights of the plaintiff under the temporary protective order or attachment.

(b) Upon the filing of a petition commencing a case under Title 11 of the United States Code (Bankruptcy), a lien terminated pursuant to this chapter is preserved for the benefit of the estate. **Leg.H.** Added Stats 1977 ch 499 §1. Amended Stats 1979 ch 177 §4, effective June 29, 1979, operative October 1, 1979.

§494. [Section repealed 1974]

Leg.H. Enacted 1872. Amended Code Amdts 1873–74 ch 383 §65; Stats 1933 ch 744 §47; Stats 1951 ch 1737 §65, operative January 1, 1952. Repealed Stats 1973 ch 20 §3.

§495. [Section repealed 1974]

Leg.H. Enacted 1872. Amended Stats 1933 ch 744 §48; Stats 1951 ch 1737 §66, operative January 1, 1952. Repealed Stats 1973 ch 20 §3.

§496. [Section repealed 1974]

Leg.H. Enacted 1872. Amended Stats 1933 ch 744 §49; Stats 1951 ch 1737 §67, operative January 1, 1952. Repealed Stats 1973 ch 20 §3.

§497. [Section repealed 1974]

Leg.H. Enacted 1872. Amended Stats 1933 ch 744 §50. Repealed Stats 1973 ch 20 §3.

§498. [Section repealed 1974]

Leg.H. Enacted 1872. Amended Stats 1933 ch 744 §51; Stats 1951 ch 1737 §68, operative January 1, 1952. Repealed Stats 1973 ch 20 §3.

§499. [Section repealed 1974]

Leg.H. Enacted 1872. Amended Stats 1933 ch 744 §52; Stats 1951 ch 1737 §69, operative January 1, 1952. Repealed Stats 1973 ch 20 §3.

ations.

TITLE 7
OTHER PROVISIONAL REMEDIES IN CIVIL ACTIONS

Chapter 1. General Provisions.
Chapter 2. Claim and Delivery of Personal Property.
Chapter 3. Injunction.
Chapter 5. Receivers.
Chapter 5A. Undertaking of Persons Handling Private Property or Funds.
Chapter 6. Deposit in Court.

CHAPTER 1
GENERAL PROVISIONS

Imprisonment for debt or tort. §501.

§500. [Section repealed 1977]

Leg.H. Added Stats 1974 ch 1516 §11, operative January 1, 1977. Repealed Stats 1977 ch 1257 §15, effective October 3, 1977. The repealed section related to limitations as to justice courts.

Prior Law: Former CCP §500, relating to disposition of deposit, was enacted 1872, amended Stats 1933 ch 744 §53, Stats 1951 ch 1737 §70, operative January 1, 1952, and repealed Stats 1973 ch 20 §3.

§501. Imprisonment for debt or tort

A person may not be imprisoned in a civil action for debt or tort, whether before or after judgment. Nothing in this section affects any power a court may have to imprison a person who violates a court order. **Leg.H.** Added Stats 1974 ch 1516 §11, operative January 1, 1977.

Prior Law: Former CCP §501, relating to liability of officer for escape, was enacted 1872, amended Stats 1933 ch 744 §54, and repealed Stats 1973 ch 20 §3.

§502. [Section repealed 1974]

Leg.H. Enacted 1872. Amended Stats 1933 ch 744 §55. Repealed Stats 1973 ch 20 §3. The repealed section related to liability of sheriff, constable, or marshal.

§503. [Section repealed 1974]

Leg.H. Enacted 1872. Amended Code Amdts 1873–74 ch 383 §66; Stats 1933 ch 744 §56; Stats 1951 ch 1737 §71, operative January 1, 1952. Repealed Stats 1973 ch 20 §3. The repealed section related to proceedings to vacate order of arrest or reduce bail.

§504. [Section repealed 1974]

Leg.H. Enacted 1872. Repealed Stats 1973 ch 20 §3. The repealed section related to when the order must be vacated or the bail reduced.

§505. [Section repealed 1974]

Leg.H. Added Stats 1969 ch 690 §4. Repealed Stats 1973 ch 20 §3. The repealed section related to defendant's right to attorney.

§509. [Section repealed 1974]

Leg.H. Added Stats 1972 ch 855 §2, effective August 14, 1972. Amended Stats 1972 ch 1324 §1, effective December 22, 1972; Stats 1973 ch 8 §1, effective March 14, 1973. Repealed Stats 1973 ch 526 §1, operative July 1, 1974. See CCP §512.010.

Prior Law: Former CCP §509, relating to plaintiff's right to claim delivery, was enacted 1872 and repealed Stats 1972 ch 855 §1, effective August 14, 1972.

§510. [Section repealed 1974]

Leg.H. Added Stats 1972 ch 855 §2, effective August 14, 1972. Amended Stats 1972 ch 1324 §1, effective December 22, 1972; Stats 1973 ch 8 §1, effective March 14, 1973. Repealed Stats 1973 ch 526 §1, operative July 1, 1974. See CCP §§512.010, 512.040, 512.060, 513.010, 513.020.

Prior Law: Former CCP §510, relating to required showing in support of plaintiff's claim, was enacted 1872 and repealed Stats 1972 ch 855 §1, effective August 14, 1972.

§511. [Section repealed 1974]

Leg.H. Added Stats 1972 ch 855 §2, effective August 14, 1972. Amended Stats 1972 ch 1324 §1, effective December 22, 1972; Stats 1973 ch 8 §1, effective March 14, 1973. Repealed Stats 1973 ch 526 §1, operative July 1, 1974. See CCP §512.060.

Prior Law: Former CCP §511, relating to seizure of property, was enacted 1872, amended Stats 1933 ch 744 §57 and repealed Stats 1972 ch 855 §1, effective August 14, 1972.

CHAPTER 2
CLAIM AND DELIVERY OF PERSONAL PROPERTY

Article 1. Words and Phrases Defined.
Article 2. Writ of Possession.
Article 3. Temporary Restraining Order.
Article 4. Levy and Custody.
Article 5. Undertakings.
Article 6. Miscellaneous Provisions.

ARTICLE 1
Words and Phrases Defined

Governing definitions. §511.010.
"Complaint". §511.020.
"Defendant". §511.030.
"Farm products". §511.040.
"Inventory". §511.050.
"Levying officer". §511.060.
"Person". §511.070.
"Plaintiff". §511.080.
"Probable validity" of claim. §511.090.
"Public entity". §511.100.

§511.010. Governing definitions

Unless the provision or context otherwise requires, the definitions in this article govern the construction of this chapter. **Leg.H.** Added Stats 1973 ch 526 §2, operative July 1, 1974.

§511.020. "Complaint"

"Complaint" includes a cross-complaint. **Leg.H.** Added Stats 1973 ch 526 §2, operative July 1, 1974.

§511.030. "Defendant"

"Defendant" includes a cross-defendant. **Leg.H.** Added Stats 1973 ch 526 §2, operative July 1, 1974.

§511.040. "Farm products"

"Farm products" means crops or livestock or supplies used or produced in farming operations or products of crops or livestock in their unmanufactured states (such as ginned cotton, wool clip, maple syrup, honey, milk, and eggs) while in the possession of a defendant engaged in raising, fattening, grazing, or other farming operations. If tangible personal property is a farm product, it is not inventory. **Leg.H.** Added Stats 1973 ch 526 §2, operative July 1, 1974.

§511.050. "Inventory"

"Inventory" means tangible personal property in the possession of a defendant who holds it for sale or lease or to be furnished under contracts of service. **Leg.H.** Added Stats 1973 ch 526 §2, operative July 1, 1974.

§511.060. "Levying officer"

"Levying officer" means the sheriff or marshal who is directed to execute a writ of possession issued under this chapter. **Leg.H.** Added Stats 1973 ch 526 §2, operative July 1, 1974. Amended Stats 1996 ch 872 §14 (AB 3472).

§511.070. "Person"

"Person" includes an individual, a corporation, a partnership or other unincorporated association, a limited liability company, and a public entity. **Leg.H.** Added Stats 1973 ch 526 §2, operative July 1, 1974. Amended Stats 1994 ch 1010 §59 (SB 2053).

§511.080. "Plaintiff"

"Plaintiff" means a person who files a complaint or cross-complaint. **Leg.H.** Added Stats 1973 ch 526 §2, operative July 1, 1974.

§511.090. "Probable validity" of claim

A claim has "probable validity" where it is more likely than not that the plaintiff will obtain a judgment against the defendant on that claim. **Leg.H.** Added Stats 1973 ch 526 §2, operative July 1, 1974.

§511.100. "Public entity"

"Public entity" includes the state, the Regents of the University of California, a county, city, district, public authority, public agency, and any other political subdivision or public corporation in the state. **Leg.H.** Added Stats 1973 ch 526 §2, operative July 1, 1974.

§512. [Section repealed 1974]

Leg.H. Added Stats 1972 ch 855 §2, effective August 14, 1972. Repealed Stats 1973 ch 526 §1, operative July 1, 1974. See CCP §§512.080, 512.090.

Prior Law: Former CCP §512, similar to later §§511, 513, was enacted 1872, amended Stats 1933 ch 744 §58, Stats 1965 ch 1973 §1, and repealed Stats 1972 ch 855 §1, effective August 14, 1972.

ARTICLE 2
Writ of Possession

Application for writ. §512.010.
Notice and hearing requirements. §512.020.
Documents served prior to hearing on noticed motion. §512.030.
Contents of Notice of Application and Hearing. §512.040.
Affidavits and points and authorities; Determination of application. §512.050.
Findings before issuance of writ at hearing; Showing for directing officer's entry. §512.060.
Order directing transfer of possession to plaintiff. §512.070.
Contents of writ. §512.080.
Court's endorsement directing seizure at place not specified in writ. §512.090.
Defendant's failures not constituting waiver of defenses or right to produce or exclude evidence. §512.100.
Limitations on effect, etc., of court's determinations. §512.110.
Unsuccessful plaintiff's redelivery of property, and liability for damages. §512.120.

§512.010. Application for writ

(a) Upon the filing of the complaint or at any time thereafter, the plaintiff may apply pursuant to this chapter for a writ of possession by filing a written application for the writ with the court in which the action is brought.

(b) The application shall be executed under oath and shall include all of the following:

(1) A showing of the basis of the plaintiff's claim and that the plaintiff is entitled to possession of the property claimed. If the basis of the plaintiff's claim is a written instrument, a copy of the instrument shall be attached.

(2) A showing that the property is wrongfully detained by the defendant, of the manner in which the defendant came into possession of the property, and, according to the best knowledge, information, and belief of the plaintiff, of the reason for the detention.

(3) A particular description of the property and a statement of its value.

(4) A statement, according to the best knowledge, information, and belief of the plaintiff, of the location of the property and, if the property, or some part of it, is within a private place which may have to be entered to take possession, a showing that there is probable cause to believe that such property is located there.

(5) A statement that the property has not been taken for a tax, assessment, or fine, pursuant to a statute; or seized under an execution against the property of the plaintiff; or, if so seized, that it is by statute exempt from such seizure.

(c) The requirements of subdivision (b) may be satisfied by one or more affidavits filed with the application. **Leg.H.** Added Stats 1973 ch 526 §2, operative July 1, 1974.

§512.020. Notice and hearing requirements

(a) Except as otherwise provided in this section, no writ shall be issued under this chapter except after a hearing on a noticed motion.

(b) A writ of possession may be issued ex parte pursuant to this subdivision if probable cause appears that any of the following conditions exists:

(1) The defendant gained possession of the property by feloniously taking the property from the plaintiff. This subdivision shall not apply where the defendant has fraudulently appropriated property entrusted to him or obtained possession by false or fraudulent representation or pretense or by embezzlement.

(2) The property is a credit card.

(3) The defendant acquired possession of the property in the ordinary course of his trade or business for commercial purposes and:

(i) The property is not necessary for the support of the defendant or his family; and

(ii) There is an immediate danger that the property will become unavailable to levy by reason of being transferred, concealed, or removed from the state or will become substantially impaired in the value by acts of destruction or by failure to take care of the property in a reasonable manner; and

(iii) The ex parte issuance of a writ of possession is necessary to protect the property.

The plaintiff's application for the writ shall satisfy the requirements of Section 512.010 and, in addition, shall include a showing that the conditions required by this subdivision exist. A writ of possession may issue if the court finds that the conditions required by this subdivision exist and the requirements of Section 512.060 are met. Where a writ of possession has been issued pursuant to this subdivision, a copy of the summons and complaint, a copy of the application and any affidavit in support thereof, and a notice which satisfies the requirements of subdivisions (c) and (d) of Section 512.040 and informs the defendant of his rights under this subdivision shall be served upon the defendant and any other person required by Section 514.020 to be served with a writ of possession. Any defendant whose property has been taken pursuant to a writ of possession issued under this subdivision may apply for an order that the writ be quashed and any property levied on pursuant to the writ be released. Such application shall be made by noticed motion, and the provisions of Section 512.050 shall apply. Pending the hearing on the defendant's application, the court may order that delivery pursuant to Section 514.030 of any property previously levied upon be stayed. If the court determines that the plaintiff is not entitled to a writ of possession, the court shall quash the writ of possession and order the release and redelivery of any property previously levied upon, and shall award the defendant any damages sustained by him which were proximately caused by the levy of the writ of possession and the loss of possession of the property pursuant to such levy. **Leg.H.** Added Stats 1973 ch 526 §2, operative July 1, 1974.

§512.030. Documents served prior to hearing on noticed motion

(a) Prior to the hearing required by subdivision (a) of Section 512.020, the defendant shall be served with all of the following:

(1) A copy of the summons and complaint.
(2) A Notice of Application and Hearing.
(3) A copy of the application and any affidavit in support thereof.

(b) If the defendant has not appeared in the action, and a writ, notice, order, or other paper is required to be personally served on the defendant under this title, service shall be made in the same manner as a summons is served under Chapter 4 (commencing with Section 413.10) of Title 5. **Leg.H.** Added Stats 1973 ch 526 §2, operative July 1, 1974. Amended Stats 2007 ch 15 §2 (AB 859), effective January 1, 2008.

§512.040. Contents of Notice of Application and Hearing

The "Notice of Application and Hearing" shall inform the defendant of all of the following:

(a) A hearing will be held at a place and at a time, to be specified in the notice, on plaintiff's application for a writ of possession.

(b) The writ will be issued if the court finds that the plaintiff's claim is probably valid and the other requirements for issuing the writ are established. The hearing is not for the purpose of determining whether the claim is actually valid. The determination of the actual validity of the claim will be made in subsequent proceedings in the action and will not be affected by the decision at the hearing on the application for the writ.

(c) If the defendant desires to oppose the issuance of the writ, he shall file with the court either an affidavit providing evidence sufficient to defeat the plaintiff's right to issuance of the writ or an undertaking to stay the delivery of the property in accordance with Section 515.020.

(d) The notice shall contain the following statement: "If you believe the plaintiff may not be entitled to possession of the property claimed, you may wish to seek the advice of an attorney. Such attorney should be consulted promptly so that he may assist you before the time set for the hearing." **Leg.H.** Added Stats 1973 ch 526 §2, operative July 1, 1974.

§512.050. Affidavits and points and authorities; Determination of application

Each party shall file with the court and serve upon the other party within the time prescribed by rule any affidavits and points and authorities intended to be relied upon at the hearing. At the hearing, the court shall make its determinations upon the basis of the pleadings and other papers in the record; but, upon good cause shown, the court may receive and consider additional evidence and authority produced at the hearing or may continue the hearing for the production of such additional evidence, oral or documentary, or the filing of other affidavits or points and authorities. **Leg.H.** Added Stats 1973 ch 526 §2, operative July 1, 1974.

§512.060. Findings before issuance of writ at hearing; Showing for directing officer's entry

(a) At the hearing, a writ of possession shall issue if both of the following are found:

(1) The plaintiff has established the probable validity of the plaintiff's claim to possession of the property.

(2) The undertaking requirements of Section 515.010 are satisfied.

(b) No writ directing the levying officer to enter a private place to take possession of any property shall be issued unless the plaintiff has established that there is probable cause to believe that the property is located there. **Leg.H.** Added Stats 1973 ch 526 §2, operative July 1, 1974. Amended Stats 2002 ch 68 §1 (SB 1322).

§512.070. Order directing transfer of possession to plaintiff

If a writ of possession is issued, the court may also issue an order directing the defendant to transfer possession of the property to the plaintiff. Such order shall contain a notice to the defendant that failure to turn over possession of such property to plaintiff may subject the defendant to being held in contempt of court. **Leg.H.** Added Stats 1973 ch 526 §2, operative July 1, 1974. Amended Stats 1976 ch 145 §1.

§512.080. Contents of writ

The writ of possession shall meet all of the following requirements:

(a) Be directed to the levying officer within whose jurisdiction the property is located.

(b) Describe the specific property to be seized.

(c) Specify any private place that may be entered to take possession of the property or some part of it.

(d) Direct the levying officer to levy on the property pursuant to Section 514.010 if found and to retain it in custody until released or sold pursuant to Section 514.030.

(e) Inform the defendant of the right to object to the plaintiff's undertaking, a copy of which shall be attached to the writ, or to obtain redelivery of the property by filing an undertaking as prescribed by Section 515.020. **Leg.H.** Added Stats 1973 ch 526 §2, operative July 1, 1974. Amended Stats 1982 ch 517 §118.

§512.090. Court's endorsement directing seizure at place not specified in writ

(a) The plaintiff may apply ex parte in writing to the court in which the action was brought for an endorsement on the writ directing the levying officer to seize the property at a private place not specified in the writ.

(b) The court shall make the endorsement if the plaintiff establishes by affidavit that there is probable cause to believe that the property or some part of it may be found at that place. **Leg.H.** Added Stats 1973 ch 526 §2, operative July 1, 1974.

§512.100. Defendant's failures not constituting waiver of defenses or right to produce or exclude evidence

Neither the failure of the defendant to oppose the issuance of a writ of possession under this chapter nor his failure to rebut any evidence produced by the plaintiff in connection with proceedings under this chapter shall constitute a waiver of any defense to plaintiff's claim in the action or any other action or have any effect on the right of the defendant to produce or exclude evidence at the trial of any such action. **Leg.H.** Added Stats 1973 ch 526 §2, operative July 1, 1974.

§512.110. Limitations on effect, etc., of court's determinations

The determinations of the court under this chapter shall have no effect on the determination of any issues in the action other than the issues relevant to proceedings under this chapter, nor shall they affect the rights of any party in any other action arising out of the same claim. The determinations of the court under this chapter shall not be given in evidence nor referred to in the trial of any such action. **Leg.H.** Added Stats 1973 ch 526 §2, operative July 1, 1974.

§512.120. Unsuccessful plaintiff's redelivery of property, and liability for damages

If the plaintiff fails to recover judgment in the action, he shall redeliver the property to the defendant and be liable for all damages sustained by the defendant which are proximately caused by operation of the temporary restraining order and preliminary injunction, if any, the levy of the writ of possession, and the loss of possession of the property pursuant to levy of the writ of possession or in compliance with an order issued under Section 512.070. **Leg.H.** Added Stats 1973 ch 526 §2, operative July 1, 1974.

§513. [Section repealed 1974]

Leg.H. Added Stats 1972 ch 855 §2, effective August 14, 1972. Amended Stats 1972 ch 1324 §2, effective December 22, 1972. Repealed Stats 1973 ch 526 §1, operative July 1, 1974. See CCP §§514.010, 514.020.

Prior Law: Former CCP §513, similar to present CCP §515.030, was enacted 1872, amended Stats 1933 ch 744 §59, Stats 1945 ch 487 §1, and repealed Stats 1972 ch 855 §1, effective August 14, 1972.

ARTICLE 3
Temporary Restraining Order

Application; Findings; Ex parte issuance. §513.010.
Defendant acts that may be prohibited. §513.020.

§513.010. Application; Findings; Ex parte issuance

(a) Except as otherwise provided by this chapter, the provisions of Chapter 3 (commencing with Section 525) of this title relating to the issuance of a temporary restraining order apply. At or after the time he files his application for writ of possession, the plaintiff may apply for a temporary restraining order by setting forth in the application a statement of grounds justifying the issuance of such order.

(b) A temporary restraining order may issue ex parte if all of the following are found:

(1) The plaintiff has established the probable validity of his claim to possession of the property.

(2) The plaintiff has provided an undertaking as required by Section 515.010.

(3) The plaintiff has established the probability that there is an immediate danger that the property claimed may become unavailable to levy by reason of being transferred, concealed, or removed or may become substantially impaired in value.

(c) If at the hearing on issuance of the writ of possession the court determines that the plaintiff is not entitled to a writ of possession, the court shall dissolve any temporary restraining order; otherwise, the court may issue a preliminary injunction to remain in effect until the property claimed is seized pursuant to the writ of possession. **Leg.H.** Added Stats 1973 ch 526 §2, operative July 1, 1974.

§513.020. Defendant acts that may be prohibited

In the discretion of the court, the temporary restraining order may prohibit the defendant from doing any or all of the following:

(a) Transferring any interest in the property by sale, pledge, or grant of security interest, or otherwise disposing of, or encumbering, the property. If the property is farm products held for sale or lease or is inventory, the order may not prohibit the defendant from transferring the property in the ordinary course of business, but the order may impose appropriate restrictions on the disposition of the proceeds from such transfer.

(b) Concealing or otherwise removing the property in such a manner as to make it less available to seizure by the levying officer.

(c) Impairing the value of the property either by acts of destruction or by failure to care for the property in a reasonable manner. **Leg.H.** Added Stats 1973 ch 526 §2, operative July 1, 1974.

§514. [Section repealed 1974]

Leg.H. Added Stats 1972 ch 855 §2, effective August 14, 1972. Repealed Stats 1973 ch 526 §1, operative July 1, 1974. See CCP §515.020.

Prior Law: Former CCP §514, similar in part to the later section, was enacted 1872, amended Stats 1933 ch 744 §60, and repealed Stats 1972 ch 855 §1, effective August 14, 1972.

ARTICLE 4
Levy and Custody

Search for property; Assumption of custody. §514.010.
Service of writ and undertaking. §514.020.
Custody of property; Delivery; Redelivery; Sale. §514.030.
Return of writ. §514.040.
Third-party claim proceedings. §514.050.

§514.010. Search for property; Assumption of custody

(a) Except as otherwise provided in this section, upon receipt of the writ of possession the levying officer shall search for and take custody of the specified property, if it be in the possession of the defendant of his agent, either be removing the property to a place of safekeeping or by installing a keeper.

(b) If the specified property is used as a dwelling, such as a mobilehome or boat, levy shall be made by placing a keeper in charge of the property for two days, at the plaintiff's expense, after which period the levying officer shall remove the occupants and any contents not specified in the writ and shall take exclusive possession of the property.

(c) If the specified property or any part of it is in a private place, the levying officer shall at the time he demands possession of the property announce his identity, purpose, and authority. If the property is not voluntarily delivered, the levying officer may cause any building or enclosure where the property may be located to be broken open in such a manner as he reasonably believes will cause the least damage and may call upon the power of the county to aid and protect him, but, if he reasonably believes that entry and seizure of the property will involve a substantial risk of death or serious bodily harm to any person, he shall refrain from seizing the property and shall promptly make a return to the court from which the writ issued setting forth the reasons for his belief that the risk exists. In such case, the court shall make such orders as may be appropriate.

(d) Nothing in this section authorizes the levying officer to enter or search any private place not specified in the writ of possession or other order of the court. **Leg.H.** Added Stats 1973 ch 526 §2, operative July 1, 1974.

§514.020. Service of writ and undertaking

(a) At the time of levy, the levying officer shall deliver to the person in possession of the property a copy of the writ of possession, a copy of the plaintiff's undertaking, if any, and a copy of the order for issuance of the writ.

(b) If no one is in possession of the property at the time of levy, the levying officer shall subsequently serve the writ and attached undertaking on the defendant. If the defendant has appeared in the action, service shall be accomplished in the manner provided by Chapter 5 (commencing with Section 1010) of Title 14. If the defendant has not appeared in the action, service shall be accomplished in the manner provided for the service of summons and complaint by Article 3 (commencing with Section 415.10) of Chapter 4 of Title 5. **Leg.H.** Added Stats 1973 ch 526 §2, operative July 1, 1974. Amended Stats 2002 ch 68 §2 (SB 1322).

§514.030. Custody of property; Delivery; Redelivery; Sale

(a) After the levying officer takes possession pursuant to a writ of possession, the levying officer shall keep the property in a secure place. Except as otherwise provided by Sections 512.020 and 514.050:

(1) If notice of the filing of an undertaking for redelivery or notice of objection to the plaintiff's undertaking is not received by the levying officer within 10 days after levy of the writ of possession, the levying officer shall deliver the property to plaintiff, upon receiving the fees for taking and necessary expenses for keeping the property.

(2) If notice of the filing of an undertaking for redelivery is received by the levying officer within 10 days after levy of the writ of possession and defendant's undertaking is not objected to, the levying officer shall redeliver the property to defendant upon expiration of the time to so object, upon receiving the fees for taking and necessary expenses for keeping the property not already paid or advanced by the plaintiff.

(3) If notice of objection to the plaintiff's undertaking or notice of the filing of an undertaking for redelivery is received within 10 days after levy of the writ of possession and defendant's undertaking is objected to, the levying officer shall not deliver or redeliver the property until the time provided in Section 515.030.

(b) Notwithstanding subdivision (a), where not otherwise provided by contract and where an undertaking for redelivery has not been filed, upon a showing that the property is perishable or will greatly deteriorate or depreciate in value or for some other reason that the interests of the parties will be best served thereby, the court may order that the property be sold and the proceeds deposited in the court to abide the judgment in the action. **Leg.H.** Added Stats 1973 ch 526 §2, operative July 1, 1974. Amended Stats 1982 ch 517 §119.

§514.040. Return of writ

The levying officer shall return the writ of possession, with his proceedings thereon, to the court in which the action is pending within 30 days after levy but in no event more than 60 days after the writ is issued. **Leg.H.** Added Stats 1973 ch 526 §2, operative July 1, 1974.

§514.050. Third-party claim proceedings

Where the property taken is claimed by a third person, the rules and proceedings applicable in cases of third-party claims under Division 4 (commencing with Section 720.010) of Title 9 apply. **Leg.H.** Added Stats 1973 ch 526 §2, operative July 1, 1974. Amended Stats 1982 ch 497 §33, operative July 1, 1983.

§515. [Section repealed 1974]

Leg.H. Added Stats 1972 ch 855 §2, effective August 14, 1972. Amended Stats 1973 ch 20 §5. Repealed Stats 1973 ch 526 §1, operative July 1, 1974. See CCP §515.030.

Prior Law: Former CCP §515, similar in part to the later section, was enacted 1872, amended Stats 1933 ch 744 §61, Stats 1951 ch 1737 §72, Stats 1955 ch 156 §1, and repealed Stats 1972 ch 855 §1, effective August 14, 1972.

ARTICLE 5
Undertakings

Undertaking prior to issuance of order or writ; Waiver. §515.010.
Undertaking to prevent levy or to regain possession. §515.020.
Objection to undertaking. §515.030.

§515.010. Undertaking prior to issuance of order or writ; Waiver

(a) Except as provided in subdivision (b), the court shall not issue a temporary restraining order or a writ of possession until the plaintiff has filed an undertaking with the court. The undertaking shall provide that the sureties are bound to the defendant for the return of the property to the defendant, if return of the property is ordered, and for the payment to the defendant of any sum recovered against the plaintiff. The undertaking shall be in an amount not less than twice the value of the defendant's interest in the property or in a greater amount. The value of the defendant's interest in the property is determined by the market value of the property less the amount due and owing on any conditional sales contract or security agreement and all liens and encumbrances on the property, and any other factors necessary to determine the defendant's interest in the property.

(b) If the court finds that the defendant has no interest in the property, the court shall waive the requirement of the plaintiff's undertaking and shall include in the order for issuance of the writ the amount of the defendant's undertaking sufficient to satisfy the requirements of subdivision (b) of Section 515.020. **Leg.H.** Added Stats 1973 ch 526 §2, operative July 1, 1974. Amended Stats 1978 ch 373 §1; Stats 1981 ch 975 §2; Stats 1982 ch 517 §120; Stats 1984 ch 538 §12; Stats 2002 ch 68 §3 (SB 1322).

§515.020. Undertaking to prevent levy or to regain possession

(a) The defendant may prevent the plaintiff from taking possession of property pursuant to a writ of possession or regain possession of property so taken by filing with the court in which the action was brought an undertaking in an amount equal to the amount of the plaintiff's undertaking pursuant to subdivision (a) of Section 515.010 or in the amount determined by the court pursuant to subdivision (b) of Section 515.010.

(b) The undertaking shall state that, if the plaintiff recovers judgment on the action, the defendant shall pay all costs awarded to the plaintiff and all damages that the plaintiff may sustain by reason of the loss of possession of the property. The damages recoverable by the plaintiff pursuant to this section shall include all damages proximately caused by the plaintiff's failure to gain or retain possession.

(c) The defendant's undertaking may be filed at any time before or after levy of the writ of possession. A copy of the undertaking shall be mailed to the levying officer.

(d) If an undertaking for redelivery is filed and the defendant's undertaking is not objected to, the levying officer shall deliver the property to the defendant, or, if the plaintiff has previously been given possession of the property, the plaintiff shall deliver the property to the defendant. If an undertaking for redelivery is filed and the defendant's undertaking is objected to, the provisions of Section 515.030 apply. **Leg.H.** Added Stats 1973 ch 526 §2, operative July 1, 1974. Amended Stats 1978 ch 373 §2; Stats 1982 ch 517 §121; Stats 1984 ch 538 §13; Stats 2002 ch 68 §4 (SB 1322).

§515.030. Objection to undertaking

(a) The defendant may object to the plaintiff's undertaking not later than 10 days after levy of the writ of possession. The defendant shall mail notice of objection to the levying officer.

(b) The plaintiff may object to the defendant's undertaking not later than 10 days after the defendant's undertaking is filed. The plaintiff shall mail notice of objection to the levying officer.

(c) If the court determines that the plaintiff's undertaking is insufficient and a sufficient undertaking is not filed within the time required by statute, the court shall vacate the temporary restraining order or preliminary injunction, if any, and the writ of possession and, if levy has occurred, order the levying officer or the plaintiff to return the property to the defendant. If the court determines that the plaintiff's undertaking is sufficient, the court shall order the levying officer to deliver the property to the plaintiff.

(d) If the court determines that the defendant's undertaking is insufficient and a sufficient undertaking is not filed within the time required by statute, the court shall order the levying officer to deliver the property to the plaintiff, or, if the plaintiff has previously been given possession of the property, the plaintiff shall retain possession. If the court determines that the defendant's undertaking is sufficient, the court shall order the levying officer or the plaintiff to deliver the property to the defendant. **Leg.H.** Added Stats 1973 ch 526 §2, operative July 1, 1974. Amended Stats 1982 ch 517 §122; Stats 1984 ch 538 §14.

§516. [Section repealed 1974]

Leg.H. Added Stats 1972 ch 855 §2, effective August 14, 1972. Repealed Stats 1973 ch 526 §1, operative July 1, 1974. See CCP §§514.030, 515.020, 515.030.

Prior Law: Former CCP §516, similar in part to later §515.030, was enacted 1872 and repealed Stats 1972 ch 855 §1, effective August 14, 1972.

ARTICLE 6
Miscellaneous Provisions

Rules. §516.010.
Forms. §516.020.
Affidavits; Verified complaint. §516.030.
Performance of "subordinate judicial duties". §516.040.
Injunctive relief. §516.050.

§516.010. Rules

The Judicial Council may provide by rule for the practice and procedure in proceedings under this chapter. **Leg.H.** Added Stats 1973 ch 526 §2, operative July 1, 1974.

§516.020. Forms

The Judicial Council shall prescribe the form of the applications, notices, orders, and other documents required by this chapter. **Leg.H.** Added Stats 1973 ch 526 §2, operative July 1, 1974.

§516.030. Affidavits; Verified complaint

The facts stated in each affidavit filed pursuant to this chapter shall be set forth with particularity. Except where matters are specifically permitted by this chapter to be shown by information and belief, each affidavit shall show affirmatively that the affiant, if sworn as a witness, can testify competently to the facts stated therein. The affiant may be any person, whether or not a party to the action, who has knowledge of the facts. A verified complaint that satisfies the requirements of this section may be used in lieu of or in addition to any ordinary affidavit. **Leg.H.** Added Stats 1973 ch 526 §2, operative July 1, 1974.

§516.040. Performance of "subordinate judicial duties"

The judicial duties to be performed under this chapter are "subordinate judicial duties" within the meaning of Section 22 of Article VI of the California Constitution and may be performed by appointed officers such as court commissioners. **Leg.H.** Added Stats 1973 ch 526 §2, operative July 1, 1974.

§516.050. Injunctive relief

Nothing in this chapter shall preclude the granting of relief pursuant to Chapter 3 (commencing with Section 525) of this title. **Leg.H.** Added Stats 1973 ch 526 §2, operative July 1, 1974.

§517. [Section repealed 1974]

Leg.H. Added Stats 1972 ch 855 §2, effective August 14, 1972. Repealed Stats 1973 ch 526 §1, operative July 1, 1974. See CCP §514.050.

Prior Law: Former CCP §517, similar in part to CCP §§514.010 et seq., was enacted 1872, amended Stats 1933 ch 744 §62, Stats 1941 ch 229 §1, and repealed Stats 1972 ch 855 §1, effective August 14, 1972.

§518. [Section repealed 1974]

Leg.H. Added Stats 1972 ch 855 §2, effective August 14, 1972. Repealed Stats 1973 ch 526 §1, operative July 1, 1974. See CCP §514.040.

Prior Law: Former CCP §518, similar to CCP §§514.030 et seq., was enacted 1872, amended Stats 1933 ch 744 §63, and repealed Stats 1972 ch 855 §1, effective August 14, 1972.

§519. [Section repealed 1974]

Leg.H. Added Stats 1972 ch 855 §2, effective August 14, 1972. Repealed Stats 1973 ch 526 §1, operative July 1, 1974. See CCP §§515.020, 515.030.

Prior Law: Former CCP §519, similar to later CCP §514.050, was enacted 1872, amended Stats 1933 ch 744 §64, and repealed Stats 1972 ch 855 §1, effective August 14, 1972.

§520. [Section repealed 1974]

Leg.H. Added Stats 1972 ch 855 §2, effective August 14, 1972. Repealed Stats 1973 ch 526 §1, operative July 1, 1974. The repealed section related to precedence of actions.

Prior Law: Former CCP §520, similar to CCP §514.040, was enacted 1872, amended Stats 1933 ch 744 §65, Stats 1951 ch 1737 §73, operative January 1, 1952, Stats 1965 ch 1975 §1, and repealed Stats 1972 ch 855 §1, effective August 14, 1972.

§521. [Section repealed 1974]

Leg.H. Added Stats 1972 ch 855 §2, effective August 14, 1972. Repealed Stats 1973 ch 526 §1, operative July 1, 1974. The repealed section related to duration of chapter's operation.

Prior Law: Former CCP §521, similar to CCP §§515.020 et seq., was added Stats 1913 ch 297 §1 and repealed Stats 1972 ch 855 §1, effective August 14, 1972.

CHAPTER 3
INJUNCTION

Injunction defined; Who may grant. §525.
Cases in which injunction may or may not be granted. §526.
Actions against officers. §526a.
Action to enjoin sale of utility bonds. §526b.
Time for granting injunction; Notice; Preliminary injunction; Temporary restraining order. §527.
Injunctions in labor disputes. §527.3.
Temporary restraining order and order after hearing prohibiting harassment; Notice, service, and hearing; Possession of firearm or ammunition by person subject to protective order; Forms, instructions, and rules. §527.6.
Action to enjoin concerted acts of violence. §527.7.
Workplace violence and threats; Right of employer to seek temporary restraining order and order after hearing; Service, notice and hearing; Possession of firearm by person subject to protective order. § 527.8.
Temporary restraining order or order after hearing for credible threat of violence against a student at postsecondary educational institution; Procedure; Duration; Forms, instructions, and rules [Repealed January 1, 2026]. §527.85.
Temporary restraining orders and orders after hearing for postsecondary educational institutions [Operative January 1, 2026]. § 527.85.
Relinquishment of firearm by person subject to temporary restraining order or injunction; Storage; Fee; Employment exemption; Sale [Repealed January 1, 2026]. §527.9.
Relinquishment of firearms and ammunition upon issuance of temporary restraining order or injunction [Operative January 1, 2026]. § 527.9.
Court order prohibiting obtaining address or location of protected party or family member. §527.10.
Court determination of possession of firearms in violation of restraining order [Operative January 1, 2026]. § 527.11.
Service of temporary restraining orders, orders after hearing, and protective orders by peace officers [Operative January 1, 2026]. § 527.12.
Injunction after answer. §528.
Undertakings. §529.
Order requiring undertaking. §529.1.
Undertakings in actions challenging housing development projects. §529.2.
Injunction to protect water rights; Notice; Effect of defendant's bond. §530.
Injunction to suspend business of corporation. §531.
Motion to dissolve or modify injunction. §532.
Modification or dissolution of injunction or temporary restraining. §533.
Injunction to protect water rights; Effect of defendant's answer; Reply; Trial; Appeal. §534.

§525. Injunction defined; Who may grant

An injunction is a writ or order requiring a person to refrain from a particular act. It may be granted by the court in which the action is brought, or by a judge thereof; and when granted by a judge, it may be enforced as an order of the court. **Leg.H.** Enacted 1872. Amended Code Amdts 1880 ch 15 §3; Stats 1907 ch 272 §1.

§526. Cases in which injunction may or may not be granted

(a) An injunction may be granted in the following cases:

(1) When it appears by the complaint that the plaintiff is entitled to the relief demanded, and the relief, or any part thereof, consists in restraining the commission or continuance of the act complained of, either for a limited period or perpetually.

(2) When it appears by the complaint or affidavits that the commission or continuance of some act during the litigation would produce waste, or great or irreparable injury, to a party to the action.

(3) When it appears, during the litigation, that a party to the action is doing, or threatens, or is about to do, or is procuring or suffering to be done, some act in violation of the rights of another party to the action respecting the subject of the action, and tending to render the judgment ineffectual.

(4) When pecuniary compensation would not afford adequate relief.

(5) Where it would be extremely difficult to ascertain the amount of compensation which would afford adequate relief.

(6) Where the restraint is necessary to prevent a multiplicity of judicial proceedings.

(7) Where the obligation arises from a trust.

(b) An injunction cannot be granted in the following cases:

(1) To stay a judicial proceeding pending at the commencement of the action in which the injunction is demanded, unless the restraint is necessary to prevent a multiplicity of proceedings.

(2) To stay proceedings in a court of the United States.

(3) To stay proceedings in another state upon a judgment of a court of that state.

(4) To prevent the execution of a public statute by officers of the law for the public benefit.

(5) To prevent the breach of a contract the performance of which would not be specifically enforced, other than a contract in writing for the rendition of personal services from one to another where the promised service is of a special, unique, unusual, extraordinary, or intellectual character, which gives it peculiar value, the loss of which cannot be reasonably or adequately compensated in damages in an action at law, and where the compensation for the personal services is as follows:

(A) As to contracts entered into on or before December 31, 1993, the minimum compensation provided in the contract for the personal services shall be at the rate of six thousand dollars ($6,000) per annum.

(B) As to contracts entered into on or after January 1, 1994, the criteria of clause (i) or (ii), as follows, are satisfied:

(i) The compensation is as follows:

(I) The minimum compensation provided in the contract shall be at the rate of nine thousand dollars ($9,000) per annum for the first year of the contract, twelve thousand dollars ($12,000) per annum for the second year of the contract, and fifteen thousand dollars ($15,000) per annum for the third to seventh years, inclusive, of the contract.

(II) In addition, after the third year of the contract, there shall actually have been paid for the services through and including the contract year during which the injunctive relief is sought, over and above the minimum contractual compensation specified in subclause (I), the amount of fifteen thousand dollars ($15,000) per annum during the fourth and fifth years of the contract, and thirty thousand dollars ($30,000) per annum during the sixth and seventh years of the contract. As a condition to petitioning for an injunction, amounts payable under this clause may be paid at any time prior to seeking injunctive relief.

(ii) The aggregate compensation actually received for the services provided under a contract that does not meet the criteria of subparagraph (A), is at least 10 times the applicable aggregate minimum amount specified in subclauses (I) and (II) of clause (i) through and including the contract year during which the injunctive relief is sought. As a condition to petitioning for an injunction, amounts payable under this subparagraph may be paid at any time prior to seeking injunctive relief.

(C) Compensation paid in any contract year in excess of the minimums specified in clauses (i) and (ii) of subparagraph (B) shall apply to reduce the compensation otherwise required to be paid under those provisions in any subsequent contract years. However, an injunction may be granted to prevent the breach of a contract entered into between any nonprofit cooperative corporation or association and a member or stockholder thereof, in respect to any provision regarding the sale or delivery to the corporation or association of the products produced or acquired by the member or stockholder.

(6) To prevent the exercise of a public or private office, in a lawful manner, by the person in possession.

(7) To prevent a legislative act by a municipal corporation. **Leg.H.** Enacted 1872. Amended Stats 1907 ch 272 §2; Stats 1919 ch 224 §1; Stats 1925 ch 408 §1; Stats 1992 ch 177 §2 (SB 1459); Stats 1993 ch 836 §2 (SB 487).

§526a. Actions against officers

(a) An action to obtain a judgment, restraining and preventing any illegal expenditure of, waste of, or injury to, the estate, funds, or other property of a local agency, may be maintained against any officer thereof, or any agent, or other person, acting in its behalf, either by a resident therein, or by a corporation, who is assessed for and is liable to pay, or, within one year before the commencement of the action, has paid, a tax that funds the defendant local agency, including, but not limited to, the following:

(1) An income tax.

(2) A sales and use tax or transaction and use tax initially paid by a consumer to a retailer.

(3) A property tax, including a property tax paid by a tenant or lessee to a landlord or lessor pursuant to the terms of a written lease.

(4) A business license tax.

(b) This section does not affect any right of action in favor of a local agency, or any public officer; provided, that no injunction shall be granted restraining the offering for sale, sale, or issuance of any municipal bonds for public improvements or public utilities.

(c) An action brought pursuant to this section to enjoin a public improvement project shall take special precedence over all civil matters on the calendar of the court except those matters to which equal precedence on the calendar is granted by law.

(d) For purposes of this section, the following definitions apply:

(1) "Local agency" means a city, town, county, or city and county, or a district, public authority, or any other political subdivision in the state.

(2) "Resident" means a person who lives, works, owns property, or attends school in the jurisdiction of the defendant local agency. **Leg.H.** Added Stats 1909 ch 348 §1. Amended Stats 1911 ch 71 §1; Stats 1967 ch 706 §1; Stats 2018 ch 319 §1 (AB 2376), effective January 1, 2019.

§526b. Action to enjoin sale of utility bonds

Every person or corporation bringing, instigating, exciting or abetting, any suit to obtain an injunction, restraining or enjoining the issuance, sale, offering for sale, or delivery, of bonds, or other securities, or the expenditure of the proceeds of the sale of such bonds or other securities, of any city, city and county, town, county or other district organized under the laws of this state, or any other political subdivision of this state, proposed to be issued, sold, offered for sale or delivered by such city, city and county, town, county, district or other political subdivision, for the purpose of acquiring, constructing, completing, improving or extending water works, electric works, gas works or other public utility works or property, shall, if the injunction sought is finally denied, and if such person or corporation owns, controls, or is operating or interested in, a public utility business of the same nature as that for which such bonds or other securities are proposed to be issued, sold, offered for sale, or delivered, be liable to the defendant for all costs, damages and necessary expenses resulting to such defendant by reason of the filing of such suit. **Leg.H.** Added Stats 1921 ch 384 §1.

§527. Time for granting injunction; Notice; Preliminary injunction; Temporary restraining order

(a) A preliminary injunction may be granted at any time before judgment upon a verified complaint, or upon affidavits if the complaint in the one case, or the affidavits in the other, show satisfactorily that sufficient grounds exist therefor. No preliminary injunction shall be granted without notice to the opposing party.

(b) A temporary restraining order or a preliminary injunction, or both, may be granted in a class action, in which one or more of the parties sues or defends for the benefit of numerous parties upon the same grounds as in other actions, whether or not the class has been certified.

(c) No temporary restraining order shall be granted without notice to the opposing party, unless both of the following requirements are satisfied:

(1) It appears from facts shown by affidavit or by the verified complaint that great or irreparable injury will result to the applicant before the matter can be heard on notice.

(2) The applicant or the applicant's attorney certifies one of the following to the court under oath:

(A) That within a reasonable time prior to the application the applicant informed the opposing party or the opposing party's attorney at what time and where the application would be made.

(B) That the applicant in good faith attempted but was unable to inform the opposing party and the opposing party's attorney, specifying the efforts made to contact them.

(C) That for reasons specified the applicant should not be required to so inform the opposing party or the opposing party's attorney.

(d) In case a temporary restraining order is granted without notice in the contingency specified in subdivision (c):

(1) The matter shall be made returnable on an order requiring cause to be shown why a preliminary injunction should not be granted, on the earliest day that the business of the court will admit of, but not later than 15 days or, if good cause appears to the court, 22 days from the date the temporary restraining order is issued.

(2) The party who obtained the temporary restraining order shall, within five days from the date the temporary restraining order is issued or two days prior to the hearing, whichever is earlier, serve on the opposing party a copy of the complaint if not previously served, the order to show cause stating the date, time, and place of the hearing, any affidavits to be used in the application, and a copy of the points and authorities in support of the application. The court may for good cause, on motion of the applicant or on its own motion, shorten the time required by this paragraph for service on the opposing party.

(3) When the matter first comes up for hearing, if the party who obtained the temporary restraining order is not ready to proceed, or if the party has failed to effect service as required by paragraph (2), the court shall dissolve the temporary restraining order.

(4) The opposing party is entitled to one continuance for a reasonable period of not less than 15 days or any shorter period requested by the opposing party, to enable the opposing party to meet the application for a preliminary injunction. If the opposing party obtains a continuance under this paragraph, the temporary restraining order shall remain in effect until the date of the continued hearing.

(5) Upon the filing of an affidavit by the applicant that the opposing party could not be served within the time required by paragraph (2), the court may reissue any temporary restraining order previously issued. The reissued order shall be made returnable as provided by paragraph (1), with the time for hearing measured from the date of reissuance. No fee shall be charged for reissuing the order.

(e) The opposing party may, in response to an order to show cause, present affidavits relating to the granting of the preliminary injunction, and if the affidavits are served on the applicant at least two days prior to the hearing, the applicant shall not be entitled to any continuance on account thereof. On the day the order is made returnable, the hearing shall take precedence over all other matters on the calendar of the day, except older matters of the same character, and matters to which special precedence may be given by law. When the cause is at issue it shall be set for trial at the earliest possible date and shall take precedence over all other cases, except older matters of the same character, and matters to which special precedence may be given by law.

(f) Notwithstanding failure to satisfy the time requirements of this section, the court may nonetheless hear the order to show cause why a preliminary injunction should not be granted if the moving and supporting papers are served within the time required by Section 1005 and one of the following conditions is satisfied:

(1) The order to show cause is issued without a temporary restraining order.

(2) The order to show cause is issued with a temporary restraining order, but is either not set for hearing within the time required by paragraph (1) of subdivision (d), or the party who obtained the temporary restraining order fails to effect service within the time required by paragraph (2) of subdivision (d).

(g) This section does not apply to an order issued under the Family Code.

(h) As used in this section:

(1) "Complaint" means a complaint or a cross-complaint.

(2) "Court" means the court in which the action is pending. **Leg.H.** Enacted 1872. Amended Stats 1895 ch 49 §1; Stats 1907 ch 272 §3; Stats 1911 ch 42 §1; Stats 1963 ch 878 §2; Stats 1970 ch 488 §1; Stats 1977 ch 720 §1; Stats 1978 ch 346 §1; Stats 1979 ch 129 §1, ch 795 §7, operative July 1, 1980; Stats 1981 ch 182 §1; Stats 1982 ch 812 §1; Stats 1992 ch 163 §23 (AB 2641), operative January 1, 1994; Stats 1993 ch 583 §1 (AB 284); Stats 1994 ch 587 §5; Stats 1994 ch 587 §5 (AB 3600); Stats 1995 ch 796 §6 (SB 45); Stats 2000 ch 688 §4 (AB 1669).

§527.3. Injunctions in labor disputes

(a) In order to promote the rights of workers to engage in concerted activities for the purpose of collective bargaining, picketing or other mutual aid or protection, and to prevent the evils which frequently occur when courts interfere with the normal processes of dispute resolution between employers and recognized employee organizations, the equity jurisdiction of the courts in cases involving or growing out of a labor dispute shall be no broader than as set forth in subdivision (b) of this section, and the provisions of subdivision (b) of this section shall be strictly construed in accordance with existing law governing labor disputes with the purpose of avoiding any unnecessary judicial interference in labor disputes.

(b) The acts enumerated in this subdivision, whether performed singly or in concert, shall be legal, and no court nor any judge nor judges thereof, shall have jurisdiction to issue any restraining order or preliminary or permanent injunction which, in specific or general terms, prohibits any person or persons, whether singly or in concert, from doing any of the following:

(1) Giving publicity to, and obtaining or communicating information regarding the existence of, or the facts involved in, any labor dispute, whether by advertising, speaking, patrolling any public street or any place where any person or persons may lawfully be, or by any other method not involving fraud, violence or breach of the peace.

(2) Peaceful picketing or patrolling involving any labor dispute, whether engaged in singly or in numbers.

(3) Assembling peaceably to do any of the acts specified in paragraphs (1) and (2) or to promote lawful interests.

(4) Except as provided in subparagraph (iv), for purposes of this section, "labor dispute" is defined as follows:

(i) A case shall be held to involve or to grow out of a labor dispute when the case involves persons who are engaged in the same industry, trade, craft, or occupation; or have direct or indirect interests therein; or who are employees of the same employer; or who are members of the same or an affiliated organization of employers or employees; whether such dispute is (a) between one or more employers or associations of employers and one or more employees or associations of employees; (b) between one or more employers or associations of employers and one or more employers or associations of employers; or (c) between one or more employees or associations of employees and one or more employees or associations of employees; or when the case involves any conflicting or competing interests in a "labor dispute" of "persons participating or interested" therein (as defined in subparagraph (ii)).

(ii) A person or association shall be held to be a person participating or interested in a labor dispute if relief is sought against him or it, and if he or it is engaged in the same industry, trade, craft, or occupation in which such dispute occurs, or has a direct or indirect interest therein, or is a member, officer, or agent of any association composed in whole or in part of employers or employees engaged in such industry, trade, craft, or occupation.

(iii) The term "labor dispute" includes any controversy concerning terms or conditions of employment, or concerning the association or representation of persons in negotiating, fixing, maintaining, changing, or seeking to arrange terms or conditions of employment regardless of whether or not the disputants stand in the proximate relation of employer and employee.

(iv) The term "labor dispute" does not include a jurisdictional strike as defined in Section 1118 of the Labor Code.

(c) Nothing contained in this section shall be construed to alter or supersede the provisions of Chapter 1 of the 1975–76 Third Extraordinary

Session, and to the extent of any conflict between the provisions of this act and that chapter, the provisions of the latter shall prevail.

(d) Nothing contained in this section shall be construed to alter the legal rights of public employees or their employers, nor shall this section alter the rights of parties to collective-bargaining agreements under the provisions of Section 1126 of the Labor Code.

(e) It is not the intent of this section to permit conduct that is unlawful including breach of the peace, disorderly conduct, the unlawful blocking of access or egress to premises where a labor dispute exists, or other similar unlawful activity. **Leg.H.** Added Stats 1975 ch 1156 §1.

§527.6. Temporary restraining order and order after hearing prohibiting harassment; Notice, service, and hearing; Possession of firearm or ammunition by person subject to protective order; Forms, instructions, and rules

(a)(1) A person who has suffered harassment as defined in subdivision (b) may seek a temporary restraining order and an order after hearing prohibiting harassment as provided in this section.

(2) An individual need not be a resident of the state to file a petition for an order under this section. A petition for an order as specified in paragraph (1) may be filed in any superior court in this state, consistent with Section 410.10 of the Code of Civil Procedure, which may include, but is not limited to:

(A) The county in which the petitioner resides or is temporarily located.

(B) The county in which the defendant resides.

(C) The county in which the offense occurred.

(D) Any other court that may have jurisdiction over the parties or the subject matter of the case.

[1] (3) A minor, under 12 years of age, accompanied by a duly appointed and acting guardian ad litem, shall be permitted to appear in court without counsel for the limited purpose of requesting or opposing a request for a temporary restraining order or order after hearing, or both, under this section as provided in Section 374.

(b) For purposes of this section, the following terms have the following meanings:

(1) "Course of conduct" is a pattern of conduct composed of a series of acts over a period of time, however short, evidencing a continuity of purpose, including following or stalking an individual, making harassing telephone calls to an individual, or sending harassing correspondence to an individual by any means, including, but not limited to, the use of public or private mails, interoffice mail, facsimile, or email. Constitutionally protected activity is not included within the meaning of "course of conduct."

(2) "Credible threat of violence" is a knowing and willful statement or course of conduct that would place a reasonable person in fear for the person's safety or the safety of the person's immediate family, and that serves no legitimate purpose.

(3) "Harassment" is unlawful violence, a credible threat of violence, or a knowing and willful course of conduct directed at a specific person that seriously alarms, annoys, or harasses the person, and that serves no legitimate purpose. The course of conduct must be that which would cause a reasonable person to suffer substantial emotional distress, and must actually cause substantial emotional distress to the petitioner.

(4) "Petitioner" means the person to be protected by the temporary restraining order and order after hearing and, if the court grants the petition, the protected person.

(5) "Respondent" means the person against whom the temporary restraining order and order after hearing are sought and, if the petition is granted, the restrained person.

(6) "Temporary restraining order" and "order after hearing" mean orders that include any of the following restraining orders, whether issued ex parte or after notice and hearing:

(A) An order enjoining a party from harassing, intimidating, molesting, attacking, striking, stalking, threatening, sexually assaulting, battering, abusing, telephoning, including, but not limited to, making annoying telephone calls, as described in Section 653m of the Penal Code, destroying personal property, contacting, either directly or indirectly, by mail or otherwise, or coming within a specified distance of, or disturbing the peace of, the petitioner. On a showing of good cause, in an order issued pursuant to this subparagraph in connection with an animal owned, possessed, leased, kept, or held by the petitioner, or residing in the residence or household of the petitioner, the court may do either or both of the following:

(i) Grant the petitioner exclusive care, possession, or control of the animal.

(ii) Order the respondent to stay away from the animal and refrain from taking, transferring, encumbering, concealing, molesting, attacking, striking, threatening, harming, or otherwise disposing of the animal.

(B) An order enjoining a party from specified behavior that the court determines is necessary to effectuate orders described in subparagraph (A).

(7) "Unlawful violence" is any assault or battery, or stalking as prohibited in Section 646.9 of the Penal Code, but does not include lawful acts of self-defense or defense of others.

(c) In the discretion of the court, on a showing of good cause, a temporary restraining order or order after hearing issued under this section may include other named family or household members.

(d) Upon filing a petition for orders under this section, the petitioner may obtain a temporary restraining order in accordance with Section 527, except to the extent this section provides an inconsistent rule. The temporary restraining order may include any of the restraining orders described in paragraph (6) of subdivision (b). A temporary restraining order may be issued with or without notice, based on a declaration that, to the satisfaction of the court, shows reasonable proof of harassment of the petitioner by the respondent, and that great or irreparable harm would result to the petitioner.

(e) A request for the issuance of a temporary restraining order without notice under this section shall be granted or denied on the same day that the petition is submitted to the court. If the petition is filed too late in the day to permit effective review, the order shall be granted or denied on the next day of judicial business in sufficient time for the order to be filed that day with the clerk of the court.

(f) A temporary restraining order issued under this section shall remain in effect, at the court's discretion, for a period not to exceed 21 days, or, if the court extends the time for hearing under subdivision (g), not to exceed 25 days, unless otherwise modified or terminated by the court.

(g) Within 21 days, or, if good cause appears to the court, 25 days from the date that a petition for a temporary order is granted or denied, a hearing shall be held on the petition. If a request for a temporary order is not made, the hearing shall be held within 21 days, or, if good cause appears to the court, 25 days, from the date that the petition is filed.

(h) The respondent may file a response that explains, excuses, justifies, or denies the alleged harassment, or may file a cross-petition under this section.

(i) At the hearing, the judge shall receive any testimony that is relevant, and may make an independent inquiry. If the judge finds by clear and convincing evidence that unlawful harassment exists, an order shall issue prohibiting the harassment.

(j)(1) In the discretion of the court, an order issued after notice and hearing under this section may have a duration of no more than five years, subject to termination or modification by further order of the court either on written stipulation filed with the court or on the motion of a party. The order may be renewed, upon the request of a party, for a duration of no more than five additional years, without a showing of any further harassment since the issuance of the original order, subject to termination or modification by further order of the court either on written stipulation filed with the court or on the motion of a party. A request for renewal may be brought any time within the three months before the order expires.

(2) The failure to state the expiration date on the face of the form creates an order with a duration of three years from the date of issuance.

(3) If an action is filed for the purpose of terminating or modifying a protective order before the expiration date specified in the order by a party other than the protected party, the party who is protected by the order shall be given notice, pursuant to subdivision (b) of Section 1005, of the proceeding by personal service or, if the protected party has satisfied the requirements of Chapter 3.1 (commencing with Section 6205) of Division 7 of Title 1 of the Government Code, by service on the Secretary of State. If the party who is protected by the order cannot be notified before the hearing for modification or termination of the protective order, the court shall deny the motion to modify or terminate the order without prejudice or continue the hearing until the party who is protected can be properly noticed and may, upon a showing of good cause, specify another method for service of process that is reasonably designed to afford actual notice to

the protected party. The protected party may waive the protected party's right to notice if the protected party is physically present in court and does not challenge the sufficiency of the notice.

(k) This section does not preclude either party from representation by private counsel or from appearing on the party's own behalf.

(*l*) In a proceeding under this section, if there are allegations of unlawful violence or credible threats of violence, a support person may accompany a party in court and, if the party is not represented by an attorney, may sit with the party at the table that is generally reserved for the party and the party's attorney. The support person is present to provide moral and emotional support for a person who alleges they are a victim of violence. The support person is not present as a legal adviser and may not provide legal advice. The support person may assist the person who alleges they are a victim of violence in feeling more confident that they will not be injured or threatened by the other party during the proceedings if the person who alleges the person is a victim of violence and the other party are required to be present in close proximity. This subdivision does not preclude the court from exercising its discretion to remove the support person from the courtroom if the court believes the support person is prompting, swaying, or influencing the party assisted by the support person.

(m)(1) Except as provided in paragraph (2), upon the filing of a petition under this section, the respondent shall be personally served with a copy of the petition, temporary restraining order, if any, and notice of hearing of the petition. Service shall be made at least five days before the hearing. The court may for good cause, on motion of the petitioner or on its own motion, shorten the time for service on the respondent.

(2) If the court determines at the hearing that, after a diligent effort, the petitioner has been unable to accomplish personal service, and that there is reason to believe that the respondent is evading service or cannot be located, then the court may specify another method of service that is reasonably calculated to give actual notice to the respondent and may prescribe the manner in which proof of service shall be made.

(n) A notice of hearing under this section shall notify the respondent that if the respondent does not attend the hearing, the court may make orders against the respondent that could last up to five years.

(o) The respondent shall be entitled, as a matter of course, to one continuance, for a reasonable period, to respond to the petition.

(p)(1) Either party may request a continuance of the hearing, which the court shall grant on a showing of good cause. The request may be made in writing before or at the hearing, or orally at the hearing. The court may also grant a continuance on its own motion.

(2) If the court grants a continuance, any temporary restraining order that has been granted shall remain in effect until the end of the continued hearing, unless otherwise ordered by the court. In granting a continuance, the court may modify or terminate a temporary restraining order.

(q)(1) If a respondent named in a restraining order issued after a hearing has not been served personally with the order but has received actual notice of the existence and substance of the order through personal appearance in court to hear the terms of the order from the court, additional proof of service is not required for enforcement of the order.

(2) If the respondent named in a temporary restraining order is personally served with the order and notice of hearing with respect to a restraining order or protective order based on the temporary restraining order, but the respondent does not appear at the hearing, either personally or by an attorney, and the terms and conditions of the restraining order or protective order issued at the hearing are identical to the temporary restraining order, except for the duration of the order, the restraining order or protective order issued at the hearing may be served on the respondent by first-class mail sent to the respondent at the most current address for the respondent available to the court.

(3) The Judicial Council form for temporary orders issued pursuant to this subdivision shall contain a statement in substantially the following form:

If you have been personally served with this temporary restraining order and notice of hearing, but you do not appear at the hearing either in person or by a lawyer, and a restraining order that is the same as this temporary restraining order except for the expiration date is issued at the hearing, a copy of the restraining order will be served on you by mail at the following address: _____.

If that address is not correct or you wish to verify that the temporary restraining order was converted to a restraining order at the hearing without substantive change and to find out the duration of that order, contact the clerk of the court.

(4) If information about a minor has been made confidential pursuant to subdivision (v), the notice shall identify the information, specifically, that has been made confidential and shall include a statement that disclosure or misuse of that information is punishable as a contempt of court.

(r)(1) Information on a temporary restraining order or order after hearing relating to civil harassment issued by a court pursuant to this section shall be transmitted to the Department of Justice in accordance with either paragraph (2) or (3).

(2) The court shall order the petitioner or the attorney for the petitioner to deliver a copy of an order issued under this section, or reissuance, extension, modification, or termination of the order, and any subsequent proof of service, by the close of the business day on which the order, reissuance, extension, modification, or termination was made, to a law enforcement agency having jurisdiction over the residence of the petitioner and to any additional law enforcement agencies within the court's discretion as are requested by the petitioner.

(3) Alternatively, the court or its designee shall transmit, within one business day, to law enforcement personnel all information required under subdivision (b) of Section 6380 of the Family Code regarding any order issued under this section, or a reissuance, extension, modification, or termination of the order, and any subsequent proof of service, by either one of the following methods:

(A) Transmitting a physical copy of the order or proof of service to a local law enforcement agency authorized by the Department of Justice to enter orders into the California Law Enforcement Telecommunications System (CLETS).

(B) With the approval of the Department of Justice, entering the order or proof of service into CLETS directly.

(4) Each appropriate law enforcement agency shall make available information as to the existence and current status of orders issued under this section to law enforcement officers responding to the scene of reported harassment.

(5) An order issued under this section shall, on request of the petitioner, be served on the respondent, whether or not the respondent has been taken into custody, by any law enforcement officer who is present at the scene of reported harassment involving the parties to the proceeding. The petitioner shall provide the officer with an endorsed copy of the order and a proof of service that the officer shall complete and send to the issuing court.

(6) Upon receiving information at the scene of an incident of harassment that a protective order has been issued under this section, or that a person who has been taken into custody is the subject of an order, if the protected person cannot produce a certified copy of the order, a law enforcement officer shall immediately attempt to verify the existence of the order.

(7) If the law enforcement officer determines that a protective order has been issued but not served, the officer shall immediately notify the respondent of the terms of the order and shall at that time also enforce the order. Verbal notice of the terms of the order shall constitute service of the order and is sufficient notice for purposes of this section and for purposes of Section 29825 of the Penal Code. Verbal notice shall include the information required pursuant to paragraph (4) of subdivision (q).

(s) The prevailing party in an action brought pursuant to this section may be awarded court costs and attorney's fees, if any.

(t) Willful disobedience of a temporary restraining order or order after hearing granted pursuant to this section is punishable pursuant to Section 273.6 of the Penal Code.

(u)(1) A person subject to a protective order issued pursuant to this section shall not own, possess, purchase, receive, or attempt to purchase or receive a firearm or ammunition while the protective order is in effect.

(2) The court shall order a person subject to a protective order issued pursuant to this section to relinquish any firearms the person owns or possesses pursuant to Section 527.9.

(3) A person who owns, possesses, purchases, or receives, or attempts to purchase or receive, a firearm or ammunition while the protective order is in effect is punishable pursuant to Section 29825 of the Penal Code.

(v)(1) A minor or the minor's legal guardian may petition the court to have information regarding the minor that was obtained in connection with a request for a protective order pursuant to this section, including, but not limited to, the minor's name, address, and the circumstances surrounding the request for a protective order with respect to that minor, be kept confidential.

(2) The court may order the information specified in paragraph (1) be kept confidential if the court expressly finds all of the following:

(A) The minor's right to privacy overcomes the right of public access to the information.

(B) There is a substantial probability that the minor's interest will be prejudiced if the information is not kept confidential.

(C) The order to keep the information confidential is narrowly tailored.

(D) No less restrictive means exist to protect the minor's privacy.

(3)(A) If the request is granted, except as provided in paragraph (4), information regarding the minor shall be maintained in a confidential case file and shall not become part of the public file in the proceeding or any other civil proceeding involving the parties. Except as provided in subparagraph (B), if the court determines that disclosure of confidential information has been made without a court order, the court may impose a sanction of up to one thousand dollars ($1,000). A minor who has alleged harassment, as defined in subdivision (b), shall not be sanctioned for disclosure of the confidential information. If the court imposes a sanction, the court shall first determine whether the person has or is reasonably likely to have the ability to pay.

(B) Confidential information may be disclosed without a court order only in the following circumstances:

(i) By the minor's legal guardian who petitioned to keep the information confidential pursuant to this subdivision or the protected party in an order pursuant to this division, provided that the disclosure is necessary to prevent harassment or is in the minor's best interest. A legal guardian or a protected party who makes a disclosure under this clause is subject to the sanction in subparagraph (A) only if the disclosure was malicious.

(ii) By a person to whom confidential information is disclosed, provided that the disclosure is necessary to prevent harassment or is in the best interest of the minor, no more information than necessary is disclosed, and a delay would be caused by first obtaining a court order to authorize the disclosure of the information. A person who makes a disclosure pursuant to this clause is subject to the sanction in subparagraph (A) if the person discloses the information in a manner that recklessly or maliciously disregards these requirements.

(4)(A) Confidential information shall be made available to both of the following:

(i) Law enforcement pursuant to subdivision (r), to the extent necessary and only for the purpose of enforcing the order.

(ii) The respondent to allow the respondent to comply with the order for confidentiality and to allow the respondent to comply with and respond to the protective order. A notice shall be provided to the respondent that identifies the specific information that has been made confidential and shall include a statement that disclosure is punishable by a monetary fine.

(B) At any time, the court on its own may authorize a disclosure of any portion of the confidential information to certain individuals or entities as necessary to prevent harassment, as defined under subdivision (b), including implementation of the protective order, or if it is in the best interest of the minor.

(C) The court may authorize a disclosure of any portion of the confidential information to any person that files a petition if necessary to prevent harassment, as defined under subdivision (b), or if it is in the best interest of the minor. The party who petitioned the court to keep the information confidential pursuant to this subdivision shall be served personally or by first-class mail with a copy of the petition and afforded an opportunity to object to the disclosure.

(w) This section does not apply to any action or proceeding covered by Title 1.6C (commencing with Section 1788) of Part 4 of Division 3 of the Civil Code or by Division 10 (commencing with Section 6200) of the Family Code. This section does not preclude a petitioner from using other existing civil remedies.

(x)(1) The Judicial Council shall develop forms, instructions, and rules relating to matters governed by this section. The petition and response forms shall be simple and concise, and their use by parties in actions brought pursuant to this section is mandatory.

(2) A temporary restraining order or order after hearing relating to civil harassment issued by a court pursuant to this section shall be issued on forms adopted by the Judicial Council and that have been approved by the Department of Justice pursuant to subdivision (i) of Section 6380 of the Family Code. However, the fact that an order issued by a court pursuant to this section was not issued on forms adopted by the Judicial Council and approved by the Department of Justice shall not, in and of itself, make the order unenforceable.

(y) There is no filing fee for a petition that alleges that a person has inflicted or threatened violence against the petitioner, stalked the petitioner, or acted or spoken in any other manner that has placed the petitioner in reasonable fear of violence, and that seeks a protective or restraining order restraining stalking, future violence, or threats of violence, in an action brought pursuant to this section. A fee shall not be paid for a subpoena filed in connection with a petition alleging these acts. A fee shall not be paid for filing a response to a petition alleging these acts.

(z)(1) Subject to paragraph (4) of subdivision (b) of Section 6103.2 of the Government Code, there shall not be a fee for the service of process by a sheriff or marshal of a protective or restraining order to be issued, if either of the following conditions apply:

(A) The protective or restraining order issued pursuant to this section is based upon stalking, as prohibited by Section 646.9 of the Penal Code.

(B) The protective or restraining order issued pursuant to this section is based upon unlawful violence or a credible threat of violence.

(2) The Judicial Council shall prepare and develop forms for persons who wish to avail themselves of the services described in this subdivision.

Leg.H. Added Stats 2013 ch 158 §2 (AB 499), effective January 1, 2014, operative July 1, 2014. Amended Stats 2015 ch 401 §1 (AB 494), effective January 1, 2016, ch 411 §1.5 (AB 1081), effective January 1, 2016; Stats 2016 ch 86 §24 (SB 1171), effective January 1, 2017; Stats 2017 ch 384 §1 (AB 953), effective January 1, 2018; Stats 2019 ch 294 §1 (AB 925), effective January 1, 2020; Stats 2021 ch 156 §1 (AB 1143), effective January 1, 2022; Stats 2024 ch 652 §1 (SB 554), effective January 1, 2025.

§527.6. 2024 Deletes. [1] (2)

Former Sections: Former CCP §527.6, similar to the present section, was added Stats 2002 ch 1009 §2, operative January 1, 2007, amended Stats 2003 ch 498 §2, operative January 1, 2007, Stats 2006 ch 476 §1, effective January 1, 2007, Stats 2010 ch 178 §20 (ch 572 prevails), ch 572 §1, effective January 1, 2011, operative January 1, 2012, Stats 2011 ch 101 §1, effective January 1, 2012, ch 285 §1 (ch 101 prevails), Stats 2012 ch 162 §12, effective January 1, 2013, Stats 2013 ch 158 §1, effective January 1, 2014, and repealed July 1, 2014, by its own terms.

Former CCP §527.6, similar to the present section, was added Stats 1978 ch 1307 §2, amended Stats 1979 ch 795 §8, operative July 1, 1980, Stats 1980 ch 1158 §5, Stats 1981 ch 182 §2, Stats 1982 ch 423 §1, Stats 1984 ch 1163 §1, Stats 1987 ch 1493 §1, Stats 1992 ch 163 §24, operative January 1, 1994, Stats 1993 ch 219 §63.5, Stats 1994 ch 587 §6, Stats 1996 ch 691 §1, Stats 1998 ch 581 §2, Stats 1999 ch 661 §1, Stats 2000 ch 688 §5, Stats 2002 ch 1008 §2, ch 1009 §1, Stats 2003 ch 498 §1, and repealed January 1, 2007, by its own terms.

2017 Note: The Legislature finds and declares that Sections 1 and 2 of this act, which amend Section 527.6 of the Code of Civil Procedure and add Section 6301.5 to the Family Code, respectively, impose a limitation on the public's right of access to the meetings of public bodies or the writings of public officials and agencies within the meaning of Section 3 of Article I of the California Constitution. Pursuant to that constitutional provision, the Legislature makes the following findings to demonstrate the interest protected by this limitation and the need for protecting that interest:

This limitation is required to protect the private information of vulnerable minors who are the victims of domestic abuse and human trafficking. Stats 2017 ch 384 (AB 953) §3.

Former Sections: Former CCP §527.6, similar to the present section, was added Stats 2002 ch 1009 §2, operative January 1, 2007, and repealed operative July 1, 2014, by its own provisions.

Former CCP §527.6, similar to the present section, was added Stats 1978 ch 1307 §2 and repealed operative January 1, 2007, by its own provisions.

§527.7. Action to enjoin concerted acts of violence

(a) It shall be unlawful for any group, association, organization, society, or other assemblage of two or more persons to meet and to advocate, and to take substantial action in furtherance of, the commission of an unlawful act of violence or force directed to and likely to produce the imminent and unlawful infliction of serious bodily injury or death of another person within this state.

(b) Whenever it reasonably appears that any group, association, society, or other assemblage of two or more persons has met and taken substantial action in furtherance of the commission of an act of violence made unlawful by subdivision (a) and will engage in those acts in the future, any aggrieved individual may bring a civil action in the superior court to enjoin the advocacy of the commission of any act of violence made unlawful by subdivision (a) at any future meeting or meetings. Upon a proper showing by clear and convincing evidence, a permanent or preliminary injunction, restraining order, or writ of mandate shall be granted.

(c) Whenever it appears that an action brought under this section was groundless and brought in bad faith for the purpose of harassment, the trial court or any appellate court may award to the defendant attorney's fees and court costs incurred for the purpose of defending the action. **Leg.H.** Added Stats 1982 ch 1624 §1.

§ 527.8. Workplace violence and threats; Right of employer to seek temporary restraining order and order after hearing; Service, notice and hearing; Possession of firearm by person subject to protective order

(a) Any employer or collective bargaining representative of an employee who has suffered harassment, unlawful violence, or a credible threat of violence from any individual, that can reasonably be construed to be carried out or to have been carried out at the workplace, may seek a temporary restraining order and an order after hearing on behalf of the employee and, at the discretion of the court, any number of other employees at the workplace, and, if appropriate, other employees at other workplaces of the employer. For purposes of this section only, a person may bring a petition for a temporary restraining order and an order after hearing on behalf of an employee as their collective bargaining representative only if the person serves as a collective bargaining representative for that employee in employment or labor matters at the employee's workplace.

(b) For purposes of this section:

(1) "Course of conduct" is a pattern of conduct composed of a series of acts over a period of time, however short, evidencing a continuity of purpose, including following or stalking an employee to or from the place of work; entering the workplace; following an employee during hours of employment; making telephone calls to an employee; or sending correspondence to an employee by any means, including, but not limited to, the use of the public or private mails, interoffice mail, facsimile, or computer email.

(2) "Credible threat of violence" is a knowing and willful statement or course of conduct that would place a reasonable person in fear for their safety, or the safety of their immediate family, and that serves no legitimate purpose.

(3) "Employer" and "employee" mean persons defined in Section 350 of the Labor Code. "Employer" also includes a federal agency, the state, a state agency, a city, county, or district, and a private, public, or quasi-public corporation, or any public agency thereof or therein. "Employee" also includes the members of boards of directors of private, public, and quasi-public corporations and elected and appointed public officers. For purposes of this section only, "employee" also includes a volunteer or independent contractor who performs services for the employer at the employer's worksite.

(4) "Harassment" is a knowing and willful course of conduct directed at a specific person that seriously alarms, annoys, or harasses the person, and that serves no legitimate purpose. The course of conduct must be that which would cause a reasonable person to suffer substantial emotional distress, and must actually cause substantial emotional distress.

(5) "Petitioner" means the employer or collective bargaining representative that petitions under subdivision (a) for a temporary restraining order and order after hearing.

(6) "Respondent" means the person against whom the temporary restraining order and order after hearing are sought and, if the petition is granted, the restrained person.

(7) "Temporary restraining order" and "order after hearing" mean orders that include any of the following restraining orders, whether issued ex parte or after notice and hearing:

(A) An order enjoining a party from harassing, intimidating, molesting, attacking, striking, stalking, threatening, sexually assaulting, battering, abusing, telephoning, including, but not limited to, making annoying telephone calls as described in Section 653m of the Penal Code, destroying personal property, contacting, either directly or indirectly, by mail or otherwise, or coming within a specified distance of, or disturbing the peace of, the employee.

(B) An order enjoining a party from specified behavior that the court determines is necessary to effectuate orders described in subparagraph (A).

(8) "Unlawful violence" is any assault or battery, or stalking as prohibited in Section 646.9 of the Penal Code, but shall not include lawful acts of self-defense or defense of others.

(c) This section does not permit a court to issue a temporary restraining order or order after hearing prohibiting speech or other activities that are constitutionally protected, protected by the National Labor Relations Act (29 U.S.C. Sec. 151 et seq.), protected by Chapter 11.5 (commencing with Section 3555) of Division 4 of Title 1 of the Government Code, or otherwise protected by Section 527.3 or any other provision of law.

(d) In the discretion of the court, on a showing of good cause, a temporary restraining order or order after hearing issued under this section may include other named family or household members, or other persons employed at the employee's workplace or workplaces.

(e) Before filing a petition under this section, an employer or collective bargaining representative of an employee shall provide the employee who has suffered harassment, unlawful violence, or a credible threat of violence from any individual, an opportunity to decline to be named in the temporary restraining order. An employee's request to not be named in the temporary restraining order shall not prohibit an employer or collective bargaining representative from seeking a temporary restraining order on behalf of other employees at the workplace, and, if appropriate, other employees at other workplaces of the employer.

(f)(1) Upon filing a petition under this section, the petitioner may obtain a temporary restraining order in accordance with subdivision (a) of Section 527, if the petitioner also files a declaration that, to the satisfaction of the court, shows one of the following:

(A) Reasonable proof that an employee has suffered unlawful violence or a credible threat of violence by the respondent, and that great or irreparable harm would result to an employee.

(B) Clear and convincing evidence of all of the following:

(i) That an employee has suffered harassment by the respondent.

(ii) That great or irreparable harm would result to an employee.

(iii) That the course of conduct at issue served no legitimate purpose.

(iv) That the issuance of the order is not prohibited by subdivision (c).

(2) The temporary restraining order may include any of the protective orders described in paragraph (7) of subdivision (b).

(g) A request for the issuance of a temporary restraining order without notice under this section shall be granted or denied on the same day that the petition is submitted to the court, unless the petition is filed too late in the day to permit effective review, in which case the order shall be granted or denied on the next day of judicial business in sufficient time for the order to be filed that day with the clerk of the court.

(h) A temporary restraining order granted under this section shall remain in effect, at the court's discretion, for a period not to exceed 21 days, or if the court extends the time for hearing under subdivision (i), not to exceed 25 days, unless otherwise modified or terminated by the court.

(i) Within 21 days, or if good cause appears to the court, 25 days from the date that a petition for a temporary order is granted or denied, a hearing shall be held on the petition. If no request for temporary orders is made, the hearing shall be held within 21 days, or, if good cause appears to the court, 25 days, from the date that the petition is filed.

(j) The respondent may file a response that explains, excuses, justifies, or denies the alleged harassment, unlawful violence, or credible threats of violence.

(k) At the hearing, the judge shall receive any testimony that is relevant and may make an independent inquiry. Moreover, if the respondent is currently employed by the employer of the employee, as described in subdivision (a), the judge shall receive evidence concerning the employer's decision to retain, terminate, or otherwise discipline the respondent. If the judge finds by clear and convincing evidence that the respondent engaged in harassment, engaged in unlawful violence, or made a credible threat of violence, an order shall issue prohibiting further harassment, unlawful violence, or threats of violence.

(*l*)(1) In the discretion of the court, an order issued after notice and hearing under this section may have a duration of not more than three years, subject to termination or modification by further order of the court either on written stipulation filed with the court or on the motion of a party. These orders may be renewed, upon the request of a party, for a duration of not more than three years, without a showing of any further harassment, unlawful violence, or credible threats of violence since the issuance of the original order, subject to termination or modification by further order of the court either on written stipulation filed with the court or on the motion of a party. The request for renewal may be brought at any time within the three months before the expiration of the order.

(2) The failure to state the expiration date on the face of the form creates an order with a duration of three years from the date of issuance.

(3) If an action is filed for the purpose of terminating or modifying a protective order prior to the expiration date specified in the order by a party other than the protected party, the party who is protected by the order shall be given notice, pursuant to subdivision (b) of Section 1005, of the proceeding by personal service or, if the protected party has satisfied the requirements of Chapter 3.1 (commencing with Section 6205) of Division 7 of Title 1 of the Government Code, by service on the Secretary of State. If the party who is protected by the order cannot be notified prior to the hearing for modification or termination of the protective order, the court shall deny the motion to modify or terminate the order without prejudice or continue the hearing until the party who is protected can be properly noticed and may, upon a showing of good cause, specify another method for service of process that is reasonably designed to afford actual notice to the protected party. The protected party may waive their right to notice if they are physically present in court and does not challenge the sufficiency of the notice.

(m) This section does not preclude any party from representation by private counsel or from appearing on the party's own behalf.

(n) Upon filing of a petition under this section, the respondent shall be personally served with a copy of the petition, temporary restraining order, if any, and notice of hearing of the petition. Service shall be made at least five days before the hearing. The court may, for good cause, on motion of the petitioner or on its own motion, shorten the time for service on the respondent.

(o) A notice of hearing under this section shall notify the respondent that, if they do not attend the hearing, the court may make orders against them that could last up to three years.

(p) The respondent shall be entitled, as a matter of course, to one continuance, for a reasonable period, to respond to the petition.

(q)(1) Any party may request a continuance of the hearing, which the court shall grant on a showing of good cause. The request may be made in writing before or at the hearing or orally at the hearing. The court may also grant a continuance on its own motion.

(2) If the court grants a continuance, any temporary restraining order that has been granted shall remain in effect until the end of the continued hearing, unless otherwise ordered by the court. In granting a continuance, the court may modify or terminate a temporary restraining order.

(r)(1) If a respondent, named in a restraining order issued under this section after a hearing, has not been served personally with the order but has received actual notice of the existence and substance of the order through personal appearance in court to hear the terms of the order from the court, no additional proof of service is required for enforcement of the order.

(2) If the respondent named in a temporary restraining order is personally served with the order and notice of hearing with respect to a restraining order or protective order based on the temporary restraining order, but the person does not appear at the hearing, either personally or by an attorney, and the terms and conditions of the restraining order or protective order issued at the hearing are identical to the temporary restraining order, except for the duration of the order, then the restraining order or protective order issued at the hearing may be served on the person by first-class mail sent to that person at the most current address for the person available to the court.

(3) The Judicial Council form for temporary orders issued pursuant to this subdivision shall contain a statement in substantially the following form:

If you have been personally served with this temporary restraining order and notice of hearing, but you do not appear at the hearing either in person or by a lawyer, and a restraining order that is the same as this restraining order except for the expiration date is issued at the hearing, a copy of the order will be served on you by mail at the following address:_____ .

If that address is not correct or you wish to verify that the temporary restraining order was converted to a restraining order at the hearing without substantive change and to find out the duration of that order, contact the clerk of the court.

(s)(1) Information on a temporary restraining order or order after hearing relating to workplace violence issued by a court pursuant to this section shall be transmitted to the Department of Justice in accordance with either paragraph (2) or (3).

(2) The court shall order the petitioner or the attorney for the petitioner to deliver a copy of any order issued under this section, or a reissuance, extension, modification, or termination of the order, and any subsequent proof of service, by the close of the business day on which the order, reissuance, extension, modification, or termination was made, to each law enforcement agency having jurisdiction over the residence of the petitioner and to any additional law enforcement agencies within the court's discretion as are requested by the petitioner.

(3) Alternatively, the court or its designee shall transmit, within one business day, to law enforcement personnel all information required under subdivision (b) of Section 6380 of the Family Code regarding any order issued under this section, or a reissuance, extension, modification, or termination of the order, and any subsequent proof of service, by either one of the following methods:

(A) Transmitting a physical copy of the order or proof of service to a local law enforcement agency authorized by the Department of Justice to enter orders into the California Law Enforcement Telecommunications System (CLETS).

(B) With the approval of the Department of Justice, entering the order or proof of service into CLETS directly.

(4) Each appropriate law enforcement agency shall make available information as to the existence and current status of these orders to law enforcement officers responding to the scene of reported harassment, unlawful violence, or a credible threat of violence.

(5) At the request of the petitioner, an order issued under this section shall be served on the respondent, regardless of whether the respondent has been taken into custody, by any law enforcement officer who is present at the scene of reported harassment, unlawful violence, or a credible threat of violence involving the parties to the proceedings. The petitioner shall provide the officer with an endorsed copy of the order and proof of service that the officer shall complete and send to the issuing court.

(6) Upon receiving information at the scene of an incident of harassment, unlawful violence, or a credible threat of violence that a protective order has been issued under this section, or that a person who has been taken into custody is the subject of an order, if the petitioner or the protected person cannot produce an endorsed copy of the order, a law enforcement officer shall immediately attempt to verify the existence of the order.

(7) If the law enforcement officer determines that a protective order has been issued but not served, the officer shall immediately notify the respondent of the terms of the order and obtain the respondent's address. The law enforcement officer shall at that time also enforce the order, but may not arrest or take the respondent into custody for acts in violation of the order that were committed prior to the verbal notice of the terms and conditions of the order. The law enforcement officer's verbal notice of the terms of the order shall constitute service of the order and constitutes sufficient notice for the purposes of this section and for the purposes of Section 29825 of the Penal Code. The petitioner shall mail an endorsed copy of the order to the respondent's mailing address provided to the law enforcement officer within one business day of the reported incident of harassment, unlawful violence, or a credible threat of violence at which a verbal notice of the terms of the order was provided by a law enforcement officer.

(t)(1) A person subject to a protective order issued under this section shall not own, possess, purchase, receive, or attempt to purchase or receive a firearm or ammunition while the protective order is in effect.

(2) The court shall order a person subject to a protective order issued under this section to relinquish any firearms they own or possess pursuant to Section 527.9.

(3) Every person who owns, possesses, purchases or receives, or attempts to purchase or receive a firearm or ammunition while the protective order is in effect is punishable pursuant to Section 29825 of the Penal Code.

(u) Any intentional disobedience of any temporary restraining order or order after hearing granted under this section is punishable pursuant to Section 273.6 of the Penal Code.

(v) This section shall not be construed as expanding, diminishing, altering, or modifying the duty, if any, of an employer to provide a safe workplace for employees and other persons.

(w)(1) The Judicial Council shall develop forms, instructions, and rules for relating to matters governed by this section. The forms for the petition and response shall be simple and concise, and their use by parties in actions brought pursuant to this section shall be mandatory.

(2) A temporary restraining order or order after hearing relating to harassment, unlawful violence, or a credible threat of violence issued by a court pursuant to this section shall be issued on forms adopted by the Judicial Council and that have been approved by the Department of Justice pursuant to subdivision (i) of Section 6380 of the Family Code. However, the fact that an order issued by a court pursuant to this section was not issued on forms adopted by the Judicial Council and approved by the Department of Justice shall not, in and of itself, make the order unenforceable.

(x) There is no filing fee for a petition that alleges that a person has inflicted or threatened violence against an employee employed or represented by the petitioner, or stalked the employee, or acted or spoken in any other manner that has placed the employee in reasonable fear of violence, and that seeks a protective or restraining order restraining stalking or future violence or threats of violence, in any action brought pursuant to this section. A fee shall not be paid for a subpoena filed in connection with a petition alleging these acts. A fee shall not be paid for filing a response to a petition alleging these acts.

(y)(1) Subject to paragraph (4) of subdivision (b) of Section 6103.2 of the Government Code, there shall be no fee for the service of process by a sheriff or marshal of a temporary restraining order or order after hearing to be issued pursuant to this section if either of the following conditions applies:

(A) The temporary restraining order or order after hearing issued pursuant to this section is based upon stalking, as prohibited by Section 646.9 of the Penal Code.

(B) The temporary restraining order or order after hearing issued pursuant to this section is based on unlawful violence or a credible threat of violence.

(2) The Judicial Council shall prepare and develop forms for persons who wish to avail themselves of the services described in this subdivision.

(z) This section shall become operative on January 1, 2025. **Leg.H.** Added Stats 2023 ch 286 §2 (SB 428), effective January 1, 2024, operative January 1, 2025; Stats 2023 ch 289 §2.5 (SB 553), effective January 1, 2024, operative January 1, 2025 (ch 289 prevails).

§527.85. Temporary restraining order or order after hearing for credible threat of violence against a student at postsecondary educational institution; Procedure; Duration; Forms, instructions, and rules [Repealed January 1, 2026]

(a) [1] A chief administrative officer of a postsecondary educational institution, or an officer or employee designated by the chief administrative officer to maintain order on the school campus or facility, a student of which has suffered a credible threat of violence made off the school campus or facility from any individual which can reasonably be construed to be carried out or to have been carried out at the school campus or facility, may, with the written consent of the student, seek a temporary restraining order and an order after hearing on behalf of the student and, at the discretion of the court, any number of other students at the campus or facility who are similarly situated.

(b) For purposes of this section, the following definitions apply:

(1) "Chief administrative officer" means the principal, president, or highest ranking official of the postsecondary educational institution.

(2) "Course of conduct" means a pattern of conduct composed of a series of acts over a period of time, however short, evidencing a continuity of purpose, including any of the following:

(A) Following or stalking a student to or from school.

(B) Entering the school campus or facility.

(C) Following a student during school hours.

(D) Making telephone calls to a student.

(E) Sending correspondence to a student by any means, including, but not limited to, the use of the public or private mails, interoffice mail, facsimile, or computer email.

(3) "Credible threat of violence" means a knowing and willful statement or course of conduct that would place a reasonable person in fear for [2] **their** safety, or the safety of [3] **their** immediate family, and that serves no legitimate purpose.

(4) "Petitioner" means the chief administrative officer, or [4] **their** designee, who petitions under subdivision (a) for a temporary restraining order and order after hearing.

(5) "Postsecondary educational institution" means a private institution of vocational, professional, or postsecondary education.

(6) "Respondent" means the person against whom the temporary restraining order and order after hearing are sought and, if the petition is granted, the restrained person.

(7) "Student" means an adult currently enrolled in or applying for admission to a postsecondary educational institution.

(8) "Temporary restraining order" and "order after hearing" mean orders that include any of the following restraining orders, whether issued ex parte, or after notice and hearing:

(A) An order enjoining a party from harassing, intimidating, molesting, attacking, striking, stalking, threatening, sexually assaulting, battering, abusing, telephoning, including, but not limited to, making annoying telephone calls as described in Section 653m of the Penal Code, destroying personal property, contacting, either directly or indirectly, by mail or otherwise, or coming within a specified distance of, or disturbing the peace of, the student.

(B) An order enjoining a party from specified behavior that the court determines is necessary to effectuate orders described in subparagraph (A).

(9) "Unlawful violence" means any assault or battery, or stalking as prohibited in Section 646.9 of the Penal Code, but shall not include lawful acts of self-defense or defense of others.

(c) This section does not permit a court to issue a temporary restraining order or order after hearing prohibiting speech or other activities that are constitutionally protected, or otherwise protected by Section 527.3 or any other [5] law.

(d) In the discretion of the court, on a showing of good cause, a temporary restraining order or order after hearing issued under this section may include other named family or household members of the student, or other students at the campus or facility.

(e) Upon filing a petition under this section, the petitioner may obtain a temporary restraining order in accordance with subdivision (a) of Section 527, if the petitioner also files a declaration that, to the satisfaction of the court, shows reasonable proof that a student has suffered a credible threat of violence made off the school campus or facility by the respondent, and that great or irreparable harm would result to the student. The temporary restraining order may include any of the protective orders described in paragraph (8) of subdivision (b).

(f) A request for the issuance of a temporary restraining order without notice under this section shall be granted or denied on the same day that the petition is submitted to the court, unless the petition is filed too late in the day to permit effective review, in which case the order shall be granted or denied on the next day of judicial business in sufficient time for the order to be filed that day with the clerk of the court.

(g) A temporary restraining order granted under this section shall remain in effect, at the court's discretion, for a period not to exceed 21 days, or if the court extends the time for hearing under subdivision (h), not to exceed 25 days, unless otherwise modified or terminated by the court.

(h) Within 21 days, or if good cause appears to the court, within 25 days, from the date that a petition for a temporary order is granted or denied, a hearing shall be held on the petition. If no request for temporary orders is made, the hearing shall be held within 21 days, or if good cause appears to the court, 25 days, from the date the petition is filed.

(i) The respondent may file a response that explains, excuses, justifies, or denies the alleged credible threats of violence.

(j) At the hearing, the judge shall receive any testimony that is relevant and may make an independent inquiry. Moreover, if the respondent is a current student of the entity requesting the order, the judge shall receive evidence concerning the decision of the postsecondary educational institution decision to retain, terminate, or otherwise discipline the respondent. If the judge finds by clear and convincing evidence that the respondent made a credible threat of violence off the school campus or facility, an order shall be issued prohibiting further threats of violence.

(k)(1) In the discretion of the court, an order issued after notice and hearing under this section may have a duration of not more than three years, subject to termination or modification by further order of the court either on written stipulation filed with the court or on the motion of a party. These orders may be renewed, upon the request of a party, for a duration of not more than three years, without a showing of any further violence or threats of violence since the issuance of the original order, subject to termination or modification by further order of the court either on written stipulation filed with the court or on the motion of a party. The request for renewal may be brought at any time within the three months before the expiration of the order.

(2) The failure to state the expiration date on the face of the form creates an order with a duration of three years from the date of issuance.

(3) If an action is filed for the purpose of terminating or modifying a protective order prior to the expiration date specified in the order by a party other than the protected party, the party who is protected by the order shall be given notice, pursuant to subdivision (b) of Section 1005, of the proceeding by personal service or, if the protected party has satisfied the requirements of Chapter 3.1 (commencing with Section 6205) of Division 7 of Title 1 of the Government Code, by service on the Secretary of State. If the party who is protected by the order cannot be notified prior to the hearing for modification or termination of the protective order, the court shall deny the motion to modify or terminate the order without prejudice or continue the hearing until the party who is protected can be properly noticed and may, upon a showing of good cause, specify another method for service of process that is reasonably designed to afford actual notice to the protected party. The protected party may waive [6] **their** right to notice if [7] **they are** physically present in court and does not challenge the sufficiency of the notice.

(l) This section does not preclude either party from representation by private counsel or from appearing on [8] **their** own behalf.

(m) Upon filing of a petition under this section, the respondent shall be personally served with a copy of the petition, temporary restraining order, if any, and notice of hearing of the petition. Service shall be made at least five days before the hearing. The court may, for good cause, on motion of the petitioner or on its own motion, shorten the time for service on the respondent.

(n) A notice of hearing under this section shall notify the respondent that if [9] **the respondent** does not attend the hearing, the court may make orders against [10] **the respondent** that could last up to three years.

(o) The respondent shall be entitled, as a matter of course, to one continuance, for a reasonable period, to respond to the petition.

(p)(1) Either party may request a continuance of the hearing, which the court shall grant on a showing of good cause. The request may be made in writing before or at the hearing or orally at the hearing. The court may also grant a continuance on its own motion.

(2) If the court grants a continuance, any temporary restraining order that has been granted shall remain in effect until the end of the continued hearing, unless otherwise ordered by the court. In granting a continuance, the court may modify or terminate a temporary restraining order.

(q)(1) If a respondent, named in an order issued under this section after a hearing, has not been served personally with the order but has received actual notice of the existence and substance of the order through personal appearance in court to hear the terms of the order from the court, no additional proof of service is required for enforcement of the order.

(2) If the respondent named in a temporary restraining order is personally served with the order and notice of hearing with respect to a restraining order or protective order based on the temporary restraining order, but the respondent does not appear at the hearing, either personally or by an attorney, and the terms and conditions of the restraining order or protective order issued at the hearing are identical to the temporary restraining order, except for the duration of the order, then the restraining order or protective order issued at the hearing may be served on the respondent by first-class mail sent to that person at the most current address for the respondent available to the court.

(3) The Judicial Council form for temporary orders issued pursuant to this subdivision shall contain a statement in substantially the following form:

If you have been personally served with a temporary restraining order and notice of hearing, but you do not appear at the hearing either in person or by a lawyer, and a restraining order that is the same as this temporary restraining order except for the expiration date is issued at the hearing, a copy of the order will be served on you by mail at the following address:____.

If that address is not correct or you wish to verify that the temporary restraining order was converted to a restraining order at the hearing without substantive change and to find out the duration of that order, contact the clerk of the court.

(r)(1) Information on a temporary restraining order or order after hearing relating to schoolsite violence issued by a court pursuant to this section shall be transmitted to the Department of Justice in accordance with either paragraph (2) or (3).

(2) The court shall order the petitioner or the attorney for the petitioner to deliver a copy of any order issued under this section, or a reissuance, extension, modification, or termination of the order, and any subsequent proof of service, by the close of the business day on which the order, reissuance, or termination of the order, and any proof of service, was made, to each law enforcement agency having jurisdiction over the residence of the petition and to any additional law enforcement agencies within the court's discretion as are requested by the petitioner.

(3) Alternatively, the court or its designee shall transmit, within one business day, to law enforcement personnel all information required under subdivision (b) of Section 6380 of the Family Code regarding any order issued under this section, or a reissuance, extension, modification, or termination of the order, and any subsequent proof of service, by either one of the following methods:

(A) Transmitting a physical copy of the order or proof of service to a local law enforcement agency authorized by the Department of Justice to enter orders into the California Law Enforcement Telecommunications System (CLETS).

(B) With the approval of the Department of Justice, entering the order of proof of service into CLETS directly.

(4) Each appropriate law enforcement agency shall make available information as to the existence and current status of these orders to law enforcement officers responding to the scene of reported unlawful violence or a credible threat of violence.

(5) At the request of the petitioner, an order issued under this section shall be served on the respondent, regardless of whether the respondent has been taken into custody, by any law enforcement officer who is present at the scene of reported unlawful violence or a credible threat of violence involving the parties to the proceedings. The petitioner shall provide the officer with an endorsed copy of the order and proof of service that the officer shall complete and send to the issuing court.

(6) Upon receiving information at the scene of an incident of unlawful violence or a credible threat of violence that a protective order has been issued under this section, or that a person who has been taken into custody is the subject of an order, if the petitioner or the protected person cannot produce an endorsed copy of the order, a law enforcement officer shall immediately attempt to verify the existence of the order.

(7) If the law enforcement officer determines that a protective order has been issued but not served, the officer shall immediately notify the respondent of the terms of the order and obtain the respondent's address. The law enforcement officer shall at that time also enforce the order, but may not arrest or take the respondent into custody for acts in violation of the order that were committed prior to the verbal notice of the terms and conditions of the order. The law enforcement officer's verbal notice of the terms of the order shall constitute service of the order and constitutes sufficient notice for the purposes of this section, and Section 29825 of the Penal Code. The petitioner shall mail an endorsed copy of the order to the respondent's mailing address provided to the law enforcement officer within one business day of the reported incident of unlawful violence or a credible threat of violence at which a verbal notice of the terms of the order was provided by a law enforcement officer.

(s)(1) A person subject to a protective order issued under this section shall not own, possess, purchase, receive, or attempt to purchase or receive a firearm or ammunition while the protective order is in effect.

(2) The court shall order a person subject to a protective order issued under this section to relinquish any firearms [11] **the person** owns or possesses pursuant to Section 527.9.

(3) Every person who owns, possesses, purchases, or receive, or attempts to purchase or receive, a firearm or ammunition while the protective order is in effect is punishable pursuant to Section 29825 of the Penal Code.

(t) Any intentional disobedience of any temporary restraining order or order after hearing granted under this section is punishable pursuant to Section 273.6 of the Penal Code.

(u) This section shall not be construed as expanding, diminishing, altering, or modifying the duty, if any, of a postsecondary educational institution to provide a safe environment for students and other persons.

(v)(1) The Judicial Council shall develop forms, instructions, and rules relating to matters governed by this section. The forms for the petition and response shall be simple and concise, and their use by parties in actions brought pursuant to this section shall be mandatory.

(2) A temporary restraining order or order after hearing relating to unlawful violence or a credible threat of violence issued by a court pursuant to this section shall be issued on forms adopted by the Judicial Council that have been approved by the Department of Justice pursuant to subdivision (i) of Section 6380 of the Family Code. However, the fact that an order issued by a court pursuant to this section was not issued on forms adopted by the Judicial Council and approved by the Department of Justice shall not, in and of itself, make the order unenforceable.

(w) There is no filing fee for a petition that alleges that a person has threatened violence against a student of the petitioner, or stalked the student, or acted or spoken in any other manner that has placed the student in reasonable fear of violence, and that seeks a protective or restraining order restraining stalking or future threats of violence, in any action brought pursuant to this section. No fee shall be paid for a subpoena filed in connection with a petition alleging these acts. No fee shall be paid for filing a response to a petition alleging these acts.

(x)(1) Subject to paragraph (4) of subdivision (b) of Section 6103.2 of the Government Code, there shall be no fee for the service of process by a sheriff or marshal of a temporary restraining order or order after hearing to be issued pursuant to this section if either of the following conditions applies:

(A) The temporary restraining order or order after hearing issued pursuant to this section is based upon stalking, as prohibited by Section 646.9 of the Penal Code.

(B) The temporary restraining order or order after hearing issued pursuant to this section is based upon a credible threat of violence.

(2) The Judicial Council shall prepare and develop forms for persons who wish to avail themselves of the services described in this subdivision.

(y) **This section shall remain in effect only until January 1, 2026, and as of that date is repealed. Leg.H.** Added Stats 2009 ch 566 §1 (SB 188), effective January 1, 2010. Amended Stats 2010 ch 178 §22 (SB 1115), effective January 1, 2011, operative January 1, 2012, ch 572 §4 (AB 1596) (ch 572 prevails), effective January 1, 2011, operative January 1, 2012; Stats 2011 ch 101 §3 (AB 454) (ch 101 prevails), effective January 1, 2012, ch 285 §3 (AB 1402), effective January 1, 2012; Stats 2012 ch 162 §14 (SB 1171), effective January 1, 2013; Stats 2015 ch 411 §3 (AB 1081), effective January 1, 2016; Stats 2024 ch 947 §1 (AB 2096), effective January 1, 2025, repealed January 1, 2026.

§527.85. 2024 Deletes. [1] Any [2] his or her [3] his or her [4] his or her [5] provision of [6] his or her [7] he or she is [8] his or her [9] he or she [10] him or her [11] he or she

§527.85. Temporary restraining orders and orders after hearing for postsecondary educational institutions [Operative January 1, 2026]

(a) A chief administrative officer of a postsecondary educational institution, or an officer or employee designated by the chief administrative officer to maintain order on the school campus or facility, a student of which has suffered unlawful violence or a credible threat of violence may, with the written consent of the student, seek a temporary restraining order and an order after hearing on behalf of the student and, at the discretion of the court, any number of other students at the campus or facility who are similarly situated.

(b) For purposes of this section, the following definitions apply:

(1) "Chief administrative officer" means the principal, president, or highest ranking official of the postsecondary educational institution.

(2) "Course of conduct" means a pattern of conduct composed of a series of acts over a period of time, however short, evidencing a continuity of purpose, including any of the following:

(A) Following or stalking a student to or from school.

(B) Entering the school campus or facility.

(C) Following a student during school hours.

(D) Making telephone calls to a student.

(E) Sending correspondence to a student by any means, including, but not limited to, the use of the public or private mails, interoffice mail, facsimile, or computer email.

(3) "Credible threat of violence" means a knowing and willful statement or course of conduct that would place a reasonable person in fear for their safety, or the safety of their immediate family, and that serves no legitimate purpose.

(4) "Petitioner" means the chief administrative officer, or their designee, who petitions under subdivision (a) for a temporary restraining order and order after hearing.

(5) "Postsecondary educational institution" means an institution of vocational, professional, or postsecondary education.

(6) "Respondent" means the person against whom the temporary restraining order and order after hearing are sought and, if the petition is granted, the restrained person.

(7) "Student" means an adult currently enrolled in or applying for admission to a postsecondary educational institution.

(8) "Temporary restraining order" and "order after hearing" mean orders that include any of the following restraining orders, whether issued ex parte, or after notice and hearing:

(A) An order enjoining a party from harassing, intimidating, molesting, attacking, striking, stalking, threatening, sexually assaulting, battering, abusing, telephoning, including, but not limited to, making annoying telephone calls as described in Section 653m of the Penal Code, destroying personal property, contacting, either directly or indirectly, by mail or otherwise, or coming within a specified distance of, or disturbing the peace of, the student.

(B) An order enjoining a party from specified behavior that the court determines is necessary to effectuate orders described in subparagraph (A).

(9) "Unlawful violence" means any assault or battery, or stalking as prohibited in Section 646.9 of the Penal Code, but shall not include lawful acts of self-defense or defense of others.

(c) This section does not permit a court to issue a temporary restraining order or order after hearing prohibiting speech or other activities that are constitutionally protected, or otherwise protected by Section 527.3 or any other law.

(d) In the discretion of the court, on a showing of good cause, a temporary restraining order or order after hearing issued under this section may include other named family or household members of the student, or other students at the campus or facility.

(e) Upon filing a petition under this section, the petitioner may obtain a temporary restraining order in accordance with subdivision (a) of Section 527, if the petitioner also files a declaration that, to the satisfaction of the court, shows reasonable proof that a student has suffered unlawful violence or a credible threat of violence by the respondent, and that great or irreparable harm would result to the student. The temporary restraining order may include any of the protective orders described in paragraph (8) of subdivision (b).

(f) A request for the issuance of a temporary restraining order without notice under this section shall be granted or denied on the same day that the petition is submitted to the court, unless the petition is filed too late in the day to permit effective review, in which case the order shall be granted or denied on the next day of judicial business in sufficient time for the order to be filed that day with the clerk of the court.

(g) A temporary restraining order granted under this section shall remain in effect, at the court's discretion, for a period not to exceed 21 days, or if the court extends the time for hearing under subdivision (h), not to exceed 25 days, unless otherwise modified or terminated by the court.

(h) Within 21 days, or if good cause appears to the court, within 25 days, from the date that a petition for a temporary order is granted or denied, a hearing shall be held on the petition. If no request for temporary orders is made, the hearing shall be held within 21 days, or if good cause appears to the court, 25 days, from the date the petition is filed.

(i) The respondent may file a response that explains, excuses, justifies, or denies the alleged unlawful violence or credible threats of violence.

(j) At the hearing, the judge shall receive any testimony that is relevant and may make an independent inquiry. Moreover, if the respondent is a current student of the entity requesting the order, the judge shall receive evidence concerning the decision of the postsecondary educational institution decision to retain, terminate, or otherwise discipline the respondent. If the judge finds by clear and convincing evidence that the respondent engaged in unlawful violence or made a credible threat of violence, an order shall be issued prohibiting further unlawful violence or threats of violence.

(k)(1) In the discretion of the court, an order issued after notice and hearing under this section may have a duration of not more than three years, subject to termination or modification by further order of the court either on written stipulation filed with the court or on the motion of a party. These orders may be renewed, upon the request of a party, for a duration of not more than three years, without a showing of any further violence or threats of violence since the issuance of the original order, subject to termination or modification by further order of the court either on written stipulation filed with the court or on the motion of a party. The request for renewal may be brought at any time within the three months before the expiration of the order.

(2) The failure to state the expiration date on the face of the form creates an order with a duration of three years from the date of issuance.

(3) If an action is filed for the purpose of terminating or modifying a protective order prior to the expiration date specified in the order by a party other than the protected party, the party who is protected by the order shall be given notice, pursuant to subdivision (b) of Section 1005, of the proceeding by personal service or, if the protected party has satisfied the requirements of Chapter 3.1 (commencing with Section 6205) of Division 7 of Title 1 of the Government Code, by service on the Secretary of State. If the party who is protected by the order cannot be notified prior to the hearing for modification or termination of the protective order, the court shall deny the motion to modify or terminate the order without prejudice or continue the hearing until the party who is protected can be properly noticed and may, upon a showing of good cause, specify another method for service of process that is reasonably designed to afford actual notice to the protected party. The protected party may waive their right to notice if they are physically present in court and does not challenge the sufficiency of the notice.

(l) This section does not preclude either party from representation by private counsel or from appearing on their own behalf.

(m) Upon filing of a petition under this section, the respondent shall be personally served with a copy of the petition, temporary restraining order, if any, and notice of hearing of the petition. Service shall be made at least five days before the hearing. The court may, for good cause, on motion of the petitioner or on its own motion, shorten the time for service on the respondent.

(n) A notice of hearing under this section shall notify the respondent that if the respondent does not attend the hearing, the court may make orders against the respondent that could last up to three years.

(o) The respondent shall be entitled, as a matter of course, to one continuance, for a reasonable period, to respond to the petition.

(p)(1) Either party may request a continuance of the hearing, which the court shall grant on a showing of good cause. The request may be made in writing before or at the hearing or orally at the hearing. The court may also grant a continuance on its own motion.

(2) If the court grants a continuance, any temporary restraining order that has been granted shall remain in effect until the end of the continued hearing, unless otherwise ordered by the court. In granting a continuance, the court may modify or terminate a temporary restraining order.

(q)(1) If a respondent, named in an order issued under this section after a hearing, has not been served personally with the order but has received actual notice of the existence and substance of the order through personal appearance in court to hear the terms of the order from the court, no additional proof of service is required for enforcement of the order.

(2) If the respondent named in a temporary restraining order is personally served with the order and notice of hearing with respect to a restraining order or protective order based on the temporary restraining order, but the respondent does not appear at the hearing, either personally or by an attorney, and the terms and conditions of the restraining order or protective order issued at the hearing are identical to the temporary restraining order, except for the duration of the order, then the restraining order or protective order issued at the hearing may be served on the respondent by first-class mail sent to that person at the most current address for the respondent available to the court.

(3) The Judicial Council form for temporary orders issued pursuant to this subdivision shall contain a statement in substantially the following form:

If you have been personally served with a temporary restraining order and notice of hearing, but you do not appear at the hearing either in person or by a lawyer, and a restraining order that is the same as this temporary restraining order except for the expiration date is issued at the hearing, a copy of the order will be served on you by mail _____ at the following address:.

If that address is not correct or you wish to verify that the temporary restraining order was converted to a restraining order at the hearing without substantive change and to find out the duration of that order, contact the clerk of the court.

(r)(1) Information on a temporary restraining order or order after hearing issued by a court pursuant to this section shall be transmitted to the Department of Justice in accordance with either paragraph (2) or (3).

(2) The court shall order the petitioner or the attorney for the petitioner to deliver a copy of any order issued under this section, or a reissuance, extension, modification, or termination of the order, and any subsequent proof of service, by the close of the business day on which the order, reissuance, or termination of the order, and any proof of service, was made, to each law enforcement agency having jurisdiction over the residence of the petition and to any additional law enforcement agencies within the court's discretion as are requested by the petitioner.

(3) Alternatively, the court or its designee shall transmit, within one business day, to law enforcement personnel all information required under subdivision (b) of Section 6380 of the Family Code regarding any order issued under this section, or a reissuance, extension, modification, or termination of the order, and any subsequent proof of service, by either one of the following methods:

(A) Transmitting a physical copy of the order or proof of service to a local law enforcement agency authorized by the Department of Justice to enter orders into the California Law Enforcement Telecommunications System (CLETS).

(B) With the approval of the Department of Justice, entering the order of proof of service into CLETS directly.

(4) Each appropriate law enforcement agency shall make available information as to the existence and current status of these orders to law enforcement officers responding to the scene of reported unlawful violence or a credible threat of violence.

(5) At the request of the petitioner, an order issued under this section shall be served on the respondent, regardless of whether the respondent has been taken into custody, by any law enforcement officer who is present at the scene of reported unlawful violence or a credible threat of violence involving the parties to the proceedings. The petitioner shall provide the officer with an endorsed copy of the order and proof of service that the officer shall complete and send to the issuing court.

(6) Upon receiving information at the scene of an incident of unlawful violence or a credible threat of violence that a protective order has been issued under this section, or that a person who has been taken into custody is the subject of an order, if the petitioner or the protected person cannot produce an endorsed copy of the order, a law enforcement officer shall immediately attempt to verify the existence of the order.

(7) If the law enforcement officer determines that a protective order has been issued but not served, the officer shall immediately notify the respondent of the terms of the order and obtain the respondent's address. The law enforcement officer shall at that time also enforce the order, but may not arrest or take the respondent into custody for acts in violation of the order that were committed prior to the verbal notice of the terms and conditions of the order. The law enforcement officer's verbal notice of the terms of the order shall constitute service of the order and constitutes sufficient notice for the purposes of this section, and Section 29825 of the Penal Code. The petitioner shall mail an endorsed copy of the order to the respondent's mailing address provided to the law enforcement officer within one business day of the reported incident of unlawful violence or a credible threat of violence at which a verbal notice of the terms of the order was provided by a law enforcement officer.

(s)(1) A person subject to a protective order issued under this section shall not own, possess, purchase, receive, or attempt to purchase or receive a firearm or ammunition while the protective order is in effect.

(2) The court shall order a person subject to a protective order issued under this section to relinquish any firearms the person owns or possesses pursuant to Section 527.9.

(3) Every person who owns, possesses, purchases, or receives, or attempts to purchase or receive, a firearm or ammunition while the protective order is in effect is punishable pursuant to Section 29825 of the Penal Code.

(t) Any intentional disobedience of any temporary restraining order or order after hearing granted under this section is punishable pursuant to Section 273.6 of the Penal Code.

(u) This section shall not be construed as expanding, diminishing, altering, or modifying the duty, if any, of a postsecondary educational institution to provide a safe environment for students and other persons.

(v)(1) The Judicial Council shall develop forms, instructions, and rules relating to matters governed by this section. The forms for the petition and response shall be simple and concise, and their use by parties in actions brought pursuant to this section shall be mandatory.

(2) A temporary restraining order or order after hearing relating to unlawful violence or a credible threat of violence issued by a court pursuant to this section shall be issued on forms adopted by the Judicial Council that have been approved by the Department of Justice pursuant to subdivision (i) of Section 6380 of the Family Code. However, the fact that an order issued by a court pursuant to this section was not issued on forms adopted by the Judicial Council and approved by the Department of Justice shall not, in and of itself, make the order unenforceable.

(w) There is no filing fee for a petition that alleges that a person has inflicted unlawful violence, including stalking, or made a credible threat against a student of the petitioner, and that seeks a protective or restraining order restraining stalking or other future unlawful violence or threats of violence, in any action brought pursuant to this section. No fee shall be paid for a subpoena filed in connection with a petition alleging these acts. No fee shall be paid for filing a response to a petition alleging these acts.

(x)(1) Subject to paragraph (4) of subdivision (b) of Section 6103.2 of the Government Code, there shall be no fee for the service of process by a sheriff or marshal of a temporary restraining order or order after hearing to be issued pursuant to this section if either of the following conditions applies:

(A) The temporary restraining order or order after hearing issued pursuant to this section is based upon unlawful violence, including stalking, as prohibited by Section 646.9 of the Penal Code.

(B) The temporary restraining order or order after hearing issued pursuant to this section is based upon a credible threat of violence.

(2) The Judicial Council shall prepare and develop forms for persons who wish to avail themselves of the services described in this subdivision.

(y) This section shall become operative on January 1, 2026. **Leg.H.** Added Stats 2024 ch 947 §2 (AB 2096), effective January 1, 2025, operative January 1, 2026.

§527.9. Relinquishment of firearm by person subject to temporary restraining order or injunction; Storage; Fee; Employment exemption; Sale [Repealed January 1, 2026]

(a) A person subject to a temporary restraining order or injunction issued pursuant to Section 527.6, 527.8, or 527.85 or subject to a restraining order issued pursuant to Section 136.2 of the Penal Code, or Section 15657.03 of the Welfare and Institutions Code, shall relinquish the firearm pursuant to this section.

(b) Upon the issuance of a protective order against a person pursuant to subdivision (a), the court shall order that person to relinquish any firearm in that person's immediate possession or control, or subject to that person's immediate possession or control, within 24 hours of being served with the order, either by surrendering the firearm to the control of local law enforcement officials, or by selling the firearm to a licensed gun dealer, as specified in Article 1 (commencing with Section 26700) and Article 2 (commencing with Section 26800) of Chapter 2 of Division 6 of Title 4 of Part 6 of the Penal Code. A person ordered to relinquish any firearm pursuant to this subdivision shall file with the court a receipt showing the firearm was surrendered to the local law enforcement agency or sold to a licensed gun dealer within 48 hours after receiving the order. In the event that it is necessary to continue the date of any hearing due to a request for a relinquishment order pursuant to this section, the court shall ensure that all applicable protective orders described in Section 6218 of the Family Code remain in effect or bifurcate the issues and grant the permanent restraining order pending the date of the hearing.

(c) A local law enforcement agency may charge the person subject to the order or injunction a fee for the storage of any firearm relinquished pursuant to this section. The fee shall not exceed the actual cost incurred by the local law enforcement agency for the storage of the firearm. For purposes of this subdivision, "actual cost" means expenses directly related to taking possession of a firearm, storing the firearm, and surrendering possession of the firearm to a licensed dealer as defined in Section 26700 of the Penal Code or to the person relinquishing the firearm.

(d) The restraining order requiring a person to relinquish a firearm pursuant to subdivision (b) shall state on its face that the respondent is prohibited from owning, possessing, purchasing, or receiving a firearm while the protective order is in effect and that the firearm shall be relinquished to the local law enforcement agency for that jurisdiction or sold to a licensed gun dealer, and that proof of surrender or sale shall be filed with the court within a specified period of receipt of the order. The order shall also state on its face the expiration date for relinquishment. Nothing in this section shall limit a respondent's right under existing law to petition the court at a later date for modification of the order.

(e) The restraining order requiring a person to relinquish a firearm pursuant to subdivision (b) shall prohibit the person from possessing or controlling any firearm for the duration of the order. At the expiration of the order, the local law enforcement agency shall return possession of any surrendered firearm to the respondent, within five days after the expiration of the relinquishment order, unless the local law enforcement agency determines that (1) the firearm has been stolen, (2) the respondent is prohibited from possessing a firearm because the respondent is in any prohibited class for the possession of firearms, as defined in Chapter 2 (commencing with Section 29800) and Chapter 3 (commencing with Section 29900) of Division 9 of Title 4 of Part 6 of the Penal Code and Sections 8100 and 8103 of the Welfare and Institutions Code, or (3) another successive restraining order is issued against the respondent under this section. If the local law enforcement agency determines that the respondent is the legal owner of any firearm deposited with the local law enforcement agency and is prohibited from possessing any firearm, the respondent shall be entitled to sell or transfer the firearm to a licensed dealer as defined in Section 26700 of the Penal Code. If the firearm has been stolen, the firearm shall be restored to the lawful owner upon [1] **their** identification of the firearm and proof of ownership.

(f) The court may, as part of the relinquishment order, grant an exemption from the relinquishment requirements of this section for a particular firearm if the respondent can show that a particular firearm is necessary as a condition of continued employment and that the current employer is unable to reassign the respondent to another position where a firearm is unnecessary. If an exemption is granted pursuant to this subdivision, the order shall provide that the firearm shall be in the physical possession of the respondent only during scheduled work hours and during travel to and from [2] **their** place of employment. In any case involving a peace officer who as a condition of employment and whose personal safety depends on the ability to carry a firearm, a court may allow the peace officer to continue to carry a firearm, either on duty or off duty, if the court finds by a preponderance of the evidence that the officer does not pose a threat of harm. Prior to making this finding, the court shall require a mandatory psychological evaluation of the peace officer and may require the peace officer to enter into counseling or other remedial treatment program to deal with any propensity for domestic violence.

(g) During the period of the relinquishment order, a respondent is entitled to make one sale of all firearms that are in the possession of a local law enforcement agency pursuant to this section. A licensed gun dealer, who presents a local law enforcement agency with a bill of sale indicating that all firearms owned by the respondent that are in the possession of the local law enforcement agency have been sold by the respondent to the licensed gun dealer, shall be given possession of those firearms, at the location where a respondent's firearms are stored, within five days of presenting the local law enforcement agency with a bill of sale.

(h) This section shall remain in effect only until January 1, 2026, and as of that date is repealed. Leg.H. Added Stats 2003 ch 498 §4 (SB 226). Amended Stats 2006 ch 474 §1 (AB 2129), effective January 1, 2007; Stats 2010 ch 178 §23 (SB 1115), effective January 1, 2011, operative January 1, 2012, ch 572 §5 (AB 1596) (ch 572 prevails), effective January 1, 2011, operative January 1, 2012; Stats 2011 ch 285 §4 (AB 1402), effective January 1, 2012; Stats 2024 ch 544 §2 (SB 899), effective January 1, 2025, repealed January 1, 2026.

§527.9. 2024 Deletes. [1] his or her [2] his or her

§ 527.9. Relinquishment of firearms and ammunition upon issuance of temporary restraining order or injunction [Operative January 1, 2026]

(a) A person subject to a temporary restraining order or injunction issued pursuant to Section 527.6, 527.8, or 527.85 or subject to a restraining order issued pursuant to Section 136.2 of the Penal Code, or Section 15657.03 of the Welfare and Institutions Code, shall relinquish the firearm and ammunition pursuant to this section.

(b) Upon the issuance of a protective order against a person pursuant to subdivision (a), the court shall order that person to relinquish any firearm and ammunition in that person's immediate possession or control, or subject to that person's immediate possession or control, within 24 hours of being served with the order, either by surrendering the firearm and ammunition to the control of local law enforcement officials, or by selling the firearm to a licensed gun dealer, as specified in Article 1 (commencing with Section 26700) and Article 2 (commencing with Section 26800) of Chapter 2 of Division 6 of Title 4 of Part 6 of the Penal Code. The court shall provide the person with information on how any firearms or ammunition still in the restrained party's possession are to be relinquished, according to local procedures, and the process for submitting a receipt to the court showing proof of relinquishment. A person ordered to relinquish any firearm and ammunition pursuant to this subdivision shall file with the court a receipt showing the firearm and ammunition were surrendered to the local law enforcement agency or sold to a licensed gun dealer within 48 hours after receiving the order. A court holding a hearing on this matter shall review the file to determine whether the receipt has been filed and inquire of the respondent whether they have complied with the requirement. Violations of the firearms prohibition of any restraining order under this section shall be reported to the prosecuting attorney in the jurisdiction where the order has been issued within two business days of the court hearing unless the restrained party provides a receipt showing compliance at a subsequent hearing or by direct filing with the clerk of the court. If the person does not file a receipt with the court within 48 hours after receiving the order for a firearm in their possession, the court shall order the clerk of the court to immediately notify, by the most effective means available, appropriate law enforcement officials of the issuance and contents of a protective order, information about the firearm or ammunition, and of any other information the court deems appropriate. In the event that it is necessary to continue the date of any hearing due to a request for a relinquishment order pursuant to this section, the court shall ensure that all applicable protective orders described in Section 6218 of the Family Code remain in effect or bifurcate the issues and grant the permanent restraining order pending the date of the hearing.

(c) A local law enforcement agency may charge the person subject to the order or injunction a fee for the storage of any firearm or ammunition relinquished pursuant to this section. The fee shall not exceed the actual cost incurred by the local law enforcement agency for the storage of the firearm or ammunition. For purposes of this subdivision, "actual cost" means expenses directly related to taking possession of a firearm and ammunition, storing the firearm and ammunition, and surrendering possession of the firearm and ammunition to a licensed dealer as defined in Section 26700 of the Penal Code or to the person relinquishing the firearm.

(d) The restraining order requiring a person to relinquish a firearm and ammunition pursuant to subdivision (b) shall state on its face that the respondent is prohibited from owning, possessing, purchasing, or receiving a firearm or ammunition while the protective order is in effect and that the firearm shall be relinquished to the local law enforcement agency for that jurisdiction or sold to a licensed gun dealer, and that proof of surrender or sale shall be filed with the court within a specified period of receipt of the order. The order shall also state on its face the expiration date for relinquishment. Nothing in this section shall limit a respondent's right under existing law to petition the court at a later date for modification of the order.

(e) The restraining order requiring a person to relinquish a firearm or ammunition pursuant to subdivision (b) shall prohibit the person from possessing or controlling any firearm for the duration of the order. At the expiration of the order, the local law enforcement agency shall return possession of any surrendered firearm and ammunition to the respondent, within five days after the expiration of the relinquishment order, unless the local law enforcement agency determines that (1) the firearm has been stolen, (2) the respondent is prohibited from possessing a firearm because the respondent is in any prohibited class for the possession of firearms, as defined in Chapter 2 (commencing with Section 29800) and Chapter 3 (commencing with Section 29900) of Division 9 of Title 4 of Part 6 of the Penal Code and Sections 8100 and 8103 of the Welfare and Institutions Code, or (3) another successive restraining order is issued against the respondent under this section. If the local law enforcement agency determines that the respondent is the legal owner of any firearm or ammunition deposited with the local law enforcement agency and is prohibited from possessing any firearm, the respondent shall be entitled to sell or transfer the firearm or ammunition to a licensed dealer as defined in Section 26700 of the Penal Code. If the firearm has been stolen, the firearm shall be restored to the lawful owner upon their identification of the firearm and proof of ownership.

(f) The court may, as part of the relinquishment order, grant an exemption from the relinquishment requirements of this section for a particular firearm or ammunition if the respondent is not otherwise prohibited from owning, possessing, controlling, or purchasing a firearm and ammunition under state or federal law and one of the following applies:

(1)(A) The respondent is currently employed as a sworn peace officer who is required, as a condition of continued employment, to carry a firearm, ammunition, or firearm and ammunition and the current employer is unable to reassign the peace officer to another position where use of a specified firearm or ammunition is unnecessary. In such a case, a court may allow the peace officer to continue to carry a specified firearm, ammunition, or firearm and ammunition, either on duty or off duty, if the court finds by a preponderance of the evidence, in writing or on the record, both of the following:

(i) The peace officer's personal safety depends on the ability to carry that specific firearm, ammunition, or firearm and ammunition outside of scheduled work hours.

(ii) The peace officer does not pose an additional threat of harm to a protected party or the public by having access to that specific firearm, ammunition, or firearm and ammunition, including whether the peace officer might use the firearm for a purpose other than as permitted under this paragraph.

(B) Prior to making the finding in subparagraph (A), the court shall require a mandatory psychological evaluation of the peace officer by a licensed mental health professional with domestic violence expertise. The court shall consider the results of an evaluation and may require the peace officer to enter into counseling or another remedial treatment program to deal with a propensity for domestic violence.

(2)(A) The respondent is not a peace officer but is required to carry a specific firearm, ammunition, or firearm and ammunition during scheduled work hours as a condition of continued employment, and the current employer is unable to reassign the respondent to another position where the firearm, ammunition, or firearm and ammunition is unnecessary. In this case, a court may grant an exemption to allow the respondent to possess a specific firearm, ammunition, or firearm and ammunition only during scheduled work hours if the court finds by a preponderance of the evidence, in writing or on the record, that the respondent does not pose an additional threat of harm to a protected party or the public by having access to the specific firearm, ammunition, or firearm and ammunition only during scheduled work hours, including whether the respondent might utilize the firearm, ammunition, or firearm and ammunition for a purpose other than as permitted under this paragraph.

(B) To assist the court in making the determination pursuant to subparagraph (A), the court may order a psychological evaluation of the respondent by a licensed mental health professional with domestic violence expertise.

(C) If the court grants an exemption pursuant to this paragraph, the order shall provide that the specific firearm, ammunition, or firearm and ammunition shall be in the physical possession of the respondent only during scheduled work hours and that the exemption does not authorize the respondent to possess any other firearm or ammunition, or to possess the specific firearm, ammunition, or firearm and ammunition outside of scheduled work hours.

(g)(1) If an exemption is granted pursuant to subdivision (f) during the pendency of a temporary restraining order and the court subsequently issues a restraining order after hearing on the same application, the court shall review and make a finding, in writing or on the record, as to whether the exemption remains appropriate, based upon the criteria set forth in paragraph (1) or (2) of subdivision (f), as applicable, in light of the issuance of the order after hearing. This review and finding shall occur at the time the restraining order after hearing is issued.

(2) If an exemption is granted and the court subsequently renews the restraining order pursuant to Section 6345 of the Family Code at the request of a party, the court shall review and make a finding, in writing or on the record, as to whether the exemption remains appropriate, based

upon the criteria set forth in paragraph (1) or (2) of subdivision (f), as applicable, in light of the renewal. This finding shall be made at the time the restraining order after hearing is renewed.

(3) The court may terminate or modify an exemption granted pursuant to this subdivision at any time if the respondent demonstrates a need to modify the specific firearm, ammunition, or firearm and ammunition authorized by the court pursuant to subdivision (f), if the respondent no longer meets the requirements in this section, or if the respondent otherwise violates the restraining order.

(h) During the period of the relinquishment order, a respondent is entitled to make one sale of all firearms that are in the possession of a local law enforcement agency pursuant to this section. A licensed gun dealer, who presents a local law enforcement agency with a bill of sale indicating that all firearms owned by the respondent that are in the possession of the local law enforcement agency have been sold by the respondent to the licensed gun dealer, shall be given possession of those firearms, at the location where a respondent's firearms are stored, within five days of presenting the local law enforcement agency with a bill of sale.

(i) If the respondent declines to relinquish possession of a firearm or ammunition based on the assertion of the right against self-incrimination, as provided by the Fifth Amendment to the United States Constitution and Section 15 of Article I of the California Constitution, the court may grant use immunity for the act of relinquishing the firearm or ammunition required under this section.

(j)(1) The relinquishment or surrender of a firearm to a law enforcement agency pursuant to this section or the return of a firearm to a person pursuant to this section shall not be subject to the requirements of Section 27545 of the Penal Code.

(2) Returns of firearms or ammunition pursuant to this section shall be governed by the applicable provisions of Chapter 2 (commencing with Section 33850) of Division 11 of Title 4 of Part 6 of the Penal Code.

(k) This section shall become operative on January 1, 2026. **Leg.H.** Added Stats 2024 ch 544 §3 (SB 899), effective January 1, 2025, operative January 1, 2026.

§527.10. Court order prohibiting obtaining address or location of protected party or family member

(a) The court shall order that any party enjoined pursuant to Section 527.6, 527.8, or 527.85 be prohibited from taking any action to obtain the address or location of any protected person, unless there is good cause not to make that order.

(b) The Judicial Council shall develop forms necessary to effectuate this section. **Leg.H.** Added Stats 2005 ch 472 §1 (AB 978), effective January 1, 2006. Amended Stats 2010 ch 572 §3 (AB 1596), effective January 1, 2011, operative January 1, 2012.

§527.11. Registration of vacant real property by owner's agent [Repealed]

Leg.H. Added Stats 2014 ch 666 §2 (AB 1513), effective January 1, 2015. Repealed January 1, 2018, by its own terms.

§ 527.11. Court determination of possession of firearms in violation of restraining order [Operative January 1, 2026]

(a) When relevant information is presented to the court at any noticed hearing that a restrained person has a firearm, the court shall consider that information to determine, by a preponderance of the evidence, whether the person subject to an order defined in Section 527.6, 527.8, or 527.85 or Section 15657.03 of the Welfare and Institutions Code, has a firearm in or subject to their immediate possession or control in violation of the order.

(b)(1) In making a determination under this section, the court may consider whether the restrained person filed a firearm relinquishment, storage, or sales receipt or if an exemption from the firearm prohibition was granted.

(2) The court may make the determination at any noticed hearing where a restraining order is issued, at a subsequent review hearing, or at any subsequent hearing while the order remains in effect.

(3) If the court makes a determination that the restrained person has a firearm in violation of the order, the court must make a written record of the determination and provide a copy to any party who is present at the hearing and, upon request, to any party not present at the hearing.

(c)(1) When presented with information under subdivision (a), the court may set a review hearing to determine whether a violation of the order has taken place.

(2) The review hearing should be held within 10 court days after the noticed hearing at which the information was presented. If the restrained person is not present when the court sets the review hearing, the protected person must provide notice of the review hearing to the restrained person at least two court days before the review hearing, in accordance with Section 414.10, by personal service or by mail to the restrained person's last known address.

(3) The court may for good cause extend the date of the review hearing for a reasonable period or remove it from the calendar.

(4) The court shall order the restrained person to appear at the review hearing.

(5) The court may conduct the review hearing in the absence of the protected person.

(6) This section does not prohibit the court from permitting a party or witness to appear through technology that enables remote appearances, as determined by the court.

(d) The determination made pursuant to this section may be considered by the court in issuing an order to show cause for contempt pursuant to paragraph (5) of subdivision (a) of Section 1209 or an order for monetary sanctions pursuant to Section 177.5.

(e) This section shall become operative on January 1, 2026. **Leg.H.** Added Stats 2024 ch 544 §4 (SB 899), effective January 1, 2025, operative January 1, 2026.

§527.12. "Declaration of Ownership" [Repealed]

Leg.H. Added Stats 2014 ch 666 §3 (AB 1513), effective January 1, 2015. Repealed January 1, 2018, by its own terms.

§ 527.12. Service of temporary restraining orders, orders after hearing, and protective orders by peace officers [Operative January 1, 2026]

(a) A peace officer shall, upon the request of a petitioner, serve any temporary restraining order, order after hearing, or protective order issued pursuant to Sections 527.6, 527.8, and 527.85, Section 136.2 of the Penal Code, or Section 15657.03 of the Welfare and Institutions Code, on the respondent, whether or not the respondent has been taken into custody.

(b)(1) The petitioner shall provide the peace officer with an endorsed copy of the order and the officer shall complete and transmit the proof of service to the issuing court. It is a rebuttable presumption that the proof of service was signed on the date of service.

(2) If the protected person cannot produce an endorsed copy of the order, the peace officer shall immediately verify the existence of the order in the California Restraining and Protective Order System.

(3) If the peace officer determines that an order subject to this section has been issued but not served, the officer shall immediately notify the respondent of the terms of the order and advise the respondent to obtain a copy of the full order from the issuing court. Upon notice, the officer shall immediately enforce the order. The officer's verbal notice of the terms of the order shall constitute service of the order and is sufficient notice for the purposes of this section and for the purposes of Sections 273.6 and 29825 of the Penal Code.

(4) If an order served pursuant to this section is subject to the reporting requirements of Section 13730 of the Penal Code, the report shall include the name and assignment of the peace officer who served the order and the case number of the order. If a report is not required, the information specified in this paragraph shall be included in the daily incident log of the officer's employing law enforcement agency.

(c) Notwithstanding any law, a fee shall not be charged to the petitioner for service of an order pursuant to this section.

(d)(1) There shall be no civil liability on the part of, and no cause of action for false arrest or false imprisonment against, a peace officer who makes an arrest pursuant to a protective or restraining order that is regular upon its face, if the peace officer, in making the arrest, acts in good faith and has reasonable cause to believe that the person against whom the order is issued has notice of the order and has committed an act in violation of the order.

(2) If there is more than one order issued and one of the orders is an emergency protective order that has precedence in enforcement pursuant to paragraph (1) of subdivision (c) of Section 136.2 of the Penal Code, the peace officer shall enforce the emergency protective order. If there is more than one order issued, none of the orders issued is an emergency protective order that has precedence in enforcement, and one of the orders issued is a no-contact order, the peace officer shall enforce the no-contact

order. If there is more than one civil order regarding the same parties and neither an emergency protective order that has precedence in enforcement nor a no-contact order has been issued, the peace officer shall enforce the order that was issued last. If there are both civil and criminal orders regarding the same parties and neither an emergency protective order that has precedence in enforcement nor a no-contact order has been issued, the peace officer shall enforce the criminal order issued last, subject to the provisions of subdivisions (h) and (i) of Section 136.2 of the Penal Code. This section does not exonerate a peace officer from liability for the unreasonable use of force in the enforcement of the order. The immunities afforded by this section shall not affect the availability of any other immunity that may apply, including, but not limited to, Sections 820.2 and 820.4 of the Government Code.

(e) For purposes of this section, "peace officer" has the same meaning as that term is defined in Section 830 of the Penal Code.

(f) This section shall become operative on January 1, 2026. **Leg.H.** Added Stats 2024 ch 544 §5 (SB 899), effective January 1, 2025, operative January 1, 2026.

§528. Injunction after answer

An injunction cannot be allowed after the defendant has answered, unless upon notice, or upon an order to show cause; but in such case the defendant may be restrained until the decision of the court or judge granting or refusing the injunction. **Leg.H.** Enacted 1872.

§529. Undertakings

(a) On granting an injunction, the court or judge must require an undertaking on the part of the applicant to the effect that the applicant will pay to the party enjoined any damages, not exceeding an amount to be specified, the party may sustain by reason of the injunction, if the court finally decides that the applicant was not entitled to the injunction. Within five days after the service of the injunction, the person enjoined may object to the undertaking. If the court determines that the applicant's undertaking is insufficient and a sufficient undertaking is not filed within the time required by statute, the order granting the injunction must be dissolved.

(b) This section does not apply to any of the following persons:

(1) Either spouse against the other in a proceeding for legal separation or dissolution of marriage.

(2) The applicant for an order described in Division 10 (commencing with Section 6200) of the Family Code.

(3) A public entity or officer described in Section 995.220.

(4) An applicant requesting an injunction under subdivision (d) of Section 1708.85 of the Civil Code.

(5) An applicant requesting an injunction under subdivision (d) of Section 1708.89 of the Civil Code. Leg.H. Enacted 1872. Amended Code Amdts 1873–74 ch 624 §1; Code Amdts 1880 ch 64 §1; Stats 1907 ch 272 §4; Stats 1931 ch 140 §1; Stats 1933 ch 744 §66; Stats 1979 ch 795 §9, operative July 1, 1980; Stats 1982 ch 517 §123; Stats 1992 ch 163 §25 (AB 2641), operative January 1, 1994; Stats 1993 ch 219 §63.7 (AB 1500); Stats 2021 ch 518 §2 (AB 514), effective January 1, 2022; Stats 2024 ch 557 §3 (AB 1979), effective January 1, 2025.

§529.1. Order requiring undertaking

(a) In all actions in which the court has granted an injunction sought by any plaintiff to enjoin a construction project which has received all legally required licenses and permits, the defendant may apply to the court by noticed motion for an order requiring the plaintiff to furnish an undertaking as security for costs and any damages that may be incurred by the defendant by the conclusion of the action or proceeding as the result of a delay in the construction of the project. The motion shall be made on the grounds that there is no reasonable possibility that the plaintiff will obtain a judgment against the moving defendant and that the plaintiff will not suffer undue economic hardship by filing the undertaking.

(b) If the court, after hearing, determines that the grounds for the motion have been established, the court shall order that the plaintiff file the undertaking in an amount specified in the court's order as security for costs and damages of the defendant. The liability of the plaintiff pursuant to this section for the costs and damages of the defendant shall not exceed five hundred thousand dollars ($500,000).

(c) As used in this section, a construction project includes, but is not restricted to, the construction, surveying, design, specifications, alteration, repair, improvement, maintenance, removal, or demolition of any building, highway, road, parking facility, bridge, railroad, airport, pier or dock, excavation or other structure, development or other improvement to real or personal property. **Leg.H.** Added Stats 1979 ch 750 §1. Amended Stats 1982 ch 517 §124; Stats 2004 ch 193 §11 (SB 111).

§529.2. Undertakings in actions challenging housing development projects

(a) In all civil actions, including, but not limited to, actions brought pursuant to Section 21167 of the Public Resources Code, brought by any plaintiff to challenge a housing project which is a development project, as defined by Section 65928 of the Government Code, and which meets or exceeds the requirements for low- or moderate-income housing as set forth in Section 65915 of the Government Code, a defendant may, if the bringing of the action or the seeking by the plaintiff of particular relief including, but not limited to, injunctions, has the effect of preventing or delaying the project from being carried out, apply to the court by noticed motion for an order requiring the plaintiff to furnish an undertaking as security for costs and any damages that may be incurred by the defendant by the conclusion of the action or proceeding as the result of a delay in carrying out the development project. The motion shall be made on the grounds that [1] **the action is without merit and that the action** was brought in bad faith, vexatiously, for the purpose of delay, or to thwart the low- or moderate-income nature of the housing development project [2].

(b) **In responding to a motion for undertaking, the plaintiff may seek to limit the amount of the undertaking by presenting admissible evidence that filing an undertaking will cause it, and in cases where the plaintiff is an unincorporated association, its members, to suffer undue economic hardship.** If the court, after hearing, determines that the grounds for the motion have been established, the court shall order that the plaintiff file the undertaking in an amount specified in the court's order, **taking into consideration any admitted evidence of plaintiff's economic hardship and avoiding causing the plaintiff to suffer undue economic hardship,** as security for costs and damages of the defendant. The liability of the plaintiff pursuant to this section for the costs and damages of the defendant shall not exceed five hundred thousand dollars ($500,000). **If the court concludes, based on all of the admissible evidence presented, that a bond in any amount would cause the plaintiff undue economic hardship, the court is authorized in its discretion to decline to impose a bond.**

(c) If at any time after the plaintiff has filed an undertaking the housing development plan is changed by the developer in bad faith so that it fails to meet or exceed the requirements for low- or moderate-income housing as set forth in Section 65915 of the Government Code, the developer shall be liable to the plaintiff for the cost of obtaining the undertaking. **Leg.H.** Added Stats 1981 ch 970 §1. Amended Stats 1982 ch 517 §124.5; Stats 2024 ch 285 §1 (SB 393), effective January 1, 2025.

§529.2. 2024 Deletes. [1] : (1) the action **[2]** , and (2) the plaintiff will not suffer undue economic hardship by filing the undertaking

§530. Injunction to protect water rights; Notice; Effect of defendant's bond

In all actions which may be hereafter brought when an injunction or restraining order may be applied for to prevent the diversion, diminution or increase of the flow of water in its natural channels, to the ordinary flow of which the plaintiff claims to be entitled, the court shall first require due notice of the application to be served upon the defendant, unless it shall appear from the verified complaint or affidavits upon which the application therefor is made, that, within ten days prior to the time of such application, the plaintiff has been in the peaceable possession of the flow of such water, and that, within such time, said plaintiff has been deprived of the flow thereof by the wrongful diversion of such flow by the defendant, or that the plaintiff, at the time of such application, is, and for ten days prior thereto, has been, in possession of the flow of said water, and that the defendant threatens to divert the flow of such water; and if such notice of such application be given and upon the hearing thereof, it be made to appear to the court that plaintiff is entitled to the injunction, but that the issuance thereof pending the litigation will entail great damage upon defendant, and that plaintiff will not be greatly damaged by the acts complained of pending the litigation, and can be fully compensated for such damage as he may suffer, the court may refuse the injunction upon the defendant giving a bond such as is provided for in section 532; and upon the trial the same proceedings shall be had, and with the same effect as in said section provided. **Leg.H.** Enacted 1872. Amended Stats 1887 ch 188; Stats 1907 ch 272 §5; Stats 1911 ch 733 §1.

§531. Injunction to suspend business of corporation

An injunction to suspend the general and ordinary business of a corporation cannot be granted without due notice of the application therefor to the proper officers or managing agent of the corporation, except when the people of this state are a party to the proceeding. **Leg.H.** Enacted 1872. Amended Stats 1907 ch 272 §6.

§532. Motion to dissolve or modify injunction

(a) If an injunction is granted without notice to the person enjoined, the person may apply, upon reasonable notice to the judge who granted the injunction, or to the court in which the action was brought, to dissolve or modify the injunction. The application may be made upon the complaint or the affidavit on which the injunction was granted, or upon affidavit on the part of the person enjoined, with or without the answer. If the application is made upon affidavits on the part of the person enjoined, but not otherwise, the person against whom the application is made may oppose the application by affidavits or other evidence in addition to that on which the injunction was granted.

(b) In all actions in which an injunction or restraining order has been or may be granted or applied for, to prevent the diversion, pending the litigation, of water used, or to be used, for irrigation or domestic purposes only, if it is made to appear to the court that great damage will be suffered by the person enjoined, in case the injunction is continued, and that the person in whose behalf it issued can be fully compensated for any damages suffered by reason of the continuance of the acts enjoined during the pendency of the litigation, the court in its discretion, may dissolve or modify the injunction. The dissolution or modification shall be subject to the person enjoined giving a bond in such amount as may be fixed by the court or judge, conditioned that the enjoined person will pay all damages which the person in whose behalf the injunction issued may suffer by reason of the continuance, during the litigation, of the acts complained of. Upon the trial the amount of the damages must be ascertained, and in case judgment is rendered for the person in whose behalf the injunction was granted, the amount fixed as damages must be included in the judgment, together with reasonable attorney's fees. In any proceedings to enforce the liability on the bond, the amount of the damages as fixed in the judgment is conclusive. **Leg.H.** Enacted 1872. Amended Stats 1887 ch 188; Stats 1907 ch 272 §7; Stats 1982 ch 517 §125.

§533. Modification or dissolution of injunction or temporary restraining

In any action, the court may on notice modify or dissolve an injunction or temporary restraining order upon a showing that there has been a material change in the facts upon which the injunction or temporary restraining order was granted, that the law upon which the injunction or temporary restraining order was granted has changed, or that the ends of justice would be served by the modification or dissolution of the injunction or temporary restraining order. **Leg.H.** Added Stats 1995 ch 796 §8 (SB 45).

Prior Law: Former CCP §533, similar to present section, was enacted 1872 and repealed Stats 1995 ch 1995 ch 796 §7.

§534. Injunction to protect water rights; Effect of defendant's answer; Reply; Trial; Appeal

In any action brought by a riparian owner to enjoin the diversion of water appropriated or proposed to be appropriated, or the use thereof, against any person or persons appropriating or proposing to appropriate such waters, the defendant may set up in his answer that the water diverted or proposed to be diverted is for the irrigation of land or other public use, and, in such case, he shall also in such answer set forth the quantity of water desired to be taken and necessary to such irrigation of land or the public use, the nature of such use, the place where the same is used or proposed to be used, the duration and extent of the diversion or the proposed diversion, including the stages of the flow of the stream at and during the time in which the water is to be diverted, and that the same may be diverted without interfering with the actual and necessary beneficial uses of the plaintiff, and that such defendant so answering desires that the court shall ascertain and fix the damages, if any, that will result to the plaintiff or to his riparian lands from the appropriation of the water so appropriated or intended to be appropriated by defendant.

The plaintiff may serve and file a reply to the defendant's answer stating plaintiff's rights to the water and the damage plaintiff will suffer by the defendant's taking of the water, and plaintiff may implead as parties to the action all persons necessary to a full determination of the rights of plaintiff to the water and the damages plaintiff will suffer by the proposed taking by defendant, and the court shall have jurisdiction to hear and determine all the rights to water of the plaintiff and other parties to the action, and said parties shall have a right to state and prove their rights, and shall be bound by the judgment rendered the same as though made parties plaintiff at the commencement of the action.

Upon the trial of the case the court shall receive and hear evidence on behalf of the respective parties, and if the court finds that the allegations of such answer are true as to the aforesaid matters, and that the appropriation and diversion of such waters is for irrigation of land or other public use and that, after allowing sufficient water for the actual and necessary beneficial uses of the plaintiff and other parties, there is water available to be beneficially appropriated by such defendant so answering, the court shall fix the time and manner and extent of such appropriation and the actual damages, if any, resulting to the plaintiff or other parties on account of the same, and in fixing such damages the court shall be guided by Article 5 (commencing with Section 1263.410) of Chapter 9 of Title 7 of Part 3, and if, upon the ascertainment and fixing of such damages the defendant, within the time allowed in Section 1268.010 for the payment of damages in proceedings in eminent domain, shall pay into court the amount of damages fixed and the costs adjudged to be paid by such defendant, or give a good and sufficient bond to pay the same upon the final settlement of the case, the injunction prayed for by the plaintiff shall be denied to the extent of the amount the defendant is permitted to appropriate, as aforesaid, and the temporary injunction, if any has been granted, shall be vacated to the extent aforesaid; provided, that any of the parties may appeal from such judgment as in other cases; and provided, further, that if such judgment is in favor of the defendant and if he upon the pending such appeal shall keep on deposit with the clerk of said court the amount of such damages and costs, or the bond, if it be given, so awarded to be paid to the plaintiff or other parties in the event such judgment shall be affirmed, no injunction against the appropriation of the amount the defendant is permitted to appropriate as aforesaid shall be granted or enforced pending such appeal, and, upon the acceptance by the plaintiff or other parties of such amount so awarded or upon the affirmation of such decision on appeal so that such judgment shall become final, the defendant shall have the right to divert and appropriate from such stream, against such plaintiff or other parties and his successors in interest, the quantity of water therein adjudged and allowed. Upon the filing of such answer as is herein provided for, the parties plaintiff or other parties and defendant shall be entitled to a jury trial upon the issues as to damages so raised, as provided in Title 7 (commencing with Section 1230.010) of Part 3, applying to proceedings in eminent domain. **Leg.H.** Added Stats 1917 ch 553 §1. Amended Stats 1975 ch 1240 §5, operative July 1, 1976.

§535. [Section repealed 1983]

Leg.H. Added Stats 1969 ch 141 §1. Repealed Stats 1982 ch 517 §126. See CCP §§995.040, 996.420, 996.440.

§537. [Section repealed 1977]

Leg.H. Added Stats 1972 ch 550 §2. Repealed Stats 1974 ch 1516 §12, operative January 1, 1977. See CCP §§484.010.

Prior Law: Former CCP §537, similar in part to the later section, was enacted 1872, amended by Code Amdts 1873–74 c 383 §68, Stats 1905 ch 363 §1, Stats 1927 ch 524 §1, Stats 1929 ch 401 §1, Stats 1933 ch 130 §1, Stats 1957 ch 1660 §1, Stats 1961 ch 589 §9, ch 1164 §2, Stats 1963 ch 50 §1, Stats 1965 ch 1375 §1, Stats 1970 ch 1523 §2, and repealed by Stats 1972 ch 550 §1.

§537.1. [Section repealed 1977]

Leg.H. Added Stats 1972 ch 550 §3. Repealed Stats 1974 ch 1516 §12, operative January 1, 1977. See CCP §§483.010, 492.010.

§537.2. [Section repealed 1977]

Leg.H. Added Stats 1972 ch 550 §4. Repealed Stats 1974 ch 1516 §12, operative January 1, 1977. See CCP §§483.010, 492.010.

§537.3. [Section repealed 1977]

Leg.H. Added Stats 1972 ch 550 §5. Repealed Stats 1974 ch 1516 §12, operative January 1, 1977. See CCP §§487.010, 487.020.

§537.5. [Section repealed 1977]

Leg.H. Added Stats 1951 ch 655 §20. Amended Stats 1957 ch 1836 §1; Stats 1959 ch 1073 §1; Stats 1972 ch 550 §6. Repealed Stats 1974 ch 1516 §12, operative January 1, 1977. See CCP §482.050.

§538. [Section repealed 1977]

Leg.H. Added Stats 1972 ch 550 §8. Repealed Stats 1974 ch 1516 §12, operative January 1, 1977. See CCP §§484.020, 484.030.

Prior Law: Former CCP §538, similar to the later section, was enacted 1872, amended Code Amdts 1873–74 ch 383 §69, Stats 1905 ch 363 §2, Stats 1927 ch 524 §2, Stats 1931 ch 916 §1, Stats 1933 ch 744 §67, Stats 1937 ch 540 §1, Stats 1951 ch 776 §1, Stats 1957 ch 1090 §1, Stats 1959 ch 1872 §1, Stats 1965 ch 668 §1, Stats 1967 ch 292 §2, Stats 1968 ch 851 §1, Stats 1970 ch 1319 §2, ch 1523 §2.7, and repealed Stats 1972 ch 550 §7.

§538.1. [Section repealed 1977]

Leg.H. Added Stats 1972 ch 550 §9. Repealed Stats 1974 ch 1516 §12, operative January 1, 1977. See CCP §§486.010, 486.070.

§538.2. [Section repealed 1977]

Leg.H. Added Stats 1972 ch 550 §10. Repealed Stats 1974 ch 1516 §12, operative January 1, 1977. See CCP §484.040.

§538.3. [Section repealed 1977]

Leg.H. Added Stats 1972 ch 550 §11. Repealed Stats 1974 ch 1516 §12, operative January 1, 1977. See CCP §§486.050, 486.060, 486.090, 486.100.

§538.4. [Section repealed 1977]

Leg.H. Added Stats 1972 ch 550 §12. Repealed Stats 1974 ch 1516 §12, operative January 1, 1977. See CCP §§484.060, 484.090.

§538.5. [Section repealed 1977]

Leg.H. Added Stats 1972 ch 550 §13. Repealed Stats 1974 ch 1516 §12, operative January 1, 1977. See CCP §§485.010, 485.210, 485.240.

§539. [Section repealed 1977]

Leg.H. Enacted 1872. Amended Code Amdts 1873–74 ch 383 §70, ch 636 §1; Stats 1907 ch 373 §1; Stats 1933 ch 744 §68; Stats 1935 ch 722 §4; Stats 1951 ch 1737 §74, operated January 1, 1952; Stats 1959 ch 892 §1; Stats 1961 ch 768 §1; Stats 1967 ch 292 §2; Stats 1972 ch 550 §14. Repealed Stats 1974 ch 1516 §12, operative January 1, 1977. See CCP §§489.210, 489.220.

§539a. [Section repealed 1977]

Leg.H. Added Stats 1941 ch 343 §2. Amended Stats 1957 ch 346 §1. Repealed Stats 1974 ch 1516 §12, operative January 1, 1977. The repealed sections related to writ of attachment.

CHAPTER 4
PREVENTION OF DOMESTIC VIOLENCE
[REPEALED]

§540. [Section repealed 1994]

Leg.H. Added Stats 1979 ch 795 §10, operative July 1, 1980. Amended Stats 1984 ch 1163 §2; Stats 1990 ch 752 §1 (AB 4000). Repealed Stats 1992 ch 162 §5 (AB 2650), operative January 1, 1994. See Fam C §6220.

Prior Law: Former CCP §540, similar to present CCP §§488.030, 489.310, was enacted 1872, amended Stats 1917 ch 608 §1, Stats 1929 ch 590 §1, Stats 1933 ch 744 §69, Stats 1935 ch 722 §5, Stats 1951 ch 1737 §75, operative January 1, 1952, Stats 1957 ch 1730 §1, Stats 1963 ch 1407 §1, Stats 1965 ch 309 §1, ch 558 §1, Stats 1967 ch 292 §3, Stats 1970 ch 1523 §3, Stats 1971 ch 529 §1, and repealed Stats 1974 ch 1516 §12, operative January 1, 1977.

§541. [Section repealed 1994]

Leg.H. Added Stats 1979 ch 795 §10, operative July 1, 1980. Repealed Stats 1992 ch 162 §5 (AB 2650), operative January 1, 1994. See Fam C §6200.

Prior Law: Former CCP §541, relating to levy on investment securities, was added Stats 1972 ch 550 §16 and repealed Stats 1974 ch 1516 §12, operative January 1, 1977.

Former CCP §541, relating to attachment and disposal of shares of stock and debts due defendant, was enacted 1872 and repealed Stats 1972 ch 550 §15.

§542. [Section repealed 1994]

Leg.H. Added Stats 1979 ch 795 §10, operative July 1, 1980. Amended Stats 1980 ch 1158 §6; Stats 1984 ch 1163 §3; Stats 1990 ch 752 §2 (AB 4000). Repealed Stats 1992 ch 162 §5 (AB 2650), operative January 1, 1994. See Fam C §§6201, 6203, 6209, 6211, 6218.

Prior Law: Former CCP §542, relating to manner in which property attached, was enacted 1872, amended Stats 1903 ch 153 §1, Stats 1923 ch 114 §1, Stats 1927 ch 507 §1, Stats 1931 ch 839 §1, Stats 1933 ch 744 §70, Stats 1935 ch 722 §6, Stats 1937 ch 576 §1, Stats 1943 ch 1122 §1, Stats 1945 ch 126 §1, ch 790 §1, Stats 1947 ch 408 §1, ch 1197 §1, Stats 1949 ch 370 §1, Stats 1951 ch 1094 §4, Stats 1955 ch 1838 §1, Stats 1957 ch 527 §1, ch 1731 §1, Stats 1959 ch 1008 §1, Stats 1963 ch 819 §25, effective January 1, 1965, Stats 1965 ch 309 §2, ch 634 §1, Stats 1970 ch 1523 §4, and repealed Stats 1974 ch 1516 §12, operative January 1, 1977.

§542.1. [Section repealed 1977]

Leg.H. Added Stats 1972 ch 550 §17. Repealed Stats 1974 ch 1516 §12, operative July 1, 1977. The repealed section related to levy on equipment and filing notice of lien.

§542.2. [Section repealed 1977]

Leg.H. Added Stats 1972 ch 550 §17.1. Repealed Stats 1974 ch 1516 §12, operative July 1, 1977. The repealed section related to fee for filing and indexing each notice of attachment lien.

§542.3. [Section repealed 1977]

Leg.H. Added Stats 1972 ch 550 §17.2. Repealed Stats 1974 ch 1516 §12, operative July 1, 1977. The repealed section related to certificate regarding filed notice of attachment lien and fee for such certificate.

§542.4. [Section repealed 1977]

Leg.H. Added Stats 1972 ch 550 §17.3. Repealed Stats 1974 ch 1516 §12, operative July 1, 1977. The repealed section related to continuation of notice of attachment lien, order for, and signing of, notice of continuation, and duration of continued notice.

§542a. [Section repealed 1977]

Leg.H. Added Stats 1909 ch 426 §1. Amended Stats 1915 ch 106 §1; Stats 1919 ch 43 §1; Stats 1931 ch 1041 §1; Stats 1933 ch 744 §71; Stats 1947 ch 408 §2. Repealed Stats 1974 ch 1516 §12, operative January 1, 1977. The repealed section related to lien on realty.

§542b. [Section repealed 1977]

Leg.H. Added Stats 1972 ch 550 §19. Repealed Stats 1974 ch 1516 §12, operative January 1, 1977. See CCP §486.110.

Prior Law: Former CCP §542b, relating to duration of attachment of personal property, was added Stats 1929 ch 278 §1, amended Stats 1931 ch 1041 §2, Stats 1971 ch 1359 §1, and repealed Stats 1972 ch 550 §18.

§542c. [Section repealed 1977]

Leg.H. Added Stats 1972 ch 550 §20. Repealed Stats 1974 ch 1516 §12, operative January 1, 1977. The repealed section related to duration of attachment of personal property.

§543. [Section repealed 1994]

Leg.H. Added Stats 1979 ch 795 §10, operative July 1, 1980. Repealed Stats 1992 ch 162 §5 (AB 2650), operative January 1, 1994. See Fam C §6226.

Prior Law: Former CCP §543, similar to present CCP §487.020, was enacted 1872, amended Stats 1933 ch 744 §72, Stats 1957 ch 496 §1, Stats 1970 ch 1523 §5, and repealed Stats 1974 ch 1516 §12, operative January 1, 1977.

§544. [Section repealed 1977]

Leg.H. Enacted 1872. Amended Stats 1931 ch 1041 §3; Stats 1933 ch 744 §73; Stats 1957 ch 935 §1. Repealed Stats 1974 ch 1516 §12, operative January 1, 1977. See CCP §§488.730, 488.740.

§545. [Section repealed 1994]

Leg.H. Added Stats 1979 ch 795 §10, operative July 1, 1980. Amended Stats 1984 ch 1163 §4; Stats 1990 ch 752 §3 (AB 4000). Repealed Stats 1992 ch 162 §5 (AB 2650), operative January 1, 1994. See Fam C §§240, 6225, 6300, 6301.

Prior Law: Former CCP §545, similar to present CCP §491.110, was enacted Stats 1872, amended Stats 1933 ch 744 §74, Stats 1951 ch 1737 §76, Stats 1969 ch 134 §1, and repealed Stats 1974 ch 1516 §12, operative January 1, 1977.

§545.1. [Section repealed 1977]

Leg.H. Added Stats 1957 ch 1596 §1. Amended Stats 1967 ch 65 §1. Repealed Stats 1974 ch 1516 §12, operative January 1, 1977. See CCP §491.150.

§545.2. [Section repealed 1977]

Leg.H. Added Stats 1957 ch 1596 §2. Repealed Stats 1974 ch 1516 §12, operative January 1, 1977. See CCP §491.150.

§545.3. [Section repealed 1977]

Leg.H. Added Stats 1957 ch 1596 §3. Repealed Stats 1974 ch 1516 §12, operative January 1, 1977. See CCP §491.120.

§545.5. [Section repealed 1994]

Leg.H. Added Stats 1990 ch 935 §4 (AB 3593). Repealed Stats 1992 ch 162 §5 (AB 2650), operative January 1, 1994 (ch 1136 prevails). Amended Stats 1992 ch 1136 §5 (SB 1541). Repealed Stats 1993 ch 219 §63.8 (AB 1500). See Fam C §6305.

§546. [Section repealed 1994]

Leg.H. Added Stats 1979 ch 795 §10, operative July 1, 1980. Amended Stats 1980 ch 1158 §7; Stats 1981 ch 182 §3; Stats 1987 ch 758 §1, operative July 1, 1988; Stats 1989 ch 850 §1, ch 1409 §1.5; Stats 1990 ch 935 §5 (AB 3593); Stats 1991 ch 866 §2, ch 953 §1 (AB 108), effective October 13, 1991, operative until January 1, 1992, ch 953 §1.5, effective October 13, 1991, operative January 1, 1992. Repealed Stats 1992 ch 162 §5 (AB 2650), operative January 1, 1994. See Fam C §§242, 243, 6226, 6241, 6250–6257, 6270–6273, 6302, 6320–6325.

Prior Law: Former CCP §546, similar to present CCP §§488.130, 488.610, was enacted Stats 1872, amended Stats 1933 ch 744 §75; Stats 1953 ch 1245 §1, and repealed Stats 1974 ch 1516 §12, operative January 1, 1977.

§546.5. [Section repealed 1994]

Leg.H. Added Stats 1986 ch 387 §1. Amended Stats 1986 ch 387 §1; Stats 1990 ch 752 §4 (AB 4000). Repealed Stats 1992 ch 162 §5 (AB 2650), operative January 1, 1994. See Fam C §6222.

§547. [Section repealed 1994]

Leg.H. Added Stats 1979 ch 795 §10, operative July 1, 1980. Amended Stats 1980 ch 1158 §8; Stats 1982 ch 578 §1, ch 1238 §1; Stats 1984 ch 439 §2; Stats 1990 ch 752 §5 (AB 4000), ch 1180 §1 (AB 1753); Stats 1991 ch 953 §2 (AB 108), effective October 13, 1991. Repealed Stats 1992 ch 162 §5 (AB 2650), operative January 1, 1994. See Fam C §§6340–6344.

Prior Law: Former CCP §547, similar to present CCP §§488.600, 488.700, 700.010, was enacted Stats 1872, amended Stats 1933 ch 744 §76, and repealed Stats 1974 ch 1516 §12, operative January 1, 1977.

§547a. [Section repealed 1974]

Leg.H. Added Stats 1933 ch 744 §76a. Repealed Stats 1974 ch 1516 §12, operative January 1, 1977. See CCP §488.700.

§547.5. [Section repealed 1994]

Leg.H. Added Stats 1982 ch 359 §3. Amended Stats 1991 ch 321 §3 (AB 370). Repealed Stats 1992 ch 162 §5 (AB 2650), operative January 1, 1994. See Fam C §6223.

§547.7. [Section repealed 1994]

Leg.H. Added Stats 1992 ch 1136 §6 (SB 1541). Repealed Stats 1993 ch 219 §63.9 (AB 1500). See Fam C §3031.

§548. [Section repealed 1994]

Leg.H. Added Stats 1979 ch 795 §10, operative July 1, 1980. Amended Stats 1982 ch 359 §4; Stats 1987 ch 391 §2. Repealed Stats 1992 ch 162 §5 (AB 2650) (ch 149 prevails). Amended Stats 1992 ch 149 §1 (AB 2634). Repealed Stats 1993 ch 219 §64 (AB 1500). See Fam C §6345.

Prior Law: Former CCP §548, similar to present CCP §488.700, was enacted Stats 1872, amended Code Amdts 1880 ch 15 §4, Stats 1927 ch 512 §1, Stats 1933 ch 744 §77, Stats 1951 ch 1737 §77, operative January 1, 1952, and repealed Stats 1974 ch 1516 §12, operative January 1, 1977.

§549. [Section repealed 1994]

Leg.H. Added Stats 1979 ch 795 §10, operative July 1, 1980. Repealed Stats 1992 ch 162 §5 (AB 2650), operative January 1, 1994. See Fam C §6227.

Prior Law: Former CCP §549, similar to present CCP §488.110, was enacted Stats 1872, amended Stats 1891 ch 32 §2, Stats 1933 ch 744 §78, and repealed Stats 1974 ch 1516 §12, operative January 1, 1977.

§550. [Section repealed 1994]

Leg.H. Added Stats 1979 ch 795 §10, operative July 1, 1980. Amended Stats 1980 ch 1158 §9; Stats 1988 ch 271 §5; Stats 1989 ch 1416 §18; Stats 1990 ch 752 §6 (AB 4000), ch 1180 §2 (AB 1753); Stats 1991 ch 953 §3 (AB 108), effective October 13, 1991. Repealed Stats 1992 ch 162 §5 (AB 2650), operative January 1, 1994. See Fam C §§6304, 6380, 6382–6385, 6387.

Prior Law: Former CCP §550, relating to satisfaction of judgment for plaintiff, was enacted Stats 1872, amended Stats 1933 ch 744 §79, and repealed Stats 1974 ch 1516 §12, operative January 1, 1977.

§551. [Section repealed 1994]

Leg.H. Added Stats 1979 ch 795 §10, operative July 1, 1980. Amended Stats 1990 ch 752 §7 (AB 4000). Repealed Stats 1992 ch 162 §5 (AB 2650), operative January 1, 1994. See Fam C §6388.

Prior Law: Former CCP §551, relating to collection of balance due or return of remaining attached property, was enacted Stats 1872, amended Stats 1933 ch 744 §80, and repealed Stats 1974 ch 1516 §12, operative January 1, 1977.

§552. [Section repealed 1994]

Leg.H. Added Stats 1979 ch 795 §10, operative July 1, 1980. Repealed Stats 1992 ch 162 §5 (AB 2650), operative January 1, 1994. See Fam C §6224.

Prior Law: Former CCP §552, relating to commencement of suits on the undertaking, was enacted Stats 1872 and repealed Stats 1974 ch 1516 §12, operative January 1, 1977.

§553. [Section repealed 1994]

Leg.H. Added Stats 1979 ch 795 §10, operative July 1, 1980. Amended Stats 1981 ch 182 §4. Repealed Stats 1992 ch 162 §5 (AB 2650), operative January 1, 1994. See Fam C §6386.

Prior Law: Former CCP §553, similar to present CCP §§488.740, 489.410, was enacted 1872, amended Stats 1907 ch 373 §2, Stats 1909 ch 631 §1, Stats 1933 ch 744 §81, Stats 1959 ch 833 §1, Stats 1968 ch 788 §1, and repealed Stats 1974 ch 1516 §12, operative January 1, 1977.

§553.5. [Section repealed 1977]

Leg.H. Added Stats 1955 ch 479 §1. Repealed Stats 1974 ch 1516 §12, operative January 1, 1977. See CCP §489.420.

§554. [Section repealed 1977]

Leg.H. Enacted Stats 1872. Amended Code Amdts 1880 ch 15 §5; Stats 1907 ch 373 §3; Stats 1917 ch 608 §2; Stats 1933 ch 744 §82; Stats 1951 ch 1737 §78, operative January 1, 1952. Repealed Stats 1974 ch 1516 §12, operative January 1, 1977. See CCP §489.310.

§555. [Section repealed 1977]

Leg.H. Enacted Stats 1872. Amended Code Amdts 1873–74 ch 383 §71; Stats 1907 ch 373 §4; Stats 1917 ch 608 §3; Stats 1933 ch 744 §83; Stats 1951 ch 1737 §79, operative January 1, 1952. Repealed Stats 1974 ch 1516 §12, operative January 1, 1977. See CCP §489.310.

§556. [Section repealed 1977]

Leg.H. Enacted Stats 1872. Amended Code Amdts 1873–74 ch 383 §72; Code Amdts 1880 ch 15 §6; Stats 1933 ch 744 §84; Stats 1951 ch 1737 §80, operative January 1, 1952. Repealed Stats 1974 ch 1516 §12, operative January 1, 1977. See CCP §§485.240, 492.050.

§557. [Section repealed 1977]

Leg.H. Enacted Stats 1872. Repealed Stats 1974 ch 1516 §12, operative January 1, 1977. The repealed section related to opposition to motion by affidavit.

§558. [Section repealed 1977]

Leg.H. Enacted Stats 1872. Amended Stats 1909 ch 153 §1. Repealed Stats 1974 ch 1516 §12, operative January 1, 1977. See CCP §§485.240, 492.050.

§559. [Section repealed 1977]

Leg.H. Enacted Stats 1872. Amended Code Amdts 1875–76 ch 122 §1; Stats 1933 ch 744 §85; Stats 1947 ch 408 §3; Stats 1955 ch 534 §1; Stats 1957 ch 1836 §2. Repealed Stats 1974 ch 1516 §12, operative January 1, 1977. The repealed section related to return of writ, and recording of discharge of release.

§559½. [Section repealed 1977]

Leg.H. Added Stats 1927 ch 476 §1. Amended Stats 1941 ch 1051 §1; Stats 1963 ch 1407 §2. Repealed Stats 1974 ch 1516 §12, operative January 1, 1977. See CCP §482.090.

§560. [Section repealed 1977]

Leg.H. Added Stats 1907 ch 373 §5. Amended Stats 1931 ch 1041 §4; Stats 1955 ch 247 §1; Stats 1957 ch 1865 §9. Repealed Stats 1974 ch 1516 §12, operative January 1, 1977. The repealed section related to release of real property from attachment.

§561. [Section repealed 1977]

Leg.H. Added Stats 1923 ch 36 §1. Repealed Stats 1974 ch 1516 §12, operative January 1, 1977. See CCP §488.485.

CHAPTER 5
RECEIVERS

Cases in which appointment of receiver is authorized. §564.
Appointment upon dissolution of corporation. §565.
Restrictions on appointment; Undertaking for ex parte application. §566.
Oath and undertaking of receiver. §567.
Powers of receivers. §568.
Deposit of securities. §568.1.
Procedures for receiver to obtain court order to assist in abatement of substandard conditions. §568.2.
Motion in receivership action seeking further court instructions. §568.3.
Authority to sell real or personal property. §568.5.
Public Utilities Commission appointed receiver. § 568.6.
Deposit of funds. §569.
Notice of unclaimed funds in receiver's hands; Disposition of funds; Recovery by owner. §570.

§564. Cases in which appointment of receiver is authorized

(a) A receiver may be appointed, in the manner provided in this chapter, by the court in which an action or proceeding is pending in any case in which the court is empowered by law to appoint a receiver.

(b) A receiver may be appointed by the court in which an action or proceeding is pending, or by a judge of that court, in the following cases:

(1) In an action by a vendor to vacate a fraudulent purchase of property, or by a creditor to subject any property or fund to the creditor's claim, or between partners or others jointly owning or interested in any property or fund, on the application of the plaintiff, or of any party whose right to or interest in the property or fund, or the proceeds of the property or fund, is probable, and where it is shown that the property or fund is in danger of being lost, removed, or materially injured.

(2) In an action by a secured lender for the foreclosure of a deed of trust or mortgage and sale of property upon which there is a lien under a deed of trust or mortgage, where it appears that the property is in danger of being lost, removed, or materially injured, or that the condition of the deed of trust or mortgage has not been performed, and that the property is probably insufficient to discharge the deed of trust or mortgage debt.

(3) After judgment, to carry the judgment into effect.

(4) After judgment, to dispose of the property according to the judgment, or to preserve it during the pendency of an appeal, or pursuant to the Enforcement of Judgments Law (Title 9 (commencing with Section 680.010)), or after sale of real property pursuant to a decree of foreclosure, during the redemption period, to collect, expend, and disburse rents as directed by the court or otherwise provided by law.

(5) Where a corporation has been dissolved, as provided in Section 565.

(6) Where a corporation is insolvent, or in imminent danger of insolvency, or has forfeited its corporate rights.

(7) In an action of unlawful detainer.

(8) At the request of the Public Utilities Commission pursuant to Section 1825 or 1826 of the Public Utilities Code.

(9) In all other cases where necessary to preserve the property or rights of any party.

(10) At the request of the Office of Statewide Health Planning and Development, or the Attorney General, pursuant to Section 129173 of the Health and Safety Code.

(11) In an action by a secured lender for specific performance of an assignment of rents provision in a deed of trust, mortgage, or separate assignment document. The appointment may be continued after entry of a judgment for specific performance if appropriate to protect, operate, or maintain real property encumbered by a deed of trust or mortgage or to collect rents therefrom while a pending nonjudicial foreclosure under power of sale in a deed of trust or mortgage is being completed.

(12) In a case brought by an assignee under an assignment of leases, rents, issues, or profits pursuant to subdivision (g) of Section 2938 of the Civil Code.

(c) A receiver may be appointed, in the manner provided in this chapter, including, but not limited to, Section 566, by the superior court in an action brought by a secured lender to enforce the rights provided in Section 2929.5 of the Civil Code, to enable the secured lender to enter and inspect the real property security for the purpose of determining the existence, location, nature, and magnitude of any past or present release or threatened release of any hazardous substance into, onto, beneath, or from the real property security. The secured lender shall not abuse the right of entry and inspection or use it to harass the borrower or tenant of the property. Except in case of an emergency, when the borrower or tenant of the property has abandoned the premises, or if it is impracticable to do so, the secured lender shall give the borrower or tenant of the property reasonable notice of the secured lender's intent to enter and shall enter only during the borrower's or tenant's normal business hours. Twenty-four hours' notice shall be presumed to be reasonable notice in the absence of evidence to the contrary.

(d) Any action by a secured lender to appoint a receiver pursuant to this section shall not constitute an action within the meaning of subdivision (a) of Section 726.

(e) For purposes of this section:

(1) "Borrower" means the trustor under a deed of trust, or a mortgagor under a mortgage, where the deed of trust or mortgage encumbers real property security and secures the performance of the trustor or mortgagor under a loan, extension of credit, guaranty, or other obligation. The term includes any successor in interest of the trustor or mortgagor to the real property security before the deed of trust or mortgage has been discharged, reconveyed, or foreclosed upon.

(2) "Hazardous substance" means any of the following:

(A) Any "hazardous substance" as defined in subdivision (h) of Section 25281 of the Health and Safety Code.

(B) Any "waste" as defined in subdivision (d) of Section 13050 of the Water Code.

(C) Petroleum including crude oil or any fraction thereof, natural gas, natural gas liquids, liquefied natural gas, or synthetic gas usable for fuel, or any mixture thereof.

(3) "Real property security" means any real property and improvements, other than a separate interest and any related interest in the common area of a residential common interest development, as the terms "separate interest," "common area," and "common interest development" are defined in Sections 4095, 4100, and 4185 of the Civil Code, or real property consisting of one acre or less that contains 1 to 15 dwelling units.

(4) "Release" means any spilling, leaking, pumping, pouring, emitting, emptying, discharging, injecting, escaping, leaching, dumping, or disposing into the environment, including continuing migration, of hazardous substances into, onto, or through soil, surface water, or groundwater.

(5) "Secured lender" means the beneficiary under a deed of trust against the real property security, or the mortgagee under a mortgage against the real property security, and any successor in interest of the beneficiary or mortgagee to the deed of trust or mortgage. **Leg.H.** Enacted Stats 1872. Amended Stats 1919 ch 166 §1; Stats 1933 ch 744 §85a; Stats 1941 ch 444 §1; Stats 1980 ch 1078 §1; Stats 1982 ch 497 §34, operative July 1, 1983; Stats 1991 ch 1167 §2 (AB 1735); Stats 1992 ch 167 §2 (AB 2750); Stats 1994 ch 414 §2 (SB 1705), effective September 1, 1994; Stats 1995 ch 384 §1 (AB 1110); Stats 1996 ch 49 §4 (SB 947), ch 1023 §29 (SB 1497), effective September 29, 1996, ch 1154 §2 (AB 3020), effective September 30, 1996, operative until January 1, 1997, ch 1154 §2.1 (AB 3030), effective September 30, 1996, operative January 1, 1997; Stats 1998 ch 931 §75 (SB 2139), effective September 28, 1998; Stats 2001 ch 44 §4 (SB 562); Stats 2002 ch 999 §3 (AB 2481); Stats 2012 ch 181 §44 (AB 806), effective January 1, 2013, operative January 1, 2014; Stats 2020 ch 27 §1 (SB 350), effective January 1, 2021.

§565. Appointment upon dissolution of corporation

Upon the dissolution of any corporation, the superior court of the county in which the corporation carries on its business or has its principal place of business, on application of any creditor of the corporation, or of any stockholder or member thereof, may appoint one or more persons to be receivers or trustees of the corporation, to take charge of the estate and effects thereof and to collect the debts and property due and belonging to the corporation, and to pay the outstanding debts thereof, and to divide the moneys and other property that shall remain over among the stockholders or members. **Leg.H.** Enacted Stats 1872. Amended Code Amdts 1880 ch 15 §7.

§566. Restrictions on appointment; Undertaking for ex parte application

(a) No party, or attorney of a party, or person interested in an action, or related to any judge of the court by consanguinity or affinity within the third degree, can be appointed receiver therein without the written consent of the parties, filed with the clerk.

(b) If a receiver is appointed upon an ex parte application, the court, before making the order, must require from the applicant an undertaking in an amount to be fixed by the court, to the effect that the applicant will pay to the defendant all damages the defendant may sustain by reason of the appointment of the receiver and the entry by the receiver upon the duties, in case the applicant shall have procured the appointment wrongfully, maliciously, or without sufficient cause. **Leg.H.** Enacted Stats 1872. Amended Code Amdts 1873–74 ch 383 §73; Stats 1897 ch 69 §1; Stats 1907 ch 374 §1; Stats 1982 ch 517 §127.

§567. Oath and undertaking of receiver

Before entering upon the duties of a receiver:

(a) The receiver must be sworn to perform the duties faithfully.

(b) The receiver shall give an undertaking to the State of California, in such sum as the court or judge may direct, to the effect that the receiver will faithfully discharge the duties of receiver in the action and obey the orders of the court therein. The receiver shall be allowed the cost of the undertaking. **Leg.H.** Enacted Stats 1872. Amended Stats 1907 ch 374 §2; Stats 1982 ch 517 §128.

§568. Powers of receivers

The receiver has, under the control of the court, power to bring and defend actions in his own name, as receiver; to take and keep possession of the property, to receive rents, collect debts, to compound for and compromise the same, to make transfers, and generally to do such acts respecting the property as the court may authorize. **Leg.H.** Enacted Stats 1872.

§568.1. Deposit of securities

Any securities in the hands of a receiver may, under the control of the court, be deposited by the receiver in a securities depository, as defined in Section 30004 of the Financial Code, which is licensed under Section 30200 of the Financial Code or exempted from licensing thereunder by Section 30005 or 30006 of the Financial Code, and such securities may be held by such securities depository in the manner authorized by Section 775 of the Financial Code. **Leg.H.** Added Stats 1972 ch 1057 §9.

§568.2. Procedures for receiver to obtain court order to assist in abatement of substandard conditions

(a) A receiver of real property containing rental housing shall notify the court of the existence of any order or notice to correct any substandard or unsafe condition, as defined in Section 17920.3 or 17920.10 of the Health and Safety Code, with which the receiver cannot comply within the time provided by the order or notice.

(b) The notice shall be filed within 30 days after the receiver's appointment or, if the substandard condition occurs subsequently, within 15 days of its occurrence.

(c) The notice shall inform the court of all of the following:

(1) The substandard conditions that exist.

(2) The threat or danger that the substandard conditions pose to any occupant of the property or the public.

(3) The approximate cost and time involved in abating the conditions. If more time is needed to approximate the cost, then the notice shall provide the date on which the approximate cost will be filed with the court and that date shall be within 10 days of the filing.

(4) Whether the receivership estate is likely to contain sufficient funds to abate the conditions.

(d) If the receivership estate does not contain sufficient funds to abate the conditions, the receiver shall request further instructions or orders from the court.

(e) The court, upon receipt of a notice pursuant to subdivision (d), shall consider appropriate orders or instructions to enable the receiver to correct the substandard conditions or to terminate or limit the period of receivership. **Leg.H.** Added Stats 2001 ch 414 §1 (AB 472). Amended Stats 2005 ch 595 §3 (SB 253), effective January 1, 2006.

§568.3. Motion in receivership action seeking further court instructions

Any tenant of real property that is subject to receivership, a tenant association or organization, or any federal, state, or local enforcement agency, may file a motion in a receivership action for the purpose of seeking further instructions or orders from the court, if either of the following is true:

(a) Substandard conditions exist, as defined by Section 17920.3 or 17920.10 of the Health and Safety Code.

(b) A dispute or controversy exists concerning the powers or duties of the receiver affecting a tenant or the public. **Leg.H.** Added Stats 2001 ch 414 §2 (AB 472). Amended Stats 2005 ch 595 §4 (SB 253), effective January 1, 2006.

§568.5. Authority to sell real or personal property

A receiver may, pursuant to an order of the court, sell real or personal property in the receiver's possession upon the notice and in the manner prescribed by Article 6 (commencing with Section 701.510) of Chapter 3 of Division 2 of Title 9. The sale is not final until confirmed by the court. **Leg.H.** Added Stats 1939 ch 374 §1. Amended Stats 1982 ch 497 §35, operative July 1, 1983.

§ 568.6. Public Utilities Commission appointed receiver

A receiver appointed at the request of the Public Utilities Commission pursuant to Section 1825 of the Public Utilities Code shall control and operate Pacific Gas and Electric Company upon such terms and conditions as the court prescribes. **Leg.H.** Added Stats 2020 ch 27 §2 (SB 350), effective January 1, 2021.

§569. Deposit of funds

Funds in the hands of a receiver may be deposited in one or more interest bearing accounts in the name and for the benefit of the receivership estate with one or more financial institutions, provided that all of the following conditions are satisfied:

(a) The deposits are fully guaranteed or insured under federal law.

(b) The financial institution in which the funds are deposited is not a party to the action in which the receiver was appointed.

(c) The receiver does not own 1 percent or more in value of the outstanding stock of the financial institution, is not an officer, director, or employee of the financial institution, and is not a sibling, whether by the whole or half-blood, spouse, aunt, uncle, nephew, niece, ancestor, or lineal descendant of an owner, officer, employee, or director. **Leg.H.** Enacted Stats 1872. Amended Stats 1998 ch 932 §16 (AB 1094).

§570. Notice of unclaimed funds in receiver's hands; Disposition of funds; Recovery by owner

A receiver having any funds in his hands belonging to a person whose whereabouts are unknown to him, shall, before receiving his discharge as such receiver, publish a notice, in one or more newspapers published in the county, at least once a week for four consecutive weeks, setting forth the name of the owner of any unclaimed funds, the last known place of residence or post office address of such owner and the amount of such unclaimed funds. Any funds remaining in his hands unclaimed for 30 days after the date of the last publication of such notice, shall be reported to the court, and upon order of the court, all such funds must be paid into the State Treasury accompanied with a copy of the order, which must set forth the facts required in the notice herein provided. Such funds shall be deemed to have been received by the State under Chapter 7 (commencing with Section 1500) of Title 10 of Part 3 of this code and may be recovered in the manner prescribed therein.

All costs and expenses connected with such advertising shall be paid out of the funds the whereabouts of whose owners are unknown. **Leg.H.** Added Stats 1913 ch 87 §1. Amended Stats 1915 ch 83 §1; Stats 1917 ch 138 §1; Stats 1963 ch 1762 §1.

CHAPTER 5A
UNDERTAKING OF PERSONS HANDLING PRIVATE PROPERTY OR FUNDS

Undertaking of referee or commissioner when duties involve personal property or moneys. §571.

§571. Undertaking of referee or commissioner when duties involve personal property or moneys

If a referee or commissioner is appointed by a court and the duties of the referee or commissioner will, or are reasonably anticipated to, involve the custody of personal property or the receipt or disbursement of moneys, the order of appointment shall provide that before entering upon the duties, the referee or commissioner shall execute an undertaking to the State of California, to the effect that the referee or commissioner will faithfully discharge the duties of referee or commissioner, as the case may be, and obey the orders of the court therein. The order of appointment shall specify the amount of the undertaking, but a failure to so specify shall not invalidate the order. **Leg.H.** Added Stats 1963 ch 575 §1. Amended Stats 1977 ch 1257 §16, effective October 3, 1977; Stats 1982 ch 517 §129.

CHAPTER 6
DEPOSIT IN COURT

Circumstances warranting order for deposit in court. §572.
Deposit with court's treasury. §573.
Enforcement of order for deposit. §574.

§572. Circumstances warranting order for deposit in court

When it is admitted by the pleadings, or shown upon the examination of a party to the action, that he or she has in his or her possession, or under his or her control, any money or other thing capable of delivery, which, being the subject of litigation, is held by him or her as trustee for another party, or which belongs or which is due to another party or which should, under the circumstances of the case be held by the court pending final disposition of the action, the court may order the same, upon motion, to be deposited in court or delivered to such party, upon those conditions that may be just, subject to the further direction of the court. **Leg.H.** Enacted Stats 1872. Amended Stats 1907 ch 375 §1; Stats 1986 ch 540 §6.

§573. Deposit with court's treasury

Whenever money is paid into or deposited in the court under this chapter, it shall be deposited with the court's treasury as provided in Section 68084 of the Government Code. **Leg.H.** Added Stats 2005 ch 75 §35 (AB 145), effective July 19, 2005, operative January 1, 2006.

Prior Law: Former CCP §573, similar to the present section, was enacted Stats 1872, amended Stats 1907 ch 375 §2, Stats 1933 ch 744 §86, Stats 1951 ch 1737 §81, operative January 1, 1952, and repealed Stats 2005 ch 75 §34, effective July 19, 2005, operative January 1, 2006.

§574. Enforcement of order for deposit

Whenever, in the exercise of its authority, a court has ordered the deposit or delivery of money, or other thing, and the order is disobeyed, the court, beside punishing the disobedience, may make an order requiring the sheriff or marshal to take the money, or thing, and deposit or deliver it in conformity with the direction of the court. **Leg.H.** Enacted Stats 1872. Amended Stats 1933 ch 744 §87; Stats 1996 ch 872 §15 (AB 3472).

TITLE 7A
PRETRIAL CONFERENCES

Authority of Judicial Council to promulgate rules. §575.
Local rules for superior courts; Preparation; Adoption; Filing; Publication. §575.1.
Imposition of penalties for failure to comply with local rules. §575.2.
Amendment of pleading or pretrial conference order; Allowance by judge before or after commencement of trial. §576.

§575. Authority of Judicial Council to promulgate rules

The Judicial Council may promulgate rules governing pretrial conferences, and the time, manner and nature thereof, in civil cases at issue, or in one or more classes thereof, in the superior courts. **Leg.H.** Added Stats 1955 ch 632 §1. Amended Stats 1977 ch 1257 §17, effective October 3, 1977; Stats 1998 ch 931 §76 (SB 2139), effective September 28, 1998; Stats 2002 ch 784 §61 (SB 1316).

§575.1. Local rules for superior courts; Preparation; Adoption; Filing; Publication

(a) The presiding judge of each superior court may prepare, with the assistance of appropriate committees of the court, proposed local rules designed to expedite and facilitate the business of the court. The rules need not be limited to those actions on the civil active list, but may provide for the supervision and judicial management of actions from the date they are filed. Rules prepared pursuant to this section shall be submitted for consideration to the judges of the court and, upon approval by a majority of the judges, the judges shall have the proposed rules published and submitted to the local bar and others, as specified by the Judicial Council, for consideration and recommendations.

(b) After a majority of the judges have officially adopted the rules, they shall be filed with the Judicial Council as required by Section 68071 of the Government Code and as specified in rules adopted by the Judicial Council. The Judicial Council shall prescribe rules to ensure that a complete current set of local rules and amendments, for each county in the state, is made available for public examination in each county. The local rules shall also be published for general distribution in accordance with rules adopted by the Judicial Council. Each court shall make its local rules available for inspection and copying in every location of the court that generally accepts filing of papers. The court may impose a reasonable charge for copying the rules and may impose a reasonable page limit on copying. The rules shall be accompanied by a notice indicating where a full set of the rules may be purchased.

(c) If a judge of a court adopts a rule that applies solely to cases in that judge's courtroom, or a particular branch or district of a court adopts a rule that applies solely to cases in that particular branch or district of a court, the court shall publish these rules as part of the general publication of rules required by the California Rules of Court. The court shall organize the rules so that rules on a common subject, whether individual, branch, district, or courtwide appear sequentially. Individual judges' rules and branch and district rules are local rules of court for purposes of this section and for purposes of the adoption, publication, comment, and filing requirements set forth in the Judicial Council rules applicable to local court rules. **Leg.H.** Added Stats 1982 ch 1402 §1. Amended Stats 1989 ch 1416 §19; Stats 1993 ch 925 §1 (SB 425), ch 926 §3.5 (AB 2205); Stats 1998 ch 931 §77 (SB 2139), effective September 28, 1998; Stats 2003 ch 149 §9 (SB 79).

§575.2. Imposition of penalties for failure to comply with local rules

(a) Local rules promulgated pursuant to Section 575.1 may provide that if any counsel, a party represented by counsel, or a party if in pro se, fails to comply with any of the requirements thereof, the court on motion of a party or on its own motion may strike out all or any part of any pleading of that party, or, dismiss the action or proceeding or any part thereof, or enter a judgment by default against that party, or impose other penalties of a lesser nature as otherwise provided by law, and may order that party or his or her counsel to pay to the moving party the reasonable expenses in making the motion, including reasonable attorney fees. No penalty may be imposed under this section without prior notice to, and an opportunity to be heard by, the party against whom the penalty is sought to be imposed.

(b) It is the intent of the Legislature that if a failure to comply with these rules is the responsibility of counsel and not of the party, any penalty shall be imposed on counsel and shall not adversely affect the party's cause of action or defense thereto. **Leg.H.** Added Stats 1982 ch 1402 §2. Amended Stats 2002 ch 806 §14 (AB 3027).

§575.5. [Section repealed 2008]

Leg.H. Added Stats 1982 ch 411 §1. Repealed Stats 2007 ch 268 §2 (AB 500), effective January 1, 2008. The repealed section related to appearances by telephone.

§575.6. [Section repealed 2008]

Leg.H. Added Stats 1993 ch 925 §2 (SB 425). Repealed Stats 2007 ch 268 §3 (AB 500), effective January 1, 2008. The repealed section related to appearance of counsel by telephone, and personal appearance of counsel for good cause.

§576. Amendment of pleading or pretrial conference order; Allowance by judge before or after commencement of trial

Any judge, at any time before or after commencement of trial, in the furtherance of justice, and upon such terms as may be proper, may allow the amendment of any pleading or pretrial conference order. **Leg.H.** Added Stats 1963 ch 882 §1.

§576.5. [Section repealed 1973]

Leg.H. Added Stats 1971 ch 1150 §1. Repealed Stats 1971 ch 1150 §5, operative December 31, 1973. The repealed section related to settlement conference in motor vehicle action for damages.

TITLE 8
OF THE TRIAL AND JUDGMENT IN CIVIL ACTIONS

Chapter 1. Judgment in General.
Chapter 1.5. Dismissal for Delay in Prosecution.
Chapter 2. Judgment Upon Failure to Answer.
Chapter 3. Issues—The Mode of Trial and Postponements.
Chapter 4. Trial by Jury.
Chapter 4.5. Voluntary Expedited Jury Trials.
Chapter 4.6. Mandatory Expedited Jury Trials in Limited Civil Cases.
Chapter 5. Trial by the Court.
Chapter 6. Of References and Trials by Referees.
Chapter 7. Provisions Relating to Trials in General.
Chapter 8. The Manner of Giving and Entering Judgment.

CHAPTER 1
JUDGMENT IN GENERAL

Judgment defined. §577.
Amount in judgment or execution upon judgment to be stated in dollars; Fractions to be rejected. §577.5.
Judgment for or against one or more parties. §578.
Judgment against one party and continuation of action against others. §579.
Relief to be awarded to plaintiff. §580.
Deficiency judgments. §580a.
Conditions under which deficiency judgment forbidden. §580b.
Limitation of liability of mortgagor or trustor. §580c.
Deficiency judgment after foreclosure under power of sale. §580d.
Deficiency under note secured solely by deed of trust or mortgage; Sale for less than remaining amount of indebtedness due; Written consent of holder of deed of trust or mortgage as obligation; Fraud; Waiver. §580e.
Obligation secured by mortgage or deed of trust and supported by letter of credit; Effect of enforcement of other obligations under letter of credit. §580.5.
Circumstances rendering letter of credit unenforceable. §580.7.
Dismissal of action or complaint by parties or court. §581.
Nonsuit. §581c.
Entry of dismissal; Effect. §581d.
Dismissal by court of action involving consumer debt; Award to defendant debtor of costs. §581.5.
Other judgments. §582.
Payment of judgment in limited civil case. §582.5.

§577. Judgment defined

A judgment is the final determination of the rights of the parties in an action or proceeding. **Leg.H.** Enacted Stats 1872.

§577.5. Amount in judgment or execution upon judgment to be stated in dollars; Fractions to be rejected

In any judgment, or execution upon such judgment, the amount shall be computed and stated in dollars and cents, rejecting fractions. **Leg.H.** Added Stats 1951 ch 655 §21.

§578. Judgment for or against one or more parties

Judgment may be given for or against one or more of several plaintiffs, and for or against one or more of several defendants; and it may, when the justice of the case requires it, determine the ultimate rights of the parties on each side, as between themselves. **Leg.H.** Enacted Stats 1872.

§579. Judgment against one party and continuation of action against others

In an action against several defendants, the Court may, in its discretion, render judgment against one or more of them, leaving the action to proceed against the others, whenever a several judgment is proper. **Leg.H.** Enacted Stats 1872.

§580. Relief to be awarded to plaintiff

(a) The relief granted to the plaintiff, if there is no answer, cannot exceed that demanded in the complaint, in the statement required by Section 425.11, or in the statement provided for by Section 425.115; but in any other case, the court may grant the plaintiff any relief consistent with the case made by the complaint and embraced within the issue. The court may impose liability, regardless of whether the theory upon which liability is sought to be imposed involves legal or equitable principles.

(b) Notwithstanding subdivision (a), the following types of relief may not be granted in a limited civil case:

(1) Relief exceeding the maximum amount in controversy for a limited civil case as provided in Section 85, exclusive of attorney's fees, interest, and costs.

(2) A permanent injunction, except as otherwise authorized by statute.

(3) A determination of title to real property.

(4) Declaratory relief, except as authorized by Section 86. **Leg.H.** Enacted Stats 1872. Amended Stats 1993 ch 456 §8 (AB 58); Stats 1995 ch 796 §9 (SB 45); Stats 1998 ch 931 §78 (SB 2139), effective September 28, 1998; Stats 2006 ch 86 §1 (AB 2126), effective January 1, 2007; Stats 2007 ch 43 §5 (SB 649), effective January 1, 2008.

Note: Sections 580.5 and 580.7 appear immediately following CCP §580e.

§580a. Deficiency judgments

Whenever a money judgment is sought for the balance due upon an obligation for the payment of which a deed of trust or mortgage with power of sale upon real property or any interest therein was given as security, following the exercise of the power of sale in such deed of trust or mortgage, the plaintiff shall set forth in his or her complaint the entire amount of the indebtedness which was secured by the deed of trust or mortgage at the time of sale, the amount for which the real property or interest therein was sold and the fair market value thereof at the date of sale and the date of that sale. Upon the application of either party made at least 10 days before the time of trial the court shall, and upon its own motion the court at any time may, appoint one of the probate referees provided for by law to appraise the property or the interest therein sold as of the time of sale. The referee shall file his or her appraisal with the clerk and that appraisal shall be admissible in evidence. The referee shall take and subscribe an oath to be attached to the appraisal that he or she has truly, honestly and impartially appraised the property to the best of his or her knowledge and ability. Any referee so appointed may be called and examined as a witness by any party or by the court itself. The court must fix the compensation of the referee in an amount as determined by the court to be reasonable, but those fees shall not exceed similar fees for similar services in the community where the services are rendered, which may be taxed and allowed in like manner as other costs. Before rendering any judgment the court shall find the fair market value of the real property, or interest therein sold, at the time of sale. The court may render judgment for not more than the amount by which the entire amount of the indebtedness due at the time of sale exceeded the fair market value of the real property or interest therein sold at the time of sale with interest thereon from the date of the sale; provided, however, that in no event shall the amount of the judgment, exclusive of interest after the date of sale, exceed the difference between the amount for which the property was sold and the entire amount of the indebtedness secured by the deed of trust or mortgage. Any such action must be brought within three months of the time of sale under the deed of trust or mortgage. No judgment shall be rendered in any such action until the real property or interest therein has first been sold pursuant to the terms of the deed of trust or mortgage, unless the real property or interest therein has become valueless. **Leg.H.** Added Stats 1933 ch 642 §4. Re-enacted Stats 1935 ch 650 §4. Amended Stats 1968 ch 450 §2; Stats 1970 ch 1282 §1, operative July 1, 1971; Stats 1982 ch 1535 §1; Stats 1988 ch 1199 §6, operative July 1, 1989.

§580b. Conditions under which deficiency judgment forbidden

(a) Except as provided in subdivision (c), no deficiency shall be owed or collected, and no deficiency judgment shall lie, for any of the following:

(1) After a sale of real property or an estate for years therein for failure of the purchaser to complete his or her contract of sale.

(2) Under a deed of trust or mortgage given to the vendor to secure payment of the balance of the purchase price of that real property or estate for years therein.

(3) Under a deed of trust or mortgage on a dwelling for not more than four families given to a lender to secure repayment of a loan that was used to pay all or part of the purchase price of that dwelling, occupied entirely or in part by the purchaser. For purposes of subdivision (b), a loan described in this paragraph is a "purchase money loan."

(b) No deficiency shall be owed or collected, and no deficiency judgment shall lie, on a loan, refinance, or other credit transaction (collectively, a "credit transaction") that is used to refinance a purchase money loan, or subsequent refinances of a purchase money loan, except to the extent that in a credit transaction the lender or creditor advances new principal (hereafter "new advance") that is not applied to an obligation owed or to be owed under the purchase money loan, or to fees, costs, or related expenses of the credit transaction. A new credit transaction shall be deemed to be a purchase money loan except as to the principal amount of a new advance. For purposes of this section, any payment of principal shall be deemed to be applied first to the principal balance of the purchase money loan, and then to the principal balance of a new advance, and interest payments shall be applied to any interest due and owing. This subdivision applies only to credit transactions that are executed on or after January 1, 2013.

(c) The fact that no deficiency shall be owed or collected under the circumstances set forth in subdivisions (a) and (b) does not affect the liability that a guarantor, pledgor, or other surety might otherwise have with respect to the deficiency, or that might otherwise be satisfied in whole or in part from other collateral pledged to secure the obligation that is the subject of the deficiency.

(d) When both a chattel mortgage and a deed of trust or mortgage have been given to secure payment of the balance of the combined purchase price of both real and personal property, no deficiency judgment shall lie under any one thereof if no deficiency judgment would lie under the deed of trust or mortgage on the real property or estate for years therein. **Leg.H.** Added Stats 1933 ch 642 §5. Re-enacted Stats 1935 ch 650 §5. Amended Stats 1935 ch 680 §1; Stats 1949 ch 1599 §1; Stats 1963 ch 2158 §1; Stats 1989 ch 698 §12; Stats 2012 ch 64 §1 (SB 1069), effective January 1, 2013; Stats 2013 ch 65 §2 (SB 426), effective January 1, 2014; Stats 2014 ch 71 §18 (SB 1304), effective January 1, 2015.

2013 Note: The Legislature finds and declares that this measure is not intended to and does not impact existing law regarding the liability a guarantor, pledgor or other surety may have with respect to a deficiency, nor does it impact existing law regarding other collateral pledged to secure an obligation that is the subject of a deficiency. Stats 2013 ch 65 (SB 426) §1.

§580c. Limitation of liability of mortgagor or trustor

In all cases where existing deeds of trust or mortgages are judicially foreclosed, unless a different amount is set up in the mortgage or deed of trust, and in all cases of mortgages and deeds of trust executed after this act takes effect, the mortgagor or trustor may be required to pay only such amount as trustee's or attorney's fees for processing the judicial foreclosure as the court may find reasonable and also the actual cost of publishing, recording, mailing and posting notices, litigation guarantee, and litigation cost of suit. **Leg.H.** Added Stats 1933 ch 642 §6. Re-enacted Stats 1935 ch 650 §6. Amended Stats 1984 ch 1730 §6.

Prior Law: There was another section of this number, identical to present CCP §580d, which was added Stats 1939 ch 586 §1 and repealed Stats 1940 1st Ex Sess ch 29 §1.

§580d. Deficiency judgment after foreclosure under power of sale

(a) Except as provided in subdivision (b), no deficiency shall be owed or collected, and no deficiency judgment shall be rendered for a deficiency on a note secured by a deed of trust or mortgage on real property or an estate for years therein executed in any case in which the real property or estate for years therein has been sold by the mortgagee or trustee under power of sale contained in the mortgage or deed of trust.

(b) The fact that no deficiency shall be owed or collected under the circumstances set forth in subdivision (a) does not affect the liability that a guarantor, pledgor, or other surety might otherwise have with respect to the deficiency, or that might otherwise be satisfied in whole or in part from other collateral pledged to secure the obligation that is the subject of the deficiency.

(c) This section does not apply to a deed of trust, mortgage, or other lien given to secure the payment of bonds or other evidences of indebtedness authorized or permitted to be issued by the Commissioner of Financial Protection and Innovation or which is made by a public utility subject to the Public Utilities Act (Part 1 (commencing with Section 201) of Division 1 of the Public Utilities Code). **Leg.H.** Added Stats 1940 1st Ex Sess ch 29 §2. Amended Stats 1989 ch 698 §13; Stats 2013 ch 65 §3 (SB 426), effective January 1, 2014; Stats 2014 ch 71 §19 (AB 1304), effective January 1, 2015, Stats 2014 ch 401 §14 (AB 2763), effective January 1, 2015 (ch 401 prevails); Stats 2022 ch 452 §38 (SB 1498), effective January 1, 2023.

2013 Note: The Legislature finds and declares that this measure is not intended to and does not impact existing law regarding the liability a guarantor, pledgor or other surety may have with respect to a deficiency, nor does it impact existing law regarding other collateral pledged to secure an obligation that is the subject of a deficiency. Stats 2013 ch 65 (SB 426) §1.

§580e. Deficiency under note secured solely by deed of trust or mortgage; Sale for less than remaining amount of indebtedness due; Written consent of holder of deed of trust or mortgage as obligation; Fraud; Waiver

(a)(1) No deficiency shall be owed or collected, and no deficiency judgment shall be requested or rendered for any deficiency upon a note secured solely by a deed of trust or mortgage for a dwelling of not more than four units, in any case in which the trustor or mortgagor sells the dwelling for a sale price less than the remaining amount of the indebtedness outstanding at the time of sale, in accordance with the written consent of the holder of the deed of trust or mortgage, provided that both of the following have occurred:

(A) Title has been voluntarily transferred to a buyer by grant deed or by other document of conveyance that has been recorded in the county where all or part of the real property is located.

(B) The proceeds of the sale have been tendered to the mortgagee, beneficiary, or the agent of the mortgagee or beneficiary, in accordance with the parties' agreement.

(2) In circumstances not described in paragraph (1), when a note is not secured solely by a deed of trust or mortgage for a dwelling of not more than four units, no judgment shall be rendered for any deficiency upon a note secured by a deed of trust or mortgage for a dwelling of not more than four units, if the trustor or mortgagor sells the dwelling for a sale price less than the remaining amount of the indebtedness outstanding at the time of sale, in accordance with the written consent of the holder of the deed of trust or mortgage. Following the sale, in accordance with the holder's written consent, the voluntary transfer of title to a buyer by grant deed or by other document of conveyance recorded in the county where all or part of the real property is located, and the tender to the mortgagee, beneficiary, or the agent of the mortgagee or beneficiary of the sale proceeds, as agreed, the rights, remedies, and obligations of any holder, beneficiary, mortgagee, trustor, mortgagor, obligor, obligee, or guarantor of the note, deed of trust, or mortgage, and with respect to any other property that secures the note, shall be treated and determined as if the dwelling had been sold through foreclosure under a power of sale contained in the deed of trust or mortgage for a price equal to the sale proceeds received by the holder, in the manner contemplated by Section 580d.

(b) A holder of a note shall not require the trustor, mortgagor, or maker of the note to pay any additional compensation, aside from the proceeds of the sale, in exchange for the written consent to the sale.

(c) If the trustor or mortgagor commits either fraud with respect to the sale of, or waste with respect to, the real property that secures the deed of trust or mortgage, this section shall not limit the ability of the holder of the deed of trust or mortgage to seek damages and use existing rights and remedies against the trustor or mortgagor or any third party for fraud or waste.

(d)(1) This section shall not apply if the trustor or mortgagor is a corporation, limited liability company, limited partnership, or political subdivision of the state.

(2) This section shall not apply to any deed of trust, mortgage, or other lien given to secure the payment of bonds or other evidence of indebtedness authorized, or permitted to be issued, by the Commissioner of Financial Protection and Innovation, or that is made by a public utility subject to the Public Utilities Act (Part 1 (commencing with Section 201) of Division 1 of the Public Utilities Code).

(e) Any purported waiver of subdivision (a) or (b) shall be void and against public policy. **Leg.H.** Added Stats 2010 ch 701 §1 (SB 931), effective January 1, 2011. Amended Stats 2011 ch 82 §1 (SB 458), effective July 15, 2011; Stats 2019 ch 143 §19 (SB 251), effective January 1, 2020; Stats 2022 ch 452 §39 (SB 1498), effective January 1, 2023.

§580.5. Obligation secured by mortgage or deed of trust and supported by letter of credit; Effect of enforcement of other obligations under letter of credit

(a) For purposes of this section:

(1) "Beneficiary" means a "beneficiary" as defined in paragraph (3) of subdivision (a) of Section 5102 of the Commercial Code.

(2) "Issuer" means an "issuer" as defined in paragraph (9) of subdivision (a) of Section 5102 of the Commercial Code.

(3) "Letter of credit" means a "letter of credit" as defined in paragraph (10) of subdivision (a) of Section 5102 of the Commercial Code whether or not the engagement is governed by Division 5 (commencing with Section 5101) of the Commercial Code.

(b) With respect to an obligation which is secured by a mortgage or a deed of trust upon real property or an estate for years therein and which is also supported by a letter of credit, neither the presentment, receipt of payment, or enforcement of a draft or demand for payment under the letter of credit by the beneficiary of the letter of credit nor the honor or payment of, or the demand for reimbursement, receipt of reimbursement or enforcement of any contractual, statutory or other reimbursement obligation relating to, the letter of credit by the issuer of the letter of credit shall, whether done before or after the judicial or nonjudicial foreclosure of the mortgage or deed of trust or conveyance in lieu thereof, constitute any of the following:

(1) An action within the meaning of subdivision (a) of Section 726, or a failure to comply with any other statutory or judicial requirement to proceed first against security.

(2) A money judgment for a deficiency or a deficiency judgment within the meaning of Section 580a, 580b, or 580d, or subdivision (b) of Section 726, or the functional equivalent of any such judgment.

(3) A violation of Section 580a, 580b, 580d, or 726. **Leg.H.** Added Stats 1994 ch 611 §2 (SB 1612), effective September 15, 1994. Amended Stats 1996 ch 176 §2 (SB 1599).

1994 Note: It is the intent of the Legislature in adding Code of Civil Procedure §580.5 to confirm the independent nature of the letter of credit engagement and to abrogate the holding in *Western Security Bank, N.A. v. The Superior Court of Los Angeles County*, 21 Cal. App. 4th 156 (1993), that presentment of a draft under a letter of credit issued in connection with a real property secured loan following foreclosure violates Section 580d of the Code of Civil Procedure and constitutes a "fraud ... or other defect not apparent on the face of the documents" under paragraph (b) of subdivision (2) of Section 5114 of the Commercial Code. The fact that a beneficiary may be precluded by applicable law from seeking a deficiency judgment respecting the underlying obligation does not permit or otherwise justify the issuer's dishonor of the draft or demand for payment under paragraph (b) of subdivision (2) of Section 5114 of the Commercial Code nor does it provide the customer with a defense to the customer's reimbursement duties under subdivision (3) of Section 5114 of the Commercial Code or under any agreement or otherwise, or provide any rights against the beneficiary as a result of performance of those duties.

The Legislature also intends to confirm the expectation of the parties to a contract that underlies a letter of credit, that the beneficiary will have available the value of the real estate collateral and the benefit of the letter of credit without regard to the order in which the beneficiary may resort to either. Stats 1994 ch 611 §5.

§580.7. Circumstances rendering letter of credit unenforceable

(a) For purposes of this section:

(1) "Beneficiary" means a "beneficiary" as defined in paragraph (3) of subdivision (a) of Section 5102 of the Commercial Code.

(2) "Customer" means an "applicant" as defined in paragraph (2) of subdivision (a) of Section 5102 of the Commercial Code.

(3) "Letter of credit" means a "letter of credit" as defined in paragraph (10) of subdivision (a) of Section 5102 of the Commercial Code whether or not the engagement is governed by Division 5 (commencing with Section 5101) of the Commercial Code.

(b) No letter of credit shall be enforceable by any party thereto in a loan transaction in which all of the following circumstances exist:

(1) The customer is a natural person.

(2) The letter of credit is issued to the beneficiary to avoid a default of the existing loan.

(3) The existing loan is secured by a purchase money deed of trust or purchase money mortgage on real property containing one to four residential units, at least one of which is owned and occupied, or was intended at the time the existing loan was made, to be occupied by the customer.

(4) The letter of credit is issued after the effective date of this section. **Leg.H.** Added Stats 1994 ch 611 §3 (SB 1612), effective September 15, 1994. Amended Stats 1996 ch 176 §3 (SB 1599).

§581. Dismissal of action or complaint by parties or court

(a) As used in this section:

(1) "Action" means any civil action or special proceeding.

(2) "Complaint" means a complaint and a cross-complaint.

(3) "Court" means the court in which the action is pending.

(4) "Defendant" includes a cross-defendant.

(5) "Plaintiff" includes a cross-complainant.

(6) "Trial." A trial shall be deemed to actually commence at the beginning of the opening statement or argument of any party or his or her counsel, or if there is no opening statement, then at the time of the administering of the oath or affirmation to the first witness, or the introduction of any evidence.

(b) An action may be dismissed in any of the following instances:

(1) With or without prejudice, upon written request of the plaintiff to the clerk, filed with papers in the case, or by oral or written request to the court at any time before the actual commencement of trial, upon payment of the costs, if any.

(2) With or without prejudice, by any party upon the written consent of all other parties.

(3) By the court, without prejudice, when no party appears for trial following 30 days' notice of time and place of trial.

(4) By the court, without prejudice, when dismissal is made pursuant to the applicable provisions of Chapter 1.5 (commencing with Section 583.110).

(5) By the court, without prejudice, when either party fails to appear on the trial and the other party appears and asks for dismissal.

(c) A plaintiff may dismiss his or her complaint, or any cause of action asserted in it, in its entirety, or as to any defendant or defendants, with or without prejudice prior to the actual commencement of trial.

(d) Except as otherwise provided in subdivision (e), the court shall dismiss the complaint, or any cause of action asserted in it, in its entirety or as to any defendant, with prejudice, when upon the trial and before the final submission of the case, the plaintiff abandons it.

(e) After the actual commencement of trial, the court shall dismiss the complaint, or any causes of action asserted in it, in its entirety or as to any defendants, with prejudice, if the plaintiff requests a dismissal, unless all affected parties to the trial consent to dismissal without prejudice or by order of the court dismissing the same without prejudice on a showing of good cause.

(f) The court may dismiss the complaint as to that defendant when:

(1) Except where Section 597 applies, after a demurrer to the complaint is sustained without leave to amend and either party moves for dismissal.

(2) Except where Section 597 applies, after a demurrer to the complaint is sustained with leave to amend, the plaintiff fails to amend it within the time allowed by the court and either party moves for dismissal.

(3) After a motion to strike the whole of a complaint is granted without leave to amend and either party moves for dismissal.

(4) After a motion to strike the whole of a complaint or portion thereof is granted with leave to amend the plaintiff fails to amend it within the time allowed by the court and either party moves for dismissal.

(g) The court may dismiss without prejudice the complaint in whole, or as to that defendant, when dismissal is made under the applicable provisions of Chapter 1.5 (commencing with Section 583.110).

(h) The court may dismiss without prejudice the complaint in whole, or as to that defendant, when dismissal is made pursuant to Section 418.10.

(i) No dismissal of an action may be made or entered, or both, under paragraph (1) of subdivision (b) where affirmative relief has been sought by the cross-complaint of a defendant or if there is a motion pending for an order transferring the action to another court under the provisions of Section 396b.

(j) No dismissal may be made or entered, or both, under paragraph (1) or (2) of subdivision (b) except upon the written consent of the attorney for the party or parties applying therefor, or if consent of the attorney is not obtained, upon order of dismissal by the court after notice to the attorney.

(k) No action may be dismissed which has been determined to be a class action under the provisions of this code unless and until notice that the court deems adequate has been given and the court orders the dismissal.

(*l*) The court may dismiss, without prejudice, the complaint in whole, or as to that defendant when either party fails to appear at the trial and the other party appears and asks for the dismissal.

(m) The provisions of this section shall not be deemed to be an exclusive enumeration of the court's power to dismiss an action or dismiss a complaint as to a defendant. **Leg.H.** Added Stats 1986 ch 540 §8. Amended Stats 1987 ch 1080 §3; Stats 1993 ch 456 §9 (AB 58).

Prior Law: Former CCP §581, similar to the present section, was enacted Stats 1872, amended Code Amdts 1877–78 ch 85 §1, Stats 1885 ch 101 §1, Stats 1889 ch 259 §1, Stats 1895 ch 26 §1, Stats 1897 ch 95 §1, Stats 1907 ch 376 §1, Stats 1919 ch 72 §1, Stats 1933 ch 744 §88, Stats 1935 ch 722 §7, Stats 1947 ch 990 §1, Stats 1951 ch 1737 §82, operative January 1, 1952, Stats 1963 ch 874 §1, Stats 1971 ch 244 §50, operative July 1, 1972, ch 1534 §1, operative until July 1, 1972, ch 1534 §2, operative July 1, 1972, Stats 1974 ch 1369 §4, Stats 1982 ch 517 §130, Stats 1983 ch 1167 §6, Stats 1984 ch 1705 §2, and repealed Stats 1986 ch 540 §7.

§581a. [Section repealed 1985]

Leg.H. Added Stats 1907 ch 376 §2. Amended Stats 1933 ch 744 §89; Stats 1949 ch 463 §1; Stats 1955 ch 1452 §5; Stats 1969 ch 1610 §24, operative July 1, 1970; Stats 1970 ch 582 §1; Stats 1971 ch 7 §1, effective February 26, 1971; Stats 1982 ch 600 §1. Repealed Stats 1984 ch 1705 §3. See CCP §§583.140, 583.210 et seq.

§581b. [Section repealed 1975]

Leg.H. Added Stats 1913 ch 163 §1. Amended Stats 1933 ch 744 §90; Stats 1943 ch 150 §1; Stats 1951 ch 1737 §83. Repealed Stats 1974 ch 1369 §5. The repealed section related to suspension or dismissal of proceedings in transferred action when fees and costs were not paid.

§581c. Nonsuit

(a) Only after, and not before, the plaintiff has completed his or her opening statement, or after the presentation of his or her evidence in a trial by jury, the defendant, without waiving his or her right to offer evidence in the event the motion is not granted, may move for a judgment of nonsuit.

(b) If it appears that the evidence presented, or to be presented, supports the granting of the motion as to some but not all of the issues involved in the action, the court shall grant the motion as to those issues and the action shall proceed as to the issues remaining. Despite the granting of the motion, no final judgment shall be entered prior to the termination of the action, but the final judgment in the action shall, in addition to any matters determined in the trial, award judgment as determined by the motion herein provided for.

(c) If the motion is granted, unless the court in its order for judgment otherwise specifies, the judgment of nonsuit operates as an adjudication upon the merits.

(d) In actions which arise out of an injury to the person or to property, when a motion for judgment of nonsuit was granted on the basis that the defendant was without fault, no other defendant during trial, over plaintiff's objection, may attempt to attribute fault to or comment on the absence or involvement of the defendant who was granted the motion. **Leg.H.** Added Stats 1947 ch 990 §2. Amended Stats 1961 ch 692 §1; Stats 1980 ch 187 §1; Stats 1982 ch 1510 §2; Stats 1998 ch 200 §1 (SB 1556).

1998 Note: The amendments made to Section 581c of the Code of Civil Procedure pursuant to Stats 1998 ch 200 §1 are not intended to affect any right of a defendant under statute or case law to move for a judgment of nonsuit upon completion of the opening statement of the plaintiff against whom the motion is made. Stats 1998 ch 200 §3.

§581d. Entry of dismissal; Effect

A written dismissal of an action shall be entered in the clerk's register and is effective for all purposes when so entered.

All dismissals ordered by the court shall be in the form of a written order signed by the court and filed in the action and those orders when so filed shall constitute judgments and be effective for all purposes, and the clerk shall note those judgments in the register of actions in the case. **Leg.H.** Added Stats 1947 ch 990 §3. Amended Stats 1951 ch 1737 §84; Stats 1959 ch 346 §1; Stats 1963 ch 875 §1; Stats 1977 ch 1257 §18, effective October 3, 1977; Stats 1998 ch 931 §79 (SB 2139), effective September 28, 1998.

§581.5. Dismissal by court of action involving consumer debt; Award to defendant debtor of costs

In a case involving consumer debt, as defined in Section 1788.2 of the Civil Code, and as regulated under Title 1.6C.5 (commencing with Section 1788.50) of Part 4 of Division 3 of the Civil Code, if the defendant debtor appears for trial on the scheduled trial date, and the plaintiff debt buyer either fails to appear or is not prepared to proceed to trial, and the court does not find a good cause for continuance, the court may, in its discretion, dismiss the action with or without prejudice. Notwithstanding any other law, in this instance, the court may award the defendant debtor's costs of preparing for trial, including, but not limited to, lost wages and transportation expenses. **Leg.H.** Added Stats 2013 ch 64 §3 (SB 233), effective January 1, 2014.

§582. Other judgments

In all other cases judgment shall be rendered on the merits. **Leg.H.** Enacted Stats 1872. Amended Stats 1907 ch 376 §3; Stats 1947 ch 990 §4.

§582.5. Payment of judgment in limited civil case

In a limited civil case in which the defendant has appeared, if the judgment or order is for the payment of money by the defendant, the defendant shall pay the judgment immediately or at any time and upon terms and conditions, including installment payments, that the court may prescribe. The court may amend the terms and conditions for payment of the judgment or order at any time to provide for installment payments for good cause upon motion by a party and notice to all affected parties, regardless of the nature of the underlying debt and regardless of whether the moving party appeared before entry of the judgment or order. In any determination regarding the imposition of terms and conditions upon the payment of the judgment, the court shall consider any factors that would be relevant to the determination of a claim for exemption pursuant to Chapter 4 (commencing with Section 703.010) of Division 2 of Title 9 of Part 2 or the examination of a debtor pursuant to Article 2 (commencing with Section 708.110) of Chapter 6 of Division 2 of Title 9. **Leg.H.** Added Stats 1998 ch 931 §80 (SB 2139), effective September 28, 1998.

§583. [Section repealed 1985]

Leg.H. Added Stats 1905 ch 271 §1. Amended Stats 1929 ch 358 §1; Stats 1931 ch 203 §1; Stats 1933 ch 286 §1; Stats 1945 ch 1310 §1; Stats 1947 ch 678 §1; Stats 1969 ch 958 §1, operative January 1, 1970; Stats 1970 ch 582 §2; Stats 1971 ch 244 §51, operative July 1, 1972; Stats 1972 ch 1014 §1; Stats 1982 ch 1402 §3. Repealed Stats 1984 ch 1705 §4. See CCP §§583.110 et seq., 583.310 et seq., 583.410, 583.420.

§583.1. [Section repealed 1980]

Leg.H. Added Stats 1968 ch 752 §1, effective July 25, 1968, effective until July 1, 1970. Repealed Stats 1979 ch 373 §50. The repealed section related to an exception to dismissal for delay in trial.

§583.5. [Section repealed 1969]

Leg.H. Added Stats 1945 ch 1285 §1, effective July 11, 1945. Repealed Stats 1969 ch 958 §2. The repealed section related to failure to bring action to trial due to war.

CHAPTER 1.5
DISMISSAL FOR DELAY IN PROSECUTION

Article 1. Definitions and General Provisions.
Article 2. Mandatory Time for Service of Summons.
Article 3. Mandatory Time for Bringing Action to Trial or New Trial.
Article 4. Discretionary Dismissal for Delay.

ARTICLE 1
Definitions and General Provisions

Definitions. §583.110.
Civil actions and special proceedings; Application of chapter under inherent authority of court. §583.120.
State policy. §583.130.
Waiver and estoppel. §583.140.
Effect of chapter on authority of court. §583.150.
Application of chapter to motions or orders that predate it. §583.160.
Conditions prohibiting dismissal of petition for dissolution of domestic partnership, judgment of nullity of marriage, dissolution of marriage or legal separation, or child custody or visitation order. §583.161.

§583.110. Definitions

As used in this chapter, unless the provision or context otherwise requires:

(a) "Action" includes an action commenced by cross-complaint or other pleading that asserts a cause of action or claim for relief.

(b) "Complaint" includes a cross-complaint or other initial pleading.

(c) "Court" means the court in which the action is pending.

(d) "Defendant" includes a cross-defendant or other person against whom an action is commenced.

(e) "Plaintiff" includes a cross-complainant or other person by whom an action is commenced.

(f) "Service" includes return of summons. **Leg.H.** Added Stats 1984 ch 1705 §5.

§583.120. Civil actions and special proceedings; Application of chapter under inherent authority of court

(a) This chapter applies to a civil action and does not apply to a special proceeding except to the extent incorporated by reference in the special proceeding.

(b) Notwithstanding subdivision (a), the court may, by rule or otherwise under inherent authority of the court, apply this chapter to a special proceeding or part of a special proceeding except to the extent such application would be inconsistent with the character of the special proceeding or the statute governing the special proceeding. **Leg.H.** Added Stats 1984 ch 1705 §5.

§583.130. State policy

It is the policy of the state that a plaintiff shall proceed with reasonable diligence in the prosecution of an action but that all parties shall cooperate in bringing the action to trial or other disposition. Except as otherwise provided by statute or by rule of court adopted pursuant to statute, the policy favoring the right of parties to make stipulations in their own interests and the policy favoring trial or other disposition of an action on the merits are generally to be preferred over the policy that requires dismissal for failure to proceed with reasonable diligence in the prosecution of an action in construing the provisions of this chapter. **Leg.H.** Added Stats 1984 ch 1705 §5.

§583.140. Waiver and estoppel

Nothing in this chapter abrogates or otherwise affects the principles of waiver and estoppel. **Leg.H.** Added Stats 1984 ch 1705 §5.

§583.150. Effect of chapter on authority of court

This chapter does not limit or affect the authority of a court to dismiss an action or impose other sanctions under a rule adopted by the court pursuant to Section 575.1 or by the Judicial Council pursuant to statute, or otherwise under inherent authority of the court. **Leg.H.** Added Stats 1984 ch 1705 §5.

§583.160. Application of chapter to motions or orders that predate it

This chapter applies to a motion for dismissal made in an action commenced before, on, or after the effective date of this chapter, except that in the case of an action commenced before the effective date of this chapter:

(a) A motion for dismissal made pursuant to notice given before, on, or within one year after the effective date of this chapter is governed by the applicable law in effect immediately before the effective date and for this purpose the law in effect immediately before the effective date continues in effect.

(b) This chapter does not affect an order dismissing an action made before the effective date of this chapter. **Leg.H.** Added Stats 1984 ch 1705 §5.

§583.161. Conditions prohibiting dismissal of petition for dissolution of domestic partnership, judgment of nullity of marriage, dissolution of marriage or legal separation, or child custody or visitation order

A petition filed pursuant to Section 299, 2250, 2330, or 7600 of the Family Code shall not be dismissed pursuant to this chapter if any of the following conditions exist:

(a) An order for child support or an order regarding child custody or visitation has been issued in connection with the proceeding and the order has not been (1) terminated by the court or (2) terminated by operation of law pursuant to Sections 3022, 3900, 3901, 4007, and 4013 of the Family Code.

(b) An order for spousal support has been issued in connection with the proceeding and the order has not been terminated by the court.

(c) A personal conduct restraining order has been issued pursuant to the Domestic Violence Prevention Act (Division 10 (commencing with Section 6200) of the Family Code) and the order has not been terminated by operation of law or by the court.

(d) An issue in the case has been bifurcated and one of the following has occurred:

(1) A separate trial has been conducted pursuant to Section 2337 of the Family Code.

(2) A separate trial has been conducted pursuant to the California Rules of Court. **Leg.H.** Added Stats 1986 ch 366 §2. Amended Stats 1992 ch 163 §26 (AB 2641), operative January 1, 1994; Stats 1993 ch 219 §65 (AB 1500); Stats 1994 ch 1269 §3 (AB 2208); Stats 2013 ch 40 §1 (AB 522), effective January 1, 2014.

ARTICLE 2
Mandatory Time for Service of Summons

Summons and complaint; Proof of service. §583.210.
Stipulation; General appearance. §583.220.
Parties' extension of time. §583.230.
Computation of time; Exclusions. §583.240.
Dismissal. §583.250.

§583.210. Summons and complaint; Proof of service

(a) The summons and complaint shall be served upon a defendant within three years after the action is commenced against the defendant. For the purpose of this subdivision, an action is commenced at the time the complaint is filed.

(b) Proof of service of the summons shall be filed within 60 days after the time the summons and complaint must be served upon a defendant. **Leg.H.** Added Stats 1984 ch 1705 §5. Amended Stats 2005 ch 300 §4 (AB 496), effective January 1, 2006.

§583.220. Stipulation; General appearance

The time within which service must be made pursuant to this article does not apply if the defendant enters into a stipulation in writing or does another act that constitutes a general appearance in the action. For the purpose of this section none of the following constitutes a general appearance in the action:

(a) A stipulation pursuant to Section 583.230 extending the time within which service must be made.

(b) A motion to dismiss made pursuant to this chapter, whether joined with a motion to quash service or a motion to set aside a default judgment, or otherwise.

(c) An extension of time to plead after a motion to dismiss made pursuant to this chapter. **Leg.H.** Added Stats 1984 ch 1705 §5.

§583.230. Parties' extension of time

The parties may extend the time within which service must be made pursuant to this article by the following means:

(a) By written stipulation. The stipulation need not be filed but, if it is not filed, the stipulation shall be brought to the attention of the court if relevant to a motion for dismissal.

(b) By oral agreement made in open court, if entered in the minutes of the court or a transcript is made. **Leg.H.** Added Stats 1984 ch 1705 §5.

§583.240. Computation of time; Exclusions

In computing the time within which service must be made pursuant to this article, there shall be excluded the time during which any of the following conditions existed:

(a) The defendant was not amenable to the process of the court.

(b) The prosecution of the action or proceedings in the action was stayed and the stay affected service.

(c) The validity of service was the subject of litigation by the parties.

(d) Service, for any other reason, was impossible, impracticable, or futile due to causes beyond the plaintiff's control. Failure to discover relevant facts or evidence is not a cause beyond the plaintiff's control for the purpose of this subdivision. **Leg.H.** Added Stats 1984 ch 1705 §5.

§583.250. Dismissal

(a) If service is not made in an action within the time prescribed in this article:

(1) The action shall not be further prosecuted and no further proceedings shall be held in the action.

(2) The action shall be dismissed by the court on its own motion or on motion of any person interested in the action, whether named as a party or not, after notice to the parties.

(b) The requirements of this article are mandatory and are not subject to extension, excuse, or exception except as expressly provided by statute. **Leg.H.** Added Stats 1984 ch 1705 §5.

ARTICLE 3
Mandatory Time for Bringing Action to Trial or New Trial

Trial; Five-year rule. §583.310.

accordance with the schedule (1) if the contract provides that attorneys' fees shall be allowed in the event of an action thereon, or (2) if the action is one in which the plaintiff is entitled by statute to recover attorneys' fees in addition to money or damages. The plaintiff shall file a written request at the time of application for entry of the default of the defendant or defendants, to have attorneys' fees fixed by the court, whereupon, after the entry of the default, the court shall hear the application for determination of the attorneys' fees and shall render judgment for the attorneys' fees and for the other relief demanded in the complaint, in the statement required by Section 425.11, or in the statement provided for in Section 425.115, or a lesser amount if credit has been acknowledged, and the costs against the defendant, or defendants, or against one or more of the defendants.

(b) In other actions, if the defendant has been served, other than by publication, and no answer, demurrer, notice of motion to strike of the character specified in subdivision (f), notice of motion to transfer pursuant to Section 396b, notice of motion to dismiss pursuant to Article 2 (commencing with Section 583.210) of Chapter 1.5 of Title 8, notice of motion to quash service of summons or to stay or dismiss the action pursuant to Section 418.10 or notice of the filing of a petition for writ of mandate as provided in Section 418.10 has been filed with the clerk of the court within the time specified in the summons, or within further time as may be allowed, the clerk, upon written application of the plaintiff, shall enter the default of the defendant. The plaintiff thereafter may apply to the court for the relief demanded in the complaint. The court shall hear the evidence offered by the plaintiff, and shall render judgment in the plaintiff's favor for that relief, not exceeding the amount stated in the complaint, in the statement required by Section 425.11, or in the statement provided for by Section 425.115, as appears by the evidence to be just. If the taking of an account, or the proof of any fact, is necessary to enable the court to give judgment or to carry the judgment into effect, the court may take the account or hear the proof, or may, in its discretion, order a reference for that purpose. If the action is for the recovery of damages, in whole or in part, the court may order the damages to be assessed by a jury; or if, to determine the amount of damages, the examination of a long account is involved, by a reference as above provided.

(c) In all actions where the service of the summons was by publication, upon the expiration of the time for answering, and upon proof of the publication and that no answer, demurrer, notice of motion to strike of the character specified in subdivision (f), notice of motion to transfer pursuant to Section 396b, notice of motion to dismiss pursuant to Article 2 (commencing with Section 583.210) of Chapter 1.5 of Title 8, notice of motion to quash service of summons or to stay or dismiss the action pursuant to Section 418.10 or notice of the filing of a petition for writ of mandate as provided in Section 418.10 has been filed, the clerk, upon written application of the plaintiff, shall enter the default of the defendant. The plaintiff thereafter may apply to the court for the relief demanded in the complaint; and the court shall hear the evidence offered by the plaintiff, and shall render judgment in the plaintiff's favor for that relief, not exceeding the amount stated in the complaint, in the statement required by Section 425.11, or in the statement provided for in Section 425.115, as appears by the evidence to be just. If the defendant is not a resident of the state, the court shall require the plaintiff, or the plaintiff's agent, to be examined, on oath, respecting any payments that have been made to the plaintiff, or to anyone for the plaintiff's use, on account of any demand mentioned in the complaint, in the statement required by Section 425.11, or in the statement provided for in Section 425.115, and may render judgment for the amount that the plaintiff is entitled to recover. In all cases affecting the title to or possession of real property, where the service of the summons was by publication and the defendant has failed to answer, no judgment shall be rendered upon proof of mere occupancy, unless the occupancy has continued for the time and has been of the character necessary to confer title by prescription. In all cases where the plaintiff bases a claim upon a paper title, the court shall require evidence establishing the plaintiff's equitable right to judgment before rendering judgment. In actions involving only the possession of real property where the complaint is verified and shows by proper allegations that no party to the action claims title to the real property involved, either by prescription, accession, transfer, will, or succession, but only the possession thereof, the court may render judgment upon proof of occupancy by plaintiff and ouster by defendant.

(d) In the cases referred to in subdivisions (b) and (c), or upon an application to have attorneys' fees fixed by the court pursuant to subdivision (a), the court in its discretion may permit the use of affidavits, in lieu of personal testimony, as to all or any part of the evidence or proof required or permitted to be offered, received, or heard in those cases. The facts stated in the affidavit or affidavits shall be within the personal knowledge of the affiant and shall be set forth with particularity, and each affidavit shall show affirmatively that the affiant, if sworn as a witness, can testify competently thereto.

(e) If a defendant files a cross-complaint against another defendant or the plaintiff, a default may be entered against that party on that cross-complaint if the plaintiff or that cross-defendant has been served with that cross-complaint and has failed to file an answer, demurrer, notice of motion to strike of the character specified in subdivision (f), notice of motion to transfer pursuant to Section 396b, notice of motion to dismiss pursuant to Article 2 (commencing with Section 583.210) of Chapter 1.5 of Title 8, notice of motion to quash service of summons or to stay or dismiss the action pursuant to Section 418.10, or notice of the filing of a petition for a writ of mandate as provided in Section 418.10 within the time specified in the summons, or within another time period as may be allowed. However, no judgment may separately be entered on that cross-complaint unless a separate judgment may, in fact, be properly awarded on that cross-complaint and the court finds that a separate judgment on that cross-complaint would not substantially delay the final disposition of the action between the parties.

(f) A notice of motion to strike within the meaning of this section is a notice of motion to strike the whole or any part of a pleading filed within the time which the moving party is required otherwise to plead to that pleading. The notice of motion to strike shall specify a hearing date set in accordance with Section 1005. The filing of a notice of motion does not extend the time within which to demur. **Leg.H.** Enacted 1872. Amended Stats 1905 ch 47 §1; Stats 1907 ch 376 §4; Stats 1915 ch 553 §1; Stats 1931 ch 285 §1; Stats 1933 ch 744 §92; Stats 1951 ch 1737 §85, operative January 1, 1952; Stats 1955 ch 512 §1, ch 1452 §6; Stats 1961 ch 393 §1; Stats 1967 ch 135 §1; Stats 1969 ch 345 §3, ch 567 §1.5, ch 1611 §6.7, operative July 1, 1970; Stats 1973 ch 312 §1; Stats 1980 ch 367 §2; Stats 1982 ch 704 §6.5; Stats 1986 ch 540 §9; Stats 1993 ch 456 §10 (AB 58); Stats 1995 ch 796 §10 (SB 45); Stats 2007 ch 263 §6 (AB 310), effective January 1, 2008.

§585.1. [Section repealed 1991]

Leg.H. Added Stats 1990 ch 207 §2 (SB 2668). Repealed Stats 1991 ch 57 §2 (SB 323), effective June 14, 1991 (ch 57 prevails). Amended Stats 1991 ch 1091 §17. See CCP §585.5.

§585.5. Affidavit required for application to enter default

(a) Every application to enter default under subdivision (a) of Section 585 shall include, or be accompanied by, an affidavit stating facts showing that the action is or is not subject to Section 1812.10 or 2984.4 of the Civil Code or subdivision (b) of Section 395.

(b) When a default or default judgment has been entered without full compliance with Section 1812.10 or 2984.4 of the Civil Code, or subdivision (b) of Section 395, the defendant may serve and file a notice of motion to set aside the default or default judgment and for leave to defend the action in the proper court. The notice of motion shall be served and filed within 60 days after the defendant first receives notice of levy under a writ of execution, or notice of any other procedure for enforcing, the default judgment.

(c) A notice of motion to set aside a default or default judgment and for leave to defend the action in the proper court shall designate as the time for making the motion a date prescribed by subdivision (b) of Section 1005, and it shall be accompanied by an affidavit showing under oath that the action was not commenced in the proper court according to Section 1812.10 or 2984.4 of the Civil Code or subdivision (b) of Section 395. The party shall serve and file with the notice a copy of the answer, motion, or other pleading proposed to be filed in the action.

(d) Upon a finding by the court that the motion was made within the period permitted by subdivision (b) and that the action was not commenced in the proper court, it shall set aside the default or default judgment on such terms as may be just and shall allow such a party to defend the action in the proper court.

(e) Unless the plaintiff can show that the plaintiff used reasonable diligence to avoid filing the action in the improper court, upon a finding that the action was commenced in the improper court the court shall award the defendant actual damages and costs, including reasonable attorney's

New trial; Three-year rule. §583.320.
Parties' extension of time. §583.330.
Tolling of period. §583.340.
Exception as to tolling or extension of time; Six-month rule. §583.350.
Dismissal. §583.360.

§583.310. Trial; Five-year rule

An action shall be brought to trial within five years after the action is commenced against the defendant. **Leg.H.** Added Stats 1984 ch 1705 §5.

§583.320. New trial; Three-year rule

(a) If a new trial is granted in the action the action shall again be brought to trial within the following times:

(1) If a trial is commenced but no judgment is entered because of a mistrial or because a jury is unable to reach a decision, within three years after the order of the court declaring the mistrial or the disagreement of the jury is entered.

(2) If after judgment a new trial is granted and no appeal is taken, within three years after the order granting the new trial is entered.

(3) If on appeal an order granting a new trial is affirmed or a judgment is reversed and the action remanded for a new trial, within three years after the remittitur is filed by the clerk of the trial court.

(b) Nothing in this section requires that an action again be brought to trial before expiration of the time prescribed in Section 583.310. **Leg.H.** Added Stats 1984 ch 1705 §5.

§583.330. Parties' extension of time

The parties may extend the time within which an action must be brought to trial pursuant to this article by the following means:

(a) By written stipulation. The stipulation need not be filed but, if it is not filed, the stipulation shall be brought to the attention of the court if relevant to a motion for dismissal.

(b) By oral agreement made in open court, if entered in the minutes of the court or a transcript is made. **Leg.H.** Added Stats 1984 ch 1705 §5.

§583.340. Tolling of period

In computing the time within which an action must be brought to trial pursuant to this article, there shall be excluded the time during which any of the following conditions existed:

(a) The jurisdiction of the court to try the action was suspended.

(b) Prosecution or trial of the action was stayed or enjoined.

(c) Bringing the action to trial, for any other reason, was impossible, impracticable, or futile. **Leg.H.** Added Stats 1984 ch 1705 §5.

§583.350. Exception as to tolling or extension of time; Six-month rule

If the time within which an action must be brought to trial pursuant to this article is tolled or otherwise extended pursuant to statute with the result that at the end of the period of tolling or extension less than six months remains within which the action must be brought to trial, the action shall not be dismissed pursuant to this article if the action is brought to trial within six months after the end of the period of tolling or extension. **Leg.H.** Added Stats 1984 ch 1705 §5.

§583.360. Dismissal

(a) An action shall be dismissed by the court on its own motion or on motion of the defendant, after notice to the parties, if the action is not brought to trial within the time prescribed in this article.

(b) The requirements of this article are mandatory and are not subject to extension, excuse, or exception except as expressly provided by statute. **Leg.H.** Added Stats 1984 ch 1705 §5.

ARTICLE 4
Discretionary Dismissal for Delay

Authority of court to dismiss; Procedure. §583.410.
Conditions for dismissal; Computation of time. §583.420.
Grant or denial of dismissal; Authority of court to enter conditional order. §583.430.

§583.410. Authority of court to dismiss; Procedure

(a) The court may in its discretion dismiss an action for delay in prosecution pursuant to this article on its own motion or on motion of the defendant if to do so appears to the court appropriate under the circumstances of the case.

(b) Dismissal shall be pursuant to the procedure and in accordance with the criteria prescribed by rules adopted by the Judicial Council. **Leg.H.** Added Stats 1984 ch 1705 §5.

§583.420. Conditions for dismissal; Computation of time

(a) The court may not dismiss an action pursuant to this article for delay in prosecution except after one of the following conditions has occurred:

(1) Service is not made within two years after the action is commenced against the defendant.

(2) The action is not brought to trial within the following times:

(A) Three years after the action is commenced against the defendant unless otherwise prescribed by rule under subparagraph (B).

(B) Two years after the action is commenced against the defendant if the Judicial Council by rule adopted pursuant to Section 583.410 so prescribes for the court because of the condition of the court calendar or for other reasons affecting the conduct of litigation or the administration of justice.

(3) A new trial is granted and the action is not again brought to trial within the following times:

(A) If a trial is commenced but no judgment is entered because of a mistrial or because a jury is unable to reach a decision, within two years after the order of the court declaring the mistrial or the disagreement of the jury is entered.

(B) If after judgment a new trial is granted and no appeal is taken, within two years after the order granting the new trial is entered.

(C) If on appeal an order granting a new trial is affirmed or a judgment is reversed and the action remanded for a new trial, within two years after the remittitur is filed by the clerk of the trial court.

(b) The times provided in subdivision (a) shall be computed in the manner provided for computation of the comparable times under Articles 2 (commencing with Section 583.210) and 3 (commencing with Section 583.310). **Leg.H.** Added Stats 1984 ch 1705 §5.

§583.430. Grant or denial of dismissal; Authority of court to enter conditional order

(a) In a proceeding for dismissal of an action pursuant to this article for delay in prosecution the court in its discretion may require as a condition of granting or denial of dismissal that the parties comply with such terms as appear to the court proper to effectuate substantial justice.

(b) The court may make any order necessary to effectuate the authority provided in this section, including, but not limited to, provisional and conditional orders. **Leg.H.** Added Stats 1984 ch 1705 §5.

CHAPTER 2
JUDGMENT UPON FAILURE TO ANSWER

Judgment if defendant fails to answer complaint. §585.
Affidavit required for application to enter default. §585.5.
Cases where proceedings and judgments treated as if defendant failed to answer. §586.
Affidavit to be filed with application by plaintiff for entry of default. §587.
Applicable terms. §587.5.

§585. Judgment if defendant fails to answer complaint

Judgment may be had, if the defendant fails to answer the complaint, as follows:

(a) In an action arising upon contract or judgment for the recovery of money or damages only, if the defendant has, or if more than one defendant, if any of the defendants have, been served, other than by publication, and no answer, demurrer, notice of motion to strike of the character specified in subdivision (f), notice of motion to transfer pursuant to Section 396b, notice of motion to dismiss pursuant to Article 2 (commencing with Section 583.210) of Chapter 1.5 of Title 8, notice of motion to quash service of summons or to stay or dismiss the action pursuant to Section 418.10, or notice of the filing of a petition for writ of mandate as provided in Section 418.10 has been filed with the clerk of the court within the time specified in the summons, or within further time as may be allowed, the clerk, upon written application of the plaintiff, and proof of the service of summons, shall enter the default of the defendant or defendants, so served, and immediately thereafter enter judgment for the principal amount demanded in the complaint, in the statement required by Section 425.11, or in the statement provided for in Section 425.115, or a lesser amount if credit has been acknowledged, together with interest allowed by law or in accordance with the terms of the contract, and the costs against the defendant, or defendants, or against one or more of the defendants. If, by rule of court, a schedule of attorneys' fees to be allowed has been adopted, the clerk may include in the judgment attorneys' fees in fees. **Leg.H.** Added Stats 1970 ch 725 §4. Amended Stats 1971 ch 1640 §2; Stats 1982 ch 497 §36, operative July 1, 1983; Stats 1983 ch 142 §6; Stats 1991 ch 1090 §3 (AB 1484).

§586. Cases where proceedings and judgments treated as if defendant failed to answer

(a) In the following cases the same proceedings shall be had, and judgment shall be rendered in the same manner, as if the defendant had failed to answer:

(1) If the complaint has been amended, and the defendant fails to answer it, as amended, or demur thereto, or file a notice of motion to strike, of the character specified in Section 585, within 30 days after service thereof or within the time allowed by the court.

(2) If the demurrer to the complaint is overruled and a motion to strike, of the character specified in Section 585, is denied, or where only one thereof is filed, if the demurrer is overruled or the motion to strike is denied, and the defendant fails to answer the complaint within the time allowed by the court.

(3) If a motion to strike, of the character specified in Section 585, is granted in whole or in part, and the defendant fails to answer the unstricken portion of the complaint within the time allowed by the court, no demurrer having been sustained or being then pending.

(4) If a motion to quash service of summons or to stay or dismiss the action has been filed, or writ of mandate sought and notice thereof given, as provided in Section 418.10, and upon denial of the motion or writ, the defendant fails to respond to the complaint within the time provided in that section or as otherwise provided by law.

(5) If the demurrer to the answer is sustained and the defendant fails to amend the answer within the time allowed by the court.

(6)(A) If a motion to transfer pursuant to Section 396b is denied and the defendant fails to respond to the complaint within the time allowed by the court pursuant to subdivision (e) of Section 396b or within the time provided in subparagraph (C).

(B) If a motion to transfer pursuant to Section 396b is granted and the defendant fails to respond to the complaint within 30 days of the mailing of notice of the filing and case number by the clerk of the court to which the action or proceeding is transferred or within the time provided in subparagraph (C).

(C) If the order granting or denying a motion to transfer pursuant to Section 396a or 396b is the subject of an appeal pursuant to Section 904.2 in which a stay is granted or of a mandate proceeding pursuant to Section 400, the court having jurisdiction over the trial, upon application or on its own motion after the appeal or mandate proceeding becomes final or upon earlier termination of a stay, shall allow the defendant a reasonable time to respond to the complaint. Notice of the order allowing the defendant further time to respond to the complaint shall be promptly served by the party who obtained the order or by the clerk if the order is made on the court's own motion.

(7) If a motion to strike the answer in whole, of the character specified in Section 585, is granted without leave to amend, or if a motion to strike the answer in whole or in part, of the character specified in Section 585, is granted with leave to amend and the defendant fails to amend the answer within the time allowed by the court.

(8) If a motion to dismiss pursuant to Section 583.250 is denied and the defendant fails to respond within the time allowed by the court.

(b) For the purposes of this section, "respond" means to answer, to demur, or to move to strike. **Leg.H.** Enacted 1872, as CCP §872. Amended Stats 1921 ch 127 §1. Amended and renumbered by Stats 1933 ch 744 §93. Amended Stats 1955 ch 1452 §7; Stats 1969 ch 345 §4, ch 1611 §7.5, operative July 1, 1970; Stats 1970 ch 587 §1; Stats 1973 ch 167 §12; Stats 1982 ch 704 §7; Stats 1983 ch 1167 §7; Stats 1991 ch 1090 §4 (AB 1484); Stats 1993 ch 456 §11 (AB 58); Stats 1995 ch 796 §11 (SB 45); Stats 2007 ch 43 §6 (SB 649), effective January 1, 2008.

§587. Affidavit to be filed with application by plaintiff for entry of default

An application by a plaintiff for entry of default under subdivision (a), (b), or (c) of Section 585 or Section 586 shall include an affidavit stating that a copy of the application has been mailed to the defendant's attorney of record or, if none, to the defendant at his or her last known address and the date on which the copy was mailed. If no such address of the defendant is known to the plaintiff or plaintiff's attorney, the affidavit shall state that fact.

No default under subdivision (a), (b), or (c) of Section 585 or Section 586 shall be entered, unless the affidavit is filed. The nonreceipt of the notice shall not invalidate or constitute ground for setting aside any judgment. **Leg.H.** Added Stats 1969 ch 567 §2. Amended Stats 1970 ch 105 §1; Stats 1983 ch 142 §7; Stats 1995 ch 796 §12 (SB 45).

§587.5. Applicable terms

As used in this chapter, unless the context otherwise specifically requires, the following terms apply:

(a) "Complaint" includes a cross-complaint.

(b) "Defendant" includes a cross-defendant.

(c) "Plaintiff" includes a cross-complainant. **Leg.H.** Added Stats 1986 ch 540 §10.

CHAPTER 3
ISSUES—THE MODE OF TRIAL AND POSTPONEMENTS

Issue defined, and the different kinds. §588.
Issue of law, how raised. §589.
Issue of fact, how raised. §590.
Trial of issue; Waiver of demurrer. §591.
Trial of issue of fact; Priority for disposition of any issues of law. §592.
Bringing issue to trial or hearing; Notice to adverse party. §594.
Grounds for postponement of trial on court's own motion. §594a.
Postponement when party, attorney, or witness is member of Legislature; Stay of proceedings; Exceptions to mandatory grant of continuance. §595.
"Proceeding in a court". §595.1.
Postponement on agreement of parties' attorneys. §595.2.
Postponement of trial of action involving title to, or trespass on, mining claims. §595.3.
Postponement on grounds of absence of evidence; Affidavit, and overruling of motion. §595.4.
Deposition of witness in case of postponement. §596.
Trial of special defenses. §597.
Answer alleging statute of limitations in suit for professional negligence; Separate trial of issues. §597.5.
Bifurcated trial of issues. §598.
Extension of deadlines in conjunction with continuance of trial date during COVID-19 pandemic. [Contingently repealed]. § 599.

§588. Issue defined, and the different kinds

Issues arise upon the pleadings when a fact or a conclusion of law is maintained by the one party and is controverted by the other. They are two kinds:

1. Of law; and,
2. Of fact. **Leg.H.** Enacted 1872.

§589. Issue of law, how raised

An issue of law arises:

(a) Upon a demurrer to the complaint, cross-complaint, or answer, or to some part thereof.

(b) Upon a motion to strike made pursuant to Section 435, 436, or 473. **Leg.H.** Enacted 1872. Amended Stats 1982 ch 704 §8; Stats 1983 ch 1167 §8.

§590. Issue of fact, how raised

An issue of fact arises:

1. Upon a material allegation in the complaint controverted by the answer; and,

2. Upon new matters in the answer, except an issue of law is joined thereon. **Leg.H.** Enacted 1872.

§591. Trial of issue; Waiver of demurrer

An issue of law must be tried by the court, unless it is referred upon consent; provided, however, that failure on the part of any person filing any demurrer to prosecute the same may be construed as a waiver of such demurrer, except as otherwise provided in Section 430.80 of this code. **Leg.H.** Enacted 1872. Amended Stats 1929 ch 484 §1; Stats 1982 ch 704 §9.

§592. Trial of issue of fact; Priority for disposition of any issues of law

In actions for the recovery of specific, real, or personal property, with or without damages, or for money claimed as due upon contract, or as damages for breach of contract, or for injuries, an issue of fact must be tried by a jury, unless a jury trial is waived, or a reference is ordered, as provided in this code. Where in these cases there are issues both of law and fact, the issue of law must be first disposed of. In other cases, issues of fact must be tried by the court, subject to its power to order any such issue to be tried by a jury, or to be referred to a referee, as provided in this code. **Leg.H.** Enacted 1872. Amended Code Amdts 1873–74 ch 383 §74.

§593. [Section repealed 1931]

Leg.H. Enacted 1872. Amended Code Amdts 1880 ch 16 §1. Repealed Stats 1931 ch 238 §1. The repealed section related to clerk's duties regarding calendaring cases.

§594. Bringing issue to trial or hearing; Notice to adverse party

(a) In superior courts either party may bring an issue to trial or to a hearing, and, in the absence of the adverse party, unless the court, for good cause, otherwise directs, may proceed with the case and take a dismissal of the action, or a verdict, or judgment, as the case may require; provided, however, if the issue to be tried is an issue of fact, proof shall first be made to the satisfaction of the court that the adverse party has had 15 days' notice of such trial or five days' notice of the trial in an unlawful detainer action as specified in subdivision (b). If the adverse party has served notice of trial upon the party seeking the dismissal, verdict, or judgment at least five days prior to the trial, the adverse party shall be deemed to have had notice.

(b) The notice to the adverse party required by subdivision (a) shall be served by mail on all the parties by the clerk of the court not less than 20 days prior to the date set for trial. In an unlawful detainer action where notice is served by mail that service shall be mailed not less than 10 days prior to the date set for trial. If notice is not served by the clerk as required by this subdivision, it may be served by mail by any party on the adverse party not less than 15 days prior to the date set for trial, and in an unlawful detainer action where notice is served by mail that service shall be mailed not less than 10 days prior to the date set for trial. The time provisions of Section 1013 shall not serve to extend the notice of trial requirements under this subdivision for unlawful detainer actions. If notice is served by the clerk, proof thereof may be made by introduction into evidence of the clerk's certificate pursuant to subdivision (3) of Section 1013a or other competent evidence. If notice is served by a party, proof may be made by introduction into evidence of an affidavit or certificate pursuant to subdivision (1) or (2) of Section 1013a or other competent evidence. The provisions of this subdivision are exclusive. **Leg.H.** Enacted 1872. Amended Stats 1899 ch 6 §1; Stats 1933 ch 744 §94; Stats 1935 ch 722 §8; Stats 1951 ch 1737 §86, operative January 1, 1952; Stats 1969 ch 85 §1; Stats 1975 ch 1001 §1; Stats 1976 ch 406 §1; Stats 1977 ch 685 §1, ch 1257 §19, effective October 3, 1977, operative until January 1, 1978, ch 1257 §19.5, effective October 3, 1977, operative January 1, 1978; Stats 1998 ch 931 §81 (SB 2139), effective September 28, 1998; Stats 2002 ch 784 §62 (SB 1316).

§594a. Grounds for postponement of trial on court's own motion

The court may, of its own motion, postpone the trial, if at the time fixed for the trial the court is engaged in the trial of another action; or if, as provided in section 473 of this code, an amendment of the pleadings, or the allowance of time to make such amendment, or to plead, renders a postponement necessary. **Leg.H.** Added Stats 1933 ch 744 §95.

§595. Postponement when party, attorney, or witness is member of Legislature; Stay of proceedings; Exceptions to mandatory grant of continuance

The trial of any civil action, or proceeding in a court, or of any administrative proceeding before a state board or commission or officer, irrespective of the date of the filing thereof or when it became at issue, or the hearing of any motion, demurrer, or other proceeding, shall be postponed to a date certain when it appears to the court, board, commission, or officer before which such action or proceeding is pending that either a party thereto, or any attorney of record therein (whether he became an attorney of record before or after the commencement of a legislative session or before or after his appointment to a legislative committee), or a principal witness, is a Member of the Legislature of this state and that the Legislature is in session or in recess (not exceeding a recess of forty (40) days) or that a legislative interim committee of which he is a duly appointed member is meeting, or is to meet within a period which the court finds does not exceed the time reasonably necessary to enable the member to reach the committee meeting by the ordinary mode of travel. When the Legislature is in session or in recess such action or proceeding shall not, without the consent of the attorney of record therein, be brought on for trial or hearing before the expiration of thirty (30) days next following final adjournment of the Legislature or the commencement of a recess of more than forty (40) days. If a date is available during recess, continuance shall be given if possible to such earlier date. When a legislative committee is meeting or is to meet within a period which the court finds does not exceed the time reasonably necessary to enable the member to reach the committee meeting by the ordinary mode of travel, such action or proceeding shall not, without the consent of the attorney of record therein, be brought on for trial or hearing before the expiration of such period necessary following the adjournment or recess of the committee meeting as the court finds is reasonably necessary to enable the member to reach the place of trial or hearing by the ordinary mode of travel from the place of the committee meeting, unless at the expiration of that period the Legislature is to be in session; and in that case the action or proceeding shall not, without such consent, be brought on for trial or hearing before the expiration of thirty (30) days next following final adjournment or the commencement of a recess of more than forty (40) days. If a date is available during the recess, continuance shall be given to such earlier date. However, any postponement granted under the provisions of this paragraph shall suspend for the same period of time as the postponement, the running of any period of time for any ruling or proceeding by a court, board, commission, or officer, or for the performance by any party of any act affected by said postponement.

Granting of a continuance pursuant to this section is mandatory unless the court determines that such continuance would defeat or abridge a right to relief pendente lite in a paternity action or a right to invoke a provisional remedy such as pendente lite support in a domestic relations controversy, attachment and sale of perishable goods, receivership of a failing business, and temporary restraining order or preliminary injunction, and that the continuance should not be granted. **Leg.H.** Enacted 1872. Amended Code Amdts 1880 ch 13 §1; Stats 1911 ch 744 §1; Stats 1931 ch 1078 §1; Stats 1933 ch 282 §1, effective May 11, 1933, ch 744 §96; Stats 1945 ch 1512 §1, effective July 18, 1945; Stats 1955 ch 926 §1; Stats 1963 ch 1468 §1; Stats 1965 ch 1989 §1; Stats 1968 ch 698 §1.

§595.1. "Proceeding in a court"

The term "proceeding in a court" as it is used in Section 595 shall include any discovery proceeding, pretrial conference, deposition, interrogatory, or any other proceeding arising out of a pending civil action.

The enactment of this section at the 1965 Regular Session of the Legislature does not constitute a change in, but is declaratory of, the preexisting law. **Leg.H.** Added Stats 1965 ch 1890 §1.

§595.2. Postponement on agreement of parties' attorneys

In all cases, the court shall postpone a trial, or the hearing of any motion or demurrer, for a period not to exceed thirty (30) days, when all attorneys of record of parties who have appeared in the action agree in writing to such postponement. **Leg.H.** Added Stats 1965 ch 1989 §3.

§595.3. Postponement of trial of action involving title to, or trespass on, mining claims

In actions involving the title to mining claims, or involving trespass for damage upon mining claims, if it be made to appear to the satisfaction of the court that, in order that justice may be done and the action fairly tried on its merits, it is necessary that further developments should be made, underground or upon the surface of the mining claims involved in such action, the court shall grant the postponement of the trial of the action, giving the party a reasonable time in which to prepare for trial and to do said development work. **Leg.H.** Added Stats 1965 ch 1989 §4.

§595.4. Postponement on grounds of absence of evidence, Affidavit, and overruling of motion

A motion to postpone a trial on the ground of the absence of evidence can only be made upon affidavit showing the materiality of the evidence expected to be obtained, and that due diligence has been used to procure it. The court may require the moving party, where application is made on account of the absence of a material witness, to state upon affidavit the evidence which he expects to obtain; and if the adverse party thereupon admits that such evidence would be given, and that it be considered as actually given on the trial, or offered and overruled as improper, the trial must not be postponed. **Leg.H.** Added Stats 1965 ch 1989 §2.

§596. Deposition of witness in case of postponement

The party obtaining a postponement of a trial, if required by the adverse party, must consent that the testimony of any witness of such adverse party, who is in attendance, be then taken by deposition before a judge or clerk of the court in which the case is pending, or before such notary public as the court may indicate, which must accordingly be done; and the testimony so taken may be read on the trial, with the same effect, and subject to the same objections, as if the witnesses were produced. **Leg.H.** Enacted 1872. Amended Stats 1933 ch 744 §97; Stats 1951 ch 1737 §87, operative January 1, 1952.

§597. Trial of special defenses

When the answer pleads that the action is barred by the statute of limitations, or by a prior judgment, or that another action is pending upon the same cause of action, or sets up any other defense not involving the merits of the plaintiff's cause of action but constituting a bar or ground of abatement to the prosecution thereof, the court may, either upon its own motion or upon the motion of any party, proceed to the trial of the special defense or defenses before the trial of any other issue in the case, and if the decision of the court, or the verdict of the jury, upon any special defense so tried (other than the defense of another action pending) is in favor of the defendant pleading the same, judgment for the defendant shall thereupon be entered and no trial of other issues in the action shall be had unless that judgment shall be reversed on appeal or otherwise set aside or vacated; and where the defense of another action pending or a demurrer based upon subdivision (c) of Section 430.10 is sustained (and no other special defense is sustained) an interlocutory judgment shall be entered in favor of the defendant pleading the same to the effect that no trial of other issues shall be had until the final determination of that other action, and the plaintiff may appeal from the interlocutory judgment in the same manner and within the same time as is now or may be hereafter provided by law for appeals from judgments. If the decision of the court, or the verdict of the jury, upon the special defense or defenses so tried is in favor of the plaintiff, trial of the other issues shall thereafter be had either upon the court's own motion or upon the motion of any party, and judgment shall be entered thereon in the same manner and with the same effect as if all the issues in the case had been tried at one time. In such an event any and all decisions or verdicts upon the special defense or defenses, and all rulings on the trial thereof shall be deemed excepted to and may be reviewed on motion for a new trial or upon appeal from the judgment.

This section also applies to the trial of special defenses pleaded in an answer to a cross-complaint or a demurrer based upon subdivision (c) of Section 430.10, and if the decision of the court or the verdict of the jury upon the special defense or defenses is in favor of the cross-defendant, no further trial shall be had upon the issues raised by the cross-complaint, but trial of the other issues in the action shall thereafter be had either upon the court's own motion or upon the motion of any party, and after the trial thereof the judgment shall be entered in the action as is justified by the decision or verdict on such other issues, considered in connection with the decision or verdict upon the trial of such an affirmative defense raised in the answer to the cross-complaint. **Leg.H.** Added Stats 1939 ch 715 §1. Amended Stats 1969 ch 201 §1; Stats 1979 ch 216 §1; Stats 1986 ch 540 §11.

§597.5. Answer alleging statute of limitations in suit for professional negligence; Separate trial of issues

In an action against a physician or surgeon, dentist, registered nurse, dispensing optician, optometrist, registered physical therapist, podiatrist, licensed psychologist, osteopathic physician and surgeon, chiropractor, clinical laboratory bioanalyst, clinical laboratory technologist, veterinarian, or a licensed hospital as the employer of any such person, based upon the person's alleged professional negligence, or for rendering professional services without consent, or for error or omission in the person's practice, if the answer pleads that the action is barred by the statute of limitations, and if any party so moves or the court upon its own motion requires, the issues raised thereby must be tried separately and before any other issues in the case are tried. If the issue raised by the statute of limitations is finally determined in favor of the plaintiff, the remaining issues shall then be tried. **Leg.H.** Added Stats 1968 ch 1104 §1. Amended Stats 1979 ch 216 §2; Stats 1993 ch 226 §5 (AB 1987).

§598. Bifurcated trial of issues

The court may, when the convenience of witnesses, the ends of justice, or the economy and efficiency of handling the litigation would be promoted thereby, on motion of a party, after notice and hearing, make an order, no later than the close of pretrial conference in cases in which such pretrial conference is to be held, or, in other cases, no later than 30 days before the trial date, that the trial of any issue or any part thereof shall precede the trial of any other issue or any part thereof in the case, except for special defenses which may be tried first pursuant to Sections 597 and 597.5. The court, on its own motion, may make such an order at any time. Where trial of the issue of liability as to all causes of action precedes the trial of other issues or parts thereof, and the decision of the court, or the verdict of the jury upon such issue so tried is in favor of any party on whom liability is sought to be imposed, judgment in favor of such party shall thereupon be entered and no trial of other issues in the action as against such party shall be had unless such judgment shall be reversed upon appeal or otherwise set aside or vacated.

If the decision of the court, or the verdict of the jury upon the issue of liability so tried shall be against any party on whom liability is sought to be imposed, or if the decision of the court or the verdict of the jury upon any other issue or part thereof so tried does not result in a judgment being entered pursuant to this chapter, then the trial of the other issues or parts thereof shall thereafter be had at such time, and if a jury trial, before the same or another jury, as ordered by the court either upon its own motion or upon the motion of any party, and judgment shall be entered in the same manner and with the same effect as if all the issues in the case had been tried at one time. **Leg.H.** Added Stats 1963 ch 1205 §1. Amended Stats 1977 ch 57 §1; Stats 1979 ch 216 §3, ch 349 §1.

§ 599. Extension of deadlines in conjunction with continuance of trial date during COVID-19 pandemic. [Contingently repealed]

(a) Notwithstanding any other law and unless ordered otherwise by a court or otherwise agreed to by the parties, a continuance or postponement of a trial or arbitration date extends any deadlines that have not already passed as of March 19, 2020, applicable to discovery, including the exchange of expert witness information, mandatory settlement conferences, and summary judgment motions in the same matter. The deadlines are extended for the same length of time as the continuance or postponement of the trial date.

(b) This section shall remain in effect only during the state of emergency proclaimed by the Governor on March 4, 2020, related to the COVID-19 pandemic and 180 days after the end, pursuant to Section 8629 of the Government Code, of that state of emergency and is repealed on that date. **Leg.H.** Added Stats 2020 ch 112 §1 (SB 1146), effective September 18, 2020, repealed September 18, 2020; contingently repealed. Amended Stats 2021 ch 214 §6 (SB 241), effective January 1, 2022.

CHAPTER 4
TRIAL BY JURY

Article 2. Conduct of the Trial.
Article 3. The Verdict.

ARTICLE 1
Formation of Jury [Repealed]

§600. [Section repealed 1989]

Leg.H. Enacted 1872. Amended Stats 1933 ch 744 §98; Stats 1951 ch 1737 §88, operative January 1, 1952. Repealed Stats 1988 ch 1245 §3. The repealed section related to drawing names of jurors from trial jury box.

§601. [Section repealed 1989]

Leg.H. Enacted 1872. Amended Code Amdts 1873–74 ch 383 §75; Stats 1919 ch 87 §1; Stats 1933 ch 744 §99; Stats 1935 ch 249 §1; Stats 1953 ch 1578 §1; Stats 1955 ch 1159 §1; Stats 1961 ch 2030 §1; Stats 1963 ch 1542 §1; Stats 1965 ch 1382 §1; Stats 1967 ch 779 §1; Stats 1975 ch 593 §7; Stats 1978 ch 98 §1. Repealed Stats 1988 ch 1245 §4. See CCP §231.

§602. [Section repealed 1989]

Leg.H. Enacted 1872. Amended Code Amdts 1873–74 ch 383 §76; Stats 1907 ch 377 §1; Stats 1909 ch 715 §1; Stats 1913 ch 277 §1; Stats 1931 ch 655 §1; Stats 1955 ch 428 §1; Stats 1968 ch 744 §1; Stats 1975 ch 469 §1; Stats 1977 ch 591 §3; Stats 1978 ch 301 §3; Stats 1979 ch 730 §21, operative January 1, 1981; Stats 1980 ch 1227 §3. Repealed Stats 1988 ch 1245 §5. See CCP §§228, 229.

§603. [Section repealed 1989]

Leg.H. Enacted 1872. Repealed Stats 1988 ch 1245 §6. See CCP §230.

§604. [Section repealed 1989]

Leg.H. Enacted 1872. Repealed Stats 1988 ch 1245 §7. The repealed section related to swearing in of jury.

§605. [Section repealed 1989]

Leg.H. Added Stats 1961 ch 618 §1. Amended Stats 1963 ch 721 §1; Stats 1977 ch 1257 §20, effective October 3, 1977. Repealed Stats 1988 ch 1245 §8. See CCP §234.

ARTICLE 2
Conduct of the Trial

Order of proceedings on trial. §607.
Proposed instructions of attorneys. §607a.
Charge to jury; Court must furnish in writing, upon request, points of law contained therein. §608.
Special instructions. §609.
Admonition when jury permitted to separate. §611.
Papers and exhibits that may be taken to jury room. §612.
Written instructions; Availability to jury. §612.5.
Conduct of deliberations. §613.
May come into court for further instructions. §614.
Judge's presence while testimony read to jury. §614.5.
Retrial where jury discharged or verdict prevented. §616.
Adjournment of court while jury is absent; Sealed verdict. §617.
Verdict. §618.
Proceedings when verdict is informal. §619.

§607. Order of proceedings on trial

When the jury has been sworn, the trial must proceed in the following order, unless the court, for special reasons otherwise directs:

1. The plaintiff may state the issue and his case;

2. The defendant may then state his defense, if he so wishes, or wait until after plaintiff has produced his evidence;

3. The plaintiff must then produce the evidence on his part;

4. The defendant may then open his defense, if he has not done so previously;

5. The defendant may then produce the evidence on his part;

6. The parties may then respectively offer rebutting evidence only, unless the court, for good reason, in furtherance of justice, permit them to offer evidence upon their original case;

7. When the evidence is concluded, unless the case is submitted to the jury on either side or on both sides without argument, the plaintiff must commence and may conclude the argument;

8. If several defendants having separate defenses, appear by different counsel, the court must determine their relative order in the evidence and argument;

9. The court may then charge the jury. **Leg.H.** Enacted 1872. Amended Stats 1933 ch 744 §100; Stats 1965 ch 841 §1.

§607a. Proposed instructions of attorneys

In every case which is being tried before the court with a jury, it shall be the duty of counsel for the respective parties, before the first witness is sworn, to deliver to the judge presiding at the trial and serve upon opposing counsel, all proposed instructions to the jury covering the law as disclosed by the pleadings. Thereafter, and before the commencement of the argument, counsel may deliver to such judge, and serve upon opposing counsel, additional proposed instructions to the jury upon questions of law developed by the evidence and not disclosed by the pleadings. All proposed instructions shall be typewritten, each on a separate sheet of paper. Before the commencement of the argument, the court, on request of counsel, must: (1) decide whether to give, refuse, or modify the proposed instructions; (2) decide which instructions shall be given in addition to those proposed, if any; and (3) advise counsel of all instructions to be given. However, if, during the argument, issues are raised which have not been covered by instructions given or refused, the court may, on request of counsel, give additional instructions on the subject matter thereof. **Leg.H.** Added Stats 1929 ch 481 §1. Amended Stats 1933 ch 744 §101; Stats 1951 ch 1737 §89, operative January 1, 1952; Stats 1957 ch 1698 §1.

§608. Charge to jury; Court must furnish in writing, upon request, points of law contained therein

In charging the jury the court may state to them all matters of law which it thinks necessary for their information in giving their verdict; and, if it state the testimony of the case, it must inform the jury that they are the exclusive judges of all questions of fact. The court must furnish to either party, at the time, upon request, a statement in writing of the points of law contained in the charge, or sign, at the time, a statement of such points prepared and submitted by the counsel of either party. **Leg.H.** Enacted 1872.

§609. Special instructions

Where either party asks special instructions to be given to the jury, the court must either give such instruction, as requested, or refuse to do so, or give the instruction with a modification, in such manner that it may distinctly appear what instructions were given in whole or in part. **Leg.H.** Enacted 1872.

§610. [Section repealed 1989]

Leg.H. Added Stats 1980 ch 1227 §4. Amended Stats 1986 ch 1171 §3. Repealed Stats 1988 ch 1245 §9. See CCP §224.

Prior Law: Former CCP §610, relating to view by jury of premises, similar to present CCP §651, was enacted 1872 and repealed Stats 1975 ch 301 §1.

§611. Admonition when jury permitted to separate

If the jury are permitted to separate, either during the trial or after the case is submitted to them, they shall be admonished by the court that it is their duty not to conduct research, disseminate information, or converse with, or permit themselves to be addressed by, any other person on any subject of the trial, and that it is their duty not to form or express an opinion thereon until the case is finally submitted to them. The court shall clearly explain, as part of the admonishment, that the prohibition on research, dissemination of information, and conversation applies to all forms of electronic and wireless communication. **Leg.H.** Enacted 1872. Amended Stats 2011 ch 181 §1 (AB 141), effective January 1, 2012.

§612. Papers and exhibits that may be taken to jury room

Upon retiring for deliberation the jury may take with them all papers which have been received as evidence in the cause, except depositions, or copies of such papers as ought not, in the opinion of the court, to be taken from the person having them in possession; and they may also take with them any exhibits which the court may deem proper, notes of the testimony or other proceedings on the trial, taken by themselves or any of them, but none taken by any other person. **Leg.H.** Enacted 1872. Amended Stats 1939 ch 753 §1.

§612.5. Written instructions; Availability to jury

Upon the jury retiring for deliberation, the court shall advise the jury of the availability of a written copy of the jury instructions. The court may, at its discretion, provide the jury with a copy of the written instructions given. However, if the jury requests the court to supply a copy of the written instructions, the court shall supply the jury with a copy. **Leg.H.** Added Stats 1975 ch 461 §1. Amended Stats 1986 ch 1045 §1.

Prior Law: Former CCP §612.5, similar to the present section, was added Stats 1971 ch 1571 §1 and repealed Stats 1971 ch 1571 §2, operative December 31, 1974.

§613. Conduct of deliberations

When the case is finally submitted to the jury, they may decide in court or retire for deliberation. If they retire, they must be kept together in some convenient place, under charge of an officer, until at least three-fourths of them agree upon a verdict or are discharged by the court. Unless by order of the court, the officer having them under his or her charge shall not permit any communication to be made to them, including any form of electronic or wireless communication, or make any himself or herself, except to ask them if they or three-fourths of them are agreed upon a verdict. The officer shall not, before their verdict is rendered, communicate to any person the state of their deliberations, or the verdict agreed upon. **Leg.H.** Enacted 1872. Amended Code Amdts 1880 ch 21 §1; Stats 2011 ch 181 §2 (AB 141), effective January 1, 2012.

§614. May come into court for further instructions

After the jury have retired for deliberation, if there be a disagreement between them as to any part of the testimony, or if they desire to be informed of any point of law arising in the cause, they may require the officer to conduct them into court. Upon their being brought into court, the information required must be given in the presence of, or after notice to, the parties or counsel. **Leg.H.** Enacted 1872.

§614.5. Judge's presence while testimony read to jury

Except for good cause shown, the judge in his or her discretion need not be present in the court while testimony previously received in evidence is read to the jury. **Leg.H.** Added Stats 1987 ch 88 §1, effective July 2, 1987.

Prior Law: Former CCP §614.5, similar to the present section, was added Stats 1983 ch 472 §1 and repealed January 1, 1987, by its own terms.

§615. [Section repealed 1989]

Leg.H. Enacted 1872. Amended Stats 1907 ch 377 §2; Stats 1961 ch 618 §2. Repealed Stats 1988 ch 1245 §10. See CCP §233.

§616. Retrial where jury discharged or verdict prevented

In all cases where the jury are discharged without having rendered a verdict, or are prevented from giving a verdict, by reason of accident or other cause, during the progress of the trial, or after the cause is submitted to them, except as provided in Section 630, the action may be again tried immediately, or at a future time, as the court may direct. **Leg.H.** Enacted 1872. Amended Stats 1947 ch 984 §1.

§617. Adjournment of court while jury is absent; Sealed verdict

While the jury are absent the court may adjourn from time to time, in respect to other business; but it is nevertheless open for every purpose connected with the cause submitted to the jury, until a verdict is rendered or the jury discharged. The court may direct the jury to bring in a sealed verdict, at the opening of the court, in case of an agreement during a recess or adjournment for the day. **Leg.H.** Enacted 1872. Amended Code Amdts 1880 ch 21 §2.

§618. Verdict

When the jury, or three-fourths of them, have agreed upon a verdict, they must be conducted into court and the verdict rendered by their foreperson. The verdict must be in writing, signed by the foreperson, and must be read to the jury by the clerk, and the inquiry made whether it is their verdict. Either party may require the jury to be polled, which is done by the court or clerk, asking each juror if it is the juror's verdict. If upon inquiry or polling, more than one-fourth of the jurors disagree thereto, the jury must be sent out again, but if no disagreement is expressed, the verdict is complete and the jury discharged from the case. **Leg.H.** Enacted 1872. Amended Code Amdts 1880 ch 221 §3; Stats 1933 ch 744 §102; Stats 1935 ch 722 §9; Stats 1978 ch 258 §1; Stats 2007 ch 263 §7 (AB 310), effective January 1, 2008.

§619. Proceedings when verdict is informal

When the verdict is announced, if it is informal or insufficient, in not covering the issue submitted, it may be corrected by the jury under the advice of the court, or the jury may be again sent out. **Leg.H.** Enacted 1872.

ARTICLE 3
The Verdict

General and special verdicts defined; Requisites of special verdict. §624.
Special verdicts; Requirements for award of punitive damages. §625.
Verdict for recovery of money. §626.
Verdict in action for recovery of specific personal property. §627.
Entry of verdict. §628.
Judgment notwithstanding the verdict. §629.
Directed verdicts. §630.

§624. General and special verdicts defined; Requisites of special verdict

The verdict of a jury is either general or special. A general verdict is that by which they pronounce generally upon all or any of the issues, either in favor of the plaintiff or defendant; a special verdict is that by which the jury find the facts only, leaving the judgment to the Court. The special verdict must present the conclusions of fact as established by the evidence, and not the evidence to prove them; and those conclusions of fact must be so presented as that nothing shall remain to the Court but to draw from them conclusions of law. **Leg.H.** Enacted 1872.

§625. Special verdicts; Requirements for award of punitive damages

In all cases the court may direct the jury to find a special verdict in writing, upon all, or any of the issues, and in all cases may instruct them, if they render a general verdict, to find upon particular questions of fact, to be stated in writing, and may direct a written finding thereon. In all cases in which the issue of punitive damages is presented to the jury the court shall direct the jury to find a special verdict in writing separating punitive damages from compensatory damages. The special verdict or finding must be filed with the clerk and entered upon the minutes. Where a special finding of facts is inconsistent with the general verdict, the former controls the latter, and the court must give judgment accordingly. **Leg.H.** Enacted 1872. Amended Stats 1905 ch 62 §1; Stats 1909 ch 121 §1; Stats 1957 ch 1443 §1; Stats 1983 ch 176 §2.

§626. Verdict for recovery of money

When a verdict is found for the plaintiff in an action for the recovery of money, or for the cross-complainant when a cross-complaint for the recovery of money is established, the jury must also find the amount of the recovery. **Leg.H.** Enacted 1872. Amended Stats 1971 ch 244 §52, operative July 1, 1972.

§627. Verdict in action for recovery of specific personal property

In an action for the recovery of specific personal property, if the property has not been delivered to the plaintiff, or the defendant, by his answer, claim a return thereof, the jury, if their verdict be in favor of the plaintiff, or, if being in favor of defendant, they also find that he is entitled to a return thereof, must find the value of the property, and, if so instructed, the value of specific portions thereof, and may at the same time assess the damages, if any are claimed in the complaint or answer, which the prevailing party has sustained by reason of the taking or detention of such property. **Leg.H.** Enacted 1872. Amended Code Amdts 1873–74 ch 383 §77.

§628. Entry of verdict

In superior courts upon receipt of a verdict, an entry must be made in the minutes of the court, specifying the time of trial, the names of the jurors and witnesses, and setting out the verdict at length; and where a special verdict is found, either the judgment rendered thereon, or if the case be reserved for argument or further consideration, the order thus reserving it. **Leg.H.** Enacted 1872. Amended Stats 1933 ch 744 §103; Stats 1951 ch 1737 §90, operative January 1, 1952; Stats 1965 ch 205 §2; Stats 1977 ch 1257 §21, effective October 3, 1977; Stats 1998 ch 931 §82 (SB 2139), effective September 28, 1998; Stats 2002 ch 784 §63 (SB 1316).

§629. Judgment notwithstanding the verdict

(a) The court, before the expiration of its power to rule on a motion for a new trial, either of its own motion, after five days' notice, or on motion of a party against whom a verdict has been rendered, shall render judgment in favor of the aggrieved party notwithstanding the verdict whenever a motion for a directed verdict for the aggrieved party should have been granted had a previous motion been made.

(b) A motion for judgment notwithstanding the verdict shall be made within the period specified by Section 659 for the filing and service of a notice of intention to move for a new trial. The moving, opposing, and reply briefs and any accompanying documents shall be filed and served within the periods specified by Section 659a, and the hearing on the motion shall be set in the same manner as the hearing on a motion for new trial under Section 660. The making of a motion for judgment notwithstanding the verdict shall not extend the time within which a party may file and serve notice of intention to move for a new trial. The court shall not rule upon the motion for judgment notwithstanding the verdict until the expiration of the time within which a motion for a new trial must be served and filed, and if a motion for a new trial has been filed with the court by the aggrieved party, the court shall rule upon both motions at the same time. The power of the court to rule on a motion for judgment notwithstanding the verdict shall not extend beyond the last date upon which it has the power to rule on a motion for a new trial. If a motion for judgment notwithstanding the verdict is not determined before that date, the effect shall be a denial of that motion without further order of the court.

(c) If the motion for judgment notwithstanding the verdict is denied and if a new trial is denied, the appellate court shall, if it appears that the motion for judgment notwithstanding the verdict should have been granted, order judgment to be so entered on appeal from the judgment or from the order denying the motion for judgment notwithstanding the verdict.

(d) If a new trial is granted to the party moving for judgment notwithstanding the verdict, and the motion for judgment notwithstanding the verdict is denied, the order denying the motion for judgment notwithstanding the verdict shall nevertheless be reviewable on appeal from that order by the aggrieved party. If the court grants the motion for judgment notwithstanding the verdict or of its own motion directs the entry of judgment notwithstanding the verdict and likewise grants the motion for a new trial, the order granting the new trial shall be effective only if, on appeal, the judgment notwithstanding the verdict is reversed, and the order granting a new trial is not appealed from or, if appealed from, is affirmed. **Leg.H.** Added Stats 1923 ch 366 §1. Amended Stats 1935 ch 722 §10; Stats 1937 ch 551 §1; Stats 1951 ch 801 §1, effective January 1, 1952; Stats 1961 ch 604 §1; Stats 1963 ch 205 §1; Stats 2014 ch 93 §1 (AB 1659), effective January 1, 2015; Stats 2015 ch 303 §40 (AB 731), effective January 1, 2016.

§630. Directed verdicts

(a) Unless the court specified an earlier time for making a motion for directed verdict, after all parties have completed the presentation of all of their evidence in a trial by jury, any party may, without waiving his or her right to trial by jury in the event the motion is not granted, move for an order directing entry of a verdict in its favor.

(b) If it appears that the evidence presented supports the granting of the motion as to some, but not all, of the issues involved in the action, the court shall grant the motion as to those issues and the action shall proceed on any remaining issues. Despite the granting of such a motion, no final judgment shall be entered prior to the termination of the action, but the final judgment, in addition to any matter determined in the trial, shall reflect the verdict ordered by the court as determined by the motion for directed verdict.

(c) If the motion is granted, unless the court in its order directing entry of the verdict specifies otherwise, it shall operate as an adjudication upon the merits.

(d) In actions which arise out of an injury to a person or property, when a motion for directed verdict was granted on the basis that a defendant was without fault, no other defendant during trial, over plaintiff's objection, shall attempt to attribute fault to or comment on the absence or involvement of the defendant who was granted the motion.

(e) The order of the court granting the motion for directed verdict is effective without any assent of the jury.

(f) When the jury for any reason has been discharged without having rendered a verdict, the court on its own motion or upon motion of a party, notice of which was given within 10 days after discharge of the jury, may order judgment to be entered in favor of a party whenever a motion for directed verdict for that party should have been granted had a previous motion been made. Except as otherwise provided in Section 12a, the power of the court to act under the provisions of this section shall expire 30 days after the day upon which the jury was discharged, and if judgment has not been ordered within that time the effect shall be the denial of any motion for judgment without further order of the court. **Leg.H.** Added Stats 1947 ch 984 §2. Amended Stats 1967 ch 625 §1; Stats 1986 ch 540 §12.

CHAPTER 4.5
VOLUNTARY EXPEDITED JURY TRIALS

Definitions. §630.01.
Applicable rules and procedures. §630.02.
Agreement to participate; Issuance of proposed consent order. §630.03.
Composition of juries; Peremptory challenges. §630.04.
Deliberation. §630.05.
Rules of evidence; Issuance of subpoenas and notices to secure attendance of witnesses or production of documents. §630.06.
Verdict. §630.07.
Waiver of specified motions; Actions by court. §630.08.
Waiver of specified rights; Grounds for new trial or appeal; Post-trial motions. §630.09.
Applicability of statutes and rules governing costs and attorney's fees. §630.10.
Adoption of rules and forms to establish uniform procedures. §630.11.

§630.01. Definitions

For purposes of this chapter:

(a) "Expedited jury trial" means a consensual, binding jury trial before a reduced jury panel and a judicial officer.

(b) "High/low agreement" means a written agreement entered into by the parties that specifies a minimum amount of damages that a plaintiff is guaranteed to receive from the defendant, and a maximum amount of damages that the defendant will be liable for, regardless of the ultimate verdict returned by the jury. Neither the existence of, nor the amounts contained in, any high/low agreements may be disclosed to the jury.

(c) "Post-trial motions" does not include motions relating to costs and attorney's fees, motions to correct a judgment for a clerical error, and motions to enforce a judgment. **Leg.H.** Added Stats 2010 ch 674 §2 (AB 2284), effective January 1, 2011, repealed January 1, 2016. Amended Stats 2011 ch 296 §37 (AB 1023), effective January 1, 2012; Stats 2015 ch 330 §4 (AB 555), effective January 1, 2016 (repealer repealed).

2010 Note: This act shall be known as the Expedited Jury Trials Act. Stats 2010 ch 674 (AB 2284) §1.

§630.02. Applicable rules and procedures

The rules and procedures applicable to expedited jury trials are as follows:

(a) The procedures in this chapter and in the implementing rules of court shall apply to expedited jury trials, unless the parties agree otherwise, as permitted under subparagraph (E) of paragraph (1) of subdivision (e) of Section 630.03, and the court so orders.

(b) Any matters not expressly addressed in this chapter, in the implementing rules of court, or in a consent order authorized by this chapter and the implementing rules, are governed by applicable statutes and rules governing civil actions. **Leg.H.** Added Stats 2010 ch 674 §2 (AB 2284), effective January 1, 2011, repealed January 1, 2016. Amended Stats 2015 ch 330 §4 (AB 555), effective January 1, 2016 (repealer repealed).

2010 Note: For citation of act, see note following CCP §630.01.

§630.03. Agreement to participate; Issuance of proposed consent order

(a) All parties agreeing to participate in an expedited jury trial and, if represented, their counsel, shall sign a proposed consent order granting an expedited jury trial.

(b) Except as provided in subdivision (d), the agreement to participate in the expedited jury trial process is binding upon the parties, unless either of the following occurs:

(1) All parties stipulate to end the agreement to participate.

(2) The court, on its own motion or at the request of a party by noticed motion, finds that good cause exists for the action not to proceed under the rules of this chapter.

(c) Any agreement to participate in an expedited jury trial under this chapter may be entered into only after a dispute has arisen and an action has been filed.

(d) The court shall approve the use of an expedited jury trial and any high/low agreements or other stipulations for an expedited jury trial involving either of the following:

(1) A self-represented litigant.

(2) A minor, an incompetent person, or a person for whom a conservator has been appointed.

(e) The proposed consent order submitted to the court shall include all of the following:

(1) A preliminary statement that each named party and any insurance carrier responsible for providing coverage or defense on behalf of that party, individually identified in the proposed consent order, have been informed of the rules and procedures for an expedited jury trial and provided with a Judicial Council information sheet regarding expedited jury trials, have agreed to take part in or, in the case of a responsible insurance carrier, not object to, the expedited jury trial process, and have agreed to all the specific provisions set forth in the consent order.

(2) The parties' agreement to all of the following:

(A) That all parties waive all rights to appeal and to move for directed verdict or make any post-trial motions, except as provided in Sections 630.08 and 630.09.

(B) That each side shall have up to five hours in which to complete voir dire and to present its case.

(C) That the jury shall be composed of eight or fewer jurors with no alternates.

(D) That each side shall be limited to three peremptory challenges, unless the court permits an additional challenge in cases with more than two sides as provided in Section 630.04.

(E) That the trial and pretrial matters will proceed under subparagraphs (A) to (D), inclusive, and, unless the parties expressly agree otherwise in the proposed consent order, under all other provisions in this chapter and in the implementing rules of court.

(f) The court shall issue the consent order as proposed by the parties, unless the court finds good cause why the action should not proceed through the expedited jury trial process, in which case the court shall deny the proposed consent order in its entirety. **Leg.H.** Added Stats 2010 ch 674 §2 (AB 2284), effective January 1, 2011, repealed January 1, 2016. Amended Stats 2015 ch 330 §§2, 4 (AB 555), effective January 1, 2016 (repealer repealed).

2010 Note: For citation of act, see note following CCP §630.01.

§630.04. Composition of juries; Peremptory challenges

(a) Juries in expedited jury trial cases shall be composed of eight jurors, unless the parties have agreed to fewer. No alternates shall be selected.

(b) The court shall allow each side three peremptory challenges. If there are more than two parties in a case and more than two sides, as determined by the court under subdivision (c) of Section 231, the parties may request one additional peremptory challenge each, which is to be granted by the court as the interests of justice may require. **Leg.H.** Added Stats 2010 ch 674 §2 (AB 2284), effective January 1, 2011, repealed January 1, 2016. Amended Stats 2015 ch 330 §4 (AB 555), effective January 1, 2016 (repealer repealed).

2010 Note: For citation of act, see note following CCP §630.01.

§630.05. Deliberation

Nothing in this chapter is intended to preclude a jury from deliberating as long as needed. **Leg.H.** Added Stats 2010 ch 674 §2 (AB 2284), effective January 1, 2011, repealed January 1, 2016. Amended Stats 2015 ch 330 §4 (AB 555), effective January 1, 2016 (repealer repealed).

2010 Note: For citation of act, see note following CCP §630.01.

§630.06. Rules of evidence; Issuance of subpoenas and notices to secure attendance of witnesses or production of documents

(a) The rules of evidence apply in expedited jury trials, unless the parties stipulate otherwise.

(b) Any stipulation by the parties to use relaxed rules of evidence may not be construed to eliminate, or in any way affect, the right of a witness or party to invoke any applicable privilege or other law protecting confidentiality.

(c) The right to issue subpoenas and notices to appear to secure the attendance of witnesses or the production of documents at trial shall be in accordance with this code. **Leg.H.** Added Stats 2010 ch 674 §2 (AB 2284), effective January 1, 2011, repealed January 1, 2016. Amended Stats 2015 ch 330 §4 (AB 555), effective January 1, 2016 (repealer repealed).

2010 Note: For citation of act, see note following CCP §630.01.

§630.07. Verdict

(a) The verdict in an expedited jury trial case is binding, subject to any written high/low agreement or other stipulations concerning the amount of the award agreed upon by the parties.

(b) A vote of six of the eight jurors is required for a verdict, unless the parties stipulate otherwise. **Leg.H.** Added Stats 2010 ch 674 §2 (AB 2284), effective January 1, 2011, repealed January 1, 2016. Amended Stats 2015 ch 330 §4 (AB 555), effective January 1, 2016 (repealer repealed).

2010 Note: For citation of act, see note following CCP §630.01.

§630.08. Waiver of specified motions; Actions by court

(a) By agreeing to participate in the expedited jury trial process, the parties agree to waive any motions for directed verdict, motions to set aside the verdict or any judgment rendered by the jury, or motions for a new trial on the basis of inadequate or excessive damages.

(b) The court shall not set aside any verdict or any judgment, shall not direct that judgment be entered in favor of a party entitled to judgment as a matter of law, and shall not order a new trial, except on the grounds stated in Section 630.09. **Leg.H.** Added Stats 2010 ch 674 §2 (AB 2284), effective January 1, 2011, repealed January 1, 2016. Amended Stats 2011 ch 296 §38 (AB 1023), effective January 1, 2012; Stats 2015 ch 330 §4 (AB 555), effective January 1, 2016 (repealer repealed).

2010 Note: For citation of act, see note following CCP §630.01.

§630.09. Waiver of specified rights; Grounds for new trial or appeal; Post-trial motions

(a) By agreeing to participate in the expedited jury trial process, the parties agree to waive the right to bring post-trial motions or to appeal from the determination of the matter, except as provided in this section. The only grounds on which a party may move for a new trial or appeal are any of the following:

(1) Judicial misconduct that materially affected the substantial rights of a party.

(2) Misconduct of the jury.

(3) Corruption, fraud, or other undue means employed in the proceedings of the court, jury, or adverse party that prevented a party from having a fair trial.

(b) Within 10 court days of the entry of a jury verdict, a party may file with the clerk and serve on each adverse party a notice of the intention to move for a new trial on any of the grounds specified in subdivision (a). The notice shall be deemed to be a motion for a new trial.

(c) Except as provided in subdivision (b), parties to an expedited jury trial shall not make any post-trial motions except for motions relating to costs and attorney's fees, motions to correct a judgment for clerical error, and motions to enforce a judgment.

(d) Before filing an appeal, a party shall make a motion for a new trial under subdivision (b). If the motion for a new trial is denied, the party may appeal the judgment to the appropriate court with appellate jurisdiction and seek a new trial on any of the grounds specified in subdivision (a). Parties to an expedited jury trial may not appeal on any other ground. **Leg.H.** Added Stats 2010 ch 674 §2 (AB 2284), effective January 1, 2011, repealed January 1, 2016. Amended Stats 2015 ch 330 §4 (AB 555), effective January 1, 2016 (repealer repealed).

2010 Note: For citation of act, see note following CCP §630.01.

§630.10. Applicability of statutes and rules governing costs and attorney's fees

All statutes and rules governing costs and attorney's fees shall apply in expedited jury trials, unless the parties agree otherwise in the consent order. **Leg.H.** Added Stats 2010 ch 674 §2 (AB 2284), effective January 1, 2011, repealed January 1, 2016. Amended Stats 2015 ch 330 §4 (AB 555), effective January 1, 2016 (repealer repealed).

2010 Note: For citation of act, see note following CCP §630.01.

§630.11. Adoption of rules and forms to establish uniform procedures

The Judicial Council shall, on or before July 1, 2016, update rules and forms to establish uniform procedures implementing the provisions of this chapter, including, but not limited to, rules for all of the following:

(a) Additional content of proposed consent orders.

(b) Pretrial exchanges and submissions.

(c) Pretrial conferences.

(d) Presentation of evidence and testimony.

(e) Any other procedures necessary to implement the provisions of this chapter. **Leg.H.** Added Stats 2010 ch 674 §2 (AB 2284), effective January 1, 2011, repealed January 1, 2016. Amended Stats 2015 ch 330 §§3, 4 (AB 555), effective January 1, 2016 (repealer repealed).

2010 Note: For citation of act, see note following CCP §630.01.

§630.12. [Section repealed 2016]

Leg.H. Added Stats 2010 ch 674 §2 (AB 2284), effective January 1, 2011, repealed January 1, 2016; Repealed Stats 2015 ch 330 §4 (AB 555), effective January 1, 2016. The repealed section related to repeal of the chapter.

CHAPTER 4.6
MANDATORY EXPEDITED JURY TRIALS IN LIMITED CIVIL CASES

Actions conducted as mandatory expedited jury trial; Opt out; Appeal. §630.20.
Definitions. §630.21.
Applicability of procedures and implementing rules of court. §630.22.
Rules and procedures for mandatory expedited jury trials. §630.23.
Jury deliberation. §630.24.
Rules of evidence; Subpoenas and notices to appear. §630.25.
Required jury vote for verdict; Appeal. §630.26.
Costs and attorney's fees. §630.27.
Adoption of rules by Judicial Council. §630.28.
Operative date of specified sections. §630.29.

§630.20. Actions conducted as mandatory expedited jury trial; Opt out; Appeal

(a) Except as provided in subdivisions (b) and (c), an action or special proceeding treated as a limited civil case pursuant to Article 1 (commencing with Section 85) of Chapter 5.1 of Title 1 of Part 1, including an action or special proceeding initially filed as a limited civil case or remanded as one thereafter, shall be conducted as a mandatory expedited jury trial pursuant to this chapter.

(b) Either party may opt out of the mandatory expedited jury trial procedures if any of the following criteria is met:

(1) Punitive damages are sought.

(2) Damages in excess of insurance policy limits are sought.

(3) A party's insurer is providing a legal defense subject to a reservation of rights.

(4) The case involves a claim reportable to a governmental entity.

(5) The case involves a claim of moral turpitude that may affect an individual's professional licensing.

(6) The case involves claims of intentional conduct.

(7) The case has been reclassified as unlimited pursuant to Section 403.020.

(8) The complaint contains a demand for attorney's fees, unless those fees are sought pursuant to Section 1717 of the Civil Code.

(9) The judge finds good cause exists for the action not to proceed under the rules of this chapter. Good cause includes, but is not limited to, a showing that a party needs more than five hours to present or defend the action and that the parties have been unable to stipulate to additional time.

(c) This chapter does not apply to a proceeding in forcible entry or forcible or unlawful detainer.

(d) A judgment in a limited civil case conducted as a mandatory expedited jury trial may be appealed to the appellate division of the superior court in which the case was tried. **Leg.H.** Added Stats 2015 ch 330 §5 (AB 555), effective January 1, 2016, operative July 1, 2016, repealed July 1, 2019. Amended Stats 2018 ch 776 §7 (AB 3250), effective January 1, 2019 (repealer repealed).

§630.21. Definitions

For purposes of this chapter:

(a) "Mandatory expedited jury trial" means a jury trial before a reduced jury panel and a judge, conducted pursuant to this chapter.

(b) "High/low agreement" means a written agreement entered into by the parties that specifies a minimum amount of damages that a plaintiff is guaranteed to receive from the defendant, and a maximum amount of damages that the defendant will be liable for, regardless of the ultimate verdict returned by the jury. Neither the existence of, nor the amounts contained in, any high/low agreements may be disclosed to the jury. **Leg.H.** Added Stats 2015 ch 330 §5 (AB 555), effective January 1, 2016, operative July 1, 2016, repealed July 1, 2019. Amended Stats 2018 ch 776 §7 (AB 3250), effective January 1, 2019 (repealer repealed).

§630.22. Applicability of procedures and implementing rules of court

(a) The procedures in this chapter and in the implementing rules of court shall apply to mandatory expedited jury trials conducted in limited civil cases, unless the parties agree otherwise, as permitted under subdivision (d) of Section 630.23, and the court so orders.

(b) Any matters not expressly addressed in this chapter, in the implementing rules of court, or in an agreement authorized by this chapter and the implementing rules, are governed by applicable statutes and rules governing civil actions. **Leg.H.** Added Stats 2015 ch 330 §5 (AB 555), effective January 1, 2016, operative July 1, 2016, repealed July 1, 2019. Amended Stats 2018 ch 776 §7 (AB 3250), effective January 1, 2019 (repealer repealed).

§630.23. Rules and procedures for mandatory expedited jury trials

The following rules and procedures apply to mandatory expedited jury trials conducted pursuant to this chapter:

(a) Each side shall have up to five hours in which to complete voir dire and to present its case.

(b) The jury shall be composed of eight jurors and one alternate, unless the parties have agreed to fewer jurors.

(c) Each side shall be limited to four peremptory challenges, unless the court permits an additional challenge in cases with more than two sides. If there are more than two parties in a case and more than two sides, as determined by the court under subdivision (c) of Section 231, the parties may request one additional peremptory challenge each, which is to be granted by the court as the interests of justice may require.

(d) The parties may agree to modify the rules and procedures specified in this chapter and the implementing rules of court, subject to the court's approval. **Leg.H.** Added Stats 2015 ch 330 §5 (AB 555), effective January 1, 2016, operative July 1, 2016, repealed July 1, 2019. Amended Stats 2018 ch 776 §7 (AB 3250), effective January 1, 2019 (repealer repealed).

§630.24. Jury deliberation

Nothing in this chapter is intended to preclude a jury from deliberating as long as needed. **Leg.H.** Added Stats 2015 ch 330 §5 (AB 555), effective January 1, 2016, operative July 1, 2016, repealed July 1, 2019. Amended Stats 2018 ch 776 §7 (AB 3250), effective January 1, 2019 (repealer repealed).

§630.25. Rules of evidence; Subpoenas and notices to appear

(a) The rules of evidence apply to mandatory expedited jury trials conducted in limited civil cases, unless the parties stipulate otherwise.

(b) Any stipulation by the parties to use relaxed rules of evidence shall not be construed to eliminate, or in any way affect, the right of a witness or party to invoke any applicable privilege or other law protecting confidentiality.

(c) The right to issue subpoenas and notices to appear to secure the attendance of witnesses or the production of documents at trial shall be in accordance with this code. **Leg.H.** Added Stats 2015 ch 330 §5 (AB 555), effective January 1, 2016, operative July 1, 2016, repealed July 1, 2019. Amended Stats 2018 ch 776 §7 (AB 3250), effective January 1, 2019 (repealer repealed).

§630.26. Required jury vote for verdict; Appeal

(a) A vote of six of the eight jurors is required for a verdict, unless the parties stipulate otherwise.

(b) The verdict in a limited civil case following a mandatory expedited jury trial case shall be appealable under subdivision (d) of Section 630.20 and subject to any written high/low agreement or other stipulations concerning the amount of the award agreed upon by the parties. **Leg.H.** Added Stats 2015 ch 330 §5 (AB 555), effective January 1, 2016, operative July 1, 2016, repealed July 1, 2019. Amended Stats 2018 ch 776 §7 (AB 3250), effective January 1, 2019 (repealer repealed).

§630.27. Costs and attorney's fees

All statutes and rules governing costs and attorney's fees shall apply in limited civil cases that are conducted as mandatory expedited jury trials, unless the parties stipulate otherwise. **Leg.H.** Added Stats 2015 ch 330 §5 (AB 555), effective January 1, 2016, operative July 1, 2016, repealed July 1, 2019. Amended Stats 2018 ch 776 §7 (AB 3250), effective January 1, 2019 (repealer repealed).

§630.28. Adoption of rules by Judicial Council

The Judicial Council shall, on or before July 1, 2016, adopt rules and forms to establish uniform procedures implementing the provisions of this chapter, including, rules for the following:

(a) Pretrial exchanges and submissions.

(b) Pretrial conferences.

(c) Opt-out procedures pursuant to subdivision (b) of Section 630.20.

(d) Presentation of evidence and testimony.

(e) Any other procedures necessary to implement the provisions of this chapter. **Leg.H.** Added Stats 2015 ch 330 §5 (AB 555), effective January 1, 2016, repealed July 1, 2019. Amended Stats 2018 ch 776 §7 (AB 3250), effective January 1, 2019 (repealer repealed).

§630.29. Operative date of specified sections

Sections 630.20 to 630.27, inclusive, shall become operative on July 1, 2016. **Leg.H.** Added Stats 2015 ch 330 §5 (AB 555), effective January 1, 2016, repealed July 1, 2019. Amended Stats 2018 ch 776 §7 (AB 3250), effective January 1, 2019 (repealer repealed).

§630.30. Repeal of chapter [Repealed]

Leg.H. Added Stats 2015 ch 330 §5 (AB 555), effective January 1, 2016, repealed July 1, 2019. Repealed Stats 2018 ch 776 §7 (AB 3250), effective January 1, 2019.

CHAPTER 5
TRIAL BY THE COURT

Demand for jury trial by adverse parties; Fees; Waiver of jury trial; Jury trial notwithstanding waiver. §631.

Payment of jury fees; Deposit of fees by party; Superior court or county's right to reimbursement; Reimbursement of superior court for jurors appearing for voir dire examination. §631.2.

When jury fees not to be refunded; Disposition of fees not refunded; Disposition of fees of juror serving on more than one case in same day. §631.3.

Party required to deposit jury fees and mileage in eminent domain cases. §631.5.

Order of proceedings. §631.7.

Motions for judgment. §631.8.

Statement of decision. §632.

Effect of failure to resolve issue. §634.

Signing order conforming to minutes. §635.

Proceedings after determination of issue of law. §636.

§631. Demand for jury trial by adverse parties; Fees; Waiver of jury trial; Jury trial notwithstanding waiver

(a) The right to a trial by jury as declared by Section 16 of Article I of the California Constitution shall be preserved to the parties inviolate. In civil cases, a jury may only be waived pursuant to subdivision (f).

(b) At least one party demanding a jury on each side of a civil case shall pay a nonrefundable fee of one hundred fifty dollars ($150), unless the fee has been paid by another party on the same side of the case. The fee shall offset the costs to the state of providing juries in civil cases. If there are more than two parties to the case, for purposes of this section only, all plaintiffs shall be considered one side of the case, and all other parties shall be considered the other side of the case. Payment of the fee by a party on one side of the case shall not relieve parties on the other side of the case from waiver pursuant to subdivision (f).

(c) The fee described in subdivision (b) shall be due on or before the date scheduled for the initial case management conference in the action, except as follows:

(1) In unlawful detainer actions, the fees shall be due at least five days before the date set for trial.

(2) If no case management conference is scheduled in a civil action, or the initial case management conference occurred before June 28, 2012, and the initial complaint was filed on or after July 1, 2011, the fee shall be due no later than 365 calendar days after the filing of the initial complaint.

(3) If the initial case management conference occurred before June 28, 2012, and the initial complaint in the case was filed before July 1, 2011, the fee shall be due at least 25 calendar days before the date initially set for trial.

(4) If the party requesting a jury has not appeared before the initial case management conference, or first appeared more than 365 calendar days after the filing of the initial complaint, the fee shall be due at least 25 calendar days before the date initially set for trial.

(d) If a party failed to timely pay the fee described in subdivision (b) that was due between June 27, 2012, and November 30, 2012, the party will be relieved of a jury waiver on that basis only if the party pays the fee on or before December 31, 2012, or 25 calendar days before the date initially set for trial, whichever is earlier.

(e) The parties demanding a jury trial shall deposit with the clerk or judge, at the beginning of the second and each succeeding day's session, a sum equal to that day's fees and mileage of the jury, including the fees and mileage for the trial jury panel if the trial jury has not yet been selected and sworn. If more than one party has demanded a jury, the respective amount to be paid daily by each party demanding a jury shall be determined by stipulation of the parties or by order of the court.

(f) A party waives trial by jury in any of the following ways:

(1) By failing to appear at the trial.

(2) By written consent filed with the clerk or judge.

(3) By oral consent, in open court, entered in the minutes.

(4) By failing to announce that a jury is required, at the time the cause is first set for trial, if it is set upon notice or stipulation, or within five days after notice of setting if it is set without notice or stipulation.

(5) By failing to timely pay the fee described in subdivision (b), unless another party on the same side of the case has paid that fee.

(6) By failing to deposit with the clerk or judge, at the beginning of the second and each succeeding day's session, the sum provided in subdivision (e).

(g) The court may, in its discretion upon just terms, allow a trial by jury although there may have been a waiver of a trial by jury.

(h) The court shall transmit the fee described in subdivision (b) to the State Treasury for deposit in the Trial Court Trust Fund within 45 calendar days after the end of the month in which the fee is paid to the court.

Leg.H. Added Stats 1988 ch 10 §3, effective February 17, 1988. Amended Stats 1988 ch 278 §1; Stats 1989 ch 15 §2, effective May 10, 1989; Stats 1998 ch 931 §83 (SB 2139), effective September 28, 1998; Stats 1999 ch 83 §24 (SB 966); Stats 2000 ch 127 §2 (AB 2866), effective July 10, 2000; Stats 2002 ch 806 §15 (AB 3027); Stats 2012 ch 41 §3 (SB 1021), effective June 27, 2012, ch 342 §1 (AB 1481), effective September 17, 2012.

Prior Law: Former CCP §631, similar to the present section, was enacted 1872, amended Code Amdts 1873–74 ch 383 §78, Stats 1915 ch 403 §1, Stats 1929 ch 490 §1, Stats 1931 ch 829 §1, Stats 1933 ch 744 §104, Stats 1941 ch 1191 §1, Stats 1951 ch 1737 §91, operative January 1, 1952, Stats 1959 ch 525 §1, Stats 1970 ch 321 §1, Stats 1979 ch 212 §4, Stats 1987 ch 1493 §1.5, and repealed Stats 1988 ch 10 §2, effective February 17, 1988.

§631.01. [Section repealed 1988]

Leg.H. Added Stats 1980 ch 1216 §1. Amended Stats 1986 ch 953 §4. Repealed January 1, 1988, by the terms of Stats 1980 ch 1216 §4, as amended Stats 1982 ch 284 §2. The repealed section related to jury trials.

§631.1. [Section repealed 2013]

Leg.H. Added Stats 1971 ch 144 §1. Repealed Stats 2012 ch 470 §5 (AB 1529), effective January 1, 2013. See CCP §631.2.

§631.2. Payment of jury fees; Deposit of fees by party; Superior court or county's right to reimbursement; Reimbursement of superior court for jurors appearing for voir dire examination

(a) Notwithstanding any other provision of law, the superior court may pay jury fees in civil cases from general funds of the court available therefor. Nothing in this section shall be construed to change the requirements for the deposit of jury fees in any civil case by the appropriate party to the litigation at the time and in the manner otherwise provided by law. Nothing in this section shall preclude the right of the superior court to be reimbursed by the party to the litigation liable therefor for any payment of jury fees pursuant to this section. Nothing in this section shall preclude the right of the county to be reimbursed by the party to the litigation liable therefor for any payment of jury fees pursuant to this section as it read in Section 4 of Chapter 10 of the Statutes of 1988, or pursuant to former Section 631.1 as it read in Section 1 of Chapter 144 of the Statutes of 1971.

(b) The party who has demanded trial by jury shall reimburse the superior court for the fees and mileage of all jurors appearing for voir dire examination, except those jurors who are excused and subsequently on the same day are called for voir dire examination in another case. **Leg.H.** Added Stats 1988 ch 10 §4, effective February 17, 1988. Amended Stats 2012 ch 470 §6 (AB 1529), effective January 1, 2013.

Prior Law: Former CCP §631.2, similar to the present section, was added Stats 1980 ch 1216 §2 and repealed January 1, 1988, by the terms of Stats 1980 ch 1216 §4, as amended Stats 1982 ch 284 §2.

§631.3. When jury fees not to be refunded; Disposition of fees not refunded; Disposition of fees of juror serving on more than one case in same day

(a) Notwithstanding any other law, when a party to the litigation has deposited jury fees with the judge or clerk and that party waives a jury or obtains a continuance of the trial, or the case is settled, none of the deposit shall be refunded if the court finds there has been insufficient time to notify the jurors that the trial would not proceed at the time set. If the jury fees so deposited are not refunded for any of these reasons, or if a refund of jury fees deposited with the judge or clerk has not been requested, in writing, by the depositing party within 20 business days from the date on which the jury is waived or the action is settled, dismissed, or a continuance thereof granted, the fees shall be transmitted to the Controller for deposit into the Trial Court Trust Fund.

(b) All jury fees and mileage fees that may accrue by reason of a juror serving on more than one case in the same day shall be transmitted to the Controller for deposit into the Trial Court Trust Fund. All jury fees that were deposited with the court in advance of trial pursuant to Section 631 prior to January 1, 1999, and that remain on deposit in cases that were settled, dismissed, or otherwise disposed of, and three years have passed since the date the case was settled, dismissed, or otherwise disposed of, shall be transmitted to the Controller for deposit into the Trial Court Trust Fund.

(c) The fee described in subdivision (b) of Section 631 shall be nonrefundable and is not subject to this section. **Leg.H.** Added Stats 1949 ch 444 §1. Amended Stats 1955 ch 511 §1; Stats 1963 ch 678 §1; Stats 1998 ch 1003 §1 (SB 1520), ch 1004 §1 (AB 1935); Stats 2000 ch 447 §2 (SB 1533); Stats 2001 ch 824 §9 (AB 1700); Stats 2012 ch 41 §4 (SB 1021), effective June 27, 2012, ch 342 §2 (AB 1481), effective September 17, 2012.

§631.5. Party required to deposit jury fees and mileage in eminent domain cases

In all cases of eminent domain the deposits of jury fees and mileage provided for in section 631 of this code shall be made by the party seeking condemnation regardless of which party shall have demanded a jury trial, and the trial shall not proceed until such deposits are made. **Leg.H.** Added Stats 1939 ch 806 §1.

§631.7. Order of proceedings

Ordinarily, unless the court otherwise directs, the trial of a civil action tried by the court without a jury shall proceed in the order specified in Section 607. **Leg.H.** Added Stats 1965 ch 299 §20, operative January 1, 1967.

§631.8. Motions for judgment

(a) After a party has completed his presentation of evidence in a trial by the court, the other party, without waiving his right to offer evidence in support of his defense or in rebuttal in the event the motion is not granted, may move for a judgment. The court as trier of the facts shall weigh the evidence and may render a judgment in favor of the moving party, in which case the court shall make a statement of decision as provided in Sections 632 and 634, or may decline to render any judgment until the close of all the evidence. The court may consider all evidence received, provided, however, that the party against whom the motion for judgment has been made shall have had an opportunity to present additional evidence to rebut evidence received during the presentation of evidence deemed by the presenting party to have been adverse to him, and to rehabilitate the testimony of a witness whose credibility has been attacked by the moving party. Such motion may also be made and granted as to any cross-complaint.

(b) If it appears that the evidence presented supports the granting of the motion as to some but not all the issues involved in the action, the court shall grant the motion as to those issues and the action shall proceed as to the issues remaining. Despite the granting of such a motion, no final judgment shall be entered prior to the termination of the action, but the final judgment in such action shall, in addition to any matters determined in the trial, award judgment as determined by the motion herein provided for.

(c) If the motion is granted, unless the court in its order for judgment otherwise specifies, such judgment operates as an adjudication upon the merits. **Leg.H.** Added Stats 1961 ch 692 §2. Amended Stats 1971 ch 244 §53, operative July 1, 1972; Stats 1978 ch 372 §1; Stats 1980 ch 187 §2; Stats 1986 ch 540 §13.

§632. Statement of decision

In superior courts, upon the trial of a question of fact by the court, written findings of fact and conclusions of law shall not be required. The court shall issue a statement of decision explaining the factual and legal basis for its decision as to each of the principal controverted issues at trial upon the request of any party appearing at the trial. The request must be made within 10 days after the court announces a tentative decision unless the trial is concluded within one calendar day or in less than eight hours over more than one day in which event the request must be made prior to the submission of the matter for decision. The request for a statement of decision shall specify those controverted issues as to which the party is requesting a statement of decision. After a party has requested the statement, any party may make proposals as to the content of the statement of decision.

The statement of decision shall be in writing, unless the parties appearing at trial agree otherwise; however, when the trial is concluded within one calendar day or in less than 8 hours over more than one day, the statement of decision may be made orally on the record in the presence of the parties. **Leg.H.** Enacted 1872. Amended Code Amdts 1873–74 ch 383 §79; Stats 1933 ch 744 §105; Stats 1951 ch 1737 §92, operative January 1, 1952; Stats 1959 ch 637 §1; Stats 1968 ch 716 §1, operative January 1, 1969; Stats 1969 ch 339 §1; Stats 1975 ch 301 §2; Stats 1977 ch 1257 §22, effective October 3, 1977; Stats 1981 ch 900 §1; Stats 1987 ch 207 §1; Stats 1998 ch 931 §84 (SB 2139), effective September 28, 1998; Stats 2002 ch 784 §64 (SB 1316).

§633. [Section repealed 1933]

Leg.H. Enacted 1872. Repealed Stats 1933 ch 744 §198. See CCP §632.

§634. Effect of failure to resolve issue

When a statement of decision does not resolve a controverted issue, or if the statement is ambiguous and the record shows that the omission or ambiguity was brought to the attention of the trial court either prior to entry of judgment or in conjunction with a motion under Section 657 or 663, it shall not be inferred on appeal or upon a motion under Section 657 or 663 that the trial court decided in favor of the prevailing party as to those facts or on that issue. **Leg.H.** Enacted 1872. Amended Stats 1913 ch 58 §1; Stats 1933 ch 744 §106; Stats 1959 ch 637 §2; Stats 1963 ch 378 §1; Stats 1968 ch 716 §2, operative January 1, 1969; Stats 1981 ch 900 §2.

§635. Signing order conforming to minutes

In all cases where the decision of the court has been entered in its minutes, and when the judge who heard or tried the case is unavailable, the formal judgment or order conforming to the minutes may be signed by the presiding judge of the court or by a judge designated by the presiding judge. **Leg.H.** Added Stats 1965 ch 1942 §1. Amended Stats 1981 ch 900 §3; Stats 1992 ch 876 §5 (AB 3296).

Prior Law: Former CCP §635, relating to how findings are prepared, was enacted 1872, amended Code Amdts 1873–74 ch 383 §80, and repealed Code Amdts 1875–76 ch 506 §1.

§636. Proceedings after determination of issue of law

On a judgment for the plaintiff upon an issue of law, he may proceed in the manner prescribed by the first two subdivisions of section five hundred and eighty-five, upon the failure of the defendant to answer. If judgment be for the defendant upon an issue of law, and the taking of an account, or the proof of any fact, be necessary to enable the court to complete the judgment, a reference may be ordered, as in that section provided. **Leg.H.** Enacted 1872.

CHAPTER 6
OF REFERENCES AND TRIALS BY REFEREES

Appointment of referee on agreement of parties. §638.
Appointment of referee in absence of consent. §639.
Designation of referees. §640.
Legislative intent; Referral to outside referee; Collection of data and report to Legislature. §640.5.
Grounds for objection to appointment. §641.
Objection to technical qualification of referee in environmental action. §641.2.
Written objections. §642.
Requirement that referees or commissioner report within twenty days. §643.
Referee's decision; Effect; Entry of judgment. §644.
Exception and review of referee's decision. §645.
Payment of fees. §645.1.
Adoption of rules. §645.2.

§638. Appointment of referee on agreement of parties

A referee may be appointed upon the agreement of the parties filed with the clerk, or judge, or entered in the minutes, or upon the motion of a party to a written contract or lease that provides that any controversy arising therefrom shall be heard by a referee if the court finds a reference agreement exists between the parties:

(a) To hear and determine any or all of the issues in an action or proceeding, whether of fact or of law, and to report a statement of decision.

(b) To ascertain a fact necessary to enable the court to determine an action or proceeding.

(c) In any matter in which a referee is appointed pursuant to this section, a copy of the order shall be forwarded to the office of the presiding judge. The Judicial Council shall, by rule, collect information on the use of these referees. The Judicial Council shall also collect information on fees paid by the parties for the use of referees to the extent that information regarding those fees is reported to the court. The Judicial Council shall report thereon to the Legislature by July 1, 2003. This subdivision shall become inoperative on January 1, 2004. **Leg.H.** Enacted 1872. Amended Stats 1933 ch 744 §107; Stats 1951 ch 1737 §93, operative January 1, 1952; Stats 1982 ch 440 §1; Stats 1984 ch 350 §1;

Stats 2000 ch 644 §1 (AB 2912); Stats 2001 ch 44 §5 (SB 562); Stats 2002 ch 1008 §4 (AB 3028).

§639. Appointment of referee in absence of consent

(a) When the parties do not consent, the court may, upon the written motion of any party, or of its own motion, appoint a referee in the following cases pursuant to the provisions of subdivision (b) of Section 640:

(1) When the trial of an issue of fact requires the examination of a long account on either side; in which case the referees may be directed to hear and decide the whole issue, or report upon any specific question of fact involved therein.

(2) When the taking of an account is necessary for the information of the court before judgment, or for carrying a judgment or order into effect.

(3) When a question of fact, other than upon the pleadings, arises upon motion or otherwise, in any stage of the action.

(4) When it is necessary for the information of the court in a special proceeding.

(5) When the court in any pending action determines that it is necessary for the court to appoint a referee to hear and determine any and all discovery motions and disputes relevant to discovery in the action and to report findings and make a recommendation thereon.

(b) In a discovery matter, a motion to disqualify an appointed referee pursuant to Section 170.6 shall be made to the court by a party either:

(A) Within 10 days after notice of the appointment, or if the party has not yet appeared in the action, a motion shall be made within 10 days after the appearance, if a discovery referee has been appointed for all discovery purposes.

(B) At least five days before the date set for hearing, if the referee assigned is known at least 10 days before the date set for hearing and the discovery referee has been assigned only for limited discovery purposes.

(c) When a referee is appointed pursuant to paragraph (5) of subdivision (a), the order shall indicate whether the referee is being appointed for all discovery purposes in the action.

(d) All appointments of referees pursuant to this section shall be by written order and shall include the following:

(1) When the referee is appointed pursuant to paragraph (1), (2), (3), or (4) of subdivision (a), a statement of the reason the referee is being appointed.

(2) When the referee is appointed pursuant to paragraph (5) of subdivision (a), the exceptional circumstances requiring the reference, which must be specific to the circumstances of the particular case.

(3) The subject matter or matters included in the reference.

(4) The name, business address, and telephone number of the referee.

(5) The maximum hourly rate the referee may charge and, at the request of any party, the maximum number of hours for which the referee may charge. Upon the written application of any party or the referee, the court may, for good cause shown, modify the maximum number of hours subject to any findings as set forth in paragraph (6).

(6)(A) Either a finding that no party has established an economic inability to pay a pro rata share of the referee's fee or a finding that one or more parties has established an economic inability to pay a pro rata share of the referee's fees and that another party has agreed voluntarily to pay that additional share of the referee's fee. A court shall not appoint a referee at a cost to the parties if neither of these findings is made.

(B) In determining whether a party has established an inability to pay the referee's fees under subparagraph (A), the court shall consider only the ability of the party, not the party's counsel, to pay these fees. If a party is proceeding in forma pauperis, the party shall be deemed by the court to have an economic inability to pay the referee's fees. However, a determination of economic inability to pay the fees shall not be limited to parties that proceed in forma pauperis. For those parties who are not proceeding in forma pauperis, the court, in determining whether a party has established an inability to pay the fees, shall consider, among other things, the estimated cost of the referral and the impact of the proposed fees on the party's ability to proceed with the litigation.

(e) In any matter in which a referee is appointed pursuant to paragraph (5) of subdivision (a), a copy of the order appointing the referee shall be forwarded to the office of the presiding judge of the court. The Judicial Council shall, by rule, collect information on the use of these references and the reference fees charged to litigants, and shall report thereon to the Legislature by July 1, 2003. This subdivision shall become inoperative on January 1, 2004. **Leg.H.** Enacted 1872. Amended Stats 1933 ch 744 §108; Stats 1951 ch 1737 §94, operative January 1, 1952; Stats 1977 ch 1257 §23, effective October 3, 1977; Stats 1981 ch 299 §1; Stats 2000 ch 644 §2 (AB 2912), ch 1011 §1.5 (SB 2153); Stats 2001 ch 362 §1 (SB 475).

§639.5. [Section repealed 1997]

Leg.H. Added Stats 1986 ch 1263 §1, effective September 29, 1986. Repealed Stats 1996 ch 957 §2 (AB 1058). The repealed section related to entry of default orders in child support matters.

§640. Designation of referees

(a) The court shall appoint as referee or referees the person or persons, not exceeding three, agreed upon by the parties.

(b) If the parties do not agree on the selection of the referee or referees, each party shall submit to the court up to three nominees for appointment as referee and the court shall appoint one or more referees, not exceeding three, from among the nominees against whom there is no legal objection. If no nominations are received from any of the parties, the court shall appoint one or more referees, not exceeding three, against whom there is no legal objection, or the court may appoint a court commissioner of the county where the cause is pending as a referee.

(c) Participation in the referee selection procedure pursuant to this section does not constitute a waiver of grounds for objection to the appointment of a referee under Section 641 or 641.2. **Leg.H.** Enacted 1872. Amended Stats 1913 ch 166 §1; Stats 1933 ch 744 §109; Stats 1951 ch 1737 §95, operative January 1, 1952; Stats 1975 ch 1240 §6, operative July 1, 1976; Stats 2000 ch 644 §3 (AB 2912).

§640.1. [Section repealed 1997]

Leg.H. Added Stats 1986 ch 1263 §2, effective September 29, 1986. Amended Stats 1987 ch 948 §2.5; Stats 1994 ch 1266 §2 (AB 3804). Repealed Stats 1996 ch 957 §3 (AB 1058). The repealed section related to referral of applications for order to establish or enforce child support.

§640.5. Legislative intent; Referral to outside referee; Collection of data and report to Legislature

It is the intent of the Legislature that the practice and cost of referring discovery disputes to outside referees be thoroughly reviewed. Therefore, in addition to the requirements of subdivision (e) of Section 639, the Judicial Council shall collect information from the trial courts on the use of referees in discovery matters pursuant to either Sections 638 and 639. The collected data shall include information on the number of referees, the cost to the parties, and the time spent by the discovery referee. The Judicial Council shall report thereon to the Legislature by July 1, 2003. **Leg.H.** Added Stats 2001 ch 362 §2 (SB 475).

§641. Grounds for objection to appointment

A party may object to the appointment of any person as referee, on one or more of the following grounds:

(a) A want of any of the qualifications prescribed by statute to render a person competent as a juror, except a requirement of residence within a particular county in the state.

(b) Consanguinity or affinity, within the third degree, to either party, or to an officer of a corporation which is a party, or to any judge of the court in which the appointment shall be made.

(c) Standing in the relation of guardian and ward, conservator and conservatee, master and servant, employer and clerk, or principal and agent, to either party; or being a member of the family of either party; or a partner in business with either party; or security on any bond or obligation for either party.

(d) Having served as a juror or been a witness on any trial between the same parties.

(e) Interest on the part of the person in the event of the action, or in the main question involved in the action.

(f) Having formed or expressed an unqualified opinion or belief as to the merits of the action.

(g) The existence of a state of mind in the potential referee evincing enmity against or bias toward either party. **Leg.H.** Enacted 1872. Amended Stats 1897 ch 69 §2; Stats 1907 ch 378 §1; Stats 1933 ch 744 §110; Stats 1951 ch 1737 §96, operative January 1, 1952; Stats 1979 ch 730 §22, operative January 1, 1981; Stats 1997 ch 724 §1 (AB 1172); Stats 2000 ch 644 §4 (AB 2912).

§641.2. Objection to technical qualification of referee in environmental action

In any action brought under Article 8 (commencing with Section 12600) of Chapter 6, Part 2, Division 3, Title 3 of the Government Code, a party may object to the appointment of any person as referee on the ground that the person is not technically qualified with respect to the particular subject matter of the proceeding. **Leg.H.** Added Stats 1971 ch 1518 §2. Amended Stats 2000 ch 644 §5 (AB 2912).

§642. Written objections

Objections, if any, to a reference or to the referee or referees appointed by the court shall be made in writing, and must be heard and disposed of by the court, not by the referee. **Leg.H.** Added Stats 2000 ch 644 §7 (AB 2912).

Former Sections: Former CCP §642, similar to the present section, was enacted 1872 and repealed Stats 2000 ch 644 §6.

Prior Law: Former CCP §642, similar to the present section, was enacted 1872 and repealed Stats 2000 ch 644 §6.

§643. Requirement that referees or commissioner report within twenty days

(a) Unless otherwise directed by the court, the referees or commissioner must report their statement of decision in writing to the court within 20 days after the hearing, if any, has been concluded and the matter has been submitted.

(b) A referee appointed pursuant to Section 638 shall report as agreed by the parties and approved by the court.

(c) A referee appointed pursuant to Section 639 shall file with the court a report that includes a recommendation on the merits of any disputed issue, a statement of the total hours spent and the total fees charged by the referee, and the referee's recommended allocation of payment. The referee shall serve the report on all parties. Any party may file an objection to the referee's report or recommendations within 10 days after the referee serves and files the report, or within another time as the court may direct. The objection shall be served on the referee and all other parties. Responses to the objections shall be filed with the court and served on the referee and all other parties within 10 days after the objection is served. The court shall review any objections to the report and any responses submitted to those objections and shall thereafter enter appropriate orders. Nothing in this section is intended to deprive the court of its power to change the terms of the referee's appointment or to modify or disregard the referee's recommendations, and this overriding power may be exercised at any time, either on the motion of any party for good cause shown or on the court's own motion. **Leg.H.** Enacted 1872. Amended Stats 1984 ch 350 §2; Stats 2000 ch 644 §8 (AB 2912).

§644. Referee's decision; Effect; Entry of judgment

(a) In the case of a consensual general reference pursuant to Section 638, the decision of the referee or commissioner upon the whole issue must stand as the decision of the court, and upon filing of the statement of decision with the clerk of the court, judgment may be entered thereon in the same manner as if the action had been tried by the court.

(b) In the case of all other references, the decision of the referee or commissioner is only advisory. The court may adopt the referee's recommendations, in whole or in part, after independently considering the referee's findings and any objections and responses thereto filed with the court. **Leg.H.** Enacted 1872. Amended Stats 1933 ch 744 §111; Stats 1951 ch 1737 §97, operative January 1, 1952; Stats 1984 ch 350 §3; Stats 2000 ch 644 §9 (AB 2912); Stats 2007 ch 263 §8 (AB 310), effective January 1, 2008.

§645. Exception and review of referee's decision

The decision of the referee appointed pursuant to Section 638 or commissioner may be excepted to and reviewed in like manner as if made by the court. When the reference is to report the facts, the decision reported has the effect of a special verdict. **Leg.H.** Enacted 1872. Amended Stats 1984 ch 350 §4; Stats 2000 ch 644 §10 (AB 2912).

§645.1. Payment of fees

(a) When a referee is appointed pursuant to Section 638, the referee's fees shall be paid as agreed by the parties. If the parties do not agree on the payment of fees and request the matter to be resolved by the court, the court may order the parties to pay the referee's fees as set forth in subdivision (b).

(b) When a referee is appointed pursuant to Section 639, at any time after a determination of ability to pay is made as specified in paragraph (6) of subdivision (d) of Section 639, the court may order the parties to pay the fees of referees who are not employees or officers of the court at the time of appointment, as fixed pursuant to Section 1023, in any manner determined by the court to be fair and reasonable, including an apportionment of the fees among the parties. For purposes of this section, the term "parties" does not include parties' counsel. **Leg.H.** Added Stats 1981 ch 299 §2. Amended Stats 2000 ch 644 §11 (AB 2912); Stats 2001 ch 159 §38.5 (SB 662).

§645.2. Adoption of rules

The Judicial Council shall adopt all rules of court necessary to implement this chapter. **Leg.H.** Added Stats 2000 ch 644 §12 (AB 2912).

CHAPTER 7
PROVISIONS RELATING TO TRIALS IN GENERAL

Article 1. Exceptions.
Article 1.5. View by Trier of Fact.
Article 2. New Trials.

ARTICLE 1
Exceptions

"Exception"; Time for exception. §646.
Matters deemed excepted to. §647.

§646. "Exception"; Time for exception

An exception is an objection upon a matter of law to a decision made, either before or after judgment, by a court, tribunal, judge, or other judicial officer, in an action or proceeding. The exception must be taken at the time the decision is made, except as provided in section six hundred and forty-seven. **Leg.H.** Enacted Stats 1872. Amended Code Amdts 1873–74 ch 383 §81; Code Amdts 1875–76 ch 517 §1.

§647. Matters deemed excepted to

All of the following are deemed excepted to: the verdict of the jury; the final decision in an action or proceeding; an interlocutory order or decision, finally determining the rights of the parties, or some of them; an order or decision from which an appeal may be taken; an order sustaining or overruling a demurrer, allowing or refusing to allow an amendment to a pleading, striking out or refusing to strike out a pleading or a portion thereof, or refusing a continuance; an order made upon ex parte application, giving an instruction, refusing to give an instruction, or modifying an instruction requested; an order or decision made in the absence of the party or an order granting or denying a nonsuit or a motion to strike out evidence or testimony; a ruling sustaining or overruling an objection to evidence; and any statement or other action of the court in commenting upon or in summarizing the evidence. If the party, at the time when the order, ruling, action or decision is sought or made, or within a reasonable time thereafter, makes known his position thereon, by objection or otherwise, all other orders, rulings, actions or decisions are deemed to have been excepted to. **Leg.H.** Enacted Stats 1872. Amended Code Amdts 1875–76 ch 517 §2; Stats 1907 ch 379 §1; Stats 1909 ch 355 §1; Stats 1939 ch 335 §1; Stats 1941 ch 1256 §1; Stats 1953 ch 715 §1; Stats 1963 ch 99 §1.

§648. [Section repealed 1945]

Leg.H. Enacted Stats 1872. Amended Code Amdts 1875–76 ch 517 §3. Repealed Stats 1945 ch 40 §16. The repealed section related to requirements for statement of exception.

§649. [Section repealed 1945]

Leg.H. Enacted Stats 1872. Amended Code Amdts 1875–76 ch 517 §4; Stats 1907 ch 379 §2; Stats 1911 ch 222 §1; Stats 1933 ch 744 §113. Repealed Stats 1945 ch 40 §16. The repealed section related to presentation of bill of exception at time of ruling.

§650. [Section repealed 1945]

Leg.H. Enacted Stats 1872. Amended Code Amdts 1873–74 ch 383 §82; Stats 1907 ch 379 §3; Stats 1909 ch 657 §1; Stats 1911 ch 221 §1; Stats 1915 ch 114 §1; Stats 1929 ch 479 §1; Stats 1933 ch 744 §114; Stats 1935 ch 722 §11. Repealed Stats 1945 ch 40 §16. The repealed section related to presentation of bill of exception subsequent to ruling.

ARTICLE 1.5
View by Trier of Fact

Subject of view; Procedure. §651.

§651. Subject of view; Procedure

(a) On its own motion or on the motion of a party, where the court finds that such a view would be proper and would aid the trier of fact in its determination of the case, the court may order a view of any of the following:

(1) The property which is the subject of litigation.

(2) The place where any relevant event occurred.

(3) Any object, demonstration, or experiment, a view of which is relevant and admissible in evidence in the case and which cannot with reasonable convenience be viewed in the courtroom.

(b) On such occasion, the entire court, including the judge, jury, if any, court reporter, if any, and any necessary officers, shall proceed to the place, property, object, demonstration, or experiment to be viewed. The court shall be in session throughout the view. At the view, the court may permit testimony of witnesses. The proceedings at the view shall be recorded to the same extent as the proceedings in the courtroom. **Leg.H.** Added Stats 1975 ch 301 §3.

Prior Law: Former CCP §651, relating to exceptions after judgment, was enacted Stats 1872, amended Code Amdts 1873–1874 ch 383 §83, Stats 1907 ch 379 §4, Stats 1919 ch 193 §1, Stats 1933 ch 744 §115, and repealed Stats 1945 ch 40 §16.

§652. [Section repealed 1965]

Leg.H. Enacted Stats 1872. Amended Stats 1907 ch 379 §5; Stats 1933 ch 744 §116. Repealed Stats 1965 ch 414 §1. The repealed section related to petition to Supreme Court to prove exception disallowed by judge.

§653. [Section repealed 1945]

Leg.H. Enacted Stats 1872. Amended Code Amdts 1875–76 ch 505 §1; Stats 1933 ch 744 §117. Repealed Stats 1945 ch 40 §16. The repealed section related to procedure for settling bill after presiding judge ceased to hold office.

ARTICLE 2
New Trials

Definition of new trial. §656.
Grounds for new trial; Requisites of order granting new trial for insufficiency of evidence. §657.
Grounds; Death or disability of reporter; Loss or destruction of notes of reporter. §657.1.
Manner of making application for new trial. §658.
Notice of motion; Filing and service; Time; Contents; Extension of time. §659.
Moving, opposing, and reply briefs and accompanying documents; Extension of service and filing deadlines. §659a.
Hearing of motion; Attendance of reporter and reading of notes; Precedence of new trial proceedings; Expiration of court's power and automatic denial of motion; Entry of order. §660.
Judge who may hear motion; Oral argument; Notice; Time for hearing. §661.
Powers of court in case tried without jury. §662.
Grant of new trial, for inadequate or excessive damages, subject to denial on consent to additur or remittitur. §662.5.
Grounds for vacation of judgment and entry of different judgment. §663.
Notice of intention to move to set aside and vacate judgment; Filing and service; Contents; Time limits; Entry of order; Moving, opposing, and reply briefs and accompanying documents; Hearing; Review. §663a.
[Section renumbered 1908]. §663½.
Right to new trial when bill of exceptions is lost or destroyed. §663.1.
Extension of time pending hearing of motion. §663.2.

§655. [Section repealed 2003]

Leg.H. Added Stats 1935 ch 722 §12. Amended Stats 1977 ch 1257 §24, effective October 3, 1977; Stats 1998 ch 931 §85 (SB 2139), effective September 28, 1998. Repealed Stats 2002 ch 784 §65 (SB 1316). The repealed section related to the application of the article to municipal or superior courts.

§656. Definition of new trial

A new trial is a re-examination of an issue of fact in the same court after a trial and decision by a jury, court or referee. **Leg.H.** Enacted Stats 1872. Amended Stats 1907 ch 380 §1.

§657. Grounds for new trial; Requisites of order granting new trial for insufficiency of evidence

The verdict may be vacated and any other decision may be modified or vacated, in whole or in part, and a new or further trial granted on all or part of the issues, on the application of the party aggrieved, for any of the following causes, materially affecting the substantial rights of such party:

1. Irregularity in the proceedings of the court, jury or adverse party, or any order of the court or abuse of discretion by which either party was prevented from having a fair trial.

2. Misconduct of the jury; and whenever any one or more of the jurors have been induced to assent to any general or special verdict, or to a finding on any question submitted to them by the court, by a resort to the determination of chance, such misconduct may be proved by the affidavit of any one of the jurors.

3. Accident or surprise, which ordinary prudence could not have guarded against.

4. Newly discovered evidence, material for the party making the application, which he could not, with reasonable diligence, have discovered and produced at the trial.

5. Excessive or inadequate damages.

6. Insufficiency of the evidence to justify the verdict or other decision, or the verdict or other decision is against law.

7. Error in law, occurring at the trial and excepted to by the party making the application.

When a new trial is granted, on all or part of the issues, the court shall specify the ground or grounds upon which it is granted and the court's reason or reasons for granting the new trial upon each ground stated.

A new trial shall not be granted upon the ground of insufficiency of the evidence to justify the verdict or other decision, nor upon the ground of excessive or inadequate damages, unless after weighing the evidence the court is convinced from the entire record, including reasonable inferences therefrom, that the court or jury clearly should have reached a different verdict or decision.

The order passing upon and determining the motion must be made and entered as provided in Section 660 and if the motion is granted must state the ground or grounds relied upon by the court, and may contain the specification of reasons. If an order granting such motion does not contain such specification of reasons, the court must, within 10 days after filing such order, prepare, sign and file such specification of reasons in writing with the clerk. The court shall not direct the attorney for a party to prepare either or both said order and said specification of reasons.

On appeal from an order granting a new trial the order shall be affirmed if it should have been granted upon any ground stated in the motion, whether or not specified in the order or specification of reasons, except that (a) the order shall not be affirmed upon the ground of the insufficiency of the evidence to justify the verdict or other decision, or upon the ground of excessive or inadequate damages, unless such ground is stated in the order granting the motion and (b) on appeal from an order granting a new trial upon the ground of the insufficiency of the evidence to justify the verdict or other decision, or upon the ground of excessive or inadequate damages, it shall be conclusively presumed that said order as to such ground was made only for the reasons specified in said order or said specification of reasons, and such order shall be reversed as to such ground only if there is no substantial basis in the record for any of such reasons. **Leg.H.** Enacted Stats 1872. Amended Stats 1919 ch 100 §1; Stats 1929 ch 479 §2; Stats 1939 ch 713 §1; Stats 1965 ch 1749 §1; Stats 1967 ch 72 §1.

§657.1. Grounds; Death or disability of reporter; Loss or destruction of notes of reporter

A new trial may also be granted as provided in Section 914 of this code. **Leg.H.** Added Stats 1968 ch 387 §1.

§658. Manner of making application for new trial

When the application is made for a cause mentioned in the first, second, third and fourth subdivisions of Section 657, it must be made upon affidavits; otherwise it must be made on the minutes of the court. **Leg.H.** Enacted Stats 1872. Amended Code Amdts 1873–74 ch 383 §84; Stats 1915 ch 107 §1; Stats 1983 ch 1167 §9.

§659. Notice of motion; Filing and service; Time; Contents; Extension of time

(a) The party intending to move for a new trial shall file with the clerk and serve upon each adverse party a notice of [1] **their** intention to move for a new trial, designating the grounds upon which the motion will be made and whether the same will be made upon affidavits or the minutes of the court, or both, either:

(1) After the decision is rendered and before the entry of judgment.

(2) Within 15 days of the date of [2] **serving** notice of entry of judgment by the clerk of the court pursuant to Section 664.5, or service upon [3] **them** by any party of written notice of entry of judgment, or within 180 days after the entry of judgment, whichever is earliest; provided, that upon the filing of the first notice of intention to move for

a new trial by a party, each other party shall have 15 days after the service of that notice upon [4] **them** to file and serve a notice of intention to move for a new trial.

(b) That notice of intention to move for a new trial shall be deemed to be a motion for a new trial on all the grounds stated in the notice. The times specified in paragraphs (1) and (2) of subdivision (a) shall not be extended by order or stipulation or by those provisions of Section 1013 that extend the time for exercising a right or doing an act where service is by mail. **Leg.H.** Enacted Stats 1872. Amended Code Amdts 1873–74 ch 383 §85; Stats 1907 ch 380 §2; Stats 1915 ch 107 §2; Stats 1923 ch 367 §1; Stats 1929 ch 479 §3; Stats 1951 ch 801 §2, effective January 1, 1952; Stats 1959 ch 469 §1; Stats 1961 ch 604 §2; Stats 1965 ch 1890 §1.5; Stats 1967 ch 169 §1; Stats 1970 ch 621 §1; Stats 2012 ch 83 §1 (AB 2106), effective January 1, 2013; Stats 2024 ch 853 §20 (AB 3281), effective January 1, 2025.

§659. 2024 Deletes. [1] his or her [2] mailing [3] him or her [4] him or her

§659a. Moving, opposing, and reply briefs and accompanying documents; Extension of service and filing deadlines

Within 10 days of filing the notice, the moving party shall serve upon all other parties and file any brief and accompanying documents, including affidavits in support of the motion. The other parties shall have 10 days after that service within which to serve upon the moving party and file any opposing briefs and accompanying documents, including counter-affidavits. The moving party shall have five days after that service to file any reply brief and accompanying documents. These deadlines may, for good cause shown by affidavit or by written stipulation of the parties, be extended by any judge for an additional period not to exceed 10 days. **Leg.H.** Added Stats 1929 ch 479 §4. Amended Stats 1933 ch 744 §118; Stats 1935 ch 722 §13; Stats 1989 ch 1416 §20; Stats 2014 ch 93 §2 (AB 1659), effective January 1, 2015.

§660. Hearing of motion; Attendance of reporter and reading of notes; Precedence of new trial proceedings; Expiration of court's power and automatic denial of motion; Entry of order

(a) On the hearing of the motion, reference may be had in all cases to the pleadings and orders of the court on file, and when the motion is made on the minutes, reference may also be had to any depositions and documentary evidence offered at the trial and to the report of the proceedings on the trial taken by the phonographic reporter, or to any certified transcript of the report or if there be no such report or certified transcript, to proceedings occurring at the trial that are within the recollection of the judge; when the proceedings at the trial have been phonographically reported, but the reporter's notes have not been transcribed, the reporter shall, upon request of the court or either party, attend the hearing of the motion and read his or her notes, or such parts thereof as the court, or either party, may require.

(b) The hearing and determination of the motion for a new trial shall have precedence over all other matters except criminal cases, probate matters, and cases actually on trial, and it shall be the duty of the court to determine the motion at the earliest possible moment.

(c) Except as otherwise provided in Section 12a of this code, the power of the court to rule on a motion for a new trial shall expire 75 days after the mailing of notice of entry of judgment by the clerk of the court pursuant to Section 664.5 or 75 days after service on the moving party by any party of written notice of entry of judgment, whichever is earlier, or if that notice has not been given, 75 days after the filing of the first notice of intention to move for a new trial. If the motion is not determined within the 75-day period, or within that period as extended, the effect shall be a denial of the motion without further order of the court. A motion for a new trial is not determined within the meaning of this section until an order ruling on the motion is entered in the permanent minutes of the court or signed by the judge and filed with the clerk. The entry of a new trial order in the permanent minutes of the court shall constitute a determination of the motion even though that minute order, as entered, expressly directs that a written order be prepared, signed, and filed. The minute entry shall in all cases show the date on which the order is entered in the permanent minutes, but failure to comply with this direction shall not impair the validity or effectiveness of the order. **Leg.H.** Enacted Stats 1872. Amended Code Amdts 1873–74 ch 383 §86; Stats 1907 ch 380 §3; Stats 1915 ch 107 §3; Stats 1917 ch 156 §1; Stats 1923 ch 105 §1; Stats 1929 ch 479 §5; Stats 1933 ch 29 §5; Stats 1959 ch 468 §1; Stats 1969 ch 87 §1; Stats 1970 ch 621 §2; Stats 2018 ch 317 §1 (AB 2230), effective January 1, 2019.

§661. Judge who may hear motion; Oral argument; Notice; Time for hearing

The motion for a new trial shall be heard and determined by the judge who presided at the trial; provided, however, that in case of the inability of such judge or if at the time noticed for hearing thereon he is absent from the county where the trial was had, the same shall be heard and determined by any other judge of the same court. Upon the expiration of the time to file counter-affidavits the clerk forthwith shall call the motion to the attention of the judge who presided at the trial, or the judge acting in his place, as the case may be, and such judge thereupon shall designate the time for oral argument, if any, to be had on said motion. Five (5) days' notice by mail shall be given of such oral argument, if any, by the clerk to the respective parties. Such motion, if heard by a judge other than the trial judge shall be argued orally or shall be submitted without oral argument, as the judge may direct, not later than ten (10) days before the expiration of the time within which the court has power to pass on the same. **Leg.H.** Added Stats 1929 ch 479 §6. Amended Stats 1931 ch 768 §1; Stats 1933 ch 744 §119.

Prior Law: Former CCP §661, relating to judge's statement on decision of motion, was enacted Stats 1872, amended Code Amdts 1873–74 ch 383 §87, and repealed Stats 1915 ch 107 §4.

§662. Powers of court in case tried without jury

In ruling on such motion, in a cause tried without a jury, the court may, on such terms as may be just, change or add to the statement of decision, modify the judgment, in whole or in part, vacate the judgment, in whole or in part, and grant a new trial on all or part of the issues, or, in lieu of granting a new trial, may vacate and set aside the statement of decision and judgment and reopen the case for further proceedings and the introduction of additional evidence with the same effect as if the case had been reopened after the submission thereof and before a decision had been filed or judgment rendered. Any judgment thereafter entered shall be subject to the provisions of sections 657 and 659. **Leg.H.** Added Stats 1929 ch 479 §7. Amended Stats 1981 ch 900 §4.

Prior Law: Former CCP §662, relating to new trial on motion of court, was added Code Amdts 1873–74 ch 383 §88 and repealed Stats 1915 ch 107 §5.

§662.5. Grant of new trial, for inadequate or excessive damages, subject to denial on consent to additur or remittitur

(a) In any civil action where after trial by jury an order granting a new trial limited to the issue of damages would be proper, the trial court may in its discretion:

(1) If the ground for granting a new trial is inadequate damages, issue a conditional order granting the new trial unless the party against whom the verdict has been rendered consents to the addition of damages in an amount the court in its independent judgment determines from the evidence to be fair and reasonable.

(2) If the ground for granting a new trial is excessive damages, issue a conditional order granting the new trial unless the party in whose favor the verdict has been rendered consents to the reduction of so much thereof as the court in its independent judgment determines from the evidence to be fair and reasonable.

(b) If a deadline for acceptance or rejection of the addition or reduction of damages is not set forth in the conditional order, the deadline is 30 days from the date the conditional order is served by the clerk of the court. Failure to respond to the order in accordance with this section shall be deemed a rejection of the addition or reduction of damages and a new trial limited to the issue of damages shall be granted automatically.

(c) A party filing and serving an acceptance of a conditionally ordered addition or reduction of damages shall concurrently serve and submit to the court a proposed amended judgment reflecting the modified judgment amount, as well as any other uncontested judgment awards. **Leg.H.** Added Stats 1967 ch 72 §2. Amended Stats 1969 ch 115 §1; Stats 2011 ch 409 §2 (AB 1403), effective January 1, 2012.

§663. Grounds for vacation of judgment and entry of different judgment

A judgment or decree, when based upon a decision by the court, or the special verdict of a jury, may, upon motion of the party aggrieved, be set aside and vacated by the same court, and another and different judgment entered, for either of the following causes, materially affecting the substantial rights of the party and entitling the party to a different judgment:

1. Incorrect or erroneous legal basis for the decision, not consistent with or not supported by the facts; and in such case when the judgment is set aside, the statement of decision shall be amended and corrected.

2. A judgment or decree not consistent with or not supported by the special verdict. **Leg.H.** Added Stats 1897 ch 67 §1. Amended Stats 1933 ch 744 §120; Stats 1981 ch 900 §5.

Prior Law: Former CCP §663, providing when motions for new trial might be brought to hearing, was added Code Amdts 1873–74 ch 383 §88, amended Code Amdts 1877–78 ch 166 §1, and repealed Code Amdts 1880 ch 70 §1.

§663a. Notice of intention to move to set aside and vacate judgment; Filing and service; Contents; Time limits; Entry of order; Moving, opposing, and reply briefs and accompanying documents; Hearing; Review

(a) A party intending to make a motion to set aside and vacate a judgment, as described in Section 663, shall file with the clerk and serve upon the adverse party a notice of his or her intention, designating the grounds upon which the motion will be made, and specifying the particulars in which the legal basis for the decision is not consistent with or supported by the facts, or in which the judgment or decree is not consistent with the special verdict, either:

(1) After the decision is rendered and before the entry of judgment.

(2) Within 15 days of the date of mailing of notice of entry of judgment by the clerk of the court pursuant to Section 664.5, or service upon him or her by any party of written notice of entry of judgment, or within 180 days after the entry of judgment, whichever is earliest.

(b) Except as otherwise provided in Section 12a, the power of the court to rule on a motion to set aside and vacate a judgment shall expire 75 days from the mailing of notice of entry of judgment by the clerk of the court pursuant to Section 664.5, or 75 days after service upon the moving party by any party of written notice of entry of the judgment, whichever is earlier, or if that notice has not been given, 75 days after the filing of the first notice of intention to move to set aside and vacate the judgment. If that motion is not determined within the 75-day period, or within that period as extended, the effect shall be a denial of the motion without further order of the court. A motion to set aside and vacate a judgment is not determined within the meaning of this section until an order ruling on the motion is entered in the permanent minutes of the court, or signed by the judge and filed with the clerk. The entry of an order to set aside and vacate the judgment in the permanent minutes of the court shall constitute a determination of the motion even though that minute order, as entered, expressly directs that a written order be prepared, signed, and filed. The minute entry shall, in all cases, show the date on which the order is entered in the permanent minutes, but failure to comply with this direction shall not impair the validity or effectiveness of the order.

(c) The provisions of Section 1013 extending the time for exercising a right or doing an act where service is by mail shall not apply to extend the times specified in paragraphs (1) and (2) of subdivision (a).

(d) The moving, opposing, and reply briefs and any accompanying documents shall be filed and served within the periods specified by Section 659a and the hearing on the motion shall be set in the same manner as the hearing on a motion for new trial under Section 660.

(e) An order of the court granting a motion may be reviewed on appeal in the same manner as a special order made after final judgment. **Leg.H.** Added Stats 1897 ch 67 §1, as CCP §663½. Amended and renumbered by Stats 1907 ch 380 §4; Amended Stats 1915 ch 108 §1; Stats 1959 ch 469 §2; Stats 1965 ch 1890 §2; Stats 1967 ch 119 §1, ch 169 §2; Stats 1983 ch 302 §1; Stats 2012 ch 83 §2 (AB 2106), effective January 1, 2013; Stats 2014 ch 93 §3 (AB 1659), effective January 1, 2015; Stats 2018 ch 317 §2 (AB 2230), effective January 1, 2019.

§663½. [Section renumbered 1908]

Leg.H. Added Stats 1897 ch 57 §1. Amended and renumbered CCP §663a by Stats 1907 ch 380 §4.

§663.1. Right to new trial when bill of exceptions is lost or destroyed

The court may grant a new trial of any action or proceeding when all of the following conditions exist:

(a) Any proposed bill of exceptions or statement of the case on motion for a new trial is lost or destroyed by reason of conflagration or other public calamity.

(b) No other record of the proceedings upon the trial thereof can be obtained.

(c) Such action or proceeding is subject to review by motion for new trial pending at the time of such loss or destruction.

(d) The court in which such action or proceeding is pending deems it impossible or impracticable to restore such proceedings and to settle a bill of exceptions or statement of the case containing such proceedings, so as to enable the court to review the judgment or order therein by motion for new trial.

(e) At the time of such loss or destruction a motion for new trial was pending.

In order to grant such new trial, it shall be unnecessary to have any bill of exceptions or statement of the case settled, but upon the facts recited in this section being shown to the satisfaction of the court by affidavit or otherwise, the court may grant such new trial. **Leg.H.** Added Stats 1953 ch 52 §2.

§663.2. Extension of time pending hearing of motion

Pending the hearing of a motion pursuant to Section 663.1 to grant a new trial, the time within which a bill of exceptions may be prepared, served, or presented for settlement shall be extended and shall not commence to run until the decision upon the motion. The motion must be made within 30 days after the loss or destruction of the records. **Leg.H.** Added Stats 1953 ch 52 §3.

CHAPTER 8
THE MANNER OF GIVING AND ENTERING JUDGMENT

Time limits for entry of judgment; Entry as condition to effectiveness of judgment. §664.
Notice of entry of judgment. §664.5.
Judgment pursuant to terms of settlement. §664.6.
Construction defect action settlement. §664.7.
Bringing case before court for argument. §665.
Judgment for defendant for excess or affirmative relief; Remission of sum exceeding court's jurisdiction. §666.
Recovery of personal property. §667.
Medical negligence actions. §667.7.
Judgment book. §668.
Exceptions from requirement of keeping judgment book. §668.5.
Death of party before judgment. §669.
Judgment roll. §670.
Assignee of record; Acknowledgment of assignment of judgment. §673.
Abstract of judgment. §674.

§664. Time limits for entry of judgment; Entry as condition to effectiveness of judgment

When trial by jury has been had, judgment must be entered by the clerk, in conformity to the verdict within 24 hours after the rendition of the verdict, whether or not a motion for judgment notwithstanding the verdict be pending, unless the court order the case to be reserved for argument or further consideration, or grant a stay of proceedings. If the trial has been had by the court, judgment must be entered by the clerk, in conformity to the decision of the court, immediately upon the filing of such decision. In no case is a judgment effectual for any purpose until entered. **Leg.H.** Enacted Stats 1872. Amended Stats 1907 ch 381 §1; Stats 1933 ch 744 §121; Stats 1951 ch 1737 §98, operative January 1, 1952; Stats 1961 ch 604 §3; Stats 1977 ch 1257 §25, effective October 3, 1977.

§664.5. Notice of entry of judgment

(a) In any contested action or special proceeding other than a small claims action or an action or proceeding in which a prevailing party is not represented by counsel, the party submitting an order or judgment for entry shall prepare and serve, a copy of the notice of entry of judgment to all parties who have appeared in the action or proceeding and shall file with the court the original notice of entry of judgment together with the proof of service. This subdivision does not apply in a proceeding for dissolution of marriage, for nullity of marriage, or for legal separation.

(b) Promptly upon entry of judgment in a contested action or special proceeding in which a prevailing party is not represented by counsel, the clerk of the court shall serve notice of entry of judgment to all parties who have appeared in the action or special proceeding and shall execute a certificate of service and place it in the court's file in the cause.

(c) For purposes of this section, "judgment" includes any judgment, decree, or signed order from which an appeal lies.

(d) Upon order of the court in any action or special proceeding, the clerk shall serve notice of entry of any judgment or ruling, whether or not appealable.

(e) The Judicial Council shall provide by rule of court that, upon entry of judgment in a contested action or special proceeding in which a state statute or regulation has been declared unconstitutional by the court, the Attorney General is promptly notified of the judgment and that a certificate of that service is placed in the court's file in the cause. **Leg.H.** Added Stats 1965 ch 1890 §3. Amended Stats 1967 ch 169 §3, ch 1428 §1; Stats 1969 ch 87 §2; Stats 1977 ch 1257 §26, effective October 3, 1977; Stats 1981 ch 904 §1; Stats 1982 ch 559 §1, effective August 24, 1982; Stats 1993 ch 158 §3.05 (AB 392), effective July 20, 1993; Stats 1996 ch 1061 §1 (SB 1033); Stats 1997 ch 259 §1 (AB 380); Stats 2016 ch 703 §8 (AB 2881), effective January 1, 2017; Stats 2017 ch 319 §1 (AB 976), effective January 1, 2018.

Prior Law: There was another section of this number which was amended Stats 1992 ch 163 §27, to become operative January 1, 1994, and repealed Stats 1993 ch 158 §3.1, effective July 20, 1993.

§664.6. Judgment pursuant to terms of settlement

(a) If parties to pending litigation stipulate, in a writing signed by the parties outside of the presence of the court or orally before the court, for settlement of the case, or part thereof, the court, upon motion, may enter judgment pursuant to the terms of the settlement. If the parties to the settlement agreement or their counsel stipulate in writing or orally before the court, the court may dismiss the case as to the settling parties without prejudice and retain jurisdiction over the parties to enforce the settlement until performance in full of the terms of the settlement.

(b) For purposes of this section, a writing is signed by a party if it is signed by any of the following:

(1) The party.

(2) An attorney who represents the party.

(3) If an insurer is defending and indemnifying a party to the action, an agent who is authorized in writing by the insurer to sign on the party's behalf. This paragraph does not apply if the party whom the insurer is defending would be liable under the terms of the settlement for any amount above the policy limits.

(c) Paragraphs (2) and (3) of subdivision (b) do not apply in a civil harassment action, an action brought pursuant to the Family Code, an action brought pursuant to the Probate Code, or a matter that is being adjudicated in a juvenile court or a dependency court.

(d) In addition to any available civil remedies, an attorney who signs a writing on behalf of a party pursuant to subdivision (b) without the party's express authorization shall, absent good cause, be subject to professional discipline.

(e)(1) If a plaintiff, cross-complainant, or other party seeking affirmative relief has filed a notice of conditional settlement, the court may, upon its own motion, without stipulation from the parties or their counsel, set an order to show cause as to why the court should not dismiss the entire action without prejudice and retain jurisdiction to enforce the settlement.

(2) This subdivision does not apply to actions brought pursuant to Chapter 5 of Title 3 of Part 2 of the Code of Civil Procedure (commencing with Section 378) and Part 13 of Division 2 of the Labor Code (commencing with Section 2698).

(f) If the Court enters judgment or dismisses the case without prejudice pursuant to this section, the following shall apply:

(1) A party may file a motion or other document pertaining to the settlement, including an application for determination of good faith settlement, a motion for the reduction or determination of a lien, a petition related to the compromise of the claim of a minor or person with a disability, or, if the terms of a settlement are not performed, a motion based upon such terms. Responsive filings and related documents may also be filed.

(2) The court shall exercise its retained jurisdiction if a party files a notice that a written settlement agreement required of all parties was not signed by all parties.

(3) A party who has paid a first appearance fee shall not be assessed a first appearance fee again for filing a motion, notice or other document pertaining to the settlement after entry of judgment or dismissal without prejudice.

(4) The clerk of the court shall accept any motion, notice, or other document properly filed by a party after entry of judgment or dismissal without prejudice.

(g) Nothing in this section shall preclude a party from filing a request for dismissal with prejudice after the court has dismissed the case without prejudice pursuant to this section.

(h) On or before January 1, 2025, the Judicial Council shall update or develop new forms or Rules of Court as necessary to implement this section.

(i) This section shall become operative on January 1, 2025. **Leg.H.** Added Stats 2023 ch 478 §13 (AB 1756), effective January 1, 2024, operative January 1, 2025.

Prior Law Former CCP §664.6, relating to judgment pursuant to terms of settlement, was added Stats 1981 ch 904 §2, amended Stats 1993 ch 768 §1 (SB 252); Stats 1994 ch 587 §7 (AB 3600); Stats 2020 ch 290 §1 (AB 2723), effective January 1, 2021; Stats 2023 ch 478 §12 (AB 1756), effective January 1, 2024, repealed January 1, 2025.

§664.7. Construction defect action settlement

(a) Notwithstanding Section 664.6, if parties to a pending construction defect action stipulate personally or, where a party's contribution is paid on its behalf pursuant to a policy of insurance, the parties stipulate through their respective counsel, in a writing signed by the parties outside the presence of the court or orally before the court, for settlement of the case, or part thereof, the court, upon motion, may enter judgment pursuant to the terms of the settlement. If requested by the parties, the court may retain jurisdiction over the parties to enforce the settlement until performance in full of the terms of the settlement.

(b) It is the intent of the Legislature that this section modify the holding of Levy v. Superior Court (1995), 10 Cal. 4th 578, regarding the authority of counsel in a construction defect action to bind a party to a settlement.

(c) For purposes of this section, "construction defect action" shall mean any civil action that seeks monetary recovery against a developer, builder, design professional, general contractor, material supplier, or subcontractor of any residential dwelling based upon a claim for alleged defects in the design or construction of the residential dwelling unit. **Leg.H.** Added Stats 1998 ch 856 §1 (AB 1950).

§665. Bringing case before court for argument

When the case is reserved for argument or further consideration, as mentioned in the last section, it may be brought by either party before the court for argument. **Leg.H.** Enacted Stats 1872.

§666. Judgment for defendant for excess or affirmative relief; Remission of sum exceeding court's jurisdiction

If a claim asserted in a cross-complaint is established at the trial and the amount so established exceeds the demand established by the party against whom the cross-complaint is asserted, judgment for the party asserting the cross-complaint must be given for the excess; or if it appears that the party asserting the cross-complaint is entitled to any other affirmative relief, judgment must be given accordingly.

When the amount found due to either party exceeds the sum for which the court is authorized to enter judgment, such party may remit the excess, and judgment may be rendered for the residue. **Leg.H.** Enacted Stats 1872. Amended Stats 1933 ch 744 §122; Stats 1971 ch 244 §54, operative July 1, 1972.

§667. Recovery of personal property

In an action to recover the possession of personal property, judgment for the plaintiff may be for the possession or the value thereof, in case a delivery cannot be had, and damages for the detention. If the property has been delivered to the plaintiff, and the defendant claim a return thereof judgment for the defendant may be for a return of the property or the value thereof, in case a return cannot be had, and damages for taking and withholding the same. **Leg.H.** Enacted Stats 1872. Amended Stats 1933 ch 744 §123; Stats 1973 ch 20 §7; Stats 1982 ch 497 §37, operative July 1, 1983.

§667a. [Section repealed 1977]

Leg.H. Added Stats 1965 ch 1890 §5. Amended Stats 1967 ch 169 §4, ch 1428 §2; Stats 1969 ch 87 §3. Repealed Stats 1977 ch 1257 §27, effective October 3, 1977. See CCP §664.5.

Prior Law: Former CCP §667a, relating to notice of judgment in justice courts, was added Stats 1933 ch 744 §123a, amended Stats 1935 ch 722 §14, Stats 1951 ch 1737 §99, operative January 1, 1952, and repealed Stats 1965 ch 1890 §4.

§667.7. Medical negligence actions

(a) In any action for injury or damages against a provider of health care services, a superior court shall, at the request of either party, enter a judgment ordering that money damages or its equivalent for future damages of the judgment creditor be paid in whole or in part by periodic payments rather than by a lump-sum payment if the award equals or exceeds two hundred fifty thousand dollars ($250,000) in future damages. In entering a judgment ordering the payment of future damages by periodic payments, the court shall make a specific finding as to the dollar amount of periodic payments which will compensate the judgment creditor for such future damages. As a condition to authorizing periodic payments of future damages, the court shall require the judgment debtor who is not adequately insured to post security adequate to assure full payment of such damages awarded by the judgment. Upon termination of periodic payments of future damages, the court shall order the return of this security, or so much as remains, to the judgment debtor.

(b)(1) The judgment ordering the payment of future damages by periodic payments shall specify the recipient or recipients of the payments, the dollar amount of the payments, the interval between payments, and the number of payments or the period of time over which payments shall be made. Such payments shall only be subject to modification in the event of the death of the judgment creditor.

(2) In the event that the court finds that the judgment debtor has exhibited a continuing pattern of failing to make the payments, as specified in paragraph (1), the court shall find the judgment debtor in contempt of court and, in addition to the required periodic payments, shall order the judgment debtor to pay the judgment creditor all damages caused by the failure to make such periodic payments, including court costs and attorney's fees.

(c) However, money damages awarded for loss of future earnings shall not be reduced or payments terminated by reason of the death of the judgment creditor, but shall be paid to persons to whom the judgment creditor owed a duty of support, as provided by law, immediately prior to their death. In such cases the court which rendered the original judgment, may, upon petition of any party in interest, modify the judgment to award and apportion the unpaid future damages in accordance with this subdivision.

(d) Following the occurrence or expiration of all obligations specified in the periodic payment judgment, any obligation of the judgment debtor to make further payments shall cease and any security given, pursuant to subdivision (a) shall revert to the judgment debtor.

(e) As used in this section:

(1) "Future damages" includes damages for future medical treatment, care or custody, loss of future earnings, loss of bodily function, or future pain and suffering of the judgment creditor.

(2) "Periodic payments" means the payment of money or delivery of other property to the judgment creditor at regular intervals.

(3) "Health care provider" means any person licensed or certified pursuant to Division 2 (commencing with Section 500) of the Business and Professions Code, or licensed pursuant to the Osteopathic Initiative Act, or the Chiropractic Initiative Act, or licensed pursuant to Chapter 2.5 (commencing with Section 1440) of Division 2 of the Health and Safety Code; and any clinic, health dispensary, or health facility, licensed pursuant to Division 2 (commencing with Section 1200) of the Health and Safety Code. "Health care provider" includes the legal representatives of a health care provider.

(4) "Professional negligence" means a negligent act or omission to act by a health care provider in the rendering of professional services, which act or omission is the proximate cause of a personal injury or wrongful death, provided that such services are within the scope of services for which the provider is licensed and which are not within any restriction imposed by the licensing agency or licensed hospital.

(f) It is the intent of the Legislature in enacting this section to authorize the entry of judgments in malpractice actions against health care providers which provide for the payment of future damages through periodic payments rather than lump-sum payments. By authorizing periodic payment judgments, it is the further intent of the Legislature that the courts will utilize such judgments to provide compensation sufficient to meet the needs of an injured plaintiff and those persons who are dependent on the plaintiff for whatever period is necessary while eliminating the potential windfall from a lump-sum recovery which was intended to provide for the care of an injured plaintiff over an extended period who then dies shortly after the judgment is paid, leaving the balance of the judgment award to persons and purposes for which it was not intended. It is also the intent of the Legislature that all elements of the periodic payment program be specified with certainty in the judgment ordering such payments and that the judgment not be subject to modification at some future time which might alter the specifications of the original judgment. **Leg.H.** Added Stats 1975 2nd Ex Sess ch 1 §26. Amended Stats 1975 2nd Ex Sess ch 2 §1.194, effective September 26, 1975, operative December 12, 1975; Stats 2022 ch 17 §4 (AB 35), effective January 1, 2023.

§668. Judgment book

Except as provided in Section 668.5, the clerk of the superior court, must keep, with the records of the court, a book called the "judgment book," in which judgments must be entered. **Leg.H.** Enacted Stats 1872. Amended Stats 1933 ch 744 §124; Stats 1951 ch 1737 §100, operative January 1, 1952; Stats 1973 ch 185 §1; Stats 1974 ch 219 §1, ch 1169 §1; Stats 1977 ch 1257 §28, effective October 3, 1977; Stats 1998 ch 931 §86 (SB 2139), effective September 28, 1998; Stats 2002 ch 784 §66 (SB 1316).

§668.5. Exceptions from requirement of keeping judgment book

In those counties where the clerk of the court places individual judgments in the file of actions and either a microfilm copy of the individual judgment is made, or the judgment is entered in the register of actions, or into the court's electronic data-processing system, prior to placement of the judgment in the file of actions, the clerk shall not be required to enter judgments in a judgment book, and the date of filing the judgment with the clerk shall constitute the date of its entry. **Leg.H.** Added Stats 1974 ch 1169 §2. Amended Stats 1983 ch 464 §1.

§669. Death of party before judgment

If a party dies after trial and submission of the case to a judge sitting without a jury for decision or after a verdict upon any issue of fact, and before judgment, the court may nevertheless render judgment thereon. **Leg.H.** Enacted Stats 1872. Amended Stats 1965 ch 1636 §1; Stats 1980 ch 124 §2.

§670. Judgment roll

In superior courts the following papers, without being attached together, shall constitute the judgment roll:

(a) In case the complaint is not answered by any defendant, the summons, with the affidavit or proof of service; the complaint; the request for entry of default with a memorandum indorsed thereon that the default of the defendant in not answering was entered, and a copy of the judgment; if defendant has appeared by demurrer, and the demurrer has been overruled, then notice of the overruling thereof served on defendant's attorney, together with proof of the service; and in case the service so made is by publication, the affidavit for publication of summons, and the order directing the publication of summons.

(b) In all other cases, the pleadings, all orders striking out any pleading in whole or in part, a copy of the verdict of the jury, the statement of decision of the court, or finding of the referee, and a copy of any order made on demurrer, or relating to a change of parties, and a copy of the judgment; if there are two or more defendants in the action, and any one of them has allowed judgment to pass against him or her by default, the summons, with proof of its service, on the defendant, and if the service on the defaulting defendant be by publication, then the affidavit for publication, and the order directing the publication of the summons. **Leg.H.** Enacted Stats 1872. Amended Code Amdts 1873–74 ch 383 §89; Code Amdts 1875–76 ch 168 §1; Stats 1895 ch 40 §1; Stats 1907 ch 381 §2; Stats 1933 ch 744 §125; Stats 1939 ch 733 §1; Stats 1970 ch 218 §1; Stats 1977 ch 1257 §29, effective October 3, 1977; Stats 1981 ch 900 §6; Stats 1998 ch 931 §87 (SB 2139), effective September 28, 1998; Stats 2002 ch 784 §67 (SB 1316).

§671. [Section repealed 1945]

Leg.H. Enacted Stats 1872. Amended Code Amdts 1873–74 ch 383 §90; Stats 1895 ch 31 §1; Stats 1917 ch 98 §1; Stats 1923 ch 368 §1; Stats 1927 ch 492 §1; Stats 1933 ch 744 §126. Repealed Stats 1945 ch 828 §1. See Gov C §69844.

§671a. [Section repealed 1923]

Leg.H. Added Stats 1917 ch 100 §1. Repealed Stats 1923 ch 368 §2. The repealed section related to filing copies of federal judgments with county.

§672. [Section repealed 1945]

Leg.H. Enacted Stats 1872. Amended Stats 1907 ch 381 §3; Stats 1921 ch 121 §1; Stats 1933 ch 744 §127. Repealed Stats 1945 ch 828 §1. The repealed section related to meaning of "docket".

§673. Assignee of record; Acknowledgment of assignment of judgment

(a) An assignee of a right represented by a judgment may become an assignee of record by filing with the clerk of the court which entered the judgment an acknowledgment of assignment of judgment.

(b) An acknowledgment of assignment of judgment shall contain all of the following:

(1) The title of the court where the judgment is entered and the cause and number of the action.

(2) The date of entry of the judgment and of any renewals of the judgment and where entered in the records of the court.

(3) The name and address of the judgment creditor and name and last known address of the judgment debtor.

(4) A statement describing the right represented by the judgment that is assigned to the assignee.

(5) The name and address of the assignee.

(c) The acknowledgment of assignment of judgment shall be:

(1) Made in the manner of an acknowledgment of a conveyance of real property.

(2) Executed and acknowledged by the judgment creditor or by the prior assignee of record if there is one.

(d)(1) If an acknowledgment of assignment of judgment purports to be executed or acknowledged by an authorized agent of the judgment creditor or an authorized agent of a prior assignee of record, then documentation sufficient to evidence that authorization shall be filed together with the acknowledgment of assignment of judgment.

(2) Notwithstanding paragraph (1), an assignee of a right represented by a judgment may also become an assignee of record by filing with the clerk of the court that entered judgment a court order or other documentation that evidences assignment of judgment by operation of law. **Leg.H.** Added Stats 1982 ch 497 §38, operative July 1, 1983. Amended Stats 2020 ch 36 §22 (AB 3364), effective January 1, 2021.

Prior Law: Former CCP §673, providing that judgment be open to public inspection, was enacted Stats 1872, amended Stats 1933 ch 744 §128, and repealed Stats 1945 ch 828 §1.

§674. Abstract of judgment

(a) Except as otherwise provided in Section 4506 of the Family Code, an abstract of a judgment or decree requiring the payment of money shall be certified by the clerk of the court where the judgment or decree was entered and shall contain all of the following:

(1) The title of the court where the judgment or decree is entered and cause and number of the action.

(2) The date of entry of the judgment or decree and of any renewals of the judgment or decree and where entered in the records of the court.

(3) The name and last known address of the judgment debtor and the address at which the summons was either personally served or mailed to the judgment debtor or the judgment debtor's attorney of record.

(4) The name and address of the judgment creditor.

(5) The amount of the judgment or decree as entered or as last renewed.

(6) The last four digits of the social security number and driver's license number of the judgment debtor if they are known to the judgment creditor. If either or both of those sets of numbers are not known to the judgment creditor, that fact shall be indicated on the abstract of judgment.

(7) Whether a stay of enforcement has been ordered by the court and, if so, the date the stay ends.

(8) The date of issuance of the abstract.

(b) An abstract of judgment, recorded after January 1, 1979, that does not list the social security number and driver's license number of the judgment debtor, or either of them, as required by subdivision (a) or by Section 4506 of the Family Code, may be amended by the recording of a document entitled "Amendment to Abstract of Judgment." The Amendment to Abstract of Judgment shall contain all of the information required by this section or by Section 4506 of the Family Code, and shall set forth the date of recording and the book and page location in the records of the county recorder of the original abstract of judgment.

A recorded Amendment to Abstract of Judgment shall have priority as of the date of recordation of the original abstract of judgment, except as to any purchaser, encumbrancer, or lessee who obtained their interest after the recordation of the original abstract of judgment but prior to the recordation of the Amendment to Abstract of Judgment without actual notice of the original abstract of judgment. The purchaser, encumbrancer, or lessee without actual notice may assert as a defense against enforcement of the abstract of judgment the failure to comply with this section or Section 4506 of the Family Code regarding the contents of the original abstract of judgment notwithstanding the subsequent recordation of an Amendment to Abstract of Judgment. With respect to an abstract of judgment recorded between January 1, 1979, and July 10, 1985, the defense against enforcement for failure to comply with this section or Section 4506 of the Family Code may not be asserted by the holder of another abstract of judgment or involuntary lien, recorded without actual notice of the prior abstract, unless refusal to allow the defense would result in prejudice and substantial injury as used in Section 475. The recordation of an Amendment to Abstract of Judgment does not extend or otherwise alter the computation of time as provided in Section 697.310.

(c)(1) The abstract of judgment shall be certified in the name of the judgment debtor as listed on the judgment and may also include the additional name or names by which the judgment debtor is known as set forth in the affidavit of identity, as defined in Section 680.135, filed by the judgment creditor with the application for issuance of the abstract of judgment. Prior to the clerk of the court certifying an abstract of judgment containing any additional name or names by which the judgment debtor is known that are not listed on the judgment, the court shall approve the affidavit of identity. If the court determines, without a hearing or a notice, that the affidavit of identity states sufficient facts upon which the judgment creditor has identified the additional names of the judgment debtor, the court shall authorize the certification of the abstract of judgment with the additional name or names.

(2) The remedies provided in Section 697.410 apply to a recorded abstract of a money judgment based upon an affidavit of identity that appears to create a judgment lien on real property of a person who is not the judgment debtor. **Leg.H.** Enacted Stats 1872. Amended Stats 1907 ch 381 §4; Stats 1923 ch 368 §3; Stats 1927 ch 493 §1; Stats 1933 ch 744 §129; Stats 1935 ch 298 §1; Stats 1947 ch 116 §1; Stats 1951 ch 1737 §101, operative January 1, 1952; Stats 1955 ch 781 §1; Stats 1957 ch 43 §6; Stats 1973 ch 797 §1; Stats 1974 ch 211 §1, ch 1169 §3; Stats 1976 ch 1000 §1, operative July 1, 1977; Stats 1977 ch 1257 §30, operative October 3, 1977; Stats 1978 ch 203 §1; Stats 1980 ch 1281 §2; Stats 1982 ch 517 §131 (ch 497 prevails), ch 497 §39, operative July 1, 1983; Stats 1988 ch 153 §6, ch 1411 §1; Stats 1992 ch 163 §28 (AB 2641), operative January 1, 1994; Stats 2000 ch 639 §1 (AB 2405); Stats 2001 ch 159 §39 (SB 662); Stats 2007 ch 189 §1 (SB 644), effective January 1, 2008.

1988 Note: The amendments made to §674 by Stats 1988 ch 1411 are intended to maintain the integrity of the recordation system for interests in real property as discussed in *Keele v. Reich*, (169 Cal. App. 3d 1129 (1985)) to preserve the reasonable expectations of all parties asserting interests in real property, and to provide a means for the amendment of abstracts of judgment recorded after the effective date of Stats 1978 ch 203. The amendments are not intended to require the amendment of abstracts of judgment recorded prior to the effective date of Stats 1978 ch 203, and are intended to prevent a windfall from being realized by the holders of junior abstracts recorded after 1978 and prior to the decision in *Keele v. Reich*. Stats 1988 ch 1411 §2.

§674.5. [Section repealed 1983]

Leg.H. Added Stats 1959 ch 2087 §1. Amended Stats 1976 ch 612 §1; Stats 1981 ch 822 §2. Repealed Stats 1982 ch 497 §40, operative July 1, 1983. See CCP §§697.320 et seq., 724.210 et seq.

§674.7. [Section repealed 1983]

Leg.H. Added Stats 1975 2nd Ex Sess ch 1 §26.4. Amended Stats 1976 ch 612 §1.5. Repealed Stats 1982 ch 497 §41, operative July 1, 1983. See CCP §§697.320 et seq.

§675. [Section repealed 1983]

Leg.H. Enacted Stats 1872. Amended Code Amdts 1873–74 ch 383 §91; Stats 1931 ch 81 §1; Stats 1933 ch 744 §130; Stats 1935 ch 298 §2; Stats 1945 ch 828 §2; Stats 1951 ch 1737 §102, operative January 1, 1952; Stats

1955 ch 247 §2; Stats 1963 ch 2084 §1; Stats 1970 ch 1004 §1; Stats 1974 ch 252 §1; Stats 1975 ch 765 §3; Stats 1976 ch 283 §1; Stats 1977 ch 1257 §31, effective October 3, 1977; Stats 1978 ch 203 §2; Stats 1980 ch 600 §1. Repealed Stats 1982 ch 497 §42, operative July 1, 1983. See CCP §§697.410, 724.010 et seq.

§675a. [Section repealed 1955]

Leg.H. Added Stats 1905 ch 269 §1. Amended Stats 1955 ch 59 §6. Repealed Stats 1955 ch 247 §3. The repealed section related to recording of satisfaction of mortgage following foreclosure.

§675b. [Section repealed 1983]

Leg.H. Added Stats 1935 ch 711 §1. Amended Stats 1945 ch 828 §3; Stats 1969 ch 902 §1. Repealed Stats 1982 ch 497 §43, operative July 1, 1983. The repealed section related to discharge of bankrupt from judgment.

§675c. [Section repealed 1983]

Leg.H. Added Stats 1969 ch 902 §2. Repealed Stats 1982 ch 497 §44, operative July 1, 1983. The repealed section related to discharge of bankrupt in proceeding to enforce judgment.

TITLE 8.5
UNIFORM FOREIGN-MONEY CLAIMS ACT

Citation of title. §676.
Definitions. §676.1.
Application of title. §676.2.
Effect of agreement of parties. §676.3.
Proper money of claim. §676.4.
Determination of amount to be paid and rate of exchange. §676.5.
Determination of proper money as question of law. §676.6.
Judgment or award on foreign-money claim. §676.7.
Rate of exchange applicable in distribution proceeding. §676.8.
Prejudgment or pre-award interest. §676.9.
Foreign judgment enforcement. §676.10.
Computations. §676.11.
Substitution of new money. §676.12.
Supplementation of title with principles of law and equity. §676.13.
Application and construction of title. §676.14.
Severability. §676.15.
Applicability of title to specified actions and distribution proceedings. §676.16.

§676. Citation of title

This title shall be known and may be cited as the Uniform Foreign-Money Claims Act. **Leg.H.** Added Stats 1991 ch 932 §1 (AB 1646).

Prior Law: Former CCP §676, similar to present CC §3446, was added Stats 1903 ch 91 §1, amended Stats 1959 ch 1472 §1, and repealed Stats 1982 ch 517 §132.

§676.1. Definitions

As used in this title:

(1) "Action" means a judicial proceeding or arbitration in which a payment in money may be awarded or enforced with respect to a foreign-money claim.

(2) "Bank-offered spot rate" means the spot rate of exchange at which a bank will sell foreign money at a spot rate.

(3) "Conversion date" means the banking day next preceding the date on which money, in accordance with this title, is (i) paid to a claimant in an action or distribution proceeding, (ii) paid to the official designated by law to enforce a judgment or award on behalf of a claimant, or (iii) used to recoup, setoff, or counterclaim in different moneys in an action or distribution proceeding.

(4) "Distribution proceeding" means a judicial or nonjudicial proceeding for the distribution of a fund in which one or more foreign-money claims is asserted and includes an accounting, an assignment for the benefit of creditors, a foreclosure, the liquidation or rehabilitation of a corporation or other entity, and the distribution of an estate, trust, or other fund.

(5) "Foreign money" means money other than money of the United States of America.

(6) "Foreign-money claim" means a claim upon an obligation to pay, or a claim for recovery of a loss, expressed in or measured by a foreign money.

(7) "Money" means a medium of exchange for the payment of obligations or a store of value authorized or adopted by a government or by intergovernmental agreement.

(8) "Money of the claim" means the money determined as proper pursuant to Section 676.4.

(9) "Person" means an individual, a corporation, government or governmental subdivision or agency, business trust, estate, trust, joint venture, partnership, association, two or more persons having a joint or common interest, or any other legal or commercial entity.

(10) "Rate of exchange" means the rate at which money of one country may be converted into money of another country in a free financial market convenient to or reasonably usable by a person obligated to pay or to state a rate of conversion. If separate rates of exchange apply to different kinds of transactions, the term means the rate applicable to the particular transaction giving rise to the foreign-money claim.

(11) "Spot rate" means the rate of exchange at which foreign money is sold by a bank or other dealer in foreign exchange for immediate or next day availability or for settlement by immediate payment in cash or equivalent, by charge to an account, or by an agreed delayed settlement not exceeding two days.

(12) "State" means a State of the United States, the District of Columbia, the Commonwealth of Puerto Rico, or a territory or insular possession subject to the jurisdiction of the United States. **Leg.H.** Added Stats 1991 ch 932 §1 (AB 1646).

§676.2. Application of title

(a) This title applies only to a foreign-money claim in an action or distribution proceeding.

(b) This title applies to foreign-money issues even if other law under the conflict-of-laws rules of this state applies to other issues in the action or distribution proceeding. **Leg.H.** Added Stats 1991 ch 932 §1 (AB 1646).

§676.3. Effect of agreement of parties

(a) The effect of this title may be varied by agreement of the parties made before or after commencement of an action or distribution proceeding or the entry of judgment.

(b) Parties to a transaction may agree upon the money to be used in a transaction giving rise to a foreign-money claim and may agree to use different moneys for different aspects of the transaction. Stating the price in a foreign money for one aspect of a transaction does not alone require the use of that money for other aspects of the transaction. **Leg.H.** Added Stats 1991 ch 932 §1 (AB 1646).

§676.4. Proper money of claim

(a) The money in which the parties to a transaction have agreed that payment is to be made is the proper money of the claim for payment.

(b) If the parties to a transaction have not otherwise agreed, the proper money of the claim, as in each case may be appropriate, is one of the following:

(1) The money regularly used between the parties as a matter of usage or course of dealing.

(2) The money used at the time of a transaction in international trade, by trade usage or common practice, for valuing or settling transactions in the particular commodity or service involved.

(3) The money in which the loss was ultimately felt or will be incurred by the party claimant. **Leg.H.** Added Stats 1991 ch 932 §1 (AB 1646).

§676.5. Determination of amount to be paid and rate of exchange

(a) If an amount contracted to be paid in a foreign money is measured by a specified amount of a different money, the amount to be paid is determined on the conversion date.

(b) If an amount contracted to be paid in a foreign money is to be measured by a different money at the rate of exchange prevailing on a date before default, that rate of exchange applies only to payments made within a reasonable time after default, not exceeding 30 days. Thereafter, conversion is made at the bank-offered spot rate on the conversion date.

(c) A monetary claim is neither usurious nor unconscionable because the agreement on which it is based provides that the amount of the debtor's obligation to be paid in the debtor's money, when received by the creditor, shall equal a specified amount of the foreign money of the country of the creditor. If, because of unexcused delay in payment of a judgment or award, the amount received by the creditor does not equal the amount of the foreign money specified in the agreement, the court or arbitrator shall amend the judgment or award accordingly. **Leg.H.** Added Stats 1991 ch 932 §1 (AB 1646).

§676.6. Determination of proper money as question of law

(a) A person may assert a claim in a specified foreign money. If a foreign-money claim is not asserted, the claimant makes the claim in United States dollars.

(b) An opposing party may allege and prove that a claim, in whole or in part, is in a different money than that asserted by the claimant.

(c) A person may assert a defense, setoff, recoupment, or counterclaim in any money without regard to the money of other claims.

(d) The determination of the proper money of the claim is a question of law. **Leg.H.** Added Stats 1991 ch 932 §1 (AB 1646).

§676.7. Judgment or award on foreign-money claim

(a) Except as provided in subdivision (c), a judgment or award on a foreign-money claim shall be stated in an amount of the money of the claim.

(b) A judgment or award on a foreign-money claim is payable in that foreign money or, at the option of the debtor, in the amount of United States dollars which will purchase that foreign money on the conversion date at a bank-offered spot rate.

(c) Assessed costs shall be entered in United States dollars.

(d) Each payment in United States dollars shall be accepted and credited on a judgment or award on a foreign-money claim in the amount of the foreign money that could be purchased by the dollars at a bank-offered spot rate of exchange at or near the close of business on the conversion date for that payment.

(e) A judgment or award made in an action or distribution proceeding on both (1) a defense, setoff, recoupment, or counterclaim and (2) the adverse party's claim, shall be netted by converting the money of the smaller into the money of the larger, and by subtracting the smaller from the larger, and specify the rates of exchange used.

(f) A judgment substantially in the following form complies with subdivision (a):

"IT IS ADJUDGED AND ORDERED, that Defendant _____ (insert name) pay to Plaintiff _____ (insert name) the sum of ____ (insert amount in the foreign money) plus interest on that sum at the rate of ____ (insert rate – see Section 676.9) percent a year or, at the option of the judgment debtor, the number of United States dollars which will purchase the _____ (insert name of foreign money) with interest due, at a bank-offered spot rate at or near the close of business on the banking day next before the day of payment, together with assessed costs of _____ (insert amount) United States dollars."

(g) If a contract claim is of the type covered by subdivision (a) or (b) of Section 676.5, the judgment or award shall be entered for the amount of money stated to measure the obligation to be paid in the money specified for payment or, at the option of the debtor, the number of United States dollars which will purchase the computed amount of the money of payment on the conversion date at a bank-offered spot rate.

(h) A judgment shall be entered in foreign money in the same manner, and has the same effect as a lien, as other judgments. It may be discharged by payment. **Leg.H.** Added Stats 1991 ch 932 §1 (AB 1646).

§676.8. Rate of exchange applicable in distribution proceeding

The rate of exchange prevailing at or near the close of business on the day the distribution proceeding is initiated governs all exchanges of foreign money in a distribution proceeding. A foreign-money claimant in a distribution proceeding shall assert its claim in the named foreign money and show the amount of United States dollars resulting from a conversion as of the date the proceeding was initiated. **Leg.H.** Added Stats 1991 ch 932 §1 (AB 1646).

§676.9. Prejudgment or pre-award interest

(a) With respect to a foreign-money claim, recovery of prejudgment or pre-award interest and the rate of interest to be applied in the action or distribution proceeding, except as provided in subdivision (b), are matters of the substantive law governing the right to recovery under the conflict-of-laws rules of this state.

(b) The court or arbitrator shall increase or decrease the amount of prejudgment or pre-award interest otherwise payable in a judgment or award in foreign money to the extent required by the law of this state governing a failure to make or accept an offer of settlement or offer of judgment, or conduct by a party or its attorney causing undue delay or expense.

(c) A judgment or award on a foreign-money claim bears interest at the rate applicable to judgments of this state. **Leg.H.** Added Stats 1991 ch 932 §1 (AB 1646).

§676.10. Foreign judgment enforcement

(a) If an action is brought to enforce a judgment of another jurisdiction expressed in a foreign money and the judgment is recognized in this state as enforceable, the enforcing judgment shall be entered as provided in Section 676.7, whether or not the foreign judgment confers an option to pay in an equivalent amount of United States dollars.

(b) A foreign judgment may be enforced in accordance with Title 11 (commencing with Section 1710.10) of Part 3.

(c) A satisfaction or partial payment made upon the foreign judgment, on proof thereof, shall be credited against the amount of foreign money specified in the judgment, notwithstanding the entry of judgment in this state.

(d) A judgment entered on a foreign-money claim only in United States dollars in another state shall be enforced in this state in United States dollars only. **Leg.H.** Added Stats 1991 ch 932 §1 (AB 1646).

§676.11. Computations

(a) Computations under this section are for the limited purposes of the section and do not affect computation of the United States dollar equivalent of the money of the judgment for the purpose of payment.

(b) For the limited purpose of facilitating the enforcement of provisional remedies in an action, the value in United States dollars of assets to be seized or restrained pursuant to a writ of attachment, garnishment, execution, or other legal process, the amount of United States dollars at issue for assessing costs, or the amount of United States dollars involved for a surety bond or other court-required undertaking, shall be ascertained as provided in subdivisions (c) and (d).

(c) A party seeking process, costs, bond, or other undertaking under subdivision (b) shall compute in United States dollars the amount of the foreign money claimed from a bank-offered spot rate prevailing at or near the close of business on the banking day next preceding the filing of a request or application for the issuance of process or for the determination of costs, or an application for a bond or other court-required undertaking.

(d) A party seeking the process, costs, bond, or other undertaking under subdivision (b) shall file with each request or application an affidavit or certificate executed in good faith by its counsel or a bank officer, stating the market quotation used and how it was obtained, and setting forth the calculation. Affected court officials incur no liability, after a filing of the affidavit or certificate, for acting as if the judgment were in the amount of United States dollars stated in the affidavit or certificate. **Leg.H.** Added Stats 1991 ch 932 §1 (AB 1646).

§676.12. Substitution of new money

(a) If, after an obligation is expressed or a loss is incurred in a foreign money, the country issuing or adopting that money substitutes a new money in place of that money, the obligation or the loss is treated as if expressed or incurred in the new money at the rate of conversion the issuing country establishes for the payment of like obligations or losses denominated in the former money.

(b) If substitution under subdivision (a) occurs after a judgment or award is entered on a foreign-money claim, the court or arbitrator shall amend the judgment or award by a like conversion of the former money. **Leg.H.** Added Stats 1991 ch 932 §1 (AB 1646).

§676.13. Supplementation of title with principles of law and equity

Unless displaced by particular provisions of this title, the principles of law and equity, including the law merchant, and the law relative to capacity to contract, principal and agent, estoppel, fraud, misrepresentation, duress, coercion, mistake, bankruptcy, or other validating or invalidating causes supplement its provisions. **Leg.H.** Added Stats 1991 ch 932 §1 (AB 1646).

§676.14. Application and construction of title

This title shall be applied and construed to effectuate its general purpose to make uniform the law with respect to the subject of this title among states enacting it. **Leg.H.** Added Stats 1991 ch 932 §1 (AB 1646).

§676.15. Severability

If any provision of this title or its application to any person or circumstance is held invalid, that invalidity does not affect other provisions or applications of this title which can be given effect without the invalid provision or application, and to this end the provisions of this title are severable. **Leg.H.** Added Stats 1991 ch 932 §1 (AB 1646).

§676.16. Applicability of title to specified actions and distribution proceedings

This title applies to actions and distribution proceedings commenced on or after January 1, 1992. **Leg.H.** Added Stats 1991 ch 932 §1 (AB 1646).

§677. [Section repealed 1983]

Leg.H. Added Stats 1903 ch 91 §2. Amended Stats 1959 ch 1472 §2. Repealed Stats 1982 ch 517 §133. See CCP §§995.310, 995.320, CC §3448.

§677½. [Section repealed 1983]
Leg.H. Added Stats 1903 ch 91 §3. Repealed Stats 1982 ch 517 §134. See CCP §§995.340, 995.370.

§678. [Section repealed 1983]
Leg.H. Added Stats 1903 ch 91 §4. Repealed Stats 1982 ch 517 §135. See CCP §§995.910 et seq.

§678½. [Section repealed 1983]
Leg.H. Added Stats 1903 ch 91 §5. Repealed Stats 1982 ch 517 §136. See CCP §§995.950, 995.960, 996.240.

§679. [Section repealed 1983]
Leg.H. Added Stats 1903 ch 91 §6. Repealed Stats 1982 ch 517 §137. See CCP §§995.320, 995.940 et seq.

§679½. [Section repealed 1983]
Leg.H. Added Stats 1903 ch 91 §7. Repealed Stats 1982 ch 517 §138. See CCP §995.910.

§680. [Section repealed 1983]
Leg.H. Added Stats 1903 ch 91 §8. Repealed Stats 1982 ch 517 §139. See CCP §995.420, CC §3449.

§680½. [Section repealed 1983]
Leg.H. Added Stats 1903 ch 91 §9. Amended Stats 1959 ch 1472 §3. Repealed Stats 1982 ch 517 §140. See CCP §996.440.

TITLE 9
ENFORCEMENT OF JUDGMENTS

Division 1. Definitions and General Provisions.
Division 2. Enforcement of Money Judgments.
Division 3. Enforcement of Nonmoney Judgments.
Division 4. Third-Party Claims and Related Procedures.
Division 5. Satisfaction of Judgment.

DIVISION 1
DEFINITIONS AND GENERAL PROVISIONS

Chapter 1. Short Title and Definitions.
Chapter 2. General Provisions.
Chapter 3. Period for Enforcement and Renewal of Judgments.
Chapter 4. Manner of Service of Writs, Notices, and Other Papers.
Chapter 5. Interest and Costs.
Chapter 6. Enforcement After Death of Judgment Creditor or Judgment Debtor.
Chapter 7. Levying Officers.
Chapter 8. Enforcement of State Tax Liability.
Chapter 9. Enforcement of Support Judgments.
Chapter 10. Enforcement of Judgments by Labor Commissioner.
Chapter 20. Transitional Provisions.

CHAPTER 1
SHORT TITLE AND DEFINITIONS

Short title. §680.010.
Application of definitions. §680.110.
"Account debtor". §680.120.
"Account receivable". §680.130.
"Affidavit of Identity". §680.135.
"Chattel paper". §680.140.
"Child support". §680.145.
"Costs". §680.150.
"Court". §680.160.
"Deposit account". §680.170.
"Document of title". §680.180.
"Equity". §680.190.
"Financial institution". §680.200.
"General intangibles". §680.210.
"Instrument". §680.220.
"Judgment". §680.230.
"Judgment creditor". §680.240.
"Judgment debtor". §680.250.
"Levying officer". §680.260.
"Money judgment". §680.270.
"Person". §680.280.
"Personal property". §680.290.
"Principal amount of the judgment". §680.300.
"Property". §680.310.
"Real property". §680.320.
"Registered process server". §680.330.
"Secured party". §680.340.
"Security". §680.345.
"Security agreement". §680.350.
"Security interest". §680.360.
"Spousal support". §680.365.
"Tangible personal property". §680.370.
"Writ". §680.380.

§680.010. Short title
This title shall be known and may be cited as the Enforcement of Judgments Law. **Leg.H.** Added Stats 1982 ch 1364 §2, operative July 1, 1983.

§680.110. Application of definitions
Unless the provision or context otherwise requires, the definitions in this chapter govern the construction of this title. **Leg.H.** Added Stats 1982 ch 1364 §2, operative July 1, 1983.

§680.120. "Account debtor"
"Account debtor" means "account debtor" as defined in paragraph (3) of subdivision (a) of Section 9102 of the Commercial Code. **Leg.H.** Added Stats 1982 ch 1364 §2, operative July 1, 1983. Amended Stats 1999 ch 991 §15.5 (SB 45), operative July 1, 2001.

§680.130. "Account receivable"
"Account receivable" means "account" as defined in paragraph (2) of subdivision (a) of Section 9102 of the Commercial Code. **Leg.H.** Added Stats 1982 ch 1364 §2, operative July 1, 1983. Amended Stats 1999 ch 991 §16 (SB 45), operative July 1, 2001.

§680.135. "Affidavit of Identity"
"Affidavit of Identity" means an affidavit or declaration executed by a judgment creditor, under penalty of perjury, that is filed with the clerk of the court in which the judgment is entered at the time the judgment creditor files for a writ of execution or an abstract of judgment. The affidavit of identity shall set forth the case name and number, the name of the judgment debtor stated in the judgment, the additional name or names by which the judgment debtor is known, and the facts upon which the judgment creditor has relied in obtaining the judgment debtor's additional name or names. The affidavit of identity shall not include the name or names of persons, including any corporations, partnerships, or any legal entities not separately named in the judgment in which the judgment debtor is a partner, shareholder, or member, other than the judgment debtor. **Leg.H.** Added Stats 2000 ch 639 §2 (AB 2405).

§680.140. "Chattel paper"
"Chattel paper" means "chattel paper" as defined in paragraph (11) of subdivision (a) of Section 9102 of the Commercial Code. **Leg.H.** Added Stats 1982 ch 1364 §2, operative July 1, 1983. Amended Stats 1999 ch 991 §16.1 (SB 45), operative July 1, 2001.

§680.145. "Child support"
"Child support" includes family support. **Leg.H.** Added Stats 1992 ch 163 §29 (AB 2641), operative January 1, 1994.

§680.150. "Costs"
"Costs" means costs and disbursements, including but not limited to statutory fees, charges, commissions, and expenses. **Leg.H.** Added Stats 1982 ch 1364 §2, operative July 1, 1983.

§680.160. "Court"
"Court" means the court where the judgment sought to be enforced was entered. **Leg.H.** Added Stats 1982 ch 1364 §2, operative July 1, 1983.

§680.170. "Deposit account"
"Deposit account" means "deposit account" as defined in paragraph (29) of subdivision (a) of Section 9102 of the Commercial Code. **Leg.H.** Added Stats 1982 ch 1364 §2, operative July 1, 1983. Amended Stats 1999 ch 991 §16.2 (SB 45), operative July 1, 2001.

§680.180. "Document of title"
"Document of title" means "document" as defined in paragraph (30) of subdivision (a) of Section 9102 of the Commercial Code. A document of title is negotiable if it is negotiable within the meaning of Section 7104 of the Commercial Code. **Leg.H.** Added Stats 1982 ch 1364 §2, operative July 1, 1983. Amended Stats 1999 ch 991 §16.3 (SB 45), operative July 1, 2001.

§680.190. "Equity"
"Equity" means the fair market value of the interest of the judgment debtor in property, or in the case of community property the fair market value of the interest of the judgment debtor and the spouse of the judgment debtor in the property, over and above all liens and encumbrances on the interest superior to the judgment creditor's lien. **Leg.H.** Added Stats 1982 ch 1364 §2, operative July 1, 1983.

§680.200. "Financial institution"
"Financial institution" means a state or national bank, state or federal savings and loan association or credit union, or like organization, and includes a corporation engaged in a safe deposit business. **Leg.H.** Added Stats 1982 ch 1364 §2, operative July 1, 1983.

§680.210. "General intangibles"
"General intangibles" means "general intangibles," as defined in paragraph (42) of subdivision (a) of Section 9102 of the Commercial Code, consisting of rights to payment. **Leg.H.** Added Stats 1982 ch 1364 §2, operative July 1, 1983. Amended Stats 1999 ch 991 §17 (SB 45), operative July 1, 2001.

§680.220. "Instrument"
"Instrument" means "instrument", as defined in paragraph (47) of subdivision (a) of Section 9102 of the Commercial Code. **Leg.H.** Added

Stats 1982 ch 1364 §2, operative July 1, 1983. Amended Stats 1999 ch 991 §17.1 (SB 45), operative July 1, 2001.

§680.230. "Judgment"

"Judgment" means a judgment, order, or decree entered in a court of this state. **Leg.H.** Added Stats 1982 ch 1364 §2, operative July 1, 1983.

§680.240. "Judgment creditor"

"Judgment creditor" means the person in whose favor a judgment is rendered or, if there is an assignee of record, means the assignee of record. Unless the context otherwise requires, the term also includes the guardian or conservator of the estate, personal representative, or other successor in interest of the judgment creditor or assignee of record. **Leg.H.** Added Stats 1982 ch 1364 §2, operative July 1, 1983.

§680.250. "Judgment debtor"

"Judgment debtor" means the person against whom a judgment is rendered. **Leg.H.** Added Stats 1982 ch 1364 §2, operative July 1, 1983.

§680.260. "Levying officer"

"Levying officer" means the sheriff or marshal. **Leg.H.** Added Stats 1982 ch 1364 §2, operative July 1, 1983. Amended Stats 1996 ch 872 §16 (AB 3472).

§680.270. "Money judgment"

"Money judgment" means that part of a judgment that requires the payment of money. **Leg.H.** Added Stats 1982 ch 1364 §2, operative July 1, 1983.

§680.280. "Person"

"Person" includes a natural person, a corporation, a partnership or other unincorporated association, a general partner of a partnership, a limited liability company, and a public entity. **Leg.H.** Added Stats 1982 ch 1364 §2, operative July 1, 1983. Amended Stats 1993 ch 1187 §1 (SB 70); Stats 1994 ch 1010 §60 (SB 2053).

§680.290. "Personal property"

"Personal property" includes both tangible and intangible personal property. **Leg.H.** Added Stats 1982 ch 1364 §2, operative July 1, 1983.

§680.300. "Principal amount of the judgment"

"Principal amount of the judgment" means the total amount of the judgment as entered or as last renewed, together with the costs thereafter added to the judgment pursuant to Section 685.090, reduced by any partial satisfactions of such amount and costs and by any amounts no longer enforceable. **Leg.H.** Added Stats 1982 ch 1364 §2, operative July 1, 1983.

§680.310. "Property"

"Property" includes real and personal property and any interest therein. **Leg.H.** Added Stats 1982 ch 1364 §2, operative July 1, 1983.

§680.320. "Real property"

"Real property" includes any right in real property, including but not limited to a leasehold interest in real property. **Leg.H.** Added Stats 1982 ch 1364 §2, operative July 1, 1983.

§680.330. "Registered process server"

"Registered process server" means a person registered as a process server pursuant to Chapter 16 (commencing with Section 22350) of Division 8 of the Business and Professions Code. **Leg.H.** Added Stats 1982 ch 1364 §2, operative July 1, 1983.

§680.340. "Secured party"

"Secured party" means "secured party" as defined in paragraph (73) of subdivision (a) of Section 9102 of the Commercial Code. **Leg.H.** Added Stats 1982 ch 1364 §2, operative July 1, 1983. Amended Stats 1999 ch 991 §17.2 (SB 45), operative July 1, 2001; Stats 2013 ch 531 §4 (AB 502), effective January 1, 2014, operative July 1, 2014.

§680.345. "Security"

"Security" means a "security" as defined in Section 8102 of the Commercial Code. **Leg.H.** Added Stats 1982 ch 1364 §2, operative July 1, 1983.

§680.350. "Security agreement"

"Security agreement" means "security agreement" as defined in paragraph (74) of subdivision (a) of Section 9102 of the Commercial Code. **Leg.H.** Added Stats 1982 ch 1364 §2, operative July 1, 1983. Amended Stats 1999 ch 991 §17.3 (SB 45), operative July 1, 2001; Stats 2013 ch 531 §5 (AB 502), effective January 1, 2014, operative July 1, 2014.

§680.360. "Security interest"

"Security interest" means "security interest" as defined in Section 1201 of the Commercial Code. **Leg.H.** Added Stats 1982 ch 1364 §2, operative July 1, 1983.

§680.365. "Spousal support"

"Spousal support" includes support for a former spouse. **Leg.H.** Added Stats 1982 ch 1364 §2, operative July 1, 1983.

§680.370. "Tangible personal property"

"Tangible personal property" includes chattel paper, documents of title, instruments, securities, and money. **Leg.H.** Added Stats 1982 ch 1364 §2, operative July 1, 1983.

§680.380. "Writ"

"Writ" includes a writ of execution, a writ of possession of personal property, a writ of possession of real property, and a writ of sale. **Leg.H.** Added Stats 1982 ch 1364 §2, operative July 1, 1983.

§681. [Section repealed 1983]

Leg.H. Enacted Stats 1872. Amended Stats 1907 ch 360 §1; Stats 1955 ch 754 §1. Repealed Stats 1982 ch 1364 §1, operative July 1, 1983. See CCP §§683.010, 683.020, 699.510, 712.010.

§681a. [Section repealed 1983]

Leg.H. Added Stats 1911 ch 220 §1. Amended Stats 1929 ch 485 §1; Stats 1933 ch 744 §131; Stats 1951 ch 1737 §103, operative January 1, 1952; Stats 1961 ch 604 §4; Stats 1977 ch 1257 §32, effective October 3, 1977; Stats 1982 ch 517 §141 (ch 1364 prevails). Repealed Stats 1982 ch 1364 §1, operative July 1, 1983. See CCP §918.

CHAPTER 2
GENERAL PROVISIONS

Provisions for enforcing judgments. §681.010.
Enforcement by assignee. §681.020.
Rules for practice and procedure; Forms. §681.030.
Continuing review of enforcement of judgments. §681.035.
Effective time of filing with levying officer. §681.040.
Severability. §681.050.

§681.010. Provisions for enforcing judgments

Except as otherwise provided by statute:

(a) A money judgment is enforceable as provided in Division 2 (commencing with Section 695.010).

(b) A judgment for possession of personal property is enforceable as provided in Chapter 2 (commencing with Section 714.010) of Division 3.

(c) A judgment for possession of real property is enforceable as provided in Chapter 3 (commencing with Section 715.010) of Division 3.

(d) A judgment for sale of real or personal property is enforceable as provided in Chapter 4 (commencing with Section 716.010) of Division 3.

(e) A judgment requiring performance of an act not described in subdivisions (a) to (d), inclusive, or requiring forbearance from performing an act, is enforceable as provided in Chapter 5 (commencing with Section 717.010) of Division 3. **Leg.H.** Added Stats 1982 ch 1364 §2, operative July 1, 1983.

§681.020. Enforcement by assignee

An assignee of a judgment is not entitled to enforce the judgment under this title unless an acknowledgment of assignment of judgment to that assignee has been filed or the assignee has otherwise become an assignee of record under Section 673. **Leg.H.** Added Stats 1982 ch 1364 §2, operative July 1, 1983. Amended Stats 2020 ch 36 §23 (AB 3364), effective January 1, 2021.

§681.030. Rules for practice and procedure; Forms

(a) The Judicial Council may provide by rule for the practice and procedure in proceedings under this title.

(b) The Judicial Council may prescribe the form of the applications, notices, orders, writs, and other papers to be used under this title. The Judicial Council may prescribe forms in languages other than English. The timely completion and return of a Judicial Council form prescribed in a language other than English has the same force and effect as the timely completion and return of an English language form.

(c) The Judicial Council shall prepare a form containing all of the following:

(1) A list of each of the federal and this state's exemptions from enforcement of a money judgment against a natural person.

(2) A citation to the relevant statute of the United States or this state which creates each of the exemptions.

(3) Information on how to obtain the list of exemption amounts published pursuant to subdivision (f) of Section 703.150. **Leg.H.** Added Stats 1982 ch 1364 §2, operative July 1, 1983. Amended Stats 1984 ch 538 §15; Stats 1985 ch 41 §3; Stats 2003 ch 379 §1 (AB 182); Stats 2023 ch 131 §19 (AB 1754), effective January 1, 2024.

§681.035. Continuing review of enforcement of judgments

The California Law Revision Commission is authorized to maintain a continuing review of and submit recommendations to the Governor and the Legislature concerning enforcement of judgments. **Leg.H.** Added Stats 2013 ch 15 §1 (AB 567), effective January 1, 2014.

§681.040. Effective time of filing with levying officer

If a paper is required or permitted to be filed with a levying officer under this title, the paper is considered filed when it is actually received by the levying officer. **Leg.H.** Added Stats 1982 ch 1364 §2, operative July 1, 1983.

§681.050. Severability

If any provision or clause of this title or application thereof to any person or circumstances is held invalid, the invalidity does not affect other provisions or applications of this title which can be given effect without the invalid provision or application, and to this end the provisions of this title are severable. **Leg.H.** Added Stats 1982 ch 1364 §2, operative July 1, 1983.

§682. [Section repealed 1983]

Leg.H. Enacted Stats 1872. Amended Stats 1933 ch 744 §132; Stats 1951 ch 1737 §104, operative January 1, 1952; Stats 1955 ch 793 §1; Stats 1971 ch 1684 §1; Stats 1973 ch 20 §8; Stats 1978 ch 1133 §1, ch 1419 §1; Stats 1979 ch 66 §1, effective May 19, 1979, operative January 1, 1980. Repealed Stats 1982 ch 1364 §1, operative July 1, 1983. See CCP §§699.510, 699.520, 699.710, 712.040, 714.010, 714.020, 715.010.

§682a. [Section repealed 1983]

Leg.H. Added Stats 1941 ch 343 §3. Amended Stats 1957 ch 346 §2; Stats 1974 ch 1516 §13, operative January 1, 1977; Stats 1977 ch 42 §1; Stats 1978 ch 1419 §2; Stats 1982 ch 517 §142 (ch 1364 prevails). Repealed Stats 1982 ch 1364 §1, operative July 1, 1983. See CCP §700.160.

§682b. [Section repealed 1977]

Leg.H. Added Stats 1974 ch 1251 §1, operative July 1, 1975. Repealed Stats 1976 ch 1000 §2, operative July 1, 1977. The repealed section related to notice of homestead exemption to be included in application for writ of execution.

§682.1. [Section repealed 1983]

Leg.H. Added Stats 1945 ch 1302 §1. Amended Stats 1957 ch 2079 §1; Stats 1959 ch 534 §1, operative January 1, 1960; Stats 1970 ch 1523 §6; Stats 1971 ch 438 §18; Stats 1978 ch 1419 §3; Stats 1979 ch 373 §50.5; Stats 1982 ch 150 §2. Repealed Stats 1982 ch 1364 §1, operative July 1, 1983. The repealed section related to statutory form of writ.

§682.2. [Section repealed 1983]

Leg.H. Added Stats 1957 ch 1734 §1. Amended Stats 1959 ch 534 §2, operative January 1, 1960. Repealed Stats 1982 ch 1364 §1, operative July 1, 1983. See CCP §§685.020, 685.030, 685.050, 699.520.

§682.3. [Section repealed 1980]

Leg.H. Added Stats 1971 ch 1684 §2. Amended Stats 1972 ch 649 §1, effective August 9, 1972. Repealed Stats 1978 ch 1133 §2, operative January 1, 1980. The repealed section related to employer's obligation to withhold from earnings following service with writ of execution.

§683. [Section repealed 1983]

Leg.H. Enacted Stats 1872. Amended Stats 1931 ch 1189 §1; Stats 1933 ch 744 §133; Stats 1949 ch 371 §1; Stats 1951 ch 1737 §106, operative January 1, 1952; Stats 1971 ch 1684 §3; Stats 1974 ch 1251 §2, operative July 1, 1975; Stats 1977 ch 42 §2, ch 305 §1, effective July 8, 1977; Stats 1978 ch 1133 §3, operative January 1, 1980. Repealed Stats 1982 ch 1364 §1, operative July 1, 1983. See CCP §§699.510, 699.530, 699.560.

CHAPTER 3
PERIOD FOR ENFORCEMENT AND RENEWAL OF JUDGMENTS

Article 1. Period for Enforcement of Judgments.
Article 2. Renewal of Judgments.
Article 3. Application of Chapter.

ARTICLE 1
Period for Enforcement of Judgments

Judgment enforceable upon entry. §683.010.
Ten-year period for enforcement of judgment. §683.020.
Time for enforcement of installment judgment. §683.030.
Application for writ more than 10 years after entry of judgment. §683.040.
Preservation of right of action on judgment. §683.050.

§683.010. Judgment enforceable upon entry

Except as otherwise provided by statute or in the judgment, a judgment is enforceable under this title upon entry. **Leg.H.** Added Stats 1982 ch 1364 §2, operative July 1, 1983.

§683.020. Ten-year period for enforcement of judgment

Except as otherwise provided by statute, upon the expiration of 10 years after the date of entry of a money judgment or a judgment for possession or sale of property:

(a) The judgment may not be enforced.

(b) All enforcement procedures pursuant to the judgment or to a writ or order issued pursuant to the judgment shall cease.

(c) Any lien created by an enforcement procedure pursuant to the judgment is extinguished. **Leg.H.** Added Stats 1982 ch 1364 §2, operative July 1, 1983.

§683.030. Time for enforcement of installment judgment

If a money judgment is payable in installments, the 10-year period of enforceability prescribed by Section 683.020 runs as to each installment from the date the installment becomes due and runs as to costs from the date the costs are added to the judgment pursuant to Section 685.090. **Leg.H.** Added Stats 1982 ch 1364 §2, operative July 1, 1983.

§683.040. Application for writ more than 10 years after entry of judgment

If the judgment creditor applies for a writ for the enforcement of a judgment and the application is made more than 10 years after the date the judgment was entered or renewed, the application shall be accompanied by an affidavit of a person having knowledge of the facts stating facts showing that the issuance of the writ sought in the application is not barred under this chapter. A copy of the affidavit shall be attached to the writ when issued. **Leg.H.** Added Stats 1982 ch 1364 §2, operative July 1, 1983.

§683.050. Preservation of right of action on judgment

(a) Except as provided in subdivision (b), nothing in this chapter limits any right the judgment creditor may have to bring an action on a judgment, but any such action shall be commenced within the period prescribed by Section 337.5.

(b) Notwithstanding subdivision (a), no action on a judgment may be brought on a judgment identified in subdivision (c) of Section 683.110. **Leg.H.** Added Stats 1982 ch 1364 §2, operative July 1, 1983. Amended Stats 2022 ch 883 §1 (SB 1200), effective January 1, 2023.

ARTICLE 2
Renewal of Judgments

Authorization for renewal; Successive renewals. §683.110.
Application for renewal; Effect of application. §683.120.
Time for filing application. §683.130.
Contents of application. §683.140.
Entry of renewal by court clerk; Fees. §683.150.
Service of notice of renewal. §683.160.
Vacation or modification of renewal. §683.170.
Extending duration of judgment lien on real property. §683.180.
Continuation of other liens. §683.190.
Continuation of enforcement proceedings. §683.200.
Renewal during stay of enforcement. §683.210.
Limitation period for action on renewed judgment. §683.220.

§683.110. Authorization for renewal; Successive renewals

(a) The period of enforceability of a money judgment or a judgment for possession or sale of property may be extended by renewal of the judgment as provided in this article.

(b) A judgment shall not be renewed under this article if the application for renewal is filed within five years from the time the judgment was previously renewed under this article.

(c) Notwithstanding subdivision (a), a judgment creditor may renew the period of enforceability of the following types of money judgments only once pursuant to subdivision (c) of Section 683.120:

(1) A judgment on a claim related to medical expenses if the principal amount of the money judgment remaining unsatisfied against a debtor is under two hundred thousand dollars ($200,000).

(2) A judgment on a claim related to personal debt if the principal amount of the money judgment remaining unsatisfied against a debtor is under fifty thousand dollars ($50,000).

(d) For purposes of this section, the following definitions apply:

(1) "Debtor" means a natural person from whom money is due or owing or alleged to be due or owing.

(2) "Due or owing" does not include debts incurred due to or obtained by tortious or fraudulent conduct or judgments for unpaid wages, damages, or penalties owed to an employee.

(3) "Personal debt" means money due or owing or alleged to be due or owing from a natural person arising out of a transaction in which the money, property, insurance, or services which are the subject of the transaction are primarily for the debtor's personal, family, or household purposes. **Leg.H.** Added Stats 1982 ch 1364 §2, operative July 1, 1983. Amended Stats 2022 ch 883 §2 (SB 1200), effective January 1, 2023; Stats 2023 ch 131 §20 (AB 1754), effective January 1, 2024.

§683.120. Application for renewal; Effect of application

(a) The judgment creditor may renew a judgment by filing an application for renewal of the judgment with the court in which the judgment was entered.

(b) Except as otherwise provided in this article, the filing of the application renews the judgment in the amount determined under Section 683.150 and extends the period of enforceability of the judgment as renewed for a period of 10 years from the date the application is filed.

(c) Notwithstanding subdivisions (a) and (b), for a judgment identified in subdivision (c) of Section 683.110, a judgment creditor may renew the judgment only once. The filing of the application under this subdivision renews the judgment in the amount determined under Section 683.150 and extends the period of enforceability of the judgment as renewed for a period of five years from the date the application is filed. No application may be filed if the judgment was renewed on or before December 31, 2022.

(d) In the case of a money judgment payable in installments, for the purposes of enforcement and of any later renewal, the amount of the judgment as renewed shall be treated as a lump-sum money judgment entered on the date the application is filed. **Leg.H.** Added Stats 1982 ch 1364 §2, operative July 1, 1983. Amended Stats 2022 ch 883 §3 (SB 1200), effective January 1, 2023.

§683.130. Time for filing application

(a) In the case of a lump-sum money judgment or a judgment for possession or sale of property, the application for renewal of the judgment may be filed at any time before the expiration of the 10-year period of enforceability provided by Section 683.020 or, if the judgment is a renewed judgment, at any time before the expiration of the 10-year period of enforceability of the renewed judgment provided by Section 683.120.

(b) In the case of a money judgment payable in installments, the application for renewal of the judgment may be filed:

(1) If the judgment has not previously been renewed, at any time as to past due amounts that at the time of filing are not barred by the expiration of the 10-year period of enforceability provided by Sections 683.020 and 683.030.

(2) If the judgment has previously been renewed, within the time specified by subdivision (a) as to the amount of the judgment as previously renewed and, as to any past due amounts that became due and payable after the previous renewal, at any time before the expiration of the 10-year period of enforceability provided by Sections 683.020 and 683.030. **Leg.H.** Added Stats 1982 ch 1364 §2, operative July 1, 1983. Amended Stats 1991 ch 110 §14 (SB 101); Stats 1992 ch 163 §30 (AB 2641), operative January 1, 1994 (ch 718 prevails), ch 718 §4 (AB 568); Stats 1993 ch 219 §66 (AB 1500), ch 876 §8 (SB 1068), effective October 6, 1993; Stats 2000 ch 808 §4 (AB 1358), effective September 28, 2000.

§683.140. Contents of application

The application for renewal of the judgment shall be executed under oath and shall include all of the following:

(a) The title of the court where the judgment is entered and the cause and number of the action.

(b) The date of entry of the judgment and of any renewals of the judgment and where entered in the records of the court.

(c) The name and address of the judgment creditor and the name and last known address of the judgment debtor. However, the judgment creditor shall omit the name of a judgment debtor from the application for a writ of execution if the liability of that judgment debtor has ceased with regard to the judgment, including either of the following occurrences:

(1) The judgment debtor has obtained a discharge of the judgment pursuant to Title 11 of the United States Code and notice thereof has been filed with the court.

(2) The judgment creditor files an acknowledgment of satisfaction of judgment with regard to the judgment debtor pursuant to Chapter 1 (commencing with Section 724.010) of Division 5.

(d) In the case of a money judgment, the information necessary to compute the amount of the judgment as renewed. In the case of a judgment for possession or sale of property, a description of the performance remaining due. **Leg.H.** Added Stats 1982 ch 1364 §2, operative July 1, 1983. Amended Stats 2013 ch 176 §1 (SB 551), effective January 1, 2014.

§683.150. Entry of renewal by court clerk; Fees

(a) Upon the filing of the application, the court clerk shall enter the renewal of the judgment in the court records.

(b) The fee for filing an application for renewal of judgment is as provided in subdivision (b) of Section 70626 of the Government Code.

(c) In the case of a money judgment, the entry of renewal shall show the amount of the judgment as renewed. Except as provided in subdivisions (d) and (e), this amount is the amount required to satisfy the judgment on the date of the filing of the application for renewal and includes the fee for the filing of the application for renewal.

(d) In the case of a money judgment payable in installments not previously renewed, the amount of the judgment as renewed is the total of the past due installments, the costs added to the judgment pursuant to Section 685.090, and the accrued interest, which remains unsatisfied and is enforceable on the date of the filing of the application for renewal and includes the fee for the filing of the application for renewal.

(e) In the case of a money judgment payable in installments previously renewed, the amount of the judgment as renewed under the latest renewal is the total of the following which remains unsatisfied and is enforceable on the date of the filing of the application for the latest renewal:

(1) The amount of the judgment as renewed under the previous renewal.

(2) The past due installments that became due and payable after the previous renewal.

(3) The costs that have been added to the judgment pursuant to Section 685.090 after the previous renewal.

(4) The interest that has accrued on the amounts described in paragraphs (1), (2), and (3) since the last renewal.

(5) The fee for filing the application for renewal.

(f) In the case of a judgment for possession or sale of property, the entry of renewal shall describe the performance remaining due. **Leg.H.** Added Stats 1982 ch 1364 §2, operative July 1, 1983. Amended Stats 2005 ch 75 §36 (AB 145), effective July 19, 2005, operative January 1, 2006.

§683.160. Service of notice of renewal

(a) The judgment creditor shall serve a notice of renewal of the judgment on the judgment debtor. Service shall be made personally or by first-class mail and proof of service shall be filed with the court clerk. The notice shall be in a form prescribed by the Judicial Council and shall inform the judgment debtor that the judgment debtor has 60 days within which to make a motion to vacate or modify the renewal.

(b) Until proof of service is filed pursuant to subdivision (a), no writ may be issued, nor may any enforcement proceedings be commenced to enforce the judgment, except to the extent that the judgment would be enforceable had it not been renewed. **Leg.H.** Added Stats 1982 ch 1364 §2, operative July 1, 1983. Amended Stats 1985 ch 41 §4; Stats 1988 ch 900 §5; Stats 2022 ch 883 §4 (SB 1200), effective January 1, 2023.

§683.170. Vacation or modification of renewal

(a) The renewal of a judgment pursuant to this article may be vacated on any ground that would be a defense to an action on the judgment, including the ground that the amount of the renewed judgment as entered pursuant to this article is incorrect, and shall be vacated if the application for renewal was filed within five years from the time the judgment was previously renewed under this article.

(b) Not later than 60 days after service of the notice of renewal pursuant to Section 683.160, the judgment debtor may apply by noticed motion under this section for an order of the court vacating the renewal of the judgment. The notice of motion shall be served on the judgment creditor. Service shall be made personally or by mail.

(c) Upon the hearing of the motion, the renewal may be ordered vacated upon any ground provided in subdivision (a), and another and different renewal may be entered, including, but not limited to, the renewal of the judgment in a different amount if the decision of the court is that the judgment creditor is entitled to renewal in a different amount. **Leg.H.** Added Stats 1982 ch 1364 §2, operative July 1, 1983. Amended Stats 2022 ch 883 §5 (SB 1200), effective January 1, 2023.

§683.180. Extending duration of judgment lien on real property

(a) If a judgment lien on an interest in real property has been created pursuant to a money judgment and the judgment is renewed pursuant to this article, the duration of the judgment lien is extended until 10 years from the date of the filing of the application for renewal if, before the expiration of the judgment lien, a certified copy of the application for renewal is recorded with the county recorder of the county where the real property subject to the judgment lien is located.

(b) A judgment lien on an interest in real property that has been transferred subject to the lien is not extended pursuant to subdivision (a) if the transfer was recorded before the application for renewal was filed unless both of the following requirements are satisfied:

(1) A copy of the application for renewal is personally served on the transferee.

(2) Proof of such service is filed with the court clerk within 90 days after the filing of the application for renewal. **Leg.H.** Added Stats 1982 ch 1364 §2, operative July 1, 1983. Amended Stats 1983 ch 155 §9.5, effective June 30, 1983, operative July 1, 1983.

§683.190. Continuation of other liens

If a lien (other than a judgment lien on an interest in real property or an execution lien) has been created by an enforcement procedure pursuant to a judgment and the judgment is renewed pursuant to this article, the duration of the lien is extended, subject to any other limitations on its duration under this title, until 10 years from the date of the filing of the application for renewal of the judgment if, before the expiration of the lien, a certified copy of the application for renewal is served on or filed with the same person and in the same manner as the notice or order that created the lien. **Leg.H.** Added Stats 1982 ch 1364 §2, operative July 1, 1983.

§683.200. Continuation of enforcement proceedings

If a judgment is renewed pursuant to this article, any enforcement proceeding previously commenced pursuant to the judgment or to a writ or order issued pursuant to the judgment that would have ceased pursuant to Section 683.020 had the judgment not been renewed may be continued, subject to any other limitations provided in this title, if, before the expiration of the prior 10-year period of enforceability, a certified copy of the application for renewal of the judgment is filed with the levying officer, receiver, or other officer acting pursuant to such writ or order or, in other cases, is filed in the enforcement proceeding. **Leg.H.** Added Stats 1982 ch 1364 §2, operative July 1, 1983.

§683.210. Renewal during stay of enforcement

A judgment may be renewed notwithstanding any stay of enforcement of the judgment, but the renewal of the judgment does not affect the stay of enforcement. **Leg.H.** Added Stats 1982 ch 1364 §2, operative July 1, 1983.

§683.220. Limitation period for action on renewed judgment

If a judgment is renewed pursuant to this article, the date of the filing of the application for renewal shall be deemed to be the date that the period for commencing an action on the renewed judgment commences to run under Section 337.5. **Leg.H.** Added Stats 1982 ch 1364 §2, operative July 1, 1983.

ARTICLE 3
Application of Chapter

Judgments enforceable under Family Code. §683.310.
Judgments against public entities. §683.320.

§683.310. Judgments enforceable under Family Code

Except as otherwise provided in the Family Code, this chapter does not apply to a judgment or order made or entered pursuant to the Family Code. **Leg.H.** Added Stats 1982 ch 1364 §2, operative July 1, 1983. Amended Stats 1991 ch 110 §15 (SB 101); Stats 1992 ch 163 §31 (AB 2641), operative January 1, 1994; Stats 2000 ch 808 §5 (AB 1358), effective September 28, 2000.

§683.320. Judgments against public entities

This chapter does not apply to a money judgment against a public entity that is subject to Section 965.5 or 970.1 of the Government Code. **Leg.H.** Added Stats 1982 ch 1364 §2, operative July 1, 1983.

§684. [Section repealed 1983]

Leg.H. Enacted Stats 1872. Amended Code Amdts 1873–74 ch 383 §92; Stats 1973 ch 20 §9. Repealed Stats 1982 ch 1364 §1, operative July 1, 1983. See CCP §681.010.

CHAPTER 4
MANNER OF SERVICE OF WRITS, NOTICES, AND OTHER PAPERS

Article 1. Service on Attorney of Creditor or Debtor.
Article 2. Manner of Service Generally.
Article 3. Proof of Service.
Article 4. Application of Chapter.

ARTICLE 1
Service on Attorney of Creditor or Debtor

Service on attorney of judgment creditor. §684.010.
Service on attorney designated by judgment debtor. §684.020.
When service on party instead of attorney required. §684.030.
Manner of service on attorney. §684.040.
Effect of service on attorney. §684.050.

§684.010. Service on attorney of judgment creditor

Subject to Chapter 1 (commencing with Section 283) of Title 5 of Part 1 of this code and Section 215 of the Family Code, when a notice, order, or other paper is required to be served under this title on the judgment creditor, it shall be served on the judgment creditor's attorney of record rather than on the judgment creditor if the judgment creditor has an attorney of record. **Leg.H.** Added Stats 1982 ch 1364 §2, operative July 1, 1983. Amended Stats 1992 ch 163 §32 (AB 2641), operative January 1, 1994.

§684.020. Service on attorney designated by judgment debtor

(a) Except as provided in subdivision (b), when a writ, notice, order, or other paper is required to be served under this title on the judgment debtor, it shall be served on the judgment debtor instead of the attorney for the judgment debtor.

(b) The writ, notice, order, or other paper shall be served on the attorney specified by the judgment debtor rather than on the judgment debtor if all of the following requirements are satisfied:

(1) The judgment debtor has filed with the court and served on the judgment creditor a request that service on the judgment debtor under this title be made by serving the attorney specified in the request. Service on the judgment creditor of the request shall be made personally or by mail. The request shall include a consent, signed by the attorney, to receive service under this title on behalf of the judgment debtor.

(2) The request has not been revoked by the judgment debtor.

(3) The consent to receive service has not been revoked by the attorney.

(c) A request or consent under subdivision (b) may be revoked by filing with the court a notice revoking the request or consent. A copy of the notice revoking the request or consent shall be served on the judgment creditor. Service shall be made personally or by mail. The judgment creditor is not bound by the revocation until the judgment creditor has received a copy of the notice revoking the request or consent. **Leg.H.** Added Stats 1982 ch 1364 §2, operative July 1, 1983.

§684.030. When service on party instead of attorney required

Sections 684.010 and 684.020 do not apply to either of the following:

(a) A subpoena or other process to require the attendance of a party.

(b) A paper to bring a party into contempt. **Leg.H.** Added Stats 1982 ch 1364 §2, operative July 1, 1983.

§684.040. Manner of service on attorney

If service on an attorney is required under this article, service on the attorney shall be made in any of the following ways:

(a) By personal delivery to the attorney.

(b) By service in the manner provided in subdivision (1) of Section 1011.

(c) By mail in the manner provided in Section 684.120. **Leg.H.** Added Stats 1982 ch 1364 §2, operative July 1, 1983.

§684.050. Effect of service on attorney

Service on the attorney for the judgment creditor or the judgment debtor pursuant to the provisions of this article constitutes service on the judgment creditor or judgment debtor for the purposes of this title. **Leg.H.** Added Stats 1982 ch 1364 §2, operative July 1, 1983.

§684.1. [Section repealed 1983]

Leg.H. Added Stats 1951 ch 777 §1. Amended Stats 1965 ch 1972 §1; Stats 1975 ch 678 §6. Repealed Stats 1982 ch 1364 §1, operative July 1, 1983. The repealed section related to enforcement of judgment for possession of personal property.

ARTICLE 2
Manner of Service Generally

Manner of personal service. §684.110.
Designation of central locations of financial institution for service of process. §684.115.
Manner of service by mail; Extension of prescribed period of notice and time for exercising right or performing act. §684.120.
Furnishing of name and address by judgment creditor. §684.130.
Service by person authorized by levying officer to make service. §684.140.

§684.110. Manner of personal service

(a)(1) Subject to subdivisions (b), (c), and (d), if legal process is required to be personally served under this title, service shall be made in the same manner as a summons is served under Chapter 4 (commencing with Section 413.10) of Title 5.

(2) For purposes of this title, the term "legal process" shall refer to each and all of the writs, notices, orders, or other papers required or permitted to be served pursuant to this title.

(b) If the legal process is required to be personally served under this title and service on an attorney is required under Article 1 (commencing with Section 684.010), service shall be made on the attorney in the manner provided in Section 684.040.

(c) If the legal process is required to be personally served on (1) a financial institution in connection with a deposit account or with property held for safekeeping, as collateral for an obligation owed to the financial institution or in a safe-deposit box, (2) a title insurer (as defined in Section 12340.4 of the Insurance Code) or underwritten title company (as defined in Section 12340.5 of the Insurance Code), or (3) an industrial loan company (as defined in Section 18003 of the Financial Code), service shall be made at the office or branch that has actual possession of the property levied upon or at which a deposit account levied upon is carried and shall be made upon the officer, manager, or other person in charge of the office or branch at the time of service. For purposes of this section, the office or branch at which a deposit account levied upon is carried shall mean the branch, office, or other location where the financial institution maintains the account.

(d) Notwithstanding subdivision (c), with respect to legal process served on a financial institution, if the financial institution has designated a central location for service of legal process pursuant to Section 684.115, unless the financial institution elects to treat legal process served at a branch or office as effective, that legal process so served on the branch or office will not reach those accounts or property and need not be reported on the financial institution's garnishee memorandum.

(e) Notwithstanding subdivision (c), a financial institution, title insurer, or industrial loan company, in its discretion and without violating any obligation to its customer, may act upon service of legal process at any of its offices or branches, whether or not the office or branch is the location wherein accounts or property that may be reached by the process is or are maintained or located. **Leg.H.** Added Stats 1982 ch 1364 §2, operative July 1, 1983. Amended Stats 2012 ch 484 §6 (AB 2364), effective January 1, 2013.

§684.115. Designation of central locations of financial institution for service of process

(a) A financial institution may, and if it has more than nine branches or offices at which it conducts its business within this state shall, designate one or more central locations for service of legal process within this state. Each designated location shall be referred to as a "central location." [1] **A financial institution may designate a third-party agent as** a central location for service of legal process. **If a financial institution designates a third-party agent as a central location**, the financial institution shall [2] **designate at least one additional central location that is not located in the same county as another designated central location. The financial institution may designate the same third-party agent as multiple central locations for service of legal process if the third-party agent maintains physical locations in multiple counties.**

(b) If a financial institution elects or is required to designate a central location for service of legal process, pursuant to subdivision (a), the financial institution shall file a notice of its designation with the Department of Financial Protection and Innovation which filing shall be effective upon filing and shall contain all of the following:

(1) The physical address of the central location.

(2) The days and hours during which service will be accepted at the central location **and, if the central location is a third-party agent, the name of the third party agent**.

(3) If the central location will not accept service of legal process directed at deposit accounts maintained or property held at all of the financial institution's branches or offices within this state, or if the service accepted at the central location will not apply to safe-deposit boxes or other property of the judgment debtor held by or for the judgment debtor, the filing shall also contain sufficient information to permit a determination of the limitation or limitations, including, in the case of a limitation applicable to certain branches or offices, an identification of the branches or offices as to which service at the central location will not apply and the nature of the limitation applicable to those branches or offices. If the limitation will apply to all branches or offices of the financial institution within this state, the filing may indicate the nature of the limitation and that it applies to all branches or offices, in lieu of an identification of branches or offices as to which the limitation applies. To the extent that a financial institution's designation of a central location for service of legal process covers the process directed at deposit accounts, safe-deposit boxes, or other property of the judgment debtor held by or for the judgment debtor at a particular branch or office located within this state, the branch or office shall be a branch or office covered by central process.

[3] **(c)** Should a financial institution required to designate a central location fail to do so, each branch of that institution located in this state shall be deemed to be a central location at which service of legal process may be made, and all of the institution's branches or offices located within this state shall be deemed to be a branch or office covered by central process.

[4] **(d)** Subject to any limitation noted pursuant to paragraph (3) of subdivision [5] **(b)**, service of legal process at a central location of a financial institution shall be effective against all deposit accounts and all property held for safekeeping, as collateral for an obligation owed to the financial institution or in a safe-deposit box if the same is described in the legal process and held by the financial institution at any branch or office covered by central process and located within this state. However, while service of legal process at the central location will establish a lien on all property, if any property other than deposit accounts is physically held by the financial institution in a county other than that in which the designated central location is located, the financial institution shall include in its garnishee's memorandum the location or locations of the property, and the judgment creditor shall obtain a writ of execution covering the property and directed to the levying officer in that county to accomplish the turnover of the property and shall forward the writ and related required documentation to the levying officer in the county in which the property is held.

[6] **(e)** A financial institution may modify or revoke any designation made pursuant to subdivision (a) by filing the modification or revocation with the Department of Financial Protection and Innovation. The modification or revocation shall be effective when the Department of Financial Protection and Innovation's records have been updated to reflect the modification or revocation, provided that the judgment creditor may rely upon the superseded designation during the 30-day period following the effective date of the revocation or modification.

[7] **(f)**(1) The Department of Financial Protection and Innovation shall update its online records to reflect a filing by a financial institution pursuant to [8] **subdivisions (a) and (b)** or a modification or revocation filed by a financial institution pursuant to subdivision [9] **(e)** within 10 business days following the filing by the financial institution. The Department of Financial Protection and Innovation's internet website shall reflect the date its online records for each financial institution have most recently been updated.

(2) The Department of Financial Protection and Innovation shall provide any person requesting it with a copy of each current filing made by a financial institution pursuant to [10] **subdivisions (a) and (b)**. The Department of Financial Protection and Innovation may satisfy its obligation under this subdivision by posting all current designations of a financial institution, or the pertinent information therein, on an internet website available to the public without charge, and if that information is made available, the Department of Financial Protection and Innovation may impose a reasonable fee for furnishing that information in any other manner.

[11] **(g)** As to deposit accounts maintained or property held for safekeeping, as collateral for an obligation owed to the financial institution or in a safe-deposit box at a branch or office covered by central process, service of legal process at a location other than a central location designated by the financial institution shall not be effective unless the financial institution, in its absolute discretion, elects to act upon the process at that location as if it were effective. In the absence of an election, the financial institution may respond to the legal process by mailing or delivery of the garnishee's memorandum to the levying officer within the time otherwise provided therefor, with a statement on the garnishee's memorandum that the legal process was not properly served at the financial institution's designated location for receiving legal process, and, therefore, was not processed, and the address at which the financial institution is to receive legal process.

[12] **(h)** If any legal process is served at a central location of a financial institution pursuant to this section, all related papers to be served on the financial institution shall be served at that location, unless agreed to the contrary between the serving party and the financial institution.

[13] **(i)** This subdivision shall apply whenever a financial institution operates within this state at least one branch or office in addition to its head office or main office, as applicable, or a financial institution headquartered in another state operates more than one branch or office within this state, and no central location has been designated or deemed to have been designated by the institution for service of legal process relating to deposit accounts maintained at the financial institution's head office or main office, as applicable, and branches located within this state. If a judgment creditor reasonably believes that, pursuant to Section 700.140 and, if applicable, Section 700.160, any act of enforcement would be effective against a specific deposit account maintained at a financial institution described in this subdivision, the judgment creditor may file with the financial institution a written request that the financial institution identify the branch or office within this state at which a specified account might be maintained by the financial institution. The written request shall contain the following statements or information:

(1) The name of the person reasonably believed by the judgment creditor to be a person in whose name the specified deposit account stands.

(2) If the name of the person reasonably believed by the judgment creditor to be a person in whose name the specified deposit account stands is not a judgment debtor identified in the writ of execution, a statement that a person reasonably believed by the judgment creditor to be a person in whose name the specified deposit account stands will be appropriately identified in the legal process to be served pursuant to Section 700.160, including any supplementary papers, such as a court order or affidavit if the same will be required by Section 700.160.

(3) The specific identifying number of the account reasonably believed to be maintained with the financial institution and standing in the name of the judgment debtor or other person.

(4) The address of the requesting party.

(5) An affidavit by the judgment creditor or the judgment creditor's counsel stating substantially the following:

"I hereby declare that this deposit account location request complies with Section 684.115 of the Code of Civil Procedure, that the account or accounts of the judgment debtor or other person or persons appropriately identified in the legal process and specified herein are subject to a valid writ of execution, or court order, that I have a reasonable belief, formed after an inquiry reasonable under the circumstances, that the financial institution receiving this deposit account location request has an account standing in the name of the judgment debtor or other person or persons appropriately identified in the legal process, and that information pertaining to the location of the account will assist the judgment creditor in enforcing the judgment."

[14] **(j)** The affidavit contemplated by subdivision [15] **(i)** shall be signed by the judgment creditor or the judgment creditor's counsel and filed at the financial institution's head office located within this state or, if the financial institution's head office is in another state, at one of its branches or offices within this state. Failure to comply with the requirements of subdivision [16] **(i)** and this subdivision shall be sufficient basis for the financial institution to refuse to produce the information that would otherwise be required by subdivision [17] **(k)**.

[18] **(k)** Within 10 banking days following receipt by a financial institution at the applicable location specified in subdivision [19] **(j)** of a request contemplated by subdivision [20] **(i)**, as to each specific deposit account identified in the request contemplated by subdivision [21] **(i)**, the financial institution shall respond by mailing, by first-class mail with postage prepaid, to the requester's address as specified in the request a response indicating the branch or office location of the financial institution at which the specified deposit account might be maintained, or, if the specified deposit account, if it exists, would not be maintained at a specific location, at least one place within this state at which legal process relating to the deposit account should or may be served. The response to be furnished pursuant to this subdivision shall not require the financial institution to determine whether an account exists or, if an account does exist, whether it would be reached by the legal process, rather, the branch or office location shall be determined and reported by the financial institution based solely upon its determination that an account with the identifying number provided by the requester would be maintained at that branch if an account did exist, and the response shall not contain any information about the name in which the account stands or any other information concerning the account, if it exists. If more than one account number is specified in the request, the financial institution's responses as to some or all of those account numbers may be combined in a single writing.

[22] **(l)** A response furnished in good faith by the financial institution pursuant to subdivision [23] **(k)** shall not be deemed to violate the privacy of any person in whose name the specified deposit account stands nor the privacy of any other person, and shall not require the consent of the person in whose name the account stands nor that of any other person.

[24] **(m)** A financial institution shall not notify the person in whose name the specified deposit account stands or any other person related to the specified account of the receipt of any request made pursuant to subdivision [25] **(i)** and affecting that person's or persons' accounts at the financial institution, provided that the financial institution shall have no liability for its failure to comply with the provisions of this subdivision.

(n) For purposes of this section, "third-party agent" means a non-financial institution entity, such as a corporation, that is in the business of accepting service of legal process on behalf of financial institutions and other businesses. Third-party agent does not include a licensed attorney or law firm acting on behalf of a financial institution. Leg.H. Added Stats 2012 ch 484 §7 (AB 2364), effective January 1, 2013. Amended Stats 2013 ch 76 §23 (AB 383), effective January 1, 2014; Stats 2014 ch 401 §15 (AB 2763), effective January 1, 2015; Stats 2022 ch 452 §40 (SB 1498), effective January 1, 2023; Stats 2024 ch 222 §2 (AB 2067), effective January 1, 2025.

§684.115. 2024 Deletes. [1] If a financial institution elects or is required to designate [2] file a notice of its designation with the Department of Financial Protection and Innovation which filing shall be effective upon filing and shall contain all of the following: [3] (b) [4] (c) [5] (a) [6] (d) [7] (e) [8] subdivision (a) [9] (d) [10] subdivision (a) [11] (f) [12] (g) [13] (h) [14] (i) [15] (h) [16] (h) [17] (j) [18] (j) [19] (i) [20] (h) [21] (h) [22] (k) [23] (j) [24] (l) [25] (h)

§684.120. Manner of service by mail; Extension of prescribed period of notice and time for exercising right or performing act

(a) Except as otherwise provided in this title, if a writ, notice, order, or other paper is to be served by mail under this title, it shall be sent by first-class mail (unless some other type of mail is specifically required) and shall be deposited in a post office, mailbox, sub-post office, substation, mail chute, or other like facility regularly maintained by the United States Postal Service, in a sealed envelope, with postage paid, addressed as follows:

(1) If an attorney is being served in place of the judgment creditor or judgment debtor as provided in Section 684.010 or 684.020, to the attorney at the last address given by the attorney on any paper filed in the proceeding and served on the party making the service.

(2) If any other person is being served, to such person at the person's current mailing address if known or, if unknown, at the address last given by the person on any paper filed in the proceeding and served on the party making the service.

(3) If the mailing cannot be made as provided in paragraph (1) or (2), to the person at the person's last known address.

(b) Service by mail is complete at the time of deposit; but, unless the court prescribes a shorter period of time, any prescribed period of notice and any right or duty to do any act or make any response within any prescribed period or on a date certain after a paper is served by mail is extended:

(1) Five days if the place of address is within the State of California.

(2) Ten days if the place of address is outside the State of California but within the United States.

(3) Twenty days if the place of address is outside the United States.

(c) The writ, notice, order, or other paper served by mail under this section shall bear a notation of the date and place of mailing or be accompanied by an unsigned copy of the affidavit or certificate of mailing. This subdivision is directory only. **Leg.H.** Added Stats 1982 ch 1364 §2, operative July 1, 1983.

§684.130. Furnishing of name and address by judgment creditor

(a) If the levying officer is required by any provision of this title to serve any writ, order, notice, or other paper on any person, the judgment creditor shall include in the instructions to the levying officer the correct name and address of the person. The judgment creditor shall use reasonable diligence to ascertain the correct name and address of the person.

(b)(1) Where the judgment upon which the writ is issued is for personal debt, as defined in subdivision (d) of Section 683.110, this subdivision shall apply.

(2) The judgment creditor shall also provide the levying officer with a declaration stating that the judgment creditor has verified using reasonable diligence within the past 12 months that the judgment debtor's address is correct to the best of the declarant's knowledge, and describing the verification dates and the methods used, which may include, but are not limited to, the following methods:

(A) Receipt of correspondence from the judgment debtor, dated no more than 12 months before the execution of the declaration, that includes a return address or other comparable verification of the judgment debtor's address.

(B) Transmittal of a letter by certified mail, or other method of transmission through the United States Postal Service providing a return receipt, to the judgment debtor's address, with a return receipt dated no more than 12 months before the execution of the declaration that is signed by the judgment debtor.

(C) Verification of the judgment debtor's current address by a commercial address verification service, including skip-tracing, or, if reasonably available, a public record database, followed by dispatch of a letter, by first-class mail to the verified address, that was not returned to sender.

(3) The levying officer shall not accept or serve any writ, order, notice, or other paper on any person if the judgment creditor fails to provide a declaration as described in paragraph (2).

(4) Upon notice by the judgment debtor that the requirements of this section have not been met, the court shall stay the notice of levy or earnings withholding order until the requirements of this section have been satisfied.

(5) The judgment creditor's cost of verification of the judgment debtor's address is not recoverable.

(6) The judgment creditor shall file with the court the signed declaration within five business days after delivering the declaration to the levying officer.

[1] (c) Unless the levying officer has actual knowledge that the name or address included in the instructions is incorrect, the levying officer shall rely on the instructions in serving the writ, order, notice, or other paper on the person. **Leg.H.** Added Stats 1982 ch 1364 §2, operative July 1, 1983. Amended Stats 2024 ch 514 §1 (AB 2837), effective January 1, 2025.

§684.130. 2024 Deletes. [1] (b)

§684.140. Service by person authorized by levying officer to make service

If a provision of this title provides for service by the levying officer of an order, notice, or other paper that runs in favor of a particular person, personal service of the paper may be made by the person or the person's agent if the levying officer gives permission. The levying officer's permission may be evidenced by a certificate signed by the levying officer. This section does not authorize the levying officer to give permission to serve a writ or notice of levy. If service is made by a person or the person's agent pursuant to this section, the cost of the service is not a recoverable cost. Nothing in this section limits the authority of a registered process server provided in this title. **Leg.H.** Added Stats 1982 ch 1364 §2, operative July 1, 1983.

§684.2. [Section repealed 1983]

Leg.H. Added Stats 1974 ch 1516 §14, operative January 1, 1977. Repealed Stats 1982 ch 1364 §1, operative July 1, 1983. The repealed section related to satisfaction of judgment involving property subject to attachment.

ARTICLE 3
Proof of Service

Proof of service of notice of court hearing. §684.210.
Proof of service, posting, or publication. §684.220.

§684.210. Proof of service of notice of court hearing

If service of notice of a court hearing is required under this title, proof of service of the notice shall be made at or before the hearing to the satisfaction of the court. **Leg.H.** Added Stats 1982 ch 1364 §2, operative July 1, 1983.

§684.220. Proof of service, posting, or publication

Proof of service or of posting or publication under this title may be made by, but is not limited to, the following means:

(a) If service is made in the same manner as a summons is served under Chapter 4 (commencing with Section 413.10) of Title 5, proof of service may be made in the manner provided in Article 5 (commencing with Section 417.10) of that chapter.

(b) If service is made in the same manner as a summons is served under Section 415.10 or 415.20, proof of service may be made by affidavit of the person making the service showing the time, place, and manner of service and the facts showing that the service was made in accordance with the applicable statutory provisions. The affidavit shall recite or in other manner show the name of the person to whom the papers served were delivered and, if appropriate, the title of the person or the capacity in which the person was served.

(c) Proof of service by mail as provided in Section 684.120 may be made in the manner prescribed in Section 1013a.

(d) Proof of posting may be made by the affidavit of the person who posted the notice, showing the time and place of posting.

(e) Proof of publication may be made by the affidavit of the publisher or printer, or the foreman or principal clerk of the publisher or printer, showing the time and place of publication.

(f) Proof of service may be made by the written admission of the person served.

(g) Proof of service however made, or of posting or publication, may be made by testimonial evidence. **Leg.H.** Added Stats 1982 ch 1364 §2, operative July 1, 1983.

ARTICLE 4
Application of Chapter

Provisions not applicable to wage garnishment. §684.310.

§684.310. Provisions not applicable to wage garnishment

Except for Sections 684.130 and 684.140, the provisions of Article 1 (commencing with Section 684.010) and Article 2 (commencing with Section 684.110) do not apply to service under Chapter 5 (commencing with Section 706.010) of Division 2 (wage garnishment). **Leg.H.** Added Stats 1982 ch 1364 §2, operative July 1, 1983.

§685. [Section repealed 1983]

Leg.H. Enacted Stats 1872. Amended Stats 1895 ch 33 §1; Stats 1933 ch 971 §1; Stats 1955 ch 754 §2; Stats 1957 ch 910 §1. Repealed Stats 1982 ch 1364 §1, operative July 1, 1983. See CCP §§683.110 et seq.

CHAPTER 5
INTEREST AND COSTS

Rate of interest on judgment. §685.010.
Commencement of interest on judgment payable in installments. §685.020.
Cessation of interest. §685.030.
Right to costs of enforcing judgment. §685.040.
Costs and interest under writ. §685.050.
Memorandum of costs enforcing judgment; Additional costs. §685.070.
Motion for costs of enforcing judgment. §685.080.
Addition of costs to judgment. §685.090.
Addition of costs for service of writs to judgment. §685.095.
Deposit of levying officer's costs. §685.100.
Law relating to prejudgment interest. §685.110.

§685.010. Rate of interest on judgment

(a)(1) Except as provided in paragraph (2), interest accrues at the rate of 10 percent per annum on the principal amount of a money judgment remaining unsatisfied.

(2)(A) For judgments entered on or after January 1, 2023, or where an application for renewal of judgment is filed on or after January 1, 2023, interest accrues at the rate of 5 percent per annum on the principal amount of a money judgment remaining unsatisfied in the following cases:

(i) The principal amount of a money judgment of under two hundred thousand dollars ($200,000) remaining unsatisfied against a debtor for a claim related to medical expenses.

(ii) The principal amount of a money judgment of under fifty thousand dollars ($50,000) remaining unsatisfied against a debtor for a claim related to personal debt.

(B) The claims specified in subparagraph (A) include, but are not limited to, a claim based on any of the following transactions:

(i) An agreement governing the use of a credit card as defined in subdivision (a) of Section 1747.02 of the Civil Code.

(ii) A conditional sale contract as defined in subdivision (a) of Section 2981 of the Civil Code.

(iii) A deferred deposit transaction as defined in subdivision (a) of Section 23001 of the Financial Code.

(C) For purposes of this paragraph, the following definitions apply:

(i) "Debtor" means a natural person from whom money is due or owing or alleged to be due or owing.

(ii) "Due or owing" does not include debts incurred due to or obtained by tortious or fraudulent conduct or judgments for unpaid wages, damages, or penalties owed to an employee.

(iii) "Personal debt" means money due or owing or alleged to be due or owing from a natural person arising out of a transaction in which the money, property, insurance, or services which are the subject of the transaction are primarily for the debtor's personal, family, or household purposes.

(b) The Legislature reserves the right to change the rate of interest provided in subdivision (a) at any time, regardless of the date of entry of the judgment or the date any obligation upon which the judgment is based was incurred. A change in the rate of interest may be made applicable only to the interest that accrues after the operative date of the statute that changes the rate. **Leg.H.** Added Stats 1982 ch 1364 §2, operative July 1, 1983. Amended Stats 2022 ch 883 §6 (SB 1200), effective January 1, 2023; Stats 2023 ch 131 §21 (AB 1754), effective January 1, 2024.

Prior Law: Former CCP §683.010, similar to the present section, was added Stats 1982 ch 150 §3 and repealed Stats 1982 ch 497 §186, operative July 1, 1983, ch 1364 §1, operative July 1, 1983.

§685.020. Commencement of interest on judgment payable in installments

(a) Except as provided in subdivision (b), interest commences to accrue on a money judgment on the date of entry of the judgment.

(b) Unless the judgment otherwise provides, if a money judgment is payable in installments, interest commences to accrue as to each installment on the date the installment becomes due. **Leg.H.** Added Stats 1982 ch 1364 §2, operative July 1, 1983. Amended Stats 1983 ch 155 §10, effective June 30, 1983, operative July 1, 1983.

§685.030. Cessation of interest

(a) If a money judgment is satisfied in full pursuant to a writ under this title, interest ceases to accrue on the judgment:

(1) If the proceeds of collection are paid in a lump sum, on the date of levy.

(2) If the money judgment is satisfied pursuant to an earnings withholding order, on the date and in the manner provided in Section 706.024 or Section 706.028.

(3) In any other case, on the date the proceeds of sale or collection are actually received by the levying officer.

(b) If a money judgment is satisfied in full other than pursuant to a writ under this title, interest ceases to accrue on the date the judgment is satisfied in full.

(c) If a money judgment is partially satisfied pursuant to a writ under this title or is otherwise partially satisfied, interest ceases to accrue as to the part satisfied on the date the part is satisfied.

(d) For the purposes of subdivisions (b) and (c), the date a money judgment is satisfied in full or in part is the earliest of the following times:

(1) The date satisfaction is actually received by the judgment creditor.

(2) The date satisfaction is tendered to the judgment creditor or deposited in court for the judgment creditor.

(3) The date of any other performance that has the effect of satisfaction.

(e) The clerk of a court may enter in the Register of Actions a writ of execution on a money judgment as returned wholly satisfied when the judgment amount, as specified on the writ, is fully collected and only an interest deficit of no more than ten dollars ($10) exists, due to automation of the continual daily interest accrual calculation. **Leg.H.** Added Stats 1982 ch 1364 §2, operative July 1, 1983. Amended Stats 1991 ch 1090 §4.5 (AB 1484); Stats 1992 ch 283 §1 (SB 1372), effective July 21, 1992; Stats 1998 ch 931 §88 (SB 2139), effective September 28, 1998; Stats 2001 ch 812 §4 (AB 223).

1992 Note: Section 685.030, as amended by ch 283, applies to all writs of execution and earnings withholding orders regardless of whether they were issued before July 21, 1992. Stats 1992 ch 283 §17.

§685.040. Right to costs of enforcing judgment

The judgment creditor is entitled to the reasonable and necessary costs of enforcing a judgment. Attorney's fees incurred in enforcing a judgment are not included in costs collectible under this title unless otherwise provided by law. Attorney's fees incurred in enforcing a judgment are included as costs collectible under this title if the underlying judgment includes an award of attorney's fees to the judgment creditor pursuant to subparagraph (A) of paragraph (10) of subdivision (a) of Section 1033.5. **Leg.H.** Added Stats 1982 ch 1364 §2, operative July 1, 1983. Amended Stats 1992 ch 1348 §3 (AB 2616).

§685.050. Costs and interest under writ

(a) If a writ is issued pursuant to this title to enforce a judgment, the costs and interest to be satisfied in a levy under the writ are the following:

(1) The statutory fee for issuance of the writ.

(2) The amount of interest that has accrued from the date of entry or renewal of the judgment to the date of issuance of the writ, as adjusted for partial satisfactions, if the judgment creditor has filed an affidavit with the court clerk stating such amount.

(3) The amount of interest that accrues on the principal amount of the judgment remaining unsatisfied from the date of issuance of the writ until the date interest ceases to accrue.

(4) The levying officer's statutory costs for performing the duties under the writ.

(b) In a levy under the writ, the levying officer shall do all of the following:

(1) Collect the amount of costs and interest entered on the writ pursuant to paragraphs (1) and (2) of subdivision (a).

(2) Compute and collect the amount of additional interest required to be collected by paragraph (3) of subdivision (a) by reference to the daily interest entered on the writ. If amounts collected periodically do not fully satisfy the money judgment, the levying officer shall adjust the amount of daily interest to reflect the partial satisfactions, and make later collections by reference to the adjusted amount of daily interest.

(3) Determine and collect the amount of additional costs pursuant to paragraph (4) of subdivision (a). **Leg.H.** Added Stats 1982 ch 1364 §2, operative July 1, 1983. Amended Stats 1992 ch 283 §2 (SB 1372), effective July 21, 1992; Stats 2010 ch 4 §1 (AB 680), effective January 1, 2011.

1992 Note: Section 685.050, as amended by ch 283, applies to all writs of execution and earnings withholding orders regardless of whether they were issued before July 21, 1992. Stats 1992 ch 283 §17.

§685.070. Memorandum of costs enforcing judgment; Additional costs

(a) The judgment creditor may claim under this section the following costs of enforcing a judgment, **which shall not include costs exempted under this title**:

(1) Statutory fees for preparing and issuing, and recording and indexing, an abstract of judgment or a certified copy of a judgment.

(2) Statutory fees for filing a notice of judgment lien on personal property.

(3) Statutory fees for issuing a writ for the enforcement of the judgment to the extent that the fees are not satisfied pursuant to Section 685.050.

(4) Statutory costs of the levying officer for performing the duties under a writ to the extent that the costs are not satisfied pursuant to Section 685.050 and the statutory fee of the levying officer for performing the duties under the Wage Garnishment Law to the extent that the fee has not been satisfied pursuant to the wage garnishment.

(5) Costs incurred in connection with any proceeding under Chapter 6 (commencing with Section 708.010) of Division 2 that have been approved as to amount, reasonableness, and necessity by the judge or referee conducting the proceeding.

(6) Attorney's fees, if allowed by Section 685.040.

(b) Before the judgment is fully satisfied but not later than two years after the costs have been incurred, the judgment creditor claiming costs under this section shall file a memorandum of costs with the court clerk and serve a copy on the judgment debtor. Service shall be made personally or by mail. The memorandum of costs shall be executed under oath by a person who has knowledge of the facts and shall state that to the person's best knowledge and belief the costs are correct, are reasonable and necessary, and have not been satisfied.

(c) Within 10 days after the memorandum of costs is served on the judgment debtor, the judgment debtor may apply to the court on noticed motion to have the costs taxed by the court. The notice of motion shall be served on the judgment creditor. Service shall be made personally or by mail. The court shall make an order allowing or disallowing the costs to the extent justified under the circumstances of the case.

(d) If no motion to tax costs is made within the time provided in subdivision (c), the costs claimed in the memorandum are allowed.

(e) If a memorandum of costs for the costs specified in subdivision (a) is filed at the same time as an application for a writ of execution, these statutory costs not already allowed by the court in an amount not to exceed one hundred dollars ($100) in the aggregate may be included in the amount specified in the writ of execution, subject to subsequent disallowance as ordered by the court pursuant to a motion to tax if filed by the debtor. The memorandum of costs shall contain the following statement: "The fees sought under this memorandum may be disallowed by a court upon a motion to tax filed by the debtor notwithstanding the fees having been included in the writ of execution." The inclusion of the above costs in the writ of execution or the pendency of the motion to tax on these costs shall not be cause for the clerk of the court to delay issuing the writ of execution or for the levying officer to delay enforcing the writ of execution.

(f) Section 1013, extending the time within which a right may be exercised or an act may be done, applies to this section. **Leg.H.** Added Stats 1982 ch 1364 §2, operative July 1, 1983. Amended Stats 1990 ch 790 §1 (SB 2099); Stats 1992 ch 1348 §4 (AB 2616); Stats 1996 ch 60 §2 (SB 52); Stats 2024 ch 514 §2 (AB 2837), effective January 1, 2025.

§685.080. Motion for costs of enforcing judgment

(a) The judgment creditor may claim costs authorized by Section 685.040 by noticed motion. The motion shall be made before the judgment is satisfied in full, but not later than two years after the costs have been incurred. The costs claimed under this section may include, but are not limited to, costs that may be claimed under Section 685.070 and costs incurred but not approved by the court or referee in a proceeding under Chapter 6 (commencing with Section 708.010) of Division 2.

(b) The notice of motion shall describe the costs claimed, shall state their amount, and shall be supported by an affidavit of a person who has knowledge of the facts stating that to the person's best knowledge and belief the costs are correct, are reasonable and necessary, and have not been satisfied. The notice of motion shall be served on the judgment debtor. Service shall be made personally or by mail.

(c) The court shall make an order allowing or disallowing the costs to the extent justified under the circumstances of the case. **Leg.H.** Added Stats 1982 ch 1364 §2, operative July 1, 1983.

§685.090. Addition of costs to judgment

(a) Costs are added to and become a part of the judgment:

(1) Upon the filing of an order allowing the costs pursuant to this chapter.

(2) If a memorandum of costs is filed pursuant to Section 685.070 and no motion to tax is made, upon the expiration of the time for making the motion.

(3) As specified in Section 685.095.

(b) The costs added to the judgment pursuant to this section are included in the principal amount of the judgment remaining unsatisfied.

(c) If a writ or earnings withholding order is outstanding at the time the costs are added to the judgment pursuant to this section, the levying officer shall add the amount of those costs to the amount to be collected pursuant to the writ or earnings withholding order if the levying officer receives either of the following before the writ or earnings withholding order is returned:

(1) A certified copy of the court order allowing the costs.

(2) A certificate from the clerk of the court that the costs have been added to the judgment where the costs have been added to the judgment after a memorandum of costs has been filed pursuant to Section 685.070 and no motion to tax has been made within the time allowed for making the motion.

(d) The levying officer shall include the costs described in subdivision (c) in the amount of the sale or collection distributed to the judgment creditor only if the levying officer receives the certified copy of the court order or the clerk's certificate before the distribution is made. **Leg.H.** Added Stats 1982 ch 1364 §2, operative July 1, 1983. Amended Stats 1992 ch 283 §3 (SB 1372), effective July 21, 1992; Stats 1995 ch 576 §3 (AB 1225).

1992 Note: Section 685.090, as amended by ch 283, applies to all writs of execution and earnings withholding orders regardless of whether they were issued before July 21, 1992. Stats 1992 ch 283 §17.

§685.095. Addition of costs for service of writs to judgment

When a writ is served by a levying officer or registered process server, the costs for that service, as determined pursuant to Section 1033.5, shall be added to and become part of the judgment. **Leg.H.** Added Stats 1984 ch 759 §3. Amended Stats 1987 ch 1080 §4.

§685.100. Deposit of levying officer's costs

(a) Except as otherwise provided by law:

(1) As a prerequisite to the performance by the levying officer of a duty under this title, the judgment creditor shall deposit a sum of money with the levying officer sufficient to pay the costs of performing the duty.

(2) As a prerequisite to the taking of property into custody by the levying officer, whether by keeper or otherwise, the judgment creditor shall deposit with the levying officer a sum of money sufficient to pay the costs of taking the property and keeping it safely for a period not to exceed 15 days. If continuation of the custody of the property is required, the levying officer shall, from time to time, demand orally or in writing that the judgment creditor deposit additional amounts to cover estimated costs for periods not to exceed 30 days each. A written demand may be mailed or delivered to the judgment creditor. The judgment creditor has not less than three business days after receipt of the demand within which to comply with the demand. If the amount demanded is not paid within the

time specified in the oral or written demand, the levying officer shall release the property.

(b) The levying officer is not liable for failure to take or hold property unless the judgment creditor has complied with the provisions of this section. **Leg.H.** Added Stats 1982 ch 1364 §2, operative July 1, 1983.

§685.110. Law relating to prejudgment interest

Nothing in this chapter affects the law relating to prejudgment interest. **Leg.H.** Added Stats 1982 ch 1364 §2, operative July 1, 1983.

§686. [Section repealed 1981]

Leg.H. Enacted Stats 1872. Repealed Stats 1980 ch 124 §3. See CCP §§686.010 and 686.020.

CHAPTER 6
ENFORCEMENT AFTER DEATH OF JUDGMENT CREDITOR OR JUDGMENT DEBTOR

Enforcement after death of judgment creditor. §686.010.
Enforcement after death of judgment debtor. §686.020.

§686.010. Enforcement after death of judgment creditor

After the death of the judgment creditor, the judgment may be enforced as provided in this title by the judgment creditor's executor or administrator or successor in interest. **Leg.H.** Added Stats 1982 ch 1364 §2, operative July 1, 1983.

Prior Law: Former CCP §686.010, similar to the present section, was added Stats 1980 ch 124 §4 and repealed Stats 1982 ch 1364 §1, operative July 1, 1983.

§686.020. Enforcement after death of judgment debtor

After the death of the judgment debtor, enforcement of a judgment against property in the judgment debtor's estate is governed by the Probate Code, and not by this title. **Leg.H.** Added Stats 1982 ch 1364 §2, operative July 1, 1983. Amended Stats 1989 ch 1416 §21.

Prior Law: Former CCP §686.020, relating to death of judgment debtor, was added Stats 1980 ch 124 §5 and repealed Stats 1982 ch 1364 §1, operative July 1, 1983.

§687. [Section repealed 1983]

Leg.H. Enacted Stats 1872. Amended Stats 1907 ch 360 §2; Stats 1933 ch 744 §134; Stats 1978 ch 1419 §4. Repealed Stats 1982 ch 1364 §1, operative July 1, 1983. See CCP §§699.080, 699.510, 712.010.

CHAPTER 7
LEVYING OFFICERS

Instructions to levying officer; Accompaniment by writ of execution. §687.010.
Endorsement and collection of certain instruments by levying officer. §687.020.
Manner of custody. §687.030.
Liability of levying officer. §687.040.
Levying officer's lien. §687.050.

§687.010. Instructions to levying officer; Accompaniment by writ of execution

(a) The judgment creditor shall give the levying officer instructions in writing. The instructions shall be signed by the judgment creditor's attorney of record or, if the judgment creditor does not have an attorney of record, by the judgment creditor. The instructions shall contain the information needed or requested by the levying officer to comply with this title, including, but not limited to, all of the following:

(1) An adequate description of any property to be levied upon.
(2) A statement whether the property is a dwelling.
(3) If the property is a dwelling, whether it is real or personal property.
(4) The name of the judgment debtor. If the judgment debtor is other than a natural person, the type of legal entity shall be stated.

(b) Subject to subdivision (c), the levying officer shall act in accordance with the written instructions to the extent the actions are taken in conformance with the provisions of this title.

(c) Except to the extent the levying officer has actual knowledge that the information is incorrect, the levying officer may rely on any information contained in the written instructions.

(d) The levying officer instructions may be transmitted electronically to the levying officer pursuant to Chapter 2 (commencing with Section 263) of Title 4 of Part 1.

(e) If the instructions directing the levying officer to perform a levy are accompanied by a writ of execution for money, possession, or sale of personal or real property issued by the court as an electronic record, as defined in subdivision (b) of Section 263.1, or a document printed from an electronic record issued by the court, the instructions shall also include all of the following information, as stated in the writ:

(1) The date of issuance of the writ.
(2) The name of each judgment creditor and judgment debtor.
(3) The amount of the total judgment for money, a description of the property subject to a judgment for possession or sale, or both the amount and the description.
(4) A statement indicating that the accompanying writ is either of the following:
(A) An original writ, or a copy of the original writ issued by the court as an electronic record, not already in the possession of the levying officer.
(B) A copy of the original writ already in possession of the levying officer.

(f) Except to the extent the levying officer has actual knowledge that the information in the electronic writ has been altered, the levying officer may proceed in the same manner as if in possession of a paper version of the original writ. **Leg.H.** Added Stats 1982 ch 1364 §2, operative July 1, 1983. Amended Stats 2010 ch 680 §5 (AB 2394), effective January 1, 2011; Stats 2013 ch 156 §1 (AB 1167), effective January 1, 2014.

§687.020. Endorsement and collection of certain instruments by levying officer

(a) As used in this section, "instrument" means a check, draft, money order, or other order for the withdrawal of money from a financial institution, the United States, any state, or any public entity within any state.

(b) If an instrument is payable to the judgment debtor on demand and comes into the possession of a levying officer pursuant to this title, the levying officer shall promptly endorse and present the instrument for payment.

(c) The levying officer shall endorse the instrument by writing on the instrument (1) the name of the judgment debtor, (2) the name and official title of the levying officer, (3) the title of the court where the judgment is entered, and (4) the date of entry of the judgment and where entered in the records of the court. The endorsement is as valid as if the instrument were endorsed by the judgment debtor. No financial institution or public entity on which the instrument is drawn is liable to any person for payment of the instrument to the levying officer rather than to the judgment debtor by reason of the endorsement. No levying officer is liable by reason of endorsing, presenting, and obtaining payment of the instrument.

(d) If it appears from the face of the instrument that it has been tendered to the judgment debtor in satisfaction of a claim or demand and that endorsement of the instrument is considered a release and satisfaction by the judgment debtor of the claim or demand, the levying officer shall not endorse the instrument unless the judgment debtor has first endorsed it to the levying officer. If the judgment debtor does not endorse the instrument to the levying officer, the levying officer shall hold the instrument for 30 days and is not liable to the judgment debtor or to any other person for delay in presenting it for payment. At the end of the 30-day holding period, the levying officer shall return the instrument to the maker. **Leg.H.** Added Stats 1982 ch 1364 §2, operative July 1, 1983.

§687.030. Manner of custody

Except as otherwise provided by statute, where the method of levy upon property requires that the property be taken into custody or where the levying officer is otherwise directed to take property into custody, the levying officer may do so by any of the following methods:

(a) Removing the property to a place of safekeeping.
(b) Installing a keeper.
(c) Otherwise obtaining possession or control of the property. **Leg.H.** Added Stats 1982 ch 1364 §2, operative July 1, 1983.

§687.040. Liability of levying officer

(a) The levying officer or registered process server is not liable for actions taken in conformance with the provisions of this title, including actions taken in conformance with the provisions of this title in reliance on information contained in the written instructions of the judgment creditor, or in reliance on information provided to the levying officer by a registered process server pursuant to subdivision (d) of Section 699.080 or subdivision (e) of Section 706.101 or subdivision (b) of Section

715.040 or other provision, except to the extent the levying officer or registered process server has actual knowledge that the information is incorrect. Nothing in this subdivision limits any liability the judgment creditor may have if the levying officer or registered process server acts on the basis of incorrect information given in the written instructions.

(b) Unless the levying officer is negligent in the care or handling of the property, the levying officer is not liable to either the judgment debtor or the judgment creditor for loss by fire, theft, injury, or damage of any kind to personal property while (1) in the possession of the levying officer either in a warehouse or other storage place or in the custody of a keeper or (2) in transit to or from a warehouse or other storage place. **Leg.H.** Added Stats 1982 ch 1364 §2, operative July 1, 1983. Amended Stats 1983 ch 155 §11, effective June 30, 1983, operative July 1, 1983.

§687.050. Levying officer's lien

The levying officer has a special lien, dependent upon possession, on personal property levied upon in the amount of the levying officer's costs for which an advance has not been made. **Leg.H.** Added Stats 1982 ch 1364 §2, operative July 1, 1983.

§688. [Section repealed 1983]

Leg.H. Enacted Stats 1872. Amended Stats 1907 ch 360 §3; Stats 1927 ch 486 §1; Stats 1937 ch 241 §1; Stats 1941 ch 1148 §1; Stats 1951 ch 175 §1; Stats 1955 ch 793 §2; Stats 1959 ch 2140 §1; Stats 1970 ch 1523 §6.5; Stats 1974 ch 1516 §15, operative January 1, 1977; Stats 1976 ch 437 §46; Stats 1977 ch 155 §1, effective June 29 1977. Repealed Stats 1982 ch 1364 §1, operative July 1, 1983. See CCP §§687.020, 687.030, 695.010–695.035, 695.060, 697.710, 699.060, 699.710, 699.720, 700.010–700.200, 708.630.

CHAPTER 8
ENFORCEMENT OF STATE TAX LIABILITY

Article 1. Enforcement Pursuant to Warrant or Notice of Levy.
Article 2. Enforcement of Judgment for Taxes.

ARTICLE 1
Enforcement Pursuant to Warrant or Notice of Levy

Conditions for treatment as limited civil case. §688.010.
Remedies of state when warrant may be issued. §688.020.
Exemptions and third-party claims. §688.030.
Meaning of terms used elsewhere for purpose of this article. §688.040.
Date of creation of tax lien. §688.050.

§688.010. Conditions for treatment as limited civil case

A proceeding for the purpose of the remedies provided under this article is a limited civil case if (a) the amount of liability sought to be collected does not exceed the maximum amount in controversy for a limited civil case provided in Section 85, and (b) the legality of the liability being enforced is not contested by the person against whom enforcement is sought. **Leg.H.** Added Stats 1982 ch 1364 §2, operative July 1, 1983. Amended Stats 1998 ch 931 §89 (SB 2139), effective September 28, 1998; Stats 2007 ch 43 §7 (SB 649), effective January 1, 2008.

§688.020. Remedies of state when warrant may be issued

(a) Except as otherwise provided by statute, if a warrant may properly be issued by the state, or by a department or agency of the state, pursuant to any provision of the Public Resources Code, Revenue and Taxation Code, or Unemployment Insurance Code, and the warrant may be levied with the same effect as a levy pursuant to a writ of execution, the state or the department or agency of the state authorized to issue the warrant may use any of the remedies available to a judgment creditor, including, but not limited to, those provided in Chapter 6 (commencing with Section 708.010) of Division 2.

(b) The proper court for the enforcement of those remedies is a court of any of the following counties:

(1) The county where the debtor resides.

(2) The county where the property against which enforcement is sought is located.

(3) If the debtor does not reside in this state, any county of this state.

(4) This section shall become operative on January 1, 2014. **Leg.H.** Added Stats 2008 ch 552 §2 (AB 2578), effective January 1, 2009, operative January 1, 2014.

Former Sections: Former CCP §688.020 was added Stats 1982 ch 1364 §2, operative July 1, 1983, and repealed operative January 1, 2014, by its own provisions. Stats 2008 ch 552 §1 (AB 2578).

Prior Law: Former CCP §688.020 was added Stats 1982 ch 1364 §2, operative July 1, 1983, and amended Stats 2008 ch 552 §1 (AB 2578), effective January 1, 2009, repealed January 1, 2014.

§688.030. Exemptions and third-party claims

(a) If pursuant to any provision of the Public Resources Code, Revenue and Taxation Code (excluding Sections 3201 to 3204, inclusive), or Unemployment Insurance Code, property is levied upon pursuant to a warrant or notice of levy issued by the state or by a department or agency of the state for the collection of a liability:

(1) If the debtor is a natural person, the debtor is entitled to the same exemptions to which a judgment debtor is entitled. Except as provided in subdivisions (b) and (c), the claim of exemption shall be made, heard, and determined as provided in Chapter 4 (commencing with Section 703.010) of Division 2 in the same manner as if the property were levied upon under a writ of execution.

(2) A third person may claim ownership or the right to possession of the property or a security interest in or lien on the property. Except as provided in subdivisions (b) and (c) or as otherwise provided by statute, the third-party claim shall be made, heard, and determined as provided in Division 4 (commencing with Section 720.010) in the same manner as if the property were levied upon under a writ of execution.

(b) In the case of a levy pursuant to a notice of levy:

(1) The claim of exemption or the third-party claim shall be filed with the state department or agency that issued the notice of levy.

(2) The state department or agency that issued the notice of levy shall perform the duties of the levying officer, except that the state department or agency need not give itself the notices that the levying officer is required to serve on a judgment creditor or creditor or the notices that a judgment creditor or creditor is required to give to the levying officer. The state department or agency in performing the duties of the levying officer under this paragraph has no obligation to search public records or otherwise seek to determine whether any lien or encumbrance exists on property sold or collected.

(c) A claim of exemption or a third-party claim pursuant to this section shall be heard and determined in the superior court in the county where the property levied upon is located.

(d) This section shall become operative on January 1, 2014. **Leg.H.** Added Stats 2008 ch 552 §4 (AB 2578), effective January 1, 2009, operative January 1, 2014.

Former Sections: Former CCP §688.030 was added Stats 1982 ch 1364 §2, operative July 1, 1983, and repealed operative January 1, 2014, by its own provisions. Stats 2008 ch 552 §3 (AB 2578).

Prior Law: Former CCP §688.030 was added Stats 1982 ch 1364 §2, operative July 1, 1983, and amended Stats 2007 ch 43 §8 (SB 649), effective January 1, 2008; Stats 2008 ch 552 §3 (AB 2578), effective January 1, 2009, repealed January 1, 2014.

§688.040. Meaning of terms used elsewhere for purpose of this article

For the purpose of this article, as used in this title:

(a) "Judgment creditor" or "creditor" means the state or the department or agency of the state seeking to collect the liability.

(b) "Judgment debtor" or "debtor" means the debtor from whom the liability is sought to be collected. **Leg.H.** Added Stats 1982 ch 1364 §2, operative July 1, 1983.

§688.050. Date of creation of tax lien

For the purpose of applying Section 694.080, 703.050, or 703.100, the date of creation of a tax lien is the earliest of the following times:

(a) The time when a notice of state tax lien is recorded or filed pursuant to Chapter 14 (commencing with Section 7150) of Division 7 of Title 1 of the Government Code.

(b) The time when the property is levied upon pursuant to a warrant or notice of levy or notice to withhold issued by the state or by a department or agency of the state.

(c) The time when any other act is performed that creates or perfects a lien on specific property as distinguished from a lien on the debtor's property generally. **Leg.H.** Added Stats 1982 ch 1364 §2, operative July 1, 1983.

§688.1. [Section repealed 1983]

Leg.H. Added Stats 1941 ch 1148 §2. Amended Stats 1943 ch 94 §1; Stats 1951 ch 1737 §105, operative January 1, 1952; Stats 1968 ch 1036 §1;

Stats 1970 ch 1245 §3, ch 1523 §7.5. Repealed Stats 1982 ch 1364 §1, operative July 1, 1983. The repealed section related to lien of judgment creditor of plaintiff in action or special proceeding, notice, order granting lien, extent of lien, enforcement of existence of lien, and statement in abstract.

ARTICLE 2
Enforcement of Judgment for Taxes

Enforcement of judgment for taxes. §688.110.

§688.110. Enforcement of judgment for taxes

Except as otherwise provided by statute, if a judgment is entered on a claim for taxes by a public entity, the judgment is enforceable pursuant to this title in the same manner as any other money judgment. **Leg.H.** Added Stats 1982 ch 1364 §2, operative July 1, 1983.

§689. [Section repealed 1983]

Leg.H. Enacted Stats 1872. Amended Stats 1891 ch 32 §1; Stats 1907 ch 360 §4; Stats 1925 ch 466 §1; Stats 1929 ch 341 §1; Stats 1933 ch 744 §135; Stats 1935 ch 722 §15; Stats 1937 ch 577 §1; Stats 1951 ch 1737 §107, operative January 1, 1952; Stats 1957 ch 422 §1; Stats 1961 ch 322 §1; Stats 1980 ch 309 §1; Stats 1982 ch 517 §143 (ch 1364 prevails). Repealed Stats 1982 ch 1364 §1, operative July 1, 1983. See CCP §§687.040, 699.070, 699.090, 720.110 et seq., 720.310 et seq., 720.400, 720.420, 720.430, 720.660, 720.760 et seq.

§689.5. [Section repealed 1983]

Leg.H. Added Stats 1941 ch 1111 §1. Amended Stats 1947 ch 721 §1; Stats 1953 ch 1796 §1. Repealed Stats 1982 ch 1364 §1, operative July 1, 1983. See CCP §§720.170, 720.270.

§689.6. [Section repealed 1953]

Leg.H. Added Stats 1947 ch 719 §1. Amended Stats 1949 ch 1543 §1. Repealed Stats 1953 ch 1796 §4. The repealed section related to handling of property levied on that was under contract for purchase.

§689a. [Section repealed 1983]

Leg.H. Added Stats 1921 ch 292 §1. Amended Stats 1945 ch 1311 §1; Stats 1953 ch 1796 §2. Repealed Stats 1982 ch 1364 §1, operative July 1, 1983. The repealed section related to levy on personal property under contract for purchase or subject to mortgage.

§689b. [Section repealed 1983]

Leg.H. Added Stats 1921 ch 292 §2. Amended Stats 1925 ch 64 §1; Stats 1945 ch 1311 §2; Stats 1947 ch 720 §1; Stats 1949 ch 373 §1; Stats 1951 ch 1073 §1; Stats 1953 ch 1796 §3; Stats 1955 ch 1401 §3; Stats 1959 ch 1147 §1, ch 1460 §1; Stats 1961 ch 1194 §1; Stats 1963 ch 1120 §1; Stats 1966 1st Ex Sess ch 61 §1; Stats 1970 ch 1428 §1; Stats 1980 ch 309 §2; Stats 1982 ch 517 §144 (ch 1364 prevails). Repealed Stats 1982 ch 1364 §1, operative July 1, 1983. See CCP §§687.040, 700.090, 720.210 et seq., 720.310, 720.390, 720.430, 720.510, 720.520, 720.550, 720.760, 720.770.

§689c. [Section repealed 1983]

Leg.H. Added Stats 1921 ch 292 §3. Amended Stats 1949 ch 368 §1. Repealed Stats 1982 ch 1364 §1, operative July 1, 1983. See CCP §701.810.

§689d. [Section repealed 1983]

Leg.H. Added Stats 1953 ch 1796 §5. Amended Stats 1959 ch 594 §5; Stats 1961 ch 72 §3, ch 1029 §1; Stats 1971 ch 873 §1. Repealed Stats 1982 ch 1364 §1, operative July 1, 1983. See CCP §§688.010, 688.030.

CHAPTER 9
ENFORCEMENT OF SUPPORT JUDGMENTS

Jurisdiction. §689.010.
Remedies. §689.020.
Levy; Claim of exemption or third-party claim. §689.030.
Writ of execution. §689.040.
Definitions. §689.050.

§689.010. Jurisdiction

For the purpose of the remedies provided under this chapter, jurisdiction is conferred upon the superior court. **Leg.H.** Added Stats 1996 ch 957 §4 (AB 1058).

§689.020. Remedies

(a) Except as otherwise provided by statute, whenever a warrant may properly be issued by a local child support agency pursuant to Section 17522 of the Family Code, and the warrant may be levied with the same effect as a levy pursuant to a writ of execution, the local child support agency may use any of the remedies available to a judgment creditor, including, but not limited to, those provided in Chapter 6 (commencing with Section 708.010) of Division 2.

(b) The proper court for the enforcement of the remedies provided under this chapter is the superior court in the county where the local child support agency enforcing the support obligation is located. **Leg.H.** Added Stats 1996 ch 957 §4 (AB 1058). Amended Stats 2000 ch 808 §6 (AB 1358), effective September 28, 2000.

§689.030. Levy; Claim of exemption or third-party claim

(a) Whenever the local child support agency, pursuant to Section 17522 of the Family Code, levies upon property pursuant to a warrant or notice of levy for the collection of a support obligation:

(1) If the debtor is a natural person, the debtor is entitled to the same exemptions to which a judgment debtor is entitled. Except as provided in subdivisions (b) and (c), the claim of exemption shall be made, heard, and determined as provided in Chapter 4 (commencing with Section 703.010) of Division 2 in the same manner as if the property were levied upon under a writ of execution.

(2) A third person may claim ownership or the right to possession of the property or a security interest in or lien on the property. Except as provided in subdivisions (b) and (c) or as otherwise provided by statute, the third-party claim shall be made, heard, and determined as provided in Division 4 (commencing with Section 720.010) in the same manner as if the property were levied upon under a writ of execution.

(b) In the case of a warrant or notice of levy issued pursuant to Section 17522 of the Family Code, the claim of exemption or the third-party claim shall be filed with the local child support agency that issued the warrant or notice of levy.

(c) A claim of exemption or a third-party claim pursuant to this section shall be heard and determined in the court specified in Section 689.010 in the county where the local child support agency enforcing the support obligation is located. **Leg.H.** Added Stats 1996 ch 957 §4 (AB 1058). Amended Stats 1997 ch 599 §1 (AB 573); Stats 2000 ch 808 §7 (AB 1358), effective September 28, 2000.

§689.040. Writ of execution

(a) Notwithstanding any other provision of law, in the case of a writ of execution issued by a court of competent jurisdiction pursuant to Chapter 3 (commencing with Section 699.010) and Chapter 5 (commencing with Section 706.010) of Division 2, the local child support agency, when enforcing a support obligation pursuant to Division 17 (commencing with Section 17000) of the Family Code, may perform the duties of the levying officer, except that the local child support agency need not give itself the notices that the levying officer is required to serve on a judgment creditor or creditor or the notices that a judgment creditor or creditor is required to give to the levying officer.

(b) Notwithstanding subdivision (a) of Section 700.140, if the writ of execution is for a deposit or credits or personal property in the possession or under the control of a bank or savings and loan association, the local child support agency may deliver or mail the writ of execution to a centralized location designated by the bank or savings and loan association. If the writ of execution is received at the designated central location, it will apply to all deposits and credits and personal property held by the bank or savings and loan association regardless of the location of that property. **Leg.H.** Added Stats 1996 ch 957 §4 (AB 1058). Amended Stats 2000 ch 808 §8 (AB 1358), effective September 28, 2000.

§689.050. Definitions

For the purpose of this chapter:

(a) "Judgment creditor" or "creditor" means the local child support agency seeking to collect a child or spousal support obligation pursuant to a support order.

(b) "Judgment debtor" or "debtor" means the debtor from whom the support obligation is sought to be collected. **Leg.H.** Added Stats 1996 ch 957 §4 (AB 1058). Amended Stats 2000 ch 808 §9 (AB 1358), effective September 28, 2000.

§690. [Section repealed 1983]

Leg.H. Enacted Stats 1872. Amended Code Amdts 1875–76 ch 483 §1; Code Amdts 1877–87 ch 579 §1; Stats 1887 ch 84 §1; Stats 1897 ch 120 §1; Stats 1899 ch 19 §1; Stats 1901 ch 28 §1; Stats 1903 ch 103 §1; Stats

1907 ch 479 §1; Stats 1927 ch 199 §1; Stats 1929 ch 45 §1; Stats 1935 ch 723 §1; Stats 1945 ch 714 §1; Stats 1949 ch 396 §1; Stats 1970 ch 1523 §8; Stats 1974 ch 1516 §16, operative January 1, 1976; Stats 1977 ch 305 §2, effective July 8, 1977; Stats 1981 ch 455 §1. Repealed Stats 1982 ch 1364 §1, operative July 1, 1983. See CCP §§680.240, 680.250, 703.010 et seq., 703.130, 703.510.

§690.1. [Section repealed 1983]
Leg.H. Added Stats 1970 ch 1523 §10. Repealed Stats 1982 ch 1364 §1, operative July 1, 1983. See CCP §§704.020, 704.040.

§690.2. [Section repealed 1983]
Leg.H. Added Stats 1976 ch 1210 §2. Amended Stats 1977 ch 683 §1. Repealed Stats 1982 ch 1364 §1, operative July 1, 1983. See CCP §§680.190, 699.060, 701.620, 701.810, 703.520, 704.010.

§690.3. [Section repealed 1983]
Leg.H. Added Stats 1970 ch 1523 §14. Amended Stats 1972 ch 418 §1; Stats 1973 ch 787 §1; Stats 1976 ch 159 §1, ch 471 §2; Stats 1978 ch 993 §2; Stats 1979 ch 373 §51; Stats 1980 ch 15 §2. Repealed Stats 1982 ch 1364 §1, operative July 1, 1983. See CCP §§680.190, 704.710 et seq.

Prior Law: Former CCP §690.3, relating to exemption of certain farming utensils, was added Stats 1935 ch 723 §4, amended Stats 1955 ch 1695 §1 and repealed Stats 1970 ch 1523 §3.

§690.4. [Section repealed 1983]
Leg.H. Added Stats 1970 ch 1523 §16. Repealed Stats 1982 ch 1364 §1, operative July 1, 1983. See CCP §§680.190, 704.060.

Prior Law: Former CCP §690.4, relating to exemption of certain tools of artisans' trades, was added Stats 1935 ch 723 §5, amended Stats 1939 ch 489 §1, Stats 1941 ch 84 §1, Stats 1961 ch 215 §36, and repealed Stats 1970 ch 1523 §15.

§690.5. [Section repealed 1983]
Leg.H. Added Stats 1953 ch 249 §1. Amended Stats 1970 ch 1523 §17. Repealed Stats 1982 ch 1364 §1, operative July 1, 1983. See CCP §704.050.

§690.6. [Section repealed 1980]
Leg.H. Added Stats 1970 ch 1523 §19. Amended Stats 1971 ch 578 §8.8, effective August 13, 1971, ch 1645 §1, ch 1684 §5; Stats 1972 ch 43 §1, effective April 6, 1972; Stats 1974 ch 1516 §17, operative January 1, 1977; Stats 1975 ch 1241 §§6.5, 7, operative January 1, 1977; Stats 1976 ch 317 §1. Repealed Stats 1978 ch 1133 §4, operative January 1, 1980. The repealed section related to garnishment of wages.

§690.7. [Section repealed 1983]
Leg.H. Added Stats 1970 ch 1523 §21. Repealed Stats 1982 ch 1364 §1, operative July 1, 1983. The repealed section related to exempt savings deposits and shares in savings and loan association.

§690.8. [Section repealed 1983]
Leg.H. Added Stats 1972 ch 861 §2. Amended Stats 1974 ch 47 §1, effective February 28, 1974. Repealed Stats 1982 ch 1364 §1, operative July 1, 1983. See CCP §704.720.

§690.8a. [Section repealed 1983]
Leg.H. Added Stats 1974 ch 47 §2, effective February 28, 1974. Repealed Stats 1982 ch 1364 §1, operative July 1, 1983. See CCP §704.180.

§690.9. [Section repealed 1983]
Leg.H. Added Stats 1935 ch 723 §19, as CCP §690.19. Amended Stats 1947 ch 1056 §1. Amended and renumbered Stats 1970 ch 1523 §39. Repealed Stats 1982 ch 1364 §1, operative July 1, 1983. See CCP §704.100.

§690.10. [Section repealed 1983]
Leg.H. Added Stats 1970 ch 1523 §26. Repealed Stats 1982 ch 1364 §1, operative July 1, 1983. See CCP §704.100.

§690.11. [Section repealed 1983]
Leg.H. Added Stats 1935 ch 723 §20, as CCP §690.20. Amended and renumbered Stats 1970 ch 1523 §41. Repealed Stats 1982 ch 1364 §1, operative July 1, 1983. See CCP §704.130.

§690.12. [Section repealed 1983]
Leg.H. Added Stats 1970 ch 1523 §29. Repealed Stats 1982 ch 1364 §1, operative July 1, 1983. The repealed section related to exempt segregated benefit funds of holder of certificates, respecting mutualized life insurance plan.

§690.125. [Section repealed 1970]
Leg.H. Added Stats 1968 ch 198 §1, as CCP §690.12. Amended and renumbered Stats 1969 ch 546 §1. Repealed Stats 1970 ch 1523 §29.5. The repealed section related to vacation credits accumulated by state employees.

§690.13. [Section repealed 1983]
Leg.H. Added Stats 1939 ch 728 §1, as CCP §690.25. Amended and renumbered Stats 1970 ch 1523 §48. Repealed Stats 1982 ch 1364 §1, operative July 1, 1983. See CCP §§704.120, 704.130.

§690.14. [Section repealed 1983]
Leg.H. Added Stats 1970 ch 1523 §32. Repealed Stats 1982 ch 1364 §1, operative July 1, 1983. See CCP §§704.100, 704.130, 704.170.

§690.15. [Section repealed 1983]
Leg.H. Added Stats 1970 ch 1523 §34. Repealed Stats 1982 ch 1364 §1, operative July 1, 1983. See CCP §704.160.

§690.16. [Section repealed 1983]
Leg.H. Added Stats 1970 ch 1523 §36. Amended Stats 1982 ch 1072 §1, effective September 15, 1982. Repealed Stats 1982 ch 1364 §1, operative July 1, 1983. See CCP §704.120.

§690.17. [Section repealed 1983]
Leg.H. Added Stats 1935 ch 723 §17. Repealed Stats 1982 ch 1364 §1, operative July 1, 1983. See CCP §§704.030, 704.060.

§690.175. [Section repealed 1983]
Leg.H. Added Stats 1970 ch 1523 §37. Amended Stats 1973 ch 1207 §3; Stats 1982 ch 1072 §2, effective September 15, 1982. Repealed Stats 1982 ch 1364 §1, operative July 1, 1983. See CCP §704.120.

§690.18. [Section repealed 1983]
Leg.H. Added Stats 1935 ch 723 §22, as CCP §690.22. Amended Stats 1937 ch 512 §1. Amended and renumbered Stats 1970 ch 1523 §44.5. Amended Stats 1975 ch 509 §1; Stats 1976 ch 948 §1; Stats 1978 ch 494 §1; Stats 1980 ch 173 §2, effective June 13, 1980; Stats 1981 ch 528 §1, effective September 16, 1981. Repealed Stats 1982 ch 1364 §1, operative July 1, 1983. See CCP §§688.030, 703.080, 704.110 et seq.

§690.19. [Section repealed 1983]
Leg.H. Added Stats 1970 ch 1523 §40. Repealed Stats 1982 ch 1364 §1, operative July 1, 1983. See CCP §704.170, W & I C §17409.

§690.20. [Section repealed 1983]
Leg.H. Added Stats 1970 ch 1523 §42. Repealed Stats 1982 ch 1364 §1, operative July 1, 1983. The repealed section related to exempt hospital endowment.

§690.21. [Section repealed 1983]
Leg.H. Added Stats 1959 ch 339 §1, as CCP §690.235. Amended and renumbered Stats 1970 ch 1523 §46. Amended Stats 1974 ch 1516 §18, operative January 1, 1977. Repealed Stats 1982 ch 1364 §1, operative July 1, 1983. See CCP §704.090.

§690.22. [Section repealed 1983]
Leg.H. Added Stats 1935 ch 723 §16, as CCP §690.16. Amended and renumbered Stats 1970 ch 1523 §35. Repealed Stats 1982 ch 1364 §1, operative July 1, 1983. The repealed section related to exemption of pension or retirement payments for public employees.

§690.23. [Section repealed 1970]
Leg.H. Added Stats 1935 ch 723 §23. Amended Stats 1937 ch 512 §2; Stats 1970 ch 913 §1. Repealed Stats 1970 ch 1523 §45. The repealed section related to exemption of money held by political subdivision of state for retirement, pension, or death benefits.

§690.235. [Section repealed 1977]
Leg.H. Added Stats 1974 ch 1251 §2.5, operative July 1, 1975. Repealed Stats 1976 ch 1000 §3, operative July 1, 1977. The repealed section related to exemption of dwelling eligible for homesteading.

§690.24. [Section repealed 1983]

Leg.H. Added Stats 1955 ch 59 §7, as CCP §690.51. Amended and renumbered Stats 1970 ch 1523 §57. Amended Stats 1974 ch 1516 §19, operative January 1, 1977. Repealed Stats 1982 ch 1364 §1, operative July 1, 1983. See CCP §704.200.

Prior Law: Former CCP §690.24, similar to present CCP §§690.2, 690.3, was added Stats 1935 ch 723 §24, amended Stats 1949 ch 628 §1, Stats 1951 ch 1094 §1, Stats 1959 ch 1474 §1, Stats 1967 ch 1241 §1, and repealed Stats 1970 ch 1523 §47.

§690.25. [Section repealed 1983]

Leg.H. Added Stats 1955 ch 59 §8, as CCP §690.52. Amended and renumbered Stats 1970 ch 1523 §58. Repealed Stats 1982 ch 1364 §1, operative July 1, 1983. The repealed section related to exempt church pews.

§690.26. [Section repealed 1983]

Leg.H. Added Stats 1970 ch 1523 §50. Repealed Stats 1982 ch 1364 §1, operative July 1, 1983. The repealed section related to exempt reclamation board and drainage district property.

§690.27. [Section repealed 1983]

Leg.H. Added Stats 1970 ch 1523 §52. Repealed Stats 1982 ch 1364 §1, operative July 1, 1983. The repealed section related to exempt housing authority realty.

§690.28. [Section repealed 1983]

Leg.H. Added Stats 1970 ch 1523 §53. Repealed Stats 1982 ch 1364 §1, operative July 1, 1983. The repealed section related to exempt educational trust property.

§690.29. [Section repealed 1983]

Leg.H. Added Stats 1970 ch 1523 §54. Repealed Stats 1982 ch 1364 §1, operative July 1, 1983. The repealed section related to exempt redevelopment agency property.

§690.30. [Section repealed 1983]

Leg.H. Added Stats 1976 ch 810 §1. Repealed Stats 1982 ch 1364 §1, operative July 1, 1983. See CCP §704.080.

§690.31. [Section repealed 1983]

Leg.H. Added Stats 1976 ch 1000 §4, operative July 1, 1977. Amended Stats 1977 ch 305 §3, effective July 8, 1977; Stats 1978 ch 684 §1; Stats 1980 ch 1372 §3. Repealed Stats 1982 ch 1364 §1, operative July 1, 1983. See former CCP §§693.050, 693.060, CCP §§703.010, 704.710–704.850.

§690.50. [Section repealed 1983]

Leg.H. Added Stats 1970 ch 1523 §56. Amended Stats 1972 ch 649 §2, effective August 9, 1972; Stats 1974 ch 1251 §3, operative July 1, 1975; Stats 1976 ch 437 §47; Stats 1977 ch 305 §4, effective July 8, 1977; Stats 1978 ch 1133 §5, operative January 1, 1980. Repealed Stats 1982 ch 1364 §1, operative July 1, 1983. See CCP §§684.110–684.140, 699.070, 703.510–703.610.

§690.51. [Section repealed 1983]

Leg.H. Added Stats 1953 ch 1796 §6, as CCP §690.27. Amended Stats 1959 ch 594 §6; Stats 1961 ch 1029 §2. Amended and renumbered Stats 1970 ch 1523 §51. Amended Stats 1971 ch 873 §2; Stats 1977 ch 305 §5, effective July 8, 1977. Repealed Stats 1982 ch 1364 §1, operative July 1, 1983. See CCP §§688.010, 688.030.

§690.52. [Section repealed 1983]

Leg.H. Added Stats 1935 ch 723 §25, as CCP §690.50. Amended and renumbered Stats 1970 ch 1523 §55. Amended Stats 1974 ch 1251 §5, operative July 1, 1975; Stats 1977 ch 305 §6, effective July 8, 1977. Repealed Stats 1982 ch 1364 §1, operative July 1, 1983. See CCP §703.010.

§690.60. [Section repealed 1983]

Leg.H. Added Stats 1979 ch 394 §1, effective July 27, 1979, operative October 1, 1979. Amended Stats 1980 ch 135 §4; Stats 1982 ch 1072 §3, effective September 15, 1982. Repealed Stats 1982 ch 1364 §1, operative July 1, 1983. See CCP §1801.

§691. [Section repealed 1983]

Leg.H. Enacted Stats 1872. Amended Code Amdts 1873–74 ch 383 §93; Stats 1933 ch 744 §136. Repealed Stats 1982 ch 1364 §1, operative July 1, 1983. See CCP §§699.530, 701.510, 701.520, 701.810–701.830.

§692. [Section repealed 1983]

Leg.H. Enacted Stats 1872. Amended Code Amdts 1873–74 ch 383 §94; Stats 1907 ch 525 §1; Stats 1923 ch 372 §1; Stats 1931 ch 117 §1, ch 1187 §1; Stats 1937 ch 502 §1; Stats 1951 ch 1737 §108, operative January 1, 1952; Stats 1957 ch 1000 §1; Stats 1959 ch 1277 §1; Stats 1963 ch 1599 §1; Stats 1967 ch 971 §11; Stats 1968 ch 243 §1, ch 391 §1, ch 1036 §3; Stats 1969 ch 149 §1; Stats 1970 ch 279 §1; Stats 1971 ch 1312 §1; Stats 1972 ch 1056 §6; Stats 1977 ch 139 §2. Repealed Stats 1982 ch 1364 §1, operative July 1, 1983. See CCP §§687.010, 699.070, 701.530, 701.540.

§692a. [Section repealed 1983]

Leg.H. Added Stats 1937 ch 502 §2. Amended Stats 1957 ch 2081 §1. Repealed Stats 1982 ch 1364 §1, operative July 1, 1983. See CCP §§699.520, 701.550.

§693. [Section repealed 1983]

Leg.H. Enacted Stats 1872. Amended Stats 1957 ch 1914 §1. Repealed Stats 1982 ch 1364 §1, operative July 1, 1983. See CCP §701.560.

CHAPTER 10
ENFORCEMENT OF JUDGMENTS BY LABOR COMMISSIONER

Jurisdiction. §690.020.
Remedies available to Labor Commissioner when warrant or notice of levy may be issued. §690.030.
Levies on property for the collection of an unsatisfied judgment or award; Exemptions of the debtor; Third party claims. §690.040.
Labor Commissioner performing duties of levying officer when collecting an unsatisfied judgment or award pursuant to Section 96.8 of the Labor Code. §690.050.

§690.020. Jurisdiction

For the purpose of the remedies provided under this chapter, jurisdiction is conferred upon the superior court. **Leg.H.** Added Stats 2015 ch 803 §1 (SB 588), effective January 1, 2016.

§690.030. Remedies available to Labor Commissioner when warrant or notice of levy may be issued

(a) Except as otherwise provided by statute, whenever a warrant or notice of levy may properly be issued by the Labor Commissioner pursuant to Section 96.8 of the Labor Code, and the warrant may be levied with the same effect as a levy pursuant to a writ of execution, the Labor Commissioner may use any of the remedies available to a judgment creditor, including, but not limited to, those provided in Chapter 6 (commencing with Section 708.010) of Division 2.

(b) The proper court for the enforcement of the remedies provided under this chapter is the superior court of any of the following counties:

(1) The county where the employee resides.
(2) The county where the judgment debtor resides.
(3) The county where the person against whom the levy or warrant was issued resides. **Leg.H.** Added Stats 2015 ch 803 §1 (SB 588), effective January 1, 2016.

§690.040. Levies on property for the collection of an unsatisfied judgment or award; Exemptions of the debtor; Third party claims

(a) Whenever the Labor Commissioner, pursuant to Section 96.8 of the Labor Code, levies upon property pursuant to a warrant or notice of levy for the collection of an unsatisfied judgment or award:

(1) If the debtor is a natural person, the debtor is entitled to the same exemptions to which a judgment debtor is entitled. Except as provided in subdivisions (b) and (c), the claim of exemption shall be made, heard, and determined as provided in Chapter 4 (commencing with Section 703.010) of Division 2 in the same manner as if the property were levied upon under a writ of execution.

(2) A third person may claim ownership or the right to possession of the property or a security interest in or lien on the property. Except as provided in subdivisions (b) and (c) or as otherwise provided by statute, the third-party claim shall be made, heard, and determined as provided in Division 4 (commencing with Section 720.010) in the same manner as if the property were levied upon under a writ of execution.

(b) In the case of a warrant or notice of levy issued pursuant to Section 96.8 of the Labor Code, the claim of exemption or the third-party claim shall be filed with the Labor Commissioner.

(c) A claim of exemption or a third-party claim pursuant to this section shall be heard and determined in a superior court specified in subdivision (b) of Section 690.030. **Leg.H.** Added Stats 2015 ch 803 §1 (SB 588), effective January 1, 2016.

§690.050. Labor Commissioner performing duties of levying officer when collecting an unsatisfied judgment or award pursuant to Section 96.8 of the Labor Code

(a) Notwithstanding any other law, in the case of a writ of execution issued by a court of competent jurisdiction pursuant to Chapter 3 (commencing with Section 699.010) and Chapter 5 (commencing with Section 706.010) of Division 2, the Labor Commissioner, when collecting an unsatisfied judgment or award pursuant to Section 96.8 of the Labor Code, may perform the duties of the levying officer, except that the Labor Commissioner need not give himself or herself the notices that the levying officer is required to serve on a judgment creditor or the notices that a judgment creditor is required to give to the levying officer.

(b) Notwithstanding subdivision (a) of Section 700.140 and Sections 700.150, 700.160, and 700.170, if the levy is for a deposit, credits, money, or property in the possession or under the control of a bank or savings and loan association or for an account receivable or other general intangible owed to the judgment debtor by an account debtor, the Labor Commissioner may deliver or mail a notice of levy to a centralized location designated by the bank or savings and loan association or, in the case of an account receivable or other general intangible, to the agent for service of process of the account debtor. If the notice of levy is received at the designated central location for the bank or savings and loan association, the notice of levy will apply to all deposits, credits, money, and personal property held by the bank or savings and loan association regardless of the location of that property. The notice of levy may be issued directly by the Labor Commissioner, whether or not a court has issued a writ of execution, and shall contain all of the information required to be included in a writ of execution under Section 699.520 and in a notice of levy under Section 699.540. **Leg.H.** Added Stats 2015 ch 803 §1 (SB 588), effective January 1, 2016.

CHAPTER 19
FORMS [REPEALED]

§§693.010–693.060. [Sections repealed 1984]

Leg.H. Added Stats 1982 ch 1364 §2, operative July 1, 1983. Repealed Stats 1984 ch 538 §16. The repealed sections related to forms.

§694. [Section repealed 1983]

Leg.H. Enacted Stats 1872. Amended Stats 1931 ch 1187 §2; Stats 1941 ch 880 §1; Stats 1949 ch 1480 §1; Stats 1972 ch 1056 §7. Repealed Stats 1982 ch 1364 §1, operative July 1, 1983. See CCP §§701.570, 701.580, 701.610.

CHAPTER 20
TRANSITIONAL PROVISIONS

Definitions. §694.010.
General rule concerning application of title. §694.020.
Period for enforcement of judgments. §694.030.
Execution and return of writs and orders. §694.040.
Redemption rights. §694.050.
Creditor's suit. §694.060.
Third-party proceedings. §694.070.
Exemptions. §694.080.
Effect of homestead declaration. §694.090.

§694.010. Definitions

As used in this chapter:
(a) "Operative date" means July 1, 1983.
(b) "Prior law" means the applicable law in effect on June 30, 1983.
Leg.H. Added Stats 1982 ch 1364 §2, operative July 1, 1983.

§694.020. General rule concerning application of title

Except as otherwise provided in this chapter, this title on and after its operative date applies to all proceedings commenced prior thereto unless in the opinion of the court application of a particular provision of this title would substantially interfere with the effective conduct of the proceedings or the rights of the parties or other interested persons, in which case the particular provision of this title does not apply and prior law applies. **Leg.H.** Added Stats 1982 ch 1364 §2, operative July 1, 1983.

§694.030. Period for enforcement of judgments

(a) Except for a judgment described in Section 683.310 or 683.320, the period for enforcement of a money judgment or a judgment for possession or sale of property entered prior to the operative date is governed on and after the operative date by Chapter 3 (commencing with Section 683.010).

(b) Notwithstanding subdivision (a), even though a judgment to which subdivision (a) applies is not renewable pursuant to Chapter 3 (commencing with Section 683.010) because the time for filing an application for renewal has expired, the judgment may be renewed under Chapter 3 (commencing with Section 683.010) if the court which entered the judgment determines, on noticed motion filed within two years after the operative date, that authority to enforce the judgment after the 10-year period provided in former Section 681 would have been granted if a motion had been made under former Section 685 and the court, in its discretion, makes an order authorizing the renewal of the judgment. The notice of motion shall be served personally or by mail on the judgment debtor. **Leg.H.** Added Stats 1982 ch 1364 §2, operative July 1, 1983.

§694.040. Execution and return of writs and orders

(a) Except as provided in subdivision (c), property levied upon or otherwise subjected to process for enforcement of a money judgment or a judgment for possession or sale of property prior to the operative date is subject to prior law relating to sale or delivery of possession.

(b) The duties to be performed in the execution of a writ or order for the enforcement of a money judgment or a judgment for possession or sale of property that is served prior to the operative date are governed by prior law.

(c) The manner of payment at a sale of property pursuant to a writ or order after the operative date is governed by Section 701.590. **Leg.H.** Added Stats 1982 ch 1364 §2, operative July 1, 1983.

§694.050. Redemption rights

(a) Except as provided in subdivision (b), property levied upon, or property to be sold upon which foreclosure or other proceedings for sale have been commenced, prior to the operative date that would have been sold subject to the right of redemption under prior law shall be sold subject to the right of redemption and may be redeemed as provided by prior law.

(b) If the judgment creditor and judgment debtor agree in writing, property described in subdivision (a) may be sold as provided in this title rather than subject to the right of redemption.

(c) Property sold prior to the operative date subject to the right of redemption under prior law may be redeemed as provided by prior law. **Leg.H.** Added Stats 1982 ch 1364 §2, operative July 1, 1983.

§694.060. Creditor's suit

Notwithstanding Section 708.230, an action may be commenced pursuant to Section 708.210 within one year after the operative date if the action could have been commenced under prior law on the day before the operative date. **Leg.H.** Added Stats 1982 ch 1364 §2, operative July 1, 1983.

§694.070. Third-party proceedings

(a) A third-party claim filed prior to the operative date is governed by prior law.

(b) A demand for a third-party claim served on a secured party prior to the operative date is governed by prior law. **Leg.H.** Added Stats 1982 ch 1364 §2, operative July 1, 1983.

§694.080. Exemptions

The exemptions from enforcement of a money judgment provided by this title do not apply to property levied upon or otherwise subjected to a lien prior to the operative date. Whether such property is exempt is determined by the exemptions provided by law at the time the lien was created. **Leg.H.** Added Stats 1982 ch 1364 §2, operative July 1, 1983.

§694.090. Effect of homestead declaration

On and after the operative date, a declaration of homestead made under prior law pursuant to Title 5 (commencing with Section 1237) of Part 4 of Division 2 of the Civil Code is effective only to the extent provided in Article 5 (commencing with Section 704.910) of Chapter 4 of Division 2. **Leg.H.** Added Stats 1982 ch 1364 §2, operative July 1, 1983.

§695. [Section repealed 1983]
Leg.H. Enacted Stats 1872. Amended Code Amdts 1873–74 ch 383 §95. Repealed Stats 1982 ch 1364 §1, operative July 1, 1983. See CCP §701.600.

DIVISION 2
ENFORCEMENT OF MONEY JUDGMENTS

Chapter 1. General Provisions.
Chapter 2. Liens.
Chapter 3. Execution.
Chapter 4. Exemptions.
Chapter 5. Wage Garnishment.
Chapter 6. Miscellaneous Creditors' Remedies.

CHAPTER 1
GENERAL PROVISIONS

Article 1. Property Subject to Enforcement of Money Judgment.
Article 2. Amount to Satisfy Money Judgment.

ARTICLE 1
Property Subject to Enforcement of Money Judgment

Property subject to enforcement of money judgment. §695.010.
Community property. §695.020.
Property not subject to enforcement of money judgment. §695.030.
Real property leases subject to enforcement. §695.035.
Release of property not subject to enforcement. §695.040.
Enforcement against public entity. §695.050.
License to engage in business. §695.060.
Property subject to lien after transfer; Death of judgment debtor. §695.070.

§695.010. Property subject to enforcement of money judgment
(a) Except as otherwise provided by law, all property of the judgment debtor is subject to enforcement of a money judgment.
(b) If property of the judgment debtor was attached in the action but was transferred before entry of the money judgment in favor of the judgment creditor, the property is subject to enforcement of the money judgment so long as the attachment lien remains effective. **Leg.H.** Added Stats 1982 ch 1364 §2, operative July 1, 1983. Amended Stats 1984 ch 538 §17.

§695.020. Community property
(a) Community property is subject to enforcement of a money judgment as provided in the Family Code.
(b) Unless the provision or context otherwise requires, if community property that is subject to enforcement of a money judgment is sought to be applied to the satisfaction of a money judgment:
(1) Any provision of this division that applies to the property of the judgment debtor or to obligations owed to the judgment debtor also applies to the community property interest of the spouse of the judgment debtor and to obligations owed to the other spouse that are community property.
(2) Any provision of this division that applies to property in the possession or under the control of the judgment debtor also applies to community property in the possession or under the control of the spouse of the judgment debtor. **Leg.H.** Added Stats 1982 ch 1364 §2, operative July 1, 1983. Amended Stats 1983 ch 155 §12, effective June 30, 1983, operative July 1, 1983; Stats 1992 ch 163 §33 (AB 2641), operative January 1, 1994.

§695.030. Property not subject to enforcement of money judgment
(a) Except as otherwise provided by statute, property of the judgment debtor that is not assignable or transferable is not subject to enforcement of a money judgment.
(b) The following property is subject to enforcement of a money judgment:
(1) An interest in a trust, to the extent provided by law.
(2) A cause of action for money or property that is the subject of a pending action or special proceeding. **Leg.H.** Added Stats 1982 ch 1364 §2, operative July 1, 1983. Amended Stats 1986 ch 820 §17, operative July 1, 1987.

§695.035. Real property leases subject to enforcement
(a) A lessee's interest in real property may be applied to the satisfaction of a money judgment in any of the following circumstances:
(1) If the lessee has the right voluntarily to sublet the property or assign the interest in the lease.
(2) If the lessee has the right voluntarily to sublet the property or assign the interest in the lease subject to standards or conditions and the purchaser at the execution sale or other assignee agrees to comply with the standards or conditions that would have had to be complied with had the lessee voluntarily sublet the property or assigned the interest in the lease.
(3) If the lessee has the right voluntarily to sublet the property or assign the interest in the lease with the consent of the lessor, in which case the obligation of the lessor to consent to the assignment is subject to the same standard that would apply had the lessee voluntarily sublet the property or assigned the interest in the lease.
(4) In any other case, if the lessor consents in writing.
(b) A provision in a lease for the termination or modification of the lease upon an involuntary transfer or assignment of the lessee's interest is ineffective to the extent that such provision would prevent the application of the lessee's interest to the satisfaction of the money judgment under subdivision (a). **Leg.H.** Added Stats 1982 ch 1364 §2, operative July 1, 1983.

§695.040. Release of property not subject to enforcement
Property that is not subject to enforcement of a money judgment may not be levied upon or in any other manner applied to the satisfaction of a money judgment. If property that is not subject to enforcement of a money judgment has been levied upon, the property may be released pursuant to the claim of exemption procedure provided in Article 2 (commencing with Section 703.510) of Chapter 4. **Leg.H.** Added Stats 1982 ch 1364 §2, operative July 1, 1983.

§695.050. Enforcement against public entity
A money judgment against a public entity is not enforceable under this division if the money judgment is subject to Chapter 1 (commencing with Section 965) of, or Article 1 (commencing with Section 970) of Chapter 2 of, Part 5 of Division 3.6 of Title 1 of the Government Code. **Leg.H.** Added Stats 1982 ch 1364 §2, operative July 1, 1983.

§695.060. License to engage in business
Except as provided in Section 708.630, a license issued by a public entity to engage in any business, profession, or activity is not subject to enforcement of a money judgment. **Leg.H.** Added Stats 1982 ch 1364 §2, operative July 1, 1983.

§695.070. Property subject to lien after transfer; Death of judgment debtor
(a) Notwithstanding the transfer or encumbrance of property subject to a lien created under this division, if the property remains subject to the lien after the transfer or encumbrance, the money judgment may be enforced against the property in the same manner and to the same extent as if it had not been transferred or encumbered.
(b) If the judgment debtor dies after the transfer of property that remains subject to a lien created under this division, the money judgment may be enforced against the property as provided in subdivision (a). **Leg.H.** Added Stats 1982 ch 1364 §2, operative July 1, 1983. Amended Stats 1989 ch 1416 §22.

ARTICLE 2
Amount to Satisfy Money Judgment

Amount required to satisfy judgment. §695.210.
Notice of interest on arrearages; Statement of account in child support action. §695.211.
Waiver of appeal. §695.215.
Order of application of money received. §695.220.
Crediting money received for support. §695.221.

§695.210. Amount required to satisfy judgment
The amount required to satisfy a money judgment is the total amount of the judgment as entered or renewed with the following additions and subtractions:
(a) The addition of costs added to the judgment pursuant to Section 685.090.
(b) The addition of interest added to the judgment as it accrues pursuant to Sections 685.010 to 685.030, inclusive.
(c) The subtraction of the amount of any partial satisfactions of the judgment.
(d) The subtraction of the amount of any portion of the judgment that is no longer enforceable. **Leg.H.** Added Stats 1982 ch 1364 §2, operative

July 1, 1983. Amended Stats 1992 ch 848 §8 (SB 1614), effective September 22, 1992; Stats 1993 ch 876 §9 (SB 1068), effective October 6, 1993.

§695.211. Notice of interest on arrearages; Statement of account in child support action

(a) Every money judgment or order for child support shall provide notice that interest on arrearages accrues at the legal rate.

(b) The notice provisions required by this section shall be incorporated in the appropriate Judicial Council forms.

(c) Upon implementation of the California Child Support Automation System prescribed in Chapter 4 (commencing with Section 10080) of Part 1 of Division 9 of the Welfare and Institutions Code and certification of the California Child Support Automation System by the United States Department of Health and Human Services, whenever a statement of account is issued by the local child support agency in any child support action, the statement shall include a statement of an amount of current support, arrears, and interest due. **Leg.H.** Added Stats 1994 ch 959 §1 (AB 3072), effective September 27, 1994. Amended Stats 2000 ch 808 §10 (AB 1358), effective September 28, 2000.

§695.215. Waiver of appeal

Payment in satisfaction of a money judgment, including payment of a severable portion of the money judgment, interest thereon, and associated costs, does not constitute a waiver of the right to appeal, except to the extent that the payment is the product of compromise or is coupled with an agreement not to appeal. Payment in satisfaction of a severable portion of a money judgment, interest thereon, and associated costs, does not constitute a waiver of the right to appeal other portions of the money judgment. **Leg.H.** Added Stats 2019 ch 48 §1 (AB 1361), effective January 1, 2020.

2019 Note: The addition of Section 695.215 of the Code of Civil Procedure made by this act does not constitute a change in, but is declaratory of, existing law. Stats 2019 ch 48 §2 (AB 1361).

§695.220. Order of application of money received

Money received in satisfaction of a money judgment, except a money judgment for support, is to be credited as follows:

(a) The money is first to be credited against the amounts described in subdivision (b) of Section 685.050 that are collected by the levying officer.

(b) Any remaining money is next to be credited against any fee due the court pursuant to Section 6103.5 or 68511.3 of the Government Code, which are to be remitted to the court by the levying officer.

(c) Any remaining money is next to be credited against the accrued interest that remains unsatisfied.

(d) Any remaining money is to be credited against the principal amount of the judgment remaining unsatisfied. If the judgment is payable in installments, the remaining money is to be credited against the matured installments in the order in which they matured. **Leg.H.** Added Stats 1982 ch 1364 §2, operative July 1, 1983. Amended Stats 1992 ch 848 §9 (SB 1614), effective September 22, 1992; Stats 1993 ch 158 §3.2 (AB 392), effective July 20, 1993, ch 876 §10 (SB 1068), effective October 6, 1993, ch 909 §1 (SB 15); Stats 1994 ch 75 §1 (AB 1702), effective May 20, 1994, ch 146 §25 (AB 3601) (ch 75 prevails).

§695.221. Crediting money received for support

Satisfaction of a money judgment for support shall be credited as follows:

(a) The money shall first be credited against the current month's support.

(b) Any remaining money shall next be credited against the principal amount of the judgment remaining unsatisfied. If the judgment is payable in installments, the remaining money shall be credited against the matured installments in the order in which they matured.

(c) Any remaining money shall be credited against the accrued interest that remains unsatisfied.

(d) In cases enforced pursuant to Part D (commencing with Section 651) of Subchapter 4 of Chapter 7 of Title 42 of the United States Code, if a lump-sum payment is collected from a support obligor who has money judgments for support owing to more than one family, effective September 1, 2006, all support collected shall be distributed pursuant to guidelines developed by the Department of Child Support Services.

(e) Support collections received between January 1, 2009, and April 30, 2020, inclusive, shall be distributed by the Department of Child Support Services as follows:

(1) Notwithstanding subdivisions (a), (b), and (c), a collection received as a result of a federal tax refund offset shall first be credited against the principal amount of past due support that has been assigned to the state pursuant to Section 11477 of the Welfare and Institutions Code and federal law and then any interest due on that past due support, prior to the principal amount of any other past due support remaining unsatisfied and then any interest due on that past due support.

(2) The following shall be the order of distribution of child support collections through September 30, 2000, except for federal tax refund offset collections, for child support received for families and children who are former recipients of Aid to Families with Dependent Children (AFDC) program benefits or former recipients of Temporary Assistance for Needy Families (TANF) program benefits:

(A) The money shall first be credited against the current month's support.

(B) Any remaining money shall next be credited against interest that accrued on arrearages owed to the family or children since leaving the AFDC program or the TANF program and then the arrearages.

(C) Any remaining money shall next be credited against interest that accrued on arrearages owed during the time the family or children received benefits under the AFDC program or the TANF program and then the arrearages.

(D) Any remaining money shall next be credited against interest that accrued on arrearages owed to the family or children prior to receiving benefits from the AFDC program or the TANF program and then the arrearages.

(f) Support collections received on or after May 1, 2020, shall be distributed by the Department of Child Support Services in accordance with Section 657(a)(2)(B) of Title 42 of the United States Code, as amended by Section 7301(b)(1) of the federal Deficit Reduction Act of 2005, in such a manner as to distribute all support collections to families first to the maximum extent permitted by federal law. **Leg.H.** Added Stats 2004 ch 305 §2 (AB 2669), operative January 1, 2009. Amended Stats 2021 ch 85 §1 (AB 135), effective July 16, 2021.

Former Sections: Former CCP §695.221, similar to the present section, was added Stats 1993 ch 876 §11, effective October 6, 1993, and repealed operative January 1, 2009, by its own terms. Stats 2004 ch 305 §1 (AB 2669).

Prior Law: Former CCP §695.221, similar to the present section, was added Stats 1993 ch 876 §11, effective October 6, 1993, amended Stats 1994 ch 75 §2, effective May 20, 1994, Stats 1996 ch 565 §1, Stats 1997 ch 599 §2, Stats 2000 ch 808 §11, effective September 28, 2000, Stats 2004 ch 305 §1, and repealed January 1, 2009, by its own terms.

§696. [Section repealed 1983]

Leg.H. Enacted Stats 1872. Amended Code Amdts 1873–74 ch 383 §96. Repealed Stats 1982 ch 1364 §1, operative July 1, 1983. See CCP §701.600.

§697. [Section repealed 1983]

Leg.H. Enacted Stats 1872. Repealed Stats 1982 ch 1364 §1, operative July 1, 1983. See CCP §687.040.

CHAPTER 2
LIENS

Article 1. General Provisions.
Article 2. Judgment Lien on Real Property.
Article 3. Judgment Lien on Personal Property.
Article 4. Execution Lien.
Article 5. Other Liens Created by Enforcement Process.

ARTICLE 1
General Provisions

Amount of lien generally. §697.010.
Relation back of liens. §697.020.
Duration of liens generally. §697.030.
Effect of stay of enforcement of judgment. §697.040.
Effect of extinction of lien. §697.050.
Judgment liens under federal judgments. §697.060.

§697.010. Amount of lien generally

Except as otherwise provided by statute, a lien created under this division or under Title 6.5 (commencing with Section 481.010) (attachment) is a lien for the amount required to satisfy the money judgment. **Leg.H.** Added Stats 1982 ch 1364 §2, operative July 1, 1983.

§697.020. Relation back of liens

(a) If a lien is created on property pursuant to Title 6.5 (commencing with Section 481.010) (attachment) and after judgment in the action a lien is created pursuant to this division on the same property under the same claim while the earlier lien is in effect, the priority of the later lien relates back to the date the earlier lien was created.

(b) If a lien is created on property pursuant to this division and a later lien of the same or a different type is created pursuant to this division on the same property under the same judgment while the earlier lien is in effect, the priority of the later lien relates back to the date the earlier lien was created.

(c) Nothing in this section affects priorities or rights of third persons established while the earlier lien was in effect under the law governing the earlier lien. **Leg.H.** Added Stats 1982 ch 1364 §2, operative July 1, 1983.

§697.030. Duration of liens generally

Subject to Sections 683.180 to 683.200, inclusive, and to Section 697.040, except where a shorter period is provided by statute, a lien created pursuant to this title is effective during the period of enforceability of the judgment. **Leg.H.** Added Stats 1982 ch 1364 §2, operative July 1, 1983.

§697.040. Effect of stay of enforcement of judgment

(a) If enforcement of the judgment is stayed on appeal by the giving of a sufficient undertaking under Chapter 2 (commencing with Section 916) of Title 13:

(1) Existing liens created under this division are extinguished.

(2) New liens may not be created under this division during the period of the stay.

(b) Unless the court otherwise expressly orders, a stay of enforcement of the judgment under Section 918 does not extinguish or prevent the creation of a lien under Article 2 (commencing with Section 697.310) or Article 3 (commencing with Section 697.510); but, unless the court otherwise expressly orders, no other liens may be created or continued under this division during the period of the stay of enforcement.

(c) Unless the court expressly orders otherwise, if enforcement of the judgment is stayed pursuant to Section 1699 or 1710.50:

(1) Existing liens created under this division are extinguished.

(2) New liens may not be created under this division during the period of the stay. **Leg.H.** Added Stats 1982 ch 1364 §2, operative July 1, 1983.

§697.050. Effect of extinction of lien

If a lien created pursuant to this division is extinguished, property held subject to the lien shall be released unless the property is to be held under another lien or the property is ordered by the court to be held pending resolution of a dispute concerning its proper disposition. **Leg.H.** Added Stats 1982 ch 1364 §2, operative July 1, 1983.

§697.060. Judgment liens under federal judgments

(a) An abstract or certified copy of a money judgment of a court of the United States that is enforceable in this state may be recorded to create a judgment lien on real property pursuant to Article 2 (commencing with Section 697.310).

(b) A notice of judgment lien based on a money judgment of a court of the United States that is enforceable in this state may be filed to create a judgment lien on personal property pursuant to Article 3 (commencing with Section 697.510). **Leg.H.** Added Stats 1982 ch 1364 §2, operative July 1, 1983.

ARTICLE 2
Judgment Lien on Real Property

Creation and duration of judgment lien on real property generally. §697.310.
Judgment lien for installments under support judgment or judgment against health care provider. §697.320.
Judgment lien for workers' compensation award. §697.330.
Interests subject to judgment lien on real property. §697.340.
Amount of judgment lien on real property. §697.350.
Effect of modification of judgment. §697.360.
Release or subordination of judgment lien. §697.370.
Priority of judgment liens. §697.380.
Effect of transfer or encumbrance of interest subject to judgment lien. §697.390.
Recording of documents extinguishing or subordinating judgment lien on real property. §697.400.
Release of erroneous judgment lien on real property. §697.410.

§697.310. Creation and duration of judgment lien on real property generally

(a) Except as otherwise provided by statute, a judgment lien on real property is created under this section by recording an abstract of a money judgment with the county recorder.

(b) Unless the money judgment is satisfied or the judgment lien is released, subject to Section 683.180 (renewal of judgment), a judgment lien created under this section continues until 10 years from the date of entry of the judgment.

(c) The creation and duration of a judgment lien under a money judgment entered pursuant to Section 117 or 582.5 of this code or Section 16380 of the Vehicle Code or under a similar judgment is governed by this section, notwithstanding that the judgment may be payable in installments. **Leg.H.** Added Stats 1982 ch 1364 §2, operative July 1, 1983. Amended Stats 1998 ch 931 §90 (SB 2139), effective September 28, 1998.

§697.320. Judgment lien for installments under support judgment or judgment against health care provider

(a) A judgment lien on real property is created under this section by recording an abstract, a notice of support judgment, an interstate lien form promulgated by the federal Secretary of Health and Human Services pursuant to Section 652(a)(11) of Title 42 of the United States Code, or a certified copy of either of the following money judgments with the county recorder:

(1) A judgment for child, family, or spousal support payable in installments.

(2) A judgment entered pursuant to Section 667.7 (judgment against health care provider requiring periodic payments).

(b) Unless the money judgment is satisfied or the judgment lien is released, a judgment lien created under paragraph (1) of subdivision (a) or by recording an interstate lien form, as described in subdivision (a), continues during the period the judgment remains enforceable. Unless the money judgment is satisfied or the judgment lien is released, a judgment lien created under paragraph (2) of subdivision (a) continues for a period of 10 years from the date of its creation. The duration of a judgment lien created under paragraph (2) of subdivision (a) may be extended any number of times by recording, during the time the judgment lien is in existence, a certified copy of the judgment in the manner provided in this section for the initial recording; this rerecording has the effect of extending the duration of the judgment lien created under paragraph (2) of subdivision (a) until 10 years from the date of the rerecording. **Leg.H.** Added Stats 1982 ch 1364 §2, operative July 1, 1983. Amended Stats 1986 ch 946 §2; Stats 1992 ch 163 §34 (AB 2641), operative January 1, 1994; Stats 1993 ch 876 §12 (SB 1068), effective October 6, 1993; Stats 1997 ch 599 §3 (AB 573); Stats 2002 ch 927 §1.5 (AB 3032).

§697.330. Judgment lien for workers' compensation award

(a) In the case of a money judgment entered on an order, decision, or award made under Division 4 (commencing with Section 3200) of the Labor Code (workers' compensation):

(1) If the judgment is for a lump sum, a judgment lien on real property is created by recording an abstract of the judgment as provided in Section 697.310 and, except as otherwise provided in Division 4 (commencing with Section 3200) of the Labor Code, the judgment lien is governed by the provisions applicable to a judgment lien created under Section 697.310.

(2) If the judgment is for the payment of money in installments, a judgment lien on real property is created by recording a certified copy of the judgment as provided in Section 697.320 and, except as otherwise provided in Division 4 (commencing with Section 3200) of the Labor Code, the lien is governed by the provisions applicable to a judgment lien created under Section 697.320.

(b) Nothing in this section limits or affects any provision of Division 4 (commencing with Section 3200) of the Labor Code. **Leg.H.** Added Stats 1982 ch 1364 §2, operative July 1, 1983.

§697.340. Interests subject to judgment lien on real property

Except as provided in Section 704.950:

(a) A judgment lien on real property attaches to all interests in real property in the county where the lien is created (whether present or future, vested or contingent, legal or equitable) that are subject to enforcement of the money judgment against the judgment debtor pursuant to Article 1 (commencing with Section 695.010) of Chapter 1 at the time the lien was created, but does not reach rental payments, a leasehold estate with an unexpired term of less than two years, the interest of a beneficiary under a trust, or real property that is subject to an attachment lien in favor of the creditor and was transferred before judgment.

(b) If any interest in real property in the county on which a judgment lien could be created under subdivision (a) is acquired after the judgment lien was created, the judgment lien attaches to such interest at the time it is acquired. **Leg.H.** Added Stats 1982 ch 1364 §2, operative July 1, 1983. Amended Stats 1984 ch 538 §18.

§697.350. Amount of judgment lien on real property

(a) Except as otherwise provided by statute, a judgment lien on real property is a lien for the amount required to satisfy the money judgment.

(b) A judgment lien on real property created under a money judgment payable in installments pursuant to Section 116.620 or 582.5 of this code or Section 16380 of the Vehicle Code or under a similar judgment is in the full amount required to satisfy the judgment, but the judgment lien may not be enforced for the amount of unmatured installments unless the court so orders.

(c) A judgment lien created pursuant to Section 697.320 is a lien for the amount of the installments as they mature under the terms of the judgment, plus accrued interest and the costs as they are added to the judgment pursuant to Chapter 5 (commencing with Section 685.010) of Division 1, and less the amount of any partial satisfactions, but does not become a lien for any installment until it becomes due and payable under the terms of the judgment. **Leg.H.** Added Stats 1982 ch 1364 §2, operative July 1, 1983. Amended Stats 1998 ch 931 §91 (SB 2139), effective September 28, 1998; Stats 2009 ch 140 §39 (AB 1164), effective January 1, 2010.

§697.360. Effect of modification of judgment

(a) If a judgment lien on real property has been created under a money judgment that is thereafter modified as to its amount, an abstract of the modified judgment or a certified copy of the order modifying the judgment may be recorded in the same manner as an abstract of judgment or a certified copy of the judgment is recorded to create a judgment lien.

(b) If a judgment lien on real property has been created under a money judgment that is thereafter modified to reduce its amount, the judgment lien continues under the terms of the judgment as modified, whether or not the modification is recorded as provided in subdivision (a).

(c) If a judgment lien on real property has been created under a money judgment that is thereafter modified to increase its amount, the judgment lien continues under the terms of the original judgment until such time as the modification is recorded as provided in subdivision (a). Upon such recording, the judgment lien extends to the judgment as modified, but the priority for the additional amount under the judgment as modified dates from the time the modification is recorded.

(d) Notwithstanding subdivision (c), if a judgment lien on real property has been created under a money judgment, by recording of an abstract of support judgment under paragraph (1) of subdivision (a) of Section 697.320, and the support order is thereafter modified to increase its amount, the judgment lien extends to the judgment as modified without the need for recording of another abstract of support judgment, but the priority for the additional amount under the judgment dates from the time the modification is effective.

(e) A support obligee shall respond in a timely manner to (1) a title or escrow company request for a demand statement needed to close an escrow relating to a support judgment lien, or (2) a support obligor who claims an error exists in the amount of alleged arrears.

(f) A support obligor who complies with the procedure specified in Division 5 (commencing with Section 724.010) shall be entitled to the remedies specified therein. **Leg.H.** Added Stats 1982 ch 1364 §2, operative July 1, 1983. Amended Stats 1995 ch 583 §1 (AB 554).

§697.370. Release or subordination of judgment lien

(a) The judgment creditor may do either of the following:

(1) Release from the judgment lien all or a part of the real property subject to the lien.

(2) Subordinate to another lien or encumbrance the judgment lien on all or a part of the real property subject to the judgment lien.

(b) A release or subordination is sufficient if it is executed by the judgment creditor in the same manner as an acknowledgment of satisfaction of judgment and contains all of the following:

(1) A description of the real property being released or on which the lien is being subordinated. If the judgment debtor does not have an interest of record in the real property, the release or subordination shall show the name of the record owner. If all of the real property of the judgment debtor in a county in which the lien is recorded is being released from the judgment lien, or if the judgment debtor has no known interest in any real property in that county, the release shall, in lieu of containing a description of the property being released, contain a statement substantially as follows: "This is a release from the judgment lien described herein of all of the interests in real property in ____ County presently owned or hereafter acquired of the herein named judgment debtor subject to the lien."

(2) The date the judgment lien was created and where in the records of the county the abstract of judgment or certified copy of the judgment was recorded to create the lien.

(3) The title of the court where the judgment is entered and the cause and number of the action.

(4) The date of entry of the judgment and of any subsequent renewals and where entered in the records of the court.

(5) The name and address of the judgment creditor, the judgment creditor's assignee, if any, and the judgment debtor whose interest in real property is released from the judgment lien or with respect to whom the judgment lien is subordinated.

(c) A release or subordination substantially complying with the requirements of this section is effective even though it contains minor errors that are not seriously misleading.

(d) The execution of a release or subordination of a judgment lien pursuant to this section does not release or subordinate the judgment lien as to judgment debtors not named in the release pursuant to paragraph (5) of subdivision (b). **Leg.H.** Added Stats 1982 ch 1364 §2, operative July 1, 1983. Amended Stats 1986 ch 271 §1; Stats 1987 ch 254 §1.

§697.380. Priority of judgment liens

(a) As used in this section:

(1) "Installment judgment lien" means a judgment lien created under Section 697.320.

(2) "Lump-sum judgment lien" means a judgment lien created under Section 697.310.

(b) Except as otherwise provided by law, the rules stated in this section govern the priorities of judgment liens on real property.

(c) A lump-sum judgment lien has priority over any other lump-sum judgment lien thereafter created.

(d) A lump-sum judgment lien has priority over an installment judgment lien as to all of the following:

(1) Installments that mature on the installment judgment after the lump-sum judgment lien is created.

(2) Interest that accrues on the installment judgment after the lump-sum judgment lien is created.

(3) Costs that are added to the installment judgment after the lump-sum judgment lien is created.

(e) An installment judgment lien has priority over a lump-sum judgment lien as to all of the following:

(1) Installments that have matured on the installment judgment before the lump-sum judgment lien is created.

(2) Interest that has accrued on the installment judgment before the lump-sum judgment lien is created.

(3) Costs that have been added to the installment judgment before the lump-sum judgment lien is created.

(f) If an installment judgment lien has been created and another installment judgment lien is thereafter created, the first installment judgment lien has priority over the second installment judgment lien as to the installments that have matured on the judgment at the time the second installment judgment lien is created, the interest that has accrued prior to that time on the judgment, and the costs that have been added prior to that time to the judgment pursuant to Chapter 5 (commencing with Section 685.010) of Division 1. Thereafter, priorities are determined by the time at which each installment matures on a judgment, the time the interest accrues on a judgment, and the time costs are added to a judgment pursuant to Chapter 5 (commencing with Section 685.010) of Division 1.

(g) For the purposes of this section, if two judgment liens attach to the same property at the same time under subdivision (b) of Section 697.340 (after-acquired property), the judgment lien that was first created has priority as to all amounts that are due and payable on that judgment at the

§697.390. Effect of transfer or encumbrance of interest subject to judgment lien

If an interest in real property that is subject to a judgment lien is transferred or encumbered without satisfying or extinguishing the judgment lien:

(a) The interest transferred or encumbered remains subject to a judgment lien created pursuant to Section 697.310 in the same amount as if the interest had not been transferred or encumbered.

(b) The interest transferred or encumbered remains subject to a judgment lien created pursuant to Section 697.320 in the amount of the lien at the time of transfer or encumbrance plus interest thereafter accruing on such amount. **Leg.H.** Added Stats 1982 ch 1364 §2, operative July 1, 1983. Amended Stats 1984 ch 538 §19.

§697.400. Recording of documents extinguishing or subordinating judgment lien on real property

(a) The judgment creditor, judgment debtor, or owner of real property subject to a judgment lien on real property created under Section 697.310, may record in the office of the county recorder an acknowledgment of satisfaction of judgment executed as provided in Section 724.060 or a court clerk's certificate of satisfaction of judgment issued pursuant to Section 724.100. Upon such recording, the judgment lien created under the judgment that has been satisfied is extinguished as a matter of record.

(b) The judgment creditor, judgment debtor, or owner of real property subject to a judgment lien on real property created under Section 697.320, may record in the office of the county recorder an acknowledgment of satisfaction of matured installments under an installment judgment if the acknowledgment is executed as provided in Section 724.250. Upon such recording, the judgment lien is extinguished as a matter of record to the extent of the satisfied installments described in the acknowledgment of satisfaction.

(c) The judgment creditor, the judgment debtor, or the owner of real property subject to a judgment lien, including a property owner described in Section 697.410, may record in the office of the county recorder a release or subordination of a judgment lien on real property if the release or subordination is executed as provided in Section 697.370. **Leg.H.** Added Stats 1982 ch 1364 §2, operative July 1, 1983.

§697.410. Release of erroneous judgment lien on real property

(a) If a recorded abstract of a money judgment or certified copy of a money judgment appears to create a judgment lien on real property of a person who is not the judgment debtor because the name of the property owner is the same as or similar to that of the judgment debtor, the erroneously identified property owner may deliver to the judgment creditor a written demand for a recordable document releasing the lien. The demand shall be accompanied by proof to the satisfaction of the judgment creditor that the property owner is not the judgment debtor and that the property is not subject to enforcement of the judgment against the judgment debtor.

(b) Within 15 days after receipt of the property owner's demand and proof satisfactory to the judgment creditor that the property owner is not the judgment debtor and that the property is not subject to enforcement of the judgment, the judgment creditor shall deliver to the property owner a recordable document releasing the lien on the property of such owner. If the judgment creditor improperly fails to deliver a recordable document releasing the lien within the time allowed, the judgment creditor is liable to the property owner for all damages sustained by reason of such failure and shall also forfeit one hundred dollars ($100) to the property owner.

(c) If the judgment creditor does not deliver a recordable document pursuant to subdivision (b), the property owner may apply to the court on noticed motion for an order releasing the judgment lien on the property of such owner. Notice of motion shall be served on the judgment creditor. Service shall be made personally or by mail. Upon presentation of evidence to the satisfaction of the court that the property owner is not the judgment debtor and that the property is not subject to enforcement of the judgment, the court shall order the judgment creditor to prepare and deliver a recordable document releasing the lien or shall itself order the release of the judgment lien on the property of such owner. The court order may be recorded in the office of the county recorder with the same effect as the recordable document demanded by the property owner.

(d) The court shall award reasonable attorney's fees to the prevailing party in any proceeding maintained pursuant to this section.

(e) The damages provided by this section are not in derogation of any other damages or penalties to which an aggrieved person may be entitled by law. **Leg.H.** Added Stats 1982 ch 1364 §2, operative July 1, 1983.

ARTICLE 3
Judgment Lien on Personal Property

Creation and duration of judgment lien on personal property; Lapse; Continuation statement; Extinguishment; Release. §697.510.
Use of other procedures. §697.520.
Property subject to judgment lien. §697.530.
Amount of judgment lien on personal property. §697.540.
Notice of judgment lien on personal property; Execution and contents. §697.550.
Service of copy of notice of judgment lien on judgment debtor. §697.560.
Filing, marking, and indexing of notice of judgment lien. §697.570.
Certificate showing liens on file; Copies of notices. §697.580.
Priority of judgment lien against security interests and agricultural liens. §697.590.
Priority of judgment lien against other judgment liens. §697.600.
Effect of disposition of property subject to judgment lien. §697.610.
Lien on identifiable cash proceeds of transferred property. §697.620.
Acknowledgment or court clerk's certificate of satisfaction of judgment; Filing and effect. §697.640.
Release or subordination of judgment lien on personal property. §697.650.
Release of erroneous judgment lien on personal property. §697.660.
Forms prescribed by Secretary of State. §697.670.

§697.510. Creation and duration of judgment lien on personal property; Lapse; Continuation statement; Extinguishment; Release

(a) A judgment lien on personal property described in Section 697.530 is created by filing a notice of judgment lien in the office of the Secretary of State pursuant to this article. A judgment lien may be created under this article only if the judgment is a money judgment that was first entered in this state after June 30, 1983. Except as provided in subdivision (b) of Section 697.540, a judgment lien may not be created under this article if the money judgment is payable in installments unless all of the installments under the judgment have become due and payable at the time the notice of judgment lien is filed.

(b) Except as otherwise provided in subdivision (c), (e), or (g), the judgment lien continues for five years from the date of filing.

(c) The effectiveness of a filed judgment lien lapses on the expiration of the period described in subdivision (b) unless, before the lapse, a continuation statement is filed pursuant to subdivision (d). Upon lapse, the judgment lien created by the filing of a notice pursuant to subdivision (a) ceases to be effective.

(d) A continuation statement may be filed only within the six-month period prior to the expiration of the five-year period specified in subdivision (b).

(e) A continuation statement that is not filed within the six-month period prescribed by subdivision (d) is ineffective. Upon timely filing of a continuation statement, the effectiveness of the initial notice of judgment lien continues for a period of five years commencing on the day on which the notice of judgment lien would have become ineffective in the absence of the filing. Upon the expiration of the five-year period, the notice of judgment lien lapses in the same manner as provided in subdivision (c), unless, before the lapse, another continuation statement is filed pursuant to subdivision (d). Succeeding continuation statements may be filed in the same manner to continue the effectiveness of the initial notice of judgment lien.

(f) For purposes of this section, "continuation statement" means an amendment of a notice of judgment lien that does both of the following:

(1) Identifies, by its file number, the initial notice of judgment lien to which it relates.

(2) Indicates that it is a continuation statement for, or that it is filed to continue the effectiveness of, the identified notice of judgment lien.

(g)(1) Notwithstanding any other provision of this section, the lien created by this section is extinguished at the earliest to occur of the following:

(A) The money judgment is satisfied.

(B) The period of enforceability of the judgment, including any extension thereof pursuant to Article 2 (commencing with Section 683.110) of Chapter 3 of Division 1, terminates.

(C) The judgment lien is terminated or released.

(2) If the lien created by this section is extinguished, the judgment creditor shall file a statement of release within 20 days after the judgment creditor receives an authenticated demand from the judgment debtor. For the purposes of this subdivision, "authenticated demand" means either a signed written demand or an executed or otherwise encrypted demand delivered electronically that identifies the judgment debtor and the demand for a statement of release.

(h) If a judgment creditor does not file a statement of release pursuant to subdivision (g), the person who made the demand may apply to the court on noticed motion for an order releasing the judgment lien. Notice of the motion shall be filed in the county where the judgment was rendered and notice of the motion shall be served on the judgment creditor. Service shall be made personally or by mail. Upon presentation of evidence to the satisfaction of the court that the judgment lien has been extinguished pursuant to subdivision (g), the court shall order the judgment creditor to prepare and file the statement of release or shall itself order the release of the judgment lien. The court order may be filed in the office of the Secretary of State and shall have the same effect as the statement of release demanded under subdivision (g).

(i) The court shall award reasonable attorney's fees to the prevailing party in any action or proceeding maintained pursuant to this section.

(j) Nothing in this section is in derogation of any other relief to which an aggrieved person may be entitled by law.

(k) The fees for filing and indexing a record under this section, or for responding to a request for information from the filing office, are as set forth in Section 9525 of the Commercial Code.

(*l*) The provisions of Sections 9522 and 9523 of the Commercial Code shall apply to a notice of judgment lien to the same extent as to a filed financing statement.

(m) Terms for which definitions are not set forth in Division 1 (commencing with Section 680.010) have the definitions set forth in the Commercial Code. **Leg.H.** Added Stats 1982 ch 1364 §2, operative July 1, 1983. Amended Stats 2009 ch 410 §1 (AB 121), effective January 1, 2010.

§697.520. Use of other procedures

A judgment lien on personal property may be created pursuant to this article as an alternative or in addition to a lien created by levy under a writ of execution pursuant to Chapter 3 (commencing with Section 699.010) or by use of an enforcement procedure provided by Chapter 6 (commencing with Section 708.010). **Leg.H.** Added Stats 1982 ch 1364 §2, operative July 1, 1983.

§697.530. Property subject to judgment lien

(a) A judgment lien on personal property is a lien on all interests in the following personal property that are subject to enforcement of the money judgment against the judgment debtor pursuant to Article 1 (commencing with Section 695.010) of Chapter 1 at the time when the lien is created if the personal property is, at that time, any of the following:

(1) Accounts receivable, and the judgment debtor is located in this state.

(2) Tangible chattel paper, as defined in paragraph (79) of subdivision (a) of Section 9102 of the Commercial Code, and the judgment debtor is located in this state.

(3) Equipment, located within this state.

(4) Farm products, located within this state.

(5) Inventory, located within this state.

(6) Negotiable documents of title, located within this state.

(b) If any interest in personal property on which a judgment lien could be created under subdivision (a) is acquired after the judgment lien was created, the judgment lien attaches to the interest at the time it is acquired.

(c) To the extent provided by Section 697.620, a judgment lien on personal property continues on the proceeds received upon the sale, collection, or other disposition of the property subject to the judgment lien.

(d) Notwithstanding any other provision of this section, the judgment lien does not attach to:

(1) A vehicle or vessel required to be registered with the Department of Motor Vehicles or a mobilehome or commercial coach required to be registered pursuant to the Health and Safety Code.

(2) As-extracted collateral, as defined in paragraph (6) of subdivision (a) of Section 9102 of the Commercial Code, and timber to be cut.

(3) The inventory of a retail merchant held for sale except to the extent that the inventory of the retail merchant consists of durable goods having a unit retail value of at least five hundred dollars ($500). For the purposes of this paragraph, "retail merchant" does not include either of the following:

(A) A person whose sales for resale exceeded 75 percent in dollar volume of the person's total sales of all goods during the 12 months preceding the filing of the notice of judgment lien on personal property.

(B) A cooperative association organized pursuant to Chapter 1 (commencing with Section 54001) of Division 20 of the Food and Agricultural Code (agricultural cooperative associations) or Part 3 (commencing with Section 13200) of Division 3 of Title 1 of the Corporations Code (Fish Marketing Act).

(e) If property subject to a lien under this article becomes a fixture, as defined in paragraph (41) of subdivision (a) of Section 9102 of the Commercial Code, the judgment lien on that property is extinguished.

(f) Notwithstanding the filing of a notice of judgment lien, subject to the provisions of Chapter 6 (commencing with Section 708.010), a person obligated on an account receivable or chattel paper is authorized to pay or compromise the amount without notice to or consent of the judgment creditor unless and until there is a levy pursuant to Chapter 3 (commencing with Section 699.010).

(g) For purposes of this section, whether a person is located in this state is determined in accordance with Section 9307 of the Commercial Code, except that the location of a registered organization, as defined in paragraph (71) of subdivision (a) of Section 9102 of the Commercial Code, that is organized under the law of another state is determined without regard to subdivision (e) of Section 9307 of the Commercial Code. **Leg.H.** Added Stats 1982 ch 1364 §2, operative July 1, 1983. Amended Stats 1999 ch 991 §17.4 (SB 45), operative July 1, 2001; Stats 2009 ch 153 §1 (AB 1549), effective January 1, 2010; Stats 2013 ch 531 §6 (AB 502), effective January 1, 2014, operative July 1, 2014.

§697.540. Amount of judgment lien on personal property

(a) Except as otherwise provided by statute, a judgment lien on personal property is a lien for the amount required to satisfy the money judgment.

(b) A judgment lien on personal property created under a money judgment payable in installments pursuant to Section 117 or 582.5 of this code or pursuant to Section 16380 of the Vehicle Code is in the full amount required to satisfy the judgment, but the judgment lien may not be enforced for the amount of unmatured installments unless the court so orders. **Leg.H.** Added Stats 1982 ch 1364 §2, operative July 1, 1983. Amended Stats 1998 ch 931 §92 (SB 2139), effective September 28, 1998.

§697.550. Notice of judgment lien on personal property; Execution and contents

The notice of judgment lien on personal property shall be executed under oath by the judgment creditor's attorney if the judgment creditor has an attorney of record or, if the judgment creditor does not have an attorney of record, by the judgment creditor and shall contain the following information:

(a) The name and mailing address of the judgment creditor.

(b) The name and last known mailing address of the judgment debtor.

(c) A statement that: "All property subject to enforcement of a money judgment against the judgment debtor to which a judgment lien on personal property may attach under Section 697.530 of the Code of Civil Procedure is subject to this judgment lien."

(d) The title of the court where the judgment is entered and the cause and number of the action.

(e) The date of entry of the judgment and of any subsequent renewals and where entered in the records of the court.

(f) The amount required to satisfy the judgment at the date of the notice.

(g) The date of the notice. **Leg.H.** Added Stats 1982 ch 1364 §2, operative July 1, 1983.

§697.560. Service of copy of notice of judgment lien on judgment debtor

At the time of filing the notice of judgment lien on personal property or promptly thereafter, the judgment creditor shall serve a copy of the notice of judgment lien on the judgment debtor. Service shall be made personally or by mail. The failure to comply with this requirement does not affect the validity of the judgment lien. **Leg.H.** Added Stats 1982 ch 1364 §2, operative July 1, 1983.

§697.570. Filing, marking, and indexing of notice of judgment lien

Upon presentation of a notice of judgment lien on personal property for filing and tender of the filing fee to the office of the Secretary of State, the notice of judgment lien shall be filed, marked, and indexed in the same manner as a financing statement. The fee for filing in the office of the Secretary of State is the same as the fee for filing a financing statement in the standard form. A notice shall not be filed if it is presented for filing more than 10 days after the date of the notice. **Leg.H.** Added Stats 1982 ch 1364 §2, operative July 1, 1983.

§697.580. Certificate showing liens on file; Copies of notices

(a) Upon the request of any person, the Secretary of State shall issue a certificate showing whether there is on file in that office on the date and hour stated therein any notice of judgment lien on personal property filed against the property of a particular person named in the request. If a notice of judgment lien is on file, the certificate shall state the date and hour of filing of each such notice and any notice affecting any such notice of judgment lien and the name and address of the judgment creditor.

(b) Upon request, the Secretary of State shall furnish a copy of any notice of judgment lien or notice affecting a notice of judgment lien. The certificate shall be issued as part of a combined certificate pursuant to Section 9528 of the Commercial Code, and the fee for the certificate and copies shall be in accordance with that section. **Leg.H.** Added Stats 1982 ch 1364 §2, operative July 1, 1983. Amended Stats 1988 ch 393 §9; Stats 1999 ch 991 §17.5 (SB 45), operative July 1, 2001.

§697.590. Priority of judgment lien against security interests and agricultural liens

(a) As used in this section:

(1) "Filing" means:

(A) With respect to a judgment lien on personal property, the filing of a notice of judgment lien in the office of the Secretary of State to create a judgment lien on personal property under this article.

(B) With respect to a security interest or agricultural lien, as defined in paragraph (5) of subdivision (a) of Section 9102 of the Commercial Code, the filing of a financing statement pursuant to Division 9 (commencing with Section 9101) of the Commercial Code.

(2) "Perfection" means perfection of a security interest or agricultural lien pursuant to Division 9 (commencing with Section 9101) of the Commercial Code.

(3) "Personal property" means:

(A) With respect to a judgment lien on personal property, the property to which a judgment lien has attached pursuant to this article.

(B) With respect to a security interest, the collateral subject to a security interest pursuant to Division 9 (commencing with Section 9101) of the Commercial Code.

(C) With respect to an agricultural lien, the farm products subject to an agricultural lien pursuant to Division 9 (commencing with Section 9101) of the Commercial Code.

(4) "Purchase money security interest" has the same meaning as used in Section 9103 of the Commercial Code.

(b) Except as provided in subdivisions (d), (e), (g), and (h), priority between a judgment lien on personal property and a conflicting security interest or agricultural lien in the same personal property shall be determined according to this subdivision. Conflicting interests rank according to priority in time of filing or perfection. In the case of a judgment lien, priority dates from the time filing is first made covering the personal property. In the case of a security interest or agricultural lien, priority dates from the earlier of the time a filing is first made covering the personal property or the time the security interest or agricultural lien is first perfected, if there is no period thereafter when there is neither filing nor perfection.

(c) For the purposes of subdivision (b), a date of filing or perfection as to personal property is also a date of filing or perfection as to proceeds.

(d) A purchase money security interest has priority over a conflicting judgment lien on the same personal property or its proceeds if the purchase money security interest is perfected at the time the judgment debtor, as a debtor under the security agreement, receives possession of the personal property or within 20 days thereafter.

(e) If a purchase money security interest in inventory has priority over a judgment lien pursuant to subdivision (d) and a conflicting security interest has priority over the purchase money security interest in the same inventory pursuant to Section 9324 of the Commercial Code, the conflicting security interest also has priority over the judgment lien on the inventory subject to the purchase money security interest, notwithstanding that the conflicting security interest would not otherwise have priority over the judgment lien.

(f) A judgment lien that has attached to personal property, and that is also subordinate under subdivision (b) to a security interest in the same personal property, is subordinate to the security interest only to the extent that the security interest secures advances made before the judgment lien attached or within 45 days thereafter or made without knowledge of the judgment lien or pursuant to a commitment entered into without knowledge of the judgment lien. For the purpose of this subdivision, a secured party shall be deemed not to have knowledge of a judgment lien on personal property until (1) the judgment creditor serves a copy of the notice of judgment lien on the secured party personally or by mail and (2) the secured party has knowledge of the judgment lien on personal property, as "knowledge" is defined in Section 1201 of the Commercial Code. If service on the secured party is by mail, it shall be sent to the secured party at the address shown in the financing statement or security agreement.

(g) A perfected agricultural lien on personal property has priority over a judgment lien on the same personal property if the statute creating the agricultural lien so provides.

(h) A security interest in personal property perfected by the filing of a financing statement under the law of a jurisdiction other than this state, or perfected by another method pursuant to the law of a jurisdiction other than this state, has priority over a judgment lien in the same personal property. **Leg.H.** Added Stats 1984 ch 538 §19.6. Amended Stats 1985 ch 41 §5; Stats 1986 ch 248 §20; Stats 1989 ch 445 §2; Stats 1999 ch 991 §18 (SB 45), operative July 1, 2001; Stats 2009 ch 153 §2 (AB 1549), effective January 1, 2010.

Prior Law: Former CCP §697.590, similar to the present section, was added Stats 1982 ch 1364 §2, operative July 1, 1983, and repealed Stats 1984 ch 538 §19.5.

§697.600. Priority of judgment lien against other judgment liens

(a) A judgment lien on personal property has priority over any other judgment lien thereafter created on the property.

(b) For the purpose of this section, if two or more judgment liens attach to after-acquired property at the same time under subdivision (b) of Section 697.530, the judgment lien first filed has priority. **Leg.H.** Added Stats 1982 ch 1364 §2, operative July 1, 1983.

§697.610. Effect of disposition of property subject to judgment lien

Except as provided in Sections 9617 and 9622 of the Commercial Code, a judgment lien on personal property continues notwithstanding the sale, exchange, or other disposition of the property, unless the person receiving the property is one of the following:

(a) A buyer in ordinary course of business (as defined in Section 1201 of the Commercial Code) who, under Section 9320 of the Commercial Code, would take free of a security interest created by the seller.

(b) A lessee in ordinary course of business (as defined in paragraph (15) of subdivision (a) of Section 10103 of the Commercial Code) who, under Section 9321 of the Commercial Code, would take free of a security interest created by the lessor.

(c) A holder to whom a negotiable document of title has been duly negotiated within the meaning of Section 7501 of the Commercial Code.

(d) A purchaser of chattel paper who, under Section 9330 of the Commercial Code, would have priority over another security interest in the chattel paper. **Leg.H.** Added Stats 1982 ch 1364 §2, operative July 1, 1983. Amended Stats 1988 ch 1368 §5, operative January 1, 1990; Stats 1994 ch 668 §5 (SB 1405); Stats 1999 ch 991 §19 (SB 45), operative July 1, 2001.

§697.620. Lien on identifiable cash proceeds of transferred property

(a) As used in this section:

(1) "Cash proceeds" means money, checks, deposit accounts, and the like.

(2) "Proceeds" means identifiable cash proceeds received upon the sale, exchange, collection, or other disposition of property subject to a judgment lien on personal property.

(b) Except as provided in subdivision (c), the judgment lien on personal property continues in the proceeds with the same priority.

(c) In the event of insolvency proceedings (as defined in Section 1201 of the Commercial Code) instituted by or against the judgment debtor, the judgment lien continues under subdivision (b) only in the following proceeds:

(1) Proceeds in a separate deposit account containing only proceeds.

(2) Proceeds in the form of money which are neither commingled with other money nor deposited in a deposit account prior to the insolvency proceedings.

(3) Proceeds in the form of checks and the like which are not deposited in a deposit account prior to the insolvency proceedings. **Leg.H.** Added Stats 1982 ch 1364 §2, operative July 1, 1983.

§697.640. Acknowledgment or court clerk's certificate of satisfaction of judgment; Filing and effect

(a) The judgment creditor, judgment debtor, owner of property subject to a judgment lien on personal property created under the judgment, or a person having a security interest in or a lien on the property subject to the judgment lien, may file in the office of the Secretary of State an acknowledgment of satisfaction of judgment executed as provided in Section 724.060 or a court clerk's certificate of satisfaction of judgment issued pursuant to Section 724.100, together with a statement containing the name of the judgment creditor, the name and address of the judgment debtor, and the file number of the notice of judgment lien. Upon such filing, the judgment lien created under the judgment that has been satisfied is extinguished as a matter of record. The fee for filing the acknowledgment or certificate is the same as the fee for filing a termination statement under Section 9404 of the Commercial Code.

(b) The filing officer shall treat an acknowledgment of satisfaction of judgment, or court clerk's certificate of satisfaction of judgment, and statement filed pursuant to this section in the same manner as a termination statement filed pursuant to Section 9525 of the Commercial Code. **Leg.H.** Added Stats 1982 ch 1364 §2, operative July 1, 1983. Amended Stats 1983 ch 155 §12.1, effective June 30, 1983, operative July 1, 1983; Stats 1999 ch 991 §20 (SB 45), operative July 1, 2001.

§697.650. Release or subordination of judgment lien on personal property

(a) The judgment creditor may by a writing do any of the following:

(1) Release the judgment lien on all the personal property subject to the lien of a sole judgment debtor or of all the judgment debtors.

(2) If the notice of judgment lien names more than one judgment debtor, release the judgment lien on all the personal property subject to the lien of one or more but of less than all the judgment debtors.

(3) Release the judgment lien on all or a part of the personal property subject to the lien.

(4) Subordinate to a security interest or other lien or encumbrance the judgment lien on all or a part of the personal property subject to the judgment lien.

(b) A statement of release or subordination is sufficient if it is signed by the judgment creditor and contains the name and address of the judgment debtor, the file number of the notice of judgment lien, and wording appropriate to bring the statement within one of the paragraphs of subdivision (a). In the case of a release under paragraph (3) of subdivision (a), the statement of release shall also describe the property being released. In the case of a subordination under paragraph (4) of subdivision (a), the statement of subordination shall also describe the property on which the judgment lien is being subordinated and describe the security interest or other lien or encumbrance to which the judgment lien is being subordinated.

(c) The filing officer shall treat the filing of a statement of release pursuant to paragraph (1) of subdivision (a) of this section in the same manner as a termination statement filed pursuant to Sections 9513 and 9519 of the Commercial Code. The filing officer shall treat the filing of a statement of release pursuant to paragraph (2) of subdivision (a) of this section in the same manner as a comparable amendment filed pursuant to Sections 9512 and 9519 of the Commercial Code. The filing officer shall treat the filing of a statement of release pursuant to paragraph (3) of subdivision (a) of this section and the filing of a statement of subordination filed pursuant to paragraph (4) of subdivision (a) of this section in the same manner as a statement of release filed pursuant to Sections 9512 and 9519 of the Commercial Code.

(d) The fee for filing the statement is the same as that provided in Section 9525 of the Commercial Code. **Leg.H.** Added Stats 1982 ch 1364 §2, operative July 1, 1983. Amended Stats 1983 ch 155 §12.2, effective June 30, 1983, operative July 1, 1983; Stats 1989 ch 445 §3; Stats 1999 ch 991 §21 (SB 45), operative July 1, 2001.

§697.660. Release of erroneous judgment lien on personal property

(a) If a notice of judgment lien on personal property filed in the office of the Secretary of State appears to create a judgment lien on personal property of a person who is not the judgment debtor because the name of the property owner is the same as or similar to that of the judgment debtor, the erroneously identified property owner or a person having a security interest in or a lien on the property may deliver to the judgment creditor a written demand that the judgment creditor file in the office of the Secretary of State a statement releasing the lien as to the property of such owner. The demand shall be accompanied by proof to the satisfaction of the judgment creditor that the property owner is not the judgment debtor and that the property is not subject to enforcement of the judgment against the judgment debtor.

(b) Within 15 days after receipt of the demand and proof satisfactory to the judgment creditor that the property owner is not the judgment debtor and that the property is not subject to enforcement of the judgment, the judgment creditor shall file in the office of the Secretary of State a statement releasing the lien on the property of such owner. If the judgment creditor improperly fails to file the statement of release within the time allowed, the judgment creditor is liable to the person who made the demand for all damages sustained by reason of such failure and shall also forfeit one hundred dollars ($100) to such person.

(c) If the judgment creditor does not file a statement of release pursuant to subdivision (b), the person who made the demand may apply to the court on noticed motion for an order releasing the judgment lien on the property of such owner. Notice of motion shall be served on the judgment creditor. Service shall be made personally or by mail. Upon presentation of evidence to the satisfaction of the court that the property owner is not the judgment debtor and that the property is not subject to enforcement of the judgment, the court shall order the judgment creditor to prepare and file the statement of release or shall itself order the release of the judgment lien on the property of such owner. The court order may be filed in the office of the Secretary of State with the same effect as the statement of release demanded under subdivision (a).

(d) The court shall award reasonable attorney's fees to the prevailing party in any action or proceeding maintained pursuant to this section.

(e) The damages provided by this section are not in derogation of any other damages or penalties to which an aggrieved person may be entitled by law.

(f) The fee for filing a statement of release or court order under this section is the same as that provided in Section 9525 of the Commercial Code. **Leg.H.** Added Stats 1982 ch 1364 §2, operative July 1, 1983. Amended Stats 1999 ch 991 §21.5 (SB 45), operative July 1, 2001.

§697.670. Forms prescribed by Secretary of State

(a) The Secretary of State may prescribe, provided that a cost-savings would be achieved thereby:

(1) The forms for the notice of judgment lien on personal property and the statement of continuation, release, or subordination provided for in this article.

(2) The form for the statement provided for in Section 697.640 and the situations when that form is required or is not required.

(b) A form prescribed by the Secretary of State for a notice or statement pursuant to subdivision (a) is deemed to comply with this article and supersedes any requirements specified in this article for the notice or statement. **Leg.H.** Added Stats 1982 ch 1364 §2, operative July 1, 1983. Amended Stats 1983 ch 155 §12.3, effective June 30, 1983, operative July 1, 1983; Stats 2009 ch 410 §2 (AB 121), effective January 1, 2010.

ARTICLE 4
Execution Lien

Creation and duration of execution lien. §697.710.
Continuation of lien on real property after transfer or encumbrance. §697.720.

Effect on lien of transfer or encumbrance of property in custody of levying officer; Rights of purchaser of business property subject to lien. §697.730.
Effect on lien of transfer or encumbrance of property not in custody of levying officer. §697.740.
Effect on lien of transfer or encumbrance on growing crops, timber to be cut, or minerals to be extracted. §697.750.

§697.710. Creation and duration of execution lien
A levy on property under a writ of execution creates an execution lien on the property from the time of levy until the expiration of two years after the date of issuance of the writ unless the judgment is sooner satisfied. **Leg.H.** Added Stats 1982 ch 1364 §2, operative July 1, 1983.

§697.720. Continuation of lien on real property after transfer or encumbrance
Subject to Section 701.630, if an interest in real property subject to an execution lien is transferred or encumbered, the interest transferred or encumbered remains subject to the lien after the transfer or encumbrance. **Leg.H.** Added Stats 1982 ch 1364 §2, operative July 1, 1983.

§697.730. Effect on lien of transfer or encumbrance of property in custody of levying officer; Rights of purchaser of business property subject to lien
(a) Subject to Section 701.630 and except as provided in subdivision (b), if tangible personal property subject to an execution lien is in the custody of a levying officer and is transferred or encumbered, the property remains subject to the lien after the transfer or encumbrance.

(b) If a levy upon tangible personal property of a going business is made by the levying officer placing a keeper in charge of the business, a purchaser or lessee of property subject to the execution lien takes the property free of the execution lien if the purchaser or lessee is one of the following:

(1) A buyer in ordinary course of business (as defined in Section 1201 of the Commercial Code) who, under Section 9320 of the Commercial Code, would take free of a security interest created by his or her seller.

(2) A lessee in ordinary course of business (as defined in paragraph (15) of subdivision (a) of Section 10103 of the Commercial Code) who, under Section 9321 of the Commercial Code, would take free of a security interest created by the lessor. **Leg.H.** Added Stats 1982 ch 1364 §2, operative July 1, 1983. Amended Stats 1983 ch 155 §12.4, effective June 30, 1983, operative July 1, 1983; Stats 1988 ch 1368 §6, operative January 1, 1990; Stats 1994 ch 668 §6 (SB 1405); Stats 1999 ch 991 §22 (SB 45), operative July 1, 2001.

§697.740. Effect on lien of transfer or encumbrance of property not in custody of levying officer
Except as provided in Sections 9617 and 9622 of the Commercial Code and in Section 701.630, if personal property subject to an execution lien is not in the custody of a levying officer and the property is transferred or encumbered, the property remains subject to the lien after the transfer or encumbrance except where the transfer or encumbrance is made to one of the following persons:

(a) A person who acquires an interest in the property under the law of this state for reasonably equivalent value without knowledge of the lien. For purposes of this subdivision, value is given for a transfer or encumbrance if, in exchange for the transfer or encumbrance, property is transferred or an antecedent debt is secured or satisfied.

(b) A buyer in ordinary course of business (as defined in Section 1201 of the Commercial Code) who, under Section 9320 of the Commercial Code, would take free of a security interest created by the seller or encumbrancer.

(c) A lessee in ordinary course of business (as defined in paragraph (15) of subdivision (a) of Section 10103 of the Commercial Code) or a licensee in the ordinary course of business (as defined in subdivision (a) of Section 9321 of the Commercial Code) who, under Section 9321 of the Commercial Code, would take free of a security interest created by the lessor or the licensor.

(d) A holder in due course (as defined in Section 3302 of the Commercial Code) of a negotiable instrument within the meaning of Section 3104 of the Commercial Code.

(e) A holder to whom a negotiable document of title has been duly negotiated within the meaning of Section 7501 of the Commercial Code.

(f) A protected purchaser (as defined in Section 8303 of the Commercial Code) of a security or a person entitled to the benefits of Section 8502 or 8510 of the Commercial Code.

(g) A purchaser of chattel paper who gives new value and takes possession of the chattel paper in good faith and in the ordinary course of the purchaser's business or a purchaser of an instrument who gives value and takes possession of the instrument in good faith.

(h) A holder of a purchase money security interest (as defined in Section 9103 of the Commercial Code).

(i) A collecting bank holding a security interest in items being collected, accompanying documents and proceeds, pursuant to Section 4210 of the Commercial Code.

(j) A person who acquires any right or interest in letters of credit, advices of credit, or money.

(k) A person who acquires any right or interest in property subject to a certificate of title statute of another jurisdiction under the law of which indication of a security interest on the certificate of title is required as a condition of perfection of the security interest. **Leg.H.** Added Stats 1982 ch 1364 §2, operative July 1, 1983. Amended Stats 1987 ch 40 §4, effective June 8, 1987; Stats 1988 ch 1368 §7, operative January 1, 1990; Stats 1994 ch 668 §7 (SB 1405); Stats 1996 ch 497 §2 (SB 1591), operative January 1, 1997; Stats 1999 ch 991 §23 (SB 45), operative July 1, 2001.

§697.750. Effect on lien of transfer or encumbrance on growing crops, timber to be cut, or minerals to be extracted
Notwithstanding Section 697.740, except as provided in Section 9617 of the Commercial Code and in Section 701.630, if (1) growing crops, (2) timber to be cut, or (3) minerals or the like (including oil or gas) to be extracted or accounts receivable resulting from the sale thereof at wellhead or minehead are subject to an execution lien and are transferred or encumbered, the property remains subject to the execution lien after the transfer or encumbrance. **Leg.H.** Added Stats 1982 ch 1364 §2, operative July 1, 1983. Amended Stats 1999 ch 991 §23.1 (SB 45), operative July 1, 2001.

ARTICLE 5
Other Liens Created by Enforcement Process

Application of article. §697.910.
Effect of transfer or encumbrance of property subject to lien. §697.920.

§697.910. Application of article
This article applies to liens created by any of the following:

(a) An examination proceeding as provided in Section 708.110, 708.120, or 708.205.

(b) A creditor's suit as provided in Section 708.250.

(c) A charging order as provided in Section 708.320. **Leg.H.** Added Stats 1982 ch 1364 §2, operative July 1, 1983.

§697.920. Effect of transfer or encumbrance of property subject to lien
Except as provided in Section 9617 of the Commercial Code and in Section 701.630, a lien described in Section 697.910 continues on property subject to the lien, notwithstanding the transfer or encumbrance of the property subject to the lien, unless the transfer or encumbrance is made to a person listed in Section 697.740. **Leg.H.** Added Stats 1982 ch 1364 §2, operative July 1, 1983. Amended Stats 1999 ch 991 §23.2 (SB 45), operative July 1, 2001.

§698. [Section repealed 1983]
Leg.H. Enacted Stats 1872. Repealed Stats 1982 ch 1364 §1, operative July 1, 1983. See CCP §§701.640, 701.650.

§699. [Section repealed 1983]
Leg.H. Enacted Stats 1872. Repealed Stats 1982 ch 1364 §1, operative July 1, 1983. See CCP §§701.640, 701.650.

CHAPTER 3
EXECUTION

Article 1. General Provisions.
Article 2. Writ of Execution and Notice of Levy.
Article 3. Property Subject to Execution.
Article 4. Methods of Levy.
Article 5. Duties and Liabilities of Third Persons After Levy.
Article 6. Sale and Collection.
Article 7. Distribution of Proceeds of Sale or Collection.

ARTICLE 1
General Provisions

Application of chapter. §699.010.

Payment by debtor of judgment debtor. §699.020.
Levy on property in private place. §699.030.
Turnover order in aid of execution. §699.040.
Release of property from lien and custody. §699.060.
Appointment of receiver, sale, or other action to preserve value of property. §699.070.
Levy by registered process server. §699.080.
Liability for levy based on record ownership. §699.090.

§699.010. Application of chapter
Except as otherwise provided by statute, this chapter governs enforcement of a money judgment by a writ of execution. **Leg.H.** Added Stats 1982 ch 1364 §2, operative July 1, 1983.

§699.020. Payment by debtor of judgment debtor
At any time after delivery of a writ of execution to a levying officer and before its return, a person indebted to the judgment debtor may pay to the levying officer the amount of the debt or so much thereof as is necessary to satisfy the money judgment. The levying officer shall give a receipt for the amount paid and such receipt is a discharge for the amount paid. **Leg.H.** Added Stats 1982 ch 1364 §2, operative July 1, 1983.

§699.030. Levy on property in private place
If personal property sought to be levied upon is located in a private place of the judgment debtor:

(a) The levying officer making the levy shall demand delivery of the property by the judgment debtor and shall advise the judgment debtor that the judgment debtor may be liable for costs and attorney's fees incurred in any further proceedings to obtain delivery of the property. If the judgment debtor does not deliver the property, the levying officer shall make no further effort to obtain custody of the property and shall promptly notify the judgment creditor of the failure to obtain custody of the property.

(b) The judgment creditor may apply to the court ex parte, or on noticed motion if the court so directs or a court rule so requires, for an order directing the levying officer to seize the property in the private place. The application may be made whether or not a writ has been issued and whether or not demand has been made pursuant to subdivision (a). The application for the order shall describe with particularity both the property sought to be levied upon, and the place where it is to be found, according to the best knowledge, information, and belief of the judgment creditor. The court may not issue the order unless the judgment creditor establishes that there is probable cause to believe that property sought to be levied upon is located in the place described. The levying officer making the levy, at the time delivery of the property pursuant to the order is demanded, shall announce his or her identity, purpose, and authority. If the property is not voluntarily delivered, the levying officer may cause the building or enclosure where the property is believed to be located to be broken open in such manner as the levying officer reasonably believes will cause the least damage, but if the levying officer reasonably believes that entry and seizure of the property will involve a substantial risk of death or serious bodily harm to any person, the levying officer shall refrain from entering and shall promptly make a return to the court setting forth the reasons for believing that the risk exists. In such a case, the court shall make such orders as may be appropriate. **Leg.H.** Added Stats 1982 ch 1364 §2, operative July 1, 1983.

§699.040. Turnover order in aid of execution
(a) If a writ of execution is issued, the judgment creditor may apply to the court ex parte, or on noticed motion if the court so directs or a court rule so requires, for an order directing the judgment debtor to transfer to the levying officer either or both of the following:

(1) Possession of the property sought to be levied upon if the property is sought to be levied upon by taking it into custody.

(2) Possession of documentary evidence of title to property of or a debt owed to the judgment debtor that is sought to be levied upon. An order pursuant to this paragraph may be served when the property or debt is levied upon or thereafter.

(b) The court may issue an order pursuant to this section upon a showing of need for the order.

(c) The order shall be personally served on the judgment debtor and shall contain a notice to the judgment debtor that failure to comply with the order may subject the judgment debtor to arrest and punishment for contempt of court. **Leg.H.** Added Stats 1982 ch 1364 §2, operative July 1, 1983.

§699.060. Release of property from lien and custody
(a) The levying officer shall release property levied upon when the levying officer receives a written direction to release the property from the judgment creditor's attorney of record or, if the judgment creditor does not have an attorney of record, from the judgment creditor, or when the levying officer receives a certified copy of a court order for release, or when otherwise required to release the property. The release shall include the signature and name of the attorney or judgment creditor issuing the release. The release extinguishes any execution lien or attachment lien in favor of the judgment creditor on the property released.

(b) If the property to be released has been taken into custody under the levy, it shall be released to the person from whom it was taken unless otherwise ordered by the court. If the person does not claim the property to be released, the levying officer shall retain custody of the property and shall serve on the person a notice of where possession of the property may be obtained. Service shall be made personally or by mail. If the person does not claim the property within 30 days after the notice is served, the levying officer shall sell the property in the manner provided by Article 6 (commencing with Section 701.510), other than cash, which does not have a value exceeding its face value. The levying officer shall deposit the proceeds of sale and cash, after first deducting the levying officer's costs, with the county treasurer of the county where the property is located, payable to the order of the person. If the amount deposited is not claimed by the person, or the legal representative of the person, within five years after the deposit is made by making application to the treasurer or other official designated by the county, it shall be paid into the general fund of the county.

(c) If the property to be released has not been taken into custody under the levy, the levying officer shall release the property by issuing a written notice of release and serving it on the person who was served with a copy of the writ and a notice of levy to create the lien. Service shall be made personally or by mail.

(d) If the property to be released was levied upon by recording or filing a copy of the writ and a notice of levy, the levying officer shall record or file a written notice of release in the same office.

(e) The levying officer is not liable for releasing property in accordance with this section nor is any other person liable for acting in conformity with the release.

(f) The written direction to release property specified in subdivision (a) may be transmitted electronically to the levying officer pursuant to Chapter 2 (commencing with Section 263) of Title 4 of Part 1. **Leg.H.** Added Stats 1982 ch 1364 §2, operative July 1, 1983. Amended Stats 2010 ch 680 §6 (AB 2394), effective January 1, 2011.

§699.070. Appointment of receiver, sale, or other action to preserve value of property
(a) The court may appoint a receiver or order the levying officer to take any action the court orders that is necessary to preserve the value of property levied upon, including but not limited to selling the property, if the court determines that the property is perishable or will greatly deteriorate or greatly depreciate in value or that for some other reason the interests of the parties will be best served by the order. An order may be made under this subdivision upon application of the judgment creditor, the judgment debtor, or a person who has filed a third-party claim pursuant to Division 4 (commencing with Section 720.010). The application shall be made on noticed motion if the court so directs or a court rule so requires. Otherwise, the application may be made ex parte.

(b) If the levying officer determines that property levied upon is extremely perishable or will greatly deteriorate or greatly depreciate in value before a court order pursuant to subdivision (a) could be obtained, the levying officer may take any action necessary to preserve the value of the property or may sell the property. The levying officer is not liable for a determination made in good faith under this subdivision.

(c) Except as otherwise provided by order of the court, a sale of property pursuant to this section shall be made in the manner provided by Article 6 (commencing with Section 701.510) and the proceeds shall be applied to the satisfaction of the money judgment in the manner provided by Article 7 (commencing with Section 701.810). Notwithstanding subdivisions (b) and (d) of Section 701.530, notice of sale shall be posted and served at a reasonable time before the sale, considering the character and condition of the property.

(d) If a receiver is appointed, the court shall fix the daily fee of the receiver and may order the judgment creditor to pay the fees and expenses of the receiver in advance or may direct that the whole or any part of the fees and expenses be paid from the proceeds of any sale of the property. Except as otherwise provided in this section, the provisions of Chapter 5 (commencing with Section 564) and Chapter 5a (commencing with Section 571) of Title 7 govern the appointment, qualifications, powers, rights, and duties of a receiver appointed under this section. **Leg.H.** Added Stats 1982 ch 1364 §2, operative July 1, 1983.

§699.080. Levy by registered process server

(a) A registered process server may levy under a writ of execution on the following types of property:

(1) Real property, pursuant to Section 700.015.

(2) Growing crops, timber to be cut, or minerals or the like including oil and gas, to be extracted or accounts receivable resulting from the sale thereof at the wellhead or minehead, pursuant to Section 700.020.

(3) Personal property in the custody of a levying officer, pursuant to Section 700.050.

(4) Personal property used as a dwelling, pursuant to subdivision (a) of Section 700.080.

(5) Deposit accounts, pursuant to Section 700.140.

(6) Property in a safe-deposit box, pursuant to Section 700.150.

(7) Accounts receivable or general intangibles, pursuant to Section 700.170.

(8) Final money judgments, pursuant to Section 700.190.

(9) Interest of a judgment debtor in personal property in the estate of a decedent, pursuant to Section 700.200.

(b) Before levying under the writ of execution, the registered process server shall cause to be deposited with the levying officer a copy of the writ and the fee, as provided by Section 26721 of the Government Code.

(c) If a registered process server levies on property pursuant to subdivision (a), the registered process server shall do both of the following:

(1) Comply with the applicable levy, posting, and service provisions of Article 4 (commencing with Section 700.010).

(2) Request any third person served to give a garnishee's memorandum to the levying officer in compliance with Section 701.030 on a form provided by the registered process server.

(d) Within five court days after levy under this section, all of the following shall be filed with the levying officer:

(1) The writ of execution.

(2) A proof of service by the registered process server stating the manner of levy performed.

(3) Proof of service of the copy of the writ and notice of levy on other persons, as required by Article 4 (commencing with Section 700.010).

(4) Instructions in writing, as required by the provisions of Section 687.010.

(e) If the fee provided by Section 26721 of the Government Code has been paid, the levying officer shall perform all other duties under the writ as if the levying officer had levied under the writ and shall return the writ to the court. If the registered process server does not comply with subdivisions (b) and (d), the levy is ineffective and the levying officer shall not be required to perform any duties under the writ, and may issue a release for any property sought to be levied upon.

(f) The fee for services of a registered process server under this section is a recoverable cost pursuant to Section 1033.5.

(g) A registered process server may levy more than once under the same writ of execution, provided that the writ is still valid. **Leg.H.** Added Stats 1982 ch 1364 §2.1, operative July 1, 1983. Amended Stats 1983 ch 155 §13, effective June 30, 1983, operative July 1, 1983; Stats 1984 ch 538 §20, ch 759 §4.5; Stats 1987 ch 1080 §5; Stats 2002 ch 197 §3 (AB 2493); Stats 2007 ch 15 §3 (AB 859), effective January 1, 2008; Stats 2016 ch 102 §2 (AB 2211), effective January 1, 2017.

§699.090. Liability for levy based on record ownership

If property that is required by law to be registered or recorded in the name of the owner is levied upon under a writ of execution and it appears at the time of the levy that the judgment debtor was the registered or record owner of the property and the judgment creditor caused the levy to be made and the lien maintained in good faith and in reliance upon such registered or recorded ownership, neither the judgment creditor, the levying officer, nor the sureties on an undertaking given by the judgment creditor pursuant to Chapter 2 (commencing with Section 720.110) or Chapter 3 (commencing with Section 720.210) of Division 4 is liable to a third person for the levy itself. **Leg.H.** Added Stats 1982 ch 1364 §2, operative July 1, 1983.

ARTICLE 2
Writ of Execution and Notice of Levy

Issuance of writ of execution; Priority to support orders. §699.510.
Contents of writ of execution. §699.520.
Delivery and execution of writ; Limitation on time for levy. §699.530.
Contents of notice of levy. §699.540.
Service of copy of original notice of levy on judgment debtor or other party. §699.545.
Effect of failure to give notice of levy or to serve list of exemptions. §699.550.
Retention or storage of writ of execution. §699.560.

§699.510. Issuance of writ of execution; Priority to support orders

(a) Subject to subdivision (b), after entry of a money judgment, a writ of execution shall be issued by the clerk of the court, upon application of the judgment creditor, and shall be directed to the levying officer in the county where the levy is to be made and to any registered process server. The clerk of the court shall give priority to the application for, and issuance of, writs of execution on orders or judgments for child support and spousal support. A separate writ shall be issued for each county where a levy is to be made. Writs may be issued successively until the money judgment is satisfied, except that a new writ may not be issued for a county until the expiration of 180 days after the issuance of a prior writ for that county unless the prior writ is first returned.

(b) If the judgment creditor seeks a writ of execution to enforce a judgment made, entered, or enforceable pursuant to the Family Code, in addition to the requirements of this article, the judgment creditor shall satisfy the requirements of any applicable provisions of the Family Code.

(c)(1) The writ of execution shall be issued in the name of the judgment debtor as listed on the judgment, except that the judgment creditor shall omit the name of a judgment debtor from the application for a writ of execution if the liability of that judgment debtor has ceased with regard to the judgment, including either of the following occurrences:

(A) The judgment debtor has obtained a discharge of the judgment pursuant to Title 11 of the United States Code and notice thereof has been filed with the court.

(B) The judgment creditor files an acknowledgment of satisfaction of judgment with regard to the judgment debtor pursuant to Chapter 1 (commencing with Section 724.010) of Division 5.

(2) The writ of execution shall include the additional name or names, and the type of legal entity, by which the judgment debtor is known, as set forth in the affidavit of identity, as defined in Section 680.135, filed by the judgment creditor with the application for issuance of the writ of execution. Prior to the clerk of the court issuing a writ of execution containing any additional name or names by which the judgment debtor is known that are not listed on the judgment, the court shall approve the affidavit of identity. If the court determines, without a hearing or a notice, that the affidavit of identity states sufficient facts upon which the judgment creditor has identified the additional names of the judgment debtor, the court shall authorize the issuance of the writ of execution with the additional name or names.

(d) In any case where the writ of execution lists any name other than that listed on the judgment, the person in possession or control of the levied property, if other than the judgment debtor, shall not pay to the levying officer the amount or deliver the property being levied upon until being notified to do so by the levying officer. The levying officer may not require the person, if other than the judgment debtor, in possession or control of the levied property to pay the amount or deliver the property levied upon until the expiration of 15 days after service of notice of levy.

(e) If a person who is not the judgment debtor has property erroneously subject to an enforcement of judgment proceeding based upon an affidavit of identity, the person shall be entitled to the recovery of reasonable attorney's fees and costs from the judgment creditor incurred in releasing the person's property from a writ of execution, in addition to any other damages or penalties to which an aggrieved person may be entitled to by law, including Division 4 (commencing with Section 720.010). **Leg.H.** Added Stats 1982 ch 1364 §2, operative July 1, 1983. Amended Stats 1992 ch 163 §35 (AB 2641), operative January 1, 1994; Stats 2000 ch 639 §3 (AB 2405), ch 808 §12.1 (AB 1358), effective September 28, 2000; Stats 2001 ch 159 §40 (SB 662); Stats 2003 ch 17 §1 (AB 308); Stats 2010 ch 680 §7 (AB 2394), effective January 1, 2011; Stats 2013 ch 176 §2 (SB 551), effective January 1, 2014.

§699.520. Contents of writ of execution

The writ of execution shall require the levying officer to whom it is directed to enforce the money judgment and shall include the following information:

(a) The date of issuance of the writ.

(b) The title of the court in which the judgment is entered and the cause and number of the action.

(c) Whether the judgment is for wages owed, child support, or spousal support. This subdivision shall become operative on September 1, 2020.

(d) The name and address of the judgment creditor and the name and last known address of the judgment debtor. If the judgment debtor is other than a natural person, the type of legal entity shall be stated.

(e) The date of the entry of the judgment and of any subsequent renewals and where entered in the records of the court.

(f) The total amount of the money judgment as entered or renewed, together with costs thereafter added to the judgment pursuant to Section 685.090 and the accrued interest on the judgment from the date of entry or renewal of the judgment to the date of issuance of the writ, reduced by any partial satisfactions and by any amounts no longer enforceable.

(g) The amount required to satisfy the money judgment on the date the writ is issued.

(h) The amount of interest accruing daily on the principal amount of the judgment from the date the writ is issued.

(i) Whether any person has requested notice of sale under the judgment and, if so, the name and mailing address of that person.

(j) The sum of the fees and costs added to the judgment pursuant to Section 6103.5 or Article 6 (commencing with Section 68630) of Chapter 2 of Title 8 of the Government Code, and which is in addition to the amount owing to the judgment creditor on the judgment.

(k) Whether the writ of execution includes any additional names of the judgment debtor pursuant to an affidavit of identity, as defined in Section 680.135.

(l) A statement indicating whether the case is limited or unlimited. **Leg.H.** Added Stats 1982 ch 1364 §2, operative July 1, 1983. Amended Stats 1993 ch 909 §2 (SB 15); Stats 2000 ch 639 §4 (AB 2405); Stats 2010 ch 680 §8 (AB 2394), effective January 1, 2011; Stats 2019 ch 552 §1 (SB 616), effective January 1, 2020; Stats 2020 ch 370 §36 (SB 1371), effective January 1, 2021.

§699.530. Delivery and execution of writ; Limitation on time for levy

(a) Upon delivery of the writ of execution to the levying officer to whom the writ is directed, together with the written instructions of the judgment creditor, the levying officer shall execute the writ in the manner prescribed by law.

(b) The levying officer may not levy upon any property under the writ after the expiration of 180 days from the date the writ was issued. **Leg.H.** Added Stats 1982 ch 1364 §2, operative July 1, 1983.

§699.540. Contents of notice of levy

The notice of levy required by Article 4 (commencing with Section 700.010) shall inform the person notified of all of the following:

(a) The capacity in which the person is notified.

(b) The property that is levied upon.

(c) The person's rights under the levy, including all of the following:

(1) The right to claim an exemption pursuant to Chapter 4 (commencing with Section 703.010).

(2) The right to make a third-party claim pursuant to Division 4 (commencing with Section 720.010).

(3) The right to, and the limitations of, the automatic exemption pursuant to Section 704.220. This paragraph shall become operative on September 1, 2020.

(d) The person's duties under the levy.

(e) All names listed in the writ of execution pursuant to an affidavit of identity, as defined in Section 680.135, if any. **Leg.H.** Added Stats 1982 ch 1364 §2, operative July 1, 1983. Amended Stats 2000 ch 639 §5 (AB 2405); Stats 2019 ch 552 §2 (SB 616), effective January 1, 2020.

§699.545. Service of copy of original notice of levy on judgment debtor or other party

A copy of the original notice of levy which has been served upon a third party holding the property sought to be levied upon and the affidavit of identity, as defined in Section 680.135, if any, if served upon the judgment debtor or any other party, shall suffice as the notice of levy to that person. **Leg.H.** Added Stats 1984 ch 759 §5. Amended Stats 2000 ch 639 §6 (AB 2405).

§699.550. Effect of failure to give notice of levy or to serve list of exemptions

In any case where property has been levied upon and, pursuant to a levy, a copy of the writ of execution and a notice of levy are required by statute to be posted or to be served on or mailed to the judgment debtor or other person, failure to post, serve, or mail the copy of the writ and the notice does not affect the execution lien created by the levy. Failure to serve on or mail to the judgment debtor a list of exemptions does not affect the execution lien created by the levy. **Leg.H.** Added Stats 1982 ch 1364 §2, operative July 1, 1983.

§699.560. Retention or storage of writ of execution

(a) Except as provided in subdivisions (b) and (c), the writ expires and the levying officer to whom the writ of execution is delivered shall return the writ to the court, or store the writ as provided in Section 263.6, and file a return with the court reporting the levying officer's actions and an accounting of amounts collected, and costs incurred, at the earliest of the following times:

(1) Two years from the date of issuance of the writ, unless paragraph (1) of subdivision (a) of Section 706.022 is applicable.

(2) Promptly after all of the duties under the writ are performed.

(3) When return is requested in writing by the judgment creditor.

(4) If no levy takes place under the writ within 180 days after its issuance, promptly after the expiration of the 180-day period.

(5) Upon expiration of the time for enforcement of the money judgment.

(b) If a levy has been made under Section 700.200 upon an interest in personal property in the estate of a decedent, the writ shall be returned within the time prescribed in Section 700.200.

(c) If a levy has been made under Section 5103 of the Family Code on the judgment debtor's right to the payment of benefits from an employee pension benefit plan, the writ shall be returned within the time prescribed in that section.

(d) If a levy has been made under the Wage Garnishment Law (Chapter 5 (commencing with Section 706.010)), and the earnings withholding order remains in effect, the writ of execution shall be returned as provided in subdivision (a) and a supplemental return shall be made as provided in Section 706.033.

(e) Subject to the limitations in subdivision (c) of Section 263, a levying officer may electronically file with the court the return, containing the information required by subdivision (a), pursuant to Chapter 2 (commencing with Section 263) of Title 4 of Part 1. **Leg.H.** Added Stats 1982 ch 1364 §2, operative July 1, 1983. Amended Stats 1985 ch 362 §5; Stats 1992 ch 163 §36 (AB 2641), operative January 1, 1994, ch 283 §4 (SB 1372), effective July 21, 1992 (ch 283 prevails); Stats 1993 ch 219 §67 (AB 1500); Stats 2010 ch 680 §9 (AB 2394), effective January 1, 2011.

1992 Note: Section 699.560, as amended by ch 283, applies to all writs of execution and earnings withholding orders regardless of whether they were issued before July 21, 1992. Stats 1992 ch 283 §17.

ARTICLE 3
Property Subject to Execution

Property subject to execution. §699.710.
Property not subject to execution. §699.720.
Principal place of residence. § 699.730.

§699.710. Property subject to execution

Except as otherwise provided by law, all property that is subject to enforcement of a money judgment pursuant to Article 1 (commencing with Section 695.010) of Chapter 1 is subject to levy under a writ of execution to satisfy a money judgment. **Leg.H.** Added Stats 1982 ch 1364 §2, operative July 1, 1983.

§699.720. Property not subject to execution

(a) The following types of property are not subject to execution:

(1) An alcoholic beverage license that is transferable under Article 5 (commencing with Section 24070) of Chapter 6 of Division 9 of the Business and Professions Code.

(2) The interest of a partner in a partnership or member in a limited liability company if the partnership or the limited liability company is not a judgment debtor.

(3) A cause of action that is the subject of a pending action or special proceeding.

(4) A judgment in favor of the judgment debtor prior to the expiration of the time for appeal from the judgment or, if an appeal is filed, prior to the final determination of the appeal.

(5) A debt (other than earnings) owing and unpaid by a public entity.

(6) The loan value of an unmatured life insurance, endowment, or annuity policy.

(7) A franchise granted by a public entity and all the rights and privileges of the franchise.

(8) The interest of a trust beneficiary.

(9) A contingent remainder, executory interest, or other interest in property that is not vested.

(10) Property in a guardianship or conservatorship estate.

(b) Nothing in subdivision (a) affects or limits the right of the judgment creditor to apply property to the satisfaction of a money judgment pursuant to any applicable procedure other than execution. **Leg.H.** Added Stats 1982 ch 1364 §2, operative July 1, 1983. Amended Stats 1996 ch 57 §1 (SB 141), effective June 6, 1996.

§ 699.730. Principal place of residence

(a) Notwithstanding any other law, the principal place of residence of a judgment debtor is not subject to sale under execution of a judgment lien based on a consumer debt unless the debt was secured by the debtor's principal place of residence at the time it was incurred. As used in this subdivision, "consumer debt" means debt incurred by an individual primarily for personal, family, or household purposes.

(b) Subdivision (a) does not apply to any of the following types of unpaid debts:

(1) Wages or employment benefits.

(2) Taxes.

(3) Child support.

(4) Spousal support.

(5) Fines and fees owed to governmental units.

(6) Tort judgments.

(7)(A) Debts, other than student loan debt, owed to a financial institution at the time of execution on the judgment lien, if both of the following requirements are met:

(i) The amount of the original judgment on which the lien is based, when entered, was greater than seventy-five thousand dollars ($75,000), as adjusted pursuant to Section 703.150.

(ii) The amount owed on the outstanding judgment at the time of execution on the judgment lien is greater than seventy-five thousand dollars ($75,000), as adjusted pursuant to Section 703.150.

(B) As used in this paragraph, the following terms have the following meanings:

(i) "Financial institution" means a financial institution, as defined in Section 680.200.

(ii) "Student loan debt" means debt based on any loan made to finance postsecondary education expenses, including tuition, fees, books, supplies, room and board, transportation, and personal expenses. Student loan debt includes debt based on a loan made to refinance a student loan, but does not include debt secured by the debtor's principal place of residence at the time it was incurred. **Leg.H.** Added Stats 2020 ch 218 §1 (AB 2463), effective January 1, 2021.

§700. [Section repealed 1983]

Leg.H. Enacted Stats 1872. Amended Stats 1907 ch 361 §1. Repealed Stats 1982 ch 1364 §1, operative July 1, 1983. See CCP §701.640.

§700a. [Section repealed 1983]

Leg.H. Added Stats 1907 ch 361 §2. Amended Stats 1971 ch 1312 §2. Repealed Stats 1982 ch 1364 §1, operative July 1, 1983. See CCP §§701.660 et seq., 726, 729.010, 729.040, 729.050.

ARTICLE 4
Methods of Levy

Service of writ, notice of levy, list of exemptions and affidavit of identity on judgment debtor. §700.010.
Real property. §700.015.
Growing crops, timber to be cut, minerals to be extracted. §700.020.
Tangible personal property in possession of judgment debtor. §700.030.
Tangible personal property in possession of third person. §700.040.
Personal property in custody of levying officer. §700.050.
Bailed goods not covered by negotiable document of title. §700.060.
Tangible personal property of going business. §700.070.
Personal property used as dwelling. §700.080.
Vehicle, vessel, manufactured home, mobilehome, or commercial coach for which certificate of ownership is issued. §700.090.
Chattel paper. §700.100.
Instruments. §700.110.
Negotiable documents of title. §700.120.
Securities. §700.130.
Deposit accounts. §700.140.
Safe deposit boxes; Service; Notice, fee and costs; Removal; Liability. §700.150.
Deposit accounts and safe deposit boxes not exclusively in name of judgment debtor. §700.160.
Accounts receivable and general intangibles. §700.170.
Levy on property that is subject of pending action or proceeding. §700.180.
Final money judgment. §700.190.
Interest in personal property of estate of decedent. §700.200.

§700.010. Service of writ, notice of levy, list of exemptions and affidavit of identity on judgment debtor

(a) At the time of levy pursuant to this article or promptly thereafter, the levying officer shall serve a copy of the following on the judgment debtor:

(1) The writ of execution.

(2) A notice of levy.

(3) If the judgment debtor is a natural person, a copy of the form listing exemptions prepared by the Judicial Council pursuant to subdivision (c) of Section 681.030, the list of exemption amounts published pursuant to subdivision (e) of Section 703.150, a copy of the form that the judgment debtor may use to make a claim of exemption pursuant to Section 703.520, and a copy of the form the judgment debtor may use to provide a financial statement pursuant to Section 703.530.

(4) Any affidavit of identity, as defined in Section 680.135, for names of the debtor listed on the writ of execution.

(b) Service under this section shall be made personally or by mail. **Leg.H.** Added Stats 1982 ch 1364 §2, operative July 1, 1983. Amended Stats 2000 ch 639 §7 (AB 2405); Stats 2003 ch 379 §2 (AB 182); Stats 2013 ch 64 §4 (SB 233), effective January 1, 2014.

§700.015. Real property

(a) To levy upon real property, the levying officer shall record with the recorder of the county where the real property is located a copy of the writ of execution and a notice of levy that describes the property levied upon and states that the judgment debtor's interest in the described property has been levied upon. If the judgment debtor's interest in the real property stands upon the records of the county in the name of a person other than the judgment debtor, the notice of levy shall identify the third person and the recorder shall index the copy of the writ and notice of levy in the names of both the judgment debtor and the third person.

(b) At the time of levy or promptly thereafter, the levying officer shall serve a copy of the writ and a notice of levy on any third person in whose name the judgment debtor's interest in the real property stands upon the records of the county. Service shall be made personally or by mail. If service on the third person is by mail, it shall be sent to the person at the address for such person, if any, shown by the records of the office of the tax assessor of the county where the real property is located or, if no address is so shown, to the person at the address used by the county recorder for the return of the instrument creating the interest of the third person in the property.

(c) At the time of levy or promptly thereafter, the levying officer shall serve a copy of the writ and a notice of levy on one occupant of the real property. Service on the occupant shall be made by leaving the copy of the writ and a notice of levy with the occupant personally or, in the occupant's absence, with a person of suitable age and discretion found upon the real property when service is attempted who is either an employee or agent of the occupant or a member of the occupant's household. If unable to serve such an occupant at the time service is attempted, the levying officer shall post the copy of the writ and the notice of levy in a conspicuous place on the real property. If the real property described in the notice of levy consists of more than one distinct lot, parcel, or governmental subdivision and any of the lots, parcels, or governmental subdivisions lies with relation to any of the others so as to form one or more continuous, unbroken tracts, only one service or posting need be made under this subdivision as to each continuous, unbroken tract. **Leg.H.** Added Stats 1982 ch 1364 §2, operative July 1, 1983.

§700.020. Growing crops, timber to be cut, minerals to be extracted

(a) To levy upon (1) growing crops, (2) timber to be cut, or (3) minerals or the like (including oil and gas) to be extracted or accounts receivable resulting from the sale thereof at the wellhead or minehead, the levying officer shall record with the recorder of the county where those crops, timber, or minerals or the like are located a copy of the writ of execution and a notice of levy that describes the property levied upon and states that the judgment debtor's interest in the described property has been levied upon and describes the real property where the crops, timber, or minerals or the like are located. If the judgment debtor's interest in the crops, timber, minerals or the like, or if the real property where the crops, timber, or minerals or the like are located, stands upon the records of the county in the name of a person other than the judgment debtor, the notice of levy shall identify the third person and the recorder shall index the copy of the writ and notice of levy in the names of both the judgment debtor and the third person.

(b) At the time of levy or promptly thereafter, the levying officer shall serve a copy of the writ and a notice of levy personally or by mail on the following persons:

(1) Any third person in whose name the judgment debtor's interest in the crops, timber, minerals or the like stands upon the records of the county and any third person in whose name the real property stands upon the records of the county. If service on the third person is by mail, it shall be sent to the person at the address for the person, if any, shown by the records of the office of the assessor of the county where the real property is located or, if no address is so shown, to the person at the address used by the county recorder for the return of the instrument creating the interest of the third person in the property.

(2) Any secured party who has filed a financing statement with respect to the crops, timber, or minerals or the like or the accounts receivable, prior to the date of levy on the property.

(c) At the time of levy or promptly thereafter, the levying officer shall serve a copy of the writ and a notice of levy on one occupant of the real property where the crops, timber, or minerals or the like are located. Service on the occupant shall be made by leaving the copy of the writ and a notice of levy with the occupant personally or, in the occupant's absence, with a person of suitable age and discretion found upon the real property when service is attempted who is either an employee or agent of the occupant or a member of the occupant's household. If he or she is unable to serve an occupant or suitable person at the time service is attempted, the levying officer shall post the copy of the writ and the notice of levy in a conspicuous place on the real property. However, the posting requirement of the preceding sentence shall not apply where the levy is made upon minerals or the like (but not including oil or gas) and no dwelling is located on the real property. If the real property described in the notice of levy consists of more than one distinct lot, parcel, or governmental subdivision and any of the lots, parcels, or governmental subdivisions lies with relation to any of the others so as to form one or more continuous, unbroken tracts, only one service or posting need be made under this subdivision as to each continuous, unbroken tract. **Leg.H.** Added Stats 1982 ch 1364 §2, operative July 1, 1983. Amended Stats 1993 ch 1187 §1.5 (SB 70).

§700.030. Tangible personal property in possession of judgment debtor

Unless another method of levy is provided by this article, to levy upon tangible personal property in the possession or under the control of the judgment debtor, the levying officer shall take the property into custody. **Leg.H.** Added Stats 1982 ch 1364 §2, operative July 1, 1983.

§700.040. Tangible personal property in possession of third person

(a) Unless another method of levy is provided by this article, to levy upon tangible personal property in the possession or under the control of a third person, the levying officer shall personally serve a copy of the writ of execution and a notice of levy on the third person.

(b) If goods are in the possession of a bailee who has issued a negotiable document of title therefor, the goods may not be levied upon but the negotiable document of title may be levied upon in the manner provided by Section 700.120. If goods are in the possession of a bailee other than one who has issued a negotiable document of title therefor, the goods may be levied upon in the manner provided by Section 700.060. As used in this subdivision, "bailee" means "bailee" as defined in Section 7102 of the Commercial Code. **Leg.H.** Added Stats 1982 ch 1364 §2, operative July 1, 1983.

§700.050. Personal property in custody of levying officer

(a) To levy upon personal property in the custody of a levying officer:

(1) If the writ of execution is directed to the levying officer having custody of the property, the judgment creditor shall deliver the writ to the levying officer.

(2) If the writ of execution is directed to a levying officer other than the levying officer having custody of the property, the levying officer to whom the writ is directed shall serve a copy of the writ and a notice of levy on the levying officer having custody. Service shall be made personally or by mail.

(b) The levying officer having custody of the property shall comply with the writs in the order they are received and is not subject to the provisions of Article 5 (commencing with Section 701.010) (duties and liabilities of third persons after levy). **Leg.H.** Added Stats 1982 ch 1364 §2, operative July 1, 1983.

§700.060. Bailed goods not covered by negotiable document of title

(a) To levy upon goods in the possession of a bailee (as defined in Section 7102 of the Commercial Code) other than one who has issued a negotiable document of title therefor, the levying officer shall personally serve a copy of the writ of execution and a notice of levy on the bailee.

(b) If the goods described in subdivision (a) are subject to a security interest, the levying officer shall, if so instructed by the judgment creditor, serve a copy of the writ of execution and a notice of levy on the secured party. Service shall be made personally or by mail. **Leg.H.** Added Stats 1982 ch 1364 §2, operative July 1, 1983.

§700.070. Tangible personal property of going business

To levy upon tangible personal property of a going business in the possession or under the control of the judgment debtor, the levying officer shall comply with Section 700.030, except to the extent that the judgment creditor instructs that levy be made in the following manner:

(a) The levying officer shall place a keeper in charge of the business for the period requested by the judgment creditor. During the period, the business may continue to operate in the ordinary course of business provided that all sales are final and are for cash or its equivalent. For the purpose of this subdivision, a check is the equivalent of cash. The levying officer is not liable for accepting payment in the form of a cash equivalent. The keeper shall take custody of the proceeds from all sales unless otherwise directed by the judgment creditor.

(b) The levying officer shall take the tangible personal property into exclusive custody at the earliest of the following times:

(1) At any time the judgment debtor objects to placement of a keeper in charge of the business.

(2) At any time when requested by the judgment creditor.

(3) At the end of 10 days from the time the keeper is placed in charge of the business.

(c) Where a keeper is placed in a business for the purpose of taking into custody tangible personal property consisting solely of money or equivalent proceeds of sales, the provisions of subdivision (b) shall not apply, and the levying officer shall take such property into exclusive custody at the end of each daily keeper period. **Leg.H.** Added Stats 1982 ch 1364 §2, operative July 1, 1983. Amended Stats 1996 ch 1159 §11 (AD 34/1).

§700.080. Personal property used as dwelling

(a) To levy upon personal property used as a dwelling, the levying officer shall serve a copy of the writ of execution and a notice of levy on one occupant of the property. Service on the occupant shall be made by leaving the copy of the writ and the notice of levy with the occupant personally or, in the occupant's absence, with a person of suitable age and discretion found at the property when service is attempted who is a member of the occupant's family or household. If unable to serve the occupant at the time service is attempted, the levying officer shall make the levy by posting the copy of the writ and the notice of levy in a conspicuous place on the property.

(b) If the judgment creditor so instructs, the levying officer shall place a keeper in charge of the property for a period requested by the judgment creditor.

(c) The judgment creditor may apply to the court on noticed motion for an order directing the levying officer to remove the occupants. The notice of motion shall be served on any legal owner and any junior lienholder who was served pursuant to Section 700.090, on the occupant, and, if the judgment debtor is not the occupant, on the judgment debtor. Service shall be made personally or by mail. At the hearing on the motion the court shall determine the occupant's right to possession and shall make an order including terms and conditions that are appropriate under the circumstances of the case.

(d) Personal property used as a dwelling shall include a mobilehome, whether the mobilehome is occupied or unoccupied at the time of the levy. **Leg.H.** Added Stats 1982 ch 1364 §2, operative July 1, 1983. Amended Stats 1983 ch 1124 §9; Stats 1995 ch 446 §2 (SB 69).

§700.090. Vehicle, vessel, manufactured home, mobilehome, or commercial coach for which certificate of ownership is issued

If a vehicle or vessel is levied upon and a certificate of ownership has been issued by the Department of Motor Vehicles for such vehicle or vessel and the certificate of ownership is still in effect, or if a manufactured home, mobilehome, or commercial coach is levied upon and a permanent title record has been established by the Department of Housing and Community Development for such manufactured home, mobilehome, or commercial coach the levying officer shall determine from the appropriate department the name and address of the legal owner and each junior lienholder of the property levied upon. If the legal owner or junior lienholder is not the judgment debtor and is not in possession of the vehicle, vessel, manufactured home, mobilehome, or commercial coach, the levying officer shall at the time of levy or promptly thereafter serve a copy of the writ of execution and a notice of levy on the legal owner or junior lienholder. Service shall be made personally or by mail. **Leg.H.** Added Stats 1982 ch 1364 §2, operative July 1, 1983. Amended Stats 1983 ch 1124 §10.

§700.100. Chattel paper

(a) To levy upon chattel paper, the levying officer shall:

(1) If the chattel paper is in the possession of the judgment debtor, take the chattel paper into custody.

(2) If the chattel paper is in the possession of a third person, personally serve a copy of the writ of execution and a notice of levy on the third person.

(b) If the levying officer obtains custody of the chattel paper or if pursuant to a security agreement the judgment debtor has liberty to collect or compromise the chattel paper or to accept the return of goods or make repossessions, the levying officer shall, if so instructed by the judgment creditor, serve a copy of the writ of execution and a notice of levy on the account debtor. Service shall be made personally or by mail.

(c) In addition to any other rights created by a levy on chattel paper, the levy creates a lien on the judgment debtor's rights in specific goods subject to the chattel paper. **Leg.H.** Added Stats 1982 ch 1364 §2, operative July 1, 1983.

§700.110. Instruments

(a) To levy upon an instrument, the levying officer shall:

(1) If the instrument is in the possession of the judgment debtor, take the instrument into custody.

(2) If the instrument is in the possession of a third person, personally serve a copy of the writ of execution and a notice of levy on the third person.

(b) If the levying officer obtains custody of the instrument, the levying officer shall, if the judgment creditor so instructs, serve a copy of the writ of execution and a notice of levy on the obligor. Service shall be made personally or by mail. **Leg.H.** Added Stats 1982 ch 1364 §2, operative July 1, 1983.

§700.120. Negotiable documents of title

To levy upon a negotiable document of title, the levying officer shall:

(a) If the negotiable document of title is in the possession of the judgment debtor, take the negotiable document of title into custody.

(b) If the negotiable document of title is in the possession of a third person, personally serve a copy of the writ of execution and a notice of levy on the third person. **Leg.H.** Added Stats 1982 ch 1364 §2, operative July 1, 1983.

§700.130. Securities

To levy upon a security, the levying officer shall comply with Section 8112 of the Commercial Code. The legal process referred to in Section 8112 of the Commercial Code means the legal process required by the state in which the chief executive office of the issuer of the security is located and, where that state is California, means personal service by the levying officer of a copy of the writ of execution and notice of levy on the person who is to be served. **Leg.H.** Added Stats 1982 ch 1364 §2, operative July 1, 1983. Amended Stats 1984 ch 927 §2; Stats 1996 ch 497 §3 (SB 1591), operative January 1, 1997.

§700.140. Deposit accounts

(a) Subject to Sections 684.115 and 700.160, to levy upon a deposit account, the levying officer shall personally serve a copy of the writ of execution and a notice of levy on the financial institution with which the deposit account is maintained.

(b) The execution lien that arises upon service of a writ of execution and notice of levy reaches only amounts in a deposit account at the time of service on the financial institution, including the amount of any deposit not yet finally collected unless the deposit is returned unpaid to the financial institution.

(c) The levying officer shall serve a copy of the writ of execution and a notice of levy on any third person in whose name any deposit account described therein stands. Service shall be made personally or by mail as follows:

(1) At the time of levy or promptly thereafter, if the party seeking the levy informs the levying officer of the person and his, her, or its residence or business address.

(2) Promptly following the levying officer's receipt of a garnishee's memorandum if service was not accomplished pursuant to paragraph (1) if the garnishee's memorandum identifies the person and his, her, or its residence or business address.

(d) The financial institution shall not honor a withdrawal request or a check or other order for the payment of money from the deposit account if presentment of the withdrawal request or item to the financial institution occurs during the time the execution lien is in effect unless, following the withdrawal or payment, sufficient funds are available to cover the levy. For these purposes, a withdrawal from the deposit account to cover the financial institution's standard fee or charge for processing the levy shall not be considered a payment of money from the account in violation of this subdivision.

(e) During the time the execution lien is in effect, the financial institution is not liable to any person for any of the following:

(1) Performance of the duties of a garnishee under the levy.

(2) Nonpayment of a check or other order for the payment or transfer of money drawn or presented against the deposit account if the nonpayment is pursuant to the requirements of subdivision (d).

(3) Refusal to pay a withdrawal from the deposit account if the refusal is pursuant to the requirements of subdivision (d).

(f) When the amount levied upon pursuant to this section is paid to the levying officer, the execution lien on the deposit account levied upon terminates.

(g) For the purposes of this section, none of the following is a third person in whose name the deposit account stands:

(1) A person who is only a person named as the beneficiary of a Totten trust account.

(2) A person who is only a payee designated in a pay-on-death provision in an account pursuant to Section 18318.5 of the Financial Code or Section 5140 of the Probate Code, or other similar provision.

(3) A person who is only acting in a representative or custodial capacity with respect to benefits paid or payable by the United States government. Rather, accounts maintained by the representative or custodian shall be deemed to stand in the beneficiary's name, and the amounts therein shall be covered by a levy against the beneficiary.

(h) For purposes of this section, final payment of a deposit shall be deemed to have occurred in accordance with Section 4215 or 11210 of the Commercial Code or with automated clearinghouse or Federal Reserve System rule, regulation, operating circular, or similar governing docu-

ment, as applicable to the deposit. If, for any reason, a deposit is returned by the financial institution upon which it is drawn, the deposit shall not be deemed finally collected for purposes of this subdivision regardless of any later payment by the financial institution upon which the deposit is drawn.
Leg.H. Added Stats 1982 ch 1364 §2, operative July 1, 1983. Amended Stats 1983 ch 155 §14, effective June 30, 1983, operative July 1, 1983; Stats 1984 ch 538 §21; Stats 2002 ch 664 §48 (AB 3034); Stats 2003 ch 110 §2 (AB 690); Stats 2009 ch 153 §3 (AB 1549), effective January 1, 2010; Stats 2012 ch 484 §8 (AB 2364), effective January 1, 2013.

§700.150. Safe deposit boxes; Service; Notice, fee and costs; Removal; Liability

(a) Subject to Section 700.160, to levy upon property in a safe-deposit box, the levying officer shall personally serve a copy of the writ of execution and a notice of levy on the financial institution with which the safe-deposit box is maintained.

(b) At the time of the levy or promptly thereafter, the levying officer shall serve a copy of the writ of execution and a notice of levy on any third person in whose name the safe-deposit box stands. Service shall be made personally or by mail.

(c) During the time the execution lien is in effect, the financial institution may not permit the removal of any of the contents of the safe-deposit box except as directed by the levying officer.

(d) Upon receipt of a garnishee's memorandum from the financial institution indicating a safe-deposit box is under levy, the levying officer shall promptly mail a written notice to the judgment creditor demanding an additional fee as required by Section 26723 of the Government Code, plus the costs to open the safe-deposit box and seize and store the contents. The levying officer shall release the levy on the safe-deposit box if the judgment creditor does not pay the required fee, plus costs, within three business days plus the extended time period specified in subdivision (a) of Section 1013 for service by mail by the levying officer.

(e) The levying officer may first give the person in whose name the safe-deposit box stands an opportunity to open the safe-deposit box to permit the removal pursuant to the levy of the property levied upon. The financial institution may refuse to permit the forcible opening of the safe-deposit box to permit the removal of the property levied upon unless the levying officer or the judgment creditor pays in advance the cost of forcibly opening the safe-deposit box and of repairing any damage caused thereby.

(f) The levying officer shall give the judgment creditor at least three court days' advance notice of the date and time the levying officer will open the safe-deposit box and seize the contents thereof, and the judgment creditor shall be entitled to be present at that time.

(g) During the time the execution lien is in effect, the financial institution is not liable to any person for any of the following:

(1) Performance of the duties of a garnishee under the levy.

(2) Refusal to permit access to the safe-deposit box by the person in whose name it stands.

(3) Removal of any of the contents of the safe-deposit box pursuant to the levy.

(h) If the levying officer removes any property from the safe-deposit box to satisfy the levy, but allows other property to remain in the safe-deposit box, the execution lien is released automatically with respect to any property that remains in the safe-deposit box. **Leg.H.** Added Stats 1982 ch 1364 §2, operative July 1, 1983. Amended Stats 1984 ch 538 §22; Stats 2003 ch 888 §2 (AB 394); Stats 2012 ch 484 §9 (AB 2364), effective January 1, 2013.

§700.160. Deposit accounts and safe deposit boxes not exclusively in name of judgment debtor

(a) Except as provided in subdivision (b), a deposit account or safe-deposit box standing in the name of a person other than the judgment debtor, either alone or together with third persons, is not subject to levy under Section 700.140 or 700.150 unless the legal process served on the third party includes a court order authorizing the levy.

(b) A court order is not required to levy on a deposit account or safe-deposit box standing in the name of any of the following:

(1) The judgment debtor, whether alone or together with third persons.

(2) The judgment debtor's spouse or registered domestic partner, whether alone or together with other persons, provided an affidavit is delivered to the financial institution at the time of levy showing that person is the judgment debtor's spouse or registered domestic partner.

(3) A fictitious business name, provided a copy of an unexpired statement certified in accordance with Section 17926 of the Business and Professions Code is delivered to the financial institution at the time of levy, the fictitious business name statement does not list any person other than the judgment debtor, the judgment debtor's spouse or the judgment debtor's registered domestic partner as the person or persons doing business under the fictitious business name, and, if a person other than the judgment debtor is listed in the statement, an affidavit stating that the other person is the judgment debtor's spouse or registered domestic partner is delivered to the financial institution at the time of the levy.

(4) The additional name of a judgment debtor listed on the legal process pursuant to an affidavit of identity as provided by Section 680.135, whether alone or together with third persons.

(c) In any case where a deposit account in the name of a person other than the judgment debtor, whether alone or together with the judgment debtor, is levied upon, the financial institution shall not pay to the levying officer the amount levied upon until being notified to do so by the levying officer. The levying officer may not require the financial institution to pay the amount levied upon until the expiration of 15 days after service of notice of levy on the third person. **Leg.H.** Added Stats 1984 ch 538 §23.5. Amended Stats 2000 ch 639 §8 (AB 2405); Stats 2011 ch 308 §3 (SB 647), effective January 1, 2012; Stats 2012 ch 484 §10 (AB 2364), effective January 1, 2013.

Prior Law: Former CCP §700.160, similar to the present section, was added Stats 1982 ch 1364 §2, amended Stats 1983 ch 18 §8, effective April 21, 1983, operative July 1, 1983, ch 155 §14.3, effective June 30, 1983, operative July 1, 1983, and repealed Stats 1984 ch 538 §23.

§700.165. [Section repealed 1985]

Leg.H. Added Stats 1983 ch 155 §14.4, effective June 30, 1983, operative July 1, 1983. Repealed Stats 1984 ch 538 §24. The repealed section related to alternative procedure and deposit account standing only in names of both judgment debtor and spouse.

§700.167. [Section repealed 1985]

Leg.H. Added Stats 1983 ch 155 §14.5, effective June 30, 1983, operative July 1, 1983. Repealed Stats 1984 ch 538 §25. The repealed section related to alternative procedure and deposit account standing in fictitious business name.

§700.170. Accounts receivable and general intangibles

(a) Unless another method of levy is provided by this article, to levy upon an account receivable or general intangible, the levying officer shall personally serve a copy of the writ of execution and a notice of levy on the account debtor.

(b) If a levy is made under subdivision (a) and payments on the account receivable or general intangible are made to a person other than the judgment debtor (whether pursuant to a security agreement, assignment for collection, or otherwise), the levying officer shall, if so instructed by the judgment creditor, personally serve a copy of the writ of execution and a notice of levy on such third person. Service of the copy of the writ and notice of levy on such third person is a levy on any amounts owed to the judgment debtor by such third person. **Leg.H.** Added Stats 1982 ch 1364 §2, operative July 1, 1983.

§700.180. Levy on property that is subject of pending action or proceeding

(a) The following property may be levied upon pursuant to this article notwithstanding that the property levied upon is the subject of a pending action or special proceeding:

(1) Real property.

(2) Growing crops, timber to be cut, or minerals or the like (including oil and gas) to be extracted or accounts receivable resulting from the sale thereof at the wellhead or minehead.

(3) Tangible personal property in the possession or under the control of the judgment debtor or in the custody of a levying officer.

(4) The interest of a judgment debtor in personal property in the estate of a decedent, whether the interest arises by testate or intestate succession.

(b) Except as provided in subdivision (a), a levy upon property that is the subject of an action or special proceeding pending at the time of the levy is not effective.

(c) If a levy is attempted but is ineffective under subdivision (b) and the levying officer has requested a garnishee's memorandum under Section 701.030 in connection with the ineffective levy, the garnishee's memorandum shall include the following information in addition to that required by Section 701.030:

(1) A statement that the levy on the property is not effective because the property is the subject of a pending action or special proceeding.

(2) The title of the court, cause, and number of the pending action or proceeding.

(d) For the purpose of this section, an action or proceeding is pending from the time the action or proceeding is commenced until judgment has been entered and the time for appeal has expired or, if an appeal is filed, until the appeal has been finally determined.

(e) Nothing in this section affects or limits the right of the judgment creditor to obtain a lien pursuant to Article 5 (commencing with Section 708.410) of Chapter 6. **Leg.H.** Added Stats 1982 ch 1364 §2, operative July 1, 1983.

§700.190. Final money judgment

(a) As used in this section, "final money judgment" means a money judgment after the time for appeal from the judgment has expired or, if an appeal is filed, after the appeal has been finally determined.

(b) To levy upon a final money judgment, the levying officer shall file a copy of the writ of execution and a notice of levy with the clerk of the court that entered the final money judgment. The court clerk shall endorse upon the judgment a statement of the existence of the execution lien and the time it was created. If an abstract of the judgment is issued, it shall include a statement of the execution lien in favor of the judgment creditor.

(c) At the time of levy or promptly thereafter, the levying officer shall serve a copy of the writ of execution and a notice of levy on the judgment debtor obligated to pay the final money judgment levied upon. Service shall be made personally or by mail. **Leg.H.** Added Stats 1982 ch 1364 §2, operative July 1, 1983. Amended Stats 1984 ch 538 §25.3.

§700.200. Interest in personal property of estate of decedent

(a) To levy upon the interest of the judgment debtor in personal property in the estate of a decedent, whether the interest arises by testate or intestate succession, the levying officer shall personally serve a copy of the writ and a notice of levy on the personal representative of the decedent. The levy does not impair the powers of the representative over the property for the purposes of administration.

(b) The personal representative shall report the levy to the court in which the estate is being administered when any petition for distribution is filed. If a decree orders distribution to the judgment debtor, the court making the decree shall order the property levied upon to be delivered to the levying officer. The property may not be delivered to the levying officer until the decree distributing the property has become final. To the extent the property delivered to the levying officer is not necessary to satisfy the money judgment, it shall be released to the judgment debtor.

(c) Promptly after the property is delivered to the levying officer pursuant to subdivision (b), the levying officer shall serve a notice describing the property on the judgment debtor. Service shall be made personally or by mail. Notwithstanding Section 703.520, a claim of exemption for the property described in the notice may be made within 10 days after the notice was served on the judgment debtor.

(d) Notwithstanding Section 697.710, an execution lien created by a levy pursuant to this section continues for a period of one year after the decree distributing the interest has become final unless the judgment is sooner satisfied.

(e) A writ under which a levy is made pursuant to this section shall be returned not later than one year after the date the decree distributing the interest has become final. **Leg.H.** Added Stats 1982 ch 1364 §2, operative July 1, 1983.

§701. [Section repealed 1983]

Leg.H. Enacted Stats 1872. Repealed Stats 1982 ch 1364 §1, operative July 1, 1983. The repealed section related to persons who had the right to redeem property sold subject to redemption.

ARTICLE 5
Duties and Liabilities of Third Persons After Levy

Duty of garnishee. §701.010.
Liability of third person for noncompliance with levy. §701.020.
Garnishee's memorandum. §701.030.
Liability of third person who gives garnishee's memorandum. §701.035.
Rights and duties of secured party. §701.040.
Duty of account debtor. §701.050.
Duty of obligor under instrument. §701.060.
Requirement that payments be made to levying officer. §701.070.

§701.010. Duty of garnishee

(a) Except as otherwise provided by statute, when a levy is made by service of a copy of the writ of execution and a notice of levy on a third person, the third person at the time of levy or promptly thereafter shall comply with this section.

(b) Unless the third person has good cause for failure or refusal to do so:

(1) The third person shall deliver to the levying officer any of the property levied upon that is in the possession or under the control of the third person at the time of levy unless the third person claims the right to possession of the property.

(2) To the extent that the third person does not deny an obligation levied upon, or claim a priority over the judgment creditor's lien, the third person shall pay to the levying officer both of the following:

(A) The amount of the obligation levied upon that is due and payable to the judgment debtor at the time of levy.

(B) Amounts that become due and payable to the judgment debtor on the obligation levied upon during the period of the execution lien.

(3) If the third person makes a delivery or payment to the levying officer pursuant to this section, the third person shall execute and deliver any documents necessary to effect the transfer of the property.

(c) For the purposes of this section, "good cause" includes, but is not limited to, a showing that the third person did not know or have reason to know of the levy from all the facts and circumstances known to the third person. **Leg.H.** Added Stats 1982 ch 1364 §2, operative July 1, 1983.

§701.020. Liability of third person for noncompliance with levy

(a) If a third person is required by this article to deliver property to the levying officer or to make payments to the levying officer and the third person fails or refuses without good cause to do so, the third person is liable to the judgment creditor for whichever of the following is the lesser amount:

(1) The value of the judgment debtor's interest in the property or the amount of the payments required to be made.

(2) The amount required to satisfy the judgment pursuant to which the levy is made.

(b) The third person's liability continues until the earliest of the following times:

(1) The time when the property levied upon is delivered to the levying officer or the payments are made to the levying officer.

(2) The time when the property levied upon is released pursuant to Section 699.060.

(3) The time when the judgment is satisfied or discharged.

(c) If the third person's liability is established, the court that determines the liability may, in its discretion, require the third person to pay the costs and reasonable attorney's fees incurred by the judgment creditor in establishing the liability. **Leg.H.** Added Stats 1982 ch 1364 §2, operative July 1, 1983.

§701.030. Garnishee's memorandum

(a) At the time of service of a copy of the legal process on a third person, the levying officer shall request the third person to give the levying officer a garnishee's memorandum containing the information required by this section. Within 10 days after the legal process is served, the third person shall mail or deliver the garnishee's memorandum to the levying officer whether or not the levy is effective.

(b) The garnishee's memorandum shall be executed under oath and shall contain the following information, as applicable:

(1) A description of any property of the judgment debtor sought to be levied upon that is not delivered to the levying officer and the reason for not delivering the property.

(2) A description of any property of the judgment debtor not sought to be levied upon that is in the possession or under the control of the third person at the time of levy.

(3) A statement of the amount and terms of any obligation to the judgment debtor sought to be levied upon that is due and payable and is not paid to the levying officer, and the reason for not paying the obligation.

(4) A statement of the amount and terms of any obligation to the judgment debtor sought to be levied upon that is not due and payable at the time of levy.

(5) A statement of the amount and terms of any obligation to the judgment debtor at the time of levy not sought to be levied upon.

(6) A description of claims and rights of other persons to the property or obligation levied upon that are known to the third person and the names and addresses of those other persons.

(7) A statement that the garnishee holds neither any property nor any obligations in favor of the judgment debtor.

(c) If a garnishee's memorandum is received from the third person, the levying officer shall retain a copy and promptly mail or deliver a copy of the memorandum to the judgment creditor.

(d) Except as provided in subdivisions (e) and (f), if a third person does not give the levying officer a garnishee's memorandum within the time provided in subdivision (a), or does not provide complete information, the third person may, in the court's discretion, be required to pay the costs and reasonable attorney's fees incurred in any proceedings to obtain the information required in the garnishee's memorandum.

(e) Notwithstanding subdivision (a), when the levy is made upon a deposit account or upon property in a safe-deposit box, the financial institution need not give a garnishee's memorandum to the levying officer if the financial institution fully complies with the levy and, if a garnishee's memorandum is required, the garnishee's memorandum needs to provide information with respect only to property that is carried on the records available at the office or branch where the levy is made provided that if a levy has been served at a central location designated by a financial institution in accordance with Section 684.115, the garnishee's memorandum shall apply to all offices and branches of the financial institution except to the extent acceptance of the levy at those central locations is limited pursuant to paragraph (3) of subdivision [1] (b) of Section 684.115.

(f) Notwithstanding subdivision (a), the third person need not give a garnishee's memorandum to the levying officer if both of the following conditions are satisfied:

(1) The third person has delivered to the levying officer all of the property sought to be levied upon.

(2) The third person has paid to the levying officer the amount due at the time of levy on any obligation to the judgment debtor that was levied upon, and there is no additional amount that thereafter will become payable on the obligation levied upon.

(g) The garnishee may electronically transmit the garnishee's memorandum to the levying officer pursuant to Chapter 2 (commencing with Section 263) of Title 4 of Part 1. **Leg.H.** Added Stats 1982 ch 1364 §2, operative July 1, 1983. Amended Stats 2010 ch 680 §10 (AB 2394), effective January 1, 2011; Stats 2012 ch 484 §11 (AB 2364), effective January 1, 2013; Stats 2024 ch 222 §3 (AB 2067), effective January 1, 2025.

§701.030. 2024 Deletes. [1] (a)

§701.035. Liability of third person who gives garnishee's memorandum

A third person who gives a garnishee's memorandum pursuant to this title is not liable to any person for the disclosure in the garnishee's memorandum of any information contained in the garnishee's memorandum. **Leg.H.** Added Stats 1983 ch 155 §14.6, effective June 30, 1983, operative July 1, 1983.

§701.040. Rights and duties of secured party

(a) Except as otherwise ordered by the court upon a determination that the judgment creditor's lien has priority over the security interest, if property levied upon is subject to a security interest that attached prior to levy, the property or obligation is subject to enforcement of the security interest without regard to the levy unless the property is in the custody of the levying officer; but, if the execution lien has priority over the security interest, the secured party is liable to the judgment creditor for any proceeds received by the secured party from the property to the extent of the execution lien.

(b) After the security interest is satisfied, the secured party shall deliver any excess property, and pay any excess payments or proceeds of property, remaining in the possession of the secured party to the levying officer for the purposes of the levy, as provided in Section 9615 of the Commercial Code, unless otherwise ordered by the court or directed by the levying officer. **Leg.H.** Added Stats 1990 ch 1125 §1.5 (AB 3881), operative January 1, 2002. Amended Stats 1999 ch 991 §24.5 (SB 45), operative July 1, 2001.

Former Sections: Former CCP §701.040 was enacted in 1982 and repealed operative January 1, 2002, by its own provisions. Stats 1999 ch 991 §24.

§701.050. Duty of account debtor

After service of a copy of the writ of execution and a notice of levy on an account debtor obligated on an account receivable, chattel paper, or general intangible:

(a) If the account debtor has been making payments or is required to make payments to the judgment debtor, the account debtor shall make payments to the levying officer as they become due unless otherwise directed by court order or by the levying officer. Payments made to the judgment debtor after the account debtor has received notice of the levy do not discharge the obligation of the account debtor to make payments as required by this subdivision.

(b) If the account debtor has been making payments to a third person or is required to make payments to a third person (whether pursuant to a security agreement, assignment for collection, or otherwise), the account debtor shall continue to make such payments to the third person notwithstanding the levy until the account debtor receives notice that the obligation to the third person is satisfied or is otherwise directed by court order or by the third person. After the account debtor receives notice that the obligation to the third person is satisfied, the account debtor shall make payments to the levying officer as they become due unless otherwise directed by court order or by the levying officer.

(c) If pursuant to a security agreement the judgment debtor has liberty to accept the return of goods or make repossessions under the account receivable or chattel paper, the account debtor shall deliver to the levying officer property returnable to the judgment debtor unless otherwise directed by court order or by the levying officer. **Leg.H.** Added Stats 1982 ch 1364 §2, operative July 1, 1983.

§701.060. Duty of obligor under instrument

If the levying officer obtains custody of an instrument levied upon and serves the obligor under the instrument pursuant to the levy, the obligor shall make payments to the levying officer as they become due. Payments made to a person other than the levying officer do not discharge the obligation of the obligor to make payments as required by this section if the payments are made after the obligor has received notice of the levy. **Leg.H.** Added Stats 1982 ch 1364 §2, operative July 1, 1983.

§701.070. Requirement that payments be made to levying officer

If a final money judgment has been levied upon and the levying officer has served the judgment debtor under the final money judgment levied upon, the judgment debtor shall make any payments due under the judgment to the levying officer. Payments made to a person other than the levying officer do not discharge the obligation of the judgment debtor under the final money judgment levied upon if the payments are made after the judgment debtor has received notice of the levy. **Leg.H.** Added Stats 1984 ch 538 §25.5.

ARTICLE 6
Sale and Collection

Sale of property levied upon. §701.510.
Collection; Sale of collectible property. §701.520.
Notice of sale of personal property. §701.530.
Notice of sale of real property. §701.540.
Period that must elapse before giving notice of sale. §701.545.
Notice to prospective bidders. §701.547.
Notice of sale to persons requesting notice. §701.550.
Advertising of sale by judgment creditor or judgment debtor. §701.555.
Effect of sale without required notice. §701.560.
Place, time, and manner of sale. §701.570.
Postponement of sale. §701.580.
Manner of payment. §701.590.
Defaulting bidder. §701.600.
Persons ineligible to purchase. §701.610.
Minimum bid. §701.620.
Extinction of liens upon sale. §701.630.
Interest acquired by purchaser. §701.640.
Delivery of possession or of certificate of sale of personal property. §701.650.
Deed of sale of real property. §701.660.
Contents of certificate or deed of sale. §701.670.

Sale as absolute; Liability; Debtor's equitable right of redemption not affected. §701.680.

§701.510. Sale of property levied upon

Subject to Sections 687.020 and 701.520, the levying officer shall sell all property that has been levied upon except:

(a) Tangible personal property may not be sold until the levying officer obtains custody of the property.

(b) Cash may not be sold unless it has a value exceeding its face value.

Leg.H. Added Stats 1982 ch 1364 §2, operative July 1, 1983.

§701.520. Collection; Sale of collectible property

(a) Except as provided in this section, any of the following property that has been levied upon shall be collected rather than sold:

(1) Accounts receivable.

(2) Chattel paper.

(3) General intangibles.

(4) Final money judgments.

(5) Instruments that are not customarily transferred in an established market.

(6) Instruments that represent an obligation arising out of the sale or lease of property, a license to use property, the furnishing of services, or the loan of money where the property sold or leased or licensed for use, the services furnished, or the money loaned was used by an individual primarily for personal, family, or household purposes.

(b) At the time of levy on property described in subdivision (a) or thereafter, the judgment creditor may serve a notice of intended sale of the property on the judgment debtor. Service shall be made personally or by mail. A copy of the notice of intended sale and proof of service on the judgment debtor shall be filed with the court and with the levying officer. The notice of intended sale shall describe the property and state that it will be sold at an execution sale unless, within the time allowed after service of the notice of intended sale, the judgment debtor applies to the court on noticed motion for an order that the property be collected rather than sold.

(c) Within 10 days after service of the notice of intended sale, the judgment debtor may apply to the court on noticed motion for an order that the property be collected rather than sold. A judgment debtor who so applies shall, within the time allowed for the application, serve a copy of the notice of motion on the judgment creditor and file a copy of the notice of motion with the levying officer. Service of the copy of the notice of motion on the judgment creditor shall be made personally or by mail. If the copy of the notice of motion is not filed with the levying officer within the time allowed, the levying officer shall proceed to sell the property. If a copy of the notice of motion is filed with the levying officer within the time allowed, the levying officer shall continue to collect the property until otherwise ordered by the court.

(d) At the hearing on the motion, the court may in its discretion order that the property be sold or be collected depending on the equities and circumstances of the particular case. If the court orders that the property be sold, the order may specify terms and conditions of sale. If the court orders that the property be collected, the court may condition its order on an assignment of the property by the judgment debtor to the judgment creditor pursuant to Article 6 (commencing with Section 708.510) of Chapter 6. **Leg.H.** Added Stats 1982 ch 1364 §2, operative July 1, 1983.

§701.530. Notice of sale of personal property

(a) Notice of sale of personal property shall be in writing, shall state the date, time, and place of sale, and shall describe the property to be sold.

(b) Not less than 10 days before a sale of personal property, notice of sale shall be posted and served on the judgment debtor by the levying officer. Service shall be made personally or by mail.

(c) Posting under this section shall be in three public places in:

(1) The city in which the property is to be sold if it is to be sold in a city.

(2) The county in which the property is to be sold if it is not to be sold in a city.

(d) A sale of personal property of an individual may not take place until the expiration of the time during which the judgment debtor may make a claim of exemption under subdivision (a) of Section 703.520.

Leg.H. Added Stats 1982 ch 1364 §2, operative July 1, 1983. Amended Stats 2002 ch 784 §68 (SB 1316).

§701.540. Notice of sale of real property

(a) Notice of sale of an interest in real property shall be in writing, shall state the date, time, and place of sale, shall describe the interest to be sold, and shall give a legal description of the real property and its street address or other common designation, if any. If the real property has no street address or other common designation, the notice of sale shall include a statement that directions to its location may be obtained from the levying officer upon oral or written request or, in the discretion of the levying officer, the notice of sale may contain directions to its location. Directions are sufficient if information as to the location of the real property is given by reference to the direction and approximate distance from the nearest crossroads, frontage road, or access road. If an accurate legal description of the real property is given, the validity of the notice and sale is not affected by the fact that the street address or other common designation, or directions to its location, are erroneous or omitted.

(b) Not less than 20 days before the date of sale, notice of sale of an interest in real property shall be served, mailed, and posted by the levying officer as provided in subdivisions (c), (d), (e), and (f).

(c) Notice of sale shall be served on the judgment debtor. Service shall be made personally or by mail.

(d) Notice of sale shall be posted in the following places:

(1) One public place in the city in which the interest in the real property is to be sold if it is to be sold in a city or, if not to be sold in a city, one public place in the county in which the interest in the real property is to be sold.

(2) A conspicuous place on the real property.

(e) At the time notice is posted pursuant to paragraph (2) of subdivision (d), notice of sale shall be served or service shall be attempted on one occupant of the real property. Service on the occupant shall be made by leaving the notice with the occupant personally or, in the occupant's absence, with any person of suitable age and discretion found upon the real property at the time service is attempted who is either an employee or agent of the occupant or a member of the occupant's household. If the levying officer is unable to serve an occupant, as specified, at the time service is attempted, the levying officer is not required to make any further attempts to serve an occupant.

(f) If the property described in the notice of sale consists of more than one distinct lot, parcel, or governmental subdivision and any of the lots, parcels, or governmental subdivisions lies with relation to any of the others so as to form one or more continuous, unbroken tracts, only one service pursuant to subdivision (e) and posting pursuant to paragraph (2) of subdivision (d) need be made as to each continuous, unbroken tract.

(g) Notice of sale shall be published pursuant to Section 6063 of the Government Code, with the first publication at least 20 days prior to the time of sale, in a newspaper of general circulation published in the city in which the real property or a part thereof is situated if any part thereof is situated in a city or, if not, in a newspaper of general circulation published in the public notice district in which the real property or a part thereof is situated. If no newspaper of general circulation is published in the city or public notice district, notice of sale shall be published in a newspaper of general circulation in the county in which the real property or a part thereof is situated.

(h) Not earlier than 30 days after the date of levy, the judgment creditor shall determine the names of all persons having liens on the real property on the date of levy that are of record in the office of the county recorder and shall instruct the levying officer to mail notice of sale to each lienholder at the address used by the county recorder for the return of the instrument creating the lien after recording. The levying officer shall mail notice to each lienholder, at the address given in the instructions, not less than 20 days before the date of sale.

(i) For the purposes of this section, publication of notice in a public notice district is governed by Chapter 1.1 (commencing with Section 6080) of Division 7 of Title 1 of the Government Code. **Leg.H.** Added Stats 1982 ch 1364 §2, operative July 1, 1983. Amended Stats 2002 ch 784 §69 (SB 1316); Stats 2016 ch 703 §9 (AB 2881), effective January 1, 2017.

§701.545. Period that must elapse before giving notice of sale

Notice of sale of an interest in real property, other than a leasehold estate with an unexpired term of less than two years at the time of levy, may not be given pursuant to Section 701.540 until the expiration of 120 days after the date notice of levy on the interest in real property was served on the judgment debtor. **Leg.H.** Added Stats 1982 ch 1364 §2, operative July 1, 1983.

§701.547. Notice to prospective bidders

A notice of sale shall contain the substance of the following statement: "Prospective bidders should refer to Sections 701.510 to 701.680, inclusive, of the Code of Civil Procedure for provisions governing the terms, conditions, and effect of the sale and the liability of defaulting bidders." **Leg.H.** Added Stats 1982 ch 1364 §2, operative July 1, 1983.

§701.550. Notice of sale to persons requesting notice

(a) In addition to the notice of sale required by this article, the levying officer shall, at the time notice of sale is posted pursuant to Section 701.530 or 701.540, mail notice of sale to any person who has requested notice of the sale pursuant to this section.

(b) A request for notice of sale under this section made prior to the issuance of the writ shall be in writing and shall be filed with the clerk of the court where the judgment is entered. The request shall specify the title of the court, the cause and number of the action in which the judgment was entered, and the date of entry thereof, and shall state the address to which the notice of sale is to be mailed. The name and address of the person requesting notice of sale under this subdivision shall be noted on the writ.

(c) A person who desires notice of sale of particular property that has been levied upon may file a request for notice of sale with the levying officer who will conduct the sale. The request shall contain the information specified by the levying officer as needed in order to comply with the request. **Leg.H.** Added Stats 1982 ch 1364 §2, operative July 1, 1983.

§701.555. Advertising of sale by judgment creditor or judgment debtor

In addition to the notice of sale required by this article, the judgment creditor may advertise the sale in the classified or other advertising section of a newspaper of general circulation or other publication and may recover reasonable costs of such advertising. The judgment debtor may also advertise the sale at the judgment debtor's own expense. **Leg.H.** Added Stats 1982 ch 1364 §2, operative July 1, 1983.

§701.560. Effect of sale without required notice

(a) Failure to give notice of sale as required by this article does not invalidate the sale.

(b) A levying officer who sells property without giving the required notice is liable to the judgment creditor and the judgment debtor for actual damages caused by failure to give notice. **Leg.H.** Added Stats 1982 ch 1364 §2, operative July 1, 1983.

§701.570. Place, time, and manner of sale

(a) A sale of property shall be held at the date, time, and place specified in the notice of sale, which shall be in the county where the property or a part thereof is situated and between the hours of nine in the morning and five in the afternoon. Subject to subdivision (d), real property consisting of one parcel, or of two or more contiguous parcels, situated in two or more counties may be sold in one county as instructed by the judgment creditor.

(b) The sale shall be made at auction to the highest bidder.

(c) If personal property capable of manual delivery is to be sold, it shall be within the view of those who attend the sale unless, upon application of the judgment creditor or the judgment debtor, the court orders otherwise.

(d) Property shall be sold separately or in such groups or lots as are likely to bring the highest price. The judgment debtor may request that the property be sold separately or together and may request that the property be sold in a particular order. If the judgment debtor is not present at the sale, the request may be made in writing and delivered to the levying officer prior to the sale. The levying officer shall honor the request if, in the opinion of the levying officer, the requested manner of sale is likely to yield an amount at least equal to any other manner of sale or the amount required to satisfy the money judgment. The levying officer is not liable for a decision made in good faith under this subdivision.

(e) After sufficient property has been sold to yield the amount required to satisfy the money judgment, no more shall be sold. **Leg.H.** Added Stats 1982 ch 1364 §2, operative July 1, 1983.

§701.580. Postponement of sale

The judgment debtor and judgment creditor together may request in writing that a sale be postponed to an agreed day and hour. The request shall be delivered to the levying officer conducting the sale, and the levying officer shall, by public declaration at the time and place originally fixed for the sale, postpone the sale to the day and hour fixed in the request. Notice of any additional postponements shall be given by public declaration by the levying officer at the time and place last appointed for the sale. No other notice of postponed sale need be given. A postponed sale shall be held at the place originally fixed for the sale. **Leg.H.** Added Stats 1982 ch 1364 §2, operative July 1, 1983.

§701.590. Manner of payment

(a) Except as otherwise provided in this section, the purchaser at a sale shall pay in cash or by certified check or cashier's check.

(b) The judgment creditor may bid by giving the levying officer a written receipt crediting all or part of the amount required to satisfy the judgment, except that the levying officer's costs remaining unsatisfied and the amount of preferred labor claims, exempt proceeds, and any other claim that is required by statute to be satisfied, shall be paid in cash or by certified check or cashier's check.

(c) If the highest bid for an interest in real property sold exceeds five thousand dollars ($5,000), the highest bidder may elect to treat the sale as a credit transaction. A person who makes the election shall deposit at least five thousand dollars ($5,000) or 10 percent of the amount bid, whichever is greater, and within 10 days after the date of the sale shall pay the balance due plus costs accruing with regard to the property sold and interest accruing at the rate on money judgments on the balance of the amount bid from the date of sale until the date of payment.

(d) If the highest bid for an item, group, or lot of personal property sold exceeds two thousand five hundred dollars ($2,500), the highest bidder may elect to treat the sale as a credit transaction. A person who makes the election shall deposit at least two thousand five hundred dollars ($2,500) or 10 percent of the amount bid, whichever is greater, and within 10 days after the date of the sale shall pay the balance due plus costs accruing with regard to the property sold and interest accruing at the rate on money judgments on the balance of the amount bid from the date of sale until the date of payment.

(e) A person who makes the election under subdivision (c) or (d) is not entitled to possession of the property sold until the amount bid, plus accruing costs and interest, have been paid. **Leg.H.** Added Stats 1982 ch 1364 §2, operative July 1, 1983.

§701.600. Defaulting bidder

If the highest bidder does not pay the amount bid as prescribed by Section 701.590:

(a) The levying officer shall sell the property:

(1) If the default occurs at the sale, either to the next highest bidder at the amount of the next highest bid if such bidder agrees or to the highest bidder at a new sale held immediately.

(2) If the default occurs after the sale to a credit bidder pursuant to subdivision (c) of Section 701.590, to the highest bidder at a new sale.

(b) The levying officer shall apply the amount of any deposit made pursuant to subdivision (c) of Section 701.590 in the following order:

(1) To the satisfaction of costs accruing with regard to the property sold from the date of the sale until the date the property is resold, including costs of resale.

(2) To the satisfaction of interest at the rate on money judgments on the amount bid from the date of the sale until the date the property is resold.

(3) To the amount required to satisfy the money judgment in the order of distribution prescribed by Section 701.810 or Section 704.850, whichever is applicable.

(c) If there is a sale to the next highest bidder or to the highest bidder at a new sale, the defaulting bidder is liable for the following amounts in an action by the judgment creditor or judgment debtor:

(1) The amount bid, less the amount obtained from the resale of the property and the amount of any deposit applied pursuant to subdivision (b). The amount recovered pursuant to this paragraph shall be distributed in the manner prescribed by Section 701.810 or Section 704.850, whichever is applicable.

(2) Any costs accruing with regard to the property sold from the date of sale until the date the property is resold, including costs of resale.

(3) Interest at the rate on money judgments on the amount bid from the date of the sale until the date the property is resold.

(4) Costs and attorney's fees incurred in the action under this subdivision.

(d) The levying officer may, in the levying officer's discretion, reject any subsequent bid of the defaulting bidder. **Leg.H.** Added Stats 1982 ch 1364 §2, operative July 1, 1983.

§701.610. Persons ineligible to purchase

The levying officer may not be a purchaser or have an interest in any purchase at a sale. **Leg.H.** Added Stats 1982 ch 1364 §2, operative July 1, 1983.

§701.620. Minimum bid

(a) Property may not be sold unless the amount bid exceeds the total of the following amounts:

(1) The amount of all preferred labor claims that are required by Section 1206 to be satisfied from the proceeds.

(2) The amount of any state tax lien (as defined in Section 7162 of the Government Code) that is superior to the judgment creditor's lien.

(3) If the purchaser is not the judgment creditor, the amount of any deposit made pursuant to Section 720.260 with interest thereon at the rate on money judgments from the date of the deposit to the date of the sale.

(b) Property for which a proceeds exemption is provided by Section 704.010 (motor vehicle), 704.020 (household furnishings and other personal effects), or 704.060 (tools of trade), may not be sold unless the amount bid exceeds the sum of any amount under subdivision (a) and the amount of the proceeds exemption.

(c) If a minimum bid required for the sale of property pursuant to this section is not received, the levying officer shall promptly release the property. **Leg.H.** Added Stats 1982 ch 1364 §2, operative July 1, 1983.

§701.630. Extinction of liens upon sale

If property is sold pursuant to this article, the lien under which it is sold, any liens subordinate thereto, and any state tax lien (as defined in Section 7162 of the Government Code) on the property sold are extinguished. **Leg.H.** Added Stats 1982 ch 1364 §2, operative July 1, 1983.

§701.640. Interest acquired by purchaser

The purchaser of property at an execution sale acquires any interest of the judgment debtor in the property sold (1) that is held on the effective date of the lien under which the property was sold or (2) that is acquired between such effective date and the date of sale. **Leg.H.** Added Stats 1982 ch 1364 §2, operative July 1, 1983.

§701.650. Delivery of possession or of certificate of sale of personal property

(a) When the purchaser of personal property pays the amount due:

(1) If the property is capable of manual delivery, the levying officer shall deliver the property to the purchaser and, if the purchaser so requests, shall execute and deliver a certificate of sale to the purchaser.

(2) If the property is not tangible personal property or if it is otherwise not capable of manual delivery, the levying officer shall execute and deliver a certificate of sale to the purchaser.

(b) If property or a certificate is delivered pursuant to subdivision (a), the levying officer shall sign or endorse any document or instrument in the levying officer's possession relating to the title to or the right to possession of the property and deliver it to the purchaser. **Leg.H.** Added Stats 1982 ch 1364 §2, operative July 1, 1983.

§701.660. Deed of sale of real property

When the purchaser of an interest in real property pays the amount due to the levying officer, including any amount required to be paid as a documentary transfer tax pursuant to Section 11911 of the Revenue and Taxation Code, the levying officer conducting the sale shall execute and deliver a deed of sale to the purchaser, record a duplicate of the deed of sale in the office of the county recorder, and forward to the county or city and county any documentary transfer tax paid by the purchaser. **Leg.H.** Added Stats 1982 ch 1364 §2, operative July 1, 1983. Amended Stats 2010 ch 680 §11 (AB 2394), effective January 1, 2011.

§701.670. Contents of certificate or deed of sale

The certificate of sale or deed of sale shall contain all of the following:

(a) The title of the court where the judgment was entered under which the sale was made and the cause and number of the action.

(b) The date of entry of the judgment and of any subsequent renewals and where entered in the records of the court.

(c) The name and address of the judgment creditor and the name and last known address of the judgment debtor.

(d) A description of the property sold.

(e) The date of sale. **Leg.H.** Added Stats 1982 ch 1364 §2, operative July 1, 1983.

§701.680. Sale as absolute; Liability; Debtor's equitable right of redemption not affected

(a) Except as provided in paragraph (1) of subdivision (c), a sale of property pursuant to this article is absolute and shall not be set aside for any reason.

(b) If the judgment is reversed, vacated, or otherwise set aside, the judgment debtor may recover from the judgment creditor the proceeds of a sale pursuant to the judgment with interest at the rate on money judgments to the extent the proceeds were applied to the satisfaction of the judgment.

(c) If the sale was improper because of irregularities in the proceedings, because the property sold was not subject to execution, or for any other reason:

(1) The judgment debtor, or the judgment debtor's successor in interest, may commence an action within 90 days after the date of sale to set aside the sale if the purchaser at the sale is the judgment creditor. Subject to paragraph (2), if the sale is set aside, the judgment of the judgment creditor is revived to reflect the amount that was satisfied from the proceeds of the sale and the judgment creditor is entitled to interest on the amount of the judgment as so revived as if the sale had not been made. Any liens extinguished by the sale of the property are revived and reattach to the property with the same priority and effect as if the sale had not been made.

(2) The judgment debtor, or the judgment debtor's successor in interest, may recover damages caused by the impropriety. If damages are recovered against the judgment creditor, they shall be offset against the judgment to the extent the judgment is not satisfied. If damages are recovered against the levying officer, they shall be applied to the judgment to the extent the judgment is not satisfied.

(d) For the purposes of subdivision (c), the purchaser of the property at the sale is not a successor in interest.

(e) This section does not affect, limit, or eliminate a judgment debtor's equitable right of redemption. **Leg.H.** Added Stats 1982 ch 1364 §2, operative July 1, 1983. Amended Stats 1985 ch 41 §6, ch 157 §3; Stats 1989 ch 1416 §23; Stats 2014 ch 183 §1 (AB 2317), effective January 1, 2015.

ARTICLE 7
Distribution of Proceeds of Sale or Collection

Distribution of proceeds of sale or collection. §701.810.
Distribution of proceeds; Ex parte application. §701.820.
Procedure where conflicting claims to proceeds. §701.830.

§701.810. Distribution of proceeds of sale or collection

Except as otherwise provided by statute, the levying officer shall distribute the proceeds of sale or collection in the following order:

(a) To persons having preferred labor claims that are required by Section 1206 to be satisfied from the proceeds, in the amounts required by Section 1206 to be satisfied.

(b) To the state department or agency having a state tax lien (as defined in Section 7162 of the Government Code) that is superior to the judgment creditor's lien, in the amount of the lien.

(c) If a deposit has been made pursuant to Section 720.260 and the purchaser at the sale is not the judgment creditor, to the judgment creditor in the amount required to repay the deposit with interest thereon at the rate on money judgments from the date of the deposit.

(d) To the judgment debtor in the amount of any applicable exemption of proceeds pursuant to Section 704.010 (motor vehicle), 704.020 (household furnishings and other personal effects), or 704.060 (tools of trade), except that such proceeds shall be used to satisfy all of the following in the order of their respective priorities:

(1) Any consensual liens and encumbrances, and any liens for labor or materials, that are subordinate to the judgment creditor's lien.

(2) Subject to Section 688.030, any state tax lien (as defined in Section 7162 of the Government Code) on the property sold if the notice of state tax lien on the property has been recorded or filed pursuant to Section 7171 of the Government Code prior to the time the levying officer received the proceeds of the sale or collection.

(e) To the levying officer for the reimbursement of the levying officer's costs for which an advance has not been made.

(f) To the judgment creditor to satisfy the following, in the following order:

(1) First, any costs and interest accruing on the judgment after issuance of the writ pursuant to which the sale or collection is conducted.

(2) Second, the principal amount due on the judgment with costs and interest, as entered on the writ.

(g) To any other judgment creditors who have delivered writs to the levying officer, accompanied by instructions to levy upon the judgment debtor's property or the proceeds of its sale or collection, or any other persons actually known by the levying officer to have a claim, lien, or other interest subordinate to the judgment creditor's lien that is extinguished by the sale and that is not otherwise satisfied pursuant to this section, in the amounts to which they are entitled in order of their respective priorities.

(h) To the judgment debtor in the amount remaining. **Leg.H.** Added Stats 1982 ch 1364 §2, operative July 1, 1983. Amended Stats 2010 ch 4 §2 (AB 680), effective January 1, 2011.

§701.820. Distribution of proceeds; Ex parte application

(a) Promptly after a sale or collection under this title, the levying officer shall distribute the proceeds to the persons entitled thereto or, in cases covered by Section 701.830, deposit the proceeds with the court.

(b) Except as otherwise provided by statute, the proceeds shall be paid to the persons entitled thereto within 30 days after the proceeds are received by the levying officer.

(c) If the proceeds are not received by the levying officer in one payment, the levying officer may accumulate proceeds received during a 30-day period and the accumulated proceeds shall be paid to the persons entitled thereto not later than 10 days after the expiration of the 30-day period.

(d) When proceeds are received by the levying officer in the form of a check or other form of noncash payment that is to be honored upon presentation by the levying officer for payment, the proceeds are not received for the purposes of this section until the check or other form of noncash payment has actually been honored upon presentation for payment.

(e) The provisions of Section 26680 of the Government Code apply to the levying officer only if all of the following conditions are satisfied:

(1) The levying officer has failed to pay the proceeds or deposit them with the court as provided in this article within the time provided in this section.

(2) Upon such failure, a person entitled to any of the proceeds has filed, in person or by certified mail, with the levying officer a written demand for the payment of the proceeds to the persons entitled thereto.

(3) The levying officer has failed within 10 days after the demand is filed to pay to the person filing the demand the proceeds to which that person is entitled.

(f) If all proceeds have not been received within 10 days after the filing of the demand specified by paragraph (3) of subdivision (e), a judgment creditor may file an ex parte application for an order directing the levying officer to show cause why relief should not be granted pursuant to Section 26680 of the Government Code. The order shall name a date and time for the levying officer to appear not less than 20 and not more than 30 days after filing of the application. If the levying officer pays all proceeds as provided in subdivision (e) of Section 701.810 to the judgment creditor no later than 10 days prior to the hearing, the judgment creditor shall notify the court of full payment no later than three days prior to the hearing and the court shall withdraw the order and vacate the hearing.

(g) An ex parte application filed pursuant to subdivision (f) shall state the date and manner of all of the following:

(1) Delivery of the writ of execution to the levying officer.

(2) Remittance of the proceeds to the levying officer.

(3) Filing of the 10-day demand pursuant to subdivision (e).

(h) If the court finds that the facts alleged in the ex parte application filed pursuant to subdivision (f) to be knowingly false, or made in bad faith, the court may award costs and reasonable attorney fees to the levying officer. **Leg.H.** Added Stats 1982 ch 1364 §2, operative July 1, 1983. Amended Stats 2010 ch 4 §3 (AB 680), effective January 1, 2011.

§701.830. Procedure where conflicting claims to proceeds

(a) If there are conflicting claims to all or a portion of the proceeds of sale or collection known to the levying officer before the proceeds are distributed, the levying officer may deposit with the court the proceeds that are the subject of the conflicting claims instead of distributing such proceeds under Section 701.810. Any interested person may apply on noticed motion for an order for the distribution of the proceeds deposited with the court. A copy of the notice of motion shall be served on such persons as the court shall by order determine in such manner as the court prescribes. Any interested person may request time for filing a response to the motion for an order for the distribution of the proceeds, for discovery proceedings in connection with the motion, or for other preparation for the hearing on the motion, and the court shall grant a continuance for a reasonable time for any of these purposes.

(b) Except as provided in subdivision (c), at the hearing on the motion the court shall determine the issues presented by the motion and make an order for the distribution of the proceeds deposited with the court.

(c) The court shall not determine the issues presented by the motion and instead shall abate the hearing until the issues presented by the motion can be determined in a civil action in the following cases if:

(1) The court is not the proper court under any other provision of law for the trial of a civil action with respect to the subject matter of the motion and any interested person at or prior to the hearing objects to the determination of the issues presented by the motion by the court.

(2) A civil action is pending with respect to the subject matter of the motion and jurisdiction has been obtained in the court in which the civil action is pending.

(3) The court determines that the matter should be determined in a civil action. **Leg.H.** Added Stats 1982 ch 1364 §2, operative July 1, 1983.

§702. [Section repealed 1983]

Leg.H. Enacted Stats 1872. Amended Code Amdts 1875–76 ch 84 §1; Stats 1895 ch 184 §1; Stats 1897 ch 44 §1; Stats 1933 ch 911 §1; Stats 1937 ch 175 §1, ch 584 §1; Stats 1963 ch 204 §1. Repealed Stats 1982 ch 1364 §1, operative July 1, 1983. The repealed section related to time limit and amounts to be paid for redemption.

§703. [Section repealed 1983]

Leg.H. Enacted Stats 1872. Amended Code Amdts 1873–74 ch 383 §97; Stats 1895 ch 184 §2; Stats 1897 ch 44 §2; Stats 1933 ch 911 §2; Stats 1957 ch 1865 §10; Stats 1963 ch 204 §2. Repealed Stats 1982 ch 1364 §1, operative July 1, 1983. The repealed section related to subsequent redemptions from redemptioners.

CHAPTER 4
EXEMPTIONS

Article 1. General Provisions.
Article 2. Procedure for Claiming Exemptions After Levy.
Article 3. Exempt Property.
Article 4. Homestead Exemption.
Article 5. Declared Homesteads.

ARTICLE 1
General Provisions

Application of exemptions. §703.010.
Persons entitled to exemptions. §703.020.
Manner of claiming exemptions; Effect of failure to claim. §703.030.
Prior waiver of exemptions. §703.040.
Statutes governing exemptions. §703.050.
Reserved power of state. §703.060.
Application of exemptions where judgment is for child, family or spousal support. §703.070.
Tracing exempt funds. §703.080.
Costs in case of subsequent levy of exempt property. §703.090.
Time for determination of exemptions. §703.100.
Application of exemptions to marital property. §703.110.
Property taken into account in determining exemption. §703.115.
Exemptions in bankruptcy. §703.130.
Election of exemptions if bankruptcy petition is filed. §703.140.
Adjustment of dollar amounts; Publication; Applicability. §703.150.

§703.010. Application of exemptions

Except as otherwise provided by statute:

(a) The exemptions provided by this chapter or by any other statute apply to all procedures for enforcement of a money judgment.

(b) The exemptions provided by this chapter or by any other statute do not apply if the judgment to be enforced is for the foreclosure of a mortgage, deed of trust, or other lien or encumbrance on the property other than a lien created pursuant to this division or pursuant to Title 6.5 (commencing with Section 481.010) (attachment). **Leg.H.** Added Stats 1982 ch 1364 §2, operative July 1, 1983.

§703.020. Persons entitled to exemptions

(a) The exemptions provided by this chapter apply only to property of a natural person.

(b) The exemptions provided in this chapter may be claimed by any of the following persons:

(1) In all cases, by the judgment debtor or a person acting on behalf of the judgment debtor.

(2) In the case of community property, by the spouse of the judgment debtor, whether or not the spouse is also a judgment debtor under the judgment.

(3) In the case of community property, by the domestic partner of the judgment debtor, as defined in Section 297 of the Family Code, whether or not the domestic partner is also a judgment debtor under the judgment. **Leg.H.** Added Stats 1982 ch 1364 §2, operative July 1, 1983. Amended Stats 2014 ch 415 §1 (AB 1945), effective January 1, 2015.

§703.030. Manner of claiming exemptions; Effect of failure to claim

(a) An exemption for property that is described in this chapter or in any other statute as exempt may be claimed within the time and in the manner prescribed in the applicable enforcement procedure. If the exemption is not so claimed, the exemption is waived and the property is subject to enforcement of a money judgment.

(b) Except as otherwise specifically provided by statute, property that is described in this chapter or in any other statute as exempt without making a claim is not subject to any procedure for enforcement of a money judgment.

(c) Nothing in this section limits the authority of the court pursuant to Section 473 to relieve a person upon such terms as may be just from failure to claim an exemption within the time and in the manner prescribed in the applicable enforcement procedure. **Leg.H.** Added Stats 1982 ch 1364 §2, operative July 1, 1983.

§703.040. Prior waiver of exemptions

A purported contractual or other prior waiver of the exemptions provided by this chapter or by any other statute, other than a waiver by failure to claim an exemption required to be claimed or otherwise made at the time enforcement is sought, is against public policy and void. **Leg.H.** Added Stats 1982 ch 1364 §2, operative July 1, 1983.

§703.050. Statutes governing exemptions

(a) The determination whether property is exempt or the amount of an exemption shall be made by application of the exemption statutes in effect (1) at the time the judgment creditor's lien on the property was created or (2) if the judgment creditor's lien on the property is the latest in a series of overlapping liens created when an earlier lien on the property in favor of the judgment creditor was in effect, at the time the earliest lien in the series of overlapping liens was created.

(b) This section applies to all judgments, whether based upon tort, contract, or other legal theory or cause of action that arose before or after the operative date of this section, and whether the judgment was entered before or after the operative date of this section.

(c) Notwithstanding subdivision (a), in the case of a levy of execution, the procedures to be followed in levying upon, selling, or releasing property, claiming, processing, opposing, and determining exemptions, and paying exemption proceeds, shall be governed by the law in effect at the time the levy of execution is made on the property. **Leg.H.** Added Stats 1982 ch 1364 §2, operative July 1, 1983.

§703.060. Reserved power of state

(a) The Legislature finds and declares that generally persons who enter into contracts do not do so in reliance on an assumption that the exemptions in effect at the time of the contract will govern enforcement of any judgment based on the contract, that liens imposed on property are imposed not as a matter of right but as a matter of privilege granted by statute for purposes of priority, that no vested rights with respect to exemptions are created by the making of a contract or imposition of a lien, that application of exemptions and exemption procedures in effect at the time of enforcement of a judgment is essential to the proper balance between the rights of judgment debtors and judgment creditors and has a minimal effect on the economic stability essential for the maintenance of private and public faith in commercial matters, and that it is the policy of the state to treat all judgment debtors equally with respect to exemptions and exemption procedures in effect at the time of enforcement of a money judgment. To this end, the Legislature reserves the right to repeal, alter, or add to the exemptions and the procedures therefor at any time and intends, unless otherwise provided by statute, that any repeals, alterations, or additions apply upon their operative date to enforcement of all money judgments, whether based upon tort, contract, or other legal theory or cause of action that arose before or after the operative date of the repeals, alterations, or additions, whether the judgment was entered before or after the operative date of the repeals, alterations, or additions.

(b) All contracts shall be deemed to have been made and all liens on property shall be deemed to have been created in recognition of the power of the state to repeal, alter, and add to statutes providing for liens and exemptions from the enforcement of money judgments. **Leg.H.** Added Stats 1982 ch 1364 §2, operative July 1, 1983.

§703.070. Application of exemptions where judgment is for child, family or spousal support

Except as otherwise provided by statute:

(a) The exemptions provided by this chapter or by any other statute apply to a judgment for child, family, or spousal support.

(b) If property is exempt without making a claim, the property is not subject to being applied to the satisfaction of a judgment for child, family, or spousal support.

(c) Except as provided in subdivision (b), if property sought to be applied to the satisfaction of a judgment for child, family, or spousal support is shown to be exempt under subdivision (a) in appropriate proceedings, the court shall, upon noticed motion of the judgment creditor, determine the extent to which the exempt property nevertheless shall be applied to the satisfaction of the judgment. In making this determination, the court shall take into account the needs of the judgment creditor, the needs of the judgment debtor and all the persons the judgment debtor is required to support, and all other relevant circumstances. The court shall effectuate its determination by an order specifying the extent to which the otherwise exempt property is to be applied to the satisfaction of the judgment. **Leg.H.** Added Stats 1982 ch 1364 §2, operative July 1, 1983. Amended Stats 1992 ch 163 §37 (AB 2641), operative January 1, 1994.

§703.080. Tracing exempt funds

(a) Subject to any limitation provided in the particular exemption, a fund that is exempt remains exempt to the extent that it can be traced into deposit accounts or in the form of cash or its equivalent.

(b) The exemption claimant has the burden of tracing an exempt fund.

(c) The tracing of exempt funds in a deposit account shall be by application of the lowest intermediate balance principle unless the exemption claimant or the judgment creditor shows that some other method of tracing would better serve the interests of justice and equity under the circumstances of the case. **Leg.H.** Added Stats 1982 ch 1364 §2, operative July 1, 1983.

§703.090. Costs in case of subsequent levy of exempt property

If a judgment creditor has failed to oppose a claim of exemption within the time allowed by Section 703.550 or if property has been determined by a court to be exempt, and the judgment creditor thereafter levies upon or otherwise seeks to apply the property toward the satisfaction of the same money judgment, the judgment creditor is not entitled to recover the subsequent costs of collection unless the property is applied to satisfaction of the judgment. **Leg.H.** Added Stats 1982 ch 1364 §2, operative July 1, 1983.

§703.100. Time for determination of exemptions

(a) Subject to subdivision (b), the determination whether property is exempt shall be made under the circumstances existing at the earliest of the following times:

(1) The time of levy on the property.

(2) The time of the commencement of court proceedings for the application of the property to the satisfaction of the money judgment.

(3) The time a lien is created under Title 6.5 (commencing with Section 481.010) (attachment) or under this title.

(b) The court, in its discretion, may take into consideration any of the following changes that have occurred between the time of levy or commencement of enforcement proceedings or creation of the lien and the time of the hearing:

(1) A change in the use of the property if the exemption is based upon the use of property and if the property was used for the exempt purpose at the time of the levy or the commencement of enforcement proceedings or the creation of the lien but is used for a nonexempt purpose at the time of the hearing.

(2) A change in the value of the property if the exemption is based upon the value of property.

(3) A change in the financial circumstances of the judgment debtor and spouse and dependents of the judgment debtor if the exemption is based upon their needs. **Leg.H.** Added Stats 1982 ch 1364 §2, operative July 1, 1983.

§703.110. Application of exemptions to marital property

If the judgment debtor is married:

(a) The exemptions provided by this chapter or by any other statute apply to all property that is subject to enforcement of a money judgment, including the interest of the spouse of the judgment debtor in community property. The fact that one or both spouses are judgment debtors under the judgment or that property sought to be applied to the satisfaction of the judgment is separate or community does not increase or reduce the number or amount of the exemptions. Where the property exempt under a particular exemption is limited to a specified maximum dollar amount, unless the exemption provision specifically provides otherwise, the two spouses together are entitled to one exemption limited to the specified maximum dollar amount, whether one or both of the spouses are judgment debtors under the judgment and whether the property sought to be applied to the satisfaction of the judgment is separate or community.

(b) If an exemption is required by statute to be applied first to property not before the court and then to property before the court, the application of the exemption to property not before the court shall be made to the community property and separate property of both spouses, whether or not such property is subject to enforcement of the money judgment.

(c) If the same exemption is claimed by the judgment debtor and the spouse of the judgment debtor for different property, and the property claimed by one spouse, but not both, is exempt, the exemption shall be applied as the spouses agree. If the spouses are unable to agree, the exemption shall be applied as directed by the court in its discretion. **Leg.H.** Added Stats 1982 ch 1364 §2, operative July 1, 1983. Amended Stats 1983 ch 155 §14.7, effective June 30, 1983, operative July 1, 1983.

§703.115. Property taken into account in determining exemption

In determining an exemption based upon the needs of the judgment debtor and the spouse and dependents of the judgment debtor or an exemption based upon the needs of the judgment debtor and the family of the judgment debtor, the court shall take into account all property of the judgment debtor and, to the extent the judgment debtor has a spouse and dependents or family, all property of such spouse and dependents or family, including community property and separate property of the spouse, whether or not such property is subject to enforcement of the money judgment. **Leg.H.** Added Stats 1983 ch 155 §15, effective June 30, 1983, operative July 1, 1983.

§703.120. [Section repealed 2014]

Leg.H. Added Stats 1982 ch 1364 §2, operative July 1, 1983. Repealed Stats 2013 ch 15 §2 (AB 567), effective January 1, 2014. The repealed section related to continuing review of exemptions. See CCP §681.035.

§703.130. Exemptions in bankruptcy

Pursuant to the authority of paragraph (2) of subsection (b) of Section 522 of Title 11 of the United States Code, the exemptions set forth in subsection (d) of Section 522 of Title 11 of the United States Code (Bankruptcy) are not authorized in this state. **Leg.H.** Added Stats 1984 ch 218 §1.5. Amended Stats 2009 ch 500 §14 (AB 1059), effective January 1, 2010.

Prior Law: Former CCP §703.130, similar to the present section, was added Stats 1982 ch 1354 §2, operative July 1, 1983, and repealed Stats 1984 ch 218 §1.

§703.140. Election of exemptions if bankruptcy petition is filed

(a) In a case under Title 11 of the United States Code, all of the exemptions provided by this chapter, including the homestead exemption, other than the provisions of subdivision (b) are applicable regardless of whether there is a money judgment against the debtor or whether a money judgment is being enforced by execution sale or any other procedure, but the exemptions provided by subdivision (b) may be elected in lieu of all other exemptions provided by this chapter, as follows:

(1) If spouses are joined in the petition, they jointly may elect to utilize the applicable exemption provisions of this chapter other than the provisions of subdivision (b), or to utilize the applicable exemptions set forth in subdivision (b), but not both.

(2)(A) If the petition is filed individually, and not jointly, for a spouse, the exemptions provided by this chapter other than the provisions of subdivision (b) are applicable, except that, if both of the spouses effectively waive in writing the right to claim, during the period the case commenced by filing the petition is pending, the exemptions provided by the applicable exemption provisions of this chapter, other than subdivision (b), in any case commenced by filing a petition for either of them under Title 11 of the United States Code, then they may elect to instead utilize the applicable exemptions set forth in subdivision (b).

(B) Notwithstanding subparagraph (A), a waiver is not required from a debtor who is living separate and apart from their spouse as of the date the petition commencing the case under Title 11 of the United States Code is filed, unless, on the petition date, the debtor and the debtor's spouse shared an ownership interest in property that could be exempted as a homestead under Article 4 of this chapter.

(3) If the petition is filed for an unmarried person, that person may elect to utilize the applicable exemption provisions of this chapter other than subdivision (b), or to utilize the applicable exemptions set forth in subdivision (b), but not both.

(b) The following exemptions may be elected as provided in subdivision (a):

(1) The debtor's aggregate interest, not to exceed twenty-nine thousand two hundred seventy-five dollars ($29,275) in value, in real property or personal property that the debtor or a dependent of the debtor uses as a residence, in a cooperative that owns property that the debtor or a dependent of the debtor uses as a residence.

(2) The debtor's interest, not to exceed seven thousand five hundred dollars ($7,500) in value, in one or more motor vehicles.

(3) The debtor's interest, not to exceed seven hundred twenty-five dollars ($725) in value in any particular item, in household furnishings, household goods, wearing apparel, appliances, books, animals, crops, or musical instruments, that are held primarily for the personal, family, or household use of the debtor or a dependent of the debtor.

(4) The debtor's aggregate interest, not to exceed one thousand seven hundred fifty dollars ($1,750) in value, in jewelry held primarily for the personal, family, or household use of the debtor or a dependent of the debtor.

(5) The debtor's aggregate interest, not to exceed one thousand five hundred fifty dollars ($1,550) in value, plus any unused amount of the exemption provided under paragraph (1), in any property.

(6) The debtor's aggregate interest, not to exceed eight thousand seven hundred twenty-five dollars ($8,725) in value, in any implements, professional books, or tools of the trade of the debtor or the trade of a dependent of the debtor.

(7) Any unmatured life insurance contract owned by the debtor, other than a credit life insurance contract.

(8) The debtor's aggregate interest, not to exceed fifteen thousand six hundred fifty dollars ($15,650) in value, in any accrued dividend or interest under, or loan value of, any unmatured life insurance contract owned by the debtor under which the insured is the debtor or an individual of whom the debtor is a dependent.

(9) Professionally prescribed health aids for the debtor, the debtor's spouse, or a dependent of the debtor, including vehicles converted for use by the debtor, the debtor's spouse, or a dependent of the debtor, who has a disability. Conversion of a vehicle for use by a person who has a disability includes altering the interior, installing steering, a wheelchair lift, or motorized steps, or modifying the operation of the vehicle.

(10) The debtor's right to receive any of the following:

(A) A social security benefit, unemployment compensation, or a local public assistance benefit.

(B) A veterans' benefit.

(C) A disability, illness, or unemployment benefit.

(D) Alimony, support, or separate maintenance, to the extent reasonably necessary for the support of the debtor and any dependent of the debtor.

(E) A payment under a stock bonus, pension, profit-sharing, annuity, or similar plan or contract on account of illness, disability, death, age, or length of service, to the extent reasonably necessary for the support of the debtor and any dependent of the debtor, unless all of the following apply:

(i) That plan or contract was established by or under the auspices of an insider that employed the debtor at the time the debtor's rights under the plan or contract arose.

(ii) The payment is on account of age or length of service.

(iii) That plan or contract does not qualify under Section 401(a), 403(a), 403(b), 408, or 408A of the Internal Revenue Code of 1986.

(F) The aggregate interest, not to exceed seven thousand five hundred dollars ($7,500), in vacation credits or accrued, or unused, vacation pay, sick leave, family leave, or wages, as defined in **Section 200 of the Labor Code.**

(11) The debtor's right to receive, or property that is traceable to, any of the following:

(A) An award under a crime victim's reparation law.

(B) A payment under a settlement agreement arising out of or regarding the debtor's employment, to the extent reasonably necessary for the support of the debtor, the debtor's spouse, or a dependent of the debtor.

(C) A payment on account of the wrongful death of an individual of whom the debtor was a dependent, to the extent reasonably necessary for the support of the debtor and any dependent of the debtor.

(D) A payment under a life insurance contract that insured the life of an individual of whom the debtor was a spouse or dependent on the date of that individual's death, to the extent reasonably necessary for the support of the debtor and any dependent of the debtor.

(E) A payment, not to exceed twenty-nine thousand two hundred seventy-five dollars ($29,275) on account of personal bodily injury of the debtor, the debtor's spouse, or an individual of whom the debtor is a dependent.

(F) A payment in compensation of loss of future earnings of the debtor or an individual of whom the debtor is or was a spouse or dependent, to the extent reasonably necessary for the support of the debtor and the debtor's spouse or a dependent of the debtor.

(12) Money held in an account owned by the judgment debtor and established pursuant to the Golden State Scholarshare Trust Act (Article 19 (commencing with Section 69980) of Chapter 2 of Part 42 of Division 5 of Title 3 of the Education Code), subject to the following limits:

(A) The amount exempted for contributions to an account during the 365-day period prior to the date of filing of the debtor's petition for bankruptcy, in the aggregate during this period, shall not exceed the amount of the annual gift tax exclusion under Section 2503(b) of the Internal Revenue Code of 1986, as amended, in effect at the time of the filing of the debtor's petition for bankruptcy.

(B) The amount exempted for contributions to an account during the period commencing 730 days prior to and ending 366 days prior to the date of filing of the debtor's petition for bankruptcy, in the aggregate during this period, shall not exceed the amount of the annual gift tax exclusion under Section 2503(b) of the Internal Revenue Code of 1986, as amended, in effect at the time of the filing of the debtor's petition for bankruptcy.

(C) For the purposes of this paragraph, "account" includes all accounts having the same beneficiary.

(D) This paragraph is not subject to the requirements of Section 703.150.

(c) In a case under Title 11 of the United States Code, the value of the property claimed as exempt and the debtor's exemptions provided by this chapter with respect to such property shall be determined as of the date the bankruptcy petition is filed. In a case where the debtor's equity in a residence is less than or equal to the amount of the debtor's allowed homestead exemption as of the date the bankruptcy petition is filed, any appreciation in the value of the debtor's interest in the property during the pendency of the case is exempt. **Leg.H.** Added Stats 1984 ch 218 §2. Amended Stats 1993 ch 1111 §1 (SB 651), effective October 10, 1993; Stats 1995 ch 196 §1 (SB 832), effective July 31, 1995; Stats 1999 ch 98 §1 (SB 469); Stats 2000 ch 135 §15 (AB 2539); Stats 2001 ch 42 §1 (AB 1704); Stats 2003 ch 379 §3 (AB 182); Stats 2012 ch 678 §1 (AB 929), effective January 1, 2013; Stats 2016 ch 50 §16 (SB 1005), effective January 1, 2017; Stats 2020 ch 81 §1 (SB 898), effective January 1, 2021; Stats 2021 ch 124 §10 (AB 938), effective January 1, 2022; Stats 2022 ch 25 §1 (SB 956), effective January 1, 2023; Stats 2022 ch 716 §2.5 (SB 1099), effective January 1, 2023 (ch 716 prevails).

2016 Note: For legislative intent, see the 2016 Note following CCP §17.

1993 Note: The Legislature finds and declares that the amendment of Section 703.140 of the Code of Civil Procedure by Section 1 of this act pertaining to exemptions in bankruptcy is not a change in, but is declaratory of, existing law. The Legislature further finds and declares that the decision in *In re Pladson*, 154 B.R. 305 (N.D. Cal. 1993), holding that the homestead exemption is not available in bankruptcy, is not a correct interpretation of California law. The Enforcement of Judgments Law provides exemptions for various forms of property, including homesteads, and contains a number of special procedural protections for special forms of property. It is not, and never has been, the intention of the Legislature to restrict any of the exemptions in bankruptcy because of technical language concerning the procedures for claiming exemptions in state money judgment enforcement proceedings under the Enforcement of Judgments Law. See, e.g., Tentative Recommendation Proposing the Enforcement of Judgments Law, 15 Cal. L. Revision Comm'n Reports 2001, 2095-96 (1980); 1982 Creditors' Remedies Legislation, 16 Cal. L. Revision Comm'n Reports 1001, 1098-99 (1982). Stats 1993 ch 1111 §2.

§703.150. Adjustment of dollar amounts; Publication; Applicability

(a) On April 1, 2004, and at each three-year interval ending on April 1 thereafter, the dollar amounts of exemptions provided in subdivision (b) of Section 703.140 in effect immediately before that date shall be adjusted as provided in subdivision (d).

(b) On April 1, 2007, and at each three-year interval ending on April 1 thereafter, the dollar amounts of exemptions provided in Article 3 (commencing with Section 704.010) in effect immediately before that date shall be adjusted as provided in subdivision (d).

(c) On April 1, 2022, and at each three-year interval ending on April 1 thereafter, the dollar amount set forth in paragraph (7) of subdivision (b) of Section 699.730 in effect immediately before that date shall be adjusted as provided in subdivision (d).

(d) The Judicial Council shall determine the amount of the adjustment based on the change in the annual California Consumer Price Index for All Urban Consumers, published by the Department of Industrial Relations, [1] for the most recent three-year period ending on December 31 preceding the adjustment, with each adjusted amount rounded to the nearest twenty-five dollars ($25).

(e) Beginning April 1, 2004, the Judicial Council shall publish a list of the current dollar amounts of exemptions provided in subdivision (b) of Section 703.140 and in Article 3 (commencing with Section 704.010), and the dollar amount set forth in paragraph (7) of subdivision (b) of Section 699.730, together with the date of the next scheduled adjustment.

(f) Adjustments made under subdivision (a) do not apply with respect to cases commenced before the date of the adjustment, subject to any contrary rule applicable under the federal Bankruptcy Code. The applicability of adjustments made under subdivisions (b), (c), and (d) is governed by Section 703.050. **Leg.H.** Added Stats 2003 ch 379 §4 (AB 182). Amended Stats 2009 ch 499 §1 (AB 1046), effective January 1, 2010; Stats 2010 ch 212 §1 (AB 2767), effective January 1, 2011; Stats 2012 ch 678 §2 (AB 929), effective January 1, 2013; Stats 2020 ch 218 §2 (AB 2463), effective January 1, 2021; Stats 2023 ch 478 §14 (AB 1756), effective January 1, 2024; Stats 2024 ch 80 §23 (SB 1525), effective January 1, 2025.

§703.150. 2024 Deletes. [1] Division of Labor Statistics.

Editor's Note: The Judicial Council updated the exemption amounts effective April 1, 2019.

Exemptions Under Section 703.140(b)

The following lists the current dollar amounts of exemptions from enforcement of judgment under Code of Civil Procedure section 703.140(b).

These amounts are effective April 1, 2019. Unless otherwise provided by statute after that date, they will be adjusted at each three-year interval, ending on March 31. The amount of the adjustment to the prior amounts is based on the change in the annual California Consumer Price Index for All Urban Consumers for the most recent three-year period ending on the preceding December 31, with each adjusted amount rounded to the nearest $25. (See Code Civ. Proc., § 703.150(d).)

Code Civ. Proc., §703.140(b)	Type of Property	Amount of Exemption
(1)	The debtor's aggregate interest in real property or personal property that the debtor or a dependent of the debtor uses as a residence, or in	$ 31,950

(2)	The debtor's interest in one or more motor vehicles	$ 6,375
(3)	The debtor's interest in household furnishings, household goods, wearing apparel, appliances, books, animals, crops, or musical instruments, that are held primarily for the personal, family, or household use of the debtor or a dependent of the debtor (value is of any particular item)	$ 800
(4)	The debtor's aggregate interest in jewelry held primarily for the personal, family, or household use of the debtor or a dependent of the debtor	$ 1,900
(5)	The debtor's aggregate interest, plus any unused amount of the exemption provided under paragraph (1), in any property	$ 1,700
(6)	The debtor's aggregate interest in any implements, professional books, or tools of the trade of the debtor or the trade of a dependent of the debtor	$ 9,525
(8)	The debtor's aggregate interest in any accrued dividend or interest under, or loan value of, any unmatured life insurance contract owned by the debtor under which the insured is the debtor or an individual of whom the debtor is a dependent	$ 17,075
7,075(11)(D)	The debtor's right to receive, or property traceable to, a payment on account of personal bodily injury of the debtor or an individual of whom the debtor is a dependent	$ 31,950

Exemptions Under Section 704.010 et seq.

The following lists the current dollar amounts of exemptions from enforcement of judgment under title 9, division 2, chapter 4, article 3 (commencing with section 704.010) of the Code of Civil Procedure.

These amounts are effective April 1, 2019. Unless otherwise provided by statute after that date, they will be adjusted at each three-year interval, ending on March 31. The amount of the adjustment to the prior amounts is based on the change in the annual California Consumer Price Index for All Urban Consumers for the most recent three-year period ending on the preceding December 31, with each adjusted amount rounded to the nearest $25. (See Code Civ. Proc., § 703.150(d).)

Code Civ. Proc. Section	Type of Property	Amount of Exemption
704.010	Motor vehicle (any combination of aggregate equity, proceeds of execution sale, and proceeds of insurance or other indemnification for loss, damage, or destruction)	$ 3,625
704.030	Material to be applied to repair or maintenance of residence	$ 3,825
704.040	Jewelry, heirlooms, art	$ 9,525
704.060	Personal property used in debtor's or debtor's spouse's trade, business, or profession (amount of exemption for commercial motor vehicle not to exceed $4,850)	$ 9,525
704.060	Personal property used in debtor's and spouse's common trade, business, or profession (amount of exemption for commercial motor vehicle not to exceed $9,700)	$ 19,050
704.080	Deposit account with direct payment of social security or public benefits (exemption without claim, section 704.080(b)) [1]	$ 1,947[3]
	• Public benefits, one depositor is designated payee	$ 1,900
	• Social security benefits, one depositor is designated payee	$ 3,825
	• Public benefits, two or more depositors are designated payees [2]	$ 2,825
	• Social security benefits, two or more depositors are designated payees [2]	$ 5,725
704.090	Inmate trust account	$ 1,900
	Inmate trust account (restitution fine or order)	$ 325[4]
704.100	Aggregate loan value of unmatured life insurance policies	$ 15,350

[1] The amount of a deposit account that exceeds exemption amounts is also exempt to the extent it consists of payments of public benefits or social security benefits. (Code Civ. Proc., § 704.080(c).)

[2] If only one joint payee is a beneficiary of the payment, the exemption is in the amount available to a single designated payee. (Code Civ. Proc., § 704.080(b)(3) and (4).)

[3] This amount is not subject to adjustments under Code Civ. Proc., § 703.150.

ARTICLE 2
Procedure for Claiming Exemptions After Levy

Application of article. §703.510.
Claim of exemption. §703.520.
Financial statement. §703.530.
Notice of claim of exemption. §703.540.
Opposition to exemption claim; Release. §703.550.
Contents of notice of opposition. §703.560.
Notice of hearing on motion. §703.570.
Hearing and order. §703.580.
Extension of time. §703.590.
Appeal. §703.600.
Disposition of property during pendency of proceedings. §703.610.

§703.510. Application of article

(a) Except as otherwise provided by statute, property that has been levied upon may be claimed to be exempt as provided in this article.

(b) If property **in a deposit account** that is exempt without making a claim, **as described in subdivision (b) of Section 704.080 or subdivision (a) of Section 704.220,** is levied upon, [1] **the property shall be released by the financial institution holding the judgment debtor's deposit account within five business days of the financial institution receiving written notice from the judgment debtor setting forth the facts supporting the exemption without the necessity of making a claim under this title. The judgment debtor's written notice to the financial institution shall be served via first-class mail on the judgment creditor or judgment creditor's attorney of record within five business days of notice being sent by the judgment debtor to the financial institution. The written notice shall be addressed to the financial institution identified pursuant to subdivision (c) or (d) of Section 684.110.**

(c) **If property that is exempt without making a claim is levied upon, other than the property in a deposit account described in subdivision (b), the property may be released pursuant to the exemption procedure provided in this article. Leg.H.** Added Stats 1982 ch 1364 §2, operative July 1, 1983. Amended Stats 2024 ch 514 §3 (AB 2837), effective January 1, 2025.

§703.510. 2024 Deletes. [1] it may be released pursuant to the exemption procedure provided in this article.

§703.520. Claim of exemption

(a) The claimant may make a claim of exemption by filing with the levying officer, either in person or by mail, a claim of exemption together with a copy of the claim. If the claimant is personally served, the claim shall be made within 15 days after the date the notice of levy on the property claimed to be exempt is served on the judgment debtor. If the claimant is served by mail, the claim shall be made within 20 days after the date the notice of levy on the property claimed to be exempt is served on the judgment debtor. If the claim is filed by mail and assigned a tracking number by the United States Postal Service or another common carrier, the filing shall be deemed complete on the date the claim is postmarked. If the claim is filed by mail and not assigned a tracking number, the filing shall be deemed complete on the date the claim is received by the levying officer.

(b) The claim of exemption shall be executed under oath and shall include all of the following:

(1) The name of the claimant and the mailing address where service of a notice of opposition to the claim may be made upon the claimant.

(2) The name and last known address of the judgment debtor if the claimant is not the judgment debtor.

(3) A description of the property claimed to be exempt. If an exemption is claimed pursuant to Section 704.010 or 704.060, the claimant shall describe all other property of the same type, including exempt proceeds of the property of the same type, owned by the judgment debtor alone or in combination with others on the date of levy and identify the property, whether or not levied upon, to which the exemption is to be applied. If an exemption is claimed pursuant to subdivision (b) of Section 704.100, the claimant shall state the nature and amount of all other property of the same type owned by the judgment debtor or the spouse of the judgment debtor alone or in combination with others on the date of levy.

(4) A financial statement if required by Section 703.530.

(5) A citation of the provision of this chapter or other statute upon which the claim is based.

(6) A statement of the facts necessary to support the claim.

(c) This section shall become operative on September 1, 2020. **Leg.H.** Added Stats 2019 ch 552 §4 (SB 616), effective January 1, 2020, operative September 1, 2020.

Prior Law: Former CCP §703.520, similar to the present section, was added Stats 1982 ch 1364 §2, operative July 1, 1983, amended Stats 2019 ch 552 §3 (SB 616), effective January 1, 2020, inoperative September 21, 2020, and repealed January 1, 2021, by its own terms.

§703.530. Financial statement

(a) If property is claimed as exempt pursuant to a provision exempting property to the extent necessary for the support of the judgment debtor and the spouse and dependents of the judgment debtor, the claim of exemption shall include a financial statement.

(b) The financial statement shall include all of the following information:

(1) The name of the spouse of the judgment debtor.

(2) The name, age, and relationship of all persons dependent upon the judgment debtor or the spouse of the judgment debtor for support.

(3) All sources and the amounts of earnings and other income of the judgment debtor and the spouse and dependents of the judgment debtor.

(4) A list of the assets of the judgment debtor and the spouse and dependents of the judgment debtor and the value of such assets.

(5) All outstanding obligations of the judgment debtor and the spouse and dependents of the judgment debtor.

(c) The financial statement shall be executed under oath by the judgment debtor and, unless the spouses are living separate and apart, by the spouse of the judgment debtor. **Leg.H.** Added Stats 1982 ch 1364 §2, operative July 1, 1983.

§703.540. Notice of claim of exemption

Promptly after the filing of the claim of exemption, the levying officer shall serve both of the following on the judgment creditor personally or by mail:

(a) A copy of the claim of exemption.

(b) A notice of claim of exemption stating that the claim of exemption has been made and that the levying officer will release the property unless, within the time allowed as specified in the notice, both of the following are filed with the levying officer:

(1) A copy of the notice of opposition to the claim of exemption.

(2) A copy of the notice of motion for an order determining the claim of exemption. **Leg.H.** Added Stats 1982 ch 1364 §2, operative July 1, 1983.

§703.550. Opposition to exemption claim; Release

(a) Within 15 days after service of the notice of claim of exemption, a judgment creditor who opposes the claim of exemption shall file with the court a notice of opposition to the claim of exemption and a notice of motion for an order determining the claim of exemption and shall file with the levying officer a copy of the notice of opposition and a copy of the notice of motion. Upon the filing of the copies of the notice of opposition and notice of motion, the levying officer shall promptly file the claim of exemption with the court. If copies of the notice of opposition and notice of motion are not filed with the levying officer within the time allowed, the levying officer shall immediately release the property to the extent it is claimed to be exempt.

(b) This section shall become operative on September 1, 2020. **Leg.H.** Added Stats 2019 ch 552 §6 (SB 616), effective January 1, 2020, operative September 1, 2020.

Prior Law: Former CCP §703.550, similar to the present section, was added Stats 1982 ch 1364 §2, operative July 1, 1983, amended Stats 2019 ch 552 §5 (SB 616), effective January 1, 2020, inoperative September 21, 2020, and repealed January 1, 2021, by its own terms.

§703.560. Contents of notice of opposition

The notice of opposition to the claim of exemption shall be executed under oath and shall include both of the following:

(a) An allegation either (1) that the property is not exempt under the provision of this chapter or other statute relied upon or (2) that the equity in the property claimed to be exempt is in excess of the amount provided in the applicable exemption.

(b) A statement of the facts necessary to support the allegation. **Leg.H.** Added Stats 1982 ch 1364 §2, operative July 1, 1983.

§703.570. Notice of hearing on motion

(a) The hearing on the motion shall be held not later than 30 days from the date the notice of motion was filed with the court unless continued by the court for good cause. **Where the judgment upon which the writ is issued is for personal debt, as defined in subdivision (d) of Section 683.110, if the hearing is delayed by the court and cannot be set within 30 days of notice of the motion, a party may seek by ex parte application, and the court shall issue, an order staying any levy or garnishment with respect to the property subject to the claim of exemption until the hearing occurs.**

(b) Not less than 10 days prior to the hearing, the judgment creditor shall serve a notice of the hearing and a copy of the notice of opposition to the claim of exemption on the claimant and on the judgment debtor, if other than the claimant. Service shall be made personally or by mail. **Leg.H.** Added Stats 1982 ch 1364 §2, operative July 1, 1983. Amended Stats 2012 ch 484 §12 (AB 2364), effective January 1, 2013; Stats 2024 ch 514 §4 (AB 2837), effective January 1, 2025.

§703.580. Hearing and order

(a) The claim of exemption and notice of opposition to the claim of exemption [1] **do not constitute an appearance pursuant to Section 1014. The** power of the court [2] **over the exemption claimant is limited to determining the claim of exemption**.

(b) At a hearing under this section, the exemption claimant has the burden of proof.

(c) The claim of exemption is deemed controverted by the notice of opposition to the claim of exemption and both shall be received in evidence. If no other evidence is offered, the court, if satisfied that sufficient facts are shown by the claim of exemption (including the financial statement if one is required) and the notice of opposition, may make its determination thereon. If **a claim of exemption asserts that money in a judgment debtor's deposit account is or was necessary for the support of the judgment debtor and the spouse and dependents of the judgment debtor as provided in Section 704.225, the court shall review the judgment debtor's financial statement and make findings thereon. If** not satisfied, the court [3] **may** order the hearing continued for the production of other evidence, oral or documentary.

(d) At the conclusion of the hearing, the court shall determine by order whether or not the property is exempt in whole or in part. [4]

(1) Subject to Section 703.600, the order is determinative of the right of the judgment creditor to apply the property to the satisfaction of the judgment.

(2) **Where the judgment upon which the writ is issued is for personal debt, as defined in subdivision (d) of Section 683.110, the court shall order the return of any property that was exempt without the need for a claim and that was levied upon within the 12 months preceding the date of the order on the claim of exemption. This paragraph does not limit a judge's authority to order, for good cause, the return of any exempt property taken more than 12 months preceding the date of the order on the claim of exemption.**

(3) **Where the judgment upon which the writ is issued is for personal debt, as defined in subdivision (d) of Section 683.110, the court shall order the return of any property that the debtor has demonstrated would have been exempt by claim of exemption and that was levied upon within the six months preceding the date of the order on the claim of exemption. This paragraph does not limit a judge's authority to order, for good cause, the return of any exempt property taken more than six months preceding the date of the order on the claim of exemption.**

(4) **If property is exempt without the need for a claim under this title or as a result of a claim of exemption, the court shall order the**

return of the exempt property from the levying officer, judgment creditor, or other person who is in possession of the property, to the judgment debtor. A levying officer shall return the exempt property within 20 business days of receipt of notice of the order. A judgment creditor shall return the exempt property within 10 business days of entry of the order.

(e) The court clerk shall promptly transmit a certified copy of the order to the levying officer. Subject to Section 703.610, the levying officer shall, in compliance with the order, release the property or apply the property to the satisfaction of the money judgment.

(f) Unless otherwise ordered by the court, if an exemption is not determined within the time provided by Section 703.570, the property claimed to be exempt shall be released. **Leg.H.** Added Stats 1982 ch 1364 §2, operative July 1, 1983. Amended Stats 2002 ch 68 §5 (SB 1322); Stats 2024 ch 229 §1 (AB 3283), effective January 1, 2025; Stats 2024 ch 514 §5.5 (AB 2837), effective January 1, 2025 (ch 514 prevails).

§703.580. 2024 Deletes. [1] constitute the pleadings, subject to the [2] to permit amendments in the interest of justice [3] shall [4] Subject to Section 703.600, the order is determinative of the right of the judgment creditor to apply the property to the satisfaction of the judgment. No findings are required in a proceeding under this section.

§703.590. Extension of time

If the court extends the time allowed for an act to be done under this article, written notice of the extension shall be filed with the levying officer and, unless notice is waived, shall be served promptly on the opposing party. Service shall be made personally or by mail. **Leg.H.** Added Stats 1982 ch 1364 §2, operative July 1, 1983.

§703.600. Appeal

An appeal lies from any order made under this article. **Leg.H.** Added Stats 1982 ch 1364 §2, operative July 1, 1983. Amended Stats 1998 ch 931 §93 (SB 2139), effective September 28, 1998.

§703.610. Disposition of property during pendency of proceedings

(a) Except as otherwise provided by statute or ordered by the court, the levying officer shall not release, sell, or otherwise dispose of the property for which an exemption is claimed until an appeal is waived, the time to file an appeal has expired, or the exemption is finally determined.

(b) At any time while the exemption proceedings are pending, upon motion of the judgment creditor or a claimant, or upon its own motion, the court may make any orders for disposition of the property that may be proper under the circumstances of the case, **except that such order may not require the release to the judgment creditor of property that would be exempt without a claim of exemption**. The order may be modified or vacated by the court at any time during the pendency of the exemption proceedings upon any terms that are just, **except that such order may not require the release to the judgment creditor of property that would be exempt without a claim of exemption**.

(c) If an appeal of the determination of a claim of exemption is taken, notice of the appeal shall be given to the levying officer and the levying officer shall hold, release, or dispose of the property in accordance with the provisions governing enforcement and stay of enforcement of money judgments pending appeal. **Where the judgment upon which the writ is issued is for personal debt, as defined in subdivision (d) of Section 683.110, if an earnings withholding order has been served upon the judgment debtor's employer, notice of the appeal shall also be given to the judgment debtor's employer who shall, upon receipt of the notice, immediately suspend any further garnishment of the judgment debtor's wages for the pendency of the appeal and until ordered by the court to resume garnishment. Leg.H.** Added Stats 1982 ch 1364 §2, operative July 1, 1983. Amended Stats 2002 ch 68 §6 (SB 1322); Stats 2024 ch 514 §6 (AB 2837), effective January 1, 2025.

§704. [Section repealed 1983]

Leg.H. Enacted Stats 1872. Repealed Stats 1982 ch 1364 §1, operative July 1, 1983. The repealed section related to procedure for making redemption payments.

ARTICLE 3
Exempt Property

Motor vehicles. §704.010.
Household furnishings and personal effects. §704.020.
Materials for repair or improvement of residence. §704.030.
Jewelry, heirlooms, works of art. §704.040.
Health aids. §704.050.
Personal property used in trade, business, or profession. §704.060.
Paid earnings. §704.070.
Deposit account in which public benefits or social security benefits are directly deposited. §704.080.
Inmate's trust account. §704.090.
Life insurance policies. §704.100.
Money held in an account established pursuant to the Golden State Scholarshare Trust Act. § 704.105.
Public retirement and related benefits and contributions. §704.110.
Alimony, support, and separate maintenance. § 704.111.
Public employee vacation credits. §704.113.
Compliance with order of earnings assignment. §704.114.
Private retirement and related benefits and contributions. §704.115.
Unemployment benefits and contributions; Strike benefits. §704.120.
Disability and health benefits. §704.130.
Damages for personal injury. §704.140.
Damages for wrongful death. §704.150.
Workers' compensation; Exceptions. §704.160.
Aid provided to needy persons. §704.170.
Relocation benefits. §704.180.
Financial aid provided to student by educational institution. §704.190.
Cemetery plot. §704.200.
Property not subject to enforcement of money judgment. §704.210.
Money in judgment debtor's deposit account; Levy requirements. §704.220.
Money exempt to support spouse and dependents. §704.225.
Money from Federal Emergency Management Agency (FEMA). §704.230.
Exemption of HOPE trust account payments from levy. § 704.235.

§704.010. Motor vehicles

(a) Any combination of the following is exempt in the amount of seven thousand five hundred dollars ($7,500):

(1) The aggregate equity in motor vehicles.

(2) The proceeds of an execution sale of a motor vehicle.

(3) The proceeds of insurance or other indemnification for the loss, damage, or destruction of a motor vehicle.

(b) Proceeds exempt under subdivision (a) are exempt for a period of 90 days after the time the proceeds are actually received by the judgment debtor.

(c) For the purpose of determining the equity, the fair market value of a motor vehicle shall be determined by reference to used car price guides customarily used by California automobile dealers unless the motor vehicle is not listed in such price guides.

(d) If the judgment debtor has only one motor vehicle and it is sold at an execution sale, the proceeds of the execution sale are exempt in the amount of seven thousand five hundred dollars ($7,500) without making a claim. The levying officer shall consult and may rely upon the records of the Department of Motor Vehicles in determining whether the judgment debtor has only one motor vehicle. In the case covered by this subdivision, the exemption provided by subdivision (a) is not available. **Leg.H.** Added Stats 1982 ch 1364 §2, operative July 1, 1983. Amended Stats 1995 ch 196 §2 (SB 832), effective July 31, 1995; Stats 2003 ch 379 §5 (AB 182); Stats 2020 ch 81 §2 (SB 898), effective January 1, 2021; Stats 2022 ch 716 §3 (SB 1099), effective January 1, 2023.

§704.020. Household furnishings and personal effects

(a) Household furnishings, appliances, provisions, wearing apparel, and other personal effects are exempt in the following cases:

(1) If ordinarily and reasonably necessary to, and personally used or procured for use by, the judgment debtor and members of the judgment debtor's family at the judgment debtor's principal place of residence.

(2) Where the judgment debtor and the judgment debtor's spouse live separate and apart, if ordinarily and reasonably necessary to, and personally used or procured for use by, the spouse and members of the spouse's family at the spouse's principal place of residence.

(b) In determining whether an item of property is "ordinarily and reasonably necessary" under subdivision (a), the court shall take into account both of the following:

(1) The extent to which the particular type of item is ordinarily found in a household.

(2) Whether the particular item has extraordinary value as compared to the value of items of the same type found in other households.

(c) If an item of property for which an exemption is claimed pursuant to this section is an item of the type ordinarily found in a household but is determined not to be exempt because the item has extraordinary value as compared to the value of items of the same type found in other households, the proceeds obtained at an execution sale of the item are exempt in the amount determined by the court to be a reasonable amount sufficient to purchase a replacement of ordinary value if the court determines that a replacement is reasonably necessary. Proceeds exempt under this subdivision are exempt for a period of 90 days after the proceeds are actually received by the judgment debtor. **Leg.H.** Added Stats 1982 ch 1364 §2, operative July 1, 1983.

§704.030. Materials for repair or improvement of residence

Material that in good faith is about to be applied to the repair or improvement of a residence is exempt if the equity in the material does not exceed three thousand five hundred dollars ($3,500) in the following cases:

(a) If purchased in good faith for use in the repair or improvement of the judgment debtor's principal place of residence.

(b) Where the judgment debtor and the judgment debtor's spouse live separate and apart, if purchased in good faith for use in the repair or improvement of the spouse's principal place of residence. **Leg.H.** Added Stats 1982 ch 1364 §2, operative July 1, 1983. Amended Stats 1995 ch 196 §3 (SB 832), effective July 31, 1995; Stats 2003 ch 379 §6 (AB 182); Stats 2020 ch 81 §3 (SB 898), effective January 1, 2021.

§704.040. Jewelry, heirlooms, works of art

Jewelry, heirlooms, and works of art are exempt to the extent that the aggregate equity therein does not exceed eight thousand seven hundred twenty-five dollars ($8,725). **Leg.H.** Added Stats 1982 ch 1364 §2, operative July 1, 1983. Amended Stats 1995 ch 196 §4 (SB 832), effective July 31, 1995; Stats 2003 ch 379 §7 (AB 182); Stats 2020 ch 81 §4 (SB 898), effective January 1, 2021.

§704.050. Health aids

(a) Health aids reasonably necessary to enable the judgment debtor or the spouse or a dependent of the judgment debtor to work or sustain health, and prosthetic and orthopedic appliances, are exempt.

(b) Health aids described in subdivision (a) include vehicles converted for use by the debtor, the debtor's spouse, or a dependent of the debtor, who has a disability. Conversion of a vehicle for use by a person who has a disability includes altering the interior, installing steering, a wheelchair lift, or motorized steps, or modifying the operation of the vehicle. **Leg.H.** Added Stats 1982 ch 1364 §2, operative July 1, 1983. Amended Stats 2022 ch 716 §4 (SB 1099), effective January 1, 2023.

§704.060. Personal property used in trade, business, or profession

(a) Tools, implements, instruments, materials, uniforms, furnishings, books, equipment, one commercial motor vehicle, one vessel, and other personal property are exempt to the extent that the aggregate equity therein does not exceed:

(1) Eight thousand seven hundred twenty-five dollars ($8,725), if reasonably necessary to and actually used by the judgment debtor in the exercise of the trade, business, or profession by which the judgment debtor earns a livelihood.

(2) Eight thousand seven hundred twenty-five dollars ($8,725), if reasonably necessary to and actually used by the spouse of the judgment debtor in the exercise of the trade, business, or profession by which the spouse earns a livelihood.

(3) Twice the amount of the exemption provided in paragraph (1), if reasonably necessary to and actually used by the judgment debtor and by the spouse of the judgment debtor in the exercise of the same trade, business, or profession by which both earn a livelihood. In the case covered by this paragraph, the exemptions provided in paragraphs (1) and (2) are not available.

(b) If property described in subdivision (a) is sold at an execution sale, or if it has been lost, damaged, or destroyed, the proceeds of the execution sale or of insurance or other indemnification are exempt for a period of 90 days after the proceeds are actually received by the judgment debtor or the judgment debtor's spouse. The amount exempt under this subdivision is the amount specified in subdivision (a) that applies to the particular case less the aggregate equity of any other property to which the exemption provided by subdivision (a) for the particular case has been applied.

(c) Notwithstanding subdivision (a), a motor vehicle is not exempt under subdivision (a) if there is a motor vehicle exempt under Section 704.010 which is reasonably adequate for use in the trade, business, or profession for which the exemption is claimed under this section.

(d) Notwithstanding subdivisions (a) and (b):

(1) The amount of the exemption for a commercial motor vehicle under paragraph (1) or (2) of subdivision (a) is limited to four thousand eight hundred fifty dollars ($4,850).

(2) The amount of the exemption for a commercial motor vehicle under paragraph (3) of subdivision (a) is limited to twice the amount of the exemption provided in paragraph (1) of this subdivision. **Leg.H.** Added Stats 1982 ch 1364 §2, operative July 1, 1983. Amended Stats 1995 ch 196 §5 (SB 832), effective July 31, 1995; Stats 2003 ch 379 §8 (AB 182); Stats 2020 ch 81 §5 (SB 898), effective January 1, 2021; Stats 2021 ch 124 §11 (AB 938), effective January 1, 2022.

2003 Note: The Legislature inadvertently left out the opening parenthesis before "$6,075)" in subsection (a)(1).

§704.070. Paid earnings

(a) As used in this section:

(1) "Earnings withholding order" means an earnings withholding order under Chapter 5 (commencing with Section 706.010) (Wage Garnishment Law).

(2) "Paid earnings" means earnings as defined in Section 706.011 that were paid to the employee during the 30-day period ending on the date of the levy. For the purposes of this paragraph, where earnings that have been paid to the employee are sought to be subjected to the enforcement of a money judgment other than by a levy, the date of levy is deemed to be the date the earnings were otherwise subjected to the enforcement of the judgment.

(3) "Earnings assignment order for support" means an earnings assignment order for support as defined in Section 706.011.

(b) Paid earnings that can be traced into deposit accounts or in the form of cash or its equivalent as provided in Section 703.080 are exempt in the following amounts:

(1) All of the paid earnings are exempt if prior to payment to the employee they were subject to an earnings withholding order or an earnings assignment order for support.

(2) Disposable earnings that would otherwise not be subject to levy under Section 706.050 that are levied upon or otherwise sought to be subjected to the enforcement of a money judgment are exempt if prior to payment to the employee they were not subject to an earnings withholding order or an earnings assignment order for support. **Leg.H.** Added Stats 1982 ch 1364 §2, operative July 1, 1983. Amended Stats 1992 ch 163 §38 (AB 2641), operative January 1, 1994; Stats 2019 ch 552 §7 (SB 616), effective January 1, 2020.

§704.080. Deposit account in which public benefits or social security benefits are directly deposited

(a) For the purposes of this section:

(1) "Deposit account" means a deposit account in which payments of public benefits or social security benefits are directly deposited by the government or its agent.

(2) "Social security benefits" means payments authorized by the Social Security Administration for regular retirement and survivors' benefits, supplemental security income benefits, coal miners' health benefits, and disability insurance benefits. "Public benefits" means aid payments authorized pursuant to subdivision (a) of Section 11450 of the Welfare and Institutions Code, payments for supportive services as described in Section 11323.2 of the Welfare and Institutions Code, and general assistance payments made pursuant to Section 17000.5 of the Welfare and Institutions Code.

(b) A deposit account is exempt without making a claim in the following amount:

(1) One thousand seven hundred fifty dollars ($1,750) where one depositor is the designated payee of the directly deposited public benefits payments.

(2) Three thousand five hundred dollars ($3,500) where one depositor is the designated payee of directly deposited social security payments.

(3) Two thousand six hundred dollars ($2,600) where two or more depositors are the designated payees of the directly deposited public benefits payments, unless those depositors are joint payees of directly deposited payments that represent a benefit to only one of the depositors, in which case the exemption under paragraph (1) applies.

(4) Five thousand two hundred fifty dollars ($5,250) where two or more depositors are the designated payees of directly deposited social security payments, unless those depositors are joint payees of directly deposited payments that represent a benefit to only one of the depositors, in which case the exemption under paragraph (2) applies.

(c) The amount of a deposit account that exceeds the exemption provided in subdivision (b) is exempt to the extent that it consists of payments of public benefits or social security benefits.

(d) Notwithstanding Article 5 (commencing with Section 701.010) of Chapter 3, when a deposit account is levied upon or otherwise sought to be subjected to the enforcement of a money judgment, the financial institution that holds the deposit account shall either place the amount that exceeds the exemption provided in subdivision (b) in a suspense account or otherwise prohibit withdrawal of that amount pending notification of the failure of the judgment creditor to file the affidavit required by this section or the judicial determination of the exempt status of the amount. Within 10 business days after the levy, the financial institution shall provide the levying officer with a written notice stating (1) that the deposit account is one in which payments of public benefits or social security benefits are directly deposited by the government or its agent and (2) the balance of the deposit account that exceeds the exemption provided by subdivision (b). Promptly upon receipt of the notice, the levying officer shall serve the notice on the judgment creditor. Service shall be made personally or by mail.

(e) Notwithstanding the procedure prescribed in Article 2 (commencing with Section 703.510), whether there is an amount exempt under subdivision (c) shall be determined as follows:

(1) Within five days after the levying officer serves the notice on the judgment creditor under subdivision (d), a judgment creditor who desires to claim that the amount is not exempt shall file with the court an affidavit alleging that the amount is not exempt and file a copy with the levying officer. The affidavit shall be in the form of the notice of opposition provided by Section 703.560, and a hearing shall be set and held, and notice given, as provided by Sections 703.570 and 703.580. For the purpose of this subdivision, the "notice of opposition to the claim of exemption" in Sections 703.570 and 703.580 means the affidavit under this subdivision.

(2) If the judgment creditor does not file the affidavit with the levying officer and give notice of hearing pursuant to Section 703.570 within the time provided in paragraph (1), the levying officer shall release the deposit account and shall notify the financial institution.

(3) The affidavit constitutes the pleading of the judgment creditor, subject to the power of the court to permit amendments in the interest of justice. The affidavit is deemed controverted and no counteraffidavit is required.

(4) At a hearing under this subdivision, the judgment debtor has the burden of proving that the excess amount is exempt.

(5) At the conclusion of the hearing, the court by order shall determine whether or not the amount of the deposit account is exempt pursuant to subdivision (c) in whole or in part and shall make an appropriate order for its prompt disposition. No findings are required in a proceeding under this subdivision.

(6) Upon determining the exemption claim for the deposit account under subdivision (c), the court shall immediately transmit a certified copy of the order of the court to the financial institution and to the levying officer. If the order determines that all or part of the excess is exempt under subdivision (c), with respect to the amount of the excess which is exempt, the financial institution shall transfer the exempt excess from the suspense account or otherwise release any restrictions on its withdrawal by the judgment debtor. The transfer or release shall be effected within three business days of the receipt of the certified copy of the court order by the financial institution.

(f) If the judgment debtor claims that a portion of the amount is exempt other than pursuant to subdivision (c), the claim of exemption shall be made pursuant to Article 2 (commencing with Section 703.510). If the judgment debtor also opposes the judgment creditor's affidavit regarding an amount exempt pursuant to subdivision (c), both exemptions shall be determined at the same hearing, provided the judgment debtor has complied with Article 2 (commencing with Section 703.510). **Leg.H.** Added Stats 1982 ch 1364 §2, operative July 1, 1983. Amended Stats 1995 ch 196 §6 (SB 832), effective July 31, 1995; Stats 1998 ch 290 §1 (AB 2724), operative January 1, 2000; Stats 2003 ch 379 §9 (AB 182); Stats 2020 ch 81 §6 (SB 898), effective January 1, 2021.

§704.090. Inmate's trust account

(a) The funds of a judgment debtor confined in a prison or facility under the jurisdiction of the Department of Corrections or the Department of the Youth Authority or confined in any county or city jail, road camp, industrial farm, or other local correctional facility, held in trust for or to the credit of the judgment debtor, in an inmate's trust account or similar account by the state, county, or city, or any agency thereof, are exempt without making a claim in the amount of one thousand seven hundred fifty dollars ($1,750). If the judgment debtor is married, each spouse is entitled to a separate exemption under this section or the spouses may combine their exemptions.

(b) Notwithstanding subdivision (a), if the judgment is for a restitution fine or order imposed pursuant to subdivision (a) of Section 13967 of the Government Code, as operative on or before September 28, 1994, or Section 1203.04 of the Penal Code, as operative on or before August 2, 1995, or Section 1202.4 of the Penal Code, the funds held in trust for, or to the credit of, a judgment debtor described in subdivision (a) are exempt in the amount of three hundred twenty-five dollars ($325) without making a claim. The exemption provided in this subdivision is not subject to adjustment under Section 703.150. **Leg.H.** Added Stats 1982 ch 1364 §2, operative July 1, 1983. Amended Stats 1996 ch 1077 §1 (AB 2898); Stats 2003 ch 379 §10 (AB 182); Stats 2020 ch 81 §7 (SB 898), effective January 1, 2021.

§704.100. Life insurance policies

(a) Unmatured life insurance policies (including endowment and annuity policies), but not the loan value of such policies, are exempt without making a claim.

(b) The aggregate loan value of unmatured life insurance policies (including endowment and annuity policies) is subject to the enforcement of a money judgment but is exempt in the amount of thirteen thousand nine hundred seventy-five dollars ($13,975). If the judgment debtor is married, each spouse is entitled to a separate exemption under this subdivision, and the exemptions of the spouses may be combined, regardless of whether the policies belong to either or both spouses and regardless of whether the spouse of the judgment debtor is also a judgment debtor under the judgment. The exemption provided by this subdivision shall be first applied to policies other than the policy before the court and then, if the exemption is not exhausted, to the policy before the court.

(c) Benefits from matured life insurance policies (including endowment and annuity policies) are exempt to the extent reasonably necessary for the support of the judgment debtor and the spouse and dependents of the judgment debtor. **Leg.H.** Added Stats 1982 ch 1364 §2, operative July 1, 1983. Amended Stats 1995 ch 196 §7 (SB 832), effective July 31, 1995; Stats 2003 ch 379 §11 (AB 182); Stats 2020 ch 81 §8 (SB 898), effective January 1, 2021.

§704.105. Money held in an account established pursuant to the Golden State Scholarshare Trust Act

Money held in an account owned by the judgment debtor and established pursuant to the Golden State Scholarshare Trust Act (Article 19 (commencing with Section 69980) of Chapter 2 of Part 42 of Division 5 of Title 3 of the Education Code) is exempt without making a claim, subject to the following limitations:

(a) The amount exempted for contributions to an account during the 365-day period prior to the date of entry of a money judgment, in the aggregate during this period, shall not exceed the amount of the annual gift tax exclusion under Section 2503(b) of the Internal Revenue Code of 1986, as amended, in effect at the time of entry of the money judgment.

(b) The amount exempted for contributions to an account during the period commencing 730 days prior to and ending 366 days prior to the date of entry of a money judgment, in the aggregate during this period, shall not exceed the amount of the annual gift tax exclusion under Section 2503(b) of the Internal Revenue Code of 1986, as amended, in effect at the time of entry of the money judgment.

(c) For the purposes of this section, "account" includes all accounts having the same beneficiary.

(d) This section is not subject to the requirements of Section 703.150. **Leg.H.** Added Stats 2020 ch 81 §9 (SB 898), effective January 1, 2021. Amended Stats 2022 ch 25 §2 (SB 956), effective January 1, 2023.

§704.110. Public retirement and related benefits and contributions

(a) As used in this section:

(1) "Public entity" means the state, or a city, city and county, county, or other political subdivision of the state, or a public trust, public corporation, or public board, or the governing body of any of them, but does not include the United States except where expressly so provided.

(2) "Public retirement benefit" means a pension or an annuity, or a retirement, disability, death, or other benefit, paid or payable by a public retirement system.

(3) "Public retirement system" means a system established pursuant to statute by a public entity for retirement, annuity, or pension purposes or payment of disability or death benefits.

(b) All amounts held, controlled, or in process of distribution by a public entity derived from contributions by the public entity or by an officer or employee of the public entity for public retirement benefit purposes, and all rights and benefits accrued or accruing to any person under a public retirement system, are exempt without making a claim.

(c) Notwithstanding subdivision (b), where an amount described in subdivision (b) becomes payable to a person and is sought to be applied to the satisfaction of a judgment for child, family, or spousal support against that person:

(1) Except as provided in paragraphs (2) and (3), the amount is exempt only to the extent that the court determines under subdivision (c) of Section 703.070.

(2) If the amount sought to be applied to the satisfaction of the judgment is payable periodically, the amount payable is subject to an earnings assignment order for support as defined in Section 706.011, or any other applicable enforcement procedure, but the amount to be withheld pursuant to the assignment order or other procedure shall not exceed the amount permitted to be withheld on an earnings withholding order for support under Section 706.052. The paying entity may deduct from the payment being made to the judgment debtor, for each payment made pursuant to an earnings assignment order under this paragraph, an amount reflecting the actual cost of administration caused by the assignment order of up to two dollars ($2) for each payment.

(3) If the intercept procedure provided for in Section 11357 of the Welfare and Institutions Code is used for benefits that are payable periodically, the amount to be withheld shall not exceed the amount permitted to be withheld on an earnings withholding order for support under Section 706.052.

(4) If the amount sought to be applied to the satisfaction of the judgment is payable as a lump-sum distribution, the amount payable is subject to the intercept procedure provided in Section 11357 of the Welfare and Institutions Code or any other applicable enforcement procedure.

(d) All amounts received by any person, a resident of the state, as a public retirement benefit or as a return of contributions and interest thereon from the United States or a public entity or from a public retirement system are exempt. **Leg.H.** Added Stats 1982 ch 1364 §2, operative July 1, 1983. Amended Stats 1992 ch 163 §39 (AB 2641), operative January 1, 1994; Stats 1996 ch 912 §1 (AB 1751), ch 927 §1.5 (SB 468).

§ 704.111. Alimony, support, and separate maintenance

Alimony, support, and separate maintenance, to the extent reasonably necessary for the support of the debtor and any dependent of the debtor, are exempt. **Leg.H.** Added Stats 2022 ch 716 §5 (SB 1099), effective January 1, 2023.

§704.113. Public employee vacation credits

(a) As used in this chapter, "vacation credits" means vacation credits accumulated by a state employee pursuant to Section 19858.1 of the Government Code or by any other public employee pursuant to any law for the accumulation of vacation credits applicable to the employee.

(b) The aggregate interest, not to exceed seven thousand five hundred dollars ($7,500), in vacation credits or accrued, or unused, vacation pay, sick leave, or family leave is exempt.

(c) Amounts paid periodically or as a lump sum representing vacation credits are subject to any earnings withholding order served under Chapter 5 (commencing with Section 706.010) or any earnings assignment order for support as defined in Section 706.011 and are exempt to the same extent as earnings of a judgment debtor. **Leg.H.** Added Stats 1982 ch 1364 §2, operative July 1, 1983. Amended Stats 1992 ch 163 §40 (AB 2641), operative January 1, 1994; Stats 2022 ch 28 §25 (SB 1380), effective January 1, 2023; Stats 2022 ch 716 §6 (SB 1099), effective January 1, 2023 (ch 716 prevails).

§704.114. Compliance with order of earnings assignment

(a) Notwithstanding any other provision of law, service of an earnings assignment order for support, or an order or notice to withhold income for child support on any public entity described in Section 704.110, other than the United States government, creates a lien on all employee contributions in the amount necessary to satisfy a support judgment as determined under Section 695.210 to the extent that the judgment remains enforceable.

(b) The public entity shall comply with any request for a return of employee contributions by an employee named in the order or notice to withhold by delivering the contributions to the clerk of the court in which the support order was awarded or last registered, unless the entity has received a certified copy of an order or administrative notice terminating the earnings assignment order for support.

(c) Upon receipt of moneys pursuant to this section, the clerk of the court, within 10 days, shall send written notice of the receipt of the deposit to the parties and to the local child support agency enforcing any order pursuant to Section 17400 of the Family Code.

(d) Moneys received pursuant to this section are subject to any procedure available to enforce an order for support, but if no enforcement procedure is commenced after 30 days have elapsed from the date the notice of receipt is sent, the clerk shall, upon request, return the moneys to the public entity that delivered the moneys to the court unless the public entity has informed the court in writing that the moneys shall be released to the employee.

(e) A court shall not directly or indirectly condition the issuance, modification, or termination of, or condition the terms or conditions of, any order for support upon the making of a request for the return of employee contributions by an employee. **Leg.H.** Added Stats 1989 ch 1359 §8. Amended Stats 1992 ch 163 §41 (AB 2641), operative January 1, 1994, ch 851 §2 (SB 1530), effective September 22, 1992 (ch 851 prevails); Stats 1993 ch 219 §68 (AB 1500); Stats 2000 ch 808 §13 (AB 1358), effective September 28, 2000.

§704.115. Private retirement and related benefits and contributions

(a) As used in this section, " [1] retirement plan" means:

(1) Private retirement plans, including, but not limited to, union retirement plans.

(2) Profit-sharing plans designed and used for retirement purposes.

(3) Self-employed retirement plans and individual retirement annuities or accounts provided for in the Internal Revenue Code of 1986, as amended, including individual retirement accounts qualified under Section 408 or 408A of that code, to the extent the amounts held in the plans, annuities, or accounts do not exceed the maximum amounts exempt from federal income taxation under that code.

(4) Retirement funds to the extent that those funds are in a fund or account that is exempt from taxation under Sections 403, 414, or 457 of the Internal Revenue Code of 1986, as amended, to the extent the amounts held in the plans, annuities, or accounts do not exceed the maximum amounts exempt from federal income taxation under that code and are not otherwise exempt under federal law.

(b) All amounts held, controlled, or in process of distribution by a [2] retirement plan, for the payment of benefits as an annuity, pension, retirement allowance, disability payment, or death benefit from a [3] retirement plan are exempt.

(c) Notwithstanding subdivision (b), where an amount described in subdivision (b) becomes payable to a person and is sought to be applied to the satisfaction of a judgment for child, family, or spousal support against that person:

(1) Except as provided in paragraph (2), the amount is exempt only to the extent that the court determines under subdivision (c) of Section 703.070.

(2) If the amount sought to be applied to the satisfaction of the judgment is payable periodically, the amount payable is subject to an earnings assignment order for support as defined in Section 706.011 or any other applicable enforcement procedure, but the amount to be withheld pursuant to the assignment order or other procedure shall not

exceed the amount permitted to be withheld on an earnings withholding order for support under Section 706.052.

(d) After payment, the amounts described in subdivision (b) and all contributions and interest thereon returned to any member of a [4] retirement plan are exempt.

(e)

(1) Notwithstanding subdivisions (b) and (d), except as provided in subdivision (f), the amounts described in [5] **paragraphs (3) and (4)** of subdivision (a) are exempt only to the extent necessary to provide for the support of the judgment debtor when the judgment debtor retires and for the support of the spouse and dependents of the judgment debtor, taking into account all resources that are likely to be available for the support of the judgment debtor when the judgment debtor retires. [6]

(2) For personal debt, as defined in subdivision (d) of Section 683.110, the amount necessary to provide for the support of the judgment debtor cannot be, unless otherwise provided by federal law, less than the amount listed in subsection (n) of Section 522 of Title 11 of the United States Code, as adjusted in accordance with subsection (b) of Section 104 of Title 11 of the United States Code. The exempt amount may be aggregated across all retirement plans in the judgment debtor's name. The exempt amount may be reduced to the extent that such value is attributable to any portion of any property the debtor disposed of with the intent to hinder, delay, or defraud a creditor, and that the debtor could not have exempted at the time the debtor so disposed of the property.

(3) In determining the amount to be exempt under this subdivision, the court shall allow the judgment debtor such additional amount as is necessary to pay any federal and state income taxes owed as a result of the application of funds in a retirement plan to the satisfaction of the money judgment.

(f) Where the amounts described in [7] **paragraphs (3) and (4)** of subdivision (a) are payable periodically, the amount of the periodic payment that may be applied to the satisfaction of a money judgment is the amount that may be withheld from a like amount of earnings under Chapter 5 (commencing with Section 706.010)(Wage Garnishment Law). To the extent a lump-sum distribution from an individual retirement account is treated differently from a periodic distribution under this subdivision, any lump-sum distribution from an account qualified under Section 408A of the Internal Revenue Code shall be treated the same as a lump-sum distribution from an account qualified under Section 408 of the Internal Revenue Code for purposes of determining whether any of that payment may be applied to the satisfaction of a money judgment. **Leg.H.** Added Stats 1982 ch 1364 §2, operative July 1, 1983. Amended Stats 1992 ch 163 §42 (AB 2641), operative January 1, 1994; Stats 1999 ch 98 §2 (SB 469); Stats 2000 ch 135 §16 (AB 2539); Stats 2024 ch 514 §7 (AB 2837), effective January 1, 2025.

§704.115. 2024 Deletes. [1] private [2] private [3] private [4] private [5] paragraph (3) [6] In determining the amount to be exempt under this subdivision, the court shall allow the judgment debtor such additional amount as is necessary to pay any federal and state income taxes payable as a result of the applying of an amount described in paragraph (3) of subdivision (a) to the satisfaction of the money judgment. [7] paragraph (3)

§704.120. Unemployment benefits and contributions; Strike benefits

(a) Contributions by workers payable to the Unemployment Compensation Disability Fund and by employers payable to the Unemployment Fund are exempt without making a claim.

(b) Before payment, amounts held for payment of the following benefits are exempt without making a claim:

(1) Benefits payable under Division 1 (commencing with Section 100) of the Unemployment Insurance Code.

(2) Incentives payable under Division 2 (commencing with Section 5000) of the Unemployment Insurance Code.

(3) Benefits payable under an employer's plan or system to supplement unemployment compensation benefits of the employees generally or for a class or group of employees.

(4) Unemployment benefits payable by a fraternal organization to its bona fide members.

(5) Benefits payable by a union due to a labor dispute.

(c) After payment, the benefits described in subdivision (b) are exempt.

(d) During the payment of benefits described in paragraph (1) of subdivision (b) to a judgment debtor under a support judgment, the judgment creditor may, through the appropriate local child support agency, seek to apply the benefit payment to satisfy the judgment as provided by Section 17518 of the Family Code.

(e) During the payment of benefits described in paragraphs (2) to (5), inclusive, of subdivision (b) to a judgment debtor under a support judgment, the judgment creditor may, directly or through the appropriate local child support agency, seek to apply the benefit payments to satisfy the judgment by an earnings assignment order for support as defined in Section 706.011 or any other applicable enforcement procedure. If the benefit is payable periodically, the amount to be withheld pursuant to the assignment order or other procedure shall be 25 percent of the amount of each periodic payment or any lower amount specified in writing by the judgment creditor or court order, rounded down to the nearest whole dollar. Otherwise the amount to be withheld shall be the amount the court determines under subdivision (c) of Section 703.070. The paying entity may deduct from each payment made pursuant to an assignment order under this subdivision an amount reflecting the actual cost of administration caused by the assignment order up to two dollars ($2) for each payment. **Leg.H.** Added Stats 1982 ch 1364 §2, operative July 1, 1983. Amended Stats 1983 ch 155 §16, effective June 30, 1983, operative July 1, 1983; Stats 1988 ch 261 §1, effective July 5, 1988; Stats 1992 ch 163 §43 (AB 2641), operative January 1, 1994; Stats 2000 ch 808 §14 (AB 1358), effective September 28, 2000.

§704.130. Disability and health benefits

(a) Before payment, benefits from a disability or health insurance policy or program are exempt without making a claim. After payment, the benefits are exempt.

(b) Subdivision (a) does not apply to benefits that are paid or payable to cover the cost of health care if the judgment creditor is a provider of health care whose claim is the basis on which the benefits are paid or payable.

(c) During the payment of disability benefits described in subdivision (a) to a judgment debtor under a support judgment, the judgment creditor or local child support agency may seek to apply the benefit payments to satisfy the judgment by an earnings assignment order for support, as defined in Section 706.011, or any other applicable enforcement procedure, but the amount to be withheld pursuant to the earnings assignment order or other procedure shall not exceed the amount permitted to be withheld on an earnings assignment order for support under Section 706.052. **Leg.H.** Added Stats 1982 ch 1364 §2, operative July 1, 1983. Amended Stats 1997 ch 599 §4 (AB 573); Stats 2000 ch 808 §15 (AB 1358), effective September 28, 2000.

§704.140. Damages for personal injury

(a) Except as provided in Article 5 (commencing with Section 708.410) of Chapter 6, a cause of action for personal injury is exempt without making a claim.

(b) Except as provided in subdivisions (c) and (d), an award of damages or a settlement arising out of personal injury is exempt to the extent necessary for the support of the judgment debtor and the spouse and dependents of the judgment debtor.

(c) Subdivision (b) does not apply if the judgment creditor is a provider of health care whose claim is based on the providing of health care for the personal injury for which the award or settlement was made.

(d) Where an award of damages or a settlement arising out of personal injury is payable periodically, the amount of such periodic payment that may be applied to the satisfaction of a money judgment is the amount that may be withheld from a like amount of earnings under Chapter 5 (commencing with Section 706.010) (Wage Garnishment Law). **Leg.H.** Added Stats 1982 ch 1364 §2, operative July 1, 1983.

§704.150. Damages for wrongful death

(a) Except as provided in Article 5 (commencing with Section 708.410) of Chapter 6, a cause of action for wrongful death is exempt without making a claim.

(b) Except as provided in subdivision (c), an award of damages or a settlement arising out of the wrongful death of the judgment debtor's spouse or a person on whom the judgment debtor or the judgment debtor's spouse was dependent is exempt to the extent reasonably necessary for support of the judgment debtor and the spouse and dependents of the judgment debtor.

(c) Where an award of damages or a settlement arising out of the wrongful death of the judgment debtor's spouse or a person on whom the judgment debtor or the judgment debtor's spouse was dependent is payable periodically, the amount of such a periodic payment that may be applied to the satisfaction of a money judgment is the amount that may be withheld from a like amount of earnings under Chapter 5 (commencing with Section 706.010) (Wage Garnishment Law). **Leg.H.** Added Stats 1982 ch 1364 §2, operative July 1, 1983.

§704.160. Workers' compensation; Exceptions

(a) Except as provided by Chapter 1 (commencing with Section 4900) of Part 3 of Division 4 of the Labor Code, before payment, a claim for workers' compensation or workers' compensation awarded or adjudged is exempt without making a claim. Except as specified in subdivision (b), after payment, the award is exempt.

(b) Notwithstanding any other provision of law, during the payment of workers' compensation temporary disability benefits described in subdivision (a) to a support judgment debtor, the support judgment creditor may, through the appropriate local child support agency, seek to apply the workers' compensation temporary disability benefit payment to satisfy the support judgment as provided by Section 17404 of the Family Code.

(c) Notwithstanding any other provision of law, during the payment of workers' compensation temporary disability benefits described in subdivision (a) to a support judgment debtor under a support judgment, including a judgment for reimbursement of public assistance, the judgment creditor may, directly or through the appropriate local child support agency, seek to apply the temporary disability benefit payments to satisfy the support judgment by an earnings assignment order for support, as defined in Section 5208 of the Family Code, or any other applicable enforcement procedure. The amount to be withheld pursuant to the earnings assignment order for support or other enforcement procedure shall be 25 percent of the amount of each periodic payment or any lower amount specified in writing by the judgment creditor or court order, rounded down to the nearest dollar. Otherwise, the amount to be withheld shall be the amount the court determines under subdivision (c) of Section 703.070. The paying entity may deduct from each payment made pursuant to an order assigning earnings under this subdivision an amount reflecting the actual cost of administration of this assignment, up to two dollars ($2) for each payment.

(d) Unless the provision or context otherwise requires, the following definitions govern the construction of this section.

(1) "Judgment debtor" or "support judgment debtor" means a person who is owing a duty of support.

(2) "Judgment creditor" or "support judgment creditor" means the person to whom support has been ordered to be paid.

(3) "Support" refers to an obligation owing on behalf of a child, spouse, or family; or an amount owing pursuant to Section 17402 of the Family Code. It also includes past due support or arrearage when it exists. **Leg.H.** Added Stats 1982 ch 1364 §2, operative July 1, 1983. Amended Stats 1992 ch 848 §10 (SB 1614), effective September 22, 1992; Stats 1993 ch 219 §69 (AB 1500); Stats 2000 ch 808 §16 (AB 1358), effective September 28, 2000.

§704.170. Aid provided to needy persons

Before payment, aid provided pursuant to Division 9 (commencing with Section 10000) of the Welfare and Institutions Code or similar aid provided by a charitable organization or a fraternal benefit society as defined in Section 10990 of the Insurance Code, is exempt without making a claim. After payment, the aid is exempt. **Leg.H.** Added Stats 1982 ch 1364 §2, operative July 1, 1983.

§704.180. Relocation benefits

Before payment, relocation benefits for displacement from a dwelling which are to be paid pursuant to Chapter 16 (commencing with Section 7260) of Division 7 of Title 1 of the Government Code or the federal "Uniform Relocation Assistance and Real Property Acquisition Policies Act of 1970" (42 U.S.C. Sec. 4601 et seq.), as amended, are exempt without making a claim. After payment, the benefits are exempt. **Leg.H.** Added Stats 1982 ch 1364 §2, operative July 1, 1983.

§704.190. Financial aid provided to student by educational institution

(a) As used in this section, "institution of higher education" means "institution of higher education" as defined in Section 1141(a) of Title 20 of the United States Code, as amended.

(b) Before payment, financial aid for expenses while attending school provided to a student by an institution of higher education is exempt without making a claim. After payment, the aid is exempt. **Leg.H.** Added Stats 1982 ch 1364 §2, operative July 1, 1983.

§704.200. Cemetery plot

(a) As used in this section:

(1) "Cemetery" has the meaning provided by Section 7003 of the Health and Safety Code.

(2) "Family plot" is a plot that satisfies the requirements of Section 8650 of the Health and Safety Code.

(3) "Plot" has the meaning provided by Section 7022 of the Health and Safety Code.

(b) A family plot is exempt without making a claim.

(c) Except as provided in subdivision (d), a cemetery plot for the judgment debtor and the spouse of the judgment debtor is exempt.

(d) Land held for the purpose of sale or disposition as cemetery plots or otherwise is not exempt. **Leg.H.** Added Stats 1982 ch 1364 §2, operative July 1, 1983.

§704.210. Property not subject to enforcement of money judgment

Property that is not subject to enforcement of a money judgment is exempt without making a claim. **Leg.H.** Added Stats 1982 ch 1364 §2, operative July 1, 1983.

§704.220. Money in judgment debtor's deposit account; Levy requirements

(a) Money in the judgment debtor's deposit account in an amount equal to or less than the minimum basic standard of adequate care for a family of four for Region 1, established by Section 11452 of the Welfare and Institutions Code and as annually adjusted by the State Department of Social Services pursuant to Section 11453 of the Welfare and Institutions Code, is exempt without making a claim.

(b)(1) Subdivision (a) does not preclude or reduce a judgment debtor's right to any other exemption provided by state or federal law.

(2) If the financial institution holding the judgment debtor's deposit account has actual knowledge that the judgment debtor is entitled to one or more exemptions that the financial institution is required to apply pursuant to federal law or state law other than that set forth in subdivision (a), the following shall apply:

(A) If the sum of the amount of money in the deposit account that would be exempt from levy under the additional exemptions is less than or equal to the amount set forth in subdivision (a), the additional exemptions described in this paragraph shall be considered encompassed within the exemption set forth in subdivision (a) and subdivision (a) shall apply.

(B) If the sum of the amount of money in the deposit account that would be exempt from levy under the additional exemptions is greater than the amount set forth in subdivision (a), subdivision (a) shall not apply and instead money in the deposit account equal to or less than the sum of the additional exemptions is exempt without making a claim.

(c) Subdivision (a) does not apply to money levied upon to satisfy any of the following:

(1) A levy to satisfy a judgment for wages owed, child support, or spousal support. For purposes of this paragraph, "wages owed" includes damages and penalties.

(2) A provision of the Public Resources Code, Revenue and Taxation Code, or Unemployment Insurance Code.

(3) A warrant or notice of levy issued by the state, or any department or agency thereof, for the collection of a liability.

(d) A levy against a judgment debtor's deposit account shall include a written description of the requirements of this section.

(e)(1) The exemption applies per debtor, not per account.

(2) If a judgment debtor holds an interest in multiple accounts at a single financial institution, the judgment creditor or judgment debtor may file an ex parte application in the superior court in which the judgment was entered for a hearing to establish how and to which account the exemption should be applied. Subject to a service of an order issued in that hearing, if any, the financial institution may determine how and to which account the exemption should be applied. This paragraph does not create a cause of action against a judgment creditor who executes a levy or against a financial institution that complies with a levy pursuant to the court's determination.

(3) If a judgment debtor holds an interest in multiple accounts at two or more financial institutions, the judgment creditor shall, and the judgment debtor may, file an ex parte application in the superior court in which the judgment was entered for a hearing to establish how and to which account the exemption should be applied. Subject to a service of an order issued in that hearing, if any, the financial institutions shall comply with the levy subject to the exemption. This paragraph does not create a cause of action against a judgment creditor who executes a levy or against a financial institution which complies with a levy pursuant to the court's determination.

(4) Notwithstanding paragraph (2), if a judgment debtor holds multiple accounts at a single financial institution, and those accounts cumulatively contain an amount less than or equal to the amount specified in subdivision (a), the financial institution shall protect the full amount in those accounts.

(5) Notwithstanding paragraph (2), if a judgment debtor holds multiple accounts at a single financial institution, and each of those accounts contains an amount less than the amount specified in subdivision (a) but the accounts cumulatively contain an amount greater than the amount specified in subdivision (a), the financial institution shall protect an aggregate amount equal to the amount specified in subdivision (a).

(f) Subdivision (e) of Section 700.140 applies to a financial institution acting under this section.

(g) The Judicial Council shall amend or adopt all forms necessary to implement this section. The forms shall clearly delineate the amount of funds exempt from levy by a financial institution, including funds exempted by this section.

(h) This section shall become operative on September 1, 2020. **Leg.H.** Added Stats 2019 ch 552 §8 (SB 616), effective January 1, 2020, operative September 1, 2020. Amended Stats 2024 ch 514 §8 (AB 2837), effective January 1, 2025, operative September 1, 2020.

§704.225. Money exempt to support spouse and dependents

Money in a judgment debtor's deposit account that is not otherwise exempt under this chapter is exempt to the extent necessary for the support of the judgment debtor and the spouse and dependents of the judgment debtor. **Leg.H.** Added Stats 2019 ch 552 §9 (SB 616), effective January 1, 2020.

§704.230. Money from Federal Emergency Management Agency (FEMA)

Money provided to the judgment debtor by the Federal Emergency Management Agency (FEMA) is exempt without making a claim. **Leg.H.** Added Stats 2019 ch 552 §10 (SB 616), effective January 1, 2020.

§704.235. Exemption of HOPE trust account payments from levy

(a) A one-time lump-sum payment made from a HOPE trust account, as defined in subdivision (a) of Section 18997.51 of the Welfare and Institutions Code, shall be exempt without making a claim, except as provided in subdivision (b).

(b) A one-time lump-sum payment described in subdivision (a) is not exempt from a levy in connection with child support, spousal support, family support, or a criminal restitution.

(c) A financial institution that receives a payment described in subdivision (a) directly from the state shall treat the payment as exempt from levy if it is designated "HOPE trust account payment" or if the payment is otherwise sufficiently identified to inform the financial institution that the payment is a HOPE trust account payment. **Leg.H.** Added Stats 2024 ch 1010 §2 (SB 242), effective January 1, 2025.

ARTICLE 4
Homestead Exemption

Definitions. §704.710.
Exemption from sale; Exemption of sale proceeds or indemnification. §704.720.
Amount of homestead exemption. §704.730.
Court order for sale; Exemption claim where court order for sale not required. §704.740.
Application for order for sale. §704.750.
Contents of application. §704.760.
Notice of hearing. §704.770.
Hearing. §704.780.
Procedure after order of sale upon default. §704.790.
Minimum bid. §704.800.
Acceleration clauses and prepayment penalties. §704.810.
Procedure where judgment debtor is co-owner or owns less than fee. §704.820.
Extensions of time and appeals. §704.830.
Costs. §704.840.
Distribution of proceeds of sale of homestead. §704.850.

§704.710. Definitions

As used in this article:

(a) "Dwelling" means a place where a person resides and may include but is not limited to the following:

(1) A house together with the outbuildings and the land upon which they are situated.

(2) A mobilehome together with the outbuildings and the land upon which they are situated.

(3) A boat or other waterborne vessel.

(4) A condominium, as defined in Section 783 of the Civil Code.

(5) A planned development, as defined in Section 11003 of the Business and Professions Code.

(6) A stock cooperative, as defined in Section 11003.2 of the Business and Professions Code.

(7) A community apartment project, as defined in Section 11004 of the Business and Professions Code.

(b) "Family unit" means any of the following:

(1) The judgment debtor and the judgment debtor's spouse if the spouses reside together in the homestead.

(2) The judgment debtor and at least one of the following persons who the judgment debtor cares for or maintains in the homestead:

(A) The minor child or minor grandchild of the judgment debtor or the judgment debtor's spouse or the minor child or grandchild of a deceased spouse or former spouse.

(B) The minor brother or sister of the judgment debtor or judgment debtor's spouse or the minor child of a deceased brother or sister of either spouse.

(C) The father, mother, grandfather, or grandmother of the judgment debtor or the judgment debtor's spouse or the father, mother, grandfather, or grandmother of a deceased spouse.

(D) An unmarried relative described in this paragraph who has attained the age of majority and is unable to take care of or support himself or herself.

(3) The judgment debtor's spouse and at least one of the persons listed in paragraph (2) who the judgment debtor's spouse cares for or maintains in the homestead.

(c) "Homestead" means the principal dwelling (1) in which the judgment debtor or the judgment debtor's spouse resided on the date the judgment creditor's lien attached to the dwelling, and (2) in which the judgment debtor or the judgment debtor's spouse resided continuously thereafter until the date of the court determination that the dwelling is a homestead. Where exempt proceeds from the sale or damage or destruction of a homestead are used toward the acquisition of a dwelling within the six-month period provided by Section 704.720, "homestead" also means the dwelling so acquired if it is the principal dwelling in which the judgment debtor or the judgment debtor's spouse resided continuously from the date of acquisition until the date of the court determination that the dwelling is a homestead, whether or not an abstract or certified copy of a judgment was recorded to create a judgment lien before the dwelling was acquired.

(d) "Spouse" does not include a married person following entry of a judgment decreeing legal separation of the parties, unless such married persons reside together in the same dwelling. **Leg.H.** Added Stats 1982 ch 1364 §2, operative July 1, 1983. Amended Stats 1983 ch 155 §17, effective June 30, 1983, operative July 1, 1983, ch 1159 §11, operative July 1, 1984.

§704.720. Exemption from sale; Exemption of sale proceeds or indemnification

(a) A homestead is exempt from sale under this division to the extent provided in Section 704.800.

(b) If a homestead is sold under this division or is damaged or destroyed or is acquired for public use, the proceeds of sale or of insurance or other indemnification for damage or destruction of the homestead or the proceeds received as compensation for a homestead acquired for public use are exempt in the amount of the homestead exemption provided in Section 704.730. The proceeds are exempt for a period of six months after the time the proceeds are actually received by the judgment debtor, except that, if a homestead exemption is applied to other property of the judgment debtor or the judgment debtor's spouse during that period, the proceeds thereafter are not exempt.

(c) If the judgment debtor and spouse of the judgment debtor reside in separate homesteads, only the homestead of one of the spouses is exempt and only the proceeds of the exempt homestead are exempt.

(d) If a judgment debtor is not currently residing in the homestead, but his or her separated or former spouse continues to reside in or exercise control over possession of the homestead, that judgment debtor continues to be entitled to an exemption under this article until entry of judgment or other legally enforceable agreement dividing the community property between the judgment debtor and the separated or former spouse, or until a later time period as specified by court order. Nothing in this subdivision shall entitle the judgment debtor to more than one exempt homestead. Notwithstanding subdivision (d) of Section 704.710, for purposes of this article, "spouse" may include a separated or former spouse consistent with this subdivision. **Leg.H.** Added Stats 1982 ch 1364 §2, operative July 1, 1983. Amended Stats 2007 ch 153 §1 (SB 433), effective January 1, 2008.

§704.730. Amount of homestead exemption

(a) The amount of the homestead exemption is the greater of the following:

(1) The countywide median sale price for a single-family home in the calendar year prior to the calendar year in which the judgment debtor claims the exemption, not to exceed six hundred thousand dollars ($600,000).

(2) Three hundred thousand dollars ($300,000).

(b) The amounts specified in this section shall adjust annually for inflation, beginning on January 1, 2022, based on the change in the annual California Consumer Price Index for All Urban Consumers, published by the Department of Industrial Relations, [1] for the most recent one-year period ending on December 31 preceding the adjustment, with each adjusted amount rounded to the nearest twenty-five dollars ($25). **Leg.H.** Added Stats 1982 ch 1364 §2, operative July 1, 1983. Amended Stats 1984 ch 454 §1; Stats 1986 ch 1000 §1, ch 1001 §1; Stats 1988 ch 1168 §1; Stats 1990 ch 155 §1 (AB 2562); Stats 1997 ch 82 §1 (AB 451); Stats 2003 ch 64 §1 (SB 804); Stats 2009 ch 499 §2 (AB 1046), effective January 1, 2010; Stats 2012 ch 678 §3 (AB 929), effective January 1, 2013; Stats 2020 ch 94 §1 (AB 1885), effective January 1, 2021; Stats 2023 ch 478 §15 (AB 1756), effective January 1, 2024; Stats 2024 ch 80 §24 (SB 1525), effective January 1, 2025.

§704.730. 2024 Deletes. [1] Division of Labor Statistics,

§704.740. Court order for sale; Exemption claim where court order for sale not required

(a) Except as provided in subdivision (b), the interest of a natural person in a dwelling may not be sold under this division to enforce a money judgment except pursuant to a court order for sale obtained under this article and the dwelling exemption shall be determined under this article.

(b) If the dwelling is personal property or is real property in which the judgment debtor has a leasehold estate with an unexpired term of less than two years at the time of levy:

(1) A court order for sale is not required and the procedures provided in this article relating to the court order for sale do not apply.

(2) An exemption claim shall be made and determined as provided in Article 2 (commencing with Section 703.510). **Leg.H.** Added Stats 1982 ch 1364 §2, operative July 1, 1983. Amended Stats 1984 ch 538 §26.

§704.750. Application for order for sale

(a) Promptly after a dwelling is levied upon (other than a dwelling described in subdivision (b) of Section 704.740), the levying officer shall serve notice on the judgment creditor that the levy has been made and that the property will be released unless the judgment creditor complies with the requirements of this section. Service shall be made personally or by mail. Within 20 days after service of the notice, the judgment creditor shall apply to the court for an order for sale of the dwelling and shall file a copy of the application with the levying officer. If the judgment creditor does not file the copy of the application for an order for sale of the dwelling within the allowed time, the levying officer shall release the dwelling.

(b) If the dwelling is located in a county other than the county where the judgment was entered:

(1) The judgment creditor shall apply to the superior court of the county where the dwelling is located.

(2) The judgment creditor shall file with the application an abstract of judgment in the form prescribed by Section 674 or, in the case of a judgment described in Section 697.320, a certified copy of the judgment.

(3) The judgment creditor shall pay the filing fee for a motion as provided in subdivision (a) of Section 70617 of the Government Code. **Leg.H.** Added Stats 1982 ch 1364 §2, operative July 1, 1983. Amended Stats 2005 ch 75 §37 (AB 145), effective July 19, 2005, operative January 01, 2006.

§704.760. Contents of application

The judgment creditor's application shall be made under oath, shall describe the dwelling, and shall contain all of the following:

(a) A statement whether or not the records of the county tax assessor indicate that there is a current homeowner's exemption or disabled veteran's exemption for the dwelling and the person or persons who claimed any such exemption.

(b) A statement, which may be based on information and belief, whether the dwelling is a homestead and the amount of the homestead exemption, if any, and a statement whether or not the records of the county recorder indicate that a homestead declaration under Article 5 (commencing with Section 704.910) that describes the dwelling has been recorded by the judgment debtor or the spouse of the judgment debtor.

(c) A statement of the amount of any liens or encumbrances on the dwelling, the name of each person having a lien or encumbrance on the dwelling, and the address of such person used by the county recorder for the return of the instrument creating such person's lien or encumbrance after recording.

(d) A statement that the judgment is based on a consumer debt, as defined in subdivision (a) of Section 699.730, or that the judgment is not based on a consumer debt, and if the judgment is based on a consumer debt, whether the judgment is based on a consumer debt that was secured by the debtor's principal place of residence at the time it was incurred or a statement indicating which of the exemptions listed in subdivision (b) of Section 699.730 are applicable. If the statement indicates that paragraph (7) of subdivision (b) is applicable, the statement shall also provide the dollar amount of the original judgment on which the lien is based. If there is more than one basis, the statement shall indicate all bases that are applicable. **Leg.H.** Added Stats 1982 ch 1364 §2, operative July 1, 1983. Amended Stats 2020 ch 218 §3 (AB 2463), effective January 1, 2021.

§704.770. Notice of hearing

(a) Upon the filing of the application by the judgment creditor, the court shall set a time and place for hearing and order the judgment debtor to show cause why an order for sale should not be made in accordance with the application. The time set for hearing shall be not later than 45 days after the application is filed or such later time as the court orders upon a showing of good cause.

(b) Not later than 30 days before the time set for hearing, the judgment creditor shall do both of the following:

(1) Serve on the judgment debtor a copy of the order to show cause, a copy of the application of the judgment creditor, and a copy of the notice of the hearing in the form prescribed by the Judicial Council. Service shall be made personally or by mail.

(2) Personally serve a copy of each document listed in paragraph (1) on an occupant of the dwelling or, if there is no occupant present at the time service is attempted, post a copy of each document in a conspicuous place at the dwelling. **Leg.H.** Added Stats 1982 ch 1364 §2, operative July 1, 1983. Amended Stats 1985 ch 41 §7.

§704.780. Hearing

(a) The burden of proof at the hearing is determined in the following manner:

(1) If the records of the county tax assessor indicate that there is a current homeowner's exemption or disabled veteran's exemption for the dwelling claimed by the judgment debtor or the judgment debtor's spouse, the judgment creditor has the burden of proof that the dwelling is not a homestead. If the records of the county tax assessor indicate that there is not a current homeowner's exemption or disabled veteran's exemption for the dwelling claimed by the judgment debtor or the judgment debtor's spouse, the burden of proof that the dwelling is a homestead is on the person who claims that the dwelling is a homestead.

(2) If the application states the amount of the homestead exemption, the person claiming the homestead exemption has the burden of proof that the amount of the exemption is other than the amount stated in the application.

(b) The court shall determine whether the dwelling is exempt. If the court determines that the dwelling is exempt, the court shall determine the amount of the homestead exemption and the fair market value of the dwelling. The court shall make an order for sale of the dwelling subject to the homestead exemption, unless the court determines that the sale of the dwelling would not be likely to produce a bid sufficient to satisfy any part of the amount due on the judgment pursuant to Section 704.800. The order for sale of the dwelling subject to the homestead exemption shall specify the amount of the proceeds of the sale that is to be distributed to each person having a lien or encumbrance on the dwelling and shall include the name and address of each such person. Subject to the provisions of this article, the sale is governed by Article 6 (commencing with Section 701.510) of Chapter 3. If the court determines that the dwelling is not exempt, the court shall make an order for sale of the property in the manner provided in Article 6 (commencing with Section 701.510) of Chapter 3.

(c) The court clerk shall transmit a certified copy of the court order (1) to the levying officer and (2) if the court making the order is not the court in which the judgment was entered, to the clerk of the court in which the judgment was entered.

(d) The court may appoint a qualified appraiser to assist the court in determining the fair market value of the dwelling. If the court appoints an appraiser, the court shall fix the compensation of the appraiser in an amount determined by the court to be reasonable, not to exceed similar fees for similar services in the community where the dwelling is located. **Leg.H.** Added Stats 1982 ch 1364 §2, operative July 1, 1983. Amended Stats 1984 ch 538 §26.5; Stats 1995 ch 196 §8 (SB 832), effective July 31, 1995.

§704.790. Procedure after order of sale upon default

(a) This section applies in any case where the court makes an order for sale of the dwelling upon a hearing at which none of the following appeared:

(1) The judgment debtor.
(2) The judgment debtor's spouse.
(3) The attorney for the judgment debtor.
(4) The attorney for the judgment debtor's spouse.

(b) Not later than 10 days after the date of the order for sale, the judgment creditor shall serve a copy of the order and a notice of the order in the form prescribed by the Judicial Council:

(1) Personally or by mail on the judgment debtor and the judgment debtor's spouse.
(2) Personally on an occupant of the dwelling or, if there is no occupant present at the time service is attempted, post a copy of the order and notice in a conspicuous place at the dwelling.

(c) Proof of service and of any posting shall be filed with the court and with the levying officer. If the judgment creditor fails to comply with this subdivision and with subdivision (b) in any case where this section applies, the dwelling may not be sold under the order for sale.

(d) If, within 10 days after service of notice of the order, the judgment debtor or the judgment debtor's spouse files with the levying officer a declaration that the absence of the judgment debtor and the judgment debtor's spouse or the attorney for the judgment debtor or the judgment debtor's spouse from the hearing was due to mistake, inadvertence, surprise, or excusable neglect and that the judgment debtor or spouse of the judgment debtor wishes to assert the homestead exemption, the levying officer shall transmit the declaration forthwith to the court. Upon receipt of the declaration, the court shall set a time and place for hearing to determine whether the determinations of the court should be modified. The time set for hearing shall be not later than 20 days after receipt of the declaration. The court clerk shall cause notice of the hearing promptly to be given to the parties. **Leg.H.** Added Stats 1982 ch 1364 §2, operative July 1, 1983. Amended Stats 1985 ch 41 §8.

§704.800. Minimum bid

(a) If no bid is received at a sale of a homestead pursuant to a court order for sale that exceeds the amount of the homestead exemption plus any additional amount necessary to satisfy all liens and encumbrances on the property, including but not limited to any attachment or judgment lien, the homestead shall not be sold and shall be released and is not thereafter subject to a court order for sale upon subsequent application by the same judgment creditor for a period of one year.

(b) If no bid is received at the sale of a homestead pursuant to a court order for sale that is 90 percent or more of the fair market value determined pursuant to Section 704.780, the homestead shall not be sold unless the court, upon motion of the judgment creditor, does one of the following:

(1) Grants permission to accept the highest bid that exceeds the amount of the minimum bid required by subdivision (a).
(2) Makes a new order for sale of the homestead. **Leg.H.** Added Stats 1982 ch 1364 §2, operative July 1, 1983.

§704.810. Acceleration clauses and prepayment penalties

Levy on a homestead that is subject to a lien or encumbrance is not by itself grounds for acceleration of the obligation secured by the lien or encumbrance, notwithstanding any provision of the obligation, lien, or encumbrance and if the homestead is sold pursuant to court order under this article the amount payable to satisfy a lien or encumbrance shall not include any penalty for prepayment. **Leg.H.** Added Stats 1982 ch 1364 §2, operative July 1, 1983.

§704.820. Procedure where judgment debtor is co-owner or owns less than fee

If the dwelling is owned by the judgment debtor as a joint tenant or tenant in common or if the interest of the judgment debtor in the dwelling is a leasehold or other interest less than a fee interest:

(a) At an execution sale of a dwelling, the interest of the judgment debtor in the dwelling and not the dwelling shall be sold. If there is more than one judgment debtor of the judgment creditor, the interests of the judgment debtors in the dwelling shall be sold together and each of the judgment debtors entitled to a homestead exemption is entitled to apply his or her exemption to his or her own interest.

(b) For the purposes of this section, all references in this article to the "dwelling" or "homestead" are deemed to be references to the interest of the judgment debtor in the dwelling or homestead. **Leg.H.** Added Stats 1982 ch 1364 §2, operative July 1, 1983.

§704.830. Extensions of time and appeals

The provisions of Sections 703.590 and 703.600 apply to proceedings under this article. **Leg.H.** Added Stats 1982 ch 1364 §2, operative July 1, 1983.

§704.840. Costs

(a) Except as provided in subdivision (b), the judgment creditor is entitled to recover reasonable costs incurred in a proceeding under this article.

(b) If no bid is received at a sale of a homestead pursuant to a court order for sale that exceeds the amount of the homestead exemption plus any additional amount necessary to satisfy all liens and encumbrances on the property, the judgment creditor is not entitled to recover costs incurred in a proceeding under this article or costs of sale. **Leg.H.** Added Stats 1982 ch 1364 §2, operative July 1, 1983.

§704.850. Distribution of proceeds of sale of homestead

(a) The levying officer shall distribute the proceeds of sale of a homestead in the following order:

(1) To the discharge of all liens and encumbrances, if any, on the property.
(2) To the judgment debtor in the amount of any applicable exemption of proceeds pursuant to Section 704.720.
(3) To the levying officer for the reimbursement of the levying officer's costs for which an advance has not been made.
(4) To the judgment creditor to satisfy the following:
  (A) First, costs and interest accruing after issuance of the writ pursuant to which the sale is conducted.
  (B) Second, the amount due on the judgment with costs and interest, as entered on the writ.
(5) To the judgment debtor in the amount remaining.

(b) Sections 701.820 and 701.830 apply to distribution of proceeds under this section. **Leg.H.** Added Stats 1982 ch 1364 §2, operative July 1, 1983.

ARTICLE 5
Declared Homesteads

Definitions. §704.910.
Manner of selection of homestead. §704.920.

Execution and contents of homestead declaration. §704.930.
Right to convey or encumber not limited; Evidentiary effect of homestead. §704.940.
Attachment of judgment lien to homestead. §704.950.
Exemption of proceeds after voluntary sale; Reinvestment of proceeds of voluntary or involuntary sale and effect of new declaration. §704.960.
Determination of amount of exemption. §704.965.
Effect of article on right of levy under writ of execution. §704.970.
Declaration of abandonment. §704.980.
Abandonment of homestead by recording homestead declaration for different property. §704.990.
Continuation of protection after death of declared homestead owner. §704.995.

§704.910. Definitions

As used in this article:

(a) "Declared homestead" means the dwelling described in a homestead declaration.

(b) "Declared homestead owner" includes both of the following:

(1) The owner of an interest in the declared homestead who is named as a declared homestead owner in a homestead declaration recorded pursuant to this article.

(2) The declarant named in a declaration of homestead recorded prior to July 1, 1983, pursuant to former Title 5 (commencing with Section 1237) of Part 4 of Division 2 of the Civil Code and the spouse of such declarant.

(c) "Dwelling" means any interest in real property (whether present or future, vested or contingent, legal or equitable) that is a "dwelling" as defined in Section 704.710, but does not include a leasehold estate with an unexpired term of less than two years or the interest of the beneficiary of a trust.

(d) "Homestead declaration" includes both of the following:

(1) A homestead declaration recorded pursuant to this article.

(2) A declaration of homestead recorded prior to July 1, 1983, pursuant to former Title 5 (commencing with former Section 1237) of Part 4 of Division 2 of the Civil Code.

(e) "Spouse" means a "spouse" as defined in Section 704.710. **Leg.H.** Added Stats 1982 ch 1364 §2, operative July 1, 1983.

§704.920. Manner of selection of homestead

A dwelling in which an owner or spouse of an owner resides may be selected as a declared homestead pursuant to this article by recording a homestead declaration in the office of the county recorder of the county where the dwelling is located. From and after the time of recording, the dwelling is a declared homestead for the purposes of this article. **Leg.H.** Added Stats 1982 ch 1364 §2, operative July 1, 1983.

§704.930. Execution and contents of homestead declaration

(a) A homestead declaration recorded pursuant to this article shall contain all of the following:

(1) The name of the declared homestead owner. Spouses both may be named as declared homestead owners in the same homestead declaration if each owns an interest in the dwelling selected as the declared homestead.

(2) A description of the declared homestead.

(3) A statement that the declared homestead is the principal dwelling of the declared homestead owner or such person's spouse, and that the declared homestead owner or such person's spouse resides in the declared homestead on the date the homestead declaration is recorded.

(b) The homestead declaration shall be executed and acknowledged in the manner of an acknowledgment of a conveyance of real property by at least one of the following persons:

(1) The declared homestead owner.

(2) The spouse of the declared homestead owner.

(3) The guardian or conservator of the person or estate of either of the persons listed in paragraph (1) or (2). The guardian or conservator may execute, acknowledge, and record a homestead declaration without the need to obtain court authorization.

(4) A person acting under a power of attorney or otherwise authorized to act on behalf of a person listed in paragraph (1) or (2).

(c) The homestead declaration shall include a statement that the facts stated in the homestead declaration are known to be true as of the personal knowledge of the person executing and acknowledging the homestead declaration. If the homestead declaration is executed and acknowledged by a person listed in paragraph (3) or (4) of subdivision (b), it shall also contain a statement that the person has authority to so act on behalf of the declared homestead owner or the spouse of the declared homestead owner and the source of the person's authority. **Leg.H.** Added Stats 1982 ch 1364 §2, operative July 1, 1983. Amended Stats 1983 ch 155 §18, effective June 30, 1983, operative July 1, 1983; Stats 2016 ch 50 §17 (SB 1005), effective January 1, 2017.

2016 Note: For legislative intent, see the 2016 Note following CCP §17.

§704.940. Right to convey or encumber not limited; Evidentiary effect of homestead

A homestead declaration does not restrict or limit any right to convey or encumber the declared homestead. A homestead declaration, when properly recorded, is prima facie evidence of the facts therein stated, and conclusive evidence thereof in favor of a purchaser or encumbrancer in good faith and for a valuable consideration. **Leg.H.** Added Stats 1982 ch 1364 §2, operative July 1, 1983.

§704.950. Attachment of judgment lien to homestead

(a) Except as provided in subdivisions (b) and (c), a judgment lien on real property created pursuant to Article 2 (commencing with Section 697.310) of Chapter 2 does not attach to a declared homestead if both of the following requirements are satisfied:

(1) A homestead declaration describing the declared homestead was recorded prior to the time the abstract or certified copy of the judgment was recorded to create the judgment lien.

(2) The homestead declaration names the judgment debtor or the spouse of the judgment debtor as a declared homestead owner.

(b) This section does not apply to a judgment lien created under Section 697.320 by recording a certified copy of a judgment for child, family, or spousal support.

(c) A judgment lien attaches to a declared homestead in the amount of any surplus over the total of the following:

(1) All liens and encumbrances on the declared homestead at the time the abstract of judgment or certified copy of the judgment is recorded to create the judgment lien.

(2) The homestead exemption set forth in Section 704.730. **Leg.H.** Added Stats 1982 ch 1364 §2, operative July 1, 1983. Amended Stats 1992 ch 163 §44 (AB 2641), operative January 1, 1994.

§704.960. Exemption of proceeds after voluntary sale; Reinvestment of proceeds of voluntary or involuntary sale and effect of new declaration

(a) If a declared homestead is voluntarily sold, the proceeds of sale are exempt in the amount provided by Section 704.730 for a period of six months after the date of sale.

(b) If the proceeds of a declared homestead are invested in a new dwelling within six months after the date of a voluntary sale or within six months after proceeds of an execution sale or of insurance or other indemnification for damage or destruction are received, the new dwelling may be selected as a declared homestead by recording a homestead declaration within the applicable six-month period. In such case, the homestead declaration has the same effect as if it had been recorded at the time the prior homestead declaration was recorded. **Leg.H.** Added Stats 1982 ch 1364 §2, operative July 1, 1983.

§704.965. Determination of amount of exemption

If a homestead declaration is recorded prior to the operative date of an amendment to Section 704.730 which increases the amount of the homestead exemption, the amount of the exemption for the purposes of subdivision (c) of Section 704.950 and Section 704.960 is the increased amount, except that, if the judgment creditor obtained a lien on the declared homestead prior to the operative date of the amendment to Section 704.730, the exemption for the purposes of subdivision (c) of Section 704.950 and Section 704.960 shall be determined as if that amendment to Section 704.730 had not been enacted. **Leg.H.** Added Stats 1984 ch 454 §2.

§704.970. Effect of article on right of levy under writ of execution

Whether or not a homestead declaration has been recorded:

(a) Nothing in this article affects the right of levy pursuant to a writ of execution.

(b) Any levy pursuant to a writ of execution on a dwelling (as defined in Section 704.710) and the sale pursuant thereto shall be made in compliance with Article 4 (commencing with Section 704.710) and the

§704.980. Declaration of abandonment

judgment debtor and the judgment creditor shall have all the rights and benefits provided by that article. **Leg.H.** Added Stats 1982 ch 1364 §2, operative July 1, 1983.

§704.980. Declaration of abandonment

(a) A declared homestead may be abandoned by a declaration of abandonment under this section, whether the homestead declaration was recorded pursuant to this article or pursuant to former Title 5 (commencing with former Section 1237) of Part 4 of Division 2 of the Civil Code.

(b) A declaration of abandonment shall be executed and acknowledged in the manner of an acknowledgment of a conveyance of real property. It shall be executed and acknowledged by a declared homestead owner or by a person authorized to act on behalf of a declared homestead owner. If it is executed and acknowledged by a person authorized to act on behalf of a declared homestead owner, the declaration shall contain a statement that the person has authority to act on behalf of the declared homestead owner and the source of the person's authority.

(c) The declaration of abandonment does not affect the declared homestead of any person other than the declared homestead owner named in the declaration of abandonment. **Leg.H.** Added Stats 1982 ch 1364 §2, operative July 1, 1983.

§704.990. Abandonment of homestead by recording homestead declaration for different property

(a) A declared homestead is abandoned by operation of law as to a declared homestead owner if the declared homestead owner or a person authorized to act on behalf of the declared homestead owner executes, acknowledges, and records a new homestead declaration for the declared homestead owner on different property. An abandonment under this subdivision does not affect the declared homestead of any person other than the declared homestead owner named in the new homestead declaration.

(b) Notwithstanding subdivision (a), if a homestead declaration is recorded which includes property described in a previously recorded homestead declaration, to the extent that the prior homestead declaration is still valid, the new homestead declaration shall not be considered an abandonment of the prior declared homestead. **Leg.H.** Added Stats 1982 ch 1364 §2, operative July 1, 1983.

§704.995. Continuation of protection after death of declared homestead owner

(a) The protection of the declared homestead from any creditor having an attachment lien, execution lien, or judgment lien on the dwelling continues after the death of the declared homestead owner if, at the time of the death, the dwelling was the principal dwelling of one or more of the following persons to whom all or part of the interest of the deceased declared homestead owner passes:

(1) The surviving spouse of the decedent.

(2) A member of the family of the decedent.

(b) The protection of the declared homestead provided by subdivision (a) continues regardless of whether the decedent was the sole owner of the declared homestead or owned the declared homestead with the surviving spouse or a member of the decedent's family and regardless of whether the surviving spouse or the member of the decedent's family was a declared homestead owner at the time of the decedent's death.

(c) The amount of the homestead exemption is determined pursuant to Section 704.730 depending on the circumstances of the case at the time the amount is required to be determined. **Leg.H.** Added Stats 1984 ch 538 §27.

§705. [Section repealed 1983]

Leg.H. Enacted Stats 1872. Amended Stats 1909 ch 632 §1; Stats 1945 ch 828 §4. Repealed Stats 1982 ch 1364 §1, operative July 1, 1983. The repealed section related to documents redemptioner was required to produce and serve.

§706. [Section repealed 1983]

Leg.H. Enacted Stats 1872. Repealed Stats 1982 ch 1364 §1, operative July 1, 1983. The repealed section related to restraint of waste during redemption period.

CHAPTER 5
WAGE GARNISHMENT

Article 1. Short Title; Definitions.
Article 2. General Provisions.
Article 3. Restrictions on Earnings Withholding.
Article 4. Earnings Withholding Order for Taxes.
Article 5. Procedure for Earnings Withholding Orders and Exemption Claims.
Article 6. Forms; Employer's Instructions.
Article 7. Administration and Enforcement.

ARTICLE 1
Short Title; Definitions

Citation of chapter. §706.010.
Definitions. §706.011.

§706.010. Citation of chapter

This chapter shall be known and may be cited as the "Wage Garnishment Law." **Leg.H.** Added Stats 1982 ch 1364 §2, operative July 1, 1983.

§706.011. Definitions

As used in this chapter:

(a) "Disposable earnings" means the portion of an individual's earnings that remains after deducting all amounts required to be withheld by law.

(b) "Earnings" means compensation payable by an employer to an employee for personal services performed by such employee, whether denominated as wages, salary, commission, bonus, or otherwise.

(c) "Earnings withholding order for elder or dependent adult financial abuse" means an earnings withholding order, made pursuant to Article 5 (commencing with Section 706.100) and based on a money judgment in an action for elder or adult dependent financial abuse under Section 15657.5 of the Welfare and Institutions Code.

(d) "Earnings assignment order for support" means an order, made pursuant to Chapter 8 (commencing with Section 5200) of Part 5 of Division 9 of the Family Code or Section 3088 of the Probate Code, which requires an employer to withhold earnings for support.

(e) "Employee" means a public officer and any individual who performs services subject to the right of the employer to control both what shall be done and how it shall be done.

(f) "Employer" means a person for whom an individual performs services as an employee.

(g) "Judgment creditor," as applied to the state, means the specific state agency seeking to collect a judgment or tax liability.

(h) "Judgment debtor" includes a person from whom the state is seeking to collect a tax liability under Article 4 (commencing with Section 706.070), whether or not a judgment has been obtained on such tax liability.

(i) "Person" includes an individual, a corporation, a partnership or other unincorporated association, a limited liability company, and a public entity. **Leg.H.** Added Stats 1982 ch 1364 §2, operative July 1, 1983. Amended Stats 1990 ch 1493 §30.5 (AB 3974); Stats 1992 ch 163 §45 (AB 2641), operative January 1, 1994; Stats 1994 ch 1010 §61 (SB 2053); Stats 2010 ch 64 §1 (AB 2619), effective January 1, 2011, operative January 1, 2012; Stats 2012 ch 474 §1 (AB 1775), effective January 1, 2013, operative July 1, 2013.

2012 Note: In order to implement the provisions of this act, the Judicial Council shall, on or before July 1, 2013, revise the instructions contained in the employer's instructions pursuant to Section 706.127 of the Code of Civil Procedure to specify the method of computation described in Section 2 of this act. Stats 2012 ch 474 (AB 1775) §4.

ARTICLE 2
General Provisions

Withholding earnings; Use of provisions of chapter. §706.020.
Levy of execution; Service of earnings withholding order. §706.021.
Employer's duty to withhold; Immunity from liability. §706.022.
Priority of earnings withholding order. §706.023.
Amount required to satisfy earnings withholding order. §706.024.
Payments to levying officer by employer. §706.025.
Receipt and account by levying officer; Payments to entitled person; Accounting. §706.026.
Satisfaction of judgment prior to termination of order; Notices. §706.027.
Final earnings withholding order for costs and interest. §706.028.
Lien created by service of earnings withholding order. §706.029.
Withholding order for support. §706.030.
Earnings assignment order for support. §706.031.
Termination of earnings withholding order. §706.032.
Supplemental return on writ. §706.033.
Deduction for payments under earnings withholding order. §706.034.

§706.020. Withholding earnings; Use of provisions of chapter

Except for an earning assignment order for support, the earnings of an employee shall not be required to be withheld by an employer for payment of a debt by means of any judicial procedure other than pursuant to this chapter. **Leg.H.** Added Stats 1982 ch 1364 §2, operative July 1, 1983. Amended Stats 1992 ch 163 §46 (AB 2641), operative January 1, 1994.

§706.021. Levy of execution; Service of earnings withholding order

Notwithstanding any other provision of this title, a levy of execution upon the earnings of an employee shall be made by service of an earnings withholding order upon the employer **and judgment debtor** in accordance with this chapter. **Leg.H.** Added Stats 1982 ch 1364 §2, operative July 1, 1983. Amended Stats 2024 ch 514 §9 (AB 2837), effective January 1, 2025.

§706.022. Employer's duty to withhold; Immunity from liability

(a) **A judgment creditor shall not enforce an earnings withholding order beyond the period of enforceability as defined in Section 683.020 or, if renewed, as provided for in subdivision (c) of Section 683.120.** As used in this section, "withholding period" means the period which commences on the [1] **30th** day after service of an earnings withholding order upon the [2] **judgment debtor. If a claim of exemption is filed with the levying officer, and the employer is given actual notice before the close of business on the 29th day after the service of the earnings withholding order on the judgment debtor, the withholding period commences on the 45th day after service of the earnings withholding order on the judgment debtor. The withholding period shall continue** until the earliest of the following dates:

(1) The date the employer has withheld the full amount required to satisfy the order.

(2) The date of termination specified in a court order served on the employer.

(3) The date of termination specified in a notice of termination served on the employer by the levying officer.

(4) The date of termination of a dormant or suspended earnings withholding order as determined pursuant to Section 706.032.

(b) Except as otherwise provided by statute, an employer shall withhold the amounts required by an earnings withholding order from all earnings of the employee payable for any pay period of the employee which ends during the withholding period.

(c) An employer is not liable for any amounts withheld and paid over to the levying officer pursuant to an earnings withholding order prior to service upon the employer pursuant to paragraph (2) or (3) of subdivision (a). **Leg.H.** Added Stats 1982 ch 1364 §2, operative July 1, 1983. Amended Stats 1989 ch 263 §1; Stats 1992 ch 283 §5 (SB 1372), effective July 21, 1992; Stats 2024 ch 514 §10 (AB 2837), effective January 1, 2025.

§706.022. 2024 Deletes. [1] 10th [2] employer and which continues

1992 Note: Section 706.022, as amended by ch 283, applies to all writs of execution and earnings withholding orders regardless of whether they were issued before July 21, 1992. Stats 1992 ch 283 §17.

§706.023. Priority of earnings withholding order

Except as otherwise provided in this chapter:

(a) An employer shall comply with the first earnings withholding order served upon the employer.

(b) If the employer is served with two or more earnings withholding orders on the same day, the employer shall comply with the order issued pursuant to the judgment first entered. If two or more orders served on the same day are based on judgments entered upon the same day, the employer shall comply with whichever one of the orders the employer selects.

(c) If an earnings withholding order is served while an employer is required to comply with another earnings withholding order with respect to the earnings of the same employee, the subsequent order is ineffective and the employer shall not withhold earnings pursuant to the subsequent order, except as provided in subdivision (d).

(d) Notwithstanding any other provisions of this section, a withholding order for elder or dependent adult financial abuse has priority over any other earning withholding order except for a withholding order for support under Section 706.030 and a withholding order for taxes under Section 706.072.

(1) An employer upon whom a withholding order for elder or dependent adult financial abuse is served shall withhold and pay over earnings of the employee pursuant to that order notwithstanding the requirements of another earnings withholding order except as provided in paragraph (2).

(2) An employer shall not withhold earnings of an employee pursuant to an earnings withholding order for elder or dependent adult financial abuse if a withholding order for support or for taxes is in effect or if a prior withholding order for elder or dependent adult financial abuse is in effect. In that case, the subsequent withholding order for elder or dependent financial abuse is ineffective.

(3) When an employer is required to cease withholding earnings pursuant to a prior earnings withholding order, the employer shall notify the levying officer who served the prior earnings withholding order that a supervening earnings withholding order for elder or dependent financial abuse is in effect. **Leg.H.** Added Stats 1982 ch 1364 §2, operative July 1, 1983. Amended Stats 2010 ch 64 §2 (AB 2619), effective January 1, 2011, operative January 1, 2012.

§706.024. Amount required to satisfy earnings withholding order

(a) The amount required to satisfy an earnings withholding order is the total amount required to satisfy the writ of execution on the date the order is issued, with the following additions and subtractions:

(1) The addition of the statutory fee for service of the order and any other statutory fees for performing duties under the order.

(2) The addition of costs added to the order pursuant to Section 685.090.

(3) The subtraction of the amount of any partial satisfactions.

(4) The addition of daily interest accruing after issuance of the order, as adjusted for partial satisfactions.

(b) From time to time the levying officer, in the levying officer's discretion, may give written notice to the employer of the amount required to satisfy the earnings withholding order and the employer shall determine the total amount to withhold based upon the levying officer's notice, notwithstanding a different amount stated in the order originally served on the employer.

(c) If the full amount required to satisfy the earnings withholding order as stated in the order or in the levying officer's notice under subdivision (b) is withheld from the judgment debtor's earnings, interest ceases to accrue on that amount. **Leg.H.** Added Stats 1992 ch 283 §6 (SB 1372), effective July 21, 1992.

1992 Note: Section 706.024, as added by ch 283, applies to all writs of execution and earnings withholding orders regardless of whether they were issued before July 21, 1992. Stats 1992 ch 283 §17.

§706.025. Payments to levying officer by employer

(a) Except as provided in subdivision (b), the amount required to be withheld pursuant to an earnings withholding order shall be paid monthly to the levying officer not later than the 15th day of each month. The initial monthly payment shall include all amounts required to be withheld from the earnings of the employee during the preceding calendar month up to the close of the employee's pay period ending closest to the last day of that month, and thereafter each monthly payment shall include amounts withheld from the employee's earnings for services rendered in the interim up to the close of the employee's pay period ending closest to the last day of the preceding calendar month.

(b) The employer may elect to pay the amounts withheld to the levying officer more frequently than monthly. If the employer so elects, payment of the amount withheld from the employee's earnings for each pay period shall be made not later than 10 days after the close of the pay period. **Leg.H.** Added Stats 1982 ch 1364 §2, operative July 1, 1983.

§706.026. Receipt and account by levying officer; Payments to entitled person; Accounting

(a) The levying officer shall receive and account for all amounts paid by the employer pursuant to Section 706.025 and shall pay the amounts so received over to the person entitled thereto at least once every 30 days.

(b) At least once every two years, the levying officer shall file an accounting with the court, as provided by Section 699.560, for all amounts collected under the earnings withholding order, including costs and interest added to the amount due. Subject to the limitations in subdivision (c) of Section 263, the levying officer may electronically file the accounting with the court, pursuant to Chapter 2 (commencing with Section 263) of Title 4 of Part 1. **Leg.H.** Added Stats 1982 ch 1364 §2, operative July 1, 1983. Amended Stats 1992 ch 283 §7 (SB 1372), effective July 21, 1992; Stats 2010 ch 680 §12 (AB 2394), effective January 1, 2011.

1992 Note: Section 706.026, as amended by ch 283, applies to all writs of execution and earnings withholding orders regardless of whether they were issued before July 21, 1992. Stats 1992 ch 283 §17.

§706.027. Satisfaction of judgment prior to termination of order; Notices

If the judgment pursuant to which the earnings withholding order is issued is satisfied before the order otherwise terminates pursuant to Section 706.022, the judgment creditor shall promptly notify the levying officer who shall promptly terminate the order by serving a notice of termination on the employer. **Leg.H.** Added Stats 1982 ch 1364 §2, operative July 1, 1983.

§706.028. Final earnings withholding order for costs and interest

(a) "Final earnings withholding order for costs and interest" means an earnings withholding order for the collection only of unsatisfied costs and interest, which is issued after an earlier earnings withholding order has been returned satisfied.

(b) After the amount stated as owing in a prior earnings withholding order is paid, the judgment creditor may obtain a final earnings withholding order for costs and interest to collect amounts of costs and interest that were not collected under the prior earnings withholding order.

(c) A final earnings withholding order for costs and interest shall be enforced in the same manner as other earnings withholding orders.

(d) Satisfaction of the amount stated as owing in a final earnings withholding order for costs and interest is equivalent to satisfaction of the money judgment. For this purpose, interest ceases to accrue on the date of issuance of the final earnings withholding order and no additional costs may be added after that date, except for the statutory fee for service of the order and any other statutory fees for performing duties under the order. **Leg.H.** Added Stats 1992 ch 283 §9, effective July 21, 1992.

Prior Law: Former CCP §706.028, similar to the present section, was added Stats 1982 ch 1364 §2, operative July 1, 1983, and repealed Stats 1992 ch 283 §8 (SB 1372), effective July 21, 1992.

1992 Note: Section 706.028, as added by ch 283, applies to all writs of execution and earnings withholding orders regardless of whether they were issued before July 21, 1992. Stats 1992 ch 283 §17.

§706.029. Lien created by service of earnings withholding order

Service of an earnings withholding order creates a lien upon the earnings of the judgment debtor that are required to be withheld pursuant to the order and upon all property of the employer subject to the enforcement of a money judgment in the amount required to be withheld pursuant to such order. The lien continues for a period of one year from the date the earnings of the judgment debtor become payable unless the amount required to be withheld pursuant to the order is paid as required by law. **Leg.H.** Added Stats 1982 ch 1364 §2, operative July 1, 1983.

§706.030. Withholding order for support

(a) A "withholding order for support" is an earnings withholding order issued on a writ of execution to collect delinquent amounts payable under a judgment for the support of a child, or spouse or former spouse, of the judgment debtor. A withholding order for support shall be denoted as such on its face.

(b) The local child support agency may issue a withholding order for support on a notice of levy pursuant to Section 17522 of the Family Code to collect a support obligation.

(1) When the local child support agency issues a withholding order for support, a reference in this chapter to a levying officer is deemed to mean the local child support agency who issues the withholding order for support.

(2) Service of a withholding order for support issued by the local child support agency may be made by first-class mail or in any other manner described in Section 706.101. Service of a withholding order for support issued by the local child support agency is complete when it is received by the employer or a person described in paragraph (1) or (2) of subdivision (a) of Section 706.101, or if service is by first-class mail, service is complete as specified in Section 1013.

(3) The local child support agency shall serve upon the employer the withholding order for support, a copy of the order, and a notice informing the support obligor of the effect of the order and of his or her right to hearings and remedies provided in this chapter and in the Family Code. The notice shall be accompanied by the forms necessary to obtain an administrative review and a judicial hearing and instructions on how to file the forms. Within 10 days from the date of service, the employer shall deliver to the support obligor a copy of the withholding order for support, the forms to obtain an administrative review and judicial hearing, and the notice. If the support obligor is no longer employed by the employer and the employer does not owe the support obligor any earnings, the employer shall inform the local child support agency that the support obligor is no longer employed by the employer.

(4) An employer who fails to comply with paragraph (3) shall be subject to a civil penalty of five hundred dollars ($500) for each occurrence.

(5) The local child support agency shall provide for an administrative review to reconsider or modify the amount to be withheld for arrearages pursuant to the withholding order for support, if the support obligor requests a review at any time after service of the withholding order. The local child support agency shall provide the review in the same manner and timeframes provided for resolution of a complaint pursuant to Section 17800 of the Family Code. The local child support agency shall notify the employer if the review results in any modifications to the withholding order for support. If the local child support agency cannot complete the administrative review within 30 calendar days of receipt of the complaint, the local child support agency shall notify the employer to suspend withholding any disputed amount pending the completion of the review and the determination by the local child support agency.

(6) Nothing in this section prohibits the support obligor from seeking a judicial determination of arrearages pursuant to subdivision (c) of Section 17256 of the Family Code or from filing a motion for equitable division of earnings pursuant to Section 706.052 either prior to or after the administrative review provided by this section. Within five business days after receiving notice of the obligor having filed for judicial relief pursuant to this section, the local child support agency shall notify the employer to suspend withholding any disputed amount pending a determination by the court. The employer shall then adjust the withholding within not more than nine days of receiving the notice from the local child support agency.

(c) Notwithstanding any other provision of this chapter:

(1) An employer shall continue to withhold pursuant to a withholding order for support until the earliest of the dates specified in paragraph (1), (2), or (3) of subdivision (a) of Section 706.022, except that a withholding order for support shall automatically terminate one year after the employment of the employee by the employer terminates.

(2) A withholding order for support has priority over any other earnings withholding order. An employer upon whom a withholding order for support is served shall withhold and pay over earnings of the employee pursuant to that order notwithstanding the requirements of another earnings withholding order.

(3) Subject to paragraph (2) and to Article 3 (commencing with Section 706.050), an employer shall withhold earnings pursuant to both a withholding order for support and another earnings withholding order simultaneously.

(4) An employer who willfully fails to withhold and forward support pursuant to a valid earnings withholding order for support issued and served upon the employer pursuant to this chapter is liable to the support obligee, as defined in Section 5214 of the Family Code, for the amount of support not withheld, forwarded, or otherwise paid to the support obligee.

(5) Notwithstanding any other provision of law, an employer shall send all earnings withheld pursuant to a withholding order for support to the levying officer or the State Disbursement Unit as described in Section 17309 of the Family Code within the time period specified by federal law.

(6) Once the State Disbursement Unit as described in Section 17309 of the Family Code is operational, all support payments made pursuant to an earnings withholding order shall be made to that unit.

(7) Earnings withheld pursuant to an earnings withholding order for support shall be credited toward satisfaction of a support judgment as specified in Section 695.221. **Leg.H.** Added Stats 1982 ch 1364 §2,

operative July 1, 1983. Amended Stats 1992 ch 283 §10 (SB 1372), effective July 21, 1992; Stats 1997 ch 599 §5 (AB 573); Stats 2000 ch 808 §17 (AB 1358), effective September 28, 2000; Stats 2001 ch 755 §1 (SB 943), effective October 12, 2001; Stats 2003 ch 387 §1 (AB 739).

§706.031. Earnings assignment order for support

(a) Nothing in this chapter affects an earnings assignment order for support.

(b) An earnings assignment order for support shall be given priority over any earnings withholding order. An employer upon whom an earnings assignment order for support is served shall withhold and pay over the earnings of the employee pursuant to the assignment order notwithstanding the requirements of any earnings withholding order. When an employer is required to cease withholding earnings pursuant to an earnings withholding order, the employer shall notify the levying officer who served the earnings withholding order that a supervening earnings assignment order for support is in effect.

(c) Subject to subdivisions (b), (d), and (e), an employer shall withhold earnings of an employee pursuant to both an earnings assignment order for support and an earnings withholding order.

(d) The employer shall withhold pursuant to an earnings withholding order only to the extent that the sum of the amount withheld pursuant to any earnings assignment order for support and the amount withheld pursuant to the earnings withholding order does not exceed the amount that may be withheld under Article 3 (commencing with Section 706.050).

(e) The employer shall withhold pursuant to an earnings withholding order for taxes only to the extent that the sum of the amount withheld pursuant to any earnings assignment order for support and the amount withheld pursuant to the earnings withholding order for taxes does not exceed the amount that may be withheld under Article 4 (commencing with Section 706.070). **Leg.H.** Added Stats 1982 ch 1364 §2, operative July 1, 1983. Amended Stats 1992 ch 163 §47 (AB 2641), operative January 1, 1994.

§706.032. Termination of earnings withholding order

(a) Except as otherwise provided by statute:

(1) If withholding under an earnings withholding order ceases because the judgment debtor's employment has terminated, the earnings withholding order terminates at the conclusion of a continuous 180-day period during which no amounts are withheld under the order.

(2) If withholding under an earnings withholding order ceases because the judgment debtor's earnings are subject to an order or assignment with higher priority, the earnings withholding order terminates at the conclusion of a continuous two-year period during which no amounts are withheld under the order.

(b) If an earnings withholding order has terminated pursuant to subdivision (a), the employer shall return the order to the levying officer along with a statement of the reasons for returning the order. **Leg.H.** Added Stats 1992 ch 283 §11 (SB 1372), effective July 21, 1992.

1992 Note: Section 706.032, as added by ch 283, applies to all writs of execution and earnings withholding orders regardless of whether they were issued before July 21, 1992. Stats 1992 ch 283 §17.

§706.033. Supplemental return on writ

If the writ is returned before the earnings withholding order terminates, on termination of the earnings withholding order the levying officer shall make a supplemental return on the writ. The supplemental return shall contain the same information as an original return pursuant to Section 699.560. **Leg.H.** Added Stats 1992 ch 283 §12 (SB 1372), effective July 21, 1992.

1992 Note: Section 706.033, as added by ch 283, applies to all writs of execution and earnings withholding orders regardless of whether they were issued before July 21, 1992. Stats 1992 ch 283 §17.

§706.034. Deduction for payments under earnings withholding order

The employer may deduct from the earnings of the employee the sum of one dollar and fifty cents ($1.50) for each payment made in accordance with an earnings withholding order issued pursuant to this chapter. **Leg.H.** Added Stats 1997 ch 137 §1 (AB 519). Amended Stats 2004 ch 520 §1 (AB 2530).

ARTICLE 3
Restrictions on Earnings Withholding

Maximum amount of disposable earnings; Use of multipliers. § 706.050.

Earnings necessary for support of judgment debtor or judgment debtor's family. §706.051.

Earnings withholding order for support. §706.052.

§ 706.050. Maximum amount of disposable earnings; Use of multipliers

(a) Except as otherwise provided in this chapter, the maximum amount of disposable earnings of an individual judgment debtor for any workweek that is subject to levy under an earnings withholding order shall not exceed the lesser of the following:

(1) Twenty percent of the individual's disposable earnings for that week.

(2) Forty percent of the amount by which the individual's disposable earnings for that week exceed 48 times the state minimum hourly wage in effect at the time the earnings are payable. If a judgment debtor works in a location where the local minimum hourly wage is greater than the state minimum hourly wage, the local minimum hourly wage in effect at the time the earnings are payable shall be used for the calculation made pursuant to this paragraph.

(b) For any pay period other than weekly, the following multipliers shall be used to determine the maximum amount of disposable earnings subject to levy under an earnings withholding order that is proportional in effect to the calculation described in paragraph (2) of subdivision (a), except as specified in paragraph (1):

(1) For a daily pay period, the amounts shall be identical to the amounts described in subdivision (a).

(2) For a biweekly pay period, multiply the applicable hourly minimum wage by 96 work hours.

(3) For a semimonthly pay period, multiply the applicable hourly minimum wage by 104 work hours.

(4) For a monthly pay period, multiply the applicable hourly minimum wage by 208 work hours.

(c) This section shall become operative on September 1, 2023. **Leg.H.** Added Stats 2022 ch 849 §2 (SB 1477), effective January 1, 2023, operative September 1, 2023.

Prior Law Former CCP §706.050, similar to the present section, was added Stats 1982 ch 1364 §2, operative July 1, 1983, amended Stats 2012 ch 474 §2 (AB 1775), effective January 1, 2013, operative July 1, 2013, Stats 2015 ch 800 §1 (SB 501), inoperative July 1, 2016, and repealed January 1, 2017, by its own terms.

Former CCP §706.050, relating to maximum amount of disposable earnings and use of multipliers, was added Stats 2015 ch 800 §2 (SB 501), effective January 1, 2016, operative July 1, 2016. Amended Stats 2022 ch 849 §1 (SB 1477), effective January 1, 2023, inoperative September 1, 2023, and repealed January 1, 2024, by its own terms.

§706.051. Earnings necessary for support of judgment debtor or judgment debtor's family

(a) For the purposes of this section, "family of the judgment debtor" includes the spouse or former spouse of the judgment debtor.

(b) Except as provided in subdivision (c), the portion of the judgment debtor's earnings that the judgment debtor proves is necessary for the support of the judgment debtor or the judgment debtor's family supported in whole or in part by the judgment debtor is exempt from levy under this chapter.

(c) The exemption provided in subdivision (b) is not available if any of the following exceptions applies:

(1) The debt was incurred pursuant to an order or award for the payment of attorney's fees under Section 2030, 3121, or 3557 of the Family Code.

(2) The debt was incurred for personal services rendered by an employee or former employee of the judgment debtor.

(3) The order is a withholding order for support under Section 706.030.

(4) The order is one governed by Article 4 (commencing with Section 706.070) (state tax order). **Leg.H.** Added Stats 1982 ch 1364 §2, operative July 1, 1983. Amended Stats 2011 ch 694 §1 (AB 1388), effective January 1, 2012.

§706.052. Earnings withholding order for support

(a) Except as provided in subdivision (b), one-half of the disposable earnings (as defined by Section 1672 of Title 15 of the United States Code) of the judgment debtor, plus any amount withheld from the judgment debtor's earnings pursuant to any earnings assignment order for support, is exempt from levy under this chapter where the earnings withholding order is a withholding order for support under Section 706.030.

(b) Except as provided in subdivision (c), upon motion of any interested party, the court shall make an equitable division of the judgment debtor's earnings that takes into account the needs of all the persons the judgment debtor is required to support and shall effectuate such division by an order determining the amount to be withheld from the judgment debtor's earnings pursuant to the withholding order for support.

(c) An order made under subdivision (b) may not authorize the withholding of an amount in excess of the amount that may be withheld for support under federal law under Section 1673 of Title 15 of the United States Code. **Leg.H.** Added Stats 1982 ch 1364 §2, operative July 1, 1983. Amended Stats 1992 ch 163 §48 (AB 2641), operative January 1, 1994.

ARTICLE 4
Earnings Withholding Order for Taxes

"State"; "State tax liability". §706.070.
Collection of state tax liability; Limitations. §706.071.
Withholding order for taxes; Issuance; Conditions. §706.072.
Application of chapter to withholding order for taxes. §706.073.
Issuance of withholding order for taxes by state; Amount to be withheld. §706.074.
Service on employer of order and notice; Delivery to employee; Administrative hearing to reconsider amount required to be withheld; Liability of employer. §706.075.
Order of court for amount in excess of order issued by state; Temporary earnings holding order. §706.076.
Priority. §706.077.
Pay periods subject to order; Jeopardy withholding order for taxes; Duration of withholding. §706.078.
Service of order or other notice or document. §706.080.
Forms; Prescription by state. §706.081.
Prohibition of review of tax liability. §706.082.
Warrant, notice of levy or notice or order to withhold served on employer deemed withholding order for taxes; Requirements. §706.084.

§706.070. "State"; "State tax liability"

As used in this article:

(a) "State" means the State of California and includes any officer, department, board, or agency thereof.

(b) "State tax liability" means an amount for which the state has a state tax lien as defined in Section 7162 of the Government Code excluding a state tax lien created pursuant to the Fish and Game Code.

(c) For purposes of an earnings withholding order for taxes issued by the Franchise Tax Board, "state tax liability" also includes any liability under Part 10 (commencing with Section 17001), Part 10.2 (commencing with Section 18401), or Part 11 (commencing with Section 23001) of Division 2 of the Revenue and Taxation Code that is due and payable within the meaning of subdivision (b) of Section 19221 of the Revenue and Taxation Code, and unpaid. The amendments to this section by the act adding this subdivision shall apply to any amount that is unpaid on or after the effective date of that act, or any amount that first becomes due and payable, and unpaid, after the effective date of that act. **Leg.H.** Added Stats 1982 ch 1364 §2, operative July 1, 1983. Amended Stats 2012 ch 37 §1 (SB 1015), effective June 27, 2012.

§706.071. Collection of state tax liability; Limitations

This chapter does not limit the state's right to collect a state tax liability except that (a) no levy upon earnings of an employee held by an employer is effective unless such levy is made in accordance with the provisions of this chapter and (b) other methods of collection may not be used to require an employer to withhold earnings of an employee in payment of a state tax liability. **Leg.H.** Added Stats 1982 ch 1364 §2, operative July 1, 1983.

§706.072. Withholding order for taxes; Issuance; Conditions

(a) A "withholding order for taxes" is an earnings withholding order issued pursuant to this article to collect a state tax liability and shall be denoted as a withholding order for taxes on its face.

(b) A withholding order for taxes may only be issued under one of the following circumstances:

(1) The existence of the state tax liability appears on the face of the taxpayer's return, including a case where such tax liability is disclosed from the taxpayer's return after errors in mathematical computations in the return have been corrected.

(2) The state tax liability has been assessed or determined as provided by statute and the taxpayer had notice of the proposed assessment or determination and had available an opportunity to have the proposed assessment or determination reviewed by appropriate administrative procedures. If the taxpayer makes a timely request for review of the assessment or determination, the state shall not issue a withholding order for taxes until the administrative review procedure is completed. If the taxpayer is given notice of the proposed assessment or determination but does not make a timely request for review, the state may issue a withholding order for taxes.

(c) In any case where a state tax liability has been assessed or determined prior to July 1, 1983, and the state determines that the requirement of subdivision (b) may not have been satisfied, the state may send a "Notice of Proposed Issuance of Withholding Order for Taxes" to the taxpayer at the taxpayer's last known address by first-class mail, postage prepaid. The notice shall advise the taxpayer that the taxpayer may have the assessment or determination reviewed by appropriate administrative procedures and state how such a review may be obtained. If the taxpayer is sent such a notice and requests such a review within 30 days from the date the notice was mailed to the taxpayer, the state shall provide appropriate administrative procedures for review of the assessment or determination and shall not issue the withholding order for taxes until the administrative review procedure is completed. If the taxpayer is sent such a notice and does not request such a review within 30 days from the date the notice was mailed to the taxpayer, the state may issue the withholding order for taxes.

(d) A withholding order for taxes may be issued whether or not the state tax liability has been reduced to judgment. **Leg.H.** Added Stats 1982 ch 1364 §2, operative July 1, 1983.

§706.073. Application of chapter to withholding order for taxes

Except as otherwise provided in this article, the provisions of this chapter govern the procedures and proceedings concerning a withholding order for taxes. For the purposes of this article, a reference in this chapter to a "levying officer" shall be deemed to mean the specific state agency seeking to collect a state tax liability under this article. **Leg.H.** Added Stats 1982 ch 1364 §2, operative July 1, 1983.

§706.074. Issuance of withholding order for taxes by state; Amount to be withheld

(a) The state may itself issue a withholding order for taxes under this section to collect a state tax liability. The order shall specify the total amount required to be withheld pursuant to the order (unpaid tax liability including any penalties, accrued interest, and costs).

(b) Unless a lesser amount is specified in the order, the amount to be withheld by the employer each pay period pursuant to an order issued under this section is the amount required to be withheld under Section 1673(a) of Title 15 of the United States Code, and is not subject to the exception provided in Section 1673(b) of Title 15 of the United States Code. **Leg.H.** Added Stats 1982 ch 1364 §2, operative July 1, 1983.

§706.075. Service on employer of order and notice; Delivery to employee; Administrative hearing to reconsider amount required to be withheld; Liability of employer

(a) This section applies to any withholding order for taxes issued under this article.

(b) Together with the withholding order for taxes, the state shall serve upon the employer an additional copy of the order and a notice informing the taxpayer of the effect of the order and of his right to hearings and remedies provided in this chapter. Within 10 days from the date of service, the employer shall deliver to the taxpayer a copy of the order and the notice, except that immediate delivery shall be made where a jeopardy withholding order for taxes has been served. If the taxpayer is no longer employed by the employer and the employer does not owe the taxpayer any earnings, the employer is not required to make such delivery.

(c) The state shall provide for an administrative hearing to reconsider or modify the amount to be withheld pursuant to the withholding order for taxes, and the taxpayer may request such a hearing at any time after service of the order. If the taxpayer requests a hearing, the hearing shall be provided, and the matter shall be determined, within 15 days after the request is received by the state. The determination of the amount to be withheld is subject to the standard provided in subdivision (b) of Section 706.051. Judicial review of the determination made pursuant to this subdivision by the state may be had only if a petition for a writ of mandate pursuant to Section 1094.5 is filed within 90 days from the date that written notice of the state's determination was delivered or mailed to the taxpayer.

(d) The employer is not subject to any civil liability for failure to comply with subdivision (b). Nothing in this subdivision limits the power of a court to hold the employer in contempt of court for failure to comply with subdivision (b). **Leg.H.** Added Stats 1982 ch 1364 §2, operative July 1, 1983.

§706.076. Order of court for amount in excess of order issued by state; Temporary earnings holding order

(a) A withholding order for taxes may be issued pursuant to this section requiring the employer of the taxpayer to withhold an amount in excess of the amount that may be required to be withheld pursuant to an order issued under Section 706.074.

(b) The state may, at any time, apply to a court of record in the county where the taxpayer was last known to reside for the issuance of a withholding order for taxes under this section to collect a state tax liability.

(c) The application for the order shall include a statement under oath that the state has served upon the taxpayer both of the following:

(1) A copy of the application.

(2) A notice informing the taxpayer of the purpose of the application and the right of the taxpayer to appear at the court hearing on the application.

(d) Upon the filing of the application, the court shall immediately set the matter for hearing and the court clerk shall send a notice of the time and place of the hearing by first-class mail, postage prepaid, to the state and the taxpayer. The notice shall be deposited in the mail at least 10 days before the day set for the hearing.

(e) After hearing, the court shall issue a withholding order for taxes which shall require the taxpayer's employer to withhold and pay over all earnings of the taxpayer other than that amount which the taxpayer proves is exempt under subdivision (b) of Section 706.051, but in no event shall the amount to be withheld be less than that permitted to be withheld under Section 706.050.

(f) The state may issue a temporary earnings holding order, which shall be denoted as such on its face, in any case where the state intends to apply for a withholding order for taxes under this section and has determined that the collection of the state tax liability will be jeopardized in whole or in part if the temporary earnings holding order is not issued. The temporary earnings holding order shall be directed to the taxpayer's employer and shall require the employer to retain in the employer's possession or under the employer's control all or such portion of the earnings of the taxpayer then or thereafter due as is specified in the order. Together with the temporary earnings holding order, the state shall serve upon the employer an additional copy of the order and a notice informing the taxpayer of the effect of the order and of the right to the remedies provided in this chapter. Upon receipt of the order, the employer shall deliver to the taxpayer a copy of the order and notice. If the taxpayer is no longer employed by the employer and the employer does not owe the taxpayer any earnings, the employer is not required to make such delivery. The temporary earnings holding order expires 15 days from the date it is served on the employer unless it is extended by the court on ex parte application for good cause shown. If a temporary earnings holding order is served on an employer, the state may not thereafter, for a period of six months, serve on the same employer another temporary earnings holding order for the same employee unless the court for good cause shown otherwise orders. Sections 706.153 and 706.154 apply to temporary earnings holding orders issued under this section. **Leg.H.** Added Stats 1982 ch 1364 §2, operative July 1, 1983.

§706.077. Priority

(a) Subject to subdivision (b), an employer upon whom a withholding order for taxes is served shall withhold and pay over earnings of the employee pursuant to such order and shall cease to withhold earnings pursuant to any prior earnings withholding order except that a withholding order for support shall be given priority as provided in Section 706.030. When an employer is required to cease withholding earnings pursuant to an earlier earnings withholding order, the employer shall notify the levying officer who served the earlier earnings withholding order that a supervening withholding order for taxes is in effect.

(b) An employer shall not withhold earnings of an employee pursuant to a withholding order for taxes if a prior withholding order for taxes is in effect, and, in such case, the subsequent withholding order for taxes is ineffective. **Leg.H.** Added Stats 1982 ch 1364 §2, operative July 1, 1983.

§706.078. Pay periods subject to order; Jeopardy withholding order for taxes; Duration of withholding

(a) Except as provided in subdivision (b), the employer shall not withhold pursuant to a withholding order for taxes from earnings of the employee payable for any pay period of such employee that ends prior to the 10th day after service of the order.

(b) A "jeopardy withholding order for taxes," which shall be denoted as such on its face, is a withholding order for taxes that requires that the employer withhold pursuant to the order from earnings due to the employee at the time of service of the order on the employer and from earnings thereafter due. A jeopardy withholding order for taxes may be issued only where the state has determined that the collection of a state tax liability will be jeopardized in whole or in part by delaying the time when withholding from earnings commences.

(c) An employer shall continue to withhold pursuant to a withholding order for taxes until the amount specified in the order has been paid in full or the order is withdrawn, except that the order automatically terminates one year after the employment of the employee by the employer terminates. The state shall promptly serve on the employer a notice terminating the withholding order for taxes if the state tax liability for which the withholding order for taxes was issued is satisfied before the employer has withheld the full amount specified in the order, and the employer shall discontinue withholding in compliance with such notice. **Leg.H.** Added Stats 1982 ch 1364 §2, operative July 1, 1983.

§706.080. Service of order or other notice or document

Service of a withholding order for taxes or of any other notice or document required under this chapter in connection with a withholding order for taxes may be made by the state by first-class mail, postage prepaid, or by any authorized state employee. Service of a withholding order for taxes is complete when it is received by the employer or a person described in paragraph (1) or (2) of subdivision (a) of Section 706.101. Service of, or the providing of, any other notice or document required to be served or provided under this chapter in connection with a withholding order for taxes is complete when the notice or document is deposited in the mail addressed to the last known address of the person on whom it is served or to whom it is to be provided. **Leg.H.** Added Stats 1982 ch 1364 §2, operative July 1, 1983.

§706.081. Forms; Prescription by state

Except for the forms referred to in Section 706.076, the state shall prescribe the form of any order, notice, or other document required by this chapter in connection with a withholding order for taxes notwithstanding Sections 706.100 and 706.120, and any form so prescribed is deemed to comply with this chapter. **Leg.H.** Added Stats 1982 ch 1364 §2, operative July 1, 1983.

§706.082. Prohibition of review of tax liability

No review of the taxpayer's tax liability shall be permitted in any court proceedings under this chapter. **Leg.H.** Added Stats 1982 ch 1364 §2, operative July 1, 1983.

§706.084. Warrant, notice of levy or notice or order to withhold served on employer deemed withholding order for taxes; Requirements

Where a warrant, notice of levy, or notice or order to withhold is served on the employer to enforce a state tax liability of a person who is an employee of that employer, it shall be deemed to be a withholding order for taxes as to any earnings that are subject to the provisions of this chapter if both of the following requirements are satisfied:

(a) The form provides notice on its face that it is to be treated as a withholding order for taxes as to any earnings that are subject to the provisions of this chapter.

(b) The form provides all the information provided in a withholding order for taxes. **Leg.H.** Added Stats 1982 ch 1364 §2, operative July 1, 1983.

ARTICLE 5
Procedure for Earnings Withholding Orders and Exemption Claims

Rules of Judicial Council. §706.100.
Manner of service of earnings withholding order and of other notices and documents. §706.101.
Application for order by judgment creditor; Issuance. §706.102.

Service on employer; Documents and instructions; Limitations. §706.103.
Duties of employer on service of order. §706.104.
Claim of exemption by judgment debtor. §706.105.
Findings in court proceedings. §706.106.
Earnings withholding orders; Issuance and service. §706.108.
Earnings withholding order. §706.109.

§706.100. Rules of Judicial Council

Notwithstanding any other provision of law, the Judicial Council may provide by rule for the practice and procedure in proceedings under this chapter except for the state's administrative hearings provided by Article 4 (commencing with Section 706.070). **Leg.H.** Added Stats 1982 ch 1364 §2, operative July 1, 1983.

§706.101. Manner of service of earnings withholding order and of other notices and documents

(a) An earnings withholding order shall be served by the levying officer upon the employer by delivery of the order to any of the following:

(1) The managing agent or person in charge, at the time of service, of the branch or office where the employee works or the office from which the employee is paid. In the case of a state employee, the office from which the employee is paid does not include the Controller's office unless the employee works directly for the Controller's office.

(2) Any person to whom a copy of the summons and of the complaint may be delivered to make service on the employer under Article 4 (commencing with Section 416.10) of Chapter 4 of Title 5.

(b) Service of an earnings withholding order shall be made by personal delivery as provided in Section 415.10 or 415.20 or by delivery by first-class mail, postage prepaid. When service is made by first-class mail, service is complete at the time of receipt of the earnings withholding order, as indicated in the employer's return, or the date of mailing if the date of receipt is not indicated on the employer's return. If the levying officer attempts service by first-class mail under this subdivision and does not receive the employer's return within 15 days from the date of mailing, the levying officer shall make service as provided in Article 3 (commencing with Section 415.10) of Chapter 4 of Title 5. For purposes of this section, "employer's return" refers to the Judicial Council-issued form specified by Section 706.126.

(c) The state may issue an earnings withholding order directly, without the use of a levying officer, for purposes of collecting overpayments of unemployment compensation or disability benefits pursuant to Article 4 (commencing with Section 1375) of Chapter 5 of Part 1 of, and Article 5 (commencing with Section 2735) of Chapter 2 of Part 2 of, Division 1 of the Unemployment Insurance Code. The earnings withholding order shall be served by registered or certified mail, postage prepaid, with return receipt requested. Service is deemed complete at the time the return receipt is executed by, or on behalf of, the recipient. If the state does not receive a return receipt within 15 days from the date of deposit in the mail of the withholding order, the state shall refer the earnings withholding order to a levying officer for service in accordance with subdivision (b).

(d) Except as provided in subdivision (b) or (c), service of any notice or document under this chapter may be made by first-class mail, postage prepaid. If service is made on the employer after the employer's return has been received by the levying officer, the service shall be made by first-class mail, postage prepaid, on the person designated in the employer's return to receive notices and at the address indicated in the employer's return, whether or not that address is within the county. This subdivision does not preclude service by personal delivery (1) on the employer before the employer's return has been received by the levying officer or (2) on the person designated in the employer's return after its receipt.

(e) Notwithstanding subdivision (b), if the judgment creditor so requests, the levying officer shall make service of the earnings withholding order by personal delivery as provided in Section 415.10 or 415.20. **Leg.H.** Added Stats 1982 ch 1364 §2.2, operative July 1, 1983. Amended Stats 1984 ch 538 §28; Stats 1989 ch 1416 §24; Stats 2002 ch 890 §1 (AB 2929); Stats 2010 ch 680 §13 (AB 2394), effective January 1, 2011.

§706.102. Application for order by judgment creditor; Issuance

(a) If a writ of execution has been issued to the county where the judgment debtor's employer is to be served and the time specified in subdivision (b) of Section 699.530 for levy on property under the writ has not expired, a judgment creditor may apply for the issuance of an earnings withholding order by filing an application with a levying officer in such county who shall promptly issue an earnings withholding order.

(b) This section does not apply where the earnings withholding order is a withholding order for taxes. **Leg.H.** Added Stats 1982 ch 1364 §2, operative July 1, 1983.

§706.103. Service on employer; Documents and instructions; Limitations

(a) The levying officer shall serve upon the designated employer all of the following:

(1) The original and one copy of the earnings withholding order.

(2) The form for the employer's return.

(3) The notice to **the** employee of **the** earnings withholding order.

(4) A copy of the form that the judgment debtor may use to make a claim of exemption.

(5) A copy of the form the judgment debtor may use to provide a financial statement.

(b) At the time the levying officer makes service pursuant to subdivision (a), the levying officer shall provide the employer with a copy of the employer's instructions referred to in Section 706.127. The Judicial Council may adopt rules prescribing the circumstances when compliance with this subdivision is not required.

(c) No earnings withholding order shall be served upon the employer after the time specified in subdivision (b) of Section 699.530. **Leg.H.** Added Stats 1982 ch 1364 §2, operative July 1, 1983. Amended Stats 2013 ch 64 §5 (SB 233), effective January 1, 2014; Stats 2024 ch 514 §11 (AB 2837), effective January 1, 2025.

§706.104. Duties of employer on service of order

Any employer who is served with an earnings withholding order shall:

(a) Deliver to the judgment debtor a copy of the earnings withholding order, the notice to employee of earnings withholding, a copy of the form that the judgment debtor may use to make a claim of exemption, and a copy of the form the judgment debtor may use to provide a financial statement within 10 days from the date of service. If the judgment debtor is no longer employed by the employer and the employer does not owe the employee any earnings, the employer is not required to make such delivery. The employer is not subject to any civil liability for failure to comply with this subdivision. Nothing in this subdivision limits the power of a court to hold the employer in contempt of court for failure to comply with this subdivision.

(b) Complete the employer's return on the form provided by the levying officer and mail it by first-class mail, postage prepaid, to the levying officer within 15 days from the date of service. If the earnings withholding order is ineffective, the employer shall state in the employer's return that the order will not be complied with for this reason and shall return the order to the levying officer with the employer's return. **Leg.H.** Added Stats 1982 ch 1364 §2, operative July 1, 1983. Amended Stats 2013 ch 64 §6 (SB 233), effective January 1, 2014.

§706.105. Claim of exemption by judgment debtor

(a) A judgment debtor may claim an exemption under Section 706.051 under either of the following circumstances:

(1) No prior hearing has been held with respect to the earnings withholding order.

(2) There has been a material change in circumstances since the time of the last prior hearing on the earnings withholding order.

(b) A claim of exemption shall be made by filing with the levying officer an original and one copy of (1) the judgment debtor's claim of exemption and (2) the judgment debtor's financial statement.

(c) Upon filing of the claim of exemption, the levying officer shall promptly send to the judgment creditor, at the address stated in the application for the earnings withholding order, by first-class mail, postage prepaid, all of the following:

(1) A copy of the claim of exemption.

(2) A copy of the financial statement.

(3) A notice of claim of exemption. The notice shall state that the claim of exemption has been filed and that the earnings withholding order will be terminated, or modified to reflect the amount of earnings claimed to be exempt in the claim of exemption, unless a notice of opposition to the claim of exemption is filed with the levying officer by the judgment creditor within 10 days after the date of the mailing of the notice of claim of exemption.

(d) A judgment creditor who desires to contest a claim of exemption shall, within 10 days after the date of the mailing of the notice of claim of exemption, file with the levying officer a notice of opposition to the claim of exemption.

(e) If a notice of opposition to the claim of exemption is filed with the levying officer within the 10-day period, the judgment creditor is entitled to a hearing on the claim of exemption. If the judgment creditor desires a hearing on the claim of exemption, the judgment creditor shall file a notice of motion for an order determining the claim of exemption with the court within 10 days after the date the levying officer mailed the notice of claim of exemption. If the notice of motion is so filed, the hearing on the motion shall be held not later than 30 days from the date the notice of motion was filed unless continued by the court for good cause. **Where the judgment upon which the writ is issued is for personal debt, as defined in subdivision (d) of Section 683.110, if the hearing is delayed by the court and cannot be set within 30 days of notice of the motion, a party may seek by ex parte application, and the court shall issue, an order staying any levy or garnishment with respect to the property subject to the claim of exemption until the hearing occurs.** At the time prescribed by subdivision (b) of Section 1005, the judgment creditor shall give written notice of the hearing to the levying officer and shall serve a notice of the hearing and a copy of the notice of opposition to the claim of exemption on the judgment debtor and, if the claim of exemption so requested, on the attorney for the judgment debtor. Service is deemed made when the notice of the hearing and a copy of the notice of opposition to the claim of exemption are deposited in the mail, postage prepaid, addressed to the judgment debtor at the address stated in the claim of exemption and, if service on the attorney for the judgment debtor was requested in the claim of exemption, to the attorney at the address stated in the claim of exemption. The judgment creditor shall file proof of the service with the court. After receiving the notice of the hearing and before the date set for the hearing, the levying officer shall file the claim of exemption and the notice of opposition to the claim of exemption with the court.

(f) If the levying officer does not receive a notice of opposition to the claim of exemption within the 10-day period after the date of mailing of the notice of claim of exemption and a notice of the hearing not later than 10 days after the filing of the notice of opposition to the claim of exemption, the levying officer shall serve on the employer one of the following:

(1) A notice that the earnings withholding order has been terminated if all of the judgment debtor's earnings were claimed to be exempt.

(2) A modified earnings withholding order that reflects the amount of earnings claimed to be exempt in the claim of exemption if only a portion of the judgment debtor's earnings was claimed to be exempt.

(g) If, after hearing, the court orders that the earnings withholding order be modified or terminated, the clerk shall promptly transmit a certified copy of the order to the levying officer who shall promptly serve on the employer of the judgment debtor (1) a copy of the modified earnings withholding order or (2) a notice that the earnings withholding order has been terminated. [1]

(1) Where the judgment debtor's wages are exempt without making a claim, the court shall terminate or modify the earnings withholding order, and shall order the return by a date certain of all of the judgment debtor's exempt wages. Where the judgment upon which the writ is issued is for personal debt, as defined in subdivision (d) of Section 683.110, the court shall order the return by a date certain of any wages that were exempt without the need for a claim and that were garnished for up to 12 months preceding the date of the order on the claim of exemption. This paragraph does not limit a judge's authority to order, for good cause, the return of any exempt property taken more than 12 months preceding the date of the order on the claim of exemption.

(2) Where the judgment debtor's wages are exempt as the result of a claim of exemption, the court shall terminate or modify the earnings withholding order, and shall order the return by a date certain of all of the judgment debtor's exempt wages. Where the judgment upon which the writ is issued is for personal debt, as defined in subdivision (d) of Section 683.110, the court shall order the return by a date certain any wages that the debtor has demonstrated would have been exempt by claim of exemption and that were garnished for up to six months preceding the date of the order on the claim of exemption. This paragraph does not limit a judge's authority to order, for good cause, the return of any exempt property taken more than six months preceding the date of the order on the claim of exemption.

(3) If the court determines that any amount withheld pursuant to the earnings withholding order should be paid to the judgment debtor, the court shall order the levying officer, judgment creditor, or other person, who is in possession of the property, to return the exempt property to the judgment debtor. A levying officer shall return the exempt property within 20 business days of receipt of notice of the order. A judgment creditor shall return the exempt property within 10 business days of entry of the order.

(h) If the earnings withholding order is terminated by the court, unless the court otherwise orders or unless there is a material change of circumstances since the time of the last prior hearing on the earnings withholding order, the judgment creditor may not apply for another earnings withholding order directed to the same employer with respect to the same judgment debtor for a period of 100 days following the date of service of the earnings withholding order or 60 days after the date of the termination of the order, whichever is later. **Where the judgment upon which the writ is issued is for personal debt, as defined in subdivision (d) of Section 683.110, the judgment creditor may not apply for another earnings withholding order directed to the same employer with respect to the same judgment debtor for a period of 100 days following the date of service of the earnings withholding order or 60 days after the date of the termination of the order, whichever is later.**

(i) If an employer has withheld and paid over amounts pursuant to an earnings withholding order after the date of termination of the order but prior to the receipt of notice of its termination, the judgment debtor may recover those amounts only from the levying officer if the levying officer still holds those amounts or, if those amounts have been paid over to the judgment creditor, from the judgment creditor. If the employer has withheld amounts pursuant to an earnings withholding order after termination of the order but has not paid over those amounts to the levying officer, the employer shall [2] pay those amounts to the judgment debtor **within five business days of the end of the next pay period**.

(j) An appeal lies from any court order under this section denying a claim of exemption or modifying or terminating an earnings withholding order. An appeal by the judgment creditor from an order modifying or terminating the earnings withholding order does not stay the order from which the appeal is taken. Notwithstanding the appeal, until the order modifying or terminating the earnings withholding order is set aside or modified, the order allowing the claim of exemption in whole or in part shall be given the same effect as if the appeal had not been taken.

(k) This section does not apply to a withholding order for support or a withholding order for taxes. **Leg.H.** Added Stats 1982 ch 1364 §2, operative July 1, 1983. Amended Stats 1989 ch 693 §3; Stats 1998 ch 931 §94 (SB 2139), effective September 28, 1998; Stats 2024 ch 514 §12 (AB 2837), effective January 1, 2025.

§706.105. 2024 Deletes. [1] The court may order that the earnings withholding order be terminated as of a date that precedes the date of hearing. If the court determines that any amount withheld pursuant to the earnings withholding order shall be paid to the judgment debtor, the court shall make an order directing the person who holds that amount to pay it promptly to the judgment debtor. [2] promptly

§706.106. Findings in court proceedings

No findings are required in court proceedings under this chapter. **Leg.H.** Added Stats 1982 ch 1364 §2, operative July 1, 1983.

§706.107. [Section repealed 1992]

Leg.H. Added Stats 1982 ch 1364 §2, operative July 1, 1983. Repealed Stats 1992 ch 283 §13 (SB 1372), effective July 21, 1992. The repealed section related to service of second earnings withholding order by same judgment creditor on same employer.

§706.108. Earnings withholding orders; Issuance and service

(a) If a writ of execution has been issued to the county where the judgment debtor's employer is to be served and the time specified in subdivision (b) of Section 699.530 for levy on property under the writ has not expired, a judgment creditor may deliver an application for issuance of an earnings withholding order to a registered process server who may then issue an earnings withholding order.

(b) If the registered process server has issued the earnings withholding order, the registered process server, before serving the earnings withholding order, shall cause to be deposited with the levying officer a copy of the writ of execution, the application for issuance of an earnings withholding order, a copy of the earnings withholding order, and the fee, as provided by Section 26750 of the Government Code.

(c) A registered process server may serve an earnings withholding order on an employer whether the earnings withholding order was issued by a levying officer or by a registered process server, but no earnings withholding order may be served after the time specified in subdivision (b) of Section 699.530. In performing this function, the registered process server shall serve upon the designated employer all of the following:

(1) The original and one copy of the earnings withholding order.

(2) The form for the employer's return.

(3) The notice to the employee of the earnings withholding order.

(4) A copy of the form that the judgment debtor may use to make a claim of exemption.

(5) A copy of the form the judgment debtor may use to provide a financial statement.

(6) A copy of the employer's instructions referred to in Section 706.127, except as otherwise prescribed in rules adopted by the Judicial Council.

(d) Within five court days after service under this section, all of the following shall be filed with the levying officer:

(1) The writ of execution, if it is not already in the hands of the levying officer.

(2) Proof of service on the employer of the papers listed in subdivision (c).

(3) Instructions in writing, as required by the provisions of Section 687.010.

(e) If the fee provided by Section 26750 of the Government Code has been paid, the levying officer shall perform all other duties required by this chapter as if the levying officer had served the earnings withholding order. If the registered process server does not comply with subdivisions (b), where applicable, and (d), the service of the earnings withholding order is ineffective and the levying officer shall not be required to perform any duties under the order, and may terminate the order and release any withheld earnings to the judgment debtor.

(f) The fee for services of a registered process server under this section is a recoverable cost pursuant to Section 1033.5. **Leg.H.** Added Stats 1984 ch 538 §29. Amended Stats 1987 ch 1080 §6; Stats 2002 ch 197 §4 (AB 2493); Stats 2009 ch 54 §6 (SB 544), effective January 1, 2010; Stats 2013 ch 64 §7 (SB 233), effective January 1, 2014; Stats 2016 ch 102 §3 (AB 2211), effective January 1, 2017.

§706.109. Earnings withholding order

An earnings withholding order may not be issued against the earnings of the spouse of the judgment debtor except by court order upon noticed motion. **Leg.H.** Added Stats 1984 ch 1671 §20.

ARTICLE 6
Forms; Employer's Instructions

Prescribing by Judicial Council. §706.120.
Application for issuance of earnings withholding order. §706.121.
Notice to employee of earnings withholding order. §706.122.
Judgment debtor's claim of exemption. §706.123.
Judgment debtor's financial statement. §706.124.
Earnings withholding order. §706.125.
Employer's return. §706.126.
Employer's instructions; Preparation, publication, and distribution. §706.127.
Judgment creditor's notice of opposition to the claim of exemption. §706.128.
Forms for judgment debtors; Availability for distribution. §706.129.

§706.120. Prescribing by Judicial Council

Except as provided in Section 706.081, the Judicial Council shall prescribe the form of the applications, notices, claims of exemption, orders, and other documents required by this chapter as provided in Section 681.030, and only such forms may be used to implement this chapter. **Leg.H.** Added Stats 1982 ch 1364 §2, operative July 1, 1983.

§706.121. Application for issuance of earnings withholding order

The "application for issuance of earnings withholding order" shall be executed under oath and shall include all of the following:

(a) The name, the last known address, and, if known, the social security number of the judgment debtor.

(b) The name and address of the judgment creditor.

(c) The court where the judgment was entered and the date the judgment was entered.

(d) Whether the judgment is based in whole or in part on a claim for elder or dependent adult financial abuse and, if in part, how much of the judgment arises from that claim.

(e) The date of issuance of a writ of execution to the county where the earnings withholding order is sought.

(f) The total amount required to satisfy the order on the date of issuance (which may not exceed the amount required to satisfy the writ of execution on the date of issuance of the order plus the levying officer's statutory fee for service of the order).

(g) The name and address of the employer to whom the order will be directed.

(h) The name and address of the person to whom the withheld money is to be paid by the levying officer. **Leg.H.** Added Stats 1982 ch 1364 §2, operative July 1, 1983. Amended Stats 1992 ch 283 §14 (SB 1372), effective July 21, 1992; Stats 2010 ch 64 §3 (AB 2619), effective January 1, 2011, operative January 1, 2012.

1992 Note: Section 706.121, as amended by ch 283, applies to all writs of execution and earnings withholding orders regardless of whether they were issued before July 21, 1992. Stats 1992 ch 283 §17.

§706.122. Notice to employee of earnings withholding order

The "notice to employee of earnings withholding order" shall contain a statement that informs the employee in simple terms of the nature of a wage garnishment, the right to an exemption, the procedure for claiming an exemption, and any other information the Judicial Council determines would be useful to the employee and appropriate for inclusion in the notice, including all of the following:

(a) The named employer has been ordered to withhold from the earnings of the judgment debtor the amounts required to be withheld under Section 706.050, or such other amounts as are specified in the earnings withholding order, and to pay these amounts over to the levying officer for transmittal to the person specified in the order in payment of the judgment described in the order.

(b) The manner of computing the amounts required to be withheld pursuant to Section 706.050.

(c) The judgment debtor may be able to keep more or all of the judgment debtor's earnings if the judgment debtor proves that the additional earnings are necessary for the support of the judgment debtor or the judgment debtor's family supported in whole or in part by the judgment debtor.

(d) If the judgment debtor wishes a court hearing to prove that amounts should not be withheld from the judgment debtor's earnings because they are necessary for the support of the judgment debtor or the judgment debtor's family supported in whole or in part by the judgment debtor, the judgment debtor shall file with the levying officer an original and one copy of the "judgment debtor's claim of exemption" and an original and one copy of the "judgment debtor's financial statement." **Leg.H.** Added Stats 1982 ch 1364 §2, operative July 1, 1983. Amended Stats 2013 ch 64 §8 (SB 233), effective January 1, 2014.

§706.123. Judgment debtor's claim of exemption

The "judgment debtor's claim of exemption" shall be executed under oath. The claim of exemption shall indicate how much the judgment debtor believes should be withheld from the judgment debtor's earnings each pay period by the employer pursuant to the earnings withholding order and shall state the judgment debtor's present mailing address. **Leg.H.** Added Stats 1982 ch 1364 §2, operative July 1, 1983.

§706.124. Judgment debtor's financial statement

The "judgment debtor's financial statement" shall be executed as provided in Section 703.530 and contain all of the information required by that section and the following additional information:

(a) Whether any earnings withholding orders are in effect with respect to the earnings of the judgment debtor or the spouse or dependents of the judgment debtor.

(b) Whether any earnings assignment orders for support are in effect with respect to the earnings of the judgment debtor or the spouse or dependents of the judgment debtor. **Leg.H.** Added Stats 1982 ch 1364 §2, operative July 1, 1983. Amended Stats 1992 ch 163 §49 (AB 2641), operative January 1, 1994.

§706.125. Earnings withholding order

The "earnings withholding order" shall include all of the following:

(a) The name, address, and, if known, the social security number of the judgment debtor.

(b) The name and address of the employer to whom the order is directed.

(c) The court where the judgment was entered, the date the judgment was entered, and the name of the judgment creditor.

(d) Whether the judgment is based in whole or in part on a claim for elder or dependent adult financial abuse and, if in part, how much of the judgment arises from the claim.

(e) The date of issuance of the writ of execution to the county where the earnings withholding order is sought.

(f) The total amount required to satisfy the order on the date of issuance (which may not exceed the amount required to satisfy the writ of execution on the date of issuance of the order plus the levying officer's statutory fee for service of the order).

(g) A description of the withholding period and an order to the employer to withhold from the earnings of the judgment debtor for each pay period the amount required to be withheld under Section 706.050 or the amount specified in the order subject to Section 706.024, as the case may be, for the pay periods ending during the withholding period.

(h) An order to the employer to pay over to the levying officer at a specified address the amount required to be withheld and paid over pursuant to the order in the manner and within the times provided by law.

(i) An order that the employer fill out the "employer's return" and return it by first-class mail, postage prepaid, to the levying officer at a specified address within 15 days after service of the earnings withholding order.

(j) An order that the employer deliver to the judgment debtor a copy of the earnings withholding order and the "notice to employee of earnings withholding order" within 10 days after service of the earnings withholding order; but, if the judgment debtor is no longer employed by the employer and the employer does not owe the employee any earnings, the employer is not required to make the delivery.

(k) The name and address of the levying officer. **Leg.H.** Added Stats 1982 ch 1364 §2, operative July 1, 1983. Amended Stats 1992 ch 283 §15 (SB 1372), effective July 21, 1992; Stats 2010 ch 64 §4 (AB 2619), effective January 1, 2011, operative January 1, 2012.

1992 Note: Section 706.125, as amended by ch 283, applies to all writs of execution and earnings withholding orders regardless of whether they were issued before July 21, 1992. Stats 1992 ch 283 §17.

§706.126. Employer's return

(a) The "employer's return" shall be executed under oath. The form for the return provided to the employer shall state all of the following information:

(1) The name and address of the levying officer to whom the form is to be returned.

(2) A direction that the form be mailed to the levying officer by first-class mail, postage prepaid, no later than 15 days after the date of service of the earnings withholding order.

(3) The name, the address, and, if known, the social security number of the judgment debtor.

(b) In addition, the employer's return form shall require the employer to supply all of the following information:

(1) The date the earnings withholding order was served on the employer.

(2) Whether the judgment debtor is employed by the employer or whether the employer otherwise owes earnings to the employee.

(3) If the judgment debtor is employed by the employer or the employer otherwise owes earnings to the employee, the amount of the employee's earnings for the last pay period and the length of this pay period.

(4) Whether the employer was required on the date of service to comply with an earlier earnings withholding order and, if so, the name of the judgment creditor who secured the earlier order, the levying officer who served such order, the date it was issued, the date it was served, the expiration date of such order, and which of the earnings withholding orders the employer is required to comply with under the applicable statutory rules concerning the priority of such orders.

(5) Whether the employer was required on the date of service to comply with an earnings assignment order for support and, if so, the court which issued such assignment order and the date it was issued and any other information the Judicial Council determines is needed to identify the order.

(6) The name and address of the person to whom notices to the employer are to be sent. **Leg.H.** Added Stats 1982 ch 1364 §2, operative July 1, 1983. Amended Stats 1992 ch 163 §50 (AB 2641), operative January 1, 1994.

§706.127. Employer's instructions; Preparation, publication, and distribution

(a) The Judicial Council shall prepare "employer's instructions" for employers and revise or supplement these instructions to reflect changes in the law or rules regulating the withholding of earnings.

(b) Except to the extent that they are included in the forms required to be provided by the employer to the levying officer, the Judicial Council shall publish and provide to the levying officers copies of the employer's instructions. **Leg.H.** Added Stats 1982 ch 1364 §2, operative July 1, 1983.

§706.128. Judgment creditor's notice of opposition to the claim of exemption

The "judgment creditor's notice of opposition to the claim of exemption" shall be executed under oath and shall include all of the following:

(a) The name, last known address, and, if known, the social security number of the judgment debtor.

(b) The name and address of the judgment creditor.

(c) The date of mailing of the notice of claim of exemption.

(d) The amount of the judgment debtor's claim of exemption which the judgment creditor claims is not exempt.

(e) The factual and legal grounds for the judgment creditor's opposition to the claim of exemption. **Leg.H.** Added Stats 1982 ch 1364 §2, operative July 1, 1983.

§706.129. Forms for judgment debtors; Availability for distribution

The levying officer shall have copies of the forms for the "judgment debtor's claim of exemption" and "judgment debtor's financial statement" available at the levying officer's office for distribution without charge to a person who desires to make a claim of exemption under Section 706.051. **Leg.H.** Added Stats 1982 ch 1364 §2, operative July 1, 1983.

ARTICLE 7
Administration and Enforcement

Exemption of state from earnings garnishment provisions of Consumer Credit Protection Act of 1968. §706.151.

Failure to pay withheld earnings by employer with intent to defraud; Misdemeanor. §706.152.

Deferment or acceleration of payment of earnings to alter rights of judgment creditor; Civil liability. §706.153.

Failure to withhold or pay over; Civil action by judgment creditor; Immunity from liability for compliance; Exception. §706.154.

§706.151. Exemption of state from earnings garnishment provisions of Consumer Credit Protection Act of 1968

The Judicial Council may perform all acts required by the Administrator of the Wage and Hour Division of the United States Department of Labor as conditions to exemption of this state from the earnings garnishment provisions of the Consumer Credit Protection Act of 1968 (15 U.S.C. Secs. 1671–1677), including, but not limited to:

(a) Representing and acting on behalf of the state in relation to the Administrator of the Wage and Hour Division and the administrator's representatives with regard to any matter relating to, or arising out of, the application, interpretation, and enforcement of the laws of this state regulating withholding of earnings.

(b) Submitting to the Administrator of the Wage and Hour Division in duplicate and on a current basis, a certified copy of every statute of this state affecting earnings withholding, and a certified copy of any decision in any case involving any of those statutes, made by the Supreme Court of this state.

(c) Submitting to the Administrator of the Wage and Hour Division any information relating to the enforcement of earnings withholding laws of

§706.152. Failure to pay withheld earnings by employer with intent to defraud; Misdemeanor

If an employer withholds earnings pursuant to this chapter and, with the intent to defraud either the judgment creditor or the judgment debtor, fails to pay such withheld earnings over to the levying officer, the employer is guilty of a misdemeanor. **Leg.H.** Added Stats 1982 ch 1364 §2, operative July 1, 1983.

§706.153. Deferment or acceleration of payment of earnings to alter rights of judgment creditor; Civil liability

(a) No employer shall defer or accelerate any payment of earnings to an employee with the intent to defeat or diminish the judgment creditor's rights under an earnings withholding order issued pursuant to the procedures provided by this chapter.

(b) If an employer violates this section, the judgment creditor may bring a civil action against the employer to recover the amount that would have been withheld and paid over pursuant to this chapter had the employer not violated this section. The remedy provided by this subdivision is not exclusive. **Leg.H.** Added Stats 1982 ch 1364 §2, operative July 1, 1983.

§706.154. Failure to withhold or pay over; Civil action by judgment creditor; Immunity from liability for compliance; Exception

(a) If an employer fails to withhold or to pay over the amount the employer is required to withhold and pay over pursuant to this chapter, the judgment creditor may bring a civil action against the employer to recover such amount. The remedy provided by this subdivision is not exclusive.

(b) Notwithstanding subdivision (a), an employer who complies with any written order or written notice which purports to be given or served in accordance with the provisions of this chapter is not subject to any civil or criminal liability for such compliance unless the employer has actively participated in a fraud. **Leg.H.** Added Stats 1982 ch 1364 §2, operative July 1, 1983.

§707. [Section repealed 1983]

Leg.H. Enacted Stats 1872. Repealed Stats 1982 ch 1364 §1, operative July 1, 1983. The repealed section related to rights of purchaser and redemptioner to rents and profits.

§708. [Section repealed 1983]

Leg.H. Enacted Stats 1872. Repealed Stats 1982 ch 1364 §1, operative July 1, 1983. See CCP §701.680.

CHAPTER 6
MISCELLANEOUS CREDITORS' REMEDIES

Article 1. Written Interrogatories to Judgment Debtor.
Article 2. Examination Proceedings.
Article 3. Creditor's Suit.
Article 4. Charging Orders.
Article 5. Lien in Pending Action or Proceeding.
Article 6. Assignment Order.
Article 7. Receiver to Enforce Judgment.
Article 8. Collection of Judgment Where Judgment Debtor Is Creditor of Public Entity.
Article 9. Enforcement Against Franchise.
Article 10. Other Enforcement Procedures.

ARTICLE 1
Written Interrogatories to Judgment Debtor

Application of article. §708.010.
Written interrogatories to judgment debtor. §708.020.
Demand for inspection of documents in aid of enforcement of judgment; Time limitations on discovery. §708.030.

§708.010. Application of article

(a) Except as provided in this section and in subdivision (b) of Section 708.020, the procedure in this article may be used at any time a money judgment is enforceable.

(b) If enforcement of the judgment is stayed on appeal by the giving of a sufficient undertaking under Chapter 2 (commencing with Section 916) of Title 13, all proceedings under this article are stayed. In any other case where the enforcement of the judgment is stayed, all proceedings under this article are stayed unless the court otherwise expressly orders. **Leg.H.** Added Stats 1982 ch 1364 §2, operative July 1, 1983.

§708.020. Written interrogatories to judgment debtor

(a) The judgment creditor may propound written interrogatories to the judgment debtor, in the manner provided in Chapter 13 (commencing with Section 2030.010) of Title 4 of Part 4, requesting information to aid in enforcement of the money judgment. The judgment debtor shall answer the interrogatories in the manner and within the time provided by Chapter 13 (commencing with Section 2030.010) of Title 4 of Part 4.

(b) The judgment creditor may not serve interrogatories pursuant to this section within 120 days after the judgment debtor has responded to interrogatories previously served pursuant to this section or within 120 days after the judgment debtor has been examined pursuant to Article 2 (commencing with Section 708.110), and the judgment debtor is not required to respond to any interrogatories so served.

(c) Interrogatories served pursuant to this section may be enforced, to the extent practicable, in the same manner as interrogatories in a civil action.

(d) The limitation provided by Chapter 13 (commencing with Section 2030.010) of Title 4 of Part 4 on the number of interrogatories that may be propounded applies to each set of interrogatories propounded from time to time pursuant to this section, but does not apply cumulatively to interrogatories propounded by the judgment creditor to the judgment debtor. **Leg.H.** Added Stats 1982 ch 1364 §2, operative July 1, 1983. Amended Stats 1992 ch 283 §16 (SB 1372), effective July 21, 1992; Stats 2004 ch 182 §11 (AB 3081), operative July 1, 2005.

§708.030. Demand for inspection of documents in aid of enforcement of judgment; Time limitations on discovery

(a) The judgment creditor may demand that any judgment debtor produce and permit the party making the demand, or someone acting on that party's behalf, to inspect and to copy a document that is in the possession, custody, or control of the party on whom the demand is made in the manner provided in Chapter 14 (commencing with Section 2031.010) of Title 4 of Part 4, if the demand requests information to aid in enforcement of the money judgment. The judgment debtor shall respond and comply with the demand in the manner and within the time provided by Chapter 14 (commencing with Section 2031.010) of Title 4 of Part 4.

(b) The judgment creditor may not serve interrogatories or inspection demands pursuant to this section or Section 708.020 within 120 days after the judgment debtor has responded to the interrogatories or demands previously served pursuant to this section or Section 708.020, or within 120 days after the judgment debtor has been examined pursuant to Article 2 (commencing with Section 708.110), and the judgment debtor is not required to respond to any discovery so served.

(c) Inspection demands served pursuant to this section may be enforced to the extent practicable, in the same manner as inspection demands in a civil action. **Leg.H.** Added Stats 1992 ch 1348 §5 (AB 2616). Amended Stats 2004 ch 182 §12 (AB 3081), operative July 1, 2005.

ARTICLE 2
Examination Proceedings

Examination of judgment debtor. §708.110.
Consumer debt awarded on or after January 1, 2025. § 708.111.
Examination of third person. §708.120.
Witnesses; Privilege of spouse of judgment debtor. §708.130.
Powers and qualifications of referee. §708.140.
Appearance at examination by representatives of organizations. §708.150.
Proper court for examination; Examination outside county where judgment entered. §708.160.
Failure to appear for examination; Penalty for unjustified arrest. §708.170.
Determination of third person's adverse claim. §708.180.
Intervention. §708.190.
Protective orders. §708.200.
Order applying property to satisfaction of judgment. §708.205.

§708.110. Examination of judgment debtor

(a) The judgment creditor may apply to the proper court for an order requiring the judgment debtor to appear before the court, or before a referee appointed by the court, at a time and place specified in the order, to furnish information to aid in enforcement of the money judgment.

(b) If the judgment creditor has not caused the judgment debtor to be examined under this section during the preceding 120 days, the court shall make the order upon ex parte application of the judgment creditor.

(c) If the judgment creditor has caused the judgment debtor to be examined under this section during the preceding 120 days, the court shall make the order if the judgment creditor by affidavit or otherwise shows good cause for the order. The application shall be made on noticed motion if the court so directs or a court rule so requires. Otherwise, it may be made ex parte.

(d) The judgment creditor shall personally serve a copy of the order on the judgment debtor not less than 30 days before the date set for the examination. Service shall be made in the manner specified in Section 415.10. Service of the order creates a lien on the personal property of the judgment debtor for a period of one year from the date of the order unless extended or sooner terminated by the court.

(e) Except as provided in section 708.111, the order shall contain the following statement in 14-point boldface type if printed or in capital letters if typed: "NOTICE TO JUDGMENT DEBTOR. If you fail to appear at the time and place specified in this order, you may be subject to arrest and punishment for contempt of court and the court may make an order requiring you to pay the reasonable attorney's fees incurred by the judgment creditor in this proceeding." **Leg.H.** Added Stats 1982 ch 1364 §2, operative July 1, 1983. Amended Stats 1984 ch 538 §30; Stats 1993 ch 793 §1 (AB 504); Stats 2023 ch 562 §1 (AB 1119), effective January 1, 2024.

§ 708.111. Consumer debt awarded on or after January 1, 2025

(a) This section applies to an application pursuant to Section 708.110 by a judgment creditor with a judgment concerning a consumer debt awarded on or after January 1, 2025.

(b) "Consumer debt" as used in this Section means any obligation or alleged obligation of a consumer to pay money arising out of a transaction in which the money, property, insurance, or services which are the subject of the transaction are primarily for personal, family, or household purposes. Consumer debt does not include debts incurred due to, or obtained by tortious or fraudulent conduct or judgments for unpaid wages, damages, or penalties owed to an employee. Consumer debt does not include rental debt, which means unpaid rent or other unpaid financial obligation of a tenant under the tenancy that has come due.

(c) Notwithstanding subdivision (e) of Section 708.110, if the order issued pursuant to section 708.110 requires a judgment debtor to appear in a case concerning consumer debt, as indicated by the judgment creditor in the application and order for appearance and examination, the order shall be accompanied by the Judicial Council form containing the list of exemptions from the enforcement judgments adopted pursuant to Section 681.030 and the notice of financial affidavit and financial affidavit forms adopted by the Judicial Council pursuant to subdivision (h). The order shall contain the following statement in 14-point boldface type if printed or in capital letters if typed: "NOTICE TO JUDGMENT DEBTOR. If you fail to appear at the time and place specified in this order, the court may make an order requiring you to pay the reasonable attorney's fees and costs incurred by the judgment creditor in this proceeding. Instead of appearing at the examination, you may file a notice of judgment debtor's financial affidavit in a form prescribed by the court and signed under penalty of perjury and serve copies of all filed documents and the financial affidavit on the judgment creditor no later than 15 days prior to the date set for the examination."

(d) If the judgment debtor in a case concerning consumer debt states in a financial affidavit, signed under penalty of perjury, that all of their income and assets are exempt, and files with the court a notice of financial affidavit with a proof of service, the court shall cancel the examination and provide notice of cancellation to the parties. If copies of the financial affidavit are not timely served or the notice and proof of service are not timely filed with the court, the court shall not cancel the examination.

(1) Within 15 days after the filing of the notice and proof of service of the financial affidavit, a judgment creditor who objects to the affidavit shall file with the court a notice of motion for an order determining the need for the debtor to appear for a debtor's examination. If the notice of motion is not timely filed with the court, the debtor's examination shall remain canceled.

(2) The notice of motion for an order determining the need for a debtor to appear for a debtor's examination shall include a declaration executed under oath and include a statement of facts showing good cause why a debtor's examination is necessary notwithstanding the debtor's financial affidavit. In an action in which the consumer debt is secured by real property or personal property, a showing of good cause is established when the plaintiff demonstrates that the debtor has not provided the plaintiff with accurate information regarding the location or condition of the security, the status of insurance on the security, or the status of the taxes due on the security.

(3) The judgment creditor shall file and serve the motion described in paragraph (1) pursuant to Section 1005 and the hearing shall be held pursuant to the same section.

(4) The financial affidavit and motion for an order determining the need for a debtor to appear for a debtor's examination, as well as any pleading filed in support of the motion and any reply by the judgment debtor, shall constitute the pleadings, subject to the power of the court to permit amendments in the interest of justice.

(5) If no other evidence is offered, the court, if satisfied that sufficient facts are shown by the financial affidavit and the notice of motion, may make its determination thereon. If not satisfied, the court shall order the hearing continued for the production of other oral or documentary evidence.

(6) At the conclusion of the hearing, the court shall determine by order whether the judgment debtor shall appear for a debtor's examination. If the judgment debtor is ordered to appear, the judgment creditor shall schedule the time and place of the examination with the court. There shall be no filing fee for the judgment creditor to refile the application and order for appearance and examination for the rescheduled exam. The judgment creditor is not required to serve the application and order by personal service, but may serve them by mail or electronic service at least 30 days before the date set for examination, pursuant to Sections 1013 and 1010.6.

(7) If the examination is canceled because the judgment creditor does not object or for another reason, the judgment creditor shall not file another application and order for appearance and examination until one year from the date of the prior filed application and order for appearance and examination.

(e) The financial affidavit shall include the following information:

(1) The number of people relying on the judgment debtor for support, including spouse, dependents, and other household members.

(2) Gross monthly income from employment, including withholdings and take home pay.

(3) Total monthly income from all sources other than employment.

(4) Property owned, including cash, bank accounts, real estate equity, vehicles (e.g., cars, motorcycles, and boats), jewelry, securities, certificates of deposit, entity ownership, life insurance policies, and tax refunds.

(5) Itemized monthly expenses.

(6) Any outstanding debts, including balance owed and to whom.

(7) Any other facts which support the claim of exemption.

(f) In a case concerning consumer debt in which the judgment debtor claims property is exempt pursuant to law exempting property to the extent necessary for the support of the judgment debtor and the spouse and dependents of the judgment debtor, the financial affidavit shall also include the following information. The financial affidavit shall also be signed under penalty of perjury by the spouse of the judgment debtor, unless the spouses are living separate and apart.

(1) The name of the spouse of the judgment debtor.

(2) The age and relationship of all persons dependent upon the judgment debtor or the spouse of the judgment debtor for support.

(3) All sources and the amounts of earnings and other income of the spouse and dependents of the judgment debtor.

(4) A list of the assets of the spouse and dependents of the judgment debtor and the value of such assets.

(5) All outstanding debts of the spouse and dependents of the judgment debtor.

(g) A judgment debtor in a case concerning consumer debt who elects to file a financial affidavit in lieu of appearing before the court for an examination shall serve a copy of all filed documents on the judgment creditor no later than 15 days prior to the date set for the examination.

(h) The Judicial Council shall adopt a notice of financial affidavit form and a financial affidavit form and revise any existing forms as necessary to implement the requirements of this section.

(i) Notwithstanding Section 708.170, 1209, or 1993, or any other applicable law or court rule, for a case involving consumer debt:

(1) No warrant for arrest or to appear shall be issued for a judgment debtor in a case concerning consumer debt who fails to appear for an examination under this section or to file and serve the judgment debtor's financial affidavit. In such cases, the court shall issue an order to show cause to determine whether to issue a warrant to compel the attendance of the judgment debtor.

(2) The court shall provide a judgment debtor who is ordered to appear pursuant to an order to show cause described in paragraph (1) with a reasonable opportunity to complete and file a judgment debtor's financial affidavit described in subdivision (e). The warrant to compel the attendance of the judgment debtor shall be satisfied by the judgment debtor's appearance or the filing of a notice of financial affidavit and proof of service pursuant to subdivision (d) certifying that the notice and financial affidavit was served on the judgment creditor. **Leg.H.** Added Stats 2023 ch 562 §2 (AB 1119), effective January 1, 2024.

§708.120. Examination of third person

(a) Upon ex parte application by a judgment creditor who has a money judgment and proof by the judgment creditor by affidavit or otherwise to the satisfaction of the proper court that a third person has possession or control of property in which the judgment debtor has an interest or is indebted to the judgment debtor in an amount exceeding two hundred fifty dollars ($250), the court shall make an order directing the third person to appear before the court, or before a referee appointed by the court, at a time and place specified in the order, to answer concerning such property or debt. The affidavit in support of the judgment creditor's application may be based on the affiant's information and belief.

(b) Not less than 10 days prior to the date set for the examination, a copy of the order shall be:

(1) Served personally on the third person.

(2) Served personally or by mail on the judgment debtor.

(c) If the property in the third person's possession or control in which the judgment debtor has an interest or the debt owed by the third person to the judgment debtor is described in the affidavit or application for an order under subdivision (a) in a manner reasonably adequate to permit it to be identified, service of the order on the third person creates a lien on the judgment debtor's interest in the property or on the debt for a period of one year from the date of the order unless extended or sooner terminated by the court.

(d) The judgment debtor may claim that all or any portion of the property or debt is exempt from enforcement of a money judgment by application to the court on noticed motion, filed with the court and personally served on the judgment creditor not later than three days before the date set for the examination. The judgment debtor shall execute an affidavit in support of the application that includes all of the matters set forth in subdivision (b) of Section 703.520. If a claim of exemption is made pursuant to this section, a notice of opposition to the claim of exemption is not required. The court shall determine any claim of exemption made pursuant to this section. Failure of the judgment debtor to make a claim of exemption does not preclude the judgment debtor from later claiming the exemption unless the property or debt is described in the order in a manner reasonably adequate to permit it to be identified and the judgment debtor receives notice of the examination proceeding at least 10 days before the date set for the examination.

(e) An order made pursuant to subdivision (a) shall contain the following statements in 14-point boldface type if printed or in capital letters if typed:

(1) "NOTICE TO PERSON SERVED. If you fail to appear at the time and place specified in this order, you may be subject to arrest and punishment for contempt of court and the court may make an order requiring you to pay the reasonable attorney's fees incurred by the judgment creditor in this proceeding."

(2) "NOTICE TO JUDGMENT DEBTOR. The person in whose favor the judgment was entered in this action claims that the person to be examined pursuant to this order has possession or control of property which is yours or owes you a debt. This property or debt is as follows: (Description of property or debt).

If you claim that all or any portion of this property or debt is exempt from enforcement of the money judgment, you must file your exemption claim in writing with the court and personally serve a copy on the judgment creditor not later than three days before the date set for the examination. You must appear at the time and place set for this examination to establish your claim of exemption or your exemption may be waived."

(f) An order made pursuant to subdivision (a) is not effective unless, at the time it is served on the third person, the person serving the order tenders to the third person fees for the mileage necessary to be traveled from the third person's residence to the place of examination. The mileage fees shall be in the same amount generally provided for witnesses when legally required to attend civil proceedings in the court where the examination proceeding is to be conducted. **Leg.H.** Added Stats 1982 ch 1364 §2, operative July 1, 1983. Amended Stats 1995 ch 576 §3.6 (AB 1225).

§708.130. Witnesses; Privilege of spouse of judgment debtor

(a) Witnesses may be required to appear and testify before the court or referee in an examination proceeding under this article in the same manner as upon the trial of an issue.

(b) The privilege prescribed by Article 4 (commencing with Section 970) of Chapter 4 of Division 8 of the Evidence Code does not apply in an examination proceeding under this article. **Leg.H.** Added Stats 1982 ch 1364 §2, operative July 1, 1983.

§708.140. Powers and qualifications of referee

(a) The examination proceedings authorized by this article may be conducted by a referee appointed by the court. The referee may issue, modify, or vacate an order authorized by Section 708.205, may make a protective order authorized by Section 708.200, and may issue a warrant authorized by Section 708.170, and has the same power as the court to grant adjournments, to preserve order, and to subpoena witnesses to attend the examination, but only the court that ordered the reference has power to do the following:

(1) Punish for contempt for disobeying an order of the referee.

(2) Make an award of attorney's fees pursuant to Section 708.170.

(3) Determine a contested claim of exemption or determine a third-party claim under Section 708.180.

(b) Only a member of the State Bar of California is eligible for appointment as a referee pursuant to this article. A person who was duly appointed as a referee prior to July 1, 1983, pursuant to the law in operation at the time of appointment, and who is available to perform the duties of a referee on July 1, 1983, shall be exempt from the requirements of this subdivision.

(c) Nothing in subdivision (a) limits the power of a court to appoint a temporary judge pursuant to Section 21 of Article VI of the California Constitution. **Leg.H.** Added Stats 1982 ch 1364 §2, operative July 1, 1983. Amended Stats 1983 ch 155 §19, effective June 30, 1983, operative July 1, 1983.

§708.150. Appearance at examination by representatives of organizations

(a)(1) If a corporation, partnership, association, trust, limited liability company, or other organization is served with an order to appear for an examination, it shall designate to appear and be examined one or more officers, directors, managing agents, or other persons who are familiar with its property and debts.

(2) If a corporation, partnership, association, trust, limited liability company, or other organization served with an order to appear for an examination fails to designate a person to appear pursuant to paragraph (1), the order to appear for an examination shall be deemed to have been made to and served upon the individuals designated in the manner described in paragraph (2) of subdivision (c).

(b) If the order to appear for an examination requires the appearance of a specified individual, the specified individual shall appear for the examination and may be accompanied by one or more officers, directors, managing agents, or other persons familiar with the property and debts of the corporation, partnership, association, trust, limited liability company, or other organization.

(c) If the order to appear for the examination does not require the appearance of a specified individual, the order shall advise the corporation, partnership, association, trust, limited liability company, or other organization of all of the following:

(1) The organization's duty to make a designation under paragraph (1) of subdivision (a).

(2) That the organization's failure to make a designation under paragraph (1) of subdivision (a) shall result in the order to appear for the

examination to be deemed to have been made to, and require the appearance of, the following:

(A) If the organization is a corporation registered with the Secretary of State, a natural person named as the chief financial officer in the corporation's most recent filing with the Secretary of State. If no one is so named, a natural person named as the chief executive officer in the corporation's most recent filing with the Secretary of State. If no one is so named, a natural person named as the secretary in the corporation's most recent filing with the Secretary of State.

(B) If the organization is a limited liability company registered with the Secretary of State, the first natural person named as a manager or member in the limited liability company's most recent filing with the Secretary of State.

(C) If the organization is a limited partnership registered with the Secretary of State, the first natural person named as a general partner in the limited partnership's most recent filing with the Secretary of State.

(D) If the organization is not registered with the Secretary of State or the organization's filings with the Secretary of State do not identify a natural person as described in subparagraph (A), (B), or (C), a natural person identified by the judgment creditor as being familiar with the property and debts of the organization, together with an affidavit or declaration signed by the judgment creditor that sets forth the factual basis for the identification of the individual. The affidavit or declaration shall be served on the organization together with the order.

(3) That service of an order to appear for an examination upon an organization by any method permitted under this code or the Corporations Code, including service on the agent of the organization for service of process, shall be deemed effective service of the order to appear upon the individuals identified under subparagraphs (A), (B), (C), and (D) of paragraph (2).

(d) A corporation, partnership, association, trust, limited liability company, or other organization, whether or not a party, may appear at an examination through any authorized officer, director, or employee, whether or not the person is an attorney.

(e) The powers of the court under Section 708.170 extend to natural persons ordered to appear and served pursuant to this section.

(f) This section shall be strictly construed and its requirements may not be varied by local rule or otherwise. **Leg.H.** Added Stats 1982 ch 1364 §2, operative July 1, 1983. Amended Stats 1984 ch 538 §30.5; Stats 2020 ch 36 §24 (AB 3364), effective January 1, 2021; Stats 2021 ch 30 §1 (AB 1580), effective January 1, 2022.

§708.160. Proper court for examination; Examination outside county where judgment entered

(a) Except as otherwise provided in this section, the proper court for examination of a person under this article is the court in which the money judgment is entered.

(b) A person sought to be examined may not be required to attend an examination before a court located outside the county in which the person resides or has a place of business unless the distance from the person's place of residence or place of business to the place of examination is less than 150 miles.

(c) If a person sought to be examined does not reside or have a place of business in the county where the judgment is entered, the superior court in the county where the person resides or has a place of business is a proper court for examination of the person.

(d) If the judgment creditor seeks an examination of a person before a court other than the court in which the judgment is entered, the judgment creditor shall file an application that shall include all of the following:

(1) An abstract of judgment in the form prescribed by Section 674.

(2) An affidavit in support of the application stating the place of residence or place of business of the person sought to be examined.

(3) Any necessary affidavit or showing for the examination as required by Section 708.110 or 708.120.

(4) The filing fee for a motion as provided in subdivision (a) of Section 70617 of the Government Code. **Leg.H.** Added Stats 1982 ch 1364 §2, operative July 1, 1983. Amended Stats 2005 ch 75 §38 (AB 145), effective July 19, 2005, operative January 1, 2006.

§708.170. Failure to appear for examination; Penalty for unjustified arrest

(a) If an order requiring a person to appear for an examination under subdivision (e) of Section 708.110 was served by a sheriff, marshal, a person specially appointed by the court in the order, or a registered process server, and the person fails to appear:

(1) The court may do either of the following:

(A) Pursuant to a warrant, have the person brought before the court to answer for the failure to appear and may punish the person for contempt.

(B) Issue a warrant for the arrest of the person who failed to appear as required by the court order, pursuant to Section 1993.

(2) If the person's failure to appear is without good cause, the judgment creditor shall be awarded reasonable attorney's fees incurred in the examination proceeding. Attorney's fees awarded against the judgment debtor shall be added to and become part of the principal amount of the judgment.

(b) A person who willfully makes an improper service of an order for an examination which subsequently results in the arrest pursuant to subdivision (a) of the person who fails to appear is guilty of a misdemeanor. **Leg.H.** Added Stats 1982 ch 1364 §2, operative July 1, 1983. Amended Stats 1996 ch 872 §17 (AB 3472); Stats 2006 ch 277 §2 (AB 2369), effective January 1, 2007; Stats 2023 ch 562 §3 (AB 1119), effective January 1, 2024.

§708.180. Determination of third person's adverse claim

(a) Subject to subdivision (b), if a third person examined pursuant to Section 708.120 claims an interest in the property adverse to the judgment debtor or denies the debt, the court may, if the judgment creditor so requests, determine the interests in the property or the existence of the debt. The determination is conclusive as to the parties to the proceeding and the third person, but an appeal may be taken from the determination. The court may grant a continuance for a reasonable time for discovery proceedings, the production of evidence, or other preparation for the hearing.

(b) The court may not make the determination provided in subdivision (a) if the third person's claim is made in good faith and any of the following conditions is satisfied:

(1) The court would not be a proper court for the trial of an independent civil action (including a creditor's suit) for the determination of the interests in the property or the existence of the debt, and the third person objects to the determination of the matter under subdivision (a).

(2) At the time an order for examination pursuant to Section 708.120 is served on the third person a civil action (including a creditor's suit) is pending with respect to the interests in the property or the existence of the debt.

(3) The court determines that the interests in the property or the existence of the debt should be determined in a creditor's suit.

(c) Upon application of the judgment creditor made ex parte, the court may make an order forbidding transfer of the property to the judgment debtor or payment of the debt to the judgment debtor until the interests in the property or the existence of the debt is determined pursuant to subdivision (a) or until a creditor's suit may be commenced and an order obtained pursuant to Section 708.240. An undertaking may be required in the discretion of the court. The court may modify or vacate the order at any time with or without a hearing on such terms as are just.

(d) Upon application of the judgment creditor upon noticed motion, the court may, if it determines that the judgment debtor probably owns an interest in the property or that the debt probably is owed to the judgment debtor, make an order forbidding the transfer or other disposition of the property to any person or forbidding payment of the debt until the interests in the property or the existence of the debt is determined pursuant to subdivision (a) or until a creditor's suit may be commenced and an order obtained pursuant to Section 708.240. The court shall require the judgment creditor to furnish an undertaking as provided in Section 529. The court may modify or vacate the order at any time after notice and hearing on such terms as are just. **Leg.H.** Added Stats 1982 ch 1364 §2, operative July 1, 1983. Amended Stats 1998 ch 931 §95 (SB 2139), effective September 28, 1998.

§708.190. Intervention

The court may permit a person claiming an interest in the property or debt sought to be applied in an examination proceeding to intervene in the proceeding and may determine the person's rights in the property or debt pursuant to Section 708.180. **Leg.H.** Added Stats 1982 ch 1364 §2, operative July 1, 1983.

§708.200. Protective orders

In any proceeding under this article, the court may, on motion of the person to be examined or on its own motion, make such protective orders as justice may require. **Leg.H.** Added Stats 1982 ch 1364 §2, operative July 1, 1983.

§708.205. Order applying property to satisfaction of judgment

(a) Except as provided in subdivision (b), at the conclusion of a proceeding pursuant to this article, the court may order the judgment debtor's interest in the property in the possession or under the control of the judgment debtor or the third person or a debt owed by the third person to the judgment debtor to be applied toward the satisfaction of the money judgment if the property is not exempt from enforcement of a money judgment. Such an order creates a lien on the property or debt.

(b) If a third person examined pursuant to Section 708.120 claims an interest in the property adverse to the judgment debtor or denies the debt and the court does not determine the matter as provided in subdivision (a) of Section 708.180, the court may not order the property or debt to be applied toward the satisfaction of the money judgment but may make an order pursuant to subdivision (c) or (d) of Section 708.180 forbidding transfer or payment to the extent authorized by that section. **Leg.H.** Added Stats 1982 ch 1364 §2, operative July 1, 1983.

ARTICLE 3
Creditor's Suit

Creditor's action against third person. §708.210.
Joinder of judgment debtor. §708.220.
Time for bringing creditor's suit. §708.230.
Order forbidding transfer of property or payment of debt. §708.240.
Lien of creditor's suit. §708.250.
Judgment debtor's claim of exemption. §708.260.
Jury trial. §708.270.
Judgment in creditor's suit. §708.280.
Costs. §708.290.

§708.210. Creditor's action against third person

If a third person has possession or control of property in which the judgment debtor has an interest or is indebted to the judgment debtor, the judgment creditor may bring an action against the third person to have the interest or debt applied to the satisfaction of the money judgment. **Leg.H.** Added Stats 1982 ch 1364 §2, operative July 1, 1983.

§708.220. Joinder of judgment debtor

The judgment debtor shall be joined in an action brought pursuant to this article but is not an indispensable party. The residence of the judgment debtor may not be considered in the determination of proper venue unless otherwise provided by contract between the judgment debtor and the third person. **Leg.H.** Added Stats 1982 ch 1364 §2, operative July 1, 1983.

§708.230. Time for bringing creditor's suit

(a) Except as provided in subdivision (b), an action shall be commenced pursuant to this article before the expiration of the later of the following times:

(1) The time when the judgment debtor may bring an action against the third person concerning the property or debt.

(2) One year after creation of a lien on the property or debt pursuant to this title if the lien is created at the time when the judgment debtor may bring an action against the third person concerning the property or debt.

(b) An action may not be commenced pursuant to this article after the period for enforcement of the money judgment has expired.

(c) Notwithstanding Section 683.020, if an action is commenced pursuant to this article within the time permitted in this section, the action may be prosecuted to judgment. **Leg.H.** Added Stats 1982 ch 1364 §2, operative July 1, 1983.

§708.240. Order forbidding transfer of property or payment of debt

The judgment creditor may apply to the court in which an action under this article is pending for either or both of the following:

(a) An order restraining the third person from transferring to the judgment debtor the property in which the judgment debtor is claimed to have an interest or from paying to the judgment debtor the alleged debt. The order shall be made on noticed motion if the court so directs or a court rule so requires. Otherwise, the order may be made on ex parte application. The order shall remain in effect until judgment is entered in the action or until such earlier time as the court may provide in the order. An undertaking may be required in the discretion of the court. The court may modify or vacate the order at any time with or without a hearing on such terms as are just.

(b) A temporary restraining order or a preliminary injunction or both, restraining the third person from transferring to any person or otherwise disposing of the property in which the judgment debtor is claimed to have an interest, pursuant to Chapter 3 (commencing with Section 525) of Title 7, and the court may make, dissolve, and modify such orders as provided therein. **Leg.H.** Added Stats 1982 ch 1364 §2, operative July 1, 1983.

§708.250. Lien of creditor's suit

Service of summons on the third person creates a lien on the interest of the judgment debtor in the property or on the debt owed to the judgment debtor that is the subject of an action under this article. **Leg.H.** Added Stats 1982 ch 1364 §2, operative July 1, 1983.

§708.260. Judgment debtor's claim of exemption

(a) In an action brought pursuant to this article, the judgment debtor may claim that all or any portion of the property or debt is exempt from enforcement of a money judgment. The claim shall be made by application to the court on noticed motion, filed with the court and served on the judgment creditor not later than 30 days before the date set for trial. Service shall be made personally or by mail. The judgment debtor shall execute an affidavit in support of the application that includes all of the matters set forth in subdivision (b) of Section 703.520. No notice of opposition to the claim of exemption is required. If the judgment debtor has not been named as a party to the action, the judgment debtor may obtain an order under Section 389 that the judgment debtor be made a party. Except as provided in subdivision (b), failure of the judgment debtor to make a claim of exemption is a waiver of the exemption.

(b) Failure of the judgment debtor to make a claim of exemption in an action brought pursuant to this article is not a waiver of the exemption if both of the following conditions are satisfied:

(1) The judgment debtor has not been served with process in the action that contains a description of the property or debt reasonably adequate to permit it to be identified.

(2) The judgment debtor does not have actual notice of the pendency of the action and the identity of the property or the nature of the debt in issue. **Leg.H.** Added Stats 1982 ch 1364 §2, operative July 1, 1983.

§708.270. Jury trial

There is no right to a jury trial in an action under this article. **Leg.H.** Added Stats 1982 ch 1364 §2, operative July 1, 1983.

§708.280. Judgment in creditor's suit

(a) The court shall determine any exemption claim made in the action. If the judgment debtor establishes to the satisfaction of the court that the property or debt is exempt from enforcement of a money judgment, the court shall so adjudge and may not make the orders referred to in subdivisions (b), (c), and (d).

(b) If the judgment creditor establishes that the third person has property in which the judgment debtor has an interest or is indebted to the judgment debtor, the court shall render judgment accordingly. The property or debt may be applied to the satisfaction of the judgment creditor's judgment against the judgment debtor as ordered by the court.

(c) If the court determines that the third person has property in which the judgment debtor has an interest, the court may order the third person not to transfer the property until it can be levied upon or otherwise applied to the satisfaction of the judgment.

(d) If the court determines that the third person has transferred property that was subject to a lien in favor of the judgment creditor or, contrary to court order of which the third person has notice, has paid the debt to the judgment debtor or has transferred the property, the court shall render judgment against the third person in an amount equal to the lesser of the following:

(1) The value of the judgment debtor's interest in the property or the amount of the debt.

(2) The amount of the judgment creditor's judgment against the judgment debtor remaining unsatisfied. **Leg.H.** Added Stats 1982 ch 1364 §2, operative July 1, 1983.

§708.290. Costs

Costs incurred by or taxed against the judgment creditor in an action under this article may not be recovered from the judgment debtor as a cost of enforcing the judgment. **Leg.H.** Added Stats 1982 ch 1364 §2, operative July 1, 1983.

ARTICLE 4
Charging Orders

Enforcement by charging order. §708.310.
Lien under terms of charging order. §708.320.

§708.310. Enforcement by charging order

If a money judgment is rendered against a partner or member but not against the partnership or limited liability company, the judgment debtor's interest in the partnership or limited liability company may be applied toward the satisfaction of the judgment by an order charging the judgment debtor's interest pursuant to Section 15907.03, 16504, or 17705.03 of the Corporations Code. **Leg.H.** Added Stats 1982 ch 1364 §2, operative July 1, 1983. Amended Stats 1985 ch 41 §9; Stats 2002 ch 451 §1 (AB 2355); Stats 2012 ch 419 §4 (AB 323), effective January 1, 2013, operative January 1, 2014; Stats 2021 ch 124 §12 (AB 938), effective January 1, 2022.

§708.320. Lien under terms of charging order

(a) A lien on a judgment debtor's interest in a partnership or limited liability company is created by service of a notice of motion for a charging order on the judgment debtor and on either of the following:

(1) All partners or the partnership.
(2) All members or the limited liability company.

(b) If a charging order is issued, the lien created pursuant to subdivision (a) continues under the terms of the order. If issuance of the charging order is denied, the lien is extinguished. **Leg.H.** Added Stats 1982 ch 1364 §2, operative July 1, 1983. Amended Stats 2002 ch 451 §2 (AB 2355).

ARTICLE 5
Lien in Pending Action or Proceeding

Judgment creditor's lien in pending action or proceeding. §708.410.
Contents of notice of lien. §708.420.
Intervention; Judgment creditor as party for certain purposes. §708.430.
Enforcement, compromise, dismissal, settlement, satisfaction. §708.440.
Judgment debtor's claim of exemption. §708.450.
Endorsement of lien on judgment and abstract. §708.460.
Orders in action or special proceeding to enforce lien. §708.470.
Enforcement of lien after final judgment. §708.480.

§708.410. Judgment creditor's lien in pending action or proceeding

(a) A judgment creditor who has a money judgment against a judgment debtor who is a party to a pending action or special proceeding may obtain a lien under this article, to the extent required to satisfy the judgment creditor's money judgment, on both of the following:

(1) Any cause of action of such judgment debtor for money or property that is the subject of the action or proceeding.
(2) The rights of such judgment debtor to money or property under any judgment subsequently procured in the action or proceeding.

(b) To obtain a lien under this article, the judgment creditor shall file a notice of lien and an abstract or certified copy of the judgment creditor's money judgment in the pending action or special proceeding.

(c) At the time of the filing under subdivision (b) or promptly thereafter, the judgment creditor shall serve on all parties who, prior thereto, have made an appearance in the action or special proceeding a copy of the notice of lien and a statement of the date when the notice of lien was filed in the action or special proceeding. Service shall be made personally or by mail. Failure to serve all parties as required by this subdivision does not affect the lien created by the filing under subdivision (b), but the rights of a party are not affected by the lien until the party has notice of the lien.

(d) For the purpose of this article, an action or special proceeding is pending until the time for appeal from the judgment has expired or, if an appeal is filed, until the appeal has been finally determined. **Leg.H.** Added Stats 1982 ch 1364 §2, operative July 1, 1983.

§708.420. Contents of notice of lien

The notice of lien under Section 708.410 shall contain all of the following:

(a) A statement that a lien has been created under this article and the title of the court and the cause and number of the pending action or proceeding in which the notice of lien is filed.
(b) The name and last known address of the judgment debtor.
(c) The name and address of the judgment creditor.
(d) The title of the court where the judgment creditor's money judgment is entered and the cause and number of the action, the date of entry of the judgment, and the date of any subsequent renewals, and where entered in the records of the court.
(e) The amount required to satisfy the judgment creditor's money judgment at the time the notice of lien is filed in the action or proceeding.
(f) A statement that the lien attaches to any cause of action of the judgment debtor that is the subject of the action or proceeding and to the judgment debtor's rights to money or property under any judgment subsequently procured in the action or proceeding.
(g) A statement that no compromise, dismissal, settlement, or satisfaction of the pending action or proceeding or any of the judgment debtor's rights to money or property under any judgment procured therein may be entered into by or on behalf of the judgment debtor, and that the judgment debtor may not enforce the judgment debtor's rights to money or property under any judgment procured in the action or proceeding by a writ or otherwise, unless one of the following requirements is satisfied:

(1) The prior approval by order of the court in which the action or proceeding is pending has been obtained.
(2) The written consent of the judgment creditor has been obtained or the judgment creditor has released the lien.
(3) The money judgment of the judgment creditor has been satisfied.

(h) A statement that the judgment debtor may claim an exemption for all or any portion of the money or property within 30 days after the judgment debtor has notice of the creation of the lien and a statement that, if the exemption is not claimed within the time allowed, the exemption is waived. **Leg.H.** Added Stats 1982 ch 1364 §2, operative July 1, 1983.

§708.430. Intervention; Judgment creditor as party for certain purposes

(a) The court in which the action or special proceeding is pending may permit a judgment creditor who has obtained a lien under this article to intervene in the action or proceeding pursuant to Section 387.

(b) For the purposes of Sections 708.450 and 708.470, a judgment creditor shall be deemed to be a party to the action or special proceeding even though the judgment creditor has not become a party to the action or proceeding under subdivision (a). **Leg.H.** Added Stats 1982 ch 1364 §2, operative July 1, 1983.

§708.440. Enforcement, compromise, dismissal, settlement, satisfaction

(a) Except as provided in subdivision (c) of Section 708.410, unless the judgment creditor's money judgment is first satisfied or the lien is released, the judgment recovered in the action or special proceeding in favor of the judgment debtor may not be enforced by a writ or otherwise, and no compromise, dismissal, settlement, or satisfaction of the pending action or special proceeding or the judgment procured therein may be entered into by or on behalf of the judgment debtor, without the written consent of the judgment creditor or authorization by order of the court obtained under subdivision (b).

(b) Upon application by the judgment debtor, the court in which the action or special proceeding is pending or the judgment procured therein is entered may, in its discretion, after a hearing, make an order described in subdivision (a) that may include such terms and conditions as the court deems necessary. The application for an order under this subdivision shall be made on noticed motion. The notice of motion shall be served on the judgment creditor. Service shall be made personally or by mail. **Leg.H.** Added Stats 1982 ch 1364 §2, operative July 1, 1983.

§708.450. Judgment debtor's claim of exemption

(a) If a lien is created under this article, the judgment debtor may claim that all or any portion of the money or property that the judgment debtor may recover in the action or special proceeding is exempt from enforcement of a money judgment. The claim shall be made by application on noticed motion to the court in which the action or special proceeding is pending, filed and served on the judgment creditor not later than 30 days after the judgment debtor has notice of the creation of the lien. Service shall be made personally or by mail. The judgment debtor shall execute an affidavit in support of the application that includes all the matters set forth in subdivision (b) of Section 703.520. No notice of opposition to the claim of exemption is required. The failure of the judgment debtor to make a claim of exemption under this section constitutes a waiver of the exemption.

(b) The court may determine the exemption claim at any time prior to the entry of judgment in the action or special proceeding or may consolidate the exemption hearing with the hearing on a motion pursuant to Section 708.470.

(c) If the judgment debtor establishes to the satisfaction of the court that the right of the judgment debtor to money or property under the judgment in the action or special proceeding is all or partially exempt from enforcement of a money judgment, the court shall order the termination of the lien created under this article on the exempt portion of the money or property. **Leg.H.** Added Stats 1982 ch 1364 §2, operative July 1, 1983. Amended Stats 1984 ch 538 §31.

§708.460. Endorsement of lien on judgment and abstract

(a) If a lien is created pursuant to this article, the court clerk shall endorse upon the judgment recovered in the action or special proceeding a statement of the existence of the lien and the time it was created.

(b) Any abstract issued upon the judgment shall include a statement of the lien in favor of the judgment creditor. **Leg.H.** Added Stats 1982 ch 1364 §2, operative July 1, 1983.

§708.470. Orders in action or special proceeding to enforce lien

(a) If the judgment debtor is entitled to money or property under the judgment in the action or special proceeding and a lien created under this article exists, upon application of any party to the action or special proceeding, the court may order that the judgment debtor's rights to money or property under the judgment be applied to the satisfaction of the lien created under this article as ordered by the court. Application for an order under this section shall be on noticed motion. The notice of motion shall be served on all other parties. Service shall be made personally or by mail.

(b) If the judgment determines that the judgment debtor has an interest in property, the court may order the party having custody or control of the property not to transfer the property until it can be levied upon or otherwise applied to the satisfaction of the lien created under this article.

(c) If the court determines that a party (other than the judgment debtor) having notice of the lien created under this article has transferred property that was subject to the lien or has paid an amount to the judgment debtor that was subject to the lien, the court shall render judgment against the party in an amount equal to the lesser of the following:

(1) The value of the judgment debtor's interest in the property or the amount paid the judgment debtor.

(2) The amount of the judgment creditor's lien created under this article. **Leg.H.** Added Stats 1982 ch 1364 §2, operative July 1, 1983.

§708.480. Enforcement of lien after final judgment

A lien created under this article may be enforced by any applicable procedure:

(a) After the judgment subject to the lien is entered and the time for appeal from the judgment has expired.

(b) If an appeal is filed from the judgment subject to the lien, after the appeal is finally determined. **Leg.H.** Added Stats 1982 ch 1364 §2, operative July 1, 1983.

ARTICLE 6
Assignment Order

Order to assign right to payment. §708.510.
Restraining assignment or other disposition. §708.520.
Effect and priority of assignment. §708.530.
Rights of person obligated. §708.540.
Exemption procedure. §708.550.
Modification or setting aside assignment order. §708.560.

§708.510. Order to assign right to payment

(a) Except as otherwise provided by law, upon application of the judgment creditor on noticed motion, the court may order the judgment debtor to assign to the judgment creditor or to a receiver appointed pursuant to Article 7 (commencing with Section 708.610) all or part of a right to payment due or to become due, whether or not the right is conditioned on future developments, including but not limited to the following types of payments:

(1) Wages due from the federal government that are not subject to withholding under an earnings withholding order.

(2) Rents.

(3) Commissions.

(4) Royalties.

(5) Payments due from a patent or copyright.

(6) Insurance policy loan value.

(b) The notice of the motion shall be served on the judgment debtor. Service shall be made personally or by mail.

(c) Subject to subdivisions (d), (e), and (f), in determining whether to order an assignment or the amount of an assignment pursuant to subdivision (a), the court may take into consideration all relevant factors, including the following:

(1) The reasonable requirements of a judgment debtor who is a natural person and of persons supported in whole or in part by the judgment debtor.

(2) Payments the judgment debtor is required to make or that are deducted in satisfaction of other judgments and wage assignments, including earnings assignment orders for support.

(3) The amount remaining due on the money judgment.

(4) The amount being or to be received in satisfaction of the right to payment that may be assigned.

(d) A right to payment may be assigned pursuant to this article only to the extent necessary to satisfy the money judgment.

(e) When earnings or periodic payments pursuant to a pension or retirement plan are assigned pursuant to subdivision (a), the amount of the earnings or the periodic payments assigned shall not exceed the amount that may be withheld from a like amount of earnings under Chapter 5 (commencing with Section 706.010) (Wage Garnishment Law).

(f) Where a specific amount of the payment or payments to be assigned is exempt by another statutory provision, the amount of the payment or payments to be assigned pursuant to subdivision (a) shall not exceed the amount by which the payment or payments exceed the exempt amount. **Leg.H.** Added Stats 1982 ch 1364 §2, operative July 1, 1983. Amended Stats 1992 ch 163 §51 (AB 2641), operative January 1, 1994.

§708.520. Restraining assignment or other disposition

(a) When an application is made pursuant to Section 708.510 or thereafter, the judgment creditor may apply to the court for an order restraining the judgment debtor from assigning or otherwise disposing of the right to payment that is sought to be assigned. The application shall be made on noticed motion if the court so directs or a court rule so requires. Otherwise, it may be made ex parte.

(b) The court may issue an order pursuant to this section upon a showing of need for the order. The court, in its discretion, may require the judgment creditor to provide an undertaking.

(c) The court may modify or vacate the order at any time with or without a hearing on such terms as are just.

(d) The order shall be personally served upon the judgment debtor and shall contain a notice to the judgment debtor that failure to comply with the order may subject the judgment debtor to being held in contempt of court. **Leg.H.** Added Stats 1982 ch 1364 §2, operative July 1, 1983.

§708.530. Effect and priority of assignment

(a) Except as provided in subdivision (b), the effect and priority of an assignment ordered pursuant to this article is governed by Section 955.1 of the Civil Code. For the purpose of priority, an assignee of a right to payment pursuant to this article shall be deemed to be a bona fide assignee for value under the terms of Section 955.1 of the Civil Code.

(b) An assignment of the right to future rent ordered under this article is recordable as an instrument affecting real property and the priority of such an assignment is governed by Section 1214 of the Civil Code. **Leg.H.** Added Stats 1982 ch 1364 §2, operative July 1, 1983. Amended Stats 1984 ch 538 §32.

§708.540. Rights of person obligated

The rights of an obligor are not affected by an order assigning the right to payment until notice of the order is received by the obligor. For the purpose of this section, "obligor" means the person who is obligated to make payments to the judgment debtor or who may become obligated to make payments to the judgment debtor depending upon future developments. **Leg.H.** Added Stats 1982 ch 1364 §2, operative July 1, 1983.

§708.550. Exemption procedure

(a) The judgment debtor may claim that all or a portion of the right to payment is exempt from enforcement of a money judgment by application to the court on noticed motion filed not later than three days before the date set for the hearing on the judgment creditor's application for an assignment order. The judgment debtor shall execute an affidavit in support of the application that includes all of the matters set forth in subdivision (b) of Section 703.520. Failure of the judgment debtor to make a claim of exemption is a waiver of the exemption.

(b) The notice of the motion shall be personally served on the judgment creditor not later than three days before the date set for the hearing.

(c) The court shall determine any claim of exemption made pursuant to this section at the hearing on issuance of the assignment order. **Leg.H.** Added Stats 1982 ch 1364 §2, operative July 1, 1983.

§708.560. Modification or setting aside assignment order

(a) Either the judgment creditor or the judgment debtor may apply to the court on noticed motion for an order to modify or set aside the assignment order. The notice of motion shall be served on the other party. Service shall be made personally or by mail.

(b) The court shall make an order modifying or setting aside the assignment order upon a showing that there has been a material change in circumstances since the time of the previous hearing on the assignment order. The court may order a reassignment of the right to payments as necessary. The order shall state whether and to what extent it applies to payments already made. **Leg.H.** Added Stats 1982 ch 1364 §2, operative July 1, 1983.

ARTICLE 7
Receiver to Enforce Judgment

Application of general provisions. §708.610.
Appointment of receiver. §708.620.
Receiver to transfer alcoholic beverage license. §708.630.

§708.610. Application of general provisions

The provisions of Chapter 5 (commencing with Section 564) and Chapter 5a (commencing with Section 571) of Title 7 govern the appointment, qualifications, powers, rights, and duties of a receiver appointed under this article. **Leg.H.** Added Stats 1982 ch 1364 §2, operative July 1, 1983.

§708.620. Appointment of receiver

The court may appoint a receiver to enforce the judgment where the judgment creditor shows that, considering the interests of both the judgment creditor and the judgment debtor, the appointment of a receiver is a reasonable method to obtain the fair and orderly satisfaction of the judgment. **Leg.H.** Added Stats 1982 ch 1364 §2, operative July 1, 1983.

§708.630. Receiver to transfer alcoholic beverage license

(a) The judgment debtor's interest in an alcoholic beverage license may be applied to the satisfaction of a money judgment only as provided in this section.

(b) The court may appoint a receiver for the purpose of transferring the judgment debtor's interest in an alcoholic beverage license that is transferable under Article 5 (commencing with Section 24070) of Chapter 6 of Division 9 of the Business and Professions Code, unless the judgment debtor shows in the proceeding to appoint a receiver that the amount of delinquent taxes described in Section 24049 of the Business and Professions Code and claims of creditors with priority over the judgment creditor pursuant to Section 24074 of the Business and Professions Code exceed the probable sale price of the license.

(c) The receiver may exercise the powers of the licensee as necessary and in exercising such powers shall comply with the applicable provisions of Division 9 (commencing with Section 23000) of the Business and Professions Code and applicable regulations of the Department of Alcoholic Beverage Control. An application shall be filed to transfer the license to the receiver and a temporary retail permit shall be obtained during the pendency of the transfer. **Leg.H.** Added Stats 1982 ch 1364 §2, operative July 1, 1983.

ARTICLE 8
Collection of Judgment Where Judgment Debtor Is Creditor of Public Entity

Definitions. §708.710.
Exclusive procedures. §708.720.
Filing and notice generally; Claim for child, family or spousal support; "Support". §708.730.
Collection where judgment debtor is creditor of state agency; Support judgment; "Support". §708.740.
Collection where judgment debtor is creditor of public entity other than state agency. §708.750.
Lien of judgment creditor against lottery prize. §708.755.
Collection where judgment debtor is contractor on public work; Subordination to claims of laborers. §708.760.
Notice of deposit with court; Exemption claim. §708.770.
Distribution of money. §708.775.
Creation of lien; Effect of filing affidavit; Notice of Support Arrearage. §708.780.
Filing fee; Deposit of fees collected by state. §708.785.
Liability of public officer. §708.790.
Limitations on procedure of this article. §708.795.

§708.710. Definitions

As used in this article:

(a) "Local public entity" means any public entity other than the state.

(b) "Public entity" means the state, a county, city, district, public authority, public agency, and any other political subdivision in the state.

(c) "State" means the State of California.

(d) "State agency" means a state office, officer, department, division, bureau, board, commission or agency claims against which are paid by warrants drawn by the Controller. **Leg.H.** Added Stats 1982 ch 1364 §2, operative July 1, 1983.

§708.720. Exclusive procedures

(a) If a public entity owes money to the judgment debtor, the obligation of the public entity may be applied to the satisfaction of the money judgment against the judgment debtor only in the manner provided by (1) this article, (2) Chapter 5 (commencing with Section 706.010) (wage garnishment), or (3) Article 5 (commencing with Section 708.410) (lien in pending action or proceeding).

(b) The earnings of a public officer or employee shall not be withheld pursuant to this article. Except as expressly provided by law, the earnings of a public officer or employee may be withheld for the payment of a money judgment only pursuant to Chapter 5 (commencing with Section 706.010).

(c) If the obligation of a public entity to pay money to the judgment debtor is the subject of a pending action or special proceeding, the procedure in this article does not apply. The payment of the obligation that is the subject of the pending action or special proceeding may be applied to the satisfaction of the money judgment against the judgment debtor only in the manner provided in Article 5 (commencing with Section 708.410). **Leg.H.** Added Stats 1982 ch 1364 §2, operative July 1, 1983.

§708.730. Filing and notice generally; Claim for child, family or spousal support; "Support"

(a) If money is owing and unpaid to the judgment debtor by a public entity, the judgment creditor may file, in the manner provided in this article, an abstract of the money judgment or a certified copy of the money judgment, together with an affidavit that states that the judgment creditor desires the relief provided by this article and states the exact amount then required to satisfy the judgment. The judgment creditor may state in the affidavit any fact tending to establish the identity of the judgment debtor.

(b) Promptly after filing the abstract or certified copy of the judgment and the affidavit with the public entity, the judgment creditor shall serve notice of the filing on the judgment debtor. Service shall be made personally or by mail.

(c) If the judgment is for support and related costs and money is owing and unpaid to the judgment debtor by a state agency, including, but not limited to, money owing and unpaid to the judgment debtor by a state agency on a claim for refund from the Franchise Tax Board under the Personal Income Tax Law, Part 10 (commencing with Section 17001) of Division 2 of the Revenue and Taxation Code, or the Bank and Corporation Tax Law, Part 11 (commencing with Section 23001) of Division 2 of the Revenue and Taxation Code or as a result of the judgment debtor's winnings in the California State Lottery, and the local child support agency is enforcing the support obligation pursuant to Section 17400 of the Family Code, the claim may be submitted as follows: The local child support agency may file the affidavit referred to in subdivision (a) without filing an abstract or certified copy of the judgment. In lieu thereof, the affidavit shall also state that an abstract of the judgment could be obtained. Where there is more than one judgment debtor, the local child support agency may include all the judgment debtors in a single affidavit. Separate affidavits need not be submitted for each judgment debtor. The affidavit need not on its face separately identify each judgment debtor or the exact amount required to satisfy the judgment, so long as it incorporates by reference forms or other automated data transmittals, as required by the Department of Child Support Services, which contain this information. Affidavits submitted pursuant to this subdivision by the local child support agency shall meet the standards and procedures prescribed by the state agency to which the affidavit is submitted, except that those affidavits submitted with respect to moneys owed and unpaid to the judgment debtor as a result of a claim for refund from the Franchise Tax Board under the Personal Income Tax Law, Part 10 (commencing with Section 17001) of Division 2 of the Revenue and Taxation Code, or the Bank and Corporation Tax Law, Part 11 (commencing with Section 23001) of Division 2 of the Revenue and Taxation Code, shall meet the standards and procedures prescribed by the Franchise Tax Board.

In serving the notice required by subdivision (b), the Director of the Department of Child Support Services or his or her designee may act in lieu of the judgment creditor as to judgments enforced under this division.

(d) If the judgment is for child, spousal, or family support and related costs and money is owing and unpaid to the judgment debtor by a state agency on a claim for refund from the Franchise Tax Board under the Personal Income Tax Law, Part 10 (commencing with Section 17001) of Division 2 of the Revenue and Taxation Code, or the Bank and Corporation Tax Law, Part 11 (commencing with Section 23001) of Division 2 of the Revenue and Taxation Code, or as a result of the judgment debtor's winnings in the California State Lottery, the judgment creditor may file with the court an abstract or a certified copy of the judgment ordering the payment of child, spousal, or family support, together with a request that the court issue a Notice of Support Arrearage, as provided in Section 708.780, to which any personal income tax refunds and lottery winnings owed the judgment debtor by the State of California will be subject. The request shall be accompanied by an affidavit, signed under penalty of perjury, which shall state that the judgment creditor desires the relief provided by this subdivision and shall state the exact amount then required to satisfy the judgment. In addition, the affidavit shall specify the beginning and ending dates of all periods during which the arrearage for support occurred, specify the arrearage for each month, and state that the support is at least 90 days overdue or is overdue in an amount equal to 90 days of support. It shall also certify that the child or children are not recipients, and during the period for which payment is requested, were not recipients, of Aid to Families with Dependent Children and there was no assignment to a state or county agency of support and shall certify on information and belief that there is not current or past action by a district attorney pending for support or support enforcement on the judgment creditor's behalf.

The request shall have attached a proof of service showing that copies of the request, the affidavit, and the abstract or certified copy of the judgment ordering the payment of support have been served on the judgment debtor and the district attorney of the county in which the support judgment is entered. Service shall be by certified mail, postage prepaid, return receipt requested, to the last known address of the party to be served, or by personal service.

This subdivision does not apply in any instance in which a district attorney initiated or participated as counsel in the action for support or if support is required to be paid through a district attorney's office.

The Department of Child Support Services shall, upon request, inform the Legislature of the use and effect of this subdivision on or before December 31, 2000.

This subdivision shall become operative on January 1, 1996, and shall become inoperative on December 31, 2000.

(e) For purposes of this section, "support" means an obligation owing on behalf of a child, spouse, or family, or combination thereof. **Leg.H.** Added Stats 1982 ch 1364 §2, operative July 1, 1983. Amended Stats 1983 ch 1010 §1; Stats 1984 ch 1007 §1; Stats 1986 ch 436 §1, effective July 22, 1986; Stats 1988 ch 1017 §1, operative July 1, 1989; Stats 1989 ch 1359 §9; Stats 1992 ch 163 §52 (AB 2641), operative January 1, 1994; Stats 1995 ch 459 §1 (AB 1515); Stats 2000 ch 808 §18 (AB 1358), effective September 28, 2000.

§708.740. Collection where judgment debtor is creditor of state agency; Support judgment; "Support"

(a) Except as provided in subdivision (e), if money is owing and unpaid to the judgment debtor by a state agency, the judgment creditor shall file the abstract or certified copy of the judgment and the affidavit with the state agency owing the money to the judgment debtor prior to the time the state agency presents the claim of the judgment debtor to the Controller. Where the affidavit is prepared under subdivision (c) of Section 708.730, the affidavit shall be filed with the Department of Child Support Services, and no abstract need be filed. Filing of the affidavit with the department shall be sufficient to require the Controller to transfer the funds claimed by the judgment debtor, notwithstanding that the claim of the judgment debtor has been filed with another state agency.

(b) When presenting the claim of the judgment debtor to the Controller, the state agency shall do all of the following:

(1) Note the fact of the filing of the abstract or certified copy of the judgment and the affidavit.

(2) State the amount required to satisfy the judgment as shown by the affidavit.

(3) State any amounts advanced to the judgment debtor by the state, or owed by the judgment debtor to the state, for expenses or for any other purpose.

(c) Except as provided in subdivisions (d) and (e), to discharge the claim of the judgment debtor, the Controller shall (1) deposit with the court, by a warrant or check payable to the court, the amount due the judgment debtor (after deducting an amount sufficient to reimburse the state for any amounts advanced to the judgment debtor or owed by the judgment debtor to the state) required to satisfy the money judgment as shown by the affidavit in full or to the greatest extent and (2) pay the balance thereof, if any, to the judgment debtor.

(d) Where an affidavit stating the existence of a judgment for support has been submitted to the Department of Child Support Services, pursuant to subdivision (c) of Section 708.730, to discharge the claim of a judgment debtor, the Controller shall direct payment to the county agency designated by the local child support agency in his or her affidavit.

(e) Where the judgment is for support and the money owed is for lottery winnings or a refund of overpayment of tax, penalty, interest, or interest allowable with respect to an overpayment under Part 10 (commencing with Section 17001) of Division 2 of the Revenue and Taxation Code, and the support obligation is not being enforced pursuant to Section 17400 of the Family Code, the judgment creditor may file the abstract or certified copy of the judgment with the local child support agency of the county in which the support judgment is entered or registered. The local child support agency shall then file the claim of the judgment creditor pursuant to subdivision (c) of Section 708.730. When funds are received by the local child support agency, it shall discharge any claim of the judgment debtor by forwarding those sums to the clerk of the court pursuant to subdivision (c) of this section. Any and all notices otherwise required of a judgment creditor or the clerk of the court, and any litigation to enforce rights under this subdivision shall be the responsibility of the judgment creditor, the same as if service had been directly on the Controller without the intervention of the local child support agency.

(f) Where the claim of the judgment debtor is less than ten dollars ($10) and the claim of the judgment creditor arises under an affidavit filed pursuant to subdivision (c) of Section 708.730, the Controller may disregard the claim of the judgment creditor and forward any and all sums due to the judgment debtor. In the event that there is more than one claimant for a refund, the Franchise Tax Board shall have discretion in allocating the overpayment among claimants.

(g) Should two or more local child support agencies submit claims on behalf of a judgment creditor, the Controller in his or her discretion may select which claim or claims he or she shall honor.

(h) Any claims which are honored in behalf of a judgment creditor shall be considered as refunds of tax overpayments to the judgment debtor.

(i) For purposes of this section, "support" means an obligation owing on behalf of a child, spouse, or family, or combination thereof. **Leg.H.** Added Stats 1982 ch 1364 §2, operative July 1, 1983. Amended Stats 1983 ch 1010 §2; Stats 1984 ch 1007 §2; Stats 1988 ch 1017 §1.5; Stats 1989 ch 1359 §9.3; Stats 2000 ch 808 §19 (AB 1358), effective September 28, 2000.

§708.750. Collection where judgment debtor is creditor of public entity other than state agency

If money is owing and unpaid to the judgment debtor by a public entity other than a state agency, the judgment creditor shall file the abstract or certified copy of the judgment and the affidavit with the auditor of the public entity or, if there is no auditor, with the official whose duty corresponds to that of auditor. To discharge the claim of the judgment debtor, the auditor or other official shall (1) deposit with the court by a warrant or check payable to the court, the amount due the judgment debtor (after deducting an amount sufficient to reimburse the public entity for any amounts advanced to the judgment debtor or owed by the judgment debtor to the public entity) required to satisfy the money judgment as shown by the affidavit in full or to the greatest extent and (2) pay the balance thereof, if any, to the judgment debtor. **Leg.H.** Added Stats 1982 ch 1364 §2, operative July 1, 1983.

Prior Law: There was another section of this number which was added Stats 1995 ch 363 §1, effective August 4, 1995 and renumbered as CCP §708.755 by Stats 1996 ch 124 §14.

§708.755. Lien of judgment creditor against lottery prize

(a) Upon compliance with this section, the lien of a judgment creditor pursuant to this article is created against a lottery prize to be paid in annual installments and shall continue in force and effect until the judgment is paid or expires, whichever occurs first. For the lien to continue in effect, the judgment creditor shall do all of the following:

(1) Commencing with the second installment against which the judgment lien creditor asserts its lien, annually file with the lottery an affidavit stating that the judgment has not been satisfied and the amount of the remaining unsatisfied judgment, including interest and costs, if any. This affidavit shall be filed with the lottery not less than 45 days, nor more than 90 days, before the annual payment due date on the prize that is the subject of the judgment lien.

(2) If the judgment lien is renewed, file with the lottery a certified copy of the renewal application, as authorized in this code not less than 45 days, nor more than 90 days, before the annual payment due date on the prize that is the subject of the judgment lien, in order for the judgment lien to be effective in continuing the existing judgment lien against the annual lottery prize payments.

(b) If the judgment lien creditor fails to file the annual statement, renewal of judgment, or renewal of abstract, the lien shall expire. Expiration of a lien for failure to comply with this section shall not preclude the judgment creditor from commencing a new procedure under this article to enforce the judgment, to the extent that the judgment otherwise continues to be enforceable under applicable law. **Leg.H.** Added Stats 1995 ch 363 §1 (AB 218), effective August 4, 1995, as CCP §708.750. Renumbered by Stats 1996 ch 124 §14 (AB 3470).

§708.760. Collection where judgment debtor is contractor on public work; Subordination to claims of laborers

(a) If the judgment debtor named in the abstract or certified copy of the judgment filed pursuant to this article is a contractor upon a public work, the cost of which is to be paid out of public moneys voted, appropriated, or otherwise set apart for such purpose, only so much of the contract price shall be deemed owing and unpaid within the meaning of Section 708.740 or 708.750 as may remain payable under the terms of the contractor's contract, upon the completion thereof, after deducting sums due and to become due to persons described in Section 9100 of the Civil Code. In ascertaining the sums due or to become due to such persons, only claims which are filed against the moneys due or to become due to the judgment debtor in accordance with Chapter 4 (commencing with Section 9350) of Title 3 of Part 6 of Division 4 of the Civil Code shall be considered.

(b) The Controller, auditor, or other public disbursing officer whose duty it is to make payments under the provisions of the contract may not deposit an amount with the court pursuant to this article until the contract is completed, but may deposit an amount with the court to satisfy the claim of the judgment debtor before the payments specified in subdivision (a) are made so long as a sufficient amount is retained for the satisfaction of the claims of persons described in Section 9100 of the Civil Code. **Leg.H.** Added Stats 1982 ch 1364 §2, operative July 1, 1983. Amended Stats 2010 ch 697 §23 (SB 189), effective January 1, 2011, operative July 1, 2012.

§708.770. Notice of deposit with court; Exemption claim

(a) Except as provided in subdivision (g), promptly after deposit with the court by the public entity, the court clerk shall cause a notice of deposit to be served on the judgment debtor. Service shall be made personally or by mail.

(b) Within 10 days after service of the notice of deposit pursuant to subdivision (a), the judgment debtor who claims an exemption shall do both of the following:

(1) File with the court a claim of exemption and a notice of motion for an order determining the claim of exemption. The claim of exemption shall include all of the matters set forth in subdivision (b) of Section 703.520.

(2) Serve on the judgment creditor a copy of the notice of motion, a copy of the claim of exemption, and a notice of hearing on the motion. Service shall be made personally or by mail.

(c) The hearing on the motion shall be held not later than 30 days from the date the notice of motion was filed with the court unless continued by the court for good cause.

(d) Within 10 days after the judgment creditor is served under subdivision (b), the judgment creditor who opposes the motion shall do both of the following:

(1) File with the court a notice of opposition to the claim of exemption. The notice of opposition to the claim of exemption shall be executed under oath and shall include all of the matters set forth in Section 703.560.

(2) Serve on the judgment debtor a copy of the notice of opposition to the claim of exemption. Service shall be made personally or by mail.

(e) Subdivisions (a) to (d), inclusive, of Section 703.580 and Sections 703.590 and 703.600 apply to a claim of exemption made pursuant to this section.

(f) The failure of the judgment debtor to make a claim of exemption under this section constitutes a waiver of the exemption.

(g) In lieu of service of the notice of deposit described herein, where a state agency has been served with an affidavit pursuant to subdivision (c) of Section 708.730 and has presented the claim of the judgment creditor to the Controller pursuant to subdivision (a) of Section 708.740, the state agency shall cause a notice of deposit to be sent to the judgment debtor instructing the judgment debtor to file any and all requests for relief with the district attorney who filed the affidavit, or the court clerk if the seizure arises under subdivision (e) of Section 708.740. Except in those cases arising under subdivision (e) of Section 708.740, the judgment debtor shall file the request for relief with the district attorney within 15 days after service of notice from the public agency, or the judgment debtor shall be deemed to have waived any claim he or she might otherwise have. If the matter cannot be resolved with the district attorney, the district attorney shall so advise the judgment debtor and the judgment debtor shall then be authorized to commence proceedings under this section or any other appropriate provision of law. The notice from the district attorney shall for any limitation have the same effect as a notice of deposit under subdivision (a). Service of any notice or request under this subdivision shall be made personally or by mail.

Claims arising from the filing of an abstract or certified copy of a judgment, under subdivision (e) of Section 708.740 shall be governed by the procedure and limitations set forth in subdivisions (a) through (f). **Leg.H.** Added Stats 1982 ch 1364 §2, operative July 1, 1983. Amended Stats 1983 ch 1010 §3.

§708.775. Distribution of money

After the expiration of the period allowed for claiming an exemption under Section 708.770 if no exemption has been claimed, or after the determination of the claim of exemption if an exemption is claimed within the period allowed for claiming the exemption under Section 708.770, the court shall pay the nonexempt portion of the money deposited to which the judgment creditor is entitled to the judgment creditor and the balance thereof, if any, to the judgment debtor, unless some other disposition is required by law. **Leg.H.** Added Stats 1982 ch 1364 §2, operative July 1, 1983.

§708.780. Creation of lien; Effect of filing affidavit; Notice of Support Arrearage

(a) Filing of the abstract or certified copy of the judgment and the affidavit pursuant to this article creates a lien on the money owing and unpaid to the judgment debtor by the public entity in an amount equal to that which may properly be applied to the satisfaction of the money judgment under this article.

(b) When an affidavit is filed pursuant to subdivision (c) of Section 708.730, it shall apply to all claims for refund from the Franchise Tax Board under the Personal Income Tax Law, Part 10 (commencing with Section 17001) of Division 2 of the Revenue and Taxation Code, or the

Bank and Corporation Tax Law, Part 11 (commencing with Section 23001) of Division 2 of the Revenue and Taxation Code, which the judgment debtor subsequently claims during a period one year after filing of the affidavit, or October 1 of the year following the filing of the affidavit, whichever occurs later, the same as if claims for these overpayments were filed by the judgment debtor with the appropriate state agency on the date the affidavit was filed.

(c) When a request is filed pursuant to subdivision (d) of Section 708.730 with the court, the clerk of the court shall issue a Notice of Support Arrearage. The clerk of the court shall issue the notice 30 days after the request was filed pursuant to subdivision (d) of Section 708.730 without a hearing if no objection has been raised by the judgment debtor pursuant to this subdivision. If an objection has been raised, the notice shall not be ordered until after a hearing. The notice shall contain the name of the person ordered to pay support and his or her social security number; the amount of the arrearage determined by the court; whether the arrearage is for child, spousal, or family support and the specific combination thereof; a statement of how the recipient may challenge the statement of arrearage; and the name, address, and social security number of the person to whom the arrearage is owed. Upon the clerk of the court issuing the Notice of Support Arrearage, a copy of the request, the affidavit, and the notice shall be served by the party who requested the court to issue the Notice of Support Arrearage upon the person ordered to pay support and the Controller. Service may be personal, in accordance with Section 1011, or by mail, in accordance with Section 1013. Service upon the Controller shall be at the Controller's office in Sacramento.

The judgment debtor may object to the request or affidavit upon any of the following grounds: (1) there is an error in the amount of the arrearage stated in the affidavit; (2) the alleged judgment debtor is not the judgment debtor from whom the support is due; (3) the amount to be intercepted exceeds that allowable under federal law; (4) a default in payment of the support for 30 days has not occurred; or (5) other necessary factual allegations contained in the affidavit are erroneous.

Upon receipt of the Notice of Support Arrearage, the Controller shall take reasonable measures to deduct from any personal income tax refunds and lottery winnings owed and processed for payment to the judgment debtor and deposit with the court a warrant, subject to Sections 708.770 and 708.775, with service of a copy of the warrant upon the local child support agency of the county in which the support judgment is entered, payable to the court, the amount due the judgment creditor (after deducting an amount sufficient to reimburse the state for any amounts advanced to the judgment debtor or owed by the judgment debtor to the state) required to satisfy the money judgment as shown by the affidavit in full or to the greatest extent, and pay the balance thereof, if any, to the judgment debtor. At any hearing pursuant to Section 708.770, the judgment debtor may challenge the distribution of these funds on exemption or other grounds, including, but not limited to, an allegation that the judgment has been satisfied or that service was improper. The notice shall not apply to any money which is exempt by law from execution. The Controller shall determine the cost of enforcing the notice and may establish a notice filing fee not to exceed five dollars ($5).

Service of the Notice of Support Arrearage and of the request and affidavit pursuant to this subdivision creates a lien on the money owing and unpaid to the judgment debtor which shall become effective 30 days following service upon the Controller. This notice shall remain in effect for four years from the date of its issuance or until the arrearage for which the notice was issued is satisfied, whichever occurs first.

Any person who files a request with the court to issue a Notice of Support Arrearage pursuant to subdivision (d) of Section 708.730 shall notify the court and the Controller of any satisfaction of the arrearage after the Notice of Support Arrearage has been issued by the clerk of the court. The notice to the court and the Controller shall be filed with the court and the Controller and served upon the local child support agency of the county in which the support judgment is entered within 30 days of the satisfaction or discharge and shall show a partial or full satisfaction of the arrearage or any other resolution of the arrearage.

Upon filing and service, the Notice of Support Arrearage shall be of no force and effect.

The State Department of Social Services shall, upon request, inform the Legislature of the use and effect of this subdivision on or before December 31, 2001.

This subdivision shall become operative on January 1, 1996, and shall become inoperative on December 31, 2001.

(d) For purposes of this section, "support" means an obligation owing on behalf of a child, spouse, or family, or combination thereof. **Leg.H.** Added Stats 1982 ch 1364 §2, operative July 1, 1983. Amended Stats 1983 ch 1010 §3.5; Stats 1988 ch 1017 §2, operative July 1, 1989; Stats 1989 ch 1359 §9.5; Stats 1990 ch 1493 §31 (AB 3974); Stats 1995 ch 459 §2 (AB 1515); Stats 1999 ch 652 §2 (SB 240).

§708.785. Filing fee; Deposit of fees collected by state

(a) The judgment creditor upon filing the abstract or certified copy of the judgment and the affidavit shall pay a fee of six dollars ($6) to the public entity with which it is filed.

(b) Fees received by the state under this section shall be deposited to the credit of the fund from which payments were, or would be, made on account of collection under this article. **Leg.H.** Added Stats 1982 ch 1364 §2, operative July 1, 1983.

§708.790. Liability of public officer

No public officer or employee is liable for failure to perform a duty imposed by this article unless sufficient information is furnished by the abstract or certified copy of the judgment together with the affidavit to enable the officer or employee in the exercise of reasonable diligence to ascertain the identity of the judgment debtor therefrom and from the papers and records on file in the office in which the officer or employee works. The word "office" as used in this section does not include any branch or subordinate office located in a different city. **Leg.H.** Added Stats 1982 ch 1364 §2, operative July 1, 1983.

§708.795. Limitations on procedure of this article

Except as to sums due and unpaid under a judgment for support, nothing in this article authorizes the filing against an overpayment of tax, penalty, or interest, or interest allowable with respect to an overpayment, under Part 10 (commencing with Section 17001), or Part 11 (commencing with Section 23001) of Division 2 of the Revenue and Taxation Code or under Division 6 (commencing with Section 13000) of the Unemployment Insurance Code. **Leg.H.** Added Stats 1982 ch 1364 §2, operative July 1, 1983. Amended Stats 1983 ch 1010 §4; Stats 1984 ch 1007 §3.

ARTICLE 9
Enforcement Against Franchise

Franchise defined. §708.910.
Court order for enforcement. §708.920.
Limitations on enforcement. §708.930.

§708.910. Franchise defined

As used in this article, "franchise" means a franchise granted by a public entity and all the rights and privileges thereof, other than the franchise of being a corporation. **Leg.H.** Added Stats 1982 ch 1364 §2, operative July 1, 1983.

§708.920. Court order for enforcement

(a) The court may, in its discretion, order a franchise applied to the satisfaction of a money judgment upon application by the judgment creditor made on noticed motion. The notice of motion shall be served on the judgment debtor and the public entity that granted the franchise. Service shall be made personally or by mail. In exercising its discretion, the court shall determine whether application of the franchise to the satisfaction of the judgment is proper taking into account all the circumstances of the case, including but not limited to the nature of the franchise, whether the franchise is by its terms transferable, and the likelihood that application of the franchise to the satisfaction of the judgment will yield a substantial amount.

(b) If the court orders application of the franchise to the satisfaction of the judgment, application shall be by such means as appears proper to the court, including but not limited to sale of the franchise, assignment of the franchise or proceeds of the franchise, or appointment of a receiver. The court may include in its order, or make additional orders containing, provisions to effectuate the application of the franchise to the satisfaction of the judgment, including but not limited to provisions relating to the place of sale of the franchise, possession of the property of the judgment debtor necessary for the exercise of the franchise, receipt of proceeds of the franchise, recovery of penalties imposed by law and recoverable for injury to the franchise or for damages or other cause, and the judgment debtor's powers, duties, and liability for penalties and forfeitures. **Leg.H.** Added Stats 1982 ch 1364 §2, operative July 1, 1983.

§708.930. Limitations on enforcement

Notwithstanding any other provision of this article, an order for application of a franchise to the satisfaction of a money judgment is subject to all applicable laws governing sale, transfer, or other actions concerning the franchise, including but not limited to any necessary approvals by the Public Utilities Commission or local public entities and compliance with statutory or administrative regulations. **Leg.H.** Added Stats 1982 ch 1364 §2, operative July 1, 1983.

§709. [Section repealed 1983]

Leg.H. Enacted Stats 1872. Repealed Stats 1983 ch 1364 §1, operative July 1, 1983. See CCP §§882, 883.

ARTICLE 10
Other Enforcement Procedures

Trusts. §709.010.
Contingent interests. §709.020.
Guardianship or conservatorship estates. §709.030.
[Section renumbered 1933]. §710½.

§709.010. Trusts

(a) As used in this section, "trust" has the meaning provided in Section 82 of the Probate Code.

(b) The judgment debtor's interest as a beneficiary of a trust is subject to enforcement of a money judgment only upon petition under this section by a judgment creditor to a court having jurisdiction over administration of the trust as prescribed in Part 5 (commencing with Section 17000) of Division 9 of the Probate Code. The judgment debtor's interest in the trust may be applied to the satisfaction of the money judgment by such means as the court, in its discretion, determines are proper, including but not limited to imposition of a lien on or sale of the judgment debtor's interest, collection of trust income, and liquidation and transfer of trust property by the trustee.

(c) Nothing in this section affects the limitations on the enforcement of a money judgment against the judgment debtor's interest in a trust under Chapter 2 (commencing with Section 15300) of Part 2 of Division 9 of the Probate Code, and the provisions of this section are subject to the limitations of that chapter. **Leg.H.** Added Stats 1982 ch 1364 §2, operative July 1, 1983. Amended Stats 1984 ch 493 §1, ch 892 §2.5; Stats 1986 ch 820 §18, operative July 1, 1987.

§709.020. Contingent interests

The judgment creditor may apply to the court on noticed motion for an order applying to the satisfaction of a money judgment a contingent remainder, executory interest, or other interest of the judgment debtor in property that is not vested in the judgment debtor. The interest of the judgment debtor may be applied to the satisfaction of the money judgment by such means as the court, in its discretion, determines are proper to protect the interests of both the judgment debtor and judgment creditor, including but not limited to the imposition of a lien on or the sale of the judgment debtor's interest. **Leg.H.** Added Stats 1982 ch 1364 §2, operative July 1, 1983.

§709.030. Guardianship or conservatorship estates

Property in a guardianship or conservatorship estate is not subject to enforcement of a money judgment by a procedure provided in this division, but the judgment creditor may apply to the court in which the guardianship or conservatorship proceeding is pending under Division 4 (commencing with Section 1400) of the Probate Code for an order requiring payment of the judgment. **Leg.H.** Added Stats 1982 ch 1364 §2, operative July 1, 1983.

§710. [Section repealed 1983]

Leg.H. Added Stats 1903 ch 263 §1. Amended Stats 1929 ch 634 §1; Stats 1933 ch 329 §1; Stats 1937 ch 211 §1; Stats 1953 ch 481 §1; Stats 1957 ch 2080 §1; Stats 1961 ch 1864 §1; Stats 1967 ch 119 §2; Stats 1969 ch 154 §1; Stats 1970 ch 241 §1, ch 1523 §58.5; Stats 1971 ch 438 §19, ch 1480 §1; Stats 1971 1st Ex Sess ch 1 §1.01; Stats 1975 ch 1240 §7, operative July 1, 1976; Stats 1976 ch 1294 §2; Stats 1978 ch 1133 §6, operative January 1, 1980; Stats 1980 ch 1007 §2, operative July 1, 1981. Repealed Stats 1982 ch 1364 §1, operative July 1, 1983. See CCP §§708.710–708.750, 708.775, 708.785, 708.790.

§710a. [Section repealed 1983]

Leg.H. Added Stats 1919 ch 276 §1. Amended Stats 1929 ch 634 §2; Stats 1961 ch 72 §4; Stats 1969 ch 1362 §2.5, operative January 1, 1971. Repealed Stats 1982 ch 1364 §1, operative July 1, 1983. See CCP §708.760.

§710b. [Section repealed 1983]

Leg.H. Added Stats 1903 ch 92 §1, as CCP §710. Renumbered by Stats 1933 ch 744 §137. Amended Stats 1965 ch 1974 §1. Repealed Stats 1982 ch 1364 §1, operative July 1, 1983. See CCP §§720.610, 720.620.

§710c. [Section repealed 1983]

Leg.H. Added Stats 1903 ch 92 §2, as CCP §710 ½. Amended and renumbered by Stats 1933 ch 744 §138. Amended Stats 1982 ch 517 §145. Repealed Stats 1982 ch 1364 §1, operative July 1, 1983 (ch 1364 prevails). See CCP §720.630.

§710½. [Section renumbered 1933]

Leg.H. Added Stats 1903 ch 92 §2. Amended and renumbered CCP §710c by Stats 1933 ch 744 §138.

§711. [Section repealed 1983]

Leg.H. Added Stats 1903 ch 92 §3. Amended Stats 1965 ch 1923 §1. Repealed Stats 1982 ch 517 §146, ch 1364 §1, operative July 1, 1983 (ch 1364 prevails). See CCP §§720.620, 720.640.

§711½. [Section repealed 1983]

Leg.H. Added Stats 1903 ch 92 §4. Repealed Stats 1982 ch 517 §148, ch 1364 §1, operative July 1, 1983 (ch 1364 prevails). See CCP §720.760.

§712. [Section repealed 1983]

Leg.H. Added Stats 1903 ch 92 §5. Amended Stats 1933 ch 744 §138a. Repealed Stats 1982 ch 517 §148, ch 1364 §1, operative July 1, 1983 (ch 1364 prevails). See CCP §720.770.

§712½. [Section repealed 1983]

Leg.H. Added Stats 1903 ch 92 §6. Repealed Stats 1982 ch 517 §149, ch 1364 §1, operative July 1, 1983 (ch 1364 prevails). See CCP §§720.770, 720.780.

DIVISION 3
ENFORCEMENT OF NONMONEY JUDGMENTS

Chapter 1. General Provisions.
Chapter 2. Judgment for Possession of Personal Property.
Chapter 3. Judgment for Possession of Real Property.
Chapter 4. Judgment for Sale of Property.
Chapter 5. Other Judgments.

CHAPTER 1
GENERAL PROVISIONS

Issuance of writ of possession or sale. §712.010.
Contents of writ of possession. §712.020.
Delivery and execution of writ. §712.030.
Collection of money amounts. §712.040.
Return of writ. §712.050.
Receiver. §712.060.
Enforcement against public entity. §712.070.

§712.010. Issuance of writ of possession or sale

After entry of a judgment for possession or sale of property, a writ of possession or sale shall be issued by the clerk of the court upon application of the judgment creditor and shall be directed to the levying officer in the county where the judgment is to be enforced. The application shall include a declaration under penalty of perjury stating the daily rental value of the property as of the date the complaint for unlawful detainer was filed. A separate writ shall be issued for each county where the judgment is to be enforced. Writs may be issued successively until the judgment is satisfied, except that a new writ may not be issued for a county until the expiration of 180 days after the issuance of a prior writ for that county unless the prior writ is first returned. **Leg.H.** Added Stats 1982 ch 1364 §2, operative July 1, 1983. Amended Stats 1988 ch 1405 §1.

§712.020. Contents of writ of possession

A writ of possession or sale issued pursuant to this division shall require the levying officer to whom it is directed to enforce the judgment and shall include the following information:

(a) The date of issuance of the writ.

(b) The title of the court where the judgment for possession or sale is entered and the cause and number of the action.

(c) The name and address of the creditor and the name and last known address of the judgment debtor. If the judgment debtor is other than a natural person, the type of legal entity shall be stated.

(d) The date the judgment was entered, and the date of any subsequent renewals, and where entered in the records of the court.

(e) If the judgment for possession or sale includes a money judgment, the amount required to satisfy the money judgment on the date the writ is issued, and the amount of interest accruing daily on the principal amount of the judgment from the date the writ is issued may be included on the writ at the option of the creditor.

(f) Whether any person has requested notice of sale under the judgment and, if so, the name and address of that person.

(g) Any other information required to be included in the particular writ.

(h) A statement indicating whether the case is limited or unlimited. **Leg.H.** Added Stats 1982 ch 1364 §2, operative July 1, 1983. Amended Stats 1988 ch 1405 §2; Stats 1989 ch 12 §1, effective April 28, 1989, operative May 1, 1989; Stats 1993 ch 926 §4 (AB 2205); Stats 2010 ch 680 §14 (AB 2394), effective January 1, 2011.

§712.030. Delivery and execution of writ

(a) Upon delivery of the writ of possession or sale to the levying officer to whom the writ is directed, together with the written instructions of the judgment creditor, the levying officer shall execute the writ in the manner prescribed by law.

(b) The levying officer may not levy upon or otherwise seize property under the writ after the expiration of 180 days from the date the writ was issued. **Leg.H.** Added Stats 1982 ch 1364 §2, operative July 1, 1983.

§712.040. Collection of money amounts

(a) A writ of possession or sale may be enforced as a writ of execution to satisfy any money judgment included in the judgment for possession or sale. If amounts due under the judgment are not satisfied pursuant to the writ of possession or sale, the judgment creditor may use a writ of execution to satisfy any money judgment included in the judgment after the writ of possession or sale has been returned or 180 days after its issuance, whichever is earlier. If the judgment creditor does not desire issuance of a writ of possession or sale (because possession has been voluntarily surrendered, the secured obligation has been voluntarily satisfied, or other reason), a writ of execution may be issued to satisfy any money judgment included in the judgment.

(b) Whether or not a writ of possession or sale has been issued, enforced, or returned, the judgment creditor may use any available remedies provided by Chapter 5 (commencing with Section 706.010) or Chapter 6 (commencing with Section 708.010) of Division 2 to satisfy any money judgment included in the judgment.

(c) Notwithstanding subdivisions (a) and (b), if so ordered in a judgment for sale, a money judgment included in the judgment may only be enforced as ordered by the court. **Leg.H.** Added Stats 1982 ch 1364 §2, operative July 1, 1983.

§712.050. Return of writ

The return of a writ of possession or sale is governed by Section 699.560 (return of writ of execution). **Leg.H.** Added Stats 1982 ch 1364 §2, operative July 1, 1983.

§712.060. Receiver

The court may appoint a receiver pursuant to Article 7 (commencing with Section 708.610) of Chapter 6 of Division 2 to enforce a judgment for possession or sale of property. **Leg.H.** Added Stats 1982 ch 1364 §2, operative July 1, 1983.

§712.070. Enforcement against public entity

Except as provided in Section 695.050, a judgment against a public entity is enforceable under this division. **Leg.H.** Added Stats 1982 ch 1364 §2, operative July 1, 1983.

§§713–713½. [Sections repealed 1983]

Leg.H. Repealed Stats 1982 ch 1364 §1, operative July 1, 1983.

§714. [Section repealed 1983]

Leg.H. Enacted 1872. Amended Code Amdts 1880 ch 17 §1; Stats 1907 ch 362 §1; Stats 1933 ch 744 §140; Stats 1945 ch 1139 §1; Stats 1951 ch 1737 §109, operative January 1, 1952; Stats 1955 ch 1191 §1; Stats 1957 ch 1194 §1; Stats 1969 ch 134 §2; Stats 1974 ch 213 §1. Repealed Stats 1982 ch 1364 §1, operative July 1, 1983. See CCP §§708.110, 708.170.

CHAPTER 2
JUDGMENT FOR POSSESSION OF PERSONAL PROPERTY

Writ of possession of personal property. §714.010.
Execution of writ of possession of personal property. §714.020.
Turnover order. §714.030.

§714.010. Writ of possession of personal property

(a) A judgment for possession of personal property may be enforced by a writ of possession of personal property issued pursuant to Section 712.010.

(b) In addition to the information required by Section 712.020, the writ of possession of personal property shall contain the following:

(1) A description of the property to be delivered to the judgment creditor in satisfaction of the judgment.

(2) The value of the property if specified in the judgment or a supplemental order. **Leg.H.** Added Stats 1982 ch 1364 §2, operative July 1, 1983.

§714.020. Execution of writ of possession of personal property

(a) To execute the writ of possession of personal property, the levying officer shall search for the property specified in the writ and, if the property is in the possession of the judgment debtor or an agent of the judgment debtor, take custody of the property in the same manner as a levy under a writ of execution on such property in the possession of the judgment debtor. Custody of personal property used as a dwelling shall be taken as provided by Section 700.080. Custody of property in a private place shall be taken as provided by Section 699.030. If the levying officer obtains possession of the property specified in the writ of possession, the levying officer shall deliver the property to the judgment creditor in satisfaction of the judgment.

(b) If the property specified in the writ of possession cannot be taken into custody, the levying officer shall make a demand upon the judgment debtor for the property if the judgment debtor can be located. If custody of the property is not then obtained, the levying officer shall so state in the return. Thereafter the judgment for the possession of the property may be enforced in the same manner as a money judgment for the value of the property as specified in the judgment or a supplemental order.

(c) The writ of possession of personal property may, under the circumstances described in subdivision (b), be treated as a writ of execution. **Leg.H.** Added Stats 1982 ch 1364 §2, operative July 1, 1983.

§714.030. Turnover order

(a) After entry of a judgment for possession of personal property, and whether or not a writ of possession of personal property has been issued, the judgment creditor may apply to the court for an order directing the judgment debtor to transfer possession of the property or documentary evidence of title to the property or both to the judgment creditor. The application shall be made on noticed motion if the court so directs or a court rule so requires. Otherwise, the application may be made ex parte.

(b) The court may issue an order pursuant to this section upon a showing of need for the order.

(c) The order shall be personally served on the judgment debtor and shall contain a notice to the judgment debtor that failure to comply with the order may subject the judgment debtor to being held in contempt of court. **Leg.H.** Added Stats 1982 ch 1364 §2, operative July 1, 1983.

§714.5. [Section repealed 1983]

Leg.H. Added Stats 1976 ch 308 §1. Repealed Stats 1982 ch 1364 §1, operative July 1, 1983. See CCP §§708.010, 708.020.

§715. [Section repealed 1983]

Leg.H. Enacted 1872. Amended Code Amdts 1880 ch 17 §2; Stats 1933 ch 744 §141; Stats 1951 ch 1737 §110, operative January 1, 1952. Repealed Stats 1982 ch 1364 §1, operative July 1, 1983. See CCP §708.110.

CHAPTER 3
JUDGMENT FOR POSSESSION OF REAL PROPERTY

Writ of possession of real property. §715.010.

Execution of writ of possession of real property. §715.020.
Disposition of personal property. §715.030.
Execution of writ by registered process server. §715.040.
Enforcement of judgment without delay. §715.050.

§715.010. Writ of possession of real property

(a) A judgment for possession of real property may be enforced by a writ of possession of real property issued pursuant to Section 712.010. The application for the writ shall provide a place to indicate that the writ applies to all tenants, subtenants, if any, name of claimants, if any, and any other occupants of the premises.

(b) In addition to the information required by Section 712.020, the writ of possession of real property shall contain the following:

(1) A description of the real property, possession of which is to be delivered to the judgment creditor in satisfaction of the judgment.

(2) A statement that if the real property is not vacated within five days from the date of service of a copy of the writ on the occupant or, if the copy of the writ is posted, within five days from the date a copy of the writ is served on the judgment debtor, the levying officer will remove the occupants from the real property and place the judgment creditor in possession.

(3) A statement that any personal property, except a mobilehome, remaining on the real property after the judgment creditor has been placed in possession will be sold or otherwise disposed of in accordance with Section 1174 unless the judgment debtor or other owner pays the judgment creditor the reasonable cost of storage and takes possession of the personal property not later than 15 days after the time the judgment creditor takes possession of the real property.

(4) The date the complaint was filed in the action that resulted in the judgment of possession.

(5) The date or dates on which the court will hear objections to enforcement of a judgment of possession that are filed pursuant to Section 1174.3, unless a summons, complaint, and prejudgment claim of right to possession were served upon the occupants in accordance with Section 415.46.

(6) The daily rental value of the property as of the date the complaint for unlawful detainer was filed unless a summons, complaint, and prejudgment claim of right of possession were served upon the occupants in accordance with Section 415.46.

(7) If a summons, complaint, and prejudgment claim of right to possession were served upon the occupants in accordance with Section 415.46, a statement that the writ applies to all tenants, subtenants, if any, named claimants, if any, and any other occupants of the premises.

(c) At the time the writ of possession is served or posted, the levying officer shall also serve or post a copy of the form for a claim of right to possession, unless a summons, complaint, and prejudgment claim of right to possession were served upon the occupants in accordance with Section 415.46. **Leg.H.** Added Stats 1982 ch 1364 §2, operative July 1, 1983. Amended Stats 1986 ch 1220 §1; Stats 1989 ch 12 §2, effective April 28, 1989, operative May 1, 1989; Stats 1990 ch 1535 §1.5 (SB 2508); Stats 1991 ch 57 §3 (SB 323), effective June 14, 1991; Stats 1995 ch 446 §3 (SB 69); Stats 2004 ch 183 §43 (AB 3082).

§715.020. Execution of writ of possession of real property

To execute the writ of possession of real property:

(a) The levying officer shall serve a copy of the writ of possession on one occupant of the property. Service on the occupant shall be made by leaving the copy of the writ with the occupant personally or, in the occupant's absence, with a person of suitable age and discretion found upon the property when service is attempted who is either an employee or agent of the occupant or a member of the occupant's household.

(b) If unable to serve an occupant described in subdivision (a) at the time service is attempted, the levying officer shall execute the writ of possession by posting a copy of the writ in a conspicuous place on the property and serving a copy of the writ of possession on the judgment debtor. Service shall be made personally or by mail. If the judgment debtor's address is not known, the copy of the writ may be served by mailing it to the address of the property.

(c) If the judgment debtor, members of the judgment debtor's household, and any other occupants holding under the judgment debtor do not vacate the property within five days from the date of service on an occupant pursuant to subdivision (a) or on the judgment debtor pursuant to subdivision (b), the levying officer shall remove the occupants from the property and place the judgment creditor in possession. The provisions of Section 684.120 extending time do not apply to the five-day period specified in this subdivision.

(d) Notwithstanding subdivision (c), unless the person is named in the writ, the levying officer may not remove any person from the property who claims a right to possession of the property accruing prior to the commencement of the unlawful detainer action or who claims to have been in possession of the property on the date of the filing of the unlawful detainer action. However, if the summons, complaint, and prejudgment claim of right to possession were served upon the occupants in accordance with Section 415.46, no occupant of the premises, whether or not the occupant is named in the judgment for possession, may object to the enforcement of the judgment as prescribed in Section 1174.3. **Leg.H.** Added Stats 1982 ch 1364 §2, operative July 1, 1983. Amended Stats 1991 ch 57 §4 (SB 323), effective June 14, 1991.

§715.030. Disposition of personal property

The disposition of personal property remaining on the real property after the judgment creditor is placed in possession thereof pursuant to the writ of possession is governed by subdivisions (e) to (m), inclusive, of Section 1174. For this purpose, references in Section 1174 and in provisions incorporated by reference in Section 1174 to the "landlord" shall be deemed to be references to the judgment creditor and references to the "tenant" shall be deemed to be references to the judgment debtor or other occupant. **Leg.H.** Added Stats 1982 ch 1364 §2, operative July 1, 1983.

§715.040. Execution of writ by registered process server

(a) A registered process server may execute the writ of possession of real property as provided in subdivisions (a) and (b) of Section 715.020 if a proper writ of possession is delivered to the sheriff or marshal and that officer does not execute the writ as provided in subdivisions (a) and (b) of Section 715.020 within three days (Saturday, Sunday, and legal holidays excluded) from the day the writ is delivered to that officer. If the writ is not executed within that time, the levying officer shall upon request give the writ to the judgment creditor or to a registered process server designated by the judgment creditor.

(b) Within five days after executing the writ under this section, all of the following shall be filed with the levying officer:

(1) The writ of possession of real property.

(2) An affidavit of the registered process server stating the manner in which the writ was executed.

(3) Proof of service of the writ.

(4) Instructions in writing, as required by the provisions of Section 687.010.

(c) If the writ is executed by a registered process server, the levying officer shall perform all other duties under the writ and shall return the writ to the court.

(d) The fee for services of a registered process server under this section may, in the court's discretion, be allowed as a recoverable cost upon a motion pursuant to Section 685.080. If allowed, the amount of the fee to be allowed is governed by Section 1033.5. **Leg.H.** Added Stats 1982 ch 1364 §2.3, operative July 1, 1983. Amended Stats 1983 ch 155 §20, effective June 30, 1983, operative July 1, 1983; Stats 1987 ch 1080 §7; Stats 1996 ch 872 §18 (AB 3472).

§715.050. Enforcement of judgment without delay

Except with respect to enforcement of a judgment for money, a writ of possession issued pursuant to a judgment for possession in an unlawful detainer action shall be enforced pursuant to this chapter without delay, notwithstanding receipt of notice of the filing by the defendant of a bankruptcy proceeding.

This section does not apply to a writ of possession issued for possession of a mobilehome or manufactured home, as those terms are defined in subdivision (a) of Section 1161a, and does not apply to a writ of possession issued for possession of real property in a mobilehome park subject to the Mobilehome Residency Law (Chapter 2.5 (commencing with Section 798) of Title 2 of Part 2 of Division 2 of the Civil Code), or to a manufactured housing community, as defined in Section 18801 of the Health and Safety Code. **Leg.H.** Added Stats 1994 ch 898 §2 (SB 690).

§716. [Section repealed 1983]

Leg.H. Enacted 1872. Amended Stats 1933 ch 744 §142. Repealed Stats 1982 ch 1364 §1, operative July 1, 1983. See CCP §699.020.

CHAPTER 4
JUDGMENT FOR SALE OF PROPERTY

Writ of sale. §716.010.
Execution of writ of sale. §716.020.
Turnover order. §716.030.

§716.010. Writ of sale
(a) A judgment for sale of real or personal property may be enforced by a writ of sale issued pursuant to Section 712.010.

(b) In addition to the information required by Section 712.020, the writ of sale shall contain a description of the property to be sold in satisfaction of the judgment for sale.

(c) The writ of sale delivered to the levying officer shall be accompanied by a certified copy of the judgment for sale. **Leg.H.** Added Stats 1982 ch 1364 §2, operative July 1, 1983.

§716.020. Execution of writ of sale
To execute the writ of sale, the levying officer shall:

(a) Levy upon the property described in the writ of sale in the manner prescribed by Article 4 (commencing with Section 700.010) of Chapter 3 of Division 2 for levy under a writ of execution.

(b) Except as otherwise ordered by the court, give notice of sale and sell the property described in the writ of sale in the manner prescribed by Article 6 (commencing with Section 701.510) of Chapter 3 of Division 2 for giving notice and selling under a writ of execution.

(c) Apply the proceeds of the sale of the property in conformity with the judgment for sale. **Leg.H.** Added Stats 1982 ch 1364 §2, operative July 1, 1983.

§716.030. Turnover order
(a) If a writ of sale is issued, the judgment creditor may apply to the court ex parte, or on noticed motion if the court so directs or a court rule so requires, for an order directing the judgment debtor to transfer to the levying officer:

(1) Possession of the property to be sold if the prescribed method of levy is by taking the property into custody.

(2) Possession of any documentary evidence of title to property to be sold. An order pursuant to this paragraph may be served when the property is levied upon or thereafter.

(b) The court may issue an order pursuant to this section upon a showing of need for the order.

(c) The order shall be personally served on the judgment debtor and shall contain a notice to the judgment debtor that failure to comply with the order may subject the judgment debtor to being held in contempt of court. **Leg.H.** Added Stats 1982 ch 1364 §2, operative July 1, 1983.

§717. [Section repealed 1983]
Leg.H. Enacted 1872. Amended Stats 1907 ch 362 §2; Stats 1933 ch 744 §143; Stats 1951 ch 1737 §111, operative January 1, 1952; Stats 1969 ch 134 §3; Stats 1972 ch 619 §1; Stats 1974 ch 214 §1. Repealed Stats 1982 ch 1364 §1, operative July 1, 1983. See CCP §§708.120, 708.130, 708.170.

CHAPTER 5
OTHER JUDGMENTS

Enforcement of other judgments. §717.010.

§717.010. Enforcement of other judgments
A judgment not otherwise enforceable pursuant to this title may be enforced by personally serving a certified copy of the judgment on the person required to obey it and invoking the power of the court to punish for contempt. **Leg.H.** Added Stats 1982 ch 1364 §2, operative July 1, 1983.

§717.1. [Section repealed 1983]
Leg.H. Added Stats 1945 ch 1139 §2. Amended Stats 1951 ch 1737 §112, operative January 1, 1952; Stats 1957 ch 1596 §4; Stats 1959 ch 196 §1; Stats 1963 ch 691 §1. Repealed Stats 1982 ch 1364 §1, operative July 1, 1983. See CCP §§708.120, 708.160.

§718. [Section repealed 1983]
Leg.H. Enacted 1872. Amended Stats 1933 ch 744 §144; Stats 1951 ch 1737 §113, operative January 1, 1952. Repealed Stats 1982 ch 1364 §1, operative July 1, 1983. See CCP §708.130.

§719. [Section repealed 1983]
Leg.H. Enacted 1872. Amended Stats 1907 ch 362 §3; Stats 1933 ch 744 §145; Stats 1951 ch 1737 §114, operative January 1, 1952. Repealed Stats 1982 ch 1364 §1, operative July 1, 1983. See CCP §§708.180, 708.205.

§720. [Section repealed 1983]
Leg.H. Enacted 1872. Amended Stats 1907 ch 362 §4; Stats 1931 ch 607 §1; Stats 1933 ch 744 §146; Stats 1951 ch 1737 §115, operative January 1, 1952. Repealed Stats 1982 ch 1364 §1, operative July 1, 1983. See CCP §§708.180, 708.210, 708.240.

DIVISION 4
THIRD-PARTY CLAIMS AND RELATED PROCEDURES

Chapter 1. Definitions.
Chapter 2. Third-Party Claims of Ownership and Possession.
Chapter 3. Third-Party Claim of Security Interest or Lien.
Chapter 4. Hearing on Third-Party Claim.
Chapter 5. Creditor's Demand for Third-Party Claim by Secured Party or Lienholder.
Chapter 6. Third-Party Undertaking to Release Property.
Chapter 7. Undertakings.

CHAPTER 1
DEFINITIONS

Application of definitions. §720.010.
"Creditor". §720.020.
"Debtor". §720.030.

§720.010. Application of definitions
Unless the provision or context otherwise requires, the definitions in this chapter govern the construction of this division. **Leg.H.** Added Stats 1982 ch 1364 §2, operative July 1, 1983.

§720.020. "Creditor"
"Creditor" means the judgment creditor or, in the case of a levy under a writ of attachment or prejudgment writ of possession of personal property, the plaintiff. **Leg.H.** Added Stats 1982 ch 1364 §2, operative July 1, 1983.

§720.030. "Debtor"
"Debtor" means the judgment debtor or, in the case of a levy under a writ of attachment or prejudgment writ of possession of personal property, the defendant. **Leg.H.** Added Stats 1982 ch 1364 §2, operative July 1, 1983.

CHAPTER 2
THIRD-PARTY CLAIMS OF OWNERSHIP AND POSSESSION

Application of chapter. §720.110.
Time and manner of making third-party claim. §720.120.
Contents of claim. §720.130.
Service on creditor and debtor of notice and copy of claim. §720.140.
Effect of filing or not filing third-party claim. §720.150.
Effect, amount, and contents of creditor's undertaking. §720.160.
Release for creditor's failure to file undertaking. §720.170.

§720.110. Application of chapter
A third person claiming ownership or the right to possession of property may make a third-party claim under this chapter in any of the following cases if the interest claimed is superior to the creditor's lien on the property:

(a) Where real property has been levied upon under a writ of attachment or a writ of execution.

(b) Where personal property has been levied upon under a writ of attachment, a writ of execution, a prejudgment or postjudgment writ of possession, or a writ of sale. **Leg.H.** Added Stats 1982 ch 1364 §2, operative July 1, 1983.

§720.120. Time and manner of making third-party claim
A person making a third-party claim under this chapter shall file the claim with the levying officer, together with two copies of the claim, after levy on the property but before the levying officer does any of the following:

(a) Sells the property.

(b) Delivers possession of the property to the creditor.

(c) Pays proceeds of collection to the creditor. **Leg.H.** Added Stats 1982 ch 1364 §2, operative July 1, 1983.

§720.130. Contents of claim

(a) The third-party claim shall be executed under oath and shall contain all of the following:

(1) The name of the third person and an address in this state where service by mail may be made on the third person.

(2) A description of the property in which an interest is claimed.

(3) A description of the interest claimed, including a statement of the facts upon which the claim is based.

(4) An estimate of the market value of the interest claimed.

(b) A copy of any writing upon which the claim is based shall be attached to the third-party claim. At a hearing on the third-party claim, the court in its discretion may exclude from evidence any writing a copy of which was not attached to the third-party claim. **Leg.H.** Added Stats 1982 ch 1364 §2, operative July 1, 1983.

§720.140. Service on creditor and debtor of notice and copy of claim

(a) Not later than five days after the third-party claim is filed with the levying officer, the levying officer shall serve the following personally or by mail on the creditor:

(1) A copy of the third-party claim.

(2) A statement whether the third person has filed an undertaking to release the property pursuant to Chapter 6 (commencing with Section 720.610).

(3) If the third person has filed an undertaking to release the property, a notice that the property will be released unless, within the time allowed as specified in the notice, the creditor objects to the undertaking.

(4) If the third person has not filed an undertaking to release the property, a notice that the property will be released unless, within the time allowed as specified in the notice, the creditor files with the levying officer an undertaking that satisfies the requirements of Section 720.160.

(b) The time allowed the creditor for objecting to the third person's undertaking to release the property or for filing an undertaking is 10 days after service under subdivision (a).

(c) Within the time allowed for service on the creditor under subdivision (a), the levying officer shall serve a copy of the papers specified in subdivision (a) on the debtor. Service shall be made personally or by mail.

(d) The levying officer may serve the copy of the third-party claim and the statement and notice pursuant to this section notwithstanding any defect, informality, or insufficiency of the claim. **Leg.H.** Added Stats 1982 ch 1364 §2, operative July 1, 1983.

§720.150. Effect of filing or not filing third-party claim

(a) Except as otherwise provided by statute, if a third-party claim is timely filed, the levying officer may not do any of the following with respect to the property in which an interest is claimed:

(1) Sell the property.

(2) Deliver possession of the property to the creditor.

(3) Pay proceeds of collection to the creditor.

(b) The interest of the third person in the property levied upon is not affected by the third person's failure to file a third-party claim under this chapter. **Leg.H.** Added Stats 1982 ch 1364 §2, operative July 1, 1983.

§720.160. Effect, amount, and contents of creditor's undertaking

(a) If the creditor files with the levying officer an undertaking that satisfies the requirements of this section within the time allowed under subdivision (b) of Section 720.140:

(1) The levying officer shall execute the writ in the manner provided by law unless the third person files an undertaking to release the property pursuant to Chapter 6 (commencing with Section 720.610).

(2) After sale, payment, or delivery of the property pursuant to the writ, the property is free of all claims of the third person for which the creditor has given the undertaking.

(b) Subject to Sections 720.770 and 996.010, unless the creditor elects to file an undertaking in a larger amount, the amount of the undertaking filed by the creditor under this section shall be in the amount of ten thousand dollars ($10,000), or twice the amount of the execution lien as of the date of levy or other enforcement lien as of the date it was created, whichever is the lesser amount.

(c) An undertaking given by the creditor under this chapter shall:

(1) Be made in favor of the third person.

(2) Indemnify the third person against any loss, liability, damages, costs, and attorney's fees, incurred by reason of the enforcement proceedings.

(3) Be conditioned on a final judgment that the third person owns or has the right of possession of the property.

(d) If the creditor is a public entity exempt from giving an undertaking, the public entity shall, in lieu of filing the undertaking, file with the levying officer a notice stating that the public entity opposes the claim of the third person. When so filed, the notice is deemed to satisfy the requirement of this section that an undertaking be filed. **Leg.H.** Added Stats 1982 ch 1364 §2, operative July 1, 1983. Amended Stats 1985 ch 41 §10; Stats 1998 ch 931 §96 (SB 2139), effective September 28, 1998; Stats 2001 ch 812 §5 (AB 223).

§720.170. Release for creditor's failure to file undertaking

(a) In a case where the third person has not filed with the levying officer an undertaking to release the property pursuant to Chapter 6 (commencing with Section 720.610), if the creditor does not within the time allowed under subdivision (b) of Section 720.140 file with the levying officer an undertaking (or file a notice if the creditor is a public entity) that satisfies the requirements of Section 720.160, the levying officer shall release the property unless it is to be held under another lien or unless otherwise ordered by the court.

(b) Except as otherwise provided in this section, release is governed by Section 699.060.

(c) If personal property that has been taken into custody is to be released to the debtor pursuant to Section 699.060 and the debtor has not claimed the property within 10 days after notice was served pursuant to Section 699.060, the levying officer shall release the property to the third person making the claim.

(d) A hearing may be had on the third-party claim pursuant to Chapter 4 (commencing with Section 720.310) notwithstanding the release of the property pursuant to this section. **Leg.H.** Added Stats 1982 ch 1364 §2, operative July 1, 1983.

CHAPTER 3
THIRD-PARTY CLAIM OF SECURITY INTEREST OR LIEN

Third-party claim. §720.210.
Time and manner of making third-party claim. §720.220.
Contents of claim. §720.230.
Service on creditor and debtor of notice and copy of claim. §720.240.
Effect of filing or not filing third-party claim. §720.250.
Effect of undertaking and statement or deposit; Amount and contents of undertaking; Notice by public entity in lieu of undertaking. §720.260.
Release for creditor's failure to make deposit or file undertaking and statement or file notice. §720.270.
Statement concerning security interest. §720.280.
Payment to secured party or lienholder. §720.290.

§720.210. Third-party claim

(a) Where personal property has been levied upon under a writ of attachment, a writ of execution, a prejudgment or postjudgment writ of possession, or a writ of sale, a third person claiming a security interest in or lien on the personal property may make a third-party claim under this chapter if the security interest or lien claimed is superior to the creditor's lien on the property.

(b) A secured party claiming a security interest in fixtures may make a third-party claim pursuant to this chapter if the security interest claimed is superior to the creditor's lien on the property. For this purpose, references in this division to "personal property" shall be deemed references to fixtures. **Leg.H.** Added Stats 1982 ch 1364 §2, operative July 1, 1983.

§720.220. Time and manner of making third-party claim

A person making a third-party claim under this chapter shall file the claim with the levying officer, together with two copies of the claim, after levy on the personal property but before the levying officer does any of the following:

(a) Sells the property.

(b) Delivers possession of the property to the creditor.

(c) Pays proceeds of collection to the creditor. **Leg.H.** Added Stats 1982 ch 1364 §2, operative July 1, 1983.

§720.230. Contents of claim

(a) The third-party claim shall be executed under oath and shall contain all of the following:

(1) The name of the secured party or lienholder and an address in this state where service by mail may be made on the secured party or lienholder.

(2) A description of the personal property in which a security interest or lien is claimed.

(3) A detailed description of the security interest or lien claimed, including a statement of the facts upon which it is based.

(4) A statement of the total amount of sums due or to accrue under the security interest or lien and the applicable rate of interest on amounts due.

(b) In the case of a security interest, a copy of the security agreement and any financing statement shall be attached to the third-party claim. In the case of a lien, a copy of any writing upon which the claim is based shall be attached to the third-party claim. At a hearing on the third-party claim, the court in its discretion may exclude from evidence any writing a copy of which was not attached to the third-party claim. **Leg.H.** Added Stats 1982 ch 1364 §2, operative July 1, 1983.

§720.240. Service on creditor and debtor of notice and copy of claim

(a) Not later than five days after the third-party claim is filed with the levying officer, the levying officer shall serve the following personally or by mail on the creditor:

(1) A copy of the third-party claim.

(2) A statement whether the third person has filed an undertaking to release the property pursuant to Chapter 6 (commencing with Section 720.610).

(3) If the third person has filed an undertaking to release the property, a notice that the property will be released unless, within the time allowed as specified in the notice, the creditor objects to the undertaking.

(4) If the third person has not filed an undertaking to release the property, a notice that the property will be released unless, within the time allowed as specified in the notice, the creditor does one of the following:

(A) Files with the levying officer an undertaking that satisfies the requirements of Section 720.260 and a statement under Section 720.280.

(B) Deposits with the levying officer the amount claimed plus interest at the applicable rate to the estimated date of tender to the secured party or lienholder.

(b) The time allowed the creditor for objecting to the third person's undertaking to release the property or for filing an undertaking and statement or making a deposit pursuant to subdivision (a) is 10 days after service under subdivision (a).

(c) Within the time allowed for service on the creditor under subdivision (a), the levying officer shall serve a copy of the papers specified in subdivision (a) on the debtor. Service shall be made personally or by mail.

(d) The levying officer may serve the copy of the third-party claim and the statement and notice pursuant to this section notwithstanding any defect, informality, or insufficiency of the claim. **Leg.H.** Added Stats 1982 ch 1364 §2, operative July 1, 1983.

§720.250. Effect of filing or not filing third-party claim

(a) Except as otherwise provided by statute, if a third-party claim is timely filed, the levying officer may not do any of the following with respect to the personal property in which the security interest or lien is claimed:

(1) Sell the property.

(2) Deliver possession of the property to the creditor.

(3) Pay proceeds of collection to the creditor.

(b) The interest of a secured party or lienholder in the property levied upon is not affected by the failure of the secured party or lienholder to file a third-party claim under this chapter. **Leg.H.** Added Stats 1982 ch 1364 §2, operative July 1, 1983.

§720.260. Effect of undertaking and statement or deposit; Amount and contents of undertaking; Notice by public entity in lieu of undertaking

(a) If the creditor within the time allowed under subdivision (b) of Section 720.240 either files with the levying officer an undertaking that satisfies the requirements of this section and a statement that satisfies the requirements of Section 720.280 or makes a deposit with the levying officer of the amount claimed under Section 720.230:

(1) The levying officer shall execute the writ in the manner provided by law unless, in a case where the creditor has filed an undertaking, the secured party or lienholder files an undertaking to release the property pursuant to Chapter 6 (commencing with Section 720.610).

(2) After sale, payment, or delivery of the property pursuant to the writ, the property is free of all claims or liens of the secured party or lienholder for which the creditor has given the undertaking or made the deposit.

(b) Subject to Sections 720.770 and 996.010, unless the creditor elects to file an undertaking in a larger amount, the amount of the undertaking filed by the creditor under this section shall be in the amount of ten thousand dollars ($10,000) or twice the amount of the execution lien as of the date of levy or other enforcement lien as of the date it was created, whichever is the lesser amount.

(c) An undertaking given by the creditor under this chapter shall:

(1) Be made in favor of the secured party or lienholder.

(2) Indemnify the secured party or lienholder against any loss, liability, damages, costs, and attorney's fees, incurred by reason of the enforcement proceedings.

(3) Be conditioned on a final judgment that the security interest or lien of the third person is entitled to priority over the creditor's lien.

(d) If the creditor is a public entity exempt from giving an undertaking, the public entity shall, in lieu of filing the undertaking, file with the levying officer a notice stating that the public entity opposes the claim of the third person. When so filed, the notice is deemed to satisfy the requirement of this section that an undertaking be filed. **Leg.H.** Added Stats 1982 ch 1364 §2, operative July 1, 1983. Amended Stats 1985 ch 41 §11; Stats 1998 ch 931 §97 (SB 2139), effective September 28, 1998; Stats 2001 ch 812 §6 (AB 223).

§720.270. Release for creditor's failure to make deposit or file undertaking and statement or file notice

(a) In a case where the third person has not filed with the levying officer an undertaking to release the property pursuant to Chapter 6 (commencing with Section 720.610), if the creditor does not within the time allowed under subdivision (b) of Section 720.240 file with the levying officer an undertaking (or file a notice if the creditor is a public entity) that satisfies the requirements of Section 720.260 and a statement under Section 720.280, or deposit with the levying officer the amount claimed under Section 720.230, the levying officer shall release the personal property unless it is to be held under another lien or unless otherwise ordered by the court.

(b) Except as otherwise provided in this section, release is governed by Section 699.060.

(c) If property that has been taken into custody is to be released to the debtor pursuant to Section 699.060 and the debtor has not claimed the property within 10 days after notice was served pursuant to Section 699.060, the levying officer shall release the property to the secured party or lienholder making the claim.

(d) A hearing may be had on the third-party claim pursuant to Chapter 4 (commencing with Section 720.310) notwithstanding the release of the property pursuant to this section. **Leg.H.** Added Stats 1982 ch 1364 §2, operative July 1, 1983.

§720.280. Statement concerning security interest

At the time the creditor files an undertaking with the levying officer in response to a third-party claim by a secured party, the creditor shall do all of the following:

(a) File with the levying officer a statement executed under oath that the security interest is invalid, that the security interest is not entitled to priority over the creditor's lien, or that the amount demanded in the claim exceeds the amount to which the secured party is entitled, for the reasons specified therein.

(b) Serve a copy of the statement on the secured party. Service shall be made personally or by mail.

(c) Serve a copy of the statement on the debtor. Service shall be made personally or by mail. **Leg.H.** Added Stats 1982 ch 1364 §2, operative July 1, 1983.

§720.290. Payment to secured party or lienholder

(a) If the levying officer receives a sufficient deposit from the creditor, the levying officer shall promptly tender or pay the deposit to the secured party or lienholder who made the third-party claim except that, if the deposit is made by personal check, the levying officer is allowed a reasonable time for the check to clear.

(b) If the tender is accepted, the interest of the secured party or lienholder in the property for which deposit is made passes to the creditor making the deposit and, on distribution of any proceeds under Section 701.810, the creditor who makes the deposit shall be entitled to the proceeds to the extent of the deposit in the priority of the interest for which the deposit is made.

(c) If the tender is refused, the amount of the deposit shall be deposited with the county treasurer payable to the order of the secured party or lienholder. **Leg.H.** Added Stats 1982 ch 1364 §2, operative July 1, 1983.

CHAPTER 4
HEARING ON THIRD-PARTY CLAIM

Application for hearing. §720.310.
Notice of hearing. §720.320.
Papers filed by levying officer. §720.330.
Filing and service of statement in opposition to claim of secured party. §720.340.
Pleadings. §720.350.
Burden of Proof. §720.360.
Dismissal. §720.370.
Stay of sale or enjoining transfer during pendency of proceedings. §720.380.
Determination of claim; Disposition of property. §720.390.
Findings. §720.400.
No right to jury trial. §720.410.
Appeal. §720.420.
Satisfaction from released property. §720.430.

§720.310. Application for hearing

(a) Not later than 15 days after the third-party claim is filed with the levying officer pursuant to Section 720.120 or 720.220, or 15 days after filing an undertaking pursuant to Section 720.610, either the creditor or the third person may petition the court for a hearing to determine the validity of the third-party claim and the proper disposition of the property that is the subject of the claim.

(b) The hearing may be held whether or not an undertaking has been filed but not if a deposit has been made pursuant to Section 720.260.

(c) The hearing shall be held within 20 days after the filing of the petition unless continued by the court for good cause shown. **Leg.H.** Added Stats 1982 ch 1364 §2, operative July 1, 1983. Amended Stats 1986 ch 672 §1.

§720.320. Notice of hearing

(a) At the time prescribed in subdivision (b) of Section 1005, the petitioner shall do both of the following:

(1) Serve notice of the time and place of the hearing on the creditor or the third person (whichever person is not the petitioner) and on the debtor. Service shall be made personally or by mail.

(2) File a copy of the notice of hearing with the levying officer.

(b) The notice of the hearing shall include a statement that the purpose of the hearing is to determine the validity of the third-party claim and the proper disposition of the property that is the subject of the third-party claim. **Leg.H.** Added Stats 1982 ch 1364 §2, operative July 1, 1983. Amended Stats 1989 ch 693 §4.

§720.330. Papers filed by levying officer

Promptly after receipt of the notice of the hearing on the third-party claim, the levying officer shall file the following papers with the court:

(a) The third-party claim that was filed with the levying officer pursuant to Section 720.120 or 720.220.

(b) Any statement filed by the creditor with the levying officer pursuant to Section 720.280 in opposition to the third-party claim of a secured party.

(c) Any undertaking of the creditor filed with the levying officer pursuant to Section 720.160 or Section 720.260.

(d) Any undertaking to release filed by a third person pursuant to Chapter 6 (commencing with section 720.610).

(e) Any notice filed by a public entity pursuant to Section 720.160 or 720.260. **Leg.H.** Added Stats 1982 ch 1364 §2, operative July 1, 1983.

§720.340. Filing and service of statement in opposition to claim of secured party

If the creditor has not filed a statement with the levying officer pursuant to Section 720.280 in opposition to a third-party claim by a secured party:

(a) In a case where the creditor petitions for a hearing on the third-party claim, the creditor shall file the statement with the court at the time the petition is filed and shall serve a copy thereof on the secured party with notice of the hearing served pursuant to Section 720.320.

(b) In a case where the secured party has petitioned for a hearing on the third-party claim, the creditor shall file the statement with the court and serve a copy of the statement on the secured party not later than five days before the date set for the hearing. Service shall be made personally or by mail. **Leg.H.** Added Stats 1982 ch 1364 §2, operative July 1, 1983.

§720.350. Pleadings

(a) Subject to the power of the court to permit an amendment in the interest of justice:

(1) The third-party claim constitutes the pleading of the third person.

(2) In the case of a third-party claim by a secured party, the creditor's statement constitutes the pleading of the creditor.

(b) A third-party claim of ownership, right to possession, or a lien, shall be deemed controverted by the creditor. **Leg.H.** Added Stats 1982 ch 1364 §2, operative July 1, 1983.

§720.360. Burden of Proof

At a hearing on a third-party claim, the third person has the burden of proof. **Leg.H.** Added Stats 1982 ch 1364 §2, operative July 1, 1983.

§720.370. Dismissal

If the petition for a hearing was made by the third person, neither the petition nor the proceedings pursuant thereto may be dismissed without the consent of the creditor. If the petition for a hearing was made by the creditor, neither the petition nor the proceedings pursuant thereto may be dismissed without the consent of the third person. **Leg.H.** Added Stats 1982 ch 1364 §2, operative July 1, 1983.

§720.380. Stay of sale or enjoining transfer during pendency of proceedings

(a) Notwithstanding any other provision of this title, the court may make an order staying the sale of the property under a writ or enjoining any transfer or other disposition of the property levied upon under a writ until proceedings for the determination of the rights of a third person can be commenced and prosecuted to termination and may require such undertaking as it considers necessary as a condition for making the order.

(b) After the filing of a third-party claim, notwithstanding Sections 720.160 and 720.260, the creditor, the debtor, or the third person may apply to the court for an order staying the sale of the property under a writ or enjoining any transfer or other disposition of the property until proceedings under this article can be commenced and prosecuted to termination. The application shall be made on noticed motion if the court so directs or a court rule otherwise so requires. Otherwise, the application may be made ex parte.

(c) An order made pursuant to this section may be modified or vacated by the court at any time prior to the termination of the proceedings upon such terms as are just. **Leg.H.** Added Stats 1982 ch 1364 §2, operative July 1, 1983.

§720.390. Determination of claim; Disposition of property

At the conclusion of the hearing, the court shall give judgment determining the validity of the third-party claim and may order the disposition of the property or its proceeds in accordance with the respective interests of the parties. Subject to Section 720.420, the judgment is conclusive between the parties to the proceeding. **Leg.H.** Added Stats 1982 ch 1364 §2, operative July 1, 1983.

§720.400. Findings

No findings are required in proceedings under this chapter. **Leg.H.** Added Stats 1982 ch 1364 §2, operative July 1, 1983.

§720.410. No right to jury trial

There is no right to a jury trial in a proceeding pursuant to this chapter. **Leg.H.** Added Stats 1982 ch 1364 §2, operative July 1, 1983.

§720.420. Appeal

An appeal may be taken from a judgment given pursuant to Section 720.390. **Leg.H.** Added Stats 1982 ch 1364 §2, operative July 1, 1983. Amended Stats 1998 ch 931 §98 (SB 2139), effective September 28, 1998.

§720.430. Satisfaction from released property

If property has been released pursuant to Section 720.170, 720.270, or 720.660, it may be levied upon or otherwise sought to be applied to the satisfaction of the judgment only if it is determined in the hearing on the third-party claim that the debtor has an interest in the property that may be levied upon or otherwise applied to the satisfaction of the judgment. **Leg.H.** Added Stats 1982 ch 1364 §2, operative July 1, 1983.

CHAPTER 5
CREDITOR'S DEMAND FOR THIRD-PARTY CLAIM BY SECURED PARTY OR LIENHOLDER

Creditor's right to demand third-party claim. §720.510.
Demand for claim; Filing and service. §720.520.
Contents of demand for claim. §720.530.
Prohibition of release, sale, or other disposition. §720.540.
Effect of failure to make third-party claim. §720.550.

§720.510. Creditor's right to demand third-party claim

A creditor may make a demand as provided in this chapter that a secured party or lienholder file a third-party claim to personal property that has been levied upon under a writ of attachment or a writ of execution. **Leg.H.** Added Stats 1982 ch 1364 §2, operative July 1, 1983.

§720.520. Demand for claim; Filing and service

(a) The creditor's demand for a third-party claim by the secured party or lienholder, together with a copy of the demand, shall be filed with the levying officer after levy on the personal property but before the levying officer sells the property or pays proceeds of collection to the creditor.

(b) Promptly after the demand and a copy thereof are filed, the levying officer shall personally serve the demand on the secured party or lienholder. Service of the demand on the secured party or lienholder shall be attested by the certificate of the levying officer and the certificate shall be filed in the action promptly after service.

(c) The demand shall be served by the levying officer who levied on the property or by any other levying officer whose office is closer to the place of service. If service is made by another levying officer, such levying officer's costs shall be paid out of the costs prepaid to the levying officer who levied on the property. **Leg.H.** Added Stats 1982 ch 1364 §2, operative July 1, 1983.

§720.530. Contents of demand for claim

The demand for a third-party claim served on a secured party or lienholder shall contain all of the following:

(a) The name and address of the secured party or lienholder.

(b) The name and address of the creditor.

(c) A detailed description of the personal property levied upon and the date of levy.

(d) A statement that if the secured party or lienholder does not file a third-party claim pursuant to Chapter 3 (commencing with Section 720.210) within 30 days after service of the demand, the secured party or lienholder shall be deemed to have waived any priority the security interest or lien may have over the creditor's lien on the property levied upon unless the property levied upon is released from the creditor's lien.

(e) A statement that if any priority of the security interest or lien is waived, the secured party or lienholder may have a right to share in any excess proceeds of an execution sale of the property as provided in Section 701.810. **Leg.H.** Added Stats 1982 ch 1364 §2, operative July 1, 1983.

§720.540. Prohibition of release, sale, or other disposition

Except as otherwise provided by statute, the levying officer may not release, sell, or otherwise dispose of the personal property described in the demand before the expiration of 30 days after service of the demand on the secured party or lienholder. **Leg.H.** Added Stats 1982 ch 1364 §2, operative July 1, 1983.

§720.550. Effect of failure to make third-party claim

(a) If the secured party or lienholder does not file a third-party claim with the levying officer pursuant to Chapter 3 (commencing with Section 720.210) within 30 days after service of the demand, the secured party or lienholder shall be deemed to have waived any priority the security interest or lien may have over the creditor's lien on the personal property levied upon and the property may be applied toward the satisfaction of the judgment free of the security interest or lien.

(b) If the secured party or lienholder is deemed to have waived any priority over the creditor's lien pursuant to subdivision (a) and the creditor's lien on the personal property is released, the security interest or lien is restored to its former position of priority. **Leg.H.** Added Stats 1982 ch 1364 §2, operative July 1, 1983.

CHAPTER 6
THIRD-PARTY UNDERTAKING TO RELEASE PROPERTY

Application of chapter. §720.610.
Filing of undertaking to release property. §720.620.
Contents of undertaking. §720.630.
Service of undertaking to release property. §720.640.
Effective date of undertaking. §720.650.
Release of property pursuant to undertaking. §720.660.

§720.610. Application of chapter

A third person may give an undertaking to release property pursuant to this chapter in the following cases:

(a) Where the third person claims ownership or the right to possession of real property that has been levied upon under a writ of attachment or a writ of execution.

(b) Where the third person claims ownership or the right to possession of personal property that has been levied upon under a writ of attachment, a writ of execution, or a writ of sale.

(c) Where the third person claims a security interest in or a lien on personal property that has been levied upon under a writ of attachment, a writ of execution, or a writ of sale. **Leg.H.** Added Stats 1982 ch 1364 §2, operative July 1, 1983.

§720.620. Filing of undertaking to release property

The third person shall file the undertaking to release property with the levying officer, together with two copies of the undertaking:

(a) At the time the third person files a third-party claim pursuant to Chapter 2 (commencing with Section 720.110) or Chapter 3 (commencing with Section 720.210).

(b) If the third person has previously filed a third-party claim to the property, at any time before the levying officer does any of the following:

(1) Sells the property.

(2) Delivers possession of the property to the creditor.

(3) Pays proceeds of collection to the creditor. **Leg.H.** Added Stats 1982 ch 1364 §2, operative July 1, 1983.

§720.630. Contents of undertaking

(a) The undertaking to release property shall contain a description of the property to be released and shall describe the interest of the third person.

(b) The undertaking shall be made in favor of the creditor and shall provide that, if the debtor is finally adjudged to have an interest in the property levied upon, the third person shall pay to the creditor the lesser of the following:

(1) The amount required to satisfy the judgment against the debtor of the creditor who had the lien on the property.

(2) A sum equal to the market value of the debtor's interest in the property levied upon.

(c) Except as provided in subdivision (d) and unless the third person elects to file an undertaking in a larger amount, the amount of the undertaking shall be the lesser of the following amounts:

(1) Twice the market value of the property sought to be released.

(2) Twice the amount of the creditor's lien on the property sought to be released.

(d) If the creditor has given an undertaking in response to the third person's claim regarding the property pursuant to Section 720.160 or 720.260, the third person's undertaking shall be in the amount of the creditor's undertaking. **Leg.H.** Added Stats 1982 ch 1364 §2, operative July 1, 1983.

§720.640. Service of undertaking to release property

(a) If the undertaking to release property is filed with the levying officer at the time the third-party claim is filed, the levying officer shall serve a copy of the undertaking on the creditor and on the debtor with the notice of the filing of the third-party claim served pursuant to Section 720.140 or 720.240.

(b) If the undertaking to release property is filed with the levying officer after the third-party claim is filed, not later than five days after the undertaking is filed, the levying officer shall serve a copy of the undertaking on the creditor and on the debtor with a notice that the property will be released unless, within the time allowed as specified in the notice, the creditor objects to the undertaking. Service shall be made personally or by mail. **Leg.H.** Added Stats 1982 ch 1364 §2, operative July 1, 1983.

§720.650. Effective date of undertaking

The third person's undertaking becomes effective when the property described therein is released pursuant to this chapter. **Leg.H.** Added Stats 1982 ch 1364 §2, operative July 1, 1983.

§720.660. Release of property pursuant to undertaking

The levying officer shall release the property described in the third person's undertaking in the manner provided by Section 720.170 promptly after the expiration of the time allowed for objecting to the undertaking, unless the creditor has objected to the undertaking, and filed with the levying officer a copy of the notice of motion as required by Section 720.760, prior to the expiration of that time. **Leg.H.** Added Stats 1982 ch 1364 §2, operative July 1, 1983. Amended Stats 1985 ch 41 §12.

CHAPTER 7
UNDERTAKINGS

Application of Bond and Undertaking Law. §720.710.
Objection to undertaking; Filing copy. §720.760.
Hearing on objection. §720.770.
Levying officer to file undertaking with court. §720.800.

§720.710. Application of Bond and Undertaking Law

The Bond and Undertaking Law (Chapter 2 (commencing with Section 995.010) of Title 14) applies to a bond given pursuant to this title, except to the extent this title prescribes a different rule or is inconsistent. **Leg.H.** Added Stats 1985 ch 41 §13.

Prior Law: Former CCP §720.710, relating to undertakings pursuant to the Enforcement of Judgments law, was added Stats 1982 ch 1364 §2, operative July 1, 1983, and repealed Stats 1983 ch 18 §9, effective April 21, 1983, operative July 1, 1983.

§720.720. [Section repealed 1983]

Leg.H. Added by Stats 1982 ch 1364 §2, operative July 1, 1983, and repealed by Stats 1983 ch 18 §10, effective April 21, 1983, operative July 1, 1983. The repealed section defined "beneficiary" and "principal".

§720.730. [Section repealed 1983]

Leg.H. Added by Stats 1982 ch 1364 §2, operative July 1, 1983, and repealed by Stats 1983 ch 18 §11, effective April 21, 1983, operative July 1, 1983. The repealed section related to the number of sureties required to execute an undertaking.

§720.740. [Section repealed 1983]

Leg.H. Added by Stats 1982 ch 1364 §2, operative July 1, 1983, and repealed by Stats 1983 ch 18 §12, effective April 21, 1983, operative July 1, 1983. The repealed section required an estimate of value for an undertaking dependent upon the value of property or an interest in property.

§720.750. [Section repealed 1983]

Leg.H. Added by Stats 1982 ch 1364 §2, operative July 1, 1983, and repealed by Stats 1983 ch 18 §13, effective April 21, 1983, operative July 1, 1983. The repealed section provided that undertakings became effective upon filing except where otherwise provided by statute.

§720.760. Objection to undertaking; Filing copy

A copy of a notice of motion objecting to an undertaking shall be filed with the levying officer. **Leg.H.** Added Stats 1982 ch 1364 §2, operative July 1, 1983. Amended Stats 1983 ch 18 §14, effective April 21, 1983, operative July 1, 1983.

§720.770. Hearing on objection

Unless the parties otherwise agree, the hearing on an objection to an undertaking shall be held not less than 10 nor more than 15 days after service of the notice of motion. The court may order the amount of the undertaking decreased below the amount prescribed by Section 720.160 or 720.260 if the court determines the amount prescribed exceeds the probable recovery of the beneficiary if the beneficiary ultimately prevails in proceedings to enforce the liability on the undertaking. **Leg.H.** Added Stats 1982 ch 1364 §2, operative July 1, 1983. Amended Stats 1983 ch 18 §15, effective April 21, 1983, operative July 1, 1983.

§720.780. [Section repealed 1983]

Leg.H. Added by Stats 1982 ch 1364 §2, operative July 1, 1983, and repealed by Stats 1983 ch 18 §16, effective April 21, 1983, operative July 1, 1983. The repealed section related to objections to estimates of market value.

§720.790. [Section repealed 1983]

Leg.H. Added by Stats 1982 ch 1364 §2, operative July 1, 1983, and repealed by Stats 1983 ch 18 §17, effective April 21, 1983, operative July 1, 1983. The repealed section related to judgments of liability on undertakings.

§720.800. Levying officer to file undertaking with court

If an undertaking has been filed with a levying officer pursuant to this division, and the undertaking remains in the levying officer's possession when the writ is to be returned, the levying officer shall file the undertaking with the court at the time the writ is returned. **Leg.H.** Added Stats 1982 ch 1364 §2, operative July 1, 1983.

§721. [Section repealed 1983]

Leg.H. Enacted 1872. Amended Stats 1933 ch 744 §147; Stats 1951 ch 1737 §116, operative January 1, 1952. Repealed Stats 1982 ch 1364 §1, operative July 1, 1983. See CCP §708.140.

§§722–724e. [Sections repealed 1983]

Leg.H. Repealed Stats 1982 ch 1364 §1, operative July 1, 1983.

DIVISION 5
SATISFACTION OF JUDGMENT

Chapter 1. Satisfaction of Judgment.
Chapter 2. Acknowledgment of Partial Satisfaction of Judgment.
Chapter 3. Acknowledgment of Satisfaction of Matured Installments Under Installment Judgment.

CHAPTER 1
SATISFACTION OF JUDGMENT

Satisfaction of money judgment. §724.010.
Entry of satisfaction of money judgment. §724.020.
Judgment creditor to file acknowledgment of satisfaction of judgment. §724.030.
Judgment creditor's duty where abstract of judgment recorded. §724.040.
Demand for filing or delivery of acknowledgment of satisfaction of judgment. §724.050.
Acknowledgment of satisfaction of judgment; Contents and execution. §724.060.
Liability for requiring additional performance or payment. §724.070.
Attorney's fees. §724.080.
Other remedies preserved. §724.090.
Certificate of satisfaction of judgment. §724.100.

§724.010. Satisfaction of money judgment

(a) A money judgment may be satisfied by payment of the full amount required to satisfy the judgment or by acceptance by the judgment creditor of a lesser sum in full satisfaction of the judgment.

(b) Where a money judgment is satisfied by levy, the obligation of the judgment creditor to give or file an acknowledgment of satisfaction arises only when the judgment creditor has received the full amount required to satisfy the judgment from the levying officer.

(c) Where a money judgment is satisfied by payment to the judgment creditor by check or other form of noncash payment that is to be honored upon presentation by the judgment creditor for payment, the obligation of the judgment creditor to give or file an acknowledgment of satisfaction of judgment arises only when the check or other form of noncash payment has actually been honored upon presentation for payment. **Leg.H.** Added Stats 1982 ch 1364 §2, operative July 1, 1983.

§724.020. Entry of satisfaction of money judgment

The court clerk shall enter satisfaction of a money judgment in the register of actions when the following occur:

(a) A writ is returned satisfied for the full amount of a lump-sum judgment.

(b) An acknowledgment of satisfaction of judgment is filed with the court.

(c) The court orders entry of satisfaction of judgment. **Leg.H.** Added Stats 1982 ch 1364 §2, operative July 1, 1983.

§724.030. Judgment creditor to file acknowledgment of satisfaction of judgment

When a money judgment is satisfied, the judgment creditor immediately shall file with the court an acknowledgment of satisfaction of judgment. This section does not apply where the judgment is satisfied in full pursuant to a writ. **Leg.H.** Added Stats 1982 ch 1364 §2, operative July 1, 1983.

§724.040. Judgment creditor's duty where abstract of judgment recorded

If an abstract of a money judgment has been recorded with the recorder of any county and the judgment is satisfied, the judgment creditor shall immediately do both of the following:

(a) File an acknowledgment of satisfaction of judgment with the court.

(b) Serve an acknowledgment of satisfaction of judgment on the judgment debtor. Service shall be made personally or by mail. **Leg.H.** Added Stats 1982 ch 1364 §2, operative July 1, 1983.

§724.050. Demand for filing or delivery of acknowledgment of satisfaction of judgment

(a) If a money judgment has been satisfied, the judgment debtor, the owner of real or personal property subject to a judgment lien created under the judgment, or a person having a security interest in or a lien on personal property subject to a judgment lien created under the judgment may serve personally or by mail on the judgment creditor a demand in writing that the judgment creditor do one or both of the following:

(1) File an acknowledgment of satisfaction of judgment with the court.

(2) Execute, acknowledge, and deliver an acknowledgment of satisfaction of judgment to the person who made the demand.

(b) The demand shall include the following statement: "Important warning. If this judgment has been satisfied, the law requires that you comply with this demand not later than 15 days after you receive it. If a court proceeding is necessary to compel you to comply with this demand, you will be required to pay my reasonable attorney's fees in the proceeding if the court determines that the judgment has been satisfied and that you failed to comply with the demand. In addition, if the court determines that you failed without just cause to comply with this demand within the 15 days allowed, you will be liable for all damages I sustain by reason of such failure and will also forfeit one hundred dollars to me."

(c) If the judgment has been satisfied, the judgment creditor shall comply with the demand not later than 15 days after actual receipt of the demand.

(d) If the judgment creditor does not comply with the demand within the time allowed, the person making the demand may apply to the court on noticed motion for an order requiring the judgment creditor to comply with the demand. The notice of motion shall be served on the judgment creditor. Service shall be made personally or by mail. If the court determines that the judgment has been satisfied and that the judgment creditor has not complied with the demand, the court shall either (1) order the judgment creditor to comply with the demand or (2) order the court clerk to enter satisfaction of the judgment.

(e) If the judgment has been satisfied and the judgment creditor fails without just cause to comply with the demand within the time allowed, the judgment creditor is liable to the person who made the demand for all damages sustained by reason of such failure and shall also forfeit one hundred dollars ($100) to such person. Liability under this subdivision may be determined in the proceedings on the motion pursuant to subdivision (d) or in an action. **Leg.H.** Added Stats 1982 ch 1364 §2, operative July 1, 1983.

§724.060. Acknowledgment of satisfaction of judgment; Contents and execution

(a) An acknowledgment of satisfaction of judgment shall contain the following information:

(1) The title of the court.

(2) The cause and number of the action.

(3) The names and addresses of the judgment creditor, the judgment debtor, and the assignee of record if any. If an abstract of the judgment has been recorded in any county, the judgment debtor's name shall appear on the acknowledgment of satisfaction of judgment as it appears on the abstract of judgment.

(4) The date of entry of judgment and of any renewals of the judgment and where entered in the records of the court.

(5) A statement either that the judgment is satisfied in full or that the judgment creditor has accepted payment or performance other than that specified in the judgment in full satisfaction of the judgment.

(6) A statement whether an abstract of the judgment has been recorded in any county and, if so, a statement of each county where the abstract has been recorded and the book and page of the county records where the abstract has been recorded, and a notice that the acknowledgment of satisfaction of judgment (or a court clerk's certificate of satisfaction of judgment) will have to be recorded with the county recorder of each county where the abstract of judgment has been recorded in order to release the judgment lien on real property in that county.

(7) A statement whether a notice of judgment lien has been filed in the office of the Secretary of State and, if such a notice has been filed, a statement of the file number of such notice, and a notice that the acknowledgment of satisfaction of judgment (or a court clerk's certificate of satisfaction of judgment) will have to be filed in that office in order to terminate the judgment lien on personal property.

(b) The acknowledgment of satisfaction of judgment shall be made in the manner of an acknowledgment of a conveyance of real property.

(c) The acknowledgment of satisfaction of judgment shall be executed and acknowledged by one of the following:

(1) The judgment creditor.

(2) The assignee of record.

(3) The attorney for the judgment creditor or assignee of record unless a revocation of the attorney's authority is filed.

(4) The local child support agency director or his or her designee, if the local child support agency has been providing child support services pursuant to Section 17400 of the Family Code. The acknowledgment of satisfaction of judgment may be recorded by the local child support agency pursuant to Section 27282 of the Government Code. **Leg.H.** Added Stats 1982 ch 1364 §2, operative July 1, 1983. Amended Stats 1983 ch 155 §21, effective June 30, 1983, operative July 1, 1983; Stats 2004 ch 339 §1 (AB 1704).

§724.070. Liability for requiring additional performance or payment

(a) If a judgment creditor intentionally conditions delivery of an acknowledgment of satisfaction of judgment upon the performance of any act or the payment of an amount in excess of that to which the judgment creditor is entitled under the judgment, the judgment creditor is liable to the judgment debtor for all damages sustained by reason of such action or two hundred fifty dollars ($250), whichever is the greater amount.

(b) Subdivision (a) does not apply if the judgment creditor has agreed to deliver an acknowledgment of satisfaction of judgment to the judgment debtor prior to full satisfaction of the judgment in consideration for the judgment debtor's agreement either to furnish security or to execute a promissory note, or both, the principal amount of which does not exceed the amount to which the judgment creditor is entitled under the judgment. **Leg.H.** Added Stats 1982 ch 1364 §2, operative July 1, 1983.

§724.080. Attorney's fees

In an action or proceeding maintained pursuant to this chapter, the court shall award reasonable attorney's fees to the prevailing party. **Leg.H.** Added Stats 1982 ch 1364 §2, operative July 1, 1983.

§724.090. Other remedies preserved

The damages recoverable pursuant to this chapter are not in derogation of any other damages or penalties to which an aggrieved person may be entitled by law. **Leg.H.** Added Stats 1982 ch 1364 §2, operative July 1, 1983.

§724.100. Certificate of satisfaction of judgment

(a) If satisfaction of a judgment has been entered in the register of actions, the court clerk shall issue a certificate of satisfaction of judgment upon application therefor and payment of the fee as provided in subdivision (a) of Section 70626 of the Government Code.

(b) The certificate of satisfaction of judgment shall contain the following information:

(1) The title of the court.

(2) The cause and number of the action.

(3) The names of the judgment creditor and the judgment debtor.

(4) The date of entry of judgment and of any renewals of the judgment and where entered in the records of the court.

(5) The date of entry of satisfaction of judgment and where it was entered in the register of actions. **Leg.H.** Added Stats 1982 ch 1364 §2,

operative July 1, 1983. Amended Stats 2005 ch 75 §39 (AB 145), effective July 19, 2005, operative January 1, 2006.

CHAPTER 2
ACKNOWLEDGMENT OF PARTIAL SATISFACTION OF JUDGMENT

Demand for delivery of acknowledgment of partial satisfaction of judgment. §724.110.

Contents and manner of execution of acknowledgment of partial satisfaction of judgment. §724.120.

§724.110. Demand for delivery of acknowledgment of partial satisfaction of judgment

(a) The judgment debtor or the owner of real or personal property subject to a judgment lien created under a money judgment may serve on the judgment creditor a demand in writing that the judgment creditor execute, acknowledge, and deliver an acknowledgment of partial satisfaction of judgment to the person who made the demand. Service shall be made personally or by mail. If the judgment has been partially satisfied, the judgment creditor shall comply with the demand not later than 15 days after actual receipt of the demand.

(b) If the judgment creditor does not comply with the demand within the time allowed, the judgment debtor or the owner of the real or personal property subject to a judgment lien created under the judgment may apply to the court on noticed motion for an order requiring the judgment creditor to comply with the demand. The notice of motion shall be served on the judgment creditor. Service shall be made personally or by mail. If the court determines that the judgment has been partially satisfied and that the judgment creditor has not complied with the demand, the court shall make an order determining the amount of the partial satisfaction and may make an order requiring the judgment creditor to comply with the demand. **Leg.H.** Added Stats 1982 ch 1364 §2, operative July 1, 1983.

§724.120. Contents and manner of execution of acknowledgment of partial satisfaction of judgment

An acknowledgment of partial satisfaction of judgment shall be made in the same manner and by the same person as an acknowledgment of satisfaction of judgment and shall contain the following information:

(a) The title of the court.

(b) The cause and number of the action.

(c) The names and addresses of the judgment creditor, the judgment debtor, and the assignee of record if any. If an abstract of the judgment has been recorded in any county, the judgment debtor's name shall appear on the acknowledgment of partial satisfaction of judgment as it appears on the abstract of judgment.

(d) The date of entry of judgment and of any renewals of the judgment and where entered in the records of the court.

(e) A statement of the amount received by the judgment creditor in partial satisfaction of the judgment.

(f) A statement whether an abstract of judgment has been recorded in any county and, if so, a statement of each county where the abstract has been recorded and the book and page of the county records where the abstract has been recorded.

(g) A statement whether a notice of judgment lien has been filed in the office of the Secretary of State and, if so, the file number of the notice. **Leg.H.** Added Stats 1982 ch 1364 §2, operative July 1, 1983.

CHAPTER 3
ACKNOWLEDGMENT OF SATISFACTION OF MATURED INSTALLMENTS UNDER INSTALLMENT JUDGMENT

Definitions. §724.210.

Demand for delivery of acknowledgment of satisfaction of matured installments. §724.220.

Proceeding to compel compliance with demand. §724.230.

Damages and penalty for failure to comply with demand. §724.240.

Contents and manner of execution of acknowledgment of satisfaction of matured installments. §724.250.

Attorney's fees. §724.260.

§724.210. Definitions

As used in this chapter:

(a) "Installment judgment" means a money judgment under which a lien may be created on an interest in real property under Section 697.320.

(b) "Matured installments" means the sum of all of the following:

(1) All amounts and installments that have matured under an installment judgment on or before the date specified in the demand for an acknowledgment of satisfaction of matured installments under an installment judgment.

(2) The interest that has accrued on the installment judgment on the date specified in the demand.

(3) The costs that have been added to the installment judgment on or before the date specified in the demand pursuant to Chapter 5 (commencing with Section 685.010) of Division 1. **Leg.H.** Added Stats 1982 ch 1364 §2, operative July 1, 1983.

§724.220. Demand for delivery of acknowledgment of satisfaction of matured installments

(a) If real property is subject to a judgment lien created under an installment judgment, the judgment debtor or the owner of real property subject to the judgment lien may serve on the judgment creditor a demand in writing that the judgment creditor execute, acknowledge, and deliver to the person who made the demand an acknowledgment of satisfaction of matured installments under an installment judgment. Service shall be made personally or by mail.

(b) The demand shall include the following statement: "Important warning. If the matured installments on this judgment have been satisfied as of date specified in this demand, the law requires that you comply with this demand not later than 15 days after you receive it. (The 'matured installments' are all amounts and installments that are due and payable on or before the date specified in this demand together with the accrued interest to that date and costs added to the judgment on or before that date.) If a court proceeding is necessary to compel you to comply with this demand, you will be required to pay my reasonable attorney's fees in the proceeding if the court determines that the matured installments have been satisfied and that you failed to comply with the demand. In addition, if the court determines that you failed without just cause to comply with this demand within the 15 days allowed, you will be liable for all damages I sustain by reason of such failure and will also forfeit one hundred dollars to me."

(c) If the matured installments have been satisfied as of the date specified in the demand, the judgment creditor shall comply with the demand not later than 15 days after actual receipt of the demand. **Leg.H.** Added Stats 1982 ch 1364 §2, operative July 1, 1983.

§724.230. Proceeding to compel compliance with demand

If the judgment creditor does not comply with the demand within the time allowed, the judgment debtor or the owner of the real property subject to a judgment lien created under the installment judgment may apply to the court on noticed motion for an order requiring the judgment creditor to comply with the demand. The notice of motion shall be served on the judgment creditor. Service shall be made personally or by mail. If the court determines that the matured installments have been satisfied as of the date specified in the demand and that the judgment creditor has not complied with the demand, the court shall either (1) order the judgment creditor to comply with the demand or (2) make an order determining that the matured installments as of the date specified in the demand have been satisfied. **Leg.H.** Added Stats 1982 ch 1364 §2, operative July 1, 1983.

§724.240. Damages and penalty for failure to comply with demand

(a) If the matured installments under the installment judgment have been satisfied as of the date specified in the demand and the judgment creditor fails without just cause to comply with the demand within the time allowed, the judgment creditor is liable to the person who made the demand for all damages sustained by reason of such failure and shall also forfeit one hundred dollars ($100) to such person. Liability under this subdivision may be determined in the proceedings on a motion pursuant to Section 724.230 or in an action.

(b) The damages recoverable pursuant to subdivision (a) are not in derogation of any other damages or penalties to which an aggrieved person may be entitled by law. **Leg.H.** Added Stats 1982 ch 1364 §2, operative July 1, 1983.

§724.250. Contents and manner of execution of acknowledgment of satisfaction of matured installments

(a) An acknowledgment of satisfaction of matured installments under an installment judgment shall be made in the same manner and by the same person as an acknowledgment of satisfaction of judgment and shall contain the following information:

(1) The title of the court.

(2) The cause and number of the action.

(3) The names and addresses of the judgment creditor, the judgment debtor, and the assignee of record if any. The judgment debtor's name shall appear on the acknowledgment of satisfaction of matured installments as it appears on the certified copy of the judgment that was recorded to create the judgment lien.

(4) The date of entry of the judgment and of any renewals of the judgment and where entered in the records of the court.

(5) A statement that the matured installments under the installment judgment had been satisfied as of a specified date.

(6) A statement whether a certified copy or abstract of the judgment has been recorded in any county and, if so, a statement of each county where the certified or abstract copy has been recorded and the book and page of the county records where the certified copy or abstract of the judgment has been recorded.

(b) If any amount of child or spousal support provided in a support order has been directed to be made to an officer designated by statute or by the court pursuant to Article 4 (commencing with Section 4200) of Chapter 2 of Part 2 of Division 9 of the Family Code or Chapter 4 (commencing with Section 4350) of Part 3 of Division 9 of the Family Code or any other provision of law and the directive is set forth in the certified copy or abstract of the judgment that was recorded to create the judgment lien on real property, or in a similarly recorded certified copy or abstract of an amended or supplemental order, the acknowledgment of satisfaction of matured installments under the installment judgment is not effective and does not affect the judgment lien unless the acknowledgment is executed by or approved in writing by the designated officer. **Leg.H.** Added Stats 1982 ch 1364 §2, operative July 1, 1983. Amended Stats 1986 ch 946 §3; Stats 1992 ch 163 §53 (AB 2641), operative January 1, 1994.

§724.260. **Attorney's fees**

In an action or proceeding maintained pursuant to this chapter, the court shall award reasonable attorney's fees to the prevailing party. **Leg.H.** Added Stats 1982 ch 1364 §2, operative July 1, 1983.

TITLE 10
ACTIONS IN PARTICULAR CASES

Chapter 1. Actions for Foreclosure of Mortgages.
Chapter 2. Actions for Nuisance, Waste, and Willful Trespass, in Certain Cases, on Real Property.
Chapter 3. Actions for the Recovery of Real Property, and Other Provisions Relating to Actions Concerning Real Property.
Chapter 3.5. Actions to Re-establish Destroyed Land Records.
Chapter 3.6. Cullen Earthquake Act.
Chapter 4. Quiet Title.
Chapter 4.5. Special Actions and Proceedings to Clear Title.
Chapter 4.6. Actions Concerning Real Property Titles Affected by Public Improvement Assessments.
Chapter 5. Actions for the Usurpation of an Office or a Franchise.
Chapter 7. Actions Relating to Groundwater Rights.
Chapter 8. Actions Against Coowners of Mines.
Chapter 9. Validating Proceedings.
Chapter 10. Good Faith Improver of Property Owned by Another.
Chapter 11. Actions to Recover COVID-19 Rental Debt [Repealed effective October 1, 2027].
Chapter 12. Actions for Restitution for or Replacement of Certain Motor Vehicles.

CHAPTER 1
ACTIONS FOR FORECLOSURE OF MORTGAGES

Persons entitled to sue. §725a.
Foreclosure of mortgage or deed of trust; Proceedings; Action based on fraud. §726.
Election between waiver of lien and exercise of specified rights and remedies; Application date of section. §726.5.
Surplus money deposited in court. §727.
Sale when secured debt falls due at different times. §728.
Deficiency judgment upon decree of foreclosure; Right of redemption. §729.010.
Persons entitled to redeem property. §729.020.
Redemption period. §729.030.
Right of redemption on sale of separate interest in common interest development arising from foreclosure. §729.035.
Certificate of sale. §729.040.
Service of notice of right of redemption. §729.050.
Deposit of redemption price. §729.060.
Petition to determine redemption price or right to redeem. §729.070.
Expiration of redemption period; Tender of redemption price. §729.080.
Rents and profits; Maintenance of property; Waste. §729.090.
Attorney's fee. §730.
Exceptions. §730.5.

§725a. Persons entitled to sue

The beneficiary or trustee named in a deed of trust or mortgagee named in a mortgage with power of sale upon real property or any interest therein to secure a debt or other obligation, or if there be a successor or successors in interest of such beneficiary, trustee or mortgagee, then such successor or successors in interest, shall have the right to bring suit to foreclose the same in the manner and subject to the provisions, rights and remedies relating to the foreclosure of a mortgage upon such property. **Leg.H.** Added Stats 1933 ch 642 §7. Re-enacted Stats 1935 ch 650 §9. Amended Stats 1939 ch 584 §1; Stats 1941 ch 446 §1; Stats 1982 ch 497 §45, operative July 1, 1983.

§726. Foreclosure of mortgage or deed of trust; Proceedings; Action based on fraud

(a) There can be but one form of action for the recovery of any debt or the enforcement of any right secured by mortgage upon real property or an estate for years therein, which action shall be in accordance with the provisions of this chapter. In the action the court may, by its judgment, direct the sale of the encumbered real property or estate for years therein (or so much of the real property or estate for years as may be necessary), and the application of the proceeds of the sale to the payment of the costs of court, the expenses of levy and sale, and the amount due plaintiff, including, where the mortgage provides for the payment of attorney's fees, the sum for attorney's fees as the court shall find reasonable, not exceeding the amount named in the mortgage.

(b) The decree for the foreclosure of a mortgage or deed of trust secured by real property or estate for years therein shall declare the amount of the indebtedness or right so secured and, unless judgment for any deficiency there may be between the sale price and the amount due with costs is waived by the judgment creditor or a deficiency judgment is prohibited by Section 580b, shall determine the personal liability of any defendant for the payment of the debt secured by the mortgage or deed of trust and shall name the defendants against whom a deficiency judgment may be ordered following the proceedings prescribed in this section. In the event of waiver, or if the prohibition of Section 580b is applicable, the decree shall so declare and there shall be no judgment for a deficiency. In the event that a deficiency is not waived or prohibited and it is decreed that any defendant is personally liable for the debt, then upon application of the plaintiff filed at any time within three months of the date of the foreclosure sale and after a hearing thereon at which the court shall take evidence and at which hearing either party may present evidence as to the fair value of the real property or estate for years therein sold as of the date of sale, the court shall render a money judgment against the defendant or defendants for the amount by which the amount of the indebtedness with interest and costs of levy and sale and of action exceeds the fair value of the real property or estate for years therein sold as of the date of sale. In no event shall the amount of the judgment, exclusive of interest from the date of sale and of costs exceed the difference between the amount for which the real property or estate for years therein was sold and the entire amount of the indebtedness secured by the mortgage or deed of trust. Notice of the hearing shall be served upon all defendants who have appeared in the action and against whom a deficiency judgment is sought, or upon their attorneys of record, at least 15 days before the date set for the hearing. Upon application of any party made at least 10 days before the date set for the hearing the court shall, and upon its own motion the court at any time may, appoint one of the probate referees provided for by law to appraise the real property or estate for years therein sold as of the time of sale. The probate referee shall file the appraisal with the clerk and the appraisal is admissible in evidence. The probate referee shall take and subscribe an oath to be attached to the appraisal that the referee has truly, honestly and impartially appraised the real property or estate for years therein to the best of the referee's knowledge and ability. Any probate referee so appointed may be called and examined as a witness by any party or by the court itself. The court shall fix the compensation, in an amount as determined by the court to be reasonable, but the fees shall not exceed similar fees for similar services in the community where the services are rendered, which may be taxed and allowed in like manner as other costs.

(c) No person holding a conveyance from or under the mortgagor of real property or estate for years therein, or having a lien thereon, which conveyance or lien does not appear of record in the proper office at the time of the commencement of the action need be made a party to the action, and the judgment therein rendered, and the proceedings therein had, are as conclusive against the person holding the unrecorded conveyance or lien as if the person had been a party to the action. Notwithstanding Section 701.630, the sale of the encumbered real property or estate for years therein does not affect the interest of a person who holds a conveyance from or under the mortgagor of the real property or estate for years therein mortgaged, or has a lien thereon, if the conveyance or lien appears of record in the proper office at the time of the commencement of the action and the person holding the recorded conveyance or lien is not made a party to the action.

(d) If the real property or estate for years therein mortgaged consists of a single parcel, or two or more parcels, situated in two or more counties, the court may, in its judgment, direct the whole thereof to be sold in one of the counties, and upon these proceedings, and with like effect, as if the whole of the property were situated in that county.

(e) If a deficiency judgment is waived or prohibited, the real property or estate for years therein shall be sold as provided in Section 716.020. If a deficiency judgment is not waived or prohibited, the real property or estate for years therein shall be sold subject to the right of redemption as provided in Sections 729.010 to 729.090, inclusive.

(f) Notwithstanding this section or any other provision of law to the contrary, any person authorized by this state to make or arrange loans secured by real property or any successor in interest thereto, that originates, acquires, or purchases, in whole or in part, any loan secured directly or collaterally, in whole or in part, by a mortgage or deed of trust on real property or an estate for years therein, may bring an action for recovery of damages, including exemplary damages not to exceed 50 percent of the actual damages, against a borrower where the action is based on fraud under Section 1572 of the Civil Code and the fraudulent conduct by the borrower induced the original lender to make that loan.

(g) Subdivision (f) does not apply to loans secured by single-family, owner-occupied residential real property, when the property is actually occupied by the borrower as represented to the lender in order to obtain the loan and the loan is for an amount of one hundred fifty thousand dollars ($150,000) or less, as adjusted annually, commencing on January 1, 1987, to the Consumer Price Index as published by the United States Department of Labor.

(h) Any action maintained pursuant to subdivision (f) for damages shall not constitute a money judgment for deficiency, or a deficiency judgment within the meaning of Section 580a, 580b, or 580d of the Code of Civil Procedure. **Leg.H.** Enacted 1872. Amended Stats 1893 ch 101 §1; Stats 1895 ch 108 §1; Stats 1901 ch 43 §1; Stats 1933 ch 793 §1; Stats 1937 ch 353 §1; Stats 1963 ch 819 §26; Stats 1967 ch 1003 §1; Stats 1968 ch 450 §3; Stats 1970 ch 1282 §2, operative July 1, 1971; Stats 1982 ch 497 §46, ch 517 §152, ch 1535 §2; Stats 1983 ch 18 §18, effective April 21, 1983, ch 155 §22, effective June 30, 1983, operative July 1, 1983; Stats 1987 ch 180 §1; Stats 1989 ch 698 §14; Stats 1992 ch 1095 §4 (AB 2734).

1989 Note: It is the intent of the Legislature in enacting this act to clarify that the "one action rule" set forth in Section 726 of the Code of Civil Procedure applies to leasehold mortgages, which is consistent with the legislative history of Section 726 and the Commercial Code and is consistent with other statutes contained in the Code of Civil Procedure, the Civil Code, and the Commercial Code regarding the creation and enforcement of mortgages and deeds of trust. This act is specifically intended to abrogate the holding in *Taylor v. Bouissiere*, 195 Cal. App. 3d 1197, that the enforcement rights in leasehold mortgages are to be governed by the rules regarding personal property, which is inconsistent with this legislative history and other statutes and would result in a gap in the method of enforcement, because the rules regarding enforcement of personal property interests are specifically made inapplicable to leasehold mortgages.

Nothing in this act shall be construed to affect the applicability of the code sections amended by this act to the lien of mortgages or deeds of trust in estates in real property specified in subdivisions (1) and (2) of Section 761 of the Civil Code. Stats 1989 ch 698 §15.

§726.5. Election between waiver of lien and exercise of specified rights and remedies; Application date of section

(a) Notwithstanding subdivision (a) of Section 726 or any other provision of law, except subdivision (d) of this section, a secured lender may elect between the following where the real property security is environmentally impaired and the borrower's obligations to the secured lender are in default:

(1)(A) Waiver of its lien against (i) any parcel of real property security that is environmentally impaired or is an affected parcel, and (ii) all or any portion of the fixtures and personal property attached to the parcels; and

(B) Exercise of (i) the rights and remedies of an unsecured creditor, including reduction of its claim against the borrower to judgment, and (ii) any other rights and remedies permitted by law.

(2) Exercise of (i) the rights and remedies of a creditor secured by a deed of trust or mortgage and, if applicable, a lien against fixtures or personal property attached to the real property security, and (ii) any other rights and remedies permitted by law.

(b) Before the secured lender may waive its lien against any parcel of real property security pursuant to paragraph (1) of subdivision (a) on the basis of the environmental impairment contemplated by paragraph (3) of subdivision (e), (i) the secured lender shall provide written notice of the default to the borrower, and (ii) the value of the subject real property security shall be established and its environmentally impaired status shall be confirmed by an order of a court of competent jurisdiction in an action brought by the secured lender against the borrower. The complaint for a valuation and confirmation action may include causes of action for a money judgment for all or part of the secured obligation, in which case the waiver of the secured lender's liens under paragraph (1) of subdivision (a) shall result only if and when a final money judgment is obtained against the borrower.

(c) If a secured lender elects the rights and remedies permitted by paragraph (1) of subdivision (a) and the borrower's obligations are also secured by other real property security, fixtures, or personal property, the secured lender shall first foreclose against the additional collateral to the extent required by applicable law in which case the amount of the judgment of the secured lender pursuant to paragraph (1) of subdivision (a) shall be limited to the extent Section 580a or 580d, or subdivision (b) of Section 726 apply to the foreclosures of additional real property security. The borrower may waive or modify the foreclosure requirements of this subdivision provided that the waiver or modification is in writing and signed by the borrower after default.

(d) Subdivision (a) shall be inapplicable if all of the following are true:

(1) The release or threatened release was not knowingly or negligently caused or contributed to, or knowingly or willfully permitted or acquiesced to, by any of the following:

(A) The borrower or any related party.

(B) Any affiliate or agent of the borrower or any related party.

(2) In conjunction with the making, renewal, or modification of the loan, extension of credit, guaranty, or other obligation secured by the real property security, neither the borrower, any related party, nor any affiliate or agent of either the borrower or any related party had actual knowledge or notice of the release or threatened release, or if a person had knowledge or notice of the release or threatened release, the borrower made written disclosure thereof to the secured lender after the secured lender's written request for information concerning the environmental condition of the real property security, or the secured lender otherwise obtained actual knowledge thereof, prior to the making, renewal, or modification of the obligation.

(e) For purposes of this section:

(1) "Affected parcel" means any portion of a parcel of real property security that is (A) contiguous to the environmentally impaired parcel, even if separated by roads, streets, utility easements, or railroad rights-of-way, (B) part of an approved or proposed subdivision within the meaning of Section 66424 of the Government Code, of which the environmentally impaired parcel is also a part, or (C) within 2,000 feet of the environmentally impaired parcel.

(2) "Borrower" means the trustor under a deed of trust, or a mortgagor under a mortgage, where the deed of trust or mortgage encumbers real property security and secures the performance of the trustor or mortgagor under a loan, extension of credit, guaranty, or other obligation. The term includes any successor-in-interest of the trustor or mortgagor to the real property security before the deed of trust or mortgage has been discharged, reconveyed, or foreclosed upon.

(3) "Environmentally impaired" means that the estimated costs to clean up and remediate a past or present release or threatened release of any hazardous substance into, onto, beneath, or from the real property security, not disclosed in writing to, or otherwise actually known by, the secured lender prior to the making of the loan or extension of credit secured by the real property security, exceeds 25 percent of the higher of the aggregate fair market value of all security for the loan or extension of credit (A) at the time of the making of the loan or extension of credit, or (B) at the time of the discovery of the release or threatened release by the secured lender. For purposes of this definition, the estimated cost to clean up and remediate the contamination caused by the release or threatened release shall include only those costs that would be incurred reasonably and in good faith, and fair market value shall be determined without giving consideration to the release or threatened release, and shall be exclusive of the amount of all liens and encumbrances against the security that are senior in priority to the lien of the secured lender. Notwithstanding the foregoing, the real property security for any loan or extension of credit secured by a single parcel of real property which is included in the National Priorities List pursuant to Section 9605 of Title 42 of the United States Code, or in any list published by the Department of Toxic Substances Control pursuant to Section 78760 of the Health and Safety Code, shall be deemed to be environmentally impaired.

(4) "Hazardous substance" means any of the following:

(A) Any "hazardous substance" as defined in subdivision (h) of Section 25281 of the Health and Safety Code.

(B) Any "waste" as defined in subdivision (d) of Section 13050 of the Water Code.

(C) Petroleum, including crude oil or any fraction thereof, natural gas, natural gas liquids, liquefied natural gas, or synthetic gas usable for fuel, or any mixture thereof.

(5) "Real property security" means any real property and improvements, other than a separate interest and any related interest in the common area of a residential common interest development, as the terms "separate interest," "common area," and "common interest development" are defined in Sections 4095, 4100, and 4185 of the Civil Code, or real property which contains only 1 to 15 dwelling units, which in either case (A) is solely used (i) for residential purposes, or (ii) if reasonably contemplated by the parties to the deed of trust or mortgage, for residential purposes as well as limited agricultural or commercial purposes incidental thereto, and (B) is the subject of an issued certificate of occupancy unless the dwelling is to be owned and occupied by the borrower.

(6) "Related party" means any person who shares an ownership interest with the borrower in the real property security, or is a partner or joint venturer with the borrower in a partnership or joint venture, the business of which includes the acquisition, development, use, lease, or sale of the real property security.

(7) "Release" means any spilling, leaking, pumping, pouring, emitting, emptying, discharging, injecting, escaping, leaching, dumping, or disposing into the environment, including continuing migration, of hazardous substances into, onto, or through soil, surface water, or groundwater. The term does not include actions directly relating to the incorporation in a lawful manner of building materials into a permanent improvement to the real property security.

(8) "Secured lender" means the beneficiary under a deed of trust against the real property security, or the mortgagee under a mortgage against the real property security, and any successor-in-interest of the beneficiary or mortgagee to the deed of trust or mortgage.

(f) This section shall not be construed to invalidate or otherwise affect in any manner any rights or obligations arising under contract in connection with a loan or extension of credit, including, without limitation, provisions limiting recourse.

(g) This section shall only apply to loans, extensions of credit, guaranties, or other obligations secured by real property security made, renewed, or modified on or after January 1, 1992. **Leg.H.** Added Stats 1991 ch 1167 §3 (AB 1735). Amended Stats 1992 ch 167 §3 (AB 2750); Stats 1999 ch 60 §1 (SB 328); Stats 2002 ch 999 §4 (AB 2481); Stats 2012 ch 181 §45 (AB 806), effective January 1, 2013, operative January 1, 2014; Stats 2022 ch 258 §8 (AB 2327), effective January 1, 2023, operative January 1, 2024.

§727. Surplus money deposited in court

If there be surplus money remaining, after payment of the amount due on the mortgage, lien, or incumbrance, with costs, the court may cause the same to be paid to the person entitled to it, and in the meantime may direct it to be deposited in court. **Leg.H.** Enacted 1872.

§728. Sale when secured debt falls due at different times

If the debt for which the mortgage, lien, or incumbrance is held is not all due, so soon as sufficient of the property has been sold to pay the amount due, with costs, the sale must cease; and afterwards, as often as more becomes due, for principal or interest, the court may, on motion, order more to be sold. But if the property cannot be sold in portions, without injury to the parties, the whole may be ordered to be sold in the first instance, and the entire debt and costs paid, there being a rebate of interest where such rebate is proper. **Leg.H.** Enacted 1872.

§729. [Section repealed 1983]

Leg.H. Added Stats 1893 ch 101 §2. Amended Stats 1927 ch 370 §1; Stats 1982 ch 517 §153 (ch 497 prevails). Repealed Stats 1982 ch 497 §47, operative July 1, 1983. The repealed section related to commissioner's oath, bond, report and compensation.

§729.010. Deficiency judgment upon decree of foreclosure; Right of redemption

(a) If the decree of foreclosure of a mortgage or deed of trust on real property pursuant to Section 726 determines that a deficiency judgment may be ordered against the defendant, the real property (other than a leasehold estate with an unexpired term of less than two years at the time of levy) shall be sold subject to the right of redemption.

(b) If the property is to be sold subject to the right of redemption, the sale is governed by Section 716.020, except that:

(1) The notice of sale of the property shall state that the property will be sold subject to the right of redemption and shall state the amount of the secured indebtedness with interest and costs.

(2) Notice of sale may be given upon entry of the judgment for sale of the property and the provision of Section 701.545 delaying notice of sale does not apply.

(3) Notice of sale may be given to persons having liens on the property upon entry of the judgment for sale of the property and the provision of subdivision (h) of Section 701.540 delaying such notice does not apply. **Leg.H.** Added Stats 1982 ch 497 §48, operative July 1, 1983.

§729.020. Persons entitled to redeem property

Property sold subject to the right of redemption may be redeemed only by the judgment debtor or the judgment debtor's successor in interest. For the purpose of this article, the purchaser of the property at the foreclosure sale is not a successor in interest. **Leg.H.** Added Stats 1982 ch 497 §49, operative July 1, 1983.

§729.030. Redemption period

The redemption period during which property may be redeemed from a foreclosure sale under this chapter ends:

(a) Three months after the date of sale if the proceeds of the sale are sufficient to satisfy the secured indebtedness with interest and costs of action and of sale.

(b) One year after the date of sale if the proceeds of the sale are not sufficient to satisfy the secured indebtedness with interest and costs of action and of sale. **Leg.H.** Added Stats 1982 ch 497 §50, operative July 1, 1983.

§729.035. Right of redemption on sale of separate interest in common interest development arising from foreclosure

Notwithstanding any provision of law to the contrary, the sale of a separate interest in a common interest development is subject to the right of redemption within 90 days after the sale if the sale arises from a foreclosure by the association of a common interest development pursuant to Sections 5700, 5710, and 5735 of the Civil Code, subject to the conditions of Sections 5705, 5715, and 5720 of the Civil Code. **Leg.H.** Added Stats 2005 ch 452 §8 (SB 137), effective January 1, 2006. Amended Stats 2012 ch 181 §46 (AB 806), effective January 1, 2013, operative January 1, 2014.

§729.040. Certificate of sale

(a) Notwithstanding Section 701.660, when the purchaser of an interest in real property sold subject to the right of redemption pays the amount due, the levying officer conducting the sale shall execute and deliver a certificate of sale to the purchaser and record a duplicate of the certificate of sale in the office of the county recorder.

(b) The certificate of sale shall contain either:

(1) In the case of a judicial foreclosure, the information required by Section 701.670.

(2) In the case of a nonjudicial foreclosure, all of the information required by subdivisions (c), (d), and (e) of Section 701.670.

(c) In addition to the information required by subdivision (b), the certificate of sale shall also contain the following:

(1) The price paid for each distinct lot or parcel of real property sold subject to the right of redemption.

(2) The total price paid.

(3) A statement that the property is subject to the right of redemption, indicating the applicable redemption period. **Leg.H.** Added Stats 1982 ch 497 §51, operative July 1, 1983. Amended Stats 2006 ch 575 §6 (AB 2624), effective January 1, 2007.

§729.050. Service of notice of right of redemption

If property is sold subject to the right of redemption, promptly after the sale the levying officer or trustee who conducted the sale shall serve notice of the right of redemption on the judgment debtor. Service shall be made personally or by mail. The notice of the right of redemption shall indicate the applicable redemption period. **Leg.H.** Added Stats 1982 ch 497 §52, operative July 1, 1983. Amended Stats 2006 ch 575 §7 (AB 2624), effective January 1, 2007.

§729.060. Deposit of redemption price

(a) A person who seeks to redeem the property shall deposit the redemption price with the levying officer who conducted the sale before the expiration of the redemption period. If a successor in interest to the judgment debtor seeks to redeem the property, the successor in interest shall, at the time the redemption price is deposited, file with the levying officer either (1) a certified copy of a recorded conveyance or (2) a copy of an assignment or any other evidence of the interest verified by an affidavit of the successor in interest or of a subscribing witness thereto.

(b) The redemption price is the total of the following amounts, less any offset allowed under subdivision (c).

(1) The purchase price at the sale.

(2) The amount of any assessments or taxes and reasonable amounts for fire insurance, maintenance, upkeep, and repair of improvements on the property.

(3) Any amount paid by the purchaser on a prior obligation secured by the property to the extent that the payment was necessary for the protection of the purchaser's interest.

(4) Interest on the amounts described in paragraphs (1), (2), and (3) at the rate of interest on money judgments from the time such amount was paid until the date the deposit is made.

(5) If the purchaser at the sale has any liens subordinate to the lien under which the property was sold, the amount of the purchaser's lien, plus interest at the rate of interest on money judgments from the date of the sale until the date the deposit is made.

(c) Rents and profits from the property paid to the purchaser or the value of the use and occupation of the property to the purchaser may be offset against the amounts described in subdivision (b). **Leg.H.** Added Stats 1982 ch 497 §53, operative July 1, 1983. Amended Stats 1984 ch 538 §32.5.

§729.070. Petition to determine redemption price or right to redeem

(a) If the purchaser and the person seeking to redeem the property disagree on the redemption price or as to whether the person is entitled to redeem the property, or if the purchaser refuses the tender of the redemption price pursuant to Section 729.080, the person seeking to redeem may file a petition with the court for an order determining the redemption price or whether the person is entitled to redeem the property. The petition shall be filed before the expiration of the redemption period. At the time the petition is filed, the petitioner shall deposit the undisputed amount of the redemption price with the levying officer, if deposit has not previously been made, and give written notice to the levying officer or trustee of the filing of the petition.

(b) The petition shall be in writing and shall include the following statements:

(1) The amounts demanded to which the person seeking to redeem objects and the reasons for the objection.

(2) Any amounts offset to which the purchaser objects and the justification for the offset.

(3) The status of the petitioner that qualifies the petitioner to redeem the property. A copy of the papers required by subdivision (a) of Section 729.060 shall be filed with the petition.

(c) The hearing on the petition shall be held not later than 20 days after the date the petition was filed unless continued by the court for good cause.

(d) Not less than 10 days before the hearing, the person seeking to redeem the property shall personally serve on the purchaser a copy of the petition together with a notice of the time and place of the hearing.

(e) At the hearing on the petition, the person seeking to redeem the property has the burden of proof.

(f) At the conclusion of the hearing, the court shall determine by order the amount required to redeem the property. The determination shall be made upon affidavit or evidence satisfactory to the court.

(g) If an amount in addition to that deposited with the levying officer is required to redeem the property, the person seeking to redeem shall, within 10 days after the issuance of the order, pay the additional amount to the levying officer. **Leg.H.** Added Stats 1982 ch 497 §54, operative July 1, 1983. Amended Stats 2006 ch 575 §8 (AB 2624), effective January 1, 2007.

§729.080. Expiration of redemption period; Tender of redemption price

(a) If the redemption price is not deposited pursuant to Section 729.060 before the expiration of the redemption period, or if no additional deposit is made pursuant to subdivision (g) of Section 729.070 before the expiration of the time provided, the levying officer who conducted the sale shall promptly execute and deliver to the purchaser a deed of sale that complies with the requirements of Section 701.670, or the nonjudicial foreclosure trustee pursuant to Section 729.035 shall deliver an executed trustee's deed and comply with the requirements of Section 2924j of the Civil Code.

(b) If the person seeking to redeem the property deposits the redemption price pursuant to Section 729.060 or 729.070 during the redemption period, the levying officer shall tender the deposit to the purchaser. If the purchaser accepts the tender or if the redemption price determined by court order is tendered, the levying officer or trustee shall promptly execute and deliver a certificate of redemption to the person seeking to redeem and shall immediately record a duplicate of the certificate in the office of the recorder of the county where the property is located.

(c) Tender of the redemption price determined by court order or agreed upon by the purchaser and the person seeking to redeem the property is equivalent to payment. If the tender is refused, the levying officer shall deposit the amount tendered with the county treasurer of the county where the property is located, payable to the order of the purchaser. If the amount deposited is not claimed by the purchaser, or the legal representative of the purchaser, within five years after the deposit is made, by making application to the treasurer or other official designated by the county, it shall be paid into the general fund of the county.

(d) Except as provided in subdivision (e), upon redemption the effect of the sale is terminated and the person who redeemed the property is restored to the estate therein sold at the sale.

(e) Liens extinguished by the sale, as provided in Section 701.630, do not reattach to the property after redemption, and the property that was subject to the extinguished lien may not be applied to the satisfaction of the claim or judgment under which the lien was created. **Leg.H.** Added Stats 1982 ch 497 §55, operative July 1, 1983. Amended Stats 2006 ch 575 §9 (AB 2624), effective January 1, 2007.

§729.090. Rents and profits; Maintenance of property; Waste

(a) From the time of the sale until a redemption, the purchaser is entitled to receive from the person in possession the rents and profits from the property or the value of the use and occupation of the property.

(b) Notwithstanding subdivision (a), the purchaser is liable to the person who redeems for any rents or profits that have been received by the purchaser pursuant to subdivision (a).

(c) The purchaser, from the time of sale until redemption, is entitled to enter the property during reasonable hours to repair and maintain the premises and is entitled to an order restraining waste on the property from the court. Such order may be granted with or without notice in the discretion of the court. **Leg.H.** Added Stats 1982 ch 497 §56, operative July 1, 1983.

§730. Attorney's fee

In all cases of foreclosure of mortgage the attorney's fee shall be fixed by the court in which the proceedings are had, any stipulation in the mortgage to the contrary notwithstanding. **Leg.H.** Added Stats 1953 ch 52 §4.

§730.5. Exceptions

Except as otherwise provided by Section 9604 of the Commercial Code, none of the provisions of this chapter or of Section 580a, 580b, 580c, or 580d applies to any security interest in personal property or fixtures governed by the Commercial Code. **Leg.H.** Added Stats 1980 ch 1156 §1. Amended Stats 1992 ch 1095 §5 (AB 2734); Stats 1999 ch 991 §25 (SB 45), operative July 1, 2001.

CHAPTER 2
ACTIONS FOR NUISANCE, WASTE, AND WILLFUL TRESPASS, IN CERTAIN CASES, ON REAL PROPERTY

Right to bring action to enjoin or abate nuisance, and to recover damages; Abatement of public nuisance. §731.
Restriction on enjoining industrial, commercial, or airport uses in zones and districts. §731a.
Evidence that airport does not constitute nuisance. §731b.
Undertaking as precluding enjoining secondary recovery operations in oil fields; Mitigation of damages. §731c.
Enjoining closure of public trail; Attorney's fees, court costs. §731.5.
Waste action against guardian or cotenant; Treble damages. §732.
Trespass for cutting or carrying away trees or timber; Treble damages. §733.
Measure of damages for taking certain timber. §734.
Treble damages in actions for forcible or unlawful entry. §735.

Secured lender's action for breach of environmental provisions relating to real property security; Damages. §736.

§731. Right to bring action to enjoin or abate nuisance, and to recover damages; Abatement of public nuisance

An action may be brought by any person whose property is injuriously affected, or whose personal enjoyment is lessened by a nuisance, as defined in Section 3479 of the Civil Code, and by the judgment in that action the nuisance may be enjoined or abated as well as damages recovered therefor. A civil action may be brought in the name of the people of the State of California to abate a public nuisance, as defined in Section 3480 of the Civil Code, by the district attorney or county counsel of any county in which the nuisance exists, or by the city attorney of any town or city in which the nuisance exists. Each of those officers shall have concurrent right to bring an action for a public nuisance existing within a town or city. The district attorney, county counsel, or city attorney of any county or city in which the nuisance exists shall bring an action whenever directed by the board of supervisors of the county, or whenever directed by the legislative authority of the town or city. **Leg.H.** Enacted 1872. Amended Stats 1905 ch 128 §1; Stats 2010 ch 570 §2 (AB 1502), effective January 1, 2011.

§731a. Restriction on enjoining industrial, commercial, or airport uses in zones and districts

Whenever any city, city and county, or county shall have established zones or districts under authority of law wherein certain manufacturing or commercial or airport uses are expressly permitted, except in an action to abate a public nuisance brought in the name of the people of the State of California, no person or persons, firm or corporation shall be enjoined or restrained by the injunctive process from the reasonable and necessary operation in any such industrial or commercial zone or airport of any use expressly permitted therein, nor shall such use be deemed a nuisance without evidence of the employment of unnecessary and injurious methods of operation. Nothing in this act shall be deemed to apply to the regulation and working hours of canneries, fertilizing plants, refineries and other similar establishments whose operation produce offensive odors. **Leg.H.** Added Stats 1935 ch 511 §1. Amended Stats 1947 ch 913 §1; Stats 1959 ch 795 §2.

§731b. Evidence that airport does not constitute nuisance

In any action or proceeding to abate the use of an airport or an airpark, proof that the airport or airpark has been in existence for three years constitutes a rebuttable presumption which shall be prima facie evidence that the operation of the airport or airpark does not constitute a nuisance. **Leg.H.** Added Stats 1953 ch 52 §5.

§731c. Undertaking as precluding enjoining secondary recovery operations in oil fields; Mitigation of damages

Injury to formations bearing oil or gas or to oil or gas wells caused by the subsurface migration of any substance as a result of secondary recovery operations for oil or gas conducted in accordance with good oilfield practices shall not be grounds for enjoining the secondary recovery operations if an undertaking is given for the payment of any compensable damages to which the owners of interests in the formations or wells may be entitled resulting from the injury. Any benefit to the injured property from the secondary recovery operation shall be considered in mitigation of damages for the injury. **Leg.H.** Added Stats 1961 ch 2200 §1. Amended Stats 1982 ch 517 §154.

§731.5. Enjoining closure of public trail; Attorney's fees, court costs

Whenever any person unlawfully closes any public trail, any person who uses such trail or would use such trail, and any association, corporation or other entity whose membership as a whole is adversely affected by such closure may bring an action to enjoin such closure.

The prevailing party in such action shall be entitled to recover reasonable attorney's fees, in addition to court costs.

As used in this section, a public trail is any trail to which the public in general has a right of access, which right is established pursuant to a recorded document conveying to a political corporation or governmental agency, specifying the nature of such public trail, specifically describing the location thereof, and naming the record owners of the real property over which such trail exists if created by a license, permit or easement. It includes, but is not limited to, pedestrian, equestrian, and boating trails, but does not include any public street, road, or highway. **Leg.H.** Added Stats 1979 ch 682 §1.

§732. Waste action against guardian or cotenant; Treble damages

If a guardian, conservator, tenant for life or years, joint tenant, or tenant in common of real property, commit waste thereon, any person aggrieved by the waste may bring an action against him therefor, in which action there may be judgment for treble damages. **Leg.H.** Enacted 1872. Amended Stats 1979 ch 730 §23, operative January 1, 1981.

§733. Trespass for cutting or carrying away trees or timber; Treble damages

Any person who cuts down or carries off any wood or underwood, tree, or timber, or girdles or otherwise injures any tree or timber on the land of another person, or on the street or highway in front of any person's house, village, or city lot, or cultivated grounds; or on the commons or public grounds of any city or town, or on the street or highway in front thereof, without lawful authority, is liable to the owner of such land, or to such city or town, for treble the amount of damages which may be assessed therefor, in a civil action, in any Court having jurisdiction. **Leg.H.** Enacted 1872.

§734. Measure of damages for taking certain timber

Nothing in the last section authorized the recovery of more than the just value of the timber taken from uncultivated woodland for the repair of a public highway or bridge upon the land, or adjoining it. **Leg.H.** Enacted 1872.

§735. Treble damages in actions for forcible or unlawful entry

If a person recover damages for a forcible or unlawful entry in or upon, or detention of any building or any cultivated real property, judgment may be entered for three times the amount at which the actual damages are assessed. **Leg.H.** Enacted 1872.

§736. Secured lender's action for breach of environmental provisions relating to real property security; Damages

(a) Notwithstanding any other provision of law, a secured lender may bring an action for breach of contract against a borrower for breach of any environmental provision made by the borrower relating to the real property security, for the recovery of damages, and for the enforcement of the environmental provision, and that action or failure to foreclose first against collateral shall not constitute an action within the meaning of subdivision (a) of Section 726, or constitute a money judgment for a deficiency or a deficiency judgment within the meaning of Section 580a, 580b, or 580d, or subdivision (b) of Section 726. No injunction for the enforcement of an environmental provision may be issued after (1) the obligation secured by the real property security has been fully satisfied, or (2) all of the borrower's rights, title, and interest in and to the real property security has been transferred in a bona fide transaction to an unaffiliated third party for fair value.

(b) The damages a secured lender may recover pursuant to subdivision (a) shall be limited to reimbursement or indemnification of the following:

(1) If not pursuant to an order of any federal, state, or local governmental agency relating to the cleanup, remediation, or other response action required by applicable law, those costs relating to a reasonable and good faith cleanup, remediation, or other response action concerning a release or threatened release of hazardous substances which is anticipated by the environmental provision.

(2) If pursuant to an order of any federal, state, or local governmental agency relating to the cleanup, remediation, or other response action required by applicable law which is anticipated by the environmental provision, all amounts reasonably advanced in good faith by the secured lender in connection therewith, provided that the secured lender negotiated, or attempted to negotiate, in good faith to minimize the amounts it was required to advance under the order.

(3) Indemnification against all liabilities of the secured lender to any third party relating to the breach and not arising from acts, omissions, or other conduct which occur after the borrower is no longer an owner or operator of the real property security, and provided the secured lender is not responsible for the environmentally impaired condition of the real property security in accordance with the standards set forth in subdivision (d) of Section 726.5. For purposes of this paragraph, the term "owner or operator" means those persons described in Section 101(20)(A) of the

Comprehensive Environmental Response, Compensation, and Liability Act of 1980, as amended (42 U.S.C. Sec. 9601, et seq.).

(4) Attorneys' fees and costs incurred by the secured lender relating to the breach.

The damages a secured lender may recover pursuant to subdivision (a) shall not include (i) any part of the principal amount or accrued interest of the secured obligation, except for any amounts advanced by the secured lender to cure or mitigate the breach of the environmental provision that are added to the principal amount, and contractual interest thereon, or (ii) amounts which relate to a release which was knowingly permitted, caused, or contributed to by the secured lender or any affiliate or agent of the secured lender.

(c) A secured lender may not recover damages against a borrower pursuant to subdivision (a) for amounts advanced or obligations incurred for the cleanup or other remediation of real property security, and related attorneys' fees and costs, if all of the following are true:

(1) The original principal amount of, or commitment for, the loan or other obligation secured by the real property security did not exceed two hundred thousand dollars ($200,000).

(2) In conjunction with the secured lender's acceptance of the environmental provision, the secured lender agreed in writing to accept the real property security on the basis of a completed environmental site assessment and other relevant information from the borrower.

(3) The borrower did not permit, cause, or contribute to the release or threatened release.

(4) The deed of trust or mortgage covering the real property security has not been discharged, reconveyed, or foreclosed upon.

(d) This section is not intended to establish, abrogate, modify, limit, or otherwise affect any cause of action other than that provided by subdivision (a) that a secured lender may have against a borrower under an environmental provision.

(e) This section shall apply only to environmental provisions contracted in conjunction with loans, extensions of credit, guaranties, or other obligations made, renewed, or modified on or after January 1, 1992. Notwithstanding the foregoing, this section shall not be construed to validate, invalidate, or otherwise affect in any manner the rights and obligations of the parties to, or the enforcement of, environmental provisions contracted before January 1, 1992.

(f) For purposes of this section:

(1) "Borrower" means the trustor under a deed of trust, or a mortgagor under a mortgage, where the deed of trust or mortgage encumbers real property security and secures the performance of the trustor or mortgagor under a loan, extension of credit, guaranty, or other obligation. The term includes any successor-in-interest of the trustor or mortgagor to the real property security before the deed of trust or mortgage has been discharged, reconveyed, or foreclosed upon.

(2) "Environmental provision" means any written representation, warranty, indemnity, promise, or covenant relating to the existence, location, nature, use, generation, manufacture, storage, disposal, handling, or past, present, or future release or threatened release, of any hazardous substance into, onto, beneath, or from the real property security, or to past, present, or future compliance with any law relating thereto, made by a borrower in conjunction with the making, renewal, or modification of a loan, extension of credit, guaranty, or other obligation involving the borrower, whether or not the representation, warranty, indemnity, promise, or covenant is or was contained in or secured by the deed of trust or mortgage, and whether or not the deed of trust or mortgage has been discharged, reconveyed, or foreclosed upon.

(3) "Hazardous substance" means any of the following:

(A) Any "hazardous substance" as defined in subdivision (h) of Section 25281 of the Health and Safety Code.

(B) Any "waste" as defined in subdivision (d) of Section 13050 of the Water Code.

(C) Petroleum, including crude oil or any fraction thereof, natural gas, natural gas liquids, liquefied natural gas, or synthetic gas usable for fuel, or any mixture thereof.

(4) "Real property security" means any real property and improvements, other than a separate interest and any related interest in the common area of a residential common interest development, as the terms "separate interest," "common area," and "common interest development" are defined in Sections 4095, 4100, and 4185 of the Civil Code, or real property which contains only 1 to 15 dwelling units, which in either case (A) is solely used (i) for residential purposes, or (ii) if reasonably contemplated by the parties to the deed of trust or mortgage, for residential purposes as well as limited agricultural or commercial purposes incidental thereto, and (B) is the subject of an issued certificate of occupancy unless the dwelling is to be owned and occupied by the borrower.

(5) "Release" means any spilling, leaking, pumping, pouring, emitting, emptying, discharging, injecting, escaping, leaching, dumping, or disposing into the environment, including continuing migration, of hazardous substances into, onto, or through soil, surface water, or groundwater. The term does not include actions directly relating to the incorporation in a lawful manner of building materials into a permanent improvement to the real property security.

(6) "Secured lender" means the beneficiary under a deed of trust against the real property security, or the mortgagee under a mortgage against the real property security, and any successor-in-interest of the beneficiary or mortgagee to the deed of trust or mortgage. **Leg.H.** Added Stats 1991 ch 1167 §4 (AB 1735). Amended Stats 1992 ch 167 §4 (AB 2750); Stats 1999 ch 60 §2 (SB 328); Stats 2002 ch 999 §5 (AB 2481); Stats 2012 ch 181 §47 (AB 806), effective January 1, 2013, operative January 1, 2014.

CHAPTER 3
ACTIONS FOR THE RECOVERY OF REAL PROPERTY, AND OTHER PROVISIONS RELATING TO ACTIONS CONCERNING REAL PROPERTY

Damages for withholding property; Recovery where plaintiff's right terminated during pendency of action. §740.
When value of improvements can be allowed as a setoff. §741.
Order allowing party to survey and measure land in dispute. §742.
Contents of order; Service. §743.
Mortgage not deemed a conveyance. §744.
Restraint of waste during foreclosure or before sale pursuant to levy. §745.
Damages for waste after sale pursuant to levy. §746.
Action not to be prejudiced by alienation, pending suit. §747.
Mining claims, actions concerning to be governed by local rules. §748.
Action by homeowner or trustor against beneficiary who forged deed. §749.
Action by assignee or successor in interest against beneficiary who forged deed. §749.5.

§738. [Section repealed 1981]

Leg.H. Enacted Stats 1872. Amended Stats 1895 ch 77 §1; Stats 1921 ch 304 §1. Repealed Stats 1980 ch 44 §4. See CCP §§760.020, 764.020.

§738.5. [Section repealed 1981]

Leg.H. Added Stats 1945 ch 1363 §1. Repealed Stats 1980 ch 44 §5. The repealed section related to action to determine escheat of property under Alien Land Law.

§739. [Section repealed 1981]

Leg.H. Enacted 1872. Repealed Stats 1980 ch 44 §6. The repealed section related to when plaintiff cannot recover costs.

§740. Damages for withholding property; Recovery where plaintiff's right terminated during pendency of action

In an action for the recovery of property, where the plaintiff shows a right to recover at the time the action was commenced, but it appears that his right has terminated during the pendency of the action, the verdict and judgment must be according to the fact, and the plaintiff may recover damages for withholding the property. **Leg.H.** Enacted 1872. Amended Stats 1907 ch 363 §1.

§741. When value of improvements can be allowed as a setoff

(a) As used in this section, "good faith improver" has the meaning given that term by Section 871.1.

(b) When damages are claimed for withholding the property recovered, and improvements have been made on the property by a defendant or his predecessor in interest as a good faith improver, the amount by which such improvements enhance the value of the land must be allowed as a set-off against such damages. **Leg.H.** Enacted 1872. Amended Stats 1968 ch 150 §2.

§742. Order allowing party to survey and measure land in dispute

The court in which an action is pending for the recovery of real property, or for damages for any injury thereto, or a judge thereof may, on motion, upon notice by either party for good cause shown, grant an order allowing to such party the right to enter upon the property and make survey and measurement thereof, and of any tunnels, shafts, or drifts therein, for the purpose of the action, even though entry for such purpose has to be made through other lands belonging to parties to the action. **Leg.H.** Enacted 1872. Amended Code Amdts 1880 ch 22 §1.

§743. Contents of order; Service

The order must describe the property, and a copy thereof must be served on the owner or occupant; and thereupon such party may enter upon the property, with necessary surveyors and assistants and make such survey and measurement; but if any unnecessary injury be done to the property he is liable therefor. **Leg.H.** Enacted 1872.

§744. Mortgage not deemed a conveyance

A mortgage of real property shall not be deemed a conveyance, whatever its terms, so as to enable the owner of the mortgage to recover possession of the real property without a foreclosure and sale. **Leg.H.** Enacted 1872.

§745. Restraint of waste during foreclosure or before sale pursuant to levy

The court may, by injunction, on good cause shown, restrain the party in possession from doing any act to the injury of real property:

(a) During the foreclosure of a mortgage on the property.

(b) After levy on the property and before the possession of the property is transferred pursuant to sale under the levy. **Leg.H.** Enacted 1872. Amended Stats 1982 ch 497 §57, operative July 1, 1983.

§746. Damages for waste after sale pursuant to levy

When real property has been sold pursuant to a levy, the purchaser of the property, or any person who has succeeded to the interest of the purchaser, may recover damages from the person causing the injury for injury to the property after levy and before possession is delivered to the purchaser or the person who has succeeded to the interest of the purchaser. **Leg.H.** Enacted 1872. Amended Stats 1982 ch 497 §58, operative July 1, 1983.

§747. Action not to be prejudiced by alienation, pending suit

An action for the recovery of real property against a person in possession cannot be prejudiced by any alienation made by such person, either before or after the commencement of the action. **Leg.H.** Enacted 1872.

§748. Mining claims, actions concerning to be governed by local rules

In actions respecting mining claims, proof must be admitted of the customs, usages, or regulations established and in force at the bar or diggings embracing such claim; and such customs, usages, or regulations, when not in conflict with the laws of this state, must govern the decision of the action. **Leg.H.** Enacted 1872.

§748.5. [Section repealed 1981]

Leg.H. Added Stats 1955 ch 563 §1. Amended Stats 1977 ch 91 §1. Repealed Stats 1980 ch 44 §7. See CCP §§771.010, 771.020.

§749. Action by homeowner or trustor against beneficiary who forged deed

(a) In an action for damages by a homeowner or trustor against a beneficiary of a trust deed on real property consisting of a single-family residence containing not more than four dwelling units, or against an assignee or successor in interest thereof, wherein it is established the trust deed was forged in whole or in part by the beneficiary, judgment may be entered for three times the amount at which the actual damages are assessed.

(b) An assignee or successor in interest of a beneficiary or a transferee of a prior assignee or of a prior successor in interest shall not be subject to treble damages unless it is established that the person purchased or obtained the deed of trust with actual knowledge of the forgery of the deed of trust.

(c) This section shall not apply to any person who does not purchase and sell four or more deeds of trust in any calendar year.

(d) This section shall not limit or affect the availability of punitive damages, if any, to the injured party.

(e) This section shall apply to any action filed on or after July 1, 1983, provided that any action filed prior to the effective date of this section is pending at that time in the court of original jurisdiction. **Leg.H.** Added Stats 1984 ch 1397 §1.

Prior Law: Former CCP §749, similar to present CCP §§760.020, 761.010, 761.020, 762.060, 763.010, was added Stats 1901 ch 183 §1, amended Stats 1903 ch 93 §1, Stats 1939 ch 404 §1, Stats 1943 ch 155 §1, and repealed Stats 1980 ch 44 §8.

There was another section of this number which was erroneously added as CCP §149 by Stats 1891 ch 195 §1 p 278 and repealed by Stats 1907 ch 364 §1 p 686.

§749.1. [Section repealed 1981]

Leg.H. Added Stats 1949 ch 1025 §1. Repealed Stats 1980 ch 44 §9. See CCP §§760.020, 761.010, 761.020, 762.060, 763.010.

§749.5. Action by assignee or successor in interest against beneficiary who forged deed

(a) In an action for damages by an assignee or a successor in interest against a beneficiary of a trust deed on real property consisting of a single-family residence containing not more than four dwelling units, wherein it is established the trust deed was forged in whole or in part by the beneficiary, judgment may be entered for three times the amount at which the actual damages are assessed.

(b) This section shall not apply to any person who does not purchase and sell four or more deeds of trust in any calendar year.

(c) This section shall not limit or affect the availability of punitive damages, if any, to the injured party.

(d) This section shall apply to any action filed on or after January 1, 1984. **Leg.H.** Added Stats 1984 ch 1397 §2.

Prior Law: Former CCP §749.5, relating to barred street improvement bond or assessment liens, was added Stats 1945 ch 1348 §1 and repealed Stats 1947 ch 410 §1.

§750. [Section repealed 1981]

Leg.H. Added Stats 1901 ch 183 §2. Amended Stats 1903 ch 93 §2; Stats 1931 ch 1174 §1; Stats 1939 ch 404 §2; Stats 1943 ch 155 §2; Stats 1951 ch 46 §1; Stats 1955 ch 776 §1; Stats 1961 ch 122 §1; Stats 1969 ch 1611 §8, operative July 1, 1970. Repealed Stats 1980 ch 44 §10. See CCP §§762.070, 763.010, 763.020, 763.030, 764.030.

§751. [Section repealed 1981]

Leg.H. Added Stats 1901 ch 183 §3. Amended Stats 1903 ch 93 §3; Stats 1943 ch 155 §3. Repealed Stats 1980 ch 44 §11. See CCP §§760.030, 763.040, 764.010, 764.030, 764.070.

§751.1. [Section repealed 1981]

Leg.H. Added Stats 1949 ch 1025 §2. Repealed Stats 1980 ch 44 §13. See CCP §§760.030, 763.040, 764.010, 764.030, 764.070.

§751.3. [Section repealed 1981]

Leg.H. Added Stats 1971 ch 1586 §1. Repealed Stats 1980 ch 44 §14. See CCP §§772.010 et seq.

§751a. [Section repealed 1981]

Leg.H. Added Stats 1931 ch 1175 §1. Amended Stats 1937 ch 325 §1; Stats 1945 ch 253 §1; Stats 1957 ch 974 §1; Stats 1967 ch 17 §13. Repealed Stats 1980 ch 44 §12. See CCP §§770.010–770.080.

CHAPTER 3.5
ACTIONS TO RE-ESTABLISH DESTROYED LAND RECORDS

Citation of chapter. §751.01.
Right to bring action; Venue. §751.02.
Any number of parcels included. §751.03.
Commencement of action; Filing of complaint. §751.04.
Issuance of summons. §751.05.
Publication of summons. §751.06.
Disclosure of adverse interest in affidavit; Memorandum appended to summons. §751.07.
Posting copy of memorandum and summons. §751.08.
Affidavit. §751.09.

Service of summons. §751.10.
Jurisdiction of court. §751.11.
Answer to complaint. §751.12.
Recording notice of pendency of action. §751.13.
Judgment not to be given by default. §751.14.
Judgment; Subject matter; Conclusiveness. §751.15.
Recordation of judgment. §751.16.
Rules of practice. §751.17.
Taking and using depositions. §751.18.
Numbering and indexing of actions. §751.19.
Successive actions respecting same property. §751.20.
Permissible plaintiffs. §751.21.
Remedies deemed cumulative. §751.22.
Notice of claim of ownership; Recordation. §751.23.
Signing and verifying notice of claim. §751.24.
Duty of recorder. §751.25.
Constructive notice. §751.26.
Plaintiff in subsequent suit must make claimant a party; Effect of failure to do so on judgment. §751.27.
Notices on behalf of others. §751.28.

§751.01. Citation of chapter
This chapter may be cited as the Destroyed Land Records Relief Law. **Leg.H.** Added Stats 1953 ch 52 §6.

§751.02. Right to bring action; Venue
Whenever the public records in the office of the county recorder of any county are lost or destroyed in whole or in any material part by flood, fire, earthquake, enemy attack, or from any other cause, any person who claims an estate of inheritance or for life in, and who is by himself, or his tenant or other person holding under him in the actual and peaceable possession of, any real property in the county may bring and maintain an action in rem against all the world, in the superior court for the county in which such real property is situate, to establish his title to such property and to determine all adverse claims thereto.

Such action may also be brought in the county in which the real property is situate if any real property is in another county, but was formerly in the county of which all or a material part of the records were so lost or destroyed, and if the lost or destroyed records included all or a material part of the public records in the office of the county recorder covering all or a material part of the time when the real property was in the county whose records were so lost or destroyed. **Leg.H.** Added Stats 1953 ch 52 §6.

§751.03. Any number of parcels included
Any number of separate parcels of land claimed by the plaintiff may be included in the same action. **Leg.H.** Added Stats 1953 ch 52 §6.

§751.04. Commencement of action; Filing of complaint
The action shall be commenced by the filing of a verified complaint. The party commencing the action shall be named as plaintiff, and the defendants shall be described as "all persons claiming any interest in, or lien upon, the real property herein described, or any part thereof." The complaint shall contain a statement of the facts enumerated in Section 751.02, a particular description of the real property, and a specification of the estate, title, or interest of the plaintiff in the property. **Leg.H.** Added Stats 1953 ch 53 §6.

§751.05. Issuance of summons
Upon the filing of the complaint, a summons shall be issued under the seal of the court. The summons shall contain the name of the court and county in which the action is brought, and the name of the plaintiff and a particular description of the real property involved, and shall be directed to "all persons claiming any interest in, or lien upon, the real property herein described, or any part thereof," as defendants, and shall be substantially in the following form:

"IN THE SUPERIOR COURT OF THE STATE OF CALIFORNIA
IN AND FOR THE COUNTY (OR CITY AND COUNTY) OF
_____

_____, Plaintiff,
vs.
All Persons Claiming Any Interest in, or Lien Upon, the Real Property Herein Described or, Any Part thereof, Defendants.

Action No. _____

The people of the State of California, to all persons claiming any interest in, or lien upon, the real property herein described, or any part thereof, defendants, greeting:

You are hereby required to appear and answer the complaint of _____, plaintiff, filed with the clerk of the above-entitled court and county, within three months after the first publication of this summons, and to set forth what interest or lien, if any, you have in or upon that certain real property or any part thereof, situated in the County (or City and County) of _____, State of California, particularly described as follows: (here insert description.)

And you are hereby notified that, unless you so appear and answer, the plaintiff will apply to the court for the relief demanded in the complaint, to wit: (here insert a statement of the relief so demanded.)

Witness my hand and the seal of said court, this ____ day of _____, A.D. ____.

(SEAL) _____, Clerk."

Leg.H. Added Stats 1953 ch 52 §6.

§751.06. Publication of summons
The summons shall be published in a newspaper of general circulation published in the county in which the action is brought. The newspaper in which publication is to be made shall be designated by an order of the court or a judge thereof to be signed and filed with the clerk. No other order for the publication of the summons shall be necessary, nor shall any affidavit therefor be required, nor need any copy of the complaint be served, except as required by this chapter. The summons shall be published pursuant to Section 6065 of the Government Code, and to each publication thereof shall be appended a memorandum in substance as follows:

"The first publication of this summons was made in _____ (here insert name) newspaper on the ____ day of _____ A.D. _____," (inserting the date). **Leg.H.** Added Stats 1953 ch 52 §6.

§751.07. Disclosure of adverse interest in affidavit; Memorandum appended to summons
If the affidavit provided for in Section 751.09 discloses the name of any person claiming an interest in the property or a lien thereon adverse to the plaintiff, that fact and the name and address, if given, of the person shall be stated in a memorandum to be appended to the summons in substance as follows:

"The following persons are said to claim an interest in, or lien upon, said property adverse to plaintiff," (giving their names and addresses as above provided.) **Leg.H.** Added Stats 1953 ch 52 §6.

§751.08. Posting copy of memorandum and summons
A copy of the summons and a copy of the memorandum shall be posted in a conspicuous place on each separate parcel of the property described in the complaint within 15 days after the first publication of the summons. **Leg.H.** Added Stats 1953 ch 52 §6.

§751.09. Affidavit
At the time of filing the complaint the plaintiff shall file with it his affidavit fully and explicitly setting forth and showing:

(a) The character of the plaintiff's estate, right, title, interest, or claim in, and possession of, the property, the period it has existed, and from whom obtained.

(b) Whether or not the plaintiff has ever made any conveyance of all or any part of the property, or any interest therein, and if so when and to whom, and a statement of any and all subsisting mortgages, deeds of trust, and other liens thereon.

(c) That the plaintiff does not know and has never been informed of any other person who claims or who may claim any interest in or lien upon all or any part of the property adversely to the plaintiff, or if the plaintiff does know or has been informed of any such person, the name and address of such person.

If the plaintiff is unable to state any of the required matters, the plaintiff shall set forth and show fully and explicitly the reasons for such inability. Such affidavit shall constitute a part of the judgment-roll. If the plaintiff is a corporation, the affidavit shall be made by an officer thereof. If the plaintiff is a person under guardianship or conservatorship, the affidavit shall be made by the guardian or conservator. **Leg.H.** Added Stats 1953 ch 52 §6. Amended Stats 1979 ch 730 §24, operative January 1, 1981.

§751.10. Service of summons
If the affidavit discloses the name of any person claiming any interest in or lien upon the property adverse to the plaintiff, a copy of the summons

and complaint and affidavit shall also be served upon such person, if he can be found, in the manner provided by law for the service of a summons in a civil action, other than by publication. Service shall be made during the period of the publication of the summons. A copy of the memorandum provided for in Section 751.07 shall be appended to the copy of the summons served upon any such person.

If such person cannot, with reasonable diligence, be served as provided above within the period of publication of the summons, a copy of the summons, memorandum, complaint, and affidavit shall be mailed, postage prepaid, addressed to him at the address given in the affidavit, or, if no address is given, at his last address known to the plaintiff, or, if none, at the county seat of the county in which the action is brought, forthwith upon the expiration of the period of publication. **Leg.H.** Added Stats 1953 ch 52 §6. Amended Stats 1969 ch 1611 §9, operative July 1, 1970.

§751.11. Jurisdiction of court

Upon the completion of the publication and posting of the summons and its service or mailing as provided for in Section 751.10, the court has complete jurisdiction over the plaintiff and the property and the person of everyone having or claiming any estate, right, title, or interest in or to, or lien upon, all or any part of the property, and shall be deemed to have obtained the possession and control of the property for the purposes of the action with complete jurisdiction to render the judgment provided for in this chapter. **Leg.H.** Added Stats 1953 ch 52 §6. Amended Stats 1969 ch 1611 §10, operative July 1, 1970.

§751.12. Answer to complaint

At any time within three months after the first publication of the summons, or such further time not exceeding 30 days as the court for good cause may grant, any person having or claiming any estate, right, title, or interest in or to, or lien upon, all or any part of the property may appear and make himself a party to the action by pleading to the complaint. All answers must be verified and must specifically set forth the estate, right, title, interest, or lien so claimed. **Leg.H.** Added Stats 1953 ch 52 §6.

§751.13. Recording notice of pendency of action

At the time of filing the complaint the plaintiff, and at the time of filing his or her answer every defendant claiming any affirmative relief, shall record in the office of the recorder of the county in which the property is situated a notice of the pendency of the action containing the object of the action or defense, and a particular description of the property affected by it. The recorder shall record the notice in the same manner as provided in Section 409. **Leg.H.** Added Stats 1953 ch 52 §6. Amended Stats 1982 ch 843 §1.

§751.14. Judgment not to be given by default

Judgment in any such action shall not be given by default, but the court must require proof of the facts alleged in the complaint and other pleadings. **Leg.H.** Added Stats 1953 ch 52 §6.

§751.15. Judgment; Subject matter; Conclusiveness

The judgment shall determine all estates, rights, titles, interests, and claims in and to such property and every part thereof, whether legal or equitable, present or future, vested or contingent, or whether they consist of mortgages or liens of any description. It shall be conclusive upon every person who at the commencement of the action had or claimed any estate, right, title, or interest in or to all or any part of such property and upon every person claiming under him by title subsequent to the commencement of the action. **Leg.H.** Added Stats 1953 ch 52 §6.

§751.16. Recordation of judgment

A certified copy of the judgment shall be recorded in the office of the recorder of the county in which the action was commenced. Any party or the successor in interest of any party to the action may file the entire judgment roll for record in the office of the county recorder. **Leg.H.** Added Stats 1953 ch 52 §6.

§751.17. Rules of practice

Except as otherwise provided in this chapter, all rules of law relating to evidence, pleading, practice, new trials, and appeals applicable to other civil actions shall apply to actions authorized by this chapter. **Leg.H.** Added Stats 1953 ch 52 §6.

§751.18. Taking and using depositions

At any time after the issuance of summons, any party to the action may take depositions in conformity to law upon notice to the adverse party sought to be bound by such depositions and who has appeared in the action and upon notice filed with the clerk. The depositions may be used by any party against any other party giving or receiving the notice, subject to all just exceptions. **Leg.H.** Added Stats 1953 ch 52 §6.

§751.19. Numbering and indexing of actions

The clerk shall number all actions authorized by this chapter consecutively in a distinct series and shall keep an index and register devoted exclusively to such actions. **Leg.H.** Added Stats 1953 ch 52 §6.

§751.20. Successive actions respecting same property

Whenever judgment in an action authorized by this chapter has been entered as to any real property, no other action relative to all or any part of the same property shall be tried until proof has first been made to the court that all persons who appeared in the first action or their successors in interest have been personally served pursuant to this chapter either within or without the State more than one month before the time to plead expired. **Leg.H.** Added Stats 1953 ch 52 §6.

§751.21. Permissible plaintiffs

An executor, administrator, guardian, conservator, or other person holding the possession of property in the right of another may maintain as plaintiff, and may appear and defend in, any action provided for by this chapter. **Leg.H.** Added Stats 1953 ch 52 §6. Amended Stats 1979 ch 730 §25, operative January 1, 1981.

§751.22. Remedies deemed cumulative

The remedies provided for by this chapter are cumulative and in addition to any other remedy provided by law for quieting or establishing title to real property. **Leg.H.** Added Stats 1953 ch 52 §6.

§751.23. Notice of claim of ownership; Recordation

Where the title to real property may be established or quieted pursuant to this chapter, any person who is or claims to be the owner of such real property or of any interest therein or lien thereon by himself or by his agent duly authorized by letter of attorney theretofore recorded in the office of the county recorder of the county where the property is situated, may sign, verify, and file for record in the office of the county recorder a notice in substantially the following form:

"Notice of Ownership and Claim to Real Property Under the Destroyed Records Relief Law

"Notice is hereby given that _____ (here insert name of claimant) _____, whose residence is at _____ (here insert street and number, city or town, county and state of residence), is the owner of an interest in the real property situated in the _____ (here insert name of city if the property be located in a city) _____, county of _____ (here insert name of county or city and county in which property is located) _____, State of California, described as follows: _____ (here insert a particular description of real property) _____.

"The character of the interest in the real property owned by the claimant is _____ (here insert description of the character of interest in or lien upon the real property) _____ and the interest was obtained from _____ (here insert the name of the party from whom the interest was obtained) _____, and at the time and in the manner following _____ (here insert time at which and manner in which the interest was acquired) _____."

Leg.H. Added Stats 1953 ch 52 §6.

§751.24. Signing and verifying notice of claim

The notice shall be signed by the claimant or by his agent and shall be verified by the oath of the party signing it, to the effect that all of the statements therein contained are true to his knowledge. **Leg.H.** Added Stats 1953 ch 52 §6.

§751.25. Duty of recorder

Upon the filing of the notice for recordation the recorder shall record the notice in the same manner as provided in Section 409. **Leg.H.** Added Stats 1953 ch 52 §6. Amended Stats 1982 ch 843 §2.

§751.26. Constructive notice

After three days after the notice has been filed for record, all persons who may begin actions pursuant to this chapter shall be deemed to have notice of the facts stated in the notice. Neither the filing of the notice for record nor its recordation constitute constructive notice to any other person or for any other purpose. The original of the notice shall be returned to the party requesting the recordation as provided in Section

27321 of the Government Code. **Leg.H.** Added Stats 1953 ch 52 §6. Amended Stats 1982 ch 843 §3.

§751.27. Plaintiff in subsequent suit must make claimant a party; Effect of failure to do so on judgment

After three days after the filing of the notice for record, any person who begins an action pursuant to this chapter to perfect or establish his title to the real property described in the notice, or any interest therein, must name, in the affidavit and memorandum appended to the summons, the claimant in the notice, or any person who is a successor in interest of such claimant under a subsequently duly recorded written instrument, judgment, or decree, as a party who claims an interest in or lien upon the property adverse to the plaintiff. He must cause such claimant, or successor in interest, to be served with summons in the action. Otherwise neither the action nor any judgment or decree made therein shall affect the title or interest in the property described in the notice and owned by the claimant at the time of the filing of the notice, or by any such successor in interest prior to the commencement of the action. The failure to name such claimant or successor in interest in the affidavit or memorandum or to serve such claimant or such successor in interest shall not affect the validity of the judgment or decree rendered in such action as to any other persons, but such judgment or decree shall be valid and binding upon all persons except such claimant or successor in interest. **Leg.H.** Added Stats 1953 ch 52 §6.

§751.28. Notices on behalf of others

An executor, administrator, guardian, conservator, or other person holding the possession of property in the right of another, may make, sign, verify, and file for record the notice and affidavit provided for in this chapter on behalf of the estate or interest which he represents. **Leg.H.** Added Stats 1953 ch 52 §6. Amended Stats 1979 ch 730 §26, operative January 1, 1981.

CHAPTER 3.6
CULLEN EARTHQUAKE ACT

Right to action to reestablish disturbed boundaries, and to quiet title to lands therein. §751.50.
Entities and persons authorized to commence action; Entities designated in complaint and given notice; Designation of unknown entities. §751.51.
Separate action by permissive plaintiff. §751.52.
Complaint's allegations. §751.53.
Provisions governing process and related matters. §751.54.
Jurisdiction on completion of process requirements. §751.55.
Answer; Service; Contents and scope; Claims unaffected by judgment. §751.56.
Notice of pendency of action. §751.57.
Vacation of public ways on offer by governmental agency and acceptance by court. §751.58.
Prohibited judgment by default. §751.59.
Determinations by judgment; Filing official map. §751.60.
Court's considerations in reaching conclusions. §751.61.
Conclusiveness of judgment. §751.62.
Recording copy of judgment; Notice therefrom. §751.63.
Cumulative remedies. §751.64.
Citation of chapter. §751.65.

§751.50. Right to action to reestablish disturbed boundaries, and to quiet title to lands therein

If the boundaries of land owned either by public or by private entities have been disturbed by earth movements such as, but not limited to, slides, subsidence, lateral or vertical displacements or similar disasters caused by man, or by earthquake or other acts of God, so that such lands are in a location different from that at which they were located prior to the disaster, an action in rem may be brought to equitably reestablish boundaries and to quiet title to land within the boundaries so reestablished. **Leg.H.** Added Stats 1972 ch 936 §2.

§751.51. Entities and persons authorized to commence action; Entities designated in complaint and given notice; Designation of unknown entities

(a) An action authorized by this chapter may be commenced by:
(1) A county in which lands were affected by a disaster described in Section 751.50 with or without the joinder of a city or cities included in the county and within the area so affected.
(2) A city, if the disaster has affected land in the city.
(3) Any other entity or person owning or having an interest in or lien upon land affected by the disaster if granted permission by the court to bring the action, and if the county in which the land is located is made a party to the action.

(b) In an action authorized by this chapter every entity in actual and peaceable possession of, or having an estate or interest in or lien upon any of the land affected by the action, whose possession or evidence of estate or interest is either recorded or known to the plaintiffs, the city, if the land is within a city, the county in which the land is located, and the State of California must be designated in the complaint of the action, and given notice in the manner required by this chapter.

(c) All unknown entities, including owners, lien or interest claimants, heirs, devisees, legatees or assigns, may be described in the caption and complaint as "all entities claiming any interest in or lien upon, the real property herein described or any part of it." **Leg.H.** Added Stats 1972 ch 936 §2.

§751.52. Separate action by permissive plaintiff

An entity which is a permissive plaintiff under this chapter, may bring a separate action with respect to separate portions of the disaster area of sufficient size to equitably reestablish boundaries without harm to other areas of the common disaster, its decision regarding the desirability of the separate action, and regarding the area to be dealt with in each action to be approved by the court. **Leg.H.** Added Stats 1972 ch 936 §2.

§751.53. Complaint's allegations

The complaint shall substantially include:
(a) A statement of the facts which make the provisions of this chapter applicable.
(b) A description of the exterior boundaries of the real property area sought to be affected by the action.
(c) A specification of the estate, title, interest or claim owned, and in the actual possession of the plaintiff or plaintiffs in described parts of the entire real property sought to be affected by the action.
(d) A specification of the estate, title, interest, or claim, so far as they are known to the plaintiffs or either of them, and so far as they are capable of being discovered by reasonably diligent search by the plaintiff or plaintiffs, in each separate part of the entire real property sought to be affected by the action.
(e) A specification of the street areas sought to be vacated or offered by the plaintiff, or plaintiffs, to be vacated in whole or in part for judicial equitable allocation to landowners for the mitigation of the losses inflicted upon the landowners by the particular disaster or disasters to which this chapter is applicable.
(f) A proposed replatting of the entire real property sought to be affected by the action, embodying the land boundaries as fixed by the disaster, except as these boundaries have been equitably and judicially readjusted, or as liberalized by judicially directed use of the vacated lands. **Leg.H.** Added Stats 1972 ch 936 §2. Amended Stats 1984 ch 193 §10.

§751.54. Provisions governing process and related matters

Summons, publication of notice, posting and related matters and procedures shall be governed by the provisions of Sections 751.05 through 751.10, inclusive, of the Code of Civil Procedure. **Leg.H.** Added Stats 1972 ch 936 §2.

§751.55. Jurisdiction on completion of process requirements

Upon the completion of the service, publication and posting of the summons, as may be required by this chapter, the court has complete jurisdiction over the parties plaintiff or plaintiffs and the entire real property described in the complaint as intended to be affected by the action, and over every entity having or claiming an estate, right, title or interest in or to, or lien upon, all or any part of the property, and shall be considered to have obtained the possession and control of the property for the purposes of the action with complete jurisdiction to render the judgment provided for in this chapter. **Leg.H.** Added Stats 1972 ch 936 §2.

§751.56. Answer; Service; Contents and scope; Claims unaffected by judgment

(a) An answer to the complaint must be served within 90 days after the first publication of the notice, or such further time not exceeding 30 days, as the court for good cause may grant.
(b) An answer must:
(1) Specifically set out the particulars in which the claimant's estate, right, title, or interest in or to, or lien upon all or any part of the property

is different from, or greater than, the interest of the claimant as it is described in the complaint.

(2) Be confined to rights based on events occurring at the time of, or since the time of the disaster.

(c) To whatever extent, if at all, the answering party has rights against anyone whatsoever, based upon facts or events which occurred before the disaster, the claims shall remain unaffected by the action brought under this chapter and shall be assertable subsequent to the conclusion of the action at any time and in any manner permitted by law, notwithstanding the judgment granted in this action, recognizing however the finality of this judgment as to the consequences, with respect to land boundaries as applicable to land in the disaster area. **Leg.H.** Added Stats 1972 ch 936 §2.

§751.57. Notice of pendency of action

A party to an action authorized by this chapter may file a notice of the pendency of the action in the form and at the place and with the effects specified by law. **Leg.H.** Added Stats 1972 ch 936 §2.

§751.58. Vacation of public ways on offer by governmental agency and acceptance by court

The vacating of streets, highways, or other public ways within or abutting the area affected by the disaster, in whole or in part, by the voluntary action of the governmental agency under whose jurisdiction the streets, highways, or ways are vested, for the purpose of making it possible for the court to mitigate the hardships suffered by entities because of the change in land boundaries caused by the disaster can be accomplished by the affected governmental agency expressing the offer in the proceedings followed by the court's acceptance thereof in an action authorized by this chapter, without complying with any other formalities of law. **Leg.H.** Added Stats 1972 ch 936 §2.

§751.59. Prohibited judgment by default

In an action of the type authorized by this chapter, judgment shall not be given by default, but the court must require proof of the facts alleged in the complaint and other pleadings. **Leg.H.** Added Stats 1972 ch 936 §2.

§751.60. Determinations by judgment; Filing official map

The judgment shall:

(a) Determine the land boundaries of each parcel of land located within the entire area of real property sought to be affected by the action, whether owned publicly or privately, as fixed by the disaster, except as these boundaries have been judicially and equitably readjusted and as liberalized by judicial equitable allocation of lands voluntarily vacated by a city, county or the state under this act.

(b) Determine the entity or entities having estates, rights, titles, interests and claims in and to each parcel, whether legal or equitable, present or future, vested or contingent, or whether they consist of mortgages or liens of any description.

(c) Approve and direct the proper filing of an official map covering the entire area of real property sought to be affected by the action, as a substitute for the plat maps previously filed, but rendered inaccurate by the disaster. **Leg.H.** Added Stats 1972 ch 936 §2.

§751.61. Court's considerations in reaching conclusions

In reaching the conclusions called for by Section 751.60, the court shall give effect to the changes in land boundaries caused by the disaster, mitigated, however, so far as can equitably be done by adjustment of land boundaries and by allocating to contiguous lots parts of the land released by a city, county or the state by its voluntary vacation of areas formerly constituting public ways, which vacatings of streets shall be approved by the judgment. **Leg.H.** Added Stats 1972 ch 936 §2.

§751.62. Conclusiveness of judgment

The judgment shall be conclusive with respect to land boundaries upon every entity who at the commencement of the action had or claimed an estate, right, title or interest in or to or lien upon a part of the entire area of real property described in the complaint as intended to be affected by the action, and upon every entity claiming under any such person by title subsequent to the commencement of the action. **Leg.H.** Added Stats 1972 ch 936 §2.

§751.63. Recording copy of judgment; Notice therefrom

A certified copy of the judgment shall be recorded, at the expense of the plaintiff or plaintiffs in the action, in the office of the recorder of the county in which the affected land is situated and shall constitute constructive notice of the findings therein and of the official plat or plats referred to therein, which findings and plats shall supersede and control all prior plats, maps and documents to the extent inconsistent therewith. **Leg.H.** Added Stats 1972 ch 936 §2.

§751.64. Cumulative remedies

The remedies provided for by this chapter are cumulative and in addition to any other remedy provided by law for quieting or establishing title to real property or the boundaries of it. **Leg.H.** Added Stats 1972 ch 936 §2.

§751.65. Citation of chapter

This chapter may be cited as the Cullen Earthquake Act. **Leg.H.** Added Stats 1972 ch 936 §2.

§752. [Section repealed 1977]

Leg.H. Enacted 1872. Amended Stats 1919 ch 216 §1; Stats 1927 ch 755 §1; Stats 1943 ch 892 §1. Repealed Stats 1976 ch 73 §4. See CCP §§872.210, 872.810, 872.820.

§752a. [Section repealed 1977]

Leg.H. Added Stats 1919 ch 49 §1. Repealed Stats 1976 ch 73 §4. See CCP §§872.020, 872.240, 872.810, 872.820.

§752b. [Section repealed 1977]

Leg.H. Added Stats 1963 ch 860 §2. Repealed Stats 1976 ch 73 §4. The repealed section related to partition action by owners of condominium.

§753. [Section repealed 1977]

Leg.H. Enacted 1872. Amended Stats 1907 ch 329 §1; Stats 1959 ch 741 §1. Repealed Stats 1976 ch 73 §4. See CCP §§872.230, 872.520.

§753.1. [Section repealed 1977]

Leg.H. Added Stats 1959 ch 741 §2. Repealed Stats 1976 ch 73 §4. See CCP §872.540.

§754. [Section repealed 1977]

Leg.H. Enacted 1872. Repealed Stats 1976 ch 73 §4. See CCP §872.510.

§755. [Section repealed 1977]

Leg.H. Enacted 1872. Amended Code Amdts 1873–74 ch 383 §98; Code Amdts 1880 ch 22 §2. Repealed Stats 1976 ch 73 §4. See CCP §§872.110, 872.250.

§756. [Section repealed 1977]

Leg.H. Enacted 1872. Amended Stats 1907 ch 329 §2. Repealed Stats 1976 ch 73 §4. See CCP §872.310, 872.520.

§757. [Section repealed 1977]

Leg.H. Enacted 1872. Amended Stats 1939 ch 516 §1; Stats 1943 ch 892 §2; Stats 1969 ch 1611 §11, operative July 1, 1970. Repealed Stats 1976 ch 73 §4. See CCP §§872.310, 872.320.

§758. [Section repealed 1977]

Leg.H. Enacted 1872. Amended Stats 1907 ch 329 §3. Repealed Stats 1976 ch 73 §4. See CCP §§872.410, 872.420.

§759. [Section repealed 1977]

Leg.H. Enacted 1872. Amended Stats 1907 ch 329 §4. Repealed Stats 1976 ch 73 §4. See CCP §§872.610, 872.620, 872.640.

§760. [Section repealed 1977]

Leg.H. Enacted 1872. Repealed Stats 1976 ch 73 §4. The repealed section related to partial partition.

CHAPTER 4
QUIET TITLE

Article 1. General Provisions.
Article 2. Commencement of Action.
Article 3. Defendants.
Article 4. Service of Process.
Article 5. Judgment.
Article 6. Liens and Encumbrances.

ARTICLE 1
General Provisions

Definitions. §760.010.
Authorization of action. §760.020.

Availability of other remedy. §760.030.
Jurisdiction. §760.040.
Venue. §760.050.
Procedure. §760.060.

§760.010. Definitions

As used in this chapter:

(a) "Claim" includes a legal or equitable right, title, estate, lien, or interest in property or cloud upon title.

(b) "Property" includes real property, and to the extent applicable, personal property. **Leg.H.** Added Stats 1980 ch 44 §15.

§760.020. Authorization of action

(a) An action may be brought under this chapter to establish title against adverse claims to real or personal property or any interest therein.

(b) An action may be brought under this chapter by parties to an agreement entered into pursuant to Section 6307 or 6357 of the Public Resources Code to confirm the validity of the agreement.

(c) Nothing in this section shall be construed to limit the right of members of the public to bring or participate in actions challenging the validity of agreements entered into pursuant to Section 6307 or 6357 of the Public Resources Code. **Leg.H.** Added Stats 1980 ch 44 §15. Amended Stats 1989 ch 1045 §1.

§760.030. Availability of other remedy

(a) The remedy provided in this chapter is cumulative and not exclusive of any other remedy, form or right of action, or proceeding provided by law for establishing or quieting title to property.

(b) In an action or proceeding in which establishing or quieting title to property is in issue the court in its discretion may, upon motion of any party, require that the issue be resolved pursuant to the provisions of this chapter to the extent practicable. **Leg.H.** Added Stats 1980 ch 44 §15.

§760.040. Jurisdiction

(a) The superior court has jurisdiction of actions under this chapter.

(b) The court has complete jurisdiction over the parties to the action and the property described in the complaint and is deemed to have obtained possession and control of the property for the purposes of the action with complete jurisdiction to render the judgment provided for in this chapter.

(c) Nothing in this chapter limits any authority the court may have to grant such equitable relief as may be proper under the circumstances of the case. **Leg.H.** Added Stats 1980 ch 44 §15.

§760.050. Venue

Subject to the power of the court to transfer actions, the proper county for the trial of an action under this chapter is:

(a) Where the subject of the action is real property or real and personal property, the county in which the real property, or some part thereof, is located.

(b) Where the subject of the action is personal property, the county in which the personal property is principally located at the commencement of the action or in which the defendants, or any of them, reside at the commencement of the action. **Leg.H.** Added Stats 1980 ch 44 §15.

§760.060. Procedure

The statutes and rules governing practice in civil actions generally apply to actions under this chapter except where they are inconsistent with the provisions of this chapter. **Leg.H.** Added Stats 1980 ch 44 §15.

§761. [Section repealed 1977]

Leg.H. Enacted 1872. Amended Stats 1907 ch 329 §5. Repealed Stats 1976 ch 73 §4. See CCP §872.630.

ARTICLE 2
Commencement of Action

Complaint; Lis pendens. §761.010.
Contents of complaint. §761.020.
Answer. §761.030.
Cross-complaint. §761.040.

§761.010. Complaint; Lis pendens

(a) An action under this chapter is commenced by filing a complaint with the court.

(b) Immediately upon commencement of the action, the plaintiff shall file a notice of the pendency of the action in the office of the county recorder of each county in which any real property described in the complaint is located. **Leg.H.** Added Stats 1980 ch 44 §15.

§761.020. Contents of complaint

The complaint shall be verified and shall include all of the following:

(a) A description of the property that is the subject of the action. In the case of tangible personal property, the description shall include its usual location. In the case of real property, the description shall include both its legal description and its street address or common designation, if any.

(b) The title of the plaintiff as to which a determination under this chapter is sought and the basis of the title. If the title is based upon adverse possession, the complaint shall allege the specific facts constituting the adverse possession.

(c) The adverse claims to the title of the plaintiff against which a determination is sought.

(d) The date as of which the determination is sought. If the determination is sought as of a date other than the date the complaint is filed, the complaint shall include a statement of the reasons why a determination as of that date is sought.

(e) A prayer for the determination of the title of the plaintiff against the adverse claims. **Leg.H.** Added Stats 1980 ch 44 §15.

§761.030. Answer

(a) The answer shall be verified and shall set forth:

(1) Any claim the defendant has.

(2) Any facts tending to controvert such material allegations of the complaint as the defendant does not wish to be taken as true.

(3) A statement of any new matter constituting a defense.

(b) If the defendant disclaims in the answer any claim, or suffers judgment to be taken without answer, the plaintiff shall not recover costs. **Leg.H.** Added Stats 1980 ch 44 §15.

§761.040. Cross-complaint

(a) The defendant may by cross-complaint seek affirmative relief in the action.

(b) If the defendant seeks a determination of title as of a date other than the date specified in the complaint, the cross-complaint shall include the date and a statement of the reasons why a determination as of that date is sought. **Leg.H.** Added Stats 1980 ch 44 §15.

§762. [Section repealed 1977]

Leg.H. Enacted 1872. Amended Stats 1969 ch 1611 §12, operative July 1, 1970. Repealed Stats 1976 ch 73 §4. See CCP §872.630.

ARTICLE 3
Defendants

Known persons. §762.010.
Unknown persons or claims. §762.020.
Decedents. §762.030.
Pretrial orders; Joinder; Title report. §762.040.
Appearance. §762.050.
Designations in complaint. §762.060.
Rights of unknown defendants. §762.070.
Guardians ad litem. §762.080.
Joinder of state. §762.090.

§762.010. Known persons

The plaintiff shall name as defendants in the action the persons having adverse claims to the title of the plaintiff against which a determination is sought. **Leg.H.** Added Stats 1980 ch 44 §15.

§762.020. Unknown persons or claims

(a) If the name of a person required to be named as a defendant is not known to the plaintiff, the plaintiff shall so state in the complaint and shall name as parties all persons unknown in the manner provided in Section 762.060.

(b) If the claim or the share or quantity of the claim of a person required to be named as a defendant is unknown, uncertain, or contingent, the plaintiff shall so state in the complaint. If the lack of knowledge, uncertainty, or contingency is caused by a transfer to an unborn or unascertained beneficiary or class member, or by a transfer in the form of a contingent remainder, vested remainder subject to defeasance, executory interest, or similar disposition, the plaintiff shall also state in the complaint, so far as is known to the plaintiff, the name, age, and legal disability (if any) of the person in being who would be entitled to the claim had the contingency upon which the claim depends occurred prior to the commencement of the action. **Leg.H.** Added Stats 1980 ch 44 §15. Amended Stats 2023 ch 260 §7 (SB 345), effective January 1, 2024.

§762.030. Decedents

(a) If a person required to be named as a defendant is dead and the plaintiff knows of a personal representative, the plaintiff shall join the personal representative as a defendant.

(b) If a person required to be named as a defendant is dead, or is believed by the plaintiff to be dead, and the plaintiff knows of no personal representative:

(1) The plaintiff shall state these facts in an affidavit filed with the complaint.

(2) Where it is stated in the affidavit that such person is dead, the plaintiff may join as defendants "the testate and intestate successors of _____ (naming the deceased person), deceased, and all persons claiming by, through, or under such decedent," naming them in that manner.

(3) Where it is stated in the affidavit that such person is believed to be dead, the plaintiff may join the person as a defendant, and may also join "the testate and intestate successors of _____ (naming the person) believed to be deceased, and all persons claiming by, through, or under such person," naming them in that manner. **Leg.H.** Added Stats 1980 ch 44 §15.

§762.040. Pretrial orders; Joinder; Title report

The court upon its own motion may, and upon motion of any party shall, make such orders as appear appropriate:

(a) For joinder of such additional parties as are necessary or proper.

(b) Requiring the plaintiff to procure a title report and designate a place where it shall be kept for inspection, use, and copying by the parties. **Leg.H.** Added Stats 1980 ch 44 §15.

§762.050. Appearance

Any person who has a claim to the property described in the complaint may appear in the proceeding. Whether or not the person is named as a defendant in the complaint, the person shall appear as a defendant. **Leg.H.** Added Stats 1980 ch 44 §15.

§762.060. Designations in complaint

(a) In addition to the persons required to be named as defendants in the action, the plaintiff may name as defendants "all persons unknown, claiming any legal or equitable right, title, estate, lien, or interest in the property described in the complaint adverse to plaintiff's title, or any cloud upon plaintiff's title thereto," naming them in that manner.

(b) In an action under this section, the plaintiff shall name as defendants the persons having adverse claims that are of record or known to the plaintiff or reasonably apparent from an inspection of the property.

(c) If the plaintiff admits the validity of any adverse claim, the complaint shall so state. **Leg.H.** Added Stats 1980 ch 44 §15.

§762.070. Rights of unknown defendants

A person named and served as an unknown defendant has the same rights as are provided by law in cases of all other defendants named and served, and the action shall proceed against unknown defendants in the same manner as against other defendants named and served, and with the same effect. **Leg.H.** Added Stats 1980 ch 44 §15.

§762.080. Guardians ad litem

The court upon its own motion may, and upon motion of any party shall, make such orders for appointment of guardians ad litem as appear necessary to protect the interest of any party. **Leg.H.** Added Stats 1980 ch 44 §15.

§762.090. Joinder of state

(a) The state may be joined as a party to an action under this chapter.

(b) This section does not constitute a change in, but is declaratory of, existing law. **Leg.H.** Added Stats 1980 ch 44 §15.

§763. [Section repealed 1977]

Leg.H. Enacted 1872. Amended Code Amdts 1880 ch 55 §1; Stats 1907 ch 329 §6; Stats 1913 ch 154 §1; Stats 1927 ch 756 §1; Stats 1931 ch 717 §1; Stats 1943 ch 892 §3; Stats 1955 ch 1501 §1; Stats 1965 ch 1687 §1. Repealed Stats 1976 ch 73 §4. See CCP §§872.710, 872.720, 872.810, 872.820, 872.840, 873.010, 873.030, 873.040, 873.050, 873.270.

ARTICLE 4
Service of Process

Manner of service; Order for publication. §763.010.
Conditions of order for publication. §763.020.
Contents of publication; Conclusiveness of judgment. §763.030.
Pre-hearing requirements. §763.040.

§763.010. Manner of service; Order for publication

(a) The form, content, and manner of the service of summons shall be the same as in civil actions generally.

(b) If upon affidavit it appears to the satisfaction of the court that the plaintiff has used reasonable diligence to ascertain the identity and residence of and to serve summons on the persons named as unknown defendants and persons joined as testate or intestate successors of a person known or believed to be dead, the court shall order service by publication pursuant to Section 415.50 and the provisions of this article. The court may, in its discretion, appoint a referee to investigate whether the plaintiff has used reasonable diligence to ascertain the identity and residence of persons sought to be served by publication, and the court may rely on the report of the referee instead of the affidavit of the plaintiff in making the order for service by publication.

(c) Nothing in this section authorizes service by publication upon any person named as an unknown defendant who is in open and actual possession of the property. **Leg.H.** Added Stats 1980 ch 44 §15.

§763.020. Conditions of order for publication

Whenever the court orders service by publication, the order is subject to the following conditions:

(a) The plaintiff shall post, not later than 10 days after the date the order is made, a copy of the summons and complaint in a conspicuous place on the real property that is the subject of the action.

(b) The plaintiff shall record, if not already recorded, a notice of the pendency of the action.

(c) The publication shall describe the property that is the subject of the action. In addition to particularly describing the property, the publication shall describe the property by giving its street address, if any, or other common designation, if any; but, if a legal description of the property is given, the validity of the publication shall not be affected by the fact that the street address or other common designation recited is erroneous or that the street address or other common designation is omitted. **Leg.H.** Added Stats 1980 ch 44 §15.

§763.030. Contents of publication; Conclusiveness of judgment

(a) Whenever the court orders service by publication, the publication may:

(1) Name only the defendants to be served thereby.

(2) Describe only the property in which the defendants to be served thereby claim interests.

(b) Judgment against a defendant who fails to appear and answer following service under this section shall be conclusive against the defendant named in respect only to property described in the publication. **Leg.H.** Added Stats 1980 ch 44 §15.

§763.040. Pre-hearing requirements

Whenever the court orders service by publication, the court before hearing the case shall require proof that the summons has been served, posted, published as required, and that the notice of pendency of action has been filed. **Leg.H.** Added Stats 1980 ch 44 §15.

§764. [Section repealed 1977]

Leg.H. Enacted 1872. Amended Code Amdts 1873–74 ch 383 §99; Code Amdts 1875–76 ch 513 §1; Stats 1907 ch 329 §7. Repealed Stats 1976 ch 73 §4. See CCP §§873.080, 873.110, 873.130, 873.210, 873.220, 873.230.

ARTICLE 5
Judgment

Hearing. §764.010.
Validity or interpretation of wills. §764.020.
Conclusiveness; Parties; Unrecorded claims. §764.030.
Claims not affected by judgment. §764.045.
Conclusiveness; third parties. §764.060.
Conclusiveness; State and federal government. §764.070.
Action for confirmation of agreement regarding boundary of tidelands. §764.080.

§764.010. Hearing

The court shall examine into and determine the plaintiff's title against the claims of all the defendants. The court shall not enter judgment by default but shall in all cases require evidence of plaintiff's title and hear such evidence as may be offered respecting the claims of any of the defendants, other than claims the validity of which is admitted by the plaintiff in the complaint. The court shall render judgment in accordance with the evidence and the law. **Leg.H.** Added Stats 1980 ch 44 §15.

§764.020. Validity or interpretation of wills

(a) If in an action under this chapter the validity or interpretation of a gift, devise, bequest, or trust, under a will or instrument purporting to be a will, whether admitted to probate or not, is involved:

(1) The will or instrument purporting to be a will is admissible in evidence.

(2) All questions concerning the validity of the gift, devise, bequest, or trust shall be finally determined in the action.

(3) If the will has been admitted to probate and the gift, devise, bequest, or trust has been interpreted by a final decree of the probate court, the interpretation is conclusive as to the proper construction thereof.

(b) Nothing in this section deprives a party of the right to a jury trial in any case where, by law, the right is now given. **Leg.H.** Added Stats 1980 ch 44 §15.

§764.030. Conclusiveness; Parties; Unrecorded claims

The judgment in the action is binding and conclusive on all of the following persons, regardless of any legal disability:

(a) All persons known and unknown who were parties to the action and who have any claim to the property, whether present or future, vested or contingent, legal or equitable, several or undivided.

(b) Except as provided in Section 764.045, all persons who were not parties to the action and who have any claim to the property which was not of record at the time the lis pendens was filed or, if none was filed, at the time the judgment was recorded. **Leg.H.** Added Stats 1980 ch 44 §15. Amended Stats 1984 ch 20 §1.

§764.040. [Section repealed 1985]

Leg.H. Added Stats 1980 ch 44 §15. Repealed Stats 1984 ch 20 §2. See CCP §764.045.

§764.045. Claims not affected by judgment

Except to the extent provided in Section 1908, the judgment does not affect a claim in the property or part thereof of any person who was not a party to the action if any of the following conditions is satisfied:

(a) The claim was of record at the time the lis pendens was filed or, if none was filed, at the time the judgment was recorded.

(b) The claim was actually known to the plaintiff or would have been reasonably apparent from an inspection of the property at the time the lis pendens was filed or, if none was filed, at the time the judgment was entered. Nothing in this subdivision shall be construed to impair the rights of a bona fide purchaser or encumbrancer for value dealing with the plaintiff or the plaintiff's successors in interest. **Leg.H.** Added Stats 1984 ch 20 §3.

§764.050. [Section repealed 1985]

Leg.H. Added Stats 1980 ch 44 §15. Repealed Stats 1984 ch 20 §4. See CCP §764.045.

§764.060. Conclusiveness; third parties

The relief granted in an action or proceeding directly or collaterally attacking the judgment in the action, whether based on lack of actual notice to a party or otherwise, shall not impair the rights of a purchaser or encumbrancer for value of the property acting in reliance on the judgment without knowledge of any defects or irregularities in the judgment or the proceedings. **Leg.H.** Added Stats 1980 ch 44 §15.

§764.070. Conclusiveness; State and federal government

Notwithstanding any other provision of this chapter, the judgment in the action is not binding or conclusive on the following:

(a) The state, unless individually joined as a party to the action.

(b) The United States, unless the United States is individually joined as a party to the action and federal law authorizes judgment in the action to be binding or conclusive as to its interests. **Leg.H.** Added Stats 1980 ch 44 §15. Amended Stats 1986 ch 271 §2.

§764.080. Action for confirmation of agreement regarding boundary of tidelands

(a) In any action brought to quiet title to land that has been subject to an agreement entered into pursuant to Section 6307 or 6357 of the Public Resources Code, at the time set for trial the court shall, at the request of any party, receive evidence on the nature of the agreement. After receiving that evidence, the court shall render a statement of decision. In the case of an agreement pursuant to Section 6357, the statement of decision shall include a recitation of the underlying facts and a determination whether the agreement meets the criteria of Section 6357 and other law applicable to the validity of boundary line agreements. In the case of an agreement pursuant to Section 6307, the statement of decision shall recite the relevant facts and shall contain a determination whether the requirements of Section 6307 of the Public Resources Code, Sections 3 and 4 of Article 10 of the California Constitution, and other applicable law have been met. If the court finds the agreement to be valid, the judgment in the action shall quiet title in the parties named in the agreement in accordance with the agreement. If the judgment is entered prior to the effective date of the agreement, the judgment shall provide that, upon the effective date, title is quieted in the parties in accordance with the agreements. However, no action may be brought pursuant to this section until the State Lands Commission has approved the agreement following a public hearing. All such actions shall be set on the trial calendar within one year from the filing of a memorandum to set, unless the court extends this time for good cause.

(b) Nothing in this section shall be construed to limit the right of members of the public to bring or participate in actions challenging the validity of agreements entered into pursuant to Section 6307 or 6357 of the Public Resources Code. Any action brought by a member of the public shall be set on the trial calendar within one year from the filing of a memorandum to set, unless the court extends this time for good cause. **Leg.H.** Added Stats 1989 ch 1045 §2.

§765. [Section repealed 1977]

Leg.H. Enacted 1872. Amended Stats 1907 ch 329 §8. Repealed Stats 1976 ch 73 §4. See CCP §§873.280, 873.290.

§766. [Section repealed 1977]

Leg.H. Enacted 1872. Amended Stats 1907 ch 329 §9; Stats 1911 ch 189 §1. Repealed Stats 1976 ch 73 §4. See CCP §§873.290, 873.840, 874.210.

§767. [Section repealed 1977]

Leg.H. Enacted 1872. Repealed Stats 1976 ch 73 §4. See CCP §§873.010, 873.110, 874.010, 874.030.

§768. [Section repealed 1977]

Leg.H. Enacted 1872. Repealed Stats 1976 ch 73 §4. See CCP §§873.010, 873.110, 874.010, 874.030.

§769. [Section repealed 1977]

Leg.H. Enacted 1872. Repealed Stats 1976 ch 73 §4. See CCP §§873.260, 874.120.

§770. [Section repealed 1977]

Leg.H. Enacted 1872. Repealed Stats 1976 ch 73 §4. See CCP §873.830.

ARTICLE 6
Liens and Encumbrances

Prohibition against filing false lawsuit, lien, or encumbrance with intent to harass or hinder public officer or employee; Petition for order striking lien or encumbrance; Hearing. §765.010.
Contents of petition; Affidavit. §765.020.
Order striking or validating lien or encumbrance; Costs and attorney's fees. §765.030.
Penalty for filing or directing filing of harassing lawsuit, lien, or other encumbrance. §765.040.
Exclusions from article's operation. §765.050.
Provision of counsel for public officer or employee. §765.060.

§765.010. Prohibition against filing false lawsuit, lien, or encumbrance with intent to harass or hinder public officer or employee; Petition for order striking lien or encumbrance; Hearing

(a) For purposes of this section:

(1) "Harass" means engage in knowing and willful conduct that serves no legitimate purpose.

(2) "Entity" includes both governmental and private entities.

(b) A person shall not file or record, or direct another to file or record, a lawsuit, lien, or other encumbrance, including a notice of lis pendens, against another person or entity knowing it is false, with the intent to harass the person or entity or to influence or hinder the person in discharging his or her official duties if the person is a public officer or employee.

(c)(1) A person or entity whose property is subject to a lien or encumbrance in violation of this section may petition the superior court of the county in which the person or entity resides or in which the property is located for an order, which may be granted ex parte, directing the lien or other encumbrance claimant to appear at a hearing before the court and show cause why the lien or other encumbrance should not be stricken and other relief provided by this article should not be granted.

(2) The court shall schedule the hearing no earlier than 14 days after the date of the order. The scheduled date of the hearing shall allow adequate time for notice of the hearing. **Leg.H.** Added Stats 2015 ch 208 §2 (AB 1267), effective January 1, 2016.

Former Sections: Former CCP §765.010, similar to the present section, was added Stats 1998 ch 779 §2 and repealed Stats 2015 ch 208 §1.

Prior Law: Former CCP §765.010, similar to the present section, was added Stats 1998 ch 779 §2 and repealed Stats 2015 ch 208 §1, effective January 1, 2016.

§765.020. Contents of petition; Affidavit

A petition under this article shall state the grounds upon which relief is requested, and shall be supported by the affidavit of the petitioner or the petitioner's attorney setting forth a concise statement of the facts upon which the motion is based.

The petition and affidavit shall be in substantially the form prescribed by the Judicial Council. **Leg.H.** Added Stats 1998 ch 779 §2 (SB 1759).

§765.030. Order striking or validating lien or encumbrance; Costs and attorney's fees

If the court determines that the lien or other encumbrance is in violation of Section 765.010, the court shall issue an order striking and releasing the lien or other encumbrance and may award costs and reasonable attorney's fees to the petitioner to be paid by the lien or other encumbrance claimant. If the court determines that the lien or other encumbrance is valid, the court shall issue an order so stating and may award costs and reasonable attorney's fees to the encumbrance claimant to be paid by the petitioner. The court may direct that an order issued pursuant to this section be recorded. **Leg.H.** Added Stats 1998 ch 779 §2 (SB 1759) Amended Stats 2015 ch 208 §3 (AB 1267), effective January 1, 2016; Stats 2016 ch 86 §25 (SB 1171), effective January 1, 2017.

§765.040. Penalty for filing or directing filing of harassing lawsuit, lien, or other encumbrance

Any lien or encumbrance claimant who records or files, or directs another to record or file, a lawsuit, lien, or other encumbrance in violation of Section 765.010 shall be liable to the person subject to the lawsuit or the owner of the property bound by the lien or other encumbrance for a civil penalty of up to five thousand dollars ($5,000). **Leg.H.** Added Stats 1998 ch 779 §2 (SB 1759). Amended Stats 2015 ch 208 §4 (AB 1267), effective January 1, 2016.

§765.050. Exclusions from article's operation

This article does not apply to a document which acts as a claim of encumbrance by a financial institution, as defined in subdivision (a) of Section 14161 of the Penal Code or Section 481.113 of this code, or a public entity, as defined in Section 481.200 of this code. **Leg.H.** Added Stats 1998 ch 779 §2 (SB 1759).

§765.060. Provision of counsel for public officer or employee

If a lien or other encumbrance is recorded or filed against a public officer or employee in violation of Section 765.010, the state or local agency that employs the public officer or employee may provide counsel for the public officer or employee in an action brought pursuant to that section. **Leg.H.** Added Stats 1998 ch 779 §2 (SB 1759). Amended Stats 2015 ch 208 §5 (AB 1267), effective January 1, 2016.

CHAPTER 4.5
SPECIAL ACTIONS AND PROCEEDINGS TO CLEAR TITLE

Article 1. Identity of Person in Chain of Title.
Article 2. Land Dedicated for Public Improvement.
Article 3. Right of Entry or Occupation of Surface Lands Under Oil or Gas Lease.

ARTICLE 1
Identity of Person in Chain of Title

Definitions. §770.010.
Proceeding to determine identity. §770.020.
Jurisdiction of proceeding. §770.030.
Parties to proceeding. §770.040.
Petition to determine identity. §770.050.
Notice of petition. §770.060.
Hearing on petition; Decree; Appeal. §770.070.
Effect of final decree of identity. §770.080.

§770.010. Definitions

As used in this article:

(a) "Acquired" means received or taken by conveyance, judgment, decree, or otherwise.

(b) "Property" means any right, title, or interest in or lien upon real property or part thereof.

(c) "Subsequent owner" means the person to whom property is transferred whether as owner, part owner, or otherwise, or the successors in interest of the person, and includes a distributee of the estate of a decedent.

(d) "Transfer" means voluntary or involuntary transfer and includes a conveyance, reconveyance, satisfaction of a lien, or divestment by judgment, decree, or otherwise. The probate of the estate of a decedent and entry of the decree of distribution is a transfer within the meaning of this subdivision. **Leg.H.** Added Stats 1980 ch 44 §16.

§770.020. Proceeding to determine identity

If property is acquired or stands of record in the name of a person who heretofore or hereafter transfers the property under a name other than or different from the name in which the property is acquired or stands of record, a proceeding is authorized to adjudicate and determine the identity of the person in whose name the property is acquired or stands of record and the person who transfers the property. **Leg.H.** Added Stats 1980 ch 44 §16.

§770.030. Jurisdiction of proceeding

The proceeding shall be brought in the superior court of the county in which the property or any part thereof is situated. **Leg.H.** Added Stats 1980 ch 44 §16.

§770.040. Parties to proceeding

(a) The proceeding may be brought by a subsequent owner of the property by filing a petition with the court.

(b) At any time before the date fixed for the hearing of the petition, any person interested in the property may answer the petition and deny any of the matters contained therein. **Leg.H.** Added Stats 1980 ch 44 §16.

§770.050. Petition to determine identity

(a) The petition shall be verified in the manner provided for verification of a complaint.

(b) The petition may be substantially entitled, "In the matter of the determination of the identity of ____" (naming all the persons sought to be identified), and may set forth:

(1) A statement of petitioner's interest in the property as subsequent owner.

(2) A particular description of the property.

(3) The name or names of the person or persons sought to be identified, setting out the name and a reference to the record of the transaction under which the property was acquired or stands of record and the name and a reference to the record of the transaction under which the property was transferred or stands of record, that the names are the names of the same person, and that the transfers affect the petitioner's title to the real property.

(4) A prayer that the identity of such persons be established.

(c) As many persons sought to be identified as appear of record in the chain of title to the property may be joined in one petition or proceeding. **Leg.H.** Added Stats 1980 ch 44 §16.

§770.060. Notice of petition

(a) Upon the filing of the petition, the clerk shall set the petition for hearing by the court.

(b) The petitioner shall give notice of the hearing by causing notices of the time and place of hearing to be posted at the courthouse of the county where the proceeding is pending and in a conspicuous place on the real property described in the petition, at least 10 days before the hearing.

(c) The special notice shall be substantially in the following form:

(Title of court and cause)

Notice is hereby given that ____ has filed a petition herein claiming to be the owner (or distributee) of the following described lands ____ (description) and praying that the identity of the following-named persons, in former conveyances (or judgments or decrees) to said lands or in decrees of distribution of said lands in probate be determined, to wit: ____ (names as J. Doe and John Doe); and that the time and place of hearing said petition has been set for ____ the ____ day of ____, 19____, at the hour of ____, ____ m. of said day at the courtroom of said court in the City of ____, County of ____, State of California.

_____

Clerk

Leg.H. Added Stats 1980 ch 44 §16.

§770.070. Hearing on petition; Decree; Appeal

(a) At the time fixed for the hearing or such time thereafter as may be fixed by the court, the court shall hear the proofs offered by the petitioner and by any persons answering the petition, and shall make and enter a decree determining the identity of the person or persons set out in the petition in accordance with the proofs.

(b) An appeal may be taken by any party aggrieved. **Leg.H.** Added Stats 1980 ch 44 §16.

§770.080. Effect of final decree of identity

(a) After the decree has become final it constitutes prima facie evidence of the matters thereby determined and it is presumed that the identity of the person or persons described in the decree is such as is stated in the decree.

(b) A certified copy of the decree shall be recorded in the office of the county recorder of every county in which any part of the property is situated. **Leg.H.** Added Stats 1980 ch 44 §16.

§771. [Section repealed 1977]

Leg.H. Enacted 1872. Amended Stats 1943 ch 892 §4. Repealed Stats 1976 ch 73 §4. See CCP §873.820.

ARTICLE 2
Land Dedicated for Public Improvement

Presumptions. §771.010.
Actions to clear title. §771.020.

§771.010. Presumptions

If a proposal is heretofore or hereafter made to dedicate real property for public improvement, there is a conclusive presumption that the proposed dedication was not accepted if all of the following conditions are satisfied:

(a) The proposal was made by filing a map only.

(b) No acceptance of the dedication was made and recorded within 25 years after the map was filed.

(c) The real property was not used for the purpose for which the dedication was proposed within 25 years after the map was filed.

(d) The real property was sold to a third person after the map was filed and used as if free of the dedication. **Leg.H.** Added Stats 1980 ch 44 §16.

§771.020. Actions to clear title

(a) An action is authorized to clear title to real property of a proposal to dedicate the property for public improvement if there is a conclusive presumption pursuant to Section 771.010 that the proposed dedication was not accepted.

(b) The action shall be pursuant to Chapter 4 (commencing with Section 760.010) and shall have the following features:

(1) The public entity to which the dedication was proposed shall be named as defendant.

(2) The judgment in the action shall clear the title of the proposed dedication and remove the cloud created by the proposed dedication. **Leg.H.** Added Stats 1980 ch 44 §16.

§772. [Section repealed 1977]

Leg.H. Enacted 1872. Repealed Stats 1976 ch 73 §4. The repealed section related to party holding other securities.

ARTICLE 3
Right of Entry or Occupation of Surface Lands Under Oil or Gas Lease

Application. §772.010.
Definitions. §772.020.
Action to terminate right of entry. §772.030.
Evidence supporting termination. §772.040.
Judgment of termination of rights; Conditions. §772.050.
Declaration of public policy. §772.060.

§772.010. Application

This article applies only to lands within a city in any county with a population exceeding 4,000,000, or with a population of more than 700,000 and less than 710,000 as determined by the 1960 Federal Decennial Census. **Leg.H.** Added Stats 1980 ch 44 §16.

§772.020. Definitions

As used in this article:

(a) "Surface zone" means the zone which lies above a plane which is 500 feet below the surface of the land.

(b) "Subject land" means that area occupied by the particular described surface and surface zone for which plaintiff seeks to terminate the leasehold right of entry and occupation.

(c) "Lease facilities" means storage tanks, wash tanks, separators, heaters, and other facilities reasonably necessary for the production of oil or gas, including secondary recovery operations. **Leg.H.** Added Stats 1980 ch 44 §16.

§772.030. Action to terminate right of entry

(a) If a mining rights lease, including a community lease, exists for the production of oil, gas, or other hydrocarbons, and a right of entry or occupation provided by the lease encumbers all or part of the surface or surface zone of the leasehold lands, any person who owns a fee interest in the surface of the leasehold lands may bring an action in the superior court to terminate the right of entry or occupation as to all or some described portion of the surface and surface zone of the leasehold lands in which the person owns an interest.

(b) No judgment rendered pursuant to this article shall change or affect the terms or operation of any valid unit agreement or valid operating agreement which comes within the provisions of Section 3301 or 3321 of the Public Resources Code. **Leg.H.** Added Stats 1980 ch 44 §16.

§772.040. Evidence supporting termination

The court may render a judgment terminating the lessee's right of entry or occupation of the surface and surface zone, subject to such conditions as the court deems fair and equitable, if the evidence shows each of the following:

(a) The document that created the leasehold interest was originally executed more than 20 years prior to filing the action under this article regardless of any amendments to the document. However, if any amendment was entered into expressly for the purpose of waiving, limiting, or rearranging surface rights of entry and occupation by the lessee, the 20-year period shall be computed as if the document were originally executed on the date of execution of the amendment.

(b) The subject land is not presently occupied by any of the following:

(1) A producing oil or gas well or well bore.

(2) A well or well bore being utilized for injection of water, gas, or other substance into geologic substrata as an aid to oil or gas production or to ameliorating subsidence.

(3) A well or well bore being utilized for the disposal injection of waste oil well brine and byproducts.

(4) A well or well bore being utilized for the production of water for use in oil field injection, waterflood, and pressure maintenance programs.

(c) Termination of the right of entry or occupation within the subject land in the manner requested by the plaintiff, or subject to such conditions as the court may impose pursuant to this section, will not significantly interfere with the right of the lessee, under the lease, to continue to conduct operations for the continued production of oil from leasehold strata beneath the surface zone in a practical and economic manner, utilizing such production techniques as will be appropriate to the leasehold area, consistent with good oilfield practice, and to gather, transport, and market the oil. **Leg.H.** Added Stats 1980 ch 44 §16.

§772.050. Judgment of termination of rights; Conditions

(a) The court may qualify the judgment terminating the surface and surface zone right of entry or occupation so as to provide for limited surface and surface zone easements that the lessee may continue to enjoy within the subject land.

(b) A judgment may be conditioned upon the relocation of pipelines, roadways, equipment, or lease facilities in such manner as will most effectively free the subject land for surface use while safeguarding continued oil and gas operations in a practical and economic manner. Any such condition of the judgment shall require the plaintiff to pay the costs of the relocation. However, the plaintiff shall be entitled to a setoff against the costs to the extent of any benefit to the lessee resulting from the installation of new equipment or material. The plaintiff has the burden of proving any benefit accruing to the lessee. **Leg.H.** Added Stats 1980 ch 44 §16.

§772.060. Declaration of public policy

It is against public policy for any oil or gas lease, at its inception, to provide for the waiver of any rights created by this article, or for such rights to be waived by amendment to any oil or gas lease within 20 years of the date of its execution by a plaintiff or the plaintiff's predecessor in interest. **Leg.H.** Added Stats 1980 ch 44 §16.

§773. [Section repealed 1977]

Leg.H. Enacted 1872. Repealed Stats 1976 ch 73 §4. See CCP §§873.630, 873.810.

§774. [Section repealed 1977]

Leg.H. Enacted 1872. Amended Stats 1907 ch 329 §10. Repealed Stats 1976 ch 73 §4. See CCP §873.850.

§775. [Section repealed 1977]

Leg.H. Enacted 1872. Amended Stats 1907 ch 329 §11; Stats 1909 ch 666 §1. Repealed Stats 1976 ch 73 §4. See CCP §§873.520, 873.530, 873.640, 873.650, 873.680.

§776. [Section repealed 1977]

Leg.H. Enacted 1872. Repealed Stats 1976 ch 73 §4. See CCP §873.630.

§777. [Section repealed 1977]

Leg.H. Enacted 1872. Repealed Stats 1976 ch 73 §4. See CCP §873.750.

§778. [Section repealed 1977]

Leg.H. Enacted 1872. Repealed Stats 1976 ch 73 §4. See CCP §873.840.

§779. [Section repealed 1977]

Leg.H. Enacted 1872. Repealed Stats 1976 ch 73 §4. See CCP §873.840.

§780. [Section repealed 1977]

Leg.H. Enacted 1872. Repealed Stats 1976 ch 73 §4. See CCP §§873.810, 873.840.

§781. [Section repealed 1977]

Leg.H. Enacted 1872. Amended Stats 1927 ch 757 §1. Repealed Stats 1976 ch 73 §4. See CCP §873.840.

§782. [Section repealed 1977]

Leg.H. Enacted 1872. Repealed Stats 1976 ch 73 §4. See CCP §§873.620, 873.650.

§783. [Section repealed 1977]

Leg.H. Enacted 1872. Repealed Stats 1976 ch 73 §4. See CCP §873.690.

§784. [Section repealed 1977]

Leg.H. Enacted 1872. Amended Stats 1907 ch 329 §12; Stats 1909 ch 667 §1; Stats 1955 ch 1501 §2; Stats 1959 ch 1320 §1. Repealed Stats 1976 ch 73 §4. See CCP §§873.640, 873.710, 873.720, 873.730, 873.740.

§785. [Section repealed 1977]

Leg.H. Enacted 1872. Amended Stats 1907 ch 329 §13. Repealed Stats 1976 ch 73 §4. See CCP §§873.750, 873.760.

§786. [Section repealed 1977]

Leg.H. Enacted 1872. Repealed Stats 1976 ch 73 §4. See CCP §873.770.

§787. [Section repealed 1977]

Leg.H. Enacted 1872. Amended Code Amdts 1873–74 ch 383 §100. Repealed Stats 1976 ch 73 §4. See CCP §§873.790, 874.210, 874.225, 874.240.

§788. [Section repealed 1977]

Leg.H. Enacted 1872. Repealed Stats 1976 ch 73 §4. See CCP §873.810.

§789. [Section repealed 1977]

Leg.H. Enacted 1872. Repealed Stats 1976 ch 73 §4. The repealed section related to investment must be made in the name of the clerk of the county.

§790. [Section repealed 1977]

Leg.H. Enacted 1872. Repealed Stats 1976 ch 73 §4. The repealed section related to when the interests of parties are ascertained, securities must be taken in their names.

§791. [Section repealed 1977]

Leg.H. Enacted 1872. Repealed Stats 1976 ch 73 §4. The repealed section related to duties of the clerk making investments.

§792. [Section repealed 1977]

Leg.H. Enacted 1872. Repealed Stats 1976 ch 73 §4. See CCP §§872.140, 873.250.

§793. [Section repealed 1977]

Leg.H. Enacted 1872. Repealed Stats 1976 ch 73 §4. The repealed section related to the share of an infant may be paid to his guardian.

§794. [Section repealed 1977]

Leg.H. Enacted 1872. Amended Code Amdts 1880 ch 22 §3. Repealed Stats 1976 ch 73 §4. The repealed section related to guardian of insane person or person incapable of conducting his own affairs may receive proceeds of such party's interest.

§795. [Section repealed 1907]

Leg.H. Enacted 1872. Repealed Stats 1907 ch 329 §14. The repealed section related to authority of guardians of infants and insane persons to consent to partition without any action.

§796. [Section repealed 1977]

Leg.H. Enacted 1872. Amended Code Amdts 1873–74 ch 383 §101. Repealed Stats 1976 ch 73 §4. See CCP §§874.010, 874.040, 874.110, 874.120, 874.140.

§797. [Section repealed 1907]

Leg.H. Enacted 1872. Repealed Stats 1907 ch 329 §15. See CCP §763.

§798. [Section repealed 1977]

Leg.H. Enacted 1872. Repealed Code Amdts 1873–74 ch 383 §102. Reenacted and amended Code Amdts 1875–76 ch 48 §1. Repealed Stats 1976 ch 73 §4. See CCP §§874.020, 874.110, 874.140.

§799. [Section repealed 1977]

Leg.H. Enacted 1872. Amended Stats 1907 ch 329 §16; Stats 1949 ch 651 §1. Repealed Stats 1976 ch 73 §4. See CCP §§872.220, 874.010.

§§800, 801. [Sections repealed 1977]

Leg.H. Enacted 1872. Repealed Stats 1976 ch 73 §4. See CCP §874.030.

CHAPTER 4.6
ACTIONS CONCERNING REAL PROPERTY TITLES AFFECTED BY PUBLIC IMPROVEMENT ASSESSMENTS

Actions to determine adverse interests, etc., in real property arising out of public improvement assessments and bonds. §801.1.
Joinder with other causes of action; Allegations and verification of complaint. §801.2.
Defendants designated in complaint; Designation of decedent and heirs and devisees. §801.3.
Unknown persons as defendants. §801.4.
Lis pendens; Filing and contents; Effect. §801.5.
Summons; Issuance and contents. §801.6.
Posting summons on property. §801.7.
Service of defendants. §801.8.
Showing of diligence to ascertain identity and residence of unknown defendants. §801.9.
Rights of unknown defendants; Effect of judgment. §801.10.
Determination of rights of parties; Proof; Presumptions; When conclusive. §801.11.
Decree. §801.12.
Manner of sale or partition of property. §801.13.
Decree as conclusive. §801.14.
Delivery of certified copy of judgment; Cancellation of assessment, bond or certificate of sale. §801.15.

§801.1. Actions to determine adverse interests, etc., in real property arising out of public improvement assessments and bonds

An action may be brought to determine adverse interests in, liens or clouds upon title to real property arising out of any public improvement assessment or any bond issued to represent such assessment where the lien of such assessment or bond is presumed to have been extinguished under the provisions of Section 2911 of the Civil Code, or to determine adverse interests in, liens or clouds upon title to real property by reason of any certificate issued on sale made to satisfy any public improvement assessment or bond where such sale was made more than four years prior to the commencement of the action and no deed pursuant thereto has been issued prior to the commencement of the action or prior to January 1, 1951, whichever is the later. **Leg.H.** Added Stats 1949 ch 1108 §1.

§801.2. Joinder with other causes of action; Allegations and verification of complaint

The action may be brought as a separate action or joined as a cause with other causes of action to determine adverse claims to and clouds upon title to real property, but the complaint shall aver the pertinent matters stated in the preceding section and shall be verified. **Leg.H.** Added Stats 1949 ch 1108 §2.

§801.3. Defendants designated in complaint; Designation of decedent and heirs and devisees

The complaint shall include as defendants to the action (a) all persons known to the plaintiff owning or claiming an interest under such public improvement assessment, bond or certificate of sale; (b) the payee, as shown by the bond representing the assessment, if any; (c) the owner of the special assessment or certificate of sale, if any, and any person claiming an interest therein, as shown by the records of the treasurer, street superintendent or other public official who is the custodian of the funds to be collected thereon or who issued such certificate of sale, and (d) such treasurer, street superintendent or other public official. If any person owning or claiming an interest under such assessment, bond or certificate of sale is known to be dead, the heirs and devisees of such person may be sued as: "the heirs and devisees of" said person, naming him, or if such person is believed to be dead and such belief is alleged in the complaint on information and belief then the heirs and devisees of such person may also be sued as "the heirs and devisees" of said person, naming him, providing that such person is also named as a defendant. **Leg.H.** Added Stats 1949 ch 1108 §3. Amended Stats 1951 ch 521 §1.

§801.4. Unknown persons as defendants

The complaint shall also include, as defendants, unknown persons owning or claiming an interest in such bond, special assessment or certificate of sale and they may be described in the complaint as: "Also the owner or any person claiming an interest (here describe the bond, special assessment or certificate of sale as it is described in the office in which it was issued)." **Leg.H.** Added Stats 1949 ch 1108 §4.

§801.5. Lis pendens; Filing and contents; Effect

Within ten days after the filing of the complaint, plaintiff shall file or cause to be filed in the office of the recorder of the county where the property is situated, a notice of the pendency of the action, containing the title and object of the action and a description of the property in that county affected thereby. From the time of filing such notice of record only, shall all persons have constructive notice thereof. **Leg.H.** Added Stats 1949 ch 1108 §5.

§801.6. Summons; Issuance and contents

Within three years after the filing of the complaint, a summons shall be issued which shall contain the matters required by Section 412.20, designating the defendants as in the complaint, and in addition, a description of the property and a statement of the object of the action. **Leg.H.** Added Stats 1949 ch 1108 §6. Amended Stats 1969 ch 1611 §13, operative July 1, 1970.

§801.7. Posting summons on property

Within thirty days after the issuance of the summons, the plaintiff shall post, or cause to be posted, a copy thereof in a conspicuous place on the property. **Leg.H.** Added Stats 1949 ch 1108 §7.

§801.8. Service of defendants

All known defendants shall be served in the manner provided by law for the service of a summons in a civil action. All unknown defendants shall be served by publication as provided in Section 750. **Leg.H.** Added Stats 1949 ch 1108 §8. Amended Stats 1969 ch 1611 §14, operative July 1, 1970.

§801.9. Showing of diligence to ascertain identity and residence of unknown defendants

In addition to the matters required to be set forth in the affidavit by the plaintiff for publication of summons, it shall appear by the affidavit that the plaintiff used reasonable diligence to ascertain the identity and residence of the unknown defendants and of any persons sued as heirs and devisees. **Leg.H.** Added Stats 1949 ch 1108 §9. Amended Stats 1951 ch 521 §2; Stats 1969 ch 1611 §15, operative July 1, 1970.

§801.10. Rights of unknown defendants; Effect of judgment

All unknown defendants, including the heirs and devisees designated in the complaint, shall have the same rights as are provided by law for other defendants upon whom summons is served, and the action shall proceed against them in the same manner. Regardless of any legal disability, any unknown defendant, including any heir or devisee designated in the complaint, who has been served, and anyone claiming under him, shall be concluded by a judgment in the action as if the action were brought against and personal service made upon that person by his or her name. **Leg.H.** Added Stats 1949 ch 1108 §10. Amended Stats 1969 ch 1611 §16, operative July 1, 1970.

§801.11. Determination of rights of parties; Proof; Presumptions; When conclusive

On the trial of the action, the court shall determine the rights of all parties thereto and shall require proof of the facts alleged. Any certificate issued on sale made to satisfy any public improvement assessment or any bond issued to represent such assessment shall be presumed to have been paid and redeemed where no deed pursuant thereto has been issued and such sale was made more than four years prior to the commencement of the action.

The presumption herein mentioned shall become and be conclusive if no deed pursuant to such sale is issued within four years after the date of sale or prior to January 1, 1953, whichever is the later; and no public official shall thereafter execute or issue any deed pursuant to such sale. **Leg.H.** Added Stats 1949 ch 1108 §11. Amended Stats 1951 ch 521 §3.

§801.12. Decree

If the court determines that none of the defendants have any right, title, interest, lien or estate in the property, it shall render its final decree quieting the plaintiff's title. If the court determines that any of the defendants have any right, title, interest, lien or estate in the property, it shall render its decree establishing these rights and may order the sale of the property or partition thereof. The decree shall direct the public officer having the record of the assessment, bond or certificate of sale to cancel the record thereof. **Leg.H.** Added Stats 1949 ch 1108 §12.

§801.13. Manner of sale or partition of property

If the court orders a sale of the property or a partition thereof, the same shall be made in accordance with the provisions of Title 10.5 (commencing with Section 872.010) of Part 2, except that proceeds of sale belonging to unknown defendants or defendants whose identities or whereabouts are unascertained shall be paid to the public officer who is the custodian of the funds collected on such public improvement assessments, bonds or certificates of sale, to be held by him as in like instances of collection. **Leg.H.** Added Stats 1949 ch 1108 §13. Amended Stats 1976 ch 73 §5.

§801.14. Decree as conclusive

The decree, after it has become final, is conclusive against all persons named in the complaint who have been served and all unknown persons and the heirs and devisees of deceased persons designated in the complaint and served as hereinbefore provided. **Leg.H.** Added Stats 1949 ch 1108 §14.

§801.15. Delivery of certified copy of judgment; Cancellation of assessment, bond or certificate of sale

After the judgment has become final, a certified copy thereof shall be delivered to the public officer having the record of the assessment, bond or certificate of sale in his office and he shall thereupon mark the record of the assessment, bond or certificate of sale as follows: "Canceled by judgment of court, superior court case number (here give number)." **Leg.H.** Added Stats 1949 ch 1108 §15.

CHAPTER 5
ACTIONS FOR THE USURPATION OF AN OFFICE OR A FRANCHISE

Scire facias abolished. §802.
Action by attorney general against usurper. §803.
Attorney General's statement. §804.
Judgment may determine rights of both incumbent and claimant. §805.
When rendered in favor of applicant. §806.
Damages may be recovered by successful applicant. §807.
Single action against several claimants. §808.
Judgment against guilty defendant. §809.
Action on information; Undertaking. §810.
Action by board of supervisors or municipal legislative body against usurper. §811.

§802. Scire facias abolished
The writ of scire facias is abolished. **Leg.H.** Enacted 1872. Amended Code Amdts 1880 ch 22 §4.

§803. Action by attorney general against usurper
An action may be brought by the attorney general, in the name of the people of this state, upon his own information, or upon a complaint of a private party, against any person who usurps, intrudes into, or unlawfully holds or exercises any public office, civil or military, or any franchise, or against any corporation, either de jure or de facto, which usurps, intrudes into, or unlawfully holds or exercises any franchise, within this state. And the attorney general must bring the action, whenever he has reason to believe that any such office or franchise has been usurped, intruded into, or unlawfully held or exercised by any person, or when he is directed to do so by the governor. **Leg.H.** Enacted 1872. Amended Stats 1907 ch 324 §1.

§804. Attorney General's statement
Whenever such action is brought, the Attorney General, in addition to the statement of the cause of action, may also set forth in the complaint the name of the person rightly entitled to the office, with a statement of his right thereto. **Leg.H.** Enacted 1872. Amended Code Amdts 1880 ch 22 §5; Stats 1973 ch 20 §10.

§805. Judgment may determine rights of both incumbent and claimant
In every such action judgment may be rendered upon the right of the defendant, and also upon the right of the party so alleged to be entitled, or only upon the right of the defendant, as justice may require. **Leg.H.** Enacted 1872.

§806. When rendered in favor of applicant
If the judgment be rendered upon the right of the person so alleged to be entitled, and the same be in favor of such person, he will be entitled, after taking the oath of office and executing such official bond as may be required by law, to take upon himself the execution of the office. **Leg.H.** Enacted 1872.

§807. Damages may be recovered by successful applicant
If judgment be rendered upon the right of the person so alleged to be entitled, in favor of such person, he may recover, by action, the damages which he may have sustained by reason of the usurpation of the office by the defendant. **Leg.H.** Enacted 1872.

§808. Single action against several claimants
When several persons claim to be entitled to the same office or franchise, one action may be brought against all such persons, in order to try their respective rights to such office or franchise. **Leg.H.** Enacted 1872.

§809. Judgment against guilty defendant
When a defendant, against whom such action has been brought, is adjudged guilty of usurping or intruding into, or unlawfully holding any office, franchise, or privilege, judgment must be rendered that such defendant be excluded from the office, franchise, or privilege, and that he pay the costs of the action. The court may also, in its discretion, impose upon the defendant a fine not exceeding five thousand dollars, which fine, when collected, must be paid into the treasury of the state. **Leg.H.** Enacted 1872.

§810. Action on information; Undertaking
If the action is brought upon the information or application of a private party, the Attorney General may require that party to enter into an undertaking, with sureties to be approved by the Attorney General, conditioned on the party or the sureties paying any judgment for costs or damages recovered against the plaintiff, and all the costs and expenses incurred in prosecuting the action. **Leg.H.** Added Code Amdts 1873–74 ch 383 §103. Amended Stats 2017 ch 561 §23 (AB 1516), effective January 1, 2018.

§811. Action by board of supervisors or municipal legislative body against usurper
The action provided for in this chapter may be maintained by the board of supervisors of any county or city and county or the legislative body of any municipal corporation, respectively, in the name of such county, city and county or municipal corporation against any person who usurps, intrudes into or unlawfully holds or exercises any franchise, or portion thereof, within the respective territorial limits of such county, city and county or municipal corporation and which is of a kind that is within the jurisdiction of such board or body to grant or withhold. **Leg.H.** Added Stats 1937 ch 575 §1.

CHAPTER 6
ACTIONS AGAINST STEAMERS, VESSELS, AND BOATS [REPEALED]

§§813, 814. [Sections repealed 1970]
Leg.H. Enacted 1872. Amended Code Amdts 1873–74 ch 383 §§104, 105. Repealed Stats 1970 ch 1341 §2. The repealed sections related to actions against steamers, vessels, and boats.

§815. [Section repealed 1970]
Leg.H. Enacted 1872. Repealed Stats 1970 ch 1341 §2. The repealed section related to actions against steamers, vessels, and boats.

§816. [Section repealed 1970]
Leg.H. Enacted 1872. Amended Code Amdts 1873–74 ch 383 §106; Code Amdts 1880 ch 22 §6. Repealed Stats 1970 ch 1341 §2. The repealed section related to actions against steamers, vessels, and boats.

§§817–823. [Sections repealed 1970]
Leg.H. Enacted 1872. Amended Code Amdts 1873–74 ch 383 §§107–113. Repealed Stats 1970 ch 1341 §2. The repealed sections related to actions against steamers, vessels, and boats.

§824. [Section repealed 1970]
Leg.H. Enacted 1872. Amended Code Amdts 1873–74 ch 383 §114; Stats 1951 ch 42 §1. Repealed Stats 1970 ch 1341 §2. The repealed section related to actions against steamers, vessels, and boats.

§825. [Section repealed 1970]
Leg.H. Enacted 1872. Repealed Stats 1970 ch 1341 §2. The repealed section related to actions against steamers, vessels, and boats.

§826. [Section repealed 1970]
Leg.H. Enacted 1872. Amended Code Amdts 1873–74 ch 383 §115; Code Amdts 1880 ch 22 §7. Repealed Stats 1970 ch 1341 §2. The repealed section related to actions against steamers, vessels, and boats.

§827. [Section repealed 1970]
Leg.H. Enacted 1872. Repealed Stats 1970 ch 1341 §2. The repealed section related to actions against steamers, vessels, and boats.

CHAPTER 7
ACTIONS RELATING TO GROUNDWATER RIGHTS

Article 1. General Provisions.
Article 2. Scope of Action.
Article 3. Notice and Service of Complaint.
Article 4. Intervention.
Article 5. Judge.
Article 6. Electronic service.
Article 7. Case Management.
Article 8. Basin Boundaries.
Article 9. Initial Disclosures.
Article 10. Expert Witnesses.
Article 11. Written Testimony.
Article 12. Special Master.

Article 13. Preliminary Injunction.
Article 14. Stay.
Article 15. Physical Solution.
Article 16. Judgment.
Article 17. Judgment Binding on Successors.
Article 18. Continuing Jurisdiction.

ARTICLE 1
General Provisions

Methods and procedures for comprehensive adjudication. §830.
Waiver of court fees and costs. §831.
Forwarding court documents to groundwater sustainability agency; Posting documents to website. § 831.5.
Definitions. §832.

§830. Methods and procedures for comprehensive adjudication

(a) This chapter establishes methods and procedures for a comprehensive adjudication.

(b) This chapter shall be applied and interpreted consistently with all of the following:

(1) Protecting water rights consistent with Section 2 of Article X of the California Constitution.

(2) Conducting a comprehensive adjudication in a manner that promotes efficiency, reduces unnecessary delays, and provides due process.

(3) Encouraging the compromise and settlement of comprehensive adjudications.

(4) Conducting a comprehensive adjudication in a manner that is consistent with the achievement of groundwater sustainability within the timeframes of the Sustainable Groundwater Management Act.

(5) Establishing procedures by which courts may conduct comprehensive determinations of all rights and priorities to groundwater in a basin.

(6) Providing for the conduct of a comprehensive adjudication consistent with Winters v. United States (1908) 207 U.S. 564, the McCarran Amendment (codified at 43 U.S.C. Sec. 666), and any other federal laws regarding the determination of federal or tribal water rights, as applicable.

(7) Providing notice and due process sufficient to enable a court in a comprehensive adjudication conducted pursuant to this chapter to determine and establish the priority for unexercised water rights. The court may consider applying the principles established in In re Waters of Long Valley Creek Stream System (1979) 25 Cal.3d 339. Except as provided in this paragraph, this chapter shall not alter groundwater rights or the law concerning groundwater rights.

(c) The other provisions of this code apply to procedures in a comprehensive adjudication to the extent they do not conflict with the provisions of this chapter. **Leg.H.** Added Stats 2015 ch 672 §1 (AB 1390), effective January 1, 2016.

Prior Law: Former CCP §830, similar to present CCP § 995.520, was added Stats 1953 ch 52 §6.5 and repealed Stats 1980 ch 114 §1.

§831. Waiver of court fees and costs

Article 6 (commencing with Section 68630) of Chapter 2 of Title 8 of the Government Code applies to a comprehensive adjudication conducted pursuant to this chapter. **Leg.H.** Added Stats 2015 ch 672 §1 (AB 1390), effective January 1, 2016.

Prior Law: Former CCP §831, relating to actions for libel and slander, was added Stats 1953 ch 52 §6.5 and repealed Stats 1980 ch 114 §1. Historical derivation: Stats 1871–72 ch 377 §2.

Former CCP §831, similar to present CCP §§392–396b, 398, was added Stats 1925 ch 436 §1, amended Stats 1927 ch 727 §1, Stats 1929 ch 809 §1, Stats 1931 ch 282 §1, and repealed Stats 1933 ch 744 §198.

§ 831.5. Forwarding court documents to groundwater sustainability agency; Posting documents to website

(a) In an adjudication action for a basin required to have a groundwater sustainability plan under the Sustainable Groundwater Management Act (Part 2.74 (commencing with Section 10720) of Division 6 of the Water Code), the court shall appoint one party to forward all case management orders, judgments, and interlocutory orders to the groundwater sustainability agency within 10 business days of issuance. The groundwater sustainability agency shall post the documents on its internet website in the interest of transparency and accessibility within 20 business days of receipt from a party. This section does not apply to any documents that have been sealed by the court.

(b) For a basin that has multiple groundwater sustainability agencies, the groundwater sustainability agencies, in consultation with the parties to the adjudication, shall select which agency will post these documents on its internet website.

(c) The court shall allocate payment of the costs incurred by the party appointed to forward all case management orders, judgments, and interlocutory orders to the groundwater sustainability agency among the parties in an amount and a manner that the court deems equitable. **Leg.H.** Added Stats 2023 ch 665 §1 (AB 779), effective January 1, 2024.

§832. Definitions

For purposes of this chapter, the following definitions apply:

(a) "Basin" has the same meaning as defined in Section 10721 of the Water Code.

(b) "Complaint" means a complaint filed in superior court to determine rights to extract groundwater and includes any cross-complaint that initiates a comprehensive adjudication in response to a plaintiff's complaint or other cross-complaint.

(c) "Comprehensive adjudication" means an action filed in superior court to comprehensively determine rights to extract groundwater in a basin.

(d) "Condition of long-term overdraft" means the condition of a groundwater basin where the average annual amount of water extracted for a long-term period, generally 10 years or more, exceeds the long-term average annual supply of water to the basin, plus any temporary surplus. Overdraft during a period of drought is not sufficient to establish a condition of long-term overdraft if extractions and recharge are managed as necessary to ensure that reductions in groundwater levels or storage during a period of drought are offset by increases in groundwater levels or storage during other periods.

(e) "Department" means the Department of Water Resources.

(f) "Expert witness" means a witness qualified pursuant to Section 720 of the Evidence Code.

(g) "Groundwater" means water beneath the surface of the earth within the zone below the water table in which the soil is completely saturated with water, but does not include water that flows in known and definite channels.

(h) "Groundwater extraction facility" means a device or method for extracting groundwater in a basin.

(i) "Groundwater recharge" means the augmentation of groundwater, by natural or artificial means.

(j) "Person" includes, but is not limited to, counties, local agencies, state agencies, federal agencies, tribes, business entities, and individuals.

(k) "Plaintiff" means the person filing the complaint initiating a comprehensive adjudication and includes a cross-complainant who initiates a comprehensive adjudication by cross-complaint.

(l) "Public water system" has the same meaning as defined in Section 116275 of the Health and Safety Code.

(m) "State small water system" has the same meaning as defined in Section 116275 of the Health and Safety Code.

(n) "Sustainable Groundwater Management Act" means Part 2.74 (commencing with Section 10720) of Division 6 of the Water Code. **Leg.H.** Added Stats 2015 ch 672 §1 (AB 1390), effective January 1, 2016; Amended Stats 2016 ch 86 §26 (SB 1171), effective January 1, 2017.

Prior Law: Former CCP §832, relating to actions for libel and slander, was added Stats 1953 ch 52 §6.5 and repealed Stats 1980 ch 114 §1. Historical derivation: Stats 1871–72 ch 377 §3, as amended Stats 1880 ch 86 §1.

Former CCP §832, similar to present CCP §§392–395, was enacted 1872, amended Code Amdts 1873-74 ch 383 §116, Stats 1907 ch 478 §1, and repealed Stats 1933 ch 744 §198.

ARTICLE 2
Scope of Action

Applicability of chapter. §833.
Determination of all groundwater rights of basin. §834.

§833. Applicability of chapter

(a) Except as provided in subdivision (b), this chapter applies to actions that would comprehensively determine rights to extract groundwater in a basin, whether based on appropriation, overlying right, or other basis of right.

(b) This chapter does not apply to any of the following:

(1) An action that concerns only allegations that a groundwater extraction facility, or group of facilities, is interfering with another

groundwater extraction facility or facilities and does not involve a comprehensive allocation of the basin's groundwater supply.

(2) An action that concerns only claims to extract, or to prevent interference with extractions of, a specific source of groundwater recharge and does not involve a comprehensive allocation of the basin's groundwater supply.

(3) An action that can be resolved among a limited number of parties and does not involve a comprehensive determination of rights to extract groundwater within the basin.

(4) An adjudicated area described in subdivisions (a) to (d), inclusive, of Section 10720.8 of the Water Code, unless a court with jurisdiction over a proposed expansion of the adjudicated area orders that the proceeding be conducted in accordance with this chapter.

(c) If the court finds that including an interconnected surface water body or subterranean stream flowing through known and definite channels is necessary for the fair and effective determination of the groundwater rights in a basin, the court may require the joinder of persons who claim rights to divert and use water from that surface water body or subterranean stream in a comprehensive adjudication conducted pursuant to this chapter.

(d) If the court finds that claims of right to extract or divert only minor quantities of water, not to exceed five acre-feet of water per year, would not have a material effect on the groundwater rights of other parties, the court may exempt those claimants with respect to those claims for only minor quantities of water, but a person who is exempted may elect to continue as a party to the comprehensive adjudication. **Leg.H.** Added Stats 2015 ch 672 §1 (AB 1390), effective January 1, 2016.

Prior Law: Former CCP §833, relating to actions for libel and slander, was added Stats 1953 ch 52 §6.5 and repealed Stats 1980 ch 114 §1. Historical derivation: Stats 1871–72 ch 377 §4.

Former CCP §833, similar to present CCP §397, was enacted 1872 and repealed Stats 1933 ch 744 §198.

§834. Determination of all groundwater rights of basin

(a) In a comprehensive adjudication conducted pursuant to this chapter, the court may determine all groundwater rights of a basin, whether based on appropriation, overlying right, or other basis of right, and use of storage space in the basin.

(b) The court's final judgment in a comprehensive adjudication, for the groundwater rights of each party, may declare the priority, amount, purposes of use, extraction location, place of use of the water, and use of storage space in the basin, together with appropriate injunctive relief, subject to terms adopted by the court to implement a physical solution in the comprehensive adjudication. **Leg.H.** Added Stats 2015 ch 672 §1 (AB 1390), effective January 1, 2016.

Prior Law: Former CCP §834, relating to actions for libel and slander, was added Stats 1953 ch 52 §6.5 and repealed Stats 1980 ch 114 §1. Historical derivation: Stats 1871–72 ch 377 §5.

Former CCP §834, similar to present CCP §398, was enacted 1872 and repealed Stats 1933 ch 744 §198.

ARTICLE 3
Notice and Service of Complaint

Provision of notice by plaintiff. §835.
Other notices to be lodged with court with complaint. §836.
Request by plaintiff to specified entities for names and addresses of persons reporting certain extractions within basin. §836.5.

§835. Provision of notice by plaintiff

(a) The plaintiff shall provide notice of the comprehensive adjudication to all of the following:

(1) A groundwater sustainability agency that overlies the basin or a portion of the basin.

(2) A city, county, or city and county that overlies the basin or a portion of the basin.

(3) A district with authority to manage or replenish groundwater resources of the basin in whole or in part.

(4) The operator of a public water system or state small water system that uses groundwater from the basin to supply water service.

(5) A California Native American tribe that is on the contact list maintained by the Native American Heritage Commission.

(6) The Attorney General, the State Water Resources Control Board, the department, and the Department of Fish and Wildlife.

(7) A federal department or agency that manages a federal reservation that overlies the basin or a portion of the basin.

(8) A person identified under Section 836.5 who is not a party to the comprehensive adjudication.

(9) A person who is on a list, maintained by a groundwater management agency, of interested parties that have requested notice under the Sustainable Groundwater Management Act.

(b) The plaintiff may provide notice under this section by first class mail or electronic mail.

(c)(1) Except as provided in paragraph (2), the plaintiff shall provide notice under this section as follows:

(A) To any person entitled to notice under paragraphs (1) to (7), inclusive, of subdivision (a) within 15 days of the filing of the complaint.

(B) To any person entitled to notice under paragraphs (8) and (9) of subdivision (a) within 30 days of receipt of the name and address of the person entitled to notice.

(2) The plaintiff may take additional time as is reasonably necessary before providing notice under this section if the plaintiff determines that additional time is necessary to identify a person entitled to notice under this section, confirm the accuracy of the name or address of a person, or to determine if the conditions requiring notice have been satisfied.

(d) The plaintiff is not required to provide notice under this section to a person who has already been served or intervened in the action. **Leg.H.** Added Stats 2015 ch 672 §1 (AB 1390), effective January 1, 2016. Amended Stats 2016 ch 86 §27 (SB 1171), effective January 1, 2017.

Prior Law: Former CCP §835, relating to actions for libel and slander, was added Stats 1953 ch 52 §6.5 and repealed Stats 1980 ch 114 §1. Historical derivation: Stats 1871–72 ch 377 §6.

Former CCP §835, similar to present CCP §398, was enacted 1872 and repealed Stats 1933 ch 744 §198.

§836. Other notices to be lodged with court with complaint

(a) When the plaintiff files the complaint, the plaintiff shall also lodge with the court both of the following:

(1)(A) A draft notice titled "NOTICE OF COMMENCEMENT OF GROUNDWATER BASIN ADJUDICATION" in no less than 20-point font and the following text printed immediately below the draft notice title in no less than 14-point font:

"THIS NOTICE IS IMPORTANT. ANY RIGHTS YOU CLAIM TO PUMP OR STORE GROUNDWATER FROM THE BASIN IDENTIFIED IN THIS NOTICE MAY BE AFFECTED BY A LAWSUIT INITIATED BY THE COMPLAINT SUMMARIZED BELOW.

A copy of the complaint may be obtained by contacting the plaintiff or the plaintiff's attorney identified in this notice. If you claim rights to pump or store groundwater within the basin, either now or in the future, you may become a party to this lawsuit by filing an answer to the lawsuit on or before the deadline specified in this notice. You may file an answer by completing the attached form answer, filing it with the court indicated in this notice, and sending a copy of the form answer to the plaintiff or the plaintiff's attorney.

Failing to participate in this lawsuit could have a significant adverse effect on any right to pump or store groundwater that you may have. You may seek the advice of an attorney in relation to this lawsuit. Such attorney should be consulted promptly. A case management conference in this groundwater basin adjudication proceeding shall occur on the date specified in this notice. If you intend to participate in the groundwater adjudication proceeding to which this notice applies, you are advised to attend the initial case management conference in person or have an attorney represent you at the initial case management conference.

Participation requires the production of all information regarding your groundwater use. You must provide this information by the date identified in this notice.

A form answer is provided for your convenience. You may fill out the form answer and file it with the court. Should you choose to file the form answer, it will serve as an answer to all complaints and cross-complaints filed in this case."

(B) The following information shall be provided immediately following the text described in subparagraph (A):

(i) The name of the basin that is the subject of the comprehensive adjudication and a link to the Internet Web site address where the department has posted a map of the basin.

(ii) A space to be completed with the case number assigned to the comprehensive adjudication, and the name and address of the court and department to which the action is assigned.

(iii) The name, address, telephone number, and email address of the plaintiff, or plaintiff's attorney, from whom the complaint may be obtained and to whom a copy of the form answer should be sent.

(iv) A summary of the causes of action alleged in the complaint and the relief sought. The summary shall not exceed 25 lines.

(v) A date by which persons receiving the notice must appear in the comprehensive adjudication.

(2)(A) A draft form answer titled "ANSWER TO ADJUDICATION COMPLAINT" in no less than 20-point font and the following text printed immediately below the draft form answer title in no less than 14-point font:

"The undersigned denies all material allegations in the complaint or cross-complaint in this action that seeks to adjudicate rights in the groundwater basin and asserts all applicable affirmative defenses to that complaint."

(B) Notwithstanding any other law, the filing of an answer in the form described in subparagraph (A) in a comprehensive adjudication is sufficient to put at issue all material allegations and applicable affirmative defenses to the complaint in the comprehensive adjudication. If a party intends to seek adjustment of the basin's boundaries, it shall disclose that intention in the form answer described in subparagraph (A).

(b) Within 30 days of the assignment of a judge by the Chairperson of the Judicial Council, the plaintiff shall file a motion for approval of the draft notice and draft form answer filed pursuant to subdivision (a). The plaintiff's motion shall include a copy of the draft notice and draft form answer filed pursuant to subdivision (a).

(c) Once the court approves the draft notice, service of that notice in accordance with this section shall substitute for the summons otherwise provided for in civil actions pursuant to Section 412.20.

(d)(1) Following a court order approving the notice and form answer and authorizing service of landowners pursuant to this section, the plaintiff shall do all of the following:

(A) Identify the assessor parcel numbers and physical addresses of all real property in the basin and the names and addresses of all holders of fee title to real property in the basin using the records of the assessor or assessors of the county or counties in which the basin to be adjudicated lies. The plaintiff shall provide the court and all parties with notice of its acquisition of, or sufficient access to, this information.

(B) Mail, by registered mail or certified mail, return receipt requested, the notice, complaint, and form answer to all holders of fee title to real property in the basin. If the physical address of the real property differs from the address of the holder of fee title, the notice, complaint, and form answer shall be mailed by registered or certified mail, return receipt requested, to the physical address of the real property and the address of the holder of fee title.

(C) If return receipt is not received for a parcel of real property, the plaintiff shall post a copy of the notice, complaint, and form answer in a conspicuous place on the real property.

(D) Within 20 days of the court order, publish the notice at least once per week for four consecutive weeks in one or more newspapers of general circulation in each county overlying the basin in whole or in part.

(2) Service pursuant to this subdivision is not required if the real property is owned by a person in a class of water users that are otherwise noticed in accordance with this chapter. If the owner is part of a class of water users proposed for certification, service is not required until the court acts on the proposal for certification.

(e) After completing the mailing pursuant to subdivision (d), the plaintiff shall file with the court a notice of the completion of the mailing.

(f) A property owner who has received notice of the comprehensive adjudication and transfers property during the pendency of the comprehensive adjudication shall disclose, on the Real Estate Transfer Disclosure Statement, that the property is subject to a comprehensive adjudication and shall attach the court-approved notice to the Real Estate Transfer Disclosure Statement.

(g) Following a court order authorizing service of landowners pursuant to this section, the plaintiff shall serve any known person that pumps groundwater who would not otherwise be served pursuant to subdivision (d) of this section, except those who have been exempted by the court pursuant to subdivision (d) of Section 833 or those who are part of a class certified pursuant to paragraph (2) of subdivision (d) of this section. Service pursuant to this subdivision shall be by personal delivery or by mail in the manner prescribed by Article 3 (commencing with Section 415.10) of Chapter 4 of Title 5.

(h) Service on the United States shall be made in accordance with Section 666 of Title 43 of the United States Code.

(i) The court may authorize any other procedures it finds appropriate and necessary to provide notice to persons who may hold groundwater rights in the basin.

(j) Compliance with the service and notice provisions of this chapter shall be deemed effective service of process of the complaint and notice on all interested parties of the comprehensive adjudication for purposes of establishing in rem jurisdiction and the comprehensive effect of the comprehensive adjudication.

(k) Whenever proceedings are instituted under this chapter, it shall be the duty of all claimants interested in the proceedings and having notice of the proceedings pursuant to this chapter to appear in the proceedings and to submit proof of their claims at the time, and in the manner, required by this chapter.

(*l*) The court may require notice to be made available in languages other than English.

(m) Within 15 days of the court order approving the notice and form answer, the plaintiff shall provide the notice and form answer to the department and each county and groundwater sustainability agency that overlies the basin or a portion of the basin. The department, and each county and groundwater sustainability agency that overlies the basin or a portion of the basin and has an Internet Web site shall do all of the following:

(1) Within 15 days of receiving the notice and form answer, post those documents on its Internet Web site.

(2) Provide a link to the notice and form answer on the home page of its Internet Web site.

(3) Maintain the posting and link described in paragraphs (1) and (2) for the entire time the comprehensive adjudication is pending. The plaintiff shall notify the department and each county and groundwater sustainability agency when the comprehensive adjudication is no longer pending. **Leg.H.** Added Stats 2015 ch 672 §1 (AB 1390), effective January 1, 2016.

Prior Law: Former CCP §836, relating to actions for libel and slander, was added Stats 1953 ch 52 §6.5 and repealed Stats 1980 ch 114 §1. Historical derivation: Stats 1871–72 ch 377 §7.

Former CCP §836, similar to present CCP §399, was enacted 1872, amended Stats 1907 ch 478 §2, and repealed Stats 1933 ch 744 §198.

§836.5. Request by plaintiff to specified entities for names and addresses of persons reporting certain extractions within basin

(a) Within 15 days of the court order approving the notice and form answer under Section 836, the plaintiff shall request from the following entities the names and addresses of persons reporting extractions within the basin under the Sustainable Groundwater Management Act, or Part 5 (commencing with Section 4999) or Part 5.2 (commencing with Section 5200) of Division 2 of the Water Code:

(1) The State Water Resources Control Board.

(2) A local agency designated under Section 5009 of the Water Code as the local agency for a board-designated local area that includes the basin or a portion of the basin.

(3) A groundwater sustainability agency for the basin or a portion of the basin.

(b) The entities described in paragraphs (1) to (3), inclusive, of subdivision (a) shall provide the plaintiff with the names, mailing addresses, and email addresses, if available, within 45 days of the plaintiff's request. The State Water Resources Control Board shall also provide the mailing address and email addresses, if available, of any person known to the board who holds a permit or license authorizing underground storage in the basin or who claims a right to divert water for underground storage in the basin.

(c) Upon request, the plaintiff shall reimburse the reasonable costs incurred under this section by an entity described in paragraphs (1) to (3), inclusive, of subdivision (a).

(d) An entity shall not be held civilly liable for complying with this section. **Leg.H.** Added Stats 2015 ch 672 §1 (AB 1390), effective January 1, 2016.

ARTICLE 4
Intervention

Intervention by groundwater sustainability agency, city, county, or city and county overlying basin, or certain persons upon filing ex parte application. §837.
State intervention in comprehensive adjudication. §837.5.

§837. Intervention by groundwater sustainability agency, city, county, or city and county overlying basin, or certain persons upon filing ex parte application

(a) A groundwater sustainability agency for the basin or a portion of the basin may intervene in a comprehensive adjudication conducted pursuant to this chapter.

(b) A city, county, or city and county that overlies the basin or a portion of the basin may intervene in a comprehensive adjudication conducted pursuant to this chapter.

(c) The court shall allow any person to intervene in a comprehensive adjudication conducted pursuant to this chapter upon an ex parte application that demonstrates that the person holds fee simple ownership in a parcel in the basin, or extracts or stores water in the basin. A person filing an ex parte application pursuant to this subdivision shall give notice to the plaintiff consistent with the California Rules of Court.

(d) A person may apply to intervene in a comprehensive adjudication conducted pursuant to this chapter pursuant to Section 387. **Leg.H.** Added Stats 2015 ch 672 §1 (AB 1390), effective January 1, 2016.

Prior Law: Former CCP §837, similar to present CCP §399, was enacted 1872 and repealed Stats 1907 ch 478 §3.

§837.5. State intervention in comprehensive adjudication

(a) The state may intervene in a comprehensive adjudication conducted pursuant to this chapter.

(b) This section does not affect substantive law. **Leg.H.** Added Stats 2015 ch 676 §1 (SB 226), effective January 1, 2016.

ARTICLE 5
Judge

Disqualification of judge of superior court of county overlying basin; Transfer, coordination, or consolidation of certain actions with comprehensive adjudication. §838.

§838. Disqualification of judge of superior court of county overlying basin; Transfer, coordination, or consolidation of certain actions with comprehensive adjudication

(a)(1) In a comprehensive adjudication conducted pursuant to this chapter, a judge of a superior court of a county that overlies the basin or any portion of the basin shall be disqualified. The Chairperson of the Judicial Council shall assign a judge to preside in all proceedings in the comprehensive adjudication.

(2) A judge of the superior court in which an action is filed may, on the court's own motion or the motion of a party, determine if the action is a comprehensive adjudication under Section 833. A motion for a determination pursuant to this paragraph shall receive calendar preference within the action and shall be resolved before other procedural or dispositive motions.

(b) A comprehensive adjudication is presumed to be a complex action under Rule 3.400 of the California Rules of Court.

(c) Sections 170.6 and 394 shall not apply in a comprehensive adjudication.

(d) Notwithstanding subdivision (b) of Section 10726.6 of the Water Code, an action against a groundwater sustainability agency that is located in a basin that is being adjudicated pursuant to this chapter shall be subject to transfer, coordination, and consolidation with the comprehensive adjudication, as appropriate, if the action concerns the adoption, substance, or implementation of a groundwater sustainability plan, or the groundwater sustainability agency's compliance with the timelines in the Sustainable Groundwater Management Act.

(e) The judge assigned by the Chairperson of the Judicial Council pursuant to subdivision (a) shall determine if transfer, coordination, or consolidation is appropriate. **Leg.H.** Added Stats 2015 ch 672 §1 (AB 1390), effective January 1, 2016.

Prior Law: Former CCP §838, similar to present CCP §396, was enacted 1872, amended Code Amdts 1880 ch 34 §1, and repealed Stats 1933 ch 744 §198.

ARTICLE 6
Electronic service

Pleadings and papers. §839.

§839. Pleadings and papers

Service of pleadings and papers in a comprehensive adjudication, other than the complaint initiating a comprehensive adjudication, shall occur electronically to the greatest extent possible. The court may provide, or authorize the use of, an electronic service system. If an electronic service system is not provided or authorized by the court, the court and the parties shall serve documents by email or other equivalent electronic means to the greatest extent possible. To enable electronic service of pleadings and papers, the attorneys of record or parties representing themselves shall include an email address for service in the captions of all pleadings they file in the comprehensive adjudication. **Leg.H.** Added Stats 2015 ch 672 §1 (AB 1390), effective January 1, 2016.

Prior Law: Former CCP §839, similar to present CCP §411.10, was enacted 1872, amended Code Amdts 1875–76 ch 182 §1, and repealed Stats 1933 ch 744 §198.

ARTICLE 7
Case Management

Case management conference. §840.

§840. Case management conference

(a) In managing a comprehensive adjudication, the court shall do both of the following:

(1) Convene a case management conference as provided by the California Rules of Court.

(2) In an adjudication action for a basin required to have a groundwater sustainability plan under the Sustainable Groundwater Management Act (Part 2.74 (commencing with Section 10720) of Division 6 of the Water Code), manage the case in accordance with Section 10737.2 of the Water Code.

(b) In an initial case management conference, or as soon as practicable, the court may consider the following in addition to other matters:

(1) Determining whether to seek adjustment of the basin boundaries pursuant to Section 841.

(2) Staying the action pursuant to Section 848.

(3) Appointing a special master pursuant to Section 845.

(4) Scheduling a hearing on a preliminary injunction pursuant to Section 847.

(5) Dividing the case into phases to resolve legal and factual issues.

(6) Issuing orders to ensure that issues resolved in one phase are not relitigated in another phase.

(7) Limiting discovery to correspond to the phases.

(8) Scheduling early resolution of claims to prescriptive rights.

(9) Forming a class or classes of overlying groundwater rights holders pursuant to the criteria specified in Section 382. **Leg.H.** Added Stats 2015 ch 672 §1 (AB 1390), effective January 1, 2016. Amended Stats 2023 ch 665 §2 (AB 779), effective January 1, 2024.

Prior Law: Former CCP §840, similar to present CCP §412.10, was enacted 1872 and repealed Stats 1933 ch 744 §198.

ARTICLE 8
Basin Boundaries

Boundaries of area subject to comprehensive adjudication; Revision of basin boundaries by court; Submission of request to department to revise basin boundaries. §841.

§841. Boundaries of area subject to comprehensive adjudication; Revision of basin boundaries by court; Submission of request to department to revise basin boundaries

(a) Except as otherwise provided in this section, the boundaries of the area subject to a comprehensive adjudication shall be consistent with the boundaries of a basin.

(b) If the department revises the boundaries of a basin pursuant to Section 10722.2, or subdivision (b) of Section 12924, of the Water Code after a comprehensive adjudication has been initiated, the court may revise the boundaries of the area subject to the comprehensive adjudication as the interests of justice and the objectives of this chapter require.

(c) Upon a showing that a revision of the basin boundaries would further a fair and effective determination of water rights, the court may direct any of the following to submit a request to the department pursuant to Section 10722.2 of the Water Code to revise the basin boundaries:

(1) A party to the comprehensive adjudication.

(2) The State Water Resources Control Board, if the court has made a reference pursuant to Part 3 (commencing with Section 2000) of Division 2 of the Water Code.

(3) A special master, if one has been appointed.

(d) A determination of the department on a submission made pursuant to subdivision (c) is subject to judicial review pursuant to Section 1085. Venue shall be in the court with jurisdiction over the comprehensive adjudication and the case shall be coordinated with the comprehensive adjudication. **Leg.H.** Added Stats 2015 ch 672 §1 (AB 1390), effective January 1, 2016.

Prior Law: Former CCP §841, similar to present CCP §412.10, was enacted 1872 and repealed Stats 1933 ch 744 §198.

ARTICLE 9
Initial Disclosures

Service of initial disclosures; Required information; Judicial Council form; Supplementation or correction of disclosure. §842.

§842. Service of initial disclosures; Required information; Judicial Council form; Supplementation or correction of disclosure

(a) Except as otherwise stipulated by the parties or ordered by the court, within six months of appearing in a comprehensive adjudication, a party shall serve on the other parties and the special master, if one is appointed, an initial disclosure that includes all of the following information:

(1) The name, address, telephone number, and email address of the party and, if applicable, the party's attorney.

(2) The quantity of any groundwater extracted from the basin by the party and the method of measurement used by the party or the party's predecessor in interest for each of the previous 10 years preceding the filing of the complaint.

(3) The type of water right or rights claimed by the party for the extraction of groundwater.

(4) A general description of the purpose to which the groundwater has been put.

(5) The location of each well or other source through which groundwater has been extracted.

(6) The area in which the groundwater has been used.

(7) Any claims for increased or future use of groundwater.

(8) The quantity of any beneficial use of any alternative water use that the party claims as its use of groundwater under any applicable law, including, but not limited to, Section 1005.1, 1005.2, or 1005.4 of the Water Code.

(9) Identification of all surface water rights and contracts that the party claims provides the basis for its water right claims in the comprehensive adjudication.

(10) The quantity of any replenishment of water to the basin that augmented the basin's native water supply, resulting from the intentional storage of imported or non-native water in the basin, managed recharge of surface water, or return flows resulting from the use of imported water or non-native water on lands overlying the basin by the party, or the party's representative or agent, during each of the 10 calendar years immediately preceding the filing of the complaint.

(11) The names, addresses, telephone numbers, and email addresses of all persons possessing information that supports the party's disclosures.

(12) Any other facts that tend to prove the party's claimed water right.

(b) The Judicial Council may develop a form for initial disclosures made pursuant to subdivision (a) to facilitate the consistent, independent, impartial, and accessible administration of comprehensive adjudications. The Judicial Council may coordinate with the department in developing the form.

(c) A party shall make its initial disclosures based on the information then reasonably available to it. A party is not excused from making its initial disclosures because it has not fully investigated the case, because it challenges the sufficiency of another party's disclosures, or because another party has not made its disclosures.

(d) A party that has made its initial disclosures, as described in subdivision (a), or that has responded to another party's discovery request, shall supplement or correct a disclosure or response in all of the following situations:

(1) In a timely manner if the party learns that in some material respect the disclosure or response is incomplete or incorrect and the additional or corrective information has not otherwise been made known to the other parties during the disclosure or discovery process.

(2) If the party extracts groundwater from the basin after the complaint is filed. A supplement filed pursuant to this paragraph shall report the quantity of water extracted and be filed within 90 days after the end of the calendar year.

(3) As ordered by the court.

(e) To the greatest extent possible, a party shall serve his or her initial disclosures electronically. If it is not possible for the party to serve his or her disclosures electronically, he or she shall serve the disclosures in an electronic format saved on a portable storage media device such as a compact disc or flash drive.

(f) A party's obligations under this section may be enforced by a court on its own motion or the motion of a party to compel disclosure.

(g) A party's disclosures under this section shall be verified under penalty of perjury as being true and correct to the best of the party's knowledge. **Leg.H.** Added Stats 2015 ch 672 §1 (AB 1390), effective January 1, 2016.

Prior Law: Former CCP §842, similar to present CCP §1014, was enacted 1872 and repealed Stats 1933 ch 744 §198.

ARTICLE 10
Expert Witnesses

Disclosure of expert witness; Expert witness's report; Time for disclosure; Supplementation or correction of disclosure. §843.

§843. Disclosure of expert witness; Expert witness's report; Time for disclosure; Supplementation or correction of disclosure

(a) In addition to all other disclosures required by this chapter, a party shall disclose to the other parties the identity of any expert witness it may use at trial to present evidence.

(b) Unless otherwise stipulated by the parties or ordered by the court, the disclosure made pursuant to subdivision (a) shall be accompanied by a written report prepared and signed by the expert witness if the witness is retained or specially employed by the party offering the expert witness to testify as an expert in the action, or if the expert witness's duties as the party's employee regularly involves giving expert testimony. The report shall include all of the following:

(1) A complete statement of all opinions the witness will express and the basis and reasons for those opinions.

(2) The facts or data considered by the witness in forming his or her opinions.

(3) Any exhibits the witness will use to summarize or support his or her opinions.

(4) The witness's qualifications, including a list of all publications authored by the witness in the previous 10 years.

(5) A list of all other cases in which the witness testified as an expert at trial or by deposition in the last five years.

(6) A statement of the compensation to be paid for the witness's work and testimony in the comprehensive adjudication.

(c) If subdivision (b) does not apply to an expert witness because of a stipulation by the parties or an order of the court, the witness's disclosure shall include both of the following:

(1) The subject matter on which the witness is expected to present evidence.

(2) A summary of the witness's opinions, and the facts or data considered by the witness in forming his or her opinions.

(d) Unless otherwise stipulated by the parties, a party shall make the disclosures of any expert witness it intends to present at trial, except for an expert witness presented solely for purposes of impeachment or rebuttal, at the times and in the sequence ordered by the court. If there is no stipulation or court order, the disclosures of an expert witness shall be made as follows:

(1) At least 30 days after the court's entry of an order establishing the scope of the relevant phase of the comprehensive adjudication.

(2) Except for a supplemental expert witness described in paragraph (3), at least 60 days before the date set for trial of the relevant phase of the comprehensive adjudication.

(3) For a supplemental expert witness who will express an opinion on a subject to be covered by another expert witness designated by an adverse party that was not among the subjects covered by an expert witness initially disclosed by the party offering the supplemental expert

witness, no more than 20 days after the initial expert witness disclosure date.

(e) The court may modify the disclosure requirements of subdivisions (b) to (d), inclusive, for expert witnesses presented solely for purposes of impeachment or rebuttal. In modifying the disclosure requirements, the court shall adopt disclosure requirements that expedite the court's consideration of the issues presented and shall ensure that expert testimony presented solely for purposes of impeachment or rebuttal is strictly limited to the scope of the testimony that it intends to impeach or rebut.

(f)(1) A party whose expert witness has made a disclosure pursuant to this section shall promptly supplement or correct the expert witness's disclosure in either of the following instances:

(A) In a timely manner if the party learns that in some material respect the disclosure is incomplete or incorrect, if the additional or corrective information has not otherwise been made known to the other parties during the disclosure or discovery process.

(B) As ordered by the court.

(2) A party's duty to supplement or correct its expert witness's disclosure includes the information included in the report and the information given during the expert witness's deposition. Unless otherwise stipulated by the parties or ordered by the court, any supplementation or correction shall occur at least 14 days before trial of the applicable phase of the comprehensive adjudication.

(3) The court may authorize a supplemental deposition of an expert witness based on a supplemental disclosure made pursuant to this subdivision. The court shall appropriately condition the authorization of a supplemental deposition of an expert witness to ensure the expeditious completion of the applicable phase of the comprehensive adjudication. The court may require the party whose expert makes the supplemental disclosure to pay some or all of the costs associated with the supplemental deposition.

(g) To the greatest extent possible, the parties shall serve expert witness disclosures electronically through an electronic service system, an electronic document repository, email, or another method of electronic transmission. If it is not possible for the party to serve his or her expert witness disclosures electronically, he or she shall serve the expert witness disclosures in an electronic format saved on a portable storage media device such as a compact disc or flash drive. **Leg.H.** Added Stats 2015 ch 672 §1 (AB 1390), effective January 1, 2016.

Prior Law: Former CCP §843, similar to present CCP §§372, 373, was enacted 1872, amended Code Amdts 1873–74 ch 383 §117, Code Amdts 1880 ch 34 §2, and repealed Stats 1933 ch 744 §198.

ARTICLE 11
Written Testimony

Submission of written testimony; Service of direct and rebuttal testimony. §844.

§844. Submission of written testimony; Service of direct and rebuttal testimony

(a) A court may require the parties in a comprehensive adjudication to submit written testimony of relevant witnesses in the forms of affidavits or declarations under penalty of perjury in lieu of presenting live testimony. The required written testimony may include, but is not limited to, expert witness opinions and testimony that authenticates documentary evidence. The court may order that the written testimony constitutes the entirety of the witness's direct testimony, require the written testimony to include any exhibits offered in support of the written testimony, and, in the case of written testimony of an expert witness, require a statement of the witness's qualifications.

(b) If the court requires the submission of written testimony pursuant to subdivision (a), a complete copy of the direct testimony shall be served at least 21 days before trial. A complete copy of any rebuttal testimony shall be served no later than the first day of trial.

(c) If the contents of the written testimony would have been admissible if the witness testified orally, the written testimony shall be received by the court as a documentary exhibit if the witness whose written testimony is being offered is made available for cross-examination by all parties. **Leg.H.** Added Stats 2015 ch 672 §1 (AB 1390), effective January 1, 2016.

Prior Law: Former CCP §844, similar to present CCP §412.20, was enacted 1872, amended Code Amdts 1875–76 ch 498 §1, Code Amdts 1880 ch 34 §3, Stats 1899 ch 84 §1, and repealed Stats 1933 ch 744 §198.

ARTICLE 12
Special Master

Appointment and duties of special master; Compensation. §845.
Draft report of special master; Objections. §846.

§845. Appointment and duties of special master; Compensation

(a) The court may appoint one or more special masters whose duties may include the following:

(1) Investigating technical and legal issues, as directed by the court. The special master shall compile a report of findings in accordance with Section 846.

(2) Conducting joint factfinding with the parties, their designees, or both.

(3) Investigating the need for, and developing a proposal for, a preliminary injunction pursuant to Article 13 (commencing with Section 847).

(4) Performing other tasks the court may deem appropriate.

(b) The court shall fix the special master's compensation on the basis and terms stated in the appointing order, and the court may set a new basis and new terms after giving the parties notice and an opportunity to be heard. The court shall allocate payment of the special master's compensation among the parties in an amount and a manner that the court deems equitable. The court may waive a party's obligations to pay the special master's compensation upon a showing of good cause.

(c) The court may request the State Water Resources Control Board or the department to recommend candidates for appointment as a special master or to review the qualifications of candidates.

(d) This section does not limit the authority of the court to make a reference pursuant to Chapter 1 (commencing with Section 2000) of Part 3 of Division 2 of the Water Code.

(e) This section does not limit the authority to appoint a watermaster pursuant to Chapter 3 (commencing with Section 4050) of Part 4 of Division 2 of the Water Code or any other law. **Leg.H.** Added Stats 2015 ch 672 §1 (AB 1390), effective January 1, 2016.

Prior Law: Former CCP §845, similar to present CCP §412.20, was enacted 1872, amended Code Amdts 1873–74 ch 523 §1, Code Amdts 1875–76 ch 498 §2, Code Amdts 1880 ch 34 §4, Stats 1899 ch 84 §1, Stats 1907 ch 478 §4, and repealed Stats 1933 ch 744 §198.

§846. Draft report of special master; Objections

(a) The special master shall make a draft report available to the parties and provide at least 60 days for the parties to submit written objections to the draft report.

(b) An objection to the draft report shall identify the specific grounds and evidence on which the objection is based.

(c) The special master may notice and hold hearings, as he or she deems appropriate, to gather information or address issues raised in the objections to the draft report.

(d) The special master shall consider the objections to the draft report and develop a final report that shall be filed with the court, together with supporting evidence. **Leg.H.** Added Stats 2015 ch 672 §1 (AB 1390), effective January 1, 2016.

Prior Law: Former CCP §846, relating to alias summons, was enacted 1872, amended Stats 1925 ch 22 §1, and repealed Stats 1933 ch 744 §198.

ARTICLE 13
Preliminary Injunction

Issuance of preliminary injunction upon showing of long-term overdraft; Evidence; Required determinations; Appointment of watermaster. §847.

§847. Issuance of preliminary injunction upon showing of long-term overdraft; Evidence; Required determinations; Appointment of watermaster

(a) Upon a showing that the basin is in a condition of long-term overdraft, the court may, upon notice and hearing, issue a preliminary injunction.

(b) Bulletins and other reports of the department, and a report of a special master indicating that a condition of long-term overdraft exists in the basin, shall be admissible as evidence of a condition of long-term overdraft. This subdivision does not limit the admissibility of other relevant evidence.

(c) The preliminary injunction may include any of the following terms:

(1) A moratorium on new or increased appropriations of water.

(2) A limitation on, or reduction in, the diversion or extraction of water.

(3) An allocation among the parties establishing amounts of extraction allowed during the pendency of the comprehensive adjudication.

(4) Procedures for voluntary transfers.

(d) The court shall issue a preliminary injunction upon determining all of the following:

(1) The basin is in a condition of long-term overdraft.

(2) The basin has been designated as a probationary basin or the planning deadlines in subdivision (a) of Section 10720.7 of the Water Code are not being complied with.

(3) There is no interim plan in effect under Section 10735.8 of the Water Code.

(e) The court may provide a schedule for further reductions in extractions over a period of years if it finds that doing so appears reasonably necessary to achieve groundwater sustainability within the timelines provided in subdivision (b) of Section 10727.2 of the Water Code.

(f) The terms of a preliminary injunction shall not determine the rights in a final judgment of the comprehensive adjudication.

(g) A bond or undertaking shall not be required for the issuance of a preliminary injunction pursuant to this section.

(h) The court may appoint a watermaster to oversee enforcement of the preliminary injunction. **Leg.H.** Added Stats 2015 ch 672 §1 (AB 1390), effective January 1, 2016.

Prior Law: Former CCP §847, relating to alias summons, was enacted 1872 and repealed Stats 1933 ch 744 §198.

ARTICLE 14
Stay

Stay of comprehensive adjudication; Required progress report for renewal. §848.

§848. Stay of comprehensive adjudication; Required progress report for renewal

(a) Upon the court's own motion or the motion of any party to a comprehensive adjudication, a court may stay a comprehensive adjudication for a period of up to one year, subject to renewal in the court's discretion upon a showing of good cause, in order to facilitate any of the following:

(1) Adoption of a groundwater sustainability plan that provides for a physical solution or otherwise addresses issues in the comprehensive adjudication.

(2) The development of technical studies that may be useful to the parties in the comprehensive adjudication.

(3) Voluntary mediation or participation in a settlement conference on all, or a portion of, the subject matters or legal questions identified in the comprehensive adjudication.

(4) Compromise and settlement of the comprehensive adjudication or issues in the comprehensive adjudication.

(b) Before renewing a stay granted pursuant to subdivision (a), the parties shall report on the progress being made on the issues that were identified as the reasons for the stay.

(c) A stay pursuant to this section shall not stay, or otherwise delay, the parties' obligations to provide initial disclosures pursuant to Section 842 unless the court determines the initial disclosures will not benefit resolution of the comprehensive adjudication. **Leg.H.** Added Stats 2015 ch 672 §1 (AB 1390), effective January 1, 2016.

Prior Law: Former CCP §848, similar to present CCP §§412.30, 413.10–415.40, 416.90, 417.30, was enacted 1872, amended Code Amdts 1873–74 ch 383 §118, Code Amdts 1875–76 ch 498 §3, Stats 1907 ch 478 §5, Stats 1909 ch 229 §1, Stats 1929 ch 57 §1, and repealed Stats 1933 ch 744 §198.

ARTICLE 15
Physical Solution

Authority and duty of court to impose physical solution. §849.

§849. Authority and duty of court to impose physical solution

(a) The court shall have the authority and the duty to impose a physical solution on the parties in a comprehensive adjudication where necessary and consistent with Article 2 of Section X of the California Constitution.

(b) Before adopting a physical solution, the court shall consider any existing groundwater sustainability plan or program. **Leg.H.** Added Stats 2015 ch 672 §1 (AB 1390), effective January 1, 2016.

Prior Law: Former CCP §849, similar to present CCP §§412.30, 413.10–415.40, 416.90, 417.30, was enacted 1872, amended Code Amdts 1873–74 ch 523 §2, Stats 1905 ch 32 §1, Stats 1929 ch 354 §1, and repealed Stats 1933 ch 744 §198.

ARTICLE 16
Judgment

Criteria for entering judgment in comprehensive adjudication; Additional criteria for action for basin with groundwater sustainability plan; Adoption of proposed stipulated judgment. §850.

§850. Criteria for entering judgment in comprehensive adjudication; Additional criteria for action for basin with groundwater sustainability plan; Adoption of proposed stipulated judgment

(a) The court may enter a judgment in a comprehensive adjudication if the court finds that the judgment meets all of the following criteria:

(1) It is consistent with Section 2 of Article X of the California Constitution.

(2) It is consistent with the water right priorities of all nonstipulating parties and any persons who have claims that are exempted pursuant to Section 833 in the basin.

(3) It treats all objecting parties and any persons who have claims that are exempted pursuant to Section 833 equitably as compared to the stipulating parties.

(4) It considers the water use of and accessibility of water for small farmers and disadvantaged communities. This consideration shall be consistent with the conditions identified in this subdivision.

(b) The court may enter judgment in an adjudication action for a basin required to have a groundwater sustainability plan under the Sustainable Groundwater Management Act (Part 2.74 (commencing with Section 10720) of Division 6 of the Water Code), if in addition to the criteria enumerated in subdivision (a), the court also finds that the judgment will not substantially impair the ability of a groundwater sustainability agency, the State Water Resources Control Board, or the department to comply with the Sustainable Groundwater Management Act and to achieve sustainable groundwater management.

(c)(1) In order to assist the court in making the findings required by this section, the court may refer the matter to the State Water Resources Control Board for investigation and report pursuant to Section 2001 of the Water Code. A party may request that the court refer the matter to the State Water Resources Control Board pursuant to this subdivision.

(2) Notwithstanding any inconsistencies with Article 2 (commencing with Section 2010) of Chapter 1 of Part 3 of Division 2 of the Water Code, for a reference undertaken by the State Water Resources Control Board under paragraph (1), the State Water Resources Control Board and Department of Water Resources shall jointly investigate and submit the report under paragraph (1).

(d) If a party or group of parties submits a proposed stipulated judgment that is supported by more than 50 percent of all parties who are groundwater extractors in the basin or use the basin for groundwater storage and is supported by groundwater extractors responsible for at least 75 percent of the groundwater extracted in the basin during the five calendar years before the filing of the complaint, the court may adopt the proposed stipulated judgment, as applied to the stipulating parties, if the proposed stipulated judgment meets the criteria described in subdivision (a). A party objecting to a proposed stipulated judgment shall demonstrate, by a preponderance of evidence, that the proposed stipulated judgment does not satisfy one or more criteria described in subdivision (a) or that it substantially violates the water rights of the objecting party. If the objecting party is unable to make this showing, the court may impose the proposed stipulated judgment on the objecting party. An objecting party may be subject to a preliminary injunction issued pursuant to Section 847 while their objections are being resolved.

(e) For purposes of this section the following definitions apply:

(1) "Disadvantaged communities" means communities identified by the California Environmental Protection Agency as disadvantaged communities pursuant to Section 39711 of the Health and Safety Code.

(2) "Small farmers" means farmers with between ten thousand dollars ($10,000) and four hundred thousand dollars ($400,000) in gross farm sales, as referenced in the Department of Food and Agriculture's California Underserved and Small Producers Program. **Leg.H.** Added Stats 2015 ch 672 §1 (AB 1390), effective January 1, 2016. Amended Stats 2016 ch

86 §28 (SB 1171), effective January 1, 2017; Stats 2023 ch 665 §3 (AB 779), effective January 1, 2024.

Former Sections: Former CCP §850 was added Stats 1953 ch 52 §7 and amended and renumbered CCP §853 by Stats 2016 ch 86 §29 (SB 1171), effective January 1, 2017.

Former CCP §850, similar to present CCP §594, was enacted 1872, amended Code Amdts 1875–76 ch 498 §4, Stats 1901 ch 191 §1, Stats 1905 ch 37 §1, Stats 1909 ch 633 §1, Stats 1913 ch 152 §1, Stats 1917 ch 127 §1, and repealed Stats 1933 ch 744 §198.

Prior Law: Former CCP §850 was added Stats 1953 ch 52 §7 and amended and renumbered CCP §853 by Stats 2016 ch 86 §29 (SB 1171), effective January 1, 2017.

Former CCP §850, similar to present CCP §594, was enacted 1872, amended Code Amdts 1875-76 ch 498 §4, Stats 1901 ch 191 §1, Stats 1905 ch 37 §1, Stats 1909 ch 633 §1, Stats 1913 ch 152 §1, Stats 1917 ch 127 §1, and repealed Stats 1933 ch 744 §198.

ARTICLE 17
Judgment Binding on Successors

Persons bound by judgment. §851.

§851. Persons bound by judgment

The judgment in a comprehensive adjudication conducted pursuant to this chapter shall be binding on the parties to the comprehensive adjudication and all their successors in interest, including, but not limited to, heirs, executors, administrators, assigns, lessees, licensees, the agents and employees of the parties to the comprehensive adjudication and all their successors in interest, and all landowners or other persons claiming rights to extract groundwater from the basin whose claims have not been exempted and are covered by the notice provided in the comprehensive adjudication. **Leg.H.** Added Stats 2015 ch 672 §1 (AB 1390), effective January 1, 2016. Amended Stats 2016 ch 86 §31 (SB 1171), effective January 1, 2017.

Former Sections: Former CCP §851 was added Stats 1953 ch 52 §7 and amended and renumbered CCP §854 by Stats 2016 ch 86 §32 (SB 1171).

Former CCP §851, similar to present CCP §422.10, was enacted in 1872 and repealed Stats 1933 ch 744 §198.

Prior Law: Former CCP §851 was added Stats 1953 ch 52 §7, amended Stats 1969 ch 1611 §17, operative July 1, 1970, and amended and renumbered CCP §854 by Stats 2016 ch 86 §32 (SB 1171), effective January 1, 2017.

Former CCP §851, similar to present CCP §422.10, was enacted 1872 and repealed Stats 1933 ch 744 §198.

ARTICLE 18
Continuing Jurisdiction

Modification or amendment of final judgment. §852.

§852. Modification or amendment of final judgment

The court shall have continuing jurisdiction to modify or amend a final judgment in a comprehensive adjudication in response to new information, changed circumstances, the interests of justice, or to ensure that the criteria of subdivision (a) of Section 850 are met. If feasible, the judge who heard the original comprehensive adjudication shall preside over actions or motions to modify or amend the final judgment. **Leg.H.** Added Stats 2015 ch 672 §1 (AB 1390), effective January 1, 2016. Amended Stats 2016 ch 86 §33 (SB 1171), effective January 1, 2017.

Former Sections: Former CCP §852 was added Stats 1953 ch 52 §7 and amended and renumbered CCP §855 by Stats 2016 ch 86 §34 (SB 1171).

Former CCP §852, similar to present CCP §422.10, was enacted 1872 and repealed Stats 1933 ch 744 §198.

Prior Law: Former CCP §852 was added Stats 1953 ch 52 §7 and amended and renumbered CCP §855 by Stats 2016 ch 86 §34 (SB 1171), effective January 1, 2017.

Former CCP §852, similar to present CCP §422.10, was enacted 1872 and repealed Stats 1933 ch 744 §198.

CHAPTER 8
ACTIONS AGAINST COOWNERS OF MINES

Service of notice of nonpayment of share of taxes. §853.
Manner of service. §854.
Petition in absence of contribution. §855.
Petition if mine or mining claim situated in more than one county. §856.
Setting petition for hearing; Notice of hearing. §857.
Evidence and judgment. §858.
Recordation of decree. §859.

§853. Service of notice of nonpayment of share of taxes

Upon the failure of a coowner of a mine or mining claim to contribute his proportionate share of the taxes that have been levied and assessed upon the mine or mining claim for the period of five years, a coowner who has paid that share may, at the expiration of the five years, serve upon the delinquent coowner notice thereof. **Leg.H.** Added Stats 1953 ch 52 §7 as CCP §850. Amended and renumbered by Stats 2016 ch 86 §29 (SB 1171), effective January 1, 2017.

Former Sections: Former CCP §853 was added Stats 1953 ch 52 §7 and amended and renumbered CCP §856 by Stats 2016 ch 86 §35 (SB 1171).

Former CCP §853, relating to pleadings in justice courts, was enacted in 1872 and repealed Stats 1933 ch 744 §198.

Prior Law: Former CCP §853 was added Stats 1953 ch 52 §7 and amended and renumbered CCP §856 by Stats 2016 ch 86 §35 (SB 1171), effective January 1, 2017.

Former CCP §853, relating to pleadings in justice courts, was enacted 1872 and repealed Stats 1933 ch 744 §198.

§854. Manner of service

The notice shall be serviced in the manner provided by law for the service of a summons in a civil action, but where service is by publication, the publication shall be in a newspaper of general circulation published in the county in which the mine or mining claim is situated or if there is no such newspaper, in such a newspaper in an adjoining county, and the publication shall be at least once a week for 90 days. **Leg.H.** Added Stats 1953 ch 52 §7, as CCP §851. Amended Stats 1969 ch 1611 §17, operative July 1, 1970. Amended and renumbered by Stats 2016 ch 86 §32 (SB 1171), effective January 1, 2017.

Former Sections: Former CCP §854 was added Stats 1953 ch 52 §7 and amended and renumbered CCP §857 by Stats 2016 ch 86 §36 (SB 1171).

Former CCP §854, similar to present CCP §§430.10, 430.30, 430.40, was enacted in 1872 and repealed Stats 1933 ch 744 §198.

Prior Law: Former CCP §854 was added Stats 1953 ch 52 §7 and amended and renumbered CCP §857 by Stats 2016 ch 86 §36 (SB 1171), effective January 1, 2017.

Former CCP §854, similar to present CCP §§430.10, 430.30, 430.40, was enacted 1872 and repealed Stats 1933 ch 744 §198.

§855. Petition in absence of contribution

If before the expiration of 90 days from the service the delinquent fails or refuses to contribute his proportionate share of the taxes, the coowner contributing such share may file in the superior court of the county in which the mine or mining claim is situated a verified petition setting forth the facts and particularly describing the mine or mining claim. **Leg.H.** Added Stats 1953 ch 52 §7, as CCP §852. Amended and renumbered from Cal Civ Code §852 by Stats 2016 ch 86 §34 (SB 1171), effective January 1, 2017.

Prior Law: Former CCP §855 was added Stats 1953 ch 52 §7 and amended and renumbered CCP §858 by Stats 2016 ch 86 §37 (SB 1171), effective January 1, 2017.

Former CCP §855, similar to present CCP §431.30, was enacted 1872, amended Stats 1907 ch 478 §7, and repealed Stats 1933 ch 744 §198.

Former Sections: Former CCP §855 was added Stats 1953 ch 52 §7 and amended and renumbered CCP §858 by Stats 2016 ch 86 §37 (SB 1171).

Former CCP §855, similar to present CCP §431.30, was enacted in 1872 and repealed Stats 1933 ch 744 §198.

§856. Petition if mine or mining claim situated in more than one county

If the mine or mining claim is situated in more than one county, the petition may be filed in the superior court of either county. **Leg.H.** Added Stats 1953 ch 52 §7, as CCP §853. Renumbered from Cal Code Civ Proc §853 by Stats 2016 ch 86 §35 (SB 1171), effective January 1, 2017.

Former Sections: Former CCP §856 was added Stats 1953 ch 52 §7 and amended and renumbered CCP §859 by Stats 2016 ch 86 §38 (SB 1171).

Former CCP §856, similar to present CCP §§426.10, 426.30- 426.60, was enacted in 1872 and repealed Stats 1933 ch 744 §198.

Prior Law: Former CCP §856 was added Stats 1953 ch 52 §7 and amended and renumbered CCP §859 by Stats 2016 ch 86 §38 (SB 1171), effective January 1, 2017.

Former CCP §856, similar to present CCP §§426.10, 426.30-426.60, was enacted 1872 and repealed Stats 1933 ch 744 §198.

§857. Setting petition for hearing; Notice of hearing

The clerk shall set the petition for hearing by the court and give notice of the hearing by causing a notice of the time and place of the hearing to be posted at the county courthouse at least 10 days before the hearing. The court may order such further notice as it deems proper. **Leg.H.** Added Stats 1953 ch 52 §7, as CCP §854. Amended and renumbered by Stats 2016 ch 86 §36 (SB 1171), effective January 1, 2017.

Prior Law Former CCP §857, similar to present CCP §§430.40, 430.50, was enacted 1872 and repealed Stats 1933 ch 744 §198.

§857a. [Section repealed 1933]

Leg.H. Added Stats 1919 ch 350 §1. Repealed Stats 1933 ch 744 §198. See CCP §666.

§858. Evidence and judgment

The court shall hear evidence for or against the petition and may order judgment on the petition vesting the interest of the delinquent in the mine or mining claim in the petitioner. **Leg.H.** Added Stats 1953 ch 52 §7, as CCP §855. Amended and renumbered by Stats 2016 ch 86 §37 (SB 1171), effective January 1, 2017.

Prior Law Former CCP §858, similar to present CCP §472(a), was enacted 1872 and repealed Stats 1933 ch 744 §198.

§859. Recordation of decree

A certified copy of the decree may be recorded in the office of the recorder of each county in which any part of the mine or mining claim is situated. **Leg.H.** Added Stats 1953 ch 52 §7, as CCP §856. Amended and renumbered from Cal Civ Code §856 by Stats 2016 ch 86 §38 (SB 1171), effective January 1, 2017.

Prior Law Former CCP §859, similar to present CCP §472(a), was enacted 1872, amended Stats 1905 ch 284 §1, and repealed Stats 1933 ch 744 §198.

CHAPTER 9
VALIDATING PROCEEDINGS

Public agency's action. §860.
Jurisdiction of interested parties; Publication of summons; Notice of pendency of proceedings. §861.
Contents of summons. §861.1.
Completion of jurisdiction; Appearance of interested party. §862.
Interested person's action; Public agency as defendant; Summons, publication, and dismissal. §863.
Authorization of bonds, warrants, contracts, obligations, and evidences of indebtedness. §864.
Consolidation of actions. §865.
Effect of error, irregularity, or omission. §866.
Setting for hearing or trial. §867.
Dismissal of action. §867.5.
Costs. §868.
Exclusive time and manner of contest; Availability of other remedy. §869.
Effect of judgment; Notice of appeal. §870.
Revenues from tax imposed by other agency. §870.5.

§860. Public agency's action

A public agency may upon the existence of any matter which under any other law is authorized to be determined pursuant to this chapter, and for 60 days thereafter, bring an action in the superior court of the county in which the principal office of the public agency is located to determine the validity of such matter. The action shall be in the nature of a proceeding in rem. **Leg.H.** Added Stats 1961 ch 1479 §1.

Prior Law: Former CCP §860, similar to present CCP §472, was enacted 1872, amended Stats 1921 ch 126 §1, and repealed Stats 1933 ch 744 §198.

§861. Jurisdiction of interested parties; Publication of summons; Notice of pendency of proceedings

Jurisdiction of all interested parties may be had by publication of summons pursuant to Section 6063 of the Government Code in a newspaper of general circulation designated by the court, published in the county where the action is pending and whenever possible within the boundaries of the public agency, and in such other counties as may be ordered by the court, and if there be no such newspaper in any such county or counties then in some adjoining county. In addition, prior to completion of such publication, the agency shall, to the extent which the court finds reasonably practicable, give notice of the pendency of the proceeding by mail or other means ordered by the court. **Leg.H.** Added Stats 1961 ch 1479 §1.

Prior Law: Former CCP §861 was enacted 1872 and repealed Stats 1933 ch 744 §198.

§861.1. Contents of summons

The summons shall be directed to "all persons interested in the matter of (specifying the matter)," and shall contain a notice to all persons interested in the matter that they may contest the legality or validity of the matter by appearing and filing a written answer to the complaint not later than the date specified in the summons, which date shall be 10 or more days after the completion of publication of the summons. The summons shall provide a detailed summary of the matter the public agency or other person seeks to validate. The summons shall also state that persons who contest the legality or validity of the matter will not be subject to punitive action, such as wage garnishment or seizure of their real or personal property. Except as otherwise specified in this section the summons shall be in the form prescribed in Section 412.20. **Leg.H.** Added Stats 1963 ch 1865 §1, effective July 19, 1963. Amended Stats 1965 ch 894 §1; Stats 1969 ch 1611 §18, operative July 1, 1970; Stats 1998 ch 529 §1 (AB 2049).

§862. Completion of jurisdiction; Appearance of interested party

Jurisdiction shall be complete after the date specified in the summons. Any party interested may, not later than the date specified in the summons, appear and contest the legality or validity of the matter sought to be determined. **Leg.H.** Added Stats 1961 ch 1479 §1. Amended Stats 1965 ch 894 §2.

Prior Law: Former CCP 2 was enacted 1872, amended code Amdts 1873–74 ch 383 §119, and repealed Stats 1933 ch 744 §198.

§863. Interested person's action; Public agency as defendant; Summons, publication, and dismissal

If no proceedings have been brought by the public agency pursuant to this chapter, any interested person may bring an action within the time and in the court specified by Section 860 to determine the validity of such matter. The public agency shall be a defendant and shall be served with the summons and complaint in the action in the manner provided by law for the service of a summons in a civil action. In any such action the summons shall be in the form prescribed in Section 861.1 except that in addition to being directed to "all persons interested in the matter of [specifying the matter]," it shall also be directed to the public agency. If the interested person bringing such action fails to complete the publication and such other notice as may be prescribed by the court in accordance with Section 861 and to file proof thereof in the action within 60 days from the filing of his complaint, the action shall be forthwith dismissed on the motion of the public agency unless good cause for such failure is shown by the interested person. **Leg.H.** Added Stats 1961 ch 1479 §1. Amended Stats 1963 ch 1865 §2, effective July 19, 1963; Stats 1969 ch 1611 §19, operative July 1, 1970.

Prior Law: Former CCP §863 was enacted 1872 and repealed Stats 1933 ch 744 §198.

§864. Authorization of bonds, warrants, contracts, obligations, and evidences of indebtedness

For purposes of this chapter, bonds, warrants, contracts, obligations, and evidences of indebtedness shall be deemed to be in existence upon their authorization. Bonds and warrants shall be deemed authorized as of the date of adoption by the governing body of the public agency of a resolution or ordinance authorizing their issuance, and contracts shall be deemed authorized as of the date of adoption by the governing body of the public agency of a resolution or ordinance approving the contract and authorizing its execution. **Leg.H.** Added Stats 1961 ch 1479 §1.

Prior Law: Former CCP §864 was enacted 1872 and repealed Stats 1933 ch 744 §198.

§865. Consolidation of actions

If more than one action is pending concerning similar contests which may be brought under this chapter, they shall be consolidated for trial. **Leg.H.** Added Stats 1961 ch 1479 §1.

Prior Law: Former CCP §865 was enacted 1872 and repealed Stats 1933 ch 744 §198.

§866. Effect of error, irregularity, or omission

The court hearing the action shall disregard any error, irregularity, or omission which does not affect the substantial rights of the parties. **Leg.H.** Added Stats 1961 ch 1479 §1.

Prior Law: Former CCP §866, similar to present CCP §§484.020, 484.030, was enacted 1872, amended Stats 1907 ch 478 §8, Stats 1911 ch 218 §1, and repealed Stats 1933 ch 744 §198.

§867. Setting for hearing or trial

Actions brought pursuant to this chapter shall be given preference over all other civil actions before the court in the matter of setting the same for hearing or trial, and in hearing the same, to the end that such actions shall be speedily heard and determined. **Leg.H.** Added Stats 1961 ch 1479 §1.

Prior Law: Former CCP §867, similar to present CCP §§489.210, 489.220, was enacted 1872, amended Stats 1907 ch 478 §9, and repealed Stats 1933 ch 744 §198.

§867.5. Dismissal of action

(a) In the event that an action is brought by a public agency pursuant to this chapter, and that public agency later dismisses the action after any party has answered, then, notwithstanding Section 863, the party that answered may file an action pursuant to this chapter within 30 days after the public agency's dismissal was filed by the court.

(b) Subdivision (a) is not applicable to a case in which a public agency has by formal act rescinded the action on the matter subject to validation. **Leg.H.** Added Stats 2000 ch 723 §2 (AB 2300).

§868. Costs

The costs of any proceeding or action pursuant to this chapter may be allowed and apportioned between the parties or taxed to the losing party in the discretion of the court. **Leg.H.** Added Stats 1961 ch 1479 §1.

Prior Law: Former CCP §868, similar to present CCP §§483.030, 489.310, 489.320, was enacted 1872, amended Stats 1905 ch 222 §1, Stats 1915 ch 88 §1, Stats 1917 ch 608 §4, Stats 1927 ch 335 §1, Stats 1929 ch 342 §1, and repealed Stats 1933 ch 744 §198.

§869. Exclusive time and manner of contest; Availability of other remedy

No contest except by the public agency or its officer or agent of any thing or matter under this chapter shall be made other than within the time and the manner herein specified. The availability to any public agency, including any local agency, or to its officers or agents, of the remedy provided by this chapter, shall not be construed to preclude the use by such public agency or its officers or agents, of mandamus or any other remedy to determine the validity of any thing or matter. **Leg.H.** Added Stats 1961 ch 1479 §1. Amended Stats 1963 ch 1865 §3, effective July 19, 1963.

Prior Law: Former CCP §869 was enacted 1872 and repealed Stats 1933 ch 744 §198.

§870. Effect of judgment; Notice of appeal

(a) The judgment, if no appeal is taken, or if taken and the judgment is affirmed, shall, notwithstanding any other provision of law including, without limitation, Sections 473 and 473.5, thereupon become and thereafter be forever binding and conclusive, as to all matters therein adjudicated or which at that time could have been adjudicated, against the agency and against all other persons, and the judgment shall permanently enjoin the institution by any person of any action or proceeding raising any issue as to which the judgment is binding and conclusive.

(b) Notwithstanding any other provision of law including, without limitation, Section 901 and any rule of court, no appeal shall be allowed from any judgment entered pursuant to this chapter unless a notice of appeal is filed within 30 days after the notice of entry of the judgment, or, within 30 days after the entry of the judgment if there is no answering party. If there is no answering party, only issues related to the jurisdiction of the court to enter a judgment in the action pursuant to this chapter may be raised on appeal. **Leg.H.** Added Stats 1961 ch 1479 §1. Amended Stats 1963 ch 1865 §4, effective July 19, 1963; Stats 1969 ch 1611 §20, operative July 1, 1970; Stats 1985 ch 229 §1; Stats 1994 ch 242 §1 (SB 2107), effective July 20, 1994.

Prior Law: Former CCP §870, similar to present CCP §512.010, was enacted 1872 and repealed Stats 1933 ch 744 §198.

§870.5. Revenues from tax imposed by other agency

Any local public agency that pledges sales or retail transaction and use tax revenues received from taxes imposed by another public agency for bond payments or payment of other security obligations shall, in any validation action it files involving those bonds or other obligations, provide written notice thereof to the public agency imposing the taxes pledged as security for the bonds or other obligations at the time it files the validation action. **Leg.H.** Added Stats 1998 ch 360 §1 (AB 1964).

§871. [Section repealed 1933]

Leg.H. Enacted 1872. Amended Code Amdts 1875–76 ch 498 §5; Code Amdts 1880 ch 106 §1. Repealed Stats 1933 ch 744 §198. See CCP §585.

CHAPTER 10
GOOD FAITH IMPROVER OF PROPERTY OWNED BY ANOTHER

"Good faith improver". §871.1.
"Person" as including unincorporated association. §871.2.
Right of good faith improver to bring action or file cross complaint; Burden of establishing right to relief; Consideration of improver's negligence. §871.3.
Denial of relief on determination that substantial justice results from exercise of right of setoff or right to remove improvement. §871.4.
Relief granted; Adjustment of equities of parties; Protection of owner against pecuniary loss; Consideration of owner's plans, etc. §871.5.
Relief when improvement encroaches. §871.6.
Inapplicability to "public entity" improver or land appropriated to public use. §871.7.
[Section renumbered 1933]. §872.

§871.1. "Good faith improver"

As used in this chapter, "good faith improver" means:

(a) A person who makes an improvement to land in good faith and under the erroneous belief, because of a mistake of law or fact, that he is the owner of the land.

(b) A successor in interest of a person described in subdivision (a). **Leg.H.** Added Stats 1968 ch 150 §3.

§871.2. "Person" as including unincorporated association

As used in this chapter, "person" includes an unincorporated association. **Leg.H.** Added Stats 1968 ch 150 §3. Amended Stats 1971 ch 244 §55, operative July 1, 1972.

§871.3. Right of good faith improver to bring action or file cross complaint; Burden of establishing right to relief; Consideration of improver's negligence

(a) An action for relief under this chapter shall be treated as an unlimited civil case, regardless of the amount in controversy and regardless of whether a defendant cross-complains for relief under this chapter. Any other case in which a defendant cross-complains for relief under this chapter shall be treated as a limited civil case if the cross-complaint is defensive and the case otherwise satisfies the amount in controversy and other requirements of Section 85.

(b) In every case, the burden is on the good faith improver to establish that the good faith improver is entitled to relief under this chapter, and the degree of negligence of the good faith improver should be taken into account by the court in determining whether the improver acted in good faith and in determining the relief, if any, that is consistent with substantial justice to the parties under the circumstances of the particular case. **Leg.H.** Added Stats 1968 ch 150 §3. Amended Stats 1971 ch 244 §56, operative July 1, 1972; Stats 1998 ch 931 §99 (SB 2139), effective September 28, 1998; Stats 1999 ch 344 §14 (SB 210), effective September 7, 1999; Stats 2000 ch 688 §7 (AB 1669).

§871.4. Denial of relief on determination that substantial justice results from exercise of right of setoff or right to remove improvement

The court shall not grant relief under this chapter if the court determines that exercise of the good faith improver's right of setoff under Section 741 of the Code of Civil Procedure or right to remove the improvement under Section 1013.5 of the Civil Code would result in substantial justice to the parties under the circumstances of the particular case. In determining whether removal of the improvement would result in substantial justice to the parties under the circumstances of the particular case, the court shall take into consideration any plans the owner of the land may have for the use or development of the land upon which the improvement was made and his need for the land upon which the improvement was made in connection with the use or development of other property owned by him. **Leg.H.** Added Stats 1968 ch 150 §3.

§871.5. Relief granted; Adjustment of equities of parties; Protection of owner against pecuniary loss; Consideration of owner's plans, etc.

When an action or cross-complaint is brought pursuant to Section 871.3, the court may, subject to Section 871.4, effect such an adjustment of the rights, equities, and interests of the good faith improver, the owner of the land, and other interested parties (including, but not limited to, lessees, lienholders, and encumbrancers) as is consistent with substantial justice to the parties under the circumstances of the particular case. The relief granted shall protect the owner of the land upon which the improvement was constructed against any pecuniary loss but shall avoid, insofar as possible, enriching him unjustly at the expense of the good faith improver. In protecting the owner of the land against pecuniary loss, the court shall take into consideration the expenses the owner of the land has incurred in the action in which relief under this chapter is sought, including but not limited to reasonable attorney fees. In determining the appropriate form of relief under this section, the court shall take into consideration any plans the owner of the land may have for the use or development of the land upon which the improvement was made and his need for the land upon which the improvement was made in connection with the use or development of other property owned by him. **Leg.H.** Added Stats 1968 ch 150 §3. Amended Stats 1971 ch 244 §57, operative July 1, 1972.

§871.6. Relief when improvement encroaches

Nothing in this chapter affects the rules of law which determine the relief, if any, to be granted when a person constructs on his own land an improvement which encroaches on adjoining land. **Leg.H.** Added Stats 1968 ch 150 §3.

§871.7. Inapplicability to "public entity" improver or land appropriated to public use

(a) This chapter does not apply where the improver is a public entity or where the improvement is made to land owned or possessed by a public entity. As used in this section, "public entity" includes the United States, a state, county, city and county, city, district, public authority, public agency, or any other political subdivision or public corporation.

(b) This chapter does not apply where the owner of the land upon which the improvement is constructed has appropriated the land to a public use and could have acquired the land for that use by exercising the power of eminent domain. **Leg.H.** Added Stats 1968 ch 150 §3.

§872. [Section renumbered 1933]

Leg.H. Enacted 1872. Amended Stat 1921 ch 127 §1. Amended and renumbered §586 by Stats 1933 ch 744 §93.

CHAPTER 11
ACTIONS TO RECOVER COVID-19 RENTAL DEBT [REPEALED EFFECTIVE OCTOBER 1, 2027]

Requirement of good faith effort to seek rental assisstance; Applicability; Commencement of action [Repealed October 1, 2027]. § 871.10.
Award of attorneys' fees [Repealed October 1, 2025]. § 871.11.
Repeal of chapter [Repealed October 1, 2027]. § 871.12.

§ 871.10. Requirement of good faith effort to seek rental assisstance; Applicability; Commencement of action [Repealed October 1, 2027]

(a) In any action seeking recovery of COVID-19 rental debt, as defined in Section 1179.02, the plaintiff shall, in addition to any other requirements provided by law, attach to the complaint documentation showing that the plaintiff has made a good faith effort to investigate whether governmental rental assistance is available to the tenant, seek governmental rental assistance for the tenant, or cooperate with the tenant's efforts to obtain rental assistance from any governmental entity, or other third party pursuant to paragraph (3) of subdivision (a) of Section 1947.3 of the Civil Code.

(b) In an action subject to subdivision (a), the court may reduce the damages awarded for any amount of COVID-19 rental debt, as defined in Section 1179.02, sought if the court determines that the landlord refused to obtain rental assistance from the state rental assistance program created pursuant to Chapter 17 (commencing with Section 50897) of Part 2 of Division 31 of the Health and Safety Code, if the tenant met the eligibility requirements and funding was available.

(c) An action to recover COVID-19 rental debt, as defined in Section 1179.02, that is subject to this section shall not be commenced before November 1, 2021.

(d) Subdivisions (a) through (c), inclusive, shall not apply to an action to recover COVID-19 rental debt, as defined in Section 1179.02, that was pending before the court as of January 29, 2021.

(e) Except as provided in subdivision(g), any action to recover COVID-19 rental debt, as defined in Section 1179.02, that is subject to this section and is pending before the court as of January 29, 2021, shall be stayed until November 1, 2021.

(f) This section shall not apply to any unlawful detainer action to recover possession pursuant to Section 1161.

(g)(1) Actions for breach of contract to recover rental debt that were filed before October 1, 2020, shall not be stayed and may proceed.

(2) This subdivision does not apply to actions filed against any person who would have qualified under the rental assistance funding provided through the Secretary of the Treasury pursuant to Section 501 of Subtitle A of Title V of Division N of the federal Consolidated Appropriations Act, 2021 (Public Law 116-260) if the person's household income is at or below 80 percent of the area median income for the 2020 or 2021 calendar year. **Leg.H.** Added Stats 2021 ch 2 §10 (SB 91), effective January 29, 2021, repealed July 1, 2027. Amended Stats 2021 ch 5 §7 (AB 81), effective February 23, 2021, repealed July 1, 2027; Stats 2021 ch 27 §§8, 10 (AB 832), effective June 28, 2021, repealed October 1, 2027 (repealer amended).

§ 871.11. Award of attorneys' fees [Repealed October 1, 2025]

(a) Notwithstanding any other law, in any action to recover COVID-19 rental debt, as defined in Section 1179.02, brought as a limited or unlimited civil case, the court shall not, under ordinary circumstances, award reasonable attorneys' fees to a prevailing party that exceed the following amounts:

(1) If the matter is uncontested, five hundred dollars ($500).

(2) If the matter is contested, one thousand dollars ($1,000).

(b) In determining whether a case was litigated under ordinary circumstances, the court may consider the following:

(1) The number and complexity of pretrial and posttrial motions.

(2) The nature and extent of any discovery performed.

(3) Whether the case was tried by jury or by the court.

(4) The length of the trial.

(5) Any other factor the court, in its discretion, finds relevant, including whether the tenant or the landlord, or both the tenant and the landlord, would have been eligible to receive a rental assistance payment from the governmental entity, or other third party pursuant to paragraph (3) of subdivision (a) of Section 1947.3 of the Civil Code.

(c) Nothing in this section shall be interpreted to entitle the prevailing party to an award of reasonable attorneys' fees if that award is not otherwise provided for by law or agreement.

(d) This section shall remain in effect until October 1, 2025, and as of that date is repealed. **Leg.H.** Added Stats 2021 ch 2 §10 (SB 91), effective January 29, 2021, repealed July 1, 2025. Amended Stats 2021 ch 27 §9 (AB 832), effective June 28, 2021, repealed October 1, 2025.

§ 871.12. Repeal of chapter [Repealed October 1, 2027]

This chapter shall remain in effect until October 1, 2027, and as of the date is repealed. **Leg.H.** Added Stats 2021 ch 2 §10 (SB 91), effective January 29, 2021, repealed July 1, 2027. Amended Stats 2021 ch 27 §10 (AB 832), effective June 28, 2021, repealed October 1, 2027.

CHAPTER 12
ACTIONS FOR RESTITUTION FOR OR REPLACEMENT OF CERTAIN MOTOR VEHICLES

Applicability. § 871.20.
Statute of Limitations. § 871.21.
Definitions. § 871.22.
Application to Distributors and Warrantors. § 871.23.
Pre-Suit Notice and Requirements for Civil Penalty Claims. § 871.24.
Standardized SBA Release. § 871.25.
Expedited Discovery and Resolution Procedures. § 871.26.
Calculation of Damages and Restitution Procedures. § 871.27.
Cumulative Remedies. § 871.28.

§ 871.20. Applicability

(a) Notwithstanding any other law, this chapter applies to an action seeking restitution or replacement of a motor vehicle pursuant to subdivision (b) or (d) of Section 1793.2, Section 1793.22, or Section 1794 of the Civil Code, or for civil penalties pursuant to subdivision (c) of Section 1794 of the Civil Code, where the request for restitution or replacement is based on noncompliance with the applicable express warranty.

(b) This chapter does not apply to service contract claims under Section 1794 of the Civil Code or any action seeking remedies that are not restitution or replacement of a motor vehicle. **Leg.H.** Added Stats 2024 ch 938 §1 (AB 1755), effective January 1, 2025.

§ 871.21. Statute of Limitations

(a) An action covered by Section 871.20 shall be commenced within one year after the expiration of the applicable express warranty.

(b) Notwithstanding subdivision (a), an action covered by Section 871.20 shall not be brought later than six years after the date of original delivery of the motor vehicle.

(c) The time periods prescribed in subdivisions (a) and (b) shall be tolled as follows:

(1) As provided by tolling requirements prescribed in subdivision (c) of Section 1793.22 of the Civil Code, as applicable.

(2) For the time the motor vehicle is out of service by reason of repair for any nonconformity.

(3) For the time period after a pre-suit notice is provided to the manufacturer in accordance with Section 871.24, which time period shall not exceed 60 days. **Leg.H.** Added Stats 2024 ch 938 §1 (AB 1755), effective January 1, 2025.

§ 871.22. Definitions

For purposes of this chapter, the following definitions apply:

(a) "Applicable express warranty" means the written warranty provided by the manufacturer at the time of delivery of the subject motor vehicle, which provides coverage for the specific nonconformity at issue in the action, subject to the terms and exclusions of that warranty.

(b) "Distributor" means any individual, partnership, corporation, association, or other legal relationship that stands between the manufacturer and the retail seller in purchases, consignments, or contracts for sale of consumer goods or motor vehicles.

(c) "Manufacturer" means any individual, partnership, corporation, association, or other legal relationship that manufactures, assembles, or produces consumer goods or motor vehicles.

(d) "Motor vehicle" includes any of the following:

(1) A motor home, as defined in paragraph (3) of subdivision (e) of Section 1793.22 of the Civil Code.

(2) A new motor vehicle, as defined in paragraph (2) of subdivision (e) of Section 1793.22 of the Civil Code.

(3) A travel trailer.

(e) "Travel trailer" means a vehicular unit without motive power that is designed to be towed or carried by a motor vehicle. "Travel trailer" does not include a mobilehome.

(f) "Warrantor" means any entity or person who gives or offers to give a written warranty or who is or may be obligated under an implied warranty. **Leg.H.** Added Stats 2024 ch 938 §1 (AB 1755), effective January 1, 2025.

§ 871.23. Application to Distributors and Warrantors

For purposes of this chapter, any reference to a manufacturer also applies to a distributor or warrantor. **Leg.H.** Added Stats 2024 ch 938 §1 (AB 1755), effective January 1, 2025.

§ 871.24. Pre-Suit Notice and Requirements for Civil Penalty Claims

(a) At least 30 days prior to the commencement of an action seeking civil penalties under subdivision (c) of Section 1794 of the Civil Code, the consumer shall do all of the following:

(1) Notify the manufacturer of the consumer's name, the accurate Vehicle Identification Number ("VIN") of the motor vehicle, and a brief summary of the repair history and problems with the motor vehicle.

(2) Demand that the manufacturer repurchase or replace the motor vehicle.

(b) Minor deviations in the notice submitted pursuant to subdivision (a) shall not disqualify consumers from seeking civil penalties.

(c) At the time that notice submitted pursuant to subdivision (a) is sent, the consumer shall have possession of the motor vehicle.

(d) The notice required by subdivision (a) shall be in writing and shall be sent either by email to the email address prominently displayed on the manufacturer's website for this purpose or by certified or registered mail, return receipt requested, to the address provided by the manufacturer in the owner's manual or warranty booklet. The notice information on the manufacturer's website, owner's manual, and warranty booklet shall be provided in both English and Spanish.

(e)(1) A request for or action seeking civil penalties under subdivision (c) of Section 1794 of the Civil Code shall not be allowed or maintained if both of the following conditions are present:

(A) Within 30 days after receipt of the notice, the manufacturer makes an offer of restitution or replacement of the motor vehicle for the amount provided by subdivision (d) of Section 1793.2 of the Civil Code and Section 871.27, plus reasonable attorneys' fees and costs, if the consumer is represented by an attorney.

(B) The motor vehicle replacement or restitution is completed within 60 days from the date of receipt of the original notice.

(2) The consumer shall comply in good faith with reasonable requests from the manufacturer for documentation required to complete the requested restitution or replacement of the motor vehicle.

(f) A prelitigation dispute as to attorney's fees and costs shall be resolved by neutral, binding arbitration. A dispute as to the amount of attorney's fees and costs shall not, by itself, be a sufficient basis to show that the manufacturer's offer is out of compliance with this section.

(g) The consumer shall maintain possession of the motor vehicle for at least 30 days after the manufacturer's receipt of written notice seeking restitution or replacement.

(1) If the manufacturer does not offer restitution or replacement of the motor vehicle within 30 days of receiving the consumer's notice, the consumer shall be permitted to sell their motor vehicle and seek remedies, including, but not limited to, civil penalties under subdivision (c) of Section 1794 of the Civil Code.

(2) If the manufacturer offers restitution or replacement of the motor vehicle, the consumer shall maintain possession of the motor vehicle for the full 60 days after the manufacturer's receipt of the consumer's notice.

(h) An action seeking restitution or replacement under Section 871.20 may be commenced without compliance with subdivision (a). In that event, the consumer shall have possession of the motor vehicle at the time of the filing of the complaint, and shall not seek civil penalties, whether by amendment of the complaint or otherwise. If, however, notice is provided pursuant to subdivision (a) and the manufacturer fails to comply with their obligations under subdivision (e), the consumer may commence an action for restitution or replacement, including, but not limited to, civil penalties under subdivision (c) of Section 1794 of the Civil Code.

(i) A consumer shall act in good faith in order to comply with this section.

(j) This section shall become operative on April 1, 2025. **Leg.H.** Added Stats 2024 ch 938 §1 (AB 1755), effective January 1, 2025.

§ 871.25. Standardized SBA Release

A remedy in compliance with this chapter shall not be contingent on the execution of any release other than the following Standardized SBA Release:

Standardized SBA Release

Release as it relates to settlements:

The parties have previously agreed to settle the case as follows and hereby memorialize all terms of their settlement as follows:

1. Within 60 days from the date of receipt of the notice requesting restitution or replacement of the Subject Vehicle [Vehicle Year/Make/Model and VIN] (hereinafter "Subject Vehicle"), [Manufacturer] (hereinafter "Defendant") will make the following payments:

a. Defendant shall pay the remaining loan balance or lease balance and residual value on the Subject Vehicle directly to the lienholder [Lender Name] in the amount necessary to relieve Plaintiff of all obligations related to Plaintiff's purchase or lease of the Subject Vehicle, excluding any late fees or penalties in the amount of [Loan Payoff Amount]. Said payment shall include interest through the date of payoff. This payment shall be expedited to the lienholder following completion of the return of the Subject Vehicle to the manufacturer or its agents.

b. Defendant shall pay to [Plaintiff's Full Name] (hereinafter "Plaintiff") a total amount of [Restitution Amount] in a check payable to Plaintiff. This payment shall be provided to Plaintiff at the time of the return of the Subject Vehicle to the manufacturer or its agents. In the event Plaintiff makes an additional payment that is not included in the above amount, Defendant shall reimburse Plaintiff for any payments made according to proof, with the exception of any late fees, within 30 days from the date proof of payment is provided to Defendant.

c. [If applicable] Defendant shall pay civil penalties in the amount of [Civil Penalties Amount] in a check payable to [Plaintiff, if not represented by counsel, or Name of Law Firm/Attorney, if Plaintiff is represented by counsel]. This payment shall be expedited following completion of the return of the Subject Vehicle to the manufacturer or its agents.

d. Defendant shall pay to Plaintiff's counsel, if Plaintiff was represented by counsel (select one option below):

(i) In the event there is an agreement as to attorney's fees and costs, a check in the amount of [Attorney's Fees and Costs] payable to [Name of Law Firm/Attorney] shall be provided to Plaintiff's counsel. This agreed upon payment shall be expedited to the attorney following completion of the return of the Subject Vehicle to the manufacturer or its agents.

(ii) In the event the matter is resolved before the filing of a lawsuit and the parties cannot agree as to the amount of attorney's fees, costs, and expenses, then reasonable attorneys' fees, costs, and expenses shall be determined by neutral, binding arbitration.

(iii) In the event the matter is resolved after the filing of a lawsuit and the parties cannot agree as to the amount of attorney's fees, costs, and expenses, then reasonable attorneys' fees, costs, and expenses pursuant to subdivision (d) of Section 1794 of the Civil Code shall be determined by the court by way of a noticed motion. Defendant agrees Plaintiff is the prevailing party for purposes of said fee motion.

2. Before transfer of the settlement funds set forth in Paragraph 1 above, Plaintiff shall execute all documents necessary for the transfer of ownership of the Subject Vehicle to Defendant or its designee.

3. The payments described above are intended as a compromise resolution of [Plaintiff's Full Name] and [Defendant] with respect to all claims relating to the purchase, lease, condition, use, or repair of the Subject Vehicle during Plaintiff's purchase or possession of the Subject Vehicle. In signing this agreement, Plaintiff hereby releases [Defendant] from all claims relating to the purchase, lease, condition, use, or repair of the Subject Vehicle that arose during Plaintiff's purchase or possession of the Subject Vehicle, including, but not limited to, all claims under Sections 1793.2, 1793.22, and 1794 of the Civil Code. All releases are to take effect once Plaintiff returns the Subject Vehicle to Defendant.

4. [If the case has gone to litigation insert this Paragraph 4] The Parties to this release agree that the court shall retain jurisdiction pursuant to Section 664.6 of the Code of Civil Procedure to enforce its terms. In the event of a breach of this agreement, the prevailing party shall be entitled to recover reasonable attorney's fees and costs incurred in the enforcement of this agreement. Within five business days of all of the above payments clearing, Plaintiff will file a Request for Dismissal with prejudice of [Plaintiff(s) v Defendant(s); Case Number/County] with the court.

_____
(signature of Plaintiff)

_____
(date)

_____
(signature of Defendant)

_____
(date)

Leg.H. Added Stats 2024 ch 938 §1 (AB 1755), effective January 1, 2025.

§ 871.26. Expedited Discovery and Resolution Procedures

(a) This section only applies to a civil action seeking restitution or replacement of a motor vehicle pursuant to Section 871.20.

(b) Within 60 days after the filing of the answer or other responsive pleading, all parties shall, without awaiting a discovery request, provide to all other parties an initial disclosure and documents pursuant to subdivisions (f), (g), and (h).

(c) Within 120 days after the filing of the answer or other responsive pleading, all parties have the right to conduct initial depositions, each not to exceed two hours, of the following deponents:

(1) The plaintiff.

(2) The defendant, and if the defendant is not a natural person, the person who is most qualified to testify on the defendant's behalf. This deposition shall be limited to the topics listed in subdivision (i).

(d) Within 90 days after filing of the answer or other responsive pleading, all parties shall schedule a mediation to occur within 150 days after filing of the answer or other responsive pleading with a court-appointed or private mediator.

(1) Costs shall be distributed equally, but costs may be recoverable by the plaintiff as part of a settlement or judgment.

(2) The plaintiff and a person with settlement authority for the manufacturer shall attend the mediation in person or by remote means.

(e) Except as provided in subdivisions (b) and (c), all other discovery shall be stayed until mediation is concluded. If the case is not resolved at the conclusion of mediation, standard discovery procedures prescribed in Title 4 (commencing with Section 2016.010) of Part 4 of the Code of Civil Procedures shall apply, including an additional deposition of the plaintiff and the defendant and, if the defendant is not a natural person, the person who is most qualified to testify on the defendant's behalf.

(f) The plaintiff shall provide the following documents to all other parties pursuant to the timeline set forth in subdivision (b):

(1) Sales or lease agreement.

(2) Copy of current registration.

(3) Any finance information, account information, including payment history and estimated payoff amount, and any loan modification agreements.

(4) Any repair orders, including to third-party repair facilities or the location of where information relating to repair orders may be found.

(5) Documents detailing all underlying claimed incidental damages.

(6) Information pertaining to the market value of the motor vehicle that is currently in the consumer's possession.

(7) Any written, pre-suit communications with the manufacturer, including, but not limited to, any restitution or replacement request.

(g) The plaintiff shall provide the following information to all other parties pursuant to the timelines set forth in subdivision (b):

(1) Mileage of the motor vehicle as of the date of the disclosure described in subdivision (b).

(2) Primary driver or drivers of the motor vehicle.

(3) If the motor vehicle is primarily used for a business purpose, whether more than five vehicles are registered to the business.

(4) Whether the plaintiff is still in possession of the motor vehicle.

(5) Address where the motor vehicle is located.

(6) Whether the plaintiff is an active or prior member of the Armed Forces.

(7) Whether the motor vehicle has been involved in a collision or accidents reported to insurance prior to the nonconformity, and if so, the approximate date of the collision, the name of the insurance company, and any applicable claim number.

(8) Whether the motor vehicle has any aftermarket modifications done after purchase of the motor vehicle, and if so, a list of each modification.

(9) Dates and mileages for presentations that are not included in the provided repair orders or the location of where the information may be found.

(10) Whether the plaintiff has had any pre-suit communications with the manufacturer, including, but not limited to, any restitution or replacement request.

(11) Any need for an interpreter for purposes of a deposition.

(h) The defendant or manufacturer shall provide the following documents to all other parties pursuant to the timelines prescribed in subdivision (b):

(1) Copy of or access to a version of the owner's manual for a motor vehicle of the same make, model, and year.

(2) Any warranties issued in conjunction with the sale of the motor vehicle.

(3) Sample brochures published for the motor vehicle.

(4) The motor vehicle's original invoice, if any, to the selling dealer.

(5) Sales or lease agreement, if the manufacturer is in possession.

(6) Motor vehicle information reports, including build documentation, component information, and delivery details.

(7) Entire warranty transaction history for the motor vehicle.

(8) Listing of required field actions applicable to the motor vehicle.

(9) Published technical service bulletins ("TSBs") for the same make, model, and year reasonably related to the nonconformities pertaining to the motor vehicle.

(10) Published information service bulletins ("ISBs") for the same make, model, and year reasonably related to the nonconformities pertaining to the motor vehicle.

(11) Records relating to communications between the manufacturer or dealership and the owner or lessee of the motor vehicle, including those related to repair orders or claims involving the motor vehicle.

(12) Warranty policies and procedure manuals.

(13) Service manuals reasonably related to the nonconformities pertaining to the motor vehicle.

(14) If a pre-suit restitution or replacement request is made, all call recordings of pre-suit communications with the consumer available at the time of service of the complaint.

(15) If a pre-suit restitution or replacement request is made, the manufacturer's written statement of policies and procedures used to evaluate customer requests for restitution or replacement pursuant to "Lemon Law" claims.

(16) If a pre-suit restitution or replacement request is made, any nonprivileged, prelitigation evaluation.

(17) Any warranty extensions or modifications issued by the manufacturer on the motor vehicle.

(i) If the defendant is not a natural person, the initial deposition of the person who is most qualified to testify on the defendant's behalf shall be limited to the following topics:

(1) All warranties that accompanied the plaintiff's motor vehicle at the time of purchase or lease.

(2) Questions relating to the nature and extent of the entire service history, warranty history, and repairs relating to the motor vehicle.

(3) Questions relating to recalls applicable to the motor vehicle.

(4) Questions relating to a reasonable number of Technical Service Bulletins or Information Service Bulletins reasonably related to the nonconformities pertaining to the motor vehicle.

(5) Questions relating to relevant diagnostic procedures consulted and followed while diagnosing the plaintiff's concerns for the motor vehicle.

(6) Questions relating to relevant repair procedures consulted and followed during the repairs for the motor vehicle.

(7) Questions relating to relevant communications between the plaintiff and defendant regarding the motor vehicle.

(8) Questions relating to relevant communications between the defendant and any dealership or other third parties regarding the motor vehicle.

(9) If a pre-suit restitution or replacement request was made, questions relating to why the defendant did not replace the motor vehicle or provide restitution.

(10) If a pre-suit restitution or replacement request was made, any nonprivileged evaluation prepared by the manufacturer.

(11) If a pre-suit restitution or replacement request was made, the manufacturer's policies and procedures regarding the restitution or replacement of vehicles in response to a consumer's request for restitution or replacement under the Song-Beverly Consumer Warranty Act, in effect from the date of the notice of the consumer's request for restitution or replacement of the vehicle to the present, and any changes thereto.

(j) Unless the party failing to comply with this section shows good cause, notwithstanding any other law and in addition to any other sanctions imposed pursuant to this chapter, a court shall impose sanctions as follows:

(1) A one-thousand-five-hundred-dollar ($1,500) sanction against the plaintiff's attorney or two-thousand-five-hundred-dollar ($2,500) sanction against the defense attorney respectively, paid within 15 business days for failure to comply with the document production requirements as prescribed in subdivision (b).

(2) A one-thousand-five-hundred-dollar ($1,500) sanction against the plaintiff's attorney or two-thousand-five-hundred-dollar ($2,500) sanction against the defense attorney respectively, paid within 15 business days for failure to comply with the provisions relating to depositions as prescribed in subdivision (c).

(3) For a plaintiff's repeated noncompliance with subdivision (b), (c), or (d), a court shall order the case dismissed without prejudice and the plaintiff's attorney to be responsible for costs awarded to the manufacturer.

(4) For a manufacturer's or defendant's repeated noncompliance with subdivision (b), (c), or (d), a court shall order that evidentiary sanctions attach precluding the manufacturer or defendant from introducing evidence at trial regarding whether the motor vehicle had a nonconformity that substantially impaired the use, value, or safety of the motor vehicle, or whether the motor vehicle was repaired to match the written warranty after a reasonable number of opportunities to do so.

(5) Notwithstanding paragraph (3) of subdivision (o) of Section 6068 of the Business and Professions Code, the court may, in its discretion, require an attorney who is sanctioned pursuant to this subdivision to report the sanction, in writing, to the State Bar of California within 30 days of the imposition of the sanction.

(k) This section does not apply to a party who is not represented by counsel.

(*l*) In addition to the requirements prescribed by subdivision (a), this section only applies to a civil action filed on or after January 1, 2025.

Leg.H. Added Stats 2024 ch 938 §1 (AB 1755), effective January 1, 2025.

§ 871.27. Calculation of Damages and Restitution Procedures

(a) This section only applies to a civil action seeking restitution or replacement of a motor vehicle pursuant to Section 871.20.

(b) The defendant is entitled to an offset in the calculation of the actual price paid or payable for optional equipment, service contracts, or GAP financing purchased by the plaintiff during the motor vehicle purchase or lease transaction from third parties, except for optional purchases for dealer-supplied equipment or services.

(1) Optional equipment and accessories, theft-deterrent devices, surface-protection products, service contracts, extended warranties, debt-cancellation agreements, and guaranteed asset protection ("GAP") financing supplied by a third party that is not the selling or leasing dealership or an authorized retail facility for the original equipment manufacturer are not recoverable as damages pursuant to this section.

(2) Optional equipment and accessories, theft-deterrent devices, surface-protection products, service contracts, extended warranties, debt-cancellation agreements, and GAP financing, if any of the foregoing constitute dealer additions supplied by the selling or leasing dealership or an authorized retail facility for the manufacturer, are recoverable as damages and do not qualify for the offset prescribed by this section.

(c) The defendant is entitled to an offset for negative equity incorporated in the transaction from prior vehicles.

(d) Noncash credits provided by the manufacturer as a form of down-payment assistance, typically referred to as a manufacturer's rebate, shall not be included in the calculation of the actual price paid or payable and shall not be used to reduce the amount of any negative equity offset.

(e) For leases, damages and civil penalties shall be calculated as follows:

(1) Amounts paid or payable by the consumer under an existing agreement to extend a lease term shall be allowable as damages.

(2) Amounts paid by the consumer for the residual value shall be allowable as damages. If the consumer has obtained financing to pay the residual value, the defendant shall pay the remaining residual value on the motor vehicle directly to the lienholder in the amount necessary to obtain title.

(3) Amounts paid or payable by the consumer to extend a lease term shall be included in civil penalty calculations if paid for or the lease extension is activated by the consumer no later than 30 days after delivering pre-suit notice or filing a lawsuit, whichever is earlier.

(4) Amounts paid by the consumer for the residual value shall only be included in civil penalty calculations if paid for or financed by the consumer no later than 30 days after delivering pre-suit notice or filing a lawsuit, whichever is earlier.

(5) The residual value shall not be included in civil penalty calculations if not paid or financed by the consumer.

(f) The defendant shall not be responsible for payment of unpaid interest or unpaid financing costs associated with the retail installment sales contract that will not be owed or paid by the consumer when the lien is paid off.

(g) The restitution payment and vehicle return procedures shall comply with all of the following conditions:

(1) A remedy in compliance with this section shall not be contingent on the execution of any release other than the Standardized SBA Release provided in Section 871.25.

(2) The defendant shall promptly process any agreed-upon motor vehicle restitution or replacement pursuant to this section and complete the restitution or replacement within 30 days from the date of receipt of a signed release from the buyer or lessee's counsel. The defendant's failure to do so shall result in a mandatory penalty of fifty dollars ($50) per day until the settlement is completed, unless the parties stipulate

otherwise. The consumer shall comply in good faith with requests from the manufacturer for reasonable documentation required to complete the requested restitution or replacement of the motor vehicle. In the event the consumer fails to comply in good faith and delays the restitution or replacement, the manufacturer shall not be subject to the daily fifty-dollar ($50) penalty.

(3) The defendant shall provide the consumer with the funds containing their restitution proceeds at the time of the vehicle return. The defendant shall also expedite the funds for the payoff of the vehicle within one business day of the vehicle return. The defendant shall expedite the funds for attorney's fees, and if applicable, civil penalties to counsel for the consumer within one business day of the vehicle return. **Leg.H.** Added Stats 2024 ch 938 §1 (AB 1755), effective January 1, 2025.

§ 871.28. Cumulative Remedies

The duties and obligations imposed by this chapter are cumulative with duties or obligations imposed under any other law and shall not be construed to relieve any party from any duties or obligations imposed under any other law. **Leg.H.** Added Stats 2024 ch 938 §1 (AB 1755), effective January 1, 2025.

TITLE 10A
CIVIL PROCEEDINGS IN MUNICIPAL COURTS [REPEALED]

TITLE 10.5
PARTITION OF REAL AND PERSONAL PROPERTY

Chapter 1. General Provisions.
Chapter 2. Commencement of Action.
Chapter 3. Trial.
Chapter 4. Referees.
Chapter 5. Division of the Property.
Chapter 6. Sale of the Property.
Chapter 7. Partition by Appraisal.
Chapter 8. Costs of Partition.
Chapter 9. Judgment.
Chapter 10. Partition of Real Property Act.

CHAPTER 1
GENERAL PROVISIONS

Article 1. Preliminary Provisions.
Article 2. Powers of Court.

ARTICLE 1
Preliminary Provisions

Definitions. §872.010.
Scope of title. §872.020.
Rules of practice in partition actions. §872.030.
Compliance with laws governing property transactions. §872.040.

§872.010. Definitions
As used in this title:
(a) "Action" means an action for partition under this title.
(b) "Lien" means a mortgage, deed of trust, or other security interest in property whether arising from contract, statute, common law, or equity.
(c) "Property" includes real and personal property.
(d) "Remainder" includes reversion, reversionary interest, right of entry, and executory interest.
(e) "Title report" includes a preliminary report, guarantee, binder, or policy of title insurance. **Leg.H.** Added Stats 1976 ch 73 §6. Amended Stats 1979 ch 730 §27, operative January 1, 1981.

§872.020. Scope of title
This title governs actions for partition of real property and, except to the extent not applicable, actions for partition of personal property. **Leg.H.** Added Stats 1976 ch 73 §6. Amended Stats 2021 ch 119 §1 (AB 633), effective January 1, 2022; Stats 2022 ch 82 §1 (AB 2245), effective January 1, 2023.

§872.030. Rules of practice in partition actions
The statutes and rules governing practice in civil actions generally apply to actions under this title except where they are inconsistent with the provisions of this title. **Leg.H.** Added Stats 1976 ch 73 §6.

§872.040. Compliance with laws governing property transactions
Nothing in this title excuses compliance with any applicable laws, regulations, or ordinances governing the division, sale, or transfer of property. **Leg.H.** Added Stats 1976 ch 73 §6.

ARTICLE 2
Powers of Court

Jurisdiction and venue. §872.110.
General authority to hear motions and make orders and decrees. §872.120.
Temporary restraining orders and injunctions. §872.130.
Compensatory adjustment. §872.140.

§872.110. Jurisdiction and venue
(a) The superior court has jurisdiction of actions under this title.
(b) Subject to the power of the court to transfer actions, the proper county for the trial of actions under this title is:
(1) Where the subject of the action is real property or real and personal property, the county in which the real property, or some part thereof, is situated.
(2) Where the subject of the action is personal property, the county in which the personal property is principally located at the commencement of the action or in which the defendants, or any of them, reside at the commencement of the action. **Leg.H.** Added Stats 1976 ch 73 §6.

§872.120. General authority to hear motions and make orders and decrees
In the conduct of the action, the court may hear and determine all motions, reports, and accounts and may make any decrees and orders necessary or incidental to carrying out the purposes of this title and to effectuating its decrees and orders. **Leg.H.** Added Stats 1976 ch 73 §6.

§872.130. Temporary restraining orders and injunctions
In the conduct of the action, the court may issue temporary restraining orders and injunctions, with or without bond, for the purpose of:
(a) Preventing waste.
(b) Protecting the property or title thereto.
(c) Restraining unlawful interference with a partition of the property ordered by the court. **Leg.H.** Added Stats 1976 ch 73 §6.

§872.140. Compensatory adjustment
The court may, in all cases, order allowance, accounting, contribution, or other compensatory adjustment among the parties according to the principles of equity. **Leg.H.** Added Stats 1976 ch 73 §6.

CHAPTER 2
COMMENCEMENT OF ACTION

Article 1. Complaint and Lis Pendens.
Article 2. Summons.
Article 3. Answer.
Article 4. Parties.

ARTICLE 1
Complaint and Lis Pendens

Persons authorized to commence partition action. §872.210.
Title report. §872.220.
Contents of complaint. §872.230.
Joinder of property. §872.240.
Lis pendens. §872.250.

§872.210. Persons authorized to commence partition action
(a) A partition action may be commenced and maintained by any of the following persons:
(1) A coowner of personal property.
(2) An owner of an estate of inheritance, an estate for life, or an estate for years in real property where such property or estate therein is owned by several persons concurrently or in successive estates.
(b) Notwithstanding subdivision (a), an action between spouses or putative spouses for partition of their community or quasi-community property or their quasi-marital interest in property may not be commenced or maintained under this title. **Leg.H.** Added Stats 1976 ch 73 §6.

§872.220. Title report
If it is necessary to have a title report:
(a) The plaintiff may, prior to commencing the action, procure a title report and shall in the complaint indicate this has been done and designate a place where it will be kept for inspection, use, and copying by the parties.
(b) The court may, upon application of a party, authorize the party to procure a title report and shall designate a place where it shall be kept for inspection, use, and copying by the parties. **Leg.H.** Added Stats 1976 ch 73 §6.

§872.230. Contents of complaint
The complaint shall set forth:
(a) A description of the property that is the subject of the action. In the case of tangible personal property, the description shall include its usual location. In the case of real property, the description shall include both its legal description and its street address or common designation, if any.
(b) All interests the plaintiff has or claims in the property.
(c) All interests of record or actually known to the plaintiff that persons other than the plaintiff have or claim in the property and that the plaintiff reasonably believes will be materially affected by the action, whether the names of such persons are known or unknown to the plaintiff.
(d) The estate as to which partition is sought and a prayer for partition of the interests therein.

(e) Where the plaintiff seeks sale of the property, an allegation of the facts justifying such relief in ordinary and concise language. **Leg.H.** Added Stats 1976 ch 73 §6.

§872.240. Joinder of property
Real and personal property may be partitioned in one action. **Leg.H.** Added Stats 1976 ch 73 §6.

§872.250. Lis pendens
(a) Immediately upon filing the complaint, the plaintiff shall record a notice of the pendency of the action in the office of the county recorder of each county in which any real property described in the complaint is located.

(b) If, thereafter, partition of other real property is sought in the same action, the plaintiff or other person seeking such relief shall immediately record a supplemental notice.

(c) If the notice is not recorded, the court, upon its own motion or upon the motion of any party at any time, shall order the plaintiff or person seeking partition of the property, or another party on behalf of the plaintiff or other person, to record the notice and shall stay the action until the notice is recorded. The expense of recordation shall be allowed to the party incurring it.

(d) From the time of filing the notice for record, all persons shall be deemed to have notice of the pendency of the action as to the property described in the notice. **Leg.H.** Added Stats 1976 ch 73 §6.

ARTICLE 2
Summons

Summons. §872.310.
Requirements where service is by publication. §872.320.
Publication as to certain defendants. §872.330.

§872.310. Summons
(a) The form, content, and manner of service of summons shall be as in civil actions generally.

(b) Service on persons named as parties pursuant to Sections 872.530(b) and 872.550, and on other persons named as unknown defendants, shall be by publication pursuant to Section 415.50 and the provisions of this article. **Leg.H.** Added Stats 1976 ch 73 §6.

§872.320. Requirements where service is by publication
Where the court orders service by publication, such order shall be subject to the following conditions:

(a) The plaintiff shall post, not later than 10 days after the date the order is made, a copy of the summons and complaint on the real property that is the subject of the action.

(b) The plaintiff shall record, if not already recorded, a notice of the pendency of the action.

(c) The publication shall describe the property that is the subject of the action. In addition to particularly describing the property, the publication shall describe the property by giving its street address, if any, or other common designation, if any; but, if a legal description of the property is given, the validity of the publication shall not be affected by the fact that the street address or other common designation recited is erroneous or that the street address or other common designation is omitted. **Leg.H.** Added Stats 1976 ch 73 §6.

§872.330. Publication as to certain defendants
(a) Where the court orders service by publication, the publication may:

(1) Name only the defendants to be served thereby.

(2) Describe only the property in which the defendants to be served thereby have or claim interests.

(b) Judgment based on failure to appear and answer following service under this section shall be conclusive against the defendants named in respect only to property described in the publication. **Leg.H.** Added Stats 1976 ch 73 §6.

ARTICLE 3
Answer

Contents of answer. §872.410.
Requirements where defendant is lienholder. §872.420.
Claim for affirmative relief. §872.430.

§872.410. Contents of answer
The answer shall set forth:

(a) Any interest the defendant has or claims in the property.

(b) Any facts tending to controvert such material allegations of the complaint as the defendant does not wish to be taken as true.

(c) Where the defendant seeks sale of the property, an allegation of the facts justifying such relief in ordinary and concise language. **Leg.H.** Added Stats 1976 ch 73 §6.

§872.420. Requirements where defendant is lienholder
Where the defendant has or claims a lien on the property, the answer shall set forth the date and character of the lien and the amount remaining due thereon. **Leg.H.** Added Stats 1976 ch 73 §6.

§872.430. Claim for affirmative relief
The answer may set forth any claim the defendant has for contribution or other compensatory adjustment. **Leg.H.** Added Stats 1976 ch 73 §6.

ARTICLE 4
Parties

Joinder of defendants. §872.510.
Where defendant is unknown or interest uncertain. §872.520.
Where defendant is deceased. §872.530.
Oil and gas interests. §872.540.
Joinder of "all persons unknown". §872.550.

§872.510. Joinder of defendants
The plaintiff shall join as defendants in the action all persons having or claiming interests of record or actually known to the plaintiff or reasonably apparent from an inspection of the property, in the estate as to which partition is sought. **Leg.H.** Added Stats 1976 ch 73 §6.

§872.520. Where defendant is unknown or interest uncertain
(a) If the name of a person described in Section 872.510 is not known to the plaintiff, the plaintiff shall so state in the complaint and shall name as parties all persons unknown in the manner provided in Section 872.550.

(b) If the ownership or the share or quantity of the interest of a person described in Section 872.510 is unknown, uncertain, or contingent, the plaintiff shall so state in the complaint. If the lack of knowledge, uncertainty, or contingency is caused by a transfer to an unborn or unascertained beneficiary or class member, or by a transfer in the form of a contingent remainder, vested remainder subject to defeasance, executory interest, or similar disposition, the plaintiff shall also state in the complaint, so far as is known to the plaintiff, the name, age, and legal disability (if any) of the person in being who would be entitled to ownership of the interest had the contingency upon which the right of such person depends occurred prior to the commencement of the action.

(c) The court shall upon its own motion or upon motion of any party make such orders for joinder of additional parties and for appointment of guardians ad litem pursuant to Sections 372, 373, and 373.5 as are necessary or proper. **Leg.H.** Added Stats 1976 ch 73 §6. Amended Stats 2023 ch 260 §8 (SB 345), effective January 1, 2024.

§872.530. Where defendant is deceased
(a) If a person described in Section 872.510 is dead and the plaintiff knows of a personal representative, the plaintiff shall join such personal representative as a defendant.

(b) If a person described in Section 872.510 is dead, or is believed by the plaintiff to be dead, and the plaintiff knows of no personal representative:

(1) The plaintiff shall state these facts in an affidavit filed with the complaint.

(2) Where it is stated in the affidavit that such person is dead, the plaintiff may join as defendants "the testate and intestate successors of _____ (naming such deceased person), deceased, and all persons claiming by, through, or under said decedent," naming them in that manner.

(3) Where it is stated in the affidavit that such person is believed to be dead, the plaintiff may join such person as a defendant, and he may also join "the testate and intestate successors of _____ (naming such person) believed to be deceased, and all persons claiming by, through, or under such person," naming them in that manner. **Leg.H.** Added Stats 1976 ch 73 §6.

§872.540. Oil and gas interests
Where property is subject to a lease, community lease, unit agreement, or other pooling arrangement with respect to oil or gas or both, the plaintiff need not join as defendants persons whose only interest in the

property is that of a lessee, royalty-owner, lessor-owner of other real property in the community, unit, or pooled area, or working interest owner, or persons claiming under them, and the judgment shall not affect the interests of such persons not joined as defendants. **Leg.H.** Added Stats 1976 ch 73 §6.

§872.550. Joinder of "all persons unknown"

Where partition is sought as to all interests in the property, the plaintiff may join as defendants "all persons unknown claiming any interest in the property," naming them in that manner. **Leg.H.** Added Stats 1976 ch 73 §6.

ARTICLE 5
Preliminary Proceedings [Repealed]

§872.570. [Section repealed 1989]

Leg.H. Added Stats 1986 ch 689 §1. Repealed operative January 1, 1989, by the terms of §872.571. The repealed section related to preliminary proceedings.

§872.571. [Section repealed 1989]

Leg.H. Added Stats 1986 ch 689 §1. Repealed operative January 1, 1989, by its own terms. The repealed section related to repeal of article.

CHAPTER 3
TRIAL

Article 1. Determination of Interests of Parties.
Article 2. Determination of Right to Partition.
Article 3. Determination of Manner of Partition.

ARTICLE 1
Determination of Interests of Parties

Court may determine interests. §872.610.
Ascertainment of state of title. §872.620.
Determination of interests of lienholders. §872.630.
Interests of unknown parties. §872.640.

§872.610. Court may determine interests

The interests of the parties, plaintiff as well as defendant, may be put in issue, tried, and determined in the action. **Leg.H.** Added Stats 1976 ch 73 §6.

§872.620. Ascertainment of state of title

To the extent necessary to grant the relief sought or other appropriate relief, the court shall upon adequate proof ascertain the state of the title to the property. **Leg.H.** Added Stats 1976 ch 73 §6.

§872.630. Determination of interests of lienholders

(a) To the extent necessary to grant the relief sought or other appropriate relief, the court shall determine the status and priority of all liens upon the property.

(b) The court may appoint a referee to ascertain the facts necessary for the determination required by this section. Upon application of the referee or a lienholder, the court shall direct the issuance of process to compel attendance of witnesses, the production of books, documents, or things, and the filing of verified claims. The report of the referee thereon shall be made in writing to the court and shall be confirmed, modified, or set aside and a new reference ordered, as the justice of the case may require. **Leg.H.** Added Stats 1976 ch 73 §6.

§872.640. Interests of unknown parties

Where two or more parties are unknown, the court may consider their interests together in the action and not as between each other. **Leg.H.** Added Stats 1976 ch 73 §6.

ARTICLE 2
Determination of Right to Partition

Court determination of right to partition. §872.710.
Interlocutory judgment. §872.720.
Partition of partnership property. §872.730.

§872.710. Court determination of right to partition

(a) At the trial, the court shall determine whether the plaintiff has the right to partition.

(b) Except as provided in Section 872.730, partition as to concurrent interests in the property shall be as of right unless barred by a valid waiver.

(c) Partition as to successive estates in the property shall be allowed if it is in the best interest of all the parties. The court shall consider whether the possessory interest has become unduly burdensome by reason of taxes or other charges, expense of ordinary or extraordinary repairs, character of the property and change in the character of the property since creation of the estates, circumstances under which the estates were created and change in the circumstances since creation of the estates, and all other factors that would be considered by a court of equity having in mind the intent of the creator of the successive estates and the interests and needs of the successive owners. **Leg.H.** Added Stats 1976 ch 73 §6.

§872.720. Interlocutory judgment

(a) If the court finds that the plaintiff is entitled to partition, it shall make an interlocutory judgment that determines the interests of the parties in the property and orders the partition of the property and, unless it is to be later determined, the manner of partition.

(b) If the court determines that it is impracticable or highly inconvenient to make a single interlocutory judgment that determines, in the first instance, the interests of all the parties in the property, the court may first ascertain the interests of the original concurrent or successive owners and thereupon make an interlocutory judgment as if such persons were the sole parties in interest and the only parties to the action. Thereafter, the court may proceed in like manner as between the original concurrent or successive owners and the parties claiming under them or may allow the interests to remain without further partition if the parties so desire. **Leg.H.** Added Stats 1976 ch 73 §6.

§872.730. Partition of partnership property

To the extent that the court determines that the provisions of this title are a suitable remedy, such provisions may be applied in a proceeding for partnership accounting and dissolution, or in an action for partition of partnership property, where the rights of unsecured creditors of the partnership will not be prejudiced. **Leg.H.** Added Stats 1976 ch 73 §6.

ARTICLE 3
Determination of Manner of Partition

Court order of division. §872.810.
Court order of sale. §872.820.
Partial division and sale. §872.830.
Disposition of property subject to express trust. §872.840.

§872.810. Court order of division

The court shall order that the property be divided among the parties in accordance with their interests in the property as determined in the interlocutory judgment. **Leg.H.** Added Stats 1976 ch 73 §6.

§872.820. Court order of sale

Notwithstanding Section 872.810, the court shall order that the property be sold and the proceeds be divided among the parties in accordance with their interests in the property as determined in the interlocutory judgment in the following situations:

(a) The parties agree to such relief, by their pleadings or otherwise.

(b) The court determines that, under the circumstances, sale and division of the proceeds would be more equitable than division of the property. For the purpose of making the determination, the court may appoint a referee and take into account his report. **Leg.H.** Added Stats 1976 ch 73 §6.

§872.830. Partial division and sale

If, in making a determination whether sale would be more equitable than division of the property, the court finds that sale and division of proceeds for part of the property would be more equitable than division of the whole property, the court may order that such part be sold and the remainder divided. **Leg.H.** Added Stats 1976 ch 73 §6.

§872.840. Disposition of property subject to express trust

(a) Where the property or an interest therein is subject to an express trust, the court may, in its discretion, order that the property be sold.

(b) Upon division or sale of such property, the property or proceeds of sale allotted to the trustee of the express trust shall be held by him upon the trust therein stated, and no further action by the court pursuant to Section 873.840 is required. **Leg.H.** Added Stats 1976 ch 73 §6.

§873. [Section repealed 1933]

Leg.H. Enacted 1872. Amended Code Amdts 1875–76 ch 498 §6. Repealed Stats 1933 ch 744 §198. See CCP §594.

CHAPTER 4
REFEREES

Article 1. General Provisions.
Article 2. Contracts of Referee.

ARTICLE 1
General Provisions

Court authority concerning referee. §873.010.
Referees for division and sale. §873.020.
Three referees in place of one. §873.030.
Appointment of person selected by parties. §873.040.
Persons disqualified as referee. §873.050.
Authority of referee. §873.060.
Petition for instructions. §873.070.
Disposition in accordance with law. §873.080.

§873.010. Court authority concerning referee

(a) The court shall appoint a referee to divide or sell the property as ordered by the court.

(b) The court may:

(1) Determine whether a referee's bond is necessary and fix the amount of the bond.

(2) Instruct the referee.

(3) Fix the reasonable compensation for the services of the referee and provide for payment of the referee's reasonable expenses.

(4) Provide for the date of commencement of the lien of the referee allowed by law.

(5) Require the filing of interim or final accounts of the referee, settle the accounts of the referee, and discharge the referee.

(6) Remove the referee.

(7) Appoint a new referee. **Leg.H.** Added Stats 1976 ch 73 §6.

§873.020. Referees for division and sale

The court in its discretion may appoint a referee for sale and a referee for division, or may appoint a single referee for both. **Leg.H.** Added Stats 1976 ch 73 §6.

§873.030. Three referees in place of one

(a) The court may, with the consent of the parties, appoint three referees to divide or sell the property as ordered by the court.

(b) The three referees so appointed shall have all the powers and may perform all the duties required of one referee. **Leg.H.** Added Stats 1976 ch 73 §6.

§873.040. Appointment of person selected by parties

(a) The court shall appoint as referee under this title any person or persons to whose appointment all parties have consented.

(b) In the case of a minor party or a party for whom a conservator of the estate has been appointed, the guardian or conservator of the estate of the party may so consent. **Leg.H.** Added Stats 1976 ch 73 §6. Amended Stats 1979 ch 730 §28, operative January 1, 1981.

§873.050. Persons disqualified as referee

None of the following persons shall be appointed a referee under this title:

(a) A clerk or deputy clerk of the court.

(b) A former or present partner or employee of the judge.

(c) A relative within the third degree of the judge or the judge's spouse or the spouse of such a relative.

(d) An owner of any interest in the property that is the subject of the action. **Leg.H.** Added Stats 1976 ch 73 §6.

§873.060. Authority of referee

The referee may perform any acts necessary to exercise the authority conferred by this title or by order of the court. **Leg.H.** Added Stats 1976 ch 73 §6.

§873.070. Petition for instructions

The referee or any party may, on noticed motion, petition the court for instructions concerning the referee's duties under this title. **Leg.H.** Added Stats 1976 ch 73 §6.

§873.080. Disposition in accordance with law

(a) In selling or dividing the property, the referee may, if it will be for the advantage of those interested, designate a portion of the property as a public or private way, road, or street. In connection therewith, the referee may also recommend the closure of any or all other roads on the property and allocation of the portion of the property occupied by such roads to the parties.

(b) Upon making such a designation and recommendation that is adequate to accommodate public and private needs, the referee shall report that fact to the court.

(c) Upon confirmation of the referee's report by the court, subject to any necessary action by the appropriate public entities:

(1) The portion of the property designated as a public way, road, or street shall not be allocated to any of the parties or sold but shall be an open and public way, road, or street.

(2) The property designated as a private way, road, or street shall be a private way for the use of the parties interested.

(3) The roads recommended to be closed shall be deemed abandoned upon the terms stated in the order of confirmation. **Leg.H.** Added Stats 1976 ch 73 §6.

ARTICLE 2
Contracts of Referee

Services of third persons. §873.110.
Employment of attorney. §873.120.
Employment of surveyor. §873.130.
Employment of auctioneer. §873.140.
Contract for third-person services may include interest. §873.150.
Referee not liable on contracts. §873.160.

§873.110. Services of third persons

Subject to the limitations of this article, the court may:

(a) Authorize or approve contracts of the referee for the services and expenses of surveyors, engineers, appraisers, attorneys, real estate brokers, auctioneers, and others.

(b) Allow and direct payment of or reject claims under such contracts.

(c) Provide for the date of commencement of any lien provided by law or contract for such claims. **Leg.H.** Added Stats 1976 ch 73 §6.

§873.120. Employment of attorney

(a) The referee may employ an attorney only with the approval of the court pursuant to Section 873.110.

(b) The application for approval shall be in writing and shall include the name of the attorney whom the referee wishes to employ and the necessity for the employment.

(c) The attorney so employed may not be attorney for, or associated with or employed by an attorney for, any party to the action except with the written consent of all the parties to the action.

(d) Any claim for compensation for the attorney shall detail the services performed by the attorney. **Leg.H.** Added Stats 1976 ch 73 §6.

§873.130. Employment of surveyor

The referee may, with the approval of the court pursuant to Section 873.110, employ a surveyor with the necessary assistants to aid in making a sale or division of property. **Leg.H.** Added Stats 1976 ch 73 §6.

§873.140. Employment of auctioneer

The referee may, with the approval of the court pursuant to Section 873.110, employ an auctioneer, authorized to act as such in the locality, to conduct a public auction and to secure purchasers by such method for any property to be sold at public auction. **Leg.H.** Added Stats 1976 ch 73 §6.

§873.150. Contract for third-person services may include interest

A contract for the services of an attorney, surveyor, auctioneer, or other third person may provide for the accrual of interest at a rate not in excess of the legal rate for amounts due under the contract that are not paid within three months after the time they become due and payable. **Leg.H.** Added Stats 1976 ch 73 §6.

§873.160. Referee not liable on contracts

The referee is not personally liable on contracts made, or for expenses incurred, except as such liability is expressly assumed by the referee in writing. **Leg.H.** Added Stats 1976 ch 73 §6.

CHAPTER 5
DIVISION OF THE PROPERTY

Division by referee. §873.210.
Division involving improvements. §873.220.
Division involving purported conveyance. §873.230.
Division by distinct lot or parcel. §873.240.

Compensation with unequal division. §873.250.
Liens. §873.260.
Unknown owners. §873.270.
Referee's report of division. §873.280.
Hearing on report and entry of judgment. §873.290.

§873.210. Division by referee

The referee appointed by the court to make a division of the property shall divide the property and allot the several portions to the parties, quality and quantity relatively considered, according to their interests in the property as determined in the interlocutory judgment. **Leg.H.** Added Stats 1976 ch 73 §6.

§873.220. Division involving improvements

As far as practical, and to the extent it can be done without material injury to the rights of the other parties, the property shall be so divided as to allot to a party any portion that embraces improvements made by that party or that party's predecessor in interest. In such division and allotment, the value of such improvements shall be excluded. **Leg.H.** Added Stats 1976 ch 73 §6.

§873.230. Division involving purported conveyance

Where prior to the commencement of the action a party has executed a deed purporting to convey to a purchaser a portion of the property to be divided, to the extent it can be done without material injury to the rights of the other parties, the property shall be so divided as to allot that portion to the purchaser, the purchaser's heirs or assigns, or such other action taken as to make the deed effectual as a conveyance of that portion of the property. **Leg.H.** Added Stats 1976 ch 73 §6.

§873.240. Division by distinct lot or parcel

Where real property consists of more than one distinct lot or parcel, the property shall be divided by such lots or parcels without other internal division to the extent that it can be done without material injury to the rights of the parties. **Leg.H.** Added Stats 1976 ch 73 §6.

§873.250. Compensation with unequal division

(a) Where division cannot be made equally among the parties according to their interests without prejudice to the rights of some, compensation may be required to be made by one party to another to correct the inequality.

(b) No compensation shall be required to be made to others by unknown owners or by minors unless it appears that a minor has personal property sufficient for that purpose and the minor's interest will be promoted thereby. **Leg.H.** Added Stats 1976 ch 73 §6.

§873.260. Liens

Where a lien is on an undivided interest of a party, the lien shall, upon division of the property, become a charge only on the share allotted to that party. **Leg.H.** Added Stats 1976 ch 73 §6.

§873.270. Unknown owners

Where the court has determined the combined interests of two or more unknown parties, the entire portion of the property allocated to such parties shall remain undivided. **Leg.H.** Added Stats 1976 ch 73 §6.

§873.280. Referee's report of division

(a) The referee shall file with the court a report of the referee's proceedings and give written notice of filing to each party who has appeared in the action.

(b) The report shall include all of the following:

(1) A specification of the manner in which the referee has executed the referee's trust.

(2) A description of the property divided and of the share allotted to each party, along with any recommendation as to owelty.

(3) Any recommendation as to opening and closing public and private ways, roads, streets, and easements. **Leg.H.** Added Stats 1976 ch 73 §6.

§873.290. Hearing on report and entry of judgment

(a) Any party, upon notice to the other parties who have appeared, may move the court to confirm, modify, or set aside the report.

(b) At the hearing, the court may either confirm the report as filed or as the court may modify and enter judgment of partition accordingly or set aside the report and order preparation of a new report and, if necessary, appoint a new referee for this purpose.

(c) The division is effective and title vests in accordance therewith upon entry of judgment of partition. **Leg.H.** Added Stats 1976 ch 73 §6.

CHAPTER 6
SALE OF THE PROPERTY

Article 1. Manner of Sale.
Article 2. Sales Procedures.
Article 3. Consummation of Sale.
Article 4. Disposition of Proceeds of Sale.

ARTICLE 1
Manner of Sale

Sale by referee. §873.510.
Determination of public or private sale. §873.520.
Public or private sale of part of property. §873.530.

§873.510. Sale by referee

The referee appointed by the court to make a sale of the property shall sell the property in the manner and following the procedures provided in this chapter. **Leg.H.** Added Stats 1976 ch 73 §6.

§873.520. Determination of public or private sale

The property shall be sold at public auction or private sale as the court determines will be more beneficial to the parties. For the purpose of making this determination, the court may refer the matter to the referee and take into account the referee's report. **Leg.H.** Added Stats 1976 ch 73 §6.

§873.530. Public or private sale of part of property

Part of the property may be sold at public auction and part at private sale if it appears that to do so will be more beneficial to the parties. **Leg.H.** Added Stats 1976 ch 73 §6.

ARTICLE 2
Sales Procedures

Procedures agreed to by parties. §873.600.
Court authority in sale. §873.610.
Sale of property separately or as unit. §873.620.
Credit sales. §873.630.
Manner of notice of sale. §873.640.
Contents of notice of sale. §873.650.
Sale of perishable property and securities. §873.660.
Conduct of sale at public auction. §873.670.
Conduct of private sale. §873.680.
Persons ineligible to purchase at sale. §873.690.

§873.600. Procedures agreed to by parties

Notwithstanding any other provision of this title, the court shall order sale by such methods and upon such terms as are expressly agreed to in writing by all the parties to the action. **Leg.H.** Added Stats 1976 ch 73 §6.

§873.610. Court authority in sale

(a) The court may, at the time of trial or thereafter, prescribe such manner, terms, and conditions of sale not inconsistent with the provisions of this chapter as it deems proper for the particular property or sale.

(b) The court may refer the manner, terms, and conditions of sale to the referee for recommendation but shall not approve the referee's report except following a hearing upon noticed motion. **Leg.H.** Added Stats 1976 ch 73 §6.

§873.620. Sale of property separately or as unit

(a) Unless the interests and rights of the parties will be materially prejudiced thereby, the court shall order that distinct lots or parcels of real property be sold separately.

(b) The court may order that the real and personal property or any portion thereof be sold as a unit. **Leg.H.** Added Stats 1976 ch 73 §6.

§873.630. Credit sales

The court may:

(a) Direct a sale on credit for the property or any part thereof.

(b) Prescribe such terms of credit as may be appropriate.

(c) Approve or prescribe the terms of security to be taken upon the sale, including the manner in which title to the security is to be taken, whether in a single instrument or several instruments, according to the interests of the parties. **Leg.H.** Added Stats 1976 ch 73 §6.

§873.640. Manner of notice of sale

(a) Notice of the sale of real or personal property shall be given in the manner required for notice of sale of like property upon execution. Such notice shall also be given to every party who has appeared in the action and to such other interested persons as may have in writing requested the referee for special notice.

(b) Where real and personal property are to be sold as a unit, notice of the sale may be in the manner required for notice of sale of real property alone.

(c) The court may order such additional notice as it deems proper.

(d) Where the court orders a new sale of property pursuant to Section 873.730 or Section 873.740, notice of sale shall be as provided in this section. **Leg.H.** Added Stats 1976 ch 73 §6.

§873.650. Contents of notice of sale

(a) The court shall prescribe the contents of the notice of sale, which shall include a description of the property, the time and place of sale, and a statement of the principal terms of sale. In place of the principal terms of sale, the notice may refer to an order of the court or to a written statement containing such information which may be inspected at the place of business of the referee or the referee's attorney.

(b) A notice of private sale shall state a place where bids or offers will be received and a day on or after which the sale will be made. **Leg.H.** Added Stats 1976 ch 73 §6.

§873.660. Sale of perishable property and securities

(a) The court may order securities listed on an established stock or bond exchange, and personal property that is perishable, that will depreciate in value if not promptly disposed of, or that will incur loss or expense by being kept, to be sold upon such notice and conditions as may be appropriate.

(b) Unless otherwise ordered by the court, title to property sold pursuant to this section passes without court confirmation. The referee is responsible for the actual value of the property until, after return and proper showing, the court approves the sale. **Leg.H.** Added Stats 1976 ch 73 §6.

§873.670. Conduct of sale at public auction

(a) A sale at public auction to the highest bidder shall be held in the county in which the action is pending or such other place as may be specified by the court.

(b) Unless otherwise ordered by the court, personal property shall be present at the sale.

(c) The sale may be postponed by the referee by public declaration as provided for sales upon execution. **Leg.H.** Added Stats 1976 ch 73 §6.

§873.680. Conduct of private sale

(a) A sale at private sale shall not be made before the day specified in the notice of sale but shall be made within one year thereafter.

(b) The bids or offers shall be in writing and left at the place designated in the notice at any time after the first publication or, if none, the posting of the notice. **Leg.H.** Added Stats 1976 ch 73 §6.

§873.690. Persons ineligible to purchase at sale

(a) The following persons shall not purchase property sold in the action directly or indirectly:

(1) The referee.
(2) The attorney of a party.
(3) The guardian or conservator of a party, unless for the benefit of the ward or conservatee.

(b) All sales contrary to this section are void except that a sale to a bona fide purchaser following a sale contrary to this section shall not be disturbed. **Leg.H.** Added Stats 1976 ch 73 §6. Amended Stats 1979 ch 730 §29, operative January 1, 1981.

ARTICLE 3
Consummation of Sale

Referee's report of sale. §873.710.
Motion to confirm or set aside sale. §873.720.
Hearing on motion. §873.730.
Increased offers. §873.740.
Agents' commissions on sale. §873.745.
Court order for collection of proceeds and transfer of property. §873.750.
Failure of purchaser to deliver proceeds. §873.760.
Taking setoff from party purchaser. §873.770.
Court authority at closing. §873.780.
Conveyance of the property. §873.790.

§873.710. Referee's report of sale

(a) Upon making a sale of property, the referee shall report the sale to the court.

(b) The referee's report shall contain, in addition to such other information as may be appropriate, all of the following information:

(1) A description of the property sold to each purchaser.
(2) The name of the purchaser.
(3) The sale price.
(4) The terms and conditions of the sale and the security, if any, taken.
(5) Any amounts payable to lienholders.
(6) A statement as to contractual or other arrangements or conditions as to agents' commissions.
(7) Any determination and recommendation as to opening and closing public and private ways, roads, streets, and easements.
(8) Other material facts relevant to the sale and the confirmation proceeding. **Leg.H.** Added Stats 1976 ch 73 §6.

§873.720. Motion to confirm or set aside sale

(a) A purchaser, the referee, or any party may move the court to confirm or set aside the sale.

(b) The moving party shall give not less than 10 days' notice of motion to:

(1) The purchaser if the purchaser is not the moving party; and
(2) All other parties who have appeared in the action. **Leg.H.** Added Stats 1976 ch 73 §6.

§873.730. Hearing on motion

(a) At the hearing, the court shall examine the report and witnesses in relation to the report.

(b) The court may confirm the sale notwithstanding a variance from the prescribed terms of sale if to do so will be beneficial to the parties and will not result in substantial prejudice to persons interested in the sale.

(c) The court may vacate the sale and direct that a new sale be made if it determines any of the following:

(1) The proceedings were unfair or notice of sale was not properly given. If there is no finding at the hearing of unfairness or improper notice, the sale may thereafter not be attacked on such grounds.
(2) The sale price is disproportionate to the value of the property.
(3) It appears that a new sale will yield a sum that exceeds the sale price by at least 10 percent on the first ten thousand dollars ($10,000) and 5 percent on the amount in excess thereof, determined after a reasonable allowance for the expenses of a new sale. **Leg.H.** Added Stats 1976 ch 73 §6.

§873.740. Increased offers

(a) If at the hearing under Section 873.730 a responsible bidder makes a written increased offer that exceeds the sale price by at least 10 percent on the first ten thousand dollars ($10,000) and 5 percent on the amount in excess thereof, the court in its discretion may do either of the following:

(1) Vacate the sale and direct that a new sale be made.
(2) Vacate the sale, accept the increased offer, and confirm the sale to the offerer.

(b) Except as provided in subdivision (c), the amount by which an increased offer exceeds the sale price is determined on the basis of the gross amount of the increased offer including any commission on the increased offer to which an agent may be entitled.

(c) Where in advance of sale the court has so ordered or the parties have so agreed, if an increased offer is made by a party to the action who is not represented by an agent, the amount by which an increased offer of a nonparty exceeds the sale price is determined on the basis of the net amount of the increased offer excluding any commission on the increased offer to which an agent may be entitled. **Leg.H.** Added Stats 1976 ch 73 §6.

§873.745. Agents' commissions on sale

The amount of agents' commissions on the sale, if any, shall be fixed by the court and divided or limited in the manner provided for private sales of real property in decedents' estates. **Leg.H.** Added Stats 1976 ch 73 §6.

§873.750. Court order for collection of proceeds and transfer of property

(a) Upon confirmation of a sale, the court shall order the referee to execute a conveyance or other instrument of transfer, to collect the proceeds, take security, and perform other acts required to consummate the sale.

(b) The order may direct the referee concerning the distribution, deposit, or securing of sale deposits and sale proceeds. **Leg.H.** Added Stats 1976 ch 73 §6.

§873.760. Failure of purchaser to deliver proceeds

If the purchaser, after the confirmation of the sale, fails to pay the sale price, the purchaser is subject to the court's jurisdiction and to further proceedings in the action. Upon such failure, a party, or the referee, may upon notice move the court to order either of the following forms of relief:

(a) Resale of the property upon notice as provided in this chapter. If any loss is occasioned thereby, the referee may recover the amount of such loss and costs and expenses incurred, including a reasonable attorney's fee, from the purchaser who failed to pay.

(b) Maintenance by the referee of an action against the purchaser for the amount of the sale price. If the referee recovers judgment, the referee shall be awarded a reasonable attorney's fee against the purchaser. **Leg.H.** Added Stats 1976 ch 73 §6.

§873.770. Taking setoff from party purchaser

Where the purchaser is a party or lienholder entitled to a share of the proceeds of sale, the referee may:

(a) Take the purchaser's receipt for so much of the proceeds of sale as belongs to the purchaser.

(b) Take security, or other arrangement satisfactory to the referee, for payment of amounts which are or may become due from the purchaser on account of the expenses of sale, general costs of the action, and costs of the reference. **Leg.H.** Added Stats 1976 ch 73 §6.

§873.780. Court authority at closing

The court may make orders relating to the closing of a sale after confirmation, including escrow and closing provisions and, if the referee and purchaser so agree and the court upon noticed motion determines it will not result in substantial prejudice to the parties, may make adjustments varying the terms of sale based on after-discovered defects. **Leg.H.** Added Stats 1976 ch 73 §6.

§873.790. Conveyance of the property

(a) Upon fulfillment of the terms of sale, the referee shall execute a conveyance or other instrument of transfer to the purchaser.

(b) The conveyance or transfer of real property and the order authorizing such conveyance or transfer shall be recorded in each county in which the property is located. **Leg.H.** Added Stats 1976 ch 73 §6.

ARTICLE 4
Disposition of Proceeds of Sale

Court order of disbursement. §873.810.
Application of proceeds of sale. §873.820.
Setoff in lieu of payment of estate for life or years. §873.830.
Treatment of successive estates. §873.840.
Where proceeds have not been allocated between parties. §873.850.

§873.810. Court order of disbursement

The court shall order the proceeds of sale and any security therefor to be paid, transferred, deposited in court, placed in trust, or invested in State of California or United States government obligations or interest-bearing accounts in an institution whose accounts are insured by an agency of the federal government, to or for the benefit of the persons in interest entitled thereto, as may be appropriate or as specifically provided in this article. **Leg.H.** Added Stats 1976 ch 73 §6.

§873.820. Application of proceeds of sale

The proceeds of sale for any property sold shall be applied in the following order:

(a) Payment of the expenses of sale.

(b) Payment of the other costs of partition in whole or in part or to secure any cost of partition later allowed.

(c) Payment of any liens on the property in their order of priority except liens which under the terms of sale are to remain on the property.

(d) Distribution of the residue among the parties in proportion to their shares as determined by the court. **Leg.H.** Added Stats 1976 ch 73 §6.

§873.830. Setoff in lieu of payment of estate for life or years

Where a part only of the property is sold, a tenant for life or years in an undivided share of the whole property may have his estate equitably set off in any part of the property not sold by way of complete or partial satisfaction of his share of the proceeds. **Leg.H.** Added Stats 1976 ch 73 §6.

§873.840. Treatment of successive estates

(a) The court shall ascertain the proportion of the proceeds of sale that will be a just and reasonable sum for the satisfaction of the estate of a tenant for life or years and shall order such amount distributed to him or held for his benefit.

(b) The court shall ascertain the proportional value of any vested or contingent future right or estate in the property and shall direct such proportion of the proceeds of sale to be distributed, secured, or held in such a manner as to protect the rights and interests of the parties.

(c) Notwithstanding any other provision of this section, in the case of an estate for life or defeasible estate with remainder over, the court may direct that the entire proceeds of sale be placed in trust as provided in this section upon a showing that the establishment of such a trust is economically feasible and will serve the best interests of the parties. The court shall appoint a trustee, upon security satisfactory to the court, who under court supervision shall invest and reinvest the proceeds, pay the income of the investments, if any, to the life tenant or owner of the defeasible interest, and upon termination of the life or defeasible estate, deliver or pay the corpus of the trust estate to the remainderman. The court shall retain jurisdiction over the settlement of the accounts of the trustee and in all matters necessary for the proper administration of the trust and the final distribution of the trust fund. **Leg.H.** Added Stats 1976 ch 73 §6.

§873.850. Where proceeds have not been allocated between parties

When the proceeds of the sale belonging to persons who are parties to the action, whether known or unknown, have not been allocated among such parties, the action may be continued as between such parties, for the determination of their respective claims thereto, which must be ascertained and adjudged by the court. Further testimony may be taken in court, or by a referee, at the discretion of the court, and the court may, if necessary, require such parties to present the facts or law in controversy, by pleadings, as in an original action. **Leg.H.** Added Stats 1976 ch 73 §6.

CHAPTER 7
PARTITION BY APPRAISAL

Agreement of parties to partition by appraisal. §873.910.
Contents of agreement. §873.920.
Court approval of agreement. §873.930.
Appointment of referee; referee's report. §873.940.
Motion to confirm, modify, or set aside report. §873.950.
Hearing on referee's report. §873.960.
Effect of agreement. §873.970.
Relation of agreement to other remedies. §873.980.

§873.910. Agreement of parties to partition by appraisal

When the interests of all parties are undisputed or have been adjudicated, the parties may agree upon a partition by appraisal pursuant to this chapter. **Leg.H.** Added Stats 1976 ch 73 §6.

§873.920. Contents of agreement

The agreement shall be in writing filed with the clerk of court and shall include:

(a) A description of the property.

(b) The names of the parties and their interests.

(c) The names of the parties who are willing to acquire the interests.

(d) The name or names of a person or persons to whose appointment as referee or referees the parties consent.

(e) The date or dates as of which the interests to be acquired are to be appraised.

(f) Other terms mutually agreed upon which may include, but are not limited to, provisions relating to abandonment of the action if the appraised value of the interest to be acquired exceeds a stated amount, required deposits on account of purchase price, terms of any credit, title and objections to title, and payment of the expenses of the procedure authorized by this chapter and of costs of the action. **Leg.H.** Added Stats 1976 ch 73 §6.

§873.930. Court approval of agreement

(a) Any party to the agreement may, upon noticed motion, apply to the court for approval of the agreement.

(b) If the court determines that the agreement complies with Section 873.920 and that the terms and conditions are equitable, it shall approve the agreement and stay any pending division or sale of the property. **Leg.H.** Added Stats 1976 ch 73 §6.

§873.940. Appointment of referee; referee's report

The court shall appoint one referee or, if provided in the agreement, three referees to appraise the property and the interests involved. The referee shall report the valuations and other findings to the court in writing filed with the clerk. **Leg.H.** Added Stats 1976 ch 73 §6.

§873.950. Motion to confirm, modify, or set aside report

Any party to the agreement or the referee, upon 10 days' notice to the referee if the referee is not the moving party and to the other parties to the agreement, may move the court to confirm, modify, or set aside the report. **Leg.H.** Added Stats 1976 ch 73 §6.

§873.960. Hearing on referee's report

At the hearing, the court shall examine the report and witnesses. If the court determines that the proceedings have been regularly conducted, that transfer of title to the interests may regularly be made, and that no facts appear which would make such transfer inequitable, it shall confirm the report and order the interests transferred to the acquiring parties in proportion to their respective interests, or in such other proportion as is set out in the agreement. The order shall be conditioned upon payment of the amounts fixed as the purchase price and any other amounts required by the agreement, the giving of any required security, and payment by the parties of the expenses of the procedure authorized by this chapter and of the general costs of the partition or an appropriate share thereof. Thereafter the court, upon motion of a party to the agreement or of the referee, made upon not less than 10 days' notice to the parties who have appeared, shall determine whether the conditions have been fulfilled and, if so, shall enter judgment confirming the transfer; otherwise, upon such further proceedings as may be ordered, the action or proceeding shall be ordered terminated. **Leg.H.** Added Stats 1976 ch 73 §6.

§873.970. Effect of agreement

The agreement binds the heirs, executors, administrators, successors, and assigns of the parties. In the event of default, the aggrieved parties may specifically enforce the agreement by further proceedings in the action or may pursue any other remedy they may have at law or in equity. **Leg.H.** Added Stats 1976 ch 73 §6.

§873.980. Relation of agreement to other remedies

The provisions of this chapter are cumulative and if, for default or other cause, interests are not transferred and acquired pursuant to this chapter, the parties may pursue their other rights of partition, subject to Section 873.970. **Leg.H.** Added Stats 1976 ch 73 §6.

§874. [Section repealed 1933]

Leg.H. Enacted 1872. Repealed Stats 1933 ch 744 §198. See CCP §594a.

CHAPTER 8
COSTS OF PARTITION

Article 1. Allowance and Apportionment of Costs of Partition.
Article 2. Payment of Costs of Partition.

ARTICLE 1
Allowance and Apportionment of Costs of Partition

Costs incurred in partition action. §874.010.
Costs incurred in related action. §874.020.
Interest on disbursements. §874.030.
Court apportionment of costs. §874.040.
Apportionment involving future interests. §874.050.

§874.010. Costs incurred in partition action

The costs of partition include:

(a) Reasonable attorney's fees incurred or paid by a party for the common benefit.

(b) The fee and expenses of the referee.

(c) The compensation provided by contract for services of a surveyor or other person employed by the referee in the action.

(d) The reasonable costs of a title report procured pursuant to Section 872.220 with interest thereon at the legal rate from the time of payment or, if paid before commencement of the action, from the time of commencement of the action.

(e) Other disbursements or expenses determined by the court to have been incurred or paid for the common benefit. **Leg.H.** Added Stats 1976 ch 73 §6.

§874.020. Costs incurred in related action

The costs of partition include reasonable expenses, including attorney's fees, necessarily incurred by a party for the common benefit in prosecuting or defending other actions or other proceedings for the protection, confirmation, or perfection of title, setting the boundaries, or making a survey of the property, with interest thereon at the legal rate from the time of making the expenditures. **Leg.H.** Added Stats 1976 ch 73 §6.

§874.030. Interest on disbursements

Where disbursements have been made by a party under the direction of the court, interest at the legal rate shall be allowed thereon from the time of making such disbursements. **Leg.H.** Added Stats 1976 ch 73 §6.

§874.040. Court apportionment of costs

Except as otherwise provided in this article, the court shall apportion the costs of partition among the parties in proportion to their interests or make such other apportionment as may be equitable. **Leg.H.** Added Stats 1976 ch 73 §6.

§874.050. Apportionment involving future interests

(a) The court may order that the share of the costs apportioned to a future interest be paid by other parties to the action or by the persons who are then the presumptive owners of the future interest.

(b) Where the court orders payment pursuant to this section, such payment is subject to a right of reimbursement, with interest at the legal rate, secured by a charge upon the future interest. **Leg.H.** Added Stats 1976 ch 73 §6.

ARTICLE 2
Payment of Costs of Partition

Payment by parties. §874.110.
Lien for costs. §874.120.
Enforcement of lien. §874.130.
Enforcement of judgment. §874.140.

§874.110. Payment by parties

(a) The costs of partition as apportioned by the court may be ordered paid in whole or in part prior to judgment.

(b) Any costs that remain unpaid shall be included and specified in the judgment. **Leg.H.** Added Stats 1976 ch 73 §6.

§874.120. Lien for costs

(a) The costs shall be a lien on the share of the party specified.

(b) A lien imposed by this section has priority over any other lien on the share except those imposed under this section. **Leg.H.** Added Stats 1976 ch 73 §6.

§874.130. Enforcement of lien

Upon application of a person entitled to a lien imposed under this article and upon a showing of good cause, the court may order a sale of all or a portion of the property before or after judgment for the benefit of all such lien claimants without priority among them. **Leg.H.** Added Stats 1976 ch 73 §6.

§874.140. Enforcement of judgment

A judgment for unpaid costs of partition may be enforced by the person entitled to the costs in the manner provided for enforcement of money judgments generally against the share of the party specified in the judgment or against other property of the party. **Leg.H.** Added Stats 1976 ch 73 §6. Amended Stats 1982 ch 497 §60, operative July 1, 1983.

CHAPTER 9
JUDGMENT

Persons bound by judgment. §874.210.
Claims not affected by judgment. §874.225.
Conveyance or transfer has binding effect of judgment. §874.240.

§874.210. Persons bound by judgment

The judgment in the action is binding and conclusive on all of the following:

(a) All persons known and unknown who were parties to the action and who have or claim any interest in the property, whether present or future, vested or contingent, legal or beneficial, several or undivided.

(b) All persons not in being or not ascertainable at the time the judgment is entered who have any remainder interest in the property, or any part thereof, after the determination of a particular estate therein and who by any contingency may be entitled to a beneficial interest in the property, provided the judge shall make appropriate provision for the protection of such interests.

(c) Except as provided in Section 874.225, all persons who were not parties to the action and who have or claim any interest in the property which was not of record at the time the lis pendens was filed, or if none was filed, at the time the judgment was recorded. **Leg.H.** Added Stats 1976 ch 73 §6. Amended Stats 1984 ch 20 §5.

§874.220. [Section repealed 1985]
Leg.H. Added Stats 1976 ch 73 §6. Repealed Stats 1984 ch 20 §6. See CCP §874.225.

§874.225. Claims not affected by judgment
Except to the extent provided in Section 1908, the judgment does not affect a claim in the property or part thereof of any person who was not a party to the action if any of the following conditions is satisfied:

(a) The claim was of record at the time the lis pendens was filed or, if none was filed, at the time the judgment was recorded.

(b) The claim was actually known to the plaintiff or would have been reasonably apparent from an inspection of the property at the time the lis pendens was filed or, if none was filed, at the time the judgment was entered. For the purpose of this subdivision, a "claim in the property or part thereof" of any person means the interest of the person in the portion of the property or proceeds of sale thereof allocated to the plaintiff. Nothing in this subdivision shall be construed to impair the rights of a bona fide purchaser or encumbrancer for value dealing with the plaintiff or the plaintiff's successors in interest. **Leg.H.** Added Stats 1984 ch 20 §7.

§874.230. [Section repealed 1985]
Leg.H. Added Stats 1976 ch 73 §6. Repealed Stats 1984 ch 20 §8. See CCP §874.225.

§874.240. Conveyance or transfer has binding effect of judgment
A conveyance or transfer pursuant to Sections 873.750 and 873.790 or Section 873.960 is binding and conclusive, in the same manner as a judgment. **Leg.H.** Added Stats 1976 ch 73 §6.

CHAPTER 10
PARTITION OF REAL PROPERTY ACT

Citation of act; Applicability. § 874.311.
Definitions. § 874.312.
Applicability. § 874.313.
Service of complaint. § 874.314.
Appointment of referees. § 874.315.
Valuation of property. § 874.316.
Cotenant's options to buy interest in partition buy sale. § 874.317.
Partition in kind. § 874.318.
Determination of prejudicial result from partition in kind. § 874.319.
Open-market sale. § 874.320.
Report requirement of broker offering heirs property for open-market sale. § 874.321.
Apportionment of costs. § 874.321.5.
Effect on the Electronic Signature in Global and National Commerce Act. § 874.323.

§ 874.311. Citation of act; Applicability
(a) This act shall be known, and may be cited, as the Partition of Real Property Act.

(b) This act applies to real property held in tenancy in common where there is no agreement in a record binding all the cotenants which governs the partition of the property.

(c) This act applies to actions for partition of real property filed on or after January 1, 2023. **Leg.H.** Added Stats 2021 ch 119 §2 (AB 633), effective January 1, 2022. Amended Stats 2022 ch 82 §3 (AB 2245), effective January 1, 2023.

§ 874.312. Definitions
For purposes of this chapter, the following definitions apply:

(a) "Determination of value" means a court order determining the fair market value of the property under Section 874.316 or 874.320 or adopting the valuation of the property agreed to by all cotenants.

(b) "Partition by sale" means a court-ordered sale of the entire property, whether by auction, sealed bids, or open-market sale conducted under Section 874.320.

(c) "Partition in kind" means the division of property into physically distinct and separately titled parcels.

(d) "Record" means information that is inscribed on a tangible medium or that is stored in an electronic or other medium and is retrievable in perceivable form. **Leg.H.** Added Stats 2021 ch 119 §2 (AB 633), effective January 1, 2022. Amended Stats 2022 ch 82 §4 (AB 2245), effective January 1, 2023.

§ 874.313. Applicability
(a) In an action to partition real property, the property shall be partitioned under this chapter unless all of the cotenants otherwise agree in a record.

(b) This chapter supplements the other provisions of this title and, if an action is governed by this chapter, this chapter shall control over any provisions of this title that are inconsistent with this chapter. **Leg.H.** Added Stats 2021 ch 119 §2 (AB 633), effective January 1, 2022. Amended Stats 2022 ch 82 §5 (AB 2245), effective January 1, 2023.

§ 874.314. Service of complaint
(a) This act does not limit or affect the method by which service of a complaint in a partition action may be made.

(b) If the plaintiff in a partition action seeks an order of notice by publication, the plaintiff, not later than 10 days after the court's determination, shall post and maintain while the action is pending a conspicuous sign on the property that is the subject of the action. The sign shall state that the action has commenced and identify the name and address of the court and the common designation by which the property is known. The court may require the plaintiff to publish on the sign the name of the plaintiff and the known defendants. **Leg.H.** Added Stats 2021 ch 119 §2 (AB 633), effective January 1, 2022. Amended Stats 2022 ch 82 §6 (AB 2245), effective January 1, 2023.

§ 874.315. Appointment of referees
If the court appoints referees pursuant to Section 873.010, each referee, in addition to any other requirements and disqualifications applicable to referees, shall be disinterested and impartial and not a party to or a participant in the action. **Leg.H.** Added Stats 2021 ch 119 §2 (AB 633), effective January 1, 2022.

§ 874.316. Valuation of property
(a) Except as otherwise provided in subdivisions (b) and (c), the court shall determine the fair market value of the property by ordering an appraisal pursuant to subdivision (d).

(b) If all cotenants have agreed to the value of the property or to another method of valuation, the court shall adopt that value or the value produced by the agreed method of valuation.

(c) If the court determines that the evidentiary value of an appraisal is outweighed by the cost of the appraisal, the court, after an evidentiary hearing, shall determine the fair market value of the property and send notice to the parties of the value.

(d) If the court orders an appraisal, the court shall appoint a disinterested real estate appraiser licensed in the State of California to determine the fair market value of the property assuming sole ownership of the fee simple estate. On completion of the appraisal, the appraiser shall file a sworn or verified appraisal with the court.

(e) If an appraisal is conducted pursuant to subdivision (d), not later than 10 days after the appraisal is filed, the court shall send notice to each party with a known address, stating all of the following:

(1) The appraised fair market value of the property.

(2) That the appraisal is available at the court clerk's office.

(3) That a party may file with the court an objection to the appraisal not later than 30 days after the notice is sent, stating the grounds for the objection.

(f) If an appraisal is filed with the court pursuant to subdivision (d), the court shall conduct a hearing to determine the fair market value of the property not sooner than 30 days after a copy of the notice of the appraisal is sent to each party under subdivision (e), whether or not an objection to the appraisal is filed under paragraph (3) of subdivision (e). In addition to the court-ordered appraisal, the court may consider any other evidence of value offered by a party.

(g) After a hearing under subdivision (f), but before considering the merits of the partition action, the court shall determine the fair market value of the property and send notice to the parties of the value. **Leg.H.** Added Stats 2021 ch 119 §2 (AB 633), effective January 1, 2022. Amended Stats 2022 ch 82 §7 (AB 2245), effective January 1, 2023.

§ 874.317. Cotenant's options to buy interest in partition buy sale
(a) If any cotenant requested partition by sale, the court shall, after the determination of value under Section 874.316, send notice to the parties

that any cotenant except a cotenant that requested partition by sale may buy all the interests of the cotenants that requested partition by sale.

(b) Not later than 45 days after the notice is sent under subdivision (a), any cotenant except a cotenant that requested partition by sale may give notice to the court that it elects to buy all the interests of the cotenants that requested partition by sale.

(c) The purchase price for each of the interests of a cotenant that requested partition by sale is the value of the entire parcel determined under Section 874.316 multiplied by the cotenant's fractional ownership of the entire parcel.

(d) After expiration of the period described in subdivision (b), the following rules apply:

(1) If only one cotenant elects to buy all the interests of the cotenants that requested partition by sale, the court shall notify all the parties of that fact.

(2) If more than one cotenant elects to buy all the interests of the cotenants that requested partition by sale, the court shall allocate the right to buy those interests among the electing cotenants based on each electing cotenant's existing fractional ownership of the entire parcel divided by the total existing fractional ownership of all cotenants electing to buy and send notice to all the parties of that fact and of the price to be paid by each electing cotenant.

(3) If no cotenant elects to buy all the interests of the cotenants that requested partition by sale, the court shall send notice to all the parties of that fact and resolve the partition action under paragraphs (a) and (b) of Section 874.318.

(e) If the court sends notice to the parties under paragraph (1) or (2) of subdivision (d), the court shall set a date, not sooner than 60 days after the date the notice was sent, by which electing cotenants shall pay their apportioned price into the court. After this date, the following rules apply:

(1) If all electing cotenants timely pay their apportioned price into court, the court shall issue an order reallocating all the interests of the cotenants and disburse the amounts held by the court to the persons entitled to them.

(2) If no electing cotenant timely pays its apportioned price, the court shall resolve the partition action under paragraphs (a) and (b) of Section 874.318 as if the interests of the cotenants that requested partition by sale were not purchased.

(3) If one or more but not all of the electing cotenants fail to pay their apportioned price on time, the court, on motion, shall give notice to the electing cotenants that paid their apportioned price of the interest remaining and the price for all that interest.

(f) Not later than 20 days after the court gives notice pursuant to paragraph (3) of subdivision (e), any cotenant that paid may elect to purchase all of the remaining interest by paying the entire price into the court. After the 20-day period, the following rules apply:

(1) If only one cotenant pays the entire price for the remaining interest, the court shall issue an order reallocating the remaining interest to that cotenant. The court shall promptly issue an order reallocating the interests of all of the cotenants and disburse the amounts held by it to the persons entitled to them.

(2) If no cotenant pays the entire price for the remaining interest, the court shall resolve the partition action under paragraphs (a) and (b) of Section 874.318 as if the interests of the cotenants that requested partition by sale were not purchased.

(3) If more than one cotenant pays the entire price for the remaining interest, the court shall reapportion the remaining interest among those paying cotenants, based on each paying cotenant's original fractional ownership of the entire parcel divided by the total original fractional ownership of all cotenants that paid the entire price for the remaining interest. The court shall issue promptly an order reallocating all of the cotenants' interests, disburse the amounts held by it to the persons entitled to them, and promptly refund any excess payment held by the court.

(g) Not later than 45 days after the court sends notice to the parties pursuant to subdivision (a), any cotenant entitled to buy an interest under this section may request the court to authorize the sale as part of the pending action of the interests of cotenants named as defendants and served with the complaint but that did not appear in the action.

(h) If the court receives a timely request under subdivision (g), the court, after a hearing, may deny the request or authorize the requested additional sale on such terms as the court determines are fair and reasonable, subject to the following limitations:

(1) A sale authorized under this subdivision may occur only after the purchase prices for all interests subject to sale under subdivisions (a) to (f), inclusive, have been paid into court and those interests have been reallocated among the cotenants as provided in those subdivisions.

(2) The purchase price for the interest of a nonappearing cotenant is based on the court's determination of value under Section 874.316. **Leg.H.** Added Stats 2021 ch 119 §2 (AB 633), effective January 1, 2022.

§ 874.318. Partition in kind

(a) If all the interests of all cotenants that requested partition by sale are not purchased by other cotenants pursuant to Section 874.317, or if after conclusion of the buyout under Section 874.317 a cotenant remains that has requested partition in kind, the court shall order partition in kind unless the court, after consideration of the factors listed in Section 874.319, finds that partition in kind will result in great prejudice to the cotenants as a group. In considering whether to order partition in kind, the court shall approve a request by two or more parties to have their individual interests aggregated.

(b) If the court does not order partition in kind under subdivision (a), the court shall order partition by sale pursuant to Section 874.320 or, if no cotenant requested partition by sale, the court shall dismiss the action.

(c) If the court orders partition in kind pursuant to subdivision (a), the court may require that one or more cotenants pay one or more other cotenants amounts so that the payments, taken together with the value of the in-kind distributions to the cotenants, will make the partition in kind just and proportionate in value to the fractional interests held.

(d) If the court orders partition in kind, the court shall allocate to the cotenants that are unknown, unlocatable, or the subject of a default judgment, if their interests were not bought out, a part of the property representing the combined interests of these cotenants as determined by the court. **Leg.H.** Added Stats 2021 ch 119 §2 (AB 633), effective January 1, 2022.

§ 874.319. Determination of prejudicial result from partition in kind

(a) In determining whether partition in kind would result in great prejudice to the cotenants as a group, the court shall consider the following:

(1) Whether the property practicably can be divided among the cotenants.

(2) Whether partition in kind would apportion the property in such a way that the aggregate fair market value of the parcels resulting from the division would be materially less than the value of the property if it were sold as a whole, taking into account the condition under which a court-ordered sale likely would occur.

(3) Evidence of the collective duration of ownership or possession of the property by a cotenant and one or more predecessors in title or predecessors in possession to the cotenant who are or were relatives of the cotenant or each other.

(4) A cotenant's sentimental attachment to the property, including any attachment arising because the property has ancestral or other unique or special value to the cotenant.

(5) The lawful use being made of the property by a cotenant and the degree to which the cotenant would be harmed if the cotenant could not continue the same use of the property.

(6) The degree to which the cotenants have contributed their pro rata share of the property taxes, insurance, and other expenses associated with maintaining ownership of the property or have contributed to the physical improvement, maintenance, or upkeep of the property.

(7) Any other relevant factor.

(b) The court shall not consider any one factor in subdivision (a) to be dispositive without weighing the totality of all relevant factors and circumstances. **Leg.H.** Added Stats 2021 ch 119 §2 (AB 633), effective January 1, 2022. Amended Stats 2022 ch 82 §8 (AB 2245), effective January 1, 2023.

§ 874.320. Open-market sale

(a) If the court orders a sale of property, the sale shall be an open-market sale unless the court finds that a sale by sealed bids or an auction would be more economically advantageous and in the best interest of the cotenants as a group.

(b) If the court orders an open-market sale and the parties, not later than 10 days after the entry of the order, agree on a real estate broker licensed in the State of California to offer the property for sale, the court shall appoint the broker and establish a reasonable commission. If the parties do not agree on a broker, the court shall appoint a disinterested real estate broker licensed in the State of California to offer the property for sale and shall establish a reasonable commission. The broker shall offer the property for sale in a commercially reasonable manner at a price no lower than the determination of value and on the terms and conditions established by the court.

(c) If the broker appointed under subdivision (b) obtains within a reasonable time an offer to purchase the property for at least the determination of value, the following requirements apply:

(1) The broker shall comply with the reporting requirements in Section 874.321.

(2) The sale shall be completed in accordance with state law.

(d) If the broker appointed under subdivision (b) does not obtain an offer to purchase the property for at least the determination of value within a reasonable time, the court, after a hearing, may do any of the following:

(1) Approve the highest outstanding offer, if any.

(2) Redetermine the value of the property and order that the property continue to be offered for an additional time.

(3) Order that the property be sold by sealed bids or at an auction.

(e) If the court orders a sale by sealed bids or an auction, the court shall set terms and conditions of the sale. If the court orders an auction, the auction shall be conducted under Chapter 6 (commencing with Section 873.510).

(f) If a purchaser is entitled to a share of the proceeds of the sale, the purchaser is entitled to a credit against the price in an amount equal to the purchaser's share of the proceeds. **Leg.H.** Added Stats 2021 ch 119 §2 (AB 633), effective January 1, 2022. Amended Stats 2022 ch 82 §9 (AB 2245), effective January 1, 2023.

§ 874.321. Report requirement of broker offering heirs property for open-market sale

(a) A broker appointed to offer property for open-market sale shall file a report with the court not later than seven days after receiving an offer to purchase the property for at least the value determined under Section 874.316 or 874.320.

(b) The report required by subdivision (a) shall contain the following information:

(1) A description of the property to be sold to each buyer.

(2) The name of each buyer.

(3) The proposed purchase price.

(4) The terms and conditions of the proposed sale, including the terms of any owner financing.

(5) The amounts to be paid to lienholders.

(6) A statement of contractual or other arrangements or conditions of the broker's commission.

(7) Other material facts relevant to the sale. **Leg.H.** Added Stats 2021 ch 119 §2 (AB 633), effective January 1, 2022. Amended Stats 2022 ch 82 §10 (AB 2245), effective January 1, 2023.

§ 874.321.5. Apportionment of costs

In an action for partition of property, the court may apportion the costs of partition, including an appraisal fee, pursuant to Section 874.040, except that the court shall not apportion the costs of partition to any party that opposes the partition unless doing so is equitable and consistent with the purposes of this chapter. **Leg.H.** Added Stats 2021 ch 119 §2 (AB 633), effective January 1, 2022. Amended Stats 2022 ch 82 §11 (AB 2245), effective January 1, 2023.

§ 874.322. Uniformity of law [Repealed]

Leg.H. Added Stats 2021 ch 119 §2 (AB 633), effective January 1, 2022. Repealed Stats 2022 ch 82 §12 (AB 2245), effective January 1, 2023.

§ 874.323. Effect on the Electronic Signature in Global and National Commerce Act

This act modifies, limits, and supersedes the Electronic Signatures in Global and National Commerce Act (15 U.S.C. Sec. 7001 et seq.), but does not modify, limit, or supersede Section 101(c) of that act (15 U.S.C. Section 7001(c)), or authorize electronic delivery of any of the notices described in Section 103(b) of that act (15 U.S.C. Section 7003(b)). **Leg.H.** Added Stats 2021 ch 119 §2 (AB 633), effective January 1, 2022.

TITLE 11
CONTRIBUTION AMONG JOINT JUDGMENT DEBTORS

Chapter 1. Releases From and Contribution Among Joint Tortfeasors.
Chapter 2. Contribution Among Other Judgment Debtors.

CHAPTER 1
RELEASES FROM AND CONTRIBUTION AMONG JOINT TORTFEASORS

Existence and incidents of right of contribution. §875.
Pro rata share. §876.
Effect of release, dismissal, or covenant not to sue or enforce judgment. §877.
Sliding scale recovery agreements. §877.5.
Hearing on issue of good faith of settlement; Review. §877.6.
Judgment for contribution. §878.
Severability and partial validity. §879.
Causes of action to which title applicable. §880.

§875. Existence and incidents of right of contribution

(a) Where a money judgment has been rendered jointly against two or more defendants in a tort action there shall be a right of contribution among them as hereinafter provided.

(b) Such right of contribution shall be administered in accordance with the principles of equity.

(c) Such right of contribution may be enforced only after one tortfeasor has, by payment, discharged the joint judgment or has paid more than his pro rata share thereof. It shall be limited to the excess so paid over the pro rata share of the person so paying and in no event shall any tortfeasor be compelled to make contribution beyond his own pro rata share of the entire judgment.

(d) There shall be no right of contribution in favor of any tortfeasor who has intentionally injured the injured person.

(e) A liability insurer who by payment has discharged the liability of a tortfeasor judgment debtor shall be subrogated to his right of contribution.

(f) This title shall not impair any right of indemnity under existing law, and where one tortfeasor judgment debtor is entitled to indemnity from another there shall be no right of contribution between them.

(g) This title shall not impair the right of a plaintiff to satisfy a judgment in full as against any tortfeasor judgment debtor. **Leg.H.** Added Stats 1957 ch 1700 §1.

Prior Law: Former CCP §875, relating to postponement of trial by consent of parties, was enacted Stats 1872 and repealed Stats 1933 ch 744 §198.

§876. Pro rata share

(a) The pro rata share of each tortfeasor judgment debtor shall be determined by dividing the entire judgment equally among all of them.

(b) Where one or more persons are held liable solely for the tort of one of them or of another, as in the case of the liability of a master for the tort of his servant, they shall contribute a single pro rata share, as to which there may be indemnity between them. **Leg.H.** Added Stats 1957 ch 1700 §1.

Prior Law: Former CCP §876, relating to postponement of trial upon application of a party, was enacted 1872 and repealed Stats 1933 ch 744 §198.

§877. Effect of release, dismissal, or covenant not to sue or enforce judgment

Where a release, dismissal with or without prejudice, or a covenant not to sue or not to enforce judgment is given in good faith before verdict or judgment to one or more of a number of tortfeasors claimed to be liable for the same tort, or to one or more other co-obligors mutually subject to contribution rights, it shall have the following effect:

(a) It shall not discharge any other such party from liability unless its terms so provide, but it shall reduce the claims against the others in the amount stipulated by the release, the dismissal or the covenant, or in the amount of the consideration paid for it, whichever is the greater.

(b) It shall discharge the party to whom it is given from all liability for any contribution to any other parties.

(c) This section shall not apply to co-obligors who have expressly agreed in writing to an apportionment of liability for losses or claims among themselves.

(d) This section shall not apply to a release, dismissal with or without prejudice, or a covenant not to sue or not to enforce judgment given to a co-obligor on an alleged contract debt where the contract was made prior to January 1, 1988. **Leg.H.** Added Stats 1957 ch 1700 §1. Amended Stats 1987 ch 677 §2; Stats 2011 ch 296 §39 (AB 1023), effective January 1, 2012.

Prior Law: Former CCP §877, relating to length of adjournments, was enacted 1872 and repealed Stats 1933 ch 744 §198.

§877.5. Sliding scale recovery agreements

(a) Where an agreement or covenant is made which provides for a sliding scale recovery agreement between one or more, but not all, alleged defendant tortfeasors and the plaintiff or plaintiffs:

(1) The parties entering into any such agreement or covenant shall promptly inform the court in which the action is pending of the existence of the agreement or covenant and its terms and provisions.

(2) If the action is tried before a jury, and a defendant party to the agreement is called as a witness at trial, the court shall, upon motion of a party, disclose to the jury the existence and content of the agreement or covenant, unless the court finds that this disclosure will create substantial danger of undue prejudice, of confusing the issues, or of misleading the jury.

The jury disclosure herein required shall be no more than necessary to inform the jury of the possibility that the agreement may bias the testimony of the witness.

(b) As used in this section, a "sliding scale recovery agreement" means an agreement or covenant between a plaintiff or plaintiffs and one or more, but not all, alleged tortfeasor defendants, which limits the liability of the agreeing tortfeasor defendants to an amount which is dependent upon the amount of recovery which the plaintiff is able to recover from the nonagreeing defendant or defendants. This includes, but is not limited to, agreements within the scope of Section 877, and agreements in the form of a loan from the agreeing tortfeasor defendant or defendants to the plaintiff or plaintiffs which is repayable in whole or in part from the recovery against the nonagreeing tortfeasor defendant or defendants.

(c) No sliding scale recovery agreement is effective unless, at least 72 hours prior to entering into the agreement, a notice of intent to enter into an agreement has been served on all nonsignatory alleged defendant tortfeasors. However, upon a showing of good cause, the court or a judge thereof may allow a shorter time. The failure to comply with the notice requirements of this subdivision shall not constitute good cause to delay commencement of trial. **Leg.H.** Added Stats 1977 ch 568 §1. Amended Stats 1987 ch 1201 §3, ch 1202 §1; Stats 1990 ch 17 §1 (AB 366).

1987 Note: Section 877.5, as amended by ch 1202, applies only to actions based upon acts or omissions occurring on or after January 1, 1988. Stats 1987 ch 1202 §2.

§877.6. Hearing on issue of good faith of settlement; Review

(a)(1) Any party to an action in which it is alleged that two or more parties are joint tortfeasors or co-obligors on a contract debt shall be entitled to a hearing on the issue of the good faith of a settlement entered into by the plaintiff or other claimant and one or more alleged tortfeasors or co-obligors, upon giving notice in the manner provided in subdivision (b) of Section 1005. Upon a showing of good cause, the court may shorten the time for giving the required notice to permit the determination of the issue to be made before the commencement of the trial of the action, or before the verdict or judgment if settlement is made after the trial has commenced.

(2) In the alternative, a settling party may give notice of settlement to all parties and to the court, together with an application for determination of good faith settlement and a proposed order. The application shall indicate the settling parties, and the basis, terms, and amount of the settlement. The notice, application, and proposed order shall be given by certified mail, return receipt requested, or by personal service. Proof of service shall be filed with the court. Within 25 days of the mailing of the notice, application, and proposed order, or within 20 days of personal service, a nonsettling party may file a notice of motion to contest the good faith of the settlement. If none of the nonsettling parties files a motion within 25 days of mailing of the notice, application, and proposed order,

or within 20 days of personal service, the court may approve the settlement. The notice by a nonsettling party shall be given in the manner provided in subdivision (b) of Section 1005. However, this paragraph shall not apply to settlements in which a confidentiality agreement has been entered into regarding the case or the terms of the settlement.

(b) The issue of the good faith of a settlement may be determined by the court on the basis of affidavits served with the notice of hearing, and any counteraffidavits filed in response, or the court may, in its discretion, receive other evidence at the hearing.

(c) A determination by the court that the settlement was made in good faith shall bar any other joint tortfeasor or co-obligor from any further claims against the settling tortfeasor or co-obligor for equitable comparative contribution, or partial or comparative indemnity, based on comparative negligence or comparative fault.

(d) The party asserting the lack of good faith shall have the burden of proof on that issue.

(e) When a determination of the good faith or lack of good faith of a settlement is made, any party aggrieved by the determination may petition the proper court to review the determination by writ of mandate. The petition for writ of mandate shall be filed within 20 days after service of written notice of the determination, or within any additional time not exceeding 20 days as the trial court may allow.

(1) The court shall, within 30 days of the receipt of all materials to be filed by the parties, determine whether or not the court will hear the writ and notify the parties of its determination.

(2) If the court grants a hearing on the writ, the hearing shall be given special precedence over all other civil matters on the calendar of the court except those matters to which equal or greater precedence on the calendar is granted by law.

(3) The running of any period of time after which an action would be subject to dismissal pursuant to the applicable provisions of Chapter 1.5 (commencing with Section 583.110) of Title 8 of Part 2 shall be tolled during the period of review of a determination pursuant to this subdivision. **Leg.H.** Added Stats 1980 ch 562 §1. Amended Stats 1984 ch 311 §1; Stats 1985 ch 621 §2; Stats 1987 ch 677 §3; Stats 1988 ch 128 §1; Stats 1989 ch 693 §5; Stats 1992 ch 876 §6 (AB 3296); Stats 1995 ch 796 §13 (SB 45); Stats 2001 ch 812 §7 (AB 223); Stats 2017 ch 64 §1 (SB 543), effective January 1, 2018.

§878. Judgment for contribution

Judgment for contribution may be entered by one tortfeasor judgment debtor against other tortfeasor judgment debtors by motion upon notice. Notice of such motion shall be given to all parties in the action, including the plaintiff or plaintiffs, at least 10 days before the hearing thereon. Such notice shall be accompanied by an affidavit setting forth any information which the moving party may have as to the assets of defendants available for satisfaction of the judgment or claim for contribution. **Leg.H.** Added Stats 1957 ch 1700 §1.

Prior Law: Former CCP §878, similar to present CCP §588, was enacted 1872 and repealed Stats 1933 ch 744 §198.

§879. Severability and partial validity

If any provision of this title or the application thereof to any person is held invalid, such invalidity shall not affect other provisions or applications of the title which can be given effect without the invalid provision or application and to this end the provisions of this title are declared to be severable. **Leg.H.** Added Stats 1957 ch 1700 §1.

Prior Law: Former CCP §879, similar to present CCP §589, was enacted 1872 and repealed Stats 1933 ch 744 §198.

§880. Causes of action to which title applicable

This title shall become effective as to causes of action accruing on or after January 1, 1958. **Leg.H.** Added Stats 1957 ch 1700 §1.

Prior Law: Former CCP §880, similar to present CCP §590, was enacted 1872 and repealed Stats 1933 ch 744 §198.

CHAPTER 2
CONTRIBUTION AMONG OTHER JUDGMENT DEBTORS

Application of chapter. §881.
Right to contribution. §882.
Procedure for compelling contribution or repayment. §883.

§881. Application of chapter

This chapter governs contribution among joint judgment debtors other than joint tortfeasors. **Leg.H.** Added Stats 1982 ch 497 §63, operative July 1, 1983.

Prior Law: Former CCP § 881, similar to present CCP §591, was enacted 1872 and repealed Stats 1933 ch 744 §198.

§882. Right to contribution

If two or more judgment debtors are jointly liable on a money judgment:

(a) A judgment debtor who has satisfied more than his or her due proportion of the judgment, whether voluntarily or through enforcement procedures, may compel contribution from another judgment debtor who has satisfied less than his or her due proportion of the judgment.

(b) If the judgment is based upon an obligation of one judgment debtor as surety for another and the surety satisfies the judgment or any part thereof, whether voluntarily or through enforcement procedures, the surety may compel repayment from the principal. **Leg.H.** Added Stats 1982 ch 497 §63, operative July 1, 1983.

Prior Law: Former CCP § 882, similar to present §592, was enacted 1872 and repealed Stats 1933 ch 744 §198.

§883. Procedure for compelling contribution or repayment

(a) A judgment debtor entitled to compel contribution or repayment pursuant to this chapter may apply on noticed motion to the court that entered the judgment for an order determining liability for contribution or repayment. The application shall be made at any time before the judgment is satisfied in full or within 30 days thereafter.

(b) The order determining liability for contribution or repayment entitles the judgment debtor to the benefit of the judgment to enforce the liability, including every remedy that the judgment creditor has against the persons liable, to the extent of the liability.

(c) Nothing in this section limits any other remedy that a judgment debtor entitled to contribution or repayment may have. **Leg.H.** Added Stats 1982 ch 497 §63, operative July 1, 1983. Amended Stats 1998 ch 77 §1 (SB 1841).

Prior Law: Former CCP §883, similar to present §631, was enacted 1872, amended Stats 1919 ch 496 §1, and repealed Stats 1933 ch 744 §198.

§§884–886. [Sections repealed 1933]

Leg.H. Enacted 1872. Repealed Stats 1933 ch 744 §198. See CCP §594.

§887. [Section repealed 1933]

Leg.H. Enacted 1872. Amended Stats 1907 ch 478 §10. Repealed Stats 1933 ch 744 §198. The repealed section related to proceedings in justices' court.

§889. [Section repealed 1933]

Leg.H. Enacted 1872. Repealed Stats 1933 ch 744 §198. See CCP §1132.

§890. [Section repealed 1933]

Leg.H. Enacted 1872. Amended Stats 1904 ch 51 §1. Repealed Stats 1933 ch 744 §198. See CCP §581.

§890a. [Section repealed 1933]

Leg.H. Added Stats 1919 ch 94 §1. Repealed Stats 1933 ch 744 §198. The repealed section related to entry of a judgment of dismissal.

§891. [Section repealed 1933]

Leg.H. Enacted 1872. Repealed Stats 1933 ch 744 §198. See CCP §664.

§892. [Section repealed 1933]

Leg.H. Enacted 1872. Amended Stats 1907 ch 478 §11, Stats 1913 ch 75 §1. Repealed Stats 1933 ch 744 §198. See CCP §664.

§893. [Section repealed 1933]

Leg.H. Enacted 1872. Amended Code Amdts 1873–74 ch 383 §120; Stats 1907 ch 478 §12; Stats 1915 ch 732 §1. Repealed Stats 1933 ch 744 §198. The repealed section related to proceedings in justices' court.

§894. [Section repealed 1933]

Leg.H. Enacted 1872. Repealed Stats 1933 ch 744 §198. See CCP §666.

§895. [Section repealed 1933]

Leg.H. Enacted 1872. Amended Code Amdts 1877–78 ch 125 §1; Stats 1907 ch 478 §13. Repealed Stats 1933 ch 744 §198. The repealed section related to proceedings in justices' court.

§896. [Section repealed 1933]
Leg.H. Enacted 1872. Repealed Stats 1933 ch 744 §198. See CCP §1033.

§897. [Section repealed 1933]
Leg.H. Enacted 1872. Amended Code Amdts 1880 ch 34 §5. Repealed Stats 1933 ch 744 §198. See CCP §674.

§898. [Section repealed 1933]
Leg.H. Enacted 1872. Amended Code Amdts 1880 ch 34 §6. Repealed Stats 1933 ch 744 §198. See CCP §674.

§899. [Section repealed 1933]
Leg.H. Enacted 1872. Amended Code Amdts 1880 ch 34 §7; Stats 1919 ch 157 §1. Repealed Stats 1933 ch 744 §198. See CCP §674.

§900. [Section repealed 1933]
Leg.H. Enacted 1872. Amended Code Amdts 1880 ch 106 §2; Stats 1911 ch 217 §1; Stats 1927 ch 322 §1. Repealed Stats 1933 ch 744 §198. See CCP §674.

§900a. [Section repealed 1933]
Leg.H. Added Stats 1919 ch 353 §1. Repealed Stats 1933 ch 744 §198. See CCP §473.

§900b. [Section repealed 1933]
Leg.H. Added Stats 1929 ch 469 §1. Repealed Stats 1933 ch 744 §198. The repealed section related to proceedings in justices' court.

TITLE 12
PROCEEDINGS IN CIVIL ACTIONS IN POLICE COURTS
[REPEALED]

TITLE 13
APPEALS IN CIVIL ACTIONS

Chapter 1. Appeals in General.
Chapter 2. Stay of Enforcement and Other Proceedings.

CHAPTER 1
APPEALS IN GENERAL

Provisions governing review; Judicial Council Rules. §901.
Right of party aggrieved; Designation of parties. §902.
Attorney General intervention in appeal. §902.1.
Notice on death of person entitled to appeal. §903.
Proceedings in which appeal available. §904.
Judgments and orders that may be appealed. §904.1.
Appeal in limited civil case. §904.2.
Appeal or review of judgment. §904.3.
Provisions governing appeals from small claims division. §904.5.
Reviewable matters. §906.
Costs on frivolous or dilatory appeal. §907.
Reversal or modification; Restitution of parties; Evidence and findings by reviewing court. §908.
Factual determinations by reviewing court; Additional evidence. §909.
Transfer to court of appeal of case on appeal to superior court. §911.
Certified copy of judgment or order of reviewing court; Remittance. §912.
Dismissal of appeal with prejudice; Exception. §913.
Phonographic report of trial. §914.
[Section renumbered 1933]. §915.

§901. Provisions governing review; Judicial Council Rules

A judgment or order in a civil action or proceeding may be reviewed as prescribed in this title. The Judicial Council shall prescribe rules for the practice and procedure on appeal not inconsistent with the provisions of this title. **Leg.H.** Added Stats 1968 ch 385 §2.

Prior Law: Former CCP §901, similar to present CCP §683.010, was added Stats 1968 ch 385 §2 and repealed Stats 1933 ch 744 §198.

§901a. [Section repealed 1933]

Leg.H. Added Stats 1906 Ex Sess ch 33 §1. Repealed Stats 1933 ch 744 §198. See CCP §918.

§902. Right of party aggrieved; Designation of parties

Any party aggrieved may appeal in the cases prescribed in this title. A party appealing is known as an appellant, and an adverse party as a respondent. **Leg.H.** Added Stats 1968 ch 385 §2.

Prior Law: Former CCP §902, similar to present CCP §682, was enacted 1872, amended Stats 1921 ch 128 §1, Stats 1929 ch 320 §1, Stats 1931 ch 1110 §1, and repealed Stats 1933 ch 744 §198.

§902.1. Attorney General intervention in appeal

In any case in which a notice was required pursuant to subdivision (e) of Section 664.5, the Attorney General shall have the right to intervene and participate in any appeal taken therefrom. These rights shall apply regardless of whether the Attorney General participated in the case in the trial court. However, the Attorney General has no direct right to appeal. If the Attorney General elects not to intervene and participate in the appeal, he or she shall file a statement with the Legislature and the Judicial Council stating the reason or reasons for the decision not to intervene and participate in the appeal. This statement may be in the form of an annual report to the Legislature and Judicial Council and that report shall be a matter of public record. **Leg.H.** Added Stats 1997 ch 259 §2 (AB 380).

§903. Notice on death of person entitled to appeal

In the event of the death of any person who would, if still alive, have a right of appeal, either the attorney of record representing the decedent in the court in which the judgment was rendered, or the executor or administrator of the estate of the decedent, may file a notice of appeal therefrom within the time within which the decedent could have filed such a notice if he had survived. **Leg.H.** Added Stats 1968 ch 385 §2.

Prior Law: Former CCP §903, similar to present CCP §683, was enacted 1872 and repealed Stats 1933 ch 744 §198.

§904. Proceedings in which appeal available

An appeal may be taken in a civil action or proceeding as provided in Sections 904.1, 904.2, 904.3, and 904.5. **Leg.H.** Added Stats 1968 ch 385 §2. Amended Stats 2007 ch 263 §9.5 (AB 310), effective January 1, 2008.

Prior Law: Former CCP §904, similar to present CCP §691, was enacted 1872 and repealed Stats 1933 ch 744 §198.

§904.1. Judgments and orders that may be appealed

(a) An appeal, other than in a limited civil case, is to the court of appeal. An appeal, other than in a limited civil case, may be taken from any of the following:

(1) From a judgment, except an interlocutory judgment, other than as provided in paragraphs (8), (9), and (11), or a judgment of contempt that is made final and conclusive by Section 1222.

(2) From an order made after a judgment made appealable by paragraph (1).

(3) From an order granting a motion to quash service of summons or granting a motion to stay the action on the ground of inconvenient forum, or from a written order of dismissal under Section 581d following an order granting a motion to dismiss the action on the ground of inconvenient forum.

(4) From an order granting a new trial or denying a motion for judgment notwithstanding the verdict.

(5) From an order discharging or refusing to discharge an attachment or granting a right to attach order.

(6) From an order granting or dissolving an injunction, or refusing to grant or dissolve an injunction.

(7) From an order appointing a receiver.

(8) From an interlocutory judgment, order, or decree, made or entered in an action to redeem real or personal property from a mortgage thereof, or a lien thereon, determining the right to redeem and directing an accounting.

(9) From an interlocutory judgment in an action for partition determining the rights and interests of the respective parties and directing partition to be made.

(10) From an order made appealable by the Probate Code or the Family Code.

(11) From an interlocutory judgment directing payment of monetary sanctions by a party or an attorney for a party if the amount exceeds five thousand dollars ($5,000).

(12) From an order directing payment of monetary sanctions by a party or an attorney for a party if the amount exceeds five thousand dollars ($5,000).

(13) From an order granting or denying a special motion to strike under Sections 425.16 and 425.19.

(14) From a final order or judgment in a bifurcated proceeding regarding child custody or visitation rights.

(b) Sanction orders or judgments of five thousand dollars ($5,000) or less against a party or an attorney for a party may be reviewed on an appeal by that party after entry of final judgment in the main action, or, at the discretion of the court of appeal, may be reviewed upon petition for an extraordinary writ. **Leg.H.** Added Stats 1968 ch 385 §2. Amended Stats 1969 ch 1611 §21, operative July 1, 1970; Stats 1971 ch 1210 §8; Stats 1978 ch 395 §1, effective July 11, 1978; Stats 1982 ch 931 §1, ch 1198 §63.2, operative July 1, 1983; Stats 1983 ch 1159 §12, operative July 1, 1984; Stats 1984 ch 29 §2; Stats 1988 ch 678 §2, ch 1199 §7, ch 1447 §1; Stats 1989 ch 1416 §25; Stats 1992 ch 163 §54 (AB 2641), operative January 1, 1994; Stats 1993 ch 456 §12 (AB 58); Stats 1998 ch 931 §100 (SB 2139), effective September 28, 1998; Stats 1999 ch 960 §2 (AB 1675), effective October 10, 1999; Stats 2006 ch 567 §8 (AB 2303), effective January 1, 2007; Stats 2007 ch 43 §9 (SB 649), effective January 1, 2008; Stats 2017 ch 41 §1 (AB 369), effective January 1, 2018; Stats 2023 ch 779 §2 (SB 439), effective January 1, 2024.

§904.2. Appeal in limited civil case

An appeal of a ruling by a superior court judge or other judicial officer in a limited civil case is to the appellate division of the superior court. An appeal of a ruling by a superior court judge or other judicial officer in a limited civil case may be taken from any of the following:

(a) From a judgment, except (1) an interlocutory judgment, or (2) a judgment of contempt that is made final and conclusive by Section 1222.

(b) From an order made after a judgment made appealable by subdivision (a).

(c) From an order changing or refusing to change the place of trial.

(d) From an order granting a motion to quash service of summons or granting a motion to stay the action on the ground of inconvenient forum, or from a written order of dismissal under Section 581d following an order granting a motion to dismiss the action on the ground of inconvenient forum.

(e) From an order granting a new trial or denying a motion for judgment notwithstanding the verdict.

(f) From an order discharging or refusing to discharge an attachment or granting a right to attach order.

(g) From an order granting or dissolving an injunction, or refusing to grant or dissolve an injunction.

(h) From an order appointing a receiver. **Leg.H.** Added Stats 1968 ch 385 §2. Amended Stats 1969 ch 1611 §22, operative July 1, 1970; Stats 1976 ch 1288 §12; Stats 1982 ch 1198 §64, operative July 1, 1983; Stats 1990 ch 1305 §5 (SB 2627); Stats 1998 ch 931 §101 (SB 2139), effective September 28, 1998; Stats 2006 ch 567 §9 (AB 2303), effective January 1, 2007; Stats 2007 ch 43 §10 (SB 649), effective January 1, 2008.

§904.3. Appeal or review of judgment

An appeal shall not be taken from a judgment of the appellate division of a superior court granting or denying a petition for issuance of a writ of mandamus or prohibition directed to the superior court, or a judge thereof, in a limited civil case or a misdemeanor or infraction case. An appellate court may, in its discretion, upon petition for extraordinary writ, review the judgment. **Leg.H.** Added Stats 2007 ch 43 §11 (SB 649), effective January 1, 2008.

Prior Law: Former CCP §904.3, relating to justice court judgments, was added Stats 1968 ch 385 §2, amended Stats 1969 ch 1611 §23, operative July 1, 1970, and repealed Stats 1976 ch 1288 §13.

§904.4. [Section repealed 1990]

Leg.H. Added Stats 1988 ch 789 §1. Repealed, effective January 1, 1990, by its own terms. The repealed section related to nonappealable judgments in San Diego County.

Prior Law: Former CCP §904.4, relating to appeal from justice court on questions of law and fact; trial de novo, was added Stats 1968 ch 385 §2, and repealed Stats 1976 ch 1288 §14.

§904.5. Provisions governing appeals from small claims division

Appeals from the small claims division of a superior court shall be governed by the Small Claims Act (Chapter 5.5 (commencing with Section 116.110) of Title 1 of Part 1). **Leg.H.** Added Stats 1968 ch 385 §2. Amended Stats 1990 ch 1305 §7 (SB 2627); Stats 1998 ch 931 §102 (SB 2139), effective September 28, 1998; Stats 2002 ch 784 §70 (SB 1316).

§905. [Section repealed 1977]

Leg.H. Added Stats 1968 ch 385 §2. Repealed Stats 1976 ch 1288 §15. The repealed section related to undertaking on appeal from justice court.

Prior Law: Former CCP §905, relating to justices' court proceedings supplementary to execution of unit, was enacted 1872, amended Stats 1907 ch 478 §14, Stats 1921 ch 128 §2, Stats 1929 ch 321 §1, and repealed Stats 1933 ch 744 §198.

§906. Reviewable matters

Upon an appeal pursuant to Section 904.1 or 904.2, the reviewing court may review the verdict or decision and any intermediate ruling, proceeding, order or decision which involves the merits or necessarily affects the judgment or order appealed from or which substantially affects the rights of a party, including, on any appeal from the judgment, any order on motion for a new trial, and may affirm, reverse or modify any judgment or order appealed from and may direct the proper judgment or order to be entered, and may, if necessary or proper, direct a new trial or further proceedings to be had. The respondent, or party in whose favor the judgment was given, may, without appealing from such judgment, request the reviewing court to and it may review any of the foregoing matters for the purpose of determining whether or not the appellant was prejudiced by the error or errors upon which he relies for reversal or modification of the judgment from which the appeal is taken. The provisions of this section do not authorize the reviewing court to review any decision or order from which an appeal might have been taken. **Leg.H.** Added Stats 1968 ch 385 §2. Amended Stats 1976 ch 1288 §16.

Prior Law: Former CCP §906, similar to present CCP §1209, was enacted 1872, amended Stats 1907 ch 478 §15, and repealed Stats 1933 ch 744 §198.

§907. Costs on frivolous or dilatory appeal

When it appears to the reviewing court that the appeal was frivolous or taken solely for delay, it may add to the costs on appeal such damages as may be just. **Leg.H.** Added Stats 1968 ch 385 §2.

Prior Law: Former CCP §907, similar to present CCP §1211, was enacted 1872 and repealed Stats 1933 ch 744 §198.

§908. Reversal or modification; Restitution of parties; Evidence and findings by reviewing court

When the judgment or order is reversed or modified, the reviewing court may direct that the parties be returned so far as possible to the positions they occupied before the enforcement of or execution on the judgment or order. In doing so, the reviewing court may order restitution on reasonable terms and conditions of all property and rights lost by the erroneous judgment or order, so far as such restitution is consistent with rights of third parties and may direct the entry of a money judgment sufficient to compensate for property or rights not restored. The reviewing court may take evidence and make findings concerning such matters or may, by order, refer such matters to the trial court for determination. **Leg.H.** Added Stats 1968 ch 385 §2.

Prior Law: Former CCP §908, similar to present CCP §1212, was enacted 1872 and repealed Stats 1933 ch 744 §198.

§909. Factual determinations by reviewing court; Additional evidence

In all cases where trial by jury is not a matter of right or where trial by jury has been waived, the reviewing court may make factual determinations contrary to or in addition to those made by the trial court. The factual determinations may be based on the evidence adduced before the trial court either with or without the taking of evidence by the reviewing court. The reviewing court may for the purpose of making the factual determinations or for any other purpose in the interests of justice, take additional evidence of or concerning facts occurring at any time prior to the decision of the appeal, and may give or direct the entry of any judgment or order and may make any further or other order as the case may require. This section shall be liberally construed to the end among others that, where feasible, causes may be finally disposed of by a single appeal and without further proceedings in the trial court except where in the interests of justice a new trial is required on some or all of the issues. **Leg.H.** Added Stats 1968 ch 385 §2. Amended Stats 1981 ch 900 §7.

Prior Law: Former CCP §909, similar to present CCP §1218, was enacted 1872 and repealed Stats 1933 ch 744 §198.

§910. [Section repealed 1977]

Leg.H. Added Stats 1968 ch 385 §2. Repealed Stats 1976 ch 1288 §17. The repealed section related to appeals to superior court from justice court.

Prior Law: Former CCP §910, similar to present CCP §1218, was enacted 1872 and repealed Stats 1933 ch 744 §198.

§911. Transfer to court of appeal of case on appeal to superior court

A court of appeal may order any case on appeal to a superior court in its district transferred to it for hearing and decision as provided by rules of the Judicial Council when the superior court certifies, or the court of appeal determines, that the transfer appears necessary to secure uniformity of decision or to settle important questions of law.

No case in which there is a right on appeal to a trial anew in the superior court shall be transferred pursuant to this section before a decision in the case becomes final therein.

A court to which any case is transferred pursuant to this section shall have similar power to review any matter and make orders and judgments as the appellate division of the superior court would have in the case, except that if the case was tried anew in the superior court, the court of appeal shall have similar power to review any matter and make orders and judgments as it has in a case appealed pursuant to Section 904.1. **Leg.H.** Added Stats 1968 ch 385 §2. Amended Stats 1998 ch 931 §103 (SB 2139), effective September 28, 1998.

Prior Law: Former CCP §911, similar to present Gov C §71614, was enacted 1872, amended Code Amdts 1873–74 ch 383 §121, and repealed Stats 1933 ch 743 §61.

§912. Certified copy of judgment or order of reviewing court; Remittance

Upon final determination of an appeal by the reviewing court, the clerk of the court shall remit to the trial court a certified copy of the judgment or order of the reviewing court and of its opinion, if any. The clerk of the trial court shall file the certified copy of the judgment and opinion of the reviewing court, shall attach that copy to the judgment roll if the appeal was from a judgment, and shall enter a note of the judgment of the reviewing court stating whether the judgment or order appealed from has been affirmed, reversed or modified, in the margin of the original entry of the judgment or order, and also in the register of actions. **Leg.H.** Added Stats 1968 ch 385 §2. Amended Stats 1998 ch 931 §104 (SB 2139), effective September 28, 1998; Stats 2001 ch 44 §6 (SB 562); Stats 2002 ch 664 §49 (AB 3034).

Prior Law: Former CCP §912, similar to present Gov C §71615, was enacted 1872, amended Code Amdts 1880 ch 34 §8, and repealed Stats 1933 ch 743 §61.

§913. Dismissal of appeal with prejudice; Exception

The dismissal of an appeal shall be with prejudice to the right to file another appeal within the time permitted, unless the dismissal is expressly made without prejudice to another appeal. **Leg.H.** Added Stats 1968 ch 385 §2.

Prior Law: Former CCP §913, similar to present Gov C §71616, was enacted 1872 and repealed Stats 1933 ch 743 §61.

§914. Phonographic report of trial

When the right to a phonographic report has not been waived and when it shall be impossible to have a phonographic report of the trial transcribed by a stenographic reporter as provided by law or by rule, because of the death or disability of a reporter who participated as a stenographic reporter at the trial or because of the loss or destruction, in whole or in substantial part, of the notes of such reporter, the trial court or a judge thereof, or the reviewing court shall have power to set aside and vacate the judgment, order or decree from which an appeal has been taken or is to be taken and to order a new trial of the action or proceeding. **Leg.H.** Added Stats 1968 ch 385 §2.

Prior Law: Former CCP §914, relating to deposit of records with judges' successor, was enacted 1872, and amended and renumbered to be CCP §113 by Stats 1933 ch 743 §24.

§915. [Section renumbered 1933]

Leg.H. Enacted 1872. Amended and renumbered as CCP §113a by Stats 1933 ch 743 §25.

CHAPTER 2
STAY OF ENFORCEMENT AND OTHER PROCEEDINGS

Stay of proceedings on perfecting appeal. §916.
[Section renumbered 1933]. §917.
Undertaking to stay enforcement of money judgment or order pending appeal. §917.1.
Appeal from certain orders concerning hazardous waste. §917.15.
Appeal from judgment or order for assignment or delivery of documents or personal property; Placing property in custody of officer of court; Furnishing undertaking; Judgment or order directing sale of perishable property. §917.2.
Appeal from judgment or order directing execution of instruments. §917.3.
Undertaking to stay enforcement of judgment or order directing disposition of real property pending appeal. §917.4.
Appeal from judgment or order appointing receiver; Undertaking. §917.5.
Appeal from judgment or order directing performance of acts specified in Sections 917.1–917.5. §917.6.
Undertaking to stay enforcement of order. §917.65.
Appeal from judgment or order affecting custody or right of visitation of minor or exclusion from family dwelling; Provisions regarding removal of minor from State. §917.7.
Undertaking to stay enforcement of judgment or order awarding attorney fees or costs in proceeding under Family Code. §917.75.
Appeal involving usurpation, etc., of public office; Order directing inspection of corporate books; Closing or discontinuance of use of building adjudged to be nuisance; Relief in certain nuisance abatement actions. §917.8.
Appeal from judgment or order in cases not otherwise provided for; Undertaking. §917.9.
Stay of enforcement of judgment or order by trial court; Limitation of power. §918.
Stay to protect possible set-off. §918.5.
Security for appeal by representative. §919.
Appeal by party levying attachment. §921.
Effect of insufficiency of undertaking. §922.
Powers of reviewing court or judge; Chapter provisions as not limiting. §923.
Notice of appeal; Indigents. §936.1.

§916. Stay of proceedings on perfecting appeal

(a) Except as provided in Sections 917.1 to 917.9, inclusive, and in Section 116.810, the perfecting of an appeal stays proceedings in the trial court upon the judgment or order appealed from or upon the matters embraced therein or affected thereby, including enforcement of the judgment or order, but the trial court may proceed upon any other matter embraced in the action and not affected by the judgment or order.

(b) When there is a stay of proceedings other than the enforcement of the judgment, the trial court shall have jurisdiction of proceedings related to the enforcement of the judgment as well as any other matter embraced in the action and not affected by the judgment or order appealed from. **Leg.H.** Added Stats 1968 ch 385 §2. Amended Stats 1975 ch 266 §5; Stats 1982 ch 497 §64, operative July 1, 1983; Stats 1990 ch 1305 §8 (SB 2627).

Prior Law: Former CCP §916 was enacted 1872, and amended and renumbered to be CCP §113b by Stats 1933 ch 743 §26.

§917. [Section renumbered 1933]

Leg.H. Enacted 1872. Amended and renumbered as CCP §113c by Stats 1933 ch 743 §27.

§917.1. Undertaking to stay enforcement of money judgment or order pending appeal

(a) Unless an undertaking is given, the perfecting of an appeal shall not stay enforcement of the judgment or order in the trial court if the judgment or order is for any of the following:

(1) Money or the payment of money, whether consisting of a special fund or not, and whether payable by the appellant or another party to the action.

(2) Costs awarded pursuant to Section 998 which otherwise would not have been awarded as costs pursuant to Section 1033.5.

(3) Costs awarded pursuant to Section 1141.21 which otherwise would not have been awarded as costs pursuant to Section 1033.5.

(b) The undertaking shall be on condition that if the judgment or order or any part of it is affirmed or the appeal is withdrawn or dismissed, the party ordered to pay shall pay the amount of the judgment or order, or the part of it as to which the judgment or order is affirmed, as entered after the receipt of the remittitur, together with any interest which may have accrued pending the appeal and entry of the remittitur, and costs which may be awarded against the appellant on appeal. This section shall not apply in cases where the money to be paid is in the actual or constructive custody of the court; and such cases shall be governed, instead, by the provisions of Section 917.2. The undertaking shall be for double the amount of the judgment or order unless given by an admitted surety insurer in which event it shall be for one and one-half times the amount of the judgment or order. The liability on the undertaking may be enforced if the party ordered to pay does not make the payment within 30 days after the filing of the remittitur from the reviewing court.

(c) If a surety on the undertaking pays the judgment, either with or without action, after the judgment is affirmed, the surety is substituted to the rights of the creditor and is entitled to control, enforce, and satisfy the judgment, in all respects as if the surety had recovered the judgment.

(d) Costs awarded by the trial court under Chapter 6 (commencing with Section 1021) of Title 14 shall be included in the amount of the judgment or order for the purpose of applying paragraph (1) of subdivision (a) and subdivision (b). However, no undertaking shall be required pursuant to this section solely for costs awarded under Chapter 6 (commencing with Section 1021) of Title 14. **Leg.H.** Added Stats 1968 ch 385 §2. Amended Stats 1972 ch 546 §1; Stats 1981 ch 196 §1; Stats 1982 ch 517 §155; Stats 1986 ch 1174 §1; Stats 1993 ch 456 §13 (AB 58).

§917.15. Appeal from certain orders concerning hazardous waste

The perfecting of an appeal shall not stay enforcement of the judgment or order in the trial court if the judgment or order appealed from, or the administrative order which is the subject of the trial court proceeding, was issued pursuant to either of the following:

(a) Section 78870 of the Health and Safety Code and ordered a responsible party to take appropriate removal or remedial actions in response to a release or a threatened release of a hazardous substance.

(b) Section 25181 of the Health and Safety Code and ordered the party to comply with Chapter 6.5 (commencing with Section 25100) of Division 20 of the Health and Safety Code or any rule, regulation, permit, covenant, standard, requirement, or order issued, adopted or executed pursuant to that Chapter 6.5. **Leg.H.** Added Stats 1985 ch 1492 §1. Amended Stats 2022 ch 258 §9 (AB 2327), effective January 1, 2023, operative January 1, 2024.

§917.2. Appeal from judgment or order for assignment or delivery of documents or personal property; Placing property in custody of officer of court; Furnishing undertaking; Judgment or order directing sale of perishable property

The perfecting of an appeal shall not stay enforcement of the judgment or order of the trial court if the judgment or order appealed from directs the assignment or delivery of personal property, including documents, whether by the appellant or another party to the action, or the sale of personal property upon the foreclosure of a mortgage, or other lien thereon, unless an undertaking in a sum and upon conditions fixed by the trial court, is given that the appellant or party ordered to assign or deliver the property will obey and satisfy the order of the reviewing court, and will not commit or suffer to be committed any damage to the property, and that if the judgment or order appealed from is affirmed, or the appeal is withdrawn or dismissed, the appellant shall pay the damage suffered to such property and the value of the use of such property for the period of the delay caused by the appeal. The appellant may cause the property to be placed in the custody of an officer designated by the court to abide the order of the reviewing court, and such fact shall be considered by the court in fixing the amount of the undertaking. If the judgment or order appealed from directs the sale of perishable property the trial court may order such property to be sold and the proceeds thereof to be deposited with the clerk of the trial court to abide the order of the reviewing court; such fact shall be considered by the court in fixing the amount of the undertaking. **Leg.H.** Added Stats 1968 ch 385 §2. Amended Stats 1972 ch 546 §2.

§917.3. Appeal from judgment or order directing execution of instruments

The perfecting of an appeal shall not stay enforcement of the judgment or order in the trial court if the judgment or order appealed from directs the execution of one or more instruments unless the instrument or instruments are executed and deposited in the office of the clerk of the court where the original judgment or order is entered to abide the order of the reviewing court. **Leg.H.** Added Stats 1968 ch 385 §2.

§917.4. Undertaking to stay enforcement of judgment or order directing disposition of real property pending appeal

The perfecting of an appeal shall not stay enforcement of the judgment or order in the trial court if the judgment or order appealed from directs the sale, conveyance or delivery of possession of real property which is in the possession or control of the appellant or the party ordered to sell, convey or deliver possession of the property, unless an undertaking in a sum fixed by the trial court is given that the appellant or party ordered to sell, convey or deliver possession of the property will not commit or suffer to be committed any waste thereon and that if the judgment or order appealed from is affirmed, or the appeal is withdrawn or dismissed, the appellant shall pay the damage suffered by the waste and the value of the use and occupancy of the property, or the part of it as to which the judgment or order is affirmed, from the time of the taking of the appeal until the delivery of the possession of the property. If the judgment or order directs the sale of mortgaged real property and the payment of any deficiency, the undertaking shall also provide for the payment of any deficiency. **Leg.H.** Added Stats 1968 ch 385 §2. Amended Stats 1982 ch 517 §156.

§917.5. Appeal from judgment or order appointing receiver; Undertaking

The perfecting of an appeal shall not stay enforcement of the judgment or order in the trial court if the judgment or order appealed from appoints a receiver, unless an undertaking in a sum fixed by the trial court is given on condition that if the judgment or order is affirmed or the appeal is withdrawn, or dismissed, the appellant will pay all damages which the respondent may sustain by reason of the stay in the enforcement of the judgment. **Leg.H.** Added Stats 1968 ch 385 §2. Amended Stats 1972 ch 546 §3; Stats 1982 ch 517 §157.

§917.6. Appeal from judgment or order directing performance of acts specified in Sections 917.1–917.5

The perfecting of an appeal shall not stay enforcement of the judgment or order in the trial court if the judgment or order appealed from directs the performance of two or more of the acts specified in Sections 917.1 through 917.5, unless the appellant complies with the requirements of each applicable section. **Leg.H.** Added Stats 1968 ch 385 §2.

§917.65. Undertaking to stay enforcement of order

The perfecting of an appeal shall not stay enforcement of a right to attach order unless an undertaking is given. The undertaking shall be in the amount specified in the right to attach order as the amount to be secured by the attachment. The undertaking shall be on condition that if the right to attach order is not reversed and the plaintiff recovers judgment in the action in which the right to attach order was issued, the appellant shall pay the amount of the judgment, together with any interest which may have accrued. The liability on the undertaking may be enforced if the judgment is not paid within 30 days after it becomes final. If a surety on the undertaking pays the judgment, either with or without action, the surety is substituted to the rights of the creditor and is entitled to control, enforce, and satisfy the judgment, in all respects as if the surety had recovered the judgment. **Leg.H.** Added Stats 1983 ch 155 §22.5, effective June 30, 1983, operative July 1, 1983.

§917.7. Appeal from judgment or order affecting custody or right of visitation of minor or exclusion from family dwelling; Provisions regarding removal of minor from State

The perfecting of an appeal shall not stay proceedings as to those provisions of a judgment or order which award, change, or otherwise affect the custody, including the right of visitation, of a minor child in any civil action, in an action filed under the Juvenile Court Law, or in a special proceeding, or the provisions of a judgment or order for the temporary exclusion of a party from a dwelling, as provided in the Family Code. However, the trial court may in its discretion stay execution of these provisions pending review on appeal or for any other period or periods that it may deem appropriate. Further, in the absence of a writ or order of a reviewing court providing otherwise, the provisions of the judgment or order allowing, or eliminating restrictions against, removal of the minor child from the state are stayed by operation of law for a period of seven calendar days from the entry of the judgment or order by a juvenile court in a dependency hearing, or for a period of 30 calendar days from the entry of judgment or order by any other trial court. The periods during which these provisions allowing, or eliminating restrictions against, removal of the minor child from the state are stayed, are subject to further stays as ordered by the trial court or by the juvenile court pursuant to this section. An order directing the return of a child to a sister state or country, including any order effectuating that return, made in a proceeding brought pursuant to the Uniform Child Custody Jurisdiction and Enforcement Act (Part 3 (commencing with Section 3400) of Division 8 of the Family Code), the Parental Kidnapping Prevention Act of 1980 (28 U.S.C. Sec. 1738A), or the Hague Convention on the Civil Aspects of International Child Abduction (implemented pursuant to the International Child Abduction Remedies Act (22 U.S.C. Secs. 9001-9011)) is not a judgment or order which awards, changes, or otherwise affects the custody of a minor child within the meaning of this section, and therefore is not subject to the automatic stay provisions of this section. **Leg.H.** Added Stats 1968 ch 385 §2. Amended Stats 1971 ch 1210 §9; Stats 1981 ch 714 §70; Stats 1992 ch 163 §55 (AB 2641), operative January 1, 1994; Stats 1993 ch 219 §69.5 (AB 1500); Stats 1999 ch 346 §1 (SB 518); Stats 2001 ch 48 §1 (SB 1151); Stats 2021 ch 124 §13 (AB 938), effective January 1, 2022.

§917.75. Undertaking to stay enforcement of judgment or order awarding attorney fees or costs in proceeding under Family Code

The perfecting of an appeal shall not stay enforcement of the judgment or order of the trial court awarding attorney's fees or costs, or both, if the judgment or order appealed from was rendered in a proceeding under the Family Code, unless an undertaking is given in a sum and upon conditions fixed by the trial court. **Leg.H.** Added Stats 2014 ch 95 §1 (AB 2154), effective January 1, 2015.

§917.8. Appeal involving usurpation, etc., of public office; Order directing inspection of corporate books; Closing or discontinuance of use of building adjudged to be nuisance; Relief in certain nuisance abatement actions

The perfecting of an appeal does not stay proceedings, in the absence of an order of the trial court providing otherwise or of a writ of supersedeas, under any of the following circumstances:

(a) If a party to the proceeding has been adjudged guilty of usurping, or intruding into, or unlawfully holding a public office, civil or military, within this state.

(b) If the judgment or order directs a corporation, or any of its officers or agents, to give to a person adjudged to be a director, stockholder, or member of that corporation a reasonable opportunity to inspect or make copies of the books, papers, or documents of the corporation as the trial court finds that the director, stockholder, or member is entitled by law to inspect or copy.

(c) If a judgment or order adjudges a building or place to be a nuisance and, as part of that judgment or order, directs the closing or discontinuance of any specific use of the building or place for any period of time.

(d) If a judgment or order, including, but not limited to, a temporary restraining order or preliminary injunction, grants relief in an action brought by a governmental agency under the provisions of Article 2 (commencing with Section 11225) of Chapter 3 of Title 1 of Part 4 of the Penal Code or Article 3 (commencing with Section 11570) of Chapter 10 of Division 10 of the Health and Safety Code. **Leg.H.** Added Stats 1968 ch 385 §2. Amended Stats 2003 ch 31 §1 (AB 1639).

§917.9. Appeal from judgment or order in cases not otherwise provided for; Undertaking

(a) The perfecting of an appeal shall not stay enforcement of the judgment or order in cases not provided for in Sections 917.1 to 917.8, inclusive, if the trial court, in its discretion, requires an undertaking and the undertaking is not given, in any of the following cases:

(1) Appellant was found to possess money or other property belonging to respondent.

(2) Appellant is required to perform an act for respondent's benefit pursuant to judgment or order under appeal.

(3) The judgment against appellant is solely for costs awarded to the respondent by the trial court pursuant to Chapter 6 (commencing with Section 1021) of Title 14.

(b) The undertaking shall be in a sum fixed by the court and shall be in an amount sufficient to cover all damages which the respondent may sustain by reason of the stay in the enforcement of the judgment or order.

(c) The undertaking shall be in the sum fixed by the court. The undertaking shall be conditioned upon the performance of the judgment or order appealed from or payment of the sums required by the judgment or order appealed from, if the judgment or order is affirmed or the appeal is withdrawn or dismissed, and it shall provide that if the judgment or order appealed from or any part of it is affirmed, or the appeal is withdrawn or dismissed, the appellant will pay all damages which the respondent may sustain by reason of the stay in the enforcement of the judgment.

(d) For the purpose of this section, "damages" means either of the following:

(1) Reasonable compensation for the loss of use of the money or property.

(2) Payment of the amounts specified in paragraph (3) of subdivision (a). **Leg.H.** Added Stats 1968 ch 385 §2. Amended Stats 1972 ch 546 §4; Stats 1982 ch 517 §158; Stats 1993 ch 456 §14 (AB 58); Stats 1994 ch 493 §3 (AB 651), effective September 11, 1994.

§918. Stay of enforcement of judgment or order by trial court; Limitation of power

(a) Subject to subdivision (b), the trial court may stay the enforcement of any judgment or order.

(b) If the enforcement of the judgment or order would be stayed on appeal only by the giving of an undertaking, a trial court shall not have power, without the consent of the adverse party, to stay the enforcement thereof pursuant to this section for a period which extends for more than 10 days beyond the last date on which a notice of appeal could be filed.

(c) This section applies whether or not an appeal will be taken from the judgment or order and whether or not a notice of appeal has been filed. **Leg.H.** Added Stats 1968 ch 385 §2. Amended Stats 1982 ch 497 §65, operative July 1, 1983.

Prior Law: Former CCP §918, relating to the duty of the County Judge to designate a successor if two or more justices are entitled, was enacted 1872, amended Code Amdts 1880 ch 34 §9 and amended and renumbered §113d by Stats 1933 ch 743 §28.

§918.5. Stay to protect possible set-off

(a) The trial court may, in its discretion, stay the enforcement of a judgment or order if the judgment debtor has another action pending on a disputed claim against the judgment creditor.

(b) In exercising its discretion under this section, the court shall consider all of the following:

(1) The likelihood of the judgment debtor prevailing in the other action.

(2) The amount of the judgment of the judgment creditor as compared to the amount of the probable recovery of the judgment debtor in the action on the disputed claim.

(3) The financial ability of the judgment creditor to satisfy the judgment if a judgment is rendered against the judgment creditor in the action on the disputed claim. **Leg.H.** Added Stats 1982 ch 497 §66, operative July 1, 1983.

§919. Security for appeal by representative

The trial court may, in its discretion, dispense with or limit the security required by any section in this chapter, when the appellant is an executor, administrator, trustee, guardian, conservator or other person acting in another's right. **Leg.H.** Added Stats 1968 ch 385 §2.

Prior Law: Former CCP §919, similar to present CCP §128, was enacted 1872 and repealed Stats 1933 ch 744 §198.

§920. [Section repealed 1983]

Leg.H. Added Stats 1968 ch 385 §2. Repealed Stats 1982 ch 517 §159. See CCP §§995.230, 995.710.

Prior Law: Former CCP §920, relating to issuance of papers by justices' courts, was enacted 1872 and repealed Stats 1933 ch 743 §61.

§921. Appeal by party levying attachment

An appeal by a party who has levied an attachment shall not continue in force the attachment, unless an undertaking is executed and filed on the part of the appellant that the appellant will pay all costs and damages which the respondent may sustain by reason of the attachment, in case the order of the court below is sustained in favor of the respondent; and unless, within five days after written notice of the entry of the order appealed from, the appeal is perfected. The amount of the undertaking on appeal required by this section shall be such amount as is fixed by the trial court on motion of the respondent as provided in Section 489.410 and if no such order has been made, the undertaking shall be in double the amount of the debt claimed by the appellant. If the respondent is not satisfied with the undertaking in double the amount of the debt or the amount fixed by order under Section 489.410, the trial court upon motion of the respondent made within 60 days after perfecting the appeal may order an increase in the amount of the undertaking in such amount as is justified by the detriment reasonably to be anticipated by continuing the attachment. If such an order is made, the attachment shall be discharged and the property released therefrom, unless the undertaking is executed and filed within 10 days after the order is made. **Leg.H.** Added Stats 1968 ch 385 §2. Amended Stats 1974 ch 1516 §20, operative January 1, 1977; Stats 1982 ch 517 §160.

Prior Law: Former CCP §921 was enacted 1872, amended Code Amdts 1880 ch 34 §10, and amended and renumbered to be CCP §108 by Stats 1933 ch 743 §20.

§922. Effect of insufficiency of undertaking

If an undertaking required or permitted by this title is objected to by the respondent and the court determines the undertaking is insufficient and a sufficient undertaking is not given within the time provided by statute, enforcement of the judgment or order appealed from is no longer stayed and property which has been levied upon under execution issued upon such judgment shall not be released from levy. **Leg.H.** Added Stats 1968 ch 385 §2. Amended Stats 1982 ch 517 §161.

Prior Law: Former CCP §922, relating to a justice's replacement in case of his disability, was enacted 1872, amended Stats 1909 ch 212 §1, Stats 1929 ch 496 §1, and repealed Stats 1933 ch 744 §198.

§923. Powers of reviewing court or judge; Chapter provisions as not limiting

The provisions of this chapter shall not limit the power of a reviewing court or of a judge thereof to stay proceedings during the pendency of an appeal or to issue a writ of supersedeas or to suspend or modify an injunction during the pendency of an appeal or to make any order appropriate to preserve the status quo, the effectiveness of the judgment subsequently to be entered, or otherwise in aid of its jurisdiction. **Leg.H.** Added Stats 1968 ch 385 §2.

Prior Law: Former CCP §923, similar to present CCP §1030, was enacted 1872 and repealed Stats 1933 ch 744 §198.

§924. [Section repealed 1933]

Leg.H. Enacted 1872. Amended Code Amdts 1873–74 ch 383 §122; Stats 1907 ch 51 §1. Repealed Stats 1933 ch 744 §198. See CCP §1031.

§925. [Section repealed 1933]

Leg.H. Enacted 1872. Repealed Stats 1933 ch 744 §198. The repealed section related to proceedings in justices' courts.

§926. [Section repealed 1933]

Leg.H. Added Code Amdts 1877–78 ch 91 §1. Repealed Stats 1933 ch 744 §198. The repealed section related to proceedings in justices' courts.

§927. [Section repealed 1933]

Leg.H. Added Stats 1921 ch 125 §1. Repealed Stats 1933 ch 743 §61. See CCP §§116.510, 116.520.

§927a. [Section repealed 1933]

Leg.H. Added Stats 1921 ch 125 §1. Amended Stats 1923 ch 236 §1. Repealed Stats 1933 ch 743 §61. See CCP §§116.320, 116.330, 116.340, 116.360.

§927b. [Section repealed 1933]

Leg.H. Added Stats 1921 ch 125 §1. Repealed Stats 1933 ch 743 §61. See CCP §§116.320, 116.330, 116.340, 116.360.

§927c. [Section repealed 1933]

Leg.H. Added Stats 1921 ch 125 §1. Amended Stats 1923 ch 449 §1. Repealed Stats 1933 ch 743 §61. See CCP §§116.320, 116.330, 116.340, 116.360.

§927d. [Section repealed 1933]

Leg.H. Added Stats 1921 ch 125 §1. Repealed Stats 1933 ch 743 §61. See CCP §§116.320, 116.330, 116.340, 116.360.

§927e. [Section repealed 1933]

Leg.H. Added Stats 1921 ch 125 §1. Repealed Stats 1933 ch 743 §61. The repealed section related to entries in docket of small claims court.

§927f. [Section repealed 1933]

Leg.H. Added Stats 1921 ch 125 §1. Repealed Stats 1933 ch 743 §61. See CCP §116.420.

§927g. [Section repealed 1933]

Leg.H. Added Stats 1921 ch 125 §1. Repealed Stats 1933 ch 743 §61. See CCP §116.530.

§927h. [Section repealed 1933]

Leg.H. Added Stats 1921 ch 125 §1. Amended Stats 1927 ch 527 §1. Repealed Stats 1933 ch 743 §61. See CCP §§116.310, 116.380, 116.510, 116.520, 116.810, 116.820.

§927i. [Section repealed 1933]

Leg.H. Added Stats 1921 ch 125 §1. Repealed Stats 1933 ch 743 §61. See CCP §§116.840, 116.850.

§927j. [Section repealed 1933]

Leg.H. Added Stats 1921 ch 125 §1. Repealed Stats 1933 ch 743 §61. See CCP §§116.730, 116.740, 116.770.

§927k. [Section repealed 1933]

Leg.H. Added Stats 1921 ch 125 §1. Repealed Stats 1933 ch 743 §61. The repealed section related to the statement of defendant's appeal.

§927l. [Section repealed 1933]

Leg.H. Added Stats 1921 ch 125 §1. Repealed Stats 1933 ch 743 §61. The repealed section related to bond on appeal, notice of filing of appeal and undertaking, exception to sureties, and justification.

§927m. [Section repealed 1933]

Leg.H. Added Stats 1921 ch 125 §1. Repealed Stats 1933 ch 743 §61. The repealed section related to abstract of judgment.

§927n. [Section repealed 1933]

Leg.H. Added Stats 1921 ch 125 §1. Repealed Stats 1933 ch 743 §61. See CCP §674.

§927o. [Section repealed 1933]

Leg.H. Added Stats 1921 ch 125 §1. Repealed Stats 1933 ch 743 §61. The repealed section related to supervisors to furnish forms, etc.

§927p. [Section repealed 1933]

Leg.H. Added Stats 1921 ch 125 §1. Amended Stats 1927 ch 361 §1. Repealed Stats 1933 ch 743 §61. See CCP 116.550.

§927q. [Section repealed 1933]

Leg.H. Added Stats 1929 ch 472 §1. Repealed Stats 1933 ch 743 §61. The repealed section related to costs.

§§929–933. [Sections repealed 1933]

Leg.H. Enacted 1872. Repealed Stats 1933 ch 743 §61. The repealed sections related to proceedings in civil actions in police courts.

§933½. [Section repealed 1933]

Leg.H. Added Stats 1929 ch 466 §1. Repealed Stats 1933 ch 743 §61. The repealed section related to application of title.

§934. [Section repealed 1968]

Leg.H. Added Stats 1955 ch 59 §9. Repealed Stats 1968 ch 385 §1. The repealed section related to statutory construction.

§936. [Section repealed 1968]

Leg.H. Enacted 1872. Amended Stats 1933 ch 744 §150; Stats 1945 ch 40 §2. Repealed Stats 1968 ch 385 §1. See CCP §901.

§936.1. Notice of appeal; Indigents

An appeal from any judgment or order in any civil commitment or other proceeding wherein the appellant would be entitled to the appointment of counsel on appeal if indigent shall be initiated by the filing of a notice of appeal in conformity with the requirements of Section 1240.1 of the Penal Code. **Leg.H.** Added Stats 1978 ch 1385 §1.

§937. [Section repealed 1968]

Leg.H. Enacted 1872. Repealed Stats 1968 ch 385 §1. The repealed section related to orders made out of court, without notice, may be reviewed by the judge.

§938. [Section repealed 1968]

Leg.H. Enacted 1872. Repealed Stats 1968 ch 385 §1. See CCP §902.

§939. [Section repealed 1945]

Leg.H. Enacted 1872. Amended Code Amdts 1880 ch 55 §2; Stats 1897 ch 62 §1; Stats 1899 ch 9 §1; Stats 1907 ch 42 §1; Stats 1915 ch 111 §1; Stats 1933 ch 29 §6. Repealed Stats 1945 ch 40 §16. See Cal R of Court 8.100-8.104, 8.750-8.752.

§940. [Section repealed 1945]

Leg.H. Enacted 1872. Amended Code Amdts 1873–74 ch 383 §123; Stats 1921 ch 185 §1. Repealed Stats 1945 ch 40 §16. See Cal R of Court 8.100, 8.750.

§941. [Section repealed 1968]

Leg.H. Enacted 1872. Amended Stats 1921 ch 185 §2. Repealed Stats 1968 ch 385 §1. See CCP §903.

§941a. [Section repealed 1921]

Leg.H. Added Stats 1907 ch 410 §1. Repealed Stats 1921 ch 185 §4. The repealed section related to appeals, alternative method.

§941b. [Section repealed 1921]

Leg.H. Added Stats 1907 ch 410 §2. Amended Stats 1915 ch 110 §1. Repealed Stats 1921 ch 185 §4. The repealed section related to notice of appeal, what to contain.

§941c. [Section repealed 1921]

Leg.H. Added Stats 1907 ch 410 §3. Repealed Stats 1921 ch 185 §4. The repealed section related to effect of appeal.

§942. [Section repealed 1968]

Leg.H. Enacted 1872. Amended Code Amdts 1873–74 ch 383 §124; Stats 1941 ch 955 §1; Stats 1967 ch 17 §14. Repealed Stats 1968 ch 385 §1. See CCP §917.1.

§943. [Section repealed 1968]

Leg.H. Enacted 1872. Amended Code Amdts 1880 ch 18 §1; Stats 1897 ch 64 §1. Repealed Stats 1968 ch 385 §1. See CCP §§917.2, 917.5.

§944. [Section repealed 1968]

Leg.H. Enacted 1872. Repealed Stats 1968 ch 385 §1. See CCP §917.3.

§945. [Section repealed 1968]

Leg.H. Enacted 1872. Repealed Stats 1968 ch 385 §1. See CCP §917.4.

§946. [Section repealed 1968]

Leg.H. Enacted 1872. Amended Code Amdts 1873–74 ch 383 §125; Stats 1913 ch 129 §1; Stats 1955 ch 1407 §1; Stats 1959 ch 833 §2. Repealed Stats 1968 ch 385 §1. See CCP §916.

§947. [Section repealed 1927]

Leg.H. Enacted 1872. Repealed Stats 1927 ch 523 §1. The repealed section related to undertaking may be in one instrument or several.

§948. [Section repealed 1968]

Leg.H. Enacted 1872. Amended Code Amdts 1873–74 ch 383 §126; Code Amdts 1880 ch 18 §2; Stats 1905 ch 162 §1; Stats 1927 ch 523 §2; Stats 1955 ch 194 §1. Repealed Stats 1968 ch 385 §1. See CCP §922.

§948a. [Section repealed 1968]

Leg.H. Added Stats 1937 ch 60 §1. Repealed Stats 1968 ch 385 §1. See CCP §922.

§949. [Section repealed 1968]

Leg.H. Enacted 1872. Amended Code Amdts 1873–74 ch 90 §1; Stats 1905 ch 29 §1; Stats 1921 ch 98 §1; Stats 1927 ch 523 §3. Repealed Stats 1968 ch 385 §1. The repealed section related to undertakings in cases not specified.

§949a. [Section repealed 1968]

Leg.H. Added Stats 1955 ch 170 §1. Amended Stats 1957 ch 2145 §2; Stats 1965 ch 1031 §1. Repealed Stats 1968 ch 385 §1. See CCP §917.7.

§§950–952. [Sections repealed 1945]

Leg.H. Enacted 1872, amended by Code Amdts 1873–74 ch 383 §§127–129, Stats 1915 ch 112 §§1–3, and repealed by Stats 1945 ch 40 §16. See Cal R of Court 8.120, 8.137.

§953. [Section repealed 1945]

Leg.H. Enacted 1872. Amended Code Amdts 1873–74 ch 383 §130; Stats 1919 ch 196 §1; Stats 1921 ch 185 §3. Repealed Stats 1945 ch 40 §16. See Cal R of Court 8.120, 8.155.

§953a. [Section repealed 1945]

Leg.H. Added Stats 1907 ch 408 §1. Amended Stats 1915 ch 113 §1; Stats 1929 ch 479 §8; Stats 1935 ch 722 §16; Stats 1937 ch 180 §1; Stats 1941 ch 1085 §1. Repealed Stats 1945 ch 40 §16. See Cal R of Court 8.120, 8.130, 8.140.

§953b. [Section repealed 1945]

Leg.H. Added Stats 1907 ch 408 §2. Amended Stats 1915 ch 113 §2. Repealed Stats 1945 ch 40 §16. See Cal R of Court 8.130.

§953c. [Section repealed 1945]

Leg.H. Added Stats 1907 ch 408 §3. Amended Stats 1919 ch 175 §1; Stats 1923 ch 364 §1; Stats 1929 ch 479 §9. Repealed Stats 1945 ch 40 §16. See Cal R of Court 8.147.

§953d. [Section repealed 1967]

Leg.H. Added Stats 1927 ch 48 §1. Amended Stats 1945 ch 40 §3; Stats 1959 ch 469 §3. Repealed Stats 1967 ch 169 §5. The repealed section related to notice of entry of judgment or order.

§953e. [Section repealed 1968]

Leg.H. Added Stats 1931 ch 239 §1. Amended Stats 1943 ch 1017 §1. Repealed Stats 1968 ch 385 §1. See CCP §914.

§954. [Section repealed 1945]

Leg.H. Enacted 1872. Amended Stats 1895 ch 63 §1; Stats 1906 Ex Sess ch 46 §1; Stats 1907 ch 307 §1. Repealed Stats 1945 ch 40 §16. See Cal R of Court 8.147.

§954a.

Leg.H. Added Stats 1935 ch 453 §1. Amended Stats 1939 ch 460 §1. Repealed Stats 1945 ch 40 §16. See Cal R of Court 8.240.

§955. [Section repealed 1968]

Leg.H. Enacted 1872. Repealed Stats 1968 ch 385 §1. See CCP §913.

§956. [Section repealed 1968]

Leg.H. Enacted 1872. Amended Code Amdts 1875–76 ch 517 §5; Stats 1915 ch 158 §1; Stats 1957 ch 1611 §1. Repealed Stats 1968 ch 385 §1. See CCP §906.

§956a. [Section repealed 1968]

Leg.H. Added Stats 1927 ch 352 §1. Amended Stats 1945 ch 40 §4; Stats 1967 ch 17 §15. Repealed Stats 1968 ch 385 §1. See CCP §909.

§957. [Section repealed 1968]

Leg.H. Enacted 1872. Amended Code Amdts 1873–74 ch 383 §131. Repealed Stats 1968 ch 385 §1. See CCP §§907, 908.

§958. [Section repealed 1968]

Leg.H. Enacted 1872. Amended Stats 1919 ch 197 §1; Stats 1945 ch 1309 §1. Repealed Stats 1968 ch 385 §1. See CCP §912.

§959. [Section repealed 1968]

Leg.H. Enacted 1872. Amended Code Amdts 1880 ch 18 §3; Stats 1933 ch 744 §151. Repealed Stats 1968 ch 385 §1. The repealed section related to provisions of this chapter not applicable to appeals to county courts.

§961. [Section repealed 1968]

Leg.H. Added Stats 1941 ch 477 §1. Amended Stats 1943 ch 4 §1, effective January 14, 1943. Repealed Stats 1968 ch 385 §1. The repealed section related to rules of judicial council to govern appeals.

§963. [Section repealed 1968]

Leg.H. Enacted 1872. Amended Code Amdts 1880 ch 33 §1; Stats 1889 ch 213 §1; Stats 1897 ch 151 §1; Stats 1899 ch 9 §2; Stats 1901 ch 69 §1; Stats 1915 ch 116 §1; Stats 1917 ch 505 §1; Stats 1923 ch 366 §2; Stats 1931 ch 922 §1; Stats 1933 ch 937 §1; Stats 1945 ch 239 §1; Stats 1951 ch 234 §1; Stats 1961 ch 1059 §2. Repealed Stats 1968 ch 385 §1. See CCP §904.1.

§964. [Section repealed 1933]

Leg.H. Added Code Amdts 1880 ch 33 §1. Repealed Stats 1933 ch 744 §198. The repealed section related to appeals; in what cases appealed from justices' courts.

§965. [Section repealed 1933]

Leg.H. Added Code Amdts 1880 ch 33 §1. Repealed Stats 1933 ch 744 §198, ch 969 §25. The repealed section related to appeals by executors, etc.

§966. [Section repealed 1933]

Leg.H. Added Code Amdts 1880 ch 33 §1. Repealed Stats 1933 ch 969 §25. See Prob C §8406.

§967. [Section repealed 1968]

Leg.H. Added Stats 1955 ch 59 §10. Repealed Stats 1968 ch 385 §1. The repealed section related to statutory construction.

§969. [Section repealed 1880]

Leg.H. Enacted 1872. Amended Code Amdts 1873–74 ch 383 §133, Code Amdts 1877–78 ch 164 §1. Repealed Code Amdts 1880 ch 71 §1. The repealed section related to circumstance permitting appeals from probate court.

§970. [Section repealed 1880]

Leg.H. Enacted 1872. Repealed Code Amdts 1880 ch 71 §1. The repealed section related to executors and administrators not required to give undertaking on appeal.

§971. [Section repealed 1880]

Leg.H. Enacted 1872. Amended Code Amdts 1873–74 ch 383 §134. Repealed Code Amdts 1880 ch 71 §1. The repealed section related to acts of acting administrator, etc., not invalidated by reversal of order appointing him.

§972. [Section repealed 1964]

Leg.H. Added Stats 1955 ch 59 §11. Repealed Stats 1963 ch 871 §15, operative July 1, 1964. The repealed section related to statutory construction.

§973. [Section repealed 1964]

Leg.H. Added Stats 1933 ch 744 §154. Amended Stats 1951 ch 1737 §119, operative January 1, 1952. Repealed Stats 1963 ch 871 §15, operative July 1, 1964. The repealed section related to appeals from justices' courts.

§974. [Section repealed 1964]

Leg.H. Enacted 1872. Amended Code Amdts 1880 ch 33 §1; Stats 1921 ch 192 §1; Stats 1951 ch 1737 §120, operative January 1, 1952. Repealed Stats 1963 ch 871 §15, operative July 1, 1964. The repealed section related to appeal from judgment of justice's or police courts.

§975. [Section repealed 1964]

Leg.H. Enacted 1872. Amended Code Amdts 1880 ch 33 §1; Stats 1921 ch 192 §2; Stats 1937 ch 517 §1; Stats 1941 ch 462 §1; Stats 1951 ch 1737 §121, operative January 1, 1952. Repealed Stats 1963 ch 871 §15, operative July 1, 1964. The repealed section related to party appealing on questions of law alone must prepare a statement.

§976. [Section repealed 1964]

Leg.H. Enacted 1872. Amended Code Amdts 1880 ch 33 §1; Stats 1937 ch 516 §1. Repealed Stats 1963 ch 871 §15, operative July 1, 1964. The repealed section related to if the appeal be upon questions of fact, or of law and fact, no statement need be made.

§977. [Section repealed 1964]

Leg.H. Enacted 1872. Amended Code Amdts 1880 ch 33 §1; Stats 1897 ch 152 §1; Stats 1941 ch 462 §2; Stats 1951 ch 1737 §122, operative January 1, 1952; Stats 1961 ch 693 §2, operative January 2, 1962. Repealed Stats 1963 ch 871 §15, operative July 1, 1964. The repealed section related to upon the appeal the justice must transmit the case to the county court.

§978. [Section repealed 1964]

Leg.H. Enacted 1872. Amended Code Amdts 1880 ch 33 §1; Stats 1909 ch 694 §1; Stats 1923 ch 365 §1; Stats 1927 ch 119 §1; Stats 1937 ch 519 §1; Stats 1951 ch 1737 §123, operative January 1, 1952; Stats 1961 ch 693 §3, operative January 2, 1962. Repealed Stats 1963 ch 871 §15, operative July 1, 1964. The repealed section related to undertaking on appeal.

§978a. [Section repealed 1964]

Leg.H. Added Stats 1909 ch 695 §1. Amended Stats 1935 ch 722 §17; Stats 1937 ch 284 §1; Stats 1951 ch 1737 §124, operative January 1, 1952. Repealed Stats 1963 ch 871 §15, operative July 1, 1964. The repealed section related to undertaking must be filed, when.

§979. [Section repealed 1964]

Leg.H. Enacted 1872. Amended Code Amdts 1880 ch 33 §1; Stats 1951 ch 1737 §125, operative January 1, 1952. Repealed Stats 1963 ch 871 §15, operative July 1, 1964. The repealed section related to on filing undertaking, execution must be stayed.

§980. [Section repealed 1964]

Leg.H. Enacted 1872. Amended Code Amdts 1880 ch 33 §1; Stats 1935 ch 722 §18; Stats 1937 ch 518 §1; Stats 1941 ch 462 §3; Stats 1961 ch 693 §4, operative January 2, 1962. Repealed Stats 1963 ch 871 §15, operative July 1, 1964. The repealed section related to miscellaneous provisions on trials in county courts.

§980a. [Section repealed 1964]

Leg.H. Added Stats 1941 ch 462 §4. Repealed Stats 1963 ch 871 §15, operative July 1, 1964. The repealed section related to trial anew.

§980b. [Section repealed 1964]

Leg.H. Added Stats 1941 ch 462 §5. Amended Stats 1953 ch 1557 §2; Stats 1961 ch 693 §5, operative January 2, 1962. Repealed Stats 1963 ch 871 §15, operative July 1, 1964. The repealed section related to failure to prosecute appeal.

§980c. [Section repealed 1964]

Leg.H. Added Stats 1941 ch 462 §6. Repealed Stats 1963 ch 871 §15, operative July 1, 1964. The repealed section related to judgment.

§981. [Section repealed 1964]

Leg.H. Added Stats 1915 ch 131 §1. Amended Stats 1951 ch 1737 §126, operative January 1, 1952. Repealed Stats 1963 ch 871 §15, operative July 1, 1964. The repealed section related to no appeal effective unless fees for filing are paid.

§981a. [Section repealed 1964]

Leg.H. Added Stats 1923 ch 373 §1. Amended Stats 1937 ch 515 §1; Stats 1953 ch 1557 §1; Stats 1961 ch 693 §6, operative January 2, 1962. Repealed Stats 1963 ch 871 §15, operative July 1, 1964. The repealed section related to dismissal of appeals from justice court where not brought to trial within one year.

§981.1. [Section repealed 1964]

Leg.H. Added Stats 1939 ch 460 §2. Repealed Stats 1963 ch 871 §15, operative July 1, 1964. The repealed section related to abandonment of appeal.

§982. [Section repealed 1964]

Leg.H. Added Stats 1919 ch 134 §1. Amended Stats 1951 ch 1737 §127, operative January 1, 1952; Stats 1961 ch 693 §7, operative January 2, 1962. Repealed Stats 1963 ch 871 §15, operative July 1, 1964. The repealed section related to papers returned on dismissal of appeal.

§982a. [Section repealed 1933]

Leg.H. Added Stats 1929 ch 471 §1. Repealed Stats 1933 ch 744 §198. The repealed section related to appeals from justices' courts in cities, etc., of 30,000 population.

§983. [Section repealed 1968]

Leg.H. Added Stats 1925 ch 433 §1. Amended Stats 1927 ch 68 §1; Stats 1933 ch 744 §156; Stats 1935 ch 722 §19; Stats 1945 ch 239 §2; Stats 1951 ch 234 §2; Stats 1963 ch 871 §4, operative July 1, 1964. Repealed Stats 1968 ch 385 §1. See CCP §§904.2, 1218.

§983a. [Section repealed 1945]

Leg.H. Added Stats 1933 ch 744 §157. Amended Stats 1935 ch 722 §20. Repealed Stats 1945 ch 39 §3. See Cal R of Court 8.751.

§984. [Section repealed 1968]

Leg.H. Added Stats 1925 ch 433 §1. Amended Stats 1927 ch 68 §2; Stats 1945 ch 39 §1. Repealed Stats 1968 ch 385 §1. The repealed section related to appellate appearance for wholly owned corporate entity by owner-attorney. See Cal R of Court 8.750.

§985. [Section repealed 1968]

Leg.H. Added Stats 1925 ch 433 §1. Amended Stats 1927 ch 68 §3; Stats 1933 ch 744 §159; Stats 1961 ch 693 §8, operative January 2, 1962; Stats 1963 ch 871 §5, operative July 1, 1964. Repealed Stats 1968 ch 385 §1. The repealed section related to powers of superior court on appeal.

§985.5. [Section repealed 1968]

Leg.H. Added Stats 1963 ch 871 §6, operative July 1, 1964. Repealed Stats 1968 ch 385 §1. See CCP §905.

§986. [Section repealed 1968]

Leg.H. Added Stats 1927 ch 68 §4. Amended Stats 1933 ch 744 §160; Stats 1963 ch 871 §7, operative July 1, 1964. Repealed Stats 1968 ch 385 §1. See CCP §922.

§987. [Section repealed 1968]

Leg.H. Added Stats 1927 ch 68 §5. Repealed Stats 1968 ch 385 §1. The repealed section related to effect of filing bond.

§988. [Section repealed 1945]

Leg.H. Added Stats 1927 ch 68 §6. Repealed Stats 1945 ch 39 §3. See Cal R of Court 8.753, 8.754.

§§988a, 988b. [Sections repealed 1945]

Leg.H. Added Stats 1927 ch 68 §§7, 8. Amended Stats 1929 ch 494 §§3, 4; Stats 1931 ch 974 §§1, 2; Stats 1933 ch 744 §§163, 164; Stats 1935 ch 722 §§21, 22. Repealed Stats 1945 ch 39 §3. See Cal R of Court 8.753–8.758.

§988c. [Section repealed 1945]

Leg.H. Added Stats 1927 ch 68 §9. Amended Stats 1929 ch 494 §5; Stats 1933 ch 744 §165; Stats 1935 ch 722 §23. Repealed Stats 1945 ch 39 §3. See Cal R of Court 8.759.

§988c-1. [Section repealed 1945]
Leg.H. Added Stats 1939 ch 460 §3. Repealed Stats 1945 ch 39 §3. See Cal R of Court 8.762.

§988d. [Section repealed 1945]
Leg.H. Added Stats 1927 ch 68 §10. Repealed Stats 1945 ch 39 §3. See Cal R of Court 8.762.

§988e. [Section repealed 1968]
Leg.H. Added Stats 1927 ch 68 §11. Repealed Stats 1968 ch 385 §1. See CCP §913.

§988f. [Section repealed 1968]
Leg.H. Added Stats 1927 ch 68 §12. Amended Stats 1961 ch 693 §9, operative January 2, 1962. Repealed Stats 1968 ch 385 §1. See CCP §908.

§988g. [Section repealed 1968]
Leg.H. Added Stats 1927 ch 68 §13. Amended Stats 1931 ch 974 §3; Stats 1945 ch 39 §2; Stats 1961 ch 693 §10, operative January 2, 1962; Stats 1963 ch 871 §8, operative July 1, 1964. Repealed Stats 1968 ch 385 §1. See CCP §912.

§988h. [Section repealed 1968]
Leg.H. Added Stats 1927 ch 68 §14. Amended Stats 1935 ch 722 §24; Stats 1957 ch 1611 §2; Stats 1961 ch 693 §11, operative January 2, 1962; Stats 1963 ch 871 §9, operative July 1, 1964. Repealed Stats 1968 ch 385 §1. See CCP §906.

§988i. [Section repealed 1968]
Leg.H. Added Stats 1931 ch 974 §4. Amended Stats 1961 ch 693 §12, operative January 2, 1962; Stats 1963 ch 871 §10, operative July 1, 1964. Repealed Stats 1968 ch 385 §1. See CCP §909.

§988j. [Section repealed 1968]
Leg.H. Added Stats 1945 ch 38 §1, effective April 18, 1945. Amended Stats 1963 ch 871 §11, operative July 1, 1964. Repealed Stats 1968 ch 385 §1. The repealed section related to appeals from municipal courts.

§988t. [Section repealed 1968]
Leg.H. Added Stats 1961 ch 693 §13, operative January 2, 1962. Amended Stats 1967 ch 17 §17. Repealed Stats 1968 ch 385 §1. See CCP §911.

TITLE 14
OF MISCELLANEOUS PROVISIONS

Chapter 1. Proceedings Against Joint Debtors.
Chapter 2. Bonds and Undertakings.
Chapter 3. Offers by a Party to Compromise.
Chapter 3.2. Time-Limited Demands.
Chapter 3.5. Confidential Settlement Agreements.
Chapter 3.6. Agreements Settling Employment Disputes.
Chapter 3.7. Enrollment Agreements.
Chapter 4. Motions and Orders.
Chapter 5. Notices, and Filing and Service of Papers.
Chapter 6. Of Costs.
Chapter 7. General Provisions.
Chapter 8. Declaratory Relief.
Chapter 9. Actions to Enforce Real Property and Mobilehome Sales Agreements.
Chapter 10. Computer Assistance.
Chapter 11. Foster Family Agency Accountability [Repealed effective January 1, 2027].

CHAPTER 1
PROCEEDINGS AGAINST JOINT DEBTORS

Summoning unserved joint debtor to show cause. §989.
Issuance, service, and return of summons. §990.
Affidavit to accompany summons. §991.
Answer's denials or defenses. §992.
Pleadings in view of answer; Amendment. §993.
Issues, how tried; Verdict, what to do. §994.

§989. Summoning unserved joint debtor to show cause

When a judgment is recovered against one or more of several persons, jointly indebted upon an obligation, by proceeding as provided in Section 410.70, those who were not originally served with the summons, and did not appear in the action, may be summoned to appear before the court in which such judgment is entered to show cause why they should not be bound by the judgment, in the same manner as though they had been originally served with the summons. **Leg.H.** Enacted 1872. Amended Stats 1933 ch 744 §170; Stats 1935 ch 722 §25; Stats 1969 ch 1611 §24, operative July 1, 1970.

§990. Issuance, service, and return of summons

The summons specified in Section 989 shall be issued by the clerk upon presentation of the affidavit specified in Section 991. The summons must describe the judgment, and require the person summoned to show cause why the person should not be bound by it, and must be served in the same manner, and returnable no later than ninety (90) days after the time specified for the return of the original summons. It is not necessary to file a new complaint. **Leg.H.** Enacted 1872. Amended Stats 1935 ch 722 §26; Stats 1951 ch 1737 §128, operative January 1, 1952; Stats 1957 ch 1195 §1; Stats 2007 ch 263 §10 (AB 310), effective January 1, 2008.

§991. Affidavit to accompany summons

The summons must be accompanied by an affidavit of the plaintiff, his agent, representative, or attorney, that the judgment, or some part thereof, remains unsatisfied, and must specify the amount due thereon. **Leg.H.** Enacted 1872.

§992. Answer's denials or defenses

Upon such summons, the defendant may answer within the time specified therein, denying the judgment, or setting up any defense which may have arisen subsequently; or he may deny his liability on the obligation upon which the judgment was recovered, by reason of any defense existing at the commencement of the action. **Leg.H.** Enacted 1872. Amended Stats 1907 ch 325 §1.

§993. Pleadings in view of answer; Amendment

If the defendant, in his answer, denies the judgment, or sets up any defense which may have arisen subsequently, the summons, with the affidavit annexed, and the answer, constitute the written allegations in the case; if he denies his liability on the obligation upon which the judgment was recovered, a copy of the original complaint and judgment, the summons, with the affidavit annexed, and the answer, constitute such written allegations, subject to the right of the parties to amend their pleadings as in other cases. **Leg.H.** Enacted 1872. Amended Stats 1907 ch 325 §2.

§994. Issues, how tried; Verdict, what to do

The issues formed may be tried as in other cases, but when the defendant denies, in his answer, any liability on the obligation upon which the judgment was rendered, if a verdict be found against him, it must be for not exceeding the amount remaining unsatisfied on such original judgment, with interest thereon. **Leg.H.** Enacted 1872.

CHAPTER 2
BONDS AND UNDERTAKINGS

Article 1. Preliminary Provisions and Definitions.
Article 2. General Provisions.
Article 3. Execution and Filing.
Article 4. Approval and Effect.
Article 5. Personal Sureties.
Article 6. Admitted Surety Insurers.
Article 7. Deposit in Lieu of Bond.
Article 8. Bonds to the State of California.
Article 9. Objections to Bonds.
Article 10. Insufficient and Excessive Bonds.
Article 11. Release or Substitution of Sureties on Bond Given in Action or Proceeding.
Article 12. New, Additional, and Supplemental Bonds.
Article 13. Cancellation of Bond or Withdrawal of Sureties.
Article 14. Liability of Principal and Sureties.
Article 15. Enforcement Lien.

ARTICLE 1
Preliminary Provisions and Definitions

Short title. §995.010.
Application of chapter. §995.020.
Manner of service. §995.030.
Affidavits. §995.040.
Extensions of time. §995.050.
Application of definitions. §995.110.
"Admitted surety insurer". §995.120.
"Beneficiary". §995.130.
"Bond". §995.140.
"Court". §995.150.
"Officer". §995.160.
"Principal". §995.170.
"Statute". §995.180.
"Surety". §995.185.
"Undertaking". §995.190.

§995.010. Short title

This chapter shall be known and may be cited as the Bond and Undertaking Law. **Leg.H.** Added Stats 1982 ch 998 §1.

§995.020. Application of chapter

(a) The provisions of this chapter apply to a bond or undertaking executed, filed, posted, furnished, or otherwise given as security pursuant to any statute of this state, except to the extent the statute prescribes a different rule or is inconsistent.

(b) The provisions of this chapter apply to a bond or undertaking given at any of the following times:

(1) On or after January 1, 1983.

(2) Before January 1, 1983, to the extent another surety is substituted for the original surety on or after January 1, 1983, or to the extent the principal gives a new, additional, or supplemental bond or undertaking on or after January 1, 1983.

Except to the extent provided in this section, the law governing a bond or undertaking given before January 1, 1983, is the law applicable to the bond or undertaking immediately before January 1, 1983, pursuant to Section 414 of Chapter 517 of the Statutes of 1982.

(c) The provisions of this chapter do not apply to a bail bond or an undertaking of bail. **Leg.H.** Added Stats 1982 ch 998 §1. Amended Stats 1983 ch 18 §18.2, effective April 21, 1983.

§995.030. Manner of service

If service of a notice, paper, or other document is required under this chapter, service shall be made in the same manner as service of process in civil actions generally. **Leg.H.** Added Stats 1982 ch 998 §1.

§995.040. Affidavits

An affidavit made under this chapter shall conform to the standards prescribed for an affidavit made pursuant to Section 437c. **Leg.H.** Added Stats 1982 ch 998 §1.

§995.050. Extensions of time

The times provided in this chapter, or in any other statute relating to a bond given in an action or proceeding, may be extended pursuant to Sections 1054 and 1054.1. **Leg.H.** Added Stats 1982 ch 998 §1.

§995.110. Application of definitions

Unless the provision or context otherwise requires, the definitions in this article govern the construction of this chapter. **Leg.H.** Added Stats 1982 ch 998 §1.

§995.120. "Admitted surety insurer"

(a) "Admitted surety insurer" means a corporate insurer or a reciprocal or interinsurance exchange to which the Insurance Commissioner has issued a certificate of authority to transact surety insurance in this state, as defined in Section 105 of the Insurance Code.

(b) For the purpose of application of this chapter to a bond given pursuant to any statute of this state, the phrases "admitted surety insurer," "authorized surety company," "bonding company," "corporate surety," and comparable phrases used in the statute mean "admitted surety insurer" as defined in this section. **Leg.H.** Added Stats 1982 ch 998 §1.

§995.130. "Beneficiary"

(a) "Beneficiary" means the person for whose benefit a bond is given, whether executed to, in favor of, in the name of, or payable to the person as an obligee.

(b) If a bond is given for the benefit of the State of California or the people of the state, "beneficiary" means the court, officer, or other person required to determine the sufficiency of the sureties or to approve the bond.

(c) For the purpose of application of this chapter to a bond given pursuant to any statute of this state, the terms "beneficiary," "obligee," and comparable terms used in the statute mean "beneficiary" as defined in this section. **Leg.H.** Added Stats 1982 ch 998 §1.

§995.140. "Bond"

(a) "Bond" includes both of the following:

(1) A surety, indemnity, fiduciary, or like bond executed by both the principal and sureties.

(2) A surety, indemnity, fiduciary, or like undertaking executed by the sureties alone.

(b) A bond provided for or given "in an action or proceeding" does not include a bond provided for, or given as, a condition of a license or permit. **Leg.H.** Added Stats 1982 ch 998 §1.

§995.150. "Court"

"Court" means, if a bond is given in an action or proceeding, the court in which the action or proceeding is pending. **Leg.H.** Added Stats 1982 ch 998 §1.

§995.160. "Officer"

"Officer" means the sheriff, marshal, clerk of court, judge or magistrate (if there is no clerk), board, commission, department, or other public official or entity to whom the bond is given or with whom a copy of the bond is filed or who is required to determine the sufficiency of the sureties or to approve the bond. **Leg.H.** Added Stats 1982 ch 998 §1. Amended Stats 1996 ch 872 §19 (AB 3472).

§995.170. "Principal"

(a) "Principal" means the person who gives a bond.

(b) For the purpose of application of this chapter to a bond given pursuant to any statute of this state, the terms "obligor," "principal," and comparable terms used in the statute mean "principal" as defined in this section. **Leg.H.** Added Stats 1982 ch 998 §1.

§995.180. "Statute"

"Statute" includes administrative regulation promulgated pursuant to statute. **Leg.H.** Added Stats 1982 ch 998 §1.

§995.185. "Surety"

(a) "Surety" has the meaning provided in Section 2787 of the Civil Code and includes personal surety and admitted surety insurer.

(b) For the purpose of application of this chapter to a bond given pursuant to any statute of this state, the terms "bail," "guarantor," "bondsman," "surety," and comparable terms used in the statute mean "surety" as defined in this section. **Leg.H.** Added Stats 1982 ch 998 §1.

§995.190. "Undertaking"

"Undertaking" means a surety, indemnity, fiduciary, or like undertaking executed by the sureties alone. **Leg.H.** Added Stats 1982 ch 998 §1.

ARTICLE 2
General Provisions

Bonds and undertakings interchangeable. §995.210.
Bond not required of public entity or officer. §995.220.
Reduction or waiver by beneficiary. §995.230.
Waiver in case of indigency. §995.240.
Cost of bond recoverable. §995.250.
Evidence of bond. §995.260.

§995.210. Bonds and undertakings interchangeable

Unless the provision or context otherwise requires:

(a) If a statute provides for a bond, an undertaking that otherwise satisfies the requirements for the bond may be given in its place with the same effect as if a bond were given, and references in the statute to the bond shall be deemed to be references to the undertaking.

(b) If a statute provides for an undertaking, a bond that otherwise satisfies the requirements for the undertaking may be given in its place with the same effect as if an undertaking were given, and references in the statute to the undertaking shall be deemed to be references to the bond. **Leg.H.** Added Stats 1982 ch 998 §1.

§995.220. Bond not required of public entity or officer

Notwithstanding any other statute, if a statute provides for a bond in an action or proceeding, including but not limited to a bond for issuance of a restraining order or injunction, appointment of a receiver, or stay of enforcement of a judgment on appeal, the following public entities and officers are not required to give the bond and shall have the same rights, remedies, and benefits as if the bond were given:

(a) The State of California or the people of the state, a state agency, department, division, commission, board, or other entity of the state, or a state officer in an official capacity or on behalf of the state.

(b) A county, city, or district, or public authority, public agency, or other political subdivision in the state, or an officer of the local public entity in an official capacity or on behalf of the local public entity.

(c) The United States or an instrumentality or agency of the United States, or a federal officer in an official capacity or on behalf of the United States or instrumentality or agency. **Leg.H.** Added Stats 1982 ch 998 §1.

§995.230. Reduction or waiver by beneficiary

The beneficiary of a bond given in an action or proceeding may in writing consent to the bond in an amount less than the amount required by statute or may waive the bond. **Leg.H.** Added Stats 1982 ch 998 §1.

§995.240. Waiver in case of indigency

The court may, in its discretion, waive a provision for a bond in an action or proceeding and make such orders as may be appropriate as if the bond were given, if the court determines that the principal is unable to give the bond because the principal is indigent and is unable to obtain sufficient sureties, whether personal or admitted surety insurers. In exercising its discretion the court shall take into consideration all factors it deems relevant, including but not limited to the character of the action or proceeding, the nature of the beneficiary, whether public or private, and the potential harm to the beneficiary if the provision for the bond is waived. **Leg.H.** Added Stats 1982 ch 998 §1.

§995.250. Cost of bond recoverable

If a statute allows costs to a party in an action or proceeding, the costs shall include all of the following:

(a) The premium on a bond reasonably paid by the party pursuant to a statute that provides for the bond in the action or proceeding.

(b) The premium on a bond reasonably paid by the party in connection with the action or proceeding, unless the court determines that the bond was unnecessary. **Leg.H.** Added Stats 1982 ch 998 §1.

§995.260. Evidence of bond

If a bond is recorded pursuant to statute, a certified copy of the record of the bond with all affidavits, acknowledgments, endorsements, and attachments may be admitted in evidence in an action or proceeding with the same effect as the original, without further proof. **Leg.H.** Added Stats 1982 ch 998 §1.

ARTICLE 3
Execution and Filing

Sureties on bond. §995.310.
Sureties on bond on public works contract; Status verification procedures. §995.311.
Contents of bond. §995.320.
Form of bond. §995.330.
Filing required. §995.340.
Entry in register of actions. §995.350.
Return of bond. §995.360.
Service of copy of bond. §995.370.
Defect in bond. §995.380.

§995.310. Sureties on bond

Unless the statute providing for the bond requires execution by an admitted surety insurer, a bond shall be executed by two or more sufficient personal sureties or by one sufficient admitted surety insurer or by any combination of sufficient personal sureties and admitted surety insurers. **Leg.H.** Added Stats 1982 ch 998 §1.

§995.311. Sureties on bond on public works contract; Status verification procedures

(a) Notwithstanding any other provision of law, any bond required on a public works contract, as defined in Section 1101 of the Public Contract Code, shall be executed by an admitted surety insurer. A public agency approving the bond on a public works contract shall have a duty to verify that the bond is being executed by an admitted surety insurer.

(b) A public agency may fulfill its duty under subdivision (a) by verifying the status of the party executing the bond in one of the following ways:

(1) Printing out information from the website of the Department of Insurance confirming the surety is an admitted surety insurer and attaching it to the bond.

(2) Obtaining a certificate from the county clerk that confirms the surety is an admitted insurer and attaching it to the bond. **Leg.H.** Added Stats 2001 ch 181 §1 (AB 263).

§995.320. Contents of bond

(a) A bond shall be in writing signed by the sureties under oath and shall include all of the following:

(1) A statement that the sureties are jointly and severally liable on the obligations of the statute providing for the bond.

(2) The address at which the principal and sureties may be served with notices, papers, and other documents under this chapter.

(3) If the amount of the bond is based upon the value of property or an interest in property, a description of the property or interest, and the principal's estimate of the value of the property or interest, or if given pursuant to the estimate of the beneficiary or court, the value as so estimated.

(b) The sureties signing the bond are jointly and severally liable on the obligations of the bond, the provisions of this chapter, and the statute providing for the bond. **Leg.H.** Added Stats 1982 ch 998 §1.

§995.330. Form of bond

A bond or undertaking given in an action or proceeding may be in the following form:

"(Title of court. Title of cause.)

Whereas the _____ desires to give (a bond) (an undertaking) for (state what) as provided by (state sections of code requiring bond or undertaking); now, therefore, the undersigned (principal and) (sureties) (surety) hereby (obligate ourselves, jointly and severally) (obligates itself) to (name who) under the statutory obligations, in the amount of _____ dollars." **Leg.H.** Added Stats 1982 ch 998 §1

§995.340. Filing required

If a bond is given in an action or proceeding:

(a) The bond shall be filed with the court unless the statute providing for the bond requires that the bond be given to another person.

(b) If the statute providing for the bond requires that the bond be given to an officer, the officer shall file the bond with the court unless the statute providing for the bond otherwise provides.

(c) A bond filed with the court shall be preserved in the office of the clerk of the court. **Leg.H.** Added Stats 1982 ch 998 §1.

§995.350. Entry in register of actions

(a) Upon the filing of a bond with the court in an action or proceeding, the clerk shall enter in the register of actions the following information:

(1) The date and amount of the bond.

(2) The names of the sureties on the bond.

(b) In the event of the loss of the bond, the entries in the register of actions are prima facie evidence of the giving of the bond in the manner required by statute. **Leg.H.** Added Stats 1982 ch 998 §1.

§995.360. Return of bond

A bond given in an action or proceeding may be withdrawn from the file and returned to the principal on order of the court only if one of the following conditions is satisfied:

(a) The beneficiary so stipulates.

(b) The bond is no longer in force and effect and the time during which the liability on the bond may be enforced has expired. **Leg.H.** Added Stats 1982 ch 998 §1.

§995.370. Service of copy of bond

At the time a bond is given, the principal shall serve a copy of the bond on the beneficiary. An affidavit of service shall be given and filed with the bond. **Leg.H.** Added Stats 1982 ch 998 §1.

§995.380. Defect in bond

(a) If a bond does not contain the substantial matter or conditions required by this chapter or by the statute providing for the bond, or if there are any defects in the giving or filing of the bond, the bond is not void so as to release the principal and sureties from liability.

(b) The beneficiary may, in proceedings to enforce the liability on the bond, suggest the defect in the bond, or its giving or filing, and enforce the liability against the principal and the persons who intended to become and were included as sureties on the bond. **Leg.H.** Added Stats 1982 ch 998 §1.

ARTICLE 4
Approval and Effect

Approval of bond. §995.410.
Time bond becomes effective. §995.420.
Term of bond. §995.430.
Term of license or permit bond. §995.440.

§995.410. Approval of bond

(a) A bond becomes effective without approval unless the statute providing for the bond requires that the bond be approved by the court or officer.

(b) If the statute providing for a bond requires that the bond be approved, the court or officer may approve or disapprove the bond on the basis of the affidavit or certificate of the sureties or may require the attendance of witnesses and the production of evidence and may examine the sureties under oath touching their qualifications.

(c) Nothing shall be construed to preclude approval of a bond in an amount greater than that required by statute. **Leg.H.** Added Stats 1982 ch 998 §1.

§995.420. Time bond becomes effective

(a) Unless the statute providing for a bond provides that the bond becomes effective at a different time, a bond is effective at the time it is given or, if the statute requires that the bond be approved, at the time it is approved.

(b) If the statute providing for a bond provides that the bond becomes effective at a time other than the time it is given or approved, the bond is effective at the time provided unless an objection is made to the bond before that time. If an objection is made to a bond before the time provided, the bond becomes effective when the court makes an order determining the sufficiency of the bond. **Leg.H.** Added Stats 1982 ch 998 §1

§995.430. Term of bond

A bond remains in force and effect until the earliest of the following events:

(a) The sureties withdraw from or cancel the bond or a new bond is given in place of the original bond.

(b) The purpose for which the bond was given is satisfied or the purpose is abandoned without any liability having been incurred.

(c) A judgment of liability on the bond that exhausts the amount of the bond is satisfied.

(d) The term of the bond expires. Unless the statute providing for the bond prescribes a fixed term, the bond is continuous. **Leg.H.** Added Stats 1982 ch 998 §1.

§995.440. Term of license or permit bond

A bond given as a condition of a license or permit shall be continuous in form, remain in full force and effect, and run concurrently with the license or permit period and any and all renewals, or until cancellation or withdrawal of the surety from the bond. **Leg.H.** Added Stats 1982 ch 998 §1.

ARTICLE 5
Personal Sureties

Qualifications of surety. §995.510.
Affidavit of surety. §995.520.

§995.510. Qualifications of surety

(a) A personal surety on a bond is sufficient if all of the following conditions are satisfied:

(1) The surety is a person other than the principal. No officer of the court or member of the State Bar shall act as a surety.

(2) The surety is a resident, and either an owner of real property or householder, within the state.

(3) The surety is worth the amount of the bond in real or personal property, or both, situated in this state, over and above all debts and liabilities, exclusive of property exempt from enforcement of a money judgment.

(b) If the amount of a bond exceeds ten thousand dollars ($10,000) and is executed by more than two personal sureties, the worth of a personal surety may be less than the amount of the bond, so long as the aggregate worth of all sureties executing the bond is twice the amount of the bond. **Leg.H.** Added Stats 1982 ch 998 §1.

§995.520. Affidavit of surety

(a) A bond executed by personal sureties shall be accompanied by an affidavit of qualifications of each surety.

(b) The affidavit shall contain all of the following information:

(1) The name, occupation, residence address, and business address (if any) of the surety.

(2) A statement that the surety is a resident, and either an owner of real property or householder, within the state.

(3) A statement that the surety is worth the amount of the bond in real or personal property, or both, situated in this state, over and above all debts and liabilities, exclusive of property exempt from enforcement of a money judgment.

(c) If the amount of the bond exceeds five thousand dollars ($5,000), the affidavit shall contain, in addition to the information required by subdivision (b), all of the following information:

(1) A description sufficient for identification of real and personal property of the surety situated in this state and the nature of the surety's interest therein that qualifies the surety on the bond.

(2) The surety's best estimate of the fair market value of each item of property.

(3) A statement of any charge or lien and its amount, known to the surety, whether of public record or not, against any item of property.

(4) Any other impediment or cloud known to the surety on the free right of possession, use, benefit, or enjoyment of the property.

(d) If the amount of the bond exceeds ten thousand dollars ($10,000) and is executed by more than two sureties, the affidavit may state that the surety is worth less than the amount of the bond and the bond may stipulate that the liability of the surety is limited to the worth of the surety stated in the affidavit, so long as the aggregate worth of all sureties executing the bond is twice the amount of the bond. **Leg.H.** Added Stats 1982 ch 998 §1.

ARTICLE 6
Admitted Surety Insurers

Admitted surety insurer in lieu of personal sureties. §995.610.
More than one surety. §995.620.
Authentication of bond. §995.630.
Certificate of authority. §995.640.
Objection to sufficiency of surety. §995.650.
Determination of sufficiency of surety. §995.660.
Admitted surety to comply only with specified requirements relating to objections to surety's sufficiency. §995.670.
Listing surety insurer. §995.675.

§995.610. Admitted surety insurer in lieu of personal sureties

(a) If a statute provides for a bond with any number of sureties, one sufficient admitted surety insurer may become and shall be accepted as sole surety on the bond.

(b) The admitted surety insurer is subject to all the liabilities and entitled to all the rights of personal sureties. **Leg.H.** Added Stats 1982 ch 998 §1.

§995.620. More than one surety

Two or more admitted surety insurers may be sureties on a bond by executing the same or separate bonds for amounts aggregating the required amount of the bond. Each admitted surety insurer is jointly and severally liable to the extent of the amount of the liability assumed by it. **Leg.H.** Added Stats 1982 ch 998 §1.

§995.630. Authentication of bond

An admitted surety insurer shall be accepted or approved by the court or officer as surety on a bond without further acknowledgment if the bond is executed in the name of the surety insurer under penalty of perjury or the fact of execution of the bond is duly acknowledged before an officer authorized to take and certify acknowledgments, and either one of the following conditions, at the option of the surety insurer, is satisfied:

(a) A copy of the transcript or record of the unrevoked appointment, power of attorney, bylaws, or other instrument, duly certified by the proper authority and attested by the seal of the insurer entitling or authorizing the person who executed the bond to do so for and in behalf of the insurer, is filed in the office of the clerk of the county in which the court or officer is located.

(b) A copy of a power of attorney is attached to the bond. **Leg.H.** Added Stats 1982 ch 998 §1. Amended Stats 1992 ch 380 §1 (SB 1521).

§995.640. Certificate of authority

Upon review of the Internet Web site of the Department of Insurance, the county clerk of any county shall, upon request of any person, do any of the following:

(a) Issue a certificate stating whether a surety is admitted or if the certificate of authority of an admitted surety insurer issued by the Insurance Commissioner authorizing the insurer to transact surety insurance has been surrendered, revoked, canceled, annulled, or suspended, and, in the event that it has, whether renewed authority has been granted. The county clerk in issuing the certificate shall rely solely upon the information furnished by the Insurance Commissioner pursuant to Article 2 (commencing with Section 12070) of Chapter 1 of Part 4 of Division 2 of the Insurance Code.

(b) Issue a certificate stating whether a copy of the transcript or record of the unrevoked appointment, power of attorney, bylaws, or other instrument, duly certified by the proper authority and attested by the seal of an admitted surety insurer entitling or authorizing the person who executed a bond to do so for and on behalf of the insurer, is filed in the office of the clerk. **Leg.H.** Added Stats 1982 ch 998 §1. Amended Stats 2004 ch 183 §44 (AB 3082); Stats 2005 ch 22 §19 (SB 1108), effective January 1, 2006; Stats 2008 ch 351 §1 (SB 1279), effective January 1, 2009.

§995.650. Objection to sufficiency of surety

If an objection is made to the sufficiency of an admitted surety insurer, the person making the objection shall attach to and incorporate in the objection one or both of the following:

(a) The certificate of the county clerk of the county in which the court is located stating that the insurer is not listed as an admitted surety insurer on the department's Internet Web site or that the certificate of authority of the insurer has been surrendered, revoked, canceled, annulled, or suspended and has not been renewed.

(b) An affidavit stating facts that establish the insufficiency of the insurer. **Leg.H.** Added Stats 1982 ch 998 §1. Amended Stats 2008 ch 351 §2 (SB 1279), effective January 1, 2009.

§995.660. Determination of sufficiency of surety

(a) If an objection is made to the sufficiency of an admitted surety insurer on a bond or if the bond is required to be approved, the insurer shall submit to the court or officer the following documents:

(1) The original, or a certified copy, of the unrevoked appointment, power of attorney, bylaws, or other instrument entitling or authorizing the

person who executed the bond to do so, within 10 calendar days of the insurer's receipt of a request to submit the instrument.

(2) A certified copy of the certificate of authority of the insurer issued by the Insurance Commissioner, within 10 calendar days of the insurer's receipt of a request to submit the copy.

(3) A certificate from the clerk of the county in which the court or officer is located that the certificate of authority of the insurer has not been surrendered, revoked, canceled, annulled, or suspended or, in the event that it has, that renewed authority has been granted, within 10 calendar days of the insurer's receipt of the certificate.

(4) Copies of the insurer's most recent annual statement and quarterly statement filed with the Department of Insurance pursuant to Article 10 (commencing with Section 900) of Chapter 1 of Part 2 of Division 1 of the Insurance Code, within 10 calendar days of the insurer's receipt of a request to submit the statements.

(b) If the admitted surety insurer complies with subdivision (a), and if it appears that the bond was duly executed, that the insurer is authorized to transact surety insurance in the state, and that its assets exceed its liabilities in an amount equal to or in excess of the amount of the bond, the insurer is sufficient and shall be accepted or approved as surety on the bond, subject to Section 12090 of the Insurance Code. **Leg.H.** Added Stats 1982 ch 998 §1. Amended Stats 1992 ch 379 §1 (SB 1502); Stats 1994 ch 487 §1 (AB 3493).

§995.670. Admitted surety to comply only with specified requirements relating to objections to surety's sufficiency

(a) This section applies to a bond executed, filed, posted, furnished, or otherwise given as security pursuant to any statute of this state or any law or ordinance of a public agency.

No public agency shall require an admitted surety insurer to comply with any requirements other than those in Section 995.660 whenever an objection is made to the sufficiency of the admitted surety insurer on the bond or if the bond is required to be approved.

(b) For the purposes of this section, "public agency" means the state, any agency or authority, any city, county, city and county, district, municipal or public corporation, or any instrumentality thereof. **Leg.H.** Added Stats 1992 ch 997 §1 (AB 2872). Amended Stats 1994 ch 487 §2 (AB 3493).

§995.675. Listing surety insurer

Notwithstanding Sections 995.660 and 995.670, the California Integrated Waste Management Board, the State Water Resources Control Board, and the Department of Toxic Substances Control may require, in order to comply with Subtitle C or Subtitle D of the federal Resource Conservation and Recovery Act of 1976, as amended (42 U.S.C. §§6901 et seq.), an admitted surety insurer to be listed in Circular 570 issued by the United States Treasury. **Leg.H.** Added Stats 1998 ch 477 §1 (AB 2353).

ARTICLE 7
Deposit in Lieu of Bond

Deposit of money, certificates, accounts, bonds, or notes. §995.710.
Valuation of bonds or notes. §995.720.
Effect of deposit. §995.730.
Interest on deposit. §995.740.
Obligation of principal. §995.750.
Enforcement against deposit. §995.760.
Return of deposit. §995.770.

§995.710. Deposit of money, certificates, accounts, bonds, or notes

(a) Except as provided in subdivision (e) or to the extent the statute providing for a bond precludes a deposit in lieu of bond or limits the form of deposit, the principal may, without prior court approval, instead of giving a bond, deposit with the officer any of the following:

(1) Lawful money of the United States or a cashier's check, made payable to the officer, issued by a bank, savings association, or credit union authorized to do business in this state. The money shall be held in trust by the officer in interest-bearing deposit or share accounts.

(2) Bonds or notes, including bearer bonds and bearer notes, of the United States or the State of California. The deposit of a bond or note pursuant to this section shall be accomplished by filing with the court, and serving upon all parties and the appropriate officer of the bank holding the bond or note, instructions executed by the person or entity holding title to the bond or note that the treasurer of the county where the judgment was entered is the custodian of that account for the purpose of staying enforcement of the judgment, and that the title holder assigns to the treasurer the right to collect, sell, or otherwise apply the bond or note to enforce the judgment debtor's liability pursuant to Section 995.760.

(3) Certificates of deposit payable to the officer, not exceeding the federally insured amount, issued by banks or savings associations authorized to do business in this state and insured by the Federal Deposit Insurance Corporation.

(4) Savings accounts assigned to the officer, not exceeding the federally insured amount, together with evidence of the deposit in the savings accounts with banks authorized to do business in this state and insured by the Federal Deposit Insurance Corporation.

(5) Investment certificates or share accounts assigned to the officer, not exceeding the federally insured amount, issued by savings associations authorized to do business in this state and insured by the Federal Deposit Insurance Corporation.

(6) Share certificates payable to the officer, not exceeding the guaranteed or insured amount, issued by a credit union, as defined in Section 14002 of the Financial Code, whose share accounts are insured by the National Credit Union Administration or guaranteed or insured by any other agency that the Commissioner of Financial Protection and Innovation has not deemed to be unsatisfactory.

(b) The deposit shall be in an amount or have a face value, or, in the case of bonds or notes, have a market value, equal to or in excess of the amount that would be required to be secured by the bond if the bond were given by an admitted surety insurer. Notwithstanding any other provision of this chapter, in the case of a deposit of bonds or notes other than in an action or proceeding, the officer may, in the officer's discretion, require that the amount of the deposit be determined not by the market value of the bonds or notes but by a formula based on the principal amount of the bonds or notes.

(c) The deposit shall be accompanied by an agreement executed by the principal authorizing the officer to collect, sell, or otherwise apply the deposit to enforce the liability of the principal on the deposit. The agreement shall include the address at which the principal may be served with notices, papers, and other documents under this chapter.

(d) The officer may prescribe terms and conditions to implement this section.

(e) This section does not apply to deposits with the Secretary of State. **Leg.H.** Added Stats 1982 ch 998 §1. Amended Stats 1983 ch 18 §18.5, effective April 21, 1983; Stats 1996 ch 1064 §6 (AB 3351), operative July 1, 1997; Stats 1998 ch 829 §16 (SB 1652); Stats 1999 ch 892 §11 (AB 1672); Stats 2014 ch 305 §1 (AB 1856), effective January 1, 2015; Stats 2022 ch 452 §41 (SB 1498), effective January 1, 2023.

§995.720. Valuation of bonds or notes

(a) The market value of bonds or notes, including bearer bonds and bearer notes, shall be agreed upon by stipulation of the principal and beneficiary or, if the bonds or notes are given in an action or proceeding and the principal and beneficiary are unable to agree, the market value shall be determined by court order in the manner prescribed in this section. A certified copy of the stipulation or court order shall be delivered to the officer at the time of the deposit of the bonds or notes.

(b) If the bonds or notes are given in an action or proceeding, the principal may file a written application with the court to determine the market value of the bonds or notes. The application shall be served upon the beneficiary and proof of service shall be filed with the application. The application shall contain all of the following:

(1) A specific description of the bonds or notes.

(2) A statement of the current market value of the bonds or notes as of the date of the filing of the application.

(3) A statement of the amount of the bonds or notes that the principal believes would be equal to the required amount of the deposit.

(c) The application pursuant to subdivision (b) shall be heard by the court not less than five days or more than 10 days after service of the application. If at the time of the hearing no objection is made to the current market value of the bonds or notes alleged in the application, the court shall fix the amount of the bonds or notes on the basis of the market value alleged in the application. If the beneficiary contends that the current market value of the bonds or notes is less than alleged in the application, the principal shall offer evidence in support of the application, and the beneficiary may offer evidence in opposition. At the conclusion of the hearing, the court shall make an order determining the market value of the bonds or notes and shall fix and determine the amount of the bonds or notes to be deposited by the principal. **Leg.H.** Added Stats 1982 ch 998 §1. Amended Stats 2014 ch 305 §2 (AB 1856), effective January 1, 2015.

§995.730. Effect of deposit

A deposit given instead of a bond has the same force and effect, is treated the same, and is subject to the same conditions, liability, and statutory provisions, including provisions for increase and decrease of amount, as the bond. **Leg.H.** Added Stats 1982 ch 998 §1.

§995.740. Interest on deposit

If no proceedings are pending to enforce the liability of the principal on the deposit, the officer shall:

(a) Pay quarterly, on demand, any interest on the deposit, when earned in accordance with the terms of the account or certificate, to the principal.

(b) Deliver to the principal, on demand, any interest coupons attached to bonds or notes, including bearer bonds and bearer notes, as the interest coupons become due and payable, or pay annually any interest payable on the bonds or notes. **Leg.H.** Added Stats 1982 ch 998 §1. Amended Stats 2014 ch 305 §3 (AB 1856), effective January 1, 2015.

§995.750. Obligation of principal

(a) The principal shall pay the amount of the liability on the deposit within 30 days after the date on which the judgment of liability becomes final.

(b) If the deposit was given to stay enforcement of a judgment on appeal, the principal shall pay the amount of the liability on the deposit, including damages and costs awarded against the principal on appeal, within 30 days after the filing of the remittitur from the appellate court in the court from which the appeal is taken. **Leg.H.** Added Stats 1982 ch 998 §1.

§995.760. Enforcement against deposit

(a) If the principal does not pay the amount of the liability on the deposit within the time prescribed in Section 995.750, the deposit shall be collected, sold, or otherwise applied to the liability upon order of the court that entered the judgment of liability, made upon five days' notice to the parties.

(b) Bonds or notes, including bearer bonds and bearer notes, without a prevailing market price shall be sold at public auction. Notice of sale shall be served on the principal. Bonds or notes having a prevailing market price may be sold at private sale at a price not lower than the prevailing market price.

(c) The deposit shall be distributed in the following order:

(1) First, to pay the cost of collection, sale, or other application of the deposit.

(2) Second, to pay the judgment of liability of the principal on the deposit.

(3) Third, the remainder, if any, shall be returned to the principal. **Leg.H.** Added Stats 1982 ch 998 §1. Amended Stats 2014 ch 305 §4 (AB 1856), effective January 1, 2015.

§995.770. Return of deposit

A deposit given pursuant to this article shall be returned to the principal at the earliest of the following times:

(a) Upon substitution of a sufficient bond for the deposit. The bond shall be in full force and effect for all liabilities incurred, and for acts, omissions, or causes existing or which arose, during the period the deposit was in effect.

(b) The time provided by Section 995.360 for return of a bond.

(c) The time provided by statute for return of the deposit. **Leg.H.** Added Stats 1982 ch 998 §1.

ARTICLE 8
Bonds to the State of California

Application of article. §995.810.
Bond by officer of court. §995.820.
Bond where no beneficiary provided. §995.830.
Court approval of bond. §995.840.
Enforcement by or for benefit of persons damaged. §995.850.

§995.810. Application of article

The provisions of this article apply to a bond executed to, in favor of, in the name of, or payable to the State of California or the people of the state, including but not limited to an official bond. **Leg.H.** Added Stats 1982 ch 998 §1.

§995.820. Bond by officer of court

Except as otherwise provided by statute, a bond given by an officer of the court for the faithful discharge of the officer's duties and obedience to the orders of the court shall be to the State of California. **Leg.H.** Added Stats 1982 ch 998 §1.

§995.830. Bond where no beneficiary provided

If a statute or court order pursuant thereto providing for a bond does not specify the beneficiary of the bond, the bond shall be to the State of California. **Leg.H.** Added Stats 1982 ch 998 §1.

§995.840. Court approval of bond

If a bond under this article is given in an action or proceeding:

(a) The bond shall be approved by the court.

(b) Any party for whose benefit the bond is given may object to the bond. **Leg.H.** Added Stats 1982 ch 998 §1.

§995.850. Enforcement by or for benefit of persons damaged

(a) The liability on a bond under this article may be enforced by or for the benefit of, and in the name of, any and all persons for whose benefit the bond is given who are damaged by breach of the condition of the bond.

(b) A person described in subdivision (a) may, in addition to any other remedy the person has, enforce the liability on the bond in the person's own name, without assignment of the bond. **Leg.H.** Added Stats 1982 ch 998 §1.

ARTICLE 9
Objections to Bonds

Article limited to actions and proceedings. §995.910.
Grounds for objection. §995.920.
Manner of making objection. §995.930.
Objection to sufficiency of bond based on market value. §995.940.
Hearing on objection. §995.950.
Determination of sufficiency of bond. §995.960.

§995.910. Article limited to actions and proceedings

This article governs objections to a bond given in an action or proceeding. **Leg.H.** Added Stats 1982 ch 998 §1.

§995.920. Grounds for objection

The beneficiary may object to a bond on any of the following grounds:

(a) The sureties are insufficient.

(b) The amount of the bond is insufficient.

(c) The bond, from any other cause, is insufficient. **Leg.H.** Added Stats 1982 ch 998 §1.

§995.930. Manner of making objection

(a) An objection shall be in writing and shall be made by noticed motion. The notice of motion shall specify the precise grounds for the objection. If a ground for the objection is that the amount of the bond is insufficient, the notice of motion shall state the reason for the insufficiency and shall include an estimate of the amount that would be sufficient.

(b) The objection shall be made within 10 days after service of a copy of the bond on the beneficiary or such other time as is required by the statute providing for the bond.

(c) If no objection is made within the time required by statute, the beneficiary is deemed to have waived all objections except upon a showing of good cause for failure to make the objection within the time required by statute or of changed circumstances. **Leg.H.** Added Stats 1982 ch 998 §1. Amended Stats 1984 ch 538 §33.

§995.940. Objection to sufficiency of bond based on market value

If a ground for the objection is that the value of property or an interest in property on which the amount of the bond is based exceeds the value estimated in the bond:

(a) The objection shall state the beneficiary's estimate of the market value of the property or interest in property.

(b) The principal may accept the beneficiary's estimate of the market value of the property or interest in property and immediately file an increased bond based on the estimate. In such case, no hearing shall be held on that ground for the objection, and the beneficiary is bound by the estimate of the market value of the property or interest in property. **Leg.H.** Added Stats 1982 ch 998 §1.

§995.950. Hearing on objection

(a) Unless the parties otherwise agree, the hearing on an objection shall be held not less than two or more than five days after service of the notice of motion.

(b) The hearing shall be conducted in such manner as the court determines is proper. The court may permit witnesses to attend and testify and evidence to be procured and introduced in the same manner as in the trial of a civil case.

(c) If the value of property or an interest in property is a ground for the objection, the court shall estimate its value. The court may appoint one or more disinterested persons to appraise property or an interest in property for the purpose of estimating its value. **Leg.H.** Added Stats 1982 ch 998 §1.

§995.960. Determination of sufficiency of bond

(a) Upon the hearing, the court shall make an order determining the sufficiency or insufficiency of the bond.

(b) If the court determines that the bond is insufficient:

(1) The court shall specify in what respect the bond is insufficient and shall order that a bond with sufficient sureties and in a sufficient amount be given within five days. If a sufficient bond is not given within the time required by the court order, all rights obtained by giving the bond immediately cease and the court shall upon ex parte motion so order.

(2) If a bond is in effect, the bond remains in effect until a bond with sufficient sureties and in a sufficient amount is given in its place, or the time in which to give the bond has expired, whichever first occurs. If the time in which to give a sufficient bond expires, the original bond remains in full force and effect for all liabilities incurred before, and for acts, omissions, or causes existing or which arose before, expiration.

(c) If the court determines that a bond is sufficient, no future objection to the bond may be made except upon a showing of changed circumstances. **Leg.H.** Added Stats 1982 ch 998 §1.

ARTICLE 10
Insufficient and Excessive Bonds

Bond in action or proceeding. §996.010.
Bond other than in action or proceeding. §996.020.
Reduced bond. §996.030.

§996.010. Bond in action or proceeding

(a) If a bond is given in an action or proceeding, the court may determine that the bond is or has from any cause become insufficient because the sureties are insufficient or because the amount of the bond is insufficient.

(b) The court determination shall be upon motion supported by affidavit or upon the court's own motion. The motion shall be deemed to be an objection to the bond. The motion shall be heard and notice of motion shall be given in the same manner as an objection to the bond.

(c) Upon the determination the court shall order that a sufficient new, additional, or supplemental bond be given within a reasonable time not less than five days. The court order is subject to any limitations in the statute providing for the bond.

(d) If a sufficient bond is not given within the time required by the court order, all rights obtained by giving the original bond immediately cease and the court shall upon ex parte motion so order. **Leg.H.** Added Stats 1982 ch 998 §1.

§996.020. Bond other than in action or proceeding

(a) If a bond is given other than in an action or proceeding and it is shown by affidavit of a credible witness or it otherwise comes to the attention of the officer that the bond is or has from any cause become insufficient because the sureties are insufficient or because the amount of the bond is insufficient, the officer may serve an order on the principal to appear and show cause why the officer should not make a determination that the bond is insufficient. The order shall name a day not less than three or more than 10 days after service.

(b) If the principal fails to appear or show good cause on the day named why a determination that the bond is insufficient should not be made, the officer may determine that the bond is insufficient and order a sufficient new, additional, or supplemental bond to be given.

(c) If a sufficient bond is not given within 10 days after the order, the officer shall make an order vacating the rights obtained by giving the original bond, including declaring vacant any office and suspending or revoking any license or certificate for which the bond was given. Any office vacated, license suspended or revoked, or any other rights lost, for failure to give a new, additional, or supplemental bond, shall not be reinstated until a new, additional, or supplemental bond is given. **Leg.H.** Added Stats 1982 ch 998 §1.

§996.030. Reduced bond

(a) The court if a bond is given or ordered in an action or proceeding, or the officer if a bond is given or ordered other than in an action or proceeding, may determine that the amount of the bond is excessive and order the amount reduced to an amount that in the discretion of the court or officer appears proper under the circumstances. The order is subject to any limitations in the statute providing for the bond.

(b) The determination shall be made upon motion or affidavit of the principal in the same manner as a motion or affidavit for a determination under this article that a bond is insufficient. The notice of motion or the order to show cause made pursuant to affidavit shall be served on the beneficiary. The determination shall be made in the same manner and pursuant to the same procedures as a determination under this article that the bond is insufficient.

(c) The principal may give a new bond for the reduced amount. The sureties may be the same sureties as on the original bond. **Leg.H.** Added Stats 1982 ch 998 §1. Amended Stats 1988 ch 309 §1.

ARTICLE 11
Release or Substitution of Sureties on Bond Given in Action or Proceeding

Application for substitution and release. §996.110.
Hearing. §996.120.
Substitution and release. §996.130.
Failure to give substitute surety. §996.140.
Liability of released surety. §996.150.

§996.110. Application for substitution and release

(a) A surety on a bond given in an action or proceeding may at any time apply to the court for an order that the surety be released from liability on the bond.

(b) The principal on a bond may, if a surety applies for release from liability on a bond, apply to the court for an order that another surety be substituted for the original surety.

(c) The applicant shall serve on the principal or surety (other than the applicant) and on the beneficiary a copy of the application and a notice of hearing on the application. Service shall be made not less than 15 days before the date set for hearing. **Leg.H.** Added Stats 1982 ch 998 §1.

§996.120. Hearing

Upon the hearing of the application, the court shall determine whether injury to the beneficiary would result from substitution or release of the surety. If the court determines that release would not reduce the amount of the bond or the number of sureties below the minimum required by the statute providing for the bond, substitution of a sufficient surety is not necessary and the court shall order the release of the surety. If the court determines that no injury would result from substitution of the surety, the court shall order the substitution of a sufficient surety within such time as appears reasonable. **Leg.H.** Added Stats 1982 ch 998 §1.

§996.130. Substitution and release

(a) If a substitute surety is given, the substitute surety is subject to all the provisions of this chapter, including but not limited to the provisions governing insufficient and excessive bonds.

(b) Upon the substitution of a sufficient surety, the court shall order the release of the original surety from liability on the bond. **Leg.H.** Added Stats 1982 ch 998 §1.

§996.140. Failure to give substitute surety

If the principal does not give a sufficient substitute surety within the time ordered by the court or such longer time as the surety consents to, all rights obtained by giving the original bond immediately cease and the court shall upon ex parte motion so order. **Leg.H.** Added Stats 1982 ch 998 §1.

§996.150. Liability of released surety

If a surety is ordered released from liability on a bond:

(a) The bond remains in full force and effect for all liabilities incurred before, and for acts, omissions, or causes existing or which arose before, the release. Legal proceedings may be had therefor in all respects as though there had been no release.

(b) The surety is not liable for any act, default, or misconduct of the principal or other breach of the condition of the bond that occurs after, or for any liabilities on the bond that arise after, the release.

(c) The release does not affect the bond as to the remaining sureties, or alter or change their liability in any respect. **Leg.H.** Added Stats 1982 ch 998 §1.

ARTICLE 12
New, Additional, and Supplemental Bonds

When bond given. §996.210.
Contents of bond. §996.220.
Provisions applicable to bond. §996.230.
Effect of new bond. §996.240.
Effect of additional or supplemental bond. §996.250.

§996.210. When bond given

(a) The principal shall give a new, additional, or supplemental bond if the court or officer orders that a new, additional, or supplemental bond be given.

(b) The principal may give a new bond if a surety withdraws from or cancels the original bond or to obtain the release of sureties from liability on the original bond. **Leg.H.** Added Stats 1982 ch 998 §1.

§996.220. Contents of bond

(a) A new, additional, or supplemental bond shall be in the same form and have the same obligation as the original bond and shall be in all other respects the same as the original bond, and shall be in such amount as is necessary for the purpose for which the new, additional, or supplemental bond is given.

(b) A supplemental bond shall, in addition to any other requirements, recite the names of the remaining original sureties, the name of the new surety, and the amount for which the new surety is liable. The supplemental bond shall be for the amount for which the original surety was liable on the original bond. **Leg.H.** Added Stats 1982 ch 998 §1.

§996.230. Provisions applicable to bond

A new, additional, or supplemental bond is subject to all the provisions applicable to the original bond and to the provisions of this chapter, including but not limited to the provisions governing giving and objecting to a bond and liabilities and enforcement procedures. **Leg.H.** Added Stats 1982 ch 998 §1.

§996.240. Effect of new bond

If a new bond is given in place of the original bond:

(a) The original bond remains in full force and effect for all liabilities incurred before, and for acts, omissions, or causes existing or which arose before, the new bond became effective.

(b) The sureties on the original bond are not liable for any act, default, or misconduct of the principal or other breach of the condition of the bond that occurs after or for any liabilities on the bond that arise after, the new bond becomes effective. **Leg.H.** Added Stats 1982 ch 998 §1.

§996.250. Effect of additional or supplemental bond

(a) An additional or supplemental bond does not discharge or affect the original bond. The original bond remains in full force and effect as if the additional or supplemental bond had not been given.

(b) After an additional or supplemental bond is given, the principal and sureties are liable upon either or both bonds for injury caused by breach of any condition of the bonds. Subject to subdivision (c), the beneficiary may enforce the liability on either bond, or may enforce the liability separately on both bonds and recover separate judgments of liability on both.

(c) If the beneficiary recovers separate judgments of liability on both bonds for the same cause of action, the beneficiary may enforce both judgments. The beneficiary may collect, by execution or otherwise, the costs of both proceedings to enforce the liability and the amount actually awarded to the beneficiary on the same cause of action in only one of the proceedings, and no double recovery shall be allowed.

(d) If the sureties on either bond have been compelled to pay any sum of money on account of the principal, they are entitled to recover from the sureties on the remaining bond a distributive part of the sum paid, in the proportion the amounts of the bonds bear one to the other and to the sums paid. **Leg.H.** Added Stats 1982 ch 998 §1.

ARTICLE 13
Cancellation of Bond or Withdrawal of Sureties

Application of article. §996.310.
Notice of cancellation or withdrawal. §996.320.
Effective date of cancellation or withdrawal. §996.330.
Effect of cancellation or withdrawal. §996.340.
New bond not required. §996.350.
Liability of surety. §996.360.

§996.310. Application of article

This article governs cancellation of or withdrawal of a surety from a bond given other than in an action or proceeding. **Leg.H.** Added Stats 1982 ch 998 §1.

§996.320. Notice of cancellation or withdrawal

A surety may cancel or withdraw from a bond by giving a notice of cancellation or withdrawal to the officer to whom the bond was given in the same manner the bond was given, notwithstanding Section 995.030. The surety shall at the same time mail or deliver a copy of the notice of cancellation or withdrawal to the principal. **Leg.H.** Added Stats 1982 ch 998 §1.

§996.330. Effective date of cancellation or withdrawal

Cancellation or withdrawal of a surety is effective at the earliest of the following times:

(a) Thirty days after notice of cancellation or withdrawal is given.

(b) If a new surety is substituted for the original surety, the date the substitution becomes effective.

(c) If a new bond is given, the date the new bond becomes effective. **Leg.H.** Added Stats 1982 ch 998 §1.

§996.340. Effect of cancellation or withdrawal

(a) If the principal does not give a new bond within 30 days after notice of cancellation or withdrawal is given, all rights obtained by giving the original bond immediately cease, any office for which the bond is given is vacant, any commission for which the bond is given is revoked, and any license or registration for which the bond is given is suspended.

(b) A person whose license or registration is suspended shall not operate or carry on business pursuant to the license or registration during the period of suspension. A license or registration that is suspended may be revived only by the giving of a new bond during the license or registration period in which the cancellation or withdrawal occurred. **Leg.H.** Added Stats 1982 ch 998 §1. Amended Stats 1983 ch 18 §19, effective April 21, 1983.

§996.350. New bond not required

If the withdrawal of a surety does not reduce the amount of the bond or the number of sureties below the minimum required by the statute providing for the bond, no new bond is required or necessary to maintain the original bond in effect. **Leg.H.** Added Stats 1982 ch 998 §1.

§996.360. Liability of surety

If a surety cancels or withdraws from a bond:

(a) The bond remains in full force and effect for all liabilities incurred before, and for acts, omissions, or causes existing or which arose before, the cancellation or withdrawal. Legal proceedings may be had therefor in all respects as though there had been no cancellation or withdrawal.

(b) The surety is not liable for any act, default, or misconduct of the principal or other breach of the condition of the bond that occurs after, or for any liabilities on the bond that arise after, the cancellation or withdrawal.

(c) The cancellation or withdrawal does not affect the bond as to the remaining sureties, or alter or change their liability in any respect. **Leg.H.** Added Stats 1982 ch 998 §1.

ARTICLE 14
Liability of Principal and Sureties

Enforcement of liability on bond. §996.410.
Surety subject to jurisdiction of court. §996.420.
Action to enforce liability. §996.430.
Motion to enforce liability. §996.440.
Statute of limitations. §996.450.
Judgment of liability. §996.460.
Limitation on liability of surety. §996.470.
Liability of surety pursuant to other statute. §996.475.
Voluntary payment by surety. §996.480.
Effect of payment by surety. §996.490.

Enforcement of judgment. §996.495.

§996.410. Enforcement of liability on bond

(a) The beneficiary may enforce the liability on a bond against both the principal and sureties.

(b) If the beneficiary is a class of persons, any person in the class may enforce the liability on a bond in the person's own name, without assignment of the bond. **Leg.H.** Added Stats 1982 ch 998 §1.

§996.420. Surety subject to jurisdiction of court

(a) A surety on a bond given in an action or proceeding submits itself to the jurisdiction of the court in all matters affecting its liability on the bond.

(b) This section does not apply to a bond of a public officer or fiduciary. **Leg.H.** Added Stats 1982 ch 998 §1.

§996.430. Action to enforce liability

(a) The liability on a bond may be enforced by civil action. Both the principal and the sureties shall be joined as parties to the action.

(b) If the bond was given in an action or proceeding, the action shall be commenced in the court in which the action or proceeding was pending. If the bond was given other than in an action or proceeding, the action shall be commenced in any court of competent jurisdiction, and the amount of damage claimed in the action, not the amount of the bond, determines the jurisdictional classification of the case.

(c) A cause of action on a bond may be transferred and assigned as other causes of action. **Leg.H.** Added Stats 1982 ch 998 §1. Amended Stats 1998 ch 931 §105 (SB 2139), effective September 28, 1998.

§996.440. Motion to enforce liability

(a) If a bond is given in an action or proceeding, the liability on the bond may be enforced on motion made in the court without the necessity of an independent action.

(b) The motion shall not be made until after entry of the final judgment in the action or proceeding in which the bond is given and the time for appeal has expired or, if an appeal is taken, until the appeal is finally determined. The motion shall not be made or notice of motion served more than one year after the later of the preceding dates.

(c) Notice of motion shall be served on the principal and sureties at least 30 days before the time set for hearing of the motion. The notice shall state the amount of the claim and shall be supported by affidavits setting forth the facts on which the claim is based. The notice and affidavits shall be served in accordance with any procedure authorized by Chapter 5 (commencing with Section 1010).

(d) Judgment shall be entered against the principal and sureties in accordance with the motion unless the principal or sureties serve and file affidavits in opposition to the motion showing such facts as may be deemed by the judge hearing the motion sufficient to present a triable issue of fact. If such a showing is made, the issues to be tried shall be specified by the court. Trial shall be by the court and shall be set for the earliest date convenient to the court, allowing sufficient time for such discovery proceedings as may be requested.

(e) The principal and sureties shall not obtain a stay of the proceedings pending determination of any conflicting claims among beneficiaries. **Leg.H.** Added Stats 1982 ch 998 §1.

§996.450. Statute of limitations

No provision in a bond is valid that attempts by contract to shorten the period prescribed by Section 337 or other statute for the commencement of an action on the bond or the period prescribed by Section 996.440 for a motion to enforce a bond. This section does not apply if the principal, beneficiary, and surety accept a provision for a shorter period in a bond. **Leg.H.** Added Stats 1982 ch 998 §1.

§996.460. Judgment of liability

(a) Notwithstanding Section 2845 of the Civil Code, a judgment of liability on a bond shall be in favor of the beneficiary and against the principal and sureties and shall obligate each of them jointly and severally.

(b) The judgment shall be in an amount determined by the court.

(c) A judgment that does not exhaust the full amount of the bond decreases the amount of the bond but does not discharge the bond. The liability on the bond may be enforced thereafter from time to time until the amount of the bond is exhausted.

(d) The judgment may be enforced by the beneficiary directly against the sureties. Nothing in this section affects any right of subrogation of a surety against the principal or any right of a surety to compel the principal to satisfy the judgment. **Leg.H.** Added Stats 1982 ch 998 §1.

§996.470. Limitation on liability of surety

(a) Notwithstanding any other statute other than Section 996.480, the aggregate liability of a surety to all persons for all breaches of the condition of a bond is limited to the amount of the bond. Except as otherwise provided by statute, the liability of the principal is not limited to the amount of the bond.

(b) If a bond is given in an amount greater than the amount required by statute or by order of the court or officer pursuant to statute, the liability of the surety on the bond is limited to the amount required by statute or by order of the court or officer, unless the amount of the bond has been increased voluntarily or by agreement of the parties to satisfy an objection to the bond made in an action or proceeding.

(c) The liability of a surety is limited to the amount stipulated in any of the following circumstances:

(1) The bond contains a stipulation pursuant to Section 995.520 that the liability of a personal surety is limited to the worth of the surety.

(2) The bond contains a stipulation that the liability of a surety is an amount less than the amount of the bond pursuant to a statute that provides that the liability of sureties in the aggregate need not exceed the amount of the bond. **Leg.H.** Added Stats 1982 ch 998 §1. Amended Stats 1993 ch 527 §2 (AB 908).

§996.475. Liability of surety pursuant to other statute

Nothing in this chapter is intended to limit the liability of a surety pursuant to any other statute. This section is declaratory of, and not a change in, existing law. **Leg.H.** Added Stats 1984 ch 538 §33.3.

§996.480. Voluntary payment by surety

(a) If the nature and extent of the liability of the principal is established by final judgment of a court and the time for appeal has expired or, if an appeal is taken, the appeal is finally determined and the judgment is affirmed:

(1) A surety may make payment on a bond without awaiting enforcement of the bond. The amount of the bond is reduced to the extent of any payment made by the surety in good faith.

(2) If the beneficiary makes a claim for payment on a bond given in an action or proceeding after the liability of the principal is so established and the surety fails to make payment, the surety is liable for costs incurred in obtaining a judgment against the surety, including a reasonable attorney's fee, and interest on the judgment from the date of the claim, notwithstanding Section 996.470.

(b) Partial payment of a claim by a surety shall not be considered satisfaction of the claim and the beneficiary may enforce the liability on the bond. If a right is affected or a license is suspended or revoked until payment of a claim, the right continues to be affected and the license continues to be suspended or revoked until the claim is satisfied in full. **Leg.H.** Added Stats 1982 ch 998 §1.

§996.490. Effect of payment by surety

(a) Payment by a surety of the amount of a bond constitutes a full discharge of all the liability of the surety on the bond.

(b) Each surety is liable to contribution to cosureties who have made payment in proportion to the amount for which each surety is liable. **Leg.H.** Added Stats 1982 ch 998 §1.

§996.495. Enforcement of judgment

A judgment of liability on a bond may be enforced in the same manner and to the same extent as other money judgments. **Leg.H.** Added Stats 1982 ch 998 §1.

ARTICLE 15
Enforcement Lien

Application of article. §996.510.
Affidavit. §996.520.
Certification by clerk. §996.530.
Recordation of certificate. §996.540.
Lien of judgment. §996.550.
Specific performance of agreement to sell property. §996.560.

§996.510. Application of article

This article applies to proceedings for the benefit of the state to enforce the liability on a bond executed to, in favor of, or payable to the state or

§996.520. Affidavit

The person enforcing the liability may file with the court in the proceedings an affidavit stating the following:

(a) The bond was executed by the defendant or one or more of the defendants (designating whom).

(b) The bond is one to which this article applies.

(c) The defendant or defendants have real property or an interest in real property (designating the county or counties in which the real property is situated).

(d) The liability is being enforced for the benefit of the state. **Leg.H.** Added Stats 1982 ch 998 §1.

§996.530. Certification by clerk

The clerk receiving the affidavit shall certify to the recorder of the county in which the real property is situated all of the following:

(a) The names of the parties.

(b) The court in which the proceedings are pending.

(c) The amount claimed.

(d) The date of commencement of the proceedings. **Leg.H.** Added Stats 1982 ch 998 §1.

§996.540. Recordation of certificate

(a) Upon receiving the certificate the county recorder shall endorse upon it the time of its receipt.

(b) The certificate shall be filed and recorded in the same manner as notice of the pendency of an action affecting real property. **Leg.H.** Added Stats 1982 ch 998 §1.

§996.550. Lien of judgment

(a) Any judgment recovered is a lien upon all real property belonging to the defendant situated in any county in which the certificate is filed, from the filing of the certificate.

(b) The lien is for the amount for which the owner of the real property is liable upon the judgment. **Leg.H.** Added Stats 1982 ch 998 §1.

§996.560. Specific performance of agreement to sell property

If an agreement to sell real property affected by the lien created by the filing of a certificate was made before the filing of the certificate and the purchase price under the agreement was not due until after the filing of the certificate, and the purchaser is otherwise entitled to specific performance of the agreement:

(a) The court in an action to compel specific performance of the agreement shall order the purchaser to pay the purchase price, or so much of the purchase price as may be due, to the State Treasurer, and to take the State Treasurer's receipt for payment.

(b) Upon payment, the purchaser is entitled to enforcement of specific performance of the agreement. The purchaser takes the real property free from the lien created by the filing of the certificate.

(c) The State Treasurer shall hold the payment pending the proceedings referred to in the certificate. The payment is subject to the lien created by the filing of the certificate. **Leg.H.** Added Stats 1982 ch 998 §1.

§997. [Section repealed 1972]

Leg.H. Enacted 1872. Amended Code Amdts 1873–74 ch 383 §135; Stats 1933 ch 744 §171; Stats 1951 ch 1737 §129, operative January 1, 1952; Stats 1967 ch 81 §1; Stats 1969 ch 277 §1. Repealed Stats 1971 ch 1679 §1. See CCP §§998.

CHAPTER 3
OFFERS BY A PARTY TO COMPROMISE

Offer to compromise; Recovery of costs; Inapplicability of law. §998.

§998. Offer to compromise; Recovery of costs; Inapplicability of law

(a) The costs allowed under Sections 1031 and 1032 shall be withheld or augmented as provided in this section.

(b) Not less than 10 days prior to commencement of trial or arbitration (as provided in Section 1281 or 1295) of a dispute to be resolved by arbitration, any party may serve an offer in writing upon any other party to the action to allow judgment to be taken or an award to be entered in accordance with the terms and conditions stated at that time. The written offer shall include a statement of the offer, containing the terms and conditions of the judgment or award, and a provision that allows the accepting party to indicate acceptance of the offer by signing a statement that the offer is accepted. Any acceptance of the offer, whether made on the document containing the offer or on a separate document of acceptance, shall be in writing and shall be signed by counsel for the accepting party or, if not represented by counsel, by the accepting party.

(1) If the offer is accepted, the offer with proof of acceptance shall be filed and the clerk or the judge shall enter judgment accordingly. In the case of an arbitration, the offer with proof of acceptance shall be filed with the arbitrator or arbitrators who shall promptly render an award accordingly.

(2) If the offer is not accepted prior to trial or arbitration or within 30 days after it is made, whichever occurs first, it shall be deemed withdrawn, and cannot be given in evidence upon the trial or arbitration.

(3) For purposes of this subdivision, a trial or arbitration shall be deemed to be actually commenced at the beginning of the opening statement of the plaintiff or counsel, or, if there is no opening statement, at the time of the administering of the oath or affirmation to the first witness, or the introduction of any evidence.

(c)(1) If an offer made by a defendant is not accepted and the plaintiff fails to obtain a more favorable judgment or award, the plaintiff shall not recover [1] **their** postoffer costs and shall pay the defendant's costs from the time of the offer. In addition, in any action or proceeding other than an eminent domain action, the court or arbitrator, in its discretion, may require the plaintiff to pay a reasonable sum to cover postoffer costs of the services of expert witnesses, who are not regular employees of any party, actually incurred and reasonably necessary in either, or both, preparation for trial or arbitration, or during trial or arbitration, of the case by the defendant.

(2)(A) In determining whether the plaintiff obtains a more favorable judgment, the court or arbitrator shall exclude the postoffer costs.

(B) It is the intent of the Legislature in enacting subparagraph (A) to supersede the holding in Encinitas Plaza Real v. Knight, 209 Cal.App.3d 996, that attorney's fees awarded to the prevailing party were not costs for purposes of this section but were part of the judgment.

(d) If an offer made by a plaintiff is not accepted and the defendant fails to obtain a more favorable judgment or award in any action or proceeding other than an eminent domain action, the court or arbitrator, in its discretion, may require the defendant to pay a reasonable sum to cover postoffer costs of the services of expert witnesses, who are not regular employees of any party, actually incurred and reasonably necessary in either, or both, preparation for trial or arbitration, or during trial or arbitration, of the case by the plaintiff, in addition to plaintiff's costs.

(e) If an offer made by a defendant is not accepted and the plaintiff fails to obtain a more favorable judgment or award, the costs under this section, from the time of the offer, shall be deducted from any damages awarded in favor of the plaintiff. If the costs awarded under this section exceed the amount of the damages awarded to the plaintiff the net amount shall be awarded to the defendant and judgment or award shall be entered accordingly.

(f) Police officers shall be deemed to be expert witnesses for the purposes of this section. For purposes of this section, "plaintiff" includes a cross-complainant and "defendant" includes a cross-defendant. Any judgment or award entered pursuant to this section shall be deemed to be a compromise settlement.

(g) This chapter does not apply to either of the following:

(1) An offer that is made by a plaintiff in an eminent domain action.

(2) Any enforcement action brought in the name of the people of the State of California by the Attorney General, **the Insurance Commissioner,** a district attorney, or a city attorney, acting as a public prosecutor.

(h) The costs for services of expert witnesses for trial under subdivisions (c) and (d) shall not exceed those specified in Section 68092.5 of the Government Code.

(i) This section shall not apply to labor arbitrations filed pursuant to memoranda of understanding under the Ralph C. Dills Act (Chapter 10.3 (commencing with Section 3512) of Division 4 of Title 1 of the Government Code). **Leg.H.** Added Stats 1971 ch 1679 §3. Amended Stats 1977 ch 458 §1; Stats 1986 ch 540 §14; Stats 1987 ch 1080 §8; Stats 1994 ch 332 §1 (SB 1324); Stats 1997 ch 892 §1 (SB 73); Stats 1999 ch 353 §1 (SB 1161); Stats 2001 ch 153 §1 (AB 732); Stats 2005 ch 706 §13 (AB 1742), effective January 1, 2006; Stats 2015 ch 345 §2 (AB 1141), effective January 1, 2016; Stats 2024 ch 444 §2 (SB 577), effective January 1, 2025.

§998. 2024 Deletes. [1] his or her

Prior Law: Former CCP §998, relating to offer of judgment prior to trial or at settlement conference, was added Stats 1969 ch 570 §1 and repealed Stats 1971 ch 1679 §2.

§1000. [Section repealed 1958]

Leg.H. Enacted 1872. Amended Code Amdts 1873–74 ch 383 §136, Code Amdts 1880 ch 75 §1; Stats 1933 ch 744 §172; Stats 1951 ch 1737 §130, operative January 1, 1952. Repealed Stats 1957 ch 1904 §1, operative January 1, 1958. See CCP §2031.

CHAPTER 3.2
TIME-LIMITED DEMANDS

Public policy declaration; Definitions. § 999.
Written requirements. § 999.1.
Delivery requirements. § 999.2.
Demand acceptance. § 999.3.
Compliance; Conflict of laws. § 999.4.
Applicability of chapter. § 999.5.

§ 999. Public policy declaration; Definitions

(a) It is declared to be the public policy of the State of California that prompt settlements of civil actions and claims are encouraged as beneficial to claimants, policyholders, and insurers.

(b) For purposes of this section, the following definitions apply:

(1) "Extracontractual damages" means any amount of damage that exceeds the total available limit of liability insurance for all of a liability insurer's liability insurance policies applicable to a claim for property damage, personal injury, bodily injury, or wrongful death.

(2) "Time-limited demand" means an offer prior to the filing of the complaint or demand for arbitration to settle any cause of action or a claim for personal injury, property damage, bodily injury, or wrongful death made by or on behalf of a claimant to a tortfeasor with a liability insurance policy for purposes of settling the claim against the tortfeasor within the insurer's limit of liability insurance, which by its terms must be accepted within a specified period of time. **Leg.H.** Added Stats 2022 ch 719 §1 (SB 1155), effective January 1, 2023.

Prior Law Former CCP §999, relating to offer to allow judgment in motor vehicle action for damages, was added Stats 1971 ch 1150 §2, operative January 1, 1972 and repealed December 31, 1973, by terms of Stats 1971 ch 1150 §5.

§ 999.1. Written requirements

A time-limited demand to settle any claim shall be in writing, be labeled as a time-limited demand or reference this section, and contain material terms, which include the following:

(a) The time period within which the demand must be accepted shall be not fewer than 30 days from date of transmission of the demand, if transmission is by email, facsimile, or certified mail, or not fewer than 33 days, if transmission is by mail.

(b) A clear and unequivocal offer to settle all claims within policy limits, including the satisfaction of all liens.

(c) An offer for a complete release from the claimant for the liability insurer's insureds from all present and future liability for the occurrence.

(d) The date and location of the loss.

(e) The claim number, if known.

(f) A description of all known injuries sustained by the claimant.

(g) Reasonable proof, which may include, if applicable, medical records or bills, sufficient to support the claim. **Leg.H.** Added Stats 2022 ch 719 §1 (SB 1155), effective January 1, 2023.

§ 999.2. Delivery requirements

(a) A claimant shall send their time-limited demand to either of the following:

(1) The email address or physical address designated by the liability insurer for receipt of time-limited demands for purposes of this chapter, if an address has been provided by the liability insurer to the Department of Insurance and the Department of Insurance has made the address publicly available.

(2) The insurance representative assigned to handle the claim, if known.

(b) To implement this section, the Department of Insurance shall post on its internet website the email address or physical address designated by a liability insurer for receipt of time-limited demands for purposes of this chapter.

(c) An act by the Department of Insurance pursuant to this section is a discretionary act for purposes of Section 820.2 of the Government Code. **Leg.H.** Added Stats 2022 ch 719 §1 (SB 1155), effective January 1, 2023.

§ 999.3. Demand acceptance

(a) The recipients of a time-limited demand may accept the demand by providing written acceptance of the material terms outlined in Section 999.1 in their entirety.

(b) Upon receipt of a time-limited demand, an attempt to seek clarification or additional information or a request for an extension due to the need for further information or investigation, made during the time within which to accept a time-limited demand, shall not, in and of itself, be deemed a counteroffer or rejection of the demand.

(c) If, for any reason, an insurer does not accept a time-limited demand, the insurer shall notify the claimant, in writing, of its decision and the basis for its decision. This notification shall be sent prior to the expiration of the time-limited demand, including any extension agreed to by the parties, and shall be relevant in any lawsuit alleging extracontractual damages against the tortfeasor's liability insurer. **Leg.H.** Added Stats 2022 ch 719 §1 (SB 1155), effective January 1, 2023.

§ 999.4. Compliance; Conflict of laws

(a) In any lawsuit filed by a claimant, or by a claimant as an assignee of the tortfeasor or by the tortfeasor for the benefit of the claimant, a time-limited demand that does not substantially comply with the terms of this chapter shall not be considered to be a reasonable offer to settle the claims against the tortfeasor for an amount within the insurance policy limits for purposes of any lawsuit alleging extracontractual damages against the tortfeasor's liability insurer.

(b) This section shall not apply to a claimant that is not represented by counsel.

(c) In the event a court determines that this chapter conflicts with the Civil Discovery Act, (Title 4 (commencing with Section 2016.010) of Part 4), the Civil Discovery Act shall prevail. **Leg.H.** Added Stats 2022 ch 719 §1 (SB 1155), effective January 1, 2023.

§ 999.5. Applicability of chapter

(a) This chapter shall only apply to causes of action and claims covered under automobile, motor vehicle, homeowner, or commercial premises liability insurance policies for property damage, personal or bodily injury, and wrongful death claims.

(b) Except as provided in this chapter, nothing shall alter existing law, including law relating to claims, damages, and defenses, that may be asserted in litigation seeking extracontractual damages.

(c) This chapter shall apply to time-limited demands transmitted on or after January 1, 2023. **Leg.H.** Added Stats 2022 ch 719 §1 (SB 1155), effective January 1, 2023.

CHAPTER 3.5
CONFIDENTIAL SETTLEMENT AGREEMENTS

No disclosure of factual information related to civil or administrative actions; Various causes of actions. §1001.
Prohibition against settlement agreement provision or court order preventing or restricting disclosure of certain factual information in civil action with factual foundation establishing cause of action for civil damages for specified sexual offenses; Failure of attorney to comply. §1002.

§1001. No disclosure of factual information related to civil or administrative actions; Various causes of actions

(a) Notwithstanding any other law, a provision within a settlement agreement that prevents or restricts the disclosure of factual information related to a claim filed in a civil action or a complaint filed in an administrative action, regarding any of the following, is prohibited:

(1) An act of sexual assault that is not governed by subdivision (a) of Section 1002.

(2) An act of sexual harassment, as defined in Section 51.9 of the Civil Code.

(3) An act of workplace harassment or discrimination, failure to prevent an act of workplace harassment or discrimination, or an act of retaliation against a person for reporting or opposing harassment or discrimination, as described in subdivisions (a), (h), (i), (j), and (k) of Section 12940 of the Government Code.

(4) An act of harassment or discrimination, or an act of retaliation against a person for reporting harassment or discrimination by the owner of a housing accommodation, as described in Section 12955 of the Government Code.

(b) Notwithstanding any other law, in a civil matter described in paragraphs (1) to (4), inclusive, of subdivision (a), a court shall not enter, by stipulation or otherwise, an order that restricts the disclosure of information in a manner that conflicts with subdivision (a).

(c) Notwithstanding subdivisions (a) and (b), a provision that shields the identity of the claimant and all facts that could lead to the discovery of the claimant's identity, including pleadings filed in court, may be included within a settlement agreement at the request of the claimant. This subdivision does not apply if a government agency or public official is a party to the settlement agreement.

(d) Except as authorized by subdivision (c), a provision within a settlement agreement that prevents or restricts the disclosure of factual information related to the claim described in subdivision (a) that is entered into on or after January 1, 2019, is void as a matter of law and against public policy.

(e) This section does not prohibit the entry or enforcement of a provision in any agreement that precludes the disclosure of the amount paid in settlement of a claim.

(f) In determining the factual foundation of a cause of action for civil damages under subdivision (a), a court may consider the pleadings and other papers in the record, or any other findings of the court.

(g) The amendments made to paragraphs (3) and (4) of subdivision (a) by Senate Bill 331 of the 2021-22 Regular Session apply only to agreements entered into on or after January 1, 2022. All other amendments made to this section by Senate Bill 331 of the 2021-22 Regular Session shall not be construed as substantive changes, but instead as merely clarifying existing law. **Leg.H.** Added Stats 2018 ch 953 §1 (SB 820), effective January 1, 2019. Amended Stats 2021 ch 638 §1 (SB 331), effective January 1, 2022; Stats 2022 ch 28 §26 (SB 1380), effective January 1, 2023.

§1002. Prohibition against settlement agreement provision or court order preventing or restricting disclosure of certain factual information in civil action with factual foundation establishing cause of action for civil damages for specified sexual offenses; Failure of attorney to comply

(a) Notwithstanding any other law, a provision within a settlement agreement that prevents the disclosure of factual information related to the action is prohibited in any civil action the factual foundation for which establishes a cause of action for civil damages for any of the following:

(1) An act that may be prosecuted as a felony sex offense.

(2) An act of childhood sexual assault, as defined in Section 340.1.

(3) An act of sexual exploitation of a minor, as defined in Section 11165.1 of the Penal Code, or conduct prohibited with respect to a minor pursuant to Section 311.1, 311.5, or 311.6 of the Penal Code.

(4) An act of sexual assault, as defined in paragraphs (1) to (8), inclusive, of subdivision (e) of Section 15610.63 of the Welfare and Institutions Code, against an elder or dependent adult, as defined in Sections 15610.23 and 15610.27 of the Welfare and Institutions Code.

(b) Notwithstanding any other law, in a civil action described in paragraphs (1) to (4), inclusive, of subdivision (a), a court shall not enter, by stipulation or otherwise, an order that restricts the disclosure of information in a manner that conflicts with subdivision (a).

(c) Subdivisions (a) and (b) do not preclude an agreement preventing the disclosure of any medical information or personal identifying information, as defined in subdivision (b) of Section 530.55 of the Penal Code, regarding the victim of the offense listed in subdivision (a) or of any information revealing the nature of the relationship between the victim and the defendant. This subdivision shall not be construed to limit the right of a crime victim to disclose this information.

(d) Except as authorized by subdivision (c), a provision within a settlement agreement that prevents the disclosure of factual information related to the action described in subdivision (a) that is entered into on or after January 1, 2017, is void as a matter of law and against public policy.

(e) An attorney's failure to comply with the requirements of this section by demanding that a provision be included in a settlement agreement that prevents the disclosure of factual information related to the action described in subdivision (a) that is not otherwise authorized by subdivision (c) as a condition of settlement, or advising a client to sign an agreement that includes such a provision, may be grounds for professional discipline and the State Bar of California shall investigate and take appropriate action in any such case brought to its attention. **Leg.H.** Added Stats 2006 ch 151 §1 (AB 2875), effective January 1, 2007. Amended Stats 2016 ch 876 §1 (AB 1682), effective January 1, 2017; Stats 2017 ch 561 §24 (AB 1516), effective January 1, 2018; Stats 2019 ch 861 §2 (AB 218), effective January 1, 2020; Stats 2023 ch 131 §22 (AB 1754), effective January 1, 2024.

CHAPTER 3.6
AGREEMENTS SETTLING EMPLOYMENT DISPUTES

Agreements settling employment disputes; Prohibition of preventing a person from obtaining future employment. §1002.5.

§1002.5. Agreements settling employment disputes; Prohibition of preventing a person from obtaining future employment

(a) An agreement to settle an employment dispute shall not contain a provision prohibiting, preventing, or otherwise restricting a settling party that is an aggrieved person from obtaining future employment with the employer against which the aggrieved person has filed a claim, or any parent company, subsidiary, division, affiliate, or contractor of the employer. A provision in an agreement entered into on or after January 1, 2020, that violates this section is void as a matter of law and against public policy.

(b) Nothing in subdivision (a) does any of the following:

(1) Preclude the employer and aggrieved person from making an agreement to do either of the following:

(A) End a current employment relationship.

(B) Prohibit or otherwise restrict the settling aggrieved person from obtaining future employment with the settling employer, if the employer has made and documented a good faith determination, before the aggrieved person filed the claim that the aggrieved person engaged in sexual harassment, sexual assault, or any criminal conduct.

(2) Require an employer to continue to employ or rehire a person if there is a legitimate non-discriminatory or non-retaliatory reason for terminating the employment relationship or refusing to rehire the person.

(c) For purposes of this section:

(1) "Aggrieved person" means a person who, in good faith, has filed a claim against the person's employer in court, before an administrative agency, in an alternative dispute resolution forum, or through the employer's internal complaint process.

(2) "Sexual assault" means conduct that would constitute a crime under Section 243.3, 261, 262, 264.1, 286, 287, or 289 of the Penal Code, assault with the intent to commit any of those crimes, or an attempt to commit any of those crimes.

(3) "Sexual harassment" has the same meaning as in subdivision (j) of Section 12940 of the Government Code. **Leg.H.** Added Stats 2019 ch 808 §1 (AB 749), effective January 1, 2020. Amended Stats 2020 ch 73 §1 (AB 2143), effective January 1, 2021; Stats 2020 ch 370 §37 (SB 1371), effective January 1, 2021 (ch 73 prevails).

CHAPTER 3.7
ENROLLMENT AGREEMENTS

Legislative findings and declarations; Definitions. § 1002.7.

§ 1002.7. Legislative findings and declarations; Definitions

(a) The Legislature finds and declares that it is unconscionable for a parent, on behalf of the parent's minor child, to be required to waive a legal right, remedy, forum, proceeding, or procedure, including the right to file and pursue a civil action, belonging to that minor child with respect to claims arising out of a criminal sexual assault or criminal sexual battery as a condition of enrollment in an educational institution.

(b) Notwithstanding Chapter 2 (commencing with Section 6710) of Part 3 of Division 11 of the Family Code, a provision in an educational institution's enrollment agreement that purports to waive a legal right, remedy, forum, proceeding, or procedure may be disaffirmed by the minor, regardless of whether a parent or legal guardian has signed the enrollment agreement on the minor's behalf, to the extent that the provision is construed to require the minor to waive a legal right, remedy, forum, proceeding, or procedure arising out of a criminal sexual assault or criminal sexual battery on that minor.

(c) The fact that a provision in an enrollment agreement has been disaffirmed by the minor pursuant to this section does not affect the validity or enforceability of any other provision of the enrollment agreement.

(d) For purposes of this section, the following definitions apply:

(1) "Criminal sexual assault" means an act that was perpetrated against a person under 18 years of age and that would be a crime under Section 261.5, 286, 287, 288, 288.7, or 289 of the Penal Code, or any predecessor statute.

(2) "Criminal sexual battery" means an act that was perpetrated against a person under 18 years of age and that would be a crime under Section 243.4 of the Penal Code.

(3) "Educational institution" means a public or private school maintaining a kindergarten or any of grades 1 through 12.

(4) "Enrollment agreement" means a written contract between a student and institution concerning an educational program. **Leg.H.** Added Stats 2021 ch 146 §1 (AB 272), effective January 1, 2022.

CHAPTER 4
MOTIONS AND ORDERS

"Order" and "motion". §1003.
Court in which motion made. §1004.
Requirement of written notice for certain motions; Time for serving and filing; Method of serving. §1005.
Proceedings on service of motion. §1005.5.
Transfer of proceeding. §1006.
Subsequent application. §1008.

§1003. "Order" and "motion"

Every direction of a court or judge, made or entered in writing, and not included in a judgment, is denominated an order. An application for an order is a motion. **Leg.H.** Enacted 1872. Amended Stats 1933 ch 744 §173; Stats 1951 ch 1737 §131, operative January 1, 1952.

§1004. Court in which motion made

Except as provided in section 166 of this code, motions must be made in the court in which the action is pending. **Leg.H.** Enacted 1872. Amended Code Amdts 1880 ch 23 §1; Stats 1933 ch 744 §173.

§1005. Requirement of written notice for certain motions; Time for serving and filing; Method of serving

(a) Written notice shall be given, as prescribed in subdivisions (b) and (c), for the following motions:

(1) Notice of Application and Hearing for Writ of Attachment under Section 484.040.

(2) Notice of Application and Hearing for Claim and Delivery under Section 512.030.

(3) Notice of Hearing for Claim of Exemption under Section 706.105.

(4) Motion to Quash Summons pursuant to subdivision (b) of Section 418.10.

(5) Motion for Determination of Good Faith Settlement pursuant to Section 877.6.

(6) Hearing for Discovery of Peace Officer Personnel Records in a civil action pursuant to Section 1043 of the Evidence Code.

(7) Notice of Hearing of Third-Party Claim pursuant to Section 720.320.

(8) Motion for an Order to Attend Deposition more than 150 miles from deponent's residence pursuant to Section 2025.260.

(9) Notice of Hearing of Application for Relief pursuant to Section 946.6 of the Government Code.

(10) Motion to Set Aside Default or Default Judgment and for Leave to Defend Actions pursuant to Section 473.5.

(11) Motion to Expunge Notice of Pendency of Action pursuant to Section 405.30.

(12) Motion to Set Aside Default and for Leave to Amend pursuant to Section 585.5.

(13) Any other proceeding under this code in which notice is required, and no other time or method is prescribed by law or by court or judge.

(b) Unless otherwise ordered or specifically provided by law, all moving and supporting papers shall be served and filed at least 16 court days before the hearing. The moving and supporting papers served shall be a copy of the papers filed or to be filed with the court. However, if the notice is served by mail, the required 16-day period of notice before the hearing shall be increased by five calendar days if the place of mailing and the place of address are within the State of California, 10 calendar days if either the place of mailing or the place of address is outside the State of California but within the United States, 12 calendar days if the place of address is the Secretary of State's address confidentiality program (Chapter 3.1 (commencing with Section 6205) of Division 7 of Title 1 of the Government Code), and 20 calendar days if either the place of mailing or the place of address is outside the United States, and if the notice is served by facsimile transmission, express mail, or another method of delivery providing for overnight delivery, the required 16-day period of notice before the hearing shall be increased by two calendar days. Section 1013, which extends the time within which a right may be exercised or an act may be done, does not apply to a notice of motion, papers opposing a motion, or reply papers governed by this section. All papers opposing a motion so noticed shall be filed with the court and a copy served on each party at least nine court days, and all reply papers at least five court days before the hearing.

The court, or a judge thereof, may prescribe a shorter time.

(c) Notwithstanding any other provision of this section, all papers opposing a motion and all reply papers shall be served by personal delivery, facsimile transmission, express mail, or other means consistent with Sections 1010, 1011, 1012, and 1013, and reasonably calculated to ensure delivery to the other party or parties not later than the close of the next business day after the time the opposing papers or reply papers, as applicable, are filed. This subdivision applies to the service of opposition and reply papers regarding motions for summary judgment or summary adjudication, in addition to the motions listed in subdivision (a).

The court, or a judge thereof, may prescribe a shorter time. **Leg.H.** Enacted 1872. Amended Code Amdts 1880 ch 23 §2; Stats 1907 ch 326 §1; Stats 1919 ch 195 §1; Stats 1933 ch 744 §175; Stats 1935 ch 658 §1, ch 722 §27; Stats 1951 ch 1737 §132, operative January 1, 1952; Stats 1963 ch 878 §3; Stats 1980 ch 196 §1; Stats 1981 ch 197 §1; Stats 1984 ch 352 §2; Stats 1986 ch 246 §1; Stats 1989 ch 693 §6; Stats 1990 ch 1491 §7 (AB 3765); Stats 1991 ch 1090 §5 (AB 1484); Stats 1992 ch 339 §2 (SB 1409); Stats 1993 ch 456 §14.5 (AB 58); Stats 1997 ch 571 §1.3 (AB 1088); Stats 1998 ch 932 §18 (AB 1094); Stats 1999 ch 43 §1 (AB 1132); Stats 2002 ch 806 §16 (AB 3027); Stats 2004 ch 171 §3 (AB 3078) (ch 171 prevails), ch 182 §13 (AB 3081); Stats 2005 ch 294 §3 (AB 333), effective January 1, 2006; Stats 2019 ch 585 §1 (AB 1600), effective January 1, 2020; Stats 2022 ch 686 §1 (AB 1726), effective January 1, 2023.

§1005.5. Proceedings on service of motion

A motion upon all the grounds stated in the written notice thereof is deemed to have been made and to be pending before the court for all purposes, upon the due service and filing of the notice of motion, but this shall not deprive a party of a hearing of the motion to which he is otherwise entitled. Procedure upon a motion for new trial shall be as otherwise provided. **Leg.H.** Added Stats 1953 ch 909 §1.

§1006. Transfer of proceeding

When a notice of motion is given, or an order to show cause is made returnable before a judge out of court, and at the time fixed for the motion, or on the return day of the order, the judge is unable to hear the parties, the matter may be transferred by his order to some other judge, before whom it might originally have been brought. **Leg.H.** Enacted 1872. Amended Stats 1933 ch 744 §176; Stats 1951 ch 1737 §133, operative January 1, 1952.

§1006.5. [Section repealed 2008]

Leg.H. Added Stats 1982 ch 411 §2. Amended Stats 1992 ch 163 §56 (AB 2641), operative January 1, 1994. Repealed Stats 2007 ch 268 §4 (AB 500), effective January 1, 2008. The repealed section related to appearance of counsel by telephone.

§1007. [Section repealed 1983]

Leg.H. Enacted 1872. Repealed Stats 1982 ch 497 §67, operative July 1, 1983. The repealed section related to enforcement of order for payment of money.

§1008. Subsequent application

(a) When an application for an order has been made to a judge, or to a court, and refused in whole or in part, or granted, or granted conditionally, or on terms, any party affected by the order may, within 10 days after service upon the party of written notice of entry of the order and based upon new or different facts, circumstances, or law, make application to the same judge or court that made the order, to reconsider the matter and modify, amend, or revoke the prior order. The party making the application shall state by affidavit what application was made before, when and to what judge, what order or decisions were made, and what new or different facts, circumstances, or law are claimed to be shown.

(b) A party who originally made an application for an order which was refused in whole or part, or granted conditionally or on terms, may make a subsequent application for the same order upon new or different facts, circumstances, or law, in which case it shall be shown by affidavit what application was made before, when and to what judge, what order or decisions were made, and what new or different facts, circumstances, or law are claimed to be shown. For a failure to comply with this subdivision, any order made on a subsequent application may be revoked or set aside on ex parte motion.

(c) If a court at any time determines that there has been a change of law that warrants it to reconsider a prior order it entered, it may do so on its own motion and enter a different order.

(d) A violation of this section may be punished as a contempt and with sanctions as allowed by Section 128.7. In addition, an order made contrary to this section may be revoked by the judge or commissioner who made it, or vacated by a judge of the court in which the action or proceeding is pending.

(e) This section specifies the court's jurisdiction with regard to applications for reconsideration of its orders and renewals of previous motions, and applies to all applications to reconsider any order of a judge or court, or for the renewal of a previous motion, whether the order deciding the previous matter or motion is interim or final. No application to reconsider any order or for the renewal of a previous motion may be considered by any judge or court unless made according to this section.

(f) For the purposes of this section, an alleged new or different law shall not include a later enacted statute without a retroactive application.

(g) An order denying a motion for reconsideration made pursuant to subdivision (a) is not separately appealable. However, if the order that was the subject of a motion for reconsideration is appealable, the denial of the motion for reconsideration is reviewable as part of an appeal from that order.

(h) This section applies to all applications for interim orders. **Leg.H.** Added Stats 1978 ch 631 §2. Amended Stats 1992 ch 460 §4 (SB 1805); Stats 1998 ch 200 §2 (SB 1556); Stats 2011 ch 78 §1 (AB 1067), effective January 1, 2012.

Prior Law: Former CCP §1008, similar to the present section, was added Stats 1933 ch 744 §177, amended Stats 1951 ch 1737 §134, operative January 1, 1952 and repealed Stats 1978 ch 631 §1.

CHAPTER 5
NOTICES, AND FILING AND SERVICE OF PAPERS

Notices and papers; Form, contents, service on party, etc. §1010.
Rules for filing by facsimile transmission; Credit card fee payment. §1010.5.
Electronic service by parties or court; Adoption of local rules; Adoption of uniform rules. §1010.6.
Personal service; Modes and requirements. §1011.
When service by mail permitted. §1012.
Manner and completion of service by mail, Express Mail, facsimile transmission, or electronically. §1013.
Proof of service by mail. §1013a.
Proof of electronic service. §1013b.
Appearance. §1014.
Service when party resides out of state. §1015.
Preceding provisions not to apply to proceeding to bring party into contempt. §1016.
Service by telegraph. §1017.
Size of type in notice or publication. §1019.
Notice of grant or denial of motion. §1019.5.
Notices by registered mail. §1020.

§1010. Notices and papers; Form, contents, service on party, etc.

Notices must be in writing, and the notice of a motion, other than for a new trial, must state when, and the grounds upon which it will be made, and the papers, if any, upon which it is to be based. If any such paper has not previously been served upon the party to be notified and was not filed by him, a copy of such paper must accompany the notice. Notices and other papers may be served upon the party or attorney in the manner prescribed in this chapter, when not otherwise provided by this code. No bill of exceptions, notice of appeal, or other notice or paper, other than amendments to the pleadings, or an amended pleading, need be served upon any party whose default has been duly entered or who has not appeared in the action or proceeding. **Leg.H.** Enacted 1872. Amended Stats 1907 ch 327 §1; Stats 1935 ch 722 §28.

§1010.5. Rules for filing by facsimile transmission; Credit card fee payment

The Judicial Council may adopt rules permitting the filing of papers by facsimile transmission, both directly with the courts and through third parties. Notwithstanding any other provision of law, the rules may provide that the facsimile transmitted document shall constitute an original document, and that notwithstanding Section 6159 of the Government Code or Title 1.3 (commencing with Section 1747) of Part 4 of Division 3 of the Civil Code, any court authorized to accept a credit card as payment pursuant to this section may add a surcharge to the amount of the transaction to be borne by the litigant to cover charges imposed on credit card transactions regarding fax filings between a litigant and the court.

If the Judicial Council adopts rules permitting the filing of papers by facsimile transmission, the consent of the Judicial Council shall not be necessary to permit the use of credit cards to pay fees for the filing of papers by facsimile transmission directly with the court, provided that the court charges a processing fee to the filing party sufficient to cover the cost to the court of processing payment by credit card. **Leg.H.** Added Stats 1992 ch 339 §3 (SB 1409). Amended Stats 2001 ch 824 §10 (AB 1700).

§1010.6. Electronic service by parties or court; Adoption of local rules; Adoption of uniform rules

(a) A document may be served electronically in an action filed with the court as provided in this section, in accordance with rules adopted pursuant to subdivision (h).

(1) For purposes of this section:

(A) "Electronic service" means service of a document, on a person, by either electronic transmission or electronic notification. Electronic service may be performed directly by a person, including a party, by a person's agent, including the person's attorney, or through an electronic filing service provider, and by a court.

(B) "Electronic transmission" means the transmission of a document by electronic means to the electronic service address at or through which a person receives electronic service.

(C) "Electronic notification" means the notification of the person that a document is served by sending an electronic message to the electronic address at or through which the person receives electronic service, specifying the exact name of the document served, and providing a hyperlink at which the served document may be viewed and downloaded.

(D) "Electronic filing" means the electronic transmission to a court of a document presented for filing in electronic form. For purposes of this section, this definition of electronic filing concerns the activity of filing and does not include the processing and review of the document and its entry into the court's records, which are necessary for a document to be officially filed.

(2) If a document is required to be served by certified or registered mail, electronic service of the document is not authorized.

(3)(A) If a document may be served by mail, express mail, overnight delivery, or facsimile transmission, electronic service of that document is deemed complete at the time of the electronic transmission of the document or at the time that the electronic notification of service of the document is sent.

(B) Any period of notice, or any right or duty to do any act or make any response within any period or on a date certain after the service of the document, which time period or date is prescribed by statute or rule of court, shall be extended after service by electronic means by two court days, but the extension shall not apply to extend the time for filing any of the following:

(i) A notice of intention to move for new trial.

(ii) A notice of intention to move to vacate judgment under Section 663a.

(iii) A notice of appeal.

(C) This extension applies in the absence of a specific exception provided by any other statute or rule of court.

(4) Any document that is served electronically between 12:00 a.m. and 11:59:59 p.m. on a court day shall be deemed served on that court day. Any document that is served electronically on a noncourt day shall be deemed served on the next court day.

(5) Confidential or sealed records shall be electronically served through encrypted methods to ensure that the documents are not improperly disclosed.

(b)(1) This subdivision applies to mandatory electronic service. The court may order electronic service on a person represented by counsel who has appeared in an action or proceeding.

(2) A person represented by counsel, who has appeared in an action or proceeding, shall accept electronic service of a notice or document that may be served by mail, express mail, overnight delivery, or facsimile transmission.

(3) Before first serving a represented person electronically, the person effecting service shall confirm the appropriate electronic service address for the counsel being served.

(4) A person represented by counsel shall, upon the request of any person who has appeared in an action or proceeding and who provides an electronic service address, electronically serve the requesting person with any notice or document that may be served by mail, express mail, overnight delivery, or facsimile transmission.

(c)(1) This subdivision applies to electronic service by consent of an unrepresented person in a civil action.

(2) An unrepresented party may consent to receive electronic service.

(3) Express consent to electronic service may be given by either of the following:

(i) Serving a notice on all parties and filing the notice with the court.

(ii) Manifesting affirmative consent through electronic means with the court or the court's electronic filing service provider, and concurrently providing the party's electronic address with that consent for the purpose of receiving electronic service. The act of electronic filing shall not be construed as express consent.

(4) A person who has provided express consent to accept service electronically may withdraw consent at any time by completing and filing with the court the appropriate Judicial Council form.

(5) Consent, or the withdrawal of consent, to receive electronic service may only be completed by a person entitled to service.

(d) On and after [1] **July 1, 2025**, in any action in which a party or other person is subject to mandatory electronic service under subdivision (b) or has consented to electronic service under subdivision (c), the court shall electronically [2] **serve**, to a person subject to mandatory electronic service or who consented to electronic service, any document issued by the court that the court is required to transmit, deliver, or serve. The electronic service of documents by the court shall have the same legal effect as service by mail, except as provided in paragraph (3) of subdivision (a).

(e) A trial court may adopt local rules permitting electronic filing of documents, subject to rules adopted by the Judicial Council pursuant to subdivision (h) and the following conditions:

(1) A document that is filed electronically shall have the same legal effect as an original paper document.

(2)(A) When a document to be filed requires the signature of any person, not under penalty of perjury, the document shall be deemed to have been signed by that person if filed electronically and if either of the following conditions is satisfied:

(i) The filer is the signer.

(ii) The person has signed the document pursuant to the procedure set forth in the California Rules of Court.

(B) When a document to be filed requires the signature, under penalty of perjury, of any person, the document shall be deemed to have been signed by that person if filed electronically and if either of the following conditions is satisfied:

(i) The person has signed a printed form of the document before, or on the same day as, the date of filing. The attorney or other person filing the document represents, by the act of filing, that the declarant has complied with this section. The attorney or other person filing the document shall maintain the printed form of the document bearing the original signature until final disposition of the case, as defined in subdivision (c) of Section 68151 of the Government Code, and make it available for review and copying upon the request of the court or any party to the action or proceeding in which it is filed.

(ii) The person has signed the document using a computer or other technology pursuant to the procedure set forth in a rule of court adopted by the Judicial Council by January 1, 2019.

(3) Any document received electronically by the court between 12:00 a.m. and 11:59:59 p.m. on a court day shall be deemed filed on that court day. Any document that is received electronically on a noncourt day shall be deemed filed on the next court day.

(4)(A) Whichever of a court, an electronic filing service provider, or an electronic filing manager is the first to receive a document submitted for electronic filing shall promptly send a confirmation of receipt of the document indicating the date and time of receipt to the party or person who submitted the document.

(B) If a document received by the court under subparagraph (A) complies with filing requirements and all required filing fees have been paid, the court shall promptly send confirmation that the document has been filed to the party or person who submitted the document.

(C) If the clerk of the court does not file a document received by the court under subparagraph (A) because the document does not comply with applicable filing requirements or the required filing fee has not been paid, the court shall promptly send notice of the rejection of the document for filing to the party or person who submitted the document. The notice of rejection shall state the reasons that the document was rejected for filing and include the date the clerk of the court sent the notice.

(D) If the court utilizes an electronic filing service provider or electronic filing manager to send the notice of rejection described in subparagraph (C), the electronic filing service provider or electronic filing manager shall promptly send the notice of rejection to the party or person who submitted the document. A notice of rejection sent pursuant to this subparagraph shall include the date the electronic filing service provider or electronic filing manager sent the notice.

(E) If the clerk of the court does not file a complaint or cross complaint because the complaint or cross complaint does not comply with applicable filing requirements or the required filing fee has not been paid, any statute of limitations applicable to the causes of action alleged in the complaint or cross complaint shall be tolled for the period beginning on the date on which the court received the document and as shown on the confirmation of receipt described in subparagraph (A), through the later of either the date on which the clerk of the court sent the notice of rejection described in subparagraph (C) or the date on which the electronic filing service provider or electronic filing manager sent the notice of rejection as described in subparagraph (D), plus one additional day if the complaint or cross complaint is subsequently submitted in a form that corrects the errors which caused the document to be rejected. The party filing the complaint or cross complaint shall not make any change to the complaint or cross complaint other than those required to correct the errors which caused the document to be rejected.

(5) Upon electronic filing of a complaint, petition, or other document that must be served with a summons, a trial court, upon request of the party filing the action, shall issue a summons with the court seal and the case number. The court shall keep the summons in its records and shall electronically transmit a copy of the summons to the requesting party. Personal service of a printed form of the electronic summons shall have the same legal effect as personal service of an original summons.

(6) The court shall permit a party or attorney to file an application for waiver of court fees and costs, in lieu of requiring the payment of the filing fee, as part of the process involving the electronic filing of a document. The court shall consider and determine the application in accordance with Article 6 (commencing with Section 68630) of Chapter 2 of Title 8 of the Government Code and shall not require the party or attorney to submit any documentation other than that set forth in Article 6 (commencing with Section 68630) of Chapter 2 of Title 8 of the Government Code. The court, an electronic filing service provider, or an electronic filing manager shall waive any fees charged to a party or the party's attorney if the party has been granted a waiver of court fees pursuant to Section 68631 of the Government Code or if the party is indigent or being represented by the public defender or court-appointed counsel. The electronic filing manager or electronic filing service provider shall not seek payment from the court of any fee waived by the court. This section does not require the court to waive a filing fee that is not otherwise waivable.

(7) If a party electronically files a filing that is exempt from the payment of filing fees under any other law, including a filing described in Section 212 of the Welfare and Institutions Code or Section 6103.9, subdivision (b) of Section 70617, or Section 70672 of the Government Code, the party shall not be required to pay any court fees associated with the electronic filing. An electronic filing service provider or an electronic filing manager shall not seek payment of these fees from the court.

(8) A fee, if any, charged by the court, an electronic filing service provider, or an electronic filing manager to process a payment for filing fees and other court fees shall not exceed the costs incurred in processing the payment.

(9) The court shall not charge fees for electronic filing and service of documents that are more than the court's actual cost of electronic filing and service of the documents.

(f)(1) Except as provided in paragraph (2), if a trial court adopts rules conforming to subdivision (e), it may provide by order, subject to the requirements and conditions stated in paragraphs (2) to (4), inclusive, of subdivision (g), and the rules adopted by the Judicial Council under subdivision (i), that all parties to an action file documents electronically in a class action, a consolidated action, a group of actions, a coordinated action, or an action that is deemed complex under Judicial Council rules, provided that the trial court's order does not cause undue hardship or significant prejudice to any party in the action.

(2) Unrepresented persons are exempt from any mandatory electronic filing imposed pursuant to this subdivision.

(g) A trial court may, by local rule, require electronic filing in civil actions, subject to the requirements and conditions stated in subdivision (e), the rules adopted by the Judicial Council under subdivision (i), and the following conditions:

(1) The court shall have the ability to maintain the official court record in electronic format for all cases where electronic filing is required.

(2) The court and the parties shall have access to more than one electronic filing service provider capable of electronically filing documents with the court or to electronic filing access directly through the court. Any fees charged by an electronic filing service provider shall be reasonable. An electronic filing manager or an electronic filing service provider shall waive any fees charged if the court deems a waiver appropriate, including in instances where a party has received a fee waiver.

(3) The court shall have a procedure for the filing of nonelectronic documents in order to prevent the program from causing undue hardship or significant prejudice to any party in an action, including, but not limited to, unrepresented parties. The Judicial Council shall make a form available to allow a party to seek an exemption from mandatory electronic filing and service on the grounds provided in this paragraph.

(4) Unrepresented persons are exempt from mandatory electronic filing imposed pursuant to this subdivision.

(5) Until January 1, 2021, a local child support agency, as defined in subdivision (h) of Section 17000 of the Family Code, is exempt from a trial court's mandatory electronic filing and service requirements, unless the Department of Child Support Services and the local child support agency determine it has the capacity and functionality to comply with the trial court's mandatory electronic filing and service requirements.

(h) The Judicial Council shall adopt uniform rules for the electronic filing and service of documents in the trial courts of the state, which shall include statewide policies on vendor contracts, privacy, and access to public records, and rules relating to the integrity of electronic service. These rules shall conform to the conditions set forth in this section, as amended from time to time.

(i) The Judicial Council shall adopt uniform rules to permit the mandatory electronic filing and service of documents for specified civil actions in the trial courts of the state, which shall include statewide policies on vendor contracts, privacy, access to public records, unrepresented parties, parties with fee waivers, hardships, reasonable exceptions to electronic filing, and rules relating to the integrity of electronic service. These rules shall conform to the conditions set forth in this section, as amended from time to time.

(j)(1) Any system for the electronic filing and service of documents, including any information technology applications, internet websites and web-based applications, used by an electronic service provider or any other vendor or contractor that provides an electronic filing and service system to a trial court, regardless of the case management system used by the trial court, shall satisfy both of the following requirements:

(A) The system shall be accessible to individuals with disabilities, including parties and attorneys with disabilities, in accordance with Section 508 of the federal Rehabilitation Act of 1973 (29 U.S.C. Sec. 794d), as amended, the regulations implementing that act set forth in Part 1194 of Title 36 of the Code of Federal Regulations and Appendices A, C, and D of that part, and the federal Americans with Disabilities Act of 1990 (42 U.S.C. Sec. 12101 et seq.).

(B) The system shall comply with the Web Content Accessibility Guidelines 2.0 at a Level AA success criteria.

(2) Commencing on June 27, 2017, the vendor or contractor shall provide an accommodation to an individual with a disability in accordance with subparagraph (D) of paragraph (3).

(3) A trial court that contracts with an entity for the provision of a system for electronic filing and service of documents shall require the entity, in the trial court's contract with the entity, to do all of the following:

(A) Test and verify that the entity's system complies with this subdivision and provide the verification to the Judicial Council no later than June 30, 2019.

(B) Respond to, and resolve, any complaints regarding the accessibility of the system that are brought to the attention of the entity.

(C) Designate a lead individual to whom any complaints concerning accessibility may be addressed and post the individual's name and contact information on the entity's internet website.

(D) Provide to an individual with a disability, upon request, an accommodation to enable the individual to file and serve documents electronically at no additional charge for any time period that the entity is not compliant with paragraph (1). Exempting an individual with a disability from mandatory electronic filing and service of documents shall not be deemed an accommodation unless the person chooses that as an accommodation. The vendor or contractor shall clearly state on its internet website that an individual with a disability may request an accommodation and the process for submitting a request for an accommodation.

(4) A trial court that provides electronic filing and service of documents directly to the public shall comply with this subdivision to the same extent as a vendor or contractor that provides electronic filing and services to a trial court.

(5)(A) The Judicial Council shall submit four reports to the appropriate committees of the Legislature relating to the trial courts that have implemented a system of electronic filing and service of documents. The first report is due by June 30, 2018; the second report is due by December 31, 2019; the third report is due by December 31, 2021; and the fourth report is due by December 31, 2023.

(B) The Judicial Council's reports shall include all of the following information:

(i) The name of each court that has implemented a system of electronic filing and service of documents.

(ii) A description of the system of electronic filing and service.

(iii) The name of the entity or entities providing the system.

(iv) A statement as to whether the system complies with this subdivision and, if the system is not fully compliant, a description of the actions that have been taken to make the system compliant.

(6) An entity that contracts with a trial court to provide a system for electronic filing and service of documents shall cooperate with the Judicial Council by providing all information, and by permitting all testing, necessary for the Judicial Council to prepare its reports to the Legislature in a complete and timely manner. **Leg.H.** Added Stats 1999 ch 514 §1 (SB 367). Amended Stats 2001 ch 824 §10.5 (AB 1700); Stats 2005 ch 300 §5 (AB 496), effective January 1, 2006; Stats 2010 ch 156 §1 (SB 1274), effective January 1, 2011; Stats 2011 ch 296 §40 (AB 1023), effective January 1, 2012; Stats 2012 ch 320 §1 (AB 2073), effective January 1, 2013; Stats 2016 ch 461 §1 (AB 2244), effective January 1, 2017; Stats 2017 ch 17 §5 (AB 103), effective June 27, 2017; Stats 2017 ch 319 §2 (AB 976), effective January 1, 2018; Stats 2018 ch 504 §1 (AB 3248), effective January 1, 2019; Stats 2020 ch 112 §2 (SB 1146), effective September 18, 2020; Stats 2020 ch 215 §1.5 (AB 2165), effective January 1, 2021; Stats 2021 ch 124 §14 (AB 938), effective January 1, 2022; Stats 2021 ch 214 §7 (SB 241), effective January 1, 2022 (ch 214 prevails); Stats 2022 ch 215 §1 (AB 2961), effective January 1, 2023; Stats 2024 ch 151 §1 (AB 2283), effective July 18, 2024.

§1010.6. 2024 Deletes. [1] July 1, 2024 [2] transmit

§1011. Personal service; Modes and requirements

The service may be personal, by delivery to the party or attorney on whom the service is required to be made, or it may be as follows:

(a) If upon an attorney, service may be made at the attorney's office, by leaving the notice or other papers in an envelope or package clearly labeled to identify the attorney being served, with a receptionist or with a person having charge thereof. If there is no person in the office with whom the notice or papers may be left for purposes of this subdivision at the time service is to be effected, service may be made by leaving them between the hours of 9 a.m. and 5 p.m., in a conspicuous place in the office, or, if the attorney's office is not open so as to admit of that service, then service may be made by leaving the notice or papers at the attorney's residence, with some person of not less than 18 years of age, if the attorney's residence is in the same county with his or her office, and, if the attorney's residence is not known or is not in the same county with his or her office, or, being in the same county, it is not open, or a person 18 years of age or older cannot be found at the attorney's residence, then service may be made by putting the notice or papers, enclosed in a sealed envelope, into the post office or a mail box, subpost office, substation, or mail chute or other like facility regularly maintained by the Government of the United States directed to the attorney at his or her office, if known, and otherwise to the attorney's residence, if known. If neither the attorney's office nor residence is known, service may be made by delivering the notice or papers to the address of the attorney or party of record as designated on the court papers, or by delivering the notice or papers to the clerk of the court, for the attorney.

(b) If upon a party, service shall be made in the manner specifically provided in particular cases, or, if no specific provision is made, service may be made by leaving the notice or other paper at the party's residence with some person 18 years of age or older.

(1) Any attempt of service upon a party at the party's residence shall be made between the hours of 8 a.m. and 8 p.m.

(2) If, at the time of service, as provided in paragraph (1), a person 18 years of age or older cannot be found at the party's residence, the notice or papers may be served by mail.

(3) If the party's residence is not known, any attempt of service pursuant to this subdivision may be made by delivering the notice or papers to the clerk of the court, for that party.

(c) If service is made by electronic service, it shall be made pursuant to Section 1010.6 and applicable rules on electric service in the California Rules of Court. **Leg.H.** Enacted 1872. Amended Stats 1907 ch 327 §2; Stats 1919 ch 194 §1; Stats 1933 ch 744 §178; Stats 1949 ch 456 §2; Stats 1951 ch 1737 §135, operative January 1, 1952; Stats 1989 ch 1105 §8; Stats 1994 ch 467 §1 (SB 1858); Stats 2007 ch 263 §11 (AB 310), effective January 1, 2008; Stats 2017 ch 319 §3 (AB 976), effective January 1, 2018; Stats 2018 ch 212 §1 (AB 2286), effective January 1, 2019.

§1012. When service by mail permitted

Service by mail may be made where the person on whom it is to be made resides or has his office at a place where there is a delivery service by mail, or where the person making the service and the person on whom it is to be made reside or have their offices in different places between which there is a regular communication by mail. **Leg.H.** Enacted 1872. Amended Code Amdts 1873–74 ch 383 §137; Stats 1931 ch 739 §1.

§1012.5. [Section repealed 2002]

Leg.H. Added Stats 1989 ch 1100 §1. Amended Stats 1991 ch 154 §1 (AB 824), effective July 22, 1991. Repealed Stats 2001 ch 115 §3 (SB 153). The repealed section related to pilot projects to assess use of service of documents by facsimile transmission.

§1013. Manner and completion of service by mail, Express Mail, facsimile transmission, or electronically

(a) In case of service by mail, the notice or other paper shall be deposited in a post office, mailbox, subpost office, substation, or mail chute, or other like facility regularly maintained by the United States Postal Service, in a sealed envelope, with postage paid, addressed to the person on whom it is to be served, at the office address as last given by that person on any document filed in the cause and served on the party making service by mail; otherwise at that party's place of residence. Service is complete at the time of the deposit, but any period of notice and any right or duty to do any act or make any response within any period or on a date certain after service of the document, which time period or date is prescribed by statute or rule of court, shall be extended five calendar days, upon service by mail, if the place of address and the place of mailing is within the State of California, 10 calendar days if either the place of mailing or the place of address is outside the State of California but within the United States, 12 calendar days if the place of address is the Secretary of State's address confidentiality program (Chapter 3.1 (commencing with Section 6205) of Division 7 of Title 1 of the Government Code), and 20 calendar days if either the place of mailing or the place of address is outside the United States, but the extension shall not apply to extend the time for filing notice of intention to move for new trial, notice of intention to move to vacate judgment pursuant to Section 663a, or notice of appeal. This extension applies in the absence of a specific exception provided for by this section or other statute or rule of court.

(b) The copy of the notice or other paper served by mail pursuant to this chapter shall bear a notation of the date and place of mailing or be accompanied by an unsigned copy of the affidavit or certificate of mailing.

(c) In case of service by Express Mail, the notice or other paper shall be deposited in a post office, mailbox, subpost office, substation, or mail chute, or other like facility regularly maintained by the United States Postal Service for receipt of Express Mail, in a sealed envelope, with Express Mail postage paid, addressed to the person on whom it is to be served, at the office address as last given by that person on any document filed in the cause and served on the party making service by Express Mail; otherwise at that party's place of residence. In case of service by another method of delivery providing for overnight delivery, the notice or other paper shall be deposited in a box or other facility regularly maintained by the express service carrier, or delivered to an authorized courier or driver authorized by the express service carrier to receive documents, in an envelope or package designated by the express service carrier with delivery fees paid or provided for, addressed to the person on whom it is to be served, at the office address as last given by that person on any document filed in the cause and served on the party making service; otherwise at that party's place of residence. Service is complete at the time of the deposit, but any period of notice and any right or duty to do any act or make any response within any period or on a date certain after service of the document served by Express Mail or other method of delivery providing for overnight delivery shall be extended by two court days. The extension shall not apply to extend the time for filing notice of intention to move for new trial, notice of intention to move to vacate judgment pursuant to Section 663a, or notice of appeal. This extension applies in the absence of a specific exception provided for by this section or other statute or rule of court.

(d) The copy of the notice or other paper served by Express Mail or another means of delivery providing for overnight delivery pursuant to this chapter shall bear a notation of the date and place of deposit or be accompanied by an unsigned copy of the affidavit or certificate of deposit.

(e) Service by facsimile transmission shall be permitted only where the parties agree and a written confirmation of that agreement is made. The Judicial Council may adopt rules implementing the service of documents by facsimile transmission and may provide a form for the confirmation of the agreement required by this subdivision. In case of service by facsimile transmission, the notice or other paper shall be transmitted to a facsimile machine maintained by the person on whom it is served at the facsimile machine telephone number as last given by that person on any document which they have filed in the cause and served on the party making the service. Service is complete at the time of transmission, but any period of notice and any right or duty to do any act or make any response within any period or on a date certain after service of the document, which time period or date is prescribed by statute or rule of court, shall be extended, after service by facsimile transmission, by two court days, but the extension shall not apply to extend the time for filing notice of intention to move for new trial, notice of intention to move to vacate judgment pursuant to Section 663a, or notice of appeal. This extension applies in the absence of a specific exception provided for by this section or other statute or rule of court.

(f) The copy of the notice or other paper served by facsimile transmission pursuant to this chapter shall bear a notation of the date and place of transmission and the facsimile telephone number to which transmitted, or to be accompanied by an unsigned copy of the affidavit or certificate of transmission which shall contain the facsimile telephone number to which the notice or other paper was transmitted.

(g) Electronic service shall be permitted pursuant to Section 1010.6 and the rules on electronic service in the California Rules of Court.

(h) Subdivisions (b), (d), and (f) are directory. **Leg.H.** Enacted 1872. Amended Code Amdts 1873–74 ch 383 §138; Stats 1907 ch 327 §3; Stats 1929 ch 480 §1; Stats 1931 ch 739 §2; Stats 1949 ch 456 §3; Stats 1967 ch 169 §6; Stats 1968 ch 166 §1; Stats 1974 ch 281 §1, ch 282 §2, effective May 28, 1974, operative January 1, 1975; Stats 1980 ch 196 §2; Stats 1992 ch 339 §4 (SB 1409); Stats 1995 ch 576 §3.8 (AB 1225); Stats 2001 ch 812 §8 (AB 223); Stats 2010 ch 156 §2 (SB 1274), effective January 1, 2011; Stats 2022 ch 686 §2 (AB 1726), effective January 1, 2023.

§1013a. Proof of service by mail

Proof of service by mail may be made by one of the following methods:

(1) An affidavit setting forth the exact title of the document served and filed in the cause, showing the name and residence or business address of the person making the service, showing that he or she is a resident of or employed in the county where the mailing occurs, that he or she is over the age of 18 years and not a party to the cause, and showing the date and place of deposit in the mail, the name and address of the person served as shown on the envelope, and also showing that the envelope was sealed and deposited in the mail with the postage thereon fully prepaid.

(2) A certificate setting forth the exact title of the document served and filed in the cause, showing the name and business address of the person making the service, showing that he or she is an active member of the State Bar of California and is not a party to the cause, and showing the date and place of deposit in the mail, the name and address of the person served as shown on the envelope, and also showing that the envelope was sealed and deposited in the mail with the postage thereon fully prepaid.

(3) An affidavit setting forth the exact title of the document served and filed in the cause, showing (A) the name and residence or business address of the person making the service, (B) that he or she is a resident of, or employed in, the county where the mailing occurs, (C) that he or she is over the age of 18 years and not a party to the cause, (D) that he or she is readily familiar with the business' practice for collection and processing of correspondence for mailing with the United States Postal Service, (E) that the correspondence would be deposited with the United States Postal Service that same day in the ordinary course of business, (F) the name and address of the person served as shown on the envelope, and the date and place of business where the correspondence was placed for deposit in the United States Postal Service, and (G) that the envelope was sealed and placed for collection and mailing on that date following ordinary business practices. Service made pursuant to this paragraph, upon motion of a party served, shall be presumed invalid if the postal cancellation date or postage meter date on the envelope is more than one day after the date of deposit for mailing contained in the affidavit.

(4) In case of service by the clerk of a court of record, a certificate by that clerk setting forth the exact title of the document served and filed in the cause, showing the name of the clerk and the name of the court of which he or she is the clerk, and that he or she is not a party to the cause, and showing the date and place of deposit in the mail, the name and address of the person served as shown on the envelope, and also showing that the envelope was sealed and deposited in the mail with the postage thereon fully prepaid. This form of proof is sufficient for service of process in which the clerk or deputy clerk signing the certificate places the document for collection and mailing on the date shown thereon, so as to cause it to be mailed in an envelope so sealed and so addressed on that date following standard court practices. Service made pursuant to this paragraph, upon motion of a party served and a finding of good cause by the court, shall be deemed to have occurred on the date of postage cancellation or postage meter imprint as shown on the envelope if that date is more than one day after the date of deposit for mailing contained in the certificate. **Leg.H.** Added Stats 1931 ch 739 §3. Amended Stats 1953 ch 1110 §1; Stats 1955 ch 779 §1; Stats 1959 ch 345 §1; Stats 1972 ch 601 §3, ch 1083 §1; Stats 1973 ch 302 §1; Stats 1974 ch 282 §3, effective May 28, 1974; Stats 1980 ch 196 §3; Stats 1987 ch 190 §24; Stats 1988 ch 160 §18; Stats 1995 ch 576 §4 (AB 1225).

§1013b. Proof of electronic service

(a) Proof of electronic service may be made by any of the following methods:

(1) An affidavit setting forth the exact title of the document served and filed in the cause, showing the name and residence or business address of the person making the service, showing that the person is a resident of or employed in the county where the electronic service occurs, and that the person is over 18 years of age.

(2) A certificate setting forth the exact title of the document served and filed in the cause, showing the name and business address of the person making the service, and showing that the person is an active member of the State Bar of California.

(3) An affidavit setting forth the exact title of the document served and filed in the cause, showing all of the following:

(A) The name and residence or business address of the person making the service.

(B) That the person is a resident of, or employed in, the county where the electronic service occurs.

(C) That the person is over 18 years of age.

(D) That the person is readily familiar with the business' practice for filing electronically.

(E) That the document would be electronically served that same day in the ordinary course of business following ordinary business practices.

(4) In case of service by the clerk of a court of record, a certificate by that clerk setting forth the exact title of the document served and filed in the cause, showing the name of the clerk and the name of the court of which they are the clerk.

(b) Proof of electronic service shall include all of the following:

(1) The electronic service address and the residence or business address of the person making the electronic service.

(2) The date of electronic service.

(3) The name and electronic service address of the person served.

(4) A statement that the document was served electronically.

(c) Proof of electronic service shall be signed as provided in subparagraph (B) of paragraph (2) of subdivision (e) of Section 1010.6.

(d) Proof of electronic service may be in electronic form and may be filed electronically with the court. **Leg.H.** Added Stats 2017 ch 319 §4 (AB 976), effective January 1, 2018. Amended Stats 2018 ch 776 §8 (AB 3250), effective January 1, 2019; Stats 2022 ch 215 §2 (AB 2961), effective January 1, 2023.

§1014. Appearance

A defendant appears in an action when the defendant answers, demurs, files a notice of motion to strike, files a notice of motion to transfer pursuant to Section 396b, moves for reclassification pursuant to Section 403.040, gives the plaintiff written notice of appearance, or when an attorney gives notice of appearance for the defendant. After appearance, a defendant or the defendant's attorney is entitled to notice of all subsequent proceedings of which notice is required to be given. Where a defendant has not appeared, service of notice or papers need not be made upon the defendant. **Leg.H.** Enacted Stats 1872. Amended Stats 1955 ch 1452 §8; Stats 1969 ch 345 §5; Stats 1973 ch 20 §11; Stats 1998 ch 931 §106 (SB 2139), effective September 28, 1998; Stats 1999 ch 344 §15 (SB 210), effective September 7, 1999.

§1015. Service when party resides out of state

When a plaintiff or a defendant, who has appeared, resides out of the state, and has no attorney in the action or proceeding, the service may be made on the clerk of the court, for that party. But in all cases where a party has an attorney in the action or proceeding, the service of papers, when required, must be upon the attorney instead of the party, except service of subpoenas, of writs, and other process issued in the suit, and of papers to bring the party into contempt. If the sole attorney for a party is removed or suspended from practice, then the party has no attorney within the meaning of this section. If the party's sole attorney has no known office in this state, notices and papers may be served by leaving a copy thereof with the clerk of the court, unless the attorney has filed in the cause an address of a place at which notices and papers may be served on the attorney, in which event they may be served at that place. **Leg.H.** Enacted 1872. Amended Stats 1907 ch 327 §4; Stats 1933 ch 744 §179; Stats 1951 ch 1737 §136, operative January 1, 1952; Stats 2007 ch 263 §12 (AB 310), effective January 1, 2008.

§1016. Preceding provisions not to apply to proceeding to bring party into contempt

The foregoing provisions of this chapter do not apply to the service of a summons or other process, or of any paper to bring a party into contempt. **Leg.H.** Enacted 1872.

§1017. Service by telegraph

Any summons, writ, or order in any civil suit or proceeding, and all other papers requiring service, may be transmitted by telegraph for service in any place, and the telegraphic copy of such writ, or order, or paper so transmitted, may be served or executed by the officer or person to whom it is sent for that purpose, and returned by him, if any return be requisite, in the same manner, and with the same force and effect in all respects, as the original thereof might be if delivered to him, and the officer or person serving or executing the same has the same authority, and is subject to the same liabilities, as if the copy were the original. The original, when a writ or order, must also be filed in the court from which it was issued, and a certified copy thereof must be preserved in the telegraph-office from which it was sent. In sending it, either the original or the certified copy may be used by the operator for that purpose. Whenever any document to be sent by telegraph bears a seal, either private or official, it is not necessary for the operator, in sending the same, to telegraph a description of the seal, or any words or device thereon, but the same may be expressed in the telegraphic copy by the letters "L.S.," or by the word "seal." **Leg.H.** Enacted 1872.

§1018. [Section repealed 2000]

Leg.H. Added Stats 1939 ch 923 §1. Amended Stats 1945 ch 753 §1; Stats 1951 ch 1065 §1; Stats 1979 ch 730 §30, operative January 1, 1981. Repealed Stats 1999 ch 1000 §12 (SB 284). The repealed section related to service on agent or Secretary of State.

§1019. Size of type in notice or publication

Whenever any notice or publication is required by a provision in this code or any other code or statute of this state to be provided in a specified size of type or printing which is to be measured by points, the size required, unless otherwise specifically defined, shall be determined by the conventional customs and practices of the printing industry and within the tolerances permitted by conventional custom and practice in that industry, except that the provisions of this section shall not be used for purposes of evasion of any requirement for notice or publication. **Leg.H.** Added Stats 1980 ch 199 §1.

Prior Law: Former CCP §1019, relating to service of pleadings when adultery is charged, was added Stats 1909 ch 640 §1, and repealed Stats 1969 ch 1608 §18, operative January 1, 1970.

§1019.5. Notice of grant or denial of motion

(a) When a motion is granted or denied, unless the court otherwise orders, notice of the court's decision or order shall be given by the prevailing party to all other parties or their attorneys, in the manner provided in this chapter, unless notice is waived by all parties in open court and is entered in the minutes.

(b) When a motion is granted or denied on the court's own motion, notice of the court's order shall be given by the court in the manner provided in this chapter, unless notice is waived by all parties in open court and is entered in the minutes. **Leg.H.** Added Stats 1982 ch 704 §10. Amended Stats 1992 ch 1348 §6 (AB 2616).

§1020. Notices by registered mail

(a) Any notice required by law, other than those required to be given to a party to an action or to his attorney, the service of which is not governed by the other sections of this chapter and which is not otherwise specifically provided for by law, may be given by sending the same by registered mail with proper postage prepaid addressed to the addressee's last known address with request for return receipt, and the production of a returned receipt purporting to be signed by the addressee shall create a disputable presumption that such notice was received by the person to whom the notice was required to be sent.

(b) Electronic service is not authorized for a notice that requires certified or registered mail. **Leg.H.** Added Stats 1939 ch 61 §1. Amended Stats 2017 ch 319 §4.5 (AB 976), effective January 1, 2018.

CHAPTER 6
OF COSTS

Compensation of attorneys; Costs to parties. §1021.
Award of attorney fees to prevailing plaintiff in damage action based on commission of felony offense. §1021.4.
Attorney fees in cases resulting in public benefit. §1021.5.
Attorney fees involving claim to implied indemnity. §1021.6.
Attorney fees in actions involving peace officers, libel, slander, bad faith. §1021.7.
Award of fees to Attorney General in certain cases. §1021.8.
Attorney fees in trespass actions. §1021.9.
Attorney's fees involving interstate sale of tobacco. §1021.10.
Attorney's fees in actions seeking to prevent enforcement of laws that regulate or restrict firearms. § 1021.11.
Costs in actions where defendants subject to joinder. §1022.
Referee's fees. §1023.
Expenses on postponement. §1024.
Effect of tender before action. §1025.
Costs in actions by or against fiduciaries. §1026.
Costs in review other than by appeal. §1027.
Costs against State. §1028.
Action between small business and regulatory agency. §1028.5.
Costs against public entity, agency, or officer. §1029.
Undertaking in malpractice action against architect, engineer, surveyor, etc. §1029.5.
Undertaking in medical malpractice action. §1029.6.
Personal injury action against unlicensed person; Award of treble damages, costs, and attorney fees. §1029.8.
Undertaking of nonresident or of foreign corporation. §1030.
Attorney fees in actions for recovery of wages. §1031.
Recovery of costs by prevailing party as matter of right. §1032.
[Section renumbered 1982]. §1032a.
[Section renumbered 1982]. §1032b.
Discretion of court where judgment could have been rendered in limited civil case. §1033.
Items allowable as costs. §1033.5.
Prejudgment costs; Costs on appeal. §1034.
Costs in unlawful detainer proceedings. §1034.5.
Costs in inverse condemnation proceedings. §1036.
Defense costs on granting of summary judgment or nonsuit. §1038.

§1021. Compensation of attorneys; Costs to parties

Except as attorney's fees are specifically provided for by statute, the measure and mode of compensation of attorneys and counselors at law is left to the agreement, express or implied, of the parties; but parties to actions or proceedings are entitled to their costs, as hereinafter provided. **Leg.H.** Enacted 1872. Amended Stats 1933 ch 744 §180; Stats 1986 ch 377 §2.

§1021.1. [Section repealed 2005]

Leg.H. Added Stats 2001 ch 719 §1 (SB 158), repealed January 1, 2005. Repealed January 1, 2005, by its own terms. The repealed section related to award of attorneys fees in certain civil actions.

Prior Law: Former CCP §1021.1, relating to discretionary award of attorney fees, was added Stats 1987 ch 1003 §2, amended Stats 1988 ch 10 §5, effective February 17, 1988, Stats 1990 ch 584 §2, Stats 1992 ch 1265 §7, Stats 1995 ch 911 §1, and repealed January 1, 2001, by its own terms.

§1021.4. Award of attorney fees to prevailing plaintiff in damage action based on commission of felony offense

In an action for damages against a defendant based upon that defendant's commission of a felony offense for which that defendant has been convicted, the court may, upon motion, award reasonable attorney's fees to a prevailing plaintiff against the defendant who has been convicted of the felony. **Leg.H.** Added Stats 1983 ch 938 §3, effective September 20, 1983.

§1021.5. Attorney fees in cases resulting in public benefit

Upon motion, a court may award attorneys' fees to a successful party against one or more opposing parties in any action which has resulted in the enforcement of an important right affecting the public interest if: (a) a significant benefit, whether pecuniary or nonpecuniary, has been conferred on the general public or a large class of persons, (b) the necessity and financial burden of private enforcement, or of enforcement by one public entity against another public entity, are such as to make the award appropriate, and (c) such fees should not in the interest of justice be paid out of the recovery, if any. With respect to actions involving public entities, this section applies to allowances against, but not in favor of, public entities, and no claim shall be required to be filed therefor, unless one or more successful parties and one or more opposing parties are public entities, in which case no claim shall be required to be filed therefor under Part 3 (commencing with Section 900) of Division 3.6 of Title 1 of the Government Code.

Attorney's fees awarded to a public entity pursuant to this section shall not be increased or decreased by a multiplier based upon extrinsic circumstances, as discussed in Serrano v. Priest, 20 Cal. 3d 25, 49. **Leg.H.** Added Stats 1977 ch 1197 §1. Amended Stats 1993 ch 645 §2 (SB 764).

§1021.6. Attorney fees involving claim to implied indemnity

Upon motion, a court after reviewing the evidence in the principal case may award attorney's fees to a person who prevails on a claim for implied indemnity if the court finds (a) that the indemnitee through the tort of the indemnitor has been required to act in the protection of the indemnitee's interest by bringing an action against or defending an action by a third person and (b) if that indemnitor was properly notified of the demand to bring the action or provide the defense and did not avail itself of the opportunity to do so, and (c) that the trier of fact determined that the indemnitee was without fault in the principal case which is the basis for the action in indemnity or that the indemnitee had a final judgment entered in his or her favor granting a summary judgment, a nonsuit, or a directed verdict. **Leg.H.** Added Stats 1979 ch 289 §1. Amended Stats 1982 ch 1383 §1.

§1021.7. Attorney fees in actions involving peace officers, libel, slander, bad faith

In any action for damages arising out of the performance of a peace officer's duties, brought against a peace officer, as defined in Chapter 4.5 (commencing with Section 830) of Title 3 of Part 2 of the Penal Code, or against a public entity employing a peace officer or in an action for libel or slander brought pursuant to Section 45 or 46 of the Civil Code, the court may, in its discretion, award reasonable attorney's fees to the defendant or defendants as part of the costs, upon a finding by the court that the action was not filed or maintained in good faith and with reasonable cause. **Leg.H.** Added Stats 1981 ch 980 §1.

§1021.8. Award of fees to Attorney General in certain cases

(a) Whenever the Attorney General prevails in a civil action to enforce Section 17537.3, 22445, 22446.5, 22958, 22962, or 22963 of the Business and Professions Code, Section 52, 52.1, 55.1, or 3494 of the Civil Code, the Corporate Securities Law of 1968 (Division 1 (commencing with Section 25000) of Title 4 of the Corporations Code) or the California Commodity Law of 1990 (Division 4.5 (commencing with Section 29500) of Title 4 of the Corporations Code), Section 1615, 2014, or 5650.1 of the Fish and Game Code, Section 4458, 12598, 12606, 12607, 12989.3, 16147, 66640, 66641, or 66641.7 of the Government Code, Section 13009, 13009.1, 19958.5, 25299, 39674, 41513, 42402, 42402.1, 42402.2, 42402.3, 42402.4, 43016, 43017, 43154, 104557, or 118950 of the Health and Safety Code, Section 308.1 or 308.3 of the Penal Code, Section 2774.1, 4601.1, 4603, 4605, 30820, 30821.6, 30822, 42847, or 48023 of the Public Resources Code, Section 30101.7 of the Revenue and Taxation Code, or Section 275, 1052, 1845, 13261, 13262, 13264, 13265, 13268, 13304, 13331, 13350, or 13385, or Part 1 (commencing with Section 6000) of Division 3, of the Water Code, the court shall award to the Attorney General all costs of investigating and prosecuting the action, including expert fees, reasonable attorney's fees, and costs. Awards under this section shall be paid to the Public Rights Law Enforcement Special Fund established by Section 12530 of the Government Code.

(b) This section applies to any action pending on the effective date of this section and to any action filed thereafter.

(c) The amendments made to this section by Chapter 227 of the Statutes of 2004 shall apply to any action pending on the effective date of these amendments and to any action filed thereafter. **Leg.H.** Added Stats 2003 ch 159 §4 (AB 1759), effective August 2, 2003. Amended Stats 2004 ch 183 §45 (AB 3082), ch 227 §12 (SB 1102), effective August 16, 2004, ch 702 §1 (AB 2104), effective September 23, 2004 (ch 702 prevails); Stats 2006 ch 538 §65 (SB 1852), effective January 1, 2007; Stats 2023 ch 51 §3 (SB 122), effective July 10, 2023.

§1021.9. Attorney fees in trespass actions

In any action to recover damages to personal or real property resulting from trespassing on lands either under cultivation or intended or used for the raising of livestock, the prevailing plaintiff shall be entitled to reasonable attorney's fees in addition to other costs, and in addition to any liability for damages imposed by law. **Leg.H.** Added Stats 1986 ch 1381 §1.

§1021.10. Attorney's fees involving interstate sale of tobacco

Notwithstanding any other provision of law, in an action brought in the name of the people of the State of California against any person for failure to comply with Chapter 10A (commencing with Section 375) of Title 15 of the United States Code, otherwise known as the "Jenkins Act," the court, to the extent not expressly prohibited by federal law, shall award fees and costs, including reasonable attorney's fees, to the people if the people succeed on any claim to enforce the Jenkins Act. Any attorney's fees awarded under this section shall be in addition to any other remedies or penalties available under all other laws of this state. **Leg.H.** Added Stats 2002 ch 686 §2 (SB 1766).

§ 1021.11. Attorney's fees in actions seeking to prevent enforcement of laws that regulate or restrict firearms

(a) Notwithstanding any other law, any person, including an entity, attorney, or law firm, who seeks declaratory or injunctive relief to prevent this state, a political subdivision, a governmental entity or public official in this state, or a person in this state from enforcing any statute, ordinance, rule, regulation, or any other type of law that regulates or restricts firearms, or that represents any litigant seeking that relief, is jointly and severally liable to pay the attorney's fees and costs of the prevailing party.

(b) For purposes of this section, a party is considered a prevailing party if a court does either of the following:

(1) Dismisses any claim or cause of action brought by the party seeking the declaratory or injunctive relief described by subdivision (a), regardless of the reason for the dismissal.

(2) Enters judgment in favor of the party opposing the declaratory or injunctive relief described by subdivision (a), on any claim or cause of action.

(c) Regardless of whether a prevailing party sought to recover attorney's fees or costs in the underlying action, a prevailing party under this section may bring a civil action to recover attorney's fees and costs against a person, including an entity, attorney, or law firm, that sought declaratory or injunctive relief described by subdivision (a) not later than the third anniversary of the date on which, as applicable:

(1) The dismissal or judgment described by subdivision (b) becomes final upon the conclusion of appellate review.

(2) The time for seeking appellate review expires.

(d) None of the following are a defense to an action brought under subdivision (c):

(1) A prevailing party under this section failed to seek recovery of attorney's fees or costs in the underlying action.

(2) The court in the underlying action declined to recognize or enforce the requirements of this section.

(3) The court in the underlying action held that any provision of this section is invalid, unconstitutional, or preempted by federal law, notwithstanding the doctrines of issue or claim preclusion.

(e) Any person, including an entity, attorney, or law firm, who seeks declaratory or injunctive relief as described in subdivision (a), shall not be deemed a prevailing party under this section or any other provision of this chapter. **Leg.H.** Added Stats 2022 ch 146 §2 (SB 1327), effective January 1, 2023.

§1022. Costs in actions where defendants subject to joinder

When several actions are brought on one bond, undertaking, promissory note, bill of exchange, or other instrument in writing, or in any other case for the same cause of action, against several parties who might have been joined as defendants in the same action, no costs can be allowed to the plaintiff in more than one of such actions, which may be at his election, if the parties proceeded against in the other actions were, at the commencement of the previous action, openly within this State; but the disbursements of the plaintiff must be allowed to him in each action. **Leg.H.** Enacted 1872 as §1023. Renumbered by Stats 1933 ch 744 §181.

Prior Law: Former CCP §1022, similar to present CCP §1032, was enacted 1872, amended Stats 1929 ch 482 §1, and repealed Stats 1933 ch 744 §198.

§1023. Referee's fees

The fees of referees are such reasonable sum as the court may fix for the time spent in the business of the reference; but the parties may agree, in writing, upon any other rate of compensation, and thereupon such rates shall be allowed. **Leg.H.** Enacted 1872 as §1028. Amended and renumbered by Stats 1933 ch 744 §182. Amended Stats 1953 ch 795 §1.

Prior Law: Former CCP §1023 was enacted 1872 and renumbered §1022 by Stats 1933 ch 744 §181.

§1024. Expenses on postponement

When an application is made to the court or referee to postpone a trial, the payment of the expenses occasioned by the postponement may be imposed, in the discretion of the court or referee, as a condition of granting the same. **Leg.H.** Enacted 1872 as §1029. Renumbered by Stats 1933 ch 744 §183. Amended Stats 1986 ch 377 §3.

Prior Law: Former CCP §1024, similar to present CCP §1032, was enacted 1872 and repealed Stats 1933 ch 744 §198.

§1025. Effect of tender before action

When, in an action for the recovery of money only, the defendant alleges in his answer that before the commencement of the action he tendered to the plaintiff the full amount to which he was entitled, and thereupon deposits in court, for plaintiff, the amount so tendered, and the allegation is found to be true, the plaintiff cannot recover costs, but must pay costs to the defendant. **Leg.H.** Enacted 1872 as §1030. Amended and renumbered by Stats 1933 ch 744 §184.

Prior Law: Former CCP §1025, similar to present CCP §1032, was enacted 1872, amended Stats 1929 ch 482 §2, and repealed Stats 1933 ch 744 §198.

§1026. Costs in actions by or against fiduciaries

(a) Except as provided in subdivision (b), in an action prosecuted or defended by a personal representative, trustee of an express trust, guardian, conservator, or a person expressly authorized by statute, costs may be recovered as in an action by or against a person prosecuting or defending in the person's own right.

(b) Costs allowed under subdivision (a) shall, by the judgment, be made chargeable only upon the estate, fund, or party represented, unless the court directs the costs to be paid by the fiduciary personally for mismanagement or bad faith in the action or defense. **Leg.H.** Enacted 1872 as §1031. Amended and renumbered by Stats 1933 ch 744 §185. Amended Stats 1988 ch 1199 §8, operative July 1, 1989.

Prior Law: Former CCP §1026, similar to present CCP §1032, was enacted 1872 and repealed Stats 1933 ch 744 §198.

§1027. Costs in review other than by appeal

When the decision of a court of inferior jurisdiction in a special proceeding is brought before a court of higher jurisdiction for a review, in any other way than by appeal, the same costs must be allowed as in cases on appeal, and may be collected in the manner provided for enforcement of money judgments generally, or in such manner as the court may direct, according to the nature of the case. **Leg.H.** Enacted 1872 as §1032. Renumbered by Stats 1933 ch 744 §186. Amended Stats 1982 ch 497 §68, operative July 1, 1983.

Prior Law: Former CCP §1027, similar to present CCP §1034, was enacted 1872, amended Stats 1913 ch 587 §1, Stats 1919 ch 50 §1, and repealed Stats 1933 ch 744 §198.

§1028. Costs against State

Notwithstanding any other provisions of law, when the State is a party, costs shall be awarded against it on the same basis as against any other party and, when awarded, must be paid out of the appropriation for the support of the agency on whose behalf the State appeared. **Leg.H.** Enacted 1872 as §1038. Renumbered by Stats 1933 ch 744 §187. Amended Stats 1943 ch 165 §1.

Prior Law: Former CCP §1028 was enacted 1872, amended and renumbered to be CCP §1023 by Stats 1933 ch 744 §182.

§1028.5. Action between small business and regulatory agency

(a) In any civil action between a small business or a licensee and a state regulatory agency, involving the regulatory functions of a state agency as applied to a small business or a licensee, if the small business or licensee prevails, and if the court determines that the action of the agency was undertaken without substantial justification, the small business or licensee may, in the discretion of the court, be awarded reasonable litigation expenses in addition to other costs. Funds for such expenses and costs shall be paid from funds in the regular operating budget of the state regulatory agency where the appropriation therefor encompasses the payment of such costs and expenses, and not from unappropriated money in the General Fund.

(b) "Reasonable litigation expenses" means any expenses not in excess of seven thousand five hundred dollars ($7,500) which the judge finds were reasonably incurred in opposing the agency action, including court costs, expenses incurred in administrative proceedings, attorney's fees, witness fees of all necessary witnesses, and such other expenses as were reasonably incurred.

(c) "Small business" means a business activity that is all of the following:

(1) Independently owned and operated.

(2) Not dominant in its field of operation.

(3) Not exceeding the following annual gross receipts or other criteria in the categories of:

(A) Agriculture, one million dollars ($1,000,000).

(B) General construction, nine million five hundred thousand dollars ($9,500,000).

(C) Special trade construction, five million dollars ($5,000,000).

(D) Retail trade, two million dollars ($2,000,000).

(E) Wholesale trade, nine million five hundred thousand dollars ($9,500,000).

(F) Services, two million dollars ($2,000,000).

(G) Transportation and warehousing, one million five hundred thousand dollars ($1,500,000).

(H) A manufacturing enterprise not exceeding 250 employees.

(I) A health care facility not exceeding 150 beds or one million five hundred thousand dollars ($1,500,000) in annual gross receipts.

(J) Generating and transmitting electric power not exceeding 4,500 megawatt hours annually.

(d) "Licensee" means any person licensed by a state agency who does not qualify as a small business, but whose annual gross receipts from the use of such license do not exceed one million dollars ($1,000,000).

(e) A small business or a licensee shall be deemed to prevail in any action in which there is no adjudication, stipulation, or acceptance of liability on the part of the small business or licensee.

(f) A small business or licensee shall not be deemed to have prevailed in actions commenced at the instance of, or on the basis of a complaint filed by, a person who is not an officer, employee, or other agent of the state regulatory agency if the action is dismissed by the agency upon a finding of no cause for the action, or is settled by the agency and small business or licensee without a finding of fault.

(g) Section 800 of the Government Code shall not apply to actions which are subject to the provisions of this section.

(h) Every state regulatory agency against which litigation expenses have been awarded under this section shall, at the time of submission of its proposed budget pursuant to Section 13320 of the Government Code, submit a report to the Department of Finance and the Legislature as to the amount of those expenses awarded and paid during the fiscal year.

(i) This section shall be known and may be cited as the Carpenter-Katz Small Business Equal Access to Justice Act of 1981. **Leg.H.** Added Stats 1981 ch 814 §1. Amended Stats 1983 ch 445 §1.

§1029. Costs against public entity, agency, or officer

When any county, city, district, or other public agency or entity, or any officer thereof in his official capacity, is a party, costs shall be awarded against it on the same basis as against any other party and, when awarded, must be paid out of the treasury thereof. **Leg.H.** Enacted 1872 as §1039. Renumbered by Stats 1933 ch 744 §188. Amended Stats 1945 ch 217 §1.

Prior Law: Former CCP §1029 was enacted 1872 and renumbered to be CCP §1024 by Stats 1933 ch 744 §183.

§1029.5. Undertaking in malpractice action against architect, engineer, surveyor, etc.

(a) Whenever a complaint for damages is filed against any architect, landscape architect, engineer, building designer, or land surveyor, duly licensed as such under the laws of this state, in an action for error, omission, or professional negligence in the creation and preparation of plans, specifications, designs, reports or surveys which are the basis for work performed or agreed to be performed on real property, any such defendant may, within 30 days after service of summons, move the court for an order, upon notice and hearing, requiring the plaintiff to file an undertaking in a sum not to exceed five hundred dollars ($500) as security for the costs of defense as provided in subdivision (d), which may be awarded against the plaintiff. The motion shall be supported by affidavit showing that the claim against the defendant is frivolous.

At the hearing upon the motion, the court shall order the plaintiff to file the undertaking if the defendant shows to the satisfaction of the court that (i) the plaintiff would not suffer undue economic hardship in filing the undertaking, and (ii) there is no reasonable possibility that the plaintiff has a cause of action against each named defendant with respect to whom the plaintiff would otherwise be required to file the undertaking. No appeal shall be taken from any order made pursuant to this subdivision to file or not to file the undertaking.

A determination by the court that the undertaking either shall or shall not be filed or shall be filed as to one or more defendants and not as to others, shall not be deemed a determination of any one or more issues in the action or of the merits thereof. If the court, upon any such motion, makes a determination that an undertaking be filed by the plaintiff as to any one or more defendants, the action shall be dismissed as to the defendant or defendants, unless the undertaking required by the court has been filed within such reasonable time as may be fixed by the court.

(b) This section does not apply to a complaint for bodily injury or for wrongful death, nor to an action commenced in a small claims court.

(c) Whenever more than one such defendant is named, the undertaking shall be increased to the extent of not to exceed five hundred dollars ($500) for each additional defendant in whose favor the undertaking is ordered not to exceed the total of three thousand dollars ($3,000).

(d) In any action requiring an undertaking as provided in this section, upon the dismissal of the action or the award of judgment to the defendant, the court shall require the plaintiff to pay the defendant's costs of defense authorized by law. Any sureties shall be liable for such costs in an amount not to exceed the sum of five hundred dollars ($500) or the amount of the undertaking, whichever is lesser, for each defendant with respect to whom the sureties have executed an undertaking. **Leg.H.** Added Stats 1967 ch 393 §1 as §405.7. Amended and renumbered by Stats 1969 ch 1610 §6, operative July 1, 1970. Amended Stats 1980 ch 114 §2; Stats 1982 ch 517 §162.

§1029.6. Undertaking in medical malpractice action

(a) Whenever a complaint for damages for personal injuries is filed against a physician and surgeon, dentist, registered nurse, dispensing optician, optometrist, pharmacist, registered physical therapist, podiatrist, licensed psychologist, osteopathic physician and surgeon, chiropractor, clinical laboratory bioanalyst, clinical laboratory technologist, or veterinarian, duly licensed as such under the laws of this state, or a licensed hospital as the employer of any such person, in an action for error, omission, or negligence in the performance of professional services, or performance of professional services without consent, any such defendant may, within six months after service of summons, move the court for an order, upon notice to plaintiff and all defendants having appeared in the action, and hearing, requiring the plaintiff to file an undertaking in a sum not to exceed five hundred dollars ($500) as security for the costs of defense as provided in subdivision (d), which may be awarded against the plaintiff. The motion shall be supported by affidavit showing that the claim against the defendant is frivolous. Any defendant having appeared in the action and within 30 days after receipt of notice may join with the moving party requesting an order under this section as to the additional defendant. The failure of any defendant to join with the moving party shall preclude that defendant from subsequently requesting an order under this section.

At the hearing upon the motion, the court shall order the plaintiff to file the undertaking if the defendant shows to the satisfaction of the court that: (i) the plaintiff would not suffer undue economic hardship in filing the undertaking and (ii) there is no reasonable possibility that the plaintiff has a cause of action against each named defendant with respect to whom the plaintiff would otherwise be required to file the undertaking.

A determination by the court that an undertaking either shall or shall not be filed or shall be filed as to one or more defendants and not as to others, shall not be deemed a determination of any one or more issues in the action or of the merits thereof. If the court, upon any such motion, makes a determination that an undertaking be filed by the plaintiff as to any one or more defendants, the action shall be dismissed as to that defendant or defendants, unless the undertaking required by the court shall have been filed within the reasonable time as may be fixed by the court.

(b) This section does not apply to a complaint in an action commenced in a small claims court.

(c) Whenever more than one defendant is named, the undertaking shall be increased to the extent of not to exceed five hundred dollars ($500) for each additional defendant in whose favor the undertaking is ordered, not to exceed the total of one thousand dollars ($1,000).

(d) In any action requiring an undertaking as provided in this section, upon the dismissal of the action or the award of judgment to the defendant, the court shall require the plaintiff to pay the defendant's court costs. Any sureties shall be liable for those costs in an amount not to exceed the sum of five hundred dollars ($500) or the amount of the undertaking, whichever is lesser, for each defendant with respect to whom the sureties have executed an undertaking. If the plaintiff prevails in the action against any defendant with respect to whom an undertaking has been filed, the defendant shall pay the costs to plaintiff incurred in defending the motion for dismissal authorized by this section.

(e) Any defendant filing a motion under this section or joining with a moving party under this section is precluded from subsequently filing a motion for summary judgment.

(f) Any defendant filing a motion for summary judgment is precluded from subsequently filing a motion, or joining with a moving party, under this section. **Leg.H.** Added Stats 1969 ch 608 §1 as §405.8. Renumbered Stats 1970 ch 910 §1. Amended Stats 1972 ch 653 §1; Stats 1980 ch 114 §3; Stats 1982 ch 517 §163; Stats 1993 ch 226 §6 (AB 1987).

§1029.8. Personal injury action against unlicensed person; Award of treble damages, costs, and attorney fees

(a) Any unlicensed person who causes injury or damage to another person as a result of providing goods or performing services for which a license is required under Division 2 (commencing with Section 500) or any initiative act referred to therein, Division 3 (commencing with Section 5000), or Chapter 2 (commencing with Section 18600) or Chapter 3 (commencing with Section 19000) of Division 8, of the Business and Professions Code, or Chapter 2 (commencing with Section 25210) or Chapter 3 (commencing with Section 25230) of Part 3 of Division 1 of Title 4 of the Corporations Code, shall be liable to the injured person for treble the amount of damages assessed in a civil action in any court having proper jurisdiction. The court may, in its discretion, award all costs and attorney's fees to the injured person if that person prevails in the action.

(b) This section shall not be construed to confer an additional cause of action or to affect or limit any other remedy, including, but not limited to, a claim for exemplary damages.

(c) The additional damages provided for in subdivision (a) shall not exceed ten thousand dollars ($10,000).

(d) For the purposes of this section, the term "unlicensed person" shall not apply to any of the following:

(1) Any person, partnership, corporation, or other entity providing goods or services under the good faith belief that they are properly licensed and acting within the proper scope of that licensure.

(2) Any person, partnership, corporation, or other entity whose license has expired for nonpayment of license renewal fees, but who is eligible to renew that license without the necessity of applying and qualifying for an original license.

(3) Any person, partnership, or corporation licensed under Chapter 6 (commencing with Section 2700) or Chapter 6.5 (commencing with Section 2840) of the Business and Professions Code, who provides professional nursing services under an existing license, if the action arises from a claim that the licensee exceeded the scope of practice authorized by his or her license.

(e) This section shall not apply to any action for unfair trade practices brought against an unlicensed person under Chapter 4 (commencing with Section 17000) of Part 2 of Division 7 of the Business and Professions Code, by a person who holds a license that is required, or closely related to the license that is required, to engage in those activities performed by the unlicensed person. **Leg.H.** Added Stats 1985 ch 895 §1. Amended Stats 2004 ch 575 §1 (AB 2167).

2004 Note: It is the intent of the Legislature that the remedies provided by this act are cumulative and that they shall not be construed as restricting any remedy that is otherwise available. Stats 2004 ch 575 (AB 2167) §4.

§1030. Undertaking of nonresident or of foreign corporation

(a) When the plaintiff in an action or special proceeding resides out of the state, or is a foreign corporation, the defendant may at any time apply to the court by noticed motion for an order requiring the plaintiff to file an undertaking to secure an award of costs and attorney's fees which may be awarded in the action or special proceeding. For the purposes of this section, "attorney's fees" means reasonable attorney's fees a party may be authorized to recover by a statute apart from this section or by contract.

(b) The motion shall be made on the grounds that the plaintiff resides out of the state or is a foreign corporation and that there is a reasonable possibility that the moving defendant will obtain judgment in the action or special proceeding. The motion shall be accompanied by an affidavit in support of the grounds for the motion and by a memorandum of points and authorities. The affidavit shall set forth the nature and amount of the costs and attorney's fees the defendant has incurred and expects to incur by the conclusion of the action or special proceeding.

(c) If the court, after hearing, determines that the grounds for the motion have been established, the court shall order that the plaintiff file the undertaking in an amount specified in the court's order as security for costs and attorney's fees.

(d) The plaintiff shall file the undertaking not later than 30 days after service of the court's order requiring it or within a greater time allowed by the court. If the plaintiff fails to file the undertaking within the time allowed, the plaintiff's action or special proceeding shall be dismissed as to the defendant in whose favor the order requiring the undertaking was made.

(e) If the defendant's motion for an order requiring an undertaking is filed not later than 30 days after service of summons on the defendant, further proceedings may be stayed in the discretion of the court upon application to the court by the defendant by noticed motion for the stay until 10 days after the motion for the undertaking is denied or, if granted, until 10 days after the required undertaking has been filed and the defendant has been served with a copy of the undertaking. The hearing on the application for the stay shall be held not later than 60 days after service of the summons. If the defendant files a motion for an order requiring an undertaking, which is granted but the defendant objects to the undertaking, the court may in its discretion stay the proceedings not longer than 10 days after a sufficient undertaking has been filed and the defendant has been served with a copy of the undertaking.

(f) The determinations of the court under this section have no effect on the determination of any issues on the merits of the action or special proceeding and may not be given in evidence nor referred to in the trial of the action or proceeding.

(g) An order granting or denying a motion for an undertaking under this section is not appealable. **Leg.H.** Enacted 1872 as §1036. Amended Stats 1903 ch 165 §1. Amended and renumbered by Stats 1933 ch 744 §189. Amended Stats 1951 ch 1737 §137, operative January 1, 1952; Stats 1980 ch 114 §4; Stats 1982 ch 517 §164; Stats 1988 ch 189 §1.

Prior Law: Former CCP §1030 was enacted 1872, amended and renumbered to be CCP §1025 by Stats 1933 ch 744 §184.

§1031. Attorney fees in actions for recovery of wages

In actions for the recovery of wages for labor performed, where the amount of the demand, exclusive of interest, does not exceed three hundred dollars ($300), the court shall add, as part of the cost, in any judgment recovered by the plaintiff or cross-complainant, an attorney's fee not exceeding 20 percent of the amount recovered. **Leg.H.** Added Stats 1933 ch 744 §190. Amended Stats 1939 ch 647 §1; Stats 1945 ch 1149 §1; Stats 1951 ch 1737 §138, operative January 1, 1952; Stats 1968 ch 71 §1; Stats 1973 ch 818 §1; Stats 1986 ch 377 §4.

Prior Law: Former CCP §1031 was enacted 1872, amended and renumbered to be CCP §1026 by Stats 1933 ch 744 §185.

§1031.5. [Section repealed 1983]

Leg.H. Added Stats 1979 ch 746 §1. Repealed January 1, 1983, by its own provisions. The repealed section related to compensation of expert appointed in civil action.

§1032. Recovery of costs by prevailing party as matter of right

(a) As used in this section, unless the context clearly requires otherwise:

(1) "Complaint" includes a cross-complaint.

(2) "Defendant" includes a cross-defendant, a person against whom a complaint is filed, or a party who files an answer in intervention.

(3) "Plaintiff" includes a cross-complainant or a party who files a complaint in intervention.

(4) "Prevailing party" includes the party with a net monetary recovery, a defendant in whose favor a dismissal is entered, a defendant where neither plaintiff nor defendant obtains any relief, and a defendant as against those plaintiffs who do not recover any relief against that defendant. If any party recovers other than monetary relief and in situations other than as specified, the "prevailing party" shall be as determined by the court, and under those circumstances, the court, in its discretion, may allow costs or not and, if allowed, may apportion costs between the parties on the same or adverse sides pursuant to rules adopted under Section 1034.

(b) Except as otherwise expressly provided by statute, a prevailing party is entitled as a matter of right to recover costs in any action or proceeding.

(c) Nothing in this section shall prohibit parties from stipulating to alternative procedures for awarding costs in the litigation pursuant to rules adopted under Section 1034. **Leg.H.** Added Stats 1986 ch 377 §6. Amended Stats 2017 ch 131 §2 (AB 1693), effective January 1, 2018.

Prior Law Former CCP §1032, similar to the present section, was added Stats 1933 ch 744 §191, amended Stats 1951 ch 1737 §139, operative January 1, 1952, Stats 1953 ch 910 §1, Stats 1957 ch 1172 §1, and repealed Stats 1986 ch 377 §5.

Former CCP §1032 was enacted 1872 and renumbered to be CCP §1027 by Stats 1933 ch 744 §186.

§1032a. [Section renumbered 1982]

Leg.H. Added Stats 1939 ch 470 §1. Amended Stats 1941 ch 1013 §1. Amended and renumbered as CCP §1032.7 by Stats 1982 ch 1354 §2.

§1032b. [Section renumbered 1982]

Leg.H. Added Stats 1969 ch 1610 §25, operative July 1, 1970. Amended Stats 1971 ch 585 §1; Stats 1976 ch 669 §1. Amended and renumbered as CCP §1032.8 by Stats 1982 ch 1354 §3.

§1032.5. [Section repealed 1987]

Leg.H. Added Stats 1939 ch 364 §1. Amended Stats 1951 ch 1737 §140, operative January 1, 1952. Repealed Stats 1986 ch 377 §7. See CCP §1033.5.

§1032.6. [Section repealed 1983]

Leg.H. Added Stats 1945 ch 1149 §2. Amended Stats 1951 ch 1737 §141, operative January 1, 1952. Repealed Stats 1982 ch 497 §69, operative July 1, 1983. See CCP §685.040.

§1032.7. [Section repealed 1987]

Leg.H. Added Stats 1939 ch 470 §1 as §1032a. Amended Stats 1941 ch 1013 §1. Amended and renumbered by Stats 1982 ch 1354 §2. Amended Stats 1985 ch 444 §1. Repealed Stats 1986 ch 377 §8. See CCP §1033.5.

§1032.8. [Section repealed 1987]

Leg.H. Added Stats 1969 ch 1610 §25, as §1032b, operative July 1, 1970. Amended Stats 1971 ch 585 §1; Stats 1976 ch 669 §1. Amended and renumbered by Stats 1982 ch 1354 §3. Repealed Stats 1986 ch 377 §9. See CCP §1033.5.

§1033. Discretion of court where judgment could have been rendered in limited civil case

(a) Costs or any portion of claimed costs shall be as determined by the court in its discretion in a case other than a limited civil case in accordance with Section 1034 where the prevailing party recovers a judgment that could have been rendered in a limited civil case.

(b) When a prevailing plaintiff in a limited civil case recovers less than the amount prescribed by law as the maximum limitation upon the jurisdiction of the small claims court, the following shall apply:

(1) When the party could have brought the action in the small claims division but did not do so, the court may, in its discretion, allow or deny costs to the prevailing party, or may allow costs in part in any amount as it deems proper.

(2) When the party could not have brought the action in the small claims court, costs and necessary disbursements shall be limited to the actual cost of the filing fee, the actual cost of service of process, and, when otherwise specifically allowed by law, reasonable attorneys' fees. However, those costs shall only be awarded to the plaintiff if the court is satisfied that prior to the commencement of the action, the plaintiff informed the defendant in writing of the intended legal action against the defendant and that legal action could result in a judgment against the defendant that would include the costs and necessary disbursements allowed by this paragraph. **Leg.H.** Added Stats 1986 ch 377 §11. Amended Stats 1987 ch 4 §2, effective March 17, 1987; Stats 1989 ch 62 §1; Stats 1998 ch 931 §107 (SB 2139), effective September 28, 1998.

Prior Law: Former CCP §1033, relating to service of memorandum of costs and disbursements, was enacted 1872, amended Code Amdts 1873–74 ch 383 §139, Stats 1899 ch 20 §1, Stats 1929 ch 482 §3, Stats 1931 ch 860 §1, Stats 1933 ch 744 §192, Stats 1937 ch 550 §1, Stats 1945 ch 828 §5, Stats 1951 ch 1737 §142, operative January 1, 1952, Stats 1955 ch 513 §1, Stats 1967 ch 1230 §2, Stats 1970 ch 602 §1, Stats 1982 ch 812 §2, and repealed Stats 1986 ch 377 §10.

§1033½. [Section repealed 1987]

Leg.H. Added Stats 1937 ch 532 §1. Amended Stats 1977 ch 1257 §34, effective October 3, 1977. Repealed Stats 1986 ch 377 §12. The repealed section related to memorandum of costs on judgment.

§1033.5. Items allowable as costs

(a) The following items are allowable as costs under Section 1032:

(1) Filing, motion, and jury fees.

(2) Juror food and lodging while they are kept together during trial and after the jury retires for deliberation.

(3)(A) Taking, video recording, and transcribing necessary depositions, including an original and one copy of those taken by the claimant and one copy of depositions taken by the party against whom costs are allowed.

(B) Fees of a certified or registered interpreter for the deposition of a party or witness who does not proficiently speak or understand the English language.

(C) Travel expenses to attend depositions.

(4) Service of process by a public officer, registered process server, or other means, as follows:

(A) When service is by a public officer, the recoverable cost is the fee authorized by law at the time of service.

(B) If service is by a process server registered pursuant to Chapter 16 (commencing with Section 22350) of Division 8 of the Business and Professions Code, the recoverable cost is the amount actually incurred in effecting service, including, but not limited to, a stakeout or other means employed in locating the person to be served, unless those charges are successfully challenged by a party to the action.

(C) When service is by publication, the recoverable cost is the sum actually incurred in effecting service.

(D) When service is by a means other than that set forth in subparagraph (A), (B), or (C), the recoverable cost is the lesser of the sum actually incurred, or the amount allowed to a public officer in this state for that service, except that the court may allow the sum actually incurred in effecting service upon application pursuant to paragraph (4) of subdivision (c).

(5) Expenses of attachment including keeper's fees.

(6) Premiums on necessary surety bonds.

(7) Ordinary witness fees pursuant to Section 68093 of the Government Code.

(8) Fees of expert witnesses ordered by the court.

(9) Transcripts of court proceedings ordered by the court.

(10) Attorney's fees, when authorized by any of the following:

(A) Contract.

(B) Statute.

(C) Law.

(11) Court reporter fees as established by statute.

(12) Court interpreter fees for a qualified court interpreter authorized by the court for an indigent person represented by a qualified legal services project, as defined in Section 6213 of the Business and Professions Code, or a pro bono attorney, as defined in Section 8030.4 of the Business and Professions Code.

(13) Models, the enlargements of exhibits and photocopies of exhibits, and the electronic presentation of exhibits, including costs of rental equipment and electronic formatting, may be allowed if they were reasonably helpful to aid the trier of fact.

(14) Fees for the electronic filing or service of documents through an electronic filing service provider if a court requires or orders electronic filing or service of documents.

(15) Fees for the hosting of electronic documents if a court requires or orders a party to have documents hosted by an electronic filing service provider. This paragraph shall become inoperative on January 1, 2022.

(16) Any other item that is required to be awarded to the prevailing party pursuant to statute as an incident to prevailing in the action at trial or on appeal.

(b) The following items are not allowable as costs, except when expressly authorized by law:

(1) Fees of experts not ordered by the court.

(2) Investigation expenses in preparing the case for trial.

(3) Postage, telephone, and photocopying charges, except for exhibits.

(4) Costs in investigation of jurors or in preparation for voir dire.

(5) Transcripts of court proceedings not ordered by the court.

(c) An award of costs shall be subject to the following:

(1) Costs are allowable if incurred, whether or not paid.

(2) Allowable costs shall be reasonably necessary to the conduct of the litigation rather than merely convenient or beneficial to its preparation.

(3) Allowable costs shall be reasonable in amount.

(4) Items not mentioned in this section and items assessed upon application may be allowed or denied in the court's discretion.

(5)(A) If a statute of this state refers to the award of "costs and attorney's fees," attorney's fees are an item and component of the costs to be awarded and are allowable as costs pursuant to subparagraph (B) of paragraph (10) of subdivision (a). A claim not based upon the court's established schedule of attorney's fees for actions on a contract shall bear the burden of proof. Attorney's fees allowable as costs pursuant to subparagraph (B) of paragraph (10) of subdivision (a) may be fixed as follows: (i) upon a noticed motion, (ii) at the time a statement of decision is rendered, (iii) upon application supported by affidavit made concurrently with a claim for other costs, or (iv) upon entry of default judgment. Attorney's fees allowable as costs pursuant to subparagraph (A) or (C) of paragraph (10) of subdivision (a) shall be fixed either upon a noticed motion or upon entry of a default judgment, unless otherwise provided by stipulation of the parties.

(B) Attorney's fees awarded pursuant to Section 1717 of the Civil Code are allowable costs under Section 1032 as authorized by subparagraph (A) of paragraph (10) of subdivision (a). **Leg.H.** Added Stats 1986 ch 377 §13. Amended Stats 1987 ch 1080 §8.5; Stats 1989 ch 1416 §26; Stats 1990 ch 804 §1 (AB 3331); Stats 1993 ch 456 §15 (AB 58); Stats 2009 ch 88 §17 (AB 176), effective January 1, 2010; Stats 2011 ch 409 §3 (AB 1403), effective January 1, 2012; Stats 2012 ch 758 §2 (AB 2684), effective January 1, 2013; Stats 2015 ch 90 §1 (AB 1002), effective January 1, 2016; Stats 2016 ch 461 §2 (AB 2244), effective January 1, 2017; Stats 2017 ch 583 §1 (AB 828), effective January 1, 2018.

1990 Note: The Legislature finds and declares that there is great uncertainty as to the procedure to be followed in awarding attorney's fees where entitlement thereto is provided by contract to the prevailing party. It is the intent of the Legislature in enacting this act to confirm that these attorney's fees are costs which are to be awarded only upon noticed motion, except where the parties stipulate otherwise or judgment is entered by default. It is further the intent of the Legislature to vest the Judicial Council with the discretion provided in Section 1034 of the Code of Civil Procedure to adopt procedural guidelines establishing the time for the hearing of these motions, but the Legislature finds and declares that the criteria set forth in Section 870.2 of the California Rules of Court provide a fair and equitable procedure for the motions. Stats 1990 ch 804 §2.

§1033.7. [Section repealed 1983]

Leg.H. Added Stats 1945 ch 1149 §3. Amended Stats 1947 ch 789 §1; Stats 1949 ch 1076 §1; Stats 1951 ch 1737 §143, operative January 1, 1952; Stats 1957 ch 1734 §2; Stats 1970 ch 602 §2. Repealed Stats 1982 ch 497 §70, operative July 1, 1983. See CCP §§685.050, 685.070, 685.080, 685.090.

§1034. Prejudgment costs; Costs on appeal

(a) Prejudgment costs allowable under this chapter shall be claimed and contested in accordance with rules adopted by the Judicial Council.

(b) The Judicial Council shall establish by rule allowable costs on appeal and the procedure for claiming those costs. **Leg.H.** Added Stats 1986 ch 377 §15.

Prior Law: Former CCP §1034, similar to the present section, was enacted 1872, amended Stats 1919 ch 198 §1, Stats 1933 ch 744 §193, Stats 1939 ch 330 §1, Stats 1945 ch 40 §5, Stats 1982 ch 497 §71, operative July 1, 1983, and repealed Stats 1986 ch 377 §14.

§1034½. [Section repealed 1967]

Leg.H. Added Stats 1945 ch 1321 §1. Repealed Stats 1967 ch 1600 §1. The repealed section related to supplemental cost bill covering eviction.

§1034.5. Costs in unlawful detainer proceedings

In unlawful detainer proceedings, the plaintiff who recovers judgment for possession of premises, and who advances or pays to the sheriff or marshal the expenses required for the eviction of any persons in possession or occupancy of the premises and the personal property of such persons, shall, after being advised by the sheriff or marshal of the exact amount necessarily used and expended to effect the eviction, be allowed to file a request for the same pursuant to rules adopted by the Judicial

§1035. [Section repealed 1983]

Leg.H. Added Stats 1951 ch 1327 §1. Repealed Stats 1982 ch 517 §165. See CCP §995.250.

Prior Law: Former CCP §1035, similar to present CCP §1033, was enacted 1872 and repealed Stats 1933 ch 744 §198.

§1036. Costs in inverse condemnation proceedings

In any inverse condemnation proceeding, the court rendering judgment for the plaintiff by awarding compensation, or the attorney representing the public entity who effects a settlement of that proceeding, shall determine and award or allow to the plaintiff, as a part of that judgment or settlement, a sum that will, in the opinion of the court, reimburse the plaintiff's reasonable costs, disbursements, and expenses, including reasonable attorney, appraisal, and engineering fees, actually incurred because of that proceeding in the trial court or in any appellate proceeding in which the plaintiff prevails on any issue in that proceeding. **Leg.H.** Added Stats 1975 ch 1240 §8, operative July 1, 1976. Amended Stats 1995 ch 181 §1 (SB 51).

Prior Law: Former CCP §1036 was enacted 1872, amended Stats 1903 ch 165 §1, and amended and renumbered to be CCP §1030 by Stats 1933 ch 744 §189.

1995 Note: It is the intent of the Legislature in enacting the amendments to Section 1036 of the Code of Civil Procedure adopted at the 1995 portion of the 1995–96 Regular Session to clarify that litigation costs are recoverable by prevailing plaintiffs in any inverse condemnation proceeding. California courts have held that Section 1036 of the Code of Civil Procedure applies to certain situations in which the plaintiff's inverse condemnation judgment is for the "damaging" of property (see, e.g., *Holtz v. San Francisco Bay Area Rapid Transit Dist.*, 17 Cal. 3d 648, 655 fn. 5; *Salton Bay Marina, Inc. v. Imperial Irrigation Dist.*, 172 Cal. App. 3d 914, 952; *Orme v. State of California ex. rel. Dept. Water Resources*, 83 Cal. App. 3d 178, 184-185; *Tilem v. City of Los Angeles*, 142 Cal. App. 3d 694), and that there are certain situations in which a plaintiff's inverse condemnation judgment may compensate for losses to personal property (see, e.g., *Imperial Cattle Co. v. Imperial Irrigation Dist.*, 167 Cal. App. 3d 263, 277 fn. 8; *Sutfin v. State of California*, 261 Cal. App. 2d 50, 53; *City of Oakland v. Oakland Raiders*, 32 Cal. 3d 60, 67).

Those changes to Section 1036 related to litigation costs on appeal are intended to abrogate the contrary ruling in *Holtz v. San Francisco Bay Area Rapid Transit Dist.*, 17 Cal. 3d 648, 658-659, and to conform Section 1036 of the Code of Civil Procedure to what the California Supreme Court has characterized as "the general rule that statutory attorney fee provisions are interpreted to apply to attorney fees on appeal unless the statute specifically provides otherwise" (*Morcos v. Board of Retirement*, 51 Cal. 3d 924, 929).

§1037. [Section repealed 1987]

Leg.H. Added Stats 1980 ch 114 §5. Repealed Stats 1986 ch 377 §17. The repealed section related to attorney fees in action for libel or slander.

Prior Law: Former CCP §1037, similar to present CCP §1030, was enacted 1872, amended Stats 1903 ch 165 §2, and repealed Stats 1933 ch 744 §198.

§1038. Defense costs on granting of summary judgment or nonsuit

(a) In any civil proceeding under the Government Claims Act (Division 3.6 (commencing with Section 810) of Title 1 of the Government Code) or for express or implied indemnity or for contribution in any civil action, the court, upon motion of the defendant or cross-defendant, shall, at the time of the granting of any summary judgment, motion for directed verdict, motion for judgment under Section 631.8, or any nonsuit dismissing the moving party other than the plaintiff, petitioner, cross-complainant, or intervenor, or at a later time set forth by rule of the Judicial Council adopted under Section 1034, determine whether or not the plaintiff, petitioner, cross-complainant, or intervenor brought the proceeding with reasonable cause and in the good faith belief that there was a justifiable controversy under the facts and law which warranted the filing of the complaint, petition, cross-complaint, or complaint or answer in intervention. If the court should determine that the proceeding was not brought in good faith and with reasonable cause, an additional issue shall be decided as to the defense costs reasonably and necessarily incurred by the party or parties opposing the proceeding, and the court shall render judgment in favor of that party in the amount of all reasonable and necessary defense costs, in addition to those costs normally awarded to the prevailing party. An award of defense costs under this section shall not be made except on notice contained in a party's papers and an opportunity to be heard.

(b) "Defense costs," as used in this section, shall include reasonable attorney's fees, expert witness fees, the expense of services of experts, advisers, and consultants in defense of the proceeding, and where reasonably and necessarily incurred in defending the proceeding.

(c) This section shall be applicable only on motion made before the discharge of the jury or entry of judgment, and any party requesting the relief pursuant to this section waives any right to seek damages for malicious prosecution. Failure to make the motion shall not be deemed a waiver of the right to pursue a malicious prosecution action.

(d) This section shall only apply if the defendant or cross-defendant has made a motion for summary judgment, judgment under Section 631.8, directed verdict, or nonsuit and the motion is granted. **Leg.H.** Added Stats 1980 ch 1209 §1. Amended Stats 1986 ch 377 §18; Stats 1989 ch 1416 §27; Stats 2012 ch 759 §2 (AB 2690), effective January 1, 2013; Stats 2017 ch 131 §3 (AB 1693), effective January 1, 2018.

Prior Law: Former CCP §1038, was enacted 1872 and renumbered to be CCP §1028 by Stats 1933 ch 744 §187.

§1039. [Section repealed 1987]

Leg.H. Added Stats 1981 ch 1034 §1. Repealed Stats 1986 ch 377 §19. The repealed section related to supplemental costs.

Prior Law: Former CCP §1039, was enacted 1872 and renumbered to be CCP §1029 by Stats 1933 ch 744 §187.

CHAPTER 7
GENERAL PROVISIONS

Lost papers, how supplied. §1045.
Papers without title of action, or with defective title, may be valid. §1046.
Filing of lost or destroyed real property records nunc pro tunc. §1046a.
Successive actions on same contract, etc. §1047.
Joint hearing or trial, and consolidation of actions; Separate trial, and right to jury. §1048.
Actions, when deemed pending. §1049.
Actions to determine adverse claims, and by sureties. §1050.
Acts by several referees. §1053.
Extension of time, by judge or on stipulation. §1054.
Extension of time when attorney is legislator. §1054.1.
Judgment in action against officer or person secured by indemnity bond or covenant. §1055.

§1041. [Section repealed 1983]

Leg.H. Added Stats 1937 ch 579 §1. Repealed Stats 1982 ch 517 §166. See CCP §§995.020, 995.320, 995.330.

§1042. [Section repealed 1983]

Leg.H. Added Stats 1933 ch 876 §1. Repealed Stats 1982 ch 517 §167. See CCP §567.

§1043. [Section repealed 1951]

Leg.H. Added Stats 1931 ch 303 §1. Repealed Stats 1951 ch 364 §50000. See Fin C §§1570–1578.

§1044. [Section repealed 1951]

Leg.H. Added Stats 1931 ch 303 §2. Repealed Stats 1951 ch 364 §50000.

§1045. Lost papers, how supplied

If an original pleading or paper be lost, the court may authorize a copy thereof to be filed and used instead of the original. **Leg.H.** Enacted 1872.

§1046. Papers without title of action, or with defective title, may be valid

An affidavit, notice, or other paper, without the title of the action or proceeding in which it is made, or with a defective title, is as valid and effectual for any purpose as if duly entitled, if it intelligibly refers to the action or proceeding. **Leg.H.** Enacted 1872. Amended Stats 1981 ch 714 §71.

§1046a. Filing of lost or destroyed real property records nunc pro tunc

In all cases brought under the provisions of any act providing for the establishment and quieting of title to real property in cases where the public records in the office of the county recorder have been, or shall hereafter be, lost or destroyed, in whole or in any material part by flood, fire or earthquake, all papers filed under order of court nunc pro tunc as of the date when they should have been filed, shall have the same force and effect as if filed on the date when they should have been filed. **Leg.H.** Added Stats 1909 ch 686 §1.

§1047. Successive actions on same contract, etc.
Successive actions may be maintained upon the same contract or transaction, whenever, after the former action, a new cause of action arises therefrom. **Leg.H.** Enacted 1872.

§1048. Joint hearing or trial, and consolidation of actions; Separate trial, and right to jury
(a) When actions involving a common question of law or fact are pending before the court, it may order a joint hearing or trial of any or all the matters in issue in the actions; it may order all the actions consolidated and it may make such orders concerning proceedings therein as may tend to avoid unnecessary costs or delay.

(b) The court, in furtherance of convenience or to avoid prejudice, or when separate trials will be conducive to expedition and economy, may order a separate trial of any cause of action, including a cause of action asserted in a cross-complaint, or of any separate issue or of any number of causes of action or issues, preserving the right of trial by jury required by the Constitution or a statute of this state or of the United States. **Leg.H.** Enacted 1872. Amended Stats 1927 ch 320 §1; Stats 1971 ch 244 §58, operative July 1, 1972.

§1049. Actions, when deemed pending
An action is deemed to be pending from the time of its commencement until its final determination upon appeal, or until the time for appeal has passed, unless the judgment is sooner satisfied. **Leg.H.** Enacted 1872.

§1050. Actions to determine adverse claims, and by sureties
An action may be brought by one person against another for the purpose of determining an adverse claim, which the latter makes against the former for money or property upon an alleged obligation; and also against two or more persons, for the purpose of compelling one to satisfy a debt due to the other, for which plaintiff is bound as a surety. **Leg.H.** Enacted 1872.

§1051. [Section repealed 1974]
Leg.H. Enacted 1872. Amended Stats 1933 ch 744 §194. Repealed Stats 1973 ch 146 §1. The repealed section related to when clerk is required to report testimony.

§1052. [Section repealed 2003]
Leg.H. Enacted 1872. Amended Stats 1933 ch 744 §195; Stats 1943 ch 847 §11; Stats 1977 ch 1257 §35, effective October 3, 1977; Stats 1984 ch 1288 §2; Stats 1998 ch 931 §108 (SB 2139), effective September 28, 1998. Repealed Stats 2002 ch 784 §71 (SB 1316). The repealed section related to the register of actions in municipal court.

§1052.5. [Section repealed 2003]
Leg.H. Added Stats 1972 ch 1083 §2. Amended Stats 1977 ch 1257 §36, effective October 3, 1977; Stats 1998 ch 931 §109 (SB 2139), effective September 28, 1998. Repealed Stats 2002 ch 784 §72 (SB 1316). The repealed section related to maintaining the register of actions by photographing, or electronically storing records.

§1053. Acts by several referees
When there are three referees all must meet, but two of them may do any act which might be done by all. **Leg.H.** Enacted 1872. Amended Stats 1961 ch 461 §3.

§1054. Extension of time, by judge or on stipulation
(a) When an act to be done, as provided in this code, relates to the pleadings in the action, or the preparation of bills of exceptions, or of amendments thereto, or to the service of notices other than of appeal and of intention to move for a new trial, the time allowed therefor, unless otherwise expressly provided, may be extended, upon good cause shown, by the judge of the court in which the action is pending, or by the judge who presided at the trial of the action; but the extension so allowed shall not exceed 30 days, without the consent of the adverse party.

(b) In all cases in which the court or judge is authorized by this section to grant an extension of time, the extension of time shall be granted when all attorneys of record of parties who have appeared in the action agree in writing to the extension of time, and any extension of time previously granted by stipulation of all attorneys of record of parties who have appeared in the action shall not be included in the computation of the 30-day limitation upon extensions of time allowed by the court or judge. **Leg.H.** Enacted 1872. Amended Code Amdts 1873–74 ch 383 §140; Code Amdts 1880 ch 19 §1; Stats 1889 ch 41 §1; Stats 1895 ch 3 §1; Stats 1906 Ex Sess ch 6 §1; Stats 1915 ch 109 §1; Stats 1931 ch 1078 §2; Stats 1933 ch 282 §2, ch 744, §196; Stats 1937 ch 525 §1; Stats 1945 ch 1512 §2, effective July 18, 1945; Stats 1947 ch 33 §1, effective February 13, 1947, ch 1097 §1, effective July 2, 1947; Stats 1951 ch 1737 §144, operative January 1, 1952; Stats 1982 ch 517 §168.

§1054.1. Extension of time when attorney is legislator
(a) When an act to be done in any action or proceeding in any court of this state or before any state administrative agency, as provided by law or rule, relates to the pleadings in the action, or the preparation of bills of exceptions, or of amendments thereto, or to the service of notices (other than of appeal, of intention to move for a new trial, and of intention to move to vacate a judgment), and such act is not a motion for a judgment notwithstanding the verdict, the time allowed therefor, unless otherwise expressly provided, shall be extended to a date certain by the judges of the court or by the agency in which the action or proceeding is pending, or by the judge who presided at the trial of the action, when it appears to the judge of any court or to the agency to whom the application is made that an attorney of record for the party applying for the extension is a Member of the Legislature of this state, and that the Legislature is in session or in recess not exceeding a recess of 40 days or that a legislative committee of which the attorney is a duly appointed member is meeting or is to meet within a period which the court or agency finds does not exceed the time reasonably necessary to enable the member to reach the committee meeting by the ordinary mode of travel. When the Legislature is in session or in recess, extension shall be to a date not less than 30 days next following the final adjournment of the Legislature or the commencement of a recess of more than 40 days. If a date is available during recess, extension shall be to such earlier date. When a legislative committee is meeting or is to meet within a period which the court or agency finds does not exceed the time reasonably necessary to enable the member to reach the committee meeting by the ordinary mode of travel, extension shall be for such period as the court or agency finds will be reasonably necessary to enable the member to perform the act to be done in the action or proceeding, unless the extension would expire when the Legislature is to be in session; and in that case the extension shall be to a date not less than 30 days following the final adjournment of the Legislature or the commencement of a recess of more than 40 days. If the act may be reasonably done by the member within the recess, continuance shall be to such earlier date. However, any postponement granted under the provisions of this section shall suspend for the same period of time as the postponement, the running of any period of time for any ruling or proceeding by a court, board, commission, or officer, or for the performance by any party of any act affected by the postponement.

(b) Extension of time pursuant to this section is mandatory unless the court determines that the extension would defeat or abridge a right to relief pendente lite in a paternity action or a right to invoke a provisional remedy such as pendente lite support in a domestic relations controversy, attachment and sale of perishable goods, receivership of a failing business, and temporary restraining order or preliminary injunction, and that the continuance should not be granted. **Leg.H.** Added Stats 1947 ch 1097 §2, effective July 2, 1947. Amended Stats 1951 ch 1737 §145, operative January 1, 1952; Stats 1959 ch 985 §1; Stats 1963 ch 1468 §2; Stats 1965 ch 1089 §5; Stats 1968 ch 698 §2; Stats 1982 ch 517 §169.

§1054a. [Section repealed 1983]
Leg.H. Added Stats 1933 ch 744 §197. Amended Stats 1937 ch 580 §1; Stats 1951 ch 1737 §146, operative January 1, 1952; Stats 1957 ch 1495 §1. Repealed Stats 1982 ch 517 §170. See CCP §§995.160, 995.710, 995.720, 995.740, 995.750.

§1055. Judgment in action against officer or person secured by indemnity bond or covenant
If an action is brought against any officer or person for an act for the doing of which he had theretofore received any valid bond or covenant of indemnity, and he gives seasonable notice thereof in writing to the persons who executed such bond or covenant, and permits them to conduct the defense of such action, the judgment recovered therein is conclusive

§1056. [Section repealed 1983]

Leg.H. Added Stats 1889 ch 181 §1. Amended Stats 1933 ch 511 §1; Stats 1963 ch 1915 §1; Stats 1976 ch 740 §1. Repealed Stats 1982 ch 517 §171. See CCP §§995.120, 995.630.

Prior Law: Former CCP §1056, relating to prosecution of actions in the Spanish language in certain counties, was enacted 1872, amended Stats 1857 ch 43 §1, Stats 1862 ch 444 §1, and repealed Code Amdts 1880 ch 98 §1.

§1057. [Section repealed 1983]

Leg.H. Enacted 1872. Amended Stats 1889 ch 181 §2; Stats 1907 ch 245 §1; Stats 1937 ch 581 §1; Stats 1939 ch 1000 §1; Stats 1953 ch 267 §1; Stats 1963 ch 137 §1. Repealed Stats 1982 ch 517 §172. See CCP §§995.260, 995.350, 995.510, 995.520, 995.610, 995.660, 996.010.

§1057a. [Section repealed 1983]

Leg.H. Added Stats 1911 ch 226 §1. Amended Stats 1921 ch 86 §1; Stats 1949 ch 1505 §1. Repealed Stats 1982 ch 517 §173. See CCP §§995.640, 995.660.

§1057b. [Section repealed 1983]

Leg.H. Added Stats 1949 ch 1501 §1. Repealed Stats 1982 ch 517 §174. See CCP §995.650.

§1058. [Section repealed 1983]

Leg.H. Enacted 1872. Amended Code Amdts 1880 ch 84 §1; Stats 1937 ch 514 §1; Stats 1939 ch 521 §1. Repealed Stats 1982 ch 517 §175. See CCP §995.220.

§1058a. [Section repealed 1983]

Leg.H. Added Stats 1972 ch 391 §2. Repealed Stats 1982 ch 517 §176. See CCP §§995.040, 995.320, 996.420, 996.440.

§1059. [Section repealed 1983]

Leg.H. Added Code Amdts 1873–74 ch 383 §141. Repealed Stats 1982 ch 517 §177. See CCP §917.1.

CHAPTER 8
DECLARATORY RELIEF

Declaratory relief. §1060.
Determination of residence for state income tax purposes. §1060.5.
When court may refuse to act. §1061.
Other remedies not affected. §1062.
[Section renumbered 1980]. §1062a.
Setting for trial. §1062.3.
Action respecting medical malpractice insurance policy. §1062.5.

§1060. Declaratory relief

Any person interested under a written instrument, excluding a will or a trust, or under a contract, or who desires a declaration of his or her rights or duties with respect to another, or in respect to, in, over or upon property, or with respect to the location of the natural channel of a watercourse, may, in cases of actual controversy relating to the legal rights and duties of the respective parties, bring an original action or cross-complaint in the superior court for a declaration of his or her rights and duties in the premises, including a determination of any question of construction or validity arising under the instrument or contract. He or she may ask for a declaration of rights or duties, either alone or with other relief; and the court may make a binding declaration of these rights or duties, whether or not further relief is or could be claimed at the time. The declaration may be either affirmative or negative in form and effect, and the declaration shall have the force of a final judgment. The declaration may be had before there has been any breach of the obligation in respect to which said declaration is sought. **Leg.H.** Added Stats 1921 ch 463 §1. Amended Stats 1965 ch 959 §2; Stats 1976 ch 1288 §18; Stats 1993 ch 1262 §6 (AB 1272); Stats 1994 ch 806 §1 (AB 3686); Stats 1998 ch 931 §110 (SB 2139), effective September 28, 1998; Stats 2002 ch 784 §73 (SB 1316).

§1060.5. Determination of residence for state income tax purposes

Any individual claiming to be a nonresident of the State of California for the purposes of the Personal Income Tax Law may commence an action in the Superior Court in the County of Sacramento, or in the County of Los Angeles, or in the City and County of San Francisco, against the Franchise Tax Board to determine the fact of his or her residence in this state under the conditions and circumstances set forth in Section 19381 of the Revenue and Taxation Code. **Leg.H.** Added Stats 1955 ch 1555 §1. Amended Stats 1996 ch 952 §1 (SB 715).

§1061. When court may refuse to act

The court may refuse to exercise the power granted by this chapter in any case where its declaration or determination is not necessary or proper at the time under all the circumstances. **Leg.H.** Added Stats 1921 ch 463 §1.

§1062. Other remedies not affected

The remedies provided by this chapter are cumulative, and shall not be construed as restricting any remedy, provisional or otherwise, provided by law for the benefit of any party to such action, and no judgment under this chapter shall preclude any party from obtaining additional relief based upon the same facts. **Leg.H.** Added Stats 1921 ch 463 §1.

§1062a. [Section renumbered 1980]

Leg.H. Added Stats 1927 ch 321 §1. Amended Stats 1976 ch 1076 §1. Amended and renumbered as CCP §1062.3 by Stats 1980 ch 676 §66.

§1062.3. Setting for trial

(a) Except as provided in subdivision (b), actions brought under the provisions of this chapter shall be set for trial at the earliest possible date and shall take precedence over all other cases, except older matters of the same character and matters to which special precedence may be given by law.

(b) Any action brought under the provisions of this chapter in which the plaintiff seeks any relief, in addition to a declaration of rights and duties, shall take such precedence only upon noticed motion and a showing that the action requires a speedy trial. **Leg.H.** Added Stats 1927 ch 321 §1, as §1062a. Amended Stats 1976 ch 1076 §1; Amended and renumbered Stats 1980 ch 676 §66.

§1062.5. Action respecting medical malpractice insurance policy

Any insurer who issues policies of professional liability insurance to health care providers for professional negligence, as defined in Chapter 1 as amended by Chapter 2, Statutes of 1975, Second Extraordinary Session, any health care provider covered by such a policy, or any potentially aggrieved person, may bring an action in the superior court for a declaration of its, his, or her rights, duties, and obligations under Chapter 1 as amended by Chapter 2, Statutes of 1975, Second Extraordinary Session.

The court shall permit any of the following persons to intervene in the action:

(1) The Attorney General.

(2) Any other person whose appearance is determined by the court to be essential to a complete determination or settlement of any issues in the action.

The action shall be commenced in the superior court in the county in which the Attorney General is required to reside and keep his office pursuant to Section 1060 of the Government Code.

The action shall be set for trial at the earliest possible date and shall take precedence over all cases other than those in which the state is a party.

The court may make a binding declaration of the rights, duties, and obligations of the insurer, whether or not further relief is or could be claimed at the time. The declaration may be affirmative or negative in form and effect and shall have the force and effect of a final judgment.

If the declaration is appealed, the appeal shall be given precedence in the court of appeal and Supreme Court and placed on the calendar in the order of its date of issue immediately following cases in which the state is a party.

The remedy established by this section is cumulative, and shall not be construed as restricting any remedy established for the benefit of any party to the action by any other provision of law. No declaration under this section shall preclude any party from obtaining additional relief based upon the same facts. **Leg.H.** Added Stats 1979 ch 373 §52.

CHAPTER 9
ACTIONS TO ENFORCE REAL PROPERTY AND MOBILEHOME SALES AGREEMENTS

Recordation of sales agreement or filing of change-in-ownership statement as prerequisite to maintenance of action. §1062.10.

§1062.10. Recordation of sales agreement or filing of change-in-ownership statement as prerequisite to maintenance of action

No person or legal entity may maintain an action in any court in this state to enforce the terms of a real property sales contract as defined in Section 2985 of the Civil Code or a conditional sale contract on a mobilehome subject to local property taxation and subject to Division 13 (commencing with Section 18000) of Part 2 of the Health and Safety Code, providing for a change in ownership of real property or of a mobilehome subject to local property taxation until the agreement is duly recorded by the county recorder or the change-in-ownership statement required by Section 480 of the Revenue and Taxation Code is filed as provided in that section.

This section shall apply to the enforcement of those agreements which are alleged to have transferred ownership of real property or of a mobilehome subject to property taxation which are entered into after January 1, 1986. **Leg.H.** Added Stats 1985 ch 911 §2. Amended Stats 1986 ch 62 §1, effective April 23, 1986.

CHAPTER 10
COMPUTER ASSISTANCE

Computer system to assist pro per litigant to prepare standardized documents. §1062.20.

§1062.20. Computer system to assist pro per litigant to prepare standardized documents

(a) In accordance with rules and policy of the Judicial Council, each court may establish and operate an interactive computer system to enable and assist a pro per litigant to prepare standardized pro per court documents for use in the following civil actions:

(1) Enforcement of court orders, including orders for visitation, child custody, and property division.

(2) Landlord and tenant actions.

(3) Uncontested dissolution of marriage.

(4) Probate of a will.

(b) The computer system may also provide standardized information to users, including, but not limited to, information regarding calculations for child and spousal support payments that meet the requirements described in Section 3830 of the Family Code, court procedures, rights and responsibilities of landlords and tenants, and alternative dispute resolution.

(c) The court may contract with a private entity to establish and operate the program and collect any fees described in subdivision (d).

(d) The court may establish and collect fees from the program not to exceed the reasonable costs to establish and operate the program. **Leg.H.** Added Stats 1995 ch 507 §1 (AB 1028).

CHAPTER 11
FOSTER FAMILY AGENCY ACCOUNTABILITY [REPEALED EFFECTIVE JANUARY 1, 2027]

Claim or lawsuit against a foster family agency [Repealed January 1, 2027]. § 1062.30.
Necessary services to vulnerable youth [Repealed January 1, 2027]. § 1062.31.
Definitions [Repealed January 1, 2027]. § 1062.32.
Liability for injury or damage [Repealed January 1, 2027]. § 1062.33.
Repeal date [Repealed January 1, 2027]. § 1062.34.

§ 1062.30. Claim or lawsuit against a foster family agency [Repealed January 1, 2027]

This chapter applies to any claim or lawsuit against a foster family agency or a noncustodial adoption agency for the acts of their employees, contractors, or volunteers brought by a recipient of those services or on the recipient's behalf. **Leg.H.** Added Stats 2024 ch 403 §1 (AB 2496), effective September 22, 2024, repealed January 1, 2027.

§ 1062.31. Necessary services to vulnerable youth [Repealed January 1, 2027]

It is the public policy of the State of California that foster family agencies or noncustodial adoption agencies, also known as FFAs, provide necessary services to vulnerable youth throughout the state and are integral to the foster care system. Consequently, FFAs are afforded the rights set forth in this chapter. **Leg.H.** Added Stats 2024 ch 403 §1 (AB 2496), effective September 22, 2024, repealed January 1, 2027.

§ 1062.32. Definitions [Repealed January 1, 2027]

For the purposes of this chapter, the following definitions apply:

(a) "FFA" means a foster family agency or a noncustodial adoption agency, as these terms are defined in Section 1502 of the Health and Safety Code.

(b) "Public entity" has the same meaning as defined in Section 811.2 of the Government Code. **Leg.H.** Added Stats 2024 ch 403 §1 (AB 2496), effective September 22, 2024, repealed January 1, 2027.

§ 1062.33. Liability for injury or damage [Repealed January 1, 2027]

(a) An FFA may be held liable for injury or damage caused by the negligence of the FFA but not for the injury or damage caused by the public entity, including its officers, employees, or volunteers, acting in its capacity. The FFA and the public entity shall each bear the cost of insuring against their respective acts and omissions and shall each bear the costs of defending itself against claims arising from those risks.

(b)(1) Notwithstanding any other law, subdivision (a) shall not be waived or suspended by any court. Any provision in a nongovernmental organization contract for child, youth, and family services in which a public entity is indemnified, held harmless, or insured for damages, claims, losses, or expenses arising from injury or damage, including, but not limited to, bodily injury, mental anguish, property damage, or economic or noneconomic damages or loss, caused by or resulting from a public entity's negligence or intentional conduct, in whole or in part, shall be void as against public policy and unenforceable.

(2) Subdivision (a) does not limit or affect the immunity provided by any other law that would otherwise be an available defense to either party. **Leg.H.** Added Stats 2024 ch 403 §1 (AB 2496), effective September 22, 2024, repealed January 1, 2027.

§ 1062.34. Repeal date [Repealed January 1, 2027]

This chapter shall remain in effect only until January 1, 2027, and as of that date is repealed. **Leg.H.** Added Stats 2024 ch 403 §1 (AB 2496), effective September 22, 2024, repealed January 1, 2027.

PART 3
OF SPECIAL PROCEEDINGS OF A CIVIL NATURE

Preliminary Provisions.
Title 1. Of Writs of Review, Mandate, and Prohibition.
Title 3. Of Summary Proceedings.
Title 4. Of the Enforcement of Liens.
Title 5. Of Contempts.
Title 7. Eminent Domain Law.
Title 8. Change of Names.
Title 9. Arbitration.
Title 9.1. Arbitration of Medical Malpractice.
Title 9.2. Public Construction Contract Arbitration.
Title 9.3. Arbitration and Conciliation of International Commercial Disputes.
Title 9.4. Real Estate Contract Arbitration.
Title 9.5. Arbitration of Firefighter and Law Enforcement Officer Labor Disputes.
Title 10. Unclaimed Property.
Title 11. Money Judgments of Other Jurisdictions.
Title 11.6. Civil Action Mediation.
Title 11b. Recovery of Preferences in an Assignment for the Benefit of Creditors [Renumbered].
Title 11.7. Recovery of Preferences and Exempt Property in an Assignment for the Benefit of Creditors.
Title 12. Tribal Injunctions.
Title 13. Inspection Warrants.

PRELIMINARY PROVISIONS

Parties, how designated. §1063.
Judgment and order same meaning as in civil actions. §1064.

§1063. Parties, how designated
The party prosecuting a special proceeding may be known as the plaintiff, and the adverse party as the defendant. **Leg.H.** Enacted 1872.

§1064. Judgment and order same meaning as in civil actions
A judgment in a special proceeding is the final determination of the rights of the parties therein. The definitions of a motion and an order in a civil action are applicable to similar acts in a special proceeding. **Leg.H.** Enacted 1872.

TITLE 1
OF WRITS OF REVIEW, MANDATE, AND PROHIBITION

Chapter 1. Writ of Review.
Chapter 2. Writ of Mandate.
Chapter 3. Writ of Prohibition.
Chapter 4. Writs of Review, Mandate, and Prohibition May Issue and Be Heard at Chambers.
Chapter 5. Rules of Practice and Appeals.

CHAPTER 1
WRIT OF REVIEW

Writ's names. §1067.
Courts that may grant writ. §1068.
Application for writ; How made. §1069.
Demurrer or answer. §1069.1.
Writ to be directed to inferior tribunal, etc. §1070.
Contents of writ. §1071.
Proceeding in inferior court may be stayed, or not. §1072.
Service of writ. §1073.
Review under writ, extent of. §1074.
A defective return of writ may be perfected; Hearing and judgment. §1075.
Copy of judgment must be sent to inferior tribunal. §1076.
Judgment rolls. §1077.

§1067. Writ's names
The writ of certiorari may be denominated the writ of review. **Leg.H.** Enacted 1872. Amended Code Amdts 1873–74 ch 383 §142.

§1068. Courts that may grant writ
(a) A writ of review may be granted by any court when an inferior tribunal, board, or officer, exercising judicial functions, has exceeded the jurisdiction of such tribunal, board, or officer, and there is no appeal, nor, in the judgment of the court, any plain, speedy, and adequate remedy.

(b) The appellate division of the superior court may grant a writ of review directed to the superior court in a limited civil case or in a misdemeanor or infraction case. Where the appellate division grants a writ of review directed to the superior court, the superior court is an inferior tribunal for purposes of this chapter. **Leg.H.** Enacted 1872. Amended Stats 1935 ch 52 §1; Stats 1951 ch 1737 §147, operative January 1, 1952; Stats 1998 ch 931 §111 (SB 2139), effective September 28, 1998; Stats 1999 ch 344 §16 (SB 210), effective September 7, 1999; Stats 2002 ch 784 §74 (SB 1316).

§1069. Application for writ; How made
The application must be made on the verified petition of the party beneficially interested, and the court may require a notice of the application to be given to the adverse party, or may grant an order to show cause why it should not be allowed, or may grant the writ without notice. **Leg.H.** Enacted 1872. Amended Stats 1907 ch 328 §1.

§1069.1. Demurrer or answer
The provisions of Section 1089 as to a return by demurrer or answer apply to a proceeding pursuant to this chapter. **Leg.H.** Added Stats 1971 ch 1475 §2.

§1070. Writ to be directed to inferior tribunal, etc.
The writ may be directed to the inferior tribunal, board, or officer, or to any other person having the custody of the record or proceedings to be certified. When directed to a tribunal, the clerk, if there be one, must return the writ with the transcript required. **Leg.H.** Enacted 1872.

§1071. Contents of writ
The writ of review must command the party to whom it is directed to certify fully to the court issuing the writ at a time and place then or thereafter specified by court order a transcript of the record and proceedings (describing or referring to them with convenient certainty), that the same may be reviewed by the court; and requiring the party, in the meantime, to desist from further proceedings in the matter to be reviewed. **Leg.H.** Enacted 1872. Amended Stats 1963 ch 461 §2.

§1072. Proceeding in inferior court may be stayed, or not
If a stay of proceedings be not intended, the words requiring the stay must be omitted from the writ; these words may be inserted or omitted, in the sound discretion of the court, but if omitted, the power of the inferior court or officer is not suspended or the proceedings stayed. **Leg.H.** Enacted 1872.

§1073. Service of writ
The writ must be served in the same manner as a summons in civil action, except when otherwise expressly directed by the court. **Leg.H.** Enacted 1872.

§1074. Review under writ, extent of
The review upon this writ cannot be extended further than to determine whether the inferior tribunal, board, or officer has regularly pursued the authority of such tribunal, board, or officer. **Leg.H.** Enacted 1872.

§1075. A defective return of writ may be perfected; Hearing and judgment
If the return of the writ be defective, the court may order a further return to be made. When a full return has been made, the court must hear the parties, or such of them as may attend for that purpose, and may thereupon give judgment, either affirming or annulling, or modifying the proceedings below. **Leg.H.** Enacted 1872.

§1076. Copy of judgment must be sent to inferior tribunal
A copy of the judgment, signed by the clerk, must be transmitted to the inferior tribunal, board, or officer having the custody of the record or proceeding certified up. **Leg.H.** Enacted 1872.

§1077. Judgment rolls
A copy of the judgment, signed by the clerk, entered upon or attached to the writ and return, constitute the judgment roll. **Leg.H.** Enacted 1872.

CHAPTER 2
WRIT OF MANDATE

Writ's names. §1084.
Writ of mandate. §1085.
Actions challenging pest control and pesticide activities; Applicable procedure for issuance of writ of mandate. §1085.5.
Issuance on petition when ordinary remedy inadequate. §1086.
Alternative or peremptory writs. §1087.
Issuance of alternative or peremptory writ in first instance; Notice and default. §1088.
Proof of service when no alternative writ is sought. §1088.5.
Return, and answer or demurrer; Judicial Council Rules. §1089.
Answer to petition for writ of mandate. §1089.5.
Order for jury trial of question of fact. §1090.
Proof in denial or avoidance. §1091.
Motion for new trial, where made. §1092.
Clerk must transmit verdict to court where motion is pending, after which hearing shall be had on motion. §1093.
Hearing by court. §1094.
Inquiry into validity of administrative order or decision. §1094.5.
Time limits for review. §1094.6.
Review of First Amendment permit or entitlement decision. §1094.8.
Applicant's recovery of damages and costs. §1095.
Service of writ. §1096.
Penalty for disobedience to writ. §1097.

§1084. Writ's names
The writ of mandamus may be denominated a writ of mandate. **Leg.H.** Enacted 1872. Amended Code Amdts 1873–74 ch 383 §143; Stats 2016 ch 86 §39 (SB 1171), effective January 1, 2017.

§1085. Writ of mandate
(a) A writ of mandate may be issued by any court to any inferior tribunal, corporation, board, or person, to compel the performance of an act which the law specially enjoins, as a duty resulting from an office, trust, or station, or to compel the admission of a party to the use and enjoyment of a right or office to which the party is entitled, and from which the party is unlawfully precluded by that inferior tribunal, corporation, board, or person.

(b) The appellate division of the superior court may grant a writ of mandate directed to the superior court in a limited civil case or in a misdemeanor or infraction case. Where the appellate division grants a writ of mandate directed to the superior court, the superior court is an inferior tribunal for purposes of this chapter. **Leg.H.** Enacted 1872. Amended Stats 1935 ch 52 §2; Stats 1951 ch 1737 §148, operative January 1, 1952; Stats 1998 ch 931 §112 (SB 2139), effective September 28, 1998; Stats 1999 ch 344 §17 (SB 210), effective September 7, 1999; Stats 2002 ch 784 §75 (SB 1316); Stats 2010 ch 212 §2 (AB 2767), effective January 1, 2011.

§1085.5. Actions challenging pest control and pesticide activities; Applicable procedure for issuance of writ of mandate

Notwithstanding this chapter, in any action or proceeding to attack, review, set aside, void, or annul the activity of the Director of Food and Agriculture under Division 4 (commencing with Section 5001) or Division 5 (commencing with Section 9101) of the Food and Agricultural Code, the procedure for issuance of a writ of mandate shall be in accordance with Chapter 1.5 (commencing with Section 5051) of Part 1 of Division 4 of that code. **Leg.H.** Added Stats 1985 ch 1282 §1. Amended Stats 1987 ch 1284 §1.

§1086. Issuance on petition when ordinary remedy inadequate

The writ must be issued in all cases where there is not a plain, speedy, and adequate remedy, in the ordinary course of law. It must be issued upon the verified petition of the party beneficially interested. **Leg.H.** Enacted 1872. Amended Stats 1907 ch 244 §1.

§1087. Alternative or peremptory writs

The writ may be either alternative or peremptory. The alternative writ must command the party to whom it is directed immediately after the receipt of the writ, or at some other specified time, to do the act required to be performed, or to show cause before the court at a time and place then or thereafter specified by court order why he has not done so. The peremptory writ must be in a similar form, except that the words requiring the party to show cause why he has not done as commanded must be omitted. **Leg.H.** Enacted 1872. Amended Stats 1907 ch 244 §2; Stats 1963 ch 461 §3.

§1088. Issuance of alternative or peremptory writ in first instance; Notice and default

When the application to the court is made without notice to the adverse party, and the writ is allowed, the alternative must be first issued; but if the application is upon due notice and with the writ is allowed, the peremptory may be issued in the first instance. With the alternative writ and also with any notice of intention to appear for the writ, there must be served on each person against whom the writ is sought a copy of the petition. The notice of the application, when given, must be at least ten days. The writ cannot be granted by default. The case must be heard by the court, whether the adverse party appears or not. **Leg.H.** Enacted 1872. Amended Stats 1907 ch 244 §3.

§1088.5. Proof of service when no alternative writ is sought

In a trial court, if no alternative writ is sought, proof of service of a copy of the petition need not accompany the application for a writ at the time of filing, but proof of service of a copy of the filed petition must be lodged with the court prior to a hearing or any action by the court. **Leg.H.** Added Stats 1982 ch 193 §1, effective May 5, 1982. Amended Stats 1983 ch 818 §1.

§1089. Return, and answer or demurrer; Judicial Council Rules

On the date for return of the alternative writ, or on which the application for the writ is noticed, or, if the Judicial Council shall adopt rules relating to the return and answer, then at the time provided by those rules, the party upon whom the writ or notice has been served may make a return by demurrer, verified answer or both. If the return is by demurrer alone, the court may allow an answer to be filed within such time as it may designate. Nothing in this section affects rules of the Judicial Council governing original writ proceedings in reviewing courts. **Leg.H.** Enacted 1872. Amended Stats 1907 ch 244 §4; Stats 1949 ch 1462 §1; Stats 1971 ch 1475 §3.

§1089.5. Answer to petition for writ of mandate

Where a petition for writ of mandate is filed in the trial court pursuant to Section 1088.5, and where a record of the proceedings to be reviewed has been filed with the petition or where no record of a proceeding is required, the respondent shall answer or otherwise respond within 30 days after service of the petition. However, where a record of the proceeding to be reviewed has been requested pursuant to Section 11523 of the Government Code, or otherwise, and has not been filed with the petition, the party upon whom the petition has been served, including any real party in interest, shall answer or otherwise respond within 30 days following receipt of a copy of the record. **Leg.H.** Added Stats 1982 ch 193 §2, effective May 5, 1982. Amended Stats 1983 ch 818 §2.

§1090. Order for jury trial of question of fact

If a return be made, which raises a question as to a matter of fact essential to the determination of the motion, and affecting the substantial rights of the parties, and upon the supposed truth of the allegation of which the application for the writ is based, the court may, in its discretion, order the question to be tried before a jury, and postpone the argument until such trial can be had, and the verdict certified to the court. The question to be tried must be distinctly stated in the order for trial, and the county must be designated in which the same shall be had. The order may also direct the jury to assess any damages which the applicant may have sustained, in case they find for him. **Leg.H.** Enacted 1872. Amended Stats 1971 ch 1475 §4.

§1091. Proof in denial or avoidance

On the trial, the applicant is not precluded by the return from any valid objection to its sufficiency, and may countervail it by proof either in direct denial or by way of avoidance. **Leg.H.** Enacted 1872. Amended Stats 1971 ch 1475 §5.

§1092. Motion for new trial, where made

The motion for new trial must be made in the court in which the issue of fact is tried. **Leg.H.** Enacted 1872.

§1093. Clerk must transmit verdict to court where motion is pending, after which hearing shall be had on motion

If no notice of a motion for a new trial be given, or if given, the motion be denied, the clerk, within five days after rendition of the verdict or denial of the motion, must transmit to the court in which the application for the writ is pending, a certified copy of the verdict attached to the order of trial; after which either party may bring on the argument of the application, upon reasonable notice to the adverse party. **Leg.H.** Enacted 1872.

§1094. Hearing by court

If no return be made, the case may be heard on the papers of the applicant. If the return raises only questions of law, or puts in issue immaterial statements, not affecting the substantial rights of the parties, the court must proceed to hear or fix a day for hearing the argument of the case.

If a petition for a writ of mandate filed pursuant to Section 1088.5 presents no triable issue of fact or is based solely on an administrative record, the matter may be determined by the court by noticed motion of any party for a judgment on the peremptory writ. **Leg.H.** Enacted 1872. Amended Code Amdts 1873–74 ch 383 §144; Stats 1971 ch 1475 §6; Stats 1982 ch 193 §3, effective May 5, 1982.

§1094.5. Inquiry into validity of administrative order or decision

(a) Where the writ is issued for the purpose of inquiring into the validity of any final administrative order or decision made as the result of a proceeding in which by law a hearing is required to be given, evidence is required to be taken, and discretion in the determination of facts is vested in the inferior tribunal, corporation, board, or officer, the case shall be heard by the court sitting without a jury. All or part of the record of the proceedings before the inferior tribunal, corporation, board, or officer may be filed with the petition, may be filed with respondent's points and authorities, or may be ordered to be filed by the court. Except when otherwise prescribed by statute, the cost of preparing the record shall be borne by the petitioner. Where the petitioner has proceeded pursuant to Article 6 (commencing with Section 68630) of Chapter 2 of Title 8 of the Government Code and the Rules of Court implementing that section and where the transcript is necessary to a proper review of the administrative proceedings, the cost of preparing the transcript shall be borne by the respondent. Where the party seeking the writ has proceeded pursuant to Section 1088.5, the administrative record shall be filed as expeditiously as possible, and may be filed with the petition, or by the respondent after payment of the costs by the petitioner, where required, or as otherwise directed by the court. If the expense of preparing all or any part of the record has been borne by the prevailing party, the expense shall be taxable as costs.

(b) The inquiry in such a case shall extend to the questions whether the respondent has proceeded without, or in excess of, jurisdiction; whether there was a fair trial; and whether there was any prejudicial abuse of discretion. Abuse of discretion is established if the respondent has not proceeded in the manner required by law, the order or decision is not supported by the findings, or the findings are not supported by the evidence.

(c) Where it is claimed that the findings are not supported by the evidence, in cases in which the court is authorized by law to exercise its independent judgment on the evidence, abuse of discretion is established if the court determines that the findings are not supported by the weight of the evidence. In all other cases, abuse of discretion is established if the court determines that the findings are not supported by substantial evidence in the light of the whole record.

(d) Notwithstanding subdivision (c), in cases arising from private hospital boards or boards of directors of districts organized pursuant to the Local Health Care District Law (Chapter 1 (commencing with Section 32000) of Division 23 of the Health and Safety Code) or governing bodies of municipal hospitals formed pursuant to Article 7 (commencing with Section 37600) or Article 8 (commencing with Section 37650) of Chapter 5 of Part 2 of Division 3 of Title 4 of the Government Code, abuse of discretion is established if the court determines that the findings are not supported by substantial evidence in the light of the whole record. However, in all cases in which the petition alleges discriminatory actions prohibited by Section 1316 of the Health and Safety Code, and the plaintiff makes a preliminary showing of substantial evidence in support of that allegation, the court shall exercise its independent judgment on the evidence and abuse of discretion shall be established if the court determines that the findings are not supported by the weight of the evidence.

(e) Where the court finds that there is relevant evidence that, in the exercise of reasonable diligence, could not have been produced or that was improperly excluded at the hearing before respondent, it may enter judgment as provided in subdivision (f) remanding the case to be reconsidered in the light of that evidence; or, in cases in which the court is authorized by law to exercise its independent judgment on the evidence, the court may admit the evidence at the hearing on the writ without remanding the case.

(f) The court shall enter judgment either commanding respondent to set aside the order or decision, or denying the writ. Where the judgment commands that the order or decision be set aside, it may order the reconsideration of the case in light of the court's opinion and judgment and may order respondent to take such further action as is specially enjoined upon it by law, but the judgment shall not limit or control in any way the discretion legally vested in the respondent.

(g) Except as provided in subdivision (h), the court in which proceedings under this section are instituted may stay the operation of the administrative order or decision pending the judgment of the court, or until the filing of a notice of appeal from the judgment or until the expiration of the time for filing the notice, whichever occurs first. However, no such stay shall be imposed or continued if the court is satisfied that it is against the public interest. The application for the stay shall be accompanied by proof of service of a copy of the application on the respondent. Service shall be made in the manner provided by Title 4.5 (commencing with Section 405) of Part 2 or Chapter 5 (commencing with Section 1010) of Title 14 of Part 2. If an appeal is taken from a denial of the writ, the order or decision of the agency shall not be stayed except upon the order of the court to which the appeal is taken. However, in cases where a stay is in effect at the time of filing the notice of appeal, the stay shall be continued by operation of law for a period of 20 days from the filing of the notice. If an appeal is taken from the granting of the writ, the order or decision of the agency is stayed pending the determination of the appeal unless the court to which the appeal is taken shall otherwise order. Where any final administrative order or decision is the subject of proceedings under this section, if the petition shall have been filed while the penalty imposed is in full force and effect, the determination shall not be considered to have become moot in cases where the penalty imposed by the administrative agency has been completed or complied with during the pendency of the proceedings.

(h)(1) The court in which proceedings under this section are instituted may stay the operation of the administrative order or decision of any licensed hospital or any state agency made after a hearing required by statute to be conducted under the Administrative Procedure Act, as set forth in Chapter 5 (commencing with Section 11500) of Part 1 of Division 3 of Title 2 of the Government Code, conducted by the agency itself or an administrative law judge on the staff of the Office of Administrative Hearings pending the judgment of the court, or until the filing of a notice of appeal from the judgment or until the expiration of the time for filing the notice, whichever occurs first. However, the stay shall not be imposed or continued unless the court is satisfied that the public interest will not suffer and that the licensed hospital or agency is unlikely to prevail ultimately on the merits. The application for the stay shall be accompanied by proof of service of a copy of the application on the respondent. Service shall be made in the manner provided by Title 4.5 (commencing with Section 405) of Part 2 or Chapter 5 (commencing with Section 1010) of Title 14 of Part 2.

(2) The standard set forth in this subdivision for obtaining a stay shall apply to any administrative order or decision of an agency that issues licenses pursuant to Division 2 (commencing with Section 500) of the Business and Professions Code or pursuant to the Osteopathic Initiative Act or the Chiropractic Initiative Act. With respect to orders or decisions of other state agencies, the standard in this subdivision shall apply only when the agency has adopted the proposed decision of the administrative law judge in its entirety or has adopted the proposed decision but reduced the proposed penalty pursuant to subdivision (c) of Section 11517 of the Government Code; otherwise the standard in subdivision (g) shall apply.

(3) If an appeal is taken from a denial of the writ, the order or decision of the hospital or agency shall not be stayed except upon the order of the court to which the appeal is taken. However, in cases where a stay is in effect at the time of filing the notice of appeal, the stay shall be continued by operation of law for a period of 20 days from the filing of the notice. If an appeal is taken from the granting of the writ, the order or decision of the hospital or agency is stayed pending the determination of the appeal unless the court to which the appeal is taken shall otherwise order. Where any final administrative order or decision is the subject of proceedings under this section, if the petition shall have been filed while the penalty imposed is in full force and effect, the determination shall not be considered to have become moot in cases where the penalty imposed by the administrative agency has been completed or complied with during the pendency of the proceedings.

(i) Any administrative record received for filing by the clerk of the court may be disposed of as provided in Sections 1952, 1952.2, and 1952.3.

(j) Effective January 1, 1996, this subdivision shall apply to state employees in State Bargaining Unit 5. For purposes of this section, the court is not authorized to review any disciplinary decisions reached pursuant to Section 19576.1 of the Government Code. **Leg.H.** Added Stats 1945 ch 868 §1. Amended Stats 1949 ch 358 §1; Stats 1974 ch 668 §1; Stats 1975 2nd Ex Sess ch 1 §26.5; Stats 1978 ch 1348 §1; Stats 1979 ch 199 §1; Stats 1982 ch 193 §4, effective May 5, 1982, ch 812 §3; Stats 1985 ch 324 §1; Stats 1991 ch 1090 §5.5 (AB 1484); Stats 1992 ch 72 §1 (AB 1525), effective May 28, 1992; Stats 1995 ch 768 §1 (SB 544), effective October 12, 1995; Stats 1998 ch 88 §5 (AB 528), effective June 30, 1998, ch 1024 §5 (AB 1291), effective September 30, 1998; Stats 1999 ch 446 §1 (AB 1013), effective September 21, 1999; Stats 2000 ch 402 §1 (AB 649), effective September 11, 2000; Stats 2008 ch 150 §1 (AB 3042), effective January 1, 2009; Stats 2011 ch 296 §41 (AB 1023), effective January 1, 2012.

§1094.6. Time limits for review

(a) Judicial review of any decision of a local agency, other than school district, as the term local agency is defined in Section 54951 of the Government Code, or of any commission, board, officer or agent thereof, may be had pursuant to Section 1094.5 of this code only if the petition for writ of mandate pursuant to such section is filed within the time limits specified in this section.

(b) Any such petition shall be filed not later than the 90th day following the date on which the decision becomes final. If there is no provision for reconsideration of the decision, or for a written decision or written findings supporting the decision, in any applicable provision of any statute, charter, or rule, for the purposes of this section, the decision is final on the date it is announced. If the decision is not announced at the close of the hearing, the date, time, and place of the announcement of the decision shall be announced at the hearing. If there is a provision for reconsideration, the decision is final for purposes of this section upon the expiration of the period during which such reconsideration can be sought; provided, that if reconsideration is sought pursuant to any such provision the decision is final for the purposes of this section on the date that reconsideration is rejected. If there is a provision for a written decision or written findings, the decision is final for purposes of this section upon the date it is mailed by first-class mail, postage prepaid, including a copy of the affidavit or certificate of mailing, to the party seeking the writ. Subdivision (a) of Section 1013 does not apply to extend the time, following deposit in the mail of the decision or findings, within which a petition shall be filed.

(c) The complete record of the proceedings shall be prepared by the local agency or its commission, board, officer, or agent which made the decision and shall be delivered to the petitioner within 190 days after he has filed a written request therefor. The local agency may recover from the petitioner its actual costs for transcribing or otherwise preparing the record. Such record shall include the transcript of the proceedings, all pleadings, all notices and orders, any proposed decision by a hearing officer, the final decision, all admitted exhibits, all rejected exhibits in the possession of the local agency or its commission, board, officer, or agent, all written evidence, and any other papers in the case.

(d) If the petitioner files a request for the record as specified in subdivision (c) within 10 days after the date the decision becomes final as provided in subdivision (b), the time within which a petition pursuant to Section 1094.5 may be filed shall be extended to not later than the 30th day following the date on which the record is either personally delivered or mailed to the petitioner or his attorney of record, if he has one.

(e) As used in this section, decision means a decision subject to review pursuant to Section 1094.5, suspending, demoting, or dismissing an officer or employee, revoking, denying an application for a permit, license, or other entitlement, imposing a civil or administrative penalty, fine, charge, or cost, or denying an application for any retirement benefit or allowance.

(f) In making a final decision as defined in subdivision (e), the local agency shall provide notice to the party that the time within which judicial review must be sought is governed by this section.

As used in this subdivision, "party" means an officer or employee who has been suspended, demoted or dismissed; a person whose permit, license, or other entitlement has been revoked or suspended, or whose application for a permit, license, or other entitlement has been denied; or a person whose application for a retirement benefit or allowance has been denied.

(g) This section shall prevail over any conflicting provision in any otherwise applicable law relating to the subject matter, unless the conflicting provision is a state or federal law which provides a shorter statute of limitations, in which case the shorter statute of limitations shall apply. **Leg.H.** Added Stats 1976 ch 276 §1. Amended Stats 1983 ch 818 §3; Stats 1991 ch 1090 §6 (AB 1484); Stats 1993 ch 926 §5 (AB 2205); Stats 1995 ch 898 §1 (SB 814).

§1094.7. [Section repealed 1999]

Leg.H. Added Stats 1998 ch 91 §5 (SB 1501), effective July 3, 1998. Repealed Stats 1999 ch 446 §2 (AB 1013), effective September 21, 1999. The repealed section related to court's authority to review.

§1094.8. Review of First Amendment permit or entitlement decision

(a) Notwithstanding anything to the contrary in this chapter, an action or proceeding to review the issuance, revocation, suspension, or denial of a permit or other entitlement for expressive conduct protected by the First Amendment to the United States Constitution shall be conducted in accordance with subdivision (d).

(b) For purposes of this section, the following definitions shall apply:

(1) The terms "permit" and "entitlement" are used interchangeably.

(2) The term "permit applicant" means both an applicant for a permit and a permitholder.

(3) The term "public agency" means a city, county, city and county, a joint powers authority or similar public entity formed pursuant to Section 65850.4 of the Government Code, or any other public entity authorized by law to issue permits for expressive conduct protected by the First Amendment to the United States Constitution.

(c) A public agency may, if it so chooses, designate the permits or entitlements to which this section applies by adopting an ordinance or resolution which contains a specific listing or other description of the permits or entitlements issued by the public agency which are eligible for expedited judicial review pursuant to this section because the permits regulate expressive conduct protected by the First Amendment to the United States Constitution.

(d) The procedure set forth in this subdivision, when applicable, shall supersede anything to the contrary set forth in this chapter.

(1) Within five court days after receipt of written notification from a permit applicant that the permit applicant will seek judicial review of a public agency's action on the permit, the public agency shall prepare, certify, and make available the administrative record to the permit applicant.

(2) Either the public agency or the permit applicant may bring an action in accordance with the procedure set forth in this section. If the permit applicant brings the action, the action shall be in the form of a petition for writ of mandate pursuant to Section 1085 or 1094.5, as appropriate.

(3) The party bringing the action pursuant to this section shall file and serve the petition on the respondent no later than 21 calendar days following the public agency's final decision on the permit. The title page of the petition shall contain the following language in 18-point type: "ATTENTION: THIS MATTER IS ENTITLED TO PRIORITY AND SUBJECT TO THE EXPEDITED HEARING AND REVIEW PROCEDURES CONTAINED IN SECTION 1094.8 OF THE CODE OF CIVIL PROCEDURE."

(4) The clerk of the court shall set a hearing for review of the petition no later than 25 calendar days from the date the petition is filed. Moving, opposition, and reply papers shall be filed as provided in the California Rules of Court. The petitioner shall lodge the administrative record with the court no later than 10 calendar days in advance of the hearing date.

(5) Following the conclusion of the hearing, the court shall render its decision in an expeditious manner consistent with constitutional requirements in view of the particular facts and circumstances. In no event shall the decision be rendered later than 20 calendar days after the matter is submitted or 50 calendar days after the date the petition is filed pursuant to paragraph (4), whichever is earlier.

(e) If the presiding judge of the court in which the action is filed determines that, as a result of either the press of other court business or other factors, the court will be unable to meet any one or more of the deadlines provided within this section, the presiding judge shall request the temporary assignment of a judicial officer to hear the petition and render a decision within the time limits contained herein, pursuant to Section 68543.8 of the Government Code. Given the short time period involved, the request shall be entitled to priority.

(f) In any action challenging the issuance, revocation, suspension, or denial of a permit or entitlement, the parties to the action shall be permitted to jointly waive the time limits provided for herein. **Leg.H.** Added Stats 1999 ch 49 §1 (SB 1165), effective June 28, 1999.

§1095. Applicant's recovery of damages and costs

If judgment be given for the applicant, the applicant may recover the damages which the applicant has sustained, as found by the jury, or as may be determined by the court or referee, upon a reference to be ordered, together with costs; and a peremptory mandate must also be awarded without delay. Damages and costs may be enforced in the manner provided for money judgments generally. In all cases where the respondent is an officer of a public entity, all damages and costs, or either, which may be recovered or awarded, shall be recovered and awarded against the public entity represented by the officer, and not against the officer so appearing in the proceeding, and are a proper claim against the public entity for which the officer appeared and shall be paid as other claims against the public entity are paid; but in all such cases, the court shall first determine that the officer appeared and made defense in the proceeding in good faith. For the purpose of this section, "public entity" includes the state, a county, city, district or other public agency or public corporation. For the purpose of this section, "officer" includes officer, agent or employee. **Leg.H.** Enacted 1872. Amended Stats 1913 ch 206 §1; Stats 1963 ch 1681 §3; Stats 1982 ch 497 §73, operative July 1, 1983.

§1096. Service of writ

The writ must be served in the same manner as a summons in a civil action, except when otherwise expressly directed by order of the court.

Service upon a majority of the members of any board or body, is service upon the board or body, whether at the time of the service the board or body was in session or not. **Leg.H.** Enacted 1872.

§1097. Penalty for disobedience to writ

If a peremptory mandate has been issued and directed to an inferior tribunal, corporation, board, or person, and it appears to the court that a member of the tribunal, corporation, or board, or the person upon whom the writ has been personally served, has, without just excuse, refused or neglected to obey the writ, the court may, upon motion, impose a fine not exceeding one thousand dollars. In case of persistence in a refusal of obedience, the court may order the party to be imprisoned until the writ is obeyed, and may make any orders necessary and proper for the complete enforcement of the writ. **Leg.H.** Enacted 1872. Amended Code Amdts 1873–74 ch 383 §145; Stats 2016 ch 86 §40 (SB 1171), effective January 1, 2017.

CHAPTER 3
WRIT OF PROHIBITION

Purpose of writ. §1102.
Issuance. §1103.
Alternative and peremptory writs. §1104.
Applicability of other provisions. §1105.

§1102. Purpose of writ

The writ of prohibition arrests the proceedings of any tribunal, corporation, board, or person exercising judicial functions, when such proceedings are without or in excess of the jurisdiction of such tribunal, corporation, board, or person. **Leg.H.** Enacted 1872. Amended Stats 1881 ch 25 §1; Stats 1919 ch 199 §1; Stats 1955 ch 971 §1.

§1103. Issuance

(a) A writ of prohibition may be issued by any court to an inferior tribunal or to a corporation, board, or person, in all cases where there is not a plain, speedy, and adequate remedy in the ordinary course of law. It is issued upon the verified petition of the person beneficially interested.

(b) The appellate division of the superior court may grant a writ of prohibition directed to the superior court in a limited civil case or in a misdemeanor or infraction case. Where the appellate division grants a writ of prohibition directed to the superior court, the superior court is an inferior tribunal for purposes of this chapter. **Leg.H.** Enacted 1872. Amended Stats 1907 ch 449 §1; Stats 1935 ch 52 §3; Stats 1951 ch 1737 §149, operative January 1, 1952; Stats 1998 ch 931 §113 (SB 2139), effective September 28, 1998; Stats 1999 ch 344 §18 (SB 210), effective September 7, 1999; Stats 2002 ch 784 §76 (SB 1316); Stats 2010 ch 212 §3 (AB 2767), effective January 1, 2011.

§1104. Alternative and peremptory writs

The writ must be either alternative or peremptory. The alternative writ must command the party to whom it is directed to desist or refrain from further proceedings in the action or matter specified therein, until the further order of the court from which it is issued, and to show cause before such court at a time and place then or thereafter specified by court order why such party should not be absolutely restrained from any further proceedings in such action or matter. The peremptory writ must be in a similar form, except that the words requiring the party to show cause why he should not be absolutely restrained must be omitted. **Leg.H.** Enacted 1872. Amended Stats 1907 ch 449 §2; Stats 1963 ch 461 §4.

§1105. Applicability of other provisions

The provisions of the preceding chapter, except of the first four sections thereof, apply to this proceeding. **Leg.H.** Enacted 1872.

CHAPTER 4
WRITS OF REVIEW, MANDATE, AND PROHIBITION MAY ISSUE AND BE HEARD AT CHAMBERS

Service; Filing; Ex parte grant. §1107.
Return; Hearing. §1108.

§1107. Service; Filing; Ex parte grant

When an application is filed for the issuance of any prerogative writ, the application shall be accompanied by proof of service of a copy thereof upon the respondent and the real party in interest named in such application. The provisions of Chapter 5 (commencing with Section 1010) of Title 14 of Part 2 shall apply to the service of the application. However, when a writ of mandate is sought pursuant to the provisions of Section 1088.5, the action may be filed and served in the same manner as an ordinary action under Part 2 (commencing with Section 307). Where the real party in respondent's interest is a board or commission, the service shall be made upon the presiding officer, or upon the secretary, or upon a majority of the members, of the board or commission. Within five days after service and filing of the application, the real party in interest or the respondent or both may serve upon the applicant and file with the court points and authorities in opposition to the granting of the writ.

The court in which the application is filed, in its discretion and for good cause, may grant the application ex parte, without notice or service of the application as herein provided.

The provisions of this section shall not be applicable to applications for the writ of habeas corpus, or to applications for writs of review of the Industrial Accident or Public Utilities Commissions. **Leg.H.** Added Stats 1941 ch 438 §1. Amended Stats 1947 ch 304 §1; Stats 1959 ch 737 §1; Stats 1982 ch 193 §5, effective May 5, 1982, ch 812 §4.

§1108. Return; Hearing

Writs of review, mandate, and prohibition issued by the Supreme Court, a court of appeal, or a superior court, may, in the discretion of the court issuing the writ, be made returnable, and a hearing thereon be had at any time. **Leg.H.** Enacted 1872. Amended Code Amdts 1873–74 ch 383 §146; Code Amdts 1880 ch 77 §1; Stats 1935 ch 52 §4; Stats 1967 ch 17 §18.

CHAPTER 5
RULES OF PRACTICE AND APPEALS

General rules of practice. §1109.
Rules for new trials and appeals. §1110.
Absence of stay or appeal from writ commanding delivery of water; Bond. §1110a.
Directing that writ of mandate not operate as stay. §1110b.

§1109. General rules of practice

Except as otherwise provided in this title, the provisions of part two of this code are applicable to and constitute the rules of practice in the proceedings mentioned in this title. **Leg.H.** Enacted 1872.

§1110. Rules for new trials and appeals

The provisions of part two of this code relative to new trials and appeals, except in so far as they are inconsistent with the provisions of this title, apply to the proceedings mentioned in this title. **Leg.H.** Enacted 1872.

§1110a. Absence of stay or appeal from writ commanding delivery of water; Bond

If an appeal be taken from an order or judgment directing the issuance of a writ of mandate commanding a party to deliver water, for irrigation purposes, such appeal shall not stay the operation of the order, judgment or writ as to the delivery of such water, but such water must until the final determination of said appeal be delivered as commanded by said writ; provided, that if any expense is necessary to be incurred by the defendant in connecting the water supply with the land to be irrigated said defendant shall not be obliged to furnish water unless the plaintiff shall provide a bond in such sum as the court may fix, conditioned that in the event of the judgment being reversed, plaintiff will pay defendant the amount of the expense so incurred not exceeding the amount of said bond. **Leg.H.** Added Stats 1919 ch 358 §1.

§1110b. Directing that writ of mandate not operate as stay

If an appeal be taken from an order or judgment granting a writ of mandate the court granting the writ, or the appellate court, may direct that the appeal shall not operate as a stay of execution if it is satisfied upon the showing made by the petitioner that he will suffer irreparable damage in his business or profession if the execution is stayed. **Leg.H.** Added Stats 1941 ch 330 §1.

TITLE 2
CONTESTING CERTAIN ELECTIONS [REPEALED]

§§1111–1127. [Sections repealed 1939]

Leg.H. Enacted 1872. Repealed Stats 1939 ch 26 §90001. See Elec C §§16000 et seq.

TITLE 3
OF SUMMARY PROCEEDINGS

Chapter 1. Confession of Judgment Without Action.
Chapter 2. Submitting a Controversy Without Action.
Chapter 2.5. Judicial Arbitration.
Chapter 4. Summary Proceedings for Obtaining Possession of Real Property in Certain Cases.
Chapter 5. COVID-19 Tenant Relief Act [Repealed effective October 1, 2025].

CHAPTER 1
CONFESSION OF JUDGMENT WITHOUT ACTION

Entry of judgment by confession. §1132.

§1132. Entry of judgment by confession

(a) A judgment by confession is unenforceable and may not be entered in any superior court.

(b) This section does not apply to a judgment by confession obtained or entered before January 1, 2023. **Leg.H.** Enacted 1872. Amended Stats 1975 ch 304 §1; Stats 1979 ch 568 §1; Stats 2002 ch 784 §77 (SB 1316); Stats 2022 ch 851 §1 (SB 688), effective January 1, 2023.

§1133. Statement in writing and form thereof [Repealed]

Leg.H. Enacted 1872. Repealed Stats 2022 ch 851 §2 (SB 688), effective January 1, 2023.

§1134. Filing and endorsement of statement; Entry of judgment; Costs [Repealed]

Leg.H. Enacted 1872. Amended Stats 1933 ch 745 §1; Stats 1951 ch 1737 §150, operative January 1, 1952; Stats 1957 ch 1982 §1; Stats 1974 ch 1285 §1; Stats 1975 ch 766 §1; Stats 1977 ch 1257 §37, effective October 3, 1977; Stats 1998 ch 931 §114 (SB 2139), effective September 28, 1998; Stats 2001 ch 812 §9 (AB 223); Stats 2005 ch 75 §40 (AB 145), effective July 19, 2005, operative January 1, 2006. Repealed Stats 2022 ch 851 §3 (SB 688), effective January 1, 2023.

§1135. [Section repealed 1977]

Leg.H. Enacted 1872. Amended Stats 1933 ch 745 §2, Stats 1951 ch 1737 §151, operative January 1, 1952, Stats 1957 ch 1982 §2. Repealed Stats 1977 ch 1257 §38, effective October 3, 1977. The repealed section related to entry of judgment in justice's court.

CHAPTER 2
SUBMITTING A CONTROVERSY WITHOUT ACTION

Procedure. §1138.
Entry of judgment. §1139.
Enforcement of judgment. §1140.

§1138. Procedure

Parties to a question in difference, which might be the subject of a civil action, may, without action, agree upon a case containing the facts upon which the controversy depends, and present a submission of the same to any court which would have jurisdiction if an action had been brought; but it must appear, by affidavit, that the controversy is real and the proceedings in good faith, to determine the rights of the parties. The court must thereupon hear and determine the case, and render judgment thereon, as if an action were depending. **Leg.H.** Enacted 1872.

§1139. Entry of judgment

Judgment must be entered as in other cases, but without costs for any proceeding prior to the trial. The case, the submission, and a copy of the judgment constitute the judgment roll. **Leg.H.** Enacted 1872. Amended Stats 1933 ch 745 §3.

§1140. Enforcement of judgment

The judgment may be enforced in the same manner as if it had been rendered in an action of the same jurisdictional classification in the same court, and is in the same manner subject to appeal. **Leg.H.** Enacted 1872. Amended Stats 1933 ch 745 §4; Stats 1998 ch 931 §115 (SB 2139), effective September 28, 1998.

CHAPTER 2.5
JUDICIAL ARBITRATION

Legislative findings and intent. §1141.10.
Mandatory submission; Local rule. §1141.11.
Uniform system of arbitration of certain causes; Stipulation of parties; Election by plaintiff. §1141.12.
Applicability of chapter. §1141.13.
Procedural rules. §1141.14.
Exceptions for cause. §1141.15.
Amount in controversy; Determination; When hearing to be held; Earlier submission to arbitration. §1141.16.
Submission as affecting dismissal for delay. §1141.17.
Selection, compensation, and disqualification of arbitrators, §1141.18.
Powers of arbitrators. §1141.19.
Production of evidence. §1141.19.5.
Finality of award; De novo trial. §1141.20.
Costs. §1141.21.
Correction, modification, or vacation of award. §1141.22.
Effect of award. §1141.23.
Discovery after award. §1141.24.
Reference to award in subsequent trial. §1141.25.
Award in excess of jurisdictional amount. §1141.26.
Public agency or entity as party. §1141.27.
Administrative costs; Actual costs. §1141.28.
Construction of provisions. §1141.30.
Operative date. §1141.31.

§1141.10. Legislative findings and intent

(a) The Legislature finds and declares that litigation involving small civil cases can be so costly and complex that efficiently resolving these civil cases is difficult, and that the resulting delays and expenses may deny parties their right to a timely resolution of minor civil disputes. The Legislature further finds and declares that arbitration has proven to be an efficient and equitable method for resolving small civil cases, and that courts should encourage or require the use of arbitration for those actions whenever possible.

(b) It is the intent of the Legislature that:

(1) Arbitration hearings held pursuant to this chapter shall provide parties with a simplified and economical procedure for obtaining prompt and equitable resolution of their disputes.

(2) Arbitration hearings shall be as informal as possible and shall provide the parties themselves maximum opportunity to participate directly in the resolution of their disputes, and shall be held during nonjudicial hours whenever possible.

(3) Members of the State Bar selected to serve as arbitrators should have experience with cases of the type under dispute and are urged to volunteer their services without compensation whenever possible. **Leg.H.** Added Stats 1978 ch 743 §2, operative July 1, 1979. Amended Stats 2003 ch 449 §9 (AB 1712).

Prior Law: Former CCP §1141.10, similar to present CCP §1141.12(b), was added Stats 1975 ch 1006 §1, operative July 1, 1976, and repealed Stats 1978 ch 743 §1, operative July 1, 1979.

§1141.105. [Section repealed 1988]

Leg.H. Added Stats 1987 ch 238 §2, effective July 23, 1987, operative January 1, 1988. Repealed Stats 1987 ch 1211 §1, operative July 1, 1988. The repealed section related to applicability of chapter.

Prior Law: Former CCP §1141.105, similar to the repealed section, was added Stats 1987 ch 134 §3, effective July 7, 1987, and repealed Stats 1987 ch 238 §1, effective July 23, 1987.

§1141.11. Mandatory submission; Local rule

(a) In each superior court with 18 or more judges, all nonexempt unlimited civil cases shall be submitted to arbitration under this chapter if the amount in controversy, in the opinion of the court, will not exceed fifty thousand dollars ($50,000) for each plaintiff.

(b) In each superior court with fewer than 18 judges, the court may provide by local rule, when it determines that it is in the best interests of justice, that all nonexempt, unlimited civil cases shall be submitted to arbitration under this chapter if the amount in controversy, in the opinion of the court, will not exceed fifty thousand dollars ($50,000) for each plaintiff.

(c) Each superior court may provide by local rule, when it is determined to be in the best interests of justice, that all nonexempt, limited civil cases shall be submitted to arbitration under this chapter. This section does not apply to any action in small claims court, or to any action maintained pursuant to Section 1781 of the Civil Code or Section 1161.

(d)(1) In each court that has adopted judicial arbitration pursuant to subdivision (c), all limited civil cases that involve a claim for money damages against a single defendant as a result of a motor vehicle collision, except those heard in the small claims division, shall be submitted to arbitration within 120 days of the filing of the defendant's answer to the complaint (except as may be extended by the court for good cause) before an arbitrator selected by the court.

(2) The court may provide by local rule for the voluntary or mandatory use of case questionnaires, established under Section 93, in any proceeding subject to these provisions. Where local rules provide for the use of case questionnaires, the questionnaires shall be exchanged by the parties upon the defendant's answer and completed and returned within 60 days.

(3) For the purposes of this subdivision, the term "single defendant" means any of the following:

(A) An individual defendant, whether a person or an entity.

(B) Two or more persons covered by the same insurance policy applicable to the motor vehicle collision.

(C) Two or more persons residing in the same household when no insurance policy exists that is applicable to the motor vehicle collision.

(4) The naming of one or more cross-defendants, not a plaintiff, shall constitute a multiple-defendant case not subject to the provisions of this subdivision. **Leg.H.** Added Stats 1978 ch 743 §2, operative July 1, 1979. Amended Stats 1979 ch 46 §1, effective May 2, 1979, operative July 1, 1979, ch 948 §1, effective September 22, 1979, 1146 §2, effective September 29, 1979; Stats 1981 ch 1110 §1; Stats 1982 ch 31 §1, effective February 17, 1982, ch 921 §1, effective September 13, 1982, ch 1522 §2; Stats 1983 ch 978 §1, effective September 21, 1983; Stats 1985 ch 1383 §3; Stats 1986 ch 287 §1; Stats 1987 ch 1201 §4, ch 1204 §1; Stats 1989 ch 894 §1; Stats 1990 ch 1305 §9 (SB 2627); Stats 1998 ch 931 §116 (SB 2139), effective September 28, 1998; Stats 2002 ch 784 §78 (SB 1316); Stats 2003 ch 449 §10 (AB 1712).

§1141.12. Uniform system of arbitration of certain causes; Stipulation of parties; Election by plaintiff

In all superior courts, the Judicial Council shall provide by rule for a uniform system of arbitration of the following causes:

(a) Any cause, regardless of the amount in controversy, upon stipulation of the parties.

(b) Upon filing of an election by the plaintiff, any cause in which the plaintiff agrees that the arbitration award shall not exceed the amount in controversy as specified in Section 1141.11. **Leg.H.** Added Stats 1978 ch 743 §2, operative July 1, 1979. Amended Stats 1981 ch 1110 §2; Stats 1983 ch 123 §1; Stats 1998 ch 931 §117 (SB 2139), effective September 28, 1998; Stats 2002 ch 784 §79 (SB 1316); Stats 2003 ch 449 §11 (AB 1712).

§1141.13. Applicability of chapter

This chapter shall not apply to any civil action which includes a prayer for equitable relief, except that if the prayer for equitable relief is frivolous or insubstantial, this chapter shall be applicable. **Leg.H.** Added Stats 1978 ch 743 §2, operative July 1, 1979.

§1141.14. Procedural rules

Notwithstanding any other provision of law except the provisions of this chapter, the Judicial Council shall provide by rule for practice and procedure for all actions submitted to arbitration under this chapter. The Judicial Council rules shall provide for and conform with the provisions of this chapter. **Leg.H.** Added Stats 1978 ch 743 §2, operative July 1, 1979.

§1141.15. Exceptions for cause

The Judicial Council rules shall provide exceptions for cause to arbitration pursuant to subdivision (a), (b), or (c) of Section 1141.11. In providing for such exceptions, the Judicial Council shall take into consideration whether the civil action might not be amenable to arbitration. **Leg.H.** Added Stats 1978 ch 743 §2, operative July 1, 1979.

§1141.16. Amount in controversy; Determination; When hearing to be held; Earlier submission to arbitration

(a) The determination of the amount in controversy, under subdivision (a) or (b) of Section 1141.11, shall be made by the court and the case referred to arbitration after all named parties have appeared or defaulted. The determination shall be made at a case management conference or based upon review of the written submissions of the parties, as provided in rules adopted by the Judicial Council. The determination shall be based on the total amount of damages, and the judge may not consider questions of liability or comparative negligence or any other defense. At that time the court shall also make a determination whether any prayer for equitable relief is frivolous or insubstantial. The determination of the amount in controversy and whether any prayer for equitable relief is frivolous or insubstantial may not be appealable. No determination pursuant to this section shall be made if all parties stipulate in writing that the amount in controversy exceeds the amount specified in Section 1141.11.

(b) The determination and any stipulation of the amount in controversy shall be without prejudice to any finding on the value of the case by an arbitrator or in a subsequent trial de novo.

(c) Except as provided in this section, the arbitration hearing may not be held until 210 days after the filing of the complaint, or 240 days after the filing of a complaint if the parties have stipulated to a continuance pursuant to subdivision (d) of Section 68616 of the Government Code. A case shall be submitted to arbitration at an earlier time upon any of the following:

(1) The stipulation of the parties to an earlier arbitration hearing.

(2) The written request of all plaintiffs, subject to a motion by a defendant for good cause shown to delay the arbitration hearing.

(3) An order of the court if the parties have stipulated, or the court has ordered under Section 1141.24, that discovery other than that permitted under Chapter 18 (commencing with Section 2034.010) of Title 4 of Part 4 will be permitted after the arbitration award is rendered. **Leg.H.** Added Stats 1978 ch 743 §2, operative July 1, 1979. Amended Stats 1979 ch 130 §1; Stats 1981 ch 181 §1, ch 1110 §3; Stats 1983 ch 123 §2; Stats 2003 ch 449 §12 (AB 1712); Stats 2004 ch 182 §14 (AB 3081), operative July 1, 2005.

§1141.17. Submission as affecting dismissal for delay

(a) Submission of an action to arbitration pursuant to this chapter shall not suspend the running of the time periods specified in Chapter 1.5 (commencing with Section 583.110) of Title 8 of Part 2, except as provided in this section.

(b) If an action is or remains submitted to arbitration pursuant to this chapter more than four years and six months after the plaintiff has filed the action, then the time beginning on the date four years and six months after the plaintiff has filed the action and ending on the date on which a request for a de novo trial is filed under Section 1141.20 shall not be included in computing the five-year period specified in Section 583.310. **Leg.H.** Added Stats 1978 ch 743 §2, operative July 1, 1979. Amended Stats 1983 ch 123 §3; Stats 1984 ch 1705 §6.

§1141.18. Selection, compensation, and disqualification of arbitrators

(a) Arbitrators shall be retired judges, retired court commissioners who were licensed to practice law prior to their appointment as a commissioner, or members of the State Bar, and shall sit individually. A judge may also serve as an arbitrator without compensation. People who are not attorneys may serve as arbitrators upon the stipulation of all parties.

(b) The Judicial Council rules shall provide for the compensation, if any, of arbitrators. Compensation for arbitrators may not be less than one hundred fifty dollars ($150) per case, or one hundred fifty dollars ($150) per day, whichever is greater. A superior court may set a higher level of compensation for that court. Arbitrators may waive compensation in whole or in part. No compensation shall be paid before the filing of the award by the arbitrator, or before the settlement of the case by the parties.

(c) In cases submitted to arbitration under Section 1141.11 or 1141.12, an arbitrator shall be assigned within 30 days from the time of submission to arbitration.

(d) Any party may request the disqualification of the arbitrator selected for his or her case on the grounds and by the procedures specified in Section 170.1 or 170.6. A request for disqualification of an arbitrator on grounds specified in Section 170.6 shall be made within five days of the naming of the arbitrator. An arbitrator shall disqualify himself or herself, upon demand of any party to the arbitration made before the conclusion of the arbitration proceedings on any of the grounds specified in Section 170.1. **Leg.H.** Added Stats 1978 ch 743 §2, operative July 1, 1979. Amended Stats 1981 ch 1110 §3.5; Stats 1993 ch 768 §2 (SB 252); Stats 1995 ch 576 §5 (AB 1225); Stats 2003 ch 449 §13 (AB 1712).

§1141.19. Powers of arbitrators

Arbitrators approved pursuant to this chapter shall have the powers necessary to perform duties pursuant to this chapter as prescribed by the Judicial Council. **Leg.H.** Added Stats 1978 ch 743 §2, operative July 1, 1979.

§1141.19.5. Production of evidence

In any arbitration proceeding under this chapter, no party may require the production of evidence specified in subdivision (a) of Section 3295 of the Civil Code at the arbitration, unless the court enters an order permitting pretrial discovery of that evidence pursuant to subdivision (c) of Section 3295 of the Civil Code. **Leg.H.** Added Stats 1993 ch 768 §3 (SB 252). Amended Stats 1994 ch 327 §1 (SB 140).

§1141.20. Finality of award; De novo trial

(a) An arbitration award shall be final unless a request for a de novo trial or a request for dismissal in the form required by the Judicial Council is filed within 60 days after the date the arbitrator files the award with the court.

(b) Any party may elect to have a de novo trial, by court or jury, both as to law and facts. Such trial shall be calendared, insofar as possible, so that the trial shall be given the same place on the active list as it had prior to arbitration, or shall receive civil priority on the next setting calendar. **Leg.H.** Added Stats 1978 ch 743 §2, operative July 1, 1979. Amended Stats 1984 ch 1249 §2; Stats 2011 ch 49 §3 (SB 731), effective January 1, 2012.

Prior Law: Former CCP §1141.20, similar in part to present §1141.18, was added Stats 1975 ch 1006 §1, operative July 1, 1976, and repealed Stats 1978 ch 743 §1, operative July 1, 1979.

§1141.21. Costs

(a)(1) If the judgment upon the trial de novo is not more favorable in either the amount of damages awarded or the type of relief granted for the party electing the trial de novo than the arbitration award, the court shall order that party to pay the following nonrefundable costs and fees, unless the court finds in writing and upon motion that the imposition of these costs and fees would create such a substantial economic hardship as not to be in the interest of justice:

(A) To the court, the compensation actually paid to the arbitrator, less any amount paid pursuant to subparagraph (D).

(B) To the other party or parties, all costs specified in Section 1033.5, and the party electing the trial de novo shall not recover his or her costs.

(C) To the other party or parties, the reasonable costs of the services of expert witnesses, who are not regular employees of any party, actually incurred or reasonably necessary in the preparation or trial of the case.

(D) To the other party or parties, the compensation paid by the other party or parties to the arbitrator, pursuant to subdivision (b) of Section 1141.28.

(2) Those costs and fees, other than the compensation of the arbitrator, shall include only those incurred from the time of election of the trial de novo.

(b) If the party electing the trial de novo has proceeded in the action in forma pauperis and has failed to obtain a more favorable judgment, the costs and fees under subparagraphs (B) and (C) of paragraph (1) of subdivision (a) shall be imposed only as an offset against any damages awarded in favor of that party.

(c) If the party electing the trial de novo has proceeded in the action in forma pauperis and has failed to obtain a more favorable judgment, the costs under subparagraph (A) of paragraph (1) of subdivision (a) shall be imposed only to the extent that there remains a sufficient amount in the judgment after the amount offset under subdivision (b) has been deducted from the judgment. **Leg.H.** Added Stats 1978 ch 743 §2, operative July 1, 1979. Amended Stats 1982 ch 1354 §4, ch 1408 §1; Stats 1986 ch 377 §20; Stats 2005 ch 706 §14 (AB 1742), effective January 1, 2006; Stats 2006 ch 538 §66 (SB 1852), effective January 1, 2007.

§1141.22. Correction, modification, or vacation of award

The Judicial Council rules shall specify the grounds upon which the arbitrator or the court, or both, may correct, modify or vacate an award. **Leg.H.** Added Stats 1978 ch 743 §2, operative July 1, 1979.

§1141.23. Effect of award

The arbitration award shall be in writing, signed by the arbitrator and filed in the court in which the action is pending. If there is no request for a de novo trial or a request for dismissal in the form required by the Judicial Council and the award is not vacated, the award shall be entered in the judgment book in the amount of the award. Such award shall have the same force and effect as a judgment in any civil action or proceeding, except that it is not subject to appeal and it may not be attacked or set aside except as provided by Section 473, 1286.2, or Judicial Council rule. **Leg.H.** Added Stats 1978 ch 743 §2, operative July 1, 1979. Amended Stats 1982 ch 621 §1; Stats 2011 ch 49 §4 (SB 731), effective January 1, 2012.

§1141.24. Discovery after award

In cases ordered to arbitration pursuant to Section 1141.11, no discovery other than that permitted by Chapter 18 (commencing with Section 2034.010) of Title 4 of Part 4 is permissible after an arbitration award except by stipulation of the parties or by leave of court upon a showing of good cause. **Leg.H.** Added Stats 1978 ch 743 §2, operative July 1, 1979. Amended Stats 1985 ch 94 §1; Stats 1990 ch 1491 §8 (AB 3765); Stats 2003 ch 449 §14 (AB 1712); Stats 2004 ch 182 §15 (AB 3081), operative July 1, 2005.

§1141.25. Reference to award in subsequent trial

Any reference to the arbitration proceedings or arbitration award during any subsequent trial shall constitute an irregularity in the proceedings of the trial for the purposes of Section 657. **Leg.H.** Added Stats 1978 ch 743 §2, operative July 1, 1979.

§1141.26. Award in excess of jurisdictional amount

Nothing in this act shall prohibit an arbitration award in excess of the amount in controversy as specified in Section 1141.11. No party electing a trial de novo after such award shall be subject to the provisions of Section 1141.21 if the judgment upon the trial de novo is in excess of the amount in controversy as specified in Section 1141.11. **Leg.H.** Added Stats 1978 ch 743 §2, operative July 1, 1979. Amended Stats 1981 ch 1110 §4.

§1141.27. Public agency or entity as party

This chapter shall apply to any civil action otherwise within the scope of this chapter in which a party to the action is a public agency or public entity. **Leg.H.** Added Stats 1978 ch 743 §2, operative July 1, 1979.

§1141.28. Administrative costs; Actual costs

(a) All administrative costs of arbitration, including compensation of arbitrators, shall be paid for by the court in which the arbitration costs are incurred, except as otherwise provided in subdivision (b) and in Section 1141.21.

(b) The actual costs of compensation of arbitrators in any proceeding which would not otherwise be subject to the provisions of this chapter but in which arbitration is conducted pursuant to this chapter solely because of the stipulation of the parties, shall be paid for in equal shares by the parties. If the imposition of these costs would create such a substantial economic hardship for any party as not to be in the interest of justice, as determined by the arbitrator, that party's share of costs shall be paid for by the court in which the arbitration costs are incurred. The determination as to substantial economic hardship may be reviewed by the court. **Leg.H.** Added Stats 1978 ch 743 §2, operative July 1, 1979. Amended Stats 1982 ch 1408 §2; Stats 2000 ch 447 §3 (SB 1533).

§1141.29. [Section repealed 2003]

Leg.H. Added Stats 1978 ch 743 §2, operative July 1, 1979. Repealed Stats 2002 ch 784 §80 (SB 1316). The repealed section related to a report to Governor and Legislature.

§1141.30. Construction of provisions

This chapter shall not be construed in derogation of Title 9 (commencing with Section 1280) of Part 3, and, to that extent, this chapter and that title, other than Section 1280.1, are mutually exclusive and independent of each other. **Leg.H.** Added Stats 1978 ch 743 §2, operative July 1, 1979. Amended Stats 1985 ch 709 §2; Stats 1990 ch 817 §1 (SB 1951).

§1141.31. Operative date

The provisions of this chapter shall become operative July 1, 1979, except that the Judicial Council shall adopt the arbitration rules for practice and procedures on or before March 31, 1979. **Leg.H.** Added Stats 1978 ch 743 §2, operative July 1, 1979.

§1141.32. [Section repealed 1986]

Leg.H. Added Stats 1978 ch 743 §2, operative July 1, 1979. Amended Stats 1983 ch 1253 §1. Repealed Stats 1985 ch 1452 §1. The repealed section related to repeal of chapter.

CHAPTER 3
DISCHARGE OF PERSONS IMPRISONED ON CIVIL PROCESS [REPEALED]

§1143. [Section repealed 1974]

Leg.H. Enacted 1872. Repealed Stats 1973 ch 20 §12. The repealed section related to conditions for discharge of person confined in jail on execution issued on judgment rendered in a civil action.

§§1144–1154. [Sections repealed 1974]

Leg.H. Enacted 1872. Repealed Stats 1973 ch 20 §12.

CHAPTER 3.5
NEIGHBORHOOD DISPUTE RESOLUTION CENTERS [REPEALED]

§1143.10. [Section repealed 1982]

Leg.H. Added Stats 1980 ch 1176 §1. Repealed January 1, 1982, by the terms of former CCP §1143.14. The repealed section related to legislative findings.

§1143.11. [Section repealed 1982]

Leg.H. Added Stats 1980 ch 1176 §1. Repealed January 1, 1982, by the terms of former CCP §1143.14. The repealed section related to legislative intent.

§1143.12. [Section repealed 1982]

Leg.H. Added Stats 1980 ch 1176 §1. Repealed January 1, 1982, by the terms of former CCP §1143.14. The repealed section related to awards of funds.

§1143.13. [Section repealed 1982]

Leg.H. Added Stats 1980 ch 1176 §1. Repealed January 1, 1982, by the terms of former CCP §1143.14. The repealed section related to federal funds.

§1143.14. [Section repealed 1982]

Leg.H. Added Stats 1980 ch 1176 §1. Repealed January 1, 1982, by its own terms. The repealed section related to repeal of chapter.

CHAPTER 4
SUMMARY PROCEEDINGS FOR OBTAINING POSSESSION OF REAL PROPERTY IN CERTAIN CASES

Forcible entry. §1159.
Forcible detainer. §1160.
Unlawful detainer [Repealed February 1, 2025]. §1161.
Unlawful detainer [Operative February 1, 2025]. § 1161.
Unlawful detainer; Commercial real property. §1161.1.
Access to court file; Notice to defendants; Fee. §1161.2.
Access to civil case records for actions seeking recovery of COVID-19 rental debt. § 1161.2.5.
Termination or renewal of tenancy; Documentation or evidence of abuse or violence; Duty of Judicial Council. §1161.3.
Prohibited conduct by landlord as it relates to immigration or citizenship status of tenant. §1161.4.
Nullification of forfeiture; Cure or waiver of breach. §1161.5.
Removal of person holding over after notice to quit. §1161a.
Written notice to quit required before removal from foreclosed property; Right to possession; Termination of tenancy; Burden of proof; Applicability. §1161b.
Service of notice. §1162.
Service of copy of deed. §1162a.
Parties defendant; Persons bound. §1164.
Parties generally. §1165.
Complaint; Contents and requirements; Attachments; Issuance of summons. §1166.
Writ of possession. §1166a.
Summons. §1167.

Proof of service. §1167.1.
Answer. §1167.3.
Motion to quash; Extension of time to plead. §1167.4.
Limitation on extension of time. §1167.5.
Default, entry; Application for relief. §1169.
Appearance. §1170.
Time for trial; Extension; Payment of damages pending termination of action. §1170.5.
Motion for summary judgment. §1170.7.
Discovery motion. §1170.8.
Adoption of rules. §1170.9.
Trial by jury. §1171.
Showing required. §1172.
Amendment of complaint; Continuance. §1173.
Judgment for possession of premises; Enforcement. §1174.
Substantial breach of warranty of habitability; Prevailing party. §1174.2.
Liability of landlord, in violation of Civil Code Section 1942.4, for attorney's fees in proceeding based upon nonpayment of rent. §1174.21.
Unlawful detainer; Occupant's right to file claim; Procedure. §1174.25.
Abuse or violence against tenant; Unlawful detainer; Remedies. § 1174.27.
Objections to enforcement of judgment; Claim of right to possession. §1174.3.
Forfeiture; No release from liability for unpaid rent. §1174.5.
Stay of judgment pending appeal; New cause of action. §1176.
Rules of practice. §1177.
New trial and appeal. §1178.
Relief against forfeiture of lease. §1179.
Precedence over other actions. §1179a.

§1159. Forcible entry

(a) Every person is guilty of a forcible entry who either:

(1) By breaking open doors, windows, or other parts of a house, or by any kind of violence or circumstance of terror enters upon or into any real property.

(2) Who, after entering peaceably upon real property, turns out by force, threats, or menacing conduct, the party in possession.

(b) For purposes of this section, "party in possession" means any person who hires real property and includes a boarder or lodger, except those persons whose occupancy is described in subdivision (b) of Section 1940 of the Civil Code. **Leg.H.** Enacted 1872. Amended Stats 1976 ch 712 §2; Stats 2018 ch 92 §42 (SB 1289), effective January 1, 2019.

§1160. Forcible detainer

(a) Every person is guilty of a forcible detainer who either:

(1) By force, or by menaces and threats of violence, unlawfully holds and keeps the possession of any real property, whether the same was acquired peaceably or otherwise.

(2) Who, in the night-time, or during the absence of the occupant of any lands, unlawfully enters upon real property, and who, after demand made for the surrender thereof, for the period of five days, refuses to surrender the same to such former occupant.

(b) The occupant of real property, within the meaning of this section is one who, within five days preceding such unlawful entry, was in the peaceable and undisturbed possession of such lands. **Leg.H.** Enacted 1872. Amended Stats 2018 ch 92 §43 (SB 1289), effective January 1, 2019.

§1161. Unlawful detainer [Repealed February 1, 2025]

A tenant of real property, for a term less than life, or the executor or administrator of the tenant's estate heretofore qualified and now acting or hereafter to be qualified and act, is guilty of unlawful detainer:

1. When the tenant continues in possession, in person or by subtenant, of the property, or any part thereof, after the expiration of the term for which it is let to the tenant; provided the expiration is of a nondefault nature however brought about without the permission of the landlord, or the successor in estate of the landlord, if applicable; including the case where the person to be removed became the occupant of the premises as a servant, employee, agent, or licensee and the relation of master and servant, or employer and employee, or principal and agent, or licensor and licensee, has been lawfully terminated or the time fixed for occupancy by the agreement between the parties has expired; but nothing in this subdivision shall be construed as preventing the removal of the occupant in any other lawful manner; but in case of a tenancy at will, it shall first be terminated by notice, as prescribed in the Civil Code.

2. When the tenant continues in possession, in person or by subtenant, without the permission of the landlord, or the successor in estate of the landlord, if applicable, after default in the payment of rent, pursuant to the

lease or agreement under which the property is held, and three days' notice, excluding Saturdays and Sundays and other judicial holidays, in writing, requiring its payment, stating the amount that is due, the name, telephone number, and address of the person to whom the rent payment shall be made, and, if payment may be made personally, the usual days and hours that person will be available to receive the payment (provided that, if the address does not allow for personal delivery, then it shall be conclusively presumed that upon the mailing of any rent or notice to the owner by the tenant to the name and address provided, the notice or rent is deemed received by the owner on the date posted, if the tenant can show proof of mailing to the name and address provided by the owner), or the number of an account in a financial institution into which the rental payment may be made, and the name and street address of the institution (provided that the institution is located within five miles of the rental property), or if an electronic funds transfer procedure has been previously established, that payment may be made pursuant to that procedure, or possession of the property, shall have been served upon the tenant and if there is a subtenant in actual occupation of the premises, also upon the subtenant.

The notice may be served at any time within one year after the rent becomes due. In all cases of tenancy upon agricultural lands, if the tenant has held over and retained possession for more than 60 days after the expiration of the term without any demand of possession or notice to quit by the landlord or the successor in estate of the landlord, if applicable, the tenant shall be deemed to be holding by permission of the landlord or successor in estate of the landlord, if applicable, and shall be entitled to hold under the terms of the lease for another full year, and shall not be guilty of an unlawful detainer during that year, and the holding over for that period shall be taken and construed as a consent on the part of a tenant to hold for another year.

An unlawful detainer action under this paragraph shall be subject to the COVID-19 Tenant Relief Act of 2020 (Chapter 5 (commencing with Section 1179.01)) if the default in the payment of rent is based upon the COVID-19 rental debt.

3. When the tenant continues in possession, in person or by subtenant, after a neglect or failure to perform other conditions or covenants of the lease or agreement under which the property is held, including any covenant not to assign or sublet, than the one for the payment of rent, and three days' notice, excluding Saturdays and Sundays and other judicial holidays, in writing, requiring the performance of those conditions or covenants, or the possession of the property, shall have been served upon the tenant, and if there is a subtenant in actual occupation of the premises, also, upon the subtenant. Within three days, excluding Saturdays and Sundays and other judicial holidays, after the service of the notice, the tenant, or any subtenant in actual occupation of the premises, or any mortgagee of the term, or other person interested in its continuance, may perform the conditions or covenants of the lease or pay the stipulated rent, as the case may be, and thereby save the lease from forfeiture; provided, if the conditions and covenants of the lease, violated by the lessee, cannot afterward be performed, then no notice, as last prescribed herein, need be given to the lessee or the subtenant, demanding the performance of the violated conditions or covenants of the lease.

A tenant may take proceedings, similar to those prescribed in this chapter, to obtain possession of the premises let to a subtenant or held by a servant, employee, agent, or licensee, in case of that person's unlawful detention of the premises underlet to or held by that person.

An unlawful detainer action under this paragraph shall be subject to the COVID-19 Tenant Relief Act of 2020 (Chapter 5 (commencing with Section 1179.01)) if the neglect or failure to perform other conditions or covenants of the lease or agreement is based upon the COVID-19 rental debt.

4. Any tenant, subtenant, or executor or administrator of that person's estate heretofore qualified and now acting, or hereafter to be qualified and act, assigning or subletting or committing waste upon the demised premises, contrary to the conditions or covenants of the lease, or maintaining, committing, or permitting the maintenance or commission of a nuisance upon the demised premises or using the premises for an unlawful purpose, thereby terminates the lease, and the landlord, or the landlord's successor in estate, shall upon service of three days' notice to quit upon the person or persons in possession, be entitled to restitution of possession of the demised premises under this chapter. For purposes of this subdivision, a person who commits or maintains a public nuisance as described in Section 3482.8 of the Civil Code, or who commits an offense described in subdivision (c) of Section 3485 of the Civil Code, or subdivision (c) of Section 3486 of the Civil Code, or uses the premises to further the purpose of that offense shall be deemed to have committed a nuisance upon the premises.

5. When the tenant gives written notice as provided in Section 1946 of the Civil Code of the tenant's intention to terminate the hiring of the real property, or makes a written offer to surrender which is accepted in writing by the landlord, but fails to deliver possession at the time specified in that written notice, without the permission of the landlord, or the successor in estate of the landlord, if applicable.

6. **A landlord or its agent shall not charge a tenant a fee for serving, posting, or otherwise delivering any notice, as described** in this section

7. As used in this section:

"COVID-19 rental debt" has the same meaning as defined in Section 1179.02.

"Tenant" includes any person who hires real property except those persons whose occupancy is described in subdivision (b) of Section 1940 of the Civil Code.

[1] 8. This section shall remain in effect until February 1, 2025, and as of that date is repealed. **Leg.H.** Added Stats 2008 ch 440 §3 (AB 2052), effective September 27, 2008. Amended Stats 2009 ch 244 §5 (AB 530), effective January 1, 2010, operative January 1, 2012; Stats 2011 ch 128 §2 (SB 426), effective January 1, 2012; Stats 2018 ch 260 §1 (AB 2343), effective January 1, 2019, operative September 1, 2019; Stats 2020 ch 37 §15 (AB 3088), effective August 31, 2020, repealed February 1, 2025; Stats 2024 ch 287 §5 (SB 611), effective January 1, 2025, repealed February 1, 2025.

§1161. 2024 Deletes. [1] 7.

Prior Law: Former CCP §1161, similar to the present section, was added Stats 1905 ch 35 §1, amended Stats 1931 ch 738 §1, Stats 1933 ch 513 §1, Stats 1943 ch 58 §1, Stats 1945 ch 1349 §1, Stats 1957 ch 1699 §1, Stats 1961 ch 782 §1, Stats 1976 ch 712 §3, Stats 1996 ch 658 §2, Stats 2001 ch 729 §6, Stats 2007 ch 456 §2, Stats 2008 ch 440 §2, effective September 27, 2008, and repealed January 1, 2012, by its own terms.

Former CCP §1161, similar to the present section, was enacted 1872, amended by Code Amdts 1873-74 ch 383 §147, Code Amdts 1875-76 ch 202 §1, Code Amdts 1877-78 ch 596 §1, ch 627 §1, and repealed Stats 1905 ch 35 §1.

§ 1161. Unlawful detainer [Operative February 1, 2025]

A tenant of real property, for a term less than life, or the executor or administrator of the tenant's estate heretofore qualified and now acting or hereafter to be qualified and act, is guilty of unlawful detainer:

1. When the tenant continues in possession, in person or by subtenant, of the property, or any part thereof, after the expiration of the term for which it is let to the tenant; provided the expiration is of a nondefault nature however brought about without the permission of the landlord, or the successor in estate of the landlord, if applicable; including the case where the person to be removed became the occupant of the premises as a servant, employee, agent, or licensee and the relation of master and servant, or employer and employee, or principal and agent, or licensor and licensee, has been lawfully terminated or the time fixed for occupancy by the agreement between the parties has expired; but nothing in this subdivision shall be construed as preventing the removal of the occupant in any other lawful manner; but in case of a tenancy at will, it shall first be terminated by notice, as prescribed in the Civil Code.

2. When the tenant continues in possession, in person or by subtenant, without the permission of the landlord, or the successor in estate of the landlord, if applicable, after default in the payment of rent, pursuant to the lease or agreement under which the property is held, and three days' notice, excluding Saturdays and Sundays and other judicial holidays, in writing, requiring its payment, stating the amount that is due, the name, telephone number, and address of the person to whom the rent payment shall be made, and, if payment may be made personally, the usual days and hours that person will be available to receive the payment (provided that, if the address does not allow for personal delivery, then it shall be conclusively presumed that upon the mailing of any rent or notice to the owner by the tenant to the name and address provided, the notice or rent is deemed received by the owner on the date posted, if the tenant can show proof of mailing to the name and address provided by the owner), or the number of an account in a financial institution into which the rental payment may be made, and the name and street address of the institution (provided that the institution is located within five miles of the rental

property), or if an electronic funds transfer procedure has been previously established, that payment may be made pursuant to that procedure, or possession of the property, shall have been served upon the tenant and if there is a subtenant in actual occupation of the premises, also upon the subtenant.

The notice may be served at any time within one year after the rent becomes due. In all cases of tenancy upon agricultural lands, if the tenant has held over and retained possession for more than 60 days after the expiration of the term without any demand of possession or notice to quit by the landlord or the successor in estate of the landlord, if applicable, the tenant shall be deemed to be holding by permission of the landlord or successor in estate of the landlord, if applicable, and shall be entitled to hold under the terms of the lease for another full year, and shall not be guilty of an unlawful detainer during that year, and the holding over for that period shall be taken and construed as a consent on the part of a tenant to hold for another year.

3. When the tenant continues in possession, in person or by subtenant, after a neglect or failure to perform other conditions or covenants of the lease or agreement under which the property is held, including any covenant not to assign or sublet, than the one for the payment of rent, and three days' notice, excluding Saturdays and Sundays and other judicial holidays, in writing, requiring the performance of those conditions or covenants, or the possession of the property, shall have been served upon the tenant, and if there is a subtenant in actual occupation of the premises, also, upon the subtenant. Within three days, excluding Saturdays and Sundays and other judicial holidays, after the service of the notice, the tenant, or any subtenant in actual occupation of the premises, or any mortgagee of the term, or other person interested in its continuance, may perform the conditions or covenants of the lease or pay the stipulated rent, as the case may be, and thereby save the lease from forfeiture; provided, if the conditions and covenants of the lease, violated by the lessee, cannot afterward be performed, then no notice, as last prescribed herein, need be given to the lessee or the subtenant, demanding the performance of the violated conditions or covenants of the lease.

A tenant may take proceedings, similar to those prescribed in this chapter, to obtain possession of the premises let to a subtenant or held by a servant, employee, agent, or licensee, in case of that person's unlawful detention of the premises underlet to or held by that person.

4. Any tenant, subtenant, or executor or administrator of that person's estate heretofore qualified and now acting, or hereafter to be qualified and act, assigning or subletting or committing waste upon the demised premises, contrary to the conditions or covenants of the lease, or maintaining, committing, or permitting the maintenance or commission of a nuisance upon the demised premises or using the premises for an unlawful purpose, thereby terminates the lease, and the landlord, or the landlord's successor in estate, shall upon service of three days' notice to quit upon the person or persons in possession, be entitled to restitution of possession of the demised premises under this chapter. For purposes of this subdivision, a person who commits or maintains a public nuisance as described in Section 3482.8 of the Civil Code, or who commits an offense described in subdivision (c) of Section 3485 of the Civil Code, or subdivision (c) of Section 3486 of the Civil Code, or uses the premises to further the purpose of that offense shall be deemed to have committed a nuisance upon the premises.

5. When the tenant gives written notice as provided in Section 1946 of the Civil Code of the tenant's intention to terminate the hiring of the real property, or makes a written offer to surrender which is accepted in writing by the landlord, but fails to deliver possession at the time specified in that written notice, without the permission of the landlord, or the successor in estate of the landlord, if applicable.

6. **A landlord or its agent shall not charge a tenant a fee for serving, posting, or otherwise delivering any notice, as described in this section.**

7. As used in this section, "tenant" includes any person who hires real property except those persons whose occupancy is described in subdivision (b) of Section 1940 of the Civil Code.

[1] 8. This section shall become operative on February 1, 2025. **Leg.H.** Added Stats 2020 ch 37 §16 (AB 3088), effective August 31, 2020, operative February 1, 2025. Amended Stats 2024 ch 287 §6 (SB 611), effective January 1, 2025, operative February 1, 2025.

§ 1161. 2024 Deletes. [1] 7

§1161.1. Unlawful detainer; Commercial real property

With respect to application of Section 1161 in cases of possession of commercial real property after default in the payment of rent:

(a) If the amount stated in the notice provided to the tenant pursuant to subdivision (2) of Section 1161 is clearly identified by the notice as an estimate and the amount claimed is not in fact correct, but it is determined upon the trial or other judicial determination that rent was owing, and the amount claimed in the notice was reasonably estimated, the tenant shall be subject to judgment for possession and the actual amount of rent and other sums found to be due. However, if (1) upon receipt of such a notice claiming an amount identified by the notice as an estimate, the tenant tenders to the landlord within the time for payment required by the notice, the amount which the tenant has reasonably estimated to be due and (2) if at trial it is determined that the amount of rent then due was the amount tendered by the tenant or a lesser amount, the tenant shall be deemed the prevailing party for all purposes. If the court determines that the amount so tendered by the tenant was less than the amount due, but was reasonably estimated, the tenant shall retain the right to possession if the tenant pays to the landlord within five days of the effective date of the judgment (1) the amount previously tendered if it had not been previously accepted, (2) the difference between the amount tendered and the amount determined by the court to be due, and (3) any other sums as ordered by the court.

(b) If the landlord accepts a partial payment of rent, including any payment pursuant to subdivision (a), after serving notice pursuant to Section 1161, the landlord, without any further notice to the tenant, may commence and pursue an action under this chapter to recover the difference between the amount demanded in that notice and the payment actually received, and this shall be specified in the complaint.

(c) If the landlord accepts a partial payment of rent after filing the complaint pursuant to Section 1166, the landlord's acceptance of the partial payment is evidence only of that payment, without waiver of any rights or defenses of any of the parties. The landlord shall be entitled to amend the complaint to reflect the partial payment without creating a necessity for the filing of an additional answer or other responsive pleading by the tenant, and without prior leave of court, and such an amendment shall not delay the matter from proceeding. However, this subdivision shall apply only if the landlord provides actual notice to the tenant that acceptance of the partial rent payment does not constitute a waiver of any rights, including any right the landlord may have to recover possession of the property.

(d) "Commercial real property" as used in this section, means all real property in this state except dwelling units made subject to Chapter 2 (commencing with Section 1940) of Title 5 of Part 4 of Division 3 of the Civil Code, mobilehomes as defined in Section 798.3 of the Civil Code, or recreational vehicles as defined in Section 799.24 of the Civil Code.

(e) For the purposes of this section, there is a presumption affecting the burden of proof that the amount of rent claimed or tendered is reasonably estimated if, in relation to the amount determined to be due upon the trial or other judicial determination of that issue, the amount claimed or tendered was no more than 20 percent more or less than the amount determined to be due. However, if the rent due is contingent upon information primarily within the knowledge of the one party to the lease and that information has not been furnished to, or has not accurately been furnished to, the other party, the court shall consider that fact in determining the reasonableness of the amount of rent claimed or tendered pursuant to subdivision (a). **Leg.H.** Added Stats 1990 ch 890 §1 (SB 2498).

§1161.2. Access to court file; Notice to defendants; Fee

(a)(1) The clerk shall allow access to limited civil case records filed under this chapter, including the court file, index, and register of actions, only as follows:

(A) To a party to the action, including a party's attorney.

(B) To a person who provides the clerk with the names of at least one plaintiff and one defendant and the address of the premises, including the apartment or unit number, if any.

(C) To a resident of the premises who provides the clerk with the name of one of the parties or the case number and shows proof of residency.

(D) To a person by order of the court, which may be granted ex parte, on a showing of good cause.

(E) Except as provided in subparagraph (G), to any person by order of the court if judgment is entered for the plaintiff after trial more than 60 days since the filing of the complaint. The court shall issue the order upon issuing judgment for the plaintiff.

(F) Except as provided in subparagraph (G), to any other person 60 days after the complaint has been filed if judgment against all defendants has been entered for the plaintiff within 60 days of the filing of the complaint, in which case the clerk shall allow access to any court records in the action. If a default or default judgment is set aside more than 60 days after the complaint has been filed, this section shall apply as if the complaint had been filed on the date the default or default judgment is set aside.

(G)(i) In the case of a complaint involving residential property based on Section 1161a as indicated in the caption of the complaint, as required in subdivision (c) of Section 1166, to any other person, if 60 days have elapsed since the complaint was filed with the court, and, as of that date, judgment against all defendants has been entered for the plaintiff, after a trial.

(ii) Subparagraphs (E) and (F) shall not apply if the plaintiff filed the action between March 4, 2020, and September 30, 2021, and the action is based on an alleged default in the payment of rent.

(2) This section shall not be construed to prohibit the court from issuing an order that bars access to the court record in an action filed under this chapter if the parties to the action so stipulate.

(b)(1) For purposes of this section, "good cause" includes, but is not limited to, both of the following:

(A) The gathering of newsworthy facts by a person described in Section 1070 of the Evidence Code.

(B) The gathering of evidence by a party to an unlawful detainer action solely for the purpose of making a request for judicial notice pursuant to subdivision (d) of Section 452 of the Evidence Code.

(2) It is the intent of the Legislature that a simple procedure be established to request the ex parte order described in subparagraph (D) of paragraph (1) of subdivision (a).

(c) Upon the filing of a case so restricted, the court clerk shall mail notice to each defendant named in the action. The notice shall be mailed to the address provided in the complaint. The notice shall contain a statement that an unlawful detainer complaint (eviction action) has been filed naming that party as a defendant, and that access to the court file will be delayed for 60 days except to a party, an attorney for one of the parties, or any other person who (1) provides to the clerk the names of at least one plaintiff and one defendant in the action and provides to the clerk the address, including any applicable apartment, unit, or space number, of the subject premises, or (2) provides to the clerk the name of one of the parties in the action or the case number and can establish through proper identification that the person lives at the subject premises. The notice shall also contain a statement that access to the court index, register of actions, or other records is not permitted until 60 days after the complaint is filed, except pursuant to an order upon a showing of good cause for access. The notice shall contain on its face the following information:

(1) The name and telephone number of the county bar association.

(2) The name and telephone number of any entity that requests inclusion on the notice and demonstrates to the satisfaction of the court that it has been certified by the State Bar of California as a lawyer referral service and maintains a panel of attorneys qualified in the practice of landlord-tenant law pursuant to the minimum standards for a lawyer referral service established by the State Bar of California and Section 6155 of the Business and Professions Code.

(3) The following statement:

"The State Bar of California certifies lawyer referral services in California and publishes a list of certified lawyer referral services organized by county. To locate a lawyer referral service in your county, go to the State Bar's internet website at www.calbar.ca.gov or call 1-866-442-2529."

(4) The name and telephone number of an office or offices funded by the federal Legal Services Corporation or qualified legal services projects that receive funds distributed pursuant to Section 6216 of the Business and Professions Code that provide legal services to low-income persons in the county in which the action is filed. The notice shall state that these telephone numbers may be called for legal advice regarding the case. The notice shall be issued between 24 and 48 hours of the filing of the complaint, excluding weekends and holidays. One copy of the notice shall be addressed to "all occupants" and mailed separately to the subject premises. The notice shall not constitute service of the summons and complaint.

(5) The following statement, for a notice sent out pursuant to this section between October 1, 2021, and March 31, 2022:

IMPORTANT NOTICE FROM THE STATE OF CALIFORNIA-YOU MUST TAKE ACTION TO AVOID AN EVICTION: As part of the state's COVID-19 relief plan, money has been set aside to help renters who have fallen behind on rent or utility payments.

If you are behind on rent or utility payments, YOU SHOULD COMPLETE A RENTAL ASSISTANCE APPLICATION IMMEDIATELY! It is free and simple to apply. Citizenship or immigration status does not matter.

You can find out how to start your application by calling 1-833-430-2122 or visiting http://housingiskey.com right away.

(d) Notwithstanding any other law, the court shall charge an additional fee of fifteen dollars ($15) for filing a first appearance by the plaintiff. This fee shall be added to the uniform filing fee for actions filed under this chapter.

[1]

(e) This section does not alter any provision of the Evidence Code.

Leg.H. Added Stats 1991 ch 1007 §3 (SB 892). Amended Stats 1992 ch 666 §2 (AB 3453), ch 876 §7 (AB 3296); Stats 1993 ch 1191 §3 (SB 236); Stats 1994 ch 587 §7.5 (AB 3600); Stats 1998 ch 931 §118 (SB 2139), effective September 28, 1998; Stats 2001 ch 824 §11 (AB 1700); Stats 2003 ch 449 §15 (AB 1712), ch 787 §2 (SB 345); Stats 2004 ch 568 §6 (SB 1145); Stats 2005 ch 75 §41 (AB 145), effective July 19, 2005, operative January 1, 2006, ch 610 §2 (AB 664), effective January 1, 2006; Stats 2010 ch 641 §1 (SB 1149), effective January 1, 2011; Stats 2012 ch 241 §1 (AB 1865), effective January 1, 2013; Stats 2016 ch 336 §3 (AB 2819), effective January 1, 2017; Stats 2020 ch 36 §25 (AB 3364), effective January 1, 2021; Stats 2020 ch 37 §17 (AB 3088), effective August 31, 2020, repealed February 1, 2021 (ch 37 prevails); Stats 2021 ch 2 §11 (SB 91), effective January 29, 2021, repealed July 1, 2021; Stats 2021 ch 27 §11 (AB 832), effective June 28, 2021; Stats 2021 ch 360 §7 (AB 1584), effective January 1, 2022; Stats 2024 ch 711 §1 (AB 2304), effective January 1, 2025.

§1161.2. 2024 Deletes. [1] (e) This section does not apply to a case that seeks to terminate a mobilehome park tenancy if the statement of the character of the proceeding in the caption of the complaint clearly indicates that the complaint seeks termination of a mobilehome park tenancy. (f)

2016 Notes: The Legislature finds and declares all of the following:

(a) It is the policy of the state to promote open access to public records. It is in the interest of the public to ensure, to the greatest extent possible, that there is open public access to court records, including civil case records.

(b) It is the policy of the state that access to public records be limited or restricted only under compelling circumstances.

(c) With the enactment of Chapter 1007 of the Statutes of 1991, the Legislature began restricting public access to civil case records in unlawful detainer proceedings. Under current law, with limited exceptions, civil case records in unlawful detainer proceedings are unavailable to the public for a period of 60 days after filing. Civil case records in unlawful detainer proceedings in which the defendant prevails within 60 days of filing are permanently unavailable to the public.

(d) The state has a housing crisis that requires revising the current restrictions on public access to civil case records in unlawful detainer proceedings. More than four decades have passed since the California Supreme Court first observed, in Green v. Superior Court (1974) 10 Cal.3d 616, 625, "a scarcity of adequate low cost housing in virtually every urban setting [in California]." Yet the shortage of affordable housing for low-income tenants has only grown. Median monthly rents in the state are now approximately 50 percent higher than the national average, but high prices have failed to spur sufficient housing construction to meet demand. As a result, households in the state in the bottom quarter of the income distribution spend an average of 67 percent of their income on housing. The recent economic and foreclosure crises have only exacerbated the challenges that low-income households face in securing affordable housing.

(e) The difficulty of securing affordable housing in competitive rental markets is also worsened by the existing law governing access to civil case records in unlawful detainer proceedings. Specifically, once unlawful detainer civil case records become public, tenant screening companies and credit reporting agencies capture and publish personal identifying information regarding tenants named as defendants in those records. This information appears in published lists, known as unlawful detainer registries, and on tenants' credit reports. So long as it is accurate, the fact that a tenant was once sued for unlawful detainer is publicly available for up to seven years and cannot be challenged under federal or state laws governing consumer credit reporting.

(f) The names of thousands of innocent tenants whose cases are resolved only after the 60-day deadline appear on unlawful detainer registries. Many of these tenants successfully settle, secure a dismissal, or win at trial, and would have escaped negative credit reporting if only they had prevailed before the deadline. In other instances, unlawful detainer complaints are filed against tenants but never served. Because these complaints are never dismissed, the tenant's name is publicly released after 60 days and negative credit reporting ensues. Because landlords, who are attempting to decide between numerous applicants for scarce rental housing, rely on unlawful detainer registries and on credit reports, landlords often choose not to rent to tenants who appear on these registries, even if the tenants were eventually found innocent of unlawful detainer. As a result, given the statewide housing shortage, these tenants may be shut out of rental markets for up to seven years through no fault of their own.

(g) This act strikes a just balance between ensuring open access to public records and protecting the credit and reputation of innocent tenants. This act also ensures that landlords will have access to timely and more accurate information regarding prospective tenants. This act is a response to the state's ongoing affordable housing crisis and is necessary to prevent tenants from being inadvertently denied an opportunity to secure housing simply as a result of being named in an unlawful detainer lawsuit. Stats 2016 ch 336 (AB 2819) §1.

It is the intent of the Legislature to amend existing statutes regarding open access to public records by making permanently unavailable to the public civil case records in unlawful detainer proceedings in which the plaintiff does not prevail within 60 days of filing instead of unlawful detainer proceedings in which the defendant prevails within 60 days of filing. Stats 2016 ch 336 (AB 2819) §2.

§ 1161.2.5. Access to civil case records for actions seeking recovery of COVID-19 rental debt

(a)(1) Except as provided in Section 1161.2, the clerk shall allow access to civil case records for actions seeking recovery of COVID-19 rental debt, as defined in Section 1179.02, including the court file, index, and register of actions, only as follows:

(A) To a party to the action, including a party's attorney.

(B) To a person who provides the clerk with the names of at least one plaintiff and one defendant.

(C) To a resident of the premises for which the COVID-19 rental debt is owed who provides the clerk with the name of one of the parties or the case number and shows proof of residency.

(D) To a person by order of the court, which may be granted ex parte, on a showing of good cause.

(2) To give the court notice that access to the records in an action is limited, any complaint or responsive pleading in a case subject to this section shall include on either the first page of the pleading or a cover page, the phrase "ACTION FOR RECOVERY OF COVID-19 RENTAL DEBT AS DEFINED UNDER SECTION 1179.02" in bold, capital letters, in 12 point or larger font.

(3) The Judicial Council shall develop forms for parties to utilize in actions brought pursuant to Section 116.223 and in civil actions for recovery of COVID-19 rental debt as defined in Section 1179.02. The forms shall provide prominent notice on the first page that access to the records in the case is limited pursuant to this section.

(b)(1) For purposes of this section, "good cause" includes, but is not limited to, both of the following:

(A) The gathering of newsworthy facts by a person described in Section 1070 of the Evidence Code.

(B) The gathering of evidence by a party to a civil action solely for the purpose of making a request for judicial notice pursuant to subdivision (d) of Section 452 of the Evidence Code.

(2) It is the intent of the Legislature that a simple procedure be established to request the ex parte order described in subparagraph (D) of paragraph (1) of subdivision (a).

(c) This section does not alter any provision of the Evidence Code.
Leg.H. Added Stats 2020 ch 37 §19 (AB 3088), effective August 31, 2020, repealed February 1, 2021. Amended Stats 2021 ch 2 §13 (SB 91), effective January 29, 2021. Repealed Stats 2021 ch 2 §13 (SB 91), effective January 29, 2021. Amended Stats 2021 ch 27 §13 (AB 832), effective June 28, 2021.

§1161.3. Termination or renewal of tenancy; Documentation or evidence of abuse or violence; Duty of Judicial Council

(a) For purposes of this section:

(1) "Abuse or violence" means domestic violence as defined in Section 6211 of the Family Code, sexual assault as defined in Section 1219, stalking as defined in Section 1708.7 of the Civil Code or Section 646.9 of the Penal Code, human trafficking as defined in Section 236.1 of the Penal Code, abuse of an elder or a dependent adult as defined in Section 15610.07 of the Welfare and Institutions Code, or any act described in paragraphs (6) to (8), inclusive, of subdivision (a) of Section 1946.7 of the Civil Code.

(2) "Documentation evidencing abuse or violence against the tenant, the tenant's immediate family member, or the tenant's household member" means any of the following:

(A) A temporary restraining order, emergency protective order, or protective order lawfully issued within the last 180 days pursuant to Section 527.6, Part 3 (commencing with Section 6240), Part 4 (commencing with Section 6300), or Part 5 (commencing with Section 6400) of Division 10 of the Family Code, Section 136.2 of the Penal Code, or Section 213.5 or 15657.03 of the Welfare and Institutions Code that protects the tenant, the tenant's immediate family member, or the tenant's household member from abuse or violence.

(B) A copy of a written report, written within the last 180 days, by a peace officer employed by a state or local law enforcement agency acting in the officer's official capacity, stating that the tenant, the tenant's immediate family member, or the tenant's household member has filed a report alleging that they are a victim of abuse or violence.

(C)(i) Documentation from a qualified third party based on information received by that third party while acting in their professional capacity to indicate that the tenant, the tenant's immediate family member, or the tenant's household member is seeking assistance for physical or mental injuries or abuse resulting from an act of abuse or violence, which shall contain, in substantially the same form, the following:

Tenant Statement and Qualified Third Party Statement
under Code of Civil Procedure Section 1161.3

Part I. Statement By Tenant

I, [insert name of tenant], state as follows:

I, my immediate family member, or a member of my household, have been a victim of:
[insert one or more of the following: domestic violence, sexual assault, stalking, human trafficking, elder abuse, dependent adult abuse, a crime that caused bodily injury or death, a crime that included the exhibition, drawing, brandishing, or use of a firearm or other deadly weapon or instrument, or a crime that included the use or threat of force against the victim.]

The most recent incident(s) happened on or about:
[insert date or dates.]

The incident(s) was/were committed by the following person(s), with these physical description(s), if known and safe to provide:
[if known and safe to provide, insert name(s) and physical description(s).]

_____
(signature of tenant)
_____
(date)

Part II. Qualified Third Party Statement

I, [insert name of qualified third party], state as follows:

My business address and phone number are:
[insert business address and phone number.]

Check and complete one of the following:

____I meet the requirements for a sexual assault counselor provided in Section 1035.2 of the Evidence Code and I am either engaged in an office, hospital, institution, or center commonly known as a rape crisis center described in that section or employed by an organization providing the programs specified in Section 13835.2 of the Penal Code.

____I meet the requirements for a domestic violence counselor provided in Section 1037.1 of the Evidence Code and I am employed, whether financially compensated or not, by a domestic violence victim service organization, as defined in that section.

____I meet the requirements for a human trafficking caseworker provided in Section 1038.2 of the Evidence Code and I am employed, whether financially compensated or not, by an organization that provides programs specified in Section 18294 of the Welfare and Institutions Code or in Section 13835.2 of the Penal Code.

____I meet the definition of "victim of violent crime advocate" provided in Section 1946.7 of the Civil Code and I am employed, whether financially compensated or not, by an agency or organization that has a documented record of providing services to victims of violent crime or provides those services under the auspices or supervision of a court or a law enforcement or prosecution agency.

____I am licensed by the State of California as a:
[insert one of the following: physician and surgeon, osteopathic physician and surgeon, registered nurse, psychiatrist, psychologist, licensed clinical social worker, licensed marriage and family therapist, or licensed professional clinical counselor.] and I am licensed by, and my license number is: [insert name of state licensing entity and license number.]

The person who signed the Statement By Tenant above stated to me that they, a member of their immediate family, or a member of their household is a victim of:
[insert one or more of the following: domestic violence, sexual assault, stalking, human trafficking, elder abuse, dependent adult abuse, a crime that caused bodily injury or death, a crime that included the exhibition, drawing, brandishing, or use of a firearm or other deadly weapon or instrument, or a crime that included the use or threat of force against the victim.]

The person further stated to me the incident(s) occurred on or about the date(s) stated above.

_____
(signature of qualified third party)
_____
(date)

(ii) The documentation may be signed by a person who meets the requirements for a sexual assault counselor, domestic violence counselor, a human trafficking caseworker, or a victim of violent crime advocate only if the documentation displays the letterhead of the office, hospital, institution, center, or organization, as appropriate, that engages or employs, whether financially compensated or not, this counselor, caseworker, or advocate.

(D) Any other form of documentation or evidence that reasonably verifies that the abuse or violence occurred.

(3) "Health practitioner" means a physician and surgeon, osteopathic physician and surgeon, psychiatrist, psychologist, registered nurse, licensed clinical social worker, licensed marriage and family therapist, or licensed professional clinical counselor.

(4) "Immediate family member" has the same meaning as defined in Section 1946.7 of the Civil Code.

(5) "Perpetrator of abuse or violence" means any of the following:
(A) The person against whom an order described in subparagraph (A) of paragraph (2) of subdivision (a) has been issued.
(B) The person who was named or referred to as causing the abuse or violence in the report described in subparagraph (B) of paragraph (2) of subdivision (a).
(C) The person who was named or referred to as causing the abuse or violence in the documentation described in subparagraph (C) of paragraph (2) of subdivision (a).
(D) The person who was named or referred to as causing the abuse or violence in the documentation described in subparagraph (D) of paragraph (2) of subdivision (a).

(6) "Qualified third party" means a health practitioner, domestic violence counselor, as defined in Section 1037.1 of the Evidence Code, a sexual assault counselor, as defined in Section 1035.2 of the Evidence Code, a human trafficking caseworker, as defined in Section 1038.2 of the Evidence Code, or a victim of violent crime advocate.

(7) "Tenant" means tenant, subtenant, lessee, or sublessee.

(8) "Tenant in residence" means a tenant who is currently residing in the unit and has full physical and legal access to the unit.

(9) "Victim of violent crime advocate" has the same meaning as defined in Section 1946.7 of the Civil Code.

(b)(1) A landlord shall not terminate a tenancy or fail to renew a tenancy based on an act of abuse or violence against a tenant, a tenant's immediate family member, or a tenant's household member if the landlord has received documentation evidencing abuse or violence against the tenant, the tenant's immediate family member, or the tenant's household member.

(2) Notwithstanding paragraph (1), a landlord may terminate a tenancy or fail to renew a tenancy based on an act of abuse or violence against a tenant, a tenant's immediate family member, or a tenant's household member even after receiving documentation of abuse or violence against the tenant, the tenant's immediate family member, or the tenant's household member if either of the following apply:
(A) The perpetrator of abuse or violence is a tenant in residence of the same dwelling unit as the tenant, the tenant's immediate family member, or household member.
(B) Both of the following apply:
(i) The perpetrator of abuse or violence's words or actions have threatened the physical safety of other tenants, guests, invitees, or licensees.
(ii) After expiration of a three-day notice requiring the tenant not to voluntarily permit or consent to the presence of the perpetrator of abuse or violence on the premises, the tenant continues to do so.

(c) Notwithstanding any provision in a lease to the contrary, a landlord shall not be liable to any other tenants for any action that arises due to the landlord's compliance with this section.

(d) A defendant in an unlawful detainer action arising from a landlord's termination of a tenancy or failure to renew a tenancy that is based on an act of abuse or violence against a tenant, a tenant's immediate family member, or a tenant's household member may raise an affirmative defense as follows:
(1) If the perpetrator of the abuse or violence is not a tenant in residence of the same dwelling unit as the tenant, the tenant's immediate family member, or household member, then the defendant shall have a complete defense as to that cause of action, unless each clause of subparagraph (B) of paragraph (2) of subdivision (b) applies.
(2) If the perpetrator of the abuse or violence is a tenant in residence of the same dwelling unit as the tenant, the tenant's immediate family member, or household member, the court shall proceed in accordance with Section 1174.27.

(e)(1) A landlord shall not disclose any information provided by a tenant under this section to a third party unless either of the following is true:
(A) The tenant has consented in writing to the disclosure.
(B) The disclosure is required by law or court order.
(2) A landlord's communication with the qualified third party who provides documentation in order to verify the contents of that documentation is not a disclosure for purposes of this subdivision.

(f) The Judicial Council shall review its forms that may be used by a party to assert in the responsive pleading the grounds set forth in this section as an affirmative defense to an unlawful detainer action and, by January 1, 2025, make any changes to those forms that the Judicial Council deems necessary to conform them to this section. **Leg.H.** Added Stats 2010 ch 626 §4 (SB 782), effective January 1, 2011. Amended Stats 2012 ch 516 §2 (SB 1403), effective January 1, 2013; Stats 2013 ch 130 §3 (SB 612), effective January 1, 2014; Stats 2018 ch 190 §2 (AB 2413), effective January 1, 2019; Stats 2022 ch 558 §2 (SB 1017), effective January 1, 2023; Stats 2023 ch 478 §16 (AB 1756), effective January 1, 2024.

§1161.4. Prohibited conduct by landlord as it relates to immigration or citizenship status of tenant

(a) A landlord shall not cause a tenant or occupant to quit involuntarily or bring an action to recover possession because of the immigration or citizenship status of a tenant, occupant, or other person known to the landlord to be associated with a tenant or occupant, unless the landlord is complying with any legal obligation under any federal government program that provides for rent limitations or rental assistance to a qualified tenant.

(b) In an unlawful detainer action, a tenant or occupant may raise, as an affirmative defense, that the landlord violated subdivision (a).

(c) It is a rebuttable presumption that a tenant or occupant has established an affirmative defense under this section in an unlawful detainer action if the landlord did both of the following:

(1) Approved the tenant or occupant to take possession of the unit before filing the unlawful detainer action.

(2) Included in the unlawful detainer action a claim based on one of the following:

(A) The failure at any time of a previously approved tenant or occupant to provide a valid social security number.

(B) The failure at any time of a previously approved tenant or occupant to provide information required to obtain a consumer credit report under Section 1785.11 of the Civil Code.

(C) The failure at any time of a previously approved tenant or occupant to provide a form of identification deemed acceptable by the landlord.

(d) This section does not create a rebuttable presumption that a tenant or occupant has established an affirmative defense under this section if a landlord has requested the information described in paragraph (2) of subdivision (c) for the purpose of complying with any legal obligation under any federal government program that provides for rent limitations or rental assistance to a qualified tenant, or any other federal law, or a subpoena, warrant, or other order issued by a court.

(e) The rebuttable presumption in this section does not limit paragraph (2) of subdivision (c) of Section 1940.3 of the Civil Code.

(f) No affirmative defense is established under subdivision (b) if a landlord files an unlawful detainer action for the purpose of complying with any legal obligation under any federal government program that provides for rent limitations or rental assistance to a qualified tenant.

(g) For purposes of this section, "immigration or citizenship status" includes a perception that the person has a particular immigration status or citizenship status, or that the person is associated with a person who has, or is perceived to have, a particular immigration status or citizenship status. **Leg.H.** Added Stats 2017 ch 489 §8 (AB 291), effective January 1, 2018.

§1161.5. Nullification of forfeiture; Cure or waiver of breach

When the notice required by Section 1161 states that the lessor or the landlord may elect to declare the forfeiture of the lease or rental agreement, that declaration shall be nullified and the lease or rental agreement shall remain in effect if the lessee or tenant performs within three days after service of the notice or if the breach is waived by the lessor or the landlord after service of the notice. **Leg.H.** Added Stats 1984 ch 174 §1.

§1161a. Removal of person holding over after notice to quit

(a) As used in this section:

(1) "Manufactured home" has the same meaning as provided in Section 18007 of the Health and Safety Code.

(2) "Mobilehome" has the same meaning as provided in Section 18008 of the Health and Safety Code.

(3) "Floating home" has the same meaning as provided in subdivision (d) of Section 18075.55 of the Health and Safety Code.

(b) In any of the following cases, a person who holds over and continues in possession of a manufactured home, mobilehome, floating home, or real property after a three-day written notice to quit the property has been served upon the person, or if there is a subtenant in actual occupation of the premises, also upon such subtenant, as prescribed in Section 1162, may be removed therefrom as prescribed in this chapter:

(1) Where the property has been sold pursuant to a writ of execution against such person, or a person under whom such person claims, and the title under the sale has been duly perfected.

(2) Where the property has been sold pursuant to a writ of sale, upon the foreclosure by proceedings taken as prescribed in this code of a mortgage, or under an express power of sale contained therein, executed by such person, or a person under whom such person claims, and the title under the foreclosure has been duly perfected.

(3) Where the property has been sold in accordance with Section 2924 of the Civil Code, under a power of sale contained in a deed of trust executed by such person, or a person under whom such person claims, and the title under the sale has been duly perfected.

(4) Where the property has been sold by such person, or a person under whom such person claims, and the title under the sale has been duly perfected.

(5) Where the property has been sold in accordance with Section 18037.5 of the Health and Safety Code under the default provisions of a conditional sale contract or security agreement executed by such person, or a person under whom such person claims, and the title under the sale has been duly perfected.

(c) Notwithstanding the provisions of subdivision (b), a tenant or subtenant in possession of a rental housing unit which has been sold by reason of any of the causes enumerated in subdivision (b), who rents or leases the rental housing unit either on a periodic basis from week to week, month to month, or other interval, or for a fixed period of time, shall be given written notice to quit pursuant to Section 1162, at least as long as the term of hiring itself but not exceeding 30 days, before the tenant or subtenant may be removed therefrom as prescribed in this chapter.

(d) For the purpose of subdivision (c), "rental housing unit" means any structure or any part thereof which is rented or offered for rent for residential occupancy in this state. **Leg.H.** Added Stats 1929 ch 393 §1. Amended Stats 1941 ch 1095 §1; Stats 1982 ch 497 §74, operative July 1, 1983; Stats 1983 ch 346 §1, ch 1124 §11, operative July 1, 1984; Stats 1991 ch 942 §11 (AB 628).

§1161b. Written notice to quit required before removal from foreclosed property; Right to possession; Termination of tenancy; Burden of proof; Applicability

(a) Notwithstanding Section 1161a, a tenant or subtenant in possession of a rental housing unit under a month-to-month lease or periodic tenancy at the time the property is sold in foreclosure shall be given 90 days' written notice to quit pursuant to Section 1162 before the tenant or subtenant may be removed from the property as prescribed in this chapter.

(b) In addition to the rights set forth in subdivision (a), tenants or subtenants holding possession of a rental housing unit under a fixed-term residential lease entered into before transfer of title at the foreclosure sale shall have the right to possession until the end of the lease term, and all rights and obligations under the lease shall survive foreclosure, except that the tenancy may be terminated upon 90 days' written notice to quit pursuant to subdivision (a) if any of the following conditions apply:

(1) The purchaser or successor in interest will occupy the housing unit as a primary residence.

(2) The lessee is the mortgagor or the child, spouse, or parent of the mortgagor.

(3) The lease was not the result of an arms' length transaction.

(4) The lease requires the receipt of rent that is substantially less than fair market rent for the property, except when rent is reduced or subsidized due to a federal, state, or local subsidy or law.

(c) The purchaser or successor in interest shall bear the burden of proof in establishing that a fixed-term residential lease is not entitled to protection under subdivision (b).

(d) This section shall not apply if any party to the note remains in the property as a tenant, subtenant, or occupant.

(e) Nothing in this section is intended to affect any local just cause eviction ordinance. This section does not, and shall not be construed to, affect the authority of a public entity that otherwise exists to regulate or monitor the basis for eviction. **Leg.H.** Added Stats 2008 ch 69 §6 (SB 1137), effective July 8, 2008, repealed January 1, 2013. Amended Stats 2012 ch 562 §3 (AB 2610), effective January 1, 2013, repealed December 31, 2019; Stats 2019 ch 134 §3 (SB 18), effective January 1, 2020.

2019 Note: This act shall be known, and may be cited, as the Keep Californians Housed Act. Stats 2019 ch 134 §1 (SB 18).

2008 Note: Nothing in this act is intended to affect any local just-cause eviction ordinance. This act does not, and shall not be construed to, affect the authority of a public entity that otherwise exists to regulate or monitor the basis for eviction. Stats 2008 ch 69 §7 (SB 1137).

§1161c. Foreclosure on residential property; Cover sheet and notice of termination of tenancy [Repealed]

(a) In the case of any foreclosure on a residential property, the immediate successor in interest in the property pursuant to the foreclosure shall attach a cover sheet, in the form as set forth in subdivision (b), to any notice of termination of tenancy served on a tenant of that property within the first year after the foreclosure sale. This notice shall not be required if any of the following apply:

(1) The tenancy is terminated pursuant to Section 1161.

(2) The successor in interest and the tenant have executed a written rental agreement or lease or a written acknowledgment of a preexisting rental agreement or lease.

(3) The tenant receiving the notice was not a tenant at the time of the foreclosure.

(b) The cover sheet shall consist of the following notice, in at least 12-point type:

Notice to Any Renters Living At
[street address of the unit]
The attached notice means that your home was recently sold in foreclosure and the new owner plans to evict you.
You should talk to a lawyer NOW to see what your rights are. You may receive court papers in a few days. If your name is on the papers it may hurt your credit if you do not respond and simply move out.
Also, if you do not respond within five days of receiving the papers, even if you are not named in the papers, you will likely lose any rights you may have. In some cases, you can respond without hurting your credit. You should ask a lawyer about it.
You may have the right to stay in your home for 90 days or longer, regardless of any deadlines stated on any attached papers. In some cases and in some cities with a "just cause for eviction law," you may not have to move at all. But you must take the proper legal steps in order to protect your rights.
How to Get Legal Help
If you cannot afford an attorney, you may be eligible for free legal services from a nonprofit legal services program. You can locate these nonprofit groups at the California Legal Services Internet Web site (www.lawhelp-ca.org), the California Courts Online Self-Help Center (www.courtinfo.ca.gov/selfhelp), or by contacting your local court or county bar association.

(c) If the notice to quit specifies an effective date of at least 90 days after the notice is served, without qualification, no cover sheet shall be required, provided that the notice incorporates the text of the cover sheet, as set forth in subdivision (b) in at least 10-point type. The incorporated text shall omit the caption and the first paragraph of the cover sheet and the fourth paragraph of the cover sheet shall be replaced by the following language:

You may have the right to stay in your home for longer than 90 days. If you have a lease that ends more than 90 days from now, the new owner must honor the lease under many circumstances. Also, in some cases and in some cities with a "just cause for eviction law," you may not have to move at all. But you must take the proper legal steps in order to protect your rights.

(d) This section shall remain in effect only until December 31, 2019, and as of that date is repealed, unless a later enacted statute, that is enacted before December 31, 2019, deletes or extends that date. **Leg.H.** Added Stats 2010 ch 641 §2 (SB 1149), effective January 1, 2011, repealed January 1, 2013. Amended Stats 2012 ch 210 §1 (SB 825), effective January 1, 2013, repealed December 31, 2019.

§1162. Service of notice

(a) Except as provided in subdivision (b), the notices required by Sections 1161 and 1161a may be served by any of the following methods:

(1) By delivering a copy to the tenant personally.

(2) If he or she is absent from his or her place of residence, and from his or her usual place of business, by leaving a copy with some person of suitable age and discretion at either place, and sending a copy through the mail addressed to the tenant at his or her place of residence.

(3) If such place of residence and business cannot be ascertained, or a person of suitable age or discretion there can not be found, then by affixing a copy in a conspicuous place on the property, and also delivering a copy to a person there residing, if such person can be found; and also sending a copy through the mail addressed to the tenant at the place where the property is situated. Service upon a subtenant may be made in the same manner.

(b) The notices required by Section 1161 may be served upon a commercial tenant by any of the following methods:

(1) By delivering a copy to the tenant personally.

(2) If he or she is absent from the commercial rental property, by leaving a copy with some person of suitable age and discretion at the property, and sending a copy through the mail addressed to the tenant at the address where the property is situated.

(3) If, at the time of attempted service, a person of suitable age or discretion is not found at the rental property through the exercise of reasonable diligence, then by affixing a copy in a conspicuous place on the property, and also sending a copy through the mail addressed to the tenant at the address where the property is situated. Service upon a subtenant may be made in the same manner.

(c) For purposes of subdivision (b), "commercial tenant" means a person or entity that hires any real property in this state that is not a dwelling unit, as defined in subdivision (c) of Section 1940 of the Civil Code, or a mobilehome, as defined in Section 798.3 of the Civil Code. **Leg.H.** Enacted 1872. Amended Code Amdts 1873–74 ch 383 §148; Stats 1935 ch 52 §5; Stats 2002 ch 664 §49.5 (AB 3034); Stats 2010 ch 144 §1 (AB 1263), effective January 1, 2011.

§1162a. Service of copy of deed

In any case in which service or exhibition of a receiver's or levying officer's deed is required, in lieu thereof service of a copy or copies of the deed may be made as provided in Section 1162. **Leg.H.** Added Stats 1939 ch 519 §1. Amended Stats 1982 ch 497 §75, operative July 1, 1983.

§1163. [Section repealed 1931]

Leg.H. Enacted 1872. Amended Code Amdts 1880 ch 20 §1, Stats 1927 ch 115 §1. Repealed Stats 1931 ch 237 §2. The repealed section related to jurisdiction of superior courts.

§1164. Parties defendant; Persons bound

No person other than the tenant of the premises and subtenant, if there be one, in the actual occupation of the premises when the complaint is filed, need be made parties defendant in the proceeding, nor shall any proceeding abate, nor the plaintiff be nonsuited for the nonjoinder of any person who might have been made party defendant, but when it appears that any of the parties served with process, or appearing in the proceeding, are guilty of the offense charged, judgment must be rendered against him or her. In case a defendant has become a subtenant of the premises in controversy, after the service of the notice provided for by subdivision 2 of Section 1161 of this code, upon the tenant of the premises, the fact that such notice was not served on each subtenant shall constitute no defense to the action. All persons who enter the premises under the tenant, after the commencement of the suit, shall be bound by the judgment, the same as if he or they had been made party to the action. **Leg.H.** Enacted 1872. Amended Code Amdts 1873–74 ch 383 §149; Stats 1885 ch 139 §1; Stats 1975 ch 1241 §8.

§1165. Parties generally

Except as provided in the preceding section, the provisions of part two of this code, relating to parties to civil actions, are applicable to this proceeding. **Leg.H.** Enacted 1872.

§1166. Complaint; Contents and requirements; Attachments; Issuance of summons

(a) The complaint shall:

(1) Be verified and include the typed or printed name of the person verifying the complaint.

(2) Set forth the facts on which the plaintiff seeks to recover.

(3) Describe the premises with reasonable certainty.

(4) If the action is based on paragraph (2) of Section 1161, state the amount of rent in default.

(5) State specifically the method used to serve the defendant with the notice or notices of termination upon which the complaint is based. This requirement may be satisfied by using and completing all items relating to service of the notice or notices in an appropriate Judicial Council form complaint, or by attaching a proof of service of the notice or notices of termination served on the defendant.

(b) The complaint may set forth any circumstances of fraud, force, or violence that may have accompanied the alleged forcible entry or forcible or unlawful detainer, and claim damages therefor.

(c) In an action regarding residential real property based on Section 1161a, the plaintiff shall state in the caption of the complaint "Action based on Code of Civil Procedure Section 1161a."

(d)(1) In an action regarding residential property, the plaintiff shall attach to the complaint the following:

(A) A copy of the notice or notices of termination served on the defendant upon which the complaint is based.

(B) A copy of any written lease or rental agreement regarding the premises. Any addenda or attachments to the lease or written agreement that form the basis of the complaint shall also be attached. The documents required by this subparagraph are not required to be attached if the complaint alleges any of the following:

(i) The lease or rental agreement is oral.

(ii) A written lease or rental agreement regarding the premises is not in the possession of the landlord or any agent or employee of the landlord.

(iii) An action based solely on subdivision (2) of Section 1161.

(2) If the plaintiff fails to attach the documents required by this subdivision, the court shall grant leave to amend the complaint for a five-day period in order to include the required attachments.

(e) Upon filing the complaint, a summons shall be issued thereon. **Leg.H.** Added Stats 2003 ch 787 §4 (SB 345), operative January 1, 2005. Amended Stats 2010 ch 641 §3 (SB 1149), effective January 1, 2011.

Former Sections: Former CCP §1166, similar to the present section, was enacted in 1872 and repealed Stats 2003 ch 787 §3. Historical derivation: Stats 1865–66 ch 550 §5.

Prior Law: Former CCP §1166, similar to the present section, was enacted 1872, amended Code Amdts 1873–74 ch 383 §150, Code Amdts 1877–78 ch 163 §1, Code Amdts 1880 ch 20 §2, Stats 1907 ch 257 §1, and repealed Stats 2003 ch 787 §3. Historical derivation: Stats 1865–66 ch 550 §5.

§1166a. Writ of possession

(a) Upon filing the complaint, the plaintiff may, upon motion, have immediate possession of the premises by a writ of possession of a manufactured home, mobilehome, or real property issued by the court and directed to the sheriff of the county or marshal, for execution, where it appears to the satisfaction of the court, after a hearing on the motion, from the verified complaint and from any affidavits filed or oral testimony given by or on behalf of the parties, that the defendant resides out of state, has departed from the state, cannot, after due diligence, be found within the state, or has concealed himself or herself to avoid the service of summons. The motion shall indicate that the writ applies to all tenants, subtenants, if any, named claimants, if any, and any other occupants of the premises.

(b) Written notice of the hearing on the motion shall be served on the defendant by the plaintiff in accordance with the provisions of Section 1011, and shall inform the defendant as follows: "You may file affidavits on your own behalf with the court and may appear and present testimony on your own behalf. However, if you fail to appear, the plaintiff will apply to the court for a writ of possession of a manufactured home, mobilehome, or real property."

(c) The plaintiff shall file an undertaking in a sum that shall be fixed and determined by the judge, to the effect that, if the plaintiff fails to recover judgment against the defendant for the possession of the premises or if the suit is dismissed, the plaintiff will pay to the defendant those damages, not to exceed the amount fixed in the undertaking, as may be sustained by the defendant by reason of that dispossession under the writ of possession of a manufactured home, mobilehome, or real property.

(d) If, at the hearing on the motion, the findings of the court are in favor of the plaintiff and against the defendant, an order shall be entered for the immediate possession of the premises.

(e) The order for the immediate possession of the premises may be enforced as provided in Division 3 (commencing with Section 712.010) of Title 9 of Part 2.

(f) For the purposes of this section, references in Division 3 (commencing with Section 712.010) of Title 9 of Part 2 and in subdivisions (e) to (m), inclusive, of Section 1174, to the "judgment debtor" shall be deemed references to the defendant, to the "judgment creditor" shall be deemed references to the plaintiff, and to the "judgment of possession or sale of property" shall be deemed references to an order for the immediate possession of the premises. **Leg.H.** Added Stats 1939 ch 751 §2. Amended Stats 1949 ch 372 §1; Stats 1951 ch 1737 §157, operative January 1, 1952; Stats 1969 ch 903 §1; Stats 1970 ch 1165 §1; Stats 1982 ch 517 §178 (ch 497 prevails), ch 497 §75.5, operative July 1, 1983; Stats 1983 ch 18 §20, effective April 21, 1983, operative July 1, 1983, ch 1124 §12, operative July 1, 1984; Stats 1990 ch 1535 §2 (SB 2508); Stats 1996 ch 872 §20 (AB 3472).

Prior Law: Former CCP §1166a, similar to the present section, was added Stats 1937 ch 232 §1 and repealed Stats 1939 ch 751 §1.

§1167. Summons

(a) The summons shall be in the form specified in Section 412.20 except that when the defendant is served, the defendant's response shall be filed within [1] **10** days, excluding Saturdays and Sundays and other judicial holidays, after the complaint is served upon the defendant.

(b) If service is completed by mail or in person through the Secretary of State's address confidentiality program under Chapter 3.1 (commencing with Section 6205) of Division 7 of Title 1 of the Government Code, the defendant shall have an additional five court days to file a response.

(c) [2] **Except as otherwise provided in this section,** the summons shall be issued and served and returned in the same manner as a summons in a civil action. **Leg.H.** Enacted 1872. Amended Code Amdts 1873–74 ch 383 §151; Code Amdts 1880 ch 20 §3; Stats 1905 ch 357 §1; Stats 1907 ch 257 §2; Stats 1969 ch 1611 §25, operative July 1, 1970; Stats 1971 ch 849 §1, ch 1127 §1; Stats 1989 ch 873 §1; Stats 2018 ch 260 §2 (AB 2343), effective January 1, 2019, operative September 1, 2019; Stats 2022 ch 686 §3 (AB 1726), effective January 1, 2023; Stats 2024 ch 512 §1 (AB 2347), effective January 1, 2025.

§1167. 2024 Deletes. [1] five [2] In all other respects

§1167.1. Proof of service

If proof of service of the summons has not been filed within 60 days of the complaint's filing, the court may dismiss the action without prejudice. **Leg.H.** Added Stats 2016 ch 336 §4 (AB 2819), effective January 1, 2017.

2016 Note: For legislative findings, declarations, and intent, see the 2016 Notes following CCP §1161.2.

§1167.2. [Section repealed 1999]

Leg.H. Added Stats 1994 ch 898 §3 (SB 690), operative July 1, 1995. Amended Stats 1996 ch 698 §2 (AB 2966); Stats 1998 ch 931 §119 (SB 2139), effective September 28, 1998, operative until December 31, 1998. Repealed July 1, 1999, by its own terms. The repealed section related to establishment of pilot project to reduce delay and abuse in unlawful detainer system.

§1167.25. [Section repealed 2002]

Leg.H. Added Stats 1995 ch 196 §9 (SB 832), effective August 1, 1995. Repealed Stats 2001 ch 115 §4 (SB 153). The repealed section related to service of prejudgment claim of right to possession.

§1167.3. Answer

In any action under this chapter, unless otherwise ordered by the court for good cause shown, the time allowed the defendant to answer the complaint, answer the complaint, if amended, or amend the answer under paragraph (2), (3), (5), (6), or (7) of subdivision (a) of Section 586 shall not exceed five days. **Leg.H.** Added Stats 1971 ch 849 §2.5. Amended Stats 1974 ch 430 §1; Stats 1984 ch 572 §3; Stats 1999 ch 83 §25 (SB 966), ch 344 §19 (SB 210) (ch 344 prevails), effective September 7, 1999.

§1167.4. Motion to quash; Extension of time to plead

Notwithstanding any other provision of law, in any action under this chapter:

(a) Where the defendant files a notice of motion as provided for in subdivision (a) of Section 418.10, the time for making the motion shall be not less than three days nor more than seven days after the filing of the notice.

(b) The service and filing of a notice of motion under subdivision (a) shall extend the defendant's time to plead until five days after service upon him of the written notice of entry of an order denying his motion, except that for good cause shown the court may extend the defendant's time to plead for an additional period not exceeding 15 days. **Leg.H.** Added Stats 1971 ch 1332 §1.

§1167.5. Limitation on extension of time

Unless otherwise ordered by the court for good cause shown, no extension of time allowed in any action under this chapter for the causes specified in Section 1054 shall exceed 10 days without the consent of the adverse party. **Leg.H.** Added Stats 1971 ch 849 §3.

§1167.6. [Section repealed 1994]

Leg.H. Added Stats 1991 ch 49 §2 (SB 1), effective June 10, 1991. Repealed Stats 1993 ch 793 §2 (AB 504), ch 926 §6 (AB 2205). The repealed section related to stay of procedures for relatives of military in active duty in Iraq-Kuwait crisis.

§1168. [Section repealed 1974]
Leg.H. Enacted 1872. Amended Code Amdts 1880 ch 20 §4, Stats 1951 ch 1737 §158, operative January 1, 1952. Repealed Stats 1973 ch 20 §13. The repealed section related to order for arrest of defendant in unlawful detainer proceeding. See CCP §501.

§1169. Default, entry; Application for relief
If, at the time appointed, any defendant served with a summons does not appear and defend, the clerk, upon written application of the plaintiff and proof of the service of summons and complaint, shall enter the default of any defendant so served, and, if requested by the plaintiff, immediately shall enter judgment for restitution of the premises and shall issue a writ of execution thereon. The application for default judgment and the default judgment shall include a place to indicate that the judgment includes tenants, subtenants, if any, named claimants, if any, and any other occupants of the premises. Thereafter, the plaintiff may apply to the court for any other relief demanded in the complaint, including the costs, against the defendant, or defendants, or against one or more of the defendants. **Leg.H.** Enacted 1872. Amended Stats 1933 ch 745 §10; Stats 1951 ch 1737 §159, operative January 1, 1952; Stats 1982 ch 1620 §1; Stats 1986 ch 953 §5; Stats 1987 ch 768 §1; Stats 1990 ch 1535 §2.6 (SB 2508); Stats 1991 ch 57 §5 (SB 323), effective June 14, 1991; Stats 2007 ch 263 §13 (AB 310), effective January 1, 2008.

§1170. Appearance
(a) On or before the day fixed for [1] **their** appearance, the defendant may appear and answer [2], **demur, or move to strike any portion of the complaint.**

(b)(1) (1)Notwithstanding any other law, in any action under this chapter in which the defendant demurs or moves to strike the complaint or any portion thereof, the hearing on the motion shall be not less than five court days nor more than seven court days after the filing of the notice of motion. For good cause shown, the court may order the hearing held on a later date on notice prescribed by the court. All moving and supporting papers shall accompany the notice of the motion and shall be served in compliance with this section and Section 1010.6 or 1013.

(2) An opposition and reply to an opposition may be made orally at the time of the hearing. If a party seeks to have a written opposition considered in advance of the hearing, the written opposition shall be filed and served on or before the court day before the hearing. Service shall be by personal delivery, electronic service, fax transmission, express mail, or other means consistent with Sections 1010, 1010.6, 1011, 1012, and 1013, and reasonably calculated to ensure delivery to the other party or parties no later than the close of business on the court day before the hearing. The court, in its discretion, may consider written opposition filed later. **Leg.H.** Enacted 1872. Amended Stats 2024 ch 512 §2 (AB 2347), effective January 1, 2025.

§1170. 2024 Deletes. [1] his [2] or demur

§1170.5. Time for trial; Extension; Payment of damages pending termination of action
(a) If the defendant appears pursuant to Section 1170, trial of the proceeding shall be held not later than the 20th day following the date that the request to set the time of the trial is made. Judgment shall be entered thereon and, if the plaintiff prevails, a writ of execution shall be issued immediately by the court upon the request of the plaintiff.

(b) The court may extend the period for trial upon the agreement of all of the parties. No other extension of the time for trial of an action under this chapter may be granted unless the court, upon its own motion or on motion of any party, holds a hearing and renders a decision thereon as specified in subdivision (c).

(c) If trial is not held within the time specified in this section, the court, upon finding that there is a reasonable probability that the plaintiff will prevail in the action, shall determine the amount of damages, if any, to be suffered by the plaintiff by reason of the extension, and shall issue an order requiring the defendant to pay that amount into court as the rent would have otherwise become due and payable or into an escrow designated by the court for so long as the defendant remains in possession pending the termination of the action.

The determination of the amount of the payment shall be based on the plaintiff's verified statement of the contract rent for rental payment, any verified objection thereto filed by the defendant, and the oral or demonstrative evidence presented at the hearing. The court's determination of the amount of damages shall include consideration of any evidence, presented by the parties, embracing the issue of diminution of value or any set off permitted by law.

(d) If the defendant fails to make a payment ordered by the court, trial of the action shall be held within 15 days of the date payment was due.

(e) Any cost for administration of an escrow account pursuant to this section shall be recoverable by the prevailing party as part of any recoverable cost in the action.

(f) After trial of the action, the court shall determine the distribution of the payment made into court or the escrow designated by the court.

(g) Where payments into court or the escrow designated by the court are made pursuant to this section, the court may order that the payments be invested in an insured interest-bearing account. Interest on the account shall be allocated to the parties in the same proportions as the original funds are allocated.

(h) If any provision of this section or the application thereof to any person or circumstances is held invalid, such invalidity shall not affect other provisions or applications of the section which can be given effect without the invalid provision or application, and to this end the provisions of this section are severable.

(i) Nothing in this section shall be construed to abrogate or interfere with the precedence given to the trial of criminal cases over the trial of civil matters by Section 1050 of the Penal Code. **Leg.H.** Added Stats 1982 ch 1620 §2.

§1170.7. Motion for summary judgment
A motion for summary judgment may be made at any time after the answer is filed upon giving five days notice. Summary judgment shall be granted or denied on the same basis as a motion under Section 437c. **Leg.H.** Added Stats 1982 ch 1620 §3.

§1170.8. Discovery motion
In any action under this chapter, a discovery motion may be made at any time upon giving five days' notice. **Leg.H.** Added Stats 2007 ch 113 §1 (AB 1126), effective January 1, 2008.

§1170.9. Adoption of rules
The Judicial Council shall adopt rules, not inconsistent with statute, prescribing the time for filing and serving opposition and reply papers, if any, relating to a motion under Section 1167.4, 1170.7, or 1170.8. **Leg.H.** Added Stats 2007 ch 113 §2 (AB 1126), effective January 1, 2008.

§1171. Trial by jury
Whenever an issue of fact is presented by the pleadings, it must be tried by a jury, unless such jury be waived as in other cases. The jury shall be formed in the same manner as other trial juries in an action of the same jurisdictional classification in the Court in which the action is pending. **Leg.H.** Enacted 1872. Amended Code Amdts 1873–74 ch 383 §152; Code Amdts 1880 ch 20 §5; Stats 1998 ch 931 §120 (SB 2139), effective September 28, 1998.

§1172. Showing required
On the trial of any proceeding for any forcible entry or forcible detainer, the plaintiff shall only be required to show, in addition to the forcible entry or forcible detainer complained of, that he was peaceably in the actual possession at the time of the forcible entry, or was entitled to the possession at the time of the forcible detainer. The defendant may show in his defense that he or his ancestors, or those whose interest in such premises he claims, have been in the quiet possession thereof for the space of one whole year together next before the commencement of the proceedings, and that his interest therein is not ended or determined; and such showing is a bar to the proceedings. **Leg.H.** Enacted 1872.

§1173. Amendment of complaint; Continuance
When, upon the trial of any proceeding under this chapter, it appears from the evidence that the defendant has been guilty of either a forcible entry or a forcible or unlawful detainer, and other than the offense charged in the complaint, the judge must order that such complaint be forthwith amended to conform to such proofs; such amendment must be made without any imposition of terms. No continuance shall be permitted upon account of such amendment unless the defendant, by affidavit filed, shows

to the satisfaction of the court good cause therefor. **Leg.H.** Enacted 1872. Amended Stats 1885 ch 121 §1.

§1174. Judgment for possession of premises; Enforcement

(a) If upon the trial, the verdict of the jury, or, if the case be tried without a jury, the findings of the court be in favor of the plaintiff and against the defendant, judgment shall be entered for the possession of the premises; and if the proceedings be for an unlawful detainer after neglect, or failure to perform the conditions or covenants of the lease or agreement under which the property is held, or after default in the payment of rent, the judgment shall also declare the forfeiture of that lease or agreement if the notice required by Section 1161 states the election of the landlord to declare the forfeiture thereof, but if that notice does not so state that election, the lease or agreement shall not be forfeited.

Except as provided in Section 1166a, in any action for unlawful detainer brought by a petroleum distributor against a gasoline dealer, possession shall not be restored to the petroleum distributor unless the court in the unlawful detainer action determines that the petroleum distributor had good cause under Section 20999.1 of the Business and Professions Code to terminate, cancel, or refuse to renew the franchise of the gasoline dealer.

In any action for unlawful detainer brought by a petroleum distributor against the gasoline dealer, the court may, at the time of request of either party, require the tenant to make rental payments into the court, for the lessor, at the contract rate, pending the resolution of the action.

(b) The jury or the court, if the proceedings be tried without a jury, shall also assess the damages occasioned to the plaintiff by any forcible entry, or by any forcible or unlawful detainer, alleged in the complaint and proved on the trial, and find the amount of any rent due, if the alleged unlawful detainer be after default in the payment of rent. If the defendant is found guilty of forcible entry, or forcible or unlawful detainer, and malice is shown, the plaintiff may be awarded statutory damages of up to six hundred dollars ($600), in addition to actual damages, including rent found due. The trier of fact shall determine whether actual damages, statutory damages, or both, shall be awarded, and judgment shall be entered accordingly.

(c) When the proceeding is for an unlawful detainer after default in the payment of rent, and the lease or agreement under which the rent is payable has not by its terms expired, and the notice required by Section 1161 has not stated the election of the landlord to declare the forfeiture thereof, the court may, and, if the lease or agreement is in writing, is for a term of more than one year, and does not contain a forfeiture clause, shall order that a writ shall not be issued to enforce the judgment until the expiration of five days after the entry of the judgment, within which time the tenant, or any subtenant, or any mortgagee of the term, or any other party interested in its continuance, may pay into the court, for the landlord, the amount found due as rent, with interest thereon, and the amount of the damages found by the jury or the court for the unlawful detainer, and the costs of the proceedings, and thereupon the judgment shall be satisfied and the tenant be restored to the tenant's estate. If payment as provided in this subdivision is not made within five days, the judgment may be enforced for its full amount and for the possession of the premises. In all other cases the judgment may be enforced immediately.

(d) Subject to subdivision (c), the judgment for possession of the premises may be enforced as provided in Division 3 (commencing with Section 712.010) of Title 9 of Part 2.

(e) Personal property remaining on the premises which the landlord reasonably believes to have been lost shall be disposed of pursuant to Article 1 (commencing with Section 2080) of Chapter 4 of Title 6 of Part 4 of Division 3 of the Civil Code. The landlord is not liable to the owner of any property which is disposed of in this manner. If the appropriate police or sheriff's department refuses to accept that property, it shall be deemed not to have been lost for the purposes of this subdivision.

(f) The landlord shall give notice pursuant to Section 1983 of the Civil Code to any person (other than the tenant) reasonably believed by the landlord to be the owner of personal property remaining on the premises unless the procedure for surrender of property under Section 1965 of the Civil Code has been initiated or completed.

(g) The landlord shall store the personal property in a place of safekeeping until it is either released pursuant to subdivision (h) or disposed of pursuant to subdivision (i).

(h) The landlord shall release the personal property pursuant to Section 1965 of the Civil Code or shall release it to the tenant or, at the landlord's option, to a person reasonably believed by the landlord to be its owner if the tenant or other person pays the costs of storage as provided in Section 1990 of the Civil Code and claims the property not later than the date specified in the writ of possession before which the tenant must make his or her claim or the date specified in the notice before which a person other than the tenant must make his or her claim.

(i) Personal property not released pursuant to subdivision (h) shall be disposed of pursuant to Section 1988 of the Civil Code.

(j) Where the landlord releases personal property to the tenant pursuant to subdivision (h), the landlord is not liable with respect to that property to any person.

(k) Where the landlord releases personal property pursuant to subdivision (h) to a person (other than the tenant) reasonably believed by the landlord to be its owner, the landlord is not liable with respect to that property to:

(1) The tenant or to any person to whom notice was given pursuant to subdivision (f); or

(2) Any other person, unless that person proves that, prior to releasing the property, the landlord believed or reasonably should have believed that the person had an interest in the property and also that the landlord knew or should have known upon reasonable investigation the address of that person.

(*l*) Where personal property is disposed of pursuant to Section 1988 of the Civil Code, the landlord is not liable with respect to that property to:

(1) The tenant or to any person to whom notice was given pursuant to subdivision (f); or

(2) Any other person, unless that person proves that, prior to disposing of the property pursuant to Section 1988 of the Civil Code, the landlord believed or reasonably should have believed that the person had an interest in the property and also that the landlord knew or should have known upon reasonable investigation the address of that person.

(m) For the purposes of subdivisions (e), (f), (h), (k), and (*l*), the terms "owner," "premises," and "reasonable belief" have the same meaning as provided in Section 1980 of the Civil Code. **Leg.H.** Enacted 1872. Amended Code Amdts 1873–74 ch 383 §153; Stats 1907 ch 37 §1; Stats 1931 ch 259 §1; Stats 1933 ch 741 §1; Stats 1939 ch 717 §1; Stats 1945 ch 593 §1; Stats 1967 ch 1600 §2; Stats 1968 ch 102 §2; Stats 1969 ch 480 §1; Stats 1970 ch 654 §1; Stats 1971 ch 1658 §1; Stats 1974 ch 331 §3, ch 1516 §21, operative January 1, 1977; Stats 1977 ch 372 §1; Stats 1982 ch 497 §76, operative July 1, 1983; Stats 1988 ch 797 §3; Stats 1993 ch 755 §2 (SB 444).

§1174.2. Substantial breach of warranty of habitability; Prevailing party

(a) In an unlawful detainer proceeding involving residential premises after default in payment of rent and in which the tenant has raised as an affirmative defense a breach of the landlord's obligations under Section 1941 of the Civil Code or of any warranty of habitability, the court shall determine whether a substantial breach of these obligations has occurred. If the court finds that a substantial breach has occurred, the court (1) shall determine the reasonable rental value of the premises in its untenantable state to the date of trial, (2) shall deny possession to the landlord and adjudge the tenant to be the prevailing party, conditioned upon the payment by the tenant of the rent that has accrued to the date of the trial as adjusted pursuant to this subdivision within a reasonable period of time not exceeding five days, from the date of the court's judgment or, if service of the court's judgment is made by mail, the payment shall be made within the time set forth in Section 1013, (3) may order the landlord to make repairs and correct the conditions which constitute a breach of the landlord's obligations, (4) shall order that the monthly rent be limited to the reasonable rental value of the premises as determined pursuant to this subdivision until repairs are completed, and (5) except as otherwise provided in subdivision (b), shall award the tenant costs and attorneys' fees if provided by, and pursuant to, any statute or the contract of the parties. If the court orders repairs or corrections, or both, pursuant to paragraph (3), the court's jurisdiction continues over the matter for the purpose of ensuring compliance. The court shall, however, award possession of the premises to the landlord if the tenant fails to pay all rent accrued to the date of trial, as determined due in the judgment, within the period prescribed by the court pursuant to this subdivision. The tenant shall, however, retain any rights conferred by Section 1174.

(b) If the court determines that there has been no substantial breach of Section 1941 of the Civil Code or of any warranty of habitability by the landlord or if the tenant fails to pay all rent accrued to the date of trial, as required by the court pursuant to subdivision (a), then judgment shall be entered in favor of the landlord, and the landlord shall be the prevailing party for the purposes of awarding costs or attorneys' fees pursuant to any statute or the contract of the parties.

(c) As used in this section, "substantial breach" means the failure of the landlord to comply with applicable building and housing code standards which materially affect health and safety.

(d) Nothing in this section is intended to deny the tenant the right to a trial by jury. Nothing in this section shall limit or supersede any provision of Chapter 12.75 (commencing with Section 7060) of Division 7 of Title 1 of the Government Code. **Leg.H.** Added Stats 1986 ch 805 §1. Amended Stats 1988 ch 1405 §3; Stats 1992 ch 488 §2 (AB 2574); Stats 1993 ch 589 §28 (AB 2211).

§1174.21. Liability of landlord, in violation of Civil Code Section 1942.4, for attorney's fees in proceeding based upon nonpayment of rent

A landlord who institutes an unlawful detainer proceeding based upon a tenant's nonpayment of rent, and who is liable for a violation of Section 1942.4 of the Civil Code, shall be liable to the tenant or lessee for reasonable attorneys' fees and costs of the suit, in an amount to be fixed by the court. **Leg.H.** Added Stats 2003 ch 109 §2 (AB 647).

§1174.25. Unlawful detainer; Occupant's right to file claim; Procedure

(a)(1) Except as provided in paragraph (2), an occupant who is served with a prejudgment claim of right to possession in accordance with Section 415.46 may file a claim as prescribed in Section 415.46, with the court within 10 days of the date of service of the prejudgment claim of right to possession as shown on the return of service, which period shall include Saturday and Sunday but exclude all other judicial holidays. If the last day for filing the claim falls on a Saturday or Sunday, the filing period shall be extended to and including the next court day. Filing the prejudgment claim of right to possession shall constitute a general appearance for which a fee shall be collected as provided in Section 70614 of the Government Code. Section 68511.3 of the Government Code applies to the prejudgment claim of right to possession.

(2) In an action as described in paragraph (2) of subdivision (e) of Section 415.46, an occupant may file a prejudgment claim of right to possession at any time before judgment is entered.

(b) At the time of filing, the claimant shall be added as a defendant in the action for unlawful detainer and the clerk shall notify the plaintiff that the claimant has been added as a defendant in the action by mailing a copy of the claim filed with the court to the plaintiff with a notation so indicating. The claimant shall answer or otherwise respond to the summons and complaint within five days, including Saturdays and Sundays, but excluding all other judicial holidays, after filing the prejudgment claim of possession. Thereafter, the name of the claimant shall be added to any pleading, filing or form filed in the action for unlawful detainer. **Leg.H.** Added Stats 1990 ch 1535 §2.8 (SB 2508). Amended Stats 1991 ch 57 §6 (SB 323), effective June 14, 1991; Stats 2005 ch 75 §42 (AB 145), effective July 19, 2005, operative January 1, 2006; Stats 2014 ch 913 §8 (AB 2747), effective January 1, 2015.

2014 Note: It is the intent of the Legislature in amending Sections 415.46, 1174.25, and 1174.3 of the Code of Civil Procedure to appropriately update statutory language and statutory forms to properly reflect the changes to law enacted by Assembly Bill 2610, Chapter 562 of the Statutes of 2012. Stats 2014 ch 913 (AB 2747) §1.

§ 1174.27. Abuse or violence against tenant; Unlawful detainer; Remedies

(a) This section shall apply to an unlawful detainer proceeding in which all of the following are true:

(1) The proceeding involves a residential premises.

(2) The complaint includes a cause of action based on an act of abuse or violence against a tenant, a tenant's immediate family member, or a tenant's household member.

(3) A defendant has invoked paragraph (2) of subdivision (d) of Section 1161.3 as an affirmative defense to the cause of action described in paragraph (2).

(b) For the purposes of this section, the definitions in subdivision (a) of Section 1161.3 apply.

(c) The court shall determine whether there is documentation evidencing abuse or violence against the tenant, the tenant's immediate family member, or the tenant's household member.

(d) If the court determines there is not documentation evidencing abuse or violence against the tenant, the court shall deny the affirmative defense.

(e) If the court determines that there is documentation evidencing abuse or violence against the tenant, the tenant's immediate family member, or the tenant's household member, and the court does not find the defendant raising the affirmative defense guilty of an unlawful detainer on any other grounds, then both of the following:

(1) The defendant raising the affirmative defense and any other occupant not found guilty of an unlawful detainer shall not be guilty of an unlawful detainer and shall not be named in any judgment in favor of the landlord.

(2) The defendant raising the affirmative defense and any other occupant not found guilty of an unlawful detainer shall not be held liable to the landlord for any amount related to the unlawful detainer, including, but not limited to, holdover damages, court costs, lease termination fees, or attorney's fees.

(f)(1) If the court makes the determination described in subdivision (e), upon a showing that any other defendant was the perpetrator of the abuse or violence on which the affirmative defense was based and is guilty of an unlawful detainer, the court shall do both of the following:

(A) Issue a partial eviction ordering the removal of the perpetrator of abuse or violence and ordering that person be immediately removed and barred from the dwelling unit, but the court shall not order the tenancy terminated.

(B) Order the landlord to change the locks and to provide the remaining occupants with the new key.

(2) If a court issues a partial eviction order as described in subparagraph (A) of paragraph (1), then only a defendant found guilty of an unlawful detainer may be liable for holdover damages, court costs, lease termination fees, or attorney's fees, as applicable.

(3) If the court makes the determination described in subdivision (e), the court may, upon a showing that any other defendant was the perpetrator of the abuse or violence on which the affirmative defense was based and is guilty of an unlawful detainer, do any of the following:

(A) Permanently bar the perpetrator of abuse or violence from entering any portion of the residential premises.

(B) Order as an express condition of the tenancy that the remaining occupants shall not give permission to or invite the perpetrator of abuse or violence to live in the dwelling unit.

(4) In exercising its discretion under this subdivision, the court shall take into account custody or visitation orders or arrangements and any other factor that may necessitate the temporary reentry of the perpetrator of abuse or violence.

(g) The Judicial Council shall develop a judgment form for use in a ruling pursuant to subdivision (e) or (f).

(h) Notwithstanding any other law, a determination that a person is a perpetrator of abuse or violence under subdivision (e) or (f) shall not constitute a finding that the person is a perpetrator of abuse or violence for any other purposes and shall not be admissible as evidence that the person committed a crime or is a perpetrator of abuse or violence in any other proceeding, including, but not limited to, a civil action or proceeding, a criminal action or proceeding, and a proceeding involving a juvenile for a criminal offense. **Leg.H.** Added Stats 2022 ch 558 §3 (SB 1017), effective January 1, 2023.

§1174.3. Objections to enforcement of judgment; Claim of right to possession

(a)(1) Except as provided in paragraph (2), unless a prejudgment claim of right to possession has been served upon occupants in accordance with Section 415.46, any occupant not named in the judgment for possession who occupied the premises on the date of the filing of the action may object to enforcement of the judgment against that occupant by filing a claim of right to possession as prescribed in this section. A claim of right to possession may be filed at any time after service or posting of the writ of possession pursuant to subdivision (a) or (b) of Section 715.020, up to and including the time at which the levying officer returns to effect the eviction of those named in the judgment of possession. Filing the claim of right to possession shall constitute a general appearance for which a fee shall be collected as provided in Section 70614 of the Government Code.

Section 68511.3 of the Government Code applies to the claim of right to possession. An occupant or tenant who is named in the action shall not be required to file a claim of right to possession to protect that occupant's right to possession of the premises.

(2) In an action as described in paragraph (2) of subdivision (e) of Section 415.46, an occupant may file a claim of right to possession at any time up to and including the time at which the levying officer returns to effect the eviction of those named in the judgment of possession, without regard to whether a prejudgment claim of right to possession has been served upon the occupant.

(b) The court issuing the writ of possession of real property shall set a date or dates when the court will hold a hearing to determine the validity of objections to enforcement of the judgment specified in subdivision (a). An occupant of the real property for which the writ is issued may make an objection to eviction to the levying officer at the office of the levying officer or at the premises at the time of the eviction.

If a claim of right to possession is completed and presented to the sheriff, marshal, or other levying officer, the officer shall forthwith (1) stop the eviction of occupants at the premises, and (2) provide a receipt or copy of the completed claim of right of possession to the claimant indicating the date and time the completed form was received, and (3) deliver the original completed claim of right to possession to the court issuing the writ of possession of real property.

(c) A claim of right to possession is effected by any of the following:

(1) Presenting a completed claim form in person with identification to the sheriff, marshal, or other levying officer as prescribed in this section, and delivering to the court within two court days after its presentation, an amount equal to 15 days' rent together with the appropriate fee or form for proceeding in forma pauperis. Upon receipt of a claim of right to possession, the sheriff, marshal, or other levying officer shall indicate thereon the date and time of its receipt and forthwith deliver the original to the issuing court and a receipt or copy of the claim to the claimant and notify the plaintiff of that fact. Immediately upon receipt of an amount equal to 15 days' rent and the appropriate fee or form for proceeding in forma pauperis, the court shall file the claim of right to possession and serve an endorsed copy with the notice of the hearing date on the plaintiff and the claimant by first-class mail. The court issuing the writ of possession shall set and hold a hearing on the claim not less than five nor more than 15 days after the claim is filed with the court.

(2) Presenting a completed claim form in person with identification to the sheriff, marshal, or other levying officer as prescribed in this section, and delivering to the court within two court days after its presentation, the appropriate fee or form for proceeding in forma pauperis without delivering the amount equivalent to 15 days' rent. In this case, the court shall immediately set a hearing on the claim to be held on the fifth day after the filing is completed. The court shall notify the claimant of the hearing date at the time the claimant completes the filing by delivering to the court the appropriate fee or form for proceeding in forma pauperis, and shall notify the plaintiff of the hearing date by first-class mail. Upon receipt of a claim of right to possession, the sheriff, marshal, or other levying officer shall indicate thereon the date and time of its receipt and forthwith deliver the original to the issuing court and a receipt or copy of the claim to the claimant and notify the plaintiff of that fact.

(d) At the hearing, the court shall determine whether there is a valid claim of possession by the claimant who filed the claim, and the court shall consider all evidence produced at the hearing, including, but not limited to, the information set forth in the claim. The court may determine the claim to be valid or invalid based upon the evidence presented at the hearing. The court shall determine the claim to be invalid if the court determines that the claimant is an invitee, licensee, guest, or trespasser. If the court determines the claim is invalid, the court shall order the return to the claimant of the amount of the 15 days' rent paid by the claimant, if that amount was paid pursuant to paragraph (1) or (3) of subdivision (c), less a pro rata amount for each day that enforcement of the judgment was delayed by reason of making the claim of right to possession, which pro rata amount shall be paid to the landlord. If the court determines the claim is valid, the amount equal to 15 days' rent paid by the claimant shall be returned immediately to the claimant.

(e) If, upon hearing, the court determines that the claim is valid, then the court shall order further proceedings as follows:

(1) If the unlawful detainer is based upon a curable breach, and the claimant was not previously served with a proper notice, if any notice is required, then the required notice may at the plaintiff's discretion be served on the claimant at the hearing or thereafter. If the claimant does not cure the breach within the required time, then a supplemental complaint may be filed and served on the claimant as defendant if the plaintiff proceeds against the claimant in the same action. For the purposes of this section only, service of the required notice, if any notice is required, and of the supplemental complaint may be made by first-class mail addressed to the claimant at the subject premises or upon his or her attorney of record and, in either case, Section 1013 shall otherwise apply. Further proceedings on the merits of the claimant's continued right to possession after service of the Summons and Supplemental Complaint as prescribed by this subdivision shall be conducted pursuant to this chapter.

(2) In all other cases, the court shall deem the unlawful detainer Summons and Complaint to be amended on their faces to include the claimant as defendant, service of the Summons and Complaint, as thus amended, may at the plaintiff's discretion be made at the hearing or thereafter, and the claimant thus named and served as a defendant in the action shall answer or otherwise respond within five days thereafter.

(f) If a claim is made without delivery to the court of the appropriate filing fee or a form for proceeding in forma pauperis, as prescribed in this section, the claim shall be immediately deemed denied and the court shall so order. Upon the denial of the claim, the court shall immediately deliver an endorsed copy of the order to the levying officer and shall serve an endorsed copy of the order on the plaintiff and claimant by first-class mail.

(g) If the claim of right to possession is denied pursuant to subdivision (f), or if the claimant fails to appear at the hearing or, upon hearing, if the court determines that there are no valid claims, or if the claimant does not prevail at a trial on the merits of the unlawful detainer action, the court shall order the levying officer to proceed with enforcement of the original writ of possession of real property as deemed amended to include the claimant, which shall be effected within a reasonable time not to exceed five days. Upon receipt of the court's order, the levying officer shall enforce the writ of possession of real property against any occupant or occupants.

(h) The claim of right to possession shall be made on the following form:

CLAIMANT OR CLAIMANT'S ATTORNEY (Name and Address):	TELEPHONE NO.	FOR COURT USE ONLY
ATTORNEY FOR (Name):		
NAME OF COURT: STREET ADDRESS: MAILING ADDRESS: CITY AND ZIP CODE: BRANCH NAME:		
PLAINTIFF:		
DEFENDANT:		
CLAIM OF RIGHT TO POSSESSION AND NOTICE OF HEARING		
		CASE NUMBER:

(For levying officer use only)
Completed form was received on

Date: _____ Time: _____
By: _____

Complete this form only if ALL of these statements are true:
1. You are NOT named in the accompanying form called Writ of Possession.
2. You occupied the premises on or before the date the unlawful detainer (eviction) action was filed.
   (The date is in the accompanying Writ of Possession.)
3. You still occupy the premises.
4. A Prejudgment Claim of Right to Possession form was NOT served with the Summons and Complaint OR this eviction results from a foreclosure.

NOTICE: If you are being evicted because of foreclosure, you have additional rights and should seek legal assistance immediately.

I DECLARE THE FOLLOWING UNDER PENALTY OF PERJURY:
1. My name is (specify):
2. I reside at (street address, unit no., city and ZIP Code):
3. The address of "the premises" subject to this claim is (address):
   Check here ☐ if this property was foreclosed on
4. On (insert date): _____, the owner, landlord, or the landlord's authorized agent filed a complaint to recover possession of the premises. (This date is in the accompanying Writ of Possession.)
5. I occupied the premises on the date the complaint was filed (the date in item 4). I have continued to occupy the premises ever since.
6. I was at least 18 years of age on the date the complaint was filed (the date in item 4).

7. I claim a right to possession of the premises because I occupied the premises on the date the complaint was filed (the date in item 4).
8. I was not named in the Writ of Possession.
9. I understand that if I make this claim of possession, a court hearing will be held to decide whether my claim will be granted.
10. (Filing fee) To obtain a court hearing on my claim, I understand that after I present this form to the levying officer I must go to the court and pay a filing fee of $ or file with the court "Application for Waiver of Court Fees and Costs." I understand that if I don't pay the filing fee or file the form for waiver of court fees within 2 court days, the court will immediately deny my claim.
11. (Immediate court hearing unless you deposit 15 days' rent) To obtain a court hearing on my claim, I understand I must also present a copy of this completed complaint form or a receipt from the levying officer. I also understand the date of my hearing will be set immediately if I do not deliver to the court an amount equal to 15 days' rent.
12. I am filing my claim in the following manner (check the box that shows how you are filing your claim. Note that you must deliver to the court a copy of the claim form or a levying officer's receipt):
    a. ☐ I presented this claim form to the sheriff, marshal, or other levying officer, and within two court days I shall deliver to the court the following: (1) a copy of this completed claim form or a receipt, (2) the court filing fee or form for proceeding in forma pauperis, and (3) an amount equal to 15 days' rent; or
    b. ☐ I presented this claim form to the sheriff, marshal, or other levying officer, and within two court days I shall deliver to the court (1) a copy of this completed claim form or a receipt, and (2) the court filing fee or form for proceeding in forma pauperis.

IMPORTANT: Do not take a copy of this claim form to the court unless you have first given the form to the sheriff, marshal, or other levying officer.

(To be completed by the court.)

Date of Hearing: Time: Dept. or Div.:   Room:

Address of court:

NOTICE: If you fail to appear at this hearing you will be evicted without further hearing.

13. Rental agreement. I have (check all that apply to you):
    a. ☐ an oral rental agreement with the landlord.
    b. ☐ a written rental agreement with the landlord.
    c. ☐ an oral rental agreement with a person other than the landlord.
    d. ☐ a written rental agreement with a person other than the landlord.
    e. ☐ a rental agreement with the former owner who lost the property through foreclosure.
    (f) ☐ other (explain):

I declare under penalty of perjury under the laws of the State of California that the foregoing is true and correct.

> WARNING: Perjury is a felony punishable by imprisonment in the state prison.

Date:

....   _____
(TYPE OR PRINT NAME)   (SIGNATURE OF CLAIMANT)

> NOTICE: If your claim to possession is found to be valid, the unlawful detainer action against you will be determined at trial. At trial, you may be found liable for rent, costs, and, in some cases, treble damages.

> NOTICE TO OCCUPANTS
>
> YOU MUST ACT AT ONCE IF ALL THE FOLLOWING ARE TRUE:
> (1) You are not named, in the accompanying form called Writ of Possession;
> (2) You occupied the premises on or before the date the unlawful detainer (eviction) action was filed; and
> (3) You still occupy the premises.
> (4) A Prejudgment Claim of Right to Possession form was NOT served with the Summons and Complaint OR you are being evicted due to foreclosure.
>
> You can complete and SUBMIT THIS CLAIM FORM
> (1) Before the date of eviction at the sheriff's or marshal's office located at: (address)
> (2) OR at the premises at the time of the eviction. (Give this form to the officer who comes to evict you.)
>
> If you do not complete and submit this form (and pay a filing fee or file the form for proceeding in forma pauperis if you cannot pay the fee), YOU WILL BE EVICTED along with the parties named in the writ.
>
> After this form is properly filed, A HEARING WILL BE HELD to decide your claim. If you do not appear at the hearing, you will be evicted without further hearing.

Leg.H. Added Stats 1986 ch 1220 §2. Amended Stats 1987 ch 720 §1; Stats 1988 ch 1405 §4; Stats 1989 ch 12 §3, effective April 28, 1989, operative May 1, 1989; Stats 1990 ch 1535 §3 (SB 2508); Stats 1991 ch 57 §7 (SB 323), effective June 14, 1991; Stats 1995 ch 196 §10 (SB 832), effective August 1, 1995; Stats 2001 ch 115 §5 (SB 153); Stats 2002 ch 664 §50 (AB 3034); Stats 2005 ch 75 §43 (AB 145), effective July 19, 2005, operative January 1, 2006; Stats 2014 ch 913 §9 (AB 2747), effective January 1, 2015.

2014 Note: It is the intent of the Legislature in amending Sections 415.46, 1174.25, and 1174.3 of the Code of Civil Procedure to appropriately update statutory language and statutory forms to properly reflect the changes to law enacted by Assembly Bill 2610, Chapter 562 of the Statutes of 2012. Stats 2014 ch 913 (AB 2747) §1.

§1174.5. Forfeiture; No release from liability for unpaid rent

A judgment in unlawful detainer declaring the forfeiture of the lease or agreement under which real property is held shall not relieve the lessee from liability pursuant to Section 1951.2 of the Civil Code. **Leg.H.** Added Stats 1982 ch 488 §1.

§1175. [Section repealed 1907]

Leg.H. Enacted 1872. Repealed Stats 1907 ch 257 §3. The repealed section related to verification of complaint and answer.

§1176. Stay of judgment pending appeal; New cause of action

(a) An appeal taken by the defendant shall not automatically stay proceedings upon the judgment. Petition for stay of the judgment pending appeal shall first be directed to the judge before whom it was rendered. Stay of judgment shall be granted when the court finds that the moving party will suffer extreme hardship in the absence of a stay and that the nonmoving party will not be irreparably injured by its issuance. If the stay is denied by the trial court, the defendant may forthwith file a petition for an extraordinary writ with the appropriate appeals court. If the trial or appellate court stays enforcement of the judgment, the court may condition the stay on whatever conditions the court deems just, but in any case it shall order the payment of the reasonable monthly rental value to the court monthly in advance as rent would otherwise become due as a condition of issuing the stay of enforcement. As used in this subdivision, "reasonable rental value" means the contract rent unless the rental value has been modified by the trial court in which case that modified rental value shall be used.

(b) A new cause of action on the same agreement for the rental of real property shall not be barred because of an appeal by any party. **Leg.H.** Enacted 1872. Amended Code Amdts 1880 ch 20 §6; Stats 1951 ch 1737 §160, operative January 1, 1952; Stats 1979 ch 958 §2; Stats 1985 ch 1279 §3.

§1177. Rules of practice

Except as otherwise provided in this chapter the provisions of part two of this code are applicable to, and constitute the rules of practice in the proceedings mentioned in this chapter. **Leg.H.** Enacted 1872.

§1178. New trial and appeal

The provisions of Part 2 of this code, relative to new trials and appeals, except insofar as they are inconsistent with the provisions of this chapter or with rules adopted by the Judicial Council apply to the proceedings mentioned in this chapter. **Leg.H.** Enacted 1872. Amended Stats 1945 ch 40 §5.

§1179. Relief against forfeiture of lease

The court may relieve a tenant against a forfeiture of a lease or rental agreement, whether written or oral, and whether or not the tenancy has terminated, and restore him or her to his or her former estate or tenancy, in case of hardship, as provided in Section 1174. The court has the discretion to relieve any person against forfeiture on its own motion.

An application for relief against forfeiture may be made at any time prior to restoration of the premises to the landlord. The application may be made by a tenant or subtenant, or a mortgagee of the term, or any person interested in the continuance of the term. It must be made upon petition, setting forth the facts upon which the relief is sought, and be verified by the applicant. Notice of the application, with a copy of the petition, must be served at least five days prior to the hearing on the plaintiff in the judgment, who may appear and contest the application. Alternatively, a person appearing without an attorney may make the application orally, if the plaintiff either is present and has an opportunity to contest the application, or has been given ex parte notice of the hearing and the purpose of the oral application. In no case shall the application or motion be granted except on condition that full payment of rent due, or full performance of conditions or covenants stipulated, so far as the same is practicable, be made. **Leg.H.** Added Code Amdts 1873–74 ch 383 §154. Amended Code Amdts 1880 ch 20 §7; Stats 2002 ch 301 §4 (SB 1403).

§1179a. Precedence over other actions

In all proceedings brought to recover the possession of real property pursuant to the provisions of this chapter all courts, wherein such actions are or may hereafter be pending, shall give such actions precedence over all other civil actions therein, except actions to which special precedence is given by law, in the matter of the setting the same for hearing or trial, and in hearing the same, to the end that all such actions shall be quickly heard and determined. **Leg.H.** Added Stats 1931 ch 885 §1.

CHAPTER 5
COVID-19 TENANT RELIEF ACT [REPEALED EFFECTIVE OCTOBER 1, 2025]

Citation of chapter [Repealed October 1, 2025]. § 1179.01.
Unlawful detainer [Repealed October 1, 2025]. § 1179.01.5.
Definitions [Repealed October 1, 2025]. § 1179.02.
High-income tenants [Repealed October 1, 2025]. § 1179.02.5.
Notice of demand for COVID-19 rental debt payment; Declaration of COVID-19-related financial distress [Repealed October 1, 2025]. § 1179.03.
Limitations on finding tenant guilty of unlawful detainer; Tenant relocation [Repealed October 1, 2025]. § 1179.03.5.
Notice to tenants with unpaid rental payments due during protected time period as of September 1, 2020 [Repealed October 1, 2025]. § 1179.04.
Limitation on application of security deposit or monthly rental payment to COVID-19 rental debt [Repealed October 1, 2025]. § 1179.04.5.
Limitations on and effect of municipal response to protect tenants from eviction related to COVID-19 pandemic [Repealed October 1, 2025]. § 1179.05.
Waivers void [Repealed October 1, 2025]. § 1179.06.
Repeal of chapter [Repealed October 1, 2025]. §1179.07.

§ 1179.01. Citation of chapter [Repealed October 1, 2025]

This chapter is known, and may be cited, as the COVID-19 Tenant Relief Act. **Leg.H.** Added Stats 2020 ch 37 §20 (AB 3088), repealed February 1, 2025. Amended Stats 2021 ch 2 §15 (SB 91), effective January 29, 2021, repealed July 1, 2025; Stats 2021 ch 27 §19 (AB 832), effective January 29, 2021, repealed October 1, 2025 (repealer amended).

§ 1179.01.5. Unlawful detainer [Repealed October 1, 2025]

(a) It is the intent of the Legislature that the Judicial Council and the courts have adequate time to prepare to implement the new procedures resulting from this chapter, including educating and training judicial officers and staff.

(b) Notwithstanding any other law, before October 5, 2020, a court shall not do any of the following:

(1) Issue a summons on a complaint for unlawful detainer in any action that seeks possession of residential real property and that is based, in whole or in part, on nonpayment of rent or other charges.

(2) Enter a default or a default judgment for restitution in an unlawful detainer action that seeks possession of residential real property and that is based, in whole or in part, on nonpayment of rent or other charges.

(c)(1) A plaintiff in an unlawful detainer action shall file a cover sheet in the form specified in paragraph (2) that indicates both of the following:

(A) Whether the action seeks possession of residential real property.

(B) If the action seeks possession of residential real property, whether the action is based, in whole or in part, on an alleged default in payment of rent or other charges.

(2) The cover sheet specified in paragraph (1) shall be in the following form:

"UNLAWFUL DETAINER SUPPLEMENTAL COVER SHEET

1. This action seeks possession of real property that is:
   a. [ ] Residential
   b. [ ] Commercial

2. (Complete only if paragraph 1(a) is checked) This action is based, in whole or in part, on an alleged default in payment of rent or other charges.
   a. [ ] Yes

b. [ ] No

Date:_____

_____   _____
Type Or Print Name   Signature Of Party Or Attorney For Party"

(3) The cover sheet required by this subdivision shall be in addition to any civil case cover sheet or other form required by law, the California Rules of Court, or a local court rule.

(4) The Judicial Council may develop a form for mandatory use that includes the information in paragraph (2).

(d) This section does not prevent a court from issuing a summons or entering default in an unlawful detainer action that seeks possession of residential real property and that is not based, in whole or in part, on nonpayment of rent or other charges. **Leg.H.** Added Stats 2020 ch 37 §20 (AB 3088), repealed February 1, 2025. Amended Stats 2021 ch 27 §19 (AB 832), effective June 28, 2021, repealed October 1, 2025 (repealer amended).

§ 1179.02. Definitions [Repealed October 1, 2025]

For purposes of this chapter:

(a) "Covered time period" means the time period between March 1, 2020, and September 30, 2021.

(b) "COVID-19-related financial distress" means any of the following:

(1) Loss of income caused by the COVID-19 pandemic.

(2) Increased out-of-pocket expenses directly related to performing essential work during the COVID-19 pandemic.

(3) Increased expenses directly related to the health impact of the COVID-19 pandemic.

(4) Childcare responsibilities or responsibilities to care for an elderly, disabled, or sick family member directly related to the COVID-19 pandemic that limit a tenant's ability to earn income.

(5) Increased costs for childcare or attending to an elderly, disabled, or sick family member directly related to the COVID-19 pandemic.

(6) Other circumstances related to the COVID-19 pandemic that have reduced a tenant's income or increased a tenant's expenses.

(c) "COVID-19 rental debt" means unpaid rent or any other unpaid financial obligation of a tenant under the tenancy that came due during the covered time period.

(d) "Declaration of COVID-19-related financial distress" means the following written statement:

I am currently unable to pay my rent or other financial obligations under the lease in full because of one or more of the following:

1. Loss of income caused by the COVID-19 pandemic.

2. Increased out-of-pocket expenses directly related to performing essential work during the COVID-19 pandemic.

3. Increased expenses directly related to health impacts of the COVID-19 pandemic.

4. Childcare responsibilities or responsibilities to care for an elderly, disabled, or sick family member directly related to the COVID-19 pandemic that limit my ability to earn income.

5. Increased costs for childcare or attending to an elderly, disabled, or sick family member directly related to the COVID-19 pandemic.

6. Other circumstances related to the COVID-19 pandemic that have reduced my income or increased my expenses.

Any public assistance, including unemployment insurance, pandemic unemployment assistance, state disability insurance (SDI), or paid family leave, that I have received since the start of the COVID-19 pandemic does not fully make up for my loss of income and/or increased expenses.

Signed under penalty of perjury:
Dated:

(e) "Landlord" includes all of the following or the agent of any of the following:

(1) An owner of residential real property.

(2) An owner of a residential rental unit.

(3) An owner of a mobilehome park.

(4) An owner of a mobilehome park space or lot.

(f) "Protected time period" means the time period between March 1, 2020, and August 31, 2020.

(g) "Rental payment" means rent or any other financial obligation of a tenant under the tenancy.

(h) "Tenant" means any natural person who hires real property except any of the following:

(1) Tenants of commercial property, as defined in subdivision (c) of Section 1162 of the Civil Code.

(2) Those persons whose occupancy is described in subdivision (b) of Section 1940 of the Civil Code.

(i) "Transition time period" means the time period between September 1, 2020, and September 30, 2021. **Leg.H.** Added Stats 2020 ch 37 §20 (AB 3088), effective May 31, 2020, repealed February 1, 2025. Amended Stats 2021 ch 2 §16 (SB 91), effective January 29, 2021, repealed July 1, 2025; Stats 2021 ch 27 §§ 14, 19 (AB 832), effective June 28, 2021, repealed October 1, 2025 (repealer amended).

§ 1179.02.5. High-income tenants [Repealed October 1, 2025]

(a) For purposes of this section:

(1)(A) "High-income tenant" means a tenant with an annual household income of 130 percent of the median income, as published by the Department of Housing and Community Development in the Official State Income Limits for 2020, for the county in which the residential rental property is located.

(B) For purposes of this paragraph, all lawful occupants of the residential rental unit, including minor children, shall be considered in determining household size.

(C) "High-income tenant" shall not include a tenant with a household income of less than one hundred thousand dollars ($100,000).

(2) "Proof of income" means any of the following:

(A) A tax return.

(B) A W-2.

(C) A written statement from a tenant's employer that specifies the tenant's income.

(D) Pay stubs.

(E) Documentation showing regular distributions from a trust, annuity, 401k, pension, or other financial instrument.

(F) Documentation of court-ordered payments, including, but not limited to, spousal support or child support.

(G) Documentation from a government agency showing receipt of public assistance benefits, including, but not limited to, social security, unemployment insurance, disability insurance, or paid family leave.

(H) A written statement signed by the tenant that states the tenant's income, including, but not limited to, a rental application.

(b)(1) This section shall apply only if the landlord has proof of income in the landlord's possession before the service of the notice showing that the tenant is a high-income tenant.

(2) This section does not do any of the following:

(A) Authorize a landlord to demand proof of income from the tenant.

(B) Require the tenant to provide proof of income for the purposes of determining whether the tenant is a high-income tenant.

(C)(i) Entitle a landlord to obtain, or authorize a landlord to attempt to obtain, confidential financial records from a tenant's employer, a government agency, financial institution, or any other source.

(ii) Confidential information described in clause (i) shall not constitute valid proof of income unless it was lawfully obtained by the landlord with the tenant's consent during the tenant screening process.

(3) Paragraph (2) does not alter a party's rights under Title 4 (commencing with Section 2016.010), Chapter 4 (commencing with Section 708.010) of Title 9, or any other law.

(c) A landlord may require a high-income tenant that is served a notice pursuant to subdivision (b) or (c) of Section 1179.03 to submit, in addition to and together with a declaration of COVID-19-related financial distress, documentation supporting the claim that the tenant has suffered COVID-19-related financial distress. Any form of objectively verifiable documentation that demonstrates the COVID-19-related financial distress the tenant has experienced is sufficient to satisfy the requirements of this subdivision, including the proof of income, as defined in subparagraphs (A) to (G), inclusive, of paragraph (2) of subdivision (a), a letter from an employer, or an unemployment insurance record.

(d) A high-income tenant is required to comply with the requirements of subdivision (c) only if the landlord has included the following language on the notice served pursuant to subdivision (b) or (c) of Section 1179.03 in at least 12-point font:

"Proof of income on file with your landlord indicates that your household makes at least 130 percent of the median income for the county where the rental property is located, as published by the Department of

Housing and Community Development in the Official State Income Limits for 2020. As a result, if you claim that you are unable to pay the amount demanded by this notice because you have suffered COVID-19-related financial distress, you are required to submit to your landlord documentation supporting your claim together with the completed declaration of COVID-19-related financial distress provided with this notice. If you fail to submit this documentation together with your declaration of COVID-19-related financial distress, and you do not either pay the amount demanded in this notice or deliver possession of the premises back to your landlord as required by this notice, you will not be covered by the eviction protections enacted by the California Legislature as a result of the COVID-19 pandemic, and your landlord can begin eviction proceedings against you as soon as this 15-day notice expires."

(e) A high-income tenant that fails to comply with subdivision (c) shall not be subject to the protections of subdivision (g) of Section 1179.03.

(f)(1) A landlord shall be required to plead compliance with this section in any unlawful detainer action based upon a notice that alleges that the tenant is a high-income tenant. If that allegation is contested, the landlord shall be required to submit to the court the proof of income upon which the landlord relied at the trial or other hearing, and the tenant shall be entitled to submit rebuttal evidence.

(2) If the court in an unlawful detainer action based upon a notice that alleges that the tenant is a high-income tenant determines that at the time the notice was served the landlord did not have proof of income establishing that the tenant is a high-income tenant, the court shall award attorney's fees to the prevailing tenant. **Leg.H.** Added Stats 2020 ch 37 §20 (AB 3088), repealed February 1, 2025. Amended Stats 2021 ch 27 §19 (AB 832), effective June 28, 2021, repealed October 1, 2025 (repealer amended).

§ 1179.03. Notice of demand for COVID-19 rental debt payment; Declaration of COVID-19-related financial distress [Repealed October 1, 2025]

(a)(1) Any notice that demands payment of COVID-19 rental debt served pursuant to subdivision (e) of Section 798.56 of the Civil Code or paragraph (2) or (3) of Section 1161 shall be modified as required by this section. A notice which does not meet the requirements of this section, regardless of when the notice was issued, shall not be sufficient to establish a cause of action for unlawful detainer or a basis for default judgment.

(2) Any case based solely on a notice that demands payment of COVID-19 rental debt served pursuant to subdivision (e) of Section 798.56 of the Civil Code or paragraph (2) or (3) of Section 1161 may be dismissed if the notice does not meet the requirements of this section, regardless of when the notice was issued.

(3) Notwithstanding paragraphs (1) and (2), this section shall have no effect if the landlord lawfully regained possession of the property or obtained a judgment for possession of the property before the operative date of this section.

(b) If the notice demands payment of rent that came due during the protected time period, as defined in Section 1179.02, the notice shall comply with all of the following:

(1) The time period in which the tenant may pay the amount due or deliver possession of the property shall be no shorter than 15 days, excluding Saturdays, Sundays, and other judicial holidays.

(2) The notice shall set forth the amount of rent demanded and the date each amount became due.

(3) The notice shall advise the tenant that the tenant cannot be evicted for failure to comply with the notice if the tenant delivers a signed declaration of COVID-19-related financial distress to the landlord on or before the date that the notice to pay rent or quit or notice to perform covenants or quit expires, by any of the methods specified in subdivision (f).

(4) The notice shall include the following text in at least 12-point font:

"NOTICE FROM THE STATE OF CALIFORNIA: If you are unable to pay the amount demanded in this notice, and have decreased income or increased expenses due to COVID-19, your landlord will not be able to evict you for this missed payment if you sign and deliver the declaration form included with your notice to your landlord within 15 days, excluding Saturdays, Sundays, and other judicial holidays, but you will still owe this money to your landlord. If you do not sign and deliver the declaration within this time period, you may lose the eviction protections available to you. You must return this form to be protected. You should keep a copy or picture of the signed form for your records.

You will still owe this money to your landlord and can be sued for the money, but you cannot be evicted from your home if you comply with these requirements. You should keep careful track of what you have paid and any amount you still owe to protect your rights and avoid future disputes. Failure to respond to this notice may result in an unlawful detainer action (eviction) being filed against you.

For information about legal resources that may be available to you, visit lawhelpca.org."

(c) If the notice demands payment of rent that came due during the transition time period, as defined in Section 1179.02, the notice shall comply with all of the following:

(1) The time period in which the tenant may pay the amount due or deliver possession of the property shall be no shorter than 15 days, excluding Saturdays, Sundays, and other judicial holidays.

(2) The notice shall set forth the amount of rent demanded and the date each amount became due.

(3) The notice shall advise the tenant that the tenant will not be evicted for failure to comply with the notice, except as allowed by this chapter, if the tenant delivers a signed declaration of COVID-19-related financial distress to the landlord on or before the date the notice to pay rent or quit or notice to perform covenants or quit expires, by any of the methods specified in subdivision (f).

(4) For notices served before February 1, 2021, the notice shall include the following text in at least 12-point type:

"NOTICE FROM THE STATE OF CALIFORNIA: If you are unable to pay the amount demanded in this notice, and have decreased income or increased expenses due to COVID-19, you may sign and deliver the declaration form included with your notice to your landlord within 15 days, excluding Saturdays, Sundays, and other judicial holidays, and your landlord will not be able to evict you for this missed payment so long as you make the minimum payment (see below). You will still owe this money to your landlord. You should keep a copy or picture of the signed form for your records.

If you provide the declaration form to your landlord as described above AND, on or before January 31, 2021, you pay an amount that equals at least 25 percent of each rental payment that came due or will come due during the period between September 1, 2020, and January 31, 2021, that you were unable to pay as a result of decreased income or increased expenses due to COVID-19, your landlord cannot evict you. Your landlord may require you to submit a new declaration form for each rental payment that you do not pay that comes due between September 1, 2020, and January 31, 2021.

For example, if you provided a declaration form to your landlord regarding your decreased income or increased expenses due to COVID-19 that prevented you from making your rental payment in September and October of 2020, your landlord could not evict you if, on or before January 31, 2021, you made a payment equal to 25 percent of September's and October's rental payment (i.e., half a month's rent). If you were unable to pay any of the rental payments that came due between September 1, 2020, and January 31, 2021, and you provided your landlord with the declarations in response to each 15-day notice your landlord sent to you during that time period, your landlord could not evict you if, on or before January 31, 2021, you paid your landlord an amount equal to 25 percent of all the rental payments due from September through January (i.e., one and a quarter month's rent).

You will still owe the full amount of the rent to your landlord, but you cannot be evicted from your home if you comply with these requirements. You should keep careful track of what you have paid and any amount you still owe to protect your rights and avoid future disputes. Failure to respond to this notice may result in an unlawful detainer action (eviction) being filed against you.

For information about legal resources that may be available to you, visit lawhelpca.org."

(5) For notices served on or after February 1, 2021, and before July 1, 2021, the notice shall include the following text in at least 12-point type:

"NOTICE FROM THE STATE OF CALIFORNIA: If you are unable to pay the amount demanded in this notice, and have decreased income or increased expenses due to COVID-19, you may sign and deliver the declaration form included with your notice to your landlord within 15 days, excluding Saturdays, Sundays, and other judicial holidays, and your landlord will not be able to evict you for this missed payment so long as you make the minimum payment (see below). You will still owe this money to your landlord. You should keep a copy or picture of the signed form for your records.

If you provide the declaration form to your landlord as described above AND, on or before June 30, 2021, you pay an amount that equals at least 25 percent of each rental payment that came due or will come due during the period between September 1, 2020, and June 30, 2021, that you were unable to pay as a result of decreased income or increased expenses due to COVID-19, your landlord cannot evict you. Your landlord may require you to submit a new declaration form for each rental payment that you do not pay that comes due between September 1, 2020, and June 30, 2021.

If you were unable to pay any of the rental payments that came due between September 1, 2020, and June 30, 2021, and you provided your landlord with the declarations in response to each 15-day notice your landlord sent to you during that time period, your landlord could not evict you if, on or before June 30, 2021, you paid your landlord an amount equal to 25 percent of all the rental payments due from September 2020 through June 2021.

You will still owe the full amount of the rent to your landlord, but you cannot be evicted from your home if you comply with these requirements. You should keep careful track of what you have paid and any amount you still owe to protect your rights and avoid future disputes. Failure to respond to this notice may result in an unlawful detainer action (eviction) being filed against you.

YOU MAY QUALIFY FOR RENTAL ASSISTANCE. In addition to extending these eviction protections, the State of California, in partnership with federal and local governments, has created an emergency rental assistance program to assist renters who have been unable to pay their rent and utility bills as a result of the COVID-19 pandemic. This program may be able to help you get caught up with past-due rent. Additionally, depending on the availability of funds, the program may also be able to assist you with making future rental payments.

While not everyone will qualify for this assistance, you can apply for it regardless of your citizenship or immigration status. There is no charge to apply for or receive this assistance.

Additional information about the extension of the COVID-19 Tenant Relief Act and new state or local rental assistance programs, including more information about how to qualify for assistance, can be found by visiting http://housingiskey.com or by calling 1-833-422-4255."

(6) For notices served on or after July 1, 2021, and before April 1, 2022, the notice shall include the following text in at least 12-point type:

"NOTICE FROM THE STATE OF CALIFORNIA-YOU MUST TAKE ACTION TO AVOID EVICTION. If you are unable to pay the amount demanded in this notice because of the COVID-19 pandemic, you should take action right away.

IMMEDIATELY: Sign and return the declaration form included with your notice to your landlord within 15 days, excluding Saturdays, Sundays, and other judicial holidays. Sign and return the declaration even if you have done this before. You should keep a copy or a picture of the signed form for your records.

BEFORE SEPTEMBER 30, 2021: Pay your landlord at least 25 percent of any rent you missed between September 1, 2020, and September 30, 2021. If you need help paying that amount, apply for rental assistance. You will still owe the rest of the rent to your landlord, but as long as you pay 25 percent by September 30, 2021, your landlord will not be able to evict you for failing to pay the rest of the rent. You should keep careful track of what you have paid and any amount you still owe to protect your rights and avoid future disputes.

AS SOON AS POSSIBLE: Apply for rental assistance! As part of California's COVID-19 relief plan, money has been set aside to help renters who have fallen behind on rent or utility payments. If you are behind on rent or utility payments, YOU SHOULD COMPLETE A RENTAL ASSISTANCE APPLICATION IMMEDIATELY! It is free and simple to apply. Citizenship or immigration status does not matter. You can find out how to start your application by calling 1-833-430-2122 or visiting http://housingiskey.com right away."

(7) For notices served on or after April 1, 2022, and before July 1, 2022, the notice shall include the following text in at least 12-point type:

"NOTICE FROM THE STATE OF CALIFORNIA:

If:

(1) Before October 1, 2021, you paid your landlord at least 25 percent of any rent you missed between September 1, 2020, and September 30, 2021, and you signed and returned on time any and all declarations of COVID-19 related financial distress that your landlord gave to you, or

(2) You completed an application for government rental assistance on or before March 31, 2022.

You may have protections against eviction.

For information about legal resources that may be available to you, visit lawhelpca.org."

(d) An unsigned copy of a declaration of COVID-19-related financial distress shall accompany each notice delivered to a tenant to which subdivision (b) or (c) is applicable. If the landlord was required, pursuant to Section 1632 of the Civil Code, to provide a translation of the rental contract or agreement in the language in which the contract or agreement was negotiated, the landlord shall also provide the unsigned copy of a declaration of COVID-19-related financial distress to the tenant in the language in which the contract or agreement was negotiated. The Department of Housing and Community Development shall make available an official translation of the text required by paragraph (4) of subdivision (b) and paragraphs (4) to (6), inclusive, of subdivision (c) in the languages specified in Section 1632 of the Civil Code by no later than July 15, 2021.

(e) If a tenant owes a COVID-19 rental debt to which both subdivisions (b) and (c) apply, the landlord shall serve two separate notices that comply with subdivisions (b) and (c), respectively.

(f) A tenant may deliver the declaration of COVID-19-related financial distress to the landlord by any of the following methods:

(1) In person, if the landlord indicates in the notice an address at which the declaration may be delivered in person.

(2) By electronic transmission, if the landlord indicates an email address in the notice to which the declaration may be delivered.

(3) Through United States mail to the address indicated by the landlord in the notice. If the landlord does not provide an address pursuant to subparagraph (1), then it shall be conclusively presumed that upon the mailing of the declaration by the tenant to the address provided by the landlord, the declaration is deemed received by the landlord on the date posted, if the tenant can show proof of mailing to the address provided by the landlord.

(4) Through any of the same methods that the tenant can use to deliver the payment pursuant to the notice if delivery of the declaration by that method is possible.

(g) Except as provided in Section 1179.02.5, the following shall apply to a tenant who, within 15 days of service of the notice specified in subdivision (b) or (c), excluding Saturdays, Sundays, and other judicial holidays, demanding payment of COVID-19 rental debt delivers a declaration of COVID-19-related financial distress to the landlord by any of the methods provided in subdivision (f):

(1) With respect to a notice served pursuant to subdivision (b), the tenant shall not then or thereafter be deemed to be in default with regard to that COVID-19 rental debt for purposes of subdivision (e) of Section 798.56 of the Civil Code or paragraphs (2) and (3) of Section 1161.

(2) With respect to a notice served pursuant to subdivision (c), the following shall apply:

(A) Except as provided by subparagraph (B), the landlord may not initiate an unlawful detainer action before October 1, 2021.

(B) A tenant shall not be guilty of unlawful detainer, now or in the future, based upon nonpayment of COVID-19 rental debt that came due during the transition period if, on or before September 30, 2021, the tenant tenders one or more payments that, when taken together, are of an amount equal to or not less than 25 percent of each transition period rental payment demanded in one or more notices served pursuant to subdivision (c) and for which the tenant complied with this subdivision by timely delivering a declaration of COVID-19-related financial distress to the landlord.

(h)(1)(A) Within the time prescribed in Section 1167, a tenant shall be permitted to file a signed declaration of COVID-19-related financial distress with the court.

(B) If the tenant files a signed declaration of COVID-19-related financial distress with the court pursuant to this subdivision, the court shall dismiss the case, pursuant to paragraph (2), if the court finds, after a noticed hearing on the matter, that the tenant's failure to return a declaration of COVID-19-related financial distress within the time required by subdivision (g) was the result of mistake, inadvertence, surprise, or excusable neglect, as those terms have been interpreted under subdivision (b) of Section 473.

(C) The noticed hearing required by this paragraph shall be held with not less than five days' notice and not more than 10 days' notice, to be given by the court, and may be held separately or in conjunction with any regularly noticed hearing in the case, other than a trial.

(2) If the court dismisses the case pursuant to paragraph (1), that dismissal shall be without prejudice as follows:

(A) If the case was based in whole or in part upon a notice served pursuant to subdivision (b), the court shall dismiss any cause of action based on the notice served pursuant to subdivision (b).

(B) Before October 1, 2021, if the case is based in whole or in part on a notice served pursuant to subdivision (c), the court shall dismiss any cause of action based on the notice served pursuant to subdivision (c).

(C) On or after October 1, 2021, if the case is based in whole or in part on a notice served pursuant to subdivision (c), the court shall dismiss any cause of action based upon the notice served pursuant to subdivision (c) if the tenant, within five days of the court's order to do so, makes the payment required by subparagraph (B) of paragraph (2) of subdivision (g), provided that if the fifth day falls on a Saturday, Sunday, or judicial holiday the last day to pay shall be extended to the next court day.

(3) If the court dismisses the case pursuant to this subdivision, the tenant shall not be considered the prevailing party for purposes of Section 1032, any attorney's fee provision appearing in contract or statute, or any other law.

(i) Notwithstanding any other law, a notice which is served pursuant to subdivision (b) or (c) that complies with the requirements of this chapter and subdivision (e) of Section 798.56 of the Civil Code or paragraphs (2) and (3) of Section 1161, as applicable, need not include specific language required by any ordinance, resolution, regulation, or administrative action adopted by a city, county, or city and county. **Leg.H.** Amended Stats 2021 ch 2 §17 (SB 91), effective January 29, 2021, repealed July 1, 2025; Stats 2021 ch 5 §8 (AB 81), effective February 23, 2021, repealed July 1, 2025; Stats 2021 ch 27 §15, 19 (AB 832), effective June 28, 2021, repealed October 1, 2025 (repealer amended); Stats 2022 ch 13 §1 (AB 2179), effective March 31, 2022, repealed October 1, 2025.

§ 1179.03.5. Limitations on finding tenant guilty of unlawful detainer; Tenant relocation [Repealed October 1, 2025]

(a) Before October 1, 2021, a court may not find a tenant guilty of an unlawful detainer unless it finds that one of the following applies:

(1) The tenant was guilty of the unlawful detainer before March 1, 2020.

(2) In response to service of a notice demanding payment of COVID-19 rental debt pursuant to subdivision (e) of Section 798.56 of the Civil Code or paragraph (2) or (3) of Section 1161, the tenant failed to comply with the requirements of Section 1179.03.

(3)(A) The unlawful detainer arises because of a termination of tenancy for any of the following:

(i) An at-fault just cause, as defined in paragraph (1) of subdivision (b) of Section 1946.2 of the Civil Code.

(ii)(I) A no-fault just cause, as defined in paragraph (2) of subdivision (b) of Section 1946.2 of the Civil Code, other than intent to demolish or to substantially remodel the residential real property, as defined in subparagraph (D) of paragraph (2) of subdivision (b) of Section 1946.2.

(II) Notwithstanding subclause (I), termination of a tenancy based on intent to demolish or to substantially remodel the residential real property shall be permitted if necessary to maintain compliance with the requirements of Section 1941.1 of the Civil Code, Section 17920.3 or 17920.10 of the Health and Safety Code, or any other applicable law governing the habitability of residential rental units.

(iii) The owner of the property has entered into a contract for the sale of that property with a buyer who intends to occupy the property, and all the requirements of paragraph (8) of subdivision (e) of Section 1946.2 of the Civil Code have been satisfied.

(B) In an action under this paragraph, other than an action to which paragraph (2) also applies, the landlord shall be precluded from recovering COVID-19 rental debt in connection with any award of damages.

(b)(1) This section does not require a landlord to assist the tenant to relocate through the payment of relocation costs if the landlord would not otherwise be required to do so pursuant to Section 1946.2 of the Civil Code or any other law.

(2) A landlord who is required to assist the tenant to relocate pursuant to Section 1946.2 of the Civil Code or any other law, may offset the tenant's COVID-19 rental debt against their obligation to assist the tenant to relocate. **Leg.H.** Amended Stats 2021 ch 2 §18 (SB 91), effective January 29, 2021. Repealed Stats 2021 ch 2 §18 (SB 91), effective July 1, 2025. Amended Stats 2021 ch 27 §§ 16, 19 (AB 832), effective June 28, 2021, repealed October 1, 2025 (repealer amended).

§ 1179.04. Notice to tenants with unpaid rental payments due during protected time period as of September 1, 2020 [Repealed October 1, 2025]

(a) On or before September 30, 2020, a landlord shall provide, in at least 12-point type, the following notice to tenants who, as of September 1, 2020, have not paid one or more rental payments that came due during the protected time period:

NOTICE FROM THE STATE OF CALIFORNIA: The California Legislature has enacted the COVID-19 Tenant Relief Act of 2020 which protects renters who have experienced COVID-19-related financial distress from being evicted for failing to make rental payments due between March 1, 2020, and January 31, 2021.

"COVID-19-related financial distress" means any of the following:

1. Loss of income caused by the COVID-19 pandemic.

2. Increased out-of-pocket expenses directly related to performing essential work during the COVID-19 pandemic.

3. Increased expenses directly related to the health impact of the COVID-19 pandemic.

4. Childcare responsibilities or responsibilities to care for an elderly, disabled, or sick family member directly related to the COVID-19 pandemic that limit your ability to earn income.

5. Increased costs for childcare or attending to an elderly, disabled, or sick family member directly related to the COVID-19 pandemic.

6. Other circumstances related to the COVID-19 pandemic that have reduced your income or increased your expenses.

This law gives you the following protections:

1. If you failed to make rental payments due between March 1, 2020, and August 31, 2020, because you had decreased income or increased expenses due to the COVID-19 pandemic, as described above, you cannot be evicted based on this nonpayment.

2. If you are unable to pay rental payments that come due between September 1, 2020, and January 31, 2021, because of decreased income or increased expenses due to the COVID-19 pandemic, as described above, you cannot be evicted if you pay 25 percent of the rental payments missed during that time period on or before January 31, 2021.

You must provide, to your landlord, a declaration under penalty of perjury of your COVID-19-related financial distress attesting to the decreased income or increased expenses due to the COVID-19 pandemic to be protected by the eviction limitations described above. Before your landlord can seek to evict you for failing to make a payment that came due between March 1, 2020, and January 31, 2021, your landlord will be required to give you a 15-day notice that informs you of the amounts owed and includes a blank declaration form you can use to comply with this requirement.

If your landlord has proof of income on file which indicates that your household makes at least 130 percent of the median income for the county where the rental property is located, as published by the Department of Housing and Community Development in the Official State Income Limits for 2020, your landlord may also require you to provide documentation which shows that you have experienced a decrease in income or increase in expenses due to the COVID-19 pandemic. Your landlord must tell you in the 15-day notice whether your landlord is requiring that documentation. Any form of objectively verifiable documentation that demonstrates the financial impact you have experienced is sufficient, including a letter from your employer, an unemployment insurance record, or medical bills, and may be provided to satisfy the documentation requirement.

It is very important you do not ignore a 15-day notice to pay rent or quit or a notice to perform covenants or quit from your landlord. If you are served with a 15-day notice and do not provide the declaration form to your landlord before the 15-day notice expires, you could be evicted. You could also be evicted beginning February 1, 2021, if you owe rental payments due between September 1, 2020, and January 31, 2021, and you do not pay an amount equal to at least 25 percent of the payments missed for that time period.

For information about legal resources that may be available to you, visit lawhelpca.org.

(b) On or before February 28, 2021, a landlord shall provide, in at least 12-point type, the following notice to tenants who, as of February 1, 2021, have not paid one or more rental payments that came due during the covered time period:

NOTICE FROM THE STATE OF CALIFORNIA: The California Legislature has enacted the COVID-19 Tenant Relief Act which protects renters who have experienced COVID-19-related financial distress from being evicted for failing to make rental payments due between March 1, 2020, and June 30, 2021.

"COVID-19-related financial distress" means any of the following:

1. Loss of income caused by the COVID-19 pandemic.
2. Increased out-of-pocket expenses directly related to performing essential work during the COVID-19 pandemic.
3. Increased expenses directly related to the health impact of the COVID-19 pandemic.
4. Childcare responsibilities or responsibilities to care for an elderly, disabled, or sick family member directly related to the COVID-19 pandemic that limit your ability to earn income.
5. Increased costs for childcare or attending to an elderly, disabled, or sick family member directly related to the COVID-19 pandemic.
6. Other circumstances related to the COVID-19 pandemic that have reduced your income or increased your expenses.

This law gives you the following protections:

1. If you failed to make rental payments due between March 1, 2020, and August 31, 2020, because you had decreased income or increased expenses due to the COVID-19 pandemic, as described above, you cannot be evicted based on this nonpayment.

2. If you are unable to pay rental payments that come due between September 1, 2020, and June 30, 2021, because of decreased income or increased expenses due to the COVID-19 pandemic, as described above, you cannot be evicted if you pay 25 percent of the rental payments missed during that time period on or before June 30, 2021.

You must provide, to your landlord, a declaration under penalty of perjury of your COVID-19-related financial distress attesting to the decreased income or increased expenses due to the COVID-19 pandemic to be protected by the eviction limitations described above. Before your landlord can seek to evict you for failing to make a payment that came due between March 1, 2020, and June 30, 2021, your landlord will be required to give you a 15-day notice that informs you of the amounts owed and includes a blank declaration form you can use to comply with this requirement.

If your landlord has proof of income on file which indicates that your household makes at least 130 percent of the median income for the county where the rental property is located, as published by the Department of Housing and Community Development in the Official State Income Limits for 2020, your landlord may also require you to provide documentation which shows that you have experienced a decrease in income or increase in expenses due to the COVID-19 pandemic. Your landlord must tell you in the 15-day notice whether your landlord is requiring that documentation. Any form of objectively verifiable documentation that demonstrates the financial impact you have experienced is sufficient, including a letter from your employer, an unemployment insurance record, or medical bills, and may be provided to satisfy the documentation requirement.

It is very important you do not ignore a 15-day notice to pay rent or quit or a notice to perform covenants or quit from your landlord. If you are served with a 15-day notice and do not provide the declaration form to your landlord before the 15-day notice expires, you could be evicted. You could also be evicted beginning July 1, 2021, if you owe rental payments due between September 1, 2020, and June 30, 2021, and you do not pay an amount equal to at least 25 percent of the payments missed for that time period.

YOU MAY QUALIFY FOR RENTAL ASSISTANCE. In addition to extending these eviction protections, the State of California, in partnership with federal and local governments, has created an emergency rental assistance program to assist renters who have been unable to pay their rent and utility bills as a result of the COVID-19 pandemic. This program may be able to help you get caught up with past-due rent. Additionally, depending on the availability of funds, the program may also be able to assist you with making future rental payments.

While not everyone will qualify for this assistance, you can apply for it regardless of your citizenship or immigration status. There is no charge to apply for or receive this assistance.

Additional information about the extension of the COVID-19 Tenant Relief Act and new state or local rental assistance programs, including more information about how to qualify for assistance, can be found by visiting http://housingiskey.comhttp://housingiskey.com or by calling 1-833-422-4255.

(c) On or before July 31, 2021, a landlord shall provide, in at least 12-point type, the following notice to tenants who, as of July 1, 2021, have not paid one or more rental payments that came due during the covered time period:

NOTICE FROM THE STATE OF CALIFORNIA: The California Legislature has extended the COVID-19 Tenant Relief Act. The law now protects renters who have experienced COVID-19-related financial distress from being evicted for failing to make rental payments due between March 1, 2020, and September 30, 2021.

"COVID-19-related financial distress" means any of the following:

1. Loss of income caused by the COVID-19 pandemic.
2. Increased out-of-pocket expenses directly related to performing essential work during the COVID-19 pandemic.
3. Increased expenses directly related to the health impact of the COVID-19 pandemic.
4. Childcare responsibilities or responsibilities to care for an elderly, disabled, or sick family member directly related to the COVID-19 pandemic that limit your ability to earn income.
5. Increased costs for childcare or attending to an elderly, disabled, or sick family member directly related to the COVID-19 pandemic.
6. Other circumstances related to the COVID-19 pandemic that have reduced your income or increased your expenses.

This law gives you the following protections:

1. If you failed to make rental payments due between March 1, 2020, and August 31, 2020, because you had decreased income or increased expenses due to the COVID-19 pandemic, as described above, you cannot be evicted based on this nonpayment.

2. If you are unable to pay rental payments that come due between September 1, 2020, and September 30, 2021, because of decreased income or increased expenses due to the COVID-19 pandemic, as described above, you cannot be evicted if you pay 25 percent of the rental payments missed during that time period on or before September 30, 2021.

You must provide, to your landlord, a declaration under penalty of perjury of your COVID-19-related financial distress attesting to the decreased income or increased expenses due to the COVID-19 pandemic to be protected by the eviction limitations described above. Before your landlord can seek to evict you for failing to make a payment that came due between March 1, 2020, and September 30, 2021, your landlord will be required to give you a 15-day notice that informs you of the amounts owed and includes a blank declaration form you can use to comply with this requirement.

If your landlord has proof of income on file that indicates that your household makes at least 130 percent of the median income for the county where the rental property is located, as published by the Department of Housing and Community Development in the Official State Income Limits for 2020, your landlord may also require you to provide documentation that shows that you have experienced a decrease in income or increase in expenses due to the COVID-19 pandemic. Your landlord must tell you in the 15-day notice whether your landlord is requiring that documentation. Any form of objectively verifiable documentation that demonstrates the financial impact you have experienced is sufficient, including a letter from your employer, an unemployment insurance record, or medical bills, and may be provided to satisfy the documentation requirement.

It is very important you do not ignore a 15-day notice to pay rent or quit or a notice to perform covenants or quit from your landlord. If you are served with a 15-day notice and do not provide the declaration form to your landlord before the 15-day notice expires, you could be evicted. You could also be evicted beginning October 1, 2021, if you owe rental payments due between September 1, 2020, and September 30, 2021, and you do not pay an amount equal to at least 25 percent of the payments missed for that time period.

YOU MAY QUALIFY FOR RENTAL ASSISTANCE. In addition to extending these eviction protections, the State of California, in partnership with federal and local governments, has created an emergency rental assistance program to assist renters who have been unable to pay their rent and utility bills as a result of the COVID-19 pandemic. This program may be able to help you get caught up with past-due rent. Additionally, depending on the availability of funds, the program may also be able to assist you with making future rental payments.

While not everyone will qualify for this assistance, you can apply for it regardless of your citizenship or immigration status. There is no charge to apply for or receive this assistance.

Additional information about the extension of the COVID-19 Tenant Relief Act and new state or local rental assistance programs, including more information about how to qualify for assistance, can be found by visiting http://housingiskey.com or by calling 1-833-430-2122.

(d) The landlord may provide the notice required by subdivisions (a) to (c), inclusive, as applicable, in the manner prescribed by Section 1162 or by mail.

(e)(1) A landlord may not serve a notice pursuant to subdivision (b) or (c) of Section 1179.03 before the landlord has provided the notice required by subdivisions (a) to (c), inclusive, as applicable.

(2) The notice required by subdivision (a) may be provided to a tenant concurrently with a notice pursuant to subdivision (b) or (c) of Section 1179.03 that is served on or before September 30, 2020.

(3) The notice required by subdivision (b) may be provided to a tenant concurrently with a notice pursuant to subdivision (b) or (c) of Section 1179.03 that is served on or before February 28, 2021.

(4) The notice required by subdivision (c) may be provided to a tenant concurrently with a notice pursuant to subdivision (b) or (c) of Section 1179.03 that is served on or before September 30, 2021. **Leg.H.** Added Stats 2020 ch 37 §20 (AB 3088), effective August 31, 2020, repealed February 1, 2025. Amended Stats 2021 ch 2 §19 (SB 91), effective January 29, 2021, repealed July 1, 2025. Repealed Stats 2021 ch 2 §19 (SB 91), effective July 1, 2025. Amended Stats 2021 ch 27 §§ 17, 19 (AB 832), effective June 28, 2021, repealed October 1, 2025 (repealer amended); Stats 2022 ch 28 §27 (SB 1380), effective January 1, 2023, repealed October 1, 2025.

§1179.04.5. Limitation on application of security deposit or monthly rental payment to COVID-19 rental debt [Repealed October 1, 2025]

Notwithstanding Sections 1470, 1947, and 1950 of the Civil Code, or any other law, for the duration of any tenancy that existed during the covered time period, the landlord shall not do either of the following:

(a) Apply a security deposit to satisfy COVID-19 rental debt, unless the tenant has agreed, in writing, to allow the deposit to be so applied. Nothing in this subdivision shall prohibit a landlord from applying a security deposit to satisfy COVID-19 rental debt after the tenancy ends, in accordance with Section 1950.5 of the Civil Code.

(b) Apply a monthly rental payment to any COVID-19 rental debt other than the prospective month's rent, unless the tenant has agreed, in writing, to allow the payment to be so applied. **Leg.H.** Added Stats 2021 ch 2 §20 (SB 91), effective January 29, 2021, repealed July 1, 2025. Amended and renumbered from Cal Civ Code §1179.04.5 by Stats 2021 ch 5 §2 (AB 81), effective February 23, 2021. Amended Stats 2021 ch 27 §19 (AB 832), effective June 28, 2021, repealed October 1, 2025 (repealer amended).

§ 1179.05. Limitations on and effect of municipal response to protect tenants from eviction related to COVID-19 pandemic [Repealed October 1, 2025]

(a) Any ordinance, resolution, regulation, or administrative action adopted by a city, county, or city and county in response to the COVID-19 pandemic to protect tenants from eviction is subject to all of the following:

(1) Any extension, expansion, renewal, reenactment, or new adoption of a measure, however delineated, that occurs between August 19, 2020, and June 30, 2022, shall have no effect before July 1, 2022.

(2) Any provision which allows a tenant a specified period of time in which to repay COVID-19 rental debt shall be subject to all of the following:

(A) If the provision in effect on August 19, 2020, required the repayment period to commence on a specific date on or before August 1, 2022 any extension of that date made after August 19, 2020, shall have no effect.

(B) If the provision in effect on August 19, 2020, required the repayment period to commence on a specific date after August 1, 2022, or conditioned commencement of the repayment period on the termination of a proclamation of state of emergency or local emergency, the repayment period is deemed to begin on August 1, 2022.

(C) The specified period of time during which a tenant is permitted to repay COVID-19 rental debt may not extend beyond the period that was in effect on August 19, 2020. In addition, a provision may not permit a tenant a period of time that extends beyond August 31, 2023, to repay COVID-19 rental debt.

(b) This section does not alter a city, county, or city and county's authority to extend, expand, renew, reenact, or newly adopt an ordinance that requires just cause for termination of a residential tenancy or amend existing ordinances that require just cause for termination of a residential tenancy, consistent with subdivision (g) of Section 1946.2, provided that a provision enacted or amended after August 19, 2020, shall not apply to rental payments that came due between March 1, 2020, and June 30, 2022.

(c) The one-year limitation provided in subdivision (2) of Section 1161 is tolled during any time period that a landlord is or was prohibited by any ordinance, resolution, regulation, or administrative action adopted by a city, county, or city and county in response to the COVID-19 pandemic to protect tenants from eviction based on nonpayment of rental payments from serving a notice that demands payment of COVID-19 rental debt pursuant to subdivision (e) of Section 798.56 of the Civil Code or paragraph (2) of Section 1161.

(d) It is the intent of the Legislature that this section be applied retroactively to August 19, 2020.

(e) The Legislature finds and declares that this section addresses a matter of statewide concern rather than a municipal affair as that term is used in Section 5 of Article XI of the California Constitution. Therefore, this section applies to all cities, including charter cities.

(f) It is the intent of the Legislature that the purpose of this section is to protect individuals negatively impacted by the COVID-19 pandemic, and that this section does not provide the Legislature's understanding of the legal validity on any specific ordinance, resolution, regulation, or administrative action adopted by a city, county, or city and county in response to the COVID-19 pandemic to protect tenants from eviction. **Leg.H.** Added Stats 2020 ch 37 §20 (AB 3088), repealed February 1, 2025. Amended Stats 2021 ch 2 §21 (SB 91), effective January 29, 2021, repealed July 1, 2025; Stats 2021 ch 5 §9 (AB 81), effective February 23, 2021, repealed July 1, 2025; Stats 2021 ch 27 §§ 18, 19 (AB 832), effective June 28, 2021, repealed October 1, 2025 (repealer amended); Stats 2022 ch 13 §2 (AB 2179), effective March 31, 2022, repealed October 1, 2025.

§ 1179.06. Waivers void [Repealed October 1, 2025]

Any provision of a stipulation, settlement agreement, or other agreement entered into on or after the effective date of this chapter, including a lease agreement, that purports to waive the provisions of this chapter is prohibited and is void as contrary to public policy. **Leg.H.** Added Stats 2020 ch 37 §20 (AB 3088), effective August 31, 2020, repealed February 1, 2025. Amended Stats 2021 ch 27 §19 (AB 832), effective June 28, 2021, repealed October 1, 2025 (repealer amended).

1179.07. Repeal of chapter [Repealed October 1, 2025]

This chapter shall remain in effect until October 1, 2025, and as of that date is repealed. **Leg.H.** Added Stats 2020 ch 37 §20 (AB 3088), repealed February 1, 2025. Amended Stats 2021 ch 2 §22 (SB 91), effective January 29, 2021, repealed July 1, 2025; Stats 2021 ch 27 §§ 19 (AB 832), effective June 28, 2021, repealed October 1, 2025 (repealer amended).

TITLE 4
OF THE ENFORCEMENT OF LIENS

Chapter 1. Liens in General.
Chapter 2.5. Oil and Gas Liens.
Chapter 3. Certain Liens and Priorities for Salaries, Wages and Consumer Deposits.
Chapter 4. Certain Liens Upon Animals.
Chapter 5. Liens on Aircraft.

CHAPTER 1
LIENS IN GENERAL

Definition of lien. §1180.

§1180. Definition of lien

A lien is a charge imposed upon specific property, by which it is made security for the performance of an act. **Leg.H.** Enacted 1872.

CHAPTER 2
LIENS OF MECHANICS AND OTHERS UPON REAL PROPERTY [REPEALED]

§§1181–1203.1. [Sections repealed 1971]

Leg.H. Added Stats 1951 ch 1159 §1. Amended Stats 1951 chs 1376, 1382, Stats 1953 ch 1402, Stats 1955 chs 945, 1511, 1750, Stats 1957 chs 1011, 1146, 1650, 1833, 1888, 2350, Stats 1959 chs 1013, 1176, 1549, 2034, Stats 1961 chs 72, 804, Stats 1963 chs 298, 1081, 1176, 1786, Stats 1965 chs 737, 1258, 1369, Stats 1967 chs 465, 542, 789, 891, Stats 1968 chs 460, 678, 777, 1298, Stats 1969 chs 1364, 1611. Repealed Stats 1969 ch 1362 §3, operative January 1, 1971, Stats 1971 ch 1284 §8. See CC §§8400 et seq.

Prior Law: Former CCP §§1183–1203 were enacted 1872, amended Code Amdts 1873–74 chs 383, 586, Code Amdts 1880 ch 67, Stats 1885 ch 152, Stats 1887 ch 137, Stats 1893 ch 171, Stats 1897 ch 141, Stats 1899 chs 23, 35, Stats 1901 ch 292, Stats 1903 chs 19, 176, Stats 1907 chs 303, 474, Stats 1909 ch 668, Stats 1911 ch 681, Stats 1913 ch 189, Stats 1919 chs 146, 277, Stats 1921 ch 144, Stats 1923 ch 106, Stats 1925 chs 155, 308, Stats 1929 chs 869-871, Stats 1931 ch 830, Stats 1933 ch 334, Stats 1935 ch 785, Stats 1939 ch 1068, Stats 1943 ch 139, Stats 1945 chs 40, 828, Stats 1947 ch 28, effective Feburary 13, 1947, Stats 1949 chs 476, 632, 1547, and repealed Stats 1951 ch 1159 §4.

CHAPTER 2.5
OIL AND GAS LIENS

Citation of chapter. §1203.50.
Definitions. §1203.51.
Right to lien. §1203.52.
Extent of liens. §1203.53.
Subcontractor's lien. §1203.54.
Liens on leasehold estate attached prior to forfeiture; Liens on equitable or legal interest prior to failure. §1203.55.
When lien arises; Priority. §1203.56.
Equality of liens; Preferred liens for labor. §1203.57.
Recording statement of lien. §1203.58.
Notice to purchaser, and withholding and using payments; Notice of claim's satisfaction. §1203.59.
Recording of bond by lessor, owner, contractor, etc., against or through whom claim is filed; Amount and condition; Action on bond. §1203.60.
Proceedings for enforcement of lien. §1203.61.
Right to maintain personal action. §1203.62.
Waiver of lien. §1203.63.
Assignments. §1203.64.
Perfection and enforcement of liens arising before and after chapter's effective date. §1203.65.
Liberal construction. §1203.66.

§1203.50. Citation of chapter

This chapter shall be known and may be cited as the Oil and Gas Lien Act. **Leg.H.** Added Stats 1959 ch 2020 §1.

§1203.51. Definitions

Unless the context otherwise requires, the definitions set forth in this section shall govern the construction of this chapter.

(a) "Person" means an individual, corporation, firm, partnership, limited liability company, or association.

(b) "Owner" means a person holding any interest in the legal or equitable title or both to any leasehold for oil or gas purposes, or his or her agent and shall include purchasers under executory contract, receivers, and trustees.

(c) "Contract" means a contract, written or oral, express or implied, or partly express and partly implied, or executory or executed, or partly executory and partly executed.

(d) "Material" means any material, machinery, appliances, buildings, structures, casing, tanks, pipelines, tools, bits, or other equipment or supplies but does not include rigs or hoists or their integral component parts except wire lines.

(e) "Labor" means work performed in return for wages.

(f) "Services" means work performed exclusive of labor, including the hauling of material, whether or not involving the furnishing of material.

(g) "Furnish" means sell or rent.

(h) "Drilling" means drilling, digging, shooting, torpedoing, perforating, fracturing, testing, logging, acidizing, cementing, completing or repairing.

(i) "Operating" means all operations conducted on the lease in connection with or necessary to the production of oil or gas, either in the development thereof or in working thereon by the subtractive process.

(j) "Construction" means construction, maintenance, operation, or repair, either in the development thereof or in working thereon by the subtractive process.

(k) "Original contractor" means any person for whose benefit a lien is prescribed under Section 1203.52. **Leg.H.** Added Stats 1959 ch 2020 §1. Amended Stats 1994 ch 1010 §62 (SB 2053).

§1203.52. Right to lien

Any person who shall, under contract with the owner of any leasehold for oil or gas purposes perform any labor or furnish any material or services used or employed, or furnished to be used or employed in the drilling or operating of any oil or gas well upon such leasehold, or in the constructing, putting together, or repairing of any material so used or employed, or furnished to be so used or employed, shall be entitled to a lien under this chapter, whether or not a producing well is obtained and whether or not such material is incorporated in or becomes a part of the completed oil or gas well, for the amount due him for any such labor performed, or materials or services furnished, within six months prior to the date of recording the statement of lien as provided in Section 1203.58, including, without limitation, shipping and mileage charges connected therewith, and interest from the date the same was due. **Leg.H.** Added Stats 1959 ch 2020 §1.

§1203.53. Extent of liens

Liens created under Section 1203.52 shall extend to:

(a) The leasehold for oil or gas purposes to which the materials or services were furnished, or for which the labor was performed, and the appurtenances thereunto belonging, exclusive of any and all royalty interest, overriding interests and production payments created by an instrument recorded prior to the date such materials or services were first furnished or such labor was first performed for which lien is claimed; and

(b) All materials and fixtures owned by the owner or owners of such leasehold and used or employed, or furnished to be used or employed in the drilling or operating of any oil or gas well located thereon; and

(c) All oil or gas wells located on such leasehold, and the oil or gas produced therefrom, and the proceeds thereof, except the interest therein owned by the owners of royalty interests, overriding royalty interests and production payments created by an instrument recorded prior to the date such materials or services were first furnished or such labor was first performed for which the lien is claimed. **Leg.H.** Added Stats 1959 ch 2020 §1.

§1203.54. Subcontractor's lien

Any person who shall, under contract, perform any labor or furnish any material or services as a subcontractor under an original contractor or for or to an original contractor or a subcontractor under an original contractor, shall be entitled to a lien upon all the property upon which the lien of an original contractor may attach to the same extent as an original contractor, and the lien provided for in this section shall further extend and attach to all materials and fixtures owned by such original contractor or subcontractor to or for whom the labor is performed or material or services furnished and used or employed, or furnished to be used or employed in the drilling or operating of such oil or gas wells. **Leg.H.** Added Stats 1959 ch 2020 §1.

§1203.55. Liens on leasehold estate attached prior to forfeiture; Liens on equitable or legal interest prior to failure

When a lien provided for in this chapter shall have attached to a leasehold estate, forfeiture of such estate shall not impair any lien as to material, appurtenances and fixtures located thereon and to which such lien has attached prior to forfeiture. If a lien provided for in this chapter attaches to an equitable interest or to a legal interest contingent upon the happening of a condition subsequent, failure of such interest to ripen into legal title or such condition subsequent to be fulfilled, shall not impair any such lien as to material, appurtenances and fixtures located thereon and to which said lien had attached prior to such failure. **Leg.H.** Added Stats 1959 ch 2020 §1.

§1203.56. When lien arises; Priority

The lien provided for in this chapter arises on the date of the furnishing of the first item of material or services or the date of performance of the first labor for which a lien is claimed under the provisions of this chapter. Upon compliance with the provisions of Section 1203.58, such lien shall be preferred to all other titles, charges, liens or encumbrances which may attach to or upon any of the property upon which a lien is given by this chapter subsequent to the date the lien herein provided for arises. **Leg.H.** Added Stats 1959 ch 2020 §1.

§1203.57. Equality of liens; Preferred liens for labor

All liens arising by virtue of this chapter upon the same property shall be of equal standing except that liens of persons for the performance of labor shall be preferred to all other liens arising by virtue of this chapter. **Leg.H.** Added Stats 1959 ch 2020 §1.

§1203.58. Recording statement of lien

Every person claiming a lien under this chapter, shall record in the office of the county recorder for the county in which such leasehold, or some part thereof, is situated, a verified statement setting forth the amount claimed and the items thereof, the dates on which labor was performed or material or services furnished, the name of the owner of the leasehold, if known, the name of the claimant and his mailing address, a description of the leasehold, and if the claimant be a claimant under Section 1203.54, the name of the person for whom the labor was immediately performed or the material or services were immediately furnished. The statement of lien must be recorded within six months after the date on which the claimant's labor was performed or his materials or services were furnished to be effective as to such labor, materials, or services. **Leg.H.** Added Stats 1959 ch 2020 §1.

§1203.59. Notice to purchaser, and withholding and using payments; Notice of claim's satisfaction

Anything in this chapter to the contrary notwithstanding, any lien claimed by virtue of this chapter, insofar as it may extend to oil or gas or the proceeds of the sale of oil or gas, shall not be effective against any purchaser of such oil or gas until written notice of such claim has been delivered to such purchaser. Such notice shall state the name of the claimant, his address, the amount for which the lien is claimed, and a description of the leasehold upon which the lien is claimed. Such notice shall be delivered personally to the purchaser or by registered letter or certified mail. Upon receipt of such notice the purchaser shall withhold payments for such oil or gas runs to the extent of the lien amount claimed until delivery of notice in writing that the claim has been paid. The funds so withheld by the purchaser shall be used in payment of the lien judgment upon foreclosure. The lien claimant shall within 10 days give notice in writing that the claim has been paid. **Leg.H.** Added Stats 1959 ch 2020 §1.

§1203.60. Recording of bond by lessor, owner, contractor, etc., against or through whom claim is filed; Amount and condition; Action on bond

(a) Whenever any lien or liens shall be claimed or recorded under the provisions of this chapter then the lessor or owner of the property on which the lien or liens are claimed or the contractor or subcontractor through whom such lien or liens are claimed, or either of them, may record a bond with the county recorder of the county in which the property is located as herein provided. Such bond shall describe the property on which lien or liens are claimed, shall refer to the lien or liens claimed in manner sufficient to identify them and shall be in an amount equal to 150 percent of the amount of the claimed lien or liens referred to and shall be payable to the party or parties claiming same. Such bond shall be executed by the party recording same as principal and by a corporate surety authorized to execute such bonds as surety and shall be conditioned substantially that the principal and surety will pay to the obligees named or their assigns the amounts of the liens so claimed by them with all costs in the event same shall be proven to be liens on such property.

(b) Such bond, when recorded, shall take the place of the property against which any claim for lien referred to in such bond is asserted. At any time within the period of time provided in Section 1203.61, any person claiming such lien may sue upon such bond but no action shall be brought upon such bond after the expiration of such period. One action upon such bond shall not exhaust the remedies thereon but each obligee or assignee of an obligee named therein may maintain a separate suit thereon in any court having jurisdiction. **Leg.H.** Added Stats 1959 ch 2020 §1.

§1203.61. Proceedings for enforcement of lien

(a) Any lien provided for by this chapter shall be enforced in the same manner as provided in Chapter 4 (commencing with Section 8400) of Title 2 of Part 6 of Division 4 of the Civil Code. The action shall be filed within 180 days from the time of the recording of the lien. If a credit is given and notice of the fact and terms of the credit is filed in the office of the county recorder subsequent to the filing of the lien and prior to the expiration of the 180-day period, then the lien continues in force until 180 days after the expiration of the credit, but no lien continues in force by reason of any agreement to give credit for a longer time than one year from the time the work is completed. If the proceedings to enforce the lien are not prosecuted to trial within two years after commencement, the court may in its discretion dismiss the action for want of prosecution, and in all cases the dismissal of the action (unless it is expressly stated that it is without prejudice) or a judgment in the action that no lien exists is equivalent to the cancellation and removal from the record of the lien.

(b) As against any purchaser or encumbrancer for value and in good faith whose rights are acquired subsequent to the expiration of the 180-day period following the filing of the lien, no giving of credit or extension of the lien or time to enforce the lien shall be effective unless evidenced by a notice or agreement filed for record in the office of the county recorder prior to the acquisition of the rights of the purchaser or encumbrancer. **Leg.H.** Added Stats 1959 ch 2020 §1. Amended Stats 1969 ch 1362 §4, operative January 1, 1971; Stats 2010 ch 697 §24 (SB 189), effective January 1, 2011, operative July 1, 2012.

§1203.62. Right to maintain personal action

Nothing in this chapter shall be construed to impair or affect the right of any person to whom any debt may be due for work performed or materials or services furnished to maintain a personal action against the person liable for such debt. **Leg.H.** Added Stats 1959 ch 2020 §1.

§1203.63. Waiver of lien

The taking of any note or any additional security by any person given a lien by this chapter shall not constitute a waiver of the lien given by this chapter unless made a waiver by express agreement of the parties in writing. The claiming of a lien under this chapter shall not constitute a waiver of any other right or security held by the claimant unless made a waiver by express agreement of the parties in writing. **Leg.H.** Added Stats 1959 ch 2020 §1.

§1203.64. Assignments

All claims for liens and likewise all actions to recover therefor under this chapter shall be assignable upon compliance with the provisions of Section 1203.58 so as to vest in the assignee all rights and remedies herein given subject to all defenses thereto that might be raised if such assignments had not been made. **Leg.H.** Added Stats 1959 ch 2020 §1.

§1203.65. Perfection and enforcement of liens arising before and after chapter's effective date

All liens granted by this chapter shall be perfected and enforced in accordance with the provisions hereof whether such liens arise before or after the effective date of this chapter; provided, however, that any unperfected lien granted under any statute in effect prior to the effective date of this chapter and which could be subsequently perfected in accordance with such prior statute were it not for the existence of this chapter may be perfected and enforced in accordance with the provisions of this chapter if the statement of lien required to be recorded under Section 1203.58 is recorded within the time therein required or within two months after the effective date of this chapter, whichever period is longer; and provided further, that the validity of any lien perfected prior to the effective date of this chapter in accordance with the requirements of any statute in effect prior to such effective date shall be determined on the basis of such prior statute but the enforcement thereof shall insofar as possible be governed by the provisions of this chapter. **Leg.H.** Added Stats 1959 ch 2020 §1.

§1203.66. Liberal construction

This chapter shall be given liberal construction in favor of all persons entitled to any lien under it. **Leg.H.** Added Stats 1959 ch 2020 §1.

CHAPTER 3
CERTAIN LIENS AND PRIORITIES FOR SALARIES, WAGES AND CONSUMER DEPOSITS

Assignment for benefit of creditors; Priorities for wages, salaries, commissions, employee benefit plan contributions. §1204.
Assignment for benefit of creditors; Priority for money deposits. §1204.5.
Preference on transfer of business or stock in trade. §1205.
Preferred labor claim. §1206.
Sworn statement denying claim or portion thereof; Costs. §1207.
Payment of preferred labor claims. §1208.

§1204. Assignment for benefit of creditors; Priorities for wages, salaries, commissions, employee benefit plan contributions

When any assignment, whether voluntary or involuntary, and whether formal or informal, is made for the benefit of creditors of the assignor, or results from any proceeding in insolvency or receivership commenced against him or her, or when any property is turned over to the creditors of a person, firm, association or corporation, or to a receiver or trustee for the benefit of creditors, the following claims have priority in the following order:

(a) Allowed unsecured claims, but only to the extent of four thousand three hundred dollars ($4,300) for each individual or corporation, as the case may be, earned within 90 days before the date of the making of such assignment or the taking over of the property or the commencement of the court proceeding or the date of the cessation of the debtor's business, whichever occurs first, for either of the following:

(1) Wages, salaries, or commissions, including vacation, severance and sick leave pay earned by an individual.

(2) Sales commissions earned by an individual, or by a corporation with only one employee, acting as an independent contractor in the sale of goods or services of the debtor in the ordinary course of the debtor's business if, and only if, during the 12 months preceding the date of the making of the assignment or the taking over of the property or the commencement of the proceeding or the date of the cessation of the debtor's business, whichever occurs first, at least 75 percent of the amount that the individual or corporation earned by acting as an independent contractor in the sale of goods or services was earned from the debtor.

(b) Allowed unsecured claims for contributions to employee benefit plans arising from services rendered within 180 days before the date of the making of the assignment or the taking over of the property or the commencement of the court proceeding or the date of the cessation of the debtor's business, whichever occurs first; but only for each employee benefit plan, to the extent of the number of employees covered by the plan multiplied by four thousand three hundred dollars ($4,300), less the aggregate amount paid to the employees under subdivision (a), plus the aggregate amount paid by the estate on behalf of the employees to any other employee benefit plan.

(c) The above claims shall be paid by the trustee, assignee or receiver before the claim of any other creditor of the assignor, insolvent, or debtor whose property is so turned over, and shall be paid as soon as the money with which to pay same becomes available. If there is insufficient money to pay all the labor claims in full, the money available shall be distributed among the claimants in proportion to the amount of their respective claims. The trustee, receiver or assignee for the benefit of creditors shall have the right to require sworn claims to be presented and shall have the right to refuse to pay any such preferred claim, either in whole or in part, if he or she has reasonable cause to believe that a claim is not valid but shall pay any part thereof that is not disputed, without prejudice to the claimant's rights, as to the balance of his or her claim, and withhold sufficient money to cover the disputed portion until the claimant in question has a reasonable opportunity to establish the validity of his or her claim by court action, either in his or her own name or through an assignee.

(d) This section is binding upon all the courts of this state and in all receivership actions the court shall order the receiver to pay promptly out of the first receipts and earnings of the receivership, after paying the current operating expenses, such preferred labor claims. **Leg.H.** Added Stats 1907 ch 256 §1. Amended Stats 1931 ch 820 §1; Stats 1933 ch 175 §1; Stats 1945 ch 1192 §1; Stats 1951 ch 476 §1; Stats 1961 ch 1082 §1; Stats 1979 ch 394 §3, effective July 27, 1979, operative October 1, 1979; Stats 1999 ch 202 §1 (SB 219).

Prior Law: Former CCP §1204, relating to preferred creditors when assignment of property is made, was enacted 1872, amended by Code Amdts 1873–74 ch 383 §157, and repealed by Stats 1907 ch 256 §1.

§1204.5. Assignment for benefit of creditors; Priority for money deposits

In any general assignment for the benefit of creditors, the following claims shall have priority, subordinate to the priorities for labor claims under Section 1204, but prior to all other unsecured claims: allowed unsecured claims of individuals, to the extent of nine hundred dollars ($900) for each such individual, arising from the deposit, before the commencement of the case, of money in connection with the purchase, lease, or rental of property, or the purchase of services, for the personal, family, or household use of such individuals, that were not delivered or provided. The priority granted by this section shall be subordinate to that granted by Sections 18933 and 26312 of the Revenue and Taxation Code. **Leg.H.** Added Stats 1979 ch 394 §4, effective July 27, 1979, operative October 1, 1979. Amended Stats 1980 ch 135 §5.

§1205. Preference on transfer of business or stock in trade

Upon the sale or transfer of any business or the stock in trade, in bulk, or a substantial part thereof, not in the ordinary and regular course of business or trade, unpaid wages of employees of the seller or transferor earned within ninety (90) days prior to the sale, transfer, or opening of an escrow for the sale thereof, shall constitute preferred claims and liens thereon as between creditors of the seller or transferor and must be paid first from the proceeds of the sale or transfer. **Leg.H.** Added Stats 1961 ch 1083 §1.

Prior Law: Former CCP §1205, relating to preference of claims against deceased employer, was added by Stats 1907 ch 256 §1 and repealed by Stats 1931 ch 281.

Former CCP §1205, relating to preferred creditors against estates, was enacted 1872, amended by Code Amdts 1873–74 ch 383 §158, Stats 1893 ch 81 §1, and repealed by Stats 1907 ch 256 §1.

§1206. Preferred labor claim

(a) Upon the levy under a writ of attachment or execution not founded upon a claim for labor, any miner, mechanic, salesman, servant, clerk, laborer or other person who has performed work or rendered personal services for the defendant within 90 days prior to the levy may file a verified statement of the claim with the officer executing the writ, file a copy with the court that issued the writ, and give copies, containing his or her address, to the plaintiff and the defendant, or any attorney, clerk or agent representing them, or mail copies to them by registered mail at their last known address, return of which by the post office undelivered shall be deemed a sufficient service if no better address is available, and that claim, not exceeding nine hundred dollars ($900), unless disputed, shall be paid by the officer, immediately upon the expiration of the time for dispute of the claim as prescribed in Section 1207, from the proceeds of the levy remaining in the officer's hands at the time of the filing of the statement or collectible by the officer on the basis of the writ.

(b) The court issuing the writ shall make a notation in the register of actions of every preferred labor claim of which it receives a copy and shall endorse on any writ of execution or abstract of judgment issued subsequently in the case that it is issued subject to the rights of a preferred labor claimant or claimants and giving the names and amounts of all preferred labor claims of which it has notice. In levying under any writ of execution the officer making the levy shall include in the amount due under the execution all preferred labor claims that have been filed in the action and of which the officer has notice, except any claims that may have been finally disallowed by the court under this procedure and of which disallowance the officer has actual notice. The amount due on preferred labor claims that have not been finally disallowed by the court shall be considered a part of the sum due under any writ of attachment or execution in augmentation of that amount and any person, firm, association, or corporation on whom a writ of attachment or execution is levied shall immediately pay to the levying officer the amount of the preferred labor claims, out of any money belonging to the defendant in the action, before paying the principal sum called for in the writ.

(c) If any claim is disputed within the time, and in the manner prescribed in Section 1207, and a copy of the dispute is mailed by registered mail to the claimant or the claimant's attorney at the address given in the statement of claim and the registry receipt is attached to the original of the dispute when it is filed with the levying officer, or is handed to the claimant or the claimant's attorney, the claimant, or the claimant's assignee, must within 10 days after the copy is deposited in the mail or is handed to the claimant or the claimant's attorney, petition the court having jurisdiction of the action on which the writ is based, for a hearing before it to determine the claim for priority, or the claim to priority is barred. If more than one attachment or execution is involved, the petition shall be filed in the court having jurisdiction over the senior attachment or execution. The hearing shall be held within 20 days from the filing of the petition, unless the court continues it for good cause. Ten days' notice of the hearing shall be given by the petitioner to the plaintiff, the defendant, and all parties claiming an interest in the property, or their attorneys. The notice may be informal and need specify only the name of the court, the names of the principal parties to the senior attachment or execution, and the name of the wage claimant or claimants on whose behalf it is filed but shall specify that the hearing is for the purpose of determining the claim for priority. The plaintiff, the defendant, or any other party claiming an interest may contest the amount or validity of the claim in spite of any confession of judgment or failure to appear or to contest the claim on the part of any other person.

(d) There shall be no cost for filing or hearing the petition. The hearing on the petition shall be informal but all parties testifying shall be sworn. Any claimant may appear on the claimant's own behalf at the hearing and may call and examine witnesses to substantiate his or her claim. An appeal may be taken from a judgment in a proceeding under this section in the manner provided for appeals from judgments of the court where the proceeding occurred, in an action of the same jurisdictional classification.

(e) The officer shall keep, until the determination of the claim for priority, any amount of the proceeds of the writ necessary to satisfy the claim. If the claim for priority is allowed, the officer shall pay the amount due, including the claimant's cost of suit, from those proceeds, immediately after the order allowing the claim becomes final. **Leg.H.** Added Stats 1907 ch 256 §1. Amended Stats 1929 ch 230 §1; Stats 1931 ch 822 §1; Stats 1935 ch 557 §1; Stats 1951 ch 476 §2; Stats 1961 ch 1085 §1; Stats 1982 ch 497 §77, operative July 1, 1983; Stats 1998 ch 931 §121 (SB 2139), effective September 28, 1998; Stats 2001 ch 44 §7 (SB 562); Stats 2002 ch 664 §51 (AB 3034).

Prior Law: Former CCP §1206, relating to preferred creditors in case of execution or attachment, was enacted Stats 1872, amended Code Amdts 1873–74 ch 383 §159, Stats 1893 ch 77 §1, and repealed Stats 1907 ch 256 §1.

§1207. Sworn statement denying claim or portion thereof; Costs

Within five days after receiving a copy of the statement provided for in the next preceding section, either the plaintiff or the defendant in the action in which the writ issued may file with the officer a sworn statement denying that any part of such claim is due for services rendered within ninety days next preceding the levy of the writ, or denying that any part of such claim, beyond a sum specified, is so due. Such sworn statement cannot be made on information and belief unless the party swearing to same has actual information and belief that the wage claim, or the portion thereof that is contested, is not justly due, and in such case the nature and source of the information must be given. If a part of the claim is admitted to be due, and the claimant nevertheless files a petition for hearing and the court does not allow more than the amount so admitted, he cannot recover costs but the costs must be adjudged against him, and the amount thereof deducted from the sum found due him. **Leg.H.** Added Stats 1907 ch 256 §1. Amended Stats 1931 ch 822 §2; Stats 1935 ch 557 §2.

Prior Law: Former CCP §1207, relating to service of statement by debtor or creditor intending to dispute claim, was added by Stats 1883 ch 25 §1 and repealed by Stats 1907 ch 256 §1.

§1208. Payment of preferred labor claims

If the claims presented under Section 1206 and not disputed, or, if disputed, established by judgment, exceed the proceeds of the writ not disposed of before their presentation, such proceeds shall be distributed among the claimants in proportion to the amount of their respective claims after the costs incurred by the senior attaching plaintiff or judgment creditor in such action have first been taken care of.

If sufficient money to pay in full all preferred labor claims filed under an attachment or execution does not become available immediately upon the expiration of the time for dispute of such claims under Section 1207, any of the claimants, or their assignees, have the right to proceed directly against the money or other property levied on in individual or joint actions by themselves or their assignees against the defendant, and the attachment or execution under which the preferred claims were filed shall be considered set aside as far as such claimants, or their assignees, are concerned so as to enable them, or any of them, or any of their assignees, to proceed directly against any or all of the money or other property in question by means of their own attachments or executions; provided, however, that any money collected on behalf of any such labor claimant, or his or her assignee, on the basis of such new attachment or execution shall be shared in by the other preferred labor claimants who have filed claims that have not been disputed, or, if disputed, established by judgment, in proportion to the amount of their respective claims, deducting only the costs in the action brought by the said labor claimant, or his or her assignee, and the costs in the original action brought by the senior attaching plaintiff or judgment creditor.

If such senior attaching plaintiff or judgment creditor requests a release of his or her original attachment or execution, and the preferred labor claims filed under same are not released, the officer who levied the writ must first mail notices of such request to release to each of the labor claimants who have filed claims, or their attorneys, which notices must specify that unless the claimants bring attachment actions of their own and levy on the money or property in question within five days from the date thereof the money or property will be released from the attachment or execution; provided, however, that such officer may instead collect sufficient money on the basis of the original writ to pay off the preferred labor claims in full and then release the attachment or execution, but in no case shall the officer release the attachment or execution without first taking care of the labor claims until the five-day period has expired, unless the officer's costs, keepers' fees or storage charges have not been immediately taken care of by some of the parties involved. In any case it shall be lawful for a garnishee to pay over to the officer levying the writ any money held by the garnishee without waiting for execution to be levied and the officer's receipt for the money shall be a sufficient quittance, and the officer shall collect such money and immediately pay off the established preferred labor claims in all cases where it is possible to do so without additional court proceedings on the officer's part. **Leg.H.** Added Stats 1907 ch 256 §1. Amended Stats 1931 ch 822 §3; Stats 1982 ch 497 §78, operative July 1, 1983.

CHAPTER 4
CERTAIN LIENS UPON ANIMALS

Lien arising from prevention of cruelty to animals, and proceedings thereon. §1208.5.

§1208.5. Lien arising from prevention of cruelty to animals, and proceedings thereon

A person having a lien upon an animal or animals under the provisions of Section 597a or 597.1 of the Penal Code may satisfy the lien in any of the following ways:

(a) If the lien is not discharged and satisfied, by the person responsible, within three days after the obligation becomes due, the person holding the lien may resort to the proper court to satisfy the claim.

(b) Three days after the charges against the property become due, sell the property, or an undivided fraction thereof as may become necessary, to defray the amount due and costs of sale, by giving three days' notice of the sale by advertising in some newspaper published in the county, or city and county, in which the lien has attached to the property.

(c) If there is no newspaper published in the county, by posting notices of the sale in three of the most public places in the town or county for three days previous to the sale. The notices shall contain an accurate description of the property to be sold, together with the terms of sale, which shall be for cash, payable on the consummation of the sale. The proceeds of the sale shall be applied to the discharge of the lien and the costs of sale; the remainder, if any, shall be paid over to the owner, if known, and if not known shall be paid into the treasury of the humane society of the county, or city and county, where the sale takes place. If there is no humane society in the county, then the remainder shall be paid into the county treasury. **Leg.H.** Added Stats 1905 ch 472 §1, as CCP §1208. Amended Stats 1935 ch 104 §1. Renumbered by Stats 1943 ch 913 §1. Amended Stats 1951 ch 1737 §161, operative January 1, 1952; Stats 1980 ch 676 §67; Stats 2002 ch 784 §81 (SB 1316); Stats 2003 ch 62 §25 (SB 600); Stats 2019 ch 256 §2 (SB 781), effective January 1, 2020.

CHAPTER 5
LIENS ON AIRCRAFT

Existence and bases of lien. §1208.61.
Liens over $250; Required notice to, and consent of, legal owner and mortgagee. §1208.62.
Assignment of lien. §1208.63.
Revival and subordination of lien or repossession of aircraft after loss through fraud. §1208.64.
Sale to satisfy lien. §1208.65.
Notice of sale. §1208.66.
Disposition of sale's proceeds. §1208.67.
Redemption after sale. §1208.68.
Fraudulent taking of aircraft subject to lien; Misdemeanor. §1208.69.
Aircraft to which chapter applicable. §1208.70.

§1208.61. Existence and bases of lien

Subject to the limitations set forth in this chapter, every person has a lien dependent upon possession for the compensation to which he is legally entitled for making repairs or performing labor upon, and furnishing supplies or materials for, and for the storage, repair, or safekeeping of, any aircraft, also for reasonable charges for the use of any landing aid furnished such aircraft and reasonable landing fees. **Leg.H.** Added Stats 1953 ch 52 §8.

§1208.62. Liens over $250; Required notice to, and consent of, legal owner and mortgagee

That portion of such lien in excess of two hundred fifty dollars ($250) for work or services rendered or performed at the request of any person other than the holder of the legal title is invalid, unless prior to commencing such work or service the person claiming the lien gives actual notice to the legal owner and the mortgagee, if any, of the aircraft, and the written consent of the legal owner and the mortgagee of the aircraft is obtained before such work or services are performed. For the purposes of this chapter the person named in the federal aircraft registration certificate issued by the Administrator of Civil Aeronautics shall be deemed to be the legal owner. **Leg.H.** Added Stats 1953 ch 52 §8.

§1208.63. Assignment of lien

Any lien for labor or materials provided for in this chapter may be assigned by written instrument accompanied by delivery of possession of the aircraft subject to the lien and the assignee may exercise the rights of a lienholder pursuant to this chapter. Any lienholder assigning a lien shall at the time of the assignment give written notice, either by personal delivery or by registered mail with return receipt requested, to the legal owner of the property covered by the lien, including the name and address of the person to whom the lien is assigned. **Leg.H.** Added Stats 1953 ch 52 §8.

§1208.64. Revival and subordination of lien or repossession of aircraft after loss through fraud

Whenever the lien upon any aircraft is lost by reason of the loss of possession through trick, fraud, or device, the repossession of such aircraft by the lienholder revives the lien, but the lien so revived is subordinate to any right, title, or interest of any person under any sale, transfer, encumbrance, lien, or other interest acquired or secured in good faith and for value between the time of the loss of possession and the time of repossession. **Leg.H.** Added Stats 1953 ch 52 §8.

§1208.65. Sale to satisfy lien

If the lienholder is not paid the amount due within 10 days after it becomes due, the lienholder may proceed to sell the property, or so much thereof as is necessary to satisfy the lien and costs of sale, at public auction. **Leg.H.** Added Stats 1953 ch 52 §8.

§1208.66. Notice of sale

Prior to any such sale the lienholder shall publish a notice of the sale pursuant to Section 6062 of the Government Code in a newspaper published in the county in which the aircraft is situated, or if there is no such newspaper, by posting notice of sale in three of the most public places in the city or place where such aircraft is to be sold for 10 days previous to the date of the sale. Prior to the sale of any aircraft to satisfy any such lien, 20 days' notice by registered mail shall be given to the legal owner as it appears in the registration certificate. **Leg.H.** Added Stats 1953 ch 52 §8. Amended Stats 1957 ch 452 §1.

§1208.67. Disposition of sale's proceeds

The proceeds of the sale must be applied to the discharge of the lien and the cost of keeping and selling the property. The remainder, if any, shall be paid to the legal owner. **Leg.H.** Added Stats 1953 ch 52 §8.

§1208.68. Redemption after sale

Within 20 days after the sale, the legal owner may redeem the aircraft so sold upon the payment of the amount of the lien, all costs and expenses of sale, and interest on such sum at the rate of 12 percent a year from the date it became due or the date when the amounts were advanced until the repayment. **Leg.H.** Added Stats 1953 ch 52 §8.

§1208.69. Fraudulent taking of aircraft subject to lien; Misdemeanor

It is a misdemeanor for any person to obtain possession of all or any part of any aircraft subject to a lien under this chapter through surreptitious removal or by trick, fraud, or device perpetrated upon the lienholder. **Leg.H.** Added Stats 1953 ch 52 §8.

§1208.70. Aircraft to which chapter applicable

This chapter shall not apply to aircraft operated exclusively by an air carrier or a foreign air carrier, as defined in subdivisions (2) and (19) of Section 1 of Chapter 601 of the Statutes of the Seventy-fifth United States Congress, Second Session (1938), engaged in air transportation as defined in subdivision (10) of the same section while there is in force a certificate by, or a foreign air carrier permit of, the Civil Aeronautics Board of the United States, or its successor, authorizing such air carrier to engage in such transportation. **Leg.H.** Added Stats 1953 ch 52 §8.

TITLE 5
OF CONTEMPTS

Acts or omissions constituting contempt. §1209.
Proof respecting parent's noncompliance with order to furnish support as evidence of contempt. §1209.5.
Re-entry on property after dispossession by court's process; Proceedings on conviction for contempt. §1210.
Summary punishment of contempt in court's presence; Affidavit or statement when contempt not committed in court's presence. §1211.
Rules for construing, amending and reviewing affidavit or statement. §1211.5.
Issuance of warrant of attachment or commitment. §1212.
Warrant's endorsement permitting undertaking. §1213.
Duties of arresting officer. §1214.
Discharge upon execution and delivery of undertaking. §1215.
Officer must return warrant and undertaking, if any. §1216.
Court's investigation and hearing. §1217.
Determination of guilt; Punishment. §1218.
Contempt for failure to pay support; Period of limitations. §1218.5.
Imprisonment for omission to perform act; Refusal of victim to testify concerning sexual assault or domestic violence. §1219.
Refusal of minor to testify; Referral to probation officer; Report and recommendation by probation officer; Placement of minor. §1219.5.
Proceedings when person does not appear; Measure of damages in action on undertaking. §1220.
Excuses for not bringing in prisoner; Person not to be unnecessarily restrained. §1221.
Judgment and orders final and conclusive. §1222.

§1209. Acts or omissions constituting contempt

(a) The following acts or omissions in respect to a court of justice, or proceedings therein, are contempts of the authority of the court:

(1) Disorderly, contemptuous, or insolent behavior toward the judge while holding the court, tending to interrupt the due course of a trial or other judicial proceeding.

(2) A breach of the peace, boisterous conduct, or violent disturbance, tending to interrupt the due course of a trial or other judicial proceeding.

(3) Misbehavior in office, or other willful neglect or violation of duty by an attorney, counsel, clerk, sheriff, coroner, or other person, appointed or elected to perform a judicial or ministerial service.

(4) Abuse of the process or proceedings of the court, or falsely pretending to act under authority of an order or process of the court.

(5) Disobedience of any lawful judgment, order, or process of the court.

(6) Willful disobedience by a juror of a court admonishment related to the prohibition on any form of communication or research about the case, including all forms of electronic or wireless communication or research.

(7) Rescuing any person or property in the custody of an officer by virtue of an order or process of that court.

(8) Unlawfully detaining a witness or party to an action while going to, remaining at, or returning from the court where the action is on the calendar for trial.

(9) Any other unlawful interference with the process or proceedings of a court.

(10) Disobedience of a subpoena duly served, or refusing to be sworn or answer as a witness.

(11) When summoned as a juror in a court, neglecting to attend or serve as a juror, or improperly conversing with a party to an action to be tried at the court, or with any other person, in relation to the merits of the action, or receiving a communication from a party or other person in respect to the action, without immediately disclosing the communication to the court.

(12) Disobedience by an inferior tribunal or judicial officer of the lawful judgment, order, or process of a superior court, or proceeding in an action or special proceeding contrary to law, after the action or special proceeding is removed from the jurisdiction of the inferior tribunal or judicial officer.

(b) A speech or publication reflecting upon or concerning a court or an officer thereof shall not be treated or punished as a contempt of the court unless made in the immediate presence of the court while in session and in such a manner as to actually interfere with its proceedings.

(c) Notwithstanding Section 1211 or any other law, if an order of contempt is made affecting an attorney, his or her agent, investigator, or any person acting under the attorney's direction, in the preparation and conduct of an action or proceeding, the execution of any sentence shall be stayed pending the filing within three judicial days of a petition for extraordinary relief testing the lawfulness of the court's order, the violation of which is the basis of the contempt, except for conduct proscribed by subdivision (b) of Section 6068 of the Business and Professions Code, relating to an attorney's duty to maintain respect due to the courts and judicial officers.

(d) Notwithstanding Section 1211 or any other law, if an order of contempt is made affecting a public safety employee acting within the scope of employment for reason of the employee's failure to comply with a duly issued subpoena or subpoena duces tecum, the execution of any sentence shall be stayed pending the filing within three judicial days of a petition for extraordinary relief testing the lawfulness of the court's order, a violation of which is the basis for the contempt.

As used in this subdivision, "public safety employee" includes any peace officer, firefighter, paramedic, or any other employee of a public law enforcement agency whose duty is either to maintain official records or to analyze or present evidence for investigative or prosecutorial purposes. **Leg.H.** Enacted 1872. Amended Stats 1891 ch 9 §1; Stats 1907 ch 255 §1; Stats 1939 ch 979 §1; Stats 1975 ch 836 §2; Stats 1982 ch 510 §2; Stats 2011 ch 181 §3 (AB 141), effective January 1, 2012.

§1209.5. Proof respecting parent's noncompliance with order to furnish support as evidence of contempt

When a court of competent jurisdiction makes an order compelling a parent to furnish support or necessary food, clothing, shelter, medical attendance, or other remedial care for his or her child, proof that the order was made, filed, and served on the parent or proof that the parent was present in court at the time the order was pronounced and proof that the parent did not comply with the order is prima facie evidence of a contempt of court. **Leg.H.** Added Stats 1955 ch 1359 §1. Amended Stats 1961 ch 1307 §1, effective July 10, 1961; Stats 1992 ch 163 §57 (AB 2641), operative January 1, 1994.

§1210. Re-entry on property after dispossession by court's process; Proceedings on conviction for contempt

Every person dispossessed or ejected from any real property by the judgment or process of any court of competent jurisdiction, who, not having right so to do, reenters into or upon or takes possession of the real property, or induces or procures any person not having right so to do, or aids or abets such a person therein, is guilty of a contempt of the court by which the judgment was rendered or from which the process issued. Upon a conviction for contempt the court must immediately issue an alias process, directed to the proper officer, and requiring the officer to restore possession to the party entitled under the original judgment or process, or to the party's lessee, grantee, or successor in interest. No appeal from the order directing the issuance of an alias writ of possession stays the execution of the writ, unless an undertaking is executed on the part of the appellant to the effect that the appellant will not commit or suffer to be committed any waste on the property, and if the order is affirmed, or the appeal dismissed, the appellant will pay the value of the use and occupation of the property from the time of the unlawful reentry until the delivery of the possession of the property, pursuant to the judgment or order, not exceeding a sum to be fixed by the judge of the court by which the order for the alias writ was made. **Leg.H.** Enacted 1872. Amended Stats 1893 ch 198 §1; Stats 1907 ch 255 §2; Stats 1982 ch 517 §179.

§1211. Summary punishment of contempt in court's presence; Affidavit or statement when contempt not committed in court's presence

(a) When a contempt is committed in the immediate view and presence of the court, or of the judge at chambers, it may be punished summarily; for which an order must be made, reciting the facts as occurring in such immediate view and presence, adjudging that the person proceeded against is thereby guilty of a contempt, and that he or she be punished as therein prescribed.

When the contempt is not committed in the immediate view and presence of the court, or of the judge at chambers, an affidavit shall be presented to the court or judge of the facts constituting the contempt, or a statement of the facts by the referees or arbitrators, or other judicial officers.

(b) In family law matters, filing of the Judicial Council form entitled "Order to Show Cause and Affidavit for Contempt (Family Law)" shall constitute compliance with this section. **Leg.H.** Enacted 1872. Amended Stats 1933 ch 745 §11; Stats 1951 ch 1737 §162, operative January 1, 1952; Stats 1995 ch 904 §1 (AB 965); Stats 2001 ch 754 §1 (AB 1697).

§1211.5. Rules for construing, amending and reviewing affidavit or statement

At all stages of all proceedings, the affidavit or statement of facts, as the case may be, required by Section 1211 shall be construed, amended, and reviewed according to the following rules:

(a) If no objection is made to the sufficiency of such affidavit or statement during the hearing on the charges contained therein, jurisdiction of the subject matter shall not depend on the averments of such affidavit or statement, but may be established by the facts found by the trial court to have been proved at such hearing, and the court shall cause the affidavit or statement to be amended to conform to proof.

(b) The court may order or permit amendment of such affidavit or statement for any defect or insufficiency at any stage of the proceedings, and the trial of the person accused of contempt shall continue as if the affidavit or statement had been originally filed as amended, unless substantial rights of such person accused would be prejudiced thereby, in which event a reasonable postponement, not longer than the ends of justice require, may be granted.

(c) No such affidavit or statement is insufficient, nor can the trial, order, judgment, or other proceeding thereon be affected by reason of any defect or imperfection in matter of form which does not prejudice a substantial right of the person accused on the merits. No order or judgment of conviction of contempt shall be set aside, nor new trial granted, for any error as to any matter of pleading in such affidavit or statement, unless, after an examination of the entire cause, including the evidence, the court shall be of the opinion that the error complained of has resulted in a miscarriage of justice. **Leg.H.** Added Stats 1970 ch 1264 §1.

§1212. Issuance of warrant of attachment or commitment

When the contempt is not committed in the immediate view and presence of the court or judge, a warrant of attachment may be issued to bring the person charged to answer, or, without a previous arrest, a warrant of commitment may, upon notice, or upon an order to show cause, be granted; and no warrant of commitment can be issued without such previous attachment to answer, or such notice or order to show cause. **Leg.H.** Enacted 1872. Amended Stats 1933 ch 745 §12; Stats 1951 ch 1737 §163, operative January 1, 1952.

§1213. Warrant's endorsement permitting undertaking

Whenever a warrant of attachment is issued pursuant to this title the court or judge must direct, by an endorsement on the warrant, that the person charged may give an undertaking for the person's appearance in an amount to be specified in such endorsement. **Leg.H.** Enacted 1872. Amended Stats 1933 ch 745 §13; Stats 1951 ch 1737 §164, operative January 1, 1952; Stats 1982 ch 517 §179.5.

§1214. Duties of arresting officer

Upon executing the warrant of attachment, the officer executing the warrant must keep the person in custody, bring him before the court or judge, and detain him until an order be made in the premises, unless the person arrested entitle himself to be discharged, as provided in the next section. **Leg.H.** Enacted 1872. Amended Stats 1933 ch 745 §14; Stats 1951 ch 1737 §165, operative January 1, 1952.

§1215. Discharge upon execution and delivery of undertaking

The person arrested must be discharged from the arrest upon executing and delivering to the officer, at any time before the return day of the warrant, an undertaking to the effect that the person arrested will appear on the return of the warrant and abide the order of the court or judge thereupon. **Leg.H.** Enacted 1872. Amended Stats 1933 ch 745 §15; Stats 1951 ch 1737 §166, operative January 1, 1952; Stats 1982 ch 517 §180.

§1216. Officer must return warrant and undertaking, if any

The officer must return the warrant of arrest and undertaking, if any, received by him from the person arrested, by the return-day specified therein. **Leg.H.** Enacted 1872.

§1217. Court's investigation and hearing

When the person arrested has been brought up or appeared, the court or judge must proceed to investigate the charge, and must hear any answer which the person arrested may make to the same, and may examine witnesses for or against him, for which an adjournment may be had from time to time if necessary. **Leg.H.** Enacted 1872. Amended Stats 1933 ch 745 §16; Stats 1951 ch 1737 §167, operative January 1, 1952.

§1218. Determination of guilt; Punishment

(a) Upon the answer and evidence taken, the court or judge shall determine whether the person proceeded against is guilty of the contempt charged, and if it be adjudged that the person is guilty of the contempt, a fine may be imposed on the person not exceeding one thousand dollars ($1,000), payable to the court, or the person may be imprisoned not exceeding five days, or both. In addition, a person who is subject to a court order as a party to the action, or any agent of this person, who is adjudged guilty of contempt for violating that court order may be ordered to pay to the party initiating the contempt proceeding the reasonable attorney's fees and costs incurred by this party in connection with the contempt proceeding.

(b) Any party, who is in contempt of a court order or judgment in a dissolution of marriage, dissolution of domestic partnership, or legal separation action, shall not be permitted to enforce such an order or judgment, by way of execution or otherwise, either in the same action or by way of a separate action, against the other party. This restriction shall not affect nor apply to the enforcement of child or spousal support orders.

(c)(1) In any court action in which a party is found in contempt of court for failure to comply with a court order pursuant to the Family Code, the court shall, subject to the sentencing option provided in paragraph (2), order the following

(A) Upon a first finding of contempt, the court shall order the contemner to perform community service of up to 120 hours, or to be imprisoned up to 120 hours, for each count of contempt.

(B) Upon the second finding of contempt, the court shall order the contemner to perform community service of up to 120 hours, in addition to ordering imprisonment of the contemner up to 120 hours, for each count of contempt.

(C) Upon the third or any subsequent finding of contempt, the court shall order that the contemner serve a term of imprisonment of up to 240 hours and perform community service of up to 240 hours, for each count of contempt. The court shall also order the contemner to pay an administrative fee, not to exceed the actual cost of the contemner's administration and supervision, while assigned to a community service program pursuant to this paragraph.

(D) The court shall take parties' employment schedules into consideration when ordering either community service or imprisonment, or both.

(2) In lieu of an order of imprisonment, community service, or both, as set forth in paragraph (1), the court may grant probation or a conditional sentence for a period not to exceed one year upon a first finding of contempt, a period not to exceed two years upon a second finding of contempt, and a period not to exceed three years upon a third or any subsequent finding of contempt.

(3) For purposes of this subdivision, "probation" and "conditional sentence" shall have the meanings set forth in subdivision (a) of Section 1203 of the Penal Code.

(d) Pursuant to Section 1211 and this section, a district attorney or city attorney may initiate and pursue a court action for contempt against a party for failing to comply with a court order entered pursuant to the Domestic Violence Protection Act (Division 10 (commencing with Section 6200) of the Family Code). Any attorney's fees and costs ordered by the court pursuant to subdivision (a) against a party who is adjudged guilty of contempt under this subdivision shall be paid to the Office of Emergency Services' account established for the purpose of funding domestic violence shelter service providers pursuant to subdivision (f) of Section 13823.15 of the Penal Code. **Leg.H.** Enacted 1872. Amended Stats 1933 ch 745 §17; Stats 1951 ch 1737 §168, operative January 1, 1952; Stats 1968 ch 938 §2; Stats 1977 ch 1257 §39, effective October 3, 1977; Stats 1983 ch 1092 §72, effective September 27, 1983, operative January 1, 1984; Stats 1988 ch 969 §2; Stats 1993 ch 745 §1 (SB 788), ch 746 §1 (AB 934); Stats 1994 ch 368 §1 (AB 2911), ch 1269 §3.3 (AB 2208); Stats 1995 ch 576 §5.5 (AB 1225); Stats 2000 ch 808 §20 (AB 1358), effective September 28, 2000; Stats 2005 ch 75 §44 (AB 145), effective July 19, 2005, operative January 1, 2006, ch 631 §1 (SB 720), effective January 1, 2006; Stats 2010 ch 618 §3 (AB 2791), effective January 1, 2011; Stats 2013 ch 352 §56 (AB 1317), effective September 26, 2013, operative July 1, 2013; Stats 2020 ch 283 §1 (AB 2338), effective January 1, 2021.

§1218.5. Contempt for failure to pay support; Period of limitations

(a) If the contempt alleged is for failure to pay child, family, or spousal support, each month for which payment has not been made in full may be alleged as a separate count of contempt and punishment imposed for each count proven.

(b) If the contempt alleged is the failure to pay child, family, or spousal support, the period of limitations for commencing a contempt action is three years from the date that the payment was due. If the action before the court is enforcement of another order under the Family Code, the period of limitations for commencing a contempt action is two years from the time that the alleged contempt occurred. **Leg.H.** Added Stats 1994 ch 1269 §3.5 (AB 2208).

§1219. Imprisonment for omission to perform act; Refusal of victim to testify concerning sexual assault or domestic violence

(a) Except as provided in subdivisions (b) and (c), if the contempt consists of the omission to perform an act which is yet in the power of the person to perform, he or she may be imprisoned until he or she has performed it, and in that case the act shall be specified in the warrant of commitment.

(b) Notwithstanding any other law, a court shall not imprison or otherwise confine or place in custody the victim of a sexual assault or domestic violence crime for contempt if the contempt consists of refusing to testify concerning that sexual assault or domestic violence crime. Before finding a victim of a domestic violence crime in contempt as described in this section, the court may refer the victim for consultation with a domestic violence counselor. All communications between the victim and the domestic violence counselor that occur as a result of that referral shall remain confidential under Section 1037.2 of the Evidence Code.

(c) Notwithstanding any other law, a court shall not imprison, hold in physical confinement, or otherwise confine or place in custody a minor for contempt if the contempt consists of the minor's failure to comply with a court order pursuant to subdivision (b) of Section 601 of, or Section 727 of, the Welfare and Institutions Code, if the minor was adjudged a ward of the court on the ground that he or she is a person described in subdivision (b) of Section 601 of the Welfare and Institutions Code. Upon a finding of contempt of court, the court may issue any other lawful order, as necessary, to secure the minor's attendance at school.

(d) As used in this section, the following terms have the following meanings:

(1) "Sexual assault" means any act made punishable by Section 261, 262, 264.1, 285, 286, 287, 288, or 289 of, or former Section 288a of, the Penal Code.

(2) "Domestic violence" means "domestic violence" as defined in Section 6211 of the Family Code.

(3) "Domestic violence counselor" means "domestic violence counselor" as defined in subdivision (a) of Section 1037.1 of the Evidence Code.

(4) "Physical confinement" has the same meaning as defined in subdivision (d) of Section 726 of the Welfare and Institutions Code. **Leg.H.** Enacted 1872. Amended Stats 1980 ch 676 §68; Stats 1984 ch 1644 §2; Stats 1991 ch 866 §4 (AB 363); Stats 1992 ch 163 §58 (AB 2641), operative January 1, 1994; Stats 1993 ch 219 §69.7 (AB 1500); Stats 2008 ch 49 §1 (SB 1356), effective January 1, 2009; Stats 2009 ch 35 §3 (SB 174), effective January 1, 2010; Stats 2012 ch 510 §1 (AB 2051), effective January 1, 2013; Stats 2014 ch 70 §1 (SB 1296), effective January 1, 2015; Stats 2018 ch 423 §9 (SB 1494), effective January 1, 2019.

§1219.5. Refusal of minor to testify; Referral to probation officer; Report and recommendation by probation officer; Placement of minor

(a) Except as provided in subdivision (d), in any case in which a contempt consists of the refusal of a minor under 16 years of age to take the oath or to testify, before imposing any sanction for the contempt, the court shall first refer the matter to the probation officer in charge of matters coming before the juvenile court for a report and recommendation as to the appropriateness of the imposition of a sanction. The probation officer shall prepare and file the report and recommendation within the time directed by the court. In making the report and recommendation, the probation officer shall consider factors such as the maturity of the minor, the reasons for the minor's refusal to take the oath or to testify, the probability that available sanctions will affect the decision of the minor not to take the oath or not to testify, the potential impact on the minor of his or her testimony, the potential impact on the pending litigation of the minor's unavailability as a witness, and the appropriateness of the various available sanctions in the minor's case. The court shall consider the report and recommendation in imposing a sanction in the case.

(b) A victim of a sex crime who is subject to subdivision (a) shall meet with a victim advocate, as defined in Section 679.04 of the Penal Code, unless the court, for good cause, finds that it is not in the best interest of the victim.

(c) In any case in which the court orders the minor to be placed outside of his or her home, the placement shall be in the least restrictive setting available. Except as provided in subdivision (e), the court shall not order the minor to be placed in a secure facility unless other placements have been made and the minor has fled the custody and control of the person under the control of whom he or she has been placed or has persistently refused to obey the reasonable and proper orders or directions of the person under the control of whom he or she has been placed.

(d) The court may impose a sanction for contempt prior to receipt of the report and recommendation required by subdivision (a) if the court enters a finding, supported by specific facts stated on the record, that the minor would be likely to flee if released before the receipt of the report and recommendation.

(e) The court may order the minor placed in a secure facility without first attempting the nonsecure placement required by subdivision (c) if the court enters a finding, supported by specific facts stated on the record, that the minor would be likely to flee if released to nonsecure placement as a prerequisite to secure confinement. **Leg.H.** Added Stats 1984 ch 1643 §1. Amended Stats 2012 ch 223 §1 (SB 1248), effective January 1, 2013.

§1220. Proceedings when person does not appear; Measure of damages in action on undertaking

When the warrant of arrest has been returned served, if the person arrested does not appear on the return day, the court or judge may issue another warrant of arrest or may order the undertaking to be enforced, or both. If the undertaking is enforced, the measure of damages is the extent of the loss or injury sustained by the aggrieved party by reason of the misconduct for which the warrant was issued. **Leg.H.** Enacted 1872. Amended Stats 1933 ch 745 §18; Stats 1951 ch 1737 §169, operative January 1, 1952; Stats 1982 ch 517 §181.

§1221. Excuses for not bringing in prisoner; Person not to be unnecessarily restrained

Whenever, by the provisions of this title, an officer is required to keep a person arrested on a warrant of attachment in custody, and to bring him before a court or judge, the inability, from illness or otherwise, of the person to attend, is a sufficient excuse for not bringing him up; and the officer must not confine a person arrested upon the warrant in a prison, or otherwise restrain him of personal liberty, except so far as may be necessary to secure his personal attendance. **Leg.H.** Enacted 1872. Amended Stats 1933 ch 745 §19; Stats 1951 ch 1737 §170, operative January 1, 1952.

§1222. Judgment and orders final and conclusive

The judgment and orders of the court or judge, made in cases of contempt, are final and conclusive. **Leg.H.** Enacted 1872. Amended Stats 1933 ch 745 §20; Stats 1951 ch 1737 §171, operative January 1, 1952.

TITLE 6
VOLUNTARY DISSOLUTION OF CORPORATIONS [REPEALED]

§§1227–1230. [Sections superseded 1931]
Leg.H. Enacted 1872. Superseded Stats 1931 ch 862 §1. See Corp C §§1900 et seq.

TITLE 7
EMINENT DOMAIN LAW

Chapter 1. General Provisions.
Chapter 2. Principles of Construction; Definitions.
Chapter 3. The Right to Take.
Chapter 4. Precondemnation Activities.
Chapter 5. Commencement of Proceeding.
Chapter 6. Deposit and Withdrawal of Probable Compensation; Possession Prior to Judgment.
Chapter 7. Discovery; Exchange of Valuation Data.
Chapter 8. Procedures for Determining Right to Take and Compensation.
Chapter 9. Compensation.
Chapter 10. Divided Interests.
Chapter 11. Postjudgment Procedure.
Chapter 12. Arbitration of Compensation In Acquisitions of Property For Public Use.

CHAPTER 1
GENERAL PROVISIONS

Title. §1230.010.
Limit on exercise of power of eminent domain. §1230.020.
Acquisition of property for public use. §1230.030.
Rules of practice. §1230.040.
Power of court in eminent domain proceeding. §1230.050.
Jurisdiction of Public Utilities Commission. §1230.060.
Operative date; Application to pending proceedings. §1230.065.
Effect on prior judgments. §1230.070.

§1230.010. Title
This title shall be known and may be cited as the Eminent Domain Law. **Leg.H.** Added Stats 1975 ch 1275 §2, operative July 1, 1976.

§1230.020. Limit on exercise of power of eminent domain
Except as otherwise specifically provided by statute, the power of eminent domain may be exercised only as provided in this title. **Leg.H.** Added Stats 1975 ch 1275 §2, operative July 1, 1976.

§1230.030. Acquisition of property for public use
Nothing in this title requires that the power of eminent domain be exercised to acquire property necessary for public use. Whether property necessary for public use is to be acquired by purchase or other means or by eminent domain is a decision left to the discretion of the person authorized to acquire the property. **Leg.H.** Added Stats 1975 ch 1275 §2, operative July 1, 1976.

§1230.040. Rules of practice
Except as otherwise provided in this title, the rules of practice that govern civil actions generally are the rules of practice for eminent domain proceedings. **Leg.H.** Added Stats 1975 ch 1275 §2, operative July 1, 1976.

§1230.050. Power of court in eminent domain proceeding
The court in which a proceeding in eminent domain is brought has the power to:

(a) Determine the right to possession of the property, as between the plaintiff and the defendant, in accordance with this title.

(b) Enforce any of its orders for possession by appropriate process. The plaintiff is entitled to enforcement of an order for possession as a matter of right. **Leg.H.** Added Stats 1975 ch 1275 §2, operative July 1, 1976.

§1230.060. Jurisdiction of Public Utilities Commission
Nothing in this title affects any other statute granting jurisdiction over any issue in eminent domain proceedings to the Public Utilities Commission. **Leg.H.** Added Stats 1975 ch 1275 §2, operative July 1, 1976.

§1230.065. Operative date; Application to pending proceedings
(a) This title becomes operative July 1, 1976.

(b) This title does not apply to an eminent domain proceeding commenced prior to January 1, 1976. Subject to subdivisions (c) and (d), in the case of an eminent domain proceeding which is commenced on or after January 1, 1976, but prior to the operative date, this title upon the operative date applies to the proceeding to the fullest extent practicable with respect to issues to be tried or retried.

(c) Chapter 3 (commencing with Section 1240.010), Chapter 4 (commencing with Section 1245.010), and Chapter 5 (commencing with Section 1250.010) do not apply to a proceeding commenced prior to the operative date.

(d) If, on the operative date, an appeal, motion to modify or vacate the verdict or judgment, or motion for new trial is pending, the law applicable thereto prior to the operative date governs the determination of the appeal or motion. **Leg.H.** Added Stats 1975 ch 1275 §2, operative July 1, 1976.

§1230.070. Effect on prior judgments
No judgment rendered prior to the operative date of this title in a proceeding to enforce the right of eminent domain is affected by the enactment of this title and the repeal of former Title 7 of this part. **Leg.H.** Added Stats 1975 ch 1275 §2, operative July 1, 1976.

CHAPTER 2
PRINCIPLES OF CONSTRUCTION; DEFINITIONS

Article 1. Construction.
Article 2. Words and Phrases Defined.

ARTICLE 1
Construction

Construction of title. §1235.010.
Chapter, article, and section headings. §1235.020.
References applicable to amendments and additions. §1235.030.
Definitions. §1235.040.
Tenses. §1235.050.
"Shall" and "may". §1235.060.
Severability. §1235.070.

§1235.010. Construction of title
Unless the provision or context otherwise requires, these preliminary provisions and rules of construction shall govern the construction of this title. **Leg.H.** Added Stats 1975 ch 1275 §2, operative July 1, 1976.

§1235.020. Chapter, article, and section headings
Chapter, article, and section headings do not in any manner affect the scope, meaning, or intent of the provisions of this title. **Leg.H.** Added Stats 1975 ch 1275 §2, operative July 1, 1976.

§1235.030. References applicable to amendments and additions
Whenever any reference is made to any portion of this title or to any other statute, such reference shall apply to all amendments and additions heretofore or hereafter made. **Leg.H.** Added Stats 1975 ch 1275 §2, operative July 1, 1976.

§1235.040. Definitions
Unless otherwise expressly stated:

(a) "Chapter" means a chapter of this title.

(b) "Article" means an article of the chapter in which that term occurs.

(c) "Section" means a section of this code.

(d) "Subdivision" means a subdivision of the section in which that term occurs.

(e) "Paragraph" means a paragraph of the subdivision in which that term occurs. **Leg.H.** Added Stats 1975 ch 1275 §2, operative July 1, 1976.

§1235.050. Tenses
The present tense includes the past and future tenses; and the future, the present. **Leg.H.** Added Stats 1975 ch 1275 §2, operative July 1, 1976.

§1235.060. "Shall" and "may"
"Shall" is mandatory and "may" is permissive. **Leg.H.** Added Stats 1975 ch 1275 §2, operative July 1, 1976.

§1235.070. Severability
If any provision or clause of this title or application thereof to any person or circumstances is held invalid, the invalidity does not affect other provisions or applications of the title that can be given effect without the invalid provision or application, and to this end the provisions of this title are severable. **Leg.H.** Added Stats 1975 ch 1275 §2, operative July 1, 1976.

ARTICLE 2
Words and Phrases Defined

Definitions governing title. §1235.110.
"Final judgment". §1235.120.
"Interest". §1235.125.
"Judgment". §1235.130.
"Litigation expenses". §1235.140.
"Local public entity". §1235.150.
"Nonprofit, special use property". §1235.155.
"Person". §1235.160.
"Proceeding". §1235.165.
"Property". §1235.170.
"Property appropriated to public use". §1235.180.
"Public entity". §1235.190.
"Electric, gas, or water public utility property". §1235.193.
"Resolution". §1235.195.
"State". §1235.200.
"Statute". §1235.210.

§1235.110. Definitions governing title

Unless the provision or context otherwise requires, these definitions govern the construction of this title. **Leg.H.** Added Stats 1975 ch 1275 §2, operative July 1, 1976.

§1235.120. "Final judgment"

"Final judgment" means a judgment with respect to which all possibility of direct attack by way of appeal, motion for a new trial, or motion under Section 663 to vacate the judgment has been exhausted. **Leg.H.** Added Stats 1975 ch 1275 §2, operative July 1, 1976.

§1235.125. "Interest"

When used with reference to property, "interest" includes any right, title, or estate in property. **Leg.H.** Added Stats 1975 ch 1275 §2, operative July 1, 1976.

§1235.130. "Judgment"

"Judgment" means the judgment determining the right to take the property by eminent domain and fixing the amount of compensation to be paid by the plaintiff. **Leg.H.** Added Stats 1975 ch 1275 §2, operative July 1, 1976.

§1235.140. "Litigation expenses"

"Litigation expenses" includes both of the following:

(a) All expenses reasonably and necessarily incurred in the proceeding in preparing for trial, during trial, and in any subsequent judicial proceedings.

(b) Reasonable attorney's fees, appraisal fees, and fees for the services of other experts where such fees were reasonably and necessarily incurred to protect the defendant's interests in the proceeding in preparing for trial, during trial, and in any subsequent judicial proceedings whether such fees were incurred for services rendered before or after the filing of the complaint. **Leg.H.** Added Stats 1975 ch 1275 §2, operative July 1, 1976.

§1235.150. "Local public entity"

"Local public entity" means any public entity other than the state. **Leg.H.** Added Stats 1975 ch 1275 §2, operative July 1, 1976.

§1235.155. "Nonprofit, special use property"

"Nonprofit, special use property" means property which is operated for a special nonprofit, tax-exempt use such as a school, church, cemetery, hospital, or similar property. "Nonprofit, special use property" does not include property owned by a public entity. **Leg.H.** Added Stats 1992 ch 7 §1 (SB 821).

1992 Note: The changes made by this act shall apply to eminent domain actions or proceedings commenced on or after January 1, 1993. Stats 1992 ch 7 §7.

§1235.160. "Person"

"Person" includes any public entity, individual, association, organization, partnership, trust, limited liability company, or corporation. **Leg.H.** Added Stats 1975 ch 1275 §2, operative July 1, 1976. Amended Stats 1994 ch 1010 §63 (SB 2053).

§1235.165. "Proceeding"

"Proceeding" means an eminent domain proceeding under this title. **Leg.H.** Added Stats 1975 ch 1275 §2, operative July 1, 1976.

§1235.170. "Property"

"Property" includes real and personal property and any interest therein. **Leg.H.** Added Stats 1975 ch 1275 §2, operative July 1, 1976.

§1235.180. "Property appropriated to public use"

"Property appropriated to public use" means property either already in use for a public purpose or set aside for a specific public purpose with the intention of using it for such purpose within a reasonable time. **Leg.H.** Added Stats 1975 ch 1275 §2, operative July 1, 1976.

§1235.190. "Public entity"

"Public entity" includes the state, a county, city, district, public authority, public agency, and any other political subdivision in the state. **Leg.H.** Added Stats 1975 ch 1275 §2, operative July 1, 1976.

§1235.193. "Electric, gas, or water public utility property"

"Electric, gas, or water public utility property" means property appropriated to a public use by a public utility, as defined in Section 218, 222, or 241 of the Public Utilities Code. **Leg.H.** Added Stats 1992 ch 812 §1 (SB 1757).

§1235.195. "Resolution"

"Resolution" includes ordinance. **Leg.H.** Added Stats 1975 ch 1275 §2, operative July 1, 1976.

§1235.200. "State"

"State" means the State of California and includes the Regents of the University of California. **Leg.H.** Added Stats 1975 ch 1275 §2, operative July 1, 1976.

§1235.210. "Statute"

"Statute" means a constitutional provision or statute, but does not include a charter provision or ordinance. **Leg.H.** Added Stats 1975 ch 1275 §2, operative July 1, 1976.

§1237. [Section repealed 1976]

Leg.H. Enacted 1872. Repealed Stats 1975 ch 1275 §1, operative July 1, 1976.

§1238. [Section repealed 1976]

Leg.H. Enacted 1872. Amended Code Amdts 1873–74 ch 383 §160; Stats 1891 ch 50 §1; Stats 1893 ch 130 §1; Stats 1895 ch 98 §1; Stats 1897 ch 77 §1; Stats 1901 ch 57 §1; Stats 1905 ch 477 §1; Stats 1906 Ex Sess ch 50 §1; Stats 1907 ch 399 §1; Stats 1909 ch 682 §1; Stats 1911 ch 251 §1, ch 635 §1; Stats 1913 ch 291 §1; Stats 1915 ch 31 §1; Stats 1917 ch 57 §1; Stats 1921 ch 141 §1; Stats 1923 ch 64 §1; Stats 1925 ch 74 §1; Stats 1929 ch 241 §1; Stats 1935 ch 569 §1; Stats 1937 ch 193 §1; Stats 1938 Ex Sess ch 3 §1; Stats 1945 ch 251 §1; Stats 1957 ch 43 §8; Stats 1970 ch 662 §1. Repealed Stats 1975 ch 1275 §1, operative July 1, 1976.

§1238.1. [Section repealed 1976]

Leg.H. Added Stats 1945 ch 649 §1. Repealed Stats 1975 ch 1275 §1, operative July 1, 1976.

§1238.2. [Section repealed 1976]

Leg.H. Added Stats 1947 ch 744 §1, effective June 14, 1947. Repealed Stats 1975 ch 1275 §1, operative July 1, 1976.

§1238.3. [Section repealed 1976]

Leg.H. Added Stats 1951 ch 791 §1. Amended Stats 1974 ch 1018 §1, effective September 23, 1974. Repealed Stats 1975 ch 1275 §1, operative July 1, 1976.

§1238.4. [Section repealed 1976]

Leg.H. Added Stats 1955 ch 804 §1. Repealed Stats 1975 ch 1275 §1, operative July 1, 1976.

§1238.5. [Section repealed 1976]

Leg.H. Added Stats 1953 ch 52 §9. Repealed Stats 1975 ch 1275 §1, operative July 1, 1976.

§1238.6. [Section repealed 1976]

Leg.H. Added Stats 1957 ch 1395 §1. Repealed Stats 1975 ch 1275 §1, operative July 1, 1976.

§1238.7. [Section repealed 1976]

Leg.H. Added Stats 1957 ch 1136 §1. Repealed Stats 1975 ch 1275 §1, operative July 1, 1976.

§1239. [Section repealed 1976]

Leg.H. Enacted 1872. Amended Code Amdts 1873–74 ch 383 §161; Stats 1911 ch 356 §1; Stats 1913 ch 394 §1; Stats 1949 ch 978 §1. Repealed Stats 1975 ch 1275 §1, operative July 1, 1976.

§1239.2. [Section repealed 1976]

Leg.H. Added Stats 1945 ch 1242 §1. Repealed Stats 1975 ch 1275 §1, operative July 1, 1976.

§1239.3. [Section repealed 1976]

Leg.H. Added Stats 1965 ch 1564 §1. Repealed Stats 1975 ch 1275 §1, operative July 1, 1976.

§1239.4. [Section repealed 1976]

Leg.H. Added Stats 1945 ch 1242 §2. Amended Stats 1961 ch 965 §1. Repealed Stats 1975 ch 1275 §1, operative July 1, 1976.

§1240. [Section repealed 1976]

Leg.H. Enacted 1872. Amended Stats 1901 ch 144 §1; Stats 1905 ch 124 §1; Stats 1907 ch 271 §1; Stats 1911 ch 115 §1, ch 358 §1; Stats 1913 ch 292 §1; Stats 1915 ch 429 §1; Stats 1933 ch 465 §1; Stats 1967 ch 751 §1. Repealed Stats 1975 ch 1275 §1, operative July 1, 1976.

CHAPTER 3
THE RIGHT TO TAKE

Article 1. General Limitations on Exercise of Power of Eminent Domain.
Article 2. Rights Included in Grant of Eminent Domain Authority.
Article 3. Future Use.
Article 4. Substitute Condemnation.
Article 5. Excess Condemnation.
Article 6. Condemnation for Compatible Use.
Article 7. Condemnation for More Necessary Public Use.

ARTICLE 1
General Limitations on Exercise of Power of Eminent Domain

Exercise of power for public use. §1240.010.
Exercise of power by authorized person. §1240.020.
Conditions precedent to exercise of power. §1240.030.
Resolution of necessity. §1240.040.
Exercise of power by local public entity; Territorial limits. §1240.050.
Exercise of power to acquire property subject to conservation easement. §1240.055.

§1240.010. Exercise of power for public use

The power of eminent domain may be exercised to acquire property only for a public use. Where the Legislature provides by statute that a use, purpose, object, or function is one for which the power of eminent domain may be exercised, such action is deemed to be a declaration by the Legislature that such use, purpose, object, or function is a public use. **Leg.H.** Added Stats 1975 ch 1275 §2, operative July 1, 1976.

§1240.020. Exercise of power by authorized person

The power of eminent domain may be exercised to acquire property for a particular use only by a person authorized by statute to exercise the power of eminent domain to acquire such property for that use. **Leg.H.** Added Stats 1975 ch 1275 §2, operative July 1, 1976.

§1240.030. Conditions precedent to exercise of power

The power of eminent domain may be exercised to acquire property for a proposed project only if all of the following are established:
(a) The public interest and necessity require the project.
(b) The project is planned or located in the manner that will be most compatible with the greatest public good and the least private injury.
(c) The property sought to be acquired is necessary for the project.
Leg.H. Added Stats 1975 ch 1275 §2, operative July 1, 1976.

§1240.040. Resolution of necessity

A public entity may exercise the power of eminent domain only if it has adopted a resolution of necessity that meets the requirements of Article 2 (commencing with Section 1245.210) of Chapter 4. **Leg.H.** Added Stats 1975 ch 1275 §2, operative July 1, 1976.

§1240.050. Exercise of power by local public entity; Territorial limits

A local public entity may acquire by eminent domain only property within its territorial limits except where the power to acquire by eminent domain property outside its limits is expressly granted by statute or necessarily implied as an incident of one of its other statutory powers. **Leg.H.** Added Stats 1975 ch 1275 §2, operative July 1, 1976.

§1240.055. Exercise of power to acquire property subject to conservation easement

(a) As used in this section, the following terms have the following meanings:
(1) "Conservation easement" means a conservation easement as defined in Section 815.1 of the Civil Code and recorded as required by Section 815.5 of the Civil Code.
(2) "Holder of a conservation easement" means the entity or organization that holds the conservation easement on the property that is proposed for acquisition and that is authorized to acquire and hold conservation easements pursuant to Section 815.3 of the Civil Code.
(3) "Property appropriated to public use," as used in Article 6 (commencing with Section 1240.510) and Article 7 (commencing with Section 1240.610), includes a conservation easement if any of the following applies:
(A) The conservation easement is held by a public entity.
(B) A public entity provided funds, not including the value of a charitable contribution for federal or state income tax purposes but including the California Natural Heritage Preservation Tax Credit, for the acquisition of that easement.
(C) A public entity imposed conditions on approval or permitting of a project that were satisfied, in whole or in part, by the conservation easement.
(b) A person authorized to acquire property for public use by eminent domain shall exercise the power of eminent domain to acquire property that is subject to a conservation easement only as provided in this section.
(c) Not later than 105 days prior to the hearing held pursuant to Section 1245.235, or at the time of the offer made to the owner or owners of record pursuant to Section 7267.2 of the Government Code, whichever occurs earlier, the person seeking to acquire property subject to a conservation easement shall give notice to the holder of the conservation easement as provided in this subdivision. If the person is not required to hold a hearing pursuant to Section 1245.235, then the notice shall be given 105 days prior to the time of the offer made to the owner or owners of record pursuant to Section 7267.2 of the Government Code.
(1) The notice required by subdivision (c) shall be sent by first-class mail and shall state all of the following:
(A) A general description, in text or by diagram, of the property subject to a conservation easement that the person proposes to acquire by eminent domain.
(B) A description of the public use or improvement that the person is considering for the property subject to a conservation easement.
(C) That written comments on the acquisition may be submitted in accordance with paragraph (3) no later than 45 days from the date the person seeking to acquire the property mailed the notice to the holder of the conservation easement.
(D) That the holder of the conservation easement, within 15 days of receipt of the notice required by subdivision (c), is required, under certain circumstances, to do all of the following:
(i) Send a copy of the notice by first-class mail to each public entity that provided funds for the purchase of the easement or that imposed conditions on approval or permitting of a project that were satisfied, in whole or in part, by the creation of the conservation easement.
(ii) Inform the public entity that written comments on the acquisition may be submitted in accordance with paragraph (3).
(iii) Notify the person seeking to acquire the property of the name and address of any public entity that was sent a copy of the notice pursuant to this paragraph.
(2)(A) The holder of the conservation easement, within 15 days of receipt of the notice required by subdivision (c), shall do all of the following:
(i) Send a copy of the notice by first-class mail to each public entity that provided funds for the purchase of the easement or that imposed conditions on approval or permitting of a project that were satisfied, in whole or in part, by the creation of the conservation easement.
(ii) Inform the public entity that written comments on the acquisition may be submitted in accordance with paragraph (3).
(iii) Notify the person seeking to acquire the property of the name and address of any public entity that was sent a copy of the notice pursuant to this paragraph.
(B) Subparagraph (A) shall apply only if one of the following applies:

(i) The holder of the easement is the original grantee of the conservation easement and there is a public entity as described in subparagraph (A).

(ii) The holder of the easement has actual knowledge of a public entity as described in subparagraph (A).

(iii) Recorded documents evidence the identity of a public entity as described in subparagraph (A).

(3) The holder of the conservation easement or the public entity receiving notice, or both, may provide to the person seeking to acquire the property written comments on the acquisition, including identifying any potential conflict between the public use proposed for the property and the purposes and terms of the conservation easement. Written comments on the acquisition may be submitted no later than 45 days from the date the person seeking to acquire the property mailed the notice to the holder of the conservation easement.

(d) The person seeking to acquire the property subject to a conservation easement, within 30 days after receipt of written comments from the holder of the conservation easement or from a public entity described in paragraph (2) of subdivision (c), shall respond in writing to the comments. The response to the comments shall be mailed by first-class mail to each easement holder or public entity that filed comments.

(e) The notice of the hearing on the resolution of necessity, pursuant to Section 1245.235, shall be sent by first-class mail to the holder of any conservation easement and to any public entity whose name and address are provided as described in paragraph (2) of subdivision (c) and shall state that they have the right to appear and be heard on the matters referred to in Sections 1240.030, 1240.510, and 1240.610. The notice shall state that, pursuant to paragraph (3) of subdivision (b) of Section 1245.235, failure to file a written request to appear and be heard within 15 days after the notice was mailed will result in waiver of the right to appear and be heard. The resolution of necessity to acquire property subject to a conservation easement shall refer specifically either to Section 1240.510 or 1240.610 as authority for the acquisition of the property.

(f) In any eminent domain proceeding to acquire property subject to a conservation easement, the holder of the conservation easement:

(1) Shall be named as a defendant, as set forth in Section 1250.220.

(2) May appear in the proceedings, as set forth in Section 1250.230.

(3) Shall have all the same rights and obligations as any other defendant in the eminent domain proceeding.

(g)(1) The holder of the conservation easement is an owner of property entitled to compensation determined pursuant to Section 1260.220 and Chapter 9 (commencing with Section 1263.010) and in accordance with all of the following:

(A) The total compensation for the acquisition of all interests in property encumbered by a conservation easement shall not be less than, and shall not exceed, the fair market value of the fee simple interest of the property as if it were not encumbered by the conservation easement.

(B) If the acquisition does not damage the conservation easement, the total compensation shall be assessed by determining the value of all interests in the property as encumbered by the conservation easement.

(C) If the acquisition damages the conservation easement in whole or in part, compensation shall be determined consistent with Section 1260.220 and the value of the fee simple interest of the property shall be assessed as if it were not encumbered by the conservation easement.

(2) This subdivision shall not apply if the requirements of Section 10261 of the Public Resources Code apply.

(h) This section shall not apply if the requirements of Section 1348.3 of the Fish and Game Code apply. **Leg.H.** Added Stats 2011 ch 589 §2 (SB 328), effective January 1, 2012.

2011 Note: It is the intent of the Legislature to encourage the parties in an eminent domain proceeding to acquire property that is subject to a conservation easement to consult early in the process to assist the parties in identifying potential significant effects of the proposed acquisition and the feasible alternatives or feasible mitigation measures that will avoid or substantially lessen significant effects on the conservation easement in order to avoid delays in the eminent domain proceeding. Stats 2011 ch 589 (SB 328) §1.

ARTICLE 2
Rights Included in Grant of Eminent Domain Authority

Interests in property which may be acquired. §1240.110.
Property necessary to carry out principal purpose; Acquisition with intent to sell or otherwise dispose of property. §1240.120.
Local public entities; Property outside territorial limits; Purpose of acquisition. §1240.125.
Acquisition of property by other means. §1240.130.
Joint exercise of power by public agencies. §1240.140.
Acquisition of remainder of property. §1240.150.
Authorizations distinct and separate. §1240.160.

§1240.110. Interests in property which may be acquired

(a) Except to the extent limited by statute, any person authorized to acquire property for a particular use by eminent domain may exercise the power of eminent domain to acquire any interest in property necessary for that use including, but not limited to, submerged lands, rights of any nature in water, subsurface rights, airspace rights, flowage or flooding easements, aircraft noise or operation easements, right of temporary occupancy, public utility facilities and franchises, and franchises to collect tolls on a bridge or highway.

(b) Where a statute authorizes the acquisition by eminent domain only of specified interests in or types of property, this section does not expand the scope of the authority so granted. **Leg.H.** Added Stats 1975 ch 1275 §2, operative July 1, 1976.

§1240.120. Property necessary to carry out principal purpose; Acquisition with intent to sell or otherwise dispose of property

(a) Subject to any other statute relating to the acquisition of property, any person authorized to acquire property for a particular use by eminent domain may exercise the power of eminent domain to acquire property necessary to carry out and make effective the principal purpose involved including but not limited to property to be used for the protection or preservation of the attractiveness, safety, and usefulness of the project.

(b) Subject to any applicable procedures governing the disposition of property, a person may acquire property under subdivision (a) with the intent to sell, lease, exchange, or otherwise dispose of the property, or an interest therein, subject to such reservations or restrictions as are necessary to protect or preserve the attractiveness, safety, and usefulness of the project. **Leg.H.** Added Stats 1975 ch 1275 §2, operative July 1, 1976.

§1240.125. Local public entities; Property outside territorial limits; Purpose of acquisition

Except as otherwise expressly provided by statute and subject to any limitations imposed by statute, a local public entity may acquire property by eminent domain outside its territorial limits for water, gas, or electric supply purposes or for airports, drainage or sewer purposes if it is authorized to acquire property by eminent domain for the purposes for which the property is to be acquired. **Leg.H.** Added Stats 1975 ch 1275 §2, operative July 1, 1976.

§1240.126. [Section repealed 1997]

Leg.H. Added Stats 1991 ch 644 §1 (AB 613), operative until January 1, 1997. Repealed January 1, 1997, by its own terms. The repealed section related to acquisition by city of unincorporated property by eminent domain for park purposes.

§1240.130. Acquisition of property by other means

Subject to any other statute relating to the acquisition of property, any public entity authorized to acquire property for a particular use by eminent domain may also acquire such property for such use by grant, purchase, lease, gift, devise, contract, or other means. **Leg.H.** Added Stats 1975 ch 1275 §2, operative July 1, 1976.

§1240.140. Joint exercise of power by public agencies

(a) As used in this section, "public agencies" includes all those agencies included within the definition of "public agency" in Section 6500 of the Government Code.

(b) Two or more public agencies may enter into an agreement for the joint exercise of their respective powers of eminent domain, whether or not possessed in common, for the acquisition of property as a single parcel. Such agreement shall be entered into and performed pursuant to the provisions of Chapter 5 (commencing with Section 6500) of Division 7 of Title 1 of the Government Code. **Leg.H.** Added Stats 1975 ch 1275 §2, operative July 1, 1976.

§1240.150. Acquisition of remainder of property

Whenever a part of a larger parcel of property is to be acquired by a public entity for public use and the remainder, or a portion of the remainder, will be left in such size, shape, or condition as to be of little value to its owners or to give rise to a claim for severance or other damages, the public entity may acquire the remainder, or portion of the remainder, by any means (including eminent domain) expressly consented to by the owner. **Leg.H.** Added Stats 1975 ch 1275 §2, operative July 1, 1976.

§1240.160. Authorizations distinct and separate

(a) None of the provisions of this article is intended to limit, or shall limit, any other provision of this article, each of which is a distinct and separate authorization.

(b) None of the provisions of Article 2 (commencing with Section 1240.110), Article 3 (commencing with Section 1240.210), Article 4 (commencing with Section 1240.310), Article 5 (commencing with Section 1240.410), Article 6 (commencing with Section 1240.510), or Article 7 (commencing with Section 1240.610) is intended to limit, or shall limit, the provisions of any other of the articles, each of which articles is a distinct and separate authorization. **Leg.H.** Added Stats 1975 ch 1275 §2, operative July 1, 1976.

ARTICLE 3
Future Use

"Date of use". §1240.210.
Acquisition of property for future use. §1240.220.
Burden of proof. §1240.230.
Consent of owner. §1240.240.
Property taken pursuant to Federal Aid Highway Act of 1973. §1240.250.

§1240.210. "Date of use"

For the purposes of this article, the "date of use" of property taken for public use is the date when the property is devoted to that use or when construction is started on the project for which the property is taken with the intent to complete the project within a reasonable time. In determining the "date of use," periods of delay caused by extraordinary litigation or by failure to obtain from any public entity any agreement or permit necessary for construction shall not be included. **Leg.H.** Added Stats 1975 ch 1275 §2, operative July 1, 1976.

§1240.220. Acquisition of property for future use

(a) Any person authorized to acquire property for a particular use by eminent domain may exercise the power of eminent domain to acquire property to be used in the future for that use, but property may be taken for future use only if there is a reasonable probability that its date of use will be within seven years from the date the complaint is filed or within such longer period as is reasonable.

(b) Unless the plaintiff plans that the date of use of property taken will be within seven years from the date the complaint is filed, the complaint, and the resolution of necessity if one is required, shall refer specifically to this section and shall state the estimated date of use. **Leg.H.** Added Stats 1975 ch 1275 §2, operative July 1, 1976.

§1240.230. Burden of proof

(a) If the defendant objects to a taking for future use, the burden of proof is as prescribed in this section.

(b) Unless the complaint states an estimated date of use that is not within seven years from the date the complaint is filed, the defendant has the burden of proof that there is no reasonable probability that the date of use will be within seven years from the date the complaint is filed.

(c) If the defendant proves that there is no reasonable probability that the date of use will be within seven years from the date the complaint is filed, or if the complaint states an estimated date of use that is not within seven years from the date the complaint is filed, the plaintiff has the burden of proof that a taking for future use satisfies the requirements of this article. **Leg.H.** Added Stats 1975 ch 1275 §2, operative July 1, 1976.

§1240.240. Consent of owner

Notwithstanding any other provision of this article, any public entity authorized to acquire property for a particular use by eminent domain may acquire property to be used in the future for that use by any means (including eminent domain) expressly consented to by its owner. **Leg.H.** Added Stats 1975 ch 1275 §2, operative July 1, 1976.

§1240.250. Property taken pursuant to Federal Aid Highway Act of 1973

Notwithstanding any other provision of this article, where property is taken pursuant to the Federal Aid Highway Act of 1973:

(a) A date of use within 10 years from the date the complaint is filed shall be deemed reasonable.

(b) The resolution of necessity and the complaint shall indicate that the taking is pursuant to the Federal Aid Highway Act of 1973 and shall state the estimated date of use.

(c) If the defendant objects to the taking, the defendant has the burden of proof that there is no reasonable probability that the date of use will be within 10 years from the date the complaint is filed. If the defendant proves that there is no reasonable probability that the date of use will be within 10 years from the date the complaint is filed, the plaintiff has the burden of proof that the taking satisfies the requirements of this article. **Leg.H.** Added Stats 1975 ch 1275 §2, operative July 1, 1976.

ARTICLE 4
Substitute Condemnation

Definitions. §1240.310.
Acquisition of substitute property. §1240.320.
Necessary property devoted to public use; Relocation. §1240.330.
Acquisition of property necessary to provide utility service or access to public road. §1240.350.

§1240.310. Definitions

As used in this article:

(a) "Necessary property" means property to be used for a public use for which the public entity is authorized to acquire property by eminent domain.

(b) "Substitute property" means property to be exchanged for necessary property. **Leg.H.** Added Stats 1975 ch 1275 §2, operative July 1, 1976.

§1240.320. Acquisition of substitute property

(a) Any public entity authorized to exercise the power of eminent domain to acquire property for a particular use may exercise the power of eminent domain to acquire for that use substitute property if all of the following are established:

(1) The owner of the necessary property has agreed in writing to the exchange.

(2) The necessary property is devoted to or held for some public use and the substitute property will be devoted to or held for the same public use by the owner of the necessary property.

(3) The owner of the necessary property is authorized to exercise the power of eminent domain to acquire the substitute property for such use.

(b) Where property is sought to be acquired pursuant to this section, the resolution of necessity and the complaint filed pursuant to such resolution shall specifically refer to this section and shall include a statement that the property is necessary for the purpose specified in this section. The determination in the resolution that the taking of the substitute property is necessary has the effect prescribed in Section 1245.250. **Leg.H.** Added Stats 1975 ch 1275 §2, operative July 1, 1976.

§1240.330. Necessary property devoted to public use; Relocation

(a) Where necessary property is devoted to public use, any public entity authorized to exercise the power of eminent domain to acquire such property for a particular use may exercise the power of eminent domain to acquire substitute property in its own name, relocate on such substitute property the public use to which necessary property is devoted, and thereafter convey the substitute property to the owner of the necessary property if all of the following are established:

(1) The public entity is required by court order or judgment in an eminent domain proceeding, or by agreement with the owner of the necessary property, to relocate the public use to which the necessary property is devoted and thereafter to convey the property upon which the public use has been relocated to the owner of the necessary property.

(2) The substitute property is necessary for compliance with the court order or judgment or agreement.

(3) The owner of the necessary property will devote the substitute property to the public use being displaced from the necessary property.

(b) Where property is sought to be acquired pursuant to this section, the resolution of necessity and the complaint filed pursuant to such resolution shall specifically refer to this section and shall include a statement that the property is necessary for the purpose specified in this section. The determination in the resolution that the taking of the substitute property is necessary has the effect prescribed in Section 1245.250. **Leg.H.** Added Stats 1975 ch 1275 §2, operative July 1, 1976.

§1240.350. Acquisition of property necessary to provide utility service or access to public road

(a) Whenever a public entity acquires property for a public use and exercises or could have exercised the power of eminent domain to acquire such property for such use, the public entity may exercise the power of eminent domain to acquire such additional property as appears reasonably necessary and appropriate (after taking into account any hardship to the owner of the additional property) to provide utility service to, or access to a public road from, any property that is not acquired for such public use but which is cut off from utility service or access to a public road as a result of the acquisition by the public entity.

(b) Where property is sought to be acquired pursuant to this section, the resolution of necessity and the complaint filed pursuant to such resolution shall specifically refer to this section and shall include a statement that the property is necessary for the purpose specified in this section. The determination in the resolution that the taking of the substitute property is necessary has the effect prescribed in Section 1245.250. **Leg.H.** Added Stats 1975 ch 1275 §2, operative July 1, 1976.

ARTICLE 5
Excess Condemnation

Acquisition of remnant. §1240.410.
Resolution of necessity and complaint. §1240.420.
Disposition of remnant. §1240.430.

§1240.410. Acquisition of remnant

(a) As used in this section, "remnant" means a remainder or portion thereof that will be left in such size, shape, or condition as to be of little market value.

(b) Whenever the acquisition by a public entity by eminent domain of part of a larger parcel of property will leave a remnant, the public entity may exercise the power of eminent domain to acquire the remnant in accordance with this article.

(c) Property may not be acquired under this section if the defendant proves that the public entity has a reasonable, practicable, and economically sound means to prevent the property from becoming a remnant. **Leg.H.** Added Stats 1975 ch 1275 §2, operative July 1, 1976.

§1240.420. Resolution of necessity and complaint

When property is sought to be acquired pursuant to Section 1240.410, the resolution of necessity and the complaint filed pursuant to such resolution shall specifically refer to that section. It shall be presumed from the adoption of the resolution that the taking of the property is authorized under Section 1240.410. This presumption is a presumption affecting the burden of producing evidence. **Leg.H.** Added Stats 1975 ch 1275 §2, operative July 1, 1976.

§1240.430. Disposition of remnant

A public entity may sell, lease, exchange, or otherwise dispose of property taken under this article and may credit the proceeds to the fund or funds available for acquisition of the property being acquired for the public work or improvement. Nothing in this section relieves a public entity from complying with any applicable statutory procedures governing the disposition of property. **Leg.H.** Added Stats 1975 ch 1275 §2, operative July 1, 1976.

ARTICLE 6
Condemnation for Compatible Use

Acquisition of property appropriated to public use for compatible use. §1240.510.
Burden of proof. §1240.520.
Terms and conditions. §1240.530.

§1240.510. Acquisition of property appropriated to public use for compatible use

Any person authorized to acquire property for a particular use by eminent domain may exercise the power of eminent domain to acquire for that use property appropriated to public use if the proposed use will not unreasonably interfere with or impair the continuance of the public use as it then exists or may reasonably be expected to exist in the future. Where property is sought to be acquired pursuant to this section, the complaint, and the resolution of necessity if one is required, shall refer specifically to this section. **Leg.H.** Added Stats 1975 ch 1275 §2, operative July 1, 1976.

§1240.520. Burden of proof

If the defendant objects to a taking under Section 1240.510, the defendant has the burden of proof that his property is appropriated to public use. If it is established that the property is appropriated to public use, the plaintiff has the burden of proof that its proposed use satisfies the requirements of Section 1240.510. **Leg.H.** Added Stats 1975 ch 1275 §2, operative July 1, 1976.

§1240.530. Terms and conditions

(a) Where property is taken under Section 1240.510, the parties shall make an agreement determining the terms and conditions upon which the property is taken and the manner and extent of its use by each of the parties. Except as otherwise provided by statute, if the parties are unable to agree, the court shall fix the terms and conditions upon which the property is taken and the manner and extent of its use by each of the parties.

(b) If the court determines that the use in the manner proposed by the plaintiff would not satisfy the requirements of Section 1240.510, the court shall further determine whether the requirements of Section 1240.510 could be satisfied by fixing terms and conditions upon which the property may be taken. If the court determines that the requirements of Section 1240.510 could be so satisfied, the court shall permit the plaintiff to take the property upon such terms and conditions and shall prescribe the manner and extent of its use by each of the parties.

(c) Where property is taken under this article, the court may order any necessary removal or relocation of structures or improvements if such removal or relocation would not require any significant alteration of the use to which the property is appropriated. Unless otherwise provided by statute, all costs and damages that result from the relocation or removal shall be paid by the plaintiff. **Leg.H.** Added Stats 1975 ch 1275 §2, operative July 1, 1976.

ARTICLE 7
Condemnation for More Necessary Public Use

Acquisition of property appropriated for public use for more necessary public use. §1240.610.
Burden of proof. §1240.620.
Continuation of use to which property is appropriated. §1240.630.
Presumption; Use by the state. §1240.640.
More necessary uses. §1240.650.
Golden State Energy acquistion of property. § 1240.655.
Presumption; Property appropriated to public use by local public entity. §1240.660.
Presumption; Appropriation for best and most necessary public use. §1240.670.
Uses giving rise to presumption of appropriation for best and most necessary public use. §1240.680.
Acquisition for state highway purposes; Declaratory relief. §1240.690.
Acquisition for city or county road, street, or highway purposes; Declaratory relief. §1240.700.

§1240.610. Acquisition of property appropriated for public use for more necessary public use

Any person authorized to acquire property for a particular use by eminent domain may exercise the power of eminent domain to acquire for that use property appropriated to public use if the use for which the property is sought to be taken is a more necessary public use than the use to which the property is appropriated. Where property is sought to be acquired pursuant to this section, the complaint, and the resolution of necessity if one is required, shall refer specifically to this section. **Leg.H.** Added Stats 1975 ch 1275 §2, operative July 1, 1976.

§1240.620. Burden of proof

If the defendant objects to a taking under Section 1240.610, the defendant has the burden of proof that his property is appropriated to public use. If it is established that the property is appropriated to public use, the plaintiff has the burden of proof that its use satisfies the requirements of Section 1240.610. **Leg.H.** Added Stats 1975 ch 1275 §2, operative July 1, 1976.

§1240.630. Continuation of use to which property is appropriated

(a) Where property is sought to be taken under Section 1240.610, the defendant is entitled to continue the public use to which the property is appropriated if the continuance of such use will not unreasonably interfere with or impair, or require a significant alteration of, the more necessary public use as it is then planned or exists or may reasonably be expected to exist in the future.

(b) If the defendant objects to a taking under this article on the ground that he is entitled under subdivision (a) to continue the public use to which the property is appropriated, upon motion of either party, the court shall determine whether the defendant is entitled under subdivision (a) to continue the use to which the property is appropriated; and, if the court determines that the defendant is so entitled, the parties shall make an agreement determining the terms and conditions upon which the defendant may continue the public use to which the property is appropriated, the terms and conditions upon which the property taken by the plaintiff is acquired, and the manner and extent of the use of the property by each of the parties. Except as otherwise provided by statute, if the parties are unable to agree, the court shall fix such terms and conditions and the manner and extent of the use of the property by each of the parties. **Leg.H.** Added Stats 1975 ch 1275 §2, operative July 1, 1976.

§1240.640. Presumption; Use by the state

(a) Where property has been appropriated to public use by any person other than the state, the use thereof by the state for the same use or any other public use is presumed to be a more necessary use than the use to which such property has already been appropriated.

(b) Where property has been appropriated to public use by the state, the use thereof by the state is presumed to be a more necessary use than any use to which such property might be put by any other person.

(c) The presumptions established by this section are presumptions affecting the burden of proof. **Leg.H.** Added Stats 1975 ch 1275 §2, operative July 1, 1976.

§1240.650. More necessary uses

(a) Where property has been appropriated to public use by any person other than a public entity, the use thereof by a public entity for the same use or any other public use is a more necessary use than the use to which such property has already been appropriated.

(b) Where property has been appropriated to public use by a public entity, the use thereof by the public entity is a more necessary use than any use to which such property might be put by any person other than a public entity.

(c) Where property which has been appropriated to a public use is electric, gas, or water public utility property which the public entity intends to put to the same use, the presumption of a more necessary use established by subdivision (a) is a rebuttable presumption affecting the burden of proof, unless the acquiring public entity is a sanitary district exercising the powers of a county water district pursuant to Section 6512.7 of the Health and Safety Code. **Leg.H.** Added Stats 1975 ch 1275 §2, operative July 1, 1976. Amended Stats 1992 ch 812 §2 (SB 1757).

§ 1240.655. Golden State Energy acquistion of property

(a) If Golden State Energy commences an eminent domain action to acquire Pacific Gas and Electric Company property, including any franchise rights and stock, pursuant to Section 713 of the Public Utilities Code, that acquisition is for a more necessary public use pursuant to Section 1240.610. Golden State Energy may exclude from the acquisition only property not directly related to providing electrical or gas service.

(b) For purposes of this section, the following definitions apply:

(1) "Golden State Energy" has the same meaning as defined in Section 222.5 of the Public Utilities Code.

(2) "Pacific Gas and Electric Company" means Pacific Gas and Electric Company, PG&E Corporation, any subsidiary or affiliate of the foregoing holding any assets related to the provision of electrical or gas service within Pacific Gas and Electric Company's service territory, and any successor to any of the foregoing. **Leg.H.** Added Stats 2020 ch 27 §3 (SB 350), effective January 1, 2021.

§1240.660. Presumption; Property appropriated to public use by local public entity

Where property has been appropriated to public use by a local public entity, the use thereof by the local public entity is presumed to be a more necessary use than any use to which such property might be put by any other local public entity. The presumption established by this section is a presumption affecting the burden of proof. **Leg.H.** Added Stats 1975 ch 1275 §2, operative July 1, 1976.

§1240.670. Presumption; Appropriation for best and most necessary public use

(a) Subject to Section 1240.690, notwithstanding any other provision of law, property is presumed to have been appropriated for the best and most necessary public use if all of the following are established:

(1) The property is owned by a nonprofit organization contributions to which are deductible for state and federal income tax purposes under the laws of this state and of the United States and having the primary purpose of preserving areas in their natural condition.

(2) The property is open to the public subject to reasonable restrictions and is appropriated, and used exclusively, for the preservation of native plants or native animals including, but not limited to, mammals, birds, and marine life, or biotic communities, or geological or geographical formations of scientific or educational interest.

(3) The property is irrevocably dedicated to such uses so that, upon liquidation, dissolution, or abandonment of or by the owner, such property will be distributed only to a fund, foundation, or corporation whose property is likewise irrevocably dedicated to such uses, or to a governmental agency holding land for such uses.

(b) The presumption established by this section is a presumption affecting the burden of proof. **Leg.H.** Added Stats 1975 ch 1275 §2, operative July 1, 1976.

§1240.680. Uses giving rise to presumption of appropriation for best and most necessary public use

(a) Subject to Sections 1240.690 and 1240.700, notwithstanding any other provision of law, property is presumed to have been appropriated for the best and most necessary public use if the property is appropriated to public use as any of the following:

(1) A state, regional, county, or city park, open space, or recreation area.

(2) A wildlife or waterfowl management area established by the Department of Fish and Game pursuant to Section 1525 of the Fish and Game Code.

(3) A historic site included in the National Register of Historic Places or state-registered landmarks.

(4) An ecological reserve as provided for in Article 4 (commencing with Section 1580) of Chapter 5 of Division 2 of the Fish and Game Code.

(b) The presumption established by this section is a presumption affecting the burden of proof. **Leg.H.** Added Stats 1975 ch 1275 §3, operative July 1, 1976.

§1240.690. Acquisition for state highway purposes; Declaratory relief

(a) When property described in Section 1240.670 or 1240.680 is sought to be acquired for state highway purposes, and the property was dedicated or devoted to a use described in those sections prior to the initiation of highway route location studies, an action for declaratory relief may be brought by the public entity or nonprofit organization owning the property in the superior court to determine the question of which public use is the best and most necessary public use for the property.

(b) The action for declaratory relief shall be filed and served within 120 days after the California Transportation Commission has published in a newspaper of general circulation pursuant to Section 6061 of the Government Code, and delivered to the public entity or nonprofit organization owning the property a written notice that a proposed route or an adopted route includes the property. In the case of nonprofit organizations, the written notice need only be given to nonprofit organizations that are on file with the Registrar of Charitable Trusts of this state.

(c) In the declaratory relief action, the resolution of the California Transportation Commission is not conclusive evidence of the matters set forth in Section 1240.030.

(d) With respect to property described in Section 1240.670 or 1240.680 which is sought to be acquired for state highway purposes:

(1) If an action for declaratory relief is not filed and served within the 120-day period established by subdivision (b), the right to bring the action is waived and Sections 1240.670 and 1240.680 do not apply.

(2) When a declaratory relief action may not be brought pursuant to this section, Sections 1240.670 and 1240.680 do not apply. **Leg.H.** Added Stats 1975 ch 1275 §2, operative July 1, 1976. Amended Stats 1982 ch 681 §2.

§1240.700. Acquisition for city or county road, street, or highway purposes; Declaratory relief

(a) When property described in Section 1240.680 is sought to be acquired for city or county road, street, or highway purposes, and such property was dedicated or devoted to regional park, recreational, or open-space purposes prior to the initiation of road, street, or highway route location studies, an action for declaratory relief may be brought in the superior court by the regional park district which operates the park, recreational, or open-space area to determine the question of which public use is the best and most necessary public use for such property.

(b) The action for declaratory relief shall be filed and served within 120 days after the city or county, as the case may be, has published in a newspaper of general circulation pursuant to Section 6061 of the Government Code, and delivered to the regional park district, a written notice that a proposed route or site or an adopted route includes such property.

(c) With respect to property dedicated or devoted to regional park, recreational, or open-space purposes which is sought to be acquired for city or county road, street, or highway purposes:

(1) If an action for declaratory relief is not filed and served within the 120-day period established by subdivision (b), the right to bring such action is waived and the provisions of Section 1240.680 do not apply.

(2) When a declaratory relief action may not be brought pursuant to this section, the provisions of Section 1240.680 do not apply. **Leg.H.** Added Stats 1975 ch 1275 §4, operative July 1, 1976.

§1241. [Section repealed 1976]

Leg.H. Enacted 1872. Amended Stats 1911 ch 115 §2, ch 358 §2; Stats 1913 ch 293 §1; Stats 1933 ch 465 §2; Stats 1935 ch 254 §1; Stats 1949 ch 802 §1; Stats 1955 ch 1036 §3; Stats 1957 ch 1616 §1; Stats 1961 ch 610 §1 Stats 1973 ch 262 §1. Repealed Stats 1975 ch 1275 §1, operative July 1, 1976.

§1241.7. [Section repealed 1976]

Leg.H. Added Stats 1968 ch 1328 §1. Amended Stats 1969 ch 357 §1; Stats 1970 ch 854 §1; Stats 1971 ch 68 §1, ch 1524 §1; Stats 1972 ch 590 §5. Repealed Stats 1975 ch 1275 §1, operative July 1, 1976.

§1241.9 [Section repealed 1976]

Leg.H. Added Stats 1970 ch 854 §2. Repealed Stats 1975 ch 1275 §1, operative July 1, 1976.

§1242. [Section repealed 1976]

Leg.H. Enacted 1872. Amended Stats 1963 ch 1681 §4; Stats 1970 ch 662 §2. Repealed Stats 1975 ch 1275 §1, operative July 1, 1976.

§1242.5. [Section repealed 1976]

Leg.H. Added Stats 1959 ch 1865 §1. Amended Stats 1970 ch 662 §3. Repealed Stats 1975 ch 1275 §1, operative July 1, 1976.

§1243. [Section repealed 1976]

Leg.H. Enacted 1872. Amended Code Amdts 1880 ch 116 §1; Stats 1913 ch 200 §1; Stats 1963 ch 70 §1; Stats 1967 ch 119 §3. Repealed Stats 1975 ch 1275 §1, operative July 1, 1976.

§1243.1. [Section repealed 1976]

Leg.H. Added Stats 1971 ch 1681 §1. Repealed Stats 1975 ch 1275 §1, operative July 1, 1976.

§1243.4. [Section repealed 1976]

Leg.H. Added Stats 1961 ch 1613 §1. Repealed Stats 1975 ch 1275 §1, operative July 1, 1976.

§1243.5. [Section repealed 1976]

Leg.H. Added Stats 1957 ch 1508 §1. Amended Stats 1961 ch 1613 §2. Repealed Stats 1975 ch 1275 §1, operative July 1, 1976.

§1243.6. [Section repealed 1976]

Leg.H. Added Stats 1957 ch 1851 §2 as §1254.5. Renumbered and amended Stats 1961 ch 1613 §3. Repealed Stats 1975 ch 1275 §1, operative July 1, 1976.

§1243.7. [Section repealed 1976]

Leg.H. Added Stats 1957 ch 2022 §1 as §1254.7. Renumbered and amended Stats 1961 ch 1613 §4. Repealed Stats 1975 ch 1275 §1, operative July 1, 1976.

§1244. [Section repealed 1976]

Leg.H. Enacted 1872. Amended Code Amdts 1873–74 ch 383 §162; Code Amdts 1880 ch 116 §2; Stats 1913 ch 298 §1; Stats 1939 ch 209 §1; Stats 1947 ch 996 §1. Repealed Stats 1975 ch 1275 §1, operative July 1, 1976.

§1245. [Section repealed 1976]

Leg.H. Enacted 1872. Amended Stats 1939 ch 209 §2. Repealed Stats 1975 ch 1275 §1, operative July 1, 1976.

§1245.2. [Section repealed 1976]

Leg.H. Added Stats 1939 ch 209 §4. Amended Stats 1969 ch 1611 §27, operative July 1, 1970. Repealed Stats 1975 ch 1275 §1, operative July 1, 1976. See CCP §§872.330, 1245.2.

§1245.3. [Section repealed 1976]

Leg.H. Added Stats 1949 ch 1145 §1. Amended Stats 1951 ch 416 §1. Repealed Stats 1975 ch 1275 §1, operative July 1, 1976.

§1245.4. [Section repealed 1976]

Leg.H. Added Stats 1949 ch 1144 §1. Amended Stats 1965 ch 371 §17. Repealed Stats 1975 ch 1275 §1, operative July 1, 1976.

CHAPTER 4
PRECONDEMNATION ACTIVITIES

Article 1. Preliminary Location, Survey, and Tests.
Article 2. Resolution of Necessity.
Article 3. Resolution Consenting to Eminent Domain Proceeding by Quasi-Public Entity.

ARTICLE 1
Preliminary Location, Survey, and Tests

Entry authorized. §1245.010.
Consent to, and order for, entry. §1245.020.
Court order permitting entry. §1245.030.
Modification of order. §1245.040.
Retention of deposit. §1245.050.
Damage to or interference with possession and use of property. §1245.060.

§1245.010. Entry authorized

Subject to requirements of this article, any person authorized to acquire property for a particular use by eminent domain may enter upon property to make photographs, studies, surveys, examinations, tests, soundings, borings, samplings, or appraisals or to engage in similar activities reasonably related to acquisition or use of the property for that use. **Leg.H.** Added Stats 1975 ch 1275 §2, operative July 1, 1976.

§1245.020. Consent to, and order for, entry

In any case in which the entry and activities mentioned in Section 1245.010 will subject the person having the power of eminent domain to liability under Section 1245.060, before making that entry and undertaking those activities, the person shall secure at least one of the following:

(a) The written consent of the owner to enter upon the owner's property and to undertake those activities.

(b) An order for entry from the superior court in accordance with Section 1245.030. **Leg.H.** Added Stats 1975 ch 1275 §2, operative July 1, 1976. Amended Stats 2021 ch 401 §3 (AB 1578), effective January 1, 2022.

§1245.030. Court order permitting entry

(a) The person seeking to enter upon the property may petition the court for an order permitting the entry and shall give such prior notice to the owner of the property as the court determines is appropriate under the circumstances of the particular case.

(b) Upon such petition and after such notice has been given, the court shall determine the purpose for the entry, the nature and scope of the activities reasonably necessary to accomplish such purpose, and the probable amount of compensation to be paid to the owner of the property for the actual damage to the property and interference with its possession and use.

(c) After such determination, the court may issue its order permitting the entry. The order shall prescribe the purpose for the entry and the nature and scope of the activities to be undertaken and shall require the person seeking to enter to deposit with the court the probable amount of compensation. **Leg.H.** Added Stats 1975 ch 1275 §2, operative July 1, 1976.

§1245.040. Modification of order

(a) The court, after notice and hearing, may modify any of the provisions of an order made under Section 1245.030.

(b) If the amount required to be deposited is increased by an order of modification, the court shall specify the time within which the additional amount shall be deposited and may direct that any further entry or that specified activities under the order as modified be stayed until the additional amount has been deposited. **Leg.H.** Added Stats 1975 ch 1275 §2, operative July 1, 1976.

§1245.050.   Retention of deposit

(a) Unless sooner disbursed by court order, the amount deposited under this article shall be retained on deposit for six months following the termination of the entry. The period of retention may be extended by the court for good cause.

(b) The deposit shall be made in the Condemnation Deposits Fund in the State Treasury or, upon written request of the plaintiff filed with the deposit, in the county treasury. If made in the State Treasury, the deposit shall be held, invested, deposited, and disbursed in accordance with Article 10 (commencing with Section 16429) of Chapter 2 of Part 2 of Division 4 of Title 2 of the Government Code. **Leg.H.** Added Stats 1975 ch 1275 §2, operative July 1, 1976.

§1245.060.   Damage to or interference with possession and use of property

(a) If the entry and activities upon property cause actual damage to or substantial interference with the possession or use of the property, whether or not a claim has been presented in compliance with Part 3 (commencing with Section 900) of Division 3.6 of Title 1 of the Government Code, the owner may recover for that damage or interference in a civil action, as a defendant in an eminent domain action affecting the property, or by application to the court under subdivision (c).

(b) The prevailing claimant in an action or proceeding under this section shall be awarded the claimant's costs and, if the court finds that any of the following occurred, the claimant's litigation expenses incurred in proceedings under this article:

(1) The entry was unlawful.

(2) The entry was lawful but the activities upon the property were abusive or lacking in due regard for the interests of the owner.

(3) There was a failure substantially to comply with the terms of an order made under Section 1245.030 or 1245.040.

(c) If funds are on deposit under this article, upon application of the owner, the court shall determine and award the amount the owner is entitled to recover under this section and shall order that amount paid out of the funds on deposit. If the funds on deposit are insufficient to pay the full amount of the award, the court shall enter judgment for the unpaid portion. In a proceeding under this subdivision, the owner has a right to a jury trial, unless waived, on the amount of compensation for actual damage or substantial interference with the possession or use of the property.

(d) Nothing in this section affects the availability of any other remedy the owner may have for the damaging of the owner's property. **Leg.H.** Added Stats 1975 ch 1275 §2, operative July 1, 1976. Amended Stats 2021 ch 401 §4 (AB 1578), effective January 1, 2022.

ARTICLE 2
Resolution of Necessity

"Governing body". §1245.210.
Resolution of necessity. §1245.220.
Contents of resolution. §1245.230.
Notice and hearing. §1245.235.
Vote required for adoption. §1245.240.
Required procedure for new public use for property subject to resolution of necessity. §1245.245.
Effect of resolution. §1245.250.
Abuse of discretion; Rescinding resolution. §1245.255.
Action by owner in inverse condemnation. §1245.260.
Effect of bribery. §1245.270.

§1245.210.   "Governing body"

As used in this article, "governing body" means:

(a) In the case of a taking by a local public entity, the legislative body of the local public entity.

(b) In the case of a taking by the Sacramento and San Joaquin Drainage District, the Central Valley Flood Protection Board.

(c) In the case of a taking by the State Public Works Board pursuant to the Property Acquisition Law (Part 11 (commencing with Section 15850) of Division 3 of Title 2 of the Government Code), the State Public Works Board.

(d) In the case of a taking by the Department of Fish and Wildlife pursuant to Section 1348 of the Fish and Game Code, the Wildlife Conservation Board.

(e) In the case of a taking by the Department of Transportation (other than a taking pursuant to Section 21633 of the Public Utilities Code or Section 30100 of the Streets and Highways Code), the California Transportation Commission.

(f) In the case of a taking by the Department of Transportation pursuant to Section 21633 of the Public Utilities Code, the California Transportation Commission.

(g) In the case of a taking by the Department of Transportation pursuant to Section 30100 of the Streets and Highways Code, the California Transportation Commission.

(h) In the case of a taking by the Department of Water Resources, the California Water Commission.

(i) In the case of a taking by the University of California, the Regents of the University of California.

(j) In the case of a taking by the State Lands Commission, the State Lands Commission.

(k) In the case of a taking by the college named in Section 92200 of the Education Code, the board of directors of that college.

(*l*) In the case of a taking by the High-Speed Rail Authority, the State Public Works Board. **Leg.H.** Added Stats 1975 ch 1275 §2, operative July 1, 1976. Amended Stats 1982 ch 681 §3; Stats 2018 ch 790 §1 (SB 1172), effective January 1, 2019; Stats 2022 ch 478 §3 (AB 1936), effective January 1, 2023.

§1245.220.   Resolution of necessity

A public entity may not commence an eminent domain proceeding until its governing body has adopted a resolution of necessity that meets the requirements of this article. **Leg.H.** Added Stats 1975 ch 1275 §2, operative July 1, 1976.

§1245.230.   Contents of resolution

In addition to other requirements imposed by law, the resolution of necessity shall contain all of the following:

(a) A general statement of the public use for which the property is to be taken and a reference to the statute that authorizes the public entity to acquire the property by eminent domain.

(b) A description of the general location and extent of the property to be taken, with sufficient detail for reasonable identification.

(c) A declaration that the governing body of the public entity has found and determined each of the following:

(1) The public interest and necessity require the proposed project.

(2) The proposed project is planned or located in the manner that will be most compatible with the greatest public good and the least private injury.

(3) The property described in the resolution is necessary for the proposed project.

(4) That either the offer required by Section 7267.2 of the Government Code has been made to the owner or owners of record, or the offer has not been made because the owner cannot be located with reasonable diligence.

If at the time the governing body of a public entity is requested to adopt a resolution of necessity and the project for which the property is needed has been determined by the public entity to be an emergency project, which project is necessary either to protect or preserve health, safety, welfare, or property, the requirements of Section 7267.2 of the Government Code need not be a prerequisite to the adoption of an authorizing resolution at the time. However, in those cases the provisions of Section 7267.2 of the Government Code shall be implemented by the public entity within a reasonable time thereafter but in any event, not later than 90 days after adoption of the resolution of necessity. **Leg.H.** Added Stats 1975 ch 1275 §2, operative July 1, 1976. Amended Stats 1982 ch 1059 §1; Stats 1983 ch 1079 §1.

§1245.235.   Notice and hearing

(a) The governing body of the public entity may adopt a resolution of necessity only after the governing body has given each person whose property is to be acquired by eminent domain and whose name and address appears on the last equalized county assessment roll notice and a reasonable opportunity to appear and be heard on the matters referred to in Section 1240.030.

(b) The notice required by subdivision (a) shall be sent by first-class mail to each person described in subdivision (a) and shall state all of the following:

(1) The intent of the governing body to adopt the resolution.

(2) The right of such person to appear and be heard on the matters referred to in Section 1240.030.

(3) Failure to file a written request to appear and be heard within 15 days after the notice was mailed will result in waiver of the right to appear and be heard.

(c) The governing body, or a committee of not less than 11 members thereof designated by the governing body if the governing body has more than 40 members, shall hold a hearing at which all persons described in subdivision (a) who filed a written request within the time specified in the notice may appear and be heard on the matters referred to in Section 1240.030. Such a committee shall be reasonably representative of the various geographical areas within the public entity's jurisdiction. The governing body need not give an opportunity to appear and be heard to any person who fails to so file a written request within the time specified in the notice. If a committee is designated by the governing body pursuant to this subdivision to hold the hearing, the committee, subsequent to the hearing, shall provide the governing body and any person described in subdivision (a) who has appeared before the committee with a written summary of the hearing and a written recommendation as to whether to adopt the resolution of necessity. Any person described in subdivision (a) who has appeared before the committee shall also be given an opportunity to appear and be heard before the governing body on the matters referred to in Section 1240.030.

(d) Notwithstanding subdivision (b), the governing body may satisfy the requirements of this section through any other procedure that has given each person described in subdivision (a) reasonable written personal notice and a reasonable opportunity to appear and be heard on the matters referred to in Section 1240.030. **Leg.H.** Added Stats 1975 ch 1275 §2, operative July 1, 1976. Amended Stats 1986 ch 358 §1.

§1245.240. Vote required for adoption

Unless a greater vote is required by statute, charter, or ordinance, the resolution shall be adopted by a vote of two-thirds of all the members of the governing body of the public entity. **Leg.H.** Added Stats 1975 ch 1275 §2, operative July 1, 1976.

§1245.245. Required procedure for new public use for property subject to resolution of necessity

(a) Property acquired by a public entity by any means set forth in subdivision (e) that is subject to a resolution of necessity adopted pursuant to this article shall only be used for the public use stated in the resolution unless the governing body of the public entity adopts a resolution authorizing a different use of the property by a vote of at least two-thirds of all members of the governing body of the public entity, or a greater vote as required by statute, charter, or ordinance. The resolution shall contain all of the following:

(1) A general statement of the new public use that is proposed for the property and a reference to the statute that would have authorized the public entity to acquire the property by eminent domain for that use.

(2) A description of the general location and extent of the property proposed to be used for the new use, with sufficient detail for reasonable identification.

(3) A declaration that the governing body has found and determined each of the following:

(A) The public interest and necessity require the proposed use.

(B) The proposed use is planned and located in the manner that will be most compatible with the greatest public good and least private injury.

(C) The property described in the resolution is necessary for the proposed use.

(b) Property acquired by a public entity by any means set forth in subdivision (e) that is subject to a resolution of necessity pursuant to this article, and is not used for the public use stated in the resolution of necessity within 10 years of the adoption of the resolution of necessity, shall be sold in accordance with the terms of subdivisions (f) and (g), unless the governing body adopts a resolution according to the terms of subdivision (a) or a resolution according to the terms of this subdivision reauthorizing the existing stated public use of the property by a vote of at least two-thirds of all members of the governing body of the public entity or a greater vote as required by statute, charter, or ordinance. A reauthorization resolution under this subdivision shall contain all of the following:

(1) A general statement of the public use that is proposed to be reauthorized for the property and a reference to the statute that authorized the public entity to acquire the property by eminent domain for that use.

(2) A description of the general location and extent of the property proposed to be used for the public use, but not yet in use for the public use, with sufficient detail for reasonable identification.

(3) A declaration that the governing body has found and determined each of the following:

(A) The public interest and necessity require the proposed use.

(B) The proposed use is planned and located in the manner that will be most compatible with the greatest public good and least private injury.

(C) The property described in the resolution is necessary for the proposed use.

(c) In addition to any notice required by law, the notice required for a new or reauthorization resolution sought pursuant to subdivision (a) or (b) shall comply with Section 1245.235 and shall be sent to each person who was given notice required by Section 1245.235 in connection with the original acquisition of the property by the public entity.

(d) Judicial review of an action pursuant to subdivision (a) or (b) may be obtained by a person who had an interest in the property described in the resolution at the time that the property was acquired by the public entity, and shall be governed by Section 1085.

(e) The following property acquisitions are subject to the requirements of this section:

(1) Any acquisition by a public entity pursuant to eminent domain.

(2) Any acquisition by a public entity following adoption of a resolution of necessity pursuant to this article for the property.

(3) Any acquisition by a public entity prior to the adoption of a resolution of necessity pursuant to this article for the property, but subsequent to a written notice that the public entity may take the property by eminent domain.

(f) If the public entity fails to adopt either a new resolution pursuant to subdivision (a) or a reauthorization resolution pursuant to subdivision (b), as required by this section, and that property was not used for the public use stated in a resolution of necessity adopted pursuant to this article or a resolution adopted pursuant to subdivision (a) or (b) between the time of its acquisition and the time of the public entity's failure to adopt a resolution pursuant to subdivision (a) or (b), the public entity shall offer the person or persons from whom the property was acquired the right of first refusal to purchase the property pursuant to this section, as follows:

(1) At the present market value, as determined by independent licensed appraisers.

(2) For property that was a single-family residence at the time of acquisition, at an affordable price, which price shall not be greater than the price paid by the agency for the original acquisition, adjusted for inflation, and shall not be greater than fair market value, if the following requirements are met:

(A) The person or persons from whom the property was acquired certify their income to the public entity as persons or families of low or moderate income.

(B) If the single-family residence is offered at a price that is less than fair market value, the public entity may verify the certifications of income in accordance with procedures used for verification of incomes of purchasers and occupants of housing financed by the California Housing Finance Agency.

(C) If the single-family residence is offered at a price that is less than fair market value, the public entity shall impose terms, conditions, and restrictions to ensure that the residence will either:

(i) Remain owner-occupied by the person or persons from whom the property was acquired for at least five years.

(ii) Remain available to persons or families of low or moderate income and households with incomes no greater than the incomes of the present occupants in proportion to the area median income for the longest feasible time, but for not less than 55 years for rental units and 45 years for home ownership units.

(D) The Department of Housing and Community Development shall provide to the public entity recommendations of standards and criteria for those prices, terms, conditions, and restrictions.

(g) If after a diligent effort the public entity is unable to locate the person from whom the property was acquired, if the person from whom the property was acquired does not choose to purchase the property as provided in subdivision (f), or if the public entity fails to adopt a resolution as required pursuant to subdivision (a) or (b) but is not required to offer a right of first refusal pursuant to subdivision (f), the public entity shall sell the property as surplus property pursuant to Article 8 (commencing with Section 54220) of Chapter 5 of Part 1 of Division 2 of Title 5 of the Government Code.

(h) If residential property acquired by a public entity by any means set forth in subdivision (e) is sold as surplus property pursuant to subdivision (g), and that property was not used for the public use stated in a resolution of necessity adopted pursuant to this article or a resolution adopted pursuant to subdivision (a) or (b) between the time of its acquisition and the time of its sale as surplus property, the public entity shall pay to the person or persons from whom the public entity acquired the property the sum of any financial gain between the original acquisition price, adjusted for inflation, and the final sale price.

(i) Upon completion of any acquisition described in subdivision (e) or upon the adoption of a resolution of necessity pursuant to this section, whichever is later, the public entity shall give written notice to the person or persons from whom the property was acquired as described in subdivision (e) stating that the notice, right of first refusal, and return of financial gain rights discussed in this section may accrue.

(j) At least 60 days before selling the property pursuant to subdivision (g), the public entity shall make a diligent effort to locate the person from whom the property was acquired. At any time before the proposed sale, the person from whom the property was acquired may exercise the rights provided by this section. As used in this section, "diligent effort" means that the public entity has done all of the following:

(1) Mailed the notice of the proposed sale by certified mail, return receipt requested, to the last known address of the person from whom the property was acquired.

(2) Mailed the notice of the proposed sale by certified mail, return receipt requested, to each person with the same name as the person from whom the property was acquired at any other address on the last equalized assessment roll.

(3) Published the notice of the proposed sale pursuant to Section 6061 of the Government Code in at least one newspaper of general circulation within the city or county in which the property is located.

(4) Posted the notice of the proposed sale in at least three public places within the city or county in which the property is located.

(5) Posted the notice of the proposed sale on the property proposed to be sold.

(k) For purposes of this section, "adjusted for inflation" means the original acquisition price increased to reflect the proportional increase in the Consumer Price Index for all items for the State of California, as determined by the United States Bureau of Labor Statistics, for the period from the date of acquisition to the date the property is offered for sale. **Leg.H.** Added Stats 2006 ch 602 §1 (SB 1650), effective January 1, 2007. Amended Stats 2007 ch 130 §36 (AB 299), effective January 1, 2008.

2006 Note: This act shall apply prospectively and shall apply to property acquired after January 1, 2007. Stats 2006 ch 602 (SB 1650) §4.

§1245.250. Effect of resolution

(a) Except as otherwise provided by statute, a resolution of necessity adopted by the governing body of the public entity pursuant to this article conclusively establishes the matters referred to in Section 1240.030.

(b) If the taking is by a local public entity, other than a sanitary district exercising the powers of a county water district pursuant to Section 6512.7 of the Health and Safety Code, and the property is electric, gas, or water public utility property, the resolution of necessity creates a rebuttable presumption that the matters referred to in Section 1240.030 are true. This presumption is a presumption affecting the burden of proof.

(c) If the taking is by a local public entity and the property described in the resolution is not located entirely within the boundaries of the local public entity, the resolution of necessity creates a presumption that the matters referred to in Section 1240.030 are true. This presumption is a presumption affecting the burden of producing evidence.

(d) For the purposes of subdivision (b), a taking by the State Reclamation Board for the Sacramento and San Joaquin Drainage District is not a taking by a local public entity. **Leg.H.** Added Stats 1975 ch 1275 §2, operative July 1, 1976. Amended Stats 1992 ch 812 §3 (SB 1757).

§1245.255. Abuse of discretion; Rescinding resolution

(a) A person having an interest in the property described in a resolution of necessity adopted by the governing body of the public entity pursuant to this article may obtain judicial review of the validity of the resolution:

(1) Before the commencement of the eminent domain proceeding, by petition for a writ of mandate pursuant to Section 1085. The court having jurisdiction of the writ of mandate action, upon motion of any party, shall order the writ of mandate action dismissed without prejudice upon commencement of the eminent domain proceeding unless the court determines that dismissal will not be in the interest of justice.

(2) After the commencement of the eminent domain proceeding, by objection to the right to take pursuant to this title.

(b) A resolution of necessity does not have the effect prescribed in Section 1245.250 to the extent that its adoption or contents were influenced or affected by gross abuse of discretion by the governing body.

(c) Nothing in this section precludes a public entity from rescinding a resolution of necessity and adopting a new resolution as to the same property subject, after the commencement of an eminent domain proceeding, to the same consequences as a conditional dismissal of the proceeding under Section 1260.120. **Leg.H.** Added Stats 1975 ch 1275 §2, operative July 1, 1976. Amended Stats 1978 ch 286 §1.

§1245.260. Action by owner in inverse condemnation

(a) If a public entity has adopted a resolution of necessity but has not commenced an eminent domain proceeding to acquire the property within six months after the date of adoption of the resolution, or has commenced such proceeding but has not within six months after the commencement of such proceeding attempted diligently to serve the complaint and the summons relating to such proceeding, the property owner may, by an action in inverse condemnation, do either or both of the following:

(1) Require the public entity to take the property and pay compensation therefor.

(2) Recover damages from the public entity for any interference with the possession and use of the property resulting from adoption of the resolution.

Service by mail pursuant to Section 415.30 shall constitute a diligent attempt at service within the meaning of this section.

(b) No claim need be presented against a public entity under Part 3 (commencing with Section 900) of Division 3.6 of Title 1 of the Government Code as a prerequisite to commencement or maintenance of an action under subdivision (a), but any such action shall be commenced within one year and six months after the date the public entity adopted the resolution of necessity.

(c) A public entity may commence an eminent domain proceeding or rescind a resolution of necessity as a matter of right at any time before the property owner commences an action under this section. If the public entity commences an eminent domain proceeding or rescinds the resolution of necessity before the property owner commences an action under this section, the property owner may not thereafter bring an action under this section.

(d) After a property owner has commenced an action under this section, the public entity may rescind the resolution of necessity and abandon the taking of the property only under the same circumstances and subject to the same conditions and consequences as abandonment of an eminent domain proceeding.

(e) Commencement of an action under this section does not affect any authority a public entity may have to commence an eminent domain proceeding, take possession of the property pursuant to Article 3 (commencing with Section 1255.410) of Chapter 6, or abandon the eminent domain proceeding.

(f) In lieu of bringing an action under subdivision (a) or if the limitations period provided in subdivision (b) has run, the property owner may obtain a writ of mandate to compel the public entity, within such time as the court deems appropriate, to rescind the resolution of necessity or to commence an eminent domain proceeding to acquire the property. **Leg.H.** Added Stats 1975 ch 1275 §2, operative July 1, 1976. Amended Stats 1978 ch 411 §1.

§1245.270. Effect of bribery

(a) A resolution of necessity does not meet the requirements of this article if the defendant establishes by a preponderance of the evidence both of the following:

(1) A member of the governing body who voted in favor of the resolution received or agreed to receive a bribe [1], **as defined in** Section 7 of the Penal Code [2], involving adoption of the resolution.

(2) But for the conduct described in paragraph (1), the resolution would not otherwise have been adopted.

(b) Where there has been a prior criminal prosecution of the member for the conduct described in paragraph (1) of subdivision (a), proof of conviction shall be conclusive evidence that the requirement of paragraph (1) of subdivision (a) is satisfied, and proof of acquittal or other dismissal of the prosecution shall be conclusive evidence that the requirement of paragraph (1) of subdivision (a) is not satisfied. Where there is a pending criminal prosecution of the member for the conduct described in paragraph (1) of subdivision (a), the court may take such action as is just under the circumstances of the case.

(c) Nothing in this section precludes a public entity from rescinding a resolution of necessity and adopting a new resolution as to the same property, subject to the same consequences as a conditional dismissal of the proceeding under Section 1260.120. **Leg.H.** Added Stats 1975 ch 1275 §2, operative July 1, 1976. Amended Stats 2024 ch 72 §1 (SB 156), effective July 2, 2024.

§1245.270. 2024 Deletes. [1] (as that term is defined in subdivision 6 of [2])

ARTICLE 3
Resolution Consenting to Eminent Domain Proceeding by Quasi-Public Entity

"Legislative body". §1245.310.
"Quasi-public entity". §1245.320.
Utility service easement; Resolution. §1245.325.
Declaration that owner seeking right of entry has met required conditions. §1245.326.
Resolution consenting to acquisition. §1245.330.
Contents of resolution. §1245.340.
Notice and hearing. §1245.350.
Vote required for adoption. §1245.360.
Costs. §1245.370.
Effect of article. §1245.380.
Liability of city or county. §1245.390.

§1245.310. "Legislative body"

As used in this article, "legislative body" means both of the following:

(a) The legislative body of each city within whose boundaries property sought to be taken by the quasi-public entity by eminent domain is located.

(b) If property sought to be taken by the quasi-public entity is not located within city boundaries, the legislative body of each county within whose boundaries such property is located. **Leg.H.** Added Stats 1975 ch 1275 §2, operative July 1, 1976.

§1245.320. "Quasi-public entity"

As used in this article, "quasi-public entity" means:

(a) An educational institution of collegiate grade not conducted for profit that seeks to take property by eminent domain under Section 94500 of the Education Code.

(b) A nonprofit hospital that seeks to take property by eminent domain under Section 1260 of the Health and Safety Code.

(c) A cemetery authority that seeks to take property by eminent domain under Section 8501 of the Health and Safety Code.

(d) A limited-dividend housing corporation that seeks to take property by eminent domain under Section 34874 of the Health and Safety Code.

(e) A land-chest corporation that seeks to take property by eminent domain under former Section 35167 of the Health and Safety Code.

(f) A mutual water company that seeks to take property by eminent domain under Section 2729 of the Public Utilities Code. **Leg.H.** Added Stats 1975 ch 1275 §2, operative July 1, 1976. Amended Stats 2006 ch 538 §67 (SB 1852), effective January 1, 2007.

§1245.325. Utility service easement; Resolution

Where an owner of real property seeks to acquire an appurtenant easement by eminent domain pursuant to Section 1001 of the Civil Code:

(a) The person seeking to exercise the power of eminent domain shall be deemed to be a "quasi-public entity" for the purposes of this article.

(b) In lieu of the requirements of subdivision (c) of Section 1245.340, the resolution required by this article shall contain a declaration that the legislative body has found and determined each of the following:

(1) There is a great necessity for the taking.

(2) The location of the easement affords the most reasonable service to the property to which it is appurtenant, consistent with the least damage to the burdened property.

(3) The hardship to the owner of the appurtenant property, if the taking is not permitted, clearly outweighs any hardship to the owner of the burdened property. **Leg.H.** Added Stats 1976 ch 994 §2.

§1245.326. Declaration that owner seeking right of entry has met required conditions

Where an owner of real property seeks to acquire by eminent domain a temporary right of entry pursuant to Section 1002 of the Civil Code:

(a) The person seeking to exercise the power of eminent domain shall be deemed to be a "quasi-public entity" for the purposes of this article.

(b) In lieu of the requirements of subdivision (c) of Section 1245.340, the resolution required by this article shall contain a declaration that the legislative body has found and determined that each of the conditions required by Section 1002 of the Civil Code appears to exist. **Leg.H.** Added Stats 1982 ch 1239 §2.

§1245.330. Resolution consenting to acquisition

Notwithstanding any other provision of law, a quasi-public entity may not commence an eminent domain proceeding to acquire any property until the legislative body has adopted a resolution consenting to the acquisition of such property by eminent domain. **Leg.H.** Added Stats 1975 ch 1275 §2, operative July 1, 1976.

§1245.340. Contents of resolution

The resolution required by this article shall contain all of the following:

(a) A general statement of the public use for which the property is to be taken and a reference to the statute that authorizes the quasi-public entity to acquire the property by eminent domain.

(b) A description of the general location and extent of the property to be taken, with sufficient detail for reasonable identification.

(c) A declaration that the legislative body has found and determined each of the following:

(1) The public interest and necessity require the proposed project.

(2) The proposed project is planned or located in the manner that will be most compatible with the greatest good and least private injury.

(3) The property described in the resolution is necessary for the proposed project.

(4) The hardship of the quasi-public entity if the acquisition of the property be eminent domain is not permitted outweighs any hardship to the owners of such property. **Leg.H.** Added Stats 1975 ch 1275 §2, operative July 1, 1976.

§1245.350. Notice and hearing

(a) The legislative body may refuse to consent to the acquisition with or without a hearing, but it may adopt the resolution required by this article only after the legislative body has held a hearing at which persons whose property is to be acquired by eminent domain have had a reasonable opportunity to appear and be heard.

(b) Notice of the hearing shall be sent by first-class mail to each person whose property is to be acquired by eminent domain if the name and address of the person appears on the last equalized county assessment roll (including the roll of state-assessed property). The notice shall state the time, place, and subject of the hearing and shall be mailed at least 15 days prior to the date of the hearing. **Leg.H.** Added Stats 1975 ch 1275 §2, operative July 1, 1976.

§1245.360. Vote required for adoption

The resolution required by this article shall be adopted by a vote of two-thirds of all the members of the legislative body. **Leg.H.** Added Stats 1975 ch 1275 §2, operative July 1, 1976.

§1245.370. Costs

The legislative body may require that the quasi-public entity pay all of the costs reasonably incurred by the legislative body under this article. The legislative body may require that such costs be secured by payment or deposit or other satisfactory security in advance of any action by the legislative body under this article. **Leg.H.** Added Stats 1975 ch 1275 §2, operative July 1, 1976.

§1245.380. Effect of article

The requirement of this article is in addition to any other requirements imposed by law. Nothing in this article relieves the quasi-public entity from satisfying the requirements of Section 1240.030 or any other requirements imposed by law. **Leg.H.** Added Stats 1975 ch 1275 §2, operative July 1, 1976.

§1245.390. Liability of city or county

The adoption of a resolution pursuant to this article does not make the city or county liable for any damages caused by the acquisition of the property or by the project for which it is acquired. **Leg.H.** Added Stats 1975 ch 1275 §2, operative July 1, 1976.

§1246. [Section repealed 1976]

Leg.H. Enacted 1872. Amended Stats 1939 ch 209 §3. Repealed Stats 1975 ch 1275 §1, operative July 1, 1976.

§1246.1. [Section repealed 1976]

Leg.H. Added Stats 1939 ch 210 §1. Repealed Stats 1975 ch 1275 §1, operative July 1, 1976.

§1246.2. [Section repealed 1976]

Leg.H. Added Stats 1967 ch 1076 §1. Amended Stats 1974 ch 530 §1. Repealed Stats 1975 ch 1275 §1, operative July 1, 1976.

§1246.3. [Section repealed 1976]

Leg.H. Added Stats 1971 ch 1574 §1. Repealed Stats 1975 ch 1275 §1, operative July 1, 1976.

§1246.4. [Section repealed 1976]

Leg.H. Added Stats 1971 ch 1574 §1.3. Repealed Stats 1975 ch 1275 §1, operative July 1, 1976.

§1247. [Section repealed 1976]

Leg.H. Enacted 1872. Amended Stats 1957 ch 43 §9. Repealed Stats 1975 ch 1275 §1, operative July 1, 1976.

§1247a. [Section repealed 1976]

Leg.H. Added Stats 1911 ch 358 §3. Amended Stats 1957 ch 43 §10. Repealed Stats 1975 ch 1275 §1, operative July 1, 1976.

§1247b. [Section repealed 1976]

Leg.H. Added Stats 1959 ch 1573 §1. Repealed Stats 1975 ch 1275 §1, operative July 1, 1976.

§1247c. [Section repealed 1976]

Leg.H. Added Stats 1957 ch 1601 §1 as §1845.5. Amended Stats 1959 ch 2107 §1; Renumbered and amended Stats 1965 ch 299 §42, operative January 1, 1967. Repealed Stats 1965 ch 1151 §5, operative January 1, 1967.

§1248. [Section repealed 1976]

Leg.H. Enacted 1872. Amended Stats 1889 ch 232 §1; Stats 1911 ch 358 §4; Stats 1915 ch 563 §1; Stats 1953 ch 462 §1; Stats 1961 ch 1612 §1, operative July 1, 1962; Stats 1965 ch 51 §1; Stats 1969 ch 1256 §1, operative July 1, 1970. Repealed Stats 1975 ch 1275 §1, operative July 1, 1976.

§1248a. [Section repealed 1976]

Leg.H. Added Stats 1911 ch 427 §1. Amended Stats 1913 ch 159 §1. Repealed Stats 1975 ch 1275 §1, operative July 1, 1976.

§1248b. [Section repealed 1976]

Leg.H. Added Stats 1957 ch 1098 §1. Repealed Stats 1975 ch 1275 §1, operative July 1, 1976.

§1249. [Section repealed 1976]

Leg.H. Enacted 1872. Amended Stats 1911 ch 417 §1; Stats 1961 ch 1613 §5. Repealed Stats 1975 ch 1275 §1, operative July 1, 1976.

§1249.1. [Section repealed 1976]

Leg.H. Added Stats 1961 ch 1613 §6. Repealed Stats 1975 ch 1275 §1, operative July 1, 1976.

§1249.2. [Section repealed 1976]

Leg.H. Added Stats 1965 ch 1434 §1. Repealed Stats 1975 ch 1275 §1, operative July 1, 1976.

§1249.3. [Section repealed 1976]

Leg.H. Added Stats 1974 ch 1469 §1. Repealed Stats 1975 ch 1275 §1, operative July 1, 1976.

§1250. [Section repealed 1976]

Leg.H. Enacted 1872. Repealed Stats 1975 ch 1275 §1, operative July 1, 1976.

CHAPTER 5
COMMENCEMENT OF PROCEEDING

Article 1. Jurisdiction and Venue.
Article 2. Commencement of Proceeding Generally.
Article 3. Parties; Joinder of Property.
Article 4. Pleadings.
Article 5. Objections to Right to Take.
Article 6. Settlement Offers and Alternative Dispute Resolution.

ARTICLE 1
Jurisdiction and Venue

Jurisdiction. §1250.010.
Venue; Commencement of proceeding. §1250.020.
Venue; Trial of proceeding. §1250.030.
Change of venue. §1250.040.

§1250.010. Jurisdiction

Except as otherwise provided in Section 1230.060 and in Chapter 12 (commencing with Section 1273.010), all eminent domain proceedings shall be commenced and prosecuted in the superior court. **Leg.H.** Added Stats 1975 ch 1275 §2, operative July 1, 1976.

§1250.020. Venue; Commencement of proceeding

(a) Except as provided in subdivision (b), the proceeding shall be commenced in the county in which the property sought to be taken is located.

(b) When property sought to be taken is situated in more than one county, the plaintiff may commence the proceeding in any one of such counties. **Leg.H.** Added Stats 1975 ch 1275 §2, operative July 1, 1976.

§1250.030. Venue; Trial of proceeding

(a) Except as provided in subdivision (b), the county in which the proceeding is commenced pursuant to Section 1250.020 is the proper county for trial of the proceeding.

(b) Where the court changes the place of trial pursuant to Section 1250.040, the county to which the proceeding is transferred is the proper county for trial of the proceeding. **Leg.H.** Added Stats 1975 ch 1275 §2, operative July 1, 1976.

§1250.040. Change of venue

The provisions of the Code of Civil Procedure for the change of place of trial of actions apply to eminent domain proceedings. **Leg.H.** Added Stats 1975 ch 1275 §2, operative July 1, 1976.

ARTICLE 2
Commencement of Proceeding Generally

Filing complaint. §1250.110.
Summons; Form and contents. §1250.120.
Service by publication. §1250.125.
Service by publication; Posting and recording. §1250.130.
Service on Attorney General. §1250.140.
Notice of pendency of proceeding. §1250.150.

§1250.110. Filing complaint

An eminent domain proceeding is commenced by filing a complaint with the court. **Leg.H.** Added Stats 1975 ch 1275 §2, operative July 1, 1976.

§1250.120. Summons; Form and contents

(a) Except as provided in subdivision (b), the form and contents of the summons shall be as in civil actions generally.

(b) Where process is served by publication, in addition to the summons, the publication shall describe the property sought to be taken in a manner reasonably calculated to give persons with an interest in the property actual notice of the pending proceeding. **Leg.H.** Added Stats 1975 ch 1275 §2, operative July 1, 1976.

§1250.125. Service by publication

(a) Where summons is served by publication, the publication may name only the defendants to be served thereby and describe only the property in which the defendants to be served thereby have or claim interests.

(b) Judgment based on failure to appear and answer following service under this section shall be conclusive against the defendants named in respect only to property described in the publication.

(c) Notwithstanding subdivision (b), a defendant who did not receive the offer required by Section 7267.2 of the Government Code because the owner could not be located with reasonable diligence, who was served by publication, and who failed to appear, may contest the amount of compensation within one year of the judgment and for good cause shown, whereupon that issue shall be litigated according to the provisions of this title. **Leg.H.** Added Stats 1975 ch 1275 §2, operative July 1, 1976. Amended Stats 1983 ch 1079 §2.

§1250.130. Service by publication; Posting and recording

Where the court orders service by publication, it shall also order the plaintiff (1) to post a copy of the summons and complaint on the property sought to be taken and (2), if not already recorded, to record a notice of the pendency of the proceeding in the manner provided by Section 1250.150. Such posting and recording shall be done not later than 10 days after the date the order is made. **Leg.H.** Added Stats 1975 ch 1275 §2, operative July 1, 1976.

§1250.140. Service on Attorney General

Where the state is a defendant, the summons and the complaint shall be served on the Attorney General. **Leg.H.** Added Stats 1975 ch 1275 §2, operative July 1, 1976.

§1250.150. Notice of pendency of proceeding

The plaintiff, at the time of the commencement of the proceeding, shall record a notice of the pendency of the proceeding in the office of the county recorder of any county in which property described in the complaint is located. A copy of the notice shall be served with the summons and complaint. **Leg.H.** Added Stats 1975 ch 1275 §2, operative July 1, 1976. Amended Stats 1983 ch 78 §2.

ARTICLE 3
Parties; Joinder of Property

Plaintiffs. §1250.210.
Defendants. §1250.220.
Appearance. §1250.230.
Joinder of property. §1250.240.
County as party; Lienholder. §1250.250.

§1250.210. Plaintiffs

Each person seeking to take property by eminent domain shall be named as a plaintiff. **Leg.H.** Added Stats 1975 ch 1275 §2, operative July 1, 1976.

§1250.220. Defendants

(a) The plaintiff shall name as defendants, by their real names, those persons who appear of record or are known by the plaintiff to have or claim an interest in the property described in the complaint.

(b) If a person described in subdivision (a) is dead and the plaintiff knows of a duly qualified and acting personal representative of the estate of such person, the plaintiff shall name such personal representative as a defendant. If a person described in subdivision (a) is dead or is believed by the plaintiff to be dead and if plaintiff knows of no duly qualified and acting personal representative of the estate of such person and states these facts in an affidavit filed with the complaint, plaintiff may name as defendants "the heirs and devises of ____ (naming such deceased person), deceased, and all persons claiming by, through, or under said decedent," naming them in that manner and, where it is stated in the affidavit that such person is believed by the plaintiff to be dead, such person also may be named as a defendant.

(c) In addition to those persons described in subdivision (a), the plaintiff may name as defendants "all persons unknown claiming an interest in the property," naming them in that manner.

(d) A judgment rendered in a proceeding under this title is binding and conclusive upon all persons named as defendants as provided in this section and properly served. **Leg.H.** Added Stats 1975 ch 1275 §2, operative July 1, 1976.

§1250.230. Appearance

Any person who claims a legal or equitable interest in the property described in the complaint may appear in the proceeding. Whether or not such person is named as a defendant in the complaint, he shall appear as a defendant. **Leg.H.** Added Stats 1975 ch 1275 §2, operative July 1, 1976.

§1250.240. Joinder of property

The plaintiff may join in one complaint all property located within the same county which is sought to be acquired for the same project. **Leg.H.** Added Stats 1975 ch 1275 §2, operative July 1, 1976.

§1250.250. County as party; Lienholder

(a) If the only interest of the county or other taxing agency in the property described in the complaint is a lien for ad valorem taxes, the county or other taxing agency need not be named as a defendant.

(b) The holder of a lien that secures a special assessment or a bond representing the special assessment shall be named as a defendant, regardless of the nature of the special assessment and the manner of collection of the special assessment. The holder of the lien may, instead of an answer, certify to the court within 30 days after service of the summons and complaint on the holder all of the following information:

(1) A complete description of the lien.

(2) A description of the property encumbered by the lien.

(3) The amount remaining due on the lien as of the date of the certificate.

(4) The date upon which each installment payable on the lien is due and the amount of each installment.

(c) A copy of the certification shall be sent by first-class mail to all parties to the proceeding at the time it is provided to the court. The filing of the certification or answer shall be considered as a general appearance. **Leg.H.** Added Stats 1979 ch 31 §1. Amended Stats 1980 ch 122 §1; Stats 1981 ch 139 §1.

ARTICLE 4
Pleadings

Complaint; Contents. §1250.310.
Answer. §1250.320.
Disclaimer. §1250.325.
Signature on pleading. §1250.330.
Amendment or supplement to pleading. §1250.340.
Waiver of objection to complaint. §1250.345.

§1250.310. Complaint; Contents

The complaint shall contain all of the following:

(a) The names of all plaintiffs and defendants.

(b) A description of the property sought to be taken. The description may, but is not required to, indicate the nature or extent of the interest of the defendant in the property.

(c) If the plaintiff claims an interest in the property sought to be taken, the nature and extent of such interest.

(d) A statement of the right of the plaintiff to take by eminent domain the property described in the complaint. The statement shall include:

(1) A general statement of the public use for which the property is to be taken.

(2) An allegation of the necessity for the taking as required by Section 1240.030; where the plaintiff is a public entity, a reference to its resolution of necessity; where the plaintiff is a quasi-public entity within the meaning of Section 1245.320, a reference to the resolution adopted pursuant to Article 3 (commencing with Section 1245.310) of Chapter 4; where the plaintiff is a nonprofit hospital, a reference to the certificate required by Section 1260 of the Health and Safety Code; where the plaintiff is a public utility and relies on a certification of the State Energy Resources Conservation and Development Commission or a requirement of that commission that development rights be acquired, a reference to such certification or requirement.

(3) A reference to the statute that authorizes the plaintiff to acquire the property by eminent domain. Specification of the statutory authority may be in the alternative and may be inconsistent.

(e) A map or diagram portraying as far as practicable the property described in the complaint and showing its location in relation to the project for which it is to be taken. **Leg.H.** Added Stats 1975 ch 1275 §2, operative July 1 1976.

§1250.320. Answer

(a) The answer shall include a statement of the nature and extent of the interest the defendant claims in the property described in the complaint.

(b) If the defendant seeks compensation provided in Article 6 (commencing with Section 1263.510) (goodwill) of Chapter 9, the answer shall include a statement that the defendant claims compensation under Section 1263.510, but the answer need not specify the amount of that compensation.

(c) If the defendant seeks compensation as provided in Article 1 (commencing with Section 1245.010) of Chapter 4, the answer shall include a statement that the defendant claims compensation under Section 1245.060, but need not specify the amount of that compensation.

(d) If the defendant seeks compensation for losses caused by the plaintiff's unreasonable conduct prior to commencing the eminent domain proceeding, the answer shall include a statement that the defendant claims compensation for that loss, but need not specify the amount of the compensation. **Leg.H.** Added Stats 1975 ch 1275 §2, operative July 1, 1976. Amended Stats 2021 ch 401 §5 (AB 1578), effective January 1, 2022.

§1250.325. Disclaimer

(a) A defendant may file a disclaimer at any time, whether or not he is in default, and the disclaimer supersedes an answer previously filed by the defendant. The disclaimer need not be in any particular form. It shall contain a statement that the defendant claims no interest in the property or in the compensation that may be awarded. Notwithstanding Section 1250.330, the disclaimer shall be signed by the defendant.

(b) Subject to subdivision (c), a defendant who has filed a disclaimer has no right to participate in further proceedings or to share in the compensation awarded.

(c) The court may implement the disclaimer by appropriate orders including, where justified, awarding costs and litigation expenses. **Leg.H.** Added Stats 1975 ch 1275 §2, operative July 1, 1976.

§1250.330. Signature on pleading

Where a party is represented by an attorney, his pleading need not be verified but shall be signed by the attorney for the party. The signature of the attorney constitutes a certificate by him that he has read the pleading and that to the best of his knowledge, information, and belief there is ground to support it. If the pleading is not signed or is signed with intent to defeat the purposes of this section, it may be stricken. **Leg.H.** Added Stats 1975 ch 1275 §2, operative July 1, 1976.

§1250.340. Amendment or supplement to pleading

(a) Subject to subdivisions (b) and (c), the court may allow upon such terms and conditions as may be just an amendment or supplement to any pleading. In the case of an amendment or supplement to the complaint, such terms and conditions may include a change in the applicable date of valuation for the proceeding and an award of costs and litigation expenses which would not have been incurred had the proceeding as originally commenced been the same as the proceeding following such amendment or supplement.

(b) A public entity may add to the property sought to be taken only if it has adopted a resolution of necessity that satisfies the requirements of Article 2 (commencing with Section 1245.210) of Chapter 4 for the property to be added.

(c) Property previously sought to be taken may be deleted from the complaint only if the plaintiff has followed the procedure for partial abandonment of the proceeding as to that property. **Leg.H.** Added Stats 1975 ch 1275 §2, operative July 1, 1976.

§1250.345. Waiver of objection to complaint

Subject to the power of the court to permit an amendment of the answer, if the defendant fails to object to the complaint, either by demurrer or answer, he is deemed to have waived the objection. **Leg.H.** Added Stats 1975 ch 1275 §2, operative July 1, 1976.

ARTICLE 5
Objections to Right to Take

Objection by demurrer or answer. §1250.350.
Grounds for objection. §1250.360.
Additional grounds for objection. §1250.370.

§1250.350. Objection by demurrer or answer

A defendant may object to the plaintiff's right to take, by demurrer or answer as provided in Section 430.30, on any ground authorized by Section 1250.360 or Section 1250.370. The demurrer or answer shall state the specific ground upon which the objection is taken and, if the objection is taken by answer, the specific facts upon which the objection is based. An objection may be taken on more than one ground, and the grounds may be inconsistent. **Leg.H.** Added Stats 1975 ch 1275 §2, operative July 1, 1976.

§1250.360. Grounds for objection

Grounds for objection to the right to take, regardless of whether the plaintiff has adopted a resolution of necessity that satisfies the requirements of Article 2 (commencing with Section 1245.210) of Chapter 4, include:

(a) The plaintiff is not authorized by statute to exercise the power of eminent domain for the purpose stated in the complaint.

(b) The stated purpose is not a public use.

(c) The plaintiff does not intend to devote the property described in the complaint to the stated purpose.

(d) There is no reasonable probability that the plaintiff will devote the described property to the stated purpose within (1) seven years, or (2) 10 years where the property is taken pursuant to the Federal Aid Highway Act of 1973, or (3) such longer period as is reasonable.

(e) The described property is not subject to acquisition by the power of eminent domain for the stated purpose.

(f) The described property is sought to be acquired pursuant to Section 1240.410 (excess condemnation), 1240.510 (condemnation for compatible use), or 1240.610 (condemnation for more necessary public use), but the acquisition does not satisfy the requirements of those provisions.

(g) The described property is sought to be acquired pursuant to Section 1240.610 (condemnation for more necessary public use), but the defendant has the right under Section 1240.630 to continue the public use to which the property is appropriated as a joint use.

(h) Any other ground provided by law. **Leg.H.** Added Stats 1975 ch 1275 §2, operative July 1, 1976.

§1250.370. Additional grounds for objection

In addition to the grounds listed in Section 1250.360, grounds for objection to the right to take where the plaintiff has not adopted a resolution of necessity that conclusively establishes the matters referred to in Section 1240.030 include:

(a) The plaintiff is a public entity and has not adopted a resolution of necessity that satisfies the requirements of Article 2 (commencing with Section 1245.210) of Chapter 4.

(b) The public interest and necessity do not require the proposed project.

(c) The proposed project is not planned or located in the manner that will be most compatible with the greatest public good and the least private injury.

(d) The property described in the complaint is not necessary for the proposed project.

(e) The plaintiff is a quasi-public entity within the meaning of Section 1245.320 and has not satisfied the requirements of Article 3 (commencing with Section 1245.310) of Chapter 4. **Leg.H.** Added Stats 1975 ch 1275 §2, operative July 1, 1976.

ARTICLE 6
Settlement Offers and Alternative Dispute Resolution

Final offer and demand; Litigation expenses. §1250.410.
Agreement to refer eminent domain proceedings to mediation or arbitration; Payment of costs and fees. §1250.420.
Postponement of eminent domain proceedings to enable resolution; Conditions. §1250.430.
[Section renumbered 1961]. §1254.5.
[Section renumbered 1961]. §1254.7.

§1250.410. Final offer and demand; Litigation expenses

(a) At least 20 days prior to the date of the trial on issues relating to compensation, the plaintiff shall file with the court and serve on the defendant its final offer of compensation in the proceeding and the defendant shall file and serve on the plaintiff its final demand for compensation in the proceeding. The offer and the demand shall include all compensation required pursuant to this title, including compensation for loss of goodwill, if any, and shall state whether interest and costs are included. These offers and demands shall be the only offers and demands considered by the court in determining the entitlement, if any, to litigation expenses. Service shall be in the manner prescribed by Chapter 5 (commencing with Section 1010) of Title 14 of Part 2.

(b) If the court, on motion of the defendant made within 30 days after entry of judgment, finds that the offer of the plaintiff was unreasonable and that the demand of the defendant was reasonable viewed in the light of the evidence admitted and the compensation awarded in the proceeding, the costs allowed pursuant to Section 1268.710 shall include the defendant's litigation expenses.

(c) In determining the amount of litigation expenses allowed under this section, the court shall consider the offer required to be made by the plaintiff pursuant to Section 7267.2 of the Government Code, any deposit made by the plaintiff pursuant to Chapter 6 (commencing with Section

1255.010), and any other written offers and demands filed and served before or during the trial.

(d) If timely made, the offers and demands as provided in subdivision (a) shall be considered by the court on the issue of determining an entitlement to litigation expenses.

(e) As used in this section, "litigation expenses" means the party's reasonable attorney's fees and costs, including reasonable expert witness and appraiser fees. **Leg.H.** Added Stats 1975 ch 1275 §2, operative July 1, 1976. Amended Stats 1982 ch 1059 §2; Stats 1999 ch 102 §1 (SB 634); Stats 2001 ch 428 §1 (AB 237); Stats 2002 ch 295 §1 (AB 1770); Stats 2006 ch 594 §1 (SB 1210), effective January 1, 2007.

2001 Note: This act applies to any proceeding commenced on or after January 1, 2002. Stats 2001 ch 428 §11.

§1250.420. Agreement to refer eminent domain proceedings to mediation or arbitration; Payment of costs and fees

The parties may by agreement refer a dispute that is the subject of an eminent domain proceeding for resolution by any of the following means:

(a) Mediation by a neutral mediator.

(b) Binding arbitration by a neutral arbitrator. The arbitration is subject to Chapter 12 (commencing with Section 1273.010).

(c) Nonbinding arbitration by a neutral arbitrator. The arbitrator's decision in a nonbinding arbitration is final unless within 30 days after service of the arbitrator's decision a party moves the court for a trial of the eminent domain proceeding. If the judgment in the eminent domain proceeding is not more favorable to the moving party, the court shall order that party to pay to the other parties the following nonrefundable costs and fees, unless the court finds in writing and on motion that the imposition of costs and fees would create such a substantial economic hardship as not to be in the interest of justice:

(1) All costs specified in Section 1033.5, limited to those incurred from the time of election of the trial de novo. Nothing in this subdivision affects the right of a defendant to recover costs otherwise allowable pursuant to Section 1268.710, incurred before election of a trial de novo, except that a defendant may recover the costs of determining the apportionment of the award made pursuant to subdivision (b) of Section 1260.220 whenever incurred.

(2) The reasonable costs of the services of expert witnesses who are not regular employees of any party, actually incurred and reasonably necessary in the preparation or trial of the case, limited to those incurred from the time of election of the trial de novo.

(3) The compensation paid by the parties to the arbitrator. **Leg.H.** Added Stats 2001 ch 428 §3 (AB 237).

2001 Note: This act applies to any proceeding commenced on or after January 1, 2002. Stats 2001 ch 428 §11.

§1250.430. Postponement of eminent domain proceedings to enable resolution; Conditions

Notwithstanding any other statute or rule of court governing the date of trial of an eminent domain proceeding, on motion of a party the court may postpone the date of trial for a period that appears adequate to enable resolution of a dispute pursuant to alternative resolution procedures, if it is demonstrated to the satisfaction of the court that all of the following conditions are satisfied:

(a) The parties are actively engaged in alternative resolution of the dispute pursuant to Section 1250.420.

(b) The parties appear to be making progress toward resolution of the dispute without the need for a trial of the matter.

(c) The parties agree that additional time for the purpose of alternative dispute resolution is desirable. **Leg.H.** Added Stats 2001 ch 428 §4 (AB 237).

2001 Note: This act applies to any proceeding commenced on or after January 1, 2002. Stats 2001 ch 428 §11.

§1251. [Section repealed 1976]

Leg.H. Enacted 1872. Amended Stats 1911 ch 80 §1; Stats 1913 ch 160 §1; Stats 1915 ch 560 §1; Stats 1937 ch 924 §1. Repealed Stats 1975 ch 1275 §1, operative July 1, 1976.

§1252. [Section repealed 1976]

Leg.H. Enacted 1872. Repealed Stats 1975 ch 1275 §1, operative July 1, 1976.

§1252.1. [Section repealed 1976]

Leg.H. Added Stats 1961 ch 1612 §2, operative July 1, 1962. Repealed Stats 1975 ch 1275 §1, operative July 1, 1976.

Prior Law: Former CCP §1252.1, relating to taxes, penalties and costs, was added by Stats 1953 ch 1792 §1 and repealed by Stats 1955 ch 1229 §1.

§1252.2. [Section repealed 1976]

Leg.H. Added Stats 1961 ch 1612 §3, operative July 2, 1962. Amended Stats 1971 ch 559 §1. Repealed Stats 1975 ch 1275 §1, operative July 1, 1976.

§1253. [Section repealed 1976]

Leg.H. Enacted 1872. Amended Stats 1961 ch 1613 §7; Stats 1963 ch 70 §1, ch 1388 §1. Repealed Stats 1975 ch 1275 §1, operative July 1, 1976.

§1254. [Section repealed 1976]

Leg.H. Enacted 1872. Amended Code Amdts 1877–78 ch 651 §1; Code Amdts 1880 ch 116 §3; Stats 1897 ch 127 §1; Stats 1903 ch 98 §1; Stats 1955 ch 929 §1; Stats 1957 ch 1851 §1; Stats 1961 ch 72 §6, ch 1613 §8 Stats 1974 ch 706 §1. Repealed Stats 1975 ch 1275 §1, operative July 1, 1976.

§1254.5. [Section renumbered 1961]

Leg.H. Added Stats 1957 ch 1851 §2. Renumbered §1243.6 and amended Stats 1961 ch 1613 §3.

§1254.7. [Section renumbered 1961]

Leg.H. Added Stats 1957 ch 2022 §1. Renumbered §1243.7 and amended Stats 1961 ch 1613 §4.

§1255. [Section repealed 1976]

Leg.H. Enacted 1872. Repealed Stats 1975 ch 1275 §1, operative July 1, 1976.

§1255a. [Section repealed 1976]

Leg.H. Added Stats 1911 ch 208 §1. Amended Stats 1933 ch 254 §1; Stats 1961 ch 1613 §9; Stats 1968 ch 133 §1. Repealed Stats 1975 ch 1275 §1, operative July 1, 1976.

§1255b. [Section repealed 1976]

Leg.H. Added Stats 1959 ch 282 §1. Amended Stats 1961 ch 1613 §10. Repealed Stats 1975 ch 1275 §1, operative July 1, 1976.

CHAPTER 6
DEPOSIT AND WITHDRAWAL OF PROBABLE COMPENSATION; POSSESSION PRIOR TO JUDGMENT

Article 1. Deposit of Probable Compensation.
Article 2. Withdrawal of Deposit.
Article 3. Possession Prior to Judgment.

ARTICLE 1
Deposit of Probable Compensation

Deposit; Appraisal. §1255.010.
Notice of deposit. §1255.020.
Details sufficient to support motion; Sufficiency of deposit; Increase of deposit. §1255.030.
Deposit where defendant resides on property. §1255.040.
Deposit where property subject to leasehold interest. §1255.050.
Amount of deposit and appraisal as evidence at trial. §1255.060.
Place of deposit. §1255.070.
Investment of deposit. §1255.075.
Rights not waived. §1255.080.

§1255.010. Deposit; Appraisal

(a) At any time before entry of judgment, the plaintiff may deposit with the State Treasury the probable amount of compensation, based on an appraisal, that will be awarded in the proceeding. The appraisal upon which the deposit is based shall be one that satisfies the requirements of subdivision (b). The deposit may be made whether or not the plaintiff applies for an order for possession or intends to do so.

(b) Before making a deposit under this section, the plaintiff shall have an expert qualified to express an opinion as to the value of the property (1) make an appraisal of the property and (2) prepare a written statement of, or summary of the basis for, the appraisal. The statement or summary shall contain detail sufficient to indicate clearly the basis for the appraisal, including, but not limited to, all of the following information:

(A) The date of valuation, highest and best use, and applicable zoning of the property.

(B) The principal transactions, reproduction or replacement cost analysis, or capitalization analysis, supporting the appraisal.

(C) If the appraisal includes compensation for damages to the remainder, the compensation for the property and for damages to the remainder separately stated, and the calculations and a narrative explanation supporting the compensation, including any offsetting benefits.

(c) On noticed motion, or upon ex parte application in an emergency, the court may permit the plaintiff to make a deposit without prior compliance with subdivision (b) if the plaintiff presents facts by affidavit showing that (1) good cause exists for permitting an immediate deposit to be made, (2) an adequate appraisal has not been completed and cannot reasonably be prepared before making the deposit, and (3) the amount of the deposit to be made is not less than the probable amount of compensation that the plaintiff, in good faith, estimates will be awarded in the proceeding. In its order, the court shall require that the plaintiff comply with subdivision (b) within a reasonable time, to be specified in the order, and also that any additional amount of compensation shown by the appraisal required by subdivision (b) be deposited within that time. **Leg.H.** Added Stats 1975 ch 1275 §2, operative July 1, 1976. Amended Stats 1990 ch 1491 §9 (AB 3765); Stats 2001 ch 428 §5 (AB 237).

2001 Note: This act applies to any proceeding commenced on or after January 1, 2002. Stats 2001 ch 428 §11.

§1255.020. Notice of deposit

(a) On making a deposit pursuant to Section 1255.010, the plaintiff shall serve a notice of deposit on all parties who have appeared in the proceeding and file with the court a proof of service together with the notice of deposit. The plaintiff shall so serve parties who appear thereafter on their appearance. The notice of deposit shall state that a deposit has been made and the date and the amount of the deposit. Service of the notice of deposit shall be made in the manner provided in Section 1255.450 for service of an order for possession.

(b) The notice of deposit shall be accompanied by a written statement or summary of the basis for the appraisal referred to in Section 1255.010.

(c) If the plaintiff has obtained an order under Section 1255.010 deferring completion of the written statement or summary, the plaintiff:

(1) On making the deposit, shall comply with subdivision (a) and include with the notice a copy of all affidavits on which the order was based.

(2) Upon completion of the written statement or summary, shall comply with subdivision (b). **Leg.H.** Added Stats 1975 ch 1275 §2, operative July 1, 1976. Amended Stats 1990 ch 1491 §10 (AB 3765).

§1255.030. Details sufficient to support motion; Sufficiency of deposit; Increase of deposit

(a) At any time after a deposit has been made pursuant to this article, the court shall, upon motion of the plaintiff or of any party having an interest in the property for which the deposit was made, determine or redetermine whether the amount deposited is the probable amount of compensation that will be awarded in the proceeding. The motion shall be supported with detail sufficient to indicate clearly the basis for the motion, including, but not limited to, the following information to the extent relevant to the motion:

(1) The date of valuation, highest and best use, and applicable zoning of the property.

(2) The principal transactions, reproduction or replacement cost analysis, or capitalization analysis, supporting the motion.

(3) The compensation for the property and for damages to the remainder separately stated, and the calculations and a narrative explanation supporting the compensation, including any offsetting benefits.

(b) If the plaintiff has not taken possession of the property and the court determines that the probable amount of compensation exceeds the amount deposited, the court may order the plaintiff to increase the deposit or may deny the plaintiff possession of the property until the amount deposited has been increased to the amount specified in the order.

(c) If the plaintiff has taken possession of the property and the court determines that the probable amount of compensation exceeds the amount deposited, the court shall order the amount deposited to be increased to the amount determined to be the probable amount of compensation. If the amount on deposit is not increased accordingly within 30 days from the date of the court's order, or any longer time as the court may have allowed at the time of making the order, the defendant may serve on the plaintiff a notice of election to treat that failure as an abandonment of the proceeding. If the plaintiff does not cure its failure within 10 days after receipt of such notice, the court shall, upon motion of the defendant, enter judgment dismissing the proceeding and awarding the defendant his or her litigation expenses and damages as provided in Sections 1268.610 and 1268.620.

(d) After any amount deposited pursuant to this article has been withdrawn by a defendant, the court may not determine or redetermine the probable amount of compensation to be less than the total amount already withdrawn. Nothing in this subdivision precludes the court from making a determination or redetermination that probable compensation is greater than the amount withdrawn.

(e) If the court determines that the amount deposited exceeds the probable amount of compensation, it may permit the plaintiff to withdraw the excess not already withdrawn by the defendant.

(f) The plaintiff may at any time increase the amount deposited without making a motion under this section. In that case, notice of the increase shall be served as provided in subdivision (a) of Section 1255.020. **Leg.H.** Added Stats 1975 ch 1275 §2, operative July 1, 1976. Amended Stats 2001 ch 428 §6 (AB 237).

2001 Note: This act applies to any proceeding commenced on or after January 1, 2002. Stats 2001 ch 428 §11.

§1255.040. Deposit where defendant resides on property

(a) If the plaintiff has not made a deposit that satisfies the requirements of this article and the property includes a dwelling containing not more than two residential units and the dwelling or one of its units is occupied as his or her residence by a defendant, the defendant may serve notice on the plaintiff requiring a deposit of the probable amount of compensation that will be awarded in the proceeding. The notice shall specify the date by which the defendant desires the deposit to be made. The date shall not be earlier than 30 days after the date of service of the notice and may be any later date.

(b) If the plaintiff deposits the probable amount of compensation, determined or redetermined as provided in this article, on or before the date specified by the defendant, the plaintiff may obtain an order for possession that authorizes the plaintiff to take possession of the property 30 days after the date for the deposit specified by the defendant or any later date as the plaintiff may request.

(c) Notwithstanding Section 1268.310, if the deposit is not made on or before the date specified by the defendant or such later date as the court specifies on motion and good cause shown by the plaintiff, the compensation awarded to the defendant in the proceeding shall draw legal interest from that date. The defendant is entitled to the full amount of such interest without offset for rents or other income received by him or her or the value of his or her continued possession of the property.

(d) If the proceeding is abandoned by the plaintiff, the interest under subdivision (c) may be recovered as costs in the proceeding in the manner provided for the recovery of litigation expenses under Section 1268.610. If, in the proceeding, the court or a jury verdict eventually determines the compensation that would have been awarded to the defendant, then the interest shall be computed on the amount of the award. If no determination is ever made, then the interest shall be computed on the probable amount of compensation as determined by the court.

(e) The serving of a notice pursuant to this section constitutes a waiver by operation of law, conditioned upon subsequent deposit by the plaintiff of the probable amount of compensation, of all claims and defenses in favor of the defendant except his or her claim for greater compensation.

(f) Notice of a deposit made under this section shall be served as provided by subdivision (a) of Section 1255.020. The defendant may withdraw the deposit as provided in Article 2 (commencing with Section 1255.210).

(g) No notice may be served by a defendant under subdivision (a) after entry of judgment unless the judgment is reversed, vacated, or set aside and no other judgment has been entered at the time the notice is served. **Leg.H.** Added Stats 1975 ch 1275 §2, operative July 1, 1976. Amended Stats 2006 ch 594 §2 (SB 1210), effective January 1, 2007.

§1255.050. Deposit where property subject to leasehold interest

If the property to be taken is subject to a leasehold interest and the plaintiff has not made a deposit that satisfies the requirements of this article, the lessor may serve notice on the plaintiff requiring a deposit of the probable amount of compensation that will be awarded in the proceeding in the same manner and subject to the same procedures and conditions as a motion pursuant to Section 1255.040 except that, if the plaintiff fails to make the deposit, the interest awarded shall be offset by the lessor's net rental profits on the property. **Leg.H.** Added Stats 1975 ch 1275 §2, operative July 1, 1976.

§1255.060. Amount of deposit and appraisal as evidence at trial

(a) The amount deposited or withdrawn pursuant to this chapter may not be given in evidence or referred to in the trial of the issue of compensation.

(b) In the trial of the issue of compensation, an appraisal report, written statement and summary of an appraisal, or other statement made in connection with a deposit or withdrawal pursuant to this chapter may not be considered to be an admission of any party.

(c) Upon objection of the party at whose request an appraisal report, written statement and summary of the appraisal, or other statement was made in connection with a deposit or withdrawal pursuant to this chapter, the person who made the report or statement and summary or other statement may not be called at the trial on the issue of compensation by any other party to give an opinion as to compensation. If the person who prepared the report, statement and summary, or other statement is called at trial to give an opinion as to compensation, the report, statement and summary, or other statement may be used for impeachment of the witness. **Leg.H.** Added Stats 1975 ch 1275 §2, operative July 1, 1976. Amended Stats 2002 ch 295 §2 (AB 1770).

§1255.070. Place of deposit

In lieu of depositing the money with the State Treasury as provided in Section 1255.010, upon written request of the plaintiff, the court shall order the money be deposited in the county treasury. If money is deposited in the State Treasury pursuant to Section 1255.010, it shall be held, invested, deposited, and disbursed in the manner specified in Article 10 (commencing with Section 16429) of Chapter 2 of Part 2 of Division 4 of Title 2 of the Government Code, and interest earned or other increment derived from its investment shall be apportioned and disbursed in the manner specified in that article. As between the parties to the proceeding, money deposited pursuant to this article shall remain at the risk of the plaintiff until paid or made payable to the defendant by order of the court. **Leg.H.** Added Stats 1975 ch 1275 §2, operative July 1, 1976. Amended Stats 1990 ch 1491 §11 (AB 3765).

§1255.075. Investment of deposit

(a) Prior to entry of judgment, a defendant who has an interest in the property for which a deposit has been made under this chapter may, upon notice to the other parties to the proceeding, move the court to have all of such deposit invested for the benefit of the defendants.

(b) At the hearing on the motion, the court shall consider the interests of the parties and the effect that investment would have upon them. The court may, in its discretion, if it finds that the interests of justice will be served, grant the motion subject to such terms and conditions as are appropriate under the circumstances of the case.

(c) An investment under this section shall be specified by the court and shall be limited to United States government obligations or interest-bearing accounts in an institution whose accounts are insured by an agency of the federal government.

(d) The investment of the deposit has the same consequences as if the deposit has been withdrawn under this chapter. **Leg.H.** Added Stats 1975 ch 1275 §2, operative July 1, 1976.

§1255.080. Rights not waived

By depositing the probable compensation pursuant to this article, the plaintiff does not waive the right to appeal from the judgment, the right to move to abandon, or the right to request a new trial. **Leg.H.** Added Stats 1975 ch 1275 §2, operative July 1, 1976.

ARTICLE 2
Withdrawal of Deposit

Application for withdrawal of deposit. §1255.210.
Order of court. §1255.220.
Objections by plaintiff. §1255.230.
Undertaking by applicant. §1255.240.
Undertaking by applicant; Where amount withdrawn exceeds amount of original deposit. §1255.250.
Waiver. §1255.260.
Withdrawal of excess amount; Judgment. §1255.280.

§1255.210. Application for withdrawal of deposit

Prior to entry of judgment, any defendant may apply to the court for the withdrawal of all or any portion of the amount deposited. The application shall be verified, set forth the applicant's interest in the property, and request withdrawal of a stated amount. The applicant shall serve a copy of the application on the plaintiff. **Leg.H.** Added Stats 1975 ch 1275 §2, operative July 1, 1976.

§1255.220. Order of court

Subject to the requirements of this article, the court shall order the amount requested in the application, or such portion of that amount as the applicant is entitled to receive, to be paid to the applicant. **Leg.H.** Added Stats 1975 ch 1275 §2, operative July 1, 1976.

§1255.230. Objections by plaintiff

(a) No withdrawal may be ordered until 20 days after service on the plaintiff of a copy of the application or until the time for all objections has expired, whichever is later.

(b) Within the 20-day period, the plaintiff may file objections to withdrawal on any one or more of the following grounds:

(1) Other parties to the proceeding are known or believed to have interests in the property.

(2) An undertaking should be filed by the applicant as provided in Section 1255.240 or 1255.250.

(3) The amount of an undertaking filed by the applicant under this chapter or the sureties thereon are insufficient.

(c) If an objection is filed on the ground that other parties are known or believed to have interests in the property, the plaintiff shall serve or attempt to serve on such other parties a notice that they may appear within 10 days after such service and object to the withdrawal. The notice shall advise such parties that their failure to object will result in waiver of any rights against the plaintiff to the extent of the amount withdrawn. The notice shall be served in the manner provided in Section 1255.450 for service of an order for possession. The plaintiff shall file, and serve on the applicant, a report setting forth (1) the names of the parties upon whom the notice was served and the dates of service and (2) the names and last known addresses of the other parties who are known or believed to have interests in the property but who were not so served. The applicant may serve parties whom the plaintiff has been unable to serve. Parties served in the manner provided in Section 1255.450 shall have no claim against the plaintiff for compensation to the extent of the amount withdrawn by all applicants. The plaintiff shall remain liable to parties having an interest of record who are not so served but, if such liability is enforced, the plaintiff shall be subrogated to the rights of such parties under Section 1255.280.

(d) If any party objects to the withdrawal, or if the plaintiff so requests, the court shall determine, upon hearing, the amounts to be withdrawn, if any, and by whom. **Leg.H.** Added Stats 1975 ch 1275 §2, operative July 1, 1976.

§1255.240. Undertaking by applicant

(a) If the court determines that an applicant is entitled to withdraw any portion of a deposit that another party claims or to which another person may be entitled, the court may require the applicant, before withdrawing such portion, to file an undertaking. The undertaking shall secure payment to such party or person of any amount withdrawn that exceeds the amount to which the applicant is entitled as finally determined in the proceeding, together with interest as provided in Section 1255.280. If withdrawal is permitted notwithstanding the lack of personal service of the application for withdrawal upon any party to the proceeding, the court may also require that the undertaking indemnify the plaintiff against any liability it may incur under Section 1255.230. The undertaking shall be in such amount as is fixed by the court, but if executed by an admitted surety insurer the amount shall not exceed the portion claimed by the adverse claimant or appearing to belong to another person. If executed by two or more sufficient sureties, the amount shall not exceed double such portion.

(b) If the undertaking is required primarily because of an issue as to title between the applicant and another party or person, the applicant filing the undertaking is not entitled to recover the premium reasonably paid for the undertaking as a part of the recoverable costs in the eminent domain proceeding. **Leg.H.** Added Stats 1975 ch 1275 §2, operative July 1, 1976. Amended Stats 1982 ch 517 §182.

§1255.250. Undertaking by applicant; Where amount withdrawn exceeds amount of original deposit

(a) If the amount originally deposited is increased pursuant to Section 1255.030 and the total amount sought to be withdrawn exceeds the amount of the original deposit, the applicant, or each applicant if there are two or more, shall file an undertaking. The undertaking shall be in favor of the plaintiff and shall secure repayment of any amount withdrawn that exceeds the amount to which the applicant is entitled as finally determined in the eminent domain proceeding, together with interest as provided in Section 1255.280. If the undertaking is executed by an admitted surety insurer, the undertaking shall be in the amount by which the total amount to be withdrawn exceeds the amount originally deposited. If the undertaking is executed by two or more sufficient sureties, the undertaking shall be in double such amount, but the maximum amount that may be recovered from such sureties is the amount by which the total amount to be withdrawn exceeds the amount originally deposited.

(b) If there are two or more applicants, the applicants, in lieu of filing separate undertakings, may jointly file a single undertaking in the amount required by subdivision (a). **Leg.H.** Added Stats 1975 ch 1275 §2, operative July 1, 1976. Amended Stats 1982 ch 517 §183.

§1255.260. Waiver

If any portion of the money deposited pursuant to this chapter is withdrawn, the receipt of any such money shall constitute a waiver by operation of law of all claims and defenses in favor of the persons receiving such payment except a claim for greater compensation. **Leg.H.** Added Stats 1975 ch 1275 §2, operative July 1, 1976.

§1255.280. Withdrawal of excess amount; Judgment

(a) Any amount withdrawn by a party pursuant to this article in excess of the amount to which he is entitled as finally determined in the eminent domain proceeding shall be paid to the parties entitled thereto. The court shall enter judgment accordingly.

(b) The judgment so entered shall not include interest except in the following cases:

(1) Any amount that is to be paid to a defendant shall include legal interest from the date of its withdrawal by another defendant.

(2) If the amount originally deposited by a plaintiff was increased pursuant to Section 1255.030 on motion of a party obligated to pay under this section, any amount that is attributable to such increase and that is to be repaid to the plaintiff shall include legal interest from the date of its withdrawal.

(c) If the judgment so entered is not paid within 30 days after its entry, the court may, on motion, enter judgment against the sureties, if any, for the amount of such judgment.

(d) The court may, in its discretion and with such security, if any, as it deems appropriate, grant a party obligated to pay under this section a stay of execution for any amount to be paid to a plaintiff. Such stay of execution shall not exceed one year following entry of judgment under this section. **Leg.H.** Added Stats 1975 ch 1275 §2, operative July 1, 1976.

ARTICLE 3
Possession Prior to Judgment

Order for possession; Application; Urgent need. §1255.410.
Vacation of order. §1255.440.
Service of order. §1255.450.
Order for possession issued under Section 1255.410. §1255.460.
Effect of taking possession. §1255.470.
Exercise of police power. §1255.480.

§1255.410. Order for possession; Application; Urgent need

(a) At the time of filing the complaint or at any time after filing the complaint and prior to entry of judgment, the plaintiff may move the court for an order for possession under this article, demonstrating that the plaintiff is entitled to take the property by eminent domain and has deposited pursuant to Article 1 (commencing with Section 1255.010) an amount that satisfies the requirements of that article.

The motion shall describe the property of which the plaintiff is seeking to take possession, which description may be by reference to the complaint, and shall state the date after which the plaintiff is seeking to take possession of the property. The motion shall include a statement substantially in the following form: "You have the right to oppose this motion for an order of possession of your property. If you oppose this motion you must serve the plaintiff and file with the court a written opposition to the motion within 30 days from the date you were served with this motion." If the written opposition asserts a hardship, it shall be supported by a declaration signed under penalty of perjury stating facts supporting the hardship.

(b) The plaintiff shall serve a copy of the motion on the record owner of the property and on the occupants, if any. The plaintiff shall set the court hearing on the motion not less than 60 days after service of the notice of motion on the record owner of unoccupied property. If the property is lawfully occupied by a person dwelling thereon or by a farm or business operation, service of the notice of motion shall be made not less than 90 days prior to the hearing on the motion.

(c) Not later than 30 days after service of the plaintiff's motion seeking to take possession of the property, any defendant or occupant of the property may oppose the motion in writing by serving the plaintiff and filing with the court the opposition. If the written opposition asserts a hardship, it shall be supported by a declaration signed under penalty of perjury stating facts supporting the hardship. The plaintiff shall serve and file any reply to the opposition not less than 15 days before the hearing.

(d)(1) If the motion is not opposed within 30 days of service on each defendant and occupant of the property, the court shall make an order for possession of the property if the court finds each of the following:

(A) The plaintiff is entitled to take the property by eminent domain.

(B) The plaintiff has deposited pursuant to Article 1 (commencing with Section 1255.010) an amount that satisfies the requirements of that article.

(2) If the motion is opposed by a defendant or occupant within 30 days of service, the court may make an order for possession of the property upon consideration of the relevant facts and any opposition, and upon completion of a hearing on the motion, if the court finds each of the following:

(A) The plaintiff is entitled to take the property by eminent domain.

(B) The plaintiff has deposited pursuant to Article 1 (commencing with Section 1255.010) an amount that satisfies the requirements of that article.

(C) There is an overriding need for the plaintiff to possess the property prior to the issuance of final judgment in the case, and the plaintiff will suffer a substantial hardship if the application for possession is denied or limited.

(D) The hardship that the plaintiff will suffer if possession is denied or limited outweighs any hardship on the defendant or occupant that would be caused by the granting of the order of possession.

(e)(1) Notwithstanding the time limits for notice prescribed by this section and Section 1255.450, a court may issue an order of possession upon an ex parte application by a water, wastewater, gas, electric, or telephone utility, as the court deems appropriate under the circumstances of the case, if the court finds each of the following:

(A) An emergency exists and as a consequence the utility has an urgent need for possession of the property. For purposes of this section, an emergency is defined to include, but is not limited to, a utility's urgent need to protect the public's health and safety or the reliability of utility service.

(B) An emergency order of possession will not displace or unreasonably affect any person in actual and lawful possession of the property to be taken or the larger parcel of which it is a part.

(2) Not later than 30 days after service of the order authorizing the plaintiff to take possession of the property, any defendant or occupant of the property may move for relief from an emergency order of possession that has been issued under this subdivision. The court may modify, stay, or vacate the order upon consideration of the relevant facts and any objections raised, and upon completion of a hearing if requested. **Leg.H.** Added Stats 1975 ch 1275 §2, operative July 1, 1976. Amended Stats 2006 ch 594 §3 (SB 1210), effective January 1, 2007; Stats 2007 ch 436 §1 (SB 698), effective January 1, 2008.

§1255.420. [Section repealed 2007]

Leg.H. Added Stats 1975 ch 1275 §2, operative July 1, 1976. Repealed Stats 2006 ch 594 §4 (SB 1210), effective January 1, 2007. The repealed section related to relief from order and hardship.

§1255.430. [Section repealed 2007]

Leg.H. Added Stats 1975 ch 1275 §2, operative July 1, 1976. Repealed Stats 2006 ch 594 §5 (SB 1210), effective January 1, 2007. The repealed section related to stay of order.

§1255.440. Vacation of order

If an order has been made under Section 1255.410 authorizing the plaintiff to take possession of property and the court subsequently determines that the conditions specified in Section 1255.410 for issuance of the order are not satisfied, the court shall vacate the order. **Leg.H.** Added Stats 1975 ch 1275 §2, operative July 1, 1976.

§1255.450. Service of order

(a) As used in this section, "record owner" means the owner of the legal or equitable title to the fee or any lesser interest in property as shown by recorded deeds or other recorded instruments.

(b) The plaintiff shall serve a copy of the order for possession issued under Section 1255.410 on the record owner of the property and on the occupants, if any. If the property is lawfully occupied by a person dwelling thereon or by a farm or business operation, service shall be made not less than 30 days prior to the time possession is to be taken pursuant to the order. In all other cases, service shall be made not less than 10 days prior to the time possession is to be taken pursuant to the order. Service may be made with or following service of summons.

(c) At least 30 days prior to the time possession is taken pursuant to an order for possession made pursuant to Section 1255.040, 1255.050, or 1255.460, the plaintiff shall serve a copy of the order on the record owner of the property and on the occupants, if any.

(d) Service of the order shall be made by personal service except that:

(1) If the person on whom service is to be made has previously appeared in the proceeding or been served with summons in the proceeding, service of the order may be made by mail upon that person and his or her attorney of record, if any.

(2) If the person on whom service is to be made resides out of the state, or has departed from the state or cannot with due diligence be found within the state, service of the order may be made by registered or certified mail addressed to that person at his or her last known address.

(e) When the record owner cannot be located, the court may, for good cause shown on ex parte application, authorize the plaintiff to take possession of unoccupied property without serving a copy of the order for possession upon a record owner.

(f) A single service upon or mailing to one of several persons having a common business or residence address is sufficient. **Leg.H.** Added Stats 1975 ch 1275 §2, operative July 1, 1976. Amended Stats 2006 ch 594 §6 (SB 1210), effective January 1, 2007.

§1255.460. Order for possession issued under Section 1255.410

An order for possession issued pursuant to Section 1255.410 shall:

(a) Recite that it has been made under this section.

(b) Describe the property to be acquired, which description may be by reference to the complaint.

(c) State the date after which plaintiff is authorized to take possession of the property. **Leg.H.** Added Stats 1975 ch 1275 §2, operative July 1, 1976. Amended Stats 2006 ch 594 §7 (SB 1210), effective January 1, 2007.

§1255.470. Effect of taking possession

By taking possession pursuant to this chapter, the plaintiff does not waive the right to appeal from the judgment, the right to move to abandon, or the right to request a new trial. **Leg.H.** Added Stats 1975 ch 1275 §2, operative July 1, 1976.

§1255.480. Exercise of police power

Nothing in this article limits the right of a public entity to exercise its police power in emergency situations. **Leg.H.** Added Stats 1975 ch 1275 §2, operative July 1, 1976.

§1256. [Section repealed 1976]

Leg.H. Enacted 1872. Repealed Stats 1975 ch 1275 §1, operative July 1, 1976.

§1256.1. [Section repealed 1976]

Leg.H. Added Stats 1951 ch 766 §1. Repealed Stats 1975 ch 1275 §1, operative July 1, 1976.

§1256.2. [Section repealed 1967]

Leg.H. Added Stats 1957 ch 1850 §1. Repealed Stats 1965 ch 299 §21, operative January 1, 1967. See Ev C §722.

§1257. [Section repealed 1976]

Leg.H. Enacted 1872. Amended Code Amdts 1877–78 ch 651 §2; Stats 1897 ch 127 §1; Stats 1903 ch 98 §2. Repealed Stats 1975 ch 1275 §1, operative July 1, 1976.

§1258. [Section repealed 1976]

Leg.H. Enacted 1872. Repealed Stats 1975 ch 1275 §1, operative July 1, 1976.

CHAPTER 7
DISCOVERY; EXCHANGE OF VALUATION DATA

Article 1. Discovery.
Article 2. Exchange of Valuation Data.

ARTICLE 1
Discovery

Effect of provisions. §1258.010.
Discovery. §1258.020.
Admissibility of evidence. §1258.030.

§1258.010. Effect of provisions

The provisions of this chapter supplement but do not replace, restrict, or prevent the use of discovery procedures or limit the matters that are discoverable in eminent domain proceedings. **Leg.H.** Added Stats 1975 ch 1275 §2, operative July 1, 1976.

§1258.020. Discovery

(a) Notwithstanding any other statute or any court rule relating to discovery, proceedings pursuant to subdivision (b) may be had without requirement of court order and may proceed until not later than 20 days prior to the day set for trial of the issue of compensation.

(b) A party to an exchange of lists of expert witnesses and statements of valuation data pursuant to Article 2 (commencing with Section 1258.210) or pursuant to court rule as provided in Section 1258.300 may after the time of the exchange obtain discovery from the other party to the exchange and from any person listed by him as an expert witness.

(c) The court, upon noticed motion by the person subjected to discovery pursuant to subdivision (b), may make any order that justice requires to protect such person from annoyance, embarrassment, or oppression. **Leg.H.** Added Stats 1975 ch 1275 §2, operative July 1, 1976. Amended Stats 1992 ch 876 §8 (AB 3296).

§1258.030. Admissibility of evidence

Nothing in this chapter makes admissible any evidence that is not otherwise admissible or permits a witness to base an opinion on any matter that is not a proper basis for such an opinion. **Leg.H.** Added Stats 1975 ch 1275 §2, operative July 1, 1976.

ARTICLE 2
Exchange of Valuation Data

Demand to exchange lists of expert witnesses and statements of valuation data. §1258.210.
"Date of exchange". §1258.220.
Deposit and service of list and statements; Duties of clerk. §1258.230.
Contents of list of expert witnesses. §1258.240.
Number of valuation data statements required. §1258.250.
Contents of statement of valuation data; Method to determine loss of goodwill. §1258.260.
Notice of additions to list and statement. §1258.270.
Failure to comply; Penalties. §1258.280.
Failure to comply; Excuse. §1258.290.
Alternative procedure. §1258.300.

§1258.210. Demand to exchange lists of expert witnesses and statements of valuation data

(a) Not later than the 10th day after the trial date is selected, any party may file and serve on any other party a demand to exchange lists of expert witnesses and statements of valuation data. Thereafter, the court may, upon noticed motion and a showing of good cause, permit any party to serve such a demand upon any other party.

(b) The demand shall:

(1) Describe the property to which it relates, which description may be by reference to the complaint.

(2) Include a statement in substantially the following form: "You are required to serve and deposit with the clerk of court a list of expert witnesses and statements of valuation data in compliance with Article 2

(commencing with Section 1258.210) of Chapter 7 of Title 7 of Part 3 of the Code of Civil Procedure not later than the date of exchange to be set in accordance with that article. Except as otherwise provided in that article, your failure to do so will constitute a waiver of your right to call unlisted expert witnesses during your case in chief and of your right to introduce on direct examination during your case in chief any matter that is required to be, but is not, set forth in your statements of valuation data."
Leg.H. Added Stats 1975 ch 1275 §2, operative July 1, 1976.

§1258.220. "Date of exchange"

(a) For the purposes of this article, the "date of exchange" is the date agreed to for the exchange of their lists of expert witnesses and statements of valuation data by the party who served a demand and the party on whom the demand was served or, failing agreement, a date 90 days prior to commencement of the trial on the issue of compensation or the date set by the court on noticed motion of either party establishing good cause therefor.

(b) Notwithstanding subdivision (a), unless otherwise agreed to by the parties, the date of exchange shall not be earlier than nine months after the date of commencement of the proceeding. **Leg.H.** Added Stats 1975 ch 1275 §2, operative July 1, 1976. Amended Stats 1999 ch 102 §2 (SB 634); Stats 2001 ch 428 §7 (AB 237).

2001 Note: This act applies to any proceeding commenced on or after January 1, 2002. Stats 2001 ch 428 §11.

§1258.230. Deposit and service of list and statements; Duties of clerk

(a) Not later than the date of exchange:

(1) Each party who served a demand and each party upon whom a demand was served shall deposit with the clerk of the court a list of expert witnesses and statements of valuation data.

(2) A party who served a demand shall serve his list and statements upon each party on whom he served his demand.

(3) Each party on whom a demand was served shall serve his list and statements upon the party who served the demand.

(b) The clerk of the court shall make an entry in the register of actions for each list of expert witnesses and statement of valuation data deposited with him pursuant to this article. The lists and statements shall not be filed in the proceeding, but the clerk shall make them available to the court at the commencement of the trial for the limited purpose of enabling the court to apply the provisions of this article. Unless the court otherwise orders, the clerk shall, at the conclusion of the trial, return all lists and statements to the attorneys for the parties who deposited them. Lists or statements ordered by the court to be retained may thereafter be destroyed or otherwise disposed of in accordance with the provisions of law governing the destruction or disposition of exhibits introduced in the trial. **Leg.H.** Added Stats 1975 ch 1275 §2, operative July 1, 1976.

§1258.240. Contents of list of expert witnesses

The list of expert witnesses shall include the name, business or residence address, and business occupation, or profession of each person intended to be called as an expert witness by the party and a statement of the subject matter to which his testimony relates. **Leg.H.** Added Stats 1975 ch 1275 §2, operative July 1, 1976.

§1258.250. Number of valuation data statements required

A statement of valuation data shall be exchanged for each person the party intends to call as a witness to testify to his opinion as to any of the following matters:

(a) The value of the property being taken.

(b) The amount of the damage, if any, to the remainder of the larger parcel from which such property is taken.

(c) The amount of the benefit, if any, to the remainder of the larger parcel from which such property is taken.

(d) The amount of any other compensation required to be paid by Chapter 9 (commencing with Section 1263.010) or Chapter 10 (commencing with Section 1265.010). **Leg.H.** Added Stats 1975 ch 1275 §2, operative July 1, 1976.

§1258.260. Contents of statement of valuation data; Method to determine loss of goodwill

(a) The statement of valuation data shall give the name and business or residence address of the witness and shall include a statement whether the witness will testify to an opinion as to any of the matters listed in Section 1258.250 and, as to each matter upon which the witness will give an opinion, what that opinion is and the following items to the extent that the opinion is based on them:

(1) The interest being valued.

(2) The date of valuation used by the witness.

(3) The highest and best use of the property.

(4) The applicable zoning and the opinion of the witness as to the probability of any change in zoning.

(5) The sales, contracts to sell and purchase, and leases supporting the opinion.

(6) The cost of reproduction or replacement of the existing improvements on the property, the depreciation or obsolescence the improvements have suffered, and the method of calculation used to determine depreciation.

(7) The gross income from the property, the deductions from gross income, and the resulting net income; the reasonable net rental value attributable to the land and existing improvements, and the estimated gross rental income and deductions upon which the reasonable net rental value is computed; the rate of capitalization used; and the value indicated by the capitalization.

(8) If the property is a portion of a larger parcel, a description of the larger parcel and its value.

(9) If the opinion concerns loss of goodwill, the method used to determine the loss, and a summary of the data supporting the opinion.

(b) With respect to each sale, contract, or lease listed under paragraph (5) of subdivision (a), the statement of valuation data shall give:

(1) The names and business or residence addresses, if known, of the parties to the transaction.

(2) The location of the property subject to the transaction.

(3) The date of the transaction.

(4) If recorded, the date of recording and the volume and page or other identification of the record of the transaction.

(5) The price and other terms and circumstances of the transaction. In lieu of stating the terms contained in any contract, lease, or other document, the statement may, if the document is available for inspection by the adverse party, state the place where and the times when it is available for inspection.

(6) The total area and shape of the property subject to the transaction.

(c) If any opinion referred to in Section 1258.250 is based in whole or in substantial part upon the opinion of another person, the statement of valuation data shall include the name and business or residence address of that other person, his business, occupation, or profession, and a statement as to the subject matter to which his or her opinion relates.

(d) Except when an appraisal report is used as a statement of valuation data as permitted by subdivision (e), the statement of valuation data shall include a statement, signed by the witness, that the witness has read the statement of valuation data and that it fairly and correctly states his or her opinions and knowledge as to the matters therein stated.

(e) An appraisal report that has been prepared by the witness which includes the information required to be included in a statement of valuation data may be used as a statement of valuation data under this article. **Leg.H.** Added Stats 1975 ch 1275 §2, operative July 1, 1976. Amended Stats 1978 ch 342 §1; Stats 2001 ch 428 §8 (AB 237).

2001 Note: This act applies to any proceeding commenced on or after January 1, 2002. Stats 2001 ch 428 §11.

§1258.270. Notice of additions to list and statement

(a) A party who is required to exchange lists of expert witnesses and statements of valuation data shall diligently give notice to the parties upon whom his list and statements were served if, after service of his list and statements, he:

(1) Determines to call an expert witness not included in his list of expert witnesses to testify on direct examination during his case in chief;

(2) Determines to have a witness called by him testify on direct examination during his case in chief to any opinion or data required to be listed in the statement of valuation data for that witness but which was not so listed; or

(3) Discovers any data required to be listed in a statement of valuation data but which was not so listed.

(b) The notice required by subdivision (a) shall include the information specified in Sections 1258.240 and 1258.260 and shall be in writing; but such notice is not required to be in writing if it is given after the commencement of the trial. **Leg.H.** Added Stats 1975 ch 1275 §2, operative July 1, 1976.

§1258.280. Failure to comply; Penalties

Except as provided in Section 1258.290, upon objection of a party who has served his list of expert witnesses and statements of valuation data in compliance with Section 1258.230:

(a) No party required to serve a list of expert witnesses on the objecting party may call an expert witness to testify on direct examination during his case in chief unless the information required by Section 1258.240 for such witness is included in the list served.

(b) No party required to serve statements of valuation data on the objecting party may call a witness to testify on direct examination during his case in chief to his opinion on any matter listed in Section 1258.250 unless a statement of valuation data for such witness was served.

(c) No witness called by a party required to serve statements of valuation data on the objecting party may testify on direct examination during the case in chief of the party who called him to any opinion or data required to be listed in the statement of valuation data for such witness unless such opinion or data is listed in the statement served except that testimony that is merely an explanation or elaboration of data so listed is not inadmissible under this subdivision. **Leg.H.** Added Stats 1975 ch 1275 §2, operative July 1, 1976.

§1258.290. Failure to comply; Excuse

(a) The court may, upon such terms as may be just (including but not limited to continuing the trial for a reasonable period of time and awarding costs and litigation expenses), permit a party to call a witness, or permit a witness called by a party to testify to an opinion or data on direct examination, during the party's case in chief where such witness, opinion, or data is required to be, but is not, included in such party's list of expert witnesses or statements of valuation data if the court finds that such party has made a good faith effort to comply with Sections 1258.210 to 1258.260, inclusive, that he has complied with Section 1258.270, and that by the date of exchange he:

(1) Would not in the exercise of reasonable diligence have determined to call such witness or discovered or listed such opinion or data; or

(2) Failed to determine to call such witness or to discover or list such opinion or data through mistake, inadvertence, surprise, or excusable neglect.

(b) In making a determination under this section, the court shall take into account the extent to which the opposing party has relied upon the list of expert witnesses and statements of valuation data and will be prejudiced if the witness is called or the testimony concerning such opinion or data is given. **Leg.H.** Added Stats 1975 ch 1275 §2, operative July 1, 1976.

§1258.300. Alternative procedure

The superior court in any county may provide by court rule a procedure for the exchange of valuation data which shall be used in lieu of the procedure provided by this article if the Judicial Council finds that such procedure serves the same purpose and is an adequate substitute for the procedure provided by this article. **Leg.H.** Added Stats 1975 ch 1275 §2, operative July 1, 1976.

§1259. [Section repealed 1976]

Leg.H. Added by unpublished act of April 1, 1872. Repealed Stats 1975 ch 1275 §1, operative July 1, 1976.

§1260. [Section repealed 1976]

Leg.H. Added by unpublished act of April 1, 1872. Repealed Stats 1975 ch 1275 §1, operative July 1, 1976.

CHAPTER 8
PROCEDURES FOR DETERMINING RIGHT TO TAKE AND COMPENSATION

Article 1. General Provisions.
Article 2. Contesting Right to Take.
Article 3. Procedures Relating to Determination of Compensation.

ARTICLE 1
General Provisions

Proceedings to be given precedence. §1260.010.
Consolidated proceedings. §1260.020.
Determination whether property is improvement pertaining to realty. §1260.030.
Evidentiary or other legal dispute motion; Postponement by court. §1260.040.

§1260.010. Proceedings to be given precedence

Proceedings under this title take precedence over all other civil actions in the matter of setting the same for hearing or trial in order that such proceedings shall be quickly heard and determined. **Leg.H.** Added Stats 1975 ch 1275 §2, operative July 1, 1976.

§1260.020. Consolidated proceedings

(a) If proceedings to acquire the same property are consolidated, the court shall first determine whether the public uses for which the property is sought are compatible within the meaning of Article 6 (commencing with Section 1240.510) of Chapter 3. If the court determines that the uses are compatible, it shall permit the proceeding to continue with the plaintiffs acting jointly. The court shall apportion the obligation to pay any award in the proceeding in proportion to the use, damage, and benefits attributable to each plaintiff.

(b) If the court determines pursuant to subdivision (a) that the uses are not all compatible, it shall further determine which of the uses is the more necessary public use within the meaning of Article 7 (commencing with Section 1240.610) of Chapter 3. The court shall permit the plaintiff alleging the more necessary public use, along with any other plaintiffs alleging compatible public uses under subdivision (a), to continue the proceeding. The court shall dismiss the proceeding as to the other plaintiffs. **Leg.H.** Added Stats 1975 ch 1275 §2, operative July 1, 1976.

§1260.030. Determination whether property is improvement pertaining to realty

(a) If there is a dispute between plaintiff and defendant whether particular property is an improvement pertaining to the realty, either party may, not later than 30 days prior to the date specified in an order for possession of the property, move the court for a determination whether the property is an improvement pertaining to the realty.

(b) A motion under this section shall be heard not sooner than 10 days and not later than 20 days after service of notice of the motion. At the hearing, the court may consider any relevant evidence, including a view of the premises and property, in making its determinations. **Leg.H.** Added Stats 1975 ch 1275 §2, operative July 1, 1976.

§1260.040. Evidentiary or other legal dispute motion; Postponement by court

(a) If there is a dispute between plaintiff and defendant over an evidentiary or other legal issue affecting the determination of compensation, either party may move the court for a ruling on the issue. The motion shall be made not later than 60 days before commencement of trial on the issue of compensation. The motion shall be heard by the judge assigned for trial of the case.

(b) Notwithstanding any other statute or rule of court governing the date of final offers and demands of the parties and the date of trial of an eminent domain proceeding, the court may postpone those dates for a period sufficient to enable the parties to engage in further proceedings before trial in response to its ruling on the motion.

(c) This section supplements, and does not replace any other pretrial or trial procedure otherwise available to resolve an evidentiary or other legal issue affecting the determination of compensation. **Leg.H.** Added Stats 2001 ch 428 §9 (AB 237).

2001 Note: This act applies to any proceeding commenced on or after January 1, 2002. Stats 2001 ch 428 §11.

ARTICLE 2
Contesting Right to Take

Objections to right to take; Hearing and determination. §1260.110.
Objections to right to take; Order. §1260.120.

§1260.110. Objections to right to take; Hearing and determination

(a) Where objections to the right to take are raised, unless the court orders otherwise, they shall be heard and determined prior to the determination of the issue of compensation.

(b) The court may, on motion of any party, after notice and hearing, specially set such objections for trial. **Leg.H.** Added Stats 1975 ch 1275 §2, operative July 1, 1976.

§1260.120. Objections to right to take; Order

(a) The court shall hear and determine all objections to the right to take.

(b) If the court determines that the plaintiff has the right to acquire by eminent domain the property described in the complaint, the court shall so order.

(c) If the court determines that the plaintiff does not have the right to acquire by eminent domain any property described in the complaint, it shall order either of the following:

(1) Immediate dismissal of the proceeding as to that property.

(2) Conditional dismissal of the proceeding as to that property unless such corrective and remedial action as the court may prescribe has been taken within the period prescribed by the court in the order. An order made under this paragraph may impose such limitations and conditions as the court determines to be just under the circumstances of the particular case including the requirement that the plaintiff pay to the defendant all or part of the reasonable litigation expenses necessarily incurred by the defendant because of the plaintiff's failure or omission which constituted the basis of the objection to the right to take. **Leg.H.** Added Stats 1975 ch 1275 §2, operative July 1, 1976.

ARTICLE 3
Procedures Relating to Determination of Compensation

Presentation of evidence; Burden of proof. §1260.210.
Dividend interests in property; Determination of rights of each defendant. §1260.220.
Items to be assessed separately. §1260.230.
Interests of persons unknown or deceased. §1260.240.
Determination of tax liability. §1260.250.

§1260.210. Presentation of evidence; Burden of proof

(a) The defendant shall present his evidence on the issue of compensation first and shall commence and conclude the argument.

(b) Except as otherwise provided by statute, neither the plaintiff nor the defendant has the burden of proof on the issue of compensation. **Leg.H.** Added Stats 1975 ch 1275 §2, operative July 1, 1976.

§1260.220. Dividend interests in property; Determination of rights of each defendant

(a) Except as provided in subdivision (b), where there are divided interests in property acquired by eminent domain, the value of each interest and the injury, if any, to the remainder of such interest shall be separately assessed and compensation awarded therefor.

(b) The plaintiff may require that the amount of compensation be first determined as between plaintiff and all defendants claiming an interest in the property. Thereafter, in the same proceeding, the trier of fact shall determine the respective rights of the defendants in and to the amount of compensation awarded and shall apportion the award accordingly. Nothing in this subdivision limits the right of a defendant to present during the first stage of the proceeding evidence of the value of, or injury to, the property or the defendant's interest in the property; and the right of a defendant to present evidence during the second stage of the proceeding is not affected by the failure to exercise the right to present evidence during the first stage of the proceeding. **Leg.H.** Added Stats 1975 ch 1275 §2, operative July 1, 1976. Amended Stats 1978 ch 294 §1.

§1260.230. Items to be assessed separately

As far as practicable, the trier of fact shall assess separately each of the following:

(a) Compensation for the property taken as required by Article 4 (commencing with Section 1263.310) of Chapter 9.

(b) When the property acquired is part of a larger parcel:

(1) The amount of the damage, if any, to the remainder as required by Article 5 (commencing with Section 1263.410) of Chapter 9.

(2) The amount of the benefit, if any, to the remainder as required by Article 5 (commencing with Section 1263.410) of Chapter 9.

(c) Compensation for loss of goodwill, if any, as required by Article 6 (commencing with Section 1263.510) of Chapter 9.

(d) Compensation claimed under subdivision (c) of Section 1250.320.

(e) Compensation claimed under subdivision (d) of Section 1250.320.
Leg.H. Added Stats 1975 ch 1275 §2, operative July 1, 1976. Amended Stats 2021 ch 401 §6 (AB 1578), effective January 1, 2022.

§1260.240. Interests of persons unknown or deceased

Where any persons unknown or any deceased persons or the heirs and devisees of any deceased persons have been properly joined as defendants but have not appeared either personally or by a personal representative, the court shall determine the extent of the interests of such defendants in the property taken or in the remainder if the property taken is part of a larger parcel and the compensation to be awarded for such interests. The court may determine the extent and value of the interests of all such defendants in the aggregate without apportionment between the respective defendants. In any event, in the case of deceased persons, the court shall determine only the extent and value of the interest of the decedent and shall not determine the extent and value of the separate interests of the heirs and devisees in such decedent's interest. **Leg.H.** Added Stats 1975 ch 1275 §2, operative July 1, 1976.

§1260.250. Determination of tax liability

(a) In a county where both the auditor and the tax collector are elected officials, the court shall by order give the auditor or tax collector the legal description of the property sought to be taken and direct the auditor or tax collector to certify to the court the information required by subdivision (c), and the auditor or tax collector shall promptly certify the required information to the court. In all other counties, the court shall by order give the tax collector the legal description of the property sought to be taken and direct the tax collector to certify to the court the information required by subdivision (c), and the tax collector shall promptly certify the required information to the court.

(b) The court order shall be made on or before the earliest of the following dates:

(1) The date the court makes an order for possession.

(2) The date set for trial.

(3) The date of entry of judgment.

(c) The court order shall require certification of the following information:

(1) The current assessed value of the property together with its assessed identification number.

(2) All unpaid taxes on the property, and any penalties and costs that have accrued thereon while on the secured roll, levied for prior tax years that constitute a lien on the property.

(3) All unpaid taxes on the property, and any penalties and costs that have accrued thereon while on the secured roll, levied for the current tax year that constitute a lien on the property prorated to, but not including, the date of apportionment determined pursuant to Section 5082 of the Revenue and Taxation Code or the date of trial, whichever is earlier. If the amount of the current taxes is not ascertainable at the time of proration, the amount shall be estimated and computed based on the assessed value for the current assessment year and the tax rate levied on the property for the immediately prior tax year.

(4) The actual or estimated amount of taxes on the property that are or will become a lien on the property in the next succeeding tax year prorated to, but not including, the date of apportionment determined pursuant to Section 5082 of the Revenue and Taxation Code or the date of trial, whichever is earlier. Any estimated amount of taxes shall be computed based on the assessed value of the property for the current assessment year and the tax rate levied on the property for the current tax year.

(5) The amount of the taxes, penalties, and costs allocable to one day of the current tax year, and where applicable, the amount allocable to one day of the next succeeding tax year, hereinafter referred to as the "daily prorate."

(6) The total of paragraphs (2), (3), and (4).

(d) If the property sought to be taken does not have a separate valuation on the assessment roll, the information required by this section shall be for the larger parcel of which the property is a part.

(e) The court, as part of the judgment, shall separately state the amount certified pursuant to this section and order that the amount be paid to the tax collector from the award. If the amount so certified is prorated to the date of trial, the order shall include, in addition to the amount so certified, an amount equal to the applicable daily prorate multiplied by the number of days commencing on the date of trial and ending on and including the day before the date of apportionment determined pursuant to Section 5082 of the Revenue and Taxation Code.

(f) Notwithstanding any other provision of this section, if the board of supervisors provides the procedure set forth in Section 5087 of the Revenue and Taxation Code, the court shall make no award of taxes in the judgment. **Leg.H.** Added Stats 1979 ch 31 §2. Amended Stats 1999 ch 892 §12 (AB 1672).

§1261. [Section repealed 1976]

Leg.H. Added by unpublished act of April 1, 1872. Repealed Stats 1975 ch 1275 §1, operative July 1, 1976.

§1262. [Section repealed 1976]

Leg.H. Added by unpublished act of April 1, 1872. Repealed Stats 1975 ch 1275 §1, operative July 1, 1976.

§1263. [Section repealed 1976]

Leg.H. Added by unpublished act of April 1, 1872. Repealed Stats 1975 ch 1275 §1, operative July 1, 1976.

CHAPTER 9
COMPENSATION

Article 1. General Provisions.
Article 2. Date of Valuation.
Article 3. Compensation for Improvements.
Article 4. Measure of Compensation for Property Taken.
Article 5. Compensation for Injury to Remainder.
Article 6. Compensation for Loss of Goodwill.
Article 7. Miscellaneous Provisions.
Article 8. Remediation of Hazardous Materials on Property to be Acquired by School Districts.

ARTICLE 1
General Provisions

Right to compensation. §1263.010.
Agreement specifying manner of payment. §1263.015.
Accrual of right to compensation. §1263.020.
Independent appraisal following offer to purchase property under threat of eminent domain. §1263.025.

§1263.010. Right to compensation

(a) The owner of property acquired by eminent domain is entitled to compensation as provided in this chapter.

(b) Nothing in this chapter affects any rights the owner of property acquired by eminent domain may have under any other statute. In any case where two or more statutes provide compensation for the same loss, the person entitled to compensation may be paid only once for that loss. **Leg.H.** Added Stats 1975 ch 1275 §2, operative July 1, 1976.

§1263.015. Agreement specifying manner of payment

At the request of an owner of property acquired by eminent domain, the public entity may enter into an agreement with the owner specifying the manner of payment of compensation to which the owner is entitled as the result of the acquisition. The agreement may provide that the compensation shall be paid by the public entity to the owner over a period not to exceed 10 years from the date the owner's right to compensation accrues. The agreement may also provide for the payment of interest by the public entity; however, the rate of interest agreed upon may not exceed the maximum rate authorized by Section 16731 or 53531 of the Government Code, as applicable, in connection with the issuance of bonds. **Leg.H.** Added Stats 1982 ch 1368 §1.

§1263.020. Accrual of right to compensation

Except as otherwise provided by law, the right to compensation shall be deemed to have accrued at the date of filing the complaint. **Leg.H.** Added Stats 1975 ch 1275 §2, operative July 1, 1976.

§1263.025. Independent appraisal following offer to purchase property under threat of eminent domain

(a) A public entity shall offer to pay the reasonable costs, not to exceed five thousand dollars ($5,000), of an independent appraisal ordered by the owner of a property that the public entity offers to purchase under a threat of eminent domain, at the time the public entity makes the offer to purchase the property. The independent appraisal shall be conducted by an appraiser licensed by the Office of Real Estate Appraisers.

(b) For purposes of this section, an offer to purchase a property "under a threat of eminent domain" is an offer to purchase a property pursuant to any of the following:

(1) Eminent domain.

(2) Following adoption of a resolution of necessity for the property pursuant to Section 1240.040.

(3) Following a statement that the public entity may take the property by eminent domain. **Leg.H.** Added Stats 2006 ch 594 §8 (SB 1210), effective January 1, 2007.

ARTICLE 2
Date of Valuation

Date of deposit. §1263.110.
Date of commencement of proceeding. §1263.120.
Date of commencement of trial. §1263.130.
Date of commencement of new trial. §1263.140.
Date of commencement of retrial. §1263.150.

§1263.110. Date of deposit

(a) Unless an earlier date of valuation is applicable under this article, if the plaintiff deposits the probable compensation in accordance with Article 1 (commencing with Section 1255.010) of Chapter 6 or the amount of the award in accordance with Article 2 (commencing with Section 1268.110) of Chapter 11, the date of valuation is the date on which the deposit is made.

(b) Whether or not the plaintiff has taken possession of the property or obtained an order for possession, if the court determines pursuant to Section 1255.030 that the probable amount of compensation exceeds the amount previously deposited pursuant to Article 1 (commencing with Section 1255.010) of Chapter 6 and the amount on deposit is not increased accordingly within the time allowed under Section 1255.030, no deposit shall be deemed to have been made for the purpose of this section. **Leg.H.** Added Stats 1975 ch 1275 §2, operative July 1, 1976.

§1263.120. Date of commencement of proceeding

If the issue of compensation is brought to trial within one year after commencement of the proceeding, the date of valuation is the date of commencement of the proceeding. **Leg.H.** Added Stats 1975 ch 1275 §2, operative July 1, 1976.

§1263.130. Date of commencement of trial

Subject to Section 1263.110, if the issue of compensation is not brought to trial within one year after commencement of the proceeding, the date of valuation is the date of the commencement of the trial unless the delay is caused by the defendant, in which case the date of valuation is the date of commencement of the proceeding. **Leg.H.** Added Stats 1975 ch 1275 §2, operative July 1, 1976.

§1263.140. Date of commencement of new trial

Subject to Section 1263.110, if a new trial is ordered by the trial or appellate court and the new trial is not commenced within one year after the commencement of the proceeding, the date of valuation is the date of the commencement of such new trial unless, in the interest of justice, the court ordering the new trial orders a different date of valuation. **Leg.H.** Added Stats 1975 ch 1275 §2, operative July 1, 1976.

§1263.150. Date of commencement of retrial

Subject to Section 1263.110, if a mistrial is declared and the retrial is not commenced within one year after the commencement of the proceeding, the date of valuation is the date of the commencement of the retrial of the case unless, in the interest of justice, the court declaring the mistrial orders a different date of valuation. **Leg.H.** Added Stats 1975 ch 1275 §2, operative July 1, 1976.

ARTICLE 3
Compensation for Improvements

Definitions. §1263.205.
Compensation for improvements. §1263.210.
Removal or destruction of improvements. §1263.230.
Subsequent improvements. §1263.240.
Crops. §1263.250.
Election to remove improvements; Notice; Costs. §1263.260.
Improvements located in part upon property not taken. §1263.270.

§1263.205. Definitions

(a) As used in this article, "improvements pertaining to the realty" include any machinery or equipment installed for use on property taken by eminent domain, or on the remainder if such property is part of a larger parcel, that cannot be removed without a substantial economic loss or without substantial damage to the property on which it is installed, regardless of the method of installation.

(b) In determining whether particular property can be removed "without a substantial economic loss" within the meaning of this section, the value of the property in place considered as a part of the realty should be compared with its value if it were removed and sold. **Leg.H.** Added Stats 1975 ch 1275 §2, operative July 1, 1976.

§1263.210. Compensation for improvements

(a) Except as otherwise provided by statute, all improvements pertaining to the realty shall be taken into account in determining compensation.

(b) Subdivision (a) applies notwithstanding the right or obligation of a tenant, as against the owner of any other interest in real property, to remove such improvement at the expiration of his term. **Leg.H.** Added Stats 1975 ch 1275 §2, operative July 1, 1976.

§1263.230. Removal or destruction of improvements

(a) Improvements pertaining to the realty shall not be taken into account in determining compensation to the extent that they are removed or destroyed before the earliest of the following times:

(1) The time the plaintiff takes title to the property.

(2) The time the plaintiff takes possession of the property.

(3) If the defendant moves from the property in compliance with an order for possession, the date specified in the order; except that, if the defendant so moves prior to such date and gives the plaintiff written notice thereof, the date 24 hours after such notice is received by the plaintiff.

(b) Where improvements pertaining to the realty are removed or destroyed by the defendant at any time, such improvements shall not be taken into account in determining compensation. Where such removal or destruction damages the remaining property, such damage shall be taken into account in determining compensation to the extent it reduces the value of the remaining property. **Leg.H.** Added Stats 1975 ch 1275 §2, operative July 1, 1976.

§1263.240. Subsequent improvements

Improvements pertaining to the realty made subsequent to the date of service of summons shall not be taken into account in determining compensation unless one of the following is established:

(a) The improvement is one required to be made by a public utility to its utility system.

(b) The improvement is one made with the written consent of the plaintiff.

(c) The improvement is one authorized to be made by a court order issued after a noticed hearing and upon a finding by the court that the hardship to the defendant of not permitting the improvement outweighs the hardship to the plaintiff of permitting the improvement. The court may, at the time it makes an order under this subdivision authorizing the improvement to be made, limit the extent to which the improvement shall be taken into account in determining compensation. **Leg.H.** Added Stats 1975 ch 1275 §2, operative July 1, 1976.

§1263.250. Crops

(a) The acquisition of property by eminent domain shall not prevent the defendant from harvesting and marketing crops planted before or after the service of summons. If the plaintiff takes possession of the property at a time that prevents the defendant from harvesting and marketing the crops, the fair market value of the crops in place at the date the plaintiff is authorized to take possession of the property shall be included in the compensation awarded for the property taken.

(b) Notwithstanding subdivision (a), the plaintiff may obtain a court order precluding the defendant from planting crops after service of summons, in which case the compensation awarded for the property taken shall include an amount sufficient to compensate for loss caused by the limitation on the defendant's right to use the property. **Leg.H.** Added Stats 1975 ch 1275 §2, operative July 1, 1976.

§1263.260. Election to remove improvements; Notice; Costs

Notwithstanding Section 1263.210, the owner of improvements pertaining to the realty may elect to remove any or all such improvements by serving on the plaintiff within 60 days after service of summons written notice of such election. If the plaintiff fails within 30 days thereafter to serve on the owner written notice of refusal to allow removal of such improvements, the owner may remove such improvements and shall be compensated for their reasonable removal and relocation cost not to exceed the market value of the improvements. Where such removal will cause damage to the structure in which the improvements are located, the defendant shall cause no more damage to the structure than is reasonably necessary in removing the improvements, and the structure shall be valued as if the removal had caused no damage to the structure. **Leg.H.** Added Stats 1975 ch 1275 §2, operative July 1, 1976.

§1263.270. Improvements located in part upon property not taken

Where an improvement pertaining to the realty is located in part upon property taken and in part upon property not taken, the court may, on motion of any party and a determination that justice so requires, direct the plaintiff to acquire the entire improvement, including the part located on property not taken, together with an easement or other interest reasonably necessary for the demolition, removal, or relocation of the improvement. **Leg.H.** Added Stats 1975 ch 1275 §2, operative July 1, 1976.

ARTICLE 4
Measure of Compensation for Property Taken

Measure of compensation. §1263.310.
Fair market value. §1263.320.
Determination of value of nonprofit, special use property. §1263.321.
Effect of changes in value. §1263.330.

§1263.310. Measure of compensation

Compensation shall be awarded for the property taken. The measure of this compensation is the fair market value of the property taken. **Leg.H.** Added Stats 1975 ch 1275 §2, operative July 1, 1976.

§1263.320. Fair market value

(a) The fair market value of the property taken is the highest price on the date of valuation that would be agreed to by a seller, being willing to sell but under no particular or urgent necessity for so doing, nor obliged to sell, and a buyer, being ready, willing, and able to buy but under no particular necessity for so doing, each dealing with the other with full knowledge of all the uses and purposes for which the property is reasonably adaptable and available.

(b) The fair market value of property taken for which there is no relevant, comparable market is its value on the date of valuation as determined by any method of valuation that is just and equitable. **Leg.H.** Added Stats 1975 ch 1275 §2, operative July 1, 1976. Amended Stats 1992 ch 7 §2 (SB 821).

1992 Note: Section 1263.320, as amended by ch 7, shall apply to eminent domain actions or proceedings commenced on or after January 1, 1993. Stats 1992 ch 7 §7.

§1263.321. Determination of value of nonprofit, special use property

A just and equitable method of determining the value of nonprofit, special use property for which there is no relevant, comparable market is as set forth in Section 824 of the Evidence Code, but subject to the exceptions set forth in subdivision (c) of Section 824 of the Evidence Code. **Leg.H.** Added Stats 1992 ch 7 §3 (SB 821).

1992 Note: Section 1263.321, as added by ch 7, shall apply to eminent domain actions or proceedings commenced on or after January 1, 1993. Stats 1992 ch 7 §7.

§1263.330. Effect of changes in value

The fair market value of the property taken shall not include any increase or decrease in the value of the property that is attributable to any of the following:

(a) The project for which the property is taken.

(b) The eminent domain proceeding in which the property is taken.

(c) Any preliminary actions of the plaintiff relating to the taking of the property. **Leg.H.** Added Stats 1975 ch 1275 §2, operative July 1, 1976.

ARTICLE 5
Compensation for Injury to Remainder

Measure of compensation. §1263.410.
Damage to remainder. §1263.420.
Benefit to remainder. §1263.430.
Time of damage or benefit. §1263.440.
Basis of compensation. §1263.450.

§1263.410. Measure of compensation

(a) Where the property acquired is part of a larger parcel, in addition to the compensation awarded pursuant to Article 4 (commencing with Section 1263.310) for the part taken, compensation shall be awarded for the injury, if any, to the remainder.

(b) Compensation for injury to the remainder is the amount of the damage to the remainder reduced by the amount of the benefit to the remainder. If the amount of the benefit to the remainder equals or exceeds the amount of the damage to the remainder, no compensation shall be awarded under this article. If the amount of the benefit to the remainder exceeds the amount of damage to the remainder, such excess shall be deducted from the compensation provided in Section 1263.510, if any, but shall not be deducted from the compensation required to be awarded for the property taken or from the other compensation required by this chapter. **Leg.H.** Added Stats 1975 ch 1275 §2, operative July 1, 1976.

§1263.420. Damage to remainder

Damage to the remainder is the damage, if any, caused to the remainder by either or both of the following:

(a) The severance of the remainder from the part taken.

(b) The construction and use of the project for which the property is taken in the manner proposed by the plaintiff whether or not the damage is caused by a portion of the project located on the part taken. **Leg.H.** Added Stats 1975 ch 1275 §2, operative July 1, 1976.

§1263.430. Benefit to remainder

Benefit to the remainder is the benefit, if any, caused by the construction and use of the project for which the property is taken in the manner proposed by the plaintiff whether or not the benefit is caused by a portion of the project located on the part taken. **Leg.H.** Added Stats 1975 ch 1275 §2, operative July 1, 1976.

§1263.440. Time of damage or benefit

(a) The amount of any damage to the remainder and any benefit to the remainder shall reflect any delay in the time when the damage or benefit caused by the construction and use of the project in the manner proposed by the plaintiff will actually be realized.

(b) The value of the remainder on the date of valuation, excluding prior changes in value as prescribed in Section 1263.330, shall serve as the base from which the amount of any damage and the amount of any benefit to the remainder shall be determined. **Leg.H.** Added Stats 1975 ch 1275 §2, operative July 1, 1976.

§1263.450. Basis of compensation

Compensation for injury to the remainder shall be based on the project as proposed. Any features of the project which mitigate the damage or provide benefit to the remainder, including but not limited to easements, crossings, underpasses, access roads, fencing, drainage facilities, and cattle guards, shall be taken into account in determining the compensation for injury to the remainder. **Leg.H.** Added Stats 1975 ch 1275 §2, operative July 1, 1976.

ARTICLE 6
Compensation for Loss of Goodwill

Burden of proof. §1263.510.
State tax returns. §1263.520.
Scope of article. §1263.530.

§1263.510. Burden of proof

(a) The owner of a business conducted on the property taken, or on the remainder if the property is part of a larger parcel, shall be compensated for loss of goodwill if the owner proves all of the following:

(1) The loss is caused by the taking of the property or the injury to the remainder.

(2) The loss cannot reasonably be prevented by a relocation of the business or by taking steps and adopting procedures that a reasonably prudent person would take and adopt in preserving the goodwill.

(3) Compensation for the loss will not be included in payments under Section 7262 of the Government Code.

(4) Compensation for the loss will not be duplicated in the compensation otherwise awarded to the owner.

(b) Within the meaning of this article, "goodwill" consists of the benefits that accrue to a business as a result of its location, reputation for dependability, skill or quality, and any other circumstances resulting in probable retention of old or acquisition of new patronage.

(c) If the public entity and the owner enter into a leaseback agreement pursuant to Section 1263.615, the following shall apply:

(1) No additional goodwill shall accrue during the lease.

(2) The entering of a leaseback agreement shall not be a factor in determining goodwill. Any liability for goodwill shall be established and paid at the time of acquisition of the property by eminent domain or subsequent to notice that the property may be taken by eminent domain. **Leg.H.** Added Stats 1975 ch 1275 §2, operative July 1, 1976. Amended Stats 2006 ch 602 §2 (SB 1650), effective January 1, 2007.

2006 Note: This act shall apply prospectively and shall apply to property acquired after January 1, 2007. Stats 2006 ch 602 (SB 1650) §4.

§1263.520. State tax returns

The owner of a business who claims compensation under this article shall make available to the court, and the court shall, upon such terms and conditions as will preserve their confidentiality, make available to the plaintiff, the state tax returns of the business for audit for confidential use solely for the purpose of determining the amount of compensation under this article. Nothing in this section affects any right a party may otherwise have to discovery or to require the production of documents, papers, books, and accounts. **Leg.H.** Added Stats 1975 ch 1275 §2, operative July 1, 1976.

§1263.530. Scope of article

Nothing in this article is intended to deal with compensation for inverse condemnation claims for temporary interference with or interruption of business. **Leg.H.** Added Stats 1975 ch 1275 §2, operative July 1, 1976.

ARTICLE 7
Miscellaneous Provisions

Agreement between public entity and owner of property. §1263.610.
Certain property acquisitions subject to offer of lease-back agreement. §1263.615.
Compensation for interrupted improvements. §1263.620.

§1263.610. Agreement between public entity and owner of property

A public entity and the owner of property to be acquired for public use may make an agreement that the public entity will:

(a) Relocate for the owner any structure if such relocation is likely to reduce the amount of compensation otherwise payable to the owner by an amount equal to or greater than the cost of such relocation.

(b) Carry out for the owner any work on property not taken, including work on any structure, if the performance of the work is likely to reduce the amount of compensation otherwise payable to the owner by an amount equal to or greater than the cost of the work. **Leg.H.** Added Stats 1975 ch 1275 §2, operative July 1, 1976.

§1263.615. Certain property acquisitions subject to offer of lease-back agreement

(a) A public entity shall offer a one-year leaseback agreement to the owner of a property to be acquired by any method set forth in subdivision (b) for that property owner's continued use of the property upon acquisition, subject to the property owner's payment of fair market rents and compliance with other conditions set forth in subdivision (c), unless the public entity states in writing that the development, redevelopment, or use of the property for its stated public use is scheduled to begin within two years of its acquisition. This section shall not apply if the public entity states in writing that a leaseback of the property would create or allow the continuation of a public nuisance to the surrounding community.

(b) The following property acquisitions are subject to the requirements of this section:

(1) Any acquisition by a public entity pursuant to eminent domain.

(2) Any acquisition by a public entity following adoption of a resolution of necessity pursuant to Article 2 (commencing with Section 1245.210) of Chapter 4 for the property.

(3) Any acquisition by a public entity prior to the adoption of a resolution of necessity pursuant to Article 2 (commencing with Section 1245.210) of Chapter 4 for the property, but subsequent to a written notice that the public entity may take the property by eminent domain.

(c) The following conditions shall apply to any leaseback offered pursuant to this section:

(1) The lessee shall be responsible for any additional waste or nuisance on the property, and for any other liability arising from the continued use of the property.

(2) The lessor may demand a security deposit to cover any potential liability arising from the leaseback. The security deposit shall be reasonable in light of the use of the leased property.

(3) The lessor shall be indemnified from any legal liability and attorney's fees resulting from any lawsuit against the lessee or lessor, arising from the operation of the lessee's business or use of the property.

(4) The lessor shall require the lessee to carry adequate insurance to cover potential liabilities arising from the lease and use of the property, and shall require that insurance to name the lessor as an additional insured.

(5) Additional goodwill shall not accrue during any lease.

(6) The lessee shall be subject to unlawful detainer proceedings as provided by law.

(d) A public entity shall offer to renew a leaseback agreement for one-year terms, subject to any rent adjustment to reflect inflation and upon compliance with other conditions set forth in subdivision (c), unless the public entity states in writing that the development, redevelopment, or use of the property for its stated public use is scheduled to begin within two years of the termination date of the lease. At least 60 days prior to the lease termination date, the public entity lessor shall either offer a one-year renewal of the lease or send a statement declaring that the lease will not be renewed because the development, redevelopment, or use of the property is scheduled to begin within two years of the lease termination date. The lessee shall either accept or reject a lease renewal offer at least 30 days prior to the lease termination date. The lessee's failure to accept a renewal offer in a timely manner shall constitute a rejection of the renewal offer. A lessor's failure to offer a renewal or give the notice as required shall extend the lease term for 60-day increments until an offer or notice is made, and if a notice of termination is given after the lease termination date, the lessee shall have no less than 60 days to vacate the property. A lessee's failure to accept within 30 days a renewal offer made subsequent to the lease termination date shall constitute a rejection of the offer.

(e) A party who holds over after expiration of the lease shall be subject to unlawful detainer proceedings and shall also be subject to the lessor for holdover damages.

(f) A leaseback entered into pursuant to this section shall not affect the amount of compensation otherwise payable to the property owner for the property to be acquired. **Leg.H.** Added Stats 2006 ch 602 §3 (SB 1650), effective January 1, 2007.

2006 Note: This act shall apply prospectively and shall apply to property acquired after January 1, 2007. Stats 2006 ch 602 (SB 1650) §4.

§1263.620. Compensation for interrupted improvements

(a) Where summons is served during construction of an improvement or installation of machinery or equipment on the property taken or on the remainder if such property is part of a larger parcel, and the owner of the property ceases the construction or installation due to such service, the owner shall be compensated for his expenses reasonably incurred for work necessary for either of the following purposes:

(1) To protect against the risk of injury to persons or to other property created by the uncompleted improvement.

(2) To protect the partially installed machinery or equipment from damage, deterioration, or vandalism.

(b) The compensation provided in this section is recoverable only if the work was preceded by notice to the plaintiff except in the case of an emergency. The plaintiff may agree with the owner (1) that the plaintiff will perform work necessary for the purposes of this section or (2) as to the amount of compensation payable under this section. **Leg.H.** Added Stats 1975 ch 1275 §2, operative July 1, 1976.

ARTICLE 8
Remediation of Hazardous Materials on Property to be Acquired by School Districts

Definitions. §1263.710.
"Hazardous material". §1263.711.
Hearing on presence of hazardous substance. §1263.720.
Insufficient funding to meet actual cost of required action. §1263.730.
Effect of hazardous substance on appraisal of property. §1263.740.
Remedies. §1263.750.
Offer to purchase as satisfying statutory requirement of offer to pay just compensation. §1263.760.
Application of article. §1263.770.

§1263.710. Definitions

(a) As used in this article, "remedial action" and "removal" shall have the meanings accorded to those terms in Sections 78125 and 78135, respectively, of the Health and Safety Code.

(b) As used in this article, "required action" means any removal or other remedial action with regard to hazardous materials that is necessary to comply with any requirement of federal, state, or local law. **Leg.H.** Added Stats 1995 ch 247 §2 (SB 231). Amended Stats 2022 ch 258 §10 (AB 2327), effective January 1, 2023, operative January 1, 2024.

Prior Law: Former CCP §1263.710, similar to present section, was added Stats 1991 ch 814 §2 and repealed Stats 1995 ch 247 §1.

§1263.711. "Hazardous material"

As used in this article, "hazardous material" shall have the same meaning as that term is defined in Section 25260 of the Health and Safety Code, except that under no circumstances shall petroleum which is naturally occurring on a site be considered a hazardous material. **Leg.H.** Added Stats 1995 ch 247 §2 (SB 231).

§1263.720. Hearing on presence of hazardous substance

(a) Upon petition of any party to the proceeding, the court in which the proceeding is brought shall specially set for hearing the issue of whether any hazardous material is present within the property to be taken.

(b) If the court determines that any hazardous material is present within the property to be taken, the court shall do all of the following:

(1) Identify those measures constituting the required action with regard to the hazardous material, the probable cost of the required action, and the party that shall be designated by the court to cause the required action to be performed.

(2) Designate a trustee to monitor the completion of the required action and to hold funds, deducted from amounts that are otherwise to be paid to the defendant pursuant to this title, to defray the probable cost of the required action.

(3) Transfer to the trustee funds necessary to defray the probable cost of the required action from amounts deposited with the court pursuant to Article 1 (commencing with Section 1255.010) of Chapter 6 or pursuant to Section 1268.110. In the case of any payment to be made directly to the defendant pursuant to Section 1268.010, the plaintiff shall first pay to the trustee the amount necessary to defray the probable cost of the required action, as identified by the court, and shall pay the remainder of the judgment to the defendant. The total amount transferred or paid to the trustee pursuant to this paragraph shall not exceed an amount equal to 75 percent of the following, as applicable:

(A) Prior to entry of judgment, the amount deposited as the probable amount of compensation pursuant to Article 1 (commencing with Section 1255.010) of Chapter 6.

(B) Subsequent to entry of judgment, the fair market value of the property taken, as determined pursuant to Article 4 (commencing with Section 1263.310). If the amount determined as fair market value pursuant to that article exceeds the amount deposited pursuant to Article 1 (commencing with Section 1255.010) of Chapter 6, that excess shall be available, subject to the 75 percent limit set forth in this paragraph, for transfer to the trustee for the purposes of this paragraph or for reimbursement of the plaintiff for payments made to the trustee pursuant to this paragraph. If the amount determined as fair market value pursuant to Article 4 (commencing with Section 1263.310) is less than the amount deposited pursuant to Article 1 (commencing with Section 1255.010) of Chapter 6, the plaintiff shall be entitled to a return of amounts thereby deposited, a judgment against the defendant, or both, as necessary to ensure that the total amount transferred or paid to the trustee pursuant to this paragraph not exceed an amount equal to 75 percent of the fair market value of the property taken, as determined pursuant to Article 4 (commencing with Section 1263.310).

(4) Establish a procedure by which the trustee shall make one or more payments from the funds it receives pursuant to paragraph (3) to the party causing the required action to be performed, upon completion of all or specified portions of the required action. Any amount of those funds that remains following the completion of all of the required action shall be applied in accordance with the provisions of this title that govern the disposition of the deposit amounts referred to in paragraph (3).

(c) The actual and reasonable costs of the trustee incurred pursuant to this section shall be paid by the plaintiff. **Leg.H.** Added Stats 1995 ch 247 §2 (SB 231).

Prior Law: Former CCP §1263.720, similar to present section, was added Stats 1991 ch 814 §2 and repealed Stats 1995 ch 247 §1.

§1263.730. Insufficient funding to meet actual cost of required action

Where the required action is caused to be performed by the plaintiff, and the amount available to the trustee under this article is insufficient to meet the actual cost incurred by the plaintiff to complete the required action, the plaintiff may either apply to the court for a new hearing regarding identification of the probable cost, or complete the required action at its own expense and bring an action against the defendant to recover the additional costs. **Leg.H.** Added Stats 1995 ch 247 §2 (SB 231).

Prior Law: Former CCP §1263.730, similar to present section, was added Stats 1991 ch 814 §2 and repealed Stats 1995 ch 247 §1.

§1263.740. Effect of hazardous substance on appraisal of property

The presence of any hazardous material within a property shall not be considered in appraising the property, for purposes of Section 1263.720, pursuant to Article 1 (commencing with Section 1255.010) of Chapter 6, or pursuant to Article 4 (commencing with Section 1263.310). **Leg.H.** Added Stats 1995 ch 247 §2 (SB 231).

Prior Law: Former CCP §1263.740, similar to present section, was added Stats 1991 ch 814 §2 and repealed Stats 1995 ch 247 §1.

§1263.750. Remedies

(a) Notwithstanding any action taken pursuant to this article, the plaintiff shall have available all remedies in law that are available to a purchaser of real property with respect to any cost, loss, or liability for which the plaintiff is not reimbursed under this article.

(b) If the plaintiff abandons the proceeding at any time, the plaintiff shall be entitled to compensation for the benefit, if any, conferred on the property by reason of the remedial action performed pursuant to this article. That benefit shall be applied as an offset to the amount of any entitlement to damages on the part of the defendant pursuant to Section 1268.620 or, if it exceeds the amount of those damages, shall constitute a lien upon the property, to the extent of that excess, when recorded with the county recorder in the county in which the real property is located. The lien shall contain the legal description of the real property, the assessor's parcel number, and the name of the owner of record as shown on the latest equalized assessment roll. The lien shall be enforceable upon the transfer or sale of the property, and the priority of the lien shall be as of the date of recording. In determining the amount of the benefit, if any, neither party shall have the burden of proof.

For the purposes of this subdivision, "benefit" means the extent to which the remedial action has enhanced the fair market value of the property. **Leg.H.** Added Stats 1995 ch 247 §2 (SB 231).

Prior Law: Former CCP §1263.750, similar to present section, was added Stats 1991 ch 814 §2 and repealed Stats 1995 ch 247 §1.

§1263.760. Offer to purchase as satisfying statutory requirement of offer to pay just compensation

An offer by the plaintiff to purchase the property subject to this article shall be deemed to satisfy the requirements of Section 7267.2 of the Government Code. **Leg.H.** Added Stats 1995 ch 247 §2 (SB 231).

Prior Law: Former CCP §1263.760, similar to present section, was added Stats 1991 ch 814 §2 and repealed Stats 1995 ch 247 §1.

§1263.770. Application of article

This article shall only apply to the acquisition of property by school districts. **Leg.H.** Added Stats 1995 ch 247 §2 (SB 231).

Prior Law: Former CCP §1263.770, similar to present section, was added Stats 1991 ch 814 §2 and repealed Stats 1995 ch 247 §1.

§1264. [Section repealed 1976]

Leg.H. Added Stats 1903 ch 150 §1. Repealed Stats 1975 ch 1275 §1, operative July 1, 1976.

§1264.1. [Section repealed 1976]

Leg.H. Added Stats 1937 ch 924 §2. Repealed Stats 1975 ch 1275 §1, operative July 1, 1976.

§1264.2. [Section repealed 1976]

Leg.H. Added Stats 1937 ch 924 §3. Repealed Stats 1975 ch 1275 §1, operative July 1, 1976.

§1264.3. [Section repealed 1976]

Leg.H. Added Stats 1937 ch 924 §4. Repealed Stats 1975 ch 1275 §1, operative July 1, 1976.

§1264.4. [Section repealed 1976]

Leg.H. Added Stats 1937 ch 924 §5. Repealed Stats 1975 ch 1275 §1, operative July 1, 1976.

§1264.5. [Section repealed 1976]

Leg.H. Added Stats 1937 ch 924 §6. Amended Stats 1967 ch 17 §19. Repealed Stats 1975 ch 1275 §1, operative July 1, 1976.

§1264.6. [Section repealed 1976]

Leg.H. Added Stats 1937 ch 924 §7. Amended Stats 1967 ch 17 §20. Repealed Stats 1975 ch 1275 §1, operative July 1, 1976.

§1264.7. [Section repealed 1976]

Leg.H. Added Stats 1937 ch 924 §8. Repealed Stats 1975 ch 1275 §1, operative July 1, 1976.

§1264.8. [Section repealed 1976]

Leg.H. Added Stats 1937 ch 924 §9. Repealed Stats 1975 ch 1275 §1, operative July 1, 1976.

§1264.9. [Section repealed 1976]

Leg.H. Added Stats 1937 ch 924 §10. Repealed Stats 1975 ch 1275 §1, operative July 1, 1976.

§1265. [Section repealed 1976]

Leg.H. Added Stats 1961 ch 2211 §1. Repealed Stats 1975 ch 1275 §1, operative July 1, 1976.

CHAPTER 10
DIVIDED INTERESTS

Article 1. General Provisions.
Article 2. Leases.
Article 3. Encumbrances.
Article 4. Future Interests.

ARTICLE 1
General Provisions

Scope of chapter. §1265.010.

§1265.010. Scope of chapter

Although this chapter provides rules governing compensation for particular interests in property, it does not otherwise limit or affect the right to compensation for any other interest in property. **Leg.H.** Added Stats 1975 ch 1275 §2, operative July 1, 1976.

ARTICLE 2
Leases

Termination of lease. §1265.110.
Partial termination of lease. §1265.120.
Court order terminating lease. §1265.130.
Time of termination of lease. §1265.140.
Right of lessee to compensation. §1265.150.
Rights and obligations of parties to lease. §1265.160.

§1265.110. Termination of lease

Where all the property subject to a lease is acquired for public use, the lease terminates. **Leg.H.** Added Stats 1975 ch 1275 §2, operative July 1, 1976.

§1265.120. Partial termination of lease

Except as provided in Section 1265.130, where part of the property subject to a lease is acquired for public use, the lease terminates as to the part taken and remains in force as to the remainder, and the rent reserved in the lease that is allocable to the part taken is extinguished. **Leg.H.** Added Stats 1975 ch 1275 §2, operative July 1, 1976.

§1265.130. Court order terminating lease

Where part of the property subject to a lease is acquired for public use, the court may, upon petition of any party to the lease, terminate the lease if the court determines that an essential part of the property subject to the lease is taken or that the remainder of the property subject to the lease is no longer suitable for the purposes of the lease. **Leg.H.** Added Stats 1975 ch 1275 §2, operative July 1, 1976.

§1265.140. Time of termination of lease

The termination or partial termination of a lease pursuant to this article shall be at the earlier of the following times:

(a) The time title to the property is taken by the person who will put it to the public use.

(b) The time the plaintiff is authorized to take possession of the property as stated in an order for possession. **Leg.H.** Added Stats 1975 ch 1275 §2, operative July 1, 1976.

§1265.150. Right of lessee to compensation

Nothing in this article affects or impairs any right a lessee may have to compensation for the taking of his lease in whole or in part or for the

§1265.160. Rights and obligations of parties to lease

Nothing in this article affects or impairs the rights and obligations of the parties to a lease to the extent that the lease provides for such rights and obligations in the event of the acquisition of all or a portion of the property for public use. **Leg.H.** Added Stats 1975 ch 1275 §2, operative July 1, 1976.

ARTICLE 3
Encumbrances

"Lien". §1265.210.
Acquisition of property encumbered by lien. §1265.220.
Partial taking of property encumbered by lien. §1265.225.
Partial taking of property encumbered by senior and junior liens. §1265.230.
Amount payable to lienholder. §1265.240.
Payment of special assessment. §1265.250.

§1265.210. "Lien"

As used in this article, "lien" means a mortgage, deed of trust, or other security interest in property whether arising from contract, statute, common law, or equity. **Leg.H.** Added Stats 1975 ch 1275 §2, operative July 1, 1976.

§1265.220. Acquisition of property encumbered by lien

Where property acquired by eminent domain is encumbered by a lien and the indebtedness secured thereby is not due at the time of the entry of judgment, the amount of such indebtedness may be, at the option of the plaintiff, deducted from the judgment and the lien shall be continued until such indebtedness is paid; but the amount for which, as between the plaintiff and the defendant, the plaintiff is liable under Article 5 (commencing with Section 1268.410) of Chapter 11 may not be deducted from the judgment. **Leg.H.** Added Stats 1975 ch 1275 §2, operative July 1, 1976.

§1265.225. Partial taking of property encumbered by lien

(a) Where there is a partial taking of property encumbered by a lien, the lienholder may share in the award only to the extent determined by the court to be necessary to prevent an impairment of the security, and the lien shall continue upon the part of the property not taken as security for the unpaid portion of the indebtedness.

(b) Notwithstanding subdivision (a), the lienholder and the property owner may at any time after commencement of the proceeding agree that some or all of the award shall be apportioned to the lienholder on the indebtedness. **Leg.H.** Added Stats 1975 ch 1275 §2, operative July 1, 1976.

§1265.230. Partial taking of property encumbered by senior and junior liens

(a) This section applies only where there is a partial taking of property encumbered by a lien and the part taken or some portion of it is also encumbered by a junior lien that extends to only a portion of the property encumbered by the senior lien. This section provides only for allocation of the portion of the award, if any, that will be available for payment to the junior and senior lienholders and does not provide for determination of the amount of such portion.

(b) As used in this section, "impairment of security" means the security of the lienholder remaining after the taking, if any, is of less value in proportion to the remaining indebtedness than the value of the security before the taking was in proportion to the indebtedness secured thereby.

(c) The portion of the award that will be available for payment to the senior and junior lienholders shall be allocated first to the senior lien up to the full amount of the indebtedness secured thereby and the remainder, if any, to the junior lien.

(d) If the allocation under subdivision (c) would result in an impairment of the junior lienholder's security, the allocation to the junior lien shall be adjusted so as to preserve the junior lienholder's security to the extent that the remaining amount allocated to the senior lien, if paid to the senior lienholder, would not result in an impairment of the senior lienholder's security.

(e) The amounts allocated to the senior and junior liens by this section are the amounts of indebtedness owing to such senior and junior lienholders that are secured by their respective liens on the property taken, and any other indebtedness owing to the senior or junior lienholders shall not be considered as secured by the property taken. If the plaintiff makes the election provided in Section 1265.220, the indebtedness that is deducted from the judgment is the indebtedness so determined, and the lien shall continue until that amount of indebtedness is paid. **Leg.H.** Added Stats 1975 ch 1275 §2, operative July 1, 1976.

§1265.240. Amount payable to lienholder

Where the property acquired for public use is encumbered by a lien, the amount payable to the lienholder shall not include any penalty for prepayment. **Leg.H.** Added Stats 1975 ch 1275 §2, operative July 1, 1976.

§1265.250. Payment of special assessment

(a) As used in this section:

(1) "Fixed lien special assessment" means a nonrecurring assessment levied on property in a fixed amount by a local public entity for the capital expenditure for a specific improvement, whether collectible in a lump sum or in installments.

(2) "Special annual assessment" means a recurring assessment levied on property annually in an indeterminate amount by a local public entity, whether for the capital expenditure for a specific improvement or for other purposes.

(b) If property acquired by eminent domain is encumbered by the lien of a fixed lien special assessment or of a bond representing the fixed lien special assessment:

(1) The amount of the lien shall be paid to the lienholder from the award or withheld from the award for payment pursuant to Section 1265.220.

(2) Where there is a partial taking of the property, the amount of the lien prescribed in Section 1265.225 shall be paid to the lienholder from the award, or at the option of the lienholder the applicable statutory procedure, if any, for segregation and apportionment of the lien may be invoked and the amount apportioned to the part taken shall be paid to the lienholder from the award.

(c) If property acquired by eminent domain is encumbered by the lien of a special annual assessment:

(1) The amount of the lien prorated to, but not including, the date of apportionment determined pursuant to Section 5082 of the Revenue and Taxation Code, shall be paid to the lienholder from the award. As between the plaintiff and defendant, the plaintiff is liable for the amount of the lien prorated from and including the date of apportionment determined pursuant to Section 5082 of the Revenue and Taxation Code.

(2) Where there is a partial taking of the property, the amount of the lien, reduced by the amount for which the plaintiff is liable pursuant to this paragraph, shall be paid to the lienholder from the award. As between the plaintiff and defendant, the plaintiff is liable for the amount of the lien allocable to the part taken for the current assessment year, determined to the extent practicable in the same manner and by the same method as the amount of the assessment on the property for the current assessment year was determined, prorated from and including the date of apportionment determined pursuant to Section 5082 of the Revenue and Taxation Code. **Leg.H.** Added Stats 1980 ch 122 §2.

ARTICLE 4
Future Interests

Acquisition in violation of use restriction. §1265.410.
Acquisition of property subject to life tenancy. §1265.420.

§1265.410. Acquisition in violation of use restriction

(a) Where the acquisition of property for public use violates a use restriction coupled with a contingent future interest granting a right to possession of the property upon violation of the use restriction:

(1) If violation of the use restriction was otherwise reasonably imminent, the owner of the contingent future interest is entitled to compensation for its value, if any.

(2) If violation of the use restriction was not otherwise reasonably imminent but the benefit of the use restriction was appurtenant to other property, the owner of the contingent future interest is entitled to compensation to the extent that the failure to comply with the use restriction damages the dominant premises to which the restriction was appurtenant and of which he was the owner.

(b) Where the acquisition of property for public use violates a use restriction coupled with a contingent future interest granting a right to possession of the property upon violation of the use restriction but the contingent future interest is not compensable under subdivision (a), if the use restriction is that the property be devoted to a particular charitable or public use, the compensation for the property shall be devoted to the same or similar use coupled with the same contingent future interest. **Leg.H.** Added Stats 1975 ch 1275 §2, operative July 1, 1976.

§1265.420. Acquisition of property subject to life tenancy

Where property acquired for public use is subject to a life tenancy, upon petition of the life tenant or any other person having an interest in the property, the court may order any of the following:

(a) An apportionment and distribution of the award based on the value of the interest of life tenant and remainderman.

(b) The compensation to be used to purchase comparable property to be held subject to the life tenancy.

(c) The compensation to be held in trust and invested and the income (and, to the extent the instrument that created the life tenancy permits, principal) to be distributed to the life tenant for the remainder of the tenancy.

(d) Such other arrangement as will be equitable under the circumstances. **Leg.H.** Added Stats 1975 ch 1275 §2, operative July 1, 1976.

§1266. [Section repealed 1976]

Leg.H. Added Stats 1941 ch 1029 §1. Repealed Stats 1975 ch 1275 §1, operative July 1, 1976.

§1266.1. [Section repealed 1976]

Leg.H. Added Stats 1941 ch 1029 §2. Repealed Stats 1975 ch 1275 §1, operative July 1, 1976.

§1266.2. [Section repealed 1976]

Leg.H. Added Stats 1953 ch 52 §10. Amended Stats 1968 ch 450 §4. Repealed Stats 1975 ch 1275 §1, operative July 1, 1976.

§1267. [Section repealed 1976]

Leg.H. Added Stats 1971 ch 1402 §1. Repealed Stats 1975 ch 1275 §1, operative July 1, 1976.

CHAPTER 11
POSTJUDGMENT PROCEDURE

Article 1. Payment of Judgment; Final Order of Condemnation.
Article 2. Deposit and Withdrawal of Award.
Article 3. Possession After Judgment.
Article 4. Interest.
Article 5. Proration of Property Taxes.
Article 6. Abandonment.
Article 7. Litigation Expenses and Damages Upon Dismissal or Defeat of Right to Take.
Article 8. Costs.

ARTICLE 1
Payment of Judgment; Final Order of Condemnation

Payment of judgment. §1268.010.
Failure to pay judgment. §1268.020.
Final order of condemnation. §1268.030.

§1268.010. Payment of judgment

(a) Not later than 30 days after final judgment, or 30 days after the conclusion of any other court proceedings, including any federal court proceedings, commenced by the defendant challenging the judgment or any of the condemnation proceedings, whichever date is later, the plaintiff shall pay the full amount required by the judgment.

(b) Payment shall be made by either or both of the following methods:

(1) Payment of money directly to the defendant. Any amount which the defendant has previously withdrawn pursuant to Article 2 (commencing with Section 1255.210) of Chapter 6 shall be credited as a payment to him on the judgment.

(2) Deposit of money with the court pursuant to Section 1268.110. Upon entry of judgment, a deposit made pursuant to Article 1 (commencing with Section 1255.010) of Chapter 6 is deemed to be a deposit made pursuant to Section 1268.110 if the full amount required by the judgment is deposited or paid. **Leg.H.** Added Stats 1975 ch 1275 §2, operative July 1, 1976. Amended Stats 1981 ch 831 §1.

§1268.020. Failure to pay judgment

(a) If the plaintiff fails to pay the full amount required by the judgment within the time specified in Section 1268.010, the defendant may:

(1) If the plaintiff is a public entity, enforce the judgment as provided in Division 3.6 (commencing with Section 810) of Title 1 of the Government Code.

(2) If the plaintiff is not a public entity, enforce the judgment as in a civil case.

(b) Upon noticed motion of the defendant, the court shall enter judgment dismissing the eminent domain proceeding if all of the following are established:

(1) The plaintiff failed to pay the full amount required by the judgment within the time specified in Section 1268.010.

(2) The defendant has filed in court and served upon the plaintiff, by registered or certified mail, a written notice of the plaintiff's failure to pay the full amount required by the judgment within the time specified in Section 1268.010.

(3) The plaintiff has failed for 20 days after service of the notice under paragraph (2) to pay the full amount required by the judgment in the manner provided in subdivision (b) of Section 1268.010.

(c) The defendant may elect to exercise the remedy provided by subdivision (b) without attempting to use the remedy provided by subdivision (a).

(d) As used in this section, "public entity" does not include the Regents of the University of California. **Leg.H.** Added Stats 1975 ch 1275 §2, operative July 1, 1976. Amended Stats 1980 ch 215 §1.

§1268.030. Final order of condemnation

(a) Upon application of any party, the court shall make a final order of condemnation if the full amount of the judgment has been paid as required by Section 1268.010 or satisfied pursuant to Section 1268.020.

(b) The final order of condemnation shall describe the property taken and identify the judgment authorizing the taking.

(c) The party upon whose application the order was made shall serve notice of the making of the order on all other parties affected thereby. Any party affected by the order may thereafter record a certified copy of the order in the office of the recorder of the county in which the property is located and shall serve notice of recordation upon all other parties affected thereby. Title to the property vests in the plaintiff upon the date of recordation. **Leg.H.** Added Stats 1975 ch 1275 §2, operative July 1, 1976.

ARTICLE 2
Deposit and Withdrawal of Award

Deposit of award. §1268.110.
Notice of deposit. §1268.120.
Deposit of additional amount. §1268.130.
Payment to defendant from deposit. §1268.140.
Place of deposit; Investment. §1268.150.
Withdrawal of excess amount; Judgment. §1268.160.
Effect of making deposit. §1268.170.

§1268.110. Deposit of award

(a) Except as provided in subdivision (b), the plaintiff may, at any time after entry of judgment, deposit with the court for the persons entitled thereto the full amount of the award, together with interest then due thereon, less any amounts previously paid directly to the defendants or deposited pursuant to Article 1 (commencing with Section 1255.010) of Chapter 6.

(b) A deposit may be made under this section notwithstanding an appeal, a motion for a new trial, or a motion to vacate or set aside the judgment but may not be made after the judgment has been reversed, vacated, or set aside.

(c) Any amount deposited pursuant to this article on a judgment that is later reversed, vacated, or set aside shall be deemed to be an amount deposited pursuant to Article 1 (commencing with Section 1255.010) of Chapter 6. **Leg.H.** Added Stats 1975 ch 1275 §2, operative July 1, 1976.

§1268.120. Notice of deposit

If the deposit is made under Section 1268.110 prior to apportionment of the award, the plaintiff shall serve a notice that the deposit has been made on all of the parties who have appeared in the proceeding. If the deposit is made after apportionment of the award, the plaintiff shall serve a notice that the deposit has been made on all of the parties to the proceeding determined by the order apportioning the award to have an interest in the money deposited. The notice of deposit shall state that a deposit has been made and the date and the amount of the deposit. Service of the notice shall be made in the manner provided in Section 1268.220 for the service of an order for possession. Service of an order for possession under

Section 1268.220 is sufficient compliance with this section. **Leg.H.** Added Stats 1975 ch 1275 §2, operative July 1, 1976.

§1268.130. Deposit of additional amount

At any time after the plaintiff has made a deposit upon the award pursuant to Section 1268.110, the court may, upon motion of any defendant, order the plaintiff to deposit such additional amount as the court determines to be necessary to secure payment of any further compensation, costs, or interest that may be recovered in the proceeding. After the making of such an order, the court may, on motion of any party, order an increase or a decrease in such additional amount. A defendant may withdraw the amount deposited under this section or a portion thereof only if it is determined that he is entitled to recover such amount in the proceeding. **Leg.H.** Added Stats 1975 ch 1275 §2, operative July 1, 1976.

§1268.140. Payment to defendant from deposit

(a) After entry of judgment, any defendant who has an interest in the property for which a deposit has been made may apply for and obtain a court order that he be paid from the deposit the amount to which he is entitled upon his filing either of the following:

(1) A satisfaction of the judgment.

(2) A receipt for the money which shall constitute a waiver by operation of law of all claims and defenses except a claim for greater compensation.

(b) If the award has not been apportioned at the time the application is made, the applicant shall give notice of the application to all the other defendants who have appeared in the proceeding and who have an interest in the property. If the award has been apportioned at the time the application is made, the applicant shall give such notice to the other defendants as the court may require.

(c) Upon objection to the withdrawal made by any party to the proceeding, the court, in its discretion, may require the applicant to file an undertaking in the same manner and upon the conditions prescribed in Section 1255.240 for withdrawal of a deposit prior to entry of judgment.

(d) If the judgment is reversed, vacated, or set aside, a defendant may withdraw a deposit only pursuant to Article 2 (commencing with Section 1255.210) of Chapter 6. **Leg.H.** Added Stats 1975 ch 1275 §2, operative July 1, 1976.

§1268.150. Place of deposit; Investment

(a) Except as provided in subdivision (b), when money is deposited as provided in this article, the court shall order the money to be deposited in the State Treasury or, upon written request of the plaintiff filed with the deposit, in the county treasury. If the money is deposited in the State Treasury pursuant to this subdivision, it shall be held, invested, deposited, and disbursed in the manner specified in Article 10 (commencing with Section 16429) of Chapter 2 of Part 2 of Division 4 of Title 2 of the Government Code, and interest earned or other increment derived from its investment shall be apportioned and disbursed in the manner specified in that article. As between the parties to the proceeding, money deposited pursuant to this subdivision shall remain at the risk of the plaintiff until paid or made payable to the defendant by order of the court.

(b) If after entry of judgment but prior to apportionment of the award the defendants are unable to agree as to the withdrawal of all or a portion of any amount deposited, the court shall upon motion of any defendant order that the amount deposited be invested in United States government obligations or interest-bearing accounts in an institution whose accounts are insured by an agency of the federal government for the benefit of the defendants who shall be entitled to the interest earned on the investments in proportion to the amount of the award they receive when the award is apportioned. **Leg.H.** Added Stats 1975 ch 1275 §2, operative July 1, 1976.

§1268.160. Withdrawal of excess amount; Judgment

(a) Any amount withdrawn by a party pursuant to this article in excess of the amount to which he is entitled as finally determined in the eminent domain proceeding shall be paid to the parties entitled thereto. The court shall enter judgment accordingly.

(b) The judgment so entered shall not include interest except that any amount that is to be paid to a defendant shall include legal interest from the date of its withdrawal by another defendant.

(c) If the judgment so entered is not paid within 30 days after its entry, the court may, on motion, enter judgment against the sureties, if any, for the amount of such judgment.

(d) The court may, in its discretion and with such security as it deems appropriate, grant a party obligated to pay under this section a stay of execution for any amount to be paid to a plaintiff. Such stay of execution shall not exceed one year following entry of judgment under this section. **Leg.H.** Added Stats 1975 ch 1275 §2, operative July 1, 1976.

§1268.170. Effect of making deposit

By making a deposit pursuant to this article, the plaintiff does not waive the right to appeal from the judgment, the right to move to abandon, or the right to request a new trial. **Leg.H.** Added Stats 1975 ch 1275 §2, operative July 1, 1976.

ARTICLE 3
Possession After Judgment

Order for possession. §1268.210.
Service of order. §1268.220.
Effect of taking possession. §1268.230.
Exercise of police power. §1268.240.

§1268.210. Order for possession

(a) If the plaintiff is not in possession of the property to be taken, the plaintiff may, at any time after entry of judgment, apply ex parte to the court for an order for possession, and the court shall authorize the plaintiff to take possession of the property pending conclusion of the litigation if:

(1) The judgment determines that the plaintiff is entitled to take the property; and

(2) The plaintiff has paid to or deposited for the defendants, pursuant to Article 1 (commencing with Section 1255.010) of Chapter 6 or Article 2 (commencing with Section 1268.110), an amount not less than the amount of the award, together with the interest then due thereon.

(b) The court's order shall state the date after which the plaintiff is authorized to take possession of the property. Where deposit is made, the order shall state such fact and the date and the amount of the deposit.

(c) Where the judgment is reversed, vacated, or set aside, the plaintiff may obtain possession of the property only pursuant to Article 3 (commencing with Section 1255.410) of Chapter 6. **Leg.H.** Added Stats 1975 ch 1275 §2, operative July 1, 1976.

§1268.220. Service of order

(a) The plaintiff shall serve a copy of the order for possession upon each defendant and his attorney, either personally or by mail:

(1) At least 30 days prior to the date possession is to be taken of property lawfully occupied by a person dwelling thereon or by a farm or business operation.

(2) At least 10 days prior to the date possession is to be taken in any case not covered by paragraph (1).

(b) A single service upon or mailing to one of several persons having a common business or residence address is sufficient. **Leg.H.** Added Stats 1975 ch 1275 §2, operative July 1, 1976.

§1268.230. Effect of taking possession

By taking possession pursuant to this article, the plaintiff does not waive the right to appeal from the judgment, the right to move to abandon, or the right to request a new trial. **Leg.H.** Added Stats 1975 ch 1275 §2, operative July 1, 1976.

§1268.240. Exercise of police power

Nothing in this article limits the right of a public entity to exercise its police power in emergency situations. **Leg.H.** Added Stats 1975 ch 1275 §2, operative July 1, 1976.

ARTICLE 4
Interest

Date interest begins. §1268.310.
Inverse condemnation proceedings. §1268.311.
Date interest ceases. §1268.320.
Offsets against interest. §1268.330.
Assessment of interest. §1268.340.
Apportionment rate for calendar quarter. §1268.350.
Compounding of interest for calendar quarter. §1268.360.

§1268.310. Date interest begins

The compensation awarded in the proceeding shall draw interest, computed as prescribed by Section 1268.350, from the earliest of the following dates:

(a) The date of entry of judgment.

(b) The date the plaintiff takes possession of the property.

(c) The date after which the plaintiff is authorized to take possession of the property as stated in an order for possession. **Leg.H.** Added Stats 1975 ch 1275 §2, operative July 1, 1976. Amended Stats 1986 ch 1372 §1.

§1268.311. Inverse condemnation proceedings

In any inverse condemnation proceeding in which interest is awarded, the interest shall be computed as prescribed by Section 1268.350. **Leg.H.** Added Stats 1986 ch 1372 §2.

§1268.320. Date interest ceases

The compensation awarded in the proceeding shall cease to draw interest at the earliest of the following dates:

(a) As to any amount deposited pursuant to Article 1 (commencing with Section 1255.010) of Chapter 6 (deposit of probable compensation prior to judgment), the date such amount is withdrawn by the person entitled thereto.

(b) As to the amount deposited in accordance with Article 2 (commencing with Section 1268.110) (deposit of amount of award), the date of such deposit.

(c) As to any amount paid to the person entitled thereto, the date of such payment. **Leg.H.** Added Stats 1975 ch 1275 §2, operative July 1, 1976.

§1268.330. Offsets against interest

If, after the date that interest begins to accrue, the defendant:

(a) Continues in actual possession of the property, the value of that possession shall be offset against the interest. For the purpose of this section, the value of possession of the property shall be presumed to be the rate of interest calculated as prescribed by Section 1268.350 on the compensation awarded. This presumption is one affecting the burden of proof.

(b) Receives rents or other income from the property attributable to the period after interest begins to accrue, the net amount of these rents and other income shall be offset against the interest. **Leg.H.** Added Stats 1975 ch 1275 §2, operative July 1, 1976. Amended Stats 1986 ch 1372 §3.

§1268.340. Assessment of interest

Interest, including interest accrued due to possession of property by the plaintiff prior to judgment, and any offset against interest as provided in Section 1268.330, shall be assessed by the court rather than by jury. **Leg.H.** Added Stats 1975 ch 1275 §2, operative July 1, 1976.

§1268.350. Apportionment rate for calendar quarter

(a) As used in this section, "apportionment rate" means the apportionment rate calculated by the Controller as the rate of earnings by the Surplus Money Investment Fund for each calendar quarter.

(b) The rate of interest payable under this article for each calendar quarter, or fraction thereof, for which interest is due, shall be the apportionment rate for the immediately preceding calendar quarter.

(c) Each district office of the Department of Transportation shall quote the apportionment rate to any person upon request. **Leg.H.** Added Stats 1986 ch 1372 §4. Amended Stats 2006 ch 311 §1 (SB 1586), effective January 1, 2007.

§1268.360. Compounding of interest for calendar quarter

The interest payable for each calendar quarter shall draw interest, computed as prescribed by Section 1268.350, in each succeeding calendar quarter for which interest is due. **Leg.H.** Added Stats 1986 ch 1372 §5. Amended Stats 2006 ch 311 §2 (SB 1586), effective January 1, 2007.

ARTICLE 5
Proration of Property Taxes

Liability of plaintiff. §1268.410.
Liability dependent on outcome of action. §1268.420.
Repayment of defendant. §1268.430.
Application to taxes previously paid. §1268.440.
Application for separate valuation. §1268.450.

§1268.410. Liability of plaintiff

As between the plaintiff and defendant, the plaintiff is liable for any ad valorem taxes, penalties, and costs upon property acquired by eminent domain prorated from and including the date of apportionment determined pursuant to Section 5082 of the Revenue and Taxation Code. **Leg.H.** Added Stats 1975 ch 1275 §2, operative July 1, 1976. Amended Stats 1979 ch 31 §3.

§1268.420. Liability dependent on outcome of action

(a) Except as provided in subdivision (b):

(1) If the acquisition of property by eminent domain will make the property exempt property as defined in Section 5081 of the Revenue and Taxation Code, any ad valorem taxes, penalties, or costs on the property for which the plaintiff is liable pursuant to Section 1268.410 are not collectible.

(2) If the acquisition of property by eminent domain will not make the property exempt property as defined in Section 5081 of the Revenue and Taxation Code, the plaintiff shall be deemed to be the assessee for the purposes of collection of any ad valorem taxes, penalties, and costs on the property for which the plaintiff is liable pursuant to Section 1268.410.

(b) To the extent there is a dismissal or partial dismissal of the eminent domain proceeding, the amount of any unpaid ad valorem taxes, penalties, and costs on the property for which the plaintiff would be liable pursuant to Section 1268.410 until the entry of judgment of dismissal shall be awarded to the defendant. The amount awarded shall be paid to the tax collector from the award or, if unpaid for any reason, are collectible from the defendant. **Leg.H.** Added Stats 1979 ch 31 §5.

Prior Law: Former CCP §1268.420, similar to present §1268.450, was added by Stats 1975 ch 1275 §2, operative July 1, 1976, and repealed by Stats 1979 ch 31 §4.

§1268.430. Repayment of defendant

(a) If the defendant has paid any amount for which, as between the plaintiff and defendant, the plaintiff is liable under this article, the plaintiff shall pay to the defendant a sum equal to such amount.

(b) The amount the defendant is entitled to be paid under this section shall be claimed in the manner provided for claiming costs and at the following times:

(1) If the plaintiff took possession of the property prior to judgment, at the time provided for claiming costs.

(2) If the plaintiff did not take possession of the property prior to judgment, not later than 30 days after the plaintiff took title to the property. **Leg.H.** Added Stats 1975 ch 1275 §2, operative July 1, 1976.

§1268.440. Application to taxes previously paid

(a) If taxes have been paid on property that is exempt property as defined in Section 5081 of the Revenue and Taxation Code, the amount of the taxes that, if unpaid, would have been subject to cancellation under Article 5 (commencing with Section 5081) of Chapter 4 of Part 9 of Division 1 of the Revenue and Taxation Code shall be deemed to be erroneously collected and shall be refunded in the manner provided in Article 1 (commencing with Section 5096) of Chapter 5 of Part 9 of Division 1 of the Revenue and Taxation Code to the person who paid the taxes.

(b) The public entity shall be deemed to be the person who paid the taxes if the public entity reimbursed the defendant for the taxes under a cost bill filed in the eminent domain proceeding pursuant to Section 1268.430. A claim for refund of taxes filed by a public entity pursuant to this section shall contain a copy of the cost bill under which taxes were reimbursed or a declaration under penalty of perjury by the public entity that the taxes were reimbursed under a cost bill.

(c) Taxes paid on either the secured or unsecured roll may be refunded pursuant to this section. **Leg.H.** Added Stats 1979 ch 31 §6.

§1268.450. Application for separate valuation

If property acquired by eminent domain does not have a separate valuation on the assessment roll, any party to the eminent domain proceeding may, at any time after the taxes on the property are subject to cancellation under Article 5 (commencing with Section 5081) of Chapter 4 of Part 9 of Division 1 of the Revenue and Taxation Code, apply to the tax collector for a separate valuation of the property in accordance with Article 3 (commencing with Section 2821) of Chapter 3 of Part 5 of Division 1 of the Revenue and Taxation Code notwithstanding any provision in that article to the contrary. **Leg.H.** Added Stats 1979 ch 31 §7.

ARTICLE 6
Abandonment

Notice; Motion; Judgment. §1268.510.

§1268.510. Notice; Motion; Judgment

(a) At any time after the filing of the complaint and before the expiration of 30 days after final judgment, the plaintiff may wholly or partially abandon the proceeding by serving on the defendant and filing in court a written notice of such abandonment.

(b) The court may, upon motion made within 30 days after the filing of such notice, set the abandonment aside if it determines that the position of the moving party has been substantially changed to his detriment in justifiable reliance upon the proceeding and such party cannot be restored to substantially the same position as if the proceeding had not been commenced.

(c) Upon denial of a motion to set aside such abandonment or, if no such motion is filed, upon the expiration of the time for filing such a motion, the court shall, on motion of any party, enter judgment wholly or partially dismissing the proceeding. **Leg.H.** Added Stats 1975 ch 1275 §2, operative July 1, 1976.

ARTICLE 7
Litigation Expenses and Damages Upon Dismissal or Defeat of Right to Take

Litigation expenses. §1268.610.
Damages upon dismissal or defeat of right to take. §1268.620.

§1268.610. Litigation expenses

(a) Subject to subdivisions (b) and (c), the court shall award the defendant his or her litigation expenses whenever:

(1) The proceeding is wholly or partly dismissed for any reason.

(2) Final judgment in the proceeding is that the plaintiff cannot acquire property it sought to acquire in the proceeding.

(b) Where there is a partial dismissal or a final judgment that the plaintiff cannot acquire a portion of the property originally sought to be acquired, or a dismissal of one or more plaintiffs pursuant to Section 1260.020, the court shall award the defendant only those litigation expenses, or portion thereof, that would not have been incurred had the property sought to be acquired following the dismissal or judgment been the property originally sought to be acquired.

(c) If the plaintiff files a notice of abandonment as to a particular defendant, or a request for dismissal of a particular defendant, and the court determines that the defendant did not own or have any interest in the property that the plaintiff sought to acquire in the proceeding, the court shall award that defendant only those litigation expenses incurred up to the time of filing the notice of abandonment or request for dismissal.

(d) Litigation expenses under this section shall be claimed in and by a cost bill to be prepared, served, filed, and taxed as in a civil action. If the proceeding is dismissed upon motion of the plaintiff, the cost bill shall be filed within 30 days after notice of entry of judgment. **Leg.H.** Added Stats 1975 ch 1275 §2, operative July 1, 1976. Amended Stats 2001 ch 192 §1 (AB 1463).

§1268.620. Damages upon dismissal or defeat of right to take

If, after the defendant moves from property in compliance with an order or agreement for possession or in reasonable contemplation of its taking by the plaintiff, the proceeding is dismissed with regard to that property for any reason or there is a final judgment that the plaintiff cannot acquire that property, the court shall:

(a) Order the plaintiff to deliver possession of the property to the persons entitled to it; and

(b) Make such provision as shall be just for the payment of all damages proximately caused by the proceeding and its dismissal as to that property. **Leg.H.** Added Stats 1975 ch 1275 §2, operative July 1, 1976.

ARTICLE 8
Costs

Costs of determining apportionment of award. §1268.710.
Costs on appeal. §1268.720.

§1268.710. Costs of determining apportionment of award

The defendants shall be allowed their costs, including the costs of determining the apportionment of the award made pursuant to subdivision (b) of Section 1260.220, except that the costs of determining any issue as to title between two or more defendants shall be borne by the defendants in such proportion as the court may direct. **Leg.H.** Added Stats 1975 ch 1275 §2, operative July 1, 1976.

§1268.720. Costs on appeal

Unless the court otherwise orders, whether or not he is the prevailing party, the defendant in the proceeding shall be allowed his costs on appeal. This section does not apply to an appeal involving issues between defendants. **Leg.H.** Added Stats 1975 ch 1275 §2, operative July 1, 1976.

CHAPTER 12
ARBITRATION OF COMPENSATION IN ACQUISITIONS OF PROPERTY FOR PUBLIC USE

Authority to agree to arbitration. §1273.010.
Payment of expenses and fees. §1273.020.
Law governing agreements; Time, effect, and enforceability of agreements; Venue. §1273.030.
Abandonment of acquisition, arbitration proceeding, and eminent domain proceeding. §1273.040.
Acknowledgment and recordation of agreement. §1273.050.

§1273.010. Authority to agree to arbitration

(a) Any person authorized to acquire property for public use may enter into an agreement to arbitrate any controversy as to the compensation to be made in connection with the acquisition of the property.

(b) Where property is already appropriated to a public use, the person authorized to compromise or settle the claim arising from a taking or damaging of such property for another public use may enter into an agreement to arbitrate any controversy as to the compensation to be made in connection with such taking or damaging.

(c) For the purposes of this section, in the case of a public entity, "person" refers to the particular department, officer, commission, board, or governing body authorized to acquire property on behalf of the public entity or to compromise or settle a claim arising from the taking or damaging of the entity's property. **Leg.H.** Added Stats 1975 ch 1275 §2, operative July 1, 1976.

§1273.020. Payment of expenses and fees

(a) Notwithstanding Sections 1283.2 and 1284.2, the party acquiring the property shall pay all of the expenses and fees of the neutral arbitrator and the statutory fees and mileage of all witnesses subpoenaed in the arbitration, together with other expenses of the arbitration incurred or approved by the neutral arbitrator, not including attorney's fees or expert witness fees or other expenses incurred by other parties for their own benefit.

(b) An agreement authorized by this chapter may require that the party acquiring the property pay reasonable attorney's fees or expert witness fees, or both, to any other party to the arbitration. If the agreement requires the payment of such fees, the amount of the fees is a matter to be determined in the arbitration proceeding unless the agreement prescribes otherwise.

(c) The party acquiring the property may pay the expenses and fees referred to in subdivisions (a) and (b) from funds available for the acquisition of the property or other funds available for the purpose. **Leg.H.** Added Stats 1975 ch 1275 §2, operative July 1, 1976.

§1273.030. Law governing agreements; Time, effect, and enforceability of agreements; Venue

(a) Except as specifically provided in this chapter, agreements authorized by this chapter are subject to Title 9 (commencing with Section 1280) of this part.

(b) An agreement authorized by this chapter may be made whether or not an eminent domain proceeding has been commenced to acquire the property. If a proceeding has been commenced or is commenced, any petition or response relating to the arbitration shall be filed and determined in the proceeding.

(c) Notwithstanding Section 1281.4, an agreement authorized by this chapter does not waive or restrict the power of any person to commence and prosecute an eminent domain proceeding, including the taking of possession prior to judgment, except that, upon motion of a party to the proceeding, the court shall stay the determination of compensation until any petition for an order to arbitrate is determined and, if arbitration is ordered, until arbitration is had in accordance with the order.

(d) The effect and enforceability of an agreement authorized by this chapter is not defeated or impaired by contention or proof by any party to the agreement that the party acquiring the property pursuant to the agreement lacks the power or capacity to take the property by eminent domain.

(e) Notwithstanding the rules as to venue provided by Sections 1292 and 1292.2, any petition relating to arbitration authorized by this chapter shall be filed in the superior court in the county in which the property, or any portion of the property, is located. **Leg.H.** Added Stats 1975 ch 1275 §2, operative July 1, 1976.

§1273.040. Abandonment of acquisition, arbitration proceeding, and eminent domain proceeding

(a) Except as provided in subdivision (b), an agreement authorized by this chapter may specify the terms and conditions under which the party acquiring the property may abandon the acquisition, the arbitration proceeding, and any eminent domain proceeding that may have been, or may be, filed. Unless the agreement provides that the acquisition may not be abandoned, the party acquiring the property may abandon the acquisition, the arbitration proceeding, and any eminent domain proceeding at any time not later than the time for filing and serving a petition or response to vacate an arbitration award under Sections 1288, 1288.2, and 1290.6.

(b) If the proceeding to acquire the property is abandoned after the arbitration agreement is executed, the party from whom the property was to be acquired is entitled to recover (1) all expenses reasonably and necessarily incurred (i) in preparing for the arbitration proceeding and for any judicial proceedings in connection with the acquisition of the property, (ii) during the arbitration proceeding and during any judicial proceedings in connection with the acquisition, and (iii) in any subsequent judicial proceedings in connection with the acquisition and (2) reasonable attorney's fees, appraisal fees, and fees for the services of other experts where such fees were reasonably and necessarily incurred to protect his interests in connection with the acquisition of the property. Unless the agreement otherwise provides, the amount of such expenses and fees shall be determined by arbitration in accordance with the agreement. **Leg.H.** Added Stats 1975 ch 1275 §2, operative July 1, 1976.

§1273.050. Acknowledgment and recordation of agreement

(a) An agreement authorized by this chapter may be acknowledged and recorded, and rerecorded, in the same manner and with the same effect as a conveyance of real property except that two years after the date the agreement is recorded, or rerecorded, the record ceases to be notice to any person for any purpose.

(b) In lieu of recording the agreement, there may be recorded a memorandum thereof, executed by the parties to the agreement, containing at least the following information: the names of the parties to the agreement, a description of the property, and a statement that an arbitration agreement affecting such property has been entered into pursuant to this chapter. Such memorandum when acknowledged and recorded, or rerecorded, in the same manner as a conveyance of real property has the same effect as if the agreement itself were recorded or rerecorded. **Leg.H.** Added Stats 1975 ch 1275 §2, operative July 1, 1976.

TITLE 7.1
EVIDENCE IN EMINENT DOMAIN AND INVERSE CONDEMNATION PROCEEDINGS [REPEALED]

§1268–1268.4. [Sections repealed 1965]

Leg.H. Added Stats 1965 ch 1151 §1. Repealed Stats 1965 ch 1151 §7, operative January 1, 1965. The repealed sections related to evidence in eminent domain proceedings and "just compensation".

Prior Law: Former CCP §1268, similar to present §1410, was added by Stats 1939 ch 213 §1, amended by Stats 1945 ch 1080 §2, Stats 1947 ch 752 §2, Stats 1951 ch 39 §1, and repealed by Stats 1951 ch 1708 §1.

§1268.5. [Section repealed 1951]

Leg.H. Added Stats 1947 ch 752 §1. Repealed Stats 1951 ch 1708 §1. See CCP §1415.

§1269. [Section repealed 1951]

Leg.H. Added Stats 1907 ch 253 §1. Amended Stats 1915 ch 557 §1, Stats 1917 ch 169 §1, Stats 1951 ch 59 §1. Repealed Stats 1951 ch 1708 §1. See CCP §1410.

§1269a. [Section repealed 1951]

Leg.H. Added Stats 1915 ch 556 §1. Amended Stats 1935 ch 52 §6. Repealed Stats 1951 ch 1708 §1. The repealed section related to an action to determine a state's right to escheated property.

§§1270–1272. [Sections repealed 1967]

Leg.H. Added Stats 1965 ch 1151 §1. Repealed Stats 1965 ch 1151 §7, operative January 1, 1967.

Prior Law: Former CCP §1270, similar to present §1422, was enacted 1872, repealed and added by Stats 1907 ch 253 §1, and repealed by Stats 1951 ch 1708 §1.

Former CCP §1271, similar to present §1423, was enacted 1872, amended by Stats 1881 ch 17 §1, repealed and added by Stats 1907 ch 253 §1, and repealed by Stats 1951 ch 1708 §1.

Former CCP §1272, similar to present CCP §1355, was enacted 1872, amended by Code Amdts 1880 ch 87 §2, repealed and added by Stats 1907 ch 253 §1; amended by Stats 1915 ch 555 §1, and repealed by Stats 1951 ch 1708 §1.

§1272a. [Section repealed 1951]

Leg.H. Added Stats 1917 ch 169 §2. Amended Stats 1923 ch 37 §1, Stats 1935 ch 52 §7, Stats 1939 ch 211 §1. Repealed Stats 1951 ch 1708 §1. The repealed section related to filing a petition showing claim to an estate.

§1272.01. [Section repealed 1976]

Leg.H. Added Stats 1967 ch 1104 §2. Repealed Stats 1975 ch 1275 §1, operative July 1, 1976.

§1272.02. [Section repealed 1976]

Leg.H. Added Stats 1967 ch 1104 §2. Repealed Stats 1975 ch 1275 §1, operative July 1, 1976.

§1272.03. [Section repealed 1976]

Leg.H. Added Stats 1967 ch 1104 §2. Repealed Stats 1975 ch 1275 §1, operative July 1, 1976.

§1272.04. [Section repealed 1976]

Leg.H. Added Stats 1967 ch 1104 §2. Repealed Stats 1975 ch 1275 §1, operative July 1, 1976.

§1272.05. [Section repealed 1976]

Leg.H. Added Stats 1967 ch 1104 §2. Repealed Stats 1975 ch 1275 §1, operative July 1, 1976.

§1272.06. [Section repealed 1976]

Leg.H. Added Stats 1967 ch 1104 §2. Repealed Stats 1975 ch 1275 §1, operative July 1, 1976.

§1272.07. [Section repealed 1976]

Leg.H. Added Stats 1967 ch 1104 §2. Repealed Stats 1975 ch 1275 §1, operative July 1, 1976.

§1272.08. [Section repealed 1976]

Leg.H. Added Stats 1967 ch 1104 §2. Repealed Stats 1975 ch 1275 §1, operative July 1, 1976.

§1272.09. [Section repealed 1976]

Leg.H. Added Stats 1967 ch 1104 §2. Repealed Stats 1975 ch 1275 §1, operative July 1, 1976.

§§1272.2, 1272.4. [Sections repealed 1967]

Leg.H. Added Stats 1965 ch 1151 §1. Repealed Stats 1965 ch 1151 §7, operative January 1, 1967. The repealed sections related to evidentiary matters in determining the value of property.

§1273. [Section repealed 1945]

Leg.H. Added Stats 1915 ch 84 §1. Repealed Stats 1945 ch 1080 §4. See CCP §§1500 et seq.

§1273.01. [Section repealed 1976]

Leg.H. Added Stats 1970 ch 417 §1. Repealed Stats 1975 ch 1275 §1, operative July 1, 1976.

§1273.02. [Section repealed 1976]

Leg.H. Added Stats 1970 ch 417 §1. Repealed Stats 1975 ch 1275 §1, operative July 1, 1976.

§1273.03. [Section repealed 1976]

Leg.H. Added Stats 1970 ch 417 §1. Repealed Stats 1975 ch 1275 §1, operative July 1, 1976.

§1273.04. [Section repealed 1976]

Leg.H. Added Stats 1970 ch 417 §1. Repealed Stats 1975 ch 1275 §1, operative July 1, 1976.

§1273.05. [Section repealed 1976]

Leg.H. Added Stats 1970 ch 417 §1. Repealed Stats 1975 ch 1275 §1, operative July 1, 1976.

§1273.06. [Section repealed 1976]

Leg.H. Added Stats 1970 ch 417 §1. Repealed Stats 1975 ch 1275 §1, operative July 1, 1976.

TITLE 8
CHANGE OF NAMES

Jurisdiction. §1275.
Application for change of name; Contents of petition. §1276.
Order to show cause; Publication or posting; Notice to nonjoining parent; Address confidentiality program. §1277.
Name to conform to gender identity. §1277.5.
Objections, hearing, order. §1278.
Denial of petition for change of name of minor. §1278.5.
Common law rights; Exceptions. §1279.5.
Refusal to do business with woman who uses her birth name or former name. §1279.6.

§1275. Jurisdiction

Applications for change of names must be determined by the Superior Courts. **Leg.H.** Enacted 1872. Amended Code Amdts 1880 ch 93 §1; Stats 1983 ch 486 §1.

§1276. Application for change of name; Contents of petition

(a)(1) All applications for change of names shall be made to the superior court of the county where the person whose name is proposed to be changed resides, except as specified in subdivision (e) or (g), either (A) by petition signed by the person or, if the person is under 18 years of age, by one of the person's parents, by any guardian of the person, or as specified in subdivision (e), or, if both parents are deceased and there is no guardian of the person, then by some near relative or friend of the person, or (B) as provided in Section 7638 of the Family Code.

(2) The petition or pleading shall specify the place of birth and residence of the person, the person's present name, the name proposed, and the reason for the change of name.

(b) In a proceeding for a change of name commenced by the filing of a petition, if the person whose name is to be changed is under 18 years of age, the petition shall, if neither parent of the person has signed the petition, name, as far as known to the person proposing the name change, the parents of the person and their place of residence, if living, or, if neither parent is living, near relatives of the person, and their place of residence.

(c) In a proceeding for a change of name commenced by the filing of a petition, if the person whose name is proposed to be changed is under 18 years of age and the petition is signed by only one parent, the petition shall specify the address, if known, of the other parent if living. If the petition is signed by a guardian, the petition shall specify the name and address, if known, of the parent or parents, if living, or the grandparents, if the addresses of both parents are unknown or if both parents are deceased, of the person whose name is proposed to be changed.

(d) In a proceeding for a change of name commenced by the filing of a petition, if the person whose name is proposed to be changed is 12 years of age or older, has been relinquished to an adoption agency by the person's parent or parents, and has not been legally adopted, the petition shall be signed by the person and the adoption agency to which the person was relinquished. The near relatives of the person and their place of residence shall not be included in the petition unless they are known to the person whose name is proposed to be changed.

(e) All petitions for the change of the name of a minor submitted by a guardian appointed by the juvenile court or the probate court, by a court-appointed dependency attorney appointed as guardian ad litem pursuant to rules adopted under Section 326.5 of the Welfare and Institutions Code, or by an attorney for a minor who is alleged or adjudged to be a person described in Section 601 or 602 of the Welfare and Institutions Code shall be made in the court having jurisdiction over the minor. All petitions for the change of name of a nonminor dependent may be made in the juvenile court.

(f) If the petition is signed by a guardian, the petition shall specify relevant information regarding the guardianship, the likelihood that the child will remain under the guardian's care until the child reaches the age of majority, and information suggesting that the child will not likely be returned to the custody of the child's parents.

(g)(1) On or after January 1, 2023, an application for a change of name may be made to a superior court for a person whose name is proposed to be changed, even if the person does not reside within the State of California, if the person is seeking to change their name on at least one of the following documents:

(A) A birth certificate that was issued within this state to the person whose name is proposed to be changed.

(B) A birth certificate that was issued within this state to the legal child of the person whose name is proposed to be changed.

(C) A marriage license and certificate or a confidential marriage license and certificate that was issued within this state to the person whose name is proposed to be changed.

(2) For the purposes of this subdivision, the superior court in the county where the birth under subparagraph (A) or (B) of paragraph (1) occurred or marriage under subparagraph (C) of paragraph (1) was entered shall be a proper venue for the proceeding. The name change shall be adjudicated in accordance with California law. **Leg.H.** Enacted 1872. Amended Code Amdts 1877–78 ch 413 §1; Code Amdts 1880 ch 113 §2; Stats 1885 ch 128 §1; Stats 1929 ch 710 §1; Stats 1945 ch 842 §1; Stats 1961 ch 1817 §1; Stats 1970 ch 651 §1; Stats 1971 ch 1748 §30; Stats 1975 ch 1241 §9; Stats 1989 ch 1105 §9; Stats 1992 ch 163 §59 (AB 2641), operative January 1, 1994; Stats 2000 ch 111 §1 (AB 2155); Stats 2006 ch 567 §10 (AB 2303), effective January 1, 2007; Stats 2018 ch 776 §9 (AB 3250), effective January 1, 2019; Stats 2021 ch 401 §7 (AB 1578), effective January 1, 2022; Stats 2021 ch 577 §1.5 (AB 218), effective January 1, 2022 (ch 577 prevails).

§1277. Order to show cause; Publication or posting; Notice to nonjoining parent; Address confidentiality program

(a)(1) If a proceeding for a change of name is commenced by the filing of a petition, except as provided in subdivisions (b), (c), (d), and (f), or Section 1277.5, the court shall thereupon make an order reciting the filing of the petition, the name of the person by whom it is filed, and the name proposed. The order shall direct all persons interested in the matter to appear before the court at a time and place specified, which shall be not less than 6 weeks nor more than 12 weeks from the time of making the order, unless the court orders a different time, to show cause why the application for change of name should not be granted. The order shall direct all persons interested in the matter to make known any objection that they may have to the granting of the petition for change of name by filing a written objection, which includes the reasons for the objection, with the court at least two court days before the matter is scheduled to be heard and by appearing in court at the hearing to show cause why the petition for change of name should not be granted. The order shall state that, if no written objection is timely filed, the court may grant the petition without a hearing.

(2)(A) A copy of the order to show cause shall be published pursuant to Section 6064 of the Government Code in a newspaper of general circulation to be designated in the order published in the county. If a newspaper of general circulation is not published in the county, a copy of the order to show cause shall be posted by the clerk of the court in three of the most public places in the county in which the court is located, for a like period. Proof shall be made to the satisfaction of the court of this publication or posting at the time of the hearing of the application.

(B)(i) On or after January 1, 2023, if the person whose name is proposed to be changed does not live in the county where the petition is filed, pursuant to subdivision (g) of Section 1276, the copy of the order to show cause shall be published pursuant to Section 6064 of the Government Code in a newspaper of general circulation published in the county of the person's residence. If a newspaper of general circulation is not published in the county of the person's residence, a copy of the order to show cause shall be posted by the clerk of the court in the county of the person's residence or a similarly situated local official in three of the most public places in the county of the person's residence, for a like period. If the place where the person seeking the name change lives does not have counties, publication shall be made according to the requirements of this paragraph in the local subdivision or territory of the person's residence. Proof shall be made to the satisfaction of the court of this publication or posting at the time of the hearing of the application.

(ii) If the person is unable to publish or post a copy of the order to show cause pursuant to clause (i), the court may allow an alternate method of publication or posting or may waive this requirement after sufficient evidence of diligent efforts to publish or post a copy of the order has been submitted to the satisfaction of the court.

(3) Four weekly publications shall be sufficient publication of the order to show cause. If the order is published in a daily newspaper, publication once a week for four successive weeks shall be sufficient.

(4) If a petition has been filed for a minor by a parent and the other parent, if living, does not join in consenting thereto, the petitioner shall cause, not less than 30 days before the hearing, to be served notice of the time and place of the hearing or a copy of the order to show cause on the other parent pursuant to Section 413.10, 414.10, 415.10, or 415.40. If notice of the hearing cannot reasonably be accomplished pursuant to Section 415.10 or 415.40, the court may order that notice be given in a manner that the court determines is reasonably calculated to give actual notice to the nonconsenting parent. In that case, if the court determines that notice by publication is reasonably calculated to give actual notice to the nonconsenting parent, the court may determine that publication of the order to show cause pursuant to this subdivision is sufficient notice to the nonconsenting parent.

(b)(1) If the petition for a change of name alleges a reason or circumstance described in paragraph (2), and the petitioner has established that the petitioner is an active participant in the address confidentiality program created pursuant to Chapter 3.1 (commencing with Section 6205) of Division 7 of Title 1 of the Government Code, and that the name the petitioner is seeking to acquire is on file with the Secretary of State, the action for a change of name is exempt from the requirement for publication of the order to show cause under subdivision (a), and the petition and the order of the court shall, in lieu of reciting the proposed name, indicate that the proposed name is confidential and is on file with the Secretary of State pursuant to the provisions of the address confidentiality program.

(2) The procedure described in paragraph (1) applies to petitions alleging any of the following reasons or circumstances:

(A) To avoid domestic violence, as defined in Section 6211 of the Family Code.

(B) To avoid stalking, as defined in Section 646.9 of the Penal Code.

(C) To avoid sexual assault, as defined in Section 1036.2 of the Evidence Code.

(D) To avoid human trafficking, as defined in Section 236.1 of the Penal Code.

(3) For any petition under this subdivision, the current legal name of the petitioner shall be kept confidential by the court and shall not be published or posted in the court's calendars, indexes, or register of actions, as required by Article 7 (commencing with Section 69840) of Chapter 5 of Title 8 of the Government Code, or by any means or in any public forum, including a hardcopy or an electronic copy, or any other type of public media or display.

(4) Notwithstanding paragraph (3), the court may, at the request of the petitioner, issue an order reciting the name of the petitioner at the time of the filing of the petition and the new legal name of the petitioner as a result of the court's granting of the petition.

(5) A petitioner may request that the court file the petition and any other papers associated with the proceeding under seal. The court may consider the request at the same time as the petition for name change, and may grant the request in any case in which the court finds that all of the following factors apply:

(A) There exists an overriding interest that overcomes the right of public access to the record.

(B) The overriding interest supports sealing the record.

(C) A substantial probability exists that the overriding interest will be prejudiced if the record is not sealed.

(D) The proposed order to seal the records is narrowly tailored.

(E) No less restrictive means exist to achieve the overriding interest.

(c) If the petition is filed for a minor or nonminor dependent who is under the jurisdiction of the juvenile court, the action for a change of name is exempt from the requirement for publication of the order to show cause under subdivision (a).

(d) A proceeding for a change of name for a witness participating in the state Witness Relocation and Assistance Program established by Title 7.5 (commencing with Section 14020) of Part 4 of the Penal Code who has been approved for the change of name by the program is exempt from the requirement for publication of the order to show cause under subdivision (a).

(e) If an application for change of name is brought as part of an action under the Uniform Parentage Act (Part 3 (commencing with Section 7600) of Division 12 of the Family Code), whether as part of a petition or cross-complaint or as a separate order to show cause in a pending action thereunder, service of the application shall be made upon all other parties to the action in a like manner as prescribed for the service of a summons, as set forth in Article 3 (commencing with Section 415.10) of Chapter 4 of Title 5 of Part 2. Upon the setting of a hearing on the issue, notice of the hearing shall be given to all parties in the action in a like manner and within the time limits prescribed generally for the type of hearing (whether trial or order to show cause) at which the issue of the change of name is to be decided.

(f) If a guardian files a petition to change the name of the guardian's minor ward pursuant to Section 1276:

(1) The guardian shall provide notice of the hearing to any living parent of the minor by personal service at least 30 days before the hearing.

(2) If either or both parents are deceased or cannot be located, the guardian shall cause, not less than 30 days before the hearing, to be served a notice of the time and place of the hearing or a copy of the order to show cause on the child's grandparents, if living, pursuant to Section 413.10, 414.10, 415.10, or 415.40. **Leg.H.** Added Stats 2017 ch 853 §4 (SB 179), effective January 1, 2018, operative September 1, 2018. Stats 2018 ch 776 §10 (AB 3250), effective January 1, 2019; Stats 2018 ch 818 §1 (AB 2201), effective January 1, 2019 (chapter 818 prevails); Stats 2021 ch 401 §8 (AB 1578), effective January 1, 2022; Stats 2021 ch 577 §2.5 (AB 218), effective January 1, 2022 (ch 577 prevails).

2017 Notes: This act shall be known and may be cited as the Gender Recognition Act. Stats 2017 ch 853 (SB 179) §1.

The Legislature finds and declares all of the following:

(a) It is the policy of the State of California that every person deserves full legal recognition and equal treatment under the law and to ensure that intersex, transgender, and nonbinary people have state-issued identification documents that provide full legal recognition of their accurate gender identity.

(b) Gender identification is fundamentally personal, and the state should endeavor to provide options on state-issued identification documents that recognize a person's accurate gender identification. It is the intent of the Legislature in enacting this legislation to provide three equally recognized gender options on state-issued identification documents—female, male, and nonbinary—and an efficient and fair process for people to amend their gender designation on state-issued identification documents so that state-issued identification documents legally recognize a person's accurate gender identification.

(c) "Intersex" is an umbrella term used to describe natural bodily variations, which can include external genitalia, internal sex organs, chromosomes, or hormonal differences that transcend typical ideas of male and female. Upper estimates of the number of intersex people are approximately 1.7 percent of the general population. In the United States, some children born with intersex traits have been subjected to involuntary and medically unnecessary surgical procedures in infancy in an attempt to erase aspects of their natural bodies, causing significant physical and psychological harm. Human rights authorities have condemned this practice as a form of torture and recognize that legal and ethical frameworks require intersex people themselves to make decisions concerning their own bodies. Thus, those human rights authorities recommended that physicians assign a provisional gender designation with the knowledge that the child may later identify differently. An option of a nonbinary gender designation on state-issued identification documents would allow intersex people, like transgender and nonbinary people, to be able to use their state-issued identification documents that accurately recognize their gender identification as female, male, or nonbinary.

(d) The binary gender designations of female and male fail to adequately represent the diversity of human experience. Nonbinary is an umbrella term for people with gender identities that fall somewhere outside of the traditional conceptions of strictly either female or male. People with nonbinary gender identities may or may not identify as transgender, may or may not have been born with intersex traits, may or may not use gender-neutral pronouns, and may or may not use more specific terms to describe their genders, such as agender, genderqueer, gender fluid, Two Spirit, bigender, pangender, gender nonconforming, or gender variant. Nonbinary gender identities have been recognized by cultures throughout history and around the world, as well as by legal systems in the United States and other countries, medical authorities, and researchers. Studies show that nonbinary people face frequent discrimination harassment, and violence in areas of life-including education, employment, health care, and law enforcement.

(e) Transgender is an umbrella term used to describe people whose gender identity or gender expression do not match the gender they were assigned at birth. Some transgender people have medically transitioned, undergoing gender affirming surgeries and hormonal treatments, while other transgender people do not choose any form of medical transition. There is no uniform set of procedures that are sought by transgender people that pursue medical transition. transgender people may identify as female, male, or nonbinary, may or may not have been born with intersex traits, may or may not use gender-neutral pronouns, and may or may not use more specific terms to describe their genders, such as agender, genderqueer, gender fluid, Two Spirit, bigender, pangender, gender nonconforming, or gender variant. Studies show that transgender people disproportionately face discrimination, harassment, and violence in areas of life including housing, education, employment, health care, and law enforcement. Stats 2017 ch 853 (SB 179) §2.

Former Sections: Former CCP §1277, similar to the present section, was added Stats 2013 ch 651 §2 (AB 1121), operative July 1, 2014, became inoperative September 1, 2018, and repealed operative January 1, 2019, by its own provisions. Stats 2017 ch 853 §3 (SB 179).

Former CCP §1277, similar to the present section, was enacted in 1872 and repealed operative July 1, 2014, by its own provisions. Stats 2013 ch 651 §1 (AB 1121).

Prior Law Former CCP §1277, similar to the present section, was added Stats 2013 ch 651 §2 (AB 1121), effective January 1, 2014, operative July 1, 2014, amended Stats 2014 ch 49 § 1 (SB 545), effective January 1, 2015; Stats 2015 ch 303 §41 (AB 731), effective January 1, 2016; Stats 2017 ch 853 §3 (SB 179), effective January 1, 2018, inoperative September 1, 2018, repealed January 1, 2019, by its own terms.

Former CCP §1277, similar to the present section, was enacted 1872, amended Stats 1905 ch 45 §1, Stats 1929 ch 710 §2, Stats 1945 ch 854 §1, Stats 1951 ch 45 §1, Stats 1961 ch 1817 §2, Stats 1989 ch 1105 §10, Stats 1990 ch 411 §6, effective July 24, 1990, Stats 1992 ch 163 §60, operative January 1, 1994, Stats 2000 ch 33 §1.5, ch 111 §4, ch 688 §8.3, Stats 2006 ch 576 §11, ch 689 §1.5, Stats 2007 ch 130 §37, Stats 2008 ch 586 §1, Stats 2013 ch 651 §1, and repealed July 1, 2014, by its own terms.

§1277.5. Name to conform to gender identity

(a)(1) If a proceeding for a change of name to conform the petitioner's name to the petitioner's gender identity is commenced by the filing of a petition, the court shall thereupon make an order reciting the filing of the petition, the name of the person by whom it is filed, and the name proposed. The order shall direct all persons interested in the matter to make known any objection to the change of name by filing a written objection, which includes any reasons for the objection, within six weeks of the making of the order, and shall state that if no objection showing good cause to oppose the name change is timely filed, the court shall, without hearing, enter the order that the change of name is granted.

(2) If a petition is filed to change the name of a minor to conform to gender identity that does not include the signatures of both living parents, the petition and the order to show cause made in accordance with paragraph (1) shall be served on the parent who did not sign the petition, pursuant to Section 413.10, 414.10, 415.10, or 415.40, within 30 days from the date on which the order is made by the court. If service cannot reasonably be accomplished pursuant to Section 415.10 or 415.40, the court may order that service be accomplished in a manner that the court determines is reasonably calculated to give actual notice to the parent who did not sign the petition.

(b) The proceeding for a change of name to conform the petitioner's name to the petitioner's gender identity is exempt from any requirement for publication.

(c) A hearing date shall not be set in the proceeding unless an objection is timely filed and shows good cause for opposing the name change. Objections based solely on concerns that the proposed change is not the petitioner's actual gender identity or gender assigned at birth shall not constitute good cause. At the hearing, the court may examine under oath any of the petitioners, remonstrants, or other persons touching the petition or application, and may make an order changing the name or dismissing the petition or application as the court may deem right and proper. **Leg.H.** Added Stats 2017 ch 853 §5 (SB 179), effective January 1, 2018, operative September 1, 2018. Amended Stats 2018 ch 776 §11 (AB 3250), effective January 1, 2019.

2017 Note: For act citation and legislative findings and declarations, see the 2017 Note following CCP §1277.

§1278. Objections, hearing, order

(a)(1) Except as provided in subdivisions (c) and (d), the petition or application shall be heard at the time designated by the court, only if objections are filed by a person who can, in those objections, show to the court good cause against the change of name. At the hearing, the court may examine on oath any of the petitioners, remonstrants, or other persons touching the petition or application, and may make an order changing the name, or dismissing the petition or application, as the court may deem right and proper.

(2) If no objection is filed at least two court days before the date set for hearing, the court may, without hearing, enter the order that the change of name is granted.

(b) If the provisions of subdivision (b) of Section 1277 apply, the court shall not disclose the proposed name unless the court finds by clear and convincing evidence that the allegations of domestic violence, stalking, or sexual assault in the petition are false.

(c) If the application for a change of name is brought as part of an action under the Uniform Parentage Act (Part 3 (commencing with Section 7600) of Division 12 of the Family Code), the hearing on the issue of the change of name shall be conducted pursuant to statutes and rules of court governing those proceedings, whether the hearing is conducted upon an order to show cause or upon trial.

(d) If the petition for a change of name is filed by a guardian on behalf of a minor ward, the court shall first find that the ward is likely to remain in the guardian's care until the age of majority and that the ward is not likely to be returned to the custody of the parents. Upon making those findings, the court shall consider the petition and may grant the petition only if it finds that the proposed name change is in the best interest of the child.

(e) This section shall become operative on September 1, 2018. **Leg.H.** Added Stats 2017 ch 853 §7 (SB 179), effective January 1, 2018, operative September 1, 2018.

2017 Note: For act citation and legislative findings and declarations, see the 2017 Note following CCP §1277.

Former Sections: Former CCP §1278, similar to the present section, was added Stats 2013 ch 651 §4 (AB 1121), operative July 1, 2014, inoperative September 1, 2018, and repealed January 1, 2019, by its own provisions. Stats 2017 ch 853 §6 (SB 179).

Former CCP §1278, similar to the present section, was enacted in 1872 and repealed operative July 1, 2014, by its own provisions. Stats 2013 ch 651 §3 (AB 1121).

Prior Law: Former CCP §1278, similar to the present section, was added Stats 2013 ch 651 §4 (AB 1121), effective January 1, 2014, operative July 1, 2014, amended Stats 2017 ch 853 §6 (SB 179), effective January 1, 2018, inoperative September 1, 2018, and repealed January 1, 2019, by its own terms.

Former CCP §1278, similar to the present section, was enacted 1872, amended Code Amdts 1880 ch 113 §3, Stats 1905 ch 103 §1, Stats 1915 ch 85 §1, Stats 1929 ch 710 §3, Stats 1983 ch 486 §2, Stats 1989 ch 1105 §11, Stats 1992 ch 163 §61, operative January 1, 1994, Stats 2000 ch 33 §2.5, ch 111 §7, Stats 2006 ch 567 §12, Stats 2013 ch 651 §3, and repealed July 1, 2014, by its own terms.

§1278.5. Denial of petition for change of name of minor

In any proceeding pursuant to this title in which a petition has been filed to change the name of a minor, and both parents, if living, do not join in consent, the court may deny the petition in whole or in part if it finds that any portion of the proposed name change is not in the best interest of the child. **Leg.H.** Added Stats 1996 ch 1061 §2 (SB 1033). Amended Stats 2006 ch 567 §13 (AB 2303), effective January 1, 2007.

§1279. [Section repealed 2001]

Leg.H. Added Code Amdts 1873–74 ch 246 §1. Amended Code Amdts 1880 ch 113 §4; Stats 1907 ch 275 §1; Stats 1929 ch 710 §4; Stats 1998 ch 829 §17 (SB 1652). Repealed Stats 2000 ch 506 §4 (SB 1350). The repealed section related to filing of copy of decree with clerk.

§1279.5. Common law rights; Exceptions

(a) Except as provided in subdivision (e) or (f), this title does not abrogate the common law right of a person to change his or her name.

(b) A person under the jurisdiction of the Department of Corrections and Rehabilitation or sentenced to county jail has the right to petition the court to obtain a name or gender change pursuant to this title or Article 7 (commencing with Section 103425) of Chapter 11 of Part 1 of Division 102 of the Health and Safety Code.

(c) A person under the jurisdiction of the Department of Corrections and Rehabilitation shall provide a copy of the petition for a name change to the department, in a manner prescribed by the department, at the time the petition is filed. A person sentenced to county jail shall provide a copy of the petition for name change to the sheriff's department, in a manner prescribed by the department, at the time the petition is filed.

(d) In all documentation of a person under the jurisdiction of the Department of Corrections and Rehabilitation or imprisoned within a county jail, the new name of a person who obtains a name change shall be used, and prior names shall be listed as an alias.

(e) Notwithstanding any other law, a court shall deny a petition for a name change pursuant to this title made by a person who is required to register as a sex offender under Section 290 of the Penal Code, unless the court determines that it is in the best interest of justice to grant the petition and that doing so will not adversely affect the public safety. If a petition for a name change is granted for an individual required to register as a sex offender, the individual shall, within five working days, notify the chief of police of the city in which he or she is domiciled, or the sheriff of the county if he or she is domiciled in an unincorporated area, and additionally with the chief of police of a campus of a University of California or California State University if he or she is domiciled upon the campus or in any of its facilities.

(f) For the purpose of this section, the court shall use the California Law Enforcement Telecommunications System (CLETS) and Criminal Justice Information System (CJIS) to determine whether or not an applicant for a name change is required to register as a sex offender pursuant to Section 290 of the Penal Code. Each person applying for a name change shall declare under penalty of perjury that he or she is not required to register as a sex offender pursuant to Section 290 of the Penal Code. If a court is not equipped with CLETS or CJIS, the clerk of the court shall contact an appropriate local law enforcement agency, which shall determine whether or not the petitioner is required to register as a sex offender pursuant to Section 290 of the Penal Code.

(g) This section shall become operative on September 1, 2018. **Leg.H.** Added Stats 2017 ch 856 §3 (SB 310), effective January 1, 2018, operative September 1, 2018.

2017 Note: For legislative findings and declarations, see the 2017 Note following CCP §1277, above.

Former Sections: Former CCP §1279.5, similar to the present section, was added Stats 1974 ch 1235 §3, inoperative September 1, 2018, and repealed January 1, 2019, by its own provisions. Stats 2017 ch 856 §2 (SB 310).

Prior Law Former CCP §1279.5, similar to the present section, was added Stats 1974 ch 1235 §3, amended Stats 1975 ch 1070 §3, Stats 1992 ch 163 §62 (AB 2641), operative January 1, 1994, Stats 1994 ch 557 §1 (AB 2782), Stats 1996 ch 730 §1 (AB 2359), Stats 1997 ch 821 §1 (AB 290), effective October 6, 1997, Stats 2006 ch 567 §14 (AB 2303), effective January 1, 2007, Stats 2017 ch 856 §2 (SB 310), effective January 1, 2018, inoperative September 1, 2018, repealed January 1, 2019, by its own terms.

§1279.6. Refusal to do business with woman who uses her birth name or former name

No person engaged in a trade or business of any kind or in the provision of a service of any kind shall do any of the following:

(a) Refuse to do business with a person, or refuse to provide the service to a person, regardless of the person's marital status, because he or she has chosen to use or regularly uses his or her birth name, former name, or name adopted upon solemnization of marriage or registration of domestic partnership.

(b) Impose, as a condition of doing business with a person, or as a condition of providing the service to a person, a requirement that the person, regardless of his or her marital status, use a name other than his or her birth name, former name, or name adopted upon solemnization of marriage or registration of domestic partnership, if the person has chosen to use or regularly uses that name. **Leg.H.** Added Stats 1992 ch 163 §63 (AB 2641), operative January 1, 1994. Amended Stats 2007 ch 567 §3 (AB 102), effective January 1, 2008.

2007 Note: This act shall be known and may be cited as the Name Equality Act of 2007. Stats 2007 ch 567 (AB 102) §1.

TITLE 8A
ABANDONED PROPERTY [REPEALED]

§§1274.1–1274.17.   [Sections repealed 1952]

Leg.H. Added Stats 1945 ch 1080 §1. Amended Stats 1947 chs 342, 1189, Stats 1951 chs 47, 352. Repealed by Stats 1951 ch 1708 §2.

TITLE 9
ARBITRATION

Chapter 1. General Provisions.
Chapter 2. Enforcement of Arbitration Agreements.
Chapter 3. Conduct of Arbitration Proceedings.
Chapter 4. Enforcement of the Award.
Chapter 5. General Provisions Relating to Judicial Proceedings.

CHAPTER 1
GENERAL PROVISIONS

Definitions. §1280.
Reference to portion of title or of any other law. §1280.2.

§1280. Definitions

As used in this title:

(a) "Agreement" includes, but is not limited to, agreements providing for valuations, appraisals, and similar proceedings and agreements between employers and employees or between their respective representatives.

(b) "Award" includes, but is not limited to, an award made pursuant to an agreement not in writing.

(c) "Consumer" means an individual who seeks, uses, or acquires, by purchase or lease, any goods or services for personal, family, or household purposes.

(d) "Controversy" means any question arising between parties to an agreement whether the question is one of law or of fact or both.

(e) "Drafting party" means the company or business that included a predispute arbitration provision in a contract with a consumer or employee. The term includes any third party relying upon, or otherwise subject to the arbitration provision, other than the employee or consumer.

(f) "Employee" means any current employee, former employee, or applicant for employment. The term includes any person who is, was, or who claims to have been misclassified as an independent contractor or otherwise improperly placed into a category other than employee or applicant for employment.

(g) "Neutral arbitrator" means an arbitrator who is (1) selected jointly by the parties or by the arbitrators selected by the parties, or (2) appointed by the court when the parties or the arbitrators selected by the parties fail to select an arbitrator who was to be selected jointly by the parties.

(h) "Party to the arbitration" means a party to the arbitration agreement, including any of the following:

(1) A party who seeks to arbitrate a controversy pursuant to the agreement.

(2) A party against whom such arbitration is sought pursuant to the agreement.

(3) A party who is made a party to the arbitration by order of the neutral arbitrator upon that party's application, upon the application of any other party to the arbitration, or upon the neutral arbitrator's own determination.

(i) "Written agreement" includes a written agreement that has been extended or renewed by an oral or implied agreement. **Leg.H.** Added Stats 1961 ch 461 §2. Amended Stats 2019 ch 870 §2 (SB 707), effective January 1, 2020.

2019 Note: It is the intent of the Legislature in enacting this measure to affirm the decisions in *Armendariz v. Foundation Health Psychcare Services, Inc., Brown v. Dillard's, Inc.,* and *Sink v. Aden Enterprises, Inc.* that a company's failure to pay arbitration fees pursuant to a mandatory arbitration provision constitutes a breach of the arbitration agreement and allows the non-breaching party to bring a claim in court. Stats 2019 ch 870 §1(f) (SB 707).

Prior Law: Former CCP §1280, similar in part to present §1281, was added by Stats 1927 ch 225 §1, amended by Stats 1935 ch 52 §9, and repealed by Stats 1961 ch 461 §1.

§1280.1. [Section repealed 1997]

Leg.H. Added Stats 1985 ch 709 §1. Amended Stats 1990 ch 817 §2 (SB 1951), operative until January 1, 1996; Stats 1995 ch 209 §2 (SB 479), operative until January 1, 1997. Repealed operative January 1, 1997, by its own terms. The repealed section related to immunity of arbitrator from civil liability.

§1280.2. Reference to portion of title or of any other law

Whenever reference is made in this title to any portion of the title or of any other law of this State, the reference applies to all amendments and additions thereto now or hereafter made. **Leg.H.** Added Stats 1961 ch 461 §2.

CHAPTER 2
ENFORCEMENT OF ARBITRATION AGREEMENTS

Requisites and validity. §1281.
Consideration of request to arbitrate as pursuant to written agreement. §1281.1.
Tolling. §1281.12.
Order to arbitrate; Determination of other issues. §1281.2.
Petition to consolidate separate arbitration proceedings. §1281.3.
Arbitration of issue involved in pending action or proceeding. §1281.4.
How right to arbitration preserved when filing action to enforce lien; Service of motion within 30 days; Waiver by defendant who fails to file petition. §1281.5.
Appointment of arbitrator. §1281.6.
Petition in lieu of answer to complaint. §1281.7.
"Provisional remedy". §1281.8.
Ethics standards; Applicability; Nonnegotiability. §1281.85.
Disclosure required of proposed nominee; Disqualification as neutral arbitrator. §1281.9.
Disqualification of arbitrator for disclosure failure; Petition to disqualify; Waiver of right to disqualify. §1281.91.
Prohibited activities by private arbitration company. §1281.92.
Restrictions on solicitation during consumer arbitration. §1281.93.
Disclosures by arbitrator in residential construction contract dispute. §1281.95.
Publication of consumer arbitration information by private arbitration company. §1281.96.
Employment or consumer arbitration; Drafting party pays fees; Drafting party breach. §1281.97.
Rights of employee or consumer when drafting party materially breaches arbitration agreement. §1281.98.
Monetary sanctions against materially breaching party. §1281.99.

§1281. Requisites and validity

A written agreement to submit to arbitration an existing controversy or a controversy thereafter arising is valid, enforceable and irrevocable, save upon such grounds as exist for the revocation of any contract. **Leg.H.** Added Stats 1961 ch 461 §2.

Prior Law: Former CCP §1281, similar in part to present CCP §§1292, 1292.2, 1292.4, was enacted Stats 1872, amended Stats 1927 ch 225 §2, and repealed Stats 1961 ch 461 §1.

§1281.1. Consideration of request to arbitrate as pursuant to written agreement

For the purposes of this article, any request to arbitrate made pursuant to subdivision (a) of Section 1299.4 shall be considered as made pursuant to a written agreement to submit a controversy to arbitration. **Leg.H.** Added Stats 2000 ch 906 §1 (SB 402).

§1281.12. Tolling

If an arbitration agreement requires that arbitration of a controversy be demanded or initiated by a party to the arbitration agreement within a period of time, the commencement of a civil action by that party based upon that controversy, within that period of time, shall toll the applicable time limitations contained in the arbitration agreement with respect to that controversy, from the date the civil action is commenced until 30 days after a final determination by the court that the party is required to arbitrate the controversy, or 30 days after the final termination of the civil action that was commenced and initiated the tolling, whichever date occurs first. **Leg.H.** Added Stats 2006 ch 266 §1 (AB 1553), effective January 1, 2007.

§1281.2. Order to arbitrate; Determination of other issues

On petition of a party to an arbitration agreement alleging the existence of a written agreement to arbitrate a controversy and that a party to the agreement refuses to arbitrate that controversy, the court shall order the petitioner and the respondent to arbitrate the controversy if it determines that an agreement to arbitrate the controversy exists, unless it determines that:

(a) The right to compel arbitration has been waived by the petitioner; or

(b) Grounds exist for rescission of the agreement.

(c) A party to the arbitration agreement is also a party to a pending court action or special proceeding with a third party, arising out of the same transaction or series of related transactions and there is a possibility of conflicting rulings on a common issue of law or fact. For purposes of this section, a pending court action or special proceeding includes an action or proceeding initiated by the party refusing to arbitrate after the petition to compel arbitration has been filed, but on or before the date of the hearing on the petition. This subdivision shall not be applicable to an agreement to arbitrate disputes as to the professional negligence of a health care provider made pursuant to Section 1295.

(d) The petitioner is a state or federally chartered depository institution that, on or after January 1, 2018, is seeking to apply a written agreement to arbitrate, contained in a contract consented to by a respondent consumer, to a purported contractual relationship with that respondent consumer that was created by the petitioner fraudulently without the respondent consumer's consent and by unlawfully using the respondent consumer's personal identifying information, as defined in Section 1798.92 of the Civil Code.

If the court determines that a written agreement to arbitrate a controversy exists, an order to arbitrate that controversy may not be refused on the ground that the petitioner's contentions lack substantive merit.

If the court determines that there are other issues between the petitioner and the respondent which are not subject to arbitration and which are the subject of a pending action or special proceeding between the petitioner and the respondent and that a determination of such issues may make the arbitration unnecessary, the court may delay its order to arbitrate until the determination of such other issues or until such earlier time as the court specifies.

If the court determines that a party to the arbitration is also a party to litigation in a pending court action or special proceeding with a third party as set forth under subdivision (c), the court (1) may refuse to enforce the arbitration agreement and may order intervention or joinder of all parties in a single action or special proceeding; (2) may order intervention or joinder as to all or only certain issues; (3) may order arbitration among the parties who have agreed to arbitration and stay the pending court action or special proceeding pending the outcome of the arbitration proceeding; or (4) may stay arbitration pending the outcome of the court action or special proceeding. **Leg.H.** Added Stats 1961 ch 461 §2. Amended Stats 1978 ch 260 §1; Stats 2017 ch 480 §1 (SB 33), effective January 1, 2018; Stats 2018 ch 106 §1 (AB 3247), effective January 1, 2019.

§1281.3. Petition to consolidate separate arbitration proceedings

A party to an arbitration agreement may petition the court to consolidate separate arbitration proceedings, and the court may order consolidation of separate arbitration proceedings when:

(1) Separate arbitration agreements or proceedings exist between the same parties; or one party is a party to a separate arbitration agreement or proceeding with a third party; and

(2) The disputes arise from the same transactions or series of related transactions; and

(3) There is common issue or issues of law or fact creating the possibility of conflicting rulings by more than one arbitrator or panel of arbitrators.

If all of the applicable arbitration agreements name the same arbitrator, arbitration panel, or arbitration tribunal, the court, if it orders consolidation, shall order all matters to be heard before the arbitrator, panel, or tribunal agreed to by the parties. If the applicable arbitration agreements name separate arbitrators, panels, or tribunals, the court, if it orders consolidation, shall, in the absence of an agreed method of selection by all parties to the consolidated arbitration, appoint an arbitrator in accord with the procedures set forth in Section 1281.6.

In the event that the arbitration agreements in consolidated proceedings contain inconsistent provisions, the court shall resolve such conflicts and determine the rights and duties of the various parties to achieve substantial justice under all the circumstances.

The court may exercise its discretion under this section to deny consolidation of separate arbitration proceedings or to consolidate separate arbitration proceedings only as to certain issues, leaving other issues to be resolved in separate proceedings.

This section shall not be applicable to an agreement to arbitrate disputes as to the professional negligence of a health care provider made pursuant to Section 1295. **Leg.H.** Added Stats 1978 ch 260 §2.

§1281.4. Arbitration of issue involved in pending action or proceeding

If a court of competent jurisdiction, whether in this State or not, has ordered arbitration of a controversy which is an issue involved in an action or proceeding pending before a court of this State, the court in which such action or proceeding is pending shall, upon motion of a party to such action or proceeding, stay the action or proceeding until an arbitration is had in accordance with the order to arbitrate or until such earlier time as the court specifies.

If an application has been made to a court of competent jurisdiction, whether in this State or not, for an order to arbitrate a controversy which is an issue involved in an action or proceeding pending before a court of this State and such application is undetermined, the court in which such action or proceeding is pending shall, upon motion of a party to such action or proceeding, stay the action or proceeding until the application for an order to arbitrate is determined and, if arbitration of such controversy is ordered, until an arbitration is had in accordance with the order to arbitrate or until such earlier time as the court specifies.

If the issue which is the controversy subject to arbitration is severable, the stay may be with respect to that issue only. **Leg.H.** Added Stats 1961 ch 461 §2.

§1281.5. How right to arbitration preserved when filing action to enforce lien; Service of motion within 30 days; Waiver by defendant who fails to file petition

(a) Any person who proceeds to record and enforce a claim of lien by commencement of an action pursuant to Chapter 4 (commencing with Section 8400) of Title 2 of Part 6 of Division 4 of the Civil Code, does not thereby waive any right of arbitration the person may have pursuant to a written agreement to arbitrate, if, in filing an action to enforce the claim of lien, the claimant does either of the following:

(1) Includes an allegation in the complaint that the claimant does not intend to waive any right of arbitration, and intends to move the court, within 30 days after service of the summons and complaint, for an order to stay further proceedings in the action.

(2) At the same time that the complaint is filed, the claimant files an application that the action be stayed pending the arbitration of any issue, question, or dispute that is claimed to be arbitrable under the agreement and that is relevant to the action to enforce the claim of lien.

(b) Within 30 days after service of the summons and complaint, the claimant shall file and serve a motion and notice of motion pursuant to Section 1281.4 to stay the action pending the arbitration of any issue, question, or dispute that is claimed to be arbitrable under the agreement and that is relevant to the action to enforce the claim of lien. The failure of a claimant to comply with this subdivision is a waiver of the claimant's right to compel arbitration.

(c) The failure of a defendant to file a petition pursuant to Section 1281.2 at or before the time the defendant answers the complaint filed pursuant to subdivision (a) is a waiver of the defendant's right to compel arbitration. **Leg.H.** Added Stats 1977 ch 135 §1. Amended Stats 1989 ch 470 §1; Stats 1998 ch 931 §122 (SB 2139), effective September 28, 1998; Stats 2002 ch 784 §82 (SB 1316); Stats 2003 ch 22 §1 (SB 113); Stats 2010 ch 697 §25 (SB 189), effective January 1, 2011, operative July 1, 2012.

§1281.6. Appointment of arbitrator

If the arbitration agreement provides a method of appointing an arbitrator, that method shall be followed. If the arbitration agreement does not provide a method for appointing an arbitrator, the parties to the agreement who seek arbitration and against whom arbitration is sought may agree on a method of appointing an arbitrator and that method shall be followed. In the absence of an agreed method, or if the agreed method fails or for any reason cannot be followed, or when an arbitrator appointed fails to act and his or her successor has not been appointed, the court, on petition of a party to the arbitration agreement, shall appoint the arbitrator.

When a petition is made to the court to appoint a neutral arbitrator, the court shall nominate five persons from lists of persons supplied jointly by the parties to the arbitration or obtained from a governmental agency concerned with arbitration or private disinterested association concerned with arbitration. The parties to the agreement who seek arbitration and against whom arbitration is sought may within five days of receipt of notice of the nominees from the court jointly select the arbitrator whether or not the arbitrator is among the nominees.

If the parties fail to select an arbitrator within the five-day period, the court shall appoint the arbitrator from the nominees. **Leg.H.** Added Stats 1961 ch 461 §2. Amended Stats 1994 ch 587 §8 (AB 3600); Stats 1997 ch 445 §1 (AB 1093); Stats 2001 ch 362 §3 (SB 475).

§1281.7. Petition in lieu of answer to complaint

A petition pursuant to Section 1281.2 may be filed in lieu of filing an answer to a complaint. The petitioning defendant shall have 15 days after any denial of the petition to plead to the complaint. **Leg.H.** Added Stats 1987 ch 1080 §9.

§1281.8. "Provisional remedy"

(a) As used in this section, "provisional remedy" includes the following:

(1) Attachments and temporary protective orders issued pursuant to Title 6.5 (commencing with Section 481.010) of Part 2.

(2) Writs of possession issued pursuant to Article 2 (commencing with Section 512.010) of Chapter 2 of Title 7 of Part 2.

(3) Preliminary injunctions and temporary restraining orders issued pursuant to Section 527.

(4) Receivers appointed pursuant to Section 564.

(b) A party to an arbitration agreement may file in the court in the county in which an arbitration proceeding is pending, or if an arbitration proceeding has not commenced, in any proper court, an application for a provisional remedy in connection with an arbitrable controversy, but only upon the ground that the award to which the applicant may be entitled may be rendered ineffectual without provisional relief. The application shall be accompanied by a complaint or by copies of the demand for arbitration and any response thereto. If accompanied by a complaint, the application shall also be accompanied by a statement stating whether the party is or is not reserving the party's right to arbitration.

(c) A claim by the party opposing issuance of a provisional remedy, that the controversy is not subject to arbitration, shall not be grounds for denial of any provisional remedy.

(d) An application for a provisional remedy under subdivision (b) shall not operate to waive any right of arbitration which the applicant may have pursuant to a written agreement to arbitrate, if, at the same time as the application for a provisional remedy is presented, the applicant also presents to the court an application that all other proceedings in the action be stayed pending the arbitration of any issue, question, or dispute which is claimed to be arbitrable under the agreement and which is relevant to the action pursuant to which the provisional remedy is sought. **Leg.H.** Added Stats 1989 ch 470 §2.

§1281.85. Ethics standards; Applicability; Nonnegotiability

(a) Beginning July 1, 2002, a person serving as a neutral arbitrator pursuant to an arbitration agreement shall comply with the ethics standards for arbitrators adopted by the Judicial Council pursuant to this section. The Judicial Council shall adopt ethical standards for all neutral arbitrators effective July 1, 2002. These standards shall be consistent with the standards established for arbitrators in the judicial arbitration program and may expand but may not limit the disclosure and disqualification requirements established by this chapter. The standards shall address the disclosure of interests, relationships, or affiliations that may constitute conflicts of interest, including prior service as an arbitrator or other dispute resolution neutral entity, disqualifications, acceptance of gifts, and establishment of future professional relationships.

(b) Subdivision (a) does not apply to an arbitration conducted pursuant to the terms of a public or private sector collective bargaining agreement.

(c) The ethics requirements and standards of this chapter are nonnegotiable and shall not be waived. **Leg.H.** Added Stats 2001 ch 362 §4 (SB 475). Amended Stats 2002 ch 176 §1 (SB 1707); Stats 2009 ch 133 §1 (AB 1090), effective January 1, 2010.

§1281.9. Disclosure required of proposed nominee; Disqualification as neutral arbitrator

(a) In any arbitration pursuant to an arbitration agreement, when a person is to serve as a neutral arbitrator, the proposed neutral arbitrator shall disclose all matters that could cause a person aware of the facts to reasonably entertain a doubt that the proposed neutral arbitrator would be able to be impartial, including all of the following:

(1) The existence of any ground specified in Section 170.1 for disqualification of a judge. For purposes of paragraph (8) of subdivision (a) of Section 170.1, the proposed neutral arbitrator shall disclose whether or not [1] **they have** a current arrangement concerning prospective employment or other compensated service as a dispute resolution neutral or [2] **are** participating in, or, within the last two years, [3] **have** participated in, discussions regarding such prospective employment or service with a party to the proceeding.

(2) Any matters required to be disclosed by the ethics standards for neutral arbitrators adopted by the Judicial Council pursuant to this chapter.

(3) The names of the parties to all prior or pending noncollective bargaining cases in which the proposed neutral arbitrator served or is serving as a party arbitrator for [4] **a** party to the arbitration proceeding or for a lawyer for a party and the results of each case arbitrated to conclusion, including the date of the arbitration award, identification of the prevailing party, the names of the parties' attorneys, and the amount of monetary damages awarded, if any. In order to preserve confidentiality, it shall be sufficient to give the name of any party who is not a party to the pending arbitration as "claimant" or "respondent" if the party is an individual and not a business or corporate entity.

(4) The names of the parties to all prior or pending noncollective bargaining cases involving [5] **a** party to the arbitration or lawyer for a party for which the proposed neutral arbitrator served or is serving as neutral arbitrator, and the results of each case arbitrated to conclusion, including the date of the arbitration award, identification of the prevailing party, the names of the parties' attorneys and the amount of monetary damages awarded, if any. In order to preserve confidentiality, it shall be sufficient to give the name of any party not a party to the pending arbitration as "claimant" or "respondent" if the party is an individual and not a business or corporate entity.

(5) Any attorney-client relationship the proposed neutral arbitrator has or had with [6] **a** party or lawyer for a party to the arbitration proceeding.

(6) Any professional or significant personal relationship the proposed neutral arbitrator or [7] **their** spouse or minor child living in the household has or has had with any party to the arbitration proceeding or lawyer for a party.

(7)(A) In a consumer arbitration case, any solicitation made after January 1, 2025, and within the last two years by, or at the direction of, the private arbitration company to a party or lawyer for a party to the consumer arbitration.

(B) This paragraph does not apply to an arbitration conducted or administered by a self-regulatory organization, as defined by the federal Securities Exchange Act of 1934 (15 U.S.C. Sec. 78a) or regulations adopted under that act.

(b) Subject only to the disclosure requirements of law, the proposed neutral arbitrator shall disclose all matters required to be disclosed pursuant to this section to all parties in writing within 10 calendar days of service of notice of the proposed nomination or appointment.

(c) For purposes of this section:

[8] **(1)** [9] "Lawyer for a party" includes any lawyer or law firm currently associated in the practice of law with the lawyer hired to represent a party.

[10] **(2)** [11] "Prior cases" means noncollective bargaining cases in which an arbitration award was rendered within five years prior to the date of the proposed nomination or appointment.

[12] **(3)** [13] "Any arbitration" does not include an arbitration conducted pursuant to the terms of a public or private sector collective bargaining agreement.

(4)(A) "Solicitation" includes either of the following:

(i) Private presentations made to a party or lawyer for a party by the private arbitration company or the arbitrator.

(ii) Oral or written discussions, meetings, or negotiations to designate the private arbitration company or the arbitrator as the arbitration provider or arbitrator for a party in specific contracts.

(B) "Solicitation" does not include any of the following:

(i) Advertising directed to the general public.

(ii) Communications indicating a general willingness to serve as an arbitrator or private arbitration company. For purposes of this clause, "communications" include, but are not limited to, standard educational materials about alternative dispute resolution or the provider organization.

(iii) Presentations made by the private arbitration company or the arbitrator at a program or seminar held open to the public.

(iv) Responding to inquiries regarding the arbitration provider's costs, rules, procedures, or standards. **Leg.H.** Added Stats 1994 ch

1202 §1 (SB 1638). Amended Stats 1997 ch 445 §2 (AB 1093); Stats 2001 ch 362 §5 (SB 475); Stats 2002 ch 1094 §2 (AB 2504); Stats 2024 ch 986 §4 (SB 940), effective January 1, 2025.

§1281.9. 2024 Deletes. [1] he or she has [2] is [3] has [4] any [5] any [6] any [7] his or her [8] (c) [9] For purposes of this section, [10] (d) [11] For purposes of this section, [12] (e) [13] For purposes of this section, any

§1281.91. Disqualification of arbitrator for disclosure failure; Petition to disqualify; Waiver of right to disqualify

(a) A proposed neutral arbitrator shall be disqualified if he or she fails to comply with Section 1281.9 and any party entitled to receive the disclosure serves a notice of disqualification within 15 calendar days after the proposed nominee or appointee fails to comply with Section 1281.9.

(b)(1) If the proposed neutral arbitrator complies with Section 1281.9, the proposed neutral arbitrator shall be disqualified on the basis of the disclosure statement after any party entitled to receive the disclosure serves a notice of disqualification within 15 calendar days after service of the disclosure statement.

(2) A party shall have the right to disqualify one court-appointed arbitrator without cause in any single arbitration, and may petition the court to disqualify a subsequent appointee only upon a showing of cause.

(c) The right of a party to disqualify a proposed neutral arbitrator pursuant to this section shall be waived if the party fails to serve the notice pursuant to the times set forth in this section, unless the proposed nominee or appointee makes a material omission or material misrepresentation in his or her disclosure. Except as provided in subdivision (d), in no event may a notice of disqualification be given after a hearing of any contested issue of fact relating to the merits of the claim or after any ruling by the arbitrator regarding any contested matter. Nothing in this subdivision shall limit the right of a party to vacate an award pursuant to Section 1286.2, or to disqualify an arbitrator pursuant to any other law or statute.

(d) If any ground specified in Section 170.1 exists, a neutral arbitrator shall disqualify himself or herself upon the demand of any party made before the conclusion of the arbitration proceeding. However, this subdivision does not apply to arbitration proceedings conducted under a collective bargaining agreement between employers and employees or their respective representatives. **Leg.H.** Added Stats 2001 ch 362 §6 (SB 475).

§1281.92. Prohibited activities by private arbitration company

(a) No private arbitration company may administer a consumer arbitration, or provide any other services related to a consumer arbitration, if the company has, or within the preceding year has had, a financial interest, as defined in Section 170.5, in any party or attorney for a party.

(b) No private arbitration company may administer a consumer arbitration, or provide any other services related to a consumer arbitration, if any party or attorney for a party has, or within the preceding year has had, any type of financial interest in the private arbitration company.

(c) This section shall operate only prospectively so as not to prohibit the administration of consumer arbitrations on the basis of financial interests held prior to January 1, 2003.

(d) This section applies to all consumer arbitration agreements subject to this article, and to all consumer arbitration proceedings conducted in California.

(e) This section shall become operative on January 1, 2003. **Leg.H.** Added Stats 2002 ch 952 §1 (AB 2574).

§1281.93. Restrictions on solicitation during consumer arbitration

(a) During the pendency of the consumer arbitration, a solicitation shall not be made of a party to the arbitration or of a lawyer for a party to the arbitration.

(b) For purposes of this section:

(1) "Lawyer for a party" has the same meaning as defined in Section 1281.9.

(2) "Solicitation" has the same meaning as defined in Section 1281.9. **Leg.H.** Added Stats 2024 ch 986 §5 (SB 940), effective January 1, 2025.

§1281.95. Disclosures by arbitrator in residential construction contract dispute

(a) In a binding arbitration of any claim for more than three thousand dollars ($3,000) pursuant to a contract for the construction or improvement of residential property consisting of one to four units, the arbitrator shall, within 10 days following his or her appointment, provide to each party a written declaration under penalty of perjury. This declaration shall disclose (1) whether the arbitrator or his or her employer or arbitration service had or has a personal or professional affiliation with either party, and (2) whether the arbitrator or his or her employer or arbitration service has been selected or designated as an arbitrator by either party in another transaction.

(b) If the arbitrator discloses an affiliation with either party, discloses that the arbitrator has been selected or designated as an arbitrator by either party in another arbitration, or fails to comply with this section, he or she may be disqualified from the arbitration by either party.

(c) A notice of disqualification shall be served within 15 days after the arbitrator makes the required disclosures or fails to comply. The right of a party to disqualify an arbitrator shall be waived if the party fails to serve the notice of disqualification pursuant to this subdivision unless the arbitration makes a material omission or material misrepresentation in his or her disclosure. Nothing in this section shall limit the right of a party to vacate an award pursuant to Section 1286.2, or to disqualify an arbitrator pursuant to any other law or statute. **Leg.H.** Added Stats 1994 ch 804 §1 (AB 3436). Amended Stats 2002 ch 1008 §5 (AB 3028).

§1281.96. Publication of consumer arbitration information by private arbitration company

(a) Except as provided in paragraph (2) of subdivision (c), a private arbitration company that administers or is otherwise involved in a consumer arbitration, shall collect, publish at least quarterly, and make available to the public on the internet website of the private arbitration company, if any, and on paper upon request, a single cumulative report that contains all of the following information regarding each consumer arbitration within the preceding five years:

(1) Whether arbitration was demanded pursuant to a pre-dispute arbitration clause and, if so, whether the pre-dispute arbitration clause designated the administering private arbitration company.

(2) The name of the nonconsumer party, if the nonconsumer party is a corporation or other business entity, and whether the nonconsumer party was the initiating party or the responding party, if known.

(3) The nature of the dispute involved as one of the following: goods; credit; other banking or finance; insurance; health care; construction; real estate; telecommunications, including software and Internet usage; debt collection; personal injury; employment; or other. If the dispute involved employment, the amount of the employee's annual wage divided into the following ranges: less than one hundred thousand dollars ($100,000), one hundred thousand dollars ($100,000) to two hundred fifty thousand dollars ($250,000), inclusive, and over two hundred fifty thousand dollars ($250,000). If the employee chooses not to provide wage information, it may be noted.

(4) Whether the consumer or nonconsumer party was the prevailing party. As used in this section, "prevailing party" includes the party with a net monetary recovery or an award of injunctive relief.

(5) The total number of occasions, if any, the nonconsumer party has previously been a party in an arbitration administered by the private arbitration company.

(6) The total number of occasions, if any, the nonconsumer party has previously been a party in a mediation administered by the private arbitration company.

(7) Whether the consumer party was represented by an attorney and, if so, the name of the attorney and the full name of the law firm that employs the attorney, if any.

(8) The date the private arbitration company received the demand for arbitration, the date the arbitrator was appointed, and the date of disposition by the arbitrator or private arbitration company.

(9) The type of disposition of the dispute, if known, identified as one of the following: withdrawal, abandonment, settlement, award after hearing, award without hearing, default, or dismissal without hearing. If a case was administered in a hearing, indicate whether the hearing was conducted in person, by telephone or video conference, or by documents only.

(10) The amount of the claim, whether equitable relief was requested or awarded, the amount of any monetary award, the amount of any attorney's fees awarded, and any other relief granted, if any.

(11) The name of the arbitrator, the arbitrator's total fee for the case, the percentage of the arbitrator's fee allocated to each party, whether a waiver of any fees was granted, and, if so, the amount of the waiver.

(12) Demographic data, reported in the aggregate, relative to ethnicity, race, disability, veteran status, gender, gender identity, and sexual orientation of all arbitrators as self-reported by the arbitrators. Demographic data disclosed or released pursuant to this paragraph shall also indicate the percentage of respondents who declined to respond.

(b) The information required by this section shall be made available in a format that allows the public to search and sort the information using readily available software, and shall be directly accessible from a conspicuously displayed link on the internet website of the private arbitration company with the identifying description: "consumer case information."

(c)(1) If the information required by subdivision (a) is provided by the private arbitration company in compliance with subdivision (b) and may be downloaded without a fee, the company may charge the actual cost of copying to any person who requests the information on paper. If the information required by subdivision (a) is not accessible by the internet in compliance with subdivision (b), the company shall provide that information without charge to any person who requests the information on paper.

(2) Notwithstanding paragraph (1), a private arbitration company that receives funding pursuant to Chapter 8 (commencing with Section 465) of Division 1 of the Business and Professions Code and that administers or conducts fewer than 50 consumer arbitrations per year may collect and publish the information required by subdivision (a) semiannually, provide the information only on paper, and charge the actual cost of copying.

(d) This section shall apply to any consumer arbitration commenced on or after January 1, 2003.

(e) A private arbitration company shall not have any liability for collecting, publishing, or distributing the information required by this section.

(f) It is the intent of the Legislature that private arbitration companies comply with all legal obligations of this section.

(g) The amendments to subdivision (a) made by the act adding this subdivision shall not apply to any consumer arbitration administered by a private arbitration company before January 1, 2015. **Leg.H.** Added Stats 2002 ch 1158 §1 (AB 2656). Amended Stats 2014 ch 870 §1 (AB 802), effective January 1, 2015; Stats 2019 ch 870 §3 (SB 707), effective January 1, 2020.

2019 Note: For legislative intent, see the 2019 Note following CCP §1280.

§1281.97. Employment or consumer arbitration; Drafting party pays fees; Drafting party breach

(a)(1) In an employment or consumer arbitration that requires, either expressly or through application of state or federal law or the rules of the arbitration provider, the drafting party to pay certain fees and costs before the arbitration can proceed, if the fees or costs to initiate an arbitration proceeding are not paid within 30 days after the due date the drafting party is in material breach of the arbitration agreement, is in default of the arbitration, and waives its right to compel arbitration under Section 1281.2.

(2) After an employee or consumer meets the filing requirements necessary to initiate an arbitration, the arbitration provider shall immediately provide an invoice for any fees and costs required before the arbitration can proceed to all of the parties to the arbitration. The invoice shall be provided in its entirety, shall state the full amount owed and the date that payment is due, and shall be sent to all parties by the same means on the same day. To avoid delay, absent an express provision in the arbitration agreement stating the number of days in which the parties to the arbitration must pay any required fees or costs, the arbitration provider shall issue all invoices to the parties as due upon receipt.

(b) If the drafting party materially breaches the arbitration agreement and is in default under subdivision (a), the employee or consumer may do either of the following:

(1) Withdraw the claim from arbitration and proceed in a court of appropriate jurisdiction.

(2) Compel arbitration in which the drafting party shall pay reasonable attorney's fees and costs related to the arbitration.

(c) If the employee or consumer withdraws the claim from arbitration and proceeds with an action in a court of appropriate jurisdiction under paragraph (1) of subdivision (b), the statute of limitations with regard to all claims brought or that relate back to any claim brought in arbitration shall be tolled as of the date of the first filing of a claim in a court, arbitration forum, or other dispute resolution forum.

(d) If the employee or consumer proceeds with an action in a court of appropriate jurisdiction, the court shall impose sanctions on the drafting party in accordance with Section 1281.99. **Leg.H.** Added Stats 2019 ch 870 §4 (SB 707), effective January 1, 2020. Amended Stats 2021 ch 222 §2 (SB 762), effective January 1, 2022.

2019 Note: For legislative intent, see the 2019 Note following CCP §1280.

§1281.98. Rights of employee or consumer when drafting party materially breaches arbitration agreement

(a)(1) In an employment or consumer arbitration that requires, either expressly or through application of state or federal law or the rules of the arbitration provider, that the drafting party pay certain fees and costs during the pendency of an arbitration proceeding, if the fees or costs required to continue the arbitration proceeding are not paid within 30 days after the due date, the drafting party is in material breach of the arbitration agreement, is in default of the arbitration, and waives its right to compel the employee or consumer to proceed with that arbitration as a result of the material breach.

(2) The arbitration provider shall provide an invoice for any fees and costs required for the arbitration proceeding to continue to all of the parties to the arbitration. The invoice shall be provided in its entirety, shall state the full amount owed and the date that payment is due, and shall be sent to all parties by the same means on the same day. To avoid delay, absent an express provision in the arbitration agreement stating the number of days in which the parties to the arbitration must pay any required fees or costs, the arbitration provider shall issue all invoices to the parties as due upon receipt. Any extension of time for the due date shall be agreed upon by all parties. Once the invoice has been paid, the arbitration provider shall provide to all parties a document that reflects the date on which the invoice was paid.

(b) If the drafting party materially breaches the arbitration agreement and is in default under subdivision (a), the employee or consumer may unilaterally elect to do any of the following:

(1) Withdraw the claim from arbitration and proceed in a court of appropriate jurisdiction. If the employee or consumer withdraws the claim from arbitration and proceeds with an action in a court of appropriate jurisdiction, the statute of limitations with regard to all claims brought or that relate back to any claim brought in arbitration shall be tolled as of the date of the first filing of a claim in any court, arbitration forum, or other dispute resolution forum.

(2) Continue the arbitration proceeding, if the arbitration provider agrees to continue administering the proceeding, notwithstanding the drafting party's failure to pay fees or costs. The neutral arbitrator or arbitration provider may institute a collection action at the conclusion of the arbitration proceeding against the drafting party that is in default of the arbitration for payment of all fees associated with the employment or consumer arbitration proceeding, including the cost of administering any proceedings after the default.

(3) Petition the court for an order compelling the drafting party to pay all arbitration fees that the drafting party is obligated to pay under the arbitration agreement or the rules of the arbitration provider.

(4) Pay the drafting party's fees and proceed with the arbitration proceeding. As part of the award, the employee or consumer shall recover all arbitration fees paid on behalf of the drafting party without regard to any findings on the merits in the underlying arbitration.

(c) If the employee or consumer withdraws the claim from arbitration and proceeds in a court of appropriate jurisdiction pursuant to paragraph (1) of subdivision (b), both of the following apply:

(1) The employee or consumer may bring a motion, or a separate action, to recover all attorney's fees and all costs associated with the abandoned arbitration proceeding. The recovery of arbitration fees, interest, and related attorney's fees shall be without regard to any findings on the merits in the underlying action or arbitration.

(2) The court shall impose sanctions on the drafting party in accordance with Section 1281.99.

(d) If the employee or consumer continues in arbitration pursuant to paragraphs (2) through (4) of subdivision (b), inclusive, the arbitrator shall impose appropriate sanctions on the drafting party, including monetary sanctions, issue sanctions, evidence sanctions, or terminating sanctions. **Leg.H.** Added Stats 2019 ch 870 §5 (SB 707), effective January

1, 2020. Amended Stats 2021 ch 222 §3 (SB 762), effective January 1, 2022; Stats 2023 ch 478 §17 (AB 1756), effective January 1, 2024.

2019 Note: For legislative intent, see the 2019 Note following CCP §1280.

§1281.99. Monetary sanctions against materially breaching party

(a) The court shall impose a monetary sanction against a drafting party that materially breaches an arbitration agreement pursuant to subdivision (a) of Section 1281.97 or subdivision (a) of Section 1281.98, by ordering the drafting party to pay the reasonable expenses, including attorney's fees and costs, incurred by the employee or consumer as a result of the material breach.

(b) In addition to the monetary sanction described in subdivision (a), the court may order any of the following sanctions against a drafting party that materially breaches an arbitration agreement pursuant to subdivision (a) of Section 1281.97 or subdivision (a) of Section 1281.98, unless the court finds that the one subject to the sanction acted with substantial justification or that other circumstances make the imposition of the sanction unjust.

(1) An evidence sanction by an order prohibiting the drafting party from conducting discovery in the civil action.

(2) A terminating sanction by one of the following orders:

(A) An order striking out the pleadings or parts of the pleadings of the drafting party.

(B) An order rendering a judgment by default against the drafting party.

(3) A contempt sanction by an order treating the drafting party as in contempt of court. **Leg.H.** Added Stats 2019 ch 870 §6 (SB 707), effective January 1, 2020.

2019 Note: For legislative intent, see the 2019 Note following CCP §1280.

CHAPTER 3
CONDUCT OF ARBITRATION PROCEEDINGS

Exercise of powers and duties of arbitrator(s). §1282.
Hearing proceedings, and incidental procedure. §1282.2.
Right to be represented by attorney at arbitration proceeding; Conditions for representation by out-of-state attorney. §1282.4.
Right to certified shorthand reporter. §1282.5.
Attendance of witnesses and production of evidence; Subpoenas. §1282.6.
Authority to administer oaths. §1282.8.
Depositions for use as evidence. §1283.
Depositions and discovery. §1283.05.
Witnesses' fees and mileage. §1283.2.
Requisites and sufficiency of award. §1283.4.
Service of award. §1283.6.
Time of making award. §1283.8.
Correction of award. §1284.
Payment of expenses and fees. §1284.2.
Fees and costs charged to consumer by private arbitration company. §1284.3.

§1282. Exercise of powers and duties of arbitrator(s)

Unless the arbitration agreement otherwise provides, or unless the parties to the arbitration otherwise provide by an agreement which is not contrary to the arbitration agreement as made or as modified by all of the parties thereto:

(a) The arbitration shall be by a single neutral arbitrator.

(b) If there is more than one arbitrator, the powers and duties of the arbitrators, other than the powers and duties of a neutral arbitrator, may be exercised by a majority of them if reasonable notice of all proceedings has been given to all arbitrators.

(c) If there is more than one neutral arbitrator:

(1) The powers and duties of a neutral arbitrator may be exercised by a majority of the neutral arbitrators.

(2) By unanimous agreement of the neutral arbitrators, the powers and duties may be delegated to one of their number but the power to make or correct the award may not be so delegated.

(d) If there is no neutral arbitrator, the powers and duties of a neutral arbitrator may be exercised by a majority of the arbitrators. **Leg.H.** Added Stats 1961 ch 461 §2. Amended Stats 1993 ch 768 §4 (SB 252); Stats 1997 ch 445 §3 (AB 1093).

Prior Law: Former CCP §1282, similar in part to present §§1281.2, 1292, was enacted 1872, amended Stats 1927 ch 225 §3, and repealed Stats 1961 ch 461 §1.

§1282.2. Hearing proceedings, and incidental procedure

Unless the arbitration agreement otherwise provides, or unless the parties to the arbitration otherwise provide by an agreement which is not contrary to the arbitration agreement as made or as modified by all the parties thereto:

(a)(1) The neutral arbitrator shall appoint a time and place for the hearing and cause notice thereof to be served personally or by registered or certified mail on the parties to the arbitration and on the other arbitrators not less than seven days before the hearing. Appearance at the hearing waives the right to notice.

(2) With the exception of matters arising out of collective-bargaining agreements, those described in Section 1283.05, actions involving personal injury or death, or as provided in the parties' agreement to arbitrate, in the event the aggregate amount in controversy exceeds fifty thousand dollars ($50,000) and the arbitrator is informed thereof by any party in writing by personal service, registered or certified mail, prior to designating a time and place of hearing pursuant to paragraph (1), the neutral arbitrator by the means prescribed in paragraph (1) shall appoint a time and place for hearing not less than 60 days before the hearing, and the following provisions shall apply:

(A) Either party shall within 15 days of receipt of the notice of hearing have the right to demand in writing, served personally or by registered or certified mail, that the other party provide a list of witnesses it intends to call designating which witnesses will be called as expert witnesses and a list of documents it intends to introduce at the hearing provided that the demanding party provides such lists at the time of its demand. A copy of such demand and the demanding party's lists shall be served on the arbitrator.

(B) Such lists shall be served personally or by registered or certified mail on the requesting party 15 days thereafter. Copies thereof shall be served on the arbitrator.

(C) Listed documents shall be made available for inspection and copying at reasonable times prior to the hearing.

(D) Time limits provided herein may be waived by mutual agreement of the parties if approved by the arbitrator.

(E) The failure to list a witness or a document shall not bar the testimony of an unlisted witness or the introduction of an undesignated document at the hearing, provided that good cause for omission from the requirements of subparagraph (A) is shown, as determined by the arbitrator.

(F) The authority of the arbitrator to administer and enforce this paragraph shall be as provided in subdivisions (b) to (e), inclusive, of Section 1283.05.

(b) The neutral arbitrator may adjourn the hearing from time to time as necessary. On request of a party to the arbitration for good cause, or upon his own determination, the neutral arbitrator may postpone the hearing to a time not later than the date fixed by the agreement for making the award, or to a later date if the parties to the arbitration consent thereto.

(c) The neutral arbitrator shall preside at the hearing, shall rule on the admission and exclusion of evidence and on questions of hearing procedure and shall exercise all powers relating to the conduct of the hearing.

(d) The parties to the arbitration are entitled to be heard, to present evidence and to cross-examine witnesses appearing at the hearing, but rules of evidence and rules of judicial procedure need not be observed. On request of any party to the arbitration, the testimony of witnesses shall be given under oath.

(e) If a court has ordered a person to arbitrate a controversy, the arbitrators may hear and determine the controversy upon the evidence produced notwithstanding the failure of a party ordered to arbitrate, who has been duly notified, to appear.

(f) If an arbitrator, who has been duly notified, for any reason fails to participate in the arbitration, the arbitration shall continue but only the remaining neutral arbitrator or neutral arbitrators may make the award.

(g) If a neutral arbitrator intends to base an award upon information not obtained at the hearing, he shall disclose the information to all parties to the arbitration and give the parties an opportunity to meet it. **Leg.H.** Added Stats 1961 ch 461 §2. Amended Stats 1979 ch 948 §2, effective September 22, 1979; Stats 1981 ch 714 §72.

§1282.4. Right to be represented by attorney at arbitration proceeding; Conditions for representation by out-of-state attorney

(a) A party to the arbitration has the right to be represented by an attorney at any proceeding or hearing in arbitration under this title. A waiver of this right may be revoked; but if a party revokes that waiver, the other party is entitled to a reasonable continuance for the purpose of procuring an attorney.

(b) Notwithstanding any other law, including Section 6125 of the Business and Professions Code, an attorney admitted to the bar of any other state may represent the parties in the course of, or in connection with, an arbitration proceeding in this state, provided that the attorney, if not admitted to the State Bar of California, satisfies all of the following:

(1) He or she timely serves the certificate described in subdivision (c).

(2) The attorney's appearance is approved in writing on that certificate by the arbitrator, the arbitrators, or the arbitral forum.

(3) The certificate bearing approval of the attorney's appearance is filed with the State Bar of California and served on the parties as described in this section.

(c) Within a reasonable period of time after the attorney described in subdivision (b) indicates an intention to appear in the arbitration, the attorney shall serve a certificate in a form prescribed by the State Bar of California on the arbitrator, arbitrators, or arbitral forum, the State Bar of California, and all other parties and counsel in the arbitration whose addresses are known to the attorney. The certificate shall state all of the following:

(1) The case name and number, and the name of the arbitrator, arbitrators, or arbitral forum assigned to the proceeding in which the attorney seeks to appear.

(2) The attorney's residence and office address.

(3) The courts before which the attorney has been admitted to practice and the dates of admission.

(4) That the attorney is currently a member in good standing of, and eligible to practice law before, the bar of those courts.

(5) That the attorney is not currently on suspension or disbarred from the practice of law before the bar of any court.

(6) That the attorney is not a resident of the State of California.

(7) That the attorney is not regularly employed in the State of California.

(8) That the attorney is not regularly engaged in substantial business, professional, or other activities in the State of California.

(9) That the attorney agrees to be subject to the jurisdiction of the courts of this state with respect to the law of this state governing the conduct of attorneys to the same extent as a member of the State Bar of California.

(10) The title of the court and the cause in which the attorney has filed an application to appear as counsel pro hac vice in this state or filed a certificate pursuant to this section in the preceding two years, the date of each application or certificate, and whether or not it was granted. If the attorney has made repeated appearances, the certificate shall reflect the special circumstances that warrant the approval of the attorney's appearance in the arbitration.

(11) The name, address, and telephone number of the active member of the State Bar of California who is the attorney of record.

(d) The arbitrator, arbitrators, or arbitral forum may approve the attorney's appearance if the attorney has complied with subdivision (c). Failure to timely file and serve the certificate described in subdivision (c) shall be grounds for disapproval of the appearance and disqualification from serving as an attorney in the arbitration in which the certificate was filed. In the absence of special circumstances, repeated appearances shall be grounds for disapproval of the appearance and disqualification from serving as an attorney in the arbitration in which the certificate was filed.

(e) Within a reasonable period of time after the arbitrator, arbitrators, or arbitral forum approves the certificate, the attorney shall file the certificate with the State Bar of California and serve the certificate as described in Section 1013a on all parties and counsel in the arbitration whose addresses are known to the attorney.

(f) An attorney who fails to file or serve the certificate required by this section or files or serves a certificate containing false information or who otherwise fails to comply with the standards of professional conduct required of members of the State Bar of California shall be subject to the disciplinary jurisdiction of the State Bar with respect to that certificate or any of his or her acts occurring in the course of the arbitration.

(g) Notwithstanding any other law, including Section 6125 of the Business and Professions Code, an attorney who is a member in good standing of the bar of any state may represent the parties in connection with rendering legal services in this state in the course of and in connection with an arbitration pending in another state.

(h) Notwithstanding any other law, including Section 6125 of the Business and Professions Code, any party to an arbitration arising under collective bargaining agreements in industries and provisions subject to either state or federal law may be represented in the course of, and in connection with, those proceedings by any person, regardless of whether that person is licensed to practice law in this state.

(i) Nothing in this section shall apply to Division 4 (commencing with Section 3200) of the Labor Code.

(j)(1) In enacting the amendments to this section made by Assembly Bill 2086 of the 1997–98 Regular Session, it is the intent of the Legislature to respond to the holding in Birbrower v. Superior Court (1998) 17 Cal.4th 119, to provide a procedure for nonresident attorneys who are not licensed in this state to appear in California arbitration proceedings.

(2) In enacting subdivision (h), it is the intent of the Legislature to make clear that any party to an arbitration arising under a collective bargaining agreement governed by the laws of this state may be represented in the course of and in connection with those proceedings by any person regardless of whether that person is licensed to practice law in this state.

(3) Except as otherwise specifically provided in this section, in enacting the amendments to this section made by Assembly Bill 2086 of the 1997–98 Regular Session, it is the Legislature's intent that nothing in this section is intended to expand or restrict the ability of a party prior to the decision in Birbrower to elect to be represented by any person in a nonjudicial arbitration proceeding, to the extent those rights or abilities existed prior to that decision. To the extent that Birbrower is interpreted to expand or restrict that right or ability pursuant to the laws of this state, it is hereby abrogated except as specifically provided in this section.

(4) In enacting subdivision (i), it is the intent of the Legislature to make clear that nothing in this section shall affect those provisions of law governing the right of injured workers to elect to be represented by any person, regardless of whether that person is licensed to practice law in this state, as set forth in Division 4 (commencing with Section 3200) of the Labor Code. **Leg.H.** Added Stats 1961 ch 461 §2. Amended Stats 1998 ch 915 §1 (AB 2086); Stats 2000 ch 1011 §2 (SB 2153); Stats 2005 ch 607 §1 (AB 415), effective October 6, 2005; Stats 2006 ch 357 §1 (AB 2482), effective January 1, 2007, repealed January 1, 2011; Stats 2010 ch 277 §1 (SB 877), effective January 1, 2011, repealed January 1, 2013; Stats 2012 ch 53 §§1, 2 (AB 1631), effective January 1, 2013; Stats 2013 ch 76 §24 (AB 383), effective January 1, 2014; Stats 2014 ch 71 §20 (SB 1304), effective January 1, 2015.

Former Sections: Former CCP §1282.4, similar to the present section, was added Stats 1998 ch 915 §2 (AB 2086) and repealed Stats 2012 ch 53 §2 (AB 1631).

Prior Law: There was another section of this number, similar to the present section, added Stats 1998 ch 915 §2 (AB 2086), amended Stats 2000 ch 1011 §3 (SB 2153), Stats 2005 ch 607 §2 (AB 415), effective October 6, 2005, Stats 2006 ch 357 §2 (AB 2482), effective January 1, 2007, operative January 1, 2011, Stats 2010 ch 277 §2 (SB 877), effective January 1, 2011, operative January 1, 2013, and repealed Stats 2012 ch 53 §2 (AB 1631), effective January 1, 2013.

§1282.5. Right to certified shorthand reporter

(a)(1) A party to an arbitration has the right to have a certified shorthand reporter transcribe any deposition, proceeding, or hearing. The transcript shall be the official record of the deposition, proceeding, or hearing.

(2) A party requesting a certified shorthand reporter shall make his or her request in or at either of the following:

(A) A demand for arbitration, or a response, answer, or counterclaim to a demand for arbitration.

(B) A pre-hearing scheduling conference at which a deposition, proceeding, or hearing is being calendared.

(b) If an arbitration agreement does not provide for a certified shorthand reporter, the party requesting the transcript shall incur the expense of the certified shorthand reporter. However, in a consumer arbitration, a certified shorthand reporter shall be provided upon request of an indigent consumer, as defined in Section 1284.3, at the expense of the nonconsumer party.

(c) If an arbitrator refuses to allow a party to have a certified shorthand reporter transcribe any deposition, proceeding, or hearing pursuant to this section, the party may petition the court for an order to compel the arbitrator to grant the party's request. The petition may include a request for an order to stay any deposition, proceeding, or hearing related to the arbitration pending the court's determination of the petition.

(d) This section does not add grounds for vacating an arbitration award pursuant to subdivision (a) of Section 1286.2 or for correcting an arbitration award pursuant to Section 1286.6. **Leg.H.** Added Stats 2016 ch 626 §1 (SB 1007), effective January 1, 2017.

§1282.6. Attendance of witnesses and production of evidence; Subpoenas

(a) A subpoena requiring the attendance of witnesses, and a subpoena duces tecum for the production of books, records, documents, and other evidence, at an arbitration proceeding or a deposition under Section 1283 [1] and 1283.05 for the purposes of discovery, shall be issued as provided in this section. In addition, the neutral arbitrator upon their own determination may issue subpoenas for the attendance of witnesses and subpoenas duces tecum for the production of books, records, documents, and other evidence.

(b) Subpoenas shall be issued, as of course, signed but otherwise in blank, to the party requesting them, by a neutral association, organization, governmental agency, or office if the arbitration agreement provides for administration of the arbitration proceedings by, or under the rules of, a neutral association, organization, governmental agency or office, or by the neutral arbitrator.

(c) The party serving the subpoena shall fill it in before service. Subpoenas shall be served and enforced in accordance with Chapter 2 (commencing with Section 1985) of Title 3 of Part 4 of this code. **Leg.H.** Added Stats 1961 ch 461 §2. Amended Stats 1982 ch 108 §1; Stats 2022 ch 420 §11 (AB 2960), effective January 1, 2023; Stats 2024 ch 986 §6 (SB 940), effective January 1, 2025.

§1282.6. 2024 Deletes. [1] , and if Section 1283.05 is applicable,

§1282.8. Authority to administer oaths

The neutral arbitrator may administer oaths. **Leg.H.** Added Stats 1961 ch 461 §2.

§1283. Depositions for use as evidence

On application of a party to the arbitration, the neutral arbitrator may order the deposition of a witness to be taken for use as evidence and not for discovery if the witness cannot be compelled to attend the hearing or if exceptional circumstances exist as to make it desirable, in the interest of justice and with due regard to the importance of presenting the testimony of witnesses orally at the hearing, to allow the deposition to be taken. The deposition shall be taken in the manner prescribed by law for the taking of depositions in civil actions. If the neutral arbitrator orders the taking of the deposition of a witness who resides outside the state, the party who applied for the taking of the deposition shall obtain a commission, letters rogatory, or a letter of request therefor from the superior court in accordance with Chapter 10 (commencing with Section 2026.010) of Title 4 of Part 4. **Leg.H.** Added Stats 1970 ch 1045 §1. Amended Stats 2005 ch 294 §4 (AB 333), effective January 1, 2006.

Prior Law: Former CCP §1283 was added by Stats 1970 ch 581 §2 and renumbered §1283.05 and amended by Stats 1970 ch 1045 §2.

Former CCP §1283, relating to depositions, was added by Stats 1961 ch 461 §2 and repealed by Stats 1970 ch 581 §1. Prior law former §1286, as amended by Stats 1927 ch 225 §7.

Original §1283, similar in part to present §§1281.6, 1282, was enacted 1872, amended by Code Amdts 1880 ch 82 §1, Stats 1927 ch 225 §4, and repealed by Stats 1961 ch 461 §1.

§1283.05. Depositions and discovery

[1] Depositions may be taken and discovery obtained in arbitration proceedings as follows:

(a) After the appointment of the arbitrator or arbitrators, the parties to the arbitration shall have the right to take depositions and to obtain discovery regarding the subject matter of the arbitration, and, to that end, to use and exercise all of the same rights, remedies, and procedures, and be subject to all of the same duties, liabilities, and obligations in the arbitration with respect to the subject matter thereof, as provided in Chapter 2 (commencing with Section 1985) of Title 3 of Part 4, and in Title 4 (commencing with Section 2016.010) of Part 4, as if the subject matter of the arbitration were pending before a superior court of this state in a civil action other than a limited civil case, subject to the limitations as to depositions set forth in subdivision (e) of this section.

(b) The arbitrator or arbitrators themselves shall have power, in addition to the power of determining the merits of the arbitration, to enforce the rights, remedies, procedures, duties, liabilities, and obligations of discovery by the imposition of the same terms, conditions, consequences, liabilities, sanctions, and penalties as can be or may be imposed in like circumstances in a civil action by a superior court of this state under the provisions of this code, except the power to order the arrest or imprisonment of a person.

(c) The arbitrator or arbitrators may consider, determine, and make such orders imposing such terms, conditions, consequences, liabilities, sanctions, and penalties, whenever necessary or appropriate at any time or stage in the course of the arbitration, and such orders shall be as conclusive, final, and enforceable as an arbitration award on the merits, if the making of any such order that is equivalent to an award or correction of an award is subject to the same conditions, if any, as are applicable to the making of an award or correction of an award.

(d) For the purpose of enforcing the duty to make discovery, to produce evidence or information, including books and records, and to produce persons to testify at a deposition or at a hearing, and to impose terms, conditions, consequences, liabilities, sanctions, and penalties upon a party for violation of any such duty, such party shall be deemed to include every affiliate of such party as defined in this section. For such purpose:

(1) The personnel of every such affiliate shall be deemed to be the officers, directors, managing agents, agents, and employees of such party to the same degree as each of them, respectively, bears such status to such affiliate; and

(2) The files, books, and records of every such affiliate shall be deemed to be in the possession and control of, and capable of production by, such party. As used in this section, "affiliate" of the party to the arbitration means and includes any party or person for whose immediate benefit the action or proceeding is prosecuted or defended, or an officer, director, superintendent, member, agent, employee, or managing agent of such party or person.

(e) Depositions for discovery shall not be taken unless leave to do so is first granted by the arbitrator or arbitrators. **Leg.H.** Added Stats 1970 ch 581 §2, as CCP §1283. Amended and Renumbered by Stats 1970 ch 1045 §2. Amended Stats 1976 ch 1185 §91.5; Stats 1998 ch 931 §123 (SB 2139), effective September 28, 1998; Stats 2004 ch 182 §16 (AB 3081), operative July 1, 2005; Stats 2024 ch 986 §7 (SB 940), effective January 1, 2025.

§1283.05. 2024 Deletes. [1] To the extent provided in Section 1283.1

§1283.1. Discovery provisions incorporated into arbitration agreement [Repealed]

Leg.H. Added Stats 1970 ch 581 §3. Amended Stats 1970 ch 1045 §3. Repealed Stats 2024 ch 986 §8 (SB 940), effective January 1, 2025.

§1283.2. Witnesses' fees and mileage

Except for the parties to the arbitration and their agents, officers and employees, all witnesses appearing pursuant to subpoena are entitled to receive fees and mileage in the same amount and under the same circumstances as prescribed by law for witnesses in civil actions in the superior court. The fee and mileage of a witness subpoenaed upon the application of a party to the arbitration shall be paid by such party. The fee and mileage of a witness subpoenaed solely upon the determination of the neutral arbitrator shall be paid in the manner provided for the payment of the neutral arbitrator's expenses. **Leg.H.** Added Stats 1961 ch 461 §2.

§1283.4. Requisites and sufficiency of award

The award shall be in writing and signed by the arbitrators concurring therein. It shall include a determination of all the questions submitted to the arbitrators the decision of which is necessary in order to determine the controversy. **Leg.H.** Added Stats 1961 ch 461 §2.

§1283.6. Service of award

The neutral arbitrator shall serve a signed copy of the award on each party to the arbitration personally or by registered or certified mail or as provided in the agreement. **Leg.H.** Added Stats 1961 ch 461 §2.

§1283.8. Time of making award

The award shall be made within the time fixed therefor by the agreement or, if not so fixed, within such time as the court orders on petition of a party to the arbitration. The parties to the arbitration may extend the time either before or after the expiration thereof. A party to the arbitration waives the objection that an award was not made within the time required unless he gives the arbitrators written notice of his objection prior to the service of a signed copy of the award on him. **Leg.H.** Added Stats 1961 ch 461 §2.

§1284. Correction of award

The arbitrators, upon written application of a party to the arbitration, may correct the award upon any of the grounds set forth in subdivisions (a) and (c) of Section 1286.6 not later than 30 days after service of a signed copy of the award on the applicant.

Application for such correction shall be made not later than 10 days after service of a signed copy of the award on the applicant. Upon or before making such application, the applicant shall deliver or mail a copy of the application to all of the other parties to the arbitration.

Any party to the arbitration may make written objection to such application. The objection shall be made not later than 10 days after the application is delivered or mailed to the objector. Upon or before making such objection, the objector shall deliver or mail a copy of the objection to the applicant and all the other parties to the arbitration.

The arbitrators shall either deny the application or correct the award. The denial of the application or the correction of the award shall be in writing and signed by the arbitrators concurring therein, and the neutral arbitrator shall serve a signed copy of such denial or correction on each party to the arbitration personally or by registered or certified mail or as provided in the agreement. If no denial of the application or correction of the award is served within the 30-day period provided in this section, the application for correction shall be deemed denied on the last day thereof. **Leg.H.** Added Stats 1961 ch 461 §2.

Prior Law: Former CCP §1284, similar in part to present §§1281.4, 1292.8, was enacted 1872, amended Stats 1927 ch 225 §5, and repealed Stats 1961 ch 461 §1.

§1284.2. Payment of expenses and fees

Unless the arbitration agreement otherwise provides or the parties to the arbitration otherwise agree, each party to the arbitration shall pay his pro rata share of the expenses and fees of the neutral arbitrator, together with other expenses of the arbitration incurred or approved by the neutral arbitrator, not including counsel fees or witness fees or other expenses incurred by a party for his own benefit. **Leg.H.** Added Stats 1961 ch 461 §2.

§1284.3. Fees and costs charged to consumer by private arbitration company

(a) No neutral arbitrator or private arbitration company shall administer a consumer arbitration under any agreement or rule requiring that a consumer who is a party to the arbitration pay the fees and costs incurred by an opposing party if the consumer does not prevail in the arbitration, including, but not limited to, the fees and costs of the arbitrator, provider organization, attorney, or witnesses.

(b)(1) All fees and costs charged to or assessed upon a consumer party by a private arbitration company in a consumer arbitration, exclusive of arbitrator fees, shall be waived for an indigent consumer. For the purposes of this section, "indigent consumer" means a person having a gross monthly income that is less than 300 percent of the federal poverty guidelines. Nothing in this section shall affect the ability of a private arbitration company to shift fees that would otherwise be charged or assessed upon a consumer party to a nonconsumer party.

(2) Prior to requesting or obtaining any fee, a private arbitration company shall provide written notice of the right to obtain a waiver of fees to a consumer or prospective consumer in a manner calculated to bring the matter to the attention of a reasonable consumer, including, but not limited to, prominently placing a notice in its first written communication to the consumer and in any invoice, bill, submission form, fee schedule, rules, or code of procedure.

(3) Any consumer requesting a waiver of fees or costs may establish his or her eligibility by making a declaration under oath on a form provided to the consumer by the private arbitration company for signature stating his or her monthly income and the number of persons living in his or her household. No private arbitration company may require a consumer to provide any further statement or evidence of indigence.

(4) Any information obtained by a private arbitration company about a consumer's identity, financial condition, income, wealth, or fee waiver request shall be kept confidential and may not be disclosed to any adverse party or any nonparty to the arbitration, except a private arbitration company may not keep confidential the number of waiver requests received or granted, or the total amount of fees waived.

(c) This section applies to all consumer arbitration agreements subject to this article, and to all consumer arbitration proceedings conducted in California. **Leg.H.** Added Stats 2002 ch 1101 §1 (AB 2915).

CHAPTER 4
ENFORCEMENT OF THE AWARD

Article 1. Confirmation, Correction or Vacation of the Award.
Article 2. Limitations of Time.

ARTICLE 1
Confirmation, Correction or Vacation of the Award

Petition for confirmation, correction or vacation of award. §1285.
Response to petition. §1285.2.
Petition's contents. §1285.4.
Response's contents. §1285.6.
Statement of grounds for relief. §1285.8.
Extent of relief. §1286.
Grounds to vacate award; Petition to vacate award. §1286.2.
Prerequisites to vacation of award. §1286.4.
Correction of award. §1286.6.
Prerequisites to correction of award. §1286.8.
Rehearing before arbitrators. §1287.
Dismissal of proceeding. §1287.2.
Entry, effect, and enforcement of judgment on confirmation. §1287.4.
Award as contract. §1287.6.

§1285. Petition for confirmation, correction or vacation of award

Any party to an arbitration in which an award has been made may petition the court to confirm, correct or vacate the award. The petition shall name as respondents all parties to the arbitration and may name as respondents any other persons bound by the arbitration award. **Leg.H.** Added Stats 1961 ch 461 §2.

Prior Law: Former CCP §1285, similar to present §1290.2, was enacted 1872, amended by Stats 1927 ch 225 §6, and repealed by Stats 1961 ch 461 §1.

§1285.2. Response to petition

A response to a petition under this chapter may request the court to dismiss the petition or to confirm, correct or vacate the award. **Leg.H.** Added Stats 1961 ch 461 §2.

§1285.4. Petition's contents

A petition under this chapter shall:

(a) Set forth the substance of or have attached a copy of the agreement to arbitrate unless the petitioner denies the existence of such an agreement.

(b) Set forth the names of the arbitrators.

(c) Set forth or have attached a copy of the award and the written opinion of the arbitrators, if any. **Leg.H.** Added Stats 1961 ch 461 §2.

§1285.6. Response's contents

Unless a copy thereof is set forth in or attached to the petition, a response to a petition under this chapter shall:

(a) Set forth the substance of or have attached a copy of the agreement to arbitrate unless the respondent denies the existence of such an agreement.

(b) Set forth the names of the arbitrators.

(c) Set forth or have attached a copy of the award and the written opinion of the arbitrators, if any. **Leg.H.** Added Stats 1961 ch 461 §2.

§1285.8. Statement of grounds for relief

A petition to correct or vacate an award, or a response requesting such relief, shall set forth the grounds on which the request for such relief is based. **Leg.H.** Added Stats 1961 ch 461 §2.

§1286. Extent of relief

If a petition or response under this chapter is duly served and filed, the court shall confirm the award as made, whether rendered in this state or another state, unless in accordance with this chapter it corrects the award and confirms it as corrected, vacates the award or dismisses the proceeding. **Leg.H.** Added Stats 1961 ch 461 §2. Amended Stats 1978 ch 260 §3.

Prior Law: Former CCP §1286, similar in part to present §§1281.2, 1282.2, 1282.6, 1282.8, 1283, 1283.2, 1283.4, 1283.8, 1284, 1284.2, was enacted 1872, amended by Stats 1927 ch 225 §7, and repealed by Stats 1961 ch 461 §1.

§1286.2. Grounds to vacate award; Petition to vacate award

(a) Subject to Section 1286.4, the court shall vacate the award if the court determines any of the following:

(1) The award was procured by corruption, fraud or other undue means.

(2) There was corruption in any of the arbitrators.

(3) The rights of the party were substantially prejudiced by misconduct of a neutral arbitrator.

(4) The arbitrators exceeded their powers and the award cannot be corrected without affecting the merits of the decision upon the controversy submitted.

(5) The rights of the party were substantially prejudiced by the refusal of the arbitrators to postpone the hearing upon sufficient cause being shown therefor or by the refusal of the arbitrators to hear evidence material to the controversy or by other conduct of the arbitrators contrary to the provisions of this title.

(6) An arbitrator making the award either: (A) failed to disclose within the time required for disclosure a ground for disqualification of which the arbitrator was then aware; or (B) was subject to disqualification upon grounds specified in Section 1281.91 but failed upon receipt of timely demand to disqualify himself or herself as required by that provision. However, this subdivision does not apply to arbitration proceedings conducted under a collective bargaining agreement between employers and employees or between their respective representatives.

(b) Petitions to vacate an arbitration award pursuant to Section 1285 are subject to the provisions of Section 128.7. **Leg.H.** Added Stats 1961 ch 461 §2. Amended Stats 1993 ch 768 §5 (SB 252); Stats 1997 ch 445 §4 (AB 1093); Stats 2001 ch 362 §7 (SB 475).

2001 Note: It is the intent of the Legislature that the grounds for vacatur added by subparagraph (A) paragraph (6) of subdivision (a) of Section 1286.2, is declarative of existing case law which provides that an arbitration award may be vacated when a neutral arbitrator fails to disclose a matter that might cause a reasonable person to question the ability of the arbitrator to conduct the arbitration proceeding impartially. Stats 2001 ch 362 §8.

§1286.4. Prerequisites to vacation of award

The court may not vacate an award unless:

(a) A petition or response requesting that the award be vacated has been duly served and filed; or

(b) A petition or response requesting that the award be corrected has been duly served and filed and:

(1) All petitioners and respondents are before the court; or

(2) All petitioners and respondents have been given reasonable notice that the court will be requested at the hearing to vacate the award or that the court on its own motion has determined to vacate the award and all petitioners and respondents have been given an opportunity to show why the award should not be vacated. **Leg.H.** Added Stats 1961 ch 461 §2.

§1286.6. Correction of award

Subject to Section 1286.8, the court, unless it vacates the award pursuant to Section 1286.2, shall correct the award and confirm it as corrected if the court determines that:

(a) There was an evident miscalculation of figures or an evident mistake in the description of any person, thing or property referred to in the award;

(b) The arbitrators exceeded their powers but the award may be corrected without affecting the merits of the decision upon the controversy submitted; or

(c) The award is imperfect in a matter of form, not affecting the merits of the controversy. **Leg.H.** Added Stats 1961 ch 461 §2.

§1286.8. Prerequisites to correction of award

The court may not correct an award unless:

(a) A petition or response requesting that the award be corrected has been duly served and filed; or

(b) A petition or response requesting that the award be vacated has been duly served and filed and;

(1) All petitioners and respondents are before the court; or

(2) All petitioners and respondents have been given reasonable notice that the court will be requested at the hearing to correct the award or that the court on its own motion has determined to correct the award and all petitioners and respondents have been given an opportunity to show why the award should not be corrected. **Leg.H.** Added Stats 1961 ch 461 §2.

§1287. Rehearing before arbitrators

If the award is vacated, the court may order a rehearing before new arbitrators. If the award is vacated on the grounds set forth in paragraph (4) or (5) of subdivision (a) of Section 1286.2, the court with the consent of the parties to the court proceeding may order a rehearing before the original arbitrators.

If the arbitration agreement requires that the award be made within a specified period of time, the rehearing may nevertheless be held and the award made within an equal period of time beginning with the date of the order for rehearing but only if the court determines that the purpose of the time limit agreed upon by the parties to the arbitration agreement will not be frustrated by the application of this provision. **Leg.H.** Added Stats 1961 ch 461 §2. Amended Stats 2012 ch 162 §15 (SB 1171), effective January 1, 2013.

Prior Law: Former CCP §1287, similar in part to present CCP §§1283.4, 1285, 1285.4, 1286, 1286.6, 1288, 1288.4, was enacted 1872, amended Stats 1927 ch 225 §8, and repealed Stats 1961 ch 461 §1.

§1287.2. Dismissal of proceeding

The court shall dismiss the proceeding under this chapter as to any person named as a respondent if the court determines that such person was not bound by the arbitration award and was not a party to the arbitration. **Leg.H.** Added Stats 1961 ch 461 §2.

§1287.4. Entry, effect, and enforcement of judgment on confirmation

If an award is confirmed, judgment shall be entered in conformity therewith. The judgment so entered has the same force and effect as, and is subject to all the provisions of law relating to, a judgment in a civil action of the same jurisdictional classification; and it may be enforced like any other judgment of the court in which it is entered, in an action of the same jurisdictional classification. **Leg.H.** Added Stats 1961 ch 461 §2. Amended Stats 1998 ch 931 §124 (SB 2139), effective September 28, 1998.

§1287.6. Award as contract

An award that has not been confirmed or vacated has the same force and effect as a contract in writing between the parties to the arbitration. **Leg.H.** Added Stats 1961 ch 461 §2.

ARTICLE 2
Limitations of Time

Service of petitions. §1288.
Service of response. §1288.2.
Service of petition after service of award. §1288.4.
Petition after application for arbitrators to correct award. §1288.6.
Dates for service of award after application for correction. §1288.8.

§1288. Service of petitions

A petition to confirm an award shall be served and filed not later than four years after the date of service of a signed copy of the award on the petitioner. A petition to vacate an award or to correct an award shall be served and filed not later than 100 days after the date of the service of a signed copy of the award on the petitioner. **Leg.H.** Added Stats 1961 ch 461 §2.

Prior Law: Former CCP §1288, similar in part to present §1286.2, was enacted 1872, amended by Stats 1927 ch 225 §9, and repealed by Stats 1961 ch 461 §1.

§1288.2. Service of response

A response requesting that an award be vacated or that an award be corrected shall be served and filed not later than 100 days after the date of service of a signed copy of the award upon:

(a) The respondent if he was a party to the arbitration; or

(b) The respondent's representative if the respondent was not a party to the arbitration. **Leg.H.** Added Stats 1961 ch 461 §2.

§1288.4. Service of petition after service of award

No petition may be served and filed under this chapter until at least 10 days after service of the signed copy of the award upon the petitioner. **Leg.H.** Added Stats 1961 ch 461 §2.

§1288.6. Petition after application for arbitrators to correct award

If an application is made to the arbitrators for correction of the award, a petition may not be served and filed under this chapter until the determination of that application. **Leg.H.** Added Stats 1961 ch 461 §2.

§1288.8. Dates for service of award after application for correction

If an application is made to the arbitrators for correction of the award, the date of the service of the award for the purposes of this article shall be deemed to be whichever of the following dates is the earlier:

(a) The date of service upon the petitioner of a signed copy of the correction of the award or of the denial of the application.

(b) The date that such application is deemed to be denied under Section 1284. **Leg.H.** Added Stats 1961 ch 461 §2.

§1289. [Section repealed 1961]

Leg.H. Enacted 1872, amended by Stats 1927 ch 225 §10, and repealed by Stats 1961 ch 461 §1. See CCP §1286.6.

CHAPTER 5
GENERAL PROVISIONS RELATING TO JUDICIAL PROCEEDINGS

Article 1. Petitions and Responses.
Article 2. Venue, Jurisdiction and Costs.
Article 3. Appeals.

ARTICLE 1
Petitions and Responses

Petition. §1290.
Summary hearing of petition; Notice of hearing. §1290.2.
Service of petition and notice. §1290.4.
Time for serving and filing response. §1290.6.
Service of response. §1290.8.
Statement of decision. §1291.
Priority of proceedings. §1291.2.

§1290. Petition

A proceeding under this title in the courts of this State is commenced by filing a petition. Any person named as a respondent in a petition may file a response thereto. The allegations of a petition are deemed to be admitted by a respondent duly served therewith unless a response is duly served and filed. The allegations of a response are deemed controverted or avoided. **Leg.H.** Added Stats 1961 ch 461 §2.

Prior Law: Former CCP §1290, relating to recovery after revocation of submission, was enacted 1872, amended by Stats 1927 ch 225 §11, and repealed by Stats 1961 ch 461 §1.

§1290.2. Summary hearing of petition; Notice of hearing

A petition under this title shall be heard in a summary way in the manner and upon the notice provided by law for the making and hearing of motions, except that not less than 10 days' notice of the date set for the hearing on the petition shall be given. **Leg.H.** Added Stats 1961 ch 461 §2.

§1290.4. Service of petition and notice

(a) A copy of the petition and a written notice of the time and place of the hearing thereof and any other papers upon which the petition is based shall be served in the manner provided in the arbitration agreement for the service of such petition and notice.

(b) If the arbitration agreement does not provide the manner in which such service shall be made and the person upon whom service is to be made has not previously appeared in the proceeding and has not previously been served in accordance with this subdivision:

(1) Service within this State shall be made in the manner provided by law for the service of summons in an action.

(2) Service outside this State shall be made by mailing the copy of the petition and notice and other papers by registered or certified mail. Personal service is the equivalent of such service by mail. Proof of service by mail shall be made by affidavit showing such mailing together with the return receipt of the United States Post Office bearing the signature of the person on whom service was made. Notwithstanding any other provision of this title, if service is made in the manner provided in this paragraph, the petition may not be heard until at least 30 days after the date of such service.

(c) If the arbitration agreement does not provide the manner in which such service shall be made and the person on whom service is to be made has previously appeared in the proceeding or has previously been served in accordance with subdivision (b) of this section, service shall be made in the manner provided in Chapter 5 (commencing with Section 1010) of Title 14 of Part 2 of this code. **Leg.H.** Added Stats 1961 ch 461 §2.

§1290.6. Time for serving and filing response

A response shall be served and filed within 10 days after service of the petition except that if the petition is served in the manner provided in paragraph (2) of subdivision (b) of Section 1290.4, the response shall be served and filed within 30 days after service of the petition. The time provided in this section for serving and filing a response may be extended by an agreement in writing between the parties to the court proceeding or, for good cause, by order of the court. **Leg.H.** Added Stats 1961 ch 461 §2.

§1290.8. Service of response

A response shall be served as provided in Chapter 5 (commencing with Section 1010) of Title 14 of Part 2 of this code. **Leg.H.** Added Stats 1961 ch 461 §2.

§1291. Statement of decision

A statement of decision shall be made by the court, if requested pursuant to Section 632, whenever an order or judgment, except a special order after final judgment, is made that is appealable under this title. **Leg.H.** Added Stats 1961 ch 461 §2. Amended Stats 1983 ch 302 §2.

Prior Law: Former CCP §1291, similar to present §§1285.4, 1286, 1287.4, was added Stats 1927 ch 225 §12 and repealed Stats 1961 ch 461 §1.

§1291.2. Priority of proceedings

In all proceedings brought under the provisions of this title, all courts wherein such proceedings are pending shall give such proceedings preference over all other civil actions or proceedings, except older matters of the same character and matters to which special precedence may be given by law, in the matter of setting the same for hearing and in hearing the same to the end that all such proceedings shall be quickly heard and determined. **Leg.H.** Added Stats 1961 ch 461 §2.

ARTICLE 2
Venue, Jurisdiction and Costs

Venue prior to commencement of arbitration. §1292.
Venue after commencement or completion of arbitration. §1292.2.
Venue where action or proceeding is pending. §1292.4.
Jurisdiction. §1292.6.
Motion for stay of action. §1292.8.
Agreement as consent to jurisdiction of courts. §1293.
Award of costs by court. §1293.2.

§1292. Venue prior to commencement of arbitration

Except as otherwise provided in this article, any petition made prior to the commencement of arbitration shall be filed in a court having jurisdiction in:

(a) The county where the agreement is to be performed or was made.

(b) If the agreement does not specify a county where the agreement is to be performed and the agreement was not made in any county in this state, the county where any party to the court proceeding resides or has a place of business.

(c) In any case not covered by subdivision (a) or (b) of this section, in any county in this state. **Leg.H.** Added Stats 1961 ch 461 §2. Amended Stats 1993 ch 1261 §2 (SB 401).

Prior Law: Former CCP §1292, similar to present §1287.4, was added by Stats 1927 ch 225 §13 and repealed by Stats 1961 ch 461 §1.

§1292.2. Venue after commencement or completion of arbitration

Except as otherwise provided in this article, any petition made after the commencement or completion of arbitration shall be filed in a court having jurisdiction in the county where the arbitration is being or has been held, or, if not held exclusively in any one county of this state, or if held outside of this state, then the petition shall be filed as provided in Section 1292. **Leg.H.** Added Stats 1961 ch 461 §2. Amended Stats 1978 ch 260 §4; Stats 1993 ch 1261 §3 (SB 401).

§1292.4. Venue where action or proceeding is pending

If a controversy referable to arbitration under an alleged agreement is involved in an action or proceeding pending in a superior court, a petition for an order to arbitrate shall be filed in such action or proceeding. **Leg.H.** Added Stats 1961 ch 461 §2.

§1292.6. Jurisdiction

After a petition has been filed under this title, the court in which such petition was filed retains jurisdiction to determine any subsequent petition involving the same agreement to arbitrate and the same controversy, and any such subsequent petition shall be filed in the same proceeding. **Leg.H.** Added Stats 1961 ch 461 §2.

§1292.8. Motion for stay of action

A motion for a stay of an action on the ground that an issue therein is subject to arbitration shall be made in the court where the action is pending. **Leg.H.** Added Stats 1961 ch 461 §2.

§1293. Agreement as consent to jurisdiction of courts

The making of an agreement in this State providing for arbitration to be had within this State shall be deemed a consent of the parties thereto to the jurisdiction of the courts of this State to enforce such agreement by the making of any orders provided for in this title and by entering of judgment on an award under the agreement. **Leg.H.** Added Stats 1961 ch 461 §2.

Prior Law: Former CCP §1293, similar in part to present §§1294, 1294.2, was added by Stats 1927 ch 225 §14 and repealed by Stats 1961 ch 461 §1.

§1293.2. Award of costs by court

The court shall award costs upon any judicial proceeding under this title as provided in Chapter 6 (commencing with Section 1021) of Title 14 of Part 2 of this code. **Leg.H.** Added Stats 1961 ch 461 §2.

ARTICLE 3
Appeals

Right to appeal. §1294.
Practice and procedure. §1294.2.
Expedited appeal process for claims under Elder and Dependent Adult Civil Protection Act; Adoption of rules of court. §1294.4.

§1294. Right to appeal

An aggrieved party may appeal from:

(a) An order dismissing or denying a petition to compel arbitration. Notwithstanding Section 916, the perfecting of such an appeal shall not automatically stay any proceedings in the trial court during the pendency of the appeal.

(b) An order dismissing a petition to confirm, correct or vacate an award.

(c) An order vacating an award unless a rehearing in arbitration is ordered.

(d) A judgment entered pursuant to this title.

(e) A special order after final judgment. **Leg.H.** Added Stats 1961 ch 461 §2. Amended Stats 2023 ch 710 §1 (SB 365), effective January 1, 2024.

Prior Law: Former CCP §1294 repealed 1931. See Probate Code.

§1294.2. Practice and procedure

The appeal shall be taken in the same manner as an appeal from an order or judgment in a civil action. Upon an appeal from any order or judgment under this title, the court may review the decision and any intermediate ruling, proceeding, order or decision which involves the merits or necessarily affects the order or judgment appealed from, or which substantially affects the rights of a party. The court may also on such appeal review any order on motion for a new trial. The respondent on the appeal, or party in whose favor the judgment or order was given may, without appealing from such judgment, request the court to and it may review any of the foregoing matters for the purpose of determining whether or not the appellant was prejudiced by the error or errors upon which he relies for reversal or modification of the judgment or order from which the appeal is taken. The provisions of this section do not authorize the court to review any decision or order from which an appeal might have been taken. **Leg.H.** Added Stats 1961 ch 461 §2.

§1294.4. Expedited appeal process for claims under Elder and Dependent Adult Civil Protection Act; Adoption of rules of court

(a) Except as provided in subdivision (b), in an appeal filed pursuant to subdivision (a) of Section 1294 involving a claim under the Elder and Dependent Adult Civil Protection Act (Chapter 11 (commencing with Section 15600) of Part 3 of Division 9 of the Welfare and Institutions Code) in which a party has been granted a preference pursuant to Section 36 of this code, the court of appeal shall issue its decision no later than 100 days after the notice of appeal is filed.

(b) The court of appeal may grant an extension of time in the appeal only if good cause is shown and the extension will promote the interests of justice.

(c) The Judicial Council shall, on or before July 1, 2017, adopt rules of court to do both of the following:

(1) Implement subdivisions (a) and (b).

(2) Establish a shortened notice of appeal period for the cases described in subdivision (a). **Leg.H.** Added Stats 2016 ch 628 §2 (SB 1065), effective January 1, 2017.

2016 Note: The Legislature finds and declares all of the following:

(a) Elders and dependent adults are vulnerable to abuse, neglect, or abandonment and this state has a responsibility to protect these persons.

(b) This state has enacted special protections for elderly persons, including the Elder and Dependent Adult Civil Protection Act (Chapter 11 (commencing with Section 15600) of Part 3 of Division 9 of the Welfare and Institutions Code).

(c) This state has also enacted Section 36 of the Code of Civil Procedure, under which a party to a civil action who is over 70 years of age may petition the court for a preference.

(d) The Legislature, therefore, consistent with the joint goals of the Elder and Dependent Adult Civil Protection Act and Section 36 of the Code of Civil Procedure, wishes to enact a limited expedited appeal process for a person filing a claim arising under the Elder and Dependent Adult Civil Protection Act who has received a court preference to expedite the claim. Stats 2016 ch 628 (SB 1065) §1.

TITLE 9.1
ARBITRATION OF MEDICAL MALPRACTICE

Contract provisions. §1295.

§1295. Contract provisions

(a) Any contract for medical services which contains a provision for arbitration of any dispute as to professional negligence of a health care provider shall have such provision as the first article of the contract and shall be expressed in the following language: "It is understood that any dispute as to medical malpractice, that is as to whether any medical services rendered under this contract were unnecessary or unauthorized or were improperly, negligently or incompetently rendered, will be determined by submission to arbitration as provided by California law, and not by a lawsuit or resort to court process except as California law provides for judicial review of arbitration proceedings. Both parties to this contract, by entering into it, are giving up their constitutional right to have any such dispute decided in a court of law before a jury, and instead are accepting the use of arbitration."

(b) Immediately before the signature line provided for the individual contracting for the medical services must appear the following in at least 10-point bold red type:

NOTICE: BY SIGNING THIS CONTRACT YOU ARE AGREEING TO
HAVE ANY ISSUE OF MEDICAL MALPRACTICE DECIDED BY NEUTRAL ARBITRATION AND YOU ARE GIVING UP YOUR RIGHT
TO A JURY OR COURT TRIAL. SEE ARTICLE 1 OF THIS CONTRACT.

(c) Once signed, such a contract governs all subsequent open-book account transactions for medical services for which the contract was signed until or unless rescinded by written notice within 30 days of signature. Written notice of such rescission may be given by a guardian or conservator of the patient if the patient is incapacitated or a minor.

(d) Where the contract is one for medical services to a minor, it shall not be subject to disaffirmance if signed by the minor's parent or legal guardian.

(e) Such a contract is not a contract of adhesion, nor unconscionable nor otherwise improper, where it complies with subdivisions (a), (b), and (c) of this section.

(f) Subdivisions (a), (b), and (c) shall not apply to any health care service plan contract offered by an organization registered pursuant to Article 2.5 (commencing with Section 12530) of Division 3 of Title 2 of the Government Code, or licensed pursuant to Chapter 2.2 (commencing with Section 1340) of Division 2 of the Health and Safety Code, which contains an arbitration agreement if the plan complies with paragraph (10) of subdivision (b) of Section 1363 of the Health and Safety Code, or otherwise has a procedure for notifying prospective subscribers of the fact that the plan has an arbitration provision, and the plan contracts conform to subdivision (h) of Section 1373 of the Health and Safety Code.

(g) For the purposes of this section:

(1) "Health care provider" means any person licensed or certified pursuant to Division 2 (commencing with Section 500) of the Business and Professions Code, or licensed pursuant to the Osteopathic Initiative Act, or the Chiropractic Initiative Act, or licensed pursuant to Chapter 2.5 (commencing with Section 1440) of Division 2 of the Health and Safety Code; and any clinic, health dispensary, or health facility, licensed pursuant to Division 2 (commencing with Section 1200) of the Health and Safety Code. "Health care provider" includes the legal representatives of a health care provider;

(2) "Professional negligence" means a negligent act or omission to act by a health care provider in the rendering of professional services, which act or omission is the proximate cause of a personal injury or wrongful death, provided that such services are within the scope of services for which the provider is licensed and which are not within any restriction imposed by the licensing agency or licensed hospital. **Leg.H.** Added Stats 1975 2nd Ex Sess ch 1 §26.6, effective December 12, 1975. Amended Stats 1975 2nd Ex Sess ch 2 §1.195, effective September 26, 1975, operative December 12, 1975, §1.196, effective September 26, 1975, operative July 1, 1976; Stats 1976 ch 1079 §5, ch 1185 §92 (ch 1185 prevails); Stats 2023 ch 42 §1 (AB 118), effective July 10, 2023.

Prior Law: Former CCP §1295 repealed 1931. See Probate Code.

TITLE 9.2
PUBLIC CONSTRUCTION CONTRACT ARBITRATION

Arbitration of public construction contracts. §1296.

§1296. Arbitration of public construction contracts

The parties to a construction contract with a public agency may expressly agree in writing that in any arbitration to resolve a dispute relating to the contract, the arbitrator's award shall be supported by law and substantial evidence. If the agreement so provides, a court shall, subject to Section 1286.4, vacate the award if after review of the award it determines either that the award is not supported by substantial evidence or that it is based on an error of law. **Leg.H.** Added Stats 1979 ch 46 §2, effective May 2, 1979.

TITLE 9.3
ARBITRATION AND CONCILIATION OF INTERNATIONAL COMMERCIAL DISPUTES

Chapter 1. Application and Interpretation.
Chapter 2. Arbitration Agreements and Judicial Measures in Aid of Arbitration.
Chapter 3. Composition of Arbitral Tribunals.
Chapter 4. Jurisdiction of Arbitral Tribunals.
Chapter 5. Manner and Conduct of Arbitration.
Chapter 6. Making of Arbitral Award and Termination of Proceedings.
Chapter 7. Conciliation.

CHAPTER 1
APPLICATION AND INTERPRETATION

Article 1. Scope of Application.
Article 2. Interpretation.
Article 3. Receipt of Written Communications.
Article 4. Waiver of Right to Object.
Article 5. Extent of Judicial Intervention.
Article 6. Functions.

ARTICLE 1
Scope of Application

Application of title. §1297.11.
Place of arbitration or conciliation. §1297.12.
International agreements. §1297.13.
Place of business. §1297.14.
Consideration of states of United States as one state. §1297.15.
Commercial agreements. §1297.16.
Effect on other provisions. §1297.17.

§1297.11. Application of title

This title applies to international commercial arbitration and conciliation, subject to any agreement which is in force between the United States and any other state or states. **Leg.H.** Added Stats 1988 ch 23 §1, effective March 7, 1988.

§1297.12. Place of arbitration or conciliation

This title, except Article 2 (commencing with Section 1297.81) of Chapter 2 and Article 3 (commencing with [1] **Section 1297.90**) of Chapter 2, applies only if the place of arbitration or conciliation is in the State of California. **Leg.H.** Added Stats 1988 ch 23 §1, effective March 7, 1988. Amended Stats 2024 ch 90 §1 (AB 1903), effective January 1, 2025.

§1297.12. 2024 Deletes. [1] Section 1297.91

§1297.13. International agreements

An arbitration or conciliation agreement is international if any of the following applies:

(a) The parties to an arbitration or conciliation agreement have, at the time of the conclusion of that agreement, their places of business in different states.

(b) One of the following places is situated outside the state in which the parties have their places of business:

(i) The place of arbitration or conciliation if determined in, or pursuant to, the arbitration or conciliation agreement.

(ii) Any place where a substantial part of the obligations of the commercial relationship is to be performed.

(iii) The place with which the subject matter of the dispute is most closely connected.

(c) The parties have expressly agreed that the subject matter of the arbitration or conciliation agreement relates to commercial interests in more than one state.

(d) The subject matter of the arbitration or conciliation agreement is otherwise related to commercial interests in more than one state. **Leg.H.** Added Stats 1988 ch 23 §1, effective March 7, 1988.

§1297.14. Place of business

For the purposes of Section 1297.13, if a party has more than one place of business, the place of business is that which has the closest relationship to the arbitration agreement, and if a party does not have a place of business, reference is to be made to his habitual residence. **Leg.H.** Added Stats 1988 ch 23 §1, effective March 7, 1988.

§1297.15. Consideration of states of United States as one state

For the purposes of Section 1297.13, the states of the United States, including the District of Columbia, shall be considered one state. **Leg.H.** Added Stats 1988 ch 23 §1, effective March 7, 1988.

§1297.16. Commercial agreements

An arbitration or conciliation agreement is commercial if it arises out of a relationship of a commercial nature including, but not limited to, any of the following:

(a) A transaction for the supply or exchange of goods or services.
(b) A distribution agreement.
(c) A commercial representation or agency.
(d) An exploitation agreement or concession.
(e) A joint venture or other, related form of industrial or business cooperation.
(f) The carriage of goods or passengers by air, sea, rail, or road.
(g) Construction.
(h) Insurance.
(i) Licensing.
(j) Factoring.
(k) Leasing.
(*l*) Consulting.
(m) Engineering.
(n) Financing.
(o) Banking.
(p) The transfer of data or technology.
(q) Intellectual or industrial property, including trademarks, patents, copyrights and software programs.
(r) Professional services. **Leg.H.** Added Stats 1988 ch 23 §1, effective March 7, 1988.

§1297.17. Effect on other provisions

This title shall not affect any other law in force in California by virtue of which certain disputes may not be submitted to arbitration or may be submitted to arbitration only in accordance with provisions other than those of this title. Notwithstanding the foregoing, this title supersedes Sections 1280 to 1284.2, inclusive, with respect to international commercial arbitration and conciliation. **Leg.H.** Added Stats 1988 ch 23 §1, effective March 7, 1988.

ARTICLE 2
Interpretation

Application of title. § 1297.20.
Definitions. §1297.21.
Parties' freedom to authorize third party to make determination. §1297.22.
Agreement as including rules referred to in agreement. §1297.23.
Reference to claim as applying to counterclaim and to defense as applying to defense to counterclaim. §1297.24.

§ 1297.20. Application of title

(a) In the application of this title, regard is to be had to its international origin and to the need to promote uniformity in its application and the observance of good faith.

(b) Questions concerning matters governed by this title that are not expressly settled in it are to be settled in conformity with the general principles embodied in this title. **Leg.H.** Added Stats 2024 ch 90 §2 (AB 1903), effective January 1, 2025.

§1297.21. Definitions

For the purposes of this title:

(a) "Arbitral award" means any decision of the arbitral tribunal on the substance of the dispute submitted to it and includes an interim, interlocutory, or partial arbitral award.

(b) "Arbitral tribunal" means a sole arbitrator or a panel of arbitrators.

(c) "Arbitration" means any arbitration whether or not administered by a permanent arbitral institution.

(d) "Conciliation" means any conciliation whether or not administered by a permanent conciliation institution.

(e) "Chief Justice" means the Chief Justice of California or his or her designee.
(f) "Court" means a body or an organ of the judicial system of a state.
(g) "Party" means a party to an arbitration or conciliation agreement.
(h) "Superior court" means the superior court in the county in this state selected pursuant to Section 1297.61.
(i) "Supreme Court" means the Supreme Court of California. **Leg.H.** Added Stats 1988 ch 23 §1, effective March 7, 1988.

§1297.22. Parties' freedom to authorize third party to make determination

Where a provision of this title, except Article 1 (commencing with Section 1297.281) of Chapter 6, leaves the parties free to determine a certain issue, such freedom includes the right of the parties to authorize a third party, including an institution, to make that determination. **Leg.H.** Added Stats 1988 ch 23 §1, effective March 7, 1988.

§1297.23. Agreement as including rules referred to in agreement

Where a provision of this title refers to the fact that the parties have agreed or that they may agree, or in any other way refers to an agreement of the parties, such agreement shall be deemed to include any arbitration or conciliation rules referred to in that agreement. **Leg.H.** Added Stats 1988 ch 23 §1, effective March 7, 1988.

§1297.24. Reference to claim as applying to counterclaim and to defense as applying to defense to counterclaim

Where this title, other than Article 8 (commencing with Section 1297.251) of Chapter 5, Article 5 (commencing with Section 1297.321) of Chapter 6, or subdivision (a) of Section 1297.322, refers to a claim, it also applies to a counterclaim, and where it refers to a defense, it also applies to a defense to that counterclaim. **Leg.H.** Added Stats 1988 ch 23 §1, effective March 7, 1988.

ARTICLE 3
Receipt of Written Communications

Receipt on delivery. §1297.31.
Receipt by registered mail. §1297.32.
Written communications in respect of court proceedings. §1297.33.

§1297.31. Receipt on delivery

Unless otherwise agreed by the parties, any written communication is deemed to have been received if it is delivered to the addressee personally or if it is delivered at his place of business, habitual residence, or mailing address, and the communication is deemed to have been received on the day it is so delivered. **Leg.H.** Added Stats 1988 ch 23 §1, effective March 7, 1988.

§1297.32. Receipt by registered mail

If none of the places referred to in Section 1297.31 can be found after making a reasonable inquiry, a written communication is deemed to have been received if it is sent to the addressee's last known place of business, habitual residence, or mailing address by registered mail or by any other means which provides a record of the attempt to deliver it. **Leg.H.** Added Stats 1988 ch 23 §1, effective March 7, 1988.

§1297.33. Written communications in respect of court proceedings

This article does not apply to written communications in respect of court proceedings. **Leg.H.** Added Stats 1988 ch 23 §1, effective March 7, 1988.

ARTICLE 4
Waiver of Right to Object

Failure to object. §1297.41.
"Any provision of this title". §1297.42.

§1297.41. Failure to object

A party who knows that any provision of this title, or any requirement under the arbitration agreement, has not been complied with and yet proceeds with the arbitration without stating his or her objection to noncompliance without undue delay or, if a time limit is provided for stating that objection, within that period of time, shall be deemed to have waived his right to object. **Leg.H.** Added Stats 1988 ch 23 §1, effective March 7, 1988.

§1297.42. "Any provision of this title"

For purposes of Section 1297.41, "any provision of this title" means any provision of this title in respect of which the parties may otherwise agree. **Leg.H.** Added Stats 1988 ch 23 §1, effective March 7, 1988.

ARTICLE 5
Extent of Judicial Intervention

Permissible intervention. §1297.51.

§1297.51. Permissible intervention

In matters governed by this title, no court shall intervene except where so provided in this title, or applicable federal law. **Leg.H.** Added Stats 1988 ch 23 §1, effective March 7, 1988.

ARTICLE 6
Functions

Performance by superior court. §1297.61.

§1297.61. Performance by superior court

The functions referred to in Sections 1297.114, 1297.115, 1297.116, 1297.134, 1297.135, 1297.136, 1297.165, 1297.166, and 1297.167 shall be performed by the superior court of the county in which the place of arbitration is located. The functions referred to in Section 1297.81 shall be performed by the superior court selected pursuant to Article 2 (commencing with Section 1292) of Chapter 5 of Title 9. **Leg.H.** Added Stats 1988 ch 23 §1, effective March 7, 1988.

CHAPTER 2
ARBITRATION AGREEMENTS AND JUDICIAL MEASURES IN AID OF ARBITRATION

Article 1. Definition and Form of Arbitration Agreements.
Article 2. Stay of Proceedings.

ARTICLE 1
Definition and Form of Arbitration Agreements

"Arbitration agreement". §1297.71.
Writing; Reference to document containing arbitration clause. §1297.72.
Writing. § 1297.73.

§1297.71. "Arbitration agreement"

An "arbitration agreement" is an agreement by the parties to submit to arbitration all or certain disputes which have arisen or which may arise between them in respect of a defined legal relationship, whether contractual or not. An arbitration agreement may be in the form of an arbitration clause in a contract or in the form of a separate agreement. **Leg.H.** Added Stats 1988 ch 23 §1, effective March 7, 1988.

§1297.72. Writing; Reference to document containing arbitration clause

An arbitration agreement shall be in writing. [1] **Leg.H.** Added Stats 1988 ch 23 §1, effective March 7, 1988. Amended Stats 2024 ch 90 §3 (AB 1903), effective January 1, 2025.

§1297.72. 2024 Deletes. [1] An agreement is in writing if it is contained in a document signed by the parties or in an exchange of letters, telex, telegrams, or other means of telecommunication which provide a record of this agreement, or in an exchange of statements of claim and defense in which the existence of an agreement is alleged by one party and not denied by another. The reference in a contract to a document containing an arbitration clause constitutes an arbitration agreement provided that the contract is in writing and the reference is such as to make that clause part of the contract.

§ 1297.73. Writing

(a) An arbitration agreement is in writing if its content is recorded in any form, including, but not limited to, in a document signed by the parties or in an exchange of letters, telex, telegrams, electronic mail, or other means of telecommunication accessible for subsequent reference that provides a record of the agreement.

(b) The requirement that an arbitration agreement be in writing is met by an electronic communication if the information contained therein is accessible so as to be usable for subsequent reference.

(1) "Electronic communication" means any communication that the parties make by means of data messages.

(2) "Data message" means information generated, sent, received, or stored by electronic, magnetic, optical, or similar means, including, but not limited to, electronic data interchange (EDI), electronic mail, telegram, telex, or telecopy.

(c) An arbitration agreement is in writing if it is contained in an exchange of statements of claim and defense in which the existence of an agreement is alleged by one party and not denied by the other.

(d) The reference in a contract to any document containing an arbitration clause constitutes an arbitration agreement in writing, provided that the reference is such as to make that clause part of the contract. **Leg.H.** Added Stats 2024 ch 90 §4 (AB 1903), effective January 1, 2025.

ARTICLE 2
Stay of Proceedings

Application for stay order and order to compel arbitration. §1297.81.
Granting of timely request. §1297.82.

§1297.81. Application for stay order and order to compel arbitration

When a party to an international commercial arbitration agreement as defined in this title commences judicial proceedings seeking relief with respect to a matter covered by the agreement to arbitrate, any other party to the agreement may apply to the superior court for an order to stay the proceedings and to compel arbitration. **Leg.H.** Added Stats 1988 ch 23 §1, effective March 7, 1988.

§1297.82. Granting of timely request

A timely request for a stay of judicial proceedings made under Section 1297.81 shall be granted. **Leg.H.** Added Stats 1988 ch 23 §1, effective March 7, 1988.

CHAPTER 3
COMPOSITION OF ARBITRAL TRIBUNALS

Article 1. Number of Arbitrators.
Article 2. Appointment of Arbitrators.
Article 3. Grounds for Challenge.
Article 4. Challenge Procedure.
Article 5. Failure or Impossibility to Act.
Article 6. Termination of Mandate and Substitution of Arbitrators.

ARTICLE 1
Number of Arbitrators

Agreement of parties; number otherwise. §1297.101.

§1297.101. Agreement of parties; number otherwise

The parties may agree on the number of arbitrators. Otherwise, there shall be one arbitrator. **Leg.H.** Added Stats 1988 ch 23 §1, effective March 7, 1988.

ARTICLE 2
Appointment of Arbitrators

Nationality of arbitrator. §1297.111.
Agreement on appointment procedure. §1297.112.
Procedure failing agreement by parties. §1297.113.
Appointment by superior court. §1297.114.
Appointment of sole arbitrator by superior court. §1297.115.
Necessary measures by superior court on request of party. §1297.116.
Finality of superior court decision. §1297.117.
Superior court's considerations in appointing arbitrator. §1297.118.
Immunity of arbitrator. §1297.119.

§1297.111. Nationality of arbitrator

A person of any nationality may be an arbitrator. **Leg.H.** Added Stats 1988 ch 23 §1, effective March 7, 1988.

§1297.112. Agreement on appointment procedure

Subject to Sections 1297.115 and 1297.116, the parties may agree on a procedure for appointing the arbitral tribunal. **Leg.H.** Added Stats 1988 ch 23 §1, effective March 7, 1988.

§1297.113. Procedure failing agreement by parties

Failing such agreement referred to in Section 1297.112, in an arbitration with three arbitrators and two parties, each party shall appoint one arbitrator, and the two appointed arbitrators shall appoint the third arbitrator. **Leg.H.** Added Stats 1988 ch 23 §1, effective March 7, 1988.

§1297.114. Appointment by superior court

If the appointment procedure in Section 1297.113 applies and either a party fails to appoint an arbitrator within 30 days after receipt of a request to do so from the other party, or the two appointed arbitrators fail to agree on the third arbitrator within 30 days after their appointment, the appointment shall be made, upon request of a party, by the superior court. **Leg.H.** Added Stats 1988 ch 23 §1, effective March 7, 1988.

§1297.115. Appointment of sole arbitrator by superior court

Failing any agreement referred to in Section 1297.112, in an arbitration with a sole arbitrator, if the parties fail to agree on the arbitrator, the appointment shall be made, upon request of a party, by the superior court. **Leg.H.** Added Stats 1988 ch 23 §1, effective March 7, 1988.

§1297.116. Necessary measures by superior court on request of party

The superior court, upon the request of a party, may take the necessary measures, unless the agreement on the appointment procedure provides other means for securing the appointment, where, under an appointment procedure agreed upon by the parties, any of the following occurs:

(a) A party fails to act as required under that procedure.

(b) The parties, or two appointed arbitrators, fail to reach an agreement expected of them under that procedure.

(c) A third party, including an institution, fails to perform any function entrusted to it under that procedure. **Leg.H.** Added Stats 1988 ch 23 §1, effective March 7, 1988.

§1297.117. Finality of superior court decision

A decision on a matter entrusted to the superior court pursuant to Sections 1297.114, 127.115, and 1297.116 is final and is not subject to appeal. **Leg.H.** Added Stats 1988 ch 23 §1, effective March 7, 1988.

1988 Note: It appears that the Legislature inadvertently referred to Section 127.115; this reference should be to Section 1297.115.

§1297.118. Superior court's considerations in appointing arbitrator

The superior court, in appointing an arbitrator, shall have due regard to all of the following:

(a) Any qualifications required of the arbitrator by the agreement of the parties.

(b) Other considerations as are likely to secure the appointment of an independent and impartial arbitrator.

(c) In the case of a sole or third arbitrator, the advisability of appointing an arbitrator of a nationality other than those of the parties. **Leg.H.** Added Stats 1988 ch 23 §1, effective March 7, 1988.

§1297.119. Immunity of arbitrator

An arbitrator has the immunity of a judicial officer from civil liability when acting in the capacity of arbitrator under any statute or contract.

The immunity afforded by this section shall supplement, and not supplant, any otherwise applicable common law or statutory immunity. **Leg.H.** Added Stats 1994 ch 228 §1 (SB 1660).

ARTICLE 3
Grounds for Challenge

Disclosures by those under consideration for appointment or designation. §1297.121.
Mandatory nature of disclosures; Waiver. §1297.122.
Continuing obligation of disclosure by arbitrator. §1297.123.
Grounds for challenge. §1297.124.
Challenge by party appointing or participating in appointment. §1297.125.

§1297.121. Disclosures by those under consideration for appointment or designation

Except as otherwise provided in this title, all persons whose names have been submitted for consideration for appointment or designation as arbitrators or conciliators, or who have been appointed or designated as such, shall, within 15 days, make a disclosure to the parties of any information which might cause their impartiality to be questioned including, but not limited to, any of the following instances:

(a) The person has a personal bias or prejudice concerning a party, or personal knowledge of disputed evidentiary facts concerning the proceeding.

(b) The person served as a lawyer in the matter in controversy, or the person is or has been associated with another who has participated in the matter during such association, or he or she has been a material witness concerning it.

(c) The person served as an arbitrator or conciliator in another proceeding involving one or more of the parties to the proceeding.

(d) The person, individually or a fiduciary, or such person's spouse or minor child residing in such person's household, has a financial interest in the subject matter in controversy or in a party to the proceeding, or any other interest that could be substantially affected by the outcome of the proceeding.

(e) The person, his or her spouse, or a person within the third degree of relationship to either of them, or the spouse of such a person meets any of the following conditions:

(i) The person is or has been a party to the proceeding, or an officer, director, or trustee of a party.

(ii) The person is acting or has acted as a lawyer in the proceeding.

(iii) The person is known to have an interest that could be substantially affected by the outcome of the proceeding.

(iv) The person is likely to be a material witness in the proceeding.

(f) The person has a close personal or professional relationship with a person who meets any of the following conditions:

(i) The person is or has been a party to the proceeding, or an officer, director, or trustee of a party.

(ii) The person is acting or has acted as a lawyer or representative in the proceeding.

(iii) The person is or expects to be nominated as an arbitrator or conciliator in the proceedings.

(iv) The person is known to have an interest that could be substantially affected by the outcome of the proceeding.

(v) The person is likely to be a material witness in the proceeding. **Leg.H.** Added Stats 1988 ch 23 §1, effective March 7, 1988.

§1297.122. Mandatory nature of disclosures; Waiver

The obligation to disclose information set forth in Section 1297.121 is mandatory and cannot be waived as to the parties with respect to persons serving either as the sole arbitrator or sole conciliator or as the chief or prevailing arbitrator or conciliator. The parties may otherwise agree to waive such disclosure. **Leg.H.** Added Stats 1988 ch 23 §1, effective March 7, 1988.

§1297.123. Continuing obligation of disclosure by arbitrator

From the time of appointment and throughout the arbitral proceedings, an arbitrator, shall, without delay, disclose to the parties any circumstances referred to in Section 1297.121 which were not previously disclosed. **Leg.H.** Added Stats 1988 ch 23 §1, effective March 7, 1988.

§1297.124. Grounds for challenge

Unless otherwise agreed by the parties or the rules governing the arbitration, an arbitrator may be challenged only if circumstances exist that give rise to justifiable doubts as to his or her independence or impartiality, or as to his or her possession of the qualifications upon which the parties have agreed. **Leg.H.** Added Stats 1988 ch 23 §1, effective March 7, 1988.

§1297.125. Challenge by party appointing or participating in appointment

A party may challenge an arbitrator appointed by it, or in whose appointment it has participated, only for reasons of which it becomes aware after the appointment has been made. **Leg.H.** Added Stats 1988 ch 23 §1, effective March 7, 1988.

ARTICLE 4
Challenge Procedure

Agreement by parties; finality of decision. §1297.131.
Written statement of reasons. §1297.132.
Decision by arbitral tribunal. §1297.133.
Judicial review of unsuccessful challenge. §1297.134.
Finality of superior court decision. §1297.135.
Continuation of arbitral proceedings pending judicial review of challenge. §1297.136.

§1297.131. Agreement by parties; finality of decision

The parties may agree on a procedure for challenging an arbitrator and the decision reached pursuant to that procedure shall be final. **Leg.H.** Added Stats 1988 ch 23 §1, effective March 7, 1988.

§1297.132. Written statement of reasons

Failing any agreement referred to in Section 1297.131, a party which intends to challenge an arbitrator shall, within 15 days after becoming aware of the constitution of the arbitral tribunal or after becoming aware of any circumstances referred to in Sections 1297.124 and 1297.125, whichever shall be later, send a written statement of the reasons for the challenge to the arbitral tribunal. **Leg.H.** Added Stats 1988 ch 23 §1, effective March 7, 1988.

§1297.133. Decision by arbitral tribunal

Unless the arbitrator challenged under Section 1297.132 withdraws from his or her office or the other party agrees to the challenge, the arbitral tribunal shall decide on the challenge. **Leg.H.** Added Stats 1988 ch 23 §1, effective March 7, 1988.

§1297.134. Judicial review of unsuccessful challenge

If a challenge following the procedure under Section 1297.133 is not successful, the challenging party may request the superior court, within 30 days after having received notice of the decision rejecting the challenge, to decide on the challenge. If a challenge is based upon the grounds set forth in Section 1297.121, and the superior court determines that the facts support a finding that such ground or grounds fairly exist, then the challenge should be sustained. **Leg.H.** Added Stats 1988 ch 23 §1, effective March 7, 1988.

§1297.135. Finality of superior court decision

The decision of the superior court under Section 1297.134 is final and is not subject to appeal. **Leg.H.** Added Stats 1988 ch 23 §1, effective March 7, 1988.

§1297.136. Continuation of arbitral proceedings pending judicial review of challenge

While a request under Section 1297.134 is pending, the arbitral tribunal, including the challenged arbitrator, may continue with the arbitral proceedings and make an arbitral award. **Leg.H.** Added Stats 1988 ch 23 §1, effective March 7, 1988.

ARTICLE 5
Failure or Impossibility to Act

Termination of arbitrator's mandate. §1297.141.
Request by party for superior court decision on termination of mandate. §1297.142.
Finality of superior court decision. §1297.143.
Withdrawal or agreement of party to termination as not implying acceptance of validity of any ground. §1297.144.

§1297.141. Termination of arbitrator's mandate

The mandate of an arbitrator terminates if he becomes de jure or de facto unable to perform his or her functions or for other reasons fails to act without undue delay, and he withdraws from his or her office or the parties agree to the termination of his or her mandate. **Leg.H.** Added Stats 1988 ch 23 §1, effective March 7, 1988.

§1297.142. Request by party for superior court decision on termination of mandate

If a controversy remains concerning any of the grounds referred to in Section 1297.141, a party may request the superior court to decide on the termination of the mandate. **Leg.H.** Added Stats 1988 ch 23 §1, effective March 7, 1988.

§1297.143. Finality of superior court decision

A decision of the superior court under Section 1297.142 is not subject to appeal. **Leg.H.** Added Stats 1988 ch 23 §1, effective March 7, 1988.

§1297.144. Withdrawal or agreement of party to termination as not implying acceptance of validity of any ground

If, under this section or Section 1297.132, an arbitrator withdraws from office or a party agrees to the termination of the mandate of an arbitrator, this does not imply acceptance of the validity of any ground referred to in Section 1297.132. **Leg.H.** Added Stats 1988 ch 23 §1, effective March 7, 1988.

ARTICLE 6
Termination of Mandate and Substitution of Arbitrators

Termination of mandate on withdrawal or agreement of parties. §1297.151.
Appointment of substitute arbitrator. §1297.152.
Repetition of hearings. §1297.153.
Validity of orders or rulings made prior to replacement of arbitrator. §1297.154.

§1297.151. Termination of mandate on withdrawal or agreement of parties

In addition to the circumstances referred to under Article 4 (commencing with Section 1297.131) and Article 5 (commencing with Section 1297.141) of this chapter, the mandate of an arbitrator terminates upon his or her withdrawal from office for any reason, or by or pursuant to

§1297.152. Appointment of substitute arbitrator

agreement of the parties. **Leg.H.** Added Stats 1988 ch 23 §1, effective March 7, 1988.

§1297.152. Appointment of substitute arbitrator

Where the mandate of an arbitrator terminates, a substitute arbitrator shall be appointed according to the rules that were applicable to the appointment of the arbitrator being replaced. **Leg.H.** Added Stats 1988 ch 23 §1, effective March 7, 1988.

§1297.153. Repetition of hearings

Unless otherwise agreed by the parties:

(a) Where the sole or presiding arbitrator is replaced, any hearings previously held shall be repeated.

(b) Where an arbitrator other than the sole or presiding arbitrator is replaced, any hearings previously held may be repeated at the discretion of the arbitral tribunal. **Leg.H.** Added Stats 1988 ch 23 §1, effective March 7, 1988.

§1297.154. Validity of orders or rulings made prior to replacement of arbitrator

Unless otherwise agreed by the parties, an order or ruling of the arbitral tribunal made prior to the replacement of an arbitrator under this section is not invalid because there has been a change in the composition of the tribunal. **Leg.H.** Added Stats 1988 ch 23 §1, effective March 7, 1988.

CHAPTER 4
JURISDICTION OF ARBITRAL TRIBUNALS

Article 1. Competence of an Arbitral Tribunal to Rule on its Jurisdiction.
Article 2. Interim Measures Ordered by Arbitral Tribunals.

ARTICLE 1
Competence of an Arbitral Tribunal to Rule on its Jurisdiction

Ruling by arbitral tribunal on own jurisdiction; Validity of arbitration clause. §1297.161.
Raising plea of lack of jurisdiction. §1297.162.
Plea that tribunal exceeding scope of authority. §1297.163.
Admission of later plea. §1297.164.
Ruling on plea as preliminary question or in award on merits. §1297.165.
Judicial review; Waiver of objection. §1297.166.
Continuation of arbitral proceedings pending judicial review. §1297.167.

§1297.161. Ruling by arbitral tribunal on own jurisdiction; Validity of arbitration clause

The arbitral tribunal may rule on its own jurisdiction, including ruling on any objections with respect to the existence or validity of the arbitration agreement, and for that purpose, an arbitration clause which forms part of a contract shall be treated as an agreement independent of the other terms of the contract, and a decision by the arbitral tribunal that the contract is null and void shall not entail ipso jure the invalidity of the arbitration clause. **Leg.H.** Added Stats 1988 ch 23 §1, effective March 7, 1988.

§1297.162. Raising plea of lack of jurisdiction

A plea that the arbitral tribunal does not have jurisdiction shall be raised not later than the submission of the statement of defense. However, a party is not precluded from raising such a plea by the fact that he or she has appointed, or participated in the appointment of, an arbitrator. **Leg.H.** Added Stats 1988 ch 23 §1, effective March 7, 1988.

§1297.163. Plea that tribunal exceeding scope of authority

A plea that the arbitral tribunal is exceeding the scope of its authority shall be raised as soon as the matter alleged to be beyond the scope of its authority is raised during the arbitral proceedings. **Leg.H.** Added Stats 1988 ch 23 §1, effective March 7, 1988.

§1297.164. Admission of later plea

The arbitral tribunal may, in either of the cases referred to in Sections 1297.162 and 1297.163, admit a later plea if it considers the delay justified. **Leg.H.** Added Stats 1988 ch 23 §1, effective March 7, 1988.

§1297.165. Ruling on plea as preliminary question or in award on merits

The arbitral tribunal may rule on a plea referred to in Sections 1297.162 and 1297.163 either as a preliminary question or in an award on the merits. **Leg.H.** Added Stats 1988 ch 23 §1, effective March 7, 1988.

§1297.166. Judicial review; Waiver of objection

If the arbitral tribunal rules as a preliminary question that it has jurisdiction, any party shall request the superior court, within 30 days after having received notice of that ruling, to decide the matter or shall be deemed to have waived objection to such finding. **Leg.H.** Added Stats 1988 ch 23 §1, effective March 7, 1988.

§1297.167. Continuation of arbitral proceedings pending judicial review

While a request under Section 1297.166 is pending, the arbitral tribunal may continue with the arbitral proceedings and make an arbitral award. **Leg.H.** Added Stats 1988 ch 23 §1, effective March 7, 1988.

ARTICLE 2
Interim Measures Ordered by Arbitral Tribunals

Order for interim measure of protection. §1297.171.
Security. §1297.172.
Application for preliminary order. §1297.173.
Preliminary order procedure. §1297.174.
Modification, suspension, or termination. §1297.175.
Security in connection with interim measure or preliminary order. §1297.176.
Disclosure of material change in circumstances. §1297.177.
Liability. §1297.178.
Recognition of interim measure. §1297.179.
Refusal of recognition or enforcement. §1297.180.

§1297.171. Order for interim measure of protection

(a) Unless otherwise agreed by the parties, the arbitral tribunal may, at the request of a party, [1] **grant interim measures of protection**.

(b) **An interim measure of protection, or interim measure, is any temporary measure, whether in the form of an award or in another form, by which, at any time prior to the issuance of the award by which the dispute is finally decided, the arbitral tribunal orders a party to do any of the following:**

(1) Maintain or restore the status quo pending determination of the dispute.

(2) Take action that would prevent, or refrain from taking action that is likely to cause, current or imminent harm or prejudice to the arbitral process itself.

(3) Provide a means of preserving assets out of which a subsequent award may be satisfied.

(4) Preserve evidence that may be relevant and material to the resolution of the dispute. **Leg.H.** Added Stats 1988 ch 23 §1, effective March 7, 1988. Amended Stats 2024 ch 90 §9 (AB 1903), effective January 1, 2025.

§1297.171. 2024 Deletes. [1] order a party to take any interim measure of protection as the arbitral tribunal may consider necessary in respect of the subject matter of the dispute

§1297.172. Security

(a) The [1] **party requesting an interim measure under paragraph (1), (2), or (3) of subdivision (b) of Section 1297.171 shall satisfy the arbitral tribunal that both of the following conditions are met:**

(1) Harm not adequately reparable by an award of damages is likely to result if the measure is not ordered, and such harm substantially outweighs the harm that is likely to result to the party against whom the measure is directed if the measure is granted.

(2) There is a reasonable possibility that the requesting party will succeed on the merits of the claim. The determination of this possibility shall not affect the discretion of the arbitral tribunal in making any subsequent determination.

(b) With regard to a request for an interim measure under paragraph (4) of subdivision (b) of Section 1297.171, the requirements in paragraphs (1) and (2) of subdivision (a) shall apply only to the extent the arbitral tribunal considers appropriate. **Leg.H.** Added Stats 1988 ch 23 §1, effective March 7, 1988. Amended Stats 2024 ch 90 §10 (AB 1903), effective January 1, 2025.

§1297.172. 2024 Deletes. [1] arbitral tribunal may require a party to provide appropriate security in connection with a measure ordered under Section 1297.171

§1297.173. Application for preliminary order

(a) Unless otherwise agreed by the parties, a party may, without notice to any other party, make a request for an interim measure together with an application for a preliminary order directing a party not to frustrate the purpose of the interim measure requested.

(b) The arbitral tribunal may grant a preliminary order provided that it considers that prior disclosure of the request for the interim measure to the party against whom it is directed risks frustrating the purpose of the measure.

(c) The conditions defined under Section 1297.172 apply to any preliminary order, provided that the harm to be assessed under paragraph (1) of subdivision (a) of Section 1297.172 is the harm likely to result from the order being granted or not. **Leg.H.** Added Stats 2024 ch 90 §11 (AB 1903), effective January 1, 2025.

§1297.174. Preliminary order procedure

(a) Immediately after the arbitral tribunal has made a determination with respect to an application for a preliminary order, the arbitral tribunal shall give notice to all parties of the request for the interim measure, the application for the preliminary order, the preliminary order, if any, and all other communications, including the content of any oral communication, between any party and the arbitral tribunal in relation thereto.

(b) At the same time, the arbitral tribunal shall give an opportunity to any party against whom a preliminary order is directed to present its case at the earliest practicable time.

(c) The arbitral tribunal shall decide promptly on any objection to the preliminary order.

(d) A preliminary order shall expire after twenty days from the date on which it was issued by the arbitral tribunal. However, the arbitral tribunal may issue an interim measure adopting or modifying the preliminary order, after the party against whom the preliminary order is directed has been given notice and an opportunity to present its case.

(e) A preliminary order shall be binding on the parties, but shall not be subject to enforcement by a court. Such a preliminary order does not constitute an award. **Leg.H.** Added Stats 2024 ch 90 §12 (AB 1903), effective January 1, 2025.

§1297.175. Modification, suspension, or termination

The arbitral tribunal may modify, suspend, or terminate an interim measure or a preliminary order it has granted upon application of any party, or in exceptional circumstances and upon prior notice to the parties, on the arbitral tribunal's own initiative. **Leg.H.** Added Stats 2024 ch 90 §13 (AB 1903), effective January 1, 2025.

§1297.176. Security in connection with interim measure or preliminary order

(a) The arbitral tribunal may require the party requesting an interim measure to provide appropriate security in connection with the measure.

(b) The arbitral tribunal shall require the party applying for a preliminary order to provide security in connection with the order unless the arbitral tribunal considers it inappropriate or unnecessary to do so. **Leg.H.** Added Stats 2024 ch 90 §14 (AB 1903), effective January 1, 2025.

§1297.177. Disclosure of material change in circumstances

(a) The arbitral tribunal may require any party to promptly disclose any material change in the circumstances on the basis of which the measure was requested or granted.

(b) The party applying for a preliminary order shall disclose to the arbitral tribunal all circumstances that are likely to be relevant to the arbitral tribunal's determination whether to grant or maintain the order, and such obligation shall continue until the party against whom the order has been requested has had an opportunity to present its case. Thereafter, subdivision (a) shall apply. **Leg.H.** Added Stats 2024 ch 90 §15 (AB 1903), effective January 1, 2025.

§1297.178. Liability

The party requesting an interim measure or applying for a preliminary order shall be liable for any costs and damages caused by the measure or the order to any party if the arbitral tribunal later determines that, in the circumstances, the measure or order should not have been granted. The arbitral tribunal may award such costs and damages at any point during the proceedings. **Leg.H.** Added Stats 2024 ch 90 §16 (AB 1903), effective January 1, 2025.

§1297.179. Recognition of interim measure

(a) An interim measure issued by an arbitral tribunal shall be recognized as final and binding, and, unless otherwise provided by the arbitral tribunal, may be enforced upon application to the superior court subject to the provisions of Section 1297.180. Nothing herein is intended to preclude enforcement of the interim measure in any other competent court.

(b) The party who is seeking or has obtained recognition or enforcement of an interim measure shall promptly inform the court of any termination, suspension, or modification of that interim measure.

(c) The superior court where recognition or enforcement is sought may, if the court considers it proper, order the requesting party to provide appropriate security if the arbitral tribunal has not already made a determination with respect to security or where such a decision is necessary to protect the rights of third parties. **Leg.H.** Added Stats 2024 ch 90 §17 (AB 1903), effective January 1, 2025.

§1297.180. Refusal of recognition or enforcement

(a) Recognition or enforcement of an interim measure may be refused only:

(1) At the request of the party against whom it is invoked if the court is satisfied that any of the following conditions are met:

(A) A party to the arbitration agreement was under some incapacity, or the said agreement is not valid under the law to which the parties have subjected it, or failing any indication thereon, under the law of the jurisdiction where the interim measure was made.

(B) The party against whom the interim measure is invoked was not given proper notice of the appointment of an arbitrator or of the arbitral proceedings or was otherwise unable to present its case.

(C) The interim measure deals with a dispute not contemplated by or not falling within the terms of the submission to arbitration, or it contains decisions on matters beyond the scope of the submission to arbitration, provided that, if the decisions on matters submitted to arbitration can be separated from those not so submitted, that part of the interim measure which contains decisions on matters submitted to arbitration may be recognized and enforced.

(D) The composition of the arbitral tribunal or the arbitral procedure was not in accordance with the agreement of the parties, or, failing such agreement, was not in accordance with the law of the jurisdiction where the arbitration took place.

(E) The arbitral tribunal's decision with respect to the provision of security in connection with the interim measure issued by the arbitral tribunal has not been complied with.

(F) The court otherwise determines that the arbitral tribunal did not have jurisdiction pursuant to Section 1297.95.

(G) The interim measure has been terminated or suspended by the arbitral tribunal, or, where so empowered, by the court of the jurisdiction in which the arbitration took place or under the law of which that interim measure was granted.

(2) If the court finds that any of the following conditions are met:

(A) The interim measure is incompatible with the powers conferred upon the court, unless the court decides to reformulate the interim measure to the extent necessary to adapt the interim measure to its own powers and procedures for the purposes of enforcing that interim measure and without modifying its substance.

(B) The subject matter of the dispute is not capable of settlement by arbitration under the law of the United States.

(C) The recognition or enforcement of the interim measure would be contrary to the public policy of the United States.

(b) Any determination made by the court on any ground in subdivision (a) shall be effective only for the purposes of the application to recognize and enforce the interim measure. The court in which recognition or enforcement is sought shall not, in making that determination, undertake a review of the substance of the interim measure. **Leg.H.** Added Stats 2024 ch 90 §18 (AB 1903), effective January 1, 2025.

CHAPTER 5
MANNER AND CONDUCT OF ARBITRATION

Article 1. Equal Treatment of Parties.
Article 1.5. Representation by Foreign and Out-of-State Attorneys.
Article 2. Determination of Rules of Procedure.
Article 3. Place of Arbitration.
Article 4. Commencement of Arbitral Proceedings.
Article 5. Language.
Article 6. Statements of Claim and Defense.
Article 7. Hearings and Written Proceedings.
Article 8. Default of a Party.
Article 9. Expert Appointed by Arbitral Tribunal.
Article 10. Court Assistance in Taking Evidence and Consolidating Arbitrations.

ARTICLE 1
Equal Treatment of Parties

Equality; Opportunity to present case. §1297.181.

§1297.181. Equality; Opportunity to present case

The parties shall be treated with equality and each party shall be given a full opportunity to present his or her case. **Leg.H.** Added Stats 1988 ch 23 §1, effective March 7, 1988.

ARTICLE 1.5
Representation by Foreign and Out-of-State Attorneys

"Qualified attorney". §1297.185.
Legal services permitted. §1297.186.
Court appearances. §1297.187.
Court jurisdiction and disciplinary authority; Complaints and disciplinary violations; Annual report. §1297.188.
Rules implementing article. §1297.189.

§1297.185. "Qualified attorney"

For purposes of this article, a "qualified attorney" means an individual who is not admitted to practice law in this state but is all of the following:

(a) Admitted to practice law in a state or territory of the United States or the District of Columbia or a member of a recognized legal profession in a foreign jurisdiction, the members of which are admitted or otherwise authorized to practice as attorneys or counselors at law or the equivalent.

(b) Subject to effective regulation and discipline by a duly constituted professional body or public authority of that jurisdiction.

(c) In good standing in every jurisdiction in which he or she is admitted or otherwise authorized to practice. **Leg.H.** Added Stats 2018 ch 134 §1 (SB 766), effective January 1, 2019.

§1297.186. Legal services permitted

(a) Notwithstanding any other law, including Section 6125 of the Business and Professions Code, a qualified attorney may provide legal services in an international commercial arbitration or related conciliation, mediation, or alternative dispute resolution proceeding, if any of the following conditions is satisfied:

(1) The services are undertaken in association with an attorney who is admitted to practice in this state and who actively participates in the matter.

(2) The services arise out of or are reasonably related to the attorney's practice in a jurisdiction in which the attorney is admitted to practice.

(3) The services are performed for a client who resides in or has an office in the jurisdiction in which the attorney is admitted or otherwise authorized to practice.

(4) The services arise out of or are reasonably related to a matter that has a substantial connection to a jurisdiction in which the attorney is admitted or otherwise authorized to practice.

(5) The services arise out of a dispute governed primarily by international law or the law of a foreign or out-of-state jurisdiction.

(b) This section does not apply to a dispute or controversy concerning any of the following:

(1) An individual's acquisition or lease of goods or services primarily for personal, family, or household use.

(2) An individual's coverage under a health insurance plan or an interaction between an individual and a healthcare provider.

(3) An application for employment in California.

(4) The terms and conditions of, or right to, employment in California, unless the dispute or controversy primarily concerns intellectual property rights, including those involving trademarks, patents, copyright, and software programs.

(c) This section does not affect the right of an attorney admitted to practice law in this state to provide legal services in an international commercial arbitration or related conciliation, mediation, or alternative dispute resolution proceeding, or the right of representation established in Section 1297.351. **Leg.H.** Added Stats 2018 ch 134 §1 (SB 766), effective January 1, 2019.

§1297.187. Court appearances

A qualified attorney rendering legal services pursuant to this article shall not appear in a court of this state unless he or she has applied for and received permission to appear as counsel pro hac vice pursuant to the California Rules of Court, as applicable. **Leg.H.** Added Stats 2018 ch 134 §1 (SB 766), effective January 1, 2019.

§1297.188. Court jurisdiction and disciplinary authority; Complaints and disciplinary violations; Annual report

(a) A qualified attorney rendering legal services pursuant to this article is subject to the jurisdiction of the courts and disciplinary authority of this state with respect to the California Rules of Professional Conduct and the laws governing the conduct of attorneys to the same extent as a member of the State Bar of California.

(b) The State Bar of California may report complaints and evidence of disciplinary violations against an attorney practicing pursuant to this article to the appropriate disciplinary authority of any jurisdiction in which the attorney is admitted or otherwise authorized to practice law. This section does not limit or affect the authority of the State Bar to report information about an attorney to authorities in any jurisdiction in which the attorney is admitted or otherwise authorized to practice law.

(c) On or before May 1 of each year, the State Bar shall submit a report to the Supreme Court that specifies the number and nature of any complaints that it has received during the prior calendar year against attorneys who provide legal services pursuant to this article and any actions it has taken in response to those complaints. **Leg.H.** Added Stats 2018 ch 134 §1 (SB 766), effective January 1, 2019.

§1297.189. Rules implementing article

The Supreme Court may issue rules implementing this article. **Leg.H.** Added Stats 2018 ch 134 §1 (SB 766), effective January 1, 2019.

ARTICLE 2
Determination of Rules of Procedure

Agreement of parties. §1297.191.
Conduct by tribunal failing agreement by parties. §1297.192.
Evidence. §1297.193.

§1297.191. Agreement of parties

Subject to this title, the parties may agree on the procedure to be followed by the arbitral tribunal in conducting the proceedings. **Leg.H.** Added Stats 1988 ch 23 §1, effective March 7, 1988.

§1297.192. Conduct by tribunal failing agreement by parties

Failing any agreement referred to in Section 1297.191, the arbitral tribunal may, subject to this title, conduct the arbitration in the manner it considers appropriate. **Leg.H.** Added Stats 1988 ch 23 §1, effective March 7, 1988.

§1297.193. Evidence

The power of the arbitral tribunal under Section 1297.192 includes the power to determine the admissibility, relevance, materiality, and weight of any evidence. **Leg.H.** Added Stats 1988 ch 23 §1, effective March 7, 1988.

ARTICLE 3
Place of Arbitration

Agreement of parties. §1297.201.
Determination by tribunal failing agreement of parties. §1297.202.
Meeting of tribunal at appropriate place notwithstanding agreement of parties. §1297.203.

§1297.201. Agreement of parties

The parties may agree on the place of arbitration. **Leg.H.** Added Stats 1988 ch 23 §1, effective March 7, 1988.

§1297.202. Determination by tribunal failing agreement of parties

Failing any agreement referred to in Section 1297.201, the place of arbitration shall be determined by the arbitral tribunal having regard to the circumstances of the case, including the convenience of the parties. **Leg.H.** Added Stats 1988 ch 23 §1, effective March 7, 1988.

§1297.203. Meeting of tribunal at appropriate place notwithstanding agreement of parties

Notwithstanding Section 1297.201, the arbitral tribunal may, unless otherwise agreed by the parties, meet at any place it considers appropriate for consultation among its members, for hearing witnesses, experts, or the parties, or for inspection of documents, goods, or other property. **Leg.H.** Added Stats 1988 ch 23 §1, effective March 7, 1988.

ARTICLE 4
Commencement of Arbitral Proceedings

Date. §1297.211.

§1297.211. Date

Unless otherwise agreed by the parties, the arbitral proceedings in respect of a particular dispute commence on the date on which a request for that dispute to be referred to arbitration is received by the respondent. **Leg.H.** Added Stats 1988 ch 23 §1, effective March 7, 1988.

ARTICLE 5
Language

Agreement of parties. §1297.221.
Determination by tribunal failing agreement of parties. §1297.222.
Application of agreement or determination. §1297.223.
Order for translation to accompany documentary evidence. §1297.224.

§1297.221. Agreement of parties

The parties may agree upon the language or languages to be used in the arbitral proceedings. **Leg.H.** Added Stats 1988 ch 23 §1, effective March 7, 1988.

§1297.222. Determination by tribunal failing agreement of parties

Failing any agreement referred to in Section 1297.221, the arbitral tribunal shall determine the language or languages to be used in the arbitral proceedings. **Leg.H.** Added Stats 1988 ch 23 §1, effective March 7, 1988.

§1297.223. Application of agreement or determination

The agreement or determination, unless otherwise specified, shall apply to any written statement by a party, any hearing, and any arbitral award, decision, or other communication by the arbitral tribunal. **Leg.H.** Added Stats 1988 ch 23 §1, effective March 7, 1988.

§1297.224. Order for translation to accompany documentary evidence

The arbitral tribunal may order that any documentary evidence shall be accompanied by a translation into the language or languages agreed upon by the parties or determined by the arbitral tribunal. **Leg.H.** Added Stats 1988 ch 23 §1, effective March 7, 1988.

ARTICLE 6
Statements of Claim and Defense

Statements by claimant and respondent. §1297.231.
Submission of documents with statements. §1297.232.
Amendment or supplement to claim or defense. §1297.233.

§1297.231. Statements by claimant and respondent

Within the period of time agreed upon by the parties or determined by the arbitral tribunal, the claimant shall state the facts supporting his or her claim, the points at issue, and the relief or remedy sought, and the respondent shall state his or her defense in respect of these particulars, unless the parties have otherwise agreed as to the required elements of those statements. **Leg.H.** Added Stats 1988 ch 23 §1, effective March 7, 1988.

§1297.232. Submission of documents with statements

The parties may submit with their statements all documents they consider to be relevant or may add a reference to the documents or other evidence they will submit. **Leg.H.** Added Stats 1988 ch 23 §1, effective March 7, 1988.

§1297.233. Amendment or supplement to claim or defense

Unless otherwise agreed by the parties, either party may amend or supplement his or her claim or defense during the course of the arbitral proceedings, unless the arbitral tribunal considers it inappropriate to allow the amendment or supplement having regard to the delay in making it. **Leg.H.** Added Stats 1988 ch 23 §1, effective March 7, 1988.

ARTICLE 7
Hearings and Written Proceedings

Determination by tribunal on oral or written nature of hearings. §1297.241.
Holding of oral hearings. §1297.242.
Notice of hearings and meetings of tribunal. §1297.243.
Communication of one party's information and applications to other party; Communication of all reports and documents relied on by tribunal to parties. §1297.244.
In camera oral hearings and meetings. §1297.245.

§1297.241. Determination by tribunal on oral or written nature of hearings

Unless otherwise agreed by the parties, the arbitral tribunal shall decide whether to hold oral hearings for the presentation of evidence or for oral argument, or whether the proceedings shall be conducted on the basis of documents and other materials. **Leg.H.** Added Stats 1988 ch 23 §1, effective March 7, 1988.

§1297.242. Holding of oral hearings

Unless the parties have agreed that no oral hearings shall be held, the arbitral tribunal shall hold oral hearings at an appropriate state of the proceedings, if so requested by a party. **Leg.H.** Added Stats 1988 ch 23 §1, effective March 7, 1988.

§1297.243. Notice of hearings and meetings of tribunal

The parties shall be given sufficient advance notice of any hearing and of any meeting of the arbitral tribunal for the purpose of inspection of documents, goods, or other property. **Leg.H.** Added Stats 1988 ch 23 §1, effective March 7, 1988.

§1297.244. Communication of one party's information and applications to other party; Communication of all reports and documents relied on by tribunal to parties

All statements, documents, or other information supplied to, or applications made to, the arbitral tribunal by one party shall be communicated to the other party, and any expert report or evidentiary document on which the arbitral tribunal may rely in making its decision shall be communicated to the parties. **Leg.H.** Added Stats 1988 ch 23 §1, effective March 7, 1988.

§1297.245. In camera oral hearings and meetings

Unless otherwise agreed by the parties, all oral hearings and meetings in arbitral proceedings shall be held in camera. **Leg.H.** Added Stats 1988 ch 23 §1, effective March 7, 1988.

ARTICLE 8
Default of a Party

Termination of proceedings for failure to communicate statement of claim. §1297.251.
Termination of proceedings for failure to communicate statement of defense. §1297.252.
Failure to appear at oral hearing or produce documentary evidence. §1297.253.

§1297.251. Termination of proceedings for failure to communicate statement of claim

Unless otherwise agreed by the parties, where, without showing sufficient cause, the claimant fails to communicate his or her statement of claim in accordance with Sections 1297.231 and 1297.232, the arbitral tribunal shall terminate the proceedings. **Leg.H.** Added Stats 1988 ch 23 §1, effective March 7, 1988.

§1297.252. Termination of proceedings for failure to communicate statement of defense

Unless otherwise agreed by the parties, where, without showing sufficient cause, the respondent fails to communicate his or her statement of defense in accordance with Sections 1297.231 and 1297.232, the arbitral tribunal shall continue the proceedings without treating that failure in itself as an admission of the claimant's allegations. **Leg.H.** Added Stats 1988 ch 23 §1, effective March 7, 1988.

§1297.253. Failure to appear at oral hearing or produce documentary evidence

Unless otherwise agreed by the parties, where, without showing sufficient cause, a party fails to appear at an oral hearing or to produce documentary evidence, the arbitral tribunal may continue with the proceedings and make the arbitral award on the evidence before it. **Leg.H.** Added Stats 1988 ch 23 §1, effective March 7, 1988.

ARTICLE 9
Expert Appointed by Arbitral Tribunal

Appointment for report of specific issues; Requiring party to give information or produce evidence. §1297.261.
Participation in oral hearing. §1297.262.

§1297.261. Appointment for report of specific issues; Requiring party to give information or produce evidence

Unless otherwise agreed by the parties, the arbitral tribunal may appoint one or more experts to report to it on specific issues to be determined by the arbitral tribunal, and require a party to give the expert any relevant information or to produce, or to provide access to, any relevant docu-

§1297.262. Participation in oral hearing

Unless otherwise agreed by the parties, if a party so requests or if the arbitral tribunal considers it necessary, the expert shall, after delivery of his or her written or oral report, participate in an oral hearing where the parties have the opportunity to question the expert and to present expert witnesses on the points at issue. **Leg.H.** Added Stats 1988 ch 23 §1, effective March 7, 1988.

ARTICLE 10
Court Assistance in Taking Evidence and Consolidating Arbitrations

Request for superior court assistance; Issuance of subpoenas. §1297.271.
Consolidation of arbitrations. §1297.272.
Parties' agreement to consolidate. §1297.273.

§1297.271. Request for superior court assistance; Issuance of subpoenas

The arbitral tribunal, or a party with the approval of the arbitral tribunal, may request from the superior court assistance in taking evidence and the court may execute the request within its competence and according to its rules on taking evidence. In addition, a subpoena may issue as provided in Section 1282.6, in which case the witness compensation provisions of Section 1283.2 shall apply. **Leg.H.** Added Stats 1988 ch 23 §1, effective March 7, 1988.

§1297.272. Consolidation of arbitrations

Where the parties to two or more arbitration agreements have agreed, in their respective arbitration agreements or otherwise, to consolidate the arbitrations arising out of those arbitration agreements, the superior court may, on application by one party with the consent of all the other parties to those arbitration agreements, do one or more of the following:

(a) Order the arbitrations to be consolidated on terms the court considers just and necessary.

(b) Where all the parties cannot agree on an arbitral tribunal for the consolidated arbitration, appoint an arbitral tribunal in accordance with Section 1297.118.

(c) Where all the parties cannot agree on any other matter necessary to conduct the consolidated arbitration, make any other order it considers necessary. **Leg.H.** Added Stats 1988 ch 23 §1, effective March 7, 1988.

§1297.273. Parties' agreement to consolidate

Nothing in this article shall be construed to prevent the parties to two or more arbitrations from agreeing to consolidate those arbitrations and taking any steps that are necessary to effect that consolidation. **Leg.H.** Added Stats 1988 ch 23 §1, effective March 7, 1988.

CHAPTER 6
MAKING OF ARBITRAL AWARD AND TERMINATION OF PROCEEDINGS

Article 1. Rules Applicable to Substance of Dispute.
Article 2. Decisionmaking by Panel of Arbitrators.
Article 3. Settlement.
Article 4. Form and Content of Arbitral Award.
Article 5. Termination of Proceedings.
Article 6. Correction and Interpretation of Awards and Additional Awards.

ARTICLE 1
Rules Applicable to Substance of Dispute

Decision in accordance with rules of law designated by parties as applicable. §1297.281.
Designation by parties of law of state as reference to substantive law. §1297.282.
Application of law by tribunal failing designation by parties. §1297.283.
Decision by tribunal ex aequo et bono or as amiable compositeur. §1297.284.
Decision in accordance with terms of contract; Usages of trade. §1297.285.

§1297.281. Decision in accordance with rules of law designated by parties as applicable

The arbitral tribunal shall decide the dispute in accordance with the rules of law designated by the parties as applicable to the substance of the dispute. **Leg.H.** Added Stats 1988 ch 23 §1, effective March 7, 1988.

§1297.282. Designation by parties of law of state as reference to substantive law

Any designation by the parties of the law or legal system of a given state shall be construed, unless otherwise expressed, as directly referring to the substantive law of that state and not to its conflict of laws rules. **Leg.H.** Added Stats 1988 ch 23 §1, effective March 7, 1988.

§1297.283. Application of law by tribunal failing designation by parties

Failing any designation of the law under Section 1297.282 by the parties, the arbitral tribunal shall apply the rules of law it considers to be appropriate given all the circumstances surrounding the dispute. **Leg.H.** Added Stats 1988 ch 23 §1, effective March 7, 1988.

§1297.284. Decision by tribunal ex aequo et bono or as amiable compositeur

The arbitral tribunal shall decide ex aequo et bono or as amiable compositeur, if the parties have expressly authorized it to do so. **Leg.H.** Added Stats 1988 ch 23 §1, effective March 7, 1988.

§1297.285. Decision in accordance with terms of contract; Usages of trade

In all cases, the arbitral tribunal shall decide in accordance with the terms of the contract and shall take into account the usages of the trade applicable to the transaction. **Leg.H.** Added Stats 1988 ch 23 §1, effective March 7, 1988.

ARTICLE 2
Decisionmaking by Panel of Arbitrators

Decision by majority; Questions of procedure. §1297.291.

§1297.291. Decision by majority; Questions of procedure

Unless otherwise agreed by the parties, in arbitral proceedings with more than one arbitrator, any decision of the arbitral tribunal shall be made by a majority of all of its members.

Notwithstanding this section, if authorized by the parties or all the members of the arbitral tribunal, questions of procedure may be decided by a presiding arbitrator. **Leg.H.** Added Stats 1988 ch 23 §1, effective March 7, 1988.

ARTICLE 3
Settlement

Encouragement of settlement. §1297.301.
Termination of proceedings on settlement; Recording of settlement as award on agreed terms. §1297.302.
Arbitral award on agreed terms. §1297.303.
Status and effect of arbitral award on agreed terms. §1297.304.

§1297.301. Encouragement of settlement

It is not incompatible with an arbitration agreement for an arbitral tribunal to encourage settlement of the dispute and, with the agreement of the parties, the arbitral tribunal may use mediation, conciliation, or other procedures at any time during the arbitral proceedings to encourage settlement. **Leg.H.** Added Stats 1988 ch 23 §1, effective March 7, 1988.

§1297.302. Termination of proceedings on settlement; Recording of settlement as award on agreed terms

If, during arbitral proceedings, the parties settle the dispute, the arbitral tribunal shall terminate the proceedings and, if requested by the parties and not objected to by the arbitral tribunal, record the settlement in the form of an arbitral award on agreed terms. **Leg.H.** Added Stats 1988 ch 23 §1, effective March 7, 1988.

§1297.303. Arbitral award on agreed terms

An arbitral award on agreed terms shall be made in accordance with Article 4 (commencing with Section 1297.311) of this chapter and shall state that it is an arbitral award. **Leg.H.** Added Stats 1988 ch 23 §1, effective March 7, 1988.

§1297.304. Status and effect of arbitral award on agreed terms

An arbitral award on agreed terms has the same status and effect as any other arbitral award on the substance of the dispute. **Leg.H.** Added Stats 1988 ch 23 §1, effective March 7, 1988.

ARTICLE 4
Form and Content of Arbitral Award

Writing; Signature. §1297.311.
Signatures of majority of tribunal members; Statement of reason for omitted signature. §1297.312.
Statement of reasons on which award based. §1297.313.
Statement of date and place of arbitration. §1297.314.

Delivery to parties after signature. §1297.315.
Interim arbitral awards; Enforcement. §1297.316.
Award of interest. §1297.317.
Costs. §1297.318.

§1297.311. Writing; Signature
An arbitral award shall be made in writing and shall be signed by the members of the arbitral tribunal. **Leg.H.** Added Stats 1988 ch 23 §1, effective March 7, 1988.

§1297.312. Signatures of majority of tribunal members; Statement of reason for omitted signature
For the purposes of Section 1297.311, in arbitral proceedings with more than one arbitrator, the signatures of the majority of all the members of the arbitral tribunal shall be sufficient so long as the reason for any omitted signature is stated. **Leg.H.** Added Stats 1988 ch 23 §1, effective March 7, 1988.

§1297.313. Statement of reasons on which award based
The arbitral award shall state the reasons upon which it is based, unless the parties have agreed that no reasons are to be given, or the award is an arbitral award on agreed terms under Article 3 (commencing with Section 1297.301) of this chapter. **Leg.H.** Added Stats 1988 ch 23 §1, effective March 7, 1988.

§1297.314. Statement of date and place of arbitration
The arbitral award shall state its date and the place of arbitration as determined in accordance with Article 3 (commencing with Section 1297.201) of Chapter 5 and the award shall be deemed to have been made at that place. **Leg.H.** Added Stats 1988 ch 23 §1, effective March 7, 1988.

§1297.315. Delivery to parties after signature
After the arbitral award is made, a signed copy shall be delivered to each party. **Leg.H.** Added Stats 1988 ch 23 §1, effective March 7, 1988.

§1297.316. Interim arbitral awards; Enforcement
The arbitral tribunal may, at any time during the arbitral proceedings, make an interim arbitral award on any matter with respect to which it may make a final arbitral award. The interim award may be enforced in the same manner as a final arbitral award. **Leg.H.** Added Stats 1988 ch 23 §1, effective March 7, 1988.

§1297.317. Award of interest
Unless otherwise agreed by the parties, the arbitral tribunal may award interest. **Leg.H.** Added Stats 1988 ch 23 §1, effective March 7, 1988.

§1297.318. Costs
(a) Unless otherwise agreed by the parties, the costs of an arbitration shall be at the discretion of the arbitral tribunal.

(b) In making an order for costs, the arbitral tribunal may include as costs any of the following:

(1) The fees and expenses of the arbitrators and expert witnesses.

(2) Legal fees and expenses.

(3) Any administration fees of the institution supervising the arbitration, if any.

(4) Any other expenses incurred in connection with the arbitral proceedings.

(c) In making an order for costs, the arbitral tribunal may specify any of the following:

(1) The party entitled to costs.

(2) The party who shall pay the costs.

(3) The amount of costs or method of determining that amount.

(4) The manner in which the costs shall be paid. **Leg.H.** Added Stats 1988 ch 23 §1, effective March 7, 1988.

ARTICLE 5
Termination of Proceedings

Manner of termination; Finality of award. §1297.321.
Issuance of order for termination. §1297.322.
Termination of tribunal's mandate. §1297.323.

§1297.321. Manner of termination; Finality of award
The arbitral proceedings are terminated by the final arbitral award or by an order of the arbitral tribunal under Section 1297.322. The award shall be final upon the expiration of the applicable periods in Article 6 (commencing with Section 1297.331) of this chapter. **Leg.H.** Added Stats 1988 ch 23 §1, effective March 7, 1988.

§1297.322. Issuance of order for termination
The arbitral tribunal shall issue an order for the termination of the arbitral proceedings where any of the following occurs:

(a) The claimant withdraws his or her claim, unless the respondent objects to the order and the arbitral tribunal recognizes a legitimate interest on the respondent's part in obtaining a final settlement of the dispute.

(b) The parties agree on the termination of the proceedings.

(c) The arbitral tribunal finds that the continuation of the proceedings has for any other reason become unnecessary or impossible. **Leg.H.** Added Stats 1988 ch 23 §1, effective March 7, 1988.

§1297.323. Termination of tribunal's mandate
Subject to Article 6 (commencing with Section 1297.331) of this chapter, the mandate of the arbitral tribunal terminates with the termination of the arbitral proceedings. **Leg.H.** Added Stats 1988 ch 23 §1, effective March 7, 1988.

ARTICLE 6
Correction and Interpretation of Awards and Additional Awards

Request for correction of errors; Request for interpretation. §1297.331.
Making of correction or giving of interpretation. §1297.332.
Tribunal's correction of error on own initiative. §1297.333.
Request for additional arbitral award. §1297.334.
Making of additional arbitral award. §1297.335.
Extension of time. §1297.336.
Form and content of correction, interpretation or additional award. §1297.337.

§1297.331. Request for correction of errors; Request for interpretation
Within 30 days after receipt of the arbitral award, unless another period of time has been agreed upon by the parties:

(a) A party may request the arbitral tribunal to correct in the arbitral award any computation errors, any clerical or typographical errors, or any other errors of a similar nature.

(b) A party may, if agreed by the parties, request the arbitral tribunal to give an interpretation of a specific point or part of the arbitral award. **Leg.H.** Added Stats 1988 ch 23 §1, effective March 7, 1988.

§1297.332. Making of correction or giving of interpretation
If the arbitral tribunal considers any request made under Section 1297.331 to be justified, it shall make the correction or give the interpretation within 30 days after receipt of the request and the interpretation shall form part of the arbitral award. **Leg.H.** Added Stats 1988 ch 23 §1, effective March 7, 1988.

§1297.333. Tribunal's correction of error on own initiative
The arbitral tribunal may correct any error of the type referred to in subdivision (a) of Section 1297.331, on its own initiative, within 30 days after the date of the arbitral award. **Leg.H.** Added Stats 1988 ch 23 §1, effective March 7, 1988.

§1297.334. Request for additional arbitral award
Unless otherwise agreed by the parties, a party may request, within 30 days after receipt of the arbitral award, the arbitral tribunal to make an additional arbitral award as to the claims presented in the arbitral proceedings but omitted from the arbitral award. **Leg.H.** Added Stats 1988 ch 23 §1, effective March 7, 1988.

§1297.335. Making of additional arbitral award
If the arbitral tribunal considers any request made under Section 1297.334 to be justified, it shall make the additional arbitral award within 60 days after receipt of the request. **Leg.H.** Added Stats 1988 ch 23 §1, effective March 7, 1988.

§1297.336. Extension of time
The arbitral tribunal may extend, if necessary, the period of time within which it shall make a correction, give an interpretation, or make an additional arbitral award under Section 1297.331 or 1297.334. **Leg.H.** Added Stats 1988 ch 23 §1, effective March 7, 1988.

§1297.337. Form and content of correction, interpretation or additional award
Article 4 (commencing with Section 1297.311) of this chapter applies to a correction or interpretation of the arbitral award or to an additional

arbitral award made under this section. **Leg.H.** Added Stats 1988 ch 23 §1, effective March 7, 1988.

CHAPTER 7
CONCILIATION

Article 1. Appointment of Conciliators.
Article 2. Representation and Assistance.
Article 3. Report of Conciliators.
Article 4. Confidentiality.
Article 5. Stay of Arbitration and Resort to Other Proceedings.
Article 6. Termination.
Article 7. Enforceability of Decree.
Article 8. Costs.
Article 9. Effect on Jurisdiction.
Article 10. Immunity of Conciliators and Parties.

ARTICLE 1
Appointment of Conciliators

State policy; Selection of conciliators. §1297.341.
Principles guiding conciliators. §1297.342.
Conduct of conciliation proceedings; Application of other provisions. §1297.343.

§1297.341. State policy; Selection of conciliators

It is the policy of the State of California to encourage parties to an international commercial agreement or transaction which qualifies for arbitration or conciliation pursuant to Section 1297.13, to resolve disputes arising from such agreements or transactions through conciliation. The parties may select or permit an arbitral tribunal or other third party to select one or more persons to serve as the conciliator or conciliators who shall assist the parties in an independent and impartial manner in their attempt to reach an amicable settlement of their dispute. **Leg.H.** Added Stats 1988 ch 23 §1, effective March 7, 1988.

§1297.342. Principles guiding conciliators

The conciliator or conciliators shall be guided by principles of objectivity, fairness, and justice, giving consideration to, among other things, the rights and obligations of the parties, the usages of the trade concerned and the circumstances surrounding the dispute, including any previous practices between the parties. **Leg.H.** Added Stats 1988 ch 23 §1, effective March 7, 1988.

§1297.343. Conduct of conciliation proceedings; Application of other provisions

The conciliator or conciliators may conduct the conciliation proceedings in such a manner as they consider appropriate, taking into account the circumstances of the case, the wishes of the parties, and the desirability of a speedy settlement of the dispute. Except as otherwise provided in this title, other provisions of this code, the Evidence Code, or the California Rules of Court, shall not apply to conciliation proceedings brought under this title. **Leg.H.** Added Stats 1988 ch 23 §1, effective March 7, 1988.

ARTICLE 2
Representation and Assistance

Appearance; Representation. §1297.351.

§1297.351. Appearance; Representation

The parties may appear in person or be represented or assisted by any person of their choice. A person assisting or representing a party need not be a member of the legal profession or licensed to practice law in California. **Leg.H.** Added Stats 1988 ch 23 §1, effective March 7, 1988.

ARTICLE 3
Report of Conciliators

Preparation of draft conciliation settlement. §1297.361.
Acceptance of settlement. §1297.362.

§1297.361. Preparation of draft conciliation settlement

At any time during the proceedings, the conciliator or conciliators may prepare a draft conciliation settlement which may include the assessment and apportionment of costs between the parties, and send copies to the parties, specifying the time within which they must signify their approval. **Leg.H.** Added Stats 1988 ch 23 §1, effective March 7, 1988.

§1297.362. Acceptance of settlement

No party may be required to accept any settlement proposed by the conciliator or conciliators. **Leg.H.** Added Stats 1988 ch 23 §1, effective March 7, 1988.

ARTICLE 4
Confidentiality

Admissibility of evidence, admissions or documents; Compelled disclosure. §1297.371.

§1297.371. Admissibility of evidence, admissions or documents; Compelled disclosure

When persons agree to participate in conciliation under this title:

(a) Evidence of anything said or of any admission made in the course of the conciliation is not admissible in evidence, and disclosure of any such evidence shall not be compelled, in any civil action in which, pursuant to law, testimony may be compelled to be given. However, this subdivision does not limit the admissibility of evidence if all parties participating in conciliation consent to its disclosure.

(b) In the event that any such evidence is offered in contravention of this section, the arbitration tribunal or the court shall make any order which it considers to be appropriate to deal with the matter, including, without limitation, orders restricting the introduction of evidence, or dismissing the case without prejudice.

(c) Unless the document otherwise provides, no document prepared for the purpose of, or in the course of, or pursuant to, the conciliation, or any copy thereof, is admissible in evidence, and disclosure of any such document shall not be compelled, in any arbitration or civil action in which, pursuant to law, testimony may be compelled to be given. **Leg.H.** Added Stats 1988 ch 23 §1, effective March 7, 1988.

ARTICLE 5
Stay of Arbitration and Resort to Other Proceedings

Agreement of parties to submit to conciliation deemed agreement to stay proceedings. §1297.381.
Tolling or extension of limitations periods; Commencement of conciliation proceedings. §1297.382.

§1297.381. Agreement of parties to submit to conciliation deemed agreement to stay proceedings

The agreement of the parties to submit a dispute to conciliation shall be deemed an agreement between or among those parties to stay all judicial or arbitral proceedings from the commencement of conciliation until the termination of conciliation proceedings. **Leg.H.** Added Stats 1988 ch 23 §1, effective March 7, 1988.

§1297.382. Tolling or extension of limitations periods; Commencement of conciliation proceedings

All applicable limitation periods including periods of prescription shall be tolled or extended upon the commencement of conciliation proceedings to conciliate a dispute under this title and all limitation periods shall remain tolled and periods of prescription extended as to all parties to the conciliation proceedings until the 10th day following the termination of conciliation proceedings. For purposes of this article, conciliation proceedings are deemed to have commenced as soon as (a) a party has requested conciliation of a particular dispute or disputes, and (b) the other party or parties agree to participate in the conciliation proceeding. **Leg.H.** Added Stats 1988 ch 23 §1, effective March 7, 1988.

ARTICLE 6
Termination

Methods of termination as to all parties. §1297.391.
Methods of termination as to particular parties. §1297.392.
Conciliator's appointment as arbitrator or participation in arbitral proceedings. §1297.393.
Waiver of rights or remedies by submission to conciliation. §1297.394.

§1297.391. Methods of termination as to all parties

The conciliation proceedings may be terminated as to all parties by any of the following:

(a) A written declaration of the conciliator or conciliators, after consultation with the parties, to the effect that further efforts at conciliation are no longer justified, on the date of the declaration.

(b) A written declaration of the parties addressed to the conciliator or conciliators to the effect that the conciliation proceedings are terminated, on the date of the declaration.

(c) The signing of a settlement agreement by all of the parties, on the date of the agreement. **Leg.H.** Added Stats 1988 ch 23 §1, effective March 7, 1988.

§1297.392. Methods of termination as to particular parties

The conciliation proceedings may be terminated as to particular parties by either of the following:

(a) A written declaration of a party to the other party and the conciliator or conciliators, if appointed, to the effect that the conciliation proceedings shall be terminated as to that particular party, on the date of the declaration.

(b) The signing of a settlement agreement by some of the parties, on the date of the agreement. **Leg.H.** Added Stats 1988 ch 23 §1, effective March 7, 1988.

§1297.393. Conciliator's appointment as arbitrator or participation in arbitral proceedings

No person who has served as conciliator may be appointed as an arbitrator for, or take part in any arbitral or judicial proceedings in, the same dispute unless all parties manifest their consent to such participation or the rules adopted for conciliation or arbitration otherwise provide. **Leg.H.** Added Stats 1988 ch 23 §1, effective March 7, 1988.

§1297.394. Waiver of rights or remedies by submission to conciliation

By submitting to conciliation, no party shall be deemed to have waived any rights or remedies which that party would have had if conciliation had not been initiated, other than those set forth in any settlement agreement which results from the conciliation. **Leg.H.** Added Stats 1988 ch 23 §1, effective March 7, 1988.

ARTICLE 7
Enforceability of Decree

Force and effect of written conciliation agreement. §1297.401.

§1297.401. Force and effect of written conciliation agreement

If the conciliation succeeds in settling the dispute, and the result of the conciliation is reduced to writing and signed by the conciliator or conciliators and the parties or their representatives, the written agreement shall be treated as an arbitral award rendered by an arbitral tribunal duly constituted in and pursuant to the laws of this state, and shall have the same force and effect as a final award in arbitration. **Leg.H.** Added Stats 1988 ch 23 §1, effective March 7, 1988.

ARTICLE 8
Costs

Fixing of costs by conciliator; Written notice to parties; "Costs". §1297.411.
Apportionment of costs; Expenses incurred by party. §1297.412.

§1297.411. Fixing of costs by conciliator; Written notice to parties; "Costs"

Upon termination of the conciliation proceedings, the conciliator shall fix the costs of the conciliation and give written notice thereof to the parties. As used in this article, "costs" includes only the following:

(a) A reasonable fee to be paid to the conciliator or conciliators.

(b) The travel and other reasonable expenses of the conciliator or conciliators.

(c) The travel and other reasonable expenses of witnesses requested by the conciliator or conciliators with the consent of the parties.

(d) The cost of any expert advice requested by the conciliator or conciliators with the consent of the parties.

(e) The cost of any court. **Leg.H.** Added Stats 1988 ch 23 §1, effective March 7, 1988.

§1297.412. Apportionment of costs; Expenses incurred by party

These costs shall be borne equally by the parties unless the settlement agreement provides for a different apportionment. All other expenses incurred by a party shall be borne by that party. **Leg.H.** Added Stats 1988 ch 23 §1, effective March 7, 1988.

ARTICLE 9
Effect on Jurisdiction

Conciliation not deemed consent to jurisdiction of court on failure of conciliation. §1297.421.

§1297.421. Conciliation not deemed consent to jurisdiction of court on failure of conciliation

Neither the request for conciliation, the consent to participate in the conciliation proceedings, the participation in such proceedings, nor the entering into a conciliation agreement or settlement shall be deemed as consent to the jurisdiction of any court in this state in the event conciliation fails. **Leg.H.** Added Stats 1988 ch 23 §1, effective March 7, 1988.

ARTICLE 10
Immunity of Conciliators and Parties

Immunity from service of process. §1297.431.
Immunity from liability for damages. §1297.432.

§1297.431. Immunity from service of process

Neither the conciliator or conciliators, the parties, nor their representatives shall be subject to service of process on any civil matter while they are present in this state for the purpose of arranging for or participating in conciliation pursuant to this title. **Leg.H.** Added Stats 1988 ch 23 §1, effective March 7, 1988.

§1297.432. Immunity from liability for damages

No person who serves as a conciliator shall be held liable in an action for damages resulting from any act or omission in the performance of his or her role as a conciliator in any proceeding subject to this title. **Leg.H.** Added Stats 1988 ch 23 §1, effective March 7, 1988.

TITLE 9.4
REAL ESTATE CONTRACT ARBITRATION

Provision in contract; Notice to precede indication of assent or nonassent; Escrow. §1298.
Waiver of rights by recording of notice of pending action. §1298.5.
Effect of arbitration provision on other causes of action. §1298.7.
Operation and application of title. §1298.8.

§1298. Provision in contract; Notice to precede indication of assent or nonassent; Escrow

(a) Whenever any contract to convey real property, or contemplated to convey real property in the future, including marketing contracts, deposit receipts, real property sales contracts as defined in Section 2985 of the Civil Code, leases together with options to purchase, or ground leases coupled with improvements, but not including powers of sale contained in deeds of trust or mortgages, contains a provision for binding arbitration of any dispute between the principals in the transaction, the contract shall have that provision clearly titled "ARBITRATION OF DISPUTES."

If a provision for binding arbitration is included in a printed contract, it shall be set out in at least 8-point bold type or in contrasting red in at least 8-point type, and if the provision is included in a typed contract, it shall be set out in capital letters.

(b) Whenever any contract or agreement between principals and agents in real property sales transactions, including, **but not limited to,** listing agreements, as defined in Section 1086 of the Civil Code, **and buyer-broker representation agreements, as defined in Section 2079.13 of the Civil Code,** contains a provision requiring binding arbitration of any dispute between the principals and agents in the transaction, the contract or agreement shall have that provision clearly titled "ARBITRATION OF DISPUTES."

If a provision for binding arbitration is included in a printed contract, it shall be set out in at least 8-point bold type or in contrasting red in at least 8-point type, and if the provision is included in a typed contract, it shall be set out in capital letters.

(c) Immediately before the line or space provided for the parties to indicate their assent or nonassent to the arbitration provision described in subdivision (a) or (b), and immediately following that arbitration provision, the following shall appear:

"NOTICE: BY INITIALLING IN THE SPACE BELOW YOU ARE AGREEING TO HAVE ANY DISPUTE ARISING OUT OF THE MATTERS INCLUDED IN THE 'ARBITRATION OF DISPUTES' PROVISION DECIDED BY NEUTRAL ARBITRATION AS PROVIDED BY CALIFORNIA LAW AND YOU ARE GIVING UP ANY RIGHTS YOU MIGHT POSSESS TO HAVE THE DISPUTE LITIGATED IN A COURT OR JURY TRIAL. BY INITIALLING IN THE SPACE BELOW YOU ARE GIVING UP YOUR JUDICIAL RIGHTS TO DISCOVERY AND APPEAL, UNLESS THOSE RIGHTS ARE SPECIFICALLY INCLUDED IN THE 'ARBITRATION OF DISPUTES' PROVISION. IF YOU REFUSE TO SUBMIT TO ARBITRATION AFTER AGREEING TO THIS PROVISION, YOU MAY BE COMPELLED TO ARBITRATE UNDER THE AUTHORITY OF THE CALIFORNIA CODE OF CIVIL PROCEDURE. YOUR AGREEMENT TO THIS ARBITRATION PROVISION IS VOLUNTARY."

"WE HAVE READ AND UNDERSTAND THE FOREGOING AND AGREE TO SUBMIT DISPUTES ARISING OUT OF THE MATTERS INCLUDED IN THE 'ARBITRATION OF DISPUTES' PROVISION TO NEUTRAL ARBITRATION."

If the above provision is included in a printed contract, it shall be set out either in at least 10-point bold type or in contrasting red print in at least 8-point bold type, and if the provision is included in a typed contract, it shall be set out in capital letters.

(d) Nothing in this section shall be construed to diminish the authority of any court of competent jurisdiction with respect to real property transactions in areas involving court supervision or jurisdiction, including, but not limited to, probate, marital dissolution, foreclosure of liens, unlawful detainer, or eminent domain.

(e) In the event an arbitration provision is contained in an escrow instruction, it shall not preclude the right of an escrowholder to institute an interpleader action. **Leg.H.** Added Stats 1988 ch 881 §1, operative July 1, 1989. Amended Stats 1989 ch 22 §1, effective May 25, 1989, operative July 1, 1989; Stats 2024 ch 516 §6 (AB 2992), effective January 1, 2025.

Prior Law: Former CCP §1298, relating to delivery of will, similar to Prob C §8200, was enacted 1872, amended Code Amdts 1880 ch 85 §2, and repealed Stats 1931 ch 281 (Prob C §1700).

§1298.5. Waiver of rights by recording of notice of pending action

Any party to an action who proceeds to record a notice of pending action pursuant to Section 409 shall not thereby waive any right of arbitration which that person may have pursuant to a written agreement to arbitrate, nor any right to petition the court to compel arbitration pursuant to Section 1281.2, if, in filing an action to record that notice, the party at the same time presents to the court an application that the action be stayed pending the arbitration of any dispute which is claimed to be arbitrable and which is relevant to the action. **Leg.H.** Added Stats 1988 ch 881 §1, operative July 1, 1989.

§1298.7. Effect of arbitration provision on other causes of action

In the event an arbitration provision is included in a contract or agreement covered by this title it shall not preclude or limit any right of action for bodily injury or wrongful death, or any right of action to which Section 337.1 or 337.15 is applicable. **Leg.H.** Added Stats 1988 ch 881 §1, operative July 1, 1989.

§1298.8. Operation and application of title

This title shall become operative on July 1, 1989, and shall only apply to contracts or agreements entered into on or after that date. **Leg.H.** Added Stats 1988 ch 881 §1, operative July 1, 1989.

TITLE 9.5
ARBITRATION OF FIREFIGHTER AND LAW ENFORCEMENT OFFICER LABOR DISPUTES

Legislative findings and declarations; Intent. §1299.
Application of title. §1299.2.
Definitions. §1299.3.
Basis for request to submit to arbitration; Panel members; Strikes; Employer's duties. §1299.4.
Meeting of arbitration panel; Powers. §1299.5.
Procedures. §1299.6.
Disclosure of decision; When binding; Right of employer to reject decision. §1299.7.
Applicable provisions. §1299.8.
Applicability of title; Costs. §1299.9.

§1299. Legislative findings and declarations; Intent

The Legislature hereby finds and declares that strikes taken by firefighters and law enforcement officers against public employers are a matter of statewide concern, are a predictable consequence of labor strife and poor morale that is often the outgrowth of substandard wages and benefits, and are not in the public interest. The Legislature further finds and declares that the dispute resolution procedures contained in this title provide the appropriate method for resolving public sector labor disputes that could otherwise lead to strikes by firefighters or law enforcement officers.

It is the intent of the Legislature to protect the health and welfare of the public by providing impasse remedies necessary to afford public employers the opportunity to safely alleviate the effects of labor strife that would otherwise lead to strikes by firefighters and law enforcement officers. It is further the intent of the Legislature that, in order to effectuate its predominant purpose, this title be construed to apply broadly to all public employers, including, but not limited to, charter cities, counties, and cities and counties in this state.

It is not the intent of the Legislature to alter the scope of issues subject to collective bargaining between public employers and employee organizations representing firefighters or law enforcement officers.

The provisions of this title are intended by the Legislature to govern the resolution of impasses reached in collective bargaining between public employers and employee organizations representing firefighters and law enforcement officers over economic issues that remain in dispute over their respective interests. However, the provisions of this title are not intended by the Legislature to be used as a procedure to determine the rights of any firefighter or law enforcement officer in any grievance initiated as a result of a disciplinary action taken by any public employer. The Legislature further intends that this title shall not apply to any law enforcement policy that pertains to how law enforcement officers interact with members of the public or pertains to police-community relations, such as policies on the use of police powers, enforcement priorities and practices, or supervision, oversight, and accountability covering officer behavior toward members of the public, to any community-oriented policing policy or to any process employed by an employer to investigate firefighter or law enforcement officer behavior that could lead to discipline against any firefighter or law enforcement officer, nor to contravene any provision of a charter that governs an employer that is a city, county, or city and county, which provision prescribes a procedure for the imposition of any disciplinary action taken against a firefighter or law enforcement officer. **Leg.H.** Added Stats 2000 ch 906 §2 (SB 402).

Prior Law: Former CCP §1299, similar to present Prob C §8000, was enacted Stats 1872 and repealed Stats 1931 ch 281 §1700.

§1299.2. Application of title

This title shall apply to all employers of firefighters and law enforcement officers. **Leg.H.** Added Stats 2000 ch 906 §2 (SB 402).

§1299.3. Definitions

As used in this title:

(a) "Employee" means any firefighter or law enforcement officer represented by an employee organization, as defined in subdivision (b).

(b) "Employee organization" means any organization recognized by the employer for the purpose of representing firefighters or law enforcement officers in matters relating to wages, hours, and other terms and conditions of employment within the scope of arbitration.

(c) "Employer" means any local agency employing employees, as defined in subdivision (a), or any entity, except the State of California, acting as an agent of any local agency, either directly or indirectly.

(d) "Firefighter" means any person who is employed to perform firefighting, fire prevention, fire training, hazardous materials response, emergency medical services, fire or arson investigation, or any related duties, without respect to the rank, job title, or job assignment of that person.

(e) "Law enforcement officer" means any person who is a peace officer, as defined in Section 830.1 of, subdivisions (b) and (d) of Section 830.31 of, subdivisions (a), (b), and (c) of Section 830.32 of, subdivisions (a), (b), and (d) of Section 830.33 of, subdivisions (a) and (b) of Section 830.35 of, subdivision (a) of Section 830.5 of, and subdivision (a) of Section 830.55 of, the Penal Code, without respect to the rank, job title, or job assignment of that person.

(f) "Local agency" means any governmental subdivision, district, public and quasi-public corporation, joint powers agency, public agency or public service corporation, town, city, county, city and county, or municipal corporation, whether incorporated or not or whether chartered or not.

(g) "Scope of arbitration" means economic issues, including salaries, wages and overtime pay, health and pension benefits, vacation and other leave, reimbursements, incentives, differentials, and all other forms of remuneration. The scope of arbitration shall not include any issue that is protected by what is commonly referred to as the "management rights" clause contained in Section 3504 of the Government Code. Notwithstanding the foregoing, any employer that is not exempt under Section 1299.9 may supersede this subdivision by adoption of an ordinance that establishes a broader definition of "scope of arbitration." **Leg.H.** Added Stats 2000 ch 906 §2 (SB 402). Amended Stats 2002 ch 664 §52 (AB 3034).

§1299.4. Basis for request to submit to arbitration; Panel members; Strikes; Employer's duties

(a) If an impasse has been declared after the parties have exhausted their mutual efforts to reach agreement over matters within the scope of arbitration, and the parties are unable to agree to the appointment of a mediator, or if a mediator agreed to by the parties is unable to effect settlement of a dispute between the parties after his or her appointment, the employee organization may, by written notification to the employer, request that their differences be submitted to an arbitration panel.

(b) Within three days after receipt of the written notification, each party shall designate a person to serve as its member of an arbitration panel. Within five days thereafter, or within additional periods to which they mutually agree, the two members of the arbitration panel appointed by the parties shall designate an impartial person with experience in labor and management dispute resolution to act as chairperson of the arbitration panel.

(c) In the event that the parties are unable or unwilling to agree upon a third person to serve as chairperson, the two members of the arbitration panel shall jointly request from the American Arbitration Association a list of seven impartial and experienced persons who are familiar with matters of employer-employee relations. The two panel members may as an alternative, jointly request a list of seven names from the California State Mediation and Conciliation Service, or a list from either entity containing more or less than seven names, so long as the number requested is an odd number. If after five days of receipt of the list, the two panel members cannot agree on which of the listed persons shall serve as chairperson, they shall, within two days, alternately strike names from the list, with the first panel member to strike names being determined by lot. The last person whose name remains on the list shall be chairperson.

(d) Employees as defined by this chapter shall not be permitted to engage in strikes that endanger public safety.

(e) No employer shall interfere with, intimidate, restrain, coerce, or discriminate against an employee organization or employee because of an exercise of rights under this title.

(f) No employer shall refuse to meet and confer or condition agreement upon a memorandum of understanding based upon an employee organization's exercise of rights under this title. **Leg.H.** Added Stats 2000 ch 906 §2 (SB 402).

§1299.5. Meeting of arbitration panel; Powers

(a) The arbitration panel shall, within 10 days after its establishment or any additional periods to which the parties agree, meet with the parties or their representatives, either jointly or separately, make inquiries and investigations, hold hearings, and take any other action including further mediation, that the arbitration panel deems appropriate.

(b) For the purpose of its hearings, investigations, or inquiries, the arbitration panel may subpoena witnesses, administer oaths, take the testimony of any person, and issue subpoenas duces tecum to require the production and examination of any employer's or employee organization's records, books, or papers relating to any subject matter before the panel. **Leg.H.** Added Stats 2000 ch 906 §2 (SB 402).

§1299.6. Procedures

(a) The arbitration panel shall direct that five days prior to the commencement of its hearings, each of the parties shall submit the last best offer of settlement as to each of the issues within the scope of arbitration, as defined in this title, made in bargaining as a proposal or counterproposal and not previously agreed to by the parties prior to any arbitration request made pursuant to subdivision (a) of Section 1299.4. The arbitration panel, within 30 days after the conclusion of the hearing, or any additional period to which the parties agree, shall separately decide on each of the disputed issues submitted by selecting, without modification, the last best offer that most nearly complies with the applicable factors described in subdivision (c). This subdivision shall be applicable except as otherwise provided in subdivision (b).

(b) Notwithstanding the terms of subdivision (a), the parties by mutual agreement may elect to submit as a package the last best offer of settlement made in bargaining as a proposal or counterproposal on those issues within the scope of arbitration, as defined in this title, not previously agreed to by the parties prior to any arbitration request made pursuant to subdivision (a) of Section 1299.4. The arbitration panel, within 30 days after the conclusion of the hearing, or any additional period to which the parties agree, shall decide on the disputed issues submitted by selecting, without modification, the last best offer package that most nearly complies with the applicable factors described in subdivision (c).

(c) The arbitration panel, unless otherwise agreed to by the parties, shall limit its findings to issues within the scope of arbitration and shall base its findings, opinions, and decisions upon those factors traditionally taken into consideration in the determination of those matters within the scope of arbitration, including but not limited to the following factors, as applicable:

(1) The stipulations of the parties.

(2) The interest and welfare of the public.

(3) The financial condition of the employer and its ability to meet the costs of the award.

(4) The availability and sources of funds to defray the cost of any changes in matters within the scope of arbitration.

(5) Comparison of matters within the scope of arbitration of other employees performing similar services in corresponding fire or law enforcement employment.

(6) The average consumer prices for goods and services, commonly known as the Consumer Price Index.

(7) The peculiarity of requirements of employment, including, but not limited to, mental, physical, and educational qualifications; job training and skills; and hazards of employment.

(8) Changes in any of the foregoing that are traditionally taken into consideration in the determination of matters within the scope of arbitration. **Leg.H.** Added Stats 2000 ch 906 §2 (SB 402).

§1299.7. Disclosure of decision; When binding; Right of employer to reject decision

(a) The arbitration panel shall mail or otherwise deliver a copy of the decision to the parties. However, the decision of the arbitration panel shall not be publicly disclosed, and shall not be binding, for a period of five days after service to the parties. During that five-day period, the parties may meet privately, attempt to resolve their differences and, by mutual agreement, amend or modify the decision of the arbitration panel.

(b) At the conclusion of the five-day period, which may be extended by the parties, the arbitration panel's decision, as may be amended or modified by the parties pursuant to subdivision (a), shall be publicly disclosed and, unless the governing body acts in accordance with subdivision (c), shall be binding on all parties, and, if specified by the arbitration panel, be incorporated into and made a part of any existing memorandum of understanding as defined in Section 3505.1 of the Government Code.

(c) The employer may by unanimous vote of all the members of the governing body reject the decision of the arbitration panel, except as specifically provided to the contrary in a city, county, or city and county charter with respect to the rejection of an arbitration award. **Leg.H.** Added Stats 2000 ch 906 §2 (SB 402). Amended Stats 2003 ch 877 §1 (SB 440).

§1299.8. Applicable provisions

Unless otherwise provided in this title, Title 9 (commencing with Section 1280) shall be applicable to any arbitration proceeding undertaken pursuant to this title. **Leg.H.** Added Stats 2000 ch 906 §2 (SB 402).

§1299.9. Applicability of title; Costs

(a) The provisions of this title shall not apply to any employer that is a city, county, or city and county, governed by a charter that was amended prior to January 1, 2004, to incorporate a procedure requiring the submission of all unresolved disputes relating to wages, hours, and other terms and conditions of employment within the scope of arbitration to an impartial and experienced neutral person or panel for final and binding determination, provided however that the charter amendment is not subsequently repealed or amended in a form that would no longer require the submission of all unresolved disputes relating to wages, hours, and other terms and conditions of employment within the scope of arbitration to an impartial and experienced neutral person or panel, for final and binding determination.

(b) Unless otherwise agreed to by the parties, the costs of the arbitration proceeding and the expenses of the arbitration panel, except those of the employer representative, shall be borne by the employee organization. **Leg.H.** Added Stats 2000 ch 906 §2 (SB 402). Amended Stats 2003 ch 877 §2 (SB 440).

TITLE 10
UNCLAIMED PROPERTY

Chapter 1. General Provisions.
Chapter 2. Receipt and Expenditure of Funds.
Chapter 3. Payment of Claims.
Chapter 4. Management of Unclaimed Property.
Chapter 5. Escheat Proceedings.
Chapter 6. Disposition of Unclaimed Property.
Chapter 7. Unclaimed Property Law.
Chapter 8. Property in Custody of Federal Officers, Agencies, and Departments.

CHAPTER 1
GENERAL PROVISIONS

Article 1. Definitions.
Article 2. Purpose and Scope.

ARTICLE 1
Definitions

Definitions. §1300.
References to sections, articles and chapters. §1301.

§1300. Definitions

For the purposes of this title, the following definitions shall apply:

(a) "Property," unless specifically qualified, includes all classes of property, real, personal and mixed.

(b) "Unclaimed property," unless specifically qualified, means all property (1) which is unclaimed, abandoned, escheated, permanently escheated, or distributed to the state, or (2) which, under any provision of law, will become unclaimed, abandoned, escheated, permanently escheated, or distributed to the state, or (3) to the possession of which the state is or will become entitled, if not claimed by the person or persons entitled thereto within the time allowed by law, whether or not there has been a judicial determination that such property is unclaimed, abandoned, escheated, permanently escheated, or distributed to the state.

(c) "Escheat," unless specifically qualified, means the vesting in the state of title to property the whereabouts of whose owner is unknown or whose owner is unknown or which a known owner has refused to accept, whether by judicial determination or by operation of law, subject to the right of claimants to appear and claim the escheated property or any portion thereof. When used in reference to the law of another state, "escheat" includes the transfer to the state of the right to the custody of such property.

(d) "Permanent escheat" means the absolute vesting in the state of title to property the whereabouts of whose owner is unknown or whose owner is unknown or which a known owner has refused to accept, pursuant to judicial determination, pursuant to a proceeding of escheat as provided by Chapter 5 (commencing with Section 1410) of this title, or pursuant to operation of law and the barring of all claims to the property by the former thereof or his successors.

(e) "Controller" means the State Controller.
(f) "Treasurer" means the State Treasurer.
(g) "Domicile," in the case of a corporation, refers to the place where The corporation is incorporated. **Leg.H.** Added Stats 1951 ch 1708 §5. Amended Stats 1968 ch 356 §1, operative January 1, 1969.

Prior Law: Former CCP §1300 repealed 1931. See Probate Code.

§1301. References to sections, articles and chapters

For the purposes of this title, unless otherwise specified, (1) a reference to a section refers to a section of this code; (2) a reference to an article refers to an article of the chapter of this title in which such reference is made; and (3) a reference to a chapter refers to a chapter of this title. **Leg.H.** Added Stats 1951 ch 1708 §5.

Prior Law: Former CCP §1301 repealed 1931. See Probate Code.

§§1302–1304. [Sections repealed 1931]

Leg.H. Enacted 1872. Repealed Stats 1931 ch 281 (Prob C §1700). See Prob C §§1000, 1201, 1215, 1217, 7050, 8003, 8100, 8110, 8111, 8201.

ARTICLE 2
Purpose and Scope

Purpose of title. §1305.
Application of title. §1306.

§1305. Purpose of title

It is the purpose of this title to provide for the receipt, custody, investment, management, disposal, escheat and permanent escheat of various classes of unclaimed property, to the possession of which the State is, or may become, entitled under the provisions of this title or under provision of law. **Leg.H.** Added Stats 1951 ch 1708 §5.

Prior Law: Former CCP §1305 repealed 1931. See Probate Code.

§1306. Application of title

The provisions of this title do not apply to money or other property held by the State or any officer thereof as trustee or bailee under the terms of an express contract to which the State or any officer thereof is a party. **Leg.H.** Added Stats 1951 ch 1708 §5.

Prior Law: Former CCP §1306 repealed 1931. See Probate Code.

§§1307–1309. [Sections repealed 1931]

Leg.H. Enacted 1872 or added Stats 1927 ch 758 §1. Repealed Stats 1931 ch 281 (Prob C §1700). See Prob C §§1043, 8002, 8004, 8220, 8221, 8250, 8251.

CHAPTER 2
RECEIPT AND EXPENDITURE OF FUNDS

Article 1. Deposit of Unclaimed Property.
Article 2. Appropriation.

ARTICLE 1
Deposit of Unclaimed Property

Transmission of unclaimed property to Treasurer or Controller. §1310.
Notice of transmittal furnished Controller. §1311.
Furnishing Controller copy of court order or decree. §1312.
Unclaimed Property Fund, creation of, and deposits in. §1313.
Unclaimed Property Fund accounts and accounting. §1314.
Record of deposits in State Treasury. §1315.
Record on deposit in State Treasury to credit, etc., of known beneficiaries. §1316.
Transfer of amounts of canceled warrants to General Fund. §1317.
Deposit of investment income in General Fund. §1318.
Depositing and account crediting of income from property held by State; Claims, and payment thereof. §1319.
Deposit of income or increment, from escheated property, in General Fund. §1320.
Immunity from claims and actions on delivery of property to Treasurer or Controller; Nonentitlement to interest. §1321.

§1310. Transmission of unclaimed property to Treasurer or Controller

Whenever, under the provisions of this title or under any other provision of law, unclaimed money or other unclaimed property is payable into the State Treasury, the person responsible for making such payment shall, if it is cash, transmit it to the Treasurer, and if it is personal property other than cash, transmit it to the Controller for deposit in the State Treasury. **Leg.H.** Added Stats 1951 ch 1708 §5.

Prior Law: Former CCP §1310 repealed 1931. See Probate Code.

§1311. Notice of transmittal furnished Controller

Any person transmitting money or other property to the Treasurer or Controller under the provisions of this title shall, at the time of such transmittal, furnish written notice thereof to the Controller, setting forth the amount of cash transmitted, the nature and description of the personal property other than cash transmitted, the name and last known address of the person entitled to such property or for whose benefit such property is transmitted, a reference to the specific statutory provision under which such property is transmitted, and if such property represents the proceeds of an estate of a decedent, or an unclaimed amount payable pursuant to an allowed and approved claim against such an estate, the name of the decedent, the county and court in which probate or escheat proceedings, if any, were held, the number of the action, if any; and, in the case of all classes of property so transmitted, such other identifying information available from the records of the person making such transmittal, as the Controller may require. **Leg.H.** Added Stats 1951 ch 1708 §5.

§1312. Furnishing Controller copy of court order or decree

Whenever money or other property is paid to the State or any officer or employee thereof under the provisions of this title, and such money or other property has been covered by a decree of distribution in a decedent's estate, or by an order or decree of a court ordering such payment, or adjudging that title to such property has vested in the State, the person transmitting such money or other property to the Treasurer or Controller shall, at the time of such transmittal, furnish to the Controller a certified copy of each court order or decree, and of each court order correcting or amending the same, covering such money or other property. **Leg.H.** Added Stats 1951 ch 1708 §5.

Prior Law: Former CCP §1312 repealed 1931. See Probate Code.

§1313. Unclaimed Property Fund, creation of, and deposits in

A fund is hereby created in the State Treasury, to be known as the Unclaimed Property Fund.

All money, except permanently escheated money, paid to the state or any officer or employee thereof for deposit in the State Treasury under the provisions of this title shall, on order of the Controller, be deposited in the Unclaimed Property Fund.

All property other than money, including the proceeds from the sale or other disposition thereof, except permanently escheated property received by, or coming into the possession of, the state or any officer or employee thereof under the provisions of this title shall, on order of the Controller, be deposited in the State Treasury to be held in the Unclaimed Property Fund. **Leg.H.** Added Stats 1951 ch 1708 §5. Amended Stats 1953 ch 218 §1; Stats 1978 ch 1183 §1.

Prior Law: Former CCP §1313 repealed 1931. See Probate Code.

§1313.1. [Section repealed 1979]

Leg.H. Added Stats 1953 ch 218 §2. Amended Stats 1963 ch 1762 §1. Repealed Stats 1978 ch 1183 §2. The repealed section related to deposits in School Land Fund.

§1314. Unclaimed Property Fund accounts and accounting

The Controller shall maintain a separate account in the Unclaimed Property Fund covering the accountability for money deposited in the Unclaimed Property Fund under each article of Chapter 6. All real and personal property distributed to the State or delivered into the possession of the State or any officer or employee thereof under the provisions of this title, shall be accounted for by the Controller in the name of the account in the Unclaimed Property Fund to which the proceeds thereof, if converted into cash, would be credited under the provisions of this title. All personal property deposited in the State Treasury under the provisions of this title shall be held by the Treasurer in the name of the same account in the Unclaimed Property Fund for which such property is accounted by the Controller, as herein provided. **Leg.H.** Added Stats 1951 ch 1708 §5.

Prior Law: Former CCP §1314 repealed 1931. See Probate Code.

§1315. Record of deposits in State Treasury

If unclaimed money or other property in an estate of a deceased person, or if any unclaimed amount payable pursuant to an allowed and approved claim against such an estate, is received by the State or any officer or employee thereof, and deposited in the State Treasury under the provisions of this title, it shall be recorded on the books of the Controller to the credit, or in the name, of such estate, for the benefit of the person entitled thereto or his successors in interest. **Leg.H.** Added Stats 1951 ch 1708 §5.

Prior Law: Former CCP §1315 repealed 1931. See Probate Code.

§1316. Record on deposit in State Treasury to credit, etc., of known beneficiaries

If unclaimed money or other property is received by the State or any officer or employee thereof and deposited in the State Treasury under the provisions of this title for the benefit of known heirs, devisees, legatees or creditors of an estate of a deceased person, or for the benefit of known claimants, payees, or other persons entitled thereto, it shall be recorded on the books of the Controller to the credit, or in the name, of such heirs, devisees, legatees, creditors, claimants, payees, or other persons entitled thereto. **Leg.H.** Added Stats 1951 ch 1708 §5.

Prior Law: Former CCP §1316 repealed 1931. See Probate Code.

§1317. Transfer of amounts of canceled warrants to General Fund

The amount of each canceled warrant credited to the Unclaimed Property Fund under the provisions of Section 17072 of the Government Code shall, on order of the Controller, be transferred to the General Fund. **Leg.H.** Added Stats 1951 ch 1708 §5. Amended Stats 1978 ch 1183 §3.

Prior Law: Former CCP §1317 repealed 1931. See Probate Code.

§1318. Deposit of investment income in General Fund

All interest received and other income derived from the investment of moneys in the Unclaimed Property Fund, as provided in Section 13470 of the Government Code, shall, on order of the Controller, be deposited in the General Fund. **Leg.H.** Added Stats 1951 ch 1708 §5. Amended Stats 1978 ch 1183 §4.

Prior Law: Former CCP §1318 repealed 1931. See Probate Code.

§1319. Depositing and account crediting of income from property held by State; Claims, and payment thereof

Except as otherwise provided in Section 1318, all rents, interest, dividends or other income or increment derived from real or personal property received and held by the State in the name of the Unclaimed Property Fund under the provisions of this title shall, on order of the Controller, be deposited in the Unclaimed Property Fund, and shall be credited by the Controller to the account maintained by him, in the name of which such property is accounted, as provided in Chapter 2. Any moneys deposited in the Unclaimed Property Fund under the provisions of this section shall be held for the benefit of the person or persons entitled to the property from which such moneys were derived, or their successors in interest; and shall be subject to claim in the same manner as such property may be claimed; but the period in which such moneys shall be available for claim by and payment to the person or persons entitled thereto shall not extend beyond the period in which the property from which such moneys were derived is available for claim and payment under the provisions of this title. **Leg.H.** Added Stats 1951 ch 1708 §5.

§1320. Deposit of income or increment, from escheated property, in General Fund

Except as otherwise provided in Section 1318, all rents, interest, dividends or other income or increment derived from real or personal property that has permanently escheated to the state, shall, on order of the Controller, be deposited in the General Fund.

All moneys deposited in the General Fund under the provisions of this section shall be deemed to have permanently escheated to the state as of the date of permanent escheat of the property from which such moneys were derived. **Leg.H.** Added Stats 1951 ch 1708 §5. Amended Stats 1978 ch 1183 §5.

§1321. Immunity from claims and actions on delivery of property to Treasurer or Controller; Nonentitlement to interest

Any person delivering money or other property to the Treasurer or Controller under the provisions of this title shall, upon such delivery, be relieved and held harmless by the State from all or any claim or claims which exist at that time with reference to such money or other property, or which may thereafter be made, or which may come into existence, on account of, or in respect to, such money or other property. No action shall be maintained against any person who is the holder of such money or other property, nor against any officer as agent thereof, for:

(a) The recovery of such money or other property delivered to the Treasurer or Controller pursuant to this title, or for interest thereon subsequent to the date of the report thereof, if any, to the Controller; or

(b) Damages alleged to have resulted from such delivery to the Treasurer or Controller.

No owner of money or other property shall be entitled to receive interest thereon or with respect thereto from and after the date on which a report of such money or other property is made to the Controller pursuant to any provision of this title, whether or not he was entitled to such interest prior to such report.

As used in this section, "person" and "holder" have the respective meanings set forth in Section 1461 of this code. **Leg.H.** Added Stats 1953 ch 279 §1.

§§1322–1324. [Sections repealed 1931]

Leg.H. Enacted 1872. Repealed Stats 1931 ch 281 (Prob C §1700). See Prob C §§7050, 12510, 12511, 12512, 12520 et seq.

ARTICLE 2
Appropriation

Unclaimed Property Fund moneys; Appropriation to, and expenditures by Controller. §1325.

§1325. Unclaimed Property Fund moneys; Appropriation to, and expenditures by Controller

Notwithstanding Section 13340 of the Government Code, all money in the Unclaimed Property Fund is hereby continuously appropriated to the Controller, without regard to fiscal years, for expenditure for any of the following purposes:

(a) For refund, to the person making such deposit, of amounts, including overpayments, deposited in error in such fund.

(b) For payment of the cost of title searches and appraisals incurred by the Controller covering real or personal property held in the name of an account in such fund.

(c) For payment of the cost incurred by the Controller covering indemnity bonds required in order to have duplicate certificates of ownership issued in order to replace lost certificates, covering personal property held in the name of an account in such fund.

(d) For payment of amounts required to be paid by the state as trustee, bailee, or successor in interest to the preceding owner, pursuant to the provisions of trust deeds, mortgages, or other hens on real property held in the name of an account in such fund.

(e) For payment of costs incurred by the Controller for the repair, maintenance and upkeep of real and personal property held in the name of an account in such fund.

(f) For payment of costs of official advertising in connection with the sale of real or personal property held in the name of an account in such fund.

(g) For payment to taxing agencies of the amounts deducted by the Controller from allowed and approved claims, in accordance with the provisions of subdivision (c) of Section 4986.5 of the Revenue and Taxation Code.

(h) For transfer to the Inheritance Tax Fund, on order of the Controller, of the amount of any inheritance taxes determined to be due and payable to the state by any claimant, with respect to any real or personal property, including cash, claimed by that person under the provisions of this title.

(i) For payment and delivery to claimants of money or other property held to the credit, or in the name, of an account in such fund, under the provisions of this title.

(j) For transfer to the General Fund, on order of the Controller, of any money or other property in the Unclaimed Property Fund which becomes permanently escheated to the state under the provisions of this title.

Any expenditure made by the Controller pursuant to the provisions of this section shall be charged against any balance credited to the particular account in the Unclaimed Property Fund, in the name of which is held the real or personal property for which the expenditure is made; and if sufficient balance is not available in such account, the expenditure may be made from any appropriation from the General Fund for the support of the Controller, or, in the case of official advertising, from any appropriation available therefor, to be reimbursed from the proceeds of any subsequent sale of the property for which such expenditure is made. **Leg.H.** Added Stats 1951 ch 1708 §5. Amended Stats 1951 ch 122 §5; Stats 1953 ch 1705 §1; Stats 1963 ch 1762 §2; Stats 1978 ch 1183 §6; Stats 1993 ch 692 §1 (AB 1854).

§1325.1. [Section repealed 1979]

Leg.H. Added Stats 1953 ch 1450 §1. Repealed Stats 1978 ch 1183 §7. The repealed section related to appropriation of School Land Fund moneys to, and expenditure thereof by, Controller.

§1326. [Section repealed 1998]

Leg.H. Added Stats 1951 ch 1708 §5. Amended Stats 1953 ch 1450 §2, ch 1705 §2; Stats 1978 ch 1183 §8. Repealed Stats 1997 ch 653 §1 (AB 1547). The repealed section related to requirement of Board of Control approval for certain expenditures by Controller for Unclaimed Property Fund that exceeded two hundred dollars $200.

§§1327–1333. [Sections repealed 1931]

Leg.H. Enacted 1872. Repealed Stats 1931 ch 281 (Prob C §1700). See Prob C §§1002, 8226, 8270 et seq.

CHAPTER 3
PAYMENT OF CLAIMS

Article 1. General.
Article 2. Refund of Erroneous Receipts.
Article 3. Claims.

ARTICLE 1
General

Nonmaintainability of suits after payment or delivery to claimant. §1335.

§1335. Nonmaintainability of suits after payment or delivery to claimant

When payment or delivery of money or other property has been made to any claimant under the provisions of this chapter, no suit shall thereafter be maintained by any other claimant against the State or any officer thereof for or on account of such property. **Leg.H.** Added Stats 1951 ch 1708 §5.

§1336. [Section repealed 1975]

Leg.H. Added Stats 1951 ch 1708 §5. Repealed Stats 1974 ch 701 §1. The repealed section related to claims of nonresident aliens.

§§1338–1344. [Sections repealed 1931]

Leg.H. Enacted 1872. Repealed Stats 1931 ch 281 (Prob C §1700). See Prob C §§8223, 8224, 9614.

ARTICLE 2
Refund of Erroneous Receipts

Property deposited or held in account in Unclaimed Property Fund. §1345.
Property deposited in, transferred to, or held in name of, General Fund. §1346.
Money transferred to, or other property held in name of, General Fund and recorded as permanently escheated; Retransfer or adjustment of records if property not permanently escheated. §1347.

§1345. Property deposited or held in account in Unclaimed Property Fund

If any person has erroneously delivered any unclaimed moneys or other unclaimed property to the state or any officer or employee thereof, and the moneys or other property is deposited in the Unclaimed Property Fund or is held by the Controller or Treasurer in the name of any account in that fund pursuant to this title, the moneys or other property delivered in error may be refunded or returned to that person on order of the Controller. **Leg.H.** Added Stats 1951 ch 1708 §5. Amended Stats 2006 ch 538 §68 (SB 1852), effective January 1, 2007; Stats 2016 ch 31 §11 (SB 836), effective June 27, 2016.

Prior Law: Former CCP §1345 repealed 1931. See Probate Code.

§1346. Property deposited in, transferred to, or held in name of, General Fund

If any person has erroneously delivered any unclaimed moneys or other unclaimed property to the state or any officer or employee thereof, and the moneys or other property is deposited in, or transferred to, the General Fund, or is held by the Controller or Treasurer in the name of that fund, pursuant to this title, the moneys or other property delivered in error, if cash, shall on order of the Controller, be transferred from the General Fund to the Unclaimed Property Fund, and, if other than cash, the records of the Controller and Treasurer shall be adjusted to show that it is held in the name of the proper account in the Unclaimed Property Fund; and the moneys or other property may be refunded or returned to that person on order of the Controller. **Leg.H.** Added Stats 1951 ch 1708 §5. Amended Stats 1978 ch 1183 §9; Stats 2006 ch 538 §69 (SB 1852), effective January 1, 2007; Stats 2016 ch 31 §12 (SB 836), effective June 27, 2016.

Prior Law: Former CCP §1346 repealed 1931. See Probate Code.

§1347. Money transferred to, or other property held in name of, General Fund and recorded as permanently escheated; Retransfer or adjustment of records if property not permanently escheated

Whenever money deposited in the Unclaimed Property Fund is transferred to the General Fund under the provisions of this title, and whenever the records of the Controller and Treasurer covering property other than money held in the name of any account in the Unclaimed Property Fund are adjusted to record such property as held in the name of the General Fund, as permanently escheated property under the provisions of this title, if it is subsequently determined that such money or other property is not, in fact, permanently escheated, such money or other property, if cash, shall, on order of the Controller, be retransferred from the General Fund to the Unclaimed Property Fund; and, if the property is other than money, the records of the Controller and Treasurer shall be adjusted to show that it is held in the name and for the benefit of the proper account in the

Unclaimed Property Fund. **Leg.H.** Added Stats 1951 ch 1708 §5. Amended Stats 1978 ch 1183 §10.

§§1348, 1349. [Sections repealed 1931]

Leg.H. Enacted 1872 or added Stats 1887 ch 26 §1. Repealed Stats 1931 ch 281 (Prob C §1700). See Prob C §§83, 300, 301, 1043, 1046, 8004, 8005, 8420, 8423, 15602.

ARTICLE 3
Claims

Right to, and time for, claim. §1350.
Escheat to State for failure to claim; Proceedings to determine State's title. §1351.
Who may present claim; Form and contents; Payment of claim; Approval; Commencement of action in superior court. §1352.
Action to determine title to property held by State; Jurisdiction and venue; Who may sue; Verification and contents of petition; Certification of court. §1353.
Claims to recover property; Proof required; Allowance of claims where only creditors exist; Application of section. §1354.
Claim to escheated property; Petition; Time for filing; What must be shown; Service, answer, trail of issues; Judgment; Failure to appear, etc.; Effect. §1355.

§1350. Right to, and time for, claim

Unless otherwise provided in this title, all money or other property deposited in the State Treasury under the provisions of this title may be claimed by the person entitled thereto at any time prior to the date on which such money or other property has become permanently escheated, as provided by this title. **Leg.H.** Added Stats 1951 ch 1708 §5.

Prior Law: Former CCP §1350 repealed 1931. See Probate Code.

§1350a. [Section repealed 1931]

Leg.H. Added Stats 1907 ch 248 §1. Repealed Stats 1931 ch 281 (Prob C §1700). See Prob C §§8440, 8552.

§1351. Escheat to State for failure to claim; Proceedings to determine State's title

Unless otherwise provided in this title, all money or other property deposited in the State Treasury under the provisions of this title, if not claimed by the person entitled thereto within five years from the date of such deposit, shall become the property of the State by escheat; and upon request by the Controller, the Attorney General shall commence a proceeding under the provisions of Section 1410, or, in lieu of such proceeding, the Controller may take action as provided by Article 2 of Chapter 5, to have it adjusted, determined or established that the title to such money or other property has vested in the State. **Leg.H.** Added Stats 1951 ch 1708 §5.

Prior Law: Former CCP §1351 repealed 1931. See Probate Code.

§1352. Who may present claim; Form and contents; Payment of claim; Approval; Commencement of action in superior court

(a) Whenever unclaimed money or other property is deposited in the State Treasury under this title, and, except as otherwise provided by law, whenever there is in the possession of the state or its officers any money or other property which is held for third persons or the title to which has vested in the state subject to the rights of third persons, and the period during which it may be claimed by a person entitled thereto has not terminated, the period and person being prescribed by law, if the value of the money or other property to which the claimant is entitled is less than sixty thousand dollars ($60,000), any such person may present his or her claim for it to the Controller.

The claim shall be made in the form prescribed by the Controller, which shall set forth the information required by Section 1355 or any other information that the Controller may deem necessary to establish right or title to the money or other property in the claimant.

(b) Property assigned or distributed to a name distributee may be claimed by the distributee himself or herself or his or her legal guardian or conservator, as provided in subdivision (a) regardless of the amount. This subdivision does not apply to the heirs or estate of a distributee, or to property distributed to the state for lack of known heirs.

(c) Any person aggrieved by a decision of the Controller may commence an action, naming the Controller as a defendant, to establish his or her claim in the superior court in any county or city and county in which the Attorney General has an office pursuant to Section 1541. **Leg.H.** Added Stats 1951 ch 1708 §5. Amended Stats 1970 ch 811 §1; Stats 1990 ch 450 §1 (SB 57), effective July 31, 1990.

Prior Law: Former CCP §1352 repealed 1931. See Probate Code.

§1353. Action to determine title to property held by State; Jurisdiction and venue; Who may sue; Verification and contents of petition; Certification of court

Except as otherwise provided in Sections 401 or 1352, whenever money or other property is deposited in the State Treasury under the provisions of this title, and, except as otherwise provided by law, when there is in the possession of the State or its officers any money or other property which is to be held for third persons or the title to which has vested in the State subject to the rights of third persons, the Superior Court of the County of Sacramento shall have full and exclusive jurisdiction to determine the title to such money or other property and all claims thereto.

If the period in which such money or other property may be claimed by a person entitled thereto has not terminated, such period and person being prescribed by law, any such person may file a petition in the Superior Court of the County of Sacramento, or as provided in Section 401, showing his claim or right to the money or other property or the proceeds thereof, or any portion thereof.

The petition shall be verified, and, among other things, must, insofar as they are applicable or material to the matters at issue, state the facts required to be stated in a petition filed under Section 1355. If the money or other property at issue did not come into the possession of the State or its officers in connection with estates of deceased persons, the petition shall, in addition to the foregoing facts, state any material facts necessary to establish a prima facie right or title in the petitioner. Upon the filing of the petition, the same proceedings shall be had as are required in Section 1355.

If, upon trial of the issues, the court is satisfied of the claimant's right or title to the money or other property claimed, it shall grant him a certificate to that effect under its seal. Upon presentation of such certificate, the Controller shall draw his warrant on the Treasurer for the amount of money covered thereby; and if the certificate covers any property other than money, a certified copy of the certificate filed with the officer of the State having possession of the property shall serve as sufficient authority to the officer for the delivery of such property to the claimant. **Leg.H.** Added Stats 1951 ch 1708 §5.

Prior Law: Former CCP §1353 repealed 1931. See Probate Code.

§1354. Claims to recover property; Proof required; Allowance of claims where only creditors exist; Application of section

Whenever any claim is made or petition filed by the representative of an estate or other person, under the provisions of this chapter, or under any other provision of law, to recover money or other property deposited in the State Treasury or held by the State or any officer thereof to the credit, or in the name, of any account in the Unclaimed Property Fund, no recovery will be allowed unless it affirmatively appears that there are heirs or legatees who will receive such money or other property or creditors of the deceased owner of the claim whose claims are valid and are not barred, and whose claims were in existence prior to the death of such deceased owner of the claim. Where only creditors exist, and there are no heirs or legatees, said claims shall be allowed only to the extent necessary to pay such claims and the reasonable costs of administration of the estate, including court costs, administrator's fees and attorney's fees. This section shall apply to all claims which are pending at the time that this section goes into effect as well as to claims arising hereafter. **Leg.H.** Added Stats 1951 ch 1708 §5.

Prior Law: Former CCP §1354 repealed 1931. See Probate Code.

§1355. Claim to escheated property; Petition; Time for filing; What must be shown; Service, answer, trail of issues; Judgment; Failure to appear, etc.; Effect

Within five years after date of entry of judgment in any proceeding had under the provisions of Chapter 5, or within five years after completion of notice by publication in an escheat action taken under the provisions of Section 1415, a person not a party or privy to such proceeding or action, if not otherwise barred, may file a petition in the Superior Court of the County of Sacramento, or as provided in Section 401, showing his claim or right to the money or other property, or the proceeds thereof.

Said petition shall be verified; and, in a proceeding for the recovery by the petitioner as heir, devisee, or legatee, or the successor in interest of an heir, devisee or legatee, of money or other property received by the State from the estate of a decedent under the provisions of Article 1 of Chapter 6, such petition, among other things must state:

The full name, and the place and date of birth of the decedent whose estate, or any part thereof, is claimed.

The full name of such decedent's father and the maiden name of his mother, the places and dates of their respective births, the place and date of their marriage, the full names of all children the issue of such marriage, with the date of birth of each, and the place and date of death of all children of such marriage who have died unmarried and without issue.

Whether or not such decedent was ever married, and if so, where, when and to whom.

How, when and where such marriage, if any, was dissolved.

Where or not said decedent was ever remarried, and, if so, where, when and to whom.

The full names, and the dates and places of birth of all lineal descendants, if any, of said decedent; the dates and places of death of any thereof who died prior to the filing of such petition; and the places of residence of all who are then surviving, with the degree of relationship of each of such survivors to said decedent.

Whether any of the brothers or sisters of such decedent ever married, and, if so, where, when and whom.

The full names, and the places and dates of birth of all children who are the issue of the marriage of any such brother or sister of the decedent, and the date and place of death of all deceased nephews and nieces of said decedent.

Whether or not said decedent, if of foreign birth, ever became a naturalized citizen of the United States, and, if so, when, where, and by what court citizenship was conferred.

The post-office names of the cities, towns or other places, each in its appropriate connection, wherein are preserved the records of the births, marriages and deaths hereinbefore enumerated, and, if known, the title of the public official or other person having custody of such records.

The nationality of each of the heirs of the decedent.

The street address of each of the heirs of the decedent.

If, for any reason, the petitioner is unable to set forth any of the matters or things hereinbefore required, he shall clearly state such reason in his petition.

At least 20 days before the hearing of the petition, a copy of the petition and notice of hearing must be served on the Attorney General and on the Controller, and the Attorney General may answer the same at his discretion.

If such claim includes a claim to real property or any interest therein, the petitioner shall record in the office of the county recorder of the county in which the real property is situated, a notice of the pendency of the petition containing the object of the action and a description of the property in the county affected thereby. From the time of filing such notice for record only, shall a purchaser or encumbrancer of the property be deemed to have constructive notice of the pendency of the action, and only of its pendency against parties designated by their real names.

The court must thereupon try the issue as issues are tried in civil actions; and if it is determined that such person is entitled to the money or other property or the proceeds thereof, it must order the property, if it has not been sold, to be delivered to him, or if it has been sold and the proceeds thereof paid into the State Treasury, it must order the Controller to draw his warrant on the Treasurer for the payment of the same, but without interest or cost to the State. A copy of such order, under the seal of the court, shall be a sufficient voucher for drawing such warrant.

All persons who fail to appear and file their petitions within the time limited are forever barred; saving, however, to infants and persons of unsound mind, the right to appear and file their petitions at any time within the time limited, or within one year after the respective disabilities cease. **Leg.H.** Added Stats 1951 ch 1708 §5. Amended Stats 1951 ch 1738 §1.

Prior Law: Former CCP §1355 repealed 1931. See Probate Code.

§1356. [Section repealed 1979]

Leg.H. Added Stats 1953 ch 218 §3. Amended Stats 1959 ch 1809 §6; Stats 1963 ch 1762 §4. Repealed Stats 1978 ch 1183 §11. The repealed section related to deduction of service charge from the amount of any approved claim.

Prior Law: Former CCP §1356 repealed 1931. See Probate Code.

CHAPTER 4
MANAGEMENT OF UNCLAIMED PROPERTY

Article 1. General Provisions.
Article 2. Powers of the Controller.
Article 3. Sale or Disposal of Property.
Article 4. Disposal of Proceeds of Sale or Lease.

ARTICLE 1
General Provisions

Definitions. §1360.
State's function and responsibility. §1361.

§1360. Definitions

For the purposes of this chapter, the following definitions shall apply:

(a) "Personal property" means personal property falling within the definition of "unclaimed property" under the provisions of this title;

(b) "Real property" means real property falling within the definition of "unclaimed property" under the provisions of this title;

(c) "Securities" includes stocks, bonds, notes, debentures, certificates of deposit, shares, and all other evidences of ownership or indebtedness, and all forms of chose in action and the interests in property represented thereby, falling within the definition of unclaimed property under the provisions of this title. **Leg.H.** Added Stats 1951 ch 1708 §5.

Prior Law: Former CCP §1360 repealed 1931. See Probate Code.

§1361. State's function and responsibility

The care and custody of all property delivered to the Treasurer or Controller pursuant to this title is assumed by the State for the benefit of those entitled thereto, and the State is responsible for the payment of all claims established thereto pursuant to law, less any lawful deductions. **Leg.H.** Added Stats 1951 ch 1708 §5.

Prior Law: Former CCP §1361 repealed 1931. See Probate Code.

§1362. [Section repealed 1931]

Leg.H. Enacted 1872. Repealed Stats 1931 ch 281 (Prob C §1700). See Prob C §§1001, 8405.

ARTICLE 2
Powers of the Controller

Safeguarding parties' interests; Incurring investments. §1365.

§1365. Safeguarding parties' interests; Incurring investments

In connection with all unclaimed property, the Controller has all of the powers necessary in order to safeguard and conserve the interests of all parties, including the State, having any vested or expectant interest in such unclaimed property. His powers include, but are not limited to, the authority to incur obligations the payment of which is authorized by the provisions of Section 1325. **Leg.H.** Added Stats 1951 ch 1708 §5.

Prior Law: Former CCP §1365 repealed 1931. See Probate Code.

§§1366–1369. [Sections repealed 1931]

Leg.H. Enacted 1872. Repealed Stats 1931 ch 281 (Prob C §1700). See Prob C §§8402, 8464, 8466, 8467.

ARTICLE 3
Sale or Disposal of Property

Sale or lease of personal property. §1370.
Disposal of securities, choses in action, etc. §1371.
Authentication of instruments for consummation of transactions; Endorsement binding against State and claimants. §1372.
Lease or sale of real property at public auction; Publication of notice. §1373.
Rejection of bids made at sales or public auctions. §1374.
Sale or lease of real property at private sale without published notice. §1375.
Execution of deed, bill of sale or leases. §1376.
Transactions not to be entered into by Controller. §1377.
No suit to be maintained against State, etc., for transaction pursuant to chapter. §1378.
Destruction or disposal of personal property other than cash; Liability of Treasurer or Controller. §1379.
Sales, etc., exempt from Gov C § 11009. §1380.
Sales, leases or other transactions conclusive; Exception. §1381.
Application of article. §1382.

§1370. Sale or lease of personal property

The Controller may sell or lease personal property at any time, and in any manner, and may execute those leases on behalf and in the name of the State of California. **Leg.H.** Added Stats 1951 ch 1708 §5. Amended Stats 2006 ch 538 §70 (SB 1852), effective January 1, 2007; Stats 2016 ch 31 §13 (SB 836), effective June 27, 2016.

Prior Law: Former CCP §1370 repealed 1931. See Probate Code.

§1371. Disposal of securities, choses in action, etc.

The Controller may sell, cash, redeem, exchange, or otherwise dispose of any securities and all other classes of personal property, and may sell, cash, redeem, exchange, compromise, adjust, settle, or otherwise dispose of any accounts, debts, contractual rights, or other choses in action if, in his or her opinion, that action on his or her part is necessary or will tend to safeguard and conserve the interests of all parties, including the state, having any vested or expectant interest in the property. **Leg.H.** Added Stats 1951 ch 1708 §5. Amended Stats 2006 ch 538 §71 (SB 1852), effective January 1, 2007; Stats 2016 ch 31 §14 (SB 836), effective June 27, 2016.

Prior Law: Former CCP §1371 repealed 1931. See Probate Code.

§1372. Authentication of instruments for consummation of transactions; Endorsement binding against State and claimants

The Controller may sign, endorse or otherwise authenticate, in the name and on behalf of the State, subscribing his name, as Controller, under such writing, any securities, bills of sale, documents, or other instruments required, under customary business practice, for the consummation of the transactions authorized by this chapter. For all purposes, such endorsement is conclusive and binding against the State and the heirs, devisees, legatees, or other claimants of the property covered by such endorsement. **Leg.H.** Added Stats 1951 ch 1708 §5.

Prior Law: Former CCP §1372 repealed 1931. See Probate Code.

§1373. Lease or sale of real property at public auction; Publication of notice

The Controller may lease or sell any real property for cash at public auction to the highest bidder.

Before such sale or lease, notice thereof shall be published pursuant to Government Code Section 6063 in a newspaper published in the county in which the real property is situated, or in an adjoining county, if there is no newspaper published in such county. The notice is sufficient for all the purposes of such lease or sale if the real property is described sufficiently to identify it. The cost of publication shall be a charge against the proceeds of the lease or sale, or, if the lease or sale is not consummated, such cost shall be a legal charge against the appropriation for official advertising.

If the value of the property to be sold does not appear to exceed one thousand dollars ($1,000) in the determination of the Controller, notice of sale thereof may be published pursuant to Government Code Section 6061. **Leg.H.** Added Stats 1951 ch 1708 §5. Amended Stats 1953 ch 281 §1.5; Stats 1963 ch 752 §1.

Prior Law: Former CCP §1373 repealed 1931. See Probate Code.

§1374. Rejection of bids made at sales or public auctions

The Controller may reject any and all bids made at sales or public auctions held under the provisions of this chapter. **Leg.H.** Added Stats 1951 ch 1708 §5.

Prior Law: Former CCP §1374 repealed 1931. See Probate Code.

§1375. Sale or lease of real property at private sale without published notice

Any real property may be sold or leased by the Controller at private sale without published notice. **Leg.H.** Added Stats 1951 ch 1708 §5. Amended Stats 2006 ch 538 §72 (SB 1852), effective January 1, 2007; Stats 2016 ch 31 §15 (SB 836), effective June 27, 2016.

Prior Law: Former CCP §1375 repealed 1931. See Probate Code.

§1376. Execution of deed, bill of sale or leases

Upon receipt of the proceeds of any sale made pursuant to this chapter, the Controller shall execute, in the name and on behalf of the State of California, a deed covering the real property, and a bill of sale covering the personal property, real property, and a bill of sale covering the personal property, sold. He may execute leases for real or personal property in the name and on behalf of the State of California. **Leg.H.** Added Stats 1951 ch 1708 §5.

Prior Law: Former CCP §1376 repealed 1931. See Probate Code.

§1377. Transactions not to be entered into by Controller

The Controller shall not enter into any transaction which shall create or impose upon the owners, heirs, devisees, legatees, or other claimants of the property involved, any obligation under an executory contract, the performance of which is not already an obligation of such owners, heirs, devisees, legatees, or other claimants prior to the consummation of the transactions authorized by this chapter. **Leg.H.** Added Stats 1951 ch 1708 §5.

Prior Law: Former CCP §1377 repealed 1931. See Probate Code.

§1378. No suit to be maintained against State, etc., for transaction pursuant to chapter

No suit shall be maintained by any person against the State or any officer thereof, for or on account of any transaction entered into by the Controller pursuant to this chapter. **Leg.H.** Added Stats 1951 ch 1708 §5.

Prior Law: Former CCP §1378 repealed 1931. See Probate Code.

§1379. Destruction or disposal of personal property other than cash; Liability of Treasurer or Controller

The Controller may destroy or otherwise dispose of any personal property other than cash deposited in the State Treasury under this title, if that property is determined by him or her to be valueless or of such little value that the costs of conducting a sale would probably exceed the amount that would be realized from the sale, and neither the Treasurer nor Controller shall be held to respond in damages at the suit of any person claiming loss by reason of that destruction or disposition. **Leg.H.** Added Stats 1951 ch 1708 §5. Amended Stats 2006 ch 538 §73 (SB 1852), effective January 1, 2007; Stats 2016 ch 31 §16 (SB 836), effective June 27, 2016.

Prior Law: Former CCP §1379 repealed 1931. See Probate Code.

§1380. Sales, etc., exempt from Gov C §11009

All sales, exchanges, or other transactions entered into by the Controller pursuant to this chapter are exempt from the provisions of Section 11009 of the Government Code. **Leg.H.** Added Stats 1951 ch 1708 §5.

Prior Law: Former CCP §1380 repealed 1931. See Probate Code.

§1381. Sales, leases or other transactions conclusive; Exception

All sales, leases or other transactions entered into by the Controller pursuant to this chapter shall be conclusive against everyone, except a purchaser or encumbrancer who in good faith and for a valuable consideration acquires a title or interest by an instrument in writing that is first duly recorded. **Leg.H.** Added Stats 1951 ch 1738 §6.

Prior Law: Former CCP §1381 repealed 1931. See Probate Code.

§1382. Application of article

Any provision of this article which authorizes the Controller to sell real property applies to any real property distributed or escheated to, or the title to which has vested in, the State of California by court order or decree of distribution, if such real property is held in the name of the Unclaimed Property Fund under the provisions of this title, whether or not such real property has permanently escheated to the State.

This section does not apply to the disposition of tax-deeded lands under Chapter 7, 8 or 9 of Part 6 of Division 1 of the Revenue and Taxation Code. **Leg.H.** Added Stats 1953 ch 281 §1.

§§1383–1389. [Sections repealed 1931]

Leg.H. Enacted 1872. Repealed Stats 1931 ch 281 (Prob C §1700). See Prob C §§8403, 8480–8482, 8500, 8503, 8520.

ARTICLE 4
Disposal of Proceeds of Sale or Lease

Proceeds from sale or lease of property not permanently escheated; Deposit in Unclaimed Property Fund; Credit to account; For whom to be held. §1390.

Proceeds from sale or lease of permanently escheated property; Deposit in General Fund; Presumption. §1391.

Proceeds of transactions of property held by State under Ch 6, Art 1; Crediting to estate or account in General Fund. §1392.

Crediting to unlocated heirs, etc., or account in General Fund. §1393.

Proceeds from transactions of property held by State for benefit of entitled persons; Crediting to such persons or account in General Fund. §1394.

§1390. Proceeds from sale or lease of property not permanently escheated; Deposit in Unclaimed Property Fund; Credit to account; For whom to be held

The Controller shall deliver to the Treasurer the proceeds of any sale or lease of property, other than permanently escheated property, made pursuant to this chapter; and, on order of the Controller, the amount thereof shall be deposited in the Unclaimed Property Fund. Such amount shall be credited by the Controller to the account in said fund, in the name of which the property sold or leased was held. All moneys deposited in the Unclaimed Property Fund under the provisions of this section shall be held for the benefit of those entitled to claim the property sold or lease; but the period in which such moneys shall be available for claim by and payment to the persons entitled thereto shall not extend beyond the period in which such property is available for claim and payment under the provisions of this title. **Leg.H.** Added Stats 1951 ch 1708 §5.

Prior Law: Former CCP §1390 repealed 1931. See Probate Code.

§1391. Proceeds from sale or lease of permanently escheated property; Deposit in General Fund; Presumption

The Controller shall deliver to the Treasurer the proceeds of any sale or lease of permanently escheated property made pursuant to this chapter; and, on order of the Controller, the amount thereof shall be deposited in the General Fund. All moneys deposited in the General Fund under the provisions of this section shall be deemed to have permanently escheated to the state as of the date of permanent escheat of the property from which such moneys were derived. **Leg.H.** Added Stats 1951 ch 1708 §5. Amended Stats 1978 ch 1183 §12.

Prior Law: Former CCP §1391 repealed 1931. See Probate Code.

§1392. Proceeds of transactions of property held by State under Ch 6, Art 1; Crediting to estate or account in General Fund

The proceeds of any transaction by the Controller under the provisions of this chapter in connection with property received and held by the state under the provisions of Article 1 (commencing with Section 1440) of Chapter 6 of this title shall be credited by the Controller to the estate from which the property affected by the transaction was received; or, if such property has permanently escheated to the state, to the account in the General Fund to which the permanently escheated cash derived from estates of deceased persons is credited. **Leg.H.** Added Stats 1951 ch 1708 §5. Amended Stats 1978 ch 1183 §13.

Prior Law: Former CCP §1392 repealed 1931. See Probate Code.

§1393. Crediting to unlocated heirs, etc., or account in General Fund

The proceeds of any transaction by the Controller under the provisions of this chapter, in connection with property received and held by the state under the provisions of Article 1 (commencing with Section 1440) of Chapter 6 of this title, for the benefit of unlocated heirs, devisees or legatees of estates of deceased persons, shall be credited by the Controller to such heirs, devisees or legatees of the property affected by such transaction; or, if such property has permanently escheated to the state, to the account in the General Fund to which the permanently escheated cash derived from estates of deceased persons is credited. **Leg.H.** Added Stats 1951 ch 1708 §5. Amended Stats 1978 ch 1183 §14.

Prior Law: Former CCP §1393 repealed 1931. See Probate Code.

§1394. Proceeds from transactions of property held by State for benefit of entitled persons; Crediting to such persons or account in General Fund

The proceeds of any transaction by the Controller under the provisions of this chapter in connection with property received and held by the state under the provisions of this title, for the benefit of the persons entitled thereto, shall be credited by the Controller to such persons; or, if the property affected by such transaction has permanently escheated to the state, to the account in the General Fund in the name of which such permanently escheated property was recorded. **Leg.H.** Added Stats 1951 ch 1708 §5. Amended Stats 1978 ch 1183 §15.

Prior Law: Former CCP §1394 repealed 1931. See Probate Code.

§§1395–1407. [Sections repealed 1931]

Leg.H. Enacted 1872 or added Code Amdts 1973–74. Repealed Stats 1931 ch 281 (Prob C §1700). See CCP §§995.030, 996.010, 996.120, 996.130, 996.140, 996.460, 996.480; Prob C §§8223, 8224, 8480, 8481, 8501, 9614.

CHAPTER 5
ESCHEAT PROCEEDINGS

Article 1. Escheat Proceedings on Unclaimed Property.
Article 2. Escheat by Notice and Publication.
Article 3. Escheat Proceedings in Decedents' Estates.
Article 4. Permanent Escheat.

ARTICLE 1
Escheat Proceedings on Unclaimed Property

Actions to adjudicate that title to unclaimed property is vested in State; Duty of Attorney General. §1410.

§1410. Actions to adjudicate that title to unclaimed property is vested in State; Duty of Attorney General

The Attorney General shall, from time to time, commence actions on behalf of the state for the purpose of having it adjudged that title to unclaimed property to which the state has become entitled by escheat has vested in the state, and for the purpose of having it adjudged that property has been actually abandoned or that the owner thereof has died and there is no person entitled thereto and the same has escheated and vested in the state. Such actions shall be brought in the Superior Court for the County of Sacramento; except that if any real property covered by the petition is not situated in the County of Sacramento, an action respecting the real property shall be commenced in the superior court for the county in which such real property or any part thereof is situated. The Attorney General shall cause to be recorded in the office of the county recorder of the county in which the real property is situated, a notice of the pendency of the petition containing the names of the parties, and the object of the action and a description of the property in the county affected thereby. From the time of filing such notice for record only, shall a purchaser or encumbrancer of the property affected thereby be deemed to have constructive notice of the pendency of the action, and only of the pendency against parties designated by their real names.

Such action shall be commenced by filing a petition. The provisions of Section 1420, relating to the facts to be set forth in the petition, joinder of parties and causes of action, and the provisions of Section 1423, relating to appearances and pleadings, shall be applicable to any proceeding had under this section.

Upon the filing of the petition, the court shall make an order requiring all persons interested in the property or estate to appear on a day not more than 90 days nor less than 60 days from the date of the order and show cause, if any they have, why title to the property should not vest in the State of California.

Service of process in such actions shall be made by delivery of a copy of the order, together with a copy of the petition, to each person who claims title to any property covered by the petition and who is known to the Attorney General or the Controller or who has theretofore filed in the office of the Controller a written request for such service of process, stating his name and address, including street number, or post-office box number, if any, and by publishing the order at least once a week for two consecutive weeks in a newspaper published in the county in which the action is filed, the last publication to be at least 10 days prior to the date set for the hearing.

Upon completion of the service of process, as provided in this section, the court shall have full and complete jurisdiction over the estate, the property, and the person of everyone having or claiming any interest in the property, and shall have full and complete jurisdiction to hear and determine the issues therein, and to render an appropriate judgment.

In addition to the foregoing publication of the order, a notice shall be given by publication, at least once a week for two successive weeks in a newspaper published in the county from which the property was forwarded to the State Treasury or is situated, of each estate and item of property from such county or situated in such county in excess of one thousand dollars ($1,000). Such notice shall state that a petition has been filed and an order made as hereinbefore provided and shall list each estate and item in excess of one thousand dollars ($1,000) and show the amount of the property, if money, or a description thereof, if other than money, and the name of the owner or claimant and his last known address. Any omission or defect in the giving of such additional notice shall not affect the jurisdiction of the court.

If it appears from the facts found or admitted that the state is entitled to the property or any part thereof mentioned in the petition, judgment shall be rendered that title to such property or part thereof, as the case may be, has vested in the state by escheat.

No costs of suit shall be allowed against any party in any action or proceeding had under this section. **Leg.H.** Added Stats 1951 ch 1708 §5.

Amended Stats 1951 ch 1738 §2; Stats 1965 ch 2066 §2; Stats 1972 ch 856 §1, operative January 1, 1973; Stats 1984 ch 268 §1, effective June 30, 1984.

§§1411–1414. [Sections repealed 1931]

Leg.H. Enacted 1872. Repealed Stats 1931 ch 281 (Prob C §1700). See Prob C §§8481, 8540–8544.

ARTICLE 2
Escheat by Notice and Publication

Alternative procedure for money or personal property of $1,000 or less. §1415.

§1415. Alternative procedure for money or personal property of $1,000 or less

Whenever any money or other personal property of a value of one thousand dollars ($1,000) or less has heretofore been, or is hereafter, deposited in the State Treasury and the same is subject to being declared escheated to the state or being declared vested in the state as abandoned property, or otherwise, under any laws of this state, in lieu of the procedure provided for elsewhere in this chapter, the Controller may, from time to time, prepare a return listing such property and give notice thereof in the manner hereinafter provided. Such return shall list each item and show (1) the amount of the property, if money, or a description thereof if other than money; (2) the name of the owner or claimant and his last known address, if known; (3) the name and address of the person delivering the property to the State Treasury, if known but where the property is received from an estate, only the name of the decedent together with the name of the county and the number of the proceeding need be given; (4) the facts and circumstances by virtue of which it is claimed the property has escheated or vested in the state; and (5) such other information as the Controller may desire to include to assist in identifying each item.

When such return has been completed, the Controller shall prepare, date, and attach thereto a notice that the property listed in the return has escheated or vested in the state. Copies of such return and notice shall then be displayed and be open to public inspection during business hours in at least three offices of the Controller, one in the City of Sacramento, one in the City and County of San Francisco, and one in the City of Los Angeles.

The Controller shall then cause notice to be given by publication in one newspaper of general circulation published in the City of Sacramento, and also by publication in one newspaper of general circulation published in the City and County of San Francisco, and also by publication in one newspaper of general circulation published in the City of Los Angeles, at least once each calendar week for two consecutive weeks, that said return and notice that the property listed in the return has escheated or vested in the state has been prepared and is on display and open to public inspection during business hours, giving the addresses and room numbers of the locations where the same may be inspected.

Such publication shall be made within 90 days after attaching the notice to the return. Notice by such publication shall be deemed completed 120 days after attaching the notice to the return.

Within five years after such notice by publication is completed, any person entitled to such property may claim it in the manner provided in Chapter 3 of this title. All persons who fail to make such claim within the time limited are forever barred; saving, however, to infants and persons of unsound mind, the right to appear and claim such property at any time within the time limited, or within one year after their respective disabilities cease. **Leg.H.** Added Stats 1951 ch 1708 §5. Amended Stats 1965 ch 1350 §1; Stats 1984 ch 268 §2, effective June 30, 1984.

Prior Law: Former CCP §1415 repealed 1931. See Probate Code.

§§1416–1418. [Sections repealed 1931]

Leg.H. Enacted 1872 or added Stats 1917 ch 72 §1. Repealed Stats 1931 ch 281 (Prob C §1700). See Prob C §§8524, 8544, 8546, 8547.

ARTICLE 3
Escheat Proceedings in Decedents' Estates

Action on behalf of State; Limitation; Petition; Order to appear; Joinder of parties and actions; Order to commence administration proceedings. §1420.
Escheated property. §1421.
Receivers of rents and profits; Appointment. §1422.
Appearance, pleadings, trial of issues and judgment; Sale of property; Confirmation, execution of conveyance and disposition of proceeds. §1423.

Judgment vesting property in State and creating trust in favor of unidentified persons as a class; Legal and equitable title vested in State; Right of claimants to appear and claim property. §1424.

§1420. Action on behalf of State; Limitation; Petition; Order to appear; Joinder of parties and actions; Order to commence administration proceedings

(a) At any time after two years after the death of any decedent who leaves property to which the state is entitled by reason of it having escheated to the state, the Attorney General shall commence a proceeding on behalf of the state in the Superior Court for the County of Sacramento to have it adjudged that the state is so entitled. The action shall be commenced by filing a petition, which shall be treated as the information elsewhere referred to in this title.

(b) The petition shall set forth a description of the property, the name of the person last in possession thereof, the name of the person, if any, claiming the property, or portion thereof, and the facts and circumstances by virtue of which it is claimed the property has escheated.

(c) Upon the filing of the petition, the court shall make an order requiring all persons interested in the estate to appear and show cause, if any, within 60 days from the date of the order, why the estate should not vest in the state. The order must be published at least once a week for four consecutive weeks in a newspaper published in the County of Sacramento, the last publication to be at least 10 days prior to the date set for the hearing. Upon the completion of the publication of the order, the court shall have full and complete jurisdiction over the estate, the property, and the person of everyone having or claiming any interest in the property, and shall have full and complete jurisdiction to hear and determine the issues therein, and render the appropriate judgment thereon.

(d) If proceedings for the administration of the estate have been instituted, a copy of the order must be filed with the papers in the estate. If proceedings for the administration of any estate of the decedent have been instituted and none of the persons entitled to succeed thereto have appeared and made claim to the property, or any portion thereof, before the decree of final distribution therein is made, or before the commencement of a proceeding by the Attorney General, or if the court shall find that the persons as have appeared are not entitled to the property of the estate, or any portion thereof, the court shall, upon final settlement of the proceedings for the administration of the estate, after the payment of all debts and expenses of administration, distribute all moneys and other property remaining to the State of California.

In any proceeding brought by the Attorney General under this chapter, any two or more parties and any two or more causes of action may be joined in the same proceedings and in the same petition without being separately stated, and it shall be sufficient to allege in the petition that the decedent left no heirs to take the estate and the failure of heirs to appear and set up their claims in any proceeding, or in any proceedings for the administration of the estate, shall be sufficient proof upon which to base the judgment in any proceeding or decree of distribution.

(e) If proceedings for the administration of any estate have not been commenced within six months from the death of any decedent the Attorney General may direct the public administrator to commence the same forthwith. **Leg.H.** Added Stats 1951 ch 1708 §5. Amended Stats 2002 ch 784 §83 (SB 1316); Stats 2003 ch 62 §26 (SB 600).

§1421. Escheated property

Whenever the Attorney General is informed that any estate has escheated or is about to escheat to the state, or that the property involved in any action or special proceeding has escheated or is about to escheat to the state, the Attorney General may commence an action on behalf of the state to determine its rights to the property or may intervene on its behalf in any action or special proceeding affecting the estate and contest the rights of any claimant or claimants thereto. The Attorney General may also apply to the superior court or any judge thereof for an order directing the county treasurer to deposit in the State Treasury all money, and to deliver to the Controller for deposit in the State Treasury, all other personal property, in the possession of the county treasurer, which may become payable to the State Treasury pursuant to Section 7643 of the Probate Code. **Leg.H.** Added Stats 1951 ch 1708 §5. Amended Stats 1988 ch 1199 §9, operative July 1, 1989.

§1422. Receivers of rents and profits; Appointment

The court, upon the information being filed, and upon application of the Attorney General, either before or after answer, upon notice to the party claiming the estate, if known, may, upon sufficient cause therefor being shown, appoint a receiver to take charge of such estate, or any part thereof, or to receive the rents, income and profits of the same until title of such estate is finally settled. **Leg.H.** Added Stats 1951 ch 1708 §5.

§1423. Appearance, pleadings, trial of issues and judgment; Sale of property; Confirmation, execution of conveyance and disposition of proceeds

All persons named in the information may appear and answer, and may traverse or deny the facts stated therein at any time before the time for answering expires, and any other person claiming an interest in such estate may appear and be made a defendant, by motion for that purpose in open court within the time allowed for answering, and if no such person appears and answers within the time, then judgment must be rendered that the State is the owner of the property in such information claimed.

If any person appears and denies the title set up by the State, or traverses any material fact set forth in the information, the issue of fact must be tried as issues of fact are tried in civil actions.

If, after the issues are tried, it appears from the facts found or admitted that the State has good title to the property in the information mentioned, or any part thereof, judgment must be rendered that the State is the owner and entitled to the possession thereof, and that it recover costs of suit against the defendants who have appeared and answered.

In any judgment rendered, or that has heretofore been rendered by any court escheating property to the State, on motion of the Attorney General, the court must make an order that such property, unless it consists of money, be sold by the sheriff of the county where it is situate, at public sale, for cash, after giving notice of the time and place of sale, as may be prescribed by the court in such order; that the sheriff, within five days after such sale, make a report thereof to the court, and upon the hearing of such report, the court may examine the report and witnesses in relation thereto, and if the proceedings were unfair, or if the sum bid disproportionate to the value, or if it appears that a sum exceeding said bid, exclusive of the expense of a new sale, may be obtained, the court may vacate the sale, and direct another to be had, of which notice must be given, and the sale in all respects conducted as if no previous sale had taken place. If an offer greater in amount than that named in the report is made to the court in writing by a responsible person, the court may, in its discretion, accept such offer and confirm the sale to such person, or order a new sale.

If it appears to the court that the sale was legally made and fairly conducted and that the sum bid is not disproportionate to the value of the property sold, and that a sum exceeding such bid, exclusive of the expense of a new sale, cannot be obtained or if the increased bid above mentioned is made and accepted by the court, the court must make an order confirming the sale and directing the sheriff, in the name of the State, to execute to the purchaser or purchasers a conveyance of said property sold; and said conveyance vests in the purchaser or purchasers all the right and title of the State therein.

The sheriff shall, out of the proceeds of such sale, pay the cost of said proceedings incurred on behalf of the State, including the expenses of making such sale, and also an attorney's fee, if additional counsel was employed in said proceedings, to be fixed by the court, not exceeding 10 percent on the amount of such sale; and the residue thereof shall be paid by said sheriff into the State Treasury. **Leg.H.** Added Stats 1951 ch 1708 §5.

Prior Law: Former CCP §1423 repealed 1931. See Probate Code.

§1424. Judgment vesting property in State and creating trust in favor of unidentified persons as a class; Legal and equitable title vested in State; Right of claimants to appear and claim property

If, in any proceeding had under this title, the judgment or decree distributes or vests unclaimed property or any portion thereof to or in the State of California, and the distributing or vesting clause contains words otherwise creating a trust in favor of certain unknown or unidentified persons as a class, such judgment or decree shall vest in the State of California both legal and equitable title to such property; saving, however, the right of claimants to appear and claim the property, as provided in this title. **Leg.H.** Added Stats 1951 ch 1708 §5.

Prior Law: Former CCP §1424 repealed 1931. See Probate Code.

§§1425–1429. [Sections repealed 1931]

Leg.H. Enacted 1872. Repealed Stats 1931 ch 281 (Prob C §1700). See Prob C §§8520–8523, 8525.

ARTICLE 4
Permanent Escheat

Period in which permanent escheat occurs; Rights of infants, persons of unsound mind, and named beneficiaries. §1430.
Transfer of permanently escheated money to General Fund. §1431.

§1430. Period in which permanent escheat occurs; Rights of infants, persons of unsound mind, and named beneficiaries

(a) Upon the expiration of five years after the date of entry of judgment in any proceeding pursuant to this chapter, or upon the expiration of five years after completion of notice by publication in an escheat action taken pursuant to Section 1415, the property covered by that proceeding or action shall permanently escheat to the state, except as provided in subdivision (b).

(b) Infants and persons of unsound mind shall have the right to appear and claim such property as provided in this title if born before the expiration of the five-year period; but it shall be presumed that there are no infants nor persons of unsound mind who are or will be entitled to claim this property unless and until they appear and claim the property as provided in this title. This presumption shall be conclusive in favor of any purchaser in good faith and for a valuable consideration from the state and everyone subsequently claiming under him or her, saving however, to infants and persons of unsound mind the right of recourse to the proceeds of any sale or other disposition of any such property by the state and as herein provided.

(c) Except as otherwise provided in this subdivision, a named beneficiary of property that escheats pursuant to this title or, if the beneficiary is deceased or a court renders a judgment that the beneficiary is dead, a blood relative of the named beneficiary may claim property described in subdivision (a) at any time within five years after the date of entry of judgment in any proceeding under this chapter. The named beneficiary or, if a court has rendered a judgment that the named beneficiary is dead, the blood relative of the named beneficiary shall be entitled to immediate payment upon this claim. If a court has not rendered a judgment that the named beneficiary is dead, payment of the claim of a blood relative of the named beneficiary shall be made on the day before the expiration of the five-year period described in this section. This subdivision shall not apply to authorize a claim by any person, including any issue or blood relative of that person, whose interest or inheritance was specifically restricted or barred by a provision in the donating or transferring instrument. **Leg.H.** Added Stats 1951 ch 1708 §5. Amended Stats 1951 ch 1738 §3; Stats 1997 ch 671 §1 (SB 999).

Prior Law: Former CCP §1430 repealed 1931. See Probate Code.

§1431. Transfer of permanently escheated money to General Fund

When money in the Unclaimed Property Fund has become permanently escheated to the state, the amount thereof shall, on order of the Controller, be transferred to the General Fund. When property other than money held by the Controller or Treasurer in the name of any account in the Unclaimed Property Fund has become permanently escheated to the state, the records of the Controller and Treasurer shall be adjusted to show that such property is held in the name of the General Fund. **Leg.H.** Added Stats 1951 ch 1708 §5. Amended Stats 1978 ch 1183 §16; Stats 1980 ch 676 §69.

Prior Law: Former CCP §1431 repealed 1931. See Probate Code.

§§1432–1439. [Sections repealed 1931]

Leg.H. Enacted 1872. Repealed Stats 1931 ch 281 (Prob C §1700). See Prob C §§7072, 8500, 8502.

CHAPTER 6
DISPOSITION OF UNCLAIMED PROPERTY

Article 1. Estates of Deceased Persons.
Article 2. Abandoned Property.

ARTICLE 1
Estates of Deceased Persons

Property in estate paid to State, etc., deemed paid under provisions of article. §1440.

Escheated property. §1441.

Right to claim property paid into State Treasury. §1442.

Payment to state. §1443.

Transfer of possession of property held for known heirs, etc., to Treasurer or Controller. §1444.

Escheat of money on deposit with county treasurer received from county public administrator in trust; Payment to State Treasurer and deposit in School Land Fund. §1444.5.

Transfer to State Treasury of undistributed funds, etc., of estate of decedent; Petition of county treasurer; Time for delivery. §1445.

Delivery for deposit and disposition of property of person dying while confined in state correctional institution. §1446.

Delivery for deposit and disposition of property of person dying while confined in state institution. §1447.

Delivery for deposit and disposition of property of person dying while confined in state institution for juvenile delinquents. §1448.

Presumption of payment or delivery. §1449.

§1440. Property in estate paid to State, etc., deemed paid under provisions of article

Whenever, under the provisions of this title or under any other provision of law, any unclaimed money or other property in an estate of a deceased person, or any unclaimed amount payable pursuant to an allowed and approved claim against such an estate, is paid to the State or any officer or employee thereof for deposit in the State Treasury, it shall be deemed to have been so paid under the provisions of this article. **Leg.H.** Added Stats 1951 ch 1708 §5.

Prior Law: Former CCP §1440 repealed 1931. See Probate Code.

§1441. Escheated property

Money or other property distributed to the state under Chapter 6 (commencing with Section 11900) of Part 10 of Division 7 of the Probate Code, if not claimed within five years from the date of the order for distribution, as provided in Chapter 3, is permanently escheated to the state without further proceeding; saving, however, to infants and persons of unsound mind, the right to appear and file their claims within the time limited pursuant to Section 1430, or within one year after their respective disabilities cease; provided, however, that any such property shall be conclusively presumed to be permanently escheated to the state as to all persons in favor of a purchaser in good faith and for a valuable consideration from the state and anyone subsequently claiming under that purchaser, saving however, to infants and persons of unsound mind the right of recourse to the proceeds of any sale or other disposition of that property by the state and as herein provided. **Leg.H.** Added Stats 1951 ch 1708 §5. Amended Stats 1951 ch 1738 §4; Stats 1988 ch 1199 §10, operative July 1, 1989; Stats 1995 ch 105 §1 (SB 481).

§1442. Right to claim property paid into State Treasury

Except as otherwise provided in Section 1441, any money or other property paid into the State Treasury under the provisions of this article may be claimed by the person entitled thereto, as provided in Chapter 3. **Leg.H.** Added Stats 1951 ch 1708 §5.

§1443. Payment to state

Notwithstanding any other provision of law, all money or other property paid or delivered to the state or any officer or employee thereof under the provisions of Section 7643 or 11428, Chapter 6 (commencing with Section 11900) of Part 10 of Division 7, or Section 6800, of the Probate Code, or under any other section of the Probate Code, or any amendment thereof adopted after the effective date of this section, shall be deemed to be paid or delivered for deposit in the State Treasury under the provisions of this article, and shall be transmitted, received, accounted for, and disposed of, as provided in this title. **Leg.H.** Added Stats 1951 ch 1708 §5. Amended Stats 1953 ch 1758 §3; Stats 1983 ch 842 §13, operative January 1, 1985; Stats 1988 ch 1199 §11, operative July 1, 1989.

Prior Law: Former CCP §1443 repealed 1931. See Probate Code.

§1444. Transfer of possession of property held for known heirs, etc., to Treasurer or Controller

At the time of the next county settlement following the expiration of one year from the date of its deposit in the county treasury, all money or other property distributed in the administration of an estate of a deceased person and heretofore or hereafter deposited in the county treasury to the credit of known heirs, legatees, or devisees, and any money or other property remaining on deposit to the credit of an estate after final distribution to such known heirs, legatees or devisees, shall be paid to the Treasurer or Controller as provided in Chapter 2. **Leg.H.** Added Stats 1951 ch 1708 §5.

Prior Law: Former CCP §1444 repealed 1931. See Probate Code.

§1444.5. Escheat of money on deposit with county treasurer received from county public administrator in trust; Payment to State Treasurer and deposit in School Land Fund

Notwithstanding any other provision of law, any money on deposit with the county treasurer of a county received from a public administrator of the county in trust and to the account of the estate of a deceased person or the creditor of a deceased person, in an amount of fifty dollars ($50) or less as to any one estate or creditor, and not covered by a decree of distribution which was received or remained on hand after the final accounting in such deceased person's estate and the discharge of such public administrator as representative of the estate, and where the money has so remained on deposit in trust for a period of 15 years or more unclaimed by any heir, devisee or legatee of such deceased person, or by any creditor having an allowed and approved claim against the deceased person's estate remaining unpaid, shall be deemed permanently escheated to the State of California. The total of any such moneys so held in trust unclaimed for such period may be paid in a lump sum by the county treasurer, from such funds as he may have on hand for the purpose, to the State Treasurer, at the time of the next county settlement after the effective date of this section, or at any county settlement thereafter. Such lump sum payment may be made by designating it to have been made under this section, without the necessity of any further report or statement of the estates or claimants concerned, without the necessity of any order of court, and without being subject to the provisions of Section 1311 or 1312. Upon receipt by the State Treasurer, any permanently escheated money received by him under this section shall forthwith be deposited in the School Land Fund, subject only to the rights of minors and persons of unsound mind saved to them by Section 1430.

This section shall also apply in all respects to any money on deposit with a county treasurer received from the coroner of the county in trust and to the account of a deceased person, and any such money shall be held, deemed permanently escheated, reported and paid over in like manner as hereinabove set forth. **Leg.H.** Added Stats 1957 ch 1375 §1.

§1445. Transfer to State Treasury of undistributed funds, etc., of estate of decedent; Petition of county treasurer; Time for delivery

If money or other property is deposited in a county treasury, and if the deposits belong (1) to known decedents' estates on which letters testamentary or letters of administration have never been issued or (2) to known decedents' estates on which letters testamentary or letters of administration have been issued but no decree of distribution has been rendered, due to the absence of any parties interested in the estate or the failure of such parties diligently to protect their interests by taking reasonable steps for the purpose of securing a distribution of the estate, the county treasurer shall, within one year following the expiration of five years from the date of such deposit, file a petition in the superior court of the county in which the deposit is held, setting forth the fact that the money or other personal property has remained in the county treasury under such circumstances for such five-year period, and petitioning the court for an order directing him to pay such money or other property into the State Treasury.

At the time of the next county settlement following the date of the making of the order by the court, unless earlier payment is required by the Controller, the county treasurer shall pay such money or other property to the Treasurer or Controller as provided in Chapter 2. **Leg.H.** Added Stats 1951 ch 1708 §5.

Prior Law: Former CCP §1445 repealed 1931. See Probate Code.

§1446. Delivery for deposit and disposition of property of person dying while confined in state correctional institution

Notwithstanding any other provision of law, all unclaimed money or other property belonging to any person who dies while confined in any state institution subject to the jurisdiction of the Director of Corrections, which is paid or delivered to the State or any officer or employee thereof under the provisions of Section 5061 of the Penal Code, or under any amendment thereof adopted after the effective date of this section, shall be deemed to be paid or delivered for deposit in the State Treasury under the provisions of this article, and shall be transmitted, received, accounted for, and disposed of, as provided in this part. **Leg.H.** Added Stats 1951 ch 1708 §5.

Prior Law: Former CCP §1446 repealed 1931. See Probate Code.

§1447. Delivery for deposit and disposition of property of person dying while confined in state institution

Notwithstanding any other law, all unclaimed money or other property belonging to a person who dies while confined in a state institution subject to the jurisdiction of the State Department of State Hospitals, which is paid or delivered to the state or an officer or employee thereof under the provisions of Section 166 of the Welfare and Institutions Code, or under any amendment thereof adopted after the effective date of Chapter 1708 of the Statutes of 1951 shall be deemed to be paid or delivered for deposit in the State Treasury under the provisions of this article, and shall be transmitted, received, accounted for, and disposed of, as provided in this part. **Leg.H.** Added Stats 1951 ch 1708 §5. Amended Stats 2014 ch 144 §7 (AB 1847), effective January 1, 2015.

Prior Law: Former CCP §1447 repealed 1931. See Probate Code.

§1448. Delivery for deposit and disposition of property of person dying while confined in state institution for juvenile delinquents

Notwithstanding any other provision of law, all unclaimed money or other property belonging to any person who dies while confined in any state institution subject to the jurisdiction of the Youth Authority, which is paid or delivered to the State or any officer thereof under the provisions of Section 1015 of the Welfare and Institutions Code or under any amendment thereof adopted after the effective date of this section, shall be deemed to be paid or delivered for deposit in the State Treasury under the provisions of this article, and shall be transmitted, received, accounted for, and disposed of, as provided in this part. **Leg.H.** Added Stats 1951 ch 1708 §5.

Prior Law: Former CCP §1448 repealed 1931. See Probate Code.

§1449. Presumption of payment or delivery

Notwithstanding any other provision of law, all presumptively abandoned money or other property paid or delivered to the Treasurer or Controller under the provisions of Section 7644 of the Probate Code shall be deemed to be paid or delivered for deposit in the State Treasury under the provisions of this article, and shall be transmitted, received, accounted for, and disposed of as provided in this title. **Leg.H.** Added Stats 1953 ch 219 §2. Amended Stats 1988 ch 1199 §12, operative July 1, 1989.

Prior Law: Former CCP §1449 repealed 1931. See Probate Code.

§§1450–1459. [Sections repealed 1931]

Leg.H. Enacted 1872 or added Stats 1907 ch 264 §1. Repealed Stats 1931 ch 281 (Prob C §1700). See Prob C §§859, 8801, 8804, 8870, 8872, 9650, 13002, 13006, 13050, 13051, 13100–13112, 13603.

ARTICLE 2
Abandoned Property

Effect of expiration of time limit for commencement of action or proceeding to secure payment of claim, etc. §1476.

§§1460–1475. [Sections repealed 1959]

Leg.H. Added Stats 1951 ch 1708 §5. Repealed Stats 1959 ch 1809 §1. See CCP §§1500 et seq.

Prior Law: Former CCP §§1460–1475 repealed 1931. See Probate Code.

§1476. Effect of expiration of time limit for commencement of action or proceeding to secure payment of claim, etc.

The expiration of any period of time specified by law, during which an action or proceeding may be commenced or enforced to secure payment of a claim for money or recovery of property, shall not prevent any such money or other property from being deemed abandoned property, nor affect any duty to file a report required by this title or to deliver to the Treasurer or Controller any such abandoned property; and shall not serve as a defense in any action or proceeding brought under the provisions of this article to compel the filing of any report or the delivery of any abandoned property required by this article or to enforce or collect any penalty provided by this article. **Leg.H.** Added Stats 1951 ch 1708 §5.

Prior Law: Former CCP §1476 repealed 1931. See Probate Code.

§1477. [Section repealed 1953]

Leg.H. Added Stats 1951 ch 1708 §5. Repealed Stats 1953 ch 279 §2. See CCP §1321.

Prior Law: Former CCP §1477 repealed 1931. See Probate Code.

§1478. [Section repealed 1959]

Leg.H. Added Stats 1951 ch 1708 §5. Repealed Stats 1959 ch 1809 §1. See CCP §§1500 et seq.

Prior Law: Former CCP §1478 repealed 1931. See Probate Code.

§§1479–1499. [Sections repealed 1931]

Leg.H. Enacted 1872. Repealed Stats 1931 ch 281 (Prob C §1700). See Prob C §§58, 1220, 6520 et seq., 7060, 7070, 7071, 7263, 9000 et seq., 11423.

ARTICLES 3–15
[Repealed]

CHAPTER 7
UNCLAIMED PROPERTY LAW

Article 1. Short Title; Definitions; Application.
Article 2. Escheat of Unclaimed Personal Property.
Article 3. Identification of Escheated Property.
Article 4. Payment of Claims.
Article 5. Administration of Unclaimed Property.
Article 6. Compliance and Enforcement.
Article 7. Miscellaneous.

ARTICLE 1
Short Title; Definitions; Application

Citation of chapter. §1500.
Definitions. §1501.
Property received by state not to escheat; Legislative intent; Notification program. §1501.5.
Property not subject to chapter. §1502.
Examination from filing reports on, and delivering, "property not subject to old act", etc. §1503.
Inapplicability of chapter to property escheated under laws of another state; Exemption from delivering "property not subject to old act", etc. §1504.
Duties enforceable by State Controller irrespective of chapter; Penalties. §1505.
Chapter as restatements and continuations of former chapter. §1506.
[Sections renumbered 1969]. §1507, 1508.

§1500. Citation of chapter

This chapter may be cited as the Unclaimed Property Law. **Leg.H.** Added Stats 1959 ch 1809 §2. Amended Stats 1968 ch 356 §4, operative January 1, 1969.

Prior Law: Former CCP §1500 repealed 1931. See Probate Code.

§1501. Definitions

As used in this chapter, unless the context otherwise requires:

(a) "Apparent owner" means the person who appears from the records of the holder to be entitled to property held by the holder.

(b) "Banking organization" means any national or state bank, trust company, banking company, land bank, savings bank, safe-deposit company, private banker, or any similar organization.

(c) "Business association" means any private corporation, joint stock company, business trust partnership, or any association for business purposes of two or more individuals, whether or not for profit, including, but not by way of limitation, a banking organization, financial organization, life insurance corporation, and utility.

(d) "Financial organization" means any federal or state savings and loan association, building and loan association, credit union, investment company, or any similar organization.

(e) "Holder" means any person in possession of property subject to this chapter belonging to another, or who is trustee in case of a trust, or is indebted to another on an obligation subject to this chapter.

(f) "Life insurance corporation" means any association or corporation transacting the business of insurance on the lives of persons or insurance appertaining thereto, including, but not by way of limitation, endowments, and annuities.

(g) "Owner" means a depositor in case of a deposit, a beneficiary in case of a trust, or creditor, claimant, or payee in case of other choses in action, or any person having a legal or equitable interest in property subject to this chapter, or his or her legal representative.

(h) "Person" means any individual, business association, government or governmental subdivision or agency, two or more persons having a joint or common interest, or any other legal or commercial entity, whether that person is acting in his or her own right or in a representative or fiduciary capacity.

(i) "Employee benefit plan distribution" means any money, life insurance, endowment or annuity policy or proceeds thereof, securities or other intangible property, or any tangible property, distributable to a participant, former participant, or the beneficiary or estate or heirs of a participant or former participant or beneficiary, from a trust or custodial fund established under a plan to provide health and welfare, pension, vacation, severance, retirement benefit, death benefit, stock purchase, profit sharing, employee savings, supplemental unemployment insurance benefits or similar benefits, or which is established under a plan by a business association functioning as or in conjunction with a labor union which receives for distribution residuals on behalf of employees working under collective-bargaining agreements.

(j) "Residuals" means payments pursuant to a collective bargaining agreement of additional compensation for domestic and foreign uses of recorded materials. **Leg.H.** Added Stats 1959 ch 1809 §2. Amended Stats 1968 ch 356 §5, operative January 1, 1969; Stats 1972 ch 856 §2, operative January 1, 1973; Stats 1976 ch 582 §1; Stats 1977 ch 579 §36; Stats 1982 ch 786 §1; Stats 1984 ch 899 §1; Stats 1990 ch 450 §2 (SB 57), effective July 31, 1990.

Prior Law: Former CCP §1501 repealed 1931. See Probate Code.

§1501.5. Property received by state not to escheat; Legislative intent; Notification program

(a) Notwithstanding any provision of law to the contrary, property received by the state under this chapter shall not permanently escheat to the state.

(b) The Legislature finds and declares that this section is declaratory of the existing law and sets forth the intent of the Legislature regarding the Uniform Disposition of Unclaimed Property Act (Chapter 1809, Statutes of 1959) and all amendments thereto and revisions thereof. Any opinions, rulings, orders, judgments, or other statements to the contrary by any court are erroneous and inconsistent with the intent of the Legislature.

(c) It is the intent of the Legislature that property owners be reunited with their property. In making changes to the unclaimed property program, the Legislature intends to adopt a more expansive notification program that will provide all of the following:

(1) Notification by the state to all owners of unclaimed property prior to escheatment.

(2) A more expansive postescheatment policy that takes action to identify those owners of unclaimed property.

(3) A waiting period of not less than seven years from delivery of property to the state prior to disposal of any unclaimed property deemed to have no commercial value. **Leg.H.** Added Stats 1988 ch 286 §1. Amended Stats 2007 ch 179 §1 (SB 86), effective August 24, 2007; Stats 2014 ch 913 §10 (AB 2747), effective January 1, 2015.

§1502. Property not subject to chapter

(a) This chapter does not apply to any of the following:

(1) Any property in the official custody of a municipal utility district.

(2) Any property in the official custody of a local agency if such property may be transferred to the general fund of such agency under the provisions of Sections 50050-50053 of the Government Code.

(3) Any property in the official custody of a court if the property may be transferred to the Trial Court Operations Fund under Section 68084.1 of the Government Code.

(b) None of the provisions of this chapter applies to any type of property received by the state under the provisions of Chapter 1 (commencing with Section 1300) to Chapter 6 (commencing with Section 1440), inclusive, of this title. **Leg.H.** Added Stats 1959 ch 1809 §2 as CCP §1526. Amended and renumbered Stats 1968 ch 356 §6, operative January 1, 1969. Amended Stats 1976 ch 582 §2; Stats 2004 ch 227 §13 (SB 1102), effective August 16, 2004; Stats 2007 ch 738 §6 (AB 1248), effective January 1, 2008.

Prior Law: Former CCP §1502 was added by Stats 1959 ch 1809 §2, amended by Stats 1961 ch 1904 §1, and amended and renumbered §1513 by Stats 1968 ch 356 §12, operative January 1, 1969.

Original §1502 repealed 1931. See Probate Code.

§1502.5. [Section repealed 1977]

Leg.H. Added Stats 1968 ch 523 §1, operative January 1, 1969. Repealed Stats 1976 ch 30 §1. The repealed section related to inapplicability of chapter to property of interstate railroad company.

§1503. Examination from filing reports on, and delivering, "property not subject to old act", etc.

(a) As used in this section:

(1) "Old act" means this chapter as it existed prior to January 1, 1969.

(2) "New act" means this chapter as it exists on and after January 1, 1969.

(3) "Property not subject to the old act" means property that was not presumed abandoned under the old act and would never have been presumed abandoned under the old act had the old act continued in existence on and after January 1, 1969, without change.

(b) The holder is not required to file a report concerning, or to pay or deliver to the Controller, any property not subject to the old act if an action by the owner against the holder to recover that property was barred by an applicable statute of limitations prior to January 1, 1969.

(c) The holder is not required to file a report concerning, or to pay or deliver to the Controller, any property not subject to the old act, or any property that was not required to be reported under the old act, unless on January 1, 1969, the property has been held by the holder for less than the escheat period. "Escheat period" means the period referred to in Sections 1513 to 1521, inclusive, of the new act, whichever is applicable to the particular property. **Leg.H.** Added Stats 1968 ch 356 §7, operative January 1, 1969. Amended Stats 1990 ch 450 §3 (SB 57), effective July 31, 1990.

Prior Law: Former CCP §1503, similar to present CCP §1515, was added by Stats 1959 ch 1809 §2 and repealed by Stats 1968 ch 356 §14, operative January 1, 1969.

Original §1503 repealed 1931. See Probate Code.

§1504. Inapplicability of chapter to property escheated under laws of another state; Exemption from delivering "property not subject to old act", etc.

(a) As used in this section:

(1) "Old act" means this chapter as it existed prior to January 1, 1969.

(2) "New act" means this chapter as it exists on and after January 1, 1969.

(3) "Property not subject to the old act" means property that was not presumed abandoned under the old act and would never have been presumed abandoned under the old act had the old act continued in existence on and after January 1, 1969, without change.

(b) This chapter does not apply to any property that was escheated under the laws of another state prior to September 18, 1959.

(c) This chapter does not require the holder to pay or deliver any property not subject to the old act to this state if the property was escheated under the laws of another state prior to January 1, 1969, and was delivered to the custody of that state prior to January 1, 1970, in compliance with the laws of that state. Nothing in this subdivision affects or limits the right of the State Controller to recover such property from the other state. **Leg.H.** Added Stats 1968 ch 356 §8, operative January 1, 1969.

Prior Law: Former CCP §1504 was added by Stats 1959 ch 1809 §2, amended by Stats 1961 ch 1904 §2, and amended and renumbered §1516 by Stats 1968 ch 356 §16, operative January 1, 1969.

Original §1504 repealed 1931. See Probate Code.

§1505. Duties enforceable by State Controller irrespective of chapter; Penalties

This chapter does not affect any duty to file a report with the State Controller or to pay or deliver any property to him that arose prior to January 1, 1969, under the provisions of this chapter as existed prior to January 1, 1969. Such duties may be enforced by the State Controller, and the penalties for failure to perform such duties may be imposed, under the provisions of this chapter as it existed prior to January 1, 1969. The provisions of this chapter as it existed prior to January 1, 1969, are continued in existence for the purposes of this section. **Leg.H.** Added Stats 1968 ch 356 §9, operative January 1, 1969.

Prior Law: Former CCP §1505, similar to present CCP §1515, was added by Stats 1959 ch 1809 §2 and repealed by Stats 1968 ch 356 §17, operative January 1, 1969.

Original §1505 repealed 1931. See Probate Code.

§1506. Chapter as restatements and continuations of former chapter

The provisions of this chapter as it exists on and after January 1, 1969, insofar as they are substantially the same as the provisions of this chapter as it existed prior to January 1, 1969, relating to the same subject matter, shall be construed as restatements and continuations thereof and not as new enactments. **Leg.H.** Added Stats 1968 ch 356 §10, operative January 1, 1969.

Prior Law: Former CCP §1506 was added by Stats 1969 ch 1809 §2, amended by Stats 1961 ch 1904 §3, and amended and renumbered §1518 by Stats 1968 ch 356 §19, operative January 1, 1969.

Original §1506 repealed 1931. See Probate Code.

§§1507, 1508. [Sections renumbered 1969]

Leg.H. Added Stats 1959 ch 1809 §2. Amended and renumbered as CCP §§1519, 1520 Stats 1968 ch 356 §§20, 21 operative January 1, 1969.

Prior Law: Former CCP §§1507, 1508 repealed 1931. See Probate Code.

§1509. [Section repealed 1969]

Leg.H. Added Stats 1959 ch 1809 §2. Repealed Stats 1968 ch 356 §22, operative January 1, 1969.

Prior Law: Former CCP §1509 repealed 1931. See Probate Code.

ARTICLE 2
Escheat of Unclaimed Personal Property

Conditions for escheat. §1510.
Record of purchase; Place of business of seller; Instruments deemed abandoned. §1511.
[Section renumbered 1969]. §1512.
Unclaimed property held by business association. §1513.
Notice to owner by banking or financial organization. §1513.5.
Contents of deposit box; Notification. §1514.
Life insurance policy; Annuity. §1515.
Distributable property deemed abandoned in demutualization or related reorganization of insurance company. §1515.5.
Unclaimed dividend, profit, distribution, or other sum held by business association. §1516.
Distributions on dissolution or liquidation of business association. §1517.
Property held in fiduciary capacity; Income or increment; Property held by agent for business association. §1518.
Funds maintained in preneed funeral trust. § 1518.5.
Property held by government or government agency. §1519.
Escheat of unclaimed sums held by business association that have been ordered refunded. §1519.5.
Property held or owing in ordinary course of business; Required notice. § 1520.
Applicability of escheat provisions to gift certificates. §1520.5.
Property held or owing in ordinary course of business; Employee benefit plan distribution; Relief from forfeiture. §1521.
Service, handling, maintenance, or other charges. §1522.
Insurance rebates to policyholders who could not be located. §1523.
[Section renumbered 1969]. §1524.
[Section renumbered 1969]. §1525.
[Section renumbered 1969]. §1526.
[Section renumbered 1969]. §1527.
Unclaimed life insurance used for scholarships. §1528.

§1510. Conditions for escheat

Unless otherwise provided by statute of this state, intangible personal property escheats to this state under this chapter if the conditions for escheat stated in Sections 1513 through 1521 exist, and if:

(a) The last known address, as shown on the records of the holder, of the apparent owner is in this state.

(b) No address of the apparent owner appears on the records of the holder and:

(1) The last known address of the apparent owner is in this state; or

(2) The holder is domiciled in this state and has not previously paid the property to the state of the last known address of the apparent owner; or

(3) The holder is a government or governmental subdivision or agency of this state and has not previously paid the property to the state of the last known address of the apparent owner.

(c) The last known address, as shown on the records of the holder, of the apparent owner is in a state that does not provide by law for the escheat of such property and the holder is (1) domiciled in this state or (2) a government or governmental subdivision or agency of this state.

(d) The last known address, as shown on the records of the holder, of the apparent owner is in a foreign nation and the holder is (1) domiciled in this state or (2) a government or governmental subdivision or agency of this state. **Leg.H.** Added Stats 1968 ch 356 §11, operative January 1, 1969. Amended Stats 1972 ch 856 §3, operative January 1, 1973; Stats 1978 ch 1183 §17.

Prior Law: Former CCP §1510 was added by Stats 1959 ch 1809 §2, amended by Stats 1961 ch 1904 §4, and amended and renumbered §1530 by Stats 1968 ch 356 §24, operative January 1, 1969.

Former CCP §1510, relating to unclaimed moneys in litigation, was added by Stats 1951 ch 1708 §5 and repealed by Stats 1959 ch 1809 §1.

Original §1510 repealed 1931. See Probate Code.

§1511. Record of purchase; Place of business of seller; Instruments deemed abandoned

(a) Any sum payable on a money order, travelers check, or other similar written instrument (other than a third-party bank check) on which a business association is directly liable escheats to this state under this chapter if the conditions for escheat stated in Section 1513 exist and if:

(1) The books and records of such business association show that such money order, travelers check, or similar written instrument was purchased in this state;

(2) The business association has its principal place of business in this state and the books and records of the business association do not show the state in which such money order, travelers check, or similar written instrument was purchased; or

(3) The business association has its principal place of business in this state, the books and records of the business association show the state in which such money order, travelers check, or similar written instrument was purchased, and the laws of the state of purchase do not provide for the escheat of the sum payable on such instrument.

(b) Notwithstanding any other provision of this chapter, this section applies to sums payable on money orders, travelers checks, and similar written instruments deemed abandoned on or after February 1, 1965, except to the extent that such sums have been paid over to a state prior to January 1, 1974. For the purposes of this subdivision, the words "deemed abandoned" have the same meaning as those words have as used in Section 604 of Public Law 93-495 (October 28, 1974), 88th Statutes at Large 1500. **Leg.H.** Added Stats 1975 ch 25 §2.

Prior Law: Former CCP §1511, relating to last known address of owner of traveler's check or money order, was added by Stats 1968 ch 356 §13, operative January 1, 1969, and repealed by Stats 1975 ch 25 §1.

Former CCP §1511 was added by Stats 1959 ch 1809 §2 and amended and renumbered §1531 by Stats 1968 ch 356 §25, operative January 1, 1969.

Former CCP §1511, relating to issuance of court order when unclaimed moneys in litigation, was added by Stats 1951 ch 1708 §5 and repealed by Stats 1959 ch 1809 §1.

Original §1511 repealed 1931. See Probate Code.

§1512. [Section renumbered 1969]

Leg.H. Added Stats 1959 ch 1809 §2. Amended Stats 1961 ch 1904 §5. Amended and renumbered CCP §1532 Stats 1968 ch 356 §26, operative January 1, 1969.

Prior Law: Former CCP §1512, relating to right to claim money paid under article into State Treasury, was added by Stats 1951 ch 1708 §5 and repealed by Stats 1959 ch 1809 §1.

Original §1512 repealed 1931. See Probate Code.

§1513. Unclaimed property held by business association

(a) Subject to Sections 1510 and 1511, the following property held or owing by a business association escheats to this state:

(1)(A) Except as provided in paragraph (6), any demand, savings, or matured time deposit, or account subject to a negotiable order of withdrawal, made with a banking organization, together with any interest or dividends thereon, excluding, from demand deposits and accounts subject to a negotiable order of withdrawal only, any reasonable service charges that may lawfully be withheld and that do not, where made in this state, exceed those set forth in schedules filed by the banking organization from time to time with the Controller, if the owner, for more than three years, has not done any of the following:

(i) Increased or decreased the amount of the deposit, cashed an interest check, or presented the passbook or other similar evidence of the deposit for the crediting of interest.

(ii) Corresponded electronically or in writing with the banking organization concerning the deposit.

(iii) Otherwise indicated an interest in the deposit as evidenced by a memorandum or other record on file with the banking organization.

(B) A deposit or account shall not, however, escheat to the state if, during the previous three years, the owner has owned another deposit or account with the banking organization or the owner has owned an individual retirement account or funds held by the banking organization under a retirement plan for self-employed individuals or a similar account or plan established pursuant to the internal revenue laws of the United States or the laws of this state, as described in paragraph (6), and, with respect to that deposit, account, or plan, the owner has done any of the acts described in clause (i), (ii), or (iii) of subparagraph (A), and the banking organization has communicated electronically or in writing with the owner, at the address to which communications regarding that deposit, account, or plan are regularly sent, with regard to the deposit or account that would otherwise escheat under subparagraph (A). For purposes of this subparagraph, "communications" includes account statements or statements required under the internal revenue laws of the United States.

(C) No banking organization may discontinue any interest or dividends on any savings deposit because of the inactivity contemplated by this section.

(2)(A) Except as provided in paragraph (6), any demand, savings, or matured time deposit, or matured investment certificate, or account subject to a negotiable order of withdrawal, or other interest in a financial organization or any deposit made therewith, and any interest or dividends thereon, excluding, from demand deposits and accounts subject to a negotiable order of withdrawal only, any reasonable service charges that may lawfully be withheld and that do not, where made in this state, exceed those set forth in schedules filed by the financial organization from time to time with the Controller, if the owner, for more than three years, has not done any of the following:

(i) Increased or decreased the amount of the funds or deposit, cashed an interest check, or presented an appropriate record for the crediting of interest or dividends.

(ii) Corresponded electronically or in writing with the financial organization concerning the funds or deposit.

(iii) Otherwise indicated an interest in the funds or deposit as evidenced by a memorandum or other record on file with the financial organization.

(B) A deposit or account shall not, however, escheat to the state if, during the previous three years, the owner has owned another deposit or account with the financial organization or the owner has owned an individual retirement account or funds held by the financial organization under a retirement plan for self-employed individuals or a similar account or plan established pursuant to the internal revenue laws of the United States or the laws of this state, as described in paragraph (6), and, with respect to that deposit, account, or plan, the owner has done any of the acts described in clause (i), (ii), or (iii) of subparagraph (A), and the financial organization has communicated electronically or in writing with the owner, at the address to which communications regarding that deposit, account, or plan are regularly sent, with regard to the deposit or account that would otherwise escheat under subparagraph (A). For purposes of this subparagraph, "communications" includes account statements or statements required under the internal revenue laws of the United States.

(C) No financial organization may discontinue any interest or dividends on any funds paid toward purchase of shares or other interest, or on any deposit, because of the inactivity contemplated by this section.

(3) Any sum payable on a traveler's check issued by a business association that has been outstanding for more than 15 years from the date of its issuance, if the owner, for more than 15 years, has not corresponded in writing with the business association concerning it, or otherwise indicated an interest as evidenced by a memorandum or other record on file with the association.

(4) Any sum payable on any other written instrument on which a banking or financial organization is directly liable, including, by way of illustration but not of limitation, any draft, cashier's check, teller's check, or certified check, that has been outstanding for more than three years from the date it was payable, or from the date of its issuance if payable on demand, if the owner, for more than three years, has not corresponded electronically or in writing with the banking or financial organization concerning it, or otherwise indicated an interest as evidenced by a memorandum or other record on file with the banking or financial organization.

(5) Any sum payable on a money order issued by a business association including a banking or financial organization, that has been outstanding for more than seven years from the date it was payable, or from the date of its issuance if payable on demand, excluding any reasonable service charges that may lawfully be withheld and that do not, when made in this state, exceed those set forth in schedules filed by the business association from time to time with the Controller, if the owner, for more than seven years, has not corresponded electronically or in writing with the business association, banking, or financial organization concerning it, or otherwise indicated an interest as evidenced by a memorandum or other record on file with the business association. For the purposes of this subdivision, "reasonable service charge" means a service charge that meets all of the following requirements:

(A) It is uniformly applied to all of the issuer's money orders.

(B) It is clearly disclosed to the purchaser at the time of purchase and to the recipient of the money order.

(C) It does not begin to accrue until three years after the purchase date, and it stops accruing after the value of the money order escheats.

(D) It is permitted by contract between the issuer and the purchaser.

(E) It does not exceed 25 cents ($0.25) per month or the aggregate amount of twenty-one dollars ($21).

(6)(A) Any funds held by a business association in an individual retirement account or under a retirement plan for self-employed individuals or similar account or plan established pursuant to the internal revenue laws of the United States or of this state, if the owner, for more than three years after the funds become payable or distributable, has not done any of the following:

(i) Increased or decreased the principal.

(ii) Accepted payment of principal or income.

(iii) Corresponded electronically or in writing concerning the property or otherwise indicated an interest.

(B) Funds held by a business association in an individual retirement account or under a retirement plan for self-employed individuals or a similar account or plan created pursuant to the internal revenue laws of the United States or the laws of this state shall not escheat to the state if, during the previous three years, the owner has owned another such account, plan, or any other deposit or account with the business association and, with respect to that deposit, account, or plan, the owner has done any of the acts described in clause (i), (ii), or (iii) of subparagraph (A), and the business association has communicated electronically or in writing with the owner, at the address to which communications regarding that deposit, account, or plan are regularly sent, with regard to the account or plan that would otherwise escheat under subparagraph (A). For purposes of this subparagraph, "communications" includes account statements or statements required under the internal revenue laws of the United States.

(C) These funds are not payable or distributable within the meaning of this subdivision unless either of the following is true:

(i) Under the terms of the account or plan, distribution of all or a part of the funds would then be mandatory.

(ii) For an account or plan not subject to mandatory distribution requirement under the internal revenue laws of the United States or the laws of this state, the owner has attained 70 1/2 years of age.

(7) Any wages or salaries that have remained unclaimed by the owner for more than one year after the wages or salaries become payable.

(b) For purposes of this section, "service charges" means service charges imposed because of the inactivity contemplated by this section.

(c) A holder shall, commencing on or before January 1, 2018, regard the following transactions that are initiated electronically and are reflected in the books and records of the banking or financial organization as evidence that an owner has increased or decreased the amount of the funds or deposit in an account, for purposes of paragraphs (1) and (2) of subdivision (a):

(1) A single or recurring debit transaction authorized by the owner.

(2) A single or recurring credit transaction authorized by the owner.

(3) Recurring transactions authorized by the owner that represent payroll deposits or deductions.

(4) Recurring credits authorized by the owner or a responsible party that represent the deposit of any federal benefits, including social security benefits, veterans' benefits, and pension payments. **Leg.H.** Added Stats 1959 ch 1809 §2 as §1502. Amended Stats 1961 ch 1904 §1; Amended and renumbered Stats 1968 ch 356 §12, operative January 1, 1969; Amended Stats 1975 ch 578 §1; Stats 1976 ch 1214 §1; Stats 1978 ch

1183 §17.5; Stats 1981 ch 831 §1.5; Stats 1982 ch 786 §2; Stats 1983 ch 104 §1; Stats 1988 ch 286 §2; Stats 1990 ch 450 §4 (SB 57), effective July 31, 1990, ch 1069 §1 (SB 1186), effective September 18, 1990; Stats 1999 ch 835 §1 (AB 777); Stats 2003 ch 304 §1 (AB 378); Stats 2009 ch 522 §1 (AB 1291), effective January 1, 2010; Stats 2011 ch 305 §1 (SB 495), effective January 1, 2012; Stats 2016 ch 463 §1 (AB 2258), effective January 1, 2017.

Prior Law: Former CCP §1513 was added Stats 1959 ch 1809 §2, amended Stats 1961 ch 1904 §6, and amended and renumbered CCP §1560 by Stats 1968 ch 356 §34, operative January 1, 1969.

Former CCP §1513, relating to application of title, was added Stats 1951 ch 1708 §5 and repealed Stats 1959 ch 1809 §1.

Original §1513 repealed 1931. See Probate Code.

1990 Note: For purposes of clarification only, the Legislature hereby declares that, by the enactment of Chapter 450 of the Statutes of 1990 and this act, the Legislature intends that all business associations holding property which on June 30, 1990, or thereafter is unclaimed for more than three years, as specified in the provisions of Chapter 450 of the Statutes of 1990 and as amended by this act, shall be reported and paid or delivered to the Controller in accordance with the applicable law as amended by Chapter 450 of the Statutes of 1990 and this act. Stats 1990 ch 1069 §5.

§1513.5. Notice to owner by banking or financial organization

(a) Except as provided in subdivision (c), if the holder has in its records an address for the apparent owner, which the holder's records do not disclose to be inaccurate, every banking or financial organization shall make reasonable efforts to notify any owner by mail or, if the owner has consented to electronic notice, electronically, that the owner's deposit, account, shares, or other interest in the banking or financial organization will escheat to the state pursuant to clause (i), (ii), or (iii) of subparagraph (A) of paragraph (1), (2), or (6) of subdivision (a) of Section 1513. The holder shall give notice either:

(1) Not less than two years nor more than two and one-half years after the date of last activity by, or communication with, the owner with respect to the account, deposit, shares, or other interest, as shown on the record of the banking or financial organization.

(2) Not less than 6 nor more than 12 months before the time the account, deposit, shares, or other interest becomes reportable to the Controller in accordance with this chapter.

(b) The notice required by this section shall specify the time that the deposit, account, shares, or other interest will escheat and the effects of escheat, including the necessity for filing a claim for the return of the deposit, account, shares, or other interest. The face of the notice shall contain a heading at the top that reads as follows: "THE STATE OF CALIFORNIA REQUIRES US TO NOTIFY YOU THAT YOUR UNCLAIMED PROPERTY MAY BE TRANSFERRED TO THE STATE IF YOU DO NOT CONTACT US," or substantially similar language. The notice required by this section shall, in boldface type or in a font a minimum of two points larger than the rest of the notice, exclusive of the heading, (1) specify that since the date of last activity, or for the last two years, there has been no owner activity on the deposit, account, shares, or other interest; (2) identify the deposit, account, shares, or other interest by number or identifier, which need not exceed four digits; (3) indicate that the deposit, account, shares, or other interest is in danger of escheating to the state; and (4) specify that the Unclaimed Property Law requires banking and financial organizations to transfer funds of a deposit, account, shares, or other interest if it has been inactive for three years. It shall also include a form, as prescribed by the Controller, by which the owner may declare an intention to maintain the deposit, account, shares, or other interest. If that form is filled out, signed by the owner, and returned to the banking or financial organization, it shall satisfy the requirement of clause (iii) of subparagraph (A) of paragraph (1), clause (iii) of subparagraph (A) of paragraph (2), or clause (iii) of subparagraph (A) of paragraph (6) of subdivision (a) of Section 1513. In lieu of returning the form, the banking or financial organization may provide a telephone number or other electronic means to enable the owner to contact that organization. The contact, as evidenced by a memorandum or other record on file with the banking or financial organization, shall satisfy the requirement of clause (iii) of subparagraph (A) of paragraph (1), clause (iii) of subparagraph (A) of paragraph (2), or clause (iii) of subparagraph (A) of paragraph (6) of subdivision (a) of Section 1513. If the deposit, account, shares, or other interest has a value greater than two dollars ($2), the banking or financial organization may impose a service charge on the deposit, account, shares, or other interest for this notice in an amount not to exceed the administrative cost of mailing or electronically sending the notice and form and in no case to exceed two dollars ($2).

(c) Notice as provided by subdivisions (a) and (b) shall not be required for deposits, accounts, shares, or other interests of less than fifty dollars ($50), and, except as provided in subdivision (b), no service charge may be made for notice on these items.

(d) In addition to the notices required pursuant to subdivision (a), the holder may give additional notice as described in subdivision (b) at any time between the date of last activity by, or communication with, the owner and the date the holder transfers the deposit, account, shares, or other interest to the Controller.

(e) At the time a new account is opened with a banking or financial organization, the organization shall provide a written notice to the person opening the account informing the person that his or her property may be transferred to the appropriate state if no activity occurs in the account within the time period specified by state law. If the person opening the account has consented to electronic notice, that notice may be provided electronically. **Leg.H.** Added Stats 1976 ch 1214 §2. Amended Stats 1981 ch 831 §2; Stats 1988 ch 286 §3; Stats 1990 ch 450 §5 (SB 57), effective July 31, 1990, ch 1069 §2 (SB 1186), effective September 18, 1990; Stats 1993 ch 692 §2 (AB 1854); Stats 1994 ch 587 §8.5 (AB 3600); Stats 1996 ch 762 §3 (SB 2014); Stats 2002 ch 813 §1 (AB 1772), operative January 1, 2004; Stats 2009 ch 522 §2 (AB 1291), effective January 1, 2010; Stats 2011 ch 305 §2 (SB 495), effective January 1, 2012; Stats 2013 ch 362 §1 (AB 212), effective January 1, 2014.

1990 Note: See note following CCP §1513.

§1514. Contents of deposit box; Notification

(a) The contents of, or the proceeds of sale of the contents of, any safe deposit box or any other safekeeping repository, held in this state by a business association, escheat to this state if unclaimed by the owner for more than three years from the date on which the lease or rental period on the box or other repository expired, or from the date of termination of any agreement because of which the box or other repository was furnished to the owner without cost, whichever last occurs.

(b) If a business association has in its records an address for an apparent owner of the contents of, or the proceeds of sale of the contents of, a safe deposit box or other safekeeping repository described in subdivision (a), and the records of the business association do not disclose the address to be inaccurate, the business association shall make reasonable efforts to notify the owner by mail, or, if the owner has consented to electronic notice, electronically, that the owner's contents, or the proceeds of the sale of the contents, will escheat to the state pursuant to this section. The business association shall give notice not less than 6 months and not more than 12 months before the time the contents, or the proceeds of the sale of the contents, become reportable to the Controller in accordance with this chapter.

(c) The face of the notice shall contain a heading at the top that reads as follows: "THE STATE OF CALIFORNIA REQUIRES US TO NOTIFY YOU THAT YOUR UNCLAIMED PROPERTY MAY BE TRANSFERRED TO THE STATE IF YOU DO NOT CONTACT US," or substantially similar language. The notice required by this subdivision shall specify the date that the property will escheat and the effects of escheat, including the necessity for filing a claim for the return of the property. The notice required by this section shall, in boldface type or in a font a minimum of two points larger than the rest of the notice, exclusive of the heading, do all of the following:

(1) Identify the safe deposit box or other safekeeping repository by number or identifier.

(2) State that the lease or rental period on the box or repository has expired or the agreement has terminated.

(3) Indicate that the contents of, or the proceeds of sale of the contents of, the safe deposit box or other safekeeping repository will escheat to the state unless the owner requests the contents or their proceeds.

(4) Specify that the Unclaimed Property Law requires business associations to transfer the contents of, or the proceeds of sale of the contents of, a safe deposit box or other safekeeping repository to the Controller if they remain unclaimed for more than three years.

(5) Advise the owner to make arrangements with the business association to either obtain possession of the contents of, or the proceeds of

sale of the contents of, the safe deposit box or other safekeeping repository, or enter into a new agreement with the business association to establish a leasing or rental arrangement. If an owner fails to establish such an arrangement prior to the end of the period described in subdivision (a), the contents or proceeds shall escheat to this state.

(d) In addition to the notice required pursuant to subdivision (b), the business association may give additional notice in accordance with subdivision (c) at any time between the date on which the lease or rental period for the safe deposit box or repository expired, or from the date of the termination of any agreement, through which the box or other repository was furnished to the owner without cost, whichever is earlier, and the date the business association transfers the contents of, or the proceeds of sale of the contents of, the safe deposit box or other safekeeping repository to the Controller.

(e) The contents of, or the proceeds of sale of the contents of, a safe deposit box or other safekeeping repository shall not escheat to the state if, as of June 30 or the fiscal yearend next preceding the date on which a report is required to be filed under Section 1530, the owner has owned, with a banking organization providing the safe deposit box or other safekeeping repository, any demand, savings, or matured time deposit, or account subject to a negotiable order of withdrawal, which has not escheated under Section 1513 and is not reportable under subdivision (d) of Section 1530.

(f) The contents of, or the proceeds of sale of the contents of, a safe deposit box or other safekeeping repository shall not escheat to the state if, as of June 30 or the fiscal yearend next preceding the date on which a report is required to be filed under Section 1530, the owner has owned, with a financial organization providing the safe deposit box or other safekeeping repository, any demand, savings, or matured time deposit, or matured investment certificate, or account subject to a negotiable order of withdrawal, or other interest in a financial organization or any deposit made therewith, and any interest or dividends thereon, which has not escheated under Section 1513 and is not reportable under subdivision (d) of Section 1530.

(g) The contents of, or the proceeds of sale of the contents of, a safe deposit box or other safekeeping repository shall not escheat to the state if, as of June 30 or the fiscal yearend next preceding the date on which a report is required to be filed under Section 1530, the owner has owned, with a banking or financial organization providing the safe deposit box or other safekeeping repository, any funds in an individual retirement account or under a retirement plan for self-employed individuals or similar account or plan pursuant to the internal revenue laws of the United States or the income tax laws of this state, which has not escheated under Section 1513 and is not reportable under subdivision (d) of Section 1530.

(h) In the event the owner is in default under the safe deposit box or other safekeeping repository agreement and the owner has owned any demand, savings, or matured time deposit, account, or plan described in subdivision (e), (f), or (g), the banking or financial organization may pay or deliver the contents of, or the proceeds of sale of the contents of, the safe deposit box or other safekeeping repository to the owner after deducting any amount due and payable from those proceeds under that agreement. Upon making that payment or delivery under this subdivision, the banking or financial organization shall be relieved of all liability to the extent of the value of those contents or proceeds.

(i) For new accounts opened for a safe deposit box or other safekeeping repository with a business association on and after January 1, 2011, the business association shall provide a written notice to the person leasing the safe deposit box or safekeeping repository informing the person that his or her property, or the proceeds of sale of the property, may be transferred to the appropriate state upon running of the time period specified by state law from the date the lease or rental period on the safe deposit box or repository expired, or from the date of termination of any agreement because of which the box or other repository was furnished to the owner without cost, whichever is earlier.

(j) A business association may directly escheat the contents of a safe deposit box or other safekeeping repository without exercising its rights under Article 2 (commencing with Section 1630) of Chapter 17 of Division 1 of the Financial Code. **Leg.H.** Added Stats 1968 ch 356 §13, operative January 1, 1969. Amended Stats 1979 ch 761 §1; Stats 1988 ch 286 §4; Stats 1990 ch 450 §6 (SB 57), effective July 31, 1990; Stats 2009 ch 522 §3 (AB 1291), effective January 1, 2010; Stats 2011 ch 305 §3 (SB 495), effective January 1, 2012; Stats 2012 ch 162 §16 (SB 1171), effective January 1, 2013.

Prior Law: Former CCP §1514 was added Stats 1959 ch 1809 §2, amended Stats 1961 ch 1904 §7, and renumbered CCP §1562 by Stats 1968 ch 356 §36, operative January 1, 1969.

Original CCP §1514 repealed 1931. See Probate Code.

§1515. Life insurance policy; Annuity

(a) Subject to Section 1510, funds held or owing by a life insurance corporation under any life or endowment insurance policy or annuity contract which has matured or terminated escheat to this state if unclaimed and unpaid for more than three years after the funds became due and payable as established from the records of the corporation.

(b) If a person other than the insured or annuitant is entitled to the funds and no address of that person is known to the corporation or if it is not definite and certain from the records of the corporation what person is entitled to the funds, it is presumed that the last known address of the person entitled to the funds is the same as the last known address of the insured or annuitant according to the records of the corporation. This presumption is a presumption affecting the burden of proof.

(c) A life insurance policy not matured by actual proof of the death of the insured according to the records of the corporation is deemed to be matured and the proceeds due and payable if:

(1) The insured has attained, or would have attained if he or she were living, the limiting age under the mortality table on which the reserve is based.

(2) The policy was in force at the time the insured attained, or would have attained, the limiting age specified in paragraph (1).

(3) Neither the insured nor any other person appearing to have an interest in the policy has, within the preceding three years, according to the records of the corporation (i) assigned, readjusted, or paid premiums on the policy, (ii) subjected the policy to loan, or (iii) corresponded in writing with the life insurance corporation concerning the policy.

(d) Any funds otherwise payable according to the records of the corporation are deemed due and payable although the policy or contract has not been surrendered as required. **Leg.H.** Added Stats 1968 ch 356 §15, operative January 1, 1969. Amended Stats 1988 ch 286 §5; Stats 1990 ch 450 §7 (SB 57), effective July 31, 1990; Stats 1993 ch 692 §3 (AB 1854).

Prior Law: Former CCP §1515 was added by Stats 1959 ch 1809 §2 and amended and renumbered §1570 by Stats 1968 ch 356 §42, operative January 1, 1969.

§1515.5. Distributable property deemed abandoned in demutualization or related reorganization of insurance company

Property distributable in the course of a demutualization or related reorganization of an insurance company is deemed abandoned as follows:

(a) On the date of the demutualization or reorganization, if the instruments or statements reflecting the distribution are not mailed to the owner because the address on the books and records for the holder is known to be incorrect.

(b) Two years after the date of the demutualization or reorganization, if instruments or statements reflecting the distribution are mailed to the owner and returned by the post office as undeliverable and the owner has done neither of the following:

(1) Communicated in writing with the holder or its agent regarding the property.

(2) Otherwise communicated with the holder or its agent regarding the property as evidenced by a memorandum or other record on file with the holder or its agent.

(c) Three years after the date of the demutualization or reorganization, if instruments or statements reflecting the distribution are mailed to the owner and not returned by the post office as undeliverable and the owner has done neither of the following:

(1) Communicated in writing with the holder or its agent regarding the property.

(2) Otherwise communicated with the holder or its agent regarding the property as evidenced by a memorandum or other record on file with the holder or its agent. **Leg.H.** Added Stats 2003 ch 304 §2 (AB 378).

§1516. Unclaimed dividend, profit, distribution, or other sum held by business association

(a) Subject to Section 1510, any dividend, profit, distribution, interest, payment on principal, or other sum held or owing by a business association for or to its shareholder, certificate holder, member, bondholder, or other security holder, or a participating patron of a cooperative, who has not claimed it, or corresponded in writing with the business association concerning it, within three years after the date prescribed for payment or delivery, escheats to this state.

(b) Subject to Section 1510, any intangible interest in a business association, as evidenced by the stock records or membership records of the association, escheats to this state if (1) the interest in the association is owned by a person who for more than three years has neither claimed a dividend or other sum referred to in subdivision (a) nor corresponded in writing with the association or otherwise indicated an interest as evidenced by a memorandum or other record on file with the association, and (2) the association does not know the location of the owner at the end of the three-year period. With respect to the interest, the business association shall be deemed the holder.

(c) Subject to Section 1510, any dividends or other distributions held for or owing to a person at the time the stock or other security to which they attach escheats to this state also escheat to this state as of the same time.

(d) If the business association has in its records an address for the apparent owner, which the business association's records do not disclose to be inaccurate, with respect to any interest that may escheat pursuant to subdivision (b), the business association shall make reasonable efforts to notify the owner by mail or, if the owner has consented to electronic notice, electronically, that the owner's interest in the business association will escheat to the state. The notice shall be given not less than 6 nor more than 12 months before the time the interest in the business association becomes reportable to the Controller in accordance with this chapter. The face of the notice shall contain a heading at the top that reads as follows: "THE STATE OF CALIFORNIA REQUIRES US TO NOTIFY YOU THAT YOUR UNCLAIMED PROPERTY MAY BE TRANSFERRED TO THE STATE IF YOU DO NOT CONTACT US," or substantially similar language. The notice required by this subdivision shall specify the time that the interest will escheat and the effects of escheat, including the necessity for filing a claim for the return of the interest. The notice required by this section shall, in boldface type or in a font a minimum of two points larger than the rest of the notice, exclusive of the heading, (1) specify that since the date of last activity, or for the last two years, there has been no owner activity on the deposit, account, shares, or other interest; (2) identify the deposit, account, shares, or other interest by number or identifier, which need not exceed four digits; (3) indicate that the deposit, account, shares, or other interest is in danger of escheating to the state; and (4) specify that the Unclaimed Property Law requires business associations to transfer funds of a deposit, account, shares, or other interest if it has been inactive for three years. It shall also include a form, as prescribed by the Controller, by which the owner may confirm the owner's current address. If that form is filled out, signed by the owner, and returned to the holder, it shall be deemed that the business association knows the location of the owner. In lieu of returning the form, the business association may provide a telephone number or other electronic means to enable the owner to contact the association. With that contact, as evidenced by a memorandum or other record on file with the business association, the business association shall be deemed to know the location of the owner. The business association may impose a service charge on the deposit, account, shares, or other interest for this notice and form in an amount not to exceed the administrative cost of mailing or electronically sending the notice and form, and in no case to exceed two dollars ($2).

(e) In addition to the notice required pursuant to subdivision (d), the holder may give additional notice as described in subdivision (d) at any time between the date of last activity by, or communication with, the owner and the date the holder transfers the deposit, shares, or other interest to the Controller.

(f) The interest that escheats pursuant to subdivision (b) shall not be reportable pursuant to Section 1530 unless and until the per share value, as set forth in Section 1172.80 of Title 2 of the California Code of Regulations, is equal to or greater than one cent ($0.01) or the aggregate value of the security held exceeds one thousand dollars ($1,000). **Leg.H.** Added Stats 1959 ch 1809 §2 as CCP §1504. Amended Stats 1961 ch 1904 §2; Amended and renumbered Stats 1968 ch 356 §16, operative January 1, 1969; Amended Stats 1975 ch 578 §1.5; Stats 1988 ch 286 §6; Stats 1990 ch 450 §8 (SB 57), effective July 31, 1990; Stats 1993 ch 692 §4 (AB 1854); Stats 2002 ch 813 §2 (AB 1772), operative January 1, 2004; Stats 2009 ch 522 §4 (AB 1291), effective January 1, 2010; Stats 2011 ch 305 §4 (SB 495), effective January 1, 2012; Stats 2022 ch 420 §12 (AB 2960), effective January 1, 2023.

Prior Law: Former CCP §1516 was added Stats 1959 ch 1809 §2, amended Stats 1963 ch 669 §1, and amended and renumbered §1563 by Stats 1968 ch 356 §37, operative January 1, 1969.

Original §1516 repealed 1931. See Probate Code.

§1517. Distributions on dissolution or liquidation of business association

(a) All property distributable in the course of a voluntary or involuntary dissolution or liquidation of a business association that is unclaimed by the owner within six months after the date of final distribution or liquidation escheats to this state.

(b) All property distributable in the course of voluntary or involuntary dissolution or liquidation of an insurer or other person brought under Article 14 (commencing with Section 1010) of Chapter 1 of Part 2 of Division 1 of the Insurance Code, that is unclaimed by the owner after six months of the date of final distribution, shall be transferred to the Department of Insurance, with any proceeds of sale of property and other funds to be deposited in the Insurance Fund for expenditure as provided in Section 12937 of the Insurance Code.

(c) This section applies to all tangible personal property located in this state and, subject to Section 1510, to all intangible personal property. **Leg.H.** Added Stats 1968 ch 356 §18, operative January 1, 1969. Amended Stats 1996 ch 187 §1 (AB 3137), effective July 19, 1996.

Prior Law: Former CCP §1517 was added Stats 1959 ch 1809 §2 and amended and renumbered §1564 by Stats 1968 ch 356 §38, operative January 1, 1969.

Original §1517 repealed 1931. See Probate Code.

§1518. Property held in fiduciary capacity; Income or increment; Property held by agent for business association

(a)(1) All tangible personal property located in this state and, subject to Section 1510, all intangible personal property, including intangible personal property maintained in a deposit or account, and the income or increment on such tangible or intangible property, held in a fiduciary capacity for the benefit of another person escheats to this state if for more than three years after it becomes payable or distributable, the owner has not done any of the following:

(A) Increased or decreased the principal.
(B) Accepted payment of principal or income.
(C) Corresponded in writing concerning the property.
(D) Otherwise indicated an interest in the property as evidenced by a memorandum or other record on file with the fiduciary.

(2) Notwithstanding paragraph (1), tangible or intangible property, and the income or increment on the tangible or intangible property, held in a fiduciary capacity for another person shall not escheat to the state if the requirements of subparagraphs (A) and (B) are satisfied.

(A) During the previous three years, the fiduciary took one of the following actions:

(i) Held another deposit or account for the benefit of the owner.
(ii) Maintained a deposit or account on behalf of the owner in an individual retirement account.
(iii) Held funds or other property under a retirement plan for a self-employed individual, or similar account or plan, established pursuant to the internal revenue laws of the United States or the laws of this state.

(B) During the previous three years, the owner has done any of the acts described in subparagraph (A), (B), (C), or (D) of paragraph (1) with respect to the deposit, account, or plan described in subparagraph (A), and the fiduciary has communicated electronically or in writing with the owner at the address to which communications regarding that deposit, account, or plan are regularly sent, with regard to the deposit, account, or plan that would otherwise escheat under this subdivision. "Communications," for purposes of this subparagraph, includes account statements or statements required under the internal revenue laws of the United States.

(b) Funds in an individual retirement account or a retirement plan for self-employed individuals or similar account or plan established pursuant to the internal revenue laws of the United States or of this state are not payable or distributable within the meaning of subdivision (a) unless either of the following is true:

(1) Under the terms of the account or plan, distribution of all or part of the funds would then be mandatory.

(2) For an account or plan not subject to mandatory distribution requirement under the internal revenue laws of the United States or the laws of this state, the owner has attained 70½ years of age.

(c) For the purpose of this section, when a person holds property as an agent for a business association, he or she is deemed to hold the property in a fiduciary capacity for the business association alone, unless the agreement between him or her and the business association clearly provides the contrary. For the purposes of this chapter, if a person holds property in a fiduciary capacity for a business association alone, he or she is the holder of the property only insofar as the interest of the business association in the property is concerned and the association is deemed to be the holder of the property insofar as the interest of any other person in the property is concerned. **Leg.H.** Added Stats 1959 ch 1809 §2 as CCP §1506. Amended Stats 1961 ch 1904 §3; Amended and renumbered Stats 1968 ch 356 §19, operative January 1, 1969; Amended Stats 1976 ch 49 §1; Stats 1982 ch 786 §3; Stats 1988 ch 286 §7; Stats 1990 ch 450 §9 (SB 57), effective July 31, 1990; Stats 2011 ch 305 §5 (SB 495), effective January 1, 2012.

Prior Law: Former CCP §1518, similar to present CCP §1540, was added by Stats 1959 ch 1809 §2 and repealed by Stats 1968 ch 356 §29, operative January 1, 1969.

§ 1518.5. Funds maintained in preneed funeral trust

(a) Subject to Section 1510, funds maintained in a preneed funeral trust or similar account or plan escheat to the state if, for more than three years after the funds became payable and distributable pursuant to subdivision (b), as established from the records of the funeral establishment or trustee, the beneficiary or trustor has not corresponded electronically or in writing concerning the property or otherwise indicated an interest, as evidenced by a memorandum or other record on file with the funeral establishment or trustee.

(b) For the purposes of this section, the corpus of a preneed funeral trust or similar account or plan, together with any income accrued, less a revocation fee not to exceed the amount reserved pursuant to Section 7735 of the Business and Professions Code, becomes payable and distributable under any of the following circumstances:

(1) The beneficiary of the trust attained, or would have attained if living, 105 years of age.

(2) Forty-five years have passed since execution of the preneed funeral agreement.

(3) The holder received notification of the death or presumed death of the beneficiary and has not provided the contracted funeral merchandise or services.

(4) The preneed funeral trust is a preneed installment trust and the amount due to the funeral establishment from the trustor has not been paid during the three preceding years and neither the trustor nor the beneficiary has communicated with either the funeral establishment or the trustee about the preneed funeral installment trust during that three-year period.

(c) For purposes of this section, except subdivision (d), the funeral establishment obligated to provide preneed funeral services under the trust or similar account or plan is the holder. For purposes of subdivision (d), the trustee is the holder.

(d)(1) All funds, including accrued income and revocation fees reserved pursuant to Section 7735 of the Business and Professions Code, maintained in a preneed funeral trust or similar account or plan held by a trustee for a funeral establishment that has been dissolved, closed, or had its license revoked shall escheat to the state if unclaimed by the funeral establishment, beneficiary, trustor, or legal representative of either the beneficiary or trustor within six months after the date of final distribution or liquidation.

(2) Notwithstanding paragraph (1), the revocation fee pursuant to Section 7735 of the Business and Professions Code shall not be retained by the funeral establishment.

(e) Escheatment of preneed funeral trust funds to the Controller shall release the funeral establishment from the obligation of furnishing the personal property, funeral merchandise, or services originally arranged in the preneed funeral agreement associated with the trust. However, if the funeral establishment provided personal property, or funeral merchandise or services to the beneficiary after funds have escheated, the funeral establishment shall be entitled to recover the escheated funds upon submission to the Controller of a death certificate and a statement detailing the personal property or funeral merchandise or services provided pursuant to Section 1560.

(f) Nothing in this section, or any other law or regulation, shall require escheatment of any funds received by a funeral establishment, cemetery, or other person from property or funeral merchandise or services provided under Chapter 4 (commencing with Section 8600) of Part 3 of Division 8 of the Health and Safety Code.

(g) A trustee or a funeral establishment shall not charge the trust, a trustor, or a beneficiary any fees or costs associated with a search or verification conducted pursuant to this section. However, a trustee or funeral establishment may incorporate fees or costs associated with a search or verification as part of the administration of the trust pursuant to Section 7735 of the Business and Professions Code.

(h) Delivery of the corpus of the trust, and the income accrued to the trust, to the funeral establishment, the trustor, the beneficiary, or the Controller pursuant to this article shall relieve the trustee of any further liability with regard to those funds.

(i) This section shall become operative on January 1, 2023. **Leg.H.** Added Stats 2021 ch 514 §5 (AB 293), effective January 1, 2022, operative January 1, 2023.

§1519. Property held by government or government agency

All tangible personal property located in this state, and, subject to Section 1510, all intangible personal property, held for the owner by any government or governmental subdivision or agency, that has remained unclaimed by the owner for more than three years escheats to this state. **Leg.H.** Added Stats 1959 ch 1809 §2 as CCP §1507. Amended and renumbered Stats 1968 ch 356 §20, operative January 1, 1969; Amended Stats 1988 ch 286 §8; Stats 1990 ch 450 §10 (SB 57), effective July 31, 1990.

Prior Law: Former CCP §1519, similar to present CCP §1540, was added by Stats 1959 ch 1809 §2 and repealed by Stats 1968 ch 356 §30, operative January 1, 1969.

§1519.5. Escheat of unclaimed sums held by business association that have been ordered refunded

Subject to Section 1510, any sums held by a business association that have been ordered to be refunded by a court or an administrative agency including, but not limited to, the Public Utilities Commission, which have remained unclaimed by the owner for more than one year after becoming payable in accordance with the final determination or order providing for the refund, whether or not the final determination or order requires any person entitled to a refund to make a claim for it, escheats to this state.

It is the intent of the Legislature that the provisions of this section shall apply retroactively to all funds held by business associations on or after January 1, 1977, and which remain undistributed by the business association as of the effective date of this act.

Further, it is the intent of the Legislature that nothing in this section shall be construed to change the authority of a court or administrative agency to order equitable remedies. **Leg.H.** Added Stats 1984 ch 1096 §1.

§ 1520. Property held or owing in ordinary course of business; Required notice

(a) All tangible personal property located in this state and, subject to Section 1510, all intangible personal property, except property of the classes mentioned in Sections 1511, 1513, 1514, 1515, 1515.5, 1516, 1517, 1518, 1518.5, 1519, and 1521, including any income or increment thereon and deducting any lawful charges, that is held or owing in the ordinary course of the holder's business and has remained unclaimed by the owner for more than three years after it became payable or distributable escheats to this state.

(b) Except as provided in subdivision (a) of Section 1513.5, subdivision (b) of Section 1514, and subdivision (d) of Section 1516, if the holder has in its records an address for the apparent owner of property valued at fifty dollars ($50) or more, which the holder's records do not disclose to be inaccurate, the holder shall make reasonable efforts to notify the owner by mail or, if the owner has consented to electronic notice, electronically, that the owner's property will escheat to the state pursuant to this chapter. The notice shall be mailed not less than 6 nor more than 12 months before the time when the owner's property held by the business becomes reportable to the Controller in accordance with this chapter. The face of the notice shall contain a heading at the top that reads as follows: "THE STATE OF CALIFORNIA REQUIRES US TO NOTIFY YOU THAT YOUR UNCLAIMED PROPERTY MAY BE TRANSFERRED TO THE STATE IF YOU DO NOT CONTACT US," or substantially similar language. The notice required by this subdivision shall specify the time when the property will escheat and the effects of escheat, including the need to file a claim in order for the owner's property to be returned to the owner. The notice required by this section shall, in boldface type or in a font a minimum of two points larger than the rest of the notice, exclusive of the heading, (1) specify that since the date of last activity, or for the last two years, there has been no owner activity on the deposit, account, shares, or other interest; (2) identify the deposit, account, shares, or other interest by number or identifier, which need not exceed four digits; (3) indicate that the deposit, account, shares, or other interest is in danger of escheating to the state; and (4) specify that the Unclaimed Property Law requires holders to transfer funds of a deposit, account, shares, or other interest if it has been inactive for three years. It shall also include a form, as prescribed by the Controller, by which the owner may confirm the owner's current address. If that form is filled out, signed by the owner, and returned to the holder, it shall be deemed that the account, or other device in which the owner's property is being held, remains currently active and recommences the escheat period. In lieu of returning the form, the holder may provide a telephone number or other electronic means to enable the owner to contact the holder. With that contact, as evidenced by a memorandum or other record on file with the holder, the account or other device in which the owner's property is being held shall be deemed to remain currently active and shall recommence the escheat period. The holder may impose a service charge on the deposit, account, shares, or other interest for this notice in an amount not to exceed the administrative cost of mailing or electronically sending the notice and form, and in no case to exceed two dollars ($2).

(c) In addition to the notice required pursuant to subdivision (b), the holder may give additional notice as described in subdivision (b) at any time between the date of last activity and the date the holder transfers the property to the Controller.

(d) For purposes of this section, "lawful charges" means charges that are specifically authorized by statute, other than the Unclaimed Property Law, or by a valid, enforceable contract.

(e) This section shall become operative on January 1, 2023. **Leg.H.** Added Stats 2021 ch 514 §7 (AB 293), effective January 1, 2022, operative January 1, 2023.

Prior Law Former CCP §1520 was added Stats 1959 ch 1809 §2 and amended and renumbered CCP §1541 by Stats 1968 ch 356 §31, operative January 1, 1969.

Former CCP §1520, relating to moneys with county treasurer as ex officio treasurer of dissolved irrigation district, was added Stats 1951 ch 1708 §5 and repealed Stats 1959 ch 1809 §1.

Former CCP §1520, relating to property held or owing in ordinary course of business, was added Stats 1959 ch 1809 §2, as CCP §1508, amended and renumbered Stats 1968 ch 356 §21, operative January 1, 1969, amended Stats 1975 ch 578 §2, Stats 1978 ch 1183 §18, Stats 1988 ch 286 §9, Stats 1990 ch 450 §11 (SB 57), effective July 31, 1990, Stats 1996 ch 762 §4 (SB 2014), Stats 2002 ch 813 §3 (AB 1772), operative January 1, 2004, Stats 2003 ch 304 §3 (AB 378), Stats 2009 ch 522 §5 (AB 1291), effective January 1, 2010, Stats 2011 ch 305 §6 (SB 495), effective January 1, 2012, and repealed January 1, 2023, by its own terms.

§1520.5. Applicability of escheat provisions to gift certificates

Section 1520 does not apply to gift certificates subject to Title 1.4A (commencing with Section 1749.45) of Part 4 of Division 3 of the Civil Code. However, Section 1520 applies to any gift certificate that has an expiration date and that is given in exchange for money or any other thing of value. **Leg.H.** Added Stats 1996 ch 933 §2 (AB 2466). Amended Stats 1997 ch 472 §2 (AB 1054); Stats 2003 ch 116 §3 (AB 1092).

2003 Note: The enactment of this act creates no inference with respect to the validity or invalidity of any service fee imposed prior to the effective date of this act. Stats 2003 ch 116 (AB 1092) §4.

§1521. Property held or owing in ordinary course of business; Employee benefit plan distribution; Relief from forfeiture

(a) Except as provided in subdivision (b), and subject to Section 1510, all employee benefit plan distributions and any income or other increment thereon escheats to the state if the owner has not, within three years after it becomes payable or distributable, accepted the distribution, corresponded in writing concerning the distribution, or otherwise indicated an interest as evidenced by a memorandum or other record on file with the fiduciary of the trust or custodial fund or administrator of the plan under which the trust or fund is established. As used in this section, "fiduciary" means any person exercising any power, authority, or responsibility of management or disposition with respect to any money or other property of a retirement system or plan, and "administrator" means the person specifically so designated by the plan, trust agreement, contract, or other instrument under which the retirement system or plan is operated, or if none is designated, the employer.

(b) Except as provided in subdivision (c), an employee benefit plan distribution and any income or other increment thereon shall not escheat to this state if, at the time the distribution shall become payable to a participant in an employee benefit plan, the plan contains a provision for forfeiture or expressly authorizes the administrator to declare a forfeiture of a distribution to a beneficiary thereof who cannot be found after a period of time specified in the plan, and the trust or fund established under the plan has not terminated prior to the date on which the distribution would become forfeitable in accordance with the provision.

(c) A participant entitled to an employee benefit plan distribution in the form of residuals shall be relieved from a forfeiture declared under subdivision (b) upon the making of a claim therefor. **Leg.H.** Added Stats 1972 ch 856 §4, operative January 1, 1973. Amended Stats 1982 ch 786 §4; Stats 1984 ch 899 §2; Stats 1988 ch 286 §10; Stats 1990 ch 450 §12 (SB 57), effective July 31, 1990.

Prior Law: Former CCP §1521 was added by Stats 1959 ch 1809 §2, amended by Stats 1961 ch 1904 §8, and amended and renumbered §1565 by Stats 1968 ch 356 §39, operative January 1, 1969.

Original §1521, relating to issuance of court order when moneys with county treasurer as ex officio treasurer of dissolved irrigation district, was added by Stats 1951 ch 1708 §5 and repealed by Stats 1959 ch 1809 §1.

§1522. Service, handling, maintenance, or other charges

No service, handling, maintenance or other charge or fee of any kind which is imposed because of the inactive or unclaimed status contemplated by this chapter, may be deducted or withheld from any property subject to escheat under this chapter, unless specifically permitted by this chapter.

Even when specifically permitted by this chapter, such charges or fees may not be excluded, withheld or deducted from property subject to this chapter if, under its policy or procedure, the holder would not have excluded, withheld or deducted such charges or fees in the event the property had been claimed by the owner prior to being reported or remitted to the Controller. **Leg.H.** Added Stats 1975 ch 578 §3. Amended Stats 1981 ch 831 §3.

Prior Law: Former CCP §1522 was added by Stats 1959 ch 1809 §2 and amended and renumbered §1571 by Stats 1968 ch 356 §43, operative January 1, 1969.

Former CCP §1522, relating to right to claim money paid under article into State Treasury, was added by Stats 1951 ch 1708 §5 and repealed by Stats 1959 ch 1809 §1.

Original §1522 repealed 1931. See Probate Code.

§1523. Insurance rebates to policyholders who could not be located

If an insurer, after a good faith effort to locate and deliver to a policyholder a Proposition 103 rebate ordered or negotiated pursuant to Section 1861.01 of the Insurance Code, determines that a policyholder cannot be located, all funds attributable to that rebate escheat to the state and shall be delivered to the Controller. The funds subject to escheat on or after July 1, 1997, shall be transferred by the Controller to the Department of Insurance for deposit in the Insurance Fund in the following amounts and for the following purposes:

(a) Up to the amount that will repay principal and interest on the General Fund loan authorized by Item 0845-001-0001 of the Budget Act of 1996 for expenditure as provided in Section 12936 of the Insurance Code.

(b) The sum of four million dollars ($4,000,000) for expenditure during the 1998–1999 fiscal year as provided in Section 12967 of the Insurance Code. **Leg.H.** Added Stats 1996 ch 187 §2 (AB 3137), effective July 19, 1996. Amended Stats 1997 ch 239 §1 (SB 18), effective August 6, 1997; Stats 1998 ch 963 §1 (SB 1530), effective September 29, 1998.

Prior Law: Former CCP §1523, similar to present CCP §1572, was added Stats 1959 ch 1809 §2, and repealed Stats 1968 ch 356 §44, operative January 1, 1969.

Former CCP §1523, similar to present Prob C §§1203, 1220, 10000, 10003, 10200, 10201, was enacted 1872, amended Code Amdts 1873–74 ch 383 §189, Code Amdts 1880 ch 85 §69, Stats 1919 ch 539 §4, Stats 1921 ch 184 §1, Stats 1927 ch 547 §1, and repealed 1931.

§1524. [Section renumbered 1969]

Leg.H. Added Stats 1959 ch 1809 §2. Amended and renumbered CCP §1576 by Stats 1968 ch 356 §49, operative January 1, 1969.

Prior Law: Former CCP §1524 repealed 1931. See Probate Code.

§1525. [Section renumbered 1969]

Leg.H. Added Stats 1959 ch 1809 §2. Amended and renumbered CCP §1580 by Stats 1968 ch 356 §51, operative January 1, 1969.

Prior Law: Former CCP §1525 repealed 1931. See Probate Code.

§1526. [Section renumbered 1969]

Leg.H. Added Stats 1959 ch 1809 §2. Amended and renumbered CCP §1502 by Stats 1968 ch 356 §6, operative January 1, 1969.

Prior Law: Former CCP §1526 repealed 1931. See Probate Code.

§1527. [Section renumbered 1969]

Leg.H. Added Stats 1959 ch 1809 §2. Amended and renumbered CCP §1582 by Stats 1968 ch 356 §53, operative January 1, 1969.

Prior Law: Former CCP §1527, relating to sale of personal property of deceased person, was added Stats 1905 p 242 and repealed Stats 1923 p 46 756.

§1528. Unclaimed life insurance used for scholarships

This chapter does not apply to unclaimed funds held by a life insurance corporation which is organized or admitted as a domestic fraternal benefit society under Chapter 10 (commencing with Section 10970) of Part 2 of Division 2 of the Insurance Code, so long as such funds are used for scholarship funds, exclusive of costs of administration thereof. **Leg.H.** Added Stats 1974 ch 1050 §1.

Prior Law: Former CCP §1528 repealed 1931. See Probate Code.

§1529. [Section repealed 1931]

Leg.H. Enacted 1872; Repealed Stats 1931 ch 281 (Prob C §1700). The repealed section related to sale of mine or interest in mine owned or held by decedent's estate.

ARTICLE 3
Identification of Escheated Property

Report by holder; Form and contents; Verification. §1530.
Notice by publication and mail required. §1531.
Notification program; Location of owner of unclaimed property. §1531.5.
Separate notice to apparent owner of United States savings bond, war bond, or military award. §1531.6.
Payment or delivery to Controller; Report of property not subject to escheat; Intangible interest in business association; Place of payment or delivery; Electronic funds transfers; Definitions. §1532.
Payment or delivery of contents of safe deposit box or safekeeping repository. §1532.1.
Controller's determination not to take custody of tangible property, and notice thereof. §1533.

§1530. Report by holder; Form and contents; Verification

(a) Every person holding funds or other property escheated to this state under this chapter shall report to the Controller as provided in this section.

(b) The report shall be on a form prescribed or approved by the Controller and shall include:

(1) Except with respect to traveler's checks and money orders, the name, if known, and last known address, if any, of each person appearing from the records of the holder to be the owner of any property of value of at least fifty dollars ($50) escheated under this chapter. This paragraph shall become inoperative on July 1, 2014.

(2) Except with respect to traveler's checks and money orders, the name, if known, and last known address, if any, of each person appearing from the records of the holder to be the owner of any property of value of at least twenty-five dollars ($25) escheated under this chapter. This paragraph shall become operative on July 1, 2014.

(3) In the case of escheated funds of life insurance corporations, the full name of the insured or annuitant, and his or her last known address, according to the life insurance corporation's records.

(4) In the case of the contents of a safe deposit box or other safekeeping repository or in the case of other tangible property, a description of the property and the place where it is held and may be inspected by the Controller. The report shall set forth any amounts owing to the holder for unpaid rent or storage charges and for the cost of opening the safe deposit box or other safekeeping repository, if any, in which the property was contained.

(5) The nature and identifying number, if any, or description of any intangible property and the amount appearing from the records to be due, except that items of value under twenty-five dollars ($25) each may be reported in aggregate.

(6) Except for any property reported in the aggregate, the date when the property became payable, demandable, or returnable, and the date of the last transaction with the owner with respect to the property.

(7) Other information which the Controller prescribes by rule as necessary for the administration of this chapter.

(c) If the holder is a successor to other persons who previously held the property for the owner, or if the holder has changed his or her name while holding the property, he or she shall file with his or her report all prior known names and addresses of each holder of the property.

(d) The report shall be filed before November 1 of each year as of June 30 or fiscal yearend next preceding, but the report of life insurance corporations, and the report of all insurance corporation demutualization proceeds subject to Section 1515.5, shall be filed before May 1 of each year as of December 31 next preceding. The initial report for property subject to Section 1515.5 shall be filed on or before May 1, 2004, with respect to conditions in effect on December 31, 2003, and all property shall be determined to be reportable under Section 1515.5 as if that section were in effect on the date of the insurance company demutualization or related reorganization. The Controller may postpone the reporting date upon his or her own motion or upon written request by any person required to file a report.

(e) The report, if made by an individual, shall be verified by the individual; if made by a partnership, by a partner; if made by an unincorporated association or private corporation, by an officer; and if made by a public corporation, by its chief fiscal officer or other employee authorized by the holder. **Leg.H.** Added Stats 1959 ch 1809 §2, as CCP §1510. Amended Stats 1961 ch 1904 §4. Amended and renumbered Stats 1968 ch 356 §24, operative January 1, 1969. Amended Stats 1990 ch 1069 §3 (SB 1186), effective September 18, 1990; Stats 1993 ch 692 §5 (AB 1854); Stats 1996 ch 762 §5 (SB 2014); Stats 2003 ch 304 §4 (AB 378); Stats 2013 ch 362 §2 (AB 212), effective January 1, 2014; Stats 2014 ch 71 §21 (SB 1304), effective January 1, 2015.

Prior Law: Former CCP §1530, relating to litigation deposits in federal court, was added Stats 1951 ch 1708 §5 and repealed Stats 1959 ch 1809 §1.

Original §1530 repealed 1931. See Probate Code.

§1531. Notice by publication and mail required

(a) Within one year after payment or delivery of escheated property as required by Section 1532, the Controller shall cause a notice to be published in a manner that the Controller determines to be reasonable, which may include, but not be limited to, newspapers, Internet Web sites, radio, television, or other media. In carrying out this duty, the Controller shall not use any of the following:

(1) Money appropriated for the Controller's audit programs.

(2) More money than the Legislature appropriates for this subdivision's purpose.

(3) A photograph in a notice.

(4) An elected official's name in a notice.

(b) Within 165 days after the final date for filing the report required by Section 1530, the Controller shall mail a notice to each person having an address listed in the report who appears to be entitled to property of the value of fifty dollars ($50) or more escheated under this chapter. If the report filed pursuant to Section 1530 includes a social security number, the Controller shall request the Franchise Tax Board to provide a current address for the apparent owner on the basis of that number. The Controller shall mail the notice to the apparent owner for whom a current address is obtained if the address is different from the address previously reported to the Controller. If the Franchise Tax Board does not provide an address or a different address, then the Controller shall mail the notice to the address listed in the report required by Section 1530.

(c) The mailed notice shall contain all of the following:

(1) A statement that, according to a report filed with the Controller, property is being held to which the addressee appears entitled.

(2) The name and address of the person holding the property and any necessary information regarding changes of name and address of the holder.

(3) A statement that, if satisfactory proof of claim is not presented by the owner to the holder by the date specified in the notice, the property will be placed in the custody of the Controller and may be sold or

destroyed pursuant to this chapter, and all further claims concerning the property or, if sold, the net proceeds of its sale, must be directed to the Controller.

(d) This section is intended to inform owners about the possible existence of unclaimed property identified pursuant to this chapter. **Leg.H.** Added Stats 1959 ch 1809 §2, as CCP §1511. Amended and renumbered Stats 1968 ch 356 §25, operative January 1, 1969. Amended Stats 1975 ch 25 §3; Stats 1978 ch 1184 §1; Stats 1979 ch 761 §2; Stats 1983 ch 323 §1, effective July 21, 1983; Stats 1990 ch 450 §13 (SB 57), effective July 31, 1990; Stats 1996 ch 762 §6 (SB 2014); Stats 2007 ch 179 §2 (SB 86), effective August 24, 2007; Stats 2017 ch 200 §1 (AB 772), effective January 1, 2018.

Prior Law: Former CCP §1531, relating to transmittal of property, was added Stats 1951 ch 1708 §5 and repealed Stats 1959 ch 1809 §1.

Former CCP §1531 repealed 1931. See Probate Code.

§1531.1. [Section repealed 1984]

Leg.H. Added Stats 1978 ch 1184 §1.5. Repealed Stats 1983 ch 323 §1.4, effective July 21, 1983. The repealed section related to establishment of procedure to locate owners of unclaimed property.

§1531.5. Notification program; Location of owner of unclaimed property

(a) The Controller shall establish and conduct a notification program designed to inform owners about the possible existence of unclaimed property received pursuant to this chapter.

(b) Any notice sent pursuant to this section shall not contain a photograph or likeness of an elected official.

(c)(1) Notwithstanding any other law, upon the request of the Controller, a state or local governmental agency may furnish to the Controller from its records the address or other identification or location information that could reasonably be used to locate an owner of unclaimed property.

(2) If the address or other identification or location information requested by the Controller is deemed confidential under any laws or regulations of this state, it shall nevertheless be furnished to the Controller. However, neither the Controller nor any officer, agent, or employee of the Controller shall use or disclose that information except as may be necessary in attempting to locate the owner of unclaimed property.

(3) This subdivision shall not be construed to require disclosure of information in violation of federal law.

(4) If a fee or charge is customarily made for the information requested by the Controller, the Controller shall pay that customary fee or charge.

(d) Costs for administering this section shall be subject to the level of appropriation in the annual Budget Act. **Leg.H.** Added Stats 2007 ch 179 §3 (SB 86), effective August 24, 2007.

§1531.6. Separate notice to apparent owner of United States savings bond, war bond, or military award

(a) In addition to the notices required pursuant to this chapter, the Controller may mail a separate notice to an apparent owner of a United States savings bond, war bond, or military award whose name is shown on or can be associated with the contents of a safe deposit box or other safekeeping repository and is different from the reported owner of the safe deposit box or other safekeeping repository.

(b) A notice sent pursuant to this section shall not contain a photograph or likeness of an elected official.

(c)(1) Notwithstanding any other law, upon request of the Controller, a state or local governmental agency may furnish to the Controller from its records the address or other identification or location information that could reasonably be used to locate an owner of unclaimed property.

(2) If the address or other identification or location information requested by the Controller is deemed confidential under any law or regulation of the state, it shall nevertheless be furnished to the Controller. However, neither the Controller nor any officer, agent, or employee of the Controller shall use or disclose that information, except as may be necessary in attempting to locate the owner of unclaimed property.

(3) This subdivision shall not be construed to require disclosure of information in violation of federal law.

(4) If a fee or charge is customarily made for the information requested by the Controller, the Controller shall pay the customary fee or charge.

(d) Costs for administering this section shall be subject to the level of appropriation in the annual Budget Act. **Leg.H.** Added Stats 2015 ch 297 §1 (AB 355), effective January 1, 2016.

§1532. Payment or delivery to Controller; Report of property not subject to escheat; Intangible interest in business association; Place of payment or delivery; Electronic funds transfers; Definitions

(a) Every person filing a report as provided by Section 1530 shall, no sooner than seven months and no later than seven months and 15 days after the final date for filing the report, pay or deliver to the Controller all escheated property specified in the report. Any payment of unclaimed cash in an amount of at least two thousand dollars ($2,000) shall be made by electronic funds transfer pursuant to regulations adopted by the Controller. The Controller may postpone the date for payment or delivery of the property, and the date for any report required by subdivision (b), upon the Controller's own motion or upon written request by any person required to pay or deliver the property or file a report as required by this section.

(b) If a person establishes their right to receive any property specified in the report to the satisfaction of the holder before that property has been delivered to the Controller, or it appears that, for any other reason, the property may not be subject to escheat under this chapter, the holder shall not pay or deliver the property to the Controller but shall instead file a report with the Controller, on a form and in a format prescribed or approved by the Controller, containing information pertaining to the property subject to escheat.

(c) Any property not paid or delivered pursuant to subdivision (b) that is later determined by the holder to be subject to escheat under this chapter shall not be subject to the interest provision of Section 1577.

(d) The holder of any interest under subdivision (b) of Section 1516 shall deliver a duplicate certificate to the Controller or shall register the securities in uncertificated form in the name of the Controller. Upon delivering a duplicate certificate or providing evidence of registration of the securities in uncertificated form to the Controller, the holder, any transfer agent, registrar, or other person acting for or on behalf of the holder in executing or delivering the duplicate certificate or registering the uncertificated securities, shall be relieved from all liability of every kind to any person including, but not limited to, any person acquiring the original certificate or the duplicate of the certificate issued to the Controller for any losses or damages resulting to that person by the issuance and delivery to the Controller of the duplicate certificate or the registration of the uncertificated securities to the Controller.

(e) Payment of any intangible property to the Controller shall be made at the office of the Controller in Sacramento or at another location as the Controller by regulation may designate. Except as otherwise agreed by the Controller and the holder, tangible personal property shall be delivered to the Controller at the place where it is held.

(f) Payment is deemed complete on the date the electronic funds transfer is initiated if the settlement to the state's demand account occurs on or before the banking day following the date the transfer is initiated. If the settlement to the state's demand account does not occur on or before the banking day following the date the transfer is initiated, payment is deemed to occur on the date settlement occurs.

(g) Any person required to pay cash by electronic funds transfer who makes the payment by means other than an authorized electronic funds transfer shall be liable for a civil penalty of 2 percent of the amount of the payment that is due pursuant to this section, in addition to any other penalty provided by law. Penalties are due at the time of payment. If the Controller finds that a holder's failure to make payment by an appropriate electronic funds transfer in accordance with the Controller's procedures is due to reasonable cause and circumstances beyond the holder's control, and occurred notwithstanding the exercise of ordinary care and in the absence of willful neglect, that holder shall be relieved of the penalties.

(h) An electronic funds transfer shall be accomplished by an automated clearinghouse debit, an automated clearinghouse credit, a Federal Reserve Wire Transfer (Fedwire), or by an international funds transfer. Banking costs incurred for the automated clearinghouse debit transaction by the holder shall be paid by the state. Banking costs incurred by the state for the automated clearinghouse credit transaction may be paid by the holder originating the credit. Banking costs incurred for the Fedwire transaction charged to the holder and the state shall be paid by the person originating the transaction. Banking costs charged to the holder and to the state for an international funds transfer may be charged to the holder.

(i) For purposes of this section:

(1) "Electronic funds transfer" means any transfer of funds, other than a transaction originated by check, draft, or similar paper instrument, that

is initiated through an electronic terminal, telephonic instrument, modem, computer, or magnetic tape, so as to order, instruct, or authorize a financial institution to credit or debit an account.

(2) "Automated clearinghouse" means any federal reserve bank, or an organization established by agreement with the National Automated Clearing House Association or any similar organization, that operates as a clearinghouse for transmitting or receiving entries between banks or bank accounts and that authorizes an electronic transfer of funds between those banks or bank accounts.

(3) "Automated clearinghouse debit" means a transaction in which the state, through its designated depository bank, originates an automated clearinghouse transaction debiting the holder's bank account and crediting the state's bank account for the amount of payment.

(4) "Automated clearinghouse credit" means an automated clearinghouse transaction in which the holder, through its own bank, originates an entry crediting the state's bank account and debiting the holder's bank account.

(5) "Fedwire" means any transaction originated by the holder and utilizing the national electronic payment system to transfer funds through federal reserve banks, pursuant to which the holder debits its own bank account and credits the state's bank account.

(6) "International funds transfer" means any transaction originated by the holder and utilizing the international electronic payment system to transfer funds, pursuant to which the holder debits its own bank account, and credits the funds to a United States bank that credits the Unclaimed Property Fund. **Leg.H.** Added Stats 1959 ch 1809 §2, as CCP §1512. Amended Stats 1961 ch 1904 §5. Amended and renumbered Stats 1968 ch 356 §26, operative January 1, 1969. Amended Stats 1978 ch 1183 §20; Stats 1990 ch 450 §14 (SB 57), effective July 31, 1990; Stats 1996 ch 762 §7 (SB 2014); Stats 2003 ch 228 §7 (AB 1756), effective August 11, 2003; Stats 2004 ch 520 §2 (AB 2530); Stats 2007 ch 179 §4 (SB 86), effective August 24, 2007; Stats 2009 ch 522 §6 (AB 1291), effective January 1, 2010; Stats 2011 ch 305 §7 (SB 495), effective January 1, 2012; Stats 2021 ch 103 §1 (SB 308), effective January 1, 2022.

Prior Law: Former CCP §1532, relating to claims in litigation deposits in federal courts, was added by Stats 1951 ch 1708 §5 and repealed by Stats 1959 ch 1809 §1.

Original §1532 repealed 1931. See Probate Code.

§1532.1. Payment or delivery of contents of safe deposit box or safekeeping repository

Notwithstanding Sections 1531 and 1532, property that escheats to the state pursuant to Section 1514 shall not be paid or delivered to the state until the earlier of (a) the time when the holder is requested to do so by the Controller or (b) within one year after the final date for filing the report required by Section 1530 as specified in subdivision (d) of Section 1530. Within one year after receipt of property as provided by this section, the Controller shall cause a notice to be published as provided in Section 1531. **Leg.H.** Added Stats 1990 ch 450 §15 (SB 57), effective July 31, 1990. Amended Stats 1990 ch 1069 §4 (SB 1186), effective September 18, 1990; Stats 1996 ch 762 §8 (SB 2014).

1990 Note: See note following CCP §1513.

§1533. Controller's determination not to take custody of tangible property, and notice thereof

Tangible personal property may be excluded from the notices required by Section 1531, shall not be delivered to the State Controller, and shall not escheat to the state, if the State Controller, in his discretion, determines that it is not in the interest of the state to take custody of the property and notifies the holder in writing, within 120 days from receipt of the report required by Section 1530, of his determination not to take custody of the property. **Leg.H.** Added Stats 1968 ch 356 §27, operative January 1, 1969.

Prior Law: Former CCP §1533 repealed 1931. See Probate Code.

§1536. [Section repealed 1931]

Leg.H. Enacted 1872. Repealed Stats 1931 ch 281 (Prob C §1700). See Prob C §10003.

ARTICLE 4
Payment of Claims

Filing of claim. §1540.
Action to establish claim. §1541.
Right of another state to recover property; Claim, and proceedings thereon. §1542.
Streamlining secure payment of claims. § 1543.

§1540. Filing of claim

(a) Any person, excluding another state, who claims to have been the owner, as defined in subdivision (d), of property paid or delivered to the Controller under this chapter may file a claim to the property or to the net proceeds from its sale. The claim shall be on a form prescribed by the Controller and shall be verified by the claimant.

(b) The Controller shall consider each claim within 180 days after it is filed to determine if the claimant is the owner, as defined in subdivision (d), and may hold a hearing and receive evidence. The Controller shall give written notice to the claimant if the Controller denies the claim in whole or in part. The notice may be given by mailing it to the address, if any, stated in the claim as the address to which notices are to be sent. If no address is stated in the claim, the notice may be mailed to the address, if any, of the claimant as stated in the claim. A notice of denial need not be given if the claim fails to state either an address to which notices are to be sent or an address of the claimant.

(c) Interest shall not be payable on any claim paid under this chapter.

(d) Notwithstanding subdivision (g) of Section 1501, for purposes of filing a claim pursuant to this section, "owner" means the person who had legal right to the property before its escheat, the person's heirs or estate representative, the person's guardian or conservator, or a public administrator acting pursuant to the authority granted in Sections 7660 and 7661 of the Probate Code. An "owner" also means a nonprofit civic, charitable, or educational organization that granted a charter, sponsorship, or approval for the existence of the organization that had the legal right to the property before its escheat but that has dissolved or is no longer in existence, if the charter, sponsorship, approval, organization bylaws, or other governing documents provide that unclaimed or surplus property shall be conveyed to the granting organization upon dissolution or cessation to exist as a distinct legal entity. Only an owner, as defined in this subdivision, may file a claim with the Controller pursuant to this article.

(e) Following a public hearing, the Controller shall adopt guidelines and forms that shall provide specific instructions to assist owners in filing claims pursuant to this article.

(f) Notwithstanding any other provision, property reported to, and received by, the Controller pursuant to this chapter in the name of a state agency, including the University of California and the California State University, or a local agency, including a school district and community college district, may be transferred by the Controller directly to the state or local agency without the filing of a claim. Property transferred pursuant to this subdivision is immune from suit pursuant to Section 1566 in the same manner as if the state or local agency had filed a claim to the property. For purposes of this subdivision, "local agency" means a city, county, city and county, or district. **Leg.H.** Added Stats 1968 ch 356 §28, operative January 1, 1969. Amended Stats 1976 ch 49 §2, ch 1151 §1; Stats 1978 ch 815 §1; Stats 1998 ch 1029 §1 (AB 698); Stats 2002 ch 1124 §3 (AB 3000), effective September 30, 2002; Stats 2003 ch 228 §8 (AB 1756), effective August 11, 2003; Stats 2005 ch 706 §15 (AB 1742), effective January 1, 2006; Stats 2013 ch 128 §1 (AB 1275), effective January 1, 2014; Stats 2014 ch 330 §1 (AB 1712), effective January 1, 2015; Stats 2019 ch 320 §1 (AB 1637), effective January 1, 2020; Stats 2020 ch 36 §26 (AB 3364), effective January 1, 2021.

Prior Law: Former CCP §1540, relating to property in custody of federal officers or agencies, was added Stats 1951 ch 1708 §5 and repealed Stats 1959 ch 1809 §1.

2003 Note: The changes made by this act to Section 1540 of the Code of Civil Procedure shall apply to any claims for which the Controller has not made a decision by the earlier of July 1, 2003, or the effective date of this act [August 11, 2003]. Stats 2003 ch 228 (AB 1756) §57.

§1541. Action to establish claim

Any person aggrieved by a decision of the Controller or as to whose claim the Controller has failed to make a decision within 180 days after the filing of the claim, may commence an action, naming the Controller as a defendant, to establish his or her claim in the superior court in any county or city and county in which the Attorney General has an office. The action shall be brought within 90 days after the decision of the Controller or within 270 days from the filing of the claim if the Controller fails to make a decision. The summons and a copy of the complaint shall be served upon the Controller and the Attorney General and the Controller shall have 60 days within which to respond by answer. The action shall be tried without a jury. **Leg.H.** Added Stats 1959 ch 1809 §2, as CCP §1520. Amended and renumbered Stats 1968 ch 356 §31, operative January 1, 1969. Amended Stats 1978 ch 1183 §21; Amended Stats 2003 ch 228 §9 (AB 1756), effective August 11, 2003.

Prior Law: Former CCP §1541, relating to transmittal of property, was added by Stats 1951 ch 1708 §5 and repealed by Stats 1959 ch 1809 §1.

Original §1541 repealed 1931. See Probate Code.

2003 Note: The changes made by this act to Section 1541 of the Code of Civil Procedure shall apply to any claims for which the Controller has not made a decision by the earlier of July 1, 2003, or the effective date of this act [August 11, 2003]. Stats 2003 ch 228 (AB 1756) §57.

§1542. Right of another state to recover property; Claim, and proceedings thereon

(a) At any time after property has been paid or delivered to the Controller under this chapter, another state is entitled to recover the property if:

(1) The property escheated to this state under subdivision (b) of Section 1510 because no address of the apparent owner of the property appeared on the records of the holder when the property was escheated under this chapter, the last known address of the apparent owner was in fact in that other state, and, under the laws of that state, the property escheated to that state.

(2) The last known address of the apparent owner of the property appearing on the records of the holder is in that other state and, under the laws of that state, the property has escheated to that state.

(3) The property is the sum payable on a travelers check, money order, or other similar instrument that escheated to this state under Section 1511, the travelers check, money order, or other similar instrument was in fact purchased in that other state, and, under the laws of that state, the property escheated to that state.

(4) The property is funds held or owing by a life insurance corporation that escheated to this state by application of the presumption provided by subdivision (b) of Section 1515, the last known address of the person entitled to the funds was in fact in that other state, and, under the laws of that state, the property escheated to that state.

(b) The claim of another state to recover escheated property under this section shall be presented in writing to the Controller, who shall consider the claim within 180 days after it is presented. The Controller may hold a hearing and receive evidence. The Controller shall allow the claim upon determination that the other state is entitled to the escheated property.

(c) Paragraphs (1) and (2) of subdivision (a) do not apply to property described in paragraph (3) or (4) of that subdivision. **Leg.H.** Added Stats 1968 ch 356 §32, operative January 1, 1969. Amended Stats 1975 ch 25 §4; Stats 1978 ch 1183 §22; Stats 2003 ch 228 §10 (AB 1756), effective August 11, 2003.

Prior Law: Former CCP §1542, relating to claims of property in custody of federal officers or agencies, was added by Stats 1951 ch 1708 §5 and repealed by Stats 1959 ch 1809 §1.

2003 Note: The changes made by this act to Section 1542 of the Code of Civil Procedure shall apply to any claims for which the Controller has not made a decision by the earlier of July 1, 2003, or the effective date of this act [August 11, 2003]. Stats 2003 ch 228 (AB 1756) §57.

§§1544–1549. [Sections repealed 1931]

Leg.H. Enacted 1872. Repealed Code Amdts 1873–74 ch 383 §195, Stats 1919 ch 538 §1, Stats 1931 ch 281 (Prob C §1700). See Prob C §§1041, 10001, 10300, 10301, 10304, 10306.

§ 1543. Streamlining secure payment of claims

Notwithstanding Section 1540, the Controller may do any of the following to streamline the secure payment of claims:

(a) Minimize the number of documents a claimant is required to submit for property valued at less than five thousand dollars ($5,000).

(b) Allow electronic submission of documentation to the Controller's internet website for any claim deemed appropriate by the Controller.

(c) Authorize direct deposit by electronic fund transfer for the payment of an approved claim. **Leg.H.** Added Stats 2022 ch 270 §1 (AB 1208), effective January 1, 2023.

Prior Law Former CCP §1543 was enacted 1872; repealed Code Amdts 1873–1874 ch 383 §195, Stats 1919 ch 538 §1, Stats 1931 ch 281 (Prob C §1700).

§1550. [Section repealed 1959]

Leg.H. Added Stats 1951 ch 1708 §5. Amended Stats 1953 ch 600 §1. Repealed Stats 1959 ch 1809 §1.

Prior Law: Former CCP §1550 repealed 1931. See Probate Code.

§§1551–1554. [Sections repealed 1931]

Leg.H. Enacted 1872. Repealed Stats 1931 ch 281 (Prob C §1700). See Prob C §§10161, 10162, 10166, 10257, 10263, 10309–10315, 10350.

§1555. [Section repealed 1959]

Leg.H. Added Stats 1951 ch 1708 §5. Amended Stats 1953 ch 600 §2. Repealed Stats 1959 ch 1809 §1.

Prior Law: Former CCP §1555 repealed 1931. See Probate Code.

§§1556–1559. [Sections repealed 1931]

Leg.H. Enacted 1872 or added Stats 1909 ch 150 §1. Repealed Stats 1931 ch 281 (Prob C §1700). See Prob C §§10150, 10160, 16161, 10164, 10165, 10261, 10263, 10305, 10310, 10312.

ARTICLE 5
Administration of Unclaimed Property

Custody by state; Reimbursement of payments by holder; Reclamation of property. § 1560.

Defense of holder against claims after delivery; Refund or redelivery of property delivered by mistake. §1561.

Crediting of dividends, interest or increments to owner's account; Disposition of income from investment of Unclaimed Property Fund. §1562.

Public sale of escheated property; Items relating to state's military history to be held in trust at California State Military Museum and Resource Center. §1563.

Deposit of money in Unclaimed Property Fund; Abandoned Property Account; Appropriation; Transfer of funds. §1564.

Deposit of money held in Interest on Lawyers' Trust Account (IOLTA) into Abandoned IOLTA Property Account; Deposit of money into IOLTA Claims Reserve Subaccount for specified payments; Annual transfer of balance to Public Interest Attorney Loan Repayment Account. §1564.5.

Retention of property with no apparent commercial value; Destruction or disposition; Immunity from liability. §1565.

Immunity of state and officers from liability. §1566.

Use of tangible personal property by Director of Parks and Recreation. §1567.

§ 1560. Custody by state; Reimbursement of payments by holder; Reclamation of property

(a) Upon the payment or delivery of escheated property to the Controller, the state shall assume custody and shall be responsible for the safekeeping of the property. Any person who pays or delivers escheated property to the Controller under this chapter and who, prior to escheat, if the person's records contain an address for the apparent owner that the holder's records do not disclose to be inaccurate, has made reasonable efforts to notify the owner by mail or, if the owner has consented to electronic notice, electronically, in substantial compliance with Sections 1513.5, 1514, 1516, and 1520, that the owner's property, deposit, account, shares, or other interest will escheat to the state, is relieved of all liability to the extent of the value of the property so paid or delivered for any claim that then exists or that thereafter may arise or be made in respect to the property. Property removed from a safe-deposit box or other safekeeping repository shall be received by the Controller subject to any valid lien of the holder for rent and other charges, the rent and other charges to be paid out of the proceeds remaining after the Controller has deducted therefrom their selling cost.

(b) Any holder who has paid moneys to the Controller pursuant to this chapter may make payment to any person appearing to that holder to be entitled thereto, and upon filing proof of the payment and proof that the payee was entitled thereto, the Controller shall forthwith reimburse the holder for the payment without deduction of any fee or other charges. Where reimbursement is sought for a payment made on a negotiable instrument, including a traveler's check or money order, the holder shall be reimbursed under this subdivision upon filing proof that the instrument was duly presented to them and that payment was made thereon to a person who appeared to the holder to be entitled to payment.

(c) The holder shall be reimbursed under this section even if they made the payment to a person whose claim against them was barred because of the expiration of any period of time as those described in Section 1570.

(d) Any holder who has delivered personal property, including a certificate of any interest in a business association, to the Controller pursuant to this chapter may reclaim the personal property if still in the possession of the Controller without payment of any fee or other charges upon filing proof that the owner thereof has claimed such personal property from the holder. The Controller may, in their discretion, accept an affidavit of the holder stating the facts that entitle the holder to reimbursement under this subdivision as sufficient proof for the purposes of this subdivision.

(e) Any holder who has delivered funds maintained under a preneed funeral trust or similar account or plan to the Controller pursuant to this chapter and has fulfilled the services of the preneed funeral trust escheated to the Controller shall be reimbursed under this section upon submission of a death certificate for the beneficiary and a statement detailing the personal property or funeral merchandise or services provided.

(f) This section shall become operative on January 1, 2023. **Leg.H.** Added Stats 2021 ch 514 §9 (AB 293), effective January 1, 2022, operative January 1, 2023.

Prior Law Former CCP §1560 repealed 1931. See Probate Code. Former CCP §1560, relating to unclaimed property in dissolved building and loan associations, was added by Stats 1951 ch 1708 §5, amended by Stats 1953 ch 600 §3, and repealed by Stats 1959 ch 1809 §1.

Former CCP §1560, relating to custody by state, holder relieved from liability, payment of safe deposit box or repository charges, reimbursement of holder paying claim, and reclaiming for owner, was added Stats 1959 ch 1809 §2, as CCP §1513, amended Stats 1961 ch 1904 §6, amended and renumbered Stats 1968 ch 356 §34, operative January 1, 1969, amended Stats 2009 ch 522 §7 (AB 1291), effective January 1, 2010 and, repealed January 1, 2023, by its own terms.

§1561. Defense of holder against claims after delivery; Refund or redelivery of property delivered by mistake

(a) If the holder pays or delivers escheated property to the State Controller in accordance with this chapter and thereafter any person claims the property from the holder or another state claims the property from the holder under that state's laws relating to escheat, the State Controller shall, upon written notice of such claim, defend the holder against the claim and indemnify him against any liability on the claim.

(b) If any holder, because of mistake of law or fact, pays or delivers any property to the State Controller that has not escheated under this chapter and thereafter claims the property from the State Controller, the State Controller shall, if he has not disposed of the property in accordance with this chapter, refund or redeliver the property to the holder without deduction for any fee or other charge.

(c) As used in this section, "escheated property" means property which this chapter provides escheats to this state, whether or not it is determined that another state had a superior right to escheat such property at the time it was paid or delivered to the State Controller or at some time thereafter. **Leg.H.** Added Stats 1968 ch 356 §35, operative January 1, 1969.

Prior Law: Former CCP §1561 repealed 1931. See Probate Code.

§1562. Crediting of dividends, interest or increments to owner's account; Disposition of income from investment of Unclaimed Property Fund

When property other than money is delivered to the State Controller under this chapter, any dividends, interest or other increments realized or accruing on such property at or prior to liquidation or conversion thereof into money, shall upon receipt be credited to the owner's account by the State Controller. Except for amounts so credited the owner is not entitled to receive income or other increments on money or other property paid or delivered to the State Controller under this chapter. All interest received and other income derived from the investment of moneys deposited in the Unclaimed Property Fund under the provisions of this chapter shall, on order of the State Controller, be transferred to the General Fund. **Leg.H.** Added Stats 1959 ch 1809 §2 as CCP §1514. Amended Stats 1961 ch 1904 §7. Renumbered Stats 1968 ch 356 §36, operative January 1, 1969.

Prior Law: Former CCP §1562 repealed 1931. See Probate Code.

§1563. Public sale of escheated property; Items relating to state's military history to be held in trust at California State Military Museum and Resource Center

(a) Except as provided in subdivisions (b) and (c), all escheated property delivered to the Controller under this chapter shall be sold by the Controller to the highest bidder at public sale in whatever city in the state affords in the Controller's judgment the most favorable market for the property involved, or the Controller may conduct the sale by electronic media, including, but not limited to, the internet, if in the Controller's judgment it is cost effective to conduct the sale of the property involved in that manner. However, no sale shall be made pursuant to this subdivision until 18 months after the final date for filing the report required by Section 1530. The Controller may decline the highest bid and reoffer the property for sale if the Controller considers the price bid insufficient. The Controller need not offer any property for sale if, in the Controller's opinion, the probable cost of sale exceeds the value of the property. Any sale of escheated property held under this section shall be preceded by a single publication of notice thereof, at least one week in advance of sale, in an English language newspaper of general circulation in the county where the property is to be sold.

(b) Securities listed on an established stock exchange shall be sold at the prevailing prices on that exchange. Other securities may be sold over the counter at prevailing prices or by any other method that the Controller may determine to be advisable. These securities shall be sold by the Controller no sooner than 18 months, but no later than 20 months, after the actual date of filing of the report required by Section 1530. If securities delivered to the Controller by a holder of the securities remain in the custody of the Controller, a person making a valid claim for those securities under this chapter shall be entitled to receive the securities from the Controller. If the securities have been sold, the person shall be entitled to receive the net proceeds received by the Controller from the sale of the securities. United States government savings bonds and United States war bonds shall be presented to the United States for payment. Subdivision (a) does not apply to the property described in this subdivision.

(c)(1) All escheated property consisting of military awards, decorations, equipment, artifacts, memorabilia, documents, photographs, films, literature, and any other item relating to the military history of California and Californians that is delivered to the Controller is exempt from subdivision (a) and may, at the discretion of the Controller, be held in trust for the Controller at the California State Military Museum and Resource Center, or successor entity. All escheated property held in trust pursuant to this subdivision is subject to the applicable regulations of the United States Army governing Army museum activities as described in Section 179 of the Military and Veterans Code. A person claiming an interest in the escheated property may file a claim to the property pursuant to Article 4 (commencing with Section 1540).

(2) The California State Military Museum and Resource Center, or successor entity, shall be responsible for the costs of storage and maintenance of escheated property delivered by the Controller under this subdivision.

(d) The purchaser at any sale conducted by the Controller pursuant to this chapter shall receive title to the property purchased, free from all claims of the owner or prior holder thereof and of all persons claiming through or under them. The Controller shall execute all documents necessary to complete the transfer of title. **Leg.H.** Added Stats 1959 ch 1809 §2 as CCP §1516. Amended Stats 1963 ch 669 §1. Amended and renumbered Stats 1968 ch 356 §37, operative January 1, 1969. Amended Stats 1972 ch 1165 §1; Stats 1993 ch 692 §6 (AB 1854); Stats 1996 ch 762 §9 (SB 2014); Stats 2000 ch 16 §2 (AB 938), effective May 5, 2000; Stats 2000 ch 924 §2 (AB 2935); Stats 2003 ch 265 §2 (AB 542); Stats 2004 ch 183 §46 (AB 3082); Stats 2007 ch 179 §5 (SB 86), effective August 24, 2007; Stats 2015 ch 297 §2 (AB 355), effective January 1, 2016; Stats 2016 ch 31 §17 (SB 836), effective June 27, 2016; Stats 2022 ch 420 §13 (AB 2960), effective January 1, 2023.

Prior Law: Former CCP §1563 repealed 1931. See Probate Code.

§1564. Deposit of money in Unclaimed Property Fund; Abandoned Property Account; Appropriation; Transfer of funds

(a) All money received under this chapter, including the proceeds from the sale of property under Section 1563, shall be deposited in the Unclaimed Property Fund in an account titled "Abandoned Property."

(b) Notwithstanding Section 13340 of the Government Code, all money in the Abandoned Property Account in the Unclaimed Property Fund is hereby continuously appropriated to the Controller, without regard to fiscal years, for expenditure in accordance with law in carrying out and enforcing the provisions of this chapter, including, but not limited to, the following purposes:

(1) For payment of claims allowed by the Controller under the provisions of this chapter.

(2) For refund, to the person making such deposit, of amounts, including overpayments, deposited in error in such fund.

(3) For payment of the cost of appraisals incurred by the Controller covering property held in the name of an account in such fund.

(4) For payment of the cost incurred by the Controller for the purchase of lost instrument indemnity bonds, or for payment to the person entitled thereto, for any unpaid lawful charges or costs which arose from holding any specific property or any specific funds which were delivered or paid to the Controller, or which arose from complying with this chapter with respect to such property or funds.

(5) For payment of amounts required to be paid by the state as trustee, bailee, or successor in interest to the preceding owner.

(6) For payment of costs incurred by the Controller for the repair, maintenance, and upkeep of property held in the name of an account in such fund.

(7) For payment of costs of official advertising in connection with the sale of property held in the name of an account in such fund.

(8) For transfer to the General Fund as provided in subdivision (c).

(9) For transfer to the Inheritance Tax Fund of the amount of any inheritance taxes determined to be due and payable to the state by any claimant with respect to any property claimed by him or her under the provisions of this chapter.

(c) At the end of each month, or more often if he or she deems it advisable, the Controller shall transfer all money in the Abandoned Property Account in excess of fifty thousand dollars ($50,000) to the General Fund. Before making this transfer, the Controller shall record the name and last known address of each person appearing from the holders' report to be entitled to the escheated property and the name and last known address of each insured person or annuitant, and with respect to each policy or contract listed in the report of a life insurance corporation, its number, and the name of the corporation. The record shall be available for public inspection at all reasonable business hours. **Leg.H.** Added Stats 1959 ch 1809 §2 as CCP §1517. Amended and renumbered Stats 1968 ch 356 §38, operative January 1, 1969; Amended Stats 1980 ch 676 §70; Stats 1993 ch 692 §7 (AB 1854).

Prior Law: Former CCP §1564 repealed 1931. See Probate Code.

§1564.5. Deposit of money held in Interest on Lawyers' Trust Account (IOLTA) into Abandoned IOLTA Property Account; Deposit of money into IOLTA Claims Reserve Subaccount for specified payments; Annual transfer of balance to Public Interest Attorney Loan Repayment Account

(a) Notwithstanding any law, including, but not limited to, Section 1564, all money received under this chapter from funds held in an Interest on Lawyers' Trust Account (IOLTA) that escheat to the state shall be administered as set forth in this section. The money shall be deposited into the Abandoned IOLTA Property Account, which is hereby established within the Unclaimed Property Fund.

(b) Twenty-five percent of the money in the Abandoned IOLTA Property Account shall be deposited into the IOLTA Claims Reserve Subaccount, which is hereby established within the Abandoned IOLTA Property Account. Notwithstanding Section 13340 of the Government Code, funds in the subaccount are continuously appropriated to the Controller for the payment of all refunds and claims pursuant to this chapter related to escheated IOLTA funds.

(c) The balance of the funds in the Abandoned IOLTA Property Account, excluding funds in the subaccount, shall be transferred on an annual basis to the Public Interest Attorney Loan Repayment Account established pursuant to Section 6032.5 of the Business and Professions Code. Before making this transfer, the Controller shall record the name and last known address of each person appearing from the holders' report to be entitled to the escheated property. The record shall be available for public inspection at all reasonable business hours. **Leg.H.** Added Stats 2015 ch 488 §2 (SB 134), effective January 1, 2016. Amended Stats 2018 ch 390 §1 (AB 2350), effective January 1, 2019.

§1565. Retention of property with no apparent commercial value; Destruction or disposition; Immunity from liability

Any property delivered to the Controller pursuant to this chapter that has no apparent commercial value shall be retained by the Controller for a period of not less than seven years from the date the property is delivered to the Controller. If the Controller determines that any property delivered to him or her pursuant to this chapter has no apparent commercial value, he or she may at any time thereafter destroy or otherwise dispose of the property, and in that event no action or proceeding shall be brought or maintained against the state or any officer thereof, or against the holder for, or on account of any action taken by, the Controller pursuant to this chapter with respect to the property. **Leg.H.** Added Stats 1959 ch 1809 §2 as CCP §1521. Amended Stats 1961 ch 1904 §8; Amended and renumbered Stats 1968 ch 356 §39, operative January 1, 1969; Amended Stats 2007 ch 179 §6 (SB 86), effective August 24, 2007; Stats 2011 ch 305 §8 (SB 495), effective January 1, 2012.

Prior Law: Former CCP §1565, relating to unclaimed property in possession of receivers, was added by Stats 1951 ch 1708 §5 and repealed by Stats 1959 ch 1809 §1.

Original §1565 repealed 1931. See Probate Code.

§1566. Immunity of state and officers from liability

(a) When payment or delivery of money or other property has been made to any claimant under the provisions of this chapter, no suit shall thereafter be maintained by any other claimant against the state or any officer or employee thereof for or on account of such property.

(b) Except as provided in Section 1541, no suit shall be maintained by any person against the state or any officer or employee thereof for or on account of any transaction entered into by the State Controller pursuant to this chapter. **Leg.H.** Added Stats 1968 ch 356 §40, operative January 1, 1969.

Prior Law: Former CCP §1566 repealed 1931. See Probate Code.

§1567. Use of tangible personal property by Director of Parks and Recreation

The Director of Parks and Recreation may examine any tangible personal property delivered to the Controller under this chapter for purposes of determining whether such property would be useful under the provisions of Section 512 of the Public Resources Code. If the director makes such a determination with respect to the property, the Controller may deliver the property to the director for use in carrying out the purposes of Section 512 of the Public Resources Code. Upon the termination of any such use, the director shall return the property to the Controller. **Leg.H.** Added Stats 1969 ch 838 §1. Amended Stats 1981 ch 714 §73.

Prior Law: Former CCP §1567 repealed 1931. See Probate Code.

§§1568, 1569. [Sections repealed 1931]

Leg.H. Enacted 1872. Repealed Stats 1931 ch 281 (Prob C §1700). See Prob C §§9251, 9253, 10314, 10361, 10362.

ARTICLE 6
Compliance and Enforcement

Inapplicability of statutes and orders limiting time for actions against holders. §1570.
Controller's right to examine records; Banking organizations and savings associations. §1571.
Permitted actions by Controller. §1572.
Agreements with other states. §1573.
Reciprocal actions to enforce laws of other states. §1574.
Request for action in other state; Costs and rewards. §1575.
Punishment for failure to render report or deliver escheated property. §1576.
Interest payable upon failure to timely report or pay over unclaimed property. §1577.
California Voluntary Compliance Program. § 1577.5.

§1570. Inapplicability of statutes and orders limiting time for actions against holders

The expiration of any period of time specified by statute or court order, during which an action or proceeding may be commenced or enforced to obtain payment of a claim for money or recovery of property from the holder, does not prevent the money or property from being escheated, nor affect any duty to file a report required by this chapter or to pay or deliver escheated property to the State Controller. **Leg.H.** Added Stats 1959 ch 1809 §2 as CCP §1515. Amended and renumbered Stats 1968 ch 356 §42, operative January 1, 1969.

Prior Law: Former CCP §1570, relating to unclaimed property in dissolved corporations, was added by Stats 1951 ch 1708 §5, amended by Stats 1953 ch 1686 §1, Stats 1957 ch 1020 §4, and repealed by Stats 1959 ch 1809 §1.

Original §1570 repealed 1931. See Probate Code.

§1571. Controller's right to examine records; Banking organizations and savings associations

(a) The Controller may at reasonable times and upon reasonable notice examine the records of any person if the Controller has reason to believe that the person is a holder who has failed to report property that should have been reported pursuant to this chapter.

(b) When requested by the Controller, the examination shall be conducted by any licensing or regulating agency otherwise empowered by the laws of this state to examine the records of the holder. For the purpose of determining compliance with this chapter, the Commissioner of Financial Protection and Innovation is vested with full authority to examine the records of any banking organization and any savings association doing business within this state but not organized under the laws of or created in this state.

(c) Following a public hearing, the Controller shall adopt guidelines as to the policies and procedures governing the activity of third-party auditors who are hired by the Controller.

(d) Following a public hearing, the Controller shall adopt guidelines, on or before July 1, 1999, establishing forms, policies, and procedures to enable a person to dispute or appeal the results of any record examination conducted pursuant to this section. **Leg.H.** Added Stats 1959 ch 1809 §2, as CCP §1522. Amended and Renumbered by Stats 1968 ch 356 §43, operative January 1, 1969; Stats 1996 ch 1064 §7 (AB 3351), operative July 1, 1997; Stats 1998 ch 1029 §2 (AB 698); Stats 2014 ch 913 §11 (AB 2747), effective January 1, 2015; Stats 2022 ch 452 §42 (SB 1498), effective January 1, 2023.

Prior Law: Former CCP §1571 was repealed 1931. See Probate Code.

1998 Note: Stats 1998 ch 1029 shall not be construed to affect any civil action or proceeding pending on or before January 1, 1999. This act shall only apply prospectively. Stats 1998 ch 1029 §3.

§1572. Permitted actions by Controller

(a) The State Controller may bring an action in a court of appropriate jurisdiction, as specified in this section, for any of the following purposes:

(1) To enforce the duty of any person under this chapter to permit the examination of the records of such person.

(2) For a judicial determination that particular property is subject to escheat by this state pursuant to this chapter.

(3) To enforce the delivery of any property to the State Controller as required under this chapter.

(b) The State Controller may bring an action under this chapter in any court of this state of appropriate jurisdiction in any of the following cases:

(1) Where the holder is any person domiciled in this state, or is a government or governmental subdivision or agency of this state.

(2) Where the holder is any person engaged in or transacting business in this state, although not domiciled in this state.

(3) Where the property is tangible personal property and is held in this state.

(c) In any case where no court of this state can obtain jurisdiction over the holder, the State Controller may bring an action in any federal or state court with jurisdiction over the holder. **Leg.H.** Added Stats 1968 ch 356 §45, operative January 1, 1969.

Prior Law: Former CCP §1572 repealed 1931. See Probate Code.

§1573. Agreements with other states

The State Controller may enter into an agreement to provide information needed to enable another state to determine unclaimed property it may be entitled to escheat if such other state or an official thereof agrees to provide this state with information needed to enable this state to determine unclaimed property it may be entitled to escheat. The State Controller may, by regulation, require the reporting of information needed to enable him to comply with agreements made pursuant to this section and may, by regulation, prescribe the form, including verification, of the information to be reported and the times for filing the reports. **Leg.H.** Added Stats 1968 ch 356 §46, operative January 1, 1969.

Prior Law: Former CCP §1573 repealed 1931. See Probate Code.

§1574. Reciprocal actions to enforce laws of other states

At the request of another state, the Attorney General of this state may bring an action in the name of the other state, in any court of appropriate jurisdiction of this state or federal court within this state, to enforce the unclaimed property laws of the other state against a holder in this state of property subject to escheat by the other state, if:

(a) The courts of the other state cannot obtain jurisdiction over the holder;

(b) The other state has agreed to bring actions in the name of this state at the request of the Attorney General of this state to enforce the provisions of this chapter against any person in the other state believed by the State Controller to hold property subject to escheat under this chapter, where the courts of this state cannot obtain jurisdiction over such person; and

(c) The other state has agreed to pay reasonable costs incurred by the Attorney General in bringing the action. **Leg.H.** Added Stats 1968 ch 356 §47, operative January 1, 1969.

Prior Law: Former CCP §1574 repealed 1931. See Probate Code.

§1575. Request for action in other state; Costs and rewards

(a) If the State Controller believes that a person in another state holds property subject to escheat under this chapter and the courts of this state cannot obtain jurisdiction over that person, the Attorney General of this state may request an officer of the other state to bring an action in the name of this state to enforce the provisions of this chapter against such person.

(b) This state shall pay all reasonable costs incurred by the other state in any action brought under the authority of this section. The State Controller may agree to pay to any state bringing such an action a reward not to exceed fifteen percent of the value, after deducting reasonable costs, of any property recovered for this state as a direct or indirect result of such action. Any costs or rewards paid pursuant to this section shall be paid from the Abandoned Property Account in the Unclaimed Property Fund and shall not be deducted from the amount that is subject to be claimed by the owner in accordance with this chapter. **Leg.H.** Added Stats 1968 ch 356 §48, operative January 1, 1969.

Prior Law: Former CCP §1575, relating to unclaimed property in dissolved insurance companies, was added by Stats 1951 ch 1708 §5, amended by Stats 1953 ch 220 §1, and repealed by Stats 1959 ch 1809 §1.

Original §1575 repealed 1931. See Probate Code.

§1576. Punishment for failure to render report or deliver escheated property

(a) Any person who willfully fails to render any report or perform other duties, including use of the report format described in Section 1530, required under this chapter shall be punished by a fine of one hundred dollars ($100) for each day such report is withheld or such duty is not performed, but not more than ten thousand dollars ($10,000).

(b) Any person who willfully refuses to pay or deliver escheated property to the Controller as required under this chapter shall be punished by a fine of not less than five thousand dollars ($5,000) nor more than fifty thousand dollars ($50,000).

(c) No person shall be considered to have willfully failed to report, pay, or deliver escheated property, or perform other duties unless he or she has failed to respond within a reasonable time after notification by certified mail by the Controller's office of his or her failure to act. **Leg.H.** Added Stats 1959 ch 1809 §2 as CCP §1524. Amended and renumbered Stats 1968 ch 356 §49, operative January 1, 1968; Amended Stats 1983 ch 1092 §73, effective September 27, 1983, operative January 1, 1984; Stats 1996 ch 762 §10 (SB 2014).

Prior Law: Former CCP §1576, relating to unclaimed property held by check sellers and cashiers, was added by Stats 1953 ch 1031 §9 and repealed by Stats 1959 ch 1809 §1.

Original §1576 repealed 1931. See Probate Code.

§1576a. [Section repealed 1931]

Leg.H. Added Stats 1929 ch 36 §1. Repealed Stats 1931 ch 281 (Prob C §1700). See Prob C §§9920–9923.

§1577. Interest payable upon failure to timely report or pay over unclaimed property

(a) In addition to any damages, penalties, or fines for which a person may be liable under other provisions of law, any person who fails to report, pay, or deliver unclaimed property within the time prescribed by this chapter, unless that failure is due to reasonable cause, shall pay to the Controller interest at the rate of 12 percent per annum on that property or value thereof from the date the property should have been reported, paid, or delivered.

(b) If a holder reports and pays or delivers unclaimed property within the time prescribed by this chapter, but files a report that is not in substantial compliance with the requirements of Section 1530 or 1532, the interest payable on the unclaimed property that is paid or delivered in the time prescribed by this chapter shall not exceed ten thousand dollars ($10,000).

(c) The Controller may waive the interest payable under this section if the holder's failure to file a report that is in substantial compliance with the requirements of Section 1530 or 1532 is due to reasonable cause.

(d) The Controller shall waive the interest payable under this section if the holder participates in and completes all of the requirements of the California Voluntary Compliance Program under Section 1577.5, subject to the right to reinstate, as specified. **Leg.H.** Added Stats 1976 ch 49 §3. Amended Stats 2003 ch 304 §5 (AB 378); Stats 2009 ch 522 §8 (AB 1291), effective January 1, 2010; Stats 2022 ch 282 §2 (AB 2280), effective January 1, 2023.

Prior Law: Former CCP §1577, relating to receipt, disposal, etc., of unclaimed property or money, was added by Stats 1953 ch 1076 §15 and repealed by Stats 1959 ch 1809 §1.

Original §1577 repealed 1931. See Probate Code.

§1577.5. California Voluntary Compliance Program

(a) This section shall be known, and may be cited, as the "California Voluntary Compliance Program."

(b) The Controller may establish a program for the voluntary compliance of holders for the purpose of resolving unclaimed property that is due and owing to the state under this chapter.

(c) A holder that has not reported unclaimed property in accordance with Section 1530 may request to enroll in the program using a form prescribed by the Controller.

(d) The Controller, in their discretion, may enroll eligible holders in the program. A holder is ineligible to participate in the program if any of the following apply:

(1) At the time the holder's request to enroll is received by the Controller, the holder is the subject of an examination of records or has received notification from the Controller of an impending examination under Section 1571.

(2) At the time the holder's request to enroll is received by the Controller, the holder is the subject of a civil or criminal prosecution involving compliance with this chapter.

(3) The Controller has notified the holder of an interest assessment under Section 1577 within the previous five years, and the interest assessment remains unpaid at the time of the holder's request to enroll. A holder subject to an outstanding interest assessment may file or refile a request to enroll in the program after resolving the outstanding interest assessment.

(4) The Controller has waived interest assessed against the holder under this section within the previous five years. Notwithstanding the foregoing, if a holder acquired or merged with another entity within the five-year period, the holder may request to enroll in the program for the purpose of resolving unclaimed property that may be due and owing to the state as a result of the acquisition or merger.

(e) The Controller shall waive interest assessed under Section 1577 for a holder enrolled in the program if the holder does all the following within the prescribed timeframes and satisfies the other requirements of this section:

(1) Enrolls and participates in an unclaimed property educational training program provided by the Controller within three months after the date on which the Controller notified the holder of their enrollment in the program, unless the Controller sets a different date.

(2) Reviews their books and records for unclaimed property for at least the previous 10 years, starting from June 30 or the fiscal yearend preceding the date on which the report required by paragraph (4) is due.

(3) Makes reasonable efforts to notify owners of reportable property by mail or electronically, as applicable, pursuant to Sections 1513.5, 1514, 1516, or 1520, no less than 30 days prior to submitting the report required by paragraph (4).

(4) Reports to the Controller as required by subdivisions (b), (c), and (e) of Section 1530 within six months after the date on which the Controller notified the holder of their enrollment in the program. Upon written request by the enrolled holder, the Controller may postpone the reporting date for a period not to exceed 18 months after the date on which the Controller notified the holder of their enrollment in the program.

(5) Submits to the Controller an updated report and pays or delivers to the Controller all escheated property specified in the report as required by Section 1532, no sooner than seven months and no later than seven months and 15 days after the Controller received the report submitted pursuant to paragraph (4).

(f) The Controller may reinstate interest waived under subdivision (d) of Section 1577 if the holder does not pay or deliver all escheated property specified in the report submitted pursuant to and within the timeframe prescribed by paragraph (5) of subdivision (e).

(g) The Controller may adopt guidelines and forms that provide specific procedures for the administration of the program.

(h) This section shall become operative only upon an appropriation by the Legislature in the annual Budget Act for this purpose. **Leg.H.** Added Stats 2022 ch 282 §4 (AB 2280), effective January 1, 2023.

Prior Law Former CCP §1577.5, relating to application of code provisions, was added Stats 2000 ch 267 §1 (AB 1888), amended Stats 2002 ch 22 §1 (AB 227), and repealed Stats 2022 ch 282 § 3 (AB 2280), effective January 1, 2023.

§1577a. [Section repealed 1931]

Leg.H. Added Stats 1921 ch 27 §1. Repealed Stats 1931 ch 281 (Prob C §1700). See Prob C §§1021, 1041, 1260, 2551–2553, 7262, 7263, 9800–9805.

§1578. [Section repealed 1959]

Leg.H. Added Stats 1953 ch 280 §1. Repealed Stats 1959 ch 1809 §1.

Prior Law: Former CCP §1578 repealed 1931. See Probate Code.

§1579. [Section repealed 1931]

Leg.H. Added Stats 1887 ch 101 §1. Repealed Stats 1931 ch 281 (Prob C §1700). See Prob C §§1021, 1041, 2553, 7262, 7263, 9943–9948.

ARTICLE 7
Miscellaneous

Controller's regulations. §1580.
Records as to traveler's check or money order sellers. §1581.
Agreement to locate reported property; Validity; Compensation. §1582.

§1580. Controller's regulations

The State Controller is hereby authorized to make necessary rules and regulations to carry out the provisions of this chapter. **Leg.H.** Added Stats 1959 ch 1809 §2 as CCP §1525. Amended and renumbered Stats 1968 ch 356 §51, operative January 1, 1969; Amended Stats 1978 ch 1183 §23.

Prior Law: Former CCP §1580 repealed 1931. See Probate Code.

§1581. Records as to traveler's check or money order sellers

(a) Any business association that sells in this state its travelers checks, money orders, or other similar written instruments (other than third-party bank checks) on which such business association is directly liable, or that provides such travelers checks, money orders, or similar written instruments to others for sale in this state, shall maintain a record indicating those travelers checks, money orders, or similar written instruments that are purchased from it in this state.

(b) The record required by this section may be destroyed after it has been retained for such reasonable time as the State Controller shall designate by regulation.

(c) Any business association that willfully fails to comply with this section is liable to the state for a civil penalty of five hundred dollars ($500) for each day of such failure to comply, which penalty may be recovered in an action brought by the State Controller. **Leg.H.** Added Stats 1968 ch 356 §52, operative January 1, 1969. Amended Stats 1975 ch 25 §5.

Prior Law: Former CCP §1581 repealed 1931. See Probate Code.

§1582. Agreement to locate reported property; Validity; Compensation

(a)(1) An agreement to locate, deliver, recover, or assist in the recovery of property reported under Section 1530 is invalid if either of the following apply:

(A) The agreement is entered into between the date a report is filed under subdivision (d) of Section 1530 and the date the property is paid or delivered under Section 1532.

(B) The agreement requires the owner to pay a fee or compensation prior to approval of the claim and payment of the recovered property to the owner by the Controller.

(2) An agreement to locate, deliver, recover, or assist in the recovery of property reported under Section 1530 made after payment or delivery under Section 1532 is valid if it meets all of the following requirements:

(A) The agreement is in writing and includes a disclosure of the nature and value of the property, that the Controller is in possession of the property, and the address where the owner can directly claim the property from the Controller.

(B) The agreement is signed by the owner after receipt of the disclosure described in subparagraph (A).

(C) The fee or compensation agreed upon is not in excess of 10 percent of the recovered property.

(3) This subdivision shall not be construed to prevent an owner from asserting, at any time, that an agreement to locate property is based upon an excessive or unjust consideration.

(b) Notwithstanding any other provision of law, records of the Controller's office pertaining to unclaimed property are not available for public inspection or copying until after publication of notice of the property or, if publication of notice of the property is not required, until one year after delivery of the property to the Controller. **Leg.H.** Added Stats 1959 ch 1809 §2 as CCP §1527. Amended and renumbered Stats 1968 ch 356 §53, operative January 1, 1969. Amended Stats 1978 ch 815 §2; Stats 1990 ch 450 §16 (SB 57), effective July 31, 1990; Stats 2022 ch 282 §5 (AB 2280), effective January 1, 2023.

Prior Law: Former CCP §1582 repealed 1931. See Probate Code.

§§1583–1599. [Sections repealed 1931]

Leg.H. Enacted 1872 or added Stats 1907 ch 384 §2. Repealed Stats 1931 ch 281 (Prob C §1700). See Prob C §§850, 851, 856, 1021, 1041, 1260, 7262, 7263, 8800, 8802, 8850, 9650, 9653, 9731, 9733, 9761, 9763, 9822, 9830, 9837, 9866, 9883.

CHAPTER 8
PROPERTY IN CUSTODY OF FEDERAL OFFICERS, AGENCIES, AND DEPARTMENTS

Declaration of policy. §1600.
Definitions. §1601.
Agreement for State's payment of share of costs. §1602.
Undertaking by State to hold the United States harmless; Intervention by Attorney General; Consent of State to suit. §1603.
Unclaimed property subject to delivery to this State; Presumptions. §1604.
Certification by Governor. §1605.
Request by Controller for report of previously unreported information. §1606.
Posting copy of report; Notice of interest and intention to claim; Determination of asserted interest. §1607.
State's right unaffected by expiration of time for proceeding. §1608.
Petition for determination of State's right to custody of unclaimed property; Venue. §1609.
Notice of proceeding. §1610.
Answer; Disposition of funds on deposit; Dismissal without prejudice. §1611.
Application for judgment relating to property not claimed by answer, and finding and declaration thereon. §1612.
Request for delivery or payment of unclaimed property described in judgment; Receipts. §1613.
Disposition of property received under this chapter; Period of limitation of claims. §1614.
Appropriation of money in abandoned property account in Unclaimed Property Fund. §1615.

§1600. Declaration of policy

It is the policy of this State:

(a) To discover property in the custody of officers, departments, and agencies of the United States, which property is unclaimed by owners whose addresses are known or presumed to be in this State;

(b) To provide a procedure for judicial determination of the right of the State to receive custody of such unclaimed property; and

(c) To authorize expenditure of state funds to pay the proportionate cost of the State in discovering such unclaimed property and to hold the United States harmless against claims concerning such property when delivered to the custody of the State in accordance with this chapter. **Leg.H.** Added Stats 1959 ch 1801 §1.

Prior Law: Former CCP §1600 repealed 1931. See Probate Code.

§1601. Definitions

As used in this chapter:

(a) "Unclaimed property" means any tangible personal property or intangible personal property, including choses in action in amounts certain, and all debts owed or entrusted funds or other property held by any federal agency or any officer or employee thereof, whether occasioned by contract or operation of law or otherwise, except bonuses and gratuities, which has remained unclaimed by the owner for:

(1) Twenty years from the date of maturity or call for payment, if arising from transactions under the public debt; or

(2) Twenty years after the last transaction concerning principal or interest, if deposits in the postal savings system; or

(3) Five years after the property first became payable, demandable, or returnable, if arising from any other transaction.

(b) "Owner" means any person, including his or her legal representative, who has or had a legal or equitable interest in unclaimed property. The owner shall be conclusively presumed to be the person to whom unclaimed property was or is payable or returnable according to the records of the United States Government. If two or more persons are interested in the property, and the extent of their respective interests is unknown, it shall be presumed that their interests in such property are equal.

(c) "Person" includes any individual, partnership, corporation, limited liability company, unincorporated association, or other legal entity. **Leg.H.** Added Stats 1959 ch 1801 §1. Amended Stats 1994 ch 1010 §64 (SB 2053).

Prior Law: Former CCP §1601, was repealed 1931. See Probate Code.

§1602. Agreement for State's payment of share of costs

The Controller is authorized to enter into agreements establishing the time and manner for payments of this State's proportionate share of the actual and necessary cost incurred by the United States in examining records and reporting information to this State as such share of such cost shall be determined pursuant to federal law. Said agreements may provide for single payments at stated times over a period of years. The State Controller shall make all payments at the time and in the manner provided in said agreements. **Leg.H.** Added Stats 1959 ch 1801 §1.

Prior Law: Former CCP §1602 repealed 1931. See Probate Code.

§1603. Undertaking by State to hold the United States harmless; Intervention by Attorney General; Consent of State to suit

The State hereby undertakes to hold the United States harmless against any claim concerning property delivered to the custody of the State in accordance with the provisions of this chapter. In the event an action or proceeding on such claim is brought against the United States the Attorney General shall intervene therein. The State consents to suit by such claimant in such contingency and any defense in favor of the United States shall be available to and urged by the State. **Leg.H.** Added Stats 1959 ch 1801 §1.

Prior Law: Former CCP §1603 repealed 1931. See Probate Code.

§1604. Unclaimed property subject to delivery to this State; Presumptions

(a) All unclaimed intangible property, together with all interest and other increments accruing thereto, is subject to delivery to this state if the last known address of the owner is in this state. If the last known address of an owner is in this state, any other owner's address which is unknown shall be presumed to be in this state. If the last known addresses of owners are in this state and in one or more other states, the addresses of other owners whose addresses are unknown shall be presumed to be within this state if the federal agency having custody of the unclaimed property initially acquired possession in this state. If the records of the United States do not disclose the address of any owner of unclaimed property, such address shall be presumed to be within this state if the federal agency having custody of such property initially acquired possession in this state. All addresses presumed to be within this state are presumed to be within the County of Sacramento. For the purposes of this chapter, it shall be presumed that the situs of unclaimed intangible property is in this state if the last known or presumed address of the owner is in this state.

(b) All unclaimed tangible property is subject to delivery to this state if the federal agency having custody of the unclaimed property initially acquired possession in this state. **Leg.H.** Added Stats 1959 ch 1801 §1. Amended Stats 1968 ch 356 §54, operative January 1, 1969.

Prior Law: Former CCP §1604 repealed 1931. See Probate Code.

§1605. Certification by Governor

The Governor shall certify to the Comptroller General or other proper officer of the United States that the law of this State provides effective means whereby the United States shall be compensated at reasonable times for this State's proportionate share of the actual and necessary cost of examining records and for reporting information and whereby the United States shall be held harmless in the event of claim for property delivered to this State in accordance with the provisions of this chapter.

Such certification shall be made on the thirtieth day of June next following the effective date of any federal statute requiring such certification. **Leg.H.** Added Stats 1959 ch 1801 §1.

Prior Law: Former CCP §1605 repealed 1931. See Probate Code.

§1606. Request by Controller for report of previously unreported information

On the thirtieth day of June next following the date of certification by the Governor, and annually thereafter, the Controller shall request the Comptroller General or other proper officer of the United States to report all previously unreported information relating to unclaimed property as determined by that officer pursuant to federal law. **Leg.H.** Added Stats 1959 ch 1801 §1.

Prior Law: Former CCP §1606 repealed 1931. See Probate Code.

§1607. Posting copy of report; Notice of interest and intention to claim; Determination of asserted interest

When a report is received from the Comptroller General or other proper officer of the United States, the Controller shall prepare and forward a copy thereof to the clerk of the superior court of each county within this state and the clerk shall post a copy at the courthouse for a period of 60 days. Any person asserting an interest in property mentioned in the report may elect to claim against the United States under the laws of the United States, in which event and within 90 days following the date of initial posting by the clerk the person shall notify the Controller of the asserted interest and intention to so claim. The Controller shall omit the property from any claim by the state until such time as the asserted interest may be finally determined against the claimant. The interest may not thereafter be asserted against the state. **Leg.H.** Added Stats 1959 ch 1801 §1. Amended Stats 2002 ch 784 §84 (SB 1316); Stats 2003 ch 62 §27 (SB 600).

Prior Law: Former CCP §1607 repealed 1931. See Probate Code.

§1608. State's right unaffected by expiration of time for proceeding

The expiration of any period of time specified by statute or court order, during which an action or proceeding may be commenced or enforced to obtain payment of a claim for funds or delivery of property shall not affect the right of this State to acquire possession of unclaimed property in accordance with the provisions of this chapter. **Leg.H.** Added Stats 1959 ch 1801 §1.

§1609. Petition for determination of State's right to custody of unclaimed property; Venue

Within 120 days following the date of initial posting by the clerk of the superior court, the Attorney General shall commence a proceeding by filing a petition to determine the state's right to custody of all property mentioned in such report and unclaimed within the time and in the manner provided by Section 1607. The proceeding shall be commenced and heard in the superior court in the County of Sacramento and venue shall not be affected by the provisions of Section 401, Code of Civil Procedure.

The petition shall name as respondents all persons known to have been interested and "all persons unknown claiming any title or interest in or to the property described or referred to in the petition." If the records of the United States fail to disclose with reasonable certainty the identity or number of owners or claimants of specific funds or other personal property, or the extent of their interests therein, such persons may be designated and described as a class, to wit, as "all unknown owners or claimants to the funds or property mentioned in or affected by ____," and, as the case may be, the petition shall identify and set forth the court actions or proceedings to the credit of which such funds or other property are held, or the accounts or other identifying references under which they are carried upon the records of the United States.

The petition shall describe or refer to the property, and may include one or more items, as the Attorney General may be advised, without prejudice to his right to commence subsequent proceedings relating to other items not included. The petition shall also state the name of the owner and his last address as known or as presumed under this chapter, and shall set forth the facts and circumstances by virtue of which it is claimed that such funds or property are subject to custody by the state. Any number of respondents may be joined whether they reside in the same or different counties, and any number of causes of action may be joined and need not be separately stated. **Leg.H.** Added Stats 1959 ch 1801 §1. Amended Stats 2002 ch 784 §85 (SB 1316).

§1610. Notice of proceeding

No summons or other process shall issue to direct the appearance and answer of a respondent. Commencing within five days after filing petition, notice of the proceeding shall be published once each week for three consecutive weeks in a newspaper of general circulation published within the County of Sacramento. At the time the notice is first published, a copy of the petition and notice shall be posted at the courthouse in the county where each defendant was last known or presumed to have had an address. Such petition and such notice shall remain posted for 45 days. The notice of proceeding shall advise that the State seeks custody of unclaimed property held by the United States. The names but not the addresses of the respondents shall be contained in the notice with a statement that such persons are believed to live or to have lived within the State and are believed to be or to have been owners of the unclaimed property. The notice shall not contain a description of the unclaimed property but shall advise that such description together with the last known or presumed addresses of owners may be determined by examining the petition filed in the proceeding. The petition and its place of filing shall be sufficiently identified and described. The notice shall advise that persons claiming an interest must answer the petition within the time prescribed by law, which time shall be stated, if they elect to pursue their claims against the United States, otherwise their rights to property shall be preserved subject to delayed delivery as provided by law. The notice shall advise that Section 1611, Code of Civil Procedure, should be consulted for the time, form, and costs of an answer.

The notice shall be deemed completed 45 days after the date of first publication, whereupon the court shall have full and complete jurisdiction over the property described in the petition and not claimed within the time or in the manner provided in Section 1611, and shall have full and complete jurisdiction to determine the right of the State to custody and to render an appropriate judgment therefor. **Leg.H.** Added Stats 1959 ch 1801 §1.

§1611. Answer; Disposition of funds on deposit; Dismissal without prejudice

Any person, whether or not named in the petition, may within 15 days after completion of notice respond to the petition by answer describing the property, asserting an interest as owner or successor, and declaring an intention to claim the same from the United States under the laws of the United States. Such answer shall not be filed unless accompanied by the sum of ten dollars ($10) for deposit in court, and no other answer or response shall be filed by or on behalf of a claimant. The court shall strike from the petition and dismiss from the proceeding all property described in the answer. The funds on deposit shall be transmitted by the court to the Controller and shall be received for deposit in the abandoned property account in the Unclaimed Property Fund as total reimbursement for costs and services expended on behalf of the claimant. Such dismissal shall be without prejudice to a subsequent petition should it appear that the claimant is not entitled to the property, and the interest asserted in said answer shall not thereafter be asserted against the State. **Leg.H.** Added Stats 1959 ch 1801 §1.

§1612. Application for judgment relating to property not claimed by answer, and finding and declaration thereon

Within 20 days following expiration of time for filing answer under Section 1611, the Attorney General shall apply to the court for a judgment relating to all property set forth in the petition and not claimed by answer. The court shall find that such property appears to be or to have been owned by persons residing within this State and remains unclaimed by such persons. The court shall declare that the property, which shall be described, is subject to custody of the State and shall be delivered to and received by the State of California to be retained until such time as it may be claimed pursuant to law. **Leg.H.** Added Stats 1959 ch 1801 §1.

Prior Law: Former CCP §1612 repealed 1931. See Probate Code.

§1613. Request for delivery or payment of unclaimed property described in judgment; Receipts

The Controller shall request delivery or payment of all unclaimed property described in the judgment declaring the right of the State to receive custody of such property. The request shall be accompanied by a certified copy of said judgment and shall be directed to such officer, agency, or department of the United States as may be designated for such purposes by federal law. The Controller shall furnish receipts for all property delivered or paid. **Leg.H.** Added Stats 1959 ch 1801 §1.

Prior Law: Former CCP §1613 repealed 1931. See Probate Code.

§1614. Disposition of property received under this chapter; Period of limitation of claims

Property received under this chapter shall be deposited or sold by the State Controller as though received under Chapter 7 (commencing with Section 1500) of this title. Property received under this chapter shall not be subject to claim within two years following the date upon which it is paid to or received by the state. Thereafter, claims shall be made in the manner provided in Chapter 7 (commencing with Section 1500) of this title. **Leg.H.** Added Stats 1959 ch 1801 §1. Amended Stats 1968 ch 356 §55, operative January 1, 1969.

Prior Law: Former CCP §1614 repealed 1931. See Probate Code.

§1615. Appropriation of money in abandoned property account in Unclaimed Property Fund

All money in the abandoned property account in the Unclaimed Property Fund is hereby continuously appropriated to the State Controller without regard to fiscal years, for expenditure in accordance with this chapter for the following purposes:

(a) For payment of the proportionate costs of this State pursuant to the terms of any contract entered with the United States;

(b) For payment of sums necessary to indemnify the United States for losses occasioned by claims to property delivered to the custody of this State. **Leg.H.** Added Stats 1959 ch 1801 §1.

Prior Law: Former CCP §1615 repealed 1931. See Probate Code.

§§1616–1649. [Sections repealed 1931]

Leg.H. Enacted 1872 or added Stats 1905 ch 235 §1, ch 561 §2. Repealed Stats 1907 ch 385 §3, 1907 ch 386 §§2–4, Stats 1931 ch 281 (Prob C §1700). See Prob C §§1041, 1303, 1304, 2630, 2632, 7250, 7622, 8502, 9731, 9733, 9839, 9880–9885, 10800–10803, 10805, 10810–10814, 10830, 10900, 10901, 10950–10953, 11000–11005, 11051, 11052, 11401, 11402, 11420–11425, 11463, 11641.

TITLE 10A
REVISED UNIFORM RECIPROCAL ENFORCEMENT OF SUPPORT ACT OF 1968 [REPEALED]

§1650. [Section repealed 1994]

Leg.H. Added Stats 1953 ch 1290 §2. Amended Stats 1970 ch 1126 §1. Repealed Stats 1992 ch 162 §6 (AB 2650), operative January 1, 1994. See Fam C §4900.

Prior Law: Former CCP §1650, similar to Fam C §4900, was added Stats 1951 ch 694 §1 and repealed Stats 1953 ch 1290 §1.

Original §1650 repealed 1931. See Probate Code.

§1651. [Section repealed 1994]

Leg.H. Added Stats 1953 ch 1290 §2. Repealed Stats 1992 ch 162 §6 (AB 2650), operative January 1, 1994. See Fam C §§3, 4975.

Prior Law: Former CCP §1651, similar to Fam C §4915, was added Stats 1951 ch 694 §1 and repealed Stats 1953 ch 1290 §1.

Original §1651 repealed 1931. See Probate Code.

§1652. [Section repealed 1994]

Leg.H. Added Stats 1953 ch 1290 §2. Repealed Stats 1992 ch 162 §6 (AB 2650), operative January 1, 1994. See Fam C §4915.

Prior Law: Former CCP §1652, similar to Fam C §§155, 4901, was added Stats 1951 ch 694 §1 and repealed Stats 1953 ch 1290 §1.

Original §1652 repealed 1931. See Probate Code.

§1653. [Section repealed 1994]

Leg.H. Added Stats 1970 ch 1126 §3. Amended Stats 1976 ch 1166 §1; Stats 1979 ch 1030 §5; Stats 1985 ch 948 §1. Repealed Stats 1992 ch 162 §6 (AB 2650), operative January 1, 1994. See Fam C §§155, 4901.

Prior Law: Former CCP §1653, similar to Fam C §§155, 4901, was added Stats 1953 ch 1290 §2, amended Stats 1959 ch 710 §1, Stats 1968 ch 1148 §1, and repealed Stats 1970 ch 1126 §2.

Former CCP §1653, similar to former Fam C §4903, was added Stats 1951 ch 694 §1 and repealed Stats 1953 ch 1290 §1.

Original §1653 repealed 1931. See Probate Code.

§1654. [Section repealed 1994]

Leg.H. Added Stats 1953 ch 1290 §2. Amended Stats 1986 ch 183 §1. Repealed Stats 1992 ch 162 §6 (AB 2650), operative January 1, 1994. See Fam C §4903.

Prior Law: Former CCP §1654, similar in part to Fam C §4905, was added Stats 1951 ch 694 §1 and repealed Stats 1953 ch 1290 §1.

§1655. [Section repealed 1994]

Leg.H. Added Stats 1953 ch 1290 §2. Repealed Stats 1992 ch 162 §6 (AB 2650), operative January 1, 1994. See Fam C §4905.

§1655.5. [Section repealed 1994]

Leg.H. Added Stats 1979 ch 1030 §6. Repealed Stats 1992 ch 162 §6 (AB 2650), operative January 1, 1994. See Fam C §4923.

§1656. [Section repealed 1994]

Leg.H. Added Stats 1970 ch 1126 §4. Repealed Stats 1992 ch 162 §6 (AB 2650), operative January 1, 1994. See Fam C §§13, 4976.

§§1658, 1659. [Sections repealed 1931]

Leg.H. Enacted 1872. Repealed Stats 1931 ch 281 (Prob C §1700). See Prob C §§11600–11602, 11620–11622, 12540.

§1660. [Section repealed 1994]

Leg.H. Added Stats 1953 ch 1290 §2. Amended Stats 1970 ch 1126 §5. Repealed Stats 1992 ch 162 §6 (AB 2650), operative January 1, 1994. See Fam C §4970.

Prior Law: Former CCP §1660, similar to Fam C §4970, was added Stats 1951 ch 694 §1 and repealed Stats 1953 ch 1290 §1.

Original §1660 repealed 1931. See Probate Code.

§1661. [Section repealed 1994]

Leg.H. Added Stats 1959 ch 710 §3. Amended Stats 1965 ch 853 §1; Stats 1970 ch 1126 §6. Repealed Stats 1992 ch 162 §6 (AB 2650), operative January 1, 1994. See Fam C §4971.

Prior Law: Former CCP §1661, similar to Fam C §4971, was added Stats 1953 ch 1290 §2 and repealed Stats 1959 ch 710 §2.

Former CCP §1661, similar to Fam C §4971, was added Stats 1951 ch 694 §1 and repealed Stats 1953 ch 1290 §1.

Original §1661 repealed 1931. See Probate Code.

§§1662–1669. [Sections repealed 1931]

Leg.H. Enacted 1872 or added Stats 1885 ch 160 §1, Stats 1889, Stats 1917 ch 492 §1. Repealed Stats 1931 ch 281 (Prob C §1700). See Prob C §§1000, 1303, 1304, 11600–11603, 11605, 11620–11622, 11624, 11640, 11642, 11700–11705, 11750, 11753, 11802, 12540, 12541.

§1670. [Section repealed 1994]

Leg.H. Added Stats 1953 ch 1290 §2. Amended Stats 1970 ch 1126 §7. Repealed Stats 1992 ch 162 §6 (AB 2650), operative January 1, 1994. See Fam C §4940.

Prior Law: Former CCP §1670, similar to Fam C §4940, was added Stats 1951 ch 694 §1 and repealed Stats 1953 ch 1290 §1.

Original §1670 repealed 1931. See Probate Code.

§1671. [Section repealed 1994]

Leg.H. Added Stats 1953 ch 1290 §2. Amended Stats 1970 ch 1126 §8. Repealed Stats 1992 ch 162 §6 (AB 2650), operative January 1, 1994. See Fam C §4910.

Prior Law: Former CCP §1671, similar to Fam C §4910, was added Stats 1951 ch 694 §1 and repealed Stats 1953 ch 1290 §1.

Original §1671 repealed 1931. See Probate Code.

§1672. [Section repealed 1994]

Leg.H. Added Stats 1953 ch 1290 §2. Amended Stats 1959 ch 710 §4; Stats 1970 ch 1126 §9. Repealed Stats 1992 ch 162 §6 (AB 2650), operative January 1, 1994. See Fam C §4929.

Prior Law: Former CCP §1672, similar to Fam C §4929, was added Stats 1951 ch 694 §1 and repealed Stats 1953 ch 1290 §1.

§1672.5. [Section repealed 1994]

Leg.H. Added Stats 1959 ch 710 §5. Repealed Stats 1992 ch 162 §6 (AB 2650), operative January 1, 1994. See Fam C §200.

§1673. [Section repealed 1994]

Leg.H. Added Stats 1953 ch 1290 §2. Amended Stats 1970 ch 1126 §10; Stats 1979 ch 1030 §7. Repealed Stats 1992 ch 162 §6 (AB 2650), operative January 1, 1994. See Fam C §4920.

Prior Law: Former CCP §1673, similar in part to Fam C §4920, was added Stats 1951 ch 694 §1 and repealed Stats 1953 ch 1290 §1.

§1674. [Section repealed 1994]

Leg.H. Added Stats 1953 ch 1290 §2. Amended Stats 1970 ch 1126 §11; Stats 1976 ch 1167 §1; Stats 1991 ch 495 §1.5 (SB 106). Repealed Stats 1992 ch 162 §6 (AB 2650), operative January 1, 1994. See Fam C §4922.

Prior Law: Former CCP §1674, similar in part to Fam C §4911, was added Stats 1951 ch 694 §1 and repealed Stats 1953 ch 1290 §1.

§1675. [Section repealed 1994]

Leg.H. Added Stats 1953 ch 1290 §2. Amended Stats 1970 ch 1126 §12. Repealed Stats 1992 ch 162 §6 (AB 2650), operative January 1, 1994. See Fam C §4915.

Prior Law: Former CCP §1675, similar to Fam C §4917, was added Stats 1951 ch 694 §1 and repealed Stats 1953 ch 1290 §1.

Original §1675 repealed 1931. See Probate Code.

§1676. [Section repealed 1994]

Leg.H. Added Stats 1953 ch 1290 §2. Amended Stats 1970 ch 1126 §13; Stats 1979 ch 1030 §8. Repealed Stats 1992 ch 162 §6 (AB 2650), operative January 1, 1994. See Fam C §4911.

Prior Law: Former CCP §1676, similar to Fam C §4940, was added Stats 1951 ch 694 §1 and repealed Stats 1953 ch 1290 §1.

Original §1676 repealed 1931. See Probate Code.

§1677. [Section repealed 1994]

Leg.H. Added Stats 1953 ch 1290 §2. Amended Stats 1959 ch 710 §6; Stats 1970 ch 1126 §14. Repealed Stats 1992 ch 162 §6 (AB 2650), operative January 1, 1994. See Fam C §4927.

Prior Law: Former CCP §1677, relating to transmission of orders, was added Stats 1951 ch 694 §1 and repealed Stats 1953 ch 1290 §1.
Original §1677, repealed 1931. See Probate Code.

§1678. [Section repealed 1994]

Leg.H. Added Stats 1953 ch 1290 §2. Amended Stats 1970 ch 1126 §15. Repealed Stats 1992 ch 162 §6 (AB 2650), operative January 1, 1994. The repealed section related to detention of defendant.

Prior Law: Former CCP §1678, relating to assurance of compliance, was added Stats 1951 ch 694 §1 and repealed Stats 1953 ch 1290 §1.
Original §1678 repealed 1931. See Probate Code.

§1679. [Section repealed 1994]

Leg.H. Added Stats 1953 ch 1290 §2. Amended Stats 1970 ch 1126 §16; Stats 1988 ch 1295 §2. Repealed Stats 1992 ch 162 §6 (AB 2650), operative January 1, 1994. See Fam C §4924.

Prior Law: Former CCP §1679, similar to Fam C §4917, was added Stats 1951 ch 694 §1 and repealed Stats 1953 ch 1290 §1.
Original §1679 repealed 1931. See Probate Code.

§1680. [Section repealed 1994]

Leg.H. Added Stats 1953 ch 1290 §2. Amended Stats 1959 ch 710 §7; Stats 1970 ch 1126 §17; Stats 1976 ch 1166 §2; Stats 1979 ch 1030 §9; Stats 1991 ch 495 §2 (SB 106). Repealed Stats 1992 ch 162 §6 (AB 2650), operative January 1, 1994. See Fam C §4917.

Prior Law: Former CCP §1680, similar to Fam C §4918, was added Stats 1951 ch 694 §1 and repealed Stats 1953 ch 1290 §1.
Original §1680 repealed 1931. See Probate Code.

§1681. [Section repealed 1994]

Leg.H. Added Stats 1959 ch 710 §9. Amended Stats 1970 ch 1126 §18; Stats 1972 ch 1118 §4; Stats 1976 ch 812 §1; Stats 1979 ch 1030 §10. Repealed Stats 1992 ch 162 §6 (AB 2650), operative January 1, 1994. The repealed section related to tracing property of defendant.

Prior Law: Former CCP §1681, relating to inability to obtain jurisdiction of defendant, was added Stats 1953 ch 1290 §2 and repealed Stats 1959 ch 710 §8.
Former CCP §1681, relating to inapplicability of privilege, was added Stats 1951 ch 694 §1 and repealed Stats 1953 ch 1290 §1.

§1682. [Section repealed 1994]

Leg.H. Added Stats 1953 ch 1290 §2 as CCP §1683. Amended Stats 1959 ch 710 §10. Amended and renumbered Stats 1970 ch 1126 §20. Repealed Stats 1992 ch 162 §6 (AB 2650), operative January 1, 1994. See Fam C §4940.

Prior Law: Former CCP §1682, relating to the manner of conducting proceedings, was added Stats 1953 ch 1290 §2 and repealed Stats 1970 ch 1126 §19.
Original §1682 repealed 1931. See Probate Code.

§1683. [Section repealed 1994]

Leg.H. Added Stats 1959 ch 710 §11 as CCP §1683.5. Amended and renumbered Stats 1970 ch 1126 §21. Repealed Stats 1992 ch 162 §6 (AB 2650), operative January 1, 1994. See Fam C §4945.

Prior Law: Former CCP §1683 was added Stats 1953 ch 1290 §2, amended Stats 1959 ch 710 §10, and amended and renumbered CCP §1682 by Stats 1970 ch 1126 §20.
Original §1683 repealed 1931. See Probate Code.

§1683.5. [Section renumbered 1970]

Leg.H. Added Stats 1959 ch 710 §11. Amended and renumbered CCP §1683 by Stats 1970 ch 1126 §21.

§1684. [Section repealed 1994]

Leg.H. Added Stats 1953 ch 1290 §2. Amended Stats 1970 ch 1126 §22; Stats 1976 ch 1167 §2; Stats 1979 ch 1030 §11. Repealed Stats 1992 ch 162 §6 (AB 2650), operative January 1, 1994. The repealed section related to sending copy of orders to the initiating state.

Prior Law: Former CCP §1684 repealed 1931. See Probate Code.

§1685. [Section repealed 1994]

Leg.H. Added Stats 1953 ch 1290 §2. Amended Stats 1959 ch 710 §12; Stats 1970 ch 1126 §23. Repealed Stats 1992 ch 162 §6 (AB 2650), operative January 1, 1994. The repealed section related to additional powers of the court.

Prior Law: Former CCP §1685 repealed 1931. See Probate Code.

§1686. [Section repealed 1994]

Leg.H. Added Stats 1953 ch 1290 §2. Amended Stats 1970 ch 1126 §24. Repealed Stats 1992 ch 162 §6 (AB 2650), operative January 1, 1994. See Fam C §4917.

Prior Law: Former CCP §1686 repealed 1931. See Probate Code.

§1687. [Section repealed 1994]

Leg.H. Added Stats 1953 ch 1290 §2. Amended Stats 1970 ch 1126 §25. Repealed Stats 1992 ch 162 §6 (AB 2650), operative January 1, 1994. See Fam C §4918.

§1688. [Section repealed 1994]

Leg.H. Added Stats 1953 ch 1290 §2. Repealed Stats 1992 ch 162 §6 (AB 2650), operative January 1, 1994. See Fam C §4930.

§1689. [Section repealed 1994]

Leg.H. Added Stats 1953 ch 1290 §2. Amended Stats 1959 ch 710 §13; Stats 1970 ch 1126 §26. Repealed Stats 1992 ch 162 §6 (AB 2650), operative January 1, 1994. See Fam C §4912.

§1690. [Section repealed 1994]

Leg.H. Added Stats 1953 ch 1290 §2. Amended Stats 1970 ch 1126 §27. Repealed Stats 1992 ch 162 §6 (AB 2650), operative January 1, 1994. See Fam C §4928.

§1691. [Section repealed 1994]

Leg.H. Added Stats 1959 ch 710 §14. Amended Stats 1970 ch 1126 §28. Repealed Stats 1992 ch 162 §6 (AB 2650), operative January 1, 1994. The repealed section related to proceedings not being stayed by divorce, etc.

Prior Law: Former CCP §1691 repealed 1931. See Probate Code.

§1692. [Section repealed 1994]

Leg.H. Added Stats 1959 ch 710 §15. Amended Stats 1970 ch 1126 §29. Repealed Stats 1992 ch 162 §6 (AB 2650), operative January 1, 1994. The repealed section related to applicability of title.

Prior Law: Former CCP §1692 repealed 1931. See Probate Code.

§1693. [Section repealed 1994]

Leg.H. Added Stats 1968 ch 1148 §2. Amended Stats 1970 ch 1126 §30. Repealed Stats 1992 ch 162 §6 (AB 2650), operative January 1, 1994. The repealed section related to declaration of a foreign jurisdiction to be a reciprocating state.

Prior Law: Former CCP §1693 repealed 1931. See Probate Code.

§1694. [Section repealed 1994]

Leg.H. Added Stats 1970 ch 1126 §31 as §1695. Renumbered Stats 1974 ch 80 §1. Repealed Stats 1992 ch 162 §6 (AB 2650), operative January 1, 1994. The repealed section related to the rules of evidence.

Prior Law: Former CCP §1694 repealed 1931. See Probate Code.

§1695. [Section repealed 1994]

Leg.H. Added Stats 1970 ch 1126 §32 as CCP §1696. Renumbered Stats 1974 ch 80 §2. Repealed Stats 1992 ch 162 §6 (AB 2650), operative January 1, 1994. See Fam C §4929.

Prior Law: Former CCP §1695 was added Stats 1970 ch 1126 §31 and renumbered CCP §1694 by Stats 1974 ch 80 §1.
Original §1695 repealed 1931. See Probate Code.

§1696. [Section repealed 1994]

Leg.H. Added Stats 1970 ch 1126 §33 as CCP §1697. Renumbered Stats 1974 ch 80 §3. Repealed Stats 1992 ch 162 §6 (AB 2650), operative January 1, 1994. See Fam C §4922.

Prior Law: Former CCP §1696 was added Stats 1970 ch 1126 §32 and renumbered CCP §1695 by Stats 1974 ch 80 §2.
Original §1696 repealed 1931. See Probate Code.

§1697. [Section repealed 1994]

Leg.H. Added Stats 1974 ch 80 §4. Amended Stats 1979 ch 1030 §12. Repealed Stats 1992 ch 162 §6 (AB 2650), operative January 1, 1994. Amended Stats 1993 ch 876 §13 (SB 1068), effective October 6, 1993, operative until January 1, 1994. Repealed January 1, 1994, by its own terms. The repealed section related to additional responsibilities.

§1698. [Section repealed 1994]

Leg.H. Added Stats 1974 ch 80 §5. Amended Stats 1985 ch 948 §2. Repealed Stats 1992 ch 162 §6 (AB 2650), operative January 1, 1994. Amended Stats 1993 ch 876 §14 (SB 1068), effective October 6, 1993, operative until January 1, 1994. Repealed January 1, 1994, by its own terms. The repealed section related to registration of a foreign support order.

Prior Law: Former CCP §1698 repealed 1931. See Probate Code.

§1698.1. [Section repealed 1994]

Leg.H. Added Stats 1974 ch 80 §6. Repealed Stats 1992 ch 162 §6 (AB 2650), operative January 1, 1994. The repealed section related to registry of foreign support orders.

§1698.2. [Section repealed 1994]

Leg.H. Added Stats 1974 ch 80 §7. Amended Stats 1991 ch 495 §3 (SB 106). Repealed Stats 1992 ch 162 §6 (AB 2650), operative January 1, 1994. See Fam C §4924.

§1698.3. [Section repealed 1994]

Leg.H. Added Stats 1974 ch 80 §8. Amended Stats 1976 ch 1166 §3. Repealed Stats 1992 ch 162 §6 (AB 2650), operative January 1, 1994. The repealed section related to registration and notice of registration of a foreign support order.

§1699. [Section repealed 1994]

Leg.H. Added Stats 1974 ch 80 §9. Amended Stats 1975 ch 678 §7; Stats 1976 ch 1166 §4; Stats 1985 ch 948 §3; Stats 1990 ch 411 §7 (AB 3973), effective and operative July 24, 1990; Stats 1991 ch 110 §16 (SB 101). Repealed Stats 1992 ch 162 §6 (AB 2650), operative January 1, 1994. Amended Stats 1992 ch 848 §11 (SB 1614), effective September 22, 1992 (ch 848 prevails). Repealed Stats 1993 ch 219 §70 (AB 1500). Amended Stats 1993 ch 876 §15 (SB 1068), effective October 6, 1993. Repealed January 1, 1994, by its own terms. The repealed section related to treatment of registered foreign support order.

Prior Law: Former CCP §1699 repealed 1931. See Probate Code.

§1699.4. [Section repealed 1994]

Leg.H. Added Stats 1985 ch 948 §4. Repealed Stats 1992 ch 162 §6 (AB 2650), operative January 1, 1994. The repealed section related to service of modification of support order on rendering court.

TITLE 10B
FIDUCIARIES' WARTIME SUBSTITUTION LAW [REPEALED]

§1700. [Section repealed 1989]

Leg.H. Added Stats 1953 ch 52 §11. Repealed Stats 1988 ch 1199 §12.5, operative July 1, 1989.

Prior Law: Former CCP §1700 repealed 1931. See Probate Code.

§1700.1. [Section repealed 1989]

Leg.H. Added Stats 1953 ch 52 §11. Repealed Stats 1988 ch 1199 §12.5, operative July 1, 1989.

§1700.2. [Section repealed 1989]

Leg.H. Added Stats 1953 ch 52 §11. Repealed Stats 1988 ch 1199 §12.5, operative July 1, 1989.

§1700.3. [Section repealed 1989]

Leg.H. Added Stats 1953 ch 52 §11. Amended Stats 1979 ch 730 §31, operative January 1, 1981. Repealed Stats 1988 ch 1199 §12.5, operative July 1, 1989.

§1700.4. [Section repealed 1989]

Leg.H. Added Stats 1953 ch 52 §11. Repealed Stats 1988 ch 1199 §12.5, operative July 1, 1989.

§1700.5. [Section repealed 1989]

Leg.H. Added Stats 1953 ch 52 §11. Repealed Stats 1988 ch 1199 §12.5, operative July 1, 1989.

§1700.6. [Section repealed 1989]

Leg.H. Added Stats 1953 ch 52 §11. Repealed Stats 1988 ch 1199 §12.5, operative July 1, 1989.

§1700.7. [Section repealed 1989]

Leg.H. Added Stats 1953 ch 52 §11. Repealed Stats 1988 ch 1199 §12.5, operative July 1, 1989.

§1700.8. [Section repealed 1989]

Leg.H. Added Stats 1953 ch 52 §11. Repealed Stats 1988 ch 1199 §12.5, operative July 1, 1989.

§1701. [Section repealed 1989]

Leg.H. Added Stats 1953 ch 52 §11. Repealed Stats 1988 ch 1199 §12.5, operative July 1, 1989.

Prior Law: Former CCP §1701 repealed 1931. See Probate Code.

§1701.1. [Section repealed 1989]

Leg.H. Added Stats 1953 ch 52 §11. Repealed Stats 1988 ch 1199 §12.5, operative July 1, 1989.

§1701.2. [Section repealed 1989]

Leg.H. Added Stats 1953 ch 52 §11. Repealed Stats 1988 ch 1199 §12.5, operative July 1, 1989.

§1701.3. [Section repealed 1989]

Leg.H. Added Stats 1953 ch 52 §11. Repealed Stats 1988 ch 1199 §12.5, operative July 1, 1989.

§1701.4. [Section repealed 1989]

Leg.H. Added Stats 1953 ch 52 §11. Repealed Stats 1988 ch 1199 §12.5, operative July 1, 1989.

§1701.5. [Section repealed 1989]

Leg.H. Added Stats 1953 ch 52 §11. Repealed Stats 1988 ch 1199 §12.5, operative July 1, 1989.

§1701.6. [Section repealed 1989]

Leg.H. Added Stats 1953 ch 52 §11. Repealed Stats 1988 ch 1199 §12.5, operative July 1, 1989.

§1701.7. [Section repealed 1989]

Leg.H. Added Stats 1953 ch 52 §11. Repealed Stats 1988 ch 1199 §12.5, operative July 1, 1989.

§1702. [Section repealed 1989]

Leg.H. Added Stats 1953 ch 52 §11. Repealed Stats 1988 ch 1199 §12.5, operative July 1, 1989.

Prior Law: Former CCP §1702 repealed 1931. See Probate Code.

§1702.1. [Section repealed 1989]

Leg.H. Added Stats 1953 ch 52 §11. Repealed Stats 1988 ch 1199 §12.5, operative July 1, 1989.

§1702.2. [Section repealed 1989]

Leg.H. Added Stats 1953 ch 52 §11. Repealed Stats 1988 ch 1199 §12.5, operative July 1, 1989.

§1702.3. [Section repealed 1989]

Leg.H. Added Stats 1953 ch 52 §11. Repealed Stats 1988 ch 1199 §12.5, operative July 1, 1989.

§1702.4. [Section repealed 1989]

Leg.H. Added Stats 1953 ch 52 §11. Repealed Stats 1988 ch 1199 §12.5, operative July 1, 1989.

§1703. [Section repealed 1989]

Leg.H. Added Stats 1953 ch 52 §11. Repealed Stats 1988 ch 1199 §12.5, operative July 1, 1989.

Prior Law: Former CCP §1703 repealed 1931. See Probate Code.

§1703½. [Section repealed 1931]

Leg.H. Added Stats 1897 ch 40 §1. Repealed Stats 1931 ch 281 (Prob C §1700). See Prob C §§11850, 11852.

§1703.1. [Section repealed 1989]

Leg.H. Added Stats 1953 ch 52 §11. Repealed Stats 1988 ch 1199 §12.5, operative July 1, 1989.

§1703.2. [Section repealed 1989]

Leg.H. Added Stats 1953 ch 52 §11. Repealed Stats 1988 ch 1199 §12.5, operative July 1, 1989.

§1703.3. [Section repealed 1989]

Leg.H. Added Stats 1953 ch 52 §11. Repealed Stats 1988 ch 1199 §12.5, operative July 1, 1989.

§1704. [Section repealed 1989]

Leg.H. Added Stats 1953 ch 52 §11. Amended Stats 1979 ch 730 §32, operative January 1, 1981. Repealed Stats 1988 ch 1199 §12.5, operative July 1, 1989.

Prior Law: Former CCP §1704 repealed 1931. See Probate Code.

§1704.1. [Section repealed 1989]

Leg.H. Added Stats 1953 ch 52 §11. Amended Stats 1979 ch 730 §33, operative January 1, 1981. Repealed Stats 1988 ch 1199 §12.5, operative July 1, 1989.

§1705. [Section repealed 1989]

Leg.H. Added Stats 1953 ch 52 §11. Repealed Stats 1988 ch 1199 §12.5, operative July 1, 1989.

Prior Law: Former CCP §1705 repealed 1931. See Probate Code.

§1706. [Section repealed 1989]

Leg.H. Added Stats 1953 ch 52 §11. Repealed Stats 1988 ch 1199 §12.5, operative July 1, 1989.

Prior Law: Former CCP §1706 repealed 1931. See Probate Code.

§§1707–1710. [Sections repealed 1931]

Leg.H. Enacted 1872. Repealed Stats 1931 ch 281 (Prob C §1700). See Prob C §§1240, 1241.

TITLE 11
MONEY JUDGMENTS OF OTHER JURISDICTIONS

Chapter 1. Sister State Money—Judgments.
Chapter 2. Foreign-Country Money Judgments.
Chapter 3. Tribal Court Civil Money Judgment Act.

CHAPTER 1
SISTER STATE MONEY—JUDGMENTS

Definitions. §1710.10.
Application for entry of judgment. §1710.15.
Venue. §1710.20.
Entry of judgment. §1710.25.
Service of notice of entry of judgment. §1710.30.
Effect and enforcement of judgments. §1710.35.
Vacation of judgment. §1710.40.
Issuance of writ of execution. §1710.45.
Stay of enforcement. §1710.50.
Limitations on entry of judgment. §1710.55.
Optional procedure. §1710.60.
Actions based on part of judgment of sister state not requiring payment of money. §1710.65.

§1710.10. Definitions

As used in this chapter:

(a) "Judgment creditor" means the person or persons who can bring an action to enforce a sister state judgment.

(b) "Judgment debtor" means the person or persons against whom an action to enforce a sister state judgment can be brought.

(c) "Sister state judgment" means that part of any judgment, decree, or order of a court of a state of the United States, other than California, which requires the payment of money, but does not include a support order as defined in Section 155 of the Family Code. **Leg.H.** Added Stats 1974 ch 211 §3. Amended Stats 1992 ch 163 §64 (AB 2641), operative January 1, 1994.

§1710.15. Application for entry of judgment

(a) A judgment creditor may apply for the entry of a judgment based on a sister state judgment by filing an application pursuant to Section 1710.20.

(b) The application shall be executed under oath and shall include all of the following:

(1) A statement that an action in this state on the sister state judgment is not barred by the applicable statute of limitations.

(2) A statement, based on the applicant's information and belief, that no stay of enforcement of the sister state judgment is currently in effect in the sister state.

(3) A statement of the amount remaining unpaid under the sister state judgment and, if accrued interest on the sister state judgment is to be included in the California judgment, a statement of the amount of interest accrued on the sister state judgment (computed at the rate of interest applicable to the judgment under the law of the sister state), a statement of the rate of interest applicable to the judgment under the law of the sister state, and a citation to the law of the sister state establishing the rate of interest.

(4) A statement that no action based on the sister state judgment is currently pending in any court in this state and that no judgment based on the sister state judgment has previously been entered in any proceeding in this state.

(5) Where the judgment debtor is an individual, a statement setting forth the name and last known residence address of the judgment debtor. Where the judgment debtor is a corporation, a statement of the corporation's name, place of incorporation, and whether the corporation, if foreign, has qualified to do business in this state under the provisions of Chapter 21 (commencing with Section 2100) of Division 1 of Title 1 of the Corporations Code. Where the judgment debtor is a partnership, a statement of the name of the partnership, whether it is a foreign partnership, and, if it is a foreign partnership, whether it has filed a statement pursuant to Section 15800 of the Corporations Code designating an agent for service of process. Except for facts which are matters of public record in this state, the statements required by this paragraph may be made on the basis of the judgment creditor's information and belief.

(6) A statement setting forth the name and address of the judgment creditor.

(c) A properly authenticated copy of the sister state judgment shall be attached to the application. **Leg.H.** Added Stats 1974 ch 211 §3. Amended Stats 1977 ch 232 §1; Stats 1982 ch 150 §4; Stats 1984 ch 311 §2; Stats 1985 ch 106 §11.

§1710.20. Venue

(a) An application for entry of a judgment based on a sister state judgment shall be filed in a superior court.

(b) Subject to the power of the court to transfer proceedings under this chapter pursuant to Title 4 (commencing with Section 392) of Part 2, the proper county for the filing of an application is any of the following:

(1) The county in which any judgment debtor resides.

(2) If no judgment debtor is a resident, any county in this state.

(c) A case in which the sister state judgment amounts to thirty-five thousand dollars ($35,000) or less is a limited civil case. **Leg.H.** Added Stats 1974 ch 211 §3. Amended Stats 1984 ch 311 §3; Stats 1988 ch 54 §1; Stats 1998 ch 931 §125 (SB 2139), effective September 28, 1998; Stats 2002 ch 784 §86 (SB 1316); Stats 2023 ch 861 §7 (SB 71), effective January 1, 2024.

§1710.25. Entry of judgment

(a) Upon the filing of the application, the clerk shall enter a judgment based upon the application for the total of the following amounts as shown therein:

(1) The amount remaining unpaid under the sister state judgment.

(2) The amount of interest accrued on the sister state judgment (computed at the rate of interest applicable to the judgment under the law of the sister state).

(3) The amount of the fee for filing the application for entry of the sister state judgment.

(b) Entry shall be made in the same manner as entry of an original judgment of the court. From the time of entry, interest shall accrue on the judgment so entered at the rate of interest applicable to a judgment entered in this state. **Leg.H.** Added Stats 1974 ch 211 §3. Amended Stats 1977 ch 232 §2; Stats 1982 ch 150 §5; Stats 1984 ch 311 §4.

§1710.30. Service of notice of entry of judgment

(a) Notice of entry of judgment shall be served promptly by the judgment creditor upon the judgment debtor in the manner provided for service of summons by Article 3 (commencing with Section 415.10) of Chapter 4 of Title 5 of Part 2. Notice shall be in a form prescribed by the Judicial Council and shall inform the judgment debtor that the judgment debtor has 30 days within which to make a motion to vacate the judgment.

(b) The fee for service of the notice of entry of judgment under this section is an item of costs recoverable in the same manner as statutory fees for service of a writ as provided in Chapter 5 (commencing with Section 685.010) of Division 1 of Title 9 of Part 2, but such fee may not exceed the amount allowed to a public officer or employee in this state for such service. **Leg.H.** Added Stats 1974 ch 211 §3. Amended Stats 1977 ch 232 §3; Stats 1982 ch 497 §79, operative July 1, 1983.

§1710.35. Effect and enforcement of judgments

Except as otherwise provided in this chapter, a judgment entered pursuant to this chapter shall have the same effect as an original money judgment of the court and may be enforced or satisfied in like manner. **Leg.H.** Added Stats 1974 ch 211 §3. Amended Stats 1984 ch 311 §5.

§1710.40. Vacation of judgment

(a) A judgment entered pursuant to this chapter may be vacated on any ground which would be a defense to an action in this state on the sister state judgment, including the ground that the amount of interest accrued on the sister state judgment and included in the judgment entered pursuant to this chapter is incorrect.

(b) Not later than 30 days after service of notice of entry of judgment pursuant to Section 1710.30, proof of which has been made in the manner provided by Article 5 (commencing with Section 417.10) of Chapter 4 of Title 5 of Part 2, the judgment debtor, on written notice to the judgment creditor, may make a motion to vacate the judgment under this section.

(c) Upon the hearing of the motion to vacate the judgment under this section, the judgment may be vacated upon any ground provided in subdivision (a) and another and different judgment entered, including, but not limited to, another and different judgment for the judgment creditor if the decision of the court is that the judgment creditor is entitled to such different judgment. The decision of the court on the motion to vacate the judgment shall be given and filed with the clerk of court in the manner provided in Sections 632, 634, and 635, except that the court is not required to make any written findings and conclusions if the amount of the judgment as entered under Section 1710.25 does not exceed one thousand dollars ($1,000). **Leg.H.** Added Stats 1974 ch 211 §3. Amended Stats 1977 ch 232 §4.

§1710.45. Issuance of writ of execution

(a) Except as otherwise provided in this section, a writ of execution on a judgment entered pursuant to this chapter shall not issue, nor may the judgment be enforced by other means, until at least 30 days after the judgment creditor serves notice of entry of the judgment upon the judgment debtor, proof of which has been made in the manner provided by Article 5 (commencing with Section 417.10) of Chapter 4 of Title 5 of Part 2.

(b) A writ of execution may be issued, or other enforcement sought, before service of the notice of entry of judgment if the judgment debtor is any of the following:

(1) An individual who does not reside in this state.

(2) A foreign corporation not qualified to do business in this state under the provisions of Chapter 21 (commencing with Section 2100) of Division 1 of Title 1 of the Corporations Code.

(3) A foreign partnership which has not filed a statement pursuant to Section 15700 of the Corporations Code designating an agent for service of process.

(c) The court may order that a writ of execution be issued, or may permit enforcement by other means, before service of the notice of entry of judgment if the court finds upon an ex parte showing that great or irreparable injury would result to the judgment creditor if issuance of the writ or enforcement were delayed as provided in subdivision (a).

(d) Property levied upon pursuant to a writ issued under subdivision (b) or (c) or otherwise sought to be applied to the satisfaction of the judgment shall not be sold or distributed before 30 days after the judgment creditor serves notice of entry of the judgment upon the judgment debtor, proof of which has been made in the manner provided by Article 5 (commencing with Section 417.10) of Chapter 4 of Title 5 of Part 2. However, if property levied upon is perishable, it may be sold in order to prevent its destruction or loss of value, but the proceeds of the sale shall not be distributed to the judgment creditor before the date sale of nonperishable property is permissible. **Leg.H.** Added Stats 1974 ch 211 §3. Amended Stats 1976 ch 641 §1.2; Stats 1982 ch 497 §80, operative July 1, 1983.

§1710.50. Stay of enforcement

(a) The court shall grant a stay of enforcement where:

(1) An appeal from the sister state judgment is pending or may be taken in the state which originally rendered the judgment. Under this paragraph, enforcement shall be stayed until the proceedings on appeal have been concluded or the time for appeal has expired.

(2) A stay of enforcement of the sister state judgment has been granted in the sister state. Under this paragraph, enforcement shall be stayed until the sister state stay of enforcement expires or is vacated.

(3) The judgment debtor has made a motion to vacate pursuant to Section 1710.40. Under this paragraph, enforcement shall be stayed until the judgment debtor's motion to vacate is determined.

(4) A money judgment or lien on real property was obtained against a person or entity for exercising a right guaranteed under the United States Constitution or a right guaranteed under the California Constitution, or against a person or entity for aiding and abetting the exercise of said rights. The stay of enforcement shall remain in place until such time as the statute of limitations in Section 1798.303 of the Civil Code has elapsed or an action prosecuted under Section 1798.303 has concluded, whichever is later.

(5) Any other circumstance exists where the interests of justice require a stay of enforcement.

(b) The court may grant a stay of enforcement under this section on its own motion, on ex parte motion, or on noticed motion.

(c) The court shall grant a stay of enforcement under this section on such terms and conditions as are just including but not limited to the following:

(1) The court may require an undertaking in an amount it determines to be just, but the amount of the undertaking shall not exceed double the amount of the judgment creditor's claim.

(2) If a writ of execution has been issued, the court may order that it remain in effect.

(3) If property of the judgment debtor has been levied upon under a writ of execution, the court may order the levying officer to retain possession of the property capable of physical possession and to maintain the levy on other property. **Leg.H.** Added Stats 1974 ch 211 §3. Amended Stats 2023 ch 260 §9 (SB 345), effective January 1, 2024.

§1710.55. Limitations on entry of judgment

No judgment based on a sister state judgment may be entered pursuant to this chapter in any of the following cases:

(a) A stay of enforcement of the sister state judgment is currently in effect in the sister state.

(b) An action based on the sister state judgment is currently pending in any court in this state.

(c) A judgment based on the sister state judgment has previously been entered in any proceeding in this state. **Leg.H.** Added Stats 1974 ch 211 §3.

§1710.60. Optional procedure

(a) Except as provided in subdivision (b), nothing in this chapter affects any right a judgment creditor may have to bring an action to enforce a sister state judgment.

(b) No action to enforce a sister state judgment may be brought where a judgment based on such sister state judgment has previously been entered pursuant to this chapter. **Leg.H.** Added Stats 1974 ch 211 §3.

§1710.65. Actions based on part of judgment of sister state not requiring payment of money

The entry of a judgment based on a sister state judgment pursuant to this chapter does not limit the right of the judgment creditor to bring an action based on the part of a judgment of a sister state which does not require the payment of money, nor does the bringing of such an action limit the right of the judgment creditor to obtain entry of judgment based on the sister state judgment pursuant to this chapter. **Leg.H.** Added Stats 1974 ch 211 §3.

§§1711, 1712. [Sections repealed 1931]

Leg.H. Enacted 1872. Repealed Stats 1931 ch 281 (Prob C §1700). See Prob C §§1240, 1242.

CHAPTER 2
FOREIGN-COUNTRY MONEY JUDGMENTS

Citation of chapter. §1713.
"Foreign country"; "Foreign-country judgment". §1714.
Applicability of chapter. §1715.
Recognition of foreign-country judgment; Burden. §1716.
Lack of personal jurisdiction. §1717.
Recognition of a foreign-country judgment sought as an original matter or in a pending action. §1718.
Conclusiveness and enforceability of judgment. §1719.
Stay on appeal. §1720.
Limitation of actions. §1721.
Construction in aid of uniformity. §1722.
Situations not covered by chapter. §1723.
Applicability of chapter to actions commenced before, on or after, the effective date of chapter. §1724.
Foreign-country defamation judgment; Declaratory relief or determination that judgment not recognizable. §1725.

§1713. Citation of chapter

This chapter may be cited as the Uniform Foreign-Country Money Judgments Recognition Act. **Leg.H.** Added Stats 2007 ch 212 §2 (SB 639), effective January 1, 2008.

Prior Law: Former CCP §1713, similar to the present section, was added Stats 1967 ch 503 §1 and repealed Stats 2007 ch 212 §1.

Former CCP §1713, similar to present Prob C §§1022, 8220, was enacted 1872 and repealed Stats 1931 ch 281 (Prob C §1700).

§1713.1. [Section repealed 2008]

Leg.H. Added Stats 1967 ch 503 §1. Amended Stats 1974 ch 211 §4. Repealed Stats 2007 ch 212 §1 (SB 639), effective January 1, 2008. The repealed section related to definitions of "foreign state" and "foreign judgment.".

§1713.2. [Section repealed 2008]
Leg.H. Added Stats 1967 ch 503 §1. Repealed Stats 2007 ch 212 §1 (SB 639), effective January 1, 2008. The repealed section related to the applicability of chapter.

§1713.3. [Section repealed 2008]
Leg.H. Added Stats 1967 ch 503 §1. Amended Stats 1974 ch 211 §5. Repealed Stats 2007 ch 212 §1 (SB 639), effective January 1, 2008. The repealed section related to the conclusiveness and enforceability of judgment.

§1713.4. [Section repealed 2008]
Leg.H. Added Stats 1967 ch 503 §1. Repealed Stats 2007 ch 212 §1 (SB 639), effective January 1, 2008. The repealed section related to when a foreign judgment is not conclusive.

§1713.5. [Section repealed 2008]
Leg.H. Added Stats 1967 ch 503 §1. Repealed Stats 2007 ch 212 §1 (SB 639), effective January 1, 2008. The repealed section related to lack of personal jurisdiction.

§1713.6. [Section repealed 2008]
Leg.H. Added Stats 1967 ch 503 §1. Repealed Stats 2007 ch 212 §1 (SB 639), effective January 1, 2008. The repealed section related to stay on appeal.

§1713.7. [Section repealed 2008]
Leg.H. Added Stats 1967 ch 503 §1. Repealed Stats 2007 ch 212 §1 (SB 639), effective January 1, 2008. The repealed section related to recognition or nonrecognition of a foreign judgment in situations not covered by the chapter.

§1713.8. [Section repealed 2008]
Leg.H. Added Stats 1967 ch 503 §1. Repealed Stats 2007 ch 212 §1 (SB 639), effective January 1, 2008. The repealed section related to construction of chapter.

§1714. "Foreign country"; "Foreign-country judgment"
As used in this chapter:

(a) "Foreign country" means a government other than any of the following:

(1) The United States.

(2) A state, district, commonwealth, territory, or insular possession of the United States.

(3) A federally recognized Indian nation, tribe, pueblo, band, or Alaska Native village.

(4) Any other government with regard to which the decision in this state as to whether to recognize a judgment of that government's courts is initially subject to determination under the Full Faith and Credit Clause of the United States Constitution.

(b) "Foreign-country judgment" means a judgment of a court of a foreign country. **Leg.H.** Added Stats 2007 ch 212 §2 (SB 639), effective January 1, 2008. Amended Stats 2014 ch 243 §2 (SB 406), effective January 1, 2015, repealed January 1, 2018; Stats 2017 ch 168 §3 (AB 905), effective January 1, 2018.

Prior Law: Former CCP §1714, similar to the present section, was added Stats 2014 ch 243 §3 (SB 406), effective January 1, 2015, operative January 1, 2018, and repealed Stats 2017 ch 168 §4 (AB 905), effective January 1, 2018.

Former CCP §1714, similar to present Prob C §7220, was enacted 1872, amended Stats 1911 ch 219 §1, Stats 1917 ch 83 §1, and repealed Stats 1931 ch 281 (Prob C §1700).

§1715. Applicability of chapter
(a) Except as otherwise provided in subdivision (b), this chapter applies to a foreign-country judgment to the extent that the judgment both:

(1) Grants or denies recovery of a sum of money.

(2) Under the law of the foreign country where rendered, is final, conclusive, and enforceable.

(b) This chapter does not apply to a foreign-country judgment, even if the judgment grants or denies recovery of a sum of money, to the extent that the judgment is any of the following:

(1) A judgment for taxes.

(2) A fine or other penalty.

(3)(A) A judgment for divorce, support, or maintenance, or other judgment rendered in connection with domestic relations.

(B) A judgment for divorce, support, or maintenance, or other judgment rendered in connection with domestic relations may be recognized by a court of this state pursuant to Section 1723.

(c) A party seeking recognition of a foreign-country judgment has the burden of establishing that the foreign-country judgment is entitled to recognition under this chapter. **Leg.H.** Added Stats 2007 ch 212 §2 (SB 639), effective January 1, 2008.

Prior Law: Former CCP §1715, relating to the time for appeal in probate proceedings, was enacted 1872, amended Stats 1911 ch 219 §1, and repealed Stats 1931 ch 281 (Prob C §1700).

§1716. Recognition of foreign-country judgment; Burden
(a) Except as otherwise provided in subdivisions (b), (c), (d), and (f), a court of this state shall recognize a foreign-country judgment to which this chapter applies.

(b) A court of this state shall not recognize a foreign-country judgment if any of the following apply:

(1) The judgment was rendered under a judicial system that does not provide impartial tribunals or procedures compatible with the requirements of due process of law.

(2) The foreign court did not have personal jurisdiction over the defendant.

(3) The foreign court did not have jurisdiction over the subject matter.

(c)(1) A court of this state shall not recognize a foreign-country judgment if any of the following apply:

(A) The defendant in the proceeding in the foreign court did not receive notice of the proceeding in sufficient time to enable the defendant to defend.

(B) The judgment was obtained by fraud that deprived the losing party of an adequate opportunity to present its case.

(C) The judgment or the cause of action or claim for relief on which the judgment is based is repugnant to the public policy of this state or of the United States.

(D) The proceeding in the foreign court was contrary to an agreement between the parties under which the dispute in question was to be determined otherwise than by proceedings in that foreign court.

(E) In the case of jurisdiction based only on personal service, the foreign court was a seriously inconvenient forum for the trial of the action.

(F) The judgment was rendered in circumstances that raise substantial doubt about the integrity of the rendering court with respect to the judgment.

(G) The specific proceeding in the foreign court leading to the judgment was not compatible with the requirements of due process of law.

(2) Notwithstanding an applicable ground for nonrecognition under paragraph (1), the court may nonetheless recognize a foreign-country judgment if the party seeking recognition of the judgment demonstrates good reason to recognize the judgment that outweighs the ground for nonrecognition.

(d) A court of this state is not required to recognize a foreign-country judgment if the judgment conflicts with another final and conclusive judgment.

(e) If the party seeking recognition of a foreign-country judgment has met its burden of establishing recognition of the foreign-country judgment pursuant to subdivision (c) of Section 1715, a party resisting recognition of a foreign-country judgment has the burden of establishing that a ground for nonrecognition stated in subdivision (b), (c), or (d) exists.

(f) A court of this state shall not recognize a foreign-country judgment for defamation if that judgment is not recognizable under Section 4102 of Title 28 of the United States Code. **Leg.H.** Added Stats 2007 ch 212 §2 (SB 639), effective January 1, 2008. Amended Stats 2009 ch 579 §1 (SB 320), effective January 1, 2010; Stats 2017 ch 168 §5 (AB 905), effective January 1, 2018.

Prior Law: Former CCP §1716, similar to present Fam C §210, Prob C §§825, 1000, 1044, 1048, 1049, 1452, 17006, was enacted 1872, amended Code Amdts 1880 ch 85 §125, and repealed Stats 1931 ch 281 (Prob C §1700).

§1717. Lack of personal jurisdiction
(a) For the purpose of paragraph (2) of subdivision (b) of Section 1716, a foreign court lacks personal jurisdiction over a defendant if either of the following conditions is met:

(1) The foreign court lacks a basis for exercising personal jurisdiction that would be sufficient according to the standards governing personal jurisdiction in this state.

(2) The foreign court lacks personal jurisdiction under its own law.

(b) A foreign-country judgment shall not be refused recognition for lack of personal jurisdiction under paragraph (1) of subdivision (a) if any of the following apply:

(1) The defendant was served with process personally in the foreign country.

(2) The defendant voluntarily appeared in the proceeding, other than for the purpose of protecting property seized or threatened with seizure in the proceeding or of contesting the jurisdiction of the court over the defendant.

(3) The defendant, before the commencement of the proceeding, had agreed to submit to the jurisdiction of the foreign court with respect to the subject matter involved.

(4) The defendant was domiciled in the foreign country when the proceeding was instituted or was a corporation or other form of business organization that had its principal place of business in, or was organized under the laws of, the foreign country.

(5) The defendant had a business office in the foreign country and the proceeding in the foreign court involved a cause of action or claim for relief arising out of business done by the defendant through that office in the foreign country.

(6) The defendant operated a motor vehicle or airplane in the foreign country and the proceeding involved a cause of action or claim for relief arising out of that operation.

(c) The list of bases for personal jurisdiction in subdivision (b) is not exclusive. The courts of this state may recognize bases of personal jurisdiction other than those listed in subdivision (b) as sufficient for the purposes of paragraph (1) of subdivision (a). **Leg.H.** Added Stats 2007 ch 212 §2 (SB 639), effective January 1, 2008. Amended Stats 2009 ch 579 §2 (SB 320), effective January 1, 2010; Stats 2017 ch 168 §6 (AB 905), effective January 1, 2018.

Prior Law: Former CCP §1714, similar to present Fam C §210, Prob C §§825, 1000, 1044, 1048, 1049, 1452, 17006, was enacted 1872, amended Stats 1907 ch 388 §1, and repealed Stats 1931 ch 281 (Prob C §1700).

§1718. Recognition of a foreign-country judgment sought as an original matter or in a pending action

(a) If recognition of a foreign-country judgment is sought as an original matter, the issue of recognition shall be raised by filing an action seeking recognition of the foreign-country judgment.

(b) If recognition of a foreign-country judgment is sought in a pending action, the issue of recognition may be raised by counterclaim, cross-claim, or affirmative defense. **Leg.H.** Added Stats 2007 ch 212 §2 (SB 639), effective January 1, 2008.

Prior Law: Former CCP §1718, relating to judicial establishment of father's death in determining child's right to state and county aid, was added Stats 1923 ch 94 §1 and repealed Stats 1931 ch 281 (Prob C §1700).

Former CCP §1718, relating to appointment of attorney at law in probate proceedings to represent interested persons who are minors, nonresidents, or underrepresented, was enacted 1872, amended Code Amdts 1873–74 ch 383 §204, Code Amdts 1880 ch 85 §126, and repealed Stats 1903 ch 206 §1.

§1719. Conclusiveness and enforceability of judgment

If the court in a proceeding under Section 1718 finds that the foreign-country judgment is entitled to recognition under this chapter then, to the extent that the foreign-country judgment grants or denies recovery of a sum of money, the foreign-country judgment is both of the following:

(a) Conclusive between the parties to the same extent as the judgment of a sister state entitled to full faith and credit in this state would be conclusive.

(b) Enforceable in the same manner and to the same extent as a judgment rendered in this state. **Leg.H.** Added Stats 2007 ch 212 §2 (SB 639), effective January 1, 2008.

Prior Law: Former CCP §1719, similar to present Prob C §7263, was enacted 1872, amended Code Amdts 1873–74 ch 383 §205, and repealed Stats 1931 ch 281 (Prob C §1700).

§1720. Stay on appeal

If a party establishes that an appeal from a foreign-country judgment is pending or will be taken in the foreign country, the court may stay any proceedings with regard to the foreign-country judgment until the appeal is concluded, the time for appeal expires, or the appellant has had sufficient time to prosecute the appeal and has failed to do so. **Leg.H.** Added Stats 2007 ch 212 §2 (SB 639), effective January 1, 2008.

Prior Law: Former CCP §1720, similar to present Prob C §1002, was enacted 1872, amended Code Amdts 1880 ch 85 §127, and repealed Stats 1931 ch 281 (Prob C §1700).

§1721. Limitation of actions

An action to recognize a foreign-country judgment shall be commenced within the earlier of the time during which the foreign-country judgment is effective in the foreign country or 10 years from the date that the foreign-country judgment became effective in the foreign country. **Leg.H.** Added Stats 2007 ch 212 §2 (SB 639), effective January 1, 2008.

Prior Law: Former CCP §1721, similar to present Prob C §§8501, 8505, was enacted 1872, amended Code Amdts 1880 ch 85 §128, and repealed Stats 1931 ch 281 (Prob C §1700).

§1722. Construction in aid of uniformity

In applying and construing this uniform act, consideration shall be given to the need to promote uniformity of the law with respect to its subject matter among states that enact it. **Leg.H.** Added Stats 2007 ch 212 §2 (SB 639), effective January 1, 2008.

Prior Law: Former CCP §1722, similar to present Prob C §1210, was added Code Amdts 1873–74 ch 383 §206, amended Code Amdts 1880 ch 85 §129, and repealed Stats 1931 ch 281 (Prob C §1700).

§1723. Situations not covered by chapter

This chapter does not prevent the recognition under principles of comity or otherwise of a foreign-country judgment not within the scope of this chapter. **Leg.H.** Added Stats 2007 ch 212 §2 (SB 639), effective January 1, 2008.

Prior Law: Former CCP §1723, similar to present Prob C §§200–204, 210, was added Stats 1881 ch 41 §1, amended Stats 1897 ch 71 §1, Stats 1901 ch 102 §432, Stats 1905 ch 149 §1, Stats 1913 ch 23 §1, Stats 1915 ch 196 §1, Stats 1917 ch 726 §1, Stats 1921 ch 327 §1, Stats 1927 ch 557 §1, Stats 1929 ch 608 §1, Stats 1931 ch 887 §1, Stats 1933 ch 152 §1, and repealed Stats 1939 ch 502 §1.

§1724. Applicability of chapter to actions commenced before, on or after, the effective date of chapter

(a) This chapter applies to all actions commenced on or after the effective date of this chapter in which the issue of recognition of a foreign-country judgment is raised.

(b) The former Uniform Foreign Money-Judgments Recognition Act (Chapter 2 (commencing with Section 1713) of Title 11 of Part 3) applies to all actions commenced before the effective date of this chapter in which the issue of recognition of a foreign-country judgment is raised. **Leg.H.** Added Stats 2007 ch 212 §2 (SB 639), effective January 1, 2008.

Prior Law: Former CCP §1724, relating to establishment of identity of heirs in cases involving interests in property, similar to present Prob C §§248 et seq., was added Stats 1909 ch 23 §1, amended Stats 1911 ch 66 §1, Stats 1921 ch 585 §1, and repealed Stats 1931 ch 281 (Prob C §1700).

§1725. Foreign-country defamation judgment; Declaratory relief or determination that judgment not recognizable

(a) If all of the following conditions are satisfied, a person against whom a foreign-country defamation judgment was rendered may seek declaratory relief with respect to liability for the judgment or a determination that the judgment is not recognizable under section 1716:

(1) The person is a resident or other person or entity amendable to jurisdiction in this state.

(2) The person either has assets in this state that may be subject to an enforcement proceeding to satisfy the foreign-country defamation judgment or may have to take actions in this state to comply with the foreign-country defamation judgment.

(3) The publication at issue was published in this state.

(b) A court of this state has jurisdiction to determine a declaratory relief action or issue a determination pursuant to this section and has personal jurisdiction over the person or entity who obtained the foreign-country defamation judgment.

(c) This section shall apply to a foreign-country defamation judgment regardless of when it was rendered. **Leg.H.** Added Stats 2017 ch 168 §7 (AB 905), effective January 1, 2018.

CHAPTER 3
TRIBAL COURT CIVIL MONEY JUDGMENT ACT

Citation of chapter. §1730.
Procedures governed by chapter; Applicability to specified tribal court money judgments; Construction. §1731.
Definitions. §1732.
Jurisdiction; Venue; Limited civil case. §1733.
Recognition of tribal court order; Application process. § 1733.1.
Application for recognition and entry of judgment. §1734.
Service of notice of filing of application; Proof of service. §1735.
Entry of judgment if no objections filed; Provisions and terms, entry, effect, and enforceability of judgment. §1736.
Service and filing of objection to recognition and entry of judgment; Reply; Hearing; Grounds for objection; Burden of proof. §1737.
Stay of enforcement. §1738.
Limitation of action to recognize or renew judgment. §1739.
Communication with tribal court judge. §1740.
Applicability of chapter to actions commenced on or after January 1, 2015. §1741.

§1730. Citation of chapter

This chapter shall be known and may be cited as the Tribal Court Civil Money Judgment Act. **Leg.H.** Added Stats 2014 ch 243 §4 (SB 406), effective January 1, 2015, repealed January 1, 2018. Amended Stats 2017 ch 168 §§10, 16 (AB 905), effective January 1, 2018 (repealer repealed).

Prior Law: Former CCP §1730, relating to establishment by Judicial Council of pilot programs in superior courts to assess the benefits of early mediation of civil cases, was added Stats 1999 ch 67 §4, effective July 6, 1999, amended Stats 2000 ch 127 §3, effective July 10, 2000, and repealed January 1, 2004, by the terms of former CCP §1743.

Former CCP §1730, similar to Fam C §1801, was added Stats 1939 ch 737 §1 and repealed Stats 1992 ch 162 §7, operative January 1, 1994.

Former CCP §1730 repealed 1931. See Probate Code.

§1731. Procedures governed by chapter; Applicability to specified tribal court money judgments; Construction

(a) This chapter governs the procedures by which the superior courts of the State of California recognize and enter tribal court money judgments of any federally recognized Indian tribe. Determinations regarding recognition and entry of a tribal court money judgment pursuant to state law shall have no effect upon the independent authority of that judgment. To the extent not inconsistent with this chapter, the Code of Civil Procedure shall apply.

(b) This chapter does not apply to any of the following tribal court money judgments:

(1) For taxes, fines, or other penalties, except for tribal taxes as described in clause 3 of subparagraph (B) of paragraph (3) of subdivision (d) of Section 1616 of Article 10 of Chapter 4 of Division 2 of Title 18 of the California Code of Regulations, and related interest or penalties.

(2) For which federal law requires that states grant full faith and credit recognition, including child support orders under the Full Faith and Credit for Child Support Orders Act (28 U.S.C. Sec. 1738B), except for the purposes of recognizing a tribal court order establishing the right of a child or other dependent of a participant in a retirement plan or other plan of deferred compensation to an assignment of all or a portion of the benefits payable.

(3) For which state law provides for recognition, including child support orders recognized under the Uniform Child Custody Jurisdiction and Enforcement Act (Part 3 (commencing with Section 3400) of Division 8 of the Family Code), other forms of family support orders under the Uniform Interstate Family Support Act (Part 6 (commencing with Section 5700.101) of Division 9 of the Family Code), except for the purposes of recognizing a tribal court order establishing the right of a spouse, former spouse, child, or other dependent of a participant in a retirement plan or other plan of deferred compensation to an assignment of all or a portion of the benefits payable.

(4) For decedents' estates, guardianships, conservatorships, internal affairs of trusts, powers of attorney, or other tribal court money judgments that arise in proceedings that are or would be governed by the Probate Code.

(c) Nothing in this chapter shall be deemed or construed to expand or limit the jurisdiction of either the state or any Indian tribe. **Leg.H.** Added Stats 2014 ch 243 §4 (SB 406), effective January 1, 2015, repealed January 1, 2018. Amended Stats 2015 ch 493 §1 (SB 646), effective January 1, 2016, repealed January 1, 2018; Stats 2017 ch 168 §§11, 16 (AB 905), effective January 1, 2018 (repealer repealed); Stats 2021 ch 58 §1 (AB 627), effective January 1, 2022; Stats 2023 ch 138 §1 (AB 1139), effective January 1, 2024.

Prior Law: Former CCP §1731, relating to definitions for former title, was added Stats 1999 ch 67 §4 (AB 1105), effective July 6, 1999, amended Stats 2000 ch 688 §9 (AB 1669), and repealed January 1, 2004, by the terms of former CCP §1743.

Former CCP §1731, similar to present Fam C §1800, was added Stats 1939 ch 737 §1, amended Stats 1955 ch 1230 §2, Stats 1980 ch 48 §1, effective March 27, 1980, and repealed Stats 1992 ch 162 §7 (AB 2650), effective January 1, 1993, operative January 1, 1994.

Former CCP §1731 repealed 1931. See Probate Code.

§1732. Definitions

For purposes of this chapter:

(a) "Applicant" means the person or persons who can bring an action to enforce a tribal court money judgment.

(b) "Civil action or proceeding" means any action or proceeding that is not criminal, except for those actions or proceedings expressly excluded by subdivision (b) of Section 1731.

(c) "Due process" includes, but is not limited to, the right to be represented by legal counsel, to receive reasonable notice and an opportunity for a hearing, to call and cross-examine witnesses, and to present evidence and argument to an impartial decisionmaker.

(d) "Good cause" means a substantial reason, taking into account the prejudice or irreparable harm a party will suffer if a hearing is not held on an objection or not held within the time periods established by this chapter.

(e) "Respondent" means the person or persons against whom an action to enforce a tribal court money judgment can be brought.

(f) "Tribal court" means any court or other tribunal of any federally recognized Indian nation, tribe, pueblo, band, or Alaska Native village, duly established under tribal or federal law, including Courts of Indian Offenses organized pursuant to Part 11 of Title 25 of the Code of Federal Regulations.

(g) "Tribal court money judgment" means any written judgment, decree, or order of a tribal court for a specified amount of money that was issued in a civil action or proceeding that is final, conclusive, and enforceable by the tribal court in which it was issued and is duly authenticated in accordance with the laws and procedures of the tribe or tribal court. **Leg.H.** Added Stats 2014 ch 243 §4 (SB 406), effective January 1, 2015, repealed January 1, 2018. Amended Stats 2017 ch 168 §§12, 16 (AB 905), effective January 1, 2018 (repealer repealed).

Prior Law: Former CCP §1732, relating to applicability of provisions to general civil cases filed in the pilot courts, was added Stats 1999 ch 67 §4, effective July 6, 1999, and repealed January 1, 2004, by the terms of former CCP §1743.

Former CCP §1732, similar to Fam C §12, was added Stats 1939 ch 737 §1, amended Stats 1955 ch 1230 §3, and repealed Stats 1992 ch 162 §7, operative January 1, 1994.

Former CCP §1732 repealed 1931. See Probate Code.

§1733. Jurisdiction; Venue; Limited civil case

(a) An application for entry of a judgment under this chapter shall be filed in a superior court.

(b) Subject to the power of the court to transfer proceedings under this chapter pursuant to Title 4 (commencing with Section 392) of Part 2, and except as provided in Section 1733.1, the proper county for the filing of an application is either of the following:

(1) The county in which any respondent resides or owns property.

(2) If no respondent is a resident, any county in this state.

(c) A case in which the tribal court money judgment amounts to thirty-five thousand dollars ($35,000) or less is a limited civil case. **Leg.H.** Added Stats 2014 ch 243 §4 (SB 406), effective January 1, 2015, repealed January 1, 2018. Amended Stats 2017 ch 168 §§13, 16 (AB 905), effective January 1, 2018 (repealer repealed); Stats 2021 ch 58 §2 (AB 627), effective January 1, 2022; Stats 2023 ch 861 §8 (SB 71), effective January 1, 2024.

Prior Law: Former CCP §1733, relating to exemption from participation in other judicially ordered arbitration or mediation, was added Stats 1999 ch 67 §4, effective July 6, 1999, and repealed January 1, 2004, by the terms of former CCP §1743.

Former CCP §1733, similar to Fam C §1802, was added Stats 1945 ch 1296 §1 and repealed Stats 1992 ch 162 §7, operative January 1, 1994.

Former CCP §1733 repealed 1931. See Probate Code.

§ 1733.1. Recognition of tribal court order; Application process

(a)(1) If the parties to the underlying tribal court proceeding agree, the parties may file a joint application for the recognition of a tribal court order that establishes a right to child support, spousal support payments, or marital property rights to such spouse, former spouse, child, or other dependent of a participant in a retirement plan or other plan of deferred compensation, which order assigns all or a portion of the benefits payable with respect to the participant to an alternate payee.

(2) If one of the parties to a tribal court order described in paragraph (1) does not agree to join in the application, the other party may proceed by having the tribal court execute a certificate in lieu of the signature of the other party. The Judicial Council shall adopt a format for the certificate.

(3) The application shall be on a form adopted by the Judicial Council, executed under penalty of perjury by parties to the proceeding submitting the application.

(4) The application shall include the name, current address, telephone number, and email address of each party, the name and mailing address of the issuing tribal court, and a certified copy of the order to be recognized.

(b) The filing fee for an application filed under this section is one hundred dollars ($100).

(c) An application filed pursuant to this section may be filed in the county in which either one of the parties resides.

(d) Entry of the tribal court order under this section does not confer any jurisdiction on a court of this state to modify or enforce the tribal court order. **Leg.H.** Added Stats 2021 ch 58 §3 (AB 627), effective January 1, 2022. Amended Stats 2022 ch 28 §29 (SB 1380), effective January 1, 2023; Stats 2022 ch 420 §14 (AB 2960), effective January 1, 2023 (ch 420 prevails).

§1734. Application for recognition and entry of judgment

(a) An applicant may apply for recognition and entry of a judgment based on a tribal court money judgment by filing an application in superior court pursuant to Section 1733.

(b) The application shall be executed under penalty of perjury and include all of the following information:

(1) The name and address of the tribal court that issued the judgment to be enforced and the date of the tribal court money judgment or any renewal thereof.

(2) The name and address of the party seeking recognition.

(3)(A) Any of the following statements, as applicable:

(i) If the respondent is an individual, the name and last known residence address of the respondent.

(ii) If the respondent is a corporation, the corporation's name, place of incorporation, and whether the corporation, if foreign, has qualified to do business in this state under the provisions of Chapter 21 (commencing with Section 2100) of Division 1 of Title 1 of the Corporations Code.

(iii) If the respondent is a partnership, the name of the partnership, whether it is a foreign partnership, and if it is a foreign partnership, whether it has filed a statement pursuant to Section 15800 of the Corporations Code designating an agent for service of process.

(iv) If the respondent is a limited liability company, the company's name, whether it is a foreign company, and if so, whether it has filed a statement pursuant to Section 17060 of the Corporations Code.

(B) Except for facts that are matters of public record in this state, the statements required by this paragraph may be made on the basis of the applicant's information and belief.

(4) A statement that an action in this state to enforce the tribal court money judgment is not barred by the applicable statute of limitations.

(5) A statement, based on the applicant's information and belief, that the tribal court money judgment is final and that no stay of enforcement of the tribal court money judgment is currently in effect.

(6) A statement that includes all of the following:

(A) The amount of the award granted in the tribal court money judgment that remains unpaid.

(B) If accrued interest on the tribal court money judgment is to be included in the California judgment, the amount of interest accrued on the tribal court money judgment, computed at the rate of interest applicable to the judgment under the law of the tribal jurisdiction in which the tribal court money judgment was issued.

(C) The rate of interest applicable to the money judgment under the law of the jurisdiction in which the tribal court money judgment was issued.

(D) A citation to the supporting authority.

(7) A statement that no action based on the tribal court money judgment is currently pending in any state court and that no judgment based on the tribal court money judgment has previously been entered in any proceeding in this state.

(c) All of the following items shall be attached to the application:

(1) An authenticated copy of the tribal court money judgment, certified by the judge or clerk of the tribal court.

(2) A copy of the tribal court rules of procedure pursuant to which the tribal court money judgment was entered.

(3) A declaration under penalty of perjury by the tribal court clerk, applicant, or applicant's attorney stating, based on personal knowledge, that the case that resulted in the entry of the judgment was conducted in compliance with the tribal court's rules of procedure. **Leg.H.** Added Stats 2014 ch 243 §4 (SB 406), effective January 1, 2015, repealed January 1, 2018. Amended Stats 2017 ch 168 §16 (AB 905), effective January 1, 2018 (repealer repealed).

Prior Law: Former CCP §1734, relating to status conference in cases subject to former title, was added Stats 1999 ch 67 §4, effective July 6, 1999, amended Stats 2000 ch 127 §4, effective July 10, 2000, and repealed January 1, 2004, by the terms of former CCP §1743.

Former CCP §1734 repealed 1931. See Probate Code.

§1735. Service of notice of filing of application; Proof of service

(a) Promptly upon the filing of an application pursuant to Section 1734, the applicant shall serve upon the respondent a notice of filing of the application to recognize and enter the tribal court money judgment, together with a copy of the application and any documents filed with the application. The notice of filing shall be in a form that shall be prescribed by the Judicial Council, and shall inform the respondent that the respondent has 30 days from service of the notice of filing to file objections to the enforcement of the tribal court money judgment. The notice shall include the name and address of the applicant and the applicant's attorney, if any, and the text of Sections 1736 and 1737.

(b) Except as provided in subdivision (c), service shall be made in the manner provided for service of summons by Article 3 (commencing with Section 415.10) of Chapter 4 of Title 5 of Part 2.

(c) If a respondent is the State of California or any of its officers, employees, departments, agencies, boards, or commissions, service of the notice of filing on that respondent may be by mail to the office of the Attorney General.

(d) The fee for service of the notice of filing under this section is an item of costs recoverable in the same manner as statutory fees for service of a writ as provided in Chapter 5 (commencing with Section 685.010) of Division 1 of Title 9 of Part 2, but the recoverable amount for that fee shall not exceed the amount allowed to a public officer or employee of this state for that service.

(e) The applicant shall file a proof of service of the notice promptly following service. **Leg.H.** Added Stats 2014 ch 243 §4 (SB 406), effective January 1, 2015, repealed January 1, 2018. Amended Stats 2017 ch 168 §16 (AB 905), effective January 1, 2018 (repealer repealed); Stats 2021 ch 58 §4 (AB 627), effective January 1, 2022.

Prior Law: Former CCP §1735, relating to requirements for panel of mediators, and selection and compensation of mediator, was added Stats 1999 ch 67 §4, effective July 6, 1999, amended Stats 2000 ch 127 §5, effective July 10, 2000, and repealed January 1, 2004, by the terms of former CCP §1743.

Former CCP §1735 repealed 1931. See Probate Code.

§1736. Entry of judgment if no objections filed; Provisions and terms, entry, effect, and enforceability of judgment

(a) If no objections are timely filed in accordance with Section 1737, the clerk shall certify that no objections were timely filed, and a judgment shall be entered.

(b) The judgment entered by the superior court shall be based on and contain the provisions and terms of the tribal court money judgment. The judgment shall be entered in the same manner, have the same effect, and be enforceable in the same manner as any civil judgment, order, or decree of a court of this state, except as provided in Section 1733.1. **Leg.H.** Added Stats 2014 ch 243 §4 (SB 406), effective January 1, 2015, repealed

January 1, 2018. Amended Stats 2017 ch 168 §16 (AB 905), effective January 1, 2018 (repealer repealed); Stats 2021 ch 58 §5 (AB 627), effective January 1, 2022.

Prior Law: Former CCP §1736, relating to scheduling early mediation, was added Stats 1999 ch 67 §4, effective July 6, 1999, and repealed January 1, 2004, by the terms of former CCP §1743.

Former CCP §1736 repealed 1931. See Probate Code.

§1737. Service and filing of objection to recognition and entry of judgment; Reply; Hearing; Grounds for objection; Burden of proof

(a) Any objection to the recognition and entry of the tribal court money judgment sought under Section 1734 shall be served and filed within 30 days of service of the notice of filing. If any objection is filed within this time period, the superior court shall set a time period for replies and set the matter for a hearing. The hearing shall be held by the superior court within 45 days from the date the objection is filed unless good cause exists for a later hearing. The only grounds for objecting to the recognition or enforcement of a tribal court money judgment are the grounds set forth in subdivisions (b), (c), and (d).

(b) A tribal court money judgment shall not be recognized and entered if the respondent demonstrates to the superior court that at least one of the following occurred:

(1) The tribal court did not have personal jurisdiction over the respondent.

(2) The tribal court did not have jurisdiction over the subject matter.

(3) The judgment was rendered under a judicial system that does not provide impartial tribunals or procedures compatible with the requirements of due process of law.

(c)(1) The superior court shall decline to recognize and enter a tribal court money judgment if any one of the following grounds applies:

(A) The defendant in the proceeding in the tribal court did not receive notice of the proceeding in sufficient time to enable the defendant to defend.

(B) The judgment was obtained by fraud that deprived the losing party of an adequate opportunity to present its case.

(C) The judgment or the cause of action or claim for relief on which the judgment is based is repugnant to the public policy of the state or of the United States.

(D) The proceeding in the tribal court was contrary to an agreement between the parties under which the dispute in question was to be determined otherwise than by proceedings in that tribal court.

(E) In the case of jurisdiction based on personal service only, the tribal court was a seriously inconvenient forum for the trial of the action.

(F) The judgment was rendered under circumstances that raise substantial doubt about the integrity of the rendering court with respect to the judgment.

(G) The specific proceeding in the tribal court leading to the judgment was not compatible with the requirements of due process of law.

(H) The judgment includes recovery for a claim of defamation, unless the court determines that the defamation law applied by the tribal court provided at least as much protection for freedom of speech and the press as provided by both the United States and California Constitutions.

(2) Notwithstanding an applicable ground for nonrecognition under paragraph (1), the court may nonetheless recognize a tribal court money judgment if the applicant demonstrates good reason to recognize the judgment that outweighs the ground for nonrecognition.

(d) The superior court may, in its discretion, decline to recognize and enter a tribal court money judgment if the judgment conflicts with another final and conclusive judgment.

(e) If objections have been timely filed, the applicant has the burden of establishing that the tribal court money judgment is entitled to recognition. If the applicant has met its burden, a party resisting recognition of the tribal court money judgment has the burden of establishing that a ground for nonrecognition exists pursuant to subdivision (b), (c), or (d). **Leg.H.** Added Stats 2014 ch 243 §4 (SB 406), effective January 1, 2015, repealed January 1, 2018. Amended Stats 2017 ch 168 §§14, 16 (AB 905), effective January 1, 2018 (repealer repealed); Stats 2021 ch 58 §6 (AB 627), effective January 1, 2022.

Prior Law: Former CCP §1737, relating to required attendance at mediation, was added Stats 1999 ch 67 §4, effective July 6, 1999, and repealed January 1, 2004, by the terms of former CCP §1743.

Former CCP §1737 repealed 1931. See Probate Code.

§1738. Stay of enforcement

The superior court shall grant a stay of enforcement if the respondent establishes one of the following to the superior court:

(a) An appeal from the tribal court money judgment is pending or may be taken in the tribal court, in which case the superior court shall stay state execution of the tribal court money judgment until the proceeding on appeal has been concluded or the time for appeal has expired.

(b) A stay of enforcement of the tribal court money judgment has been granted by the tribal court, in which case the superior court shall stay enforcement of the tribal court money judgment until the stay of execution expires or is vacated.

(c) Any other circumstance exists where the interests of justice require a stay of enforcement. **Leg.H.** Added Stats 2014 ch 243 §4 (SB 406), effective January 1, 2015, repealed January 1, 2018. Amended Stats 2017 ch 168 §16 (AB 905), effective January 1, 2018 (repealer repealed).

Prior Law: Former CCP §1738, relating to application of provisions of Evidence Code to statements made during mediation and references to mediation in a subsequent trial, was added Stats 1999 ch 67 §4, effective July 6, 1999, amended Stats 2000 ch 688 §10, and repealed January 1, 2004, by the terms of former CCP §1743.

Former CCP §1738 repealed 1931. See Probate Code.

§1739. Limitation of action to recognize or renew judgment

An action to recognize a tribal court money judgment or any renewal thereof shall be commenced within the earlier of the following periods:

(a) The time during which the tribal court money judgment is effective within the territorial jurisdiction of the tribal court.

(b) Ten years from the date that the tribal court money judgment became effective in the tribal jurisdiction. **Leg.H.** Added Stats 2014 ch 243 §4 (SB 406), effective January 1, 2015, repealed January 1, 2018. Amended Stats 2017 ch 168 §16 (AB 905), effective January 1, 2018 (repealer repealed).

Prior Law: Former CCP §1739, relating to filing of statement of nonagreement, was added Stats 1999 ch 67 §4, effective July 6, 1999, and repealed January 1, 2004, by the terms of former CCP §1743.

Former CCP §1739 repealed 1931. See Probate Code.

§1740. Communication with tribal court judge

(a) The superior court may, after notice to all parties, attempt to resolve any issues raised regarding a tribal court money judgment by contacting the tribal court judge who issued the judgment.

(b) The superior court shall allow the parties to participate in, and shall prepare a record of, any communication made with the tribal court judge pursuant to this section. **Leg.H.** Added Stats 2014 ch 243 §4 (SB 406), effective January 1, 2015, repealed January 1, 2018. Amended Stats 2017 ch 168 §16 (AB 905), effective January 1, 2018 (repealer repealed).

Prior Law: Former CCP §1740, relating to effect of submission of action to mediation on time limitations, was added Stats 1999 ch 67 §4, effective July 6, 1999, and repealed January 1, 2004, by the terms of former CCP §1743.

Former CCP §1740, similar to Fam C §1810, was added Stats 1980 ch 48 §2, effective March 27, 1980, and repealed Stats 1992 ch 162 §7, operative January 1, 1994.

Former CCP §1740, similar to Fam C §1810, was added Stats 1939 ch 737 §1, amended Stats 1955 ch 1230 §5, and repealed Stats 1980 ch 48 §1.5, effective March 27, 1980.

Former CCP §1740 repealed 1931. See Probate Code.

§1741. Applicability of chapter to actions commenced on or after January 1, 2015

(a) The Uniform Foreign-Country Money Judgments Recognition Act (Chapter 2 (commencing with Section 1713) applies to all actions commenced in superior court before January 1, 2015, in which the issue of recognition of a tribal court money judgment is raised.

(b) This chapter applies to all actions to enforce tribal court money judgments as defined herein commenced in superior court on or after January 1, 2015. A judgment entered under this chapter shall not limit the right of a party to seek enforcement of any part of a judgment, order, or decree entered by a tribal court that is not encompassed by the judgment entered under this chapter. **Leg.H.** Added Stats 2014 ch 243 §4 (SB 406), effective January 1, 2015, repealed January 1, 2018. Amended Stats 2017 ch 168 §§15, 16 (AB 905), effective January 1, 2018 (repealer repealed).

Prior Law: Former CCP §1741, relating to retention of right to discovery, was added Stats 1999 ch 67 §4 (AB 1105), effective July 6, 1999, and repealed January 1, 2004, by the terms of former CCP §1743.

Former CCP §1741, similar to present Fam C §1811, was added Stats 1980 ch 48 §2, effective March 27, 1980, and repealed Stats 1992 ch 162 §7 (AB 2650), effective January 1, 1993, operative January 1, 1994.

Former CCP §1741, similar to Fam C §1811, was added Stats 1939 ch 737 §1, amended Stats 1957 ch 704 §1, and repealed Stats 1980 ch 48 §1.5, effective March 27, 1980.

Former CCP §1741 repealed 1931. See Probate Code.

§1742. Repeal of title [Repealed]

Leg.H. Added Stats 2014 ch 243 §4 (SB 406), effective January 1, 2015, repealed January 1, 2018. Repealed Stats 2017 ch 168 §16 (AB 905), effective January 1, 2018. The repealed section related to repeal of former Title 11.5, Tribal Court Civil Money Judgment Act.

Prior Law: Former CCP §1742, relating to report by Judicial Council to Legislature and Governor concerning mediation pilot programs, was added Stats 1999 ch 67 §4 (AB 1105), effective July 6, 1999, amended Stats 2000 ch 127 §6 (AB 2866), effective July 10, 2000, and repealed January 1, 2004, by the terms of former CCP §1743.

Former CCP §1742, similar to present Fam C §1812, was added Stats 1980 ch 48 §2, effective March 27, 1980, and repealed Stats 1992 ch 162 §7 (AB 2650), effective January 1, 1993, operative January 1, 1994.

Former CCP §1742, similar to present Fam C §1812, was added Stats 1939 ch 737 §1 and repealed Stats 1980 ch 48 §1.5, effective March 27, 1980.

Former CCP §1742 repealed 1931. See Probate Code.

TITLE 11.5
TRIBAL COURT CIVIL MONEY JUDGMENT ACT [REPEALED]

§1743. [Section repealed 2004]

Leg.H. Added Stats 1999 ch 67 §4 (AB 1105), effective July 6, 1999. Repealed January 1, 2004, by its own terms. The repealed section related to repeal of title.

Prior Law: Former CCP §1743, similar to Fam C §1813, was added Stats 1980 ch 48 §2, effective March 27, 1980, and repealed Stats 1992 ch 162 §7, operative January 1, 1994.

Former CCP §1743, similar to Fam C §1813, was added Stats 1939 ch 737 §1 and repealed Stats 1980 ch 48 §1.5, effective March 27, 1980.

Original §1743 repealed 1931. See Probate Code.

§1744. [Section repealed 1994]

Leg.H. Added Stats 1980 ch 48 §2, effective March 27, 1980. Repealed Stats 1992 ch 162 §7 (AB 2650), operative January 1, 1994. See Fam C §1814.

Prior Law: Former CCP §1744, similar to Fam C §1814, was added Stats 1961 ch 1943 §1, amended Stats 1963 ch 829 §1, and repealed Stats 1980 ch 48 §1.5, effective March 27, 1980.

Former CCP §1744, relating to court assistants, Gov C §69894.1, was added Stats 1939 ch 737 §1, amended Stats 1945 ch 536 §3, Stats 1947 ch 814 §1, Stats 1941 ch 1132 §1, Stats 1951 ch 1132, Stats 1953 ch 915 §1, Stats 1955 ch 1230 §6, Stats 1957 ch 705 §1, and repealed Stats 1959 ch 1843 §2.

Original §1744 repealed 1931. See Probate Code.

§1744.1. [Section repealed 1980]

Leg.H. Added Stats 1959 ch 208 §1. Amended Stats 1961 ch 27 §1; Stats 1963 ch 242 §1; Stats 1966 1st Ex Sess ch 87 §1. Repealed Stats 1980 ch 48 §1.5, effective March 27, 1980. See Fam C §1814.

§1744.2. [Section repealed 1980]

Leg.H. Added Stats 1963 ch 195 §1. Amended Stats 1972 ch 727 §Repealed Stats 1980 ch 48 §1.5, effective March 27, 1980. See Fam C §1814.

§1744.3. [Section repealed 1980]

Leg.H. Added Stats 1967 ch 724 §1. Amended Stats 1979 ch 134 §1, effective June 20, 1979. Repealed Stats 1980 ch 48 §1.5, effective March 20, 1980. See Fam C §1814.

§1744.4. [Section repealed 1980]

Leg.H. Added Stats 1979 ch 134 §2, effective June 20, 1979. Repealed Stats 1980 ch 48 §1.5, effective March 20, 1980. See Fam C §1814.

§1745. [Section repealed 1994]

Leg.H. Added Stats 1980 ch 48 §2, effective March 27, 1980. Amended Stats 1984 ch 792 §1. Repealed Stats 1992 ch 162 §7 (AB 2650), operative January 1, 1994. See Fam C §1815.

Prior Law: Former CCP §1745, similar in part to Fam C §1814, was added Stats 1939 ch 737 §1, amended Stats 1955 ch 1230 §7, Stats 1957 ch 705 §2, and repealed Stats 1980 ch 48 §1.5, effective March 27, 1980.

§1745.5. [Section repealed 1994]

Leg.H. Added Stats 1984 ch 792 §2. Repealed Stats 1992 ch 162 §7 (AB 2650), operative January 1, 1994. See Fam C §1816.

§1746. [Section repealed 1994]

Leg.H. Added Stats 1980 ch 48 §2, effective March 27, 1980. Repealed Stats 1992 ch 162 §7 (AB 2650), operative January 1, 1994. See Fam C §1817.

Prior Law: Former CCP §1746, similar to Fam C §1817, was added Stats 1939 ch 737 §1, amended Stats 1955 ch 1230 §8, and repealed Stats 1980 ch 48 §1.5, effective March 27, 1980.

§1747. [Section repealed 1994]

Leg.H. Added Stats 1980 ch 48 §2, effective March 27, 1980. Repealed Stats 1992 ch 162 §7 (AB 2650), operative January 1, 1994. See Fam C §1818.

Prior Law: Former CCP §1747, similar to Fam C §1818, was added Stats 1955 ch 1230 §10, amended Stats 1965 ch 299 §22, operative January 1, 1967, and repealed Stats 1980 ch 48 §1.5, effective March 27, 1980.

Former CCP §1747, similar to Fam C §1818, was added Stats 1939 ch 737 §1 and repealed Stats 1955 ch 1230 §9.

Original §1747 repealed 1931. See Probate Code.

§1748. [Section repealed 1994]

Leg.H. Added Stats 1980 ch 48 §2, effective March 27, 1980. Repealed Stats 1992 ch 162 §7 (AB 2650), operative January 1, 1994. See Fam C §1819.

Prior Law: Former CCP §1748, similar to Fam C §1819, was added Stats 1967 ch 884 §1, amended Stats 1978 ch 274 §1, and repealed Stats 1980 ch 48 §1.5, effective March 27, 1980.

Original §1748 repealed 1931. See Probate Code.

§1749. [Section repealed 1994]

Leg.H. Added Stats 1980 ch 48 §2, effective March 27, 1980. Repealed Stats 1992 ch 162 §7 (AB 2650), operative January 1, 1994. See Fam C §1820.

Prior Law: Former CCP §1749 repealed 1931. See Probate Code.

§§1750–1759. [Sections repealed 1931]

Leg.H. Enacted 1872. Repealed Stats 1931 ch 281 (Prob C §1700). See Prob C §§1510, 1600, 1601, 2108, 2300, 2310, 2311, 2320, 2324, 2351, 2352, 2356, 2358, 2401, 2402, 2422.

§1760. [Section repealed 1994]

Leg.H. Added Stats 1980 ch 48 §4, effective March 27, 1980. Repealed Stats 1992 ch 162 §7 (AB 2650), operative January 1, 1994. See Fam C §1830.

Prior Law: Former CCP §1760, similar to Fam C §1830, was added Stats 1939 ch 737 §1, amended Stats 1955 ch 1230 §11, and repealed Stats 1980 ch 48 §3, effective March 27, 1980.

Original §1760 repealed 1931. See Probate Code.

§1761. [Section repealed 1994]

Leg.H. Added Stats 1980 ch 48 §4, effective March 27, 1980. Repealed Stats 1992 ch 162 §7 (AB 2650), operative January 1, 1994. See Fam C §1831.

Prior Law: Former CCP §1761, similar to Fam C §1831, was added Stats 1939 ch 737 §1, amended Stats 1969 ch 1608 §19, operative January 1, 1971, and repealed Stats 1980 ch 48 §3, effective March 27, 1980.

Original §1761 repealed 1931. See Probate Code.

§1762. [Section repealed 1994]

Leg.H. Added Stats 1980 ch 48 §4, effective March 27, 1980. Repealed Stats 1992 ch 162 §7 (AB 2650), operative January 1, 1994. See Fam C §1832.

Prior Law: Former CCP §1762, similar to Fam C §1832, was added Stats 1939 ch 737 §1, amended Stats 1955 ch 1230 §12, and repealed Stats 1980 ch 48 §3, effective March 27, 1980.

§1763. [Section repealed 1994]

Leg.H. Added Stats 1980 ch 48 §4, effective March 27, 1980. Repealed Stats 1992 ch 162 §7 (AB 2650), operative January 1, 1994. See Fam C §1833.

Prior Law: Former CCP §1763, similar to Fam C §1833, was added Stats 1939 ch 737 §1 and repealed Stats 1980 ch 48 §3, effective March 27, 1980.

Original §1763 repealed 1931. See Probate Code.

§1764. [Section repealed 1994]

Leg.H. Added Stats 1980 ch 48 §4, effective March 27, 1980. Repealed Stats 1992 ch 162 §7 (AB 2650), operative January 1, 1994. See Fam C §1834.

Prior Law: Former CCP §1764, similar to Fam C §1834, was added Stats 1939 ch 737 §1 and repealed Stats 1980 ch 48 §3, effective March 27, 1980.

Original §1764 repealed 1931. See Probate Code.

§1764a. [Section repealed 1931]

Leg.H. Added Stats 1917 ch 510 §1. Repealed Stats 1931 ch 281 (Prob C §1700). The repealed section related to appointment of guardian of insane or incompetent person.

§1765. [Section repealed 1994]

Leg.H. Added Stats 1980 ch 48 §4, effective March 27, 1980. Repealed Stats 1992 ch 162 §7 (AB 2650), operative January 1, 1994. See Fam C §1835.

Prior Law: Former CCP §1765, similar to Fam C §1835, was added Stats 1939 ch 737 §1 and repealed Stats 1980 ch 48 §3, effective March 27, 1980.
Original §1765 repealed 1931. See Probate Code.

§1766. [Section repealed 1994]

Leg.H. Added Stats 1980 ch 48 §4, effective March 27, 1980. Repealed Stats 1992 ch 162 §7 (AB 2650), operative January 1, 1994. See Fam C §1836.

Prior Law: Former CCP §1766, similar to Fam C §1836, was added Stats 1939 ch 737 §1 and repealed Stats 1980 ch 48 §3, effective March 27, 1980.
Original §1766 repealed 1931. See Probate Code.

§1767. [Section repealed 1994]

Leg.H. Added Stats 1980 ch 48 §4, effective March 27, 1980. Repealed Stats 1992 ch 162 §7 (AB 2650), operative January 1, 1994. See Fam C §1837.

Prior Law: Former CCP §1767, similar to Fam C §1837, was added Stats 1939 ch 737 §1 and repealed Stats 1980 ch 48 §3, effective March 27, 1980.
Original §1767 repealed 1931. See Probate Code.

§1768. [Section repealed 1994]

Leg.H. Added Stats 1980 ch 48 §4, effective March 27, 1980. Repealed Stats 1992 ch 162 §7 (AB 2650), operative January 1, 1994. See Fam C §1838.

Prior Law: Former CCP §1768, similar to Fam C §1838, was added Stats 1939 ch 737 §1 and repealed Stats 1980 ch 48 §3, effective March 27, 1980.
Original §1768 repealed 1931. See Probate Code.

§1769. [Section repealed 1994]

Leg.H. Added Stats 1980 ch 48 §4, effective March 27, 1980. Repealed Stats 1992 ch 162 §7 (AB 2650), operative January 1, 1994. See Fam C §1839.

Prior Law: Former CCP §1769, similar to Fam C §1839, was added Stats 1939 ch 737 §1, amended Stats 1955 ch 230 §13, Stats 1969 ch 1608 §20, Stats 1972 ch 1118 §5, and repealed Stats 1980 ch 48 §3, effective March 27, 1980.

§1770. [Section repealed 1994]

Leg.H. Added Stats 1980 ch 48 §4, effective March 27, 1980. Repealed Stats 1992 ch 162 §7 (AB 2650), operative January 1, 1994. See Fam C §1840.

Prior Law: Former CCP §1770, similar to Fam C §1840, was added Stats 1939 ch 737 §1, amended Stats 1955 ch 1230 §14, Stats 1957 ch 1262 §1, Stats 1969 ch 1608 §21, operative January 1, 1970, and repealed Stats 1980 ch 48 §3, effective March 27, 1980.
Original §1770 repealed 1931. See Probate Code.

§1771. [Section repealed 1994]

Leg.H. Added Stats 1980 ch 48 §4, effective March 27, 1980. Repealed Stats 1992 ch 162 §7 (AB 2650), operative January 1, 1994. See Fam C §1841.

Prior Law: Former CCP §1771, similar to Fam C §1841, was added Stats 1939 ch 737 §1, amended Stats 1955 ch 1230 §15, Stats 1969 ch 1608 §22, operative January 1, 1970, and repealed Stats 1980 ch 48 §3, effective March 27, 1980.
Original §1771 repealed 1931. See Probate Code.

§1772. [Section repealed 1994]

Leg.H. Added Stats 1980 ch 48 §4, effective March 27, 1980. Repealed Stats 1992 ch 162 §7 (AB 2650), operative January 1, 1994. See Fam C §1842.

Prior Law: Former CCP §1772, similar to Fam C §1842, was added Stats 1939 ch 737 §1, amended Stats 1955 ch 1230 §16, Stats 1969 ch 1608 §23, operative January 1, 1970, and repealed Stats 1980 ch 48 §3, effective March 27, 1980.
Original §1772 repealed 1931. See Probate Code.

§§1773–1799. [Sections repealed 1931]

Leg.H. Enacted 1872. Repealed Stats 1931 ch 281 (Prob C §1700). See Prob C §§1461, 1510, 1820, 2107, 2200, 2202, 2203, 2330, 2403, 2420, 2540–2543, 2547, 2550, 2570, 2573, 2610–2613, 2615, 2621, 2623, 2630, 2632, 2640, 2806, 3800–3803.

TITLE 11.6
CIVIL ACTION MEDIATION

Legislative findings and declarations. §1775.
"Mediation"; Acts performed by counsel. §1775.1.
Courts to which title applies; Election to apply title. §1775.2.
Actions to be submitted to mediation. §1775.3.
Actions ordered into arbitration or mediation. §1775.4.
Amount in controversy. §1775.5.
Selection of mediator. §1775.6.
Effect of submission to mediation on running of time periods. §1775.7.
Compensation of court-appointed mediators; Administrative costs. §1775.8.
Statement of nonagreement. §1775.9.
Applicability of Evidence Code provisions regarding statements made in mediation. §1775.10.
Discovery rights. §1775.11.
Reference to mediation or statement of nonagreement as grounds for new trial. §1775.12.
Effect of title on other alternative dispute resolution programs. §1775.13.
Report to Legislature. §1775.14.
Judicial Council rules. §1775.15.

§1775. Legislative findings and declarations

The Legislature finds and declares that:

(a) The peaceful resolution of disputes in a fair, timely, appropriate, and cost-effective manner is an essential function of the judicial branch of state government under Article VI of the California Constitution.

(b) In the case of many disputes, litigation culminating in a trial is costly, time consuming, and stressful for the parties involved. Many disputes can be resolved in a fair and equitable manner through less formal processes.

(c) Alternative processes for reducing the cost, time, and stress of dispute resolution, such as mediation, have been effectively used in California and elsewhere. In appropriate cases mediation provides parties with a simplified and economical procedure for obtaining prompt and equitable resolution of their disputes and a greater opportunity to participate directly in resolving these disputes. Mediation may also assist to reduce the backlog of cases burdening the judicial system. It is in the public interest for mediation to be encouraged and used where appropriate by the courts.

(d) Mediation and similar alternative processes can have the greatest benefit for the parties in a civil action when used early, before substantial discovery and other litigation costs have been incurred. Where appropriate, participants in disputes should be encouraged to utilize mediation and other alternatives to trial for resolving their differences in the early stages of a civil action.

(e) As a pilot project in Los Angeles County and in other counties which elect to apply this title, courts should be able to refer cases to appropriate dispute resolution processes such as judicial arbitration and mediation as an alternative to trial, consistent with the parties' right to obtain a trial if a dispute is not resolved through an alternative process.

(f) The purpose of this title is to encourage the use of court-annexed alternative dispute resolution methods in general, and mediation in particular. It is estimated that the average cost to the court for processing a civil case of the kind described in Section 1775.3 through judgment is three thousand nine hundred forty-three dollars ($3,943) for each judge day, and that a substantial portion of this cost can be saved if these cases are resolved before trial.

The Judicial Council, through the Administrative Office of the Courts, shall conduct a survey to determine the number of cases resolved by alternative dispute resolution authorized by this title, and shall estimate the resulting savings realized by the courts and the parties. The results of the survey shall be included in the report submitted pursuant to Section 1775.14. The programs authorized by this title shall be deemed successful if they result in estimated savings of at least two hundred fifty thousand dollars ($250,000) to the courts and corresponding savings to the parties. **Leg.H.** Added Stats 1993 ch 1261 §4 (SB 401).

§1775.1. "Mediation"; Acts performed by counsel

(a) As used in this title, "mediation" means a process in which a neutral person or persons facilitate communication between the disputants to assist them in reaching a mutually acceptable agreement.

(b) Unless otherwise specified in this title or ordered by the court, any act to be performed by a party may also be performed by his or her counsel of record. **Leg.H.** Added Stats 1993 ch 1261 §4 (SB 401). Amended Stats 1998 ch 931 §126 (SB 2139), effective September 28, 1998; Stats 2002 ch 784 §87 (SB 1316).

§1775.2. Courts to which title applies; Election to apply title

(a) This title shall apply to the courts of the County of Los Angeles.

(b) A court of any county, at the option of the presiding judge, may elect whether or not to apply this title to eligible actions filed in that court, and this title shall not apply in any court which has not so elected. An election under this subdivision may be revoked by the court at any time.

(c) Courts are authorized to apply this title to all civil actions pending or commenced on or after January 1, 1994. **Leg.H.** Added Stats 1993 ch 1261 §4 (SB 401).

§1775.3. Actions to be submitted to mediation

(a) In the courts of the County of Los Angeles and in other courts that elect to apply this title, all at-issue civil actions in which arbitration is otherwise required pursuant to Section 1141.11, whether or not the action includes a prayer for equitable relief, may be submitted to mediation by the presiding judge or the judge designated under this title as an alternative to judicial arbitration pursuant to Chapter 2.5 (commencing with Section 1141.10) of Title 3.

(b) Any civil action otherwise within the scope of this title in which a party to the action is a public agency or public entity may be submitted to mediation pursuant to subdivision (a). **Leg.H.** Added Stats 1993 ch 1261 §4 (SB 401).

§1775.4. Actions ordered into arbitration or mediation

An action that has been ordered into arbitration pursuant to Section 1141.11 or 1141.12 may not be ordered into mediation under this title, and an action that has been ordered into mediation pursuant to Section 1775.3 may not be ordered into arbitration pursuant to Section 1141.11. **Leg.H.** Added Stats 1993 ch 1261 §4 (SB 401).

§1775.5. Amount in controversy

The court shall not order a case into mediation where the amount in controversy exceeds fifty thousand dollars ($50,000). The determination of the amount in controversy shall be made in the same manner as provided in Section 1141.16 and, in making this determination, the court shall not consider the merits of questions of liability, defenses, or comparative negligence. **Leg.H.** Added Stats 1993 ch 1261 §4 (SB 401).

§1775.6. Selection of mediator

In actions submitted to mediation pursuant to Section 1775.3, a mediator shall be selected for the action within 30 days of its submission to mediation. The method of selection and qualification of the mediator shall be as the parties determine. If the parties are unable to agree on a mediator within 15 days of the date of submission of the action to mediation, the court may select a mediator pursuant to standards adopted by the Judicial Council. **Leg.H.** Added Stats 1993 ch 1261 §4 (SB 401).

§1775.7. Effect of submission to mediation on running of time periods

(a) Submission of an action to mediation pursuant to this title shall not suspend the running of the time periods specified in Chapter 1.5 (commencing with Section 583.110) of Title 8 of Part 2, except as provided in this section.

(b) If an action is or remains submitted to mediation pursuant to this title more than four years and six months after the plaintiff has filed the action, then the time beginning on the date four years and six months after the plaintiff has filed the action and ending on the date on which a statement of nonagreement is filed pursuant to Section 1775.9 shall not be included in computing the five-year period specified in Section 583.310. **Leg.H.** Added Stats 1993 ch 1261 §4 (SB 401).

§1775.8. Compensation of court-appointed mediators; Administrative costs

(a) The compensation of court-appointed mediators shall be the same as the compensation of arbitrators pursuant to Section 1141.18, except that no compensation shall be paid prior to the filing of a statement of nonagreement by the mediator pursuant to Section 1775.9 or prior to settlement of the action by the parties.

(b) All administrative costs of mediation, including compensation of mediators, shall be paid in the same manner as for arbitration pursuant to Section 1141.28. Funds allocated for the payment of arbitrators under the judicial arbitration program shall be equally available for the payment of mediators under this title. **Leg.H.** Added Stats 1993 ch 1261 §4 (SB 401).

§1775.9. Statement of nonagreement

(a) In the event that the parties to mediation are unable to reach a mutually acceptable agreement and any party to the mediation wishes to terminate the mediation, then the mediator shall file a statement of nonagreement. This statement shall be in a form to be developed by the Judicial Council.

(b) Upon the filing of a statement of nonagreement, the matter shall be calendared for trial, by court or jury, both as to law and fact, insofar as possible, so that the trial shall be given the same place on the active list as it had prior to mediation, or shall receive civil priority on the next setting calendar. **Leg.H.** Added Stats 1993 ch 1261 §4 (SB 401).

§1775.10. Applicability of Evidence Code provisions regarding statements made in mediation

All statements made by the parties during the mediation shall be subject to Sections 703.5 and 1152, and Chapter 2 (commencing with Section 1115) of Division 9, of the Evidence Code. **Leg.H.** Added Stats 1993 ch 1261 §4 (SB 401). Amended Stats 1997 ch 772 §2 (AB 939).

§1775.11. Discovery rights

Any party who participates in mediation pursuant to Section 1775.3 shall retain the right to obtain discovery to the extent available under the Civil Discovery Act, Title 4 (commencing with Section 2016.010) of Part 4. **Leg.H.** Added Stats 1993 ch 1261 §4 (SB 401). Amended Stats 2004 ch 182 §17 (AB 3081), operative July 1, 2005.

§1775.12. Reference to mediation or statement of nonagreement as grounds for new trial

Any reference to the mediation or the statement of nonagreement filed pursuant to Section 1775.9 during any subsequent trial shall constitute an irregularity in the proceedings of the trial for the purposes of Section 657. **Leg.H.** Added Stats 1993 ch 1261 §4 (SB 401).

§1775.13. Effect of title on other alternative dispute resolution programs

It is the intent of the Legislature that nothing in this title be construed to preempt other current or future alternative dispute resolution programs operating in the trial courts. **Leg.H.** Added Stats 1993 ch 1261 §4 (SB 401).

§1775.14. Report to Legislature

(a) On or before January 1, 1998, the Judicial Council shall submit a report to the Legislature concerning court alternative dispute resolution programs. This report shall include, but not be limited to, a review of programs operated in Los Angeles County and other courts that have elected to apply this title, and shall examine, among other things, the effect of this title on the judicial arbitration programs of courts that have participated in that program.

(b) The Judicial Council shall, by rule, require that each court applying this title file with the Judicial Council data that will enable the Judicial Council to submit the report required by subdivision (a). **Leg.H.** Added Stats 1993 ch 1261 §4 (SB 401). Amended Stats 2006 ch 538 §74 (SB 1852), effective January 1, 2007.

§1775.15. Judicial Council rules

Notwithstanding any other provision of law except the provisions of this title, the Judicial Council shall provide by rule for all of the following:

(a) The procedures to be followed in submitting actions to mediation under this act.

(b) Coordination of the procedures and processes under this act with those under the trial Court Delay Reduction Act, Article 5 (commencing with Section 68600) of Chapter 2 of Title 8 of the Government Code.

(c) Exceptions for cause from provisions of this title. In providing for exceptions, the Judicial Council shall take into consideration whether the civil action might not be amenable to mediation. **Leg.H.** Added Stats 1993 ch 1261 §4 (SB 401).

§1775.16. [Section repealed 1999]

Leg.H. Added Stats 1993 ch 1261 §4 (SB 401). Repealed Stats 1998 ch 618 §1 (SB 19). The repealed section related to repeal of title.

TITLE 11.65
ALTERNATIVE DISPUTE RESOLUTION ACT [INOPERATIVE]

TITLE 11B
RECOVERY OF PREFERENCES IN AN ASSIGNMENT FOR THE BENEFIT OF CREDITORS [RENUMBERED]

TITLE 11.7
RECOVERY OF PREFERENCES AND EXEMPT PROPERTY IN AN ASSIGNMENT FOR THE BENEFIT OF CREDITORS

Right of assignee of general assignment for benefit of creditors to recover transfer of property. §1800.
General assignment for benefit of creditors; Exempt property. §1801.
Notice of assignment. §1802.

§1800. Right of assignee of general assignment for benefit of creditors to recover transfer of property

(a) As used in this section, the following terms have the following meanings:

(1) "Insolvent" means:

(A) With reference to a person other than a partnership, a financial condition such that the sum of the person's debts is greater than all of the person's property, at a fair valuation, exclusive of both of the following:

(i) Property transferred, concealed, or removed with intent to hinder, delay, or defraud the person's creditors.

(ii) Property that is exempt from property of the estate pursuant to the election of the person made pursuant to Section 1801.

(B) With reference to a partnership, financial condition such that the sum of the partnership's debts are greater than the aggregate of, at a fair valuation, both of the following:

(i) All of the partnership's property, exclusive of property of the kind specified in clause (i) of subparagraph (A).

(ii) The sum of the excess of the value of each general partner's separate property, exclusive of property of the kind specified in clause (ii) of subparagraph (A), over the partner's separate debts.

(2) "Inventory" means personal property leased or furnished, held for sale or lease, or to be furnished under a contract for service, raw materials, work in process, or materials used or consumed in a business, including farm products such as crops or livestock, held for sale or lease.

(3) "Insider" means:

(A) If the assignor is an individual, any of the following:

(i) A relative of the assignor or of a general partner of the assignor.

(ii) A partnership in which the assignor is a general partner.

(iii) A general partner of the assignor.

(iv) A corporation of which the assignor is a director, officer, or person in control.

(B) If the assignor is a corporation, any of the following:

(i) A director of the assignor.

(ii) An officer of the assignor.

(iii) A person in control of the assignor.

(iv) A partnership in which the assignor is a general partner.

(v) A general partner of the assignor.

(vi) A relative of a general partner, director, officer, or person in control of the assignor.

(C) If the assignor is a partnership, any of the following:

(i) A general partner in the assignor.

(ii) A relative of a general partner in, general partner of, or person in control of the assignor.

(iii) A partnership in which the assignor is a general partner.

(iv) A general partner of the assignor.

(v) A person in control of the assignor.

(D) An affiliate of the assignor or an insider of an affiliate as if the affiliate were the assignor.

(E) A managing agent of the assignor.

As used in this paragraph, the following terms have the following meanings:

"Relative" means an individual related by affinity or consanguinity within the third degree as determined by the common law, or an individual in a step or adoptive relationship within the third degree.

An "affiliate" means a person that directly or indirectly owns, controls, or holds, with power to vote, 20 percent or more of the outstanding voting securities of the assignor, or 20 percent or more of whose outstanding voting securities are directly or indirectly owned, controlled, or held with power to vote by the assignor, excluding securities held in a fiduciary or agency capacity without sole discretionary power to vote, or held solely to secure a debt if the holder has not in fact exercised the power to vote, or a person who operates the business of the assignor under a lease or operating agreement or whose business is operated by the assignor under a lease or operating agreement.

(4) "Judicial lien" means a lien obtained by judgment, levy, sequestration, or other legal or equitable process or proceeding.

(5) "New value" means money or money's worth in goods, services, or new credit, or release by a transferee of property previously transferred to the transferee in a transaction that is neither void nor voidable by the assignor or the assignee under any applicable law, but does not include an obligation substituted for an existing obligation.

(6) "Receivable" means a right to payment, whether or not the right has been earned by performance.

(7) "Security agreement" means an agreement that creates or provides for a security interest.

(8) "Security interest" means a lien created by an agreement.

(9) "Statutory lien" means a lien arising solely by force of a statute on specified circumstances or conditions, or lien of distress for rent, whether or not statutory, but does not include a security interest or judicial lien, whether or not the interest or lien is provided by or is dependent on a statute and whether or not the interest or lien is made fully effective by statute.

(10) "Transfer" means every mode, direct or indirect, absolute or conditional, voluntary or involuntary, or disposing of or parting with property or with an interest in property, including retention of title as a security interest.

(b) Except as provided in subdivision (c), the assignee of any general assignment for the benefit of creditors, as defined in Section 493.010, may recover any transfer of property of the assignor that is all of the following:

(1) To or for the benefit of a creditor.

(2) For or on account of an antecedent debt owed by the assignor before the transfer was made.

(3) Made while the assignor was insolvent.

(4) Made on or within 90 days before the date of the making of the assignment or made between 90 days and one year before the date of making the assignment if the creditor, at the time of the transfer, was an insider and had reasonable cause to believe the debtor was insolvent at the time of the transfer.

(5) Enables the creditor to receive more than another creditor of the same class.

(c) The assignee may not recover under this section a transfer as follows:

(1) To the extent that the transfer was both of the following:

(A) Intended by the assignor and the creditor to or for whose benefit the transfer was made to be a contemporaneous exchange for new value given to the assignor.

(B) In fact a substantially contemporaneous exchange.

(2) To the extent that the transfer was all of the following:

(A) In payment of a debt incurred in the ordinary course of business or financial affairs of the assignor and the transferee.

(B) Made in the ordinary course of business or financial affairs of the assignor and the transferee.

(C) Made according to ordinary business terms.

(3) Of a security interest in property acquired by the assignor that meets both of the following:

(A) To the extent the security interest secures new value that was all of the following:

(i) Given at or after the signing of a security agreement that contains a description of the property as collateral.

(ii) Given by or on behalf of the secured party under the agreement.

(iii) Given to enable the assignor to acquire the property.

(iv) In fact used by the assignor to acquire the property.

(B) That is perfected within 20 days after the security interest attaches.

(4) To or for the benefit of a creditor, to the extent that, after the transfer, the creditor gave new value to or for the benefit of the assignor that meets both of the following:

(A) Not secured by an otherwise unavoidable security interest.

(B) On account of which new value the assignor did not make an otherwise unavoidable transfer to or for the benefit of the creditor.

(5) Of a perfected security interest in inventory or a receivable or the proceeds of either, except to the extent that the aggregate of all the transfers to the transferee caused a reduction, as of the date of the making of the assignment and to the prejudice of other creditors holding unsecured claims, of any amount by which the debt secured by the security interest exceeded the value of all security interest for the debt on the later of the following:

(A) Ninety days before the date of the making of the assignment.

(B) The date on which new value was first given under the security agreement creating the security interest.

(6) That is the fixing of a statutory lien.

(7) That is payment to a claimant, as defined in Section 8004 of the Civil Code, in exchange for the claimant's waiver or release of any potential or asserted claim of lien, stop payment notice, or right to recover on a payment bond, or any combination thereof.

(8) To the extent that the transfer was a bona fide payment of a debt to a spouse, former spouse, or child of the debtor, for alimony to, maintenance for, or support of, the spouse or child, in connection with a separation agreement, divorce decree, or other order of a court of record, or a determination made in accordance with state or territorial law by a governmental unit, or property settlement agreement; but not to the extent that either of the following occurs:

(A) The debt is assigned to another entity voluntarily, by operation of law or otherwise, in which case the assignee may not recover that portion of the transfer that is assigned to the state or any political subdivision of the state pursuant to Part D of Title IV of the Social Security Act (42 U.S.C. Sec. 601 et seq.) and passed on to the spouse, former spouse, or child of the debtor.

(B) The debt includes a liability designated as alimony, maintenance, or support, unless the liability is actually in the nature of alimony, maintenance, or support.

(d) An assignee of any general assignment for the benefit of creditors, as defined in Section 493.010, may avoid a transfer of property of the assignor transferred to secure reimbursement of a surety that furnished a bond or other obligation to dissolve a judicial lien that would have been avoidable by the assignee under subdivision (b). The liability of the surety under the bond or obligation shall be discharged to the extent of the value of the property recovered by the assignee or the amount paid to the assignee.

(e)(1) For the purposes of this section:

(A) A transfer of real property other than fixtures, but including the interest of a seller or purchaser under a contract for the sale of real property, is perfected when a bona fide purchaser of the property from the debtor, against whom applicable law permits the transfer to be perfected, cannot acquire an interest that is superior to the interest of the transferee.

(B) A transfer of a fixture or property other than real property is perfected when a creditor on a simple contract cannot acquire a judicial lien that is superior to the interest of the transferee.

(2) For the purposes of this section, except as provided in paragraph (3), a transfer is made at any of the following times:

(A) At the time the transfer takes effect between the transferor and the transferee, if the transfer is perfected at, or within 10 days after, the time, except as provided in subparagraph (B) of paragraph (3) of subdivision (c).

(B) At the time the transfer is perfected, if the transfer is perfected after the 10 days.

(C) Immediately before the date of making the assignment if the transfer is not perfected at the later of:

(i) The making of the assignment.

(ii) Ten days after the transfer takes effect between the transferor and the transferee.

(3) For the purposes of this section, a transfer is not made until the assignor has acquired rights in the property transferred.

(f) For the purposes of this section, the assignor is presumed to have been insolvent on and during the 90 days immediately preceding the date of making the assignment.

(g) An action by an assignee under this section must be commenced within one year after making the assignment. **Leg.H.** Added Stats 1979 ch 394 §5, effective July 27, 1979, operative October 1, 1979. Amended Stats 1980 ch 135 §6; Stats 1982 ch 35 §3, effective February 17, 1982, ch 497 §81.5, effective July 1, 1983; Stats 1992 ch 1348 §7 (AB 2616); Stats 1995 ch 152 §1 (AB 1156); Stats 1999 ch 202 §2 (SB 219); Stats 2006 ch 538 §75 (SB 1852), effective January 1, 2007; Stats 2010 ch 697 §26 (SB 178), effective January 1, 2011, operative July 1, 2012.

Prior Law: Former CCP §1800 repealed 1931. See Probate Code.

§1801. General assignment for benefit of creditors; Exempt property

In any general assignment for the benefit of creditors (as defined in Section 493.010), the assignor, if an individual, may choose to retain as exempt property either the property which is otherwise exempt under Chapter 4 (commencing with Section 703.010) of Division 2 of Title 9 of Part 2 or, in the alternative, the following property:

(a) The assignor's aggregate interest, not to exceed seven thousand five hundred dollars ($7,500) in value, in real property or personal property that the assignor or a dependent of the assignor uses as a residence, in a cooperative that owns property that the assignor or a dependent of the assignor uses as a residence, or in a burial plot for the assignor or a dependent of the assignor.

(b) The assignor's interest, not to exceed one thousand two hundred dollars ($1,200) in value, in one motor vehicle.

(c) The assignor's interest, not to exceed two hundred dollars ($200) in value in any particular item, in household furnishings, household goods, wearing apparel, appliances, books, animals, crops, or musical instruments, that are held primarily for the personal, family, or household use of the assignor or a dependent of the assignor.

(d) The assignor's aggregate interest, not to exceed five hundred dollars ($500) in value, in jewelry held primarily for the personal, family, or household use of the assignor or a dependent of the assignor.

(e) The assignor's aggregate interest, not to exceed in value four hundred dollars ($400) plus any unused amount of the exemption provided under subdivision (a), in any property.

(f) The assignor's aggregate interest, not to exceed seven hundred fifty dollars ($750) in value, in any implements, professional books, or tools, of the trade of the assignor or the trade of a dependent of the assignor.

(g) Any unmatured life insurance contract owned by the assignor, other than a credit life insurance contract.

(h) The assignor's aggregate interest, not to exceed in value four thousand dollars ($4,000) in any accrued dividend or interest under, or loan value of, any unmatured life insurance contract owned by the assignor under which the insured is the assignor or an individual of whom the assignor is a dependent.

(i) Professionally prescribed health aids for the assignor or a dependent of the assignor.

(j) The assignor's right to receive any of the following:

(1) A social security benefit, unemployment compensation, or a local public assistance benefit except that this paragraph does not preclude the application of Section 1255.7 of the Unemployment Insurance Code.

(2) A veterans' benefit.

(3) A disability, illness, or unemployment benefit except that this paragraph does not preclude the application of Section 1255.7 of the Unemployment Insurance Code.

(4) Alimony, support, or separate maintenance, to the extent reasonably necessary for the support of the assignor and any dependent of the assignor.

(5) A payment under a stock bonus, pension, profit sharing, annuity, or similar plan or contract on account of illness, disability, death, age, or length of service, to the extent reasonably necessary for the support of the assignor and any dependent of the assignor, unless:

(i) The plan or contract was established by or under the auspices of an employer of which the assignor was a partner, officer, director or controlling person at the time the assignor's rights under the plan or contract arose;

(ii) The payment is on account of age or length of service; and

(iii) Such plan or contract does not qualify under Section 401(a), 403(a), 403(b), 408, or 409 of the Internal Revenue Code of 1954 (26 U.S.C. 401(a), 403(a), 403(b), 408, or 409).

(k) The assignor's right to receive, or property that is traceable to any of the following:

(1) An award under a crime victim's reparation law.

(2) A payment on account of the wrongful death of an individual of whom the assignor was a dependent, to the extent reasonably necessary for the support of the assignor and any dependent of the assignor.

(3) A payment under a life insurance contract that insured the life of an individual of whom the assignor was a dependent on the date of such individual's death, to the extent reasonably necessary for the support of the assignor and any dependent of the assignor.

(4) A payment, not to exceed seven thousand five hundred dollars ($7,500), on account of personal bodily injury, as compensation for pain and suffering or actual pecuniary loss (other than loss of future earnings), of the assignor or an individual of whom the assignor is a dependent.

(5) A payment in compensation of loss of future earnings of the assignor or an individual of whom the assignor is or was a dependent, to the extent reasonably necessary for the support of the assignor and any dependent of the assignor.

In this section, "dependent" includes spouse, whether or not actually dependent, "assignor" means each spouse, if the assignment is made by a married couple, and "value" means fair market value as of the date of the making of the assignment. **Leg.H.** Added Stats 1982 ch 497 §82, operative July 1, 1983. Amended Stats 1983 ch 155 §23, effective June 30, 1983, operative July 1, 1983.

§1802. Notice of assignment

(a) In any general assignment for the benefit of creditors, as defined in Section 493.010, the assignee shall, within 30 days after the assignment has been accepted in writing, give written notice of the assignment to the assignor's creditors, equityholders, and other parties in interest as set forth on the list provided by the assignor pursuant to subdivision (c).

(b) In the notice given pursuant to subdivision (a), the assignee shall establish a date by which creditors must file their claims to be able to share in the distribution of proceeds of the liquidation of the assignor's assets. That date shall be not less than 150 days and not greater than 180 days after the date of the first giving of the written notice to creditors and parties in interest.

(c) The assignor shall provide to the assignee at the time of the making of the assignment a list of creditors, equityholders, and other parties in interest, signed under penalty of perjury, which shall include the names, addresses, cities, states, and ZIP Codes for each person together with the amount of that person's anticipated claim in the assignment proceedings. **Leg.H.** Added Stats 1992 ch 1348 §8 (AB 2616).

§§1803–1810c. [Sections repealed 1931]

Leg.H. Enacted 1872 or added Stats 1903 ch 152 §1, Stats 1911 ch 190 §1, Stats 1913 ch 33 §1, Stats 1919 ch 330 §1. Repealed Stats 1931 ch 281 (Prob C §1700). See CCP 995.340, 995.350, 995.520, 995.630, 995.840; Fam C §6602; Prob C §§23, 1446, 2100, 2105, 2326, 2333, 2334, 2528, 2548, 3302, 3500, 3600–3603, 3610.

TITLE 12
TRIBAL INJUNCTIONS

Right to seek injunction against impairment of gaming rights; Legislative finding; Petition for writ of mandate. §1811.

§1811. Right to seek injunction against impairment of gaming rights; Legislative finding; Petition for writ of mandate

(a) Following the issuance of the bonds as specified in Section 63048.65 of the Government Code and during the term of the bonds, if it reasonably appears that the exclusive right of an Indian tribe with a designated tribal compact, as defined in subdivision (b) of Section 63048.6 of the Government Code, pursuant to Section 3.2(a) of that compact has been violated, the tribe may seek a preliminary and permanent injunction against that gaming or the authorization of that gaming as a substantial impairment of the rights specified in Section 3.2(a), in order to afford the tribe stability in its gaming operation and to maintain the bargained-for source of payment and security of the bonds. However, no remedy other than an injunction shall be available against the state or any of its political subdivisions for a violation of Section 3.2(a). The Legislature hereby finds and declares that any such violation of the exclusive right to gaming under Section 3.2(a) is a substantial impairment of the rights specified in that section and will cause irreparable harm that cannot be adequately remedied by damages. No undertaking shall be required on the part of the tribes in connection with any action to seek the preliminary or permanent injunction.

(b) Notwithstanding any other provision of law, the parties to an action brought pursuant to subdivision (a) may petition the Supreme Court for a writ of mandate from any order granting or denying a preliminary injunction. Any such petition shall be filed within 15 days following the notice of entry of the superior court order, and no extension of that period shall be allowed. In any case in which a petition has been filed within the time allowed therefor, the Supreme Court shall make any orders, as it may deem proper in the circumstances. **Leg.H.** Added Stats 2004 ch 91 §2 (AB 687), effective July 1, 2004.

Prior Law: Former CCP §1811, relating to married women as sole traders, was enacted 1872 and repealed Stats 1980 ch 123 §1.

§§1812–1821. [Sections repealed 1981]

Leg.H. Enacted 1872. Amended Stats 1881 ch 15 §§1, 2; Stats 1951 ch 60 §1; Stats 1967 ch 857 §§1, 2. Repealed Stats 1980 ch 123 §1.

TITLE 13
INSPECTION WARRANTS

Definition. §1822.50.
Affidavit for issuance of warrant. §1822.51.
Grounds for issuance. §1822.52.
Examination of witnesses. §1822.53.
Issuance and contents of warrant. §1822.54.
Duration, and extension or renewal of warrant; Execution and return. §1822.55.
Manner of inspection; Notice. §1822.56.
Misdemeanor. §1822.57.
Inspections by personnel of Fish and Game Department. §1822.58.
Inspections for purpose of animal or plant pest or disease eradication. §1822.59.
Warrant for inspections. §1822.60.

§1822. [Section repealed 1935]

Leg.H. Added Stats 1907 ch 390 §1. Repealed Stats 1935 ch 712 §3. The repealed section related to estates of missing persons.

Prior Law: Former CCP §1822, relating to insolvency proceedings, was enacted 1872 and repealed by Stats 1907 ch 390 §1.

§1822.50. Definition

An inspection warrant is an order, in writing, in the name of the people, signed by a judge of a court of record, directed to a state or local official, commanding him to conduct any inspection required or authorized by state or local law or regulation relating to building, fire, safety, plumbing, electrical, health, labor, or zoning. **Leg.H.** Added Stats 1968 ch 1097 §1. Amended Stats 1980 ch 230 §1.

§1822.51. Affidavit for issuance of warrant

An inspection warrant shall be issued upon cause, unless some other provision of state or federal law makes another standard applicable. An inspection warrant shall be supported by an affidavit, particularly describing the place, dwelling, structure, premises, or vehicle to be inspected and the purpose for which the inspection is made. In addition, the affidavit shall contain either a statement that consent to inspect has been sought and refused or facts or circumstances reasonably justifying the failure to seek such consent. **Leg.H.** Added Stats 1968 ch 1097 §1. Amended Stats 1970 ch 241 §2; Stats 1971 ch 438 §20; Stats 1984 ch 476 §2.

§1822.52. Grounds for issuance

Cause shall be deemed to exist if either reasonable legislative or administrative standards for conducting a routine or area inspection are satisfied with respect to the particular place, dwelling, structure, premises, or vehicle, or there is reason to believe that a condition of nonconformity exists with respect to the particular place, dwelling, structure, premises, or vehicle. **Leg.H.** Added Stats 1968 ch 1097 §1.

§1822.53. Examination of witnesses

Before issuing an inspection warrant, the judge may examine on oath the applicant and any other witness, and shall satisfy himself of the existence of grounds for granting such application. **Leg.H.** Added Stats 1968 ch 1097 §1.

§1822.54. Issuance and contents of warrant

If the judge is satisfied that the proper standard for issuance of the warrant has been met, he or she shall issue the warrant particularly describing each place, dwelling, structure, premises, or vehicle to be inspected and designating on the warrant the purpose and limitations of the inspection, including the limitations required by this title. **Leg.H.** Added Stats 1968 ch 1097 §1. Amended Stats 1984 ch 476 §3.

§1822.55. Duration, and extension or renewal of warrant; Execution and return

An inspection warrant shall be effective for the time specified therein, but not for a period of more than 14 days, unless extended or renewed by the judge who signed and issued the original warrant, upon satisfying himself that such extension or renewal is in the public interest. Such inspection warrant must be executed and returned to the judge by whom it was issued within the time specified in the warrant or within the extended or renewed time. After the expiration of such time, the warrant, unless executed, is void. **Leg.H.** Added Stats 1968 ch 1097 §1.

§1822.56. Manner of inspection; Notice

An inspection pursuant to this warrant may not be made between 6:00 p.m. of any day and 8:00 a.m. of the succeeding day, nor in the absence of an owner or occupant of the particular place, dwelling, structure, premises, or vehicle unless specifically authorized by the judge upon a showing that such authority is reasonably necessary to effectuate the purpose of the regulation being enforced. An inspection pursuant to a warrant shall not be made by means of forcible entry, except that the judge may expressly authorize a forcible entry where facts are shown sufficient to create a reasonable suspicion of a violation of a state or local law or regulation relating to building, fire, safety, plumbing, electrical, health, labor, or zoning, which, if such violation existed, would be an immediate threat to health or safety, or where facts are shown establishing that reasonable attempts to serve a previous warrant have been unsuccessful. Where prior consent has been sought and refused, notice that a warrant has been issued must be given at least 24 hours before the warrant is executed, unless the judge finds that immediate execution is reasonably necessary in the circumstances shown. **Leg.H.** Added Stats 1968 ch 1097 §1. Amended Stats 1980 ch 230 §2.

§1822.57. Misdemeanor

Any person who willfully refuses to permit an inspection lawfully authorized by warrant issued pursuant to this title is guilty of a misdemeanor. **Leg.H.** Added Stats 1968 ch 1097 §1.

§1822.58. Inspections by personnel of Fish and Game Department

A warrant may be issued under the requirements of this title to authorize personnel of the Department of Fish and Game to conduct inspections of locations where fish, amphibia, or aquatic plants are held or stored under Division 12 (commencing with Section 15000) of the Fish and Game Code. **Leg.H.** Added Stats 1982 ch 1486 §1.

§1822.59. Inspections for purpose of animal or plant pest or disease eradication

(a) Notwithstanding the provisions of Section 1822.54, for purposes of an animal or plant pest or disease eradication effort pursuant to Division 4 (commencing with Section 5001) or Division 5 (commencing with Section 9101) of the Food and Agricultural Code, the judge may issue a warrant under the requirements of this title describing a specified geographic area to be inspected by authorized personnel of the Department of Food and Agriculture.

(b) A warrant issued pursuant to this section may only authorize the inspection of the exterior of places, dwellings, structures, premises or vehicles, and only in areas urban in character. The warrant shall state the geographical area which it covers and the purpose of and limitations on the inspection.

(c) A warrant may be issued pursuant to this section whether or not the property owners in the area have refused to consent to the inspection. A peace officer may use reasonable force to enter a property to be inspected if so authorized by the warrant. **Leg.H.** Added Stats 1984 ch 476 §4.

§1822.60. Warrant for inspections

A warrant may be issued under the requirements of this title to authorize personnel of the Department of Justice to conduct inspections as provided in subdivision (a) of Section 19827 of the Business and Professions Code. **Leg.H.** Added Stats 1997 ch 867 §53 (SB 8). Amended Stats 2004 ch 183 §47 (AB 3082); Stats 2007 ch 176 §51 (SB 82), effective August 24, 2007.

§§1822a–1822bb. [Sections repealed 1935]

Leg.H. Added Stats 1907 ch 390 §1, Stats 1929 ch 326 §1. Amended Stats 1935 ch 52 §§10, 11, ch 70 §1. Repealed Stats 1935 ch 712 §3. The repealed sections related to estates of missing persons.

TITLE 14
PROCEEDINGS FOR THE ADJUSTMENT, SETTLEMENT, AND PAYMENT OF ANY INDEBTEDNESS EXISTING AGAINST ANY CITY OR MUNICIPAL CORPORATION AT THE TIME OF EXCLUSION OF TERRITORY THEREFROM, AND THE DIVISION OF THE PROPERTY THEREOF [REPEALED]

§§1822c–1822f. [Sections repealed 1950]

Leg.H. Added Stats 1907 ch 383 §1. Repealed Stats 1949 ch 79 §3 (Gov C §500042). The repealed sections related to settlement of a city's indebtedness when territory has been excluded from the city pursuant to alteration of the city's boundaries.

PART 3.5
OF ALTERNATIVE PROCEDURES [REPEALED]
TITLE 1
PILOT PROJECTS [REPEALED]

§1823. **[Section repealed 1995]**

Leg.H. Added Stats 1976 ch 960 §1. Repealed Stats 1994 ch 146 §26 (AB 3601). The repealed section related to legislative findings and declarations on pilot projects.

Prior Law: Former CCP §1823, similar to present Ev C §140, was enacted 1872 and repealed Stats 1965 ch 299 §24, operative January 1, 1967.

§1823.1. **[Section repealed 1995]**

Leg.H. Added Stats 1976 ch 960 §1. Amended Stats 1980 ch 71 §1. Repealed Stats 1994 ch 146 §26 (AB 3601). The repealed section related to courts selected by Judicial Council.

§1823.15. **[Section repealed 1995]**

Leg.H. Added Stats 1982 ch 1581 §2. Repealed Stats 1994 ch 146 §26 (AB 3601). The repealed section related to termination date of pilot project in municipal courts.

§1823.2. **[Section repealed 1995]**

Leg.H. Added Stats 1976 ch 960 §1. Repealed Stats 1994 ch 146 §26 (AB 3601). The repealed section related to jurisdiction of municipal courts in pilot project.

§1823.3. **[Section repealed 1995]**

Leg.H. Added Stats 1976 ch 960 §1. Repealed Stats 1994 ch 146 §26 (AB 3601). The repealed section related to jurisdiction of superior courts in pilot project.

§1823.4. **[Section repealed 1995]**

Leg.H. Added Stats 1976 ch 960 §1. Repealed Stats 1994 ch 146 §26 (AB 3601). The repealed section related to adoption of pilot project rules by Judicial Council.

§1823.5. **[Section repealed 1995]**

Leg.H. Added Stats 1976 ch 960 §1. Repealed Stats 1994 ch 146 §26 (AB 3601). The repealed section related to laws applicable to pilot projects.

§1823.6. **[Section repealed 1995]**

Leg.H. Added Stats 1976 ch 960 §1. Repealed Stats 1994 ch 146 §26 (AB 3601). The repealed section related to collection and evaluation of pilot project data.

§1823.7. **[Section repealed 1995]**

Leg.H. Added Stats 1976 ch 960 §1. Repealed Stats 1994 ch 146 §26 (AB 3601). The repealed section related to advisory committee for pilot projects.

§1824. **[Section repealed 1995]**

Leg.H. Added Stats 1976 ch 960 §1. Amended Stats 1977 ch 579 §37. Repealed Stats 1994 ch 146 §26 (AB 3601). The repealed section related to pleadings and motions in pilot projects.

Prior Law: Former CCP §1824, similar to present Ev C §190, was enacted 1872 and repealed Stats 1965 ch 299 §25, operative January 1, 1967.

§1824.1. **[Section repealed 1995]**

Leg.H. Added Stats 1976 ch 960 §1. Repealed Stats 1994 ch 146 §26 (AB 3601). The repealed section related to contents and construction of pleadings.

§1825. **[Section repealed 1995]**

Leg.H. Added Stats 1976 ch 960 §1. Repealed Stats 1994 ch 146 §26 (AB 3601). The repealed section related to discovery in pilot projects.

Prior Law: Former CCP §1825, defining the law of evidence, was enacted 1872 and repealed Stats 1965 ch 299 §26, operative January 1, 1967.

§1825.1. **[Section repealed 1995]**

Leg.H. Added Stats 1976 ch 960 §1. Repealed Stats 1994 ch 146 §26 (AB 3601). The repealed section related to statement of witnesses and physical evidence in pilot projects.

§1825.2. **[Section repealed 1995]**

Leg.H. Added Stats 1976 ch 960 §1. Repealed Stats 1994 ch 146 §26 (AB 3601). The repealed section related to procedure regarding statements in pilot projects.

§1825.3. **[Section repealed 1995]**

Leg.H. Added Stats 1976 ch 960 §1. Repealed Stats 1994 ch 146 §26 (AB 3601). The repealed section related to limitation of evidence in pilot projects.

§1825.4. **[Section repealed 1995]**

Leg.H. Added Stats 1976 ch 960 §1. Repealed Stats 1994 ch 146 §26 (AB 3601). The repealed section related to pretrial conferences in pilot projects.

§1825.5. **[Section repealed 1995]**

Leg.H. Added Stats 1976 ch 960 §1. Repealed Stats 1994 ch 146 §26 (AB 3601). The repealed section related to demurrers and pretrial motions for pilot projects.

§1826. **[Section repealed 1995]**

Leg.H. Added Stats 1976 ch 960 §1. Repealed Stats 1994 ch 146 §26 (AB 3601). The repealed section related to trial dates in pilot projects.

Prior Law: Former CCP §1826, similar to Ev C §§500 et seq., was enacted 1872 and repealed Stats 1965 ch 299 §27, operative January 1, 1967.

§1826.1. **[Section repealed 1995]**

Leg.H. Added Stats 1976 ch 960 §1. Repealed Stats 1994 ch 146 §26 (AB 3601). The repealed section related to jury trials in pilot projects.

§1826.2. **[Section repealed 1995]**

Leg.H. Added Stats 1976 ch 960 §1. Repealed Stats 1994 ch 146 §26 (AB 3601). The repealed section related to opening statements in pilot projects.

§1826.3. **[Section repealed 1995]**

Leg.H. Added Stats 1976 ch 960 §1. Repealed Stats 1994 ch 146 §26 (AB 3601). The repealed section related to trial briefs in pilot projects.

§1826.4. **[Section repealed 1995]**

Leg.H. Added Stats 1976 ch 960 §1. Repealed Stats 1994 ch 146 §26 (AB 3601). The repealed section related to interrogation of witnesses and narrative testimony in pilot projects.

§1826.5. **[Section repealed 1995]**

Leg.H. Added Stats 1976 ch 960 §1. Repealed Stats 1994 ch 146 §26 (AB 3601). The repealed section related to order of proceeding in pilot projects.

§1826.6. **[Section repealed 1995]**

Leg.H. Added Stats 1976 ch 960 §1. Repealed Stats 1994 ch 146 §26 (AB 3601). The repealed section related to written submission of testimony for pilot projects.

§1826.7. **[Section repealed 1995]**

Leg.H. Added Stats 1976 ch 960 §1. Repealed Stats 1994 ch 146 §26 (AB 3601). The repealed section related to record of proceedings in pilot projects.

§1826.8. **[Section repealed 1995]**

Leg.H. Added Stats 1976 ch 960 §1. Repealed Stats 1994 ch 146 §26 (AB 3601). The repealed section related to admissibility and weight of evidence in pilot projects.

§1826.9. [Section repealed 1995]

Leg.H. Added Stats 1976 ch 960 §1. Repealed Stats 1994 ch 146 §26 (AB 3601). The repealed section related to amendment of pleadings in pilot projects.

§1826.10. [Section repealed 1995]

Leg.H. Added Stats 1976 ch 960 §1. Repealed Stats 1994 ch 146 §26 (AB 3601). The repealed section related to closing arguments in pilot projects.

§1826.11. [Section repealed 1995]

Leg.H. Added Stats 1976 ch 960 §1. Repealed Stats 1994 ch 146 §26 (AB 3601). The repealed section related to findings of fact and conclusions of law in pilot projects.

§1826.12. [Section repealed 1995]

Leg.H. Added Stats 1976 ch 960 §1. Repealed Stats 1994 ch 146 §26 (AB 3601). The repealed section related to post-trial motions pilot projects.

§1826.13. [Section repealed 1995]

Leg.H. Added Stats 1976 ch 960 §1. Repealed Stats 1994 ch 146 §26 (AB 3601). The repealed section related to conclusiveness of judgment or final order in pilot projects.

§1826.14. [Section repealed 1995]

Leg.H. Added Stats 1976 ch 960 §1. Repealed Stats 1994 ch 146 §26 (AB 3601). The repealed section related to appeals in pilot projects.

§§1827–1832. [Sections repealed 1967]

Leg.H. Enacted 1872. Amended Stats 1873–74 ch 383 §§211 et seq. Repealed Stats 1965 ch 299 §§24 et seq., operative January 1, 1967.

§1833. [Section repealed 1995]

Leg.H. Added Stats 1976 ch 960 §1. Repealed Stats 1994 ch 146 §26 (AB 3601). The repealed section related to study of pilot project and annual report.

Prior Law: Former CCP §1833, defining prima facie evidence, was enacted 1872, amended Code Amdts 1873–74 ch 383 §214, and repealed Stats 1965 ch 299 §34, operative January 1, 1967.

§1833.1. [Section repealed 1995]

Leg.H. Added Stats 1976 ch 960 §1. Repealed Stats 1994 ch 146 §26 (AB 3601). The repealed section related to implementation of Title 1 on pilot projects.

§1833.2. [Section repealed 1995]

Leg.H. Added Stats 1976 ch 960 §1. Repealed Stats 1994 ch 146 §26 (AB 3601). The repealed section related to operative date of Title 1 on pilot projects.

PART 4
MISCELLANEOUS PROVISIONS

Title 1. Of the General Principles of Evidence.
Title 2. Of the Kinds and Degrees of Evidence.
Title 3. Of the Production of Evidence.
Title 4. Civil Discovery Act.
Title 5. Of the Rights and Duties of Witnesses.
Title 6. Of Evidence in Particular Cases, and Miscellaneous and General Provisions.
Title 7. Uniform Federal Lien Registration Act.

GENERAL DEFINITIONS AND DIVISIONS [REPEALED]

§1834. [Section repealed 1967]

Leg.H. Enacted 1872. Repealed Stats 1965 ch 299 §35, operative January 1, 1967. The repealed section defined partial evidence.

§1835. [Section repealed 1923]

Leg.H. Enacted 1872. Repealed Stats 1923 ch 110 §1. The repealed section defined satisfactory evidence and slight evidence.

§§1836–1839. [Sections repealed 1967]

Leg.H. Enacted in 1872. Repealed Stats 1965 ch 299 §§36–39, operative January 1, 1967. The repealed sections related to definitions of evidence.

TITLE 1
OF THE GENERAL PRINCIPLES OF EVIDENCE

Map and plat restoration; Recordation of copy. §1855.
[Section renumbered 1988]. §1855b.
Parol evidence rule. §1856.
Construction of language as relating to place of execution. §1857.
Construction of statutes and instruments; General rule. §1858.
The intention of the Legislature or parties. §1859.
Circumstances considered. §1860.
Terms presumed used in general acceptation; Evidence of local, etc., use. §1861.
Written words control those printed in a blank form. §1862.
Of two constructions, which preferred. §1864.
Notice construed according to ordinary acceptation of terms; What notice of protest imports. §1865.
Construction in favor of natural right preferred. §1866.

§§1844–1854. [Sections repealed 1967]

Leg.H. Enacted 1872 or added Stats 1957 ch 1601 §1, Amended Code Admts 1873–74 ch 383 §§215, 216, Stats 1959 ch 2107 §1, Stats 1965 ch 299 §42, operative January 1, 1967. Repealed Stats 1965 ch 299 §§40, 41, 43–51, operative January 1, 1967, Stats 1965 ch 1151 §2. The repealed sections related to general principles of evidence.

§1855. Map and plat restoration; Recordation of copy

When any map which has been recorded in the office of the recorder of any county is injured, destroyed, lost, or stolen, any person interested may file in the superior court of the county in which the map was originally filed or recorded a verified petition in writing alleging that the map has been injured, destroyed, lost, or stolen without fault of the person making the application, and that the petitioner has a true and correct copy of the original map which he or she offers for record in the place of the original map. The petition shall be accompanied by a copy of the true copy offered for recording.

Upon the filing of the petition the clerk shall set it for hearing by the court, and give notice of the hearing by causing notice of the time and place of the hearing to be posted at the courthouse in the county where the court is held at least 10 days prior to the hearing. A copy of the petition and a copy of the true copy offered for record shall be served upon the recorder of the county in which the proceedings are brought at least 10 days prior to the hearing. The court may order any further notice to be given as it deems proper. At the time set for the hearing the court shall take evidence for and against the petition, and if it appears to the court from the evidence presented that the copy of the map submitted is a true copy of the original map, it shall decree that the copy is a true copy of the original map, and order the copy placed of record in the office of the recorder in the place of the original map.

A certified copy of the decree shall accompany the true copy of the map for record. When presented to the county recorder for record, he or she shall place of record the copy of the map in the place of the original map.

When placed of record the copy shall have the same effect as the original map, and conveyances of property referring to the original map shall have the same effect as though the original map had not been injured, destroyed, lost, or stolen, and conveyances thereafter made referring to the copy of the original map shall be deemed to refer also to the original map. **Leg.H.** Added Stats 1953 ch 52 §12 as CCP §1855b. Amended and renumbered by Stats 1987 ch 56 §23.

Prior Law: Former CCP §1855, relating to proving the contents of a writing, was enacted 1872, amended Code Amdts 1873–74 ch 383 §217, and repealed Stats 1965 ch 299 §52, operative January 1, 1967.

§1855a. [Section repealed 1967]

Leg.H. Enacted 1872. Repealed Stats 1965 ch 299 §53, operative January 1, 1967. See Ev C §1601.

§1855b. [Section renumbered 1988]

Leg.H. Added Stats 1953 ch 52 §12. Amended and renumbered CCP §1855 by Stats 1987 ch 56 §23.

§1856. Parol evidence rule

(a) Terms set forth in a writing intended by the parties as a final expression of their agreement with respect to the terms included therein may not be contradicted by evidence of a prior agreement or of a contemporaneous oral agreement.

(b) The terms set forth in a writing described in subdivision (a) may be explained or supplemented by evidence of consistent additional terms unless the writing is intended also as a complete and exclusive statement of the terms of the agreement.

(c) The terms set forth in a writing described in subdivision (a) may be explained or supplemented by course of dealing or usage of trade or by course of performance.

(d) The court shall determine whether the writing is intended by the parties as a final expression of their agreement with respect to the terms included therein and whether the writing is intended also as a complete and exclusive statement of the terms of the agreement.

(e) Where a mistake or imperfection of the writing is put in issue by the pleadings, this section does not exclude evidence relevant to that issue.

(f) Where the validity of the agreement is the fact in dispute, this section does not exclude evidence relevant to that issue.

(g) This section does not exclude other evidence of the circumstances under which the agreement was made or to which it relates, as defined in Section 1860, or to explain an extrinsic ambiguity or otherwise interpret the terms of the agreement, or to establish illegality or fraud.

(h) As used in this section, "agreement" includes trust instruments, deeds, wills, and contracts between parties. **Leg.H.** Enacted 1872. Amended Stats 1978 ch 150 §1; Stats 2013 ch 81 §1 (AB 824), effective January 1, 2014.

§1857. Construction of language as relating to place of execution

The language of a writing is to be interpreted according to the meaning it bears in the place of its execution, unless the parties have reference to a different place. **Leg.H.** Enacted 1872.

§1858. Construction of statutes and instruments; General rule

In the construction of a statute or instrument, the office of the Judge is simply to ascertain and declare what is in terms or in substance contained therein, not to insert what has been omitted, or to omit what has been inserted; and where there are several provisions or particulars, such a construction is, if possible, to be adopted as will give effect to all. **Leg.H.** Enacted 1872.

§1859. The intention of the Legislature or parties

In the construction of a statute the intention of the Legislature, and in the construction of the instrument the intention of the parties, is to be pursued, if possible; and when a general and [a] particular provision are inconsistent, the latter is paramount to the former. So a particular intent will control a general one that is inconsistent with it. **Leg.H.** Enacted 1872.

§1860. Circumstances considered

For the proper construction of an instrument, the circumstances under which it was made, including the situation of the subject of the instrument, and of the parties to it, may also be shown, so that the Judge be placed in the position of those whose language he is to interpret. **Leg.H.** Enacted 1872.

§1861. Terms presumed used in general acceptation; Evidence of local, etc., use

The terms of a writing are presumed to have been used in their primary and general acceptation, but evidence is nevertheless admissible that they have a local, technical, or otherwise peculiar signification, and were so used and understood in the particular instance, in which case the agreement must be construed accordingly. **Leg.H.** Enacted 1872.

§1862. Written words control those printed in a blank form

When an instrument consists partly of written words and partly of a printed form, and the two are inconsistent, the former controls the latter. **Leg.H.** Enacted 1872.

§1863. [Section repealed 1967]

Leg.H. Enacted 1872. Repealed Stats 1965 ch 299 §54, operative January 1, 1967. See Ev C §753.

§1864. Of two constructions, which preferred

When the terms of an agreement have been intended in a different sense by the different parties to it, that sense is to prevail against either party in which he supposed the other understood it, and when different constructions of a provision are otherwise equally proper, that is to be taken which is most favorable to the party in whose favor the provision was made. **Leg.H.** Enacted 1872.

§1865. Notice construed according to ordinary acceptation of terms; What notice of protest imports

A written notice, as well as every other writing, is to be construed according to the ordinary acceptation of its terms. Thus a notice to the drawers or indorsers of a bill of exchange or promissory note, that it has been protested for want of acceptance or payment, must be held to import that the same has been duly presented for acceptance or payment and the same refused, and that the holder looks for payment to the person to whom the notice is given. **Leg.H.** Enacted 1872.

§1866. Construction in favor of natural right preferred

When a statute or instrument is equally susceptible of two interpretations, one in favor of natural right, and the other against it, the former is to be adopted. **Leg.H.** Enacted 1872.

§1867. [Section repealed 1967]

Leg.H. Enacted 1872. Repealed Stats 1965 ch 299 §55, operative January 1, 1967.

§1868. [Section repealed 1967]

Leg.H. Enacted 1872. Repealed Stats 1965 ch 299 §56, operative January 1, 1967. See Ev C §§210, 350, 352.

§1869. [Section repealed 1967]

Leg.H. Enacted 1872. Repealed Stats 1965 ch 299 §57, operative January 1, 1967. See Ev C §§500, 550.

§1870. [Section repealed 1967]

Leg.H. Enacted 1872. Repealed Stats 1965 ch 299 §58, operative January 1, 1967. See Ev C §§210, 351, 720, 780, 800, 801, 870, 1220–1225, 1230, 1240–1242, 1290–1292, 1310–1314, 1320–1322, 1416.

§1871. [Section repealed 1967]

Leg.H. Added Stats 1925 ch 156 §1. Amended Stats 1941 ch 254 §1, Stats 1959 ch 1408 §1, Stats 1961 ch 1100 §1. Repealed Stats 1965 ch 299 §59, operative January 1, 1967. See Ev C §§723, 730–733.

§1872. [Section repealed 1967]

Leg.H. Added Stats 1937 ch 565 §1. Repealed Stats 1965 ch 299 §60, operative January 1, 1967. See Ev C §§721, 802.

TITLE 2
OF THE KINDS AND DEGREES OF EVIDENCE

Chapter 2. Witnesses.
Chapter 3. Writings.
Chapter 6. Indispensable Evidence.

CHAPTER 1
KNOWLEDGE OF THE COURT [REPEALED]

§1875. [Section repealed 1967]

Leg.H. Enacted 1872. Amended Stats 1927 ch 62, Stats 1957 ch 249 §1. Repealed Stats 1965 ch 299 §61, operative January 1, 1967. See Ev C §§311, 450–459, 1452, 1453.

CHAPTER 2
WITNESSES

Witness defined. §1878.

§1878. Witness defined

A witness is a person whose declaration under oath is received as evidence for any purpose, whether such declaration be made on oral examination, or by deposition or affidavit. **Leg.H.** Enacted 1872.

§1879. [Section repealed 1967]

Leg.H. Enacted 1872. Repealed Stats 1965 ch 299 §62, operative January 1, 1967. See Ev C §§700–702.

§1880. [Section repealed 1967]

Leg.H. Enacted 1872. Amended Code Amdts 1873–74 ch 383 §218; Code Amdts 1880 ch 99 §1. Repealed Stats 1965 ch 299 §63, operative January 1, 1967. See Ev C §§701, 702.

§1881. [Section repealed 1981]

Leg.H. Enacted 1872. Amended Stats 1893 ch 217 §1; Stats 1907 ch 68 §1; Stats 1911 ch 603 §1; Stats 1917 ch 611 §1; Stats 1927 ch 683 §1; Stats 1933 ch 536 §1; Stats 1935 ch 532 §1; Stats 1939 ch 129 §5; Stats 1957 ch 1961 §1; Stats 1961 ch 629 §1. Repealed Stats 1965 ch 299 §64, operative January 1, 1967. Amended Stats 1965 ch 922 §1, ch 923 §1. Repealed Stats 1980 ch 676 §72. See Ev C §§950–962, 970–973, 980–987, 990–1006, 1010–1026, 1030–1034, 1040–1042, 1070.

§1881.1. [Section repealed 1967]

Leg.H. Added Stats 1965 ch 937 §1. Repealed Stats 1965 ch 937 §3, operative January 1, 1967. See Ev C §1042.

§1882. [Section repealed]

Leg.H. Enacted 1872. Repealed Code Amdts 1875–76 ch 107 §1. The repealed section related to examination of witnesses.

§1883. [Section repealed 1967]

Leg.H. Enacted 1872. Repealed Stats 1965 ch 299 §65, operative January 1, 1967. See Ev C §§703, 704.

§1884. [Section repealed 1967]

Leg.H. Enacted 1872. Repealed Stats 1965 ch 299 §66, operative January 1, 1967. See Ev C §752.

§1885. [Section repealed 1967]

Leg.H. Added Stats 1959 ch 1262 §1, effective June 30, 1959. Repealed Stats 1965 ch 299 §67, operative January 1, 1967. See Ev C §§751, 754.

Prior Law: Former CCP §1885, incorporated in Gov C §§68093–68096, was added by Stats 1951 ch 655 §18 and repealed by Stats 1953 ch 206 §7.

§§1885.1, 1885.2. [Sections repealed 1953]

Leg.H. Added Stats 1951 ch 655 §18. Repealed Stats 1953 ch 206 §7. See Gov C §§68097, 68098.

CHAPTER 3
WRITINGS

Article 2. Public Writings.
Article 3. Private Writings.
Article 4. Records Destroyed in Fire or Calamity.
Article 4.5. Private Records Destroyed in Disaster or Calamity.

ARTICLE 1
Writings in General [Repealed]

§§1887–1889. [Sections repealed 1968]

Leg.H. Enacted 1872. Repealed Stats 1968 ch 1473 §24. See Gov C §§6250 et seq.

ARTICLE 2
Public Writings

Laws, written or unwritten. §1895.
Written laws defined. §1896.
Constitution and statutes. §1897.
Public and private statutes defined. §1898.
Unwritten law defined. §1899.
Judicial record defined. §1904.
Conclusive effect of judgment in various cases. §1908.
Pleading and proof of conclusive judgment or order. §1908.5.
Judicial orders creating disputable presumption. §1909.
When parties are to be deemed the same as in judgment. §1910.
What deemed adjudged in a judgment. §1911.
Where sureties bound, principal is also. §1912.
Sister state judicial records. §1913.
Record of a foreign court of admiralty, effect. §1914.
Impeachment of judicial record. §1916.
The jurisdiction necessary to a judgment. §1917.

§1892. [Section repealed 1968]

Leg.H. Enacted 1872. Repealed Stats 1968 ch 1473 §25. See Gov C §§6250 et seq.

§1893. [Section repealed 1968]

Leg.H. Enacted 1872. Amended Code Amdts 1873–74 ch 383 §219; Stats 1965 ch 299 §68, operative January 1, 1967. Repealed Stats 1968 ch 1473 §26. See Gov C §§6250 et seq.

§1894. [Section repealed 1968]

Leg.H. Enacted 1872. Repealed Stats 1968 ch 1473 §27. See Gov C §§6250 et seq.

§1895. Laws, written or unwritten

Laws, whether organic or ordinary, are either written or unwritten. **Leg.H.** Enacted 1872.

§1896. Written laws defined

A written law is that which is promulgated in writing, and of which a record is in existence. **Leg.H.** Enacted 1872.

§1897. Constitution and statutes

The organic law is the constitution of government, and is altogether written. Other written laws are denominated statutes. The written law of this State is therefore contained in its Constitution and statutes, and in the Constitution and statutes of the United States. **Leg.H.** Enacted 1872.

§1898. Public and private statutes defined

Statutes are public or private. A private statute is one which concerns only certain designated individuals, and affects only their private rights. All other statutes are public, in which are included statutes creating or affecting corporations. **Leg.H.** Enacted 1872.

§1899. Unwritten law defined

Unwritten law is the law not promulgated and recorded, as mentioned in Section 1896, but which is, nevertheless, observed and administered in the courts of the country. It has no certain repository, but is collected from the reports of the decisions of the courts, and the treatises of learned men. **Leg.H.** Enacted 1872.

§1900. [Section repealed 1957]

Leg.H. Enacted 1872. Repealed Stats 1957 ch 249 §2. See Ev C §452.

§1901. [Section repealed 1967]

Leg.H. Enacted 1872. Amended Code Amdts 1873–74 ch 383 §220; Stats 1957 ch 249 §3. Repealed Stats 1965 ch 299 §69, operative January 1, 1967. See Ev C §§1452–1454, 1530.

§1902. [Section repealed 1957]
Leg.H. Enacted 1872. Repealed Stats 1957 ch 249 §2. See Ev C §452.

§1903. [Section repealed 1967]
Leg.H. Enacted 1872. Repealed Stats 1965 ch 299 §70, operative January 1, 1967. See Ev C §1530.

§1904. Judicial record defined
A judicial record is the record or official entry of the proceedings in a court of justice, or of the official act of a judicial officer, in an action or special proceeding. **Leg.H.** Enacted 1872.

§1905. [Section repealed 1967]
Leg.H. Enacted 1872. Repealed Stats 1965 ch 299 §71, operative January 1, 1967. See Ev C §§1452, 1453, 1530.

§1906. [Section repealed 1967]
Leg.H. Enacted 1872. Amended Code Amdts 1873–74 ch 383 §221. Repealed Stats 1965 ch 299 §72, operative January 1, 1967. See Ev C §§1452, 1454, 1530.

§1907. [Section repealed 1967]
Leg.H. Enacted 1872. Repealed Stats 1965 ch 299 §73, operative January 1, 1967. See Ev C §§1400, 1401, 1410, 1452, 1454, 1530.

§1908. Conclusive effect of judgment in various cases
(a) The effect of a judgment or final order in an action or special proceeding before a court or judge of this state, or of the United States, having jurisdiction to pronounce the judgment or order, is as follows:

(1) In case of a judgment or order against a specific thing, or in respect to the probate of a will, or the administration of the estate of a decedent, or in respect to the personal, political, or legal condition or relation of a particular person, the judgment or order is conclusive upon the title to the thing, the will, or administration, or the condition or relation of the person.

(2) In other cases, the judgment or order is, in respect to the matter directly adjudged, conclusive between the parties and their successors in interest by title subsequent to the commencement of the action or special proceeding, litigating for the same thing under the same title and in the same capacity, provided they have notice, actual or constructive, of the pendency of the action or proceeding.

(b) A person who is not a party but who controls an action, individually or in cooperation with others, is bound by the adjudications of litigated matters as if he were a party if he has a proprietary or financial interest in the judgment or in the determination of a question of fact or of a question of law with reference to the same subject matter or transaction; if the other party has notice of his participation, the other party is equally bound.

At any time prior to a final judgment, as defined in Section 577, a determination of whether the judgment, verdict upon which it was entered, or a finding upon which it was entered is to be binding upon a nonparty pursuant to this subdivision or whether such nonparty is entitled to the benefit of this subdivision may, on the noticed motion of any party or any nonparty that may be affected by this subdivision, be made in the court in which the action was tried or in which the action is pending on appeal. If no such motion is made before the judgment becomes final, the determination may be made in a separate action. If appropriate, a judgment may be entered or ordered to be entered pursuant to such determination. **Leg.H.** Enacted 1872. Amended Code Amdts 1873–74 ch 383 §222; Stats 1975 ch 225 §1.

§1908.5. Pleading and proof of conclusive judgment or order
When a judgment or order of a court is conclusive, the judgment or order must be alleged in the pleadings if there be an opportunity to do so; if there be no such opportunity, the judgment or order may be used as evidence. **Leg.H.** Added Stats 1965 ch 299 §74, operative January 1, 1967.

§1909. Judicial orders creating disputable presumption
Other judicial orders of a court or judge of this State, or of the United States, create a disputable presumption, according to the matter directly determined, between the same parties and their representatives and successors in interest by title subsequent to the commencement of the action or special proceeding, litigating for the same thing under the same title and in the same capacity. **Leg.H.** Enacted 1872.

§1910. When parties are to be deemed the same as in judgment
The parties are deemed to be the same when those between whom the evidence is offered were on opposite sides in the former case, and a judgment or other determination could in that case have been made between them alone, though other parties were joined with both or either. **Leg.H.** Enacted 1872.

§1911. What deemed adjudged in a judgment
That only is deemed to have been adjudged in a former judgment which appears upon its face to have been so adjudged, or which was actually and necessarily included therein or necessary thereto. **Leg.H.** Enacted 1872.

§1912. Where sureties bound, principal is also
Whenever, pursuant to the last four sections, a party is bound by a record, and such party stands in the relation of a surety for another, the latter is also bound from the time that he has notice of the action or proceeding, and an opportunity at the surety's request to join in the defense. **Leg.H.** Enacted 1872.

§1913. Sister state judicial records
(a) Subject to subdivision (b), the effect of a judicial record of a sister state is the same in this state as in the state where it was made, except that it can only be enforced in this state by an action or special proceeding.

(b) The authority of a guardian, conservator, or committee, or of a personal representative, does not extend beyond the jurisdiction of the government under which that person was invested with authority, except to the extent expressly authorized by Article 4 (commencing with Section 2011) of Chapter 8 of Part 3 of Division 4 of the Probate Code or another statute. **Leg.H.** Added 1872. Amended Stats 1979 ch 730 §34, operative January 1, 1981; Stats 1988 ch 1199 §13, operative July 1, 1989; Stats 2014 ch 553 §1 (SB 940), effective January 1, 2015, operative January 1, 2016.

§1914. Record of a foreign court of admiralty, effect
The effect of the judicial record of a court of admiralty of a foreign country is the same as if it were the record of a court of admiralty of the United States. **Leg.H.** Enacted 1872.

§1915. [Section repealed 1975]
Leg.H. Enacted 1872. Amended Stats 1907 ch 178 §1; Stats 1967 ch 503 §2. Repealed Stats 1974 ch 211 §6. The repealed section related to effect of judgment of foreign country.

§1916. Impeachment of judicial record
Any judicial record may be impeached by evidence of a want of jurisdiction in the court or judicial officer, of collusion between the parties, or of fraud in the party offering the record, in respect to the proceedings. **Leg.H.** Enacted 1872.

§1917. The jurisdiction necessary to a judgment
The jurisdiction sufficient to sustain a record is jurisdiction over the cause, over the parties, and over the thing, when a specific thing is the subject of the judgment. **Leg.H.** Enacted 1872.

§1918. [Section repealed 1967]
Leg.H. Enacted 1872. Amended Code Amdts 1873–74 §223, Stats 1931 ch 266 §1. Repealed Stats 1965 ch 299 §75, operative January 1, 1967. See Ev C 1270, 1271, 1280, 1400–1402, 1410, 1452–1454, 1530.

§1919. [Section repealed 1967]
Leg.H. Enacted 1872. Repealed Stats 1965 ch 299 §76, operative January 1, 1967. See Ev C §§1453, 1530, 1532, 1600.

§1919a. [Section repealed 1967]
Leg.H. Added Stats 1931 ch 267 §1. Repealed Stats 1965 ch 299 §77, operative January 1, 1967. See Ev C §§1315, 1316.

§1919b. [Section repealed 1967]
Leg.H. Added Stats 1931 ch 267 §2. Repealed Stats 1965 ch 299 §78, operative January 1, 1967. See Ev C §§1315, 1316.

§1920. [Section repealed 1967]
Leg.H. Enacted 1872. Amended Code Amdts 1873–74 ch 383 §224. Repealed Stats 1965 ch 299 §79, operative January 1, 1967. See Ev C §§1270, 1271, 1280.

§1920a. [Section repealed 1967]

Leg.H. Added Stats 1937 ch 574 §1. Repealed Stats 1965 ch 299 §80, operative January 1, 1967. See Ev C §1530.

§1920b. [Section repealed 1967]

Leg.H. Added Stats 1943 ch 1126 §1. Amended Stats 1947 ch 818 §1. Repealed Stats 1965 ch 299 §81, operative January 1, 1967. See Ev C §1551.

§1921. [Section repealed 1967]

Leg.H. Enacted 1872. Repealed Stats 1965 ch 299 §82, operative January 1, 1967. See Ev C §§1270, 1271, 1280, 1452, 1453, 1530.

§1922. [Section repealed 1967]

Leg.H. Enacted 1872. Repealed Stats 1965 ch 299 §83, operative January 1, 1967. See Ev C §§1270, 1271, 1280, 1452, 1453, 1530.

§1923. [Section repealed 1967]

Leg.H. Enacted 1872. Amended Code Amdts 1873–74 §225. Repealed Stats 1965 ch 299 §84, operative January 1, 1967. See Ev C §1531.

§1924. [Section repealed 1967]

Leg.H. Enacted 1872. Amended Code Amdts 1873–74 ch 383. Repealed Stats 1965 ch 299 §85, operative January 1, 1967. The repealed section related to the applicability of provisions relating to public writings.

§1925. [Section repealed 1967]

Leg.H. Enacted 1872. Repealed Stats 1965 ch 299 §86, operative January 1, 1967. See Ev C §1604.

§1927. [Section repealed 1967]

Leg.H. Added Stats 1905 ch 81 §1. Repealed Stats 1965 ch 299 §88, operative January 1, 1967. The repealed section related to writings affecting mineral lands.

§1927.5. [Section repealed 1967]

Leg.H. Added Stats 1955 ch 59 §12. Repealed Stats 1965 ch 299 §89, operative January 1, 1967. See Ev C §1605.

ARTICLE 2.1
Official Reports [Repealed]

§1928.1. [Section repealed 1967]

Leg.H. Added Stats 1953 §13. Repealed Stats 1965 ch 299 §91, operative January 1, 1967. See Ev C §1282.

§1928.2. [Section repealed 1967]

Leg.H. Added Stats 1953 ch 52 §13. Repealed Stats 1965 ch 299 §91, operative January 1, 1967. See Ev C §1283.

§1928.3. [Section repealed 1967]

Leg.H. Added Stats 1953 ch 52 §13. Repealed Stats 1965 ch 299 §91, operative January 1, 1967. See Ev C §§1452, 1453, 1530.

§1928.4. [Section repealed 1967]

Leg.H. Added Stats 1953 ch 52 §13. Repealed Stats 1965 ch 299 §91, operative January 1, 1967. See Ev C §3.

ARTICLE 3
Private Writings

Private writings classified. §1929.
Seal defined. §1930.
Public and private seals; Recognition of seals in sister states or foreign countries. §1931.
Distinction between sealed and unsealed instruments abolished. §1932.
Execution of an instrument defined. §1933.
Compromise of a debt without seal good. §1934.
Subscribing witness defined. §1935.
Removal of public records for evidence. §1950.
Disposition of exhibits or depositions; Notice to parties. §1952.
Return of exhibits introduced in trial. §1952.2.
Destruction of exhibit or deposition introduced at trial; Conditions and time limits; Sealed files. §1952.3.

§1929. Private writings classified

Private writings are either:
1. Sealed; or,
2. Unsealed. **Leg.H.** Enacted 1872.

§1930. Seal defined

A seal is a particular sign, made to attest, in the most formal manner, the execution of an instrument. **Leg.H.** Enacted 1872.

§1931. Public and private seals; Recognition of seals in sister states or foreign countries

A public seal in this State is a stamp or impression made by a public officer with an instrument provided by law, to attest the execution of an official or public document, upon the paper, or upon any substance attached to the paper, which is capable of receiving a visible impression. A private seal may be made in the same manner by any instrument, or it may be made by the scroll of a pen, or by writing the word "seal" against the signature of the writer. A scroll or other sign, made in a sister state or foreign country, and there recognized as a seal, must be so regarded in this State. **Leg.H.** Enacted 1872. Amended Code Amdts 1873–74 ch 383 §228.

§1932. Distinction between sealed and unsealed instruments abolished

There shall be no difference hereafter, in this State, between sealed and unsealed writings. A writing under seal may therefore be changed, or altogether discharged by a writing not under seal. **Leg.H.** Enacted 1872. Amended Code Amdts 1873–74 ch 383 §229.

§1933. Execution of an instrument defined

The execution of an instrument is the subscribing and delivering it, with or without affixing a seal. **Leg.H.** Enacted 1872.

§1934. Compromise of a debt without seal good

An agreement, in writing, without a seal, for the compromise or settlement of a debt, is as obligatory as if a seal were affixed. **Leg.H.** Enacted 1872.

§1935. Subscribing witness defined

A subscribing witness is one who sees a writing executed or hears it acknowledged, and at the request of the party thereupon signs his name as a witness. **Leg.H.** Enacted 1872.

§1936. [Section repealed 1967]

Leg.H. Enacted 1872. Amended Code Amdts 1873–74, ch 383 §230. Repealed Stats 1965 ch 299 §92, operative January 1, 1967. See Ev C §1341.

§1936.1. [Section repealed 1967]

Leg.H. Added Stats 1963 ch 1558 §1. Repealed Stats 1965 ch 299 §93, operative January 1, 1967. See Ev C §1156.

§1937. [Section repealed 1967]

Leg.H. Enacted 1872. Repealed Stats 1965 ch 299 §94 operative January 1, 1967. See Ev C §§1520 et seq.

§1938. [Section repealed 1967]

Leg.H. Enacted 1872. Repealed Stats 1965 ch 299 §95 operative January 1, 1967. The repealed section related to writings under the control of a proponent.

§1939. [Section repealed 1967]

Leg.H. Enacted 1872. Repealed Stats 1965 ch 299 §96 operative January 1, 1967. See Ev C §§1520 et seq.

§1940. [Section repealed 1967]

Leg.H. Enacted 1872. Amended Code Amdts 1873–74 ch 383 §231. Repealed Stats 1965 ch 299 §97, operative January 1, 1967. See Ev C §§1413, 1415.

§1941. [Section repealed 1967]

Leg.H. Enacted 1872. Repealed Stats 1965 ch 299 §98, operative January 1, 1967. See Ev C §1412.

§1942. [Section repealed 1967]

Leg.H. Enacted 1872. Repealed Stats 1965 ch 299 §99, operative January 1, 1967. See Ev C §1414.

§1943. [Section repealed 1967]

Leg.H. Enacted 1872. Repealed Stats 1965 ch 299 §100, operative January 1, 1967. See Ev C §1416.

§1944. [Section repealed 1967]

Leg.H. Enacted 1872. Amended Code Amdts 1873–74 ch 383 §232. Repealed Stats 1965 ch 299 §101, operative January 1, 1967. See Ev C §§1417, 1418.

§1945. [Section repealed 1967]
Leg.H. Enacted 1872. Repealed Stats 1965 ch 299 §103, operative January 1, 1967. See Ev C §1419.

§1946. [Section repealed 1967]
Leg.H. Enacted 1872. Amended Code Amdts 1873–74 ch 383 §233. Repealed Stats 1965 ch 299 §103, operative January 1, 1967. See Ev C §§1230, 1270, 1271, 1280.

§1947. [Section repealed 1967]
Leg.H. Enacted 1872. Repealed Stats 1965 ch 299 §104, operative January 1, 1967. See Ev C §§1270, 1271.

§1948. [Section repealed 1967]
Leg.H. Enacted 1872. Amended Code Amdts 1873–74 ch 383 §234. Repealed Stats 1965 ch 299 §105, operative January 1, 1967. See Ev C §1451.

§1949. [Section repealed 1874]
Leg.H. Enacted 1872. Repealed Stats 1873–74 ch 383 §235. See Gov C §§27201 et seq.

§1950. Removal of public records for evidence
The record of a conveyance of real property, or any other record, a transcript of which is admissible in evidence, must not be removed from the office where it is kept, except upon the order of a court, in cases where the inspection of the record is shown to be essential to the just determination of the cause or proceeding pending, or where the court is held in the same building with such office. **Leg.H.** Enacted 1872. Amended Code Amdts 1873–74 ch 383 §236.

§1951. [Section repealed 1967]
Leg.H. Added Code Amdts 1873–74 ch 383 §237. Amended Stats 1889 ch 42 §1. Repealed Stats 1965 ch 299 §106, operative January 1, 1967. See Ev C §§1451, 1532, 1600.

§1952. Disposition of exhibits or depositions; Notice to parties
(a) The clerk shall retain in his or her custody any exhibit, deposition, or administrative record introduced in the trial of a civil action or proceeding or filed in the action or proceeding until the final determination thereof or the dismissal of the action or proceeding, except that the court may order the exhibit, deposition, or administrative record returned to the respective party or parties at any time upon oral stipulation in open court or by written stipulation by the parties or for good cause shown.

(b) No exhibit or deposition shall be ordered destroyed or otherwise disposed of pursuant to this section where a party to the action or proceeding files a written notice with the court requesting the preservation of any exhibit, deposition, or administrative record for a stated time, but not to exceed one year.

(c) Upon the conclusion of the trial of a civil action or proceeding at which any exhibit or deposition has been introduced, the court shall order that the exhibit or deposition be destroyed or otherwise disposed of by the clerk. The operative destruction or disposition date shall be 60 days following final determination of the action or proceeding. Final determination includes final determination on appeal. Written notice of the order shall be sent by first-class mail to the parties by the clerk.

(d) Upon the conclusion of any posttrial hearing at which any exhibit, deposition, or administrative record has been introduced, the court shall order that the exhibit or deposition be destroyed or otherwise disposed of by the clerk. The operative date of destruction or disposition shall be 60 days following the conclusion of the hearing, or if an appeal is taken, upon final determination of the appeal. Written notice of the order shall be sent by first-class mail to the parties by the clerk. **Leg.H.** Added Stats 1984 ch 27 §2. Amended Stats 1990 ch 382 §1 (AB 3408); Stats 1991 ch 1090 §7 (AB 1484).

Prior Law: Former CCP §1952, similar to the present section, was added Stats 1931 ch 235 §1, amended Stats 1945 ch 1043 §1, Stats 1947 ch 679 §1, Stats 1951 ch 678 §1, Stats 1967 ch 85 §1, Stats 1978 ch 423 §1, Stats 1981 ch 714 §74, and repealed Stats 1984 ch 27 §1.

§1952.1. [Section repealed 1967]
Leg.H. Added Stats 1959 ch 344 §1. Amended Stats 1963 ch 837 §1. Repealed Stats 1967 ch 85 §2. The repealed section related to the destruction of documents.

§1952.2. Return of exhibits introduced in trial
Notwithstanding any other provisions of law, upon a judgment becoming final, at the expiration of the appeal period, unless an appeal is pending, the court, in its discretion, and on its own motion by a written order signed by the judge, filed in the action, and an entry thereof made in the register of actions, may order the clerk to return all of the exhibits, depositions, and administrative records introduced or filed in the trial of a civil action or proceeding to the attorneys for the parties introducing or filing the same. **Leg.H.** Added Stats 1959 ch 343 §1. Amended Stats 1969 ch 44 §1; Stats 1984 ch 27 §3; Stats 1991 ch 1090 §8 (AB 1484).

§1952.3. Destruction of exhibit or deposition introduced at trial; Conditions and time limits; Sealed files
Notwithstanding any other provision of the law, the court, on its own motion, may order the destruction or other disposition of any exhibit, deposition, or administrative record introduced in the trial or posttrial hearing of a civil action or proceeding or filed in the action or proceeding that, if appeal has not been taken from the decision of the court in the action or proceeding, remains in the custody of the court or clerk five years after time for appeal has expired, or, if appeal has been taken, remains in the custody of the court or clerk five years after final determination thereof, or that remains in the custody of the court or clerk for a period of five years after any of the following:

(a) A motion for a new trial has been granted and a memorandum to set the case for trial has not been filed, or a motion to set for trial has not been made within five years.

(b) The dismissal of the action or proceeding.

In addition, the court on its own motion, may order the destruction or other disposition of any exhibit, deposition, or administrative record that remains in the custody of the court or clerk for a period of 10 years after the introduction or filing of the action or proceeding if, in the discretion of the court, the exhibit, deposition, or administrative record should be disposed of or destroyed.

The order shall be entered in the register of actions of each case in which the order is made.

No exhibit, deposition, or administrative record shall be ordered destroyed or otherwise disposed of pursuant to this section if a party to the action or proceeding files a written notice with the court requesting the preservation of any exhibit, deposition, or administrative record for a stated time, but not to exceed one year.

Any sealed file shall be retained for at least two years after the date on which destruction would otherwise be authorized pursuant to this section. **Leg.H.** Added Stats 1984 ch 250 §3. Amended Stats 1985 ch 875 §1; Stats 1990 ch 382 §2 (AB 3408); Stats 1991 ch 1090 §9 (AB 1484).

Prior Law: Former CCP §1952.3, similar to the present section, was added Stats 1965 ch 1003 §1, amended Stats 1969 ch 48 §1, Stats 1979 ch 908 §1, and repealed Stats 1984 ch 27 §4.

ARTICLE 4
Records Destroyed in Fire or Calamity

"Record". §1953.
Application for order for certified copy of lost, injured, or destroyed record. §1953.01.
Notice showing, and order. §1953.02.
Application to court when certified copy of records cannot be obtained, and notice thereof. §1953.03.
Issuance and effect of order. §1953.04.
Supplying record; Notice; Effect of restored record. §1953.05.
Appeal. §1953.06.

§1953. "Record"
As used in this article "record" includes all or any part of any judgment, decree, order, document, paper, process, or file. **Leg.H.** Added Stats 1953 ch 52 §14.

§1953.01. Application for order for certified copy of lost, injured, or destroyed record
Whenever in any action or special proceeding, civil or criminal, in any court of this State any record is lost, injured, or destroyed by reason of conflagration or other public calamity, any person interested therein may apply by a duly verified petition in writing to the court for an order

authorizing such defect to be supplied by a duly certified copy of the original, where such copy can be obtained. **Leg.H.** Added Stats 1953 ch 52 §14.

§1953.02. Notice showing, and order

Upon notice given pursuant to Sections 1010 to 1020, inclusive, of this code, and its being shown to the satisfaction of the court that the record has been so lost, injured, or destroyed, the court shall make an order that the certified copy shall thereafter have the same effect in all respects as the original would have had. **Leg.H.** Added Stats 1953 ch 52 §14.

§1953.03. Application to court when certified copy of records cannot be obtained, and notice thereof

Whenever in any action or special proceeding, civil or criminal, in any court of this State any record is lost, injured, or destroyed by reason of conflagration or other public calamity, and a certified copy of the original cannot be supplied, any person interested therein may make written application to the court, verified by affidavit, showing such loss, injury, or destruction, and that a certified copy of the record cannot be obtained by the person making the application, and that such loss, injury, or destruction occurred by conflagration, or other calamity, without the fault or neglect of the person making the application, and that such loss, injury, or destruction, unless supplied or remedied may result in damage to the person making the application. Thereupon the court shall cause notice of the application to be given pursuant to Sections 1010 to 1020, inclusive, of this code. **Leg.H.** Added Stats 1953 ch 52 §14.

§1953.04. Issuance and effect of order

Upon the hearing if the court is satisfied that the statements contained in the written application are true, it shall make an order reciting the substance and effect of the lost, injured, or destroyed record. The order shall have the same effect that the original would have had if it had not been lost, injured, or destroyed, so far as concerns the person making the application, and the persons who have been notified, pursuant to Section 1953.03. **Leg.H.** Added Stats 1953 ch 52 §14.

§1953.05. Supplying record; Notice; Effect of restored record

The record in all cases where the proceeding is in rem, including probate, guardianship, conservatorship, and insolvency proceedings, may be supplied in like manner upon like notice to all persons who have appeared therein, and upon notice by publication or postings for not less than 10 days, as the court may order, to all persons who have not appeared. When restored the record shall have the same effect as the original upon all persons who have been personally served with notice of the application, and as to all other persons it shall be prima facie evidence of the contents of the original. **Leg.H.** Added Stats 1953 ch 52 §14. Amended Stats 1979 ch 730 §35, operative January 1, 1981.

§1953.06. Appeal

If an appeal to a reviewing court has been taken in any action or special proceeding in any trial court in which the record has been subsequently lost or destroyed by conflagration or other public calamity and a transcript of such record has been filed in the reviewing court, any person interested in the action or special proceeding may obtain a certified copy of all or any portion of the transcript from the clerk of the reviewing court and may file such certified copy in the office of the clerk of the court from which the appeal was taken. Thereupon the certified copy may be made the basis of any further proceedings or processes in the trial court in such action or special proceeding to all intents and purposes as if the original record were on file. **Leg.H.** Added Stats 1953 ch 52 §14. Amended Stats 1967 ch 17 §21.

ARTICLE 4.5
Private Records Destroyed in Disaster or Calamity

Petition for establishing destroyed or damaged records. §1953.10.
Notice of filing and hearing, on order therefor; Proof of notice. §1953.11.
Evidence; Order reciting existence, substance, or authenticity of memorandum or other document. §1953.12.
Reference in order to memorandum or other writing; Effect of order. §1953.13.

§1953.10. Petition for establishing destroyed or damaged records

Any person, corporation, copartnership, organization, institution, business, member of profession or calling interested in establishing the existence, substance, genuineness, or authenticity of any memorandum, book, map, chart, manuscript, writing, account, entry, record, print, document, representation, or combination thereof that has been damaged, rendered wholly or partially illegible, destroyed in whole or in part or lost by explosion, conflagration, earthquake, disaster or other public calamity, may apply by duly verified petition to the court for an order establishing, reciting, or declaring the existence, substance, genuineness or authenticity of the same. **Leg.H.** Added Stats 1961 ch 1311 §1.

§1953.11. Notice of filing and hearing, on order therefor; Proof of notice

Notice of the filing of the petition and of the time and place of the hearing thereof shall be given to such persons, if any, as the court shall designate by its order. Such order shall specify how such notice shall be given and may be by publication, posting, personal service or otherwise as the court shall direct. Upon the hearing of the petition proof shall be submitted to the court that notice has been given as prescribed in such order. **Leg.H.** Added Stats 1961 ch 1311 §1.

§1953.12. Evidence; Order reciting existence, substance, or authenticity of memorandum or other document.

Upon the hearing the court shall receive such evidence as may be required and if the court is satisfied that the statements contained in the petition are true, it shall make an order reciting the existence, substance, genuineness or authenticity of the destroyed or lost memorandum, book, map, chart, manuscript, writing, account, entry, print, document, representation or combination thereof. **Leg.H.** Added Stats 1961 ch 1311 §1.

§1953.13. Reference in order to memorandum or other writing; Effect of order

The order of court made upon such hearing shall refer to the memorandum, book, map, chart, manuscript, writing, account, entry, record, print, document, representation or combination thereof which is the subject of said petition and such court order shall be deemed in lieu of the original and have the same effect as if the original had not been damaged, destroyed or otherwise rendered wholly or partially illegible. **Leg.H.** Added Stats 1961 ch 1311 §1.

ARTICLE 5
Uniform Business Records as Evidence Act [Repealed]

§§1953e, 1953f. [Sections repealed 1967]

Leg.H. Added Stats 1941 ch 482 §1. Repealed Stats 1965 ch 299 §107, operative January 1, 1967. See Ev C §§1270–1272.

§1953f.5 [Section repealed 1967]

Leg.H. Added Stats 1959 ch 1009 §1. Repealed Stats 1965 ch 299 §107, operative January 1, 1967. See Ev C §§1270–1272.

§§1953g, 1953h. [Sections repealed 1967]

Leg.H. Added Stats 1941 ch 482 §1. Repealed Stats 1965 ch 299 §107, and operative January 1, 1967. See Ev C §§1270–1272.

ARTICLE 6
Uniform Photographic Copies of Business and Public Records as Evidence Act [Repealed]

§1953i. [Section repealed 1967]

Leg.H. Added Stats 1951 ch 346 §1. Amended Stats 1953 ch 294 §1. Repealed Stats 1965 ch 299 §108, operative January 1, 1967. See Ev C §1550.

§§1953j–1953*l*. [Sections repealed 1967]

Leg.H. Added Stats 1951 ch 346 §1. Repealed Stats 1965 ch 299 §108, operative January 1, 1967. See Ev C §1550.

CHAPTER 4
MATERIAL OBJECTS PRESENTED TO THE SENSES OTHER THAN WRITINGS [REPEALED]

§1954. [Section repealed 1967]

Leg.H. Enacted 1872. Repealed Stats 1965 ch 299 §109, operative January 1, 1967. See Ev C §§140, 210, 351, 352.

CHAPTER 5
INDIRECT EVIDENCE, INFERENCES, AND PRESUMPTIONS [REPEALED]

§1957. **[Section repealed 1967]**

Leg.H. Enacted 1872. Repealed Stats 1965 ch 299 §109, operative January 1, 1967. See Ev C §§140, 210.

§1958. **[Section repealed 1967]**

Leg.H. Enacted 1872. Repealed Stats 1965 ch 299 §109, operative January 1, 1967. See Ev C §600 subd (b).

§1959. **[Section repealed 1967]**

Leg.H. Enacted 1872. Repealed Stats 1965 ch 299 §109, operative January 1, 1967. See Ev C §600 subd (a).

§1960. **[Section repealed 1967]**

Leg.H. Enacted 1872. Repealed Stats 1965 ch 299 §109, operative January 1, 1967. See Ev C §600 subd (b).

§1961. **[Section repealed 1967]**

Leg.H. Enacted 1872. Repealed Stats 1965 ch 299 §109, operative January 1, 1967. See Ev C §601.

§1962. **[Section repealed 1967]**

Leg.H. Enacted 1872. Amended Stats 1955 ch 948 §3. Repealed Stats 1965 ch 299 §109, operative January 1, 1967. See Ev C §§620–624.

§1963. **[Section repealed 1967]**

Leg.H. Enacted 1872. Amended Stats 1945 ch 988 §2, Stats 1955 ch 860 §1. Repealed Stats 1965 ch 299 §109, operative January 1, 1967. See CC §§3545–3548, Ev C §§412, 413, 520, 521, 631–634, 636–645, 664, 666, 667, 1314, Fam C §7611.

CHAPTER 6
INDISPENSABLE EVIDENCE

Creation and transfer of estate or interest in, or trust or power relating to, realty. §1971.
Creation of trust; Specific performance; Trusts arising or extinguished by implication. §1972.
Writing necessary for charge on representation as to another's credit. §1974.

§1967. **[Section repealed 1967]**

Leg.H. Enacted 1872. Repealed Stats 1965 ch 299 §111, operative January 1, 1967. The repealed section defined indispensable evidence.

§1968. **[Section repealed 1967]**

Leg.H. Enacted 1872. Repealed Stats 1965 ch 299 §112, operative January 1, 1967. The repealed section related to treason and perjury.

§1969. **[Section repealed 1967]**

Leg.H. Enacted 1872. Amended Code Amdts 1873–74 ch 383 §228. Repealed Stats 1933 ch 969 §25. See Prob C §50.

§1970. **[Section repealed 1967]**

Leg.H. Enacted 1872. Amended Code Amdts 1873–74 ch 383 §239. Repealed Stats 1933 ch 969 §25. See Prob C §§70 et seq.

§1971. Creation and transfer of estate or interest in, or trust or power relating to, realty

No estate or interest in real property, other than for leases for a term not exceeding one year, nor any power over or concerning it, or in any manner relating thereto, can be created, granted, assigned, surrendered, or declared, otherwise than by operation of law, or a conveyance or other instrument in writing, subscribed by the party creating, granting, assigning, surrendering, or declaring the same, or by the party's lawful agent thereunto authorized by writing. **Leg.H.** Enacted 1872. Amended Stats 1986 ch 820 §19, operative July 1, 1987.

§1972. Creation of trust; Specific performance; Trusts arising or extinguished by implication

(a) Section 1971 shall not be construed to abridge the power of any court to compel the specific performance of an agreement, in case of part performance thereof.

(b) Section 1971 does not affect the creation of a trust under Division 9 (commencing with Section 15000) of the Probate Code nor prevent any trust from arising or being extinguished by implication or operation of law. **Leg.H.** Enacted 1872. Amended Stats 1986 ch 820 §20, operative July 1, 1987.

§1973. **[Section repealed 1967]**

Leg.H. Enacted 1872. Amended Stats 1907 ch 291 §1; Stats 1931 ch 1071 §1; Stats 1937 ch 316 §1; Stats 1963 ch 814 §2. Repealed Stats 1965 ch 299 §113, operative January 1, 1967. See CC §1624.

§1973a. **[Section repealed 1965]**

Leg.H. Added Stats 1931 ch 1071 §2. Repealed Stats 1963 ch 819 §27, effective January 1, 1965. See UCC §2201.

§1974. Writing necessary for charge on representation as to another's credit

No evidence is admissible to charge a person upon a representation as to the credit of a third person, unless such representation, or some memorandum thereof, be in writing, and either subscribed by or in the handwriting of the party to be charged. This section is a Statute of Frauds provision and is to be applied in a manner that is consistent with the manner in which subdivision 2 of Section 1624 of the Civil Code is applied. **Leg.H.** Enacted 1872. Amended Stats 1965 ch 299 §114; Stats 1970 ch 720 §1.

CHAPTER 7
CONCLUSIVE OR UNANSWERABLE EVIDENCE [REPEALED]

§1978. **[Section repealed 1967]**

Leg.H. Enacted 1872. Repealed Stats 1965 ch 299 §115, operative January 1, 1967. The repealed section related to conclusive evidence.

CHAPTER 8
UNIFORM ACT ON BLOOD TESTS TO DETERMINE PATERNITY [REPEALED]

§§1980.1–1980.7. **[Sections repealed 1967]**

Leg.H. Added Stats 1953 ch 1426 §1. Repealed Stats 1965 ch 299 §116, operative January 1, 1967. See Fam C §§7550 et seq.

TITLE 3
OF THE PRODUCTION OF EVIDENCE

Chapter 2. Means of Production.
Chapter 3. Manner of Production.

CHAPTER 1
BY WHOM TO BE PRODUCED [REPEALED]

§1981. [Section repealed 1967]

Leg.H. Enacted 1872. Repealed Stats 1965 ch 299 §117, operative January 1, 1967. See Ev C §§500, 550.

§1982. [Section repealed 1967]

Leg.H. Enacted 1872. Repealed Stats 1965 ch 299 §117, operative January 1, 1967. See Ev C §1402.

§1983. [Section repealed 1967]

Leg.H. Added Stats 1927 ch 244 §1. Repealed Stats 1965 ch 299 §117, operative January 1, 1967. The repealed section related to burden of proof.

CHAPTER 2
MEANS OF PRODUCTION

"Subpoena"; Issuance; Affidavit. §1985.
Agreement to appear at time not specified in subpoena. §1985.1.
Subpoena requiring attendance of witness; Notice. §1985.2.
Subpoena duces tecum for production of personal records; Definitions; Application of section. §1985.3.
Production of consumer records maintained by state or local agency. §1985.4.
Subpoena provision where witness to appear out of court. §1985.5.
Subpoena duces tecum for production of employment records; Definitions, Procedures and requirements; Application of section and exceptions. §1985.6.
Order to show cause against medical provider. §1985.7.
Procedure for subpoena of electronically stored information. §1985.8.
Obtaining subpoenas. §1986.
Testimony or other evidence given by journalist. §1986.1.
Rights of person subpoenaed, for deposition to receive fees and mileage. §1986.5.
Service of subpoena, or of written notice. §1987.
Order to quash, modify or limit subpoena. §1987.1.
Expenses in making or opposing motion; Exception to sanctions for failure to provide certain electronic information. §1987.2.
Exemption of custodian of business records from attendance requirement. §1987.3.
Filing and service of affidavit for subpoena duces tecum. §1987.5.
Service if witness concealed. §1988.
Attendance of non-resident witnesses. §1989.
Compelling person to testify. §1990.
Punishment of disobedient witness for contempt. §1991.
Punishment for disobedience of witness in deposition proceeding. §1991.1.
Contempt provisions inapplicable to depositions. §1991.2.
Forfeiture and damages; Recovery in civil action. §1992.
Issuance of warrant to arrest witness; Failure to appear notice. §1993.
Arrest of witness; Requirements for release. §1993.1.
Failure to appear; Civil assessment. §1993.2.
Contents of warrant of commitment; Direction and execution of warrants. §1994.
Order for examination or production of witness confined in jail. §1995.
Motion and affidavit for order as to confined witness. §1996.
Production or deposition of confined witness. §1997.

§1985. "Subpoena"; Issuance; Affidavit

(a) The process by which the attendance of a witness is required is the subpoena. It is a writ or order directed to a person and requiring the person's attendance at a particular time and place to testify as a witness. It may also require a witness to bring any books, documents, electronically stored information, or other things under the witness's control which the witness is bound by law to produce in evidence. When a county recorder is using the microfilm system for recording, and a witness is subpoenaed to present a record, the witness shall be deemed to have complied with the subpoena if the witness produces a certified copy thereof.

(b) A copy of an affidavit shall be served with a subpoena duces tecum issued before trial, showing good cause for the production of the matters and things described in the subpoena, specifying the exact matters or things desired to be produced, setting forth in full detail the materiality thereof to the issues involved in the case, and stating that the witness has the desired matters or things in his or her possession or under his or her control.

(c) The clerk, or a judge, shall issue a subpoena or subpoena duces tecum signed and sealed but otherwise in blank to a party requesting it, who shall fill it in before service. An attorney at law who is the attorney of record in an action or proceeding, may sign and issue a subpoena to require attendance before the court in which the action or proceeding is pending or at the trial of an issue therein, or upon the taking of a deposition in an action or proceeding pending therein; the subpoena in such a case need not be sealed. An attorney at law who is the attorney of record in an action or proceeding, may sign and issue a subpoena duces tecum to require production of the matters or things described in the subpoena. **Leg.H.** Enacted 1872. Amended Stats 1933 ch 567 §1; Stats 1961 ch 496 §1; Stats 1967 ch 431 §1; Stats 1968 ch 95 §1; Stats 1979 ch 458 §1; Stats 1982 ch 452 §1; Stats 1986 ch 603 §3; Stats 1990 ch 511 §1 (SB 163); Stats 2012 ch 72 §1 (SB 1574), effective January 1, 2013.

§1985.1. Agreement to appear at time not specified in subpoena

Any person who is subpoenaed to appear at a session of court, or at the trial of an issue therein, may, in lieu of appearance at the time specified in the subpoena, agree with the party at whose request the subpoena was issued to appear at another time or upon such notice as may be agreed upon. Any failure to appear pursuant to such agreement may be punished as a contempt by the court issuing the subpoena. The facts establishing or disproving such agreement and the failure to appear may be proved by an affidavit of any person having personal knowledge of the facts. **Leg.H.** Added Stats 1969 ch 140 §1.

§1985.2. Subpoena requiring attendance of witness; Notice

Any subpoena which requires the attendance of a witness at any civil trial shall contain the following notice in a type face designed to call attention to the notice:

Contact the attorney requesting this subpoena, listed above, before the date on which you are required to be in court, if you have any question about the time or date for you to appear, or if you want to be certain that your presence in court is required. **Leg.H.** Added Stats 1978 ch 431 §1, operative July 1, 1979.

§1985.3. Subpoena duces tecum for production of personal records; Definitions; Application of section

(a) For purposes of this section, the following definitions apply:

(1) "Personal records" means the original, any copy of books, documents, other writings, or electronically stored information pertaining to a consumer and which are maintained by any "witness" which is a physician, dentist, ophthalmologist, optometrist, chiropractor, physical therapist, acupuncturist, podiatrist, veterinarian, veterinary hospital, veterinary clinic, pharmacist, pharmacy, hospital, medical center, clinic, radiology or MRI center, clinical or diagnostic laboratory, state or national bank, state or federal association (as defined in Section 5102 of the Financial Code), state or federal credit union, trust company, anyone authorized by this state to make or arrange loans that are secured by real property, security brokerage firm, insurance company, title insurance company, underwritten title company, escrow agent licensed pursuant to Division 6 (commencing with Section 17000) of the Financial Code or exempt from licensure pursuant to Section 17006 of the Financial Code, attorney, accountant, institution of the Farm Credit System, as specified in Section 2002 of Title 12 of the United States Code, or telephone corporation which is a public utility, as defined in Section 216 of the Public Utilities Code, or psychotherapist, as defined in Section 1010 of the Evidence Code, or a private or public preschool, elementary school, secondary school, or postsecondary school as described in Section 76244 of the Education Code.

(2) "Consumer" means any individual, partnership of five or fewer persons, association, or trust which has transacted business with, or has used the services of, the witness or for whom the witness has acted as agent or fiduciary.

(3) "Subpoenaing party" means the person or persons causing a subpoena duces tecum to be issued or served in connection with any civil

action or proceeding pursuant to this code, but shall not include the state or local agencies described in Section 7465 of the Government Code, or any entity provided for under Article VI of the California Constitution in any proceeding maintained before an adjudicative body of that entity pursuant to Chapter 4 (commencing with Section 6000) of Division 3 of the Business and Professions Code.

(4) "Deposition officer" means a person who meets the qualifications specified in Section 2020.420.

(b) Prior to the date called for in the subpoena duces tecum for the production of personal records, the subpoenaing party shall serve or cause to be served on the consumer whose records are being sought a copy of the subpoena duces tecum, of the affidavit supporting the issuance of the subpoena, if any, and of the notice described in subdivision (e), and proof of service as indicated in paragraph (1) of subdivision (c). This service shall be made as follows:

(1) To the consumer personally, or at his or her last known address, or in accordance with Chapter 5 (commencing with Section 1010) of Title 14 of Part 3, or, if he or she is a party, to his or her attorney of record. If the consumer is a minor, service shall be made on the minor's parent, guardian, conservator, or similar fiduciary, or if one of them cannot be located with reasonable diligence, then service shall be made on any person having the care or control of the minor or with whom the minor resides or by whom the minor is employed, and on the minor if the minor is at least 12 years of age.

(2) Not less than 10 days prior to the date for production specified in the subpoena duces tecum, plus the additional time provided by Section 1013 if service is by mail.

(3) At least five days prior to service upon the custodian of the records, plus the additional time provided by Section 1013 if service is by mail.

(c) Prior to the production of the records, the subpoenaing party shall do either of the following:

(1) Serve or cause to be served upon the witness a proof of personal service or of service by mail attesting to compliance with subdivision (b).

(2) Furnish the witness a written authorization to release the records signed by the consumer or by his or her attorney of record. The witness may presume that any attorney purporting to sign the authorization on behalf of the consumer acted with the consent of the consumer, and that any objection to release of records is waived.

(d) A subpoena duces tecum for the production of personal records shall be served in sufficient time to allow the witness a reasonable time, as provided in Section 2020.410, to locate and produce the records or copies thereof.

(e) Every copy of the subpoena duces tecum and affidavit, if any, served on a consumer or his or her attorney in accordance with subdivision (b) shall be accompanied by a notice, in a typeface designed to call attention to the notice, indicating that (1) records about the consumer are being sought from the witness named on the subpoena; (2) if the consumer objects to the witness furnishing the records to the party seeking the records, the consumer must file papers with the court or serve a written objection as provided in subdivision (g) prior to the date specified for production on the subpoena; and (3) if the party who is seeking the records will not agree in writing to cancel or limit the subpoena, an attorney should be consulted about the consumer's interest in protecting his or her rights of privacy. If a notice of taking of deposition is also served, that other notice may be set forth in a single document with the notice required by this subdivision.

(f) A subpoena duces tecum for personal records maintained by a telephone corporation which is a public utility, as defined in Section 216 of the Public Utilities Code, shall not be valid or effective unless it includes a consent to release, signed by the consumer whose records are requested, as required by Section 2891 of the Public Utilities Code.

(g) Any consumer whose personal records are sought by a subpoena duces tecum and who is a party to the civil action in which this subpoena duces tecum is served may, prior to the date for production, bring a motion under Section 1987.1 to quash or modify the subpoena duces tecum. Notice of the bringing of that motion shall be given to the witness and deposition officer at least five days prior to production. The failure to provide notice to the deposition officer shall not invalidate the motion to quash or modify the subpoena duces tecum but may be raised by the deposition officer as an affirmative defense in any action for liability for improper release of records.

Any other consumer or nonparty whose personal records are sought by a subpoena duces tecum may, prior to the date of production, serve on the subpoenaing party, the witness, and the deposition officer, a written objection that cites the specific grounds on which production of the personal records should be prohibited.

No witness or deposition officer shall be required to produce personal records after receipt of notice that the motion has been brought by a consumer, or after receipt of a written objection from a nonparty consumer, except upon order of the court in which the action is pending or by agreement of the parties, witnesses, and consumers affected.

The party requesting a consumer's personal records may bring a motion under Section 1987.1 to enforce the subpoena within 20 days of service of the written objection. The motion shall be accompanied by a declaration showing a reasonable and good faith attempt at informal resolution of the dispute between the party requesting the personal records and the consumer or the consumer's attorney.

(h) Upon good cause shown and provided that the rights of witnesses and consumers are preserved, a subpoenaing party shall be entitled to obtain an order shortening the time for service of a subpoena duces tecum or waiving the requirements of subdivision (b) where due diligence by the subpoenaing party has been shown.

(i) Nothing contained in this section shall be construed to apply to any subpoena duces tecum which does not request the records of any particular consumer or consumers and which requires a custodian of records to delete all information which would in any way identify any consumer whose records are to be produced.

(j) This section shall not apply to proceedings conducted under Division 1 (commencing with Section 50), Division 4 (commencing with Section 3200), Division 4.5 (commencing with Section 6100), or Division 4.7 (commencing with Section 6200), of the Labor Code.

(k) Failure to comply with this section shall be sufficient basis for the witness to refuse to produce the personal records sought by a subpoena duces tecum.

(*l*) If the subpoenaing party is the consumer, and the consumer is the only subject of the subpoenaed records, notice to the consumer, and delivery of the other documents specified in subdivision (b) to the consumer, is not required under this section. **Leg.H.** Added Stats 1980 ch 976 §1, operative July 1, 1981. Amended Stats 1981 ch 227 §1, effective July 20, 1981, operative July 1, 1981, ch 1014 §1; Stats 1982 ch 666 §1; Stats 1984 ch 603 §1; Stats 1985 ch 983 §1, effective September 26, 1985; Stats 1986 ch 248 §21, ch 605 §1, ch 1209 §2; Stats 1987 ch 20 §1, ch 149 §1, effective July 10, 1987, ch 1080 §10, ch 1492 §2; Stats 1988 ch 184 §1; Stats 1990 ch 1220 §1 (AB 2980); Stats 1996 ch 679 §1 (SB 1821); Stats 1997 ch 442 §10 (AB 758); Stats 1998 ch 932 §19 (AB 1094); Stats 1999 ch 444 §1 (AB 794); Stats 2004 ch 182 §18 (AB 3081), operative July 1, 2005; Stats 2005 ch 300 §6 (AB 496), effective January 1, 2006; Stats 2012 ch 72 §2 (SB 1574), effective January 1, 2013.

§1985.4. Production of consumer records maintained by state or local agency

The procedures set forth in Section 1985.3 are applicable to a subpoena duces tecum for records containing "personal information," as defined in Section 1798.3 of the Civil Code that are otherwise exempt from public disclosure under a provision listed in Section 7920.505 of the Government Code that are maintained by a state or local agency as defined in Section 7920.510 or 7920.540 of the Government Code. For the purposes of this section, "witness" means a state or local agency as defined in Section 7920.510 or 7920.540 of the Government Code and "consumer" means any employee of any state or local agency as defined in Section 7920.510 or 7920.540 of the Government Code, or any other natural person. Nothing in this section shall pertain to personnel records as defined in Section 832.8 of the Penal Code. **Leg.H.** Added Stats 1984 ch 437 §1. Amended Stats 1988 ch 441 §1; Stats 2021 ch 615 §57 (AB 474), effective January 1, 2022.

§1985.5. Subpoena provision where witness to appear out of court

If a subpena requires the attendance of a witness before an officer or commissioner out of court, it shall, for a refusal to be sworn, or to answer as a witness, or to subscribe an affidavit or deposition when required, also require the witness to attend a session of the court issuing the subpena at a time and place thereof to be fixed by said officer or commissioner. **Leg.H.** Added Stats 1941 ch 405 §1.

§1985.6. Subpoena duces tecum for production of employment records; Definitions, Procedures and requirements; Application of section and exceptions

(a) For purposes of this section, the following terms have the following meanings:

(1) "Deposition officer" means a person who meets the qualifications specified in Section 2020.420.

(2) "Employee" means any individual who is or has been employed by a witness subject to a subpoena duces tecum. "Employee" also means any individual who is or has been represented by a labor organization that is a witness subject to a subpoena duces tecum.

(3) "Employment records" means the original or any copy of books, documents, other writings, or electronically stored information pertaining to the employment of any employee maintained by the current or former employer of the employee, or by any labor organization that has represented or currently represents the employee.

(4) "Labor organization" has the meaning set forth in Section 1117 of the Labor Code.

(5) "Subpoenaing party" means the person or persons causing a subpoena duces tecum to be issued or served in connection with any civil action or proceeding, but does not include the state or local agencies described in Section 7465 of the Government Code, or any entity provided for under Article VI of the California Constitution in any proceeding maintained before an adjudicative body of that entity pursuant to Chapter 4 (commencing with Section 6000) of Division 3 of the Business and Professions Code.

(b) Prior to the date called for in the subpoena duces tecum of the production of employment records, the subpoenaing party shall serve or cause to be served on the employee whose records are being sought a copy of: the subpoena duces tecum; the affidavit supporting the issuance of the subpoena, if any; the notice described in subdivision (e); and proof of service as provided in paragraph (1) of subdivision (c). This service shall be made as follows:

(1) To the employee personally, or at his or her last known address, or in accordance with Chapter 5 (commencing with Section 1010) of Title 14 of Part 2, or, if he or she is a party, to his or her attorney of record. If the employee is a minor, service shall be made on the minor's parent, guardian, conservator, or similar fiduciary, or if one of them cannot be located with reasonable diligence, then service shall be made on any person having the care or control of the minor, or with whom the minor resides, and on the minor if the minor is at least 12 years of age.

(2) Not less than 10 days prior to the date for production specified in the subpoena duces tecum, plus the additional time provided by Section 1013 if service is by mail.

(3) At least five days prior to service upon the custodian of the employment records, plus the additional time provided by Section 1013 if service is by mail.

(c) Prior to the production of the records, the subpoenaing party shall either:

(1) Serve or cause to be served upon the witness a proof of personal service or of service by mail attesting to compliance with subdivision (b).

(2) Furnish the witness a written authorization to release the records signed by the employee or by his or her attorney of record. The witness may presume that the attorney purporting to sign the authorization on behalf of the employee acted with the consent of the employee, and that any objection to the release of records is waived.

(d) A subpoena duces tecum for the production of employment records shall be served in sufficient time to allow the witness a reasonable time, as provided in Section 2020.410, to locate and produce the records or copies thereof.

(e) Every copy of the subpoena duces tecum and affidavit served on an employee or his or her attorney in accordance with subdivision (b) shall be accompanied by a notice, in a typeface designed to call attention to the notice, indicating that (1) employment records about the employee are being sought from the witness named on the subpoena; (2) the employment records may be protected by a right of privacy; (3) if the employee objects to the witness furnishing the records to the party seeking the records, the employee shall file papers with the court prior to the date specified for production on the subpoena; and (4) if the subpoenaing party does not agree in writing to cancel or limit the subpoena, an attorney should be consulted about the employee's interest in protecting his or her rights of privacy. If a notice of taking of deposition is also served, that other notice may be set forth in a single document with the notice required by this subdivision.

(f)(1) Any employee whose employment records are sought by a subpoena duces tecum may, prior to the date for production, bring a motion under Section 1987.1 to quash or modify the subpoena duces tecum. Notice of the bringing of that motion shall be given to the witness and the deposition officer at least five days prior to production. The failure to provide notice to the deposition officer does not invalidate the motion to quash or modify the subpoena duces tecum but may be raised by the deposition officer as an affirmative defense in any action for liability for improper release of records.

(2) Any nonparty employee whose employment records are sought by a subpoena duces tecum may, prior to the date of production, serve on the subpoenaing party, the deposition officer, and the witness a written objection that cites the specific grounds on which production of the employment records should be prohibited.

(3) No witness or deposition officer shall be required to produce employment records after receipt of notice that the motion has been brought by an employee, or after receipt of a written objection from a nonparty employee, except upon order of the court in which the action is pending or by agreement of the parties, witnesses, and employees affected.

(4) The party requesting an employee's employment records may bring a motion under subdivision (c) of Section 1987 to enforce the subpoena within 20 days of service of the written objection. The motion shall be accompanied by a declaration showing a reasonable and good faith attempt at informal resolution of the dispute between the party requesting the employment records and the employee or the employee's attorney.

(g) Upon good cause shown and provided that the rights of witnesses and employees are preserved, a subpoenaing party shall be entitled to obtain an order shortening the time for service of a subpoena duces tecum or waiving the requirements of subdivision (b) if due diligence by the subpoenaing party has been shown.

(h) This section may not be construed to apply to any subpoena duces tecum that does not request the records of any particular employee or employees and that requires a custodian of records to delete all information that would in any way identify any employee whose records are to be produced.

(i) This section does not apply to proceedings conducted under Division 1 (commencing with Section 50), Division 4 (commencing with Section 3200), Division 4.5 (commencing with Section 6100), or Division 4.7 (commencing with Section 6200), of the Labor Code.

(j) Failure to comply with this section shall be sufficient basis for the witness to refuse to produce the employment records sought by subpoena duces tecum.

(k) If the subpoenaing party is the employee, and the employee is the only subject of the subpoenaed records, notice to the employee, and delivery of the other documents specified in subdivision (b) to the employee, are not required under this section. **Leg.H.** Added Stats 1995 ch 299 §1 (AB 617). Amended Stats 1996 ch 679 §1 (SB 1821); Stats 1997 ch 442 §11 (AB 758); Stats 1998 ch 932 §20 (AB 1094); Stats 1999 ch 444 §2 (AB 794); Stats 2004 ch 101 §1 (SB 1465) (ch 101 prevails), ch 182 §19 (AB 3081), operative July 1, 2005; Stats 2005 ch 22 §20 (SB 1108), ch 294 §5 (AB 333), ch 300 §7.5 (AB 496), effective January 1, 2006; Stats 2006 ch 538 §76 (SB 1852), effective January 1, 2007; Stats 2012 ch 72 §3 (SB 1574), effective January 1, 2013.

§1985.7. Order to show cause against medical provider

When a medical provider fails to comply with Section 1158 of the Evidence Code, in addition to any other available remedy, the demanding party may apply to the court for an order to show cause why the records should not be produced.

Any order to show cause issued pursuant to this section shall be served upon respondent in the same manner as a summons. It shall be returnable no sooner than 20 days after issuance unless ordered otherwise upon a showing of substantial hardship. The court shall impose monetary sanctions pursuant to Section 1158 of the Evidence Code unless it finds that the person subject to the sanction acted with substantial justification or that other circumstances make the imposition of the sanction unjust. **Leg.H.** Added Stats 1996 ch 1159 §12 (AB 3471).

§1985.8. Procedure for subpoena of electronically stored information

(a)(1) A subpoena in a civil proceeding may require that electronically stored information, as defined in Section 2016.020, be produced and that the party serving the subpoena, or someone acting on the party's request, be permitted to inspect, copy, test, or sample the information.

(2) Any subpoena seeking electronically stored information shall comply with the requirements of this chapter.

(b) A party serving a subpoena requiring production of electronically stored information may specify the form or forms in which each type of information is to be produced.

(c) If a person responding to a subpoena for production of electronically stored information objects to the specified form or forms for producing the information, the subpoenaed person may provide an objection stating the form or forms in which it intends to produce each type of information.

(d) Unless the subpoenaing party and the subpoenaed person otherwise agree or the court otherwise orders, the following shall apply:

(1) If a subpoena requiring production of electronically stored information does not specify a form or forms for producing a type of electronically stored information, the person subpoenaed shall produce the information in the form or forms in which it is ordinarily maintained or in a form that is reasonably usable.

(2) A subpoenaed person need not produce the same electronically stored information in more than one form.

(e) The subpoenaed person opposing the production, inspection, copying, testing, or sampling of electronically stored information on the basis that information is from a source that is not reasonably accessible because of undue burden or expense shall bear the burden of demonstrating that the information is from a source that is not reasonably accessible because of undue burden or expense.

(f) If the person from whom discovery of electronically stored information is subpoenaed establishes that the information is from a source that is not reasonably accessible because of undue burden or expense, the court may nonetheless order discovery if the subpoenaing party shows good cause, subject to any limitations imposed under subdivision (i).

(g) If the court finds good cause for the production of electronically stored information from a source that is not reasonably accessible, the court may set conditions for the discovery of the electronically stored information, including allocation of the expense of discovery.

(h) If necessary, the subpoenaed person, at the reasonable expense of the subpoenaing party, shall, through detection devices, translate any data compilations included in the subpoena into a reasonably usable form.

(i) The court shall limit the frequency or extent of discovery of electronically stored information, even from a source that is reasonably accessible, if the court determines that any of the following conditions exists:

(1) It is possible to obtain the information from some other source that is more convenient, less burdensome, or less expensive.

(2) The discovery sought is unreasonably cumulative or duplicative.

(3) The party seeking discovery has had ample opportunity by discovery in the action to obtain the information sought.

(4) The likely burden or expense of the proposed discovery outweighs the likely benefit, taking into account the amount in controversy, the resources of the parties, the importance of the issues in the litigation, and the importance of the requested discovery in resolving the issues.

(j) If a subpoenaed person notifies the subpoenaing party that electronically stored information produced pursuant to a subpoena is subject to a claim of privilege or of protection as attorney work product, as described in Section 2031.285, the provisions of Section 2031.285 shall apply.

(k) A party serving a subpoena requiring the production of electronically stored information shall take reasonable steps to avoid imposing undue burden or expense on a person subject to the subpoena.

(*l*) An order of the court requiring compliance with a subpoena issued under this section shall protect a person who is neither a party nor a party's officer from undue burden or expense resulting from compliance.

(m)(1) Absent exceptional circumstances, the court shall not impose sanctions on a subpoenaed person or any attorney of a subpoenaed person for failure to provide electronically stored information that has been lost, damaged, altered, or overwritten as the result of the routine, good faith operation of an electronic information system.

(2) This subdivision shall not be construed to alter any obligation to preserve discoverable information. **Leg.H.** Added Stats 2009 ch 5 §2 (AB 5), effective June 29, 2009. Amended Stats 2012 ch 72 §4 (SB 1574), effective January 1, 2013.

2009 Note: This act shall be known as the Electronic Discovery Act. Stats 2009 ch 5 (AB 5) §1.

§1986. Obtaining subpoenas

A subpoena is obtainable as follows:

(a) To require attendance before a court, or at the trial of an issue therein, or upon the taking of a deposition in an action or proceeding pending therein, it is obtainable from the clerk of the court in which the action or proceeding is pending.

(b) To require attendance before a commissioner appointed to take testimony by a court of a foreign country, or of the United States, or of any other state in the United States, or before any officer or officers empowered by the laws of the United States to take testimony, it may be obtained from the clerk of the superior court of the county in which the witness is to be examined.

(c) To require attendance out of court, in cases not provided for in subdivision (a), before a judge, justice, or other officer authorized to administer oaths or take testimony in any matter under the laws of this state, it is obtainable from the judge, justice, or other officer before whom the attendance is required.

If the subpoena is to require attendance before a court, or at the trial of an issue therein, it is obtainable from the clerk, as of course, upon the application of the party desiring it. If it is obtained to require attendance before a commissioner or other officer upon the taking of a deposition, it must be obtained, as of course, from the clerk of the superior court of the county wherein the attendance is required upon the application of the party requiring it. **Leg.H.** Enacted 1872. Amended Stats 1907 ch 391 §1; Stats 1929 ch 110 §1; Stats 1957 ch 1904 §2, operative January 1, 1958; Stats 1979 ch 458 §2; Stats 2007 ch 263 §14 (AB 310), effective January 1, 2008.

§1986.1. Testimony or other evidence given by journalist

(a) No testimony or other evidence given by a journalist under subpoena in a civil or criminal proceeding may be construed as a waiver of the immunity rights provided by subdivision (b) of Section 2 of Article I of the California Constitution.

(b)(1) Because important constitutional rights of a third-party witness are adjudicated when rights under subdivision (b) of Section 2 of Article I of the California Constitution are asserted, except in circumstances that pose a clear and substantial threat to the integrity of the criminal investigation or present an imminent risk of death or serious bodily harm, a journalist who is subpoenaed in any civil or criminal proceeding shall be given at least five days' notice by the party issuing the subpoena that his or her appearance will be required.

(2) To protect against the inadvertent disclosure by a third party of information protected by Section 2 of Article I of the California Constitution, a party issuing a subpoena in any civil or criminal proceeding to a third party that seeks the records of a journalist shall, except in circumstances that pose a clear and substantial threat to the integrity of the criminal investigation or present an imminent risk of death or serious bodily harm, provide notice of the subpoena to the journalist and the publisher of the newspaper, magazine, or other publication or station operations manager of the broadcast station that employs or contracts with the journalist, as applicable, at least five days prior to issuing the subpoena. The party issuing the subpoena shall include in the notice, at a minimum, an explanation of why the requested records will be of material assistance to the party seeking them and why alternate sources of information are not sufficient to avoid the need for the subpoena.

(c) If a trial court holds a journalist in contempt of court in a criminal proceeding notwithstanding subdivision (b) of Section 2 of Article I of the California Constitution, the court shall set forth findings, either in writing or on the record, stating at a minimum, why the information will be of material assistance to the party seeking the evidence, and why alternate sources of the information are not sufficient to satisfy the defendant's right to a fair trial under the Sixth Amendment to the United States Constitution and Section 15 of Article I of the California Constitution.

(d) As used in this section, "journalist" means the persons specified in subdivision (b) of Section 2 of Article I of the California Constitution. **Leg.H.** Added Stats 2000 ch 377 §1 (AB 1860). Amended Stats 2013 ch 519 §1 (SB 558), effective January 1, 2014.

§1986.5. Rights of person subpoenaed, for deposition to receive fees and mileage

Any person who is subpoenaed and required to give a deposition shall be entitled to receive the same witness fees and mileage as if the subpoena required him or her to attend and testify before a court in which the action or proceeding is pending. Notwithstanding this requirement, the only fees owed to a witness who is required to produce business records under Section 1560 of the Evidence Code pursuant to a subpoena duces tecum, but who is not required to personally attend a deposition away from his or her place of business, shall be those prescribed in Section 1563 of the Evidence Code. **Leg.H.** Added Stats 1961 ch 1386 §1. Amended Stats 1986 ch 603 §4.

§1987. Service of subpoena, or of written notice

(a) Except as provided in Sections 68097.1 to 68097.8, inclusive, of the Government Code, the service of a subpoena is made by delivering a copy, or a ticket containing its substance, to the witness personally, giving or offering to the witness at the same time, if demanded by him or her, the fees to which he or she is entitled for travel to and from the place designated, and one day's attendance there. The service shall be made so as to allow the witness a reasonable time for preparation and travel to the place of attendance. The service may be made by any person. If service is to be made on a minor, service shall be made on the minor's parent, guardian, conservator, or similar fiduciary, or if one of those persons cannot be located with reasonable diligence, service shall be made on any person having the care or control of the minor or with whom the minor resides or by whom the minor is employed, and on the minor if the minor is 12 years of age or older. If the minor is alleged to come within the description of Section 300, 601, or 602 of the Welfare and Institutions Code and the minor is not in the custody of a parent or guardian, regardless of the age of the minor, service also shall be made upon the designated agent for service of process at the county child welfare department or the probation department under whose jurisdiction the minor has been placed.

(b) In the case of the production of a party to the record of any civil action or proceeding or of a person for whose immediate benefit an action or proceeding is prosecuted or defended or of anyone who is an officer, director, or managing agent of any such party or person, the service of a subpoena upon any such witness is not required if written notice requesting the witness to attend before a court, or at a trial of an issue therein, with the time and place thereof, is served upon the attorney of that party or person. The notice shall be served at least 10 days before the time required for attendance unless the court prescribes a shorter time. If entitled thereto, the witness, upon demand, shall be paid witness fees and mileage before being required to testify. The giving of the notice shall have the same effect as service of a subpoena on the witness, and the parties shall have those rights and the court may make those orders, including the imposition of sanctions, as in the case of a subpoena for attendance before the court.

(c) If the notice specified in subdivision (b) is served at least 20 days before the time required for attendance, or within any shorter period of time as the court may order, it may include a request that the party or person bring with him or her books, documents, electronically stored information, or other things. The notice shall state the exact materials or things desired and that the party or person has them in his or her possession or under his or her control. Within five days thereafter, or any other time period as the court may allow, the party or person of whom the request is made may serve written objections to the request or any part thereof, with a statement of grounds. Thereafter, upon noticed motion of the requesting party, accompanied by a showing of good cause and of materiality of the items to the issues, the court may order production of items to which objection was made, unless the objecting party or person establishes good cause for nonproduction or production under limitations or conditions. The procedure of this subdivision is alternative to the procedure provided by Sections 1985 and 1987.5 in the cases herein provided for, and no subpoena duces tecum shall be required.

Subject to this subdivision, the notice provided in this subdivision shall have the same effect as is provided in subdivision (b) as to a notice for attendance of that party or person. **Leg.H.** Enacted 1872. Amended Stats 1963 ch 1485 §3; Stats 1968 ch 933 §1; Stats 1969 ch 311 §1, ch 1034 §1.5; Stats 1981 ch 184 §2; Stats 1986 ch 605 §2; Stats 1989 ch 1416 §28; Stats 2002 ch 1008 §6 (AB 3028); Stats 2012 ch 72 §5 (SB 1574), effective January 1, 2013.

§1987.1. Order to quash, modify or limit subpoena

(a) If a subpoena requires the attendance of a witness or the production of books, documents, electronically stored information, or other things before a court, or at the trial of an issue therein, or at the taking of a deposition, the court, upon motion reasonably made by any person described in subdivision (b), or upon the court's own motion after giving counsel notice and an opportunity to be heard, may make an order quashing the subpoena entirely, modifying it, or directing compliance with it upon those terms or conditions as the court shall declare, including protective orders. In addition, the court may make any other order as may be appropriate to protect the person from unreasonable or oppressive demands, including unreasonable violations of the right of privacy of the person.

(b) The following persons may make a motion pursuant to subdivision (a):

(1) A party.
(2) A witness.
(3) A consumer described in Section 1985.3.
(4) An employee described in Section 1985.6.
(5) A person whose personally identifying information, as defined in subdivision (b) of Section 1798.79.8 of the Civil Code, is sought in connection with an underlying action involving that person's exercise of free speech rights.

(c) Nothing in this section shall require any person to move to quash, modify, or condition any subpoena duces tecum of personal records of any consumer served under paragraph (1) of subdivision (b) of Section 1985.3 or employment records of any employee served under paragraph (1) of subdivision (b) of Section 1985.6. **Leg.H.** Added Stats 1976 ch 1168 §1. Amended Stats 1980 ch 976 §2, operative July 1, 1981; Stats 1997 ch 442 §12 (AB 758); Stats 2007 ch 113 §3 (AB 1126), effective January 1, 2008; Stats 2008 ch 742 §1 (AB 2433), effective January 1, 2009; Stats 2012 ch 72 §6 (SB 1574), effective January 1, 2013.

§1987.2. Expenses in making or opposing motion; Exception to sanctions for failure to provide certain electronic information

(a) Except as specified in subdivision (c), in making an order pursuant to motion made under subdivision (c) of Section 1987 or under Section 1987.1, the court may in its discretion award the amount of the reasonable expenses incurred in making or opposing the motion, including reasonable attorney's fees, if the court finds the motion was made or opposed in bad faith or without substantial justification or that one or more of the requirements of the subpoena was oppressive.

(b)(1) Notwithstanding subdivision (a), absent exceptional circumstances, the court shall not impose sanctions on a subpoenaed person or the attorney of a subpoenaed person for failure to provide electronically stored information that has been lost, damaged, altered, or overwritten as the result of the routine, good faith operation of an electronic information system.

(2) This subdivision shall not be construed to alter any obligation to preserve discoverable information.

(c) If a motion is filed under Section 1987.1 for an order to quash or modify a subpoena from a court of this state for personally identifying information, as defined in subdivision (b) of Section 1798.79.8 of the Civil Code, for use in an action pending in another state, territory, or district of the United States, or in a foreign nation, and that subpoena has been served on any Internet service provider, or on the provider of any other interactive computer service, as defined in Section 230(f)(2) of Title 47 of the United States Code, if the moving party prevails, and if the underlying action arises from the moving party's exercise of free speech rights on the Internet and the respondent has failed to make a prima facie showing of a cause of action, the court shall award the amount of the reasonable expenses incurred in making the motion, including reasonable attorney's fees. **Leg.H.** Added Stats 1976 ch 1168 §2. Amended Stats 2008 ch 742 §2 (AB 2433), effective January 1, 2009; Stats 2012 ch 72 §7 (SB 1574), effective January 1, 2013.

§1987.3. Exemption of custodian of business records from attendance requirement

When a subpoena duces tecum is served upon a custodian of records or other qualified witness as provided in Article 4 (commencing with Section 1560) of Chapter 2 of Division 11 of the Evidence Code, and his personal attendance is not required by the terms of the subpoena, Section 1989 shall not apply. **Leg.H.** Added Stats 1970 ch 590 §1.

§1987.4. [Section repealed 1982]

Leg.H. Added Stats 1980 ch 830 §1. Repealed Stats 1981 ch 1014 §1.5. See Ev C §1563.

§1987.5. Filing and service of affidavit for subpoena duces tecum

The service of a subpoena duces tecum is invalid unless at the time of such service a copy of the affidavit upon which the subpoena is based is served on the person served with the subpoena. In the case of a subpoena duces tecum which requires appearance and the production of matters and things at the taking of a deposition, the subpoena shall not be valid unless a copy of the affidavit upon which the subpoena is based and the designation of the materials to be produced, as set forth in the subpoena, is attached to the notice of taking the deposition served upon each party or its attorney as provided in Chapter 3 (commencing with Section 2002) and in Title 4 (commencing with Section 2016.010). If matters and things are produced pursuant to a subpoena duces tecum in violation of this section, any other party to the action may file a motion for, and the court may grant, an order providing appropriate relief, including, but not limited to, exclusion of the evidence affected by the violation, a retaking of the deposition notwithstanding any other limitation on discovery proceedings, or a continuance. The party causing the subpoena to be served shall retain the original affidavit until final judgment in the action, and shall file the affidavit with the court only upon reasonable request by any party or witness affected thereby. This section does not apply to deposition subpoenas commanding only the production of business records for copying under Article 4 (commencing with Section 2020.410) of Chapter 6 of Title 4. **Leg.H.** Added Stats 1951 ch 1413 §1. Amended Stats 1968 ch 95 §2; Stats 1981 ch 189 §1; Stats 1982 ch 452 §2; Stats 1985 ch 1239 §1; Stats 1993 ch 926 §7 (AB 2205); Stats 2004 ch 182 §20 (AB 3081), operative July 1, 2005.

§1988. Service if witness concealed

If a witness is concealed in a building or vessel, so as to prevent the service of a subpena upon him, any court or judge, or any officer issuing the subpena, may, upon proof by affidavit of the concealment, and of the materiality of the witness, make an order that the sheriff of the county serve the subpena; and the sheriff must serve it accordingly, and for that purpose may break into the building or vessel where the witness is concealed. **Leg.H.** Enacted 1872.

§1989. Attendance of non-resident witnesses

A witness, including a witness specified in subdivision (b) of Section 1987, is not obliged to attend as a witness before any court, judge, justice or any other officer, unless the witness is a resident within the state at the time of service. **Leg.H.** Enacted 1872. Amended Stats 1915 ch 162 §1; Stats 1935 ch 257 §1; Stats 1957 ch 1560 §1; Stats 1980 ch 591 §1; Stats 1981 ch 184 §3.

§1990. Compelling person to testify

A person present in court, or before a judicial officer, may be required to testify in the same manner as if he were in attendance upon a subpoena issued by such court or officer. **Leg.H.** Enacted 1872.

§1991. Punishment of disobedient witness for contempt

Disobedience to a subpoena, or a refusal to be sworn, or to answer as a witness, or to subscribe an affidavit or deposition when required, may be punished as a contempt by the court issuing the subpoena.

When the subpoena, in any such case, requires the attendance of the witness before an officer or commissioner out of court, it is the duty of the officer or commissioner to report any disobedience or refusal to be sworn or to answer a question or to subscribe an affidavit or deposition when required, to the court issuing the subpoena. The witness shall not be punished for any refusal to be sworn or to answer a question or to subscribe an affidavit or deposition, unless, after a hearing upon notice, the court orders the witness to be sworn, or to so answer or subscribe and then only for disobedience to the order.

Any judge, justice, or other officer mentioned in subdivision (c) of Section 1986, may report any disobedience or refusal to be sworn or to answer a question or to subscribe an affidavit or deposition when required to the superior court of the county in which attendance was required; and the court thereupon has power, upon notice, to order the witness to perform the omitted act, and any refusal or neglect to comply with the order may be punished as a contempt of court.

In lieu of the reporting of the refusal as hereinabove provided, the party seeking to obtain the deposition or to have the deposition or affidavit signed, at the time of the refusal may request the officer or commissioner to notify the witness that at a time stated, not less than five days nor more than 20 days from the date of the refusal, he or she will report the refusal of the witness to the court and that the party will, at that time, or as soon thereafter as he or she may be heard, apply to the court for an order directing the witness to be sworn, or to answer as a witness, or subscribe the deposition or affidavit, as the case may be, and that the witness is required to attend that session of the court.

The officer or commissioner shall enter in the record of the proceedings an exact transcription of the request made of him or her that he or she notify the witness that the party will apply for an order directing the witness to be sworn or to answer as a witness or subscribe the deposition or affidavit, and of his or her notice to the witness, and the transcription shall be attached to his or her report to the court of the refusal of the witness. The report shall be filed by the officer with the clerk of the court issuing the subpoena, and the witness shall attend that session of the court, and for failure or refusal to do so may be punished for contempt.

At the time so specified by the officer, or at a subsequent time to which the court may have continued the matter, if the officer has theretofore filed a report showing the refusal of the witness, the court shall hear the matter, and without further notice to the witness, may order the witness to be sworn or to answer as a witness or subscribe the deposition or affidavit, as the case may be, and may in the order specify the time and place at which compliance shall be made or to which the taking of the deposition is continued. Thereafter if the witness refuses to comply with the order he or she may be punished for contempt. **Leg.H.** Enacted 1872. Amended Stats 1907 ch 391 §2; Stats 1941 ch 406 §1; Stats 1987 ch 56 §24.

§1991.1. Punishment for disobedience of witness in deposition proceeding

Disobedience to a subpoena requiring attendance of a witness before an officer out of court in a deposition taken pursuant to Title 4 (commencing with Section 2016.010), or refusal to be sworn as a witness at that deposition, may be punished as contempt, as provided in subdivision (e) of Section 2023.030, without the necessity of a prior order of court directing compliance by the witness. **Leg.H.** Added Stats 1959 ch 1590 §13. Amended Stats 1996 ch 124 §15.5 (AB 3470); Stats 2004 ch 182 §21 (AB 3081), operative July 1, 2005.

§1991.2. Contempt provisions inapplicable to depositions

The provisions of Section 1991 do not apply to any act or omission occurring in a deposition taken pursuant to Title 4 (commencing with Section 2016.010). The provisions of Chapter 7 (commencing with Section 2023.010) of Title 4 are exclusively applicable. **Leg.H.** Added Stats 1959 ch 1590 §14. Amended Stats 2005 ch 294 §6 (AB 333), effective January 1, 2006.

§1992. Forfeiture and damages; Recovery in civil action

A person failing to appear pursuant to a subpoena or a court order also forfeits to the party aggrieved the sum of five hundred dollars ($500), and all damages that he or she may sustain by the failure of the person to appear pursuant to the subpoena or court order, which forfeiture and damages may be recovered in a civil action. **Leg.H.** Enacted 1872. Amended Stats 1978 ch 479 §1; Stats 2005 ch 474 §1 (AB 1150), effective January 1, 2006.

§1993. Issuance of warrant to arrest witness; Failure to appear notice

(a)(1) As an alternative to issuing a warrant for contempt pursuant to paragraph (5) or (9) of subdivision (a) of Section 1209, the court may issue a warrant for the arrest of a witness who failed to appear pursuant to a subpoena or a person who failed to appear pursuant to a court order. The court, upon proof of the service of the subpoena or order, may issue a warrant to the sheriff of the county in which the witness or person may be located and the sheriff shall, upon payment of fees as provided in Section 26744.5 of the Government Code, arrest the witness or person and bring him or her before the court.

(2) Before issuing a warrant for a failure to appear pursuant to a subpoena pursuant to this section, the court shall issue a "failure to appear" notice informing the person subject to the subpoena that a failure to appear in response to the notice may result in the issuance of a warrant. This notice requirement may be omitted only upon a showing that the appearance of the person subject to the subpoena is material to the case and that urgency dictates the person's immediate appearance.

(b) The warrant shall contain all of the following:
(1) The title and case number of the action.
(2) The name and physical description of the person to be arrested.
(3) The last known address of the person to be arrested.
(4) The date of issuance and county in which it is issued.
(5) The signature or name of the judicial officer issuing the warrant, the title of his or her office, and the name of the court.
(6) A command to arrest the person for failing to appear pursuant to the subpoena or court order, and specifying the date of service of the subpoena or court order.
(7) A command to bring the person to be arrested before the issuing court, or the nearest court if in session, for the setting of bail in the amount of the warrant or to release on the person's own recognizance. Any person so arrested shall be released from custody if he or she cannot be brought before the court within 12 hours of arrest, and the person shall not be arrested if the court will not be in session during the 12-hour period following the arrest.
(8) A statement indicating the expiration date of the warrant as determined by the court.
(9) The amount of bail.
(10) An endorsement for nighttime service if good cause is shown, as provided in Section 840 of the Penal Code.
(11) A statement indicating whether the person may be released upon a promise to appear, as provided by Section 1993.1. The court shall permit release upon a promise to appear, unless it makes a written finding that the urgency and materiality of the person's appearance in court precludes use of the promise to appear process.
(12) The date and time to appear in court if arrested and released pursuant to paragraph (11). **Leg.H.** Added 2005 ch 474 §3 (AB 1150), effective January 1, 2006. Amended Stats 2006 ch 277 §3 (AB 2369), effective January 1, 2007; Stats 2010 ch 680 §15 (AB 2394), effective January 1, 2011.

Former Sections: Former CCP §1993, similar to the present section, was enacted in 1872 and repealed Stats 2005 ch 474 §2.

Prior Law: Former CCP §1993, similar to the present section, was enacted Stats 1872 and repealed Stats 2005 ch 474 §2.

§1993.1. Arrest of witness; Requirements for release

(a) If authorized by the court as provided by paragraph (11) of subdivision (b) of Section 1993, the sheriff may release the person arrested upon his or her promise to appear as provided in this section.

(b) The sheriff shall prepare in duplicate a written notice to appear in court, containing the title of the case, case number, name and address of the person, the offense charged, and the time when, and place where, the person shall appear in court. In addition, the notice shall advise the person arrested of the provisions of Section 1992.

(c) The date and time specified in the notice to appear in court shall be that determined by the issuing court pursuant to paragraph (12) of subdivision (b) of Section 1993.

(d) The sheriff shall deliver one copy of the notice to appear to the arrested person, and the arrested person, in order to secure release, shall give his or her written promise to appear in court as specified in the notice by signing the duplicate notice, which shall be retained by the sheriff, and the sheriff may require the arrested person, if he or she has no satisfactory identification, to place a right thumbprint, or a left thumbprint or fingerprint if the person has a missing or disfigured right thumb, on the notice to appear. Except for law enforcement purposes relating to the identity of the arrestee, no person or entity may sell, give away, allow the distribution of, include in a database, or create a database with, this print. Upon the signing of the duplicate notice, the arresting officer shall immediately release the person arrested from custody.

(e) The sheriff shall, as soon as practicable, file the original notice with the issuing court. The notice may be electronically transmitted to the court.

(f) The person arrested shall be released unless one of the following is a reason for nonrelease, in which case the arresting officer either may release the person or shall indicate, on a form to be established by his or her employing law enforcement agency, which of the following was a reason for the nonrelease:

(1) The person arrested was so intoxicated that he or she could have been a danger to himself or herself or to others.

(2) The person arrested required medical examination or medical care or was otherwise unable to care for his or her own safety.

(3) There were one or more additional outstanding arrest warrants for the person.

(4) The person arrested demanded to be taken before a magistrate or refused to sign the notice to appear. **Leg.H.** Added Stats 2005 ch 474 §4 (AB 1150), effective January 1, 2006.

§1993.2. Failure to appear; Civil assessment

If a person arrested on a civil bench warrant issued pursuant to Section 1993 fails to appear after being released on a promise to appear, the court may issue another warrant to bring the person before the court or assess a civil assessment in the amount of not more than one thousand dollars ($1,000), which shall be collected as follows:

(a) The assessment shall not become effective until at least 10 calendar days after the court mails a warning notice to the person by first-class mail to the address shown on the promise to appear or to the person's last known address. If the person appears within the time specified in the notice and shows good cause for the failure to appear or for the failure to pay a fine, the court shall vacate the assessment.

(b) The assessment imposed under subdivision (a) may be enforced in the same manner as a money judgment in a limited civil case, and shall be subject to the due process requirements governing defense of actions and collection of civil money judgments generally. **Leg.H.** Added Stats 2005 ch 474 §5 (AB 1150), effective January 1, 2006.

§1994. Contents of warrant of commitment; Direction and execution of warrants

Every warrant of commitment, issued by a court or officer pursuant to this chapter, shall specify therein, particularly, the cause of the commitment, and if it be for refusing to answer a question, that question shall be stated in the warrant. **Leg.H.** Enacted 1872. Amended Code Amdts 1880 ch 111 §1; Stats 2005 ch 474 §6 (AB 1150), effective January 1, 2006.

§1995. Order for examination or production of witness confined in jail

If the witness be a prisoner, confined in a jail within this state, an order for his examination in the jail upon deposition, or for his temporary removal and production before a court or officer may be made as follows:

1. By the court itself in which the action or special proceeding is pending, unless it be a small claims court.

2. By a justice of the Supreme Court, or a judge of the superior court of the county where the action or proceeding is pending, if pending before a small claims court, or before a judge or other person out of court. **Leg.H.** Enacted 1872. Amended Code Amdts 1880 ch 111 §2; Stats 1941 ch 802 §6; Stats 1951 ch 1737 §172, operative January 1, 1952; Stats 1977 ch 1257 §40, effective October 3, 1977.

§1996. Motion and affidavit for order as to confined witness

Such order can only be made on the motion of a party, upon affidavit showing the nature of the action or proceeding, the testimony expected from the witness, and its materiality. **Leg.H.** Enacted 1872.

§1997. Production or deposition of confined witness

If the witness be imprisoned in a jail in the county where the action or proceeding is pending, his production may be required. In all other cases his examination, when allowed, must be taken upon deposition. **Leg.H.** Enacted 1872. Amended Stats 1941 ch 802 §7.

§1998. [Section repealed 1967]

Leg.H. Added Stats 1959 ch 1059 §1. Amended Stats 1961 ch 1034 §1. Repealed Stats 1965 ch 299 §118, operative January 1, 1967. See Ev C §1560.

§1998.1. [Section repealed 1967]

Leg.H. Added Stats 1959 ch 1059 §2. Repealed Stats 1965 ch 299 §119, operative January 1, 1967. See Ev C §1561.

§1998.2. [Section repealed 1967]

Leg.H. Added Stats 1959 ch 1059 §3. Repealed Stats 1965 ch 299 §120, operative January 1, 1967. See Ev C §1562.

§1998.3. [Section repealed 1967]

Leg.H. Added Stats 1959 ch 1059 §4. Repealed Stats 1965 ch 299 §121, operative January 1, 1967. See Ev C §1563.

§1998.4. [Section repealed 1967]
Leg.H. Added Stats 1959 ch 1059 §5. Repealed Stats 1965 ch 299 §122, operative January 1, 1967. See Ev C §1564.

§1998.5. [Section repealed 1967]
Leg.H. Added Stats 1959 ch 1059 §6. Repealed Stats 1965 ch 299 §123, operative January 1, 1967. See Ev C §1565.

CHAPTER 3
MANNER OF PRODUCTION

Article 1. Mode of Taking the Testimony of Witnesses.
Article 2. Affidavits.
Article 3. Discovery [Repealed].

ARTICLE 1
Mode of Taking the Testimony of Witnesses

Testimony, in what mode taken. §2002.
Affidavit defined. §2003.
Deposition defined; Waiver of notice. §2004.
Oral examination defined. §2005.

§2002. Testimony, in what mode taken
The testimony of witnesses is taken in three modes:
1. By affidavit;
2. By deposition;
3. By oral examination. **Leg.H.** Enacted 1872.

§2003. Affidavit defined
An affidavit is a written declaration under oath, made without notice to the adverse party. **Leg.H.** Enacted 1872.

§2004. Deposition defined; Waiver of notice
A deposition is a written declaration, under oath, made upon notice to the adverse party, for the purpose of enabling him to attend and cross-examine. In all actions and proceedings where the default of the defendant has been duly entered, and in all proceedings where the default of the defendant has been duly entered, and in all proceedings to obtain letters of administration, or for the probate of wills and the issuance of letters testamentary thereon, where, after due and legal notice, those entitled to contest the application have failed to appear, the entry of said defaults, and the failure of said persons to appear after notice, shall be deemed to be a waiver of the right to any further notice of any application or proceeding to take testimony by deposition in such action or proceeding. **Leg.H.** Enacted 1872. Amended Stats 1907 ch 527 §1.

§2005. Oral examination defined
An oral examination is an examination in presence of the jury or tribunal which is to decide the fact or act upon it, the testimony being heard by the jury or tribunal from the lips of the witness. **Leg.H.** Enacted 1872.

§2006. [Section repealed 1958]
Leg.H. Enacted 1872. Amended Stats 1907 ch 392 §1 Stats 1929 ch 474 §1. Repealed Stats 1957 ch 1904 §1, operative January 1, 1958. See CCP §§2019.010 et seq.

ARTICLE 2
Affidavits

Use of affidavits. §2009.
Affidavit of publication or of other notice. §2010.
Filing, and evidentiary effect of affidavit. §2011.
Officers in this state before whom affidavits taken. §2012.
Officers in another state before whom affidavits taken. §2013.
Officers in foreign country before whom affidavits taken. §2014.
Clerk's certificate where affidavit is taken before judge of out-of-state court. §2015.
Effect of certificate of peace officer or court clerk. §2015.3.
Use of unsworn statements; Form. §2015.5.
Affirmation in lieu of oath. §2015.6.

§2009. Use of affidavits
An affidavit may be used to verify a pleading or a paper in a special proceeding, to prove the service of a summons, notice, or other paper in an action or special proceeding, to obtain a provisional remedy, the examination of a witness, or a stay of proceedings, and in uncontested proceedings to establish a record of birth, or upon a motion, and in any other case expressly permitted by statute. **Leg.H.** Enacted 1872. Amended Stats 1927 ch 242 §1; Stats 1929 ch 493 §1; Stats 1943 ch 11 §1; effective February 5, 1943, ch 821 §2, effective May 28, 1943; Stats 1965 ch 299 §124, operative January 1, 1967.

§2010. Affidavit of publication or of other notice
Evidence of the publication of a document or notice required by law, or by an order of a court or judge, to be published in a newspaper, may be given by the affidavit of the printer of the newspaper, or his foreman or principal clerk, annexed to a copy of the document or notice, specifying the times when, and the paper in which, the publication was made. **Leg.H.** Enacted 1872.

§2011. Filing, and evidentiary effect of affidavit
If such affidavit be made in an action or special proceeding pending in a court, it may be filed with the court or a clerk thereof. If not so made, it may be filed with the clerk of the county where the newspaper is printed. In either case the original affidavit, or a copy thereof, certified by the judge of the court or clerk having it in custody, is prima facie evidence of the facts stated therein. **Leg.H.** Enacted 1872. Amended Code Amdts 1873–74 Ch 383 §240.

§2012. Officers in this state before whom affidavits taken
An affidavit to be used before any court, judge, or officer of this state may be taken before any officer authorized to administer oaths. **Leg.H.** Enacted 1872. Amended Stats 1907 ch 393 §1.

§2013. Officers in another state before whom affidavits taken
An affidavit taken in another state of the United States, to be used in this State, may be taken before a commissioner appointed by the governor of this State to take affidavits and depositions in such other state, or before any notary public in another state, or before any judge or clerk of a court of record having a seal. **Leg.H.** Enacted 1872. Amended Code Amdts 1873–74 Ch 383 §241.

§2014. Officers in foreign country before whom affidavits taken
An affidavit taken in a foreign country to be used in this State, may be taken before an ambassador, minister, consul, vice consul, or consular agent of the United States, or before any judge of a court of record having a seal in such foreign country. **Leg.H.** Enacted 1872. Amended Code Amdts 1873–74 Ch 383 §242.

§2015. Clerk's certificate where affidavit is taken before judge of out-of-state court
(a) When an affidavit is taken before a [1] **judge** or a [2] **court** in another [3] **state** or in a foreign country, the genuineness of the signature of the [4] **judge**, the existence of the [5] **court**, and the fact that such [6] **judge** is a member thereof, must be certified by the [7] **clerk** of the [8] **court** under the seal thereof.
(b) **This section shall not apply to oaths administered for admission to the State Bar of California pursuant to Section 6067 of the Business and Professions Code. Leg.H.** Enacted 1872. Amended Stats 2024 ch 227 §28 (AB 3279), effective January 1, 2025.

§2015. 2024 Deletes. [1] Judge [2] Court [3] State, [4] Judge [5] Court [6] Judge [7] Clerk [8] Court,

§2015.3. Effect of certificate of peace officer or court clerk
The certificate of a sheriff, marshal, or the clerk of the superior court, has the same force and effect as his or her affidavit. **Leg.H.** Added Stats 1969 ch 1611 §28, operative July 1, 1970. Amended Stats 1982 ch 834 §1; Stats 1996 ch 872 §21 (AB 3472); Stats 1998 ch 931 §127 (SB 2139), effective September 28, 1998; Stats 2002 ch 784 §88 (SB 1316).

§2015.5. Use of unsworn statements; Form
Whenever, under any law of this state or under any rule, regulation, order or requirement made pursuant to the law of this state, any matter is required or permitted to be supported, evidenced, established, or proved by the sworn statement, declaration, verification, certificate, oath, or affidavit, in writing of the person making the same (other than a deposition, or an oath of office, or an oath required to be taken before a specified official other than a notary public), such matter may with like force and effect be supported, evidenced, established or proved by the unsworn statement, declaration, verification, or certificate, in writing of such person which recites that it is certified or declared by him or her to be true under penalty of perjury, is subscribed by him or her, and (1), if executed within this state, states the date and place of execution, or (2), if

executed at any place, within or without this state, states the date of execution and that it is so certified or declared under the laws of the State of California. The certification or declaration may be in substantially the following form:

(a) If executed within this state:

"I certify (or declare) under penalty of perjury that the foregoing is true and correct":

(Date and (Signature)_____
Place)

(b) If executed at any place, within or without this state:

"I certify (or declare) under penalty of perjury under the laws of the State of California that the foregoing is true and correct":

(Date)_____ (Signature)_____

Leg.H. Added Stats 1957 ch 1612 §1. Amended Stats 1961 ch 495 §1; Stats 1963 ch 2080 §1; Stats 1975 ch 666 §1, operative January 1, 1977; Stats 1980 ch 889 §1, operative July 1, 1981.

§2015.6. Affirmation in lieu of oath

Whenever, under any law of this State or under any rule, regulation, order or requirement made pursuant to law, an oath is required to be taken by a person appointed to discharge specific duties in a particular action, proceeding or matter, whether or not pending in court, including but not limited to a person appointed as executor, administrator, guardian, conservator, appraiser, receiver, or elisor, an unsworn written affirmation may be made and executed, in lieu of such oath. Such affirmation shall commence "I solemnly affirm," shall state the substance of the other matter required by the oath, the date and place of execution and shall be subscribed by him. **Leg.H.** Added Stats 1961 ch 1364 §1.

ARTICLE 3
Discovery [Repealed]

ARTICLE 4
Discovery of Expert Witnesses [Repealed]

ARTICLE 5
Manner of Taking Depositions in This State [Repealed]

ARTICLE 6
General Rules of Examination [Repealed]

TITLE 4
CIVIL DISCOVERY ACT

Chapter 1. General Provisions.
Chapter 2. Scope of Discovery.
Chapter 3. Use of Technology in Conducting Discovery in a Complex Case.
Chapter 4. Attorney Work Product.
Chapter 5. Methods and Sequence of Discovery.
Chapter 6. Nonparty Discovery.
Chapter 7. Sanctions.
Chapter 8. Time for Completion of Discovery.
Chapter 9. Oral Deposition Inside California.
Chapter 10. Oral Deposition Outside California.
Chapter 11. Deposition by Written Questions.
Chapter 12. Discovery in Action Pending Outside California.
Chapter 13. Written Interrogatories.
Chapter 14. Inspection, Copying, Testing, Sampling, and Production of Documents, Electronically Stored Information, Tangible Things, Land, and Other Property.
Chapter 15. Physical or Mental Examination.
Chapter 16. Requests for Admission.
Chapter 17. Form Interrogatories and Requests for Admission.
Chapter 18. Simultaneous Exchange of Expert Witness Information.
Chapter 19. Perpetuation of Testimony or Preservation of Evidence Before Filing Action.
Chapter 20. Perpetuation of Testimony or Preservation of Information Pending Appeal.

CHAPTER 1
GENERAL PROVISIONS

Citation of title. §2016.010.
Definitions. §2016.020.
Modification by written stipulation. §2016.030.
What meet and confer declaration in support of motion must show. §2016.040.
Applicability of Sections 1011 and 1013. §2016.050.
Specified date falling on Saturday, Sunday or holiday; Extension of time limit. §2016.060.
Applicability of title to enforcement of money judgment. §2016.070.
Applicability to civil action; Initial disclosure [Repealed January 1, 2027]. §2016.090.
Applicability to civil action; Initial disclosure [Operative January 1, 2027]. § 2016.090.

§2016. [Section repealed 2005]

Leg.H. Added Stats 1986 ch 1334 §2, operative July 1, 1987. Amended Stats 1987 ch 86 §1.8, operative July 1, 1987. Repealed Stats 2004 ch 182 §22 (AB 3081), operative July 1, 2005. The repealed section related to coverage of the former Civil Discovery Act. See CCP §§2016.010, 2016.020, 2016.070.

Prior Law: Former CCP §2016 was added Stats 1957 ch 1904 §3, operative January 1, 1958, amended Stats 1959 ch 1590 §1, Stats 1961 ch 496 §2, Stats 1963 ch 1744 §1, Stats 1965 ch 299 §125, operative January 1, 1967, Stats 1982 ch 848 §1, effective September 10, 1982, Stats 1984 ch 1127 §1, and repealed Stats 1986 ch 1334 §1, operative July 1, 1987.

§2016.010. Citation of title

This title may be cited as the "Civil Discovery Act." **Leg.H.** Added Stats 2004 ch 182 §23 (AB 3081), operative July 1, 2005.

§2016.020. Definitions

As used in this title:
(a) "Action" includes a civil action and a special proceeding of a civil nature.
(b) "Court" means the trial court in which the action is pending, unless otherwise specified.
(c) "Document" and "writing" mean a writing, as defined in Section 250 of the Evidence Code.
(d) "Electronic" means relating to technology having electrical, digital, magnetic, wireless, optical, electromagnetic, or similar capabilities.
(e) "Electronically stored information" means information that is stored in an electronic medium. **Leg.H.** Added Stats 2004 ch 182 §23 (AB 3081), operative July 1, 2005. Amended Stats 2009 ch 5 §3 (AB 5), effective June 29, 2009.

2009 Note: This act shall be known as the Electronic Discovery Act. Stats 2009 ch 5 (AB 5) §1.

§2016.030. Modification by written stipulation

Unless the court orders otherwise, the parties may by written stipulation modify the procedures provided by this title for any method of discovery permitted under Section 2019.010. **Leg.H.** Added Stats 2004 ch 182 §23 (AB 3081), operative July 1, 2005.

§2016.040. What meet and confer declaration in support of motion must show

A meet and confer declaration in support of a motion shall state facts showing a reasonable and good faith attempt at an informal resolution of each issue presented by the motion. **Leg.H.** Added Stats 2004 ch 182 §23 (AB 3081), operative July 1, 2005.

§2016.050. Applicability of Sections 1011 and 1013

Sections 1011 and 1013 apply to any method of discovery or service of a motion provided for in this title. **Leg.H.** Added Stats 2004 ch 182 §23 (AB 3081), operative July 1, 2005. Amended Stats 2017 ch 64 §2 (SB 543), effective January 1, 2018.

§2016.060. Specified date falling on Saturday, Sunday or holiday; Extension of time limit

When the last day to perform or complete any act provided for in this title falls on a Saturday, Sunday, or holiday as specified in Section 10, the time limit is extended until the next court day closer to the trial date. **Leg.H.** Added Stats 2004 ch 182 §23.5 (AB 3081), operative July 1, 2005.

§2016.070. Applicability of title to enforcement of money judgment

This title applies to discovery in aid of enforcement of a money judgment only to the extent provided in Article 1 (commencing with Section 708.010) of Chapter 6 of Title 9 of Part 2. **Leg.H.** Added Stats 2004 ch 182 §23 (AB 3081), operative July 1, 2005.

§2016.080. Informal discovery conference [Repealed]

Leg.H. Added Stats 2017 ch 189 §1 (AB 383), effective January 1, 2018, repealed January 1, 2023. Amended Stats 2018 ch 92 §44 (SB 1289), effective January 1, 2019, repealed January 1, 2023.

§2016.090. Applicability to civil action; Initial disclosure [Repealed January 1, 2027]

(a) The following shall apply in a civil action unless modified by stipulation by all parties to the action:
(1) Within 60 days of a demand by any party to the action, each party that has appeared in the action, including the party that made the demand, shall provide to the other parties an initial disclosure that includes all of the following information:
(A) The names, addresses, telephone numbers, and email addresses of all persons likely to have discoverable information, along with the subjects of that information, that the disclosing party may use to support its claims or defenses, or that is relevant to the subject matter of the action or the order on any motion made in that action, unless the use would be solely for impeachment. The disclosure required by this subparagraph is not required to include persons who are expert trial witnesses or are retained as consultants who may later be designated as expert trial witnesses, as that term is described in Chapter 18 (commencing with Section 2034.010) of Title 4 of Part 4.
(B) A copy, or a description by category and location, of all documents, electronically stored information, and tangible things that the disclosing party has in its possession, custody, or control and may use to support its claims or defenses, or that is relevant to the subject matter of the action or the order on any motion made in that action, unless the use would be solely for impeachment.
(C) Any contractual agreement and any insurance policy under which an insurance company may be liable to satisfy, in whole or in part, a judgment entered in the action or to indemnify or reimburse for payments made to satisfy the judgment.
(D) Any and all contractual agreements and any and all insurance policies under which a person, as defined in Section 175 of the Evidence Code, may be liable to satisfy, in whole or in part, a judgment entered in the action or to indemnify or reimburse for payments made to satisfy the

judgment. Only those provisions of an agreement that are material to the terms of the insurance, indemnification, or reimbursement are required to be included in the initial disclosure. Material provisions include, but are not limited to, the identities of parties to the agreement, the nature and limits of the coverage, and any and all documents regarding whether any insurance carrier is disputing the agreement's or policy's coverage of the claim involved in the action.

(2) A party shall make its initial disclosures based on the information then reasonably available to it. A party is not excused from making its initial disclosures because it has not fully investigated the case, because it challenges the sufficiency of another party's disclosures, or because another party has not made its disclosures.

(3)(A) A party that has made, or responded to, a demand for an initial disclosure pursuant to paragraph (1) may propound a supplemental demand on any other party to elicit any later-acquired information bearing on all disclosures previously made by any party.

(B) A party may propound a supplemental demand twice before the initial setting of a trial date, and, subject to the time limits on discovery proceedings and motions provided in Chapter 8 (commencing with Section 2024.010) of Title 4 of Part 4, once after the initial setting of a trial date.

(C) Notwithstanding subparagraphs (A) and (B), on motion, for good cause shown, the court may grant leave to a party to propound one additional supplemental demand.

(4) A party's obligations under this section may be enforced by a court on its own motion or the motion of a party to compel disclosure.

(5) A party's disclosures under this section shall be verified either in a written declaration by the party or the party's authorized representative, or signed by the party's counsel.

(b) Notwithstanding subdivision (a), this section does not apply to the following actions:

(1) An unlawful detainer action, as defined in Section 1161.

(2) An action in the small claims division of a court, as defined in Section 116.210.

(3) An action or proceeding commenced in whole or in part under the Family Code.

(4) An action or proceeding commenced in whole or in part under the Probate Code.

(5) An action in which a party has been granted preference pursuant to Section 36.

(c) This section does not apply to any party in the action who is not represented by counsel.

(d) The changes made to this section by the act adding this subdivision apply only to civil actions filed on or after January 1, 2024.

(e) This section shall remain in effect until January 1, 2027, and as of that date is repealed. **Leg.H.** Added Stats 2019 ch 836 §1 (SB 17), effective January 1, 2020. Amended Stats 2023 ch 284 §1 (SB 235), effective January 1, 2024, repealed January 1, 2027.

§2016.090. Applicability to civil action; Initial disclosure [Operative January 1, 2027]

(a) The following shall apply only to a civil action upon an order of the court following stipulation by all parties to the action:

(1) Within 45 days of the order of the court, a party shall, without awaiting a discovery request, provide to the other parties an initial disclosure that includes all of the following information:

(A) The names, addresses, telephone numbers, and email addresses of all persons likely to have discoverable information, along with the subjects of that information, that the disclosing party may use to support its claims or defenses, unless the use would be solely for impeachment.

(B) A copy, or a description by category and location, of all documents, electronically stored information, and tangible things that the disclosing party has in its possession, custody, or control and may use to support its claims or defenses, unless the use would be solely for impeachment.

(C) Any agreement under which an insurance company may be liable to satisfy, in whole or in part, a judgment entered in the action or to indemnify or reimburse for payments made to satisfy the judgment.

(D) Any agreement under which a person, as defined in Section 175 of the Evidence Code, may be liable to satisfy, in whole or in part, a judgment entered in the action or to indemnify or reimburse for payments made to satisfy the judgment. Only those provisions of an agreement that are material to the terms of the insurance, indemnification, or reimbursement are required to be included in the initial disclosure. Material provisions include, but are not limited to, the identities of parties to the agreement and the nature and limits of the coverage.

(2) A party shall make its initial disclosures based on the information then reasonably available to it. A party is not excused from making its initial disclosures because it has not fully investigated the case, because it challenges the sufficiency of another party's disclosures, or because another party has not made its disclosures.

(3) A party that has made its initial disclosures, as described in paragraph (1), or that has responded to another party's discovery request, shall supplement or correct a disclosure or response in the following situations:

(A) In a timely manner if the party learns that in some material respect the disclosure or response is incomplete or incorrect and the additional or corrective information has not otherwise been made known to the other parties during the disclosure or discovery process.

(B) As ordered by the court.

(4) A party's obligations under this section may be enforced by a court on its own motion or the motion of a party to compel disclosure.

(5) A party's disclosures under this section shall be verified under penalty of perjury as being true and correct to the best of the party's knowledge.

(b) Notwithstanding subdivision (a), this section does not apply to the following actions:

(1) An unlawful detainer action, as defined in Section 1161.

(2) An action in the small claims division of a court, as defined in Section 116.210.

(c) This section shall become operative on January 1, 2027. **Leg.H.** Added Stats 2023 ch 249 §2 (SB 235), effective January 1, 2024, operative January 1, 2027.

CHAPTER 2
SCOPE OF DISCOVERY

Article 1. **General Provisions.**
Article 2. **Scope of Discovery in Specific Contexts.**
Article 3. **Violation of the Elder Abuse and Dependent Adult Civil Protection Act.**

ARTICLE 1
General Provisions

Matters subject to discovery. §2017.010.
When court may limit scope of discovery; Motion for protective order; Monetary sanction. §2017.020.

§2017. [Section repealed 2005]

Leg.H. Added Stats 1986 ch 1334 §2, operative July 1, 1987. Amended Stats 1987 ch 86 §2, operative July 1, 1987; Stats 1988 ch 160 §19, ch 553 §1 (ch 553 prevails); Stats 2001 ch 812 §9.4 (AB 223). Repealed Stats 2004 ch 182 §22 (AB 3081), operative July 1, 2005. The repealed section related to scope of discovery. See Cal Code Civ Proc §§2017.010 et seq.

Prior Law: Former CCP §2017 was added Stats 1957 ch 1904 §1, operative January 1, 1958, and repealed Stats 1986 ch 1334 §1, operative July 1, 1987.

§2017.010. Matters subject to discovery

Unless otherwise limited by order of the court in accordance with this title, any party may obtain discovery regarding any matter, not privileged, that is relevant to the subject matter involved in the pending action or to the determination of any motion made in that action, if the matter either is itself admissible in evidence or appears reasonably calculated to lead to the discovery of admissible evidence. Discovery may relate to the claim or defense of the party seeking discovery or of any other party to the action. Discovery may be obtained of the identity and location of persons having knowledge of any discoverable matter, as well as of the existence, description, nature, custody, condition, and location of any document, electronically stored information, tangible thing, or land or other property. **Leg.H.** Added Stats 2004 ch 182 §23 (AB 3081), operative July 1, 2005. Amended Stats 2012 ch 72 §8 (SB 1574), effective January 1, 2013.

§2017.020. When court may limit scope of discovery; Motion for protective order; Monetary sanction

(a) The court shall limit the scope of discovery if it determines that the burden, expense, or intrusiveness of that discovery clearly outweighs the likelihood that the information sought will lead to the discovery of admissible evidence. The court may make this determination pursuant to a motion for protective order by a party or other affected person. This motion shall be accompanied by a meet and confer declaration under Section 2016.040.

(b) The court shall impose a monetary sanction under Chapter 7 (commencing with Section 2023.010) against any party, person, or attorney who unsuccessfully makes or opposes a motion for a protective order, unless it finds that the one subject to the sanction acted with substantial justification or that other circumstances make the imposition of the sanction unjust.

(c)(1) Notwithstanding subdivision (b), or any other section of this title, absent exceptional circumstances, the court shall not impose sanctions on a party or any attorney of a party for failure to provide electronically stored information that has been lost, damaged, altered, or overwritten as the result of the routine, good faith operation of an electronic information system.

(2) This subdivision shall not be construed to alter any obligation to preserve discoverable information. **Leg.H.** Added Stats 2004 ch 182 §23 (AB 3081), operative July 1, 2005. Amended Stats 2012 ch 72 §9 (SB 1574), effective January 1, 2013.

ARTICLE 2
Scope of Discovery in Specific Contexts

Information concerning insurance. §2017.210.
Discovery regarding plaintiff's sexual conduct in certain actions; Showing of good cause; Monetary sanction. §2017.220.

§2017.210. Information concerning insurance

A party may obtain discovery of the existence and contents of any agreement under which any insurance carrier may be liable to satisfy in whole or in part a judgment that may be entered in the action or to indemnify or reimburse for payments made to satisfy the judgment. This discovery may include the identity of the carrier and the nature and limits of the coverage. A party may also obtain discovery as to whether that insurance carrier is disputing the agreement's coverage of the claim involved in the action, but not as to the nature and substance of that dispute. Information concerning the insurance agreement is not by reason of disclosure admissible in evidence at trial. **Leg.H.** Added Stats 2004 ch 182 §23 (AB 3081), operative July 1, 2005.

§2017.220. Discovery regarding plaintiff's sexual conduct in certain actions; Showing of good cause; Monetary sanction

(a) In any civil action alleging conduct that constitutes sexual harassment, sexual assault, or sexual battery, any party seeking discovery concerning the plaintiff's sexual conduct with individuals other than the alleged perpetrator shall establish specific facts showing that there is good cause for that discovery, and that the matter sought to be discovered is relevant to the subject matter of the action and reasonably calculated to lead to the discovery of admissible evidence. This showing shall be made by a noticed motion, accompanied by a meet and confer declaration under Section 2016.040, and shall not be made or considered by the court at an ex parte hearing.

(b) The court shall impose a monetary sanction under Chapter 7 (commencing with Section 2023.010) against any party, person, or attorney who unsuccessfully makes or opposes a motion for discovery under subdivision (a), unless it finds that the one subject to the sanction acted with substantial justification or that other circumstances make the imposition of the sanction unjust. **Leg.H.** Added Stats 2004 ch 182 §23 (AB 3081), operative July 1, 2005.

ARTICLE 3
Violation of the Elder Abuse and Dependent Adult Civil Protection Act

Confidential settlement agreements; Policy; When recognized. §2017.310.
Information protected from disclosure by protective order; Redaction and filing of information; Notice; Showing of good cause; When stipulated protective order may be recognized. §2017.320.

§2017.310. Confidential settlement agreements; Policy; When recognized

(a) Notwithstanding any other provision of law, it is the policy of the State of California that confidential settlement agreements are disfavored in any civil action the factual foundation for which establishes a cause of action for a violation of the Elder Abuse and Dependent Adult Civil Protection Act (Chapter 11 (commencing with Section 15600) of Part 3 of Division 9 of the Welfare and Institutions Code).

(b) Provisions of a confidential settlement agreement described in subdivision (a) may not be recognized or enforced by the court absent a showing of any of the following:

(1) The information is privileged under existing law.

(2) The information is not evidence of abuse of an elder or dependent adult, as described in Sections 15610.30, 15610.57, and 15610.63 of the Welfare and Institutions Code.

(3) The party seeking to uphold the confidentiality of the information has demonstrated that there is a substantial probability that prejudice will result from the disclosure and that the party's interest in the information cannot be adequately protected through redaction.

(c) Nothing in paragraph (1), (2), or (3) of subdivision (b) permits the sealing or redacting of a defendant's name in any information made available to the public.

(d) Except as expressly provided in this section, nothing in this section is intended to alter, modify, or amend existing law.

(e) Nothing in this section may be deemed to prohibit the entry or enforcement of that part of a confidentiality agreement, settlement agreement, or stipulated agreement between the parties that requires the nondisclosure of the amount of any money paid in a settlement of a claim.

(f) Nothing in this section applies to or affects an action for professional negligence against a health care provider. **Leg.H.** Added Stats 2004 ch 182 §23 (AB 3081), operative July 1, 2005.

§2017.320. Information protected from disclosure by protective order; Redaction and filing of information; Notice; Showing of good cause; When stipulated protective order may be recognized

(a) In any civil action the factual foundation for which establishes a cause of action for a violation of the Elder Abuse and Dependent Adult Civil Protection Act (Chapter 11 (commencing with Section 15600) of Part 3 of Division 9 of the Welfare and Institutions Code), any information that is acquired through discovery and is protected from disclosure by a stipulated protective order shall remain subject to the protective order, except for information that is evidence of abuse of an elder or dependent adult as described in Sections 15610.30, 15610.57, and 15610.63 of the Welfare and Institutions Code.

(b) In that instance, after redacting information in the document that is not evidence of abuse of an elder or dependent adult as described in Sections 15610.30, 15610.57, and 15610.63 of the Welfare and Institutions Code, a party may file that particularized information with the court. The party proposing to file the information shall offer to meet and confer with the party from whom the information was obtained at least one week prior to filing that information with the court.

(c) The filing party shall give concurrent notice of the filing with the court and its basis to the party from whom the information was obtained.

(d) Any filed information submitted to the court shall remain confidential under any protective order for 30 days after the filing and shall be part of the public court record thereafter, unless an affected party petitions the court and shows good cause for a court protective order.

(e) The burden of showing good cause shall be on the party seeking the court protective order.

(f) A stipulated protective order may not be recognized or enforced by the court to prevent disclosure of information filed with the court pursuant to subdivision (b), absent a showing of any of the following:

(1) The information is privileged under existing law.

(2) The information is not evidence of abuse of an elder or dependent adult as described in Sections 15610.30, 15610.57, and 15610.63 of the Welfare and Institutions Code.

(3) The party seeking to uphold the confidentiality of the information has demonstrated that there is a substantial probability that prejudice will result from the disclosure and that the party's interest in the information cannot be adequately protected through redaction.

(g) If the court denies the petition for a court protective order, it shall redact any part of the filed information it finds is not evidence of abuse of an elder or dependent adult, as described in Sections 15610.30, 15610.57, and 15610.63 of the Welfare and Institutions Code. Nothing in this subdivision or in paragraph (1), (2), or (3) of subdivision (f) permits the sealing or redacting of a defendant's name in any information made available to the public.

(h) Nothing in this section applies to or affects an action for professional negligence against a health care provider. **Leg.H.** Added Stats 2004 ch 182 §23 (AB 3081), operative July 1, 2005.

CHAPTER 3
USE OF TECHNOLOGY IN CONDUCTING DISCOVERY IN A COMPLEX CASE

§2017.710. [Section repealed 2013]

Leg.H. Added Stats 2004 ch 182 §23 (AB 3081), operative July 1, 2005. Repealed Stats 2012 ch 72 §10 (SB 1574), effective January 1, 2013. The repealed section related to meaning of "technology".

§2017.720. [Section repealed 2013]

Leg.H. Added Stats 2004 ch 182 §23 (AB 3081), operative July 1, 2005. Repealed Stats 2012 ch 72 §11 (SB 1574), effective January 1, 2013. The repealed section related to the effect of chapter on rights, duties and responsibilities of parties, and the use of stenographic court reporter.

§2017.730. [Section repealed 2013]

Leg.H. Added Stats 2004 ch 182 §23 (AB 3081), operative July 1, 2005. Repealed Stats 2012 ch 72 §12 (SB 1574), effective January 1, 2013. The repealed section related to order authorizing the use of technology in conducting discovery, criteria, and promulgation of rules and standards.

§2017.740. [Section repealed 2013]

Leg.H. Added Stats 2004 ch 182 §23 (AB 3081), operative July 1, 2005. Repealed Stats 2012 ch 72 §13 (SB 1574), effective January 1, 2013. The repealed section related to use and compensation of a service provider in discovery, selection and appointment, removal, and periodic review of service.

CHAPTER 4
ATTORNEY WORK PRODUCT

Meaning of "client" for purposes of chapter. §2018.010.
Policy of state. §2018.020.
Certain writings not discoverable; When other work product may be subject to discovery. §2018.030.
Restatement of existing law. §2018.040.
Work product enabling commission of crime not protected in official investigations. §2018.050.
Right to request in camera hearing. §2018.060.
Discovery for purposes of State Bar disciplinary proceedings; Protective order; Client approval. §2018.070.
No privilege when work product relevant to issue of breach of attorney-client relationship. §2018.080.

§2018. [Section repealed 2005]

Leg.H. Added Stats 1987 ch 86 §3.5, operative July 1, 1987. Amended Stats 1988 ch 1159 §34; Stats 1990 ch 207 §1 (SB 2668); Stats 2002 ch 1059 §1 (AB 2055), effective September 29, 2002. Repealed Stats 2004 ch 182 §22 (AB 3081), operative July 1, 2005. The repealed section related to protection for attorney's work product. See CCP §§2018.010 et seq.

Prior Law: Former CCP §2018 was added Stats 1986 ch 1334 §2, operative July 1, 1987, and repealed Stats 1987 ch 86 §3, effective and operative July 1, 1987.

Former CCP §2018 was added Stats 1957 ch 1904 §1, operative January 1, 1958, amended Stats 1961 ch 192 §1, and repealed Stats 1986 ch 1334 §1, operative July 1, 1987.

§2018.010. Meaning of "client" for purposes of chapter

For purposes of this chapter, "client" means a "client" as defined in Section 951 of the Evidence Code. **Leg.H.** Added Stats 2004 ch 182 §23 (AB 3081), operative July 1, 2005.

§2018.020. Policy of state

It is the policy of the state to do both of the following:

(a) Preserve the rights of attorneys to prepare cases for trial with that degree of privacy necessary to encourage them to prepare their cases thoroughly and to investigate not only the favorable but the unfavorable aspects of those cases.

(b) Prevent attorneys from taking undue advantage of their adversary's industry and efforts. **Leg.H.** Added Stats 2004 ch 182 §23 (AB 3081), operative July 1, 2005.

§2018.030. Certain writings not discoverable; When other work product may be subject to discovery

(a) A writing that reflects an attorney's impressions, conclusions, opinions, or legal research or theories is not discoverable under any circumstances.

(b) The work product of an attorney, other than a writing described in subdivision (a), is not discoverable unless the court determines that denial of discovery will unfairly prejudice the party seeking discovery in preparing that party's claim or defense or will result in an injustice. **Leg.H.** Added Stats 2004 ch 182 §23 (AB 3081), operative July 1, 2005.

§2018.040. Restatement of existing law

This chapter is intended to be a restatement of existing law relating to protection of work product. It is not intended to expand or reduce the extent to which work product is discoverable under existing law in any action. **Leg.H.** Added Stats 2004 ch 182 §23 (AB 3081), operative July 1, 2005.

§2018.050. Work product enabling commission of crime not protected in official investigations

Notwithstanding Section 2018.040, when a lawyer is suspected of knowingly participating in a crime or fraud, there is no protection of work product under this chapter in any official investigation by a law enforcement agency or proceeding or action brought by a public prosecutor in the name of the people of the State of California if the services of the lawyer were sought or obtained to enable or aid anyone to commit or plan to commit a crime or fraud. **Leg.H.** Added Stats 2004 ch 182 §23 (AB 3081), operative July 1, 2005.

§2018.060. Right to request in camera hearing

Nothing in this chapter is intended to limit an attorney's ability to request an in camera hearing as provided for in People v. Superior Court (Laff) (2001) 25 Cal.4th 703. **Leg.H.** Added Stats 2004 ch 182 §23 (AB 3081), operative July 1, 2005.

§2018.070. Discovery for purposes of State Bar disciplinary proceedings; Protective order; Client approval

(a) The State Bar may discover the work product of an attorney against whom disciplinary charges are pending when it is relevant to issues of breach of duty by the lawyer and requisite client approval has been granted.

(b) Where requested and for good cause, discovery under this section shall be subject to a protective order to ensure the confidentiality of the work product except for its use by the State Bar in disciplinary investigations and its consideration under seal in State Bar Court proceedings.

(c) For purposes of this chapter, whenever a client has initiated a complaint against an attorney, the requisite client approval shall be deemed to have been granted. **Leg.H.** Added Stats 2004 ch 182 §23 (AB 3081), operative July 1, 2005.

§2018.080. No privilege when work product relevant to issue of breach of attorney-client relationship

In an action between an attorney and a client or a former client of the attorney, no work product privilege under this chapter exists if the work product is relevant to an issue of breach by the attorney of a duty to the client arising out of the attorney-client relationship. **Leg.H.** Added Stats 2004 ch 182 §23 (AB 3081), operative July 1, 2005.

CHAPTER 5
METHODS AND SEQUENCE OF DISCOVERY

Article 1. General Provisions.
Article 2. Methods and Sequence of Discovery in Specific Contexts.

ARTICLE 1
General Provisions

Methods of discovery. §2019.010.
Sequence and timing of discovery. §2019.020.
When frequency or extent of discovery may be restricted; Motion for protective order; Monetary sanction. §2019.030.
Electronically stored information. §2019.040.

§2019. [Section repealed 2005]

Leg.H. Added Stats 1986 ch 1334 §2, operative July 1, 1987. Amended Stats 1987 ch 86 §4, operative July 1, 1987; Stats 1988 ch 553 §2; Stats 1995 ch 576 §6 (AB 1225). Repealed Stats 2004 ch 182 §22 (AB 3081), operative July 1, 2005. The repealed section related to methods for discovery. See CCP §§2016.050, 2019.010 et seq.

Prior Law: Former CCP §2019 was added Stats 1957 ch 1904 §3, operative January 1, 1958, amended Stats 1959 ch 1590 §2, Stats 1961 ch 192 §2, Stats 1963 ch 519 §1, Stats 1968 ch 918 §1, Stats 1969 ch 1034 §2, Stats 1976 ch 79 §1, Stats

1978 ch 1384 §1, Stats 1979 ch 19 §1, effective April 3, 1979, Stats 1980 ch 677 §1, ch 970 §2, Stats 1982 ch 192 §1, Stats 1985 ch 444 §2, and repealed Stats 1986 ch 1334 §1, operative July 1, 1987.

Original CCP §2019, relating to use of depositions, was enacted 1872 and repealed Stats 1957 ch 1904 §1, operative January 1, 1958.

§2019.010. Methods of discovery

Any party may obtain discovery by one or more of the following methods:

(a) Oral and written depositions.
(b) Interrogatories to a party.
(c) Inspections of documents, things, and places.
(d) Physical and mental examinations.
(e) Requests for admissions.
(f) Simultaneous exchanges of expert trial witness information. **Leg.H.** Added Stats 2004 ch 182 §23 (AB 3081), operative July 1, 2005.

§2019.020. Sequence and timing of discovery

(a) Except as otherwise provided by a rule of the Judicial Council, a local court rule, or a local uniform written policy, the methods of discovery may be used in any sequence, and the fact that a party is conducting discovery, whether by deposition or another method, shall not operate to delay the discovery of any other party.

(b) Notwithstanding subdivision (a), on motion and for good cause shown, the court may establish the sequence and timing of discovery for the convenience of parties and witnesses and in the interests of justice. **Leg.H.** Added Stats 2004 ch 182 §23 (AB 3081), operative July 1, 2005.

§2019.030. When frequency or extent of discovery may be restricted; Motion for protective order; Monetary sanction

(a) The court shall restrict the frequency or extent of use of a discovery method provided in Section 2019.010 if it determines either of the following:

(1) The discovery sought is unreasonably cumulative or duplicative, or is obtainable from some other source that is more convenient, less burdensome, or less expensive.

(2) The selected method of discovery is unduly burdensome or expensive, taking into account the needs of the case, the amount in controversy, and the importance of the issues at stake in the litigation.

(b) The court may make these determinations pursuant to a motion for a protective order by a party or other affected person. This motion shall be accompanied by a meet and confer declaration under Section 2016.040.

(c) The court shall impose a monetary sanction under Chapter 7 (commencing with Section 2023.010) against any party, person, or attorney who unsuccessfully makes or opposes a motion for a protective order, unless it finds that the one subject to the sanction acted with substantial justification or that other circumstances make the imposition of the sanction unjust. **Leg.H.** Added Stats 2004 ch 182 §23 (AB 3081), operative July 1, 2005.

§2019.040. Electronically stored information

(a) When any method of discovery permits the production, inspection, copying, testing, or sampling of documents or tangible things, that method shall also permit the production, inspection, copying, testing, or sampling of electronically stored information.

(b) All procedures available under this title to compel, prevent, or limit the production, inspection, copying, testing, or sampling of documents or tangible things shall be available to compel, prevent, or limit the production, inspection, copying, testing, or sampling of electronically stored information. **Leg.H.** Added Stats 2012 ch 72 §14 (SB 1574), effective January 1, 2013.

ARTICLE 2
Methods and Sequence of Discovery in Specific Contexts

Misappropriation of trade secret. §2019.210.

§2019.210. Misappropriation of trade secret

In any action alleging the misappropriation of a trade secret under the Uniform Trade Secrets Act (Title 5 (commencing with Section 3426) of Part 1 of Division 4 of the Civil Code), before commencing discovery relating to the trade secret, the party alleging the misappropriation shall identify the trade secret with reasonable particularity subject to any orders that may be appropriate under Section 3426.5 of the Civil Code. **Leg.H.** Added Stats 2004 ch 182 §23 (AB 3081), operative July 1, 2005.

CHAPTER 6
NONPARTY DISCOVERY

Article 1. General Provisions.
Article 2. Procedures Applicable to All Types of Deposition Subpoenas.
Article 3. Subpoena Commanding Only Attendance and Testimony of the Deponent.
Article 4. Subpoena Commanding Only Production of Business Records for Copying.
Article 5. Subpoena Commanding Both Production of Business Records and Attendance and Testimony of the Deponent.

ARTICLE 1
General Provisions

Methods for discovery within state from nonparty. §2020.010.
Service of deposition subpoena; Discovery of electronically stored information; Sanctions. §2020.020.
Provisions applicable to deposition subpoena. §2020.030.

§2020. [Section repealed 2005]

Leg.H. Added Stats 1986 ch 1334 §2, operative July 1, 1987. Amended Stats 1987 ch 86 §5, operative July 1, 1987; Stats 1992 ch 876 §9 (AB 3296); Stats 1993 ch 926 §8 (AB 2205); Stats 1999 ch 444 §3 (AB 794); Stats 2002 ch 1068 §1 (AB 2842). Repealed Stats 2004 ch 182 §22 (AB 3081), operative July 1, 2005. The repealed section related to discovery from a non-party. See CCP §§2020.010 et seq.

Prior Law: Former CCP §2020 was added Stats 1957 ch 1904 §1, operative January 1, 1958, amended Stats 1959 ch 1590 §3, Stats 1963 ch 519 §2, and repealed Stats 1986 ch 1334 §1, operative July 1, 1987.

Former CCP §2020 was enacted 1872, amended Stats 1909 ch 628 §1, and repealed Stats 1957 ch 1904 §1, operative January 1, 1958.

§2020.010. Methods for discovery within state from nonparty

(a) Any of the following methods may be used to obtain discovery within the state from a person who is not a party to the action in which the discovery is sought:

(1) An oral deposition under Chapter 9 (commencing with Section 2025.010).

(2) A written deposition under Chapter 11 (commencing with Section 2028.010).

(3) A deposition for production of business records and things under Article 4 (commencing with Section 2020.410) or Article 5 (commencing with Section 2020.510).

(b) Except as provided in subdivision (a) of Section 2025.280, the process by which a nonparty is required to provide discovery is a deposition subpoena. **Leg.H.** Added Stats 2004 ch 182 §23 (AB 3081), operative July 1, 2005.

§2020.020. Service of deposition subpoena; Discovery of electronically stored information; Sanctions

A deposition subpoena may command any of the following:

(a) Only the attendance and the testimony of the deponent, under Article 3 (commencing with Section 2020.310).

(b) Only the production of business records for copying, under Article 4 (commencing with Section 2020.410).

(c) The attendance and the testimony of the deponent, as well as the production of business records, other documents, electronically stored information, and tangible things, under Article 5 (commencing with Section 2020.510). **Leg.H.** Added Stats 2004 ch 182 §23 (AB 3081), operative July 1, 2005. Amended Stats 2012 ch 72 §15 (SB 1574), effective January 1, 2013.

§2020.030. Provisions applicable to deposition subpoena

Except as modified in this chapter, the provisions of Chapter 2 (commencing with Section 1985) of Title 3 of Part 4 of this code, and of Article 4 (commencing with Section 1560) of Chapter 2 of Division 11 of the Evidence Code, apply to a deposition subpoena. **Leg.H.** Added Stats 2004 ch 182 §23 (AB 3081), operative July 1, 2005.

ARTICLE 2
Procedures Applicable to All Types of Deposition Subpoenas

Issuance of deposition subpoena by clerk of court or attorney of record. §2020.210.
Service of deposition subpoena; Subpoena seeking electronically stored information. §2020.220.

Witness fee and mileage. §2020.230.
Punishment for disobeying deposition subpoena; Contempt; Forfeiture and damages. §2020.240.

§2020.210. Issuance of deposition subpoena by clerk of court or attorney of record

(a) The clerk of the court in which the action is pending shall issue a deposition subpoena signed and sealed, but otherwise in blank, to a party requesting it, who shall fill it in before service.

(b) Instead of a court-issued deposition subpoena, an attorney of record for any party may sign and issue a deposition subpoena. A deposition subpoena issued under this subdivision need not be sealed. A copy may be served on the nonparty, and the attorney may retain the original. **Leg.H.** Added Stats 2004 ch 182 §23 (AB 3081), operative July 1, 2005.

§2020.220. Service of deposition subpoena; Subpoena seeking electronically stored information

(a) Subject to subdivision (c) of Section 2020.410, service of a deposition subpoena shall be effected a sufficient time in advance of the deposition to provide the deponent a reasonable opportunity to locate and produce any designated business records, documents, electronically stored information, and tangible things, as described in Article 4 (commencing with Section 2020.410), and, where personal attendance is commanded, a reasonable time to travel to the place of deposition.

(b) Any person may serve the subpoena by personal delivery of a copy of it as follows:

(1) If the deponent is a natural person, to that person.

(2) If the deponent is an organization, to any officer, director, custodian of records, or to any agent or employee authorized by the organization to accept service of a subpoena.

(c) Personal service of any deposition subpoena is effective to require all of the following of any deponent who is a resident of California at the time of service:

(1) Personal attendance and testimony, if the subpoena so specifies.

(2) Any specified production, inspection, testing, and sampling.

(3) The deponent's attendance at a court session to consider any issue arising out of the deponent's refusal to be sworn, or to answer any question, or to produce specified items, or to permit inspection or photocopying, if the subpoena so specifies, or specified testing and sampling of the items produced.

(d) Unless the subpoenaing party and the subpoenaed person otherwise agree or the court otherwise orders, the following shall apply:

(1) If a subpoena requiring production of electronically stored information does not specify a form or forms for producing a type of electronically stored information, the person subpoenaed shall produce the information in the form or forms in which it is ordinarily maintained or in a form that is reasonably usable.

(2) A subpoenaed person need not produce the same electronically stored information in more than one form.

(e) The subpoenaed person opposing the production, inspection, copying, testing, or sampling of electronically stored information on the basis that the information is from a source that is not reasonably accessible because of undue burden or expense shall bear the burden of demonstrating that the information is from a source that is not reasonably accessible because of undue burden or expense.

(f) If the person from whom discovery of electronically stored information is subpoenaed establishes that the information is from a source that is not reasonably accessible because of undue burden or expense, the court may nonetheless order discovery if the subpoenaing party shows good cause, subject to any limitations imposed under subdivision (i).

(g) If the court finds good cause for the production of electronically stored information from a source that is not reasonably accessible, the court may set conditions for the discovery of the electronically stored information, including allocation of the expense of discovery.

(h) If necessary, the subpoenaed person, at the reasonable expense of the subpoenaing party, shall, through detection devices, translate any data compilations included in the subpoena into a reasonably usable form.

(i) The court shall limit the frequency or extent of discovery of electronically stored information, even from a source that is reasonably accessible, if the court determines that any of the following conditions exists:

(1) It is possible to obtain the information from some other source that is more convenient, less burdensome, or less expensive.

(2) The discovery sought is unreasonably cumulative or duplicative.

(3) The party seeking discovery has had ample opportunity by discovery in the action to obtain the information sought.

(4) The likely burden or expense of the proposed discovery outweighs the likely benefit, taking into account the amount in controversy, the resources of the parties, the importance of the issues in the litigation, and the importance of the requested discovery in resolving the issues.

(j) If a subpoenaed person notifies the subpoenaing party that electronically stored information produced pursuant to a subpoena is subject to a claim of privilege or of protection as attorney work product, as described in Section 2031.285, the provisions of Section 2031.285 shall apply.

(k) A party serving a subpoena requiring the production of electronically stored information shall take reasonable steps to avoid imposing undue burden or expense on a person subject to the subpoena.

(*l*) An order of the court requiring compliance with a subpoena issued under this section shall protect a person who is neither a party nor a party's officer from undue burden or expense resulting from compliance.

(m)(1) Absent exceptional circumstances, the court shall not impose sanctions on a subpoenaed person or any attorney of a subpoenaed person for failure to provide electronically stored information that has been lost, damaged, altered, or overwritten as the result of the routine, good faith operation of an electronic information system.

(2) The subdivision shall not be construed to alter any obligation to preserve discoverable information. **Leg.H.** Added Stats 2004 ch 182 §23 (AB 3081), operative July 1, 2005. Amended Stats 2012 ch 72 §16 (SB 1574), effective January 1, 2013.

§2020.230. Witness fee and mileage

(a) If a deposition subpoena requires the personal attendance of the deponent, under Article 3 (commencing with Section 2020.310) or Article 5 (commencing with Section 2020.510), the party noticing the deposition shall pay to the deponent in cash or by check the same witness fee and mileage required by Chapter 1 (commencing with Section 68070) of Title 8 of the Government Code for attendance and testimony before the court in which the action is pending. This payment, whether or not demanded by the deponent, shall be made, at the option of the party noticing the deposition, either at the time of service of the deposition subpoena, or at the time the deponent attends for the taking of testimony.

(b) Service of a deposition subpoena that does not require the personal attendance of a custodian of records or other qualified person, under Article 4 (commencing with Section 2020.410), shall be accompanied, whether or not demanded by the deponent, by a payment in cash or by check of the witness fee required by paragraph (6) of subdivision (b) of Section 1563 of the Evidence Code. **Leg.H.** Added Stats 2004 ch 182 §23 (AB 3081), operative July 1, 2005.

§2020.240. Punishment for disobeying deposition subpoena; Contempt; Forfeiture and damages

A deponent who disobeys a deposition subpoena in any manner described in subdivision (c) of Section 2020.220 may be punished for contempt under Chapter 7 (commencing with Section 2023.010) without the necessity of a prior order of court directing compliance by the witness. The deponent is also subject to the forfeiture and the payment of damages set forth in Section 1992. **Leg.H.** Added Stats 2004 ch 182 §23 (AB 3081), operative July 1, 2005.

ARTICLE 3
Subpoena Commanding Only Attendance and Testimony of the Deponent

Rules applicable to deposition subpoena commanding only attendance and testimony. §2020.310.

§2020.310. Rules applicable to deposition subpoena commanding only attendance and testimony

The following rules apply to a deposition subpoena that commands only the attendance and the testimony of the deponent:

(a) The subpoena shall specify the time when and the place where the deponent is commanded to attend the deposition.

(b) The subpoena shall set forth a summary of all of the following:

(1) The nature of a deposition.

(2) The rights and duties of the deponent.

(3) The penalties for disobedience of a deposition subpoena, as described in Section 2020.240.

(c) If the deposition will be recorded using audio or video technology by, or at the direction of, the noticing party under Section 2025.340, the subpoena shall state that it will be recorded in that manner.

(d) If the deposition testimony will be conducted using instant visual display, the subpoena shall state that it will be conducted in that manner.

(e) If the deponent is an organization, the subpoena shall describe with reasonable particularity the matters on which examination is requested. The subpoena shall also advise the organization of its duty to make the designation of employees or agents who will attend the deposition, as described in Section 2025.230. **Leg.H.** Added Stats 2004 ch 182 §23 (AB 3081), operative July 1, 2005.

ARTICLE 4
Subpoena Commanding Only Production of Business Records for Copying

What deposition subpoena commanding only production of business records to contain; Description of records; Records pertaining to consumer. §2020.410.
Deposition officer. §2020.420.
Delivery to deposition officer; Copy of records and affidavit; Duties of custodian; Date for delivery; Applicability of specified provisions. §2020.430.
Deposition officer to provide copies to specified parties. §2020.440.

§2020.410. What deposition subpoena commanding only production of business records to contain; Description of records; Records pertaining to consumer

(a) A deposition subpoena that commands only the production of business records for copying shall designate the business records to be produced either by specifically describing each individual item or by reasonably particularizing each category of item, and shall specify the form in which any electronically stored information is to be produced, if a particular form is desired.

(b) Notwithstanding subdivision (a), specific information identifiable only to the deponent's records system, like a policy number or the date when a consumer interacted with the witness, is not required.

(c) A deposition subpoena that commands only the production of business records for copying need not be accompanied by an affidavit or declaration showing good cause for the production of the business records designated in it. It shall be directed to the custodian of those records or another person qualified to certify the records. It shall command compliance in accordance with Section 2020.430 on a date that is no earlier than 20 days after the issuance, or 15 days after the service, of the deposition subpoena, whichever date is later.

(d) If, under Section 1985.3 or 1985.6, the one to whom the deposition subpoena is directed is a witness, and the business records described in the deposition subpoena are personal records pertaining to a consumer, the service of the deposition subpoena shall be accompanied either by a copy of the proof of service of the notice to the consumer described in subdivision (e) of Section 1985.3, or subdivision (b) of Section 1985.6, as applicable, or by the consumer's written authorization to release personal records described in paragraph (2) of subdivision (c) of Section 1985.3, or paragraph (2) of subdivision (c) of Section 1985.6, as applicable. **Leg.H.** Added Stats 2004 ch 182 §23 (AB 3081), operative July 1, 2005. Amended Stats 2012 ch 72 §17 (SB 1574), effective January 1, 2013.

§2020.420. Deposition officer

The officer for a deposition seeking discovery only of business records for copying under this article shall be a professional photocopier registered under Chapter 20 (commencing with Section 22450) of Division 8 of the Business and Professions Code, or a person exempted from the registration requirements of that chapter under Section 22451 of the Business and Professions Code. This deposition officer shall not be financially interested in the action, or a relative or employee of any attorney of the parties. Any objection to the qualifications of the deposition officer is waived unless made before the date of production or as soon thereafter as the ground for that objection becomes known or could be discovered by reasonable diligence. **Leg.H.** Added Stats 2004 ch 182 §23 (AB 3081), operative July 1, 2005.

§2020.430. Delivery to deposition officer; Copy of records and affidavit; Duties of custodian; Date for delivery; Applicability of specified provisions

(a) Except as provided in subdivision (e), if a deposition subpoena commands only the production of business records for copying, the custodian of the records or other qualified person shall, in person, by messenger, or by mail, deliver both of the following only to the deposition officer specified in the subpoena:

(1) A true, legible, and durable copy of the records.

(2) An affidavit in compliance with Section 1561 of the Evidence Code.

(b) If the delivery required by subdivision (a) is made to the office of the deposition officer, the records shall be enclosed, sealed, and directed as described in subdivision (c) of Section 1560 of the Evidence Code.

(c) If the delivery required by subdivision (a) is made at the office of the business whose records are the subject of the deposition subpoena, the custodian of those records or other qualified person shall do one of the following:

(1) Permit the deposition officer specified in the deposition subpoena to make a copy of the originals of the designated business records during normal business hours, as defined in subdivision (e) of Section 1560 of the Evidence Code.

(2) Deliver to the deposition officer a true, legible, and durable copy of the records on receipt of payment in cash or by check, by or on behalf of the party serving the deposition subpoena, of the reasonable costs of preparing that copy, together with an itemized statement of the cost of preparation, as determined under subdivision (b) of Section 1563 of the Evidence Code. This copy need not be delivered in a sealed envelope.

(d) Unless the parties, and if the records are those of a consumer as defined in Section 1985.3 or 1985.6, the consumer, stipulate to an earlier date, the custodian of the records shall not deliver to the deposition officer the records that are the subject of the deposition subpoena prior to the date and time specified in the deposition subpoena. The following legend shall appear in boldface type on the deposition subpoena immediately following the date and time specified for production: "Do not release the requested records to the deposition officer prior to the date and time stated above."

(e) This section does not apply if the subpoena directs the deponent to make the records available for inspection or copying by the subpoenaing party's attorney or a representative of that attorney at the witness' business address under subdivision (e) of Section 1560 of the Evidence Code.

(f) The provisions of Section 1562 of the Evidence Code concerning the admissibility of the affidavit of the custodian or other qualified person apply to a deposition subpoena served under this article. **Leg.H.** Added Stats 2004 ch 182 §23 (AB 3081), operative July 1, 2005.

§2020.440. Deposition officer to provide copies to specified parties

Promptly on or after the deposition date and after the receipt or the making of a copy of business records under this article, the deposition officer shall provide that copy to the party at whose instance the deposition subpoena was served, and a copy of those records to any other party to the action who then or subsequently, within a period of six months following the settlement of the case, notifies the deposition officer that the party desires to purchase a copy of those records. **Leg.H.** Added Stats 2004 ch 182 §23 (AB 3081), operative July 1, 2005.

ARTICLE 5
Subpoena Commanding Both Production of Business Records and Attendance and Testimony of the Deponent

Requirements for deposition subpoena that commands attendance, testimony and production of business records, etc.; Records pertaining to consumer. §2020.510.

§2020.510. Requirements for deposition subpoena that commands attendance, testimony and production of business records, etc.; Records pertaining to consumer

(a) A deposition subpoena that commands the attendance and the testimony of the deponent, as well as the production of business records, documents, electronically stored information, and tangible things, shall:

(1) Comply with the requirements of Section 2020.310.

(2) Designate the business records, documents, electronically stored information, and tangible things to be produced either by specifically describing each individual item or by reasonably particularizing each category of item.

(3) Specify any testing or sampling that is being sought.

(4) Specify the form in which any electronically stored information is to be produced, if a particular form is desired.

(b) A deposition subpoena under subdivision (a) need not be accompanied by an affidavit or declaration showing good cause for the production of the documents and things designated.

(c) If, as described in Section 1985.3, the person to whom the deposition subpoena is directed is a witness, and the business records described in the deposition subpoena are personal records pertaining to a consumer, the service of the deposition subpoena shall be accompanied either by a copy of the proof of service of the notice to the consumer described in subdivision (e) of Section 1985.3, or by the consumer's written authorization to release personal records described in paragraph (2) of subdivision (c) of Section 1985.3.

(d) If, as described in Section 1985.6, the person to whom the deposition subpoena is directed is a witness and the business records described in the deposition subpoena are employment records pertaining to an employee, the service of the deposition subpoena shall be accompanied either by a copy of the proof of service of the notice to the employee described in subdivision (e) of Section 1985.6, or by the employee's written authorization to release personal records described in paragraph (2) of subdivision (c) of Section 1985.6. **Leg.H.** Added Stats 2004 ch 182 §23 (AB 3081), operative July 1, 2005. Amended Stats 2007 ch 113 §4 (AB 1126), effective January 1, 2008; Stats 2012 ch 72 §18 (SB 1574), effective January 1, 2013.

§2021. [Section repealed 2005]

Leg.H. Added Stats 1986 ch 1334 §2, operative July 1, 1987. Repealed Stats 2004 ch 182 §22 (AB 3081), operative July 1, 2005. The repealed section related to stipulations modifying discovery procedures. See CCP §2016.030.

Prior Law: Former CCP §2021 was added Stats 1957 ch 1904 §3, operative January 1, 1958, amended Stats 1959 ch 1590 §4, Stats 1961 ch 192 §3, and repealed Stats 1986 ch 1334 §1, operative July 1, 1987.

Former CCP §2021, relating to testimony of witness in the state, was enacted 1872, amended Code Amdts 1875–76 ch 220 §1, Code Amdts 1877–78 ch 167, Stats 1905 ch 134 §1, Stats 1935 ch 58 §1, Stats 1939 ch 195 §1, Stats 1955 ch 1133 §1, and repealed Stats 1957 ch 1904 §1, operative January 1, 1958.

§2022. [Section repealed 1958]

Leg.H. Added Stats 1907 ch 392 §2. Repealed Stats 1957 ch 1904 §1, operative January 1, 1958. The repealed section related to use of depositions as evidence.

CHAPTER 7
SANCTIONS

Misuses of discovery process. §2023.010.
Monetary sanction for failure to confer. §2023.020.
Sanctions for misuse of discovery process; Failure to provide electronically stored information. §2023.030.
Request for sanction and notice of motion. §2023.040.
Sanctions. §2023.050.

§2023. [Section repealed 2005]

Leg.H. Added Stats 1986 ch 1334 §2, operative July 1, 1987. Amended Stats 1987 ch 86 §6, operative July 1, 1987. Repealed Stats 2004 ch 182 §22 (AB 3081), operative July 1, 2005 (ch 182 prevails), ch 183 §48 (AB 3082). The repealed section related to sanctions for misuse of discovery. See CCP §§2023.010 et seq.

Prior Law: Former CCP §2023 added Stats 1959 ch 1590 §5 and repealed Stat 1986 ch 1334 §1, operative July 1, 1987.

Former CCP §2023 added Stats 1907 ch 392 §3 and repealed Stats 1957 ch 1904 §1, operative January 1, 1958.

§2023.010. Misuses of discovery process

Misuses of the discovery process include, but are not limited to, the following:

(a) Persisting, over objection and without substantial justification, in an attempt to obtain information or materials that are outside the scope of permissible discovery.

(b) Using a discovery method in a manner that does not comply with its specified procedures.

(c) Employing a discovery method in a manner or to an extent that causes unwarranted annoyance, embarrassment, or oppression, or undue burden and expense.

(d) Failing to respond or to submit to an authorized method of discovery.

(e) Making, without substantial justification, an unmeritorious objection to discovery.

(f) Making an evasive response to discovery.

(g) Disobeying a court order to provide discovery.

(h) Making or opposing, unsuccessfully and without substantial justification, a motion to compel or to limit discovery.

(i) Failing to confer in person, by telephone, or by letter with an opposing party or attorney in a reasonable and good faith attempt to resolve informally any dispute concerning discovery, if the section governing a particular discovery motion requires the filing of a declaration stating facts showing that an attempt at informal resolution has been made. **Leg.H.** Added Stats 2004 ch 182 §23 (AB 3081), operative July 1, 2005.

§2023.020. Monetary sanction for failure to confer

Notwithstanding the outcome of the particular discovery motion, the court shall impose a monetary sanction ordering that any party or attorney who fails to confer as required pay the reasonable expenses, including attorney's fees, incurred by anyone as a result of that conduct. **Leg.H.** Added Stats 2004 ch 182 §23 (AB 3081), operative July 1, 2005.

§2023.030. Sanctions for misuse of discovery process; Failure to provide electronically stored information

To the extent authorized by the chapter governing any particular discovery method or any other provision of this title, the court, after notice to any affected party, person, or attorney, and after opportunity for hearing, may impose the following sanctions against anyone engaging in conduct that is a misuse of the discovery process:

(a) The court may impose a monetary sanction ordering that one engaging in the misuse of the discovery process, or any attorney advising that conduct, or both pay the reasonable expenses, including attorney's fees, incurred by anyone as a result of that conduct. The court may also impose this sanction on one unsuccessfully asserting that another has engaged in the misuse of the discovery process, or on any attorney who advised that assertion, or on both. If a monetary sanction is authorized by any provision of this title, the court shall impose that sanction unless it finds that the one subject to the sanction acted with substantial justification or that other circumstances make the imposition of the sanction unjust.

(b) The court may impose an issue sanction ordering that designated facts shall be taken as established in the action in accordance with the claim of the party adversely affected by the misuse of the discovery process. The court may also impose an issue sanction by an order prohibiting any party engaging in the misuse of the discovery process from supporting or opposing designated claims or defenses.

(c) The court may impose an evidence sanction by an order prohibiting any party engaging in the misuse of the discovery process from introducing designated matters in evidence.

(d) The court may impose a terminating sanction by one of the following orders:

(1) An order striking out the pleadings or parts of the pleadings of any party engaging in the misuse of the discovery process.

(2) An order staying further proceedings by that party until an order for discovery is obeyed.

(3) An order dismissing the action, or any part of the action, of that party.

(4) An order rendering a judgment by default against that party.

(e) The court may impose a contempt sanction by an order treating the misuse of the discovery process as a contempt of court.

(f)(1) Notwithstanding subdivision (a), or any other section of this title, absent exceptional circumstances, the court shall not impose sanctions on a party or any attorney of a party for failure to provide electronically stored information that has been lost, damaged, altered, or overwritten as the result of the routine, good faith operation of an electronic information system.

(2) This subdivision shall not be construed to alter any obligation to preserve discoverable information. **Leg.H.** Added Stats 2004 ch 182 §23 (AB 3081), operative July 1, 2005. Amended Stats 2012 ch 72 §19 (SB 1574), effective January 1, 2013.

§2023.040. Request for sanction and notice of motion

A request for a sanction shall, in the notice of motion, identify every person, party, and attorney against whom the sanction is sought, and specify the type of sanction sought. The notice of motion shall be supported by a memorandum of points and authorities, and accompanied by a declaration setting forth facts supporting the amount of any monetary sanction sought. **Leg.H.** Added Stats 2004 ch 182 §23 (AB 3081), operative July 1, 2005.

§2023.050. Sanctions

(a) Notwithstanding any other law, and in addition to any other sanctions imposed pursuant to this chapter, a court shall impose a one-thousand-dollar ($1,000) sanction, payable to the requesting party, upon a party, person, or attorney if, upon reviewing a request for a sanction made pursuant to Section 2023.040, the court finds any of the following:

(1) The party, person, or attorney did not respond in good faith to a request for the production of documents made pursuant to Section 2020.010, 2020.410, 2020.510, or 2025.210, or to an inspection demand made pursuant to Section 2031.010.

(2) The party, person, or attorney produced requested documents within seven days before the court was scheduled to hear a motion to compel production of the records pursuant to Section 2025.450, 2025.480, or 2031.320 that is filed by the requesting party as a result of the other party's, person's, or attorney's failure to respond in good faith.

(3) The party, person, or attorney failed to confer in person, by telephone, letter, or other means of communication in writing, as defined in Section 250 of the Evidence Code, with the party or attorney requesting the documents in a reasonable and good faith attempt to resolve informally any dispute concerning the request.

(b) Notwithstanding paragraph (3) of subdivision (o) of Section 6068 of the Business and Professions Code, the court may, in its discretion, require an attorney who is sanctioned pursuant to subdivision (a) to report the sanction, in writing, to the State Bar within 30 days of the imposition of the sanction.

(c) The court may excuse the imposition of the sanction required by subdivision (a) if the court makes written findings that the one subject to the sanction acted with substantial justification or that other circumstances make the imposition of the sanction unjust.

(d) Sanctions pursuant to this section shall be imposed only after notice to the party, person, or attorney against whom the sanction is proposed to be imposed and opportunity for that party, person, or attorney to be heard.

(e) For purposes of this section, there is a rebuttable presumption that a natural person acted in good faith if that person was not represented by an attorney in the action at the time the conduct that is sanctionable under subdivision (a) occurred. This presumption may only be overcome by clear and convincing evidence. **Leg.H.** Added Stats 2019 ch 836 §2 (SB 17), effective January 1, 2020. Amended Stats 2023 ch 284 §3 (SB 235), effective January 1, 2024.

CHAPTER 8
TIME FOR COMPLETION OF DISCOVERY

Discovery completion date. §2024.010.
Cutoff of discovery proceedings. §2024.020.
Discovery cutoff for expert witness. §2024.030.
Time limit for completing discovery in action subject to judicial arbitration; Summary proceedings for obtaining real property; Eminent domain. §2024.040.
Motion for leave to complete discovery closer to trial date or to reopen discovery after new trial date set; Monetary sanction. §2024.050.
Agreement to extend time for completion of discovery or to reopen discovery; Written confirmation. §2024.060.

§2024. [Section repealed 2005]

Leg.H. Added Stats 1986 ch 1334 §2, operative July 1, 1987. Amended Stats 1987 ch 86 §7, operative July 1, 1987; Stats 1991 ch 1090 §9.5 (AB 1484); Stats 1998 ch 932 §21 (AB 1094); Stats 2000 ch 688 §11 (AB 1669); Stats 2004 ch 171 §5 (AB 3078), operative until July 1, 2005. Repealed Stats 2004 ch 182 §22 (AB 3081), operative July 1, 2005. The repealed section related to time limit on discovery. See CCP §§2016.060, 2024.010 et seq.

Prior Law: Former CCP §2024 was added Stats 1961 ch 192 §5 and repealed Stats 1986 ch 1334 §1, operative July 1, 1987.

Former CCP §2024, relating to deposition of witness out of state, was added Stats 1957 ch 1904 §3, operative January 1, 1958, amended Stats 1959 ch 1590 §6, and repealed Stats 1961 ch 192 §4.

Former CCP §2024, relating to deposition of witness out of State, was enacted 1872, amended Code Amdts 1873-74 ch 383 §243, Code Amdts 1880 ch 111 §3, Stats 1891 ch 52 §1, Stats 1907 ch 392 §4, Stats 1909 ch 627 §1, Stats 1917 ch 190 §1, Stats 1951 ch 1737 §173, operative January 1, 1952, and repealed Stats 1957 ch 1904 §1, operative January 1, 1958.

§2024.010. Discovery completion date

As used in this chapter, discovery is considered completed on the day a response is due or on the day a deposition begins. **Leg.H.** Added Stats 2004 ch 182 §23 (AB 3081), operative July 1, 2005.

§2024.020. Cutoff of discovery proceedings

(a) Except as otherwise provided in this chapter, any party shall be entitled as a matter of right to complete discovery proceedings on or before the 30th day, and to have motions concerning discovery heard on or before the 15th day, before the date initially set for the trial of the action.

(b) Except as provided in Section 2024.050, a continuance or postponement of the trial date does not operate to reopen discovery proceedings. **Leg.H.** Added Stats 2004 ch 182 §23 (AB 3081), operative July 1, 2005.

§2024.030. Discovery cutoff for expert witness

Any party shall be entitled as a matter of right to complete discovery proceedings pertaining to a witness identified under Chapter 18 (commencing with Section 2034.010) on or before the 15th day, and to have motions concerning that discovery heard on or before the 10th day, before the date initially set for the trial of the action. **Leg.H.** Added Stats 2004 ch 182 §23 (AB 3081), operative July 1, 2005.

§2024.040. Time limit for completing discovery in action subject to judicial arbitration; Summary proceedings for obtaining real property; Eminent domain

(a) The time limit on completing discovery in an action to be arbitrated under Chapter 2.5 (commencing with Section 1141.10) of Title 3 of Part 3 is subject to Judicial Council Rule. After an award in a case ordered to judicial arbitration, completion of discovery is limited by Section 1141.24.

(b) This chapter does not apply to either of the following:

(1) Summary proceedings for obtaining possession of real property governed by Chapter 4 (commencing with Section 1159) of Title 3 of Part 3. Except as provided in Sections 2024.050 and 2024.060, discovery in these proceedings shall be completed on or before the fifth day before the date set for trial.

(2) Eminent domain proceedings governed by Title 7 (commencing with Section 1230.010) of Part 3. **Leg.H.** Added Stats 2004 ch 182 §23 (AB 3081), operative July 1, 2005. Amended Stats 2012 ch 162 §17 (SB 1171), effective January 1, 2013.

§2024.050. Motion for leave to complete discovery closer to trial date or to reopen discovery after new trial date set; Monetary sanction

(a) On motion of any party, the court may grant leave to complete discovery proceedings, or to have a motion concerning discovery heard, closer to the initial trial date, or to reopen discovery after a new trial date has been set. This motion shall be accompanied by a meet and confer declaration under Section 2016.040.

(b) In exercising its discretion to grant or deny this motion, the court shall take into consideration any matter relevant to the leave requested, including, but not limited to, the following:

(1) The necessity and the reasons for the discovery.

(2) The diligence or lack of diligence of the party seeking the discovery or the hearing of a discovery motion, and the reasons that the discovery was not completed or that the discovery motion was not heard earlier.

(3) Any likelihood that permitting the discovery or hearing the discovery motion will prevent the case from going to trial on the date set, or otherwise interfere with the trial calendar, or result in prejudice to any other party.

(4) The length of time that has elapsed between any date previously set, and the date presently set, for the trial of the action.

(c) The court shall impose a monetary sanction under Chapter 7 (commencing with Section 2023.010) against any party, person, or attorney who unsuccessfully makes or opposes a motion to extend or to reopen discovery, unless it finds that the one subject to the sanction acted with substantial justification or that other circumstances make the imposition of the sanction unjust. **Leg.H.** Added Stats 2004 ch 182 §23 (AB 3081), operative July 1, 2005.

§2024.060. Agreement to extend time for completion of discovery or to reopen discovery; Written confirmation

Parties to an action may, with the consent of any party affected by it, enter into an agreement to extend the time for the completion of discovery proceedings or for the hearing of motions concerning discovery, or to reopen discovery after a new date for trial of the action has been set. This agreement may be informal, but it shall be confirmed in a writing that specifies the extended date. In no event shall this agreement require a court to grant a continuance or postponement of the trial of the action. **Leg.H.** Added Stats 2004 ch 182 §23 (AB 3081), operative July 1, 2005.

CHAPTER 9
ORAL DEPOSITION INSIDE CALIFORNIA

Article 1. General Provisions.
Article 2. Deposition Notice.
Article 3. Conduct of Deposition.
Article 4. Objections, Sanctions, Protective Orders, Motions to Compel, and Suspension of Depositions.
Article 5. Transcript or Recording.
Article 6. Post-Deposition Procedures.

ARTICLE 1
General Provisions

Oral deposition in state of any person by any party. §2025.010.

§2025. [Section repealed 2005]

Leg.H. Added Stats 1986 ch 1334 §2, operative July 1, 1987. Amended Stats 1987 ch 86 §8, operative July 1, 1987; Stats 1988 ch 160 §20 (ch 553 prevails), ch 553 §3; Stats 1989 ch 1137 §1, ch 1360 §13, ch 1416 §29.5; Stats 1990 ch 1491 §11.5 (AB 3765); Stats 1991 ch 1090 §10 (AB 1484); Stats 1993 ch 926 §9 (AB 2205); Stats 1994 ch 660 §5 (AB 3670); Stats 1995 ch 576 §7 (AB 1225); Stats 1997 ch 395 §1 (SB 544); Stats 1998 ch 875 §1 (SB 2145), ch 932 §22 (AB 1094), ch 974 §4 (AB 2150); Stats 1999 ch 892 §13 (AB 1672); Stats 2000 ch 474 §1 (SB 877); Stats 2001 ch 812 §9.6 (AB 223); Stats 2002 ch 1068 §2 (AB 2842). Repealed Stats 2004 ch 182 §22 (AB 3081), operative July 1, 2005. The repealed section related to oral depositions in California. See CCP §§2025.010 et seq.

Prior Law: Former CCP §2025, relating to postponement of trial for nonreturn of deposition taken out of state, was added Stats 1961 ch 192 §7 and repealed Stats 1986 ch 1334 §1, operative July 1, 1987.

Former CCP §2025, relating to interrogatories, was added Stats 1957 ch 1904 §3, operative January 1, 1958, amended Stats 1959 ch 1590 §7, and repealed Stats 1961 ch 192 §6.

Original CCP §2025, relating to preparation or waiver of interrogatories, was enacted 1872, amended Stats 1907 ch 392 §5, and repealed Stats 1957 ch 1904 §1, operative January 1, 1958.

§2025.010. Oral deposition in state of any person by any party

Any party may obtain discovery within the scope delimited by Chapter 2 (commencing with Section 2017.010), and subject to the restrictions set forth in Chapter 5 (commencing with Section 2019.010), by taking in California the oral deposition of any person, including any party to the action. The person deposed may be a natural person, an organization such as a public or private corporation, a partnership, an association, or a governmental agency. **Leg.H.** Added Stats 2004 ch 182 §23 (AB 3081), operative July 1, 2005. Amended Stats 2016 ch 86 §41 (SB 1171), effective January 1, 2017.

ARTICLE 2
Deposition Notice

Time for service of notice. §2025.210.
Contents of deposition notice. §2025.220.
Contents of deposition notice if deponent not a natural person. §2025.230.
Notice to parties to the action; Duties of subpoenaing party if deponent to produce personal records of consumer or employment records. §2025.240.
Place of taking deposition. §2025.250.
Motion for deposition at more distant place; Monetary sanction. §2025.260.
Date of oral deposition; Motion to shorten or extend time or for stay. §2025.270.
Effect of service of deposition notice; When deposition subpoena is required; Access to password protected or otherwise inaccessible information. §2025.280.
Appropriate time limit for depositions; Additional time; Exclusion; Construction. §2025.290.
Deposition examination; Time limitation for testimony; Mesothelioma or silicosis. §2025.295.

§2025.210. Time for service of notice

Subject to Sections 2025.270 and 2025.610, an oral deposition may be taken as follows:

(a) The defendant may serve a deposition notice without leave of court at any time after that defendant has been served or has appeared in the action, whichever occurs first.

(b) The plaintiff may serve a deposition notice without leave of court on any date that is 20 days after the service of the summons on, or appearance by, any defendant. On motion with or without notice, the court, for good cause shown, may grant to a plaintiff leave to serve a deposition notice on an earlier date. **Leg.H.** Added Stats 2004 ch 182 §23 (AB 3081), operative July 1, 2005.

§2025.220. Contents of deposition notice

(a) A party desiring to take the oral deposition of any person shall give notice in writing. The deposition notice shall state all of the following, in at least 12-point type:

(1) The address where the deposition will be taken.

(2) The date of the deposition, selected under Section 2025.270, and the time it will commence.

(3) The name of each deponent, and the address and telephone number, if known, of any deponent who is not a party to the action. If the name of the deponent is not known, the deposition notice shall set forth instead a general description sufficient to identify the person or particular class to which the person belongs.

(4) The specification with reasonable particularity of any materials or category of materials, including any electronically stored information, to be produced by the deponent.

(5) Any intention by the party noticing the deposition to record the testimony by audio or video technology, in addition to recording the testimony by the stenographic method as required by Section 2025.330 and any intention to record the testimony by stenographic method through the instant visual display of the testimony. If the deposition will be conducted using instant visual display, a copy of the deposition notice shall also be given to the deposition officer. Any offer to provide the instant visual display of the testimony or to provide rough draft transcripts to any party which is accepted prior to, or offered at, the deposition shall also be made by the deposition officer at the deposition to all parties in attendance. Any party or attorney requesting the provision of the instant visual display of the testimony, or rough draft transcripts, shall pay the reasonable cost of those services, which may be no greater than the costs charged to any other party or attorney.

(6) Any intention to reserve the right to use at trial a video recording of the deposition testimony of a treating or consulting physician or of an expert witness under subdivision (d) of Section 2025.620. In this event, the operator of the video camera shall be a person who is authorized to administer an oath, and shall not be financially interested in the action or be a relative or employee of any attorney of any of the parties.

(7) The form in which any electronically stored information is to be produced, if a particular form is desired.

(8)(A) A statement disclosing the existence of a contract, if any is known to the noticing party, between the noticing party or a third party who is financing all or part of the action and either of the following for any service beyond the noticed deposition:

(i) The deposition officer.

(ii) The entity providing the services of the deposition officer.

(B) A statement disclosing that the party noticing the deposition, or a third party financing all or part of the action, directed his or her attorney to use a particular officer or entity to provide services for the deposition, if applicable.

(b) Notwithstanding subdivision (a), where under Article 4 (commencing with Section 2020.410) only the production by a nonparty of business records for copying is desired, a copy of the deposition subpoena shall serve as the notice of deposition. **Leg.H.** Added Stats 2004 ch 182 §23 (AB 3081), operative July 1, 2005. Amended Stats 2012 ch 72 §20 (SB 1574), effective January 1, 2013; Stats 2015 ch 346 §2 (AB 1197), effective January 1, 2016; Stats 2018 ch 268 §1 (AB 3019), effective January 1, 2019.

2015 Note: This act shall be known and may be cited as the John Zandonella Act of 2015. Stats 2015 ch 346 (AB 1197) §1.

§2025.230. Contents of deposition notice if deponent not a natural person

If the deponent named is not a natural person, the deposition notice shall describe with reasonable particularity the matters on which examination is requested. In that event, the deponent shall designate and produce at the deposition those of its officers, directors, managing agents, employees, or agents who are most qualified to testify on its behalf as to those matters to the extent of any information known or reasonably available to the deponent. **Leg.H.** Added Stats 2004 ch 182 §23 (AB 3081), operative July 1, 2005.

§2025.240. Notice to parties to the action; Duties of subpoenaing party if deponent to produce personal records of consumer or employment records

(a) The party who prepares a notice of deposition shall give the notice to every other party who has appeared in the action. The deposition notice, or the accompanying proof of service, shall list all the parties or attorneys for parties on whom it is served.

(b) If, as defined in subdivision (a) of Section 1985.3 or subdivision (a) of Section 1985.6, the party giving notice of the deposition is a subpoenaing party, and the deponent is a witness commanded by a deposition subpoena to produce personal records of a consumer or employment records of an employee, the subpoenaing party shall serve on that consumer or employee all of the following:

(1) A notice of the deposition.

(2) The notice of privacy rights specified in subdivision (e) of Section 1985.3 or in subdivision (e) of Section 1985.6.

(3) A copy of the deposition subpoena.

(c) If the attendance of the deponent is to be compelled by service of a deposition subpoena under Chapter 6 (commencing with Section 2020.010), an identical copy of that subpoena shall be served with the deposition notice. **Leg.H.** Added Stats 2004 ch 182 §23 (AB 3081), operative July 1, 2005. Amended Stats 2007 ch 113 §5 (AB 1126), effective January 1, 2008.

§2025.250. Place of taking deposition

(a) Unless the court orders otherwise under Section 2025.260, the deposition of a natural person, whether or not a party to the action, shall be taken at a place that is, at the option of the party giving notice of the deposition, either within 75 miles of the deponent's residence, or within the county where the action is pending and within 150 miles of the deponent's residence.

(b) The deposition of an organization that is a party to the action shall be taken at a place that is, at the option of the party giving notice of the deposition, either within 75 miles of the organization's principal executive or business office in California, or within the county where the action is pending and within 150 miles of that office.

(c) Unless the organization consents to a more distant place, the deposition of any other organization shall be taken within 75 miles of the organization's principal executive or business office in California.

(d) If an organization has not designated a principal executive or business office in California, the deposition shall be taken at a place that is, at the option of the party giving notice of the deposition, either within the county where the action is pending, or within 75 miles of any executive or business office in California of the organization. **Leg.H.** Added Stats 2004 ch 182 §23 (AB 3081), operative July 1, 2005. Amended Stats 2005 ch 294 §7 (AB 333), effective January 1, 2006.

§2025.260. Motion for deposition at more distant place; Monetary sanction

(a) A party desiring to take the deposition of a natural person who is a party to the action or an officer, director, managing agent, or employee of a party may make a motion for an order that the deponent attend for deposition at a place that is more distant than that permitted under Section 2025.250. This motion shall be accompanied by a meet and confer declaration under Section 2016.040.

(b) In exercising its discretion to grant or deny this motion, the court shall take into consideration any factor tending to show whether the interests of justice will be served by requiring the deponent's attendance at that more distant place, including, but not limited to, the following:

(1) Whether the moving party selected the forum.

(2) Whether the deponent will be present to testify at the trial of the action.

(3) The convenience of the deponent.

(4) The feasibility of conducting the deposition by written questions under Chapter 11 (commencing with Section 2028.010), or of using a discovery method other than a deposition.

(5) The number of depositions sought to be taken at a place more distant than that permitted under Section 2025.250.

(6) The expense to the parties of requiring the deposition to be taken within the distance permitted under Section 2025.250.

(7) The whereabouts of the deponent at the time for which the deposition is scheduled.

(c) The order may be conditioned on the advancement by the moving party of the reasonable expenses and costs to the deponent for travel to the place of deposition.

(d) The court shall impose a monetary sanction under Chapter 7 (commencing with Section 2023.010) against any party, person, or attorney who unsuccessfully makes or opposes a motion to increase the travel limits for a party deponent, unless it finds that the one subject to the sanction acted with substantial justification or that other circumstances make the imposition of the sanction unjust. **Leg.H.** Added Stats 2004 ch 182 §23 (AB 3081), operative July 1, 2005.

§2025.270. Date of oral deposition; Motion to shorten or extend time or for stay

(a) An oral deposition shall be scheduled for a date at least 10 days after service of the deposition notice.

(b) Notwithstanding subdivision (a), in an unlawful detainer action or other proceeding under Chapter 4 (commencing with Section 1159) of Title 3 of Part 3, an oral deposition shall be scheduled for a date at least five days after service of the deposition notice, but not later than five days before trial.

(c) Notwithstanding subdivisions (a) and (b), if, as defined in Section 1985.3 or 1985.6, the party giving notice of the deposition is a subpoenaing party, and the deponent is a witness commanded by a deposition subpoena to produce personal records of a consumer or employment records of an employee, the deposition shall be scheduled for a date at least 20 days after issuance of that subpoena.

(d) On motion or ex parte application of any party or deponent, for good cause shown, the court may shorten or extend the time for scheduling a deposition, or may stay its taking until the determination of a motion for a protective order under Section 2025.420. **Leg.H.** Added Stats 2004 ch 182 §23 (AB 3081), operative July 1, 2005. Amended Stats 2007 ch 113 §6 (AB 1126), effective January 1, 2008.

§2025.280. Effect of service of deposition notice; When deposition subpoena is required; Access to password protected or otherwise inaccessible information

(a) The service of a deposition notice under Section 2025.240 is effective to require any deponent who is a party to the action or an officer, director, managing agent, or employee of a party to attend and to testify, as well as to produce any document, electronically stored information, or tangible thing for inspection and copying.

(b) The attendance and testimony of any other deponent, as well as the production by the deponent of any document, electronically stored information, or tangible thing for inspection and copying, requires the service on the deponent of a deposition subpoena under Chapter 6 (commencing with Section 2020.010).

(c) A deponent required by notice or subpoena to produce electronically stored information shall provide a means of gaining direct access to, or a translation into a reasonably usable form of, any electronically stored information that is password protected or otherwise inaccessible. **Leg.H.** Added Stats 2004 ch 182 §23 (AB 3081), operative July 1, 2005. Amended Stats 2012 ch 72 §21 (SB 1574), effective January 1, 2013; Stats 2016 ch 467 §2 (AB 2427), effective January 1, 2017.

§2025.290. Appropriate time limit for depositions; Additional time; Exclusion; Construction

(a) Except as provided in subdivision (b), or by any court order, including a case management order, a deposition examination of the witness by all counsel, other than the witness' counsel of record, shall be limited to seven hours of total testimony. The court shall allow additional time, beyond any limits imposed by this section, if needed to fairly examine the deponent or if the deponent, another person, or any other circumstance impedes or delays the examination.

(b) This section shall not apply under any of the following circumstances:

(1) If the parties have stipulated that this section will not apply to a specific deposition or to the entire proceeding.

(2) To any deposition of a witness designated as an expert pursuant to Sections 2034.210 to 2034.310, inclusive.

(3) To any case designated as complex by the court pursuant to Rule 3.400 of the California Rules of Court, unless a licensed physician attests in a declaration served on the parties that the deponent suffers from an illness or condition that raises substantial medical doubt of survival of the deponent beyond six months, in which case the deposition examination of the witness by all counsel, other than the witness' counsel of record, shall be limited to two days of no more than seven hours of total testimony each day, or 14 hours of total testimony.

(4) To any case brought by an employee or applicant for employment against an employer for acts or omissions arising out of or relating to the employment relationship.

(5) To any deposition of a person who is designated as the most qualified person to be deposed under Section 2025.230.

(6) To any party who appeared in the action after the deposition has concluded, in which case the new party may notice another deposition subject to the requirements of this section.

(c) It is the intent of the Legislature that any exclusions made by this section shall not be construed to create any presumption or any substantive change to existing law relating to the appropriate time limit for depositions falling within the exclusion. Nothing in this section shall be construed to affect the existing right of any party to move for a protective order or the court's discretion to make any order that justice requires to limit a deposition in order to protect any party, deponent, or other natural person or organization from unwarranted annoyance, embarrassment, oppression, undue burden, or expense. **Leg.H.** Added Stats 2012 ch 346 §1 (AB 1875), effective January 1, 2013.

§2025.295. Deposition examination; Time limitation for testimony; Mesothelioma or silicosis

(a) Notwithstanding Section 2025.290, in any civil action for injury or illness that results in mesothelioma or silicosis, a deposition examination of the plaintiff by all counsel, other than the plaintiff's counsel of record, shall be limited to seven hours of total testimony if a licensed physician attests in a declaration served on the parties that the deponent suffers from mesothelioma or silicosis, raising substantial medical doubt of the survival of the deponent beyond six months.

(b) Notwithstanding the presumptive time limit in subdivision (a), upon request by a defendant, a court may, in its discretion, grant one of the following up to:

(1) An additional three hours of deposition testimony for no more than 10 hours of total deposition conducted by the defendants if there are more than 10 defendants appearing at the deposition.

(2) An additional seven hours of deposition testimony for no more than 14 hours of total deposition conducted by the defendants if there are more than 20 defendants appearing at the deposition.

(c) The court may grant the additional time provided for in paragraphs (1) and (2) of subdivision (b) only if it finds that an extension, in the instant case, is in the interest of fairness, which includes consideration of the number of defendants appearing at the deposition, and determines that the health of the deponent does not appear to be endangered by the grant of additional time. **Leg.H.** Added Stats 2019 ch 212 §1 (SB 645), effective January 1, 2020.

ARTICLE 3
Conduct of Deposition

Deposition via remote means; Who must appear in person; Procedures. §2025.310.
Supervision of deposition by deposition officer; Qualifications and requirements; Objections; Penalty for violations. §2025.320.
Deponents to be under oath; Taking of testimony and objections stenographically; Recording of testimony; Examination and cross-examination; Written questions. §2025.330.
Procedure for audio or video recording of deposition; Notice and objections. §2025.340.

§2025.310. Deposition via remote means; Who must appear in person; Procedures

(a) At the election of the deponent or the deposing party, the deposition officer may attend the deposition at a different location than the deponent via remote means. A deponent is not required to be physically present with the deposition officer when being sworn in at the time of the deposition.

(b) Subject to Section 2025.420, any party or attorney of record may, but is not required to, be physically present at the deposition at the location of the deponent. If a party or attorney of record elects to be physically present at the location of the deponent, all physically present participants in the deposition shall comply with local health and safety ordinances, rules, and orders.

(c) The procedures to implement this section shall be established by court order in the specific action or proceeding or by the California Rules of Court.

(d) An exercise of the authority granted by subdivision (a) or (b) does not waive any other provision of this title, including, but not limited to, provisions regarding the time, place, or manner in which a deposition shall be conducted.

(e) This section does not alter or amend who may lawfully serve as a deposition officer pursuant to this title or who otherwise may administer oaths pursuant to Sections 2093 and 2094 of this code or Section 8201 of the Government Code. **Leg.H.** Added Stats 2004 ch 182 §23 (AB 3081), operative July 1, 2005. Amended Stats 2020 ch 112 §3 (SB 1146), effective September 18, 2020; Stats 2022 ch 92 §1 (SB 1037), effective January 1, 2023.

§2025.320. Supervision of deposition by deposition officer; Qualifications and requirements; Objections; Penalty for violations

Except as provided in Section 2020.420, the deposition shall be conducted under the supervision of an officer who is authorized to administer an oath and is subject to all of the following requirements:

(a) The officer shall not be financially interested in the action and shall not be a relative or employee of any attorney of the parties, or of any of the parties.

(b) Services and products offered or provided by the deposition officer or the entity providing the services of the deposition officer to any party or to any party's attorney or third party who is financing all or part of the action shall be offered to all parties or their attorneys attending the deposition. No service or product may be offered or provided by the deposition officer or by the entity providing the services of the deposition officer to any party or any party's attorney or third party who is financing all or part of the action unless the service or product is offered or provided to all parties or their attorneys attending the deposition. All services and products offered or provided shall be made available at the same time to all parties or their attorneys.

(c) The deposition officer or the entity providing the services of the deposition officer shall not provide to any party or any party's attorney or third party who is financing all or part of the action any service or product consisting of the deposition officer's notations or comments regarding the demeanor of any witness, attorney, or party present at the deposition. The deposition officer or entity providing the services of the deposition officer shall not collect any personal identifying information about the witness as a service or product to be provided to any party or third party who is financing all or part of the action.

(d) Upon the request of any party or any party's attorney attending a deposition, any party or any party's attorney attending the deposition shall enter in the record of the deposition all services and products made available to that party or party's attorney or third party who is financing all or part of the action by the deposition officer or by the entity providing the services of the deposition officer. A party in the action who is not represented by an attorney shall be informed by the noticing party or the party's attorney that the unrepresented party may request this statement.

(e) Any objection to the qualifications of the deposition officer is waived unless made before the deposition begins or as soon thereafter as the ground for that objection becomes known or could be discovered by reasonable diligence.

(f) Violation of this section by any person may result in a civil penalty of up to five thousand dollars ($5,000) imposed by a court of competent jurisdiction. **Leg.H.** Added Stats 2004 ch 182 §23 (AB 3081), operative July 1, 2005.

§2025.330. Deponents to be under oath; Taking of testimony and objections stenographically; Recording of testimony; Examination and cross-examination; Written questions

(a) The deposition officer shall put the deponent under oath or affirmation.

(b) Unless the parties agree or the court orders otherwise, the testimony, as well as any stated objections, shall be taken stenographically. If taken stenographically, it shall be by a person certified pursuant to Article 3 (commencing with Section 8020) of Chapter 13 of Division 3 of the Business and Professions Code.

(c) The party noticing the deposition may also record the testimony by audio or video technology if the notice of deposition stated an intention also to record the testimony by either of those methods, or if all the parties agree that the testimony may also be recorded by either of those methods. Any other party, at that party's expense, may make an audio or video record of the deposition, provided that the other party promptly, and in no event less than three calendar days before the date for which the deposition is scheduled, serves a written notice of this intention to make an audio or video record of the deposition testimony on the party or attorney who noticed the deposition, on all other parties or attorneys on whom the deposition notice was served under Section 2025.240, and on any deponent whose attendance is being compelled by a deposition subpoena under Chapter 6 (commencing with Section 2020.010). If this notice is given three calendar days before the deposition date, it shall be made by personal service under Section 1011.

(d) Examination and cross-examination of the deponent shall proceed as permitted at trial under the provisions of the Evidence Code.

(e) In lieu of participating in the oral examination, parties may transmit written questions in a sealed envelope to the party taking the deposition for delivery to the deposition officer, who shall unseal the envelope and propound them to the deponent after the oral examination has been completed. **Leg.H.** Added Stats 2004 ch 182 §23 (AB 3081), operative July 1, 2005. Amended Stats 2005 ch 294 §8 (AB 333), effective January 1, 2006.

§2025.340. Procedure for audio or video recording of deposition; Notice and objections

If a deposition is being recorded by means of audio or video technology by, or at the direction of, any party, the following procedure shall be observed:

(a) The area used for recording the deponent's oral testimony shall be suitably large, adequately lighted, and reasonably quiet.

(b) The operator of the recording equipment shall be competent to set up, operate, and monitor the equipment in the manner prescribed in this section. Except as provided in subdivision (c), the operator may be an employee of the attorney taking the deposition unless the operator is also the deposition officer.

(c) If a video recording of deposition testimony is to be used under subdivision (d) of Section 2025.620, the operator of the recording equipment shall be a person who is authorized to administer an oath, and shall not be financially interested in the action or be a relative or employee of any attorney of any of the parties, unless all parties attending the deposition agree on the record to waive these qualifications and restrictions.

(d) Services and products offered or provided by the deposition officer or the entity providing the services of the deposition officer to any party or to any party's attorney or third party who is financing all or part of the action shall be offered or provided to all parties or their attorneys attending the deposition. No service or product may be offered or provided by the deposition officer or by the entity providing the services of the deposition officer to any party or any party's attorney or third party who is financing all or part of the action unless the service or product is offered or provided to all parties or their attorneys attending the deposition. All services and products offered or provided shall be made available at the same time to all parties or their attorneys.

(e) The deposition officer or the entity providing the services of the deposition officer shall not provide to any party or any other person or entity any service or product consisting of the deposition officer's notations or comments regarding the demeanor of any witness, attorney, or party present at the deposition. The deposition officer or the entity providing the services of the deposition officer shall not collect any personal identifying information about the witness as a service or product to be provided to any party or third party who is financing all or part of the action.

(f) Upon the request of any party or any party's attorney attending a deposition, any party or any party's attorney attending the deposition shall enter in the record of the deposition all services and products made available to that party or party's attorney or third party who is financing all or part of the action by the deposition officer or by the entity providing the services of the deposition officer. A party in the action who is not represented by an attorney shall be informed by the noticing party that the unrepresented party may request this statement.

(g) The operator shall not distort the appearance or the demeanor of participants in the deposition by the use of camera or sound recording techniques.

(h) The deposition shall begin with an oral or written statement on camera or on the audio recording that includes the operator's name and business address, the name and business address of the operator's employer, the date, time, and place of the deposition, the caption of the case, the name of the deponent, a specification of the party on whose behalf the deposition is being taken, and any stipulations by the parties.

(i) Counsel for the parties shall identify themselves on camera or on the audio recording.

(j) The oath shall be administered to the deponent on camera or on the audio recording.

(k) If the length of a deposition requires the use of more than one unit of tape or electronic storage, the end of each unit and the beginning of each succeeding unit shall be announced on camera or on the audio recording.

(*l*) At the conclusion of a deposition, a statement shall be made on camera or on the audio recording that the deposition is ended and shall set forth any stipulations made by counsel concerning the custody of the audio or video recording and the exhibits, or concerning other pertinent matters.

(m) A party intending to offer an audio or video recording of a deposition in evidence under Section 2025.620 shall notify the court and all parties in writing of that intent and of the parts of the deposition to be offered. That notice shall be given within sufficient time for objections to be made and ruled on by the judge to whom the case is assigned for trial or hearing, and for any editing of the recording. Objections to all or part of the deposition shall be made in writing. The court may permit further designations of testimony and objections as justice may require. With respect to those portions of an audio or video record of deposition testimony that are not designated by any party or that are ruled to be objectionable, the court may order that the party offering the recording of the deposition at the trial or hearing suppress those portions, or that an edited version of the deposition recording be prepared for use at the trial or hearing. The original audio or video record of the deposition shall be preserved unaltered. If no stenographic record of the deposition testimony has previously been made, the party offering an audio or video recording of that testimony under Section 2025.620 shall accompany that offer with a stenographic transcript prepared from that recording. **Leg.H.** Added Stats 2004 ch 182 §23 (AB 3081), operative July 1, 2005.

ARTICLE 4
Objections, Sanctions, Protective Orders, Motions to Compel, and Suspension of Depositions

Service of written objection; Time for serving; Motion for stay; Monetary sanction; Exception. §2025.410.

Motion for protective order; What order may include; Discovery of electronically stored information; Denial of protective order; Monetary sanction. §2025.420.

Imposition of monetary sanction for failure of party giving notice of deposition to attend or proceed; Exception. §2025.430.

Imposition of monetary sanction where deponent does not appear due to failure to be served deposition subpoena; Sanction where deponent who has been served fails to appear or refuses to be sworn in. §2025.440.

Failure to comply with deposition notice; Motion for order compelling compliance; Requirements; Discovery of electronically stored information; Monetary and other sanctions. §2025.450.

Privileged and protected information; Waiver absent objection; Objection to errors and irregularities; Certain matters not waived by failure to object. §2025.460.

Suspension of taking of testimony; Stipulation; Motion for protective order. §2025.470.

Motion for order compelling answer or production; Time for motion; Notice; Discovery of electronically stored information; Certified copy of relevant parts of transcript; Monetary and other sanctions. §2025.480.

§2025.410. Service of written objection; Time for serving; Motion for stay; Monetary sanction; Exception

(a) Any party served with a deposition notice that does not comply with Article 2 (commencing with Section 2025.210) waives any error or irregularity unless that party promptly serves a written objection specifying that error or irregularity at least three calendar days prior to the date for which the deposition is scheduled, on the party seeking to take the deposition and any other attorney or party on whom the deposition notice was served.

(b) If an objection is made three calendar days before the deposition date, the objecting party shall make personal service of that objection pursuant to Section 1011 on the party who gave notice of the deposition. Any deposition taken after the service of a written objection shall not be used against the objecting party under Section 2025.620 if the party did not attend the deposition and if the court determines that the objection was a valid one.

(c) In addition to serving this written objection, a party may also move for an order staying the taking of the deposition and quashing the deposition notice. This motion shall be accompanied by a meet and confer declaration under Section 2016.040. The taking of the deposition is stayed pending the determination of this motion.

(d) The court shall impose a monetary sanction under Chapter 7 (commencing with Section 2023.010) against any party, person, or attorney who unsuccessfully makes or opposes a motion to quash a deposition notice, unless it finds that the one subject to the sanction acted with substantial justification or that other circumstances make the imposition of the sanction unjust.

(e)(1) Notwithstanding subdivision (d), absent exceptional circumstances, the court shall not impose sanctions on any party, person, or attorney for failure to provide electronically stored information that has been lost, damaged, altered, or overwritten as the result of the routine, good faith operation of an electronic information system.

(2) This subdivision shall not be construed to alter any obligation to preserve discoverable information. **Leg.H.** Added Stats 2004 ch 182 §23 (AB 3081), operative July 1, 2005. Amended Stats 2012 ch 72 §22 (SB 1574), effective January 1, 2013.

§2025.420. Motion for protective order; What order may include; Discovery of electronically stored information; Denial of protective order; Monetary sanction

(a) Before, during, or after a deposition, any party, any deponent, or any other affected natural person or organization may promptly move for a protective order. The motion shall be accompanied by a meet and confer declaration under Section 2016.040.

(b) The court, for good cause shown, may make any order that justice requires to protect any party, deponent, or other natural person or organization from unwarranted annoyance, embarrassment, or oppression, or undue burden and expense. This protective order may include, but is not limited to, one or more of the following directions:

(1) That the deposition not be taken at all.

(2) That the deposition be taken at a different time.

(3) That a video recording of the deposition testimony of a treating or consulting physician or of any expert witness, intended for possible use at trial under subdivision (d) of Section 2025.620, be postponed until the moving party has had an adequate opportunity to prepare, by discovery deposition of the deponent, or other means, for cross-examination.

(4) That the deposition be taken at a place other than that specified in the deposition notice, if it is within a distance permitted by Sections 2025.250 and 2025.260.

(5) That the deposition be taken only on certain specified terms and conditions.

(6) That the deponent's testimony be taken by written, instead of oral, examination.

(7) That the method of discovery be interrogatories to a party instead of an oral deposition.

(8) That the testimony be recorded in a manner different from that specified in the deposition notice.

(9) That certain matters not be inquired into.

(10) That the scope of the examination be limited to certain matters.

(11) That all or certain of the writings or tangible things designated in the deposition notice not be produced, inspected, copied, tested, or sampled, or that conditions be set for the production of electronically stored information designated in the deposition notice.

(12) That designated persons, other than the parties to the action and their officers and counsel, be excluded from attending the deposition.

(13) That a trade secret or other confidential research, development, or commercial information not be disclosed or be disclosed only to specified persons or only in a specified way.

(14) That the parties simultaneously file specified documents enclosed in sealed envelopes to be opened as directed by the court.

(15) That the deposition be sealed and thereafter opened only on order of the court.

(16) That examination of the deponent be terminated. If an order terminates the examination, the deposition shall not thereafter be resumed, except on order of the court.

(c) The party, deponent, or any other affected natural person or organization that seeks a protective order regarding the production, inspection, copying, testing, or sampling of electronically stored information on the basis that the information is from a source that is not reasonably accessible because of undue burden or expense shall bear the burden of demonstrating that the information is from a source that is not reasonably accessible because of undue burden or expense.

(d) If the party or affected person from whom discovery of electronically stored information is sought establishes that the information is from a source that is not reasonably accessible because of undue burden or expense, the court may nonetheless order discovery if the demanding party shows good cause, subject to any limitations imposed under subdivision (f).

(e) If the court finds good cause for the production of electronically stored information from a source that is not reasonably accessible, the court may set conditions for the discovery of the electronically stored information, including allocation of the expense of discovery.

(f) The court shall limit the frequency or extent of discovery of electronically stored information, even from a source that is reasonably accessible, if the court determines that any of the following conditions exist:

(1) It is possible to obtain the information from some other source that is more convenient, less burdensome, or less expensive.

(2) The discovery sought is unreasonably cumulative or duplicative.

(3) The party seeking discovery has had ample opportunity by discovery in the action to obtain the information sought.

(4) The likely burden or expense of the proposed discovery outweighs the likely benefit, taking into account the amount in controversy, the resources of the parties, the importance of the issues in the litigation, and the importance of the requested discovery in resolving the issues.

(g) If the motion for a protective order is denied in whole or in part, the court may order that the deponent provide or permit the discovery against which protection was sought on those terms and conditions that are just.

(h) The court shall impose a monetary sanction under Chapter 7 (commencing with Section 2023.010) against any party, person, or attorney who unsuccessfully makes or opposes a motion for a protective order, unless it finds that the one subject to the sanction acted with substantial justification or that other circumstances make the imposition of the sanction unjust.

(i)(1) Notwithstanding subdivision (h), absent exceptional circumstances, the court shall not impose sanctions on any party, deponent, or other affected natural person or organization or any of their attorneys for failure to provide electronically stored information that has been lost, damaged, altered, or overwritten as the result of the routine, good faith operation of an electronic information system.

(2) This subdivision shall not be construed to alter any obligation to preserve discoverable information. **Leg.H.** Added Stats 2004 ch 182 §23 (AB 3081), operative July 1, 2005. Amended Stats 2012 ch 72 §23 (SB 1574), effective January 1, 2013.

§2025.430. Imposition of monetary sanction for failure of party giving notice of deposition to attend or proceed; Exception

If the party giving notice of a deposition fails to attend or proceed with it, the court shall impose a monetary sanction under Chapter 7 (commencing with Section 2023.010) against that party, or the attorney for that party, or both, and in favor of any party attending in person or by attorney, unless it finds that the one subject to the sanction acted with substantial justification or that other circumstances make the imposition of the sanction unjust. **Leg.H.** Added Stats 2004 ch 182 §23 (AB 3081), operative July 1, 2005.

§2025.440. Imposition of monetary sanction where deponent does not appear due to failure to be served deposition subpoena; Sanction where deponent who has been served fails to appear or refuses to be sworn in

(a) If a deponent does not appear for a deposition because the party giving notice of the deposition failed to serve a required deposition subpoena, the court shall impose a monetary sanction under Chapter 7 (commencing with Section 2023.010) against that party, or the attorney for that party, or both, in favor of any other party who, in person or by attorney, attended at the time and place specified in the deposition notice in the expectation that the deponent's testimony would be taken, unless the court finds that the one subject to the sanction acted with substantial justification or that other circumstances make the imposition of the sanction unjust.

(b) If a deponent on whom a deposition subpoena has been served fails to attend a deposition or refuses to be sworn as a witness, the court may impose on the deponent the sanctions described in Section 2020.240. **Leg.H.** Added Stats 2004 ch 182 §23 (AB 3081), operative July 1, 2005.

§2025.450. Failure to comply with deposition notice; Motion for order compelling compliance; Requirements; Discovery of electronically stored information; Monetary and other sanctions

(a) If, after service of a deposition notice, a party to the action or an officer, director, managing agent, or employee of a party, or a person designated by an organization that is a party under Section 2025.230, without having served a valid objection under Section 2025.410, fails to appear for examination, or to proceed with it, or to produce for inspection any document, electronically stored information, or tangible thing described in the deposition notice, the party giving the notice may move for an order compelling the deponent's attendance and testimony, and the production for inspection of any document, electronically stored information, or tangible thing described in the deposition notice.

(b) A motion under subdivision (a) shall comply with both of the following:

(1) The motion shall set forth specific facts showing good cause justifying the production for inspection of any document, electronically stored information, or tangible thing described in the deposition notice.

(2) The motion shall be accompanied by a meet and confer declaration under Section 2016.040, or, when the deponent fails to attend the deposition and produce the documents, electronically stored information, or things described in the deposition notice, by a declaration stating that the petitioner has contacted the deponent to inquire about the nonappearance.

(c) In a motion under subdivision (a) relating to the production of electronically stored information, the party or party-affiliated deponent objecting to or opposing the production, inspection, copying, testing, or sampling of electronically stored information on the basis that the information is from a source that is not reasonably accessible because of the undue burden or expense shall bear the burden of demonstrating that the information is from a source that is not reasonably accessible because of undue burden or expense.

(d) If the party or party-affiliated deponent from whom discovery of electronically stored information is sought establishes that the information is from a source that is not reasonably accessible because of the undue burden or expense, the court may nonetheless order discovery if the demanding party shows good cause, subject to any limitations imposed under subdivision (f).

(e) If the court finds good cause for the production of electronically stored information from a source that is not reasonably accessible, the court may set conditions for the discovery of the electronically stored information, including allocation of the expense of discovery.

(f) The court shall limit the frequency or extent of discovery of electronically stored information, even from a source that is reasonably accessible, if the court determines that any of the following conditions exists:

(1) It is possible to obtain the information from some other source that is more convenient, less burdensome, or less expensive.

(2) The discovery sought is unreasonably cumulative or duplicative.

(3) The party seeking discovery has had ample opportunity by discovery in the action to obtain the information sought.

(4) The likely burden or expense of the proposed discovery outweighs the likely benefit, taking into account the amount in controversy, the resources of the parties, the importance of the issues in the litigation, and the importance of the requested discovery in resolving the issues.

(g)(1) If a motion under subdivision (a) is granted, the court shall impose a monetary sanction under Chapter 7 (commencing with Section 2023.010) in favor of the party who noticed the deposition and against the deponent or the party with whom the deponent is affiliated, unless the court finds that the one subject to the sanction acted with substantial justification or that other circumstances make the imposition of the sanction unjust.

(2) On motion of any other party who, in person or by attorney, attended at the time and place specified in the deposition notice in the expectation that the deponent's testimony would be taken, the court shall impose a monetary sanction under Chapter 7 (commencing with Section 2023.010) in favor of that party and against the deponent or the party with whom the deponent is affiliated, unless the court finds that the one subject to the sanction acted with substantial justification or that other circumstances make the imposition of the sanction unjust.

(h) If that party or party-affiliated deponent then fails to obey an order compelling attendance, testimony, and production, the court may make those orders that are just, including the imposition of an issue sanction, an evidence sanction, or a terminating sanction under Chapter 7 (commencing with Section 2023.010) against that party deponent or against the party with whom the deponent is affiliated. In lieu of, or in addition to, this sanction, the court may impose a monetary sanction under Chapter 7 (commencing with Section 2023.010) against that deponent or against the party with whom that party deponent is affiliated, and in favor of any party who, in person or by attorney, attended in the expectation that the deponent's testimony would be taken pursuant to that order.

(i)(1) Notwithstanding subdivisions (g) and (h), absent exceptional circumstances, the court shall not impose sanctions on a party or any attorney of a party for failure to provide electronically stored information that has been lost, damaged, altered, or overwritten as the result of the routine, good faith operation of an electronic information system.

(2) This subdivision shall not be construed to alter any obligation to preserve discoverable information. **Leg.H.** Added Stats 2004 ch 182 §23 (AB 3081), operative July 1, 2005. Amended Stats 2012 ch 72 §24 (SB 1574), effective January 1, 2013.

§2025.460. Privileged and protected information; Waiver absent objection; Objection to errors and irregularities; Certain matters not waived by failure to object

(a) The protection of information from discovery on the ground that it is privileged or that it is a protected work product under Chapter 4 (commencing with Section 2018.010) is waived unless a specific objection to its disclosure is timely made during the deposition.

(b) Errors and irregularities of any kind occurring at the oral examination that might be cured if promptly presented are waived unless a specific objection to them is timely made during the deposition. These errors and irregularities include, but are not limited to, those relating to the manner of taking the deposition, to the oath or affirmation administered, to the conduct of a party, attorney, deponent, or deposition officer, or to the form of any question or answer. Unless the objecting party demands that the taking of the deposition be suspended to permit a motion for a protective order under Sections 2025.420 and 2025.470, the deposition shall proceed subject to the objection.

(c) Objections to the competency of the deponent, or to the relevancy, materiality, or admissibility at trial of the testimony or of the materials produced are unnecessary and are not waived by failure to make them before or during the deposition.

(d) If a deponent objects to the production of electronically stored information on the grounds that it is from a source that is not reasonably accessible because of undue burden or expense and that the deponent will not search the source in the absence of an agreement with the deposing party or court order, the deponent shall identify in its objection the types or categories of sources of electronically stored information that it asserts are not reasonably accessible. By objecting and identifying information of a type or category of source or sources that are not reasonably accessible, the deponent preserves any objections it may have relating to that electronically stored information.

(e) If a deponent fails to answer any question or to produce any document, electronically stored information, or tangible thing under the deponent's control that is specified in the deposition notice or a deposition subpoena, the party seeking that answer or production may adjourn the deposition or complete the examination on other matters without waiving the right at a later time to move for an order compelling that answer or production under Section 2025.480.

(f) Notwithstanding subdivision (a), if a deponent notifies the party that took a deposition that electronically stored information produced pursuant to the deposition notice or subpoena is subject to a claim of privilege or of protection as attorney work product, as described in Section 2031.285, the provisions of Section 2031.285 shall apply. **Leg.H.** Added Stats 2004 ch 182 §23 (AB 3081), operative July 1, 2005. Amended Stats 2012 ch 72 §25 (SB 1574), effective January 1, 2013.

§2025.470. Suspension of taking of testimony; Stipulation; Motion for protective order

The deposition officer may not suspend the taking of testimony without the stipulation of all parties present unless any party attending the deposition, including the deponent, demands that the deposition officer suspend taking the testimony to enable that party or deponent to move for a protective order under Section 2025.420 on the ground that the examination is being conducted in bad faith or in a manner that unreasonably annoys, embarrasses, or oppresses that deponent or party. **Leg.H.** Added Stats 2004 ch 182 §23 (AB 3081), operative July 1, 2005.

§2025.480. Motion for order compelling answer or production; Time for motion; Notice; Discovery of electronically stored information; Certified copy of relevant parts of transcript; Monetary and other sanctions

(a) If a deponent fails to answer any question or to produce any document, electronically stored information, or tangible thing under the deponent's control that is specified in the deposition notice or a deposition subpoena, the party seeking discovery may move the court for an order compelling that answer or production.

(b) This motion shall be made no later than 60 days after the completion of the record of the deposition, and shall be accompanied by a meet and confer declaration under Section 2016.040.

(c) Notice of this motion shall be given to all parties and to the deponent either orally at the examination, or by subsequent service in writing. If the notice of the motion is given orally, the deposition officer shall direct the deponent to attend a session of the court at the time specified in the notice.

(d) In a motion under subdivision (a) relating to the production of electronically stored information, the deponent objecting to or opposing the production, inspection, copying, testing, or sampling of electronically stored information on the basis that the information is from a source that is not reasonably accessible because of the undue burden or expense shall bear the burden of demonstrating that the information is from a source that is not reasonably accessible because of undue burden or expense.

(e) If the deponent from whom discovery of electronically stored information is sought establishes that the information is from a source that is not reasonably accessible because of the undue burden or expense, the court may nonetheless order discovery if the deposing party shows good cause, subject to any limitations imposed under subdivision (g).

(f) If the court finds good cause for the production of electronically stored information from a source that is not reasonably accessible, the court may set conditions for the discovery of the electronically stored information, including allocation of the expense of discovery.

(g) The court shall limit the frequency or extent of discovery of electronically stored information, even from a source that is reasonably accessible, if the court determines that any of the following conditions exists:

(1) It is possible to obtain the information from some other source that is more convenient, less burdensome, or less expensive.

(2) The discovery sought is unreasonably cumulative or duplicative.

(3) The party seeking discovery has had ample opportunity by discovery in the action to obtain the information sought.

(4) The likely burden or expense of the proposed discovery outweighs the likely benefit, taking into account the amount in controversy, the resources of the parties, the importance of the issues in the litigation, and the importance of the requested discovery in resolving the issues.

(h) Not less than five days prior to the hearing on this motion, the moving party shall lodge with the court a certified copy of any parts of the stenographic transcript of the deposition that are relevant to the motion. If a deposition is recorded by audio or video technology, the moving party is required to lodge a certified copy of a transcript of any parts of the deposition that are relevant to the motion.

(i) If the court determines that the answer or production sought is subject to discovery, it shall order that the answer be given or the production be made on the resumption of the deposition.

(j) The court shall impose a monetary sanction under Chapter 7 (commencing with Section 2023.010) against any party, person, or attorney who unsuccessfully makes or opposes a motion to compel an answer or production, unless it finds that the one subject to the sanction acted with substantial justification or that other circumstances make the imposition of the sanction unjust.

(k) If a deponent fails to obey an order entered under this section, the failure may be considered a contempt of court. In addition, if the disobedient deponent is a party to the action or an officer, director, managing agent, or employee of a party, the court may make those orders that are just against the disobedient party, or against the party with whom the disobedient deponent is affiliated, including the imposition of an issue sanction, an evidence sanction, or a terminating sanction under Chapter 7 (commencing with Section 2023.010). In lieu of or in addition to this sanction, the court may impose a monetary sanction under Chapter 7 (commencing with Section 2023.010) against that party deponent or against any party with whom the deponent is affiliated.

(*l*)(1) Notwithstanding subdivisions (j) and (k), absent exceptional circumstances, the court shall not impose sanctions on a deponent or any attorney of a deponent for failure to provide electronically stored information that has been lost, damaged, altered, or overwritten as the result of the routine, good faith operation of an electronic information system.

(2) This subdivision shall not be construed to alter any obligation to preserve discoverable information. **Leg.H.** Added Stats 2004 ch 182 §23 (AB 3081), operative July 1, 2005. Amended Stats 2005 ch 22 §21 (SB 1108), effective January 1, 2006, ch 294 §21 (AB 333), effective January 1, 2006; Stats 2012 ch 72 §26 (SB 1574), effective January 1, 2013.

ARTICLE 5
Transcript or Recording

Transcription of testimony; Costs; Who may obtain copies and when; Retention of stenographic notes; Access to recorded testimony; Stenographic testimony as official record. §2025.510.

Written notice when original transcript becomes available for reading, correcting and signing; Exception; Time period for deponent to change answers and approve or refuse to approve transcript; Motion to suppress transcript; Monetary sanction. §2025.520.

Written notice when audio or video recording becomes available for review; Exception; Time period for deponent to change answers; Identification of deposition as deponent's own or failure to do so; Motion to suppress deposition; Monetary sanction. §2025.530.

Certification by deposition officer; Use of rough draft transcript not permitted. §2025.540.

Transmittal of transcript to attorney; Time period for retention. §2025.550.

Retention of audio or video recording of deposition testimony by operator; Access of parties to hearing or viewing or copy of recording; Cost; Timeframe for retention. §2025.560.

Furnishing of copies of transcript or recording by deposition officer; Charge; Notice to parties of right to seek protective order; Applicability of section. §2025.570.

§2025.5. [Section repealed 2005]

Leg.H. Added Stats 1997 ch 395 §2 (SB 544). Amended Stats 2000 ch 474 §2 (SB 877); Stats 2002 ch 1068 §3 (AB 2842). Repealed Stats 2004 ch 182 §22 (AB 3081), operative July 1, 2005. The repealed section related to copies of depositions. See CCP §2025.570.

§2025½. [Section repealed 1958]

Leg.H. Added Stats 1903 ch 255 §1. Repealed Stats 1957 ch 1904 §1, operative January 1, 1958. The repealed section related to deposition of nonresident witness.

§2025.510. Transcription of testimony; Costs; Who may obtain copies and when; Retention of stenographic notes; Access to recorded testimony; Stenographic testimony as official record

(a) Unless the parties agree otherwise, the testimony at a deposition recorded by stenographic means shall be transcribed.

(b) The party noticing the deposition shall bear the cost of the transcription, unless the court, on motion and for good cause shown, orders that the cost be borne or shared by another party.

(c) Notwithstanding subdivision (b) of Section 2025.320, any other party or the deponent, at the expense of that party or deponent, may obtain a copy of the transcript.

(d) If the deposition officer receives a request from a party for an original or a copy of the deposition transcript, or any portion thereof, and the full or partial transcript will be available to that party prior to the time the original or copy would be available to any other party, the deposition officer shall immediately notify all other parties attending the deposition of the request, and shall, upon request by any party other than the party making the original request, make that copy of the full or partial deposition transcript available to all parties at the same time.

(e) Stenographic notes of depositions shall be retained by the reporter for a period of not less than eight years from the date of the deposition, where no transcript is produced, and not less than one year from the date on which the transcript is produced. The notes may be either on paper or electronic media, as long as it allows for satisfactory production of a transcript at any time during the periods specified.

(f) At the request of any other party to the action, including a party who did not attend the taking of the deposition testimony, any party who records or causes the recording of that testimony by means of audio or video technology shall promptly do both of the following:

(1) Permit that other party to hear the audio recording or to view the video recording.

(2) Furnish a copy of the audio or video recording to that other party on receipt of payment of the reasonable cost of making that copy of the recording.

(g) If the testimony at the deposition is recorded both stenographically and by audio or video technology, the stenographic transcript shall be the official record of that testimony for the purpose of the trial and any subsequent hearing or appeal.

(h)(1) The requesting attorney or party appearing in propria persona shall timely pay the deposition officer or the entity providing the services of the deposition officer for the transcription or copy of the transcription described in subdivision (b) or (c), and any other deposition product or service that is requested either orally or in writing.

(2) This subdivision shall apply unless responsibility for the payment is otherwise provided by law or unless the deposition officer or entity is notified in writing at the time the services or products are requested that the party or another identified person will be responsible for payment.

(3) This subdivision does not prohibit or supersede an agreement between an attorney and a party allocating responsibility for the payment of deposition costs to the party.

(4) Nothing in the case of Serrano v. Stefan Merli Plastering Co., Inc. (2008) 162 Cal.App.4th 1014 shall be construed to alter the standards by which a court acquires personal jurisdiction over a nonparty to an action.

(5) The requesting attorney or party appearing in propria persona, upon the written request of a deposition officer who has obtained a final judgment for payment of services provided pursuant to this subdivision, shall provide to the deposition officer an address that can be used to effectuate service for the purpose of Section 708.110 in the manner specified in Section 415.10.

(i) For purposes of this section, "deposition product or service" means any product or service provided in connection with a deposition that qualifies as shorthand reporting, as described in Section 8017 of the Business and Professions Code, and any product or service derived from that shorthand reporting. **Leg.H.** Added Stats 2004 ch 182 §23 (AB 3081), operative July 1, 2005. Amended Stats 2007 ch 115 §1 (AB 1211), effective January 1, 2008; Stats 2012 ch 125 §1 (AB 2372), effective January 1, 2013; Stats 2014 ch 913 §12 (AB 2747), effective January 1, 2015.

§2025.520. Written notice when original transcript becomes available for reading, correcting and signing; Exception; Time period for deponent to change answers and approve or refuse to approve transcript; Motion to suppress transcript; Monetary sanction

(a) If the deposition testimony is stenographically recorded, the deposition officer shall send written notice to the deponent and to all parties attending the deposition when the original transcript of the testimony for each session of the deposition is available for reading, correcting, and signing, unless the deponent and the attending parties agree on the record that the reading, correcting, and signing of the transcript of the testimony will be waived or that the reading, correcting, and signing of a transcript of the testimony will take place after the entire deposition has been concluded or at some other specific time.

(b) For 30 days following each notice under subdivision (a), unless the attending parties and the deponent agree on the record or otherwise in writing to a longer or shorter time period, the deponent may change the form or the substance of the answer to a question, and may either approve the transcript of the deposition by signing it, or refuse to approve the transcript by not signing it.

(c) Alternatively, within this same period, the deponent may change the form or the substance of the answer to any question and may approve or refuse to approve the transcript by means of a letter to the deposition officer signed by the deponent which is mailed by certified or registered mail with return receipt requested. A copy of that letter shall be sent by first-class mail to all parties attending the deposition.

(d) For good cause shown, the court may shorten the 30-day period for making changes, approving, or refusing to approve the transcript.

(e) The deposition officer shall indicate on the original of the transcript, if the deponent has not already done so at the office of the deposition officer, any action taken by the deponent and indicate on the original of the transcript, the deponent's approval of, or failure or refusal to approve, the transcript. The deposition officer shall also notify in writing the parties attending the deposition of any changes which the deponent timely made in person.

(f) If the deponent fails or refuses to approve the transcript within the allotted period, the deposition shall be given the same effect as though it had been approved, subject to any changes timely made by the deponent.

(g) Notwithstanding subdivision (f), on a seasonable motion to suppress the deposition, accompanied by a meet and confer declaration under Section 2016.040, the court may determine that the reasons given for the failure or refusal to approve the transcript require rejection of the deposition in whole or in part.

(h) The court shall impose a monetary sanction under Chapter 7 (commencing with Section 2023.010) against any party, person, or attorney who unsuccessfully makes or opposes a motion to suppress a deposition under this section, unless the court finds that the one subject to the sanction acted with substantial justification or that other circumstances make the imposition of the sanction unjust. **Leg.H.** Added Stats 2004 ch 182 §23 (AB 3081), operative July 1, 2005.

§2025.530. Written notice when audio or video recording becomes available for review; Exception; Time period for deponent to change answers; Identification of deposition as deponent's own or failure to do so; Motion to suppress deposition; Monetary sanction

(a) If there is no stenographic transcription of the deposition, the deposition officer shall send written notice to the deponent and to all parties attending the deposition that the audio or video recording made by, or at the direction of, any party, is available for review, unless the deponent and all these parties agree on the record to waive the hearing or viewing of the audio or video recording of the testimony.

(b) For 30 days following a notice under subdivision (a), the deponent, either in person or by signed letter to the deposition officer, may change the substance of the answer to any question.

(c) The deposition officer shall set forth in a writing to accompany the recording any changes made by the deponent, as well as either the deponent's signature identifying the deposition as the deponent's own, or a statement of the deponent's failure to supply the signature, or to contact the officer within the period prescribed by subdivision (b).

(d) When a deponent fails to contact the officer within the period prescribed by subdivision (b), or expressly refuses by a signature to identify the deposition as the deponent's own, the deposition shall be given the same effect as though signed.

(e) Notwithstanding subdivision (d), on a reasonable motion to suppress the deposition, accompanied by a meet and confer declaration under Section 2016.040, the court may determine that the reasons given for the refusal to sign require rejection of the deposition in whole or in part.

(f) The court shall impose a monetary sanction under Chapter 7 (commencing with Section 2023.010) against any party, person, or attorney who unsuccessfully makes or opposes a motion to suppress a deposition under this section, unless it finds that the one subject to the sanction acted with substantial justification or that other circumstances make the imposition of the sanction unjust. **Leg.H.** Added Stats 2004 ch 182 §23 (AB 3081), operative July 1, 2005.

§2025.540. Certification by deposition officer; Use of rough draft transcript not permitted

(a) The deposition officer shall certify on the transcript of the deposition, or in a writing accompanying an audio or video record of deposition testimony, as described in Section 2025.530, that the deponent was duly sworn and that the transcript or recording is a true record of the testimony given.

(b) When prepared as a rough draft transcript, the transcript of the deposition may not be certified and may not be used, cited, or transcribed as the certified transcript of the deposition proceedings. The rough draft transcript may not be cited or used in any way or at any time to rebut or contradict the certified transcript of deposition proceedings as provided by the deposition officer. **Leg.H.** Added Stats 2004 ch 182 §23 (AB 3081), operative July 1, 2005.

§2025.550. Transmittal of transcript to attorney; Time period for retention

(a) The certified transcript of a deposition shall not be filed with the court. Instead, the deposition officer shall securely seal that transcript in an envelope or package endorsed with the title of the action and marked: "Deposition of (here insert name of deponent)," and shall promptly transmit it to the attorney for the party who noticed the deposition. This attorney shall store it under conditions that will protect it against loss, destruction, or tampering.

(b) The attorney to whom the transcript of a deposition is transmitted shall retain custody of it until six months after final disposition of the action. At that time, the transcript may be destroyed, unless the court, on motion of any party and for good cause shown, orders that the transcript be preserved for a longer period. **Leg.H.** Added Stats 2004 ch 182 §23 (AB 3081), operative July 1, 2005.

§2025.560. Retention of audio or video recording of deposition testimony by operator; Access of parties to hearing or viewing or copy of recording; Cost; Timeframe for retention

(a) An audio or video recording of deposition testimony made by, or at the direction of, any party, including a certified recording made by an operator qualified under subdivisions (b) to (f), inclusive, of Section 2025.340, shall not be filed with the court. Instead, the operator shall retain custody of that recording and shall store it under conditions that will protect it against loss, destruction, or tampering, and preserve as far as practicable the quality of the recording and the integrity of the testimony and images it contains.

(b) At the request of any party to the action, including a party who did not attend the taking of the deposition testimony, or at the request of the deponent, that operator shall promptly do both of the following:

(1) Permit the one making the request to hear or to view the recording on receipt of payment of a reasonable charge for providing the facilities for hearing or viewing the recording.

(2) Furnish a copy of the audio or video recording to the one making the request on receipt of payment of the reasonable cost of making that copy of the recording.

(c) The attorney or operator who has custody of an audio or video recording of deposition testimony made by, or at the direction of, any party, shall retain custody of it until six months after final disposition of the action. At that time, the audio or video recording may be destroyed or erased, unless the court, on motion of any party and for good cause shown, orders that the recording be preserved for a longer period. **Leg.H.** Added Stats 2004 ch 182 §23 (AB 3081), operative July 1, 2005. Amended Stats 2009 ch 88 §18 (AB 176), effective January 1, 2010.

§2025.570. Furnishing of copies of transcript or recording by deposition officer; Charge; Notice to parties of right to seek protective order; Applicability of section

(a) Notwithstanding subdivision (b) of Section 2025.320, unless the court issues an order to the contrary, a copy of the transcript of the deposition testimony made by, or at the direction of, any party, or an audio or video recording of the deposition testimony, if still in the possession of the deposition officer, shall be made available by the deposition officer to any person requesting a copy, on payment of a reasonable charge set by the deposition officer.

(b) If a copy is requested from the deposition officer, the deposition officer shall mail a notice to all parties attending the deposition and to the deponent at the deponent's last known address advising them of all of the following:

(1) The copy is being sought.

(2) The name of the person requesting the copy.

(3) The right to seek a protective order under Section 2025.420.

(c) If a protective order is not served on the deposition officer within 30 days of the mailing of the notice, the deposition officer shall make the copy available to the person requesting the copy.

(d) This section shall apply only to recorded testimony taken at depositions occurring on or after January 1, 1998. **Leg.H.** Added Stats 2004 ch 182 §23 (AB 3081), operative July 1, 2005.

ARTICLE 6
Post-Deposition Procedures

Subsequent depositions; When permitted. §2025.610.
Use of deposition as evidence; Requirements. §2025.620.

§2025.610. Subsequent depositions; When permitted

(a) Once any party has taken the deposition of any natural person, including that of a party to the action, neither the party who gave, nor any other party who has been served with a deposition notice pursuant to Section 2025.240 may take a subsequent deposition of that deponent.

(b) Notwithstanding subdivision (a), for good cause shown, the court may grant leave to take a subsequent deposition, and the parties, with the consent of any deponent who is not a party, may stipulate that a subsequent deposition be taken.

(c) This section does not preclude taking one subsequent deposition of a natural person who has previously been examined under either or both of the following circumstances:

(1) The person was examined as a result of that person's designation to testify on behalf of an organization under Section 2025.230.

(2) The person was examined pursuant to a court order under Section 485.230, for the limited purpose of discovering pursuant to Section 485.230 the identity, location, and value of property in which the deponent has an interest.

(d) This section does not authorize the taking of more than one subsequent deposition for the limited purpose of Section 485.230. **Leg.H.** Added Stats 2004 ch 182 §23 (AB 3081), operative July 1, 2005.

§2025.620. Use of deposition as evidence; Requirements

At the trial or any other hearing in the action, any part or all of a deposition may be used against any party who was present or represented at the taking of the deposition, or who had due notice of the deposition and did not serve a valid objection under Section 2025.410, so far as admissible under the rules of evidence applied as though the deponent were then present and testifying as a witness, in accordance with the following provisions:

(a) Any party may use a deposition for the purpose of contradicting or impeaching the testimony of the deponent as a witness, or for any other purpose permitted by the Evidence Code.

(b) An adverse party may use for any purpose, a deposition of a party to the action, or of anyone who at the time of taking the deposition was an officer, director, managing agent, employee, agent, or designee under Section 2025.230 of a party. It is not ground for objection to the use of a deposition of a party under this subdivision by an adverse party that the deponent is available to testify, has testified, or will testify at the trial or other hearing.

(c) Any party may use for any purpose the deposition of any person or organization, including that of any party to the action, if the court finds any of the following:

(1) The deponent resides more than 150 miles from the place of the trial or other hearing.

(2) The deponent, without the procurement or wrongdoing of the proponent of the deposition for the purpose of preventing testimony in open court, is any of the following:

(A) Exempted or precluded on the ground of privilege from testifying concerning the matter to which the deponent's testimony is relevant.

(B) Disqualified from testifying.

(C) Dead or unable to attend or testify because of existing physical or mental illness or infirmity.

(D) Absent from the trial or other hearing and the court is unable to compel the deponent's attendance by its process.

(E) Absent from the trial or other hearing and the proponent of the deposition has exercised reasonable diligence but has been unable to procure the deponent's attendance by the court's process.

(3) Exceptional circumstances exist that make it desirable to allow the use of any deposition in the interests of justice and with due regard to the importance of presenting the testimony of witnesses orally in open court.

(d) Any party may use a video recording of the deposition testimony of a treating or consulting physician or of any expert witness even though the deponent is available to testify if the deposition notice under Section 2025.220 reserved the right to use the deposition at trial, and if that party has complied with subdivision (m) of Section 2025.340.

(e) Subject to the requirements of this chapter, a party may offer in evidence all or any part of a deposition, and if the party introduces only part of the deposition, any other party may introduce any other parts that are relevant to the parts introduced.

(f) Substitution of parties does not affect the right to use depositions previously taken.

(g) When an action has been brought in any court of the United States or of any state, and another action involving the same subject matter is subsequently brought between the same parties or their representatives or successors in interest, all depositions lawfully taken and duly filed in the initial action may be used in the subsequent action as if originally taken in that subsequent action. A deposition previously taken may also be used as permitted by the Evidence Code. **Leg.H.** Added Stats 2004 ch 182 §23 (AB 3081), operative July 1, 2005.

CHAPTER 10
ORAL DEPOSITION OUTSIDE CALIFORNIA

Taking of oral deposition in another state or in a territory or insular possession; Procedures and process; Issuance of commission. §2026.010.

Taking of oral deposition in foreign nation; Procedures and process; Issuance of commission. §2027.010.

§2026. [Section repealed 2005]

Leg.H. Added Stats 1986 ch 1334 §2, operative July 1, 1987. Amended Stats 1987 ch 86 §9, operative July 1, 1987; Stats 2000 ch 474 §3 (SB 877); Stats 2001 ch 812 §10 (AB 223). Repealed Stats 2004 ch 182 §22 (AB 3081), operative July 1, 2005. The repealed section related to oral depositions in another state. See CCP §2026.010.

Prior Law: Former CCP §2026 was added Stats 1957 ch 1904 §3, operative January 1, 1958, amended Stats 1959 ch 1590 §8, and repealed Stats 1961 ch 192 §8.

Former CCP §2026, relating to authority of commissioner, was enacted 1872, amended Stats 1907 ch 392 §6, and repealed Stats 1957 ch 1904 §1, operative January 1, 1958.

§2026.010. Taking of oral deposition in another state or in a territory or insular possession; Procedures and process; Issuance of commission

(a) Any party may obtain discovery by taking an oral deposition, as described in Section 2025.010, in another state of the United States, or in a territory or an insular possession subject to its jurisdiction. Except as modified in this section, the procedures for taking oral depositions in California set forth in Chapter 9 (commencing with Section 2025.010) apply to an oral deposition taken in another state of the United States, or in a territory or an insular possession subject to its jurisdiction.

(b) If a deponent is a party to the action or an officer, director, managing agent, or employee of a party, the service of the deposition notice is effective to compel that deponent to attend and to testify, as well as to produce any document, electronically stored information, or tangible thing for inspection, copying, testing, or sampling. The deposition notice shall specify a place in the state, territory, or insular possession of the United States that is within 75 miles of the residence or a business office of a deponent.

(c) If the deponent is not a party to the action or an officer, director, managing agent, or employee of a party, a party serving a deposition notice under this section shall use any process and procedures required and available under the laws of the state, territory, or insular possession where the deposition is to be taken to compel the deponent to attend and to testify, as well as to produce any document, electronically stored information, or tangible thing for inspection, copying, testing, sampling, and any related activity.

(d) A deposition taken under this section shall be conducted in either of the following ways:

(1) Under the supervision of a person who is authorized to administer oaths by the laws of the United States or those of the place where the examination is to be held, and who is not otherwise disqualified under Section 2025.320 and subdivisions (b) to (f), inclusive, of Section 2025.340.

(2) Before a person appointed by the court.

(e) An appointment under subdivision (d) is effective to authorize that person to administer oaths and to take testimony.

(f) On request, the clerk of the court shall issue a commission authorizing the deposition in another state or place. The commission shall request that process issue in the place where the examination is to be held, requiring attendance and enforcing the obligations of the deponents to produce documents and electronically stored information and answer questions. The commission shall be issued by the clerk to any party in any action pending in its venue without a noticed motion or court order. The commission may contain terms that are required by the foreign jurisdiction to initiate the process. If a court order is required by the foreign jurisdiction, an order for a commission may be obtained by ex parte application. **Leg.H.** Added Stats 2004 ch 182 §23 (AB 3081), operative July 1, 2005. Amended Stats 2012 ch 72 §27 (SB 1574), effective January 1, 2013.

§2027. [Section repealed 2005]

Leg.H. Added Stats 1986 ch 1334 §2, operative July 1, 1987. Amended Stats 1987 ch 86 §10, operative July 1, 1987; Stats 2000 ch 474 §4 (SB 877). Repealed Stats 2004 ch 182 §22 (AB 3081), operative July 1, 2005. The repealed section related to oral deposition in another nation. See CCP §2027.010.

Prior Law: Former CCP §2027 was added Stats 1957 ch 1904 §3, operative January 1, 1958, and repealed Stats 1961 ch 192 §9.

Former CCP §2027, relating to postponement of proceedings by reason of nonreturn of commission, was enacted 1872 and repealed Stats 1957 ch 1904 §1, operative January 1, 1958.

§2027.010. Taking of oral deposition in foreign nation; Procedures and process; Issuance of commission

(a) Any party may obtain discovery by taking an oral deposition, as described in Section 2025.010, in a foreign nation. Except as modified in this section, the procedures for taking oral depositions in California set forth in Chapter 9 (commencing with Section 2025.010) apply to an oral deposition taken in a foreign nation.

(b) If a deponent is a party to the action or an officer, director, managing agent, or employee of a party, the service of the deposition notice is effective to compel the deponent to attend and to testify, as well as to produce any document, electronically stored information, or tangible thing for inspection, copying, testing, or sampling.

(c) If a deponent is not a party to the action or an officer, director, managing agent or employee of a party, a party serving a deposition notice under this section shall use any process and procedures required and available under the laws of the foreign nation where the deposition is to be taken to compel the deponent to attend and to testify, as well as to produce any document, electronically stored information, or tangible thing for inspection, copying, testing, sampling, and any related activity.

(d) A deposition taken under this section shall be conducted under the supervision of any of the following:

(1) A person who is authorized to administer oaths or their equivalent by the laws of the United States or of the foreign nation, and who is not otherwise disqualified under Section 2025.320 and subdivisions (b) to (f), inclusive, of Section 2025.340.

(2) A person or officer appointed by commission or under letters rogatory.

(3) Any person agreed to by all the parties.

(e) On motion of the party seeking to take an oral deposition in a foreign nation, the court in which the action is pending shall issue a commission, letters rogatory, or a letter of request, if it determines that one is necessary or convenient. The commission, letters rogatory, or letter of request may include any terms and directions that are just and appropriate. The deposition officer may be designated by name or by descriptive title in the deposition notice and in the commission. Letters rogatory or a letter of request may be addressed: "To the Appropriate Judicial Authority in [name of foreign nation]." **Leg.H.** Added Stats 2004 ch 182 §23 (AB 3081), operative July 1, 2005. Amended Stats 2012 ch 72 §28 (SB 1574), effective January 1, 2013.

CHAPTER 11
DEPOSITION BY WRITTEN QUESTIONS

Taking of deposition by written questions. §2028.010.

Notice of written deposition. §2028.020.
Questions to accompany notice; Time for service of cross questions and redirect questions. §2028.030.
Objection to form of question; Motion; Monetary sanction. §2028.040.
Objection to question on grounds of privilege or protection as work product; Motion to overrule; Monetary sanction. §2028.050.
What questions may be forwarded to deponent prior to deposition. §2028.060.
Orders which court may issue. §2028.070.
Delivery of deposition notice and questions to deposition officer and taking of testimony. §2028.080.

§2028. [Section repealed 2005]

Leg.H. Added Stats 1986 ch 1334 §2, operative July 1, 1987. Amended Stats 1987 ch 86 §11, operative July 1, 1987. Repealed Stats 2004 ch 182 §22 (AB 3081), operative July 1, 2005. The repealed section related to deposition by written questions rather than by oral examination. See CCP §§2028.010 et seq.

Prior Law: Former CCP §2028 was added Stats 1957 ch 1904 §3, operative January 1, 1958, and repealed Stats 1961 ch 192 §10.

Former CCP §2028, relating to use of depositions, was enacted 1872 and repealed Stats 1957 ch 1904 §1, operative January 1, 1958.

§2028.010. Taking of deposition by written questions

Any party may obtain discovery by taking a deposition by written questions instead of by oral examination. Except as modified in this chapter, the procedures for taking oral depositions set forth in Chapters 9 (commencing with Section 2025.010) and 10 (commencing with Section 2026.010) apply to written depositions. **Leg.H.** Added Stats 2004 ch 182 §23 (AB 3081), operative July 1, 2005.

§2028.020. Notice of written deposition

The notice of a written deposition shall comply with Sections 2025.220 and 2025.230, and with subdivision (c) of Section 2020.240, except as follows:

(a) The name or descriptive title, as well as the address, of the deposition officer shall be stated.

(b) The date, time, and place for commencement of the deposition may be left to future determination by the deposition officer. **Leg.H.** Added Stats 2004 ch 182 §23 (AB 3081), operative July 1, 2005.

§2028.030. Questions to accompany notice; Time for service of cross questions and redirect questions

(a) The questions to be propounded to the deponent by direct examination shall accompany the notice of a written deposition.

(b) Within 30 days after the deposition notice and questions are served, a party shall serve any cross questions on all other parties entitled to notice of the deposition.

(c) Within 15 days after being served with cross questions, a party shall serve any redirect questions on all other parties entitled to notice of the deposition.

(d) Within 15 days after being served with redirect questions, a party shall serve any recross questions on all other parties entitled to notice of the deposition.

(e) The court may, for good cause shown, extend or shorten the time periods for the interchange of cross, redirect, and recross questions. **Leg.H.** Added Stats 2004 ch 182 §23 (AB 3081), operative July 1, 2005.

§2028.040. Objection to form of question; Motion; Monetary sanction

(a) A party who objects to the form of any question shall serve a specific objection to that question on all parties entitled to notice of the deposition within 15 days after service of the question. A party who fails to timely serve an objection to the form of a question waives it.

(b) The objecting party shall promptly move the court to sustain the objection. This motion shall be accompanied by a meet and confer declaration under Section 2016.040. Unless the court has sustained that objection, the deposition officer shall propound to the deponent that question subject to that objection as to its form.

(c) The court shall impose a monetary sanction under Chapter 7 (commencing with Section 2023.010) against any party, person, or attorney who unsuccessfully makes or opposes a motion to sustain an objection, unless it finds that the one subject to the sanction acted with substantial justification or that other circumstances make the imposition of the sanction unjust. **Leg.H.** Added Stats 2004 ch 182 §23 (AB 3081), operative July 1, 2005.

§2028.050. Objection to question on grounds of privilege or protection as work product; Motion to overrule; Monetary sanction

(a) A party who objects to any question on the ground that it calls for information that is privileged or is protected work product under Chapter 4 (commencing with Section 2018.010) shall serve a specific objection to that question on all parties entitled to notice of the deposition within 15 days after service of the question. A party who fails to timely serve that objection waives it.

(b) The party propounding any question to which an objection is made on those grounds may then move the court for an order overruling that objection. This motion shall be accompanied by a meet and confer declaration under Section 2016.040. The deposition officer shall not propound to the deponent any question to which a written objection on those grounds has been served unless the court has overruled that objection.

(c) The court shall impose a monetary sanction under Chapter 7 (commencing with Section 2023.010) against any party, person, or attorney who unsuccessfully makes or opposes a motion to overrule an objection, unless it finds that the one subject to the sanction acted with substantial justification or that other circumstances make the imposition of the sanction unjust. **Leg.H.** Added Stats 2004 ch 182 §23 (AB 3081), operative July 1, 2005.

§2028.060. What questions may be forwarded to deponent prior to deposition

(a) The party taking a written deposition may forward to the deponent a copy of the questions on direct examination for study prior to the deposition.

(b) No party or attorney shall permit the deponent to preview the form or the substance of any cross, redirect, or recross questions. **Leg.H.** Added Stats 2004 ch 182 §23 (AB 3081), operative July 1, 2005.

§2028.070. Orders which court may issue

In addition to any appropriate order listed in Section 2025.420, the court may order any of the following:

(a) That the deponent's testimony be taken by oral, instead of written, examination.

(b) That one or more of the parties receiving notice of the written deposition be permitted to attend in person or by attorney and to propound questions to the deponent by oral examination.

(c) That objections under Sections 2028.040 and 2028.050 be sustained or overruled.

(d) That the deposition be taken before an officer other than the one named or described in the deposition notice. **Leg.H.** Added Stats 2004 ch 182 §23 (AB 3081), operative July 1, 2005.

§2028.080. Delivery of deposition notice and questions to deposition officer and taking of testimony

The party taking a written deposition shall deliver to the officer designated in the deposition notice a copy of that notice and of all questions served under Section 2028.030. The deposition officer shall proceed promptly to propound the questions and to take and record the testimony of the deponent in response to the questions. **Leg.H.** Added Stats 2004 ch 182 §23 (AB 3081), operative July 1, 2005.

CHAPTER 12
DISCOVERY IN ACTION PENDING OUTSIDE CALIFORNIA

Article 1. Interstate and International Depositions and Discovery Act.

ARTICLE 1
Interstate and International Depositions and Discovery Act

Citation of article. §2029.100.
Definitions. §2029.200.
Issuance of subpoena by clerk of court. §2029.300.
Issuance of subpoena by local counsel. §2029.350.
Judicial Council forms. §2029.390.
Service of subpoena. §2029.400.
Deposition, production, and inspection. §2029.500.
Discovery dispute. §2029.600.
Fees and format of papers relating to discovery dispute. §2029.610.
Subsequent discovery dispute in same case and county. §2029.620.

Hearing date and briefing schedule. §2029.630.
Discovery on notice or agreement. §2029.640.
Writ petition. §2029.650.
Uniformity of application and construction. §2029.700.
Application to pending action. §2029.800.
Operative date. §2029.900.

§2029. [Section repealed 2005]

Leg.H. Added Stats 1986 ch 1334 §2, operative July 1, 1987. Amended Stats 1989 ch 1416 §30. Repealed Stats 2004 ch 182 §22 (AB 3081), operative July 1, 2005. The repealed section related to depositions in actions pending outside California. See CCP §2029.100.

Prior Law: Former CCP §2029 was added Stats 1957 ch 1904 §3, operative January 1, 1958, and repealed Stats 1961 ch 192 §11.

Former CCP §2029, providing that notice dispensed with when defendant served by publication, was added Stats 1907 ch 87 §1 and repealed Stats 1957 ch 1904 §1, operative January 1, 1958.

§2029.010. [Section repealed 2009]

Leg.H. Added Stats 2004 ch 182 §23 (AB 3081), operative July 1, 2005. Repealed Stats 2008 ch 231 §2 (AB 2193), effective January 1, 2009. See CCP §§2029.100 et seq.

§2029.100. Citation of article

This article may be cited as the Interstate and International Depositions and Discovery Act. **Leg.H.** Added Stats 2008 ch 231 §3 (AB 2193), effective January 1, 2009, operative January 1, 2010.

2008 Note: See CCP §2029.900 for operative date information.

§2029.200. Definitions

In this article:

(a) "Foreign jurisdiction" means either of the following:

(1) A state other than this state.

(2) A foreign nation.

(b) "Foreign penal civil action" means a civil action authorized by the law of a state other than this state in which the sole purpose is to punish an offense against the public justice of that state.

(c) "Foreign subpoena" means a subpoena issued under authority of a court of record of a foreign jurisdiction.

(d) "Person" means an individual, corporation, business trust, estate, trust, partnership, limited liability company, association, joint venture, public corporation, government, or governmental subdivision, agency, or instrumentality, or any other legal or commercial entity.

(e) "State" means a state of the United States, the District of Columbia, Puerto Rico, the Virgin Islands, a federally recognized Indian tribe, or any territory or insular possession subject to the jurisdiction of the United States.

(f) "Subpoena" means a document, however denominated, issued under authority of a court of record requiring a person to do any of the following:

(1) Attend and give testimony at a deposition.

(2) Produce and permit inspection, copying, testing, or sampling of designated books, documents, records, electronically stored information, or tangible things in the possession, custody, or control of the person.

(3) Permit inspection of premises under the control of the person.

Leg.H. Added Stats 2008 ch 231 §3 (AB 2193), effective January 1, 2009, operative January 1, 2010. Amended Stats 2012 ch 72 §29 (SB 1574), effective January 1, 2013; Stats 2022 ch 628 §3 (AB 2091), effective September 27, 2022.

2008 Note: See CCP §2029.900 for operative date information.

§2029.300. Issuance of subpoena by clerk of court

(a) To request issuance of a subpoena under this section, a party shall submit the original or a true and correct copy of a foreign subpoena to the clerk of the superior court in the county in which discovery is sought to be conducted in this state. A request for the issuance of a subpoena under this section does not constitute making an appearance in the courts of this state.

(b) In addition to submitting a foreign subpoena under subdivision (a), a party seeking discovery shall do both of the following:

(1) Submit an application requesting that the superior court issue a subpoena with the same terms as the foreign subpoena. The application shall be on a form prescribed by the Judicial Council pursuant to Section 2029.390. No civil case cover sheet is required.

(2) Pay the fee specified in Section 70626 of the Government Code.

(c) When a party submits a foreign subpoena to the clerk of the superior court in accordance with subdivision (a), and satisfies the requirements of subdivision (b), the clerk shall promptly issue a subpoena for service upon the person to which the foreign subpoena is directed.

(d) A subpoena issued under this section shall satisfy all of the following conditions:

(1) It shall incorporate the terms used in the foreign subpoena.

(2) It shall contain or be accompanied by the names, addresses, and telephone numbers of all counsel of record in the proceeding to which the subpoena relates and of any party not represented by counsel.

(3) It shall bear the caption and case number of the out-of-state case to which it relates.

(4) It shall state the name of the court that issues it.

(5) It shall be on a form prescribed by the Judicial Council pursuant to Section 2029.390.

(e) Notwithstanding subdivision (a), a subpoena shall not be issued pursuant to this section in any of the following circumstances:

(1) If the foreign subpoena is based on a violation of another state's laws that interfere with a person's right to allow a child to receive gender-affirming health care or gender-affirming mental health care. For the purpose of this paragraph, "gender-affirming health care" and "gender-affirming mental health care" shall have the same meaning as provided in Section 16010.2 of the Welfare and Institutions Code.

(2) If the submitted foreign subpoena relates to a foreign penal civil action and would require disclosure of information related to sensitive services. For purposes of this paragraph, "sensitive services" has the same meaning as defined in Section 791.02 of the Insurance Code. **Leg.H.** Added Stats 2008 ch 231 §3 (AB 2193), effective January 1, 2009, operative January 1, 2010. Amended Stats 2022 ch 628 §4 (AB 2091), effective September 27, 2022; Stats 2022 ch 810 §2.5 (SB 107), effective January 1, 2023.

2008 Note: See CCP §2029.900 for operative date information.

§2029.350. Issuance of subpoena by local counsel

(a) Notwithstanding Sections 1986 and 2029.300, if a party to a proceeding pending in a foreign jurisdiction retains an attorney licensed to practice in this state, who is an active member of the State Bar, and that attorney receives the original or a true and correct copy of a foreign subpoena, the attorney may issue a subpoena under this article.

(b)(1) Notwithstanding subdivision (a), an authorized attorney shall not issue a subpoena pursuant to subdivision (a) if the foreign subpoena is based on a violation of another state's laws that interfere with a person's right to allow a child to receive gender-affirming health care or gender-affirming mental health care.

(2) For the purpose of this subdivision, "gender-affirming health care" and "gender-affirming mental health care" shall have the same meaning as provided in Section 16010.2 of the Welfare and Institutions Code.

(c) Notwithstanding subdivision (a), an attorney shall not issue a subpoena under this article based on a foreign subpoena that relates to a foreign penal civil action and that would require disclosure of information related to sensitive services. For purposes of this subdivision, "sensitive services" has the same meaning as defined in Section 791.02 of the Insurance Code.

(d) A subpoena issued under this section shall satisfy all of the following conditions:

(1) It shall incorporate the terms used in the foreign subpoena.

(2) It shall contain or be accompanied by the names, addresses, and telephone numbers of all counsel of record in the proceeding to which the subpoena relates and of any party not represented by counsel.

(3) It shall bear the caption and case number of the out-of-state case to which it relates.

(4) It shall state the name of the superior court of the county in which the discovery is to be conducted.

(5) It shall be on a form prescribed by the Judicial Council pursuant to Section 2029.390. **Leg.H.** Added Stats 2008 ch 231 §3 (AB 2193), effective January 1, 2009, operative January 1, 2010. Amended Stats 2022 ch 628 §5 (AB 2091), effective September 27, 2022; Stats 2022 ch 810 §3.5 (SB 107), effective January 1, 2023.

2008 Note: See CCP §2029.900 for operative date information.

§2029.390. Judicial Council forms

On or before January 1, 2010, the Judicial Council shall do all of the following:

(a) Prepare an application form to be used for purposes of Section 2029.300.

(b) Prepare one or more new subpoena forms that include clear instructions for use in issuance of a subpoena under Section 2029.300 or 2029.350. Alternatively, the Judicial Council may modify one or more existing subpoena forms to include clear instructions for use in issuance of a subpoena under Section 2029.300 or 2029.350. **Leg.H.** Added Stats 2008 ch 231 §3 (AB 2193), effective and operative January 1, 2009.

2008 Note: See CCP §2029.900 for operative date information.

§2029.400. Service of subpoena

A subpoena issued under this article shall be personally served in compliance with the law of this state, including, without limitation, Section 1985. **Leg.H.** Added Stats 2008 ch 231 §3 (AB 2193), effective January 1, 2009, operative January 1, 2010.

2008 Note: See CCP §2029.900 for operative date information.

§2029.500. Deposition, production, and inspection

Titles 3 (commencing with Section 1985) and 4 (commencing with Section 2016.010) of Part 4, and any other law or court rule of this state governing a deposition, a production of documents or other tangible items, or an inspection of premises, including any law or court rule governing payment of court costs or sanctions, apply to discovery under this article. **Leg.H.** Added Stats 2008 ch 231 §3 (AB 2193), effective January 1, 2009, operative January 1, 2010.

2008 Note: See CCP §2029.900 for operative date information.

§2029.600. Discovery dispute

(a) If a dispute arises relating to discovery under this article, any request for a protective order or to enforce, quash, or modify a subpoena, or for other relief may be filed in the superior court in the county in which discovery is to be conducted and, if so filed, shall comply with the applicable rules or statutes of this state.

(b) A request for relief pursuant to this section shall be referred to as a petition notwithstanding any statute under which a request for the same relief would be referred to as a motion or by another term if it was brought in a proceeding pending in this state.

(c) A petition for relief pursuant to this section shall be accompanied by a civil case cover sheet. **Leg.H.** Added Stats 2008 ch 231 §3 (AB 2193), effective January 1, 2009, operative January 1, 2010.

2008 Note: See CCP §2029.900 for operative date information.

§2029.610. Fees and format of papers relating to discovery dispute

(a) On filing a petition under Section 2029.600, a petitioner who is a party to the out-of-state proceeding shall pay a first appearance fee as specified in Section 70611 of the Government Code. A petitioner who is not a party to the out-of-state proceeding shall pay the fee specified in subdivision (c) of Section 70626 of the Government Code.

(b) The court in which the petition is filed shall assign it a case number.

(c) On responding to a petition under Section 2029.600, a party to the out-of-state proceeding shall pay a first appearance fee as specified in Section 70612 of the Government Code. A person who is not a party to the out-of-state proceeding may file a response without paying a fee.

(d) Any petition, response, or other document filed under this section shall satisfy all of the following conditions:

(1) It shall bear the caption and case number of the out-of-state case to which it relates.

(2) The first page shall state the name of the court in which the document is filed.

(3) The first page shall state the case number assigned by the court under subdivision (b).

(4) The first page shall state whether or not the person filing the document is a party to the out-of-state case. **Leg.H.** Added Stats 2008 ch 231 §3 (AB 2193), effective January 1, 2009, operative January 1, 2010. Amended Stats 2011 ch 308 §4 (SB 647), effective January 1, 2012.

2008 Note: See CCP §2029.900 for operative date information.

§2029.620. Subsequent discovery dispute in same case and county

(a) If a petition has been filed under Section 2029.600 and another dispute later arises relating to discovery being conducted in the same county for purposes of the same out-of-state proceeding, the deponent or other disputant may file a petition for appropriate relief in the same superior court as the previous petition.

(b) The first page of the petition shall clearly indicate that it is not the first petition filed in that court that relates to the out-of-state case.

(c)(1) If the petitioner in the new dispute is a party to the out-of-state case who previously paid a first appearance fee under this article, the petitioner shall pay a motion fee as specified in subdivision (a) of Section 70617 of the Government Code. If the petitioner in the new dispute is a party to the out-of-state case but has not previously paid a first appearance fee under this article, the petitioner shall pay a first appearance fee as specified in Section 70611 of the Government Code.

(2) If the petitioner in the new dispute is not a party to the out-of-state case, the petitioner shall pay the fee specified in subdivision (c) of Section 70626 of the Government Code, unless the petitioner previously paid that fee. If the petitioner previously paid the fee specified in subdivision (c) of Section 70626 of the Government Code, the petitioner shall pay a motion fee as specified in subdivision (a) of Section 70617 of the Government Code.

(d) If a person responding to the new petition is not a party to the out-of-state case, or is a party who previously paid a first appearance fee under this article, that person does not have to pay a fee for responding. If a person responding to the new petition is a party to the out-of-state case but has not previously paid a first appearance fee under this article, that person shall pay a first appearance fee as specified in Section 70612 of the Government Code.

(e) Any petition, response, or other document filed under this section shall satisfy all of the following conditions:

(1) It shall bear the caption and case number of the out-of-state case to which it relates.

(2) The first page shall state the name of the court in which the document is filed.

(3) The first page shall state the same case number that the court assigned to the first petition relating to the out-of-state case.

(4) The first page shall state whether or not the person filing the document is a party to the out-of-state case.

(f) A petition for relief pursuant to this section shall be accompanied by a civil case cover sheet. **Leg.H.** Added Stats 2008 ch 231 §3 (AB 2193), effective January 1, 2009, operative January 1, 2010. Amended Stats 2011 ch 308 §5 (SB 647), effective January 1, 2012.

2008 Note: See CCP §2029.900 for operative date information.

§2029.630. Hearing date and briefing schedule

A petition under Section 2029.600 or Section 2029.620 is subject to the requirements of Section 1005 relating to notice and to filing and service of papers. **Leg.H.** Added Stats 2008 ch 231 §3 (AB 2193), effective January 1, 2009, operative January 1, 2010.

2008 Note: See CCP §2029.900 for operative date information.

§2029.640. Discovery on notice or agreement

If a party to a proceeding pending in a foreign jurisdiction seeks discovery from a witness in this state by properly issued notice or by agreement, it is not necessary for that party to obtain a subpoena under this article to be able to seek relief under Section 2029.600 or 2029.620. The deponent or any other party may also seek relief under Section 2029.600 or 2029.620 in those circumstances, regardless of whether the deponent was subpoenaed under this article. **Leg.H.** Added Stats 2008 ch 231 §3 (AB 2193), effective January 1, 2009, operative January 1, 2010.

2008 Note: See CCP §2029.900 for operative date information.

§2029.650. Writ petition

(a) If a superior court issues an order granting, denying, or otherwise resolving a petition under Section 2029.600 or 2029.620, a person aggrieved by the order may petition the appropriate court of appeal for an extraordinary writ. No order or other action of a court under this article is appealable in this state.

(b) Pending its decision on the writ petition, the court of appeal may stay the order of the superior court, the discovery that is the subject of that order, or both. **Leg.H.** Added Stats 2008 ch 231 §3 (AB 2193), effective January 1, 2009, operative January 1, 2010.

2008 Note: See CCP §2029.900 for operative date information.

§2029.700. Uniformity of application and construction

(a) Sections 2029.100, 2029.200, 2029.300, 2029.400, 2029.500, 2029.600, 2029.800, 2029.900, and this section, collectively, constitute and may be referred to as the "California version of the Uniform Interstate Depositions and Discovery Act."

(b) In applying and construing this uniform act, consideration shall be given to the need to promote uniformity of the law with respect to its subject matter among the states that enact it. **Leg.H.** Added Stats 2008 ch 231 §3 (AB 2193), effective January 1, 2009, operative January 1, 2010.

2008 Note: See CCP §2029.900 for operative date information.

§2029.800. Application to pending action

This article applies to requests for discovery in cases pending on or after the operative date of this section. **Leg.H.** Added Stats 2008 ch 231 §3 (AB 2193), effective January 1, 2009, operative January 1, 2010.

2008 Note: See CCP §2029.900 for operative date information.

§2029.900. Operative date

Section 2029.390 is operative on January 1, 2009. The remainder of this article is operative on January 1, 2010. **Leg.H.** Added Stats 2008 ch 231 §3 (AB 2193), effective January 1, 2009, operative January 1, 2010.

CHAPTER 13
WRITTEN INTERROGATORIES

Article 1. Propounding Interrogatories.
Article 2. Response to Interrogatories.
Article 3. Use of Interrogatory Answer.

ARTICLE 1
Propounding Interrogatories

Use of written interrogatories to obtain discovery. §2030.010.
When interrogatories may be propounded. §2030.020.
Number of specially prepared and official form interrogatories that may be propounded; Number to which party must respond. §2030.030.
Additional specially prepared interrogatories with supporting declaration; Grounds; Burden of justification. §2030.040.
Format for declaration supporting additional interrogatories. §2030.050.
Numbering, style and format of interrogatories. §2030.060.
Supplemental interrogatory to elicit later acquired information bearing on previous answers; When permitted. §2030.070.
Service of interrogatories. §2030.080.
Motion for protective order; What protective order may provide; Denial of protective order; Monetary sanction. §2030.090.

§2030. [Section repealed 2005]

Leg.H. Added Stats 1986 ch 1334 §2, operative July 1, 1987. Amended Stats 1987 ch 86 §12, operative July 1, 1987; Stats 1988 ch 553 §4, ch 575 §1; Stats 1991 ch 1090 §11 (AB 1484). Repealed Stats 2004 ch 182 §22 (AB 3081), operative July 1, 2005. The repealed section related to written interrogatories. See CCP §§2030.010 et seq.

Prior Law: Former CCP §2030 was added Stats 1978 ch 12 §2, effective February 18, 1978, amended Stats 1980 ch 186 §1, ch 677 §2, Stats 1983 ch 141 §1, and repealed Stats 1986 ch 1334 §1, operative July 1, 1987.

Former CCP §2030 was added Stats 1957 ch 1904 §3, operative January 1, 1958, amended Stats 1959 ch 1590 §9, Stats 1961 ch 249 §1, Stats 1963 ch 450 §1, Stats 1967 ch 841 §1, Stats 1968 ch 188 §1, Stats 1971 ch 1643 §1, Stats 1974 ch 732 §1, Stats 1977 ch 500 §1, and repealed Stats 1978 ch 12 §1, effective February 18, 1978.

§2030.010. Use of written interrogatories to obtain discovery

(a) Any party may obtain discovery within the scope delimited by Chapter 2 (commencing with Section 2017.010), and subject to the restrictions set forth in Chapter 5 (commencing with Section 2019.010), by propounding to any other party to the action written interrogatories to be answered under oath.

(b) An interrogatory may relate to whether another party is making a certain contention, or to the facts, witnesses, and writings on which a contention is based. An interrogatory is not objectionable because an answer to it involves an opinion or contention that relates to fact or the application of law to fact, or would be based on information obtained or legal theories developed in anticipation of litigation or in preparation for trial. **Leg.H.** Added Stats 2004 ch 182 §23 (AB 3081), operative July 1, 2005. Amended Stats 2015 ch 303 §42 (AB 731), effective January 1, 2016.

§2030.020. When interrogatories may be propounded

(a) A defendant may propound interrogatories to a party to the action without leave of court at any time.

(b) A plaintiff may propound interrogatories to a party without leave of court at any time that is 10 days after the service of the summons on, or appearance by, that party, whichever occurs first.

(c) Notwithstanding subdivision (b), in an unlawful detainer action or other proceeding under Chapter 4 (commencing with Section 1159) of Title 3 of Part 3, a plaintiff may propound interrogatories to a party without leave of court at any time that is five days after service of the summons on, or appearance by, that party, whichever occurs first.

(d) Notwithstanding subdivisions (b) and (c), on motion with or without notice, the court, for good cause shown, may grant leave to a plaintiff to propound interrogatories at an earlier time. **Leg.H.** Added Stats 2004 ch 182 §23 (AB 3081), operative July 1, 2005. Amended Stats 2007 ch 113 §7 (AB 1126), effective January 1, 2008.

§2030.030. Number of specially prepared and official form interrogatories that may be propounded; Number to which party must respond

(a) A party may propound to another party either or both of the following:

(1) Thirty-five specially prepared interrogatories that are relevant to the subject matter of the pending action.

(2) Any additional number of official form interrogatories, as described in Chapter 17 (commencing with Section 2033.710), that are relevant to the subject matter of the pending action.

(b) Except as provided in Section 2030.070, no party shall, as a matter of right, propound to any other party more than 35 specially prepared interrogatories. If the initial set of interrogatories does not exhaust this limit, the balance may be propounded in subsequent sets.

(c) Unless a declaration as described in Section 2030.050 has been made, a party need only respond to the first 35 specially prepared interrogatories served, if that party states an objection to the balance, under Section 2030.240, on the ground that the limit has been exceeded. **Leg.H.** Added Stats 2004 ch 182 §23 (AB 3081), operative July 1, 2005.

§2030.040. Additional specially prepared interrogatories with supporting declaration; Grounds; Burden of justification

(a) Subject to the right of the responding party to seek a protective order under Section 2030.090, any party who attaches a supporting declaration as described in Section 2030.050 may propound a greater number of specially prepared interrogatories to another party if this greater number is warranted because of any of the following:

(1) The complexity or the quantity of the existing and potential issues in the particular case.

(2) The financial burden on a party entailed in conducting the discovery by oral deposition.

(3) The expedience of using this method of discovery to provide to the responding party the opportunity to conduct an inquiry, investigation, or search of files or records to supply the information sought.

(b) If the responding party seeks a protective order on the ground that the number of specially prepared interrogatories is unwarranted, the propounding party shall have the burden of justifying the number of these interrogatories. **Leg.H.** Added Stats 2004 ch 182 §23 (AB 3081), operative July 1, 2005.

§2030.050. Format for declaration supporting additional interrogatories

Any party who is propounding or has propounded more than 35 specially prepared interrogatories to any other party shall attach to each set of those interrogatories a declaration containing substantially the following:

DECLARATION FOR ADDITIONAL DISCOVERY

I, _____, declare:

1. I am (a party to this action or proceeding appearing in propria persona) (presently the attorney for _____, a party to this action or proceeding).

2. I am propounding to _____ the attached set of interrogatories.

3. This set of interrogatories will cause the total number of specially prepared interrogatories propounded to the party to whom they are directed to exceed the number of specially prepared interrogatories permitted by Section 2030.030 of the Code of Civil Procedure.

4. I have previously propounded a total of ____ interrogatories to this party, of which ____ interrogatories were not official form interrogatories.

5. This set of interrogatories contains a total of ____ specially prepared interrogatories.

6. I am familiar with the issues and the previous discovery conducted by all of the parties in the case.

7. I have personally examined each of the questions in this set of interrogatories.

8. This number of questions is warranted under Section 2030.040 of the Code of Civil Procedure because _____ . (Here state each factor described in Section 2030.040 that is relied on, as well as the reasons why any factor relied on is applicable to the instant lawsuit.)

9. None of the questions in this set of interrogatories is being propounded for any improper purpose, such as to harass the party, or the attorney for the party, to whom it is directed, or to cause unnecessary delay or needless increase in the cost of litigation.

I declare under penalty of perjury under the laws of California that the foregoing is true and correct, and that this declaration was executed on _____ .

_____
(Signature)
Attorney for _____

Leg.H. Added Stats 2004 ch 182 §23 (AB 3081), operative July 1, 2005. Amended Stats 2005 ch 22 §22 (SB 1108), effective January 1, 2006.

§2030.060. Numbering, style and format of interrogatories

(a) A party propounding interrogatories shall number each set of interrogatories consecutively.

(b) In the first paragraph immediately below the title of the case, there shall appear the identity of the propounding party, the set number, and the identity of the responding party.

(c) Each interrogatory in a set shall be separately set forth and identified by number or letter.

(d) Each interrogatory shall be full and complete in and of itself. No preface or instruction shall be included with a set of interrogatories unless it has been approved under Chapter 17 (commencing with Section 2033.710).

(e) Any term specially defined in a set of interrogatories shall be typed with all letters capitalized wherever that term appears.

(f) No specially prepared interrogatory shall contain subparts, or a compound, conjunctive, or disjunctive question.

(g) An interrogatory may not be made a continuing one so as to impose on the party responding to it a duty to supplement an answer to it that was initially correct and complete with later acquired information. **Leg.H.** Added Stats 2004 ch 182 §23 (AB 3081), operative July 1, 2005.

§2030.070. Supplemental interrogatory to elicit later acquired information bearing on previous answers; When permitted

(a) In addition to the number of interrogatories permitted by Sections 2030.030 and 2030.040, a party may propound a supplemental interrogatory to elicit any later acquired information bearing on all answers previously made by any party in response to interrogatories.

(b) A party may propound a supplemental interrogatory twice before the initial setting of a trial date, and, subject to the time limits on discovery proceedings and motions provided in Chapter 8 (commencing with Section 2024.010), once after the initial setting of a trial date.

(c) Notwithstanding subdivisions (a) and (b), on motion, for good cause shown, the court may grant leave to a party to propound an additional number of supplemental interrogatories. **Leg.H.** Added Stats 2004 ch 182 §23 (AB 3081), operative July 1, 2005.

§2030.080. Service of interrogatories

(a) The party propounding interrogatories shall serve a copy of them on the party to whom the interrogatories are directed.

(b) The propounding party shall also serve a copy of the interrogatories on all other parties who have appeared in the action. On motion, with or without notice, the court may relieve the party from this requirement on its determination that service on all other parties would be unduly expensive or burdensome. **Leg.H.** Added Stats 2004 ch 182 §23 (AB 3081), operative July 1, 2005.

§2030.090. Motion for protective order; What protective order may provide; Denial of protective order; Monetary sanction

(a) When interrogatories have been propounded, the responding party, and any other party or affected natural person or organization may promptly move for a protective order. This motion shall be accompanied by a meet and confer declaration under Section 2016.040.

(b) The court, for good cause shown, may make any order that justice requires to protect any party or other natural person or organization from unwarranted annoyance, embarrassment, or oppression, or undue burden and expense. This protective order may include, but is not limited to, one or more of the following directions:

(1) That the set of interrogatories, or particular interrogatories in the set, need not be answered.

(2) That, contrary to the representations made in a declaration submitted under Section 2030.050, the number of specially prepared interrogatories is unwarranted.

(3) That the time specified in Section 2030.260 to respond to the set of interrogatories, or to particular interrogatories in the set, be extended.

(4) That the response be made only on specified terms and conditions.

(5) That the method of discovery be an oral deposition instead of interrogatories to a party.

(6) That a trade secret or other confidential research, development, or commercial information not be disclosed or be disclosed only in a certain way.

(7) That some or all of the answers to interrogatories be sealed and thereafter opened only on order of the court.

(c) If the motion for a protective order is denied in whole or in part, the court may order that the party provide or permit the discovery against which protection was sought on terms and conditions that are just.

(d) The court shall impose a monetary sanction under Chapter 7 (commencing with Section 2023.010) against any party, person, or attorney who unsuccessfully makes or opposes a motion for a protective order under this section, unless it finds that the one subject to the sanction acted with substantial justification or that other circumstances make the imposition of the sanction unjust. **Leg.H.** Added Stats 2004 ch 182 §23 (AB 3081), operative July 1, 2005.

ARTICLE 2
Response to Interrogatories

Written responses to interrogatories; Content of response; Format and method of transmission. §2030.210.
Completeness of responses to interrogatories. §2030.220.
Specification of writings from which answer may be derived; Access to documents. §2030.230.
Answer to unobjectionable portion of interrogatory; Objection and grounds therefor. §2030.240.
Signing of responses to interrogatories. §2030.250.
Time for response to interrogatories; Unlawful detainer actions; Service on parties. §2030.260.
Extension of time for response; Confirmation of agreement in writing. §2030.270.
Retention of interrogatories, proof of service and response by propounding party. §2030.280.
Effect of failure to serve timely response to interrogatories; Waiver; Monetary sanction. §2030.290.
Motion for order compelling further response; Grounds; Waiver; Monetary and other sanctions. §2030.300.
Amended answer to interrogatory; Use and effect; Motion that initial order be deemed binding; Monetary sanction. §2030.310.

§2030.210. Written responses to interrogatories; Content of response; Format and method of transmission

(a) The party to whom interrogatories have been propounded shall respond in writing under oath separately to each interrogatory by any of the following:

(1) An answer containing the information sought to be discovered.

(2) An exercise of the party's option to produce writings.

(3) An objection to the particular interrogatory.

(b) In the first paragraph of the response immediately below the title of the case, there shall appear the identity of the responding party, the set number, and the identity of the propounding party.

(c) Each answer, exercise of option, or objection in the response shall bear the same identifying number or letter and be in the same sequence as the corresponding interrogatory. The text of that interrogatory need not be repeated, except as provided in paragraph (6) of subdivision (d).

(d) In order to facilitate the discovery process:

(1) Except as provided in paragraph (5), upon request by the responding party, the propounding party shall provide the interrogatories in an

electronic format to the responding party within three court days of the request.

(2) Except as provided in paragraph (5), upon request by the propounding party after receipt of the responses to the interrogatories, the responding party shall provide the responses in an electronic format to the propounding party within three court days of the request.

(3) A party may provide the interrogatories or responses to the interrogatories requested pursuant to paragraphs (1) and (2) in any format agreed upon by the parties. If the parties are unable to agree on a format, the interrogatories or responses to interrogatories shall be provided in plain text format.

(4) A party may transmit the interrogatories or responses to the interrogatories requested pursuant to paragraphs (1) and (2) by any method agreed upon by the parties. If the parties are unable to agree on a method of transmission, the interrogatories or responses to interrogatories shall be transmitted by electronic mail to an email address provided by the requesting party.

(5) If the interrogatories or responses to interrogatories were not created in an electronic format, a party is not required to create the interrogatories or response to interrogatories in an electronic format for the purpose of transmission to the requesting party.

(6) A responding party who has requested and received the interrogatories in an electronic format pursuant to paragraph (1) shall include the text of the interrogatory immediately preceding the response. **Leg.H.** Added Stats 2004 ch 182 §23 (AB 3081), operative July 1, 2005. Amended Stats 2019 ch 190 §1 (AB 1349), effective January 1, 2020.

§2030.220. Completeness of responses to interrogatories

(a) Each answer in a response to interrogatories shall be as complete and straightforward as the information reasonably available to the responding party permits.

(b) If an interrogatory cannot be answered completely, it shall be answered to the extent possible.

(c) If the responding party does not have personal knowledge sufficient to respond fully to an interrogatory, that party shall so state, but shall make a reasonable and good faith effort to obtain the information by inquiry to other natural persons or organizations, except where the information is equally available to the propounding party. **Leg.H.** Added Stats 2004 ch 182 §23 (AB 3081), operative July 1, 2005.

§2030.230. Specification of writings from which answer may be derived; Access to documents

If the answer to an interrogatory would necessitate the preparation or the making of a compilation, abstract, audit, or summary of or from the documents of the party to whom the interrogatory is directed, and if the burden or expense of preparing or making it would be substantially the same for the party propounding the interrogatory as for the responding party, it is a sufficient answer to that interrogatory to refer to this section and to specify the writings from which the answer may be derived or ascertained. This specification shall be in sufficient detail to permit the propounding party to locate and to identify, as readily as the responding party can, the documents from which the answer may be ascertained. The responding party shall then afford to the propounding party a reasonable opportunity to examine, audit, or inspect these documents and to make copies, compilations, abstracts, or summaries of them. **Leg.H.** Added Stats 2004 ch 182 §23 (AB 3081), operative July 1, 2005.

§2030.240. Answer to unobjectionable portion of interrogatory; Objection and grounds therefor

(a) If only a part of an interrogatory is objectionable, the remainder of the interrogatory shall be answered.

(b) If an objection is made to an interrogatory or to a part of an interrogatory, the specific ground for the objection shall be set forth clearly in the response. If an objection is based on a claim of privilege, the particular privilege invoked shall be clearly stated. If an objection is based on a claim that the information sought is protected work product under Chapter 4 (commencing with Section 2018.010), that claim shall be expressly asserted. **Leg.H.** Added Stats 2004 ch 182 §23 (AB 3081), operative July 1, 2005.

§2030.250. Signing of responses to interrogatories

(a) The party to whom the interrogatories are directed shall sign the response under oath unless the response contains only objections.

(b) If that party is a public or private corporation, or a partnership, association, or governmental agency, one of its officers or agents shall sign the response under oath on behalf of that party. If the officer or agent signing the response on behalf of that party is an attorney acting in that capacity for the party, that party waives any lawyer-client privilege and any protection for work product under Chapter 4 (commencing with Section 2018.010) during any subsequent discovery from that attorney concerning the identity of the sources of the information contained in the response.

(c) The attorney for the responding party shall sign any responses that contain an objection. **Leg.H.** Added Stats 2004 ch 182 §23 (AB 3081), operative July 1, 2005.

§2030.260. Time for response to interrogatories; Unlawful detainer actions; Service on parties

(a) Within 30 days after service of interrogatories, the party to whom the interrogatories are propounded shall serve the original of the response to them on the propounding party, unless on motion of the propounding party the court has shortened the time for response, or unless on motion of the responding party the court has extended the time for response.

(b) Notwithstanding subdivision (a), in an unlawful detainer action or other proceeding under Chapter 4 (commencing with Section 1159) of Title 3 of Part 3, the party to whom the interrogatories are propounded shall have five days from the date of service to respond, unless on motion of the propounding party the court has shortened the time for response, or unless on motion of the responding party the court has extended the time for response.

(c) The party to whom the interrogatories are propounded shall also serve a copy of the response on all other parties who have appeared in the action. On motion, with or without notice, the court may relieve the party from this requirement on its determination that service on all other parties would be unduly expensive or burdensome. **Leg.H.** Added Stats 2004 ch 182 §23 (AB 3081), operative July 1, 2005. Amended Stats 2007 ch 113 §8 (AB 1126), effective January 1, 2008.

§2030.270. Extension of time for response; Confirmation of agreement in writing

(a) The party propounding interrogatories and the responding party may agree to extend the time for service of a response to a set of interrogatories, or to particular interrogatories in a set, to a date beyond that provided in Section 2030.260.

(b) This agreement may be informal, but it shall be confirmed in a writing that specifies the extended date for service of a response.

(c) Unless this agreement expressly states otherwise, it is effective to preserve to the responding party the right to respond to any interrogatory to which the agreement applies in any manner specified in Sections 2030.210, 2030.220, 2030.230, and 2030.240. **Leg.H.** Added Stats 2004 ch 182 §23 (AB 3081), operative July 1, 2005.

§2030.280. Retention of interrogatories, proof of service and response by propounding party

(a) The interrogatories and the response thereto shall not be filed with the court.

(b) The propounding party shall retain both the original of the interrogatories, with the original proof of service affixed to them, and the original of the sworn response until six months after final disposition of the action. At that time, both originals may be destroyed, unless the court on motion of any party and for good cause shown orders that the originals be preserved for a longer period. **Leg.H.** Added Stats 2004 ch 182 §23 (AB 3081), operative July 1, 2005.

§2030.290. Effect of failure to serve timely response to interrogatories; Waiver; Monetary sanction

If a party to whom interrogatories are directed fails to serve a timely response, the following rules apply:

(a) The party to whom the interrogatories are directed waives any right to exercise the option to produce writings under Section 2030.230, as well as any objection to the interrogatories, including one based on privilege or on the protection for work product under Chapter 4 (commencing with Section 2018.010). The court, on motion, may relieve that party from this waiver on its determination that both of the following conditions are satisfied:

(1) The party has subsequently served a response that is in substantial compliance with Sections 2030.210, 2030.220, 2030.230, and 2030.240.

(2) The party's failure to serve a timely response was the result of mistake, inadvertence, or excusable neglect.

(b) The party propounding the interrogatories may move for an order compelling response to the interrogatories.

(c) The court shall impose a monetary sanction under Chapter 7 (commencing with Section 2023.010) against any party, person, or attorney who unsuccessfully makes or opposes a motion to compel a response to interrogatories, unless it finds that the one subject to the sanction acted with substantial justification or that other circumstances make the imposition of the sanction unjust. If a party then fails to obey an order compelling answers, the court may make those orders that are just, including the imposition of an issue sanction, an evidence sanction, or a terminating sanction under Chapter 7 (commencing with Section 2023.010). In lieu of or in addition to that sanction, the court may impose a monetary sanction under Chapter 7 (commencing with Section 2023.010). **Leg.H.** Added Stats 2004 ch 182 §23 (AB 3081), operative July 1, 2005.

§2030.300. Motion for order compelling further response; Grounds; Waiver; Monetary and other sanctions

(a) On receipt of a response to interrogatories, the propounding party may move for an order compelling a further response if the propounding party deems that any of the following apply:

(1) An answer to a particular interrogatory is evasive or incomplete.

(2) An exercise of the option to produce documents under Section 2030.230 is unwarranted or the required specification of those documents is inadequate.

(3) An objection to an interrogatory is without merit or too general.

(b)(1) A motion under subdivision (a) shall be accompanied by a meet and confer declaration under Section 2016.040.

(2) In lieu of a separate statement required under the California Rules of Court, the court may allow the moving party to submit a concise outline of the discovery request and each response in dispute.

(c) Unless notice of this motion is given within 45 days of the service of the verified response, or any supplemental verified response, or on or before any specific later date to which the propounding party and the responding party have agreed in writing, the propounding party waives any right to compel a further response to the interrogatories.

(d) The court shall impose a monetary sanction under Chapter 7 (commencing with Section 2023.010) against any party, person, or attorney who unsuccessfully makes or opposes a motion to compel a further response to interrogatories, unless it finds that the one subject to the sanction acted with substantial justification or that other circumstances make the imposition of the sanction unjust.

(e) If a party then fails to obey an order compelling further response to interrogatories, the court may make those orders that are just, including the imposition of an issue sanction, an evidence sanction, or a terminating sanction under Chapter 7 (commencing with Section 2023.010). In lieu of, or in addition to, that sanction, the court may impose a monetary sanction under Chapter 7 (commencing with Section 2023.010). **Leg.H.** Added Stats 2004 ch 182 §23 (AB 3081), operative July 1, 2005. Amended Stats 2013 ch 18 §1 (AB 1183), effective January 1, 2014; Stats 2018 ch 317 §3 (AB 2230), effective January 1, 2019, operative January 1, 2020.

§2030.310. Amended answer to interrogatory; Use and effect; Motion that initial order be deemed binding; Monetary sanction

(a) Without leave of court, a party may serve an amended answer to any interrogatory that contains information subsequently discovered, inadvertently omitted, or mistakenly stated in the initial interrogatory. At the trial of the action, the propounding party or any other party may use the initial answer under Section 2030.410, and the responding party may then use the amended answer.

(b) The party who propounded an interrogatory to which an amended answer has been served may move for an order that the initial answer to that interrogatory be deemed binding on the responding party for the purpose of the pending action. This motion shall be accompanied by a meet and confer declaration under Section 2016.040.

(c) The court shall grant a motion under subdivision (b) if it determines that all of the following conditions are satisfied:

(1) The initial failure of the responding party to answer the interrogatory correctly has substantially prejudiced the party who propounded the interrogatory.

(2) The responding party has failed to show substantial justification for the initial answer to that interrogatory.

(3) The prejudice to the propounding party cannot be cured either by a continuance to permit further discovery or by the use of the initial answer under Section 2030.410.

(d) The court shall impose a monetary sanction under Chapter 7 (commencing with Section 2023.010) against any party, person, or attorney who unsuccessfully makes or opposes a motion to deem binding an initial answer to an interrogatory, unless it finds that the one subject to the sanction acted with substantial justification or that other circumstances make the imposition of the sanction unjust. **Leg.H.** Added Stats 2004 ch 182 §23 (AB 3081), operative July 1, 2005.

ARTICLE 3
Use of Interrogatory Answer

Use of answers to interrogatories as evidence. §2030.410.

§2030.410. Use of answers to interrogatories as evidence

At the trial or any other hearing in the action, so far as admissible under the rules of evidence, the propounding party or any party other than the responding party may use any answer or part of an answer to an interrogatory only against the responding party. It is not ground for objection to the use of an answer to an interrogatory that the responding party is available to testify, has testified, or will testify at the trial or other hearing. **Leg.H.** Added Stats 2004 ch 182 §23 (AB 3081), operative July 1, 2005.

CHAPTER 14
INSPECTION, COPYING, TESTING, SAMPLING, AND PRODUCTION OF DOCUMENTS, ELECTRONICALLY STORED INFORMATION, TANGIBLE THINGS, LAND, AND OTHER PROPERTY

Article 1. Inspection Demand.
Article 2. Response to Inspection Demand.
Article 3. Inspection and Production of Documents and Other Property in Specific Contexts.

ARTICLE 1
Inspection Demand

Right to discovery by inspecting, copying, testing, or sampling documents, tangible things, land or other property, and electronically stored information. §2031.010.
When demand for inspection, copying, testing or sampling authorized. §2031.020.
Format and requirements for demands for inspection, copying, testing, or sampling. §2031.030.
Service of demand. §2031.040.
When supplemental demand may be propounded. §2031.050.
Motion for protective order; What protective order may provide; Denial of protective order; Monetary sanction. §2031.060.

§2031. [Section repealed 2005]

Leg.H. Added Stats 1986 ch 1334 §2, operative July 1, 1987. Amended Stats 1987 ch 86 §13, operative July 1, 1987; Stats 1988 ch 575 §2; Stats 1991 ch 1090 §12 (AB 1484); Stats 1998 ch 932 §23 (AB 1094); Stats 1999 ch 48 §1 (SB 447); Stats 2000 ch 688 §12 (AB 1669). Repealed Stats 2004 ch 182 §22 (AB 3081), operative July 1, 2005. The repealed section related to inspections of documents, tangible things, and land or other property. See CCP §§2031.010 et seq.

Prior Law: Former CCP §2031 was added Stats 1957 ch 1904 §3, operative January 1, 1958, amended Stats 1971 ch 1706 §1, Stats 1974 ch 592 §1, Stats 1980 ch 23 §1, and repealed Stats 1986 ch 1334 §1, operative July 1, 1987.

Original CCP §2031, relating to taking of depositions, was enacted 1872, amended Stats 1929 ch 488 §1, and repealed Stats 1957 ch 1904 §1, operative January 1, 1958.

§2031.010. Right to discovery by inspecting, copying, testing, or sampling documents, tangible things, land or other property, and electronically stored information

(a) Any party may obtain discovery within the scope delimited by Chapter 2 (commencing with Section 2017.010), and subject to the restrictions set forth in Chapter 5 (commencing with Section 2019.010), by inspecting, copying, testing, or sampling documents, tangible things, land or other property, and electronically stored information in the possession, custody, or control of any other party to the action.

(b) A party may demand that any other party produce and permit the party making the demand, or someone acting on the demanding party's behalf, to inspect and to copy a document that is in the possession, custody, or control of the party on whom the demand is made.

(c) A party may demand that any other party produce and permit the party making the demand, or someone acting on the demanding party's behalf, to inspect and to photograph, test, or sample any tangible things that are in the possession, custody, or control of the party on whom the demand is made.

(d) A party may demand that any other party allow the party making the demand, or someone acting on the demanding party's behalf, to enter on any land or other property that is in the possession, custody, or control of the party on whom the demand is made, and to inspect and to measure, survey, photograph, test, or sample the land or other property, or any designated object or operation on it.

(e) A party may demand that any other party produce and permit the party making the demand, or someone acting on the demanding party's behalf, to inspect, copy, test, or sample electronically stored information in the possession, custody, or control of the party on whom demand is made. **Leg.H.** Added Stats 2004 ch 182 §23 (AB 3081), operative July 1, 2005. Amended Stats 2009 ch 5 §4 (AB 5), effective June 29, 2009; Stats 2016 ch 86 §42 (SB 1171), effective January 1, 2017.

2009 Note: This act shall be known as the Electronic Discovery Act. Stats 2009 ch 5 (AB 5) §1.

§2031.020. When demand for inspection, copying, testing or sampling authorized

(a) A defendant may make a demand for inspection, copying, testing, or sampling without leave of court at any time.

(b) A plaintiff may make a demand for inspection, copying, testing, or sampling without leave of court at any time that is 10 days after the service of the summons on, or appearance by, the party to whom the demand is directed, whichever occurs first.

(c) Notwithstanding subdivision (b), in an unlawful detainer action or other proceeding under Chapter 4 (commencing with Section 1159) of Title 3 of Part 3, a plaintiff may make a demand for inspection, copying, testing, or sampling without leave of court at any time that is five days after service of the summons on, or appearance by, the party to whom the demand is directed, whichever occurs first.

(d) Notwithstanding subdivisions (b) and (c), on motion with or without notice, the court, for good cause shown, may grant leave to a plaintiff to make a demand for inspection, copying, testing, or sampling at an earlier time. **Leg.H.** Added Stats 2004 ch 182 §23 (AB 3081), operative July 1, 2005. Amended Stats 2007 ch 113 §9 (AB 1126), effective January 1, 2008; Stats 2009 ch 5 §5 (AB 5), effective June 29, 2009.

2009 Note: This act shall be known as the Electronic Discovery Act. Stats 2009 ch 5 (AB 5) §1.

§2031.030. Format and requirements for demands for inspection, copying, testing, or sampling

(a)(1) A party demanding inspection, copying, testing, or sampling shall number each set of demands consecutively.

(2) A party demanding inspection, copying, testing, or sampling of electronically stored information may specify the form or forms in which each type of electronically stored information is to be produced.

(b) In the first paragraph immediately below the title of the case, there shall appear the identity of the demanding party, the set number, and the identity of the responding party.

(c) Each demand in a set shall be separately set forth, identified by number or letter, and shall do all of the following:

(1) Designate the documents, tangible things, land or other property, or electronically stored information to be inspected, copied, tested, or sampled either by specifically describing each individual item or by reasonably particularizing each category of item.

(2) Specify a reasonable time for the inspection, copying, testing, or sampling that is at least 30 days after service of the demand, unless the court for good cause shown has granted leave to specify an earlier date. In an unlawful detainer action or other proceeding under Chapter 4 (commencing with Section 1159) of Title 3 of Part 3, the demand shall specify a reasonable time for the inspection, copying, testing, or sampling that is at least five days after service of the demand, unless the court, for good cause shown, has granted leave to specify an earlier date.

(3) Specify a reasonable place for making the inspection, copying, testing, or sampling, and performing any related activity.

(4) Specify any inspection, copying, testing, sampling, or related activity that is being demanded, as well as the manner in which that activity will be performed, and whether that activity will permanently alter or destroy the item involved. **Leg.H.** Added Stats 2004 ch 182 §23 (AB 3081), operative July 1, 2005. Amended Stats 2007 ch 113 §10 (AB 1126), effective January 1, 2008; Stats 2009 ch 5 §6 (AB 5), effective June 29, 2009.

2009 Note: This act shall be known as the Electronic Discovery Act. Stats 2009 ch 5 (AB 5) §1.

§2031.040. Service of demand

The party making a demand for inspection, copying, testing, or sampling shall serve a copy of the demand on the party to whom it is directed and on all other parties who have appeared in the action. **Leg.H.** Added Stats 2004 ch 182 §23 (AB 3081), operative July 1, 2005. Amended Stats 2009 ch 5 §7 (AB 5), effective June 29, 2009.

2009 Note: This act shall be known as the Electronic Discovery Act. Stats 2009 ch 5 (AB 5) §1.

§2031.050. When supplemental demand may be propounded

(a) In addition to the demands for inspection, copying, testing, or sampling permitted by this chapter, a party may propound a supplemental demand to inspect, copy, test, or sample any later acquired or discovered documents, tangible things, land or other property, or electronically stored information in the possession, custody, or control of the party on whom the demand is made.

(b) A party may propound a supplemental demand for inspection, copying, testing, or sampling twice before the initial setting of a trial date, and, subject to the time limits on discovery proceedings and motions provided in Chapter 8 (commencing with Section 2024.010), once after the initial setting of a trial date.

(c) Notwithstanding subdivisions (a) and (b), on motion, for good cause shown, the court may grant leave to a party to propound an additional number of supplemental demands for inspection, copying, testing, or sampling. **Leg.H.** Added Stats 2004 ch 182 §23 (AB 3081), operative July 1, 2005. Amended Stats 2009 ch 5 §8 (AB 5), effective June 18, 2009.

2009 Note: This act shall be known as the Electronic Discovery Act. Stats 2009 ch 5 (AB 5) §1.

§2031.060. Motion for protective order; What protective order may provide; Denial of protective order; Monetary sanction

(a) When an inspection, copying, testing, or sampling of documents, tangible things, places, or electronically stored information has been demanded, the party to whom the demand has been directed, and any other party or affected person, may promptly move for a protective order. This motion shall be accompanied by a meet and confer declaration under Section 2016.040.

(b) The court, for good cause shown, may make any order that justice requires to protect any party or other person from unwarranted annoyance, embarrassment, or oppression, or undue burden and expense. This protective order may include, but is not limited to, one or more of the following directions:

(1) That all or some of the items or categories of items in the demand need not be produced or made available at all.

(2) That the time specified in Section 2031.260 to respond to the set of demands, or to a particular item or category in the set, be extended.

(3) That the place of production be other than that specified in the demand.

(4) That the inspection, copying, testing, or sampling be made only on specified terms and conditions.

(5) That a trade secret or other confidential research, development, or commercial information not be disclosed, or be disclosed only to specified persons or only in a specified way.

(6) That the items produced be sealed and thereafter opened only on order of the court.

(c) The party or affected person who seeks a protective order regarding the production, inspection, copying, testing, or sampling of electronically stored information on the basis that the information is from a source that is not reasonably accessible because of undue burden or expense shall bear the burden of demonstrating that the information is from a source that is not reasonably accessible because of undue burden or expense.

(d) If the party or affected person from whom discovery of electronically stored information is sought establishes that the information is from a source that is not reasonably accessible because of undue burden or expense, the court may nonetheless order discovery if the demanding party shows good cause, subject to any limitations imposed under subdivision (f).

(e) If the court finds good cause for the production of electronically stored information from a source that is not reasonably accessible, the court may set conditions for the discovery of the electronically stored information, including allocation of the expense of discovery.

(f) The court shall limit the frequency or extent of discovery of electronically stored information, even from a source that is reasonably accessible, if the court determines that any of the following conditions exist:

(1) It is possible to obtain the information from some other source that is more convenient, less burdensome, or less expensive.

(2) The discovery sought is unreasonably cumulative or duplicative.

(3) The party seeking discovery has had ample opportunity by discovery in the action to obtain the information sought.

(4) The likely burden or expense of the proposed discovery outweighs the likely benefit, taking into account the amount in controversy, the resources of the parties, the importance of the issues in the litigation, and the importance of the requested discovery in resolving the issues.

(g) If the motion for a protective order is denied in whole or in part, the court may order that the party to whom the demand was directed provide or permit the discovery against which protection was sought on terms and conditions that are just.

(h) Except as provided in subdivision (i), the court shall impose a monetary sanction under Chapter 7 (commencing with Section 2023.010) against any party, person, or attorney who unsuccessfully makes or opposes a motion for a protective order, unless it finds that the one subject to the sanction acted with substantial justification or that other circumstances make the imposition of the sanction unjust.

(i)(1) Notwithstanding subdivision (h), absent exceptional circumstances, the court shall not impose sanctions on a party or any attorney of a party for failure to provide electronically stored information that has been lost, damaged, altered, or overwritten as the result of the routine, good faith operation of an electronic information system.

(2) This subdivision shall not be construed to alter any obligation to preserve discoverable information. **Leg.H.** Added Stats 2004 ch 182 §23 (AB 3081), operative July 1, 2005. Amended Stats 2009 ch 5 §9 (AB 5), effective June 29, 2009; Stats 2021 ch 124 §15 (AB 938), effective January 1, 2022.

2009 Notes: This act shall be known as the Electronic Discovery Act. Stats 2009 ch 5 (AB 5) §1.

It appears the Legislature inadvertently referred to "Section 2030.260" in subdivision (b)(2). It is the Publisher's belief that the correct reference should be "Section 2031.260."

§2031.1. [Section repealed 2005]

Leg.H. Added Stats 2003 ch 242 §1 (AB 634). Repealed Stats 2004 ch 182 §22 (AB 3081), operative July 1, 2005. The repealed section related to confidential settlement agreements involving elder and dependent adult abuse. See CCP §2017.310.

ARTICLE 2
Response to Inspection Demand

Nature and format of response. §2031.210.
Statement regarding compliance in whole or in part. §2031.220.
Representation of inability to comply. §2031.230.
Statement of compliance or inability to comply when part of demand objectionable; Legislative intent regarding privilege log. §2031.240.
Signing of response to demand. §2031.250.
Time for service of response; Unlawful detainer actions. §2031.260.
Extension of time for service of response; Written confirmation of agreement. §2031.270.
Form in which documents to be produced; Form for producing electronically stored information; Translation of data. §2031.280.
Claim of privilege or protection as attorney work product for electronically stored information. §2031.285.

Retention of inspection demand, proof of service, and response by demanding party. §2031.290.
Effect of failure to serve timely response to demand; Motion for order; Monetary and other sanctions; Failure to provide electronically stored information. §2031.300.
Motion for order compelling further response; Notice; Electronically stored information; Sanctions. §2031.310.
Motion for order compelling compliance upon failure to permit inspection, copying, testing, or sampling; Sanctions; Failure to provide electronically stored information. §2031.320.

§2031.2. [Section repealed 2005]

Leg.H. Added Stats 2003 ch 242 §2 (AB 634). Repealed Stats 2004 ch 182 §22 (AB 3081), operative July 1, 2005. The repealed section related to disclosure of certain information covered by stipulated protective order in action involving elder and dependent adult abuse. See CCP §2017.320.

§2031.210. Nature and format of response

(a) The party to whom a demand for inspection, copying, testing, or sampling has been directed shall respond separately to each item or category of item by any of the following:

(1) A statement that the party will comply with the particular demand for inspection, copying, testing, or sampling by the date set for the inspection, copying, testing, or sampling pursuant to paragraph (2) of subdivision (c) of Section 2031.030 and any related activities.

(2) A representation that the party lacks the ability to comply with the demand for inspection, copying, testing, or sampling of a particular item or category of item.

(3) An objection to the particular demand for inspection, copying, testing, or sampling.

(b) In the first paragraph of the response immediately below the title of the case, there shall appear the identity of the responding party, the set number, and the identity of the demanding party.

(c) Each statement of compliance, each representation, and each objection in the response shall bear the same number and be in the same sequence as the corresponding item or category in the demand, but the text of that item or category need not be repeated.

(d) If a party objects to the discovery of electronically stored information on the grounds that it is from a source that is not reasonably accessible because of undue burden or expense and that the responding party will not search the source in the absence of an agreement with the demanding party or court order, the responding party shall identify in its response the types or categories of sources of electronically stored information that it asserts are not reasonably accessible. By objecting and identifying information of a type or category of source or sources that are not reasonably accessible, the responding party preserves any objections it may have relating to that electronically stored information. **Leg.H.** Added Stats 2004 ch 182 §23 (AB 3081), operative July 1, 2005. Amended Stats 2007 ch 738 §7 (AB 1248), effective January 1, 2008; Stats 2009 ch 5 §10 (AB 5), effective June 29, 2009.

2009 Note: This act shall be known as the Electronic Discovery Act. Stats 2009 ch 5 (AB 5) §1.

§2031.220. Statement regarding compliance in whole or in part

A statement that the party to whom a demand for inspection, copying, testing, or sampling has been directed will comply with the particular demand shall state that the production, inspection, copying, testing, or sampling, and related activity demanded, will be allowed either in whole or in part, and that all documents or things in the demanded category that are in the possession, custody, or control of that party and to which no objection is being made will be included in the production. **Leg.H.** Added Stats 2004 ch 182 §23 (AB 3081), operative July 1, 2005. Amended Stats 2009 ch 5 §11 (AB 5), effective June 29, 2009.

2009 Note: This act shall be known as the Electronic Discovery Act. Stats 2009 ch 5 (AB 5) §1.

§2031.230. Representation of inability to comply

A representation of inability to comply with the particular demand for inspection, copying, testing, or sampling shall affirm that a diligent search and a reasonable inquiry has been made in an effort to comply with that demand. This statement shall also specify whether the inability to comply is because the particular item or category has never existed, has been destroyed, has been lost, misplaced, or stolen, or has never been, or is no longer, in the possession, custody, or control of the responding party. The statement shall set forth the name and address of any natural person or organization known or believed by that party to have possession, custody, or control of that item or category of item. **Leg.H.** Added Stats 2004 ch 182 §23 (AB 3081), operative July 1, 2005. Amended Stats 2009 ch 5 §12 (AB 5), effective June 29, 2009.

2009 Note: This act shall be known as the Electronic Discovery Act. Stats 2009 ch 5 (AB 5) §1.

§2031.240. Statement of compliance or inability to comply when part of demand objectionable; Legislative intent regarding privilege log

(a) If only part of an item or category of item in a demand for inspection, copying, testing, or sampling is objectionable, the response shall contain a statement of compliance, or a representation of inability to comply with respect to the remainder of that item or category.

(b) If the responding party objects to the demand for inspection, copying, testing, or sampling of an item or category of item, the response shall do both of the following:

(1) Identify with particularity any document, tangible thing, land, or electronically stored information falling within any category of item in the demand to which an objection is being made.

(2) Set forth clearly the extent of, and the specific ground for, the objection. If an objection is based on a claim of privilege, the particular privilege invoked shall be stated. If an objection is based on a claim that the information sought is protected work product under Chapter 4 (commencing with Section 2018.010), that claim shall be expressly asserted.

(c)(1) If an objection is based on a claim of privilege or a claim that the information sought is protected work product, the response shall provide sufficient factual information for other parties to evaluate the merits of that claim, including, if necessary, a privilege log.

(2) It is the intent of the Legislature to codify the concept of a privilege log as that term is used in California case law. Nothing in this subdivision shall be construed to constitute a substantive change in case law. **Leg.H.** Added Stats 2004 ch 182 §23 (AB 3081), operative July 1, 2005. Amended Stats 2009 ch 5 §13 (AB 5), effective June 29, 2009; Stats 2012 ch 232 §1 (AB 1354), effective January 1, 2013.

2009 Note: This act shall be known as the Electronic Discovery Act. Stats 2009 ch 5 (AB 5) §1.

§2031.250. Signing of response to demand

(a) The party to whom the demand for inspection, copying, testing, or sampling is directed shall sign the response under oath unless the response contains only objections.

(b) If that party is a public or private corporation or a partnership or association or governmental agency, one of its officers or agents shall sign the response under oath on behalf of that party. If the officer or agent signing the response on behalf of that party is an attorney acting in that capacity for a party, that party waives any lawyer-client privilege and any protection for work product under Chapter 4 (commencing with Section 2018.010) during any subsequent discovery from that attorney concerning the identity of the sources of the information contained in the response.

(c) The attorney for the responding party shall sign any responses that contain an objection. **Leg.H.** Added Stats 2004 ch 182 §23 (AB 3081), operative July 1, 2005. Amended Stats 2009 ch 5 §14 (AB 5), effective June 29, 2009.

2009 Note: This act shall be known as the Electronic Discovery Act. Stats 2009 ch 5 (AB 5) §1.

§2031.260. Time for service of response; Unlawful detainer actions

(a) Within 30 days after service of a demand for inspection, copying, testing, or sampling, the party to whom the demand is directed shall serve the original of the response to it on the party making the demand, and a copy of the response on all other parties who have appeared in the action, unless on motion of the party making the demand, the court has shortened the time for response, or unless on motion of the party to whom the demand has been directed, the court has extended the time for response.

(b) Notwithstanding subdivision (a), in an unlawful detainer action or other proceeding under Chapter 4 (commencing with Section 1159) of Title 3 of Part 3, the party to whom a demand for inspection, copying, testing, or sampling is directed shall have at least five days from the date of service of the demand to respond, unless on motion of the party making the demand, the court has shortened the time for the response, or unless on motion of the party to whom the demand has been directed, the court has extended the time for response. **Leg.H.** Added Stats 2004 ch 182 §23 (AB 3081), operative July 1, 2005. Amended Stats 2007 ch 113 §11 (AB 1126), effective January 1, 2008; Stats 2009 ch 5 §15 (AB 5), effective June 29, 2009.

2009 Note: This act shall be known as the Electronic Discovery Act. Stats 2009 ch 5 (AB 5) §1.

§2031.270. Extension of time for service of response; Written confirmation of agreement

(a) The party demanding inspection, copying, testing, or sampling and the responding party may agree to extend the date for the inspection, copying, testing, or sampling or the time for service of a response to a set of demands, or to particular items or categories of items in a set, to a date or dates beyond those provided in Sections 2031.030, 2031.210, 2031.260, and 2031.280.

(b) This agreement may be informal, but it shall be confirmed in a writing that specifies the extended date for inspection, copying, testing, or sampling, or for the service of a response.

(c) Unless this agreement expressly states otherwise, it is effective to preserve to the responding party the right to respond to any item or category of item in the demand to which the agreement applies in any manner specified in Sections 2031.210, 2031.220, 2031.230, 2031.240, and 2031.280. **Leg.H.** Added Stats 2004 ch 182 §23 (AB 3081), operative July 1, 2005. Amended Stats 2007 ch 738 §8 (AB 1248), effective January 1, 2008; Stats 2009 ch 5 §16 (AB 5), effective June 29, 2009.

2009 Note: This act shall be known as the Electronic Discovery Act. Stats 2009 ch 5 (AB 5) §1.

§2031.280. Form in which documents to be produced; Form for producing electronically stored information; Translation of data

(a) Any documents or category of documents produced in response to a demand for inspection, copying, testing, or sampling shall be identified with the specific request number to which the documents respond.

(b) The documents shall be produced on the date specified in the demand pursuant to paragraph (2) of subdivision (c) of Section 2031.030, unless an objection has been made to that date. If the date for inspection has been extended pursuant to Section 2031.270, the documents shall be produced on the date agreed to pursuant to that section.

(c) If a party responding to a demand for production of electronically stored information objects to a specified form for producing the information, or if no form is specified in the demand, the responding party shall state in its response the form in which it intends to produce each type of information.

(d) Unless the parties otherwise agree or the court otherwise orders, the following shall apply:

(1) If a demand for production does not specify a form or forms for producing a type of electronically stored information, the responding party shall produce the information in the form or forms in which it is ordinarily maintained or in a form that is reasonably usable.

(2) A party need not produce the same electronically stored information in more than one form.

(e) If necessary, the responding party at the reasonable expense of the demanding party shall, through detection devices, translate any data compilations included in the demand into reasonably usable form. **Leg.H.** Added Stats 2004 ch 182 §23 (AB 3081), operative July 1, 2005. Amended Stats 2007 ch 738 §9 (AB 1248), effective January 1, 2008; Stats 2009 ch 5 §17 (AB 5), effective June 29, 2009; Stats 2019 ch 208 §1 (SB 370), effective January 1, 2020.

2009 Note: This act shall be known as the Electronic Discovery Act. Stats 2009 ch 5 (AB 5) §1.

§2031.285. Claim of privilege or protection as attorney work product for electronically stored information

(a) If electronically stored information produced in discovery is subject to a claim of privilege or of protection as attorney work product, the party making the claim may notify any party that received the information of the claim and the basis for the claim.

(b) After being notified of a claim of privilege or of protection under subdivision (a), a party that received the information shall immediately sequester the information and either return the specified information and any copies that may exist or present the information to the court conditionally under seal for a determination of the claim.

(c)(1) Prior to the resolution of the motion brought under subdivision (d), a party shall be precluded from using or disclosing the specified information until the claim of privilege is resolved.

(2) A party who received and disclosed the information before being notified of a claim of privilege or of protection under subdivision (a) shall, after that notification, immediately take reasonable steps to retrieve the information.

(d)(1) If the receiving party contests the legitimacy of a claim of privilege or protection, he or she may seek a determination of the claim from the court by making a motion within 30 days of receiving the claim and presenting the information to the court conditionally under seal.

(2) Until the legitimacy of the claim of privilege or protection is resolved, the receiving party shall preserve the information and keep it confidential and shall be precluded from using the information in any manner. **Leg.H.** Added Stats 2009 ch 5 §18 (AB 5), effective June 29, 2009.

2009 Note: This act shall be known as the Electronic Discovery Act. Stats 2009 ch 5 (AB 5) §1.

§2031.290. Retention of inspection demand, proof of service, and response by demanding party

(a) The demand for inspection, copying, testing, or sampling, and the response to it, shall not be filed with the court.

(b) The party demanding an inspection, copying, testing, or sampling shall retain both the original of the demand, with the original proof of service affixed to it, and the original of the sworn response until six months after final disposition of the action. At that time, both originals may be destroyed, unless the court, on motion of any party and for good cause shown, orders that the originals be preserved for a longer period. **Leg.H.** Added Stats 2004 ch 182 §23 (AB 3081), operative July 1, 2005. Amended Stats 2009 ch 5 §19 (AB 5), effective June 29, 2009.

2009 Note: This act shall be known as the Electronic Discovery Act. Stats 2009 ch 5 (AB 5) §1.

§2031.300. Effect of failure to serve timely response to demand; Motion for order; Monetary and other sanctions; Failure to provide electronically stored information

If a party to whom a demand for inspection, copying, testing, or sampling is directed fails to serve a timely response to it, the following rules shall apply:

(a) The party to whom the demand for inspection, copying, testing, or sampling is directed waives any objection to the demand, including one based on privilege or on the protection for work product under Chapter 4 (commencing with Section 2018.010). The court, on motion, may relieve that party from this waiver on its determination that both of the following conditions are satisfied:

(1) The party has subsequently served a response that is in substantial compliance with Sections 2031.210, 2031.220, 2031.230, 2031.240, and 2031.280.

(2) The party's failure to serve a timely response was the result of mistake, inadvertence, or excusable neglect.

(b) The party making the demand may move for an order compelling response to the demand.

(c) Except as provided in subdivision (d), the court shall impose a monetary sanction under Chapter 7 (commencing with Section 2023.010) against any party, person, or attorney who unsuccessfully makes or opposes a motion to compel a response to a demand for inspection, copying, testing, or sampling, unless it finds that the one subject to the sanction acted with substantial justification or that other circumstances make the imposition of the sanction unjust. If a party then fails to obey the order compelling a response, the court may make those orders that are just, including the imposition of an issue sanction, an evidence sanction, or a terminating sanction under Chapter 7 (commencing with Section 2023.010). In lieu of or in addition to this sanction, the court may impose a monetary sanction under Chapter 7 (commencing with Section 2023.010).

(d)(1) Notwithstanding subdivision (c), absent exceptional circumstances, the court shall not impose sanctions on a party or any attorney of a party for failure to provide electronically stored information that has been lost, damaged, altered, or overwritten as a result of the routine, good faith operation of an electronic information system.

(2) This subdivision shall not be construed to alter any obligation to preserve discoverable information. **Leg.H.** Added Stats 2004 ch 182 §23 (AB 3081), operative July 1, 2005. Amended Stats 2005 ch 22 §23 (SB 1108), effective January 1, 2006; Stats 2009 ch 5 §20 (AB 5), effective June 29, 2009.

2009 Note: This act shall be known as the Electronic Discovery Act. Stats 2009 ch 5 (AB 5) §1.

§2031.310. Motion for order compelling further response; Notice; Electronically stored information; Sanctions

(a) On receipt of a response to a demand for inspection, copying, testing, or sampling, the demanding party may move for an order compelling further response to the demand if the demanding party deems that any of the following apply:

(1) A statement of compliance with the demand is incomplete.

(2) A representation of inability to comply is inadequate, incomplete, or evasive.

(3) An objection in the response is without merit or too general.

(b) A motion under subdivision (a) shall comply with each of the following:

(1) The motion shall set forth specific facts showing good cause justifying the discovery sought by the demand.

(2) The motion shall be accompanied by a meet and confer declaration under Section 2016.040.

(3) In lieu of a separate statement required under the California Rules of Court, the court may allow the moving party to submit a concise outline of the discovery request and each response in dispute.

(c) Unless notice of this motion is given within 45 days of the service of the verified response, or any supplemental verified response, or on or before any specific later date to which the demanding party and the responding party have agreed in writing, the demanding party waives any right to compel a further response to the demand.

(d) In a motion under subdivision (a) relating to the production of electronically stored information, the party or affected person objecting to or opposing the production, inspection, copying, testing, or sampling of electronically stored information on the basis that the information is from a source that is not reasonably accessible because of the undue burden or expense shall bear the burden of demonstrating that the information is from a source that is not reasonably accessible because of undue burden or expense.

(e) If the party or affected person from whom discovery of electronically stored information is sought establishes that the information is from a source that is not reasonably accessible because of the undue burden or expense, the court may nonetheless order discovery if the demanding party shows good cause, subject to any limitations imposed under subdivision (g).

(f) If the court finds good cause for the production of electronically stored information from a source that is not reasonably accessible, the court may set conditions for the discovery of the electronically stored information, including allocation of the expense of discovery.

(g) The court shall limit the frequency or extent of discovery of electronically stored information, even from a source that is reasonably accessible, if the court determines that any of the following conditions exists:

(1) It is possible to obtain the information from some other source that is more convenient, less burdensome, or less expensive.

(2) The discovery sought is unreasonably cumulative or duplicative.

(3) The party seeking discovery has had ample opportunity by discovery in the action to obtain the information sought.

(4) The likely burden or expense of the proposed discovery outweighs the likely benefit, taking into account the amount in controversy, the resources of the parties, the importance of the issues in the litigation, and the importance of the requested discovery in resolving the issues.

(h) Except as provided in subdivision (j), the court shall impose a monetary sanction under Chapter 7 (commencing with Section 2023.010) against any party, person, or attorney who unsuccessfully makes or opposes a motion to compel further response to a demand, unless it finds that the one subject to the sanction acted with substantial justification or that other circumstances make the imposition of the sanction unjust.

(i) Except as provided in subdivision (j), if a party fails to obey an order compelling further response, the court may make those orders that are just, including the imposition of an issue sanction, an evidence sanction, or a terminating sanction under Chapter 7 (commencing with Section 2023.010). In lieu of, or in addition to, that sanction, the court may impose a monetary sanction under Chapter 7 (commencing with Section 2023.010).

(j)(1) Notwithstanding subdivisions (h) and (i), absent exceptional circumstances, the court shall not impose sanctions on a party or any attorney of a party for failure to provide electronically stored information that has been lost, damaged, altered, or overwritten as the result of the routine, good faith operation of an electronic information system.

(2) This subdivision shall not be construed to alter any obligation to preserve discoverable information. **Leg.H.** Added Stats 2004 ch 182 §23 (AB 3081), operative July 1, 2005. Amended Stats 2009 ch 5 §21 (AB 5), effective June 29, 2009; Stats 2013 ch 18 §2 (AB 1183), effective January 1, 2014; Stats 2018 ch 317 §4 (AB 2230), effective January 1, 2019, operative January 1, 2020.

2009 Note: This act shall be known as the Electronic Discovery Act. Stats 2009 ch 5 (AB 5) §1.

§2031.320. Motion for order compelling compliance upon failure to permit inspection, copying, testing, or sampling; Sanctions; Failure to provide electronically stored information

(a) If a party filing a response to a demand for inspection, copying, testing, or sampling under Sections 2031.210, 2031.220, 2031.230, 2031.240, and 2031.280 thereafter fails to permit the inspection, copying, testing, or sampling in accordance with that party's statement of compliance, the demanding party may move for an order compelling compliance.

(b) Except as provided in subdivision (d), the court shall impose a monetary sanction under Chapter 7 (commencing with Section 2023.010) against any party, person, or attorney who unsuccessfully makes or opposes a motion to compel compliance with a demand, unless it finds that the one subject to the sanction acted with substantial justification or that other circumstances make the imposition of the sanction unjust.

(c) Except as provided in subdivision (d), if a party then fails to obey an order compelling inspection, copying, testing, or sampling, the court may make those orders that are just, including the imposition of an issue sanction, an evidence sanction, or a terminating sanction under Chapter 7 (commencing with Section 2023.010). In lieu of or in addition to that sanction, the court may impose a monetary sanction under Chapter 7 (commencing with Section 2023.010).

(d)(1) Notwithstanding subdivisions (b) and (c), absent exceptional circumstances, the court shall not impose sanctions on a party or any attorney of a party for failure to provide electronically stored information that has been lost, damaged, altered, or overwritten as the result of the routine, good faith operation of an electronic information system.

(2) This subdivision shall not be construed to alter any obligation to preserve discoverable information. **Leg.H.** Added Stats 2004 ch 182 §23 (AB 3081), operative July 1, 2005. Amended Stats 2009 ch 5 §22 (AB 5), effective June 29, 2009.

ARTICLE 3
Inspection and Production of Documents and Other Property in Specific Contexts

Boundary of land granted by state or validity of certain state patents or grants; Duty to disclose nonprivileged relevant written information. §2031.510.

§2031.5. [Section repealed 2005]

Leg.H. Added Stats 1994 ch 128 §1 (SB 1429). Repealed Stats 2004 ch 182 §22 (AB 3081), operative July 1, 2005. The repealed section related to duty to disclose relevant evidence in action involving land patented or granted by state. See CCP §2031.510.

§2031.510. Boundary of land granted by state or validity of certain state patents or grants; Duty to disclose nonprivileged relevant written information

(a) In any action, regardless of who is the moving party, where the boundary of land patented or otherwise granted by the state is in dispute, or the validity of any state patent or grant dated before 1950 is in dispute, all parties shall have the duty to disclose to all opposing parties all nonprivileged relevant written evidence then known and available, including evidence against interest, relating to the above issues.

(b) This evidence shall be disclosed within 120 days after the filing with the court of proof of service upon all named defendants. Thereafter, the parties shall have the continuing duty to make all subsequently discovered relevant and nonprivileged written evidence available to the opposing parties. **Leg.H.** Added Stats 2004 ch 182 §23 (AB 3081), operative July 1, 2005.

CHAPTER 15
PHYSICAL OR MENTAL EXAMINATION

Article 1. General Provisions.
Article 2. Physical Examination of Personal Injury Plaintiff.
Article 3. Motion for Physical or Mental Examination.
Article 4. Failure to Submit to or Produce Another for Physical or Mental Examination.
Article 5. Conduct of Examination.
Article 6. Reports of Examination.

ARTICLE 1
General Provisions

Certain matters not affected by chapter. §2032.010.
Right to discovery by physical or mental examination; By whom performed. §2032.020.

§2032. [Section repealed 2005]

Leg.H. Added Stats 1986 ch 1336 §1, operative July 1, 1987. Amended Stats 1987 ch 86 §14, operative July 1, 1987; Stats 1988 ch 553 §5; Stats 1992 ch 163 §65 (AB 2641), operative January 1, 1994, ch 615 §6 (SB 1804) (ch 615 prevails); Stats 1993 ch 219 §71 (AB 1500). Repealed Stats 2004 ch 182 §22 (AB 3081), operative July 1, 2005. The repealed section related to physical and mental examinations. See CCP §§2032.010 et seq.

Prior Law: Former CCP §2032 was added Stats 1957 ch 1904 §3, operative January 1, 1958, amended Stats 1959 ch 1590 §10, Stats 1980 ch 1206 §1, and repealed Stats 1986 ch 1334 §1, operative July 1, 1987.

Original CCP §2032, relating to use of depositions at trial, was enacted 1872, amended Stats 1929 ch 474 §2, and repealed Stats 1957 ch 1904 §1, operative January 1, 1958.

§2032.010. Certain matters not affected by chapter

(a) This chapter does not affect genetic testing under Chapter 2 (commencing with Section 7550) of Part 2 of Division 12 of the Family Code.

(b) This chapter does not require the disclosure of the identity of an expert consulted by an attorney in order to make the certification required in an action for professional negligence under Section 411.35. **Leg.H.** Added Stats 2004 ch 182 §23 (AB 3081), operative July 1, 2005. Amended Stats 2018 ch 876 §2 (AB 2684), effective January 1, 2019.

§2032.020. Right to discovery by physical or mental examination; By whom performed

(a) Any party may obtain discovery, subject to the restrictions set forth in Chapter 5 (commencing with Section 2019.010), by means of a physical or mental examination of (1) a party to the action, (2) an agent of any party, or (3) a natural person in the custody or under the legal control of a party, in any action in which the mental or physical condition (including the blood group) of that party or other person is in controversy in the action.

(b) A physical examination conducted under this chapter shall be performed only by a licensed physician or other appropriate licensed health care practitioner.

(c)(1) A mental examination conducted under this chapter shall be performed only by a licensed physician, or by a licensed clinical psychologist who holds a doctoral degree in psychology and has had at least five years of postgraduate experience in the diagnosis of emotional and mental disorders.

(2) If an action involves allegations of sexual abuse of a minor, including any act listed in paragraphs (1) to (3), inclusive, of subdivision (a) of Section 1002, and the examinee is less than 15 years of age, the licensed physician or clinical psychologist shall have expertise in child abuse and trauma. **Leg.H.** Added Stats 2004 ch 182 §23 (AB 3081), operative July 1, 2005. Amended Stats 2017 ch 133 §1 (SB 755), effective January 1, 2018.

ARTICLE 2
Physical Examination of Personal Injury Plaintiff

Meaning of "plaintiff" for purposes of article. §2032.210.
When defendant in personal injury action may seek physical examination of plaintiff; Requirements; Service of demand. §2032.220.

Response of plaintiff to demand. §2032.230.
Effect of failure to serve timely response; Waiver; Relief from waiver; Motion for order compelling compliance; Monetary and other sanctions. §2032.240.
Motion for compliance on receipt of response; Monetary sanction. §2032.250.
Retention by defendant of demand, proof of service and response. §2032.260.

§2032.210. Meaning of "plaintiff" for purposes of article

As used in this article, "plaintiff" includes a cross-complainant, and "defendant" includes a cross-defendant. **Leg.H.** Added Stats 2004 ch 182 §23 (AB 3081), operative July 1, 2005.

§2032.220. When defendant in personal injury action may seek physical examination of plaintiff; Requirements; Service of demand

(a) In any case in which a plaintiff is seeking recovery for personal injuries, any defendant may demand one physical examination of the plaintiff, if both of the following conditions are satisfied:

(1) The examination does not include any diagnostic test or procedure that is painful, protracted, or intrusive.

(2) The examination is conducted at a location within 75 miles of the residence of the examinee.

(b) A defendant may make a demand under this article without leave of court after that defendant has been served or has appeared in the action, whichever occurs first.

(c) A demand under subdivision (a) shall specify the time, place, manner, conditions, scope, and nature of the examination, as well as the identity and the specialty, if any, of the physician who will perform the examination.

(d) A physical examination demanded under subdivision (a) shall be scheduled for a date that is at least 30 days after service of the demand. On motion of the party demanding the examination, the court may shorten this time.

(e) The defendant shall serve a copy of the demand under subdivision (a) on the plaintiff and on all other parties who have appeared in the action. **Leg.H.** Added Stats 2004 ch 182 §23 (AB 3081), operative July 1, 2005.

§2032.230. Response of plaintiff to demand

(a) The plaintiff to whom a demand for a physical examination under this article is directed shall respond to the demand by a written statement that the examinee will comply with the demand as stated, will comply with the demand as specifically modified by the plaintiff, or will refuse, for reasons specified in the response, to submit to the demanded physical examination.

(b) Within 20 days after service of the demand the plaintiff to whom the demand is directed shall serve the original of the response to it on the defendant making the demand, and a copy of the response on all other parties who have appeared in the action. On motion of the defendant making the demand, the court may shorten the time for response. On motion of the plaintiff to whom the demand is directed, the court may extend the time for response. **Leg.H.** Added Stats 2004 ch 182 §23 (AB 3081), operative July 1, 2005.

§2032.240. Effect of failure to serve timely response; Waiver; Relief from waiver; Motion for order compelling compliance; Monetary and other sanctions

(a) If a plaintiff to whom a demand for a physical examination under this article is directed fails to serve a timely response to it, that plaintiff waives any objection to the demand. The court, on motion, may relieve that plaintiff from this waiver on its determination that both of the following conditions are satisfied:

(1) The plaintiff has subsequently served a response that is in substantial compliance with Section 2032.230.

(2) The plaintiff's failure to serve a timely response was the result of mistake, inadvertence, or excusable neglect.

(b) The defendant may move for an order compelling response and compliance with a demand for a physical examination.

(c) The court shall impose a monetary sanction under Chapter 7 (commencing with Section 2023.010) against any party, person, or attorney who unsuccessfully makes or opposes a motion to compel response and compliance with a demand for a physical examination, unless it finds that the one subject to the sanction acted with substantial justification or that other circumstances make the imposition of the sanction unjust.

(d) If a plaintiff then fails to obey the order compelling response and compliance, the court may make those orders that are just, including the imposition of an issue sanction, an evidence sanction, or a terminating sanction under Chapter 7 (commencing with Section 2023.010). In lieu of or in addition to that sanction the court may impose a monetary sanction under Chapter 7 (commencing with Section 2023.010). **Leg.H.** Added Stats 2004 ch 182 §23 (AB 3081), operative July 1, 2005.

§2032.250. Motion for compliance on receipt of response; Monetary sanction

(a) If a defendant who has demanded a physical examination under this article, on receipt of the plaintiff's response to that demand, deems that any modification of the demand, or any refusal to submit to the physical examination is unwarranted, that defendant may move for an order compelling compliance with the demand. This motion shall be accompanied by a meet and confer declaration under Section 2016.040.

(b) The court shall impose a monetary sanction under Chapter 7 (commencing with Section 2023.010) against any party, person, or attorney who unsuccessfully makes or opposes a motion to compel compliance with a demand for a physical examination, unless it finds that the one subject to the sanction acted with substantial justification or that other circumstances make the imposition of the sanction unjust. **Leg.H.** Added Stats 2004 ch 182 §23 (AB 3081), operative July 1, 2005.

§2032.260. Retention by defendant of demand, proof of service and response

(a) The demand for a physical examination under this article and the response to it shall not be filed with the court.

(b) The defendant shall retain both the original of the demand, with the original proof of service affixed to it, and the original response until six months after final disposition of the action. At that time, the original may be destroyed, unless the court, on motion of any party and for good cause shown, orders that the originals be preserved for a longer period. **Leg.H.** Added Stats 2004 ch 182 §23 (AB 3081), operative July 1, 2005.

ARTICLE 3
Motion for Physical or Mental Examination

Leave of court for physical examination other than that described in Sections 2032.210 et seq. or mental examination; Motion and notice. §2032.310.
When motion to be granted; Stipulation as to mental and emotional distress; Order; Mileage limitation. §2032.320.
Mental examination of child less than 15 years of age in action involving allegations of sexual abuse of minor. §2032.340.

§2032.310. Leave of court for physical examination other than that described in Sections 2032.210 et seq. or mental examination; Motion and notice

(a) If any party desires to obtain discovery by a physical examination other than that described in Article 2 (commencing with Section 2032.210), or by a mental examination, the party shall obtain leave of court.

(b) A motion for an examination under subdivision (a) shall specify the time, place, manner, conditions, scope, and nature of the examination, as well as the identity and the specialty, if any, of the person or persons who will perform the examination. The motion shall be accompanied by a meet and confer declaration under Section 2016.040.

(c) Notice of the motion shall be served on the person to be examined and on all parties who have appeared in the action. **Leg.H.** Added Stats 2004 ch 182 §23 (AB 3081), operative July 1, 2005.

§2032.320. When motion to be granted; Stipulation as to mental and emotional distress; Order; Mileage limitation

(a) The court shall grant a motion for a physical or mental examination under Section 2032.310 only for good cause shown.

(b) If a party stipulates as provided in subdivision (c), the court shall not order a mental examination of a person for whose personal injuries a recovery is being sought except on a showing of exceptional circumstances.

(c) A stipulation by a party under this subdivision shall include both of the following:

(1) A stipulation that no claim is being made for mental and emotional distress over and above that usually associated with the physical injuries claimed.

(2) A stipulation that no expert testimony regarding this usual mental and emotional distress will be presented at trial in support of the claim for damages.

(d) An order granting a physical or mental examination shall specify the person or persons who may perform the examination, as well as the time, place, manner, diagnostic tests and procedures, conditions, scope, and nature of the examination.

(e) If the place of the examination is more than 75 miles from the residence of the person to be examined, an order to submit to it shall be entered only if both of the following conditions are satisfied:

(1) The court determines that there is good cause for the travel involved.

(2) The order is conditioned on the advancement by the moving party of the reasonable expenses and costs to the examinee for travel to the place of examination. **Leg.H.** Added Stats 2004 ch 182 §23 (AB 3081), operative July 1, 2005.

§2032.340. Mental examination of child less than 15 years of age in action involving allegations of sexual abuse of minor

(a) If any action involving allegations of sexual abuse of a minor, including any act listed in paragraphs (1) to (3), inclusive, of subdivision (a) of Section 1002, the mental examination of a child less than 15 years of age shall not exceed three hours, inclusive of breaks.

(b) Notwithstanding subdivision (a), the court may grant an extension of the three-hour limit for good cause. **Leg.H.** Added Stats 2017 ch 133 §2 (SB 755), effective January 1, 2018.

ARTICLE 4
Failure to Submit to or Produce Another for Physical or Mental Examination

Effect of failure to submit to examination; Sanctions. §2032.410.
Effect of failure to produce another for examination; Sanctions. §2032.420.

§2032.410. Effect of failure to submit to examination; Sanctions

If a party is required to submit to a physical or mental examination under Articles 2 (commencing with Section 2032.210) or 3 (commencing with Section 2032.310), or under Section 2016.030, but fails to do so, the court, on motion of the party entitled to the examination, may make those orders that are just, including the imposition of an issue sanction, an evidence sanction, or a terminating sanction under Chapter 7 (commencing with Section 2023.010). In lieu of or in addition to that sanction, the court may, on motion of the party, impose a monetary sanction under Chapter 7 (commencing with Section 2023.010). **Leg.H.** Added Stats 2004 ch 182 §23 (AB 3081), operative July 1, 2005.

§2032.420. Effect of failure to produce another for examination; Sanctions

If a party is required to produce another for a physical or mental examination under Articles 2 (commencing with Section 2032.210) or 3 (commencing with Section 2032.310), or under Section 2032.030, but fails to do so, the court, on motion of the party entitled to the examination, may make those orders that are just, including the imposition of an issue sanction, an evidence sanction, or a terminating sanction under Chapter 7 (commencing with Section 2023.010), unless the party failing to comply demonstrates an inability to produce that person for examination. In lieu of or in addition to that sanction, the court may impose a monetary sanction under Chapter 7 (commencing with Section 2023.010). **Leg.H.** Added Stats 2004 ch 182 §23 (AB 3081), operative July 1, 2005.

ARTICLE 5
Conduct of Examination

Attendance of attorney for examinee or attorney's representative at physical examination; Recording and monitoring; Right to suspend examination pending motion for protective order; Monetary sanction. §2032.510.
Consent of examinee to additional X-rays. §2032.520.
Right of examiner and examinee to record mental examination; Presence of attorney and others. §2032.530.

§2032.510. Attendance of attorney for examinee or attorney's representative at physical examination; Recording and monitoring; Right to suspend examination pending motion for protective order; Monetary sanction

(a) The attorney for the examinee or for a party producing the examinee, or that attorney's representative, shall be permitted to attend and observe any physical examination conducted for discovery purposes, and to record stenographically or by audio technology any words spoken to or by the examinee during any phase of the examination.

(b) The observer under subdivision (a) may monitor the examination, but shall not participate in or disrupt it.

(c) If an attorney's representative is to serve as the observer, the representative shall be authorized to so act by a writing subscribed by the attorney which identifies the representative.

(d) If in the judgment of the observer the examiner becomes abusive to the examinee or undertakes to engage in unauthorized diagnostic tests and procedures, the observer may suspend it to enable the party being examined or producing the examinee to make a motion for a protective order.

(e) If the observer begins to participate in or disrupt the examination, the person conducting the physical examination may suspend the examination to enable the party at whose instance it is being conducted to move for a protective order.

(f) The court shall impose a monetary sanction under Chapter 7 (commencing with Section 2023.010) against any party, person, or attorney who unsuccessfully makes or opposes a motion for a protective order under this section, unless it finds that the one subject to the sanction acted with substantial justification or that other circumstances make the imposition of the sanction unjust. **Leg.H.** Added Stats 2004 ch 182 §23 (AB 3081), operative July 1, 2005. Amended Stats 2005 ch 294 §10 (AB 333), effective January 1, 2006.

§2032.520. Consent of examinee to additional X-rays

If an examinee submits or authorizes access to X-rays of any area of his or her body for inspection by the examining physician, no additional X-rays of that area may be taken by the examining physician except with consent of the examinee or on order of the court for good cause shown. **Leg.H.** Added Stats 2004 ch 182 §23 (AB 3081), operative July 1, 2005.

§2032.530. Right of examiner and examinee to record mental examination; Presence of attorney and others

(a) The examiner and examinee shall have the right to record a mental examination by audio technology.

(b) Nothing in this title shall be construed to alter, amend, or affect existing case law with respect to the presence of the attorney for the examinee or other persons during the examination by agreement or court order. **Leg.H.** Added Stats 2004 ch 182 §23 (AB 3081), operative July 1, 2005. Amended Stats 2005 ch 294 §11 (AB 333), effective January 1, 2006.

ARTICLE 6
Reports of Examination

Right of party to demand reports; Waiver of work product privilege. §2032.610.
Failure to timely deliver reports demanded under Section 2032.610; Motion to compel delivery; Monetary and other sanctions. §2032.620.
Waiver of privilege and protection of work product by demanding and obtaining report of examination. §2032.630.
Right of party receiving demand for report to existing and later reports of same condition. §2032.640.
Failure to deliver existing and later reports under Section 2032.640; Motion for order compelling delivery; Monetary and other sanctions. §2032.650.

§2032.610. Right of party to demand reports; Waiver of work product privilege

(a) If a party submits to, or produces another for, a physical or mental examination in compliance with a demand under Article 2 (commencing with Section 2032.210), an order of court under Article 3 (commencing with Section 2032.310), or an agreement under Section 2016.030, that party has the option of making a written demand that the party at whose instance the examination was made deliver both of the following to the demanding party:

(1) A copy of a detailed written report setting out the history, examinations, findings, including the results of all tests made, diagnoses, prognoses, and conclusions of the examiner.

(2) A copy of reports of all earlier examinations of the same condition of the examinee made by that or any other examiner.

(b) If the option under subdivision (a) is exercised, a copy of the requested reports shall be delivered within 30 days after service of the demand, or within 15 days of trial, whichever is earlier.

(c) In the circumstances described in subdivision (a), the protection for work product under Chapter 4 (commencing with Section 2018.010) is waived, both for the examiner's writings and reports and to the taking of

§2032.620. Failure to timely deliver reports demanded under Section 2032.610; Motion to compel delivery; Monetary and other sanctions

(a) If the party at whose instance an examination was made fails to make a timely delivery of the reports demanded under Section 2032.610, the demanding party may move for an order compelling their delivery. This motion shall be accompanied by a meet and confer declaration under Section 2016.040.

(b) The court shall impose a monetary sanction under Chapter 7 (commencing with Section 2023.010) against any party, person, or attorney who unsuccessfully makes or opposes a motion to compel delivery of medical reports under this section, unless it finds that the one subject to the sanction acted with substantial justification or that other circumstances make the imposition of the sanction unjust.

(c) If a party then fails to obey an order compelling delivery of demanded medical reports, the court may make those orders that are just, including the imposition of an issue sanction, an evidence sanction, or a terminating sanction under Chapter 7 (commencing with Section 2023.010). In lieu of or in addition to those sanctions, the court may impose a monetary sanction under Chapter 7 (commencing with Section 2023.010). The court shall exclude at trial the testimony of any examiner whose report has not been provided by a party. **Leg.H.** Added Stats 2004 ch 182 §23 (AB 3081), operative July 1, 2005.

§2032.630. Waiver of privilege and protection of work product by demanding and obtaining report of examination

By demanding and obtaining a report of a physical or mental examination under Section 2032.610 or 2032.620, or by taking the deposition of the examiner, other than under Article 3 (commencing with Section 2034.410) of Chapter 18, the party who submitted to, or produced another for, a physical or mental examination waives in the pending action, and in any other action involving the same controversy, any privilege, as well as any protection for work product under Chapter 4 (commencing with Section 2018.010), that the party or other examinee may have regarding reports and writings as well as the testimony of every other physician, psychologist, or licensed health care practitioner who has examined or may thereafter examine the party or other examinee in respect of the same physical or mental condition. **Leg.H.** Added Stats 2004 ch 182 §23 (AB 3081), operative July 1, 2005.

§2032.640. Right of party receiving demand for report to existing and later reports of same condition

A party receiving a demand for a report under Section 2032.610 is entitled at the time of compliance to receive in exchange a copy of any existing written report of any examination of the same condition by any other physician, psychologist, or licensed health care practitioner. In addition, that party is entitled to receive promptly any later report of any previous or subsequent examination of the same condition, by any physician, psychologist, or licensed health care practitioner. **Leg.H.** Added Stats 2004 ch 182 §23 (AB 3081), operative July 1, 2005.

§2032.650. Failure to deliver existing and later reports under Section 2032.640; Motion for order compelling delivery; Monetary and other sanctions

(a) If a party who has demanded and received delivery of medical reports under Section 2032.610 fails to deliver existing or later reports of previous or subsequent examinations under Section 2032.640, a party who has complied with Section 2032.610 may move for an order compelling delivery of medical reports. This motion shall be accompanied by a meet and confer declaration under Section 2016.040.

(b) The court shall impose a monetary sanction under Chapter 7 (commencing with Section 2023.010) against any party, person, or attorney who unsuccessfully makes or opposes a motion to compel delivery of medical reports under this section, unless it finds that the one subject to the sanction acted with substantial justification or that other circumstances make the imposition of the sanction unjust.

(c) If a party then fails to obey an order compelling delivery of medical reports, the court may make those orders that are just, including the imposition of an issue sanction, an evidence sanction, or a terminating sanction under Chapter 7 (commencing with Section 2023.010). In lieu of or in addition to the sanction, the court may impose a monetary sanction under Chapter 7 (commencing with Section 2023.010). The court shall exclude at trial the testimony of any health care practitioner whose report has not been provided by a party ordered to do so by the court. **Leg.H.** Added Stats 2004 ch 182 §23 (AB 3081), operative July 1, 2005.

CHAPTER 16
REQUESTS FOR ADMISSION

Article 1. Requests for Admission.
Article 2. Response to Requests for Admission.
Article 3. Effect of Admission.

ARTICLE 1
Requests for Admission

Request for admissions; Scope and restrictions. §2033.010.
Time when defendant or plaintiff may make requests for admission. §2033.020.
Number of admission requests permitted; Genuineness of documents. §2033.030.
Greater number of admission requests when accompanied by supporting declaration; Protective order; Burden of justification. §2033.040.
Form of declaration for additional discovery. §2033.050.
Style and format for requests for admission; Copies of documents. §2033.060.
Service of requests for admission. §2033.070.
Motion for protective order; Grounds; Denial of order; Monetary sanction. §2033.080.

§2033. [Section repealed 2005]

Leg.H. Added Stats 1986 ch 1334 §2, operative July 1, 1987. Amended Stats 1987 ch 86 §15, operative July 1, 1987; Stats 1988 ch 553 §6, ch 575 §3; Stats 1991 ch 1090 §13 (AB 1484). Repealed Stats 2004 ch 182 §22 (AB 3081), operative July 1, 2005. The repealed section related to requests for admission. See CCP §§2033.010 et seq.

Prior Law: Former CCP §2033 was added Stats 1978 ch 12 §3, effective February 18, 1978, amended Stats 1978 ch 265 §1, Stats 1981 ch 225 §1, Stats 1983 ch 141 §2, and repealed Stats 1986 ch 1334 §1, operative July 1, 1987.

Former CCP §2033 was added Stats 1957 ch 1904 §3, operative January 1, 1958, amended Stats 1959 ch 1590 §11, Stats 1967 ch 610 §1, Stats 1968 ch 188 §2, Stats 1974 ch 723 §2, and repealed Stats 1977 ch 500 §2.

Original CCP §2033, relating to exclusion of depositions, was enacted 1872 and repealed Stats 1907 ch 392 §1.

§2033.010. Request for admissions; Scope and restrictions

Any party may obtain discovery within the scope delimited by Chapter 2 (commencing with Section 2017.010), and subject to the restrictions set forth in Chapter 5 (commencing with Section 2019.010), by a written request that any other party to the action admit the genuineness of specified documents, or the truth of specified matters of fact, opinion relating to fact, or application of law to fact. A request for admission may relate to a matter that is in controversy between the parties. **Leg.H.** Added Stats 2004 ch 182 §23 (AB 3081), operative July 1, 2005. Amended Stats 2016 ch 86 §43 (SB 1171), effective January 1, 2017.

§2033.020. Time when defendant or plaintiff may make requests for admission

(a) A defendant may make requests for admission by a party without leave of court at any time.

(b) A plaintiff may make requests for admission by a party without leave of court at any time that is 10 days after the service of the summons on, or appearance by, that party, whichever occurs first.

(c) Notwithstanding subdivision (b), in an unlawful detainer action or other proceeding under Chapter 4 (commencing with Section 1159) of Title 3 of Part 3, a plaintiff may make requests for admission by a party without leave of court at any time that is five days after service of the summons on, or appearance by, that party, whichever occurs first.

(d) Notwithstanding subdivisions (b) and (c), on motion with or without notice, the court, for good cause shown, may grant leave to a plaintiff to make requests for admission at an earlier time. **Leg.H.** Added Stats 2004 ch 182 §23 (AB 3081), operative July 1, 2005. Amended Stats 2007 ch 113 §12 (AB 1126), effective January 1, 2008.

§2033.030. Number of admission requests permitted; Genuineness of documents

(a) No party shall request, as a matter of right, that any other party admit more than 35 matters that do not relate to the genuineness of documents. If the initial set of admission requests does not exhaust this limit, the balance may be requested in subsequent sets.

(b) Unless a declaration as described in Section 2033.050 has been made, a party need only respond to the first 35 admission requests served that do not relate to the genuineness of documents, if that party states an objection to the balance under Section 2033.230 on the ground that the limit has been exceeded.

(c) The number of requests for admission of the genuineness of documents is not limited except as justice requires to protect the responding party from unwarranted annoyance, embarrassment, oppression, or undue burden and expense. **Leg.H.** Added Stats 2004 ch 182 §23 (AB 3081), operative July 1, 2005.

§2033.040. Greater number of admission requests when accompanied by supporting declaration; Protective order; Burden of justification

(a) Subject to the right of the responding party to seek a protective order under Section 2033.080, any party who attaches a supporting declaration as described in Section 2033.050 may request a greater number of admissions by another party if the greater number is warranted by the complexity or the quantity of the existing and potential issues in the particular case.

(b) If the responding party seeks a protective order on the ground that the number of requests for admission is unwarranted, the propounding party shall have the burden of justifying the number of requests for admission. **Leg.H.** Added Stats 2004 ch 182 §23 (AB 3081), operative July 1, 2005.

§2033.050. Form of declaration for additional discovery

Any party who is requesting or who has already requested more than 35 admissions not relating to the genuineness of documents by any other party shall attach to each set of requests for admissions a declaration containing substantially the following words:

DECLARATION FOR ADDITIONAL DISCOVERY

I, _____, declare:

1. I am (a party to this action or proceeding appearing in propria persona) (presently the attorney for _____, a party to this action or proceeding).

2. I am propounding to _____ the attached set of requests for admission.

3. This set of requests for admission will cause the total number of requests propounded to the party to whom they are directed to exceed the number of requests permitted by Section 2033.030 of the Code of Civil Procedure.

4. I have previously propounded a total of _____ requests for admission to this party.

5. This set of requests for admission contains a total of _____ requests.

6. I am familiar with the issues and the previous discovery conducted by all of the parties in this case.

7. I have personally examined each of the requests in this set of requests for admission.

8. This number of requests for admission is warranted under Section 2033.040 of the Code of Civil Procedure because _____. (Here state the reasons why the complexity or the quantity of issues in the instant lawsuit warrant this number of requests for admission.)

9. None of the requests in this set of requests is being propounded for any improper purpose, such as to harass the party, or the attorney for the party, to whom it is directed, or to cause unnecessary delay or needless increase in the cost of litigation.

I declare under penalty of perjury under the laws of California that the foregoing is true and correct, and that this declaration was executed on _____.

_____
(Signature)
Attorney for _____

Leg.H. Added Stats 2004 ch 182 §23 (AB 3081), operative July 1, 2005.

§2033.060. Style and format for requests for admission; Copies of documents

(a) A party requesting admissions shall number each set of requests consecutively.

(b) In the first paragraph immediately below the title of the case, there shall appear the identity of the party requesting the admissions, the set number, and the identity of the responding party.

(c) Each request for admission in a set shall be separately set forth and identified by letter or number.

(d) Each request for admission shall be full and complete in and of itself. No preface or instruction shall be included with a set of admission requests unless it has been approved under Chapter 17 (commencing with Section 2033.710).

(e) Any term specially defined in a request for admission shall be typed with all letters capitalized whenever the term appears.

(f) No request for admission shall contain subparts, or a compound, conjunctive, or disjunctive request unless it has been approved under Chapter 17 (commencing with Section 2033.710).

(g) A party requesting an admission of the genuineness of any documents shall attach copies of those documents to the requests, and shall make the original of those documents available for inspection on demand by the party to whom the requests for admission are directed.

(h) No party shall combine in a single document requests for admission with any other method of discovery. **Leg.H.** Added Stats 2004 ch 182 §23 (AB 3081), operative July 1, 2005.

§2033.070. Service of requests for admission

The party requesting admissions shall serve a copy of them on the party to whom they are directed and on all other parties who have appeared in the action. **Leg.H.** Added Stats 2004 ch 182 §23 (AB 3081), operative July 1, 2005.

§2033.080. Motion for protective order; Grounds; Denial of order; Monetary sanction

(a) When requests for admission have been made, the responding party may promptly move for a protective order. This motion shall be accompanied by a meet and confer declaration under Section 2016.040.

(b) The court, for good cause shown, may make any order that justice requires to protect any party from unwarranted annoyance, embarrassment, oppression, or undue burden and expense. This protective order may include, but is not limited to, one or more of the following directions:

(1) That the set of admission requests, or particular requests in the set, need not be answered at all.

(2) That, contrary to the representations made in a declaration submitted under Section 2033.050, the number of admission requests is unwarranted.

(3) That the time specified in Section 2033.250 to respond to the set of admission requests, or to particular requests in the set, be extended.

(4) That a trade secret or other confidential research, development, or commercial information not be admitted or be admitted only in a certain way.

(5) That some or all of the answers to requests for admission be sealed and thereafter opened only on order of the court.

(c) If the motion for a protective order is denied in whole or in part, the court may order that the responding party provide or permit the discovery against which protection was sought on terms and conditions that are just.

(d) The court shall impose a monetary sanction under Chapter 7 (commencing with Section 2023.010) against any party, person, or attorney who unsuccessfully makes or opposes a motion for a protective order under this section, unless it finds that the one subject to the sanction acted with substantial justification or that other circumstances make the imposition of the sanction unjust. **Leg.H.** Added Stats 2004 ch 182 §23 (AB 3081), operative July 1, 2005.

ARTICLE 2
Response to Requests for Admission

Response in writing; Format and method of transmission. §2033.210.
Completeness of responses; Reasonable inquiry. §2033.220.
Objections to part of request; Grounds for objections. §2033.230.
Signing of response. §2033.240.
Time for service of response; Unlawful detainer actions. §2033.250.
Extension of time for response; Written confirmation of agreement; Effect; Notice. §2033.260.
Retention of requests for admission, proof of service and response. §2033.270.
Failure to serve timely response; Waiver; Motion for order that matters be deemed admitted; Finding of court; Monetary sanction. §2033.280.
Motion for order compelling further response; Grounds; Time for motion; Monetary sanction; Order that matters be deemed admitted. §2033.290.
Withdrawal or amendment of admission: When permitted; Grounds; Conditions. §2033.300.

§2033.210. Response in writing; Format and method of transmission

(a) The party to whom requests for admission have been directed shall respond in writing under oath separately to each request.

(b) Each response shall answer the substance of the requested admission, or set forth an objection to the particular request.

(c) In the first paragraph of the response immediately below the title of the case, there shall appear the identity of the responding party, the set number, and the identity of the requesting party.

(d) Each answer or objection in the response shall bear the same identifying number or letter and be in the same sequence as the corresponding request. The text of that request need not be repeated, except as provided in paragraph (6) of subdivision (e).

(e) In order to facilitate the discovery process:

(1) Except as provided in paragraph (5), upon request by the responding party, the propounding party shall provide the requests for admission in an electronic format to the responding party within three court days of the request.

(2) Except as provided in paragraph (5), upon request by the propounding party after receipt of the responses to the requests for admission, the responding party shall provide the responses in an electronic format to the propounding party within three court days of the request.

(3) A party may provide the requests for admission or responses to the requests for admission requested pursuant to paragraphs (1) and (2) in any format agreed upon by the parties. If the parties are unable to agree on a format, the requests for admission or responses to the requests for admission shall be provided in plain text format.

(4) A party may transmit the requests for admission or responses to the requests for admission requested pursuant to paragraphs (1) and (2) by any method agreed upon by the parties. If the parties are unable to agree on a method of transmission, the requests for admission or responses to the requests for admission shall be transmitted by electronic mail to an email address provided by the requesting party.

(5) If the requests for admission or responses to the requests for admission were not created in an electronic format, a party is not required to create the requests for admission or responses in an electronic format for the purpose of transmission to the requesting party.

(6) A responding party who has requested and received requests for admission in an electronic format pursuant to paragraph (1) shall include the text of the request immediately preceding the response. **Leg.H.** Added Stats 2004 ch 182 §23 (AB 3081), operative July 1, 2005. Amended Stats 2019 ch 190 §2 (AB 1349), effective January 1, 2020.

§2033.220. Completeness of responses; Reasonable inquiry

(a) Each answer in a response to requests for admission shall be as complete and straightforward as the information reasonably available to the responding party permits.

(b) Each answer shall:

(1) Admit so much of the matter involved in the request as is true, either as expressed in the request itself or as reasonably and clearly qualified by the responding party.

(2) Deny so much of the matter involved in the request as is untrue.

(3) Specify so much of the matter involved in the request as to the truth of which the responding party lacks sufficient information or knowledge.

(c) If a responding party gives lack of information or knowledge as a reason for a failure to admit all or part of a request for admission, that party shall state in the answer that a reasonable inquiry concerning the matter in the particular request has been made, and that the information known or readily obtainable is insufficient to enable that party to admit the matter. **Leg.H.** Added Stats 2004 ch 182 §23 (AB 3081), operative July 1, 2005. Amended Stats 2005 ch 22 §24 (SB 1108), effective January 1, 2006.

§2033.230. Objections to part of request; Grounds for objections

(a) If only a part of a request for admission is objectionable, the remainder of the request shall be answered.

(b) If an objection is made to a request or to a part of a request, the specific ground for the objection shall be set forth clearly in the response. If an objection is based on a claim of privilege, the particular privilege invoked shall be clearly stated. If an objection is based on a claim that the matter as to which an admission is requested is protected work product under Chapter 4 (commencing with Section 2018.010), that claim shall be expressly asserted. **Leg.H.** Added Stats 2004 ch 182 §23 (AB 3081), operative July 1, 2005.

§2033.240. Signing of response

(a) The party to whom the requests for admission are directed shall sign the response under oath, unless the response contains only objections.

(b) If that party is a public or private corporation, or a partnership or association or governmental agency, one of its officers or agents shall sign the response under oath on behalf of that party. If the officer or agent signing the response on behalf of that party is an attorney acting in that capacity for the party, that party waives any lawyer-client privilege and any protection for work product under Chapter 4 (commencing with Section 2018.010) during any subsequent discovery from that attorney concerning the identity of the sources of the information contained in the response.

(c) The attorney for the responding party shall sign any response that contains an objection. **Leg.H.** Added Stats 2004 ch 182 §23 (AB 3081), operative July 1, 2005.

§2033.250. Time for service of response; Unlawful detainer actions

(a) Within 30 days after service of requests for admission, the party to whom the requests are directed shall serve the original of the response to them on the requesting party, and a copy of the response on all other parties who have appeared, unless on motion of the requesting party the court has shortened the time for response, or unless on motion of the responding party the court has extended the time for response.

(b) Notwithstanding subdivision (a), in an unlawful detainer action or other proceeding under Chapter 4 (commencing with Section 1159) of Title 3 of Part 3, the party to whom the request is directed shall have at least five days from the date of service to respond, unless on motion of the requesting party the court has shortened the time for response, or unless on motion of the responding party the court has extended the time for response. **Leg.H.** Added Stats 2004 ch 182 §23 (AB 3081), operative July 1, 2005. Amended Stats 2007 ch 113 §13 (AB 1126), effective January 1, 2008.

§2033.260. Extension of time for response; Written confirmation of agreement; Effect; Notice

(a) The party requesting admissions and the responding party may agree to extend the time for service of a response to a set of admission requests, or to particular requests in a set, to a date beyond that provided in Section 2033.250.

(b) This agreement may be informal, but it shall be confirmed in a writing that specifies the extended date for service of a response.

(c) Unless this agreement expressly states otherwise, it is effective to preserve to the responding party the right to respond to any request for admission to which the agreement applies in any manner specified in Sections 2033.210, 2033.220, and 2033.230.

(d) Notice of this agreement shall be given by the responding party to all other parties who were served with a copy of the request. **Leg.H.** Added Stats 2004 ch 182 §23 (AB 3081), operative July 1, 2005.

§2033.270. Retention of requests for admission, proof of service and response

(a) The requests for admission and the response to them shall not be filed with the court.

(b) The party requesting admissions shall retain both the original of the requests for admission, with the original proof of service affixed to them, and the original of the sworn response until six months after final disposition of the action. At that time, both originals may be destroyed, unless the court, on motion of any party and for good cause shown, orders that the originals be preserved for a longer period. **Leg.H.** Added Stats 2004 ch 182 §23 (AB 3081), operative July 1, 2005.

§2033.280. Failure to serve timely response; Waiver; Motion for order that matters be deemed admitted; Finding of court; Monetary sanction

If a party to whom requests for admission are directed fails to serve a timely response, the following rules apply:

(a) The party to whom the requests for admission are directed waives any objection to the requests, including one based on privilege or on the protection for work product under Chapter 4 (commencing with Section 2018.010). The court, on motion, may relieve that party from this waiver on its determination that both of the following conditions are satisfied:

(1) The party has subsequently served a response that is in substantial compliance with Sections 2033.210, 2033.220, and 2033.230.

(2) The party's failure to serve a timely response was the result of mistake, inadvertence, or excusable neglect.

(b) The requesting party may move for an order that the genuineness of any documents and the truth of any matters specified in the requests be deemed admitted, as well as for a monetary sanction under Chapter 7 (commencing with Section 2023.010).

(c) The court shall make this order, unless it finds that the party to whom the requests for admission have been directed has served, before the hearing on the motion, a proposed response to the requests for admission that is in substantial compliance with Section 2033.220. It is mandatory that the court impose a monetary sanction under Chapter 7 (commencing with Section 2023.010) on the party or attorney, or both, whose failure to serve a timely response to requests for admission necessitated this motion. **Leg.H.** Added Stats 2004 ch 182 §23 (AB 3081), operative July 1, 2005. Amended Stats 2005 ch 294 §12 (AB 333), effective January 1, 2006.

§2033.290. Motion for order compelling further response; Grounds; Time for motion; Monetary sanction; Order that matters be deemed admitted

(a) On receipt of a response to requests for admissions, the party requesting admissions may move for an order compelling a further response if that party deems that either or both of the following apply:

(1) An answer to a particular request is evasive or incomplete.

(2) An objection to a particular request is without merit or too general.

(b)(1) A motion under subdivision (a) shall be accompanied by a meet and confer declaration under Section 2016.040.

(2) In lieu of a separate statement required under the California Rules of Court, the court may allow the moving party to submit a concise outline of the discovery request and each response in dispute.

(c) Unless notice of this motion is given within 45 days of the service of the verified response, or any supplemental verified response, or any specific later date to which the requesting party and the responding party have agreed in writing, the requesting party waives any right to compel further response to the requests for admission.

(d) The court shall impose a monetary sanction under Chapter 7 (commencing with Section 2023.010) against any party, person, or attorney who unsuccessfully makes or opposes a motion to compel further response, unless it finds that the one subject to the sanction acted with substantial justification or that other circumstances make the imposition of the sanction unjust.

(e) If a party then fails to obey an order compelling further response to requests for admission, the court may order that the matters involved in the requests be deemed admitted. In lieu of, or in addition to, this order, the court may impose a monetary sanction under Chapter 7 (commencing with Section 2023.010). **Leg.H.** Added Stats 2004 ch 182 §23 (AB 3081), effective January 1, 2005, operative July 1, 2005. Amended Stats 2013 ch 18 §3 (AB 1183), effective January 1, 2014; Stats 2018 ch 317 §5 (AB 2230), effective January 1, 2019, operative January 1, 2020.

§2033.300. Withdrawal or amendment of admission: When permitted; Grounds; Conditions

(a) A party may withdraw or amend an admission made in response to a request for admission only on leave of court granted after notice to all parties.

(b) The court may permit withdrawal or amendment of an admission only if it determines that the admission was the result of mistake, inadvertence, or excusable neglect, and that the party who obtained the admission will not be substantially prejudiced in maintaining that party's action or defense on the merits.

(c) The court may impose conditions on the granting of the motion that are just, including, but not limited to, the following:

(1) An order that the party who obtained the admission be permitted to pursue additional discovery related to the matter involved in the withdrawn or amended admission.

(2) An order that the costs of any additional discovery be borne in whole or in part by the party withdrawing or amending the admission. **Leg.H.** Added Stats 2004 ch 182 §23 (AB 3081), operative July 1, 2005.

ARTICLE 3
Effect of Admission

Effect of admission in pending action; Other proceedings. §2033.410.

Expenses incurred in proving matters which party to whom request was directed failed to admit; When court to require payment. §2033.420.

§2033.410. Effect of admission in pending action; Other proceedings

(a) Any matter admitted in response to a request for admission is conclusively established against the party making the admission in the pending action, unless the court has permitted withdrawal or amendment of that admission under Section 2033.300.

(b) Notwithstanding subdivision (a), any admission made by a party under this section is binding only on that party and is made for the purpose of the pending action only. It is not an admission by that party for any other purpose, and it shall not be used in any manner against that party in any other proceeding. **Leg.H.** Added Stats 2004 ch 182 §23 (AB 3081), operative July 1, 2005.

§2033.420. Expenses incurred in proving matters which party to whom request was directed failed to admit; When court to require payment

(a) If a party fails to admit the genuineness of any document or the truth of any matter when requested to do so under this chapter, and if the party requesting that admission thereafter proves the genuineness of that document or the truth of that matter, the party requesting the admission may move the court for an order requiring the party to whom the request was directed to pay the reasonable expenses incurred in making that proof, including reasonable attorney's fees.

(b) The court shall make this order unless it finds any of the following:

(1) An objection to the request was sustained or a response to it was waived under Section 2033.290.

(2) The admission sought was of no substantial importance.

(3) The party failing to make the admission had reasonable ground to believe that that party would prevail on the matter.

(4) There was other good reason for the failure to admit. **Leg.H.** Added Stats 2004 ch 182 §23 (AB 3081), operative July 1, 2005.

§2033.5. [Section repealed 2005]

Leg.H. Added Stats 1998 ch 587 §2 (SB 1768), operative January 1, 2000. Amended Stats 2001 ch 812 §11 (AB 223). Repealed Stats 2004 ch 182 §22 (AB 3081), operative July 1, 2005. The repealed section related to official forms of interrogatories and requests for admission. See CCP §§2033.710 et seq.

Prior Law: Former CCP §2033.5 was added Stats 1986 ch 1334 §2, operative July 1, 1987, amended Stats 1987 ch 86 §16, effective and operative July 1, 1987, Stats 1988 ch 71 §1, effective April 8, 1988, Stats 1998 ch 587 §1, and repealed, operative January 1, 2000, by its own terms.

CHAPTER 17
FORM INTERROGATORIES AND REQUESTS FOR ADMISSION

Development by Judicial Council of form interrogatories and requests for admission. §2033.710.

Form interrogatories for use of victim who has not received complete payment of restitution order; How often propounded; Duty of defendant. §2033.720.

Consultation with representative advisory committee; Use of nontechnical language. §2033.730.

Optional use of form interrogatories and requests for admission; Availability; Rules. §2033.740.

§2033.710. Development by Judicial Council of form interrogatories and requests for admission

The Judicial Council shall develop and approve official form interrogatories and requests for admission of the genuineness of any relevant documents or of the truth of any relevant matters of fact for use in any civil action in a state court based on personal injury, property damage, wrongful death, unlawful detainer, breach of contract, family law, or fraud and for any other civil actions the Judicial Council deems appropriate. **Leg.H.** Added Stats 2004 ch 182 §23 (AB 3081), operative July 1, 2005.

§2033.720. Form interrogatories for use of victim who has not received complete payment of restitution order; How often propounded; Duty of defendant

(a) The Judicial Council shall develop and approve official form interrogatories for use by a victim who has not received complete payment of a restitution order made pursuant to Section 1202.4 of the Penal Code.

(b) Notwithstanding whether a victim initiates or maintains an action to satisfy the unpaid restitution order, a victim may propound the form interrogatories approved pursuant to this section once each calendar year. The defendant subject to the restitution order shall, in responding to the interrogatories propounded, provide current information regarding the nature, extent, and location of any assets, income, and liabilities in which the defendant claims a present or future interest. **Leg.H.** Added Stats 2004 ch 182 §23 (AB 3081), operative July 1, 2005.

§2033.730. Consultation with representative advisory committee; Use of nontechnical language

(a) In developing the form interrogatories and requests for admission required by Sections 2033.710 and 2033.720, the Judicial Council shall consult with a representative advisory committee which shall include, but not be limited to, representatives of all of the following:

(1) The plaintiff's bar.
(2) The defense bar.
(3) The public interest bar.
(4) Court administrators.
(5) The public.

(b) The form interrogatories and requests for admission shall be drafted in nontechnical language. **Leg.H.** Added Stats 2004 ch 182 §23 (AB 3081), operative July 1, 2005.

§2033.740. Optional use of form interrogatories and requests for admission; Availability; Rules

(a) Use of the form interrogatories and requests for admission approved by the Judicial Council shall be optional.

(b) The form interrogatories and requests for admission shall be made available through the office of the clerk of the appropriate trial court.

(c) The Judicial Council shall promulgate any necessary rules to govern the use of the form interrogatories and requests for admission. **Leg.H.** Added Stats 2004 ch 182 §23 (AB 3081), operative July 1, 2005.

CHAPTER 18
SIMULTANEOUS EXCHANGE OF EXPERT WITNESS INFORMATION

Article 1. General Provisions.
Article 2. Demand for Exchange of Expert Witness Information.
Article 3. Deposition of Expert Witness.
Article 4. Motion to Augment or Amend Expert Witness List or Declaration.
Article 5. Motion to Submit Tardy Expert Witness Information.

ARTICLE 1
General Provisions

Applicability to eminent domain proceedings. §2034.010.

§2034. [Section repealed 2005]

Leg.H. Added Stats 1986 ch 1336 §2, operative July 1, 1987. Amended Stats 1987 ch 86 §17, operative July 1, 1987; Stats 1988 ch 553 §7; Stats 1990 ch 771 §2 (SB 247), ch 1392 §2 (AB 3136); Stats 1992 1301 §1 (AB 2913); Stats 1993 ch 3 §1 (AB 240), operative March 25, 1993, ch 678 §1 (AB 907); Stats 1995 ch 797 §1 (AB 1204); Stats 2004 ch 171 §6 (AB 3078). Repealed Stats 2004 ch 182 §22 (AB 3081), operative July 1, 2005. The repealed section related to exchanges of expert trial witness information. See CCP §§2034.210 et seq.

Prior Law: Former CCP §2034 was added Stats 1957 ch 1904 §3, amended 1959 ch 1590 §12, Stats 1961 ch 496 §3, Stats 1965 ch 126 §1, Stats 1968 ch 188 §3, Stats 1974 ch 592 §2, ch 732 §4, Stats 1980 ch 23 §2, Stats 1981 ch 714 §25, Stats 1982 ch 138 §1, and repealed Stats 1986 ch 1334 §1.

Original CCP §2034, providing that deposition once taken could be read at any time, was enacted 1872, and repealed Stats 1907 ch 392 §8.

§2034.010. Applicability to eminent domain proceedings

This chapter does not apply to exchanges of lists of experts and valuation data in eminent domain proceedings under Chapter 7 (commencing with Section 1258.010) of Title 7 of Part 3. **Leg.H.** Added Stats 2004 ch 182 §23 (AB 3081), operative July 1, 2005.

ARTICLE 2
Demand for Exchange of Expert Witness Information

Demand for simultaneous exchange of expert trial witness information; List; Expert witness declaration; Discoverable reports and writings. §2034.210.
Leave of court not required; Time for making demand. §2034.220.
Form and content of demand for exchange of expert witness information. §2034.230.
Service of demand. §2034.240.
Motion for protective order; Grounds; What order may include; Denial of order; Monetary sanction. §2034.250.
How information to be exchanged; What information to be included; When expert witness declaration required; Contents. §2034.260.
Production of discoverable reports and writings. §2034.270.
Submission of supplemental expert witness list; When permitted; Expert witness declaration; Availability of experts for deposition. §2034.280.
Retention of demand, proof of service, lists and declarations; When lodged with court. §2034.290.
Exclusion of expert testimony for failure to comply. §2034.300.
When party may call expert witness who has not been previously designated. §2034.310.

§2034.210. Demand for simultaneous exchange of expert trial witness information; List; Expert witness declaration; Discoverable reports and writings

After the setting of the initial trial date for the action, any party may obtain discovery by demanding that all parties simultaneously exchange information concerning each other's expert trial witnesses to the following extent:

(a) Any party may demand a mutual and simultaneous exchange by all parties of a list containing the name and address of any natural person, including one who is a party, whose oral or deposition testimony in the form of an expert opinion any party expects to offer in evidence at the trial.

(b) If any expert designated by a party under subdivision (a) is a party or an employee of a party, or has been retained by a party for the purpose of forming and expressing an opinion in anticipation of the litigation or in preparation for the trial of the action, the designation of that witness shall include or be accompanied by an expert witness declaration under Section 2034.260.

(c) Any party may also include a demand for the mutual and simultaneous production for inspection and copying of all discoverable reports and writings, if any, made by any expert described in subdivision (b) in the course of preparing that expert's opinion. **Leg.H.** Added Stats 2004 ch 182 §23 (AB 3081), operative July 1, 2005.

§2034.220. Leave of court not required; Time for making demand

Any party may make a demand for an exchange of information concerning expert trial witnesses without leave of court. A party shall make this demand no later than the 10th day after the initial trial date has been set, or 70 days before that trial date, whichever is closer to the trial date. **Leg.H.** Added Stats 2004 ch 182 §23 (AB 3081), operative July 1, 2005.

§2034.230. Form and content of demand for exchange of expert witness information

(a) A demand for an exchange of information concerning expert trial witnesses shall be in writing and shall identify, below the title of the case, the party making the demand. The demand shall state that it is being made under this chapter.

(b) The demand shall specify the date for the exchange of lists of expert trial witnesses, expert witness declarations, and any demanded production of writings. The specified date of exchange shall be 50 days before the initial trial date, or 20 days after service of the demand, whichever is closer to the trial date, unless the court, on motion and a showing of good cause, orders an earlier or later date of exchange. **Leg.H.** Added Stats 2004 ch 182 §23 (AB 3081), operative July 1, 2005.

§2034.240. Service of demand

The party demanding an exchange of information concerning expert trial witnesses shall serve the demand on all parties who have appeared in the action. **Leg.H.** Added Stats 2004 ch 182 §23 (AB 3081), operative July 1, 2005.

§2034.250. Motion for protective order; Grounds; What order may include; Denial of order; Monetary sanction

(a) A party who has been served with a demand to exchange information concerning expert trial witnesses may promptly move for a protective order. This motion shall be accompanied by a meet and confer declaration under Section 2016.040.

(b) The court, for good cause shown, may make any order that justice requires to protect any party from unwarranted annoyance, embarrassment, oppression, or undue burden and expense. The protective order may include, but is not limited to, one or more of the following directions:

(1) That the demand be quashed because it was not timely served.

(2) That the date of exchange be earlier or later than that specified in the demand.

(3) That the exchange be made only on specified terms and conditions.

(4) That the production and exchange of any reports and writings of experts be made at a different place or at a different time than specified in the demand.

(5) That some or all of the parties be divided into sides on the basis of their identity of interest in the issues in the action, and that the designation of any experts as described in subdivision (b) of Section 2034.210 be made by any side so created.

(6) That a party or a side reduce the list of employed or retained experts designated by that party or side under subdivision (b) of Section 2034.210.

(c) If the motion for a protective order is denied in whole or in part, the court may order that the parties against whom the motion is brought, provide or permit the discovery against which the protection was sought on those terms and conditions that are just.

(d) The court shall impose a monetary sanction under Chapter 7 (commencing with Section 2023.010) against any party, person, or attorney who unsuccessfully makes or opposes a motion for a protective order under this section, unless it finds that the one subject to the sanction acted with substantial justification or that other circumstances make the imposition of the sanction unjust. **Leg.H.** Added Stats 2004 ch 182 §23 (AB 3081), operative July 1, 2005.

§2034.260. How information to be exchanged; What information to be included; When expert witness declaration required; Contents

(a) All parties who have appeared in the action shall exchange information concerning expert witnesses in writing on or before the date of exchange specified in the demand. The exchange of information may occur at a meeting of the attorneys for the parties involved or by serving the information on the other party by any method specified in Section 1011 or 1013, on or before the date of exchange.

(b) The exchange of expert witness information shall include either of the following:

(1) A list setting forth the name and address of a person whose expert opinion that party expects to offer in evidence at the trial.

(2) A statement that the party does not presently intend to offer the testimony of an expert witness.

(c) If a witness on the list is an expert as described in subdivision (b) of Section 2034.210, the exchange shall also include or be accompanied by an expert witness declaration signed only by the attorney for the party designating the expert, or by that party if that party has no attorney. This declaration shall be under penalty of perjury and shall contain all of the following:

(1) A brief narrative statement of the qualifications of each expert.

(2) A brief narrative statement of the general substance of the testimony that the expert is expected to give.

(3) A representation that the expert has agreed to testify at the trial.

(4) A representation that the expert will be sufficiently familiar with the pending action to submit to a meaningful oral deposition concerning the specific testimony, including an opinion and its basis, that the expert is expected to give at trial.

(5) A statement of the expert's hourly and daily fee for providing deposition testimony and for consulting with the retaining attorney. **Leg.H.** Added Stats 2004 ch 182 §23 (AB 3081), operative July 1, 2005. Amended Stats 2017 ch 64 §3 (SB 543), effective January 1, 2018; Stats 2018 ch 92 §45 (SB 1289), effective January 1, 2019.

§2034.270. Production of discoverable reports and writings

If a demand for an exchange of information concerning expert trial witnesses includes a demand for production of reports and writings as described in subdivision (c) of Section 2034.210, all parties shall produce and exchange, at the place and on the date specified in the demand, all discoverable reports and writings, if any, made by any designated expert described in subdivision (b) of Section 2034.210. **Leg.H.** Added Stats 2004 ch 182 §23 (AB 3081), operative July 1, 2005.

§2034.280. Submission of supplemental expert witness list; When permitted; Expert witness declaration; Availability of experts for deposition

(a) Within 20 days after the exchange described in Section 2034.260, any party who engaged in the exchange may submit a supplemental expert witness list containing the name and address of any experts who will express an opinion on a subject to be covered by an expert designated by an adverse party to the exchange, if the party supplementing an expert witness list has not previously retained an expert to testify on that subject.

(b) This supplemental list shall be accompanied by an expert witness declaration under subdivision (c) of Section 2034.260 concerning those additional experts, and by all discoverable reports and writings, if any, made by those additional experts.

(c) The party shall also make those experts available immediately for a deposition under Article 3 (commencing with Section 2034.410), which deposition may be taken even though the time limit for discovery under Chapter 8 (commencing with Section 2024.010) has expired. **Leg.H.** Added Stats 2004 ch 182 §23 (AB 3081), operative July 1, 2005.

§2034.290. Retention of demand, proof of service, lists and declarations; When lodged with court

(a) A demand for an exchange of information concerning expert trial witnesses, and any expert witness lists and declarations exchanged shall not be filed with the court.

(b) The party demanding the exchange shall retain both the original of the demand, with the original proof of service affixed, and the original of all expert witness lists and declarations exchanged in response to the demand until six months after final disposition of the action. At that time, all originals may be destroyed unless the court, on motion of any party and for good cause shown, orders that the originals be preserved for a longer period.

(c) Notwithstanding subdivisions (a) and (b), a demand for exchange of information concerning expert trial witnesses, and all expert witness lists and declarations exchanged in response to it, shall be lodged with the court when their contents become relevant to an issue in any pending matter in the action. **Leg.H.** Added Stats 2004 ch 182 §23 (AB 3081), operative July 1, 2005.

§2034.300. Exclusion of expert testimony for failure to comply

Except as provided in Section 2034.310 and in Articles 4 (commencing with Section 2034.610) and 5 (commencing with Section 2034.710), on objection of any party who has made a complete and timely compliance with Section 2034.260, the trial court shall exclude from evidence the expert opinion of any witness that is offered by any party who has unreasonably failed to do any of the following:

(a) List that witness as an expert under Section 2034.260.

(b) Submit an expert witness declaration.

(c) Produce reports and writings of expert witnesses under Section 2034.270.

(d) Make that expert available for a deposition under Article 3 (commencing with Section 2034.410). **Leg.H.** Added Stats 2004 ch 182 §23 (AB 3081), operative July 1, 2005.

§2034.310. When party may call expert witness who has not been previously designated

A party may call as a witness at trial an expert not previously designated by that party if either of the following conditions is satisfied:

(a) That expert has been designated by another party and has thereafter been deposed under Article 3 (commencing with Section 2034.410).

(b) That expert is called as a witness to impeach the testimony of an expert witness offered by any other party at the trial. This impeachment may include testimony to the falsity or nonexistence of any fact used as the foundation for any opinion by any other party's expert witness, but may not include testimony that contradicts the opinion. **Leg.H.** Added Stats 2004 ch 182 §23 (AB 3081), operative July 1, 2005.

ARTICLE 3
Deposition of Expert Witness

Right to depose persons on expert witness list; Procedure. §2034.410.
Production of materials called for by deposition notice. §2034.415.
Place of taking deposition of expert. §2034.420.
Payment of certain experts' reasonable and customary hourly or daily fees for time spent at deposition; Tardy counsel; Worker's compensation cases. §2034.430.
Fees for which party designating expert is responsible. §2034.440.
Tender of expert's fee by party taking deposition; Payment of balance. §2034.450.
Service of deposition notice accompanied by tender of fee as effective to require production of expert; Effect of failure to tender fee. §2034.460.
Motion for order setting compensation of expert; Notice; Evidence and factors; Monetary sanction. §2034.470.

§2034.410. Right to depose persons on expert witness list; Procedure

On receipt of an expert witness list from a party, any other party may take the deposition of any person on the list. The procedures for taking oral and written depositions set forth in Chapters 9 (commencing with Section 2025.010), 10 (commencing with Section 2026.010), and 11 (commencing with Section 2028.010) apply to a deposition of a listed trial expert witness except as provided in this article. **Leg.H.** Added Stats 2004 ch 182 §23 (AB 3081), operative July 1, 2005.

§2034.415. Production of materials called for by deposition notice

An expert described in subdivision (b) of Section 2034.210 whose deposition is noticed pursuant to Section 2025.220 shall, no later than three business days before his or her deposition, produce any materials or category of materials, including any electronically stored information, called for by the deposition notice. **Leg.H.** Added Stats 2016 ch 467 §3 (AB 2427), effective January 1, 2017.

§2034.420. Place of taking deposition of expert

The deposition of any expert described in subdivision (b) of Section 2034.210 shall be taken at a place that is within 75 miles of the courthouse where the action is pending. On motion for a protective order by the party designating an expert witness, and on a showing of exceptional hardship, the court may order that the deposition be taken at a more distant place from the courthouse. **Leg.H.** Added Stats 2004 ch 182 §23 (AB 3081), operative July 1, 2005. Amended Stats 2008 ch 303 §1 (AB 2619), effective January 1, 2009.

§2034.430. Payment of certain experts' reasonable and customary hourly or daily fees for time spent at deposition; Tardy counsel; Worker's compensation cases

(a) Except as provided in subdivision (f), this section applies to an expert witness, other than a party or an employee of a party, who is any of the following:

(1) An expert described in subdivision (b) of Section 2034.210.

(2) A treating physician and surgeon or other treating health care practitioner who is to be asked during the deposition to express opinion testimony, including opinion or factual testimony regarding the past or present diagnosis or prognosis made by the practitioner or the reasons for a particular treatment decision made by the practitioner, but not including testimony requiring only the reading of words and symbols contained in the relevant medical record or, if those words and symbols are not legible to the deponent, the approximation by the deponent of what those words or symbols are.

(3) An architect, professional engineer, or licensed land surveyor who was involved with the original project design or survey for which that person is asked to express an opinion within the person's expertise and relevant to the action or proceeding.

(b) A party desiring to depose an expert witness described in subdivision (a) shall pay the expert's reasonable and customary hourly or daily fee for any time spent at the deposition from the time noticed in the deposition subpoena, or from the time of the arrival of the expert witness should that time be later than the time noticed in the deposition subpoena, until the time the expert witness is dismissed from the deposition, regardless of whether the expert is actually deposed by any party attending the deposition.

(c) If any counsel representing the expert or a nonnoticing party is late to the deposition, the expert's reasonable and customary hourly or daily fee for the time period determined from the time noticed in the deposition subpoena until the counsel's late arrival, shall be paid by that tardy counsel.

(d) Notwithstanding subdivision (c), the hourly or daily fee charged to the tardy counsel shall not exceed the fee charged to the party who retained the expert, except where the expert donated services to a charitable or other nonprofit organization.

(e) A daily fee shall only be charged for a full day of attendance at a deposition or where the expert was required by the deposing party to be available for a full day and the expert necessarily had to forgo all business that the expert would otherwise have conducted that day but for the request that the expert be available all day for the scheduled deposition.

(f) In a worker's compensation case arising under Division 4 (commencing with Section 3201) or Division 4.5 (commencing with Section 6100) of the Labor Code, a party desiring to depose any expert on another party's expert witness list shall pay the fee under this section. **Leg.H.** Added Stats 2004 ch 182 §23 (AB 3081), operative July 1, 2005. Amended Stats 2008 ch 303 §2 (AB 2619), effective January 1, 2009.

§2034.440. Fees for which party designating expert is responsible

The party designating an expert is responsible for any fee charged by the expert for preparing for a deposition and for traveling to the place of the deposition, as well as for any travel expenses of the expert. **Leg.H.** Added Stats 2004 ch 182 §23 (AB 3081), operative July 1, 2005.

§2034.450. Tender of expert's fee by party taking deposition; Payment of balance

(a) The party taking the deposition of an expert witness shall either accompany the service of the deposition notice with a tender of the expert's fee based on the anticipated length of the deposition, or tender that fee at the commencement of the deposition.

(b) The expert's fee shall be delivered to the attorney for the party designating the expert.

(c) If the deposition of the expert takes longer than anticipated, the party giving notice of the deposition shall pay the balance of the expert's fee within five days of receipt of an itemized statement from the expert. **Leg.H.** Added Stats 2004 ch 182 §23 (AB 3081), operative July 1, 2005.

§2034.460. Service of deposition notice accompanied by tender of fee as effective to require production of expert; Effect of failure to tender fee

(a) The service of a proper deposition notice accompanied by the tender of the expert witness fee described in Section 2034.430 is effective to require the party employing or retaining the expert to produce the expert for the deposition.

(b) If the party noticing the deposition fails to tender the expert's fee under Section 2034.430, the expert shall not be deposed at that time unless the parties stipulate otherwise. **Leg.H.** Added Stats 2004 ch 182 §23 (AB 3081), operative July 1, 2005.

§2034.470. Motion for order setting compensation of expert; Notice; Evidence and factors; Monetary sanction

(a) If a party desiring to take the deposition of an expert witness under this article deems that the hourly or daily fee of that expert for providing deposition testimony is unreasonable, that party may move for an order setting the compensation of that expert. Notice of this motion shall also be given to the expert.

(b) A motion under subdivision (a) shall be accompanied by a meet and confer declaration under Section 2016.040. In any attempt at an informal resolution under Section 2016.040, either the party or the expert shall provide the other with all of the following:

(1) Proof of the ordinary and customary fee actually charged and received by that expert for similar services provided outside the subject litigation.

(2) The total number of times the presently demanded fee has ever been charged and received by that expert.

(3) The frequency and regularity with which the presently demanded fee has been charged and received by that expert within the two-year period preceding the hearing on the motion.

(c) In addition to any other facts or evidence, the expert or the party designating the expert shall provide, and the court's determination as to the reasonableness of the fee shall be based on, proof of the ordinary and customary fee actually charged and received by that expert for similar services provided outside the subject litigation.

(d) In an action filed after January 1, 1994, the expert or the party designating the expert shall also provide, and the court's determination as to the reasonableness of the fee shall also be based on, both of the following:

(1) The total number of times the presently demanded fee has ever been charged and received by that expert.

(2) The frequency and regularity with which the presently demanded fee has been charged and received by that expert within the two-year period preceding the hearing on the motion.

(e) The court may also consider the ordinary and customary fees charged by similar experts for similar services within the relevant community and any other factors the court deems necessary or appropriate to make its determination.

(f) Upon a determination that the fee demanded by that expert is unreasonable, and based upon the evidence and factors considered, the court shall set the fee of the expert providing testimony.

(g) The court shall impose a monetary sanction under Chapter 7 (commencing with Section 2023.010) against any party, person, or attorney who unsuccessfully makes or opposes a motion to set the expert witness fee, unless it finds that the one subject to the sanction acted with substantial justification or that other circumstances make the imposition of the sanction unjust. **Leg.H.** Added Stats 2004 ch 182 §23 (AB 3081), operative July 1, 2005.

ARTICLE 4
Motion to Augment or Amend Expert Witness List or Declaration

Power of court to allow motion to augment or amend expert witness list and declaration; Time of motion. §2034.610.
Conditions for granting leave to augment or amend expert witness list or declaration. §2034.620.
Monetary sanction for unsuccessfully making or opposing motion to augment or amend expert witness information. §2034.630.

§2034.610. Power of court to allow motion to augment or amend expert witness list and declaration; Time of motion

(a) On motion of any party who has engaged in a timely exchange of expert witness information, the court may grant leave to do either or both of the following:

(1) Augment that party's expert witness list and declaration by adding the name and address of any expert witness whom that party has subsequently retained.

(2) Amend that party's expert witness declaration with respect to the general substance of the testimony that an expert previously designated is expected to give.

(b) A motion under subdivision (a) shall be made at a sufficient time in advance of the time limit for the completion of discovery under Chapter 8 (commencing with Section 2024.010) to permit the deposition of any expert to whom the motion relates to be taken within that time limit. Under exceptional circumstances, the court may permit the motion to be made at a later time.

(c) The motion shall be accompanied by a meet and confer declaration under Section 2016.040. **Leg.H.** Added Stats 2004 ch 182 §23 (AB 3081), operative July 1, 2005.

§2034.620. Conditions for granting leave to augment or amend expert witness list or declaration

The court shall grant leave to augment or amend an expert witness list or declaration only if all of the following conditions are satisfied:

(a) The court has taken into account the extent to which the opposing party has relied on the list of expert witnesses.

(b) The court has determined that any party opposing the motion will not be prejudiced in maintaining that party's action or defense on the merits.

(c) The court has determined either of the following:

(1) The moving party would not in the exercise of reasonable diligence have determined to call that expert witness or have decided to offer the different or additional testimony of that expert witness.

(2) The moving party failed to determine to call that expert witness, or to offer the different or additional testimony of that expert witness as a result of mistake, inadvertence, surprise, or excusable neglect, and the moving party has done both of the following:

(A) Sought leave to augment or amend promptly after deciding to call the expert witness or to offer the different or additional testimony.

(B) Promptly thereafter served a copy of the proposed expert witness information concerning the expert or the testimony described in Section 2034.260 on all other parties who have appeared in the action.

(d) Leave to augment or amend is conditioned on the moving party making the expert available immediately for a deposition under Article 3 (commencing with Section 2034.410), and on any other terms as may be just, including, but not limited to, leave to any party opposing the motion to designate additional expert witnesses or to elicit additional opinions from those previously designated, a continuance of the trial for a reasonable period of time, and the awarding of costs and litigation expenses to any party opposing the motion. **Leg.H.** Added Stats 2004 ch 182 §23 (AB 3081), operative July 1, 2005.

§2034.630. Monetary sanction for unsuccessfully making or opposing motion to augment or amend expert witness information

The court shall impose a monetary sanction under Chapter 7 (commencing with Section 2023.010) against any party, person, or attorney who unsuccessfully makes or opposes a motion to augment or amend expert witness information, unless it finds that the one subject to the sanction acted with substantial justification or that other circumstances make the imposition of the sanction unjust. **Leg.H.** Added Stats 2004 ch 182 §23 (AB 3081), operative July 1, 2005.

ARTICLE 5
Motion to Submit Tardy Expert Witness Information

Power of court to allow motion to submit tardy expert witness information; Time of motion. §2034.710.
When leave to submit tardy expert witness information may be granted. §2034.720.
Monetary sanction for unsuccessfully making or opposing motion to submit tardy witness information. §2034.730.

§2034.710. Power of court to allow motion to submit tardy expert witness information; Time of motion

(a) On motion of any party who has failed to submit expert witness information on the date specified in a demand for that exchange, the court may grant leave to submit that information on a later date.

(b) A motion under subdivision (a) shall be made a sufficient time in advance of the time limit for the completion of discovery under Chapter 8 (commencing with Section 2024.010) to permit the deposition of any expert to whom the motion relates to be taken within that time limit. Under exceptional circumstances, the court may permit the motion to be made at a later time.

(c) The motion shall be accompanied by a meet and confer declaration under Section 2016.040. **Leg.H.** Added Stats 2004 ch 182 §23 (AB 3081), operative July 1, 2005.

§2034.720. When leave to submit tardy expert witness information may be granted

The court shall grant leave to submit tardy expert witness information only if all of the following conditions are satisfied:

(a) The court has taken into account the extent to which the opposing party has relied on the absence of a list of expert witnesses.

(b) The court has determined that any party opposing the motion will not be prejudiced in maintaining that party's action or defense on the merits.

(c) The court has determined that the moving party did all of the following:

(1) Failed to submit the information as the result of mistake, inadvertence, surprise, or excusable neglect.

(2) Sought leave to submit the information promptly after learning of the mistake, inadvertence, surprise, or excusable neglect.

(3) Promptly thereafter served a copy of the proposed expert witness information described in Section 2034.260 on all other parties who have appeared in the action.

(d) The order is conditioned on the moving party making the expert available immediately for a deposition under Article 3 (commencing with Section 2034.410), and on any other terms as may be just, including, but not limited to, leave to any party opposing the motion to designate additional expert witnesses or to elicit additional opinions from those previously designated, a continuance of the trial for a reasonable period of time, and the awarding of costs and litigation expenses to any party opposing the motion. **Leg.H.** Added Stats 2004 ch 182 §23 (AB 3081), operative July 1, 2005.

§2034.730. Monetary sanction for unsuccessfully making or opposing motion to submit tardy witness information

The court shall impose a monetary sanction under Chapter 7 (commencing with Section 2023.010) against any party, person, or attorney who unsuccessfully makes or opposes a motion to submit tardy expert witness information, unless it finds that the one subject to the sanction acted with substantial justification or that other circumstances make the imposition of the sanction unjust. **Leg.H.** Added Stats 2004 ch 182 §23 (AB 3081), operative July 1, 2005.

CHAPTER 19
PERPETUATION OF TESTIMONY OR PRESERVATION OF EVIDENCE BEFORE FILING ACTION

Right to obtain discovery to perpetuate testimony or preserve evidence for use if action is filed; Certain purposes not permissible. §2035.010.
Available methods for perpetuation of testimony or preservation of evidence. §2035.020.
Verified petition; Contents; Request for order. §2035.030.
Service of notice of petition; Time for service; Service by publication; Appointment of attorney to represent expected adverse party served by publication and not appearing at hearing. §2035.040.
When court to order discovery. §2035.050.
Use of deposition to perpetuate testimony taken under this chapter or under comparable provisions of other jurisdictions. §2035.060.

§2035. [Section repealed 2005]

Leg.H. Added Stats 1986 ch 1334 §2, operative July 1, 1987. Amended Stats 1987 ch 86 §18, operative July 1, 1987. Repealed Stats 2004 ch 182 §22 (AB 3081), operative July 1, 2005. The repealed section related to discovery for the purpose of perpetuating testimony or preserving evidence for use in subsequent action. See CCP §§2035.010 et seq.

Prior Law: Former CCP §2035, defining "action", was added by Stats 1957 ch 1904 §3, operative January 1, 1958, and repealed by Stats 1986 ch 1334 §1, operative July 1, 1987.

Original CCP §2035, relating to use of deposition taken in this state in other states, was enacted 1872 and repealed by Stats 1957 ch 1904 §1, operative January 1, 1958.

§2035.010. Right to obtain discovery to perpetuate testimony or preserve evidence for use if action is filed; Certain purposes not permissible

(a) One who expects to be a party or expects a successor in interest to be a party to an action that may be cognizable in a court of the state, whether as a plaintiff, or as a defendant, or in any other capacity, may obtain discovery within the scope delimited by Chapter 2 (commencing with Section 2017.010), and subject to the restrictions set forth in Chapter 5 (commencing with Section 2019.010), for the purpose of perpetuating that person's own testimony or that of another natural person or organization, or of preserving evidence for use in the event an action is subsequently filed.

(b) One shall not employ the procedures of this chapter for purposes of either ascertaining the possible existence of a cause of action or a defense to it, or of identifying those who might be made parties to an action not yet filed. **Leg.H.** Added Stats 2004 ch 182 §23 (AB 3081), operative July 1, 2005. Amended Stats 2005 ch 294 §13 (AB 333), effective January 1, 2006; Stats 2016 ch 86 §44 (SB 1171), effective January 1, 2017.

§2035.020. Available methods for perpetuation of testimony or preservation of evidence

The methods available for discovery conducted for the purposes set forth in Section 2035.010 are all of the following:

(a) Oral and written depositions.
(b) Inspections of documents, things, and places.
(c) Physical and mental examinations. **Leg.H.** Added Stats 2004 ch 182 §23 (AB 3081), operative July 1, 2005.

§2035.030. Verified petition; Contents; Request for order

(a) One who desires to perpetuate testimony or preserve evidence for the purposes set forth in Section 2035.010 shall file a verified petition in the superior court of the county of the residence of at least one expected adverse party, or, if no expected adverse party is a resident of the State of California, in the superior court of a county where the action or proceeding may be filed.

(b) The petition shall be titled in the name of the one who desires the perpetuation of testimony or the preservation of the evidence. The petition shall set forth all of the following:

(1) The expectation that the petitioner or the petitioner's successor in interest will be a party to an action cognizable in a court of the State of California.

(2) The present inability of the petitioner and, if applicable, the petitioner's successor in interest either to bring that action or to cause it to be brought.

(3) The subject matter of the expected action and the petitioner's involvement. A copy of any written instrument the validity or construction of which may be called into question, or which is connected with the subject matter of the proposed discovery, shall be attached to the petition.

(4) The particular discovery methods described in Section 2035.020 that the petitioner desires to employ.

(5) The facts that the petitioner desires to establish by the proposed discovery.

(6) The reasons for desiring to perpetuate or preserve these facts before an action has been filed.

(7) The name or a description of those whom the petitioner expects to be adverse parties so far as known.

(8) The name and address of those from whom the discovery is to be sought.

(9) The substance of the information expected to be elicited from each of those from whom discovery is being sought.

(c) The petition shall request the court to enter an order authorizing the petitioner to engage in discovery by the described methods for the purpose of perpetuating the described testimony or preserving the described evidence. **Leg.H.** Added Stats 2004 ch 182 §23 (AB 3081), operative July 1, 2005. Amended Stats 2005 ch 294 §14 (AB 333), effective January 1, 2006.

§2035.040. Service of notice of petition; Time for service; Service by publication; Appointment of attorney to represent expected adverse party served by publication and not appearing at hearing

(a) The petitioner shall cause service of a notice of the petition under Section 2035.030 to be made on each natural person or organization named in the petition as an expected adverse party. This service shall be made in the same manner provided for the service of a summons.

(b) The service of the notice shall be accompanied by a copy of the petition. The notice shall state that the petitioner will apply to the court at a time and place specified in the notice for the order requested in the petition.

(c) This service shall be effected at least 20 days prior to the date specified in the notice for the hearing on the petition.

(d) If after the exercise of due diligence, the petitioner is unable to cause service to be made on any expected adverse party named in the petition, the court in which the petition is filed shall make an order for service by publication.

(e) If any expected adverse party served by publication does not appear at the hearing, the court shall appoint an attorney to represent that party for all purposes, including the cross-examination of any person whose testimony is taken by deposition. The court shall order that the petitioner pay the reasonable fees and expenses of any attorney so appointed. **Leg.H.** Added Stats 2004 ch 182 §23 (AB 3081), operative July 1, 2005.

§2035.050. When court to order discovery

(a) If the court determines that all or part of the discovery requested under this chapter may prevent a failure or delay of justice, it shall make an order authorizing that discovery. In determining whether to authorize discovery by a petitioner who expects a successor in interest to be a party to an action, the court shall consider, in addition to other appropriate factors, whether the requested discovery could be conducted by the petitioner's successor in interest, instead of by the petitioner.

(b) The order shall identify any witness whose deposition may be taken, and any documents, things, or places that may be inspected, and any person whose physical or mental condition may be examined.

(c) Any authorized depositions, inspections, and physical or mental examinations shall then be conducted in accordance with the provisions of this title relating to those methods of discovery in actions that have been filed. **Leg.H.** Added Stats 2004 ch 182 §23 (AB 3081), operative July 1, 2005. Amended Stats 2005 ch 294 §15 (AB 333), effective January 1, 2006.

§2035.060. Use of deposition to perpetuate testimony taken under this chapter or under comparable provisions of other jurisdictions

If a deposition to perpetuate testimony has been taken either under the provisions of this chapter, or under comparable provisions of the laws of the state in which it was taken, or the federal courts, or a foreign nation in which it was taken, that deposition may be used, in any action involving the same subject matter that is brought in a court of the State of California, in accordance with Section 2025.620 against any party, or the successor in interest of any party, named in the petition as an expected adverse party. **Leg.H.** Added Stats 2004 ch 182 §23 (AB 3081), operative July 1, 2005. Amended Stats 2005 ch 294 §16 (AB 333), effective January 1, 2006.

CHAPTER 20
PERPETUATION OF TESTIMONY OR PRESERVATION OF INFORMATION PENDING APPEAL

Right to discovery to perpetuate testimony or preserve information for use in further proceedings. §2036.010.
Methods of discovery available. §2036.020.
Motion for leave to conduct discovery pending appeal. §2036.030.
When court to authorize discovery under this chapter. §2036.040.
Use of deposition taken under this chapter in later proceeding. §2036.050.

§2036. [Section repealed 2005]

Leg.H. Added Stats 1986 ch 1334 §2, operative July 1, 1987. Amended Stats 1987 ch 86 §19, operative July 1, 1987. Repealed Stats 2004 ch 182 §22 (AB 3081), operative July 1, 2005. The repealed section related to discovery for the purpose of perpetuating testimony or preserving evidence pending appeal. See CCP §§2036.010 et seq.

Prior Law: Former CCP §2036, relating to showing "good cause", was added Stats 1963 ch 1744 §2, amended Stats 1971 ch 1649 §1, and repealed Stats 1986 ch 1334 §1, operative July 1, 1987.

Original CCP §2036, relating to procuring witnesses on commission, was enacted 1872, amended by Code Amdts 1880 ch 111 §4, and repealed by Stats 1957 ch 1904 §1, operative January 1, 1958.

§2036.010. Right to discovery to perpetuate testimony or preserve information for use in further proceedings

If an appeal has been taken from a judgment entered by a court of the state, or if the time for taking an appeal has not expired, a party may obtain discovery within the scope delimited by Chapter 2 (commencing with Section 2017.010), and subject to the restrictions set forth in Chapter 5 (commencing with Section 2019.010), for purposes of perpetuating testimony or preserving information for use in the event of further proceedings in that court. **Leg.H.** Added Stats 2004 ch 182 §23 (AB 3081), operative July 1, 2005. Amended Stats 2016 §45 (SB 1171), effective January 1, 2017.

§2036.020. Methods of discovery available

The methods available for discovery for the purpose set forth in Section 2036.010 are all of the following:

(a) Oral and written depositions.
(b) Inspections of documents, things, and places.
(c) Physical and mental examinations. **Leg.H.** Added Stats 2004 ch 182 §23 (AB 3081), operative July 1, 2005.

§2036.030. Motion for leave to conduct discovery pending appeal

(a) A party who desires to obtain discovery pending appeal shall obtain leave of the court that entered the judgment. This motion shall be made on the same notice to and service of parties as is required for discovery sought in an action pending in that court.

(b) The motion for leave to conduct discovery pending appeal shall set forth all of the following:

(1) The names and addresses of the natural persons or organizations from whom the discovery is being sought.

(2) The particular discovery methods described in Section 2036.020 for which authorization is being sought.

(3) The reasons for perpetuating testimony or preserving evidence. **Leg.H.** Added Stats 2004 ch 182 §23 (AB 3081), operative July 1, 2005.

§2036.040. When court to authorize discovery under this chapter

(a) If the court determines that all or part of the discovery requested under this chapter may prevent a failure or delay of justice in the event of further proceedings in the action in that court, it shall make an order authorizing that discovery.

(b) The order shall identify any witness whose deposition may be taken, and any documents, things, or places that may be inspected, and any person whose physical or mental condition may be examined.

(c) Any authorized depositions, inspections, and physical and mental examinations shall then be conducted in accordance with the provisions of this title relating to these methods of discovery in a pending action. **Leg.H.** Added Stats 2004 ch 182 §23 (AB 3081), operative July 1, 2005.

§2036.050. Use of deposition taken under this chapter in later proceeding

If a deposition to perpetuate testimony has been taken under the provisions of this chapter, it may be used in any later proceeding in accordance with Section 2025.620. **Leg.H.** Added Stats 2004 ch 182 §23 (AB 3081), operative July 1, 2005.

§2036.1. [Section repealed 1987]

Leg.H. Added Stats 1985 ch 1328 §2. Repealed Stats 1986 ch 1334 §1, operative July 1, 1987. See CCP §2017.220.

§2036.2. [Section repealed 1987]

Leg.H. Added Stats 1984 ch 1724 §2. Repealed Stats 1986 ch 1334 §1, operative July 1, 1987. See CCP §2019.210.

§2036.5. [Section repealed 1987]

Leg.H. Added Stats 1980 ch 1263 §1. Repealed Stats 1986 ch 1334 §1, operative July 1, 1987. See CCP §§2033.710 et seq.

§2036a. [Section repealed 1958]

Leg.H. Added Stats 1923 ch 39 §1. Repealed Stats 1957 ch 1904 §1, operative January 1, 1958. The repealed section related to compelling California residents to testify in out-of-state proceedings. See CCP §§2029.100 et seq.

§2037. [Section repealed 1987]

Leg.H. Added Stats 1978 ch 1069 §1. Amended Stats 1982 ch 1400 §1; Stats 1986 ch 248 §22 (ch 1336 prevails). Repealed Stats 1986 ch 1336 §3, operative July 1, 1987. See CCP §§2034.210 et seq.

Prior Law: Former CPP §2037, relating to taking depositions in this state, was enacted 1872, amended by Code Amdts 1880 ch 1 111 §5, Stats 1907 ch 392 §10, Stats 1951 ch 1737 §174, operative January 1, 1952, and repealed by Stats 1957 ch 1904 §1, operative January 1, 1958.

§§2037.1–2037.5. [Sections repealed 1987]

Leg.H. Added Stats 1978 ch 1069 §1. Amended Stats 1982 ch 1400 §§2-5. Repealed Stats 1986 ch 1336 §3, operative July 1, 1987. See CCP §§2034.210 et seq.

§2037.6. [Section repealed 1987]

Leg.H. Added Stats 1978 ch 1069 §1. Repealed Stats 1986 ch 1336 §3, operative July 1, 1987. See CCP §§2034.210 et seq.

§2037.7. [Section repealed 1987]

Leg.H. Added Stats 1978 ch 1069 §1. Amended Stats 1980 ch 552 §1; Stats 1986 ch 560 §1. Repealed Stats 1986 ch 1336 §3, operative July 1, 1987. See CCP §§2034.210 et seq.

§§2037.8, 2037.9. [Sections repealed 1987]

Leg.H. Added Stats 1978 ch 1069 §1. Repealed Stats 1986 ch 1336 §3, operative July 1, 1987. See CCP §§2034.210 et seq.

§2038. [Section repealed 1958]

Leg.H. Enacted 1872. Amended Stats 1951 ch 1737 §175, operative January 1, 1952. Repealed Stats 1957 ch 1904 §1, operative January 1, 1958. The repealed section related to taking testimony of witness in this state for proceeding out of this state.

§2042. [Section repealed 1967]

Leg.H. Enacted 1872. Repealed Stats 1965 ch 299 §126, operative January 1, 1967. The repealed section related to the order of proof.

§2043. [Section repealed 1967]

Leg.H. Enacted 1872. Amended Stats 1907 ch 394 §1. Repealed Stats 1965 ch 299 §126, operative January 1, 1967. The repealed section related to exclusion from courtroom of adverse party's witness not at the time under examination.

§§2044–2050. [Sections repealed 1967]

Leg.H. Enacted 1872. Repealed Stats 1965 ch 299 §126, operative January 1, 1967. The repealed sections related to the examination of witnesses.

§2051. [Section repealed 1967]

Leg.H. Enacted 1872. Amended Stats 1949 ch 333 §1. Repealed Stats 1965 ch 299 §126, operative January 1, 1967. The repealed section related to the impeachment of a witness.

§§2052, 2053. [Sections repealed 1967]

Leg.H. Enacted 1872. Repealed Stats 1965 ch 299 §126, operative January 1, 1967. The repealed sections related to the credibility of witnesses.

§2054. [Section repealed 1967]

Leg.H. Enacted 1872. Amended Stats 1907 ch 194 §2. Repealed Stats 1965 ch 299 §126, operative January 1, 1967. The repealed section related to inspection by opposite party of writing shown to witness.

§2055. [Section repealed 1967]

Leg.H. Added Stats 1917 ch 55 §1. Amended Stats 1947 ch 442 §1; Stats 1951 ch 1176 §1; Stats 1957 ch 1209 §1. Repealed Stats 1965 ch 299 §126, operative January 1, 1967. The repealed section related to examination of an adverse party.

§2056. [Section repealed 1967]

Leg.H. Added Stats 1935 ch 57 §1. Repealed Stats 1965 ch 299 §126, operative January 1, 1967. The repealed section related to nonresponsive answer of witness.

§2061. [Section repealed 1967]

Leg.H. Enacted 1872. Repealed Stats 1965 ch 299 §127, operative January 1, 1967. The repealed section related to jury as judges of effect and value of evidence.

TITLE 5
OF THE RIGHTS AND DUTIES OF WITNESSES

Duty to attend and answer when subpoenaed. §2064.
Notice of witness' entitlement to fees and mileage. §2065.

§2064. Duty to attend and answer when subpoenaed

A witness, served with a subpoena, must attend at the time appointed, with any papers under his control lawfully required by the subpoena, and answer all pertinent and legal questions; and, unless sooner discharged, must remain until the testimony is closed. **Leg.H.** Enacted 1872. Amended Stats 1907 ch 395 §1.

§2065. Notice of witness' entitlement to fees and mileage

Any witness who is subpoenaed in any civil or administrative action or proceeding shall be given written notice on the subpoena that the witness may be entitled to receive fees and mileage. Such notice shall indicate generally the manner in which the request for fees and mileage should be made. **Leg.H.** Added Stats 1979 ch 67 §1, operative July 1, 1980.

Prior Law: Former CCP §2065, similar to Ev C §§351, 911, was enacted 1872, amended by Stats 1949 ch 333 §2, and repealed by Stats 1965 ch 299 §128, operative January 1, 1967.

§2066. [Section repealed 1967]

Leg.H. Enacted 1872. Repealed Stats 1965 ch 299 §129, operative January 1, 1967.

§§2067–2070. [Sections repealed 1986]

Leg.H. Enacted 1872. Amended Code Amdts 1880 ch 111 §6; Stats 1907 ch 395 §2. Repealed Stats 1985 ch 41 §§14–17.

TITLE 6
OF EVIDENCE IN PARTICULAR CASES, AND MISCELLANEOUS AND GENERAL PROVISIONS

Chapter 1. Evidence in Particular Cases.
Chapter 3. Administration of Oaths and Affirmations.

CHAPTER 1
EVIDENCE IN PARTICULAR CASES

Offer to pay or deliver as equivalent to actual tender. §2074.
Whoever pays entitled to receipt. §2075.
Objections to tender must be specified. §2076.
Rules for construing description of lands in conveyances. §2077.

§2074. Offer to pay or deliver as equivalent to actual tender

An offer in writing to pay a particular sum of money, or to deliver a written instrument or specific personal property, is, if not accepted, equivalent to the actual production and tender of the money, instrument, or property. **Leg.H.** Enacted 1872.

§2075. Whoever pays entitled to receipt

Whoever pays money, or delivers an instrument or property, is entitled to a receipt therefor from the person to whom the payment or delivery is made, and may demand a proper signature to such receipt as a condition of the payment or delivery. **Leg.H.** Enacted 1872.

§2076. Objections to tender must be specified

The person to whom a tender is made must, at the time, specify any objection he may have to the money, instrument, or property, or he must be deemed to have waived it; and if the objection be to the amount of money, the terms of the instrument, or the amount or kind of property, he must specify the amount, terms, or kind which he requires, or be precluded from objecting afterwards. **Leg.H.** Enacted 1872.

§2077. Rules for construing description of lands in conveyances

The following are the rules for construing the descriptive part of a conveyance of real property, when the construction is doubtful and there are no other sufficient circumstances to determine it:

1. Where there are certain definite and ascertained particulars in the description, the addition of others which are indefinite, unknown, or false, does not frustrate the conveyance, but it is to be construed by the first mentioned particulars.
2. When permanent and visible or ascertained boundaries or monuments are inconsistent with the measurement, either of lines, angles, or surfaces, the boundaries or monuments are paramount.
3. Between different measurements which are inconsistent with each other, that of angles is paramount to that of surfaces, and that of lines paramount to both.
4. When a road, or stream of water not navigable, is the boundary, the rights of the grantor to the middle of the road or the thread of the stream are included in the conveyance, except where the road or thread of the stream is held under another title.
5. When tide water is the boundary, the rights of the grantor to ordinary high-water mark are included in the conveyance. When a navigable lake, where there is no tide, is the boundary, the rights of the grantor to low-mark are included in the conveyance.
6. When the description refers to a map, and that reference is inconsistent with other particulars, it controls them if it appear that the parties acted with reference to the map; otherwise the map is subordinate to other definite and ascertained particulars. **Leg.H.** Enacted 1872. Amended Code Amdts 1873–74 ch 383 §244.

§§2078, 2079. [Sections repealed 1967]

Leg.H. Enacted 1872. Repealed Stats 1965 ch 299 §§130, 131, operative January 1, 1967. The repealed sections related to offer of compromise as admission and confession of adultery as justification for judgment of civil divorce.

CHAPTER 2
PROCEEDINGS TO PERPETUATE TESTIMONY
[REPEALED]

§2083. [Section repealed 1958]

Leg.H. Enacted 1872. Repealed Stats 1957 ch 1904 §1, operative January 1, 1958. The repealed section related to authority to take and perpetuate testimony.

§2084. [Section repealed 1958]

Leg.H. Enacted 1872. Amended Code Amdts 1873–74 ch 383 §245; Code Amdts 1880 ch 111 §2; Stats 1953 ch 1077 §1. Repealed Stats 1957 ch 1904 §1, operative January 1, 1958. The repealed section related to petition and its contents.

§§2084.1, 2084.2. [Sections repealed 1958]

Leg.H. Added Stats 1953 ch 1077 §§4, 5. Repealed Stats 1957 ch 1904 §1, operative January 1, 1958. The repealed sections related to order allowing examination and protection of party and witness from abuse of process.

§§2085, 2086. [Sections repealed 1958]

Leg.H. Enacted 1872. Amended Code Amdts 1873–74 ch 383 §§246, 247; Stats 1953 ch 1077 §§2, 3. Repealed Stats 1957 ch 1904 §1, operative January 1, 1958. The repealed sections related to authority to take depositions and the taking of depositions in or out of state.

§§2087, 2088. [Sections repealed 1958]

Leg.H. Enacted 1872. Amended Code Amdts 1873–74 ch 383 §§248, 249. Repealed Stats 1957 ch 1904 §1, operative January 1, 1958. The repealed sections related to petition and order as prima facie evidence of compliance with chapter and the use of depositions.

§2089. [Section repealed 1958]

Leg.H. Enacted 1872. Repealed Stats 1957 ch 1904 §1, operative January 1, 1958. The repealed section related to the effect of depositions.

§2090. [Section repealed 1958]

Leg.H. Added Stats 1953 ch 1077 §8. Repealed Stats 1957 ch 1904 §1, operative January 1, 1958. The repealed section related to issuance of subpoena duces tecum.

CHAPTER 3
ADMINISTRATION OF OATHS AND AFFIRMATIONS

Authority to administer oaths and affirmations. §2093.
Form of oath, affirmation, or declaration. §2094.

§2093. Authority to administer oaths and affirmations

(a) A court, judge or clerk of a court, justice, notary public, and officer or person authorized to take testimony in an action or proceeding, or to decide upon evidence, has the power to administer oaths and affirmations.

(b)(1) A shorthand reporter certified pursuant to Article 3 (commencing with Section 8020) of Chapter 13 of Division 3 of the Business and Professions Code has the power to administer oaths and affirmations and may perform the duties of the deposition officer pursuant to Chapter 9 (commencing with Section 2025.010) of Title 4. The certified shorthand reporter is entitled to receive fees for services rendered during a deposition, including fees for deposition services, as specified in subdivision (c) of Section 8211 of the Government Code.

(2) This subdivision also applies to depositions taken by telephone or other remote electronic means as specified in Chapter 2 (commencing with Section 2017.010) and Chapter 9 (commencing with Section 2025.010) of Title 4.

(c)(1) A former judge or justice of a court of record in the state who retired or resigned from office may administer oaths and affirmations, if the former judge or justice requests and receives a certification from the Commission on Judicial Performance pursuant to paragraph (2).

(2) The Commission on Judicial Performance shall issue a certification enabling a former judge or justice to administer oaths and affirmations if the following conditions are satisfied:

(A) The former judge or justice was not removed from office; was not censured and barred from receiving an assignment, appointment, or reference of work from any California state court; did not retire or resign from office with an agreement with the commission that the former judge or justice would not receive an assignment, appointment or reference of work from any California state court; and, at the time of the former judge or justice's retirement, resignation, or request for certification, a formal disciplinary proceeding was not pending or was resolved on the merits in the judge or justice's favor after his or her retirement or resignation and before the request for certification.

(B) A medical certification provided to the commission by the former judge or justice pursuant to paragraph (3) establishes one of the following:

(i) The former judge or justice does not have a medical condition that would impair his or her ability to administer oaths or affirmations.

(ii) The former judge or justice has a medical condition that may impair his or her ability to administer oaths and affirmations, but the condition does not impair his or her ability at the present time.

(3) The Commission on Judicial Performance may require an applicant to obtain a medical certification in order to receive or renew a certification to administer oaths and affirmations if, at the time of resignation or retirement, there is evidence in a disability application file or in a disciplinary investigation file of possible cognitive impairment affecting the judge or justice, or if the former judge or justice previously received a two-year certification to administer oaths and affirmations from the commission. The commission shall supply the required forms to an applicant upon request.

(4) If an applicant's medical certification indicates that the applicant has a medical condition that may impair his or her ability to administer oaths and affirmations, but the condition does not impair his or her ability at the time the medical certification is submitted with the application, the Commission on Judicial Performance shall issue a certification to administer oaths and affirmations pursuant to paragraph (2), but the certification is only valid for a period of two years from the date of issuance.

(5) Notwithstanding paragraph (1), a former judge or justice of a court of record who received a certification to administer oaths and affirmations from the Commission on Judicial Performance prior to January 1, 2018, may continue to administer oaths and affirmations until the expiration of the certification, at which time he or she may reapply for certification pursuant to paragraph (2).

(6) The Commission on Judicial Performance may charge a regulatory fee not to exceed fifteen dollars ($15) for each certification application submitted pursuant to this subdivision to cover its costs, including costs to review a medical certification.

(d) A rule or regulation regarding the confidentiality of proceedings of the Commission on Judicial Performance does not prohibit the commission from issuing a certificate as provided for in this section.

(e) The administration of an oath or affirmation pursuant to this section without pay does not violate Section 75060.6 of the Government Code.
Leg.H. Enacted 1872. Amended Stats 1986 ch 1417 §3, ch 1418 §1.3; Stats 1988 ch 1032 §1; Stats 2001 ch 812 §12 (AB 223); Stats 2004 ch 182 §24 (AB 3081), operative July 1, 2005; Stats 2015 ch 308 §1 (AB 1028), effective January 1, 2016; Stats 2016 ch 86 §46 (SB 1171), effective January 1, 2017; Stats 2017 ch 82 §1 (AB 740), effective January 1, 2018; Stats 2018 ch 92 §46 (SB 1289), effective January 1, 2019.

§2094. Form of oath, affirmation, or declaration

(a) An oath, affirmation, or declaration in an action or a proceeding, may be administered by obtaining an affirmative response to one of the following questions:

(1) "Do you solemnly state that the evidence you shall give in this issue (or matter) shall be the truth, the whole truth, and nothing but the truth, so help you God?"

(2) "Do you solemnly state, under penalty of perjury, that the evidence that you shall give in this issue (or matter) shall be the truth, the whole truth, and nothing but the truth?"

(b) In the alternative to the forms prescribed in subdivision (a), the court may administer an oath, affirmation, or declaration in an action or a proceeding in a manner that is calculated to awaken the person's conscience and impress the person's mind with the duty to tell the truth. The court shall satisfy itself that the person testifying understands that his or her testimony is being given under penalty of perjury. **Leg.H.** Enacted 1872. Amended Code Amdts 1873–74 ch 383 §250; Stats 2000 ch 688 §13 (AB 1669); Stats 2002 ch 806 §17 (AB 3027).

§2095. [Section repealed 2001]

Leg.H. Enacted 1872. Repealed Stats 2000 ch 688 §14 (AB 1669). The repealed section related to varying form of administering oath.

§2096. [Section repealed 2001]

Leg.H. Enacted 1872. Repealed Stats 2000 ch 688 §15 (AB 1669). The repealed section related to administration of oath to witness according to ceremonies of religion.

§2097. [Section repealed 2001]

Leg.H. Enacted 1872. Repealed Stats 2000 ch 688 §16 (AB 1669). The repealed section related to option to affirm or declare.

CHAPTER 4
GENERAL PROVISIONS [REPEALED]

TITLE 7
UNIFORM FEDERAL LIEN REGISTRATION ACT

Application of title. §2100.
Filing of notices. §2101.
Certification of notices. §2102.
Filing procedure. §2103.
Recording fee; Filing fee; Billing for documents recorded or filed by county recorder of Secretary of State. §2104.
Maintenance of file. §2105.
Construction; General purpose. §2106.
Information technology for tax liens. §2106.5.
Popular title. §2107.

§2100. Application of title

This title applies only to federal tax liens and to other federal liens notices of which under any Act of Congress or any regulation adopted pursuant thereto are required or permitted to be filed in the same manner as notices of federal tax liens. **Leg.H.** Added Stats 1979 ch 330 §1.

§2101. Filing of notices

(a) Notices of liens, certificates, and other notices affecting federal tax liens or other federal liens must be filed in accordance with this title.

(b) Notices of liens upon real property for obligations payable to the United States and certificates and notices affecting the liens shall be filed for record in the office of the recorder of the county in which the real property subject to the liens is situated.

(c) Notices of federal liens upon personal property, whether tangible or intangible, for obligations payable to the United States and certificates and notices affecting the liens shall be filed as follows:

(1) If the person against whose interest the lien applies is a corporation, a limited liability company, or a partnership whose principal executive office is in this state, as these entities are defined in the internal revenue laws of the United States, in the office of the Secretary of State.

(2) If the person against whose interest the lien applies is a trust that is not covered by paragraph (1), in the office of the Secretary of State.

(3) If the person against whose interest the lien applies is the estate of a decedent, in the office of the Secretary of State.

(4) In all other cases, in the office of the recorder of the county where the person against whose interest the lien applies resides at the time of filing of the notice of lien. **Leg.H.** Added Stats 1979 ch 330 §1. Amended Stats 1991 ch 932 §2 (AB 1646); Stats 1997 ch 892 §2 (SB 73).

Prior Law: Former CCP §2101, relating to questions of fact, was enacted 1872, amended by Code Amdts 1873-74 ch 383 §251, and repealed by Stats 1965 ch 299 §192, operative January 1, 1967.

§2102. Certification of notices

Certification of notices of liens, certificates, or other notices affecting federal liens by the Secretary of the Treasury of the United States or his or her delegate, or by any official or entity of the United States responsible for filing or certifying of notice of any other lien, entitles them to be filed and no other attestation, certification, or acknowledgment is necessary. **Leg.H.** Added Stats 1979 ch 330 §1.

Prior Law: Former CCP §2102, relating to questions of law, was enacted 1872 and repealed by Stats 1965 ch 299 §k32m operative January 1, 1967.

§2103. Filing procedure

(a) If a notice of federal lien, a refiling of a notice of federal lien, or a notice of revocation of any certificate described in subdivision (b) is presented to a filing officer who is:

(1) The Secretary of State, he or she shall cause the notice to be filed, indexed, and marked in accordance with the provisions of Sections 9515, 9516, and 9522 of the Commercial Code as if the notice were a financing statement within the meaning of that code; or

(2) A county recorder, he or she shall accept for filing, file for record in the manner set forth in Section 27320 of the Government Code, and index the document by the name of the person against whose interest the lien applies in the general index.

(b) If a certificate of release, nonattachment, discharge, or subordination of any lien is presented to the Secretary of State for filing he or she shall:

(1) Cause a certificate of release or nonattachment to be filed, indexed, and marked as if the certificate were a termination statement within the meaning of the Commercial Code.

(2) Cause a certificate of discharge or subordination to be filed, indexed, and marked as if the certificate were a release of collateral within the meaning of the Commercial Code.

(c) If a refiled notice of federal lien referred to in subdivision (a) or any of the certificates or notices referred to in subdivision (b) is presented for filing to a county recorder, he or she shall accept for filing, file for record in the manner set forth in Section 27320 of the Government Code, and index the document by the name of the person against whose interest the lien applies in the general index.

(d) Upon request of any person, the filing officer shall issue his or her certificate showing whether there is on file, on the date and hour stated therein, any notice of lien or certificate or notice affecting any lien filed after January 1, 1968, under this title or former Chapter 14 (commencing with Section 7200) of Division 7 of Title 1 of the Government Code, naming a particular person, and if a notice or certificate is on file, giving the date and hour of filing of each notice or certificate. Upon request, the filing officer shall furnish a copy of any notice of federal lien, or notice or certificate affecting a federal lien. If the filing officer is a county recorder, the fee for a certificate for each name searched shall be set by the filing officer in an amount that covers actual costs, and the fee for copies shall be in accordance with Section 27366 of the Government Code. If the filing officer is the Secretary of State, the certificate shall be issued as part of a combined certificate pursuant to Section 9528 of the Commercial Code, and the fee for the certificate and copies shall be in accordance with that section. **Leg.H.** Added Stats 1979 ch 330 §1. Amended Stats 1982 ch 865 §1; Stats 1988 ch 393 §10; Stats 1999 ch 991 §25.5 (SB 45), operative July 1, 2001; Stats 2009 ch 606 §1 (SB 676), effective January 1, 2010; Stats 2012 ch 494 §2 (SB 1532), effective January 1, 2013.

Prior Law: Former CCP §2103, relating to questions of fact, was enacted 1872 and repealed Stats 1965 ch 299 §132, operative January 1, 1967.

§2104. Recording fee; Filing fee; Billing for documents recorded or filed by county recorder of Secretary of State

The fee charged for recording and indexing each notice of lien or certificate or notice affecting the lien filed with the county recorder shall be the same as those established by Article 5 (commencing with Section 27360) of Chapter 6 of Part 3 of Division 2 of Title 3 of the Government Code for the recording and indexing of documents.

The fee for filing and indexing each notice of lien or certificate or notice affecting the lien with the office of the Secretary of State is set forth in subdivision (a) of Section 12194 of the Government Code.

The officer shall bill the district directors of internal revenue or other appropriate federal officials on a monthly basis for fees for documents recorded or filed by the county recorder or the Secretary of State. **Leg.H.** Added Stats 1995 ch 656 §3.5 (SB 888), operative January 1, 2000. Amended Stats 1999 ch 1000 §13 (SB 284).

Prior Law: Former CCP §2104, similar to the present section, was added Stats 1979 ch 330 §1, amended Stats 1987 ch 1348 §8, Stats 1988 ch 487 §1, Stats 1995 ch 656 §4, and repealed January 1, 2000, by its own terms.

Former CCP §2104 was added Code Amdts 1873-74 ch 383 §252 and repealed Stats 1907 ch 375 §3, ch 396 §1.

§2105. Maintenance of file

Filing officers with whom notices of federal tax liens, certificates and notices affecting such liens have been filed on or before January 1, 1968, shall, after that date, continue to maintain a file labeled "federal tax lien notices filed prior to January 2, 1968" containing notices and certificates filed in numerical order of receipt. If a notice of lien was filed on or before January 1, 1968, any certificate or notice affecting the lien shall be filed in the same office. **Leg.H.** Added Stats 1979 ch 330 §1.

§2106. Construction; General purpose

This title shall be applied and construed to effectuate its general purpose to make uniform the law with respect to the subject of this title among states enacting it. **Leg.H.** Added Stats 1979 ch 330 §1.

§2106.5. Information technology for tax liens

This title shall be applied and construed to permit the transmission, filing, recording, and indexing of notices of federal tax liens and all certificates that relate to or affect those liens, including, but not limited to, certificates of release, discharge, subordination, and nonattachment, by electronic or magnetic means, using computerized data processing, telecommunications, and other similar information technologies available to the filing offices. **Leg.H.** Added Stats 1998 ch 463 §1 (AB 1906).

§2107. Popular title

This title may be cited as the Uniform Federal Lien Registration Act. **Leg.H.** Added Stats 1979 ch 330 §1.

The STANDARD EVIDENCE CODE

of the

STATE OF CALIFORNIA

2025 EDITION

The Original Evidence Code
Approved May 18, 1965—Effective January 1, 1967
With All Subsequent Legislative Enactments

Table Showing 2024 Changes in the Evidence Code

Effective January 1, 2025, unless otherwise noted at end of section.

Section	Effect	Chapter
1106	Amended	993
1157	Amended	329

CONTENTS

	Sections
DIVISION 1. PRELIMINARY PROVISIONS AND CONSTRUCTION	1 – 12
DIVISION 2. WORDS AND PHRASES DEFINED	100 – 260
DIVISION 3. GENERAL PROVISIONS	
Chapter 1. Applicability of Code	300
Chapter 2. Province of Court and Jury	310 – 312
Chapter 3. Order of Proof	320
Chapter 4. Admitting and Excluding Evidence	350 – 406
Chapter 5. Weight of Evidence Generally	410 – 413
DIVISION 4. JUDICIAL NOTICE	450 – 460
DIVISION 5. BURDEN OF PROOF; BURDEN OF PRODUCING EVIDENCE; PRESUMPTIONS & INFERENCES	
Chapter 1. Burden of Proof	500 – 524
Chapter 2. Burden of Producing Evidence	550
Chapter 3. Presumptions and Inferences	600 – 670
DIVISION 6. WITNESSES	
Chapter 1. Competency	700 – 704
Chapter 2. Oath and Confrontation	710 – 712
Chapter 3. Expert Witnesses	720 – 733
Chapter 4. Interpreters and Translators	750 – 757
Chapter 5. Method and Scope of Examination	760 – 778
Chapter 6. Credibility of Witnesses	780 – 791
Chapter 7. Hypnosis of Witnesses	795
DIVISION 7. OPINION TESTIMONY AND SCIENTIFIC EVIDENCE	
Chapter 1. Expert and Other Opinion Testimony	800 – 870
DIVISION 8. PRIVILEGES	
Chapter 1. Definitions	900 – 905
Chapter 2. Applicability of Division	910
Chapter 3. General Provisions Relating to Privileges	911 – 920
Chapter 4. Particular Privileges	930 – 1063
Chapter 5. Immunity of Newsman from Citation for Contempt	1070
DIVISION 9. EVIDENCE AFFECTED OR EXCLUDED BY EXTRINSIC POLICIES	
Chapter 1. Evidence of Character, Habit, or Custom	1100 – 1109
Chapter 2. Mediation	1115 – 1129
Chapter 3. Other Evidence Affected or Excluded by Extrinsic Policies	1150 – 1162
DIVISION 10. HEARSAY EVIDENCE	
Chapter 1. General Provisions	1200 – 1205
Chapter 2. Exceptions to the Hearsay Rule	1220 – 1390
DIVISION 11. WRITINGS	
Chapter 1. Authentication and Proof of Writings	1400 – 1454
Chapter 2. Secondary Evidence of Writings	1520 – 1567
Chapter 3. Official Writings Affecting Property	1600 – 1605

EVIDENCE CODE

An Act to establish an Evidence Code, thereby consolidating and revising the law relating to evidence; amending various sections of the Business and Professions Code, Civil Code, Code of Civil Procedure, Corporations Code, Government Code, Health and Safety Code, Penal Code, and Public Utilities Code to make them consistent therewith; adding Sections 164.5, 3544, 3545, 3546, 3547, and 3548 to the Civil Code; adding Sections 631.7 and 1908.5 to the Code of Civil Procedure; and repealing legislation inconsistent therewith.

DIVISION 1
PRELIMINARY PROVISIONS AND CONSTRUCTION

§ 1. Short title
Common law construing code abrogated. §2.
Constitutionality. §3.
Construction of code. §4.
Effect of headings. §5.
References to statutes. §6.
"Division," "chapter," "article," "section," "subdivision," and "paragraph". §7.
Construction of tenses. §8.
Construction of genders. §9.
Construction of singular and plural. §10.
"Shall" and "may". §11.
Code becomes operative January 1, 1967; Effect on pending proceedings. §12.

§1. Short title
This code shall be known as the Evidence Code. **Leg.H.** Enacted Stats 1965 ch 299 §2, operative January 1, 1967.

§2. Common law construing code abrogated
The rule of the common law, that statutes in derogation thereof are to be strictly construed, has no application to this code. This code establishes the law of this state respecting the subject to which it relates, and its provisions are to be liberally construed with a view to effecting its objects and promoting justice. **Leg.H.** Enacted Stats 1965 ch 299 §2, operative January 1, 1967.

§3. Constitutionality
If any provision or clause of this code or application thereof to any person or circumstances is held invalid, such invalidity shall not affect other provisions or applications of the code which can be given effect without the invalid provision or application, and to this end the provisions of this code are declared to be severable. **Leg.H.** Enacted Stats 1965 ch 299 §2, operative January 1, 1967.

§4. Construction of code
Unless the provision or context otherwise requires, these preliminary provisions and rules of construction shall govern the construction of this code. **Leg.H.** Enacted Stats 1965 ch 299 §2, operative January 1, 1967.

§5. Effect of headings
Division, chapter, article, and section headings do not in any manner affect the scope, meaning, or intent of the provisions of this code. **Leg.H.** Enacted Stats 1965 ch 299 §2, operative January 1, 1967.

§6. References to statutes
Whenever any reference is made to any portion of this code or of any other statute, such reference shall apply to all amendments and additions heretofore or hereafter made. **Leg.H.** Enacted Stats 1965 ch 299 §2, operative January 1, 1967.

§7. "Division," "chapter," "article," "section," "subdivision," and "paragraph"
Unless otherwise expressly stated:
(a) "Division" means a division of this code.
(b) "Chapter" means a chapter of the division in which that term occurs.
(c) "Article" means an article of the chapter in which that term occurs.
(d) "Section" means a section of this code.
(e) "Subdivision" means a subdivision of the section in which that term occurs.
(f) "Paragraph" means a paragraph of the subdivision in which that term occurs. **Leg.H.** Enacted Stats 1965 ch 299 §2, operative January 1, 1967.

§8. Construction of tenses
The present tense includes the past and future tenses; and the future, the present. **Leg.H.** Enacted Stats 1965 ch 299 §2, operative January 1, 1967.

§9. Construction of genders
The masculine gender includes the feminine and neuter. **Leg.H.** Enacted Stats 1965 ch 299 §2, operative January 1, 1967.

§10. Construction of singular and plural
The singular number includes the plural; and the plural, the singular. **Leg.H.** Enacted Stats 1965 ch 299 §2, operative January 1, 1967.

§11. "Shall" and "may"
"Shall" is mandatory and "may" is permissive. **Leg.H.** Enacted Stats 1965 ch 299 §2, operative January 1, 1967.

§12. Code becomes operative January 1, 1967; Effect on pending proceedings
(a) This code shall become operative on January 1, 1967, and shall govern proceedings in actions brought on or after that date and, except as provided in subdivision (b), further proceedings in actions pending on that date.
(b) Subject to subdivision (c), a trial commenced before January 1, 1967, shall not be governed by this code. For the purpose of this subdivision:
(1) A trial is commenced when the first witness is sworn or the first exhibit is admitted into evidence and is terminated when the issue upon which such evidence is received is submitted to the trier of fact. A new trial, or a separate trial of a different issue, commenced on or after January 1, 1967, shall be governed by this code.
(2) If an appeal is taken from a ruling made at a trial commenced before January 1, 1967, the appellate court shall apply the law applicable at the time of the commencement of the trial.
(c) The provisions of Division 8 (commencing with Section 900) relating to privileges shall govern any claim of privilege made after December 31, 1966. **Leg.H.** Enacted Stats 1965 ch 299 §2, operative January 1, 1967.

DIVISION 2
WORDS AND PHRASES DEFINED

Application of definitions. §100.
"Action". §105.
"Burden of producing evidence". §110.
"Burden of proof". §115.
"Civil action". §120.
"Conduct". §125.
"Criminal action". §130.
"Declarant". §135.
"Evidence". §140.
"The hearing". §145.
"Hearsay evidence". §150.
"Law". §160.
"Oath". §165.
"Perceive". §170.
"Person". §175.
"Dependent person". §177.
"Personal property". §180.
"Property". §185.
"Proof". §190.
"Public employee". §195.
"Public entity". §200.
"Real property". §205.
"Relevant evidence". §210.
"Spouse" to include registered domestic partner. §215.
"State". §220.
"Statement". §225.
"Statute". §230.
"Trier of fact". §235.
"Unavailable as a witness". §240.
"Writing". §250.
"Original". §255.
"Duplicate". §260.

§100. Application of definitions
Unless the provision or context otherwise requires, these definitions govern the construction of this code. **Leg.H.** Enacted Stats 1965 ch 299 §2, operative January 1, 1967.

§105. "Action"
"Action" includes a civil action and a criminal action. **Leg.H.** Enacted Stats 1965 ch 299 §2, operative January 1, 1967.

§110. "Burden of producing evidence"
"Burden of producing evidence" means the obligation of a party to introduce evidence sufficient to avoid a ruling against him on the issue. **Leg.H.** Enacted Stats 1965 ch 299 §2, operative January 1, 1967.

§115. "Burden of proof"
"Burden of proof" means the obligation of a party to establish by evidence a requisite degree of belief concerning a fact in the mind of the trier of fact or the court. The burden of proof may require a party to raise a reasonable doubt concerning the existence or nonexistence of a fact or that he establish the existence or nonexistence of a fact by a preponderance of the evidence, by clear and convincing proof, or by proof beyond a reasonable doubt.

Except as otherwise provided by law, the burden of proof requires proof by a preponderance of the evidence. **Leg.H.** Enacted Stats 1965 ch 299 §2, operative January 1, 1967.

§120. "Civil action"
"Civil action" includes civil proceedings. **Leg.H.** Enacted Stats 1965 ch 299 §2, operative January 1, 1967.

§125. "Conduct"
"Conduct" includes all active and passive behavior, both verbal and nonverbal. **Leg.H.** Enacted Stats 1965 ch 299 §2, operative January 1, 1967.

§130. "Criminal action"
"Criminal action" includes criminal proceedings. **Leg.H.** Enacted Stats 1965 ch 299 §2, operative January 1, 1967.

§135. "Declarant"
"Declarant" is a person who makes a statement. **Leg.H.** Enacted Stats 1965 ch 299 §2, operative January 1, 1967.

§140. "Evidence"
"Evidence" means testimony, writings, material objects, or other things presented to the senses that are offered to prove the existence or nonexistence of a fact. **Leg.H.** Enacted Stats 1965 ch 299 §2, operative January 1, 1967.

§145. "The hearing"
"The hearing" means the hearing at which a question under this code arises, and not some earlier or later hearing. **Leg.H.** Enacted Stats 1965 ch 299 §2, operative January 1, 1967.

§150. "Hearsay evidence"
"Hearsay evidence" is defined in Section 1200. **Leg.H.** Enacted Stats 1965 ch 299 §2, operative January 1, 1967.

§160. "Law"
"Law" includes constitutional, statutory, and decisional law. **Leg.H.** Enacted Stats 1965 ch 299 §2, operative January 1, 1967.

§165. "Oath"
"Oath" includes affirmation or declaration under penalty of perjury. **Leg.H.** Enacted Stats 1965 ch 299 §2, operative January 1, 1967.

§170. "Perceive"
"Perceive" means to acquire knowledge through one's senses. **Leg.H.** Enacted Stats 1965 ch 299 §2, operative January 1, 1967.

§175. "Person"
"Person" includes a natural person, firm, association, organization, partnership, business trust, corporation, limited liability company, or public entity. **Leg.H.** Enacted Stats 1965 ch 299 §2, operative January 1, 1967. Amended Stats 1994 ch 1010 §103 (SB 2053).

§177. "Dependent person"
"Dependent person" means a person, regardless of whether the person lives independently, who has a physical or mental impairment that substantially restricts his or her ability to carry out normal activities or to protect his or her rights, including, but not limited to, persons who have physical or developmental disabilities or whose physical or mental abilities have significantly diminished because of age. "Dependent person" includes any person who is admitted as an inpatient to a 24-hour health facility, as defined in Sections 1250, 1250.2, and 1250.3 of the Health and Safety Code. **Leg.H.** Added Stats 2004 ch 823 §2 (AB 20). Amended Stats 2018 ch 70 §1 (AB 1934), effective January 1, 2019.

§180. "Personal property"
"Personal property" includes money, goods, chattels, things in action, and evidences of debt. **Leg.H.** Enacted Stats 1965 ch 299 §2, operative January 1, 1967.

§185. "Property"
"Property" includes both real and personal property. **Leg.H.** Enacted Stats 1965 ch 299 §2, operative January 1, 1967.

§190. "Proof"
"Proof" is the establishment by evidence of a requisite degree of belief concerning a fact in the mind of the trier of fact or the court. **Leg.H.** Enacted Stats 1965 ch 299 §2, operative January 1, 1967.

§195. "Public employee"
"Public employee" means an officer, agent, or employee of a public entity. **Leg.H.** Enacted Stats 1965 ch 299 §2, operative January 1, 1967.

§200. "Public entity"
"Public entity" includes a nation, state, county, city and county, city, district, public authority, public agency, or any other political subdivision or public corporation, whether foreign or domestic. **Leg.H.** Enacted Stats 1965 ch 299 §2, operative January 1, 1967.

§205. "Real property"
"Real property" includes lands, tenements, and hereditaments. **Leg.H.** Enacted Stats 1965 ch 299 §2, operative January 1, 1967.

§210. "Relevant evidence"
"Relevant evidence" means evidence, including evidence relevant to the credibility of a witness or hearsay declarant, having any tendency in

reason to prove or disprove any disputed fact that is of consequence to the determination of the action. **Leg.H.** Enacted Stats 1965 ch 299 §2, operative January 1, 1967.

§215. "Spouse" to include registered domestic partner
"Spouse" includes "registered domestic partner," as required by Section 297.5 of the Family Code. **Leg.H.** Added Stats 2016 ch 50 §32 (SB 1005), effective January 1, 2017.

2016 Note: It is the intent of the Legislature that the changes made by this act have only technical and nonsubstantive effect. Hence, no change made by this act shall create any new right, duty, or other obligation that did not exist immediately preceding the effective date of this act, or result in the limitation or termination of any right, duty, or other obligation that existed immediately preceding the effective date of this act. Stats 2016 ch 50 (SB 1005) §125.

§220. "State"
"State" means the State of California, unless applied to the different parts of the United States. In the latter case, it includes any state, district, commonwealth, territory, or insular possession of the United States. **Leg.H.** Enacted Stats 1965 ch 299 §2, operative January 1, 1967.

§225. "Statement"
"Statement" means (a) oral or written verbal expression or (b) nonverbal conduct of a person intended by him as a substitute for oral or written verbal expression. **Leg.H.** Enacted Stats 1965 ch 299 §2, operative January 1, 1967.

§230. "Statute"
"Statute" includes a treaty and a constitutional provision. **Leg.H.** Enacted Stats 1965 ch 299 §2, operative January 1, 1967.

§235. "Trier of fact"
"Trier of fact" includes (a) the jury and (b) the court when the court is trying an issue of fact other than one relating to the admissibility of evidence. **Leg.H.** Enacted Stats 1965 ch 299 §2, operative January 1, 1967.

§240. "Unavailable as a witness"
(a) Except as otherwise provided in subdivision (b), "unavailable as a witness" means that the declarant is any of the following:

(1) Exempted or precluded on the ground of privilege from testifying concerning the matter to which his or her statement is relevant.

(2) Disqualified from testifying to the matter.

(3) Dead or unable to attend or to testify at the hearing because of then-existing physical or mental illness or infirmity.

(4) Absent from the hearing and the court is unable to compel his or her attendance by its process.

(5) Absent from the hearing and the proponent of his or her statement has exercised reasonable diligence but has been unable to procure his or her attendance by the court's process.

(6) Persistent in refusing to testify concerning the subject matter of the declarant's statement despite having been found in contempt for refusal to testify.

(b) A declarant is not unavailable as a witness if the exemption, preclusion, disqualification, death, inability, or absence of the declarant was brought about by the procurement or wrongdoing of the proponent of his or her statement for the purpose of preventing the declarant from attending or testifying.

(c) Expert testimony that establishes that physical or mental trauma resulting from an alleged crime has caused harm to a witness of sufficient severity that the witness is physically unable to testify or is unable to testify without suffering substantial trauma may constitute a sufficient showing of unavailability pursuant to paragraph (3) of subdivision (a). As used in this section, the term "expert" means a physician and surgeon, including a psychiatrist, or any person described by subdivision (b), (c), or (e) of Section 1010.

The introduction of evidence to establish the unavailability of a witness under this subdivision shall not be deemed procurement of unavailability, in absence of proof to the contrary. **Leg.H.** Enacted Stats 1965 ch 299 §2, operative January 1, 1967. Amended Stats 1984 ch 401 §1; Stats 1988 ch 485 §1; Stats 2010 ch 537 §1 (AB 1723), effective January 1, 2011.

§250. "Writing"
"Writing" means handwriting, typewriting, printing, photostating, photographing, photocopying, transmitting by electronic mail or facsimile, and every other means of recording upon any tangible thing, any form of communication or representation, including letters, words, pictures, sounds, or symbols, or combinations thereof, and any record thereby created, regardless of the manner in which the record has been stored. **Leg.H.** Enacted Stats 1965 ch 299 §2, operative January 1, 1967. Amended Stats 2002 ch 945 §1 (AB 1962).

§255. "Original"
"Original" means the writing itself or any counterpart intended to have the same effect by a person executing or issuing it. An "original" of a photograph includes the negative or any print therefrom. If data are stored in a computer or similar device, any printout or other output readable by sight, shown to reflect the data accurately, is an "original." **Leg.H.** Added Stats 1977 ch 708 §1.

§260. "Duplicate"
A "duplicate" is a counterpart produced by the same impression as the original, or from the same matrix, or by means of photography, including enlargements and miniatures, or by mechanical or electronic rerecording, or by chemical reproduction, or by other equivalent technique which accurately reproduces the original. **Leg.H.** Added Stats 1977 ch 708 §2.

DIVISION 3
GENERAL PROVISIONS

Chapter 1. Applicability of Code.
Chapter 2. Province of Court and Jury.
Chapter 3. Order of Proof.
Chapter 4. Admitting and Excluding Evidence.
Chapter 5. Weight of Evidence Generally.

CHAPTER 1
APPLICABILITY OF CODE

Applicability of code. §300.

§300. Applicability of code

Except as otherwise provided by statute, this code applies in every action before the Supreme Court or a court of appeal or superior court, including proceedings in such actions conducted by a referee, court commissioner, or similar officer, but does not apply in grand jury proceedings. **Leg.H.** Enacted Stats 1965 ch 299 §2, operative January 1, 1967. Amended Stats 1967 ch 17 §35; Stats 1998 ch 931 §141 (SB 2139), effective September 28, 1998; Stats 2002 ch 784 §101 (SB 1316).

CHAPTER 2
PROVINCE OF COURT AND JURY

Questions of law for court. §310.
Procedure when foreign or sister-state law cannot be determined. §311.
Jury as trier of fact. §312.

§310. Questions of law for court

(a) All questions of law (including but not limited to questions concerning the construction of statutes and other writings, the admissibility of evidence, and other rules of evidence) are to be decided by the court. Determination of issues of fact preliminary to the admission of evidence are to be decided by the court as provided in Article 2 (commencing with Section 400) of Chapter 4.

(b) Determination of the law of an organization of nations or of the law of a foreign nation or a public entity in a foreign nation is a question of law to be determined in the manner provided in Division 4 (commencing with Section 450). **Leg.H.** Enacted Stats 1965 ch 299 §2, operative January 1, 1967.

§311. Procedure when foreign or sister-state law cannot be determined

If the law of an organization of nations, a foreign nation or a state other than this state, or a public entity in a foreign nation or a state other than this state, is applicable and such law cannot be determined, the court may, as the ends of justice require, either:

(a) Apply the law of this state if the court can do so consistently with the Constitution of the United States and the Constitution of this state; or

(b) Dismiss the action without prejudice or, in the case of a reviewing court, remand the case to the trial court with directions to dismiss the action without prejudice. **Leg.H.** Enacted Stats 1965 ch 299 §2, operative January 1, 1967.

§312. Jury as trier of fact

Except as otherwise provided by law, where the trial is by jury:

(a) All questions of fact are to be decided by the jury.

(b) Subject to the control of the court, the jury is to determine the effect and value of the evidence addressed to it, including the credibility of witnesses and hearsay declarants. **Leg.H.** Enacted Stats 1965 ch 299 §2, operative January 1, 1967.

CHAPTER 3
ORDER OF PROOF

Power of court to regulate order of proof. §320.

§320. Power of court to regulate order of proof

Except as otherwise provided by law, the court in its discretion shall regulate the order of proof. **Leg.H.** Enacted Stats 1965 ch 299 §2, operative January 1, 1967.

CHAPTER 4
ADMITTING AND EXCLUDING EVIDENCE

Article 1. General Provisions.
Article 2. Preliminary Determinations on Admissibility of Evidence.

ARTICLE 1
General Provisions

Only relevant evidence admissible. §350.
Admissibility of relevant evidence. §351.
Exclusion of results of polygraph examination. §351.1.
Immigration status inadmissible in civil action for personal injury or wrongful death. §351.2.
Disclosure of immigration status in civil action. § 351.3.
Disclosure of immigration status in criminal action. § 351.4.
Discretion of court to exclude evidence. §352.
Address and telephone number of victim of criminal sex act. §352.1.
Admission of creative expressions. § 352.2.
Effect of erroneous admission of evidence. §353.
Effect of erroneous exclusion of evidence. §354.
Limited admissibility. §355.
Entire act, declaration, conversation, or writing may be brought out to elucidate part offered. §356.

§350. Only relevant evidence admissible

No evidence is admissible except relevant evidence. **Leg.H.** Enacted Stats 1965 ch 299 §2, operative January 1, 1967.

§351. Admissibility of relevant evidence

Except as otherwise provided by statute, all relevant evidence is admissible. **Leg.H.** Enacted Stats 1965 ch 299 §2, operative January 1, 1967.

§351.1. Exclusion of results of polygraph examination

(a) Notwithstanding any other provision of law, the results of a polygraph examination, the opinion of a polygraph examiner, or any reference to an offer to take, failure to take, or taking of a polygraph examination, shall not be admitted into evidence in any criminal proceeding, including pretrial and post conviction motions and hearings, or in any trial or hearing of a juvenile for a criminal offense, whether heard in juvenile or adult court, unless all parties stipulate to the admission of such results.

(b) Nothing in this section is intended to exclude from evidence statements made during a polygraph examination which are otherwise admissible. **Leg.H.** Added Stats 1983 ch 202 §1, effective July 12, 1983.

§351.2. Immigration status inadmissible in civil action for personal injury or wrongful death

(a) In a civil action for personal injury or wrongful death, evidence of a person's immigration status shall not be admitted into evidence, nor shall discovery into a person's immigration status be permitted.

(b) This section does not affect the standards of relevance, admissibility, or discovery prescribed by Section 3339 of the Civil Code, Section 7285 of the Government Code, Section 24000 of the Health and Safety Code, and Section 1171.5 of the Labor Code. **Leg.H.** Added Stats 2016 ch 132 §1 (AB 2159), effective January 1, 2017.

§351.3. Disclosure of immigration status in civil action other than personal injury or wrongful death action [Repealed]

Leg.H. Added Stats 2018 ch 12 §1 (SB 785), effective May 17, 2018, repealed January 1, 2022.

§ 351.3. Disclosure of immigration status in civil action

(a) In a civil action not governed by Section 351.2, evidence of a person's immigration status shall not be disclosed in open court by a party or their attorney unless the judge presiding over the matter first determines that the evidence is admissible in an in camera hearing requested by the party seeking disclosure of the person's immigration status.

(b) This section does not do any of the following:

(1) Apply to cases in which a person's immigration status is necessary to prove an element of a claim or an affirmative defense.

(2) Impact otherwise applicable laws governing the relevance of immigration status to liability or the standards applicable to inquiries regarding immigration status in discovery or proceedings in a civil action, including Section 3339 of the Civil Code, Section 7285 of the Government Code, Section 24000 of the Health and Safety Code, and Section 1171.5 of the Labor Code.

(3) Prohibit a person or their attorney from voluntarily revealing the person's immigration status to the court. **Leg.H.** Added Stats 2022 ch 168 §1 (SB 836), effective August 22, 2022.

Prior Law: Former Ev C §351.3, relating to disclosure of immigration status in civil action other than personal injury or wrongful death action, was added Stats 2018 ch 12 §1 (SB 785), effective May 17, 2018, and repealed January 1, 2022, by its own terms.

§ 351.4. Disclosure of immigration status in criminal action

(a) In a criminal action, evidence of a person's immigration status shall not be disclosed in open court by a party or their attorney unless the judge presiding over the matter first determines that the evidence is admissible in an in camera hearing requested by the party seeking disclosure of the person's immigration status.

(b) This section does not do any of the following:

(1) Apply to cases in which a person's immigration status is necessary to prove an element of an offense or an affirmative defense.

(2) Limit discovery in a criminal action.

(3) Prohibit a person or their attorney from voluntarily revealing the person's immigration status to the court. **Leg.H.** Added Stats 2022 ch 168 §2 (SB 836), effective August 22, 2022.

Prior Law Former Ev C §351.4, relating to disclosure of immigration status in criminal action, was added Stats 2018 ch 12 §2 (SB 785), effective May 17, 2018, and repealed January 1, 2022, by its own terms.

§352. Discretion of court to exclude evidence

The court in its discretion may exclude evidence if its probative value is substantially outweighed by the probability that its admission will (a) necessitate undue consumption of time or (b) create substantial danger of undue prejudice, of confusing the issues, or of misleading the jury. **Leg.H.** Enacted Stats 1965 ch 299 §2, operative January 1, 1967.

§352.1. Address and telephone number of victim of criminal sex act

In any criminal proceeding under Section 261, 262, or 264.1, subdivision (d) of Section 286, or subdivision (d) of Section 287 of, or former Section 288a of, the Penal Code, or in any criminal proceeding under subdivision (c) of Section 286 or subdivision (c) of Section 287 of, or former Section 288a of, the Penal Code in which the defendant is alleged to have compelled the participation of the victim by force, violence, duress, menace, or threat of great bodily harm, the district attorney may, upon written motion with notice to the defendant or the defendant's attorney, if he or she is represented by an attorney, within a reasonable time prior to any hearing, move to exclude from evidence the current address and telephone number of any victim at the hearing.

The court may order that evidence of the victim's current address and telephone number be excluded from any hearings conducted pursuant to the criminal proceeding if the court finds that the probative value of the evidence is outweighed by the creation of substantial danger to the victim.

Nothing in this section shall abridge or limit the defendant's right to discover or investigate the information. **Leg.H.** Added Stats 1985 ch 335 §3. Amended Stats 1996 ch 1075 §5 (SB 1444); Stats 2018 ch 423 §18 (SB 1494), effective January 1, 2019.

Prior Law: Former Ev C §352.1, similar to the present section, was added Stats 1977 ch 34 §1 and repealed Stats 1985 ch 335 §2.

1985 Note: The Legislature finds and declares that the provisions of §352.1 of the Evidence Code have been in continuous effect since the passage of Proposition 8 and this bill is a reaffirmation of that fact. Stats 1985 ch 335 §1.

§ 352.2. Admission of creative expressions

(a) In any criminal proceeding where a party seeks to admit as evidence a form of creative expression, the court, while balancing the probative value of that evidence against the substantial danger of undue prejudice under Section 352, shall consider, in addition to the factors listed in Section 352, that: (1) the probative value of such expression for its literal truth or as a truthful narrative is minimal unless that expression is created near in time to the charged crime or crimes, bears a sufficient level of similarity to the charged crime or crimes, or includes factual detail not otherwise publicly available; and (2) undue prejudice includes, but is not limited to, the possibility that the trier of fact will, in violation of Section 1101, treat the expression as evidence of the defendant's propensity for violence or general criminal disposition as well as the possibility that the evidence will explicitly or implicitly inject racial bias into the proceedings.

(b) If proffered and relevant to the issues in the case, the court shall consider the following as well as any additional relevant evidence offered by either party:

(1) Credible testimony on the genre of creative expression as to the social or cultural context, rules, conventions, and artistic techniques of the expression.

(2) Experimental or social science research demonstrating that the introduction of a particular type of expression explicitly or implicitly introduces racial bias into the proceedings.

(3) Evidence to rebut such research or testimony.

(c) For purposes of this section, "creative expression" means the expression or application of creativity or imagination in the production or arrangement of forms, sounds, words, movements, or symbols, including, but not limited to, music, dance, performance art, visual art, poetry, literature, film, and other such objects or media.

(d) The question of the admissibility of a form of creative expression shall be heard in limine and determined by the court, outside the presence and hearing of the jury, pursuant to Section 402. The court shall state on the record its ruling and its reasons therefor. **Leg.H.** Added Stats 2022 ch 973 §2 (AB 2799), effective January 1, 2023.

§353. Effect of erroneous admission of evidence

A verdict or finding shall not be set aside, nor shall the judgment or decision based thereon be reversed, by reason of the erroneous admission of evidence unless:

(a) There appears of record an objection to or a motion to exclude or to strike the evidence that was timely made and so stated as to make clear the specific ground of the objection or motion; and

(b) The court which passes upon the effect of the error or errors is of the opinion that the admitted evidence should have been excluded on the ground stated and that the error or errors complained of resulted in a miscarriage of justice. **Leg.H.** Enacted Stats 1965 ch 299 §2, operative January 1, 1967.

§354. Effect of erroneous exclusion of evidence

A verdict or finding shall not be set aside, nor shall the judgment or decision based thereon be reversed, by reason of the erroneous exclusion of evidence unless the court which passes upon the effect of the error or errors is of the opinion that the error or errors complained of resulted in a miscarriage of justice and it appears of record that:

(a) The substance, purpose, and relevance of the excluded evidence was made known to the court by the questions asked, an offer of proof, or by any other means;

(b) The rulings of the court made compliance with subdivision (a) futile; or

(c) The evidence was sought by questions asked during cross-examination or recross-examination. **Leg.H.** Enacted Stats 1965 ch 299 §2, operative January 1, 1967.

§355. Limited admissibility

When evidence is admissible as to one party or for one purpose and is inadmissible as to another party or for another purpose, the court upon request shall restrict the evidence to its proper scope and instruct the jury accordingly. **Leg.H.** Enacted Stats 1965 ch 299 §2, operative January 1, 1967.

§356. Entire act, declaration, conversation, or writing may be brought out to elucidate part offered

Where part of an act, declaration, conversation, or writing is given in evidence by one party, the whole on the same subject may be inquired into by an adverse party; when a letter is read, the answer may be given; and when a detached act, declaration, conversation, or writing is given in evidence, any other act, declaration, conversation, or writing which is necessary to make it understood may also be given in evidence. **Leg.H.** Enacted Stats 1965 ch 299 §2, operative January 1, 1967.

ARTICLE 2
Preliminary Determinations on Admissibility of Evidence

"Preliminary fact". §400.
"Proffered evidence". §401.
Procedure for determining foundational and other preliminary facts. §402.
Determination of foundational and other preliminary facts where relevancy, personal knowledge, or authenticity is disputed. §403.
Determination of whether proffered evidence is incriminatory. §404.

Determination of foundational and other preliminary facts in other cases. §405.
Evidence affecting weight or credibility. §406.

§400. "Preliminary fact"

As used in this article, "preliminary fact" means a fact upon the existence or nonexistence of which depends the admissibility or inadmissibility of evidence. The phrase "the admissibility or inadmissibility of evidence" includes the qualification or disqualification of a person to be a witness and the existence or nonexistence of a privilege. **Leg.H.** Enacted Stats 1965 ch 299 §2, operative January 1, 1967.

§401. "Proffered evidence"

As used in this article, "proffered evidence" means evidence, the admissibility or inadmissibility of which is dependent upon the existence or nonexistence of a preliminary fact. **Leg.H.** Enacted Stats 1965 ch 299 §2, operative January 1, 1967.

§402. Procedure for determining foundational and other preliminary facts

(a) When the existence of a preliminary fact is disputed, its existence or nonexistence shall be determined as provided in this article.

(b) The court may hear and determine the question of the admissibility of evidence out of the presence or hearing of the jury; but in a criminal action, the court shall hear and determine the question of the admissibility of a confession or admission of the defendant out of the presence and hearing of the jury if any party so requests.

(c) A ruling on the admissibility of evidence implies whatever finding of fact is prerequisite thereto; a separate or formal finding is unnecessary unless required by statute. **Leg.H.** Enacted Stats 1965 ch 299 §2, operative January 1, 1967.

§403. Determination of foundational and other preliminary facts where relevancy, personal knowledge, or authenticity is disputed

(a) The proponent of the proffered evidence has the burden of producing evidence as to the existence of the preliminary fact, and the proffered evidence is inadmissible unless the court finds that there is evidence sufficient to sustain a finding of the existence of the preliminary fact, when:

(1) The relevance of the proffered evidence depends on the existence of the preliminary fact;

(2) The preliminary fact is the personal knowledge of a witness concerning the subject matter of his testimony;

(3) The preliminary fact is the authenticity of a writing; or

(4) The proffered evidence is of a statement or other conduct of a particular person and the preliminary fact is whether that person made the statement or so conducted himself.

(b) Subject to Section 702, the court may admit conditionally the proffered evidence under this section, subject to evidence of the preliminary fact being supplied later in the course of the trial.

(c) If the court admits the proffered evidence under this section, the court:

(1) May, and on request shall, instruct the jury to determine whether the preliminary fact exists and to disregard the proffered evidence unless the jury finds that the preliminary fact does exist.

(2) Shall instruct the jury to disregard the proffered evidence if the court subsequently determines that a jury could not reasonably find that the preliminary fact exists. **Leg.H.** Enacted Stats 1965 ch 299 §2, operative January 1, 1967.

§404. Determination of whether proffered evidence is incriminatory

Whenever the proffered evidence is claimed to be privileged under Section 940, the person claiming the privilege has the burden of showing that the proffered evidence might tend to incriminate him; and the proffered evidence is inadmissible unless it clearly appears to the court that the proffered evidence cannot possibly have a tendency to incriminate the person claiming the privilege. **Leg.H.** Enacted Stats 1965 ch 299 §2, operative January 1, 1967.

§405. Determination of foundational and other preliminary facts in other cases

With respect to preliminary fact determinations not governed by Section 403 or 404:

(a) When the existence of a preliminary fact is disputed, the court shall indicate which party has the burden of producing evidence and the burden of proof on the issue as implied by the rule of law under which the question arises. The court shall determine the existence or nonexistence of the preliminary fact and shall admit or exclude the proffered evidence as required by the rule of law under which the question arises.

(b) If a preliminary fact is also a fact in issue in the action:

(1) The jury shall not be informed of the court's determination as to the existence or nonexistence of the preliminary fact.

(2) If the proffered evidence is admitted, the jury shall not be instructed to disregard the evidence if its determination of the fact differs from the court's determination of the preliminary fact. **Leg.H.** Enacted Stats 1965 ch 299 §2, operative January 1, 1967.

§406. Evidence affecting weight or credibility

This article does not limit the right of a party to introduce before the trier of fact evidence relevant to weight or credibility. **Leg.H.** Enacted Stats 1965 ch 299 §2, operative January 1, 1967.

CHAPTER 5
WEIGHT OF EVIDENCE GENERALLY

"Direct evidence". §410.
Direct evidence of one witness sufficient. §411.
Party having power to produce better evidence. §412.
Party's failure to explain or deny evidence. §413.

§410. "Direct evidence"

As used in this chapter, "direct evidence" means evidence that directly proves a fact, without an inference or presumption, and which in itself, if true, conclusively establishes that fact. **Leg.H.** Enacted Stats 1965 ch 299 §2, operative January 1, 1967.

§411. Direct evidence of one witness sufficient

Except where additional evidence is required by statute, the direct evidence of one witness who is entitled to full credit is sufficient for proof of any fact. **Leg.H.** Enacted Stats 1965 ch 299 §2, operative January 1, 1967.

§412. Party having power to produce better evidence

If weaker and less satisfactory evidence is offered when it was within the power of the party to produce stronger and more satisfactory evidence, the evidence offered should be viewed with distrust. **Leg.H.** Enacted Stats 1965 ch 299 §2, operative January 1, 1967.

§413. Party's failure to explain or deny evidence

In determining what inferences to draw from the evidence or facts in the case against a party, the trier of fact may consider, among other things, the party's failure to explain or to deny by his testimony such evidence or facts in the case against him, or his willful suppression of evidence relating thereto, if such be the case. **Leg.H.** Enacted Stats 1965 ch 299 §2, operative January 1, 1967.

DIVISION 4
JUDICIAL NOTICE

Judicial notice may be taken only as authorized by law. §450.
Matters which must be judicially noticed. §451.
Matters which may be judicially noticed. §452.
Computer-generated records or electronically digitized copies; Seal, signature, or other indicia of court as adequate showing. §452.5.
Compulsory judicial notice upon request. §453.
Information that may be used in taking judicial notices. §454.
Opportunity to present information to court. §455.
Noting for record denial of request to take judicial notice. §456.
Instructing jury on matter judicially noticed. §457.
Judicial notice by trial court in subsequent proceedings. §458.
Judicial notice by reviewing court. §459.
Appointment of expert by court. §460.

§450. Judicial notice may be taken only as authorized by law

Judicial notice may not be taken of any matter unless authorized or required by law. **Leg.H.** Enacted Stats 1965 ch 299 §2, operative January 1, 1967.

§451. Matters which must be judicially noticed

Judicial notice shall be taken of the following:

(a) The decisional, constitutional, and public statutory law of this state and of the United States and the provisions of any charter described in Section 3, 4, or 5 of Article XI of the California Constitution.

(b) Any matter made a subject of judicial notice by Section 11343.6, 11344.6, or 18576 of the Government Code or by Section 1507 of Title 44 of the United States Code.

(c) Rules of professional conduct for members of the bar adopted pursuant to Section 6076 of the Business and Professions Code and rules of practice and procedure for the courts of this state adopted by the Judicial Council.

(d) Rules of pleading, practice, and procedure prescribed by the United States Supreme Court, such as the Rules of the United States Supreme Court, the Federal Rules of Civil Procedure, the Federal Rules of Criminal Procedure, the Admiralty Rules, the Rules of the Court of Claims, the Rules of the Customs Court, and the General Orders and Forms in Bankruptcy.

(e) The true signification of all English words and phrases and of all legal expressions.

(f) Facts and propositions of generalized knowledge that are so universally known that they cannot reasonably be the subject of dispute. **Leg.H.** Enacted Stats 1965 ch 299 §2, operative January 1, 1967. Amended Stats 1971 ch 438 §88; Stats 1972 ch 764 §1; Stats 1982 ch 454 §20; Stats 1985 ch 106 §32; Stats 1986 ch 248 §43.

§452. Matters which may be judicially noticed

Judicial notice may be taken of the following matters to the extent that they are not embraced within Section 451:

(a) The decisional, constitutional, and statutory law of any state of the United States and the resolutions and private acts of the Congress of the United States and of the Legislature of this state.

(b) Regulations and legislative enactments issued by or under the authority of the United States or any public entity in the United States.

(c) Official acts of the legislative, executive, and judicial departments of the United States and of any state of the United States.

(d) Records of (1) any court of this state or (2) any court of record of the United States or of any state of the United States.

(e) Rules of court of (1) any court of this state or (2) any court of record of the United States or of any state of the United States.

(f) The law of an organization of nations and of foreign nations and public entities in foreign nations.

(g) Facts and propositions that are of such common knowledge within the territorial jurisdiction of the court that they cannot reasonably be the subject of dispute.

(h) Facts and propositions that are not reasonably subject to dispute and are capable of immediate and accurate determination by resort to sources of reasonably indisputable accuracy. **Leg.H.** Enacted Stats 1965 ch 299 §2, operative January 1, 1967.

§452.5. Computer-generated records or electronically digitized copies; Seal, signature, or other indicia of court as adequate showing

(a) The official acts and records specified in subdivisions (c) and (d) of Section 452 include any computer-generated official court records, as specified by the Judicial Council, that relate to criminal convictions, when the record is certified by a clerk of the superior court pursuant to Section 69844.5 of the Government Code at the time of computer entry.

(b)(1) An official record of conviction certified in accordance with subdivision (a) of Section 1530, or an electronically digitized copy thereof, is admissible under Section 1280 to prove the commission, attempted commission, or solicitation of a criminal offense, prior conviction, service of a prison term, or other act, condition, or event recorded by the record.

(2) For purposes of this subdivision, "electronically digitized copy" means a copy that is made by scanning, photographing, or otherwise exactly reproducing a document, is stored or maintained in a digitized format, and meets either of the following requirements:

(A) The copy bears an electronic signature or watermark unique to the entity responsible for certifying the document.

(B) The copied document is an official record of conviction, certified in accordance with subdivision (a) of Section 1530, that is transmitted by the clerk of the superior court in a manner showing that the copy was prepared and transmitted by that clerk of the superior court. A seal, signature, or other indicia of the court shall constitute adequate showing. **Leg.H.** Added Stats 1996 ch 642 §3 (AB 1387). Amended Stats 2002 ch 784 §102 (SB 1316); Stats 2013 ch 150 §1 (SB 378), effective January 1, 2014; Stats 2016 ch 126 §1 (AB 1867), effective January 1, 2017; Stats 2017 ch 561 §55 (AB 1516), effective January 1, 2018.

§453. Compulsory judicial notice upon request

The trial court shall take judicial notice of any matter specified in Section 452 if a party requests it and:

(a) Gives each adverse party sufficient notice of the request, through the pleadings or otherwise, to enable such adverse party to prepare to meet the request; and

(b) Furnishes the court with sufficient information to enable it to take judicial notice of the matter. **Leg.H.** Enacted Stats 1965 ch 299 §2, operative January 1, 1967.

§454. Information that may be used in taking judicial notices

(a) In determining the propriety of taking judicial notice of a matter, or the tenor thereof:

(1) Any source of pertinent information, including the advice of persons learned in the subject matter, may be consulted or used, whether or not furnished by a party.

(2) Exclusionary rules of evidence do not apply except for Section 352 and the rules of privilege.

(b) Where the subject of judicial notice is the law of an organization of nations, a foreign nation, or a public entity in a foreign nation and the court resorts to the advice of persons learned in the subject matter, such advice, if not received in open court, shall be in writing. **Leg.H.** Enacted Stats 1965 ch 299 §2, operative January 1, 1967.

§455. Opportunity to present information to court

With respect to any matter specified in Section 452 or in subdivision (f) of Section 451 that is of substantial consequence to the determination of the action:

(a) If the trial court has been requested to take or has taken or proposes to take judicial notice of such matter, the court shall afford each party reasonable opportunity, before the jury is instructed or before the cause is submitted for decision by the court, to present to the court information relevant to (1) the propriety of taking judicial notice of the matter and (2) the tenor of the matter to be noticed.

(b) If the trial court resorts to any source of information not received in open court, including the advice of persons learned in the subject matter, such information and its source shall be made a part of the record in the action and the court shall afford each party reasonable opportunity to meet such information before judicial notice of the matter may be taken. **Leg.H.** Enacted Stats 1965 ch 299 §2, operative January 1, 1967.

§456. Noting for record denial of request to take judicial notice

If the trial court denies a request to take judicial notice of any matter, the court shall at the earliest practicable time so advise the parties and indicate for the record that it has denied the request. **Leg.H.** Enacted Stats 1965 ch 299 §2, operative January 1, 1967.

§457. Instructing jury on matter judicially noticed

If a matter judicially noticed is a matter which would otherwise have been for determination by the jury, the trial court may, and upon request shall, instruct the jury to accept as a fact the matter so noticed. **Leg.H.** Enacted Stats 1965 ch 299 §2, operative January 1, 1967.

§458. Judicial notice by trial court in subsequent proceedings

The failure or refusal of the trial court to take judicial notice of a matter, or to instruct the jury with respect to the matter, does not preclude the trial court in subsequent proceedings in the action from taking judicial notice of the matter in accordance with the procedure specified in this division. **Leg.H.** Enacted Stats 1965 ch 299 §2, operative January 1, 1967.

§459. Judicial notice by reviewing court

(a) The reviewing court shall take judicial notice of (1) each matter properly noticed by the trial court and (2) each matter that the trial court was required to notice under Section 451 or 453. The reviewing court may take judicial notice of any matter specified in Section 452. The reviewing court may take judicial notice of a matter in a tenor different from that noticed by the trial court.

(b) In determining the propriety of taking judicial notice of a matter, or the tenor thereof, the reviewing court has the same power as the trial court under Section 454.

(c) When taking judicial notice under this section of a matter specified in Section 452 or in subdivision (f) of Section 451 that is of substantial consequence to the determination of the action, the reviewing court shall comply with the provisions of subdivision (a) of Section 455 if the matter was not theretofore judicially noticed in the action.

(d) In determining the propriety of taking judicial notice of a matter specified in Section 452 or in subdivision (f) of Section 451 that is of substantial consequence to the determination of the action, or the tenor thereof, if the reviewing court resorts to any source of information not received in open court or not included in the record of the action, including the advice of persons learned in the subject matter, the reviewing court shall afford each party reasonable opportunity to meet such information before judicial notice of the matter may be taken. **Leg.H.** Enacted Stats 1965 ch 299 §2, operative January 1, 1967.

§460. Appointment of expert by court

Where the advice of persons learned in the subject matter is required in order to enable the court to take judicial notice of a matter, the court on its own motion or on motion of any party may appoint one or more such persons to provide such advice. If the court determines to appoint such a person, he shall be appointed and compensated in the manner provided in Article 2 (commencing with Section 730) of Chapter 3 of Division 6. **Leg.H.** Enacted Stats 1965 ch 299 §2, operative January 1, 1967.

DIVISION 5
BURDEN OF PROOF; BURDEN OF PRODUCING EVIDENCE; PRESUMPTIONS & INFERENCES

Chapter 1. Burden of Proof.
Chapter 2. Burden of Producing Evidence.
Chapter 3. Presumptions and Inferences.

CHAPTER 1
BURDEN OF PROOF

Article 1. General.
Article 2. Burden of Proof on Specific Issues.

ARTICLE 1
General

Party who has the burden of proof. §500.
Burden of proof in criminal action generally. §501.
Instructions on burden of proof. §502.

§500. Party who has the burden of proof

Except as otherwise provided by law, a party has the burden of proof as to each fact the existence or nonexistence of which is essential to the claim for relief or defense that he is asserting. **Leg.H.** Enacted Stats 1965 ch 299 §2, operative January 1, 1967.

§501. Burden of proof in criminal action generally

Insofar as any statute, except Section 522, assigns the burden of proof in a criminal action, such statute is subject to Penal Code Section 1096. **Leg.H.** Enacted Stats 1965 ch 299 §2, operative January 1, 1967.

§502. Instructions on burden of proof

The court on all proper occasions shall instruct the jury as to which party bears the burden of proof on each issue and as to whether that burden requires that a party raise a reasonable doubt concerning the existence or nonexistence of a fact or that he establish the existence or nonexistence of a fact by a preponderance of the evidence, by clear and convincing proof, or by proof beyond a reasonable doubt. **Leg.H.** Enacted Stats 1965 ch 299 §2, operative January 1, 1967.

ARTICLE 2
Burden of Proof on Specific Issues

Claim that person guilty of crime or wrongdoing. §520.
Claim that person did not exercise care. §521.
Claim that person is or was insane. §522.
Claim regarding land patented or granted by state. §523.
Burden of proof on State Board of Equalization; Standard. §524.

§520. Claim that person guilty of crime or wrongdoing

The party claiming that a person is guilty of crime or wrongdoing has the burden of proof on that issue. **Leg.H.** Enacted Stats 1965 ch 299 §2, operative January 1, 1967.

§521. Claim that person did not exercise care

The party claiming that a person did not exercise a requisite degree of care has the burden of proof on that issue. **Leg.H.** Enacted Stats 1965 ch 299 §2, operative January 1, 1967.

§522. Claim that person is or was insane

The party claiming that any person, including himself, is or was insane has the burden of proof on that issue. **Leg.H.** Enacted Stats 1965 ch 299 §2, operative January 1, 1967.

§523. Claim regarding land patented or granted by state

In any action where the state is a party, regardless of who is the moving party, where (a) the boundary of land patented or otherwise granted by the state is in dispute, or (b) the validity of any state patent or grant dated prior to 1950 is in dispute, the state shall have the burden of proof on all issues relating to the historic locations of rivers, streams, and other water bodies and the authority of the state in issuing the patent or grant.

This section is not intended to nor shall it be construed to supersede existing statutes governing disputes where the state is a party and regarding title to real property. **Leg.H.** Added Stats 1994 ch 128 §2 (SB 1429).

§524. Burden of proof on State Board of Equalization; Standard

(a) Notwithstanding any other provision of law, in a civil proceeding to which the State Board of Equalization is a party, that board shall have the burden of proof by clear and convincing evidence in sustaining its assertion of a penalty for intent to evade or fraud against a taxpayer, with respect to any factual issue relevant to ascertaining the liability of a taxpayer.

(b) Nothing in this section shall be construed to override any requirement for a taxpayer to substantiate any item on a return or claim filed with the State Board of Equalization.

(c) Nothing in this section shall subject a taxpayer to unreasonable search or access to records in violation of the United States Constitution, the California Constitution, or any other law.

(d) For purposes of this section, "taxpayer" includes a person on whom fees administered by the State Board of Equalization are imposed. **Leg.H.** Added Stats 2010 ch 168 §1 (AB 2195), effective January 1, 2011.

CHAPTER 2
BURDEN OF PRODUCING EVIDENCE

Party who has the burden of producing evidence. §550.

§550. Party who has the burden of producing evidence

(a) The burden of producing evidence as to a particular fact is on the party against whom a finding on that fact would be required in the absence of further evidence.

(b) The burden of producing evidence as to a particular fact is initially on the party with the burden of proof as to that fact. **Leg.H.** Enacted Stats 1965 ch 299 §2, operative January 1, 1967.

CHAPTER 3
PRESUMPTIONS AND INFERENCES

Article 1. General.
Article 2. Conclusive Presumptions.
Article 3. Presumptions Affecting the Burden of Producing Evidence.
Article 4. Presumptions Affecting the Burden of Proof.

ARTICLE 1
General

Presumption and inference defined. §600.
Classification of presumptions. §601.
Statute making one fact prima facie evidence of another fact. §602.
Presumption affecting the burden of producing evidence defined. §603.
Effect of presumption affecting burden of producing evidence. §604.
Presumption affecting the burden of proof defined. §605.
Effect of presumption affecting burden of proof. §606.
Effect of certain presumption in a criminal action. §607.

§600. Presumption and inference defined

(a) A presumption is an assumption of fact that the law requires to be made from another fact or group of facts found or otherwise established in the action. A presumption is not evidence.

(b) An inference is a deduction of fact that may logically and reasonably be drawn from another fact or group of facts found or otherwise established in the action. **Leg.H.** Enacted Stats 1965 ch 299 §2, operative January 1, 1967.

§601. Classification of presumptions

A presumption is either conclusive or rebuttable. Every rebuttable presumption is either (a) a presumption affecting the burden of producing evidence or (b) a presumption affecting the burden of proof. **Leg.H.** Enacted Stats 1965 ch 299 §2, operative January 1, 1967.

§602. Statute making one fact prima facie evidence of another fact

A statute providing that a fact or group of facts is prima facie evidence of another fact establishes a rebuttable presumption. **Leg.H.** Enacted Stats 1965 ch 299 §2, operative January 1, 1967.

§603. Presumption affecting the burden of producing evidence defined

A presumption affecting the burden of producing evidence is a presumption established to implement no public policy other than to facilitate the determination of the particular action in which the presumption is applied. **Leg.H.** Enacted Stats 1965 ch 299 §2, operative January 1, 1967.

§604. Effect of presumption affecting burden of producing evidence

The effect of a presumption affecting the burden of producing evidence is to require the trier of fact to assume the existence of the presumed fact unless and until evidence is introduced which would support a finding of its nonexistence, in which case the trier of fact shall determine the existence or nonexistence of the presumed fact from the evidence and without regard to the presumption. Nothing in this section shall be construed to prevent the drawing of any inference that may be appropriate. **Leg.H.** Enacted Stats 1965 ch 299 §2, operative January 1, 1967.

§605. Presumption affecting the burden of proof defined

A presumption affecting the burden of proof is a presumption established to implement some public policy other than to facilitate the determination of the particular action in which the presumption is applied, such as the policy in favor of establishment of a parent and child relationship, the validity of marriage, the stability of titles to property, or the security of those who entrust themselves or their property to the administration of others. **Leg.H.** Enacted Stats 1965 ch 299 §2, operative January 1, 1967. Amended Stats 1975 ch 1244 §12.

§606. Effect of presumption affecting burden of proof

The effect of a presumption affecting the burden of proof is to impose upon the party against whom it operates the burden of proof as to the nonexistence of the presumed fact. **Leg.H.** Enacted Stats 1965 ch 299 §2, operative January 1, 1967.

§607. Effect of certain presumption in a criminal action

When a presumption affecting the burden of proof operates in a criminal action to establish presumptively any fact that is essential to the defendant's guilt, the presumption operates only if the facts that give rise to the presumption have been found or otherwise established beyond a reasonable doubt and, in such case, the defendant need only raise a reasonable doubt as to the existence of the presumed fact. **Leg.H.** Enacted Stats 1965 ch 299 §2, operative January 1, 1967.

ARTICLE 2
Conclusive Presumptions

Conclusive presumptions. §620.
Facts recited in written instrument. §622.
Estoppel by own statement or conduct. §623.
Estoppel of tenant to deny title of landlord. §624.

§620. Conclusive presumptions

The presumptions established by this article, and all other presumptions declared by law to be conclusive, are conclusive presumptions. **Leg.H.** Enacted Stats 1965 ch 299 §2, operative January 1, 1967.

§621. [Section repealed 1994]

Leg.H. Enacted Stats 1965 ch 299 §2, operative January 1, 1967. Amended Stats 1975 ch 1244 §13; Stats 1980 ch 1310 §1, effective September 30, 1980; Stats 1981 ch 1180 §1; Stats 1990 ch 543 §2 (SB 2015). Repealed Stats 1992 ch 162 §8 (AB 2650), operative January 1, 1994. See Fam C §§7540, 7541.

§621.1. [Section repealed 1994.]

Leg.H. Added Stats 1992 ch 849 §2 (SB 1959). Repealed Stats 1993 ch 219 §76 (AB 1500), effective January 1, 1994. See Fam C §§7570–7577.

§622. Facts recited in written instrument

The facts recited in a written instrument are conclusively presumed to be true as between the parties thereto, or their successors in interest; but this rule does not apply to the recital of a consideration. **Leg.H.** Enacted Stats 1965 ch 299 §2, operative January 1, 1967.

§623. Estoppel by own statement or conduct

Whenever a party has, by his own statement or conduct, intentionally and deliberately led another to believe a particular thing true and to act upon such belief, he is not, in any litigation arising out of such statement or conduct, permitted to contradict it. **Leg.H.** Enacted Stats 1965 ch 299 §2, operative January 1, 1967.

§624. Estoppel of tenant to deny title of landlord

A tenant is not permitted to deny the title of his landlord at the time of the commencement of the relation. **Leg.H.** Enacted Stats 1965 ch 299 §2, operative January 1, 1967.

ARTICLE 3
Presumptions Affecting the Burden of Producing Evidence

Presumption affecting the burden of producing evidence. §630.
Money delivered by one to another. §631.
Thing delivered by one to another. §632.
Obligation delivered up to the debtor. §633.
Person in possession of order on himself. §634.
Obligation possessed by creditor. §635.
Payment of earlier rent or installments. §636.
Ownership of things possessed. §637.
Ownership of property by person who exercises acts of ownership. §638.
Judgment correctly determines rights of parties. §639.
Writing truly dated. §640.
Letter received in ordinary course of mail. §641.
Conveyance by person having duty to convey real property. §642.
Authenticity of ancient document. §643.
Book purporting to be published by public authority. §644.
Book purporting to contain reports of cases. §645.
Printed materials purporting to be particular newspaper or periodical. §645.1.
Res ipsa loquitur; Instructions to jury. §646.
Return of registered process server. §647.

§630. Presumption affecting the burden of producing evidence

The presumptions established by this article, and all other rebuttable presumptions established by law that fall within the criteria of Section 603, are presumptions affecting the burden of producing evidence. **Leg.H.** Enacted Stats 1965 ch 299 §2, operative January 1, 1967.

§631. Money delivered by one to another

Money delivered by one to another is presumed to have been due to the latter. **Leg.H.** Enacted Stats 1965 ch 299 §2, operative January 1, 1967.

§632. Thing delivered by one to another

A thing delivered by one to another is presumed to have belonged to the latter. **Leg.H.** Enacted Stats 1965 ch 299 §2, operative January 1, 1967.

§633. Obligation delivered up to the debtor

An obligation delivered up to the debtor is presumed to have been paid. **Leg.H.** Enacted Stats 1965 ch 299 §2, operative January 1, 1967.

§634. Person in possession of order on himself

A person in possession of an order on himself for the payment of money, or delivery of a thing, is presumed to have paid the money or delivered the thing accordingly. **Leg.H.** Enacted Stats 1965 ch 299 §2, operative January 1, 1967.

§635. Obligation possessed by creditor

An obligation possessed by the creditor is presumed not to have been paid. **Leg.H.** Enacted Stats 1965 ch 299 §2, operative January 1, 1967.

§636. Payment of earlier rent or installments

The payment of earlier rent or installments is presumed from a receipt for later rent or installments. **Leg.H.** Enacted Stats 1965 ch 299 §2, operative January 1, 1967.

§637. Ownership of things possessed

The things which a person possesses are presumed to be owned by him. **Leg.H.** Enacted Stats 1965 ch 299 §2, operative January 1, 1967.

§638. Ownership of property by person who exercises acts of ownership

A person who exercises acts of ownership over property is presumed to be the owner of it. **Leg.H.** Enacted Stats 1965 ch 299 §2, operative January 1, 1967.

§639. Judgment correctly determines rights of parties

A judgment, when not conclusive, is presumed to correctly determine or set forth the rights of the parties, but there is no presumption that the facts essential to the judgment have been correctly determined. **Leg.H.** Enacted Stats 1965 ch 299 §2, operative January 1, 1967.

§640. Writing truly dated

A writing is presumed to have been truly dated. **Leg.H.** Enacted Stats 1965 ch 299 §2, operative January 1, 1967.

§641. Letter received in ordinary course of mail

A letter correctly addressed and properly mailed is presumed to have been received in the ordinary course of mail. **Leg.H.** Enacted Stats 1965 ch 299 §2, operative January 1, 1967.

§642. Conveyance by person having duty to convey real property

A trustee or other person, whose duty it was to convey real property to a particular person, is presumed to have actually conveyed to him when such presumption is necessary to perfect title of such person or his successor in interest. **Leg.H.** Enacted Stats 1965 ch 299 §2, operative January 1, 1967.

§643. Authenticity of ancient document

A deed or will or other writing purporting to create, terminate, or affect an interest in real or personal property is presumed to be authentic if it:

(a) Is at least 30 years old;

(b) Is in such condition as to create no suspicion concerning its authenticity;

(c) Was kept, or if found was found, in a place where such writing, if authentic, would be likely to be kept or found; and

(d) Has been generally acted upon as authentic by persons having an interest in the matter. **Leg.H.** Enacted Stats 1965 ch 299 §2, operative January 1, 1967.

§644. Book purporting to be published by public authority

A book, purporting to be printed or published by public authority, is presumed to have been so printed or published. **Leg.H.** Enacted Stats 1965 ch 299 §2, operative January 1, 1967.

§645. Book purporting to contain reports of cases

A book, purporting to contain reports of cases adjudged in the tribunals of the state or nation where the book is published, is presumed to contain correct reports of such cases. **Leg.H.** Enacted Stats 1965 ch 299 §2, operative January 1, 1967.

§645.1. Printed materials purporting to be particular newspaper or periodical

Printed materials, purporting to be a particular newspaper or periodical, are presumed to be that newspaper or periodical if regularly issued at average intervals not exceeding three months. **Leg.H.** Added Stats 1986 ch 330 §1.

§646. Res ipsa loquitur; Instructions to jury

(a) As used in this section, "defendant" includes any party against whom the res ipsa loquitur presumption operates.

(b) The judicial doctrine of res ipsa loquitur is a presumption affecting the burden of producing evidence.

(c) If the evidence, or facts otherwise established, would support a res ipsa loquitur presumption and the defendant has introduced evidence which would support a finding that he was not negligent or that any negligence on his part was not a proximate cause of the occurrence, the court may, and upon request shall, instruct the jury to the effect that:

(1) If the facts which would give rise to a res ipsa loquitur presumption are found or otherwise established, the jury may draw the inference from such facts that a proximate cause of the occurrence was some negligent conduct on the part of the defendant; and

(2) The jury shall not find that a proximate cause of the occurrence was some negligent conduct on the part of the defendant unless the jury believes, after weighing all the evidence in the case and drawing such inferences therefrom as the jury believes are warranted, that it is more probable than not that the occurrence was caused by some negligent conduct on the part of the defendant. **Leg.H.** Added Stats 1970 ch 69 §1.

§647. Return of registered process server

The return of a process server registered pursuant to Chapter 16 (commencing with Section 22350) of Division 8 of the Business and Professions Code upon process or notice establishes a presumption, affecting the burden of producing evidence, of the facts stated in the return. **Leg.H.** Added Stats 1978 ch 528 §1.

ARTICLE 4
Presumptions Affecting the Burden of Proof

Presumptions affecting the burden of proof. §660.
Owner of legal title to property is owner of beneficial title. §662.
Ceremonial marriage. §663.
Official duty regularly performed. §664.
Ordinary consequences of voluntary act. §665.
Judicial action lawful exercise of jurisdiction. §666.
Death of person not heard from in five years. §667.
Unlawful intent. §668.
Failure to exercise due care. §669.
Governmental rule or guideline for standards of conduct for public employees. §669.1.
Ordinances. §669.5.
Presumption that check has been paid. §670.

§660. Presumptions affecting the burden of proof

The presumptions established by this article, and all other rebuttable presumptions established by law that fall within the criteria of Section 605, are presumptions affecting the burden of proof. **Leg.H.** Enacted Stats 1965 ch 299 §2, operative January 1, 1967.

§661. [Section repealed 1976]

Leg.H. Enacted Stats 1965 ch 299 §2, operative January 1, 1967. Repealed Stats 1975 ch 1244 §14, effective January 1, 1976. See Fam C §§7611, 7611.5, 7612.

§662. Owner of legal title to property is owner of beneficial title

The owner of the legal title to property is presumed to be the owner of the full beneficial title. This presumption may be rebutted only by clear and convincing proof. **Leg.H.** Enacted Stats 1965 ch 299 §2, operative January 1, 1967.

§663. Ceremonial marriage

A ceremonial marriage is presumed to be valid. **Leg.H.** Enacted Stats 1965 ch 299 §2, operative January 1, 1967.

§664. Official duty regularly performed

It is presumed that official duty has been regularly performed. This presumption does not apply on an issue as to the lawfulness of an arrest if it is found or otherwise established that the arrest was made without a warrant. **Leg.H.** Enacted Stats 1965 ch 299 §2, operative January 1, 1967.

§665. Ordinary consequences of voluntary act

A person is presumed to intend the ordinary consequences of his voluntary act. This presumption is inapplicable in a criminal action to establish the specific intent of the defendant where specific intent is an element of the crime charged. **Leg.H.** Enacted Stats 1965 ch 299 §2, operative January 1, 1967.

§666. Judicial action lawful exercise of jurisdiction

Any court of this state or the United States, or any court of general jurisdiction in any other state or nation, or any judge of such a court, acting as such, is presumed to have acted in the lawful exercise of its jurisdiction. This presumption applies only when the act of the court or judge is under collateral attack. **Leg.H.** Enacted Stats 1965 ch 299 §2, operative January 1, 1967.

§667. Death of person not heard from in five years

A person not heard from in five years is presumed to be dead. **Leg.H.** Enacted Stats 1965 ch 299 §2, operative January 1, 1967. Amended Stats 1983 ch 201 §1.

§668. Unlawful intent

An unlawful intent is presumed from the doing of an unlawful act. This presumption is inapplicable in a criminal action to establish the specific intent of the defendant where specific intent is an element of the crime charged. **Leg.H.** Enacted Stats 1965 ch 299 §2, operative January 1, 1967.

§669. Failure to exercise due care

(a) The failure of a person to exercise due care is presumed if:

(1) He violated a statute, ordinance, or regulation of a public entity;

(2) The violation proximately caused death or injury to person or property;

(3) The death or injury resulted from an occurrence of the nature which the statute, ordinance, or regulation was designed to prevent; and

(4) The person suffering the death or the injury to his person or property was one of the class of persons for whose protection the statute, ordinance, or regulation was adopted.

(b) This presumption may be rebutted by proof that:

(1) The person violating the statute, ordinance, or regulation did what might reasonably be expected of a person of ordinary prudence, acting under similar circumstances, who desired to comply with the law; or

(2) The person violating the statute, ordinance, or regulation was a child and exercised the degree of care ordinarily exercised by persons of his maturity, intelligence, and capacity under similar circumstances, but the presumption may not be rebutted by such proof if the violation

occurred in the course of an activity normally engaged in only by adults and requiring adult qualifications. **Leg.H.** Added Stats 1967 ch 650 §1.

§669.1. Governmental rule or guideline for standards of conduct for public employees

A rule, policy, manual, or guideline of state or local government setting forth standards of conduct or guidelines for its employees in the conduct of their public employment shall not be considered a statute, ordinance, or regulation of that public entity within the meaning of Section 669, unless the rule, manual, policy, or guideline has been formally adopted as a statute, as an ordinance of a local governmental entity in this state empowered to adopt ordinances, or as a regulation by an agency of the state pursuant to the Administrative Procedure Act (Chapter 3.5 (commencing with Section 11340) of Division 3 of Title 2 of the Government Code), or by an agency of the United States government pursuant to the federal Administrative Procedure Act (Chapter 5 (commencing with Section 5001) of Title 5 of the United States Code). This section affects only the presumption set forth in Section 669, and is not otherwise intended to affect the admissibility or inadmissibility of the rule, policy, manual, or guideline under other provisions of law. **Leg.H.** Added Stats 1987 ch 1201 §13, ch 1207 §2.

Prior Law: Former Ev C §669.1, similar to the present section, was added Stats 1983 ch 168 §1, amended Stats 1986 ch 695 §1, and repealed Stats 1987 ch 1201 §12, ch 1207 §1.

1987 Notes: Section 669.1, as added by 1987 ch 1207, applies only to actions based on acts or commissions occurring on or after January 1, 1988. Stats 1987 ch 1208 §4.

In repealing and adding Section 669.1 of the Evidence Code, the Legislature intends to clarify Instruction No. 3.45 of the Book of Approved California Jury Instructions, 7th Edition. Stats 1987 ch 1207 §5.

§669.5. Ordinances

(a) Any ordinance enacted by the governing body of a city, county, or city and county which (1) directly limits, by number, the building permits that may be issued for residential construction or the buildable lots which may be developed for residential purposes, or (2) changes the standards of residential development on vacant land so that the governing body's zoning is rendered in violation of Section 65913.1 of the Government Code is presumed to have an impact on the supply of residential units available in an area which includes territory outside the jurisdiction of the city, county, or city and county.

(b) With respect to any action which challenges the validity of an ordinance specified in subdivision (a) the city, county, or city and county enacting the ordinance shall bear the burden of proof that the ordinance is necessary for the protection of the public health, safety, or welfare of the population of the city, county, or city and county.

(c) This section does not apply to state and federal building code requirements or local ordinances which (1) impose a moratorium, to protect the public health and safety, on residential construction for a specified period of time, if, under the terms of the ordinance, the moratorium will cease when the public health or safety is no longer jeopardized by the construction, (2) create agricultural preserves under Chapter 7 (commencing with Section 51200) of Part 1 of Division 1 of Title 5 of the Government Code, or (3) restrict the number of buildable parcels or designate lands within a zone for nonresidential uses in order to protect agricultural uses as defined in subdivision (b) of Section 51201 of the Government Code or open-space land as defined in subdivision (h) of Section 65560 of the Government Code.

(d) This section shall not apply to a voter approved ordinance adopted by referendum or initiative prior to the effective date of this section which (1) requires the city, county, or city and county to establish a population growth limit which represents its fair share of each year's statewide population growth, or (2) which sets a growth rate of no more than the average population growth rate experienced by the state as a whole. Paragraph (2) of subdivision (a) does not apply to a voter-approved ordinance adopted by referendum or initiative which exempts housing affordable to persons and families of low or moderate income, as defined in Section 50093 of the Health and Safety Code, or which otherwise provides low- and moderate-income housing sites equivalent to such an exemption. **Leg.H.** Added Stats 1980 ch 1144 §2. Amended Stats 1988 ch 541 §1; Stats 2017 ch 434 §2 (SB 732), effective January 1, 2018.

§670. Presumption that check has been paid

(a) In any dispute concerning payment by means of a check, a copy of the check produced in accordance with Section 1550 of the Evidence Code, together with the original bank statement that reflects payment of the check by the bank on which it was drawn or a copy thereof produced in the same manner, creates a presumption that the check has been paid.

(b) As used in this section:

(1) "Bank" means any person engaged in the business of banking and includes, in addition to a commercial bank, a savings and loan association, savings bank, or credit union.

(2) "Check" means a draft, other than a documentary draft, payable on demand and drawn on a bank, even though it is described by another term, such as "share draft" or "negotiable order of withdrawal." **Leg.H.** Added Stats 1992 ch 914 §51 (SB 833). Amended Stats 2001 ch 854 §3 (SB 205).

DIVISION 6
WITNESSES

Chapter 1. Competency.
Chapter 2. Oath and Confrontation.
Chapter 3. Expert Witnesses.
Chapter 4. Interpreters and Translators.
Chapter 5. Method and Scope of Examination.
Chapter 6. Credibility of Witnesses.
Chapter 7. Hypnosis of Witnesses.

CHAPTER 1
COMPETENCY

General rule as to competency. §700.
Disqualification of witness. §701.
Personal knowledge of witness. §702.
Judge as witness. §703.
Judge, arbitrator or mediator as witness in subsequent proceeding. §703.5.
Juror as witness. §704.

§700. General rule as to competency

Except as otherwise provided by statute, every person, irrespective of age, is qualified to be a witness and no person is disqualified to testify to any matter. **Leg.H.** Enacted Stats 1965 ch 299 §2, operative January 1, 1967. Amended Stats 1985 ch 884 §1.

§701. Disqualification of witness

(a) A person is disqualified to be a witness if he or she is:

(1) Incapable of expressing himself or herself concerning the matter so as to be understood, either directly or through interpretation by one who can understand him; or

(2) Incapable of understanding the duty of a witness to tell the truth.

(b) In any proceeding held outside the presence of a jury, the court may reserve challenges to the competency of a witness until the conclusion of the direct examination of that witness. **Leg.H.** Enacted Stats 1965 ch 299 §2, operative January 1, 1967. Amended Stats 1985 ch 884 §2.

§702. Personal knowledge of witness

(a) Subject to Section 801, the testimony of a witness concerning a particular matter is inadmissible unless he has personal knowledge of the matter. Against the objection of a party, such personal knowledge must be shown before the witness may testify concerning the matter.

(b) A witness' personal knowledge of a matter may be shown by any otherwise admissible evidence, including his own testimony. **Leg.H.** Enacted Stats 1965 ch 299 §2, operative January 1, 1967.

§703. Judge as witness

(a) Before the judge presiding at the trial of an action may be called to testify in that trial as a witness, he shall, in proceedings held out of the presence and hearing of the jury, inform the parties of the information he has concerning any fact or matter about which he will be called to testify.

(b) Against the objection of a party, the judge presiding at the trial of an action may not testify in that trial as a witness. Upon such objection, the judge shall declare a mistrial and order the action assigned for trial before another judge.

(c) The calling of the judge presiding at a trial to testify in that trial as a witness shall be deemed a consent to the granting of a motion for mistrial, and an objection to such calling of a judge shall be deemed a motion for mistrial.

(d) In the absence of objection by a party, the judge presiding at the trial of an action may testify in that trial as a witness. **Leg.H.** Enacted Stats 1965 ch 299 §2, operative January 1, 1967.

§703.5. Judge, arbitrator or mediator as witness in subsequent proceeding

No person presiding at any judicial or quasi-judicial proceeding, and no arbitrator or mediator, shall be competent to testify, in any subsequent civil proceeding, as to any statement, conduct, decision, or ruling, occurring at or in conjunction with the prior proceeding, except as to a statement or conduct that could (a) give rise to civil or criminal contempt, (b) constitute a crime, (c) be the subject of investigation by the State Bar or Commission on Judicial Performance, or (d) give rise to disqualification proceedings under paragraph (1) or (6) of subdivision (a) of Section 170.1 of the Code of Civil Procedure. However, this section does not apply to a mediator with regard to any mediation under Chapter 11 (commencing with Section 3160) of Part 2 of Division 8 of the Family Code. **Leg.H.** Added Stats 1979 ch 205 §1. Amended Stats 1980 ch 290 §1; Stats 1988 ch 281 §1; Stats 1990 ch 1491 §13 (AB 3765); Stats 1993 ch 114 §1 (AB 1757), ch 1261 §5 (SB 401); Stats 1994 ch 1269 §7 (AB 2208).

§704. Juror as witness

(a) Before a juror sworn and impaneled in the trial of an action may be called to testify before the jury in that trial as a witness, he shall, in proceedings conducted by the court out of the presence and hearing of the remaining jurors, inform the parties of the information he has concerning any fact or matter about which he will be called to testify.

(b) Against the objection of a party, a juror sworn and impaneled in the trial of an action may not testify before the jury in that trial as a witness. Upon such objection, the court shall declare a mistrial and order the action assigned for trial before another jury.

(c) The calling of a juror to testify before the jury as a witness shall be deemed a consent to the granting of a motion for mistrial, and an objection to such calling of a juror shall be deemed a motion for mistrial.

(d) In the absence of objection by a party, a juror sworn and impaneled in the trial of an action may be compelled to testify in that trial as a witness. **Leg.H.** Enacted Stats 1965 ch 299 §2, operative January 1, 1967.

CHAPTER 2
OATH AND CONFRONTATION

Oath required; Exception for child or dependent person with cognitive impairment. §710.
Confrontation. §711.
Blood sample affidavits. §712.

§710. Oath required; Exception for child or dependent person with cognitive impairment

Every witness before testifying shall take an oath or make an affirmation or declaration in the form provided by law, except that a child under the age of 10 or a dependent person with a substantial cognitive impairment, in the court's discretion, may be required only to promise to tell the truth. **Leg.H.** Enacted Stats 1965 ch 299 §2, operative January 1, 1967. Amended Stats 1988 ch 486 §1; Stats 2004 ch 823 §3 (AB 20).

§711. Confrontation

At the trial of an action, a witness can be heard only in the presence and subject to the examination of all the parties to the action, if they choose to attend and examine. **Leg.H.** Enacted Stats 1965 ch 299 §2, operative January 1, 1967.

§712. Blood sample affidavits

Notwithstanding Sections 711 and 1200, at the trial of a criminal action, evidence of the technique used in taking blood samples may be given by a registered nurse, licensed vocational nurse, or licensed clinical laboratory technologist or clinical laboratory bioanalyst, by means of an affidavit. The affidavit shall be admissible, provided the party offering the affidavit as evidence has served all other parties to the action, or their counsel, with a copy of the affidavit no less than 10 days prior to trial. Nothing in this section shall preclude any party or his counsel from objecting to the introduction of the affidavit at any time, and requiring the attendance of the affiant, or compelling attendance by subpoena. **Leg.H.** Added Stats 1978 ch 93 §1.

CHAPTER 3
EXPERT WITNESSES

Article 1. Expert Witnesses Generally.
Article 2. Appointment of Expert Witness by Court.

ARTICLE 1
Expert Witnesses Generally

Qualification as an expert witness. §720.
Cross-examination of expert witness. §721.
Credibility of expert witness. §722.
Limit on number of expert witnesses. §723.

§720. Qualification as an expert witness

(a) A person is qualified to testify as an expert if he has special knowledge, skill, experience, training, or education sufficient to qualify him as an expert on the subject to which his testimony relates. Against the objection of a party, such special knowledge, skill, experience, training, or education must be shown before the witness may testify as an expert.

(b) A witness' special knowledge, skill, experience, training, or education may be shown by any otherwise admissible evidence, including his own testimony. **Leg.H.** Enacted Stats 1965 ch 299 §2, operative January 1, 1967.

§721. Cross-examination of expert witness

(a) Subject to subdivision (b), a witness testifying as an expert may be cross-examined to the same extent as any other witness and, in addition, may be fully cross-examined as to (1) his or her qualifications, (2) the subject to which his or her expert testimony relates, and (3) the matter upon which his or her opinion is based and the reasons for his or her opinion.

(b) If a witness testifying as an expert testifies in the form of an opinion, he or she may not be cross-examined in regard to the content or tenor of any scientific, technical, or professional text, treatise, journal, or similar publication unless any of the following occurs:

(1) The witness referred to, considered, or relied upon such publication in arriving at or forming his or her opinion.

(2) The publication has been admitted in evidence.

(3) The publication has been established as a reliable authority by the testimony or admission of the witness or by other expert testimony or by judicial notice.

If admitted, relevant portions of the publication may be read into evidence but may not be received as exhibits. **Leg.H.** Enacted Stats 1965 ch 299 §2, operative January 1, 1967. Amended Stats 1997 ch 892 §11 (SB 73).

§722. Credibility of expert witness

(a) The fact of the appointment of an expert witness by the court may be revealed to the trier of fact.

(b) The compensation and expenses paid or to be paid to an expert witness by the party calling him is a proper subject of inquiry by any adverse party as relevant to the credibility of the witness and the weight of his testimony. **Leg.H.** Enacted Stats 1965 ch 299 §2, operative January 1, 1967.

§723. Limit on number of expert witnesses

The court may, at any time before or during the trial of an action, limit the number of expert witnesses to be called by any party. **Leg.H.** Enacted Stats 1965 ch 299 §2, operative January 1, 1967.

ARTICLE 2
Appointment of Expert Witness by Court

Appointment by court of expert; Construction regarding requirement of license. §730.
Payment of court-appointed expert. §731.
Calling and examining court-appointed expert. §732.
Right to produce other expert evidence. §733.

§730. Appointment by court of expert; Construction regarding requirement of license

When it appears to the court, at any time before or during the trial of an action, that expert evidence is or may be required by the court or by any party to the action, the court on its own motion or on motion of any party may appoint one or more experts to investigate, to render a report as may be ordered by the court, and to testify as an expert at the trial of the action relative to the fact or matter as to which the expert evidence is or may be required. The court may fix the compensation for these services, if any, rendered by any person appointed under this section, in addition to any service as a witness, at the amount as seems reasonable to the court.

Nothing in this section shall be construed to permit a person to perform any act for which a license is required unless the person holds the appropriate license to lawfully perform that act. **Leg.H.** Added Stats 1979 ch 746 §3, operative January 1, 1983. Amended Stats 1990 ch 295 §1 (AB 3371).

Prior Law: Former §730, similar to the present section, was enacted Stats 1965 ch 299 §2, operative January 1, 1967, amended Stats 1979 ch 746 §2, and repealed, January 1, 1983, by its own terms.

§731. Payment of court-appointed expert

(a)(1) In all criminal actions and juvenile court proceedings, the compensation fixed under Section 730 shall be a charge against the county in which the action or proceeding is pending and shall be paid out of the treasury of that county on order of the court.

(2) Notwithstanding paragraph (1), if the expert is appointed for the court's needs, the compensation shall be a charge against the court.

(b) In any county in which the superior court so provides, the compensation fixed under Section 730 for medical experts appointed for the court's needs in civil actions shall be a charge against the court. In any county in which the board of supervisors so provides, the compensation fixed under Section 730 for medical experts appointed in civil actions, for purposes other than the court's needs, shall be a charge against and paid out of the treasury of that county on order of the court.

(c) Except as otherwise provided in this section, in all civil actions, the compensation fixed under Section 730 shall, in the first instance, be apportioned and charged to the several parties in a proportion as the court may determine and may thereafter be taxed and allowed in like manner as other costs. **Leg.H.** Added Stats 1979 ch 746 §5, operative January 1, 1983. Amended Stats 2012 ch 470 §8 (AB 1529), effective January 1, 2013.

Prior Law: Former Ev C §731, similar to the present section, was enacted Stats 1965 ch 299 §2, operative January 1, 1967, amended Stats 1979 ch 746 §4, and repealed January 1, 1983, by its own terms.

§732. Calling and examining court-appointed expert

Any expert appointed by the court under Section 730 may be called and examined by the court or by any party to the action. When such witness is called and examined by the court, the parties have the same right as is expressed in Section 775 to cross-examine the witness and to object to the questions asked and the evidence adduced. **Leg.H.** Enacted Stats 1965 ch 299 §2, operative January 1, 1967.

§733. Right to produce other expert evidence

Nothing contained in this article shall be deemed or construed to prevent any party to any action from producing other expert evidence on the same fact or matter mentioned in Section 730; but, where other expert witnesses are called by a party to the action, their fees shall be paid by the party calling them and only ordinary witness fees shall be taxed as costs in the action. **Leg.H.** Enacted Stats 1965 ch 299 §2, operative January 1, 1967.

CHAPTER 4
INTERPRETERS AND TRANSLATORS

Rules relating to witnesses apply to interpreters and translators. §750.
Oath required of interpreters and translators. §751.
Interpreters for witnesses. §752.
Translators of writings. §753.
Interpreters for deaf or hard of hearing in civil and criminal cases. §754.
Effect of interpreter on privilege. §754.5.
Interpreter's presence in medical examination. §755.5.
Reimbursement to courts for court interpreter services in civil actions and proceedings. §756.
Interpreter in proceeding to determine special immigrant juvenile status. §757.

§750. Rules relating to witnesses apply to interpreters and translators

A person who serves as an interpreter or translator in any action is subject to all the rules of law relating to witnesses. **Leg.H.** Enacted Stats 1965 ch 299 §2, operative January 1, 1967.

§751. Oath required of interpreters and translators

(a) An interpreter shall take an oath that he or she will make a true interpretation to the witness in a language that the witness understands and that he or she will make a true interpretation of the witness' answers to questions to counsel, court, or jury, in the English language, with his or her best skill and judgment.

(b) In any proceeding in which a deaf or hard-of-hearing person is testifying under oath, the interpreter certified pursuant to subdivision (f) of Section 754 shall advise the court whenever he or she is unable to comply with his or her oath taken pursuant to subdivision (a).

(c) A translator shall take an oath that he or she will make a true translation in the English language of any writing he or she is to decipher or translate.

(d) An interpreter regularly employed by the court and certified or registered in accordance with Article 4 (commencing with Section 68560) of Chapter 2 of Title 8 of the Government Code, or a translator regularly employed by the court, may file an oath as prescribed by this section with the clerk of the court. The filed oath shall serve for all subsequent court proceedings until the appointment is revoked by the court. **Leg.H.** Enacted Stats 1965 ch 299 §2, operative January 1, 1967. Amended Stats 1984 ch 30 §1, effective March 7, 1984; Stats 1990 ch 1450 §1 (SB 2046); Stats 1997 ch 376 §1 (AB 1445).

§752. Interpreters for witnesses

(a) When a witness is incapable of understanding the English language or is incapable of expressing himself or herself in the English language so as to be understood directly by counsel, court, and jury, an interpreter whom the witness can understand and who can understand the witness shall be sworn to interpret for the witness.

(b) The record shall identify the interpreter, who may be appointed and compensated as provided in Article 2 (commencing with Section 730) of Chapter 3, with that compensation charged as follows:

(1) In all criminal actions and juvenile court proceedings, the compensation for an interpreter under this section shall be a charge against the court.

(2) In all civil actions, the compensation for an interpreter under this section shall, in the first instance, be apportioned and charged to the several parties in a proportion as the court may determine and may thereafter be taxed and allowed in a like manner as other costs. **Leg.H.** Enacted Stats 1965 ch 299 §2, operative January 1, 1967. Amended Stats 1984 ch 30 §2, effective March 7, 1984, ch 768 §1; Stats 2012 ch 470 §9 (AB 1529), effective January 1, 2013.

§753. Translators of writings

(a) When the written characters in a writing offered in evidence are incapable of being deciphered or understood directly, a translator who can decipher the characters or understand the language shall be sworn to decipher or translate the writing.

(b) The record shall identify the translator, who may be appointed and compensated as provided in Article 2 (commencing with Section 730) of Chapter 3, with that compensation charged as follows:

(1) In all criminal actions and juvenile court proceedings, the compensation for a translator under this section shall be a charge against the court.

(2) In all civil actions, the compensation for a translator under this section shall, in the first instance, be apportioned and charged to the several parties in a proportion as the court may determine and may thereafter be taxed and allowed in like manner as other costs. **Leg.H.** Enacted Stats 1965 ch 299 §2, operative January 1, 1967. Amended Stats 1984 ch 30 §3, effective March 7, 1984; Stats 2012 ch 470 §10 (AB 1529), effective January 1, 2013.

§754. Interpreters for deaf or hard of hearing in civil and criminal cases

(a) As used in this section, "individual who is deaf or hard of hearing" means an individual with a hearing loss so great as to prevent his or her understanding language spoken in a normal tone, but does not include an individual who is hard of hearing provided with, and able to fully participate in the proceedings through the use of, an assistive listening system or computer-aided transcription equipment provided pursuant to Section 54.8 of the Civil Code.

(b) In a civil or criminal action, including an action involving a traffic or other infraction, a small claims court proceeding, a juvenile court proceeding, a family court proceeding or service, or a proceeding to determine the mental competency of a person, in a court-ordered or court-provided alternative dispute resolution, including mediation and arbitration, or in an administrative hearing, where a party or witness is an individual who is deaf or hard of hearing and the individual who is deaf or hard of hearing is present and participating, the proceeding shall be interpreted in a language that the individual who is deaf or hard of hearing understands by a qualified interpreter appointed by the court or other appointing authority, or as agreed upon.

(c) For purposes of this section, "appointing authority" means a court, department, board, commission, agency, licensing or legislative body, or other body for proceedings requiring a qualified interpreter.

(d) For purposes of this section, "interpreter" includes an oral interpreter, a sign language interpreter, or a deaf-blind interpreter, depending upon the needs of the individual who is deaf or hard of hearing.

(e) For purposes of this section, "intermediary interpreter" means an individual who is deaf or hard of hearing, or a hearing individual who is able to assist in providing an accurate interpretation between spoken English and sign language or between variants of sign language or between American Sign Language and other foreign languages by acting as an intermediary between the individual who is deaf or hard of hearing and the qualified interpreter.

(f) For purposes of this section, "qualified interpreter" means an interpreter who has been certified as competent to interpret court proceedings by a testing organization, agency, or educational institution approved by the Judicial Council as qualified to administer tests to court interpreters for individuals who are deaf or hard of hearing.

(g) If the appointed interpreter is not familiar with the use of particular signs by the individual who is deaf or hard of hearing or his or her particular variant of sign language, the court or other appointing authority shall, in consultation with the individual who is deaf or hard of hearing or his or her representative, appoint an intermediary interpreter.

(h)(1) Before July 1, 1992, the Judicial Council shall conduct a study to establish the guidelines pursuant to which it shall determine which testing organizations, agencies, or educational institutions will be approved to administer tests for certification of court interpreters for individuals who are deaf or hard of hearing. It is the intent of the Legislature that the study obtain the widest possible input from the public, including, but not limited to, educational institutions, the judiciary, linguists, members of the State Bar of California, court interpreters, members of professional interpreting organizations, and members of the deaf and hard of hearing communities. After obtaining public comment and completing its study, the Judicial Council shall publish these guidelines. By January 1, 1997, the Judicial Council shall approve one or more entities to administer testing for court interpreters for individuals who are deaf or hard of hearing. Testing entities may include educational institutions, testing organizations, joint powers agencies, or public agencies.

(2) Commencing July 1, 1997, court interpreters for individuals who are deaf or hard of hearing shall meet the qualifications specified in subdivision (f).

(i) Persons appointed to serve as interpreters under this section shall be paid, in addition to actual travel costs, the prevailing rate paid to persons employed by the court to provide other interpreter services unless such service is considered to be a part of the person's regular duties as an employee of the state, county, or other political subdivision of the state. Except as provided in subdivision (j), payment of the interpreter's fee shall be a charge against the court. Payment of the interpreter's fee in administrative proceedings shall be a charge against the appointing board or authority.

(j) Whenever a peace officer or any other person having a law enforcement or prosecutorial function in a criminal or quasi-criminal investigation or non-court proceeding questions or otherwise interviews an alleged victim or witness who demonstrates or alleges deafness or hearing loss, a good faith effort to secure the services of an interpreter shall be made without any unnecessary delay, unless either the individual who is deaf or hard of hearing affirmatively indicates that he or she does not need or cannot use an interpreter, or an interpreter is not otherwise required by Title II of the federal Americans with Disabilities Act of 1990 (Public Law 101-336) and federal regulations adopted thereunder. Payment of the interpreter's fee shall be a charge against the county, or other political subdivision of the state, in which the action is pending.

(k) A statement, written or oral, made by an individual who the court finds is deaf or hard of hearing in reply to a question of a peace officer, or any other person having a law enforcement or prosecutorial function in a criminal or quasi-criminal investigation or proceeding, shall not be used against that individual who is deaf or hard of hearing unless the question was accurately interpreted and the statement was made knowingly, voluntarily, and intelligently and was accurately interpreted, or the court finds that either the individual could not have used an interpreter or an interpreter was not otherwise required by Title II of the federal Americans with Disabilities Act of 1990 (Public Law 101-336) and federal regulations adopted thereunder and that the statement was made knowingly, voluntarily, and intelligently.

(*l*) In obtaining services of an interpreter for purposes of subdivision (j) or (k), priority shall be given to first obtaining a qualified interpreter.

(m) Subdivisions (j) and (k) shall not be deemed to supersede the requirement of subdivision (b) for use of a qualified interpreter for an individual who is deaf or hard of hearing participating as a party or witness in a trial or hearing.

(n) In an action or proceeding in which an individual who is deaf or hard of hearing is a participant, the appointing authority shall not commence the action or proceeding until the appointed interpreter is in full view of and spatially situated to assure proper communication with the participating individual who is deaf or hard of hearing.

(o) Each superior court shall maintain a current roster of qualified interpreters certified pursuant to subdivision (f). **Leg.H.** Enacted Stats 1965 ch 299 §2, operative January 1, 1967. Amended Stats 1977 ch 1182 §1; Stats 1984 ch 768 §2; Stats 1989 ch 1002 §2; Stats 1990 ch 1450 §2 (SB 2046); Stats 1991 ch 883 §1 (SB 585); Stats 1992 ch 118 §1 (SB 16), effective July 6, 1992, ch 913 §14 (AB 1077); Stats 1995 ch 143 §1 (AB 1833), effective July 18, 1995; Stats 2012 ch 470 §11 (AB 1529), effective January 1, 2013; Stats 2016 ch 94 §7 (AB 1709), effective January 1, 2017; Stats 2017 ch 561 §56 (AB 1516), effective January 1, 2018.

§754.5. Effect of interpreter on privilege

Whenever an otherwise valid privilege exists between an individual who is deaf or hard of hearing and another person, that privilege is not waived merely because an interpreter was used to facilitate their communication. **Leg.H.** Added Stats 1990 ch 1450 §3 (SB 2046). Amended Stats 1992 ch 913 §15 (AB 1077); Stats 2016 ch 94 §8 (AB 1709), effective January 1, 2017.

§755. [Section repealed 2015]

Leg.H. Added Stats 1995 ch 888 §1 (SB 982). Repealed Stats 2014 ch 721 §1 (AB 1657), effective January 1, 2015. The repealed section related to interpreters in domestic violence, parental rights, dissolution of marriage or separation proceedings.

Former Sections: Former Ev C §755, relating to interpreters in specified proceedings and medical examinations, was added Stats 1991 ch 883 §2 and repealed January 1, 1993, by its own terms.

§755.5. Interpreter's presence in medical examination

(a) During any medical examination, requested by an insurer or by the defendant, of a person who is a party to a civil action and who does not proficiently speak or understand the English language, conducted for the purpose of determining damages in a civil action, an interpreter shall be present to interpret the examination in a language that the person understands. The interpreter shall be certified pursuant to Article 8 (commencing with Section 11435.05) of Chapter 4.5 of Part 1 of Division 3 of Title 2 of the Government Code.

(b) The fees of interpreters used under subdivision (a) shall be paid by the insurer or defendant requesting the medical examination.

(c) The record of, or testimony concerning, any medical examination conducted in violation of subdivision (a) shall be inadmissible in the civil action for which it was conducted or any other civil action.

(d) This section does not prohibit the presence of any other person to assist a party.

(e) In the event that interpreters certified pursuant to Article 8 (commencing with Section 11435.05) of Chapter 4.5 of Part 1 of Division 3 of Title 2 of the Government Code cannot be present at the medical examination, upon stipulation of the parties the requester specified in subdivision (a) shall have the discretionary authority to provisionally qualify and use other interpreters. **Leg.H.** Added Stats 1992 ch 1302 §5 (AB 3107), effective September 30, 1992. Amended Stats 1995 ch 938 §8 (SB 523), operative July 1, 1997.

§756. Reimbursement to courts for court interpreter services in civil actions and proceedings

(a) To the extent required by other state or federal laws, the Judicial Council shall reimburse courts for court interpreter services provided in civil actions and proceedings to any party who is present in court and who does not proficiently speak or understand the English language for the purpose of interpreting the proceedings in a language the party understands, and assisting communications between the party, the party's attorney, and the court.

(b) If sufficient funds are not appropriated to provide an interpreter to every party that meets the standard of eligibility, court interpreter services in civil cases reimbursed by the Judicial Council, pursuant to subdivision (a), shall be prioritized by case type by each court in the following order:

(1) Actions and proceedings under Division 10 (commencing with Section 6200) of the Family Code, actions or proceedings under the Uniform Parentage Act (Part 3 (commencing with Section 7600) of Division 12 of the Family Code) in which a protective order has been granted or is being sought pursuant to Section 6221 of the Family Code, and actions and proceedings for dissolution or nullity of marriage or legal separation of the parties in which a protective order has been granted or is being sought pursuant to Section 6221 of the Family Code; actions and proceedings under subdivision (y) of Section 527.6 of the Code of Civil Procedure; and actions and proceedings for physical abuse or neglect under the Elder Abuse and Dependent Adult Civil Protection Act (Chapter 11 (commencing with Section 15600) of Part 3 of Division 9 of the Welfare and Institutions Code).

(2) Actions and proceedings relating to unlawful detainer.

(3) Actions and proceedings to terminate parental rights.

(4) Actions and proceedings relating to conservatorship or guardianship, including the appointment or termination of a probate guardian or conservator.

(5) Actions and proceedings by a parent to obtain sole legal or physical custody of a child or rights to visitation.

(6) All other actions and proceedings under Section 527.6 of the Code of Civil Procedure or the Elder Abuse and Dependent Adult Civil Protection Act (Chapter 11 (commencing with Section 15600) of Part 3 of Division 9 of the Welfare and Institutions Code).

(7) All other actions and proceedings related to family law.

(8) All other civil actions or proceedings.

(c)(1) If funds are not available to provide an interpreter to every party that meets the standard of eligibility, preference shall be given for parties proceeding in forma pauperis pursuant to Section 68631 of the Government Code in any civil action or proceeding described in paragraph (3), (4), (5), (6), (7), or (8) of subdivision (b).

(2) Courts may provide an interpreter to a party outside the priority order listed in subdivision (b) when a qualified interpreter is present and available at the court location and no higher priority action that meets the standard of eligibility described in subdivision (a) is taking place at that location during the period of time for which the interpreter has already been compensated.

(d) A party shall not be charged a fee for the provision of a court interpreter.

(e) In seeking reimbursement for court interpreter services, the court shall identify to the Judicial Council the case types for which the interpretation to be reimbursed was provided. Courts shall regularly certify that in providing the interpreter services, they have complied with the priorities and preferences set forth in subdivisions (b) and (c), which shall be subject to review by the Judicial Council.

(f) This section shall not be construed to alter, limit, or negate any right to an interpreter in a civil action or proceeding otherwise provided by state or federal law, or the right to an interpreter in criminal, traffic, or other infraction, juvenile, or mental competency actions or proceedings.

(g) This section shall not result in a reduction in staffing or compromise the quality of interpreting services in criminal, juvenile, or other types of matters in which interpreters are provided. **Leg.H.** Added Stats 2014 ch 721 §2 (AB 1657), effective January 1, 2015. Amended Stats 2019 ch 497 §109 (AB 991), effective January 1, 2020.

§757. Interpreter in proceeding to determine special immigrant juvenile status

Pursuant to this chapter, other applicable law, and existing Judicial Council policy, including the policy adopted on January 23, 2014, existing authority to provide interpreters in civil court includes the authority to provide an interpreter in a proceeding in which a petitioner requests an order from the superior court to make the findings regarding special immigrant juvenile status pursuant to Section 1101(a)(27)(J) of Title 8 of the United States Code. **Leg.H.** Added Stats 2014 ch 685 §2 (SB 873), effective September 27, 2014.

CHAPTER 5
METHOD AND SCOPE OF EXAMINATION

Article 1. **Definitions.**
Article 2. **Examination of Witnesses.**

ARTICLE 1
Definitions

"Direct examination". §760.
"Cross-examination". §761.

"Redirect examination". §762.
"Recross-examination". §763.
"Leading question". §764.

§760. "Direct examination"
"Direct examination" is the first examination of a witness upon a matter that is not within the scope of a previous examination of the witness. **Leg.H.** Enacted Stats 1965 ch 299 §2, operative January 1, 1967.

§761. "Cross-examination"
"Cross-examination" is the examination of a witness by a party other than the direct examiner upon a matter that is within the scope of the direct examination of the witness. **Leg.H.** Enacted Stats 1965 ch 299 §2, operative January 1, 1967.

§762. "Redirect examination"
"Redirect examination" is an examination of a witness by the direct examiner subsequent to the cross-examination of the witness. **Leg.H.** Enacted Stats 1965 ch 299 §2, operative January 1, 1967.

§763. "Recross-examination"
"Recross-examination" is an examination of a witness by a cross-examiner subsequent to a redirect examination of the witness. **Leg.H.** Enacted Stats 1965 ch 299 §2, operative January 1, 1967.

§764. "Leading question"
A "leading question" is a question that suggests to the witness the answer that the examining party desires. **Leg.H.** Enacted Stats 1965 ch 299 §2, operative January 1, 1967.

ARTICLE 2
Examination of Witnesses

Court to control mode of interrogation. §765.
Responsive answers. §766.
Leading questions. §767.
Writings. §768.
Inconsistent statement or conduct. §769.
Evidence of inconsistent statement of witness. §770.
Production of writing used to refresh memory. §771.
Order of examination. §772.
Cross-examination. §773.
Reexamination. §774.
Court may call witnesses. §775.
Examination of adverse party or witness. §776.
Exclusion of witness. §777.
Recall of witness. §778.

§765. Court to control mode of interrogation
(a) The court shall exercise reasonable control over the mode of interrogation of a witness so as to make interrogation as rapid, as distinct, and as effective for the ascertainment of the truth, as may be, and to protect the witness from undue harassment or embarrassment.

(b) With a witness under the age of 14 or a dependent person with a substantial cognitive impairment, the court shall take special care to protect him or her from undue harassment or embarrassment, and to restrict the unnecessary repetition of questions. The court shall also take special care to ensure that questions are stated in a form which is appropriate to the age or cognitive level of the witness. The court may, in the interests of justice, on objection by a party, forbid the asking of a question which is in a form that is not reasonably likely to be understood by a person of the age or cognitive level of the witness. **Leg.H.** Enacted Stats 1965 ch 299 §2, operative January 1, 1967. Amended Stats 1985 ch 884 §3; Stats 1986 ch 1051 §1; Stats 2004 ch 823 §4 (AB 20).

§766. Responsive answers
A witness must give responsive answers to questions, and answers that are not responsive shall be stricken on motion of any party. **Leg.H.** Enacted Stats 1965 ch 299 §2, operative January 1, 1967.

§767. Leading questions
(a) Except under special circumstances where the interests of justice otherwise require:

(1) A leading question may not be asked of a witness on direct or redirect examination.

(2) A leading question may be asked of a witness on cross-examination or recross-examination.

(b) The court may, in the interests of justice permit a leading question to be asked of a child under 10 years of age or a dependent person with a substantial cognitive impairment in a case involving a prosecution under Section 273a, 273d, 288.5, 368, or any of the acts described in Section 11165.1 or 11165.2 of the Penal Code. **Leg.H.** Enacted Stats 1965 ch 299 §2, operative January 1, 1967. Amended Stats 1984 ch 1423 §1, effective September 26, 1984; Stats 1995 ch 87 §1 (AB 355); Stats 2004 ch 823 §5 (AB 20), effective January 1, 2005.

§768. Writings
(a) In examining a witness concerning a writing, it is not necessary to show, read, or disclose to him any part of the writing.

(b) If a writing is shown to a witness, all parties to the action must be given an opportunity to inspect it before any question concerning it may be asked of the witness. **Leg.H.** Enacted Stats 1965 ch 299 §2, operative January 1, 1967.

§769. Inconsistent statement or conduct
In examining a witness concerning a statement or other conduct by him that is inconsistent with any part of his testimony at the hearing, it is not necessary to disclose to him any information concerning the statement or other conduct. **Leg.H.** Enacted Stats 1965 ch 299 §2, operative January 1, 1967.

§770. Evidence of inconsistent statement of witness
Unless the interests of justice otherwise require, extrinsic evidence of a statement made by a witness that is inconsistent with any part of his testimony at the hearing shall be excluded unless:

(a) The witness was so examined while testifying as to give him an opportunity to explain or to deny the statement; or

(b) The witness has not been excused from giving further testimony in the action. **Leg.H.** Enacted Stats 1965 ch 299 §2, operative January 1, 1967.

§771. Production of writing used to refresh memory
(a) Subject to subdivision (c), if a witness, either while testifying or prior thereto, uses a writing to refresh his memory with respect to any matter about which he testifies, such writing must be produced at the hearing at the request of an adverse party and, unless the writing is so produced, the testimony of the witness concerning such matter shall be stricken.

(b) If the writing is produced at the hearing, the adverse party may, if he chooses, inspect the writing, cross-examine the witness concerning it, and introduce in evidence such portion of it as may be pertinent to the testimony of the witness.

(c) Production of the writing is excused, and the testimony of the witness shall not be stricken, if the writing:

(1) Is not in the possession or control of the witness or the party who produced his testimony concerning the matter; and

(2) Was not reasonably procurable by such party through the use of the court's process or other available means. **Leg.H.** Enacted Stats 1965 ch 299 §2, operative January 1, 1967.

§772. Order of examination
(a) The examination of a witness shall proceed in the following phases: direct examination, cross-examination, redirect examination, recross-examination, and continuing thereafter by redirect and recross-examination.

(b) Unless for good cause the court otherwise directs, each phase of the examination of a witness must be concluded before the succeeding phase begins.

(c) Subject to subdivision (d), a party may, in the discretion of the court, interrupt his cross-examination, redirect examination, or recross-examination of a witness, in order to examine the witness upon a matter not within the scope of a previous examination of the witness.

(d) If the witness is the defendant in a criminal action, the witness may not, without his consent, be examined under direct examination by another party. **Leg.H.** Enacted Stats 1965 ch 299 §2, operative January 1, 1967.

§773. Cross-examination
(a) A witness examined by one party may be cross-examined upon any matter within the scope of the direct examination by each other party to the action in such order as the court directs.

(b) The cross-examination of a witness by any party whose interest is not adverse to the party calling him is subject to the same rules that are applicable to the direct examination. **Leg.H.** Enacted Stats 1965 ch 299 §2, operative January 1, 1967.

§774. Reexamination

A witness once examined cannot be reexamined as to the same matter without leave of the court, but he may be reexamined as to any new matter upon which he has been examined by another party to the action. Leave may be granted or withheld in the court's discretion. **Leg.H.** Enacted Stats 1965 ch 299 §2, operative January 1, 1967.

§775. Court may call witnesses

The court, on its own motion or on the motion of any party, may call witnesses and interrogate them the same as if they had been produced by a party to the action, and the parties may object to the questions asked and the evidence adduced the same as if such witnesses were called and examined by an adverse party. Such witnesses may be cross-examined by all parties to the action in such order as the court directs. **Leg.H.** Enacted Stats 1965 ch 299 §2, operative January 1, 1967.

§776. Examination of adverse party or witness

(a) A party to the record of any civil action, or a person identified with such a party, may be called and examined as if under cross-examination by any adverse party at any time during the presentation of evidence by the party calling the witness.

(b) A witness examined by a party under this section may be cross-examined by all other parties to the action in such order as the court directs; but, subject to subdivision (e), the witness may be examined only as if under redirect examination by:

(1) In the case of a witness who is a party, his own counsel and counsel for a party who is not adverse to the witness.

(2) In the case of a witness who is not a party, counsel for the party with whom the witness is identified and counsel for a party who is not adverse to the party with whom the witness is identified.

(c) For the purpose of this section, parties represented by the same counsel are deemed to be a single party.

(d) For the purpose of this section, a person is identified with a party if he is:

(1) A person for whose immediate benefit the action is prosecuted or defended by the party.

(2) A director, officer, superintendent, member, agent, employee, or managing agent of the party or of a person specified in paragraph (1), or any public employee of a public entity when such public entity is the party.

(3) A person who was in any of the relationships specified in paragraph (2) at the time of the act or omission giving rise to the cause of action.

(4) A person who was in any of the relationships specified in paragraph (2) at the time he obtained knowledge of the matter concerning which he is sought to be examined under this section.

(e) Paragraph (2) of subdivision (b) does not require counsel for the party with whom the witness is identified and counsel for a party who is not adverse to the party with whom the witness is identified to examine the witness as if under redirect examination if the party who called the witness for examination under this section:

(1) Is also a person identified with the same party with whom the witness is identified.

(2) Is the personal representative, heir, successor, or assignee of a person identified with the same party with whom the witness is identified. **Leg.H.** Enacted Stats 1965 ch 299 §2, operative January 1, 1967. Amended Stats 1967 ch 650 §2.

§777. Exclusion of witness

(a) Subject to subdivisions (b) and (c), the court may exclude from the courtroom any witness not at the time under examination so that such witness cannot hear the testimony of other witnesses.

(b) A party to the action cannot be excluded under this section.

(c) If a person other than a natural person is a party to the action, an officer or employee designated by its attorney is entitled to be present. **Leg.H.** Enacted Stats 1965 ch 299 §2, operative January 1, 1967.

§778. Recall of witness

After a witness has been excused from giving further testimony in the action, he cannot be recalled without leave of the court. Leave may be granted or withheld in the court's discretion. **Leg.H.** Enacted Stats 1965 ch 299 §2, operative January 1, 1967.

CHAPTER 6
CREDIBILITY OF WITNESSES

Article 1. Credibility Generally.
Article 2. Attacking or Supporting Credibility.

ARTICLE 1
Credibility Generally

General rule as to credibility. §780.
Evidence of sexual conduct of complaining witness; Written motion; Offer of proof; Affidavit; Procedure. §782.
Possession of condom as evidence not admissible if offense related to prostitution. §782.1.
Evidence of sexual conduct to attack credibility of plaintiff in civil action alleging sexual harassment; Procedure. §783.

§780. General rule as to credibility

Except as otherwise provided by statute, the court or jury may consider in determining the credibility of a witness any matter that has any tendency in reason to prove or disprove the truthfulness of his testimony at the hearing, including but not limited to any of the following:

(a) His demeanor while testifying and the manner in which he testifies.

(b) The character of his testimony.

(c) The extent of his capacity to perceive, to recollect, or to communicate any matter about which he testifies.

(d) The extent of his opportunity to perceive any matter about which he testifies.

(e) His character for honesty or veracity or their opposites.

(f) The existence or nonexistence of a bias, interest, or other motive.

(g) A statement previously made by him that is consistent with his testimony at the hearing.

(h) A statement made by him that is inconsistent with any part of his testimony at the hearing.

(i) The existence or nonexistence of any fact testified to by him.

(j) His attitude toward the action in which he testifies or toward the giving of testimony.

(k) His admission of untruthfulness. **Leg.H.** Enacted Stats 1965 ch 299 §2, operative January 1, 1967.

§782. Evidence of sexual conduct of complaining witness; Written motion; Offer of proof; Affidavit; Procedure

(a) In any of the circumstances described in subdivision (c), if evidence of sexual conduct of the complaining witness is offered to attack the credibility of the complaining witness under Section 780, the following procedure shall be followed:

(1) A written motion shall be made by the defendant to the court and prosecutor stating that the defense has an offer of proof of the relevance of evidence of the sexual conduct of the complaining witness that is proposed to be presented and of its relevance in attacking the credibility of the complaining witness.

(2) The written motion shall be accompanied by an affidavit in which the offer of proof shall be stated. The affidavit shall be filed under seal and only unsealed by the court to determine if the offer of proof is sufficient to order a hearing pursuant to paragraph (3). After that determination, the affidavit shall be resealed by the court.

(3) If the court finds that the offer of proof is sufficient, the court shall order a hearing out of the presence of the jury, if any, and at the hearing allow the questioning of the complaining witness regarding the offer of proof made by the defendant.

(4) At the conclusion of the hearing, if the court finds that evidence proposed to be offered by the defendant regarding the sexual conduct of the complaining witness is relevant pursuant to Section 780, and is not inadmissible pursuant to Section 352, the court may make an order stating what evidence may be introduced by the defendant, and the nature of the questions to be permitted. The defendant may then offer evidence pursuant to the order of the court.

(5) An affidavit resealed by the court pursuant to paragraph (2) shall remain sealed, unless the defendant raises an issue on appeal or collateral review relating to the offer of proof contained in the sealed document. If the defendant raises that issue on appeal, the court shall allow the Attorney General and appellate counsel for the defendant access to the sealed affidavit. If the issue is raised on collateral review, the court shall allow the district attorney and defendant's counsel access to the sealed affidavit. The use of the information contained in the affidavit shall be limited solely to the pending proceeding.

(b)(1) As used in this section, "complaining witness" means:

(A) The alleged victim of the crime charged, the prosecution of which is subject to this section, pursuant to paragraph (1) of subdivision (c).

(B) An alleged victim offering testimony pursuant to paragraph (2) or (3) of subdivision (c).

(2) As used in this section, "evidence of sexual conduct" includes those portions of a social media account about the complaining witness, including any text, image, video, or picture, which depict sexual content, sexual history, nudity or partial nudity, intimate sexual activity, communications about sex, sexual fantasies, and other information that appeals to a prurient interest, unless it is related to the alleged offense.

(c) The procedure provided by subdivision (a) shall apply in any of the following circumstances:

(1) In a prosecution under Section 261, 262, 264.1, 286, 287, 288, 288.5, or 289 of, or former Section 288a of, the Penal Code, or for assault with intent to commit, attempt to commit, or conspiracy to commit any crime defined in any of those sections, except if the crime is alleged to have occurred in a local detention facility, as defined in Section 6031.4 of the Penal Code, or in the state prison, as defined in Section 4504.

(2) When an alleged victim testifies pursuant to subdivision (b) of Section 1101 as a victim of a crime listed in Section 243.4, 261, 261.5, 269, 285, 286, 287, 288, 288.5, 289, 314, or 647.6 of, or former Section 288a of, the Penal Code, except if the crime is alleged to have occurred in a local detention facility, as defined in Section 6031.4 of the Penal Code, or in the state prison, as defined in Section 4504 of the Penal Code.

(3) When an alleged victim of a sexual offense testifies pursuant to Section 1108, except if the crime is alleged to have occurred in a local detention facility, as defined in Section 6031.4 of the Penal Code, or in the state prison, as defined in Section 4504 of the Penal Code. **Leg.H.** Added Stats 1974 ch 569 §1. Amended Stats 1981 ch 726 §1; Stats 1987 ch 177 §1; Stats 1989 ch 1402 §2; Stats 1996 ch 1075 §6 (SB 1444); Stats 2004 ch 61 §1 (AB 2829); Stats 2006 ch 225 §1 (AB 1996), effective January 1, 2007; Stats 2007 ch 130 §83 (AB 299), effective January 1, 2008; Stats 2018 ch 423 §19 (SB 1494), effective January 1, 2019; Stats 2021 ch 24 §1 (AB 341), effective January 1, 2022.

§782.1. Possession of condom as evidence not admissible if offense related to prostitution

The possession of a condom is not admissible as evidence in the prosecution of a violation of Section 372 of, or subdivision (a) or (b) of Section 647 of, or former Section 653.22 of, the Penal Code, if the offense is related to prostitution. **Leg.H.** Added Stats 2019 ch 141 §2 (SB 233), effective January 1, 2020. Amended Stats 2022 ch 86 §1 (SB 357), effective January 1, 2023.

Prior Law: Former Ev C §782.1, relating to condoms as evidence, was added Stats 2014 ch 403 §1 (AB 336), effective January 1, 2015, and repealed Stats 2019 ch 141 §1 (SB 233), effective January 1, 2020.

Former Sections: Former Ev C §782.1, relating to condoms as evidence, was added Stats 2014 ch 403 §1 (AB 336) and repealed Stats 2019 ch 141 §1 (SB 233), effective January 1, 2020.

§783. Evidence of sexual conduct to attack credibility of plaintiff in civil action alleging sexual harassment; Procedure

In any civil action alleging conduct which constitutes sexual harassment, sexual assault, or sexual battery, if evidence of sexual conduct of the plaintiff is offered to attack credibility of the plaintiff under Section 780, the following procedures shall be followed:

(a) A written motion shall be made by the defendant to the court and the plaintiff's attorney stating that the defense has an offer of proof of the relevancy of evidence of the sexual conduct of the plaintiff proposed to be presented.

(b) The written motion shall be accompanied by an affidavit in which the offer of proof shall be stated.

(c) If the court finds that the offer of proof is sufficient, the court shall order a hearing out of the presence of the jury, if any, and at the hearing allow the questioning of the plaintiff regarding the offer of proof made by the defendant.

(d) At the conclusion of the hearing, if the court finds that evidence proposed to be offered by the defendant regarding the sexual conduct of the plaintiff is relevant pursuant to Section 780, and is not inadmissible pursuant to Section 352, the court may make an order stating what evidence may be introduced by the defendant, and the nature of the questions to be permitted. The defendant may then offer evidence pursuant to the order of the court. **Leg.H.** Added Stats 1985 ch 1328 §3.

ARTICLE 2
Attacking or Supporting Credibility

Parties may attack or support credibility. §785.
Character evidence generally. §786.
Specific instances of conduct. §787.
Prior felony conviction. §788.
Religious belief. §789.
Good character of witness. §790.
Prior consistent statement of witness. §791.

§785. Parties may attack or support credibility

The credibility of a witness may be attacked or supported by any party, including the party calling him. **Leg.H.** Enacted Stats 1965 ch 299 §2, operative January 1, 1967.

§786. Character evidence generally

Evidence of traits of his character other than honesty or veracity, or their opposites, is inadmissible to attack or support the credibility of a witness. **Leg.H.** Enacted Stats 1965 ch 299 §2, operative January 1, 1967.

1989 Note: See the 1989 Note following Ev C §790.

§787. Specific instances of conduct

Subject to Section 788, evidence of specific instances of his conduct relevant only as tending to prove a trait of his character is inadmissible to attack or support the credibility of a witness. **Leg.H.** Enacted Stats 1965 ch 299 §2, operative January 1, 1967.

1989 Note: See the 1989 Note following Ev C §790.

§788. Prior felony conviction

For the purpose of attacking the credibility of a witness, it may be shown by the examination of the witness or by the record of the judgment that he has been convicted of a felony unless:

(a) A pardon based on his innocence has been granted to the witness by the jurisdiction in which he was convicted.

(b) A certificate of rehabilitation and pardon has been granted to the witness under the provisions of Chapter 3.5 (commencing with Section 4852.01) of Title 6 of Part 3 of the Penal Code.

(c) The accusatory pleading against the witness has been dismissed under the provisions of Penal Code Section 1203.4, but this exception does not apply to any criminal trial where the witness is being prosecuted for a subsequent offense.

(d) The conviction was under the laws of another jurisdiction and the witness has been relieved of the penalties and disabilities arising from the conviction pursuant to a procedure substantially equivalent to that referred to in subdivision (b) or (c). **Leg.H.** Enacted Stats 1965 ch 299 §2, operative January 1, 1967.

§789. Religious belief

Evidence of his religious belief or lack thereof is inadmissible to attack or support the credibility of a witness. **Leg.H.** Enacted Stats 1965 ch 299 §2, operative January 1, 1967.

§790. Good character of witness

Evidence of the good character of a witness is inadmissible to support his credibility unless evidence of his bad character has been admitted for the purpose of attacking his credibility. **Leg.H.** Enacted Stats 1965 ch 299 §2, operative January 1, 1967.

1989 Note: The California Supreme Court, in *People v. Harris* (47 Cal. 3d 1047, 1081–1082, 255 Cal. Rptr. 352, 767 P.2d 619 (1989)), held that California Constitution Art. I §28(d) effected a pro tanto repeal of Evidence Code §790, and suggested that Evidence Code §§786 and 787 were similarly repealed.

§791. Prior consistent statement of witness

Evidence of a statement previously made by a witness that is consistent with his testimony at the hearing is inadmissible to support his credibility unless it is offered after:

(a) Evidence of a statement made by him that is inconsistent with any part of his testimony at the hearing has been admitted for the purpose of attacking his credibility, and the statement was made before the alleged inconsistent statement; or

(b) An express or implied charge has been made that his testimony at the hearing is recently fabricated or is influenced by bias or other improper motive, and the statement was made before the bias, motive for fabrication, or other improper motive is alleged to have arisen. **Leg.H.** Enacted Stats 1965 ch 299 §2, operative January 1, 1967.

CHAPTER 7
HYPNOSIS OF WITNESSES

Admissibility of testimony in criminal proceeding. §795.

§795. Admissibility of testimony in criminal proceeding

(a) The testimony of a witness is not inadmissible in a criminal proceeding by reason of the fact that the witness has previously undergone hypnosis for the purpose of recalling events that are the subject of the witness's testimony, if all of the following conditions are met:

(1) The testimony is limited to those matters that the witness recalled and related prior to the hypnosis.

(2) The substance of the prehypnotic memory was preserved in a writing, audio recording, or video recording prior to the hypnosis.

(3) The hypnosis was conducted in accordance with all of the following procedures:

(A) A written record was made prior to hypnosis documenting the subject's description of the event, and information that was provided to the hypnotist concerning the subject matter of the hypnosis.

(B) The subject gave informed consent to the hypnosis.

(C) The hypnosis session, including the pre- and post-hypnosis interviews, was video recorded for subsequent review.

(D) The hypnosis was performed by a licensed physician and surgeon, psychologist, licensed clinical social worker, licensed marriage and family therapist, or licensed professional clinical counselor experienced in the use of hypnosis and independent of and not in the presence of law enforcement, the prosecution, or the defense.

(4) Prior to admission of the testimony, the court holds a hearing pursuant to Section 402 at which the proponent of the evidence proves by clear and convincing evidence that the hypnosis did not so affect the witness as to render the witness's prehypnosis recollection unreliable or to substantially impair the ability to cross-examine the witness concerning the witness's prehypnosis recollection. At the hearing, each side shall have the right to present expert testimony and to cross-examine witnesses.

(b) Nothing in this section shall be construed to limit the ability of a party to attack the credibility of a witness who has undergone hypnosis, or to limit other legal grounds to admit or exclude the testimony of that witness. **Leg.H.** Added Stats 1984 ch 479 §1. Amended Stats 1987 ch 285 §1; Stats 1996 ch 67 §1 (AB 2296); Stats 2002 ch 1013 §77 (SB 2026); Stats 2009 ch 88 §34 (AB 176), effective January 1, 2010; Stats 2011 ch 381 §20 (SB 146), effective January 1, 2012.

DIVISION 7
OPINION TESTIMONY AND SCIENTIFIC EVIDENCE

Chapter 1. Expert and Other Opinion Testimony.
Chapter 2. Blood Tests to Determine Paternity [Repealed].

CHAPTER 1
EXPERT AND OTHER OPINION TESTIMONY

Article 1. Expert and Other Opinion Testimony Generally.
Article 2. Evidence of Market Value of Property.
Article 3. Opinion Testimony on Particular Subjects.

ARTICLE 1
Expert and Other Opinion Testimony Generally

Opinion testimony by lay witness. §800.
Opinion testimony by expert witness. §801.
Expert testimony regarding medical causation. § 801.1.
Statement of basis of opinion. §802.
Opinion based on improper matter. §803.
Opinion based on opinion or statement of another. §804.
Opinion on ultimate issue. §805.

§800. Opinion testimony by lay witness

If a witness is not testifying as an expert, his testimony in the form of an opinion is limited to such an opinion as is permitted by law, including but not limited to an opinion that is:

(a) Rationally based on the perception of the witness; and

(b) Helpful to a clear understanding of his testimony. **Leg.H.** Enacted Stats 1965 ch 299 §2, operative January 1, 1967.

§801. Opinion testimony by expert witness

If a witness is testifying as an expert, his testimony in the form of an opinion is limited to such an opinion as is:

(a) Related to a subject that is sufficiently beyond common experience that the opinion of an expert would assist the trier of fact; and

(b) Based on matter (including his special knowledge, skill, experience, training, and education) perceived by or personally known to the witness or made known to him at or before the hearing, whether or not admissible, that is of a type that reasonably may be relied upon by an expert in forming an opinion upon the subject to which his testimony relates, unless an expert is precluded by law from using such matter as a basis for his opinion. **Leg.H.** Enacted Stats 1965 ch 299 §2, operative January 1, 1967.

§ 801.1. Expert testimony regarding medical causation

(a) In a general civil case, as defined in Rule 1.6 of the California Rules of Court, where the party bearing the burden of proof proffers expert testimony regarding medical causation and where that party's expert is required as a condition of testifying to opine that causation exists to a reasonable medical probability, the party not bearing the burden of proof may offer a contrary expert only if its expert is able to opine that the proffered alternative cause or causes each exists to a reasonable medical probability, except as provided in subdivision (b).

(b) Subdivision (a) does not preclude a witness testifying as an expert from testifying that a matter cannot meet a reasonable degree of probability in the applicable field, and providing the basis for that opinion. **Leg.H.** Added Stats 2023 ch 75 §1 (SB 652), effective January 1, 2024. Amended Stats 2023 ch 190 §1 (SB 135), effective September 13, 2023, operative January 1, 2024.

§802. Statement of basis of opinion

A witness testifying in the form of an opinion may state on direct examination the reasons for his opinion and the matter (including, in the case of an expert, his special knowledge, skill, experience, training, and education) upon which it is based, unless he is precluded by law from using such reasons or matter as a basis for his opinion. The court in its discretion may require that a witness before testifying in the form of an opinion be first examined concerning the matter upon which his opinion is based. **Leg.H.** Enacted Stats 1965 ch 299 §2, operative January 1, 1967.

§803. Opinion based on improper matter

The court may, and upon objection shall, exclude testimony in the form of an opinion that is based in whole or in significant part on matter that is not a proper basis for such an opinion. In such case, the witness may, if there remains a proper basis for his opinion, then state his opinion after excluding from consideration the matter determined to be improper. **Leg.H.** Enacted Stats 1965 ch 299 §2, operative January 1, 1967.

§804. Opinion based on opinion or statement of another

(a) If a witness testifying as an expert testifies that his opinion is based in whole or in part upon the opinion or statement of another person, such other person may be called and examined by any adverse party as if under cross-examination concerning the opinion or statement.

(b) This section is not applicable if the person upon whose opinion or statement the expert witness has relied is (1) a party, (2) a person identified with a party within the meaning of subdivision (d) of Section 776, or (3) a witness who has testified in the action concerning the subject matter of the opinion or statement upon which the expert witness has relied.

(c) Nothing in this section makes admissible an expert opinion that is inadmissible because it is based in whole or in part on the opinion or statement of another person.

(d) An expert opinion otherwise admissible is not made inadmissible by this section because it is based on the opinion or statement of a person who is unavailable for examination pursuant to this section. **Leg.H.** Enacted Stats 1965 ch 299 §2, operative January 1, 1967.

§805. Opinion on ultimate issue

Testimony in the form of an opinion that is otherwise admissible is not objectionable because it embraces the ultimate issue to be decided by the trier of fact. **Leg.H.** Enacted Stats 1965 ch 299 §2, operative January 1, 1967.

ARTICLE 2
Evidence of Market Value of Property

Application. §810.
"Value of property". §811.
Concept of "market value" not affected. §812.
Opinion testimony. §813.
Basis for opinion. §814.
Sales of subject property. §815.
Comparable sales. §816.
Leases of subject property. §817.
Comparable leases. §818.
Capitalization of income. §819.
Reproduction cost. §820.
Conditions in general vicinity of subject property. §821.
Inadmissible evidence. §822.
Property with no relevant market. §823.
Method for determining value of nonprofit, special use property; Application. §824.

§810. Application

(a) Except where another rule is provided by statute, this article provides special rules of evidence applicable to any action in which the value of property is to be ascertained.

(b) This article does not govern ad valorem property tax assessment or equalization proceedings. **Leg.H.** Added Stats 1965 ch 1151 §4, operative January 1, 1967. Amended Stats 1978 ch 294 §3; Stats 1980 ch 381 §1.

§811. "Value of property"

As used in this article, "value of property" means market value of any of the following:

(a) Real property or any interest therein.

(b) Real property or any interest therein and tangible personal property valued as a unit. **Leg.H.** Added Stats 1965 ch 1151 §4, operative January 1, 1967. Amended Stats 1975 ch 1240 §15, operative July 1, 1976; Stats 1978 ch 294 §4; Stats 1980 ch 381 §2.

§812. Concept of "market value" not affected

This article is not intended to alter or change the existing substantive law, whether statutory or decisional, interpreting the meaning of "market value," whether denominated "fair market value" or otherwise. **Leg.H.** Added Stats 1965 ch 1151 §4, operative January 1, 1967. Amended Stats 1975 ch 1240 §16, operative July 1, 1976; Stats 1978 ch 294 §5.

§813. Opinion testimony

(a) The value of property may be shown only by the opinions of any of the following:

(1) Witnesses qualified to express such opinions.

(2) The owner or the spouse of the owner of the property or property interest being valued.

(3) An officer, regular employee, or partner designated by a corporation, partnership, or unincorporated association that is the owner of the property or property interest being valued, if the designee is knowledgeable as to the value of the property or property interest.

(b) Nothing in this section prohibits a view of the property being valued or the admission of any other admissible evidence (including but not limited to evidence as to the nature and condition of the property and, in an eminent domain proceeding, the character of the improvement proposed to be constructed by the plaintiff) for the limited purpose of enabling the court, jury, or referee to understand and weigh the testimony given under subdivision (a); and such evidence, except evidence of the character of the improvement proposed to be constructed by the plaintiff in an eminent domain proceeding, is subject to impeachment and rebuttal.

(c) For the purposes of subdivision (a), "owner of the property or property interest being valued" includes, but is not limited to, the following persons:

(1) A person entitled to possession of the property.

(2) Either party in an action or proceeding to determine the ownership of the property between the parties if the court determines that it would not be in the interest of efficient administration of justice to determine the issue of ownership prior to the admission of the opinion of the party. **Leg.H.** Added Stats 1965 ch 1151 §4, operative January 1, 1967. Amended Stats 1978 ch 294 §6; Stats 1980 ch 381 §3.

§814. Basis for opinion

The opinion of a witness as to the value of property is limited to such an opinion as is based on matter perceived by or personally known to the witness or made known to the witness at or before the hearing, whether or not admissible, that is of a type that reasonably may be relied upon by an expert in forming an opinion as to the value of property, including but not limited to the matters listed in Sections 815 to 821, inclusive, unless a witness is precluded by law from using such matter as a basis for an opinion. **Leg.H.** Added Stats 1965 ch 1151 §4, operative January 1, 1967. Amended Stats 1975 ch 1240 §17, operative July 1, 1976; Stats 1980 ch 381 §4.

§814.5. [Section repealed 1972]

Leg.H. Added Stats 1971 ch 515 §1, effective August 10, 1971. Repealed Stats 1971 ch 1574 §1.4, effective March 4, 1972. The repealed section related to any increase or decrease in the value of property.

§815. Sales of subject property

When relevant to the determination of the value of property, a witness may take into account as a basis for an opinion the price and other terms and circumstances of any sale or contract to sell and purchase which included the property or property interest being valued or any part thereof if the sale or contract was freely made in good faith within a reasonable time before or after the date of valuation, except that in an eminent domain proceeding where the sale or contract to sell and purchase includes only the property or property interest being taken or a part thereof, such sale or contract to sell and purchase may not be taken into account if it occurs after the filing of the lis pendens. **Leg.H.** Added Stats 1965 ch 1151 §4, operative January 1, 1967. Amended Stats 1978 ch 294 §7.

§816. Comparable sales

When relevant to the determination of the value of property, a witness may take into account as a basis for his opinion the price and other terms and circumstances of any sale or contract to sell and purchase comparable property if the sale or contract was freely made in good faith within a reasonable time before or after the date of valuation. In order to be considered comparable, the sale or contract must have been made sufficiently near in time to the date of valuation, and the property sold must be located sufficiently near the property being valued, and must be sufficiently alike in respect to character, size, situation, usability, and improvements, to make it clear that the property sold and the property being valued are comparable in value and that the price realized for the property sold may fairly be considered as shedding light on the value of the property being valued. **Leg.H.** Added Stats 1965 ch 1151 §4, operative January 1, 1967.

§817. Leases of subject property

(a) Subject to subdivision (b), when relevant to the determination of the value of property, a witness may take into account as a basis for an opinion the rent reserved and other terms and circumstances of any lease which included the property or property interest being valued or any part thereof which was in effect within a reasonable time before or after the date of valuation, except that in an eminent domain proceeding where the lease includes only the property or property interest being taken or a part thereof, such lease may not be taken into account in the determination of the value of property if it is entered into after the filing of the lis pendens.

(b) A witness may take into account a lease providing for a rental fixed by a percentage or other measurable portion of gross sales or gross income from a business conducted on the leased property only for the purpose of arriving at an opinion as to the reasonable net rental value attributable to the property or property interest being valued as provided in Section 819 or determining the value of a leasehold interest. **Leg.H.** Added Stats 1965 ch 1151 §4, operative January 1, 1967. Amended Stats 1978 ch 294 §8.

§818. Comparable leases

For the purpose of determining the capitalized value of the reasonable net rental value attributable to the property or property interest being valued as provided in Section 819 or determining the value of a leasehold interest, a witness may take into account as a basis for his opinion the rent reserved and other terms and circumstances of any lease of comparable property if the lease was freely made in good faith within a reasonable time before or after the date of valuation. **Leg.H.** Added Stats 1965 ch 1151 §4, operative January 1, 1967.

§819. Capitalization of income

When relevant to the determination of the value of property, a witness may take into account as a basis for his opinion the capitalized value of the reasonable net rental value attributable to the land and existing improvements thereon (as distinguished from the capitalized value of the income or profits attributable to the business conducted thereon). **Leg.H.** Added Stats 1965 ch 1151 §4, operative January 1, 1967.

§820. Reproduction cost

When relevant to the determination of the value of property, a witness may take into account as a basis for his opinion the value of the property or property interest being valued as indicated by the value of the land together with the cost of replacing or reproducing the existing improvements thereon, if the improvements enhance the value of the property or property interest for its highest and best use, less whatever depreciation or obsolescence the improvements have suffered. **Leg.H.** Added Stats 1965 ch 1151 §4, operative January 1, 1967.

§821. Conditions in general vicinity of subject property

When relevant to the determination of the value of property, a witness may take into account as a basis for his opinion the nature of the improvements on properties in the general vicinity of the property or property interest being valued and the character of the existing uses being made of such properties. **Leg.H.** Added Stats 1965 ch 1151 §4, operative January 1, 1967.

§822. Inadmissible evidence

(a) In an eminent domain or inverse condemnation proceeding, notwithstanding the provisions of Sections 814 to 821, inclusive, the following matter is inadmissible as evidence and shall not be taken into account as a basis for an opinion as to the value of property:

(1) The price or other terms and circumstances of an acquisition of property or a property interest if the acquisition was for a public use for which the property could have been taken by eminent domain.

The price or other terms and circumstances shall not be excluded pursuant to this paragraph if the proceeding relates to the valuation of all or part of a water system as defined in Section 240 of the Public Utilities Code.

(2) The price at which an offer or option to purchase or lease the property or property interest being valued or any other property was made, or the price at which the property or interest was optioned, offered, or listed for sale or lease, except that an option, offer, or listing may be introduced by a party as an admission of another party to the proceeding; but nothing in this subdivision permits an admission to be used as direct evidence upon any matter that may be shown only by opinion evidence under Section 813.

(3) The value of any property or property interest as assessed for taxation purposes or the amount of taxes which may be due on the property, but nothing in this subdivision prohibits the consideration of actual or estimated taxes for the purpose of determining the reasonable net rental value attributable to the property or property interest being valued.

(4) An opinion as to the value of any property or property interest other than that being valued.

(5) The influence upon the value of the property or property interest being valued of any noncompensable items of value, damage, or injury.

(6) The capitalized value of the income or rental from any property or property interest other than that being valued.

(b) In an action other than an eminent domain or inverse condemnation proceeding, the matters listed in subdivision (a) are not admissible as evidence, and may not be taken into account as a basis for an opinion as to the value of property, except to the extent permitted under the rules of law otherwise applicable. **Leg.H.** Added Stats 1965 ch 1151 §4, operative January 1, 1967. Amended Stats 1978 ch 294 §9; Stats 1980 ch 381 §5; Stats 1986 ch 1238 §2; Stats 1987 ch 1278 §1; Stats 2000 ch 948 §1 (AB 321).

§823. Property with no relevant market

Notwithstanding any other provision of this article, the value of property for which there is no relevant, comparable market may be determined by any method of valuation that is just and equitable. **Leg.H.** Added Stats 1980 ch 381 §6. Amended Stats 1992 ch 7 §4 (SB 821).

1992 Note: The changes made by this act shall apply to eminent domain actions or proceedings commenced on or after January 1, 1993. Stats 1992 ch 7 §7.

§824. Method for determining value of nonprofit, special use property; Application

(a) Notwithstanding any other provision of this article, a just and equitable method of determining the value of nonprofit, special use property, as defined by Section 1235.155 of the Code of Civil Procedure, for which there is no relevant, comparable market, is the cost of purchasing land and the reasonable cost of making it suitable for the conduct of the same nonprofit, special use, together with the cost of constructing similar improvements. The method for determining compensation for improvements shall be as set forth in subdivision (b).

(b) Notwithstanding any other provision of this article, a witness providing opinion testimony on the value of nonprofit, special use property, as defined by Section 1235.155 of the Code of Civil Procedure, for which there is no relevant, comparable market, shall base his or her opinion on the value of reproducing the improvements without taking into consideration any depreciation or obsolescence of the improvements.

(c) This section does not apply to actions or proceedings commenced by a public entity or public utility to acquire real property or any interest in real property for the use of water, sewer, electricity, telephone, natural gas, or flood control facilities or rights-of-way where those acquisitions neither require removal or destruction of existing improvements, nor render the property unfit for the owner's present or proposed use. **Leg.H.** Added Stats 1992 ch 7 §5 (SB 821).

1992 Note: The changes made by this act shall apply to eminent domain actions or proceedings commenced on or after January 1, 1993. Stats 1992 ch 7 §7.

ARTICLE 3
Opinion Testimony on Particular Subjects

Opinion as to sanity. §870.

§870. Opinion as to sanity

A witness may state his opinion as to the sanity of a person when:

(a) The witness is an intimate acquaintance of the person whose sanity is in question;

(b) The witness was a subscribing witness to a writing, the validity of which is in dispute, signed by the person whose sanity is in question and the opinion relates to the sanity of such person at the time the writing was signed; or

(c) The witness is qualified under Section 800 or 801 to testify in the form of an opinion. **Leg.H.** Enacted Stats 1965 ch 299 §2, operative January 1, 1967.

CHAPTER 2
BLOOD TESTS TO DETERMINE PATERNITY [REPEALED]

§890. [Section repealed 1994]

Leg.H. Enacted Stats 1965 ch 299 §2, operative January 1, 1967. Repealed Stats 1992 ch 162 §9 (AB 2650), operative January 1, 1994. See Fam C §7550.

§891. [Section repealed 1994]

Leg.H. Enacted Stats 1965 ch 299 §2, operative January 1, 1967. Repealed Stats 1992 ch 162 §9 (AB 2650), operative January 1, 1994. See Fam C §3.

§892. [Section repealed 1994]

Leg.H. Enacted Stats 1965 ch 299 §2, operative January 1, 1967. Amended Stats 1983 ch 253 §1. Repealed Stats 1992 ch 162 §9 (AB 2650), operative January 1, 1994. See Fam C §7551.

§893. [Section repealed 1994]

Leg.H. Enacted Stats 1965 ch 299 §2, operative January 1, 1967. Repealed Stats 1992 ch 162 §9 (AB 2650), operative January 1, 1994. See Fam C §7552.

§894. [Section repealed 1994]

Leg.H. Enacted Stats 1965 ch 299 §2, operative January 1, 1967. Repealed Stats 1992 ch 162 §9 (AB 2650), operative January 1, 1994. See Fam C §7553.

§895. [Section repealed 1994]

Leg.H. Enacted Stats 1965 ch 299 §2, operative January 1, 1967. Amended Stats 1981 ch 266 §1. Repealed Stats 1992 ch 162 §9 (AB 2650), operative January 1, 1994. See Fam C §7554.

§895.5. [Section repealed 1994]

Leg.H. Added Stats 1986 ch 629 §2. Repealed Stats 1992 ch 162 §9 (AB 2650), operative January 1, 1994 (ch 851 prevails). Amended Stats 1992 ch 851 §3 (SB 1530), effective September 22, 1992. Repealed Stats 1993 ch 219 §77 (AB 1500), effective January 1, 1994. See Fam C §7555.

§896. [Section repealed 1994]

Leg.H. Enacted Stats 1965 ch 299 §2, operative January 1, 1967. Repealed Stats 1992 ch 162 §9 (AB 2650), operative January 1, 1994. See Fam C §7556.

§897. [Section repealed 1994]

Leg.H. Enacted Stats 1965 ch 299 §2, operative January 1, 1967. Repealed Stats 1992 ch 162 §9 (AB 2650), operative January 1, 1994. See Fam C §7557.

DIVISION 8
PRIVILEGES

Chapter 1. Definitions.
Chapter 2. Applicability of Division.
Chapter 3. General Provisions Relating to Privileges.
Chapter 4. Particular Privileges.
Chapter 5. Immunity of Newsman from Citation for Contempt.

CHAPTER 1
DEFINITIONS

Application of definitions. §900.
"Proceeding". §901.
"Civil proceeding". §902.
"Criminal proceeding". §903.
"Presiding officer". §905.

§900. Application of definitions
Unless the provision or context otherwise requires, the definitions in this chapter govern the construction of this division. They do not govern the construction of any other division. **Leg.H.** Enacted Stats 1965 ch 299 §2, operative January 1, 1967.

§901. "Proceeding"
"Proceeding" means any action, hearing, investigation, inquest, or inquiry (whether conducted by a court, administrative agency, hearing officer, arbitrator, legislative body, or any other person authorized by law) in which, pursuant to law, testimony can be compelled to be given. **Leg.H.** Enacted Stats 1965 ch 299 §2, operative January 1, 1967.

§902. "Civil proceeding"
"Civil proceeding" means any proceeding except a criminal proceeding. **Leg.H.** Enacted Stats 1965 ch 299 §2, operative January 1, 1967.

§903. "Criminal proceeding"
"Criminal proceeding" means:
(a) A criminal action; and
(b) A proceeding pursuant to Article 3 (commencing with Section 3060) of Chapter 7 of Division 4 of Title 1 of the Government Code to determine whether a public officer should be removed from office for willful or corrupt misconduct in office. **Leg.H.** Enacted Stats 1965 ch 299 §2, operative January 1, 1967.

§905. "Presiding officer"
"Presiding officer" means the person authorized to rule on a claim of privilege in the proceeding in which the claim is made. **Leg.H.** Enacted Stats 1965 ch 299 §2, operative January 1, 1967.

CHAPTER 2
APPLICABILITY OF DIVISION

Applicability of division. §910.

§910. Applicability of division
Except as otherwise provided by statute, the provisions of this division apply in all proceedings. The provisions of any statute making rules of evidence inapplicable in particular proceedings, or limiting the applicability of rules of evidence in particular proceedings, do not make this division inapplicable to such proceedings. **Leg.H.** Enacted Stats 1965 ch 299 §2, operative January 1, 1967.

CHAPTER 3
GENERAL PROVISIONS RELATING TO PRIVILEGES

General rule as to privileges. §911.
Waiver of privilege. §912.
Comment on, and inferences from, exercise of privilege. §913.
Determination of claim of privilege; Limitation on punishment for contempt. §914.
Disclosure of privileged information in ruling on claim of privilege. §915.
Exclusion of privileged information where persons authorized to claim privilege are not present. §916.
Presumption that certain communications are confidential. §917.
Effect of error in overruling claim of privilege. §918.
Admissibility where disclosure erroneously compelled. §919.
No implied repeal. §920.

§911. General rule as to privileges
Except as otherwise provided by statute:
(a) No person has a privilege to refuse to be a witness.
(b) No person has a privilege to refuse to disclose any matter or to refuse to produce any writing, object, or other thing.
(c) No person has a privilege that another shall not be a witness or shall not disclose any matter or shall not produce any writing, object, or other thing. **Leg.H.** Enacted Stats 1965 ch 299 §2, operative January 1, 1967.

§912. Waiver of privilege
(a) Except as otherwise provided in this section, the right of any person to claim a privilege provided by Section 954 (lawyer-client privilege), 966 (lawyer referral service-client privilege), 980 (privilege for confidential marital communications), 994 (physician-patient privilege), 1014 (psychotherapist-patient privilege), 1033 (privilege of penitent), 1034 (privilege of clergy member), 1035.8 (sexual assault counselor-victim privilege), 1037.5 (domestic violence counselor-victim privilege), or 1038 (human trafficking caseworker-victim privilege) is waived with respect to a communication protected by the privilege if any holder of the privilege, without coercion, has disclosed a significant part of the communication or has consented to disclosure made by anyone. Consent to disclosure is manifested by any statement or other conduct of the holder of the privilege indicating consent to the disclosure, including failure to claim the privilege in any proceeding in which the holder has legal standing and the opportunity to claim the privilege.
(b) Where two or more persons are joint holders of a privilege provided by Section 954 (lawyer-client privilege), 966 (lawyer referral service-client privilege), 994 (physician-patient privilege), 1014 (psychotherapist-patient privilege), 1035.8 (sexual assault counselor-victim privilege), 1037.5 (domestic violence counselor-victim privilege), or 1038 (human trafficking caseworker-victim privilege), a waiver of the right of a particular joint holder of the privilege to claim the privilege does not affect the right of another joint holder to claim the privilege. In the case of the privilege provided by Section 980 (privilege for confidential marital communications), a waiver of the right of one spouse to claim the privilege does not affect the right of the other spouse to claim the privilege.
(c) A disclosure that is itself privileged is not a waiver of any privilege.
(d) A disclosure in confidence of a communication that is protected by a privilege provided by Section 954 (lawyer-client privilege), 966 (lawyer referral service-client privilege), 994 (physician-patient privilege), 1014 (psychotherapist-patient privilege), 1035.8 (sexual assault counselor-victim privilege), 1037.5 (domestic violence counselor-victim privilege), or 1038 (human trafficking caseworker-victim privilege), when disclosure is reasonably necessary for the accomplishment of the purpose for which the lawyer, lawyer referral service, physician, psychotherapist, sexual assault counselor, domestic violence counselor, or human trafficking caseworker was consulted, is not a waiver of the privilege. **Leg.H.** Enacted Stats 1965 ch 299 §2, operative January 1, 1967. Amended Stats 1980 ch 917 §1; Stats 2002 ch 72 §1 (SB 2061); Stats 2004 ch 405 §1 (SB 1796); Stats 2013 ch 123 §1 (AB 267), effective January 1, 2014; Stats 2014 ch 913 §13 (AB 2747), effective January 1, 2015.

§913. Comment on, and inferences from, exercise of privilege
(a) If in the instant proceeding or on a prior occasion a privilege is or was exercised not to testify with respect to any matter, or to refuse to disclose or to prevent another from disclosing any matter, neither the presiding officer nor counsel may comment thereon, no presumption shall arise because of the exercise of the privilege, and the trier of fact may not draw any inference therefrom as to the credibility of the witness or as to any matter at issue in the proceeding.
(b) The court, at the request of a party who may be adversely affected because an unfavorable inference may be drawn by the jury because a privilege has been exercised, shall instruct the jury that no presumption arises because of the exercise of the privilege and that the jury may not draw any inference therefrom as to the credibility of the witness or as to

any matter at issue in the proceeding. **Leg.H.** Enacted Stats 1965 ch 299 §2, operative January 1, 1967.

§914. Determination of claim of privilege; Limitation on punishment for contempt

(a) The presiding officer shall determine a claim of privilege in any proceeding in the same manner as a court determines such a claim under Article 2 (commencing with Section 400) of Chapter 4 of Division 3.

(b) No person may be held in contempt for failure to disclose information claimed to be privileged unless he has failed to comply with an order of a court that he disclose such information. This subdivision does not apply to any governmental agency that has constitutional contempt power, nor does it apply to hearings and investigations of the Industrial Accident Commission, nor does it impliedly repeal Chapter 4 (commencing with Section 9400) of Part 1 of Division 2 of Title 2 of the Government Code. If no other statutory procedure is applicable, the procedure prescribed by Section 1991 of the Code of Civil Procedure shall be followed in seeking an order of a court that the person disclose the information claimed to be privileged. **Leg.H.** Enacted Stats 1965 ch 299 §2, operative January 1, 1967.

§915. Disclosure of privileged information in ruling on claim of privilege

(a) Subject to subdivision (b), the presiding officer may not require disclosure of information claimed to be privileged under this division or attorney work product under subdivision (a) of Section 2018.030 of the Code of Civil Procedure in order to rule on the claim of privilege; provided, however, that in any hearing conducted pursuant to subdivision (c) of Section 1524 of the Penal Code in which a claim of privilege is made and the court determines that there is no other feasible means to rule on the validity of the claim other than to require disclosure, the court shall proceed in accordance with subdivision (b).

(b) When a court is ruling on a claim of privilege under Article 9 (commencing with Section 1040) of Chapter 4 (official information and identity of informer) or under Section 1060 (trade secret) or under subdivision (b) of Section 2018.030 of the Code of Civil Procedure (attorney work product) and is unable to do so without requiring disclosure of the information claimed to be privileged, the court may require the person from whom disclosure is sought or the person authorized to claim the privilege, or both, to disclose the information in chambers out of the presence and hearing of all persons except the person authorized to claim the privilege and any other persons as the person authorized to claim the privilege is willing to have present. If the judge determines that the information is privileged, neither the judge nor any other person may ever disclose, without the consent of a person authorized to permit disclosure, what was disclosed in the course of the proceedings in chambers. **Leg.H.** Enacted Stats 1965 ch 299 §2, operative January 1, 1967. Amended Stats 1979 ch 1034 §1; Stats 2001 ch 812 §13 (AB 223); Stats 2004 ch 182 §29 (AB 3081), operative July 1, 2005.

§916. Exclusion of privileged information where persons authorized to claim privilege are not present

(a) The presiding officer, on his own motion or on the motion of any party, shall exclude information that is subject to a claim of privilege under this division if:

(1) The person from whom the information is sought is not a person authorized to claim the privilege; and

(2) There is no party to the proceeding who is a person authorized to claim the privilege.

(b) The presiding officer may not exclude information under this section if:

(1) He is otherwise instructed by a person authorized to permit disclosure; or

(2) The proponent of the evidence establishes that there is no person authorized to claim the privilege in existence. **Leg.H.** Enacted Stats 1965 ch 299 §2, operative January 1, 1967.

§917. Presumption that certain communications are confidential

(a) If a privilege is claimed on the ground that the matter sought to be disclosed is a communication made in confidence in the course of the lawyer-client, lawyer referral service-client, physician-patient, psychotherapist-patient, clergy-penitent, marital or domestic partnership, sexual assault counselor-victim, domestic violence counselor-victim, or human trafficking caseworker-victim relationship, the communication is presumed to have been made in confidence and the opponent of the claim of privilege has the burden of proof to establish that the communication was not confidential.

(b) A communication between persons in a relationship listed in subdivision (a) does not lose its privileged character for the sole reason that it is communicated by electronic means or because persons involved in the delivery, facilitation, or storage of electronic communication may have access to the content of the communication.

(c) For purposes of this section, "electronic" has the same meaning provided in Section 1633.2 of the Civil Code. **Leg.H.** Enacted Stats 1965 ch 299 §2, operative January 1, 1967. Amended Stats 2002 ch 72 §2 (SB 2061); Stats 2003 ch 468 §2 (SB 851); Stats 2004 ch 183 §93 (AB 3082); Stats 2006 ch 689 §2 (SB 1743), effective January 1, 2007; Stats 2014 ch 913 §14 (AB 2747), effective January 1, 2015; Stats 2016 ch 50 §33 (SB 1005), effective January 1, 2017.

2016 Note: For legislative intent, see the 2016 Note following Ev C §215.

§918. Effect of error in overruling claim of privilege

A party may predicate error on a ruling disallowing a claim of privilege only if he is the holder of the privilege, except that a party may predicate error on a ruling disallowing a claim of privilege by his spouse under Section 970 or 971. **Leg.H.** Enacted Stats 1965 ch 299 §2, operative January 1, 1967.

§919. Admissibility where disclosure erroneously compelled

(a) Evidence of a statement or other disclosure of privileged information is inadmissible against a holder of the privilege if:

(1) A person authorized to claim the privilege claimed it but nevertheless disclosure erroneously was required to be made; or

(2) The presiding officer did not exclude the privileged information as required by Section 916.

(b) If a person authorized to claim the privilege claimed it, whether in the same or a prior proceeding, but nevertheless disclosure erroneously was required by the presiding officer to be made, neither the failure to refuse to disclose nor the failure to seek review of the order of the presiding officer requiring disclosure indicates consent to the disclosure or constitutes a waiver and, under these circumstances, the disclosure is one made under coercion. **Leg.H.** Enacted Stats 1965 ch 299 §2, operative January 1, 1967. Amended Stats 1974 ch 227 §1.

§920. No implied repeal

Nothing in this division shall be construed to repeal by implication any other statute relating to privileges. **Leg.H.** Enacted Stats 1965 ch 299 §2, operative January 1, 1967.

CHAPTER 4
PARTICULAR PRIVILEGES

Article 1. Privilege of Defendant in Criminal Case.
Article 2. Privilege Against Self-Incrimination.
Article 3. Lawyer-Client Privilege.
Article 3.5. Lawyer Referral Service-Client Privilege.
Article 4. Privilege Not to Testify Against Spouse.
Article 5. Privilege for Confidential Marital Communications.
Article 6. Physician-Patient Privilege.
Article 7. Psychotherapist-Patient Privilege.
Article 8. Clergy Penitent Privileges.
Article 8.5. Sexual Assault Counselor-Victim Privilege.
Article 8.7. Domestic Violence Counselor-Victim Privilege.
Article 8.8. Human Trafficking Caseworker-Victim Privilege.
Article 9. Official Information and Identity of Informer.
Article 10. Political Vote.
Article 11. Trade Secret.

ARTICLE 1
Privilege of Defendant in Criminal Case

Privilege not to be called as a witness and not to testify. §930.

§930. Privilege not to be called as a witness and not to testify

To the extent that such privilege exists under the Constitution of the United States or the State of California, a defendant in a criminal case has a privilege not to be called as a witness and not to testify. **Leg.H.** Enacted Stats 1965 ch 299 §2, operative January 1, 1967.

ARTICLE 2
Privilege Against Self-Incrimination

Privilege against self-incrimination. §940.

§940. Privilege against self-incrimination

To the extent that such privilege exists under the Constitution of the United States or the State of California, a person has a privilege to refuse to disclose any matter that may tend to incriminate him. **Leg.H.** Enacted Stats 1965 ch 299 §2, operative January 1, 1967.

ARTICLE 3
Lawyer-Client Privilege

"Lawyer". §950.
"Client". §951.
"Confidential communication between client and lawyer". §952.
"Holder of the privilege". §953.
Lawyer-client privilege. §954.
When lawyer required to claim privilege. §955.
Crime or fraud. §956.
Disclosure necessary to prevent criminal act likely to result in death or bodily harm. §956.5.
Parties claiming through deceased client. §957.
Breach of duty arising out of lawyer-client relationship. §958.
Lawyer as attesting witness. §959.
Intention of deceased client concerning writing affecting property interest. §960.
Validity of writing affecting property interest. §961.
Joint clients. §962.

§950. "Lawyer"

As used in this article, "lawyer" means a person authorized, or reasonably believed by the client to be authorized, to practice law in any state or nation. **Leg.H.** Enacted Stats 1965 ch 299 §2, operative January 1, 1967.

§951. "Client"

As used in this article, "client" means a person who, directly or through an authorized representative, consults a lawyer for the purpose of retaining the lawyer or securing legal service or advice from him in his professional capacity, and includes an incompetent (a) who himself so consults the lawyer or (b) whose guardian or conservator so consults the lawyer in behalf of the incompetent. **Leg.H.** Enacted Stats 1965 ch 299 §2, operative January 1, 1967.

§952. "Confidential communication between client and lawyer"

As used in this article, "confidential communication between client and lawyer" means information transmitted between a client and his or her lawyer in the course of that relationship and in confidence by a means which, so far as the client is aware, discloses the information to no third persons other than those who are present to further the interest of the client in the consultation or those to whom disclosure is reasonably necessary for the transmission of the information or the accomplishment of the purpose for which the lawyer is consulted, and includes a legal opinion formed and the advice given by the lawyer in the course of that relationship. **Leg.H.** Enacted Stats 1965 ch 299 §2, operative January 1, 1967. Amended Stats 1967 ch 650 §3; Stats 1994 ch 186 §1 (AB 2662), ch 587 §9 (AB 3600); Stats 2002 ch 72 §3 (SB 2061).

§953. "Holder of the privilege"

As used in this article, "holder of the privilege" means:
(a) The client, if the client has no guardian or conservator.
(b)(1) A guardian or conservator of the client, if the client has a guardian or conservator, except as provided in paragraph (2).
(2) If the guardian or conservator has an actual or apparent conflict of interest with the client, then the guardian or conservator does not hold the privilege.
(c) The personal representative of the client if the client is dead, including a personal representative appointed pursuant to Section 12252 of the Probate Code.
(d) A successor, assign, trustee in dissolution, or any similar representative of a firm, association, organization, partnership, business trust, corporation, or public entity that is no longer in existence. **Leg.H.** Enacted Stats 1965 ch 299 §2, operative January 1, 1967. Amended Stats 2009 ch 8 §1 (AB 1163), effective January 1, 2010; Stats 2018 ch 475 §1 (AB 1290), effective January 1, 2019.

§954. Lawyer-client privilege

Subject to Section 912 and except as otherwise provided in this article, the client, whether or not a party, has a privilege to refuse to disclose, and to prevent another from disclosing, a confidential communication between client and lawyer if the privilege is claimed by:
(a) The holder of the privilege;
(b) A person who is authorized to claim the privilege by the holder of the privilege; or
(c) The person who was the lawyer at the time of the confidential communication, but such person may not claim the privilege if there is no holder of the privilege in existence or if he is otherwise instructed by a person authorized to permit disclosure.

The relationship of attorney and client shall exist between a law corporation as defined in Article 10 (commencing with Section 6160) of Chapter 4 of Division 3 of the Business and Professions Code and the persons to whom it renders professional services, as well as between such persons and members of the State Bar employed by such corporation to render services to such persons. The word "persons" as used in this subdivision includes partnerships, corporations, limited liability companies, associations and other groups and entities. **Leg.H.** Enacted Stats 1965 ch 299 §2, operative January 1, 1967. Amended Stats 1968 ch 1375 §2; Stats 1994 ch 1010 §104 (SB 2053), effective January 1, 1995.

§955. When lawyer required to claim privilege

The lawyer who received or made a communication subject to the privilege under this article shall claim the privilege whenever he is present when the communication is sought to be disclosed and is authorized to claim the privilege under subdivision (c) of Section 954. **Leg.H.** Enacted Stats 1965 ch 299 §2, operative January 1, 1967.

§956. Crime or fraud

(a) There is no privilege under this article if the services of the lawyer were sought or obtained to enable or aid anyone to commit or plan to commit a crime or a fraud.
(b) This exception to the privilege granted by this article shall not apply to legal services rendered in compliance with state and local laws on medicinal cannabis or adult-use cannabis, and confidential communications provided for the purpose of rendering those services are confidential communications between client and lawyer, as defined in Section 952, provided the lawyer also advises the client on conflicts with respect to federal law. **Leg.H.** Enacted Stats 1965 ch 299 §2, operative January 1, 1967. Amended Stats 2017 ch 530 §2 (AB 1159), effective January 1, 2018.

§956.5. Disclosure necessary to prevent criminal act likely to result in death or bodily harm

There is no privilege under this article if the lawyer reasonably believes that disclosure of any confidential communication relating to representation of a client is necessary to prevent a criminal act that the lawyer reasonably believes is likely to result in the death of, or substantial bodily harm to, an individual. **Leg.H.** Added Stats 1993 ch 982 §8 (SB 645). Amended Stats 2003 ch 765 §2 (AB 1101), operative July 1, 2004; Stats 2004 ch 183 §94 (AB 3082).

§957. Parties claiming through deceased client

There is no privilege under this article as to a communication relevant to an issue between parties all of whom claim through a deceased client, regardless of whether the claims are by testate or intestate succession, nonprobate transfer, or inter vivos transaction. **Leg.H.** Enacted Stats 1965 ch 299 §2, operative January 1, 1967. Amended Stats 2009 ch 8 §2 (AB 1163), effective January 1, 2010.

§958. Breach of duty arising out of lawyer-client relationship

There is no privilege under this article as to a communication relevant to an issue of breach, by the lawyer or by the client, of a duty arising out of the lawyer-client relationship. **Leg.H.** Enacted Stats 1965 ch 299 §2, operative January 1, 1967.

§959. Lawyer as attesting witness

There is no privilege under this article as to a communication relevant to an issue concerning the intention or competence of a client executing an attested document of which the lawyer is an attesting witness, or concerning the execution or attestation of such a document. **Leg.H.** Enacted Stats 1965 ch 299 §2, operative January 1, 1967.

§960. Intention of deceased client concerning writing affecting property interest

There is no privilege under this article as to a communication relevant to an issue concerning the intention of a client, now deceased, with respect to a deed of conveyance, will, or other writing, executed by the client, purporting to affect an interest in property. **Leg.H.** Enacted Stats 1965 ch 299 §2, operative January 1, 1967.

§961. Validity of writing affecting property interest
There is no privilege under this article as to a communication relevant to an issue concerning the validity of a deed of conveyance, will, or other writing, executed by a client, now deceased, purporting to affect an interest in property. **Leg.H.** Enacted Stats 1965 ch 299 §2, operative January 1, 1967.

§962. Joint clients
Where two or more clients have retained or consulted a lawyer upon a matter of common interest, none of them, nor the successor in interest of any of them, may claim a privilege under this article as to a communication made in the course of that relationship when such communication is offered in a civil proceeding between one of such clients (or his successor in interest) and another of such clients (or his successor in interest). **Leg.H.** Enacted Stats 1965 ch 299 §2, operative January 1, 1967.

ARTICLE 3.5
Lawyer Referral Service-Client Privilege

Definitions. §965.
Privilege for confidential communication between client and lawyer referral service; Who may claim privilege. §966.
When lawyer referral service must claim privilege. §967.
Crime or fraud; Disclosure necessary to prevent criminal act likely to result in death or bodily harm. §968.

§965. Definitions
For purposes of this article, the following terms have the following meanings:

(a) "Client" means a person who, directly or through an authorized representative, consults a lawyer referral service for the purpose of retaining, or securing legal services or advice from, a lawyer in his or her professional capacity, and includes an incompetent who consults the lawyer referral service himself or herself or whose guardian or conservator consults the lawyer referral service on his or her behalf.

(b) "Confidential communication between client and lawyer referral service" means information transmitted between a client and a lawyer referral service in the course of that relationship and in confidence by a means that, so far as the client is aware, does not disclose the information to third persons other than those who are present to further the interests of the client in the consultation or those to whom disclosure is reasonably necessary for the transmission of the information or the accomplishment of the purpose for which the lawyer referral service is consulted.

(c) "Holder of the privilege" means any of the following:

(1) The client, if the client has no guardian or conservator.

(2) A guardian or conservator of the client, if the client has a guardian or conservator.

(3) The personal representative of the client if the client is dead, including a personal representative appointed pursuant to Section 12252 of the Probate Code.

(4) A successor, assign, trustee in dissolution, or any similar representative of a firm, association, organization, partnership, business trust, corporation, or public entity that is no longer in existence.

(d) "Lawyer referral service" means a lawyer referral service certified under, and operating in compliance with, Section 6155 of the Business and Professions Code or an enterprise reasonably believed by the client to be a lawyer referral service certified under, and operating in compliance with, Section 6155 of the Business and Professions Code. **Leg.H.** Added Stats 2013 ch 123 §2 (AB 267), effective January 1, 2014.

§966. Privilege for confidential communication between client and lawyer referral service; Who may claim privilege
(a) Subject to Section 912 and except as otherwise provided in this article, the client, whether or not a party, has a privilege to refuse to disclose, and to prevent another from disclosing, a confidential communication between client and lawyer referral service if the privilege is claimed by any of the following:

(1) The holder of the privilege.

(2) A person who is authorized to claim the privilege by the holder of the privilege.

(3) The lawyer referral service or a staff person thereof, but the lawyer referral service or a staff person thereof may not claim the privilege if there is no holder of the privilege in existence or if the lawyer referral service or a staff person thereof is otherwise instructed by a person authorized to permit disclosure.

(b) The relationship of lawyer referral service and client shall exist between a lawyer referral service, as defined in Section 965, and the persons to whom it renders services, as well as between such persons and anyone employed by the lawyer referral service to render services to such persons. The word "persons" as used in this subdivision includes partnerships, corporations, limited liability companies, associations, and other groups and entities. **Leg.H.** Added Stats 2013 ch 123 §2 (AB 267), effective January 1, 2014.

§967. When lawyer referral service must claim privilege
A lawyer referral service that has received or made a communication subject to the privilege under this article shall claim the privilege if the communication is sought to be disclosed and the client has not consented to the disclosure. **Leg.H.** Added Stats 2013 ch 123 §2 (AB 267), effective January 1, 2014.

§968. Crime or fraud; Disclosure necessary to prevent criminal act likely to result in death or bodily harm
There is no privilege under this article if either of the following applies:

(a) The services of the lawyer referral service were sought or obtained to enable or aid anyone to commit or plan to commit a crime or a fraud.

(b) A staff person of the lawyer referral service who receives a confidential communication in processing a request for legal assistance reasonably believes that disclosure of the confidential communication is necessary to prevent a criminal act that the staff person of the lawyer referral service reasonably believes is likely to result in the death of, or substantial bodily harm to, an individual. **Leg.H.** Added Stats 2013 ch 123 §2 (AB 267), effective January 1, 2014.

ARTICLE 4
Privilege Not to Testify Against Spouse

Privilege not to testify against spouse. §970.
Privilege not to be called as a witness against spouse. §971.
When privilege not applicable. §972.
Waiver of privilege. §973.

§970. Privilege not to testify against spouse
Except as otherwise provided by statute, a married person has a privilege not to testify against his spouse in any proceeding. **Leg.H.** Enacted Stats 1965 ch 299 §2, operative January 1, 1967.

§971. Privilege not to be called as a witness against spouse
Except as otherwise provided by statute, a married person whose spouse is a party to a proceeding has a privilege not to be called as a witness by an adverse party to that proceeding without the prior express consent of the spouse having the privilege under this section unless the party calling the spouse does so in good faith without knowledge of the marital relationship. **Leg.H.** Enacted Stats 1965 ch 299 §2, operative January 1, 1967.

§972. When privilege not applicable
A married person does not have a privilege under this article in:

(a) A proceeding brought by or on behalf of one spouse against the other spouse.

(b) A proceeding to commit or otherwise place his or her spouse or his or her spouse's property, or both, under the control of another because of the spouse's alleged mental or physical condition.

(c) A proceeding brought by or on behalf of a spouse to establish his or her competence.

(d) A proceeding under the Juvenile Court Law, Chapter 2 (commencing with Section 200) of Part 1 of Division 2 of the Welfare and Institutions Code.

(e) A criminal proceeding in which one spouse is charged with:

(1) A crime against the person or property of the other spouse or of a child, parent, relative, or cohabitant of either, whether committed before or during marriage.

(2) A crime against the person or property of a third person committed in the course of committing a crime against the person or property of the other spouse, whether committed before or during marriage.

(3) Bigamy.

(4) A crime defined by Section 270 or 270a of the Penal Code.

(f) A proceeding resulting from a criminal act which occurred prior to legal marriage of the spouses to each other regarding knowledge acquired prior to that marriage if prior to the legal marriage the witness spouse was aware that his or her spouse had been arrested for or had been formally charged with the crime or crimes about which the spouse is called to testify.

(g) A proceeding brought against the spouse by a former spouse so long as the property and debts of the marriage have not been adjudicated, or in order to establish, modify, or enforce a child, family or spousal support obligation arising from the marriage to the former spouse; in a proceeding brought against a spouse by the other parent in order to establish, modify, or enforce a child support obligation for a child of a nonmarital relationship of the spouse; or in a proceeding brought against a spouse by the guardian of a child of that spouse in order to establish, modify, or enforce a child support obligation of the spouse. The married person does not have a privilege under this subdivision to refuse to provide information relating to the issues of income, expenses, assets, debts, and employment of either spouse, but may assert the privilege as otherwise provided in this article if other information is requested by the former spouse, guardian, or other parent of the child.

Any person demanding the otherwise privileged information made available by this subdivision, who also has an obligation to support the child for whom an order to establish, modify, or enforce child support is sought, waives his or her marital privilege to the same extent as the spouse as provided in this subdivision. **Leg.H.** Enacted Stats 1965 ch 299 §2, operative January 1, 1967. Amended Stats 1975 ch 71 §2; Stats 1982 ch 256 §1; Stats 1983 ch 244 §1; Stats 1986 ch 769 §1, effective September 15, 1986; Stats 1989 ch 1359 §9.7.

§973. Waiver of privilege

(a) Unless erroneously compelled to do so, a married person who testifies in a proceeding to which his spouse is a party, or who testifies against his spouse in any proceeding, does not have a privilege under this article in the proceeding in which such testimony is given.

(b) There is no privilege under this article in a civil proceeding brought or defended by a married person for the immediate benefit of his spouse or of himself and his spouse. **Leg.H.** Enacted Stats 1965 ch 299 §2, operative January 1, 1967.

ARTICLE 5
Privilege for Confidential Marital Communications

Privilege for confidential marital communications. §980.
Crime or fraud. §981.
Commitment or similar proceeding. §982.
Proceeding to establish competence. §983.
Proceeding between spouses. §984.
Certain criminal proceedings. §985.
Juvenile court proceedings. §986.
Communication offered by spouse who is criminal defendant. §987.

§980. Privilege for confidential marital communications

Subject to Section 912 and except as otherwise provided in this article, a spouse (or his or her guardian or conservator when he or she has a guardian or conservator), whether or not a party, has a privilege during the marital or domestic partnership relationship and afterwards to refuse to disclose, and to prevent another from disclosing, a communication if he or she claims the privilege and the communication was made in confidence between him or her and the other spouse while they were spouses. **Leg.H.** Enacted Stats 1965 ch 299 §2, operative January 1, 1967. Amended Stats 2016 ch 50 §34 (SB 1005), effective January 1, 2017; Stats 2016 ch 86 §125 (SB 1171), effective January 1, 2017 (ch 50 prevails; ch 86 not effective).

2016 Note: For legislative intent, see the 2016 Note following Ev C §215.

§981. Crime or fraud

There is no privilege under this article if the communication was made, in whole or in part, to enable or aid anyone to commit or plan to commit a crime or a fraud. **Leg.H.** Enacted Stats 1965 ch 299 §2, operative January 1, 1967.

§982. Commitment or similar proceeding

There is no privilege under this article in a proceeding to commit either spouse or otherwise place him or his property, or both, under the control of another because of his alleged mental or physical condition. **Leg.H.** Enacted Stats 1965 ch 299 §2, operative January 1, 1967.

§983. Proceeding to establish competence

There is no privilege under this article in a proceeding brought by or on behalf of either spouse to establish his competence. **Leg.H.** Enacted Stats 1965 ch 299 §2, operative January 1, 1967.

§984. Proceeding between spouses

There is no privilege under this article in:

(a) A proceeding brought by or on behalf of one spouse against the other spouse.

(b) A proceeding between a surviving spouse and a person who claims through the deceased spouse, regardless of whether such claim is by testate or intestate succession or by inter vivos transaction. **Leg.H.** Enacted Stats 1965 ch 299 §2, operative January 1, 1967.

§985. Certain criminal proceedings

There is no privilege under this article in a criminal proceeding in which one spouse is charged with:

(a) A crime committed at any time against the person or property of the other spouse or of a child of either.

(b) A crime committed at any time against the person or property of a third person committed in the course of committing a crime against the person or property of the other spouse.

(c) Bigamy.

(d) A crime defined by Section 270 or 270a of the Penal Code. **Leg.H.** Enacted Stats 1965 ch 299 §2, operative January 1, 1967. Amended Stats 1975 ch 71 §3.

§986. Juvenile court proceedings

There is no privilege under this article in a proceeding under the Juvenile Court Law, Chapter 2 (commencing with Section 200) of Part 1 of Division 2 of the Welfare and Institutions Code. **Leg.H.** Enacted Stats 1965 ch 299 §2, operative January 1, 1967. Amended Stats 1982 ch 256 §2.

§987. Communication offered by spouse who is criminal defendant

There is no privilege under this article in a criminal proceeding in which the communication is offered in evidence by a defendant who is one of the spouses between whom the communication was made. **Leg.H.** Enacted Stats 1965 ch 299 §2, operative January 1, 1967.

ARTICLE 6
Physician-Patient Privilege

"Physician". §990.
"Patient". §991.
"Confidential communication between patient and physician". §992.
"Holder of the privilege". §993.
Physician-patient privilege. §994.
When physician required to claim privilege. §995.
Patient-litigant exception. §996.
Crime or tort. §997.
Criminal proceeding. §998.
Proceeding to recover damages on account of conduct of patient. §999.
Parties claiming through deceased patient. §1000.
Breach of duty arising out of physician-patient relationship. §1001.
Intention of deceased patient concerning writing affecting property interest. §1002.
Validity of writing affecting property interest. §1003.
Commitment or similar proceeding. §1004.
Proceeding to establish competence. §1005.
Required report. §1006.
Proceeding to terminate right, license, or privilege. §1007.

§990. "Physician"

As used in this article, "physician" means a person authorized, or reasonably believed by the patient to be authorized, to practice medicine in any state or nation. **Leg.H.** Enacted Stats 1965 ch 299 §2, operative January 1, 1967.

§991. "Patient"

As used in this article, "patient" means a person who consults a physician or submits to an examination by a physician for the purpose of securing a diagnosis or preventive, palliative, or curative treatment of his physical or mental or emotional condition. **Leg.H.** Enacted Stats 1965 ch 299 §2, operative January 1, 1967.

§992. "Confidential communication between patient and physician"

As used in this article, "confidential communication between patient and physician" means information, including information obtained by an examination of the patient, transmitted between a patient and his physician in the course of that relationship and in confidence by a means which, so far as the patient is aware, discloses the information to no third persons other than those who are present to further the interest of the patient in the consultation or those to whom disclosure is reasonably necessary for the transmission of the information or the accomplishment of the purpose for which the physician is consulted, and includes a diagnosis made and the advice given by the physician in the course of that relationship. **Leg.H.** Enacted Stats 1965 ch 299 §2, operative January 1, 1967. Amended Stats 1967 ch 650 §4.

§993. "Holder of the privilege"
As used in this article, "holder of the privilege" means:
(a) The patient when he has no guardian or conservator.
(b) A guardian or conservator of the patient when the patient has a guardian or conservator.
(c) The personal representative of the patient if the patient is dead.
Leg.H. Enacted Stats 1965 ch 299 §2, operative January 1, 1967.

§994. Physician-patient privilege
Subject to Section 912 and except as otherwise provided in this article, the patient, whether or not a party, has a privilege to refuse to disclose, and to prevent another from disclosing, a confidential communication between patient and physician if the privilege is claimed by:
(a) The holder of the privilege;
(b) A person who is authorized to claim the privilege by the holder of the privilege; or
(c) The person who was the physician at the time of the confidential communication, but such person may not claim the privilege if there is no holder of the privilege in existence or if he or she is otherwise instructed by a person authorized to permit disclosure.
The relationship of a physician and patient shall exist between a medical or podiatry corporation as defined in the Medical Practice Act and the patient to whom it renders professional services, as well as between such patients and licensed physicians and surgeons employed by such corporation to render services to such patients. The word "persons" as used in this subdivision includes partnerships, corporations, limited liability companies, associations, and other groups and entities. **Leg.H.** Enacted Stats 1965 ch 299 §2, operative January 1, 1967. Amended Stats 1968 ch 1375 §3; Stats 1980 ch 1313 §12; Stats 1994 ch 1010 §105 (SB 2053).

§995. When physician required to claim privilege
The physician who received or made a communication subject to the privilege under this article shall claim the privilege whenever he is present when the communication is sought to be disclosed and is authorized to claim the privilege under subdivision (c) of Section 994. **Leg.H.** Enacted Stats 1965 ch 299 §2, operative January 1, 1967.

§996. Patient-litigant exception
There is no privilege under this article as to a communication relevant to an issue concerning the condition of the patient if such issue has been tendered by:
(a) The patient;
(b) Any party claiming through or under the patient;
(c) Any party claiming as a beneficiary of the patient through a contract to which the patient is or was a party; or
(d) The plaintiff in an action brought under Section 376 or 377 of the Code of Civil Procedure for damages for the injury or death of the patient.
Leg.H. Enacted Stats 1965 ch 299 §2, operative January 1, 1967.

§997. Crime or tort
There is no privilege under this article if the services of the physician were sought or obtained to enable or aid anyone to commit or plan to commit a crime or a tort or to escape detection or apprehension after the commission of a crime or a tort. **Leg.H.** Enacted Stats 1965 ch 299 §2, operative January 1, 1967.

§998. Criminal proceeding
There is no privilege under this article in a criminal proceeding. **Leg.H.** Enacted Stats 1965 ch 299 §2, operative January 1, 1967.

§999. Proceeding to recover damages on account of conduct of patient
There is no privilege under this article as to a communication relevant to an issue concerning the condition of the patient in a proceeding to recover damages on account of the conduct of the patient if good cause for disclosure of the communication is shown. **Leg.H.** Enacted Stats 1965 ch 299 §2, operative January 1, 1967. Amended Stats 1975 ch 318 §1.

§1000. Parties claiming through deceased patient
There is no privilege under this article as to a communication relevant to an issue between parties all of whom claim through a deceased patient, regardless of whether the claims are by testate or intestate succession or by inter vivos transaction. **Leg.H.** Enacted Stats 1965 ch 299 §2, operative January 1, 1967.

§1001. Breach of duty arising out of physician-patient relationship
There is no privilege under this article as to a communication relevant to an issue of breach, by the physician or by the patient, of a duty arising out of the physician-patient relationship. **Leg.H.** Enacted Stats 1965 ch 299 §2, operative January 1, 1967.

§1002. Intention of deceased patient concerning writing affecting property interest
There is no privilege under this article as to a communication relevant to an issue concerning the intention of a patient, now deceased, with respect to a deed of conveyance, will, or other writing, executed by the patient, purporting to affect an interest in property. **Leg.H.** Enacted Stats 1965 ch 299 §2, operative January 1, 1967.

§1003. Validity of writing affecting property interest
There is no privilege under this article as to a communication relevant to an issue concerning the validity of a deed of conveyance, will, or other writing, executed by a patient, now deceased, purporting to affect an interest in property. **Leg.H.** Enacted Stats 1965 ch 299 §2, operative January 1, 1967.

§1004. Commitment or similar proceeding
There is no privilege under this article in a proceeding to commit the patient or otherwise place him or his property, or both, under the control of another because of his alleged mental or physical condition. **Leg.H.** Enacted Stats 1965 ch 299 §2, operative January 1, 1967.

§1005. Proceeding to establish competence
There is no privilege under this article in a proceeding brought by or on behalf of the patient to establish his competence. **Leg.H.** Enacted Stats 1965 ch 299 §2, operative January 1, 1967.

§1006. Required report
There is no privilege under this article as to information that the physician or the patient is required to report to a public employee, or as to information required to be recorded in a public office, if such report or record is open to public inspection. **Leg.H.** Enacted Stats 1965 ch 299 §2, operative January 1, 1967.

§1007. Proceeding to terminate right, license, or privilege
There is no privilege under this article in a proceeding brought by a public entity to determine whether a right, authority, license, or privilege (including the right or privilege to be employed by the public entity or to hold a public office) should be revoked, suspended, terminated, limited, or conditioned. **Leg.H.** Enacted Stats 1965 ch 299 §2, operative January 1, 1967.

ARTICLE 7
Psychotherapist-Patient Privilege

"Psychotherapist". §1010.
Communication between patient and educational psychologist. §1010.5.
"Patient". §1011.
"Confidential communication between patient and psychotherapist". §1012.
"Holder of the privilege". §1013.
Psychotherapist-patient privilege. §1014.
When psychotherapist required to claim privilege. §1015.
Patient-litigant exception. §1016.
Exception where psychotherapist is appointed by court or Board of Prison Terms. §1017.
Crime or tort. §1018.
Parties claiming through deceased patient. §1019.
Breach of duty arising out of psychotherapist-patient relationship. §1020.
Intention of deceased patient concerning writing affecting property interest. §1021.
Validity of writing affecting property interest. §1022.
Proceeding to determine sanity of criminal defendant. §1023.
Patient dangerous to self or others. §1024.
Proceeding to establish competence. §1025.
Required report. §1026.

Exception; Patient under 16 who is victim of crime. §1027.

§1010. "Psychotherapist"

As used in this article, "psychotherapist" means a person who is, or is reasonably believed by the patient to be:

(a) A person authorized to practice medicine in any state or nation who devotes, or is reasonably believed by the patient to devote, a substantial portion of their time to the practice of psychiatry.

(b) A person licensed as a psychologist under Chapter 6.6 (commencing with Section 2900) of Division 2 of the Business and Professions Code.

(c) A person licensed as a clinical social worker under Chapter 14 (commencing with Section 4991) of Division 2 of the Business and Professions Code, when they are engaged in applied psychotherapy of a nonmedical nature.

(d) A person who is serving as a school psychologist and holds a credential authorizing that service issued by the state.

(e) A person licensed as a marriage and family therapist under Chapter 13 (commencing with Section 4980) of Division 2 of the Business and Professions Code.

(f) A person registered as a registered psychological associate who is under the supervision of a licensed psychologist as required by Section 2913 of the Business and Professions Code, or a person registered as an associate marriage and family therapist who is under the supervision of a licensed marriage and family therapist, a licensed clinical social worker, a licensed professional clinical counselor, a licensed psychologist, or a licensed physician and surgeon certified in psychiatry, as specified in Section 4980.44 of the Business and Professions Code.

(g) A person registered as an associate clinical social worker who is under supervision as specified in Section 4996.23 of the Business and Professions Code.

(h) A psychological intern as defined in Section 2911 of the Business and Professions Code who is under the primary supervision of a licensed psychologist.

(i) A trainee, as defined in subdivision (c) of Section 4980.03 of the Business and Professions Code, who is fulfilling their supervised practicum required by subparagraph (B) of paragraph (1) of subdivision (d) of Section 4980.36 of, or subdivision (c) of Section 4980.37 of, the Business and Professions Code and is supervised by a licensed psychologist, a board certified psychiatrist, a licensed clinical social worker, a licensed marriage and family therapist, or a licensed professional clinical counselor.

(j) A person licensed as a registered nurse pursuant to Chapter 6 (commencing with Section 2700) of Division 2 of the Business and Professions Code, who possesses a master's degree in psychiatric-mental health nursing and is listed as a psychiatric-mental health nurse by the Board of Registered Nursing.

(k) An advanced practice registered nurse who is certified as a clinical nurse specialist pursuant to Article 9 (commencing with Section 2838) of Chapter 6 of Division 2 of the Business and Professions Code and who participates in expert clinical practice in the specialty of psychiatric-mental health nursing.

(l) A person rendering mental health treatment or counseling services as authorized pursuant to Section 6924 of the Family Code.

(m) A person licensed as a professional clinical counselor under Chapter 16 (commencing with Section 4999.10) of Division 2 of the Business and Professions Code.

(n) A person registered as an associate professional clinical counselor who is under the supervision of a licensed professional clinical counselor, a licensed marriage and family therapist, a licensed clinical social worker, a licensed psychologist, or a licensed physician and surgeon certified in psychiatry, as specified in Sections 4999.42 to 4999.48, inclusive, of the Business and Professions Code.

(o) A clinical counselor trainee, as defined in subdivision (g) of Section 4999.12 of the Business and Professions Code, who is fulfilling their supervised practicum required by paragraph (3) of subdivision (c) of Section 4999.32 of, or paragraph (3) of subdivision (c) of Section 4999.33 of, the Business and Professions Code, and is supervised by a licensed psychologist, a board-certified psychiatrist, a licensed clinical social worker, a licensed marriage and family therapist, or a licensed professional clinical counselor. **Leg.H.** Enacted Stats 1965 ch 299 §2, operative January 1, 1967. Amended Stats 1967 ch 1677 §3; Stats 1970 ch 1396 §1.5, ch 1397 §1.5; Stats 1972 ch 888 §1; 1974 ch 546 §6; Stats 1983 ch 928 §8; Stats 1987 ch 724 §1; Stats 1988 ch 488 §1; Stats 1989 ch 1104 §37; Stats 1990 ch 662 §1 (AB 3613); Stats 1992 ch 308 §2 (AB 3035); Stats 1994 ch 1270 §1 (AB 2659); Stats 2001 ch 142 §1 (SB 716), ch 420 §1 (AB 1253), effective October 2, 2001, inoperative January 1, 2002, ch 420 §1.5 (AB 1253), effective October 2, 2001, operative January 1, 2002; Stats 2009 ch 26 §21 (SB 33), effective January 1, 2010; Stats 2011 ch 381 §21 (SB 146), effective January 1, 2012; Stats 2015 ch 529 §4 (AB 1374), effective January 1, 2016; Stats 2016 ch 86 §126 (SB 1171), effective January 1, 2017; Stats 2017 ch 573 §75 (SB 800), effective January 1, 2018; Stats 2018 ch 389 §10 (AB 2296), effective January 1, 2019; Stats 2021 ch 647 §74 (SB 801), effective January 1, 2022.

§1010.5. Communication between patient and educational psychologist

A communication between a patient and an educational psychologist, licensed under Chapter 13.5 (commencing with Section 4989.10) of Division 2 of the Business and Professions Code, shall be privileged to the same extent, and subject to the same limitations, as a communication between a patient and a psychotherapist described in subdivisions (c), (d), and (e) of Section 1010. **Leg.H.** Added Stats 1985 ch 545 §1. Amended Stats 2020 ch 370 §113 (SB 1371), effective January 1, 2021.

§1011. "Patient"

As used in this article, "patient" means a person who consults a psychotherapist or submits to an examination by a psychotherapist for the purpose of securing a diagnosis or preventive, palliative, or curative treatment of his mental or emotional condition or who submits to an examination of his mental or emotional condition for the purpose of scientific research on mental or emotional problems. **Leg.H.** Enacted Stats 1965 ch 299 §2, operative January 1, 1967.

§1012. "Confidential communication between patient and psychotherapist"

As used in this article, "confidential communication between patient and psychotherapist" means information, including information obtained by an examination of the patient, transmitted between a patient and his psychotherapist in the course of that relationship and in confidence by a means which, so far as the patient is aware, discloses the information to no third persons other than those who are present to further the interest of the patient in the consultation, or those to whom disclosure is reasonably necessary for the transmission of the information or the accomplishment of the purpose for which the psychotherapist is consulted, and includes a diagnosis made and the advice given by the psychotherapist in the course of that relationship. **Leg.H.** Enacted Stats 1965 ch 299 §2, operative January 1, 1967. Amended Stats 1967 ch 650 §5; Stats 1970 ch 1396 §2, ch 1397 §2.

§1013. "Holder of the privilege"

As used in this article, "holder of the privilege" means:

(a) The patient when he has no guardian or conservator.

(b) A guardian or conservator of the patient when the patient has a guardian or conservator.

(c) The personal representative of the patient if the patient is dead.
Leg.H. Enacted Stats 1965 ch 299 §2, operative January 1, 1967.

§1014. Psychotherapist-patient privilege

Subject to Section 912 and except as otherwise provided in this article, the patient, whether or not a party, has a privilege to refuse to disclose, and to prevent another from disclosing, a confidential communication between patient and psychotherapist if the privilege is claimed by:

(a) The holder of the privilege.

(b) A person who is authorized to claim the privilege by the holder of the privilege.

(c) The person who was the psychotherapist at the time of the confidential communication, but the person may not claim the privilege if there is no holder of the privilege in existence or if he or she is otherwise instructed by a person authorized to permit disclosure.

The relationship of a psychotherapist and patient shall exist between a psychological corporation as defined in Article 9 (commencing with Section 2995) of Chapter 6.6 of Division 2 of the Business and Professions Code, a marriage and family therapist corporation as defined in Article 6 (commencing with Section 4987.5) of Chapter 13 of Division 2 of the Business and Professions Code, a licensed clinical social workers corporation as defined in Article 5 (commencing with Section 4998) of Chapter 14 of Division 2 of the Business and Professions Code, or a professional clinical counselor corporation as defined in Article 7 (commencing with Section 4999.123) of Chapter 16 of Division 2 of the Business and Professions Code, and the patient to whom it renders professional services, as well as between those patients and psychotherapists employed by those corporations to render services to those patients. The word "persons" as used in this subdivision includes partnerships, corporations, limited liability companies, associations, and other groups and entities. **Leg.H.** Enacted Stats 1965 ch 299 §2, operative January 1, 1967. Amended Stats 1969 ch 871 §1; Stats 1972 ch 1286 §6; Stats 1989 ch 1104 §38; Stats 1990 ch 605 §1 (SB 2245); Stats 1994 ch 1010 §106 (SB 2053); Stats 2002 ch 1013 §78 (SB 2026); Stats 2011 ch 381 §22 (SB 146), effective January 1, 2012.

§1014.5. [Section repealed 1995]

Leg.H. Added Stats 1979 ch 832 §2. Amended Stats 1994 ch 1269 §7.5 (AB 2208). Repealed Stats 1994 ch 1270 §2 (AB 2659), effective January 1, 1995. The repealed section related to privilege regarding mental health treatment of minors under former Civil Code §25.9.

§1015. When psychotherapist required to claim privilege

The psychotherapist who received or made a communication subject to the privilege under this article shall claim the privilege whenever he is present when the communication is sought to be disclosed and is authorized to claim the privilege under subdivision (c) of Section 1014. **Leg.H.** Enacted Stats 1965 ch 299 §2, operative January 1, 1967.

§1016. Patient-litigant exception

There is no privilege under this article as to a communication relevant to an issue concerning the mental or emotional condition of the patient if such issue has been tendered by:

(a) The patient;
(b) Any party claiming through or under the patient;
(c) Any party claiming as a beneficiary of the patient through a contract to which the patient is or was a party; or
(d) The plaintiff in an action brought under Section 376 or 377 of the Code of Civil Procedure for damages for the injury or death of the patient.
Leg.H. Enacted Stats 1965 ch 299 §2, operative January 1, 1967.

§1017. Exception where psychotherapist is appointed by court or Board of Prison Terms

(a) There is no privilege under this article if the psychotherapist is appointed by order of a court to examine the patient, but this exception does not apply where the psychotherapist is appointed by order of the court upon the request of the lawyer for the defendant in a criminal proceeding in order to provide the lawyer with information needed so that he or she may advise the defendant whether to enter or withdraw a plea based on insanity or to present a defense based on his or her mental or emotional condition.

(b) There is no privilege under this article if the psychotherapist is appointed by the Board of Prison Terms to examine a patient pursuant to the provisions of Article 4 (commencing with Section 2960) of Chapter 7 of Title 1 of Part 3 of the Penal Code. **Leg.H.** Enacted Stats 1965 ch 299 §2, operative January 1, 1967. Amended Stats 1967 ch 650 §6; Stats 1987 ch 687 §1.

§1018. Crime or tort

There is no privilege under this article if the services of the psychotherapist were sought or obtained to enable or aid anyone to commit or plan to commit a crime or a tort or to escape detection or apprehension after the commission of a crime or a tort. **Leg.H.** Enacted Stats 1965 ch 299 §2, operative January 1, 1967.

§1019. Parties claiming through deceased patient

There is no privilege under this article as to a communication relevant to an issue between parties all of whom claim through a deceased patient, regardless of whether the claims are by testate or intestate succession or by inter vivos transaction. **Leg.H.** Enacted Stats 1965 ch 299 §2, operative January 1, 1967.

§1020. Breach of duty arising out of psychotherapist-patient relationship

There is no privilege under this article as to a communication relevant to an issue of breach, by the psychotherapist or by the patient, of a duty arising out of the psychotherapist-patient relationship. **Leg.H.** Enacted Stats 1965 ch 299 §2, operative January 1, 1967.

§1021. Intention of deceased patient concerning writing affecting property interest

There is no privilege under this article as to a communication relevant to an issue concerning the intention of a patient, now deceased, with respect to a deed of conveyance, will, or other writing, executed by the patient, purporting to affect an interest in property. **Leg.H.** Enacted Stats 1965 ch 299 §2, operative January 1, 1967.

§1022. Validity of writing affecting property interest

There is no privilege under this article as to a communication relevant to an issue concerning the validity of a deed of conveyance, will, or other writing, executed by a patient, now deceased, purporting to affect an interest in property. **Leg.H.** Enacted Stats 1965 ch 299 §2, operative January 1, 1967.

§1023. Proceeding to determine sanity of criminal defendant

There is no privilege under this article in a proceeding under Chapter 6 (commencing with Section 1367) of Title 10 of Part 2 of the Penal Code initiated at the request of the defendant in a criminal action to determine his sanity. **Leg.H.** Enacted Stats 1965 ch 299 §2, operative January 1, 1967.

§1024. Patient dangerous to self or others

There is no privilege under this article if the psychotherapist has reasonable cause to believe that the patient is in such mental or emotional condition as to be dangerous to himself or to the person or property of another and that disclosure of the communication is necessary to prevent the threatened danger. **Leg.H.** Enacted Stats 1965 ch 299 §2, operative January 1, 1967.

§1025. Proceeding to establish competence

There is no privilege under this article in a proceeding brought by or on behalf of the patient to establish his competence. **Leg.H.** Enacted Stats 1965 ch 299 §2, operative January 1, 1967.

§1026. Required report

There is no privilege under this article as to information that the psychotherapist or the patient is required to report to a public employee or as to information required to be recorded in a public office, if such report or record is open to public inspection. **Leg.H.** Enacted Stats 1965 ch 299 §2, operative January 1, 1967.

§1027. Exception; Patient under 16 who is victim of crime

There is no privilege under this article if all of the following circumstances exist:

(a) The patient is a child under the age of 16.
(b) The psychotherapist has reasonable cause to believe that the patient has been the victim of a crime and that disclosure of the communication is in the best interest of the child. **Leg.H.** Added Stats 1970 ch 1397 §3.

Prior Law: There was another section of this number, identical to the present section, which was added Stats 1970 ch 1396 §3 and repealed Stats 1990 ch 216 §23.

§1028. [Section repealed 1986]

Leg.H. Added Stats 1970 ch 1396 §4, ch 1397 §4. Repealed Stats 1985 ch 1077 §§1, 2, effective January 1, 1986. The repealed section related to the restriction on a psychotherapist's privilege in criminal proceedings.

ARTICLE 8
Clergy Penitent Privileges

"Member of the clergy". §1030.
"Penitent". §1031.
"Penitential communication". §1032.
Privilege of penitent. §1033.
Privilege of clergy member. §1034.

§1030. "Member of the clergy"

As used in this article, a "member of the clergy" means a priest, minister, religious practitioner, or similar functionary of a church or of a religious denomination or religious organization. **Leg.H.** Enacted Stats 1965 ch 299 §2, operative January 1, 1967. Amended Stats 2002 ch 806 §19 (AB 3027).

§1031. "Penitent"

As used in this article, "penitent" means a person who has made a penitential communication to a member of the clergy. **Leg.H.** Enacted

Stats 1965 ch 299 §2, operative January 1, 1967. Amended Stats 2002 ch 806 §20 (AB 3027).

§1032. "Penitential communication"

As used in this article, "penitential communication" means a communication made in confidence, in the presence of no third person so far as the penitent is aware, to a member of the clergy who, in the course of the discipline or practice of the clergy member's church, denomination, or organization, is authorized or accustomed to hear those communications and, under the discipline or tenets of his or her church, denomination, or organization, has a duty to keep those communications secret. **Leg.H.** Enacted Stats 1965 ch 299 §2, operative January 1, 1967. Amended Stats 2002 ch 806 §21 (AB 3027).

§1033. Privilege of penitent

Subject to Section 912, a penitent, whether or not a party, has a privilege to refuse to disclose, and to prevent another from disclosing, a penitential communication if he or she claims the privilege. **Leg.H.** Enacted Stats 1965 ch 299 §2, operative January 1, 1967. Amended Stats 2002 ch 806 §22 (AB 3027).

§1034. Privilege of clergy member

Subject to Section 912, a member of the clergy, whether or not a party, has a privilege to refuse to disclose a penitential communication if he or she claims the privilege. **Leg.H.** Enacted Stats 1965 ch 299 §2, operative January 1, 1967. Amended Stats 2002 ch 806 §23 (AB 3027).

ARTICLE 8.5
Sexual Assault Counselor-Victim Privilege

"Victim". §1035.
"Sexual assault counselor". §1035.2.
"Confidential communication between the sexual assault counselor and the victim". §1035.4.
"Holder of the privilege". §1035.6.
Victim's privilege. §1035.8.
Counselor's privilege. §1036.
"Sexual assault". §1036.2.

§1035. "Victim"

As used in this article, "victim" means a person who consults a sexual assault counselor for the purpose of securing advice or assistance concerning a mental, physical, or emotional condition caused by a sexual assault. **Leg.H.** Added Stats 1980 ch 917 §2. Amended Stats 2006 ch 689 §4 (SB 1743), effective January 1, 2007.

§1035.2. "Sexual assault counselor"

As used in this article, "sexual assault counselor" means any of the following:

(a) A person who is engaged in any office, hospital, institution, or center commonly known as a rape crisis center, whose primary purpose is the rendering of advice or assistance to victims of sexual assault and who has received a certificate evidencing completion of a training program in the counseling of sexual assault victims issued by a counseling center that meets the criteria for the award of a grant established pursuant to Section 13837 of the Penal Code and who meets one of the following requirements:

(1) Is a psychotherapist as defined in Section 1010; has a master's degree in counseling or a related field; or has one year of counseling experience, at least six months of which is in rape crisis counseling.

(2) Has 40 hours of training as described below and is supervised by an individual who qualifies as a counselor under paragraph (1). The training, supervised by a person qualified under paragraph (1), shall include, but not be limited to, the following areas:

(A) Law.
(B) Medicine.
(C) Societal attitudes.
(D) Crisis intervention and counseling techniques.
(E) Role playing.
(F) Referral services.
(G) Sexuality.

(b) A person who is engaged in a program on the campus of a public or private institution of higher education, whose primary purpose is the rendering of advice or assistance to victims of sexual assault and who has received a certificate evidencing completion of a training program in the counseling of sexual assault victims issued by a counseling center that meets the criteria for the award of a grant established pursuant to Section 13837 of the Penal Code and who meets one of the following requirements:

(1) Is a psychotherapist as defined in Section 1010; has a master's degree in counseling or a related field; or has one year of counseling experience, at least six months of which is in rape crisis counseling.

(2) Has 40 hours of training as described below and is supervised by an individual who qualifies as a counselor under paragraph (1). The training, supervised by a person qualified under paragraph (1), shall include, but not be limited to, the following areas:

(A) Law.
(B) Medicine.
(C) Societal attitudes.
(D) Crisis intervention and counseling techniques.
(E) Role playing.
(F) Referral services.
(G) Sexuality.

(c) A person who is employed by any organization providing the programs specified in Section 13835.2 of the Penal Code, whether financially compensated or not, for the purpose of counseling and assisting sexual assault victims, and who meets one of the following requirements:

(1) Is a psychotherapist as defined in Section 1010; has a master's degree in counseling or a related field; or has one year of counseling experience, at least six months of which is in rape assault counseling.

(2) Has the minimum training for sexual assault counseling required by guidelines established by the employing agency pursuant to subdivision (c) of Section 13835.10 of the Penal Code, and is supervised by an individual who qualifies as a counselor under paragraph (1). The training, supervised by a person qualified under paragraph (1), shall include, but not be limited to, the following areas:

(A) Law.
(B) Victimology.
(C) Counseling.
(D) Client and system advocacy.
(E) Referral services. **Leg.H.** Added Stats 1980 ch 917 §2. Amended Stats 1983 ch 580 §1, ch 1072 §1; Stats 1990 ch 1342 §1 (SB 2501); Stats 2006 ch 689 §5 (SB 1743), effective January 1, 2007; Stats 2018 ch 123 §2 (AB 1896), effective January 1, 2019.

2018 Notes: The amendments to Section 1035.2 of the Evidence Code made by this act do not establish or support in any way that the privilege was not conferred on sexual assault counselors who practiced on college campuses before the enactment of those amendments. Stats 2018 ch 123 §1(j) (AB 1896).

This act is intended as a signal that the privilege existed previously and will continue to exist after its enactment. Stats 2018 ch 123 §1(k) (AB 1896).

§1035.4. "Confidential communication between the sexual assault counselor and the victim"

As used in this article, "confidential communication between the sexual assault counselor and the victim" means information transmitted between the victim and the sexual assault counselor in the course of their relationship and in confidence by a means which, so far as the victim is aware, discloses the information to no third persons other than those who are present to further the interests of the victim in the consultation or those to whom disclosures are reasonably necessary for the transmission of the information or an accomplishment of the purposes for which the sexual assault counselor is consulted. The term includes all information regarding the facts and circumstances involving the alleged sexual assault and also includes all information regarding the victim's prior or subsequent sexual conduct, and opinions regarding the victim's sexual conduct or reputation in sexual matters.

The court may compel disclosure of information received by the sexual assault counselor which constitutes relevant evidence of the facts and circumstances involving an alleged sexual assault about which the victim is complaining and which is the subject of a criminal proceeding if the court determines that the probative value outweighs the effect on the victim, the treatment relationship, and the treatment services if disclosure is compelled. The court may also compel disclosure in proceedings related to child abuse if the court determines the probative value outweighs the effect on the victim, the treatment relationship, and the treatment services if disclosure is compelled.

When a court is ruling on a claim of privilege under this article, the court may require the person from whom disclosure is sought or the person authorized to claim the privilege, or both, to disclose the information in chambers out of the presence and hearing of all persons except the person authorized to claim the privilege and such other persons as the person authorized to claim the privilege is willing to have present. If the judge determines that the information is privileged and must not be disclosed, neither he or she nor any other person may ever disclose, without the consent of a person authorized to permit disclosure, what was disclosed in the course of the proceedings in chambers.

If the court determines certain information shall be disclosed, the court shall so order and inform the defendant. If the court finds there is a reasonable likelihood that particular information is subject to disclosure pursuant to the balancing test provided in this section, the following procedure shall be followed:

(1) The court shall inform the defendant of the nature of the information which may be subject to disclosure.

(2) The court shall order a hearing out of the presence of the jury, if any, and at the hearing allow the questioning of the sexual assault counselor regarding the information which the court has determined may be subject to disclosure.

(3) At the conclusion of the hearing, the court shall rule which items of information, if any, shall be disclosed. The court may make an order stating what evidence may be introduced by the defendant and the nature of questions to be permitted. The defendant may then offer evidence pursuant to the order of the court. Admission of evidence concerning the sexual conduct of the complaining witness is subject to Sections 352, 782, and 1103. **Leg.H.** Added Stats 1980 ch 917 §2. Amended Stats 1983 ch 1072 §2.

§1035.6. "Holder of the privilege"

As used in this article, "holder of the privilege" means:

(a) The victim when such person has no guardian or conservator.

(b) A guardian or conservator of the victim when the victim has a guardian or conservator.

(c) The personal representative of the victim if the victim is dead. **Leg.H.** Added Stats 1980 ch 917 §2.

§1035.8. Victim's privilege

A victim of a sexual assault, whether or not a party, has a privilege to refuse to disclose, and to prevent another from disclosing, a confidential communication between the victim and a sexual assault counselor if the privilege is claimed by any of the following:

(a) The holder of the privilege;

(b) A person who is authorized to claim the privilege by the holder of the privilege; or

(c) The person who was the sexual assault counselor at the time of the confidential communication, but that person may not claim the privilege if there is no holder of the privilege in existence or if he or she is otherwise instructed by a person authorized to permit disclosure. **Leg.H.** Added Stats 1980 ch 917 §2. Amended Stats 2006 ch 689 §6 (SB 1743), effective January 1, 2007.

§1036. Counselor's privilege

The sexual assault counselor who received or made a communication subject to the privilege under this article shall claim the privilege if he or she is present when the communication is sought to be disclosed and is authorized to claim the privilege under subdivision (c) of Section 1035.8. **Leg.H.** Added Stats 1980 ch 917 §2. Amended Stats 2006 ch 689 §7 (SB 1743), effective January 1, 2007.

§1036.2. "Sexual assault"

As used in this article, "sexual assault" includes all of the following:

(a) Rape, as defined in Section 261 of the Penal Code.

(b) Unlawful sexual intercourse, as defined in Section 261.5 of the Penal Code.

(c) Rape in concert with force and violence, as defined in Section 264.1 of the Penal Code.

(d) Sodomy, as defined in Section 286 of the Penal Code, except a violation of subdivision (e) of that section.

(e) A violation of Section 288 of the Penal Code.

(f) Oral copulation, as defined in Section 287 of, or former Section 288a of, the Penal Code, except a violation of subdivision (e) of those sections.

(g) Sexual penetration, as defined in Section 289 of the Penal Code.

(h) Annoying or molesting a child under 18 years of age, as defined in Section 647a of the Penal Code.

(i) Any attempt to commit any of the acts listed in this section. **Leg.H.** Added Stats 1980 ch 917 §2. Amended Stats 1988 ch 102 §1; Stats 2001 ch 854 §4 (SB 205); Stats 2018 ch 423 §20 (SB 1494), effective January 1, 2019; Stats 2021 ch 626 §7 (AB 1171), effective January 1, 2022.

ARTICLE 8.7
Domestic Violence Counselor-Victim Privilege

"Victim". §1037.
"Domestic violence counselor"; "Domestic violence victim service organization". §1037.1.
"Confidential communication"; Compelling disclosure. §1037.2.
Effect of article on obligation to report child abuse. §1037.3.
"Holder of the privilege". §1037.4.
Who may claim privilege. §1037.5.
When domestic violence counselor must claim privilege. §1037.6.
"Domestic violence". §1037.7.
Informing victim of limitations on confidentiality of communications. §1037.8.

§1037. "Victim"

As used in this article, "victim" means any person who suffers domestic violence, as defined in Section 1037.7. **Leg.H.** Added Stats 1986 ch 854 §1.

§1037.1. "Domestic violence counselor"; "Domestic violence victim service organization"

(a)(1) As used in this article, "domestic violence counselor" means a person who is employed by a domestic violence victim service organization, as defined in this article, whether financially compensated or not, for the purpose of rendering advice or assistance to victims of domestic violence and who has at least 40 hours of training as specified in paragraph (2).

(2) The 40 hours of training shall be supervised by an individual who qualifies as a counselor under paragraph (1), and who has at least one year of experience counseling domestic violence victims for the domestic violence victim service organization. The training shall include, but need not be limited to, the following areas: history of domestic violence, civil and criminal law as it relates to domestic violence, the domestic violence victim-counselor privilege and other laws that protect the confidentiality of victim records and information, societal attitudes towards domestic violence, peer counseling techniques, housing, public assistance and other financial resources available to meet the financial needs of domestic violence victims, and referral services available to domestic violence victims.

(3) A domestic violence counselor who has been employed by the domestic violence victim service organization for a period of less than six months shall be supervised by a domestic violence counselor who has at least one year of experience counseling domestic violence victims for the domestic violence victim service organization.

(b) As used in this article, "domestic violence victim service organization" means either of the following:

(1) A nongovernmental organization or entity that provides shelter, programs, or services to victims of domestic violence and their children, including, but not limited to, either of the following:

(A) Domestic violence shelter-based programs, as described in Section 18294 of the Welfare and Institutions Code.

(B) Other programs with the primary mission to provide services to victims of domestic violence whether or not that program exists in an agency that provides additional services.

(2) Programs on the campus of a public or private institution of higher education with the primary mission to provide support or advocacy services to victims of domestic violence. **Leg.H.** Added Stats 1986 ch 854 §1. Amended Stats 1990 ch 1342 §2 (SB 2501); Stats 2007 ch 206 §2 (SB 407), effective January 1, 2008; Stats 2017 ch 178 §1 (SB 331), effective January 1, 2018.

§1037.2. "Confidential communication"; Compelling disclosure

(a) As used in this article, "confidential communication" means any information, including, but not limited to, written or oral communication, transmitted between the victim and the counselor in the course of their relationship and in confidence by a means which, so far as the victim is aware, discloses the information to no third persons other than those who are present to further the interests of the victim in the consultation or those to whom disclosures are reasonably necessary for the transmission of the information or an accomplishment of the purposes for which the domestic violence counselor is consulted. The term includes all information regarding the facts and circumstances involving all incidences of domestic violence, as well as all information about the children of the victim or abuser and the relationship of the victim with the abuser.

(b) The court may compel disclosure of information received by a domestic violence counselor which constitutes relevant evidence of the facts and circumstances involving a crime allegedly perpetrated against the victim or another household member and which is the subject of a criminal proceeding, if the court determines that the probative value of the information outweighs the effect of disclosure of the information on the victim, the counseling relationship, and the counseling services. The court may compel disclosure if the victim is either dead or not the complaining witness in a criminal action against the perpetrator. The court may also compel disclosure in proceedings related to child abuse if the court determines that the probative value of the evidence outweighs the effect of the disclosure on the victim, the counseling relationship, and the counseling services.

(c) When a court rules on a claim of privilege under this article, it may require the person from whom disclosure is sought or the person authorized to claim the privilege, or both, to disclose the information in chambers out of the presence and hearing of all persons except the person authorized to claim the privilege and such other persons as the person authorized to claim the privilege consents to have present. If the judge determines that the information is privileged and shall not be disclosed, neither he nor she nor any other person may disclose, without the consent of a person authorized to permit disclosure, any information disclosed in the course of the proceedings in chambers.

(d) If the court determines that information shall be disclosed, the court shall so order and inform the defendant in the criminal action. If the court finds there is a reasonable likelihood that any information is subject to disclosure pursuant to the balancing test provided in this section, the procedure specified in subdivisions (1), (2), and (3) of Section 1035.4 shall be followed. **Leg.H.** Added Stats 1986 ch 854 §1. Amended Stats 2007 ch 206 §3 (SB 407), effective January 1, 2008.

§1037.3. Effect of article on obligation to report child abuse

Nothing in this article shall be construed to limit any obligation to report instances of child abuse as required by Section 11166 of the Penal Code. **Leg.H.** Added Stats 1986 ch 854 §1.

§1037.4. "Holder of the privilege"

As used in this article, "holder of the privilege" means:

(a) The victim when he or she has no guardian or conservator.

(b) A guardian or conservator of the victim when the victim has a guardian or conservator, unless the guardian or conservator is accused of perpetrating domestic violence against the victim. **Leg.H.** Added Stats 1986 ch 854 §1. Amended Stats 2007 ch 206 §4 (SB 407), effective January 1, 2008.

§1037.5. Who may claim privilege

A victim of domestic violence, whether or not a party to the action, has a privilege to refuse to disclose, and to prevent another from disclosing, a confidential communication between the victim and a domestic violence counselor in any proceeding specified in Section 901 if the privilege is claimed by any of the following persons:

(a) The holder of the privilege.

(b) A person who is authorized to claim the privilege by the holder of the privilege.

(c) The person who was the domestic violence counselor at the time of the confidential communication. However, that person may not claim the privilege if there is no holder of the privilege in existence or if he or she is otherwise instructed by a person authorized to permit disclosure. **Leg.H.** Added Stats 1986 ch 854 §1. Amended Stats 2007 ch 206 §5 (SB 407), effective January 1, 2008.

§1037.6. When domestic violence counselor must claim privilege

The domestic violence counselor who received or made a communication subject to the privilege granted by this article shall claim the privilege whenever he or she is present when the communication is sought to be disclosed and he or she is authorized to claim the privilege under subdivision (c) of Section 1037.5. **Leg.H.** Added Stats 1986 ch 854 §1.

§1037.7. "Domestic violence"

As used in this article, "domestic violence" means "domestic violence" as defined in Section 6211 of the Family Code. **Leg.H.** Added Stats 1993 ch 219 §77.4 (AB 1500).

Prior Law: Former Ev C §1037.7, similar to the present section, was added Stats 1986 ch 854 §1, amended Stats 1992 ch 163 §71, operative January 1, 1994, and repealed Stats 1993 ch 219 §77.3.

§1037.8. Informing victim of limitations on confidentiality of communications

A domestic violence counselor shall inform a domestic violence victim of any applicable limitations on confidentiality of communications between the victim and the domestic violence counselor. This information may be given orally. **Leg.H.** Added Stats 2002 ch 629 §1 (SB 1735).

ARTICLE 8.8
Human Trafficking Caseworker-Victim Privilege

Right to prevent disclosure of confidential communication between victim and caseworker; Who may claim privilege; Notice to victim. §1038.
When court may compel disclosure; Ruling on claim of privilege. §1038.1.
Definitions. §1038.2.
No limitation on obligation to report child abuse. §1038.3.

§1038. Right to prevent disclosure of confidential communication between victim and caseworker; Who may claim privilege; Notice to victim

(a) A trafficking victim, whether or not a party to the action, has a privilege to refuse to disclose, and to prevent another from disclosing, a confidential communication, whether made orally, in writing, or otherwise conveyed, between the victim and a human trafficking caseworker if the privilege is claimed by any of the following persons:

(1) The holder of the privilege.

(2) A person who is authorized to claim the privilege by the holder of the privilege.

(3) The person who was the human trafficking caseworker at the time of the confidential communication or is presently the human trafficking caseworker for the victim. However, that person may not claim the privilege if there is no holder of the privilege in existence or if the person is otherwise instructed by the court or by another person authorized to permit disclosure.

(b) The human trafficking caseworker shall claim the privilege whenever the caseworker is present when the communication is sought to be disclosed and the caseworker is authorized to claim the privilege under this section.

(c) A human trafficking caseworker shall inform a trafficking victim of any applicable limitations on confidentiality of communications between the victim and the caseworker. This information may be given orally. **Leg.H.** Added Stats 2005 ch 240 §4 (AB 22), effective January 1, 2006. Amended Stats 2019 ch 197 §1 (AB 1735), effective January 1, 2020.

2005 Note: See the 2005 Note following Ev C §1038.2.

§1038.1. When court may compel disclosure; Ruling on claim of privilege

(a) The court may compel disclosure of information received by a human trafficking caseworker that constitutes relevant evidence of the facts and circumstances involving a crime allegedly perpetrated against the victim and that is the subject of a criminal proceeding, if the court determines that the probative value of the information outweighs the effect of disclosure of the information on the victim, the counseling relationship, and the counseling services.

(b) When a court rules on a claim of privilege under this article, it may require the person from whom disclosure is sought or the person authorized to claim the privilege, or both, to disclose the information in chambers out of the presence and hearing of all persons except the person authorized to claim the privilege and those other persons that the person authorized to claim the privilege consents to have present.

(c) If the judge determines that the information is privileged and shall not be disclosed, no person shall disclose, without the consent of a person authorized to permit disclosure, any information disclosed in the course of the proceedings in chambers. If the court determines that information shall be disclosed, the court shall so order and inform the defendant in the criminal action. If the court finds there is a reasonable likelihood that any information is subject to disclosure pursuant to the balancing test provided in this section, the procedure specified in paragraphs (1), (2), and (3) of

Section 1035.4 shall be followed. **Leg.H.** Added Stats 2005 ch 240 §4 (AB 22), effective January 1, 2006. Amended Stats 2019 ch 197 §2 (AB 1735), effective January 1, 2020.

2005 Note: See the 2005 Note following Ev C §1038.2.

§1038.2. Definitions

As used in this article, the following terms have the following meanings:

(a) "Confidential communication" means all information, including, but not limited to, written and oral communication, transmitted between the victim and the human trafficking caseworker in the course of their relationship and in confidence by a means which, so far as the victim is aware, discloses the information to no third persons other than those who are present to further the interests of the victim in the consultation or those to whom disclosures are reasonably necessary for the transmission of the information or an accomplishment of the purposes for which the human trafficking caseworker is consulted and made with the victim's knowledge and consent. "Confidential communication" includes all information regarding the facts and circumstances relating to all incidences of human trafficking, as well as all information about the children of the victim and the relationship of the victim to the human trafficker.

(b) "Holder of the privilege" means:

(1) The victim if the victim has no guardian or conservator.

(2) A guardian or conservator of the victim if the victim has a guardian or conservator.

(3) The personal representative of the victim if the victim is deceased.

(c) "Human trafficking caseworker" means a person working for a human trafficking victim service organization, whether financially compensated or not, for the purpose of rendering advice or assistance to victims of human trafficking, who meets the requirements of paragraph (1) or (2) and who also meets the requirements of paragraph (3), if applicable:

(1) Has an advanced degree or license, such as a master's degree in counseling, social work, or a related field and at least one year of experience in a caseworker role working directly with victims of human trafficking.

(2) Has at least 40 hours of training as specified in this paragraph and is supervised by an individual who qualifies as a human trafficking caseworker under paragraph (1). The training, supervised by a person qualified under paragraph (1), shall include, but need not be limited to, the following areas:

(A) History of human trafficking.

(B) Civil and criminal law relating to human trafficking.

(C) Systems of oppression.

(D) Peer counseling techniques.

(E) Resources available to victims of human trafficking.

(F) Crisis intervention and counseling techniques.

(G) Role playing.

(H) Intersections of human trafficking and other crimes.

(I) Client and system advocacy.

(J) Referral services.

(K) Connecting to local, regional, and national human trafficking coalitions.

(L) Explaining privileged communications.

(3) If the caseworker has been employed by a human trafficking service organization for a period of less than six months, that caseworker is supervised by another human trafficking caseworker who has at least one year of experience working with human trafficking victims.

(d) "Human trafficking victim service organization" means a nongovernmental organization or entity that provides shelter, program, or other support services to victims of human trafficking and their children and that does all of the following:

(1) Employs staff that meet the requirements of a human trafficking caseworker as set forth in this section.

(2) Operates a telephone hotline, advertised to the public, for survivor crisis calls.

(3) Offers psychological support and peer counseling provided in accordance with this section.

(4) Makes staff available during normal business hours to assist victims of human trafficking who need shelter, programs, or other support services.

(e) "Victim" means a person who consults a human trafficking caseworker for the purpose of securing advice or assistance concerning a mental, physical, emotional, or other condition related to their experience as a victim of human trafficking. **Leg.H.** Added Stats 2005 ch 240 §4 (AB 22), effective January 1, 2006. Amended Stats 2014 ch 913 §15 (AB 2747), effective January 1, 2015; Stats 2019 ch 197 §3 (AB 1735), effective January 1, 2020; Stats 2020 ch 370 §114 (SB 1371), effective January 1, 2021.

2005 Note: Nothing in this act shall be construed as prohibiting or precluding prosecution under any other provision of law or to prevent punishment pursuant to any other provision of law that imposes a greater or more severe punishment than provided for in this act. Stats 2005 ch 240 (AB 22) §13.

§1038.3. No limitation on obligation to report child abuse

Nothing in this article shall be construed as limiting any obligation to report instances of child abuse as required by Section 11166 of the Penal Code. **Leg.H.** Added Stats 2019 ch 197 §4 (AB 1735), effective January 1, 2020.

ARTICLE 9
Official Information and Identity of Informer

Privilege for official information. §1040.
Privilege for identity of informer. §1041.
Adverse order or finding in certain cases. §1042.
Discovery or disclosure of peace or custodial officer's personnel records. §1043.
Access to medical or psychological history. §1044.
Access to records of complaints where investigations or discipline concern peace officer. §1045.
Motion to include copy of police report in excessive force case. §1046.
Police records not subject to disclosure; Disclosure of supervisorial officer's records. §1047.

§1040. Privilege for official information

(a) As used in this section, "official information" means information acquired in confidence by a public employee in the course of his or her duty and not open, or officially disclosed, to the public prior to the time the claim of privilege is made.

(b) A public entity has a privilege to refuse to disclose official information, and to prevent another from disclosing official information, if the privilege is claimed by a person authorized by the public entity to do so and either of the following apply:

(1) Disclosure is forbidden by an act of the Congress of the United States or a statute of this state.

(2) Disclosure of the information is against the public interest because there is a necessity for preserving the confidentiality of the information that outweighs the necessity for disclosure in the interest of justice; but no privilege may be claimed under this paragraph if any person authorized to do so has consented that the information be disclosed in the proceeding. In determining whether disclosure of the information is against the public interest, the interest of the public entity as a party in the outcome of the proceeding may not be considered.

(c) Notwithstanding any other law, the Employment Development Department shall disclose to law enforcement agencies, in accordance with subdivision (i) of Section 1095 of the Unemployment Insurance Code, information in its possession relating to any person if an arrest warrant has been issued for the person for commission of a felony. **Leg.H.** Enacted Stats 1965 ch 299 §2, operative January 1, 1967. Amended Stats 1984 ch 1127 §2; Stats 2015 ch 20 §1 (SB 79), effective June 24, 2015.

§1041. Privilege for identity of informer

(a) Except as provided in this section, a public entity has a privilege to refuse to disclose the identity of a person who has furnished information as provided in subdivision (b) purporting to disclose a violation of a law of the United States or of this state or of a public entity in this state, and to prevent another from disclosing the person's identity, if the privilege is claimed by a person authorized by the public entity to do so and either of the following apply:

(1) Disclosure is forbidden by an act of the Congress of the United States or a statute of this state.

(2) Disclosure of the identity of the informer is against the public interest because the necessity for preserving the confidentiality of his or her identity outweighs the necessity for disclosure in the interest of justice. The privilege shall not be claimed under this paragraph if a person authorized to do so has consented that the identity of the informer be disclosed in the proceeding. In determining whether disclosure of the identity of the informer is against the public interest, the interest of the

public entity as a party in the outcome of the proceeding shall not be considered.

(b) The privilege described in this section applies only if the information is furnished in confidence by the informer to any of the following:

(1) A law enforcement officer.

(2) A representative of an administrative agency charged with the administration or enforcement of the law alleged to be violated.

(3) Any person for the purpose of transmittal to a person listed in paragraph (1) or (2). As used in this paragraph, "person" includes a volunteer or employee of a crime stopper organization.

(c) The privilege described in this section shall not be construed to prevent the informer from disclosing his or her identity.

(d) As used in this section, "crime stopper organization" means a private, nonprofit organization that accepts and expends donations used to reward persons who report to the organization information concerning alleged criminal activity, and forwards the information to the appropriate law enforcement agency. **Leg.H.** Enacted Stats 1965 ch 299 §2, operative January 1, 1967. Amended Stats 2013 ch 19 §1 (AB 1250), effective January 1, 2014.

§1042. Adverse order or finding in certain cases

(a) Except where disclosure is forbidden by an act of the Congress of the United States, if a claim of privilege under this article by the state or a public entity in this state is sustained in a criminal proceeding, the presiding officer shall make such order or finding of fact adverse to the public entity bringing the proceeding as is required by law upon any issue in the proceeding to which the privileged information is material.

(b) Notwithstanding subdivision (a), where a search is made pursuant to a warrant valid on its face, the public entity bringing a criminal proceeding is not required to reveal to the defendant official information or the identity of an informer in order to establish the legality of the search or the admissibility of any evidence obtained as a result of it.

(c) Notwithstanding subdivision (a), in any preliminary hearing, criminal trial, or other criminal proceeding, any otherwise admissible evidence of information communicated to a peace officer by a confidential informant, who is not a material witness to the guilt or innocence of the accused of the offense charged, is admissible on the issue of reasonable cause to make an arrest or search without requiring that the name or identity of the informant be disclosed if the judge or magistrate is satisfied, based upon evidence produced in open court, out of the presence of the jury, that such information was received from a reliable informant and in his discretion does not require such disclosure.

(d) When, in any such criminal proceeding, a party demands disclosure of the identity of the informant on the ground the informant is a material witness on the issue of guilt, the court shall conduct a hearing at which all parties may present evidence on the issue of disclosure. Such hearing shall be conducted outside the presence of the jury, if any. During the hearing, if the privilege provided for in Section 1041 is claimed by a person authorized to do so or if a person who is authorized to claim such privilege refuses to answer any question on the ground that the answer would tend to disclose the identity of the informant, the prosecuting attorney may request that the court hold an in camera hearing. If such a request is made, the court shall hold such a hearing outside the presence of the defendant and his counsel. At the in camera hearing, the prosecution may offer evidence which would tend to disclose or which discloses the identity of the informant to aid the court in its determination whether there is a reasonable possibility that nondisclosure might deprive the defendant of a fair trial. A reporter shall be present at the in camera hearing. Any transcription of the proceedings at the in camera hearing, as well as any physical evidence presented at the hearing, shall be ordered sealed by the court, and only a court may have access to its contents. The court shall not order disclosure, nor strike the testimony of the witness who invokes the privilege, nor dismiss the criminal proceeding, if the party offering the witness refuses to disclose the identity of the informant, unless, based upon the evidence presented at the hearing held in the presence of the defendant and his counsel and the evidence presented at the in camera hearing, the court concludes that there is a reasonable possibility that nondisclosure might deprive the defendant of a fair trial. **Leg.H.** Enacted Stats 1965 ch 299 §2, operative January 1, 1967. Amended Stats 1969 ch 1412 §1.

§1043. Discovery or disclosure of peace or custodial officer's personnel records

(a) In any case in which discovery or disclosure is sought of peace or custodial officer personnel records or records maintained pursuant to Section 832.5 of the Penal Code or information from those records, the party seeking the discovery or disclosure shall file a written motion with the appropriate court or administrative body upon written notice to the governmental agency that has custody and control of the records, as follows:

(1) In a civil action, the written notice shall be given at the times prescribed by subdivision (b) of Section 1005 of the Code of Civil Procedure.

(2) In a criminal action, the written notice shall be served and filed at least 10 court days before the hearing. All papers opposing a motion so noticed shall be filed with the court at least five court days, and all reply papers at least two court days, before the hearing. Proof of service of the notice shall be filed no later than five court days before the hearing.

(b) The motion shall include all of the following:

(1) Identification of the proceeding in which discovery or disclosure is sought, the party seeking discovery or disclosure, the peace or custodial officer whose records are sought, the governmental agency that has custody and control of the records, and the time and place at which the motion for discovery or disclosure shall be heard.

(2) A description of the type of records or information sought.

(3) Affidavits showing good cause for the discovery or disclosure sought, setting forth the materiality thereof to the subject matter involved in the pending litigation and stating upon reasonable belief that the governmental agency identified has the records or information from the records.

(c) Upon receipt of a notice served pursuant to subdivision (a), the governmental agency shall immediately notify the individual whose records are sought.

(d) No hearing upon a motion for discovery or disclosure shall be held without full compliance with the notice provisions of this section except upon a showing by the moving party of good cause for noncompliance, or upon a waiver of the hearing by the governmental agency identified as having the records. **Leg.H.** Added Stats 1978 ch 630 §1. Amended Stats 1989 ch 693 §7; Stats 2002 ch 391 §1 (AB 2040); Stats 2019 ch 585 §2 (AB 1600), effective January 1, 2020.

§1044. Access to medical or psychological history

Nothing in this article shall be construed to affect the right of access to records of medical or psychological history where such access would otherwise be available under Section 996 or 1016. **Leg.H.** Added Stats 1978 ch 630 §2.

§1045. Access to records of complaints where investigations or discipline concern peace officer

(a) This article does not affect the right of access to records of complaints, or investigations of complaints, or discipline imposed as a result of those investigations, concerning an event or transaction in which the peace officer or custodial officer, as defined in Section 831.5 of the Penal Code, participated, or which the officer perceived, and pertaining to the manner in which the officer performed the officer's duties, provided that information is relevant to the subject matter involved in the pending litigation.

(b) In determining relevance, the court shall examine the information in chambers in conformity with Section 915, and shall exclude from disclosure both of the following:

(1) In any criminal proceeding the conclusions of any officer investigating a complaint filed pursuant to Section 832.5 of the Penal Code.

(2) Facts sought to be disclosed that are so remote as to make disclosure of little or no practical benefit.

(c) In determining relevance where the issue in litigation concerns the policies or pattern of conduct of the employing agency, the court shall consider whether the information sought may be obtained from other records maintained by the employing agency in the regular course of agency business which would not necessitate the disclosure of individual personnel records.

(d) Upon motion seasonably made by the governmental agency which has custody or control of the records to be examined or by the officer whose records are sought, and upon good cause showing the necessity thereof, the court may make any order which justice requires to protect the officer or agency from unnecessary annoyance, embarrassment or oppression.

(e) The court shall, in any case or proceeding permitting the disclosure or discovery of any peace or custodial officer records requested pursuant to Section 1043, order that the records disclosed or discovered may not be used for any purpose other than a court proceeding pursuant to applicable law. **Leg.H.** Added Stats 1978 ch 630 §3. Amended Stats 1982 ch 946 §1; Stats 2002 ch 391 §2 (AB 2040); Stats 2021 ch 402 §1 (SB 16), effective January 1, 2022.

§1046. Motion to include copy of police report in excessive force case

In any case, otherwise authorized by law, in which the party seeking disclosure is alleging excessive force by a peace officer or custodial officer, as defined in Section 831.5 of the Penal Code, in connection with the arrest of that party, or for conduct alleged to have occurred within a jail facility, the motion shall include a copy of the police report setting forth the circumstances under which the party was stopped and arrested, or a copy of the crime report setting forth the circumstances under which the conduct is alleged to have occurred within a jail facility. **Leg.H.** Added Stats 1985 ch 539 §1. Amended Stats 2002 ch 391 §3 (AB 2040).

§1047. Police records not subject to disclosure; Disclosure of supervisorial officer's records

(a) Records of peace officers or custodial officers, as defined in Section 831.5 of the Penal Code, including supervisorial officers, who either were not present during the arrest or had no contact with the party seeking disclosure from the time of the arrest until the time of booking, or who were not present at the time the conduct at issue is alleged to have occurred within a jail facility, shall not be subject to disclosure.

(b) Notwithstanding subdivision (a), if a supervisorial officer whose records are being sought had direct oversight of a peace officer or a custodial officer, as defined in Section 831.5 of the Penal Code and issued command directives or had command influence over the circumstances at issue, the supervisorial officer's records shall be subject to disclosure pursuant to Section 1045 if the peace officer or custodial officer under supervision was present during the arrest, had contact with the party seeking disclosure from the time of the arrest until the time of booking, or was present at the time the conduct at issue is alleged to have occurred within a jail facility. **Leg.H.** Added Stats 1985 ch 539 §2. Amended Stats 2002 ch 391 §4 (AB 2040); Stats 2019 ch 585 §3 (AB 1600), effective January 1, 2020.

ARTICLE 10
Political Vote

Privilege to protect secrecy of vote. §1050.

§1050. Privilege to protect secrecy of vote

If he claims the privilege, a person has a privilege to refuse to disclose the tenor of his vote at a public election where the voting is by secret ballot unless he voted illegally or he previously made an unprivileged disclosure of the tenor of his vote. **Leg.H.** Enacted Stats 1965 ch 299 §2, operative January 1, 1967.

ARTICLE 11
Trade Secret

Privilege to protect trade secret. §1060.
"Trade secret"; "Article"; Procedure for assertion of trade secret privilege; Protective order. §1061.
Exclusion of public from portion of criminal proceeding in which trade secret may be disclosed. §1062.
Provisions governing requests to seal articles. §1063.

§1060. Privilege to protect trade secret

If he or his agent or employee claims the privilege, the owner of a trade secret has a privilege to refuse to disclose the secret, and to prevent another from disclosing it, if the allowance of the privilege will not tend to conceal fraud or otherwise work injustice. **Leg.H.** Enacted Stats 1965 ch 299 §2, operative January 1, 1967.

§1061. "Trade secret"; "Article"; Procedure for assertion of trade secret privilege; Protective order

(a) For purposes of this section, and Sections 1062 and 1063:

(1) "Trade secret" means "trade secret," as defined in subdivision (d) of Section 3426.1 of the Civil Code, or paragraph (9) of subdivision (a) of Section 499c of the Penal Code.

(2) "Article" means "article," as defined in paragraph (2) of subdivision (a) of Section 499c of the Penal Code.

(b) In addition to Section 1062, the following procedure shall apply whenever the owner of a trade secret wishes to assert his or her trade secret privilege, as provided in Section 1060, during a criminal proceeding:

(1) The owner of the trade secret shall file a motion for a protective order, or the people may file the motion on the owner's behalf and with the owner's permission. The motion shall include an affidavit based upon personal knowledge listing the affiant's qualifications to give an opinion concerning the trade secret at issue, identifying, without revealing, the alleged trade secret and articles which disclose the secret, and presenting evidence that the secret qualifies as a trade secret under either subdivision (d) of Section 3426.1 of the Civil Code or paragraph (9) of subdivision (a) of Section 499c of the Penal Code. The motion and affidavit shall be served on all parties in the proceeding.

(2) Any party in the proceeding may oppose the request for the protective order by submitting affidavits based upon the affiant's personal knowledge. The affidavits shall be filed under seal, but shall be provided to the owner of the trade secret and to all parties in the proceeding. Neither the owner of the trade secret nor any party in the proceeding may disclose the affidavit to persons other than to counsel of record without prior court approval.

(3) The movant shall, by a preponderance of the evidence, show that the issuance of a protective order is proper. The court may rule on the request without holding an evidentiary hearing. However, in its discretion, the court may choose to hold an in camera evidentiary hearing concerning disputed articles with only the owner of the trade secret, the people's representative, the defendant, and defendant's counsel present. If the court holds such a hearing, the parties' right to examine witnesses shall not be used to obtain discovery, but shall be directed solely toward the question of whether the alleged trade secret qualifies for protection.

(4) If the court finds that a trade secret may be disclosed during any criminal proceeding unless a protective order is issued and that the issuance of a protective order would not conceal a fraud or work an injustice, the court shall issue a protective order limiting the use and dissemination of the trade secret, including, but not limited to, articles disclosing that secret. The protective order may, in the court's discretion, include the following provisions:

(A) That the trade secret may be disseminated only to counsel for the parties, including their associate attorneys, paralegals, and investigators, and to law enforcement officials or clerical officials.

(B) That the defendant may view the secret only in the presence of his or her counsel, or if not in the presence of his or her counsel, at counsel's offices.

(C) That any party seeking to show the trade secret, or articles containing the trade secret, to any person not designated by the protective order shall first obtain court approval to do so:

(i) The court may require that the person receiving the trade secret do so only in the presence of counsel for the party requesting approval.

(ii) The court may require the person receiving the trade secret to sign a copy of the protective order and to agree to be bound by its terms. The order may include a provision recognizing the owner of the trade secret to be a third-party beneficiary of that agreement.

(iii) The court may require a party seeking disclosure to an expert to provide that expert's name, employment history, and any other relevant information to the court for examination. The court shall accept that information under seal, and the information shall not be disclosed by any court except upon termination of the action and upon a showing of good cause to believe the secret has been disseminated by a court-approved expert. The court shall evaluate the expert and determine whether the expert poses a discernible risk of disclosure. The court shall withhold approval if the expert's economic interests place the expert in a competitive position with the victim, unless no other experts are available. The court may interview the expert in camera in aid of its ruling. If the court rejects the expert, it shall state its reasons for doing so on the record and a transcript of those reasons shall be prepared and sealed.

(D) That no articles disclosing the trade secret shall be filed or otherwise made a part of the court record available to the public without approval of the court and prior notice to the owner of the secret. The owner of the secret may give either party permission to accept the notice on the owner's behalf.

(E) Other orders as the court deems necessary to protect the integrity of the trade secret.

(c) A ruling granting or denying a motion for a protective order filed pursuant to subdivision (b) shall not be construed as a determination that the alleged trade secret is or is not a trade secret as defined by subdivision (d) of Section 3426.1 of the Civil Code or paragraph (9) of subdivision (a) of Section 499c of the Penal Code. Such a ruling shall not have any effect on any civil litigation.

(d) This section shall have prospective effect only and shall not operate to invalidate previously entered protective orders. **Leg.H.** Added Stats 1990 ch 149 §1 (AB 2986). Amended Stats 1990 ch 714 §1 (AB 2553); Stats 2002 ch 784 §103 (SB 1316).

§1062. Exclusion of public from portion of criminal proceeding in which trade secret may be disclosed

(a) Notwithstanding any other provision of law, in a criminal case, the court, upon motion of the owner of a trade secret, or upon motion by the People with the consent of the owner, may exclude the public from any portion of a criminal proceeding where the proponent of closure has demonstrated a substantial probability that the trade secret would otherwise be disclosed to the public during that proceeding and a substantial probability that the disclosure would cause serious harm to the owner of the secret, and where the court finds that there is no overriding public interest in an open proceeding. No evidence, however, shall be excluded during a criminal proceeding pursuant to this section if it would conceal a fraud, work an injustice, or deprive the People or the defendant of a fair trial.

(b) The motion made pursuant to subdivision (a) shall identify, without revealing, the trade secrets which would otherwise be disclosed to the public. A showing made pursuant to subdivision (a) shall be made during an in camera hearing with only the owner of the trade secret, the People's representative, the defendant, and defendant's counsel present. A court reporter shall be present during the hearing. Any transcription of the proceedings at the in camera hearing, as well as any articles presented at that hearing, shall be ordered sealed by the court and only a court may allow access to its contents upon a showing of good cause. The court, in ruling upon the motion made pursuant to subdivision (a), may consider testimony presented or affidavits filed in any proceeding held in that action.

(c) If, after the in camera hearing described in subdivision (b), the court determines that exclusion of trade secret information from the public is appropriate, the court shall close only that portion of the criminal proceeding necessary to prevent disclosure of the trade secret. Before granting the motion, however, the court shall find and state for the record that the moving party has met its burden pursuant to subdivision (b), and that the closure of that portion of the proceeding will not deprive the People or the defendant of a fair trial.

(d) The owner of the trade secret, the People, or the defendant may seek relief from a ruling denying or granting closure by petitioning a higher court for extraordinary relief.

(e) Whenever the court closes a portion of a criminal proceeding pursuant to this section, a transcript of that closed proceeding shall be made available to the public as soon as practicable. The court shall redact any information qualifying as a trade secret before making that transcript available.

(f) The court, subject to Section 867 of the Penal Code, may allow witnesses who are bound by a protective order entered in the criminal proceeding protecting trade secrets, pursuant to Section 1061, to remain within the courtroom during the closed portion of the proceeding. **Leg.H.** Added Stats 1990 ch 149 §2 (AB 2986). Amended Stats 1990 ch 714 §2 (AB 2553).

§1063. Provisions governing requests to seal articles

The following provisions shall govern requests to seal articles which are protected by a protective order entered pursuant to Evidence Code Section 1060 or 1061:

(a) The People shall request sealing of articles reasonably expected to be filed or admitted into evidence as follows:

(1) No less than 10 court days before trial, and no less than five court days before any other criminal proceeding, the People shall file with the court a list of all articles which the People reasonably expect to file with the court, or admit into evidence, under seal at that proceeding. That list shall be available to the public. The People may be relieved from providing timely notice upon showing that exigent circumstances prevent that notice.

(2) The court shall not allow the listed articles to be filed, admitted into evidence, or in any way made a part of the court record otherwise open to the public before holding a hearing to consider any objections to the People's request to seal the articles. The court at that hearing shall allow those objecting to the sealing to state their objections.

(3) After hearing any objections to sealing, the court shall conduct an in camera hearing with only the owner of the trade secret contained within those articles, the People's representative, defendant, and defendant's counsel present. The court shall review the articles sought to be sealed, evaluate objections to sealing, and determine whether the People have satisfied the constitutional standards governing public access to articles which are part of the judicial record. The court may consider testimony presented or affidavits filed in any proceeding held in that action. The People, defendant, and the owner of the trade secret may file affidavits based on the affiant's personal knowledge to be considered at that hearing. Those affidavits are to be sealed and not released to the public, but shall be made available to the parties. The court may rule on the request to seal without taking testimony. If the court takes testimony, examination of witnesses shall not be used to obtain discovery, but shall be directed solely toward whether sealing is appropriate.

(4) If the court finds that the movant has satisfied appropriate constitutional standards with respect to sealing particular articles, the court shall seal those articles if and when they are filed, admitted into evidence, or in any way made a part of the court record otherwise open to the public. The articles shall not be unsealed absent an order of a court upon a showing of good cause. Failure to examine the court file for notice of a request to seal shall not constitute good cause to consider objections to sealing.

(b) The following procedure shall apply to other articles made a part of the court record:

(1) Where any articles protected by a protective order entered pursuant to Section 1060 or 1061 are filed, admitted into evidence, or in any way made a part of the court record in such a way as to be otherwise open to the public, the People, a defendant, or the owner of a trade secret contained within those articles may request the court to seal those articles.

(2) The request to seal shall be made by noticed motion filed with the court. It may also be made orally in court at the time the articles are made a part of the court record. Where the request is made orally, the movant must file within 24 hours a written description of that request, including a list of the articles which are the subject of that request. These motions and lists shall be available to the public.

(3) The court shall promptly conduct hearings as provided in paragraphs (2), (3), and (4) of subdivision (a). The court shall, pending the hearings, seal those articles which are the subject of the request. Where a request to seal is made orally, the court may conduct hearings at the time the articles are made a part of the court record, but shall reconsider its ruling in light of additional objections made by objectors within two court days after the written record of the request to seal is made available to the public.

(4) Any articles sealed pursuant to these hearings shall not be unsealed absent an order of a court upon a showing of good cause. Failure to examine the court file for notice of a request to seal shall not constitute good cause to consider objections to sealing. **Leg.H.** Added Stats 1990 ch 714 §3 (AB 2553).

CHAPTER 5
IMMUNITY OF NEWSMAN FROM CITATION FOR CONTEMPT

Newsman's refusal to disclose news source. §1070.

§1070. Newsman's refusal to disclose news source

(a) A publisher, editor, reporter, or other person connected with or employed upon a newspaper, magazine, or other periodical publication, or by a press association or wire service, or any person who has been so connected or employed, cannot be adjudged in contempt by a judicial, legislative, administrative body, or any other body having the power to issue subpoenas, for refusing to disclose, in any proceeding as defined in Section 901, the source of any information procured while so connected or employed for publication in a newspaper, magazine or other periodical publication, or for refusing to disclose any unpublished information obtained or prepared in gathering, receiving or processing of information for communication to the public.

(b) Nor can a radio or television news reporter or other person connected with or employed by a radio or television station, or any person who has been so connected or employed, be so adjudged in contempt for refusing to disclose the source of any information procured while so connected or employed for news or news commentary purposes on radio or television, or for refusing to disclose any unpublished information obtained or prepared in gathering, receiving or processing of information for communication to the public.

(c) As used in this section, "unpublished information" includes information not disseminated to the public by the person from whom disclosure is sought, whether or not related information has been disseminated and includes, but is not limited to, all notes, outtakes, photographs, tapes or other data of whatever sort not itself disseminated to the public through a medium of communication, whether or not published information based upon or related to such material has been disseminated. **Leg.H.** Enacted Stats 1965 ch 299 §2, operative January 1, 1967. Amended Stats 1971 ch 1717 §1; Stats 1972 ch 1431 §1; Stats 1974 ch 1456 §2.

DIVISION 9
EVIDENCE AFFECTED OR EXCLUDED BY EXTRINSIC POLICIES

Chapter 1. Evidence of Character, Habit, or Custom.
Chapter 2. Mediation.
Chapter 3. Other Evidence Affected or Excluded by Extrinsic Policies.

CHAPTER 1
EVIDENCE OF CHARACTER, HABIT, OR CUSTOM

Manner of proof of character. §1100.
Evidence of character to prove conduct. §1101.
Opinion and reputation evidence of character of criminal defendant to prove conduct. §1102.
Evidence of character of victim of crime. §1103.
Character trait for care or skill. §1104.
Habit or custom to prove specific behavior. §1105.
Specific instances of plaintiff's sexual conduct in civil action alleging sexual harassment. §1106.
Admissibility of expert evidence regarding intimate partner battering. §1107.
Human trafficking; Admissibility of expert testimony. §1107.5.
Evidence of another sexual offense. §1108.
Domestic violence, abuse of elder or dependent person, and child abuse; When evidence of other acts is admissible; Disclosure to defendant. §1109.

§1100. Manner of proof of character

Except as otherwise provided by statute, any otherwise admissible evidence (including evidence in the form of an opinion, evidence of reputation, and evidence of specific instances of such person's conduct) is admissible to prove a person's character or a trait of his character. **Leg.H.** Enacted Stats 1965 ch 299 §2, operative January 1, 1967.

§1101. Evidence of character to prove conduct

(a) Except as provided in this section and in Sections 1102, 1103, 1108, and 1109, evidence of a person's character or a trait of his or her character (whether in the form of an opinion, evidence of reputation, or evidence of specific instances of his or her conduct) is inadmissible when offered to prove his or her conduct on a specified occasion.

(b) Nothing in this section prohibits the admission of evidence that a person committed a crime, civil wrong, or other act when relevant to prove some fact (such as motive, opportunity, intent, preparation, plan, knowledge, identity, absence of mistake or accident, or whether a defendant in a prosecution for an unlawful sexual act or attempted unlawful sexual act did not reasonably and in good faith believe that the victim consented) other than his or her disposition to commit such an act.

(c) Nothing in this section affects the admissibility of evidence offered to support or attack the credibility of a witness. **Leg.H.** Enacted Stats 1965 ch 299 §2, operative January 1, 1967. Amended Stats 1986 ch 1432 §1; Stats 1995 ch 439 §1 (AB 882); Stats 1996 ch 261 §1 (SB 1876).

1986 Note: It is the intent of the Legislature in enacting this act to clarify the holding in *People v. Tassell* (36 Cal. 3d 77) to the extent an inference can be drawn from that holding that evidence of another act is ipso facto inadmissible or irrelevant to the issue of a defendant's reasonable and good faith belief that the victim consented, by rejecting that inference and making it clear that that evidence can be relevant on that issue in a particular case, depending upon the circumstances there present. Stats 1986 ch 1432 §2.

§1102. Opinion and reputation evidence of character of criminal defendant to prove conduct

In a criminal action, evidence of the defendant's character or a trait of his character in the form of an opinion or evidence of his reputation is not made inadmissible by Section 1101 if such evidence is:

(a) Offered by the defendant to prove his conduct in conformity with such character or trait of character.

(b) Offered by the prosecution to rebut evidence adduced by the defendant under subdivision (a). **Leg.H.** Enacted Stats 1965 ch 299 §2, operative January 1, 1967.

§1103. Evidence of character of victim of crime

(a) In a criminal action, evidence of the character or a trait of character (in the form of an opinion, evidence of reputation, or evidence of specific instances of conduct) of the victim of the crime for which the defendant is being prosecuted is not made inadmissible by Section 1101 if the evidence is:

(1) Offered by the defendant to prove conduct of the victim in conformity with the character or trait of character.

(2) Offered by the prosecution to rebut evidence adduced by the defendant under paragraph (1).

(b) In a criminal action, evidence of the defendant's character for violence or trait of character for violence (in the form of an opinion, evidence of reputation, or evidence of specific instances of conduct) is not made inadmissible by Section 1101 if the evidence is offered by the prosecution to prove conduct of the defendant in conformity with the character or trait of character and is offered after evidence that the victim had a character for violence or a trait of character tending to show violence has been adduced by the defendant under paragraph (1) of subdivision (a).

(c)(1) Notwithstanding any other provision of this code to the contrary, and except as provided in this subdivision, in any prosecution under Section 261 or 264.1 of the Penal Code, or under Section 286, 287, or 289 of, or former Section 262 or 288a of, the Penal Code, or for assault with intent to commit, attempt to commit, or conspiracy to commit a crime defined in any of those sections, except where the crime is alleged to have occurred in a local detention facility, as defined in Section 6031.4, or in a state prison, as defined in Section 4504, opinion evidence, reputation evidence, and evidence of specific instances of the complaining witness' sexual conduct, or any of that evidence, is not admissible by the defendant in order to prove consent by the complaining witness.

(2) Notwithstanding paragraph (3), evidence of the manner in which the victim was dressed at the time of the commission of the offense is not admissible when offered by either party on the issue of consent in any prosecution for an offense specified in paragraph (1). For the purposes of this paragraph, "manner of dress" does not include the condition of the victim's clothing before, during, or after the commission of the offense.

(3) Paragraph (1) does not apply to evidence of the complaining witness' sexual conduct with the defendant.

(4) If the prosecutor introduces evidence, including testimony of a witness, or the complaining witness as a witness gives testimony, and that evidence or testimony relates to the complaining witness' sexual conduct, the defendant may cross-examine the witness who gives the testimony and offer relevant evidence limited specifically to the rebuttal of the evidence introduced by the prosecutor or given by the complaining witness.

(5) This subdivision does not make inadmissible any evidence offered to attack the credibility of the complaining witness as provided in Section 782.

(6) As used in this subdivision, "complaining witness" means the alleged victim of the crime charged, the prosecution of which is subject to this subdivision. **Leg.H.** Enacted Stats 1965 ch 299 §2, operative January 1, 1967. Amended Stats 1974 ch 569 §2; Stats 1981 ch 726 §2; Stats 1990 ch 268 §1 (AB 2615); Stats 1991 ch 16 §1 (AB 263), effective March 18, 1991; Stats 1996 ch 1075 §7 (SB 1444); Stats 1998 ch 127 §1 (AB 1926); Stats 2018 ch 423 §21 (SB 1494), effective January 1, 2019; Stats 2021 ch 529 §2 (AB 939), effective January 1, 2022; Stats 2021 ch 626 §8.1 (AB 1171), effective January 1, 2022 (ch 626 prevails); Stats 2022 ch 197 §1 (SB 1493), effective January 1, 2023.

§1104. Character trait for care or skill

Except as provided in Sections 1102 and 1103, evidence of a trait of a person's character with respect to care or skill is inadmissible to prove the quality of his conduct on a specified occasion. **Leg.H.** Enacted Stats 1965 ch 299 §2, operative January 1, 1967.

§1105. Habit or custom to prove specific behavior

Any otherwise admissible evidence of habit or custom is admissible to prove conduct on a specified occasion in conformity with the habit or custom. **Leg.H.** Enacted Stats 1965 ch 299 §2, operative January 1, 1967.

§1106. Specific instances of plaintiff's sexual conduct in civil action alleging sexual harassment

(a) In any civil action alleging conduct which constitutes sexual harassment, sexual assault, or sexual battery, opinion evidence, reputation evidence, and evidence of specific instances of the plaintiff's sexual conduct, or any of that evidence, is not admissible by the defendant in order to [1]:

(1) Prove consent by the plaintiff.

(2) Prove absence of injury suffered by the plaintiff, unless the injury alleged by the plaintiff is in the nature of loss of consortium.

(3) Attack the credibility of the plaintiff's testimony on consent or the absence of injury suffered by the plaintiff.

(b) Subdivision (a) does not apply to evidence of the plaintiff's sexual conduct with the alleged perpetrator.

(c) Notwithstanding subdivision (b), in any civil action brought pursuant to Section 1708.5 of the Civil Code involving a minor and **an** adult as described in Section 1708.5.5 of the Civil Code, evidence of the plaintiff minor's sexual conduct with the defendant adult shall not be admissible to prove consent by the plaintiff or the absence of injury to the plaintiff. [2]

(d) If the plaintiff introduces evidence, including testimony of a witness, or the plaintiff as a witness gives testimony, and the evidence or testimony relates to the plaintiff's sexual conduct, the defendant may cross-examine the witness who gives the testimony and offer relevant evidence limited specifically to the rebuttal of the evidence introduced by the plaintiff or given by the plaintiff.

(e) This section shall not be construed to make inadmissible any evidence offered to attack the credibility of the [3] **plaintiff's testimony as to something other than consent or absence of injury as** provided in Section 783. **Leg.H.** Added Stats 1985 ch 1328 §4. Amended Stats 2015 ch 128 §2 (SB 14), effective January 1, 2016; Stats 2016 ch 86 §127 (SB 1171), effective January 1, 2017; Stats 2024 ch 993 §1 (SB 1386), effective January 1, 2025.

§1106. 2024 Deletes. [1] prove consent by the plaintiff or the absence of injury to the plaintiff, unless the injury alleged by the plaintiff is in the nature of loss of consortium. **[2]** Such evidence of the plaintiff's sexual conduct may only be introduced to attack the credibility of the plaintiff in accordance with Section 783 or to prove something other than consent by the plaintiff if, upon a hearing of the court out of the presence of the jury, the defendant proves that the probative value of that evidence outweighs the prejudice to the plaintiff consistent with Section 352. **[3]** plaintiff as

§1107. Admissibility of expert evidence regarding intimate partner battering

(a) In a criminal action, expert testimony is admissible by either the prosecution or the defense regarding intimate partner battering and its effects, including the nature and effect of physical, emotional, or mental abuse on the beliefs, perceptions, or behavior of victims of domestic violence, except when offered against a criminal defendant to prove the occurrence of the act or acts of abuse which form the basis of the criminal charge.

(b) The foundation shall be sufficient for admission of this expert testimony if the proponent of the evidence establishes its relevancy and the proper qualifications of the expert witness. Expert opinion testimony on intimate partner battering and its effects shall not be considered a new scientific technique whose reliability is unproven.

(c) For purposes of this section, "abuse" is defined in Section 6203 of the Family Code, and "domestic violence" is defined in Section 6211 of the Family Code and may include acts defined in Section 242, subdivision (e) of Section 243, Section 261, 273.5, 273.6, 422, or 653m of, or former Section 262 of, the Penal Code.

(d) This section is intended as a rule of evidence only and no substantive change affecting the Penal Code is intended.

(e) This section shall be known, and may be cited, as the Expert Witness Testimony on Intimate Partner Battering and Its Effects Section of the Evidence Code.

(f) The changes in this section that become effective on January 1, 2005, are not intended to impact any existing decisional law regarding this section, and that decisional law should apply equally to this section as it refers to "intimate partner battering and its effects" in place of "battered women's syndrome." **Leg.H.** Added Stats 1991 ch 812 §1. Amended Stats 1992 ch 163 §72 (AB 2641), operative January 1, 1994; Stats 1993 ch 219 §77.5 (AB 1500), ch 589 §60 (AB 2211) (ch 219 prevails); Stats 2000 ch 1001 §1 (SB 1944); Stats 2004 ch 609 §1 (SB 1385); Stats 2021 ch 626 §9 (AB 1171), effective January 1, 2022; Stats 2022 ch 197 §2 (SB 1493), effective January 1, 2023.

1991 Note: The Legislature does not intend Section 1107 of the Evidence Code to preclude the admissibility of evidence of battered women's syndrome under other statutory or case law. Stats 1991 ch 812 §2.

§1107.5. Human trafficking; Admissibility of expert testimony

(a) In a criminal action, expert testimony is admissible by either the prosecution or the defense regarding the effects of human trafficking on human trafficking victims, including the nature and effect of physical, emotional, or mental abuse on the beliefs, perceptions, or behavior of human trafficking victims.

(b) The foundation shall be sufficient for admission of this expert testimony if the proponent of the evidence establishes its relevancy and the proper qualifications of the expert witness.

(c) For purposes of this section, "human trafficking victim" is defined as a victim of an offense described in Section 236.1 of the Penal Code.

(d) This section is intended as a rule of evidence only and no substantive change affecting the Penal Code is intended. **Leg.H.** Added Stats 2016 ch 636 §1 (AB 1761), effective January 1, 2017. Amended Stats 2017 ch 269 §1 (SB 811), effective January 1, 2018.

§1108. Evidence of another sexual offense

(a) In a criminal action in which the defendant is accused of a sexual offense, evidence of the defendant's commission of another sexual offense or offenses is not made inadmissible by Section 1101, if the evidence is not inadmissible pursuant to Section 352.

(b) In an action in which evidence is to be offered under this section, the people shall disclose the evidence to the defendant, including statements of witnesses or a summary of the substance of any testimony that is expected to be offered in compliance with the requirements of Section 1054.7 of the Penal Code.

(c) This section does not limit the admission or consideration of evidence under any other section of this code.

(d) As used in this section, the following definitions shall apply:

(1) "Sexual offense" means a crime under the law of a state or of the United States that involved any of the following:

(A) Any conduct proscribed by subdivision (b) or (c) of Section 236.1, Section 243.4, 261, 261.5, 262, 264.1, 266c, 269, 286, 287, 288, 288.2, 288.5, or 289, or subdivision (b), (c), or (d) of Section 311.2 or Section 311.3, 311.4, 311.10, 311.11, 314, or 647.6 of, or former Section 288a of, the Penal Code.

(B) Any conduct proscribed by Section 220 of the Penal Code, except assault with intent to commit mayhem.

(C) Contact, without consent, between any part of the defendant's body or an object and the genitals or anus of another person.

(D) Contact, without consent, between the genitals or anus of the defendant and any part of another person's body.

(E) Deriving sexual pleasure or gratification from the infliction of death, bodily injury, or physical pain on another person.

(F) An attempt or conspiracy to engage in conduct described in this paragraph.

(2) "Consent" shall have the same meaning as provided in Section 261.6 of the Penal Code, except that it does not include consent which is legally ineffective because of the age, mental disorder, or developmental or physical disability of the victim. **Leg.H.** Added Stats 1995 ch 439 §2 (AB 882). Amended Stats 2001 ch 517 §1 (AB 380); Stats 2002 ch 194 §1 (AB 2252), ch 828 §1 (AB 2499); Stats 2017 ch 805 §1 (SB 230), effective January 1, 2018; Stats 2018 ch 423 §22 (SB 1494), effective January 1, 2019.

§1109. Domestic violence, abuse of elder or dependent person, and child abuse; When evidence of other acts is admissible; Disclosure to defendant

(a)(1) Except as provided in subdivision (e) or (f), in a criminal action in which the defendant is accused of an offense involving domestic violence, evidence of the defendant's commission of other domestic violence is not made inadmissible by Section 1101 if the evidence is not inadmissible pursuant to Section 352.

(2) Except as provided in subdivision (e) or (f), in a criminal action in which the defendant is accused of an offense involving abuse of an elder or dependent person, evidence of the defendant's commission of other abuse of an elder or dependent person is not made inadmissible by Section 1101 if the evidence is not inadmissible pursuant to Section 352.

(3) Except as provided in subdivision (e) or (f) and subject to a hearing conducted pursuant to Section 352, which shall include consideration of any corroboration and remoteness in time, in a criminal action in which the defendant is accused of an offense involving child abuse, evidence of the defendant's commission of child abuse is not made inadmissible by Section 1101 if the evidence is not inadmissible pursuant to Section 352. Nothing in this paragraph prohibits or limits the admission of evidence pursuant to subdivision (b) of Section 1101.

(b) In an action in which evidence is to be offered under this section, the people shall disclose the evidence to the defendant, including statements of witnesses or a summary of the substance of any testimony that is expected to be offered, in compliance with the provisions of Section 1054.7 of the Penal Code.

(c) This section shall not be construed to limit or preclude the admission or consideration of evidence under any other statute or case law.

(d) As used in this section:

(1) "Abuse of an elder or dependent person" means physical or sexual abuse, neglect, financial abuse, abandonment, isolation, abduction, or other treatment that results in physical harm, pain, or mental suffering, the deprivation of care by a caregiver, or other deprivation by a custodian or provider of goods or services that are necessary to avoid physical harm or mental suffering.

(2) "Child abuse" means an act proscribed by Section 273d of the Penal Code.

(3) "Domestic violence" has the meaning set forth in Section 13700 of the Penal Code. Subject to a hearing conducted pursuant to Section 352, which shall include consideration of any corroboration and remoteness in time, "domestic violence" has the further meaning as set forth in Section 6211 of the Family Code, if the act occurred no more than five years before the charged offense.

(e) Evidence of acts occurring more than 10 years before the charged offense is inadmissible under this section, unless the court determines that the admission of this evidence is in the interest of justice.

(f) Evidence of the findings and determinations of administrative agencies regulating the conduct of health facilities licensed under Section 1250 of the Health and Safety Code is inadmissible under this section. **Leg.H.** Added Stats 1996 ch 261 §2 (SB 1876). Amended Stats 1998 ch 707 §1 (SB 1682); Stats 2000 ch 97 §1 (AB 2063); Stats 2004 ch 116 §1 (AB 141), ch 823 §6.5 (AB 20); Stats 2005 ch 464 §1 (AB 114), effective January 1, 2006.

CHAPTER 2
MEDIATION

Definitions. §1115.
Effect of chapter. §1116.
Applicability of chapter. §1117.
Oral agreement. §1118.
Admissibility, discovery, or disclosure of evidence; Confidentiality. §1119.
Exceptions to inadmissibility or protection from disclosure. §1120.
Reports. §1121.
Conditions for admissibility of communication or writing. §1122.
Admissibility or disclosure of written settlement agreement. §1123.
Admissibility or disclosure of oral agreement. §1124.
Conditions constituting end of mediation. §1125.
Confidentiality after end of mediation. §1126.
Attorney fees for compelling mediator to testify or produce writing. §1127.
Reference to mediation during subsequent proceedings. §1128.
Printed disclosure and acknowledgment requirements. §1129.

§1115. Definitions

For purposes of this chapter:

(a) "Mediation" means a process in which a neutral person or persons facilitate communication between the disputants to assist them in reaching a mutually acceptable agreement.

(b) "Mediator" means a neutral person who conducts a mediation. "Mediator" includes any person designated by a mediator either to assist in the mediation or to communicate with the participants in preparation for a mediation.

(c) "Mediation consultation" means a communication between a person and a mediator for the purpose of initiating, considering, or reconvening a mediation or retaining the mediator. **Leg.H.** Added Stats 1997 ch 772 §3 (AB 939).

§1116. Effect of chapter

(a) Nothing in this chapter expands or limits a court's authority to order participation in a dispute resolution proceeding. Nothing in this chapter authorizes or affects the enforceability of a contract clause in which parties agree to the use of mediation.

(b) Nothing in this chapter makes admissible evidence that is inadmissible under Section 1152 or any other statute. **Leg.H.** Added Stats 1997 ch 772 §3 (AB 939).

§1117. Applicability of chapter

(a) Except as provided in subdivision (b), this chapter applies to a mediation as defined in Section 1115.

(b) This chapter does not apply to either of the following:

(1) A proceeding under Part 1 (commencing with Section 1800) of Division 5 of the Family Code or Chapter 11 (commencing with Section 3160) of Part 2 of Division 8 of the Family Code.

(2) A settlement conference pursuant to Rule 3.1380 of the California Rules of Court. **Leg.H.** Added Stats 1997 ch 772 §3 (AB 939). Amended Stats 2007 ch 130 §84 (AB 299), effective January 1, 2008.

§1118. Oral agreement

An oral agreement "in accordance with Section 1118" means an oral agreement that satisfies all of the following conditions:

(a) The oral agreement is recorded by a court reporter or reliable means of audio recording.

(b) The terms of the oral agreement are recited on the record in the presence of the parties and the mediator, and the parties express on the record that they agree to the terms recited.

(c) The parties to the oral agreement expressly state on the record that the agreement is enforceable or binding, or words to that effect.

(d) The recording is reduced to writing and the writing is signed by the parties within 72 hours after it is recorded. **Leg.H.** Added Stats 1997 ch 772 §3 (AB 939). Amended Stats 2009 ch 88 §35 (AB 176), effective January 1, 2010; Stats 2010 ch 328 §64 (SB 1330), effective January 1, 2011.

§1119. Admissibility, discovery, or disclosure of evidence; Confidentiality

Except as otherwise provided in this chapter:

(a) No evidence of anything said or any admission made for the purpose of, in the course of, or pursuant to, a mediation or a mediation consultation is admissible or subject to discovery, and disclosure of the evidence shall not be compelled, in any arbitration, administrative adjudication, civil action, or other noncriminal proceeding in which, pursuant to law, testimony can be compelled to be given.

(b) No writing, as defined in Section 250, that is prepared for the purpose of, in the course of, or pursuant to, a mediation or a mediation consultation, is admissible or subject to discovery, and disclosure of the writing shall not be compelled, in any arbitration, administrative adjudication, civil action, or other noncriminal proceeding in which, pursuant to law, testimony can be compelled to be given.

(c) All communications, negotiations, or settlement discussions by and between participants in the course of a mediation or a mediation consultation shall remain confidential. **Leg.H.** Added Stats 1997 ch 772 §3 (AB 939).

§1120. Exceptions to inadmissibility or protection from disclosure

(a) Evidence otherwise admissible or subject to discovery outside of a mediation or a mediation consultation shall not be or become inadmissible or protected from disclosure solely by reason of its introduction or use in a mediation or a mediation consultation.

(b) This chapter does not limit any of the following:

(1) The admissibility of an agreement to mediate a dispute.

(2) The effect of an agreement not to take a default or an agreement to extend the time within which to act or refrain from acting in a pending civil action.

(3) Disclosure of the mere fact that a mediator has served, is serving, will serve, or was contacted about serving as a mediator in a dispute.

(4) The admissibility of declarations of disclosure required by Sections 2104 and 2105 of the Family Code, even if prepared for the purpose of, in the course of, or pursuant to, a mediation or a mediation consultation. **Leg.H.** Added Stats 1997 ch 772 §3 (AB 939). Amended Stats 2017 ch 60 §1 (SB 217), effective January 1, 2018.

2017 Note: It is the intent of the Legislature that this act codify the holding of *Lappe v. Superior Court* (2014) 232 Cal.App.4th 774. Stats 2017 ch 60 (SB 217) §2.

§1121. Reports

Neither a mediator nor anyone else may submit to a court or other adjudicative body, and a court or other adjudicative body may not consider, any report, assessment, evaluation, recommendation, or finding of any kind by the mediator concerning a mediation conducted by the mediator, other than a report that is mandated by court rule or other law and that states only whether an agreement was reached, unless all parties to the mediation expressly agree otherwise in writing, or orally in accordance with Section 1118. **Leg.H.** Added Stats 1997 ch 772 §3 (AB 939).

§1122. Conditions for admissibility of communication or writing

(a) A communication or a writing, as defined in Section 250, that is made or prepared for the purpose of, or in the course of, or pursuant to, a mediation or a mediation consultation, is not made inadmissible, or protected from disclosure, by provisions of this chapter if any of the following conditions are satisfied:

(1) All persons who conduct or otherwise participate in the mediation expressly agree in writing, or orally in accordance with Section 1118, to disclosure of the communication, document, or writing.

(2) The communication, document, or writing was prepared by or on behalf of fewer than all the mediation participants, those participants expressly agree in writing, or orally in accordance with Section 1118, to its disclosure, and the communication, document, or writing does not disclose anything said or done or any admission made in the course of the mediation.

(3) The communication, document, or writing is related to an attorney's compliance with the requirements described in Section 1129 and does not disclose anything said or done or any admission made in the course of the mediation, in which case the communication, document, or writing may be used in an attorney disciplinary proceeding to determine whether the attorney has complied with Section 1129.

(b) For purposes of subdivision (a), if the neutral person who conducts a mediation expressly agrees to disclosure, that agreement also binds any other person described in subdivision (b) of Section 1115. **Leg.H.** Added Stats 1997 ch 772 §3 (AB 939). Amended Stats 2018 ch 350 §1 (SB 954), effective January 1, 2019.

§1123. Admissibility or disclosure of written settlement agreement

A written settlement agreement prepared in the course of, or pursuant to, a mediation, is not made inadmissible, or protected from disclosure, by provisions of this chapter if the agreement is signed by the settling parties and any of the following conditions are satisfied:

(a) The agreement provides that it is admissible or subject to disclosure, or words to that effect.

(b) The agreement provides that it is enforceable or binding or words to that effect.

(c) All parties to the agreement expressly agree in writing, or orally in accordance with Section 1118, to its disclosure.

(d) The agreement is used to show fraud, duress, or illegality that is relevant to an issue in dispute. **Leg.H.** Added Stats 1997 ch 772 §3 (AB 939).

§1124. Admissibility or disclosure of oral agreement

An oral agreement made in the course of, or pursuant to, a mediation is not made inadmissible, or protected from disclosure, by the provisions of this chapter if any of the following conditions are satisfied:

(a) The agreement is in accordance with Section 1118.

(b) The agreement is in accordance with subdivisions (a), (b), and (d) of Section 1118, and all parties to the agreement expressly agree, in writing or orally in accordance with Section 1118, to disclosure of the agreement.

(c) The agreement is in accordance with subdivisions (a), (b), and (d) of Section 1118, and the agreement is used to show fraud, duress, or illegality that is relevant to an issue in dispute. **Leg.H.** Added Stats 1997 ch 772 §3 (AB 939).

§1125. Conditions constituting end of mediation

(a) For purposes of confidentiality under this chapter, a mediation ends when any one of the following conditions is satisfied:

(1) The parties execute a written settlement agreement that fully resolves the dispute.

(2) An oral agreement that fully resolves the dispute is reached in accordance with Section 1118.

(3) The mediator provides the mediation participants with a writing signed by the mediator that states that the mediation is terminated, or words to that effect, which shall be consistent with Section 1121.

(4) A party provides the mediator and the other mediation participants with a writing stating that the mediation is terminated, or words to that effect, which shall be consistent with Section 1121. In a mediation involving more than two parties, the mediation may continue as to the remaining parties or be terminated in accordance with this section.

(5) For 10 calendar days, there is no communication between the mediator and any of the parties to the mediation relating to the dispute. The mediator and the parties may shorten or extend this time by agreement.

(b) For purposes of confidentiality under this chapter, if a mediation partially resolves a dispute, mediation ends when either of the following conditions is satisfied:

(1) The parties execute a written settlement agreement that partially resolves the dispute.

(2) An oral agreement that partially resolves the dispute is reached in accordance with Section 1118.

(c) This section does not preclude a party from ending a mediation without reaching an agreement. This section does not otherwise affect the extent to which a party may terminate a mediation. **Leg.H.** Added Stats 1997 ch 772 §3 (AB 939).

§1126. Confidentiality after end of mediation

Anything said, any admission made, or any writing that is inadmissible, protected from disclosure, and confidential under this chapter before a mediation ends, shall remain inadmissible, protected from disclosure, and confidential to the same extent after the mediation ends. **Leg.H.** Added Stats 1997 ch 772 §3 (AB 939).

§1127. Attorney fees for compelling mediator to testify or produce writing

If a person subpoenas or otherwise seeks to compel a mediator to testify or produce a writing, as defined in Section 250, and the court or other adjudicative body determines that the testimony or writing is inadmissible under this chapter, or protected from disclosure under this chapter, the court or adjudicative body making the determination shall award reasonable attorney's fees and costs to the mediator against the person seeking the testimony or writing. **Leg.H.** Added Stats 1997 ch 772 §3 (AB 939).

§1128. Reference to mediation during subsequent proceedings

Any reference to a mediation during any subsequent trial is an irregularity in the proceedings of the trial for the purposes of Section 657 of the Code of Civil Procedure. Any reference to a mediation during any other subsequent noncriminal proceeding is grounds for vacating or modifying the decision in that proceeding, in whole or in part, and granting a new or further hearing on all or part of the issues, if the reference materially affected the substantial rights of the party requesting relief. **Leg.H.** Added Stats 1997 ch 772 §3 (AB 939).

§1129. Printed disclosure and acknowledgment requirements

(a) Except in the case of a class or representative action, an attorney representing a client participating in a mediation or a mediation consultation shall, as soon as reasonably possible before the client agrees to participate in the mediation or mediation consultation, provide that client with a printed disclosure containing the confidentiality restrictions described in Section 1119 and obtain a printed acknowledgment signed by that client stating that he or she has read and understands the confidentiality restrictions.

(b) An attorney who is retained after an individual agrees to participate in the mediation or mediation consultation shall, as soon as reasonably possible after being retained, comply with the printed disclosure and acknowledgment requirements described in subdivision (a).

(c) The printed disclosure required by subdivision (a) shall:

(1) Be printed in the preferred language of the client in at least 12-point font.

(2) Be printed on a single page that is not attached to any other document provided to the client.

(3) Include the names of the attorney and the client and be signed and dated by the attorney and the client.

(d) If the requirements in subdivision (c) are met, the following disclosure shall be deemed to comply with the requirements of subdivision (a):

Mediation Disclosure Notification and Acknowledgment

To promote communication in mediation, California law generally makes mediation a confidential process. California's mediation confidentiality laws are laid out in Sections 703.5 and 1115 to 1129, inclusive, of the Evidence Code. Those laws establish the confidentiality of mediation and limit the disclosure, admissibility, and a court's consideration of communications, writings, and conduct in connection with a mediation. In general, those laws mean the following:

• All communications, negotiations, or settlement offers in the course of a mediation must remain confidential.

• Statements made and writings prepared in connection with a mediation are not admissible or subject to discovery or compelled disclosure in noncriminal proceedings.

• A mediator's report, opinion, recommendation, or finding about what occurred in a mediation may not be submitted to or considered by a court or another adjudicative body.

• A mediator cannot testify in any subsequent civil proceeding about any communication or conduct occurring at, or in connection with, a mediation.

This means that all communications between you and your attorney made in preparation for a mediation, or during a mediation, are confidential and cannot be disclosed or used (except in extremely limited circumstances), even if you later decide to sue your attorney for malpractice because of something that happens during the mediation.

I, _____ [Name of Client], understand that, unless all participants agree otherwise, no oral or written communication made during a mediation, or in preparation for a mediation, including communications between me and my attorney, can be used as evidence in any subsequent noncriminal legal action including an action against my attorney for malpractice or an ethical violation.

NOTE: This disclosure and signed acknowledgment does not limit your attorney's potential liability to you for professional malpractice, or prevent you from (1) reporting any professional misconduct by your attorney to the State Bar of California or (2) cooperating with any disciplinary investigation or criminal prosecution of your attorney.

[Name of Client] _____ [Date signed] _____
[Name of Attorney] _____ [Date signed] _____

(e) Failure of an attorney to comply with this section is not a basis to set aside an agreement prepared in the course of, or pursuant to, a mediation. **Leg.H.** Added Stats 2018 ch 350 §2 (SB 954), effective January 1, 2019.

CHAPTER 3
OTHER EVIDENCE AFFECTED OR EXCLUDED BY EXTRINSIC POLICIES

Evidence to test a verdict. §1150.
Subsequent remedial conduct. §1151.
Admissibility of evidence of offer to compromise. §1152.
Offer to plead guilty or withdraw plea of guilty by criminal defendant. §1153.
Offer to resolve offense against property by civil process. §1153.5.
Offer to discount a claim. §1154.
Liability insurance. §1155.
Records of medical or dental study of in-hospital staff committee. §1156.
Medical or psychiatric studies undertaken by quality assurance committee. §1156.1.
Person suffered or experienced excited delirium. § 1156.5.
Exemption from discovery of proceedings and records of specified committees and bodies. §1157.
Proceedings or records of nonprofit medical care foundation or professional standards review organization. §1157.5.
Proceedings and records of mental health quality assurance committees. §1157.6.
Proceedings and records of committee reporting on specialty health care services. §1157.7.
Inspection and copying of records upon patient's written authorization; Authorization form. §1158.
Admissibility of live animal experimentation evidence in motor vehicle product liability action. §1159.
Statement of benevolence. §1160.
Admissibility of evidence relating to victim of human trafficking. §1161.
Admissibility of evidence; Serious felony, assault, extortion, sexual battery, or stalking; Prostitution. §1162.

§1150. Evidence to test a verdict

(a) Upon an inquiry as to the validity of a verdict, any otherwise admissible evidence may be received as to statements made, or conduct, conditions, or events occurring, either within or without the jury room, of such a character as is likely to have influenced the verdict improperly. No evidence is admissible to show the effect of such statement, conduct, condition, or event upon a juror either in influencing him to assent to or dissent from the verdict or concerning the mental processes by which it was determined.

(b) Nothing in this code affects the law relating to the competence of a juror to give evidence to impeach or support a verdict. **Leg.H.** Enacted Stats 1965 ch 299 §2, operative January 1, 1967.

§1151. Subsequent remedial conduct

When, after the occurrence of an event, remedial or precautionary measures are taken, which, if taken previously, would have tended to make the event less likely to occur, evidence of such subsequent measures is inadmissible to prove negligence or culpable conduct in connection with the event. **Leg.H.** Enacted Stats 1965 ch 299 §2, operative January 1, 1967.

§1152. Admissibility of evidence of offer to compromise

(a) Evidence that a person has, in compromise or from humanitarian motives, furnished or offered or promised to furnish money or any other thing, act, or service to another who has sustained or will sustain or claims that he or she has sustained or will sustain loss or damage, as well as any conduct or statements made in negotiation thereof, is inadmissible to prove his or her liability for the loss or damage or any part of it.

(b) In the event that evidence of an offer to compromise is admitted in an action for breach of the covenant of good faith and fair dealing or violation of subdivision (h) of Section 790.03 of the Insurance Code, then at the request of the party against whom the evidence is admitted, or at the request of the party who made the offer to compromise that was admitted, evidence relating to any other offer or counteroffer to compromise the same or substantially the same claimed loss or damage shall also be admissible for the same purpose as the initial evidence regarding settlement. Other than as may be admitted in an action for breach of the covenant of good faith and fair dealing or violation of subdivision (h) of Section 790.03 of the Insurance Code, evidence of settlement offers shall not be admitted in a motion for a new trial, in any proceeding involving an additur or remittitur, or on appeal.

(c) This section does not affect the admissibility of evidence of any of the following:

(1) Partial satisfaction of an asserted claim or demand without questioning its validity when such evidence is offered to prove the validity of the claim.

(2) A debtor's payment or promise to pay all or a part of his or her preexisting debt when such evidence is offered to prove the creation of a new duty on his or her part or a revival of his or her preexisting duty. **Leg.H.** Enacted Stats 1965 ch 299 §2, operative January 1, 1967. Amended Stats 1967 ch 650 §7; Stats 1987 ch 496 §1.

§1152.5. [Section repealed 1998]

Leg.H. Added Stats 1985 ch 731 §1. Amended Stats 1992 ch 163 §73 (AB 2641), operative January 1, 1994; Stats 1993 ch 219 §77.7 (AB 1500), ch 1261 §6 (SB 401); Stats 1994 ch 1269 §8 (AB 2208); Stats 1996 ch 174 §1 (SB 1522). Repealed Stats 1997 ch 772 §5 (AB 939). See Ev C §1119.

§1152.6. [Section repealed 1998]

Leg.H. Added Stats 1995 ch 576 §8 (AB 1225). Repealed Stats 1997 ch 772 §6 (AB 939). See Ev C §1121.

§1153. Offer to plead guilty or withdraw plea of guilty by criminal defendant

Evidence of a plea of guilty, later withdrawn, or of an offer to plead guilty to the crime charged or to any other crime, made by the defendant in a criminal action is inadmissible in any action or in any proceeding of any nature, including proceedings before agencies, commissions, boards, and tribunals. **Leg.H.** Enacted Stats 1965 ch 299 §2, operative January 1, 1967.

§1153.5. Offer to resolve offense against property by civil process

Evidence of an offer for civil resolution of a criminal matter pursuant to the provisions of Section 33 of the Code of Civil Procedure, or admissions made in the course of or negotiations for the offer shall not be admissible in any action. **Leg.H.** Added Stats 1982 ch 1518 §2.

§1154. Offer to discount a claim

Evidence that a person has accepted or offered or promised to accept a sum of money or any other thing, act, or service in satisfaction of a claim, as well as any conduct or statements made in negotiation thereof, is inadmissible to prove the invalidity of the claim or any part of it. **Leg.H.** Enacted Stats 1965 ch 299 §2, operative January 1, 1967.

§1155. Liability insurance

Evidence that a person was, at the time a harm was suffered by another, insured wholly or partially against loss arising from liability for that harm is inadmissible to prove negligence or other wrongdoing. **Leg.H.** Enacted Stats 1965 ch 299 §2, operative January 1, 1967.

§1156. Records of medical or dental study of in-hospital staff committee

(a) In-hospital medical or medical-dental staff committees of a licensed hospital may engage in research and medical or dental study for the purpose of reducing morbidity or mortality, and may make findings and recommendations relating to such purpose. Except as provided in subdivision (b), the written records of interviews, reports, statements, or memoranda of such in-hospital medical or medical-dental staff committees relating to such medical or dental studies are subject to Title 4 (commencing with Section 2016.010) of Part 4 of the Code of Civil Procedure (relating to discovery proceedings) but, subject to subdivisions (c) and (d), shall not be admitted as evidence in any action or before any administrative body, agency, or person.

(b) The disclosure, with or without the consent of the patient, of information concerning him to such in-hospital medical or medical-dental staff committee does not make unprivileged any information that would otherwise be privileged under Section 994 or 1014; but, notwithstanding Sections 994 and 1014, such information is subject to discovery under subdivision (a) except that the identity of any patient may not be discovered under subdivision (a) unless the patient consents to such disclosure.

(c) This section does not affect the admissibility in evidence of the original medical or dental records of any patient.

(d) This section does not exclude evidence which is relevant evidence in a criminal action. **Leg.H.** Enacted Stats 1965 ch 299 §2, operative January 1, 1967. Amended Stats 1975 ch 674 §1; Stats 2004 ch 182 §30 (AB 3081), operative July 1, 2005.

§1156.1. Medical or psychiatric studies undertaken by quality assurance committee

(a) A committee established in compliance with Sections 4070 and 5624 of the Welfare and Institutions Code may engage in research and medical or psychiatric study for the purpose of reducing morbidity or mortality, and may make findings and recommendations to the county and state relating to such purpose. Except as provided in subdivision (b), the written records of interviews, reports, statements, or memoranda of such committees relating to such medical or psychiatric studies are subject to Title 4 (commencing with Section 2016.010) of Part 4 of the Code of Civil Procedure but, subject to subdivisions (c) and (d), shall not be admitted as evidence in any action or before any administrative body, agency, or person.

(b) The disclosure, with or without the consent of the patient, of information concerning him or her to such committee does not make unprivileged any information that would otherwise be privileged under Section 994 or 1014. However, notwithstanding Sections 994 and 1014, such information is subject to discovery under subdivision (a) except that the identity of any patient may not be discovered under subdivision (a) unless the patient consents to such disclosure.

(c) This section does not affect the admissibility in evidence of the original medical or psychiatric records of any patient.

(d) This section does not exclude evidence which is relevant evidence in a criminal action. **Leg.H.** Added Stats 1982 ch 234 §4, effective June 2, 1982. Amended Stats 2004 ch 182 §31 (AB 3081), operative July 1, 2005.

§1156.5. Person suffered or experienced excited delirium

(a) Evidence that a person suffered or experienced excited delirium shall not be admitted in any civil action.

(b) A party or witness may describe the factual circumstances surrounding the case, including a person's demeanor, conduct, and physical and mental condition at issue, including, but not limited to, a person's state of agitation, excitability, paranoia, extreme aggression, physical violence, and apparent immunity to pain, but shall not describe or diagnose such demeanor, conduct, or condition by use of the term excited delirium, or attribute such demeanor, conduct, or physical and mental condition to that term.

(c) For the purposes of this section, "excited delirium" means a term used to describe a person's state of agitation, excitability, paranoia, extreme aggression, physical violence, and apparent immunity to pain that is not listed in the most current version of the Diagnostic and Statistical Manual of Mental Disorders, or for which the court finds there is insufficient scientific evidence or diagnostic criteria to be recognized as a medical condition. Excited delirium also includes excited delirium syndrome, excited delirium, hyperactive delirium, agitated delirium, and exhaustive mania. **Leg.H.** Added Stats 2023 ch 431 §1 (AB 360), effective January 1, 2024.

§1157. Exemption from discovery of proceedings and records of specified committees and bodies

(a) Neither the proceedings nor the records of organized committees of medical, medical-dental, podiatric, registered dietitian, psychological, marriage and family therapist, licensed clinical social worker, professional clinical counselor, pharmacist, [1] **prehospital emergency medical care person or personnel, or veterinary staffs**, or of a peer review body, as defined in Section 805 of the Business and Professions Code, having the responsibility of evaluation and improvement of the quality of care rendered in the hospital, or for that peer review body, or medical or dental review or dental hygienist review or chiropractic review or podiatric review or registered dietitian review or pharmacist review or veterinary review or acupuncturist review or licensed midwife review **or prehospital emergency medical care person or personnel review** committees of local medical, dental, dental hygienist, podiatric, dietetic, pharmacist, veterinary, acupuncture, [2] **chiropractic, or prehospital emergency medical care person or personnel** societies, marriage and family therapist, licensed clinical social worker, professional clinical counselor, or psychological review committees of state or local marriage and family therapist, state or local licensed clinical social worker, state or local licensed professional clinical counselor, or state or local psychological associations or societies or licensed midwife associations or societies having the responsibility of evaluation and improvement of the quality of care, shall be subject to discovery.

(b) Except as hereinafter provided, a person in attendance at a meeting of any of the committees described in subdivision (a) shall not be required to testify as to what transpired at that meeting.

(c) The prohibition relating to discovery or testimony does not apply to the statements made by a person in attendance at a meeting of any of the committees described in subdivision (a) if that person is a party to an action or proceeding the subject matter of which was reviewed at that meeting, to a person requesting hospital staff privileges, or in an action against an insurance carrier alleging bad faith by the carrier in refusing to accept a settlement offer within the policy limits.

(d) The prohibitions in this section do not apply to medical, dental, dental hygienist, podiatric, dietetic, psychological, marriage and family therapist, licensed clinical social worker, professional clinical counselor, pharmacist, veterinary, acupuncture, midwifery, [3] **chiropractic, or prehospital emergency medical care person or personnel** society committees that exceed 10 percent of the membership of the society, nor to any of those committees if a person serves upon the committee when his or her own conduct or practice is being reviewed.

(e) The amendments made to this section by Chapter 1081 of the Statutes of 1983, or at the 1985 portion of the 1985-86 Regular Session of the Legislature, at the 1990 portion of the 1989-90 Regular Session of the Legislature, at the 2000 portion of the 1999-2000 Regular Session of the Legislature, at the 2011 portion of the 2011-12 Regular Session of the Legislature, [4] at the 2015 portion of the 2015-16 Regular Session of the

Legislature, **or at the 2024 portion of the 2023-24 Regular Session of the Legislature,** do not exclude the discovery or use of relevant evidence in a criminal action.

(f) For purposes of this section, "prehospital emergency medical care person or personnel" has the same meaning as defined in paragraph (1) of subdivision (a) of Section 1797.188 of the Health and Safety Code. **Leg.H.** Added Stats 1968 ch 1122 §1. Amended Stats 1975 ch 674 §2; Stats 1978 ch 7 §1, effective February 10, 1978, ch 503 §2; Stats 1982 ch 705 §3; Stats 1983 ch 289 §3, ch 422 §1, ch 1081 §2.5; Stats 1985 ch 725 §1; Stats 1990 ch 196 §2 (AB 1565); Stats 1994 ch 815 §3 (SB 1279); Stats 2000 ch 136 §1 (AB 2374); Stats 2011 ch 381 §23 (SB 146), effective January 1, 2012; Stats 2015 ch 274 §1 (SB 672), effective January 1, 2016; Stats 2016 ch 86 §128 (SB 1171), effective January 1, 2017; Stats 2017 ch 775 §109 (SB 798), effective January 1, 2018; Stats 2024 ch 329 §1 (AB 2225), effective January 1, 2025.

§1157. 2024 Deletes. [1] or veterinary staffs in hospitals [2] or chiropractic [3] or chiropractic [4] or

§1157.5. Proceedings or records of nonprofit medical care foundation or professional standards review organization

Except in actions involving a claim of a provider of health care services for payment for such services, the prohibition relating to discovery or testimony provided by Section 1157 shall be applicable to the proceedings or records of an organized committee of any nonprofit medical care foundation or professional standards review organization which is organized in a manner which makes available professional competence to review health care services with respect to medical necessity, quality of care, or economic justification of charges or level of care. **Leg.H.** Added Stats 1973 ch 848 §1. Amended Stats 1980 ch 524 §1.

§1157.6. Proceedings and records of mental health quality assurance committees

Neither the proceedings nor the records of a committee established in compliance with Sections 4070 and 5624 of the Welfare and Institutions Code having the responsibility of evaluation and improvement of the quality of mental health care rendered in county operated and contracted mental health facilities shall be subject to discovery. Except as provided in this section, no person in attendance at a meeting of any such committee shall be required to testify as to what transpired thereat. The prohibition relating to discovery or testimony shall not apply to the statements made by any person in attendance at such a meeting who is a party to an action or proceeding the subject matter of which was reviewed at such meeting, or to any person requesting facility staff privileges. **Leg.H.** Added Stats 1982 ch 234 §5, effective June 2, 1982.

Editor's Note: W & I C §5624, referred to in the first sentence of this section, was repealed by Stats 1991 ch 89 §108 (AB 1288).

§1157.7. Proceedings and records of committee reporting on specialty health care services

The prohibition relating to discovery or testimony provided in Section 1157 shall be applicable to proceedings and records of any committee established by a local governmental agency to monitor, evaluate, and report on the necessity, quality, and level of specialty health services, including, but not limited to, trauma care services, provided by a general acute care hospital that has been designated or recognized by that governmental agency as qualified to render specialty health care services. The provisions of Division 10 (commencing with Section 7920.000) of Title 1 of the Government Code and Chapter 9 (commencing with Section 54950) of Division 2 of Title 5 of the Government Code shall not be applicable to the committee records and proceedings. **Leg.H.** Added Stats 1983 ch 1237 §1. Amended Stats 2021 ch 615 §105 (AB 474), effective January 1, 2022.

§1158. Inspection and copying of records upon patient's written authorization; Authorization form

(a) For purposes of this section, "medical provider" means physician and surgeon, dentist, registered nurse, dispensing optician, registered physical therapist, podiatrist, licensed psychologist, osteopathic physician and surgeon, chiropractor, clinical laboratory bioanalyst, clinical laboratory technologist, or pharmacist or pharmacy, duly licensed as such under the laws of the state, or a licensed hospital.

(b) Before the filing of any action or the appearance of a defendant in an action, if an attorney at law or his or her representative presents a written authorization therefor signed by an adult patient, by the guardian or conservator of his or her person or estate, or, in the case of a minor, by a parent or guardian of the minor, or by the personal representative or an heir of a deceased patient, or a copy thereof, to a medical provider, the medical provider shall promptly make all of the patient's records under the medical provider's custody or control available for inspection and copying by the attorney at law or his or her representative.

(c) Copying of medical records shall not be performed by a medical provider, or by an agent thereof, when the requesting attorney has employed a professional photocopier or anyone identified in Section 22451 of the Business and Professions Code as his or her representative to obtain or review the records on his or her behalf. The presentation of the authorization by the agent on behalf of the attorney shall be sufficient proof that the agent is the attorney's representative.

(d) Failure to make the records available during business hours, within five days after the presentation of the written authorization, may subject the medical provider having custody or control of the records to liability for all reasonable expenses, including attorney's fees, incurred in any proceeding to enforce this section.

(e)(1) All reasonable costs incurred by a medical provider in making patient records available pursuant to this section may be charged against the attorney who requested the records.

(2) "Reasonable cost," as used in this section, shall include, but not be limited to, the following specific costs: ten cents ($0.10) per page for standard reproduction of documents of a size 8½ by 14 inches or less; twenty cents ($0.20) per page for copying of documents from microfilm; actual costs for the reproduction of oversize documents or the reproduction of documents requiring special processing which are made in response to an authorization; reasonable clerical costs incurred in locating and making the records available to be billed at the maximum rate of sixteen dollars ($16) per hour per person, computed on the basis of four dollars ($4) per quarter hour or fraction thereof; actual postage charges; and actual costs, if any, charged to the witness by a third person for the retrieval and return of records held by that third person.

(f) If the records are delivered to the attorney or the attorney's representative for inspection or photocopying at the record custodian's place of business, the only fee for complying with the authorization shall not exceed fifteen dollars ($15), plus actual costs, if any, charged to the record custodian by a third person for retrieval and return of records held offsite by the third person.

(g) If the records requested pursuant to subdivision (b) are maintained electronically and if the requesting party requests an electronic copy of such information, the medical provider shall provide the requested medical records in the electronic form and format requested by the requesting party, if it is readily producible in such form and format, or, if not, in a readable form and format as agreed to by the medical provider and the requesting party.

(h) A medical provider shall accept a signed and completed authorization form for the disclosure of health information if both of the following conditions are satisfied:

(1) The medical provider determines that the form is valid.

(2) The form is printed in a typeface no smaller than 14-point type and is in substantially the following form:

AUTHORIZATION FOR DISCLOSURE OF HEALTH INFORMATION PURSUANT TO EVIDENCE CODE SECTION 1158

The undersigned authorizes the medical provider designated below to disclose specified medical records to a designated recipient. The medical provider shall not condition treatment, payment, enrollment, or eligibility for benefits on the submission of this authorization.

Medical provider: _____

Patient name: _____

Medical record number: _____

Date of birth: _____

Address: _____

Telephone number: _____

Email: _____

Recipient name: _____

Recipient address: _____

Recipient telephone number: _____

Recipient email: _____

Health information requested (check all that apply):

___ Records dated from _____ to _____.

__ Radiology records: _____ images or films _____ reports _____ digital/CD, if available.
__ Laboratory results dated.
__ Laboratory results regarding specific test(s) only (specify) _____.
__ All records.
__ Records related to a specific injury, treatment, or other purpose (specify): _____.
Note: records may include information related to mental health, alcohol or drug use, and HIV or AIDS. However, treatment records from mental health and alcohol or drug departments and results of HIV tests will not be disclosed unless specifically requested (check all that apply):
__ Mental health records.
__ Alcohol or drug records.
__ HIV test results.
Method of delivery of requested records:
__ Mail
__ Pick up
__ Electronic delivery, recipient email: _____
This authorization is effective for one year from the date of the signature unless a different date is specified here: _____.
This authorization may be revoked upon written request, but any revocation will not apply to information disclosed before receipt of the written request.
A copy of this authorization is as valid as the original. The undersigned has the right to receive a copy of this authorization.
Notice: Once the requested health information is disclosed, any disclosure of the information by the recipient may no longer be protected under the federal Health Insurance Portability and Accountability Act of 1996 (HIPAA).
Patient signature*: _____
Date: _____
Print name: _____
*If not signed by the patient, please indicate relationship to the patient (check one, if applicable):
__ Parent or guardian of minor patient who could not have consented to health care.
__ Guardian or conservator of an incompetent patient.
__ Beneficiary or personal representative of deceased patient.

Leg.H. Added Stats 1968 ch 1122 §2. Amended Stats 1970 ch 556 §1; Stats 1974 ch 250 §1, ch 667 §1; Stats 1975 ch 563 §1; Stats 1978 ch 493 §1; Stats 1980 ch 697 §1; Stats 1986 ch 603 §5; Stats 1987 ch 19 §1, effective May 12, 1987; Stats 1993 ch 226 §9 (AB 1987); Stats 1997 ch 442 §15 (AB 758); Stats 2015 ch 528 §1 (AB 1337), effective January 1, 2016.

§1159. Admissibility of live animal experimentation evidence in motor vehicle product liability action

(a) No evidence pertaining to live animal experimentation, including, but not limited to, injury, impact, or crash experimentation, shall be admissible in any product liability action involving a motor vehicle or vehicles.

(b) This section shall apply to cases for which a trial has not actually commenced, as described in paragraph (6) of subdivision (a) of Section 581 of the Code of Civil Procedure, on January 1, 1993. **Leg.H.** Added Stats 1992 ch 188 §1 (AB 3691).

§1160. Statement of benevolence

(a) The portion of statements, writings, or benevolent gestures expressing sympathy or a general sense of benevolence relating to the pain, suffering, or death of a person involved in an accident and made to that person or to the family of that person shall be inadmissible as evidence of an admission of liability in a civil action. A statement of fault, however, which is part of, or in addition to, any of the above shall not be inadmissible pursuant to this section.

(b) For purposes of this section:

(1) "Accident" means an occurrence resulting in injury or death to one or more persons which is not the result of willful action by a party.

(2) "Benevolent gestures" means actions which convey a sense of compassion or commiseration emanating from humane impulses.

(3) "Family" means the spouse, parent, grandparent, stepmother, stepfather, child, grandchild, brother, sister, half brother, half sister, adopted children of parent, or spouse's parents of an injured party. **Leg.H.** Added Stats 2000 ch 195 §1 (AB 2804).

§1161. Admissibility of evidence relating to victim of human trafficking

(a) Evidence that a victim of human trafficking, as defined in Section 236.1 of the Penal Code, has engaged in any commercial sexual act as a result of being a victim of human trafficking is inadmissible to prove the victim's criminal liability for the commercial sexual act.

(b) Evidence of sexual history or history of any commercial sexual act of a victim of human trafficking, as defined in Section 236.1 of the Penal Code, is inadmissible to attack the credibility or impeach the character of the victim in any civil or criminal proceeding. **Leg.H.** Adopted by voters, Prop. 35 §4, effective November 6, 2012. Amended Stats 2013 ch 126 §1 (AB 694), effective January 1, 2014.

2012 Notes: This measure shall be known and may be cited as the "Californians Against Sexual Exploitation Act" ("CASE Act"). Prop. 35 §1, November 6, 2012, General Election.

The people of the State of California declare their purpose and intent in enacting the CASE Act to be as follows:

1. To combat the crime of human trafficking and ensure just and effective punishment of people who promote or engage in the crime of human trafficking.

2. To recognize trafficked individuals as victims and not criminals, and to protect the rights of trafficked victims.

3. To strengthen laws regarding sexual exploitation, including sex offender registration requirements, to allow law enforcement to track and prevent online sex offenses and human trafficking. Prop. 35 §3, November 6, 2012, General Election.

§1162. Admissibility of evidence; Serious felony, assault, extortion, sexual battery, or stalking; Prostitution

Evidence that a victim of, or a witness to, a serious felony as defined in subdivision (c) of Section 1192.7 of, an assault in violation of subdivision (a) of Section 245 of, domestic violence in violation of Section 273.5 of, extortion in violation of Section 518 of, human trafficking in violation of Section 236.1 of, sexual battery in violation of subdivision (a) of Section 243.4 of, or stalking in violation of Section 646.9 of, the Penal Code, has engaged in an act of prostitution at or around the time they were the victim of or witness to the crime is inadmissible in a separate prosecution of that victim or witness to prove criminal liability for the act of prostitution. **Leg.H.** Added Stats 2018 ch 27 §1 (AB 2243), effective January 1, 2019. Amended Stats 2019 ch 141 §3 (SB 233), effective January 1, 2020.

DIVISION 10
HEARSAY EVIDENCE

Chapter 1. General Provisions.
Chapter 2. Exceptions to the Hearsay Rule.

CHAPTER 1
GENERAL PROVISIONS

The hearsay rule. §1200.
Multiple hearsay. §1201.
Credibility of hearsay declarant. §1202.
Cross-examination of hearsay declarant. §1203.
Hearsay statements admissible at preliminary hearing. §1203.1.
Hearsay statement offered against criminal defendant. §1204.
No implied repeal. §1205.

§1200. The hearsay rule

(a) "Hearsay evidence" is evidence of a statement that was made other than by a witness while testifying at the hearing and that is offered to prove the truth of the matter stated.

(b) Except as provided by law, hearsay evidence is inadmissible.

(c) This section shall be known and may be cited as the hearsay rule.
Leg.H. Enacted Stats 1965 ch 299 §2, operative January 1, 1967.

§1201. Multiple hearsay

A statement within the scope of an exception to the hearsay rule is not inadmissible on the ground that the evidence of such statement is hearsay evidence if such hearsay evidence consists of one or more statements each of which meets the requirements of an exception to the hearsay rule.
Leg.H. Enacted Stats 1965 ch 299 §2, operative January 1, 1967. Amended Stats 1967 ch 650 §8.

§1202. Credibility of hearsay declarant

Evidence of a statement or other conduct by a declarant that is inconsistent with a statement by such declarant received in evidence as hearsay evidence is not inadmissible for the purpose of attacking the credibility of the declarant though he is not given and has not had an opportunity to explain or to deny such inconsistent statement or other conduct. Any other evidence offered to attack or support the credibility of the declarant is admissible if it would have been admissible had the declarant been a witness at the hearing. For the purposes of this section, the deponent of a deposition taken in the action in which it is offered shall be deemed to be a hearsay declarant. **Leg.H.** Enacted Stats 1965 ch 299 §2, operative January 1, 1967.

§1203. Cross-examination of hearsay declarant

(a) The declarant of a statement that is admitted as hearsay evidence may be called and examined by any adverse party as if under cross-examination concerning the statement.

(b) This section is not applicable if the declarant is (1) a party, (2) a person identified with a party within the meaning of subdivision (d) of Section 776, or (3) a witness who has testified in the action concerning the subject matter of the statement.

(c) This section is not applicable if the statement is one described in Article 1 (commencing with Section 1220), Article 3 (commencing with Section 1235), or Article 10 (commencing with Section 1300) of Chapter 2 of this division.

(d) A statement that is otherwise admissible as hearsay evidence is not made inadmissible by this section because the declarant who made the statement is unavailable for examination pursuant to this section. **Leg.H.** Enacted Stats 1965 ch 299 §2, operative January 1, 1967.

§1203.1. Hearsay statements admissible at preliminary hearing

Section 1203 is not applicable if the hearsay statement is offered at a preliminary examination, as provided in Section 872 of the Penal Code. **Leg.H.** Addition adopted by voters, Prop 115 §8, effective June 5, 1990.

1991 Note: Section 1203.1 may be applied to any case regardless of the date on which the crime was committed (*Tapia v. Superior Court* (1991) 53 Cal. 3d 282, 299–300, 279 Cal. Rptr. 592, 807 P.2d 434).

§1204. Hearsay statement offered against criminal defendant

A statement that is otherwise admissible as hearsay evidence is inadmissible against the defendant in a criminal action if the statement was made, either by the defendant or by another, under such circumstances that it is inadmissible against the defendant under the Constitution of the United States or the State of California. **Leg.H.** Enacted Stats 1965 ch 299 §2, operative January 1, 1967.

§1205. No implied repeal

Nothing in this division shall be construed to repeal by implication any other statute relating to hearsay evidence. **Leg.H.** Enacted Stats 1965 ch 299 §2, operative January 1, 1967.

CHAPTER 2
EXCEPTIONS TO THE HEARSAY RULE

Article 1. Confessions and Admissions.
Article 2. Declarations Against Interest.
Article 2.5. Sworn Statements Regarding Gang-Related Crimes.
Article 3. Prior Statements of Witnesses.
Article 4. Spontaneous, Contemporaneous, and Dying Declarations.
Article 5. Statements of Mental or Physical State.
Article 6. Statements Relating to Wills and to Claims Against Estates.
Article 7. Business Records.
Article 8. Official Records and Other Official Writings.
Article 9. Former Testimony.
Article 10. Judgments.
Article 11. Family History.
Article 12. Reputation and Statements Concerning Community History, Property Interests, and Character.
Article 13. Dispositive Instruments and Ancient Writings.
Article 14. Commercial, Scientific, and Similar Publications.
Article 15. Declarant Unavailable as Witness.
Article 16. Statements by Children Under the Age of 12 in Child Neglect and Abuse Proceedings.
Article 17. Physical Abuse.

ARTICLE 1
Confessions and Admissions

Admission of party. §1220.
Adoptive admission. §1221.
Authorized admission. §1222.
Admission of co-conspirator. §1223.
Statement of declarant whose liability or breach of duty is in issue. §1224.
Statement of declarant whose right or title is in issue. §1225.
Statement of minor child in parent's action for child's injury. §1226.
Wrongful death action—Statements by deceased. §1227.
Statement of minor child as victim of sexual abuse. §1228.
Signature of parent or guardian on child welfare services case plan; Acceptance of services. §1228.1.

§1220. Admission of party

Evidence of a statement is not made inadmissible by the hearsay rule when offered against the declarant in an action to which he is a party in either his individual or representative capacity, regardless of whether the statement was made in his individual or representative capacity. **Leg.H.** Enacted Stats 1965 ch 299 §2, operative January 1, 1967.

§1221. Adoptive admission

Evidence of a statement offered against a party is not made inadmissible by the hearsay rule if the statement is one of which the party, with knowledge of the content thereof, has by words or other conduct manifested his adoption or his belief in its truth. **Leg.H.** Enacted Stats 1965 ch 299 §2, operative January 1, 1967.

§1222. Authorized admission

Evidence of a statement offered against a party is not made inadmissible by the hearsay rule if:

(a) The statement was made by a person authorized by the party to make a statement or statements for him concerning the subject matter of the statement; and

(b) The evidence is offered either after admission of evidence sufficient to sustain a finding of such authority or, in the court's discretion as to the order of proof, subject to the admission of such evidence. **Leg.H.** Enacted Stats 1965 ch 299 §2, operative January 1, 1967.

§1223. Admission of co-conspirator

Evidence of a statement offered against a party is not made inadmissible by the hearsay rule if:

(a) The statement was made by the declarant while participating in a conspiracy to commit a crime or civil wrong and in furtherance of the objective of that conspiracy;

(b) The statement was made prior to or during the time that the party was participating in that conspiracy; and

(c) The evidence is offered either after admission of evidence sufficient to sustain a finding of the facts specified in subdivisions (a) and (b) or, in the court's discretion as to the order of proof, subject to the admission of such evidence. **Leg.H.** Enacted Stats 1965 ch 299 §2, operative January 1, 1967.

§1224. Statement of declarant whose liability or breach of duty is in issue

When the liability obligation, or duty of a party to a civil action is based in whole or in part upon the liability, obligation, or duty of the declarant, or when the claim or right asserted by a party to a civil action is barred or diminished by a breach of duty by the declarant, evidence of a statement made by the declarant is as admissible against the party as it would be if offered against the declarant in an action involving that liability, obligation, duty, or breach of duty. **Leg.H.** Enacted Stats 1965 ch 299 §2, operative January 1, 1967.

§1225. Statement of declarant whose right or title is in issue

When a right, title, or interest in any property or claim asserted by a party to a civil action requires a determination that a right, title, or interest exists or existed in the declarant, evidence of a statement made by the declarant during the time the party now claims the declarant was the holder of the right, title, or interest is as admissible against the party as it would be if offered against the declarant in an action involving that right, title, or interest. **Leg.H.** Enacted Stats 1965 ch 299 §2, operative January 1, 1967.

§1226. Statement of minor child in parent's action for child's injury

Evidence of a statement by a minor child is not made inadmissible by the hearsay rule if offered against the plaintiff in an action brought under Section 376 of the Code of Civil Procedure for injury to such minor child. **Leg.H.** Enacted Stats 1965 ch 299 §2, operative January 1, 1967.

§1227. Wrongful death action—Statements by deceased

Evidence of a statement by the deceased is not made inadmissible by the hearsay rule if offered against the plaintiff in an action for wrongful death brought under Article 6 (commencing with Section 377.60) of Chapter 4 of Title 3 of Part 2 of the Code of Civil Procedure. **Leg.H.** Enacted Stats 1965 ch 299 §2, operative January 1, 1967. Amended Stats 2023 ch 131 §58 (AB 1754), effective January 1, 2024.

Editor's Note: Section 377 of the Code of Civil Procedure, referred to in this section, was repealed by Stats 1992 ch 178 §19 (SB 1496).

§1228. Statement of minor child as victim of sexual abuse

Notwithstanding any other provision of law, for the purpose of establishing the elements of the crime in order to admit as evidence the confession of a person accused of violating Section 261, 264.1, 285, 286, 287, 288, 289, or 647a of, or former Section 288a of, the Penal Code, a court, in its discretion, may determine that a statement of the complaining witness is not made inadmissible by the hearsay rule if it finds all of the following:

(a) The statement was made by a minor child under the age of 12, and the contents of the statement were included in a written report of a law enforcement official or an employee of a county welfare department.

(b) The statement describes the minor child as a victim of sexual abuse.

(c) The statement was made prior to the defendant's confession. The court shall view with caution the testimony of a person recounting hearsay where there is evidence of personal bias or prejudice.

(d) There are no circumstances, such as significant inconsistencies between the confession and the statement concerning material facts establishing any element of the crime or the identification of the defendant, that would render the statement unreliable.

(e) The minor child is found to be unavailable pursuant to paragraph (2) or (3) of subdivision (a) of Section 240 or refuses to testify.

(f) The confession was memorialized in a trustworthy fashion by a law enforcement official.

If the prosecution intends to offer a statement of the complaining witness pursuant to this section, the prosecution shall serve a written notice upon the defendant at least 10 days prior to the hearing or trial at which the prosecution intends to offer the statement.

If the statement is offered during trial, the court's determination shall be made out of the presence of the jury. If the statement is found to be admissible pursuant to this section, it shall be admitted out of the presence of the jury and solely for the purpose of determining the admissibility of the confession of the defendant. **Leg.H.** Added Stats 1984 ch 1421 §1. Amended Stats 1985 ch 1572 §1, effective October 2, 1985; Stats 2018 ch 423 §23 (SB 1494), effective January 1, 2019.

§1228.1. Signature of parent or guardian on child welfare services case plan; Acceptance of services

(a) Except as provided in subdivision (b), neither the signature of any parent or legal guardian on a child welfare services case plan nor the acceptance of any services prescribed in the child welfare services case plan by any parent or legal guardian shall constitute an admission of guilt or be used as evidence against the parent or legal guardian in a court of law.

(b) A parent's or guardian's failure to cooperate, except for good cause, in the provision of services specified in the child welfare services case plan may be used as evidence, if relevant, in any hearing held pursuant to Section 366.21, 366.22, or 388 of the Welfare and Institutions Code and at any jurisdictional or dispositional hearing held on a petition filed pursuant to Section 300, 342, or 387 of the Welfare and Institutions Code. **Leg.H.** Added Stats 1995 ch 540 §1 (AB 1523). Amended Stats 1997 ch 793 §1 (AB 1544).

ARTICLE 2
Declarations Against Interest

Declarations against interest. §1230.

§1230. Declarations against interest

Evidence of a statement by a declarant having sufficient knowledge of the subject is not made inadmissible by the hearsay rule if the declarant is unavailable as a witness and the statement, when made, was so far contrary to the declarant's pecuniary or proprietary interest, or so far subjected him to the risk of civil or criminal liability, or so far tended to render invalid a claim by him against another, or created such a risk of making him an object of hatred, ridicule, or social disgrace in the community, that a reasonable man in his position would not have made the statement unless he believed it to be true. **Leg.H.** Enacted Stats 1965 ch 299 §2, operative January 1, 1967.

ARTICLE 2.5
Sworn Statements Regarding Gang-Related Crimes

Exception to hearsay rule. §1231.
Intent to offer statement. §1231.1.
Peace officer administering oath. §1231.2.
Law enforcement experience requirement. §1231.3.
Statement to jury. §1231.4.

§1231. Exception to hearsay rule

Evidence of a prior statement made by a declarant is not made inadmissible by the hearsay rule if the declarant is deceased and the proponent of introducing the statement establishes each of the following:

(a) The statement relates to acts or events relevant to a criminal prosecution under provisions of the California Street Terrorism Enforcement and Prevention Act (Chapter 11 (commencing with Section 186.20) of Title 7 of Part 1 of the Penal Code).

(b) A verbatim transcript, copy, or record of the statement exists. A record may include a statement preserved by means of an audio or video recording or equivalent technology.

(c) The statement relates to acts or events within the personal knowledge of the declarant.

(d) The statement was made under oath or affirmation in an affidavit; or was made at a deposition, preliminary hearing, grand jury hearing, or other proceeding in compliance with law, and was made under penalty of perjury.

(e) The declarant died from other than natural causes.

(f) The statement was made under circumstances that would indicate its trustworthiness and render the declarant's statement particularly worthy of belief. For purposes of this subdivision, circumstances relevant to the issue of trustworthiness include, but are not limited to, all of the following:

(1) Whether the statement was made in contemplation of a pending or anticipated criminal or civil matter, in which the declarant had an interest, other than as a witness.

(2) Whether the declarant had a bias or motive for fabricating the statement, and the extent of any bias or motive.

(3) Whether the statement is corroborated by evidence other than statements that are admissible only pursuant to this section.

(4) Whether the statement was a statement against the declarant's interest. **Leg.H.** Added Stats 1997 ch 499 §1 (SB 941).

1997 Note: Article 2.5, §§1231–1231.4, as added by Stats 1997 ch 499, shall not affect other evidentiary requirements, including, but not limited to, Sections 351 and 352 of the Evidence Code, shall not impair a party's right to attack the credibility of the declarant pursuant to Section 1202 of the Evidence Code, shall not affect the defendant's right to discovery for purposes of producing rebuttal evidence attacking the declarant's credibility, and shall not be used in a manner inconsistent with the defendant's right to due process and to confront witnesses under the United States or California Constitution. Stats 1997 ch 499 §2.

§1231.1. Intent to offer statement

A statement is admissible pursuant to Section 1231 only if the proponent of the statement makes known to the adverse party the intention to offer the statement and the particulars of the statement sufficiently in advance of the proceedings to provide the adverse party with a fair opportunity to prepare to meet the statement. **Leg.H.** Added Stats 1997 ch 499 §1 (SB 941).

1997 Note: For legislative intent, see the 1997 Note following Ev C §1231.

§1231.2. Peace officer administering oath

A peace officer may administer and certify oaths for purposes of this article. **Leg.H.** Added Stats 1997 ch 499 §1 (SB 941). Amended Stats 1998 ch 606 §2 (SB 1880).

1997 Note: For legislative intent, see the 1997 Note following Ev C §1231.

§1231.3. Law enforcement experience requirement

Any law enforcement officer testifying as to any hearsay statement pursuant to this article shall either have five years of law enforcement experience or have completed a training course certified by the Commission on Peace Officer Standards and Training which includes training in the investigation and reporting of cases and testifying at preliminary hearings and trials. **Leg.H.** Added Stats 1997 ch 499 §1 (SB 941).

1997 Note: For legislative intent, see the 1997 Note following Ev C §1231.

§1231.4. Statement to jury

If evidence of a prior statement is introduced pursuant to this article, the jury may not be told that the declarant died from other than natural causes, but shall merely be told that the declarant is unavailable. **Leg.H.** Added Stats 1997 ch 499 §1 (SB 941).

1997 Note: For legislative intent, see the 1997 Note following Ev C §1231.

ARTICLE 3
Prior Statements of Witnesses

Inconsistent statement. §1235.
Prior consistent statement. §1236.
Past recollection recorded. §1237.
Prior identification. §1238.

§1235. Inconsistent statement

Evidence of a statement made by a witness is not made inadmissible by the hearsay rule if the statement is inconsistent with his testimony at the hearing and is offered in compliance with Section 770. **Leg.H.** Enacted Stats 1965 ch 299 §2, operative January 1, 1967.

§1236. Prior consistent statement

Evidence of a statement previously made by a witness is not made inadmissible by the hearsay rule if the statement is consistent with his testimony at the hearing and is offered in compliance with Section 791. **Leg.H.** Enacted Stats 1965 ch 299 §2, operative January 1, 1967.

§1237. Past recollection recorded

(a) Evidence of a statement previously made by a witness is not made inadmissible by the hearsay rule if the statement would have been admissible if made by him while testifying, the statement concerns a matter as to which the witness has insufficient present recollection to enable him to testify fully and accurately, and the statement is contained in a writing which:

(1) Was made at a time when the fact recorded in the writing actually occurred or was fresh in the witness' memory;

(2) Was made (i) by the witness himself or under his direction or (ii) by some other person for the purpose of recording the witness' statement at the time it was made;

(3) Is offered after the witness testifies that the statement he made was a true statement of such fact; and

(4) Is offered after the writing is authenticated as an accurate record of the statement.

(b) The writing may be read into evidence, but the writing itself may not be received in evidence unless offered by an adverse party. **Leg.H.** Enacted Stats 1965 ch 299 §2, operative January 1, 1967.

§1238. Prior identification

Evidence of a statement previously made by a witness is not made inadmissible by the hearsay rule if the statement would have been admissible if made by him while testifying and:

(a) The statement is an identification of a party or another as a person who participated in a crime or other occurrence;

(b) The statement was made at a time when the crime or other occurrence was fresh in the witness' memory; and

(c) The evidence of the statement is offered after the witness testifies that he made the identification and that it was a true reflection of his opinion at that time. **Leg.H.** Enacted Stats 1965 ch 299 §2, operative January 1, 1967.

ARTICLE 4
Spontaneous, Contemporaneous, and Dying Declarations

Spontaneous statement. §1240.
Contemporaneous statement. §1241.
Dying declaration. §1242.

§1240. Spontaneous statement

Evidence of a statement is not made inadmissible by the hearsay rule if the statement:

(a) Purports to narrate, describe, or explain an act, condition, or event perceived by the declarant; and

(b) Was made spontaneously while the declarant was under the stress of excitement caused by such perception. **Leg.H.** Enacted Stats 1965 ch 299 §2, operative January 1, 1967.

§1241. Contemporaneous statement

Evidence of a statement is not made inadmissible by the hearsay rule if the statement:

(a) Is offered to explain, qualify, or make understandable conduct of the declarant; and

(b) Was made while the declarant was engaged in such conduct. **Leg.H.** Enacted Stats 1965 ch 299 §2, operative January 1, 1967.

§1242. Dying declaration

Evidence of a statement made by a dying person respecting the cause and circumstances of his death is not made inadmissible by the hearsay rule if the statement was made upon his personal knowledge and under a sense of immediately impending death. **Leg.H.** Enacted Stats 1965 ch 299 §2, operative January 1, 1967.

ARTICLE 5
Statements of Mental or Physical State

Statement of declarant's then existing mental or physical state. §1250.
Statement of declarant's previously existing mental or physical state. §1251.
Limitation on admissibility of statement of mental or physical state. §1252.
Statement describing medical history, symptoms, or pain, made for purposes of medical diagnosis or treatment. §1253.

§1250. Statement of declarant's then existing mental or physical state

(a) Subject to Section 1252, evidence of a statement of the declarant's then existing state of mind, emotion, or physical sensation (including a statement of intent, plan, motive, design, mental feeling, pain, or bodily health) is not made inadmissible by the hearsay rule when:

(1) The evidence is offered to prove the declarant's state of mind, emotion, or physical sensation at that time or at any other time when it is itself an issue in the action; or

(2) The evidence is offered to prove or explain acts or conduct of the declarant.

(b) This section does not make admissible evidence of a statement of memory or belief to prove the fact remembered or believed. **Leg.H.** Enacted Stats 1965 ch 299 §2, operative January 1, 1967.

§1251. Statement of declarant's previously existing mental or physical state

Subject to Section 1252, evidence of a statement of the declarant's state of mind, emotion, or physical sensation (including a statement of intent, plan, motive, design, mental feeling, pain, or bodily health) at a time prior to the statement is not made inadmissible by the hearsay rule if:

(a) The declarant is unavailable as a witness; and

(b) The evidence is offered to prove such prior state of mind, emotion, or physical sensation when it is itself an issue in the action and the evidence is not offered to prove any fact other than such state of mind, emotion, or physical sensation. **Leg.H.** Enacted Stats 1965 ch 299 §2, operative January 1, 1967.

§1252. Limitation on admissibility of statement of mental or physical state

Evidence of a statement is inadmissible under this article if the statement was made under circumstances such as to indicate its lack of trustworthiness. **Leg.H.** Enacted Stats 1965 ch 299 §2, operative January 1, 1967.

§1253. Statement describing medical history, symptoms, or pain, made for purposes of medical diagnosis or treatment

Subject to Section 1252, evidence of a statement is not made inadmissible by the hearsay rule if the statement was made for purposes of medical diagnosis or treatment and describes medical history, or past or present symptoms, pain, or sensations, or the inception or general character of the cause or external source thereof insofar as reasonably pertinent to diagnosis or treatment. This section applies only to a statement made by a victim who is a minor at the time of the proceedings, provided the statement was made when the victim was under the age of 12 describing any act, or attempted act, of child abuse or neglect. "Child abuse" and "child neglect," for purposes of this section, have the meanings provided in subdivision (c) of Section 1360. In addition, "child abuse" means any act proscribed by Chapter 5 (commencing with Section 281) of Title 9 of Part 1 of the Penal Code committed against a minor. **Leg.H.** Added Stats 1995 ch 87 §2 (AB 355).

ARTICLE 6
Statements Relating to Wills and to Claims Against Estates

Statement concerning declarant's will or revocable trust; Trustworthiness of statement. §1260.
Statement of decedent offered in action against estate. §1261.

§1260. Statement concerning declarant's will or revocable trust; Trustworthiness of statement

(a) Except as provided in subdivision (b), evidence of any of the following statements made by a declarant who is unavailable as a witness is not made inadmissible by the hearsay rule:

(1) That the declarant has or has not made a will or established or amended a revocable trust.

(2) That the declarant has or has not revoked his or her will, revocable trust, or an amendment to a revocable trust.

(3) That identifies the declarant's will, revocable trust, or an amendment to a revocable trust.

(b) Evidence of a statement is inadmissible under this section if the statement was made under circumstances that indicate its lack of trustworthiness. **Leg.H.** Enacted Stats 1965 ch 299 §2, operative January 1, 1967. Amended Stats 2010 ch 106 §1 (SB 1041), effective January 1, 2011.

§1261. Statement of decedent offered in action against estate

(a) Evidence of a statement is not made inadmissible by the hearsay rule when offered in an action upon a claim or demand against the estate of the declarant if the statement was made upon the personal knowledge of the declarant at a time when the matter had been recently perceived by him and while his recollection was clear.

(b) Evidence of a statement is inadmissible under this section if the statement was made under circumstances such as to indicate its lack of trustworthiness. **Leg.H.** Enacted Stats 1965 ch 299 §2, operative January 1, 1967.

ARTICLE 7
Business Records

"A business". §1270.
Business record. §1271.
Absence of entry in business records. §1272.

§1270. "A business"

As used in this article, "a business" includes every kind of business, governmental activity, profession, occupation, calling, or operation of institutions, whether carried on for profit or not. **Leg.H.** Enacted Stats 1965 ch 299 §2, operative January 1, 1967.

§1271. Business record

Evidence of a writing made as a record of an act, condition, or event is not made inadmissible by the hearsay rule when offered to prove the act, condition, or event if:

(a) The writing was made in the regular course of a business;

(b) The writing was made at or near the time of the act, condition, or event;

(c) The custodian or other qualified witness testifies to its identity and the mode of its preparation; and

(d) The sources of information and method and time of preparation were such as to indicate its trustworthiness. **Leg.H.** Enacted Stats 1965 ch 299 §2, operative January 1, 1967.

§1272. Absence of entry in business records

Evidence of the absence from the records of a business of a record of an asserted act, condition, or event is not made inadmissible by the hearsay rule when offered to prove the nonoccurrence of the act or event, or the nonexistence of the condition, if:

(a) It was the regular course of that business to make records of all such acts, conditions, or events at or near the time of the act, condition, or event and to preserve them; and

(b) The sources of information and method and time of preparation of the records of that business were such that the absence of a record of an act, condition, or event is a trustworthy indication that the act or event did not occur or the condition did not exist. **Leg.H.** Enacted Stats 1965 ch 299 §2, operative January 1, 1967.

ARTICLE 8
Official Records and Other Official Writings

Record by public employee. §1280.
Record of vital statistic. §1281.
Finding of presumed death by authorized federal employee. §1282.
Record by federal employee that person is missing, captured, or the like. §1283.
Statement of absence of public record. §1284.
Statements at civil hearing for person convicted of sexual offense. § 1285.

§1280. Record by public employee

Evidence of a writing made as a record of an act, condition, or event is not made inadmissible by the hearsay rule when offered in any civil or criminal proceeding to prove the act, condition, or event if all of the following applies:

(a) The writing was made by and within the scope of duty of a public employee.

(b) The writing was made at or near the time of the act, condition, or event.

(c) The sources of information and method and time of preparation were such as to indicate its trustworthiness. **Leg.H.** Enacted Stats 1965 ch 299 §2, operative January 1, 1967. Amended Stats 1996 ch 642 §4 (AB 1387).

§1281. Record of vital statistic

Evidence of a writing made as a record of a birth, fetal death, death, or marriage is not made inadmissible by the hearsay rule if the maker was required by law to file the writing in a designated public office and the writing was made and filed as required by law. **Leg.H.** Enacted Stats 1965 ch 299 §2, operative January 1, 1967.

§1282. Finding of presumed death by authorized federal employee

A written finding of presumed death made by an employee of the United States authorized to make such finding pursuant to the Federal Missing Persons Act (56 Stats. 143, 1092, and P.L. 408, Ch. 371, 2d Sess.

78th Cong.; 50 U.S.C. App. 1001–1016), as enacted or as heretofore or hereafter amended, shall be received in any court, office, or other place in this state as evidence of the death of the person therein found to be dead and of the date, circumstances, and place of his disappearance. **Leg.H.** Enacted Stats 1965 ch 299 §2, operative January 1, 1967.

§1283. Record by federal employee that person is missing, captured, or the like

An official written report or record that a person is missing, missing in action, interned in a foreign country, captured by a hostile force, beleaguered by a hostile force, besieged by a hostile force, or detained in a foreign country against his will, or is dead or is alive, made by an employee of the United States authorized by any law of the United States to make such report or record shall be received in any court, office, or other place in this state as evidence that such person is missing, missing in action, interned in a foreign country, captured by a hostile force, beleaguered by a hostile force, besieged by a hostile force, or detained in a foreign country against his will, or is dead or is alive. **Leg.H.** Enacted Stats 1965 ch 299 §2, operative January 1, 1967.

§1284. Statement of absence of public record

Evidence of a writing made by the public employee who is the official custodian of the records in a public office, reciting diligent search and failure to find a record, is not made inadmissible by the hearsay rule when offered to prove the absence of a record in that office. **Leg.H.** Enacted Stats 1965 ch 299 §2, operative January 1, 1967.

§ 1285. Statements at civil hearing for person convicted of sexual offense

Within an official written report or record of a law enforcement officer regarding a sexual offense that resulted in a person's conviction, the following statements are not made inadmissible by the hearsay rule at the civil hearing described in Section 6602 of the Welfare and Institutions Code when offered to prove the truth of the matter stated:

(a) A statement from a victim of the sexual offense.

(b) A statement from an eyewitness to the sexual offense.

(c) A statement from a sexual assault medical examiner who examined a victim of the sexual offense. **Leg.H.** Added Stats 2023 ch 363 §1 (AB 1253), effective January 1, 2024.

ARTICLE 9
Former Testimony

"Former testimony". §1290.
Former testimony offered against party to former proceeding. §1291.
Former testimony offered against person not a party to former proceeding. §1292.
Former testimony of minor against parent or guardian as exception to hearsay rule;
   Challenge to testimony. §1293.
Inconsistent statement hearsay exception. §1294.

§1290. "Former testimony"

As used in this article, "former testimony" means testimony given under oath in:

(a) Another action or in a former hearing or trial of the same action;

(b) A proceeding to determine a controversy conducted by or under the supervision of an agency that has the power to determine such a controversy and is an agency of the United States or a public entity in the United States;

(c) A deposition taken in compliance with law in another action; or

(d) An arbitration proceeding if the evidence of such former testimony is a verbatim transcript thereof. **Leg.H.** Enacted Stats 1965 ch 299 §2, operative January 1, 1967.

§1291. Former testimony offered against party to former proceeding

(a) Evidence of former testimony is not made inadmissible by the hearsay rule if the declarant is unavailable as a witness and:

(1) The former testimony is offered against a person who offered it in evidence in his own behalf on the former occasion or against the successor in interest of such person; or

(2) The party against whom the former testimony is offered was a party to the action or proceeding in which the testimony was given and had the right and opportunity to cross-examine the declarant with an interest and motive similar to that which he has at the hearing.

(b) The admissibility of former testimony under this section is subject to the same limitations and objections as though the declarant were testifying at the hearing, except that former testimony offered under this section is not subject to:

(1) Objections to the form of the question which were not made at the time the former testimony was given.

(2) Objections based on competency or privilege which did not exist at the time the former testimony was given. **Leg.H.** Enacted Stats 1965 ch 299 §2, operative January 1, 1967.

§1292. Former testimony offered against person not a party to former proceeding

(a) Evidence of former testimony is not made inadmissible by the hearsay rule if:

(1) The declarant is unavailable as a witness;

(2) The former testimony is offered in a civil action; and

(3) The issue is such that the party to the action or proceeding in which the former testimony was given had the right and opportunity to cross-examine the declarant with an interest and motive similar to that which the party against whom the testimony is offered has at the hearing.

(b) The admissibility of former testimony under this section is subject to the same limitations and objections as though the declarant were testifying at the hearing, except that former testimony offered under this section is not subject to objections based on competency or privilege which did not exist at the time the former testimony was given. **Leg.H.** Enacted Stats 1965 ch 299 §2, operative January 1, 1967.

§1293. Former testimony of minor against parent or guardian as exception to hearsay rule; Challenge to testimony

(a) Evidence of former testimony made at a preliminary examination by a minor child who was the complaining witness is not made inadmissible by the hearsay rule if:

(1) The former testimony is offered in a proceeding to declare the minor a dependent child of the court pursuant to Section 300 of the Welfare and Institutions Code.

(2) The issues are such that a defendant in the preliminary examination in which the former testimony was given had the right and opportunity to cross-examine the minor child with an interest and motive similar to that which the parent or guardian against whom the testimony is offered has at the proceeding to declare the minor a dependent child of the court.

(b) The admissibility of former testimony under this section is subject to the same limitations and objections as though the minor child were testifying at the proceeding to declare him or her a dependent child of the court.

(c) The attorney for the parent or guardian against whom the former testimony is offered or, if none, the parent or guardian may make a motion to challenge the admissibility of the former testimony upon a showing that new substantially different issues are present in the proceeding to declare the minor a dependent child than were present in the preliminary examination.

(d) As used in this section, "complaining witness" means the alleged victim of the crime for which a preliminary examination was held.

(e) This section shall apply only to testimony made at a preliminary examination on and after January 1, 1990. **Leg.H.** Added Stats 1989 ch 322 §1.

§1294. Inconsistent statement hearsay exception

(a) The following evidence of prior inconsistent statements of a witness properly admitted in a conditional examination, preliminary hearing, or trial of the same criminal matter pursuant to Section 1235 is not made inadmissible by the hearsay rule if the witness is unavailable and former testimony of the witness is admitted pursuant to Section 1291:

(1) A video or audio recorded statement introduced at a conditional examination, preliminary hearing, or prior proceeding concerning the same criminal matter.

(2) A transcript, containing the statements, of the conditional examination, preliminary hearing, or prior proceeding concerning the same criminal matter.

(b) The party against whom the prior inconsistent statements are offered, at his or her option, may examine or cross-examine any person who testified at the conditional examination, preliminary hearing, or prior proceeding, as to the prior inconsistent statements of the witness.

(c) As used in this section, "conditional examination" has the same meaning as in Chapter 4 (commencing with Section 1335) of Title 10 of

Part 2 of the Penal Code. **Leg.H.** Added Stats 1996 ch 560 §1 (AB 2483). Amended Stats 2009 ch 88 §36 (AB 176), effective January 1, 2010; Stats 2018 ch 64 §1 (AB 1736), effective January 1, 2019.

ARTICLE 10
Judgments

Judgment of conviction of crime punishable as felony. §1300.
Judgment against person entitled to indemnity. §1301.
Judgment determining liability of third person. §1302.

§1300. Judgment of conviction of crime punishable as felony

Evidence of a final judgment adjudging a person guilty of a crime punishable as a felony is not made inadmissible by the hearsay rule when offered in a civil action to prove any fact essential to the judgment whether or not the judgment was based on a plea of nolo contendere. **Leg.H.** Enacted Stats 1965 ch 299 §2, operative January 1, 1967. Amended Stats 1982 ch 390 §2.

§1301. Judgment against person entitled to indemnity

Evidence of a final judgment is not made inadmissible by the hearsay rule when offered by the judgment debtor to prove any fact which was essential to the judgment in an action in which he seeks to:

(a) Recover partial or total indemnity or exoneration for money paid or liability incurred because of the judgment;

(b) Enforce a warranty to protect the judgment debtor against the liability determined by the judgment; or

(c) Recover damages for breach of warranty substantially the same as the warranty determined by the judgment to have been breached. **Leg.H.** Enacted Stats 1965 ch 299 §2, operative January 1, 1967.

§1302. Judgment determining liability of third person

When the liability, obligation, or duty of a third person is in issue in a civil action, evidence of a final judgment against that person is not made inadmissible by the hearsay rule when offered to prove such liability, obligation, or duty. **Leg.H.** Enacted Stats 1965 ch 299 §2, operative January 1, 1967.

ARTICLE 11
Family History

Statement concerning declarant's own family history. §1310.
Statement concerning family history of another. §1311.
Entries in family records and the like. §1312.
Reputation in family concerning family history. §1313.
Reputation in community concerning family history. §1314.
Church records concerning family history. §1315.
Marriage, baptismal, and similar certificates. §1316.

§1310. Statement concerning declarant's own family history

(a) Subject to subdivision (b), evidence of a statement by a declarant who is unavailable as a witness concerning his own birth, marriage, divorce, a parent and child relationship, relationship by blood or marriage, race, ancestry, or other similar fact of his family history is not made inadmissible by the hearsay rule, even though the declarant had no means of acquiring personal knowledge of the matter declared.

(b) Evidence of a statement is inadmissible under this section if the statement was made under circumstances such as to indicate its lack of trustworthiness. **Leg.H.** Enacted Stats 1965 ch 299 §2, operative January 1, 1967. Amended Stats 1975 ch 1244 §15.

§1311. Statement concerning family history of another

(a) Subject to subdivision (b), evidence of a statement concerning the birth, marriage, divorce, death, parent and child relationship, race, ancestry, relationship by blood or marriage, or other similar fact of the family history of a person other than the declarant is not made inadmissible by the hearsay rule if the declarant is unavailable as a witness and:

(1) The declarant was related to the other by blood or marriage; or

(2) The declarant was otherwise so intimately associated with the other's family as to be likely to have had accurate information concerning the matter declared and made the statement (i) upon information received from the other or from a person related by blood or marriage to the other or (ii) upon repute in the other's family.

(b) Evidence of a statement is inadmissible under this section if the statement was made under circumstances such as to indicate its lack of trustworthiness. **Leg.H.** Enacted Stats 1965 ch 299 §2, operative January 1, 1967. Amended Stats 1975 ch 1244 §16.

§1312. Entries in family records and the like

Evidence of entries in family Bibles or other family books or charts, engravings on rings, family portraits, engravings on urns, crypts, or tombstones, and the like, is not made inadmissible by the hearsay rule when offered to prove the birth, marriage, divorce, death, parent and child relationship, race, ancestry, relationship by blood or marriage, or other similar fact of the family history of a member of the family by blood or marriage. **Leg.H.** Enacted Stats 1965 ch 299 §2, operative January 1, 1967. Amended Stats 1975 ch 1244 §17.

§1313. Reputation in family concerning family history

Evidence of reputation among members of a family is not made inadmissible by the hearsay rule if the reputation concerns the birth, marriage, divorce, death, parent and child relationship, race, ancestry, relationship by blood or marriage, or other similar fact of the family history of a member of the family by blood or marriage. **Leg.H.** Enacted Stats 1965 ch 299 §2, operative January 1, 1967. Amended Stats 1975 ch 1244 §18.

§1314. Reputation in community concerning family history

Evidence of reputation in a community concerning the date or fact of birth, marriage, divorce, or death of a person resident in the community at the time of the reputation is not made inadmissible by the hearsay rule. **Leg.H.** Enacted Stats 1965 ch 299 §2, operative January 1, 1967.

§1315. Church records concerning family history

Evidence of a statement concerning a person's birth, marriage, divorce, death, parent and child relationship, race, ancestry, relationship by blood or marriage, or other similar fact of family history which is contained in a writing made as a record of a church, religious denomination, or religious society is not made inadmissible by the hearsay rule if:

(a) The statement is contained in a writing made as a record of an act, condition, or event that would be admissible as evidence of such act, condition, or event under Section 1271; and

(b) The statement is of a kind customarily recorded in connection with the act, condition, or event recorded in the writing. **Leg.H.** Enacted Stats 1965 ch 299 §2, operative January 1, 1967. Amended Stats 1975 ch 1244 §19.

§1316. Marriage, baptismal, and similar certificates

Evidence of a statement concerning a person's birth, marriage, divorce, death, parent and child relationship, race, ancestry, relationship by blood or marriage, or other similar fact of family history is not made inadmissible by the hearsay rule if the statement is contained in a certificate that the maker thereof performed a marriage or other ceremony or administered a sacrament and:

(a) The maker was a clergyman, civil officer, or other person authorized to perform the acts reported in the certificate by law or by the rules, regulations, or requirements of a church, religious denomination, or religious society; and

(b) The certificate was issued by the maker at the time and place of the ceremony or sacrament or within a reasonable time thereafter. **Leg.H.** Enacted Stats 1965 ch 299 §2, operative January 1, 1967. Amended Stats 1975 ch 1244 §20.

ARTICLE 12
Reputation and Statements Concerning Community History, Property Interests, and Character

Reputation concerning community history. §1320.
Reputation concerning public interest in property. §1321.
Reputation concerning boundary or custom affecting land. §1322.
Statement concerning boundary. §1323.
Reputation concerning character. §1324.

§1320. Reputation concerning community history

Evidence of reputation in a community is not made inadmissible by the hearsay rule if the reputation concerns an event of general history of the community or of the state or nation of which the community is a part and the event was of importance to the community. **Leg.H.** Enacted Stats 1965 ch 299 §2, operative January 1, 1967.

§1321. Reputation concerning public interest in property

Evidence of reputation in a community is not made inadmissible by the hearsay rule if the reputation concerns the interest of the public in property in the community and the reputation arose before controversy. **Leg.H.** Enacted Stats 1965 ch 299 §2, operative January 1, 1967.

§1322. Reputation concerning boundary or custom affecting land

Evidence of reputation in a community is not made inadmissible by the hearsay rule if the reputation concerns boundaries of, or customs affecting, land in the community and the reputation arose before controversy. **Leg.H.** Enacted Stats 1965 ch 299 §2, operative January 1, 1967.

§1323. Statement concerning boundary

Evidence of a statement concerning the boundary of land is not made inadmissible by the hearsay rule if the declarant is unavailable as a witness and had sufficient knowledge of the subject, but evidence of a statement is not admissible under this section if the statement was made under circumstances such as to indicate its lack of trustworthiness. **Leg.H.** Enacted Stats 1965 ch 299 §2, operative January 1, 1967.

§1324. Reputation concerning character

Evidence of a person's general reputation with reference to his character or a trait of his character at a relevant time in the community in which he then resided or in a group with which he then habitually associated is not made inadmissible by the hearsay rule. **Leg.H.** Enacted Stats 1965 ch 299 §2, operative January 1, 1967.

ARTICLE 13
Dispositive Instruments and Ancient Writings

Recitals in writings affecting property. §1330.
Recitals in ancient writings. §1331.

§1330. Recitals in writings affecting property

Evidence of a statement contained in a deed of conveyance or a will or other writing purporting to affect an interest in real or personal property is not made inadmissible by the hearsay rule if:

(a) The matter stated was relevant to the purpose of the writing;

(b) The matter stated would be relevant to an issue as to an interest in the property; and

(c) The dealings with the property since the statement was made have not been inconsistent with the truth of the statement. **Leg.H.** Enacted Stats 1965 ch 299 §2, operative January 1, 1967.

§1331. Recitals in ancient writings

Evidence of a statement is not made inadmissible by the hearsay rule if the statement is contained in a writing more than 30 years old and the statement has been since generally acted upon as true by persons having an interest in the matter. **Leg.H.** Enacted Stats 1965 ch 299 §2, operative January 1, 1967.

ARTICLE 14
Commercial, Scientific, and Similar Publications

Commercial lists and the like. §1340.
Publications concerning facts of general notoriety and interest. §1341.

§1340. Commercial lists and the like

Evidence of a statement, other than an opinion, contained in a tabulation, list, directory, register, or other published compilation is not made inadmissible by the hearsay rule if the compilation is generally used and relied upon as accurate in the course of a business as defined in Section 1270. **Leg.H.** Enacted Stats 1965 ch 299 §2, operative January 1, 1967.

§1341. Publications concerning facts of general notoriety and interest

Historical works, books of science or art, and published maps or charts, made by persons indifferent between the parties, are not made inadmissible by the hearsay rule when offered to prove facts of general notoriety and interest. **Leg.H.** Enacted Stats 1965 ch 299 §2, operative January 1, 1967.

ARTICLE 15
Declarant Unavailable as Witness

Admissibility of statement in serious felony prosecutions. §1350.

§1350. Admissibility of statement in serious felony prosecutions

(a) In a criminal proceeding charging a serious felony, evidence of a statement made by a declarant is not made inadmissible by the hearsay rule if the declarant is unavailable as a witness, and all of the following are true:

(1) There is clear and convincing evidence that the declarant's unavailability was knowingly caused by, aided by, or solicited by the party against whom the statement is offered for the purpose of preventing the arrest or prosecution of the party and is the result of the death by homicide or the kidnapping of the declarant.

(2) There is no evidence that the unavailability of the declarant was caused by, aided by, solicited by, or procured on behalf of, the party who is offering the statement.

(3) The statement has been memorialized in a tape recording made by a law enforcement official, or in a written statement prepared by a law enforcement official and signed by the declarant and notarized in the presence of the law enforcement official, prior to the death or kidnapping of the declarant.

(4) The statement was made under circumstances which indicate its trustworthiness and was not the result of promise, inducement, threat, or coercion.

(5) The statement is relevant to the issues to be tried.

(6) The statement is corroborated by other evidence which tends to connect the party against whom the statement is offered with the commission of the serious felony with which the party is charged. The corroboration is not sufficient if it merely shows the commission of the offense or the circumstances thereof.

(b) If the prosecution intends to offer a statement pursuant to this section, the prosecution shall serve a written notice upon the defendant at least 10 days prior to the hearing or trial at which the prosecution intends to offer the statement, unless the prosecution shows good cause for the failure to provide that notice. In the event that good cause is shown, the defendant shall be entitled to a reasonable continuance of the hearing or trial.

(c) If the statement is offered during trial, the court's determination shall be made out of the presence of the jury. If the defendant elects to testify at the hearing on a motion brought pursuant to this section, the court shall exclude from the examination every person except the clerk, the court reporter, the bailiff, the prosecutor, the investigating officer, the defendant and his or her counsel, an investigator for the defendant, and the officer having custody of the defendant. Notwithstanding any other provision of law, the defendant's testimony at the hearing shall not be admissible in any other proceeding except the hearing brought on the motion pursuant to this section. If a transcript is made of the defendant's testimony, it shall be sealed and transmitted to the clerk of the court in which the action is pending.

(d) As used in this section, "serious felony" means any of the felonies listed in subdivision (c) of Section 1192.7 of the Penal Code or any violation of Section 11351, 11352, 11378, or 11379 of the Health and Safety Code.

(e) If a statement to be admitted pursuant to this section includes hearsay statements made by anyone other than the declarant who is unavailable pursuant to subdivision (a), those hearsay statements are inadmissible unless they meet the requirements of an exception to the hearsay rule. **Leg.H.** Added Stats 1985 ch 783 §1. Amended Stats 2001 ch 854 §5 (SB 205).

ARTICLE 16
Statements by Children Under the Age of 12 in Child Neglect and Abuse Proceedings

Statement describing child abuse or neglect made by child under age of 12. §1360.

§1360. Statement describing child abuse or neglect made by child under age of 12

(a) In a criminal prosecution where the victim is a minor, a statement made by the victim when under the age of 12 describing any act of child abuse or neglect performed with or on the child by another, or describing any attempted act of child abuse or neglect with or on the child by another, is not made inadmissible by the hearsay rule if all of the following apply:

(1) The statement is not otherwise admissible by statute or court rule.

(2) The court finds, in a hearing conducted outside the presence of the jury, that the time, content, and circumstances of the statement provide sufficient indicia of reliability.

(3) The child either:

(A) Testifies at the proceedings.

(B) Is unavailable as a witness, in which case the statement may be admitted only if there is evidence of the child abuse or neglect that corroborates the statement made by the child.

(b) A statement may not be admitted under this section unless the proponent of the statement makes known to the adverse party the intention to offer the statement and the particulars of the statement sufficiently in advance of the proceedings in order to provide the adverse party with a fair opportunity to prepare to meet the statement.

(c) For purposes of this section, "child abuse" means an act proscribed by Section 273a, 273d, or 288.5 of the Penal Code, or any of the acts described in Section 11165.1 of the Penal Code, and "child neglect" means any of the acts described in Section 11165.2 of the Penal Code. **Leg.H.** Added Stats 1995 ch 87 §3 (AB 355).

ARTICLE 17
Physical Abuse

Hearsay exception. §1370.
Effect of hearsay rule. §1380.
Evidence of statement; Elements; Conduct of foundational hearing; Considerations; Applicability; Effect of repeal. §1390.

§1370. Hearsay exception

(a) Evidence of a statement by a declarant is not made inadmissible by the hearsay rule if all of the following conditions are met:

(1) The statement purports to narrate, describe, or explain the infliction or threat of physical injury upon the declarant.

(2) The declarant is unavailable as a witness pursuant to Section 240.

(3) The statement was made at or near the time of the infliction or threat of physical injury. Evidence of statements made more than five years before the filing of the current action or proceeding shall be inadmissible under this section.

(4) The statement was made under circumstances that would indicate its trustworthiness.

(5) The statement was made in writing, was electronically recorded, or made to a physician, nurse, paramedic, or to a law enforcement official.

(b) For purposes of paragraph (4) of subdivision (a), circumstances relevant to the issue of trustworthiness include, but are not limited to, the following:

(1) Whether the statement was made in contemplation of pending or anticipated litigation in which the declarant was interested.

(2) Whether the declarant has a bias or motive for fabricating the statement, and the extent of any bias or motive.

(3) Whether the statement is corroborated by evidence other than statements that are admissible only pursuant to this section.

(c) A statement is admissible pursuant to this section only if the proponent of the statement makes known to the adverse party the intention to offer the statement and the particulars of the statement sufficiently in advance of the proceedings in order to provide the adverse party with a fair opportunity to prepare to meet the statement. **Leg.H.** Added Stats 1996 ch 416 §2 (AB 2068), effective September 4, 1996. Amended Stats 2000 ch 1001 §2 (SB 1944).

1996 Note: It is the intent of the Legislature that enactment of this statute shall not affect other evidentiary requirements, including, but not limited to, Sections 351 and 352, shall not impair a party's right to attack the credibility of the declarant pursuant to Section 1202, shall not affect the defendant's right to discovery for purposes of producing rebuttal evidence attacking the declarant's credibility, and shall not be used in a manner inconsistent with the defendant's right to due process and to confront witnesses under the United States or California Constitution. Stats 1996 ch 416 §1.

§1380. Effect of hearsay rule

(a) In a criminal proceeding charging a violation, or attempted violation, of Section 368 of the Penal Code, evidence of a statement made by a declarant is not made inadmissible by the hearsay rule if the declarant is unavailable as a witness, as defined in subdivisions (a) and (b) of Section 240, and all of the following are true:

(1) The party offering the statement has made a showing of particularized guarantees of trustworthiness regarding the statement, the statement was made under circumstances which indicate its trustworthiness, and the statement was not the result of promise, inducement, threat, or coercion. In making its determination, the court may consider only the circumstances that surround the making of the statement and that render the declarant particularly worthy of belief.

(2) There is no evidence that the unavailability of the declarant was caused by, aided by, solicited by, or procured on behalf of, the party who is offering the statement.

(3) The entire statement has been memorialized in a videotape recording made by a law enforcement official, prior to the death or disabling of the declarant.

(4) The statement was made by the victim of the alleged violation.

(5) The statement is supported by corroborative evidence.

(6) The victim of the alleged violation is an individual who meets both of the following requirements:

(A) Was 65 years of age or older or was a dependent adult when the alleged violation or attempted violation occurred.

(B) At the time of any criminal proceeding, including, but not limited to, a preliminary hearing or trial, regarding the alleged violation or attempted violation, is either deceased or suffers from the infirmities of aging as manifested by advanced age or organic brain damage, or other physical, mental, or emotional dysfunction, to the extent that the ability of the person to provide adequately for the person's own care or protection is impaired.

(b) If the prosecution intends to offer a statement pursuant to this section, the prosecution shall serve a written notice upon the defendant at least 10 days prior to the hearing or trial at which the prosecution intends to offer the statement, unless the prosecution shows good cause for the failure to provide that notice. In the event that good cause is shown, the defendant shall be entitled to a reasonable continuance of the hearing or trial.

(c) If the statement is offered during trial, the court's determination as to the availability of the victim as a witness shall be made out of the presence of the jury. If the defendant elects to testify at the hearing on a motion brought pursuant to this section, the court shall exclude from the examination every person except the clerk, the court reporter, the bailiff, the prosecutor, the investigating officer, the defendant and his or her counsel, an investigator for the defendant, and the officer having custody of the defendant. Notwithstanding any other provision of law, the defendant's testimony at the hearing shall not be admissible in any other proceeding except the hearing brought on the motion pursuant to this section. If a transcript is made of the defendant's testimony, it shall be sealed and transmitted to the clerk of the court in which the action is pending. **Leg.H.** Added Stats 1999 ch 383 §1 (AB 526).

§1390. Evidence of statement; Elements; Conduct of foundational hearing; Considerations; Applicability; Effect of repeal

(a) Evidence of a statement is not made inadmissible by the hearsay rule if the statement is offered against a party that has engaged, or aided and abetted, in the wrongdoing that was intended to, and did, procure the unavailability of the declarant as a witness.

(b)(1) The party seeking to introduce a statement pursuant to subdivision (a) shall establish, by a preponderance of the evidence, that the elements of subdivision (a) have been met at a foundational hearing.

(2) The hearsay evidence that is the subject of the foundational hearing is admissible at the foundational hearing. However, a finding that the elements of subdivision (a) have been met shall not be based solely on the unconfronted hearsay statement of the unavailable declarant, and shall be supported by independent corroborative evidence.

(3) The foundational hearing shall be conducted outside the presence of the jury. However, if the hearing is conducted after a jury trial has begun, the judge presiding at the hearing may consider evidence already presented to the jury in deciding whether the elements of subdivision (a) have been met.

(4) In deciding whether or not to admit the statement, the judge may take into account whether it is trustworthy and reliable.

(c) This section shall apply to any civil, criminal, or juvenile case or proceeding initiated or pending as of January 1, 2011. **Leg.H.** Added Stats 2010 ch 537 §2 (AB 1723), effective January 1, 2011, repealed January 1, 2016. Amended Stats 2011 ch 296 §90 (AB 1023), effective January 1, 2012, repealed January 1, 2016; Stats 2015 ch 55 §1 (AB 593), effective January 1, 2016.

DIVISION 11
WRITINGS

Chapter 1. Authentication and Proof of Writings.
Chapter 2. Secondary Evidence of Writings.
Chapter 3. Official Writings Affecting Property.

CHAPTER 1
AUTHENTICATION AND PROOF OF WRITINGS

Article 1. Requirement of Authentication.
Article 2. Means of Authenticating and Proving Writings.
Article 3. Presumptions Affecting Acknowledged Writings and Official Writings.

ARTICLE 1
Requirement of Authentication

Authentication defined. §1400.
Authentication required. §1401.
Authentication of altered writing. §1402.

§1400. Authentication defined

Authentication of a writing means (a) the introduction of evidence sufficient to sustain a finding that it is the writing that the proponent of the evidence claims it is or (b) the establishment of such facts by any other means provided by law. **Leg.H.** Enacted Stats 1965 ch 299 §2, operative January 1, 1967.

§1401. Authentication required

(a) Authentication of a writing is required before it may be received in evidence.

(b) Authentication of a writing is required before secondary evidence of its content may be received in evidence. **Leg.H.** Enacted Stats 1965 ch 299 §2, operative January 1, 1967.

§1402. Authentication of altered writing

The party producing a writing as genuine which has been altered, or appears to have been altered, after its execution, in a part material to the question in dispute, must account for the alteration or appearance thereof. He may show that the alteration was made by another, without his concurrence, or was made with the consent of the parties affected by it, or otherwise properly or innocently made, or that the alteration did not change the meaning or language of the instrument. If he does that, he may give the writing in evidence, but not otherwise. **Leg.H.** Enacted Stats 1965 ch 299 §2, operative January 1, 1967.

ARTICLE 2
Means of Authenticating and Proving Writings

Article not exclusive. §1410.
Vandalism; Evidence of graffiti. §1410.5.
Subscribing witness' testimony unnecessary. §1411.
Use of other evidence when subscribing witness' testimony required. §1412.
Witness to the execution of a writing. §1413.
Authentication by admission. §1414.
Authentication by handwriting evidence. §1415.
Proof of handwriting by person familiar therewith. §1416.
Comparison of handwriting by trier of fact. §1417.
Comparison of writing by expert witness. §1418.
Exemplars when writing is 30 years old. §1419.
Authentication by evidence of reply. §1420.
Authentication by content. §1421.

§1410. Article not exclusive

Nothing in this article shall be construed to limit the means by which a writing may be authenticated or proved. **Leg.H.** Enacted Stats 1965 ch 299 §2, operative January 1, 1967.

§1410.5. Vandalism; Evidence of graffiti

(a) For purposes of this chapter, a writing shall include any graffiti consisting of written words, insignia, symbols, or any other markings which convey a particular meaning.

(b) Any writing described in subdivision (a), or any photograph thereof, may be admitted into evidence in an action for vandalism, for the purpose of proving that the writing was made by the defendant.

(c) The admissibility of any fact offered to prove that the writing was made by the defendant shall, upon motion of the defendant, be ruled upon outside the presence of the jury, and is subject to the requirements of Sections 1416, 1417, and 1418. **Leg.H.** Added Stats 1989 ch 660 §1.

§1411. Subscribing witness' testimony unnecessary

Except as provided by statute, the testimony of a subscribing witness is not required to authenticate a writing. **Leg.H.** Enacted Stats 1965 ch 299 §2, operative January 1, 1967.

§1412. Use of other evidence when subscribing witness' testimony required

If the testimony of a subscribing witness is required by statute to authenticate a writing and the subscribing witness denies or does not recollect the execution of the writing, the writing may be authenticated by other evidence. **Leg.H.** Enacted Stats 1965 ch 299 §2, operative January 1, 1967.

§1413. Witness to the execution of a writing

A writing may be authenticated by anyone who saw the writing made or executed, including a subscribing witness. **Leg.H.** Enacted Stats 1965 ch 299 §2, operative January 1, 1967.

§1414. Authentication by admission

A writing may be authenticated by evidence that:

(a) The party against whom it is offered has at any time admitted its authenticity; or

(b) The writing has been acted upon as authentic by the party against whom it is offered. **Leg.H.** Enacted Stats 1965 ch 299 §2, operative January 1, 1967.

§1415. Authentication by handwriting evidence

A writing may be authenticated by evidence of the genuineness of the handwriting of the maker. **Leg.H.** Enacted Stats 1965 ch 299 §2, operative January 1, 1967.

§1416. Proof of handwriting by person familiar therewith

A witness who is not otherwise qualified to testify as an expert may state his opinion whether a writing is in the handwriting of a supposed writer if the court finds that he has personal knowledge of the handwriting of the supposed writer. Such personal knowlegde may be acquired from:

(a) Having seen the supposed writer write;

(b) Having seen a writing purporting to be in the handwriting of the supposed writer and upon which the supposed writer has acted or been charged;

(c) Having received letters in the due course of mail purporting to be from the supposed writer in response to letters duly addressed and mailed by him to the supposed writer; or

(d) Any other means of obtaining personal knowledge of the handwriting of the supposed writer. **Leg.H.** Enacted Stats 1965 ch 299 §2, operative January 1, 1967.

§1417. Comparison of handwriting by trier of fact

The genuineness of handwriting, or the lack thereof, may be proved by a comparison made by the trier of fact with handwriting (a) which the court finds was admitted or treated as genuine by the party against whom the evidence is offered or (b) otherwise proved to be genuine to the satisfaction of the court. **Leg.H.** Enacted Stats 1965 ch 299 §2, operative January 1, 1967.

§1418. Comparison of writing by expert witness

The genuineness of writing, or the lack thereof, may be proved by a comparison made by an expert witness with writing (a) which the court finds was admitted or treated as genuine by the party against whom the evidence is offered or (b) otherwise proved to be genuine to the satisfaction of the court. **Leg.H.** Enacted Stats 1965 ch 299 §2, operative January 1, 1967.

§1419. Exemplars when writing is 30 years old

Where a writing whose genuineness is sought to be proved is more than 30 years old, the comparison under Section 1417 or 1418 may be made with writing purporting to be genuine, and generally respected and acted upon as such, by persons having an interest in knowing whether it is genuine. **Leg.H.** Enacted Stats 1965 ch 299 §2, operative January 1, 1967.

§1420. Authentication by evidence of reply

A writing may be authenticated by evidence that the writing was received in response to a communication sent to the person who is claimed by the proponent of the evidence to be the author of the writing. **Leg.H.** Enacted Stats 1965 ch 299 §2, operative January 1, 1967.

§1421. Authentication by content

A writing may be authenticated by evidence that the writing refers to or states matters that are unlikely to be known to anyone other than the person who is claimed by the proponent of the evidence to be the author of the writing. **Leg.H.** Enacted Stats 1965 ch 299 §2, operative January 1, 1967.

ARTICLE 3
Presumptions Affecting Acknowledged Writings and Official Writings

Classification of presumptions in article. §1450.
Acknowledged writings. §1451.
Official seals. §1452.
Domestic official signatures. §1453.
Foreign official signatures. §1454.

§1450. Classification of presumptions in article

The presumptions established by this article are presumptions affecting the burden of producing evidence. **Leg.H.** Enacted Stats 1965 ch 299 §2, operative January 1, 1967.

§1451. Acknowledged writings

A certificate of the acknowledgment of a writing other than a will, or a certificate of the proof of such a writing, is prima facie evidence of the facts recited in the certificate and the genuineness of the signature of each person by whom the writing purports to have been signed if the certificate meets the requirements of Article 3 (commencing with Section 1180) of Chapter 4, Title 4, Part 4, Division 2 of the Civil Code. **Leg.H.** Enacted Stats 1965 ch 299 §2, operative January 1, 1967.

§1452. Official seals

A seal is presumed to be genuine and its use authorized if it purports to be the seal of:

(a) The United States or a department, agency, or public employee of the United States.
(b) A public entity in the United States or a department, agency, or public employee of such public entity.
(c) A nation recognized by the executive power of the United States or a department, agency, or officer of such nation.
(d) A public entity in a nation recognized by the executive power of the United States or a department, agency, or officer of such public entity.
(e) A court of admiralty or maritime jurisdiction.
(f) A notary public within any state of the United States. **Leg.H.** Enacted Stats 1965 ch 299 §2, operative January 1, 1967.

§1453. Domestic official signatures

A signature is presumed to be genuine and authorized if it purports to be the signature, affixed in his official capacity, of:

(a) A public employee of the United States.
(b) A public employee of any public entity in the United States.
(c) A notary public within any state of the United States. **Leg.H.** Enacted Stats 1965 ch 299 §2, operative January 1, 1967.

§1454. Foreign official signatures

A signature is presumed to be genuine and authorized if it purports to be the signature, affixed in his official capacity, of an officer, or deputy of an officer, of a nation or public entity in a nation recognized by the executive power of the United States and the writing to which the signature is affixed is accompanied by a final statement certifying the genuineness of the signature and the official position of (a) the person who executed the writing or (b) any foreign official who has certified either the genuineness of the signature and official position of the person executing the writing or the genuineness of the signature and official position of another foreign official who has executed a similar certificate in a chain of such certificates beginning with a certificate of the genuineness of the signature and official position of the person executing the writing. The final statement may be made only by a secretary of an embassy or legation, consul general, consul, vice consul, consular agent, or other officer in the foreign service of the United States stationed in the nation, authenticated by the seal of his office. **Leg.H.** Enacted Stats 1965 ch 299 §2, operative January 1, 1967.

CHAPTER 2
SECONDARY EVIDENCE OF WRITINGS

Article 1. Proof of the Content of a Writing.
Article 2. Official Writings and Recorded Writings.
Article 3. Photographic Copies and Printed Representations of Writings.
Article 4. Production of Business Records.

ARTICLE 1
Proof of the Content of a Writing

Proof by original. §1520.
Secondary Evidence Rule. §1521.
Additional grounds for exclusion in criminal actions; Request to exclude secondary evidence. §1522.
Use of oral testimony. §1523.

§1500. [Section repealed 1999]

Leg.H. Enacted Stats 1965 ch 299 §2, operative January 1, 1967. Amended Stats 1977 ch 708 §3. Repealed Stats 1998 ch 100 §1 (SB 177). The repealed section related to statement of the best evidence rule.

1998 Notes: Stats 1998 ch 100 applies in an action or proceeding commenced before, on, or after January 1, 1999. Stats 1998 ch 100 §9(b).

Nothing in Stats 1998 ch 100 invalidates an evidentiary determination made before January 1, 1999, that evidence is inadmissible pursuant to former Article 1 (commencing with Section 1500) of Chapter 2 of Division 11 of the Evidence Code. However, if an action or proceeding is pending on January 1, 1999, the proponent of evidence excluded pursuant to former Article 1 (commencing with Section 1500) of Chapter 2 of Division 11 of the Evidence Code may, on or after January 1, 1999, and before entry of judgment in the action or proceeding, make a new request for admission of the evidence on the basis of this act. Stats 1998 ch 100 §9(c).

§1500.5. [Section repealed 1999]

Leg.H. Added Stats 1983 ch 933 §1. Amended Stats 1996 ch 642 §5 (AB 1387). Repealed Stats 1998 ch 100 §1 (SB 177). See Ev C §1552.

1998 Note: For applicability and effect of repeal on pending proceedings, see the 1998 Note following Ev C §1500.

§1500.6. [Section repealed 1999]

Leg.H. Added Stats 1996 ch 345 §1 (AB 2897). Repealed Stats 1998 ch 100 §1 (SB 177). See Ev C §1553.

1998 Note: For applicability and effect of repeal on pending proceedings, see the 1998 Note following Ev C §1500.

§1501. [Section repealed 1999]

Leg.H. Enacted Stats 1965 ch 299 §2, operative January 1, 1967. Repealed Stats 1998 ch 100 §1 (SB 177). The repealed section related to lost or destroyed writing.

1998 Note: For applicability and effect of repeal on pending proceedings, see the 1998 Note following Ev C §1500.

§1502. [Section repealed 1999]

Leg.H. Enacted Stats 1965 ch 299 §2, operative January 1, 1967. Repealed Stats 1998 ch 100 §1 (SB 177). The repealed section related to writing not reasonably procurable by proponent.

1998 Note: For applicability and effect of repeal on pending proceedings, see the 1998 Note following Ev C §1500.

§1503. [Section repealed 1999]

Leg.H. Enacted Stats 1965 ch 299 §2, operative January 1, 1967. Repealed Stats 1998 ch 100 §1 (SB 177). The repealed section related to writing under control of proponent.

1998 Note: For applicability and effect of repeal on pending proceedings, see the 1998 Note following Ev C §1500.

§1504. [Section repealed 1999]

Leg.H. Enacted Stats 1965 ch 299 §2, operative January 1, 1967. Repealed Stats 1998 ch 100 §1 (SB 177). The repealed section related to collateral writings.

1998 Note: For applicability and effect of repeal on pending proceedings, see the 1998 Note following Ev C §1500.

§1505. [Section repealed 1999]

Leg.H. Enacted Stats 1965 ch 299 §2, operative January 1, 1967. Repealed Stats 1998 ch 100 §1 (SB 177). The repealed section related to secondary evidence other than copy of writing.

1998 Note: For applicability and effect of repeal on pending proceedings, see the 1998 Note following Ev C §1500.

§1506. [Section repealed 1999]

Leg.H. Enacted Stats 1965 ch 299 §2, operative January 1, 1967. Repealed Stats 1998 ch 100 §1 (SB 177). The repealed section related to writing in custody of public entity.

1998 Note: For applicability and effect of repeal on pending proceedings, see the 1998 Note following Ev C §1500.

§1507. [Section repealed 1999]

Leg.H. Enacted Stats 1965 ch 299 §2, operative January 1, 1967. Repealed Stats 1998 ch 100 §1 (SB 177). The repealed section related to writing recorded in public records.

1998 Note: For applicability and effect of repeal on pending proceedings, see the 1998 Note following Ev C §1500.

§1508. [Section repealed 1999]

Leg.H. Enacted Stats 1965 ch 299 §2, operative January 1, 1967. Repealed Stats 1998 ch 100 §1 (SB 177). The repealed section related to secondary evidence other than copy of public or publicly recorded writing.

1998 Note: For applicability and effect of repeal on pending proceedings, see the 1998 Note following Ev C §1500.

§1509. [Section repealed 1999]

Leg.H. Enacted Stats 1965 ch 299 §2, operative January 1, 1967. Repealed Stats 1998 ch 100 §1 (SB 177). The repealed section related to voluminous writings.

1998 Note: For applicability and effect of repeal on pending proceedings, see the 1998 Note following Ev C §1500.

§1510. [Section repealed 1999]

Leg.H. Enacted Stats 1965 ch 299 §2, operative January 1, 1967. Repealed Stats 1998 ch 100 §1 (SB 177). The repealed section related to writing produced at hearing.

1998 Note: For applicability and effect of repeal on pending proceedings, see the 1998 Note following Ev C §1500.

§1511. [Section repealed 1999]

Leg.H. Added Stats 1985 ch 100 §2. Repealed Stats 1998 ch 100 §1 (SB 177). The repealed section related to duplicates.

Prior Law: Former Ev C §1511, relating to duplicates, was added Stats 1977 ch 708 §4 and repealed Stats 1985 ch 100 §1.

1998 Note: For applicability and effect of repeal on pending proceedings, see the 1998 Note following Ev C §1500.

§1520. Proof by original

The content of a writing may be proved by an otherwise admissible original. **Leg.H.** Added Stats 1998 ch 100 §2 (SB 177).

1998 Note: Stats 1998 ch 100 applies in an action or proceeding commenced before, on, or after January 1, 1999. Stats 1998 ch 100 §9(b).

§1521. Secondary Evidence Rule

(a) The content of a writing may be proved by otherwise admissible secondary evidence. The court shall exclude secondary evidence of the content of writing if the court determines either of the following:

(1) A genuine dispute exists concerning material terms of the writing and justice requires the exclusion.

(2) Admission of the secondary evidence would be unfair.

(b) Nothing in this section makes admissible oral testimony to prove the content of a writing if the testimony is inadmissible under Section 1523 (oral testimony of the content of a writing).

(c) Nothing in this section excuses compliance with Section 1401 (authentication).

(d) This section shall be known as the "Secondary Evidence Rule." **Leg.H.** Added Stats 1998 ch 100 §2 (SB 177).

1998 Note: For applicability, see the 1998 Note following Ev C §1520.

§1522. Additional grounds for exclusion in criminal actions; Request to exclude secondary evidence

(a) In addition to the grounds for exclusion authorized by Section 1521, in a criminal action the court shall exclude secondary evidence of the content of a writing if the court determines that the original is in the proponent's possession, custody, or control, and the proponent has not made the original reasonably available for inspection at or before trial. This section does not apply to any of the following:

(1) A duplicate as defined in Section 260.

(2) A writing that is not closely related to the controlling issues in the action.

(3) A copy of a writing in the custody of a public entity.

(4) A copy of a writing that is recorded in the public records, if the record or a certified copy of it is made evidence of the writing by statute.

(b) In a criminal action, a request to exclude secondary evidence of the content of a writing, under this section or any other law, shall not be made in the presence of the jury. **Leg.H.** Added Stats 1998 ch 100 §2 (SB 177).

1998 Note: For applicability, see the 1998 Note following Ev C §1520.

§1523. Use of oral testimony

(a) Except as otherwise provided by statute, oral testimony is not admissible to prove the content of a writing.

(b) Oral testimony of the content of a writing is not made inadmissible by subdivision (a) if the proponent does not have possession or control of a copy of the writing and the original is lost or has been destroyed without fraudulent intent on the part of the proponent of the evidence.

(c) Oral testimony of the content of a writing is not made inadmissible by subdivision (a) if the proponent does not have possession or control of the original or a copy of the writing and either of the following conditions is satisfied:

(1) Neither the writing nor a copy of the writing was reasonably procurable by the proponent by use of the court's process or by other available means.

(2) The writing is not closely related to the controlling issues and it would be inexpedient to require its production.

(d) Oral testimony of the content of a writing is not made inadmissible by subdivision (a) if the writing consists of numerous accounts or other writings that cannot be examined in court without great loss of time, and the evidence sought from them is only the general result of the whole. **Leg.H.** Added Stats 1998 ch 100 §2 (SB 177).

1998 Note: For applicability, see the 1998 Note following Ev C §1520.

ARTICLE 2
Official Writings and Recorded Writings

Copy of writing in official custody. §1530.
Certification of copy for evidence. §1531.
Official record of recorded writing. §1532.

§1530. Copy of writing in official custody

(a) A purported copy of a writing in the custody of a public entity, or of an entry in such a writing, is prima facie evidence of the existence and content of such writing or entry if:

(1) The copy purports to be published by the authority of the nation or state, or public entity therein in which the writing is kept;

(2) The office in which the writing is kept is within the United States or within the Panama Canal Zone, the Trust Territory of the Pacific Islands, or the Ryukyu Islands, and the copy is attested or certified as a correct copy of the writing or entry by a public employee, or a deputy of a public employee, having the legal custody of the writing; or

(3) The office in which the writing is kept is not within the United States or any other place described in paragraph (2) and the copy is attested as a correct copy of the writing or entry by a person having authority to make attestation. The attestation must be accompanied by a final statement certifying the genuineness of the signature and the official position of (i) the person who attested the copy as a correct copy or (ii) any foreign official who has certified either the genuineness of the signature and official position of the person attesting the copy or the genuineness of the signature and official position of another foreign official who has executed a similar certificate in a chain of such certificates beginning with a certificate of the genuineness of the signature and official position of the person attesting the copy. Except as provided in the next sentence, the final statement may be made only by a secretary of an embassy or legation, consul general, consul, vice consul, or consular agent of the United States, or a diplomatic or consular official of the foreign country assigned or accredited to the United States. Prior to January 1, 1971, the final statement may also be made by a secretary of an embassy or legation, consul general, consul, vice consul, consular

agent, or other officer in the foreign service of the United States stationed in the nation in which the writing is kept, authenticated by the seal of his office. If reasonable opportunity has been given to all parties to investigate the authenticity and accuracy of the documents, the court may, for good cause shown, (i) admit an attested copy without the final statement or (ii) permit the writing or entry in foreign custody to be evidenced by an attested summary with or without a final statement.

(b) The presumptions established by this section are presumptions affecting the burden of producing evidence. **Leg.H.** Enacted Stats 1965 ch 299 §2, operative January 1, 1967. Amended Stats 1970 ch 41 §1, effective April 1, 1970.

§1531. Certification of copy for evidence

For the purpose of evidence, whenever a copy of a writing is attested or certified, the attestation or certificate must state in substance that the copy is a correct copy of the original, or of a specified part thereof, as the case may be. **Leg.H.** Enacted Stats 1965 ch 299 §2, operative January 1, 1967.

§1532. Official record of recorded writing

(a) The official record of a writing is prima facie evidence of the existence and content of the original recorded writing if:

(1) The record is in fact a record of an office of a public entity; and

(2) A statute authorized such a writing to be recorded in that office.

(b) The presumption established by this section is a presumption affecting the burden of producing evidence. **Leg.H.** Enacted Stats 1965 ch 299 §2, operative January 1, 1967.

ARTICLE 3
Photographic Copies and Printed Representations of Writings

Photographic copies made as business records [First of two; Operative term contingent]. §1550.
Photographic copies made as business records [Second of two; Operative date contingent]. §1550.
Admissibility of reproduced files, records, writings, photographs, fingerprints or other instruments. §1550.1.
Photographic copies where original destroyed or lost. §1551.
Printed representation of computer information or computer program. §1552.
Printed representation of images stored on video or digital medium. §1553.

§1550. Photographic copies made as business records [First of two; Operative term contingent]

A nonerasable optical image reproduction provided that additions, deletions, or changes to the original document are not permitted by the technology, a photostatic, microfilm, microcard, miniature photographic, or other photographic copy or reproduction, or an enlargement thereof, of a writing is as admissible as the writing itself if the copy or reproduction was made and preserved as a part of the records of a business (as defined by Section 1270) in the regular course of that business. The introduction of the copy, reproduction, or enlargement does not preclude admission of the original writing if it is still in existence. A court may require the introduction of a hard copy printout of the document. **Leg.H.** Enacted Stats 1965 ch 299 §2, operative January 1, 1967. Amended Stats 1992 ch 876 §10 (AB 3296).

§1550. Photographic copies made as business records [Second of two; Operative date contingent]

(a) If made and preserved as a part of the records of a business, as defined in Section 1270, in the regular course of that business, the following types of evidence of a writing are as admissible as the writing itself:

(1) A nonerasable optical image reproduction or any other reproduction of a public record by a trusted system, as defined in Section 12168.7 of the Government Code, if additions, deletions, or changes to the original document are not permitted by the technology.

(2) A photostatic copy or reproduction.

(3) A microfilm, microcard, or miniature photographic copy, reprint, or enlargement.

(4) Any other photographic copy or reproduction, or an enlargement thereof.

(b) The introduction of evidence of a writing pursuant to subdivision (a) does not preclude admission of the original writing if it is still in existence. A court may require the introduction of a hard copy printout of the document. **Leg.H.** Amended Stats 2002 ch 124 §1 (AB 2033).

2002 Note: This act shall become operative on the date the Secretary of State adopts uniform standards for storing and recording permanent and nonpermanent documents in electronic media, as required by Section 12168.7 of the Government Code. Stats 2002 ch 124 (AB 2033) §2.

§1550.1. Admissibility of reproduced files, records, writings, photographs, fingerprints or other instruments

Reproductions of files, records, writings, photographs, fingerprints or other instruments in the official custody of a criminal justice agency that were microphotographed or otherwise reproduced in a manner that conforms with the provisions of Section 11106.1, 11106.2, or 11106.3 of the Penal Code shall be admissible to the same extent and under the same circumstances as the original file, record, writing or other instrument would be admissible. **Leg.H.** Added Stats 2004 ch 65 §1 (AB 883).

2004 Note: The addition of §1550.1 is declarative of existing law. Stats 2004 ch 65 (AB 883) §3.

§1551. Photographic copies where original destroyed or lost

A print, whether enlarged or not, from a photographic film (including a photographic plate, microphotographic film, photostatic negative, or similar reproduction) of an original writing destroyed or lost after such film was taken or a reproduction from an electronic recording of video images on magnetic surfaces is admissible as the original writing itself if, at the time of the taking of such film or electronic recording, the person under whose direction and control it was taken attached thereto, or to the sealed container in which it was placed and has been kept, or incorporated in the film or electronic recording, a certification complying with the provisions of Section 1531 and stating the date on which, and the fact that, it was so taken under his direction and control. **Leg.H.** Enacted Stats 1965 ch 299 §2, operative January 1, 1967. Amended Stats 1969 ch 646 §1.

§1552. Printed representation of computer information or computer program

(a) A printed representation of computer information or a computer program is presumed to be an accurate representation of the computer information or computer program that it purports to represent. This presumption is a presumption affecting the burden of producing evidence. If a party to an action introduces evidence that a printed representation of computer information or computer program is inaccurate or unreliable, the party introducing the printed representation into evidence has the burden of proving, by a preponderance of evidence, that the printed representation is an accurate representation of the existence and content of the computer information or computer program that it purports to represent.

(b) Subdivision (a) applies to the printed representation of computer-generated information stored by an automated traffic enforcement system.

(c) Subdivision (a) shall not apply to computer-generated official records certified in accordance with Section 452.5 or 1530. **Leg.H.** Added Stats 1998 ch 100 §4 (SB 177). Amended Stats 2012 ch 735 §1 (SB 1303), effective January 1, 2013.

1998 Note: For applicability, see the 1998 Note following Ev C §1520.

§1553. Printed representation of images stored on video or digital medium

(a) A printed representation of images stored on a video or digital medium is presumed to be an accurate representation of the images it purports to represent. This presumption is a presumption affecting the burden of producing evidence. If a party to an action introduces evidence that a printed representation of images stored on a video or digital medium is inaccurate or unreliable, the party introducing the printed representation into evidence has the burden of proving, by a preponderance of evidence, that the printed representation is an accurate representation of the existence and content of the images that it purports to represent.

(b) Subdivision (a) applies to the printed representation of video or photographic images stored by an automated traffic enforcement system. **Leg.H.** Added Stats 1998 ch 100 §5 (SB 177). Amended Stats 2012 ch 735 §2 (SB 1303), effective January 1, 2013.

1998 Note: For applicability, see the 1998 Note following Ev C §1520.

ARTICLE 4
Production of Business Records

Compliance with subpoena duces tecum for business records; Alternative procedure in civil actions; Sufficiency of compliance by nonparty business. §1560.
Affidavit accompanying records. §1561.

Admissibility of affidavit and copy of records. §1562.
Witness and mileage fees; Recovery of "reasonable costs". §1563.
Personal attendance of custodian and production of original records. §1564.
Service of more than one subpoena duces tecum. §1565.
Applicability of article. §1566.
Form for income and benefit information. §1567.

§1560. Compliance with subpoena duces tecum for business records; Alternative procedure in civil actions; Sufficiency of compliance by nonparty business

(a) As used in this article:

(1) "Business" includes every kind of business described in Section 1270.

(2) "Record" includes every kind of record maintained by a business.

(b) Except as provided in Section 1564, when a subpoena duces tecum is served upon the custodian of records or other qualified witness of a business in an action in which the business is neither a party nor the place where any cause of action is alleged to have arisen, and the subpoena requires the production of all or any part of the records of the business, it is sufficient compliance therewith if the custodian or other qualified witness delivers by mail or otherwise a true, legible, and durable copy of all of the records described in the subpoena to the clerk of the court or to another person described in subdivision (d) of Section 2026.010 of the Code of Civil Procedure, together with the affidavit described in Section 1561, within one of the following time periods:

(1) In any criminal action, five days after the receipt of the subpoena.

(2) In any civil action, within 15 days after the receipt of the subpoena.

(3) Within the time agreed upon by the party who served the subpoena and the custodian or other qualified witness.

(c) The copy of the records shall be separately enclosed in an inner envelope or wrapper, sealed, with the title and number of the action, name of witness, and date of subpoena clearly inscribed thereon; the sealed envelope or wrapper shall then be enclosed in an outer envelope or wrapper, sealed, and directed as follows:

(1) If the subpoena directs attendance in court, to the clerk of the court.

(2) If the subpoena directs attendance at a deposition, to the officer before whom the deposition is to be taken, at the place designated in the subpoena for the taking of the deposition or at the officer's place of business.

(3) In other cases, to the officer, body, or tribunal conducting the hearing, at a like address.

(d) Unless the parties to the proceeding otherwise agree, or unless the sealed envelope or wrapper is returned to a witness who is to appear personally, the copy of the records shall remain sealed and shall be opened only at the time of trial, deposition, or other hearing, upon the direction of the judge, officer, body, or tribunal conducting the proceeding, in the presence of all parties who have appeared in person or by counsel at the trial, deposition, or hearing. Records that are original documents and that are not introduced in evidence or required as part of the record shall be returned to the person or entity from whom received. Records that are copies may be destroyed.

(e) As an alternative to the procedures described in subdivisions (b), (c), and (d), the subpoenaing party in a civil action may direct the witness to make the records available for inspection or copying by the party's attorney, the attorney's representative, or deposition officer as described in Section 2020.420 of the Code of Civil Procedure, at the witness' business address under reasonable conditions during normal business hours. Normal business hours, as used in this subdivision, means those hours that the business of the witness is normally open for business to the public. When provided with at least five business days' advance notice by the party's attorney, attorney's representative, or deposition officer, the witness shall designate a time period of not less than six continuous hours on a date certain for copying of records subject to the subpoena by the party's attorney, attorney's representative, or deposition officer. It shall be the responsibility of the attorney's representative to deliver any copy of the records as directed in the subpoena. Disobedience to the deposition subpoena issued pursuant to this subdivision is punishable as provided in Section 2020.240 of the Code of Civil Procedure.

(f) If a search warrant for business records is served upon the custodian of records or other qualified witness of a business in compliance with Section 1524 of the Penal Code regarding a criminal investigation in which the business is neither a party nor the place where any crime is alleged to have occurred, and the search warrant provides that the warrant will be deemed executed if the business causes the delivery of records described in the warrant to the law enforcement agency ordered to execute the warrant, it is sufficient compliance therewith if the custodian or other qualified witness delivers by mail or otherwise a true, legible, and durable copy of all of the records described in the search warrant to the law enforcement agency ordered to execute the search warrant, together with the affidavit described in Section 1561, within five days after the receipt of the search warrant or within such other time as is set forth in the warrant. This subdivision does not abridge or limit the scope of search warrant procedures set forth in Chapter 3 (commencing with Section 1523) of Title 12 of Part 2 of the Penal Code or invalidate otherwise duly executed search warrants. **Leg.H.** Enacted Stats 1965 ch 299 §2, operative January 1, 1967. Amended Stats 1969 ch 199 §2; Stats 1982 ch 452 §2.5; Stats 1984 ch 481 §2; Stats 1986 ch 603 §6; Stats 1991 ch 1090 §14 (AB 1484); Stats 1997 ch 442 §16 (AB 758); Stats 1999 ch 444 §4 (AB 794); Stats 2000 ch 287 §1 (SB 1955); Stats 2004 ch 162 §1 (AB 1249) (ch 162 prevails), ch 182 §32 (AB 3081), operative July 1, 2005, ch 294 §18 (AB 333), effective January 1, 2006; Stats 2006 ch 538 §155 (SB 1852), effective January 1, 2007; Stats 2016 ch 85 §1 (SB 1087), effective January 1, 2017.

§1561. Affidavit accompanying records

(a) The records shall be accompanied by the affidavit of the custodian or other qualified witness, stating in substance each of the following:

(1) The affiant is the duly authorized custodian of the records or other qualified witness and has authority to certify the records.

(2) The copy is a true copy of all the records described in the subpoena duces tecum or search warrant, or pursuant to subdivision (e) of Section 1560, the records were delivered to the attorney, the attorney's representative, or deposition officer for copying at the custodian's or witness' place of business, as the case may be.

(3) The records were prepared by the personnel of the business in the ordinary course of business at or near the time of the act, condition, or event.

(4) The identity of the records.

(5) A description of the mode of preparation of the records.

(b) If the business has none of the records described, or only part thereof, the custodian or other qualified witness shall so state in the affidavit, and deliver the affidavit and those records that are available in one of the manners provided in Section 1560.

(c) If the records described in the subpoena were delivered to the attorney or his or her representative or deposition officer for copying at the custodian's or witness' place of business, in addition to the affidavit required by subdivision (a), the records shall be accompanied by an affidavit by the attorney or his or her representative or deposition officer stating that the copy is a true copy of all the records delivered to the attorney or his or her representative or deposition officer for copying. **Leg.H.** Enacted Stats 1965 ch 299 §2, operative January 1, 1967. Amended Stats 1969 ch 199 §3; Stats 1986 ch 603 §7; Stats 1987 ch 19 §2, effective May 12, 1987; Stats 1996 ch 146 §1 (AB 3001); Stats 1999 ch 444 §5 (AB 794); Stats 2016 ch 85 §2 (SB 1087), effective January 1, 2017.

§1562. Admissibility of affidavit and copy of records

If the original records would be admissible in evidence if the custodian or other qualified witness had been present and testified to the matters stated in the affidavit, and if the requirements of Section 1271 have been met, the copy of the records is admissible in evidence. The affidavit is admissible as evidence of the matters stated therein pursuant to Section 1561 and the matters so stated are presumed true. When more than one person has knowledge of the facts, more than one affidavit may be made. The presumption established by this section is a presumption affecting the burden of producing evidence. **Leg.H.** Enacted Stats 1965 ch 299 §2, operative January 1, 1967. Amended Stats 1989 ch 1416 §31; Stats 1996 ch 146 §2 (AB 3001).

§1563. Witness and mileage fees; Recovery of "reasonable costs"

(a) This article does not require tender or payment of more than one witness fee and one mileage fee or other charge, to a witness or witness' business, unless there is an agreement to the contrary between the witness and the requesting party.

(b) All reasonable costs incurred in a civil proceeding by a witness who is not a party with respect to the production of all or any part of business records requested pursuant to a subpoena duces tecum shall be charged against the party serving the subpoena duces tecum.

(1) "Reasonable costs," as used in this section, includes, but is not limited to, the following specific costs: ten cents ($0.10) per page for standard reproduction of documents of a size 8½ by 14 inches or less; twenty cents ($0.20) per page for copying of documents from microfilm; actual costs for the reproduction of oversize documents or the reproduction of documents requiring special processing which are made in response to a subpoena; reasonable clerical costs incurred in locating and making the records available to be billed at the maximum rate of twenty-four dollars ($24) per hour per person, computed on the basis of six dollars ($6) per quarter hour or fraction thereof; actual postage charges; and the actual cost, if any, charged to the witness by a third person for the retrieval and return of records held offsite by that third person.

(2) The requesting party, or the requesting party's deposition officer, shall not be required to pay the reasonable costs or any estimate thereof before the records are available for delivery pursuant to the subpoena, but the witness may demand payment of costs pursuant to this section simultaneous with actual delivery of the subpoenaed records, and until payment is made, the witness is under no obligation to deliver the records.

(3) The witness shall submit an itemized statement for the costs to the requesting party, or the requesting party's deposition officer, setting forth the reproduction and clerical costs incurred by the witness. If the costs exceed those authorized in paragraph (1), or if the witness refuses to produce an itemized statement of costs as required by paragraph (3), upon demand by the requesting party, or the requesting party's deposition officer, the witness shall furnish a statement setting forth the actions taken by the witness in justification of the costs.

(4) The requesting party may petition the court in which the action is pending to recover from the witness all or a part of the costs paid to the witness, or to reduce all or a part of the costs charged by the witness, pursuant to this subdivision, on the grounds that those costs were excessive. Upon the filing of the petition the court shall issue an order to show cause and from the time the order is served on the witness the court has jurisdiction over the witness. The court may hear testimony on the order to show cause and if it finds that the costs demanded and collected, or charged but not collected, exceed the amount authorized by this subdivision, it shall order the witness to remit to the requesting party, or reduce its charge to the requesting party by an amount equal to, the amount of the excess. If the court finds the costs were excessive and charged in bad faith by the witness, the court shall order the witness to remit the full amount of the costs demanded and collected, or excuse the requesting party from any payment of costs charged but not collected, and the court shall also order the witness to pay the requesting party the amount of the reasonable expenses incurred in obtaining the order, including attorney's fees. If the court finds the costs were not excessive, the court shall order the requesting party to pay the witness the amount of the reasonable expenses incurred in defending the petition, including attorney's fees.

(5) If a subpoena is served to compel the production of business records and is subsequently withdrawn, or is quashed, modified, or limited on a motion made other than by the witness, the witness shall be entitled to reimbursement pursuant to paragraph (1) for all reasonable costs incurred in compliance with the subpoena to the time that the requesting party has notified the witness that the subpoena has been withdrawn or quashed, modified, or limited. If the subpoena is withdrawn or quashed, if those costs are not paid within 30 days after demand therefor, the witness may file a motion in the court in which the action is pending for an order requiring payment, and the court shall award the payment of expenses and attorney's fees in the manner set forth in paragraph (4).

(6) If records requested pursuant to a subpoena duces tecum are delivered to the attorney, the attorney's representative, or the deposition officer for inspection or photocopying at the witness' place of business, the only fee for complying with the subpoena shall not exceed fifteen dollars ($15), plus the actual cost, if any, charged to the witness by a third person for retrieval and return of records held offsite by that third person. If the records are retrieved from microfilm, the reasonable costs, as defined in paragraph (1), applies.

(c) If the personal attendance of the custodian of a record or other qualified witness is required pursuant to Section 1564, in a civil proceeding, he or she shall be entitled to the same witness fees and mileage permitted in a case where the subpoena requires the witness to attend and testify before a court in which the action or proceeding is pending and to any additional costs incurred as provided by subdivision (b). **Leg.H.** Enacted Stats 1965 ch 299 §2, operative January 1, 1967. Amended Stats 1972 ch 396 §1; Stats 1981 ch 1014 §2; Stats 1982 ch 452 §3; Stats 1986 ch 603 §8; Stats 1987 ch 19 §3, effective May 12, 1987; Stats 1997 ch 442 §17 (AB 758); Stats 1999 ch 444 §6 (AB 794); Stats 2016 ch 85 §3 (SB 1087), effective January 1, 2017.

§1564. Personal attendance of custodian and production of original records

The personal attendance of the custodian or other qualified witness and the production of the original records is not required unless, at the discretion of the requesting party, the subpoena duces tecum contains a clause which reads:

"The personal attendance of the custodian or other qualified witness and the production of the original records are required by this subpoena. The procedure authorized pursuant to subdivision (b) of Section 1560, and Sections 1561 and 1562, of the Evidence Code will not be deemed sufficient compliance with this subpoena." **Leg.H.** Enacted Stats 1965 ch 299 §2, operative January 1, 1967. Amended Stats 1984 ch 603 §2; Stats 1986 ch 603 §9; Stats 1987 ch 19 §4, effective May 12, 1987.

§1565. Service of more than one subpoena duces tecum

If more than one subpoena duces tecum is served upon the custodian of records or other qualified witness and the personal attendance of the custodian or other qualified witness is required pursuant to Section 1564, the witness shall be deemed to be the witness of the party serving the first such subpoena duces tecum. **Leg.H.** Enacted Stats 1965 ch 299 §2, operative January 1, 1967. Amended Stats 1969 ch 199 §4.

§1566. Applicability of article

This article applies in any proceeding in which testimony can be compelled. **Leg.H.** Added Stats 1965 ch 299 §2, operative January 1, 1967.

§1567. Form for income and benefit information

A completed form described in Section 3664 of the Family Code for income and benefit information provided by the employer may be admissible in a proceeding for modification or termination of an order for child, family, or spousal support if both of the following requirements are met:

(a) The completed form complies with Sections 1561 and 1562.

(b) A copy of the completed form and notice was served on the employee named therein pursuant to Section 3664 of the Family Code. **Leg.H.** Added Stats 1995 ch 506 §1 (AB 413).

CHAPTER 3
OFFICIAL WRITINGS AFFECTING PROPERTY

Official record of document affecting property interest. §1600.
Proof of content of lost official record affecting property. §1601.
Deed by officer in pursuance of court process. §1603.
Certificate of purchase or of location of lands. §1604.
Authenticated Spanish title records. §1605.

§1600. Official record of document affecting property interest

(a) The record of an instrument or other document purporting to establish or affect an interest in property is prima facie evidence of the existence and content of the original recorded document and its execution and delivery by each person by whom it purports to have been executed if:

(1) The record is in fact a record of an office of a public entity; and
(2) A statute authorized such a document to be recorded in that office.

(b) The presumption established by this section is a presumption affecting the burden of proof. **Leg.H.** Enacted Stats 1965 ch 299 §2, operative January 1, 1967. Amended Stats 1967 ch 650 §9.

§1601. Proof of content of lost official record affecting property

(a) Subject to subdivisions (b) and (c), when in any action it is desired to prove the contents of the official record of any writing lost or destroyed by conflagration or other public calamity, after proof of such loss or destruction, the following may, without further proof, be admitted in evidence to prove the contents of such record:

(1) Any abstract of title made and issued and certified as correct prior to such loss or destruction, and purporting to have been prepared and made in the ordinary course of business by any person engaged in the business of preparing and making abstracts of title prior to such loss or destruction; or

(2) Any abstract of title, or of any instrument affecting title, made, issued, and certified as correct by any person engaged in the business of insuring titles or issuing abstracts of title to real estate, whether the same was made, issued, or certified before or after such loss or destruction and whether the same was made from the original records or from abstract and notes, or either, taken from such records in the preparation and upkeeping of its plant in the ordinary course of its business.

(b) No proof of the loss of the original writing is required other than the fact that the original is not known to the party desiring to prove its contents to be in existence.

(c) Any party desiring to use evidence admissible under this section shall give reasonable notice in writing to all other parties to the action who have appeared therein, of his intention to use such evidence at the trial of the action, and shall give all such other parties a reasonable opportunity to inspect the evidence, and also the abstracts, memoranda, or notes from which it was compiled, and to take copies thereof. **Leg.H.** Enacted Stats 1965 ch 299 §2, operative January 1, 1967.

§1602. [Section repealed 1967]

Leg.H. Enacted Stats 1965 ch 299 §2, operative January 1, 1967. Repealed Stats 1967 ch 650 §10. The repealed section related to mineral lands.

§1603. Deed by officer in pursuance of court process

A deed of conveyance of real property, purporting to have been executed by a proper officer in pursuance of legal process of any of the courts of record of this state, acknowledged and recorded in the office of the recorder of the county wherein the real property therein described is situated, or the record of such deed, or a certified copy of such record, is prima facie evidence that the property or interest therein described was thereby conveyed to the grantee named in such deed. The presumption established by this section is a presumption affecting the burden of proof. **Leg.H.** Enacted Stats 1965 ch 299 §2, operative January 1, 1967. Amended Stats 1967 ch 650 §11.

§1604. Certificate of purchase or of location of lands

A certificate of purchase, or of location, of any lands in this state, issued or made in pursuance of any law of the United States or of this state, is prima facie evidence that the holder or assignee of such certificate is the owner of the land described therein; but this evidence may be overcome by proof that, at the time of the location, or time of filing a preemption claim on which the certificate may have been issued, the land was in the adverse possession of the adverse party, or those under whom he claims, or that the adverse party is holding the land for mining purposes. **Leg.H.** Enacted Stats 1965 ch 299 §2, operative January 1, 1967.

§1605. Authenticated Spanish title records

Duplicate copies and authenticated translations of original Spanish title papers relating to land claims in this state, derived from the Spanish or Mexican governments, prepared under the supervision of the Keeper of Archives, authenticated by the Surveyor-General or his successor and by the Keeper of Archives, and filed with a county recorder, in accordance with Chapter 281 of the Statutes of 1865–66, are admissible as evidence with like force and effect as the originals and without proving the execution of such originals. **Leg.H.** Enacted Stats 1965 ch 299 §2, operative January 1, 1967. Amended Stats 1967 ch 650 §12.

The FAMILY CODE

of the

STATE OF CALIFORNIA

2025 EDITION

As Enacted by Stats. 1992 ch. 162—Operative January 1, 1994
With All Subsequent Legislative Enactments

Table Showing 2024 Changes in the Family Code

Effective January 1, 2025, unless otherwise noted at end of section.

Section	Effect	Chapter	Section	Effect	Chapter
1816	Amended	303	6380	Amended	169
Ch. 7 (comm. w/2080)	Amended	780	6389	Amended	544
2080	Amended	780	6389	Repealed & Added	544
2081	Amended	780	Pt. 2.5 (comm. w/6650)	Added	611
2082	Amended	780	6650–6656	Added	611
2331	Amended	190	6650	Added	611
2342	Amended	190	6651	Added	611
2342.5	Added	190	6652	Added	611
2342.51	Added	190	6653	Added	611
2401	Amended	190	6654	Added	611
2402	Amended	190	6655	Added	611
2330	Amended	190	6656	Added	611
3044	Amended & Added	544	6750	Amended	610
3064	Amended	317	7950	Amended	845
3100	Amended	317	8616.5	Amended	80
3910	Amended	25	17400	Amended	853
6228	Amended	495	17561	Repealed	46
6300	Amended	648	17706	Repealed	46
6301	Added	652			
6306	Repealed & Added	541			

CONTENTS

Sections

DIVISION 1. PRELIMINARY PROVISIONS AND DEFINITIONS
- Part 1. Preliminary Provisions ... 1 – 13
- Part 2. Definitions ... 50 – 155
- Part 3. Indian Children ... 170 – 185

DIVISION 2. GENERAL PROVISIONS
- Part 1. Jurisdiction ... 200
- Part 2. General Procedural Provisions ... 210 – 218
- Part 3. Temporary Restraining Order in Summons ... 231 – 235
- Part 4. Ex Parte Temporary Restraining Orders ... 240 – 246
- Part 5. Attorney's Fees and Costs ... 270 – 274
- Part 6. Enforcement of Judgments and Orders ... 290 – 292
- Part 7. Tribal Marriages and Divorces ... 295

DIVISION 2.5. DOMESTIC PARTNER REGISTRATION
- Part 1. Definitions ... 297 – 297.5
- Part 2. Registration ... 298 – 298.8
- Part 3. Termination ... 299
- Part 4. Legal Effect ... 299.2
- Part 5. Preemption ... 299.6

DIVISION 3. MARRIAGE
- Part 1. Validity of Marriage ... 300 – 310
- Part 2. Marriage License ... 350 – 360
- Part 3. Solemnization of Marriage ... 400 – 426
- Part 4. Confidential Marriage ... 500 – 536
- Part 5. Remote Marriage License Issuance and Solemnization ... 550 – 560

DIVISION 4. RIGHTS AND OBLIGATIONS DURING MARRIAGE
- Part 1. General Provisions ... 700 – 755
- Part 2. Characterization of Marital Property ... 760 – 853
- Part 3. Liability of Marital Property ... 900 – 1000
- Part 4. Management and Control of Marital Property ... 1100 – 1103
- Part 5. Marital Agreements ... 1500 – 1620

DIVISION 5. CONCILIATION PROCEEDINGS
- Part 1. Family Conciliation Court Law ... 1800 – 1842
- Part 2. Statewide Coordination of Family Mediation and Conciliation Services ... 1850 – 1852

DIVISION 6. NULLITY, DISSOLUTION, AND LEGAL SEPARATION
- Part 1. General Provisions ... 2000 – 2129
- Part 2. Judicial Determination of Void or Voidable Marriage ... 2200 – 2255
- Part 3. Dissolution of Marriage and Legal Separation ... 2300 – 2452

DIVISION 7. DIVISION OF PROPERTY
- Part 1. Definitions ... 2500 – 2502
- Part 2. General Provisions ... 2550 – 2556
- Part 3. Presumption Concerning Property Held in Joint Form ... 2580 – 2581
- Part 4. Special Rules for Division of Community Estate ... 2600 – 2605
- Part 5. Retirement Plan Benefits ... 2610 – 2611
- Part 6. Debts and Liabilities ... 2620 – 2628
- Part 7. Reimbursements ... 2640 – 2641
- Part 8. Jointly Held Separate Property ... 2650
- Part 9. Real Property Located in Another State ... 2660

DIVISION 8. CUSTODY OF CHILDREN
- Part 1. Definitions and General Provisions ... 3000 – 3012
- Part 2. Right to Custody of Minor Child ... 3020 – 3204
- Part 3. Uniform Child Custody Jurisdiction and Enforcement Act ... 3400 – 3465

DIVISION 9. SUPPORT
Part 1.	Definitions and General Provisions	3500 – 3830
Part 2.	Child Support	3900 – 4253
Part 3.	Spousal Support	4300 – 4360
Part 4.	Support of Parents	4400 – 4414
Part 5.	Enforcement of Support Orders	4500 – 5616
Part 6.	Uniform Interstate Family Support Act	5700.101 – 5700.905

DIVISION 10. PREVENTION OF DOMESTIC VIOLENCE
Part 1.	Short Title and Definitions	6200 – 6219
Part 2.	General Provisions	6220 – 6229
Part 3.	Emergency Protective Orders	6240 – 6275
Part 4.	Protective Orders and Other Domestic Violence Prevention Orders	6300 – 6389
Part 5.	Uniform Interstate Enforcement of Domestic Violence Protection Orders Act	6400 – 6409
Part 6.	Uniform Recognition and Enforcement of Canadian Domestic Violence Protection Orders Act	6450 – 6460

DIVISION 11. MINORS
Part 1.	Age of Majority	6500 – 6502
Part 1.5.	Caregivers	6550 – 6552
Part 2.	Rights and Liabilities; Civil Actions and Proceedings	6600 – 6602
Part 2.5.	ONLINE PLATFORMS	6650 – 6656
Part 3.	Contracts	6700 – 6753
Part 4.	Medical Treatment	6900 – 6930
Part 5.	Enlistment in Armed Forces	6950
Part 6.	Emancipation of Minors Law	7000 – 7143

DIVISION 12. PARENT AND CHILD RELATIONSHIP
Part 1.	Rights of Parents	7500 – 7507
Part 2.	Presumption Concerning Child of Marriage and Genetic Testing to Determine Parentage	7540 – 7581
Part 3.	Uniform Parentage Act	7600 – 7730
Part 4.	Freedom From Parental Custody and Control	7800 – 7895
Part 5.	Interstate Compact on Placement of Children	7900 – 7913
Part 6.	Foster Care Placement Considerations	7950 – 7952
Part 7.	Surrogacy and Donor Facilitators, Assisted Reproduction Agreements for Gestational Carriers, and Oocyte Donations	7960 – 7962

DIVISION 13. ADOPTION
Part 1.	Definitions	8500 – 8548
Part 2.	Adoption of Unmarried Minors	8600 – 9213
Part 3.	Adoption of Adults and Married Minors	9300 – 9340

DIVISION 14. FAMILY LAW FACILITATOR ACT
10000 – 10015

DIVISION 17. SUPPORT SERVICES
Chapter 1.	Department of Child Support Services	17000 – 17393
Chapter 2.	Child Support Enforcement	17400 – 17714
Chapter 5.	Complaint Resolution	17800 – 17804

DIVISION 20. PILOT PROJECTS
Part 1.	Family Law Pilot Projects	20000 – 20043

FAMILY CODE

An act to repeal Part 2.7 (commencing with Section 60) and Part 3 (commencing with Section 196) of Division 1 of, and to repeal Part 5 (commencing with Section 4000) and Part 7 (commencing with Section 7000) of Division 4 of, the Civil Code, to repeal Chapter 4 (commencing with Section 540) of Title 7 of Part 2 of, to repeal Title 10a (commencing with Section 1650) and Title 11.5 (commencing with Section 1730) of Part 3 of, the Code of Civil Procedure, to repeal Section 621 of, and to repeal Chapter 2 (commencing with Section 890) of Division 7 of, the Evidence Code, to enact the Family Code, and to repeal Sections 3301 and 3302 of the Probate Code, relating to family law.

DIVISION 1
PRELIMINARY PROVISIONS AND DEFINITIONS

Part 1. Preliminary Provisions.
Part 2. Definitions.
Part 3. Indian Children.

PART 1
PRELIMINARY PROVISIONS

Title of code. §1.
Continuation of existing law. §2.
Construction of provision drawn from uniform act. §3.
Transitional provision for amendments, additions, and repeals. §4.
Effect of headings in code. §5.
Construction of code. §6.
Reference to statute includes amendments and additions. §7.
Reference to division, part, chapter, article, section, or part of section. §8.
Construction of tenses. §9.
Construction of singular and plural. §10.
Reference to married person includes formerly married person. §11.
Meaning of shall, may, shall not, and may not. §12.
Severability of provisions. §13.

§1. Title of code

This code shall be known as the Family Code. **Leg.H.** Enacted Stats 1992 ch 162 §10 (AB 2650), operative January 1, 1994.

§2. Continuation of existing law

A provision of this code, insofar as it is substantially the same as a previously existing provision relating to the same subject matter, shall be considered as a restatement and continuation thereof and not as a new enactment, and a reference in a statute to the provision of this code shall be deemed to include a reference to the previously existing provision unless a contrary intent appears. **Leg.H.** Enacted Stats 1992 ch 162 §10 (AB 2650), operative January 1, 1994. Amended Stats 1993 ch 219 §78 (AB 1500).

§3. Construction of provision drawn from uniform act

A provision of this code, insofar as it is the same in substance as a provision of a uniform act, shall be construed to effectuate the general purpose to make uniform the law in those states which enact that provision. **Leg.H.** Enacted Stats 1992 ch 162 §10 (AB 2650), operative January 1, 1994.

§4. Transitional provision for amendments, additions, and repeals

(a) As used in this section:

(1) "New law" means either of the following, as the case may be:

(A) The act that enacted this code.

(B) The act that makes a change in this code, whether effectuated by amendment, addition, or repeal of a provision of this code.

(2) "Old law" means the applicable law in effect before the operative date of the new law.

(3) "Operative date" means the operative date of the new law.

(b) This section governs the application of the new law except to the extent otherwise expressly provided in the new law.

(c) Subject to the limitations provided in this section, the new law applies on the operative date to all matters governed by the new law, regardless of whether an event occurred or circumstance existed before, on, or after the operative date, including, but not limited to, commencement of a proceeding, making of an order, or taking of an action.

(d) If a document or paper is filed before the operative date, the contents, execution, and notice thereof are governed by the old law and not by the new law; but subsequent proceedings taken after the operative date concerning the document or paper, including an objection or response, a hearing, an order, or other matter relating thereto is governed by the new law and not by the old law.

(e) If an order is made before the operative date, or an action on an order is taken before the operative date, the validity of the order or action is governed by the old law and not by the new law. Nothing in this subdivision precludes proceedings after the operative date to modify an order made, or alter a course of action commenced, before the operative date to the extent proceedings for modification of an order or alteration of a course of action of that type are otherwise provided in the new law.

(f) No person is liable for an action taken before the operative date that was proper at the time the action was taken, even though the action would be improper if taken on or after the operative date, and the person has no duty, as a result of the enactment of the new law, to take any step to alter the course of action or its consequences.

(g) If the new law does not apply to a matter that occurred before the operative date, the old law continues to govern the matter notwithstanding its repeal or amendment by the new law.

(h) If a party shows, and the court determines, that application of a particular provision of the new law or of the old law in the manner required by this section or by the new law would substantially interfere with the effective conduct of the proceedings or the rights of the parties or other interested persons in connection with an event that occurred or circumstance that existed before the operative date, the court may, notwithstanding this section or the new law, apply either the new law or the old law to the extent reasonably necessary to mitigate the substantial interference. **Leg.H.** Enacted Stats 1992 ch 162 §10 (AB 2650), operative January 1, 1994.

§5. Effect of headings in code

Division, part, chapter, article, and section headings do not in any manner affect the scope, meaning, or intent of this code. **Leg.H.** Enacted Stats 1992 ch 162 §10 (AB 2650), operative January 1, 1994.

§6. Construction of code

Unless the provision or context otherwise requires, the general provisions and rules of construction in this part govern the construction of this code. **Leg.H.** Enacted Stats 1992 ch 162 §10 (AB 2650), operative January 1, 1994.

§7. Reference to statute includes amendments and additions

Whenever a reference is made to a portion of this code or to another law, the reference applies to all amendments and additions regardless of when made. **Leg.H.** Enacted Stats 1992 ch 162 §10 (AB 2650), operative January 1, 1994.

§8. Reference to division, part, chapter, article, section, or part of section

Unless otherwise expressly stated:

(a) "Division" means a division of this code.

(b) "Part" means a part of the division in which that term occurs.

(c) "Chapter" means a chapter of the division or part, as the case may be, in which that term occurs.

(d) "Article" means an article of the chapter in which that term occurs.

(e) "Section" means a section of this code.

(f) "Subdivision" means a subdivision of the section in which that term occurs.

(g) "Paragraph" means a paragraph of the subdivision in which that term occurs.

(h) "Subparagraph" means a subparagraph of the paragraph in which that term occurs. **Leg.H.** Enacted Stats 1992 ch 162 §10 (AB 2650), operative January 1, 1994.

§9. Construction of tenses

The present tense includes the past and future tenses, and the future, the present. **Leg.H.** Enacted Stats 1992 ch 162 §10 (AB 2650), operative January 1, 1994.

§10. Construction of singular and plural

The singular number includes the plural, and the plural, the singular. **Leg.H.** Enacted Stats 1992 ch 162 §10 (AB 2650), operative January 1, 1994.

§11. Reference to married person includes formerly married person

A reference to "husband" and "wife," "spouses," or "married persons," or a comparable term, includes persons who are lawfully married to each other and persons who were previously lawfully married to each other, as is appropriate under the circumstances of the particular case. **Leg.H.** Enacted Stats 1992 ch 162 §10 (AB 2650), operative January 1, 1994.

§12. Meaning of shall, may, shall not, and may not

"Shall" is mandatory and "may" is permissive. "Shall not" and "may not" are prohibitory. **Leg.H.** Enacted Stats 1992 ch 162 §10 (AB 2650), operative January 1, 1994.

§13. Severability of provisions

If a provision or clause of this code or its application to any person or circumstances is held invalid, the invalidity does not affect other provisions or applications of the code which can be given effect without the invalid provision or application, and to this end the provisions of this code are severable. **Leg.H.** Enacted Stats 1992 ch 162 §10 (AB 2650), operative January 1, 1994.

PART 2
DEFINITIONS

Application of definitions. §50.
"Child for whom support may be ordered". §58.
"Community estate". §63.
"Community property". §65.
"County". §67.
"Date of separation". §70.
"Employee benefit plan". §80.
"Family support". §92.
"Income and expense declaration". §95.
"Judgment" and "order". §100.
"Person". §105.
"Proceeding". §110.
"Property". §113.
"Property declaration". §115.
"Quasi-community property". §125.
"Petitioner". §126.
"Respondent". §127.
"Separate property". §130.
"Spousal support". §142.
"Spouse" to include registered domestic partner. §143.
"State". §145.
"Support". §150.
"Support order". §155.

§50. Application of definitions
Unless the provision or context otherwise requires, the definitions and rules of construction in this part govern the construction of this code. **Leg.H.** Enacted Stats 1992 ch 162 §10 (AB 2650), operative January 1, 1994.

§55. [Section repealed 1993]
Leg.H. Enacted Stats 1992 ch 162 §10 (AB 2650), operative January 1, 1994. Repealed Stats 1993 ch 219 §78.5 (AB 1500). See Fam C §6203.

§57. [Section repealed 1993]
Leg.H. Enacted Stats 1992 ch 162 §10 (AB 2650), operative January 1, 1994. Repealed Stats 1993 ch 219 §78.7 (AB 1500). See Fam C §6205.

§58. "Child for whom support may be ordered"
"Child for whom support may be ordered" means a minor child and a child for whom support is authorized under Section 3587, 3901, or 3910. **Leg.H.** Added Stats 1993 ch 219 §79 (AB 1500).

§60. [Section repealed 1993]
Leg.H. Enacted Stats 1992 ch 162 §10 (AB 2650), operative January 1, 1994. Repealed Stats 1993 ch 219 §79.1 (AB 1500). See Fam C §6209.

§63. "Community estate"
"Community estate" includes both community property and quasi-community property. **Leg.H.** Added Stats 1993 ch 219 §79.3 (AB 1500).

§65. "Community property"
"Community property" is property that is community property under Part 2 (commencing with Section 760) of Division 4. **Leg.H.** Enacted Stats 1992 ch 162 §10 (AB 2650), operative January 1, 1994.

§67. "County"
"County" includes city and county. **Leg.H.** Enacted Stats 1992 ch 162 §10 (AB 2650), operative January 1, 1994.

§70. "Date of separation"
(a) "Date of separation" means the date that a complete and final break in the marital relationship has occurred, as evidenced by both of the following:
(1) The spouse has expressed to the other spouse the intent to end the marriage.
(2) The conduct of the spouse is consistent with the intent to end the marriage.
(b) In determining the date of separation, the court shall take into consideration all relevant evidence.
(c) It is the intent of the Legislature in enacting this section to abrogate the decisions in In re Marriage of Davis (2015) 61 Cal.4th 846 and In re Marriage of Norviel (2002) 102 Cal.App.4th 1152. **Leg.H.** Added Stats 2016 ch 114 §1 (SB 1255), effective January 1, 2017. Amended Stats 2019 ch 115 §1 (AB 1817), effective January 1, 2020.

Prior Law: Former Fam C §70, similar to present Fam C §6211, was enacted Stats 1992 ch 162 §10 (AB 2650), effective January 1, 1993, operative January 1, 1994, and repealed Stats 1993 ch 219 §79.5 (AB 1500), effective January 1, 1994.

§75. [Section repealed 1993]
Leg.H. Enacted Stats 1992 ch 162 §10 (AB 2650), operative January 1, 1994. Repealed Stats 1993 ch 219 §79.7 (AB 1500). The repealed section related to domestic violence prevention order.

§80. "Employee benefit plan"
"Employee benefit plan" includes public and private retirement, pension, annuity, savings, profit sharing, stock bonus, stock option, thrift, vacation pay, and similar plans of deferred or fringe benefit compensation, whether of the defined contribution or defined benefit type whether or not such plan is qualified under the Employee Retirement Income Security Act of 1974 (P.L. 93-406) (ERISA), as amended. The term also includes "employee benefit plan" as defined in Section 3 of ERISA (29 U.S.C.A. Sec. 1002(3)). **Leg.H.** Enacted Stats 1992 ch 162 §10 (AB 2650), operative January 1, 1994. Amended Stats 1994 ch 1269 §9 (AB 2208).

§92. "Family support"
"Family support" means an agreement between the parents, or an order or judgment, that combines child support and spousal support without designating the amount to be paid for child support and the amount to be paid for spousal support. **Leg.H.** Enacted Stats 1992 ch 162 §10 (AB 2650), operative January 1, 1994.

§95. "Income and expense declaration"
"Income and expense declaration" means the form for an income and expense declaration in family law matters adopted by the Judicial Council. **Leg.H.** Enacted Stats 1992 ch 162 §10 (AB 2650), operative January 1, 1994.

§100. "Judgment" and "order"
"Judgment" and "order" include a decree, as appropriate under the circumstances. **Leg.H.** Enacted Stats 1992 ch 162 §10 (AB 2650), operative January 1, 1994.

§105. "Person"
"Person" includes a natural person, firm, association, organization, partnership, business trust, corporation, limited liability company, or public entity. **Leg.H.** Added Stats 1993 ch 219 §80 (AB 1500). Amended Stats 1994 ch 1010 §107 (SB 2053).

§110. "Proceeding"
"Proceeding" includes an action. **Leg.H.** Added Stats 1993 ch 219 §81 (AB 1500).

§113. "Property"
"Property" includes real and personal property and any interest therein. **Leg.H.** Added Stats 2000 ch 808 §21 (AB 1358), effective September 28, 2000.

§115. "Property declaration"
"Property declaration" means the form for a property declaration in family law matters adopted by the Judicial Council. **Leg.H.** Enacted Stats 1992 ch 162 §10 (AB 2650), operative January 1, 1994.

§125. "Quasi-community property"
"Quasi-community property" means all real or personal property, wherever situated, acquired before or after the operative date of this code in any of the following ways:
(a) By either spouse while domiciled elsewhere which would have been community property if the spouse who acquired the property had been domiciled in this state at the time of its acquisition.
(b) In exchange for real or personal property, wherever situated, which would have been community property if the spouse who acquired the property so exchanged had been domiciled in this state at the time of its acquisition. **Leg.H.** Enacted Stats 1992 ch 162 §10 (AB 2650), operative January 1, 1994.

§126. "Petitioner"

"Petitioner" includes plaintiff, where appropriate. **Leg.H.** Added Stats 1999 ch 980 §1 (AB 1671).

§127. "Respondent"

"Respondent" includes defendant, where appropriate. **Leg.H.** Enacted Stats 1992 ch 162 §10 (AB 2650), operative January 1, 1994.

§130. "Separate property"

"Separate property" is property that is separate property under Part 2 (commencing with Section 760) of Division 4. **Leg.H.** Enacted Stats 1992 ch 162 §10 (AB 2650), operative January 1, 1994.

§142. "Spousal support"

"Spousal support" means support of the spouse of the obligor. **Leg.H.** Enacted Stats 1992 ch 162 §10 (AB 2650), operative January 1, 1994.

§143. "Spouse" to include registered domestic partner

"Spouse" includes "registered domestic partner," as required by Section 297.5. **Leg.H.** Added Stats 2016 ch 50 §35 (SB 1005), effective January 1, 2017.

2016 Note: It is the intent of the Legislature that the changes made by this act have only technical and nonsubstantive effect. Hence, no change made by this act shall create any new right, duty, or other obligation that did not exist immediately preceding the effective date of this act, or result in the limitation or termination of any right, duty, or other obligation that existed immediately preceding the effective date of this act. Stats 2016 ch 50 (SB 1005) §125.

§145. "State"

"State" means a state of the United States, the District of Columbia, or a commonwealth, territory, or insular possession subject to the jurisdiction of the United States. **Leg.H.** Enacted Stats 1992 ch 162 §10 (AB 2650), operative January 1, 1994. Amended Stats 1999 ch 661 §3 (AB 825).

§150. "Support"

"Support" refers to a support obligation owing on behalf of a child, spouse, or family, or an amount owing pursuant to Section 17402. It also includes past due support or arrearage when it exists. "Support," when used with reference to a minor child or a child described in Section 3901, includes maintenance and education. **Leg.H.** Enacted Stats 1992 ch 162 §10 (AB 2650), operative January 1, 1994. Amended Stats 1993 ch 219 §82 (AB 1500); Stats 2000 ch 808 §22 (AB 1358), effective September 28, 2000.

§155. "Support order"

"Support order" means a judgment or order of support in favor of an obligee, whether temporary or final, or subject to modification, termination, or remission, regardless of the kind of action or proceeding in which it is entered. For the purposes of Section 685.020 of the Code of Civil Procedure, only the initial support order, whether temporary or final, whether or not the order is contained in a judgment, shall be considered an installment judgment. No support order or other order or notice issued, which sets forth the amount of support owed for prior periods of time or establishes a periodic payment to liquidate the support owed for prior periods, shall be considered a money judgment for purposes of subdivision (b) of Section 685.020 of the Code of Civil Procedure. **Leg.H.** Enacted Stats 1992 ch 162 §10 (AB 2650), operative January 1, 1994. Amended Stats 2002 ch 539 §2 (SB 97).

2002 Note: (a) The Legislature finds and declares the following:

(1) The California Court of Appeal held in *Dupont v. Dupont* (2001) 88 Cal.App.4th 192, that a child support order which calculates the amount of past due support owed under a prior order and sets a monthly amount to reduce the past due support constitutes a new installment judgment.

(2) The decision in *Dupont* has resulted in disparate application of the rules regarding accrual of interest from order to order, court to court, and county to county for the purpose of calculating interest under Section 685.020 of the Code of Civil Procedure.

(3) It is therefore the intent of the Legislature to abrogate the holding of the California Court of Appeal in *Dupont v. Dupont*, to reaffirm that the legislative intent is that no support order or notice issued, which sets forth the amount of support owed for prior periods of time or establishes a periodic payment to liquidate the support owed for prior periods, be considered a money judgment for the purposes of subdivision (b) of Section 685.020 of the Code of Civil Procedure. It is further the intent of the Legislature to ensure the consistent treatment of parents and their support obligations, and to allow the Department of Child Support Services to address the issue of interest as part of a comprehensive approach to maximize collections for families. Stats 2002 ch 539 (SB 97) §1(a).

PART 3
INDIAN CHILDREN

Definitions; Determination as to Indian tribe. §170.
Legislative findings and declarations. §175.
Indian child custody proceeding; Applicable law. §177.
Indian child custody proceeding; Notice. §180.
Indian child custody proceeding; Tribal participation. §185.

§170. Definitions; Determination as to Indian tribe

(a) As used in this code, unless the context otherwise requires, the terms "Indian," "Indian child," "Indian child's tribe," "Indian custodian," "Indian organization," "Indian tribe," "reservation," and "tribal court" shall be defined as provided in Section 1903 of the Indian Child Welfare Act (25 U.S.C. Sec. 1901 et seq.).

(b) When used in connection with an Indian child custody proceeding, the terms "extended family member" and "parent" shall be defined as provided in Section 1903 of the Indian Child Welfare Act.

(c) "Indian child custody proceeding" means a "child custody proceeding" within the meaning of Section 1903 of the Indian Child Welfare Act, including a voluntary or involuntary proceeding that may result in an Indian child's temporary or long-term foster care or guardianship placement if the parent or Indian custodian cannot have the child returned upon demand, termination of parental rights, or adoptive placement. An "Indian child custody proceeding" does not include a proceeding under this code commenced by the parent of an Indian child to determine the custodial rights of the child's parents, unless the proceeding involves a petition to declare an Indian child free from the custody or control of a parent or involves a grant of custody to a person or persons other than a parent, over the objection of a parent.

(d) If an Indian child is a member of more than one tribe or is eligible for membership in more than one tribe, the court shall make a determination, in writing together with the reasons for it, as to which tribe is the Indian child's tribe for purposes of the Indian child custody proceeding. The court shall make that determination as follows:

(1) If the Indian child is or becomes a member of only one tribe, that tribe shall be designated as the Indian child's tribe, even though the child is eligible for membership in another tribe.

(2) If an Indian child is or becomes a member of more than one tribe, or is not a member of any tribe but is eligible for membership in more than one tribe, the tribe with which the child has the more significant contacts shall be designated as the Indian child's tribe. In determining which tribe the child has the more significant contacts with, the court shall consider, among other things, the following factors:

(A) The length of residence on or near the reservation of each tribe and frequency of contact with each tribe.

(B) The child's participation in activities of each tribe.

(C) The child's fluency in the language of each tribe.

(D) Whether there has been a previous adjudication with respect to the child by a court of one of the tribes.

(E) Residence on or near one of the tribes' reservations by the child's parents, Indian custodian or extended family members.

(F) Tribal membership of custodial parent or Indian custodian.

(G) Interest asserted by each tribe in response to the notice specified in Section 180.

(H) The child's self identification.

(3) If an Indian child becomes a member of a tribe other than the one designated by the court as the Indian child's tribe under paragraph (2), actions taken based on the court's determination prior to the child's becoming a tribal member shall continue to be valid. **Leg.H.** Added Stats 2006 ch 838 §1 (SB 678), effective January 1, 2007.

§175. Legislative findings and declarations

(a) The Legislature finds and declares the following:

(1) There is no resource that is more vital to the continued existence and integrity of recognized Indian tribes than their children, and the State of California has an interest in protecting Indian children who are members of, or are eligible for membership in, an Indian tribe. The state is committed to protecting the essential tribal relations and best interest of an Indian child by promoting practices, in accordance with the Indian Child Welfare Act (25 U.S.C. Sec. 1901 et seq.) and other applicable law, designed to prevent the child's involuntary out-of-home placement and, whenever the placement is necessary or ordered, by placing the child, whenever possible, in a placement that reflects the unique values of the child's tribal culture and is best able to assist the child in establishing, developing, and maintaining a political, cultural, and social relationship with the child's tribe and tribal community.

(2) It is in the interest of an Indian child that the child's membership in the child's Indian tribe and connection to the tribal community be encouraged and protected, regardless of any of the following:

(A) Whether the child is in the physical custody of an Indian parent or Indian custodian at the commencement of a child custody proceeding.

(B) Whether the parental rights of the child's parents have been terminated.

(C) Where the child has resided or been domiciled.

(b) In all Indian child custody proceedings the court shall consider all of the findings contained in subdivision (a), strive to promote the stability and security of Indian tribes and families, comply with the federal Indian Child Welfare Act, and seek to protect the best interest of the child. Whenever an Indian child is removed from a foster care home or institution, guardianship, or adoptive placement for the purpose of further foster care, guardianship, or adoptive placement, placement of the child shall be in accordance with the Indian Child Welfare Act.

(c) A determination by an Indian tribe that an unmarried person, who is under the age of 18 years, is either (1) a member of an Indian tribe or (2) eligible for membership in an Indian tribe and a biological child of a member of an Indian tribe shall constitute a significant political affiliation with the tribe and shall require the application of the federal Indian Child Welfare Act to the proceedings.

(d) In any case in which this code or other applicable state or federal law provides a higher standard of protection to the rights of the parent or Indian custodian of an Indian child, or the Indian child's tribe, than the rights provided under the Indian Child Welfare Act, the court shall apply the higher standard.

(e) Any Indian child, the Indian child's tribe, or the parent or Indian custodian from whose custody the child has been removed, may petition the court to invalidate an action in an Indian child custody proceeding for foster care, guardianship placement, or termination of parental rights if the action violated Sections 1911, 1912, and 1913 of the Indian Child Welfare Act (25 U.S.C. Sec. 1901 et seq.). Nothing in this section is intended to prohibit, restrict, or otherwise limit any rights under Section 1914 of the Indian Child Welfare Act (25 U.S.C. Sec. 1901 et seq.). **Leg.H.** Added Stats 2006 ch 838 §1 (SB 678), effective January 1, 2007.

§177. Indian child custody proceeding; Applicable law

(a) In an Indian child custody proceeding, the court shall apply Sections 224.2 to 224.6, inclusive, and Sections 305.5, 361.31, and 361.7 of the Welfare and Institutions Code, and the following rules from the California Rules of Court, as they read on January 1, 2007:

(1) Paragraph (7) of subdivision (b) of Rule 5.530.

(2) Subdivision (i) of Rule 5.534.

(b) In the provisions cited in subdivision (a), references to social workers, probation officers, county welfare department, or probation department shall be construed as meaning the party seeking a foster care placement, guardianship, or adoption under this code.

(c) This section shall only apply to proceedings involving an Indian child. **Leg.H.** Added Stats 2006 ch 838 §1 (SB 678), effective January 1, 2007. Amended Stats 2007 ch 130 §85 (AB 299), effective January 1, 2008.

§180. Indian child custody proceeding; Notice

(a) In an Indian child custody proceeding notice shall comply with subdivision (b) of this section.

(b) Any notice sent under this section shall be sent to the minor's parent or legal guardian, Indian custodian, if any, and the Indian child's tribe and shall comply with all of the following requirements:

(1) Notice shall be sent by registered or certified mail with return receipt requested. Additional notice by first-class mail is recommended, but not required.

(2) Notice to the tribe shall be to the tribal chairperson, unless the tribe has designated another agent for service.

(3) Notice shall be sent to all tribes of which the child may be a member or eligible for membership until the court makes a determination as to which tribe is the Indian child's tribe in accordance with subdivision (d) of Section 170, after which notice need only be sent to the tribe determined to be the Indian child's tribe.

(4) Notice, to the extent required by federal law, shall be sent to the Secretary of the Interior's designated agent, the Sacramento Area Director, Bureau of Indian Affairs. If the identity or location of the Indian child's tribe is known, a copy of the notice shall also be sent directly to the Secretary of the Interior unless the Secretary of the Interior has waived that notice in writing and the person responsible for giving notice under this section has filed proof of the waiver with the court.

(5) In addition to the information specified in other sections of this article, notice shall include all of the following information:

(A) The name, birthdate, and birthplace of the Indian child, if known.

(B) The name of any Indian tribe in which the child is a member or may be eligible for membership, if known.

(C) All names known of the Indian child's biological parents, grandparents, and great-grandparents, or Indian custodians, including maiden, married, and former names or aliases, as well as their current and former addresses, birthdates, places of birth and death, tribal enrollment numbers, and any other identifying information, if known.

(D) A copy of the petition by which the proceeding was initiated.

(E) A copy of the child's birth certificate, if available.

(F) The location, mailing address, and telephone number of the court and all parties notified pursuant to this section.

(G) A statement of the following:

(i) The absolute right of the child's parents, Indian custodians, and tribe to intervene in the proceeding.

(ii) The right of the child's parents, Indian custodians, and tribe to petition the court to transfer the proceeding to the tribal court of the Indian child's tribe, absent objection by either parent and subject to declination by the tribal court.

(iii) The right of the child's parents, Indian custodians, and tribe to, upon request, be granted up to an additional 20 days from the receipt of the notice to prepare for the proceeding.

(iv) The potential legal consequences of the proceedings on the future custodial rights of the child's parents or Indian custodians.

(v) That if the parents or Indian custodians are unable to afford counsel, counsel will be appointed to represent the parents or Indian custodians pursuant to Section 1912 of the Indian Child Welfare Act (25 U.S.C. Sec. 1901 et seq.).

(vi) That the information contained in the notice, petition, pleading, and other court documents is confidential, so any person or entity notified shall maintain the confidentiality of the information contained in the notice concerning the particular proceeding and not reveal it to anyone who does not need the information in order to exercise the tribe's rights under the Indian Child Welfare Act (25 U.S.C. Sec. 1901 et seq.).

(c) Notice shall be sent whenever it is known or there is reason to know that an Indian child is involved, and for every hearing thereafter, including, but not limited to, the hearing at which a final adoption order is to be granted. After a tribe acknowledges that the child is a member or eligible for membership in that tribe, or after the Indian child's tribe intervenes in a proceeding, the information set out in subparagraphs (C), (D), (E), and (G) of paragraph (5) of subdivision (b) need not be included with the notice.

(d) Proof of the notice, including copies of notices sent and all return receipts and responses received, shall be filed with the court in advance of the hearing except as permitted under subdivision (e).

(e) No proceeding shall be held until at least 10 days after receipt of notice by the parent, Indian custodian, the tribe, or the Bureau of Indian Affairs. The parent, Indian custodian, or the tribe shall, upon request, be granted up to 20 additional days to prepare for the proceeding. Nothing herein shall be construed as limiting the rights of the parent, Indian custodian, or tribe to 10 days' notice if a lengthier notice period is required under this code.

(f) With respect to giving notice to Indian tribes, a party shall be subject to court sanctions if that person knowingly and willfully falsifies or conceals a material fact concerning whether the child is an Indian child, or counsels a party to do so.

(g) The inclusion of contact information of any adult or child that would otherwise be required to be included in the notification pursuant to this section, shall not be required if that person is at risk of harm as a result of domestic violence, child abuse, sexual abuse, or stalking. **Leg.H.** Added Stats 2006 ch 838 §1 (SB 678), effective January 1, 2007.

§185. Indian child custody proceeding; Tribal participation

(a) In a custody proceeding involving a child who would otherwise be an Indian child based on the definition contained in paragraph (4) of Section 1903 of the federal Indian Child Welfare Act (25 U.S.C. Sec. 1901 et seq.), but is not an Indian child based on status of the child's tribe, as defined in paragraph (8) of Section 1903 of the federal Indian Child Welfare Act (25 U.S.C. Sec. 1901 et seq.), the court may permit the tribe from which the child is descended to participate in the proceeding upon request of the tribe.

(b) If the court permits a tribe to participate in a proceeding, the tribe may do all of the following, upon consent of the court:

(1) Be present at the hearing.

(2) Address the court.

(3) Request and receive notice of hearings.

(4) Request to examine court documents relating to the proceeding.

(5) Present information to the court that is relevant to the proceeding.

(6) Submit written reports and recommendations to the court.

(7) Perform other duties and responsibilities as requested or approved by the court.

(c) If more than one tribe requests to participate in a proceeding under subdivision (a), the court may limit participation to the tribe with which the child has the most significant contacts, as determined in accordance with paragraph (2) of subdivision (d) of Section 170.

(d) This section is intended to assist the court in making decisions that are in the best interest of the child by permitting a tribe in the circumstances set out in subdivision (a) to inform the court and parties to the proceeding about placement options for the child within the child's extended family or the tribal community, services and programs available to the child and the child's parents as Indians, and other unique interests the child or the child's parents may have as Indians. This section shall not be construed to make the Indian Child Welfare Act (25 U.S.C. Sec. 1901 et seq.), or any state law implementing the Indian Child Welfare Act, applicable to the proceedings, or to limit the court's discretion to permit other interested persons to participate in these or any other proceedings.

(e) This section shall only apply to proceedings involving an Indian child. **Leg.H.** Added Stats 2006 ch 838 §1 (SB 678), effective January 1, 2007.

DIVISION 2
GENERAL PROVISIONS

Part 1. Jurisdiction.
Part 2. General Procedural Provisions.
Part 3. Temporary Restraining Order in Summons.
Part 4. Ex Parte Temporary Restraining Orders.
Part 5. Attorney's Fees and Costs.
Part 6. Enforcement of Judgments and Orders.
Part 7. Tribal Marriages and Divorces.

PART 1
JURISDICTION

Jurisdiction in superior court, §200.

§200. Jurisdiction in superior court
The superior court has jurisdiction in proceedings under this code.

Leg.H. Enacted Stats 1992 ch 162 §10 (AB 2650), operative January 1, 1994.

PART 2
GENERAL PROCEDURAL PROVISIONS

General rules of practice and procedure. §210.
Judicial Council rules of practice and procedure. §211.
Veterans. § 211.5.
Verification of pleadings. §212.
Responding party's request for affirmative relief. §213.
Private trial. §214.
Service of notice prerequisite to validity of modification of judgment or subsequent order; Service of postjudgment motion to modify custody, visitation, or child support order; Service when bifurcated judgment. §215.
Ex parte communications involving court-appointed or court-connected evaluators or mediators prohibited; Exceptions; Responsibilities not limited; Judicial Council to adopt rule. §216.
Finding of good cause to refuse to receive live testimony; Adoption of statewide rule of court regarding factors a court shall consider. §217.
Discovery in postjudgment proceedings. §218.

§210. General rules of practice and procedure

Except to the extent that any other statute or rules adopted by the Judicial Council provide applicable rules, the rules of practice and procedure applicable to civil actions generally, including the provisions of Title 3a (commencing with Section 391) of Part 2 of the Code of Civil Procedure, apply to, and constitute the rules of practice and procedure in, proceedings under this code. **Leg.H.** Enacted Stats 1992 ch 162 §10 (AB 2650), operative January 1, 1994. Amended Stats 2002 ch 1118 §2 (AB 1938).

§211. Judicial Council rules of practice and procedure

Notwithstanding any other provision of law, the Judicial Council may provide by rule for the practice and procedure in proceedings under this code. **Leg.H.** Enacted Stats 1992 ch 162 §10 (AB 2650), operative January 1, 1994.

§211.5. Veterans

(a)(1) Commencing January 1, 2024, in proceedings under this code, a court shall provide self-identified veterans with a list of resources for veterans, including information about how to contact the local office of the Department of Veterans Affairs.

(2) The veteran may, at their discretion, provide the information about their veteran status on the Judicial Council military service form, file the form with the court, and serve it on the other parties to the action.

(b)(1) When a person files a form identifying the person as a veteran pursuant to paragraph (2) of subdivision (a), the court shall transmit a copy of the form to the Department of Veterans Affairs.

(2) Upon receipt of a copy of the form, the Department of Veterans Affairs shall, within a reasonable time, contact the person using the information provided on the form.

(c) On or before January 1, 2024, the Judicial Council may amend or develop the rules and forms necessary to implement this section. **Leg.H.** Added Stats 2022 ch 385 §2 (SB 1182), effective January 1, 2023.

§212. Verification of pleadings

A petition, response, application, opposition, or other pleading filed with the court under this code shall be verified. **Leg.H.** Enacted Stats 1992 ch 162 §10 (AB 2650), operative January 1, 1994.

§213. Responding party's request for affirmative relief

(a) In a hearing on an order to show cause, or on a modification thereof, or in a hearing on a motion, other than for contempt, the responding party may seek affirmative relief alternative to that requested by the moving party, on the same issues raised by the moving party, by filing a responsive declaration within the time set by statute or rules of court.

(b) This section applies in any of the following proceedings:

(1) A proceeding for dissolution of marriage, for nullity of marriage, or for legal separation of the parties.

(2) A proceeding relating to a protective order described in Section 6218.

(3) Any other proceeding in which there is at issue the visitation, custody, or support of a child. **Leg.H.** Enacted Stats 1992 ch 162 §10 (AB 2650), operative January 1, 1994. Amended Stats 1993 ch 219 §82 (AB 1500).

§214. Private trial

Except as otherwise provided in this code or by court rule, the court may, when it considers it necessary in the interests of justice and the persons involved, direct the trial of any issue of fact joined in a proceeding under this code to be private, and may exclude all persons except the officers of the court, the parties, their witnesses, and counsel. **Leg.H.** Enacted Stats 1992 ch 162 §10 (AB 2650), operative January 1, 1994.

§215. Service of notice prerequisite to validity of modification of judgment or subsequent order; Service of postjudgment motion to modify custody, visitation, or child support order; Service when bifurcated judgment

(a) Except as provided in subdivision (b) or (c), after entry of a judgment of dissolution of marriage, nullity of marriage, legal separation of the parties, or paternity, or after a permanent order in any other proceeding in which there was at issue the visitation, custody, or support of a child, no modification of the judgment or order, and no subsequent order in the proceedings, is valid unless any prior notice otherwise required to be given to a party to the proceeding is served, in the same manner as the notice is otherwise permitted by law to be served, upon the party. For the purposes of this section, service upon the attorney of record is not sufficient.

(b) A postjudgment motion to modify a custody, visitation, or child support order may be served on the other party or parties by first-class mail or airmail, postage prepaid, to the persons to be served. For any party served by mail, the proof of service shall include an address verification.

(c) This section does not apply if the court has ordered an issue or issues bifurcated for separate trial in advance of the disposition of the entire case. In those cases, service of a motion on any outstanding matter shall be served either upon the attorney of record, if the parties are represented, or upon the parties, if unrepresented. However, if there has been no pleading filed in the action for a period of six months after the entry of the bifurcated judgment, service shall be upon both the party, at the party's last known address, and the attorney of record. **Leg.H.** Enacted Stats 1992 ch 162 §10 (AB 2650), operative January 1, 1994. Amended Stats 1993 ch 219 §84 (AB 1500); Stats 1999 ch 980 §2 (AB 1671); Stats 2010 ch 352 §2 (AB 939), effective January 1, 2011; Stats 2016 ch 67 §1 (AB 1735), effective January 1, 2017.

§216. Ex parte communications involving court-appointed or court-connected evaluators or mediators prohibited; Exceptions; Responsibilities not limited; Judicial Council to adopt rule

(a) In the absence of a stipulation by the parties to the contrary, there shall be no ex parte communication between the attorneys for any party to an action and any court-appointed or court-connected evaluator or mediator, or between a court-appointed or court-connected evaluator or mediator and the court, in any proceedings under this code, except with regard to the scheduling of appointments.

(b) There shall be no ex parte communications between counsel appointed by the court pursuant to Section 3150 and a court-appointed or court-connected evaluator or mediator, except when it is expressly authorized by the court or undertaken pursuant to paragraph (5) of subdivision (c) of Section 3151.

(c) Subdivisions (a) and (b) shall not apply in the following situations:

(1) To allow a mediator or evaluator to address a case involving allegations of domestic violence as set forth in Sections 3113, 3181, and 3192.

(2) To allow a mediator or evaluator to address a case involving allegations of domestic violence as set forth in Rule 5.215 of the California Rules of Court.

(3) If the mediator or evaluator determines that ex parte communication is needed to inform the court of the mediator's or evaluator's belief that a restraining order is necessary to prevent an imminent risk to the physical safety of the child or the party.

(d) This section shall not be construed to limit the responsibilities a mediator or evaluator may have as a mandated reporter pursuant to Section 11165.9 of the Penal Code or the responsibilities a mediator or evaluator have to warn under Tarasoff v. Regents of the University of California (1976) 17 Cal.3d 425, Hedlund v. Superior Court (1983) 34 Cal.3d 695, and Section 43.92 of the Civil Code.

(e) The Judicial Council shall, by July 1, 2006, adopt a rule of court to implement this section. **Leg.H.** Added Stats 2005 ch 489 §1 (SB 1088), effective January 1, 2006. Amended Stats 2007 ch 130 §86 (AB 299), effective January 1, 2008; Stats 2019 ch 115 §2 (AB 1817), effective January 1, 2020.

§217. Finding of good cause to refuse to receive live testimony; Adoption of statewide rule of court regarding factors a court shall consider

(a) At a hearing on any order to show cause or notice of motion brought pursuant to this code, absent a stipulation of the parties or a finding of good cause pursuant to subdivision (b), the court shall receive any live, competent testimony that is relevant and within the scope of the hearing and the court may ask questions of the parties.

(b) In appropriate cases, a court may make a finding of good cause to refuse to receive live testimony and shall state its reasons for the finding on the record or in writing. The Judicial Council shall, by January 1, 2012, adopt a statewide rule of court regarding the factors a court shall consider in making a finding of good cause.

(c) A party seeking to present live testimony from witnesses other than the parties shall, prior to the hearing, file and serve a witness list with a brief description of the anticipated testimony. If the witness list is not served prior to the hearing, the court may, on request, grant a brief continuance and may make appropriate temporary orders pending the continued hearing. **Leg.H.** Added Stats 2010 ch 352 §3 (AB 939), effective January 1, 2011.

§218. Discovery in postjudgment proceedings

With respect to the ability to conduct formal discovery in family law proceedings, when a request for order or other motion is filed and served after entry of judgment, discovery shall automatically reopen as to the issues raised in the postjudgment pleadings currently before the court. The date initially set for trial of the action specified in subdivision (a) of Section 2024.020 of the Code of Civil Procedure shall mean the date the postjudgment proceeding is set for hearing on the motion or any continuance thereof, or evidentiary trial, whichever is later. **Leg.H.** Added Stats 2014 ch 169 §1 (AB 2586), effective January 1, 2015.

PART 3
TEMPORARY RESTRAINING ORDER IN SUMMONS

Application of part. §231.
Statement in summons concerning enforcement of order. §232.
Enforcement of order. §233.
Order not evidence of proscribed conduct. §234.
Modification or revocation of order; Other orders. §235.

§231. Application of part

This part applies to a temporary restraining order in a summons issued under any of the following provisions:

(a) Section 2040 (proceeding for dissolution of marriage, for nullity of marriage, or for legal separation of the parties).

(b) Section 7700 (proceeding under Uniform Parentage Act). **Leg.H.** Enacted Stats 1992 ch 162 §10 (AB 2650), operative January 1, 1994. Amended Stats 1993 ch 219 §84.5 (AB 1500).

§232. Statement in summons concerning enforcement of order

The summons shall state on its face that the order is enforceable in any place in this state by any law enforcement agency that has received mailed notice of the order or has otherwise received a copy of the order and any officer who has been shown a copy of the order. **Leg.H.** Enacted Stats 1992 ch 162 §10 (AB 2650), operative January 1, 1994.

§233. Enforcement of order

(a) Upon filing the petition and issuance of the summons and upon personal service of the petition and summons on the respondent or upon waiver and acceptance of service by the respondent, the temporary restraining order under this part shall be in effect against the parties until the final judgment is entered or the petition is dismissed, or until further order of the court.

(b) The temporary restraining order is enforceable in any place in this state, but is not enforceable by a law enforcement agency of a political subdivision unless that law enforcement agency has received mailed notice of the order or has otherwise received a copy of the order or the officer enforcing the order has been shown a copy of the order.

(c) A willful and knowing violation of the order included in the summons by removing a child from the state without the written consent of the other party or an order of the court is punishable as provided in Section 278.5 of the Penal Code. A willful and knowing violation of any of the other orders included in the summons is punishable as provided in Section 273.6 of the Penal Code. **Leg.H.** Enacted Stats 1992 ch 162 §10 (AB 2650), operative January 1, 1994.

§234. Order not evidence of proscribed conduct

The automatic granting of the ex parte temporary restraining order under this part is not a court determination or competent evidence in any proceeding of any prior history of the conduct so proscribed occurring between the parties. **Leg.H.** Enacted Stats 1992 ch 162 §10 (AB 2650), operative January 1, 1994.

§235. Modification or revocation of order; Other orders

Nothing in this part precludes either party from applying to the court for modification or revocation of the temporary restraining order provided for in this part or for further temporary orders or an expanded temporary ex parte order. **Leg.H.** Enacted Stats 1992 ch 162 §10 (AB 2650), operative January 1, 1994.

PART 4
EX PARTE TEMPORARY RESTRAINING ORDERS

Application of part. §240.
Granting temporary order without notice. §241.
Order to show cause. §242.
Service on respondent; Response. §243.
Precedence for hearing and trial. §244.
Continuance to respond to petition; Continuance of hearing; Extension of temporary restraining order. §245.
Time for grant or denial of temporary restraining order issued without notice. §246.

§240. Application of part

This part applies where a temporary restraining order, including a protective order as defined in Section 6218, is issued under any of the following provisions:

(a) Article 2 (commencing with Section 2045) of Chapter 4 of Part 1 of Division 6 (dissolution of marriage, nullity of marriage, or legal separation of the parties).

(b) Article 3 (commencing with Section 4620) of Chapter 3 of Part 5 of Division 9 (deposit of assets to secure future child support payments).

(c) Article 1 (commencing with Section 6320) of Chapter 2 of Part 4 of Division 10 (Domestic Violence Prevention Act), other than an order under Section 6322.5.

(d) Article 2 (commencing with Section 7710) of Chapter 6 of Part 3 of Division 12 (Uniform Parentage Act). **Leg.H.** Added Stats 1993 ch 219 §85.1 (AB 1500). Amended Stats 1998 ch 511 §1 (AB 1900).

Prior Law: Former §240, similar to the present section, was enacted Stats 1992 ch 162 §10, to become operative January 1, 1994, and repealed Stats 1993 ch 219 §85.

§240.5. [Section repealed 2002]

Leg.H. Added Stats 1995 ch 907 §1 (AB 935). Repealed Stats 2002 ch 784 §104 (SB 1316). The repealed section related to issuance of an order by municipal court judge.

§241. Granting temporary order without notice

Except as provided in Section 6300, an order described in Section 240 may not be granted without notice to the respondent unless it appears from facts shown by the declaration in support of the petition for the order, or in the petition for the order, that great or irreparable injury would result to the petitioner before the matter can be heard on notice. **Leg.H.** Enacted Stats 1992 ch 162 §10 (AB 2650), operative January 1, 1994. Amended Stats 1993 ch 219 §85.2 (AB 1500); Stats 2010 ch 572 §6 (AB 1596), effective January 1, 2011, operative January 1, 2012.

§242. Order to show cause

(a) Within 21 days, or, if good cause appears to the court, 25 days from the date that a temporary restraining order is granted or denied, a hearing shall be held on the petition. If no request for a temporary restraining order is made, the hearing shall be held within 21 days, or, if good cause appears to the court, 25 days from the date that the petition is filed.

(b) If a hearing is not held within the time provided in subdivision (a), the court may nonetheless hear the matter, but the temporary restraining order shall no longer be enforceable unless it is extended under Section 245. **Leg.H.** Added Stats 1993 ch 219 §85.4 (AB 1500). Amended Stats 2010 ch 572 §7 (AB 1596), effective January 1, 2011, operative January 1, 2012; Stats 2015 ch 411 §4 (AB 1081), effective January 1, 2016.

Prior Law: Former §242, similar to the present section, was enacted Stats 1992 ch 162 §10 (AB 2650), to become operative January 1, 1994, and repealed Stats 1993 ch 219 §85.3 (AB 1500).

§243. Service on respondent; Response

(a) If a petition under this part has been filed, the respondent shall be personally served with a copy of the petition, the temporary restraining order, if any, and the notice of hearing on the petition. Service shall be made at least five days before the hearing.

(b) On motion of the petitioner or on its own motion, the court may shorten the time for service on the respondent.

(c) If service on the respondent is made, the respondent may file a response that explains or denies the allegations in the petition. **Leg.H.** Enacted Stats 1992 ch 162 §10 (AB 2650), operative January 1, 1994. Amended Stats 1993 ch 219 §85.5 (AB 1500); Stats 1999 ch 980 §3 (AB 1671); Stats 2000 ch 90 §1 (AB 2914), effective July 5, 2000, ch 135 §56 (AB 2539) (ch 90 prevails; ch 135 not effective); Stats 2010 ch 572 §8 (AB 1596), effective January 1, 2011, operative January 1, 2012; Stats 2015 ch 411 §5 (AB 1081), effective January 1, 2016.

§244. Precedence for hearing and trial

(a) On the day of the hearing, the hearing on the petition shall take precedence over all other matters on the calendar that day, except older matters of the same character, and matters to which special precedence may be given by law.

(b) The hearing on the petition shall be set for trial at the earliest possible date and shall take precedence over all other matters, except older matters of the same character, and matters to which special precedence may be given by law. **Leg.H.** Enacted Stats 1992 ch 162 §10 (AB 2650), operative January 1, 1994. Amended Stats 2010 ch 572 §9 (AB 1596), effective January 1, 2011, operative January 1, 2012.

§245. Continuance to respond to petition; Continuance of hearing; Extension of temporary restraining order

(a) The respondent shall be entitled, as a matter of course, to one continuance for a reasonable period, to respond to the petition.

(b) Either party may request a continuance of the hearing, which the court shall grant on a showing of good cause. The request may be made in writing before or at the hearing or orally at the hearing. The court may also grant a continuance on its own motion.

(c) If the court grants a continuance, any temporary restraining order that has been issued shall remain in effect until the end of the continued hearing, unless otherwise ordered by the court. In granting a continuance, the court may modify or terminate a temporary restraining order.

(d) If the court grants a continuance, the extended temporary restraining order shall state on its face the new date of expiration of the order.

(e) A fee shall not be charged for the extension of the temporary restraining order. **Leg.H.** Enacted Stats 1992 ch 162 §10 (AB 2650), operative January 1, 1994. Amended Stats 2010 ch 572 §10 (AB 1596), effective January 1, 2011, operative January 1, 2012; Stats 2015 ch 411 §6 (AB 1081), effective January 1, 2016.

§246. Time for grant or denial of temporary restraining order issued without notice

A request for a temporary restraining order described in Section 240, issued without notice, shall be granted or denied on the same day that the petition is submitted to the court, unless the petition is filed too late in the day to permit effective review, in which case the order shall be granted or denied on the next day of judicial business in sufficient time for the order to be filed that day with the clerk of the court. **Leg.H.** Added Stats 1993 ch 148 §1 (AB 1331). Amended Stats 2010 ch 572 §11 (AB 1596), effective January 1, 2011, operative January 1, 2012.

PART 5
ATTORNEY'S FEES AND COSTS

Determination of ability to pay. §270.
Basis and effect of award. §271.
Order for direct payment; Enforcement. §272.
Award of attorney's fees against governmental agency in family law matter. §273.
Attorney's fees and costs as sanction; Notice. §274.

§270. Determination of ability to pay

If a court orders a party to pay attorney's fees or costs under this code, the court shall first determine that the party has or is reasonably likely to have the ability to pay. **Leg.H.** Added Stats 1993 ch 219 §87 (AB 1500).

Prior Law: Former §270, similar to present Fam C §2030, was enacted Stats 1992 ch 162 §10, to become operative January 1, 1994, and repealed Stats 1993 ch 219 §86.

§271. Basis and effect of award

(a) Notwithstanding any other provision of this code, the court may base an award of attorney's fees and costs on the extent to which any conduct of each party or attorney furthers or frustrates the policy of the law to promote settlement of litigation and, where possible, to reduce the cost of litigation by encouraging cooperation between the parties and attorneys. An award of attorney's fees and costs pursuant to this section is in the nature of a sanction. In making an award pursuant to this section, the court shall take into consideration all evidence concerning the parties' incomes, assets, and liabilities. The court shall not impose a sanction pursuant to this section that imposes an unreasonable financial burden on the party against whom the sanction is imposed. In order to obtain an award under this section, the party requesting an award of attorney's fees and costs is not required to demonstrate any financial need for the award.

(b) An award of attorney's fees and costs as a sanction pursuant to this section shall be imposed only after notice by the requesting party or the court to the party against whom the sanction is proposed and opportunity for that party to be heard is provided by the court.

(c) An award of attorney's fees and costs as a sanction pursuant to this section is payable only from the property or income of the party against whom the sanction is imposed, except that the award may be against the sanctioned party's share of the community property. **Leg.H.** Added Stats 1993 ch 219 §87 (AB 1500). Amended Stats 2023 ch 67 §1 (AB 1179), effective January 1, 2024.

Prior Law: Former §271, similar to present §2031, was enacted Stats 1992 ch 162 §10, to become operative January 1, 1994, and repealed Stats 1993 ch 219 §86.

§272. Order for direct payment; Enforcement

(a) Where the court orders one of the parties to pay attorney's fees and costs for the benefit of the other party, the fees and costs may, in the discretion of the court, be made payable in whole or in part to the attorney entitled thereto.

(b) Subject to subdivision (c), the order providing for payment of the attorney's fees and costs may be enforced directly by the attorney in the attorney's own name or by the party in whose behalf the order was made.

(c) If the attorney has ceased to be the attorney for the party in whose behalf the order was made, the attorney may enforce the order only if it appears of record that the attorney has given to the former client or successor counsel 10 days' written notice of the application for enforcement of the order. During the 10-day period, the client may file in the proceeding a motion directed to the former attorney for partial or total reallocation of fees and costs to cover the services and cost of successor counsel. On the filing of the motion, the enforcement of the order by the former attorney shall be stayed until the court has resolved the motion. **Leg.H.** Added Stats 1993 ch 219 §87 (AB 1500).

Prior Law: Former §272, similar to present §2032, was enacted Stats 1992 ch 162 §10, to become operative January 1, 1994, and repealed Stats 1993 ch 219 §86.

§273. Award of attorney's fees against governmental agency in family law matter

Notwithstanding any other provision of this code, the court shall not award attorney's fees against any governmental agency involved in a family law matter or child support proceeding except when sanctions are appropriate pursuant to Section 128.5 of the Code of Civil Procedure or Section 271 of this code. **Leg.H.** Added Stats 1994 ch 1269 §10 (AB 2208).

Prior Law: Former §273, relating to attorney's fees for enforcement of support order or civil penalty for child support delinquency, was enacted Stats 1992 ch 162 §10, to become operative January 1, 1994, and repealed Stats 1993 ch 219 §86, effective January 1, 1994.

§274. Attorney's fees and costs as sanction; Notice

(a) Notwithstanding any other provision of law, if the injured spouse is entitled to a remedy authorized pursuant to Section 4324, the injured spouse shall be entitled to an award of reasonable attorney's fees and costs as a sanction pursuant to this section.

(b) An award of attorney's fees and costs as a sanction pursuant to this section shall be imposed only after notice to the party against whom the sanction is proposed to be imposed and opportunity for that party to be heard.

(c) An award of attorney's fees and costs as a sanction pursuant to this section is payable only from the property or income of the party against whom the sanction is imposed, except that the award may be against the sanctioned party's share of the community property. In order to obtain an award under this section, the party requesting an award of attorney's fees and costs is not required to demonstrate any financial need for the award. **Leg.H.** Added Stats 1995 ch 364 §1 (AB 16). Amended Stats 2006 ch 538 §156 (SB 1852), effective January 1, 2007.

Prior Law: Former §274 was enacted Stats 1992 ch 162 §10, to become operative January 1, 1994, and repealed Stats 1993 ch 219 §86.

§275. [Section repealed 1993]

Leg.H. Enacted Stats 1992 ch 162 §10 (AB 2650), to become operative January 1, 1994. Repealed Stats 1993 ch 219 §86 (AB 1500).

PART 6
ENFORCEMENT OF JUDGMENTS AND ORDERS

Methods of enforcement. §290.
Judgment, enforcement and renewal; Defense of laches; Effect of death; Self-help materials. §291.
Judicial Council Forms; Order to Show Cause and Affidavit for Contempt; Affidavit of Facts Constituting Contempt. §292.

§290. Methods of enforcement

A judgment or order made or entered pursuant to this code may be enforced by the court by execution, the appointment of a receiver, or contempt, or by any other order as the court in its discretion determines from time to time to be necessary. **Leg.H.** Enacted Stats 1992 ch 162 §10 (AB 2650), operative January 1, 1994. Amended Stats 2000 ch 808 §23 (AB 1358), effective September 28, 2000; Stats 2006 ch 86 §2 (AB 2126), effective January 1, 2007.

§291. Judgment, enforcement and renewal; Defense of laches; Effect of death; Self-help materials

(a) A money judgment or judgment for possession or sale of property that is made or entered under this code, including a judgment for child, family, or spousal support, is enforceable until paid in full or otherwise satisfied.

(b) A judgment described in this section is exempt from any requirement that a judgment be renewed. Failure to renew a judgment described in this section has no effect on the enforceability of the judgment.

(c) A judgment described in this section may be renewed pursuant to Article 2 (commencing with Section 683.110) of Chapter 3 of Division 1 of Title 9 of Part 2 of the Code of Civil Procedure. An application for renewal of a judgment described in this section, whether or not payable in installments, may be filed:

(1) If the judgment has not previously been renewed as to past due amounts, at any time.

(2) If the judgment has previously been renewed, the amount of the judgment as previously renewed and any past due amount that became due and payable after the previous renewal may be renewed at any time after a period of at least five years has elapsed from the time the judgment was previously renewed.

(d) In an action to enforce a judgment for child, family, or spousal support, the defendant may raise, and the court may consider, the defense of laches only with respect to any portion of the judgment that is owed to the state.

(e) Nothing in this section supersedes the law governing enforcement of a judgment after the death of the judgment creditor or judgment debtor.

(f) On or before January 1, 2008, the Judicial Council shall develop self-help materials that include: (1) a description of the remedies available for enforcement of a judgment under this code, and (2) practical advice on how to avoid disputes relating to the enforcement of a support obligation. The self-help materials shall be made available to the public through the Judicial Council self-help Internet Web site.

(g) As used in this section, "judgment" includes an order. **Leg.H.** Added Stats 2006 ch 86 §4 (AB 2126), effective January 1, 2007. Amended Stats 2007 ch 130 §87 (AB 299), effective January 1, 2008.

Prior Law: Former Fam C §291, relating to judgment or order for possession or sale, was added Stats 2000 ch 808 §25 (AB 1358), and repealed Stats 2006, ch 86 (AB 2126), §3.

Former Fam C §291, relating to effect of lack of diligence in seeking enforcement, was enacted Stats 1992 ch 162 §10, operative January 1, 1994 and repealed Stats 2000 ch 808 §24, effective September 28, 2000.

Former Sections: Former Fam C §291, relating to judgment or order for possession or sale, was added Stats 2000 ch 808 §25 (AB 1358) and repealed Stats 2006 ch 86 (AB 2126) §3.

Former Fam C §291, relating to effect of lack of diligence in seeking enforcement, was enacted Stats 1992 ch 162 §10, operative January 1, 1994, and repealed Stats 2000 ch 808 §24, effective September 28, 2000.

§292. Judicial Council Forms; Order to Show Cause and Affidavit for Contempt; Affidavit of Facts Constituting Contempt

(a) The Judicial Council shall modify the title of its existing form, "Order to Show Cause and Declaration for Contempt (Family Law)," to "Order to Show Cause and Affidavit for Contempt (Family Law)."

(b) The Judicial Council shall prescribe a form entitled "Affidavit of Facts Constituting Contempt" that a party seeking to enforce a judgment or order made or entered pursuant to this code by contempt may use as an attachment to the Judicial Council form entitled "Order to Show Cause and Affidavit for Contempt (Family Law)." The form shall provide in the simplest language possible:

(1) The basic information needed to sustain a cause of action for contempt, including, but not limited to, the elements of a cause of action for contempt.

(2) Instructions on how to prepare and submit the Order to Show Cause and Affidavit for Contempt (Family Law) and the Affidavit of Facts Constituting Contempt.

(3) Lines for the date and a signature made under penalty of perjury.

(c) Section 1211.5 of the Code of Civil Procedure shall apply to the Order to Show Cause and Affidavit for Contempt (Family Law) and the Affidavit of Facts Constituting Contempt. **Leg.H.** Added Stats 1995 ch 904 §2 (AB 965).

PART 7
TRIBAL MARRIAGES AND DIVORCES

Tribal marriages and divorces. §295.

§295. Tribal marriages and divorces

(a) For the purpose of application of the laws of succession set forth in the Probate Code to a decedent, and for the purpose of determining the validity of a marriage under the laws of this state, an alliance entered into before 1958, which, by custom of the Indian tribe, band, or group of which the parties to the alliance, or either of them, are members, is commonly recognized in the tribe, band, or group as marriage, is deemed a valid marriage under the laws of this state.

(b) In the case of these marriages and for the purposes described in subdivision (a), a separation, which, by custom of the Indian tribe, band, or group of which the separating parties, or either of them, are members, is commonly recognized in the tribe, band, or group as a dissolution of marriage, is deemed a valid divorce under the laws of this state. **Leg.H.** Enacted Stats 1992 ch 162 §10 (AB 2650), operative January 1, 1994.

DIVISION 2.5
DOMESTIC PARTNER REGISTRATION

Part 1. Definitions.
Part 2. Registration.
Part 3. Termination.
Part 4. Legal Effect.
Part 5. Preemption.

PART 1
DEFINITIONS

Domestic partners defined; Requirements for establishing domestic partnership. §297.
Domestic partnership for person under 18 years of age; Requirements prior to court order granting permission; Factors considered. §297.1.
Rights, protections, benefits and responsibilities of present, former, and surviving registered domestic partners; Federal provisions; Long-term care plans; Constitutional provisions and provisions adopted by initiative. §297.5.

§297. Domestic partners defined; Requirements for establishing domestic partnership

(a) Domestic partners are two adults who have chosen to share one another's lives in an intimate and committed relationship of mutual caring.

(b) A domestic partnership shall be established in California when both persons file a Declaration of Domestic Partnership with the Secretary of State pursuant to this division, and, at the time of filing, all of the following requirements are met:

(1) Neither person is married to someone else or is a member of another domestic partnership with someone else that has not been terminated, dissolved, or adjudged a nullity.

(2) The two persons are not related by blood in a way that would prevent them from being married to each other in this state.

(3) Both persons are at least 18 years of age, except as provided in Section 297.1.

(4) Both persons are capable of consenting to the domestic partnership.

Leg.H. Added Stats 1999 ch 588 §2 (AB 26). Amended Stats 2001 ch 893 §3 (AB 25); Stats 2003 ch 421 §3 (AB 205), operative January 1, 2005; Stats 2011 ch 721 §1 (SB 651), effective January 1, 2012; Stats 2019 ch 135 §1 (SB 30), effective January 1, 2020.

2003 Note: This act shall be construed liberally in order to secure to eligible couples who register as domestic partners the full range of legal rights, protections and benefits, as well as all of the responsibilities, obligations, and duties to each other, to their children, to third parties and to the state, as the laws of California extend to and impose upon spouses. Stats 2003 ch 421 (AB 205) §15.

§297.1. Domestic partnership for person under 18 years of age; Requirements prior to court order granting permission; Factors considered

(a) A person under 18 years of age who, together with the other proposed domestic partner, otherwise meets the requirements for a domestic partnership other than the requirement of being at least 18 years of age, may establish a domestic partnership upon obtaining a court order granting permission to the underage person or persons to establish a domestic partnership.

(b)(1) The court order and written consent of the parents of each person under 18 years of age or of one of the parents or the guardian of each person under 18 years of age, except as provided in paragraph (2), shall be filed with the clerk of the court, and a certified copy of the order shall be filed with the Secretary of State with the Declaration of Domestic Partnership.

(2) If it appears to the satisfaction of the court by application of a person under 18 years of age that the person requires a written consent to establish a domestic partnership and that the minor has no parent or guardian, or has no parent or guardian capable of consenting, the court may make an order consenting to establishing the domestic partnership. The order shall be filed with the clerk of the court and a certified copy of the order shall be filed with the Secretary of State with the Declaration of Domestic Partnership.

(3) Notwithstanding any other law, immediately after the Secretary of State creates or updates the document described in Section 298.8 using the information required for the document and that is contained in a certified copy of a court order filed with the Secretary of State with the Declaration of Domestic Partnership pursuant to this subdivision, the Secretary of State may dispose of the certified copy of the court order.

(c) In determining whether to issue a court order granting permission to establish a domestic partnership, the court shall do all of the following:

(1) Require Family Court Services to separately interview the parties intending to establish a domestic partnership and, if applicable, at least one of the parents or the guardian of each party who is a minor. If more than one parent or guardian is interviewed, the parents or guardians shall be interviewed separately.

(2) Require Family Court Services to prepare and submit to the court a written report, containing any assessment of potential force, threat, persuasion, fraud, coercion, or duress by either of the parties or their family members relating to the intended domestic partnership. The report shall also contain recommendations of Family Court Services for either granting or denying the parties permission to establish a domestic partnership. If Family Court Services knows or reasonably suspects that either party is a victim of child abuse or neglect, Family Court Services shall submit a report of the known or suspected child abuse or neglect to the county child protective services agency.

(3) After receiving the report of the assessments of Family Court Services, as described in paragraph (2), separately interview in camera each of the parties prior to making a final determination regarding the court order.

(4) Consider whether there is evidence of coercion or undue influence on the minor.

(d) If the court issues an order granting the parties permission to establish a domestic partnership, and if one or both of the parties are 17 years of age or younger, the parties shall be eligible to file a Declaration of Domestic Partnership with the Secretary of State no earlier than 30 days from the time the court order was issued.

(e) As part of the court order granting permission to establish a domestic partnership, the court shall, if it considers it necessary, require the parties to the prospective domestic partnership of a minor to participate, before the domestic partnership is established, in counseling concerning social, economic, and personal responsibilities incident to the domestic partnership. The parties shall not be required to confer with counselors provided by religious organizations of any denomination. In determining whether to order the parties to participate in the counseling, the court shall consider, among other factors, the ability of the parties to pay for the counseling. The court may impose a reasonable fee to cover the cost of counseling provided by the county or the court. The fees shall be used exclusively to cover the cost of the counseling services authorized by this section.

(f)(1) Only for purposes of completing the document described in Section 298.8, and not for purposes of making a determination regarding the court order, the gender of each party intending to establish a domestic partnership, if provided, shall be documented on the court order granting permission to establish the domestic partnership.

(2) The date of birth of each party intending to establish a domestic partnership shall also be documented on the court order granting permission to establish the domestic partnership.

(g) Upon issuance of the order granting permission to establish a domestic partnership, the minor shall be provided with the following information:

(1) The rights and responsibilities of an emancipated minor, including, but not limited to, the effects of emancipation as described in Chapter 2 (commencing with Section 7050) of Part 6 of Division 11.

(2)(A) The circumstances under which a domestic partnership may be determined by a court to be void or voidable and adjudged a nullity and the procedure for obtaining that judicial determination.

(B) The procedures for termination of a domestic partnership.

(3) Telephone numbers for the National Domestic Violence Hotline and the National Sexual Assault Hotline.

(4) The conditions under which an unemancipated minor may leave home and seek to remain in a shelter or otherwise live separately from the minor's parent or guardian, and whether the consent or acquiescence of a parent or guardian is required to remain away from the home of the parent or guardian, the rights of an unemancipated minor to apply for a protective or restraining order to prevent abuse, and the rights of a minor to enter into contracts, including contracts for legal services and mental health counseling.

(h)(1) Subdivisions (c) and (d) do not apply to a minor who is 17 years of age and who has achieved a high school diploma or a high school equivalency certificate.

(2) Subdivision (d) does not apply to a minor who is 16 or 17 years of age and who is pregnant or whose prospective domestic partner is pregnant. **Leg.H.** Added Stats 2011 ch 721 §2 (SB 651), effective January 1, 2012. Amended Stats 2018 ch 660 §1 (SB 273), effective January 1, 2019; Stats 2019 ch 115 §3 (AB 1817), effective January 1, 2020; Stats 2019 ch 135 §2 (SB 30), effective January 1, 2020 (ch 135 prevails).

§297.5. Rights, protections, benefits and responsibilities of present, former, and surviving registered domestic partners; Federal provisions; Long-term care plans; Constitutional provisions and provisions adopted by initiative

(a) Registered domestic partners shall have the same rights, protections, and benefits, and shall be subject to the same responsibilities, obligations, and duties under law, whether they derive from statutes, administrative regulations, court rules, government policies, common law, or any other provisions or sources of law, as are granted to and imposed upon spouses.

(b) Former registered domestic partners shall have the same rights, protections, and benefits, and shall be subject to the same responsibilities, obligations, and duties under law, whether they derive from statutes, administrative regulations, court rules, government policies, common law, or any other provisions or sources of law, as are granted to and imposed upon former spouses.

(c) A surviving registered domestic partner, following the death of the other partner, shall have the same rights, protections, and benefits, and shall be subject to the same responsibilities, obligations, and duties under law, whether they derive from statutes, administrative regulations, court rules, government policies, common law, or any other provisions or sources of law, as are granted to and imposed upon a widow or a widower.

(d) The rights and obligations of registered domestic partners with respect to a child of either of them shall be the same as those of spouses. The rights and obligations of former or surviving registered domestic partners with respect to a child of either of them shall be the same as those of former or surviving spouses.

(e) To the extent that provisions of California law adopt, refer to, or rely upon, provisions of federal law in a way that otherwise would cause registered domestic partners to be treated differently than spouses, registered domestic partners shall be treated by California law as if federal law recognized a domestic partnership in the same manner as California law.

(f) Registered domestic partners shall have the same rights regarding nondiscrimination as those provided to spouses.

(g) No public agency in this state may discriminate against any person or couple on the ground that the person is a registered domestic partner rather than a spouse or that the couple are registered domestic partners rather than spouses, except that nothing in this section applies to modify eligibility for long-term care plans pursuant to Chapter 15 (commencing with Section 21660) of Part 3 of Division 5 of Title 2 of the Government Code.

(h) This act does not preclude any state or local agency from exercising its regulatory authority to implement statutes providing rights to, or imposing responsibilities upon, domestic partners.

(i) This section does not amend or modify any provision of the California Constitution or any provision of any statute that was adopted by initiative.

(j) Where necessary to implement the rights of registered domestic partners under this act, gender-specific terms referring to spouses shall be construed to include domestic partners.

(k)(1) For purposes of the statutes, administrative regulations, court rules, government policies, common law, and any other provision or source of law governing the rights, protections, and benefits, and the responsibilities, obligations, and duties of registered domestic partners in this state, as effectuated by this section, with respect to community property, mutual responsibility for debts to third parties, the right in particular circumstances of either partner to seek financial support from the other following the dissolution of the partnership, and other rights and duties as between the partners concerning ownership of property, any reference to the date of a marriage shall be deemed to refer to the date of registration of a domestic partnership with the state.

(2) Notwithstanding paragraph (1), for domestic partnerships registered with the state before January 1, 2005, an agreement between the domestic partners that the partners intend to be governed by the requirements set forth in Sections 1600 to 1620, inclusive, and which complies with those sections, except for the agreement's effective date, shall be enforceable as provided by Sections 1600 to 1620, inclusive, if that agreement was fully executed and in force as of June 30, 2005. **Leg.H.** Added Stats 2003 ch 421 §4 (AB 205), operative January 1, 2005. Amended Stats 2004 ch 947 §2 (AB 2580); Stats 2006 ch 802 §2 (SB 1827), effective January 1, 2007.

2003 Note: This act shall be construed liberally in order to secure to eligible couples who register as domestic partners the full range of legal rights, protections and benefits, as well as all of the responsibilities, obligations, and duties to each other, to their children, to third parties and to the state, as the laws of California extend to and impose upon spouses. Stats 2003 ch 421 (AB 205) §15.

PART 2
REGISTRATION

Declaration of Domestic Partnership and Notice of Termination of Domestic Partnership; Forms; Fees; Requirements; Change in name. §298.
Registration of domestic partnership; Registry; Copy; Termination prior to filing of new declaration or marriage. §298.5.
Election to change names; Middle or last names; Documents establishing a true, full name for purposes of Vehicle Code Section 12800.7. §298.6.
Establishment of process to enter into confidential domestic partnership. §298.7.
Document regarding domestic partnerships. §298.8.

§298. Declaration of Domestic Partnership and Notice of Termination of Domestic Partnership; Forms; Fees; Requirements; Change in name

(a)(1) The Secretary of State shall prepare forms entitled "Declaration of Domestic Partnership" and "Notice of Termination of Domestic Partnership" to meet the requirements of this division. These forms shall require the signature and seal of an acknowledgment by a notary public to be binding and valid.

(2) The instructions on the "Declaration of Domestic Partnership" form shall include both of the following:

(A) An explanation that registered domestic partners have the same rights, protections, and benefits, and are subject to the same responsibilities, obligations, and duties under law as are granted to and imposed upon spouses.

(B) An explanation of how to terminate a registered domestic partnership.

(3) When funding allows, the Secretary of State shall include on the form notice that a lesbian, gay, bisexual, and transgender specific domestic abuse brochure is available upon request.

(b)(1) These forms shall be available to the public at the office of the Secretary of State or on the Secretary of State's internet website. The Secretary of State's internet website shall include all of the information required in paragraph (2) of subdivision (a).

(2) The Secretary of State shall, by regulation, establish fees for the actual costs of processing each of these forms and shall charge these fees to persons filing the forms.

(3) There is hereby established a fee of twenty-three dollars ($23) to be charged in addition to the existing fees established by regulation to persons filing domestic partner registrations pursuant to Section 297 for development and support of a lesbian, gay, bisexual, and transgender curriculum for training workshops on domestic violence, conducted pursuant to Section 13823.15 of the Penal Code, and for the support of a grant program to promote healthy nonviolent relationships in the lesbian, gay, bisexual, and transgender community. This paragraph does not apply to persons filing a domestic partner registration when one or both of the domestic partners are 62 years of age or older.

(4) The fee established by paragraph (3) shall be deposited in the Equality in Prevention and Services for Domestic Abuse Fund, which is hereby established. The fund shall be administered by the Office of Emergency Services, and expenditures from the fund shall be used to support the purposes of paragraph (3).

(c) The Declaration of Domestic Partnership shall require each person who wants to become a domestic partner to (1) state that the person meets the requirements of Section 297 at the time the form is signed, (2) provide a mailing address, (3) state that the person consents to the jurisdiction of the Superior Courts of California for the purpose of a proceeding to obtain a judgment of dissolution or nullity of the domestic partnership or for legal separation of partners in the domestic partnership, or for any other proceeding related to the partners' rights and obligations, even if one or both partners ceases to be a resident of, or to maintain a domicile in, this state, (4) sign the form with a declaration that representations made therein are true, correct, and contain no material omissions of fact to the best knowledge and belief of the applicant, and (5) have a notary public acknowledge the signature. Both partners' signatures shall be affixed to one Declaration of Domestic Partnership form, which shall then be transmitted to the Secretary of State according to the instructions provided on the form. Filing an intentionally and materially false Declaration of Domestic Partnership shall be punishable as a misdemeanor.

(d) The Declaration of Domestic Partnership form shall contain an optional section for either party or both parties to indicate a change in name pursuant to Section 298.6. The optional section shall require a party indicating a change in name to provide the person's date of birth. **Leg.H.** Added Stats 1999 ch 588 §2 (AB 26). Amended Stats 2003 ch 421 §5 (AB 205), operative January 1, 2005; Stats 2006 ch 856 §2 (AB 2051), effective January 1, 2007; Stats 2007 ch 179 §7 (SB 86), effective August 24, 2007, ch 567 §4 (AB 102), effective January 1, 2008; Stats 2010 ch 618 §14 (AB 2791), effective January 1, 2011; Stats 2013 ch 352 §78 (AB 1317), effective September 26, 2013, operative July 1, 2013; Stats 2019 ch 115 §4 (AB 1817), effective January 1, 2020; Stats 2019 ch 135 §3 (SB 30), effective January 1, 2020 (ch 135 prevails).

Editor's Notes— 2007 Note: This act shall be known and may be cited as the Name Equality Act of 2007. Stats 2007 ch 567 (AB 102) §1.

2006 Note: This act shall be known and may be cited as the "Equality in Prevention and Services for Domestic Abuse Act." Stats 2006 ch 856 (AB 2051) §1.

2003 Note: This act shall be construed liberally in order to secure to eligible couples who register as domestic partners the full range of legal rights, protections and benefits, as well as all of the responsibilities, obligations, and duties to each other, to their children, to third parties and to the state, as the laws of California extend to and impose upon spouses. Stats 2003 ch 421 (AB 205) §15.

§298.5. Registration of domestic partnership; Registry; Copy; Termination prior to filing of new declaration or marriage

(a) Two persons desiring to become domestic partners may complete and file a Declaration of Domestic Partnership with the Secretary of State.

(b) The Secretary of State shall register the Declaration of Domestic Partnership in a registry for those partnerships, and shall return a copy of the registered form, a Certificate of Registered Domestic Partnership, and a copy of the brochure that is made available to county clerks and the Secretary of State by the State Department of Public Health pursuant to Section 358 and distributed to individuals receiving a confidential marriage license pursuant to Section 503, to the domestic partners at the mailing address provided by the domestic partners.

(c) A person who has filed a Declaration of Domestic Partnership may not file a new Declaration of Domestic Partnership or enter a civil marriage with someone other than their registered domestic partner unless the most recent domestic partnership has been terminated or a final judgment of dissolution or nullity of the most recent domestic partnership has been entered. This prohibition does not apply if the previous domestic partnership ended because one of the partners died.

(d) When funding allows, the Secretary of State shall print and make available upon request, pursuant to Section 358, a lesbian, gay, bisexual, and transgender specific domestic abuse brochure developed by the State Department of Public Health and made available to the Secretary of State to domestic partners who qualify pursuant to Section 297.

(e) The Certificate of Registered Domestic Partnership shall include the name used by each party before registration of the domestic partnership and the new name, if any, selected by each party upon registration of the domestic partnership. **Leg.H.** Added Stats 1999 ch 588 §2 (AB 26). Amended Stats 2003 ch 421 §6 (AB 205), operative January 1, 2005; Stats 2006 ch 856 §3 (AB 2051), effective January 1, 2007; Stats 2007 ch 483 §8 (SB 1039), effective January 1, 2008; Stats 2007 ch 567 §5 (AB 102) (ch 567 prevails), effective January 1, 2008; Stats 2019 ch 135 §4 (SB 30), effective January 1, 2020.

2007 Note: This act shall be known and may be cited as the Name Equality Act of 2007. Stats 2007 ch 567 (AB 102) §1.

2006 Note: This act shall be known and may be cited as the "Equality in Prevention and Services for Domestic Abuse Act." Stats 2006 ch 856 (AB 2051) §1.

2003 Note: This act shall be construed liberally in order to secure to eligible couples who register as domestic partners the full range of legal rights, protections and benefits, as well as all of the responsibilities, obligations, and duties to each other, to their children, to third parties and to the state, as the laws of California extend to and impose upon spouses. Stats 2003 ch 421 (AB 205) §15.

§298.6. Election to change names; Middle or last names; Documents establishing a true, full name for purposes of Vehicle Code Section 12800.7

(a) Parties to a registered domestic partnership shall not be required to have the same name. Neither party shall be required to change their name.

A person's name shall not change upon registration as a domestic partner unless that person elects to change their name pursuant to subdivision (b).

(b)(1) One party or both parties to a registered domestic partnership may elect to change the middle or last names by which that party wishes to be known after registration of the domestic partnership by entering the new name in the space provided on the Declaration of Domestic Partnership form without intent to defraud.

(2) A person may adopt any of the following middle or last names pursuant to paragraph (1):

(A) The current last name of the other domestic partner.

(B) The last name of either domestic partner given at birth.

(C) A name combining into a single last name all or a segment of the current last name or the last name of either domestic partner given at birth.

(D) A hyphenated combination of last names.

(3)(A) An election by a person to change the person's name pursuant to paragraph (1) shall serve as a record of the name change. A certified copy of the Declaration of Domestic Partnership containing the new name, or retaining the former name, shall constitute proof that the use of the new name or retention of the former name is lawful.

(B) A certified copy of a Declaration of Domestic Partnership shall be accepted as identification establishing a true, full name for purposes of Section 12800.7 of the Vehicle Code.

(C) This section does not prohibit the Department of Motor Vehicles from accepting as identification other documents establishing a true, full name for purposes of Section 12800.7 of the Vehicle Code. Those documents may include, without limitation, a certified copy of a document that is substantially equivalent to a Certificate of Registered Domestic Partnership that records either of the following:

(i) A legal union of two persons that was validly formed in another jurisdiction and is recognized as a valid domestic partnership in this state pursuant to Section 299.2.

(ii) A legal union of domestic partners as defined by a local jurisdiction pursuant to Section 299.6.

(D) This section shall be applied in a manner consistent with the requirements of Sections 1653.5 and 12801 of the Vehicle Code.

(4) The adoption of a new name, or the choice not to adopt a new name, by means of a Declaration of Domestic Partnership pursuant to paragraph (1) shall not abrogate the right of either party to adopt a different name through usage at a future date, or to petition the superior court for a change of name pursuant to Title 8 (commencing with Section 1275) of Part 3 of the Code of Civil Procedure.

(c) This section does not abrogate the common law right of a person to change the person's name, or the right of a person to petition the superior court for a change of name pursuant to Title 8 (commencing with Section 1275) of Part 3 of the Code of Civil Procedure. **Leg.H.** Added Stats 2007 ch 567 §6 (AB 102), effective January 1, 2008. Amended Stats 2019 ch 115 §5 (AB 1817), effective January 1, 2020; Stats 2019 ch 135 §5 (SB 30), effective January 1, 2020 (ch 135 prevails).

Editor's Notes— 2007 Note: This act shall be known and may be cited as the Name Equality Act of 2007. Stats 2007 ch 567 §1 (AB 102).

§298.7. Establishment of process to enter into confidential domestic partnership

The Secretary of State shall establish a process by which two persons, who have been living together as domestic partners and who meet the requirements of paragraphs (1) to (4), inclusive, of subdivision (b) of Section 297, may enter into a confidential domestic partnership. This process shall do all of the following:

(a) Maintain each confidential Declaration of Domestic Partnership as a permanent record that is not open to public inspection except upon order of the court issued upon a showing of good cause.

(b) Authorize the Secretary of State to charge a reasonable fee to offset costs directly connected with maintaining confidentiality of a Declaration of Domestic Partnership. **Leg.H.** Added Stats 2011 ch 721 §3 (SB 651), effective January 1, 2012. Amended Stats 2019 ch 135 §6 (SB 30), effective January 1, 2020.

§298.8. Document regarding domestic partnerships

(a) The Secretary of State shall create a document no later than March 1, 2020, with annual updates no later than March 1 of each year thereafter, disaggregated by county, containing only the following information concerning domestic partnerships that were registered during the preceding calendar year and in which one or both of the parties were minors at the time the domestic partnership was established:

(1) The total number of those registered domestic partnerships.

(2) Itemized for each of those registered domestic partnerships, the age of each party at the time the domestic partnership was established.

(3) Itemized for each of those registered domestic partnerships, the gender of each party as documented on the court order pursuant to Section 297.1, unless the court order does not include the gender.

(b) The document shall not contain the names, addresses, or other personal identifying information of parties to a registered domestic partnership, or any information identifying a registered domestic partnership. The document shall not contain a registered domestic partnership or a copy of the court order described in Section 297.1.

(c) The Secretary of State shall make the document available to the public upon request. **Leg.H.** Added Stats 2018 ch 660 §2 (SB 273), effective January 1, 2019.

PART 3
TERMINATION

Notice of Termination of Domestic Partnership; Filing; Conditions; Effective. §299.

§299. Notice of Termination of Domestic Partnership; Filing; Conditions; Effective

(a) A registered domestic partnership may be terminated without filing a proceeding for dissolution of domestic partnership by the filing of a Notice of Termination of Domestic Partnership with the Secretary of State pursuant to this section, provided that all of the following conditions exist at the time of the filing:

(1) The Notice of Termination of Domestic Partnership is signed by both registered domestic partners.

(2) There are no children of the relationship of the parties born before or after registration of the domestic partnership or adopted by the parties after registration of the domestic partnership, and neither of the registered domestic partners, to their knowledge, is pregnant.

(3) The registered domestic partnership is not more than five years in duration.

(4) Neither party has any interest in real property wherever situated, with the exception of the lease of a residence occupied by either party which satisfies the following requirements:

(A) The lease does not include an option to purchase.

(B) The lease terminates within one year from the date of filing of the Notice of Termination of Domestic Partnership.

(5) There are no unpaid obligations in excess of the amount described in paragraph (6) of subdivision (a) of Section 2400, as adjusted by subdivision (b) of Section 2400, incurred by either or both of the parties after registration of the domestic partnership, excluding the amount of any unpaid obligation with respect to an automobile.

(6) The total fair market value of community property assets, excluding all encumbrances and automobiles, including any deferred compensation or retirement plan, is less than the amount described in paragraph (7) of subdivision (a) of Section 2400, as adjusted by subdivision (b) of Section 2400, and neither party has separate property assets, excluding all encumbrances and automobiles, in excess of that amount.

(7) The parties have executed an agreement setting forth the division of assets and the assumption of liabilities of the community property, and have executed any documents, title certificates, bills of sale, or other evidence of transfer necessary to effectuate the agreement.

(8) The parties waive any rights to support by the other domestic partner.

(9) The parties have read and understand a brochure prepared by the Secretary of State describing the requirements, nature, and effect of terminating a domestic partnership.

(10) Both parties desire that the domestic partnership be terminated.

(b) The registered domestic partnership shall be terminated effective six months after the date of filing of the Notice of Termination of Domestic Partnership with the Secretary of State pursuant to this section, provided that neither party has, before that date, filed with the Secretary of State a notice of revocation of the termination of domestic partnership, in the form and content as shall be prescribed by the Secretary of State, and sent to the other party a copy of the notice of revocation by first-class mail, postage prepaid, at the other party's last known address. The effect of termination of a domestic partnership pursuant to this section shall be the same as, and shall be treated for all purposes as, the entry of a judgment of dissolution of a domestic partnership.

(c) The termination of a domestic partnership pursuant to subdivision (b) does not prejudice nor bar the rights of either of the parties to institute an action in the superior court to set aside the termination for fraud, duress, mistake, or any other ground recognized at law or in equity. A court may set aside the termination of domestic partnership and declare the termination of the domestic partnership null and void upon proof that the parties did not meet the requirements of subdivision (a) at the time of the filing of the Notice of Termination of Domestic Partnership with the Secretary of State.

(d) The superior courts shall have jurisdiction over all proceedings relating to the dissolution of domestic partnerships, nullity of domestic partnerships, and legal separation of partners in a domestic partnership. The dissolution of a domestic partnership, nullity of a domestic partnership, and legal separation of partners in a domestic partnership shall follow the same procedures, and the partners shall possess the same rights, protections, and benefits, and be subject to the same responsibilities, obligations, and duties, as apply to the dissolution of marriage, nullity of marriage, and legal separation of spouses in a marriage, respectively, except as provided in subdivision (a), and except that, in accordance with the consent acknowledged by domestic partners in the Declaration of Domestic Partnership form, proceedings for dissolution, nullity, or legal separation of a domestic partnership registered in this state may be filed in the superior courts of this state even if neither domestic partner is a resident of, or maintains a domicile in, the state at the time the proceedings are filed.

(e) Parties to a registered domestic partnership who are also married to one another may petition the court to dissolve both their domestic partnership and their marriage in a single proceeding, in a form that shall be prescribed by the Judicial Council. **Leg.H.** Added Stats 2003 ch 421 §8 (AB 205), operative January 1, 2005. Amended Stats 2004 ch 947 §3 (AB 2580); Stats 2010 ch 397 §1 (AB 2700), effective January 1, 2011.

Prior Law: Former §299, similar to present section, was added Stats 1999 ch 588 §2 and repealed Stats 2003 ch 421 §7, operative January 1, 2005.

2003 Note: This act shall be construed liberally in order to secure to eligible couples who register as domestic partners the full range of legal rights, protections and benefits, as well as all of the responsibilities, obligations, and duties to each other, to their children, to third parties and to the state, as the laws of California extend to and impose upon spouses. Stats 2003 ch 421 (AB 205) §15.

Former Sections: Former Fam C §299, similar to present section, was added Stats 1999 ch 588 §2 and repealed Stats 2003 ch 421 §7, operative January 1, 2005.

PART 4
LEGAL EFFECT

Recognition of legal unions in other states. §299.2.

§299.2. Recognition of legal unions in other states

A legal union of two persons, other than a marriage, that was validly formed in another jurisdiction, and that is substantially equivalent to a domestic partnership as defined in this part, shall be recognized as a valid domestic partnership in this state regardless of whether it bears the name domestic partnership. **Leg.H.** Added Stats 2003 ch 421 §9 (AB 205), operative January 1, 2005. Amended Stats 2019 ch 135 §7 (SB 30), effective January 1, 2020.

2003 Note: This act shall be construed liberally in order to secure to eligible couples who register as domestic partners the full range of legal rights, protections and benefits, as well as all of the responsibilities, obligations, and duties to each other, to their children, to third parties and to the state, as the laws of California extend to and impose upon spouses. Stats 2003 ch 421 (AB 205) §15.

§299.3. Letter to be sent to registered domestic partners; Notice to potential domestic partner registrants [Repealed]

Leg.H. Added Stats 2003 ch 421 §10 (AB 205). Amended Stats 2004 ch 947 §4 (AB 2580); Stats 2005 ch 22 §59 (SB 1108), effective January 1, 2006. Repealed Stats 2019 ch 135 §8 (SB 30), effective January 1, 2020.

§299.5. [Section repealed 2005]

Leg.H. Added Stats 1999 ch 588 §2 (AB 26). Amended Stats 2001 ch 893 §4 (AB 25). Repealed Stats 2003 ch 421 §11 (AB 205), operative January 1, 2005. The repealed section related to effect of domestic partnership.

PART 5
PREEMPTION

Preemption of ordinances and laws. §299.6.

§299.6. Preemption of ordinances and laws

(a) Any local ordinance or law that provides for the creation of a "domestic partnership" shall be preempted on and after July 1, 2000, except as provided in subdivision (c).

(b) Domestic partnerships created under any local domestic partnership ordinance or law before July 1, 2000, shall remain valid. On and after July 1, 2000, domestic partnerships previously established under a local ordinance or law shall be governed by this division and the rights and duties of the partners shall be those set out in this division, except as provided in subdivision (c), provided a Declaration of Domestic Partnership is filed by the domestic partners under Section 298.5.

(c) Any local jurisdiction may retain or adopt ordinances, policies, or laws that offer rights within that jurisdiction to domestic partners as defined by Section 297 or as more broadly defined by the local jurisdiction's ordinances, policies, or laws, or that impose duties upon third parties regarding domestic partners as defined by Section 297 or as more broadly defined by the local jurisdiction's ordinances, policies, or laws, that are in addition to the rights and duties set out in this division, and the local rights may be conditioned upon the agreement of the domestic partners to assume the additional obligations set forth in this division. **Leg.H.** Added Stats 1999 ch 588 §2 (AB 26).

DIVISION 3
MARRIAGE

Part 1. Validity of Marriage.
Part 2. Marriage License.
Part 3. Solemnization of Marriage.
Part 4. Confidential Marriage.
Part 5. Remote Marriage License Issuance and Solemnization.

PART 1
VALIDITY OF MARRIAGE

Marriage relation; Consent, license, and solemnization; License becomes certificate. §300.
Capacity of adult to consent to and consummate marriage. §301.
Issuance of a marriage license to a minor. §302.
Consent of court where minor has no parent. §303.
Interview of parties; Premarital counseling; Emancipated minors. §304.
Proof of consent and solemnization. §305.
Procedural requirements; Effect of noncompliance. §306.
Election to change names; Middle or last names; Documents establishing a true, full name for purposes of Vehicle Code Section 12800.7. §306.5.
Requirements for marriage of members of religious society or denomination. §307.
Validity of foreign marriage. §308.
Action to have validity of marriage determined. §309.
Methods of dissolution. §310.

§300. Marriage relation; Consent, license, and solemnization; License becomes certificate

(a) Marriage is a personal relation arising out of a civil contract between two persons, to which the consent of the parties capable of making that contract is necessary. Consent alone does not constitute marriage. Consent must be followed by the issuance of a license and solemnization as authorized by this division, except as provided by Section 425 and Part 4 (commencing with Section 500).

(b) For purposes of this part, the document issued by the county clerk is a marriage license until it is registered with the county recorder, at which time the license becomes a marriage certificate. **Leg.H.** Enacted Stats 1992 ch 162 §10 (AB 2650), operative January 1, 1994. Amended Stats 1993 ch 219 §88 (AB 1500); Stats 2006 ch 816 §1 (AB 1102), effective January 1, 2007, operative January 1, 2008; Stats 2014 ch 82 §2 (SB 1306), effective January 1, 2015.

§301. Capacity of adult to consent to and consummate marriage

Two unmarried persons 18 years of age or older, who are not otherwise disqualified, are capable of consenting to and consummating marriage. **Leg.H.** Enacted Stats 1992 ch 162 §10 (AB 2650), operative January 1, 1994. Amended Stats 2014 ch 82 §3 (SB 1306), effective January 1, 2015.

§302. Issuance of a marriage license to a minor

(a) An unmarried person under 18 years of age may be issued a marriage license upon obtaining a court order granting permission to the underage person or persons to marry, in accordance with the requirements described in Section 304.

(b) The court order and written consent of at least one of the parents or the guardian of each underage person shall be filed with the clerk of the court, and a certified copy of the order shall be presented to the county clerk at the time the marriage license is issued. **Leg.H.** Enacted Stats 1992 ch 162 §10 (AB 2650), operative January 1, 1994. Amended Stats 2006 ch 816 §2 (AB 1102), effective January 1, 2007, operative January 1, 2008; Stats 2014 ch 82 §4 (SB 1306), effective January 1, 2015; Stats 2016 ch 474 §1 (AB 2882), effective January 1, 2017; Stats 2018 ch 660 §3 (SB 273), effective January 1, 2019.

§303. Consent of court where minor has no parent

If it appears to the satisfaction of the court by application of a minor that the minor requires a written consent to marry and that the minor has no parent or has no parent capable of consenting, the court may make an order consenting to the issuance of a marriage license and granting permission to the minor to marry, in accordance with the requirements described in Section 304. The order shall be filed with the clerk of the court and a certified copy of the order shall be presented to the county clerk at the time the marriage license is issued. **Leg.H.** Enacted Stats 1992 ch 162 §10 (AB 2650), operative January 1, 1994. Amended Stats 2006 ch 816 §3 (AB 1102), effective January 1, 2007, operative January 1, 2008; Stats 2018 ch 660 §4 (SB 273), effective January 1, 2019.

§304. Interview of parties; Premarital counseling; Emancipated minors

(a) In determining whether to issue a court order granting permission to marry pursuant to Section 302 or 303, the court shall do all of the following:

(1) Require Family Court Services to separately interview the parties intending to marry and, if applicable, at least one of the parents or the guardian of each party who is a minor. If more than one parent or guardian is interviewed, the parents or guardians shall be interviewed separately.

(2) Require Family Court Services to prepare and submit to the court a written report, containing any assessment of potential force, threat, persuasion, fraud, coercion, or duress by either of the parties or their family members relating to the intended marriage. The report shall also contain recommendations of Family Court Services for either granting or denying the parties permission to marry. If Family Court Services knows or reasonably suspects that either party is a victim of child abuse or neglect, Family Court Services shall submit a report of the known or suspected child abuse or neglect to the county child protective services agency.

(3) After receiving the report of the assessments of Family Court Services, as described in paragraph (2), separately interview in camera each of the parties prior to making a final determination regarding the court order.

(4) Consider whether there is evidence of coercion or undue influence on the minor.

(b) If the court issues an order granting the parties permission to marry pursuant to Section 302 or 303, and if one or both of the parties are 17 years of age or younger, the parties shall be eligible to request a marriage license no earlier than 30 days from the time the court order was issued.

(c) As part of the court order granting permission to marry under Section 302 or 303, the court shall, if it considers it necessary, require the parties to the prospective marriage of a minor to participate in premarital counseling concerning social, economic, and personal responsibilities incident to marriage. The parties shall not be required to confer with counselors provided by religious organizations of any denomination. In determining whether to order the parties to participate in the premarital counseling, the court shall consider, among other factors, the ability of the parties to pay for the counseling. The court may impose a reasonable fee to cover the cost of premarital counseling provided by the county or the court. The fees shall be used exclusively to cover the cost of the counseling services authorized by this section.

(d)(1) Only for purposes of completing the document described in Section 102233 of the Health and Safety Code, and not for purposes of making a determination regarding the court order, the gender of each party intending to marry, if provided, shall be documented on the court order granting permission to marry.

(2) The date of birth of each party intending to marry shall also be documented on the court order granting permission to marry.

(3) For purposes of the requirements on the person solemnizing the marriage under subdivision (b) of Section 423, and the requirements on the local registrar under subdivision (a) of Section 102356 of the Health and Safety Code, the court shall provide parties who are granted permission to marry with a copy of the court order granting permission to marry.

(e) Upon issuance of the order granting permission to marry, the minor shall be provided with the following information:

(1) The rights and responsibilities of an emancipated minor, including, but not limited to, the effects of emancipation as described in Chapter 2 (commencing with Section 7050) of Part 6 of Division 11.

(2)(A) The circumstances under which a marriage may be determined by a court to be void or voidable and adjudged a nullity and the procedure for obtaining that judicial determination.

(B) The procedures for legal separation or dissolution of marriage.

(3) Telephone numbers for the National Domestic Violence Hotline and the National Sexual Assault Hotline.

(4) The conditions under which an unemancipated minor may leave home and seek to remain in a shelter or otherwise live separately from the minor's parent or guardian, and whether the consent or acquiescence of a parent or guardian is required to remain away from the home of the parent or guardian, the rights of an unemancipated minor to apply for a protective or restraining order to prevent abuse, and the rights of a minor to enter into contracts, including contracts for legal services and mental health counseling.

(f)(1) Subdivisions (a) and (b) do not apply to a minor who is 17 years of age and who has achieved a high school diploma or a high school equivalency certificate.

(2) Subdivision (b) does not apply to a minor who is 16 or 17 years of age and who is pregnant or whose prospective spouse is pregnant. **Leg.H.** Enacted Stats 1992 ch 162 §10 (AB 2650), operative January 1, 1994. Amended Stats 2007 ch 738 §12 (AB 1248), effective January 1, 2008; Stats 2016 ch 474 §2 (AB 2882), effective January 1, 2017; Stats 2018 ch 660 §5 (SB 273), effective January 1, 2019; Stats 2019 ch 115 §6 (AB 1817), effective January 1, 2020.

§305. Proof of consent and solemnization

Consent to and solemnization of marriage may be proved under the same general rules of evidence as facts are proved in other cases. **Leg.H.** Enacted Stats 1992 ch 162 §10 (AB 2650), operative January 1, 1994.

§306. Procedural requirements; Effect of noncompliance

Except as provided in Section 307, a marriage shall be licensed, solemnized, and authenticated, and the authenticated marriage license shall be returned to the county recorder of the county where the marriage license was issued, as provided in this part. Noncompliance with this part by a nonparty to the marriage does not invalidate the marriage. **Leg.H.** Enacted Stats 1992 ch 162 §10 (AB 2650), operative January 1, 1994. Amended Stats 1993 ch 219 §89 (AB 1500); Stats 2006 ch 816 §4 (AB 1102), effective January 1, 2007, operative January 1, 2008.

§306.5. Election to change names; Middle or last names; Documents establishing a true, full name for purposes of Vehicle Code Section 12800.7

(a) Parties to a marriage shall not be required to have the same name. Neither party shall be required to change their name. A person's name shall not change upon marriage unless that person elects to change their name pursuant to subdivision (b).

(b)(1) One party or both parties to a marriage may elect to change the middle or last names, or both, by which that party wishes to be known after solemnization of the marriage by entering the new name in the spaces provided on the marriage license application without intent to defraud.

(2) A person may adopt any of the following last names pursuant to paragraph (1):

(A) The current last name of the other spouse.

(B) The last name of either spouse given at birth.

(C) A name combining into a single last name all or a segment of the current last name or the last name of either spouse given at birth.

(D) A combination of last names.

(3) A person may adopt any of the following middle names pursuant to paragraph (1):

(A) The current last name of either spouse.

(B) The last name of either spouse given at birth.

(C) A combination of the current middle name and the current last name of the person or spouse.

(D) A combination of the current middle name and the last name given at birth of the person or spouse.

(4)(A) An election by a person to change their name pursuant to paragraph (1) shall serve as a record of the name change. A certified copy of a marriage certificate containing the new name, or retaining the former name, shall constitute proof that the use of the new name or retention of the former name is lawful.

(B) A certified copy of a marriage certificate shall be accepted as identification establishing a true, full name for purposes of Section 12800.7 of the Vehicle Code.

(C) This section does not prohibit the Department of Motor Vehicles from accepting as identification other documents establishing a true, full name for purposes of Section 12800.7 of the Vehicle Code. Those documents may include, without limitation, a certified copy of a marriage certificate recording a marriage outside of this state.

(D) This section shall be applied in a manner consistent with the requirements of Sections 1653.5 and 12801 of the Vehicle Code.

(5) The adoption of a new name, or the choice not to adopt a new name, by means of a marriage license application pursuant to paragraph (1) shall only be made at the time the marriage license is issued. After a marriage certificate is registered by the local registrar, the certificate shall not be amended to add a new name or change the name adopted pursuant to paragraph (1). An amendment may be issued to correct a clerical error in the new name fields on the marriage license. In this instance, the amendment shall be signed by one of the parties to the marriage and the county clerk or a deputy clerk, and the reason for the amendment shall be stated as correcting a clerical error. A clerical error as used in this part is an error made by the county clerk, a deputy clerk, or a notary authorized to issue confidential marriage licenses, whereby the information shown in the new name field does not match the information shown on the marriage license application. This requirement does not abrogate the right of either party to adopt a different name through usage at a future date, or to petition the superior court for a change of name pursuant to Title 8 (commencing with Section 1275) of Part 3 of the Code of Civil Procedure.

(c) This section does not abrogate the common law right of a person to change their name, or the right of a person to petition the superior court for a change of name pursuant to Title 8 (commencing with Section 1275) of Part 3 of the Code of Civil Procedure. **Leg.H.** Added Stats 2007 ch 567 §7 (AB 102), effective January 1, 2008, operative January 1, 2009. Amended Stats 2009 ch 512 §1 (AB 1143), effective January 1, 2010; Stats 2016 ch 474 §3 (AB 2882), effective January 1, 2017; Stats 2019 ch 115 §7 (AB 1817), effective January 1, 2020.

2007 Note: This act shall be known and may be cited as the Name Equality Act of 2007. Stats 2007 ch 567 (AB 102) §1.

§307. Requirements for marriage of members of religious society or denomination

This division, so far as it relates to the solemnizing of marriage, is not applicable to members of a particular religious society or denomination not having clergy for the purpose of solemnizing marriage or entering the marriage relation, if all of the following requirements are met:

(a) The parties to the marriage sign and endorse on the form prescribed by the State Department of Public Health, showing all of the following:

(1) The fact, time, and place of entering into the marriage.

(2) The printed names, signatures, and mailing addresses of two witnesses to the ceremony.

(3) The religious society or denomination of the parties to the marriage, and that the marriage was entered into in accordance with the rules and customs of that religious society or denomination. The statement of the parties to the marriage that the marriage was entered into in accordance with the rules and customs of the religious society or denomination is conclusively presumed to be true.

(b) The License and Certificate of Non-Clergy Marriage, endorsed pursuant to subdivision (a), is returned to the county recorder of the county in which the license was issued within 10 days after the ceremony. **Leg.H.** Enacted Stats 1992 ch 162 §10 (AB 2650), operative January 1, 1994. Amended Stats 1993 ch 219 §90 (AB 1500); Stats 2006 ch 816 §5 (AB 1102), effective January 1, 2007, operative January 1, 2008; Stats 2007 ch 483 §9 (SB 1039), effective January 1, 2008.

§308. Validity of foreign marriage

A marriage contracted outside this state that would be valid by laws of the jurisdiction in which the marriage was contracted is valid in California. **Leg.H.** Added Stats 2014 ch 82 §6 (SB 1306), effective January 1, 2015. Amended Stats 2016 ch 474 §4 (AB 2882), effective January 1, 2017.

Prior Law: Former Fam C §308, similar to the present section, was enacted Stats 1992 ch 162 §10, operative January 1, 1994, amended Stats 2009 ch 625 §1, effective January 1, 2010, and repealed Stats 2014 ch 82 §5, effective January 1, 2015.

Former Sections: Former Fam C §308, similar to the present section, was enacted Stats 1992 ch 162 §10, operative January 1, 1994, and repealed Stats 2014 ch 82 §5, effective January 1, 2015.

§308.5. [Section repealed 2015]

Leg.H. Adopted by voters, Prop 22 §2, effective March 8, 2000. Repealed Stats 2014 ch 82 §7 (SB 1306), effective January 1, 2015. The repealed section related to marriage between a man and a woman as the only valid or recognized marriage in California.

§309. Action to have validity of marriage determined

If either party to a marriage denies the marriage, or refuses to join in a declaration of the marriage, the other party may proceed, by action pursuant to Section 103450 of the Health and Safety Code, to have the validity of the marriage determined and declared. **Leg.H.** Enacted Stats 1992 ch 162 §10 (AB 2650), operative January 1, 1994. Amended Stats 2006 ch 816 §6 (AB 1102), effective January 1, 2007, operative January 1, 2008.

§310. Methods of dissolution

Marriage is dissolved only by one of the following:

(a) The death of one of the parties.

(b) A judgment of dissolution of marriage.

(c) A judgment of nullity of marriage. **Leg.H.** Enacted Stats 1992 ch 162 §10 (AB 2650), operative January 1, 1994.

PART 2
MARRIAGE LICENSE

Marriage license required; Armed Forces personnel stationed overseas. §350.
Contents of license. §351.
Contents, optional address provision. §351.5.
Mailing address. §351.6.
Denial of license. §352.
Requiring proof of facts; Compliance by attorney in fact for overseas armed services personnel. §354.
Forms; Signature by attorney in fact for overseas armed services personnel. §355.
Expiration of license. §356.
Duties of county clerk and county recorder. §357.
Informational brochure. §358.
Marriage license; Preparation and filing. § 359.
Replacement of lost, damaged, or destroyed marriage license. §360.

§350. Marriage license required; Armed Forces personnel stationed overseas

(a) Before entering a marriage, or declaring a marriage pursuant to Section 425, the parties shall first obtain a marriage license from a county clerk.

(b) If a marriage is to be entered into pursuant to subdivision (b) of Section 420, the attorney-in-fact shall appear before the county clerk on behalf of the party who is overseas, as prescribed in subdivision (a). **Leg.H.** Enacted Stats 1992 ch 162 §10 (AB 2650), operative January 1, 1994. Amended Stats 2004 ch 476 §1 (SB 7), effective September 10, 2004.

§351. Contents of license

The marriage license shall show all of the following:

(a) The identity of the parties to the marriage.

(b) The parties' full given names at birth or by court order, and mailing addresses.

(c) The parties' dates of birth. **Leg.H.** Enacted Stats 1992 ch 162 §10 (AB 2650), operative January 1, 1994. Amended Stats 2006 ch 816 §8 (AB 1102), effective January 1, 2007, operative January 1, 2008.

§351.5. Contents, optional address provision

Notwithstanding subdivision (b) of Section 351 or 359 of this code, or Section 103175 of the Health and Safety Code, if either of the applicants for, or any witness to, a certificate of registry of marriage and a marriage license requests, the certificate of registry and the marriage license shall show the business address or United States Postal Service post office box for that applicant or witness instead of the residential address of that person. **Leg.H.** Added Stats 2006 ch 60 §1 (SB 1364), effective January 1, 2007.

§351.6. Mailing address

Notwithstanding Section 307, 351, 351.5, 359, or 422 of this code, or Section 103175 or 103180 of the Health and Safety Code, a mailing address used by an applicant, witness, or person solemnizing or performing the marriage ceremony shall be a residential address, a business address, or a United States Postal Service post office box. **Leg.H.** Added Stats 2006 ch 816 §8.5 (AB 1102), effective January 1, 2007, operative January 1, 2007.

§352. Denial of license

No marriage license shall be granted if either of the applicants lacks the capacity to enter into a valid marriage or is, at the time of making the application for the license, under the influence of an intoxicating liquor or narcotic drug. **Leg.H.** Enacted Stats 1992 ch 162 §10 (AB 2650), operative January 1, 1994.

§353. [Section repealed 2008]

Leg.H. Enacted Stats 1992 ch 162 §10 (AB 2650), operative January 1, 1994. Repealed Stats 2006 ch 816 §9 (AB 1102), effective January 1, 2007, operative January 1, 2008. The repealed section related to underage applicant.

§354. Requiring proof of facts; Compliance by attorney in fact for overseas armed services personnel

(a) Each applicant for a marriage license shall be required to present authentic photo identification acceptable to the county clerk as to name and date of birth. A credible witness affidavit or affidavits may be used in lieu of authentic photo identification.

(b) For the purpose of ascertaining the facts mentioned or required in this part, if the clerk deems it necessary, the clerk may examine the applicants for a marriage license on oath at the time of the application. The clerk shall reduce the examination to writing and the applicants shall sign it.

(c) If necessary, the clerk may request additional documentary proof as to the accuracy of the facts stated.

(d) Applicants for a marriage license shall not be required to state, for any purpose, their race or color.

(e) If a marriage is to be entered into pursuant to subdivision (b) of Section 420, the attorney-in-fact shall comply with the requirements of this section on behalf of the applicant who is overseas, if necessary. **Leg.H.** Enacted Stats 1992 ch 162 §10 (AB 2650), operative January 1, 1994. Amended Stats 2004 ch 476 §2 (SB 7), effective September 10, 2004; Stats 2006 ch 816 §10 (AB 1102), effective January 1, 2007, operative January 1, 2008.

§355. Forms; Signature by attorney in fact for overseas armed services personnel

(a) The forms for the marriage license shall be prescribed by the State Department of Public Health, and shall be adapted to set forth the facts required in this part.

(b) The marriage license shall include an affidavit, which the applicants shall sign, affirming that they have received the brochure provided for in Section 358. If the marriage is to be entered into pursuant to subdivision (b) of Section 420, the attorney in fact shall sign the affidavit on behalf of the applicant who is overseas.

(c) The forms for the marriage license shall contain spaces for either party or both parties to indicate a change in name pursuant to Section 306.5. **Leg.H.** Enacted Stats 1992 ch 162 §10 (AB 2650), operative January 1, 1994. Amended Stats 2004 ch 476 §3 (SB 7), effective September 10, 2004; Stats 2006 ch 816 §11 (AB 1102), effective January 1, 2007, operative January 1, 2008; Stats 2007 ch 483 §10 (SB 1039), effective January 1, 2008; Stats 2007 ch 567 §8 (AB 102), effective January 1, 2008, operative January 1, 2009 (ch 567 prevails).

2007 Note: This act shall be known and may be cited as the Name Equality Act of 2007. Stats 2007 ch 567 (AB 102) §1.

§356. Expiration of license

A marriage license issued pursuant to this part expires 90 days after its issuance. The calendar date of expiration shall be clearly noted on the face of the license. **Leg.H.** Enacted Stats 1992 ch 162 §10 (AB 2650), operative January 1, 1994.

§357. Duties of county clerk and county recorder

(a) The county clerk shall number each marriage license issued and shall transmit at periodic intervals to the county recorder a list or copies of the licenses issued.

(b) Not later than 60 days after the date of issuance, the county recorder shall notify licenseholders whose marriage license has not been returned of that fact and that the marriage license will automatically expire on the date shown on its face.

(c) The county recorder shall notify the licenseholders of the obligation of the person solemnizing their marriage to return the marriage license to the recorder's office within 10 days after the ceremony. **Leg.H.** Enacted Stats 1992 ch 162 §10 (AB 2650), operative January 1, 1994. Amended Stats 1993 ch 219 §91 (AB 1500); Stats 2001 ch 39 §1 (AB 1323); Stats 2006 ch 816 §12 (AB 1102), effective January 1, 2007, operative January 1, 2008.

§358. Informational brochure

(a) The State Department of Public Health shall prepare and publish a brochure that shall contain the following:

(1) Information concerning the possibilities of genetic defects and diseases and a listing of centers available for the testing and treatment of genetic defects and diseases.

(2) Information concerning acquired immunodeficiency syndrome (AIDS) and the availability of testing for antibodies to the probable causative agent of AIDS.

(3) Information concerning domestic violence, including resources available to victims and a statement that physical, emotional, psychological, and sexual abuse, and assault and battery, are against the law.

(4) Information concerning options for changing a name upon solemnization of marriage pursuant to Section 306.5, or upon registration of a domestic partnership pursuant to Section 298.6. That information shall include a notice that the recording of a change in name or the absence of a change in name on a marriage license application and certificate pursuant to Section 306.5 may not be amended once the marriage license is issued, but that options to adopt a change in name in the future through usage, common law, or petitioning the superior court are preserved, as set forth in Section 306.5.

(b) The State Department of Public Health shall make the brochures available to county clerks who shall distribute a copy of the brochure to each applicant for a marriage license, including applicants for a confidential marriage license and notaries public receiving a confidential marriage license pursuant to Section 503. The department shall also make the brochure available to the Secretary of State, who shall distribute a copy of the brochure to persons who qualify as domestic partners pursuant to Section 297 and shall make the brochure available electronically on the Internet Web site of the Secretary of State.

(c) The department shall prepare a lesbian, gay, bisexual, and transgender specific domestic abuse brochure and make the brochure available to the Secretary of State who shall print and make available the brochure, as funding allows, pursuant to Section 298.5.

(d) Each notary public issuing a confidential marriage license under Section 503 shall distribute a copy of the brochure to the applicants for a confidential marriage license.

(e) To the extent possible, the State Department of Public Health shall seek to combine in a single brochure all statutorily required information for marriage license applicants. **Leg.H.** Enacted Stats 1992 ch 162 §10 (AB 2650), operative January 1, 1994. Amended Stats 1996 ch 1075 §8 (SB 1444); Stats 2006 ch 816 §13 (AB 1102), effective January 1, 2007, ch 856 §4.5 (AB 2051), effective January 1, 2007; Stats 2007 ch 483 §11 (SB 1039), effective January 1, 2008; Stats 2007 ch 567 §9 (AB 102) (ch 567 prevails), effective January 1, 2008.

2007 Note: This act shall be known and may be cited as the Name Equality Act of 2007. Stats 2007 ch 567 (AB 102) §1.

§ 359. Marriage license; Preparation and filing

(a) Except as provided in Sections 420 and 426, applicants to be married shall first appear together in person before the county clerk to obtain a marriage license.

(b) The contents of the marriage license are provided in Part 1 (commencing with Section 102100) of Division 102 of the Health and Safety Code.

(c) The issued marriage license shall be presented to the person solemnizing the marriage by the parties to be married.

(d) The person solemnizing the marriage shall complete the solemnization sections on the marriage license, and shall cause to be entered on the marriage license the printed name, signature, and mailing address of at least one, and no more than two, witnesses to the marriage ceremony.

(e) The marriage license shall be returned by the person solemnizing the marriage to the county recorder of the county in which the license was issued within 10 days after the ceremony.

(f) As used in this division, "returned" means presented to the appropriate person in person, or postmarked, before the expiration of the specified time period.

(g) This section shall become operative on January 1, 2024. **Leg.H.** Added Stats 2021 ch 620 §2 (AB 583), effective October 7, 2021, operative January 1, 2024.

Prior Law. Former Fam C §359, similar to the present section, was enacted Stats 1992 ch 162 §10 (AB 2650), operative January 1, 1994, amended Stats 1993 ch 219 §92 (AB 1500), Stats 1996 ch 1023 §44 (SB 1497), effective September 29, 1996, Stats 2001 ch 39 §2 (AB 1323), Stats 2006 ch 816 §14 (AB 1102), effective January 1, 2007, operative January 1, 2008, Stats 2021 ch 620 §1 (AB 583), effective October 7, 2021, and repealed effective January 1, 2024 by its own provision.

§360. Replacement of lost, damaged, or destroyed marriage license

(a) If a marriage license is lost, damaged, or destroyed after the marriage ceremony, but before it is returned to the county recorder, or deemed unacceptable for registration by the county recorder, the person solemnizing the marriage, in order to comply with Section 359, shall obtain a duplicate marriage license by filing an affidavit setting forth the facts with the county clerk of the county in which the license was issued.

(b) The duplicate marriage license shall not be issued later than one year after the date of marriage and shall be returned by the person solemnizing the marriage to the county recorder within one year of the date of marriage.

(c) The county clerk may charge a fee to cover the actual costs of issuing a duplicate marriage license.

(d) If a marriage license is lost, damaged, or destroyed before a marriage ceremony takes place, the applicants shall purchase a new marriage license and the old license shall be voided. **Leg.H.** Enacted Stats 1992 ch 162 §10 (AB 2650), operative January 1, 1994. Amended Stats 1993 ch 219 §93 (AB 1500); Stats 2001 ch 39 §3 (AB 1323); Stats 2006 ch 816 §15 (AB 1102), effective January 1, 2007, operative January 1, 2008; Stats 2016 ch 474 §5 (AB 2882), effective January 1, 2017.

PART 3
SOLEMNIZATION OF MARRIAGE

Chapter 1. Persons Authorized to Solemnize Marriage.
Chapter 2. Solemnization of Marriage.

CHAPTER 1
PERSONS AUTHORIZED TO SOLEMNIZE MARRIAGE

Solemnization of marriage. §400.
Commissioner of civil marriages; Deputies. §401.
Officials of nonprofit religious institutions. §402.

§400. Solemnization of marriage

(a) Although marriage is a personal relation arising out of a civil, and not a religious, contract, a marriage may be solemnized by a priest, minister, rabbi, or authorized person of any religious denomination who is 18 years of age or older. A person authorized by this subdivision shall not be required to solemnize a marriage that is contrary to the tenets of the person's faith. Refusal to solemnize a marriage under this subdivision, either by an individual or by a religious denomination, shall not affect the tax-exempt status of any entity.

(b) Consistent with Section 94.5 of the Penal Code and provided that any compensation received is reasonable, including payment of actual expenses, a marriage may also be solemnized by any of the following persons:

(1) A judge or retired judge, commissioner of civil marriages or retired commissioner of civil marriages, commissioner or retired commissioner, or assistant commissioner of a court of record in this state.

(2) A judge or magistrate who has resigned from office.

(3) Any of the following judges or magistrates of the United States:

(A) A justice or retired justice of the United States Supreme Court.

(B) A judge or retired judge of a court of appeals, a district court, or a court created by an act of the United States Congress the judges of which are entitled to hold office during good behavior.

(C) A judge or retired judge of a bankruptcy court or a tax court.

(D) A United States magistrate or retired magistrate.

(c) Except as provided in subdivision (d), a marriage may also be solemnized by any of the following persons who are 18 years of age or older:

(1) A Member of the Legislature or constitutional officer of this state or a Member of Congress of the United States who represents a district within this state, or a former Member of the Legislature or constitutional officer of this state or a former Member of Congress of the United States who represented a district within this state.

(2) A person that holds or formerly held an elected office of a city, county, or city and county.

(3) A city clerk of a charter city or serving in accordance with subdivision (b) of Section 36501 of the Government Code, while that person holds office.

(d)(1) A person listed in subdivision (c) shall not accept compensation for solemnizing a marriage while holding office.

(2) A person listed in subdivision (c) shall not solemnize a marriage pursuant to this section if they have been removed from office due to committing an offense or have been convicted of an offense that involves moral turpitude, dishonesty, or fraud. **Leg.H.** Enacted Stats 1992 ch 162 §10 (AB 2650), operative January 1, 1994. Amended Stats 1998 ch 931 §142 (SB 2139), effective September 28, 1998, ch 932 §31.5 (AB 1094); Stats 2006 ch 816 §16 (AB 1102), effective January 1, 2007, operative January 1, 2008; Stats 2012 ch 834 §1 (SB 1140), effective January 1, 2013; Stats 2016 ch 211 §1 (SB 875), effective January 1, 2017; Stats 2016 ch 528 §1 (AB 2761), effective January 1, 2017; Stats 2017 ch 42 §1 (AB 430), effective July 10, 2017; Stats 2019 ch 115 §8 (AB 1817), effective January 1, 2020.

§400.1. Other person authorized to solemnize [Repealed]

Leg.H. Added Stats 2010 ch 268 §1 (AB 2600), effective September 24, 2010. Amended Stats 2012 ch 63 §1 (SB 991), effective January 1, 2013; Stats 2014 ch 450 §1 (AB 1525), effective January 1, 2015. Repealed Stats 2016 ch 211 §2 (SB 875), effective January 1, 2017; Stats 2016 ch 528 §2 (AB 2761), effective January 1, 2017 (ch 528 prevails). The repealed section related to authorization of county supervisor, city clerk, or elected city mayor to solemnize a marriage.

§401. Commissioner of civil marriages; Deputies

(a) For each county, the county clerk is designated as a commissioner of civil marriages.

(b) The commissioner of civil marriages may appoint deputy commissioners of civil marriages who may solemnize marriages under the direction of the commissioner of civil marriages and shall perform other duties directed by the commissioner. **Leg.H.** Enacted Stats 1992 ch 162 §10 (AB 2650), operative January 1, 1994.

§402. Officials of nonprofit religious institutions

In addition to the persons permitted to solemnize marriages under Section 400, a county may license officials of a nonprofit religious institution, whose articles of incorporation are registered with the Secretary of State, to solemnize the marriages of persons who are affiliated with or are members of the religious institution. The licensee shall possess the degree of doctor of philosophy and must perform religious services or rites for the institution on a regular basis. The marriages shall be performed without fee to the parties. **Leg.H.** Enacted Stats 1992 ch 162 §10 (AB 2650), operative January 1, 1994.

CHAPTER 2
SOLEMNIZATION OF MARRIAGE

Solemnization; Appearance of attorney–in–fact for overseas armed services personnel. §420.
Determining correctness of facts stated in license. §421.
Statement of person solemnizing marriage. §422.
Return of license and statement to local registrar. §423.
Unrecorded marriage; Filing license and certificate of declaration of marriage. §425.
Issuance of marriage license where party unable to appear. §426.

§420. Solemnization; Appearance of attorney–in–fact for overseas armed services personnel

(a) No particular form for the ceremony of marriage is required for solemnization of the marriage, but the parties shall declare, in the physical presence of the person solemnizing the marriage and necessary witnesses, that they take each other as spouses.

(b) Notwithstanding subdivision (a), a member of the Armed Forces of the United States who is stationed overseas and serving in a conflict or a war and is unable to appear for the licensure and solemnization of the marriage may enter into that marriage by the appearance of an attorney in fact, commissioned and empowered in writing for that purpose through a power of attorney. The attorney in fact shall personally appear at the county clerk's office with the party who is not stationed overseas and present the original power of attorney duly signed by the party stationed overseas and acknowledged before a notary or witnessed by two officers of the United States Armed Forces. Copies in any form, including by facsimile, are not acceptable. The power of attorney shall state the full given names at birth, or by court order, of the parties to be married, and that the power of attorney is solely for the purpose of authorizing the attorney in fact to obtain a marriage license on the person's behalf and participate in the solemnization of the marriage. The original power of attorney shall be a part of the marriage certificate upon registration. The completion of a power of attorney shall be the sole determinant as to whether the county clerk's office and the State Registrar will accept the power of attorney.

(c) A contract of marriage, if otherwise duly made, shall not be invalidated for want of conformity to the requirements of any religious sect. **Leg.H.** Enacted Stats 1992 ch 162 §10 (AB 2650), operative January 1, 1994. Amended Stats 1993 ch 219 §94 (AB 1500); Stats 2004 ch 476 §4 (SB 7), effective September 10, 2004; Stats 2005 ch 22 §60 (SB 1108), effective January 1, 2006; Stats 2006 ch 816 §17 (AB 1102), effective January 1, 2007, operative January 1, 2008; Stats 2014 ch 82 §8 (SB 1306), effective January 1, 2015; Stats 2016 ch 130 §1 (AB 2128), effective January 1, 2017.

§421. Determining correctness of facts stated in license

Before solemnizing a marriage, the person solemnizing the marriage shall require the presentation of the marriage license. If the person solemnizing the marriage has reason to doubt the correctness of the statement of facts in the marriage license, the person must be satisfied as to the correctness of the statement of facts before solemnizing the marriage. For this purpose, the person may administer oaths and examine the parties and witnesses in the same manner as the county clerk does before issuing the license. **Leg.H.** Enacted Stats 1992 ch 162 §10 (AB 2650), operative January 1, 1994.

§422. Statement of person solemnizing marriage

The person solemnizing a marriage shall sign and print or type upon the marriage license a statement, in the form prescribed by the State Department of Public Health, showing all of the following:

(a) The fact, date (month, day, year), and place (city and county) of solemnization.

(b) The printed names, signatures, and mailing addresses of at least one, and no more than two, witnesses to the ceremony.

(c) The official position of the person solemnizing the marriage, or of the denomination of which that person is a priest, minister, rabbi, or other authorized person of any religious denomination.

(d) The person solemnizing the marriage shall also type or print their name and mailing address. **Leg.H.** Enacted Stats 1992 ch 162 §10 (AB 2650), operative January 1, 1994. Amended Stats 1993 ch 219 §95 (AB 1500); Stats 2006 ch 816 §18 (AB 1102), effective January 1, 2007, operative January 1, 2008; Stats 2007 ch 483 §12 (SB 1039), effective January 1, 2008; Stats 2019 ch 115 §9 (AB 1817), effective January 1, 2020.

§423. Return of license and statement to local registrar

(a) The person solemnizing the marriage shall return the marriage license, endorsed as required in Section 422, to the county recorder of the county in which the license was issued within 10 days after the ceremony.

(b) For purposes of Section 102356 of the Health and Safety Code, the person solemnizing the marriage shall include with the marriage license described in subdivision (a) a copy of the court order granting permission to marry described in Section 304, if one or both of the parties to the marriage were minors at the time of solemnization of the marriage. **Leg.H.** Enacted Stats 1992 ch 162 §10 (AB 2650), operative January 1, 1994. Amended Stats 1993 ch 219 §96 (AB 1500); Stats 2001 ch 39 §4 (AB 1323); Stats 2018 ch 660 §6 (SB 273), effective January 1, 2019.

§424. [Section repealed 2008]

Leg.H. Enacted Stats 1992 ch 162 §10 (AB 2650), operative January 1, 1994. Repealed Stats 2006 ch 816 §19 (AB 1102), effective January 1, 2007, operative January 1, 2008. The repealed section related to issuance of marriage certificate.

§425. Unrecorded marriage; Filing license and certificate of declaration of marriage

If no record of the solemnization of a California marriage previously contracted under this division for that marriage is known to exist, the parties may purchase a License and Certificate of Declaration of Marriage from the county clerk in the parties' county of residence one year or more from the date of the marriage. The license and certificate shall be returned to the county recorder of the county in which the license was issued. **Leg.H.** Enacted Stats 1992 ch 162 §10 (AB 2650), operative January 1, 1994. Amended Stats 1993 ch 219 §97 (AB 1500); Stats 2006 ch 816 §20 (AB 1102), effective January 1, 2007, operative January 1, 2008.

§426. Issuance of marriage license where party unable to appear

If for sufficient reason, as described in subdivision (d), either or both of the parties to be married are physically unable to appear in person before the county clerk, a marriage license may be issued by the county clerk to the person solemnizing the marriage if the following requirements are met:

(a) The person solemnizing the marriage physically presents an affidavit to the county clerk explaining the reason for the inability to appear.

(b) The affidavit is signed under penalty of perjury by the person solemnizing the marriage and by both parties.

(c) The signature of any party to be married who is unable to appear in person before the county clerk is authenticated by a notary public or a court prior to the county clerk issuing the marriage license.

(d) Sufficient reason includes proof of hospitalization, incarceration, or any other reason proved to the satisfaction of the county clerk. **Leg.H.** Added Stats 2006 ch 816 §21 (AB 1102), effective January 1, 2007, operative January 1, 2008.

PART 4
CONFIDENTIAL MARRIAGE

Chapter 1. General Provisions.
Chapter 2. Approval of Notaries to Authorize Confidential Marriages.

CHAPTER 1
GENERAL PROVISIONS

Requirements for confidential marriage generally. §500.
Marriage license becomes marriage certificate upon registration. §500.5.
Issuance of confidential marriage license. § 501.
Issuance of license where party unable to personally appear. §502.
Issuance of license on request of approved notary public. §503.
Duration of license. §504.
Form of confidential marriage license; Form to include affidavit. §505.
Preparation and filing of marriage license. §506.
Application for certified copy of certificate. §508.
Issuance of certified copy of certificate. §509.
Replacement of lost, damaged, or destroyed license. §510.
Record of confidential marriage; Disclosing information concerning confidential marriage. §511.

§500. Requirements for confidential marriage generally

When two unmarried people, not minors, have been living together as spouses, they may be married pursuant to this chapter by a person authorized to solemnize a marriage under Chapter 1 (commencing with Section 400) of Part 3. **Leg.H.** Enacted Stats 1992 ch 162 §10 (AB 2650), operative January 1, 1994. Amended Stats 2014 ch 82 §9 (SB 1306), effective January 1, 2015; Stats 2016 ch 474 §6 (AB 2882), effective January 1, 2017.

§500.5. Marriage license becomes marriage certificate upon registration

For purposes of this part, the document issued by the county clerk is a marriage license until it is registered with the county clerk, at which time the license becomes a marriage certificate. **Leg.H.** Added Stats 2006 ch 816 §22 (AB 1102), effective January 1, 2007, operative January 1, 2008.

§ 501. Issuance of confidential marriage license

(a) Except as provided in Section 502, a confidential marriage license shall be issued by the county clerk upon the personal appearance together of the parties to be married and their payment of the fees required by Sections 26840.1 and 26840.8 of the Government Code and any fee imposed pursuant to the authorization of Section 26840.3 of the Government Code.

(b) This section shall become operative on January 1, 2024. **Leg.H.** Added Stats 2021 ch 620 §4 (AB 583), effective October 7, 2021, operative January 1, 2024.

Prior Law Former Fam C §501, similar to the present section, was enacted Stats 1992 ch 162 §10 (AB 2650), operative January 1, 1994, amended Stats 2006 ch 816 §23 (AB 1102), effective January 1, 2007, operative January 1, 2008, Stats 2021 ch 620 §3 (AB 583), effective October 7, 2021, and repealed effective January 1, 2024 by its own provision.

§502. Issuance of license where party unable to personally appear

If for sufficient reason, as described in subdivision (d), either or both of the parties to be married are physically unable to appear in person before the county clerk, a confidential marriage license may be issued by the county clerk to the person solemnizing the marriage if the following requirements are met:

(a) The person solemnizing the marriage physically presents an affidavit to the county clerk explaining the reason for the inability to appear.

(b) The affidavit is signed under penalty of perjury by the person solemnizing the marriage and by both parties.

(c) The signature of any party to be married who is unable to appear in person before the county clerk is authenticated by a notary public or a court prior to the county clerk issuing the confidential marriage license.

(d) Sufficient reason includes proof of hospitalization, incarceration, or any other reason proved to the satisfaction of the county clerk. **Leg.H.** Enacted Stats 1992 ch 162 §10 (AB 2650), operative January 1, 1994. Amended Stats 2006 ch 816 §24 (AB 1102), effective January 1, 2007, operative January 1, 2008.

§503. Issuance of license on request of approved notary public

The county clerk shall issue a confidential marriage license upon the request of a notary public approved by the county clerk to issue confidential marriage licenses pursuant to Chapter 2 (commencing with Section 530) and upon payment by the notary public of the fees specified in Sections 26840.1 and 26840.8 of the Government Code. The parties shall reimburse a notary public who issues a confidential marriage license for the amount of the fees. **Leg.H.** Enacted Stats 1992 ch 162 §10 (AB 2650), operative January 1, 1994. Amended Stats 2006 ch 816 §25 (AB 1102), effective January 1, 2007, operative January 1, 2008.

§504. Duration of license

A confidential marriage license is valid only for a period of 90 days after its issuance by the county clerk. **Leg.H.** Enacted Stats 1992 ch 162 §10 (AB 2650), operative January 1, 1994. Amended Stats 2014 ch 913 §16 (AB 2747), effective January 1, 2015.

§505. Form of confidential marriage license; Form to include affidavit

(a) The form of the confidential marriage license shall be prescribed by the State Registrar of Vital Statistics.

(b) The form shall be designed to require that the parties to be married declare or affirm that they meet all of the requirements of this chapter.

(c) The form shall include an affidavit, which the bride and groom shall sign, affirming that they have received the brochure provided for in Section 358. **Leg.H.** Enacted Stats 1992 ch 162 §10 (AB 2650), operative January 1, 1994. Amended Stats 2006 ch 816 §26 (AB 1102), effective January 1, 2007, operative January 1, 2008.

§506. Preparation and filing of marriage license

(a) The confidential marriage license shall be presented to the person solemnizing the marriage.

(b) Upon performance of the ceremony, the solemnization section on the confidential marriage license shall be completed by the person solemnizing the marriage.

(c) The confidential marriage license shall be returned by the person solemnizing the marriage to the office of the county clerk in the county in which the license was issued within 10 days after the ceremony. **Leg.H.** Enacted Stats 1992 ch 162 §10 (AB 2650), operative January 1, 1994. Amended Stats 1993 ch 219 §98 (AB 1500); Stats 2001 ch 39 §5 (AB 1323); Stats 2006 ch 816 §27 (AB 1102), effective January 1, 2007, operative January 1, 2008.

§507. [Section repealed 2001]

Leg.H. Enacted Stats 1992 ch 162 §10 (AB 2650), operative January 1, 1994. Repealed Stats 2001 ch 39 §6 (AB 1323). The repealed section related to delivery of copy of certificate to parties.

§508. Application for certified copy of certificate

Upon issuance of a confidential marriage license, parties shall be provided with an application to obtain a certified copy of the confidential marriage certificate from the county clerk. **Leg.H.** Enacted Stats 1992 ch 162 §10 (AB 2650), operative January 1, 1994. Amended Stats 2001 ch 39 §7 (AB 1323); Stats 2006 ch 816 §28 (AB 1102), effective January 1, 2007, operative January 1, 2008.

§509. Issuance of certified copy of certificate

(a) A party to a confidential marriage may obtain a certified copy of the confidential marriage certificate from the county clerk of the county in which the certificate is filed by submitting an application that satisfies the requirements of Chapter 14 (commencing with Section 103525) of Part 1 of Division 102 of the Health and Safety Code.

(b) Copies of a confidential marriage certificate may be issued to the parties to the marriage upon payment of the fee equivalent to that charged for copies of a marriage certificate. **Leg.H.** Enacted Stats 1992 ch 162 §10 (AB 2650), operative January 1, 1994. Amended Stats 2001 ch 39 §8 (AB 1323); Stats 2006 ch 816 §29 (AB 1102), effective January 1, 2007, operative January 1, 2008; Stats 2009 ch 412 §2 (AB 130), effective January 1, 2010.

2009 Note: The Legislature finds and declares that Sections 2, 3, and 6 of this act impose a limitation on the public's right of access to the writings of public officials within the meaning of Section 3 of Article 1 of the California Constitution. Pursuant to that constitutional provision, the Legislature makes the following findings to demonstrate the interest protected by this limitation and the need for protecting that interest:

In order to protect personal privacy and reduce the risk of identity theft when marriage records maintained by county recorders contain personal identifying information, including, but not limited to, an individual's date of birth and mother's maiden name, it is necessary to enact legislation that generally restricts access to, and release of, marriage records. Stats 2009 ch 412 (AB 130) §10.

§510. Replacement of lost, damaged, or destroyed license

(a) If a confidential marriage license is lost, damaged, or destroyed after the performance of the marriage, but before it is returned to the county clerk, or deemed unacceptable for registration by the county clerk, the person solemnizing the marriage, in order to comply with Section 506, shall obtain a duplicate marriage license by filing an affidavit setting forth the facts with the county clerk of the county in which the license was issued.

(b) The duplicate license may not be issued later than one year after the date of the marriage and shall be returned by the person solemnizing the marriage to the county clerk within one year of the date of the marriage.

(c) The county clerk may charge a fee to cover the actual costs of issuing a duplicate marriage license.

(d) If a marriage license is lost, damaged, or destroyed before a marriage ceremony takes place, the applicants shall purchase a new marriage license and the old license shall be voided. **Leg.H.** Enacted Stats 1992 ch 162 §10 (AB 2650), operative January 1, 1994. Amended Stats 1993 ch 219 §99 (AB 1500); Stats 2001 ch 39 §9 (AB 1323); Stats 2006 ch 816 §30 (AB 1102), effective January 1, 2007, operative January 1, 2008; Stats 2020 ch 36 §27 (AB 3364), effective January 1, 2021.

§511. Record of confidential marriage; Disclosing information concerning confidential marriage

(a) Except as provided in subdivision (b), the county clerk shall maintain confidential marriage certificates filed pursuant to Section 506 as permanent records which shall not be open to public inspection except upon order of the court issued upon a showing of good cause. The confidential marriage license is a confidential record and not open to public inspection without an order from the court.

(b) The county clerk shall keep all original certificates of confidential marriages for one year from the date of filing. After one year, the clerk may reproduce the certificates pursuant to Section 26205 of the Government Code, and dispose of the original certificates. The county clerk shall promptly seal and store at least one original negative of each microphotographic film made in a manner and place as reasonable to ensure its preservation indefinitely against loss, theft, defacement, or destruction. The microphotograph shall be made in a manner that complies with the minimum standards or guidelines, or both, recommended by the American National Standards Institute or the Association for Information and Image Management. Every reproduction shall be deemed and considered an original. A certified copy of any reproduction shall be deemed and considered a certified copy of the original.

(c) The county clerk may conduct a search for a confidential marriage certificate for the purpose of confirming the existence of a marriage, but the date of the marriage and any other information contained in the certificate shall not be disclosed except upon order of the court.

(d) The county clerk shall, not less than quarterly, transmit copies of all original confidential marriage certificates retained, or originals of reproduced confidential marriage certificates filed after January 1, 1982, to the State Registrar of Vital Statistics. The registrar may destroy the copies so transmitted after they have been indexed. The registrar may respond to an inquiry as to the existence of a marriage performed pursuant to this chapter, but shall not disclose the date of the marriage. **Leg.H.** Enacted Stats 1992 ch 162 §10 (AB 2650), operative January 1, 1994. Amended Stats 1994 ch 1269 §11 (AB 2208); Stats 2006 ch 816 §31 (AB 1102), effective January 1, 2007, operative January 1, 2008.

CHAPTER 2
APPROVAL OF NOTARIES TO AUTHORIZE CONFIDENTIAL MARRIAGES

Only approved notary may authorize confidential marriage. §530.
Application by notary for approval to authorize confidential marriages. §531.
Required course of instruction before approval. §532.
Approval valid one year; Renewal. §533.
List of notaries approved to authorize confidential marriages. §534.
Suspending or revoking approval of notary. §535.
Fees; Use of money received. §536.

§530. Only approved notary may authorize confidential marriage

(a) No notary public shall issue a confidential marriage license pursuant to this part unless the notary public is approved by the county clerk to issue confidential marriage licenses pursuant to this chapter.

(b) A violation of subdivision (a) is a misdemeanor punishable by a fine not to exceed one thousand dollars ($1,000) or six months in jail. **Leg.H.** Enacted Stats 1992 ch 162 §10 (AB 2650), operative January 1, 1994. Amended Stats 2006 ch 816 §32 (AB 1102), effective January 1, 2007, operative January 1, 2008.

§531. Application by notary for approval to authorize confidential marriages

(a) An application for approval to authorize confidential marriages pursuant to this part shall be submitted to the county clerk in the county in which the notary public who is applying for the approval resides. The county clerk shall exercise reasonable discretion as to whether to approve applications.

(b) The application shall include all of the following:

(1) The full name of the applicant.

(2) The date of birth of the applicant.

(3) The applicant's current residential address and telephone number.

(4) The address and telephone number of the place where the applicant will issue confidential marriage licenses.

(5) The full name of the applicant's employer if the applicant is employed by another person.

(6) Whether or not the applicant has engaged in any of the acts specified in Section 8214.1 of the Government Code.

(c) The application shall be accompanied by the fee provided for in Section 536. **Leg.H.** Enacted Stats 1992 ch 162 §10 (AB 2650), operative January 1, 1994. Amended Stats 2001 ch 39 §10 (AB 1323); Stats 2006 ch 816 §33 (AB 1102), effective January 1, 2007, operative January 1, 2008.

§532. Required course of instruction before approval

No approval, or renewal of the approval, shall be granted pursuant to this chapter unless the notary public shows evidence of successful completion of a course of instruction concerning the issuance of confidential marriage licenses that was conducted by the county clerk in the county of registration. The course of instruction shall not exceed six hours in duration. **Leg.H.** Enacted Stats 1992 ch 162 §10 (AB 2650), operative January 1, 1994. Amended Stats 2006 ch 816 §34 (AB 1102), effective January 1, 2007, operative January 1, 2008.

§533. Approval valid one year; Renewal

An approval to issue confidential marriage licenses pursuant to this chapter is valid for one year. The approval may be renewed for additional one-year periods provided the following conditions are met:

(a) The applicant has not violated any of the provisions provided for in Section 531.

(b) The applicant has successfully completed the course prescribed in Section 532.

(c) The applicant has paid the renewal fee provided for in Section 536. **Leg.H.** Enacted Stats 1992 ch 162 §10 (AB 2650), operative January 1, 1994. Amended Stats 2006 ch 816 §35 (AB 1102), effective January 1, 2007, operative January 1, 2008.

§534. List of notaries approved to authorize confidential marriages

(a) The county clerk shall maintain a list of the notaries public who are approved to issue confidential marriage licenses. The list shall be available for inspection by the public.

(b) It is the responsibility of a notary public approved to issue confidential marriage licenses pursuant to this chapter to keep current the information required in paragraphs (1), (3), (4), and (5) of subdivision (b) of Section 531. This information shall be used by the county clerk to update the list required to be maintained by this section. **Leg.H.** Enacted Stats 1992 ch 162 §10 (AB 2650), operative January 1, 1994. Amended

Stats 2006 ch 816 §36 (AB 1102), effective January 1, 2007, operative January 1, 2008.

§535. Suspending or revoking approval of notary

(a) If, after an approval to issue confidential marriage licenses is granted pursuant to this chapter, it is discovered that the notary public has engaged in any of the actions specified in Section 8214.1 of the Government Code, the approval shall be revoked, and the county clerk shall notify the Secretary of State for whatever action the Secretary of State deems appropriate. Any fees paid by the notary public shall be retained by the county clerk.

(b) If a notary public who is approved to authorize confidential marriages pursuant to this chapter is alleged to have violated a provision of this division, the county clerk shall conduct a hearing to determine if the approval of the notary public should be suspended or revoked. The notary public may present any evidence as is necessary in the notary public's defense. If the county clerk determines that the notary public has violated a provision of this division, the county clerk may place the notary public on probation or suspend or revoke the notary public's registration, and any fees paid by the notary public shall be retained by the county clerk. The county clerk shall report the findings of the hearing to the Secretary of State for whatever action the Secretary of State deems appropriate. **Leg.H.** Enacted Stats 1992 ch 162 §10 (AB 2650), operative January 1, 1994. Amended Stats 2006 ch 816 §37 (AB 1102), effective January 1, 2007, operative January 1, 2008.

§536. Fees; Use of money received

(a) The fee for an application for approval to authorize confidential marriages pursuant to this chapter is three hundred dollars ($300).

(b) The fee for renewal of an approval is three hundred dollars ($300).

(c) Fees received pursuant to this chapter shall be deposited in a trust fund established by the county clerk. The money in the trust fund shall be used exclusively for the administration of the programs described in this chapter. **Leg.H.** Enacted Stats 1992 ch 162 §10 (AB 2650), operative January 1, 1994, Amended Stats 2006 ch 816 §38 (AB 1102), effective January 1, 2007, operative January 1, 2008.

PART 5
REMOTE MARRIAGE LICENSE ISSUANCE AND SOLEMNIZATION

Issuance of license using remote technology. § 550.
Photo identification and additional documentary proof. § 552.
Physical location of applicants, person solemnizing marriage, witnesses, and county clerk. § 554.
Signatures on marriage license; Transmittal of license to county clerk. § 556.
Guidance. § 558.
Definitions. § 560.

§ 550. Issuance of license using remote technology

Notwithstanding any other law, including, but not limited to, Section 420, a county clerk may issue a marriage license, including a confidential marriage license, or solemnize or witness a marriage ceremony under state law using remote technology pursuant to this part, except for a marriage of a minor, as set forth in Sections 302 to 304, inclusive, or any successor provisions. **Leg.H.** Added Stats 2021 ch 620 §5 (AB 583), effective October 7, 2021, repealed January 1, 2024. Amended Stats 2023 ch 478 §21 (AB 1756), effective January 1, 2024 (repealer repealed).

§ 552. Photo identification and additional documentary proof

A couple seeking a marriage license or solemnization pursuant to this part shall present, in the manner requested by the county clerk, a copy of a valid government-issued photo identification to verify their identity and any additional documentary proof requested by the county clerk. **Leg.H.** Added Stats 2021 ch 620 §5 (AB 583), effective October 7, 2021, repealed January 1, 2024. Amended Stats 2023 ch 478 §21 (AB 1756), effective January 1, 2024 (repealer repealed).

§ 554. Physical location of applicants, person solemnizing marriage, witnesses, and county clerk

(a) Each member of the couple shall be physically located in the State of California while using remote technology to obtain a marriage license pursuant to this part.

(b)(1) Each member of the couple shall be in the same physical location in the State of California while using remote technology to solemnize their marriage pursuant to this part.

(2) The person solemnizing the marriage, any necessary witnesses, and the county clerk shall all be physically located in the State of California, but may be at separate physical locations from each other and the couple solemnizing their marriage.

(c) The county clerk may require a couple to complete an affidavit, in a form provided by the county clerk, affirming that they and each individual participating in a marriage solemnization using remote technology are physically present within the State of California in compliance with this part. **Leg.H.** Added Stats 2021 ch 620 §5 (AB 583), effective October 7, 2021, repealed January 1, 2024. Amended Stats 2023 ch 478 §21 (AB 1756), effective January 1, 2024 (repealer repealed).

§ 556. Signatures on marriage license; Transmittal of license to county clerk

(a) At the discretion of the county clerk, a couple applying for a marriage license using remote technology may sign their marriage license electronically or by original wet signature. The couple shall transmit a signed, legible copy of their marriage license by United States mail, fax, or electronic means directly to the county clerk, in the manner required by the county clerk.

(b) At the discretion of the county clerk, a marriage license issued using the procedure described in this part may be transmitted to the applicants by United States mail, fax, or electronic means.

(c) Before the solemnization of a marriage pursuant to this part, one or both of the parties to be married shall transmit the marriage license by United States mail, fax, or electronic means to the person solemnizing the marriage and any necessary witnesses, in the manner required by the county clerk.

(d) At the discretion of the county clerk, the person solemnizing the marriage or any necessary witnesses may sign the marriage license electronically or by original wet signature and transmit the signed marriage license by United States mail, fax, or electronic means, in the manner required by the county clerk.

(e) A county clerk who witnesses a marriage solemnized by someone other than the county clerk using remote technology may apply an electronic signature to the marriage license as a witness, and transmit the signed license to the person solemnizing the marriage by United States mail, fax, or electronic means. **Leg.H.** Added Stats 2021 ch 620 §5 (AB 583), effective October 7, 2021, repealed January 1, 2024. Amended Stats 2023 ch 478 §21 (AB 1756), effective January 1, 2024 (repealer repealed).

§ 558. Guidance

A county clerk may provide guidance relating to marriage license applications, marriage license issuance, and the witnessing or solemnizing of the marriage ceremony when the guidance relates to the use of their remote technology pursuant to this part. **Leg.H.** Added Stats 2021 ch 620 §5 (AB 583), effective October 7, 2021, repealed January 1, 2024. Amended Stats 2023 ch 478 §21 (AB 1756), effective January 1, 2024 (repealer repealed).

§ 560. Definitions

For purposes of this part, "remote technology" means audiovideo technology that is provided by a county clerk and allows the couple, or the couple and others participating in a marriage solemnization, as applicable, to appear together from the same physical location and directly interact with each other and the county clerk. **Leg.H.** Added Stats 2021 ch 620 §5 (AB 583), effective October 7, 2021, repealed January 1, 2024. Amended Stats 2023 ch 478 §21 (AB 1756), effective January 1, 2024 (repealer repealed).

§ 562. Repeal of part [Repealed]

Leg.H. Added Stats 2021 ch 620 §5 (AB 583), effective October 7, 2021, repealed January 1, 2024. Repealed Stats 2023 ch 478 §21 (AB 1756), effective January 1, 2024.

DIVISION 4
RIGHTS AND OBLIGATIONS DURING MARRIAGE

Part 1. General Provisions.
Part 2. Characterization of Marital Property.
Part 3. Liability of Marital Property.
Part 4. Management and Control of Marital Property.
Part 5. Marital Agreements.

PART 1
GENERAL PROVISIONS

Chapter 1. Definitions.
Chapter 2. Relation of Spouses.
Chapter 3. Property Rights During Marriage.

CHAPTER 1
DEFINITIONS

Leasehold interest in real property defined. §700.

§700. Leasehold interest in real property defined

For the purposes of this division, a leasehold interest in real property is real property, not personal property. **Leg.H.** Enacted Stats 1992 ch 162 §10 (AB 2650), operative January 1, 1994.

CHAPTER 2
RELATION OF SPOUSES

Mutual obligations. §720.
Transactions with each other and third parties; Fiduciary relationship of spouses. §721.

§720. Mutual obligations

Spouses contract toward each other obligations of mutual respect, fidelity, and support. **Leg.H.** Enacted Stats 1992 ch 162 §10 (AB 2650), operative January 1, 1994. Amended Stats 2014 ch 82 §11 (SB 1306), effective January 1, 2015.

§721. Transactions with each other and third parties; Fiduciary relationship of spouses

(a) Subject to subdivision (b), either spouse may enter into any transaction with the other, or with any other person, respecting property, which either might if unmarried.

(b) Except as provided in Sections 143, 144, 146, 16040, 16047, and 21385 of the Probate Code, in transactions between themselves, spouses are subject to the general rules governing fiduciary relationships that control the actions of persons occupying confidential relations with each other. This confidential relationship imposes a duty of the highest good faith and fair dealing on each spouse, and neither shall take any unfair advantage of the other. This confidential relationship is a fiduciary relationship subject to the same rights and duties of nonmarital business partners, as provided in Sections 16403, 16404, and 16503 of the Corporations Code, including, but not limited to, the following:

(1) Providing each spouse access at all times to any books kept regarding a transaction for the purposes of inspection and copying.

(2) Rendering upon request, true and full information of all things affecting any transaction that concerns the community property. Nothing in this section is intended to impose a duty for either spouse to keep detailed books and records of community property transactions.

(3) Accounting to the spouse, and holding as a trustee, any benefit or profit derived from any transaction by one spouse without the consent of the other spouse that concerns the community property. **Leg.H.** Enacted Stats 1992 ch 162 §10 (AB 2650), operative January 1, 1994. Amended Stats 2002 ch 310 §1 (SB 1936); Stats 2014 ch 82 §12 (SB 1306), effective January 1, 2015; Stats 2019 ch 43 §1 (AB 327), effective January 1, 2020.

2002 Note: It is the intent of the Legislature in enacting this act to clarify that Section 721 of the Family Code provides that the fiduciary relationship between spouses includes all of the same rights and duties in the management of community property as the rights and duties of unmarried business partners managing partnership property, as provided in Sections 16403, 16404, and 16503 of the Corporations Code, and to abrogate the ruling in *In re Marriage of Duffy* (2001) 91 Cal.App.4th 923, to the extent that it is in conflict with this clarification. Stats 2002 ch 310 (SB 1936) §2.

CHAPTER 3
PROPERTY RIGHTS DURING MARRIAGE

Methods of holding property. §750.
Interests of spouses in community property. §751.
Interest of spouses in separate property. §752.
Excluding one spouse from other's dwelling. §753.
Limitation on disposition of separate property residence if notice of pendency of proceeding recorded. §754.
Payment or refund from employee benefit plan; Discharge of adverse claims. §755.

§750. Methods of holding property

Spouses may hold property as joint tenants or tenants in common, or as community property, or as community property with a right of survivorship. **Leg.H.** Enacted Stats 1992 ch 162 §10 (AB 2650), operative January 1, 1994. Amended Stats 2001 ch 754 §2 (AB 1697); Stats 2014 ch 82 §13 (SB 1306), effective January 1, 2015.

§751. Interests of spouses in community property

The respective interests of each spouse in community property during continuance of the marriage relation are present, existing, and equal interests. **Leg.H.** Enacted Stats 1992 ch 162 §10 (AB 2650), operative January 1, 1994. Amended Stats 2014 ch 82 §14 (SB 1306), effective January 1, 2015.

§752. Interest of spouses in separate property

Except as otherwise provided by statute, neither spouse has any interest in the separate property of the other. **Leg.H.** Enacted Stats 1992 ch 162 §10 (AB 2650), operative January 1, 1994. Amended Stats 2014 ch 82 §15 (SB 1306), effective January 1, 2015.

§753. Excluding one spouse from other's dwelling

Notwithstanding Section 752 and except as provided in Article 2 (commencing with Section 2045), Article 3 (commencing with Section 2047), or Article 4 (commencing with Section 2049) of Chapter 4 of Part 1 of Division 6, neither spouse may be excluded from the other's dwelling. **Leg.H.** Enacted Stats 1992 ch 162 §10 (AB 2650), operative January 1, 1994. Amended Stats 1993 ch 219 §99.5 (AB 1500).

§754. Limitation on disposition of separate property residence if notice of pendency of proceeding recorded

If notice of the pendency of a proceeding for dissolution of the marriage, for nullity of the marriage, or for legal separation of the parties is recorded in any county in which either spouse resides on real property that is the separate property of the other, the real property shall not for a period of three months thereafter be transferred, encumbered, or otherwise disposed of voluntarily or involuntarily without the joinder of both spouses, unless the court otherwise orders. **Leg.H.** Enacted Stats 1992 ch 162 §10 (AB 2650), operative January 1, 1994. Amended Stats 2014 ch 82 §16 (SB 1306), effective January 1, 2015.

§755. Payment or refund from employee benefit plan; Discharge of adverse claims

(a) The terms "participant," "beneficiary," "employer," "employee organization," "named fiduciary," "fiduciary," and "administrator," as used in subdivision (b), have the same meaning as provided in Section 3 of the Employee Retirement Income Security Act of 1974 (P.L. 93-406) (ERISA), as amended (29 U.S.C.A. Sec. 1002). The term "employee benefit plan" has the same meaning as provided in Section 80 of this code. The term "trustee" shall include a "named fiduciary" as that term is employed in ERISA. The term "plan sponsor" shall include an "employer" or "employee organization," as those terms are used in ERISA (29 U.S.C.A. Sec. 1002).

(b) Notwithstanding Sections 751 and 1100, if payment or refund is made to a participant or the participant's, employee's, or former employee's beneficiary or estate pursuant to an employee benefit plan including a plan governed by the Employee Retirement Income Security Act of 1974 (P.L. 93-406), as amended, the payment or refund fully discharges the plan sponsor and the administrator, trustee, or insurance company making the payment or refund from all adverse claims thereto unless, before the payment or refund is made, the plan sponsor or the administrator of the plan has received written notice by or on behalf of some other person that the other person claims to be entitled to the payment or refund or some part thereof. Nothing in this section affects or releases the participant from claims which may exist against the participant by a person other than the plan sponsor, trustee, administrator, or other person making the benefit payment. **Leg.H.** Enacted Stats 1992 ch 162 §10 (AB 2650), operative January 1, 1994. Amended Stats 1994 ch 1269 §12 (AB 2208).

PART 2
CHARACTERIZATION OF MARITAL PROPERTY

Chapter 1. Community Property.
Chapter 2. Separate Property.
Chapter 3. Damages for Injuries to Married Person.
Chapter 4. Presumptions Concerning Nature of Property.
Chapter 5. Transmutation of Property.

CHAPTER 1
COMMUNITY PROPERTY

Community property. §760.
Property in certain revocable trusts as community property. §761.

§760. Community property

Except as otherwise provided by statute, all property, real or personal, wherever situated, acquired by a married person during the marriage while domiciled in this state is community property. **Leg.H.** Enacted Stats 1992 ch 162 §10 (AB 2650), operative January 1, 1994.

§761. Property in certain revocable trusts as community property

(a) Unless the trust instrument or the instrument of transfer expressly provides otherwise, community property that is transferred in trust remains community property during the marriage, regardless of the identity of the trustee, if the trust, originally or as amended before or after the transfer, provides that the trust is revocable as to that property during the marriage and the power, if any, to modify the trust as to the rights and interests in that property during the marriage may be exercised only with the joinder or consent of both spouses.

(b) Unless the trust instrument expressly provides otherwise, a power to revoke as to community property may be exercised by either spouse acting alone. Community property, including any income or appreciation, that is distributed or withdrawn from a trust by revocation, power of withdrawal, or otherwise, remains community property unless there is a valid transmutation of the property at the time of distribution or withdrawal.

(c) The trustee may convey and otherwise manage and control the trust property in accordance with the provisions of the trust without the joinder or consent of either spouse unless the trust expressly requires the joinder or consent of one or both spouses.

(d) This section applies to a transfer made before, on, or after July 1, 1987.

(e) Nothing in this section affects the community character of property that is transferred before, on, or after July 1, 1987, in any manner or to a trust other than described in this section. **Leg.H.** Enacted Stats 1992 ch 162 §10 (AB 2650), operative January 1, 1994. Amended Stats 2014 ch 82 §17 (SB 1306), effective January 1, 2015.

CHAPTER 2
SEPARATE PROPERTY

Separate property of married person. §770.
Earnings and accumulations after date of separation; Minor child's earnings under specified types of contracts. §771.
Earnings and accumulations after judgment of legal separation. §772.

§770. Separate property of married person

(a) Separate property of a married person includes all of the following:
(1) All property owned by the person before marriage.
(2) All property acquired by the person after marriage by gift, bequest, devise, or descent.
(3) The rents, issues, and profits of the property described in this section.

(b) A married person may, without the consent of the person's spouse, convey the person's separate property. **Leg.H.** Enacted Stats 1992 ch 162 §10 (AB 2650), operative January 1, 1994.

§771. Earnings and accumulations after date of separation; Minor child's earnings under specified types of contracts

(a) The earnings and accumulations of a spouse and the minor children living with, or in the custody of, the spouse, after the date of separation of the spouses, are the separate property of the spouse.

(b) Notwithstanding subdivision (a), the earnings and accumulations of an unemancipated minor child related to a contract of a type described in Section 6750 shall remain the sole legal property of the minor child. **Leg.H.** Enacted Stats 1992 ch 162 §10 (AB 2650), operative January 1, 1994. Amended Stats 1999 ch 940 §1 (SB 1162); Stats 2016 ch 114 §2 (SB 1255), effective January 1, 2017.

§772. Earnings and accumulations after judgment of legal separation

After entry of a judgment of legal separation of the parties, the earnings or accumulations of each party are the separate property of the party acquiring the earnings or accumulations. **Leg.H.** Enacted Stats 1992 ch 162 §10 (AB 2650), operative January 1, 1994.

CHAPTER 3
DAMAGES FOR INJURIES TO MARRIED PERSON

Damages for personal injury to married person as community property. §780.
Cases where damages for personal injury are separate property. §781.
Injuries to married person by spouse. §782.
Conviction of attempted murder or solicitation of murder; Retirement and pension benefits to injured spouse. §782.5.
Injuries to married person by third party; Extent concurring negligence of spouse allowable as defense. §783.

§780. Damages for personal injury to married person as community property

Except as provided in Section 781 and subject to the rules of allocation set forth in Section 2603, money and other property received or to be received by a married person in satisfaction of a judgment for damages for personal injuries, or pursuant to an agreement for the settlement or compromise of a claim for such damages, is community property if the cause of action for the damages arose during the marriage. **Leg.H.** Enacted Stats 1992 ch 162 §10 (AB 2650), operative January 1, 1994.

§781. Cases where damages for personal injury are separate property

(a) Money or other property received or to be received by a married person in satisfaction of a judgment for damages for personal injuries, or pursuant to an agreement for the settlement or compromise of a claim for those damages, is the separate property of the injured person if the cause of action for the damages arose as follows:
(1) After the entry of a judgment of dissolution of a marriage or legal separation of the parties.
(2) While the injured spouse is living separate from the other spouse.

(b) Notwithstanding subdivision (a), if the spouse of the injured person has paid expenses by reason of the personal injuries from separate property or from the community property, the spouse is entitled to reimbursement of the separate property or the community property for those expenses from the separate property received by the injured person under subdivision (a).

(c) Notwithstanding subdivision (a), if one spouse has a cause of action against the other spouse that arose during the marriage of the parties, money or property paid or to be paid by or on behalf of a party to the party's spouse of that marriage in satisfaction of a judgment for damages for personal injuries to that spouse, or pursuant to an agreement for the settlement or compromise of a claim for the damages, is the separate property of the injured spouse. **Leg.H.** Enacted Stats 1992 ch 162 §10 (AB 2650), operative January 1, 1994. Amended Stats 2019 ch 115 §10 (AB 1817), effective January 1, 2020.

§782. Injuries to married person by spouse

(a) Where an injury to a married person is caused in whole or in part by the negligent or wrongful act or omission of the person's spouse, the community property may not be used to discharge the liability of the tortfeasor spouse to the injured spouse or the liability to make contribution to a joint tortfeasor until the separate property of the tortfeasor spouse, not exempt from enforcement of a money judgment, is exhausted.

(b) This section does not prevent the use of community property to discharge a liability referred to in subdivision (a) if the injured spouse gives written consent thereto after the occurrence of the injury.

(c) This section does not affect the right to indemnity provided by an insurance or other contract to discharge the tortfeasor spouse's liability, whether or not the consideration given for the contract consisted of community property. **Leg.H.** Enacted Stats 1992 ch 162 §10 (AB 2650), operative January 1, 1994.

§782.5. Conviction of attempted murder or solicitation of murder; Retirement and pension benefits to injured spouse

In addition to any other remedy authorized by law, when a spouse is convicted of attempting to murder the other spouse, as punishable pursuant to subdivision (a) of Section 664 of the Penal Code, or of soliciting the murder of the other spouse, as punishable pursuant to subdivision (b) of Section 653f of the Penal Code, the injured spouse shall be entitled to an award to the injured spouse of 100 percent of the community property interest in the retirement and pension benefits of the injured spouse.

As used in this section, "injured spouse" has the same meaning as defined in Section 4324. **Leg.H.** Added Stats 1995 ch 364 §2 (AB 16). Amended Stats 2010 ch 65 §1 (AB 2674), effective January 1, 2010.

§783. Injuries to married person by third party; Extent concurring negligence of spouse allowable as defense

If a married person is injured by the negligent or wrongful act or omission of a person other than the married person's spouse, the fact that the negligent or wrongful act or omission of the spouse of the injured person was a concurring cause of the injury is not a defense in an action brought by the injured person to recover damages for the injury except in cases where the concurring negligent or wrongful act or omission would be a defense if the marriage did not exist. **Leg.H.** Enacted Stats 1992 ch 162 §10 (AB 2650), operative January 1, 1994.

CHAPTER 4
PRESUMPTIONS CONCERNING NATURE OF PROPERTY

Presumption not applicable where marriage terminated by dissolution more than four years before death. §802.
Property acquired by married woman before January 1, 1975. §803.

§802. Presumption not applicable where marriage terminated by dissolution more than four years before death

The presumption that property acquired during marriage is community property does not apply to any property to which legal or equitable title is held by a person at the time of the person's death if the marriage during which the property was acquired was terminated by dissolution of marriage more than four years before the death. **Leg.H.** Enacted Stats 1992 ch 162 §10 (AB 2650), operative January 1, 1994.

§803. Property acquired by married woman before January 1, 1975

Notwithstanding any other provision of this part, whenever any real or personal property, or any interest therein or encumbrance thereon, was acquired before January 1, 1975, by a married woman by an instrument in writing, the following presumptions apply, and are conclusive in favor of any person dealing in good faith and for a valuable consideration with the married woman or her legal representatives or successors in interest, regardless of any change in her marital status after acquisition of the property:

(a) If acquired by the married woman, the presumption is that the property is the married woman's separate property.

(b) If acquired by the married woman and any other person, the presumption is that the married woman takes the part acquired by her as tenant in common, unless a different intention is expressed in the instrument.

(c) If acquired by husband and wife by an instrument in which they are described as husband and wife, the presumption is that the property is the community property of the husband and wife, unless a different intention is expressed in the instrument. **Leg.H.** Enacted Stats 1992 ch 162 §10 (AB 2650), operative January 1, 1994.

CHAPTER 5
TRANSMUTATION OF PROPERTY

Transmutation of property by agreement or transfer. §850.
Fraudulent transfers laws apply. §851.
Form of transmutation. §852.
Effect of will statement, waiver of specified benefits, or written joinder or consent to nonprobate transfer of property on transmutation of property. §853.

§850. Transmutation of property by agreement or transfer

Subject to Sections 851 to 853, inclusive, married persons may by agreement or transfer, with or without consideration, do any of the following:

(a) Transmute community property to separate property of either spouse.

(b) Transmute separate property of either spouse to community property.

(c) Transmute separate property of one spouse to separate property of the other spouse. **Leg.H.** Enacted Stats 1992 ch 162 §10 (AB 2650), operative January 1, 1994.

§851. Fraudulent transfers laws apply

A transmutation is subject to the laws governing fraudulent transfers. **Leg.H.** Enacted Stats 1992 ch 162 §10 (AB 2650), operative January 1, 1994.

§852. Form of transmutation

(a) A transmutation of real or personal property is not valid unless made in writing by an express declaration that is made, joined in, consented to, or accepted by the spouse whose interest in the property is adversely affected.

(b) A transmutation of real property is not effective as to third parties without notice thereof unless recorded.

(c) This section does not apply to a gift between the spouses of clothing, wearing apparel, jewelry, or other tangible articles of a personal nature that is used solely or principally by the spouse to whom the gift is made and that is not substantial in value taking into account the circumstances of the marriage.

(d) Nothing in this section affects the law governing characterization of property in which separate property and community property are commingled or otherwise combined.

(e) This section does not apply to or affect a transmutation of property made before January 1, 1985, and the law that would otherwise be applicable to that transmutation shall continue to apply. **Leg.H.** Enacted Stats 1992 ch 162 §10 (AB 2650), operative January 1, 1994.

§853. Effect of will statement, waiver of specified benefits, or written joinder or consent to nonprobate transfer of property on transmutation of property

(a) A statement in a will of the character of property is not admissible as evidence of a transmutation of the property in a proceeding commenced before the death of the person who made the will.

(b) A waiver of a right to a joint and survivor annuity or survivor's benefits under the federal Retirement Equity Act of 1984 (Public Law 98-397) is not a transmutation of the community property rights of the person executing the waiver.

(c) A written joinder or written consent to a nonprobate transfer of community property on death that satisfies Section 852 is a transmutation and is governed by the law applicable to transmutations and not by Chapter 2 (commencing with Section 5010) of Part 1 of Division 5 of the Probate Code. **Leg.H.** Enacted Stats 1992 ch 162 §10 (AB 2650), operative January 1, 1994. Amended Stats 1993 ch 219 §100 (AB 1500).

PART 3
LIABILITY OF MARITAL PROPERTY

Chapter 1. Definitions.
Chapter 2. General Rules of Liability.
Chapter 3. Reimbursement.
Chapter 4. Transitional Provisions.
Chapter 5. Liability for Death or Injury.

CHAPTER 1
DEFINITIONS

Application of definitions. §900.
Debt. §902.
Time debt incurred. §903.

§900. Application of definitions
Unless the provision or context otherwise requires, the definitions in this chapter govern the construction of this part. **Leg.H.** Enacted Stats 1992 ch 162 §10 (AB 2650), operative January 1, 1994.

§901. [Section repealed 1993]
Leg.H. Enacted Stats 1992 ch 162 §10 (AB 2650), operative January 1, 1994. Repealed Stats 1993 ch 219 §100.3 (AB 1500). The repealed section defined "community estate".

§902. Debt
"Debt" means an obligation incurred by a married person before or during marriage, whether based on contract, tort, or otherwise. **Leg.H.** Enacted Stats 1992 ch 162 §10 (AB 2650), operative January 1, 1994.

§903. Time debt incurred
A debt is "incurred" at the following time:
(a) In the case of a contract, at the time the contract is made.
(b) In the case of a tort, at the time the tort occurs.
(c) In other cases, at the time the obligation arises. **Leg.H.** Enacted Stats 1992 ch 162 §10 (AB 2650), operative January 1, 1994.

CHAPTER 2
GENERAL RULES OF LIABILITY

Community estate liable for debt of either spouse. §910.
Liability of married person's earnings for premarital debt of spouse. §911.
Liability of quasi-community property. §912.
Liability of separate property. §913.
Liability for necessaries; Statute of limitations. §914.
Liability for support obligation. §915.
Liability after property division. §916.

§910. Community estate liable for debt of either spouse
(a) Except as otherwise expressly provided by statute, the community estate is liable for a debt incurred by either spouse before or during marriage, regardless of which spouse has the management and control of the property and regardless of whether one or both spouses are parties to the debt or to a judgment for the debt.
(b) "During marriage" for purposes of this section does not include the period after the date of separation, as defined in Section 70, and before a judgment of dissolution of marriage or legal separation of the parties. **Leg.H.** Enacted Stats 1992 ch 162 §10 (AB 2650), operative January 1, 1994. Amended Stats 2016 ch 114 §3 (SB 1255), effective January 1, 2017.

§911. Liability of married person's earnings for premarital debt of spouse
(a) The earnings of a married person during marriage are not liable for a debt incurred by the person's spouse before marriage. After the earnings of the married person are paid, they remain not liable so long as they are held in a deposit account in which the person's spouse has no right of withdrawal and are uncommingled with other property in the community estate, except property insignificant in amount.
(b) As used in this section:
(1) "Deposit account" has the meaning prescribed in paragraph (29) of subdivision (a) of Section 9102 of the Commercial Code.
(2) "Earnings" means compensation for personal services performed, whether as an employee or otherwise. **Leg.H.** Enacted Stats 1992 ch 162 §10 (AB 2650), operative January 1, 1994. Amended Stats 1999 ch 991 §42.5 (SB 45), operative July 1, 2001.

§912. Liability of quasi-community property
For the purposes of this part, quasi-community property is liable to the same extent, and shall be treated the same in all other respects, as community property. **Leg.H.** Enacted Stats 1992 ch 162 §10 (AB 2650), operative January 1, 1994.

§913. Liability of separate property
(a) The separate property of a married person is liable for a debt incurred by the person before or during marriage.
(b) Except as otherwise provided by statute:
(1) The separate property of a married person is not liable for a debt incurred by the person's spouse before or during marriage.
(2) The joinder or consent of a married person to an encumbrance of community estate property to secure payment of a debt incurred by the person's spouse does not subject the person's separate property to liability for the debt unless the person also incurred the debt. **Leg.H.** Enacted Stats 1992 ch 162 §10 (AB 2650), operative January 1, 1994.

§914. Liability for necessaries; Statute of limitations
(a) Notwithstanding Section 913, a married person is personally liable for the following debts incurred by the person's spouse during marriage:
(1) A debt incurred for necessaries of life of the person's spouse before the date of separation of the spouses.
(2) Except as provided in Section 4302, a debt incurred for common necessaries of life of the person's spouse after the date of separation of the spouses.
(b) The separate property of a married person may be applied to the satisfaction of a debt for which the person is personally liable pursuant to this section. If separate property is so applied at a time when nonexempt property in the community estate or separate property of the person's spouse is available but is not applied to the satisfaction of the debt, the married person is entitled to reimbursement to the extent such property was available.
(c)(1) Except as provided in paragraph (2), the statute of limitations set forth in Section 366.2 of the Code of Civil Procedure shall apply if the spouse for whom the married person is personally liable dies.
(2) If the surviving spouse had actual knowledge of the debt prior to expiration of the period set forth in Section 366.2 of the Code of Civil Procedure and the personal representative of the deceased spouse's estate failed to provide the creditor asserting the claim under this section with a timely written notice of the probate administration of the estate in the manner provided for pursuant to Section 9050 of the Probate Code, the statute of limitations set forth in Section 337 or 339 of the Code of Civil Procedure, as applicable, shall apply.
(d) For purposes of this section, "date of separation" has the same meaning as set forth in Section 70. **Leg.H.** Enacted Stats 1992 ch 162 §10 (AB 2650), operative January 1, 1994. Amended Stats 1993 ch 219 §100.4 (AB 1500); Stats 2001 ch 702 §1 (AB 539); Stats 2014 ch 71 §53 (SB 1304), effective January 1, 2015; Stats 2016 ch 114 §4 (SB 1255), effective January 1, 2017.

§915. Liability for support obligation
(a) For the purpose of this part, a child or spousal support obligation of a married person that does not arise out of the marriage shall be treated as a debt incurred before marriage, regardless of whether a court order for support is made or modified before or during marriage and regardless of whether any installment payment on the obligation accrues before or during marriage.
(b) If property in the community estate is applied to the satisfaction of a child or spousal support obligation of a married person that does not arise out of the marriage, at a time when nonexempt separate income of the person is available but is not applied to the satisfaction of the obligation, the community estate is entitled to reimbursement from the person in the amount of the separate income, not exceeding the property in the community estate so applied.
(c) Nothing in this section limits the matters a court may take into consideration in determining or modifying the amount of a support order, including, but not limited to, the earnings of the spouses of the parties.

Leg.H. Enacted Stats 1992 ch 162 §10 (AB 2650), operative January 1, 1994. Amended Stats 1993 ch 219 §100.5 (AB 1500).

§916. Liability after property division

(a) Notwithstanding any other provision of this chapter, after division of community and quasi-community property pursuant to Division 7 (commencing with Section 2500):

(1) The separate property owned by a married person at the time of the division and the property received by the person in the division is liable for a debt incurred by the person before or during marriage and the person is personally liable for the debt, whether or not the debt was assigned for payment by the person's spouse in the division.

(2) The separate property owned by a married person at the time of the division and the property received by the person in the division is not liable for a debt incurred by the person's spouse before or during marriage, and the person is not personally liable for the debt, unless the debt was assigned for payment by the person in the division of the property. Nothing in this paragraph affects the liability of property for the satisfaction of a lien on the property.

(3) The separate property owned by a married person at the time of the division and the property received by the person in the division is liable for a debt incurred by the person's spouse before or during marriage, and the person is personally liable for the debt, if the debt was assigned for payment by the person in the division of the property. If a money judgment for the debt is entered after the division, the property is not subject to enforcement of the judgment and the judgment may not be enforced against the married person, unless the person is made a party to the judgment for the purpose of this paragraph.

(b) If property of a married person is applied to the satisfaction of a money judgment pursuant to subdivision (a) for a debt incurred by the person that is assigned for payment by the person's spouse, the person has a right of reimbursement from the person's spouse to the extent of the property applied, with interest at the legal rate, and may recover reasonable attorney's fees incurred in enforcing the right of reimbursement. **Leg.H.** Enacted Stats 1992 ch 162 §10 (AB 2650), operative January 1, 1994.

CHAPTER 3
REIMBURSEMENT

General provisions. §920.

§920. General provisions

A right of reimbursement provided by this part is subject to the following provisions:

(a) The right arises regardless of which spouse applies the property to the satisfaction of the debt, regardless of whether the property is applied to the satisfaction of the debt voluntarily or involuntarily, and regardless of whether the debt to which the property is applied is satisfied in whole or in part. The right is subject to an express written waiver of the right by the spouse in whose favor the right arises.

(b) The measure of reimbursement is the value of the property or interest in property at the time the right arises.

(c) The right shall be exercised not later than the earlier of the following times:

(1) Within three years after the spouse in whose favor the right arises has actual knowledge of the application of the property to the satisfaction of the debt.

(2) In proceedings for division of community and quasi-community property pursuant to Division 7 (commencing with Section 2500) or in proceedings upon the death of a spouse. **Leg.H.** Enacted Stats 1992 ch 162 §10 (AB 2650), operative January 1, 1994.

CHAPTER 4
TRANSITIONAL PROVISIONS

Enforcement of debts. §930.
Reimbursement rights. §931.

§930. Enforcement of debts

Except as otherwise provided by statute, this part governs the liability of separate property and property in the community estate and the personal liability of a married person for a debt enforced on or after January 1, 1985, regardless of whether the debt was incurred before, on, or after that date. **Leg.H.** Enacted Stats 1992 ch 162 §10 (AB 2650), operative January 1, 1994. Amended Stats 1993 ch 219 §100.6 (AB 1500).

§931. Reimbursement rights

The provisions of this part that govern reimbursement apply to all debts, regardless of whether satisfied before, on, or after January 1, 1985. **Leg.H.** Enacted Stats 1992 ch 162 §10 (AB 2650), operative January 1, 1994.

CHAPTER 5
LIABILITY FOR DEATH OR INJURY

Liability for death or injury. §1000.

§1000. Liability for death or injury

(a) A married person is not liable for any injury or damage caused by the other spouse except in cases where the married person would be liable therefor if the marriage did not exist.

(b) The liability of a married person for death or injury to person or property shall be satisfied as follows:

(1) If the liability of the married person is based upon an act or omission which occurred while the married person was performing an activity for the benefit of the community, the liability shall first be satisfied from the community estate and second from the separate property of the married person.

(2) If the liability of the married person is not based upon an act or omission which occurred while the married person was performing an activity for the benefit of the community, the liability shall first be satisfied from the separate property of the married person and second from the community estate.

(c) This section does not apply to the extent the liability is satisfied out of proceeds of insurance for the liability, whether the proceeds are from property in the community estate or from separate property. Notwithstanding Section 920, no right of reimbursement under this section shall be exercised more than seven years after the spouse in whose favor the right arises has actual knowledge of the application of the property to the satisfaction of the debt. **Leg.H.** Enacted Stats 1992 ch 162 §10 (AB 2650), operative January 1, 1994. Amended Stats 1993 ch 219 §100.7 (AB 1500).

PART 4
MANAGEMENT AND CONTROL OF MARITAL PROPERTY

Management and control of community personal property; Fiduciary duty. §1100.
Remedies for breach of fiduciary duty between spouses. §1101.
Management and control of community real property. §1102.
Management and control where spouse has conservator or lacks legal capacity. §1103.

§1100. Management and control of community personal property; Fiduciary duty

(a) Except as provided in subdivisions (b), (c), and (d) and Sections 761 and 1103, either spouse has the management and control of the community personal property, whether acquired prior to or on or after January 1, 1975, with like absolute power of disposition, other than testamentary, as the spouse has of the separate estate of the spouse.

(b) A spouse may not make a gift of community personal property, or dispose of community personal property for less than fair and reasonable value, without the written consent of the other spouse. This subdivision does not apply to gifts mutually given by both spouses to third parties and to gifts given by one spouse to the other spouse.

(c) A spouse may not sell, convey, or encumber community personal property used as the family dwelling, or the furniture, furnishings, or fittings of the home, or the clothing or wearing apparel of the other spouse or minor children which is community personal property, without the written consent of the other spouse.

(d) Except as provided in subdivisions (b) and (c), and in Section 1102, a spouse who is operating or managing a business or an interest in a business that is all or substantially all community personal property has the primary management and control of the business or interest. Primary management and control means that the managing spouse may act alone in all transactions but shall give prior written notice to the other spouse of any sale, lease, exchange, encumbrance, or other disposition of all or substantially all of the personal property used in the operation of the business (including personal property used for agricultural purposes), whether or not title to that property is held in the name of only one spouse. Written notice is not, however, required when prohibited by the law otherwise applicable to the transaction.

Remedies for the failure by a managing spouse to give prior written notice as required by this subdivision are only as specified in Section 1101. A failure to give prior written notice shall not adversely affect the validity of a transaction nor of any interest transferred.

(e) Each spouse shall act with respect to the other spouse in the management and control of the community assets and liabilities in accordance with the general rules governing fiduciary relationships which control the actions of persons having relationships of personal confidence as specified in Section 721, until such time as the assets and liabilities have been divided by the parties or by a court. This duty includes the obligation to make full disclosure to the other spouse of all material facts and information regarding the existence, characterization, and valuation of all assets in which the community has or may have an interest and debts for which the community is or may be liable, and to provide equal access to all information, records, and books that pertain to the value and character of those assets and debts, upon request. **Leg.H.** Enacted Stats 1992 ch 162 §10 (AB 2650), operative January 1, 1994. Amended Stats 1993 ch 219 §100.8 (AB 1500).

§1101. Remedies for breach of fiduciary duty between spouses

(a) A spouse has a claim against the other spouse for any breach of the fiduciary duty that results in impairment to the claimant spouse's present undivided one-half interest in the community estate, including, but not limited to, a single transaction or a pattern or series of transactions, which transaction or transactions have caused or will cause a detrimental impact to the claimant spouse's undivided one-half interest in the community estate.

(b) A court may order an accounting of the property and obligations of the parties to a marriage and may determine the rights of ownership in, the beneficial enjoyment of, or access to, community property, and the classification of all property of the parties to a marriage.

(c) A court may order that the name of a spouse shall be added to community property held in the name of the other spouse alone or that the title of community property held in some other title form shall be reformed to reflect its community character, except with respect to any of the following:

(1) A partnership interest held by the other spouse as a general partner.

(2) An interest in a professional corporation or professional association.

(3) An asset of an unincorporated business if the other spouse is the only spouse involved in operating and managing the business.

(4) Any other property, if the revision would adversely affect the rights of a third person.

(d)(1) Except as provided in paragraph (2), any action under subdivision (a) shall be commenced within three years of the date a petitioning spouse had actual knowledge that the transaction or event for which the remedy is being sought occurred.

(2) An action may be commenced under this section upon the death of a spouse or in conjunction with an action for legal separation, dissolution of marriage, or nullity without regard to the time limitations set forth in paragraph (1).

(3) The defense of laches may be raised in any action brought under this section.

(4) Except as to actions authorized by paragraph (2), remedies under subdivision (a) apply only to transactions or events occurring on or after July 1, 1987.

(e) In any transaction affecting community property in which the consent of both spouses is required, the court may, upon the motion of a spouse, dispense with the requirement of the other spouse's consent if both of the following requirements are met:

(1) The proposed transaction is in the best interest of the community.

(2) Consent has been arbitrarily refused or cannot be obtained due to the physical incapacity, mental incapacity, or prolonged absence of the nonconsenting spouse.

(f) Any action may be brought under this section without filing an action for dissolution of marriage, legal separation, or nullity, or may be brought in conjunction with the action or upon the death of a spouse.

(g) Remedies for breach of the fiduciary duty by one spouse, including those set out in Sections 721 and 1100, shall include, but not be limited to, an award to the other spouse of 50 percent, or an amount equal to 50 percent, of any asset undisclosed or transferred in breach of the fiduciary duty plus attorney's fees and court costs. The value of the asset shall be determined to be its highest value at the date of the breach of the fiduciary duty, the date of the sale or disposition of the asset, or the date of the award by the court.

(h) Remedies for the breach of the fiduciary duty by one spouse, as set forth in Sections 721 and 1100, when the breach falls within the ambit of Section 3294 of the Civil Code shall include, but not be limited to, an award to the other spouse of 100 percent, or an amount equal to 100 percent, of any asset undisclosed or transferred in breach of the fiduciary duty. **Leg.H.** Enacted Stats 1992 ch 162 §10 (AB 2650), operative January 1, 1994. Amended Stats 2001 ch 703 §1 (AB 583).

2001 Note: This act shall apply to any judgment that becomes final on or after January 1, 2002. Stats 2001 ch 703 §8.

§1102. Management and control of community real property

(a) Except as provided in Sections 761 and 1103, either spouse has the management and control of the community real property, whether acquired prior to, or on or after January 1, 1975, but both spouses, either personally or by a duly authorized agent, are required to join in executing an instrument by which that community real property or an interest therein is leased for a longer period than one year, or is sold, conveyed, or encumbered.

(b) This section does not apply to a lease, mortgage, conveyance, or transfer of real property, or of an interest in real property, between spouses.

(c) Notwithstanding subdivision (b), both of the following shall apply:

(1) The sole lease, contract, mortgage, or deed of the husband, holding the record title to community real property, to a lessee, purchaser, or

encumbrancer, in good faith without knowledge of the marriage relation, shall be presumed to be valid if executed prior to January 1, 1975.

(2) The sole lease, contract, mortgage, or deed of either spouse, holding the record title to community real property to a lessee, purchaser, or encumbrancer, in good faith without knowledge of the marriage relation, shall be presumed to be valid if executed on or after January 1, 1975.

(d) An action to avoid an instrument mentioned in this section, affecting any property standing of record in the name of either spouse alone, executed by the spouse alone, shall not be commenced after the expiration of one year from the filing for record of that instrument in the recorder's office in the county in which the land is situated.

(e) This section does not preclude either spouse from encumbering that spouse's interest in community real property, as provided in Section 2033, to pay reasonable attorney's fees in order to retain or maintain legal counsel in a proceeding for dissolution of marriage, for nullity of marriage, or for legal separation of the parties. **Leg.H.** Enacted Stats 1992 ch 162 §10 (AB 2650), operative January 1, 1994. Amended Stats 1993 ch 219 §101 (AB 1500); Stats 2014 ch 82 §18 (SB 1306), effective January 1, 2015; Stats 2019 ch 115 §11 (AB 1817), effective January 1, 2020.

§1103. Management and control where spouse has conservator or lacks legal capacity

(a) Where one or both of the spouses either has a conservator of the estate or lacks legal capacity to manage and control community property, the procedure for management and control (which includes disposition) of the community property is that prescribed in Part 6 (commencing with Section 3000) of Division 4 of the Probate Code.

(b) Where one or both spouses either has a conservator of the estate or lacks legal capacity to give consent to a gift of community personal property or a disposition of community personal property without a valuable consideration as required by Section 1100 or to a sale, conveyance, or encumbrance of community personal property for which a consent is required by Section 1100, the procedure for that gift, disposition, sale, conveyance, or encumbrance is that prescribed in Part 6 (commencing with Section 3000) of Division 4 of the Probate Code.

(c) Where one or both spouses either has a conservator of the estate or lacks legal capacity to join in executing a lease, sale, conveyance, or encumbrance of community real property or any interest therein as required by Section 1102, the procedure for that lease, sale, conveyance, or encumbrance is that prescribed in Part 6 (commencing with Section 3000) of Division 4 of the Probate Code. **Leg.H.** Enacted Stats 1992 ch 162 §10 (AB 2650), operative January 1, 1994.

PART 5
MARITAL AGREEMENTS

Chapter 1. General Provisions.
Chapter 2. Uniform Premarital Agreement Act.
Chapter 3. Agreements Between Spouses.

CHAPTER 1
GENERAL PROVISIONS

Effect of premarital or other marital property agreement. §1500.
Premarital agreements and marital property agreements of minors. §1501.
Recording of agreements. §1502.
Law applicable to premarital agreements made before January 1, 1986. §1503.

§1500. Effect of premarital or other marital property agreement

The property rights of spouses prescribed by statute may be altered by a premarital agreement or other marital property agreement. **Leg.H.** Enacted Stats 1992 ch 162 §10 (AB 2650), operative January 1, 1994. Amended Stats 2014 ch 82 §19 (SB 1306), effective January 1, 2015.

§1501. Premarital agreements and marital property agreements of minors

A minor may make a valid premarital agreement or other marital property agreement if the minor is emancipated, is otherwise capable of contracting marriage pursuant to Section 302 or 303, or has entered or is entering a marriage that is valid in the jurisdiction where the marriage is solemnized. **Leg.H.** Enacted Stats 1992 ch 162 §10 (AB 2650), operative January 1, 1994. Amended Stats 2018 ch 660 §7 (SB 273), effective January 1, 2019.

§1502. Recording of agreements

(a) A premarital agreement or other marital property agreement that is executed and acknowledged or proved in the manner that a grant of real property is required to be executed and acknowledged or proved may be recorded in the office of the recorder of each county in which real property affected by the agreement is situated.

(b) Recording or nonrecording of a premarital agreement or other marital property agreement has the same effect as recording or nonrecording of a grant of real property. **Leg.H.** Enacted Stats 1992 ch 162 §10 (AB 2650), operative January 1, 1994.

§1503. Law applicable to premarital agreements made before January 1, 1986

Nothing in this chapter affects the validity or effect of premarital agreements made before January 1, 1986, and the validity and effect of those agreements shall continue to be determined by the law applicable to the agreements before January 1, 1986. **Leg.H.** Enacted Stats 1992 ch 162 §10 (AB 2650), operative January 1, 1994.

CHAPTER 2
UNIFORM PREMARITAL AGREEMENT ACT

Article 1. Preliminary Provisions.
Article 2. Premarital Agreements.

ARTICLE 1
Preliminary Provisions

Short title. §1600.
Application of chapter. §1601.

§1600. Short title

This chapter may be cited as the Uniform Premarital Agreement Act. **Leg.H.** Enacted Stats 1992 ch 162 §10 (AB 2650), operative January 1, 1994.

§1601. Application of chapter

This chapter is effective on and after January 1, 1986, and applies to any premarital agreement executed on or after that date. **Leg.H.** Enacted Stats 1992 ch 162 §10 (AB 2650), operative January 1, 1994.

ARTICLE 2
Premarital Agreements

Definitions. §1610.
Formalities; Consideration. §1611.
Subject matter of premarital agreement; Spousal support waiver requirements. §1612.
Agreement becomes effective upon marriage. §1613.
Amendment; Revocation. §1614.
Enforcement; Specified court finding requirements. §1615.
Effect of void marriage. §1616.
Limitation of actions. §1617.

§1610. Definitions

As used in this chapter:

(a) "Premarital agreement" means an agreement between prospective spouses made in contemplation of marriage and to be effective upon marriage.

(b) "Property" means an interest, present or future, legal or equitable, vested or contingent, in real or personal property, including income and earnings. **Leg.H.** Enacted Stats 1992 ch 162 §10 (AB 2650), operative January 1, 1994.

§1611. Formalities; Consideration

A premarital agreement shall be in writing and signed by both parties. It is enforceable without consideration. **Leg.H.** Enacted Stats 1992 ch 162 §10 (AB 2650), operative January 1, 1994.

§1612. Subject matter of premarital agreement; Spousal support waiver requirements

(a) Parties to a premarital agreement may contract with respect to all of the following:

(1) The rights and obligations of each of the parties in any of the property of either or both of them whenever and wherever acquired or located.

(2) The right to buy, sell, use, transfer, exchange, abandon, lease, consume, expend, assign, create a security interest in, mortgage, encumber, dispose of, or otherwise manage and control property.

(3) The disposition of property upon separation, marital dissolution, death, or the occurrence or nonoccurrence of any other event.

(4) The making of a will, trust, or other arrangement to carry out the provisions of the agreement.

(5) The ownership rights in and disposition of the death benefit from a life insurance policy.

(6) The choice of law governing the construction of the agreement.

(7) Any other matter, including their personal rights and obligations, not in violation of public policy or a statute imposing a criminal penalty.

(b) The right of a child to support may not be adversely affected by a premarital agreement.

(c) Any provision in a premarital agreement regarding spousal support, including, but not limited to, a waiver of it, is not enforceable if the party against whom enforcement of the spousal support provision is sought was not represented by independent counsel at the time the agreement containing the provision was signed, or if the provision regarding spousal support is unconscionable at the time of enforcement. An otherwise unenforceable provision in a premarital agreement regarding spousal support may not become enforceable solely because the party against whom enforcement is sought was represented by independent counsel. **Leg.H.** Enacted Stats 1992 ch 162 §10 (AB 2650), operative January 1, 1994. Amended Stats 2001 ch 286 §1 (SB 78).

§1613. Agreement becomes effective upon marriage

A premarital agreement becomes effective upon marriage. **Leg.H.** Enacted Stats 1992 ch 162 §10 (AB 2650), operative January 1, 1994.

§1614. Amendment; Revocation

After marriage, a premarital agreement may be amended or revoked only by a written agreement signed by the parties. The amended agreement or the revocation is enforceable without consideration. **Leg.H.** Enacted Stats 1992 ch 162 §10 (AB 2650), operative January 1, 1994.

§1615. Enforcement; Specified court finding requirements

(a) A premarital agreement is not enforceable if the party against whom enforcement is sought proves either of the following:

(1) That party did not execute the agreement voluntarily.

(2) The agreement was unconscionable when it was executed and, before execution of the agreement, all of the following applied to that party:

(A) That party was not provided a fair, reasonable, and full disclosure of the property or financial obligations of the other party.

(B) That party did not voluntarily and expressly waive, in writing, any right to disclosure of the property or financial obligations of the other party beyond the disclosure provided.

(C) That party did not have, or reasonably could not have had, an adequate knowledge of the property or financial obligations of the other party.

(b) An issue of unconscionability of a premarital agreement shall be decided by the court as a matter of law.

(c) For the purposes of subdivision (a), it shall be deemed that a premarital agreement was not executed voluntarily unless the court finds in writing or on the record all of the following:

(1) The party against whom enforcement is sought was represented by independent legal counsel at the time of signing the agreement or, after being advised to seek independent legal counsel, expressly waived, in a separate writing, representation by independent legal counsel. The advisement to seek independent legal counsel shall be made at least seven calendar days before the final agreement is signed.

(2) One of the following:

(A) For an agreement executed between January 1, 2002, and January 1, 2020, the party against whom enforcement is sought had not less than seven calendar days between the time that party was first presented with the final agreement and advised to seek independent legal counsel and the time the agreement was signed. This requirement does not apply to nonsubstantive amendments that do not change the terms of the agreement.

(B) For an agreement executed on or after January 1, 2020, the party against whom enforcement is sought had not less than seven calendar days between the time that party was first presented with the final agreement and the time the agreement was signed, regardless of whether the party is represented by legal counsel. This requirement does not apply to nonsubstantive amendments that do not change the terms of the agreement.

(3) The party against whom enforcement is sought, if unrepresented by legal counsel, was fully informed of the terms and basic effect of the agreement as well as the rights and obligations the party was giving up by signing the agreement, and was proficient in the language in which the explanation of the party's rights was conducted and in which the agreement was written. The explanation of the rights and obligations relinquished shall be memorialized in writing and delivered to the party prior to signing the agreement. The unrepresented party shall, on or before the signing of the premarital agreement, execute a document declaring that the party received the information required by this paragraph and indicating who provided that information.

(4) The agreement and the writings executed pursuant to paragraphs (1) and (3) were not executed under duress, fraud, or undue influence, and the parties did not lack capacity to enter into the agreement.

(5) Any other factors the court deems relevant. **Leg.H.** Enacted Stats 1992 ch 162 §10 (AB 2650), operative January 1, 1994. Amended Stats 2001 ch 286 §2 (SB 78); Stats 2019 ch 115 §12 (AB 1817), effective January 1, 2020; Stats 2019 ch 193 §1 (AB 1380), effective January 1, 2020 (ch 193 prevails).

§1616. Effect of void marriage

If a marriage is determined to be void, an agreement that would otherwise have been a premarital agreement is enforceable only to the extent necessary to avoid an inequitable result. **Leg.H.** Enacted Stats 1992 ch 162 §10 (AB 2650), operative January 1, 1994.

§1617. Limitation of actions

Any statute of limitations applicable to an action asserting a claim for relief under a premarital agreement is tolled during the marriage of the parties to the agreement. However, equitable defenses limiting the time for enforcement, including laches and estoppel, are available to either party. **Leg.H.** Enacted Stats 1992 ch 162 §10 (AB 2650), operative January 1, 1994.

CHAPTER 3
AGREEMENTS BETWEEN SPOUSES

Restrictions on contract altering spouse's legal relations. §1620.

§1620. Restrictions on contract altering spouse's legal relations

Except as otherwise provided by law, spouses cannot, by a contract with each other, alter their legal relations, except as to property. **Leg.H.** Enacted Stats 1992 ch 162 §10 (AB 2650), operative January 1, 1994. Amended Stats 2014 ch 82 §21 (SB 1306), effective January 1, 2015.

DIVISION 5
CONCILIATION PROCEEDINGS

Part 1. Family Conciliation Court Law.
Part 2. Statewide Coordination of Family Mediation and Conciliation Services.

PART 1
FAMILY CONCILIATION COURT LAW

Chapter 1. General Provisions.
Chapter 2. Family Conciliation Courts.
Chapter 3. Proceedings for Conciliation.

CHAPTER 1
GENERAL PROVISIONS

Short title. §1800.
Purposes of part. §1801.
Applicability of part. §1802.

§1800. Short title

This part may be cited as the Family Conciliation Court Law. **Leg.H.** Enacted Stats 1992 ch 162 §10 (AB 2650), operative January 1, 1994.

§1801. Purposes of part

The purposes of this part are to protect the rights of children and to promote the public welfare by preserving, promoting, and protecting family life and the institution of matrimony, and to provide means for the reconciliation of spouses and the amicable settlement of domestic and family controversies. **Leg.H.** Enacted Stats 1992 ch 162 §10 (AB 2650), operative January 1, 1994.

§1802. Applicability of part

(a) This part applies only in counties in which the superior court determines that the social conditions in the county and the number of domestic relations cases in the courts render the procedures provided in this part necessary to the full and proper consideration of those cases and the effectuation of the purposes of this part.

(b) The determination under subdivision (a) shall be made annually in the month of January by:

(1) The judge of the superior court in counties having only one superior court judge.

(2) A majority of the judges of the superior court in counties having more than one superior court judge. **Leg.H.** Enacted Stats 1992 ch 162 §10 (AB 2650), operative January 1, 1994.

CHAPTER 2
FAMILY CONCILIATION COURTS

Jurisdiction; Court to be known as family conciliation court. §1810.
Designation of judge or judges to hear cases. §1811.
Transfer of cases. §1812.
Substitute judge. §1813.
Appointment of supervising counselor, secretary, and other assistants. §1814.
Qualifications of supervising and associate counselors. §1815.
Continuing instruction programs for evaluators; Duties of eligible providers. §1816.
Probation officers; Duties. §1817.
Persons present at hearings and conferences; Communications with court; Files to be closed; Inspection. §1818.
Destruction of records. §1819.
Agreement between courts for joint family conciliation court services. §1820.

§1810. Jurisdiction; Court to be known as family conciliation court

Each superior court shall exercise the jurisdiction conferred by this part. While sitting in the exercise of this jurisdiction, the court shall be known and referred to as the "family conciliation court." **Leg.H.** Enacted Stats 1992 ch 162 §10 (AB 2650), operative January 1, 1994.

§1811. Designation of judge or judges to hear cases

The presiding judge of the superior court shall annually, in the month of January, designate at least one judge to hear all cases under this part. **Leg.H.** Enacted Stats 1992 ch 162 §10 (AB 2650), operative January 1, 1994. Amended Stats 2003 ch 149 §11 (SB 79).

§1812. Transfer of cases

(a) The judge of the family conciliation court may transfer any case before the family conciliation court pursuant to this part to the department of the presiding judge of the superior court for assignment for trial or other proceedings by another judge of the court, whenever in the opinion of the judge of the family conciliation court the transfer is necessary to expedite the business of the family conciliation court or to ensure the prompt consideration of the case.

(b) When a case is transferred pursuant to subdivision (a), the judge to whom it is transferred shall act as the judge of the family conciliation court in the matter. **Leg.H.** Enacted Stats 1992 ch 162 §10 (AB 2650), operative January 1, 1994.

§1813. Substitute judge

(a) The presiding judge of the superior court may appoint a judge of the superior court other than the judge of the family conciliation court to act as judge of the family conciliation court during any period when the judge of the family conciliation court is on vacation, absent, or for any reason unable to perform the duties as judge of the family conciliation court.

(b) The judge appointed under subdivision (a) has all of the powers and authority of a judge of the family conciliation court in cases under this part. **Leg.H.** Enacted Stats 1992 ch 162 §10 (AB 2650), operative January 1, 1994.

§1814. Appointment of supervising counselor, secretary, and other assistants

(a) In each county in which a family conciliation court is established, the superior court may appoint one supervising counselor of conciliation and one secretary to assist the family conciliation court in disposing of its business and carrying out its functions. When superior courts by contract have established joint family conciliation court services, the contracting courts jointly may make the appointments under this subdivision.

(b) The supervising counselor of conciliation has the power to do all of the following:

(1) Hold conciliation conferences with parties to, and hearings in, proceedings under this part, and make recommendations concerning the proceedings to the judge of the family conciliation court.

(2) Provide supervision in connection with the exercise of the counselor's jurisdiction as the judge of the family conciliation court may direct.

(3) Cause reports to be made, statistics to be compiled, and records to be kept as the judge of the family conciliation court may direct.

(4) Hold hearings in all family conciliation court cases as may be required by the judge of the family conciliation court, and make investigations as may be required by the court to carry out the intent of this part.

(5) Make recommendations relating to marriages where one or both parties are underage.

(6) Make investigations, reports, and recommendations as provided in Section 281 of the Welfare and Institutions Code under the authority provided the probation officer in that code.

(7) Act as domestic relations cases investigator.

(8) Conduct mediation of child custody and visitation disputes.

(c) The superior court, or contracting superior courts, may also appoint associate counselors of conciliation and other office assistants as may be necessary to assist the family conciliation court in disposing of its business. The associate counselors shall carry out their duties under the supervision of the supervising counselor of conciliation and have the powers of the supervising counselor of conciliation. Office assistants shall work under the supervision and direction of the supervising counselor of conciliation.

(d) The classification and salaries of persons appointed under this section shall be determined by:

(1) The superior court of the county in which a noncontracting family conciliation court operates.

(2) The superior court of the county which by contract has the responsibility to administer funds of the joint family conciliation court service. **Leg.H.** Enacted Stats 1992 ch 162 §10 (AB 2650), operative January 1, 1994. Amended Stats 2012 ch 470 §12 (AB 1529), effective January 1, 2013.

§1815. Qualifications of supervising and associate counselors

(a) A person employed as a supervising counselor of conciliation or as an associate counselor of conciliation shall have all of the following minimum qualifications:

(1) A master's degree in psychology, social work, marriage, family and child counseling, or other behavioral science substantially related to marriage and family interpersonal relationships.

(2) At least two years of experience in counseling or psychotherapy, or both, preferably in a setting related to the areas of responsibility of the family conciliation court and with the ethnic population to be served.

(3) Knowledge of the court system of California and the procedures used in family law cases.

(4) Knowledge of other resources in the community that clients can be referred to for assistance.

(5) Knowledge of adult psychopathology and the psychology of families.

(6) Knowledge of child development, child abuse, clinical issues relating to children, the effects of divorce on children, the effects of domestic violence on children, and child custody research sufficient to enable a counselor to assess the mental health needs of children.

(7) Training in domestic violence issues as described in Section 1816.

(b) The family conciliation court may substitute additional experience for a portion of the education, or additional education for a portion of the experience, required under subdivision (a).

(c) This section does not apply to any supervising counselor of conciliation who was in office on March 27, 1980. **Leg.H.** Enacted Stats 1992 ch 162 §10 (AB 2650), operative January 1, 1994. Amended Stats 2006 ch 130 §1 (AB 2853), effective January 1, 2007.

§1816. Continuing instruction programs for evaluators; Duties of eligible providers

(a) For purposes of this section, the following definitions apply:

(1) "Eligible provider" means the Administrative Office of the Courts or an educational institution, professional association, professional continuing education group, a group connected to the courts, or a public or private group that has been authorized by the Administrative Office of the Courts to provide domestic violence training.

(2) "Evaluator" means a supervising or associate counselor described in Section 1815, a mediator described in Section 3164, a court-connected or private child custody evaluator described in Section 3110.5, or a court-appointed investigator or evaluator as described in Section 3110 or Section 730 of the Evidence Code.

(b) An evaluator shall participate in a program of continuing instruction in domestic violence, including child abuse, as may be arranged and provided to that evaluator. This training may utilize domestic violence training programs conducted by nonprofit community organizations with an expertise in domestic violence issues.

(c) Areas of basic instruction shall include, but are not limited to, the following:

(1) The effects of domestic violence on children.

(2) The nature and extent of domestic violence.

(3) The social and family dynamics of domestic violence.

(4) Techniques for identifying and assisting families affected by domestic violence.

(5) Interviewing, documentation of, and appropriate recommendations for, families affected by domestic violence.

(6) The legal rights of, and remedies available to, victims.

(7) Availability of community and legal domestic violence resources.

(d) An evaluator shall also complete 16 hours of advanced training within a 12-month period. Four hours of that advanced training shall include community resource networking intended to acquaint the evaluator with domestic violence resources in the geographical communities where the family being evaluated may reside. Twelve hours of instruction, as approved by the Administrative Office of the Courts, shall include all of the following:

(1) The appropriate structuring of the child custody evaluation process, including, but not limited to, all of the following:

(A) Maximizing safety for clients, evaluators, and court personnel.

(B) Maintaining objectivity.

(C) Providing and gathering balanced information from the parties and controlling for bias.

(D) Providing separate sessions at separate times as described in Section 3113.

(E) Considering the impact of the evaluation report and recommendations with particular attention to the dynamics of domestic violence.

(2) The relevant sections of local, state, and federal laws, rules, or regulations.

(3) The range, availability, and applicability of domestic violence resources available to victims, including, but not limited to, all of the following:

(A) Domestic violence shelter-based programs.

(B) Counseling, including drug and alcohol counseling.

(C) Legal assistance.

(D) Job training.

(E) Parenting classes.

(F) Resources for a victim who is an immigrant.

(4) The range, availability, and applicability of domestic violence intervention available to perpetrators, including, but not limited to, all of the following:

(A) Certified treatment programs described in subdivision (c) of Section 1203.097 of the Penal Code.

(B) Drug and alcohol counseling.

(C) Legal assistance.

(D) Job training.

(E) Parenting classes.

(5) The unique issues in a family and psychological assessment in a domestic violence case, including all of the following:

(A) The effects of exposure to domestic violence and psychological trauma on children, the relationship between child physical abuse, child sexual abuse, and domestic violence, the differential family dynamics related to parent-child attachments in families with domestic violence, intergenerational transmission of familial violence, and manifestations of post-traumatic stress disorders in children.

(B) The nature and extent of domestic violence, and the relationship of gender, class, race, culture, and sexual orientation to domestic violence.

(C) Current legal, psychosocial, public policy, and mental health research related to the dynamics of family violence, the impact of victimization, the psychology of perpetration, and the dynamics of power and control in battering relationships.

(D) The assessment of family history based on the type, severity, and frequency of violence.

(E) The impact on parenting abilities of being a victim or perpetrator of domestic violence.

(F) The uses and limitations of psychological testing and psychiatric diagnosis in assessing parenting abilities in domestic violence cases.

(G) The influence of alcohol and drug use and abuse on the incidence of domestic violence.

(H) Understanding the dynamics of high conflict relationships and relationships between an abuser and victim.

(I) The importance of, and procedures for, obtaining collateral information from a probation department, children's protective services, police incident report, a pleading regarding a restraining order, medical records, a school, and other relevant sources.

(J) Accepted methods for structuring safe and enforceable child custody and parenting plans that ensure the health, safety, welfare, and best interest of the child, and safeguards for the parties.

(K) The importance of discouraging participants in child custody matters from blaming victims of domestic violence for the violence and from minimizing allegations of domestic violence, child abuse, or abuse against a family member.

(L) The risks associated with access to firearms and ways to reduce those risks.

(e) After an evaluator has completed the advanced training described in subdivision (d), that evaluator shall complete four hours of updated training annually that shall include, but is not limited to, all of the following:

(1) Changes in local court practices, case law, and state and federal legislation related to domestic violence.

(2) An update of current social science research and theory, including the impact of exposure to domestic violence on children.

(f) Training described in this section shall be acquired from an eligible provider and that eligible provider shall comply with all of the following:

(1) Ensure that a training instructor or consultant delivering the education and training programs either meets the training requirements of this section or is an expert in the subject matter.

(2) Monitor and evaluate the quality of courses, curricula, training, instructors, and consultants.

(3) Emphasize the importance of focusing child custody evaluations on the health, safety, welfare, and best interest of the child.

(4) Develop a procedure to verify that an evaluator completes the education and training program.

(5) Distribute a certificate of completion to each evaluator who has completed the training. That certificate shall document the number of hours of training offered, the number of hours the evaluator completed, the dates of the training, and the name of the training provider.

(g)(1) If there is a local court rule regarding the procedure to notify the court that an evaluator has completed training as described in this section, the evaluator shall comply with that local court rule.

(2) Except as provided in paragraph (1), an evaluator shall attach copies of the certificates of completion of the training described in subdivision (d) and the most recent updated training described in subdivision (e).

(h) An evaluator may satisfy the requirement for 12 hours of instruction described in subdivision (d) by training from an eligible provider that was obtained on or after January 1, 1996. The advanced training of that evaluator shall not be complete until that evaluator completes the four hours of community resource networking described in subdivision (d).

(i) The Judicial Council shall develop standards for the training programs. The Judicial Council shall solicit the assistance of community organizations concerned with domestic violence and child abuse and shall seek to develop training programs that will maximize coordination between conciliation courts and local agencies concerned with domestic violence. **Leg.H.** Enacted Stats 1992 ch 162 §10 (AB 2650), operative January 1, 1994. Amended Stats 1993 ch 219 §101.5 (AB 1500); Stats 2000 ch 926 §1 (SB 1716); Stats 2006 ch 130 §2 (AB 2853), effective January 1, 2007; Stats 2007 ch 130 §88 (AB 299), effective January 1, 2008; Stats 2019 ch 115 §13 (AB 1817), effective January 1, 2020; Stats 2022 ch 197 §3 (SB 1493), effective January 1, 2023; Stats 2024 ch 303 §1 (AB 1974), effective January 1, 2025.

§1817. Probation officers; Duties

The probation officer in every county shall do all of the following:

(a) Give assistance to the family conciliation court that the court may request to carry out the purposes of this part, and to that end shall, upon request, make investigations and reports as requested.

(b) In cases pursuant to this part, exercise all the powers and perform all the duties granted or imposed by the laws of this state relating to probation or to probation officers. **Leg.H.** Enacted Stats 1992 ch 162 §10 (AB 2650), operative January 1, 1994.

§1818. Persons present at hearings and conferences; Communications with court; Files to be closed; Inspection

(a) All superior court hearings or conferences in proceedings under this part shall be held in private and the court shall exclude all persons except the officers of the court, the parties, their counsel, and witnesses. The court shall not allow ex parte communications, except as authorized by Section 216. All communications, verbal or written, from parties to the judge, commissioner, or counselor in a proceeding under this part shall be deemed to be official information within the meaning of Section 1040 of the Evidence Code.

(b) The files of the family conciliation court shall be closed. The petition, supporting affidavit, conciliation agreement, and any court order made in the matter may be opened to inspection by a party or the party's counsel upon the written authority of the judge of the family conciliation court. **Leg.H.** Enacted Stats 1992 ch 162 §10 (AB 2650), operative January 1, 1994. Amended Stats 2005 ch 489 §2 (SB 1088), effective January 1, 2006.

§1819. Destruction of records

(a) Except as provided in subdivision (b), upon order of the judge of the family conciliation court, the supervising counselor of conciliation may destroy any record, paper, or document filed or kept in the office of the supervising counselor of conciliation which is more than two years old.

(b) Records described in subdivision (a) of child custody or visitation mediation may be destroyed when the minor or minors involved are 18 years of age.

(c) In the judge's discretion, the judge of the family conciliation court may order the microfilming of any record, paper, or document described in subdivision (a) or (b). **Leg.H.** Enacted Stats 1992 ch 162 §10 (AB 2650), operative January 1, 1994.

§1820. Agreement between courts for joint family conciliation court services

(a) A court may contract with any other court or courts to provide joint family conciliation court services.

(b) An agreement between two or more courts for the operation of a joint family conciliation court service may provide that one participating court shall be the custodian of moneys made available for the purposes of the joint services, and that the custodian court may make payments from the moneys upon audit of the appropriate auditing officer or body of the court.

(c) An agreement between two or more courts for the operation of a joint family conciliation court service may also provide:

(1) For the joint provision or operation of services and facilities or for the provision or operation of services and facilities by one participating court under contract for the other participating courts.

(2) For appointments of members of the staff of the family conciliation court including the supervising counselor.

(3) That, for specified purposes, the members of the staff of the family conciliation court including the supervising counselor, but excluding the judges of the family conciliation court, shall be considered to be employees of one participating court.

(4) For other matters that are necessary or proper to effectuate the purposes of the Family Conciliation Court Law.

(d) The provisions of this part relating to family conciliation court services provided by a single court shall be equally applicable to courts which contract, pursuant to this section, to provide joint family conciliation court services. **Leg.H.** Enacted Stats 1992 ch 162 §10 (AB 2650), operative January 1, 1994. Amended Stats 2012 ch 470 §13 (AB 1529), effective January 1, 2013.

CHAPTER 3
PROCEEDINGS FOR CONCILIATION

Jurisdiction of family conciliation court. §1830.
Purpose of petition. §1831.
Caption of petition. §1832.
Contents of petition. §1833.
Assistance in preparing and presenting petition; Coextensive jurisdiction in cases of domestic violence. §1834.
Fees. §1835.
Notice of hearing; Citation. §1836.
Time and place of hearings. §1837.
Informal hearings; Aid of experts. §1838.
Temporary orders; Reconciliation agreement. §1839.
Stay of right to file other proceeding; Effect of pendency of other proceeding. §1840.
Transfer of other pending proceeding involving minor child. §1841.
Transfer where no minor child involved in other proceedings. §1842.

§1830. Jurisdiction of family conciliation court

(a) When a controversy exists between spouses, or when a controversy relating to child custody or visitation exists between parents regardless of their marital status, and the controversy may, unless a reconciliation is achieved, result in dissolution of the marriage, nullity of the marriage, or legal separation of the parties, or in the disruption of the household, and there is a minor child of the spouses or parents or of either of them whose welfare might be affected thereby, the family conciliation court has jurisdiction as provided in this part over the controversy and over the parties to the controversy and over all persons having any relation to the controversy.

(b) The family conciliation court also has jurisdiction over the controversy, whether or not there is a minor child of the parties or either of them, where the controversy involves domestic violence. **Leg.H.** Enacted Stats 1992 ch 162 §10 (AB 2650), operative January 1, 1994.

§1831. Purpose of petition

Before the filing of a proceeding for determination of custody or visitation rights, for dissolution of marriage, for nullity of a voidable marriage, or for legal separation of the parties, either spouse or parent, or both, may file in the family conciliation court a petition invoking the jurisdiction of the court for the purpose of preserving the marriage by effecting a reconciliation between the parties, or for amicable settlement of the controversy between the spouses or parents, so as to avoid further litigation over the issue involved. **Leg.H.** Enacted Stats 1992 ch 162 §10 (AB 2650), operative January 1, 1994.

§1832. Caption of petition

The petition shall be captioned substantially as follows:

In the Superior Court of the State of California in and for the County of _____

Upon the petition of
_____
(Petitioner)
And concerning
_____ and
_____ , Respondents

Petition for Conciliation (Under the Family Conciliation Court Law)

To the Family Conciliation Court:

Leg.H. Enacted Stats 1992 ch 162 §10 (AB 2650), operative January 1, 1994.

§1833. Contents of petition

The petition shall:

(a) Allege that a controversy exists between the spouses or parents and request the aid of the court to effect a reconciliation or an amicable settlement of the controversy.

(b) State the name and age of each minor child whose welfare may be affected by the controversy.

(c) State the name and address of the petitioner or the names and addresses of the petitioners.

(d) If the petition is presented by one spouse or parent only, the name of the other spouse or parent as a respondent, and state the address of that spouse or parent.

(e) Name as a respondent any other person who has any relation to the controversy, and state the address of the person if known to the petitioner.

(f) If the petition arises out of an instance of domestic violence, so state generally and without specific allegations as to the incident.

(g) State any other information the court by rule requires. **Leg.H.** Enacted Stats 1992 ch 162 §10 (AB 2650), operative January 1, 1994.

§1834. Assistance in preparing and presenting petition; Coextensive jurisdiction in cases of domestic violence

(a) The clerk of the court shall provide, at the expense of the court, blank forms for petitions for filing pursuant to this part.

(b) The probation officers of the county and the attachés and employees of the family conciliation court shall assist a person in the preparation and presentation of a petition under this part if the person requests assistance.

(c) All public officers in each county shall refer to the family conciliation court all petitions and complaints made to them in respect to controversies within the jurisdiction of the family conciliation court.

(d) The jurisdiction of the family conciliation court in respect to controversies arising out of an instance of domestic violence is not exclusive but is coextensive with any other remedies either civil or criminal in nature that may be available. **Leg.H.** Enacted Stats 1992 ch 162 §10 (AB 2650), operative January 1, 1994. Amended Stats 2012 ch 470 §14 (AB 1529), effective January 1, 2013.

§1835. Fees

No fee shall be charged by any officer for filing the petition. **Leg.H.** Enacted Stats 1992 ch 162 §10 (AB 2650), operative January 1, 1994.

§1836. Notice of hearing; Citation

(a) The court shall fix a reasonable time and place for hearing on the petition. The court shall cause notice to be given to the respondents of the filing of the petition and of the time and place of the hearing that the court deems necessary.

(b) The court may, when it deems it necessary, issue a citation to a respondent requiring the respondent to appear at the time and place stated in the citation. The court may require the attendance of witnesses as in other civil cases. **Leg.H.** Enacted Stats 1992 ch 162 §10 (AB 2650), operative January 1, 1994.

§1837. Time and place of hearings

(a) Except as provided in subdivision (b), for the purpose of conducting hearings pursuant to this part, the family conciliation court may be convened at any time and place within the county, and the hearing may be had in chambers or otherwise.

(b) The time and place for hearing shall not be different from the time and place provided by law for the trial of civil actions if any party, before the hearing, objects to any different time or place. **Leg.H.** Enacted Stats 1992 ch 162 §10 (AB 2650), operative January 1, 1994.

§1838. Informal hearings; Aid of experts

(a) The hearing shall be conducted informally as a conference or a series of conferences to effect a reconciliation of the spouses or an amicable adjustment or settlement of the issues in controversy.

(b) To facilitate and promote the purposes of this part, the court may, with the consent of both parties to the proceeding, recommend or invoke the aid of medical or other specialists or scientific experts, or of the pastor or director of any religious denomination to which the parties may belong. Aid under this subdivision shall not be at the expense of the court unless the presiding judge specifically authorizes the aid, nor at the expense of the county unless the board of supervisors of the county specifically provides and authorizes the aid. **Leg.H.** Enacted Stats 1992 ch 162 §10 (AB 2650), operative January 1, 1994. Amended Stats 2012 ch 470 §15 (AB 1529), effective January 1, 2013.

§1839. Temporary orders; Reconciliation agreement

(a) At or after the hearing, the court may make orders in respect to the conduct of the spouses or parents and the subject matter of the controversy that the court deems necessary to preserve the marriage or to implement the reconciliation of the spouses. No such order shall be effective for more than 30 days from the hearing of the petition unless the parties mutually consent to a continuation of the time the order remains effective.

(b) A reconciliation agreement between the parties may be reduced to writing and, with the consent of the parties, a court order may be made requiring the parties to comply fully with the agreement.

(c) During the pendency of a proceeding under this part, the superior court may order a spouse or parent, as the case may be, to pay an amount necessary for the support and maintenance of the other spouse and for the support, maintenance, and education of the minor children, as the case may be. In determining the amount, the superior court may take into consideration the recommendations of a financial referee if one is available to the court. An order made pursuant to this subdivision shall not prejudice the rights of the parties or children with respect to any subsequent order that may be made. An order made pursuant to this subdivision may be modified or terminated at any time except as to an amount that accrued before the date of filing of the notice of motion or order to show cause to modify or terminate. **Leg.H.** Enacted Stats 1992 ch 162 §10 (AB 2650), operative January 1, 1994. Amended Stats 1993 ch 219 §102 (AB 1500); Stats 2014 ch 82 §22 (SB 1306), effective January 1, 2015.

§1840. Stay of right to file other proceeding; Effect of pendency of other proceeding

(a) During a period beginning upon the filing of the petition for conciliation and continuing until 30 days after the hearing of the petition for conciliation, neither spouse shall file a petition for dissolution of marriage, for nullity of a voidable marriage, or for legal separation of the parties.

(b) After the expiration of the period under subdivision (a), if the controversy between the spouses, or the parents, has not been terminated, either spouse may institute a proceeding for dissolution of marriage, for nullity of a voidable marriage, or for legal separation of the parties, or a proceeding to determine custody or visitation of the minor child or children.

(c) The pendency of a proceeding for dissolution of marriage, for nullity of marriage, or for legal separation of the parties, or a proceeding to determine custody or visitation of the minor child or children, does not operate as a bar to the instituting of proceedings for conciliation under this part. **Leg.H.** Enacted Stats 1992 ch 162 §10 (AB 2650), operative January 1, 1994.

§1841. Transfer of other pending proceeding involving minor child

If a petition for dissolution of marriage, for nullity of marriage, or for legal separation of the parties is filed, the case may be transferred at any time during the pendency of the proceeding to the family conciliation court for proceedings for reconciliation of the spouses or amicable settlement of issues in controversy in accordance with this part if both of the following appear to the court:

(a) There is a minor child of the spouses, or of either of them, whose welfare may be adversely affected by the dissolution of the marriage or the disruption of the household or a controversy involving child custody.

(b) There is some reasonable possibility of a reconciliation being effected. **Leg.H.** Enacted Stats 1992 ch 162 §10 (AB 2650), operative January 1, 1994.

§1842. Transfer where no minor child involved in other proceedings

(a) If an application is made to the family conciliation court for conciliation proceedings in respect to a controversy between spouses, or a contested proceeding for dissolution of marriage, for nullity of a voidable marriage, or for legal separation of the parties, but there is no minor child whose welfare may be affected by the results of the controversy, and it appears to the court that reconciliation of the spouses or amicable adjustment of the controversy can probably be achieved, and that the work of the court in cases involving children will not be seriously impeded by acceptance of the case, the court may accept and dispose of the case in the same manner as similar cases involving the welfare of children are disposed of.

(b) If the court accepts the case under subdivision (a), the court has the same jurisdiction over the controversy and the parties to the controversy and those having a relation to the controversy that it has under this part in similar cases involving the welfare of children. **Leg.H.** Enacted Stats 1992 ch 162 §10 (AB 2650), operative January 1, 1994.

PART 2
STATEWIDE COORDINATION OF FAMILY MEDIATION AND CONCILIATION SERVICES

Judicial Council duties. §1850.
Advisory committee. §1851.
Family Law Trust Fund. §1852.

§1850. Judicial Council duties

The Judicial Council shall do all of the following:

(a) Assist courts in implementing mediation and conciliation proceedings under this code.

(b) Establish and implement a uniform statistical reporting system relating to proceedings brought for dissolution of marriage, for nullity of marriage, or for legal separation of the parties, including, but not limited to, a custody disposition survey.

(c) Administer a program of grants to public and private agencies submitting proposals for research, study, and demonstration projects in the area of family law, including, but not limited to, all of the following:

(1) The development of conciliation and mediation and other newer dispute resolution techniques, particularly as they relate to child custody and to avoidance of litigation.

(2) The establishment of criteria to ensure that a child support order is adequate.

(3) The development of methods to ensure that a child support order is paid.

(4) The study of the feasibility and desirability of guidelines to assist judges in making custody decisions.

(d) Administer a program for the training of court personnel involved in family law proceedings, which shall be available to the court personnel and which shall be totally funded from funds specified in Section 1852. The training shall include, but not be limited to, the order of preference for custody of minor children and the meaning of the custody arrangements under Part 2 (commencing with Section 3020) of Division 8.

(e) Conduct research on the effectiveness of current family law for the purpose of shaping future public policy. **Leg.H.** Enacted Stats 1992 ch 162 §10 (AB 2650), operative January 1, 1994. Amended Stats 1993 ch 219 §102.5 (AB 1500); Stats 2012 ch 470 §16 (AB 1529), effective January 1, 2013.

§1851. Advisory committee

The Judicial Council shall establish an advisory committee of persons representing a broad spectrum of interest in and knowledge about family law. The committee shall recommend criteria for determining grant recipients pursuant to subdivision (c) of Section 1850, which shall include proposal evaluation guidelines and procedures for submission of the results to the Legislature, the Governor, and family law courts. In accordance with established criteria, the committee shall receive grant proposals and shall recommend the priority of submitted proposals. **Leg.H.** Enacted Stats 1992 ch 162 §10 (AB 2650), operative January 1, 1994.

§1852. Family Law Trust Fund

(a) There is in the State Treasury the Family Law Trust Fund.

(b) Moneys collected by the state pursuant to subdivision (c) of Section 103625 of the Health and Safety Code, Section 70674 of the Government Code, and grants, gifts, or devises made to the state from private sources to be used for the purposes of this part shall be deposited into the Family Law Trust Fund.

(c) Moneys deposited in the Family Law Trust Fund shall be placed in an interest bearing account. Any interest earned shall accrue to the fund and shall be disbursed pursuant to subdivision (d).

(d) Money deposited in the Family Law Trust Fund shall be disbursed for purposes specified in this part and for other family law related activities.

(e) Moneys deposited in the Family Law Trust Fund shall be administered by the Judicial Council. The Judicial Council may, with appropriate guidelines, delegate the administration of the fund to the Administrative Office of the Courts.

(f) Any moneys in the Family Law Trust Fund that are unencumbered at the end of the fiscal year are automatically appropriated to the Family Law Trust Fund of the following year.

(g) In order to defray the costs of collection of these funds, pursuant to this section, the local registrar, county clerk, or county recorder may retain a percentage of the funds collected, not to exceed 10 percent of the fee payable to the state pursuant to subdivision (c) of Section 103625 of the Health and Safety Code. **Leg.H.** Enacted Stats 1992 ch 162 §10 (AB 2650), operative January 1, 1994. Amended Stats 1996 ch 1023 §45 (SB 1497), effective September 29, 1996; Stats 1997 ch 850 §5 (AB 233); Stats 2005 ch 75 §45 (AB 145), effective July 19, 2005, operative January 1, 2006.

DIVISION 6
NULLITY, DISSOLUTION, AND LEGAL SEPARATION

Part 1. General Provisions.
Part 2. Judicial Determination of Void or Voidable Marriage.
Part 3. Dissolution of Marriage and Legal Separation.

PART 1
GENERAL PROVISIONS

Chapter 1. Application of Part.
Chapter 2. Jurisdiction.
Chapter 3. Procedural Provisions.
Chapter 3.5. Attorney's Fees and Costs.
Chapter 4. Protective and Restraining Orders.
Chapter 5. Notice to Insurance Carriers.
Chapter 6. Employee Pension Benefit Plan as Party.
Chapter 7. Restoration of Spouse's Former Name.
Chapter 8. Uniform Divorce Recognition Act.
Chapter 9. Disclosure of Assets and Liabilities.
Chapter 10. Relief From Judgment.

CHAPTER 1
APPLICATION OF PART

Application to dissolution, nullity, and legal separation proceedings. §2000.

§2000. Application to dissolution, nullity, and legal separation proceedings

This part applies to a proceeding for dissolution of marriage, for nullity of marriage, or for legal separation of the parties. **Leg.H.** Enacted Stats 1992 ch 162 §10 (AB 2650), operative January 1, 1994.

CHAPTER 2
JURISDICTION

Authority of court. §2010.
Jurisdiction over property of spouse served by publication. §2011.
Special appearance in opposition to order made during pendency of objection to jurisdiction. §2012.
Collaborative law process. §2013.

§2010. Authority of court

In a proceeding for dissolution of marriage, for nullity of marriage, or for legal separation of the parties, the court has jurisdiction to inquire into and render any judgment and make orders that are appropriate concerning the following:

(a) The status of the marriage, including any marriage under subdivision (c) of Section 308.

(b) The custody of minor children of the marriage.

(c) The support of children for whom support may be ordered, including children born after the filing of the initial petition or the final decree of dissolution.

(d) The support of either party.

(e) The settlement of the property rights of the parties.

(f) The award of attorney's fees and costs. **Leg.H.** Enacted Stats 1992 ch 162 §10 (AB 2650), operative January 1, 1994. Amended Stats 1993 ch 219 §103 (AB 1500); Stats 1994 ch 1269 §12.5 (AB 2208); Stats 2010 ch 397 §2 (AB 2700), effective January 1, 2011.

§2011. Jurisdiction over property of spouse served by publication

When service of summons on a spouse is made pursuant to Section 415.50 of the Code of Civil Procedure, the court, without the aid of attachment or the appointment of a receiver, shall have and may exercise the same jurisdiction over:

(a) The community real property of the spouse so served situated in this state as it has or may exercise over the community real property of a spouse who is personally served with process within this state.

(b) The quasi-community real property of the spouse so served situated in this state as it has or may exercise over the quasi-community real property of a spouse who is personally served with process within this state. **Leg.H.** Enacted Stats 1992 ch 162 §10 (AB 2650), operative January 1, 1994.

§2012. Special appearance in opposition to order made during pendency of objection to jurisdiction

(a) During the time a motion pursuant to Section 418.10 of the Code of Civil Procedure is pending, the respondent may appear in opposition to an order made during the pendency of the proceeding and the appearance shall not be deemed a general appearance by the respondent.

(b) As used in this section, a motion pursuant to Section 418.10 of the Code of Civil Procedure is pending from the time notice of motion is served and filed until the time within which to petition for a writ of mandate has expired or, if a petition is made, until the time final judgment in the mandate proceeding is entered. **Leg.H.** Enacted Stats 1992 ch 162 §10 (AB 2650), operative January 1, 1994.

§2013. Collaborative law process

(a) If a written agreement is entered into by the parties, the parties may utilize a collaborative law process to resolve any matter governed by this code over which the court is granted jurisdiction pursuant to Section 2000.

(b) "Collaborative law process" means the process in which the parties and any professionals engaged by the parties to assist them agree in writing to use their best efforts and to make a good faith attempt to resolve disputes related to the family law matters as referenced in subdivision (a) on an agreed basis without resorting to adversary judicial intervention. **Leg.H.** Added Stats 2006 ch 496 §2 (AB 402), effective January 1, 2007.

2006 Note: This act shall be known and may be cited as the Collaborative Family Law Act. Stats 2006 ch 496 (AB 402) §1.

CHAPTER 3
PROCEDURAL PROVISIONS

Responsive pleading. §2020.
Joinder of interested person and employee benefit plan as parties. §2021.
Evidence collected by eavesdropping. §2022.
Payment of obligation directly to creditor. §2023.
Notice concerning effect of judgment on will, insurance, and other matters. §2024.
Redaction of social security numbers from court documents. §2024.5.
Petition to seal pleadings as to information about financial assets and liabilities. §2024.6.
Notice of eligibility for reduced-cost coverage through California Health Benefit Exchange or no-cost coverage through Medi-Cal. §2024.7.
Appeal of bifurcated issue. §2025.
Effect of reconciliation of parties. §2026.

§2020. Responsive pleading

A responsive pleading, if any, shall be filed and a copy served on the petitioner within 30 days of the date of the service on the respondent of a copy of the petition and summons. **Leg.H.** Enacted Stats 1992 ch 162 §10 (AB 2650), operative January 1, 1994. Amended Stats 1998 ch 581 §4 (AB 2801).

§2021. Joinder of interested person and employee benefit plan as parties

(a) Subject to subdivision (b), the court may order that a person who claims an interest in the proceeding be joined as a party to the proceeding in accordance with rules adopted by the Judicial Council pursuant to Section 211.

(b) An employee benefit plan may be joined as a party only in accordance with Chapter 6 (commencing with Section 2060). **Leg.H.** Enacted Stats 1992 ch 162 §10 (AB 2650), operative January 1, 1994. Amended Stats 1996 ch 1061 §3 (SB 1033).

§2022. Evidence collected by eavesdropping

(a) Evidence collected by eavesdropping in violation of Chapter 1.5 (commencing with Section 630) of Title 15 of Part 1 of the Penal Code is inadmissible.

(b) If it appears that a violation described in subdivision (a) exists, the court may refer the matter to the proper authority for investigation and prosecution. **Leg.H.** Enacted Stats 1992 ch 162 §10 (AB 2650), operative January 1, 1994.

§2023. Payment of obligation directly to creditor

(a) On a determination that payment of an obligation of a party would benefit either party or a child for whom support may be ordered, the court may order one of the parties to pay the obligation, or a portion thereof, directly to the creditor.

(b) The creditor has no right to enforce the order made under this section, nor are the creditor's rights affected by the determination made under this section. **Leg.H.** Enacted Stats 1992 ch 162 §10 (AB 2650), operative January 1, 1994. Amended Stats 1993 ch 219 §104 (AB 1500).

§2024. Notice concerning effect of judgment on will, insurance, and other matters

(a) A petition for dissolution of marriage, nullity of marriage, or legal separation of the parties, or a joint petition for summary dissolution of marriage, shall contain the following notice:

"Dissolution or annulment of your marriage may automatically cancel your spouse's rights under your will, trust, retirement benefit plan, power of attorney, pay on death bank account, transfer on death vehicle registration, survivorship rights to any property owned in joint tenancy, and any other similar thing. It does not automatically cancel your spouse's rights as beneficiary of your life insurance policy. If these are not the results that you want, you must change your will, trust, account agreement, or other similar document to reflect your actual wishes.

Dissolution or annulment of your marriage may also automatically cancel your rights under your spouse's will, trust, retirement benefit plan, power of attorney, pay on death bank account, transfer on death vehicle registration, and survivorship rights to any property owned in joint tenancy, and any other similar thing. It does not automatically cancel your rights as beneficiary of your spouse's life insurance policy.

You should review these matters, as well as any credit cards, other credit accounts, insurance policies, retirement benefit plans, and credit reports to determine whether they should be changed or whether you should take any other actions in view of the dissolution or annulment of your marriage, or your legal separation. However, some changes may require the agreement of your spouse or a court order (see Part 3 (commencing with Section 231) of Division 2 of the Family Code)."

(b) A judgment for dissolution of marriage, for nullity of marriage, or for legal separation of the parties shall contain the following notice:

"Dissolution or annulment of your marriage may automatically cancel your spouse's rights under your will, trust, retirement benefit plan, power of attorney, pay on death bank account, transfer on death vehicle registration, survivorship rights to any property owned in joint tenancy, and any other similar thing. It does not automatically cancel your spouse's rights as beneficiary of your life insurance policy. If these are not the results that you want, you must change your will, trust, account agreement, or other similar document to reflect your actual wishes.

Dissolution or annulment of your marriage may also automatically cancel your rights under your spouse's will, trust, retirement benefit plan, power of attorney, pay on death bank account, transfer on death vehicle registration, survivorship rights to any property owned in joint tenancy, and any other similar thing. It does not automatically cancel your rights as beneficiary of your spouse's life insurance policy.

You should review these matters, as well as any credit cards, other credit accounts, insurance policies, retirement benefit plans, and credit reports to determine whether they should be changed or whether you should take any other actions in view of the dissolution or annulment of your marriage, or your legal separation." **Leg.H.** Enacted Stats 1992 ch 162 §10 (AB 2650), operative January 1, 1994. Amended Stats 1993 ch 219 §105 (AB 1500); Stats 2001 ch 417 §1 (AB 873).

§2024.5. Redaction of social security numbers from court documents

(a) Except as provided in subdivision (b), the petitioner or respondent may redact any social security number from any pleading, attachment, document, or other written material filed with the court pursuant to a petition for dissolution of marriage, nullity of marriage, or legal separation. The Judicial Council form used to file such a petition, or a response to such a petition, shall contain a notice that the parties may redact any social security numbers from those pleadings, attachments, documents, or other material filed with the court.

(b) An abstract of support judgment, the form required pursuant to subdivision (b) of Section 4014, or any similar form created for the purpose of collecting child or spousal support payments may not be redacted pursuant to subdivision (a). **Leg.H.** Added Stats 2004 ch 45 §2 (AB 782), effective June 7, 2004.

Prior Law: Former §2024.5, similar to present section, was added Stats 2003 ch 154 §1 and repealed Stats 2004 ch 45 §1, effective June 7, 2004.

Former Sections: Former Fam C §2024.5, similar to present section, was added Stats 2003 ch 154 §1 and repealed Stats 2004 ch 45 §1, effective June 7, 2004.

§2024.6. Petition to seal pleadings as to information about financial assets and liabilities

(a) Upon request by a party to a petition for dissolution of marriage, nullity of marriage, or legal separation, the court shall order a pleading that lists the parties' financial assets and liabilities and provides the location or identifying information about those assets and liabilities sealed. The request may be made by ex parte application. Nothing sealed pursuant to this section may be unsealed except upon petition to the court and good cause shown.

(b) Commencing not later than July 1, 2005, the Judicial Council form used to declare assets and liabilities of the parties in a proceeding for dissolution of marriage, nullity of marriage, or legal separation of the parties shall require the party filing the form to state whether the declaration contains identifying information on the assets and liabilities listed therein. If the party making the request uses a pleading other than the Judicial Council form, the pleading shall exhibit a notice on the front page, in bold capital letters, that the pleading lists and identifies financial information and is therefore subject to this section.

(c) For purposes of this section, "pleading" means a document that sets forth or declares the parties' assets and liabilities, income and expenses, a marital settlement agreement that lists and identifies the parties' assets and liabilities, or any document filed with the court incidental to the declaration or agreement that lists and identifies financial information.

(d) The party making the request to seal a pleading pursuant to subdivision (a) shall serve a copy of the pleading on the other party to the proceeding and file a proof of service with the request to seal the pleading.

(e) Nothing in this section precludes a party to a proceeding described in this section from using any document or information contained in a sealed pleading in any manner that is not otherwise prohibited by law. **Leg.H.** Added Stats 2004 ch 45 §3 (AB 782), effective June 7, 2004. Amended Stats 2005 ch 22 §61 (SB 1108), effective January 1, 2006.

§2024.7. Notice of eligibility for reduced-cost coverage through California Health Benefit Exchange or no-cost coverage through Medi-Cal

On and after January 1, 2014, upon the filing of a petition for dissolution of marriage, nullity of marriage, or legal separation, the court shall provide to the petitioner and the respondent a notice informing them that they may be eligible for reduced-cost coverage through the California Health Benefit Exchange established under Title 22 (commencing with Section 100500) of the Government Code or no-cost coverage through Medi-Cal. The notice shall include information on obtaining coverage pursuant to those programs, and shall be developed by the California Health Benefit Exchange. **Leg.H.** Added Stats 2012 ch 851 §1 (AB 792), effective January 1, 2013. Amended Stats 2019 ch 115 §14 (AB 1817), effective January 1, 2020.

§2025. Appeal of bifurcated issue

Notwithstanding any other provision of law, if the court has ordered an issue or issues bifurcated for separate trial or hearing in advance of the disposition of the entire case, a court of appeal may order an issue or issues transferred to it for hearing and decision when the court that heard the issue or issues certifies that the appeal is appropriate. Certification by the court shall be in accordance with rules promulgated by the Judicial Council. **Leg.H.** Enacted Stats 1992 ch 162 §10 (AB 2650), operative January 1, 1994.

§2026. Effect of reconciliation of parties

The reconciliation of the parties, whether conditional or unconditional, is an ameliorating factor to be considered by the court in considering a contempt of an existing court order. **Leg.H.** Enacted Stats 1992 ch 162 §10 (AB 2650), operative January 1, 1994.

CHAPTER 3.5
ATTORNEY'S FEES AND COSTS

Ordering party to pay to ensure other party's access to legal representation. §2030.
Application for temporary order making, augmenting, or modifying award. §2031.
Award to be just and reasonable. §2032.
Family law attorney's real property lien. §2033.
Denial or limitation of family law attorney's real property lien. §2034.

§2030. Ordering party to pay to ensure other party's access to legal representation

(a)(1) In a proceeding for dissolution of marriage, nullity of marriage, or legal separation of the parties, and in any proceeding subsequent to entry of a related judgment, the court shall ensure that each party has access to legal representation, including access early in the proceedings, to preserve each party's rights by ordering, if necessary based on the income and needs assessments, one party, except a governmental entity, to pay to the other party, or to the other party's attorney, whatever amount is reasonably necessary for attorney's fees and for the cost of maintaining or defending the proceeding during the pendency of the proceeding.

(2) When a request for attorney's fees and costs is made, the court shall make findings on whether an award of attorney's fees and costs under this section is appropriate, whether there is a disparity in access to funds to retain counsel, and whether one party is able to pay for legal representation of both parties. If the findings demonstrate disparity in access and ability to pay, the court shall make an order awarding attorney's fees and costs. A party who lacks the financial ability to hire an attorney may request, as an in pro per litigant, that the court order the other party, if that other party has the financial ability, to pay a reasonable amount to allow the unrepresented party to retain an attorney in a timely manner before proceedings in the matter go forward.

(b) Attorney's fees and costs within this section may be awarded for legal services rendered or costs incurred before or after the commencement of the proceeding.

(c) The court shall augment or modify the original award for attorney's fees and costs as may be reasonably necessary for the prosecution or defense of the proceeding, or any proceeding related thereto, including after any appeal has been concluded.

(d) Any order requiring a party who is not the spouse of another party to the proceeding to pay attorney's fees or costs shall be limited to an amount reasonably necessary to maintain or defend the action on the issues relating to that party.

(e) The Judicial Council shall, by January 1, 2012, adopt a statewide rule of court to implement this section and develop a form for the information that shall be submitted to the court to obtain an award of attorney's fees under this section. **Leg.H.** Added Stats 1993 ch 219 §106.1 (AB 1500). Amended Stats 2004 ch 472 §1 (AB 2148); Stats 2010 ch 352 §4 (AB 939), effective January 1, 2011.

Prior Law: Former §2030, similar to present §2040, was enacted Stats 1992 ch 162 §10, to become operative January 1, 1994, and repealed Stats 1993 ch 219 §106.

§2031. Application for temporary order making, augmenting, or modifying award

(a)(1) Except as provided in subdivision (b), during the pendency of a proceeding for dissolution of marriage, for nullity of marriage, for legal separation of the parties, or any proceeding subsequent to entry of a related judgment, an application for a temporary order making, augmenting, or modifying an award of attorney's fees, including a reasonable retainer to hire an attorney, or costs or both shall be made by motion on notice or by an order to show cause.

(2) The court shall rule on an application within 15 days of the hearing on the motion or order to show cause.

(b) An order described in subdivision (a) may be made without notice by an oral motion in open court at either of the following times:

(1) At the time of the hearing of the cause on the merits.

(2) At any time before entry of judgment against a party whose default has been entered pursuant to Section 585 or 586 of the Code of Civil Procedure. The court shall rule on any motion made pursuant to this subdivision within 15 days and prior to the entry of any judgment. **Leg.H.** Added Stats 1993 ch 219 §106.1 (AB 1500). Amended Stats 2004 ch 472 §2 (AB 2148).

Prior Law: Former §2031, similar to present §2041, was enacted Stats 1992 ch 162 §10, to become operative January 1, 1994, and repealed Stats 1993 ch 219 §106.

§2032. Award to be just and reasonable

(a) The court may make an award of attorney's fees and costs under Section 2030 or 2031 where the making of the award, and the amount of the award, are just and reasonable under the relative circumstances of the respective parties.

(b) In determining what is just and reasonable under the relative circumstances, the court shall take into consideration the need for the award to enable each party, to the extent practical, to have sufficient financial resources to present the party's case adequately, taking into consideration, to the extent relevant, the circumstances of the respective parties described in Section 4320. The fact that the party requesting an award of attorney's fees and costs has resources from which the party could pay the party's own attorney's fees and costs is not itself a bar to an order that the other party pay part or all of the fees and costs requested. Financial resources are only one factor for the court to consider in determining how to apportion the overall cost of the litigation equitably between the parties under their relative circumstances.

(c) The court may order payment of an award of attorney's fees and costs from any type of property, whether community or separate, principal or income.

(d) Either party may, at any time before the hearing of the cause on the merits, on noticed motion, request the court to make a finding that the case involves complex or substantial issues of fact or law related to property rights, visitation, custody, or support. Upon that finding, the court may in its discretion determine the appropriate, equitable allocation of attorney's fees, court costs, expert fees, and consultant fees between the parties. The court order may provide for the allocation of separate or community assets, security against these assets, and for payments from income or anticipated income of either party for the purpose described in this subdivision and for the benefit of one or both parties. Payments shall be authorized only on agreement of the parties or, in the absence thereof, by court order. The court may order that a referee be appointed pursuant to Section 639 of the Code of Civil Procedure to oversee the allocation of fees and costs. **Leg.H.** Added Stats 1993 ch 219 §106.1 (AB 1500). Amended Stats 2010 ch 352 §5 (AB 939), effective January 1, 2011.

§2033. Family law attorney's real property lien

(a) Either party may encumber the party's interest in community real property to pay reasonable attorney's fees in order to retain or maintain legal counsel in a proceeding for dissolution of marriage, for nullity of marriage, or for legal separation of the parties. This encumbrance shall be known as a "family law attorney's real property lien" and attaches only to the encumbering party's interest in the community real property.

(b) Notice of a family law attorney's real property lien shall be served either personally or on the other party's attorney of record at least 15 days before the encumbrance is recorded. This notice shall contain a declaration signed under penalty of perjury containing all of the following:

(1) A full description of the real property.

(2) The party's belief as to the fair market value of the property and documentation supporting that belief.

(3) Encumbrances on the property as of the date of the declaration.

(4) A list of community assets and liabilities and their estimated values as of the date of the declaration.

(5) The amount of the family law attorney's real property lien.

(c) The nonencumbering party may file an ex parte objection to the family law attorney's real property lien. The objection shall include a request to stay the recordation until further notice of the court and shall contain a copy of the notice received. The objection shall also include a declaration signed under penalty of perjury as to all of the following:

(1) Specific objections to the family law attorney's real property lien and to the specific items in the notice.

(2) The objector's belief as to the appropriate items or value and documentation supporting that belief.

(3) A declaration specifically stating why recordation of the encumbrance at this time would likely result in an unequal division of property or would otherwise be unjust under the circumstances of the case.

(d) Except as otherwise provided by this section, general procedural rules regarding ex parte motions apply.

(e) An attorney for whom a family law attorney's real property lien is obtained shall comply with Rule 3-300 of the Rules of Professional Conduct of the State Bar of California. **Leg.H.** Added Stats 1993 ch 219 §106.1 (AB 1500). Amended Stats 2019 ch 115 §15 (AB 1817), effective January 1, 2020.

§2034. Denial or limitation of family law attorney's real property lien

(a) On application of either party, the court may deny the family law attorney's real property lien described in Section 2033 based on a finding that the encumbrance would likely result in an unequal division of property because it would impair the encumbering party's ability to meet the party's fair share of the community obligations or would otherwise be unjust under the circumstances of the case. The court may also, for good cause, limit the amount of the family law attorney's real property lien. A limitation by the court is not to be construed as a determination of reasonable attorney's fees.

(b) On receiving an objection to the establishment of a family law attorney's real property lien, the court may, on its own motion, determine whether the case involves complex or substantial issues of fact or law related to property rights, visitation, custody, or support. If the court finds that the case involves one or more of these complex or substantial issues, the court may determine the appropriate, equitable allocation of fees and costs as provided in subdivision (d) of Section 2032.

(c) The court has jurisdiction to resolve any dispute arising from the existence of a family law attorney's real property lien. **Leg.H.** Added Stats 1993 ch 219 §106.1 (AB 1500). Amended Stats 2010 ch 352 §6 (AB 939), effective January 1, 2011; Stats 2019 ch 115 §16 (AB 1817), effective January 1, 2020.

§2035. [Section repealed 1993]

Leg.H. Enacted Stats 1992 ch 162 §10 (AB 2650), operative January 1, 1994. Repealed Stats 1993 ch 219 §106 (AB 1500). See Fam C §2045.

§2036. [Section repealed 1993]

Leg.H. Enacted Stats 1992 ch 162 §10 (AB 2650), operative January 1, 1994. Repealed Stats 1993 ch 219 §106 (AB 1500). See Fam C §6305.

§2036.5. [Section repealed 1993]

Leg.H. Enacted Stats 1992 ch 162 §10 (AB 2650), operative January 1, 1994. Repealed Stats 1993 ch 219 §106 (AB 1500). See Fam C §6340.

§2037. [Section repealed 1993]

Leg.H. Enacted Stats 1992 ch 162 §10 (AB 2650), operative January 1, 1994. Repealed Stats 1993 ch 219 §106 (AB 1500). See Fam C §§6224, 6302.

§2038. [Section repealed 1993]

Leg.H. Enacted Stats 1992 ch 162 §10 (AB 2650), operative January 1, 1994. Repealed Stats 1993 ch 219 §106 (AB 1500). See Fam C §6380.

§2039. [Section repealed 1993]

Leg.H. Enacted Stats 1992 ch 162 §10 (AB 2650), operative January 1, 1994. Repealed Stats 1993 ch 219 §106 (AB 1500). See Fam C §6382.

CHAPTER 4
PROTECTIVE AND RESTRAINING ORDERS

Article 1. Orders in Summons.
Article 2. Ex Parte Orders.
Article 3. Orders After Notice and Hearing.
Article 4. Orders Included in Judgment.

ARTICLE 1
Orders in Summons

Temporary restraining order in summons. §2040.
Rights, title, and interest of purchaser for value. §2041.

§2040. Temporary restraining order in summons

(a) In addition to the contents required by Section 412.20 of the Code of Civil Procedure, the summons shall contain a temporary restraining order:

(1) Restraining both parties from removing the minor child or children of the parties, if any, from the state, or from applying for a new or replacement passport for the minor child or children, without the prior written consent of the other party or an order of the court.

(2)(A) Restraining both parties from transferring, encumbering, hypothecating, concealing, or in any way disposing of, any property, real or personal, whether community, quasi-community, or separate, without the written consent of the other party or an order of the court, except in the usual course of business or for the necessities of life, and requiring each party to notify the other party of proposed extraordinary expenditures at least five business days before incurring those expenditures and to account to the court for all extraordinary expenditures made after service of the summons on that party.

(B) Notwithstanding subparagraph (A), the restraining order shall not preclude a party from using community property, quasi-community property, or the party's own separate property to pay reasonable attorney's fees and costs in order to retain legal counsel in the proceeding. A party who uses community property or quasi-community property to pay the party's attorney's retainer for fees and costs under this provision shall account to the community for the use of the property. A party who uses other property that is subsequently determined to be the separate property of the other party to pay the party's attorney's retainer for fees and costs under this provision shall account to the other party for the use of the property.

(3) Restraining both parties from cashing, borrowing against, canceling, transferring, disposing of, or changing the beneficiaries of insurance or other coverage, including life, health, automobile, and disability, held for the benefit of the parties and their child or children for whom support may be ordered.

(4) Restraining both parties from creating a nonprobate transfer or modifying a nonprobate transfer in a manner that affects the disposition of property subject to the transfer, without the written consent of the other party or an order of the court.

(b) This section does not restrain any of the following:
(1) Creation, modification, or revocation of a will.
(2) Revocation of a nonprobate transfer, including a revocable trust, pursuant to the instrument, provided that notice of the change is filed and served on the other party before the change takes effect.
(3) Elimination of a right of survivorship to property, provided that notice of the change is filed and served on the other party before the change takes effect.
(4) Creation of an unfunded revocable or irrevocable trust.
(5) Execution and filing of a disclaimer pursuant to Part 8 (commencing with Section 260) of Division 2 of the Probate Code.

(c) In all actions filed on and after January 1, 1995, the summons shall contain the following notice:

"WARNING: California law provides that, for purposes of division of property upon dissolution of marriage or legal separation, property acquired by the parties during marriage in joint form is presumed to be community property. If either party to this action should die before the jointly held community property is divided, the language of how title is held in the deed (i.e., joint tenancy, tenants in common, or community property) will be controlling and not the community property presumption. You should consult your attorney if you want the community property presumption to be written into the recorded title to the property."

(d) For the purposes of this section:
(1) "Nonprobate transfer" means an instrument, other than a will, that makes a transfer of property on death, including a revocable trust, pay on death account in a financial institution, Totten trust, transfer on death registration of personal property, revocable transfer on death deed, or other instrument of a type described in Section 5000 of the Probate Code.
(2) "Nonprobate transfer" does not include a provision for the transfer of property on death in an insurance policy or other coverage held for the benefit of the parties and their child or children for whom support may be ordered, to the extent that the provision is subject to paragraph (3) of subdivision (a).

(e) The restraining order included in the summons shall include descriptions of the notices required by paragraphs (2) and (3) of subdivision (b). **Leg.H.** Added Stats 1993 ch 219 §106.7 (AB 1500). Amended Stats 1994 ch 1269 §13 (AB 2208); Stats 1999 ch 118 §1 (SB 357); Stats 2000 ch 135 §57 (AB 2539); Stats 2001 ch 417 §2 (AB 873); Stats 2012 ch 276 §2 (SB 1206), effective January 1, 2013; Stats 2015 ch 293 §2 (AB 139), effective January 1, 2016; Stats 2019 ch 115 §17 (AB 1817), effective January 1, 2020.

Prior Law: Former §2040, similar to present Fam C §6381, was enacted Stats 1992 ch 162 §10, to become operative January 1, 1994, and repealed Stats 1993 ch 219 §106.

2012 Note: This act shall be known and may be cited as Keisuke's Law. Stats 2012 ch 276 (SB 1206) §1.

§2041. Rights, title, and interest of purchaser for value

Nothing in Section 2040 adversely affects the rights, title, and interest of a purchaser for value, encumbrancer for value, or lessee for value who is without actual knowledge of the restraining order. **Leg.H.** Added Stats 1993 ch 219 §106.7 (AB 1500).

Prior Law: Former §2041, similar to present §6383, was enacted Stats 1992 ch 162 §10, to become operative January 1, 1994, and repealed Stats 1993 ch 219 §106.

§2042. [Section repealed 1993]

Leg.H. Enacted Stats 1992 ch 162 §10 (AB 2650), operative January 1, 1994. Repealed Stats 1993 ch 219 §106 (AB 1500). See Fam C §6388.

§2043. [Section repealed 1993]

Leg.H. Enacted Stats 1992 ch 162 §10 (AB 2650), operative January 1, 1994. Repealed Stats 1993 ch 219 §106 (AB 1500). See Fam C §6226.

ARTICLE 2
Ex Parte Orders

Protective and restraining orders. §2045.

§2045. Protective and restraining orders

During the pendency of the proceeding, on application of a party in the manner provided by Part 4 (commencing with Section 240) of Division 2, the court may issue ex parte any of the following orders:

(a) An order restraining any person from transferring, encumbering, hypothecating, concealing, or in any way disposing of any property, real or personal, whether community, quasi-community, or separate, except in the usual course of business or for the necessities of life, and if the order is directed against a party, requiring that party to notify the other party of any proposed extraordinary expenditures and to account to the court for all extraordinary expenditures.

(b) A protective order, as defined in Section 6218, and any other order as provided in Article 1 (commencing with Section 6320) of Chapter 2 of Part 4 of Division 10. **Leg.H.** Added Stats 1993 ch 219 §106.7 (AB 1500).

Prior Law: Former §2045, relating to protective orders included in judgment, was enacted Stats 1992 ch 162 §10, to become operative January 1, 1994, and repealed Stats 1993 ch 219 §106.

ARTICLE 3
Orders After Notice and Hearing

Issuance of orders. §2047.

§2047. Issuance of orders

(a) After notice and a hearing, the court may issue a protective order, as defined in Section 6218, and any other restraining order as provided in Article 2 (commencing with Section 6340) of Chapter 2 of Part 4 of Division 10.

(b) The court may not issue a mutual protective order pursuant to subdivision (a) unless it meets the requirements of Section 6305. **Leg.H.** Added Stats 1993 ch 219 §106.7 (AB 1500). Amended Stats 1995 ch 246 §1 (SB 591).

ARTICLE 4
Orders Included in Judgment

Includable orders. §2049.

§2049. Includable orders

A judgment may include a protective order, as defined in Section 6218, and any other restraining order as provided in Article 3 (commencing with Section 6360) of Chapter 2 of Part 4 of Division 10. **Leg.H.** Added Stats 1993 ch 219 §106.7.

CHAPTER 5
NOTICE TO INSURANCE CARRIERS

Notice of pending proceeding. §2050.
Notice of entry and requirements of judgment. §2051.
Manner of giving notice. §2052.
Policyholder to furnish other party with name and address of insurer. §2053.

§2050. Notice of pending proceeding

Upon filing of the petition, or at any time during the proceeding, a party may transmit to, or the court may order transmittal to, a health, life, or disability insurance carrier or plan the following notice in substantially the following form:

"YOU ARE HEREBY NOTIFIED, PURSUANT TO A PENDING PROCEEDING, IN RE MARRIAGE OF ____, CASE NUMBER ____, FILED IN THE SUPERIOR COURT OF THE STATE OF CALIFORNIA, COUNTY OF ____, THAT OWNERSHIP OF, OR BENEFITS PAYABLE UNDER, A POLICY OF HEALTH, LIFE, OR DISABILITY INSURANCE WHICH YOU HAVE ISSUED TO ONE OF THE PARTIES TO THIS PROCEEDING, POLICY NO. ____, IS AT ISSUE OR MAY BE AT ISSUE IN THE PROCEEDING.

YOU ARE HEREBY INSTRUCTED TO MAINTAIN THE NAMED BENEFICIARIES OR COVERED DEPENDENTS UNDER THE POLICY, UNLESS THE TERMS OF THE POLICY OR OTHER PROVISIONS OF LAW REQUIRE OTHERWISE, OR UNTIL RECEIPT OF A COURT ORDER, JUDGMENT, OR STIPULATION BETWEEN THE PARTIES PROVIDING OTHER INSTRUCTIONS.

YOU ARE FURTHER INSTRUCTED TO SEND NOTICE TO THE NAMED BENEFICIARIES, COVERED DEPENDENTS, OR OTHER SPECIFIED PERSONS UPON CANCELLATION, LAPSE, OR CHANGE OF THE COVERAGE, OR CHANGE OF DESIGNATED BENEFICIARIES UNDER THE POLICY." **Leg.H.** Enacted Stats 1992 ch 162 §10 (AB 2650), operative January 1, 1994.

§2051. Notice of entry and requirements of judgment

Upon the entry of an order or judgment in the proceeding requiring a party to maintain existing health, life, or disability insurance coverage for a spouse or children or after an order or judgment in the proceeding requiring a party to purchase life or disability insurance and name the spouse or children as beneficiaries and upon receipt of the name, title, and address of the insurer, or the name of the plan's trustee, administrator, or agent for service of process, a party may transmit to, or the court may order transmittal to, the insurer or plan a copy of the order or judgment endorsed by the court, together with the following notice in substantially the following form:

"PURSUANT TO A PROCEEDING, IN RE MARRIAGE OF ____, CASE NUMBER ____, IN THE SUPERIOR COURT OF THE STATE OF CALIFORNIA, COUNTY OF ____, YOUR INSURED, ____, HAS BEEN ORDERED TO MAINTAIN THE EXISTING (HEALTH) (LIFE) (DISABILITY) INSURANCE COVERAGE, POLICY NO. ____, IN FORCE FOR THE NAMED BENEFICIARIES OR COVERED DEPENDENTS AS SPECIFIED IN THE ATTACHED ORDER OR JUDGMENT.

THE ATTACHED ORDER OR JUDGMENT REQUIRES YOU TO MAINTAIN THE NAMED BENEFICIARIES UNDER THE POLICY AS IRREVOCABLE BENEFICIARIES OR COVERED DEPENDENTS OF THE POLICY AND YOU MUST ADMINISTER THE COVERAGE ACCORDINGLY, UNTIL THE DATE SPECIFIED, IF ANY, IN THE ORDER OR JUDGMENT, OR UNTIL THE RECEIPT OF A COURT ORDER, JUDGMENT, OR STIPULATION PROVIDING OTHER INSTRUCTIONS.

YOU ARE FURTHER INSTRUCTED TO SEND NOTICE TO THE NAMED BENEFICIARIES, COVERED DEPENDENTS, OR OTHER SPECIFIED PERSONS UPON ANY CANCELLATION, LAPSE, OR CHANGE OF COVERAGE, OR CHANGE OF DESIGNATED BENEFICIARIES UNDER THIS POLICY." **Leg.H.** Enacted Stats 1992 ch 162 §10 (AB 2650), operative January 1, 1994.

§2052. Manner of giving notice

Notice pursuant to this chapter may be sent by first-class mail, postage prepaid, to the last known address of the covered dependents, named beneficiaries, or other specified persons who have requested receipt of notification. **Leg.H.** Enacted Stats 1992 ch 162 §10 (AB 2650), operative January 1, 1994.

§2053. Policyholder to furnish other party with name and address of insurer

The insured or policyholder who is a party to the proceeding shall furnish to the other party the name, title, and address of the insurer or the insurer's agent for service of process. **Leg.H.** Enacted Stats 1992 ch 162 §10 (AB 2650), operative January 1, 1994.

CHAPTER 6
EMPLOYEE PENSION BENEFIT PLAN AS PARTY

Article 1. Joinder of Plan.
Article 2. Proceedings After Joinder.

ARTICLE 1
Joinder of Plan

Application and order for joinder of plan. §2060.
Pleading of party requesting joinder. §2061.

Service upon trustee, administrator, or agent of plan. §2062.
Notice of appearance and responsive pleading by plan. §2063.
Plan need not pay filing fees. §2064.
Entry of default of plan. §2065.

§2060. Application and order for joinder of plan

(a) Upon written application by a party, the clerk shall enter an order joining as a party to the proceeding any employee benefit plan in which either party to the proceeding claims an interest that is or may be subject to disposition by the court.

(b) An order or judgment in the proceeding is not enforceable against an employee benefit plan unless the plan has been joined as a party to the proceeding. **Leg.H.** Enacted Stats 1992 ch 162 §10 (AB 2650), operative January 1, 1994. Amended Stats 1996 ch 1061 §4 (SB 1033).

§2061. Pleading of party requesting joinder

Upon entry of the order under Section 2060, the party requesting joinder shall file an appropriate pleading setting forth the party's claim against the plan and the nature of the relief sought. **Leg.H.** Enacted Stats 1992 ch 162 §10 (AB 2650), operative January 1, 1994.

§2062. Service upon trustee, administrator, or agent of plan

(a) The party requesting joinder shall serve all of the following upon the employee benefit plan:

(1) A copy of the pleading on joinder.

(2) A copy of the request for joinder and order of joinder.

(3) A copy of the summons (joinder).

(4) A blank copy of a notice of appearance in form and content approved by the Judicial Council.

(b) Service shall be made in the same manner as service of papers generally. Service of the summons upon a trustee or administrator of the plan in its capacity as trustee or administrator, or upon an agent designated by the plan for service of process in its capacity as agent, constitutes service upon the plan.

(c) To facilitate identification and service, the employee spouse shall furnish to the nonemployee spouse within 30 days after written request, as to each employee benefit plan covering the employee, the name of the plan, the name, title, address, and telephone number of the plan's trustee, administrator, or agent for service of process. If necessary, the employee shall obtain the information from the plan or plan sponsor. **Leg.H.** Enacted Stats 1992 ch 162 §10 (AB 2650), operative January 1, 1994. Amended Stats 1994 ch 1269 §15 (AB 2208).

§2063. Notice of appearance and responsive pleading by plan

(a) The employee benefit plan shall file and serve a copy of a notice of appearance upon the party requesting joinder within 30 days of the date of the service upon the plan of a copy of the joinder request and summons.

(b) The employee benefit plan may, but need not, file an appropriate responsive pleading with its notice of appearance. If the plan does not file a responsive pleading, all statements of fact and requests for relief contained in any pleading served on the plan are deemed to be controverted by the plan's notice of appearance. **Leg.H.** Enacted Stats 1992 ch 162 §10 (AB 2650), operative January 1, 1994. Amended Stats 1994 ch 1269 §16 (AB 2208).

§2064. Plan need not pay filing fees

Notwithstanding any contrary provision of law, the employee benefit plan is not required to pay any fee to the clerk of the court as a condition to filing the notice of appearance or any subsequent paper in the proceeding. **Leg.H.** Enacted Stats 1992 ch 162 §10 (AB 2650), operative January 1, 1994. Amended Stats 1994 ch 1269 §17 (AB 2208).

§2065. Entry of default of plan

If the employee benefit plan has been served and no notice of appearance, notice of motion to quash service of summons pursuant to Section 418.10 of the Code of Civil Procedure, or notice of the filing of a petition for writ of mandate as provided in that section, has been filed with the clerk of the court within the time specified in the summons or such further time as may be allowed, the clerk, upon written application of the party requesting joinder, shall enter the default of the employee benefit plan in accordance with Chapter 2 (commencing with Section 585) of Title 8 of Part 2 of the Code of Civil Procedure. **Leg.H.** Enacted Stats 1992 ch 162 §10 (AB 2650), operative January 1, 1994. Amended Stats 1994 ch 1269 §18 (AB 2208).

ARTICLE 2
Proceedings After Joinder

Provisions governing proceeding in which plan has been joined. §2070.
Notice to plan of proposed property settlement; Response by plan. §2071.
Appearance by plan at hearing. §2072.
Order affecting plan made at hearing not attended by plan. §2073.
Motion to set aside or modify order. §2074.

§2070. Provisions governing proceeding in which plan has been joined

(a) This article governs a proceeding in which an employee benefit plan has been joined as a party.

(b) To the extent not in conflict with this article and except as otherwise provided by rules adopted by the Judicial Council pursuant to Section 211, all provisions of law applicable to civil actions generally apply, regardless of nomenclature, to the portion of the proceeding as to which an employee benefit plan has been joined as a party if those provisions would otherwise apply to the proceeding without reference to this article. **Leg.H.** Enacted Stats 1992 ch 162 §10 (AB 2650), operative January 1, 1994. Amended Stats 1994 ch 1269 §19 (AB 2208).

§2071. Notice to plan of proposed property settlement; Response by plan

Either party or their representatives may notify the employee benefit plan of any proposed property settlement as it concerns the plan before any hearing at which the proposed property settlement will be a matter before the court. If so notified, the plan may stipulate to the proposed settlement or advise the representative that it will contest the proposed settlement. **Leg.H.** Enacted Stats 1992 ch 162 §10 (AB 2650), operative January 1, 1994. Amended Stats 1994 ch 1269 §20 (AB 2208).

§2072. Appearance by plan at hearing

The employee benefit plan is not required to, but may, appear at any hearing in the proceeding. For purposes of the Code of Civil Procedure, the plan shall be considered a party appearing at the trial with respect to any hearing at which the interest of the parties in the plan is an issue before the court. **Leg.H.** Enacted Stats 1992 ch 162 §10 (AB 2650), operative January 1, 1994. Amended Stats 1994 ch 1269 §21 (AB 2208).

§2073. Order affecting plan made at hearing not attended by plan

(a) Subject to subdivisions (b) and (c), the provisions of an order entered by stipulation of the parties or entered at or as a result of a hearing not attended by the employee benefit plan (whether or not the plan received notice of the hearing) which affect the plan or which affect any interest either the petitioner or respondent may have or claim under the plan, shall be stayed until 30 days after the order has been served upon the plan.

(b) The plan may waive all or any portion of the 30-day period under subdivision (a).

(c) If within the 30-day period, the plan files in the proceeding a motion to set aside or modify those provisions of the order affecting it, those provisions shall be stayed until the court has resolved the motion.

(d) The duration of the stay described in subdivision (a), and the time period for filing the motion to set aside or modify provisions of the order, shall be extended to 60 days if the plan files with the court and serves on all affected parties a request for extension within the 30-day period.

(e) Either spousal party may seek an order staying any other provisions of the order and associated orders or judgments related to or affected by the provisions to which the plan has objected, until the court has resolved the motion, in order to protect the right of the party to seek relief under subdivision (c) of Section 2074. **Leg.H.** Enacted Stats 1992 ch 162 §10 (AB 2650), operative January 1, 1994. Amended Stats 1994 ch 1269 §22 (AB 2208).

§2074. Motion to set aside or modify order

(a) At any hearing on a motion to set aside or modify an order pursuant to Section 2073, any party may present further evidence on any issue relating to the rights of the parties under the employee benefit plan or the extent of the parties' community or quasi-community property interest in the plan, except where the parties have agreed in writing to the contrary.

(b) Any statement of decision issued by the court with respect to the order which is the subject of the motion shall take account of the evidence referred to in subdivision (a).

(c) If the provisions of the order affecting the employee benefit plan are modified or set aside, the court, on motion by either party, may set aside or modify other provisions of the order and associated orders or judgments related to or affected by the provisions affecting the plan. **Leg.H.** Enacted Stats 1992 ch 162 §10 (AB 2650), operative January 1, 1994. Amended Stats 1994 ch 1269 §23 (AB 2208).

CHAPTER 7
RESTORATION OF SPOUSE'S FORMER NAME

Restoration of party's birth name or former name. §2080.
Restoration not to be denied for any reason other than fraud. §2081.
Common law right to change name not limited. §2082.

§2080. Restoration of party's birth name or former name

In a proceeding for dissolution of marriage or for nullity of marriage, but not in a proceeding for legal separation of the parties, the court, upon the request of a party, shall restore the birth name or former name of that party, regardless of whether [1] a request for restoration of the name was included in the petition. **Leg.H.** Enacted Stats 1992 ch 162 §10 (AB 2650), operative January 1, 1994. Amended Stats 1996 ch 1061 §5 (SB 1033); Stats 2024 ch 780 §2 (SB 1150), effective January 1, 2025.

§2080. 2024 Deletes. [1] or not

§2081. Restoration not to be denied for any reason other than fraud

The restoration of a former name or birth name requested under Section 2080 shall not be denied [1] on the basis that the party has custody of a minor child who bears a different [2] **name,** or [3] for any other reason [4] **except** fraud. **Leg.H.** Enacted Stats 1992 ch 162 §10 (AB 2650), operative January 1, 1994. Amended Stats 1996 ch 1061 §6 (SB 1033); Stats 2024 ch 780 §3 (SB 1150), effective January 1, 2025.

§2081. 2024 Deletes. [1] (a) [2] name [3] (b) [4] other than

§2082. Common law right to change name not limited

[1] **This code does not** abrogate the common law right of any person to change one's name. **Leg.H.** Enacted Stats 1992 ch 162 §10 (AB 2650), operative January 1, 1994. Amended Stats 2024 ch 780 §4 (SB 1150), effective January 1, 2025.

§2082. 2024 Deletes. [1] Nothing in this code shall be construed to

CHAPTER 8
UNIFORM DIVORCE RECOGNITION ACT

Short title. §2090.
Effect of foreign divorce of parties domiciled in this state. §2091.
Prima facie evidence of domicile. §2092.
Full faith and credit limitation. §2093.

§2090. Short title

This chapter may be cited as the Uniform Divorce Recognition Act. **Leg.H.** Enacted Stats 1992 ch 162 §10 (AB 2650), operative January 1, 1994.

§2091. Effect of foreign divorce of parties domiciled in this state

A divorce obtained in another jurisdiction shall be of no force or effect in this state if both parties to the marriage were domiciled in this state at the time the proceeding for the divorce was commenced. **Leg.H.** Enacted Stats 1992 ch 162 §10 (AB 2650), operative January 1, 1994.

§2092. Prima facie evidence of domicile

Proof that a person hereafter obtaining a divorce from the bonds of matrimony in another jurisdiction was (a) domiciled in this state within 12 months before the commencement of the proceeding therefor, and resumed residence in this state within 18 months after the date of the person's departure therefrom, or (b) at all times after the person's departure from this state and until the person's return maintained a place of residence within this state, shall be prima facie evidence that the person was domiciled in this state when the divorce proceeding was commenced. **Leg.H.** Enacted Stats 1992 ch 162 §10 (AB 2650), operative January 1, 1994.

§2093. Full faith and credit limitation

The application of this chapter is limited by the requirement of the Constitution of the United States that full faith and credit shall be given in each state to the public acts, records, and judicial proceedings of every other state. **Leg.H.** Enacted Stats 1992 ch 162 §10 (AB 2650), operative January 1, 1994.

CHAPTER 9
DISCLOSURE OF ASSETS AND LIABILITIES

Legislative findings and declarations. §2100.
Definitions. §2101.
Fiduciary duties. §2102.
Service of preliminary and final disclosure declarations. §2103.
Preliminary declaration of disclosure; Income and expense declaration; Manner of service. §2104.
Final disclosure declaration; Income and expense declaration. §2105.
Execution and filing of final declaration. §2106.
Remedies for noncompliance; Setting aside judgment; Waiver for good cause. §2107.
Court's authority to liquidate assets. §2108.
Disclosure declarations required for summary dissolution. §2109.
Disclosure declarations required in default judgment. §2110.
Effect of disclosure on attorney work product privilege or power to issue protective orders. §2111.
Judicial Council forms. §2112.
Application of chapter. §2113.

§2100. Legislative findings and declarations

The Legislature finds and declares the following:

(a) It is the policy of the State of California (1) to marshal, preserve, and protect community and quasi-community assets and liabilities that exist at the date of separation so as to avoid dissipation of the community estate before distribution, (2) to ensure fair and sufficient child and spousal support awards, and (3) to achieve a division of community and quasi-community assets and liabilities on the dissolution or nullity of marriage or legal separation of the parties as provided under California law.

(b) Sound public policy further favors the reduction of the adversarial nature of marital dissolution and the attendant costs by fostering full disclosure and cooperative discovery.

(c) In order to promote this public policy, a full and accurate disclosure of all assets and liabilities in which one or both parties have or may have an interest must be made in the early stages of a proceeding for dissolution of marriage or legal separation of the parties, regardless of the characterization as community or separate, together with a disclosure of all income and expenses of the parties. Moreover, each party has a continuing duty to immediately, fully, and accurately update and augment that disclosure to the extent there have been any material changes so that at the time the parties enter into an agreement for the resolution of any of these issues, or at the time of trial on these issues, each party will have a full and complete knowledge of the relevant underlying facts. **Leg.H.** Added Stats 1993 ch 219 §107 (AB 1500). Amended Stats 1993 ch 1101 §3 (AB 1469), effective October 11, 1993, operative January 1, 1994; Stats 2001 ch 703 §2 (AB 583).

2001 Note: This act shall apply to any judgment that becomes final on or after January 1, 2002. Stats 2001 ch 703 §8.

§2101. Definitions

Unless the provision or context otherwise requires, the following definitions apply to this chapter:

(a) "Asset" includes, but is not limited to, any real or personal property of any nature, whether tangible or intangible, and whether currently existing or contingent.

(b) "Default judgment" does not include a stipulated judgment or any judgment pursuant to a marital settlement agreement.

(c) "Earnings and accumulations" includes income from whatever source derived, as provided in Section 4058.

(d) "Expenses" includes, but is not limited to, all personal living expenses, but does not include business related expenses.

(e) "Income and expense declaration" includes the Income and Expense Declaration forms approved for use by the Judicial Council, and any other financial statement that is approved for use by the Judicial Council in lieu of the Income and Expense Declaration, if the financial statement form satisfies all other applicable criteria.

(f) "Liability" includes, but is not limited to, any debt or obligation, whether currently existing or contingent. **Leg.H.** Added Stats 1993 ch 219 §107 (AB 1500). Amended Stats 1993 ch 1101 §4 (AB 1469), effective October 11, 1993, operative January 1, 1994; Stats 1998 ch 581 §5 (AB 2801).

§2102. Fiduciary duties

(a) From the date of separation to the date of the distribution of the community or quasi-community asset or liability in question, each party is subject to the standards provided in Section 721, as to all activities that affect the assets and liabilities of the other party, including, but not limited to, the following activities:

(1) The accurate and complete disclosure of all assets and liabilities in which the party has or may have an interest or obligation and all current earnings, accumulations, and expenses, including an immediate, full, and accurate update or augmentation to the extent there have been material changes.

(2) The accurate and complete written disclosure of any investment opportunity, business opportunity, or other income-producing opportunity that presents itself after the date of separation, but that results from any investment, significant business activity outside the ordinary course of business, or other income-producing opportunity of either spouse from the date of marriage to the date of separation, inclusive. The written disclosure shall be made in sufficient time for the other spouse to make an informed decision as to whether the spouse desires to participate in the investment opportunity, business, or other potential income-producing opportunity, and for the court to resolve any dispute regarding the right of the other spouse to participate in the opportunity. In the event of nondisclosure of an investment opportunity, the division of any gain resulting from that opportunity is governed by the standard provided in Section 2556.

(3) The operation or management of a business or an interest in a business in which the community may have an interest.

(b) From the date that a valid, enforceable, and binding resolution of the disposition of the asset or liability in question is reached, until the asset or liability has actually been distributed, each party is subject to the standards provided in Section 721 as to all activities that affect the assets or liabilities of the other party. Once a particular asset or liability has been distributed, the duties and standards set forth in Section 721 shall end as to that asset or liability.

(c) From the date of separation to the date of a valid, enforceable, and binding resolution of all issues relating to child or spousal support and professional fees, each party is subject to the standards provided in Section 721 as to all issues relating to the support and fees, including immediate, full, and accurate disclosure of all material facts and information regarding the income or expenses of the party. **Leg.H.** Added Stats 1993 ch 219 §107 (AB 1500). Amended Stats 1993 ch 1101 §5 (AB 1469), effective October 11, 1993, operative January 1, 1994; Stats 2001 ch 703 §3 (AB 583); Stats 2019 ch 115 §18 (AB 1817), effective January 1, 2020.

2001 Note: This act shall apply to any judgment that becomes final on or after January 1, 2002. Stats 2001 ch 703 §8.

§2103. Service of preliminary and final disclosure declarations

In order to provide full and accurate disclosure of all assets and liabilities in which one or both parties may have an interest, each party to a proceeding for dissolution of the marriage or legal separation of the parties shall serve on the other party a preliminary declaration of disclosure under Section 2104, unless service of the preliminary declaration of disclosure is waived as provided in Section 2107 or is not required pursuant to Section 2110, and a final declaration of disclosure under Section 2105, unless service of the final declaration of disclosure is waived pursuant to Section 2105, 2107, or 2110, and shall file proof of service of each with the court. **Leg.H.** Added Stats 1993 ch 219 §107 (AB 1500). Amended Stats 1998 ch 581 §6 (AB 2801); Stats 2015 ch 46 §1 (SB 340), effective January 1, 2016; Stats 2016 ch 474 §7 (AB 2882), effective January 1, 2017.

§2104. Preliminary declaration of disclosure; Income and expense declaration; Manner of service

(a) Except by court order for good cause, as provided in Section 2107, or when service of the preliminary declaration of disclosure is not required pursuant to Section 2110, in the time period set forth in subdivision (f), each party shall serve on the other party a preliminary declaration of disclosure, executed under penalty of perjury on a form prescribed by the Judicial Council. The commission of perjury on the preliminary declaration of disclosure may be grounds for setting aside the judgment, or any part or parts thereof, pursuant to Chapter 10 (commencing with Section 2120), in addition to any and all other remedies, civil or criminal, that otherwise are available under law for the commission of perjury. The preliminary declaration of disclosure shall include all tax returns filed by the declarant within the two years prior to the date that the party served the declaration.

(b) The preliminary declaration of disclosure shall not be filed with the court, except on court order. However, the parties shall file proof of service of the preliminary declaration of disclosure with the court.

(c) The preliminary declaration of disclosure shall set forth with sufficient particularity, that a person of reasonable and ordinary intelligence can ascertain, all of the following:

(1) The identity of all assets in which the declarant has or may have an interest and all liabilities for which the declarant is or may be liable, regardless of the characterization of the asset or liability as community, quasi-community, or separate.

(2) The declarant's percentage of ownership in each asset and percentage of obligation for each liability when property is not solely owned by one or both of the parties. The preliminary declaration may also set forth the declarant's characterization of each asset or liability.

(d) A declarant may amend the preliminary declaration of disclosure without leave of the court. Proof of service of an amendment shall be filed with the court.

(e) Along with the preliminary declaration of disclosure, each party shall provide the other party with a completed income and expense declaration unless an income and expense declaration has already been provided and is current and valid.

(f) The petitioner shall serve the other party with the preliminary declaration of disclosure either concurrently with the petition for dissolution or legal separation, or within 60 days of filing the petition. When a petitioner serves the summons and petition by publication or posting pursuant to court order and the respondent files a response prior to a default judgment being entered, the petitioner shall serve the other party with the preliminary declaration of disclosure within 30 days of the response being filed. The respondent shall serve the other party with the preliminary declaration of disclosure either concurrently with the response to the petition, or within 60 days of filing the response. The time periods specified in this subdivision may be extended by written agreement of the parties or by court order. **Leg.H.** Added Stats 1993 ch 219 §107 (AB 1500). Amended Stats 1993 ch 1101 §6 (AB 1469), effective October 11, 1993, operative January 1, 1994; Stats 1998 ch 581 §7 (AB 2801); Stats 2009 ch 110 §1 (AB 459), effective January 1, 2010; Stats 2012 ch 107 §1 (AB 1406), effective January 1, 2013; Stats 2015 ch 46 §2 (SB 340), effective January 1, 2016, ch 416 §1.5 (AB 1519), effective January 1, 2016; Stats 2019 ch 115 §19 (AB 1817), effective January 1, 2020.

§2105. Final disclosure declaration; Income and expense declaration

(a) Except by court order for good cause, before or at the time the parties enter into an agreement for the resolution of property or support issues other than pendente lite support, or, if the case goes to trial, no later than 45 days before the first assigned trial date, each party, or the attorney for the party in this matter, shall serve on the other party a final declaration of disclosure and a current income and expense declaration, executed under penalty of perjury on a form prescribed by the Judicial Council, unless the parties mutually waive the final declaration of disclosure. The commission of perjury on the final declaration of disclosure by a party may be grounds for setting aside the judgment, or any part or parts thereof, pursuant to Chapter 10 (commencing with Section 2120), in addition to any and all other remedies, civil or criminal, that otherwise are available under law for the commission of perjury.

(b) The final declaration of disclosure shall include all of the following information:

(1) All material facts and information regarding the characterization of all assets and liabilities.

(2) All material facts and information regarding the valuation of all assets that are contended to be community property or in which it is contended the community has an interest.

(3) All material facts and information regarding the amounts of all obligations that are contended to be community obligations or for which it is contended the community has liability.

(4) All material facts and information regarding the earnings, accumulations, and expenses of each party that have been set forth in the income and expense declaration.

(c) In making an order setting aside a judgment for failure to comply with this section, the court may limit the set aside to those portions of the judgment materially affected by the nondisclosure.

(d) The parties may stipulate to a mutual waiver of the requirements of subdivision (a) concerning the final declaration of disclosure, by execution of a waiver under penalty of perjury entered into in open court or by separate stipulation. The waiver shall include all of the following representations:

(1) Both parties have complied with Section 2104 and the preliminary declarations of disclosure have been completed and exchanged.

(2) Both parties have completed and exchanged a current income and expense declaration, that includes all material facts and information regarding that party's earnings, accumulations, and expenses.

(3) Both parties have fully complied with Section 2102 and have fully augmented the preliminary declarations of disclosure, including disclosure of all material facts and information regarding the characterization of all assets and liabilities, the valuation of all assets that are contended to be community property or in which it is contended the community has an interest, and the amounts of all obligations that are contended to be community obligations or for which it is contended the community has liability.

(4) The waiver is knowingly, intelligently, and voluntarily entered into by each of the parties.

(5) Each party understands that this waiver does not limit the legal disclosure obligations of the parties, but rather is a statement under penalty of perjury that those obligations have been fulfilled. Each party further understands that noncompliance with those obligations will result in the court setting aside the judgment. **Leg.H.** Added Stats 1993 ch 219 §107 (AB 1500). Amended Stats 1993 ch 1101 §7 (AB 1469), effective October 11, 1993, operative January 1, 1994; Stats 1995 ch 233 §1 (AB 806); Stats 1996 ch 1061 §7 (SB 1033); Stats 1998 ch 581 §8 (AB 2801); Stats 2001 ch 703 §4 (AB 583).

2001 Note: This act shall apply to any judgment that becomes final on or after January 1, 2002. Stats 2001 ch 703 §8.

§2106. Execution and filing of final declaration

Except as provided in subdivision (d) of Section 2105, Section 2110, or absent good cause as provided in Section 2107, judgment shall not be entered with respect to the parties' property rights without each party, or the attorney for that party in this matter, having executed and served a copy of the final declaration of disclosure and current income and expense declaration. Each party, or the party's attorney, shall execute and file with the court a declaration signed under penalty of perjury stating that service of the final declaration of disclosure and current income and expense declaration was made on the other party or that service of the final declaration of disclosure has been waived pursuant to subdivision (d) of Section 2105 or in Section 2110. **Leg.H.** Added Stats 1993 ch 219 §107 (AB 1500). Amended Stats 1993 ch 1101 §8 (AB 1469), effective October 11, 1993, operative January 1, 1994; Stats 1995 ch 233 §2 (AB 806); Stats 1996 ch 1061 §8 (SB 1033); Stats 1998 ch 581 §9 (AB 2801); Stats 2001 ch 703 §5 (AB 583); Stats 2002 ch 1008 §15 (AB 3028); Stats 2009 ch 110 §2 (AB 459), effective January 1, 2010; Stats 2019 ch 115 §20 (AB 1817), effective January 1, 2020.

§2107. Remedies for noncompliance; Setting aside judgment; Waiver for good cause

(a) If one party fails to serve on the other party a preliminary declaration of disclosure under Section 2104, unless that party is not required to serve a preliminary declaration of disclosure pursuant to Section 2110, or a final declaration of disclosure under Section 2105, or fails to provide the information required in the respective declarations with sufficient particularity, and if the other party has served the respective declaration of disclosure on the noncomplying party, the complying party may, within a reasonable time, request preparation of the appropriate declaration of disclosure or further particularity.

(b) If the noncomplying party fails to comply with a request under subdivision (a), the complying party may do one or more of the following:

(1) File a motion to compel a further response.

(2) File a motion for an order preventing the noncomplying party from presenting evidence on issues that should have been covered in the declaration of disclosure.

(3) File a motion showing good cause for the court to grant the complying party's voluntary waiver of receipt of the noncomplying party's preliminary declaration of disclosure pursuant to Section 2104 or final declaration of disclosure pursuant to Section 2105. The voluntary waiver does not affect the rights enumerated in subdivision (d).

(c) If a party fails to comply with any provision of this chapter, the court shall, in addition to any other remedy provided by law, impose money sanctions against the noncomplying party. Sanctions shall be in an amount sufficient to deter repetition of the conduct or comparable conduct, and shall include reasonable attorney's fees, costs incurred, or both, unless the court finds that the noncomplying party acted with substantial justification or that other circumstances make the imposition of the sanction unjust.

(d) Except as otherwise provided in this subdivision, if a court enters a judgment when the parties have failed to comply with all disclosure requirements of this chapter, the court shall set aside the judgment. The failure to comply with the disclosure requirements does not constitute harmless error. If the court granted the complying party's voluntary waiver of receipt of the noncomplying party's preliminary declaration of disclosure pursuant to paragraph (3) of subdivision (b), the court shall set aside the judgment only at the request of the complying party, unless the motion to set aside the judgment is based on one of the following:

(1) Actual fraud if the defrauded party was kept in ignorance or in some other manner was fraudulently prevented from fully participating in the proceeding.

(2) Perjury, as defined in Section 118 of the Penal Code, in the preliminary or final declaration of disclosure, in the waiver of the final declaration of disclosure, or in the current income and expense statement.

(e) Upon the motion to set aside judgment, the court may order the parties to provide the preliminary and final declarations of disclosure that were exchanged between them. Absent a court order to the contrary, the disclosure declarations shall not be filed with the court and shall be returned to the parties. **Leg.H.** Added Stats 1993 ch 219 §107 (AB 1500). Amended Stats 1993 ch 1101 §9 (AB 1469), effective October 11, 1993, operative January 1, 1994; Stats 2001 ch 703 §6 (AB 583); Stats 2009 ch 110 §3 (AB 459), effective January 1, 2010; Stats 2015 ch 46 §3 (SB 340), effective January 1, 2016.

2001 Note: This act shall apply to any judgment that becomes final on or after January 1, 2002. Stats 2001 ch 703 §8.

§2108. Court's authority to liquidate assets

At any time during the proceeding, the court has the authority, on application of a party and for good cause, to order the liquidation of community or quasi-community assets so as to avoid unreasonable market or investment risks, given the relative nature, scope, and extent of the community estate. However, in no event shall the court grant the application unless, as provided in this chapter, the appropriate declaration of disclosure has been served by the moving party. **Leg.H.** Added Stats 1993 ch 219 §107 (AB 1500).

§2109. Disclosure declarations required for summary dissolution

The provisions of this chapter requiring a final declaration of disclosure do not apply to a summary dissolution of marriage, but a preliminary declaration of disclosure is required. **Leg.H.** Added Stats 1993 ch 1101 §11 (AB 1469), effective October 11, 1993, operative January 1, 1994.

§2110. Disclosure declarations required in default judgment

In the case of a default judgment, the petitioner may waive the final declaration of disclosure requirements provided in this chapter, and shall not be required to serve a final declaration of disclosure on the respondent nor receive a final declaration of disclosure from the respondent. However, a preliminary declaration of disclosure by the petitioner is required unless the petitioner served the summons and petition by publication or posting pursuant to court order and the respondent has defaulted. **Leg.H.** Added Stats 1993 ch 1101 §12 (AB 1469), effective October 11, 1993, operative January 1, 1994. Amended Stats 1994 ch 146 §41 (AB 3601); Stats 1998 ch 581 §10 (AB 2801); Stats 2015 ch 46 §4 (SB 340), effective January 1, 2016.

§2111. Effect of disclosure on attorney work product privilege or power to issue protective orders

A disclosure required by this chapter does not abrogate the attorney work product privilege or impede the power of the court to issue protective orders. **Leg.H.** Added Stats 1993 ch 1101 §13 (AB 1469), effective October 11, 1993, operative January 1, 1994.

§2112. Judicial Council forms

The Judicial Council shall adopt appropriate forms and modify existing forms to effectuate the purposes of this chapter. **Leg.H.** Added Stats 1993 ch 1101 §14 (AB 1469), effective October 11, 1993, operative January 1, 1994.

§2113. Application of chapter

This chapter applies to any proceeding commenced on or after January 1, 1993. **Leg.H.** Added Stats 1993 ch 219 §107 (AB 1500) as §2109. Amended and renumbered by Stats 1993 ch 1101 §10 (AB 1469), effective October 11, 1993, operative January 1, 1994.

CHAPTER 10
RELIEF FROM JUDGMENT

Legislative findings and declarations. §2120.
Relief of spouse from adjudication of support or division of property. §2121.
Grounds and time limits for motion to set aside judgment. §2122.
Setting aside judgment. §2123.
Negligence of attorney. §2124.
Scope of relief. §2125.
Date of valuation. §2126.
Statement of decision. §2127.
Effect on other law. §2128.
Application of chapter. §2129.

§2120. Legislative findings and declarations

The Legislature finds and declares the following:

(a) The State of California has a strong policy of ensuring the division of community and quasi-community property in the dissolution of a marriage as set forth in Division 7 (commencing with Section 2500), and of providing for fair and sufficient child and spousal support awards. These policy goals can only be implemented with full disclosure of community, quasi-community, and separate assets, liabilities, income, and expenses, as provided in Chapter 9 (commencing with Section 2100), and decisions freely and knowingly made.

(b) It occasionally happens that the division of property or the award of support, whether made as a result of agreement or trial, is inequitable when made due to the nondisclosure or other misconduct of one of the parties.

(c) The public policy of assuring finality of judgments must be balanced against the public interest in ensuring proper division of marital property, in ensuring sufficient support awards, and in deterring misconduct.

(d) The law governing the circumstances under which a judgment can be set aside, after the time for relief under Section 473 of the Code of Civil Procedure has passed, has been the subject of considerable confusion which has led to increased litigation and unpredictable and inconsistent decisions at the trial and appellate levels. **Leg.H.** Added Stats 1993 ch 219 §108 (AB 1500).

§2121. Relief of spouse from adjudication of support or division of property

(a) In proceedings for dissolution of marriage, for nullity of marriage, or for legal separation of the parties, the court may, on any terms that may be just, relieve a spouse from a judgment, or any part or parts thereof, adjudicating support or division of property, after the six-month time limit of Section 473 of the Code of Civil Procedure has run, based on the grounds, and within the time limits, provided in this chapter.

(b) In all proceedings under this chapter, before granting relief, the court shall find that the facts alleged as the grounds for relief materially affected the original outcome and that the moving party would materially benefit from the granting of the relief. **Leg.H.** Added Stats 1993 ch 219 §108 (AB 1500).

§2122. Grounds and time limits for motion to set aside judgment

The grounds and time limits for a motion to set aside a judgment, or any part or parts thereof, are governed by this section and shall be one of the following:

(a) Actual fraud where the defrauded party was kept in ignorance or in some other manner was fraudulently prevented from fully participating in the proceeding. An action or motion based on fraud shall be brought within one year after the date on which the complaining party either did discover, or should have discovered, the fraud.

(b) Perjury. An action or motion based on perjury in the preliminary or final declaration of disclosure, the waiver of the final declaration of disclosure, or in the current income and expense statement shall be brought within one year after the date on which the complaining party either did discover, or should have discovered, the perjury.

(c) Duress. An action or motion based upon duress shall be brought within two years after the date of entry of judgment.

(d) Mental incapacity. An action or motion based on mental incapacity shall be brought within two years after the date of entry of judgment.

(e) As to stipulated or uncontested judgments or that part of a judgment stipulated to by the parties, mistake, either mutual or unilateral, whether mistake of law or mistake of fact. An action or motion based on mistake shall be brought within one year after the date of entry of judgment.

(f) Failure to comply with the disclosure requirements of Chapter 9 (commencing with Section 2100). An action or motion based on failure to comply with the disclosure requirements shall be brought within one year after the date on which the complaining party either discovered, or should have discovered, the failure to comply. **Leg.H.** Added Stats 1993 ch 219 §108 (AB 1500). Amended Stats 1993 ch 1101 §15 (AB 1469), effective October 11, 1993, operative January 1, 1994; Stats 2001 ch 703 §7 (AB 583).

2001 Note: This act shall apply to any judgment that becomes final on or after January 1, 2002. Stats 2001 ch 703 §8.

§2123. Setting aside judgment

Notwithstanding any other provision of this chapter, or any other law, a judgment may not be set aside simply because the court finds that it was inequitable when made, nor simply because subsequent circumstances caused the division of assets or liabilities to become inequitable, or the support to become inadequate. **Leg.H.** Added Stats 1993 ch 219 §108 (AB 1500).

§2124. Negligence of attorney

The negligence of an attorney shall not be imputed to a client to bar an order setting aside a judgment, unless the court finds that the client knew, or should have known, of the attorney's negligence and unreasonably failed to self-protect. **Leg.H.** Added Stats 1993 ch 219 §108 (AB 1500). Amended Stats 2019 ch 115 §21 (AB 1817), effective January 1, 2020.

§2125. Scope of relief

When ruling on an action or motion to set aside a judgment, the court shall set aside only those provisions materially affected by the circumstances leading to the court's decision to grant relief. However, the court has discretion to set aside the entire judgment, if necessary, for equitable considerations. **Leg.H.** Added Stats 1993 ch 219 §108 (AB 1500). Amended Stats 1993 ch 1101 §16 (AB 1469), effective October 11, 1993, operative January 1, 1994.

§2126. Date of valuation

As to assets or liabilities for which a judgment or part of a judgment is set aside, the date of valuation shall be subject to equitable considerations. The court shall equally divide the asset or liability, unless the court finds upon good cause shown that the interests of justice require an unequal division. **Leg.H.** Added Stats 1993 ch 219 §108 (AB 1500).

§2127. Statement of decision

As to actions or motions filed under this chapter, if a timely request is made, the court shall render a statement of decision where the court has resolved controverted factual evidence. **Leg.H.** Added Stats 1993 ch 219 §108 (AB 1500). Amended Stats 1993 ch 1101 §17 (AB 1469), effective October 11, 1993, operative January 1, 1994.

§2128. Effect on other law

(a) Nothing in this chapter prohibits a party from seeking relief under Section 2556.

(b) Nothing in this chapter changes existing law with respect to contract remedies where the contract has not been merged or incorporated into a judgment.

(c) Nothing in this chapter is intended to restrict a family law court from acting as a court of equity.

(d) Nothing in this chapter is intended to limit existing law with respect to the modification or enforcement of support orders.

(e) Nothing in this chapter affects the rights of a bona fide lessee, purchaser, or encumbrancer for value of real property. **Leg.H.** Added Stats 1993 ch 219 §108 (AB 1500).

§2129. Application of chapter

This chapter applies to judgments entered on or after January 1, 1993.

Leg.H. Added Stats 1993 ch 219 §108 (AB 1500).

PART 2
JUDICIAL DETERMINATION OF VOID OR VOIDABLE MARRIAGE

Chapter 1. Void Marriage.
Chapter 2. Voidable Marriage.
Chapter 3. Procedural Provisions.

CHAPTER 1
VOID MARRIAGE

Incestuous marriages. §2200.
Bigamous and polygamous marriages. §2201.

§2200. Incestuous marriages

Marriages between parents and children, ancestors and descendants of every degree, and between siblings of the half as well as the whole blood, and between uncles or aunts and nieces or nephews, are incestuous, and void from the beginning, whether the relationship is legitimate or illegitimate. **Leg.H.** Enacted Stats 1992 ch 162 §10 (AB 2650), operative January 1, 1994. Amended Stats 2014 ch 82 §23 (SB 1306), effective January 1, 2015.

§2201. Bigamous and polygamous marriages

(a) A subsequent marriage contracted by a person during the life of his or her former spouse, with a person other than the former spouse, is illegal and void, unless:

(1) The former marriage has been dissolved or adjudged a nullity before the date of the subsequent marriage.

(2) The former spouse (A) is absent, and not known to the person to be living for the period of five successive years immediately preceding the subsequent marriage, or (B) is generally reputed or believed by the person to be dead at the time the subsequent marriage was contracted.

(b) In either of the cases described in paragraph (2) of subdivision (a), the subsequent marriage is valid until its nullity is adjudged pursuant to subdivision (b) of Section 2210. **Leg.H.** Enacted Stats 1992 ch 162 §10 (AB 2650), operative January 1, 1994. Amended Stats 2014 ch 82 §24 (SB 1306), effective January 1, 2015.

CHAPTER 2
VOIDABLE MARRIAGE

Grounds for nullity. §2210.
Limitations on obtaining judgment of nullity. §2211.
Effect of judgment of nullity of marriage. §2212.

§2210. Grounds for nullity

A marriage is voidable and may be adjudged a nullity if any of the following conditions existed at the time of the marriage:

(a) The party who commences the proceeding or on whose behalf the proceeding is commenced was under 18 years of age, unless the party entered into the marriage pursuant to Section 302 or 303.

(b) The spouse of either party was living and the marriage with that spouse was then in force and that spouse (1) was absent and not known to the party commencing the proceeding to be living for a period of five successive years immediately preceding the subsequent marriage for which the judgment of nullity is sought or (2) was generally reputed or believed by the party commencing the proceeding to be dead at the time the subsequent marriage was contracted.

(c) Either party was of unsound mind, unless the party of unsound mind, after coming to reason, freely cohabited with the other as his or her spouse.

(d) The consent of either party was obtained by fraud, unless the party whose consent was obtained by fraud afterwards, with full knowledge of the facts constituting the fraud, freely cohabited with the other as his or her spouse.

(e) The consent of either party was obtained by force, unless the party whose consent was obtained by force afterwards freely cohabited with the other as his or her spouse.

(f) Either party was, at the time of marriage, physically incapable of entering into the marriage state, and that incapacity continues, and appears to be incurable. **Leg.H.** Enacted Stats 1992 ch 162 §10 (AB 2650), operative January 1, 1994. Amended Stats 2014 ch 82 §25 (SB 1306), effective January 1, 2015; Stats 2018 ch 660 §8 (SB 273), effective January 1, 2019.

§2211. Limitations on obtaining judgment of nullity

A proceeding to obtain a judgment of nullity of marriage, for causes set forth in Section 2210, must be commenced within the periods and by the parties, as follows:

(a) For causes mentioned in subdivision (a) of Section 2210, by any of the following:

(1) The party to the marriage who was married under the age of legal consent, within four years after arriving at the age of consent.

(2) A parent, guardian, conservator, or other person having charge of the minor, at any time before the married minor has arrived at the age of legal consent.

(b) For causes mentioned in subdivision (b) of Section 2210, by either of the following:

(1) Either party during the life of the other.

(2) The former spouse.

(c) For causes mentioned in subdivision (c) of Section 2210, by the party injured, or by a relative or conservator of the party of unsound mind, at any time before the death of either party.

(d) For causes mentioned in subdivision (d) of Section 2210, by the party whose consent was obtained by fraud, within four years after the discovery of the facts constituting the fraud.

(e) For causes mentioned in subdivision (e) of Section 2210, by the party whose consent was obtained by force, within four years after the marriage.

(f) For causes mentioned in subdivision (f) of Section 2210, by the injured party, within four years after the marriage. **Leg.H.** Enacted Stats 1992 ch 162 §10 (AB 2650), operative January 1, 1994. Amended Stats 2014 ch 82 §26 (SB 1306), effective January 1, 2015.

§2212. Effect of judgment of nullity of marriage

(a) The effect of a judgment of nullity of marriage is to restore the parties to the status of unmarried persons.

(b) A judgment of nullity of marriage is conclusive only as to the parties to the proceeding and those claiming under them. **Leg.H.** Enacted Stats 1992 ch 162 §10 (AB 2650), operative January 1, 1994.

CHAPTER 3
PROCEDURAL PROVISIONS

Petition for judgment of nullity. §2250.
Status of putative spouse; Division of quasi-marital property. §2251.
Liability of quasi-marital property for debts. §2252.
Custody of children. §2253.
Support of putative spouse. §2254.
Attorney's fees and costs. §2255.

§2250. Petition for judgment of nullity

(a) A proceeding based on void or voidable marriage is commenced by filing a petition entitled "In re the marriage of ____ and ____" which shall state that it is a petition for a judgment of nullity of the marriage.

(b) A copy of the petition together with a copy of a summons in form and content approved by the Judicial Council shall be served upon the other party to the marriage in the same manner as service of papers in civil actions generally. **Leg.H.** Enacted Stats 1992 ch 162 §10 (AB 2650), operative January 1, 1994.

§2251. Status of putative spouse; Division of quasi-marital property

(a) If a determination is made that a marriage is void or voidable and the court finds that either party or both parties believed in good faith that the marriage was valid, the court shall:

(1) Declare the party or parties, who believed in good faith that the marriage was valid, to have the status of a putative spouse.

(2) If the division of property is in issue, divide, in accordance with Division 7 (commencing with Section 2500), that property acquired during the union that would have been community property or quasi-

community property if the union had not been void or voidable, only upon request of a party who is declared a putative spouse under paragraph (1). This property is known as "quasi-marital property."

(b) If the court expressly reserves jurisdiction, it may make the property division at a time after the judgment. **Leg.H.** Enacted Stats 1992 ch 162 §10 (AB 2650), operative January 1, 1994. Amended Stats 2015 ch 196 §1 (AB 380), effective January 1, 2016.

§2252. Liability of quasi-marital property for debts

The property divided pursuant to Section 2251 is liable for debts of the parties to the same extent as if the property had been community property or quasi-community property. **Leg.H.** Enacted Stats 1992 ch 162 §10 (AB 2650), operative January 1, 1994.

§2253. Custody of children

In a proceeding under this part, custody of the children shall be determined according to Division 8 (commencing with Section 3000). **Leg.H.** Enacted Stats 1992 ch 162 §10 (AB 2650), operative January 1, 1994.

§2254. Support of putative spouse

The court may, during the pendency of a proceeding for nullity of marriage or upon judgment of nullity of marriage, order a party to pay for the support of the other party in the same manner as if the marriage had not been void or voidable if the party for whose benefit the order is made is found to be a putative spouse. **Leg.H.** Enacted Stats 1992 ch 162 §10 (AB 2650), operative January 1, 1994.

§2255. Attorney's fees and costs

The court may grant attorney's fees and costs in accordance with Chapter 3.5 (commencing with Section 2030) of Part 1 in proceedings to have the marriage adjudged void and in those proceedings based upon voidable marriage in which the party applying for attorney's fees and costs is found to be innocent of fraud or wrongdoing in inducing or entering into the marriage, and free from knowledge of the then existence of any prior marriage or other impediment to the contracting of the marriage for which a judgment of nullity is sought. **Leg.H.** Enacted Stats 1992 ch 162 §10 (AB 2650), operative January 1, 1994. Amended Stats 1993 ch 219 §108.5 (AB 1500).

PART 3
DISSOLUTION OF MARRIAGE AND LEGAL SEPARATION

Chapter 1. Effect of Dissolution.
Chapter 2. Grounds for Dissolution or Legal Separation.
Chapter 3. Residence Requirements.
Chapter 4. General Procedural Provisions.
Chapter 5. Summary Dissolution.
Chapter 6. Case Management.

CHAPTER 1
EFFECT OF DISSOLUTION

Effect of dissolution. §2300.

§2300. Effect of dissolution
The effect of a judgment of dissolution of marriage when it becomes final is to restore the parties to the state of unmarried persons. **Leg.H.** Enacted Stats 1992 ch 162 §10 (AB 2650), operative January 1, 1994.

CHAPTER 2
GROUNDS FOR DISSOLUTION OR LEGAL SEPARATION

Grounds for dissolution or legal separation. §2310.
Irreconcilable differences. §2311.
Proof required for dissolution on grounds of permanent legal incapacity to make decisions. §2312.
Duty of support not affected by dissolution on ground of permanent legal incapacity to make decisions. §2313.

§2310. Grounds for dissolution or legal separation
Dissolution of the marriage or legal separation of the parties may be based on either of the following grounds, which shall be pleaded generally:
(a) Irreconcilable differences, which have caused the irremediable breakdown of the marriage.
(b) Permanent legal incapacity to make decisions. **Leg.H.** Enacted Stats 1992 ch 162 §10 (AB 2650), operative January 1, 1994. Amended Stats 2014 ch 144 §9 (AB 1847), effective January 1, 2015.

§2311. Irreconcilable differences
Irreconcilable differences are those grounds which are determined by the court to be substantial reasons for not continuing the marriage and which make it appear that the marriage should be dissolved. **Leg.H.** Enacted Stats 1992 ch 162 §10 (AB 2650), operative January 1, 1994.

§2312. Proof required for dissolution on grounds of permanent legal incapacity to make decisions
A marriage may be dissolved on the grounds of permanent legal incapacity to make decisions only upon proof, including competent medical or psychiatric testimony, that the spouse was at the time the petition was filed, and remains, permanently lacking the legal capacity to make decisions. **Leg.H.** Enacted Stats 1992 ch 162 §10 (AB 2650), operative January 1, 1994. Amended Stats 2014 ch 144 §10 (AB 1847), effective January 1, 2015.

§2313. Duty of support not affected by dissolution on ground of permanent legal incapacity to make decisions
No dissolution of marriage granted on the ground of permanent legal incapacity to make decisions relieves a spouse from any obligation imposed by law as a result of the marriage for the support of the spouse who lacks legal capacity to make decisions, and the court may make an order for support, or require a bond therefor, as the circumstances require. **Leg.H.** Enacted Stats 1992 ch 162 §10 (AB 2650), operative January 1, 1994. Amended Stats 2014 ch 144 §11 (AB 1847), effective January 1, 2015.

CHAPTER 3
RESIDENCE REQUIREMENTS

Residence requirement for dissolution judgment. §2320.
Conversion of separation proceeding to dissolution proceeding. §2321.
Separate domicile or residence. §2322.

§2320. Residence requirement for dissolution judgment
(a) Except as provided in subdivision (b), a judgment of dissolution of marriage may not be entered unless one of the parties to the marriage has been a resident of this state for six months and of the county in which the proceeding is filed for three months next preceding the filing of the petition.
(b)(1) A judgment for dissolution, nullity, or legal separation of a marriage between persons of the same sex may be entered, even if neither spouse is a resident of, or maintains a domicile in, this state at the time the proceedings are filed, if the following apply:
(A) The marriage was entered in California.
(B) Neither party to the marriage resides in a jurisdiction that will dissolve the marriage. If the jurisdiction does not recognize the marriage, there shall be a rebuttable presumption that the jurisdiction will not dissolve the marriage.
(2) For the purposes of this subdivision, the superior court in the county where the marriage was entered shall be the proper court for the proceeding. The dissolution, nullity, or legal separation shall be adjudicated in accordance with California law. **Leg.H.** Enacted Stats 1992 ch 162 §10 (AB 2650), operative January 1, 1994. Amended Stats 2011 ch 721 §4 (SB 651), effective January 1, 2012.

§2321. Conversion of separation proceeding to dissolution proceeding
(a) In a proceeding for legal separation of the parties in which neither party, at the time the proceeding was commenced, has complied with the residence requirements of Section 2320, either party may, upon complying with the residence requirements, amend the party's petition or responsive pleading in the proceeding to request that a judgment of dissolution of the marriage be entered. The date of the filing of the amended petition or pleading shall be deemed to be the date of commencement of the proceeding for the dissolution of the marriage for the purposes only of the residence requirements of Section 2320.
(b) If the other party has appeared in the proceeding, notice of the amendment shall be given to the other party in the manner provided by rules adopted by the Judicial Council. If no appearance has been made by the other party in the proceeding, notice of the amendment may be given to the other party by mail to the last known address of the other party, or by personal service, if the intent of the party to so amend upon satisfaction of the residence requirements of Section 2320 is set forth in the initial petition or pleading in the manner provided by rules adopted by the Judicial Council. **Leg.H.** Enacted Stats 1992 ch 162 §10 (AB 2650), operative January 1, 1994.

§2322. Separate domicile or residence
For the purpose of a proceeding for dissolution of marriage, each spouse may have a separate domicile or residence depending upon proof of the fact and not upon legal presumptions. **Leg.H.** Enacted Stats 1992 ch 162 §10 (AB 2650), operative January 1, 1994. Amended Stats 2014 ch 82 §27 (SB 1306), effective January 1, 2015.

CHAPTER 4
GENERAL PROCEDURAL PROVISIONS

Petition for dissolution or legal separation. §2330.
Supplemental complaint for paternity or child support. §2330.1.
Judicial officer. §2330.3.
Financial declarations not required in certain default cases. §2330.5.
Service on other spouse. §2331.
Representation of spouse who is determined to have permanent legal incapacity to make decisions by guardian, conservator, or guardian ad litem. §2332.
Court finding and order where grounds is irreconcilable differences. §2333.
Continuance for reconciliation. §2334.
Evidence of specific acts of misconduct. §2335.
Stamped envelope. §2335.5.
Proof required for default. §2336.
Severance and grant of early trial on issue of dissolution of status of marriage; Preliminary declaration of disclosure. §2337.
Decisions; Judgments. §2338.
Default. §2338.5.
Waiting period before dissolution judgment becomes final. §2339.
Statement in judgment of date marriage terminates. §2340.
Effect of appeal or motion for new trial. §2341.

Calculating date judgment becomes final where joint petition for summary dissolution is revoked. §2342.

Procedure for joint petitioners [Operative January 1, 2026]. § 2342.5.

Implementation of joint petitioner procedure. § 2342.51.

Retention of jurisdiction over date of termination; Order for termination at future specified date. §2343.

Effect of death of either party after entry of judgment. §2344.

Consent of parties to legal separation. §2345.

Entry of judgment nunc pro tunc. §2346.

Legal separation judgment does not bar subsequent dissolution judgment. §2347.

Report of number of judgments. §2348.

§2330. Petition for dissolution or legal separation

(a) A proceeding for dissolution of marriage or for legal separation of the parties is commenced by filing a petition **or joint petition** entitled "In re the marriage of ____ and ____," which shall state whether it is a petition for dissolution of the marriage or for legal separation of the parties.

(b) In a proceeding for dissolution of marriage or for legal separation of the parties, the petition shall set forth, among other matters, as nearly as can be ascertained, the following facts:

(1) The date of marriage.

(2) The date of separation.

(3) The number of years from marriage to separation.

(4) The number of children of the marriage, if any, and if none a statement of that fact.

(5) The age and birth date of each minor child of the marriage.

(c) In a joint petition proceeding for dissolution of marriage or for legal separation of the parties, the joint petition shall set forth, among other matters, as nearly as can be ascertained, the following facts:

(1) The date of the marriage.

(2)(A) If there are children of the marriage, all of the following information:

(i) The number of children.

(ii) The age of each child.

(iii) The date of birth of each child.

(B) If there are no children of the marriage, a statement of that fact.

(3)(A) A list of issues upon which the parties intend to resolve by agreement, which may include, but is not limited to, the following:

(i) The legal grounds for dissolution or legal separation.

(ii) The date of separation.

(iii) Child custody.

(iv) Child support.

(v) Spousal support or domestic partner support.

(vi) Separate property.

(vii) Community and quasi-community property.

(viii) Restoration of former name.

(ix) Attorney's fees and costs.

(B) The list of issues required by subparagraph (A) shall represent all of the matters at issue in the dissolution. If the parties have an issue that they do not intend to resolve by agreement, they shall file a petition pursuant to subdivision (b). Leg.H. Enacted Stats 1992 ch 162 §10 (AB 2650), operative January 1, 1994. Amended Stats 1998 ch 581 §11 (AB 2801); Stats 2024 ch 190 §1 (SB 1427), effective January 1, 2025.

§2330.1. Supplemental complaint for paternity or child support

In any proceeding for dissolution of marriage, for legal separation of the parties, or for the support of children, the petition or complaint may list children born before the marriage to the same parties and, pursuant to the terms of the Uniform Parentage Act, a determination of paternity may be made in the action. In addition, a supplemental complaint may be filed, in any of those proceedings, pursuant to Section 464 of the Code of Civil Procedure, seeking a judgment or order of paternity or support for a child of the mother and father of the child whose paternity and support are already in issue before the court. A supplemental complaint for paternity or support of children may be filed without leave of court either before or after final judgment in the underlying action. Service of the supplemental summons and complaint shall be made in the manner provided for the initial service of a summons by this code. **Leg.H.** Added Stats 1994 ch 1269 §23.5 (AB 2208). Amended Stats 1998 ch 581 §12 (AB 2801).

§2330.3. Judicial officer

(a) All dissolution actions, to the greatest extent possible, shall be assigned to the same superior court department for all purposes, in order that all decisions in a case through final judgment shall be made by the same judicial officer. However, if the assignment will result in a significant delay of any family law matter, the dissolution action need not be assigned to the same superior court department for all purposes, unless the parties stipulate otherwise.

(b) The Judicial Council shall adopt a standard of judicial administration prescribing a minimum length of assignment of a judicial officer to a family law assignment.

(c) This section shall be operative on July 1, 1997. **Leg.H.** Added Stats 1996 ch 56 §2 (SB 389), operative July 1, 1997. Amended Stats 2010 ch 352 §7 (AB 939), effective January 1, 2011.

§2330.5. Financial declarations not required in certain default cases

Notwithstanding any other provision of law, if no demand for money, property, costs, or attorney's fees is contained in the petition and the judgment of dissolution of marriage is entered by default, the filing of income and expense declarations and property declarations in connection therewith shall not be required. **Leg.H.** Enacted Stats 1992 ch 162 §10 (AB 2650), operative January 1, 1994.

§2331. Service on other spouse

(a) A copy of the petition, together with a copy of a summons, in **a form and content approved by the Judicial Council,** shall be served upon the other party to the marriage in the same manner as service of papers in civil actions generally.

(b) If the parties file a joint petition and joint summons, in a form and content approved by the Judicial Council, the joint petition shall be deemed to be served on both parties upon the filing of the joint petition with the court and both parties shall be determined to have appeared in the matter. Leg.H. Enacted Stats 1992 ch 162 §10 (AB 2650), operative January 1, 1994. Amended Stats 2024 ch 190 §2 (SB 1427), effective January 1, 2025.

§2332. Representation of spouse who is determined to have permanent legal incapacity to make decisions by guardian, conservator, or guardian ad litem

(a) If the petition for dissolution of the marriage is based on the ground of permanent legal incapacity to make decisions and the spouse who lacks legal capacity to make decisions has a guardian or conservator, other than the spouse filing the petition, the petition and summons shall be served upon the spouse and the guardian or conservator. The guardian or conservator shall defend and protect the interests of the spouse who lacks legal capacity to make decisions.

(b) If the spouse who lacks legal capacity to make decisions has no guardian or conservator, or if the spouse filing the petition is the guardian or conservator, the court shall appoint a guardian ad litem, who may be the district attorney or the county counsel, if any, to defend and protect the interests of the spouse who lacks legal capacity to make decisions. If a district attorney or county counsel is appointed guardian ad litem pursuant to this subdivision, the successor in the office of district attorney or county counsel, as the case may be, succeeds as guardian ad litem, without further action by the court or parties.

(c) "Guardian or conservator" as used in this section means:

(1) With respect to the issue of the dissolution of the marriage relationship, the guardian or conservator of the person.

(2) With respect to support and property division issues, the guardian or conservator of the estate. **Leg.H.** Enacted Stats 1992 ch 162 §10 (AB 2650), operative January 1, 1994. Amended Stats 2014 ch 144 §12 (AB 1847), effective January 1, 2015.

§2333. Court finding and order where grounds is irreconcilable differences

Subject to Section 2334, if from the evidence at the hearing the court finds that there are irreconcilable differences which have caused the irremediable breakdown of the marriage, the court shall order the dissolution of the marriage or a legal separation of the parties. **Leg.H.** Enacted Stats 1992 ch 162 §10 (AB 2650), operative January 1, 1994.

§2334. Continuance for reconciliation

(a) If it appears that there is a reasonable possibility of reconciliation, the court shall continue the proceeding for the dissolution of the marriage or for a legal separation of the parties for a period not to exceed 30 days.

(b) During the period of the continuance, the court may make orders for the support and maintenance of the parties, the custody of the minor children of the marriage, the support of children for whom support may be ordered, attorney's fees, and for the preservation of the property of the parties.

(c) At any time after the termination of the period of the continuance, either party may move for the dissolution of the marriage or a legal separation of the parties, and the court may enter a judgment of dissolution of the marriage or legal separation of the parties. **Leg.H.** Enacted Stats 1992 ch 162 §10 (AB 2650), operative January 1, 1994. Amended Stats 1993 ch 219 §109 (AB 1500).

§2335. Evidence of specific acts of misconduct

Except as otherwise provided by statute, in a pleading or proceeding for dissolution of marriage or legal separation of the parties, including depositions and discovery proceedings, evidence of specific acts of misconduct is improper and inadmissible. **Leg.H.** Enacted Stats 1992 ch 162 §10 (AB 2650), operative January 1, 1994. Amended Stats 1993 ch 219 §110 (AB 1500).

§2335.5. Stamped envelope

In a proceeding for dissolution of marriage or legal separation of the parties, where the judgment is to be entered by default, the petitioner shall provide the court clerk with a stamped envelope bearing sufficient postage addressed to the spouse who has defaulted, with the address of the court clerk as the return address, and the court clerk shall mail a copy of the request to enter default to that spouse in the envelope provided. A judgment of dissolution or legal separation, including relief requested in the petition, shall not be denied solely on the basis that the request to enter default was returned unopened to the court. The court clerk shall maintain any such document returned by the post office as part of the court file in the case. **Leg.H.** Added Stats 1996 ch 810 §1 (AB 2149).

§2336. Proof required for default

(a) No judgment of dissolution or of legal separation of the parties may be granted upon the default of one of the parties or upon a statement or finding of fact made by a referee; but the court shall, in addition to the statement or finding of the referee, require proof of the grounds alleged, and the proof, if not taken before the court, shall be by affidavit. In all cases where there are minor children of the parties, each affidavit or offer of proof shall include an estimate by the declarant or affiant of the monthly gross income of each party. If the declarant or affiant has no knowledge of the estimated monthly income of a party, the declarant or affiant shall state why he or she has no knowledge. In all cases where there is a community estate, each affidavit or offer of proof shall include an estimate of the value of the assets and the debts the declarant or affiant proposes to be distributed to each party, unless the declarant or affiant has filed, or concurrently files, a complete and accurate property declaration with the court.

(b) If the proof is by affidavit, the personal appearance of the affiant is required only when it appears to the court that any of the following circumstances exist:

(1) Reconciliation of the parties is reasonably possible.

(2) A proposed child custody order is not in the best interest of the child.

(3) A proposed child support order is less than a noncustodial parent is capable of paying.

(4) A personal appearance of a party or interested person would be in the best interests of justice.

(c) An affidavit submitted pursuant to this section shall contain a stipulation by the affiant that the affiant understands that proof will be by affidavit and that the affiant will not appear before the court unless so ordered by the court. **Leg.H.** Enacted Stats 1992 ch 162 §10 (AB 2650), operative January 1, 1994. Amended Stats 1996 ch 810 §2 (AB 2149); Stats 1998 ch 581 §13 (AB 2801).

§2337. Severance and grant of early trial on issue of dissolution of status of marriage; Preliminary declaration of disclosure

(a) In a proceeding for dissolution of marriage, the court, upon noticed motion, may sever and grant an early and separate trial on the issue of the dissolution of the status of the marriage apart from other issues.

(b) A preliminary declaration of disclosure with a completed schedule of assets and debts shall be served on the nonmoving party with the noticed motion unless it has been served previously, or unless the parties stipulate in writing to defer service of the preliminary declaration of disclosure until a later time.

(c) The court may impose upon a party any of the following conditions on granting a severance of the issue of the dissolution of the status of the marriage, and in case of that party's death, an order of any of the following conditions continues to be binding upon that party's estate:

(1) The party shall indemnify and hold the other party harmless from any taxes, reassessments, interest, and penalties payable by the other party in connection with the division of the community estate that would not have been payable if the parties were still married at the time the division was made.

(2) Until judgment has been entered on all remaining issues and has become final, the party shall maintain all existing health and medical insurance coverage for the other party and any minor children as named dependents, so long as the party is eligible to do so. If at any time during this period the party is not eligible to maintain that coverage, the party shall, at the party's sole expense, provide and maintain health and medical insurance coverage that is comparable to the existing health and medical insurance coverage to the extent it is available. To the extent that coverage is not available, the party shall be responsible to pay, and shall demonstrate to the court's satisfaction the ability to pay, for the health and medical care for the other party and the minor children, to the extent that care would have been covered by the existing insurance coverage but for the dissolution of marital status, and shall otherwise indemnify and hold the other party harmless from any adverse consequences resulting from the loss or reduction of the existing coverage. For purposes of this subdivision, "health and medical insurance coverage" includes any coverage for which the parties are eligible under any group or individual health or other medical plan, fund, policy, or program.

(3) Until judgment has been entered on all remaining issues and has become final, the party shall indemnify and hold the other party harmless from any adverse consequences to the other party if the bifurcation results in a termination of the other party's right to a probate homestead in the residence in which the other party resides at the time the severance is granted.

(4) Until judgment has been entered on all remaining issues and has become final, the party shall indemnify and hold the other party harmless from any adverse consequences to the other party if the bifurcation results in the loss of the rights of the other party to a probate family allowance as the surviving spouse of the party.

(5) Until judgment has been entered on all remaining issues and has become final, the party shall indemnify and hold the other party harmless from any adverse consequences to the other party if the bifurcation results in the loss of the other party's rights with respect to any retirement, survivor, or deferred compensation benefits under any plan, fund, or arrangement, or to any elections or options associated therewith, to the extent that the other party would have been entitled to those benefits or elections as the spouse or surviving spouse of the party.

(6) The party shall indemnify and hold the other party harmless from any adverse consequences if the bifurcation results in the loss of rights to social security benefits or elections to the extent the other party would have been entitled to those benefits or elections as the surviving spouse of the party.

(7)(A) The court may make an order pursuant to paragraph (3) of subdivision (b) of Section 5040 of the Probate Code, if appropriate, that a party maintain a beneficiary designation for a nonprobate transfer, as described in Section 5000 of the Probate Code, for a spouse or domestic partner for up to one-half of or, upon a showing of good cause, for all of a nonprobate transfer asset until judgment has been entered with respect to the community ownership of that asset, and until the other party's interest therein has been distributed to him or her.

(B) Except upon a showing of good cause, this paragraph does not apply to any of the following:

(i) A nonprobate transfer described in Section 5000 of the Probate Code that was not created by either party or that was acquired by either party by gift, descent, or devise.

(ii) An irrevocable trust.

(iii) A trust of which neither party is the grantor.

(iv) Powers of appointment under a trust instrument that was not created by either party or of which neither party is a grantor.

(v) The execution and filing of a disclaimer pursuant to Part 8 (commencing with Section 260) of Division 2 of the Probate Code.

(vi) The appointment of a party as a trustee.

(8) In order to preserve the ability of the party to defer the distribution of the Individual Retirement Account or annuity (IRA) established under Section 408 or 408A of the Internal Revenue Code of 1986, as amended, (IRC) upon the death of the other party, the court may require that one-half, or all upon a showing of good cause, of the community interest in any IRA, by or for the benefit of the party, be assigned and transferred to the other party pursuant to Section 408(d)(6) of the Internal Revenue Code. This paragraph does not limit the power granted pursuant to subdivision (g).

(9) Upon a showing that circumstances exist that would place a substantial burden of enforcement upon either party's community property rights or would eliminate the ability of the surviving party to enforce his or her community property rights if the other party died before the division and distribution or compliance with any court-ordered payment of any community property interest therein, including, but not limited to, a situation in which preemption under federal law applies to an asset of a party, or purchase by a bona fide purchaser has occurred, the court may order a specific security interest designed to reduce or eliminate the likelihood that a postmortem enforcement proceeding would be ineffective or unduly burdensome to the surviving party. For this purpose, those orders may include, but are not limited to, any of the following:

(A) An order that the party provide an undertaking.

(B) An order to provide a security interest by Qualified Domestic Relations Order from that party's share of a retirement plan or plans.

(C) An order for the creation of a trust as defined in paragraph (2) of subdivision (a) of Section 82 of the Probate Code.

(D) An order for other arrangements as may be reasonably necessary and feasible to provide appropriate security in the event of the party's death before judgment has been entered with respect to the community ownership of that asset, and until the other party's interest therein has been distributed to him or her.

(E) If a retirement plan is not subject to an enforceable court order for the payment of spousal survivor benefits to the other party, an interim order requiring the party to pay or cause to be paid, and to post adequate security for the payment of, any survivor benefit that would have been payable to the other party on the death of the party but for the judgment granting a dissolution of the status of the marriage, pending entry of judgment on all remaining issues.

(10) Any other condition the court determines is just and equitable.

(d) Prior to, or simultaneously with, entry of judgment granting dissolution of the status of the marriage, all of the following shall occur:

(1) The party's retirement or pension plan shall be joined as a party to the proceeding for dissolution, unless joinder is precluded or made unnecessary by Title 1 of the federal Employee Retirement Income Security Act of 1974 (29 U.S.C. Sec. 1001 et seq.), as amended (ERISA), or any other applicable law.

(2) To preserve the claims of each spouse in all retirement plan benefits upon entry of judgment granting a dissolution of the status of the marriage, the court shall enter one of the following in connection with the judgment for each retirement plan in which either party is a participant:

(A) An order pursuant to Section 2610 disposing of each party's interest in retirement plan benefits, including survivor and death benefits.

(B) An interim order preserving the nonemployee party's right to retirement plan benefits, including survivor and death benefits, pending entry of judgment on all remaining issues.

(C) An attachment to the judgment granting a dissolution of the status of the marriage, as follows:

EACH PARTY (insert names and addresses) IS PROVISIONALLY AWARDED WITHOUT PREJUDICE AND SUBJECT TO ADJUSTMENT BY A SUBSEQUENT DOMESTIC RELATIONS ORDER, A SEPARATE INTEREST EQUAL TO ONE-HALF OF ALL BENEFITS ACCRUED OR TO BE ACCRUED UNDER THE PLAN (name each plan individually) AS A RESULT OF EMPLOYMENT OF THE OTHER PARTY DURING THE MARRIAGE OR DOMESTIC PARTNERSHIP AND PRIOR TO THE DATE OF SEPARATION. IN ADDITION, PENDING FURTHER NOTICE, THE PLAN SHALL, AS ALLOWED BY LAW, OR IN THE CASE OF A GOVERNMENTAL PLAN, AS ALLOWED BY THE TERMS OF THE PLAN, CONTINUE TO TREAT THE PARTIES AS MARRIED OR DOMESTIC PARTNERS FOR PURPOSES OF ANY SURVIVOR RIGHTS OR BENEFITS AVAILABLE UNDER THE PLAN TO THE EXTENT NECESSARY TO PROVIDE FOR PAYMENT OF AN AMOUNT EQUAL TO THAT SEPARATE INTEREST OR FOR ALL OF THE SURVIVOR BENEFIT IF AT THE TIME OF THE DEATH OF THE PARTICIPANT, THERE IS NO OTHER ELIGIBLE RECIPIENT OF THE SURVIVOR BENEFIT.

(e) The moving party shall promptly serve a copy of any order, interim order, or attachment entered pursuant to paragraph (2) of subdivision (d), and a copy of the judgment granting a dissolution of the status of the marriage, on the retirement or pension plan administrator.

(f) A judgment granting a dissolution of the status of the marriage shall expressly reserve jurisdiction for later determination of all other pending issues.

(g) If the party dies after the entry of judgment granting a dissolution of marriage, any obligation imposed by this section shall be enforceable against any asset, including the proceeds thereof, against which these obligations would have been enforceable prior to the person's death. **Leg.H.** Enacted Stats 1992 ch 162 §10 (AB 2650), operative January 1, 1994. Amended Stats 1994 ch 1269 §24 (AB 2208); Stats 1997 ch 56 §1 (AB 1098); Stats 1998 ch 581 §14 (AB 2801); Stats 2007 ch 141 §1 (AB 861), effective January 1, 2008; Stats 2015 ch 293 §1 (AB 139), effective January 1, 2016.

§2338. Decisions; Judgments

(a) In a proceeding for dissolution of the marriage or legal separation of the parties, the court shall file its decision and any statement of decision as in other cases.

(b) If the court determines that no dissolution should be granted, a judgment to that effect only shall be entered.

(c) If the court determines that a dissolution should be granted, a judgment of dissolution of marriage shall be entered. After the entry of the judgment and before it becomes final, neither party has the right to dismiss the proceeding without the consent of the other. **Leg.H.** Enacted Stats 1992 ch 162 §10 (AB 2650), operative January 1, 1994.

§2338.5. Default

Where a judgment of dissolution or nullity of marriage or legal separation of the parties is to be granted upon the default of one of the parties:

(a) The signature of the spouse who has defaulted on any marital settlement agreement or on any stipulated judgment shall be notarized.

(b) The court clerk shall give notice of entry of judgment of dissolution of marriage, nullity of marriage, or legal separation to the attorney for each party or to the party, if unrepresented.

(c) For the purpose of mailing the notice of entry of judgment, the party submitting the judgment shall provide the court clerk with a stamped envelope bearing sufficient postage addressed to the attorney for the other party or to the party, if unrepresented, with the address of the court clerk as the return address. The court clerk shall maintain any such document returned by the post office as part of the court file in the case. **Leg.H.** Added Stats 1996 ch 810 §3 (AB 2149).

§2339. Waiting period before dissolution judgment becomes final

(a) Subject to subdivision (b) and to Sections 2340 to 2344, inclusive, no judgment of dissolution is final for the purpose of terminating the marriage relationship of the parties until six months have expired from the date of service of a copy of summons and petition or the date of appearance of the respondent, whichever occurs first.

(b) The court may extend the six-month period described in subdivision (a) for good cause shown. **Leg.H.** Enacted Stats 1992 ch 162 §10 (AB 2650), operative January 1, 1994.

§2340. Statement in judgment of date marriage terminates

A judgment of dissolution of marriage shall specify the date on which the judgment becomes finally effective for the purpose of terminating the marriage relationship of the parties. **Leg.H.** Enacted Stats 1992 ch 162 §10 (AB 2650), operative January 1, 1994.

§2341. Effect of appeal or motion for new trial

(a) Notwithstanding Section 2340, if an appeal is taken from the judgment or a motion for a new trial is made, the dissolution of marriage does not become final until the motion or appeal has been finally disposed of, nor then, if the motion has been granted or judgment reversed.

(b) Notwithstanding any other provision of law, the filing of an appeal or of a motion for a new trial does not stay the effect of a judgment insofar as it relates to the dissolution of the marriage status and restoring the parties to the status of unmarried persons, unless the appealing or moving party specifies in the notice of appeal or motion for new trial an objection to the termination of the marriage status. No party may make such an objection to the termination of the marriage status unless such an objection was also made at the time of trial. **Leg.H.** Enacted Stats 1992 ch 162 §10 (AB 2650), operative January 1, 1994.

§2342. Calculating date judgment becomes final where joint petition for summary dissolution is revoked

Where a joint petition **for summary dissolution** under Chapter 5 (commencing with Section 2400) is thereafter revoked and either party commences a proceeding pursuant to Section 2330 within 90 days from the date of the filing of the revocation, the date the judgment becomes a final judgment under Section 2339 shall be calculated by deducting the period of time [1] **that** has elapsed from the date of filing the joint petition to the date of filing the revocation. **Leg.H.** Enacted Stats 1992 ch 162 §10 (AB 2650), operative January 1, 1994. Amended Stats 2024 ch 190 §3 (SB 1427), effective January 1, 2025.

§2342. 2024 Deletes. [1] which

§2342.5. Procedure for joint petitioners [Operative January 1, 2026]

(a)(1) If the parties file a joint petition for dissolution of marriage or for legal separation of the parties and joint summons in accordance with Sections 2330 and 2331, for identification purposes, including, but not limited to, identification on a Judicial Council form, the first joint petitioner shall be deemed petitioner and the other joint petitioner shall be deemed respondent.

(2) A joint summons shall include the temporary restraining order required by Section 2040.

(3) Section 412.20 of the Code of Civil Procedure does not apply to a joint summons.

(b)(1) At any time before the entry of judgment on the joint petition, without leave of court, in a form and content approved by the Judicial Council, a petitioner may file an amended petition or the respondent may file an amended response.

(2)(A) If either party is served with an amended petition or amended response, the party served shall file and serve an amended petition or amended response, as applicable, within 30 days, in accordance with Section 2020, in a form and content approved by the Judicial Council.

(B) Subject to the court's discretion to regulate the order of proof, pursuant to Section 320 of the Evidence Code, the order of proof shall be determined by the order of service of the amended pleadings.

(3) If an amended petition or amended response is filed pursuant to paragraph (1), the joint petition for dissolution or for legal separation of the parties is deemed revoked and the proceeding shall proceed as a petition for dissolution or for legal separation of the parties under Section 2330. The filing date of the joint petition shall be considered the filing date for the action and all relevant deadlines, including, but not limited to, the deadlines set forth in Section 2339.

(4) A temporary restraining order included in the summons shall remain in effect if a party files an amended petition or amended response.

(c) The parties may file an amended joint petition. The filing of an amended joint petition does not affect the parties' ability to proceed pursuant to a joint petition.

(d) Either party may seek discovery, as set forth in the Code of Civil Procedure, under the joint petition process.

(e) If either party files a request for order, including, but not limited to, a request for a motion to compel or other discovery motion, or request for trial setting with the court, that party shall file an amended petition or amended response, pursuant to subdivision (b), before making, or simultaneously with, the request.

(f) A judgment based on the agreement of the parties shall be in the same form as if one party had filed a petition for dissolution of marriage or legal separation and the other party had filed a response to the petition for dissolution of marriage or legal separation or otherwise appeared prior to entry of judgment because both joint petitioners will have appeared in the matter pursuant to subdivision (b) of Section 2331 due to the filing of a joint petition.

(g) The provisions of Division 6 (commencing with Section 2000) of this code that apply to a petition for dissolution of marriage or for the legal separation of the parties also apply to a joint petition for dissolution of marriage or for legal separation of the parties unless otherwise provided for by this section, in which case the provisions of this section shall supersede.

(h) The filing of a joint petition shall be accompanied by the fees provided in subdivisions (b) and (d) of Section 70670 of the Government Code and the supplemental fees provided in Sections 70602.5 and 70602.6 of the Government Code unless both parties have been granted a fee waiver pursuant to Section 68632 of the Government Code.

(i) This section shall become operative on January 1, 2026. **Leg.H.** Added Stats 2024 ch 190 §4 (SB 1427), effective January 1, 2025, operative January 1, 2026.

§2342.51. Implementation of joint petitioner procedure

The Judicial Council shall adopt or amend any rules or forms necessary to implement Section 2342.5 on or before January 1, 2026. **Leg.H.** Added Stats 2024 ch 190 §5 (SB 1427), effective January 1, 2025.

§2343. Retention of jurisdiction over date of termination; Order for termination at future specified date

The court may, upon notice and for good cause shown, or on stipulation of the parties, retain jurisdiction over the date of termination of the marital status, or may order that the marital status be terminated at a future specified date. On the date of termination of the marital status, the parties are restored to the status of unmarried persons. **Leg.H.** Enacted Stats 1992 ch 162 §10 (AB 2650), operative January 1, 1994.

§2344. Effect of death of either party after entry of judgment

(a) The death of either party after entry of the judgment does not prevent the judgment from becoming a final judgment under Sections 2339 to 2343, inclusive.

(b) Subdivision (a) does not validate a marriage by either party before the judgment becomes final, nor does it constitute a defense in a criminal prosecution against either party. **Leg.H.** Enacted Stats 1992 ch 162 §10 (AB 2650), operative January 1, 1994.

§2345. Consent of parties to legal separation

The court may not render a judgment of the legal separation of the parties without the consent of both parties unless one party has not made a general appearance and the petition is one for legal separation. **Leg.H.** Enacted Stats 1992 ch 162 §10 (AB 2650), operative January 1, 1994.

§2346. Entry of judgment nunc pro tunc

(a) If the court determines that a judgment of dissolution of the marriage should be granted, but by mistake, negligence, or inadvertence, the judgment has not been signed, filed, and entered, the court may cause the judgment to be signed, dated, filed, and entered in the proceeding as of the date when the judgment could have been signed, dated, filed, and entered originally, if it appears to the satisfaction of the court that no appeal is to be taken in the proceeding or motion made for a new trial, to annul or set aside the judgment, or for relief under Chapter 8 (commencing with Section 469) of Title 6 of Part 2 of the Code of Civil Procedure.

(b) The court may act under subdivision (a) on its own motion or upon the motion of either party to the proceeding. In contested cases, the motion of a party shall be with notice to the other party.

(c) The court may cause the judgment to be entered nunc pro tunc as provided in this section, even though the judgment may have been previously entered, where through mistake, negligence, or inadvertence the judgment was not entered as soon as it could have been entered under the law if applied for.

(d) The court shall not cause a judgment to be entered nunc pro tunc as provided in this section as of a date before trial in the matter, before the date of an uncontested judgment hearing in the matter, or before the date of submission to the court of an application for judgment on affidavit pursuant to Section 2336. Upon the entry of the judgment, the parties have the same rights with regard to the dissolution of marriage becoming final on the date that it would have become final had the judgment been entered upon the date when it could have been originally entered. **Leg.H.** Enacted Stats 1992 ch 162 §10 (AB 2650), operative January 1, 1994.

§2347. Legal separation judgment does not bar subsequent dissolution judgment

A judgment of legal separation of the parties does not bar a subsequent judgment of dissolution of the marriage granted pursuant to a petition for dissolution filed by either party. **Leg.H.** Enacted Stats 1992 ch 162 §10 (AB 2650), operative January 1, 1994.

§2348. Report of number of judgments

(a) In addition to the requirements of Section 103200 of the Health and Safety Code, the clerk of the superior court of each county shall report annually to the Judicial Council the number of judgments entered in the county during the preceding calendar year or other 12-month period as required by the Judicial Council for each of the following:

(1) Dissolution of marriage.

(2) Legal separation of the parties.

(3) Nullity of marriage.

(b) After the Judicial Branch Statistical Information System (JBSIS) is operational statewide, the clerk of the superior court of each county shall also report annually to the Judicial Council the number of each of those judgments specified in paragraphs (1), (2), and (3) of subdivision (a), entered in the county during the preceding calendar year or other 12-month period as required by the Judicial Council, that include orders relating to child custody, visitation, or support.

(c) The Judicial Council shall include in its annual report to the Legislature on court statistics the number of each of the types of judgments entered in the state reported pursuant to subdivisions (a) and (b).

(d) The Judicial Council shall establish the applicable 12-month reporting period, the due date, and forms to be used, for submission of data pursuant to subdivisions (a) and (b). Until the Judicial Branch Statistical Information System (JBSIS) is operational statewide, the clerk of the superior court may report the data described in subdivision (a) using existing data collection systems, according to current Judicial Council statistical reporting regulations. **Leg.H.** Added Stats 1998 ch 225 §1 (AB 913).

CHAPTER 5
SUMMARY DISSOLUTION

Conditions necessary at commencement of proceeding. §2400.
Joint petition. §2401.
Revocation of joint petition and termination of proceeding. §2402.
Entry of judgment of dissolution. §2403.
Effect of entry of judgment. §2404.
Action to set aside judgment. §2405.
Brochure describing summary dissolution proceedings. §2406.

§2400. Conditions necessary at commencement of proceeding

(a) A marriage may be dissolved by the summary dissolution procedure provided in this chapter if all of the following conditions exist at the time the proceeding is commenced:

(1) Either party has met the jurisdictional requirements of Chapter 3 (commencing with Section 2320) with regard to dissolution of marriage.

(2) Irreconcilable differences have caused the irremediable breakdown of the marriage and the marriage should be dissolved.

(3) There are no children of the relationship of the parties born before or during the marriage or adopted by the parties during the marriage, and neither party, to that party's knowledge, is pregnant.

(4) The marriage is not more than five years in duration as of the date of separation of the parties.

(5) Neither party has any interest in real property wherever situated, with the exception of the lease of a residence occupied by either party which satisfies the following requirements:

(A) The lease does not include an option to purchase.

(B) The lease terminates within one year from the date of the filing of the petition.

(6) There are no unpaid obligations in excess of four thousand dollars ($4,000) incurred by either or both of the parties after the date of their marriage, excluding the amount of any unpaid obligation with respect to an automobile.

(7) The total fair market value of community property assets, excluding all encumbrances and automobiles, including any deferred compensation or retirement plan, is less than twenty-five thousand dollars ($25,000), and neither party has separate property assets, excluding all encumbrances and automobiles, in excess of twenty-five thousand dollars ($25,000).

(8) The parties have executed an agreement setting forth the division of assets and the assumption of liabilities of the community, and have executed any documents, title certificates, bills of sale, or other evidence of transfer necessary to effectuate the agreement.

(9) The parties waive any rights to spousal support.

(10) The parties, upon entry of the judgment of dissolution of marriage pursuant to Section 2403, irrevocably waive their respective rights to appeal and their rights to move for a new trial.

(11) The parties have read and understand the summary dissolution brochure provided for in Section 2406.

(12) The parties desire that the court dissolve the marriage.

(b) On January 1, 1985, and on January 1 of each odd-numbered year thereafter, the amounts in paragraph (6) of subdivision (a) shall be adjusted to reflect any change in the value of the dollar. On January 1, 1993, and on January 1 of each odd-numbered year thereafter, the amounts in paragraph (7) of subdivision (a) shall be adjusted to reflect any change in the value of the dollar. The adjustments shall be made by multiplying the base amounts by the percentage change in the California Consumer Price Index as compiled by the Department of Industrial Relations, with the result rounded to the nearest thousand dollars. The Judicial Council shall compute and publish the amounts. **Leg.H.** Enacted Stats 1992 ch 162 §10 (AB 2650), operative January 1, 1994. Amended Stats 1993 ch 219 §110.2 (AB 1500); Stats 2010 ch 352 §8 (AB 939), effective January 1, 2011; Stats 2014 ch 82 §28 (SB 1306), effective January 1, 2015.

§2401. Joint petition

(a) A proceeding for summary dissolution of the marriage shall be commenced by filing a joint petition **for summary dissolution** in the form prescribed by the Judicial Council.

(b) The petition shall be signed under oath by both spouses [1] and shall include all of the following:

(1) A statement that as of the date of the filing of the joint petition all of the conditions set forth in Section 2400 have been met.

(2) The mailing address of each spouse.

(3) A statement whether a spouse elects to have [2] **their** former name restored [3] and, if so, the name to be restored. **Leg.H.** Enacted Stats 1992 ch 162 §10 (AB 2650), operative January 1, 1994. Amended Stats 2014 ch 82 §29 (SB 1306), effective January 1, 2015; Stats 2024 ch 190 §6 (SB 1427), effective January 1, 2025.

§2401. 2024 Deletes. [1] , [2] his or her [3] ,

§2402. Revocation of joint petition and termination of proceeding

(a) At any time before the filing of application for judgment pursuant to Section 2403, either party to the marriage may revoke the joint petition **for summary dissolution** and thereby terminate the summary dissolution proceeding filed pursuant to this chapter.

(b) The revocation shall be effected by filing with the clerk of the court where the proceeding was commenced a notice of revocation in [1] **a** form and content as shall be prescribed by the Judicial Council.

(c) The revoking party shall send a copy of the notice of revocation to the other party by first-class mail, postage prepaid, at the other party's last known address. **Leg.H.** Enacted Stats 1992 ch 162 §10 (AB 2650), operative January 1, 1994. Amended Stats 2024 ch 190 §7 (SB 1427), effective January 1, 2025.

§2402. 2024 Deletes. [1] such

§2403. Entry of judgment of dissolution

When six months have expired from the date of the filing of the joint petition for summary dissolution, the court shall, unless a revocation has been filed pursuant to Section 2402, enter the judgment dissolving the marriage. The judgment restores to the parties the status of single persons, and either party may marry after the entry of the judgment. The clerk shall send a notice of entry of judgment to each of the parties at the party's last known address. **Leg.H.** Enacted Stats 1992 ch 162 §10 (AB 2650), operative January 1, 1994. Amended Stats 2010 ch 352 §9 (AB 939), effective January 1, 2011.

§2404. Effect of entry of judgment

Entry of the judgment pursuant to Section 2403 constitutes:

(a) A final adjudication of the rights and obligations of the parties with respect to the status of the marriage and property rights.

(b) A waiver of their respective rights to spousal support, rights to appeal, and rights to move for a new trial. **Leg.H.** Enacted Stats 1992 ch 162 §10 (AB 2650), operative January 1, 1994.

§2405. Action to set aside judgment

(a) Entry of the judgment pursuant to Section 2403 does not prejudice nor bar the rights of either of the parties to institute an action to set aside the judgment for fraud, duress, accident, mistake, or other grounds recognized at law or in equity or to make a motion pursuant to Section 473 of the Code of Civil Procedure.

(b) The court shall set aside a judgment entered pursuant to Section 2403 regarding all matters except the status of the marriage, upon proof that the parties did not meet the requirements of Section 2400 at the time the petition was filed. **Leg.H.** Enacted Stats 1992 ch 162 §10 (AB 2650), operative January 1, 1994.

§2406. Brochure describing summary dissolution proceedings

(a) Each superior court shall make available a brochure, the contents and form of which shall be prescribed by the Judicial Council, describing the requirements, nature, and effect of proceedings under this chapter. The brochure shall be printed and distributed by the Judicial Council in both English and Spanish.

(b) The brochure shall state, in nontechnical language, all the following:

(1) It is in the best interests of the parties to consult an attorney regarding the dissolution of their marriage. The services of an attorney may be obtained through lawyer referral services, group or prepaid legal services, or legal aid organizations.

(2) The parties should not rely exclusively on this brochure which is not intended as a guide for self-representation in proceedings under this chapter.

(3) A concise summary of the provisions and procedures of this chapter and Sections 2320 and 2322 and Sections 2339 to 2344, inclusive.

(4) The nature of services of the conciliation court, where available.

(5) Neither party to the marriage can in the future obtain spousal support from the other.

(6) A statement in boldface type to the effect that upon entry of the judgment, the rights and obligations of the parties to the marriage with respect to the marriage, including property and spousal support rights, will be permanently adjudicated without right of appeal, except that neither party will be barred from instituting an action to set aside the judgment for fraud, duress, accident, mistake, or other grounds at law or in equity, or to make a motion pursuant to Section 473 of the Code of Civil Procedure.

(7) The parties to the marriage retain the status of married persons and cannot remarry until the judgment dissolving the marriage is entered.

(8) Other matters as the Judicial Council considers appropriate. **Leg.H.** Enacted Stats 1992 ch 162 §10 (AB 2650), operative January 1, 1994.

CHAPTER 6
CASE MANAGEMENT

Purpose. §2450.
Plan; Adoption of statewide rule of court. §2451.
Judicial Council authority to convert judicial officer positions to judgeships. §2452.

§2450. Purpose

(a) The purpose of family centered case resolution is to benefit the parties by providing judicial assistance and management to the parties in actions for dissolution of marriage for the purpose of expediting the processing of the case, reducing the expense of litigation, and focusing on early resolution by settlement. Family centered case resolution is a tool to allow the courts to better assist families. It does not increase the authority of the court to appoint any third parties to the case.

(b) The court may order a family centered case resolution plan as provided in Section 2451. If the court orders family centered case resolution, it shall state the family centered case resolution plan in writing or on the record. **Leg.H.** Added Stats 1996 ch 56 §3 (SB 389). Amended Stats 2010 ch 352 §10 (AB 939), effective January 1, 2011.

§2451. Plan; Adoption of statewide rule of court

(a) A court-ordered family centered case resolution plan must be in conformance with due process requirements and may include, but is not limited to, all of the following:

(1) Early neutral case evaluation.

(2) Alternative dispute resolution consistent with the requirements of subdivision (a) of Section 3181.

(3) Limitations on discovery, including temporary suspension pending exploration of settlement. There is a rebuttable presumption that an attorney who carries out discovery as provided in a family centered case resolution plan has fulfilled his or her duty of care to the client as to the existence of community property.

(4) Use of telephone conference calls to ascertain the status of the case, encourage cooperation, and assist counsel in reaching agreement. However, if the court is required to issue an order other than by stipulation, a hearing shall be held.

(5) If stipulated by the parties, modification or waiver of the requirements of procedural statutes.

(6) A requirement that any expert witness be selected by the parties jointly or be appointed by the court. However, if at any time the court determines that the issues for which experts are required cannot be settled under these conditions, the court shall permit each party to employ his or her own expert.

(7) Bifurcation of issues for trial.

(b) This section does not provide any additional authority to the court to appoint experts beyond that permitted under other provisions of law.

(c) The Judicial Council shall, by January 1, 2012, adopt a statewide rule of court to implement this section.

(d) The changes made to this section by the act adding this subdivision shall become operative on January 1, 2012. **Leg.H.** Added Stats 1996 ch 56 §3 (SB 389). Amended Stats 2010 ch 352 §11 (AB 939), effective January 1, 2011, operative January 1, 2012.

§2452. Judicial Council authority to convert judicial officer positions to judgeships

The Judicial Council may, by rule, increase the procedures set forth in this chapter. **Leg.H.** Added Stats 1996 ch 56 §3 (SB 389). Amended Stats 2014 ch 311 §1 (AB 2745), effective January 1, 2015.

DIVISION 7
DIVISION OF PROPERTY

Part 1. Definitions.
Part 2. General Provisions.
Part 3. Presumption Concerning Property Held in Joint Form.
Part 4. Special Rules for Division of Community Estate.
Part 5. Retirement Plan Benefits.
Part 6. Debts and Liabilities.
Part 7. Reimbursements.
Part 8. Jointly Held Separate Property.
Part 9. Real Property Located in Another State.

PART 1
DEFINITIONS

Application of definitions. §2500.
Separate property. §2502.

§2500. Application of definitions

Unless the provision or context otherwise requires, the definitions in this part govern the construction of this division. **Leg.H.** Enacted Stats 1992 ch 162 §10 (AB 2650), operative January 1, 1994.

§2501. [Section repealed 1993]

Leg.H. Enacted Stats 1992 ch 162 §10 (AB 2650), operative January 1, 1994. Repealed Stats 1993 ch 219 §110.5 (AB 1500). See Fam C §63.

§2502. Separate property

"Separate property" does not include quasi-community property.
Leg.H. Enacted Stats 1992 ch 162 §10 (AB 2650), operative January 1, 1994.

PART 2
GENERAL PROVISIONS

Equal division of community estate. §2550.
Characterization of liabilities as separate or community and confirming or assigning them to parties. §2551.
Valuation date for assets and liabilities. §2552.
Orders necessary to carry out purposes of this division. §2553.
Arbitration where parties do not voluntarily agree to division. §2554.
Revision of property disposition on appeal. §2555.
Continuing jurisdiction to award community estate assets or liabilities. §2556.

§2550. Equal division of community estate

Except upon the written agreement of the parties, or on oral stipulation of the parties in open court, or as otherwise provided in this division, in a proceeding for dissolution of marriage or for legal separation of the parties, the court shall, either in its judgment of dissolution of the marriage, in its judgment of legal separation of the parties, or at a later time if it expressly reserves jurisdiction to make such a property division, divide the community estate of the parties equally. **Leg.H.** Enacted Stats 1992 ch 162 §10 (AB 2650), operative January 1, 1994.

§2551. Characterization of liabilities as separate or community and confirming or assigning them to parties

For the purposes of division and in confirming or assigning the liabilities of the parties for which the community estate is liable, the court shall characterize liabilities as separate or community and confirm or assign them to the parties in accordance with Part 6 (commencing with Section 2620). **Leg.H.** Enacted Stats 1992 ch 162 §10 (AB 2650), operative January 1, 1994.

§2552. Valuation date for assets and liabilities

(a) For the purpose of division of the community estate upon dissolution of marriage or legal separation of the parties, except as provided in subdivision (b), the court shall value the assets and liabilities as near as practicable to the time of trial.

(b) Upon 30 days' notice by the moving party to the other party, the court for good cause shown may value all or any portion of the assets and liabilities at a date after separation and before trial to accomplish an equal division of the community estate of the parties in an equitable manner. **Leg.H.** Enacted Stats 1992 ch 162 §10 (AB 2650), operative January 1, 1994.

§2553. Orders necessary to carry out purposes of this division

The court may make any orders the court considers necessary to carry out the purposes of this division. **Leg.H.** Enacted Stats 1992 ch 162 §10 (AB 2650), operative January 1, 1994.

§2554. Arbitration where parties do not voluntarily agree to division

(a) Notwithstanding any other provision of this division, in any case in which the parties do not agree in writing to a voluntary division of the community estate of the parties, the issue of the character, the value, and the division of the community estate may be submitted by the court to arbitration for resolution pursuant to Chapter 2.5 (commencing with Section 1141.10) of Title 3 of Part 3 of the Code of Civil Procedure, if the total value of the community and quasi-community property in controversy in the opinion of the court does not exceed fifty thousand dollars ($50,000). The decision of the court regarding the value of the community and quasi-community property for purposes of this section is not appealable.

(b) The court may submit the matter to arbitration at any time it believes the parties are unable to agree upon a division of the property. **Leg.H.** Enacted Stats 1992 ch 162 §10 (AB 2650), operative January 1, 1994.

§2555. Revision of property disposition on appeal

The disposition of the community estate, as provided in this division, is subject to revision on appeal in all particulars, including those which are stated to be in the discretion of the court. **Leg.H.** Enacted Stats 1992 ch 162 §10 (AB 2650), operative January 1, 1994.

§2556. Continuing jurisdiction to award community estate assets or liabilities

In a proceeding for dissolution of marriage, for nullity of marriage, or for legal separation of the parties, the court has continuing jurisdiction to award community estate assets or community estate liabilities to the parties that have not been previously adjudicated by a judgment in the proceeding. A party may file a postjudgment motion or order to show cause in the proceeding in order to obtain adjudication of any community estate asset or liability omitted or not adjudicated by the judgment. In these cases, the court shall equally divide the omitted or unadjudicated community estate asset or liability, unless the court finds upon good cause shown that the interests of justice require an unequal division of the asset or liability. **Leg.H.** Enacted Stats 1992 ch 162 §10 (AB 2650), operative January 1, 1994. Amended Stats 1993 ch 219 §111 (AB 1500).

PART 3
PRESUMPTION CONCERNING PROPERTY HELD IN JOINT FORM

Legislative findings and declarations. §2580.
Community property presumption of property acquired during marriage in joint form. §2581.

§2580. Legislative findings and declarations

The Legislature hereby finds and declares as follows:

(a) It is the public policy of this state to provide uniformly and consistently for the standard of proof in establishing the character of property acquired by spouses during marriage in joint title form, and for the allocation of community and separate interests in that property between the spouses.

(b) The methods provided by case and statutory law have not resulted in consistency in the treatment of spouses' interests in property they hold in joint title, but rather, have created confusion as to which law applies to property at a particular point in time, depending on the form of title, and, as a result, spouses cannot have reliable expectations as to the characterization of their property and the allocation of the interests therein, and attorneys cannot reliably advise their clients regarding applicable law.

(c) Therefore, a compelling state interest exists to provide for uniform treatment of property. Thus, former Sections 4800.1 and 4800.2 of the Civil Code, as operative on January 1, 1987, and as continued in Sections 2581 and 2640 of this code, apply to all property held in joint title regardless of the date of acquisition of the property or the date of any agreement affecting the character of the property, and those sections apply in all proceedings commenced on or after January 1, 1984. However, those sections do not apply to property settlement agreements executed before January 1, 1987, or proceedings in which judgments were rendered before January 1, 1987, regardless of whether those judgments have become final. **Leg.H.** Added Stats 1993 ch 219 §111.6 (AB 1500). Amended Stats 1993 ch 876 §15.2 (SB 1068), effective October 6, 1993, operative January 1, 1994.

Prior Law: Former §2580, similar to present §2581, was enacted Stats 1992 ch 162 §10 (AB 2650), to become operative January 1, 1994, and repealed Stat 1993 ch 219 §111.5.

§2581. Community property presumption of property acquired during marriage in joint form

For the purpose of division of property on dissolution of marriage or legal separation of the parties, property acquired by the parties during marriage in joint form, including property held in tenancy in common, joint tenancy, or tenancy by the entirety, or as community property, is presumed to be community property. This presumption is a presumption affecting the burden of proof and may be rebutted by either of the following:

(a) A clear statement in the deed or other documentary evidence of title by which the property is acquired that the property is separate property and not community property.

(b) Proof that the parties have made a written agreement that the property is separate property. **Leg.H.** Added Stats 1993 ch 219 §111.7 (AB 1500).

PART 4
SPECIAL RULES FOR DIVISION OF COMMUNITY ESTATE

Special rules for division of community estate. §2600.
Awarding asset to one party to effect substantially equal division. §2601.
Award or offset of amount deliberately misappropriated by party. §2602.
Community estate personal injury damages. §2603.
Judgment of spousal abuse enforced against abusive spouse's community property. §2603.5.
Award where community estate less than $5,000 and one party cannot be located. §2604.
Division of ownership of pets upon dissolution of marriage. §2605.

§2600. Special rules for division of community estate

Notwithstanding Sections 2550 to 2552, inclusive, the court may divide the community estate as provided in this part. **Leg.H.** Enacted Stats 1992 ch 162 §10 (AB 2650), operative January 1, 1994.

§2601. Awarding asset to one party to effect substantially equal division

Where economic circumstances warrant, the court may award an asset of the community estate to one party on such conditions as the court deems proper to effect a substantially equal division of the community estate. **Leg.H.** Enacted Stats 1992 ch 162 §10 (AB 2650), operative January 1, 1994.

§2602. Award or offset of amount deliberately misappropriated by party

As an additional award or offset against existing property, the court may award, from a party's share, the amount the court determines to have been deliberately misappropriated by the party to the exclusion of the interest of the other party in the community estate. **Leg.H.** Enacted Stats 1992 ch 162 §10 (AB 2650), operative January 1, 1994.

§2603. Community estate personal injury damages

(a) "Community estate personal injury damages" as used in this section means all money or other property received or to be received by a person in satisfaction of a judgment for damages for the person's personal injuries or pursuant to an agreement for the settlement or compromise of a claim for the damages, if the cause of action for the damages arose during the marriage but is not separate property as described in Section 781, unless the money or other property has been commingled with other assets of the community estate.

(b) Community estate personal injury damages shall be assigned to the party who suffered the injuries unless the court, after taking into account the economic condition and needs of each party, the time that has elapsed since the recovery of the damages or the accrual of the cause of action, and all other facts of the case, determines that the interests of justice require another disposition. In such a case, the community estate personal injury damages shall be assigned to the respective parties in such proportions as the court determines to be just, except that at least one-half of the damages shall be assigned to the party who suffered the injuries. **Leg.H.** Enacted Stats 1992 ch 162 §10 (AB 2650), operative January 1, 1994.

§2603.5. Judgment of spousal abuse enforced against abusive spouse's community property

The court may, if there is a judgment for civil damages for an act of domestic violence perpetrated by one spouse against the other spouse, enforce that judgment against the abusive spouse's share of community property, if a proceeding for dissolution of marriage or legal separation of the parties is pending prior to the entry of final judgment. **Leg.H.** Added Stats 2004 ch 299 §1 (AB 2018).

§2604. Award where community estate less than $5,000 and one party cannot be located

If the net value of the community estate is less than five thousand dollars ($5,000) and one party cannot be located through the exercise of reasonable diligence, the court may award all the community estate to the other party on conditions the court deems proper in its judgment of dissolution of marriage or legal separation of the parties. **Leg.H.** Enacted Stats 1992 ch 162 §10 (AB 2650), operative January 1, 1994.

§2605. Division of ownership of pets upon dissolution of marriage

(a) The court, at the request of a party to proceedings for dissolution of marriage or for legal separation of the parties, may enter an order, prior to the final determination of ownership of a pet animal, to require a party to care for the pet animal. The existence of an order providing for the care of a pet animal during the course of proceedings for dissolution of marriage or for legal separation of the parties shall not have any impact on the court's final determination of ownership of the pet animal.

(b) Notwithstanding any other law, including, but not limited to, Section 2550, the court, at the request of a party to proceedings for dissolution of marriage or for legal separation of the parties, may assign sole or joint ownership of a pet animal taking into consideration the care of the pet animal.

(c) For purposes of this section, the following definitions shall apply:

(1) "Care" includes, but is not limited to, the prevention of acts of harm or cruelty, as described in Section 597 of the Penal Code, and the provision of food, water, veterinary care, and safe and protected shelter.

(2) "Pet animal" means any animal that is community property and kept as a household pet. **Leg.H.** Added Stats 2018 ch 820 §1 (AB 2274), effective January 1, 2019.

PART 5
RETIREMENT PLAN BENEFITS

Division of retirement plan benefits. §2610.
Payment of benefits pursuant to tribal court order. § 2611.

§2610. Division of retirement plan benefits

(a) Except as provided in subdivision (b), the court shall make whatever orders are necessary or appropriate to ensure that each party receives the party's full community property share in any retirement plan, whether public or private, including all survivor and death benefits, including, but not limited to, any of the following:

(1) Order the disposition of retirement benefits payable upon or after the death of either party in a manner consistent with Section 2550.

(2) Order a party to elect a survivor benefit annuity or other similar election for the benefit of the other party, as specified by the court, when a retirement plan provides for that election, provided that no court shall order a retirement plan to provide increased benefits determined on the basis of actuarial value.

(3) Upon the agreement of the nonemployee spouse, order the division of accumulated community property contributions and service credit as provided in the following or similar enactments:

(A) Article 2 (commencing with Section 21290) of Chapter 9 of Part 3 of Division 5 of Title 2 of the Government Code.

(B) Chapter 12 (commencing with Section 22650) of Part 13 of Division 1 of Title 1 of the Education Code.

(C) Article 8.4 (commencing with Section 31685) of Chapter 3 of Part 3 of Division 4 of Title 3 of the Government Code.

(D) Article 2.5 (commencing with Section 75050) of Chapter 11 of Title 8 of the Government Code.

(E) Chapter 15 (commencing with Section 27400) of Part 14 of Division 1 of Title 1 of the Education Code.

(4) Order a retirement plan to make payments directly to a nonmember party of the nonmember party's community property interest in retirement benefits.

(b) A court shall not make an order that requires a retirement plan to do either of the following:

(1) Make payments in a manner that will result in an increase in the amount of benefits provided by the plan.

(2) Make the payment of benefits to a party at any time before the member retires, except as provided in paragraph (3) of subdivision (a), unless the plan so provides.

(c) This section shall not be applied retroactively to payments made by a retirement plan to a person who retired or died prior to January 1, 1987, or to payments made to a person who retired or died prior to June 1, 1988, for plans subject to paragraph (3) of subdivision (a). **Leg.H.** Enacted Stats 1992 ch 162 §10 (AB 2650), operative January 1, 1994. Amended Stats 1993 ch 219 §112 (AB 1500); Stats 1994 ch 670 §1 (SB 1500), ch 1269 §25.5 (AB 2208); Stats 1998 ch 965 §322 (AB 2765); Stats 2009 ch 130 §1 (AB 966), effective January 1, 2010; Stats 2019 ch 115 §22 (AB 1817), effective January 1, 2020.

§ 2611. Payment of benefits pursuant to tribal court order

(a) A final order of a tribal court that creates or recognizes the existence of the right of a spouse, former spouse, child, or other dependent of a participant in a retirement plan or other plan of deferred compensation to receive all or a portion of the benefits payable with respect to such plan participant, and that relates to the provision of child support, spousal support payments, or marital property rights to such spouse, former spouse, child, or other dependent, that is filed in accordance with Section 1733.1 of the Code of Civil Procedure shall be recognized as an order made pursuant to the domestic relations laws of this state.

(b) The filing of the tribal court order does not confer any jurisdiction on a court of this state to modify or enforce the tribal court order. **Leg.H.** Added Stats 2021 ch 58 §7 (AB 627), effective January 1, 2022.

PART 6
DEBTS AND LIABILITIES

Confirmation or division of community estate debts. §2620.
Debts incurred before marriage. §2621.
Debts incurred after marriage but before separation. §2622.
Debts incurred after separation but before judgment. §2623.
Debts incurred after entry of judgment. §2624.
Separate debts. §2625.
Reimbursement for debts paid after separation but before trial. §2626.
Educational loans and tort liability. §2627.
Revision of joint income tax liability by court. §2628.

§2620. Confirmation or division of community estate debts

The debts for which the community estate is liable which are unpaid at the time of trial, or for which the community estate becomes liable after trial, shall be confirmed or divided as provided in this part. **Leg.H.** Enacted Stats 1992 ch 162 §10 (AB 2650), operative January 1, 1994.

§2621. Debts incurred before marriage

Debts incurred by either spouse before the date of marriage shall be confirmed without offset to the spouse who incurred the debt. **Leg.H.** Enacted Stats 1992 ch 162 §10 (AB 2650), operative January 1, 1994.

§2622. Debts incurred after marriage but before separation

(a) Except as provided in subdivision (b), debts incurred by either spouse after the date of marriage but before the date of separation shall be divided as set forth in Sections 2550 to 2552, inclusive, and Sections 2601 to 2604, inclusive.

(b) To the extent that community debts exceed total community and quasi-community assets, the excess of debt shall be assigned as the court deems just and equitable, taking into account factors such as the parties' relative ability to pay. **Leg.H.** Enacted Stats 1992 ch 162 §10 (AB 2650), operative January 1, 1994.

§2623. Debts incurred after separation but before judgment

Debts incurred by either spouse after the date of separation but before entry of a judgment of dissolution of marriage or legal separation of the parties shall be confirmed as follows:

(a) Debts incurred by either spouse for the common necessaries of life of either spouse or the necessaries of life of the children of the marriage for whom support may be ordered, in the absence of a court order or written agreement for support or for the payment of these debts, shall be confirmed to either spouse according to the parties' respective needs and abilities to pay at the time the debt was incurred.

(b) Debts incurred by either spouse for nonnecessaries of that spouse or children of the marriage for whom support may be ordered shall be confirmed without offset to the spouse who incurred the debt. **Leg.H.** Enacted Stats 1992 ch 162 §10 (AB 2650), operative January 1, 1994. Amended Stats 1993 ch 219 §113 (AB 1500).

§2624. Debts incurred after entry of judgment

Debts incurred by either spouse after entry of a judgment of dissolution of marriage but before termination of the parties' marital status or after entry of a judgment of legal separation of the parties shall be confirmed without offset to the spouse who incurred the debt. **Leg.H.** Enacted Stats 1992 ch 162 §10 (AB 2650), operative January 1, 1994.

§2625. Separate debts

Notwithstanding Sections 2620 to 2624, inclusive, all separate debts, including those debts incurred by a spouse during marriage and before the date of separation that were not incurred for the benefit of the community, shall be confirmed without offset to the spouse who incurred the debt. **Leg.H.** Enacted Stats 1992 ch 162 §10 (AB 2650), operative January 1, 1994.

§2626. Reimbursement for debts paid after separation but before trial

The court has jurisdiction to order reimbursement in cases it deems appropriate for debts paid after separation but before trial. **Leg.H.** Enacted Stats 1992 ch 162 §10 (AB 2650), operative January 1, 1994.

§2627. Educational loans and tort liability

Notwithstanding Sections 2550 to 2552, inclusive, and Sections 2620 to 2624, inclusive, educational loans shall be assigned pursuant to Section 2641 and liabilities subject to paragraph (2) of subdivision (b) of Section 1000 shall be assigned to the spouse whose act or omission provided the basis for the liability, without offset. **Leg.H.** Enacted Stats 1992 ch 162 §10 (AB 2650), operative January 1, 1994.

§2628. Revision of joint income tax liability by court

Notwithstanding Sections 2550 to 2552, inclusive, and Sections 2620 to 2624, inclusive, joint California income tax liabilities may be revised by a court in a proceeding for dissolution of marriage, provided the requirements of Section 19006 of the Revenue and Taxation Code are satisfied. **Leg.H.** Added Stats 2002 ch 374 §1 (AB 2979).

Prior Law: Former §2628, relating to notice in judgment that creditor could be able to collect debt or obligation notwithstanding assignment to other party, was enacted Stats 1992 ch 162 §10 and repealed Stats 1993 ch 219 §114.

PART 7
REIMBURSEMENTS

Contributions to acquisition of property; Amount of reimbursement; Waiver. §2640.
Community contributions for education or training. §2641.

§2640. Contributions to acquisition of property; Amount of reimbursement; Waiver

(a) "Contributions to the acquisition of property," as used in this section, include downpayments, payments for improvements, and payments that reduce the principal of a loan used to finance the purchase or improvement of the property but do not include payments of interest on the loan or payments made for maintenance, insurance, or taxation of the property.

(b) In the division of the community estate under this division, unless a party has made a written waiver of the right to reimbursement or has signed a writing that has the effect of a waiver, the party shall be reimbursed for the party's contributions to the acquisition of property of the community property estate to the extent the party traces the contributions to a separate property source. The amount reimbursed shall be without interest or adjustment for change in monetary values and may not exceed the net value of the property at the time of the division.

(c) A party shall be reimbursed for the party's separate property contributions to the acquisition of property of the other spouse's separate property estate during the marriage, unless there has been a transmutation in writing pursuant to Chapter 5 (commencing with Section 850) of Part 2 of Division 4, or a written waiver of the right to reimbursement. The amount reimbursed shall be without interest or adjustment for change in monetary values and may not exceed the net value of the property at the time of the division. **Leg.H.** Enacted Stats 1992 ch 162 §10 (AB 2650), operative January 1, 1994. Amended Stats 1993 ch 219 §114.5 (AB 1500); Stats 2004 ch 119 §1 (SB 1407).

§2641. Community contributions for education or training

(a) "Community contributions to education or training" as used in this section means payments made with community or quasi-community property for education or training or for the repayment of a loan incurred for education or training, whether the payments were made while the parties were resident in this state or resident outside this state.

(b) Subject to the limitations provided in this section, upon dissolution of marriage or legal separation of the parties:

(1) The community shall be reimbursed for community contributions to education or training of a party that substantially enhances the earning capacity of the party. The amount reimbursed shall be with interest at the legal rate, accruing from the end of the calendar year in which the contributions were made.

(2) A loan incurred during marriage for the education or training of a party shall not be included among the liabilities of the community for the purpose of division pursuant to this division but shall be assigned for payment by the party.

(c) The reimbursement and assignment required by this section shall be reduced or modified to the extent circumstances render such a disposition unjust, including, but not limited to, any of the following:

(1) The community has substantially benefited from the education, training, or loan incurred for the education or training of the party. There is a rebuttable presumption, affecting the burden of proof, that the community has not substantially benefited from community contributions to the education or training made less than 10 years before the commencement of the proceeding, and that the community has substantially benefited from community contributions to the education or training made more than 10 years before the commencement of the proceeding.

(2) The education or training received by the party is offset by the education or training received by the other party for which community contributions have been made.

(3) The education or training enables the party receiving the education or training to engage in gainful employment that substantially reduces the need of the party for support that would otherwise be required.

(d) Reimbursement for community contributions and assignment of loans pursuant to this section is the exclusive remedy of the community or a party for the education or training and any resulting enhancement of the earning capacity of a party. However, nothing in this subdivision limits consideration of the effect of the education, training, or enhancement, or the amount reimbursed pursuant to this section, on the circumstances of the parties for the purpose of an order for support pursuant to Section 4320.

(e) This section is subject to an express written agreement of the parties to the contrary. **Leg.H.** Enacted Stats 1992 ch 162 §10 (AB 2650), operative January 1, 1994.

PART 8
JOINTLY HELD SEPARATE PROPERTY

Division of jointly held separate property. §2650.

§2650. Division of jointly held separate property

In a proceeding for division of the community estate, the court has jurisdiction, at the request of either party, to divide the separate property interests of the parties in real and personal property, wherever situated and whenever acquired, held by the parties as joint tenants or tenants in common. The property shall be divided together with, and in accordance with the same procedure for and limitations on, division of community estate. **Leg.H.** Enacted Stats 1992 ch 162 §10 (AB 2650), operative January 1, 1994.

PART 9
REAL PROPERTY LOCATED IN ANOTHER STATE

Division where community estate includes real property located in another state. §2660.

§2660. Division where community estate includes real property located in another state

(a) Except as provided in subdivision (b), if the property subject to division includes real property situated in another state, the court shall, if possible, divide the community property and quasi-community property as provided for in this division in such a manner that it is not necessary to change the nature of the interests held in the real property situated in the other state.

(b) If it is not possible to divide the property in the manner provided for in subdivision (a), the court may do any of the following in order to effect a division of the property as provided for in this division:

(1) Require the parties to execute conveyances or take other actions with respect to the real property situated in the other state as are necessary.

(2) Award to the party who would have been benefited by the conveyances or other actions the money value of the interest in the property that the party would have received if the conveyances had been executed or other actions taken. **Leg.H.** Enacted Stats 1992 ch 162 §10 (AB 2650), operative January 1, 1994.

DIVISION 8
CUSTODY OF CHILDREN

Part 1. Definitions and General Provisions.
Part 2. Right to Custody of Minor Child.
Part 3. Uniform Child Custody Jurisdiction and Enforcement Act.

PART 1
DEFINITIONS AND GENERAL PROVISIONS

Chapter 1. Definitions.
Chapter 2. General Provisions.

CHAPTER 1
DEFINITIONS

Application of definitions. §3000.
Joint custody. §3002.
Joint legal custody. §3003.
Joint physical custody. §3004.
Sole legal custody. §3006.
Sole physical custody. §3007.

§3000. Application of definitions

Unless the provision or context otherwise requires, the definitions in this chapter govern the construction of this division. **Leg.H.** Enacted Stats 1992 ch 162 §10 (AB 2650), operative January 1, 1994.

§3002. Joint custody

"Joint custody" means joint physical custody and joint legal custody. **Leg.H.** Enacted Stats 1992 ch 162 §10 (AB 2650), operative January 1, 1994.

§3003. Joint legal custody

"Joint legal custody" means that both parents shall share the right and the responsibility to make the decisions relating to the health, education, and welfare of a child. **Leg.H.** Enacted Stats 1992 ch 162 §10 (AB 2650), operative January 1, 1994.

§3004. Joint physical custody

"Joint physical custody" means that each of the parents shall have significant periods of physical custody. Joint physical custody shall be shared by the parents in such a way so as to assure a child of frequent and continuing contact with both parents, subject to Sections 3011 and 3020. **Leg.H.** Enacted Stats 1992 ch 162 §10 (AB 2650), operative January 1, 1994. Amended Stats 1997 ch 849 §1 (AB 200).

§3006. Sole legal custody

"Sole legal custody" means that one parent shall have the right and the responsibility to make the decisions relating to the health, education, and welfare of a child. **Leg.H.** Enacted Stats 1992 ch 162 §10 (AB 2650), operative January 1, 1994.

§3007. Sole physical custody

"Sole physical custody" means that a child shall reside with and be under the supervision of one parent, subject to the power of the court to order visitation. **Leg.H.** Enacted Stats 1992 ch 162 §10 (AB 2650), operative January 1, 1994.

CHAPTER 2
GENERAL PROVISIONS

Right of parent to custody of child. §3010.
Factors considered in determining best interest of child. §3011.
Presentation of testimony and evidence and participation in mediation by electronic means. §3012.

§3010. Right of parent to custody of child

(a) The mother of an unemancipated minor child and the father, if presumed to be the father under Section 7611, are equally entitled to the custody of the child.

(b) If one parent is dead, is unable or refuses to take custody, or has abandoned the child, the other parent is entitled to custody of the child. **Leg.H.** Added Stats 1993 ch 219 §115.5 (AB 1500).

Prior Law: Former §3010, similar to the present section and Fam C §7501, was enacted Stats 1992 ch 162 §10, to become operative January 1, 1994, and repealed Stats 1993 ch 219 §115.

§3011. Factors considered in determining best interest of child

(a) In making a determination of the best interests of the child in a proceeding described in Section 3021, the court shall, among any other factors it finds relevant and consistent with Section 3020, consider all of the following:

(1) The health, safety, and welfare of the child.

(2)(A) A history of abuse by one parent or any other person seeking custody against any of the following:

(i) A child to whom the parent or person seeking custody is related by blood or affinity or with whom the parent or person seeking custody has had a caretaking relationship, no matter how temporary.

(ii) The other parent.

(iii) A parent, current spouse, or cohabitant, of the parent or person seeking custody, or a person with whom the parent or person seeking custody has a dating or engagement relationship.

(B) As a prerequisite to considering allegations of abuse, the court may require independent corroboration, including, but not limited to, written reports by law enforcement agencies, child protective services or other social welfare agencies, courts, medical facilities, or other public agencies or private nonprofit organizations providing services to victims of sexual assault or domestic violence. As used in this paragraph, "abuse against a child" means "child abuse and neglect" as defined in Section 11165.6 of the Penal Code and abuse against any other person described in clause (ii) or (iii) of subparagraph (A) means "abuse" as defined in Section 6203.

(3) The nature and amount of contact with both parents, including as provided in Sections 3046 and 3100.

(4) The habitual or continual illegal use of controlled substances, the habitual or continual abuse of alcohol, or the habitual or continual abuse of prescribed controlled substances by either parent. Before considering these allegations, the court may first require independent corroboration, including, but not limited to, written reports from law enforcement agencies, courts, probation departments, social welfare agencies, medical facilities, rehabilitation facilities, or other public agencies or nonprofit organizations providing drug and alcohol abuse services. As used in this paragraph, "controlled substances" has the same meaning as defined in the California Uniform Controlled Substances Act (Division 10 (commencing with Section 11000) of the Health and Safety Code).

(5)(A) When allegations about a parent pursuant to paragraph (2) or (4) have been brought to the attention of the court in the current proceeding, and the court makes an order for sole or joint custody or unsupervised visitation to that parent, the court shall state its reasons in writing or on the record that the order is in the best interest of the child and protects the safety of the parties and the child. In these circumstances, the court shall ensure that any order regarding custody or visitation is specific as to time, day, place, and manner of transfer of the child as set forth in subdivision (c) of Section 6323.

(B) Nothing in this paragraph eliminates the requirement that the contents of the stipulation be in the best interest of the child and be specific as to time, day, place, and manner of transfer of the child if the parties do stipulate in writing or on the record regarding custody or visitation.

(b) Notwithstanding subdivision (a), the court shall not consider the sex, gender identity, gender expression, or sexual orientation of a parent, legal guardian, or relative in determining the best interests of the child. **Leg.H.** Added Stats 1993 ch 219 §115.5 (AB 1500). Amended Stats 1996 ch 835 §1 (AB 2474), ch 836 §1.5 (SB 384); Stats 1997 ch 849 §2 (AB 200); Stats 1999 ch 980 §4 (AB 1671); Stats 2012 ch 258 §1 (AB 2365), effective January 1, 2013; Stats 2018 ch 941 §1 (AB 2044), effective January 1, 2019; Stats 2019 ch 115 §23 (AB 1817), effective January 1, 2020; Stats 2019 ch 551 §1 (SB 495), effective January 1, 2020 (ch 551 prevails); Stats 2020 ch 370 §115 (SB 1371), effective January 1, 2021; Stats 2021 ch 768 §1 (SB 654), effective January 1, 2022; Stats 2022 ch 28 §45 (SB 1380), effective January 1, 2023; Stats 2023 ch 493 §2 (SB 599), effective January 1, 2024.

Prior Law: Former §3011, similar to present Fam C §7501, was enacted Stats 1992 ch 162 §10, to become operative January 1, 1994, and repealed Stats 1993 ch 219 §115.

§3012. Presentation of testimony and evidence and participation in mediation by electronic means

(a) If a party's deportation or detention by the United States Immigration and Customs Enforcement of the Department of Homeland Security will have a material effect on the person's ability, or anticipated ability, to appear in person at a child custody proceeding, the court shall, upon motion of the party, allow the party to present testimony and evidence and participate in mandatory child custody mediation by electronic means, including, but not limited to, telephone, video teleconferencing, or other electronic means that provide remote access to the hearing, to the extent that this technology is reasonably available to the court and protects the due process rights of all parties.

(b) This section does not authorize the use of electronic recording for the purpose of taking the official record of these proceedings. **Leg.H.** Added Stats 2015 ch 69 §1 (AB 365), effective January 1, 2016. Amended Stats 2019 ch 115 §24 (AB 1817), effective January 1, 2020.

Prior Law: Former Fam C §3012, similar to present Fam C §7502, was enacted Stats 1992 ch 162 §10, operative January 1, 1994, and repealed Stats 1993 ch 219 §115, effective January 1, 1994.

§3013. [Section repealed 1993]

Leg.H. Enacted Stats 1992 ch 162 §10 (AB 2650), operative January 1, 1994. Repealed Stats 1993 ch 219 §115 (AB 1500). See Fam C §7503.

§3014. [Section repealed 1993]

Leg.H. Enacted Stats 1992 ch 162 §10 (AB 2650), operative January 1, 1994. Repealed Stats 1993 ch 219 §115 (AB 1500). See Fam C §7504.

§3015. [Section repealed 1993]

Leg.H. Enacted Stats 1992 ch 162 §10 (AB 2650), operative January 1, 1994. Repealed Stats 1993 ch 219 §115 (AB 1500). See Fam C §7505.

§3016. [Section repealed 1993]

Leg.H. Enacted Stats 1992 ch 162 §10 (AB 2650), operative January 1, 1994. Repealed Stats 1993 ch 219 §115 (AB 1500). See Fam C §7506.

§3017. [Section repealed 1993]

Leg.H. Enacted Stats 1992 ch 162 §10 (AB 2650), operative January 1, 1994. Repealed Stats 1993 ch 219 §115 (AB 1500). See Fam C §3029.

§3018. [Section repealed 1993]

Leg.H. Enacted Stats 1992 ch 162 §10 (AB 2650), operative January 1, 1994. Repealed Stats 1993 ch 219 §115 (AB 1500). See Fam C §7507.

PART 2
RIGHT TO CUSTODY OF MINOR CHILD

Chapter 1. General Provisions.
Chapter 2. Matters To Be Considered in Granting Custody.
Chapter 3. Temporary Custody Order During Pendency of Proceeding.
Chapter 4. Joint Custody.
Chapter 5. Visitation Rights.
Chapter 6. Custody Investigation and Report.
Chapter 7. Action for Exclusive Custody.
Chapter 8. Location of Missing Party or Child.
Chapter 9. Check to Determine Whether Child Is Missing Person.
Chapter 10. Appointment of Counsel to Represent Child.
Chapter 11. Mediation of Custody and Visitation Issues.
Chapter 12. Counseling of Parents and Child.
Chapter 13. Supervised Visitation and Exchange Services, Education, and Counseling.

CHAPTER 1
GENERAL PROVISIONS

Legislative findings and declarations. §3020.
Application of part. §3021.
Authority of court to make custody order. §3022.
Statement explaining basis of decision by court. §3022.3.
Motion for reconsideration of existing custody order based on conviction of other parent of crime of false accusation of child abuse against moving parent. §3022.5.
Preference for trial on issue of custody. §3023.
Notice to other parent of change of residence of child. §3024.
Parental access to records. §3025.
Confidentiality of psychological evaluations of child involved in custody or visitation rights proceedings. §3025.5.
Family reunification services. §3026.
Allegations made during child custody proceedings. §3027.
Monetary sanction for false accusation of child abuse or neglect. §3027.1.
Supervised visitation or denial of custody based on parent's actions regarding suspicion of sexual abuse or seeking treatment for child; Necessary findings. §3027.5.
Compensation for failure to assume caretaker responsibility or for thwarting other parent's visitation or custody rights. §3028.
Order for support where custodial parent receiving public assistance. §3029.
Persons not entitled to custody or unsupervised visitation; Determination of risk; Child support paid through local agency; Confidentiality. §3030.
Modification or termination of custody or unsupervised visitation with sex offender. §3030.5.
Effect of civil restraining orders or criminal protective orders concerning parties or minor. §3031.
Interpreter for child custody proceedings. §3032.

§3020. Legislative findings and declarations

(a) The Legislature finds and declares that it is the public policy of this state to ensure that the health, safety, and welfare of children shall be the court's primary concern in determining the best interests of children when making any orders regarding the physical or legal custody or visitation of children. The Legislature further finds and declares that children have the right to be safe and free from abuse, and that the perpetration of child abuse or domestic violence in a household where a child resides is detrimental to the health, safety, and welfare of the child.

(b) The Legislature finds and declares that it is the public policy of this state to ensure that children have frequent and continuing contact with both parents after the parents have separated or dissolved their marriage, or ended their relationship, and to encourage parents to share the rights and responsibilities of child rearing in order to effect this policy, except when the contact would not be in the best interests of the child, as provided in subdivisions (a) and (c) of this section and Section 3011.

(c) When the policies set forth in subdivisions (a) and (b) of this section are in conflict, a court's order regarding physical or legal custody or visitation shall be made in a manner that ensures the health, safety, and welfare of the child and the safety of all family members.

(d) The Legislature finds and declares that it is the public policy of this state to ensure that the sex, gender identity, gender expression, or sexual orientation of a parent, legal guardian, or relative is not considered in determining the best interests of the child. **Leg.H.** Enacted Stats 1992 ch 162 §10 (AB 2650), operative January 1, 1994. Amended Stats 1993 ch 219 §116 (AB 1500); Stats 1997 ch 849 §3 (AB 200); Stats 1999 ch 980 §5 (AB 1671); Stats 2018 ch 941 §2 (AB 2044), effective January 1, 2019; Stats 2019 ch 551 §2 (SB 495), effective January 1, 2020.

§3021. Application of part

This part applies in any of the following:
(a) A proceeding for dissolution of marriage.
(b) A proceeding for nullity of marriage.
(c) A proceeding for legal separation of the parties.
(d) An action for exclusive custody pursuant to Section 3120.
(e) A proceeding to determine physical or legal custody or for visitation in a proceeding pursuant to the Domestic Violence Prevention Act (Division 10 (commencing with Section 6200)).

In an action under Section 6323, nothing in this subdivision shall be construed to authorize physical or legal custody, or visitation rights, to be granted to any party to a Domestic Violence Prevention Act proceeding who has not established a parent and child relationship pursuant to paragraph (2) of subdivision (a) of Section 6323.

(f) A proceeding to determine physical or legal custody or visitation in an action pursuant to the Uniform Parentage Act (Part 3 (commencing with Section 7600) of Division 12).

(g) A proceeding to determine physical or legal custody or visitation in an action brought by the district attorney pursuant to Section 17404. **Leg.H.** Added Stats 1993 ch 219 §116.11 (AB 1500). Amended Stats 1996 ch 1075 §9 (SB 1444); Stats 1997 ch 396 §1 (SB 564); Stats 1999 ch 980 §6 (AB 1671); Stats 2000 ch 135 §58 (AB 2539).

Prior Law: Former §3021 was enacted Stats 1992 ch 162 §10, to become operative January 1, 1994, and amended and renumbered to be Fam C §3022 by Stats 1993 ch 219 §116.12.

§3022. Authority of court to make custody order

The court may, during the pendency of a proceeding or at any time thereafter, make an order for the custody of a child during minority that seems necessary or proper. **Leg.H.** Enacted Stats 1992 ch 162 §10 (AB 2650), operative January 1, 1994, as §3021. Amended and renumbered by Stats 1993 ch 219 §116.12 (AB 1500).

Prior Law: Former §3022, similar to present Fam C §3011, was enacted Stats 1992 ch 162 §10, to become operative January 1, 1994, and repealed Stats 1993 ch 219 §116.23.

§3022.3. Statement explaining basis of decision by court

Upon the trial of a question of fact in a proceeding to determine the custody of a minor child, the court shall, upon the request of either party, issue a statement of the decision explaining the factual and legal basis for its decision pursuant to Section 632 of the Code of Civil Procedure. **Leg.H.** Added Stats 2006 ch 496 §3 (AB 402), effective January 1, 2007.

2006 Note: This act shall be known and may be cited as the Collaborative Family Law Act. Stats 2006 ch 496 (AB 402) §1.

§3022.5. Motion for reconsideration of existing custody order based on conviction of other parent of crime of false accusation of child abuse against moving parent

A motion by a parent for reconsideration of an existing child custody order shall be granted if the motion is based on the fact that the other parent was convicted of a crime in connection with falsely accusing the moving parent of child abuse. **Leg.H.** Added Stats 1995 ch 406 §1 (SB 558).

§3023. Preference for trial on issue of custody

(a) If custody of a minor child is the sole contested issue, the case shall be given preference over other civil cases, except matters to which special precedence may be given by law, for assigning a trial date and shall be given an early hearing.

(b) If there is more than one contested issue and one of the issues is the custody of a minor child, the court, as to the issue of custody, shall order a separate trial. The separate trial shall be given preference over other civil cases, except matters to which special precedence may be given by law, for assigning a trial date. **Leg.H.** Enacted Stats 1992 ch 162 §10 (AB 2650), operative January 1, 1994. Amended Stats 1993 ch 219 §116.14 (AB 1500).

§3024. Notice to other parent of change of residence of child

In making an order for custody, if the court does not consider it inappropriate, the court may specify that a parent shall notify the other parent if the parent plans to change the residence of the child for more than 30 days, unless there is prior written agreement to the removal. The notice shall be given before the contemplated move, by mail, return receipt requested, postage prepaid, to the last known address of the parent to be notified. A copy of the notice shall also be sent to that parent's counsel of record. To the extent feasible, the notice shall be provided within a minimum of 45 days before the proposed change of residence so as to allow time for mediation of a new agreement concerning custody. This section does not affect orders made before January 1, 1989. **Leg.H.** Enacted Stats 1992 ch 162 §10 (AB 2650), operative January 1, 1994.

§3025. Parental access to records

Notwithstanding any other provision of law, access to records and information pertaining to a minor child, including, but not limited to, medical, dental, and school records, shall not be denied to a parent because that parent is not the child's custodial parent. **Leg.H.** Enacted Stats 1992 ch 162 §10 (AB 2650), operative January 1, 1994.

§3025.5. Confidentiality of psychological evaluations of child involved in custody or visitation rights proceedings

(a) In a proceeding involving child custody or visitation rights, if a report containing psychological evaluations of a child or recommendations regarding custody of, or visitation with, a child is submitted to the court, including, but not limited to, a report created pursuant to Chapter 6 (commencing with Section 3110) of this part and a recommendation made to the court pursuant to Section 3183, that information shall be contained in a document that shall be placed in the confidential portion of the court file of the proceeding, and may not be disclosed, except to the following persons:

(1) A party to the proceeding and the party's attorney.

(2) A federal or state law enforcement officer, the licensing entity of a child custody evaluator, a judicial officer, court employee, or family court facilitator of the superior court of the county in which the action was filed, or an employee or agent of that facilitator, acting within the scope of the facilitator's duties.

(3) Counsel appointed for the child pursuant to Section 3150.

(4) Any other person upon order of the court for good cause.

(b) Confidential information contained in a report prepared pursuant to Section 3111 that is disclosed to the licensing entity of a child custody evaluator pursuant to subdivision (a) shall remain confidential and shall only be used for purposes of investigating allegations of unprofessional conduct by the child custody evaluator, or in a criminal, civil, or administrative proceeding involving the child custody evaluator. All confidential information, including, but not limited to, the identity of any minors, shall retain their confidential nature in a criminal, civil, or administrative proceeding resulting from the investigation of unprofessional conduct and shall be sealed at the conclusion of the proceeding and shall not subsequently be released. Names that are confidential shall be listed in attachments separate from the general pleadings. If the confidential information does not result in a criminal, civil, or administrative proceeding, it shall be sealed after the licensing entity decides that no further action will be taken in the matter of suspected licensing violations. **Leg.H.** Added Stats 2004 ch 102 §1 (SB 1284). Amended Stats 2012 ch 470 §17 (AB 1529), effective January 1, 2013; Stats 2014 ch 283 §2 (AB 1843), effective January 1, 2015; Stats 2019 ch 115 §25 (AB 1817), effective January 1, 2020.

§3026. Family reunification services

Family reunification services shall not be ordered as a part of a child custody or visitation rights proceeding. Nothing in this section affects the applicability of Section 16507 of the Welfare and Institutions Code. **Leg.H.** Enacted Stats 1992 ch 162 §10 (AB 2650), operative January 1, 1994. Amended Stats 1993 ch 219 §116.16 (AB 1500).

§3027. Allegations made during child custody proceedings

(a) If allegations of child abuse, including child sexual abuse, are made during a child custody proceeding and the court has concerns regarding the child's safety, the court may take any reasonable, temporary steps as the court, in its discretion, deems appropriate under the circumstances to protect the child's safety until an investigation can be completed. Nothing in this section shall affect the applicability of Section 16504 or 16506 of the Welfare and Institutions Code.

(b) If allegations of child abuse, including child sexual abuse, are made during a child custody proceeding, the court may request that the local child welfare services agency conduct an investigation of the allegations pursuant to Section 328 of the Welfare and Institutions Code. Upon completion of the investigation, the agency shall report its findings to the court. **Leg.H.** Added Stats 2000 ch 926 §3 (SB 1716). Amended Stats 2010 ch 352 §12 (AB 939), effective January 1, 2011.

Prior Law: There was another section of this number which was enacted Stats 1992 ch 162 §10, operative January 1, 1994, amended Stats 1993 ch 219 §116.17, Stats 1994 ch 688 §1, and renumbered Fam C §3027.1 by Stats 2000 ch 926 §2.

Former Sections: Former Fam C §3027 was enacted Stats 1992 ch 162 §10, operative January 1, 1994, and renumbered Fam C §3027.1 by Stats 2000 ch 926 §2.

§3027.1. Monetary sanction for false accusation of child abuse or neglect

(a) If a court determines, based on the investigation described in Section 3027 or other evidence presented to it, that an accusation of child abuse or neglect made during a child custody proceeding is false and the person making the accusation knew it to be false at the time the accusation was made, the court may impose reasonable money sanctions, not to exceed all costs incurred by the party accused as a direct result of defending the accusation, and reasonable attorney's fees incurred in recovering the sanctions, against the person making the accusation. For the purposes of this section, "person" includes a witness, a party, or a party's attorney.

(b) On motion by any person requesting sanctions under this section, the court shall issue its order to show cause why the requested sanctions should not be imposed. The order to show cause shall be served on the person against whom the sanctions are sought and a hearing thereon shall be scheduled by the court to be conducted at least 15 days after the order is served.

(c) The remedy provided by this section is in addition to any other remedy provided by law. **Leg.H.** Enacted Stats 1992 ch 162 §10 (AB 2650), operative January 1, 1994, as Fam C §3027. Amended Stats 1993 ch 219 §116.17 (AB 1500); Stats 1994 ch 688 §1 (AB 2845). Amended and renumbered Stats 2000 ch 926 §2 (SB 1716).

§3027.5. Supervised visitation or denial of custody based on parent's actions regarding suspicion of sexual abuse or seeking treatment for child; Necessary findings

(a) A parent shall not be placed on supervised visitation, or be denied custody of or visitation with the parent's child, and custody or visitation rights shall not be limited, solely because the parent did any of the following:

(1) Lawfully reported suspected sexual abuse of the child.

(2) Otherwise acted lawfully, based on a reasonable belief, to determine if the child was the victim of sexual abuse.

(3) Sought treatment for the child from a licensed mental health professional for suspected sexual abuse.

(b) The court may order supervised visitation or limit a parent's custody or visitation if the court finds substantial evidence that the parent, with the intent to interfere with the other parent's lawful contact with the child, made a report of child sexual abuse, during a child custody proceeding or at any other time, that the reporting parent knew was false at the time it was made. A limitation of custody or visitation, including an order for supervised visitation, pursuant to this subdivision, or a statute regarding the making of a false child abuse report, shall be imposed only after the court has determined that the limitation is necessary to protect the health, safety, and welfare of the child, and the court has considered the state's policy of ensuring that children have frequent and continuing contact with both parents as declared in subdivision (b) of Section 3020. **Leg.H.** Added Stats 1999 ch 985 §1 (SB 792). Amended Stats 2019 ch 115 §26 (AB 1817), effective January 1, 2020.

§3028. Compensation for failure to assume caretaker responsibility or for thwarting other parent's visitation or custody rights

(a) The court may order financial compensation for periods when a parent fails to assume the caretaker responsibility or when a parent has been thwarted by the other parent when attempting to exercise custody or visitation rights contemplated by a custody or visitation order, including, but not limited to, an order for joint physical custody, or by a written or oral agreement between the parents.

(b) The compensation shall be limited to (1) the reasonable expenses incurred for or on behalf of a child, resulting from the other parent's failure to assume caretaker responsibility or (2) the reasonable expenses incurred by a parent for or on behalf of a child, resulting from the other parent's thwarting of the parent's efforts to exercise custody or visitation rights. The expenses may include the value of caretaker services but are not limited to the cost of services provided by a third party during the relevant period.

(c) The compensation may be requested by noticed motion or an order to show cause, which shall allege, under penalty of perjury, (1) a minimum of one hundred dollars ($100) of expenses incurred or (2) at least three occurrences of failure to exercise custody or visitation rights or (3) at least three occurrences of the thwarting of efforts to exercise custody or visitation rights within the six months before filing of the motion or order.

(d) Attorney's fees shall be awarded to the prevailing party upon a showing of the nonprevailing party's ability to pay as required by Section 270. **Leg.H.** Enacted Stats 1992 ch 162 §10 (AB 2650), operative January 1, 1994. Amended Stats 1993 ch 219 §116.18 (AB 1500).

§3029. Order for support where custodial parent receiving public assistance

An order granting custody to a parent who is receiving, or in the opinion of the court is likely to receive, assistance pursuant to the Family Economic Security Act of 1982 (Chapter 2 (commencing with Section 11200) of Part 3 of Division 9 of the Welfare and Institutions Code) for the maintenance of the child shall include an order pursuant to Chapter 2 (commencing with Section 4000) of Part 2 of Division 9 of this code, directing the noncustodial parent to pay any amount necessary for the support of the child, to the extent of the noncustodial parent's ability to pay. **Leg.H.** Added Stats 1993 ch 219 §116.19 (AB 1500).

§3030. Persons not entitled to custody or unsupervised visitation; Determination of risk; Child support paid through local agency; Confidentiality

(a)(1) No person shall be granted physical or legal custody of, or unsupervised visitation with, a child if the person is required to be registered as a sex offender under Section 290 of the Penal Code where the victim was a minor, or if the person has been convicted under Section 273a, 273d, or 647.6 of the Penal Code, unless the court finds that there is no significant risk to the child and states its reasons in writing or on the record. The child may not be placed in a home in which that person resides, nor permitted to have unsupervised visitation with that person, unless the court states the reasons for its findings in writing or on the record.

(2) No person shall be granted physical or legal custody of, or unsupervised visitation with, a child if anyone residing in the person's household is required, as a result of a felony conviction in which the victim was a minor, to register as a sex offender under Section 290 of the Penal Code, unless the court finds there is no significant risk to the child and states its reasons in writing or on the record. The child may not be placed in a home in which that person resides, nor permitted to have unsupervised visitation with that person, unless the court states the reasons for its findings in writing or on the record.

(3) The fact that a child is permitted unsupervised contact with a person who is required, as a result of a felony conviction in which the victim was a minor, to be registered as a sex offender under Section 290 of the Penal Code, shall be prima facie evidence that the child is at significant risk. When making a determination regarding significant risk to the child, the prima facie evidence shall constitute a presumption affecting the burden of producing evidence. However, this presumption shall not apply if there are factors mitigating against its application, including whether the party seeking custody or visitation is also required, as the result of a felony conviction in which the victim was a minor, to register as a sex offender under Section 290 of the Penal Code.

(b) No person shall be granted custody of, or visitation with, a child if the person has been convicted under Section 261 of the Penal Code and the child was conceived as a result of that violation.

(c) No person shall be granted custody of, or unsupervised visitation with, a child if the person has been convicted of murder in the first degree, as defined in Section 189 of the Penal Code, and the victim of the murder was the other parent of the child who is the subject of the order, unless the court finds that there is no risk to the child's health, safety, and welfare, and states the reasons for its finding in writing or on the record. In making its finding, the court may consider, among other things, the following:

(1) The wishes of the child, if the child is of sufficient age and capacity to reason so as to form an intelligent preference.

(2) Credible evidence that the convicted parent was a victim of abuse, as defined in Section 6203, committed by the deceased parent. That evidence may include, but is not limited to, written reports by law enforcement agencies, child protective services or other social welfare agencies, courts, medical facilities, or other public agencies or private nonprofit organizations providing services to victims of domestic abuse.

(3) Testimony of an expert witness, qualified under Section 1107 of the Evidence Code, that the convicted parent experiences intimate partner battering.

Unless and until a custody or visitation order is issued pursuant to this subdivision, no person shall permit or cause the child to visit or remain in the custody of the convicted parent without the consent of the child's custodian or legal guardian.

(d) The court may order child support that is to be paid by a person subject to subdivision (a), (b), or (c) to be paid through the local child support agency, as authorized by Section 4573 of the Family Code and Division 17 (commencing with Section 17000) of this code.

(e) The court shall not disclose, or cause to be disclosed, the custodial parent's place of residence, place of employment, or the child's school, unless the court finds that the disclosure would be in the best interest of the child. **Leg.H.** Added Stats 1993 ch 219 §116.2 (AB 1500). Amended Stats 1994 1st Ex Sess 1993–1994 ch 5 §1 (SBX1-25), effective November 30, 1994; Stats 1997 ch 594 §1 (AB 1222); Stats 1998 ch 131 §1 (AB 1645), ch 485 §64 (AB 2803), ch 704 §1.5 (AB 2745), ch 705 §1.5 (AB 2386); Stats 2000 ch 808 §26 (AB 1358), effective September 28, 2000; Stats 2005 ch 215 §2 (AB 220), effective January 1, 2006, ch 483 §2.5 (SB 594), effective January 1, 2006; Stats 2006 ch 207 §1 (AB 2893), effective January 1, 2007.

§3030.5. Modification or termination of custody or unsupervised visitation with sex offender

(a) Upon the motion of one or both parents, or the legal guardian or custodian, or upon the court's own motion, an order granting physical or legal custody of, or unsupervised visitation with, a child may be modified or terminated if either of the following circumstances has occurred since the order was entered, unless the court finds that there is no significant risk to the child and states its reasons in writing or on the record:

(1) The person who has been granted physical or legal custody of, or unsupervised visitation with the child is required, as a result of a felony conviction in which the victim was a minor, to be registered as a sex offender under Section 290 of the Penal Code.

(2) The person who has been granted physical or legal custody of, or unsupervised visitation with, the child resides with another person who is required, as a result of a felony conviction in which the victim was a minor, to be registered as a sex offender under Section 290 of the Penal Code.

(b) The fact that a child is permitted unsupervised contact with a person who is required, as a result of a felony conviction in which the victim was a minor, to be registered as a sex offender under Section 290 of the Penal Code, shall be prima facie evidence that the child is at significant risk. When making a determination regarding significant risk to the child, the prima facie evidence shall constitute a presumption affecting the burden of producing evidence. However, this presumption shall not apply if there are factors mitigating against its application, including whether the party seeking custody or visitation is also required, as the result of a felony conviction in which the victim was a minor, to register as a sex offender under Section 290 of the Penal Code.

(c) The court shall not modify an existing custody or visitation order upon the ex parte petition of one party pursuant to this section without providing notice to the other party and an opportunity to be heard. This notice provision applies only when the motion for custody or visitation change is based solely on the fact that the child is allowed unsupervised contact with a person required, as a result of a felony conviction in which the victim was a minor, to register as a sex offender under Section 290 of the Penal Code and does not affect the court's ability to remove a child upon an ex parte motion when there is a showing of immediate harm to the child. **Leg.H.** Added Stats 2005 ch 483 §3 (SB 594), effective January 1, 2006.

§3031. Effect of civil restraining orders or criminal protective orders concerning parties or minor

(a) Where the court considers the issue of custody or visitation the court is encouraged to make a reasonable effort to ascertain whether or not any emergency protective order, protective order, or other restraining order is in effect that concerns the parties or the minor. The court is encouraged not to make a custody or visitation order that is inconsistent with the emergency protective order, protective order, or other restraining order, unless the court makes both of the following findings:

(1) The custody or visitation order cannot be made consistent with the emergency protective order, protective order, or other restraining order.

(2) The custody or visitation order is in the best interest of the minor.

(b) Whenever custody or visitation is granted to a parent in a case in which domestic violence is alleged and an emergency protective order, protective order, or other restraining order has been issued, the custody or visitation order shall specify the time, day, place, and manner of transfer of the child for custody or visitation to limit the child's exposure to potential domestic conflict or violence and to ensure the safety of all family members. Where the court finds a party is staying in a place designated as a shelter for victims of domestic violence or other confidential location, the court's order for time, day, place, and manner of transfer of the child for custody or visitation shall be designed to prevent disclosure of the location of the shelter or other confidential location.

(c) When making an order for custody or visitation in a case in which domestic violence is alleged and an emergency protective order, protective order, or other restraining order has been issued, the court shall consider whether the best interest of the child, based upon the circumstances of the case, requires that any custody or visitation arrangement shall be limited to situations in which a third person, specified by the court, is present, or whether custody or visitation shall be suspended or denied. **Leg.H.** Added Stats 1993 ch 219 §116.30 (AB 1500). Amended Stats 1994 ch 320 §1 (AB 356).

§3032. Interpreter for child custody proceedings

(a) The Judicial Council shall establish a state-funded one-year pilot project beginning July 1, 1999, in at least two counties, including Los Angeles County, pursuant to which, in any child custody proceeding, including mediation proceedings pursuant to Section 3170, any action or proceeding under Division 10 (commencing with Section 6200), any action or proceeding under the Uniform Parentage Act (Part 3 (commencing with Section 7600) of Division 12), and any proceeding for dissolution or nullity of marriage or legal separation of the parties in which a protective order as been granted or is being sought pursuant to Section 6221, the court shall, notwithstanding Section 68092 of the Government Code, appoint an interpreter to interpret the proceedings at court expense, if both of the following conditions are met:

(1) One or both of the parties is unable to participate fully in the proceeding due to a lack of proficiency in the English language.

(2) The party who needs an interpreter appears in forma pauperis, pursuant to Section 68511.3 of the Government Code, or the court otherwise determines that the parties are financially unable to pay the cost of an interpreter. In all other cases where an interpreter is required pursuant to this section, interpreter fees shall be paid as provided in Section 68092 of the Government Code.

(3) This section shall not prohibit the court doing any of the following when an interpreter is not present:

(A) Issuing an order when the necessity for the order outweighs the necessity for an interpreter.

(B) Extending the duration of a previously issued temporary order if an interpreter is not readily available.

(C) Issuing a permanent order where a party who requires an interpreter fails to make appropriate arrangements for an interpreter after receiving proper notice of the hearing, including notice of the requirement to have an interpreter present, along with information about obtaining an interpreter.

(b) The Judicial Council shall submit its findings and recommendations with respect to the pilot project to the Legislature by January 31, 2001. Measurable objectives of the program may include increased utilization of the court by parties not fluent in English, increased efficiency in proceedings, increased compliance with orders, enhanced coordination between courts and culturally relevant services in the community, increased client satisfaction, and increased public satisfaction. **Leg.H.** Added Stats 1998 ch 981 §2 (AB 1884).

CHAPTER 2
MATTERS TO BE CONSIDERED IN GRANTING CUSTODY

Order of preference in granting custody. §3040.
Additional requirements for custody granted to nonparent. §3041.
Testing for alcohol or use of illegal substance in certain custody, visitation or guardianship proceedings; Confidentiality; Use; Costs. §3041.5.
Wishes of child to be given due weight; Examination of child as witness; Alternative means of obtaining input; Change in preference. §3042.
Nomination of guardian by parent. §3043.
Rebuttable presumption from showing that person seeking custody has perpetrated domestic violence; Factors; Finding; Evidence; Copy of section [Repealed January 1, 2026]. §3044.
Presumption against custody to perpetrator of domestic violence [Effective January 1, 2026]. § 3044.
Absence or relocation as custody or visitation factor. §3046.
Absence, relocation or failure to comply due to military duty or temporary duty, mobilization in support of combat or other military operation, or military deployment outside state; Review of temporary custody order; Visitation rights to family members; Scheduled hearings; Relocation by nondeploying parent. §3047.
Contents of child custody or visitation order; Determination of risk of abduction. §3048.
Custody and visitation where parent is disabled. §3049.

§3040. Order of preference in granting custody

(a) Custody should be granted in the following order of preference according to the best interest of the child as provided in Sections 3011 and 3020:

(1) To both parents jointly pursuant to Chapter 4 (commencing with Section 3080) or to either parent. In making an order granting custody to either parent, the court shall consider, among other factors, which parent is more likely to allow the child frequent and continuing contact with the noncustodial parent, consistent with Sections 3011 and 3020. The court, in its discretion, may require the parents to submit to the court a plan for the implementation of the custody order.

(2) If to neither parent, to the person or persons in whose home the child has been living in a wholesome and stable environment.

(3) To any other person or persons deemed by the court to be suitable and able to provide adequate and proper care and guidance for the child.

(b) The immigration status of a parent, legal guardian, or relative shall not disqualify the parent, legal guardian, or relative from receiving custody under subdivision (a).

(c) The court shall not consider the sex, gender identity, gender expression, or sexual orientation of a parent, legal guardian, or relative in determining the best interest of the child under subdivision (a).

(d)(1) Commencing January 1, 2024, if a court finds that the effects of a parent's, legal guardian's, or relative's history of or current mental illness are a factor in determining the best interest of the child under subdivision (a), the court shall do both of the following:

(A) Provide the parent, legal guardian, or relative with a list of local resources for mental health treatment.

(B) State its reasons for the finding in writing or on the record.

(2) This subdivision does not relieve a court from ensuring that the health, safety, and welfare of the child is the court's primary concern in determining the best interests of children when making any order regarding the physical or legal custody, or visitation, of the child.

(e) This section establishes neither a preference nor a presumption for or against joint legal custody, joint physical custody, or sole custody, but allows the court and the family the widest discretion to choose a parenting plan that is in the best interest of the child, consistent with this section.

(f) In cases where a child has more than two parents, the court shall allocate custody and visitation among the parents based on the best interest of the child, including, but not limited to, addressing the child's need for continuity and stability by preserving established patterns of care and emotional bonds. The court may order that not all parents share legal or physical custody of the child if the court finds that it would not be in the best interest of the child as provided in Sections 3011 and 3020. **Leg.H.** Added Stats 1993 ch 219 §116.50 (AB 1500). Amended Stats

1997 ch 849 §4 (AB 200); Stats 2012 ch 845 §1 (SB 1064), effective January 1, 2013; Stats 2013 ch 564 §2 (SB 274), effective January 1, 2014; Stats 2019 ch 551 §3 (SB 495), effective January 1, 2020; Stats 2022 ch 385 §3 (SB 1182), effective January 1, 2023.

Prior Law: Former §3040, similar to the present section, was enacted Stats 1992 ch 162 §10, to become operative January 1, 1994, and repealed Stats 1993 ch 219 §116.40.

§3041. Additional requirements for custody granted to nonparent

(a) Before making an order granting custody to a person other than a parent, over the objection of a parent, the court shall make a finding that granting custody to a parent would be detrimental to the child and that granting custody to the nonparent is required to serve the best interest of the child. Allegations that parental custody would be detrimental to the child, other than a statement of that ultimate fact, shall not appear in the pleadings. The court may, in its discretion, exclude the public from the hearing on this issue.

(b) Subject to subdivision (d), a finding that parental custody would be detrimental to the child shall be supported by clear and convincing evidence.

(c) As used in this section, "detriment to the child" includes the harm of removal from a stable placement of a child with a person who has assumed, on a day-to-day basis, the role of the child's parent, fulfilling both the child's physical needs and the child's psychological needs for care and affection, and who has assumed that role for a substantial period of time. A finding of detriment does not require a finding of unfitness of the parents.

(d) Notwithstanding subdivision (b), if the court finds by a preponderance of the evidence that the person to whom custody may be given is a person described in subdivision (c), this finding shall constitute a finding that the custody is in the best interest of the child and that parental custody would be detrimental to the child absent a showing by a preponderance of the evidence to the contrary.

(e) Notwithstanding subdivisions (a) to (d), inclusive, if the child is an Indian child, when an allegation is made that parental custody would be detrimental to the child, before making an order granting custody to a person other than a parent, over the objection of a parent, the court shall apply the evidentiary standards described in subdivisions (d), (e), and (f) of Section 1912 of the Indian Child Welfare Act (25 U.S.C. Sec. 1901 et seq.) and Sections 224.6 and 361.7 of the Welfare and Institutions Code and the placement preferences and standards set out in Section 361.31 of the Welfare and Institutions Code and Section 1922 of the Indian Child Welfare Act (25 U.S.C. Sec. 1901 et seq.). **Leg.H.** Added Stats 1993 ch 219 §116.50 (AB 1500). Amended Stats 2002 ch 1118 §3 (AB 1938); Stats 2006 ch 838 §2 (SB 678), effective January 1, 2007; Stats 2019 ch 115 §27 (AB 1817), effective January 1, 2020.

Prior Law: Former §3041, similar to the present section, was enacted Stats 1992 ch 162 §10, to become operative January 1, 1994, and repealed Stats 1993 ch 219 §116.40.

§3041.5. Testing for alcohol or use of illegal substance in certain custody, visitation or guardianship proceedings; Confidentiality; Use; Costs

In any custody or visitation proceeding brought under this part, as described in Section 3021, or any guardianship proceeding brought under the Probate Code, the court may order any person who is seeking custody of, or visitation with, a child who is the subject of the proceeding to undergo testing for the illegal use of controlled substances and the use of alcohol if there is a judicial determination based upon a preponderance of evidence that there is the habitual, frequent, or continual illegal use of controlled substances or the habitual or continual abuse of alcohol by the parent, legal custodian, person seeking guardianship, or person seeking visitation in a guardianship. This evidence may include, but may not be limited to, a conviction within the last five years for the illegal use or possession of a controlled substance. The court shall order the least intrusive method of testing for the illegal use of controlled substances or the habitual or continual abuse of alcohol by either or both parents, the legal custodian, person seeking guardianship, or person seeking visitation in a guardianship. If substance abuse testing is ordered by the court, the testing shall be performed in conformance with procedures and standards established by the United States Department of Health and Human Services for drug testing of federal employees. The parent, legal custodian, person seeking guardianship, or person seeking visitation in a guardianship who has undergone drug testing shall have the right to a hearing, if requested, to challenge a positive test result. A positive test result, even if challenged and upheld, shall not, by itself, constitute grounds for an adverse custody or guardianship decision. Determining the best interests of the child requires weighing all relevant factors. The court shall also consider any reports provided to the court pursuant to the Probate Code. The results of this testing shall be confidential, shall be maintained as a sealed record in the court file, and may not be released to any person except the court, the parties, their attorneys, the Judicial Council, until completion of its authorized study of the testing process, and any person to whom the court expressly grants access by written order made with prior notice to all parties. Any person who has access to the test results may not disseminate copies or disclose information about the test results to any person other than a person who is authorized to receive the test results pursuant to this section. Any breach of the confidentiality of the test results shall be punishable by civil sanctions not to exceed two thousand five hundred dollars ($2,500). The results of the testing may not be used for any purpose, including any criminal, civil, or administrative proceeding, except to assist the court in determining, for purposes of the proceeding, the best interest of the child pursuant to Section 3011 and the content of the order or judgment determining custody or visitation. The court may order either party, or both parties, to pay the costs of the drug or alcohol testing ordered pursuant to this section. As used in this section, "controlled substances" has the same meaning as defined in the California Uniform Controlled Substances Act (Division 10 (commencing with Section 11000) of the Health and Safety Code). **Leg.H.** Added Stats 2004 ch 19 §1 (AB 1108), effective February 23, 2004. Amended Stats 2005 ch 302 §1 (AB 541), effective January 1, 2006, repealed January 1, 2008. Stats 2007 ch 152 §1 (SB 403), effective January 1, 2008, repealed January 1, 2009; Stats 2008 ch 57 §1 (SB 1255), effective January 1, 2009, repealed January 1, 2013; Stats 2009 ch 140 §66 (AB 1164), effective January 1, 2010; Stats 2012 ch 258 §2 (AB 2365), effective January 1, 2013.

§3042. Wishes of child to be given due weight; Examination of child as witness; Alternative means of obtaining input; Change in preference

(a) If a child is of sufficient age and capacity to reason so as to form an intelligent preference as to custody or visitation, the court shall consider, and give due weight to, the wishes of the child in making an order granting or modifying custody or visitation.

(b) In addition to the requirements of subdivision (b) of Section 765 of the Evidence Code, the court shall control the examination of a child witness so as to protect the best interest of the child.

(c) If the child is 14 years of age or older and wishes to address the court regarding custody or visitation, the child shall be permitted to do so, unless the court determines that doing so is not in the child's best interest, in which case, the court shall state its reasons for that finding on the record.

(d) This section does not prevent a child who is less than 14 years of age from addressing the court regarding custody or visitation, if the court determines that is appropriate pursuant to the child's best interest.

(e) If the court precludes the calling of a child as a witness, the court shall provide alternative means of obtaining input from the child and other information regarding the child's preferences.

(f)(1) Except as provided in paragraph (2), the court shall not permit a child addressing the court regarding custody or visitation to do so in the presence of the parties. The court shall provide an alternative to having the child address the court in the presence of the parties in order to obtain input directly from the child.

(2) Notwithstanding paragraph (1), the court may permit the child addressing the court regarding custody or visitation to do so in the presence of the parties if the court determines that doing so is in the child's best interest and states its reasons for that finding on the record. In determining the child's best interest under this paragraph, the court shall consider whether addressing the court regarding custody or visitation in the presence of the parties is likely to be detrimental to the child.

(g) To assist the court in determining whether the child wishes to express a preference or to provide other input regarding custody or visitation to the court, a minor's counsel, an evaluator, an investigator, or a child custody recommending counselor shall indicate to the judge that the child wishes to address the court, or the judge may make that inquiry in the absence of that request. A party or a party's attorney may also indicate to the judge that the child wishes to address the court or judge.

(h) If a child informs the minor's counsel, an evaluator, an investigator, or a child custody recommending counselor at any point that the child has changed their choice with respect to addressing the court, the minor's counsel, evaluator, investigator, or child custody recommending counselor shall, as soon as feasible, indicate to the judge, the parties or their attorneys, and other professionals serving on the case that the child has changed their preference.

(i) This section does not require the child to express to the court a preference or to provide other input regarding custody or visitation.

(j) The Judicial Council shall, no later than January 1, 2023, develop or amend rules as necessary to implement this section. **Leg.H.** Added Stats 1993 ch 219 §116.50 (AB 1500). Amended Stats 1994 ch 596 §1 (SB 1700); Stats 1995 ch 91 §38 (SB 975); Stats 2010 ch 187 §1 (AB 1050), effective January 1, 2011, operative January 1, 2012; Stats 2019 ch 115 §28 (AB 1817), effective January 1, 2020; Stats 2021 ch 768 §2 (SB 654), effective January 1, 2022.

Prior Law: Former §3042, similar to the present section, was enacted Stats 1992 ch 162 §10, to become operative January 1, 1994, and repealed Stats 1993 ch 219 §116.40.

§3043. Nomination of guardian by parent

In determining the person or persons to whom custody should be granted under paragraph (2) or (3) of subdivision (a) of Section 3040, the court shall consider and give due weight to the nomination of a guardian of the person of the child by a parent under Article 1 (commencing with Section 1500) of Chapter 1 of Part 2 of Division 4 of the Probate Code. **Leg.H.** Added Stats 1993 ch 219 §116.50 (AB 1500).

Prior Law: Former §3043, similar to the present section, was enacted Stats 1992 ch 162 §10, to become operative January 1, 1994, and repealed Stats 1993 ch 219 §116.40.

§3044. Rebuttable presumption from showing that person seeking custody has perpetrated domestic violence; Factors; Finding; Evidence; Copy of section [Repealed January 1, 2026]

(a) Upon a finding by the court that a party seeking custody of a child has perpetrated domestic violence within the previous five years against the other party seeking custody of the child, or against the child or the child's siblings, or against a person in subparagraph (A) of paragraph (2) of subdivision (a) of Section 3011 with whom the party has a relationship, there is a rebuttable presumption that an award of sole or joint physical or legal custody of a child to a person who has perpetrated domestic violence is detrimental to the best interest of the child, pursuant to Sections 3011 and 3020. This presumption may only be rebutted by a preponderance of the evidence.

(b) To overcome the presumption set forth in subdivision (a), the court shall find that paragraph (1) is satisfied and shall find that the factors in paragraph (2), on balance, support the legislative findings in Section 3020.

(1) The perpetrator of domestic violence has demonstrated that giving sole or joint physical or legal custody of a child to the perpetrator is in the best interest of the child pursuant to Sections 3011 and 3020. In determining the best interest of the child, the preference for frequent and continuing contact with both parents, as set forth in subdivision (b) of Section 3020, or with the noncustodial parent, as set forth in paragraph (1) of subdivision (a) of Section 3040, may not be used to rebut the presumption, in whole or in part.

(2) Additional factors:

(A) The perpetrator has successfully completed a batterer's treatment program that meets the criteria outlined in subdivision (c) of Section 1203.097 of the Penal Code.

(B) The perpetrator has successfully completed a program of alcohol or drug abuse counseling, if the court determines that counseling is appropriate.

(C) The perpetrator has successfully completed a parenting class, if the court determines the class to be appropriate.

(D) The perpetrator is on probation or parole, and has or has not complied with the terms and conditions of probation or parole.

(E) The perpetrator is restrained by a protective order or restraining order, and has or has not complied with its terms and conditions.

(F) The perpetrator of domestic violence has committed further acts of domestic violence.

(G) The court has determined, pursuant to Section 6322.5, that the perpetrator is a restrained person in possession or control of a firearm or ammunition in violation of Section 6389.

(c) For purposes of this section, a person has "perpetrated domestic violence" when the person is found by the court to have intentionally or recklessly caused or attempted to cause bodily injury, or sexual assault, or to have placed a person in reasonable apprehension of imminent serious bodily injury to that person or to another, or to have engaged in behavior involving, but not limited to, threatening, striking, harassing, destroying personal property, or disturbing the peace of another, for which a court may issue an ex parte order pursuant to Section 6320 to protect the other party seeking custody of the child or to protect the child and the child's siblings.

(d)(1) For purposes of this section, the requirement of a finding by the court shall be satisfied by, among other things, and not limited to, evidence that a party seeking custody has been convicted within the previous five years, after a trial or a plea of guilty or no contest, of a crime against the other party that comes within the definition of domestic violence contained in Section 6211 and of abuse contained in Section 6203, including, but not limited to, a crime described in subdivision (e) of Section 243 of, or Section 261, 273.5, 422, or 646.9 of, or former Section 262 of, the Penal Code.

(2) The requirement of a finding by the court shall also be satisfied if a court, whether that court hears or has heard the child custody proceedings or not, has made a finding pursuant to subdivision (a) based on conduct occurring within the previous five years.

(e) When a court makes a finding that a party has perpetrated domestic violence, the court may not base its findings solely on conclusions reached by a child custody evaluator or on the recommendation of the Family Court Services staff, but shall consider any relevant, admissible evidence submitted by the parties.

(f)(1) It is the intent of the Legislature that this subdivision be interpreted consistently with the decision in Jaime G. v. H.L. (2018) 25 Cal.App.5th 794, which requires that the court, in determining that the presumption in subdivision (a) has been overcome, make specific findings on each of the factors in subdivision (b).

(2) If the court determines that the presumption in subdivision (a) has been overcome, the court shall state its reasons in writing or on the record as to why paragraph (1) of subdivision (b) is satisfied and why the factors in paragraph (2) of subdivision (b), on balance, support the legislative findings in Section 3020.

(g) In an evidentiary hearing or trial in which custody orders are sought and where there has been an allegation of domestic violence, the court shall make a determination as to whether this section applies prior to issuing a custody order, unless the court finds that a continuance is necessary to determine whether this section applies, in which case the court may issue a temporary custody order for a reasonable period of time, provided the order complies with Sections 3011 and 3020.

(h) In a custody or restraining order proceeding in which a party has alleged that the other party has perpetrated domestic violence in accordance with the terms of this section, the court shall inform the parties of the existence of this section and shall give them a copy of this section prior to custody mediation in the case.

(i) This section shall remain in effect only until January 1, 2026, and as of that date is repealed. Leg.H. Added Stats 1999 ch 445 §1 (AB 840). Amended Stats 2003 ch 243 §1 (SB 265); Stats 2018 ch 941 §3 (AB 2044), effective January 1, 2019; Stats 2019 ch 115 §29 (AB 1817), effective January 1, 2020; Stats 2021 ch 124 §26 (AB 938), effective January 1, 2022; Stats 2021 ch 213 §1 (AB 1579), effective January 1, 2022; Stats 2021 ch 626 §10 (AB 1171), effective January 1, 2022; Stats 2021 ch 685 §2.7 (SB 320), effective January 1, 2022 (ch 685 prevails); Stats 2024 ch 544 §6 (SB 899), effective January 1, 2025, repealed January 1, 2026.

Prior Law: Former §3044, similar to present Fam C §3030, was enacted Stats 1992 ch 162 §10, operative January 1, 1994, and repealed Stats 1993 ch 219 §116.40, effective January 1, 1994.

§ 3044. Presumption against custody to perpetrator of domestic violence [Effective January 1, 2026]

(a) Upon a finding by the court that a party seeking custody of a child has perpetrated domestic violence within the previous five years against the other party seeking custody of the child, or against the child or the child's siblings, or against a person in subparagraph (A) of paragraph (2) of subdivision (a) of Section 3011 with whom the party has a relationship, there is a rebuttable presumption that an award of sole or joint physical or legal custody of a child to a person who has perpetrated domestic violence is detrimental to the best interest of the child, pursuant to Sections 3011 and 3020. This presumption may only be rebutted by a preponderance of the evidence.

(b) To overcome the presumption set forth in subdivision (a), the court shall find that paragraph (1) is satisfied and shall find that the factors in paragraph (2), on balance, support the legislative findings in Section 3020.

(1) The perpetrator of domestic violence has demonstrated that giving sole or joint physical or legal custody of a child to the perpetrator is in the best interest of the child pursuant to Sections 3011 and 3020. In determining the best interest of the child, the preference for frequent and continuing contact with both parents, as set forth in subdivision (b) of Section 3020, or with the noncustodial parent, as set forth in paragraph (1) of subdivision (a) of Section 3040, may not be used to rebut the presumption, in whole or in part.

(2) Additional factors:

(A) The perpetrator has successfully completed a batterer's treatment program that meets the criteria outlined in subdivision (c) of Section 1203.097 of the Penal Code.

(B) The perpetrator has successfully completed a program of alcohol or drug abuse counseling, if the court determines that counseling is appropriate.

(C) The perpetrator has successfully completed a parenting class, if the court determines the class to be appropriate.

(D) The perpetrator is on probation or parole, and has or has not complied with the terms and conditions of probation or parole.

(E) The perpetrator is restrained by a protective order or restraining order, and has or has not complied with its terms and conditions.

(F) The perpetrator of domestic violence has committed further acts of domestic violence.

(G) The court has determined, pursuant to Section 6322.5, that the perpetrator is a restrained person in possession or control of a firearm or ammunition in violation of Section 6389, Section 527.9 of the Code of Civil Procedure, or Section 18120 of the Penal Code.

(c) For purposes of this section, a person has "perpetrated domestic violence" when the person is found by the court to have intentionally or recklessly caused or attempted to cause bodily injury, or sexual assault, or to have placed a person in reasonable apprehension of imminent serious bodily injury to that person or to another, or to have engaged in behavior involving, but not limited to, threatening, striking, harassing, destroying personal property, or disturbing the peace of another, for which a court may issue an ex parte order pursuant to Section 6320 to protect the other party seeking custody of the child or to protect the child and the child's siblings.

(d)(1) For purposes of this section, the requirement of a finding by the court shall be satisfied by, among other things, and not limited to, evidence that a party seeking custody has been convicted within the previous five years, after a trial or a plea of guilty or no contest, of a crime against the other party that comes within the definition of domestic violence contained in Section 6211 and of abuse contained in Section 6203, including, but not limited to, a crime described in subdivision (e) of Section 243 of, or Section 261, 273.5, 422, or 646.9 of, or former Section 262 of, the Penal Code.

(2) The requirement of a finding by the court shall also be satisfied if a court, whether that court hears or has heard the child custody proceedings or not, has made a finding pursuant to subdivision (a) based on conduct occurring within the previous five years.

(e) When a court makes a finding that a party has perpetrated domestic violence, the court may not base its findings solely on conclusions reached by a child custody evaluator or on the recommendation of the Family Court Services staff, but shall consider any relevant, admissible evidence submitted by the parties.

(f)(1) It is the intent of the Legislature that this subdivision be interpreted consistently with the decision in Jaime G. v. H.L. (2018) 25 Cal.App.5th 794, which requires that the court, in determining that the presumption in subdivision (a) has been overcome, make specific findings on each of the factors in subdivision (b).

(2) If the court determines that the presumption in subdivision (a) has been overcome, the court shall state its reasons in writing or on the record as to why paragraph (1) of subdivision (b) is satisfied and why the factors in paragraph (2) of subdivision (b), on balance, support the legislative findings in Section 3020.

(g) In an evidentiary hearing or trial in which custody orders are sought and where there has been an allegation of domestic violence, the court shall make a determination as to whether this section applies prior to issuing a custody order, unless the court finds that a continuance is necessary to determine whether this section applies, in which case the court may issue a temporary custody order for a reasonable period of time, provided the order complies with Sections 3011 and 3020.

(h) In a custody or restraining order proceeding in which a party has alleged that the other party has perpetrated domestic violence in accordance with the terms of this section, the court shall inform the parties of the existence of this section and shall give them a copy of this section prior to custody mediation in the case.

(i) This section shall become effective on January 1, 2026. **Leg.H.** Added Stats 2024 ch 544 §7 (SB 899), effective January 1, 2026.

§3046. Absence or relocation as custody or visitation factor

(a) If a party is absent or relocates from the family residence, the court shall not consider the absence or relocation as a factor in determining custody or visitation in either of the following circumstances:

(1) The absence or relocation is of short duration and the court finds that, during the period of absence or relocation, the party has demonstrated an interest in maintaining custody or visitation, the party maintains, or makes reasonable efforts to maintain, regular contact with the child, and the party's behavior demonstrates no intent to abandon the child.

(2) The party is absent or relocates because of an act or acts of actual or threatened domestic or family violence by the other party.

(b) The court may consider attempts by one party to interfere with the other party's regular contact with the child in determining if the party has satisfied the requirements of subdivision (a).

(c) This section does not apply to either of the following:

(1) A party against whom a protective or restraining order has been issued excluding the party from the dwelling of the other party or the child, or otherwise enjoining the party from assault or harassment against the other party or the child, including, but not limited to, orders issued under Part 4 (commencing with Section 6300) of Division 10, orders preventing civil harassment or workplace violence issued pursuant to Section 527.6 or 527.8 of the Code of Civil Procedure, and criminal protective orders issued pursuant to Section 136.2 of the Penal Code.

(2) A party who abandons a child as provided in Section 7822. **Leg.H.** Added Stats 1999 ch 980 §7 (AB 1671). Amended Stats 2006 ch 538 §157 (SB 1852), effective January 1, 2007.

§3047. Absence, relocation or failure to comply due to military duty or temporary duty, mobilization in support of combat or other military operation, or military deployment outside state; Review of temporary custody order; Visitation rights to family members; Scheduled hearings; Relocation by nondeploying parent

(a) A party's absence, relocation, or failure to comply with custody and visitation orders shall not, by itself, be sufficient to justify a modification of a custody or visitation order if the reason for the absence, relocation, or failure to comply is the party's activation to military duty or temporary duty, mobilization in support of combat or other military operation, or military deployment out of state.

(b)(1) If a party with sole or joint physical custody or visitation receives temporary duty, deployment, or mobilization orders from the military that require the party to move a substantial distance from the party's residence or otherwise has a material effect on the ability of the party to exercise custody or visitation rights, any necessary modification of the existing custody order shall be deemed a temporary custody order made without prejudice, which shall be subject to review and reconsideration upon the return of the party from military deployment, mobilization, or temporary duty.

(2) If the temporary order is reviewed upon return of the party from military deployment, mobilization, or temporary duty, there shall be a presumption that the custody order shall revert to the order that was in place before the modification, unless the court determines that it is not in

the best interest of the child. The court shall not, as part of its review of the temporary order upon the return of the deploying party, order a child custody evaluation under Section 3111 of this code or Section 730 of the Evidence Code, unless the party opposing reversion of the order makes a prima facie showing that reversion is not in the best interest of the child.

(3)(A) If the court makes a temporary custody order, it shall consider any appropriate orders to ensure that the relocating party can maintain frequent and continuing contact with the child by means that are reasonably available.

(B) Upon a motion by the relocating party, the court may grant reasonable visitation rights to a stepparent, grandparent, or other family member if the court does all of the following:

(i) Finds that there is a preexisting relationship between the family member and the child that has engendered a bond such that visitation is in the best interest of the child.

(ii) Finds that the visitation will facilitate the child's contact with the relocating party.

(iii) Balances the interest of the child in having visitation with the family member against the right of the parents to exercise parental authority.

(C) This paragraph does not increase the authority of the persons described in subparagraph (B) to seek visitation orders independently.

(D) The granting of visitation rights to a nonparent pursuant to subparagraph (B) shall not impact the calculation of child support.

(c) If a party's deployment, mobilization, or temporary duty will have a material effect on the party's ability, or anticipated ability, to appear in person at a regularly scheduled hearing, the court shall do either of the following:

(1) Upon motion of the party, hold an expedited hearing to determine custody and visitation issues prior to the departure of the party.

(2) Upon motion of the party, allow the party to present testimony and evidence and participate in court-ordered child custody mediation by electronic means, including, but not limited to, telephone, video teleconferencing, or the internet, to the extent that this technology is reasonably available to the court and protects the due process rights of all parties.

(d) A relocation by a nondeploying parent during a period of a deployed parent's absence while a temporary modification order for a parenting plan is in effect shall not, by itself, terminate the exclusive and continuing jurisdiction of the court for purposes of later determining custody or parenting time under this chapter.

(e) When a court of this state has issued a custody or visitation order, the absence of a child from this state during the deployment of a parent shall be considered a "temporary absence" for purposes of the Uniform Child Custody Jurisdiction and Enforcement Act (Part 3 (commencing with Section 3400)), and the court shall retain exclusive continuing jurisdiction under Section 3422.

(f) The deployment of a parent shall not be used as a basis to assert inconvenience of the forum under Section 3427.

(g) For purposes of this section, the following terms have the following meanings:

(1) "Deployment" means the temporary transfer of a member of the Armed Forces in active-duty status in support of combat or some other military operation.

(2) "Mobilization" means the transfer of a member of the National Guard or Military Reserve to extended active-duty status, but does not include National Guard or Military Reserve annual training.

(3) "Temporary duty" means the transfer of a servicemember from one military base to a different location, usually another base, for a limited period of time to accomplish training or to assist in the performance of a noncombat mission.

(h) It is the intent of the Legislature that this section provide a fair, efficient, and expeditious process to resolve child custody and visitation issues when a party receives temporary duty, deployment, or mobilization orders from the military, as well as at the time that the party returns from service and files a motion to revert back to the custody order in place before the deployment. The Legislature intends that family courts shall, to the extent feasible within existing resources and court practices, prioritize the calendaring of these cases, avoid unnecessary delay or continuances, and ensure that parties who serve in the military are not penalized for their service by a delay in appropriate access to their children. **Leg.H.** Added Stats 2005 ch 154 §1 (SB 1082), effective August 30, 2005. Amended Stats 2010 ch 466 §1 (AB 2416), effective January 1, 2011; Stats 2012 ch 116 §1 (AB 1807), effective January 1, 2013; Stats 2013 ch 76 §59 (AB 383), effective January 1, 2014; Stats 2019 ch 115 §30 (AB 1817), effective January 1, 2020.

§3048. Contents of child custody or visitation order; Determination of risk of abduction

(a) Notwithstanding any other law, in a proceeding to determine child custody or visitation with a child, every custody or visitation order shall contain all of the following:

(1) The basis for the court's exercise of jurisdiction.

(2) The manner in which notice and opportunity to be heard were given.

(3) A clear description of the custody and visitation rights of each party.

(4) A provision stating that a violation of the order may subject the party in violation to civil or criminal penalties, or both.

(5) Identification of the country of habitual residence of the child or children.

(b)(1) In cases in which the court becomes aware of facts that may indicate that there is a risk of abduction of a child, the court shall, either on its own motion or at the request of a party, determine whether measures are needed to prevent the abduction of the child by one parent. To make that determination, the court shall consider the risk of abduction of the child, obstacles to location, recovery, and return if the child is abducted, and potential harm to the child if the child is abducted. To determine whether there is a risk of abduction, the court shall consider the following factors:

(A) Whether a party has previously taken, enticed away, kept, withheld, or concealed a child in violation of the right of custody or of visitation of a person.

(B) Whether a party has previously threatened to take, entice away, keep, withhold, or conceal a child in violation of the right of custody or of visitation of a person.

(C) Whether a party lacks strong ties to this state.

(D) Whether a party has strong familial, emotional, or cultural ties to another state or country, including foreign citizenship. This factor shall be considered only if evidence exists in support of another factor specified in this section.

(E) Whether a party has no financial reason to stay in this state, including whether the party is unemployed, is able to work anywhere, or is financially independent.

(F) Whether a party has engaged in planning activities that would facilitate the removal of a child from the state, including quitting a job, selling the primary residence, terminating a lease, closing a bank account, liquidating other assets, hiding or destroying documents, applying for a passport, applying to obtain a birth certificate or school or medical records, or purchasing airplane or other travel tickets, with consideration given to whether a party is carrying out a safety plan to flee from domestic violence.

(G) Whether a party has a history of a lack of parental cooperation or child abuse, or there is substantiated evidence that a party has perpetrated domestic violence.

(H) Whether a party has a criminal record.

(2) If the court makes a finding that there is a need for preventative measures after considering the factors listed in paragraph (1), the court shall consider taking one or more of the following measures to prevent the abduction of the child:

(A) Ordering supervised visitation.

(B) Requiring a parent to post a bond in an amount sufficient to serve as a financial deterrent to abduction, the proceeds of which may be used to offset the cost of recovery of the child in the event there is an abduction.

(C) Restricting the right of the custodial or noncustodial parent to remove the child from the county, the state, or the country.

(D) Restricting the right of the custodial parent to relocate with the child, unless the custodial parent provides advance notice to, and obtains the written agreement of, the noncustodial parent, or obtains the approval of the court, before relocating with the child.

(E) Requiring the surrender of passports and other travel documents.

(F) Prohibiting a parent from applying for a new or replacement passport for the child.

(G) Requiring a parent to notify a relevant foreign consulate or embassy of passport restrictions and to provide the court with proof of that notification.

(H) Requiring a party to register a California order in another state as a prerequisite to allowing a child to travel to that state for visits, or to obtain an order from another country containing terms identical to the custody and visitation order issued in the United States (recognizing that these orders may be modified or enforced pursuant to the laws of the other country), as a prerequisite to allowing a child to travel to that country for visits.

(I) Obtaining assurances that a party will return from foreign visits by requiring the traveling parent to provide the court or the other parent or guardian with any of the following:

(i) The travel itinerary of the child.

(ii) Copies of round trip airline tickets.

(iii) A list of addresses and telephone numbers where the child can be reached at all times.

(iv) An open airline ticket for the left-behind parent in case the child is not returned.

(J) Including provisions in the custody order to facilitate use of the Uniform Child Custody Jurisdiction and Enforcement Act (Part 3 (commencing with Section 3400)) and the Hague Convention on the Civil Aspects of International Child Abduction (implemented pursuant to 42 U.S.C. Sec. 11601 et seq.), such as identifying California as the home state of the child or otherwise defining the basis for the California court's exercise of jurisdiction under Part 3 (commencing with Section 3400), identifying the United States as the country of habitual residence of the child pursuant to the Hague Convention, defining custody rights pursuant to the Hague Convention, obtaining the express agreement of the parents that the United States is the country of habitual residence of the child, or that California or the United States is the most appropriate forum for addressing custody and visitation orders.

(K) Authorizing the assistance of law enforcement.

(3) If the court imposes any or all of the conditions listed in paragraph (2), those conditions shall be specifically noted on the minute order of the court proceedings.

(4) If the court determines there is a risk of abduction that is sufficient to warrant the application of one or more of the prevention measures authorized by this section, the court shall inform the parties of the telephone number and address of the Child Abduction Unit in the office of the district attorney in the county where the custody or visitation order is being entered.

(c) The Judicial Council shall make the changes to its child custody order forms that are necessary for the implementation of subdivision (b).

(d) This section does not affect the applicability of Section 278.7 of the Penal Code. **Leg.H.** Added Stats 2002 ch 856 §2 (AB 2441). Amended Stats 2003 ch 52 §1 (AB 1516), effective July 14, 2003, ch 62 §86 (SB 600) (ch 52 prevails; ch 62 not effective); Stats 2019 ch 115 §31 (AB 1817), effective January 1, 2020.

2002 Note: This act shall be known and may be cited as the Synclair-Cannon Child Abduction Prevention Act of 2002. Stats 2002 ch 856 (AB 2441) §1.

§3049. Custody and visitation where parent is disabled

It is the intent of the Legislature in enacting this section to codify the decision of the California Supreme Court in In re Marriage of Carney (1979) 24 Cal.3d 725, with respect to custody and visitation determinations by the court involving a disabled parent. **Leg.H.** Added Stats 2010 ch 179 §1 (SB 1188), effective January 1, 2011.

CHAPTER 3
TEMPORARY CUSTODY ORDER DURING PENDENCY OF PROCEEDING

Petition for temporary custody order. §3060.
Order for temporary custody in accordance with agreement or understanding of parties. §3061.
Ex parte order and order to show cause. §3062.
Order restraining removal of child from state. §3063.
Limitation on ex parte order granting or modifying custody order. §3064.

§3060. Petition for temporary custody order

A petition for a temporary custody order, containing the statement required by Section 3429, may be included with the initial filing of the petition or action or may be filed at any time after the initial filing. **Leg.H.** Enacted Stats 1992 ch 162 §10 (AB 2650), operative January 1, 1994. Amended Stats 1993 ch 219 §116.60 (AB 1500); Stats 2019 ch 497 §110 (AB 991), effective January 1, 2020.

§3061. Order for temporary custody in accordance with agreement or understanding of parties

If the parties have agreed to or reached an understanding on the custody or temporary custody of their children, a copy of the agreement or an affidavit as to their understanding shall be attached to the petition or action. As promptly as possible after this filing, the court shall, except in exceptional circumstances, enter an order granting temporary custody in accordance with the agreement or understanding or in accordance with any stipulation of the parties. **Leg.H.** Enacted Stats 1992 ch 162 §10 (AB 2650), operative January 1, 1994. Amended Stats 1993 ch 219 §116.61 (AB 1500).

§3062. Ex parte order and order to show cause

(a) In the absence of an agreement, understanding, or stipulation, the court may, if jurisdiction is appropriate, enter an ex parte temporary custody order, set a hearing date within 20 days, and issue an order to show cause on the responding party. If the responding party does not appear or respond within the time set, the temporary custody order may be extended as necessary, pending the termination of the proceedings.

(b) If, despite good faith efforts, service of the ex parte order and order to show cause has not been effected in a timely fashion and there is reason to believe, based on an affidavit, or other manner of proof made under penalty of perjury, by the petitioner, that the responding party has possession of the minor child and seeks to avoid the jurisdiction of the court or is concealing the whereabouts of the child, then the hearing date may be reset and the ex parte order extended up to an additional 90 days. After service has been effected, either party may request ex parte that the hearing date be advanced or the ex parte order be dissolved or modified. **Leg.H.** Enacted Stats 1992 ch 162 §10 (AB 2650), operative January 1, 1994.

§3063. Order restraining removal of child from state

In conjunction with any ex parte order seeking or modifying an order of custody, the court shall enter an order restraining the person receiving custody from removing the child from the state pending notice and a hearing on the order seeking or modifying custody. **Leg.H.** Enacted Stats 1992 ch 162 §10 (AB 2650), operative January 1, 1994.

§3064. Limitation on ex parte order granting or modifying custody order

(a) The court shall refrain from making an order granting or modifying a custody order on an ex parte basis unless there has been a showing of immediate harm to the child or immediate risk that the child will be removed from the State of California.

(b)**(1)** "Immediate harm to the child" includes, but is not limited to, **either of** the following:

[1] **(A)** Having a parent who has committed acts of domestic violence, [2] **if** the court determines that the acts of domestic violence are of recent origin or are a part of a demonstrated and continuing pattern of acts of domestic violence.

[3] **(B)** Sexual abuse of the child, [4] **if** the court determines that the acts of sexual abuse are of recent origin or are [5] part of a demonstrated and continuing pattern of acts of sexual abuse.

(2)(A) In determining whether there is a showing of immediate harm to the child, the court shall consider a parent's illegal access to firearms and ammunition, including, but not limited to, whether a parent is prohibited from having firearms and ammunition.

(B) "Illegal access to firearms and ammunition" includes the possession, purchase, or receipt of a firearm or ammunition in violation of state or federal law, a restraining order, a protective order, or an injunction, or a condition of probation or parole. **Leg.H.** Enacted Stats 1992 ch 162 §10 (AB 2650), operative January 1, 1994. Amended Stats 2008 ch 54 §1 (AB 2960), effective January 1, 2009; Stats 2024 ch 317 §1 (AB 3072), effective January 1, 2025.

§3064. 2024 Deletes. [1] (1) [2] where [3] (2) [4] where [5] a

CHAPTER 4
JOINT CUSTODY

Presumption for joint custody where parents agree to joint custody. §3080.
Grant of joint custody absent agreement of parents. §3081.
Statement by court of reasons for grant or denial of joint custody request. §3082.
Content and effect of joint legal custody order. §3083.
Content of joint physical custody order. §3084.
Grant of joint legal custody without joint physical custody. §3085.

Order may specify one parent as primary caretaker of child. §3086.
Modification or termination of joint custody order. §3087.
Modification to make custody order a joint custody order. §3088.
Consultation with conciliation court. §3089.

§3080. Presumption for joint custody where parents agree to joint custody

There is a presumption, affecting the burden of proof, that joint custody is in the best interest of a minor child, subject to Section 3011, where the parents have agreed to joint custody or so agree in open court at a hearing for the purpose of determining the custody of the minor child. **Leg.H.** Enacted Stats 1992 ch 162 §10 (AB 2650), operative January 1, 1994. Amended Stats 1993 ch 219 §116.70 (AB 1500).

§3081. Grant of joint custody absent agreement of parents

On application of either parent, joint custody may be ordered in the discretion of the court in cases other than those described in Section 3080, subject to Section 3011. For the purpose of assisting the court in making a determination whether joint custody is appropriate under this section, the court may direct that an investigation be conducted pursuant to Chapter 6 (commencing with Section 3110). **Leg.H.** Enacted Stats 1992 ch 162 §10 (AB 2650), operative January 1, 1994. Amended Stats 1993 ch 219 §116.71 (AB 1500).

§3082. Statement by court of reasons for grant or denial of joint custody request

When a request for joint custody is granted or denied, the court, upon the request of any party, shall state in its decision the reasons for granting or denying the request. A statement that joint physical custody is, or is not, in the best interest of the child is not sufficient to satisfy the requirements of this section. **Leg.H.** Enacted Stats 1992 ch 162 §10 (AB 2650), operative January 1, 1994.

§3083. Content and effect of joint legal custody order

In making an order of joint legal custody, the court shall specify the circumstances under which the consent of both parents is required to be obtained in order to exercise legal control of the child and the consequences of the failure to obtain mutual consent. In all other circumstances, either parent acting alone may exercise legal control of the child. An order of joint legal custody shall not be construed to permit an action that is inconsistent with the physical custody order unless the action is expressly authorized by the court. **Leg.H.** Enacted Stats 1992 ch 162 §10 (AB 2650), operative January 1, 1994.

§3084. Content of joint physical custody order

In making an order of joint physical custody, the court shall specify the rights of each parent to physical control of the child in sufficient detail to enable a parent deprived of that control to implement laws for relief of child snatching and kidnapping. **Leg.H.** Enacted Stats 1992 ch 162 §10 (AB 2650), operative January 1, 1994.

§3085. Grant of joint legal custody without joint physical custody

In making an order for custody with respect to both parents, the court may grant joint legal custody without granting joint physical custody. **Leg.H.** Enacted Stats 1992 ch 162 §10 (AB 2650), operative January 1, 1994. Amended Stats 1993 ch 219 §116.72 (AB 1500).

§3086. Order may specify one parent as primary caretaker of child

In making an order of joint physical custody or joint legal custody, the court may specify one parent as the primary caretaker of the child and one home as the primary home of the child, for the purposes of determining eligibility for public assistance. **Leg.H.** Enacted Stats 1992 ch 162 §10 (AB 2650), operative January 1, 1994.

§3087. Modification or termination of joint custody order

An order for joint custody may be modified or terminated upon the petition of one or both parents or on the court's own motion if it is shown that the best interest of the child requires modification or termination of the order. If either parent opposes the modification or termination order, the court shall state in its decision the reasons for modification or termination of the joint custody order. **Leg.H.** Enacted Stats 1992 ch 162 §10 (AB 2650), operative January 1, 1994.

§3088. Modification to make custody order a joint custody order

An order for the custody of a minor child entered by a court in this state or any other state may, subject to the jurisdictional requirements in Sections 3403 and 3414, be modified at any time to an order for joint custody in accordance with this chapter. **Leg.H.** Enacted Stats 1992 ch 162 §10 (AB 2650), operative January 1, 1994. Amended Stats 1993 ch 219 §116.73 (AB 1500).

§3089. Consultation with conciliation court

In counties having a conciliation court, the court or the parties may, at any time, pursuant to local rules of court, consult with the conciliation court for the purpose of assisting the parties to formulate a plan for implementation of the custody order or to resolve a controversy which has arisen in the implementation of a plan for custody. **Leg.H.** Enacted Stats 1992 ch 162 §10 (AB 2650), operative January 1, 1994.

CHAPTER 5
VISITATION RIGHTS

Visitation rights generally; Protective orders; Confidentiality regarding shelter location. §3100.
Visitation rights of stepparent in dissolution, nullity, or legal separation proceedings. §3101.
Visitation rights of close relatives where parent of unemancipated minor child is deceased. §3102.
Visitation rights of grandparents in specified proceedings. §3103.
Prerequisite findings for grant of visitation rights to grandparent. §3104.
Visitation rights of former legal guardian. §3105.

§3100. Visitation rights generally; Protective orders; Confidentiality regarding shelter location

(a) In making an order pursuant to Chapter 4 (commencing with Section 3080), the court shall grant reasonable visitation rights to a parent when it is shown that the visitation would be in the best interest of the child, as defined in Section 3011, and consistent with Section 3020. In the discretion of the court, reasonable visitation rights may be granted to any other person having an interest in the welfare of the child.

(b)(1)(A) If a protective order, as defined in Section 6218 of this code or Section 136.2 of the Penal Code, has been issued restraining a parent, the court shall consider whether the best interest of the child requires that [1] visitation by that parent be suspended, denied, or limited to situations in which a third person, specified by the court, is present, including virtual visitation. [2]

(B) A parent may submit to the court the name of a person who the parent deems suitable to be present during visitation.

(C) The court may order supervised visitation with the person whose name was submitted, but the submission of a name does not require the court to order supervised visitation if it is not in the best interest of the child, nor does a parent's submission of a name constitute agreement or stipulation to supervised visitation.

(2) In determining [3] **the** type of visitation with the restrained party, if any, is in the best interest of the child pursuant to paragraph (1), the court shall consider the nature of the acts that led to the protective order, the period of time that has elapsed since that order, and whether the restrained party has committed further acts of abuse.

(c)(1)(A) If the court has found that circumstances warrant making an order granting or modifying a custody order on an ex parte basis under Section 3064, the court shall consider whether the best interest of the child requires that visitation by the party whose conduct presents a risk of immediate harm to the child or immediate risk that the child will be removed from the State of California should be suspended, denied, or limited to situations in which a third person, specified by the court, is present, including virtual visitation.

(B) A parent may submit to the court the name of a person who the parent deems suitable to be present during visitation, which may be accepted or rejected by the court as set forth in subparagraph (C) of paragraph (1) of subdivision (b).

(2) In determining the type of visitation with the party whose conduct presents a risk of immediate harm to the child or immediate risk that the child will be removed from the State of California, if any, is in the best interest of the child pursuant to paragraph (1), the court shall consider the nature of the acts that led to the finding of the risk of immediate harm or immediate risk of removal.

[4] **(d)** If visitation is ordered in a case in which domestic violence is alleged and an emergency protective order, protective order, or other restraining order has been issued, the visitation order shall specify the time, day, place, and manner of the visitation, including virtual visitation, or any transfer of the child, so as to limit the child's exposure to potential

domestic conflict or abuse, to ensure the safety of all family members, and to minimize any opportunity for the use of abuse, including coercive control. If a criminal protective order has been issued pursuant to Section 136.2 of the Penal Code, the visitation order shall make reference to, and, unless there is an emergency protective order that has precedence in enforcement pursuant to paragraph (1) of subdivision (c) of Section 136.2 of the Penal Code or a no-contact order, as described in Section 6320, acknowledge the precedence of enforcement of, an appropriate criminal protective order.

[5] **(e)**(1) If the court finds a party is staying in a place designated as a shelter for victims of domestic violence or other confidential location, the court's order shall be designed to prevent disclosure of the location of the shelter or other confidential location and to protect all adults and children living in that location.

(2) If a court finds that a parent is residing in a confidential shelter due to domestic violence or fear of domestic violence from the other parent, the court shall order in-person visitation with the other parent only if the court finds that in-person visitation is in the best interest of the child, taking into account all of the following:

(A) The other parent's access to firearms and ammunition, including, but not limited to, whether the other parent is prohibited from having firearms and ammunition.

(B) If a parent is the subject of an emergency protective order, protective order, or other restraining order, whether that parent has violated that order, and the nature of any violation.

(C) Information obtained pursuant to Section 6306, the requirements of this section, and the information obtained pursuant to Section 3011.

(D) The potential for disclosure of the confidential location.

(3) A court shall make its findings pursuant to paragraphs (1) and (2) in writing or on the record.

[6] **(f)** For purposes of this section, "virtual visitation" means use of audiovisual electronic communication tools to provide contact between a parent and their children as part of a parenting plan or custody order. Virtual visitation may be supervised or unsupervised, based on the court's determination of what is in the best interest of the child. **Leg.H.** Enacted Stats 1992 ch 162 §10 (AB 2650), operative January 1, 1994. Amended Stats 1993 ch 219 §116.74 (AB 1500); Stats 1994 ch 320 §2 (AB 356); Stats 2005 ch 465 §1 (AB 118), effective January 1, 2006; Stats 2013 ch 263 §1 (AB 176), effective January 1, 2014, operative July 1, 2014; Stats 2018 ch 941 §4 (AB 2044), effective January 1, 2019; Stats 2023 ch 493 §3 (SB 599), effective January 1, 2024; Stats 2024 ch 317 §2 (AB 3072), effective January 1, 2025.

§3100. 2024 Deletes. [1] any [2] A parent may submit to the court the name of a person that the parent deems suitable to be present during visitation. The court may order supervised visitation with the person whose name was submitted, but the submission of a name does not require the court to order supervised visitation if it is not in the best interest of the child, nor does a parent's submission of a name constitute agreement or stipulation to supervised visitation. [3] what [4] (c) [5] (d) [6] (e)

§3101. Visitation rights of stepparent in dissolution, nullity, or legal separation proceedings

(a) Notwithstanding any other provision of law, the court may grant reasonable visitation to a stepparent, if visitation by the stepparent is determined to be in the best interest of the minor child.

(b) If a protective order, as defined in Section 6218, has been directed to a stepparent to whom visitation may be granted pursuant to this section, the court shall consider whether the best interest of the child requires that any visitation by the stepparent be denied.

(c) Visitation rights may not be ordered under this section that would conflict with a right of custody or visitation of a birth parent who is not a party to the proceeding.

(d) As used in this section:

(1) "Birth parent" means "birth parent" as defined in Section 8512.

(2) "Stepparent" means a person who is a party to the marriage that is the subject of the proceeding, with respect to a minor child of the other party to the marriage. **Leg.H.** Added Stats 1993 ch 219 §116.76 (AB 1500).

Prior Law: Former §3101, similar to the present section and §3103, was enacted Stats 1992 ch 162 §10, to become operative January 1, 1994, and repealed Stats 1993 ch 219 §116.75.

§3102. Visitation rights of close relatives where parent of unemancipated minor child is deceased

(a) If either parent of an unemancipated minor child is deceased, the children, siblings, parents, and grandparents of the deceased parent may be granted reasonable visitation with the child during the child's minority upon a finding that the visitation would be in the best interest of the minor child.

(b) In granting visitation pursuant to this section to a person other than a grandparent of the child, the court shall consider the amount of personal contact between the person and the child before the application for the visitation order.

(c) This section does not apply if the child has been adopted by a person other than a stepparent or grandparent of the child. Any visitation rights granted pursuant to this section before the adoption of the child automatically terminate if the child is adopted by a person other than a stepparent or grandparent of the child. **Leg.H.** Enacted Stats 1992 ch 162 §10 (AB 2650), operative January 1, 1994. Amended Stats 1993 ch 219 §116.77 (AB 1500); Stats 1994 ch 164 §1 (AB 3042).

§3103. Visitation rights of grandparents in specified proceedings

(a) Notwithstanding any other provision of law, in a proceeding described in Section 3021, the court may grant reasonable visitation to a grandparent of a minor child of a party to the proceeding if the court determines that visitation by the grandparent is in the best interest of the child.

(b) If a protective order as defined in Section 6218 has been directed to the grandparent during the pendency of the proceeding, the court shall consider whether the best interest of the child requires that visitation by the grandparent be denied.

(c) The petitioner shall give notice of the petition to each of the parents of the child, any stepparent, and any person who has physical custody of the child, by certified mail, return receipt requested, postage prepaid, to the person's last known address, or to the attorneys of record of the parties to the proceeding.

(d) There is a rebuttable presumption affecting the burden of proof that the visitation of a grandparent is not in the best interest of a minor child if the child's parents agree that the grandparent should not be granted visitation rights.

(e) Visitation rights may not be ordered under this section if that would conflict with a right of custody or visitation of a birth parent who is not a party to the proceeding.

(f) Visitation ordered pursuant to this section shall not create a basis for or against a change of residence of the child, but shall be one of the factors for the court to consider in ordering a change of residence.

(g) When a court orders grandparental visitation pursuant to this section, the court in its discretion may, based upon the relevant circumstances of the case:

(1) Allocate the percentage of grandparental visitation between the parents for purposes of the calculation of child support pursuant to the statewide uniform guideline (Article 2 (commencing with Section 4050) of Chapter 2 of Part 2 of Division 9).

(2) Notwithstanding Sections 3930 and 3951, order a parent or grandparent to pay to the other, an amount for the support of the child or grandchild. For purposes of this paragraph, "support" means costs related to visitation such as any of the following:

(A) Transportation.

(B) Provision of basic expenses for the child or grandchild, such as medical expenses, day care costs, and other necessities.

(h) As used in this section, "birth parent" means "birth parent" as defined in Section 8512. **Leg.H.** Added Stats 1993 ch 219 §116.78 (AB 1500). Amended Stats 1993 ch 832 §1 (SB 306).

§3104. Prerequisite findings for grant of visitation rights to grandparent

(a) On petition to the court by a grandparent of a minor child, the court may grant reasonable visitation rights to the grandparent if the court does both of the following:

(1) Finds that there is a preexisting relationship between the grandparent and the grandchild that has engendered a bond such that visitation is in the best interest of the child.

(2) Balances the interest of the child in having visitation with the grandparent against the right of the parents to exercise their parental authority.

(b) A petition for visitation under this section shall not be filed while the natural or adoptive parents are married, unless one or more of the following circumstances exist:

(1) The parents are currently living separately and apart on a permanent or indefinite basis.

(2) One of the parents has been absent for more than one month without the other spouse knowing the whereabouts of the absent spouse.

(3) One of the parents joins in the petition with the grandparents.

(4) The child is not residing with either parent.

(5) The child has been adopted by a stepparent.

(6) One of the parents is incarcerated or involuntarily institutionalized.

At any time that a change of circumstances occurs such that none of these circumstances exist, the parent or parents may move the court to terminate grandparental visitation and the court shall grant the termination.

(c) The petitioner shall give notice of the petition to each of the parents of the child, any stepparent, and any person who has physical custody of the child, by personal service pursuant to Section 415.10 of the Code of Civil Procedure.

(d) If a protective order as defined in Section 6218 has been directed to the grandparent during the pendency of the proceeding, the court shall consider whether the best interest of the child requires that any visitation by that grandparent should be denied.

(e) There is a rebuttable presumption that the visitation of a grandparent is not in the best interest of a minor child if the natural or adoptive parents agree that the grandparent should not be granted visitation rights.

(f) There is a rebuttable presumption affecting the burden of proof that the visitation of a grandparent is not in the best interest of a minor child if the parent who has been awarded sole legal and physical custody of the child in another proceeding, or the parent with whom the child resides if there is currently no operative custody order objects to visitation by the grandparent.

(g) Visitation rights may not be ordered under this section if that would conflict with a right of custody or visitation of a birth parent who is not a party to the proceeding.

(h) Visitation ordered pursuant to this section shall not create a basis for or against a change of residence of the child, but shall be one of the factors for the court to consider in ordering a change of residence.

(i) When a court orders grandparental visitation pursuant to this section, the court in its discretion may, based upon the relevant circumstances of the case:

(1) Allocate the percentage of grandparental visitation between the parents for purposes of the calculation of child support pursuant to the statewide uniform guideline (Article 2 (commencing with Section 4050) of Chapter 2 of Part 2 of Division 9).

(2) Notwithstanding Sections 3930 and 3951, order a parent or grandparent to pay to the other, an amount for the support of the child or grandchild. For purposes of this paragraph, "support" means costs related to visitation such as any of the following:

(A) Transportation.

(B) Provision of basic expenses for the child or grandchild, such as medical expenses, day care costs, and other necessities.

(j) As used in this section, "birth parent" means "birth parent" as defined in Section 8512. **Leg.H.** Added Stats 1993 ch 832 §2 (SB 306). Amended Stats 2006 ch 138 §1 (AB 2517), effective January 1, 2007; Stats 2014 ch 328 §1 (AB 1628), effective January 1, 2015.

§3105. Visitation rights of former legal guardian

(a) The Legislature finds and declares that a parent's fundamental right to provide for the care, custody, companionship, and management of the parent's children, while compelling, is not absolute. Children have a fundamental right to maintain healthy, stable relationships with a person who has served in a significant, judicially approved parental role.

(b) The court may grant reasonable visitation rights to a person who previously served as the legal guardian of a child, if visitation is determined to be in the best interest of the minor child.

(c) In the absence of a court order granting or denying visitation between a former legal guardian and a former minor ward, and if a dependency proceeding is not pending, a former legal guardian may maintain an independent action for visitation with the former minor ward. If the child does not have at least one living parent, visitation shall not be determined in a proceeding under the Family Code, but shall instead be determined in a guardianship proceeding that may be initiated for that purpose. **Leg.H.** Added Stats 2004 ch 301 §1 (AB 2292). Amended Stats 2019 ch 115 §32 (AB 1817), effective January 1, 2020.

CHAPTER 6
CUSTODY INVESTIGATION AND REPORT

"Court-appointed investigator". §3110.
Qualifications for child custody evaluator. §3110.5.
Appointment of child custody evaluator; Evaluation and report; Availability; Use in evidence; Unwarranted disclosure; Adoption of form. §3111.
Ability to repay county expenses for investigation or visitation work. §3112.
Separate meetings where domestic violence history between parties or domestic violence prevention orders. §3113.
Recommendation for appointment of counsel for minor child. §3114.
Testimony of investigator. §3115.
Limitation on investigator's duty to assist court. §3116.
Investigations. §3117.
Evaluation of child abuse allegation in contested proceeding for child custody or visitation. §3118.

§3110. "Court-appointed investigator"

As used in this chapter, "court-appointed investigator" means a probation officer, domestic relations investigator, or court-appointed evaluator directed by the court to conduct an investigation pursuant to this chapter. **Leg.H.** Added Stats 1993 ch 219 §116.81 (AB 1500).

Prior Law: Former §3110, similar to present §3111, was enacted Stats 1992 ch 162 §10, operative January 1, 1994, and repealed Stats 1993 ch 219 §116.80.

§3110.5. Qualifications for child custody evaluator

(a) A person may be a court-connected or private child custody evaluator under this chapter only if the person has completed the domestic violence and child abuse training program described in Section 1816 and has complied with Rules 5.220 and 5.230 of the California Rules of Court.

(b)(1) On or before January 1, 2002, the Judicial Council shall formulate a statewide rule of court that establishes education, experience, and training requirements for all child custody evaluators appointed pursuant to this chapter, Section 730 of the Evidence Code, or Chapter 15 (commencing with Section 2032.010) of Title 4 of Part 4 of the Code of Civil Procedure.

(A) The rule shall require a child custody evaluator to declare under penalty of perjury that the evaluator meets all of the education, experience, and training requirements specified in the rule and, if applicable, possesses a license in good standing. The Judicial Council shall establish forms to implement this section. The rule shall permit court-connected evaluators to conduct evaluations if they meet all of the qualifications established by the Judicial Council. The education, experience, and training requirements to be specified for court-connected evaluators shall include, but not be limited to, knowledge of the psychological and developmental needs of children and parent and child relationships.

(B) The rule shall require all evaluators to utilize comparable interview, assessment, and testing procedures for all parties that are consistent with generally accepted clinical, forensic, scientific, diagnostic, or medical standards. The rule shall also require evaluators to inform each adult party of the purpose, nature, and method of the evaluation.

(C) The rule may allow courts to permit the parties to stipulate to an evaluator of their choosing with the approval of the court under the circumstances set forth in subdivision (d). The rule may require courts to provide general information about how parties can contact qualified child custody evaluators in their county.

(2) On or before January 1, 2004, the Judicial Council shall include in the statewide rule of court created pursuant to this section a requirement that all court-connected and private child custody evaluators receive training in the nature of child sexual abuse. The Judicial Council shall develop standards for this training that shall include, but not be limited to, the following:

(A) Children's patterns of hiding and disclosing sexual abuse occurring in a family setting.

(B) The effects of sexual abuse on children.

(C) The nature and extent of child sexual abuse.

(D) The social and family dynamics of child sexual abuse.

(E) Techniques for identifying and assisting families affected by child sexual abuse.

(F) Legal rights, protections, and remedies available to victims of child sexual abuse.

(c) In addition to the education, experience, and training requirements established by the Judicial Council pursuant to subdivision (b), on or after January 1, 2005, a person may be a child custody evaluator under this chapter, Section 730 of the Evidence Code, or Chapter 15 (commencing with Section 2032.010) of Title 4 of Part 4 of the Code of Civil Procedureonly if the person meets one of the following criteria:

(1) The person is licensed as a physician under Chapter 5 (commencing with Section 2000) of Division 2 of the Business and Professions Code and either is a board certified psychiatrist or has completed a residency in psychiatry.

(2) The person is licensed as a psychologist under Chapter 6.6 (commencing with Section 2900) of Division 2 of the Business and Professions Code.

(3) The person is licensed as a marriage and family therapist under Chapter 13 (commencing with Section 4980) of Division 2 of the Business and Professions Code.

(4) The person is licensed as a clinical social worker under Article 4 (commencing with Section 4996) of Chapter 14 of Division 2 of the Business and Professions Code.

(5) The person is licensed as a professional clinical counselor under Chapter 16 (commencing with Section 4999.10) of Division 2 of the Business and Professions Code.

(6) The person is a court-connected evaluator who has been certified by the court as meeting all of the qualifications for court-connected evaluators as specified by the Judicial Council pursuant to subdivision (b).

(d) Subdivision (c) does not apply in a case in which the court determines that there are no evaluators who meet the criteria of subdivision (c) who are willing and available, within a reasonable period of time, to perform child custody evaluations. In those cases, the parties may stipulate to an individual who does not meet the criteria of subdivision (c), subject to approval by the court.

(e) A child custody evaluator who is licensed by the Medical Board of California, the Board of Psychology, or the Board of Behavioral Sciences shall be subject to disciplinary action by that board for unprofessional conduct, as defined in the licensing law applicable to that licensee.

(f) On or after January 1, 2005, a court-connected or private child custody evaluator may not evaluate, investigate, or mediate an issue of child custody in a proceeding pursuant to this division unless that person has completed child sexual abuse training as required by this section. **Leg.H.** Added Stats 1999 ch 932 §1 (SB 433). Amended Stats 2000 ch 926 §4 (SB 1716); Stats 2004 ch 811 §1 (AB 3079), operative until July 1, 2005; Stats 2004 ch 182 §33 (AB 3081), operative July 1, 2005, ch 811 §1.5 (AB 3079) (ch 811 prevails), operative July 1, 2005; Stats 2018 ch 389 §11 (AB 2296), effective January 1, 2019; Stats 2019 ch 115 §33 (AB 1817), effective January 1, 2020; Stats 2021 ch 440 §6 (AB 462), effective January 1, 2022.

§3111. Appointment of child custody evaluator; Evaluation and report; Availability; Use in evidence; Unwarranted disclosure; Adoption of form

(a) In a contested proceeding involving child custody or visitation rights, the court may appoint a child custody evaluator to conduct a child custody evaluation in cases where the court determines it is in the best interest of the child. The child custody evaluation shall be conducted in accordance with the standards adopted by the Judicial Council pursuant to Section 3117, and all other standards adopted by the Judicial Council regarding child custody evaluations. If directed by the court, the court-appointed child custody evaluator shall file a written confidential report on the evaluation. At least 10 days before a hearing regarding custody of the child, the report shall be filed with the clerk of the court in which the custody hearing will be conducted and served on the parties or their attorneys, and any other counsel appointed for the child pursuant to Section 3150. A child custody evaluation, investigation, or assessment, and a resulting report, may be considered by the court only if it is conducted in accordance with the requirements set forth in the standards adopted by the Judicial Council pursuant to Section 3117; however, this does not preclude the consideration of a child custody evaluation report that contains nonsubstantive or inconsequential errors or both.

(b) The report shall not be made available other than as provided in subdivision (a) or Section 3025.5, or as described in Section 204 of the Welfare and Institutions Code or Section 1514.5 of the Probate Code. Any information obtained from access to a juvenile court case file, as defined in subdivision (e) of Section 827 of the Welfare and Institutions Code, is confidential and shall only be disseminated as provided by paragraph (4) of subdivision (a) of Section 827 of the Welfare and Institutions Code.

(c) The report may be received in evidence on stipulation of all interested parties and is competent evidence as to all matters contained in the report.

(d) If the court determines that an unwarranted disclosure of a written confidential report has been made, the court may impose a monetary sanction against the disclosing party. The sanction shall be in an amount sufficient to deter repetition of the conduct, and may include reasonable attorney's fees, costs incurred, or both, unless the court finds that the disclosing party acted with substantial justification or that other circumstances make the imposition of the sanction unjust. The court shall not impose a sanction pursuant to this subdivision that imposes an unreasonable financial burden on the party against whom the sanction is imposed.

(e) The Judicial Council shall, by January 1, 2010, do the following:

(1) Adopt a form to be served with every child custody evaluation report that informs the report recipient of the confidentiality of the report and the potential consequences for the unwarranted disclosure of the report.

(2) Adopt a rule of court to require that, when a court-ordered child custody evaluation report is served on the parties, the form specified in paragraph (1) shall be included with the report.

(f) For purposes of this section, a disclosure is unwarranted if it is done either recklessly or maliciously, and is not in the best interest of the child. **Leg.H.** Added Stats 1993 ch 219 §116.81 (AB 1500). Amended Stats 1996 ch 761 §1 (SB 1995); Stats 1999 ch 932 §2 (SB 433); Stats 2002 ch 1008 §16 (AB 3028); Stats 2004 ch 574 §1 (AB 2228); Stats 2005 ch 22 §62 (SB 1108), effective January 1, 2006; Stats 2008 ch 215 §1 (AB 1877), effective January 1, 2009; Stats 2014 ch 283 §3 (AB 1843), effective January 1, 2015; Stats 2015 ch 130 §1 (SB 594), effective January 1, 2016; Stats 2019 ch 115 §34 (AB 1817), effective January 1, 2020.

Prior Law: Former §3111, similar to present §3113, was enacted Stats 1992 ch 162 §10, operative January 1, 1994, and repealed Stats 1993 ch 219 §116.80.

§3112. Ability to repay county expenses for investigation or visitation work

(a) Where a court-appointed investigator is directed by the court to conduct a custody investigation or evaluation pursuant to this chapter or to undertake visitation work, including necessary evaluation, supervision, and reporting, the court shall inquire into the financial condition of the parent, guardian, or other person charged with the support of the minor. If the court finds the parent, guardian, or other person able to pay all or part of the expense of the investigation, report, and recommendation, the court may make an order requiring the parent, guardian, or other person to repay the court the amount the court determines proper.

(b) The repayment shall be made to the court. The court shall keep suitable accounts of the expenses and repayments and shall deposit the collections as directed by the Judicial Council. **Leg.H.** Added Stats 1993 ch 219 §116.81 (AB 1500). Amended Stats 2000 ch 926 §5 (SB 1716).

Prior Law: Former §3112, similar to the present section, was enacted Stats 1992 ch 162 §10, operative January 1, 1994, and repealed Stats 1993 ch 219 §116.80.

§3113. Separate meetings where domestic violence history between parties or domestic violence prevention orders

Where there has been a history of domestic violence between the parties, or where a protective order as defined in Section 6218 is in effect, at the request of the party alleging domestic violence in a written declaration under penalty of perjury or at the request of a party who is protected by the order, the parties shall meet with the court-appointed investigator separately and at separate times. **Leg.H.** Added Stats 1993 ch 219 §116.81 (AB 1500).

Prior Law: Former §3113, similar to present Fam C §3114, was enacted Stats 1992 ch 162 §10, operative January 1, 1994, and repealed Stats 1993 ch 219 §116.80.

§3114. Recommendation for appointment of counsel for minor child

Nothing in this chapter prohibits a court-appointed investigator from recommending to the court that counsel be appointed pursuant to Chapter 10 (commencing with Section 3150) to represent the minor child. In making that recommendation, the court-appointed investigator shall inform the court of the reasons why it would be in the best interest of the child to have counsel appointed. **Leg.H.** Added Stats 1993 ch 219 §116.81 (AB 1500).

§3115. Testimony of investigator

A statement, whether written or oral, or conduct shall not be held to constitute a waiver by a party of the right to cross-examine the court-appointed investigator, unless the statement is made, or the conduct occurs, after the report has been received by a party or the party's attorney. **Leg.H.** Added Stats 1993 ch 219 §116.81 (AB 1500). Amended Stats 1996 ch 761 §2 (SB 1995); Stats 2019 ch 115 §35 (AB 1817), effective January 1, 2020.

§3116. Limitation on investigator's duty to assist court

Nothing in this chapter limits the duty of a court-appointed investigator to assist the appointing court in the transaction of the business of the court. **Leg.H.** Added Stats 1993 ch 219 §116.81 (AB 1500).

§3117. Investigations

The Judicial Council shall, by January 1, 1999, do both of the following:

(a) Adopt standards for full and partial court-connected evaluations, investigations, and assessments related to child custody.

(b) Adopt procedural guidelines for the expeditious and cost-effective cross-examination of court-appointed investigators, including, but not limited to, the use of electronic technology whereby the court-appointed investigator may not need to be present in the courtroom. These guidelines shall in no way limit the requirement that the court-appointed investigator be available for the purposes of cross-examination. These guidelines shall also provide for written notification to the parties of the right to cross-examine these investigators after the parties have had a reasonable time to review the investigator's report. **Leg.H.** Added Stats 1996 ch 761 §3 (SB 1995).

§3118. Evaluation of child abuse allegation in contested proceeding for child custody or visitation

(a) In any contested proceeding involving child custody or visitation rights, where the court has appointed a child custody evaluator or has referred a case for a full or partial court-connected evaluation, investigation, or assessment, and the court determines that there is a serious allegation of child sexual abuse, the court shall require an evaluation, investigation, or assessment pursuant to this section. When the court has determined that there is a serious allegation of child sexual abuse, any child custody evaluation, investigation, or assessment conducted subsequent to that determination shall be considered by the court only if the evaluation, investigation, or assessment is conducted in accordance with the minimum requirements set forth in this section in determining custody or visitation rights, except as specified in paragraph (1). For purposes of this section, a serious allegation of child sexual abuse means an allegation of child sexual abuse, as defined in Section 11165.1 of the Penal Code, that is based in whole or in part on statements made by the child to law enforcement, a child welfare services agency investigator, any person required by statute to report suspected child abuse, or any other court-appointed personnel, or that is supported by substantial independent corroboration as provided for in subparagraph (B) of paragraph (2) of subdivision (a) of Section 3011. When an allegation of child abuse arises in any other circumstances in any proceeding involving child custody or visitation rights, the court may require an evaluator or investigator to conduct an evaluation, investigation, or assessment pursuant to this section. The order appointing a child custody evaluator or investigator pursuant to this section shall provide that the evaluator or investigator have access to all juvenile court records pertaining to the child who is the subject of the evaluation, investigation, or assessment. The order shall also provide that any juvenile court records or information gained from those records remain confidential and shall only be released as specified in Section 3111.

(1) This section does not apply to any emergency court-ordered partial investigation that is conducted for the purpose of assisting the court in determining what immediate temporary orders may be necessary to protect and meet the immediate needs of a child. This section does apply when the emergency is resolved and the court is considering permanent child custody or visitation orders.

(2) This section does not prohibit a court from considering evidence relevant to determining the safety and protection needs of the child.

(3) Any evaluation, investigation, or assessment conducted pursuant to this section shall be conducted by an evaluator or investigator who meets the qualifications set forth in Section 3110.5.

(b) The evaluator or investigator shall, at a minimum, do all of the following:

(1) Consult with the agency providing child welfare services and law enforcement regarding the allegations of child sexual abuse, and obtain recommendations from these professionals regarding the child's safety and the child's need for protection.

(2) Review and summarize the child welfare services agency file. No document contained in the child welfare services agency file may be photocopied, but a summary of the information in the file, including statements made by the children and the parents, and the recommendations made or anticipated to be made by the child welfare services agency to the juvenile court, may be recorded by the evaluator or investigator, except for the identity of the reporting party. The evaluator's or investigator's notes summarizing the child welfare services agency information shall be stored in a file separate from the evaluator's or investigator's file and may only be released to either party under order of the court.

(3) Obtain from a law enforcement investigator all available information obtained from criminal background checks of the parents and any suspected perpetrator that is not a parent, including information regarding child abuse, domestic violence, or substance abuse.

(4) Review the results of a multidisciplinary child interview team (hereafter MDIT) interview if available, or if not, or if the evaluator or investigator believes the MDIT interview is inadequate for purposes of the evaluation, investigation, or assessment, interview the child or request an MDIT interview, and shall wherever possible avoid repeated interviews of the child.

(5) Request a forensic medical examination of the child from the appropriate agency, or include in the report required by paragraph (6) a written statement explaining why the examination is not needed.

(6) File a confidential written report with the clerk of the court in which the custody hearing will be conducted and which shall be served on the parties or their attorneys at least 10 days prior to the hearing. On and after January 1, 2021, this report shall be made on the form adopted pursuant to subdivision (i). This report may not be made available other than as provided in this subdivision. This report shall address the safety of the child and shall include, but not be limited to, the following:

(A) Documentation of material interviews, including any MDIT interview of the child or the evaluator or investigator, written documentation of interviews with both parents by the evaluator or investigator, and interviews with other witnesses who provided relevant information.

(B) A summary of any law enforcement investigator's investigation, including information obtained from the criminal background check of the parents and any suspected perpetrator that is not a parent, including information regarding child abuse, domestic violence, or substance abuse.

(C) Relevant background material, including, but not limited to, a summary of a written report from any therapist treating the child for suspected child sexual abuse, excluding any communication subject to Section 1014 of the Evidence Code, reports from other professionals, and the results of any forensic medical examination and any other medical examination or treatment that could help establish or disprove whether the child has been the victim of sexual abuse.

(D) The written recommendations of the evaluator or investigator regarding the therapeutic needs of the child and how to ensure the safety of the child.

(E) A summary of the following information: whether the child and the child's parents are or have been the subject of a child abuse investigation and the disposition of that investigation; the name, location, and telephone number of the children's services worker; the status of the investigation and the recommendations made or anticipated to be made regarding the child's safety; and any dependency court orders or findings that might have a bearing on the custody dispute.

(F) Any information regarding the presence of domestic violence or substance abuse in the family that has been obtained from a child protective agency in accordance with paragraphs (1) and (2), a law enforcement agency, medical personnel or records, prior or currently treating therapists, excluding any communication subject to Section 1014 of the Evidence Code, or from interviews conducted or reviewed for this evaluation, investigation, or assessment.

(G) Which, if any, family members are known to have been deemed eligible for assistance from the Victims of Crime Program due to child abuse or domestic violence.

(H) Any other information the evaluator or investigator believes would be helpful to the court in determining what is in the best interests of the child.

(c) If the evaluator or investigator obtains information as part of a family court mediation, that information shall be maintained in the family court file, which is not subject to subpoena by either party. If, however, the members of the family are the subject of an ongoing child welfare services investigation, or the evaluator or investigator has made a child welfare services referral, the evaluator or investigator shall so inform the family law judicial officer in writing and this information shall become part of the family law file. This subdivision may not be construed to authorize or require a mediator to disclose any information not otherwise authorized or required by law to be disclosed.

(d) In accordance with subdivision (d) of Section 11167 of the Penal Code, the evaluator or investigator may not disclose any information regarding the identity of any person making a report of suspected child abuse. This section is not intended to limit any disclosure of information by any agency that is otherwise required by law or court order.

(e) The evaluation, investigation, or assessment standards set forth in this section represent minimum requirements of evaluation and the court shall order further evaluation beyond these minimum requirements when necessary to determine the safety needs of the child.

(f) If the court orders an evaluation, investigation, or assessment pursuant to this section, the court shall consider whether the best interests of the child require that a temporary order be issued that limits visitation with the parent against whom the allegations have been made to situations in which a third person specified by the court is present or whether visitation will be suspended or denied in accordance with Section 3011.

(g) An evaluation, investigation, or assessment pursuant to this section shall be suspended if a petition is filed to declare the child a dependent child of the juvenile court pursuant to Section 300 of the Welfare and Institutions Code, and all information gathered by the evaluator or investigator shall be made available to the juvenile court.

(h) This section shall not be construed to authorize a court to issue any orders in a proceeding pursuant to this division regarding custody or visitation with respect to a minor child who is the subject of a dependency hearing in juvenile court or to otherwise supersede Section 302 of the Welfare and Institutions Code.

(i) On or before January 1, 2021, the Judicial Council shall adopt a mandatory form that shall be used for all evaluations, investigations, or assessments conducted pursuant to this section. The form shall provide a standardized template for all information necessary to provide a full and complete analysis of the allegations raised in the proceeding. **Leg.H.** Added Stats 2000 ch 926 §6 (SB 1716). Amended Stats 2002 ch 305 §1 (SB 1704); Stats 2003 ch 62 §87 (SB 600); Stats 2019 ch 115 §36 (AB 1817), effective January 1, 2020; Stats 2019 ch 127 §1 (AB 1179), effective January 1, 2020 (ch 127 prevails); Stats 2021 ch 124 §27 (AB 938), effective January 1, 2022.

CHAPTER 7
ACTION FOR EXCLUSIVE CUSTODY

Independent action for exclusive custody. §3120.
Ordering party to pay to ensure other party's access to legal representation; Adoption of statewide rule of court; Development of form for submission of information. §3121.

§3120. Independent action for exclusive custody

Without filing a petition for dissolution of marriage or legal separation of the parties, a spouse may bring an action for the exclusive custody of the children of the marriage. The court may, during the pendency of the action, or at the final hearing thereof, or afterwards, make such order regarding the support, care, custody, education, and control of the children of the marriage as may be just and in accordance with the natural rights of the parents and the best interest of the children. The order may be modified or terminated at any time thereafter as the natural rights of the parties and the best interest of the children may require. **Leg.H.** Enacted Stats 1992 ch 162 §10 (AB 2650), operative January 1, 1994. Amended Stats 2014 ch 82 §30 (SB 1306), effective January 1, 2015.

§3121. Ordering party to pay to ensure other party's access to legal representation; Adoption of statewide rule of court; Development of form for submission of information

(a) In any proceeding pursuant to Section 3120, and in any proceeding subsequent to entry of a related judgment, the court shall ensure that each party has access to legal representation, including access early in the proceedings, to preserve each party's rights by ordering, if necessary based on the income and needs assessments, one party, except a government entity, to pay to the other party, or to the other party's attorney, whatever amount is reasonably necessary for attorney's fees and for the cost of maintaining or defending the proceeding during the pendency of the proceeding.

(b) When a request for attorney's fees and costs is made, the court shall make findings on whether an award of attorney's fees and costs under this section is appropriate, whether there is a disparity in access to funds to retain counsel, and whether one party is able to pay for legal representation of both parties. If the findings demonstrate disparity in access and ability to pay, the court shall make an order awarding attorney's fees and costs. A party who lacks the financial ability to hire an attorney may request, as an in pro per litigant, that the court order the other party, if that other party has the financial ability, to pay a reasonable amount to allow the unrepresented party to retain an attorney in a timely manner before proceedings in the matter go forward.

(c) Attorney's fees and costs within this section may be awarded for legal services rendered or costs incurred before or after the commencement of the proceeding.

(d) The court shall augment or modify the original award for attorney's fees and costs as may be reasonably necessary for the prosecution or defense of a proceeding described in Section 3120, or any proceeding related thereto, including after any appeal has been concluded.

(e) Except as provided in subdivision (f), an application for a temporary order making, augmenting, or modifying an award of attorney's fees, including a reasonable retainer to hire an attorney, or costs, or both, shall be made by motion on notice or by an order to show cause during the pendency of any proceeding described in Section 3120.

(f) The court shall rule on an application for fees under this section within 15 days of the hearing on the motion or order to show cause. An order described in subdivision (a) may be made without notice by an oral motion in open court at either of the following times:

(1) At the time of the hearing of the cause on the merits.

(2) At any time before entry of judgment against a party whose default has been entered pursuant to Section 585 or 586 of the Code of Civil Procedure. The court shall rule on any motion made pursuant to this subdivision within 15 days and prior to the entry of any judgment.

(g) The Judicial Council shall, by January 1, 2012, adopt a statewide rule of court to implement this section and develop a form for the information that shall be submitted to the court to obtain an award of attorney's fees under this section. **Leg.H.** Added Stats 2004 ch 472 §3 (AB 2148). Amended Stats 2006 ch 538 §158 (SB 1852), effective January 1, 2007; Stats 2010 ch 352 §13 (AB 939), effective January 1, 2011.

CHAPTER 8
LOCATION OF MISSING PARTY OR CHILD

Action by district attorney to locate missing party and child and to procure compliance with order to appear. §3130.
Action by district attorney where child taken or detained in violation of custody or visitation order. §3131.
District attorney acts on behalf of court. §3132.
Temporary custody order upon request of district attorney. §3133.
Payment of district attorney's expenses. §3134.
Protective custody warrant. §3134.5.
Effect of Uniform Child Custody Jurisdiction and Enforcement Act on authority of district attorney. §3135.

§3130. Action by district attorney to locate missing party and child and to procure compliance with order to appear

If a petition to determine custody of a child has been filed in a court of competent jurisdiction, or if a temporary order pending determination of custody has been entered in accordance with Chapter 3 (commencing with Section 3060), and the whereabouts of a party in possession of the child are not known, or there is reason to believe that the party may not appear in the proceedings although ordered to appear personally with the child pursuant to Section 3430, the district attorney shall take all actions necessary to locate the party and the child and to procure compliance with the order to appear with the child for purposes of adjudication of custody. The petition to determine custody may be filed by the district attorney. **Leg.H.** Enacted Stats 1992 ch 162 §10 (AB 2650), operative January 1,

1994. Amended Stats 2008 ch 699 §2 (SB 1241), effective January 1, 2009.

§3131. Action by district attorney where child taken or detained in violation of custody or visitation order

If a custody or visitation order has been entered by a court of competent jurisdiction and the child is taken or detained by another person in violation of the order, the district attorney shall take all actions necessary to locate and return the child and the person who violated the order and to assist in the enforcement of the custody or visitation order or other order of the court by use of an appropriate civil or criminal proceeding. **Leg.H.** Enacted Stats 1992 ch 162 §10 (AB 2650), operative January 1, 1994.

§3132. District attorney acts on behalf of court

In performing the functions described in Sections 3130 and 3131, the district attorney shall act on behalf of the court and shall not represent any party to the custody proceedings. **Leg.H.** Enacted Stats 1992 ch 162 §10 (AB 2650), operative January 1, 1994.

§3133. Temporary custody order upon request of district attorney

If the district attorney represents to the court, by a written declaration under penalty of perjury, that a temporary custody order is needed to recover a child who is being detained or concealed in violation of a court order or a parent's right to custody, the court may issue an order, placing temporary sole physical custody in the parent or person recommended by the district attorney to facilitate the return of the child to the jurisdiction of the court, pending further hearings. If the court determines that it is not in the best interest of the child to place temporary sole physical custody in the parent or person recommended by the district attorney, the court shall appoint a person to take charge of the child and return the child to the jurisdiction of the court. **Leg.H.** Enacted Stats 1992 ch 162 §10 (AB 2650), operative January 1, 1994.

§3134. Payment of district attorney's expenses

(a) When the district attorney incurs expenses pursuant to this chapter, including expenses incurred in a sister state, payment of the expenses may be advanced by the county subject to reimbursement by the state, and shall be audited by the Controller and paid by the State Treasury according to law.

(b) The court in which the custody proceeding is pending or which has continuing jurisdiction shall, if appropriate, allocate liability for the reimbursement of actual expenses incurred by the district attorney to either or both parties to the proceedings, and that allocation shall constitute a judgment for the state for the funds advanced pursuant to this section. The county shall take reasonable action to enforce that liability and shall transmit all recovered funds to the state. **Leg.H.** Enacted Stats 1992 ch 162 §10 (AB 2650), operative January 1, 1994.

§3134.5. Protective custody warrant

(a) Upon request of the district attorney, the court may issue a protective custody warrant to secure the recovery of an unlawfully detained or concealed child. The request by the district attorney shall include a written declaration under penalty of perjury that a warrant for the child is necessary in order for the district attorney to perform the duties described in Sections 3130 and 3131. The protective custody warrant for the child shall contain an order that the arresting agency shall place the child in protective custody, or return the child as directed by the court. The protective custody warrant for the child may also contain an order to freeze the California assets of the party alleged to be in possession of the child. The protective custody warrant may be served in any county in the same manner as a warrant of arrest and may be served at any time of the day or night. For purposes of this subdivision, "assets" means funds held in a depository institution, as defined in subdivision (a) of Section 1420 of the Financial Code, in California.

(b) Upon a declaration of the district attorney that the child has been recovered or that the warrant is otherwise no longer required, the court may dismiss the warrant without further court proceedings.

(c) Upon noticed motion, any order to freeze assets pursuant to subdivision (a) may be terminated, modified, or vacated by the court upon a finding that the release of the assets will not jeopardize the safety or best interest of the child.

(d) If an asset freeze order is entered pursuant to subdivision (a), and the court subsequently dismisses the warrant pursuant to subdivision (b), notice of the dismissal shall be immediately served on the depository institutions holding any assets pursuant to the freeze order. **Leg.H.** Added Stats 1996 ch 988 §1.5 (AB 2936). Amended Stats 2012 ch 276 §3 (SB 1206), effective January 1, 2013.

2012 Note: This act shall be known and may be cited as Keisuke's Law. Stats 2012 ch 276 (SB 1206) §1.

§3135. Effect of Uniform Child Custody Jurisdiction and Enforcement Act on authority of district attorney

Part 3 (commencing with Section 3400) does not limit the authority of a district attorney or arresting agency to act pursuant to this chapter, Section 279.6 of the Penal Code, or any other applicable law. **Leg.H.** Added Stats 1999 ch 867 §1 (SB 668).

CHAPTER 9
CHECK TO DETERMINE WHETHER CHILD IS MISSING PERSON

Submission of child's birth certificate to court if parent has not appeared in proceeding; Check to determine if child is missing person. §3140.

§3140. Submission of child's birth certificate to court if parent has not appeared in proceeding; Check to determine if child is missing person

(a) Subject to subdivisions (b) and (c), before granting or modifying a custody order in a case in which one or both parents of the child have not appeared either personally or by counsel, the court shall require the parent, petitioner, or other party appearing in the case to submit a certified copy of the child's birth certificate to the court. The court or its designee shall forward the certified copy of the birth certificate to the local police or sheriff's department which shall check with the National Crime Information Center Missing Person System to ascertain whether the child has been reported missing or is the victim of an abduction and shall report the results of the check to the court.

(b) If the custody matter before the court also involves a petition for the dissolution of marriage or the adjudication of paternity rights or duties, this section applies only to a case in which there is no proof of personal service of the petition on the absent parent.

(c) For good cause shown, the court may waive the requirements of this section. **Leg.H.** Enacted Stats 1992 ch 162 §10 (AB 2650), operative January 1, 1994.

CHAPTER 10
APPOINTMENT OF COUNSEL TO REPRESENT CHILD

Appointment of private counsel to represent child in custody or visitation proceeding. §3150.
Rights and duties of appointed counsel. §3151.
Release to counsel of reports and files of child protective agency. §3152.
Compensation of appointed counsel. §3153.

§3150. Appointment of private counsel to represent child in custody or visitation proceeding

(a) If the court determines that it would be in the best interest of the minor child, the court may appoint private counsel to represent the interests of the child in a custody or visitation proceeding, provided that the court and counsel comply with the requirements set forth in Rules 5.240, 5.241, and 5.242 of the California Rules of Court.

(b) Upon entering an appearance on behalf of a child pursuant to this chapter, counsel shall continue to represent that child unless relieved by the court upon the substitution of other counsel by the court or for cause. **Leg.H.** Enacted Stats 1992 ch 162 §10 (AB 2650), operative January 1, 1994. Amended Stats 1993 ch 219 §116.85 (AB 1500); Stats 2010 ch 352 §14 (AB 939), effective January 1, 2011.

§3151. Rights and duties of appointed counsel

(a) The child's counsel appointed under this chapter is charged with the representation of the child's best interests. The role of the child's counsel is to gather evidence that bears on the best interests of the child, and present that admissible evidence to the court in any manner appropriate for the counsel of a party. If the child so desires, the child's counsel shall present the child's wishes to the court. The counsel's duties, unless under the circumstances it is inappropriate to exercise the duty, include interviewing the child, reviewing the court files and all accessible relevant records available to both parties, and making any further investigations as the counsel considers necessary to ascertain evidence relevant to the custody or visitation hearings.

(b) Counsel shall serve notices and pleadings on all parties, consistent with requirements for parties. Counsel shall not be called as a witness in the proceeding. Counsel may introduce and examine counsel's own witnesses, present arguments to the court concerning the child's welfare, and participate further in the proceeding to the degree necessary to represent the child adequately.

(c) The child's counsel shall have the following rights:

(1) Reasonable access to the child.

(2) Standing to seek affirmative relief on behalf of the child.

(3) Notice of any proceeding, and all phases of that proceeding, including a request for examination affecting the child.

(4) The right to take any action that is available to a party to the proceeding, including, but not limited to, the following: filing pleadings, making evidentiary objections, and presenting evidence and being heard in the proceeding, which may include, but shall not be limited to, presenting motions and orders to show cause, and participating in settlement conferences, trials, seeking writs, appeals, and arbitrations.

(5) Access to the child's medical, dental, mental health, and other health care records, school and educational records, and the right to interview school personnel, caretakers, health care providers, mental health professionals, and others who have assessed the child or provided care to the child. The release of this information to counsel shall not constitute a waiver of the confidentiality of the reports, files, and any disclosed communications. Counsel may interview mediators; however, the provisions of Sections 3177 and 3182 shall apply.

(6) The right to reasonable advance notice of and the right to refuse any physical or psychological examination or evaluation, for purposes of the proceeding, which has not been ordered by the court.

(7) The right to assert or waive any privilege on behalf of the child.

(8) The right to seek independent psychological or physical examination or evaluation of the child for purposes of the pending proceeding, upon approval by the court. **Leg.H.** Enacted Stats 1992 ch 162 §10 (AB 2650), operative January 1, 1994. Amended Stats 1997 ch 449 §1 (AB 1526); Stats 2010 ch 352 §15 (AB 939), effective January 1, 2011.

§3151.5. [Section repealed 2013]

Leg.H. Added Stats 1997 ch 449 §2 (AB 1526). Repealed Stats 2012 ch 107 §2 (AB 1406), effective January 1, 2013. The repealed section related to judicial determination regarding custody or visitation, statement of issues and contentions of child's counsel, and subpoena of persons providing information to attorney.

§3152. Release to counsel of reports and files of child protective agency

(a) The child's counsel may, upon noticed motion to all parties and the local child protective services agency, request the court to authorize release of relevant reports or files, concerning the child represented by the counsel, of the relevant local child protective services agency.

(b) The court shall review the reports or files in camera in order to determine whether they are relevant to the pending action and whether and to what extent they should be released to the child's counsel.

(c) Neither the review by the court nor the release to counsel shall constitute a waiver of the confidentiality of the reports and files. Counsel shall not disclose the contents or existence of the reports or files to anyone unless otherwise permitted by law. **Leg.H.** Enacted Stats 1992 ch 162 §10 (AB 2650), operative January 1, 1994.

§3153. Compensation of appointed counsel

(a) If the court appoints counsel under this chapter to represent the child, counsel shall receive a reasonable sum for compensation and expenses, the amount of which shall be determined by the court. Except as provided in subdivision (b), this amount shall be paid by the parties in the proportions the court deems just.

(b) Upon its own motion or that of a party, the court shall determine whether both parties together are financially unable to pay all or a portion of the cost of counsel appointed pursuant to this chapter, and the portion of the cost of that counsel which the court finds the parties are unable to pay shall be paid by the county. The Judicial Council shall adopt guidelines to assist in determining financial eligibility for county payment of counsel appointed by the court pursuant to this chapter. **Leg.H.** Enacted Stats 1992 ch 162 §10 (AB 2650), operative January 1, 1994.

§3155. [Section repealed 1993]

Leg.H. Enacted Stats 1992 ch 162 §10 (AB 2650), operative January 1, 1994. Repealed Stats 1993 ch 219 §116.86 (AB 1500). See Fam C §3160.

§3156. [Section repealed 1993]

Leg.H. Enacted Stats 1992 ch 162 §10 (AB 2650), operative January 1, 1994. Repealed Stats 1993 ch 219 §116.86 (AB 1500). See Fam C §3177.

§3157. [Section repealed 1993]

Leg.H. Enacted Stats 1992 ch 162 §10 (AB 2650), operative January 1, 1994. Repealed Stats 1993 ch 219 §116.86 (AB 1500). See Fam C §3180.

§3158. [Section repealed 1993]

Leg.H. Enacted Stats 1992 ch 162 §10 (AB 2650), operative January 1, 1994. Repealed Stats 1993 ch 219 §116.86 (AB 1500). See Fam C §3182.

§3159. [Section repealed 1993]

Leg.H. Enacted Stats 1992 ch 162 §10 (AB 2650), operative January 1, 1994. Repealed Stats 1993 ch 219 §116.86 (AB 1500). See Fam C §3183.

CHAPTER 11
MEDIATION OF CUSTODY AND VISITATION ISSUES

Article 1. General Provisions.
Article 2. Availability of Mediation.
Article 3. Mediation Proceedings.

ARTICLE 1
General Provisions

Availability of mediators. §3160.
Purpose of mediation proceeding. §3161.
Uniform standards of practice for mediation. §3162.
Local court rules. §3163.
Qualifications of mediator. §3164.
Continuing education. §3165.

§3160. Availability of mediators

Each superior court shall make a mediator available. The court is not required to institute a family conciliation court in order to provide mediation services. **Leg.H.** Added Stats 1993 ch 219 §116.87 (AB 1500).

Prior Law: Former §3160, similar to present §3186, was enacted Stats 1992 ch 162 §10, to become operative January 1, 1994, and repealed Stats 1993 ch 219 §116.86.

§3161. Purpose of mediation proceeding

The purposes of a mediation proceeding are as follows:

(a) To reduce acrimony that may exist between the parties.

(b) To develop an agreement assuring the child close and continuing contact with both parents that is in the best interest of the child, consistent with Sections 3011 and 3020.

(c) To effect a settlement of the issue of visitation rights of all parties that is in the best interest of the child. **Leg.H.** Added Stats 1993 ch 219 §116.87 (AB 1500). Amended Stats 1997 ch 849 §5 (AB 200).

Prior Law: Former §3161, similar to present §3162, was enacted Stats 1992 ch 162 §10, to become operative January 1, 1994, and repealed Stats 1993 ch 219 §116.86.

§3162. Uniform standards of practice for mediation

(a) Mediation of cases involving custody and visitation concerning children shall be governed by uniform standards of practice adopted by the Judicial Council.

(b) The standards of practice shall include, but not be limited to, all of the following:

(1) Provision for the best interest of the child and the safeguarding of the rights of the child to frequent and continuing contact with both parents, consistent with Sections 3011 and 3020.

(2) Facilitation of the transition of the family by detailing factors to be considered in decisions concerning the child's future.

(3) The conducting of negotiations in such a way as to equalize power relationships between the parties.

(c) In adopting the standards of practice, the Judicial Council shall consider standards developed by recognized associations of mediators and attorneys and other relevant standards governing mediation of proceedings for the dissolution of marriage.

(d) The Judicial Council shall offer training with respect to the standards to mediators. **Leg.H.** Added Stats 1993 ch 219 §116.87 (AB 1500). Amended Stats 1997 ch 849 §6 (AB 200).

Prior Law: Former §3162, similar to present §3163, was enacted Stats 1992 ch 162 §10, to become operative January 1, 1994, and repealed Stats 1993 ch 219 §116.86.

§3163. Local court rules

Courts shall develop local rules to respond to requests for a change of mediators or to general problems relating to mediation. **Leg.H.** Added Stats 1993 ch 219 §116.87 (AB 1500).

§3164. Qualifications of mediator

(a) The mediator may be a member of the professional staff of a family conciliation court, probation department, or mental health services agency, or may be any other person or agency designated by the court.

(b) The mediator shall meet the minimum qualifications required of a counselor of conciliation as provided in Section 1815. **Leg.H.** Added Stats 1993 ch 219 §116.87 (AB 1500).

§3165. Continuing education

Any person, regardless of administrative title, hired on or after January 1, 1998, who is responsible for clinical supervision of evaluators, investigators, or mediators or who directly supervises or administers the Family Court Services evaluation or mediation programs shall meet the same continuing education requirements specified in Section 1816 for supervising and associate counselors of conciliation. **Leg.H.** Added Stats 1996 ch 761 §4 (SB 1995).

ARTICLE 2
Availability of Mediation

Setting contested issues for mediation; Domestic violence cases. §3170.
Purpose of mediation; Parties; Waiver. §3171.
Availability of mediation notwithstanding paternity disputes. §3172.
Mediation of dispute concerning existing order. §3173.

§3170. Setting contested issues for mediation; Domestic violence cases

(a) If it appears on the face of a petition, application, or other pleading to obtain or modify a temporary or permanent custody or visitation order that custody, visitation, or both are contested, the court shall set the contested issues for mediation.

(b) Domestic violence cases shall be handled by Family Court Services in accordance with a separate written protocol approved by the Judicial Council. The Judicial Council shall adopt guidelines for services, other than services provided under this chapter, that courts or counties may offer to parents who have been unable to resolve their disputes. These services may include, but are not limited to, parent education programs, booklets, video recordings, or referrals to additional community resources.

(c) This section shall become operative on January 1, 2020. **Leg.H.** Added Stats 2017 ch 330 §2 (AB 1692), effective January 1, 2018, operative January 1, 2020.

Prior Law: Former Fam C §3170, similar to the present section, was added Stats 1993 ch 219 §116.87 (AB 1500), amended Stats 1996 ch 761 §5 (SB 1995), Stats 2009 ch 88 §37 (AB 176), effective January 1, 2010, Stats 2012 ch 470 §18 (AB 1529), effective January 1, 2013, Stats 2017 ch 330 §1 (AB 1692), effective January 1, 2018, and repealed January 1, 2020, by its own terms.

§3171. Purpose of mediation; Parties; Waiver

(a) If a stepparent or grandparent has petitioned, or otherwise applied, for a visitation order pursuant to Chapter 5 (commencing with Section 3100), the court shall set the matter for mediation.

(b) A natural or adoptive parent who is not a party to the proceeding is not required to participate in the mediation proceeding, but failure to participate is a waiver of that parent's right to object to a settlement reached by the other parties during mediation or to require a hearing on the matter. **Leg.H.** Added Stats 1993 ch 219 §116.87 (AB 1500).

Prior Law: Former §3171, similar to present Fam C §3173, was enacted Stats 1992 ch 162 §10, to become operative January 1, 1994, and repealed Stats 1993 ch 219 §116.86.

§3172. Availability of mediation notwithstanding paternity disputes

Mediation shall not be denied to the parties on the basis that paternity is at issue in a proceeding before the court. **Leg.H.** Added Stats 1993 ch 219 §116.87 (AB 1500).

Prior Law: Former §3172, similar to present §§3161, 3180, was enacted Stats 1992 ch 162 §10, to become operative January 1, 1994, and repealed Stats 1993 ch 219 §116.86.

§3173. Mediation of dispute concerning existing order

(a) Upon an order of the presiding judge of a superior court authorizing the procedure in that court, a petition may be filed pursuant to this chapter for mediation of a dispute relating to an existing order for custody, visitation, or both.

(b) The mediation of a dispute concerning an existing order shall be set not later than 60 days after the filing of the petition. **Leg.H.** Added Stats 1993 ch 219 §116.87 (AB 1500). Amended Stats 2012 ch 470 §19 (AB 1529), effective January 1, 2013.

Prior Law: Former §3173, similar to present §3172, was enacted Stats 1992 ch 162 §10, to become operative January 1, 1994, and repealed Stats 1993 ch 219 §116.86.

§3174. [Section repealed 1993]

Leg.H. Enacted Stats 1992 ch 162 §10 (AB 2650), operative January 1, 1994. Repealed Stats 1993 ch 219 §116.86 (AB 1500).

ARTICLE 3
Mediation Proceedings

Setting mediation before or concurrent with hearing. §3175.
Notice of mediation or hearing. §3176.
Confidentiality of proceedings. §3177.
Scope of mediation agreements. §3178.
Modification of agreement resulting from mediation. §3179.
Assessment of needs and interests of child. §3180.
Separate mediation following history of domestic violence. §3181.
Exclusion of counsel from participation. §3182.
Recommendations to court. §3183.
Recommendations that counsel be appointed for minor child. §3184.
Hearing on unresolved issues. §3185.
Confirmation of agreement reached by parties as result of mediation. §3186.
Adoption of confidential mediation program by court. §3188.

§3175. Setting mediation before or concurrent with hearing

If a matter is set for mediation pursuant to this chapter, the mediation shall be set before or concurrent with the setting of the matter for hearing. **Leg.H.** Added Stats 1993 ch 219 §116.87 (AB 1500).

Prior Law: Former §3175, similar to present §§3178, 3179, was enacted Stats 1992 ch 162 §10, to become operative January 1, 1994, and repealed Stats 1993 ch 219 §116.86.

§3176. Notice of mediation or hearing

(a) Notice of mediation and of any hearing to be held pursuant to this chapter shall be given to the following persons:

(1) Where mediation is required to settle a contested issue of custody or visitation, to each party and to each party's counsel of record.

(2) Where a stepparent or grandparent seeks visitation rights, to the stepparent or grandparent seeking visitation rights, to each parent of the child, and to each parent's counsel of record.

(b) Notice shall be given by certified mail, return receipt requested, postage prepaid, to the last known address.

(c) Notice of mediation pursuant to Section 3188 shall state that all communications involving the mediator shall be kept confidential between the mediator and the disputing parties. **Leg.H.** Added Stats 1993 ch 219 §116.87 (AB 1500). Amended Stats 2002 ch 1077 §1 (SB 174).

Prior Law: Former §3176, similar to present Fam C §3181, was enacted Stats 1992 ch 162 §10, to become operative January 1, 1994, and repealed Stats 1993 ch 219 §116.86.

§3177. Confidentiality of proceedings

Mediation proceedings pursuant to this chapter shall be held in private and shall be confidential. All communications, verbal or written, from the parties to the mediator made in the proceeding are official information within the meaning of Section 1040 of the Evidence Code. **Leg.H.** Added Stats 1993 ch 219 §116.87 (AB 1500).

Prior Law: Former §3176, similar to present Fam C §3181, was enacted Stats 1992 ch 162 §10, to become operative January 1, 1994, and repealed Stats 1993 ch 219 §116.86.

§3178. Scope of mediation agreements

An agreement reached by the parties as a result of mediation shall be limited as follows:

(a) Where mediation is required to settle a contested issue of custody or visitation, the agreement shall be limited to the resolution of issues relating to parenting plans, custody, visitation, or a combination of these issues.

(b) Where a stepparent or grandparent seeks visitation rights, the agreement shall be limited to the resolution of issues relating to visitation. **Leg.H.** Added Stats 1993 ch 219 §116.87 (AB 1500).

§3179. Modification of agreement resulting from mediation

A custody or visitation agreement reached as a result of mediation may be modified at any time at the discretion of the court, subject to Chapter 1 (commencing with Section 3020), Chapter 2 (commencing with Section 3040), Chapter 4 (commencing with Section 3080), and Chapter 5 (commencing with Section 3100). **Leg.H.** Added Stats 1993 ch 219 §116.87 (AB 1500).

§3180. Assessment of needs and interests of child

(a) In mediation proceedings pursuant to this chapter, the mediator has the duty to assess the needs and interests of the child involved in the controversy, and is entitled to interview the child when the mediator considers the interview appropriate or necessary.

(b) The mediator shall use their best efforts to effect a settlement of the custody or visitation dispute that is in the best interest of the child, as provided in Section 3011. **Leg.H.** Added Stats 1993 ch 219 §116.87 (AB 1500). Amended Stats 2019 ch 115 §37 (AB 1817), effective January 1, 2020.

Prior Law: Former §3180, similar to present Fam C §§3161, 3171, was enacted Stats 1992 ch 162 §10, to become operative January 1, 1994, and repealed Stats 1993 ch 219 §116.86.

§3181. Separate mediation following history of domestic violence

(a) In a proceeding in which mediation is required pursuant to this chapter, where there has been a history of domestic violence between the parties or where a protective order as defined in Section 6218 is in effect, at the request of the party alleging domestic violence in a written declaration under penalty of perjury or protected by the order, the mediator appointed pursuant to this chapter shall meet with the parties separately and at separate times.

(b) Any intake form that an agency charged with providing family court services requires the parties to complete before the commencement of mediation shall state that, if a party alleging domestic violence in a written declaration under penalty of perjury or a party protected by a protective order so requests, the mediator will meet with the parties separately and at separate times. **Leg.H.** Added Stats 1993 ch 219 §116.87 (AB 1500).

Prior Law: Former §3181, similar to present §3179, was enacted Stats 1992 ch 162 §10, to become operative January 1, 1994, and repealed Stats 1993 ch 219 §116.86.

§3182. Exclusion of counsel from participation

(a) The mediator has authority to exclude counsel from participation in the mediation proceedings pursuant to this chapter if, in the mediator's discretion, exclusion of counsel is appropriate or necessary.

(b) The mediator has authority to exclude a domestic violence support person from a mediation proceeding as provided in Section 6303. **Leg.H.** Added Stats 1993 ch 219 §116.87 (AB 1500).

Prior Law: Former §3182, similar to present Fam C §3185, was enacted Stats 1992 ch 162 §10, to become operative January 1, 1994, and repealed Stats 1993 ch 219 §116.86.

§3183. Recommendations to court

(a) Except as provided in Section 3188, the mediator may, consistent with local court rules, submit a recommendation to the court as to the custody of or visitation with the child, if the mediator has first provided the parties and their attorneys, including counsel for any minor children, with the recommendations in writing in advance of the hearing. The court shall make an inquiry at the hearing as to whether the parties and their attorneys have received the recommendations in writing. If the mediator is authorized to submit a recommendation to the court pursuant to this subdivision, the mediation and recommendation process shall be referred to as "child custody recommending counseling" and the mediator shall be referred to as a "child custody recommending counselor." Mediators who make those recommendations are considered mediators for purposes of Chapter 11 (commencing with Section 3160), and shall be subject to all requirements for mediators for all purposes under this code and the California Rules of Court. On and after January 1, 2012, all court communications and information regarding the child custody recommending counseling process shall reflect the change in the name of the process and the name of the providers.

(b) If the parties have not reached agreement as a result of the mediation proceedings, the mediator may recommend to the court that an investigation be conducted pursuant to Chapter 6 (commencing with Section 3110) or that other services be offered to assist the parties to effect a resolution of the controversy before a hearing on the issues.

(c) In appropriate cases, the mediator may recommend that restraining orders be issued, pending determination of the controversy, to protect the well-being of the child involved in the controversy. **Leg.H.** Added Stats 1993 ch 219 §116.87 (AB 1500). Amended Stats 1996 ch 761 §6 (SB 1995); Stats 2002 ch 1077 §2 (SB 174); Stats 2010 ch 352 §16 (AB 939), effective January 1, 2011.

Prior Law: Former §3183, similar to present Fam C §3176, was enacted Stats 1992 ch 162 §10, to become operative January 1, 1994, and repealed Stats 1993 ch 219 §116.86.

§3184. Recommendations that counsel be appointed for minor child

Except as provided in Section 3188, nothing in this chapter prohibits the mediator from recommending to the court that counsel be appointed, pursuant to Chapter 10 (commencing with Section 3150), to represent the minor child. In making this recommendation, the mediator shall inform the court of the reasons why it would be in the best interest of the minor child to have counsel appointed. **Leg.H.** Added Stats 1993 ch 219 §116.87 (AB 1500). Amended Stats 2002 ch 1077 §3 (SB 174).

§3185. Hearing on unresolved issues

(a) If issues that may be resolved by agreement pursuant to Section 3178 are not resolved by an agreement of all the parties who participate in mediation, the mediator shall inform the court in writing and the court shall set the matter for hearing on the unresolved issues.

(b) Where a stepparent or grandparent requests visitation, each natural or adoptive parent and the stepparent or grandparent shall be given an opportunity to appear and be heard on the issue of visitation. **Leg.H.** Added Stats 1993 ch 219 §116.87 (AB 1500).

§3186. Confirmation of agreement reached by parties as result of mediation

(a) An agreement reached by the parties as a result of mediation shall be reported to counsel for the parties by the mediator on the day set for mediation or as soon thereafter as practical, but before the agreement is reported to the court.

(b) An agreement may not be confirmed or otherwise incorporated in an order unless each party, in person or by counsel of record, has affirmed and assented to the agreement in open court or by written stipulation.

(c) An agreement may be confirmed or otherwise incorporated in an order if a party fails to appear at a noticed hearing on the issue involved in the agreement. **Leg.H.** Added Stats 1993 ch 219 §116.87 (AB 1500).

§3188. Adoption of confidential mediation program by court

(a) Any court selected by the Judicial Council under subdivision (c) may voluntarily adopt a confidential mediation program that provides for all of the following:

(1) The mediator may not make a recommendation as to custody or visitation to anyone other than the disputing parties, except as otherwise provided in this section.

(2) If total or partial agreement is reached in mediation, the mediator may report this fact to the court. If both parties consent in writing, where there is a partial agreement, the mediator may report to the court a description of the issues still in dispute, without specific reference to either party.

(3) In making the recommendation described in Section 3184, the mediator may not inform the court of the reasons why it would be in the best interest of the minor child to have counsel appointed.

(4) If the parties have not reached agreement as a result of the initial mediation, this section does not prohibit the court from requiring subsequent mediation that may result in a recommendation as to custody or visitation with the child if the subsequent mediation is conducted by a different mediator with no prior involvement with the case or knowledge

of any communications, as defined in Section 1040 of the Evidence Code, with respect to the initial mediation. The court, however, shall inform the parties that the mediator will make a recommendation to the court regarding custody or visitation in the event that the parties cannot reach agreement on these issues.

(5) If an initial screening or intake process indicates that the case involves serious safety risks to the child, such as domestic violence, sexual abuse, or serious substance abuse, the mediator may provide an initial emergency assessment service that includes a recommendation to the court concerning temporary custody or visitation orders in order to expeditiously address those safety issues.

(b) This section shall become operative upon the appropriation of funds in the annual Budget Act sufficient to implement this section.

(c) This section shall apply only in four or more superior courts selected by the Judicial Council that currently allow a mediator to make custody recommendations to the court and have more than 1,000 family law case filings per year. The Judicial Council may also make this section applicable to additional superior courts that have fewer than 1,000 family law case filings per year. **Leg.H.** Added Stats 2002 ch 1077 §4 (SB 174). Amended Stats 2012 ch 470 §20 (AB 1529), effective January 1, 2013.

CHAPTER 12
COUNSELING OF PARENTS AND CHILD

Order requiring counseling. §3190.
Purpose of counseling. §3191.
Separate counseling where protective order against domestic violence. §3192.
Limitations on court ordered family reunification treatments, programs, or services. § 3193.

§3190. Order requiring counseling

(a) The court may require parents or any other party involved in a custody or visitation dispute, and the minor child, to participate in outpatient counseling with a licensed mental health professional, or through other community programs and services that provide appropriate counseling, including, but not limited to, mental health or substance abuse services, for not more than one year, provided that the program selected has counseling available for the designated period of time, if the court finds both of the following:

(1) The dispute between the parents, between the parent or parents and the child, between the parent or parents and another party seeking custody or visitation rights with the child, or between a party seeking custody or visitation rights and the child, poses a substantial danger to the best interest of the child.

(2) The counseling is in the best interest of the child.

(b) In determining whether a dispute, as described in paragraph (1) of subdivision (a), poses a substantial danger to the best interest of the child, the court shall consider, in addition to any other factors the court determines relevant, any history of domestic violence, as defined in Section 6211, within the past five years between the parents, between the parent or parents and the child, between the parent or parents and another party seeking custody or visitation rights with the child, or between a party seeking custody or visitation rights and the child.

(c) Subject to Section 3192, if the court finds that the financial burden created by the order for counseling does not otherwise jeopardize a party's other financial obligations, the court shall fix the cost and shall order the entire cost of the services to be borne by the parties in the proportions the court deems reasonable.

(d) The court, in its finding, shall set forth reasons why it has found both of the following:

(1) The dispute poses a substantial danger to the best interest of the child and the counseling is in the best interest of the child.

(2) The financial burden created by the court order for counseling does not otherwise jeopardize a party's other financial obligations.

(e) The court shall not order the parties to return to court upon the completion of counseling. Any party may file a new order to show cause or motion after counseling has been completed, and the court may again order counseling consistent with this chapter. **Leg.H.** Enacted Stats 1992 ch 162 §10 (AB 2650), operative January 1, 1994. Amended Stats 1993 ch 219 §116.90 (AB 1500), ch 301 §1 (AB 197), ch 876 §15.4 (SB 1068), effective October 6, 1993, operative January 1, 1994; Stats 1994 ch 1269 §30 (AB 2208); Stats 1998 ch 229 §1 (AB 1837).

§3191. Purpose of counseling

The counseling pursuant to this chapter shall be specifically designed to facilitate communication between the parties regarding their minor child's best interest, to reduce conflict regarding custody or visitation, and to improve the quality of parenting skills of each parent. **Leg.H.** Enacted Stats 1992 ch 162 §10 (AB 2650), operative January 1, 1994. Amended Stats 1993 ch 219 §116.91 (AB 1500).

§3192. Separate counseling where protective order against domestic violence

In a proceeding in which counseling is ordered pursuant to this chapter, where there has been a history of abuse by either parent against the child or by one parent against the other parent and a protective order, as defined in Section 6218, is in effect, the court may order the parties to participate in counseling separately and at separate times. Each party shall bear the cost of the party's own counseling separately, unless good cause is shown for a different apportionment. The costs associated with a minor child participating in counseling shall be apportioned in accordance with Section 4062. **Leg.H.** Enacted Stats 1992 ch 162 §10 (AB 2650), operative January 1, 1994. Amended Stats 1993 ch 219 §116.92 (AB 1500); Stats 1994 ch 1269 §31 (AB 2208); Stats 2019 ch 115 §38 (AB 1817), effective January 1, 2020.

§ 3193. Limitations on court ordered family reunification treatments, programs, or services

(a) Notwithstanding any other law, a court shall not order family reunification treatments, programs, or services, including, but not limited to, camps, workshops, therapeutic vacations, or educational programs that, as a condition of enrollment or participation, require or result in any of the following:

(1) A no-contact order.
(2) An overnight, out-of-state, or multiday stay.
(3) A transfer of physical or legal custody of the child.
(4) The use of private youth transporters or private transportation agents engaged in the use of force, threat of force, physical obstruction, acutely distressing circumstances, or circumstances that place the safety of the child at risk.
(5) The use of threats of physical force, undue coercion, verbal abuse, isolation from the child's family, community, or other sources of support, or other acutely distressing circumstances.

(b) This section does not affect the applicability of Section 16507 of the Welfare and Institutions Code. **Leg.H.** Added Stats 2023 ch 865 §3 (SB 331), effective January 1, 2024.

CHAPTER 13
SUPERVISED VISITATION AND EXCHANGE SERVICES, EDUCATION, AND COUNSELING

Standards. §3200.
Standards for supervised visitation providers to conform to statute. §3200.5.
Administration of supervised visitation maintained or imposed by court. §3201.
Administration of programs; Definitions. §3201.5.
Compliance with requirements; Definitions. §3202.
Programs and counseling administered by family law division. §3203.
Administration of grant funds. §3204.

§3200. Standards

The Judicial Council shall develop standards for supervised visitation providers in accordance with the guidelines set forth in this section. For the purposes of the development of these standards, the term "provider" shall include any individual who functions as a visitation monitor, as well as supervised visitation centers, including those housed in superior court locations. Provisions shall be made within the standards to allow for the diversity of supervised visitation providers.

(a) When developing standards, the Judicial Council shall consider all of the following issues:

(1) The provider's qualifications, experience, and education.
(2) Safety and security procedures, including ratios of children per supervisor.
(3) Any conflict of interest.
(4) Maintenance and disclosure of records, including confidentiality policies.
(5) Procedures for screening, delineation of terms and conditions, and termination of supervised visitation services.
(6) Procedures for emergency or extenuating situations.
(7) Orientation to and guidelines for cases in which there are allegations of domestic violence, child abuse, substance abuse, or special circumstances.

(8) The legal obligations and responsibilities of supervisors.

(b) The Judicial Council shall consult with visitation centers, mothers' groups, fathers' groups, judges, the State Bar of California, children's advocacy groups, domestic violence prevention groups, Family Court Services, and other groups it regards as necessary in connection with these standards.

(c) It is the intent of the Legislature that the safety of children, adults, and visitation supervisors be a precondition to providing visitation services. Once safety is assured, the best interest of the child is the paramount consideration at all stages and particularly in deciding the manner in which supervision is provided.

(d) Superior court locations may serve as supervised visitation and exchange locations. Superior courts may designate employees and contractors to provide supervised visitation and exchange services or assistance with those services. **Leg.H.** Added Stats 1996 ch 387 §1 (SB 1643). Amended Stats 2004 ch 193 §17 (SB 111); Stats 2023 ch 493 §4 (SB 599), effective January 1, 2024.

§3200.5. Standards for supervised visitation providers to conform to statute

(a) Any standards for supervised visitation providers adopted by the Judicial Council pursuant to Section 3200 shall conform to this section. A provider, as described in Section 3200, shall be a professional provider or nonprofessional provider.

(b) In any case in which the court has determined that there is domestic violence or child abuse or neglect, as defined in Section 11165.6 of the Penal Code, and the court determines supervision is necessary, the court shall consider whether to use a professional or nonprofessional provider based upon the child's best interest.

(c) For the purposes of this section, the following definitions apply:

(1) "Nonprofessional provider" means any person who is not paid for providing supervised visitation services.

(2) "Professional provider" means any person paid for providing supervised visitation services, or an independent contractor, employee, intern, or volunteer operating independently or through a supervised visitation center or agency.

(d) Unless otherwise ordered by the court or stipulated by the parties, a nonprofessional provider shall:

(1) Have no record of a conviction for child molestation, child abuse, or other crimes against a person.

(2) Have proof of automobile insurance if transporting the child.

(3) Have no current or past court order in which the provider is the person being supervised.

(4) Agree to adhere to and enforce the court order regarding supervised visitation.

(e) A professional provider shall:

(1) Be at least 21 years of age.

(2) Have no record of a conviction for driving under the influence (DUI) within the last five years.

(3) Not have been on probation or parole for the last 10 years.

(4) Have no record of a conviction for child molestation, child abuse, or other crimes against a person.

(5) Have proof of automobile insurance if transporting the child.

(6) Have no civil, criminal, or juvenile restraining orders within the last 10 years.

(7) Have no current or past court order in which the provider is the person being supervised.

(8) Be able to speak the language of the party being supervised and of the child, or the provider must provide a neutral interpreter over 18 years of age who is able to do so.

(9) Agree to adhere to and enforce the court order regarding supervised visitation.

(10)(A) Complete 24 hours of training prior to providing visitation services, including at least 12 hours of classroom instruction in the following subjects:

(i) The role of a professional provider.

(ii) Child abuse reporting laws.

(iii) Recordkeeping procedures.

(iv) Screening, monitoring, and termination of visitation.

(v) Developmental needs of children.

(vi) Legal responsibilities and obligations of a provider.

(vii) Cultural sensitivity.

(viii) Conflicts of interest, including the acceptance of gifts.

(ix) Confidentiality.

(x) Issues relating to substance abuse, child abuse, sexual abuse, and domestic violence.

(xi) Basic knowledge of family and juvenile law.

(B) Of the 24 hours of training required pursuant to subparagraph (A), at a minimum, three hours shall be on the screening, monitoring, and termination of visitation, three hours shall be on the developmental needs of children, three hours shall be on issues relating to substance abuse, child abuse, sexual abuse, and domestic violence, and one hour shall be on basic knowledge of family law.

(C) Notwithstanding the requirement for classroom instruction in subparagraph (A), on and after January 1, 2021, a professional provider shall complete the training required pursuant to clause (ii) of subparagraph (A), relating to child abuse reporting laws, by completing an online training course required for mandated reporters that is provided by the State Department of Social Services. This online training requirement is not intended to increase the total number of training hours required by this paragraph.

(11) Complete a Live Scan criminal background check, at the expense of the provider or the supervised visitation center or agency, prior to providing visitation services.

(12) Sign the Judicial Council Declaration of Supervised Visitation Provider form that the person meets the training and qualifications of a provider. A professional provider shall sign a separate, updated form each time the professional provider submits a report to the court.

(13)(A) Beginning January 1, 2021, be registered as a trustline provider pursuant to Chapter 3.35 (commencing with Section 1596.60) of Division 2 of the Health and Safety Code.

(B) Notwithstanding any other law, if a person is denied trustline registration by the State Department of Social Services pursuant to Section 1596.605 or 1596.607 of the Health and Safety Code, or if the State Department of Social Services revokes a person's trustline registration pursuant to Section 1596.608 of the Health and Safety Code, that person shall be ineligible to be a professional provider.

(f) The ratio of children to a professional provider shall be contingent on:

(1) The degree of risk factors present in each case.

(2) The nature of supervision required in each case.

(3) The number and ages of the children to be supervised during a visit.

(4) The number of people visiting the child during the visit.

(5) The duration and location of the visit.

(6) The experience of the provider.

(g) Professional providers of supervised visitation shall:

(1) Advise the parties before commencement of supervised visitation that no confidential privilege exists.

(2) Report suspected child abuse to the appropriate agency, as provided by law, and inform the parties of the provider's obligation to make those reports.

(3) Suspend or terminate visitation under subdivision (h).

(h) Professional providers shall:

(1) Prepare a written contract to be signed by the parties before commencement of the supervised visitation. The contract should inform each party of the terms and conditions of supervised visitation.

(2) Review custody and visitation orders relevant to the supervised visitation.

(3) Keep a record for each case, including, at least, all of the following:

(A) A written record of each contact and visit.

(B) Who attended the visit.

(C) Any failure to comply with the terms and conditions of the visitation.

(D) Any incidence of abuse, as required by law.

(i)(1) Each provider shall make every reasonable effort to provide a safe visit for the child and the noncustodial party.

(2) If a provider determines that the rules of the visit have been violated, the child has become acutely distressed, or the safety of the child or the provider is at risk, the visit may be temporarily interrupted, rescheduled at a later date, or terminated.

(3) All interruptions or terminations of visits shall be recorded in the case file.

(4) All providers shall advise both parties of the reasons for the interruption or termination of a visit.

(j) A professional provider shall state the reasons for temporary suspension or termination of supervised visitation in writing and shall provide the written statement to both parties, their attorneys, the attorney for the child, and the court. **Leg.H.** Added Stats 2012 ch 692 §1 (AB 1674), effective January 1, 2013. Amended Stats 2013 ch 76 §60 (AB 383), effective January 1, 2014; Stats 2019 ch 823 §1 (AB 1165), effective January 1, 2020.

§3201. Administration of supervised visitation maintained or imposed by court

Any supervised visitation maintained or imposed by the court shall be administered in accordance with Standard 5.20 of the California Standards of Judicial Administration recommended by the Judicial Council. **Leg.H.** Added Stats 1999 ch 985 §2 (SB 792). Amended Stats 2021 ch 213 §2 (AB 1579), effective January 1, 2022.

Prior Law: Former Fam C §3201 was added Stats 1999 ch 1004 §2, effective January 1, 2000, and amended and renumbered Fam C §3201.5 by Stats 2015 ch 303 §145, effective January 1, 2016.

Former Sections: Former Fam C §3201 was added Stats 1999 ch 1004 §2 and amended and renumbered Fam C §3201.5 by Stats 2015 ch 303 §145.

§3201.5. Administration of programs; Definitions

(a) The programs described in this chapter shall be administered by the family law division of the superior court in the county.

(b) For purposes of this chapter, "education about protecting children during family disruption" includes education on parenting skills and the impact of parental conflict on children, how to put a parenting agreement into effect, and the responsibility of both parents to comply with custody and visitation orders. **Leg.H.** Added Stats 1999 ch 1004 §2 (AB 673), as Fam C §3201. Amended and renumbered by Stats 2015 ch 303 §145 (AB 731), effective January 1, 2016.

§3202. Compliance with requirements; Definitions

(a) All supervised visitation and exchange programs funded pursuant to this chapter shall comply with all requirements of the Uniform Standards of Practice for Providers of Supervised Visitation set forth in Standard 5.20 of the Standards of Judicial Administration as amended. The family law division of the superior court may contract with eligible providers of supervised visitation and exchange services, education, and group counseling to provide services under this chapter.

(b) As used in this section, "eligible provider" means:

(1) For providers of supervised visitation and exchange services, a local public agency or nonprofit entity that satisfies the Uniform Standards of Practice for Providers of Supervised Visitation.

(2) For providers of group counseling, a professional licensed to practice psychotherapy in this state, including, but not limited to, a licensed psychiatrist, licensed psychologist, licensed clinical social worker, licensed marriage and family therapist, or licensed professional clinical counselor; or a mental health intern working under the direct supervision of a professional licensed to practice psychotherapy.

(3) For providers of education, a professional with a bachelor's or master's degree in human behavior, child development, psychology, counseling, family-life education, or a related field, having specific training in issues relating to child and family development, substance abuse, child abuse, domestic violence, effective parenting, and the impact of divorce and interparental conflict on children; or an intern working under the supervision of that professional. **Leg.H.** Added Stats 1999 ch 1004 §3 (AB 673). Amended Stats 2011 ch 381 §24 (SB 146), effective January 1, 2012; Stats 2013 ch 61 §1 (SB 826), effective January 1, 2014.

§3203. Programs and counseling administered by family law division

Subject to the availability of federal funding for the purposes of this chapter, the family law division of the superior court in each county may establish and administer a supervised visitation and exchange program, programs for education about protecting children during family disruption, and group counseling programs for parents and children under this chapter. The programs shall allow parties and children to participate in supervised visitation between a custodial party and a noncustodial party or joint custodians, and to participate in the education and group counseling programs, irrespective of whether the parties are or are not married to each other or are currently living separately and apart on a permanent or temporary basis. **Leg.H.** Added Stats 1999 ch 1004 §4 (AB 673).

§3204. Administration of grant funds

(a) The Judicial Council shall annually submit an application to the federal Administration for Children and Families, pursuant to Section 669B of the "1996 Federal Personal Responsibility and Work Opportunity Recovery Act" (PRWORA), for a grant to fund child custody and visitation programs pursuant to this chapter.

The Judicial Council shall be charged with the administration of the grant funds.

(b)(1) It is the intention of the Legislature that, effective October 1, 2000, the grant funds described in subdivision (a) shall be used to fund the following three types of programs: supervised visitation and exchange services, education about protecting children during family disruption, and group counseling for parents and children, as set forth in this chapter. Contracts shall follow a standard request for proposal procedure, that may include multiple year funding. Requests for proposals shall meet all state and federal requirements for receiving access and visitation grant funds.

(2) The grant funds shall be awarded with the intent of approving as many requests for proposals as possible while assuring that each approved proposal would provide beneficial services and satisfy the overall goals of the program under this chapter. The Judicial Council shall determine the final number and amount of grants. Requests for proposals shall be evaluated based on the following criteria:

(A) Availability of services to a broad population of parties.
(B) The ability to expand existing services.
(C) Coordination with other community services.
(D) The hours of service delivery.
(E) The number of counties or regions participating.
(F) Overall cost-effectiveness.
(G) The purpose of the program to promote and encourage healthy parent and child relationships between noncustodial parents and their children, while ensuring the health, safety, and welfare of the children.

(3) Special consideration for grant funds shall be given to proposals that coordinate supervised visitation and exchange services, education, and group counseling with existing court-based programs and services.

(c) The family law division of the superior court in each county shall approve sliding scale fees that are based on the ability to pay for all parties, including low-income families, participating in a supervised visitation and exchange, education, and group counseling programs under this chapter.

(d) The Judicial Council shall, on March 1, 2002, and on the first day of March of each subsequent even-numbered year, report to the Legislature on the programs funded pursuant to this chapter and whether and to what extent those programs are achieving the goal of promoting and encouraging healthy parent and child relationships between noncustodial or joint custodial parents and their children while ensuring the health, safety, and welfare of children, and the other goals described in this chapter. **Leg.H.** Added Stats 1999 ch 1004 §5 (AB 673). Amended Stats 2007 ch 738 §13 (AB 1248), effective January 1, 2008.

PART 3
UNIFORM CHILD CUSTODY JURISDICTION AND ENFORCEMENT ACT

Chapter 1. General Provisions.
Chapter 2. Jurisdiction.
Chapter 3. Enforcement.
Chapter 4. Miscellaneous Provisions.

CHAPTER 1
GENERAL PROVISIONS

Citation of part. §3400.
Definitions. §3402.
Adoption proceedings; Authorization of emergency medical care. §3403.
Custody proceedings involving Indian children. §3404.
Effect of custody determination in foreign country. §3405.
Binding force and res judicata effect of custody determination. §3406.
Priority for challenge to jurisdiction. §3407.
Notice to person outside state; Submission to jurisdiction. §3408.
Effect of participation in proceeding on personal jurisdiction. §3409.
Communication with court in another state concerning proceeding. §3410.
Testimony of witnesses located in another state; Transmission of documentary evidence. §3411.
Request for hearings or evaluations in another state; Assistance to courts of other states; Preservation of records; Forwarding to another state. §3412.

§3400. Citation of part

This part may be cited as the Uniform Child Custody Jurisdiction and Enforcement Act. **Leg.H.** Added Stats 1999 ch 867 §3 (SB 668).

Prior Law: Former §3400, similar to the present section, was enacted Stats 1992 ch 162 §10, operative January 1, 1994, and repealed Stats 1999 ch 867 §2.

§3401. [Section repealed 1999]

Leg.H. Enacted Stats 1992 ch 162 §10 (AB 2650), operative January 1, 1994. Repealed Stats 1999 ch 867 §2 (SB 668). The repealed section related to purposes of act.

§3402. Definitions

As used in this part:

(a) "Abandoned" means left without provision for reasonable and necessary care or supervision.

(b) "Child" means an individual who has not attained 18 years of age.

(c) "Child custody determination" means a judgment, decree, or other order of a court providing for the legal custody, physical custody, or visitation with respect to a child. The term includes a permanent, temporary, initial, and modification order. The term does not include an order relating to child support or other monetary obligation of an individual.

(d) "Child custody proceeding" means a proceeding in which legal custody, physical custody, or visitation with respect to a child is an issue. The term includes a proceeding for dissolution of marriage, legal separation of the parties, neglect, abuse, dependency, guardianship, paternity, termination of parental rights, and protection from domestic violence, in which the issue may appear. The term does not include a proceeding involving juvenile delinquency, contractual emancipation, or enforcement under Chapter 3 (commencing with Section 3441).

(e) "Commencement" means the filing of the first pleading in a proceeding.

(f) "Court" means an entity authorized under the law of a state to establish, enforce, or modify a child custody determination.

(g) "Home state" means the state in which a child lived with a parent or a person acting as a parent for at least six consecutive months immediately before the commencement of a child custody proceeding. In the case of a child less than six months of age, the term means the state in which the child lived from birth with any of the persons mentioned. A period of temporary absence of any of the mentioned persons is part of the period.

(h) "Initial determination" means the first child custody determination concerning a particular child.

(i) "Issuing court" means the court that makes a child custody determination for which enforcement is sought under this part.

(j) "Issuing state" means the state in which a child custody determination is made.

(k) "Modification" means a child custody determination that changes, replaces, supersedes, or is otherwise made after a previous determination concerning the same child, whether or not it is made by the court that made the previous determination.

(*l*) "Person" means an individual, corporation, business trust, estate, trust, partnership, limited liability company, association, joint venture, or government; governmental subdivision, agency, or instrumentality; public corporation; or any other legal or commercial entity.

(m) "Person acting as a parent" means a person, other than a parent, who: (1) has physical custody of the child or has had physical custody for a period of six consecutive months, including any temporary absence, within one year immediately before the commencement of a child custody proceeding; and (2) has been awarded legal custody by a court or claims a right to legal custody under the law of this state.

(n) "Physical custody" means the physical care and supervision of a child.

(o) "State" means a state of the United States, the District of Columbia, Puerto Rico, the United States Virgin Islands, or any territory or insular possession subject to the jurisdiction of the United States.

(p) "Tribe" means an Indian tribe or band, or Alaskan Native village, that is recognized by federal law or formally acknowledged by a state.

(q) "Warrant" means an order issued by a court authorizing law enforcement officers to take physical custody of a child. **Leg.H.** Added Stats 1999 ch 867 §3 (SB 668).

Prior Law: Former §3402, similar to the present section, was enacted Stats 1992 ch 162 §10, operative January 1, 1994, and repealed Stats 1999 ch 867 §2.

§3403. Adoption proceedings; Authorization of emergency medical care

This part does not govern an adoption proceeding or a proceeding pertaining to the authorization of emergency medical care for a child. **Leg.H.** Added Stats 1999 ch 867 §3 (SB 668).

Prior Law: Former §3403, similar to present Fam C §§3421, 3423, 3424, was enacted Stats 1992 ch 162 §10, operative January 1, 1994, amended Stats 1993 ch 219 §117, and repealed Stats 1999 ch 867 §2.

§3404. Custody proceedings involving Indian children

(a) A child custody proceeding that pertains to an Indian child as defined in the Indian Child Welfare Act (25 U.S.C. Sec. 1901 et seq.) is not subject to this part to the extent that it is governed by the Indian Child Welfare Act.

(b) A court of this state shall treat a tribe as if it were a state of the United States for the purpose of applying this chapter and Chapter 2 (commencing with Section 3421).

(c) A child custody determination made by a tribe under factual circumstances in substantial conformity with the jurisdictional standards of this part must be recognized and enforced under Chapter 3 (commencing with Section 3441). **Leg.H.** Added Stats 1999 ch 867 §3 (SB 668).

Prior Law: Former §3404, similar to present Fam C §3425, was enacted Stats 1992 ch 162 §10, operative January 1, 1994, and repealed Stats 1999 ch 867 §2.

§3405. Effect of custody determination in foreign country

(a) A court of this state shall treat a foreign country as if it were a state of the United States for the purpose of applying this chapter and Chapter 2 (commencing with Section 3421).

(b) Except as otherwise provided in subdivision (c), a child custody determination made in a foreign country under factual circumstances in substantial conformity with the jurisdictional standards of this part must be recognized and enforced under Chapter 3 (commencing with Section 3441).

(c) A court of this state need not apply this part if the child custody law of a foreign country violates fundamental principles of human rights. **Leg.H.** Added Stats 1999 ch 867 §3 (SB 668).

Prior Law: Former §3405, similar to present Fam C §3408, was enacted Stats 1992 ch 162 §10, operative January 1, 1994, and repealed Stats 1999 ch 867 §2.

§3406. Binding force and res judicata effect of custody determination

A child custody determination made by a court of this state that had jurisdiction under this part binds all persons who have been served in accordance with the laws of this state or notified in accordance with Section 3408 or who have submitted to the jurisdiction of the court, and who have been given an opportunity to be heard. As to those persons, the determination is conclusive as to all decided issues of law and fact except to the extent the determination is modified. **Leg.H.** Added Stats 1999 ch 867 §3 (SB 668).

Prior Law: Former §3406, similar to present Fam C §3426, was enacted Stats 1992 ch 162 §10, operative January 1, 1994, and repealed Stats 1999 ch 867 §2.

§3407. Priority for challenge to jurisdiction

If a question of existence or exercise of jurisdiction under this part is raised in a child custody proceeding, the question, upon request of a party, must be given priority on the calendar and handled expeditiously. **Leg.H.** Added Stats 1999 ch 867 §3 (SB 668).

Prior Law: Former §3407, similar to present Fam C §3427, was enacted Stats 1992 ch 162 §10, operative January 1, 1994, and repealed Stats 1999 ch 867 §2.

§3408. Notice to person outside state; Submission to jurisdiction

(a) Notice required for the exercise of jurisdiction when a person is outside this state may be given in a manner prescribed by the law of this state for service of process or by the law of the state in which the service is made. Notice must be given in a manner reasonably calculated to give actual notice but may be by publication if other means are not effective.

(b) Proof of service may be made in the manner prescribed by the law of this state or by the law of the state in which the service is made.

(c) Notice is not required for the exercise of jurisdiction with respect to a person who submits to the jurisdiction of the court. **Leg.H.** Added Stats 1999 ch 867 §3 (SB 668).

Prior Law: Former §3408, similar to present Fam C §3428, was enacted Stats 1992 ch 162 §10, operative January 1, 1994, amended Stats 1993 ch 219 §118, and repealed Stats 1999 ch 867 §2.

§3409. Effect of participation in proceeding on personal jurisdiction

(a) A party to a child custody proceeding, including a modification proceeding, or a petitioner or respondent in a proceeding to enforce or register a child custody determination, is not subject to personal jurisdiction in this state for another proceeding or purpose solely by reason of having participated, or of having been physically present for the purpose of participating, in the proceeding.

(b) A person who is subject to personal jurisdiction in this state on a basis other than physical presence is not immune from service of process in this state. A party present in this state who is subject to the jurisdiction of another state is not immune from service of process allowable under the laws of that state.

(c) The immunity granted by subdivision (a) does not extend to civil litigation based on acts unrelated to the participation in a proceeding under this part committed by an individual while present in this state. **Leg.H.** Added Stats 1999 ch 867 §3 (SB 668).

Prior Law: Former §3409, similar to present Fam C §3429, was enacted Stats 1992 ch 162 §10), operative January 1, 1994, amended Stats 1993 ch 219 §119, and repealed Stats 1999 ch 867 §2.

§3410. Communication with court in another state concerning proceeding

(a) A court of this state may communicate with a court in another state concerning a proceeding arising under this part.

(b) The court may allow the parties to participate in the communication. If the parties are not able to participate in the communication, they must be given the opportunity to present facts and legal arguments before a decision on jurisdiction is made.

(c) Communication between courts on schedules, calendars, court records, and similar matters may occur without informing the parties. A record need not be made of the communication.

(d) Except as otherwise provided in subdivision (c), a record must be made of a communication under this section. The parties must be informed promptly of the communication and granted access to the record.

(e) For the purposes of this section, "record" means information that is inscribed on a tangible medium or that is stored in an electronic or other medium and is retrievable in perceivable form. **Leg.H.** Added Stats 1999 ch 867 §3 (SB 668).

Prior Law: Former §3410, relating to court's right to join additional parties, was enacted Stats 1992 ch 162 §10, operative January 1, 1994, and repealed Stats 1999 ch 867 §2. Historical derivation: Former CC §5159, as added Stats 1973 ch 693 §1.

§3411. Testimony of witnesses located in another state; Transmission of documentary evidence

(a) In addition to other procedures available to a party, a party to a child custody proceeding may offer testimony of witnesses who are located in another state, including testimony of the parties and the child, by deposition or other means allowable in this state for testimony taken in another state. The court, on its own motion, may order that the testimony of a person be taken in another state and may prescribe the manner in which and the terms upon which the testimony is taken.

(b) A court of this state may permit an individual residing in another state to be deposed or to testify by telephone, audiovisual means, or other electronic means before a designated court or at another location in that state. A court of this state shall cooperate with courts of other states in designating an appropriate location for the deposition or testimony.

(c) Documentary evidence transmitted from another state to a court of this state by technological means that do not produce an original writing may not be excluded from evidence on an objection based on the means of transmission. **Leg.H.** Added Stats 1999 ch 867 §3 (SB 668).

Prior Law: Former §3411, similar to present Fam C §3430, was enacted Stats 1992 ch 162 §10, operative January 1, 1994, amended Stats 1996 ch 988 §2, and repealed Stats 1999 ch 867 §2.

§3412. Request for hearings or evaluations in another state; Assistance to courts of other states; Preservation of records; Forwarding to another state

(a) A court of this state may request the appropriate court of another state to do all of the following:

(1) Hold an evidentiary hearing.

(2) Order a person to produce or give evidence pursuant to procedures of that state.

(3) Order that an evaluation be made with respect to the custody of a child involved in a pending proceeding.

(4) Forward to the court of this state a certified copy of the transcript of the record of the hearing, the evidence otherwise presented, and any evaluation prepared in compliance with the request.

(5) Order a party to a child custody proceeding or any person having physical custody of the child to appear in the proceeding with or without the child.

(b) Upon request of a court of another state, a court of this state may hold a hearing or enter an order described in subdivision (a).

(c) Travel and other necessary and reasonable expenses incurred under subdivisions (a) and (b) may be assessed against the parties according to the law of this state.

(d) A court of this state shall preserve the pleadings, orders, decrees, records of hearings, evaluations, and other pertinent records with respect to a child custody proceeding until the child attains 18 years of age. Upon appropriate request by a court or law enforcement official of another state, the court shall forward a certified copy of those records. **Leg.H.** Added Stats 1999 ch 867 §3 (SB 668).

Prior Law: Former §3412, similar to present Fam C §3406, was enacted Stats 1992 ch 162 §10 and repealed Stats 1999 ch 867 §2.

§3413. [Section repealed 1999]

Leg.H. Enacted Stats 1992 ch 162 §10 (AB 2650), operative January 1, 1994. Repealed Stats 1999 ch 867 §2 (SB 668). See Fam C §3443.

§3414. [Section repealed 1999]

Leg.H. Enacted Stats 1992 ch 162 §10 (AB 2650), operative January 1, 1994. Repealed Stats 1999 ch 867 §2 (SB 668.) See Fam C §3423.

§3415. [Section repealed 1999]

Leg.H. Enacted Stats 1992 ch 162 §10 (AB 2650), operative January 1, 1994. Repealed Stats 1999 ch 867 §2 (SB 668). The repealed section related to check to determine whether child was missing person.

§3416. [Section repealed 1999]

Leg.H. Enacted Stats 1992 ch 162 §10 (AB 2650), operative January 1, 1994. Repealed Stats 1999 ch 867 §2 (SB 668). See Fam C §3445.

§3417. [Section repealed 1999]

Leg.H. Enacted Stats 1992 ch 162 §10 (AB 2650), operative January 1, 1994. Repealed Stats 1999 ch 867 §2 (SB 668). See Fam C §3445.

§3418. [Section repealed 1999]

Leg.H. Enacted Stats 1992 ch 162 §10 (AB 2650), operative January 1, 1994. Repealed Stats 1999 ch 867 §2 (SB 668). The repealed section related to clerk's obligation to forward certified copy of custody decree.

§3419. [Section repealed 1999]

Leg.H. Enacted Stats 1992 ch 162 §10 (AB 2650), operative January 1, 1994. Repealed Stats 1999 ch 867 §2 (SB 668). See Fam C §3411.

§3420. [Section repealed 1999]

Leg.H. Enacted Stats 1992 ch 162 §10 (AB 2650), operative January 1, 1994. Repealed Stats 1999 ch 867 §2 (SB 668). See Fam C §3412.

CHAPTER 2
JURISDICTION

Jurisdiction of court to make custody determination. §3421.
Extent of exclusive and continuing jurisdiction. §3422.
Modification of determination made by another state. §3423.
Temporary emergency jurisdiction; Effect of determination; Communication with other court in which proceeding has been commenced or determination has been made. §3424.
Notice and opportunity to be heard; Joinder; Intervention. §3425.
Simultaneous proceedings in other states. §3426.
Inconvenient forum. §3427.
Declining jurisdiction on ground of unjustifiable conduct. §3428.
Provision of information to court. §3429.
Appearance of parties and child. §3430.

§3421. Jurisdiction of court to make custody determination

(a) Except as otherwise provided in Section 3424, a court of this state has jurisdiction to make an initial child custody determination only if any of the following are true:

(1) This state is the home state of the child on the date of the commencement of the proceeding, or was the home state of the child within six months before the commencement of the proceeding and the child is absent from this state but a parent or person acting as a parent continues to live in this state.

(2) A court of another state does not have jurisdiction under paragraph (1), or a court of the home state of the child has declined to exercise jurisdiction on the grounds that this state is the more appropriate forum under Section 3427 or 3428, and both of the following are true:

(A) The child and the child's parents, or the child and at least one parent or a person acting as a parent, have a significant connection with this state other than mere physical presence.

(B) Substantial evidence is available in this state concerning the child's care, protection, training, and personal relationships.

(3) All courts having jurisdiction under paragraph (1) or (2) have declined to exercise jurisdiction on the ground that a court of this state is the more appropriate forum to determine the custody of the child under Section 3427 or 3428.

(4) No court of any other state would have jurisdiction under the criteria specified in paragraph (1), (2), or (3).

(b) Subdivision (a) is the exclusive jurisdictional basis for making a child custody determination by a court of this state.

(c) Physical presence of, or personal jurisdiction over, a party or a child is not necessary or sufficient to make a child custody determination.

(d) The presence of a child in this state for the purpose of obtaining gender-affirming health care or gender-affirming mental health care, as defined by Section 16010.2 of the Welfare and Institutions Code, is sufficient to meet the requirements of paragraph (2) of subdivision (a). **Leg.H.** Added Stats 1999 ch 867 §3 (SB 668). Amended Stats 2022 ch 810 §4 (SB 107), effective January 1, 2023.

Prior Law: Former §3421, similar to present Fam C §3412, was enacted Stats 1992 ch 162 §10 and repealed Stats 1999 ch 867 §2.

§3422. Extent of exclusive and continuing jurisdiction

(a) Except as otherwise provided in Section 3424, a court of this state that has made a child custody determination consistent with Section 3421 or 3423 has exclusive, continuing jurisdiction over the determination until either of the following occurs:

(1) A court of this state determines that neither the child, nor the child and one parent, nor the child and a person acting as a parent have a significant connection with this state and that substantial evidence is no longer available in this state concerning the child's care, protection, training, and personal relationships.

(2) A court of this state or a court of another state determines that the child, the child's parents, and any person acting as a parent do not presently reside in this state.

(b) A court of this state that has made a child custody determination and does not have exclusive, continuing jurisdiction under this section may modify that determination only if it has jurisdiction to make an initial determination under Section 3421. **Leg.H.** Added Stats 1999 ch 867 §3 (SB 668).

Prior Law: Former §3422, similar to present Fam C §3412, was enacted Stats 1992 ch 162 §10 and repealed Stats 1999 ch 867 §2.

§3423. Modification of determination made by another state

Except as otherwise provided in Section 3424, a court of this state may not modify a child custody determination made by a court of another state unless a court of this state has jurisdiction to make an initial determination under paragraph (1) or (2) of subdivision (a) of Section 3421 and either of the following determinations is made:

(a) The court of the other state determines it no longer has exclusive, continuing jurisdiction under Section 3422 or that a court of this state would be a more convenient forum under Section 3427.

(b) A court of this state or a court of the other state determines that the child, the child's parents, and any person acting as a parent do not presently reside in the other state. **Leg.H.** Added Stats 1999 ch 867 §3 (SB 668).

Prior Law: Former §3423, relating to request for documents from another state, was enacted Stats 1992 ch 162 §10, operative January 1, 1994, and repealed Stats 1999 ch 867 §2. Historical derivation: Former CC §5171, as added Stats 1973 ch 693 §1.

§3424. Temporary emergency jurisdiction; Effect of determination; Communication with other court in which proceeding has been commenced or determination has been made

(a) A court of this state has temporary emergency jurisdiction if the child is present in this state and the child has been abandoned or it is necessary in an emergency to protect the child because the child, or a sibling or parent of the child, is subjected to, or threatened with, mistreatment or abuse, or because the child has been unable to obtain gender-affirming health care or gender-affirming mental health care, as defined by Section 16010.2 of the Welfare and Institutions Code.

(b) If there is no previous child custody determination that is entitled to be enforced under this part and a child custody proceeding has not been commenced in a court of a state having jurisdiction under Sections 3421 to 3423, inclusive, a child custody determination made under this section remains in effect until an order is obtained from a court of a state having jurisdiction under Sections 3421 to 3423, inclusive. If a child custody proceeding has not been or is not commenced in a court of a state having jurisdiction under Sections 3421 to 3423, inclusive, a child custody determination made under this section becomes a final determination, if it so provides and this state becomes the home state of the child.

(c) If there is a previous child custody determination that is entitled to be enforced under this part, or a child custody proceeding has been commenced in a court of a state having jurisdiction under Sections 3421 to 3423, inclusive, any order issued by a court of this state under this section must specify in the order a period that the court considers adequate to allow the person seeking an order to obtain an order from the state having jurisdiction under Sections 3421 to 3423, inclusive. The order issued in this state remains in effect until an order is obtained from the other state within the period specified or the period expires.

(d) A court of this state that has been asked to make a child custody determination under this section, upon being informed that a child custody proceeding has been commenced in, or a child custody determination has been made by, a court of a state having jurisdiction under Sections 3421 to 3423, inclusive, shall immediately communicate with the other court. A court of this state which is exercising jurisdiction pursuant to Sections 3421 to 3423, inclusive, upon being informed that a child custody proceeding has been commenced in, or a child custody determination has been made by, a court of another state under a statute similar to this section shall immediately communicate with the court of that state to resolve the emergency, protect the safety of the parties and the child, and determine a period for the duration of the temporary order.

(e) It is the intent of the Legislature in enacting subdivision (a) that the grounds on which a court may exercise temporary emergency jurisdiction be expanded. It is further the intent of the Legislature that these grounds include those that existed under Section 3403 of the Family Code as that section read on December 31, 1999, particularly including cases involving domestic violence. **Leg.H.** Added Stats 1999 ch 867 §3 (SB 668). Amended Stats 2022 ch 810 §5 (SB 107), effective January 1, 2023.

Prior Law: Former §3424, relating to application of part to international area and legal institutions, was enacted Stats 1992 ch 162 §10, operative January 1, 1994, and repealed Stats 1999 ch 867 §2. Historical derivation: Former CC §5172, as added Stats 1973 ch 693 §1.

§3425. Notice and opportunity to be heard; Joinder; Intervention

(a) Before a child custody determination is made under this part, notice and an opportunity to be heard in accordance with the standards of Section 3408 must be given to all persons entitled to notice under the law of this state as in child custody proceedings between residents of this state, any parent whose parental rights have not been previously terminated, and any person having physical custody of the child.

(b) This part does not govern the enforceability of a child custody determination made without notice or an opportunity to be heard.

(c) The obligation to join a party and the right to intervene as a party in a child custody proceeding under this part are governed by the law of this state as in child custody proceedings between residents of this state. **Leg.H.** Added Stats 1999 ch 867 §3 (SB 668). Amended Stats 2008 ch 699 §3 (SB 1241), effective January 1, 2009.

Prior Law: Former §3425, similar to present Fam C §3407, was enacted Stats 1992 ch 162 §10 and repealed Stats 1999 ch 867 §2.

§3426. Simultaneous proceedings in other states

(a) Except as otherwise provided in Section 3424, a court of this state may not exercise its jurisdiction under this chapter if, at the time of the commencement of the proceeding, a proceeding concerning the custody of the child has been commenced in a court of another state having jurisdiction substantially in conformity with this part, unless the proceeding has been terminated or is stayed by the court of the other state because a court of this state is a more convenient forum under Section 3427.

(b) Except as otherwise provided in Section 3424, a court of this state, before hearing a child custody proceeding, shall examine the court documents and other information supplied by the parties pursuant to Section 3429. If the court determines that a child custody proceeding has been commenced in a court in another state having jurisdiction substantially in accordance with this part, the court of this state shall stay its proceeding and communicate with the court of the other state. If the court of the state having jurisdiction substantially in accordance with this part does not determine that the court of this state is a more appropriate forum, the court of this state shall dismiss the proceeding.

(c) In a proceeding to modify a child custody determination, a court of this state shall determine whether a proceeding to enforce the determination has been commenced in another state. If a proceeding to enforce a child custody determination has been commenced in another state, the court may do any of the following:

(1) Stay the proceeding for modification pending the entry of an order of a court of the other state enforcing, staying, denying, or dismissing the proceeding for enforcement.

(2) Enjoin the parties from continuing with the proceeding for enforcement.

(3) Proceed with the modification under conditions it considers appropriate. **Leg.H.** Added Stats 1999 ch 867 §3 (SB 668).

§3427. Inconvenient forum

(a) A court of this state that has jurisdiction under this part to make a child custody determination may decline to exercise its jurisdiction at any time if it determines that it is an inconvenient forum under the circumstances and that a court of another state is a more appropriate forum. The issue of inconvenient forum may be raised upon motion of a party, the court's own motion, or request of another court.

(b) Before determining whether it is an inconvenient forum, a court of this state shall consider whether it is appropriate for a court of another state to exercise jurisdiction. For this purpose, the court shall allow the parties to submit information and shall consider all relevant factors, including:

(1) Whether domestic violence has occurred and is likely to continue in the future and which state could best protect the parties and the child.

(2) The length of time the child has resided outside this state.

(3) The distance between the court in this state and the court in the state that would assume jurisdiction.

(4) The degree of financial hardship to the parties in litigating in one forum over the other.

(5) Any agreement of the parties as to which state should assume jurisdiction.

(6) The nature and location of the evidence required to resolve the pending litigation, including testimony of the child.

(7) The ability of the court of each state to decide the issue expeditiously and the procedures necessary to present the evidence.

(8) The familiarity of the court of each state with the facts and issues in the pending litigation.

(c) If a court of this state determines that it is an inconvenient forum and that a court of another state is a more appropriate forum, it shall stay the proceedings upon condition that a child custody proceeding be promptly commenced in another designated state and may impose any other condition the court considers just and proper.

(d) A court of this state may decline to exercise its jurisdiction under this part if a child custody determination is incidental to an action for dissolution of marriage or another proceeding while still retaining jurisdiction over the dissolution of marriage or other proceeding.

(e) If it appears to the court that it is clearly an inappropriate forum, the court may require the party who commenced the proceeding to pay, in addition to the costs of the proceeding in this state, necessary travel and other expenses, including attorney's fees, incurred by the other parties or their witnesses. Payment is to be made to the clerk of the court for remittance to the proper party.

(f)(1) In a case where the provision of gender-affirming health care or gender-affirming mental health care to the child is at issue, a court of this state shall not determine that it is an inconvenient forum where the law or policy of the other state that may take jurisdiction limits the ability of a parent to obtain gender-affirming health care or gender-affirming mental health care for their child.

(2) For the purposes of this section, "gender-affirming health care" and "gender-affirming mental health care" have the same meaning as defined by Section 16010.2 of the Welfare and Institutions Code. **Leg.H.** Added Stats 1999 ch 867 §3 (SB 668). Amended Stats 2022 ch 810 §6 (SB 107), effective January 1, 2023.

§3428. Declining jurisdiction on ground of unjustifiable conduct

(a) Except as otherwise provided in Section 3424 or by any other law of this state, if a court of this state has jurisdiction under this part because a person seeking to invoke its jurisdiction has engaged in unjustifiable conduct, the court shall decline to exercise its jurisdiction unless one of the following are true:

(1) The parents and all persons acting as parents have acquiesced in the exercise of jurisdiction.

(2) A court of the state otherwise having jurisdiction under Sections 3421 to 3423, inclusive, determines that this state is a more appropriate forum under Section 3427.

(3) No court of any other state would have jurisdiction under the criteria specified in Sections 3421 to 3423, inclusive.

(b) If a court of this state declines to exercise its jurisdiction pursuant to subdivision (a), it may fashion an appropriate remedy to ensure the safety of the child and prevent a repetition of the unjustifiable conduct, including staying the proceeding until a child custody proceeding is commenced in a court having jurisdiction under Sections 3421 to 3423, inclusive.

(c) If a court dismisses a petition or stays a proceeding because it declines to exercise its jurisdiction pursuant to subdivision (a), it shall assess against the party seeking to invoke its jurisdiction necessary and reasonable expenses including costs, communication expenses, attorney's fees, investigative fees, expenses for witnesses, travel expenses, and child care during the course of the proceedings, unless the party from whom fees are sought establishes that the assessment would be clearly inappropriate. The court may not assess fees, costs, or expenses against this state unless authorized by law other than this part.

(d) In making a determination under this section, a court shall not consider as a factor weighing against the petitioner any taking of the child, or retention of the child after a visit or other temporary relinquishment of physical custody, from the person who has legal custody, if there is evidence that the taking or retention of the child was a result of domestic violence against the petitioner, as defined in Section 6211, or for the purposes of obtaining gender-affirming health care or gender-affirming mental health care, as defined by Section 16010.2 of the Welfare and Institutions Code, for the child and the law or policy of the other state limits the ability of a parent to obtain gender-affirming health care or gender-affirming mental health care for their child. **Leg.H.** Added Stats 1999 ch 867 §3 (SB 668). Amended Stats 2022 ch 810 §7 (SB 107), effective January 1, 2023.

§3429. Provision of information to court

(a) In a child custody proceeding, each party, in its first pleading or in an attached affidavit, shall give information, if reasonably ascertainable, under oath as to the child's present address or whereabouts, the places where the child has lived during the last five years, and the names and present addresses of the persons with whom the child has lived during that period. However, where there are allegations of domestic violence or child abuse, any addresses of the party alleging violence or abuse and of the child which are unknown to the other party are confidential and may not be disclosed in the pleading or affidavit. The pleading or affidavit must state whether the party:

(1) Has participated, as a party or witness or in any other capacity, in any other proceeding concerning the custody of, or visitation with, the child and, if so, identify the court, the case number, and the date of the child custody determination, if any.

(2) Knows of any proceeding that could affect the current proceeding, including proceedings for enforcement and proceedings relating to domestic violence, protective orders, termination of parental rights, and adoptions and, if so, identify the court, the case number, and the nature of the proceeding.

(3) Knows the names and addresses of any person not a party to the proceeding who has physical custody of the child or claims rights of legal custody or physical custody of, or visitation with, the child and, if so, the names and addresses of those persons.

(b) If the information required by subdivision (a) is not furnished, the court, upon motion of a party or its own motion, may stay the proceeding until the information is furnished.

(c) If the declaration as to any of the items described in paragraphs (1) to (3), inclusive, of subdivision (a) is in the affirmative, the declarant shall give additional information under oath as required by the court. The court may examine the parties under oath as to details of the information furnished and other matters pertinent to the court's jurisdiction and the disposition of the case.

(d) Each party has a continuing duty to inform the court of any proceeding in this or any other state that could affect the current proceeding. **Leg.H.** Added Stats 1999 ch 867 §3 (SB 668).

§3430. Appearance of parties and child

(a) In a child custody proceeding in this state, the court may order a party to the proceeding who is in this state to appear before the court in person with or without the child. The court may order any person who is in this state and who has physical custody or control of the child to appear in person with the child.

(b) If a party to a child custody proceeding whose presence is desired by the court is outside this state, the court may order that a notice given pursuant to Section 3408 include a statement directing the party to appear in person with or without the child and informing the party that failure to appear may result in a decision adverse to the party.

(c) The court may enter any orders necessary to ensure the safety of the child and of any person ordered to appear under this section.

(d) If a party to a child custody proceeding who is outside this state is directed to appear under subdivision (b) or desires to appear personally before the court with or without the child, the court may require another party to pay reasonable and necessary travel and other expenses of the party so appearing and of the child. **Leg.H.** Added Stats 1999 ch 867 §3 (SB 668).

CHAPTER 3
ENFORCEMENT

"Petitioner"; "Respondent". §3441.
Order under Hague Convention on Civil Aspects of International Child Abduction. §3442.
Recognition of another state's custody determination. §3443.
Temporary order by court lacking jurisdiction to modify. §3444.
Registration of determination by court of another state; Notice of registration and its consequences; Hearing; Confirmation of order. §3445.
Recognition and enforcement of determination by another state. §3446.
Enforcement proceeding that is contemporaneous with modification proceeding in another state. §3447.
Verification of petition; Contents; Orders; Hearing. §3448.
Service of petition and order. §3449.
Custody order; Fees, costs, and expenses; Inference from refusal to testify; Privilege. §3450.
Warrant to take physical custody of child. §3451.
Costs and expenses for prevailing party. §3452.
Full faith and credit; Enforcement of another state's custody determination. §3453.
Unenforceability of out-of-state law authorizing removal of child based on parent or guardian allowing child to receive gender-affirming health care or gender-affirming mental health care. § 3453.5.
Appeal. §3454.
District attorney's authority to locate missing party or child. §3455.
Assistance by law enforcement officer in finding party or child. §3456.
Costs and expenses incurred by district attorney. §3457.

§3441. "Petitioner"; "Respondent"

In this chapter:

(a) "Petitioner" means a person who seeks enforcement of an order for return of a child under the Hague Convention on the Civil Aspects of International Child Abduction or enforcement of a child custody determination.

(b) "Respondent" means a person against whom a proceeding has been commenced for enforcement of an order for return of a child under the Hague Convention on the Civil Aspects of International Child Abduction or enforcement of a child custody determination. **Leg.H.** Added Stats 1999 ch 867 §3 (SB 668).

§3442. Order under Hague Convention on Civil Aspects of International Child Abduction

Under this chapter, a court of this state may enforce an order for the return of a child made under the Hague Convention on the Civil Aspects of International Child Abduction as if it were a child custody determination. **Leg.H.** Added Stats 1999 ch 867 §3 (SB 668).

§3443. Recognition of another state's custody determination

(a) A court of this state shall recognize and enforce a child custody determination of a court of another state if the latter court exercised jurisdiction in substantial conformity with this part or the determination was made under factual circumstances meeting the jurisdictional standards of this part and the determination has not been modified in accordance with this part.

(b) A court of this state may utilize any remedy available under other laws of this state to enforce a child custody determination made by a court of another state. The remedies provided in this chapter are cumulative and do not affect the availability of other remedies to enforce a child custody determination. **Leg.H.** Added Stats 1999 ch 867 §3 (SB 668).

§3444. Temporary order by court lacking jurisdiction to modify

(a) A court of this state which does not have jurisdiction to modify a child custody determination may issue a temporary order enforcing either:

(1) A visitation schedule made by a court of another state.

(2) The visitation provisions of a child custody determination of another state that does not provide for a specific visitation schedule.

(b) If a court of this state makes an order under paragraph (2) of subdivision (a), it shall specify in the order a period that it considers adequate to allow the petitioner to obtain an order from a court having jurisdiction under the criteria specified in Chapter 2 (commencing with Section 3421). The order remains in effect until an order is obtained from the other court or the period expires. **Leg.H.** Added Stats 1999 ch 867 §3 (SB 668).

§3445. Registration of determination by court of another state; Notice of registration and its consequences; Hearing; Confirmation of order

(a) A child custody determination issued by a court of another state may be registered in this state, with or without a simultaneous request for enforcement, by sending all of the following to the appropriate court in this state:

(1) A letter or other document requesting registration.

(2) Two copies, including one certified copy, of the determination sought to be registered, and a statement under penalty of perjury that to the best of the knowledge and belief of the person seeking registration the order has not been modified.

(3) Except as otherwise provided in Section 3429, the name and address of the person seeking registration and any parent or person acting as a parent who has been awarded custody or visitation in the child custody determination sought to be registered.

(b) On receipt of the documents required by subdivision (a), the registering court shall do both of the following:

(1) Cause the determination to be filed as a foreign judgment, together with one copy of any accompanying documents and information, regardless of their form.

(2) Serve notice upon the persons named pursuant to paragraph (3) of subdivision (a) and provide them with an opportunity to contest the registration in accordance with this section.

(c) The notice required by paragraph (2) of subdivision (b) shall state all of the following:

(1) That a registered determination is enforceable as of the date of the registration in the same manner as a determination issued by a court of this state.

(2) That a hearing to contest the validity of the registered determination must be requested within 20 days after service of the notice.

(3) That failure to contest the registration will result in confirmation of the child custody determination and preclude further contest of that determination with respect to any matter that could have been asserted.

(d) A person seeking to contest the validity of a registered order must request a hearing within 20 days after service of the notice. At that hearing, the court shall confirm the registered order unless the person contesting registration establishes any of the following:

(1) That the issuing court did not have jurisdiction under Chapter 2 (commencing with Section 3421).

(2) That the child custody determination sought to be registered has been vacated, stayed, or modified by a court having jurisdiction to do so under Chapter 2 (commencing with Section 3421).

(3) That the person contesting registration was entitled to notice, but notice was not given in accordance with the standards of Section 3408, in the proceedings before the court that issued the order for which registration is sought.

(e) If a timely request for a hearing to contest the validity of the registration is not made, the registration is confirmed as a matter of law and the person requesting registration and all persons served shall be notified of the confirmation.

(f) Confirmation of a registered order, whether by operation of law or after notice and hearing, precludes further contest of the order with respect to any matter that could have been asserted at the time of registration. **Leg.H.** Added Stats 1999 ch 867 §3 (SB 668).

§3446. Recognition and enforcement of determination by another state

(a) A court of this state may grant any relief normally available under the law of this state to enforce a registered child custody determination made by a court of another state.

(b) A court of this state shall recognize and enforce, but may not modify, except in accordance with Chapter 2 (commencing with Section 3421), a registered child custody determination of a court of another state. **Leg.H.** Added Stats 1999 ch 867 §3 (SB 668).

§3447. Enforcement proceeding that is contemporaneous with modification proceeding in another state

If a proceeding for enforcement under this chapter is commenced in a court of this state and the court determines that a proceeding to modify the determination is pending in a court of another state having jurisdiction to modify the determination under Chapter 2 (commencing with Section 3421), the enforcing court shall immediately communicate with the modifying court. The proceeding for enforcement continues unless the enforcing court, after consultation with the modifying court, stays or dismisses the proceeding. **Leg.H.** Added Stats 1999 ch 867 §3 (SB 668).

§3448. Verification of petition; Contents; Orders; Hearing

(a) A petition under this chapter must be verified. Certified copies of all orders sought to be enforced and of any order confirming registration must be attached to the petition. A copy of a certified copy of an order may be attached instead of the original.

(b) A petition for enforcement of a child custody determination must state all of the following:

(1) Whether the court that issued the determination identified the jurisdictional basis it relied upon in exercising jurisdiction and, if so, what the basis was.

(2) Whether the determination for which enforcement is sought has been vacated, stayed, or modified by a court whose decision must be enforced under this part and, if so, identify the court, the case number, and the nature of the proceeding.

(3) Whether any proceeding has been commenced that could affect the current proceeding, including proceedings relating to domestic violence, protective orders, termination of parental rights, and adoptions and, if so, identify the court, the case number, and the nature of the proceeding.

(4) The present physical address of the child and the respondent, if known.

(5) Whether relief in addition to the immediate physical custody of the child and attorney's fees is sought, including a request for assistance from law enforcement officials and, if so, the relief sought.

(6) If the child custody determination has been registered and confirmed under Section 3445, the date and place of registration.

(c) Upon the filing of a petition, the court shall issue an order directing the respondent to appear in person with or without the child at a hearing and may enter any order necessary to ensure the safety of the parties and the child. The hearing must be held on the next judicial day after service of the order unless that date is impossible. In that event, the court shall hold the hearing on the first judicial day possible. The court may extend the date of hearing at the request of the petitioner.

(d) An order issued under subdivision (c) must state the time and place of the hearing and advise the respondent that, at the hearing, the court will order that the petitioner may take immediate physical custody of the child and the payment of fees, costs, and expenses under Section 3452, and may schedule a hearing to determine whether further relief is appropriate, unless the respondent appears and establishes either of the following:

(1) That the child custody determination has not been registered and confirmed under Section 3445 and all of the following are true:

(A) The issuing court did not have jurisdiction under Chapter 2 (commencing with Section 3421).

(B) The child custody determination for which enforcement is sought has been vacated, stayed, or modified by a court having jurisdiction to do so under Chapter 2 (commencing with Section 3421).

(C) The respondent was entitled to notice, but notice was not given in accordance with the standards of Section 3408, in the proceedings before the court that issued the order for which enforcement is sought.

(2) That the child custody determination for which enforcement is sought was registered and confirmed under Section 3445, but has been vacated, stayed, or modified by a court of a state having jurisdiction to do so under Chapter 2 (commencing with Section 3421). **Leg.H.** Added Stats 1999 ch 867 §3 (SB 668). Amended Stats 2008 ch 699 §4 (SB 1241), effective January 1, 2009.

§3449. Service of petition and order

Except as otherwise provided in Section 3451, the petition and order shall be served, by any method authorized by the law of this state, upon the respondent and any person who has physical custody of the child. **Leg.H.** Added Stats 1999 ch 867 §3 (SB 668).

§3450. Custody order; Fees, costs, and expenses; Inference from refusal to testify; Privilege

(a) Unless the court issues a temporary emergency order pursuant to Section 3424, upon a finding that a petitioner is entitled to immediate physical custody of the child, the court shall order that the petitioner may take immediate physical custody of the child unless the respondent establishes either of the following:

(1) That the child custody determination has not been registered and confirmed under Section 3445 and one of the following is true:

(A) The issuing court did not have jurisdiction under Chapter 2 (commencing with Section 3421).

(B) The child custody determination for which enforcement is sought has been vacated, stayed, or modified by a court of a state having jurisdiction to do so under Chapter 2 (commencing with Section 3421).

(C) The respondent was entitled to notice, but notice was not given in accordance with the standards of Section 3408, in the proceedings before the court that issued the order for which enforcement is sought.

(2) That the child custody determination for which enforcement is sought was registered and confirmed under Section 3445 but has been vacated, stayed, or modified by a court of a state having jurisdiction to do so under Chapter 2 (commencing with Section 3421).

(b) The court shall award the fees, costs, and expenses authorized under Section 3452 and may grant additional relief, including a request for the assistance of law enforcement officials, and set a further hearing to determine whether additional relief is appropriate.

(c) If a party called to testify refuses to answer on the ground that the testimony may be self-incriminating, the court may draw an adverse inference from the refusal.

(d) A privilege against disclosure of communications between spouses and a defense of immunity based on the relationship of spouses or parent and child may not be invoked in a proceeding under this chapter. **Leg.H.** Added Stats 1999 ch 867 §3 (SB 668). Amended Stats 2014 ch 82 §31 (SB 1306), effective January 1, 2015.

§3451. Warrant to take physical custody of child

(a) Upon the filing of a petition seeking enforcement of a child custody determination, the petitioner may file a verified application for the issuance of a warrant to take physical custody of the child if the child is imminently likely to suffer serious physical harm or be removed from this state.

(b) If the court, upon the testimony of the petitioner or other witness, finds that the child is imminently likely to suffer serious physical harm or be removed from this state, it may issue a warrant to take physical custody of the child. The petition must be heard on the next judicial day after the warrant is executed unless that date is impossible. In that event, the court shall hold the hearing on the first judicial day possible. The application for the warrant must include the statements required by subdivision (b) of Section 3448.

(c) A warrant to take physical custody of a child must do all of the following:

(1) Recite the facts upon which a conclusion of imminent serious physical harm or removal from the jurisdiction is based.

(2) Direct law enforcement officers to take physical custody of the child immediately.

(3) Provide for the placement of the child pending final relief.

(d) The respondent must be served with the petition, warrant, and order immediately after the child is taken into physical custody.

(e) A warrant to take physical custody of a child is enforceable throughout this state. If the court finds on the basis of the testimony of the petitioner or other witness that a less intrusive remedy is not effective, it may authorize law enforcement officers to enter private property to take physical custody of the child. If required by exigent circumstances of the case, the court may authorize law enforcement officers to make a forcible entry at any hour.

(f) The court may impose conditions upon placement of a child to ensure the appearance of the child and the child's custodian. **Leg.H.** Added Stats 1999 ch 867 §3 (SB 668).

§3452. Costs and expenses for prevailing party

(a) The court shall award the prevailing party, including a state, necessary and reasonable expenses incurred by or on behalf of the party, including costs, communication expenses, attorney's fees, investigative fees, expenses for witnesses, travel expenses, and child care during the course of the proceedings, unless the party from whom fees or expenses are sought establishes that the award would be clearly inappropriate.

(b) The court may not assess fees, costs, or expenses against a state unless authorized by law other than this part. **Leg.H.** Added Stats 1999 ch 867 §3 (SB 668).

§3453. Full faith and credit; Enforcement of another state's custody determination

A court of this state shall accord full faith and credit to an order issued by another state, and consistent with this part, enforce a child custody determination by a court of another state unless the order has been vacated, stayed, or modified by a court having jurisdiction to do so under Chapter 2 (commencing with Section 3421). **Leg.H.** Added Stats 1999 ch 867 §3 (SB 668).

§ 3453.5. Unenforceability of out-of-state law authorizing removal of child based on parent or guardian allowing child to receive gender-affirming health care or gender-affirming mental health care

(a) A law of another state that authorizes a state agency to remove a child from their parent or guardian based on the parent or guardian allowing their child to receive gender-affirming health care or gender-affirming mental health care is against the public policy of this state and shall not be enforced or applied in a case pending in a court in this state.

(b) For the purpose of this subdivision, "gender-affirming health care" and "gender-affirming mental health care" shall have the same meaning as provided in Section 16010.2 of the Welfare and Institutions Code. **Leg.H.** Added Stats 2022 ch 810 §8 (SB 107), effective January 1, 2023.

§3454. Appeal

An appeal may be taken from a final order in a proceeding under this chapter in accordance with expedited appellate procedures in other civil cases. Unless the court enters a temporary emergency order under Section 3424, the enforcing court may not stay an order enforcing a child custody determination pending appeal. **Leg.H.** Added Stats 1999 ch 867 §3 (SB 668).

§3455. District attorney's authority to locate missing party or child

(a) In a case arising under this part or involving the Hague Convention on the Civil Aspects of International Child Abduction, a district attorney is authorized to proceed pursuant to Chapter 8 (commencing with Section 3130) of Part 2.

(b) A district attorney acting under this section acts on behalf of the court and may not represent any party. **Leg.H.** Added Stats 1999 ch 867 §3 (SB 668).

§3456. Assistance by law enforcement officer in finding party or child

At the request of a district attorney acting under Section 3455, a law enforcement officer may take any lawful action reasonably necessary to locate a child or a party and assist the district attorney with responsibilities under Section 3455. **Leg.H.** Added Stats 1999 ch 867 §3 (SB 668).

§3457. Costs and expenses incurred by district attorney

The court may assess all direct expenses and costs incurred by a district attorney under Section 3455 or 3456 pursuant to the provisions of Section 3134. **Leg.H.** Added Stats 1999 ch 867 §3 (SB 668).

CHAPTER 4
MISCELLANEOUS PROVISIONS

Need for uniformity of law. §3461.
Severability. §3462.
Governing law. §3465.

§3461. Need for uniformity of law

In applying and construing this Uniform Child Custody Jurisdiction and Enforcement Act, consideration shall be given to the need to promote uniformity of the law with respect to its subject matter among states that enact it. **Leg.H.** Added Stats 1999 ch 867 §3 (SB 668).

§3462. Severability

If any provision of this part or its application to any person or circumstance is held invalid, the invalidity does not affect other provisions or applications of this part that can be given effect without the invalid provision or application, and to this end the provisions of this part are severable. **Leg.H.** Added Stats 1999 ch 867 §3 (SB 668).

§3465. Governing law

A motion or other request for relief made in a child custody proceeding or to enforce a child custody determination that was commenced before the effective date of this part is governed by the law in effect at the time the motion or other request was made. **Leg.H.** Added Stats 1999 ch 867 §3 (SB 668).

DIVISION 9
SUPPORT

Part 1. Definitions and General Provisions.
Part 2. Child Support.
Part 3. Spousal Support.
Part 4. Support of Parents.
Part 5. Enforcement of Support Orders.
Part 6. Uniform Interstate Family Support Act.

PART 1
DEFINITIONS AND GENERAL PROVISIONS

Chapter 1. Definitions.
Chapter 2. General Provisions.
Chapter 3. Support Agreements.
Chapter 4. Spousal and Child Support During Pendency of Proceeding.
Chapter 6. Modification, Termination, or Set Aside of Support Orders.
Chapter 7. Health Insurance.
Chapter 8. Deferred Sale of Home Order.
Chapter 9. Software Used to Determine Support.

CHAPTER 1
DEFINITIONS

Application of definitions. §3500.
Separate property. §3515.

§3500. Application of definitions

Unless the provision or context otherwise requires, the definitions in this chapter govern the construction of this division. **Leg.H.** Enacted Stats 1992 ch 162 §10 (AB 2650), operative January 1, 1994.

§3515. Separate property

"Separate property" does not include quasi-community property. **Leg.H.** Enacted Stats 1992 ch 162 §10 (AB 2650), operative January 1, 1994.

CHAPTER 2
GENERAL PROVISIONS

Presence or residence of obligor in state. §3550.
Competency of spouse to testify. §3551.
Tax returns of parties. §3552.
Appeals. §3554.
Forwarding support paid through designated county officer. §3555.
Effect of failure to implement custody or visitation rights. §3556.
Attorney's fees for enforcement of support order or civil penalty for child support delinquency. §3557.
Work programs. §3558.

§3550. Presence or residence of obligor in state

(a) As used in this section:
(1) "Obligee" means a person to whom a duty of support is owed.
(2) "Obligor" means a person who owes a duty of support.
(b) An obligor present or resident in this state has the duty of support as defined in Sections 3900, 3901, 3910, 4300, and 4400, regardless of the presence or residence of the obligee. **Leg.H.** Enacted Stats 1992 ch 162 §10 (AB 2650), operative January 1, 1994.

§3551. Competency of spouse to testify

Laws attaching a privilege against the disclosure of communications between spouses are inapplicable under this division. Spouses are competent witnesses to testify to any relevant matter, including marriage and parentage. **Leg.H.** Enacted Stats 1992 ch 162 §10 (AB 2650), operative January 1, 1994. Amended Stats 2014 ch 82 §32 (SB 1306), effective January 1, 2015.

§3552. Tax returns of parties

(a) In a proceeding involving child, family, or spousal support, no party to the proceeding may refuse to submit copies of the party's state and federal income tax returns to the court, whether individual or joint.

(b) The tax returns may be examined by the other party and are discoverable by the other party. A party also may be examined by the other party as to the contents of a tax return submitted pursuant to this section.

(c) If the court finds that it is relevant to the case to retain the tax return, the tax return shall be sealed and maintained as a confidential record of the court. If the court finds that the tax return is not relevant to disposition of the case, all copies of the tax return shall be returned to the party who submitted it. **Leg.H.** Enacted Stats 1992 ch 162 §10 (AB 2650), operative January 1, 1994.

§3554. Appeals

An appeal may be taken from an order or judgment under this division as in other civil actions. **Leg.H.** Enacted Stats 1992 ch 162 §10 (AB 2650), operative January 1, 1994.

§3555. Forwarding support paid through designated county officer

Where support is ordered to be paid through the county officer designated by the court on behalf of a child or other party not receiving public assistance pursuant to the Family Economic Security Act of 1982 (Chapter 2 (commencing with Section 11200) of Part 3 of Division 9 of the Welfare and Institutions Code), the designated county officer shall forward the support received to the designated payee within the time standards prescribed by federal law and the Department of Child Support Services. **Leg.H.** Enacted Stats 1992 ch 162 §10 (AB 2650), operative January 1, 1994. Amended Stats 1993 ch 219 §120 (AB 1500); Stats 2000 ch 808 §27 (AB 1358), effective September 28, 2000.

§3556. Effect of failure to implement custody or visitation rights

The existence or enforcement of a duty of support owed by a noncustodial parent for the support of a minor child is not affected by a failure or refusal by the custodial parent to implement any rights as to custody or visitation granted by a court to the noncustodial parent. **Leg.H.** Enacted Stats 1992 ch 162 §10 (AB 2650), operative January 1, 1994.

§3557. Attorney's fees for enforcement of support order or civil penalty for child support delinquency

(a) Notwithstanding any other provision of law, absent good cause to the contrary, the court, in order to ensure that each party has access to legal representation to preserve each party's rights, upon determining (1) an award of attorney's fees and cost under this section is appropriate, (2) there is a disparity in access to funds to retain counsel, and (3) one party is able to pay for legal representation for both parties, shall award reasonable attorney's fees to any of the following persons:

(1) A custodial parent or other person to whom payments should be made in any action to enforce any of the following:

(A) An existing order for child support.

(B) A penalty incurred pursuant to Chapter 5 (commencing with Section 4720) of Part 5 of Division 9.

(2) A supported spouse in an action to enforce an existing order for spousal support.

(b) This section shall not be construed to allow an award of attorney's fees to or against a governmental entity. **Leg.H.** Added Stats 1993 ch 219 §120.3 (AB 1500). Amended Stats 1994 ch 1269 §31.2 (AB 2208); Stats 2010 ch 352 §17 (AB 939), effective January 1, 2011.

§3558. Work programs

In a proceeding involving child or family support, a court may require either parent to attend job training, job placement and vocational rehabilitation, and work programs, as designated by the court, at regular intervals and times and for durations specified by the court, and provide documentation of participation in the programs, in a format that is acceptable to the court, in order to enable the court to make a finding that good faith attempts at job training and placement have been undertaken by the parent. **Leg.H.** Added Stats 1996 ch 490 §1 (AB 932).

CHAPTER 3
SUPPORT AGREEMENTS

Article 1. General Provisions.
Article 2. Child Support.
Article 3. Spousal Support.

ARTICLE 1
General Provisions

Provisions for spousal and child support in separation agreement. §3580.

§3580. Provisions for spousal and child support in separation agreement

Subject to this chapter and to Section 3651, spouses may agree, in writing, to an immediate separation, and may provide in the agreement for the support of either of them and of their children during the separation or upon the dissolution of their marriage. The mutual consent of the parties is sufficient consideration for the agreement. **Leg.H.** Enacted Stats 1992 ch 162 §10 (AB 2650), operative January 1, 1994. Amended Stats 2014 ch 82 §33 (SB 1306), effective January 1, 2015.

ARTICLE 2
Child Support

Support order based on agreement between parents. §3585.
Court order to effectuate family support agreement. §3586.
Court order to effectuate agreement for support for adult child. §3587.

§3585. Support order based on agreement between parents

The provisions of an agreement between the parents for child support shall be deemed to be separate and severable from all other provisions of the agreement relating to property and support of either spouse. An order for child support based on the agreement shall be imposed by law and shall be made under the power of the court to order child support. **Leg.H.** Enacted Stats 1992 ch 162 §10 (AB 2650), operative January 1, 1994. Amended Stats 2014 ch 82 §34 (SB 1306), effective January 1, 2015.

§3586. Court order to effectuate family support agreement

If an agreement between the parents combines child support and spousal support without designating the amount to be paid for child support and the amount to be paid for spousal support, the court is not required to make a separate order for child support. **Leg.H.** Enacted Stats 1992 ch 162 §10 (AB 2650), operative January 1, 1994.

§3587. Court order to effectuate agreement for support for adult child

Notwithstanding any other provision of law, the court has the authority to approve a stipulated agreement by the parents to pay for the support of an adult child or for the continuation of child support after a child attains the age of 18 years and to make a support order to effectuate the agreement. **Leg.H.** Enacted Stats 1992 ch 162 §10 (AB 2650), operative January 1, 1994.

ARTICLE 3
Spousal Support

Support agreement severable and enforceable by court. §3590.
Authority to modify or terminate spousal support agreement. §3591.
Agreement discharged in bankruptcy. §3592.
Applicability of Sections 3590 and 3591. §3593.

§3590. Support agreement severable and enforceable by court

The provisions of an agreement for support of either party shall be deemed to be separate and severable from the provisions of the agreement relating to property. An order for support of either party based on the agreement shall be law-imposed and shall be made under the power of the court to order spousal support. **Leg.H.** Enacted Stats 1992 ch 162 §10 (AB 2650), operative January 1, 1994.

§3591. Authority to modify or terminate spousal support agreement

(a) Except as provided in subdivisions (b) and (c), the provisions of an agreement for the support of either party are subject to subsequent modification or termination by court order.

(b) An agreement may not be modified or terminated as to an amount that accrued before the date of the filing of the notice of motion or order to show cause to modify or terminate.

(c) An agreement for spousal support may not be modified or revoked to the extent that a written agreement, or, if there is no written agreement, an oral agreement entered into in open court between the parties, specifically provides that the spousal support is not subject to modification or termination. **Leg.H.** Enacted Stats 1992 ch 162 §10 (AB 2650), operative January 1, 1994.

§3592. Agreement discharged in bankruptcy

If an obligation under an agreement for settlement of property to a spouse or for support of a spouse is discharged in bankruptcy, the court may make all proper orders for the support of the spouse, as the court determines are just, having regard for the circumstances of the parties and the amount of the obligations under the agreement that are discharged. **Leg.H.** Enacted Stats 1992 ch 162 §10 (AB 2650), operative January 1, 1994.

§3593. Applicability of Sections 3590 and 3591

Sections 3590 and 3591 are effective only with respect to a property settlement agreement entered into on or after January 1, 1970, and do not affect an agreement entered into before January 1, 1970, as to which Chapter 1308 of the Statutes of 1967 shall apply. **Leg.H.** Enacted Stats 1992 ch 162 §10 (AB 2650), operative January 1, 1994.

CHAPTER 4
SPOUSAL AND CHILD SUPPORT DURING PENDENCY OF PROCEEDING

Order for support during pendency of proceeding. §3600.
Child support order continues in effect until terminated by court or by operation of law. §3601.
Order not enforceable where parties are reconciled and living together. §3602.
Modification or termination of order. §3603.
Rights with respect to subsequent order not prejudiced. §3604.

§3600. Order for support during pendency of proceeding

During the pendency of any proceeding for dissolution of marriage or for legal separation of the parties or under Division 8 (commencing with Section 3000) (custody of children) or in any proceeding where there is at issue the support of a minor child or a child for whom support is authorized under Section 3901 or 3910, the court may order (a) either spouse to pay any amount that is necessary for the support of the other spouse, consistent with the requirements of subdivisions (i) and (m) of Section 4320 and Section 4325, or (b) either or both parents to pay any amount necessary for the support of the child, as the case may be. **Leg.H.** Enacted Stats 1992 ch 162 §10 (AB 2650), operative January 1, 1994. Amended Stats 2001 ch 293 §1 (SB 1221); Stats 2002 ch 759 §1 (AB 3033); Stats 2014 ch 82 §35 (SB 1306), effective January 1, 2015.

§3601. Child support order continues in effect until terminated by court or by operation of law

(a) An order for child support entered pursuant to this chapter continues in effect until the order (1) is terminated by the court or (2) terminates by operation of law pursuant to Sections 3900, 3901, 4007, and 4013.

(b) Subject to Section 3602, subdivision (a) applies notwithstanding any other provision of law and notwithstanding that the proceeding has not been brought to trial within the time limits specified in Chapter 1.5 (commencing with Section 583.110) of Title 8 of Part 2 of the Code of Civil Procedure. **Leg.H.** Enacted Stats 1992 ch 162 §10 (AB 2650), operative January 1, 1994. Amended Stats 1993 ch 219 §121 (AB 1500).

§3602. Order not enforceable where parties are reconciled and living together

Unless the order specifies otherwise, an order made pursuant to this chapter is not enforceable during any period in which the parties have reconciled and are living together. **Leg.H.** Enacted Stats 1992 ch 162 §10 (AB 2650), operative January 1, 1994.

§3603. Modification or termination of order

An order made pursuant to this chapter may be modified or terminated at any time except as to an amount that accrued before the date of the filing of the notice of motion or order to show cause to modify or terminate. **Leg.H.** Enacted Stats 1992 ch 162 §10 (AB 2650), operative January 1, 1994.

§3604. Rights with respect to subsequent order not prejudiced

An order made pursuant to this chapter does not prejudice the rights of the parties or the child with respect to any subsequent order which may be made. **Leg.H.** Enacted Stats 1992 ch 162 §10 (AB 2650), operative January 1, 1994.

CHAPTER 5
EXPEDITED CHILD SUPPORT ORDER
[REPEALED]

§3620. Designation of order as expedited support order [Repealed]

Leg.H. Enacted Stats 1992 ch 162 §10 (AB 2650), operative January 1, 1994. Repealed Stats 2023 ch 213 §1 (SB 343), effective January 1, 2024.

§3621. Child support order during pendency of action [Repealed]

Leg.H. Enacted Stats 1992 ch 162 §10 (AB 2650), operative January 1, 1994. Amended Stats 1993 ch 219 §122 (AB 1500). Repealed Stats 2023 ch 213 §1 (SB 343), effective January 1, 2024.

§3622. Application for order [Repealed]

Leg.H. Enacted Stats 1992 ch 162 §10 (AB 2650), operative January 1, 1994. Amended Stats 1993 ch 219 §123 (AB 1500); Stats 1997 ch 14 §2 (AB 239), effective May 30, 1997. Repealed Stats 2023 ch 213 §1 (SB 343), effective January 1, 2024.

§3623. Jurisdiction of court on application [Repealed]

Leg.H. Enacted Stats 1992 ch 162 §10 (AB 2650), operative January 1, 1994. Amended Stats 1993 ch 219 §124 (AB 1500). Repealed Stats 2023 ch 213 §1 (SB 343), effective January 1, 2024.

§3624. Order automatically effective 30 days after service unless response served [Repealed]

Leg.H. Enacted Stats 1992 ch 162 §10 (AB 2650), operative January 1, 1994. Repealed Stats 2023 ch 213 §1 (SB 343), effective January 1, 2024.

§3625. Obligated parent's response to application [Repealed]

Leg.H. Enacted Stats 1992 ch 162 §10 (AB 2650), operative January 1, 1994. Repealed Stats 2023 ch 213 §1 (SB 343), effective January 1, 2024.

§3626. Setting application for hearing [Repealed]

Leg.H. Enacted Stats 1992 ch 162 §10 (AB 2650), operative January 1, 1994. Repealed Stats 2023 ch 213 §1 (SB 343), effective January 1, 2024.

§3627. Giving notice of hearing [Repealed]

Leg.H. Enacted Stats 1992 ch 162 §10 (AB 2650), operative January 1, 1994. Repealed Stats 2023 ch 213 §1 (SB 343), effective January 1, 2024.

§3628. Effect of failure to give notice of hearing [Repealed]

Leg.H. Enacted Stats 1992 ch 162 §10 (AB 2650), operative January 1, 1994. Repealed Stats 2023 ch 213 §1 (SB 343), effective January 1, 2024.

§3629. Production of tax returns at hearing [Repealed]

Leg.H. Enacted Stats 1992 ch 162 §10 (AB 2650), operative January 1, 1994. Repealed Stats 2023 ch 213 §1 (SB 343), effective January 1, 2024.

§3630. Amount of support [Repealed]

Leg.H. Enacted Stats 1992 ch 162 §10 (AB 2650), operative January 1, 1994. Repealed Stats 2023 ch 213 §1 (SB 343), effective January 1, 2024.

§3631. Order after hearing [Repealed]

Leg.H. Enacted Stats 1992 ch 162 §10 (AB 2650), operative January 1, 1994. Repealed Stats 2023 ch 213 §1 (SB 343), effective January 1, 2024.

§3632. Effective date of order after hearing [Repealed]

Leg.H. Enacted Stats 1992 ch 162 §10 (AB 2650), operative January 1, 1994. Repealed Stats 2023 ch 213 §1 (SB 343), effective January 1, 2024.

§3633. Modification or termination of order [Repealed]

Leg.H. Enacted Stats 1992 ch 162 §10 (AB 2650), operative January 1, 1994. Repealed Stats 2023 ch 213 §1 (SB 343), effective January 1, 2024.

§3634. Judicial Council to prepare necessary forms [Repealed]

Leg.H. Enacted Stats 1992 ch 162 §10 (AB 2650), operative January 1, 1994. Repealed Stats 2023 ch 213 §1 (SB 343), effective January 1, 2024.

§ 3635. Repeal of chapter [Repealed]

This chapter shall remain in effect only until January 1, 2024, and as of that date is repealed. **Leg.H.** Added Stats 2023 ch 213 §1 (SB 343), effective January 1, 2023, repealed January 1, 2024.

Prior Law Former Fam C §3635, relating to Repeal of chapter, was added Stats 2023 ch 213 §1 (SB 343), effective January 1, 2024, repealed January 1, 2024.

CHAPTER 6
MODIFICATION, TERMINATION, OR SET ASIDE OF SUPPORT ORDERS

Article 1. General Provisions.
Article 2. Discovery Before Commencing Modification or Termination Proceeding.
Article 3. Simplified Procedure for Modification of Support Order.
Article 4. Relief From Orders.

ARTICLE 1
General Provisions

Support order defined. §3650.
Modification or termination of support order; Military deployment outside state. §3651.
Attorney's fees and court costs. §3652.
Retroactivity of modification or termination. §3653.
Statement of decision. §3654.

§3650. Support order defined

Unless the provision or context otherwise requires, as used in this chapter, "support order" means a child, family, or spousal support order. **Leg.H.** Enacted Stats 1992 ch 162 §10 (AB 2650), operative January 1, 1994. Amended Stats 1993 ch 219 §124.5 (AB 1500).

§3651. Modification or termination of support order; Military deployment outside state

(a) Except as provided in subdivisions (c) and (d) and subject to Article 3 (commencing with Section 3680) and Sections 3552, 3587, and 4004, a support order may be modified or terminated at any time as the court determines to be necessary.

(b) Upon the filing of a supplemental complaint pursuant to Section 2330.1, a child support order in the original proceeding may be modified in conformity with the statewide uniform guideline for child support to provide for the support of all of the children of the same parents who were named in the initial and supplemental pleadings, to consolidate arrearages and wage assignments for children of the parties, and to consolidate orders for support.

(c)(1) Except as provided in paragraph (2) and subdivision (b), a support order may not be modified or terminated as to an amount that accrued before the date of the filing of the notice of motion or order to show cause to modify or terminate.

(2) If a party to a support order is activated to United States military duty or National Guard service and deployed out of state, the servicemember may file and serve a notice of activation of military service and request to modify a support order, in lieu of a notice of motion or order to show cause, by informing the court and the other party of the request to modify the support order based on the change in circumstance. The servicemember shall indicate the date of deployment and, if possible, the court shall schedule the hearing prior to that date. If the court cannot hear the matter prior to the date of deployment out of state, and the servicemember complies with the conditions set forth in the Servicemembers Civil Relief Act, Section 522 of the Appendix of Title 50 of the United States Code, the court shall grant a stay of proceedings consistent with the timelines for stays set forth in that section. If, after granting the mandatory stay required by Section 522 of the Appendix of Title 50 of the United States Code, the court fails to grant the discretionary stay described under the law, it shall comply with the federal mandate to appoint counsel to represent the interests of the deployed servicemember. The court may not proceed with the matter if it does not appoint counsel, unless the servicemember is represented by other counsel. If the court stays the proceeding until after the return of the service member, the servicemember shall request the court to set the matter for hearing within 90 days of return from deployment or the matter shall be taken off calendar and the existing order may not be made retroactive pursuant to subdivision (c) of Section 3653.

(3) A servicemember who does not file a notice of activation of military service and request to modify a support order or order to show cause or notice of motion prior to deployment out of state nonetheless

shall not be subject to penalties otherwise authorized by Chapter 5 (commencing with Section 4720) of Part 5 on the amount of child support that would not have accrued if the order had been modified pursuant to paragraph (2), absent a finding by the court of good cause. Any such finding shall be stated on the record.

(4) Notwithstanding any other law, interest shall not accrue on that amount of a child support obligation that would not have become due and owing if the activated servicemember modified the support order upon activation to reflect the change in income due to the activation. Upon a finding by the court that good cause did not exist for the servicemember's failure to seek, or delay in seeking, the modification, interest shall accrue as otherwise allowed by law.

(d) An order for spousal support may not be modified or terminated to the extent that a written agreement or, if there is no written agreement, an oral agreement entered into in open court between the parties, specifically provides that the spousal support is not subject to modification or termination.

(e) This section applies whether or not the support order is based upon an agreement between the parties.

(f) This section is effective only with respect to a property settlement agreement entered into on or after January 1, 1970, and does not affect an agreement entered into before January 1, 1970, as to which Chapter 1308 of the Statutes of 1967 shall apply.

(g)(1) The Judicial Council, no later than 90 days after the effective date of the act adding this section, shall develop forms and procedures necessary to implement paragraph (2) of subdivision (c). The Judicial Council shall ensure that all forms adopted pursuant to this section are in plain language.

(2) The form developed by the Judicial Council, in addition to other items the Judicial Council determines to be necessary or appropriate, shall include the following:

(A) The date of deployment and all information relevant to the determination of the amount of child support, including whether the servicemember's employer will supplement the servicemember's income during the deployment.

(B) A notice informing the opposing party that, absent a finding of good cause, the order will be made retroactive to the date of service of the form or the date of deployment, whichever is later.

(C) Notice that the requesting party must notify the court and the other party upon return from military duty and seek to bring any unresolved request for modification to hearing within 90 days of return, or else lose the right to modify the order pursuant to this section. **Leg.H.** Enacted Stats 1992 ch 162 §10 (AB 2650), operative January 1, 1994. Amended Stats 1994 ch 1269 §31.4 (AB 2208); Stats 1997 ch 599 §6 (AB 573); Stats 2005 ch 154 §2 (SB 1082), effective August 30, 2005; Stats 2019 ch 115 §39 (AB 1817), effective January 1, 2020.

§3652. Attorney's fees and court costs

Except as against a governmental agency, an order modifying, terminating, or setting aside a support order may include an award of attorney's fees and court costs to the prevailing party. **Leg.H.** Enacted Stats 1992 ch 162 §10 (AB 2650), operative January 1, 1994. Amended Stats 1994 ch 1269 §31.6 (AB 2208); Stats 1999 ch 653 §3 (AB 380).

§3653. Retroactivity of modification or termination

(a) An order modifying or terminating a support order may be made retroactive to the date of the filing of the notice of motion or order to show cause to modify or terminate, or to any subsequent date, except as provided in subdivision (b) or by federal law (42 U.S.C. Sec. 666(a)(9)).

(b) If an order modifying or terminating a support order is entered due to the unemployment of either the support obligor or the support obligee, the order shall be made retroactive to the later of the date of the service on the opposing party of the notice of motion or order to show cause to modify or terminate or the date of unemployment, subject to the notice requirements of federal law (42 U.S.C. Sec. 666(a)(9)), unless the court finds good cause not to make the order retroactive and states its reasons on the record.

(c) If an order modifying or terminating a support order is entered due to a change in income resulting from the activation to United States military service or National Guard duty and deployment out of state for either the support obligor or the support obligee, the order shall be made retroactive to the later of the date of the service on the opposing party of the notice of activation, notice of motion, order to show cause to modify or terminate, or the date of activation, subject to the notice requirements of federal law (42 U.S.C. Sec. 666(a)(9)), unless the court finds good cause not to make the order retroactive and states its reasons on the record. Good cause shall include, but not be limited to, a finding by the court that the delay in seeking the modification was not reasonable under the circumstances faced by the service member.

(d) If an order decreasing or terminating a support order is entered retroactively pursuant to this section, the support obligor may be entitled to, and the support obligee may be ordered to repay, according to the terms specified in the order, any amounts previously paid by the support obligor pursuant to the prior order that are in excess of the amounts due pursuant to the retroactive order. The court may order that the repayment by the support obligee shall be made over any period of time and in any manner, including, but not limited to, by an offset against future support payments or wage assignment, as the court deems just and reasonable. In determining whether to order a repayment, and in establishing the terms of repayment, the court shall consider all of the following factors:

(1) The amount to be repaid.

(2) The duration of the support order prior to modification or termination.

(3) The financial impact on the support obligee of any particular method of repayment such as an offset against future support payments or wage assignment.

(4) Any other facts or circumstances that the court deems relevant. **Leg.H.** Enacted Stats 1992 ch 162 §10 (AB 2650), operative January 1, 1994. Amended Stats 1998 ch 854 §1 (AB 960); Stats 1999 ch 653 §4 (AB 380); Stats 2005 ch 154 §3 (SB 1082), effective August 30, 2005.

§3654. Statement of decision

At the request of either party, an order modifying, terminating, or setting aside a support order shall include a statement of decision. **Leg.H.** Enacted Stats 1992 ch 162 §10 (AB 2650), operative January 1, 1994. Amended Stats 1999 ch 653 §5 (AB 380).

ARTICLE 2
Discovery Before Commencing Modification or Termination Proceeding

Purpose of article. §3660.
Limitation on use of other methods of discovery. §3662.
Limitation on use of discovery under this article. §3663.
Request for production of income and expense declaration. §3664.
Tax returns. §3665.
Enforcement. §3666.
Sanctions. §3667.
Forms. §3668.

§3660. Purpose of article

The purpose of this article is to permit inexpensive discovery of facts before the commencement of a proceeding for modification or termination of an order for child, family, or spousal support. **Leg.H.** Enacted Stats 1992 ch 162 §10 (AB 2650), operative January 1, 1994.

§3662. Limitation on use of other methods of discovery

Methods of discovery other than that described in this article may only be used if a motion for modification or termination of the support order is pending. **Leg.H.** Enacted Stats 1992 ch 162 §10 (AB 2650), operative January 1, 1994.

§3663. Limitation on use of discovery under this article

In the absence of a pending motion for modification or termination of a support order, a request for discovery pursuant to this article may be undertaken not more frequently than once every 12 months. **Leg.H.** Enacted Stats 1992 ch 162 §10 (AB 2650), operative January 1, 1994.

§3664. Request for production of income and expense declaration

(a) At any time following a judgment of dissolution of marriage or legal separation of the parties, or a determination of parentage, that provides for payment of support, either the party ordered to pay support or the party to whom support was ordered to be paid or that party's assignee, without leave of court, may serve a request on the other party for the production of a completed current income and expense declaration in the form adopted by the Judicial Council.

(b) If there is no response within 35 days of service of the request or if the responsive income and expense declaration is incomplete as to any wage information, including the attachment of pay stubs and income tax returns, the requesting party may serve a request on the employer of the other party for information limited to the income and benefits provided to the party in the form adopted by the Judicial Council. The employer may require the requesting party to pay the reasonable costs of copying this information for the requesting party. The date specified in the request served on the employer for the production of income and benefit information shall not be less than 15 days from the date this request is issued.

(c) The requesting party shall serve or cause to be served on the employee described in this section, or on the employee's attorney, a copy of the request served on the employer prior to the date specified in the request served on the employer for the production of income and benefit information. This copy shall be accompanied by a notice, in a typeface that is intended to call attention to its terms, that indicates all of the following:

(1) That information limited to the income and benefits provided to the employee by the employer is being sought from the employer named in the request for production.

(2) That the information may be protected by right of privacy.

(3) That, if the employee objects to the production of this information by the employer to the requesting party, the employee shall notify the court, in writing, of this objection prior to the date specified in the request served on the employer for the production of income and benefit information.

(4) That, if the requesting party does not agree, in writing, to cancel or narrow the scope of the request for the production of this information by the employer, the employee should consult an attorney regarding the employee's right to privacy and how to protect this right.

(d) The employee described in this section may, prior to the date specified in the request served on the employer for the production of income and benefit information, bring a motion pursuant to Section 1987.1 of the Code of Civil Procedure to quash or modify this request in the same manner as a subpoena duces tecum. Notice of this motion shall be given to the employer prior to the date specified in the request served on the employer for the production of income and benefit information. An employer is not required to produce information limited to the income and benefits of the employee, except upon order of the court or upon agreement of the parties, employers, and employee affected.

(e) Service of a request for production of an income and expense declaration or for income and benefit information pursuant to this section or a copy thereof shall be by certified mail, postage prepaid, return receipt requested, to the last known address of the party to be served, or by personal service.

(f) The form adopted by the Judicial Council for purposes of the request on an employer described in subdivision (b) shall state that compliance with the request is voluntary, except upon order of the court or upon agreement of the parties, employers, and employee affected. **Leg.H.** Enacted Stats 1992 ch 162 §10 (AB 2650), operative January 1, 1994. Amended Stats 1995 ch 506 §2 (AB 413); Stats 2019 ch 115 §40 (AB 1817), effective January 1, 2020.

§3665. Tax returns

(a) A copy of the prior year's federal and state personal income tax returns shall be attached to the income and expense declaration of each party.

(b) A party shall not disclose the contents or provide copies of the other party's tax returns to anyone except the court, the party's attorney, the party's accountant, or other financial consultant assisting with matters relating to the proceeding, or any other person permitted by the court.

(c) The tax returns shall be controlled by the court as provided in Section 3552. **Leg.H.** Enacted Stats 1992 ch 162 §10 (AB 2650), operative January 1, 1994.

§3666. Enforcement

This article may be enforced in the manner specified in Sections 1991, 1991.1, 1991.2, 1992, and 1993 of the Code of Civil Procedure and in the Civil Discovery Act (Title 4 (commencing with Section 2016.010) of Part 4 of the Code of Civil Procedure), and any other statutes applicable to the enforcement of procedures for discovery. **Leg.H.** Enacted Stats 1992 ch 162 §10 (AB 2650), operative January 1, 1994. Amended Stats 2004 ch 182 §34 (AB 3081), operative July 1, 2005.

§3667. Sanctions

Upon the subsequent filing of a motion for modification or termination of the support order by the requesting party, if the court finds that the income and expense declaration submitted by the responding party pursuant to this article was incomplete, inaccurate, or missing the prior year's federal and state personal income tax returns, or that the declaration was not submitted in good faith, the court may order sanctions against the responding party in the form of payment of all costs of the motion, including the filing fee and the costs of the depositions and subpoenas necessary to be utilized in order to obtain complete and accurate information. This section is applicable regardless of whether a party has utilized subdivision (b) of Section 3664. **Leg.H.** Enacted Stats 1992 ch 162 §10 (AB 2650), operative January 1, 1994. Amended Stats 1995 ch 506 §3 (AB 413).

§3668. Forms

The Judicial Council shall adopt forms which shall be used in the procedure provided by this article. **Leg.H.** Enacted Stats 1992 ch 162 §10 (AB 2650), operative January 1, 1994.

ARTICLE 3
Simplified Procedure for Modification of Support Order

Findings. §3680.
Local agency's duty to monitor child support cases; Periodic review of CalWORKs cases. §3680.5.

§3680. Findings

(a) The Legislature finds and declares the following:

(1) There is currently no simple method available to parents to quickly modify their support orders when circumstances warrant a change in the amount of support.

(2) The lack of a simple method for parents to use to modify support orders has led to orders in which the amount of support ordered is inappropriate based on the parents' financial circumstances.

(3) Parents should not have to incur significant costs or experience significant delays in obtaining an appropriate support order.

(b) Therefore, it is the intent of the Legislature that the Judicial Council adopt rules of court and forms for a simplified method to modify support orders. This simplified method should be designed to be used by parents who are not represented by counsel. **Leg.H.** Added Stats 1996 ch 957 §5 (AB 1058).

Prior Law: Former §3680, relating to purpose of article, was enacted Stats 1992 ch 162 §10, operative January 1, 1994, amended Stats 1993 ch 219 §124.6, and repealed Stats 1994 ch 415 §1.

§3680.5. Local agency's duty to monitor child support cases; Periodic review of CalWORKs cases

(a) The local child support agency shall monitor child support cases and seek modifications, when needed.

(b) At least once every three years, the local child support agency shall review, and, if appropriate, seek modification of, each child support case for which assistance is being provided under the CalWORKs program, pursuant to Chapter 2 (commencing with Section 11200) of Part 3 of Division 9 of the Welfare and Institutions Code. **Leg.H.** Added Stats 1999 ch 652 §3 (SB 240). Amended Stats 2007 ch 488 §1 (AB 176), effective January 1, 2008.

§3681. [Section repealed 1994]

Leg.H. Enacted Stats 1992 ch 162 §10 (AB 2650), operative January 1, 1994. Repealed Stats 1994 ch 415 §1 (SB 1715). The repealed section related to notifying other party of address changes.

§3682. [Section repealed 1994]

Leg.H. Enacted Stats 1992 ch 162 §10 (AB 2650), operative January 1, 1994. Repealed Stats 1994 ch 415 §1 (SB 1715). The repealed section related to limitation on use of procedure under article.

§3683. [Section repealed 1994]

Leg.H. Enacted Stats 1992 ch 162 §10 (AB 2650), operative January 1, 1994. Repealed Stats 1994 ch 415 §1 (SB 1715). The repealed section related to notice of motion to modify support order.

§3684. [Section repealed 1994]

Leg.H. Enacted Stats 1992 ch 162 §10 (AB 2650), operative January 1, 1994. Amended Stats 1993 ch 219 §124.9 (AB 1500). Repealed Stats 1994 ch 415 §1 (SB 1715). The repealed section related to objection and request for hearing.

§3685. [Section repealed 1994]

§3686. [Section repealed 1994]

Leg.H. Enacted Stats 1992 ch 162 §10 (AB 2650), operative January 1, 1994. Repealed Stats 1994 ch 415 §1 (SB 1715). The repealed section related to lawyers and other nonparties not allowed to appear.

§3686. [Section repealed 1994]

Leg.H. Enacted Stats 1992 ch 162 §10 (AB 2650), operative January 1, 1994. Repealed Stats 1994 ch 415 §1 (SB 1715), ch 1269 §32 (AB 2208). The repealed section related to consideration of age increase factor in modification of child support order.

§3687. [Section repealed 1994]

Leg.H. Enacted Stats 1992 ch 162 §10 (AB 2650), operative January 1, 1994. Amended Stats 1993 ch 219 §125 (AB 1500). Repealed Stats 1994 ch 415 §1 (SB 1715). The repealed section related to modification without showing of changed circumstances.

§3688. [Section repealed 1994]

Leg.H. Enacted Stats 1992 ch 162 §10 (AB 2650), operative January 1, 1994. Amended Stats 1993 ch 219 §126 (AB 1500). Repealed Stats 1994 ch 415 §1 (SB 1715). The repealed section related to modification based on significant decrease in income.

§3689. [Section repealed 1994]

Leg.H. Enacted Stats 1992 ch 162 §10 (AB 2650), operative January 1, 1994. Repealed Stats 1994 ch 415 §1 (SB 1715). The repealed section related to tax returns and other documents.

ARTICLE 4
Relief From Orders

Relief from support order. §3690.
Grounds and time limits. §3691.
Finding of inequitable order. §3692.
Provisions materially affected by circumstances. §3693.

§3690. Relief from support order

(a) The court may, on any terms that may be just, relieve a party from a support order, or any part or parts thereof, after the six-month time limit of Section 473 of the Code of Civil Procedure has run, based on the grounds, and within the time limits, provided in this article.

(b) In all proceedings under this division, before granting relief, the court shall find that the facts alleged as the grounds for relief materially affected the original order and that the moving party would materially benefit from the granting of the relief.

(c) Nothing in this article shall limit or modify the provisions of Section 17432 or 17433.

(d) This section shall only be operative if Assembly Bill 196, of the 1999–2000 Regular Session, is enacted and becomes operative. **Leg.H.** Added Stats 1999 ch 653 §6 (AB 380) (2nd), effective January 1, 2000.

Former Sections: Former Fam C §3690, similar to the present section, was added Stats 1999 ch 653 §6 (1st) and repealed Stats 2015 ch 303 §146.

Former Fam C §3690, relating to manner of service of notice, was enacted Stats 1992 ch 162 §10, operative January 1, 1994, and repealed Stats 1994 ch 415 §1.

Prior Law: Former §3690, similar to the present section, was added Stats 1999 ch 653 §6 (1st), effective January 1, 2000, and repealed Stats 2015 ch 303 §146, effective January 1, 2016.

Former §3690, relating to manner of service of notice, was enacted Stats 1992 ch 162 §10, operative January 1, 1994, and repealed Stats 1994 ch 415 §1.

§3691. Grounds and time limits

The grounds and time limits for an action or motion to set aside a support order, or part thereof, are governed by this section and shall be one of the following:

(a) Actual fraud. Where the defrauded party was kept in ignorance or in some other manner, other than through the party's own lack of care or attention, was fraudulently prevented from fully participating in the proceeding. An action or motion based on fraud shall be brought within six months after the date on which the complaining party discovered or reasonably should have discovered the fraud.

(b) Perjury. An action or motion based on perjury shall be brought within six months after the date on which the complaining party discovered or reasonably should have discovered the perjury.

(c) Lack of Notice.

(1) When service of a summons has not resulted in notice to a party in time to defend the action for support and a default or default judgment has been entered against the party in the action, the party may serve and file a notice of motion to set aside the default and for leave to defend the action. The notice of motion shall be served and filed within a reasonable time, but in no event later than six months after the party obtains or reasonably should have obtained notice (A) of the support order, or (B) that the party's income and assets are subject to attachment pursuant to the order.

(2) A notice of motion to set aside a support order pursuant to this subdivision shall be accompanied by an affidavit showing, under oath, that the party's lack of notice in time to defend the action was not caused by avoidance of service or inexcusable neglect. The party shall serve and file with the notice a copy of the answer, motion, or other pleading proposed to be filed in the action.

(3) The court may not set aside or otherwise relieve a party from a support order pursuant to this subdivision if service of the summons was accomplished in accordance with existing requirements of law regarding service of process. **Leg.H.** Added Stats 1999 ch 653 §6 (AB 380). Amended Stats 2019 ch 115 §41 (AB 1817), effective January 1, 2020.

Prior Law: Former Fam C §3691, relating to notice to district attorney, was enacted Stats 1992 ch 162 §10, operative January 1, 1994, amended Stats 1993 ch 219 §126.5, and repealed Stats 1994 ch 415 §1. Historical derivation: (a) Former CC §4700.1, as added Stats 1983 ch 1036 §1, amended Stats 1987 ch 57 §2. (b) Former CC §4801.9, as added Stats 1987 ch 1086 §3.

§3692. Finding of inequitable order

Notwithstanding any other provision of this article, or any other law, a support order may not be set aside simply because the court finds that it was inequitable when made, nor simply because subsequent circumstances caused the support ordered to become excessive or inadequate. **Leg.H.** Added Stats 1999 ch 653 §6 (AB 380).

Prior Law: Former §3692, relating to compliance with federal requirements, was enacted Stats 1992 ch 162 §10, operative January 1, 1994, and repealed Stats 1994 ch 415 §1. Historical derivation: (a) Former CC §4700.1, as added Stats 1983 ch 1036 §1, amended Stats 1987 ch 57 §2. (b) Former CC §4801.9, as added Stats 1987 ch 1086 §3.

§3693. Provisions materially affected by circumstances

When ruling on an action or motion to set aside a support order, the court shall set aside only those provisions materially affected by the circumstances leading to the court's decision to grant relief. However, the court has discretion to set aside the entire order, if necessary, for equitable considerations. **Leg.H.** Added Stats 1999 ch 653 §6 (AB 380).

Prior Law: Former §3693, relating to election to be represented by counsel, was enacted Stats 1992 ch 162 §10, operative January 1, 1994, and repealed Stats 1994 ch 415 §1. Historical derivation: (a) Former CC §4700.1, as added Stats 1983 ch 1036 §1, amended Stats 1987 ch 57 §2. (b) Former CC §4801.9, as added Stats 1987 ch 1086 §3.

§3694. [Section repealed 1994]

Leg.H. Enacted Stats 1992 ch 162 §10 (AB 2650), operative January 1, 1994. Repealed Stats 1994 ch 415 §1 (SB 1715). The repealed section related to Judicial Council forms.

CHAPTER 7
HEALTH INSURANCE

Article 1. Health Insurance Coverage for Supported Child.
Article 2. Health Insurance Coverage Assignment.
Article 3. Assignment of Reimbursement Rights Under Health Plan [Repealed].

ARTICLE 1
Health Insurance Coverage for Supported Child

Health insurance coverage defined. §3750.
Health insurance for supported child. §3751.
Prohibited grounds for denial of coverage for child; Employer's or insurer's obligations when parent is required to provide coverage. §3751.5.
District attorney designated as assigned payee; Information on policy for custodial parent. §3752.
Health insurance policy information to be provided to support obligor. §3752.5.
Health insurance cost in addition to child support amount. §3753.

§3750. Health insurance coverage defined

"Health insurance coverage" as used in this article includes all of the following:

(a) Vision care and dental care coverage whether the vision care or dental care coverage is part of existing health insurance coverage or is issued as a separate policy or plan.

(b) Provision for the delivery of health care services by a fee for service, health maintenance organization, preferred provider organization, or any other type of health care delivery system under which medical services could be provided to a dependent child of an absent parent. **Leg.H.** Enacted Stats 1992 ch 162 §10 (AB 2650), operative January 1, 1994. Amended Stats 1994 ch 147 §1 (AB 2377), effective July 9, 1994; Stats 1996 ch 1062 §1 (AB 1832).

§3751. Health insurance for supported child

(a)(1) Support orders issued or modified pursuant to this chapter shall include a provision requiring the child support obligor to keep the agency designated under Title IV-D of the Social Security Act (42 U.S.C. Sec. 651 et seq.) informed of whether the obligor has health insurance coverage at a reasonable cost and, if so, the health insurance policy information.

(2) When an amount is set for current support, the court shall require that health insurance coverage for a supported child shall be maintained by either or both parents if that insurance is available at no cost or at a reasonable cost to the parent. Health insurance coverage shall be rebuttably presumed to be reasonable in cost if the cost to the responsible parent providing medical support does not exceed 5 percent of the parent's gross income. In applying the 5 percent for the cost of health insurance, the cost is the difference between self-only and family coverage, If the obligor is entitled to a low-income adjustment as provided in paragraph (7) of subdivision (b) of Section 4055, medical support shall be deemed not reasonable, unless the court determines that not requiring medical support would be unjust and inappropriate in the particular case. If the court determines that the cost of health insurance coverage is not reasonable, the court shall state its reasons on the record. If the court determines that, although the obligor is entitled to a low-income adjustment, not requiring medical support would be unjust and inappropriate, the court shall state its reasons on the record.

(b) If the court determines that health insurance coverage is not available at no cost or at a reasonable cost, the court's order for support shall contain a provision that specifies that health insurance coverage shall be obtained if it becomes available at no cost or at a reasonable cost. Upon health insurance coverage at no cost or at a reasonable cost becoming available to a parent, the parent shall apply for that coverage.

(c) The court's order for support shall require the parent who, at the time of the order or subsequently, provides health insurance coverage for a supported child to seek continuation of coverage for the child upon attainment of the limiting age for a dependent child under the health insurance coverage if the child meets the criteria specified under Section 1373 of the Health and Safety Code or Section 10277 or 10278 of the Insurance Code and that health insurance coverage is available at no cost or at a reasonable cost to the parent or parents, as applicable. **Leg.H.** Enacted Stats 1992 ch 162 §10 (AB 2650), operative January 1, 1994. Amended Stats 1993 ch 876 §16 (SB 1068), effective October 6, 1993, operative January 1, 1994; Stats 1994 ch 1269 §33 (AB 2208); Stats 2007 ch 617 §1 (AB 910), effective January 1, 2008; Stats 2010 ch 103 §1 (SB 580), effective January 1, 2011; Stats 2019 ch 115 §42 (AB 1817), effective January 1, 2020.

§3751.5. Prohibited grounds for denial of coverage for child; Employer's or insurer's obligations when parent is required to provide coverage

(a) Notwithstanding any other provision of law, an employer or insurer shall not deny enrollment of a child under the health insurance coverage of a child's parent on any of the following grounds:

(1) The child was born out of wedlock.

(2) The child is not claimed as a dependent on the parent's federal income tax return.

(3) The child does not reside with the parent or within the insurer's service area.

(b) Notwithstanding any other provision of law, in any case in which a parent is required by a court or administrative order to provide health insurance coverage for a child and the parent is eligible for family health coverage through an employer or an insurer, the employer or insurer shall do all of the following, as applicable:

(1) Permit the parent to enroll under health insurance coverage any child who is otherwise eligible to enroll for that coverage, without regard to any enrollment period restrictions.

(2) If the parent is enrolled in health insurance coverage but fails to apply to obtain coverage of the child, enroll that child under the health coverage upon presentation of the court order or request by the local child support agency, the other parent or person having custody of the child, or the Medi-Cal program.

(3) The employer or insurer shall not disenroll or eliminate coverage of a child unless either of the following applies:

(A) The employer has eliminated family health insurance coverage for all of the employer's employees.

(B) The employer or insurer is provided with satisfactory written evidence that either of the following apply:

(i) The court order or administrative order is no longer in effect or is terminated pursuant to Section 3770.

(ii) The child is or will be enrolled in comparable health insurance coverage through another insurer that will take effect not later than the effective date of the child's disenrollment.

(c) In any case in which health insurance coverage is provided for a child pursuant to a court or administrative order, the insurer shall do all of the following:

(1) Provide any information, including, but not limited to, the health insurance membership or identification card regarding the child, the evidence of coverage and disclosure form, and any other information provided to the covered parent about the child's health care coverage to the noncovered parent having custody of the child or any other person having custody of the child and to the local child support agency when requested by the local child support agency.

(2) Permit the noncovered parent or person having custody of the child, or a provider with the approval of the noncovered parent or person having custody, to submit claims for covered services without the approval of the covered parent.

(3) Make payment on claims submitted in accordance with subparagraph (2) directly to the noncovered parent or person having custody, the provider, or to the Medi-Cal program. Payment on claims for services provided to the child shall be made to the covered parent for claims submitted or paid by the covered parent.

(d) For purposes of this section, "insurer" includes every health care service plan, self-insured welfare benefit plan, including those regulated pursuant to the Employee Retirement Income Security Act of 1974 (29 U.S.C. Sec. 1001, et seq.), self-funded employer plan, disability insurer, nonprofit hospital service plan, labor union trust fund, employer, and any other similar plan, insurer, or entity offering a health coverage plan.

(e) For purposes of this section, "person having custody of the child" is defined as a legal guardian, a caregiver who is authorized to enroll the child in school or to authorize medical care for the child pursuant to Section 6550, or a person with whom the child resides.

(f) For purposes of this section, "employer" has the meaning provided in Section 5210.

(g) For purposes of this section, the insurer shall notify the covered parent and noncovered parent having custody of the child or any other person having custody of the child in writing at any time that health insurance for the child is terminated.

(h) The requirements of subdivision (g) shall not apply unless the court, employer, or person having custody of the child provides the insurer with one of the following:

(1) A qualified medical child support order that meets the requirements of subdivision (a) of Section 1169 of Title 29 of the United States Code.

(2) A health insurance coverage assignment or assignment order made pursuant to Section 3761.

(3) A national medical support notice made pursuant to Section 3773.

(i) The noncovered parent or person having custody of the child may contact the insurer, by telephone or in writing, and request information about the health insurance coverage for the child. Upon request of the noncovered parent or person having custody of the child, the insurer shall provide the requested information that is specific to the health insurance coverage for the child. **Leg.H.** Added Stats 1996 ch 1062 §2 (AB 1832). Amended Stats 1997 ch 599 §7 (AB 573); Stats 2000 ch 808 §28 (AB 1358), effective September 28, 2000, ch 809 §1 (AB 2130); Stats 2001 ch 755 §2 (SB 943), effective October 12, 2001.

§3752. District attorney designated as assigned payee; Information on policy for custodial parent

(a) If the local child support agency has been designated as the assigned payee for child support, the court shall order the parent to notify the local child support agency upon applying for and obtaining health insurance coverage for the child within a reasonable period of time.

(b) The local child support agency shall obtain a completed medical form from the parent in accordance with Section 17422 and shall forward the completed form to the State Department of Health Services.

(c) In those cases where the local child support agency is providing medical support enforcement services, the local child support agency shall provide the parent or person having custody of the child with information pertaining to the health insurance policy that has been secured for the child. **Leg.H.** Enacted Stats 1992 ch 162 §10 (AB 2650), operative January 1, 1994. Amended Stats 2000 ch 808 §30 (AB 1358), effective September 28, 2000.

§3752.5. Health insurance policy information to be provided to support obligor

(a) A child support order issued or modified pursuant to this division shall include a provision requiring the child support obligor to keep the obligee informed of whether the obligor has health insurance made available through the obligor's employer or has other group health insurance and, if so, the health insurance policy information. The support obligee under a child support order shall inform the support obligor of whether the obligee has health insurance made available through the employer or other group health insurance and, if so, the health insurance policy information.

(b) A child support order issued or modified pursuant to this division shall include a provision requiring the child support obligor and obligee to provide the information described in subdivision (a) for a child or an adult who meets the criteria for continuation of health insurance coverage upon attaining the limiting age pursuant to Section 1373 of the Health and Safety Code or Section 10277 or 10278 of the Insurance Code.

(c) The Judicial Council shall modify the form of the order for health insurance coverage (family law) to notify child support obligors of the requirements of this section and of Section 3752. Notwithstanding any other provision of law, the Judicial Council shall not be required to modify the form of the order for health insurance coverage (family law) to include the provisions described in subdivision (b) until January 1, 2010. **Leg.H.** Added Stats 1993 ch 876 §17 (SB 1068), effective October 6, 1993, operative January 1, 1994. Amended Stats 2007 ch 617 §2 (AB 910), effective January 1, 2008.

§3753. Health insurance cost in addition to child support amount

The cost of the health insurance shall be in addition to the child support amount ordered under Article 2 (commencing with Section 4050), with allowance for the costs of health insurance actually obtained given due consideration under subdivision (d) of Section 4059. **Leg.H.** Added Stats 1994 ch 1269 §36 (AB 2208).

Prior Law: Former §3753, relating to applicability of article in all cases, was enacted Stats 1992 ch 162 §10, operative January 1, 1994, and repealed Stats 1994 ch 1269 §35.

ARTICLE 2
Health Insurance Coverage Assignment

Definitions. §3760.
Application and order for health insurance coverage assignment; Notice of intent to seek order. §3761.
Good cause for not making assignment order. §3762.
Time of making and effect of assignment order; Modification of order. §3763.
Service of assignment order; Delivery of copy and information to obligor. §3764.
Motion to quash assignment. §3765.
Selection of plans. §3766.
Notice of commencement of coverage; Providing evidence of coverage. §3767.
Liability for failure to comply with assignment. §3768.
Civil penalty for adverse action against employee. §3769.
Termination of assignment. §3770.
Employer providing information. §3771.
Judicial Council forms. §3772.
Notice of health insurance coverage assignment. §3773.

§3760. Definitions

As used in this article, unless the provision or context otherwise requires:

(a) "Employer" includes the United States government and any public entity as defined in Section 811.2 of the Government Code.

(b) "Health insurance," "health insurance plan," "health insurance coverage," "health care services," or "health insurance coverage assignment" includes vision care and dental care coverage whether the vision care or dental care coverage is part of existing health insurance coverage or is issued as a separate policy or plan.

(c) "Health insurance coverage assignment" or "assignment order" means an order made under Section 3761.

(d) "National medical support notice" means the notice required by Section 666(a)(19) of Title 42 of the United States Code with respect to an order made pursuant to Section 3773. **Leg.H.** Enacted Stats 1992 ch 162 §10 (AB 2650), operative January 1, 1994. Amended Stats 2000 ch 119 §1 (SB 2045).

§3761. Application and order for health insurance coverage assignment; Notice of intent to seek order

(a) Upon application by a party or local child support agency in any proceeding where the court has ordered either or both parents to maintain health insurance coverage under Article 1 (commencing with Section 3750), the court shall order the employer of the obligor parent or other person providing health insurance to the obligor to enroll the supported child in the health insurance plan available to the obligor through the employer or other person and to deduct the appropriate premium or costs, if any, from the earnings of the obligor unless the court makes a finding of good cause for not making the order.

(b)(1) The application shall state that the party or local child support agency seeking the assignment order has given the obligor a written notice of the intent to seek a health insurance coverage assignment order in the event of a default in instituting coverage required by court order on behalf of the parties' child and that the notice was transmitted by first-class mail, postage prepaid, or personally served at least 15 days before the date of the filing of the application for the order. The written notice of the intent to seek an assignment order required by this subdivision may be given at the time of filing a petition or complaint for support or at any later time, but shall be given at least 15 days before the date of filing the application under this section. The obligor may at any time waive the written notice required by this subdivision.

(2) The party or local child support agency seeking the assignment order shall file a certificate of service showing the method and date of service of the order and the statements required under Section 3772 upon the employer or provider of health insurance.

(c) The total amount that may be withheld from earnings for all obligations, including health insurance assignments, is limited by subdivision (a) of Section 706.052 of the Code of Civil Procedure or Section 1673 of Title 15 of the United States Code, whichever is less. **Leg.H.** Enacted Stats 1992 ch 162 §10 (AB 2650), operative January 1, 1994. Amended Stats 1993 ch 219 §127 (AB 1500); Stats 1994 ch 1269 §37 (AB 2208); Stats 2000 ch 808 §31 (AB 1358), effective September 28, 2000.

§3762. Good cause for not making assignment order

Good cause for not making a health insurance coverage assignment order shall be limited to either of the following:

(a) The court finds that one of the conditions listed in subdivision (a) of Section 3765 or in Section 3770 exists.

(b) The court finds that the health insurance coverage assignment order would cause extraordinary hardship to the obligor. The court shall specify the nature of the extraordinary hardship and, whenever possible, a date by which the obligor shall obtain health insurance coverage or be subject to a health insurance coverage assignment. **Leg.H.** Enacted Stats 1992 ch 162 §10 (AB 2650), operative January 1, 1994. Amended Stats 1994 ch 1269 §38 (AB 2208).

§3763. Time of making and effect of assignment order; Modification of order

(a) The health insurance coverage assignment order may be ordered at the time of trial or entry of a judgment ordering health insurance coverage. The order operates as an assignment and is binding on any existing or future employer of the obligor parent, or other person providing health insurance to the obligor, upon whom a copy of the order has been served.

(b) The order of assignment may be modified at any time by the court. **Leg.H.** Enacted Stats 1992 ch 162 §10 (AB 2650), operative January 1, 1994. Amended Stats 1994 ch 1269 §39 (AB 2208).

§3764. Service of assignment order; Delivery of copy and information to obligor

(a) A health insurance coverage assignment order does not become effective until 20 days after service by the applicant of the assignment order on the employer.

(b) Within 10 days after service of the order, the employer or other person providing health insurance to the obligor shall deliver a copy of the order to the obligor, together with a written statement of the obligor's rights and the relevant procedures under the law to move to quash the order.

(c) Service of a health insurance coverage assignment order on any employer or other person providing health insurance may be made by first class mail in the manner prescribed in Section 1013 of the Code of Civil Procedure. **Leg.H.** Enacted Stats 1992 ch 162 §10 (AB 2650), operative January 1, 1994. Amended Stats 1994 ch 1269 §40 (AB 2208).

§3765. Motion to quash assignment

(a) The obligor may move to quash a health insurance coverage assignment order as provided in this section if the obligor declares under penalty of perjury that there is error on any of the following grounds:

(1) No order to maintain health insurance has been issued under Article 1 (commencing with Section 3750).

(2) The amount to be withheld for premiums is greater than that permissible under Article 1 (commencing with Section 3750) or greater than the amount otherwise ordered by the court.

(3) The amount of the increased premium is unreasonable.

(4) The alleged obligor is not the obligor from whom health insurance coverage is due.

(5) The child is or will be otherwise provided health care coverage.

(6) The employer's choice of coverage is inappropriate.

(b) The motion and notice of motion to quash the assignment order, including the declaration required by subdivision (a), shall be filed with the court issuing the assignment order within 15 days after delivery of a copy of the order to the obligor pursuant to subdivision (b) of Section 3764. The court clerk shall set the motion for hearing not less than 15 days, nor more than 30 days, after receipt of the notice of motion. The clerk shall, within five days after receipt of the notice of motion, deliver a copy of the notice of motion to (1) the district attorney personally or by first-class mail, and (2) the applicant and the employer or other person providing health insurance, at the appropriate addresses contained in the application, by first-class mail.

(c) Upon a finding of error described in subdivision (a), the court shall quash the assignment. **Leg.H.** Enacted Stats 1992 ch 162 §10 (AB 2650), operative January 1, 1994. Amended Stats 1994 ch 1269 §41 (AB 2208).

§3766. Selection of plans

(a) The employer, or other person providing health insurance, shall take steps to commence coverage, consistent with the order for the health insurance coverage assignment, within 30 days after service of the assignment order upon the obligor under Section 3764 unless the employer or other person providing health insurance coverage receives an order issued pursuant to Section 3765 to quash the health insurance coverage assignment. The employer, or the person providing health insurance, shall commence coverage at the earliest possible time and, if applicable, consistent with the group plan enrollment rules.

(b) If the obligor has made a selection of health coverage prior to the issuance of the court order, the selection shall not be superseded unless the child to be enrolled in the plan will not be provided benefits or coverage where the child resides or the court order specifically directs other health coverage.

(c) If the obligor has not enrolled in an available health plan, there is a choice of coverage, and the court has not ordered coverage by a specific plan, the employer or other person providing health insurance shall enroll the child in the plan that will provide reasonable benefits or coverage where the child resides. If that coverage is not available, the employer or other person providing health insurance shall, within 20 days, return the assignment order to the attorney or person initiating the assignment.

(d) If an assignment order is served on an employer or other person providing health insurance and no coverage is available for the supported child, the employer or other person shall, within 20 days, return the assignment to the attorney or person initiating the assignment. **Leg.H.** Enacted Stats 1992 ch 162 §10 (AB 2650), operative January 1, 1994. Amended Stats 1994 ch 1269 §42 (AB 2208); Stats 2002 ch 927 §2 (AB 3032).

§3767. Notice of commencement of coverage; Providing evidence of coverage

The employer or other person providing health insurance shall do all of the following:

(a) Notify the applicant for the assignment order or notice of assignment of the commencement date of the coverage of the child.

(b) Provide evidence of coverage and any information necessary for the child to obtain benefits through the coverage to both parents or the person having custody of the child and to the local child support agency when requested by the local child support agency.

(c) Upon request by the parents or person having custody of the child, provide all forms and other documentation necessary for the purpose of submitting claims to the insurance carrier which the employer or other person providing health insurance usually provides to insureds. **Leg.H.** Enacted Stats 1992 ch 162 §10 (AB 2650), operative January 1, 1994. Amended Stats 1996 ch 1062 §3 (AB 1832); Stats 1997 ch 599 §8 (AB 573); Stats 2001 ch 755 §3 (SB 943), effective October 12, 2001.

§3768. Liability for failure to comply with assignment

(a) An employer or other person providing health insurance who willfully fails to comply with a valid health insurance coverage assignment order entered and served on the employer or other person pursuant to this article is liable to the applicant for the amount incurred in health care services that would otherwise have been covered under the insurance policy but for the conduct of the employer or other person that was contrary to the assignment order.

(b) Willful failure of an employer or other person providing health insurance to comply with a health insurance coverage assignment order is punishable as contempt of court under Section 1218 of the Code of Civil Procedure. **Leg.H.** Enacted Stats 1992 ch 162 §10 (AB 2650), operative January 1, 1994. Amended Stats 1994 ch 1269 §43 (AB 2208).

§3769. Civil penalty for adverse action against employee

No employer shall use a health insurance coverage assignment order as grounds for refusing to hire a person or for discharging or taking disciplinary action against an employee. An employer who violates this section may be assessed a civil penalty of a maximum of five hundred dollars ($500). **Leg.H.** Enacted Stats 1992 ch 162 §10 (AB 2650), operative January 1, 1994. Amended Stats 1994 ch 1269 §44 (AB 2208).

§3770. Termination of assignment

Upon notice of motion by the obligor, the court shall terminate a health insurance coverage assignment order if any of the following conditions exist:

(a) A new order has been issued under Article 1 (commencing with Section 3750) that is inconsistent with the existing assignment.

(b) The employer or other person providing health insurance has discontinued that coverage to the obligor.

(c) The court determines that there is good cause, consistent with Section 3762, to terminate the assignment.

(d) The death or emancipation of the child for whom the health insurance has been obtained. **Leg.H.** Enacted Stats 1992 ch 162 §10 (AB 2650), operative January 1, 1994. Amended Stats 1994 ch 1269 §45 (AB 2208).

§3771. Employer providing information

Upon request of the local child support agency the employer shall provide the following information to the local child support agency within 30 days:

(a) The social security number of the absent parent.

(b) The home address of the absent parent.

(c) Whether the absent parent has a health insurance policy and, if so, the policy names and numbers, and the names of the persons covered.

(d) Whether the health insurance policy provides coverage for dependent children of the absent parent who do not reside in the absent parent's home.

(e) If there is a subsequent lapse in health insurance coverage, the employer shall notify the local child support agency, giving the date the coverage ended, the reason for the lapse in coverage and, if the lapse is temporary, the date upon which coverage is expected to resume. **Leg.H.** Enacted Stats 1992 ch 162 §10 (AB 2650), operative January 1, 1994. Amended Stats 2000 ch 808 §32 (AB 1358), effective September 28, 2000.

§3772. Judicial Council forms

The Judicial Council shall adopt forms for the health insurance coverage assignment required or authorized by this article, including, but not limited to, the application, the order, the statement of the obligor's rights, and an employer's return form which shall include information on the limitations on the total amount that may be withheld from earnings for obligations, including health insurance assignments, under subdivision (a) of Section 706.052 of the Code of Civil Procedure and Section 1673 of Title 15 of the United States Code, and the information required by Section 3771. The parties and child shall be sufficiently identified on the forms by the inclusion of birth dates, social security numbers, and any other information the Judicial Council determines is necessary. **Leg.H.** Enacted Stats 1992 ch 162 §10 (AB 2650), operative January 1, 1994. Amended Stats 1994 ch 1269 §46 (AB 2208).

§3773. Notice of health insurance coverage assignment

(a) This section applies only to Title IV-D cases where support enforcement services are being provided by the local child support agency pursuant to Section 17400.

(b) After the court has ordered that a parent provide health insurance coverage, the local child support agency shall serve on the employer a national medical support notice in lieu of the health insurance coverage assignment order. The national medical support notice may be combined with the order/notice to withhold income for child support that is authorized by Section 5246.

(c) A national medical support notice shall have the same force and effect as a health insurance coverage assignment order.

(d) The obligor shall have the same right to move to quash or terminate a national medical support notice as provided in this article for a health insurance coverage assignment order. **Leg.H.** Added Stats 1997 ch 599 §9 (AB 573). Amended Stats 1998 ch 858 §1 (AB 2169); Stats 2000 ch 119 §2 (SB 2045).

ARTICLE 3
Assignment of Reimbursement Rights Under Health Plan [Repealed]

§3780. [Section repealed 1997]

Leg.H. Enacted Stats 1992 ch 162 §10 (AB 2650), operative January 1, 1994. Repealed Stats 1997 ch 599 §10 (AB 573). The repealed section related to definition of health plan.

§3781. [Section repealed 1997]

Leg.H. Enacted Stats 1992 ch 162 §10 (AB 2650), operative January 1, 1994. Repealed Stats 1997 ch 599 §11 (AB 573). The repealed section related to assignment of rights to reimbursement under health plan.

§3782. [Section repealed 1997]

Leg.H. Enacted Stats 1992 ch 162 §10 (AB 2650), operative January 1, 1994. Repealed Stats 1997 ch 599 §12 (AB 573). The repealed section related to provision of information and forms by party covered by health plan.

CHAPTER 8
DEFERRED SALE OF HOME ORDER

Definitions. §3800.
Determination of economic feasibility. §3801.
Matters to be considered by court in determining whether to grant order. §3802.
Contents of order. §3803.
Recording order. §3804.
Order concerning maintenance and capital improvements. §3806.
Modification or termination or order. §3807.
Presumption arising upon remarriage or other change in circumstances. §3808.
Reservation of jurisdiction by court. §3809.
Chapter applies to preexisting orders. §3810.

§3800. Definitions

As used in this chapter:

(a) "Custodial parent" means a party awarded physical custody of a child.

(b) "Deferred sale of home order" means an order that temporarily delays the sale and awards the temporary exclusive use and possession of the family home to a custodial parent of a minor child or child for whom support is authorized under Sections 3900 and 3901 or under Section 3910, whether or not the custodial parent has sole or joint custody, in order to minimize the adverse impact of dissolution of marriage or legal separation of the parties on the welfare of the child.

(c) "Resident parent" means a party who has requested or who has already been awarded a deferred sale of home order. **Leg.H.** Enacted Stats 1992 ch 162 §10 (AB 2650), operative January 1, 1994.

§3801. Determination of economic feasibility

(a) If one of the parties has requested a deferred sale of home order pursuant to this chapter, the court shall first determine whether it is economically feasible to maintain the payments of any note secured by a deed of trust, property taxes, insurance for the home during the period the sale of the home is deferred, and the condition of the home comparable to that at the time of trial.

(b) In making this determination, the court shall consider all of the following:

(1) The resident parent's income.

(2) The availability of spousal support, child support, or both spousal and child support.

(3) Any other sources of funds available to make those payments.

(c) It is the intent of the Legislature, by requiring the determination under this section, to do all of the following:

(1) Avoid the likelihood of possible defaults on the payments of notes and resulting foreclosures.

(2) Avoid inadequate insurance coverage.

(3) Prevent deterioration of the condition of the family home.

(4) Prevent any other circumstance which would jeopardize both parents' equity in the home. **Leg.H.** Enacted Stats 1992 ch 162 §10 (AB 2650), operative January 1, 1994.

§3802. Matters to be considered by court in determining whether to grant order

(a) If the court determines pursuant to Section 3801 that it is economically feasible to consider ordering a deferred sale of the family home, the court may grant a deferred sale of home order to a custodial parent if the court determines that the order is necessary in order to minimize the adverse impact of dissolution of marriage or legal separation of the parties on the child.

(b) In exercising its discretion to grant or deny a deferred sale of home order, the court shall consider all of the following:

(1) The length of time the child has resided in the home.

(2) The child's placement or grade in school.

(3) The accessibility and convenience of the home to the child's school and other services or facilities used by and available to the child, including child care.

(4) Whether the home has been adapted or modified to accommodate any physical disabilities of a child or a resident parent in a manner that a change in residence may adversely affect the ability of the resident parent to meet the needs of the child.

(5) The emotional detriment to the child associated with a change in residence.

(6) The extent to which the location of the home permits the resident parent to continue employment.

(7) The financial ability of each parent to obtain suitable housing.

(8) The tax consequences to the parents.

(9) The economic detriment to the nonresident parent in the event of a deferred sale of home order.

(10) Any other factors the court deems just and equitable. **Leg.H.** Enacted Stats 1992 ch 162 §10 (AB 2650), operative January 1, 1994.

§3803. Contents of order

A deferred sale of home order shall state the duration of the order and may include the legal description and assessor's parcel number of the real property which is subject to the order. **Leg.H.** Enacted Stats 1992 ch 162 §10 (AB 2650), operative January 1, 1994.

§3804. Recording order

A deferred sale of home order may be recorded in the office of the county recorder of the county in which the real property is located. **Leg.H.** Enacted Stats 1992 ch 162 §10 (AB 2650), operative January 1, 1994.

§3805. [Section repealed 1993]

Leg.H. Enacted Stats 1992 ch 162 §10 (AB 2650), operative January 1, 1994. Repealed Stats 1993 ch 219 §128 (AB 1500). The repealed section related to deferred sale of home order as additonal child support.

§3806. Order concerning maintenance and capital improvements

The court may make an order specifying the parties' respective responsibilities for the payment of the costs of routine maintenance and capital improvements. **Leg.H.** Enacted Stats 1992 ch 162 §10 (AB 2650), operative January 1, 1994.

§3807. Modification or termination or order

Except as otherwise agreed to by the parties in writing, a deferred sale of home order may be modified or terminated at any time at the discretion of the court. **Leg.H.** Enacted Stats 1992 ch 162 §10 (AB 2650), operative January 1, 1994.

§3808. Presumption arising upon remarriage or other change in circumstances

Except as otherwise agreed to by the parties in writing, if the party awarded the deferred sale of home order remarries, or if there is otherwise a change in circumstances affecting the determinations made pursuant to Section 3801 or 3802 or affecting the economic status of the parties or the children on which the award is based, a rebuttable presumption, affecting the burden of proof, is created that further deferral of the sale is no longer an equitable method of minimizing the adverse impact of the dissolution of marriage or legal separation of the parties on the children. **Leg.H.** Enacted Stats 1992 ch 162 §10 (AB 2650), operative January 1, 1994.

§3809. Reservation of jurisdiction by court

In making an order pursuant to this chapter, the court shall reserve jurisdiction to determine any issues that arise with respect to the deferred sale of home order including, but not limited to, the maintenance of the home and the tax consequences to each party. **Leg.H.** Enacted Stats 1992 ch 162 §10 (AB 2650), operative January 1, 1994.

§3810. Chapter applies to preexisting orders

This chapter is applicable regardless of whether the deferred sale of home order is made before or after January 1, 1989. **Leg.H.** Enacted Stats 1992 ch 162 §10 (AB 2650), operative January 1, 1994.

CHAPTER 9
SOFTWARE USED TO DETERMINE SUPPORT

Software to conform to court rules. §3830.

§3830. Software to conform to court rules

(a) On and after January 1, 1994, no court shall use any computer software to assist in determining the appropriate amount of child support or spousal support obligations, unless the software conforms to rules of court adopted by the Judicial Council prescribing standards for the software, which shall ensure that it performs in a manner consistent with the applicable statutes and rules of court for determination of child support or spousal support.

(b) The Judicial Council may contract with an outside agency or organization to analyze software to ensure that it conforms to the standards established by the Judicial Council. The cost of this analysis shall be paid by the applicant software producers and fees therefor shall be established by the Judicial Council in an amount that in the aggregate will defray its costs of administering this section. **Leg.H.** Added Stats 1993 ch 219 §129 (AB 1500).

PART 2
CHILD SUPPORT

Chapter 1. Duty of Parent to Support Child.
Chapter 2. Court-Ordered Child Support.

CHAPTER 1
DUTY OF PARENT TO SUPPORT CHILD

Article 1. Support of Minor Child.
Article 2. Support of Adult Child.
Article 3. Support of Grandchild.
Article 4. Liability to Others Who Provide Support for Child.

ARTICLE 1
Support of Minor Child

Duty of parents. §3900.
Duration of duty. §3901.
Support out of child's property. §3902.

§3900. Duty of parents

Subject to this division, the father and mother of a minor child have an equal responsibility to support their child in the manner suitable to the child's circumstances. **Leg.H.** Enacted Stats 1992 ch 162 §10 (AB 2650), operative January 1, 1994.

§3901. Duration of duty

(a)(1) The duty of support imposed by Section 3900 continues as to an unmarried child who has attained 18 years of age, is a full-time high school student, unless excused pursuant to paragraph (2), and who is not self-supporting, until the time the child completes the 12th grade or attains 19 years of age, whichever occurs first.

(2) A child is excused from the requirement to be a full-time high school student for purposes of paragraph (1) if the child has a medical condition documented by a physician that prevents full-time school attendance.

(b) This section does not limit a parent's ability to agree to provide additional support or the court's power to inquire whether an agreement to provide additional support has been made. **Leg.H.** Enacted Stats 1992 ch 162 §10 (AB 2650), operative January 1, 1994. Amended Stats 1993 ch 219 §130 (AB 1500); Stats 2018 ch 504 §2 (AB 3248), effective January 1, 2019.

§3902. Support out of child's property

The court may direct that an allowance be made to the parent of a child for whom support may be ordered out of the child's property for the child's past or future support, on conditions that are proper, if the direction is for the child's benefit. **Leg.H.** Enacted Stats 1992 ch 162 §10 (AB 2650), operative January 1, 1994. Amended Stats 1993 ch 219 §131 (AB 1500).

ARTICLE 2
Support of Adult Child

Duty to maintain incapacitated child. §3910.

§3910. Duty to maintain incapacitated child

(a) [1] **Each parent of a child has** an equal responsibility to maintain, to the extent of their ability, [2] **their** child of whatever age who is incapacitated from earning a living and without sufficient means.

(b) **The court may order that a support payment be paid to a special needs trust. For purposes of this section, "special needs trust" means a trust that meets the requirements described in subparagraph (A) or (C) of paragraph (4) of subsection (d) of Section 1396p of Title 42 of the United States Code and paragraph (3) or (4) of subdivision (a) of Section 50489.9 of Title 22 of the California Code of Regulations.**

[3] (c) [4] **This section does not limit** the duty of support under Sections 3900 and 3901. **Leg.H.** Enacted Stats 1992 ch 162 §10 (AB 2650), operative January 1, 1994. Amended Stats 2024 ch 25 §1 (AB 2397), effective January 1, 2025.

§3910. 2024 Deletes. [1] The father and mother have [2] a [3] (b) [4] Nothing in this section limits

ARTICLE 3
Support of Grandchild

Support of grandchild. §3930.

§3930. Support of grandchild

A parent does not have the duty to support a child of the parent's child. **Leg.H.** Enacted Stats 1992 ch 162 §10 (AB 2650), operative January 1, 1994. Amended Stats 1993 ch 219 §132 (AB 1500).

ARTICLE 4
Liability to Others Who Provide Support for Child

Necessaries provided to child. §3950.
When reimbursement not required. §3951.
Support of public charge out of estate of parent. §3952.

§3950. Necessaries provided to child

If a parent neglects to provide articles necessary for the parent's child who is under the charge of the parent, according to the circumstances of the parent, a third person may in good faith supply the necessaries and recover their reasonable value from the parent. **Leg.H.** Enacted Stats 1992 ch 162 §10 (AB 2650), operative January 1, 1994.

§3951. When reimbursement not required

(a) A parent is not bound to compensate the other parent, or a relative, for the voluntary support of the parent's child, without an agreement for compensation.

(b) A parent is not bound to compensate a stranger for the support of a child who has abandoned the parent without just cause.

(c) Nothing in this section relieves a parent of the obligation to support a child during any period in which the state, county, or other governmental entity provides support for the child. **Leg.H.** Enacted Stats 1992 ch 162 §10 (AB 2650), operative January 1, 1994.

§3952. Support of public charge out of estate of parent

If a parent chargeable with the support of a child dies leaving the child chargeable to the county or leaving the child confined in a state institution to be cared for in whole or in part at the expense of the state, and the parent leaves an estate sufficient for the child's support, the supervisors of the county or the director of the state department having jurisdiction over the institution may claim provision for the child's support from the parent's estate, and for this purpose has the same remedies as a creditor against the estate of the parent and may obtain reimbursement from the successor of the deceased parent to the extent provided in Division 8 (commencing with Section 13000) of the Probate Code. **Leg.H.** Enacted Stats 1992 ch 162 §10 (AB 2650), operative January 1, 1994.

CHAPTER 2
COURT-ORDERED CHILD SUPPORT

Article 1. General Provisions.
Article 2. Statewide Uniform Guideline.
Article 3. Payment to Court Designated County Officer; Enforcement by District Attorney.
Article 4. Child Support Commissioners.

ARTICLE 1
General Provisions

Civil action to enforce parent's duty to support. §4000.
Order for child support. §4001.
Enforcement by county on behalf of child. §4002.
Preference for trial on issue of support. §4003.
Child receiving public assistance. §4004.
Findings on circumstances for order of child support. §4005.
Health insurance coverage as factor. §4006.
Support for contingent period of time. §4007.
Suspension of money judgment or child support order; Conditions. § 4007.5.
Property available for child support. §4008.
Retroactivity of order. §4009.
Notice of modification procedures. §4010.
Priority of child support payments. §4011.
Security for payment. §4012.
Obligation discharged in bankruptcy. §4013.
Notice of current employer; Personal information; Filing and updating; Forms. §4014.

§4000. Civil action to enforce parent's duty to support

If a parent has the duty to provide for the support of the parent's child and willfully fails to so provide, the other parent, or the child by a guardian ad litem, may bring an action against the parent to enforce the duty. **Leg.H.** Enacted Stats 1992 ch 162 §10 (AB 2650), operative January 1, 1994.

§4001. Order for child support

In any proceeding where there is at issue the support of a minor child or a child for whom support is authorized under Section 3901 or 3910, the court may order either or both parents to pay an amount necessary for the support of the child. **Leg.H.** Enacted Stats 1992 ch 162 §10 (AB 2650), operative January 1, 1994.

§4002. Enforcement by county on behalf of child

(a) The county may proceed on behalf of a child to enforce the child's right of support against a parent.

(b) If the county furnishes support to a child, the county has the same right as the child to secure reimbursement and obtain continuing support. The right of the county to reimbursement is subject to any limitation otherwise imposed by the law of this state.

(c) The court may order the parent to pay the county reasonable attorney's fees and court costs in a proceeding brought by the county pursuant to this section. **Leg.H.** Enacted Stats 1992 ch 162 §10 (AB 2650), operative January 1, 1994.

§4003. Preference for trial on issue of support

In any case in which the support of a child is at issue, the court may, upon a showing of good cause, order a separate trial on that issue. The separate trial shall be given preference over other civil cases, except matters to which special precedence may be given by law, for assigning a trial date. If the court has also ordered a separate trial on the issue of custody pursuant to Section 3023, the two issues shall be tried together. **Leg.H.** Enacted Stats 1992 ch 162 §10 (AB 2650), operative January 1, 1994. Amended Stats 1993 ch 219 §133 (AB 1500).

§4004. Child receiving public assistance

In a proceeding where there is at issue the support of a child, the court shall require the parties to reveal whether a party is currently receiving, or intends to apply for, public assistance under the Family Economic Security Act of 1982 (Chapter 2 (commencing with Section 11200) of Part 3 of Division 9 of the Welfare and Institutions Code) for the maintenance of the child. **Leg.H.** Enacted Stats 1992 ch 162 §10 (AB 2650), operative January 1, 1994. Amended Stats 1993 ch 219 §134 (AB 1500).

§4005. Findings on circumstances for order of child support

At the request of either party, the court shall make appropriate findings with respect to the circumstances on which the order for support of a child is based. **Leg.H.** Added Stats 1994 ch 1269 §47 (AB 2208).

§4006. Health insurance coverage as factor

In a proceeding for child support under this code, including, but not limited to, Division 17 (commencing with Section 17000), the court shall consider the health insurance coverage, if any, of the parties to the proceeding. **Leg.H.** Enacted Stats 1992 ch 162 §10 (AB 2650), operative January 1, 1994. Amended Stats 2000 ch 808 §33 (AB 1358), effective September 28, 2000.

§4007. Support for contingent period of time

(a) If a court orders a person to make specified payments for support of a child during the child's minority, or until the child is married or otherwise emancipated, or until the death of, or the occurrence of a specified event as to, a child for whom support is authorized under Section 3901 or 3910, the obligation of the person ordered to pay support terminates on the happening of the contingency. The court may, in the original order for support, order the custodial parent or other person to whom payments are to be made to notify the person ordered to make the payments, or the person's attorney of record, of the happening of the contingency.

(b) If the custodial parent or other person having physical custody of the child, to whom payments are to be made, fails to notify the person ordered to make the payments, or the attorney of record of the person ordered to make the payments, of the happening of the contingency and continues to accept support payments, the person shall refund all moneys received that accrued after the happening of the contingency, except that the overpayments shall first be applied to any support payments that are then in default. **Leg.H.** Enacted Stats 1992 ch 162 §10 (AB 2650), operative January 1, 1994.

§ 4007.5. Suspension of money judgment or child support order; Conditions

(a) Every money judgment or order for support of a child shall be suspended, by operation of law, for any period exceeding 90 consecutive days in which the person ordered to pay support is incarcerated or involuntarily institutionalized, unless the person owing support has the means to pay support while incarcerated or involuntarily institutionalized.

(b)(1) The child support obligation shall be suspended effective on the first day of the first full month of incarceration or involuntary institutionalization.

(2) For persons owing support who are released from incarceration or involuntary institutionalization on or after January 1, 2024, the child support obligation shall resume on the first day of the 10th month after release from incarceration or involuntary institutionalization of the person owing support.

(3) If the person owing support obtains employment prior to the date set for reinstatement, the person to whom the support is owed or the local child support agency may seek a court order reinstating child support obligations at the amount determined by the court pursuant to Article 2 (commencing with Section 4050).

(4) This section does not preclude a person owing support or the local child support agency from seeking a modification of the child support order pursuant to Section 3651, based on a change in circumstances or any other appropriate reason.

(c)(1) A local child support agency enforcing a child support order under Title IV-D of the Social Security Act (42 U.S.C. Sec. 651 et seq.) may, upon written notice of the proposed adjustment to the support obligor and obligee along with a blank form provided for the support obligor or obligee to object to the administrative adjustment to the local child support agency, administratively adjust account balances for a money judgment or order for support of a child suspended pursuant to subdivision (a) if all of the following occurs:

(A) The agency verifies that arrears and interest were accrued in violation of this section.

(B) The agency verifies that, to the extent known to the agency, the person owing support does not have the means to pay support while incarcerated or involuntarily institutionalized.

(C) Neither the support obligor nor obligee objects, within 30 days of receipt of the notice of proposed adjustment, whether in writing or by telephone, to the administrative adjustment by the local child support agency.

(2) If either the support obligor or obligee objects to the administrative adjustment set forth in this subdivision, the agency shall not adjust the order, but shall file a motion with the court to seek to adjust the arrears and shall serve copies of the motion on the parties, who may file an objection to the agency's motion with the court. The obligor's arrears shall not be adjusted unless the court approves the adjustment.

(3) The agency may perform this adjustment without regard to whether it was enforcing the child support order at the time the parent owing support qualified for relief under this section.

(d) This section does not prohibit the local child support agency or a party from petitioning a court for a determination of child support or arrears amounts.

(e) For purposes of this section, the following definitions shall apply:

(1) "Incarcerated or involuntarily institutionalized" includes, but is not limited to, involuntary confinement to a federal or state prison, a county jail, a juvenile facility operated by the Division of Juvenile Facilities in the Department of Corrections and Rehabilitation, or a mental health facility.

(2) "Suspend" means that the payment due on the current child support order, an arrears payment on a preexisting arrears balance, or interest on arrears created during a qualifying period of incarceration pursuant to this section is, by operation of law, set to zero dollars ($0) for the period in which the person owing support is incarcerated or involuntarily institutionalized.

(f) This section applies to any child support obligation that accrues on or after the enactment of this section regardless of when the child support order was established.

(g) The Department of Child Support Services shall, by July 1, 2023, and in consultation with the Judicial Council, develop forms to implement this section.

(h) On or before January 1, 2026, the Department of Child Support Services, in consultation with the Judicial Council, shall conduct an evaluation of the effectiveness of the administrative adjustment process authorized by this section and shall report the results of the review, as well as any recommended changes, to the Assembly Judiciary Committee and the Senate Judiciary Committee. The evaluation shall include a review of the ease of the process to both the obligor and obligee, as well as an analysis of the number of cases administratively adjusted, the number of cases adjusted in court, and the number of cases not adjusted.

(i) It is the intent of the Legislature to ensure qualified persons are provided the support suspension by operation of law for qualified periods of incarceration or involuntary institutionalization that existed during the operative terms of the earlier versions of this statute regardless of whether the judicial or administrative determination of arrears is made before or after the repeal of the statute, if the earlier version of the statute provided for the money judgment or order for support to be suspended by operation of law. This subdivision is declarative of existing law. **Leg.H.** Added Stats 2020 ch 217 §2 (AB 2325), effective January 1, 2021. Amended Stats 2022 ch 573 §2 (AB 207), effective September 27, 2022; Stats 2023 ch 565 §1 (AB 1148), effective January 1, 2024.

Prior Law Former Fam C §4007.5, relating to suspension of support obligation due to incarceration or involuntary institutionalization, adjustment of balance, applicability, and evaluation of adjustment process, was added Stats 2015 ch 629 §2 (AB 610), effective October 8, 2015, and repealed January 1, 2020, by its own terms.

§4008. Property available for child support

The community property, the quasi-community property, and the separate property may be subjected to the support of the children in the proportions the court determines are just. **Leg.H.** Enacted Stats 1992 ch 162 §10 (AB 2650), operative January 1, 1994.

§4009. Retroactivity of order

An original order for child support may be made retroactive to the date of filing the petition, complaint, or other initial pleading. If the parent ordered to pay support was not served with the petition, complaint, or other initial pleading within 90 days after filing and the court finds that the parent was not intentionally evading service, the child support order shall be effective no earlier than the date of service. **Leg.H.** Enacted Stats 1992 ch 162 §10 (AB 2650), operative January 1, 1994. Amended Stats 1999 ch 653 §8 (AB 380); Stats 2000 ch 808 §34 (AB 1358), effective September 28, 2000; Stats 2004 ch 305 §3 (AB 2669).

§4010. Notice of modification procedures

In a proceeding in which the court orders a payment for the support of a child, the court shall, at the time of providing written notice of the order, provide the parties with a document describing the procedures by which the order may be modified. **Leg.H.** Enacted Stats 1992 ch 162 §10 (AB 2650), operative January 1, 1994. Amended Stats 1993 ch 219 §136 (AB 1500).

§4011. Priority of child support payments

Payment of child support ordered by the court shall be made by the person owing the support payment before payment of any debts owed to creditors. **Leg.H.** Enacted Stats 1992 ch 162 §10 (AB 2650), operative January 1, 1994.

§4012. Security for payment

Upon a showing of good cause, the court may order a parent required to make a payment of child support to give reasonable security for the payment. **Leg.H.** Enacted Stats 1992 ch 162 §10 (AB 2650), operative January 1, 1994.

§4013. Obligation discharged in bankruptcy

If obligations for support of a child are discharged in bankruptcy, the court may make all proper orders for the support of the child that the court determines are just. **Leg.H.** Enacted Stats 1992 ch 162 §10 (AB 2650), operative January 1, 1994.

§4014. Notice of current employer; Personal information; Filing and updating; Forms

(a) An order for child support issued or modified pursuant to this chapter shall include a provision requiring the obligor and child support obligee to notify the other parent or, if the order requires payment through an agency designated under Title IV-D of the Social Security Act (42 U.S.C. Sec. 651 et seq.), the agency named in the order, of the name and address of the person's current employer.

(b) The requirements set forth in this subdivision apply only in cases when the local child support agency is not providing child support services pursuant to Section 17400. To the extent required by federal law, and subject to applicable confidentiality provisions of state or federal law, a judgment for paternity and an order for child support entered or modified pursuant to any law shall include a provision requiring the child support obligor and obligee to file with the court all of the following information:

(1) Residential and mailing address.

(2) Social security number, individual taxpayer identification number, or other uniform identification number.

(3) Telephone number.

(4) Driver's license number or identification card number issued by the Department of Motor Vehicles.

(5) Name, address, and telephone number of the employer.

(6) Any other information prescribed by the Judicial Council.

The judgment or order shall specify that each parent is responsible for providing the parent's own information, that the information must be filed with the court within 10 days of the court order, and that new or different information must be filed with the court within 10 days after any event causing a change in the previously provided information.

(c) The requirements set forth in this subdivision shall only apply in cases in which the local child support agency is not providing child support services pursuant to Section 17400. Once the child support registry, as described in Section 17391 is operational, a judgment for parentage and an order for child support entered or modified pursuant to any law shall include a provision requiring the child support obligor and obligee to file and keep updated the information specified in subdivision (b) with the child support registry.

(d) The Judicial Council shall develop forms to implement this section. The forms shall be developed so as not to delay the implementation of the Statewide Child Support Registry described in Section 17391 and shall be available no later than 30 days prior to the implementation of the Statewide Child Support Registry. **Leg.H.** Added Stats 1993 ch 876 §18 (SB 1068), effective October 6, 1993, operative January 1, 1994. Amended Stats 1997 ch 599 §13 (AB 573); Stats 1998 ch 858 §2 (AB 2169); Stats 2004 ch 339 §2 (AB 1704); Stats 2016 ch 474 §8 (AB 2882), effective January 1, 2017; Stats 2018 ch 838 §5 (SB 695), effective January 1, 2019; Stats 2019 ch 115 §43 (AB 1817), effective January 1, 2020.

ARTICLE 2
Statewide Uniform Guideline

Legislative intent. §4050.
Adherence to guidelines. §4052.
Applicability of guideline to cases involving child with more than two parents. §4052.5.
Child support according to parent's circumstances and station in life. §4053.
Periodic review by Judicial Council. §4054.
Formula for statewide uniform guideline for determining child support. § 4055.
Information in writing or on record. §4056.
Presumption of amount of award established by formula. § 4057.
Income of subsequent spouse or nonmarital partner. §4057.5.
Annual gross income of each parent. § 4058.
Annual net disposable income of each parent. §4059.
Monthly net disposable income. §4060.
Additional child support. § 4061.
Allocation of additional expenses. § 4062.
Payment or reimbursement of costs. § 4063.
Adjustment for seasonal or fluctuating income. §4064.
Stipulated child support agreement. §4065.
Order or stipulation designating family support. §4066.
Continuing review by Legislature. §4067.
Judicial Council worksheets and forms. §4068.
Establishment of guideline as change of circumstances. §4069.
Financial hardship deductions. §4070.
Circumstances evidencing hardship. §4071.
Statement of reasons for and duration of hardship deductions. §4072.
Consideration of legislative goals when ordering hardship deductions. §4073.
Application to family support awards. §4074.
Treatment of spousal support payments under federal tax law. §4075.
Modification of order to comply with statewide guideline; Two-step phase-in. §4076.

Department of Child Support Services and Judicial Council meeting; Report on federal child support regulations compliance. § 4077.

§4050. Legislative intent

In adopting the statewide uniform guideline provided in this article, it is the intention of the Legislature to ensure that this state remains in compliance with federal regulations for child support guidelines. **Leg.H.** Added Stats 1993 ch 219 §138 (AB 1500).

Prior Law: Former §4050, similar to the present section and §4051, was enacted Stats 1992 ch 162 §10, to become operative January 1, 1994, and repealed, operative January 1, 1994, by the terms of §4067, Stats 1993 ch 219 §137.

§4051. [Section repealed 2016]

Leg.H. Added Stats 1993 ch 219 §138 (AB 1500). Repealed Stats 2015 ch 303 §148 (AB 731), effective January 1, 2016. The repealed section related to the operative date of the article.

Prior Law: Former Fam C §4051, similar to present Fam C §4053, was enacted Stats 1992 ch 162 §10, operative January 1, 1994, and repealed January 1, 1994, by the terms of former Fam C §4067, Stats 1993 ch 219 §137. Historical derivation: (a) former Fam C §4050, as enacted Stats 1992 ch 162 §10; (b) former CC §4720, as added Stats 1992 ch 46 §5, amended Stats 1992 ch 848 §5; (c) former CC §4720, as added Stats 1990 ch 1493 §10; (d) former CC §4720, as added Stats 1984 ch 1605 §4, amended Stats 1990 ch 1493 §9; (e) former CC §4720.1, as added Stats 1990 ch 1493 §12.

§4052. Adherence to guidelines

The court shall adhere to the statewide uniform guideline and may depart from the guideline only in the special circumstances set forth in this article. **Leg.H.** Added Stats 1993 ch 219 §138 (AB 1500).

Prior Law: Former §4052, similar to the present section, was enacted Stats 1992 ch 162 §10, to become operative January 1, 1994, and repealed, operative January 1, 1994, by the terms of §4067, Stats 1993 ch 219 §137.

§4052.5. Applicability of guideline to cases involving child with more than two parents

(a) The statewide uniform guideline, as required by federal regulations, shall apply in any case in which a child has more than two parents. The court shall apply the guideline by dividing child support obligations among the parents based on income and amount of time spent with the child by each parent, pursuant to Section 4053.

(b) Consistent with federal regulations, after calculating the amount of support owed by each parent under the guideline, the presumption that the guideline amount of support is correct may be rebutted if the court finds that the application of the guideline in that case would be unjust or inappropriate due to special circumstances, pursuant to Section 4057. If the court makes that finding, the court shall divide child support obligations among the parents in a manner that is just and appropriate based on income and amount of time spent with the child by each parent, applying the principles set forth in Section 4053 and this article.

(c) Nothing in this section shall be construed to require reprogramming of the California Child Support Enforcement System, a change to the statewide uniform guideline for determining child support set forth in Section 4055, or a revision by the Department of Child Support Services of its regulations, policies, procedures, forms, or training materials. **Leg.H.** Added Stats 2013 ch 564 §3 (SB 274), effective January 1, 2014. Amended Stats 2016 ch 474 §9 (AB 2882), effective January 1, 2017.

§4053. Child support according to parent's circumstances and station in life

In implementing the statewide uniform guideline, the courts shall adhere to the following principles:

(a) A parent's first and principal obligation is to support the parent's minor children according to the parent's circumstances and station in life.

(b) Both parents are mutually responsible for the support of their children.

(c) The guideline takes into account each parent's actual income and level of responsibility for the children.

(d) Each parent should pay for the support of the children according to the parent's ability.

(e) The guideline seeks to place the interests of children as the state's top priority.

(f) Children should share in the standard of living of both parents. Child support may therefore appropriately improve the standard of living of the custodial household to improve the lives of the children.

(g) Child support orders in cases in which both parents have high levels of responsibility for the children should reflect the increased costs of raising the children in two homes and should minimize significant disparities in the children's living standards in the two homes.

(h) The financial needs of the children should be met through private financial resources as much as possible.

(i) It is presumed that a parent having primary physical responsibility for the children contributes a significant portion of available resources for the support of the children.

(j) The guideline seeks to encourage fair and efficient settlements of conflicts between parents and seeks to minimize the need for litigation.

(k) The guideline is intended to be presumptively correct in all cases, and only under special circumstances should child support orders fall below the child support mandated by the guideline formula.

(*l*) Child support orders shall ensure that children actually receive fair, timely, and sufficient support reflecting the state's high standard of living and high costs of raising children compared to other states. **Leg.H.** Added Stats 1993 ch 219 §138 (AB 1500). Amended Stats 2019 ch 115 §44 (AB 1817), effective January 1, 2020.

Prior Law: Former §4053, similar to present Fam C §4055, was enacted Stats 1992 ch 162 §10, to become operative January 1, 1994, and repealed Stats 1993 ch 219 §137.

§4054. Periodic review by Judicial Council

(a) The Judicial Council shall periodically review the statewide uniform guideline to recommend to the Legislature appropriate revisions.

(b) The review shall include all of the following:

(1) Economic data on the cost of raising children.

(2) Labor market data, such as unemployment rates, employment rates, hours worked, and earnings, by occupation and skill level for the state and local job markets.

(3) The impact of guideline policies and amounts on custodial and noncustodial parents who have family incomes below 200 percent of the federal poverty level.

(4) Factors that influence employment rates among custodial and noncustodial parents and compliance with child support orders.

(5) An analysis of case data, gathered through sampling or other methods, on the actual application of, and deviations from, the guideline after the guideline's operative date, as well as the rates of orders entered by default, orders entered based on presumed income and earning capacity, and orders determined using the low-income adjustment.

(6) An analysis of guidelines and studies from other states, and other research and studies available to or undertaken by the Judicial Council.

(7) A comparison of payments on child support orders by case characteristics, including whether the order was entered by default, based on earning capacity or presumed income, or determined using the low-income adjustment.

(8) Any additional factors required by federal regulations.

(c) Any recommendations for revisions to the guideline shall be made to ensure that the guideline results in appropriate child support orders, to limit deviations from the guideline, or otherwise to help ensure that the guideline is in compliance with federal law.

(d) The Judicial Council may also review and report on other matters, including, but not limited to, the following:

(1) The treatment of the income of a subsequent spouse or nonmarital partner.

(2) The treatment of children from prior or subsequent relationships.

(3) The application of the guideline in a case where a payer parent has extraordinarily low or extraordinarily high income, or where each parent has primary physical custody of one or more of the children of the marriage.

(4) The benefits and limitations of a uniform statewide spousal support guideline and the interrelationship of that guideline with the state child support guideline.

(5) Whether the use of gross or net income in the guideline is preferable.

(6) Whether the guideline affects child custody litigation or the efficiency of the judicial process.

(7) Whether the various assumptions used in computer software used by some courts to calculate child support comport with state law and should be made available to parties and counsel.

(e) The initial review by the Judicial Council shall be submitted to the Legislature and to the Department of Child Support Services on or before

December 31, 1993, and subsequent reviews shall occur at least every four years thereafter unless federal law requires a different interval.

(f) In developing its recommendations, the Judicial Council shall consult with a broad cross-section of groups involved in child support issues, including, but not limited to, the following:

(1) Custodial and noncustodial parents.

(2) Representatives of established women's rights and fathers' rights groups.

(3) Representatives of established organizations that advocate for the economic well-being of children.

(4) Members of the judiciary, district attorney's offices, the Attorney General's office, and the Department of Child Support Services.

(5) Certified family law specialists.

(6) Academicians specializing in family law.

(7) Persons representing low-income parents.

(8) Persons representing recipients of assistance under the CalWORKs program seeking child support services.

(9) Persons representing currently or formerly incarcerated parents.

(g) In developing its recommendations, the Judicial Council shall seek public comment and shall be guided by the legislative intent that children share in the standard of living of both of their parents. **Leg.H.** Added Stats 1993 ch 219 §138 (AB 1500). Amended Stats 2002 ch 927 §2.5 (AB 3032); Stats 2022 ch 573 §3 (AB 207), effective September 27, 2022.

Prior Law: Former §4054, similar to present Fam C §4057, was enacted Stats 1992 ch 162 §10, to become operative January 1, 1994, and repealed Stats 1993 ch 219 §137.

§ 4055. Formula for statewide uniform guideline for determining child support

(a) The statewide uniform guideline for determining child support orders is as follows: $CS = K[HN - (H\%)(TN)]$.

(b)(1) The components of the formula are as follows:

(A) CS = child support amount.

(B) K = amount of both parents' income to be allocated for child support as set forth in paragraph (3).

(C) HN = high earner's net monthly disposable income.

(D) $H\%$ = approximate percentage of time that the high earner has or will have primary physical responsibility for the children compared to the other parent. In cases in which parents have different time-sharing arrangements for different children, $H\%$ equals the average of the approximate percentages of time the high earner parent spends with each child.

(E) TN = total net monthly disposable income of both parties.

(2) To compute net disposable income, see Section 4059.

(3) K (amount of both parents' income allocated for child support) equals one plus $H\%$ (if $H\%$ is less than or equal to 50 percent) or two minus $H\%$ (if $H\%$ is greater than 50 percent) times the following fraction:

Total Net Disposable Income Per Month	K
$0-2,900	0.165 + tn/82,857
$2,901-5,000	0.131 + tn/42,149
$5,001-10,000	0.250
$10,001-15,000	0.10 + 1,499/tn
Over $15,000	0.12 + 1,200/tn

For example, if $H\%$ equals 20 percent and the total monthly net disposable income of the parents is $1,000, $K = (1 + 0.20) \times (0.165 + 1,000/82,857)$, or 0.21. If $H\%$ equals 80 percent and the total monthly net disposable income of the parents is $1,000, $K = (2 - 0.80) \times (0.165 + 1,000/82,857)$, or 0.21.

(4) For more than one child, multiply CS by:

2 children	1.6
3 children	2
4 children	2.3
5 children	2.5
6 children	2.625
7 children	2.75
8 children	2.813
9 children	2.844
10 children	2.86

(5) If the amount calculated under the formula results in a positive number, the higher earner shall pay that amount to the lower earner. If the amount calculated under the formula results in a negative number, the lower earner shall pay the absolute value of that amount to the higher earner.

(6) In any default proceeding where proof is by affidavit pursuant to Section 2336, or in any proceeding for child support in which a party fails to appear after being duly noticed, $H\%$ shall be set at zero in the formula if the noncustodial parent is the higher earner or at 100 if the custodial parent is the higher earner, where there is no evidence presented demonstrating the percentage of time that the noncustodial parent has primary physical responsibility for the children. $H\%$ shall not be set as described in paragraph (3) if the moving party in a default proceeding is the noncustodial parent or if the party who fails to appear after being duly noticed is the custodial parent. A statement by the party who is not in default as to the percentage of time that the noncustodial parent has primary physical responsibility for the children shall be deemed sufficient evidence.

(7) In all cases in which the net disposable income per month of the obligor is less than the amount of monthly gross income earned from full-time minimum wage, established by Section 1182.12 of the Labor Code, at 40 hours per week, 52 weeks per year, there is a rebuttable presumption that the obligor is entitled to a low-income adjustment. The presumption may be rebutted by evidence showing that the application of the lowest amount of child support permitted pursuant to this paragraph would be unjust and inappropriate in the particular case. In determining whether the presumption is rebutted, the court shall consider the principles provided in Section 4053, and the impact of the contemplated adjustment on the respective net incomes of the obligor and the obligee. The low-income adjustment shall reduce the child support amount otherwise determined under this section by an amount that is no greater than the amount calculated by multiplying the child support amount otherwise determined under this section by a fraction, the numerator of which is the amount of monthly gross income earned from full-time minimum wage, established by Section 1182.12 of the Labor Code, at 40 hours per week, 52 weeks per year, minus the obligor's net disposable income per month, and the denominator of which is the amount of monthly gross income earned from full-time minimum wage, established by Section 1182.12 of the Labor Code, at 40 hours per week, 52 weeks per year.

(8) Unless the court orders otherwise, the order for child support shall allocate the support amount so that the amount of support for the youngest child is the amount of support for one child, and the amount for the next youngest child is the difference between that amount and the amount for two children, with similar allocations for additional children. However, this paragraph does not apply to cases in which there are different time-sharing arrangements for different children or where the court determines that the allocation would be inappropriate in the particular case.

(c) If a court uses a computer to calculate the child support order and the obligor's income qualifies for a low-income adjustment, the computer program shall provide the range of the adjustment permitted by paragraph (7) of subdivision (b).

(d) This section shall be operative September 1, 2024. **Leg.H.** Added Stats 2023 ch 213 §3 (SB 343), effective January 1, 2024, operative September 1, 2024.

Prior Law Former Fam C §4055, relating to Formula for statewide uniform guideline for determining child support, was added Stats 1993 ch 219 §138 (AB 1500), amended Stats 1993 ch 1156 §1 (SB 541); Stats 1994 ch 906 §1.5 (AB 923); Stats 1998 ch 581 §15 (AB 2801); Stats 2003 ch 225 §1 (AB 1752), effective August 11, 2003; Stats 2012 ch 646 §1(AB 2393), effective January 1, 2013, repealed January 1, 2018; Stats 2013 ch 76 §61 (AB 383), effective January 1, 2014, repealed January 1, 2018; Stats 2017 ch 730 §1 (SB 469), effective January 1, 2018, repealed January 1, 2021; Stats 2020 ch 36 §28 (AB 3364), effective January 1, 2021; Stats 2023 ch 213 §2 (SB 343), effective January 1, 2024, inoperative September 1, 2024, repealed January 1, 2025.

§4056. Information in writing or on record

(a) To comply with federal law, the court shall state, in writing or on the record, the following information whenever the court is ordering an amount for support that differs from the statewide uniform guideline formula amount under this article:

(1) The amount of support that would have been ordered under the guideline formula.

(2) The reasons the amount of support ordered differs from the guideline formula amount.

(3) The reasons the amount of support ordered is consistent with the best interests of the children.

(b) At the request of any party, the court shall state in writing or on the record the following information used in determining the guideline amount under this article:

(1) The net monthly disposable income of each parent.

(2) The actual federal income tax filing status of each parent (for example, single, married, married filing separately, or head of household and number of exemptions).

(3) Deductions from gross income for each parent.

(4) The approximate percentage of time pursuant to paragraph (1) of subdivision (b) of Section 4055 that each parent has primary physical responsibility for the children compared to the other parent. **Leg.H.** Added Stats 1993 ch 219 §138 (AB 1500). Amended Stats 1993 ch 1156 §2 (SB 541).

Prior Law: Former §4056, similar to the present section, was enacted Stats 1992 ch 162 §10, to become operative January 1, 1994, and repealed Stats 1993 ch 219 §137.

§ 4057. Presumption of amount of award established by formula

(a) The amount of child support established by the formula provided in subdivision (a) of Section 4055 is presumed to be the correct amount of child support to be ordered.

(b) The presumption of subdivision (a) is a rebuttable presumption affecting the burden of proof and may be rebutted by admissible evidence showing that application of the formula would be unjust or inappropriate in the particular case, consistent with the principles set forth in Section 4053, because one or more of the following factors is found to be applicable by a preponderance of the evidence, and the court states in writing or on the record the information required in subdivision (a) of Section 4056:

(1) The parties have stipulated to a different amount of child support under subdivision (a) of Section 4065.

(2) The sale of the family residence is deferred pursuant to Chapter 8 (commencing with Section 3800) of Part 1 and the rental value of the family residence where the children reside exceeds the mortgage payments, homeowner's insurance, and property taxes. The amount of any adjustment pursuant to this paragraph shall not be greater than the excess amount.

(3) The parent being ordered to pay child support has an extraordinarily high income and the amount determined under the formula would exceed the needs of the children.

(4) A party is not contributing to the needs of the children at a level commensurate with that party's custodial time.

(5) A support obligor qualifies for the low-income adjustment pursuant to paragraph (7) of subdivision (b) of Section 4055 and the amount of child support established by the formula exceeds 50 percent of the support obligor's net disposable income as defined in Section 4059 after application of the low-income adjustment. The amount of any adjustment pursuant to this paragraph shall not be greater than the amount exceeding 50 percent of the support obligor's net disposable income.

(6) Application of the formula would be unjust or inappropriate due to special circumstances in the particular case. These special circumstances include, but are not limited to, the following:

(A) Cases in which the parents have different time-sharing arrangements for different children.

(B) Cases in which both parents have substantially equal time-sharing of the children and one parent has a much lower or higher percentage of income used for housing than the other parent.

(C) Cases in which the children have special medical or other needs that could require child support that would be greater than the formula amount.

(D) Cases in which a child is found to have more than two parents.

(c) If the court is made aware that a parent is subject to multiple court orders to pay child support arising from a different case or cases, the court may take steps to determine how to allocate the parent's income and support obligation appropriately across the cases. A court that continues a hearing based on a party's representation that it will file an appropriate request to modify support in a related case may issue a temporary support order.

(d) This section shall be operative September 1, 2024. **Leg.H.** Added Stats 2023 ch 213 §5 (SB 343), effective January 1, 2024, operative September 1, 2024.

Prior Law Former Fam C §4057, relating to Presumption of amount of award established by formula, was added Stats 1993 ch 219 §138 (AB 1500), amended Stats 1993 ch 935 §1 (SB 145), ch 1156 §3.5 (SB 541); Stats 2013 ch 564 §4 (SB 274), effective January 1, 2014; Stats 2023 ch 213 §4 (SB 343), effective January 1, 2024, inoperative September 1, 2024, repealed January 1, 2025.

§4057.5. Income of subsequent spouse or nonmarital partner

(a)(1) The income of the obligor parent's subsequent spouse or nonmarital partner shall not be considered when determining or modifying child support, except in an extraordinary case where excluding that income would lead to extreme and severe hardship to any child subject to the child support award, in which case the court shall also consider whether including that income would lead to extreme and severe hardship to any child supported by the obligor or by the obligor's subsequent spouse or nonmarital partner.

(2) The income of the obligee parent's subsequent spouse or nonmarital partner shall not be considered when determining or modifying child support, except in an extraordinary case where excluding that income would lead to extreme and severe hardship to any child subject to the child support award, in which case the court shall also consider whether including that income would lead to extreme and severe hardship to any child supported by the obligee or by the obligee's subsequent spouse or nonmarital partner.

(b) For purposes of this section, an extraordinary case may include a parent who voluntarily or intentionally quits work or reduces income, or who intentionally remains unemployed or underemployed and relies on a subsequent spouse's income.

(c) If any portion of the income of either parent's subsequent spouse or nonmarital partner is allowed to be considered pursuant to this section, discovery for the purposes of determining income shall be based on W2 and 1099 income tax forms, except where the court determines that application would be unjust or inappropriate.

(d) If any portion of the income of either parent's subsequent spouse or nonmarital partner is allowed to be considered pursuant to this section, the court shall allow a hardship deduction based on the minimum living expenses for one or more stepchildren of the party subject to the order.

(e) The enactment of this section constitutes cause to bring an action for modification of a child support order entered prior to the operative date of this section. **Leg.H.** Added Stats 1993 ch 935 §2 (SB 145). Amended Stats 1994 ch 1140 §1 (SB 279), ch 1269 §47.5 (AB 2208).

1994 Note: It is the intent of the Legislature that the restrictions in Section 4057.5 of the Family Code on considering the income of a subsequent spouse or nonmarital partner is not subject to court standardization, but is subject to judgment on a case-by-case basis. It is further the intent of the Legislature that Section 4057.5 of the Family Code prohibit the establishment or use of any formula or local court guideline devised to determine when consideration of a subsequent spouse or nonmarital partner's income is relevant. Stats 1994 ch 1140 §3, 1995 ch 91 §191.

§ 4058. Annual gross income of each parent

(a) The annual gross income of each parent means income from whatever source derived, except as specified in subdivision (c) and includes, but is not limited to, the following:

(1) Income such as commissions, salaries, royalties, wages, bonuses, rents, dividends, pensions, interest, trust income, annuities, workers' compensation benefits, unemployment insurance benefits, disability insurance benefits, social security benefits, severance pay, veterans benefits that are not based on need, military allowances for housing and food, and spousal support actually received from a person not a party to the proceeding to establish a child support order pursuant to this article.

(2) Income from the proprietorship of a business, such as gross receipts from the business reduced by expenditures required for the operation of the business.

(3) In the discretion of the court, employee benefits or self-employment benefits, taking into consideration the benefit to the employee, any corresponding reduction in living expenses, and other relevant facts.

(b)(1)(A) In a case when a parent's annual gross income is unknown, the court shall consider the earning capacity of the parent.

(B) In a case when a parent's annual gross income is known, the court may, in its discretion, consider the earning capacity of a parent in lieu of the parent's income, consistent with the best interests of the children, taking into consideration the overall welfare and developmental needs of the children, and the time that parent spends with the children.

(2) When determining the earning capacity of the parent pursuant to this subdivision, the court shall consider the specific circumstances of the parent, to the extent known. Those circumstances include, but are not limited to, evidence of the parent's assets, residence, employment and earnings history, job skills, educational attainment, literacy, age, health, criminal record and other employment barriers, and record of seeking work, as well as the local job market, the availability of employers willing to hire the parent, prevailing earnings levels in the local community, and other relevant background factors affecting the parent's ability to earn.

(3) Notwithstanding any other law, the incarceration or involuntary institutionalization of a parent shall not be treated as voluntary unemployment in establishing or modifying support orders regardless of the nature of the offense. "Incarcerated or involuntarily institutionalized" has the same meaning as subdivision (e) of Section 4007.5.

(c) Annual gross income does not include any income derived from child support payments actually received, and income derived from any public assistance program, eligibility for which is based on a determination of need. Child support received by a party for children from another relationship shall not be included as part of that party's gross or net income.

(d) This section shall be operative September 1, 2024. **Leg.H.** Added Stats 2023 ch 213 §7 (SB 343), effective January 1, 2024, operative September 1, 2024.

Prior Law Former Fam C §4058, relating to Annual gross income of each parent, was added Stats 1993 ch 219 §138 (AB 1500), amended Stats 2018 ch 178 §1 (AB 2780), effective January 1, 2019; Stats 2022 ch 573 §4(AB 207), effective September 27, 2022; Stats 2023 ch 213 §6 (SB 343), effective January 1, 2024, inoperative September 1, 2024, repealed January 1, 2025.

§4059. Annual net disposable income of each parent

The annual net disposable income of each parent shall be computed by deducting from the parent's annual gross income the actual amounts attributable to the following items or other items permitted under this article:

(a) The state and federal income tax liability resulting from the parties' taxable income. Federal and state income tax deductions shall bear an accurate relationship to the tax status of the parties (that is, single, married, married filing separately, or head of household) and number of dependents. State and federal income taxes shall be those actually payable (not necessarily current withholding) after considering appropriate filing status, all available exclusions, deductions, and credits. Unless the parties stipulate otherwise, the tax effects of spousal support shall not be considered in determining the net disposable income of the parties for determining child support, but shall be considered in determining spousal support consistent with Chapter 3 (commencing with Section 4330) of Part 3.

(b) Deductions attributed to the employee's contribution or the self-employed worker's contribution pursuant to the Federal Insurance Contributions Act (FICA), or an amount not to exceed that allowed under FICA for persons not subject to FICA, provided that the deducted amount is used to secure retirement or disability benefits for the parent.

(c) Deductions for mandatory union dues and retirement benefits, provided that they are required as a condition of employment.

(d) Deductions for health insurance or health plan premiums for the parent and for any children the parent has an obligation to support and deductions for state disability insurance premiums.

(e) Any child or spousal support actually being paid by the parent pursuant to a court order, to or for the benefit of a person who is not a subject of the order to be established by the court. In the absence of a court order, child support actually being paid, not to exceed the amount established by the guideline, for natural or adopted children of the parent not residing in that parent's home, who are not the subject of the order to be established by the court, and of whom the parent has a duty of support. Unless the parent proves payment of the support, a deduction shall not be allowed under this subdivision.

(f) Job-related expenses, if allowed by the court after consideration of whether the expenses are necessary, the benefit to the employee, and any other relevant facts.

(g) A deduction for hardship, as defined by Sections 4070 to 4073, inclusive, and applicable published appellate court decisions. The amount of the hardship shall not be deducted from the amount of child support, but shall be deducted from the income of the party to whom it applies. In applying any hardship under paragraph (2) of subdivision (a) of Section 4071, the court shall seek to provide equity between competing child support orders. The Judicial Council shall develop a formula for calculating the maximum hardship deduction and shall submit it to the Legislature for its consideration on or before July 1, 1995. **Leg.H.** Added Stats 1993 ch 219 §138 (AB 1500). Amended Stats 1994 ch 1056 §1 (AB 3258); Stats 2019 ch 115 §45 (AB 1817), effective January 1, 2020.

Prior Law: Former §4059, similar to the present section, was enacted Stats 1992 ch 162 §10, to become operative January 1, 1994, and repealed Stats 1993 ch 219 §137.

§4060. Monthly net disposable income

The monthly net disposable income shall be computed by dividing the annual net disposable income by 12. If the monthly net disposable income figure does not accurately reflect the actual or prospective earnings of the parties at the time the determination of support is made, the court may adjust the amount appropriately. **Leg.H.** Added Stats 1993 ch 219 §138 (AB 1500).

Prior Law: Former §4060, similar to the present section, was enacted Stats 1992 ch 162 §10, to become operative January 1, 1994, and repealed Stats 1993 ch 219 §137.

§ 4061. Additional child support

The amounts in Section 4062 shall be considered additional support for the children and shall be computed in accordance with the following:

(a) If there needs to be an apportionment of expenses pursuant to Section 4062, the expenses shall be divided in proportion to the parents' net incomes as adjusted pursuant to subdivisions (c) and (d), unless a party requests or the court finds on its own motion that expenses should be divided in a different manner.

(b)(1) The basic child support obligation shall first be computed using the formula set forth in subdivision (a) of Section 4055, as adjusted for any appropriate rebuttal factors in subdivision (b) of Section 4057.

(2) Any additional child support required for expenses pursuant to Section 4062 shall thereafter be ordered to be paid by the parents in proportion to their net disposable incomes as adjusted pursuant to subdivisions (c) and (d).

(c) In cases when spousal support is or has been ordered to be paid by one parent to the other, for purposes of allocating additional expenses pursuant to Section 4062, the gross income of the parent paying spousal support shall be decreased by the amount of the spousal support paid and the gross income of the parent receiving the spousal support shall be increased by the amount of the spousal support received for as long as the spousal support order is in effect and is paid.

(d) For purposes of computing the adjusted net disposable income of the parent paying child support for allocating any additional expenses pursuant to Section 4062, the net disposable income of the parent paying child support shall be reduced by the amount of any basic child support ordered to be paid under subdivision (a) of Section 4055. However, the net disposable income of the parent receiving child support shall not be increased by any amount of child support received.

(e) This section shall be operative September 1, 2024. **Leg.H.** Added Stats 2023 ch 213 §9 (SB 343), effective January 1, 2024, operative September 1, 2024.

Prior Law Former Fam C §4061, relating to additional child support, was added Stats 1993 ch 219 §138 (AB 1500), amended Stats 2010 ch 103 §2 (SB 580), effective January 1, 2011; Stats 2023 ch 213 §8, (SB 343), effective January 1, 2024, inoperative September 1, 2024, repealed January 1, 2025.

§ 4062. Allocation of additional expenses

(a) The court shall order the following as additional child support:

(1) Childcare costs, if those expenses are actually incurred, related to employment or to reasonably necessary education or training for employment skills, as described in Section 4063, unless those costs are specifically included in the guideline calculation itself.

(2) The reasonable uninsured health care costs for the children as provided in Section 4063.

(b) The court may order the following as additional child support:

(1) Costs related to the educational or other special needs of the children.

(2) Travel expenses for visitation.

(c) This section shall be operative September 1, 2024. **Leg.H.** Added Stats 2023 ch 213 §11 (SB 343), effective January 1, 2024, operative September 1, 2024.

Prior Law Former Fam C §4062, relating to Allocation of additional expenses, was added Stats 1993 ch 219 §138 (AB 1500), amended Stats 1994 ch 466 §1 (SB 1807); Stats 2023 ch 213 §10 (SB 343), effective January 1, 2024, inoperative September 1, 2024, repealed January 1, 2025.

§ 4063. Payment or reimbursement of costs

(a) When making an order pursuant to subdivision (a) of Section 4062, the court shall:

(1) Advise each parent, in writing or on the record, of the parent's rights and liabilities, including financial responsibilities.

(2) Include in its order the time period for a parent to reimburse the other parent for the reimbursing parent's share of the reasonable additional child support costs subject to the requirements of this section.

(b) Unless there has been an assignment of rights pursuant to Section 11477 of the Welfare and Institutions Code, when either parent accrues or pays costs pursuant to an order under this section, that parent shall provide the other parent with an itemized statement of the costs within a reasonable time, but not more than 90 days after accruing the costs. These costs shall then be paid as follows:

(1) If a parent has already paid all of these costs, that parent shall provide proof of payment and a request for reimbursement of that parent's court-ordered share to the other parent.

(2) If a parent has paid the parent's court-ordered share of the costs only, that parent shall provide proof of payment to the other parent, request the other parent to pay the remainder of the costs directly to the provider, and provide the reimbursing parent with any necessary information about how to make the payment to the provider.

(3) The other parent shall make the reimbursement or pay the remaining costs within the time period specified by the court, or, if no period is specified, within a reasonable time not to exceed 30 days from notification of the amount due, or according to any payment schedule set by the health care provider for either parent unless the parties agree in writing to another payment schedule or the court finds good cause for setting another payment schedule.

(4) If the reimbursing parent disputes a request for payment, that parent shall pay the requested amount and thereafter may seek judicial relief under this section and Section 290. If the reimbursing parent fails to pay the other parent as required by this subdivision, the other parent may seek judicial relief under this section and Section 290.

(c) Either parent may file a noticed motion to enforce an order issued pursuant to this section. In addition to the court's powers under Section 290, the court may award filing costs and reasonable attorney's fees if it finds that either party acted without reasonable cause regarding the party's obligations pursuant to this section.

(d) There is a rebuttable presumption that the costs actually paid for the uninsured health care needs of the children and for childcare that is for employment or reasonably necessary for education or training for employment skills are reasonable, except as provided in subdivision (e).

(e) Except as provided in subdivision (g):

(1) The health care insurance coverage, including, but not limited to, coverage for emergency treatment, provided by a parent pursuant to a court order, shall be the coverage to be utilized at all times, consistent with the requirements of that coverage, unless the other parent can show that the health care insurance coverage is inadequate to meet the child's needs.

(2) If either parent obtains health care insurance coverage in addition to that provided pursuant to the court order, that parent shall bear sole financial responsibility for the costs of that additional coverage and the costs of any care or treatment obtained pursuant thereto in excess of the costs that would have been incurred under the health care insurance coverage provided for in the court order.

(f) Except as provided in subdivision (g):

(1) If the health care insurance coverage provided by a parent pursuant to a court order designates a preferred health care provider, that preferred provider shall be used at all times, consistent with the terms and requirements of that coverage.

(2) If either parent uses a health care provider other than the preferred provider inconsistent with the terms and requirements of the court-ordered health care insurance coverage, the parent obtaining that care shall bear the sole responsibility for any nonreimbursable health care costs in excess of the costs that would have been incurred under the court-ordered health care insurance coverage had the preferred provider been used.

(g) When ruling on a motion made pursuant to this section, in order to ensure that the health care needs of the child and the need for childcare for employment or reasonably necessary for education or training for employment skills pursuant to this section are met, the court shall consider all relevant facts, on both of the following categories:

(1) With regard to health care, the court shall consider all relevant facts, including, but not limited to, the following:

(A) The geographic access and reasonable availability of necessary health care for the child that complies with the terms of the health care insurance coverage paid for by either parent pursuant to a court order. Health insurance shall be rebuttably presumed to be accessible if services to be provided are within 50 miles of the residence of the child subject to the support order. If the court determines that health insurance is not accessible, the court shall state the reason on the record.

(B) The necessity of emergency medical treatment that may have precluded the use of the health care insurance, or the preferred health care provider required under the insurance, provided by either parent pursuant to a court order.

(C) The special medical needs of the child.

(D) The reasonable inability of a parent to pay the full amount of reimbursement within a 30-day period and the resulting necessity for a court-ordered payment schedule.

(2) With regard to childcare costs for employment or that are reasonably necessary for education or training for employment skills, the court shall consider all relevant facts, including, but not limited to, the following:

(A) The nature and extent of job-related childcare needs, including, but not limited to, work schedule needs and the duration of education or training for employment skills.

(B) The necessity and reasonableness of the cost under the circumstances of the case.

(C) The special needs of the child.

(D) The reasonable inability of a parent to pay the full amount of reimbursement within a 30-day period and the resulting necessity for a court-ordered payment schedule.

(h) This section shall become operative September 1, 2024. **Leg.H.** Added Stats 2023 ch 213 §13 (SB 343), effective January 1, 2024, operative September 1, 2024.

Prior Law Former Fam C §4063, relating to payment or reimbursement of costs, was added Stats 1994 ch 466 §3 (SB 1807), amended Stats 2010 ch 103 §3 (SB 580), effective January 1, 2011; Stats 2019 ch 115 §46 (AB 1817), effective January 1, 2020; Stats 2023 ch 213 §12 (SB 343), effective January 1, 2024, inoperative September 1, 2024, repealed January 1, 2025.

§4064. Adjustment for seasonal or fluctuating income

The court may adjust the child support order as appropriate to accommodate seasonal or fluctuating income of either parent. **Leg.H.** Added Stats 1993 ch 219 §138 (AB 1500).

Prior Law: Former §4064, similar to present §4061, was enacted Stats 1992 ch 162 §10, to become operative January 1, 1994, and repealed Stats 1993 ch 219 §137.

§4065. Stipulated child support agreement

(a) Unless prohibited by applicable federal law, the parties may stipulate to a child support amount subject to approval of the court. However, the court shall not approve a stipulated agreement for child support below the guideline formula amount unless the parties declare all of the following:

(1) They are fully informed of their rights concerning child support.

(2) The order is being agreed to without coercion or duress.

(3) The agreement is in the best interests of the children involved.

(4) The needs of the children will be adequately met by the stipulated amount.

(5) The right to support has not been assigned to the county pursuant to Section 11477 of the Welfare and Institutions Code and no public assistance application is pending.

(b) The parties may, by stipulation, require the child support obligor to designate an account for the purpose of paying the child support obligation by electronic funds transfer pursuant to Section 4508.

(c) A stipulated agreement of child support is not valid unless the local child support agency has joined in the stipulation by signing it in any case in which the local child support agency is providing services pursuant to Section 17400. The local child support agency shall not stipulate to a child support order below the guideline amount if the children are receiving assistance under the CalWORKs program, if an application for public assistance is pending, or if the parent receiving support has not consented to the order.

(d) If the parties to a stipulated agreement stipulate to a child support order below the amount established by the statewide uniform guideline, no change of circumstances need be demonstrated to obtain a modification of the child support order to the applicable guideline level or above. **Leg.H.** Added Stats 1993 ch 219 §138 (AB 1500). Amended Stats 1993 ch 1156 §4 (SB 541); Stats 1999 ch 980 §8 (AB 1671); Stats 2000 ch 135 §59 (AB 2539), ch 808 §35 (AB 1358) (ch 808 prevails), effective September 28, 2000.

Prior Law: Former §4065, similar to present §4066, was enacted Stats 1992 ch 162 §10, to become operative January 1, 1994, and repealed Stats 1993 ch 219 §137.

§4066. Order or stipulation designating family support

Orders and stipulations otherwise in compliance with the statewide uniform guideline may designate as "family support" an unallocated total sum for support of the spouse and any children without specifically labeling all or any portion as "child support" as long as the amount is adjusted to reflect the effect of additional deductibility. The amount of the order shall be adjusted to maximize the tax benefits for both parents. **Leg.H.** Added Stats 1993 ch 219 §138 (AB 1500).

Prior Law: Former §4066, similar to present §4054, was enacted Stats 1992 ch 162 §10, to become operative January 1, 1994, and repealed, operative January 1, 1994, by the terms of §4067, Stats 1993 ch 219 §137.

§4067. Continuing review by Legislature

It is the intent of the Legislature that the statewide uniform guideline shall be reviewed by the Legislature at least every four years and shall be revised by the Legislature as appropriate to ensure that its application results in the determination of appropriate child support amounts. The review shall include consideration of changes required by applicable federal laws and regulations or recommended from time to time by the Judicial Council pursuant to Section 4054. **Leg.H.** Added Stats 1993 ch 219 §138 (AB 1500).

Prior Law: Former §4067, relating to duration of former Fam C §§4050, 4051, 4052, and 4066, was enacted Stats 1992 ch 162 §10, to become operative January 1, 1994, and repealed Stats 1993 ch 219 §137.

§4068. Judicial Council worksheets and forms

(a) The Judicial Council may develop the following:

(1) Model worksheets to assist parties in determining the approximate amount of child support due under the formula provided in subdivision (a) of Section 4055 and the approximate percentage of time each parent has primary physical responsibility for the children.

(2) A form to assist the courts in making the findings and orders required by this article.

(b) The Judicial Council, in consultation with representatives of the State Department of Social Services, the California Family Support Council, the Senate Judiciary Committee, the Assembly Judiciary Committee, the Family Law Section of the State Bar of California, a legal services organization providing representation on child support matters, a custodial parent group, and a noncustodial parent group, shall develop a simplified income and expense form for determining child support under the formula provided in subdivision (a) of Section 4055, by June 1, 1995. The Judicial Council, also in consultation with these groups, shall develop factors to use to determine when the simplified income and expense form may be used and when the standard income and expense form must be used. **Leg.H.** Added Stats 1993 ch 219 §138 (AB 1500). Amended Stats 1994 ch 415 §2 (SB 1715), ch 953 §1 (AB 2142).

Prior Law: Former §4068, similar to present §4067, was enacted Stats 1992 ch 162 §10, to become operative January 1, 1994, and repealed Stats 1993 ch 219 §137.

§4069. Establishment of guideline as change of circumstances

The establishment of the statewide uniform guideline constitutes a change of circumstances. **Leg.H.** Added Stats 1993 ch 219 §138 (AB 1500). Amended Stats 1993 ch 1156 §5 (SB 541).

§4070. Financial hardship deductions

If a parent is experiencing extreme financial hardship due to justifiable expenses resulting from the circumstances enumerated in Section 4071, on the request of a party, the court may allow the income deductions under Section 4059 that may be necessary to accommodate those circumstances. **Leg.H.** Added Stats 1993 ch 219 §138 (AB 1500).

§4071. Circumstances evidencing hardship

(a) Circumstances evidencing hardship include the following:

(1) Extraordinary health expenses for which the parent is financially responsible, and uninsured catastrophic losses.

(2) The minimum basic living expenses of either parent's natural or adopted children for whom the parent has the obligation to support from other marriages or relationships who reside with the parent. The court, on its own motion or on the request of a party, may allow these income deductions as necessary to accommodate these expenses after making the deductions allowable under paragraph (1).

(b) The maximum hardship deduction under paragraph (2) of subdivision (a) for each child who resides with the parent may be equal to, but shall not exceed, the support allocated each child subject to the order. For purposes of calculating this deduction, the amount of support per child established by the statewide uniform guideline shall be the total amount ordered divided by the number of children and not the amount established under paragraph (8) of subdivision (b) of Section 4055.

(c) The Judicial Council may develop tables in accordance with this section to reflect the maximum hardship deduction, taking into consideration the parent's net disposable income before the hardship deduction, the number of children for whom the deduction is being given, and the number of children for whom the support award is being made. **Leg.H.** Added Stats 1993 ch 219 §138 (AB 1500). Amended Stats 1993 ch 1156 §6 (SB 541).

§4071.5. [Section repealed 1999]

Leg.H. Added Stats 1994 ch 146 §42 (AB 3601). Repealed Stats 1999 ch 653 §9 (AB 380). The repealed section related to effect of Aid to Families with Dependent Children payments to either parent on determination of hardship.

§4072. Statement of reasons for and duration of hardship deductions

(a) If a deduction for hardship expenses is allowed, the court shall do both of the following:

(1) State the reasons supporting the deduction in writing or on the record.

(2) Document the amount of the deduction and the underlying facts and circumstances.

(b) Whenever possible, the court shall specify the duration of the deduction. **Leg.H.** Added Stats 1993 ch 219 §138 (AB 1500).

§4073. Consideration of legislative goals when ordering hardship deductions

The court shall be guided by the goals set forth in this article when considering whether or not to allow a financial hardship deduction, and, if allowed, when determining the amount of the deduction. **Leg.H.** Added Stats 1993 ch 219 §138 (AB 1500).

§4074. Application to family support awards

This article applies to an award for the support of children, including those awards designated as "family support," that contain provisions for the support of children as well as for the support of the spouse. **Leg.H.** Added Stats 1993 ch 219 §138 (AB 1500).

§4075. Treatment of spousal support payments under federal tax law

This article shall not be construed to affect the treatment of spousal support and separate maintenance payments pursuant to Section 71 of the Internal Revenue Code of 1954 (26 U.S.C. Sec. 71). **Leg.H.** Added Stats 1993 ch 219 §138 (AB 1500).

§4076. Modification of order to comply with statewide guideline; Two-step phase-in

(a) When the court is requested to modify a child support order issued prior to July 1, 1992, for the purpose of conforming to the statewide child support guideline, and it is not using its discretionary authority to depart from the guideline pursuant to paragraph (3), (4), or (5) of subdivision (b) of Section 4057, and the amount of child support to be ordered is the amount provided under the guideline formula in subdivision (a) of Section 4055, the court may, in its discretion, order a two-step phase-in of the formula amount of support to provide the obligor with time for transition to the full formula amount if all of the following are true:

(1) The period of the phase-in is carefully limited to the time necessary for the obligor to rearrange the obligor's financial obligations in order to meet the full formula amount of support.

(2) The obligor is immediately being ordered to pay not less than 30 percent of the amount of the child support increase, in addition to the amount of child support required under the prior order.

(3) The obligor has not unreasonably increased their financial obligations following notice of the motion for modification of support, has no arrearages owing, and has a history of good faith compliance with prior support orders.

(b) When the court grants a request for a phase-in pursuant to this section, the court shall state the following in writing:

(1) The specific reasons why (A) the immediate imposition of the full formula amount of support would place an extraordinary hardship on the obligor, and (B) this extraordinary hardship on the obligor would outweigh the hardship caused the supported children by the temporary phase-in of the full formula amount of support.

(2) The full guideline amount of support, the date and amount of each phase-in, and the date that the obligor must commence paying the full formula amount of support, which shall not be later than one year after the filing of the motion for modification of support.

(c) When the court orders a phase-in pursuant to this section, and the court thereafter determines that the obligor has violated the phase-in schedule or has intentionally lowered the income available for the payment of child support during the phase-in period, the court may order the immediate payment of the full formula amount of child support and the difference in the amount of support that would have been due without the phase-in and the amount of support due with the phase-in, in addition to any other penalties provided for by law. **Leg.H.** Added Stats 1993 ch 1156 §7.5 (SB 541). Amended Stats 2019 ch 115 §47 (AB 1817), effective January 1, 2020.

§ 4077. Department of Child Support Services and Judicial Council meeting; Report on federal child support regulations compliance

The Department of Child Support Services and the Judicial Council shall meet and confer, no later than November 21, 2022, and each entity shall submit its own report to the Assembly Committee on Budget and the Senate Committee on Budget and Fiscal Review and the Assembly and Senate Committees on Judiciary on what additional legislative changes are required to comply with the federal child support regulations revised in 81 Federal Register 93492 (Dec. 20, 2016), if any, which shall consider the most recent review of the statewide child support guideline completed pursuant to Section 4054, and identify any points of agreement and any difference of interpretation, perspective, or opinion between the entities regarding the legislative changes required. **Leg.H.** Added Stats 2022 ch 573 §5 (AB 207), effective September 27, 2022.

§4100. [Section repealed 1993]

Leg.H. Enacted Stats 1992 ch 162 §10 (AB 2650)Enacted Stats 1992 ch 162 §10 (AB 2650). Repealed Stats 1993 ch 219 §139 (AB 1500). The repealed section related to recovery for cost of support provided before filing proceeding.

§4101. [Section repealed 1993]

Leg.H. Enacted Stats 1992 ch 162 §10 (AB 2650)Enacted Stats 1992 ch 162 §10 (AB 2650). Repealed Stats 1993 ch 219 §139 (AB 1500). The repealed section related to recovery for cost of support provided before filing proceeding.

§4102. [Section repealed 1993]

Leg.H. Enacted Stats 1992 ch 162 §10 (AB 2650)Enacted Stats 1992 ch 162 §10 (AB 2650). Repealed Stats 1993 ch 219 §139 (AB 1500). The repealed section related to recovery for cost of support provided before filing proceeding.

§4103. [Section repealed 1993]

Leg.H. Enacted Stats 1992 ch 162 §10 (AB 2650)Enacted Stats 1992 ch 162 §10 (AB 2650). Repealed Stats 1993 ch 219 §139 (AB 1500). The repealed section related to recovery for cost of support provided before filing proceeding.

§4104. [Section repealed 1993]

Leg.H. Enacted Stats 1992 ch 162 §10 (AB 2650)Enacted Stats 1992 ch 162 §10 (AB 2650). Repealed Stats 1993 ch 219 §139 (AB 1500). The repealed section related to recovery for cost of support provided before filing proceeding.

§4105. [Section repealed 1993]

Leg.H. Enacted Stats 1992 ch 162 §10 (AB 2650)Enacted Stats 1992 ch 162 §10 (AB 2650). Repealed Stats 1993 ch 219 §139 (AB 1500). The repealed section related to recovery for cost of support provided before filing proceeding.

ARTICLE 3
Payment to Court Designated County Officer; Enforcement by District Attorney

Child support payable to parent receiving welfare. §4200.
Child support payable to person having custody of child. §4201.
Custodial and supporting parents reside in different counties. §4202.
County responsible for expenses and fees. §4203.
Child support payment where support is assigned to county, or where district attorney is requested to provide enforcement services. §4204.
Support obligor's right to attorney. §4205.

§4200. Child support payable to parent receiving welfare

In any proceeding where a court makes or has made an order requiring the payment of child support to a parent receiving welfare moneys for the maintenance of children for whom support may be ordered, the court shall do both of the following:

(a) Direct that the payments of support shall be made to the county officer designated by the court for that purpose. Once the State Disbursement Unit is implemented pursuant to Section 17309, all payments shall be directed to the State Disbursement Unit instead of the county officer designated by the court.

(b) Direct the local child support agency to appear on behalf of the welfare recipient in any proceeding to enforce the order. **Leg.H.** Enacted Stats 1992 ch 162 §10 (AB 2650), operative January 1, 1994. Amended Stats 1993 ch 219 §140 (AB 1500); Stats 1997 ch 599 §14 (AB 573); Stats 2000 ch 808 §36 (AB 1358), effective September 28, 2000; Stats 2003 ch 387 §2 (AB 739).

§4201. Child support payable to person having custody of child

In any proceeding where a court makes or has made an order requiring the payment of child support to the person having custody of a child for whom support may be ordered, the court may do either or both of the following:

(a) Direct that the payments shall be made to the county officer designated by the court for that purpose. Once the State Disbursement Unit is implemented pursuant to Section 17309, all payments shall be directed to the State Disbursement Unit instead of the county officer designated by the court.

(b) Direct the local child support agency to appear on behalf of the minor children in any proceeding to enforce the order. **Leg.H.** Enacted Stats 1992 ch 162 §10 (AB 2650), operative January 1, 1994. Amended Stats 1993 ch 219 §141 (AB 1500); Stats 1997 ch 599 §15 (AB 573); Stats 2000 ch 808 §37 (AB 1358), effective September 28, 2000; Stats 2003 ch 387 §3 (AB 739).

§4202. Custodial and supporting parents reside in different counties

(a) Notwithstanding any other provision of law, in a proceeding where the custodial parent resides in one county and the parent ordered to pay support resides in another county, the court may direct payment to be made to the county officer designated by the court for those purposes in the county of residence of the custodial parent, and may direct the local child support agency of either county to enforce the order.

(b) If the court directs the local child support agency of the county of residence of the noncustodial parent to enforce the order, the expenses of the local child support agency with respect to the enforcement is a charge upon the county of residence of the noncustodial parent. **Leg.H.** Enacted Stats 1992 ch 162 §10 (AB 2650), operative January 1, 1994. Amended Stats 2000 ch 808 §38 (AB 1358), effective September 28, 2000; Stats 2004 ch 339 §3 (AB 1704).

§4203. County responsible for expenses and fees

(a) Except as provided in Section 4202, expenses of the county officer designated by the court, and expenses of the local child support agency incurred in the enforcement of an order of the type described in Section 4200 or 4201, are a charge upon the county where the proceedings are pending.

(b) Fees for service of process in the enforcement of an order of the type described in Section 4200 or 4201 are a charge upon the county where the process is served. **Leg.H.** Enacted Stats 1992 ch 162 §10 (AB 2650), operative January 1, 1994. Amended Stats 2000 ch 808 §39 (AB 1358), effective September 28, 2000.

§4204. Child support payment where support is assigned to county, or where district attorney is requested to provide enforcement services

Notwithstanding any other law, in any proceeding where the court has made an order requiring the payment of child support and the child support is subsequently assigned to the county pursuant to Section 11477 of the Welfare and Institutions Code or the support obligor or obligee has requested a local child support agency to provide child support enforcement services pursuant to Section 17400, the local child support agency shall issue a notice directing that the payments shall be made to the local child support agency, another county office, or the State Disbursement Unit pursuant to Section 17309. Additionally, the local child support agency shall provide notice when it is no longer providing services under Part D of Title IV of the federal Social Security Act (42 U.S.C. Sec. 651 et seq.). The local child support agency shall serve the notice on both the support obligor and obligee in compliance with Section 1013 of the Code of Civil Procedure and file the notice with the court. **Leg.H.** Added Stats 1997 ch 599 §16 (AB 573). Amended Stats 2000 ch 808 §40 (AB 1358), effective September 28, 2000; Stats 2003 ch 387 §4 (AB 739); Stats 2022 ch 420 §15 (AB 2960), effective January 1, 2023.

§4205. Support obligor's right to attorney

Any notice from the local child support agency requesting a meeting with the support obligor for any purpose authorized under this part shall contain a statement advising the support obligor of the obligor's right to have an attorney present at the meeting. **Leg.H.** Added Stats 1998 ch 854 §2 (AB 960). Amended Stats 2000 ch 808 §41 (AB 1358), effective September 28, 2000; Stats 2019 ch 115 §48 (AB 1817), effective January 1, 2020.

ARTICLE 4
Child Support Commissioners

Findings. §4250.
Provision of sufficient commissioners; Commissioner as temporary judge; Duties; Notice to local child support agency. §4251.
Responsibility and qualifications. §4252.
Default. §4253.

§4250. Findings

(a) The Legislature finds and declares the following:

(1) Child and spousal support are serious legal obligations.

(2) The current system for obtaining, modifying, and enforcing child and spousal support orders is inadequate to meet the future needs of California's children due to burgeoning caseloads within local child support agencies and the growing number of parents who are representing themselves in family law actions.

(3) The success of California's child support enforcement program depends upon its ability to establish and enforce child support orders quickly and efficiently.

(4) There is a compelling state interest in creating an expedited process in the courts that is cost-effective and accessible to families, for establishing and enforcing child support orders in cases being enforced by the local child support agency.

(5) There is a compelling state interest in having a simple, speedy, conflict-reducing system, that is both cost-effective and accessible to families, for resolving all issues concerning children, including support, health insurance, custody, and visitation in family law cases that do not involve enforcement by the local child support agency.

(b) Therefore, it is the intent of the Legislature to: (1) provide for commissioners to hear child support cases being enforced by the local child support agency; (2) adopt uniform and simplified procedures for all child support cases; and (3) create an Office of the Family Law Facilitator in the courts to provide education, information, and assistance to parents with child support issues. **Leg.H.** Added Stats 1996 ch 957 §6 (AB 1058). Amended Stats 2000 ch 808 §42 (AB 1358), effective September 28, 2000.

§4251. Provision of sufficient commissioners; Commissioner as temporary judge; Duties; Notice to local child support agency

(a) Commencing July 1, 1997, each superior court shall provide sufficient commissioners to hear Title IV-D child support cases filed by the local child support agency. The number of child support commissioners required in each county shall be determined by the Judicial Council as prescribed by paragraph (3) of subdivision (b) of Section 4252. All actions or proceedings filed by the local child support agency in a support action or proceeding in which enforcement services are being provided pursuant to Section 17400, for an order to establish, modify, or enforce child or spousal support, including actions to establish parentage, shall be referred for hearing to a child support commissioner unless a child support commissioner is not available due to exceptional circumstances, as prescribed by the Judicial Council pursuant to paragraph (7) of subdivision (b) of Section 4252. All actions or proceedings filed by a party other than the local child support agency to modify or enforce a support order established by the local child support agency or for which enforcement services are being provided pursuant to Section 17400 shall be referred for hearing to a child support commissioner unless a child support commissioner is not available due to exceptional circumstances, as prescribed by the Judicial Council pursuant to paragraph (7) of subdivision (b) of Section 4252.

(b) The commissioner shall act as a temporary judge unless an objection is made by the local child support agency or any other party. The Judicial Council shall develop a notice that shall be included on all forms and pleadings used to initiate a child support action or proceeding that advises the parties of their right to review by a superior court judge and how to exercise that right. The parties shall also be advised by the court prior to the commencement of the hearing that the matter is being heard by a commissioner who shall act as a temporary judge unless any party objects to the commissioner acting as a temporary judge. While acting as a temporary judge, the commissioner shall receive no compensation other than compensation as a commissioner.

(c) If a party objects to the commissioner acting as a temporary judge, the commissioner may hear the matter and make findings of fact and a recommended order. Within 10 court days, a judge shall ratify the recommended order unless either party objects to the recommended order, or where a recommended order is in error. In both cases, the judge shall issue a temporary order and schedule a hearing de novo within 10 court days. A party may waive the right to the review hearing at any time.

(d) The commissioner, where appropriate, shall do any of the following:

(1) Review and determine ex parte applications for orders and writs.

(2) Take testimony.

(3) Establish a record, evaluate evidence, and make recommendations or decisions.

(4) Enter judgments or orders based upon voluntary acknowledgments of support liability and parentage and stipulated agreements respecting the amount of child support to be paid.

(5) Enter default orders and judgments pursuant to Section 4253.

(6) In actions in which parentage is at issue, order the mother, child, and alleged father to submit to genetic tests.

(e) The commissioner shall, upon application of a party, join issues concerning custody, visitation, and protective orders in the action filed by the local child support agency, subject to Section 17404. After joinder, the commissioner shall:

(1) Refer the parents for mediation of disputed custody or visitation issues pursuant to Section 3170.

(2) Accept stipulated agreements concerning custody, visitation, and protective orders and enter orders pursuant to the agreements.

(3) Refer contested issues of custody, visitation, and protective orders to a judge or to another commissioner for hearing. A child support commissioner may hear contested custody, visitation, and restraining order issues only if the court has adopted procedures to segregate the costs of hearing Title IV-D child support issues from the costs of hearing other issues pursuant to applicable federal requirements.

(f) The local child support agency shall be served notice by the moving party of any proceeding under this section in which support is at issue. An order for support that is entered without the local child support agency having received proper notice shall be voidable upon the motion of the local child support agency. **Leg.H.** Added Stats 1996 ch 957 §6 (AB 1058). Amended Stats 1998 ch 932 §32 (AB 1094); Stats 2000 ch 808 §43 (AB 1358), effective September 28, 2000; Stats 2019 ch 115 §49 (AB 1817), effective January 1, 2020.

§4252. Responsibility and qualifications

(a) The superior court shall appoint one or more subordinate judicial officers as child support commissioners to perform the duties specified in Section 4251. The child support commissioners' first priority always shall be to hear Title IV-D child support cases. The child support commissioners shall specialize in hearing child support cases, and their primary responsibility shall be to hear Title IV-D child support cases. Notwithstanding Section 71622 of the Government Code, the number of child support commissioner positions allotted to each court shall be determined by the Judicial Council in accordance with caseload standards developed pursuant to paragraph (3) of subdivision (b), subject to appropriations in the annual Budget Act.

(b) The Judicial Council shall do all of the following:

(1) Establish minimum qualifications for child support commissioners.

(2) Establish minimum educational and training requirements for child support commissioners and other court personnel that are assigned to Title IV–D child support cases. Training programs shall include both federal and state laws concerning child support and related issues.

(3) Establish caseload, case processing, and staffing standards for child support commissioners on or before April 1, 1997, which shall set forth the maximum number of cases that each child support commissioner can process. These standards shall be reviewed and, if appropriate, revised by the Judicial Council every two years.

(4) Adopt uniform rules of court and forms for use in Title IV-D child support cases.

(5) Offer technical assistance to courts regarding issues relating to implementation and operation of the child support commissioner system, including assistance related to funding, staffing, and the sharing of resources between courts.

(6) Establish procedures for the distribution of funding to the courts for child support commissioners, family law facilitators pursuant to Division 14 (commencing with Section 10000), and related allowable costs.

(7) Adopt rules that define the exceptional circumstances in which judges may hear Title IV-D child support matters as provided in subdivision (a) of Section 4251.

(8) Undertake other actions as appropriate to ensure the successful implementation and operation of child support commissioners in the counties.

(c) As used in this article, "Title IV-D" means Title IV-D of the federal Social Security Act (42 U.S.C. Sec. 651 et seq.). **Leg.H.** Added Stats 1996 ch 957 §6 (AB 1058). Amended Stats 1998 ch 249 §1 (AB 2498); Stats 1999 ch 83 §49 (SB 966); Stats 2002 ch 784 §105 (SB 1316).

§4253. Default

Notwithstanding any other provision of law, when hearing child support matters, a commissioner or referee may enter default orders if the defendant does not respond to notice or other process within the time prescribed to respond to that notice. **Leg.H.** Added Stats 1996 ch 957 §6 (AB 1058).

PART 3
SPOUSAL SUPPORT

Chapter 1. Duty to Support Spouse.
Chapter 2. Factors to be Considered in Ordering Support.
Chapter 3. Spousal Support Upon Dissolution or Legal Separation.
Chapter 4. Payment to Court-Designated Officer; Enforcement by District Attorney.
Chapter 5. Provision for Support After Death of Supporting Party.

CHAPTER 1
DUTY TO SUPPORT SPOUSE

Duty to support spouse. §4300.
Use of separate property for support while living together. §4301.
Spouse living separate by agreement. §4302.
Civil action to enforce spouse's right to support. §4303.

§4300. Duty to support spouse

Subject to this division, a person shall support the person's spouse. **Leg.H.** Enacted Stats 1992 ch 162 §10 (AB 2650), operative January 1, 1994.

§4301. Use of separate property for support while living together

Subject to Section 914, a person shall support the person's spouse while they are living together out of the separate property of the person when there is no community property or quasi-community property. **Leg.H.** Enacted Stats 1992 ch 162 §10 (AB 2650), operative January 1, 1994.

§4302. Spouse living separate by agreement

A person is not liable for support of the person's spouse when the person is living separate from the spouse by agreement unless support is stipulated in the agreement. **Leg.H.** Enacted Stats 1992 ch 162 §10 (AB 2650), operative January 1, 1994.

§4303. Civil action to enforce spouse's right to support

(a) The obligee spouse, or the county on behalf of the obligee spouse, may bring an action against the obligor spouse to enforce the duty of support.

(b) If the county furnishes support to a spouse, the county has the same right as the spouse to whom the support was furnished to secure reimbursement and obtain continuing support. The right of the county to reimbursement is subject to any limitation otherwise imposed by the law of this state.

(c) The court may order the obligor to pay the county reasonable attorney's fees and court costs in a proceeding brought by the county under this section. **Leg.H.** Enacted Stats 1992 ch 162 §10 (AB 2650), operative January 1, 1994.

CHAPTER 2
FACTORS TO BE CONSIDERED IN ORDERING SUPPORT

Circumstances to be considered in ordering spousal support. §4320.
Denial of support from separate property of other party. §4321.
No support order where no children and other party's separate estate sufficient. §4322.
Effect of cohabitation on support. §4323.
Conviction of attempted murder or solicitation of murder; Spousal support and insurance benefits. §4324.
Proceeding for dissolution of marriage considering criminal conviction for violent sexual felony; Applicability. §4324.5.
Rebuttable presumption for conviction of domestic violence. §4325.
Modification of spousal support based on termination of child support as change of circumstances; Filing of motion. §4326.

§4320. Circumstances to be considered in ordering spousal support

In ordering spousal support under this part, the court shall consider all of the following circumstances:

(a) The extent to which the earning capacity of each party is sufficient to maintain the standard of living established during the marriage, taking into account all of the following:

(1) The marketable skills of the supported party; the job market for those skills; the time and expenses required for the supported party to acquire the appropriate education or training to develop those skills; and the possible need for retraining or education to acquire other, more marketable skills or employment.

(2) The extent to which the supported party's present or future earning capacity is impaired by periods of unemployment that were incurred during the marriage to permit the supported party to devote time to domestic duties.

(b) The extent to which the supported party contributed to the attainment of an education, training, a career position, or a license by the supporting party.

(c) The ability of the supporting party to pay spousal support, taking into account the supporting party's earning capacity, earned and unearned income, assets, and standard of living.

(d) The needs of each party based on the standard of living established during the marriage.

(e) The obligations and assets, including the separate property, of each party.

(f) The duration of the marriage.

(g) The ability of the supported party to engage in gainful employment without unduly interfering with the interests of dependent children in the custody of the party.

(h) The age and health of the parties.

(i) All documented evidence of any history of domestic violence, as defined in Section 6211, between the parties or perpetrated by either party against either party's child, including, but not limited to, consideration of:

(1) A plea of nolo contendere.

(2) Emotional distress resulting from domestic violence perpetrated against the supported party by the supporting party.

(3) Any history of violence against the supporting party by the supported party.

(4) Issuance of a protective order after a hearing pursuant to Section 6340.

(5) A finding by a court during the pendency of a divorce, separation, or child custody proceeding, or other proceeding under Division 10 (commencing with Section 6200), that the spouse has committed domestic violence.

(j) The immediate and specific tax consequences to each party.

(k) The balance of the hardships to each party.

(*l*) The goal that the supported party shall be self-supporting within a reasonable period of time. Except in the case of a marriage of long duration as described in Section 4336, a "reasonable period of time" for purposes of this section generally shall be one-half the length of the marriage. However, nothing in this section is intended to limit the court's discretion to order support for a greater or lesser length of time, based on any of the other factors listed in this section, Section 4336, and the circumstances of the parties.

(m) The criminal conviction of an abusive spouse shall be considered in making a reduction or elimination of a spousal support award in accordance with Section 4324.5 or 4325.

(n) Any other factors the court determines are just and equitable. **Leg.H.** Enacted Stats 1992 ch 162 §10 (AB 2650), operative January 1, 1994. Amended Stats 1996 ch 1163 §1 (SB 509); Stats 1999 ch 284 §1 (AB 808), ch 846 §1.5 (AB 391); Stats 2001 ch 293 §2 (SB 1221); Stats 2012 ch 718 §1 (AB 1522), effective January 1, 2013; Stats 2013 ch 455 §1 (AB 681), effective January 1, 2014; Stats 2015 ch 137 §1 (SB 28), effective January 1, 2016; Stats 2018 ch 938 §1 (AB 929), effective January 1, 2019.

§4321. Denial of support from separate property of other party

In a judgment of dissolution of marriage or legal separation of the parties, the court may deny support to a party out of the separate property of the other party in any of the following circumstances:

(a) The party has separate property, or is earning the party's own livelihood, or there is community property or quasi-community property sufficient to give the party proper support.

(b) The custody of the children has been awarded to the other party, who is supporting them. **Leg.H.** Enacted Stats 1992 ch 162 §10 (AB

2650), operative January 1, 1994. Amended Stats 1993 ch 219 §141.5 (AB 1500).

§4322. No support order where no children and other party's separate estate sufficient

In an original or modification proceeding, where there are no children, and a party has or acquires a separate estate, including income from employment, sufficient for the party's proper support, no support shall be ordered or continued against the other party. **Leg.H.** Enacted Stats 1992 ch 162 §10 (AB 2650), operative January 1, 1994.

§4323. Effect of cohabitation on support

(a)(1) Except as otherwise agreed to by the parties in writing, there is a rebuttable presumption, affecting the burden of proof, of decreased need for spousal support if the supported party is cohabiting with a nonmarital partner. Upon a determination that circumstances have changed, the court may modify or terminate the spousal support as provided for in Chapter 6 (commencing with Section 3650) of Part 1.

(2) Holding oneself out to be the spouse of the person with whom one is cohabiting is not necessary to constitute cohabitation as the term is used in this subdivision.

(b) The income of a supporting spouse's subsequent spouse or nonmarital partner shall not be considered when determining or modifying spousal support.

(c) Nothing in this section precludes later modification or termination of spousal support on proof of change of circumstances. **Leg.H.** Enacted Stats 1992 ch 162 §10 (AB 2650), operative January 1, 1994. Amended Stats 1993 ch 935 §3 (SB 145); Stats 2014 ch 82 §36 (SB 1306), effective January 1, 2015.

§4324. Conviction of attempted murder or solicitation of murder; Spousal support and insurance benefits

In addition to any other remedy authorized by law, when a spouse is convicted of attempting to murder the other spouse, as punishable pursuant to subdivision (a) of Section 664 of the Penal Code, or of soliciting the murder of the other spouse, as punishable pursuant to subdivision (b) of Section 653f of the Penal Code, the injured spouse shall be entitled to a prohibition of any temporary or permanent award for spousal support or medical, life, or other insurance benefits or payments from the injured spouse to the other spouse.

As used in this section, "injured spouse" means the spouse who has been the subject of the attempted murder or the solicitation of murder for which the other spouse was convicted, whether or not actual physical injury occurred. **Leg.H.** Added Stats 1995 ch 364 §3 (AB 16). Amended Stats 2010 ch 65 §2 (AB 2674), effective January 1, 2011.

§4324.5. Proceeding for dissolution of marriage considering criminal conviction for violent sexual felony; Applicability

(a) In any proceeding for dissolution of marriage where there is a criminal conviction for a violent sexual felony or a domestic violence felony perpetrated by one spouse against the other spouse and the petition for dissolution is filed before five years following the conviction and any time served in custody, on probation, or on parole, the following shall apply:

(1) An award of spousal support to the convicted spouse from the injured spouse is prohibited.

(2) If economic circumstances warrant, the court shall order the attorney's fees and costs incurred by the parties to be paid from the community assets. The injured spouse shall not be required to pay any attorney's fees of the convicted spouse out of the injured spouse's separate property.

(3) At the request of the injured spouse, the date of separation, as defined in Section 70, shall be the date of the incident giving rise to the conviction, or earlier, if the court finds circumstances that justify an earlier date.

(4) The injured spouse shall be entitled to 100 percent of the community property interest in the retirement and pension benefits of the injured spouse.

(b) As used in this section, the following definitions apply:

(1) "Domestic violence felony" means a felony offense for an act of abuse, as described in Section 6203, perpetrated by one spouse against the other spouse.

(2) "Injured spouse" means the spouse who has been the subject of the violent sexual felony or domestic violence felony for which the other spouse was convicted.

(3) "Violent sexual felony" means those offenses described in paragraphs (3), (4), (5), (11), and (18) of subdivision (c) of Section 667.5 of the Penal Code.

(c) If a convicted spouse presents documented evidence of the convicted spouse's history as a victim of a violent sexual offense, as described in paragraphs (3), (4), (5), (11), and (18) of subdivision (c) of Section 667.5 of the Penal Code, or domestic violence, as defined in Section 6211, perpetrated by the other spouse, the court may determine, based on the facts of the particular case, that one or more of paragraphs (1) to (4), inclusive, of subdivision (a) do not apply.

(d) The changes made to this section by the bill that added this subdivision shall only apply to convictions that occur on or after January 1, 2019. **Leg.H.** Added Stats 2012 ch 718 §2 (AB 1522), effective January 1, 2013. Amended Stats 2018 ch 850 §1 (SB 1129), effective January 1, 2019.

§4325. Rebuttable presumption for conviction of domestic violence

(a) In a proceeding for dissolution of marriage where there is a criminal conviction for a domestic violence misdemeanor or a criminal conviction for a misdemeanor that results in a term of probation pursuant to Section 1203.097 of the Penal Code perpetrated by one spouse against the other spouse entered by the court within five years prior to the filing of the dissolution proceeding or during the course of the dissolution proceeding, there shall be a rebuttable presumption that the following shall apply:

(1) An award of spousal support to the convicted spouse from the injured spouse is prohibited.

(2) If economic circumstances warrant, the court shall order the attorney's fees and costs incurred by the parties to be paid from the community assets. The injured spouse shall not be required to pay any attorney's fees of the convicted spouse out of the injured spouse's separate property.

(3) At the request of the injured spouse, the date of separation, as defined in Section 70, shall be the date of the incident giving rise to the conviction, or earlier, if the court finds circumstances that justify an earlier date.

(b) The court may consider documented evidence of a convicted spouse's history as a victim of domestic violence, as defined in Section 6211, perpetrated by the other spouse, or any other factors the court deems just and equitable, as conditions for rebutting this presumption.

(c) The rebuttable presumption created in this section may be rebutted by a preponderance of the evidence.

(d) The court may determine, based on the facts of a particular case, that the injured spouse is entitled to up to 100 percent of the community property interest in the injured spouse's retirement and pension benefits. In determining whether and how to apportion the community property interest in the retirement and pension benefits of the injured spouse, the court shall consider all of the following factors:

(1) The misdemeanor domestic violence conviction, as well as documented evidence of other instances of domestic violence, as defined in Section 6211, between the parties or perpetrated by either party against either party's child, including, but not limited to, consideration of emotional distress resulting from domestic violence. The court shall also consider documented evidence of a convicted spouse's history as a victim of domestic violence, as defined in Section 6211, perpetrated by the other spouse.

(2) The duration of the marriage and when, based on documented evidence, incidents of domestic violence, as defined in Section 6211, occurred.

(3) The extent to which the convicted spouse's present or future earning capacity is impaired by periods of unemployment that were incurred during the marriage to permit the convicted spouse to devote time to domestic duties.

(4) The extent to which the convicted spouse contributed to the attainment of an education, training, a career position, or a license by the injured spouse.

(5) The balance of the hardships to each party.

(6) Any other factors the court determines are just and equitable.

(e) As used in this section, the following definitions apply:

(1) "Domestic violence misdemeanor" means a misdemeanor offense for an act of abuse, as described in paragraphs (1) to (3), inclusive, of

subdivision (a) of Section 6203, perpetrated by one spouse against the other spouse.

(2) "Injured spouse" means the spouse who has been the subject of the domestic violence misdemeanor for which the other spouse was convicted.

(f) The changes made to this section by the bill that added this subdivision shall only apply to convictions that occur on or after January 1, 2019. **Leg.H.** Added Stats 2001 ch 293 §3 (SB 1221). Amended Stats 2018 ch 850 §2 (SB 1129), effective January 1, 2019; Stats 2019 ch 115 §50 (AB 1817), effective January 1, 2020.

§4326. Modification of spousal support based on termination of child support as change of circumstances; Filing of motion

(a) Except as provided in subdivision (d), in a proceeding in which a spousal support order exists or in which the court has retained jurisdiction over a spousal support order, if a companion child support order is in effect, the termination of child support pursuant to subdivision (a) of Section 3901 constitutes a change of circumstances that may be the basis for a request by either party for modification of spousal support.

(b) A motion to modify spousal support based on the change of circumstances described in subdivision (a) shall be filed by either party no later than six months from the date the child support order terminates.

(c) If a motion to modify a spousal support order pursuant to subdivision (a) is filed, either party may request the appointment of a vocational training counselor pursuant to Section 4331.

(d) Notwithstanding subdivision (a), termination of the child support order does not constitute a change of circumstances under subdivision (a) in any of the following circumstances:

(1) The child and spousal support orders are the result of a marital settlement agreement or judgment and the marital settlement agreement or judgment contains a provision regarding what is to occur when the child support order terminates.

(2) The child and spousal support orders are the result of a marital settlement agreement or judgment, which provides that the spousal support order is nonmodifiable or that spousal support is waived and the court's jurisdiction over spousal support has been terminated.

(3) The court's jurisdiction over spousal support was previously terminated.

(e) Notwithstanding subdivision (b), a party whose six-month deadline to file expired between January 1, 2014, and September 30, 2014, may file a motion pursuant to this section until December 31, 2014. **Leg.H.** Added Stats 2014 ch 202 §1 (AB 414), effective August 15, 2014.

Prior Law: Former Fam C §4326, similar to the present section, was added Stats 2007 ch 247 §1, effective January 1, 2008, repealed January 1, 2011, amended Stats 2010 ch 297 §1, effective January 1, 2011, repealed January 1, 2014, Stats 2011 ch 296 §91, effective January 1, 2012, and repealed January 1, 2014, by its own terms.

Former Sections: Former Fam C §4326, similar to the present section, was added Stats 2007 ch 247 §1 and repealed operative January 1, 2014, by its own provisions.

CHAPTER 3
SPOUSAL SUPPORT UPON DISSOLUTION OR LEGAL SEPARATION

Order for spousal support in dissolution or legal separation proceeding. §4330.
Examination by vocational training counselor. §4331.
Court findings concerning circumstances. §4332.
Retroactivity of order. §4333.
Support for contingent period of time. §4334.
Support for fixed period of time. §4335.
Retention of jurisdiction. §4336.
Effect of death or remarriage. §4337.
Order of resort to property for payment of spousal support. §4338.
Security for payment. §4339.

§4330. Order for spousal support in dissolution or legal separation proceeding

(a) In a judgment of dissolution of marriage or legal separation of the parties, the court may order a party to pay for the support of the other party an amount, for a period of time, that the court determines is just and reasonable, based on the standard of living established during the marriage, taking into consideration the circumstances as provided in Chapter 2 (commencing with Section 4320).

(b) When making an order for spousal support, the court may advise the recipient of support that the recipient should make reasonable efforts to assist in providing for their support needs, taking into account the particular circumstances considered by the court pursuant to Section 4320, unless, in the case of a marriage of long duration as provided for in Section 4336, the court decides this warning is inadvisable. **Leg.H.** Enacted Stats 1992 ch 162 §10 (AB 2650), operative January 1, 1994. Amended Stats 1996 ch 1163 §2 (SB 509); Stats 1999 ch 846 §2 (AB 391); Stats 2019 ch 115 §51 (AB 1817), effective January 1, 2020.

§4331. Examination by vocational training counselor

(a) In a proceeding for dissolution of marriage or for legal separation of the parties, the court may order a party to submit to an examination by a vocational training counselor. The examination shall include an assessment of the party's ability to obtain employment based upon the party's age, health, education, marketable skills, employment history, and the current availability of employment opportunities. The focus of the examination shall be on an assessment of the party's ability to obtain employment that would allow the party to maintain their marital standard of living.

(b) The order may be made only on motion, for good cause, and on notice to the party to be examined and to all parties. The order shall specify the time, place, manner, conditions, scope of the examination, and the person or persons by whom it is to be made.

(c) A party who does not comply with an order under this section is subject to the same consequences provided for failure to comply with an examination ordered pursuant to Chapter 15 (commencing with Section 2032.010) of Title 4 of Part 4 of the Code of Civil Procedure.

(d) "Vocational training counselor" for the purpose of this section means an individual with sufficient knowledge, skill, experience, training, or education in interviewing, administering, and interpreting tests for analysis of marketable skills, formulating career goals, planning courses of training and study, and assessing the job market, to qualify as an expert in vocational training under Section 720 of the Evidence Code.

(e) A vocational training counselor shall have at least the following qualifications:

(1) A master's degree in the behavioral sciences, or other postgraduate degree that the court finds provides sufficient training to perform a vocational evaluation.

(2) Qualification to administer and interpret inventories for assessing career potential.

(3) Demonstrated ability in interviewing clients and assessing marketable skills with an understanding of age constraints, physical and mental health, previous education and experience, and time and geographic mobility constraints.

(4) Knowledge of current employment conditions, job market, and wages in the indicated geographic area.

(5) Knowledge of education and training programs in the area with costs and time plans for these programs.

(f) The court may order the supporting spouse to pay, in addition to spousal support, the necessary expenses and costs of the counseling, retraining, or education. **Leg.H.** Enacted Stats 1992 ch 162 §10 (AB 2650), operative January 1, 1994. Amended Stats 2004 ch 182 §35 (AB 3081), operative July 1, 2005; Stats 2018 ch 178 §2 (AB 2780), effective January 1, 2019; Stats 2019 ch 115 §52 (AB 1817), effective January 1, 2020.

§4332. Court findings concerning circumstances

In a proceeding for dissolution of marriage or for legal separation of the parties, the court shall make specific factual findings with respect to the standard of living during the marriage, and, at the request of either party, the court shall make appropriate factual determinations with respect to other circumstances. **Leg.H.** Enacted Stats 1992 ch 162 §10 (AB 2650), operative January 1, 1994.

§4333. Retroactivity of order

An order for spousal support in a proceeding for dissolution of marriage or for legal separation of the parties may be made retroactive to the date of filing the notice of motion or order to show cause, or to any subsequent date. **Leg.H.** Enacted Stats 1992 ch 162 §10 (AB 2650), operative January 1, 1994.

§4334. Support for contingent period of time

(a) If a court orders spousal support for a contingent period of time, the obligation of the supporting party terminates on the happening of the contingency. The court may, in the order, order the supported party to notify the supporting party, or the supporting party's attorney of record, of the happening of the contingency.

(b) If the supported party fails to notify the supporting party, or the attorney of record of the supporting party, of the happening of the contingency and continues to accept spousal support payments, the supported party shall refund payments received that accrued after the happening of the contingency, except that the overpayments shall first be applied to spousal support payments that are then in default. **Leg.H.** Enacted Stats 1992 ch 162 §10 (AB 2650), operative January 1, 1994.

§4335. Support for fixed period of time

An order for spousal support terminates at the end of the period provided in the order and shall not be extended unless the court retains jurisdiction in the order or under Section 4336. **Leg.H.** Enacted Stats 1992 ch 162 §10 (AB 2650), operative January 1, 1994.

§4336. Retention of jurisdiction

(a) Except on written agreement of the parties to the contrary or a court order terminating spousal support, the court retains jurisdiction indefinitely in a proceeding for dissolution of marriage or for legal separation of the parties where the marriage is of long duration.

(b) For the purpose of retaining jurisdiction, there is a presumption affecting the burden of producing evidence that a marriage of 10 years or more, from the date of marriage to the date of separation, is a marriage of long duration. However, the court may consider periods of separation during the marriage in determining whether the marriage is in fact of long duration. Nothing in this subdivision precludes a court from determining that a marriage of less than 10 years is a marriage of long duration.

(c) Nothing in this section limits the court's discretion to terminate spousal support in later proceedings on a showing of changed circumstances.

(d) This section applies to the following:

(1) A proceeding filed on or after January 1, 1988.

(2) A proceeding pending on January 1, 1988, in which the court has not entered a permanent spousal support order or in which the court order is subject to modification. **Leg.H.** Enacted Stats 1992 ch 162 §10 (AB 2650), operative January 1, 1994.

§4337. Effect of death or remarriage

Except as otherwise agreed by the parties in writing, the obligation of a party under an order for the support of the other party terminates upon the death of either party or the remarriage of the other party. **Leg.H.** Enacted Stats 1992 ch 162 §10 (AB 2650), operative January 1, 1994.

§4338. Order of resort to property for payment of spousal support

In the enforcement of an order for spousal support, the court shall resort to the property described below in the order indicated:

(a) The earnings, income, or accumulations of either spouse after the date of separation, as defined in Section 70, which would have been community property if the spouse had not been separated from the other spouse.

(b) The community property.

(c) The quasi-community property.

(d) The other separate property of the party required to make the support payments. **Leg.H.** Enacted Stats 1992 ch 162 §10 (AB 2650), operative January 1, 1994. Amended Stats 2016 ch 114 §5 (SB 1255), effective January 1, 2017.

§4339. Security for payment

The court may order the supporting party to give reasonable security for payment of spousal support. **Leg.H.** Enacted Stats 1992 ch 162 §10 (AB 2650), operative January 1, 1994.

CHAPTER 4
PAYMENT TO COURT-DESIGNATED OFFICER; ENFORCEMENT BY DISTRICT ATTORNEY

Payment of support payments to designated county officer. §4350.
Referral of enforcement to local child support agency. §4351.
County responsible for expenses and fees. §4352.

§4350. Payment of support payments to designated county officer

In any proceeding where a court makes or has made an order requiring the payment of spousal support, the court may direct that payment shall be made to the county officer designated by the court for that purpose. The court may include in its order made pursuant to this section any service charge imposed under the authority of Section 279 of the Welfare and Institutions Code. **Leg.H.** Enacted Stats 1992 ch 162 §10 (AB 2650), operative January 1, 1994.

§4351. Referral of enforcement to local child support agency

(a) In a proceeding where the court has entered an order pursuant to Section 4350, the court may also refer the matter of enforcement of the spousal support order to the local child support agency. The local child support agency may bring those enforcement proceedings it determines to be appropriate.

(b) Notwithstanding subdivision (a), when the local child support agency is required to appear on behalf of a welfare recipient in a proceeding to enforce an order requiring payment of child support, the local child support agency shall also enforce any order requiring payment to the welfare recipient of spousal support that is in arrears.

(c) This section does not prohibit the district attorney or the local child support agency from bringing an action or initiating process to enforce or punish the failure to obey an order for spousal support under any law that empowers the district attorney or the local child support agency to bring an action or initiate a process, whether or not there has been a referral by the court pursuant to this chapter.

(d) Any notice from the district attorney or the local child support agency requesting a meeting with the support obligor for any purpose authorized under this part shall contain a statement advising the support obligor of the obligor's right to have an attorney present at the meeting. **Leg.H.** Enacted Stats 1992 ch 162 §10 (AB 2650), operative January 1, 1994. Amended Stats 1998 ch 854 §3 (AB 960); Stats 1999 ch 83 §50 (SB 966); Stats 2000 ch 808 §44 (AB 1358), effective September 28, 2000; Stats 2019 ch 115 §53 (AB 1817), effective January 1, 2020.

§4352. County responsible for expenses and fees

(a) Insofar as expenses of the county officer designated by the court and expenses of the local child support agency incurred in the enforcement of an order referred by the court under this chapter exceed any service charge imposed under Section 279 of the Welfare and Institutions Code, the expenses are a charge upon the county where the proceedings are pending.

(b) Fees for service of process in the enforcement of an order referred by the court under this chapter are a charge upon the county where the process is served. **Leg.H.** Enacted Stats 1992 ch 162 §10 (AB 2650), operative January 1, 1994. Amended Stats 2000 ch 808 §45 (AB 1358), effective September 28, 2000.

CHAPTER 5
PROVISION FOR SUPPORT AFTER DEATH OF SUPPORTING PARTY

Annuity, life insurance, or trust for support. §4360.

§4360. Annuity, life insurance, or trust for support

(a) For the purpose of Section 4320, where it is just and reasonable in view of the circumstances of the parties, the court, in determining the needs of a supported spouse, may include an amount sufficient to purchase an annuity for the supported spouse or to maintain insurance for the benefit of the supported spouse on the life of the spouse required to make the payment of support, or may require the spouse required to make the payment of support to establish a trust to provide for the support of the supported spouse, so that the supported spouse will not be left without means of support in the event that the spousal support is terminated by the death of the party required to make the payment of support.

(b) Except as otherwise agreed to by the parties in writing, an order made under this section may be modified or terminated at the discretion of the court at any time before the death of the party required to make the payment of support. **Leg.H.** Enacted Stats 1992 ch 162 §10 (AB 2650), operative January 1, 1994.

PART 4
SUPPORT OF PARENTS

Chapter 1. General Provisions.
Chapter 2. Relief From Duty to Support Parent Who Abandoned Child.

CHAPTER 1
GENERAL PROVISIONS

Duty to support parent in need. §4400.
Promise to pay for previous support. §4401.
Duty cumulative. §4402.
Civil action to enforce parent's right to support. §4403.
Determination of amount of support. §4404.
Modification or termination of order. §4405.

§4400. Duty to support parent in need

Except as otherwise provided by law, an adult child shall, to the extent of the adult child's ability, support a parent who is in need and unable to self-maintain by work. **Leg.H.** Enacted Stats 1992 ch 162 §10 (AB 2650), operative January 1, 1994. Amended Stats 2019 ch 115 §54 (AB 1817), effective January 1, 2020.

§4401. Promise to pay for previous support

The promise of an adult child to pay for necessaries previously furnished to a parent described in Section 4400 is binding. **Leg.H.** Enacted Stats 1992 ch 162 §10 (AB 2650), operative January 1, 1994.

§4402. Duty cumulative

The duty of support under this part is cumulative and not in substitution for any other duty. **Leg.H.** Enacted Stats 1992 ch 162 §10 (AB 2650), operative January 1, 1994.

§4403. Civil action to enforce parent's right to support

(a) Subject to subdivision (b):
(1) A parent, or the county on behalf of the parent, may bring an action against the child to enforce the duty of support under this part.
(2) If the county furnishes support to a parent, the county has the same right as the parent to whom the support was furnished to secure reimbursement and obtain continuing support.
(b) The right of the county to proceed on behalf of the parent or to obtain reimbursement is subject to any limitation otherwise imposed by the law of this state.
(c) The court may order the child to pay the county reasonable attorney's fees and court costs in a proceeding by the county under this section. **Leg.H.** Enacted Stats 1992 ch 162 §10 (AB 2650), operative January 1, 1994.

§4404. Determination of amount of support

In determining the amount to be ordered for support, the court shall consider the following circumstances of each party:
(a) Earning capacity and needs.
(b) Obligations and assets.
(c) Age and health.
(d) Standard of living.
(e) Other factors the court deems just and equitable. **Leg.H.** Enacted Stats 1992 ch 162 §10 (AB 2650), operative January 1, 1994.

§4405. Modification or termination of order

The court retains jurisdiction to modify or terminate an order for support where justice requires. **Leg.H.** Enacted Stats 1992 ch 162 §10 (AB 2650), operative January 1, 1994.

CHAPTER 2
RELIEF FROM DUTY TO SUPPORT PARENT WHO ABANDONED CHILD

Proceeding to obtain relief from obligation to support parent. §4410.
Requirements for order granting relief. §4411.
Citation and notice of hearing. §4412.
Notice to district attorney or county counsel. §4413.
Hearing and order. §4414.

§4410. Proceeding to obtain relief from obligation to support parent

An adult child may file a petition in the county where a parent of the child resides requesting that the court make an order freeing the petitioner from the obligation otherwise imposed by law to support the parent. If the parent does not reside in this state, the petition shall be filed in the county where the adult child resides. **Leg.H.** Enacted Stats 1992 ch 162 §10 (AB 2650), operative January 1, 1994.

§4411. Requirements for order granting relief

The court shall make the order requested pursuant to Section 4410 only if the petition alleges and the court finds all of the following:
(a) The child was abandoned by the parent when the child was a minor.
(b) The abandonment continued for a period of two or more years before the time the child attained the age of 18 years.
(c) During the period of abandonment the parent was physically and mentally able to provide support for the child. **Leg.H.** Enacted Stats 1992 ch 162 §10 (AB 2650), operative January 1, 1994.

§4412. Citation and notice of hearing

On the filing of a petition under this chapter, the clerk shall set the matter for hearing by the court and shall issue a citation, stating the time and place of the hearing, directed to the parent and to the parent's conservator, if any, or, if the parent is deceased, the personal representative of the parent's estate. At least five days before the date of the hearing, the citation and a copy of the petition shall be personally served on each person to whom it is directed, in the same manner as provided by law for the service of summons. **Leg.H.** Enacted Stats 1992 ch 162 §10 (AB 2650), operative January 1, 1994.

§4413. Notice to district attorney or county counsel

If the parent is a resident of this state, the court does not have jurisdiction to make an order under this chapter until 30 days after the county counsel, or the district attorney in a county not having a county counsel, of the county in which the parent resides has been served with notice of the pendency of the proceeding. **Leg.H.** Enacted Stats 1992 ch 162 §10 (AB 2650), operative January 1, 1994.

§4414. Hearing and order

(a) If, upon hearing, the court determines that the requirements of Section 4411 are satisfied, the court shall make an order that the petitioner is relieved from the obligation otherwise imposed by law to support the parent.
(b) An order under this section also releases the petitioner with respect to any state law under which a child is required to do any of the following:
(1) Pay for the support, care, maintenance, and the like of a parent.
(2) Reimburse the state or a local public agency for furnishing the support, care, maintenance, or the like of a parent. **Leg.H.** Enacted Stats 1992 ch 162 §10 (AB 2650), operative January 1, 1994.

PART 5
ENFORCEMENT OF SUPPORT ORDERS

Chapter 1. General Provisions.
Chapter 2. Deposit of Money to Secure Future Child Support Payments.
Chapter 3. Deposit of Assets to Secure Future Child Support Payments.
Chapter 4. Child Support Delinquency Reporting.
Chapter 5. Civil Penalty for Child Support Delinquency.
Chapter 6. Uniform Interstate Family Support Act [Repealed].
Chapter 7. Enforcement by Writ of Execution.
Chapter 8. Earnings Assignment Order.
Chapter 9. Private Child Support Collectors.

CHAPTER 1
GENERAL PROVISIONS

Support orders enforceable under this code. §4500.
Enforcement of family support order. §4501.
Applicability of section 291 to enforcement and renewal of judgment or order. §4502.
Limitation period for recovery of arrearages in child support not affected by child attaining age of 18. §4503.
Applying for benefits and crediting payments made pursuant to Social Security or Railroad Retirement Acts, or from Department of Veterans Affairs against amount of court-ordered support. §4504.
Submitting list of places applied for employment where default in support due to unemployment. §4505.
Abstract of judgment; Notice of support judgment. §4506.
Recording of abstract of support judgment. §4506.1.
Recording of substitution of payee. §4506.2.
Forms by Judicial Council. §4506.3.
Order for payment under Government Code § 1151.5. §4507.
Designation of account to pay child support by electronic funds transfer. §4508.

§4500. Support orders enforceable under this code
An order for child, family, or spousal support that is made, entered, or enforceable in this state is enforceable under this code, whether or not the order was made or entered pursuant to this code. **Leg.H.** Enacted Stats 1992 ch 162 §10 (AB 2650), operative January 1, 1994.

§4501. Enforcement of family support order
A family support order is enforceable in the same manner and to the same extent as a child support order. **Leg.H.** Enacted Stats 1992 ch 162 §10 (AB 2650), operative January 1, 1994.

§4502. Applicability of section 291 to enforcement and renewal of judgment or order
The period for enforcement and procedure for renewal of a judgment or order for child, family, or spousal support is governed by Section 291. **Leg.H.** Added Stats 2006 ch 86 §6 (AB 2126), effective January 1, 2007.

Prior Law: Former Fam C §4502, similar to the present section, was enacted Stats 1992 ch 162 §10, to become operative January 1, 1994, and repealed Stats 1993 ch 219 §142.

Former §4502, relating to exceptions from renewal of judgment for support and the defense of laches, was added Stats 1993 ch 219 §143 (AB 1500), amended Stats 2000 ch 808 §45.5 (AB 1358), effective September 28, 2000, Stats 2002 ch 304 §1 (SB 1658), and repealed Stats 2006 ch 86 §5 (AB 2126).

Former Sections: Former Fam C §4502, relating to exceptions from renewal of judgment for support and the defense of laches, was added Stats 1993 ch 219 §143 (AB 1500) and repealed Stats 2006 ch 86 §5 (AB 2126).

Former Fam C §4502, similar to the present section, was enacted Stats 1992 ch 162 §10, operative January 1, 1994, and repealed Stats 1993 ch 219 §142.

§4503. Limitation period for recovery of arrearages in child support not affected by child attaining age of 18
If a parent has been ordered to make payments for the support of a minor child, an action to recover an arrearage in those payments may be maintained at any time within the period otherwise specified for the enforcement of such a judgment, notwithstanding the fact that the child has attained the age of 18 years. **Leg.H.** Enacted Stats 1992 ch 162 §10 (AB 2650), operative January 1, 1994.

§4504. Applying for benefits and crediting payments made pursuant to Social Security or Railroad Retirement Acts, or from Department of Veterans Affairs against amount of court-ordered support
(a) If the noncustodial parent is receiving payments from the federal government pursuant to the Social Security Act or Railroad Retirement Act, or from the Department of Veterans Affairs because of the retirement or disability of the noncustodial parent and the noncustodial parent notifies the custodial person, or notifies the local child support agency in a case being enforced by the local child support agency pursuant to Title IV-D of the Social Security Act, then the custodial parent or other child support obligee shall contact the appropriate federal agency within 30 days of receiving notification that the noncustodial parent is receiving those payments to verify eligibility for each child to receive payments from the federal government because of the disability of the noncustodial parent. If the child is potentially eligible for those payments, the custodial parent or other child support obligee shall apply for and cooperate with the appropriate federal agency for the receipt of those benefits on behalf of each child. The noncustodial parent shall cooperate with the custodial parent or other child support obligee in making that application and shall provide any information necessary to complete the application.

(b) If the court has ordered a noncustodial parent to pay for the support of a child, payments for the support of the child made by the federal government pursuant to the Social Security Act or Railroad Retirement Act, or by the Department of Veterans Affairs because of the retirement or disability of the noncustodial parent and received by the custodial parent or other child support obligee shall be credited toward the amount ordered by the court to be paid by the noncustodial parent for support of the child unless the payments made by the federal government were taken into consideration by the court in determining the amount of support to be paid. Any payments shall be credited in the order set forth in Section 695.221 of the Code of Civil Procedure.

(c) If the custodial parent or other child support obligee refuses to apply for those benefits or fails to cooperate with the appropriate federal agency in completing the application but the child or children otherwise are eligible to receive those benefits, the noncustodial parent shall be credited toward the amount ordered by the court to be paid for that month by the noncustodial parent for support of the child or children in the amount of payment that the child or children would have received that month had the custodial parent or other child support obligee completed an application for the benefits if the noncustodial parent provides evidence to the local child support agency indicating the amount the child or children would have received. The credit for those payments shall continue until the child or children would no longer be eligible for those benefits or the order for child support for the child or children is no longer in effect, whichever occurs first. **Leg.H.** Enacted Stats 1992 ch 162 §10 (AB 2650), operative January 1, 1994. Amended Stats 1996 ch 912 §2 (AB 1751); Stats 2001 ch 651 §1 (AB 891); Stats 2004 ch 305 §4 (AB 2669).

§4505. Submitting list of places applied for employment where default in support due to unemployment
(a) A court may require a parent who alleges that the parent's default in a child or family support order is due to the parent's unemployment to submit to the appropriate child support enforcement agency or any other entity designated by the court, including, but not limited to, the court itself, each two weeks, or at a frequency deemed appropriate by the court, a list of at least five different places the parent has applied for employment.

(b) This section shall become operative on January 1, 2011. **Leg.H.** Added Stats 2007 ch 249 §2 (SB 523), effective January 1, 2008, operative January 1, 2011.

Prior Law: Former Fam C §4505, similar to the present section, was added Stats 1992 ch 162 §10 and repealed Stats 2007 ch 249 §1.

Former Sections: Former Fam C §4505, similar to the present section, was added Stats 1992 ch 162 §10 and repealed Stats 2007 ch 249 §1.

§4506. Abstract of judgment; Notice of support judgment
(a) An abstract of a judgment ordering a party to pay spousal, child, or family support to the other party shall be certified by the clerk of the court where the judgment was entered and shall contain all of the following:

(1) The title of the court where the judgment is entered and the cause and number of the proceeding.

(2) The date of entry of the judgment and of any renewal of the judgment.

(3) Where the judgment and any renewals are entered in the records of the court.

(4) The name and last known address of the party ordered to pay support.

(5) The name and address of the party to whom support payments are ordered to be paid.

(6) Only the last four digits of the social security number, birth date, and driver's license number of the party who is ordered to pay support. If any of those numbers are not known to the party to whom support payments are to be paid, that fact shall be indicated on the abstract of the court judgment. This paragraph shall not apply to documents created prior to January 1, 2010.

(7) Whether a stay of enforcement has been ordered by the court and, if so, the date the stay ends.

(8) The date of issuance of the abstract.

(9) Any other information deemed reasonable and appropriate by the Judicial Council.

(b) The Judicial Council may develop a form for an abstract of a judgment ordering a party to pay child, family, or spousal support to another party which contains the information required by subdivision (a).

(c) Notwithstanding any other provision of law, when a support obligation is being enforced pursuant to Title IV-D of the Social Security Act, the agency enforcing the obligation may record a notice of support judgment. The notice of support judgment shall contain the same information as the form adopted by the Judicial Council pursuant to subdivision (b) and Section 4506.1. The notice of support judgment shall have the same force and effect as an abstract of judgment certified by the clerk of the court where the judgment was entered. The local child support agency or other Title IV-D agency shall not be subject to any civil liability as a consequence of causing a notice of support judgment to be recorded.

(d) As used in this section, "judgment" includes an order for child, family, or spousal support. **Leg.H.** Enacted Stats 1992 ch 162 §10 (AB 2650), operative January 1, 1994. Amended Stats 2002 ch 927 §3 (AB 3032); Stats 2009 ch 552 §3 (SB 40), effective January 1, 2010.

§4506.1. Recording of abstract of support judgment

Notwithstanding any other provision of law, when a support obligation is being enforced pursuant to Title IV-D of the Social Security Act, the agency enforcing the obligation may file and record an abstract of support judgment as authorized by Section 4506 and substitute the office address of the agency designated to receive support payments for the address of the party to whom support was ordered to be paid. **Leg.H.** Added Stats 1994 ch 1269 §48 (AB 2208).

§4506.2. Recording of substitution of payee

(a) Notwithstanding any other provision of law, when a support obligation is being enforced pursuant to Title IV-D of the Social Security Act, the agency enforcing the obligation may file and record a substitution of payee, if a judgment or abstract of judgment has previously been recorded pursuant to Section 697.320 of the Code of Civil Procedure by the support obligee or by a different governmental agency.

(b) Notwithstanding any other provision of law, when the Title IV-D agency ceases enforcement of a support obligation at the request of the support obligee, the agency may file and record a substitution of payee, if a judgment or abstract of judgment has been previously recorded pursuant to Section 697.320 of the Code of Civil Procedure.

(c) The substitution of payee shall contain all of the following:

(1) The name and address of the governmental agency or substituted payee filing the substitution and a notice that the substituted payee is to be contacted when notice to a lienholder may or must be given.

(2) The title of the court, the cause, and number of the proceeding where the substituted payee has registered the judgment.

(3) The name and last known address of the party ordered to pay support.

(4) The recorder identification number or book and page of the recorded document to which the substitution of payee applies.

(5) Any other information deemed reasonable and appropriate by the Judicial Council.

(d) The recorded substitution of payee shall not affect the priorities created by earlier recordations of support judgments or abstracts of support judgments.

(e) An agency enforcing the support obligation pursuant to Title IV-D of the Social Security Act is not required to obtain prior court approval or a clerk's certification when filing and recording a substitution of payee under this section. **Leg.H.** Added Stats 1994 ch 1269 §48.2 (AB 2208). Amended Stats 1997 ch 599 §17 (AB 573).

§4506.3. Forms by Judicial Council

The Judicial Council, in consultation with the California Family Support Council, the Department of Child Support Services, and title insurance industry representatives, shall develop a single form, which conforms with the requirements of Section 27361.6 of the Government Code, for the substitution of payee, for notice directing payment of support to the local child support agency pursuant to Section 4204, and for notice that support has been assigned pursuant to Section 11477 of the Welfare and Institutions Code. The form shall be available no later than July 1, 1998. **Leg.H.** Added Stats 1994 ch 1269 §48.4 (AB 2208). Amended Stats 1996 ch 957 §7 (AB 1058); Stats 1997 ch 599 §18 (AB 573); Stats 2000 ch 808 §46 (AB 1358), effective September 28, 2000.

§4507. Order for payment under Government Code §1151.5

When a court orders a person to make payment for child support or family support, the court may order that individual to make that payment as provided in Section 1151.5 of the Government Code. **Leg.H.** Added Stats 1993 ch 176 §1 (AB 877).

§4508. Designation of account to pay child support by electronic funds transfer

(a) This section does not apply to any child support obligor who is subject to an earnings assignment order pursuant to Chapter 8 (commencing with Section 5200).

(b) Except as provided in subdivision (a), every order or judgment to pay child support may require a child support obligor to designate an account for the purpose of paying the child support obligation by electronic funds transfer, as defined in subdivision (a) of Section 6479.5 of the Revenue and Taxation Code. The order or judgment may require the obligor to deposit funds in an interest-bearing account with a state or federally chartered commercial bank, a savings and loan association, or in shares of a federally insured credit union doing business in this state, and shall require the obligor to maintain funds in the account sufficient to pay the monthly child support obligation. The court may order that each payment be electronically transferred to either the obligee's account or the local child support agency account. The obligor shall be required to notify the obligee if the depository institution or the account number is changed. No interest shall accrue on any amount subject to electronic funds transfer as long as funds are maintained in the account that are sufficient to pay the monthly child support obligation. **Leg.H.** Added Stats 1994 ch 906 §2 (AB 923). Amended Stats 1999 ch 980 §9 (AB 1671); Stats 2001 ch 755 §4 (SB 943), effective October 12, 2001.

CHAPTER 2
DEPOSIT OF MONEY TO SECURE FUTURE CHILD SUPPORT PAYMENTS

Article 1. General Provisions.
Article 2. Order for Deposit of Money.
Article 3. Application to Reduce or Eliminate Deposit.
Article 4. Use of Deposit to Make Delinquent Support Payment.

ARTICLE 1
General Provisions

"Child support obligee". §4550.
Application of chapter. §4551.
Judicial Council rules and forms. §4552.
Compliance with requirements of federal law. §4553.
Chapter applies notwithstanding any other law. §4554.

§4550. "Child support obligee"

"Child support obligee" as used in this chapter means either the parent, guardian, or other person to whom child support has been ordered to be paid or the local child support agency designated by the court to receive the payment. The local child support agency is the "child support obligee" for the purposes of this chapter for all cases in which an application for services has been filed under Part D of Title IV of the Social Security Act (42 U.S.C. Sec. 651 et seq.). **Leg.H.** Enacted Stats 1992 ch 162 §10 (AB

2650), operative January 1, 1994. Amended Stats 2001 ch 755 §5 (SB 943), effective October 12, 2001.

§4551. Application of chapter
Except as provided in this section, this chapter:

(a) Does not apply to a temporary child support order.

(b) Applies to an application for modification of child support filed on or after January 1, 1992, but this chapter does not constitute the basis for the modification.

(c) Applies to an application for modification of child support in a case where the child support obligee has previously waived the establishment of a child support trust account pursuant to subdivision (b) of Section 4560 and now seeks the establishment of the child support trust account.

(d) Applies to an order or judgment entered by the court on or after January 1, 1993, ordering a child support obligor to pay a then existing child support arrearage that the child support obligor has unlawfully failed to pay as of the date of that order or judgment, including the arrearages which were incurred before January 1, 1992. **Leg.H.** Enacted Stats 1992 ch 162 §10 (AB 2650), operative January 1, 1994.

§4552. Judicial Council rules and forms
The Judicial Council shall promulgate such rules of court and publish such related judicial forms as the Judicial Council determines are necessary and appropriate to implement this chapter. In taking these steps, the Judicial Council shall ensure the uniform statewide application of this chapter and compliance with Part D of Title IV of the Social Security Act (42 U.S.C. Sec. 651 et seq.) and any regulations promulgated thereunder. **Leg.H.** Enacted Stats 1992 ch 162 §10 (AB 2650), operative January 1, 1994.

§4553. Compliance with requirements of federal law
Nothing in this chapter shall be construed to permit any action or omission by the state or any of its political subdivisions that would place the state in noncompliance with any requirement of federal law, including, but not limited to, the state reimbursement requirements of Part D of Title IV of the Social Security Act (42 U.S.C. Sec. 651 et seq.) and any regulations promulgated thereunder. **Leg.H.** Enacted Stats 1992 ch 162 §10 (AB 2650), operative January 1, 1994.

§4554. Chapter applies notwithstanding any other law
This chapter applies notwithstanding any other law. **Leg.H.** Enacted Stats 1992 ch 162 §10 (AB 2650), operative January 1, 1994.

ARTICLE 2
Order for Deposit of Money
Order for child support security deposit. §4560.
Deposit in court controlled account. §4561.
Child support obligor to provide evidence of deposit. §4562.
Dissolution of account and disposition of remaining funds. §4563.

§4560. Order for child support security deposit
(a) Except as provided in subdivision (b) or in Article 3 (commencing with Section 4565), every order or judgment to pay child support may also require the payment by the child support obligor of up to one year's child support or such lesser amount as is equal to the child support amount due to be paid by the child support obligor between the time of the date of the order and the date when the support obligation will be terminated by operation of law. This amount shall be known as the "child support security deposit."

(b) Unless expressly waived by the child support obligee, the court may order the establishment of a child support trust account pursuant to this chapter in every proceeding in which a child support obligation is imposed by order of the court. Among other reasons, the court may decline to establish a child support trust account upon its finding that an adequately funded child support trust account already exists pursuant to this chapter for the benefit of the child or children involved in the proceeding or that the child support obligor has provided adequate alternative security which is equivalent to the child support security deposit otherwise required by this chapter. **Leg.H.** Enacted Stats 1992 ch 162 §10 (AB 2650), operative January 1, 1994.

§4561. Deposit in court controlled account
If a child support security deposit is ordered, the court shall order that the moneys be deposited by the child support obligor in an interest-bearing account with a state or federally chartered commercial bank, a trust company authorized to transact trust business in this state, or a savings and loan association, or in shares of a federally insured credit union doing business in this state and having a trust department, subject to withdrawal only upon authorization of the court. The moneys so deposited shall be used exclusively to guarantee the monthly payment of child support. **Leg.H.** Enacted Stats 1992 ch 162 §10 (AB 2650), operative January 1, 1994.

§4562. Child support obligor to provide evidence of deposit
The court shall also order that evidence of the deposit shall be provided by the child support obligor in the form specified by the court, which shall be served upon the child support obligee and filed with the court within a reasonable time specified by the court, not to exceed 30 days. **Leg.H.** Enacted Stats 1992 ch 162 §10 (AB 2650), operative January 1, 1994.

§4563. Dissolution of account and disposition of remaining funds
An account established pursuant to this chapter shall be dissolved and any remaining funds in the account shall be returned to the support obligor, with any interest earned thereon, upon the full payment and cessation of the child support obligation as provided by court order or operation of law. **Leg.H.** Enacted Stats 1992 ch 162 §10 (AB 2650), operative January 1, 1994.

ARTICLE 3
Application to Reduce or Eliminate Deposit
Application by child support obligor; Service. §4565.
Filing information in opposition to application. §4566.
Hearing and court order. §4567.

§4565. Application by child support obligor; Service
(a) Before entry of a child support order pursuant to Section 4560, the court shall give the child support obligor reasonable notice and opportunity to file an application to reduce or eliminate the child support security deposit on either of the following grounds:

(1) The obligor has provided adequate alternative equivalent security to assure timely payment of the amount required by Section 4560.

(2) The obligor is unable, without undue financial hardship, to pay the support deposit required by Section 4560.

(b) The application shall be supported by all reasonable and necessary financial and other information required by the court to establish the existence of either ground for relief.

(c) After the filing of an application, the child support obligor shall also serve the application and supporting financial and other information submitted pursuant to subdivision (b) upon the child support obligee and any other party to the proceeding. **Leg.H.** Enacted Stats 1992 ch 162 §10 (AB 2650), operative January 1, 1994. Amended Stats 2007 ch 441 §1 (SB 892), effective January 1, 2008.

§4566. Filing information in opposition to application
Upon the filing of an application under Section 4565 with the court and the service of the application upon the child support obligee and any other party to the proceedings, the court shall provide notice and opportunity for any party opposing the application to file responsive financial and other information setting forth the factual and legal bases for the party's opposition. **Leg.H.** Enacted Stats 1992 ch 162 §10 (AB 2650), operative January 1, 1994.

§4567. Hearing and court order
The court shall then provide an opportunity for hearing, and shall thereafter enter its order exercising its discretion under all the facts and circumstances as disclosed in the admissible evidence before it so as to maximize the payment and deposit of the amount required by Section 4560, or an equivalent adequate security for the payment thereof, without imposition of undue financial hardship on the support obligor. If the court finds that the deposit of the amount required by Section 4560 would impose an undue financial hardship upon the child support obligor, the court shall reduce this amount to an amount that the child support obligor can pay as the child support security deposit without undue financial hardship. **Leg.H.** Enacted Stats 1992 ch 162 §10 (AB 2650), operative January 1, 1994.

ARTICLE 4
Use of Deposit to Make Delinquent Support Payment
Court order for disbursement and for replenishment of account. §4570.
Service on support obligor. §4571.
Service on depository institution and child support agency with jurisdiction. §4572.

Payment where support paid through district attorney for child not receiving public assistance. §4573.

§4570. Court order for disbursement and for replenishment of account

(a) Upon the application of the child support obligee stating that the support payment is 10 or more days late, the court shall immediately order disbursement of funds from the account established pursuant to this chapter solely for the purpose of providing the amount of child support then in arrears.

(b) Funds so disbursed shall be used exclusively for the support, maintenance, and education of the child or children subject to the child support order.

(c) The court shall also order the account to be replenished by the child support obligor in the same amounts as are expended from the account to pay the amount of child support which the child support obligor has failed to pay the child support obligee in a timely manner. **Leg.H.** Enacted Stats 1992 ch 162 §10 (AB 2650), operative January 1, 1994.

§4571. Service on support obligor

The court shall cause a copy of the application, as well as its order to disburse and replenish funds, to be served upon the child support obligor, who shall be subject to contempt of court for failure to comply with the order. **Leg.H.** Enacted Stats 1992 ch 162 §10 (AB 2650), operative January 1, 1994.

§4572. Service on depository institution and child support agency with jurisdiction

The court shall cause a copy of its order to disburse and replenish funds to be served upon the depository institution where the child support security deposit is maintained, and upon the child support agency with jurisdiction over the case. **Leg.H.** Enacted Stats 1992 ch 162 §10 (AB 2650), operative January 1, 1994. Amended Stats 2001 ch 755 §6 (SB 943), effective October 12, 2001.

§4573. Payment where support paid through district attorney for child not receiving public assistance

If support is ordered to be paid through the local child support agency on behalf of a child not receiving public assistance pursuant to the Family Economic Security Act of 1982 (Chapter 2 (commencing with Section 11200) of Part 3 of Division 9 of the Welfare and Institutions Code), the local child support agency shall forward the support received pursuant to this chapter to the custodial parent or other person having care or control of the child or children involved. **Leg.H.** Enacted Stats 1992 ch 162 §10 (AB 2650), operative January 1, 1994. Amended Stats 1993 ch 219 §144 (AB 1500); Stats 2000 ch 808 §47 (AB 1358), effective September 28, 2000.

CHAPTER 3
DEPOSIT OF ASSETS TO SECURE FUTURE CHILD SUPPORT PAYMENTS

Article 1. General Provisions.
Article 2. Order for Deposit of Assets.
Article 3. Ex Parte Restraining Orders.
Article 4. Use or Sale of Assets to Make Support Payments.
Article 5. Return of Assets of Obligor.

ARTICLE 1
General Provisions

Purpose of chapter. §4600.
Deposit holder defined. §4601.
Statement of receipts and disbursements. §4602.
Protection of deposit holder from liability. §4603.
Reimbursement of deposit holder for fees or costs not otherwise compensated. §4604.

§4600. Purpose of chapter

The purpose of this chapter is to provide an extraordinary remedy for cases of bad faith failure to pay child support obligations. **Leg.H.** Enacted Stats 1992 ch 162 §10 (AB 2650), operative January 1, 1994.

§4601. Deposit holder defined

"Deposit holder" as used in this chapter means the district attorney, county officer, or trustee designated by the court to receive assets deposited pursuant to this chapter to secure future support payments. **Leg.H.** Enacted Stats 1992 ch 162 §10 (AB 2650), operative January 1, 1994.

§4602. Statement of receipts and disbursements

If requested by an obligor-parent, the deposit holder shall prepare a statement setting forth disbursements and receipts made under this chapter. **Leg.H.** Enacted Stats 1992 ch 162 §10 (AB 2650), operative January 1, 1994.

§4603. Protection of deposit holder from liability

The deposit holder who is responsible for any money or property and for any disbursements under this chapter is not liable for any action undertaken in good faith and in conformance with this chapter. **Leg.H.** Enacted Stats 1992 ch 162 §10 (AB 2650), operative January 1, 1994.

§4604. Reimbursement of deposit holder for fees or costs not otherwise compensated

(a) If the deposit holder incurs fees or costs under this chapter which are not compensated by the deduction under subdivision (c) of Section 4630 (including, but not limited to, fees or costs incurred in a sale of assets pursuant to this chapter and in the preparation of a statement pursuant to Section 4602), the court shall, after a hearing, order the obligor-parent to pay the reasonable fees and costs incurred by the deposit holder. The hearing shall be held not less than 20 days after the deposit holder serves notice of motion or order to show cause upon the obligor-parent.

(b) Fees and costs ordered to be paid under this section shall be in addition to any deposit made under this chapter but shall not exceed whichever of the following is less:

(1) Five percent of one year's child support obligation.
(2) The total amount ordered deposited under Section 4614. **Leg.H.** Enacted Stats 1992 ch 162 §10 (AB 2650), operative January 1, 1994.

ARTICLE 2
Order for Deposit of Assets

Issuance of order for deposit of assets. §4610.
Presumptions. §4611.
Grounds for defense to allegation that obligor-parent in arrears. §4612.
Determination by court of need for deposit order. §4613.
Designation by court of assets subject to order. §4614.
Providing bond in lieu of depositing cash or other assets. §4615.
Order for sale of deposited asset and deposit of proceeds. §4616.
Deposit of real property. §4617.

§4610. Issuance of order for deposit of assets

(a) Subject to Sections 4613, 4614, and 4615, in any proceeding where the court has ordered either or both parents to pay any amount for the support of a child for whom support may be ordered, upon an order to show cause or notice of motion, application, and declaration signed under penalty of perjury by the person or county officer to whom support has been ordered to have been paid stating that the parent or parents so ordered is in arrears in payment in a sum equal to the amount of 60 days of payments, the court shall issue to the parent or parents ordered to pay support, following notice and opportunity for a hearing, an order requiring that the parent or parents deposit assets to secure future support payments with the deposit holder designated by the court.

(b) In a proceeding under this article, upon request of any party, the court may also issue an ex parte restraining order as specified in Section 4620. **Leg.H.** Enacted Stats 1992 ch 162 §10 (AB 2650), operative January 1, 1994. Amended Stats 1993 ch 219 §145 (AB 1500).

§4611. Presumptions

In a proceeding under this chapter, an obligor-parent shall rebut both of the following presumptions:

(a) The nonpayment of child support was willful, without good faith.
(b) The obligor had the ability to pay the support. **Leg.H.** Enacted Stats 1992 ch 162 §10 (AB 2650), operative January 1, 1994.

§4612. Grounds for defense to allegation that obligor-parent in arrears

An obligor-parent alleged to be in arrears may use any of the following grounds as a defense to the motion filed pursuant to this article or as a basis for filing a motion to stop a sale or use of assets under Section 4631:

(a) Child support payments are not in arrears.
(b) Laches.
(c) There has been a change in the custody of the children.

(d) There is a pending motion for reduction in support due to a reduction in income.
(e) Illness or disability.
(f) Unemployment.
(g) Serious adverse impact on the immediate family of the obligor-parent residing with the obligor-parent that outweighs the impact of denial of the motion or stopping the sale on obligee.
(h) Serious impairment of the ability of the obligor-parent to generate income.
(i) Other emergency conditions. **Leg.H.** Enacted Stats 1992 ch 162 §10 (AB 2650), operative January 1, 1994.

§4613. Determination by court of need for deposit order

The court shall not issue an order pursuant to this article unless the court determines that one or more of the following conditions exist:
(a) The obligor-parent is not receiving salary or wages subject to an assignment pursuant to Chapter 8 (commencing with Section 5200) and there is reason to believe that the obligor-parent has earned income from some source of employment.
(b) An assignment of a portion of salary or wages pursuant to Chapter 8 (commencing with Section 5200) would not be sufficient to meet the amount of the support obligation, for reasons other than a change of circumstances which would qualify for a reduction in the amount of child support ordered.
(c) The job history of the obligor-parent shows that an assignment of a portion of salary or wages pursuant to Chapter 8 (commencing with Section 5200), would be difficult to enforce or would not be a practical means for securing the payment of the support obligation, due to circumstances including, but not limited to, multiple concurrent or consecutive employers. **Leg.H.** Enacted Stats 1992 ch 162 §10 (AB 2650), operative January 1, 1994.

§4614. Designation by court of assets subject to order

The designation of assets subject to an order pursuant to this article shall be based upon concern for maximizing the liquidity and ready conversion into cash of the deposited asset. In all instances, the assets shall include a sum of money up to or equal in value to one year of support payments or six thousand dollars ($6,000) whichever is less, or any other assets, personal or real, designated by the court which equal in value up to one year of payments for support of the child, or six thousand dollars ($6,000), whichever is less, subject to Section 703.070 of the Code of Civil Procedure. **Leg.H.** Enacted Stats 1992 ch 162 §10 (AB 2650), operative January 1, 1994. Amended Stats 1993 ch 219 §146 (AB 1500).

§4615. Providing bond in lieu of depositing cash or other assets

In lieu of depositing cash or other assets as provided in Section 4614, the obligor-parent may, if approved by the court, provide a performance bond secured by real property or other assets of the obligor-parent and equal in value to one year of payments. **Leg.H.** Enacted Stats 1992 ch 162 §10 (AB 2650), operative January 1, 1994.

§4616. Order for sale of deposited asset and deposit of proceeds

Upon deposit of an asset which is not readily convertible into money, the court may, after a hearing, order the sale of that asset and the deposit of the proceeds with the deposit holder. Not less than 20 days written notice of the hearing shall be served on the obligor-parent. **Leg.H.** Enacted Stats 1992 ch 162 §10 (AB 2650), operative January 1, 1994.

§4617. Deposit of real property

(a) If the asset ordered to be deposited is real property, the order shall be certified as an abstract of judgment in accordance with Section 674 of the Code of Civil Procedure.
(b) A deposit of real property is made effective by recordation of the certified abstract with the county recorder.
(c) The deposited real property and the rights, benefits, and liabilities attached to that property shall continue in the possession of the legal owner.
(d) For purposes of Section 701.545 of the Code of Civil Procedure, the date of the issuance of the order to deposit assets shall be construed as the date notice of levy on an interest in real property was served on the judgment debtor. **Leg.H.** Enacted Stats 1992 ch 162 §10 (AB 2650), operative January 1, 1994.

ARTICLE 3
Ex Parte Restraining Orders

Ex parte restraining orders. §4620.

§4620. Ex parte restraining orders

(a) During the pendency of a proceeding under this chapter, upon the application of either party in the manner provided by Part 4 (commencing with Section 240) of Division 2, the court may, without a hearing, issue ex parte orders restraining any person from transferring, encumbering, hypothecating, concealing, or in any way disposing of any property, real or personal, whether community, quasi-community, or separate, except in the usual course of business or for the necessities of life, and if the order is directed against a party, requiring the party to notify the other party of any proposed extraordinary expenditures and to account to the court for all such extraordinary expenditures.
(b) The matter shall be made returnable not later than 20 days, or if good cause appears to the court, 25 days from the date of the order at which time the ex parte order shall expire.
(c) The court, at the hearing, shall determine for which property the obligor-parent shall be required to report extraordinary expenditures and shall specify what is deemed an extraordinary expenditure for purposes of this subdivision.
(d) An order issued pursuant to this section after the hearing shall state on its face the date of expiration of the order, which shall expire in one year or upon deposit of assets or money pursuant to Article 2 (commencing with Section 4610), whichever first occurs. **Leg.H.** Enacted Stats 1992 ch 162 §10 (AB 2650), operative January 1, 1994.

ARTICLE 4
Use or Sale of Assets to Make Support Payments

Use or sale of assets. §4630.
Motion to stop sale or use of assets. §4631.
Grounds for defense to allegation that obligor-parent in arrears. §4632.

§4630. Use or sale of assets

(a) Upon an obligor-parent's failure, within the time specified by the court, to make reasonable efforts to cure the default in child support payments or to comply with a court-approved payment plan, if payments continue in arrears, the deposit holder shall, not less than 25 days after providing the obligor-parent or parents with a written notice served personally or with return receipt requested, unless a motion or order to show cause has been filed to stop the use or sale, use the money or sell or otherwise process the deposited assets for an amount sufficient to pay the arrearage and the amount ordered by the court for the support currently due for the child for whom support may be ordered.
(b) Assets deposited pursuant to an order issued under Article 2 (commencing with Section 4610) shall be construed as being assets subject to levy pursuant to Article 6 (commencing with Section 701.510) of Chapter 3 of Division 2 of Title 9 of Part 2 of the Code of Civil Procedure. The sale of assets shall be conducted in accordance with Article 6 (commencing with Section 701.510) and Article 7 (commencing with Section 701.810) of Chapter 3 of Division 2 of Title 9 of Part 2 of the Code of Civil Procedure.
(c) The deposit holder may deduct from the deposited money the sum of one dollar ($1) for each payment made pursuant to this section. **Leg.H.** Enacted Stats 1992 ch 162 §10 (AB 2650), operative January 1, 1994. Amended Stats 1993 ch 219 §147 (AB 1500).

§4631. Motion to stop sale or use of assets

(a) An obligor-parent may file a motion to stop the use of the money or the sale of the asset under this article within 15 days after service of notice on the obligor-parent pursuant to Section 4630.
(b) The clerk of the court shall set the motion for hearing not less than 20 days after service of the notice of motion and the motion on the person or county officer to whom support has been ordered to have been paid. **Leg.H.** Enacted Stats 1992 ch 162 §10 (AB 2650), operative January 1, 1994.

§4632. Grounds for defense to allegation that obligor-parent in arrears

An obligor-parent alleged to be in arrears under this article may use any ground set forth in Section 4612 as a basis for filing a motion under Section 4631 to stop a sale or use of assets under this article. **Leg.H.** Enacted Stats 1992 ch 162 §10 (AB 2650), operative January 1, 1994.

ARTICLE 5
Return of Assets of Obligor

Conditions for return of assets to obligor. §4640.
Release of real property. §4641.

§4640. Conditions for return of assets to obligor

The deposit holder shall return all assets subject to court order under Article 2 (commencing with Section 4610) to the obligor-parent when both of the following occur:

(a) One year has elapsed since the court issued the order described under Article 2 (commencing with Section 4610).

(b) The obligor-parent has made all support payments on time during that one-year period. **Leg.H.** Enacted Stats 1992 ch 162 §10 (AB 2650), operative January 1, 1994.

§4641. Release of real property

If the deposited asset is real property and the requirements of Section 4640 have been satisfied, the deposit holder shall do all of the following:

(a) Prepare a release in accordance with Section 697.370 of the Code of Civil Procedure.

(b) Request the clerk of the court where the order to deposit assets was made to certify the release.

(c) Record the certified release in the office of the county recorder where the certified abstract was recorded under Section 4617. **Leg.H.** Enacted Stats 1992 ch 162 §10 (AB 2650), operative January 1, 1994.

CHAPTER 4
CHILD SUPPORT DELINQUENCY REPORTING

Short title. §4700.
Child support delinquency reporting. §4701.

§4700. Short title

This chapter may be cited as the Child Support Delinquency Reporting Law. **Leg.H.** Enacted Stats 1992 ch 162 §10 (AB 2650), operative January 1, 1994.

§4701. Child support delinquency reporting

(a) The Department of Child Support Services shall administer a statewide automated system for the reporting of court-ordered child support obligations to credit reporting agencies.

(b) The department shall design and develop standards for the system in conjunction with representatives of the California Family Support Council and the credit reporting industry.

(c) The standards for the system shall be consistent with credit reporting industry standards and reporting format and with the department's statewide central automated system for support enforcement.

(d) The standards shall include, but not be limited to, all of the following:

(1) Court-ordered child support obligations and delinquent payments, including amounts owed and by whom. The California local child support agencies, on a monthly basis, shall update this information, and then submit it to the department which, in turn, shall consolidate and transmit it to the credit reporting agencies.

(2) Before the initial reporting of a court-ordered child support obligation or a delinquent payment, the local child support agency shall attempt to notify the obligor parent of the proposed action and give 30 days to contest in writing the accuracy of the information, or to pay the arrearage, if any, in compliance with the due process requirements of the laws of this state.

(e) The department and the local child support agencies are responsible for the accuracy of information provided pursuant to this section, and the information shall be based upon the data available at the time the information is provided. Each of these organizations and the credit reporting agencies shall follow reasonable procedures to ensure maximum possible accuracy of the information provided. Neither the department, nor the local child support agencies are liable for any consequences of the failure of a parent to contest the accuracy of the information within the time allowed under paragraph (2) of subdivision (d). **Leg.H.** Enacted Stats 1992 ch 162 §10 (AB 2650), operative January 1, 1994. Amended Stats 2000 ch 808 §48 (AB 1358), effective September 28, 2000.

CHAPTER 5
CIVIL PENALTY FOR CHILD SUPPORT DELINQUENCY

"Support". §4720.
Application of chapter; Legislative intent. §4721.
Notice of delinquency; Financial penalty for failure to pay delinquent amount. §4722.
Contents of notice of delinquency. §4723.
Service of notice of delinquency. §4724.
Motion to obtain judgment; Enforcement of judgment. §4725.
Showing required to avoid imposition of penalties. §4726.
Limit on amount of penalty. §4727.
Enforcement of penalties. §4728.
Utilization of penalties by agencies. §4729.
Penalties not considered at hearing to set or modify amount of current support. §4730.
Subsequent notice of delinquency. §4731.
Judicial Council forms. §4732.
Payment of penalties to custodian. §4733.

§4720. "Support"

"Support" for the purposes of this chapter means support as defined in Section 150. **Leg.H.** Enacted Stats 1992 ch 162 §10 (AB 2650), operative January 1, 1994.

§4721. Application of chapter; Legislative intent

(a) This chapter applies only to installments of child support that are due on or after January 1, 1992.

(b) It is the intent of the Legislature that the penalties provided under this chapter shall be applied in egregious instances of noncompliance with child support orders.

(c) It is the intent of the Legislature that for the purposes of this chapter, payments made through wage assignments are considered timely regardless of the date of receipt by the local child support agency or obligee. **Leg.H.** Enacted Stats 1992 ch 162 §10 (AB 2650), operative January 1, 1994. Amended Stats 1994 ch 959 §2 (AB 3072), effective September 28, 1994; Stats 2000 ch 808 §49 (AB 1358), effective September 28, 2000.

§4722. Notice of delinquency; Financial penalty for failure to pay delinquent amount

(a) Any person with a court order for child support, the payments on which are more than 30 days in arrears, may file and then serve a notice of delinquency, as described in this chapter.

(b) Except as provided in Section 4726, and subject to Section 4727, any amount of child support specified in a notice of delinquency that remains unpaid for more than 30 days after the notice of delinquency has been filed and served shall incur a penalty of 6 percent of the delinquent payment for each month that it remains unpaid, up to a maximum of 72 percent of the unpaid balance due. **Leg.H.** Enacted Stats 1992 ch 162 §10 (AB 2650), operative January 1, 1994.

§4723. Contents of notice of delinquency

(a) The notice of delinquency shall be signed under penalty of perjury by the support obligee.

(b) The notice of delinquency shall state all of the following:

(1) The amount that the child support obligor is in arrears.

(2) The installments of support due, the amounts, if any, that have been paid, and the balance due.

(3) That any unpaid installment of child support will incur a penalty of 6 percent of the unpaid support per month until paid, to a maximum of 72 percent of the original amount of the unpaid support, unless the support arrearage is paid within 30 days of the date of service of the notice of delinquency.

(c) In the absence of a protective order prohibiting the support obligor from knowing the whereabouts of the child or children for whom support is payable, or otherwise excusing the requirements of this subdivision, the notice of delinquency shall also include a current address and telephone number of all of the children for whom support is due and, if different from that of the support obligee, the address at which court papers may be served upon the support obligee. **Leg.H.** Enacted Stats 1992 ch 162 §10 (AB 2650), operative January 1, 1994.

§4724. Service of notice of delinquency

The notice of delinquency may be served personally or by certified mail or in any manner provided for service of summons. **Leg.H.** Enacted Stats 1992 ch 162 §10 (AB 2650), operative January 1, 1994.

§4725. Motion to obtain judgment; Enforcement of judgment

If the child support owed, or any arrearages, interest, or penalty, remains unpaid more than 30 days after serving the notice of delinquency, the support obligee may file a motion to obtain a judgment for the amount owed, which shall be enforceable in any manner provided by law for the enforcement of judgments. **Leg.H.** Enacted Stats 1992 ch 162 §10 (AB 2650), operative January 1, 1994.

§4726. Showing required to avoid imposition of penalties

No penalties may be imposed pursuant to this chapter if, in the discretion of the court, all of the following conditions are met:

(a) Within a timely fashion after service of the notice of delinquency, the support obligor files and serves a motion to determine arrearages and to show cause why the penalties provided in this chapter should not be imposed.

(b) At the hearing on the motion filed by the support obligor, the court finds that the support obligor has proved any of the following:

(1) The child support payments were not 30 days in arrears as of the date of service of the notice of delinquency and are not in arrears as of the date of the hearing.

(2) The support obligor suffered serious illness, disability, or unemployment which substantially impaired the ability of the support obligor to comply fully with the support order and the support obligor has made every possible effort to comply with the support order.

(3) The support obligor is a public employee and for reasons relating to fiscal difficulties of the employing entity the obligor has not received a paycheck for 30 or more days.

(4) It would not be in the interests of justice to impose a penalty. **Leg.H.** Enacted Stats 1992 ch 162 §10 (AB 2650), operative January 1, 1994.

§4727. Limit on amount of penalty

Any penalty due under this chapter shall not be greater than 6 percent per month of the original amount of support arrearages or support installment, nor may the penalties on any arrearage amount or support installment exceed 72 percent of the original amount due, regardless of whether or not the installments have been listed on more than one notice of delinquency. **Leg.H.** Enacted Stats 1992 ch 162 §10 (AB 2650), operative January 1, 1994.

§4728. Enforcement of penalties

Penalties due pursuant to this chapter may be enforced by the issuance of a writ of execution in the same manner as a writ of execution may be issued for unpaid installments of child support, as described in Chapter 7 (commencing with Section 5100), except that payment of penalties under this chapter may not take priority over payment of arrearages or current support. **Leg.H.** Enacted Stats 1992 ch 162 §10 (AB 2650), operative January 1, 1994.

§4729. Utilization of penalties by agencies

The local child support agency or any other agency providing support enforcement services pursuant to Title IV-D of the federal Social Security Act may not enforce child support obligations utilizing the penalties provided for by this chapter. **Leg.H.** Enacted Stats 1992 ch 162 §10 (AB 2650), operative January 1, 1994. Amended Stats 1993 ch 219 §148 (AB 1500); Stats 1994 ch 959 §3 (AB 3072), effective September 28, 1994; Stats 2000 ch 808 §50 (AB 1358), effective September 28, 2000.

§4730. Penalties not considered at hearing to set or modify amount of current support

At any hearing to set or modify the amount payable for the support of a child, the court shall not consider any penalties imposed under this chapter in determining the amount of current support to be paid. **Leg.H.** Enacted Stats 1992 ch 162 §10 (AB 2650), operative January 1, 1994. Amended Stats 1993 ch 219 §149 (AB 1500).

§4731. Subsequent notice of delinquency

A subsequent notice of delinquency may be served and filed at any time. The subsequent notice shall indicate those child support arrearages and ongoing installments that have been listed on a previous notice. **Leg.H.** Enacted Stats 1992 ch 162 §10 (AB 2650), operative January 1, 1994.

§4732. Judicial Council forms

The Judicial Council shall adopt forms or notices for the use of the procedures provided by this chapter. **Leg.H.** Enacted Stats 1992 ch 162 §10 (AB 2650), operative January 1, 1994.

§4733. Payment of penalties to custodian

Penalties collected pursuant to this chapter shall be paid to the custodian of the child who is the subject of the child support judgment or order, whether or not the child is a recipient of public assistance. **Leg.H.** Added Stats 1993 ch 219 §150 (AB 1500).

§4800. [Section repealed 1997]

Leg.H. Enacted Stats 1992 ch 162 §10 (AB 2650), operative January 1, 1994. Repealed Stats 1997 ch 194 §1 (SB 568). See Fam C §4900.

§4801. [Section repealed 1997]

Leg.H. Enacted Stats 1992 ch 162 §10 (AB 2650), operative January 1, 1994. Repealed Stats 1997 ch 194 §1 (SB 568). See Fam C §4915.

§4802. [Section repealed 1997]

Leg.H. Enacted Stats 1992 ch 162 §10 (AB 2650), operative January 1, 1994. Repealed Stats 1997 ch 194 §1 (SB 568). See Fam C §4901.

§4803. [Section repealed 1997]

Leg.H. Enacted Stats 1992 ch 162 §10 (AB 2650), operative January 1, 1994. Repealed Stats 1997 ch 194 §1 (SB 568). See Fam C §4903.

§4804. [Section repealed 1997]

Leg.H. Enacted Stats 1992 ch 162 §10 (AB 2650), operative January 1, 1994. Repealed Stats 1997 ch 194 §1 (SB 568). See Fam C §4905.

§4805. [Section repealed 1997]

Leg.H. Enacted Stats 1992 ch 162 §10 (AB 2650), operative January 1, 1994. Repealed Stats 1997 ch 194 §1 (SB 568). See Fam C §4923.

§4810. [Section repealed 1997]

Leg.H. Enacted Stats 1992 ch 162 §10 (AB 2650), operative January 1, 1994. Repealed Stats 1997 ch 194 §1 (SB 568). See Fam C §4970.

§4811. [Section repealed 1997]

Leg.H. Enacted Stats 1992 ch 162 §10 (AB 2650), operative January 1, 1994. Repealed Stats 1997 ch 194 §1 (SB 568). See Fam C §4971.

§4820. [Section repealed 1997]

Leg.H. Enacted Stats 1992 ch 162 §10 (AB 2650), operative January 1, 1994. Repealed Stats 1997 ch 194 §1 (SB 568). See Fam C §4940.

§4821. [Section repealed 1997]

Leg.H. Enacted Stats 1992 ch 162 §10 (AB 2650), operative January 1, 1994. Repealed Stats 1997 ch 194 §1 (SB 568). See Fam C §4910.

§4822. [Section repealed 1997]

Leg.H. Enacted Stats 1992 ch 162 §10 (AB 2650), operative January 1, 1994. Repealed Stats 1997 ch 194 §1 (SB 568). See Fam C §4929.

§4824. [Section repealed 1997]

Leg.H. Enacted Stats 1992 ch 162 §10 (AB 2650), operative January 1, 1994. Repealed Stats 1997 ch 194 §1 (SB 568). See Fam C §4920.

§4825. [Section repealed 1997]

Leg.H. Enacted Stats 1992 ch 162 §10 (AB 2650), operative January 1, 1994. Repealed Stats 1997 ch 194 §1 (SB 568). See Fam C §4922.

§4826. [Section repealed 1997]

Leg.H. Enacted Stats 1992 ch 162 §10 (AB 2650), operative January 1, 1994. Repealed Stats 1997 ch 194 §1 (SB 568). See Fam C §4915.

§4827. [Section repealed 1997]

Leg.H. Enacted Stats 1992 ch 162 §10 (AB 2650), operative January 1, 1994. Repealed Stats 1997 ch 194 §1 (SB 568). See Fam C §4911.

§4828. [Section repealed 1997]

Leg.H. Enacted Stats 1992 ch 162 §10 (AB 2650), operative January 1, 1994. Repealed Stats 1997 ch 194 §1 (SB 568). See Fam C §4927.

§4829. [Section repealed 1997]

Leg.H. Enacted Stats 1992 ch 162 §10 (AB 2650), operative January 1, 1994. Repealed Stats 1997 ch 194 §1 (SB 568). The repealed section related to arrest of family support obligor.

§4830. [Section repealed 1997]

Leg.H. Enacted Stats 1992 ch 162 §10 (AB 2650), operative January 1, 1994. Repealed Stats 1997 ch 194 §1 (SB 568). See Fam C §4924.

§4831. [Section repealed 1997]

§4832. [Section repealed 1997]

Leg.H. Enacted Stats 1992 ch 162 §10 (AB 2650), operative January 1, 1994. Repealed Stats 1997 ch 194 §1 (SB 568). The repealed section related to tracing a support obligor's property and making reports to the initiating court.

§4833. [Section repealed 1997]

Leg.H. Enacted Stats 1992 ch 162 §10 (AB 2650), operative January 1, 1994. Repealed Stats 1997 ch 194 §1 (SB 568). See Fam C §4940.

§4834. [Section repealed 1997]

Leg.H. Enacted Stats 1992 ch 162 §10 (AB 2650), operative January 1, 1994. Repealed Stats 1997 ch 194 §1 (SB 568). See Fam C §4945.

§4835. [Section repealed 1997]

Leg.H. Enacted Stats 1992 ch 162 §10 (AB 2650), operative January 1, 1994. Repealed Stats 1997 ch 194 §1 (SB 568). The repealed section related to copies of support order to initiating court and obligor.

§4836. [Section repealed 1997]

Leg.H. Enacted Stats 1992 ch 162 §10 (AB 2650), operative January 1, 1994. Repealed Stats 1997 ch 194 §1 (SB 568). The repealed section related to terms and conditions to ensure obligor's compliance with support order.

§4837. [Section repealed 1997]

Leg.H. Enacted Stats 1992 ch 162 §10 (AB 2650), operative January 1, 1994. Repealed Stats 1997 ch 194 §1 (SB 568). See Fam C §4917.

§4838. [Section repealed 1997]

Leg.H. Enacted Stats 1992 ch 162 §10 (AB 2650), operative January 1, 1994. Repealed Stats 1997 ch 194 §1 (SB 568). See Fam C §4918.

§4839. [Section repealed 1997]

Leg.H. Enacted Stats 1992 ch 162 §10 (AB 2650), operative January 1, 1994. Repealed Stats 1997 ch 194 §1 (SB 568). See Fam C §4930.

§4840. [Section repealed 1997]

Leg.H. Enacted Stats 1992 ch 162 §10 (AB 2650), operative January 1, 1994. Repealed Stats 1997 ch 194 §1 (SB 568). See Fam C §4912.

§4841. [Section repealed 1997]

Leg.H. Enacted Stats 1992 ch 162 §10 (AB 2650), operative January 1, 1994. Repealed Stats 1997 ch 194 §1 (SB 568). See Fam C §4928.

§4842. [Section repealed 1997]

Leg.H. Enacted Stats 1992 ch 162 §10 (AB 2650), operative January 1, 1994. Repealed Stats 1997 ch 194 §1 (SB 568). The repealed section related to stay of support proceedings.

§4843. [Section repealed 1997]

Leg.H. Enacted Stats 1992 ch 162 §10 (AB 2650), operative January 1, 1994. Repealed Stats 1997 ch 194 §1 (SB 568). The repealed section related to support obligor and obligee in different counties.

§4844. [Section repealed 1997]

Leg.H. Enacted Stats 1992 ch 162 §10 (AB 2650), operative January 1, 1994. Repealed Stats 1997 ch 194 §1 (SB 568). The repealed section related to declaration of foreign jurisdiction as reciprocating state for support enforcement.

§4845. [Section repealed 1997]

Leg.H. Enacted Stats 1992 ch 162 §10 (AB 2650), operative January 1, 1994. Repealed Stats 1997 ch 194 §1 (SB 568). The repealed section related to rules of evidence and interference with custody and visitation in enforcing support orders.

§4846. [Section repealed 1997]

Leg.H. Enacted Stats 1992 ch 162 §10 (AB 2650), operative January 1, 1994. Amended Stats 1994 ch 1266 §3 (AB 3804). Repealed Stats 1997 ch 194 §1 (SB 568). See Fam C §4929.

§4847. [Section repealed 1997]

Leg.H. Enacted Stats 1992 ch 162 §10 (AB 2650), operative January 1, 1994. Amended Stats 1994 ch 1269 §48.6 (AB 2208). Repealed Stats 1997 ch 194 §1 (SB 568). See Fam C §4922.

§4848. [Section repealed 1997]

Leg.H. Enacted Stats 1992 ch 162 §10 (AB 2650), operative January 1, 1994. Amended Stats 1993 ch 876 §19 (SB 1068), effective October 6, 1993, operative January 1, 1994. Repealed Stats 1997 ch 194 §1 (SB 568). The repealed section related to additional remedies for foreign support orders and registration of a support order made in this state.

§4849. [Section repealed 1997]

Leg.H. Enacted Stats 1992 ch 162 §10 (AB 2650), operative January 1, 1994. Amended Stats 1993 ch 219 §151 (AB 1500), ch 876 §20 (SB 1068), effective October 6, 1993, operative January 1, 1994. Repealed Stats 1997 ch 194 §1 (SB 568). The repealed section related to registration of foreign support orders.

§4850. [Section repealed 1997]

Leg.H. Enacted Stats 1992 ch 162 §10 (AB 2650), operative January 1, 1994. Repealed Stats 1997 ch 194 §1 (SB 568). The repealed section related to registry of foreign support orders.

§4851. [Section repealed 1997]

Leg.H. Enacted Stats 1992 ch 162 §10 (AB 2650), operative January 1, 1994. Repealed Stats 1997 ch 194 §1 (SB 568). See Fam C §4924.

§4852. [Section repealed 1997]

Leg.H. Enacted Stats 1992 ch 162 §10 (AB 2650), operative January 1, 1994. Repealed Stats 1997 ch 194 §1 (SB 568). The repealed section related to procedure for registration of foreign support order and enforcement of registered orders.

§4852.1. [Section repealed 1997]

Leg.H. Added Stats 1994 ch 1269 §48.8 (AB 2208). Amended Stats 1996 ch 912 §3 (AB 1751). Repealed Stats 1997 ch 194 §1 (SB 568). The repealed section related to registration of a support order made in another county.

§4853. [Section repealed 1997]

Leg.H. Enacted Stats 1992 ch 162 §10 (AB 2650), operative January 1, 1994. Amended Stats 1993 ch 219 §152 (AB 1500), ch 876 §20.5 (SB 1068), effective October 6, 1993, operative January 1, 1994; Stats 1994 ch 1269 §49 (AB 2208). Repealed Stats 1997 ch 194 §1 (SB 568). The repealed section related to effect of registration of a foreign support or assignment order and enforcement of a registered order.

§4854. [Section repealed 1997]

Leg.H. Enacted Stats 1992 ch 162 §10 (AB 2650), operative January 1, 1994. Repealed Stats 1997 ch 194 §1 (SB 568). The repealed section related to support orders registered in a court of a county other than that of the rendering court, and service of a copy by mail.

CHAPTER 6
UNIFORM INTERSTATE FAMILY SUPPORT ACT [REPEALED]

Article 4. Establishment of Support Order [Repealed].
Article 6. Enforcement and Modification of Support Order After Registration [Repealed].

ARTICLE 1
General Provisions [Repealed]

§4900. [Section repealed 2016]

Leg.H. Added Stats 1997 ch 194 §2 (SB 568). Repealed Stats 2015 ch 493 §2 (SB 646), effective January 1, 2016. The repealed section related to citation of the chapter as the Uniform Interstate Family Support Act. See Fam C §5700.101.

§4901. [Section repealed 2016]

Leg.H. Added Stats 1997 ch 194 §2 (SB 568). Amended Stats 1998 ch 485 §65 (AB 2803); Stats 1999 ch 83 §51 (SB 966). Repealed Stats 2015 ch 493 §2 (SB 646), effective January 1, 2016. The repealed section related to definitions for the chapter. See Fam C §5700.102.

2015 Note: Stats 2002 ch 349 §1 amended this section, operative upon federal government action specified in Stats 2002 ch 349 §47; however, Stats 2015 ch 493 §16, effective January 1, 2016, repealed Stats 2002 ch 349 prior to the federal government taking the specified action, thereby deleting the amendment, which had not yet, and never will, become operative.

§4902. [Section repealed 2016]

Leg.H. Added Stats 1997 ch 194 §2 (SB 568). Repealed Stats 2015 ch 493 §2 (SB 646), effective January 1, 2016. The repealed section related to the superior court as tribunal of state. See Fam C §5700.103.

§4903. [Section repealed 2016]

Leg.H. Added Stats 1997 ch 194 §2 (SB 568). Repealed Stats 2015 ch 493 §2 (SB 646), effective January 1, 2016. The repealed section related to remedies provided by chapter. See Fam C §5700.104.

2015 Note: Stats 2002 ch 349 §2 amended this section, operative upon federal government action specified in Stats 2002 ch 349 §47; however, Stats 2015 ch 493 §16, effective January 1, 2016, repealed Stats 2002 ch 349 prior to the federal government taking the specified action, thereby deleting the amendment, which had not yet, and never will, become operative.

ARTICLE 2
Jurisdiction [Repealed]

§4905. [Section repealed 2016]

Leg.H. Added Stats 1997 ch 194 §2 (SB 568). Repealed Stats 2015 ch 493 §2 (SB 646), effective January 1, 2016. The repealed section related to personal jurisdiction over nonresidents. See Fam C §5700.201.

2015 Note: Stats 2002 ch 349 §3 amended this section, operative upon federal government action specified in Stats 2002 ch 349 §47; however, Stats 2015 ch 493 §16, effective January 1, 2016, repealed Stats 2002 ch 349 prior to the federal government taking the specified action, thereby deleting the amendment, which had not yet, and never will, become operative.

§4906. [Section repealed 2016]

Leg.H. Added Stats 1997 ch 194 §2 (SB 568). Repealed Stats 2015 ch 493 §2 (SB 646), effective January 1, 2016. The repealed section related to receipt of evidence from, and obtaining discovery through tribunal of, another state. See Fam C §5700.210.

2015 Note: Stats 2002 ch 349 §4 amended this section, operative upon federal government action specified in Stats 2002 ch 349 §47; however, Stats 2015 ch 493 §16, effective January 1, 2016, repealed Stats 2002 ch 349 prior to the federal government taking the specified action, thereby deleting the amendment, which had not yet, and never will, become operative.

§4907. [Section repealed 2016]

Leg.H. Added Stats 1997 ch 194 §2 (SB 568). Repealed Stats 2015 ch 493 §2 (SB 646), effective January 1, 2016. The repealed section related to tribunal of state serving as an initiating tribunal and a responding tribunal. See Fam C §5700.203.

§4908. [Section repealed 2016]

Leg.H. Added Stats 1997 ch 194 §2 (SB 568). Repealed Stats 2015 ch 493 §2 (SB 646), effective January 1, 2016. The repealed section related to conditions for the exercise of jurisdiction to establish support order. See Fam C §5700.204.

§4909. [Section repealed 2016]

Leg.H. Added Stats 1997 ch 194 §2 (SB 568). Repealed Stats 2015 ch 493 §2 (SB 646), effective January 1, 2016. The repealed section related to continuing jurisdiction. See Fam C §5700.205.

2015 Note: Stats 2002 ch 349 §5 amended this section, operative upon federal government action specified in Stats 2002 ch 349 §47; however, Stats 2015 ch 493 §16, effective January 1, 2016, repealed Stats 2002 ch 349 prior to the federal government taking the specified action, thereby deleting the amendment, which had not yet, and never will, become operative.

§4910. [Section repealed 2016]

Leg.H. Added Stats 1997 ch 194 §2 (SB 568). Repealed Stats 2015 ch 493 §2 (SB 646), effective January 1, 2016. The repealed section related to the relationship of continuing jurisdiction to modification and enforcement. See Fam C §5700.206.

2015 Note: Stats 2002 ch 349 §6 amended this section, operative upon federal government action specified in Stats 2002 ch 349 §47; however, Stats 2015 ch 493 §16, effective January 1, 2016, repealed Stats 2002 ch 349 prior to the federal government taking the specified action, thereby deleting the amendment, which had not yet, and never will, become operative.

§4911. [Section repealed 2016]

Leg.H. Added Stats 1997 ch 194 §2 (SB 568). Repealed Stats 2015 ch 493 §2 (SB 646), effective January 1, 2016. The repealed section related to multiple support orders. See Fam C §5700.207.

2015 Note: Stats 2002 ch 349 §7 amended this section, operative upon federal government action specified in Stats 2002 ch 349 §47; however, Stats 2015 ch 493 §16, effective January 1, 2016, repealed Stats 2002 ch 349 prior to the federal government taking the specified action, thereby deleting the amendment, which had not yet, and never will, become operative.

§4912. [Section repealed 2016]

Leg.H. Added Stats 1997 ch 194 §2 (SB 568). Repealed Stats 2015 ch 493 §2 (SB 646), effective January 1, 2016. The repealed section related to enforcement of multiple orders. See Fam C §5700.208.

2015 Note: Stats 2002 ch 349 §8 amended this section, operative upon federal government action specified in Stats 2002 ch 349 §47; however, Stats 2015 ch 493 §16, effective January 1, 2016, repealed Stats 2002 ch 349 prior to the federal government taking the specified action, thereby deleting the amendment, which had not yet, and never will, become operative.

§4913. [Section repealed 2016]

Leg.H. Added Stats 1997 ch 194 §2 (SB 568). Repealed Stats 2015 ch 493 §2 (SB 646), effective January 1, 2016. The repealed section related to crediting amounts collected. See Fam C §5700.209.

2015 Note: Stats 2002 ch 349 §9 amended this section, operative upon federal government action specified in Stats 2002 ch 349 §47; however, Stats 2015 ch 493 §16, effective January 1, 2016, repealed Stats 2002 ch 349 prior to the federal government taking the specified action, thereby deleting the amendment, which had not yet, and never will, become operative.

§4913.5. [Section repealed 2016]

Leg.H. Added Stats 2002 ch 349 §10, effective January 1, 2003, operative date contingent. Repealed Stats 2015 ch 493 §2 (SB 646), effective January 1, 2016. The repealed section related to evidence, communication, and discovery from another state in proceedings relating to support order involving nonresident.

2015 Note: Stats 2002 ch 349 §10 added this section, operative upon federal government action specified in Stats 2002 ch 349 §47; however, Stats 2015 ch 493 §16, effective January 1, 2016, repealed Stats 2002 ch 349 prior to the federal government taking the specified action, thereby deleting the amendment, which had not yet, and never will, become operative.

§4914. [Section repealed 2016]

Leg.H. Added Stats 2002 ch 349 §11, effective January 1, 2003, operative date contingent. Repealed Stats 2015 ch 493 §2 (SB 646), effective January 1, 2016. The repealed section related to jurisdiction over spousal support orders.

2015 Note: Stats 2002 ch 349 §11 added this section, operative upon federal government action specified in Stats 2002 ch 349 §47; however, Stats 2015 ch 493 §16, effective January 1, 2016, repealed Stats 2002 ch 349 prior to the federal government taking the specified action, thereby deleting the amendment, which had not yet, and never will, become operative.

ARTICLE 3
Civil Provisions of General Application [Repealed]

§4915. [Section repealed 2016]

Leg.H. Added Stats 1997 ch 194 §2 (SB 568). Repealed Stats 2015 ch 493 §2 (SB 646), effective January 1, 2016. The repealed section related to proceedings under chapter. See Fam C §5700.301.

2015 Note: Stats 2002 ch 349 §12 amended this section, operative upon federal government action specified in Stats 2002 ch 349 §47; however, Stats 2015 ch 493 §16, effective January 1, 2016, repealed Stats 2002 ch 349 prior to the federal government taking the specified action, thereby deleting the amendment, which had not yet, and never will, become operative.

§4916. [Section repealed 2016]

Leg.H. Added Stats 1997 ch 194 §2 (SB 568). Repealed Stats 2015 ch 493 §2 (SB 646), effective January 1, 2016. The repealed section related to minor parent or guardian maintaining proceeding on behalf of the minor's child. See Fam C §5700.302.

§4917. [Section repealed 2016]

Leg.H. Added Stats 1997 ch 194 §2 (SB 568). Repealed Stats 2015 ch 493 §2 (SB 646), effective January 1, 2016. The repealed section related to responding tribunals. See Fam C §5700.303.

2015 Note: Stats 2002 ch 349 §13 amended this section, operative upon federal government action specified in Stats 2002 ch 349 §47; however, Stats 2015 ch 493 §16, effective January 1, 2016, repealed Stats 2002 ch 349 prior to the federal government taking the specified action, thereby deleting the amendment, which had not yet, and never will, become operative.

§4918. [Section repealed 2016]

Leg.H. Added Stats 1997 ch 194 §2 (SB 568). Repealed Stats 2015 ch 493 §2 (SB 646), effective January 1, 2016. The repealed section related to forwarding of petition by initiating tribunal. See Fam C §5700.304.

2015 Note: Stats 2002 ch 349 §14 amended this section, operative upon federal government action specified in Stats 2002 ch 349 §47; however, Stats 2015 ch 493 §16, effective January 1, 2016, repealed Stats 2002 ch 349 prior to the federal government taking the specified action, thereby deleting the amendment, which had not yet, and never will, become operative.

§4919. [Section repealed 2016]

Leg.H. Added Stats 1997 ch 194 §2 (SB 568). Repealed Stats 2015 ch 493 §2 (SB 646), effective January 1, 2016. The repealed section related to responding tribunal authority and duties. See Fam C §5700.305.

2015 Note: Stats 2002 ch 349 §15 amended this section, operative upon federal government action specified in Stats 2002 ch 349 §47; however, Stats 2015 ch 493 §16, effective January 1, 2016, repealed Stats 2002 ch 349 prior to the federal government taking the specified action, thereby deleting the amendment, which had not yet, and never will, become operative.

§4920. [Section repealed 2016]

Leg.H. Added Stats 1997 ch 194 §2 (SB 568). Repealed Stats 2015 ch 493 §2 (SB 646), effective January 1, 2016. The repealed section related to inappropriate tribunals. See Fam C §5700.306.

2015 Note: Stats 2002 ch 349 §16 amended this section, operative upon federal government action specified in Stats 2002 ch 349 §47; however, Stats 2015 ch 493 §16, effective January 1, 2016, repealed Stats 2002 ch 349 prior to the federal government taking the specified action, thereby deleting the amendment, which had not yet, and never will, become operative.

§4921. [Section repealed 2016]

Leg.H. Added Stats 1997 ch 194 §2 (SB 568). Amended Stats 1998 ch 511 §2 (AB 1900). Repealed Stats 2015 ch 493 §2 (SB 646), effective January 1, 2016. The repealed section related to provision of services by support enforcement agency to petitioners. See Fam C §5700.307.

2015 Note: Stats 2002 ch 349 §17 amended this section, operative upon federal government action specified in Stats 2002 ch 349 §47; however, Stats 2015 ch 493 §16, effective January 1, 2016, repealed Stats 2002 ch 349 prior to the federal government taking the specified action, thereby deleting the amendment, which had not yet, and never will, become operative.

§4922. [Section repealed 2016]

Leg.H. Added Stats 1997 ch 194 §2 (SB 568). Repealed Stats 2015 ch 493 §2 (SB 646), effective January 1, 2016. The repealed section related to provision of services by the Attorney General if support enforcement agency is neglecting or refusing to provide services. See Fam C §5700.308.

2015 Note: Stats 2002 ch 349 §18 amended this section, operative upon federal government action specified in Stats 2002 ch 349 §47; however, Stats 2015 ch 493 §16, effective January 1, 2016, repealed Stats 2002 ch 349 prior to the federal government taking the specified action, thereby deleting the amendment, which had not yet, and never will, become operative.

§4923. [Section repealed 2016]

Leg.H. Added Stats 1997 ch 194 §2 (SB 568). Repealed Stats 2015 ch 493 §2 (SB 646), effective January 1, 2016. The repealed section related to employment of private counsel. See Fam C §5700.309.

§4924. [Section repealed 2016]

Leg.H. Added Stats 1997 ch 194 §2 (SB 568). Repealed Stats 2015 ch 493 §2 (SB 646), effective January 1, 2016. The repealed section related to state information agency. See Fam C §5700.310.

2015 Note: Stats 2002 ch 349 §19 amended this section, operative upon federal government action specified in Stats 2002 ch 349 §47; however, Stats 2015 ch 493 §16, effective January 1, 2016, repealed Stats 2002 ch 349 prior to the federal government taking the specified action, thereby deleting the amendment, which had not yet, and never will, become operative.

§4925. [Section repealed 2016]

Leg.H. Added Stats 1997 ch 194 §2 (SB 568). Repealed Stats 2015 ch 493 §2 (SB 646), effective January 1, 2016. The repealed section related to contents of petition. See Fam C §5700.311.

2015 Note: Stats 2002 ch 349 §20 amended this section, operative upon federal government action specified in Stats 2002 ch 349 §47; however, Stats 2015 ch 493 §16, effective January 1, 2016, repealed Stats 2002 ch 349 prior to the federal government taking the specified action, thereby deleting the amendment, which had not yet, and never will, become operative.

§4926. [Section repealed 2016]

Leg.H. Added Stats 1997 ch 194 §2 (SB 568). Repealed Stats 2002 ch 349 §21 (AB 2934), repeal date contingent; Stats 2015 ch 493 §2 (SB 646), effective January 1, 2016. The repealed section related to disclosure of identifying information. See Fam C §5700.312.

2015 Note: Stats 2002 ch 349 §21 repealed this section, operative upon federal government action specified in Stats 2002 ch 349 §47; however, Stats 2015 ch 493 §16, effective January 1, 2016, repealed Stats 2002 ch 349 prior to the federal government taking the specified action, thereby deleting the amendment, which had not yet, and never will, become operative.

§4927. [Section repealed 2016]

Leg.H. Added Stats 1997 ch 194 §2 (SB 568). Repealed Stats 2015 ch 493 §2 (SB 646), effective January 1, 2016. The repealed section related to costs and fees. See Fam C §5700.313.

§4928. [Section repealed 2016]

Leg.H. Added Stats 1997 ch 194 §2 (SB 568). Repealed Stats 2015 ch 493 §2 (SB 646), effective January 1, 2016. The repealed section related to the physical presence of petitioner. See Fam C §5700.314.

2015 Note: Stats 2002 ch 349 §23 amended this section, operative upon federal government action specified in Stats 2002 ch 349 §47; however, Stats 2015 ch 493 §16, effective January 1, 2016, repealed Stats 2002 ch 349 prior to the federal government taking the specified action, thereby deleting the amendment, which had not yet, and never will, become operative.

§4929. [Section repealed 2016]

Leg.H. Added Stats 1997 ch 194 §2 (SB 568). Repealed Stats 2015 ch 493 §2 (SB 646), effective January 1, 2016. The repealed section related to nonparentage as a defense. See Fam C §5700.315.

§4930. [Section repealed 2016]

Leg.H. Added Stats 1997 ch 194 §2 (SB 568). Amended Stats 2014 ch 82 §37 (SB 1306), effective January 1, 2015. Repealed Stats 2015 ch 493 §2 (SB 646), effective January 1, 2016. The repealed section related to special evidentiary rules. See Fam C §5700.316.

2015 Note: Stats 2002 ch 349 §24 amended this section, operative upon federal government action specified in Stats 2002 ch 349 §47; however, Stats 2015 ch 493 §16, effective January 1, 2016, repealed Stats 2002 ch 349 prior to the federal government taking the specified action, thereby deleting the amendment, which had not yet, and never will, become operative.

§4931. [Section repealed 2016]

Leg.H. Added Stats 1997 ch 194 §2 (SB 568). Repealed Stats 2015 ch 493 §2 (SB 646), effective January 1, 2016. The repealed section related to communications with tribunal of another state. See Fam C §5700.317.

2015 Note: Stats 2002 ch 349 §25 amended this section, operative upon federal government action specified in Stats 2002 ch 349 §47; however, Stats 2015 ch 493 §16, effective January 1, 2016, repealed Stats 2002 ch 349 prior to the federal government taking the specified action, thereby deleting the amendment, which had not yet, and never will, become operative.

§4932. [Section repealed 2016]

Leg.H. Added Stats 1997 ch 194 §2 (SB 568). Repealed Stats 2015 ch 493 §2 (SB 646), effective January 1, 2016. The repealed section related to discovery. See Fam C §5700.318.

§4933. [Section repealed 2016]

Leg.H. Added Stats 1997 ch 194 §2 (SB 568). Repealed Stats 2015 ch 493 §2 (SB 646), effective January 1, 2016. The repealed section related to payments received pursuant to a support order. See Fam C §5700.319.

2015 Note: Stats 2002 ch 349 §26 amended this section, operative upon federal government action specified in Stats 2002 ch 349 §47; however, Stats 2015 ch 493

ARTICLE 4
Establishment of Support Order [Repealed]

§4935. [Section repealed 2016]

Leg.H. Added Stats 1997 ch 194 §2 (SB 568). Repealed Stats 2015 ch 493 §2 (SB 646), effective January 1, 2016. The repealed section related to conditions for issuing support order. See Fam C §5700.401.

2015 Note: Stats 2002 ch 349 §27 amended this section, operative upon federal government action specified in Stats 2002 ch 349 §47; however, Stats 2015 ch 493 §16, effective January 1, 2016, repealed Stats 2002 ch 349 prior to the federal government taking the specified action, thereby deleting the amendment, which had not yet, and never will, become operative.

ARTICLE 5
Enforcement of Order of Another State Without Registration [Repealed]

§4940. [Section repealed 2016]

Leg.H. Added Stats 1997 ch 194 §2 (SB 568). Repealed Stats 2015 ch 493 §2 (SB 646), effective January 1, 2016. The repealed section related to sending of income-withholding order to obligor's employer. See Fam C §5700.501.

2015 Note: Stats 2002 ch 349 §28 amended this section, operative upon federal government action specified in Stats 2002 ch 349 §47; however, Stats 2015 ch 493 §16, effective January 1, 2016, repealed Stats 2002 ch 349 prior to the federal government taking the specified action, thereby deleting the amendment, which had not yet, and never will, become operative.

§4941. [Section repealed 2016]

Leg.H. Added Stats 1997 ch 194 §2 (SB 568). Repealed Stats 2015 ch 493 §2 (SB 646), effective January 1, 2016. The repealed section related to employer's duties upon receipt of income-withholding order. See Fam C §5700.502.

2015 Note: Stats 2002 ch 349 §29 amended this section, operative upon federal government action specified in Stats 2002 ch 349 §47; however, Stats 2015 ch 493 §16, effective January 1, 2016, repealed Stats 2002 ch 349 prior to the federal government taking the specified action, thereby deleting the amendment, which had not yet, and never will, become operative.

§4942. [Section repealed 2016]

Leg.H. Added Stats 1997 ch 194 §2 (SB 568). Repealed Stats 2015 ch 493 §2 (SB 646), effective January 1, 2016. The repealed section related to receipt of multiple income-withholding orders by obligor's employer. See Fam C §5700.503.

2015 Note: Stats 2002 ch 349 §30 amended this section, operative upon federal government action specified in Stats 2002 ch 349 §47; however, Stats 2015 ch 493 §16, effective January 1, 2016, repealed Stats 2002 ch 349 prior to the federal government taking the specified action, thereby deleting the amendment, which had not yet, and never will, become operative.

§4943. [Section repealed 2016]

Leg.H. Added Stats 1997 ch 194 §2 (SB 568). Repealed Stats 2015 ch 493 §2 (SB 646), effective January 1, 2016. The repealed section related to liability of employer for complying with income-withholding order. See Fam C §5700.504.

§4944. [Section repealed 2016]

Leg.H. Added Stats 1997 ch 194 §2 (SB 568). Repealed Stats 2015 ch 493 §2 (SB 646), effective January 1, 2016. The repealed section related to penalties for noncompliance by employer with income-withholding order. See Fam C §5700.505.

§4945. [Section repealed 2016]

Leg.H. Added Stats 1997 ch 194 §2 (SB 568). Repealed Stats 2015 ch 493 §2 (SB 646), effective January 1, 2016. The repealed section related to contesting income-withholding order. See Fam C §5700.506.

2015 Note: Stats 2002 ch 349 §31 amended this section, operative upon federal government action specified in Stats 2002 ch 349 §47; however, Stats 2015 ch 493 §16, effective January 1, 2016, repealed Stats 2002 ch 349 prior to the federal government taking the specified action, thereby deleting the amendment, which had not yet, and never will, become operative.

§4946. [Section repealed 2016]

Leg.H. Added Stats 1997 ch 194 §2 (SB 568). Repealed Stats 2015 ch 493 §2 (SB 646), effective January 1, 2016. The repealed section related to sending documents required to register support or income-withholding order to support enforcement agency and administrative enforcement or registration of order. See Fam C §5700.507.

2015 Note: Stats 2002 ch 349 §32 amended this section, operative upon federal government action specified in Stats 2002 ch 349 §47; however, Stats 2015 ch 493 §16, effective January 1, 2016, repealed Stats 2002 ch 349 prior to the federal government taking the specified action, thereby deleting the amendment, which had not yet, and never will, become operative.

See §5700.507.

ARTICLE 6
Enforcement and Modification of Support Order After Registration [Repealed]

§4950. [Section repealed 2016]

Leg.H. Added Stats 1997 ch 194 §2 (SB 568). Repealed Stats 2015 ch 493 §2 (SB 646), effective January 1, 2016. The repealed section related to registration of support or income-withholding order issued by another state for enforcement. See Fam C §5700.601.

2015 Note: Stats 2002 ch 349 §33 amended this section, operative upon federal government action specified in Stats 2002 ch 349 §47; however, Stats 2015 ch 493 §16, effective January 1, 2016, repealed Stats 2002 ch 349 prior to the federal government taking the specified action, thereby deleting the amendment, which had not yet, and never will, become operative.

§4951. [Section repealed 2016]

Leg.H. Added Stats 1997 ch 194 §2 (SB 568). Repealed Stats 2015 ch 493 §2 (SB 646), effective January 1, 2016. The repealed section related to documents and information required to register support or income-withholding order in state. See Fam C §5700.602.

2015 Note: Stats 2002 ch 349 §34 amended this section, operative upon federal government action specified in Stats 2002 ch 349 §47; however, Stats 2015 ch 493 §16, effective January 1, 2016, repealed Stats 2002 ch 349 prior to the federal government taking the specified action, thereby deleting the amendment, which had not yet, and never will, become operative.

See §5700.602.

§4952. [Section repealed 2016]

Leg.H. Added Stats 1997 ch 194 §2 (SB 568). Repealed Stats 2015 ch 493 §2 (SB 646), effective January 1, 2016. The repealed section related to registered order issued in another state. See Fam C §5700.603.

§4953. [Section repealed 2016]

Leg.H. Added Stats 1997 ch 194 §2 (SB 568). Repealed Stats 2015 ch 493 §2 (SB 646), effective January 1, 2016. The repealed section related to governing law. See Fam C §5700.604.

2015 Note: Stats 2002 ch 349 §35 amended this section, operative upon federal government action specified in Stats 2002 ch 349 §47; however, Stats 2015 ch 493 §16, effective January 1, 2016, repealed Stats 2002 ch 349 prior to the federal government taking the specified action, thereby deleting the amendment, which had not yet, and never will, become operative.

§4954. [Section repealed 2016]

Leg.H. Added Stats 1997 ch 194 §2 (SB 568). Repealed Stats 2015 ch 493 §2 (SB 646), effective January 1, 2016. The repealed section related to notification of registration of support or income-withholding order. See Fam C §5700.605.

2015 Note: Stats 2002 ch 349 §36 amended this section, operative upon federal government action specified in Stats 2002 ch 349 §47; however, Stats 2015 ch 493 §16, effective January 1, 2016, repealed Stats 2002 ch 349 prior to the federal government taking the specified action, thereby deleting the amendment, which had not yet, and never will, become operative.

See §5700.605.

§4955. [Section repealed 2016]

Leg.H. Added Stats 1997 ch 194 §2 (SB 568). Repealed Stats 2015 ch 493 §2 (SB 646), effective January 1, 2016. The repealed section related to contesting a registered order. See Fam C §5700.606.

§4956. [Section repealed 2016]

Leg.H. Added Stats 1997 ch 194 §2 (SB 568). Repealed Stats 2015 ch 493 §2 (SB 646), effective January 1, 2016. The repealed section related to burden of proving specified defenses. See Fam C §5700.607.

§4957. [Section repealed 2016]

Leg.H. Added Stats 1997 ch 194 §2 (SB 568). Repealed Stats 2015 ch 493 §2 (SB 646), effective January 1, 2016. The repealed section related to preclusion of further contest by confirmation of registered order. See Fam C §5700.608.

§4958. [Section repealed 2016]

Leg.H. Added Stats 1997 ch 194 §2 (SB 568). Repealed Stats 2015 ch 493 §2 (SB 646), effective January 1, 2016. The repealed section related to modification of child support order issued in another state. See Fam C §5700.609.

§4959. [Section repealed 2016]

Leg.H. Added Stats 1997 ch 194 §2 (SB 568). Repealed Stats 2015 ch 493 §2 (SB 646), effective January 1, 2016. The repealed section related to the enforcement of child support order of another state registered for modification. See Fam C §5700.610.

2015 Note: Stats 2002 ch 349 §38 amended this section, operative upon federal government action specified in Stats 2002 ch 349 §47; however, Stats 2015 ch 493 §16, effective January 1, 2016, repealed Stats 2002 ch 349 prior to the federal government taking the specified action, thereby deleting the amendment, which had not yet, and never will, become operative.

§4960. [Section repealed 2016]

Leg.H. Added Stats 1997 ch 194 §2 (SB 568). Repealed Stats 2015 ch 493 §2 (SB 646), effective January 1, 2016. The repealed section related to requirements for modification of child support order. See Fam C §5700.611.

2015 Note: Stats 2002 ch 349 §39 amended this section, operative upon federal government action specified in Stats 2002 ch 349 §47; however, Stats 2015 ch 493 §16, effective January 1, 2016, repealed Stats 2002 ch 349 prior to the federal government taking the specified action, thereby deleting the amendment, which had not yet, and never will, become operative.

See §5700.611.

§4961. [Section repealed 2016]

Leg.H. Added Stats 1997 ch 194 §2 (SB 568). Repealed Stats 2015 ch 493 §2 (SB 646), effective January 1, 2016. The repealed section related to recognition of modification of child support order. See Fam C §5700.612.

2015 Note: Stats 2002 ch 349 §40 amended this section, operative upon federal government action specified in Stats 2002 ch 349 §47; however, Stats 2015 ch 493 §16, effective January 1, 2016, repealed Stats 2002 ch 349 prior to the federal government taking the specified action, thereby deleting the amendment, which had not yet, and never will, become operative.

§4962. [Section repealed 2016]

Leg.H. Added Stats 1997 ch 194 §2 (SB 568). Amended Stats 2004 ch 183 §95 (AB 3082). Repealed Stats 2015 ch 493 §2 (SB 646), effective January 1, 2016. The repealed section related to jurisdiction to enforce and modify child support order when child does not reside in issuing state. See Fam C §5700.613.

§4963. [Section repealed 2016]

Leg.H. Added Stats 1997 ch 194 §2 (SB 568). Repealed Stats 2015 ch 493 §2 (SB 646), effective January 1, 2016. The repealed section related to filing certified copy of modified child support order. See Fam C §5700.614.

§4964. [Section repealed 2016]

Leg.H. Added Stats 2002 ch 349 §41, effective January 1, 2003, operative date contingent. Repealed Stats 2015 ch 493 §2 (SB 646), effective January 1, 2016. The repealed section related to assumption of jurisdiction to modify foreign child support order.

2015 Note: Stats 2002 ch 349 §41 added this section, operative upon federal government action specified in Stats 2002 ch 349 §47; however, Stats 2015 ch 493 §16, effective January 1, 2016, repealed Stats 2002 ch 349 prior to the federal government taking the specified action, thereby deleting the amendment, which had not yet, and never will, become operative.

ARTICLE 7
Determination of Parentage [Repealed]

§4965. [Section repealed 2016]

Leg.H. Added Stats 1997 ch 194 §2 (SB 568). Repealed Stats 2015 ch 493 §2 (SB 646), effective January 1, 2016. The repealed section related to tribunal of state acting as initiating or responding tribunal to determine parentage of child and application of Uniform Parentage Act. See Fam C §5700.402.

2015 Note: Stats 2002 ch 349 §42 amended this section, operative upon federal government action specified in Stats 2002 ch 349 §47; however, Stats 2015 ch 493 §16, effective January 1, 2016, repealed Stats 2002 ch 349 prior to the federal government taking the specified action, thereby deleting the amendment, which had not yet, and never will, become operative.

ARTICLE 8
Interstate Rendition [Repealed]

§4970. [Section repealed 2016]

Leg.H. Added Stats 1997 ch 194 §2 (SB 568). Repealed Stats 2015 ch 493 §2 (SB 646), effective January 1, 2016. The repealed section related to the governor's extradition powers. See Fam C §5700.801.

2015 Note: Stats 2002 ch 349 §43 amended this section, operative upon federal government action specified in Stats 2002 ch 349 §47; however, Stats 2015 ch 493 §16, effective January 1, 2016, repealed Stats 2002 ch 349 prior to the federal government taking the specified action, thereby deleting the amendment, which had not yet, and never will, become operative.

§4971. [Section repealed 2016]

Leg.H. Added Stats 1997 ch 194 §2 (SB 568). Repealed Stats 2015 ch 493 §2 (SB 646), effective January 1, 2016. The repealed section related to rights of governor with respect to extradition demands. See Fam C §5700.802.

2015 Note: Stats 2002 ch 349 §44 amended this section, operative upon federal government action specified in Stats 2002 ch 349 §47; however, Stats 2015 ch 493 §16, effective January 1, 2016, repealed Stats 2002 ch 349 prior to the federal government taking the specified action, thereby deleting the amendment, which had not yet, and never will, become operative.

ARTICLE 9
Miscellaneous Provisions [Repealed]

§4975. [Section repealed 2016]

Leg.H. Added Stats 1997 ch 194 §2 (SB 568). Repealed Stats 2015 ch 493 §2 (SB 646), effective January 1, 2016. The repealed section related to uniformity of laws. See Fam C §5700.901.

§4976. [Section repealed 2016]

Leg.H. Added Stats 1997 ch 194 §2 (SB 568). Repealed Stats 2015 ch 493 §2 (SB 646), effective January 1, 2016. The repealed section related to severability of provisions. See Fam C §5700.903.

§4977. [Section repealed 2016]

Leg.H. Added Stats 1998 ch 511 §3 (AB 1900). Repealed Stats 2015 ch 493 §2 (SB 646), effective January 1, 2016. The repealed section related to order of nondisclosure of applicant's address or other identifying information.

§4978. [Section repealed 2016]

Leg.H. Added Stats 1998 ch 511 §4 (AB 1900). Repealed Stats 2015 ch 493 §2 (SB 646), effective January 1, 2016. The repealed section related to the duties of support enforcement agency.

§5000. [Section repealed 2016]

Leg.H. Added Stats 1999 ch 980 §10 (AB 1671). Amended Stats 2000 ch 808 §51 (AB 1358), effective September 28, 2000. Repealed Stats 2015 ch 493 §2 (SB 646), effective January 1, 2016. The repealed section related to a summons or order to show cause. See Fam C §17404.1.

§5001. [Section repealed 2016]

Leg.H. Added Stats 1999 ch 980 §11 (AB 1671). Amended Stats 2000 ch 808 §52 (AB 1358), effective September 28, 2000. Repealed Stats 2015 ch 493 §2 (SB 646), effective January 1, 2016. The repealed section related to transfers of actions. See Fam C §17404.2.

§5002. [Section repealed 2016]

Leg.H. Added Stats 1999 ch 980 §12 (AB 1671). Amended Stats 2000 ch 135 §60 (AB 2539), ch 808 §53 (AB 1358) (ch 808 prevails), effective September 28, 2000; Stats 2004 ch 339 §4 (AB 1704). Repealed Stats

2015 ch 493 §2 (SB 646), effective January 1, 2016. The repealed section related to judgment pursuant to presumed income.

§5003. [Section repealed 2016]

Leg.H. Added Stats 2004 ch 339 §5 (AB 1704). Repealed Stats 2015 ch 493 §2 (SB 646), effective January 1, 2016. The repealed section related to the implementation of provisions for hearings by telephone, audiovisual, or other electronic means and application to child support cases. See Fam C §17404.3.

§5005. [Section repealed 2016]

Leg.H. Added Stats 1999 ch 652 §4 (SB 240). Repealed Stats 2015 ch 493 §2 (SB 646), effective January 1, 2016. The repealed section related to the declaration of foreign jurisdiction as reciprocating state. See Fam C §17407.5.

CHAPTER 7
ENFORCEMENT BY WRIT OF EXECUTION

Enforcement of child or family support without prior court approval. §5100.
Enforcement of support against employee pension benefit plan. §5103.
Application for writ. §5104.

§5100. Enforcement of child or family support without prior court approval

Notwithstanding Section 290, a child, family, or spousal support order may be enforced by a writ of execution or a notice of levy pursuant to Section 706.030 of the Code of Civil Procedure or Section 17522 of this code without prior court approval. **Leg.H.** Enacted Stats 1992 ch 162 §10 (AB 2650), operative January 1, 1994. Amended Stats 1993 ch 876 §21 (SB 1068), effective October 6, 1993, operative January 1, 1994; Stats 1994 ch 1269 §49.2 (AB 2208); Stats 1997 ch 599 §19 (AB 573); Stats 2000 ch 808 §54 (AB 1358), effective September 28, 2000.

§5101. [Section repealed 2000]

Leg.H. Enacted Stats 1992 ch 162 §10 (AB 2650), operative January 1, 1994. Amended Stats 1993 ch 876 §22 (SB 1068), effective October 6, 1993, operative January 1, 1994; Stats 1994 ch 1269 §49.4 (AB 2208); Stats 1997 ch 599 §20 (AB 573). Repealed Stats 2000 ch 808 §55 (AB 1358), effective September 28, 2000. The repealed section related to enforcement of spousal support without prior court approval.

§5102. [Section repealed 2000]

Leg.H. Enacted Stats 1992 ch 162 §10 (AB 2650), operative January 1, 1994. Repealed Stats 2000 ch 808 §56 (AB 1358), effective September 28, 2000. The repealed section related to period for enforcement of installment payments.

§5103. Enforcement of support against employee pension benefit plan

(a) Notwithstanding Section 2060, an order for the payment of child, family, or spousal support may be enforced against an employee benefit plan regardless of whether the plan has been joined as a party to the proceeding in which the support order was obtained.

(b) Notwithstanding Section 697.710 of the Code of Civil Procedure, an execution lien created by a levy on the judgment debtor's right to payment of benefits from an employee benefit plan to enforce an order for the payment of child, family, or spousal support continues until the date the plan has withheld and paid over to the levying officer, as provided in Section 701.010 of the Code of Civil Procedure, the full amount specified in the notice of levy, unless the plan is directed to stop withholding and paying over before that time by court order or by the levying officer.

(c) A writ of execution pursuant to which a levy is made on the judgment debtor's right to payment of benefits from an employee benefit plan under an order for the payment of child, family, or spousal support shall be returned not later than one year after the date the execution lien expires under subdivision (b). **Leg.H.** Enacted Stats 1992 ch 162 §10 (AB 2650), operative January 1, 1994. Amended Stats 1994 ch 1269 §50 (AB 2208).

§5104. Application for writ

(a) The application for a writ of execution shall be accompanied by an affidavit stating the total amount due and unpaid that is authorized to be enforced pursuant to Sections 5100 to 5103, inclusive, on the date of the application.

(b) If interest on the overdue installments is sought, the affidavit shall state the total amount of the interest and the amount of each due and unpaid installment and the date it became due.

(c) The affidavit shall be filed in the action and a copy shall be attached to the writ of execution delivered to the levying officer. The levying officer shall serve the copy of the affidavit on the judgment debtor when the writ of execution is first served on the judgment debtor pursuant to a levy under the writ. **Leg.H.** Enacted Stats 1992 ch 162 §10 (AB 2650), operative January 1, 1994.

CHAPTER 8
EARNINGS ASSIGNMENT ORDER

Article 1. Definitions.
Article 2. General Provisions.
Article 3. Support Orders Issued or Modified Before July 1, 1990.
Article 4. Stay of Service of Assignment Order.
Article 5. Motion to Quash Assignment Order.
Article 6. Information Concerning Address and Employment of Obligor.
Article 7. Prohibited Practices.
Article 8. Judicial Council Forms.
Article 9. Intercounty Support Obligations.

ARTICLE 1
Definitions

Definitions to govern construction. §5200.
"Arrearage" or "arrearages". §5201.
"Assignment order". §5202.
"Due date of support payments". §5204.
"Earnings". §5206.
"Earnings assignment order for support". §5208.
"Employer". §5210.
"IV-D Case". §5212.
"Obligee"; "Assigned obligee". §5214.
"Obligor". §5216.
"Timely payment". §5220.

§5200. Definitions to govern construction

Unless the provision or context otherwise requires, the definitions in this article govern the construction of this chapter. **Leg.H.** Enacted Stats 1992 ch 162 §10 (AB 2650), operative January 1, 1994.

§5201. "Arrearage" or "arrearages"

"Arrearage" or "arrearages" is the amount necessary to satisfy a support judgment or order pursuant to Section 695.210 of the Code of Civil Procedure. **Leg.H.** Added Stats 1997 ch 599 §21 (AB 573).

§5202. "Assignment order"

"Assignment order" has the same meaning as "earnings assignment order for support." **Leg.H.** Enacted Stats 1992 ch 162 §10 (AB 2650), operative January 1, 1994.

§5204. "Due date of support payments"

"Due date of support payments" is the date specifically stated in the order of support or, if no date is stated in the support order, the last day of the month in which the support payment is to be paid. **Leg.H.** Enacted Stats 1992 ch 162 §10 (AB 2650), operative January 1, 1994.

§5206. "Earnings"

"Earnings," to the extent that they are subject to an earnings assignment order for support under Chapter 4 (commencing with Section 703.010) of Division 2 of Title 9 of Part 2 of the Code of Civil Procedure, include:

(a) Wages, salary, bonus, money, and benefits described in Sections 704.110, 704.113, and 704.115 of the Code of Civil Procedure.

(b) Payments due for services of independent contractors, interest, dividends, rents, royalties, residuals, patent rights, or mineral or other natural resource rights.

(c) Payments or credits due or becoming due as a result of written or oral contracts for services or sales whether denominated as wages, salary, commission, bonus, or otherwise.

(d) Payments due for workers' compensation temporary disability benefits.

(e) Payments due as a result of disability from benefits described in Section 704.130 of the Code of Civil Procedure.

(f) Any other payments or credits due or becoming due, regardless of source. **Leg.H.** Enacted Stats 1992 ch 162 §10 (AB 2650), operative January 1, 1994. Amended Stats 1993 ch 219 §152.5 (AB 1500); Stats 1997 ch 599 §22 (AB 573).

§5208. "Earnings assignment order for support"

(a) "Earnings assignment order for support" means an order that assigns to an obligee a portion of the earnings of a support obligor due or to become due in the future.

(b) Commencing January 1, 2000, all earnings assignment orders for support in any action in which child support or family support is ordered shall be issued on an "order/notice to withhold income for child support" mandated by Section 666 of Title 42 of the United States Code. **Leg.H.** Enacted Stats 1992 ch 162 §10 (AB 2650), operative January 1, 1994. Amended Stats 1999 ch 480 §1 (SB 542).

§5210. "Employer"

"Employer" includes all of the following:

(a) A person for whom an individual performs services as an employee, as defined in Section 706.011 of the Code of Civil Procedure.

(b) The United States government and any public entity as defined in Section 811.2 of the Government Code.

(c) Any person or entity paying earnings as defined under Section 5206. **Leg.H.** Enacted Stats 1992 ch 162 §10 (AB 2650), operative January 1, 1994.

§5212. "IV-D Case"

"IV-D Case" means any case being established, modified, or enforced by the local child support agency pursuant to Section 654 of Title 42 of the United States Code (Section 454 of the Social Security Act). **Leg.H.** Enacted Stats 1992 ch 162 §10 (AB 2650), operative January 1, 1994. Amended Stats 1999 ch 480 §2 (SB 542).

§5214. "Obligee"; "Assigned obligee"

"Obligee" or "assigned obligee" means either the person to whom support has been ordered to be paid, the local child support agency, or other person designated by the court to receive the payment. The local child support agency is the obligee for all Title IV-D cases as defined under Section 5212 or in which an application for services has been filed under Part D (commencing with Section 651) and Part E (commencing with Section 670) of Subchapter IV of Chapter 7 of Title 42 of the United States Code (Title IV-D or IV-E of the Social Security Act). **Leg.H.** Enacted Stats 1992 ch 162 §10 (AB 2650), operative January 1, 1994. Amended Stats 2000 ch 808 §57 (AB 1358), effective September 28, 2000; Stats 2001 ch 755 §7 (SB 943), effective October 12, 2001.

§5216. "Obligor"

"Obligor" means a person owing a duty of support. **Leg.H.** Enacted Stats 1992 ch 162 §10 (AB 2650), operative January 1, 1994.

§5220. "Timely payment"

"Timely payment" means receipt of support payments by the obligee or assigned obligee within five days of the due date. **Leg.H.** Enacted Stats 1992 ch 162 §10 (AB 2650), operative January 1, 1994.

ARTICLE 2
General Provisions

Support order to include earnings assignment order. §5230.
Earnings assignment or income withholding order for support from another state. §5230.1.
Specification of amount of arrearages in child support; Perjury. §5230.5.
Order binds existing and future employers. §5231.
Manner of service on employer. §5232.
Commencement of withholding by employer. §5233.
Delivery of copy of order and statement of rights to obligor. §5234.
Employer to withhold and forward support. §5235.
Consolidated check by employer. §5236.
Obligee's notice of change of address. §5237.
Priorities where order includes both current support and arrearages; Multiple assignment orders for same employee. §5238.
Manner of computing arrearages of support payments. §5239.
Termination of order; Ex parte relief. §5240.
Penalty for employer failing to comply with order. §5241.
Service of order creates lien. §5242.
Priority of order over attachment, execution, or other assignment. §5243.
Application of chapter to local child support agency. §5244.
Use of other civil and criminal remedies not limited. §5245.
Order/notice to withhold income for child support; Hearing. §5246.
Civil liability of local child support agency and employer. §5247.

§5230. Support order to include earnings assignment order

(a) When the court orders a party to pay an amount for support or orders a modification of the amount of support to be paid, the court shall include in its order an earnings assignment order for support that orders the employer of the obligor to pay to the obligee that portion of the obligor's earnings due or to become due in the future as will be sufficient to pay an amount to cover both of the following:

(1) The amount ordered by the court for support.

(2) An amount which shall be ordered by the court to be paid toward the liquidation of any arrearage.

(b) An earnings assignment order for support shall be issued, and shall be effective and enforceable pursuant to Section 5231, notwithstanding the absence of the name, address, or other identifying information regarding the obligor's employer. **Leg.H.** Enacted Stats 1992 ch 162 §10 (AB 2650), operative January 1, 1994. Amended Stats 1993 ch 876 §22.5 (SB 1068), effective October 6, 1993, operative January 1, 1994; Stats 1997 ch 599 §23 (AB 573); Stats 2000 ch 808 §57.3 (AB 1358), effective September 28, 2000.

§5230.1. Earnings assignment or income withholding order for support from another state

(a) An earnings assignment or income withholding order for support issued by a court or administrative agency of another state is binding upon an employer of the obligor to the same extent as an earnings assignment order made by a court of this state.

(b) When an employer receives an earnings assignment order or an income withholding order for support from a court or administrative agency in another state, all of the provisions of this chapter shall apply. **Leg.H.** Added Stats 1997 ch 599 §24 (AB 573).

§5230.5. Specification of amount of arrearages in child support; Perjury

Any obligee alleging arrearages in child support shall specify the amount thereof under penalty of perjury. **Leg.H.** Added Stats 1994 ch 1140 §2 (SB 279).

§5231. Order binds existing and future employers

Unless stayed pursuant to Article 4 (commencing with Section 5260), an assignment order is effective and binding upon any existing or future employer of the obligor upon whom a copy of the order is served in compliance with Sections 5232 and 5233, notwithstanding the absence of the name, address, or other identifying information regarding the obligor's employer, or the inclusion of incorrect information regarding the support obligor's employer. **Leg.H.** Enacted Stats 1992 ch 162 §10 (AB 2650), operative January 1, 1994. Amended Stats 2000 ch 808 §57.5 (AB 1358), effective September 28, 2000.

§5232. Manner of service on employer

Service on an employer of an assignment order may be made by first-class mail in the manner prescribed in Section 1013 of the Code of Civil Procedure. The obligee shall serve the documents specified in Section 5234. **Leg.H.** Enacted Stats 1992 ch 162 §10 (AB 2650), operative January 1, 1994. Amended Stats 1997 ch 599 §25 (AB 573).

§5233. Commencement of withholding by employer

Unless the order states a later date, beginning as soon as possible after service of the order on the employer but not later than 10 days after service of the order on the employer, the employer shall commence withholding pursuant to the assignment order from all earnings payable to the employee. **Leg.H.** Enacted Stats 1992 ch 162 §10 (AB 2650), operative January 1, 1994.

§5234. Delivery of copy of order and statement of rights to obligor

Within 10 days of service of an assignment order or an order/notice to withhold income for child support on an employer, the employer shall deliver both of the following to the obligor:

(a) A copy of the assignment order or the order/notice to withhold income for child support.

(b) A written statement of the obligor's rights under the law to seek to quash, modify, or stay service of the earnings assignment order, together with a blank form that the obligor can file with the court to request a hearing to quash, modify, or stay service of the earnings assignment order with instructions on how to file the form and obtain a hearing date. **Leg.H.** Enacted Stats 1992 ch 162 §10 (AB 2650), operative January 1, 1994. Amended Stats 1997 ch 599 §26 (AB 573); Stats 1999 ch 480 §3 (SB 542).

§5235. Employer to withhold and forward support

(a) The employer shall continue to withhold and forward support as required by the assignment order until served with notice terminating the assignment order. If an employer withholds support as required by the assignment order, the obligor shall not be held in contempt or subject to criminal prosecution for nonpayment of the support that was withheld by the employer but not received by the obligee. If the employer withheld the support but failed to forward the payments to the obligee, the employer shall be liable for the payments, including interest, as provided in Section 5241.

(b) Within 10 days of service of a substitution of payee on the employer, the employer shall forward all subsequent support to the governmental entity or other payee that sent the substitution.

(c) The employer shall send the amounts withheld to the obligee within the timeframe specified in federal law and shall report to the obligee the date on which the amount was withheld from the obligor's wages.

(d) The employer may deduct from the earnings of the employee the sum of one dollar and fifty cents ($1.50) for each payment made pursuant to the order.

(e) Once the State Disbursement Unit as required by Section 17309 is operational, the employer shall send all earnings withheld pursuant to this chapter to the State Disbursement Unit instead of the obligee. **Leg.H.** Enacted Stats 1992 ch 162 §10 (AB 2650), operative January 1, 1994. Amended Stats 1993 ch 876 §23 (SB 1068), effective October 6, 1993, operative January 1, 1994; Stats 1994 ch 1269 §50.2 (AB 2208); Stats 1997 ch 599 §27 (AB 573); Stats 1998 ch 854 §4 (AB 960); Stats 2000 ch 808 §58 (AB 1358), effective September 28, 2000; Stats 2003 ch 387 §5 (AB 739); Stats 2004 ch 520 §3 (AB 2530).

§5236. Consolidated check by employer

The state agency or the local agency, designated to enforce support obligations as required by federal law, shall allow employers to simplify the process of assignment order withholding by forwarding, as ordered by the court, the amounts of support withheld under more than one order in a consolidated check, accompanied by an itemized accounting providing names, social security number or other identifying number, and the amount attributable to each obligor. **Leg.H.** Enacted Stats 1992 ch 162 §10 (AB 2650), operative January 1, 1994.

§5237. Obligee's notice of change of address

(a) Except as provided in subdivisions (b) and (c), the obligee shall notify the employer of the obligor, by first-class mail, postage prepaid, of any change of address within a reasonable period of time after the change.

(b) Where payments have been ordered to be made to a county officer designated by the court, the obligee who is the parent, guardian, or other person entitled to receive payment through the designated county officer shall notify the designated county officer by first-class mail, postage prepaid, of any address change within a reasonable period of time after the change.

(c) If the obligee is receiving support payments from the State Disbursement Unit as required by Section 17309, the obligee shall notify the State Disbursement Unit instead of the employer of the obligor as provided in subdivision (a).

(d)(1) Except as set forth in paragraph (2), if the employer, designated county officer, or the State Disbursement Unit is unable to deliver payments under the assignment order for a period of six months due to the failure of the obligee to notify the employer, designated county officer, or State Disbursement Unit, of a change of address, the employer, designated county officer, or State Disbursement Unit shall not make any further payments under the assignment order and shall return all undeliverable payments to the obligor.

(2) If payments are being directed to the State Disbursement Unit pursuant to subdivision (e) of Section 5235, but the case is not otherwise receiving services from the Title IV-D agency, and the State Disbursement Unit is unable to deliver payments under the assignment order for a period of 45 days due to the failure of the obligee to notify the employer, designated county officer, or State Disbursement Unit of a change of address, the Title IV-D agency shall take the following actions:

(A) Immediately return the undeliverable payments to the obligor if the obligee cannot be located.

(B) Notify the employer to suspend withholding pursuant to the wage assignment until the employer or Title IV-D agency is notified of the obligee's whereabouts. **Leg.H.** Enacted Stats 1992 ch 162 §10 (AB 2650), operative January 1, 1994. Amended Stats 1997 ch 599 §28 (AB 573); Stats 2000 ch 808 §59 (AB 1358), effective September 28, 2000; Stats 2003 ch 387 §6 (AB 739); Stats 2004 ch 806 §1 (AB 2358).

§5238. Priorities where order includes both current support and arrearages; Multiple assignment orders for same employee

(a) Where an assignment order or assignment orders include both current support and payments towards the liquidation of arrearages, priority shall be given first to the current child support obligation, then the current spousal support obligation, and thereafter to the liquidation of child and then spousal support arrearages.

(b) Where there are multiple assignment orders for the same employee, the employer shall prorate the withheld payments as follows:

(1) If the obligor has more than one assignment for support, the employer shall add together the amount of support due for each assignment.

(2) If 50 percent of the obligor's net disposable earnings will not pay in full all of the assignments for support, the employer shall prorate it first among all of the current support assignments in the same proportion that each assignment bears to the total current support owed.

(3) The employer shall apply any remainder to the assignments for arrearage support in the same proportion that each assignment bears to the total arrearage owed. **Leg.H.** Enacted Stats 1992 ch 162 §10 (AB 2650), operative January 1, 1994. Amended Stats 1997 ch 599 §29 (AB 573).

§5239. Manner of computing arrearages of support payments

Arrearages of support payments shall be computed on the basis of the payments owed and unpaid on the date that the obligor has been given notice of the assignment order as required by Section 5234. **Leg.H.** Enacted Stats 1992 ch 162 §10 (AB 2650), operative January 1, 1994.

§5240. Termination of order; Ex parte relief

(a) Upon the filing and service of a motion and a notice of motion by the obligor, the court shall terminate the service of an assignment order if past due support has been paid in full, including any interest due, and if any of the following conditions exist:

(1) With regard to orders for spousal support, the death or remarriage of the spouse to whom support is owed.

(2) With regard to orders for child support, the death or emancipation of the child for whom support is owed.

(3) The court determines that there is good cause, as defined in Section 5260, to terminate the assignment order. This subdivision does not apply if there has been more than one application for an assignment order.

(4) The obligor meets the conditions of an alternative arrangement specified in paragraph (2) of subdivision (b) of Section 5260, and a wage assignment has not been previously terminated and subsequently initiated.

(5) There is no longer a current order for support.

(6) The termination of the stay of an assignment order under Section 5261 was improper, but only if that termination was based upon the obligor's failure to make timely support payments as described in subdivision (b) of Section 5261.

(7) The employer or agency designated to provide services under Title IV-D of the Social Security Act or the State Disbursement Unit is unable to deliver payment for a period of six months due to the failure of the obligee to notify that employer or agency or the State Disbursement Unit of a change in the obligee's address.

(b) In lieu of filing and serving a motion and a notice of motion pursuant to subdivision (a), an obligor may request ex parte relief, except ex parte relief shall not be available in the circumstances described in paragraphs (3) and (4) of subdivision (a). **Leg.H.** Enacted Stats 1992 ch 162 §10 (AB 2650), operative January 1, 1994. Amended Stats 1993 ch 876 §24 (SB 1068), effective October 6, 1993, operative January 1, 1994; Stats 1997 ch 599 §30 (AB 573); Stats 2003 ch 387 §7 (AB 739); Stats 2012 ch 77 §1 (AB 1727), effective January 1, 2013.

§5241. Penalty for employer failing to comply with order

(a) An employer who willfully fails to withhold and forward support pursuant to a currently valid assignment order entered and served upon the employer pursuant to this chapter is liable to the obligee for the amount of support not withheld, forwarded, or otherwise paid to the obligee, including any interest thereon.

(b) If an employer withholds support as required by the assignment order, the obligor shall not be held in contempt or subject to criminal prosecution for nonpayment of the support that was withheld by the employer but not received by the obligee. In addition, the employer is liable to the obligee for any interest incurred as a result of the employer's failure to timely forward the withheld support pursuant to an assignment earnings order.

(c) In addition to any other penalty or liability provided by law, willful failure by an employer to comply with an assignment order is punishable as a contempt pursuant to Section 1218 of the Code of Civil Procedure.

(d) If an employer withholds support, as required by the assignment order, but fails to forward the support to the obligee, the local child support agency shall take appropriate action to collect the withheld sums from the employer. The child support obligee or the local child support agency upon application may obtain an order requiring payment of support by electronic transfer from the employer's bank account if the employer has willfully failed to comply with the assignment order or if the employer has failed to comply with the assignment order on three separate occasions within a 12-month period. Where a court finds that an employer has willfully failed to comply with the assignment order or has otherwise failed to comply with the assignment order on three separate occasions within a 12-month period, the court may impose a civil penalty, in addition to any other penalty required by law, of up to 50 percent of the support amount that has not been received by the obligee.

(e) To facilitate employer awareness, the local child support agency shall make reasonable efforts to notify any employer subject to an assignment order pursuant to this chapter of the electronic fund transfer provision and enhanced penalties provided by this act.

(f) Notwithstanding any other provision of law, any penalty payable pursuant to this subdivision shall be payable directly to the obligee. The local child support agency shall not be required to establish or collect this penalty on behalf of the obligee. The penalty shall not be included when determining the income of the obligee for the purpose of determining the eligibility of the obligee for benefits payable pursuant to state supplemental income programs. A court may issue the order requiring payment of support by electronic transfer from the employer's bank account and impose the penalty described in this subdivision, after notice and hearing. This provision shall not be construed to expand or limit the duties and obligations of the Labor Commissioner, as set forth in Section 200 and following of the Labor Code. **Leg.H.** Enacted Stats 1992 ch 162 §10 (AB 2650), operative January 1, 1994. Amended Stats 1993 ch 745 §2 (SB 788), ch 876 §25 (SB 1068), effective October 6, 1993, operative January 1, 1994; Stats 1998 ch 854 §5 (AB 960); Stats 2000 ch 808 §60 (AB 1358), effective September 28, 2000; Stats 2001 ch 371 §1 (AB 1426); Stats 2003 ch 308 §2 (AB 738).

§5242. Service of order creates lien

Service of the assignment order creates a lien on the earnings of the employee and the property of the employer to the same extent as the service of an earnings withholding order as provided in Section 706.029 of the Code of Civil Procedure. **Leg.H.** Enacted Stats 1992 ch 162 §10 (AB 2650), operative January 1, 1994.

§5243. Priority of order over attachment, execution, or other assignment

An assignment order for support has priority as against any attachment, execution, or other assignment as specified in Section 706.031 of the Code of Civil Procedure. **Leg.H.** Enacted Stats 1992 ch 162 §10 (AB 2650), operative January 1, 1994. Amended Stats 1993 ch 876 §26 (SB 1068), effective October 6, 1993, operative January 1, 1994.

§5244. Application of chapter to local child support agency

A reference to the local child support agency in this chapter applies only when the local child support agency is otherwise ordered or required to act pursuant to law. Nothing in this chapter shall be deemed to mandate additional enforcement or collection duties upon the local child support agency beyond those otherwise imposed by law. **Leg.H.** Enacted Stats 1992 ch 162 §10 (AB 2650), operative January 1, 1994. Amended Stats 2000 ch 808 §61 (AB 1358), effective September 28, 2000.

§5245. Use of other civil and criminal remedies not limited

Nothing in this chapter limits the authority of the local child support agency to use any other civil and criminal remedies to enforce support obligations, regardless of whether or not the child or the obligee who is the parent, guardian, or other person entitled to receive payment is the recipient of welfare moneys. **Leg.H.** Enacted Stats 1992 ch 162 §10 (AB 2650), operative January 1, 1994. Amended Stats 1993 ch 219 §153 (AB 1500); Stats 2000 ch 808 §62 (AB 1358), effective September 28, 2000.

§5246. Order/notice to withhold income for child support; Hearing

(a) This section applies only to Title IV-D cases where support enforcement services are being provided by the local child support agency pursuant to Section 17400.

(b) In lieu of an earnings assignment order signed by a judicial officer, the local child support agency may serve on the employer a notice of assignment in the manner specified in Section 5232. An order/notice to withhold income for child support shall have the same force and effect as an earnings assignment order signed by a judicial officer. An order/notice to withhold income for child support, when used under this section, shall be considered a notice and shall not require the signature of a judicial officer.

(c) Pursuant to Section 666 of Title 42 of the United States Code, the federally mandated order/notice to withhold income for child support shall be used for the purposes described in this section.

(d)(1) An order/notice to withhold income may not reduce the current amount withheld for court-ordered child support.

(2) If the underlying court order for support does not provide for an arrearage payment, or if an additional arrearage accrues after the date of the court order for support, the local child support agency may send an order/notice to withhold income for child support that shall be used for the purposes described in this section directly to the employer that specifies the updated arrearage amount and directs the employer to withhold an additional amount to be applied towards liquidation of the arrearages not to exceed the maximum amount permitted by Section 1673(b) of Title 15 of the United States Code.

(3) Notwithstanding paragraph (2), if an obligor is disabled, meets the SSI resource test, and is receiving Supplemental Security Income/State Supplementary Payments (SSI/SSP) or, but for excess income as described in Section 416.1100 et seq. of Part 416 of Title 20 of the Code of Federal Regulations, would be eligible to receive SSI/SSP, pursuant to Section 12200 of the Welfare and Institutions Code, and the obligor has supplied the local child support agency with proof of eligibility for and, if applicable, receipt of, SSI/SSP or Social Security Disability Insurance benefits, then the order/notice to withhold income issued by the local child support agency for the liquidation of the arrearage shall not exceed 5 percent of the obligor's total monthly Social Security Disability payments under Title II of the Social Security Act.

(e) If the obligor requests a hearing, a hearing date shall be scheduled within 20 days of the filing of the request with the court. The clerk of the court shall provide notice of the hearing to the local child support agency and the obligor no later than 10 days prior to the hearing.

(1) If, at the hearing, the obligor establishes that they are not the obligor or good cause or an alternative arrangement as provided in Section 5260, the court may order that service of the order/notice to withhold income for child support be quashed. If the court quashes service of the order/notice to withhold income for child support, the local child support agency shall notify the employer within 10 days.

(2) If the obligor contends at the hearing that the payment of arrearages at the rate specified in the order/notice to withhold income for child support is excessive or that the total arrearages owing is incorrect, and if it is determined that payment of the arrearages at the rate specified in this section creates an undue hardship upon the obligor or that the withholding would exceed the maximum amount permitted by Section 1673(b) of Title 15 of the United States Code Annotated, the rate at which the arrearages must be paid shall be reduced to a rate that is fair and reasonable considering the circumstances of the parties and the best interest of the child. If it is determined at a hearing that the total amount of arrearages calculated is erroneous, the court shall modify the amount calculated to the correct amount. If the court modifies the total amount of arrearages owed or reduces the monthly payment due on the arrearages, the local child support agency shall serve the employer with an amended order/notice to withhold income for child support within 10 days.

(f) If an obligor's current support obligation has terminated by operation of law, the local child support agency may serve an order/notice to withhold income for child support on the employer that directs the employer to continue withholding from the obligor's earnings an amount to be applied towards liquidation of the arrearages, not to exceed the maximum amount permitted by Section 1673(b) of Title 15 of the United States Code, until the employer is notified by the local child support agency that the arrearages have been paid in full. The employer shall provide the obligor with a copy of the order/notice to withhold income for child support and a blank form that the obligor may file with the court to request a hearing to modify or quash the assignment with instructions on how to file the form and obtain a hearing date. The obligor shall be entitled to the same rights to a hearing as specified in subdivision (e).

(g) The local child support agency shall retain a copy of the order/notice to withhold income for child support and shall file a copy with the court whenever a hearing concerning the order/notice to withhold income for child support is requested.

(h) The local child support agency may transmit an order/notice to withhold income for child support and other forms required by this section to the employer through electronic means. **Leg.H.** Added Stats 1996 ch 957 §8 (AB 1058). Amended Stats 1997 ch 599 §31 (AB 573); Stats 1999 ch 480 §4 (SB 542); Stats 2000 ch 808 §62.3 (AB 1358), effective September 28, 2000; Stats 2001 ch 111 §1 (AB 429), effective July 30, 2001, ch 651 §2 (AB 891); Stats 2019 ch 115 §55 (AB 1817), effective January 1, 2020.

§5247. Civil liability of local child support agency and employer

Neither the local child support agency nor an employer shall be subject to any civil liability for any amount withheld and paid to the obligee, the local child support agency, or the State Disbursement Unit pursuant to an earnings assignment order or notice of assignment. **Leg.H.** Added Stats 1997 ch 599 §32 (AB 573). Amended Stats 2000 ch 808 §63 (AB 1358), effective September 28, 2000; Stats 2003 ch 387 §8 (AB 739).

ARTICLE 3
Support Orders Issued or Modified Before July 1, 1990

Article applies to support orders first issued or modified before July 1, 1990. §5250.
Procedures available for obtaining assignment order. §5251.
Application for order under this article. §5252.
Issuance of assignment order. §5253.

§5250. Article applies to support orders first issued or modified before July 1, 1990

For a support order first issued or modified before July 1, 1990, this article provides a procedure for obtaining an earnings assignment order for support when the court in ordering support or modification of support did not issue an assignment order. **Leg.H.** Enacted Stats 1992 ch 162 §10 (AB 2650), operative January 1, 1994.

§5251. Procedures available for obtaining assignment order

The obligee seeking issuance of an assignment order to enforce a support order described in Section 5250 may use the procedure set forth in this article by filing an application under Section 5252, or by notice of motion or order to show cause, or pursuant to subdivision (b) of Section 5230. **Leg.H.** Enacted Stats 1992 ch 162 §10 (AB 2650), operative January 1, 1994.

§5252. Application for order under this article

(a) An assignment order under this article may be issued only upon an application signed under penalty of perjury by the obligee that the obligor is in default in support payments in a sum equal to the amount of support payable for one month, for any other occurrence specified by the court in the support order, or earlier by court order if requested by the local child support agency or the obligor.

(b) If the order for support does not contain a provision for an earnings assignment order for support, the application shall state that the obligee has given the obligor a written notice of the obligee's intent to seek an assignment order if there is a default in support payments and that the notice was transmitted by first-class mail, postage prepaid, or personally served at least 15 days before the date of the filing of the application. The written notice of the intent to seek an assignment order may be given at any time, including at the time of filing a petition or complaint in which support is requested or at any time subsequent thereto. The obligor may at any time waive the written notice required by this subdivision.

(c) In addition to any other penalty provided by law, the filing of the application with knowledge of the falsity of the declaration or notice is punishable as a contempt pursuant to Section 1209 of the Code of Civil Procedure. **Leg.H.** Enacted Stats 1992 ch 162 §10 (AB 2650), operative January 1, 1994. Amended Stats 2000 ch 808 §64 (AB 1358), effective September 28, 2000.

§5253. Issuance of assignment order

Upon receipt of the application, the court shall issue, without notice to the obligor, an assignment order requiring the employer of the obligor to pay to the obligee or the State Disbursement Unit that portion of the earnings of the obligor due or to become due in the future as will be sufficient to pay an amount to cover both of the following:

(a) The amount ordered by the court for support.

(b) An amount which shall be ordered by the court to be paid toward the liquidation of any arrearage or past due support amount. **Leg.H.** Enacted Stats 1992 ch 162 §10 (AB 2650), operative January 1, 1994. Amended Stats 1997 ch 599 §33 (AB 573); Stats 2003 ch 387 §9 (AB 739).

ARTICLE 4
Stay of Service of Assignment Order

Grounds for stay of assignment. §5260.
Termination of stay. §5261.

§5260. Grounds for stay of assignment

(a) The court may order that service of the assignment order be stayed only if the court makes a finding of good cause or if an alternative arrangement exists for payment in accordance with paragraph (2) of subdivision (b). Notwithstanding any other provision of law, service of wage assignments issued for foreign orders for support, and service of foreign orders for the assignment of wages registered pursuant to Chapter 6 (commencing with Section 5700.601) of Part 6 shall not be stayed pursuant to this subdivision.

(b) For purposes of this section, good cause or an alternative arrangement for staying an assignment order is as follows:

(1) Good cause for staying a wage assignment exists only when all of the following conditions exist:

(A) The court provides a written explanation of why the stay of the wage assignment would be in the best interests of the child.

(B) The obligor has a history of uninterrupted, full, and timely payment, other than through a wage assignment or other mandatory process of previously ordered support, during the previous 12 months.

(C) The obligor does not owe an arrearage for prior support.

(D) The obligor proves, and the court finds, by clear and convincing evidence that service of the wage assignment would cause extraordinary hardship upon the obligor. Whenever possible, the court shall specify a date that any stay ordered under this section will automatically terminate.

(2) An alternative arrangement for staying a wage assignment order shall require a written agreement between the parties that provides for payment of the support obligation as ordered other than through the immediate service of a wage assignment. Any agreement between the parties which includes the staying of a service of a wage assignment shall include the concurrence of the local child support agency in any case in which support is ordered to be paid through a county officer designated for that purpose. The execution of an agreement pursuant to this paragraph shall not preclude a party from thereafter seeking a wage assignment in accordance with the procedures specified in Section 5261 upon violation of the agreement. **Leg.H.** Enacted Stats 1992 ch 162 §10 (AB 2650), operative January 1, 1994. Amended Stats 1993 ch 219 §153.2 (AB 1500), ch 876 §27 (SB 1068), effective October 6, 1993, operative January 1, 1994; Stats 1994 ch 1269 §50.4 (AB 2208); Stats 2000 ch 808 §65 (AB 1358), effective September 28, 2000; Stats 2001 ch 755 §8 (SB 943), effective October 12, 2001; Stats 2015 ch 493 §3 (SB 646), effective January 1, 2016.

§5261. Termination of stay

(a) If service of the assignment order has been ordered stayed, the stay shall terminate pursuant to subdivision (b) upon the obligor's failure to make timely support payments or earlier by court order if requested by the local child support agency or by the obligor. The stay shall terminate earlier by court order if requested by any other obligee who can establish that good cause, as defined in Section 5260, no longer exists.

(b) To terminate a stay of the service of the assignment order, the obligee shall file a declaration signed under penalty of perjury by the obligee that the obligor is in arrears in payment of any portion of the support. At the time of filing the declaration, the stay shall terminate by operation of law without notice to the obligor.

(c) In addition to any other penalty provided by law, the filing of a declaration under subdivision (b) with knowledge of the falsity of its contents is punishable as a contempt pursuant to Section 1209 of the Code of Civil Procedure. **Leg.H.** Enacted Stats 1992 ch 162 §10 (AB 2650), operative January 1, 1994. Amended Stats 2000 ch 808 §66 (AB 1358), effective September 28, 2000.

ARTICLE 5
Motion to Quash Assignment Order

Grounds for motion to quash. §5270.
Procedure for notice and motion to quash. §5271.
Modification of order to reflect correct or allowable amount. §5272.

§5270. Grounds for motion to quash

(a) An obligor may move to quash an assignment order on any of the following grounds:

(1) The assignment order does not correctly state the amount of current or overdue support ordered by the courts.

(2) The alleged obligor is not the obligor from whom support is due.

(3) The amount to be withheld exceeds that allowable under federal law in subsection (b) of Section 1673 of Title 15 of the United States Code.

(b) If an assignment order is sought under Article 3 (commencing with Section 5250), the party ordered to pay support may also move to quash the service of the order based upon Section 5260.

(c) The obligor shall state under oath the ground on which the motion to quash is made.

(d) If an assignment order which has been issued and served on a prior employer is served on the obligor's new employer, the obligor does not have the right to move to quash the assignment order on any grounds which the obligor previously raised when the assignment order was served on the prior employer or on any grounds which the obligor could have raised when the assignment order was served on the prior employer but failed to raise. **Leg.H.** Enacted Stats 1992 ch 162 §10 (AB 2650), operative January 1, 1994.

§5271. Procedure for notice and motion to quash

(a) The motion and notice of motion to quash the assignment order shall be filed with the court issuing the order within 10 days after delivery of the copy of the assignment order to the obligor by the employer.

(b) The clerk of the court shall set the motion to quash for hearing within not less than 15 days, nor more than 20 days, after receipt of the notice of motion.

(c) The obligor shall serve personally or by first-class mail, postage prepaid, a copy of the motion and notice of motion on the obligee named in the assignment order no less than 10 days before the date of the hearing. **Leg.H.** Enacted Stats 1992 ch 162 §10 (AB 2650), operative January 1, 1994.

§5272. Modification of order to reflect correct or allowable amount

A finding of error in the amount of the current support or arrearage or that the amount exceeds federal or state limits is not grounds to vacate the assignment order. The court shall modify the order to reflect the correct or allowable amount of support or arrearages. The fact that the obligor may have subsequently paid the arrearages does not relieve the court of its duty to enter the assignment order. **Leg.H.** Enacted Stats 1992 ch 162 §10 (AB 2650), operative January 1, 1994.

ARTICLE 6
Information Concerning Address and Employment of Obligor

Use of California parent locator service. §5280.
Obligor to inform obligee of change of employment. §5281.
Employer to notify obligee when obligor leaves employment. §5282.

§5280. Use of California parent locator service

If the obligee making the application under this chapter also states that the whereabouts of the obligor or the identity of the obligor's employer is unknown to the party to whom support has been ordered to be paid, the local child support agency shall do both of the following:

(a) Contact the California parent locator service maintained by the Department of Justice in the manner prescribed in Section 17506.

(b) Upon receiving the requested information, notify the court of the last known address of the obligor and the name and address of the obligor's last known employer. **Leg.H.** Enacted Stats 1992 ch 162 §10 (AB 2650), operative January 1, 1994. Amended Stats 2000 ch 808 §67 (AB 1358), effective September 28, 2000.

§5281. Obligor to inform obligee of change of employment

An assignment order required or authorized by this chapter shall include a requirement that the obligor notify the obligee of any change of employment and of the name and address of the obligor's new employer within 10 days of obtaining new employment. **Leg.H.** Enacted Stats 1992 ch 162 §10 (AB 2650), operative January 1, 1994.

§5282. Employer to notify obligee when obligor leaves employment

After the obligor has left employment with the employer, the employer, at the time the next payment is due on the assignment order, shall notify the obligee designated in the assignment order by first-class mail, postage prepaid, to the last known address of the obligee that the obligor has left employment. **Leg.H.** Enacted Stats 1992 ch 162 §10 (AB 2650), operative January 1, 1994.

§5283. [Section repealed 1997]

Leg.H. Enacted Stats 1992 ch 162 §10 (AB 2650), operative January 1, 1994. Amended Stats 1996 ch 1062 §3.5 (AB 1832). Repealed Stats 1997 ch 599 §34 (AB 573). The repealed section related to information provided to district attorney by employer.

ARTICLE 7
Prohibited Practices

Assignment order not grounds for refusal to hire, discharge, or disciplinary action; Civil penalty. §5290.

§5290. Assignment order not grounds for refusal to hire, discharge, or disciplinary action; Civil penalty

No employer shall use an assignment order authorized by this chapter as grounds for refusing to hire a person, or for discharging, taking disciplinary action against, denying a promotion to, or for taking any other action adversely affecting the terms and conditions of employment of, an employee. An employer who engages in the conduct prohibited by this section may be assessed a civil penalty of a maximum of five hundred dollars ($500). **Leg.H.** Enacted Stats 1992 ch 162 §10 (AB 2650), operative January 1, 1994. Amended Stats 2004 ch 369 §1 (AB 1706).

ARTICLE 8
Judicial Council Forms

Forms to implement statute. §5295.

§5295. Forms to implement statute

The Judicial Council shall prescribe forms necessary to carry out the requirements of this chapter, including the following:

(a) The written statement of the obligor's rights.

(b) The earnings assignment order for support.

(c) The instruction guide for obligees and obligors.

(d) The application forms required under Sections 5230, 5252, and 5261.

(e) The notice form required under Section 5252.

(f) Revised judgment and assignment order forms as necessary. **Leg.H.** Enacted Stats 1992 ch 162 §10 (AB 2650), operative January 1, 1994.

§5500. [Section repealed 1993]

Leg.H. Enacted Stats 1992 ch 162 §10 (AB 2650), operative January 1, 1994. Repealed Stats 1993 ch 219 §153.5 (AB 1500). See Fam C §6201.

§5501. [Section repealed 1993]

Leg.H. Enacted Stats 1992 ch 162 §10 (AB 2650), operative January 1, 1994. Repealed Stats 1993 ch 219 §153.5 (AB 1500). See Fam C §§6203, 6211, 6218.

§5505. [Section repealed 1993]

Leg.H. Enacted Stats 1992 ch 162 §10 (AB 2650), operative January 1, 1994. Repealed Stats 1993 ch 219 §153.5 (AB 1500). See Fam C §6218.

§5510. [Section repealed 1993]

Leg.H. Enacted Stats 1992 ch 162 §10 (AB 2650), operative January 1, 1994. Repealed Stats 1993 ch 219 §153.5 (AB 1500). See Fam C §6200.

§5511. [Section repealed 1993]
Leg.H. Enacted Stats 1992 ch 162 §10 (AB 2650), operative January 1, 1994. Repealed Stats 1993 ch 219 §153.5 (AB 1500). See Fam C §6220.

§5512. [Section repealed 1993]
Leg.H. Enacted Stats 1992 ch 162 §10 (AB 2650), operative January 1, 1994. Repealed Stats 1993 ch 219 §153.5 (AB 1500). See Fam C §6222.

§5513. [Section repealed 1993]
Leg.H. Enacted Stats 1992 ch 162 §10 (AB 2650), operative January 1, 1994. Repealed Stats 1993 ch 219 §153.5 (AB 1500). See Fam C §6223.

§5514. [Section repealed 1993]
Leg.H. Enacted Stats 1992 ch 162 §10 (AB 2650), operative January 1, 1994. Repealed Stats 1993 ch 219 §153.5 (AB 1500). See Fam C §6305.

§5515. [Section repealed 1993]
Leg.H. Enacted Stats 1992 ch 162 §10 (AB 2650), operative January 1, 1994. Repealed Stats 1993 ch 219 §153.5 (AB 1500). See Fam C §6224.

§5516. [Section repealed 1993]
Leg.H. Enacted Stats 1992 ch 162 §10 (AB 2650), operative January 1, 1994. Repealed Stats 1993 ch 219 §153.5 (AB 1500). See Fam C §6304.

§5517. [Section repealed 1993]
Leg.H. Enacted Stats 1992 ch 162 §10 (AB 2650), operative January 1, 1994. Repealed Stats 1993 ch 219 §153.5 (AB 1500). See Fam C §6225.

§5518. [Section repealed 1993]
Leg.H. Enacted Stats 1992 ch 162 §10 (AB 2650), operative January 1, 1994. Repealed Stats 1993 ch 219 §153.5 (AB 1500). See Fam C §6227.

§5519. [Section repealed 1993]
Leg.H. Enacted Stats 1992 ch 162 §10 (AB 2650), operative January 1, 1994. Repealed Stats 1993 ch 219 §153.5 (AB 1500). See Fam C §6303.

§5520. [Section repealed 1993]
Leg.H. Enacted Stats 1992 ch 162 §10 (AB 2650), operative January 1, 1994. Repealed Stats 1993 ch 219 §153.5 (AB 1500). See Fam C §6226.

§5530. [Section repealed 1993]
Leg.H. Enacted Stats 1992 ch 162 §10 (AB 2650), operative January 1, 1994. Repealed Stats 1993 ch 219 §153.5 (AB 1500). See Fam C §6300.

§5531. [Section repealed 1993]
Leg.H. Enacted Stats 1992 ch 162 §10 (AB 2650), operative January 1, 1994. Repealed Stats 1993 ch 219 §153.5 (AB 1500). See Fam C §6301.

§5550. [Section repealed 1993]
Leg.H. Enacted Stats 1992 ch 162 §10 (AB 2650), operative January 1, 1994. Repealed Stats 1993 ch 219 §153.5 (AB 1500). See Fam C §§6320–6327.

§5551. [Section repealed 1993]
Leg.H. Enacted Stats 1992 ch 162 §10 (AB 2650), operative January 1, 1994. Repealed Stats 1993 ch 219 §153.5 (AB 1500). See Fam C §6302.

§5552. [Section repealed 1993]
Leg.H. Enacted Stats 1992 ch 162 §10 (AB 2650), operative January 1, 1994. Repealed Stats 1993 ch 219 §153.5 (AB 1500). See Fam C §6321.

ARTICLE 9
Intercounty Support Obligations

Registration of order obtained in other county. §5600.
Registration by local child support agency responsible for enforcement of support order; Filing of documents as registration; Service of copies of documents; Notice; Registration of other orders. §5601.
Registration by obligee other than local child support agency; Filing; Notice. §5602.
Motion for vacation of registration or for other relief; Hearing. §5603.
Effect of previous determination of paternity by another state. §5604.

§5600. Registration of order obtained in other county

(a) A local child support agency or obligee may register an order for support or earnings withholding, or both, obtained in another county of the state.

(b) An obligee may register a support order in the court of another county of this state in the manner, with the effect, and for the purposes provided in this part. The orders may be registered in any county in which the obligor, the obligee, or the child who is the subject of the order resides, or in any county in which the obligor has income, assets, or any other property. **Leg.H.** Added Stats 1997 ch 599 §35 (AB 573). Amended Stats 2000 ch 808 §68 (AB 1358), effective September 28, 2000.

Prior Law: Former §5600, relating to application of provisions of chapter, was enacted Stats 1992 ch 162 §10, operative January 1, 1994, and repealed Stats 1993 ch 219 §153.5.

§5601. Registration by local child support agency responsible for enforcement of support order; Filing of documents as registration; Service of copies of documents; Notice; Registration of other orders

(a) When the local child support agency is responsible for the enforcement of a support order pursuant to Section 17400, the local child support agency may register a support order made in another county by utilizing the procedures set forth in Section 5602 or by filing all of the following in the superior court of the agency's county:

(1) An endorsed file copy of the most recent support order or a copy thereof.

(2) A statement of arrearages, including an accounting of amounts ordered and paid each month, together with any added costs, fees, and interest.

(3) A statement prepared by the local child support agency showing the post office address of the local child support agency, the last known place of residence or post office address of the obligor; the most recent address of the obligor set forth in the licensing records of the Department of Motor Vehicles, if known; and a list of other states and counties in California that are known to the local child support agency in which the original order of support and any modifications are registered.

(b) The filing of the documents described in subdivision (a) constitutes registration under this chapter.

(c) Promptly upon registration, the local child support agency, in compliance with the requirements of Section 1013 of the Code of Civil Procedure, or in any other manner as provided by law, shall serve the obligor with copies of the documents described in subdivision (a).

(d) If a motion to vacate registration is filed under Section 5603, a party may introduce into evidence copies of pleadings, documents, or orders that have been filed in the original court or other courts where the support order has been registered or modified. Certified copies of the documents shall not be required unless a party objects to the authenticity or accuracy of the document, in which case it shall be the responsibility of the party who is asserting the authenticity of the document to obtain a certified copy of the questioned document.

(e) Upon registration, the clerk of the court shall forward a notice of registration to the courts in other counties and states in which the original order for support and any modifications were issued or registered. Further proceedings regarding the obligor's support obligations shall not be filed in other counties.

(f) The procedure prescribed by this section may also be used to register support or wage and earnings assignment orders of other California jurisdictions that previously have been registered for purposes of enforcement only pursuant to the Uniform Interstate Family Support Act (Part 6 (commencing with Section 5700.101)) in another California county. The local child support agency may register such an order by filing an endorsed file copy of the registered California order plus any subsequent orders, including procedural amendments.

(g) The Judicial Council shall develop the forms necessary to effectuate this section. These forms shall be available no later than July 1, 1998. **Leg.H.** Added Stats 1997 ch 599 §35 (AB 573). Amended Stats 2000 ch 808 §69 (AB 1358), effective September 28, 2000; Stats 2015 ch 493 §4 (SB 646), effective January 1, 2016; Stats 2019 ch 115 §56 (AB 1817), effective January 1, 2020.

Prior Law: Former §5601, similar to present Fam C §6241, was enacted Stats 1992 ch 162 §10, operative January 1, 1994, and repealed Stats 1993 ch 219 §153.5.

§5602. Registration by obligee other than local child support agency; Filing; Notice

(a) An obligee other than the local child support agency may register an order issued in this state using the same procedures specified in subdivision (a) of Section 5601, except that the obligee shall prepare and file the statement of registration. The statement shall be verified and signed by the obligee showing the mailing address of the obligee, the last known place of residence or mailing address of the obligor, and a list of other states and counties in California in which, to the obligee's knowledge, the original order of support and any modifications are registered.

(b) Upon receipt of the documents described in subdivision (a) of Section 5601, the clerk of the court shall file them without payment of a filing fee or other cost to the obligee. The filing constitutes registration under this chapter.

(c) Promptly upon registration, the clerk of the court shall send, by any form of mail requiring a return receipt from the addressee only, to the obligor at the address given a notice of the registration with a copy of the registered support order and the post office address of the obligee. Proof shall be made to the satisfaction of the court that the obligor personally received the notice of registration by mail or other method of service. A return receipt signed by the obligor shall be satisfactory evidence of personal receipt. **Leg.H.** Added Stats 1997 ch 599 §35 (AB 573). Amended Stats 2000 ch 808 §70 (AB 1358), effective September 28, 2000.

Prior Law: Former §5602, similar to present Fam C §6270, was enacted Stats 1992 ch 162 §10, operative January 1, 1994, and repealed Stats 1993 ch 219 §153.5.

§5603. Motion for vacation of registration or for other relief; Hearing

(a) An obligor shall have 20 days after the service of notice of the registration of a California order of support in which to file a noticed motion requesting the court to vacate the registration or for other relief. In an action under this section, there shall be no joinder of actions, coordination of actions, or cross-complaints, and the claims or defenses shall be limited strictly to the identity of the obligor, the validity of the underlying California support order, or the accuracy of the obligee's statement of the amount of support remaining unpaid unless the amount has been previously established by a judgment or order. The obligor shall serve a copy of the motion, personally or by first-class mail, on the local child support agency, private attorney representing the obligee, or obligee who is self-representing who filed the request for registration of the order, not less than 15 days prior to the date on which the motion is to be heard. If service is by mail, Section 1013 of the Code of Civil Procedure applies. If the obligor does not file the motion within 20 days, the registered California support order and all other documents filed pursuant to subdivision (a) of Section 5601 or Section 5602 are confirmed.

(b) At the hearing on the motion to vacate the registration of the order, the obligor may present only matters that would be available to the obligor as defenses in an action to enforce a support judgment. If the obligor shows, and the court finds, that an appeal from the order is pending or that a stay of execution has been granted, the court shall stay enforcement of the order until the appeal is concluded, the time for appeal has expired, or the order is vacated, upon satisfactory proof that the obligor has furnished security for payment of the support ordered. If the obligor shows, and the court finds, any ground upon which enforcement of a California support order may be stayed, the court shall stay enforcement of the order for an appropriate period if the obligor furnishes security for payment of support. **Leg.H.** Added Stats 1997 ch 599 §35 (AB 573). Amended Stats 2000 ch 808 §71 (AB 1358), effective September 28, 2000; Stats 2019 ch 115 §57 (AB 1817), effective January 1, 2020.

Prior Law: Former §5603, similar to present Fam C §6256, was enacted Stats 1992 ch 162 §10, operative January 1, 1994, and repealed Stats 1993 ch 219 §153.5.

§5604. Effect of previous determination of paternity by another state

A previous determination of paternity made by another state, whether established through voluntary acknowledgment procedures in effect in that state or through an administrative or judicial process shall be given full faith and credit by the courts in this state, and shall have the same effect as a paternity determination made in this state and may be enforced and satisfied in a like manner. **Leg.H.** Added Stats 1997 ch 599 §35 (AB 573).

Prior Law: Former §5604, similar to present Fam C §6273, was enacted Stats 1992 ch 162 §10, operative January 1, 1994, and repealed Stats 1993 ch 219 §153.5.

§5605. [Section repealed 1993]

Leg.H. Enacted Stats 1992 ch 162 §10 (AB 2650), operative January 1, 1994. Repealed Stats 1993 ch 219 §153.5 (AB 1500). See Fam C §6271.

§5606. [Section repealed 1993]

Leg.H. Enacted Stats 1992 ch 162 §10 (AB 2650), operative January 1, 1994. Repealed Stats 1993 ch 219 §153.5 (AB 1500). See Fam C §6272.

§5650. [Section repealed 1993]

Leg.H. Enacted Stats 1992 ch 162 §10 (AB 2650), operative January 1, 1994. Repealed Stats 1993 ch 219 §153.5 (AB 1500). See Fam C §§6250, 6252, 6255.

§5651. [Section repealed 1993]

Leg.H. Enacted Stats 1992 ch 162 §10 (AB 2650), operative January 1, 1994. Repealed Stats 1993 ch 219 §153.5 (AB 1500). See Fam C §6251.

§5652. [Section repealed 1993]

Leg.H. Enacted Stats 1992 ch 162 §10 (AB 2650), operative January 1, 1994. Repealed Stats 1993 ch 219 §153.5 (AB 1500). See Fam C §6253.

§5700. [Section repealed 1993]

Leg.H. Enacted Stats 1992 ch 162 §10 (AB 2650), operative January 1, 1994. Repealed Stats 1993 ch 219 §153.5 (AB 1500). See Fam C §§6250, 6252, 6255.

§5701. [Section repealed 1993]

Leg.H. Enacted Stats 1992 ch 162 §10 (AB 2650), operative January 1, 1994. Repealed Stats 1993 ch 219 §153.5 (AB 1500). See Fam C §§6251, 6254.

§5702. [Section repealed 1993]

Leg.H. Enacted Stats 1992 ch 162 §10 (AB 2650), operative January 1, 1994. Repealed Stats 1993 ch 219 §153.5 (AB 1500). See Fam C §6253.

§5703. [Section repealed 1993]

Leg.H. Enacted Stats 1992 ch 162 §10 (AB 2650), operative January 1, 1994. Repealed Stats 1993 ch 219 §153.5 (AB 1500). See Fam C §6257.

§5750. [Section repealed 1993]

Leg.H. Enacted Stats 1992 ch 162 §10 (AB 2650), operative January 1, 1994. Repealed Stats 1993 ch 219 §153.5 (AB 1500). See Fam C §6340.

§5751. [Section repealed 1993]

Leg.H. Enacted Stats 1992 ch 162 §10 (AB 2650), operative January 1, 1994. Repealed Stats 1993 ch 219 §153.5 (AB 1500). See Fam C §6340.

§5752. [Section repealed 1993]

Leg.H. Enacted Stats 1992 ch 162 §10 (AB 2650), operative January 1, 1994. Repealed Stats 1993 ch 219 §153.5 (AB 1500). See Fam C §6341.

§5753. [Section repealed 1993]

Leg.H. Enacted Stats 1992 ch 162 §10 (AB 2650), operative January 1, 1994. Repealed Stats 1993 ch 219 §153.5 (AB 1500). See Fam C §6342.

§5754. [Section repealed 1993]

Leg.H. Enacted Stats 1992 ch 162 §10 (AB 2650), operative January 1, 1994. Repealed Stats 1993 ch 219 §153.5 (AB 1500). Amended Stats 1993 ch 301 §2 (AB 197). Repealed Stats 1993 ch 876 §27.1 (SB 1068), effective October 6, 1993. See Fam C §6343.

§5755. [Section repealed 1993]

Leg.H. Enacted Stats 1992 ch 162 §10 (AB 2650), operative January 1, 1994. Repealed Stats 1993 ch 219 §153.5 (AB 1500). See Fam C §6344.

§5756. [Section repealed 1993]

Leg.H. Enacted Stats 1992 ch 162 §10 (AB 2650), operative January 1, 1994. Repealed Stats 1993 ch 219 §153.5 (AB 1500). See Fam C §6345.

§5800. [Section repealed 1993]

Leg.H. Enacted Stats 1992 ch 162 §10 (AB 2650), operative January 1, 1994. Repealed Stats 1993 ch 219 §153.5 (AB 1500). See Fam C §6380.

§5801. [Section repealed 1993]

Leg.H. Enacted Stats 1992 ch 162 §10 (AB 2650), operative January 1, 1994. Repealed Stats 1993 ch 219 §153.5 (AB 1500). See Fam C §6382.

§5802. [Section repealed 1993]

Leg.H. Enacted Stats 1992 ch 162 §10 (AB 2650), operative January 1, 1994. Repealed Stats 1993 ch 219 §153.5 (AB 1500). See Fam C §6383.

§5803. [Section repealed 1993]

Leg.H. Enacted Stats 1992 ch 162 §10 (AB 2650), operative January 1, 1994. Repealed Stats 1993 ch 219 §153.5 (AB 1500). See Fam C §6384.

§5804. [Section repealed 1993]

Leg.H. Enacted Stats 1992 ch 162 §10 (AB 2650), operative January 1, 1994. Repealed Stats 1993 ch 219 §153.5 (AB 1500). See Fam C §6385.

§5805. [Section repealed 1993]

Leg.H. Enacted Stats 1992 ch 162 §10 (AB 2650), operative January 1, 1994. Repealed Stats 1993 ch 219 §153.5 (AB 1500). See Fam C §6386.

§5806. [Section repealed 1993]

Leg.H. Enacted Stats 1992 ch 162 §10 (AB 2650), operative January 1, 1994. Repealed Stats 1993 ch 219 §153.5 (AB 1500). See Fam C §6387.

§5807. [Section repealed 1993]

Leg.H. Enacted Stats 1992 ch 162 §10 (AB 2650), operative January 1, 1994. Repealed Stats 1993 ch 219 §153.5 (AB 1500). See Fam C §6388.

CHAPTER 9
PRIVATE CHILD SUPPORT COLLECTORS

"Private child support collector". §5610.
Contract terms. §5611.
Disclosure. §5612.
Cancellation. §5613.
Duties and prohibitions. §5614.
Violations; Waiver; Attorney private child support collectors. §5615.
Money judgment in court order. §5616.

§5610. "Private child support collector"

For the purposes of this chapter, "private child support collector" means any individual, corporation, attorney, nonprofit organization, or other nongovernmental entity who is engaged by an obligee to collect child support ordered by a court or other tribunal for a fee or other consideration. The term does not include any attorney who addresses issues of ongoing child support or child support arrearages in the course of an action to establish parentage or a child support obligation, a proceeding under Division 10 (commencing with Section 6200), a proceeding for dissolution of marriage, legal separation, or nullity of marriage, or in postjudgment or modification proceedings related to any of those actions. A "private child support collector" includes any private, nongovernmental attorney whose business is substantially comprised of the collection or enforcement of child support. As used in this section, substantially means that at least 50 percent of the attorney's business, either in terms of remuneration or time spent, is comprised of the activity of seeking to collect or enforce child support obligations for other individuals. **Leg.H.** Added Stats 2006 ch 797 §1 (AB 2781), effective January 1, 2007.

§5611. Contract terms

(a) A contract for the collection of child support between a private child support collector and an obligee shall be in writing and written in simple language, in at least 10-point type, signed by the private child support collector and the obligee. The contract shall be delivered to the obligee in a paper form that the obligee may retain for their records. The contract shall include all of the following:

(1) An explanation of the fees imposed by contract and otherwise permitted by law and an example of how they are calculated and deducted.

(2) A statement that the amount of fees to be charged is set by the agency and is not set by state law.

(3) A statement that the private child support collector cannot charge fees on current support if the obligee received any current child support during the 6 months preceding execution of the contract with the private collector.

(4) An explanation of the nature of the services to be provided.

(5) The expected duration of the contract, stated as a length of time or as an amount to be collected by the collection agency.

(6) An explanation of the opportunities available to the obligee or private child support collector to cancel the contract or other conditions under which the contract terminates.

(7) The mailing address, street address, telephone numbers, facsimile numbers, and internet address or location of the private child support collector.

(8) A statement that the private child support collector is not a governmental entity and that governmental entities in California provide child support collection and enforcement services free of charge.

(9) A statement that the private child support collector collects only money owed to the obligee and not support assigned to the state or county due to the receipt of CalWORKs or Temporary Assistance to Needy Families.

(10) A statement that the private child support collector will not retain fees from collections that are primarily attributable to the actions of a governmental entity or any other person or entity and is required by law to refund any fees improperly retained.

(11) A statement that the obligee may continue to receive, or may pursue, services through a governmental entity to collect support, and the private child support collection agency will not require or request that the obligee cease or refrain from engaging those services.

(12) A notice that the private child support collector is required to keep and maintain case records for a period of four years and four months, after the expiration of the contract and may thereafter destroy or otherwise dispose of the records. The obligee may, prior to destruction or disposal, retrieve those portions of the records that are not confidential.

(13) A "Notice of Cancellation," which shall be included with the contract and which shall contain, in the same size font as the contract, the following statement, written in the same language as the contract:

"Notice of Cancellation

You may cancel this contract, without any penalty or obligation, within 15 business days from the date the contract is signed or you receive this notice, whichever is later, or at any time if the private child support collector commits a material breach of any provision of the contract or a material violation of any provision of this chapter with respect to the obligee or the obligor, or _____ (all other reasons for cancellation permitted).

To cancel this contract, mail or deliver a signed copy of this cancellation notice or any other written notice to _____ (name of private child support collector) at _____ (address for mail or delivery) no later than midnight on _____ .

I am canceling this contract. _____ (date) _____ (signature)"

(14) The following statement by the obligee on the first page of the contract:

"I understand that this contract calls for (name of private child support collector) to collect money owed to me, and not money owed to the state or county. If child support is owed to the state or county because I am receiving or have received program benefits from CalWORKs or Temporary Assistance to Needy Families, then (name of private child support collector) cannot collect that money for me. If I start to receive program benefits from CalWORKs or Temporary Assistance to Needy Families during this contract, I must notify (name of private child support collector) in writing."

"I declare by my signature below that the child support to be collected for me pursuant to this contract is not assigned to the state or county as of the time I sign this contract. I agree that I will give written notice to the private child support collector if I apply for program benefits under CalWORKs or Temporary Assistance to Needy Families during the term of this contract."

(15)(A) The following statement by the obligee immediately above the signature line of the contract:

"I understand that (name of private child support collector) will charge a fee for all the current child support and arrears it collects for me until the entire contract amount is collected or the contract terminates for another reason. I also understand that depending on the frequency and size of payments, it could take years for the amount specified in my contract to be collected. This means that if (name of private child support collector) is collecting my current support by wage withholding or other means, I will not receive the full amount of my periodic court-ordered current support until the contract terminates since (name of private child support collector) will be deducting its fee from the periodic court-ordered current support it collects for me."

(B) The statement required by subparagraph (A) shall:

(i) Be in a type size that is at least equal to one-quarter of the largest type size used in the contract. In no event shall the disclosure be printed in less than 8-point type.

(ii) Be in a contrasting style, and contrasting color or bold type, that is equally or more visible than the type used in the contract.

(b) The disclosures required by paragraph (1) of subdivision (a) of Section 5612 shall be printed in the contract, as follows:

(1) In a type size that is at least equal to one-quarter of the largest type size used in the contract. In no event shall the disclosure be printed in less than 8-point type.

(2) In a contrasting style, and contrasting color or bold type that is equally or more visible than the type used in the contract.

(3) Immediately above, below, or beside the stated fee without any intervening words, pictures, marks, or symbols.

(4) In the same language as the contract. **Leg.H.** Added Stats 2006 ch 797 §1 (AB 2781), effective January 1, 2007. Amended Stats 2019 ch 115 §58 (AB 1817), effective January 1, 2020.

§5612. Disclosure

(a) Each private child support collector:

(1) That charges any initial fee, processing fee, application fee, filing fee, or other fee or assessment that must be paid by an obligee regardless of whether any child support collection is made on behalf of the obligee shall make the following disclosure in every radio, television, or print advertisement intended for a target audience consisting primarily of California residents:

"(Name of private child support collector) is not a governmental entity and charges an upfront fee for its services even if it does not collect anything."

(2) That does not charge any fee or assessment specified in paragraph (1) shall make the following disclosure in every radio, television, or print advertisement aired for a target audience consisting primarily of California residents:

"(Name of private child support collector) is not a governmental entity and charges a fee for its services."

(b) The disclosures required in subdivision (a) shall also be stated during the first 30 seconds of any initial telephone conversation with an obligee and in the private child support collector's contract. **Leg.H.** Added Stats 2006 ch 797 §1 (AB 2781), effective January 1, 2007.

§5613. Cancellation

(a) An obligee shall have the right to cancel a contract with a private support collector under either of the following circumstances:

(1) Within 15 business days of the later of signing the contract, or receiving a blank notice of cancellation form, or at any time if the private child support collector commits a material breach of any provision of the contract or a material violation of any provision of this chapter with respect to the obligee or the obligor.

(2) At the end of any 12-month period in which the total amount collected by the private child support collector is less than 50 percent of the amount scheduled to be paid under a payment plan.

(b) A contract shall automatically terminate when the contract term has expired or the contract amount has been collected, whichever occurs first. **Leg.H.** Added Stats 2006 ch 797 §1 (AB 2781), effective January 1, 2007.

§5614. Duties and prohibitions

(a) A private child support collector shall do all of the following:

(1)(A) Provide to an obligee all of the following information:

(i) The name of, and any other identifying information relating to, an obligor who made child support payments collected by the private child support collector.

(ii) The amount of support collected by the private child support collector.

(iii) The date on which each amount was received by the private child support collector.

(iv) The date on which each amount received by the private child support collector was sent to the obligee.

(v) The amount of the payment sent to the obligee.

(vi) The source of payment of support collected and the actions affirmatively taken by the private child support collector that resulted in the payment.

(vii) The amount and percentage of each payment kept by the private child support collector as its fee.

(B) The information required by subparagraph (A) shall be made available, at the option of the obligee, by mail, telephone, or via secure Internet access. If provided by mail, the notice shall be sent at least quarterly and, if provided by any other method, the information shall be updated and made available at least monthly. Information accessed by telephone and the Internet shall be up to date.

(2) Maintain records of all child support collections made on behalf of a client who is an obligee. The records required under this section shall be maintained by the private child support collector for the duration of the contract plus a period of four years and four months from the date of the last child support payment collected by the private child support collector on behalf of an obligee. In addition to information required by paragraph (1), the private child support collector shall maintain the following:

(A) A copy of the order establishing the child support obligation under which a collection was made by the private child support collector.

(B) Records of all correspondence between the private child support collector and the obligee or obligor in a case.

(C) Any other pertinent information relating to the child support obligation, including any case, cause, or docket number of the court having jurisdiction over the matter and official government payment records obtained by the private child support collector on behalf of, and at the request of, the obligee.

(3) Safeguard case records in a manner reasonably expected to prevent intentional or accidental disclosure of confidential information pertaining to the obligee or obligor, including providing necessary protections for records maintained in an automated system.

(4) Ensure that every person who contracts with a private child support collector has the right to review all files and documents, both paper and electronic, in the possession of the private child support collector for the information specified in this paragraph regarding that obligee's case that are not required by law to be kept confidential. The obligee, during regular business hours, shall be provided reasonable access to and copies of the files and records of the private child support collector regarding all moneys received, collection attempts made, fees retained or paid to the private child support collector, and moneys disbursed to the obligee. The private child support collector may not charge a fee for access to the files and records, but may require the obligee to pay up to three cents ($0.03) per page for the copies prior to their release.

(5) Provide, prior to commencing collection activities, written notice of a contract with an obligee to the local child support agency that is enforcing the obligee's support order, if known, or the local child support agency for the county in which the obligee resides as of the time the contract is signed by the obligee. The notice shall identify the obligee, the obligor, and the amount of the arrearage claimed by the obligee.

(b) A private child support collector shall not do any of the following:

(1) Charge fees on current support if the obligee received any current child support during the six months preceding execution of the contract with the private child support collector. A private child support collector shall inquire of the obligee and record the month and year of the last current support payment and may rely on information provided by the obligee in determining whether a fee may be charged on current support.

(2) Improperly retain fees from collections that are primarily attributable to the actions of a governmental entity. The private child support collector shall refund all of those fees to the obligee immediately upon discovery or notice of the improper retention of fees.

(3) Collect or attempt to collect child support by means of conduct that is prohibited of a debt collector collecting a consumer debt under Sections 1788.10 to 1788.16, inclusive, of the Civil Code. This chapter does not modify, alter, or amend the definition of a debt or a debt collector under the Rosenthal Fair Debt Collection Practices Act (Title 1.6C (commencing with Section 1788) of Part 4 of Division 3 of the Civil Code).

(4) Misstate the amount of the fee that may be lawfully paid to the private child support collector for the performance of the contract or the identity of the person who is obligated to pay that fee.

(5) Make a false representation of the amount of child support to be collected. A private child support collector is not in violation of this paragraph if it reasonably relied on sufficient documentation provided by the government entity collecting child support, a court with jurisdiction over the support obligation, or from the obligee, or upon sufficient documentation provided by the obligor.

(6) Ask a party other than the obligor to pay the child support obligation, unless that party is legally responsible for the obligation or is the legal representative of the obligor.

(7) On or after January 1, 2007, require, as a condition of providing services to the obligee, that the obligee waive any right or procedure provided for in state law regarding the right to file and pursue a civil action, or that the obligee agree to resolve disputes in a jurisdiction outside of California or to the application of laws other than those of California, as provided by law. Any waiver by the obligee of the right to file and pursue a civil action, the right to file and pursue a civil action in California, or the right to rely upon California law as provided by law must be knowing, voluntary, and not made a condition of doing business with the private child support collector. Any waiver, including, but not limited to, an agreement to arbitrate or regarding choice of forum or choice of law, that is required as a condition of doing business with the private child support collector, shall be presumed involuntary, unconscionable, against public policy, and unenforceable. The private child support collector has the burden of proving that any waiver of rights, including an agreement to arbitrate a claim or regarding choice of forum or choice of law, was knowing, voluntary, and not made a condition of the contract with the obligee. **Leg.H.** Added Stats 2006 ch 797 §1 (AB 2781), effective January 1, 2007. Amended Stats 2007 ch 130 §89 (AB 299), effective January 1, 2008; Stats 2018 ch 504 §3 (AB 3248), effective January 1, 2019.

§5615. Violations; Waiver; Attorney private child support collectors

(a)(1) A person may bring an action for actual damages incurred as a result of a violation of this chapter.

(2) In addition to actual damages, a private child support collector who willfully and knowingly violates the provisions of this chapter shall be liable for a civil penalty in an amount determined by the court, which may not be less than one hundred dollars ($100) nor more than one thousand dollars ($1,000).

(3)(A) The prevailing party in any action pursuant to this chapter shall be entitled to recover the costs of the action. Reasonable attorney's fees, which shall be based on the time necessarily expended to enforce the liability, shall be awarded to a prevailing party, other than the private child support collector, asserting rights under this chapter. Reasonable attorney's fees may be awarded to a prevailing private child support collector if the court finds that the party bringing the action did not prosecute the action in good faith.

(B) In an action by an obligor under this chapter, the private child support collector shall have no civil liability under this chapter to the obligor under any circumstance in which a debt collector would not have civil liability under Section 1788.30 of the Civil Code.

(4) A private child support collector is not in violation of this chapter if the private child support collector shows, by a preponderance of the evidence, that the action complained of was not intentional and resulted from a bona fide error that occurred notwithstanding the use of reasonable procedures to avoid the error.

(5) The remedies provided in this section are cumulative and are in addition to any other procedures, rights, or remedies available under any other law.

(b) Any waiver of the rights, requirements, and remedies provided by this chapter violates public policy and is void.

(c) Notwithstanding any other provision of this chapter, including provisions establishing a right of cancellation and requiring notice thereof, any contract for the collection of child support between an attorney who is a "private child support collector" pursuant to Section 5610 shall conform to the statutes, rules, and case law governing attorney conduct, including the provisions of law providing that a contract with an attorney is cancelable by the attorney's client at any time. Upon cancellation of that contract, the attorney may seek compensation as provided by law, including, if applicable, a claim for the reasonable value of any services rendered to the attorney's client pursuant to the doctrine of quantum meruit, provided those services lead to the collection of support and the compensation is limited to what would have been collected had the contract been in effect. To the extent that the provisions of this chapter are in conflict with the provisions of state law governing the conduct of attorneys, this chapter shall control. If there is no conflict, an attorney who is a "private child support collector" pursuant to Section 5610 shall conform to the provisions of this chapter. **Leg.H.** Added Stats 2006 ch 797 §1 (AB 2781), effective January 1, 2007.

§5616. Money judgment in court order

(a) Every court order for child support issued on or after January 1, 2010, and every child support agreement providing for the payment of child support approved by a court on or after January 1, 2010, shall include a separate money judgment owed by the child support obligor to pay a fee not to exceed 33 and ⅓ percent of the total amount in arrears, and not to exceed 50 percent of the fee as charged by a private child support collector pursuant to a contract complying with this chapter and any other child support collections costs expressly permitted by the child support order for the collection efforts undertaken by the private child support collector. The money judgment shall be in favor of the private child support collector and the child support obligee, jointly, but shall not constitute a private child support collector lien on real property unless an abstract of judgment is recorded pursuant to subdivision (d). Except as provided in subdivision (c), the money judgment may be enforced by the private child support collector by any means available to the obligee for the enforcement of the child support order without any additional action or order by the court. Nothing in this chapter shall be construed to grant the private child support collector any enforcement remedies beyond those authorized by federal or state law. Any fee collected from the obligor pursuant to a contract complying with this chapter, shall not constitute child support.

(b) If the child support order makes the obligor responsible for payment of collection fees and costs, fees that are deducted by a private child support collector may not be credited against child support arrearages or interest owing on arrearages or any other money owed by the obligor to the obligee.

(c) If the order for child support requires payment of collection fees and costs by the obligor, then not later than five days after the date that the private child support collector makes its first collection, written notice shall be provided to the obligor of (1) the amount of arrearages subject to collection, (2) the amount of the collection that shall be applied to the arrearage, and (3) the amount of the collection that shall be applied to the fees and costs of collection. The notice shall provide that, in addition to any other procedures available, the obligor has 30 days to file a motion to contest the amount of collection fees and costs assessed against the obligor.

(d) Any fees or monetary obligations resulting from the contract between an obligee parent and a private child support collector, or moneys owed to a private child support collector by the obligor parent or obligee parent as a result of the private child support collector's efforts, does not create a lien on real property, unless an abstract of judgment is obtained from the court and recorded by the private child support collector against the real property in the county in which it is located, nor shall that amount be added to any existing lien created by a recorded abstract of support or be added to an obligation on any abstract of judgment. A private child support collector lien shall have the force, effect, and priority of a judgment lien.

(e) An assignment to a private child support collector is a voluntary assignment for the purpose of collecting the domestic support obligation as defined in Section 101 of Title 11 of the United States Bankruptcy Code (11 U.S.C. Sec. 101 (14 A)). **Leg.H.** Added Stats 2006 ch 797 §1 (AB 2781), effective January 1, 2007. Amended Stats 2011 ch 296 §92 (AB 1023), effective January 1, 2012.

PART 6
UNIFORM INTERSTATE FAMILY SUPPORT ACT

Chapter 1. General Provisions.
Chapter 2. Jurisdiction.
Chapter 3. Civil Provisions of General Application.
Chapter 4. Establishment of Support Order or Determination of Parentage.
Chapter 5. Enforcement of Support Order Without Registration.
Chapter 6. Registration, Enforcement, and Modification of Support Order.
Chapter 7. Support Proceeding Under Convention.
Chapter 8. Interstate Rendition.
Chapter 9. Miscellaneous Provisions.

CHAPTER 1
GENERAL PROVISIONS

Citation of part; Adoption of act. §5700.101.
Definitions. §5700.102.
Tribunal. §5700.103.
Remedies. §5700.104.
Applicability to support proceedings. §5700.105.

§5700.101. Citation of part; Adoption of act

(a) This part may be cited as the Uniform Interstate Family Support Act.

(b) There is a federal mandate set forth in Section 666(f) of Title 42 of the United States Code requiring California to adopt and have in effect the Uniform Interstate Family Support Act, including any amendments officially adopted by the National Council of Commissioners on Uniform State Laws as of September 30, 2008. **Leg.H.** Added Stats 2015 ch 493 §5 (SB 646), effective January 1, 2016.

§5700.102. Definitions

In this part:

(1) "Child" means an individual, whether over or under the age of majority, who is or is alleged to be owed a duty of support by the individual's parent or who is or is alleged to be the beneficiary of a support order directed to the parent.

(2) "Child-support order" means a support order for a child, including a child who has attained the age of majority under the law of the issuing state or foreign country.

(3) "Convention" means the Convention on the International Recovery of Child Support and Other Forms of Family Maintenance, concluded at The Hague on November 23, 2007.

(4) "Duty of support" means an obligation imposed or imposable by law to provide support for a child, spouse, or former spouse, including an unsatisfied obligation to provide support.

(5) "Foreign country" means a country, including a political subdivision thereof, other than the United States, that authorizes the issuance of support orders and:

(A) Which has been declared under the law of the United States to be a foreign reciprocating country;

(B) Which has established a reciprocal arrangement for child support with this state as provided in Section 5700.308;

(C) Which has enacted a law or established procedures for the issuance and enforcement of support orders which are substantially similar to the procedures under this part; or

(D) In which the Convention is in force with respect to the United States.

(6) "Foreign support order" means a support order of a foreign tribunal.

(7) "Foreign tribunal" means a court, administrative agency, or quasi-judicial entity of a foreign country which is authorized to establish, enforce, or modify support orders or to determine parentage of a child. The term includes a competent authority under the Convention.

(8) "Home state" means the state or foreign country in which a child lived with a parent or a person acting as parent for at least six consecutive months immediately preceding the time of filing of a petition or comparable pleading for support and, if a child is less than six months old, the state or foreign country in which the child lived from birth with any of them. A period of temporary absence of any of them is counted as part of the six-month or other period.

(9) "Income" includes earnings or other periodic entitlements to money from any source and any other property subject to withholding for support under the law of this state.

(10) "Income-withholding order" means an order or other legal process directed to an obligor's employer, or other debtor, as defined by Section 5208, to withhold support from the income of the obligor.

(11) "Initiating tribunal" means the tribunal of a state or foreign country from which a petition or comparable pleading is forwarded or in which a petition or comparable pleading is filed for forwarding to another state or foreign country.

(12) "Issuing foreign country" means the foreign country in which a tribunal issues a support order or a judgment determining parentage of a child.

(13) "Issuing state" means the state in which a tribunal issues a support order or a judgment determining parentage of a child.

(14) "Issuing tribunal" means the tribunal of a state or foreign country that issues a support order or a judgment determining parentage of a child.

(15) "Law" includes decisional and statutory law and rules and regulations having the force of law.

(16) "Obligee" means:

(A) an individual to whom a duty of support is or is alleged to be owed or in whose favor a support order or a judgment determining parentage of a child has been issued;

(B) a foreign country, state, or political subdivision of a state to which the rights under a duty of support or support order have been assigned or which has independent claims based on financial assistance provided to an individual obligee in place of child support;

(C) an individual seeking a judgment determining parentage of the individual's child; or

(D) a person that is a creditor in a proceeding under Chapter 7.

(17) "Obligor" means an individual, or the estate of a decedent that:

(A) owes or is alleged to owe a duty of support;

(B) is alleged but has not been adjudicated to be a parent of a child;

(C) is liable under a support order; or

(D) is a debtor in a proceeding under Chapter 7.

(18) "Outside this state" means a location in another state or a country other than the United States, whether or not the country is a foreign country.

(19) "Person" means an individual, corporation, business trust, estate, trust, partnership, limited liability company, association, joint venture, public corporation, government or governmental subdivision, agency, or instrumentality, or any other legal or commercial entity.

(20) "Record" means information that is inscribed on a tangible medium or that is stored in an electronic or other medium and is retrievable in perceivable form.

(21) "Register" means to file in a tribunal of this state a support order or judgment determining parentage of a child issued in another state or a foreign country.

(22) "Registering tribunal" means a tribunal in which a support order or judgment determining parentage of a child is registered.

(23) "Responding state" means a state in which a petition or comparable pleading for support or to determine parentage of a child is filed or to which a petition or comparable pleading is forwarded for filing from another state or a foreign country.

(24) "Responding tribunal" means the authorized tribunal in a responding state or foreign country.

(25) "Spousal-support order" means a support order for a spouse or former spouse of the obligor.

(26) "State" means a state of the United States, the District of Columbia, Puerto Rico, the United States Virgin Islands, or any territory or insular possession under the jurisdiction of the United States. The term includes an Indian nation or tribe.

(27) "Support enforcement agency" means a public official, governmental entity, or private agency authorized to:

(A) seek enforcement of support orders or laws relating to the duty of support;

(B) seek establishment or modification of child support;

(C) request determination of parentage of a child;

(D) attempt to locate obligors or their assets; or

(E) request determination of the controlling child-support order.

(28) "Support order" means a judgment, decree, order, decision, or directive, whether temporary, final, or subject to modification, issued in a state or foreign country for the benefit of a child, a spouse, or a former spouse, which provides for monetary support, health care, arrearages, retroactive support, or reimbursement for financial assistance provided to an individual obligee in place of child support. The term may include related costs and fees, interest, income withholding, automatic adjustment, reasonable attorney's fees, and other relief.

(29) "Tribunal" means a court, administrative agency, or quasi-judicial entity authorized to establish, enforce, or modify support orders or to determine parentage of a child. **Leg.H.** Added Stats 2015 ch 493 §5 (SB 646), effective January 1, 2016.

§5700.103. Tribunal

(a) The superior court is the tribunal of this state.

(b) The Department of Child Support Services is the support enforcement agency of this state. **Leg.H.** Added Stats 2015 ch 493 §5 (SB 646), effective January 1, 2016.

§5700.104. Remedies

(a) Remedies provided by this part are cumulative and do not affect the availability of remedies under other law or the recognition of a foreign support order on the basis of comity.

(b) This part does not:

(1) provide the exclusive method of establishing or enforcing a support order under the law of this state; or

(2) grant a tribunal of this state jurisdiction to render judgment or issue an order relating to child custody or visitation in a proceeding under this part. **Leg.H.** Added Stats 2015 ch 493 §5 (SB 646), effective January 1, 2016.

§5700.105. Applicability to support proceedings

(a) A tribunal of this state shall apply Chapters 1 through 6 and, as applicable, Chapter 7, to a support proceeding involving:

(1) a foreign support order;

(2) a foreign tribunal; or

(3) an obligee, obligor, or child residing in a foreign country.

(b) A tribunal of this state that is requested to recognize and enforce a support order on the basis of comity may apply the procedural and substantive provisions of Chapters 1 through 6.

(c) Chapter 7 applies only to a support proceeding under the Convention. In such a proceeding, if a provision of Chapter 7 is inconsistent with Chapters 1 through 6, Chapter 7 controls. **Leg.H.** Added Stats 2015 ch 493 §5 (SB 646), effective January 1, 2016.

CHAPTER 2
JURISDICTION

Nonresidents. §5700.201.
Personal jurisdiction. §5700.202.
Initiating and responding tribunals. §5700.203.
Conditions for establishing support orders. §5700.204.
Continuing jurisdiction. §5700.205.
State tribunal as initiating or responding tribunal to enforce child support order. §5700.206.
Multiple support orders. §5700.207.
Enforcement of multiple orders. §5700.208.
Crediting amounts collected. §5700.209.
Evidence, discovery, and communication with tribunal outside state. §5700.210.
Jurisdiction over spousal support orders. §5700.211.

§5700.201. Nonresidents

(a) In a proceeding to establish or enforce a support order or to determine parentage of a child, a tribunal of this state may exercise personal jurisdiction over a nonresident individual or the individual's guardian or conservator if:

(1) the individual is personally served with notice within this state;

(2) the individual submits to the jurisdiction of this state by consent in a record, by entering a general appearance, or by filing a responsive document having the effect of waiving any contest to personal jurisdiction;

(3) the individual resided with the child in this state;

(4) the individual resided in this state and provided prenatal expenses or support for the child;

(5) the child resides in this state as a result of the acts or directives of the individual;

(6) the individual engaged in sexual intercourse in this state and the child may have been conceived by that act of intercourse;

(7) the individual has filed a declaration of paternity pursuant to Chapter 3 (commencing with Section 7570) of Part 2 of Division 12, maintained in this state by the Department of Child Support Services; or

(8) there is any other basis consistent with the constitutions of this state and the United States for the exercise of personal jurisdiction.

(b) The bases of personal jurisdiction set forth in subsection (a) or in any other law of this state may not be used to acquire personal jurisdiction for a tribunal of this state to modify a child-support order of another state unless the requirements of Section 5700.611 are met, or, in the case of a foreign support order, unless the requirements of Section 5700.615 are met. **Leg.H.** Added Stats 2015 ch 493 §5 (SB 646), effective January 1, 2016.

§5700.202. Personal jurisdiction

Personal jurisdiction acquired by a tribunal of this state in a proceeding under this part or other law of this state relating to a support order continues as long as a tribunal of this state has continuing, exclusive jurisdiction to modify its order or continuing jurisdiction to enforce its order as provided by Sections 5700.205, 5700.206, and 5700.211. **Leg.H.** Added Stats 2015 ch 493 §5 (SB 646), effective January 1, 2016.

§5700.203. Initiating and responding tribunals

Under this part, a tribunal of this state may serve as an initiating tribunal to forward proceedings to a tribunal of another state, and as a responding tribunal for proceedings initiated in another state or a foreign country. **Leg.H.** Added Stats 2015 ch 493 §5 (SB 646), effective January 1, 2016.

§5700.204. Conditions for establishing support orders

(a) A tribunal of this state may exercise jurisdiction to establish a support order if the petition or comparable pleading is filed after a pleading is filed in another state or a foreign country only if:

(1) the petition or comparable pleading in this state is filed before the expiration of the time allowed in the other state or the foreign country for filing a responsive pleading challenging the exercise of jurisdiction by the other state or the foreign country;

(2) the contesting party timely challenges the exercise of jurisdiction in the other state or the foreign country; and

(3) if relevant, this state is the home state of the child.

(b) A tribunal of this state may not exercise jurisdiction to establish a support order if the petition or comparable pleading is filed before a petition or comparable pleading is filed in another state or a foreign country if:

(1) the petition or comparable pleading in the other state or foreign country is filed before the expiration of the time allowed in this state for filing a responsive pleading challenging the exercise of jurisdiction by this state;

(2) the contesting party timely challenges the exercise of jurisdiction in this state; and

(3) if relevant, the other state or foreign country is the home state of the child. **Leg.H.** Added Stats 2015 ch 493 §5 (SB 646), effective January 1, 2016.

§5700.205. Continuing jurisdiction

(a) A tribunal of this state that has issued a child-support order consistent with the law of this state has and shall exercise continuing, exclusive jurisdiction to modify its child-support order if the order is the controlling order and:

(1) at the time of the filing of a request for modification this state is the residence of the obligor, the individual obligee, or the child for whose benefit the support order is issued; or

(2) even if this state is not the residence of the obligor, the individual obligee, or the child for whose benefit the support order is issued, the parties consent in a record or in open court that the tribunal of this state may continue to exercise jurisdiction to modify its order.

(b) A tribunal of this state that has issued a child-support order consistent with the law of this state may not exercise continuing, exclusive jurisdiction to modify the order if:

(1) all of the parties who are individuals file consent in a record with the tribunal of this state that a tribunal of another state that has jurisdiction over at least one of the parties who is an individual or that is located in the

state of residence of the child may modify the order and assume continuing, exclusive jurisdiction; or

(2) its order is not the controlling order.

(c) If a tribunal of another state has issued a child-support order pursuant to the Uniform Interstate Family Support Act or a law substantially similar to that Act which modifies a child-support order of a tribunal of this state, tribunals of this state shall recognize the continuing, exclusive jurisdiction of the tribunal of the other state.

(d) A tribunal of this state that lacks continuing, exclusive jurisdiction to modify a child-support order may serve as an initiating tribunal to request a tribunal of another state to modify a support order issued in that state.

(e) A temporary support order issued ex parte or pending resolution of a jurisdictional conflict does not create continuing, exclusive jurisdiction in the issuing tribunal. **Leg.H.** Added Stats 2015 ch 493 §5 (SB 646), effective January 1, 2016.

§5700.206. State tribunal as initiating or responding tribunal to enforce child support order

(a) A tribunal of this state that has issued a child-support order consistent with the law of this state may serve as an initiating tribunal to request a tribunal of another state to enforce:

(1) the order if the order is the controlling order and has not been modified by a tribunal of another state that assumed jurisdiction pursuant to the Uniform Interstate Family Support Act; or

(2) a money judgment for arrears of support and interest on the order accrued before a determination that an order of a tribunal of another state is the controlling order.

(b) A tribunal of this state having continuing jurisdiction over a support order may act as a responding tribunal to enforce the order. **Leg.H.** Added Stats 2015 ch 493 §5 (SB 646), effective January 1, 2016.

§5700.207. Multiple support orders

(a) If a proceeding is brought under this part and only one tribunal has issued a child-support order, the order of that tribunal controls and must be recognized.

(b) If a proceeding is brought under this part, and two or more child-support orders have been issued by tribunals of this state, another state, or a foreign country with regard to the same obligor and same child, a tribunal of this state having personal jurisdiction over both the obligor and individual obligee shall apply the following rules and by order shall determine which order controls and must be recognized:

(1) If only one of the tribunals would have continuing, exclusive jurisdiction under this part, the order of that tribunal controls.

(2) If more than one of the tribunals would have continuing, exclusive jurisdiction under this part:

(A) an order issued by a tribunal in the current home state of the child controls; or

(B) if an order has not been issued in the current home state of the child, the order most recently issued controls.

(3) If none of the tribunals would have continuing, exclusive jurisdiction under this part, the tribunal of this state shall issue a child-support order, which controls.

(c) If two or more child-support orders have been issued for the same obligor and same child, upon request of a party who is an individual or that is a support enforcement agency, a tribunal of this state having personal jurisdiction over both the obligor and the obligee who is an individual shall determine which order controls under subsection (b). The request may be filed with a registration for enforcement or registration for modification pursuant to Chapter 6, or may be filed as a separate proceeding.

(d) A request to determine which is the controlling order must be accompanied by a copy of every child-support order in effect and the applicable record of payments. The requesting party shall give notice of the request to each party whose rights may be affected by the determination.

(e) The tribunal that issued the controlling order under subsection (a), (b), or (c) has continuing jurisdiction to the extent provided in Section 5700.205 or 5700.206.

(f) A tribunal of this state that determines by order which is the controlling order under subsection (b)(1) or (2) or (c), or that issues a new controlling order under subsection (b)(3), shall state in that order:

(1) the basis upon which the tribunal made its determination;

(2) the amount of prospective support, if any; and

(3) the total amount of consolidated arrears and accrued interest, if any, under all of the orders after all payments made are credited as provided by Section 5700.209.

(g) Within 30 days after issuance of an order determining which is the controlling order, the party obtaining the order shall file a certified copy of it in each tribunal that issued or registered an earlier order of child support. A party or support enforcement agency obtaining the order that fails to file a certified copy is subject to appropriate sanctions by a tribunal in which the issue of failure to file arises. The failure to file does not affect the validity or enforceability of the controlling order.

(h) An order that has been determined to be the controlling order, or a judgment for consolidated arrears of support and interest, if any, made pursuant to this section must be recognized in proceedings under this part. **Leg.H.** Added Stats 2015 ch 493 §5 (SB 646), effective January 1, 2016.

§5700.208. Enforcement of multiple orders

In responding to registrations or petitions for enforcement of two or more child-support orders in effect at the same time with regard to the same obligor and different individual obligees, at least one of which was issued by a tribunal of another state or a foreign country, a tribunal of this state shall enforce those orders in the same manner as if the orders had been issued by a tribunal of this state. **Leg.H.** Added Stats 2015 ch 493 §5 (SB 646), effective January 1, 2016.

§5700.209. Crediting amounts collected

A tribunal of this state shall credit amounts collected for a particular period pursuant to any child-support order against the amounts owed for the same period under any other child-support order for support of the same child issued by a tribunal of this state, another state, or a foreign country. **Leg.H.** Added Stats 2015 ch 493 §5 (SB 646), effective January 1, 2016.

§5700.210. Evidence, discovery, and communication with tribunal outside state

A tribunal of this state exercising personal jurisdiction over a nonresident in a proceeding under this part, under other law of this state relating to a support order, or recognizing a foreign support order may receive evidence from outside this state pursuant to Section 5700.316, communicate with a tribunal outside this state pursuant to Section 5700.317, and obtain discovery through a tribunal outside this state pursuant to Section 5700.318. In all other respects, Chapters 3 through 6 do not apply, and the tribunal shall apply the procedural and substantive law of this state. **Leg.H.** Added Stats 2015 ch 493 §5 (SB 646), effective January 1, 2016.

§5700.211. Jurisdiction over spousal support orders

(a) A tribunal of this state issuing a spousal-support order consistent with the law of this state has continuing, exclusive jurisdiction to modify the spousal-support order throughout the existence of the support obligation.

(b) A tribunal of this state may not modify a spousal-support order issued by a tribunal of another state or a foreign country having continuing, exclusive jurisdiction over that order under the law of that state or foreign country.

(c) A tribunal of this state that has continuing, exclusive jurisdiction over a spousal-support order may serve as:

(1) an initiating tribunal to request a tribunal of another state to enforce the spousal-support order issued in this state; or

(2) a responding tribunal to enforce or modify its own spousal-support order. **Leg.H.** Added Stats 2015 ch 493 §5 (SB 646), effective January 1, 2016.

CHAPTER 3
CIVIL PROVISIONS OF GENERAL APPLICATION

Proceedings under chapter. §5700.301.
Minor parents. §5700.302.
Responding tribunals. §5700.303.
Initiating tribunal to forward copies of petition. §5700.304.
Responding tribunal authority and duties. §5700.305.
Inappropriate tribunals. §5700.306.
Providing services to petitioners. §5700.307.
Attorney General services. §5700.308.
Private counsel. §5700.309.
State information agency. §5700.310.

Contents of petition. §5700.311.
Disclosure of identifying information. §5700.312.
Costs and fees. §5700.313.
Physical presence of petitioner. §5700.314.
Nonparentage as a defense. §5700.315.
Special evidentiary rules. §5700.316.
Communications with tribunal of another state. §5700.317.
Discovery. §5700.318.
Payments received. §5700.319.

§5700.301. Proceedings under chapter

(a) Except as otherwise provided in this part, this chapter applies to all proceedings under this part.

(b) An individual petitioner or a support enforcement agency may initiate a proceeding authorized under this part by filing a petition in an initiating tribunal for forwarding to a responding tribunal or by filing a petition or a comparable pleading directly in a tribunal of another state or a foreign country which has or can obtain personal jurisdiction over the respondent. **Leg.H.** Added Stats 2015 ch 493 §5 (SB 646), effective January 1, 2016.

§5700.302. Minor parents

A minor parent, or a guardian or other legal representative of a minor parent, may maintain a proceeding on behalf of or for the benefit of the minor's child. **Leg.H.** Added Stats 2015 ch 493 §5 (SB 646), effective January 1, 2016.

§5700.303. Responding tribunals

Except as otherwise provided in this part, a responding tribunal of this state shall:

(1) apply the procedural and substantive law generally applicable to similar proceedings originating in this state and may exercise all powers and provide all remedies available in those proceedings; and

(2) determine the duty of support and the amount payable in accordance with the law and support guidelines of this state. **Leg.H.** Added Stats 2015 ch 493 §5 (SB 646), effective January 1, 2016.

§5700.304. Initiating tribunal to forward copies of petition

(a) Upon the filing of a petition authorized by this part, an initiating tribunal of this state shall forward the petition and its accompanying documents:

(1) to the responding tribunal or appropriate support enforcement agency in the responding state; or

(2) if the identity of the responding tribunal is unknown, to the state information agency of the responding state with a request that they be forwarded to the appropriate tribunal and that receipt be acknowledged.

(b) If requested by the responding tribunal, a tribunal of this state shall issue a certificate or other document and make findings required by the law of the responding state. If the responding tribunal is in a foreign country, upon request the tribunal of this state shall specify the amount of support sought, convert that amount into the equivalent amount in the foreign currency under applicable official or market exchange rate as publicly reported, and provide any other documents necessary to satisfy the requirements of the responding foreign tribunal. **Leg.H.** Added Stats 2015 ch 493 §5 (SB 646), effective January 1, 2016.

§5700.305. Responding tribunal authority and duties

(a) When a responding tribunal of this state receives a petition or comparable pleading from an initiating tribunal or directly pursuant to Section 5700.301(b), it shall cause the petition or pleading to be filed and notify the petitioner where and when it was filed.

(b) A responding tribunal of this state, to the extent not prohibited by other law, may do one or more of the following:

(1) establish or enforce a support order, modify a child-support order, determine the controlling child-support order, or determine parentage of a child;

(2) order an obligor to comply with a support order, specifying the amount and the manner of compliance;

(3) order income withholding;

(4) determine the amount of any arrearages, and specify a method of payment;

(5) enforce orders by civil or criminal contempt, or both;

(6) set aside property for satisfaction of the support order;

(7) place liens and order execution on the obligor's property;

(8) order an obligor to keep the tribunal informed of the obligor's current residential address, electronic-mail address, telephone number, employer, address of employment, and telephone number at the place of employment;

(9) issue a bench warrant for an obligor who has failed after proper notice to appear at a hearing ordered by the tribunal and enter the bench warrant in any local and state computer systems for criminal warrants;

(10) order the obligor to seek appropriate employment by specified methods;

(11) award reasonable attorney's fees and other fees and costs; and

(12) grant any other available remedy.

(c) A responding tribunal of this state shall include in a support order issued under this part, or in the documents accompanying the order, the calculations on which the support order is based.

(d) A responding tribunal of this state may not condition the payment of a support order issued under this part upon compliance by a party with provisions for visitation.

(e) If a responding tribunal of this state issues an order under this part, the tribunal shall send a copy of the order to the petitioner and the respondent and to the initiating tribunal, if any.

(f) If requested to enforce a support order, arrears, or judgment or modify a support order stated in a foreign currency, a responding tribunal of this state shall convert the amount stated in the foreign currency to the equivalent amount in dollars under the applicable official or market exchange rate as publicly reported. **Leg.H.** Added Stats 2015 ch 493 §5 (SB 646), effective January 1, 2016.

§5700.306. Inappropriate tribunals

If a petition or comparable pleading is received by an inappropriate tribunal of this state, the tribunal shall forward the pleading and accompanying documents to an appropriate tribunal of this state or another state and notify the petitioner where and when the pleading was sent. **Leg.H.** Added Stats 2015 ch 493 §5 (SB 646), effective January 1, 2016.

§5700.307. Providing services to petitioners

(a) A support enforcement agency of this state, upon request, shall provide services to a petitioner in a proceeding under this part.

(b) A support enforcement agency of this state that is providing services to the petitioner shall:

(1) take all steps necessary to enable an appropriate tribunal of this state, another state, or a foreign country to obtain jurisdiction over the respondent;

(2) request an appropriate tribunal to set a date, time, and place for a hearing;

(3) make a reasonable effort to obtain all relevant information, including information as to income and property of the parties;

(4) within 14 days, exclusive of Saturdays, Sundays, and legal holidays, after receipt of notice in a record from an initiating, responding, or registering tribunal, send a copy of the notice to the petitioner;

(5) within 14 days, exclusive of Saturdays, Sundays, and legal holidays, after receipt of communication in a record from the respondent or the respondent's attorney, send a copy of the communication to the petitioner; and

(6) notify the petitioner if jurisdiction over the respondent cannot be obtained.

(c) A support enforcement agency of this state that requests registration of a child-support order in this state for enforcement or for modification shall make reasonable efforts:

(1) to ensure that the order to be registered is the controlling order; or

(2) if two or more child-support orders exist and the identity of the controlling order has not been determined, to ensure that a request for such a determination is made in a tribunal having jurisdiction to do so.

(d) A support enforcement agency of this state that requests registration and enforcement of a support order, arrears, or judgment stated in a foreign currency shall convert the amounts stated in the foreign currency into the equivalent amounts in dollars under the applicable official or market exchange rate as publicly reported.

(e) A support enforcement agency of this state shall issue or request a tribunal of this state to issue a child-support order and an income-withholding order that redirect payment of current support, arrears, and interest if requested to do so by a support enforcement agency of another state pursuant to Section 5700.319.

(f) This part does not create or negate a relationship of attorney and client or other fiduciary relationship between a support enforcement

§5700.308. Attorney General services

(a) If the Attorney General or the Department of Child Support Services determines that the support enforcement agency is neglecting or refusing to provide services to an individual, the Attorney General or the department may order the agency to perform its duties under this part or may provide those services directly to the individual.

(b) The Department of Child Support Services, in consultation with the Attorney General, may determine that a foreign country has established a reciprocal arrangement for child support with this state and take appropriate action for notification of the determination. **Leg.H.** Added Stats 2015 ch 493 §5 (SB 646), effective January 1, 2016.

§5700.309. Private counsel

An individual may employ private counsel to represent the individual in proceedings authorized by this part. **Leg.H.** Added Stats 2015 ch 493 §5 (SB 646), effective January 1, 2016.

§5700.310. State information agency

(a) The Department of Child Support Services is the state information agency under this part.

(b) The state information agency shall:

(1) compile and maintain a current list, including addresses, of the tribunals in this state which have jurisdiction under this part and any support enforcement agencies in this state and transmit a copy to the state information agency of every other state;

(2) maintain a register of names and addresses of tribunals and support enforcement agencies received from other states;

(3) forward to the appropriate tribunal in the county in this state in which the obligee who is an individual or the obligor resides, or in which the obligor's property is believed to be located, all documents concerning a proceeding under this part received from another state or a foreign country; and

(4) obtain information concerning the location of the obligor and the obligor's property within this state not exempt from execution, by such means as postal verification and federal or state locator services, examination of telephone directories, requests for the obligor's address from employers, and examination of governmental records, including, to the extent not prohibited by other law, those relating to real property, vital statistics, law enforcement, taxation, motor vehicles, driver's licenses, and social security. **Leg.H.** Added Stats 2015 ch 493 §5 (SB 646), effective January 1, 2016.

§5700.311. Contents of petition

(a) In a proceeding under this part, a petitioner seeking to establish a support order, to determine parentage of a child, or to register and modify a support order of a tribunal of another state or a foreign country must file a petition. Unless otherwise ordered under Section 5700.312, the petition or accompanying documents must provide, so far as known, the name, residential address, and social security numbers of the obligor and the obligee or the parent and alleged parent, and the name, sex, residential address, social security number, and date of birth of each child for whose benefit support is sought or whose parentage is to be determined. Unless filed at the time of registration, the petition must be accompanied by a copy of any support order known to have been issued by another tribunal. The petition may include any other information that may assist in locating or identifying the respondent.

(b) The petition must specify the relief sought. The petition and accompanying documents must conform substantially with the requirements imposed by the forms mandated by federal law for use in cases filed by a support enforcement agency. **Leg.H.** Added Stats 2015 ch 493 §5 (SB 646), effective January 1, 2016.

§5700.312. Disclosure of identifying information

If a party alleges in an affidavit or a pleading under oath that the health, safety, or liberty of a party or child would be jeopardized by disclosure of specific identifying information, that information must be sealed and may not be disclosed to the other party or the public. After a hearing in which a tribunal takes into consideration the health, safety, or liberty of the party or child, the tribunal may order disclosure of information that the tribunal determines to be in the interest of justice. **Leg.H.** Added Stats 2015 ch 493 §5 (SB 646), effective January 1, 2016.

§5700.313. Costs and fees

(a) The petitioner may not be required to pay a filing fee or other costs.

(b) If an obligee prevails, a responding tribunal of this state may assess against an obligor filing fees, reasonable attorney's fees, other costs, and necessary travel and other reasonable expenses incurred by the obligee and the obligee's witnesses. The tribunal may not assess fees, costs, or expenses against the obligee or the support enforcement agency of either the initiating or responding state or foreign country, except as provided by other law. Attorney's fees may be taxed as costs, and may be ordered paid directly to the attorney, who may enforce the order in the attorney's own name. Payment of support owed to the obligee has priority over fees, costs, and expenses.

(c) The tribunal shall order the payment of costs and reasonable attorney's fees if it determines that a hearing was requested primarily for delay. In a proceeding under Chapter 6, a hearing is presumed to have been requested primarily for delay if a registered support order is confirmed or enforced without change. **Leg.H.** Added Stats 2015 ch 493 §5 (SB 646), effective January 1, 2016.

§5700.314. Physical presence of petitioner

(a) Participation by a petitioner in a proceeding under this part before a responding tribunal, whether in person, by private attorney, or through services provided by the support enforcement agency, does not confer personal jurisdiction over the petitioner in another proceeding.

(b) A petitioner is not amenable to service of civil process while physically present in this state to participate in a proceeding under this part.

(c) The immunity granted by this section does not extend to civil litigation based on acts unrelated to a proceeding under this part committed by a party while physically present in this state to participate in the proceeding. **Leg.H.** Added Stats 2015 ch 493 §5 (SB 646), effective January 1, 2016.

§5700.315. Nonparentage as a defense

A party whose parentage of a child has been previously determined by or pursuant to law may not plead nonparentage as a defense to a proceeding under this part. **Leg.H.** Added Stats 2015 ch 493 §5 (SB 646), effective January 1, 2016.

§5700.316. Special evidentiary rules

(a) The physical presence of a nonresident party who is an individual in a tribunal of this state is not required for the establishment, enforcement, or modification of a support order or the rendition of a judgment determining parentage of a child.

(b) An affidavit, a document substantially complying with federally mandated forms, or a document incorporated by reference in any of them, which would not be excluded under the hearsay rule if given in person, is admissible in evidence if given under penalty of perjury by a party or witness residing outside this state.

(c) A copy of the record of child-support payments certified as a true copy of the original by the custodian of the record may be forwarded to a responding tribunal. The copy is evidence of facts asserted in it, and is admissible to show whether payments were made.

(d) Copies of bills for testing for parentage of a child, and for prenatal and postnatal health care of the mother and child, furnished to the adverse party at least 10 days before trial, are admissible in evidence to prove the amount of the charges billed and that the charges were reasonable, necessary, and customary.

(e) Documentary evidence transmitted from outside this state to a tribunal of this state by telephone, telecopier, or other electronic means that do not provide an original record may not be excluded from evidence on an objection based on the means of transmission.

(f) In a proceeding under this part, a tribunal of this state shall permit a party or witness residing outside this state to be deposed or to testify under penalty of perjury by telephone, audiovisual means, or other electronic means at a designated tribunal or other location. A tribunal of this state shall cooperate with other tribunals in designating an appropriate location for the deposition or testimony.

(g) If a party called to testify at a civil hearing refuses to answer on the ground that the testimony may be self-incriminating, the trier of fact may draw an adverse inference from the refusal.

(h) A privilege against disclosure of communications between spouses does not apply in a proceeding under this part.

(i) The defense of immunity based on the relationship of husband and wife or parent and child does not apply in a proceeding under this part.

(j) A voluntary acknowledgment of paternity, certified as a true copy, is admissible to establish parentage of the child. **Leg.H.** Added Stats 2015 ch 493 §5 (SB 646), effective January 1, 2016.

§5700.317. Communications with tribunal of another state

A tribunal of this state may communicate with a tribunal outside this state in a record or by telephone, electronic mail, or other means, to obtain information concerning the laws, the legal effect of a judgment, decree, or order of that tribunal, and the status of a proceeding. A tribunal of this state may furnish similar information by similar means to a tribunal outside this state. **Leg.H.** Added Stats 2015 ch 493 §5 (SB 646), effective January 1, 2016.

§5700.318. Discovery

A tribunal of this state may:

(1) request a tribunal outside this state to assist in obtaining discovery; and

(2) upon request, compel a person over which it has jurisdiction to respond to a discovery order issued by a tribunal outside this state. **Leg.H.** Added Stats 2015 ch 493 §5 (SB 646), effective January 1, 2016.

§5700.319. Payments received

(a) A support enforcement agency or tribunal of this state shall disburse promptly any amounts received pursuant to a support order, as directed by the order. The agency or tribunal shall furnish to a requesting party or tribunal of another state or a foreign country a certified statement by the custodian of the record of the amounts and dates of all payments received.

(b) If neither the obligor, nor the obligee who is an individual, nor the child resides in this state, upon request from the support enforcement agency of this state or another state, the Department of Child Support Services or a tribunal of this state shall:

(1) direct that the support payment be made to the support enforcement agency in the state in which the obligee is receiving services; and

(2) issue and send to the obligor's employer a conforming income-withholding order or an administrative notice of change of payee, reflecting the redirected payments.

(c) The support enforcement agency of this state receiving redirected payments from another state pursuant to a law similar to subsection (b) shall furnish to a requesting party or tribunal of the other state a certified statement by the custodian of the record of the amount and dates of all payments received. **Leg.H.** Added Stats 2015 ch 493 §5 (SB 646), effective January 1, 2016.

CHAPTER 4
ESTABLISHMENT OF SUPPORT ORDER OR DETERMINATION OF PARENTAGE

Conditions for issuing support order. §5700.401.
Responding tribunal in proceeding to determine parentage. §5700.402.

§5700.401. Conditions for issuing support order

(a) If a support order entitled to recognition under this part has not been issued, a responding tribunal of this state with personal jurisdiction over the parties may issue a support order if:

(1) the individual seeking the order resides outside this state; or

(2) the support enforcement agency seeking the order is located outside this state.

(b) The tribunal may issue a temporary child-support order if the tribunal determines that such an order is appropriate and the individual ordered to pay is:

(1) a presumed father of the child;

(2) petitioning to have his paternity adjudicated;

(3) identified as the father of the child through genetic testing;

(4) an alleged father who has declined to submit to genetic testing;

(5) shown by clear and convincing evidence to be the father of the child;

(6) an acknowledged father as provided by applicable state law;

(7) the mother of the child; or

(8) an individual who has been ordered to pay child support in a previous proceeding and the order has not been reversed or vacated.

(c) Upon finding, after notice and opportunity to be heard, that an obligor owes a duty of support, the tribunal shall issue a support order directed to the obligor and may issue other orders pursuant to Section 5700.305. **Leg.H.** Added Stats 2015 ch 493 §5 (SB 646), effective January 1, 2016.

§5700.402. Responding tribunal in proceeding to determine parentage

A tribunal of this state authorized to determine parentage of a child may serve as a responding tribunal in a proceeding to determine parentage of a child brought under this part or a law or procedure substantially similar to this part. **Leg.H.** Added Stats 2015 ch 493 §5 (SB 646), effective January 1, 2016.

CHAPTER 5
ENFORCEMENT OF SUPPORT ORDER WITHOUT REGISTRATION

Income-withholding order. §5700.501.
Employer's duties. §5700.502.
Multiple income-withholding orders. §5700.503.
Liability of employer. §5700.504.
Penalties for noncompliance. §5700.505.
Contesting the order. §5700.506.
Documentation and registration. §5700.507.

§5700.501. Income-withholding order

An income-withholding order issued in another state may be sent by or on behalf of the obligee, or by the support enforcement agency, to the person defined as the obligor's employer under Section 5210 without first filing a petition or comparable pleading or registering the order with a tribunal of this state. **Leg.H.** Added Stats 2015 ch 493 §5 (SB 646), effective January 1, 2016.

§5700.502. Employer's duties

(a) Upon receipt of an income-withholding order, the obligor's employer shall immediately provide a copy of the order to the obligor.

(b) The employer shall treat an income-withholding order issued in another state which appears regular on its face as if it had been issued by a tribunal of this state.

(c) Except as otherwise provided in subsection (d) and Section 5700.503, the employer shall withhold and distribute the funds as directed in the withholding order by complying with terms of the order which specify:

(1) the duration and amount of periodic payments of current child support, stated as a sum certain;

(2) the person designated to receive payments and the address to which the payments are to be forwarded;

(3) medical support, whether in the form of periodic cash payment, stated as a sum certain, or ordering the obligor to provide health insurance coverage for the child under a policy available through the obligor's employment;

(4) the amount of periodic payments of fees and costs for a support enforcement agency, the issuing tribunal, and the obligee's attorney, stated as sums certain; and

(5) the amount of periodic payments of arrearages and interest on arrearages, stated as sums certain.

(d) An employer shall comply with the law of the state of the obligor's principal place of employment for withholding from income with respect to:

(1) the employer's fee for processing an income-withholding order;

(2) the maximum amount permitted to be withheld from the obligor's income; and

(3) the times within which the employer must implement the withholding order and forward the child-support payment. **Leg.H.** Added Stats 2015 ch 493 §5 (SB 646), effective January 1, 2016.

§5700.503. Multiple income-withholding orders

If an obligor's employer receives two or more income-withholding orders with respect to the earnings of the same obligor, the employer satisfies the terms of the orders if the employer complies with the law of the state of the obligor's principal place of employment to establish the priorities for withholding and allocating income withheld for two or more child-support obligees. **Leg.H.** Added Stats 2015 ch 493 §5 (SB 646), effective January 1, 2016.

§5700.504. Liability of employer

An employer that complies with an income-withholding order issued in another state in accordance with this chapter is not subject to civil liability to an individual or agency with regard to the employer's withholding of child support from the obligor's income. **Leg.H.** Added Stats 2015 ch 493 §5 (SB 646), effective January 1, 2016.

§5700.505. Penalties for noncompliance

An employer that willfully fails to comply with an income-withholding order issued in another state and received for enforcement is subject to the same penalties that may be imposed for noncompliance with an order issued by a tribunal of this state. **Leg.H.** Added Stats 2015 ch 493 §5 (SB 646), effective January 1, 2016.

§5700.506. Contesting the order

(a) An obligor may contest the validity or enforcement of an income-withholding order issued in another state and received directly by an employer in this state by registering the order in a tribunal of this state and filing a contest to that order as provided in Chapter 6, or otherwise contesting the order in the same manner as if the order had been issued by a tribunal of this state.

(b) The obligor shall give notice of the contest to:

(1) a support enforcement agency providing services to the obligee;

(2) each employer that has directly received an income-withholding order relating to the obligor; and

(3) the person designated to receive payments in the income-withholding order or, if no person is designated, to the obligee. **Leg.H.** Added Stats 2015 ch 493 §5 (SB 646), effective January 1, 2016.

§5700.507. Documentation and registration

(a) A party or support enforcement agency seeking to enforce a support order or an income-withholding order, or both, issued in another state or a foreign support order may send the documents required for registering the order to a support enforcement agency of this state.

(b) Upon receipt of the documents, the support enforcement agency, without initially seeking to register the order, shall consider and, if appropriate, use any administrative procedure authorized by the law of this state to enforce a support order or an income-withholding order, or both. If the obligor does not contest administrative enforcement, the order need not be registered. If the obligor contests the validity or administrative enforcement of the order, the support enforcement agency shall register the order pursuant to this part. **Leg.H.** Added Stats 2015 ch 493 §5 (SB 646), effective January 1, 2016.

CHAPTER 6
REGISTRATION, ENFORCEMENT, AND MODIFICATION OF SUPPORT ORDER

Article 1. Registration for Enforcement of Support Order.
Article 2. Contest of Validity or Enforcement.
Article 3. Registration and Modification of Child-Support Order of Another State.
Article 4. Registration and Modification of Foreign Child-Support Order.

ARTICLE 1
Registration for Enforcement of Support Order

Registration for enforcement. §5700.601.
Documents and information required to register. §5700.602.
Order issued in other state. §5700.603.
Governing law. §5700.604.

§5700.601. Registration for enforcement

A support order or income-withholding order issued in another state or a foreign support order may be registered in this state for enforcement. **Leg.H.** Added Stats 2015 ch 493 §5 (SB 646), effective January 1, 2016.

§5700.602. Documents and information required to register

(a) Except as otherwise provided in Section 5700.706, a support order or income-withholding order of another state or a foreign support order may be registered in this state by sending the following records to the appropriate tribunal in this state:

(1) a letter of transmittal to the tribunal requesting registration and enforcement;

(2) two copies, including one certified copy, of the order to be registered, including any modification of the order;

(3) a sworn statement by the person requesting registration or a certified statement by the custodian of the records showing the amount of any arrearage;

(4) the name of the obligor and, if known:

(A) the obligor's address and social security number;

(B) the name and address of the obligor's employer and any other source of income of the obligor; and

(C) a description and the location of property of the obligor in this state not exempt from execution; and

(5) except as otherwise provided in Section 5700.312, the name and address of the obligee and, if applicable, the person to whom support payments are to be remitted.

(b) On receipt of a request for registration, the registering tribunal shall cause the order to be filed as an order of a tribunal of another state or a foreign support order, together with one copy of the documents and information, regardless of their form.

(c) A petition or comparable pleading seeking a remedy that must be affirmatively sought under other law of this state may be filed at the same time as the request for registration or later. The pleading must specify the grounds for the remedy sought.

(d) If two or more orders are in effect, the person requesting registration shall:

(1) furnish to the tribunal a copy of every support order asserted to be in effect in addition to the documents specified in this section;

(2) specify the order alleged to be the controlling order, if any; and

(3) specify the amount of consolidated arrears, if any.

(e) A request for a determination of which is the controlling order may be filed separately or with a request for registration and enforcement or for registration and modification. The person requesting registration shall give notice of the request to each party whose rights may be affected by the determination. **Leg.H.** Added Stats 2015 ch 493 §5 (SB 646), effective January 1, 2016.

§5700.603. Order issued in other state

(a) A support order or income-withholding order issued in another state or a foreign support order is registered when the order is filed in the registering tribunal of this state.

(b) A registered support order issued in another state or a foreign country is enforceable in the same manner and is subject to the same procedures as an order issued by a tribunal of this state.

(c) Except as otherwise provided in this part, a tribunal of this state shall recognize and enforce, but may not modify, a registered support order if the issuing tribunal had jurisdiction. **Leg.H.** Added Stats 2015 ch 493 §5 (SB 646), effective January 1, 2016.

§5700.604. Governing law

(a) Except as otherwise provided in subsection (d), the law of the issuing state or foreign country governs:

(1) the nature, extent, amount, and duration of current payments under a registered support order;

(2) the computation and payment of arrearages and accrual of interest on the arrearages under the support order; and

(3) the existence and satisfaction of other obligations under the support order.

(b) In a proceeding for arrears under a registered support order, the statute of limitation of this state, or of the issuing state or foreign country, whichever is longer, applies.

(c) A responding tribunal of this state shall apply the procedures and remedies of this state to enforce current support and collect arrears and interest due on a support order of another state or a foreign country registered in this state.

(d) After a tribunal of this state or another state determines which is the controlling order and issues an order consolidating arrears, if any, a tribunal of this state shall prospectively apply the law of the state or foreign country issuing the controlling order, including its law on interest on arrears, on current and future support, and on consolidated arrears. **Leg.H.** Added Stats 2015 ch 493 §5 (SB 646), effective January 1, 2016.

ARTICLE 2
Contest of Validity or Enforcement

Notification of registration. §5700.605.
Contesting a registered order. §5700.606.
Burden of proof and defenses. §5700.607.
Precluding a contest. §5700.608.

§5700.605. Notification of registration

(a) When a support order or income-withholding order issued in another state or a foreign support order is registered, the registering tribunal of this state shall notify the nonregistering party. The notice must

(2) the other party resides outside the United States. **Leg.H.** Added Stats 2015 ch 493 §5 (SB 646), effective January 1, 2016.

§5700.612. Recognition of modifications

If a child-support order issued by a tribunal of this state is modified by a tribunal of another state which assumed jurisdiction pursuant to the Uniform Interstate Family Support Act, a tribunal of this state:

(1) may enforce its order that was modified only as to arrears and interest accruing before the modification;

(2) may provide appropriate relief for violations of its order which occurred before the effective date of the modification; and

(3) shall recognize the modifying order of the other state, upon registration, for the purpose of enforcement. **Leg.H.** Added Stats 2015 ch 493 §5 (SB 646), effective January 1, 2016.

§5700.613. Child not residing in issuing state

(a) If all of the parties who are individuals reside in this state and the child does not reside in the issuing state, a tribunal of this state has jurisdiction to enforce and to modify the issuing state's child-support order in a proceeding to register that order.

(b) A tribunal of this state exercising jurisdiction under this section shall apply the provisions of Chapters 1 and 2, and this chapter, and the procedural and substantive law of this state to the proceeding for enforcement or modification. Chapters 3, 4, 5, 7, and 8 do not apply. **Leg.H.** Added Stats 2015 ch 493 §5 (SB 646), effective January 1, 2016.

§5700.614. Filing copy of modified order

Within 30 days after issuance of a modified child-support order, the party obtaining the modification shall file a certified copy of the order with the issuing tribunal that had continuing, exclusive jurisdiction over the earlier order, and in each tribunal in which the party knows the earlier order has been registered. A party who obtains the order and fails to file a certified copy is subject to appropriate sanctions by a tribunal in which the issue of failure to file arises. The failure to file does not affect the validity or enforceability of the modified order of the new tribunal having continuing, exclusive jurisdiction. **Leg.H.** Added Stats 2015 ch 493 §5 (SB 646), effective January 1, 2016.

ARTICLE 4
Registration and Modification of Foreign Child-Support Order

Assumption of jurisdiction to modify foreign support order. §5700.615.
Modification of foreign support order. §5700.616.

§5700.615. Assumption of jurisdiction to modify foreign support order

(a) Except as otherwise provided in Section 5700.711, if a foreign country lacks or refuses to exercise jurisdiction to modify its child-support order pursuant to its laws, a tribunal of this state may assume jurisdiction to modify the child-support order and bind all individuals subject to the personal jurisdiction of the tribunal whether the consent to modification of a child-support order otherwise required of the individual pursuant to Section 5700.611 has been given or whether the individual seeking modification is a resident of this state or of the foreign country.

(b) An order issued by a tribunal of this state modifying a foreign child-support order pursuant to this section is the controlling order. **Leg.H.** Added Stats 2015 ch 493 §5 (SB 646), effective January 1, 2016.

§5700.616. Modification of foreign support order

A party or support enforcement agency seeking to modify, or to modify and enforce, a foreign child-support order not under the Convention may register that order in this state under Sections 5700.601 through 5700.608 if the order has not been registered. A petition for modification may be filed at the same time as a request for registration, or at another time. The petition must specify the grounds for modification. **Leg.H.** Added Stats 2015 ch 493 §5 (SB 646), effective January 1, 2016.

CHAPTER 7
SUPPORT PROCEEDING UNDER CONVENTION

Definitions. §5700.701.
Applicability of chapter. §5700.702.
Department as designated agency. §5700.703.
Duties of department. §5700.704.
Direct request for establishment, modification, or enforcement of support order; Parentage determination. §5700.705.
Registration of support order. §5700.706.
Contest of support order. §5700.707.
Recognition and enforcement of support order; Grounds for refusal. §5700.708.
Severability or partial enforcement of support order. §5700.709.
Recognition and enforcement of foreign support order; Grounds for refusal. §5700.710.
Modification of support order involving foreign obligee. §5700.711.
Use of personal information. §5700.712.
Language of filed record. §5700.713.

§5700.701. Definitions

In this chapter:

(1) "Application" means a request under the Convention by an obligee or obligor, or on behalf of a child, made through a central authority for assistance from another central authority.

(2) "Central authority" means the entity designated by the United States or a foreign country described in Section 5700.102(5)(D) to perform the functions specified in the Convention.

(3) "Convention support order" means a support order of a tribunal of a foreign country described in Section 5700.102(5)(D).

(4) "Direct request" means a petition filed by an individual in a tribunal of this state in a proceeding involving an obligee, obligor, or child residing outside the United States.

(5) "Foreign central authority" means the entity designated by a foreign country described in Section 5700.102(5)(D) to perform the functions specified in the Convention.

(6) "Foreign support agreement":

(A) means an agreement for support in a record that:

(i) is enforceable as a support order in the country of origin;

(ii) has been:

(I) formally drawn up or registered as an authentic instrument by a foreign tribunal; or

(II) authenticated by, or concluded, registered, or filed with a foreign tribunal; and

(iii) may be reviewed and modified by a foreign tribunal; and

(B) includes a maintenance arrangement or authentic instrument under the Convention.

(7) "United States central authority" means the Secretary of the United States Department of Health and Human Services. **Leg.H.** Added Stats 2015 ch 493 §5 (SB 646), effective January 1, 2016.

§5700.702. Applicability of chapter

This chapter applies only to a support proceeding under the Convention. In such a proceeding, if a provision of this chapter is inconsistent with Chapters 1 through 6, this chapter controls. **Leg.H.** Added Stats 2015 ch 493 §5 (SB 646), effective January 1, 2016.

§5700.703. Department as designated agency

The Department of Child Support Services is recognized as the agency designated by the United States central authority to perform specific functions under the Convention. **Leg.H.** Added Stats 2015 ch 493 §5 (SB 646), effective January 1, 2016.

§5700.704. Duties of department

(a) In a support proceeding under this chapter, the Department of Child Support Services shall:

(1) transmit and receive applications; and

(2) initiate or facilitate the institution of a proceeding regarding an application in a tribunal of this state.

(b) The following support proceedings are available to an obligee under the Convention:

(1) recognition or recognition and enforcement of a foreign support order;

(2) enforcement of a support order issued or recognized in this state;

(3) establishment of a support order if there is no existing order, including, if necessary, determination of parentage of a child;

(4) establishment of a support order if recognition of a foreign support order is refused under Section 5700.708(b)(2), (4), or (9);

(5) modification of a support order of a tribunal of this state; and

(6) modification of a support order of a tribunal of another state or a foreign country.

(c) The following support proceedings are available under the Convention to an obligor against which there is an existing support order:

be accompanied by a copy of the registered order and the documents and relevant information accompanying the order.

(b) A notice must inform the nonregistering party:

(1) that a registered support order is enforceable as of the date of registration in the same manner as an order issued by a tribunal of this state;

(2) that a hearing to contest the validity or enforcement of the registered order must be requested within 20 days after notice unless the registered order is under Section 5700.707;

(3) that failure to contest the validity or enforcement of the registered order in a timely manner will result in confirmation of the order and enforcement of the order and the alleged arrearages; and

(4) of the amount of any alleged arrearages.

(c) If the registering party asserts that two or more orders are in effect, a notice must also:

(1) identify the two or more orders and the order alleged by the registering party to be the controlling order and the consolidated arrears, if any;

(2) notify the nonregistering party of the right to a determination of which is the controlling order;

(3) state that the procedures provided in subsection (b) apply to the determination of which is the controlling order; and

(4) state that failure to contest the validity or enforcement of the order alleged to be the controlling order in a timely manner may result in confirmation that the order is the controlling order.

(d) Upon registration of an income-withholding order for enforcement, the support enforcement agency or the registering tribunal shall notify the obligor's employer pursuant to Chapter 8 (commencing with Section 5200) of Part 5. **Leg.H.** Added Stats 2015 ch 493 §5 (SB 646), effective January 1, 2016.

§5700.606. Contesting a registered order

(a) A nonregistering party seeking to contest the validity or enforcement of a registered support order in this state shall request a hearing within the time required by Section 5700.605. The nonregistering party may seek to vacate the registration, to assert any defense to an allegation of noncompliance with the registered order, or to contest the remedies being sought or the amount of any alleged arrearages pursuant to Section 5700.607.

(b) If the nonregistering party fails to contest the validity or enforcement of the registered support order in a timely manner, the order is confirmed by operation of law.

(c) If a nonregistering party requests a hearing to contest the validity or enforcement of the registered support order, the registering tribunal shall schedule the matter for hearing and give notice to the parties of the date, time, and place of the hearing. **Leg.H.** Added Stats 2015 ch 493 §5 (SB 646), effective January 1, 2016.

§5700.607. Burden of proof and defenses

(a) A party contesting the validity or enforcement of a registered support order or seeking to vacate the registration has the burden of proving one or more of the following defenses:

(1) the issuing tribunal lacked personal jurisdiction over the contesting party;

(2) the order was obtained by fraud;

(3) the order has been vacated, suspended, or modified by a later order;

(4) the issuing tribunal has stayed the order pending appeal;

(5) there is a defense under the law of this state to the remedy sought;

(6) full or partial payment has been made;

(7) the statute of limitation under Section 5700.604 precludes enforcement of some or all of the alleged arrearages; or

(8) the alleged controlling order is not the controlling order.

(b) If a party presents evidence establishing a full or partial defense under subsection (a), a tribunal may stay enforcement of a registered support order, continue the proceeding to permit production of additional relevant evidence, and issue other appropriate orders. An uncontested portion of the registered support order may be enforced by all remedies available under the law of this state.

(c) If the contesting party does not establish a defense under subsection (a) to the validity or enforcement of a registered support order, the registering tribunal shall issue an order confirming the order. **Leg.H.** Added Stats 2015 ch 493 §5 (SB 646), effective January 1, 2016.

§5700.608. Precluding a contest

Confirmation of a registered support order, whether by operation of law or after notice and hearing, precludes further contest of the order with respect to any matter that could have been asserted at the time of registration. **Leg.H.** Added Stats 2015 ch 493 §5 (SB 646), effective January 1, 2016.

ARTICLE 3
Registration and Modification of Child-Support Order of Another State

Modification of support order. §5700.609.
Enforcement of order registered for modification. §5700.610.
Requirements for modification. §5700.611.
Recognition of modifications. §5700.612.
Child not residing in issuing state. §5700.613.
Filing copy of modified order. §5700.614.

§5700.609. Modification of support order

A party or support enforcement agency seeking to modify, or to modify and enforce, a child-support order issued in another state shall register that order in this state in the same manner provided in Sections 5700.601 through 5700.608 if the order has not been registered. A petition for modification may be filed at the same time as a request for registration, or later. The pleading must specify the grounds for modification. **Leg.H.** Added Stats 2015 ch 493 §5 (SB 646), effective January 1, 2016.

§5700.610. Enforcement of order registered for modification

A tribunal of this state may enforce a child-support order of another state registered for purposes of modification, in the same manner as if the order had been issued by a tribunal of this state, but the registered support order may be modified only if the requirements of Section 5700.611 or 5700.613 have been met. **Leg.H.** Added Stats 2015 ch 493 §5 (SB 646), effective January 1, 2016.

§5700.611. Requirements for modification

(a) If Section 5700.613 does not apply, upon petition a tribunal of this state may modify a child-support order issued in another state which is registered in this state if, after notice and hearing, the tribunal finds that:

(1) the following requirements are met:

(A) neither the child, nor the obligee who is an individual, nor the obligor resides in the issuing state;

(B) a petitioner who is a nonresident of this state seeks modification; and

(C) the respondent is subject to the personal jurisdiction of the tribunal of this state; or

(2) this state is the residence of the child, or a party who is an individual is subject to the personal jurisdiction of the tribunal of this state, and all of the parties who are individuals have filed consents in a record in the issuing tribunal for a tribunal of this state to modify the support order and assume continuing, exclusive jurisdiction.

(b) Modification of a registered child-support order is subject to the same requirements, procedures, and defenses that apply to the modification of an order issued by a tribunal of this state and the order may be enforced and satisfied in the same manner.

(c) A tribunal of this state may not modify any aspect of a child-support order that may not be modified under the law of the issuing state, including the duration of the obligation of support. If two or more tribunals have issued child-support orders for the same obligor and same child, the order that controls and must be so recognized under Section 5700.207 establishes the aspects of the support order which are nonmodifiable.

(d) In a proceeding to modify a child-support order, the law of the state that is determined to have issued the initial controlling order governs the duration of the obligation of support. The obligor's fulfillment of the duty of support established by that order precludes imposition of a further obligation of support by a tribunal of this state.

(e) On the issuance of an order by a tribunal of this state modifying a child-support order issued in another state, the tribunal of this state becomes the tribunal having continuing, exclusive jurisdiction.

(f) Notwithstanding subsections (a) through (e) and Section 5700.201(b), a tribunal of this state retains jurisdiction to modify an order issued by a tribunal of this state if:

(1) one party resides in another state; and

(1) recognition of an order suspending or limiting enforcement of an existing support order of a tribunal of this state;

(2) modification of a support order of a tribunal of this state; and

(3) modification of a support order of a tribunal of another state or a foreign country.

(d) A tribunal of this state may not require security, bond, or deposit, however described, to guarantee the payment of costs and expenses in proceedings under the Convention. **Leg.H.** Added Stats 2015 ch 493 §5 (SB 646), effective January 1, 2016.

§5700.705. Direct request for establishment, modification, or enforcement of support order; Parentage determination

(a) A petitioner may file a direct request seeking establishment or modification of a support order or determination of parentage of a child. In the proceeding, the law of this state applies.

(b) A petitioner may file a direct request seeking recognition and enforcement of a support order or support agreement. In the proceeding, Sections 5700.706 through 5700.713 apply.

(c) In a direct request for recognition and enforcement of a Convention support order or foreign support agreement:

(1) a security, bond, or deposit is not required to guarantee the payment of costs and expenses; and

(2) an obligee or obligor that in the issuing country has benefited from free legal assistance is entitled to benefit, at least to the same extent, from any free legal assistance provided for by the law of this state under the same circumstances.

(d) A petitioner filing a direct request is not entitled to assistance from the Department of Child Support Services.

(e) This chapter does not prevent the application of laws of this state that provide simplified, more expeditious rules regarding a direct request for recognition and enforcement of a foreign support order or foreign support agreement. **Leg.H.** Added Stats 2015 ch 493 §5 (SB 646), effective January 1, 2016.

§5700.706. Registration of support order

(a) Except as otherwise provided in this chapter, a party who is an individual or a support enforcement agency seeking recognition of a Convention support order shall register the order in this state as provided in Chapter 6.

(b) Notwithstanding Sections 5700.311 and 5700.602(a), a request for registration of a Convention support order must be accompanied by:

(1) a complete text of the support order or an abstract or extract of the support order drawn up by the issuing foreign tribunal, which may be in the form recommended by the Hague Conference on Private International Law;

(2) a record stating that the support order is enforceable in the issuing country;

(3) if the respondent did not appear and was not represented in the proceedings in the issuing country, a record attesting, as appropriate, either that the respondent had proper notice of the proceedings and an opportunity to be heard or that the respondent had proper notice of the support order and an opportunity to be heard in a challenge or appeal on fact or law before a tribunal;

(4) a record showing the amount of arrears, if any, and the date the amount was calculated;

(5) a record showing a requirement for automatic adjustment of the amount of support, if any, and the information necessary to make the appropriate calculations; and

(6) if necessary, a record showing the extent to which the applicant received free legal assistance in the issuing country.

(c) A request for registration of a Convention support order may seek recognition and partial enforcement of the order.

(d) A tribunal of this state may vacate the registration of a Convention support order without the filing of a contest under Section 5700.707 only if, acting on its own motion, the tribunal finds that recognition and enforcement of the order would be manifestly incompatible with public policy.

(e) The tribunal shall promptly notify the parties of the registration or the order vacating the registration of a Convention support order. **Leg.H.** Added Stats 2015 ch 493 §5 (SB 646), effective January 1, 2016.

§5700.707. Contest of support order

(a) Except as otherwise provided in this chapter, Sections 5700.605 through 5700.608 apply to a contest of a registered Convention support order.

(b) A party contesting a registered Convention support order shall file a contest not later than 30 days after notice of the registration, but if the contesting party does not reside in the United States, the contest must be filed not later than 60 days after notice of the registration.

(c) If the nonregistering party fails to contest the registered Convention support order by the time specified in subsection (b), the order is enforceable.

(d) A contest of a registered Convention support order may be based only on grounds set forth in Section 5700.708. The contesting party bears the burden of proof.

(e) In a contest of a registered Convention support order, a tribunal of this state:

(1) is bound by the findings of fact on which the foreign tribunal based its jurisdiction; and

(2) may not review the merits of the order.

(f) A tribunal of this state deciding a contest of a registered Convention support order shall promptly notify the parties of its decision.

(g) A challenge or appeal, if any, does not stay the enforcement of a Convention support order unless there are exceptional circumstances. **Leg.H.** Added Stats 2015 ch 493 §5 (SB 646), effective January 1, 2016.

§5700.708. Recognition and enforcement of support order; Grounds for refusal

(a) Except as otherwise provided in subsection (b), a tribunal of this state shall recognize and enforce a registered Convention support order.

(b) The following grounds are the only grounds on which a tribunal of this state may refuse recognition and enforcement of a registered Convention support order:

(1) recognition and enforcement of the order is manifestly incompatible with public policy, including the failure of the issuing tribunal to observe minimum standards of due process, which include notice and an opportunity to be heard;

(2) the issuing tribunal lacked personal jurisdiction consistent with Section 5700.201;

(3) the order is not enforceable in the issuing country;

(4) the order was obtained by fraud in connection with a matter of procedure;

(5) a record transmitted in accordance with Section 5700.706 lacks authenticity or integrity;

(6) a proceeding between the same parties and having the same purpose is pending before a tribunal of this state and that proceeding was the first to be filed;

(7) the order is incompatible with a more recent support order involving the same parties and having the same purpose if the more recent support order is entitled to recognition and enforcement under this part in this state;

(8) payment, to the extent alleged arrears have been paid in whole or in part;

(9) in a case in which the respondent neither appeared nor was represented in the proceeding in the issuing foreign country:

(A) if the law of that country provides for prior notice of proceedings, the respondent did not have proper notice of the proceedings and an opportunity to be heard; or

(B) if the law of that country does not provide for prior notice of the proceedings, the respondent did not have proper notice of the order and an opportunity to be heard in a challenge or appeal on fact or law before a tribunal; or

(10) the order was made in violation of Section 5700.711.

(c) If a tribunal of this state does not recognize a Convention support order under subsection (b)(2), (4), or (9):

(1) the tribunal may not dismiss the proceeding without allowing a reasonable time for a party to request the establishment of a new Convention support order; and

(2) the Department of Child Support Services shall take all appropriate measures to request a child-support order for the obligee if the application for recognition and enforcement was received under Section 5700.704. **Leg.H.** Added Stats 2015 ch 493 §5 (SB 646), effective January 1, 2016.

§5700.709. Severability or partial enforcement of support order

If a tribunal of this state does not recognize and enforce a Convention support order in its entirety, it shall enforce any severable part of the order. An application or direct request may seek recognition and partial

§5700.710. Recognition and enforcement of foreign support order; Grounds for refusal

(a) Except as otherwise provided in subsections (c) and (d), a tribunal of this state shall recognize and enforce a foreign support agreement registered in this state.

(b) An application or direct request for recognition and enforcement of a foreign support agreement must be accompanied by:

(1) a complete text of the foreign support agreement; and

(2) a record stating that the foreign support agreement is enforceable as an order of support in the issuing country.

(c) A tribunal of this state may vacate the registration of a foreign support agreement only if, acting on its own motion, the tribunal finds that recognition and enforcement would be manifestly incompatible with public policy.

(d) In a contest of a foreign support agreement, a tribunal of this state may refuse recognition and enforcement of the agreement if it finds:

(1) recognition and enforcement of the agreement is manifestly incompatible with public policy;

(2) the agreement was obtained by fraud or falsification;

(3) the agreement is incompatible with a support order involving the same parties and having the same purpose in this state, another state, or a foreign country if the support order is entitled to recognition and enforcement under this act in this state; or

(4) the record submitted under subsection (b) lacks authenticity or integrity.

(e) A proceeding for recognition and enforcement of a foreign support agreement must be suspended during the pendency of a challenge to or appeal of the agreement before a tribunal of another state or a foreign country. **Leg.H.** Added Stats 2015 ch 493 §5 (SB 646), effective January 1, 2016.

§5700.711. Modification of support order involving foreign obligee

(a) A tribunal of this state may not modify a Convention child-support order if the obligee remains a resident of the foreign country where the support order was issued unless:

(1) the obligee submits to the jurisdiction of a tribunal of this state, either expressly or by defending on the merits of the case without objecting to the jurisdiction at the first available opportunity; or

(2) the foreign tribunal lacks or refuses to exercise jurisdiction to modify its support order or issue a new support order.

(b) If a tribunal of this state does not modify a Convention child-support order because the order is not recognized in this state, Section 5700.708(c) applies. **Leg.H.** Added Stats 2015 ch 493 §5 (SB 646), effective January 1, 2016.

§5700.712. Use of personal information

Personal information gathered or transmitted under this chapter may be used only for the purposes for which it was gathered or transmitted. **Leg.H.** Added Stats 2015 ch 493 §5 (SB 646), effective January 1, 2016.

§5700.713. Language of filed record

A record filed with a tribunal of this state under this chapter must be in the original language and, if not in English, must be accompanied by an English translation. **Leg.H.** Added Stats 2015 ch 493 §5 (SB 646), effective January 1, 2016.

CHAPTER 8
INTERSTATE RENDITION

Governor's extradition powers. §5700.801.
Rights with respect to extradition demands. §5700.802.

§5700.801. Governor's extradition powers

(a) For purposes of this chapter, "governor" includes an individual performing the functions of governor or the executive authority of a state covered by this part.

(b) The Governor may:

(1) demand that the governor of another state surrender an individual found in the other state who is charged criminally in this state with having failed to provide for the support of an obligee; or

(2) on the demand of the governor of another state, surrender an individual found in this state who is charged criminally in the other state with having failed to provide for the support of an obligee.

(c) A provision for extradition of individuals not inconsistent with this act applies to the demand even if the individual whose surrender is demanded was not in the demanding state when the crime was allegedly committed and has not fled therefrom. **Leg.H.** Added Stats 2015 ch 493 §5 (SB 646), effective January 1, 2016.

§5700.802. Rights with respect to extradition demands

(a) Before making a demand that the governor of another state surrender an individual charged criminally in this state with having failed to provide for the support of an obligee, the Governor may require a prosecutor of this state to demonstrate that at least 60 days previously the obligee had initiated proceedings for support pursuant to this act or that the proceeding would be of no avail.

(b) If, under this act or a law substantially similar to this act, the Governor of another state makes a demand that the Governor of this state surrender an individual charged criminally in that state with having failed to provide for the support of a child or other individual to whom a duty of support is owed, the Governor may require a prosecutor to investigate the demand and report whether a proceeding for support has been initiated or would be effective. If it appears that a proceeding would be effective but has not been initiated, the Governor may delay honoring the demand for a reasonable time to permit the initiation of a proceeding.

(c) If a proceeding for support has been initiated and the individual whose rendition is demanded prevails, the Governor may decline to honor the demand. If the petitioner prevails and the individual whose rendition is demanded is subject to a support order, the Governor may decline to honor the demand if the individual is complying with the support order. **Leg.H.** Added Stats 2015 ch 493 §5 (SB 646), effective January 1, 2016.

CHAPTER 9
MISCELLANEOUS PROVISIONS

Uniformity of laws. §5700.901.
Applicability of part. §5700.902.
Severability of provisions. §5700.903.
Adoption of emergency regulations. §5700.905.

§5700.901. Uniformity of laws

In applying and construing this uniform act, consideration must be given to the need to promote uniformity of the law with respect to its subject matter among states that enact it. **Leg.H.** Added Stats 2015 ch 493 §5 (SB 646), effective January 1, 2016.

§5700.902. Applicability of part

This part applies to proceedings begun on or after January 1, 2016, to establish a support order or determine parentage of a child or to register, recognize, enforce, or modify a prior support order, determination, or agreement, whenever issued or entered. **Leg.H.** Added Stats 2015 ch 493 §5 (SB 646), effective January 1, 2016.

§5700.903. Severability of provisions

If any provision of this part or its application to any person or circumstance is held invalid, the invalidity does not affect other provisions or applications of this part which can be given effect without the invalid provision or application, and to this end the provisions of this part are severable. **Leg.H.** Added Stats 2015 ch 493 §5 (SB 646), effective January 1, 2016.

§5700.905. Adoption of emergency regulations

The Department of Child Support Services may adopt emergency regulations as appropriate to implement this part. **Leg.H.** Added Stats 2015 ch 493 §5 (SB 646), effective January 1, 2016.

PART 2
GENERAL PROVISIONS

Purpose of division. §6220.
Application of division. §6221.
No fees in specified circumstances. §6222.
Matters to be considered where custody or visitation order issued pursuant to this division. §6223.
Required statements in order. §6224.
Explicit statement of address not required. §6225.
Judicial Council forms and instructions. §6226.
Amendment of Judicial Council form "Can a Domestic Violence Restraining Order Help Me?". § 6226.5.
Cumulative remedies. §6227.
Provision of incident reports to victims of specified crimes. §6228.
Minor allowed access to court for requesting or opposing request for temporary restraining order or injunction. §6229.

§6220. Purpose of division
The purpose of this division is to prevent acts of domestic violence, abuse, and sexual abuse and to provide for a separation of the persons involved in the domestic violence for a period sufficient to enable these persons to seek a resolution of the causes of the violence. **Leg.H.** Added Stats 1993 ch 219 §154 (AB 1500). Amended Stats 2014 ch 635 §3 (AB 2089), effective January 1, 2015.

§6221. Application of division
(a) Unless the provision or context otherwise requires, this division applies to any order described in this division, whether the order is issued in a proceeding brought pursuant to this division, in an action brought pursuant to the Uniform Parentage Act (Part 3 (commencing with Section 7600) of Division 12), or in a proceeding for dissolution of marriage, for nullity of marriage, or for legal separation of the parties.

(b) Nothing in this division affects the jurisdiction of the juvenile court.

(c) Any order issued by a court to which this division applies shall be issued on forms adopted by the Judicial Council of California and that have been approved by the Department of Justice pursuant to subdivision (i) of Section 6380. However, the fact that an order issued by a court pursuant to this section was not issued on forms adopted by the Judicial Council and approved by the Department of Justice shall not, in and of itself, make the order unenforceable. **Leg.H.** Added Stats 1993 ch 219 §154 (AB 1500). Amended Stats 1999 ch 661 §4 (AB 825).

§6222. No fees in specified circumstances
There is no filing fee for an application, a responsive pleading, or an order to show cause that seeks to obtain, modify, or enforce a protective order or other order authorized by this division when the request for the other order is necessary to obtain or give effect to a protective order. There is no fee for a subpoena filed in connection with that application, responsive pleading, or order to show cause. There is no fee for any filings related to a petition filed pursuant to Part 4 (commencing with 6300) of this division. **Leg.H.** Added Stats 2002 ch 1009 §4 (AB 2030), operative January 1, 2007. Amended Stats 2006 ch 476 §3 (AB 2695), effective January 1, 2007; Stats 2021 ch 686 §1 (SB 538), effective January 1, 2022.

Prior Law: Former Fam C §6222, relating to fees, was added Stats 1993 ch 219 §154 (AB 1500), amended Stats 1993 ch 583 §2 (AB 284); Stats 1995 ch 904 §3 (AB 965); Stats 2000 ch 1001 §3 (SB 1944); Stats 2002 ch 1009 §3 (AB 2030); Stats 2004 ch 811 §2 (AB 3079), and repealed January 1, 2007 by its own terms.

Former Sections: Former Fam C §6222, relating to fees, was added Stats 1993 ch 219 §154 (AB 1500) and repealed operative January 1, 2007, by its own provisions.

§6223. Matters to be considered where custody or visitation order issued pursuant to this division
A custody or visitation order issued in a proceeding brought pursuant to this division is subject to Part 2 (commencing with Section 3020) of Division 8 (custody of children). **Leg.H.** Added Stats 1993 ch 219 §154 (AB 1500).

§6224. Required statements in order
An order described in this division shall state on its face the date of expiration of the order and the following statements in substantially the following form:

"This order is effective when made. The law enforcement agency shall enforce it immediately on receipt. It is enforceable anywhere in California by any law enforcement agency that has received the order or is shown a copy of the order. If proof of service on the restrained person has not been received, the law enforcement agency shall advise the restrained person of the terms of the order and then shall enforce it." **Leg.H.** Added Stats 1993 ch 219 §154 (AB 1500).

§6225. Explicit statement of address not required
A petition for an order described in this division is valid and the order is enforceable without explicitly stating the address of the petitioner or the petitioner's place of residence, school, employment, the place where the petitioner's child is provided child care services, or the child's school. **Leg.H.** Added Stats 1993 ch 219 §154 (AB 1500).

§6226. Judicial Council forms and instructions
The Judicial Council shall prescribe the form of the orders and any other documents required by this division and shall promulgate forms and instructions for applying for orders described in this division. **Leg.H.** Added Stats 1993 ch 219 §154 (AB 1500).

§ 6226.5. Amendment of Judicial Council form "Can a Domestic Violence Restraining Order Help Me?"
(a) On or before January 1, 2023, the Judicial Council shall amend the Judicial Council form entitled "Can a Domestic Violence Restraining Order Help Me?" to include a brief description of the address confidentiality program established under Chapter 3.1 (commencing with Section 6205) of Division 7 of Title 1 of the Government Code, the benefits of enrollment in the program for victims of domestic violence, and the internet address for the Secretary of State's internet web page that contains more detailed information about the program.

(b) On or before January 1, 2023, the Judicial Council shall make the Judicial Council form available in English and in at least the other languages described in Section 1632 of the Civil Code. The Judicial Council may make the form available in additional languages. **Leg.H.** Added Stats 2021 ch 457 §1 (AB 277), effective January 1, 2022.

§6227. Cumulative remedies
The remedies provided in this division are in addition to any other civil or criminal remedies that may be available to the petitioner. **Leg.H.** Added Stats 1993 ch 219 §154 (AB 1500).

§6228. Provision of incident reports to victims of specified crimes
(a) State and local law enforcement agencies shall provide, upon request and without charging a fee, one copy of all incident report face sheets, one copy of all incident reports, a copy of any accompanying or related photographs of a victim's injuries, property damage, or any other photographs that are noted in the incident report, and a copy of 911 recordings, if any, to a victim, or the victim's representative as defined in subdivision (g), of a crime that constitutes an act of any of the following:

(1) Domestic violence, as defined in Section 6211.

(2) Sexual assault, as defined in Sections 261, 261.5, [1] **265, 266,** 266a, 266b, 266c, 266g, 266j, 267, 269, 273.4, 285, 286, 287, 288, 288.5, 289, or 311.4 of, or former Section [2] **262** or 288a of, the Penal Code.

(3) Stalking, as defined in Section 1708.7 of the Civil Code or Section 646.9 of the Penal Code.

(4) Human trafficking, as defined in Section 236.1 of the Penal Code.

(5) Abuse of an elder or a dependent adult, as defined in Section 15610.07 of the Welfare and Institutions Code.

(b)(1) A copy of an incident report face sheet shall be made available during regular business hours to a victim or the victim's representative no later than 48 hours after being requested, unless the state or local law enforcement agency informs the victim or the victim's representative of the reasons why, for good cause, the incident report face sheet is not available, in which case the incident report face sheet shall be made available no later than five working days after the request is made.

(2) A copy of the incident report, any accompanying or related photographs of a victim's injuries, property damage, or any other photographs that are noted in the incident report, and a copy of 911

DIVISION 10
PREVENTION OF DOMESTIC VIOLENCE

Part 1. Short Title and Definitions.
Part 2. General Provisions.
Part 3. Emergency Protective Orders.
Part 4. Protective Orders and Other Domestic Violence Prevention Orders.
Part 5. Uniform Interstate Enforcement of Domestic Violence Protection Orders Act.
Part 6. Uniform Recognition and Enforcement of Canadian Domestic Violence Protection Orders Act.

PART 1
SHORT TITLE AND DEFINITIONS

Citation of division. §6200.
Definitions to govern construction. §6201.
"Abuse". §6203.
"Affinity". §6205.
"Cohabitant". §6209.
"Dating relationship". §6210.
"Domestic violence". §6211.
"Emergency protective order". §6215.
"Firearm"; "Firearm precursor part". § 6216.
"Protective order". §6218.
Development of demonstration project to identify best practices in certain court cases; Report. §6219.

§6200. Citation of division
This division may be cited as the Domestic Violence Prevention Act. **Leg.H.** Added Stats 1993 ch 219 §154 (AB 1500).

§6201. Definitions to govern construction
Unless the provision or context otherwise requires, the definitions in this part govern the construction of this code. **Leg.H.** Added Stats 1993 ch 219 §154 (AB 1500).

§6203. "Abuse"
(a) For purposes of this act, "abuse" means any of the following:
(1) To intentionally or recklessly cause or attempt to cause bodily injury.
(2) Sexual assault.
(3) To place a person in reasonable apprehension of imminent serious bodily injury to that person or to another.
(4) To engage in any behavior that has been or could be enjoined pursuant to Section 6320.
(b) Abuse is not limited to the actual infliction of physical injury or assault. **Leg.H.** Added Stats 1993 ch 219 §154 (AB 1500). Amended Stats 1998 ch 581 §16 (AB 2801); Stats 2014 ch 635 §2 (AB 2089), effective January 1, 2015; Stats 2015 ch 303 §149 (AB 731), effective January 1, 2016.

§6205. "Affinity"
"Affinity," when applied to the marriage relation, signifies the connection existing in consequence of marriage between each of the married persons and the blood relatives of the other. **Leg.H.** Added Stats 1993 ch 219 §154 (AB 1500).

§6209. "Cohabitant"
"Cohabitant" means a person who regularly resides in the household. "Former cohabitant" means a person who formerly regularly resided in the household. **Leg.H.** Added Stats 1993 ch 219 §154 (AB 1500).

§6210. "Dating relationship"
"Dating relationship" means frequent, intimate associations primarily characterized by the expectation of affection or sexual involvement independent of financial considerations. **Leg.H.** Added Stats 2001 ch 110 §1 (AB 362).

§6211. "Domestic violence"
"Domestic violence" is abuse perpetrated against any of the following persons:
(a) A spouse or former spouse.
(b) A cohabitant or former cohabitant, as defined in Section 6209.
(c) A person with whom the respondent is having or has had a dating or engagement relationship.
(d) A person with whom the respondent has had a child, where the presumption applies that the male parent is the father of the child of the female parent under the Uniform Parentage Act (Part 3 (commencing with Section 7600) of Division 12).
(e) A child of a party or a child who is the subject of an action under the Uniform Parentage Act, where the presumption applies that the male parent is the father of the child to be protected.
(f) Any other person related by consanguinity or affinity within the second degree. **Leg.H.** Added Stats 1993 ch 219 §154 (AB 1500).

§6215. "Emergency protective order"
"Emergency protective order" means an order issued under Part 3 (commencing with Section 6240). **Leg.H.** Added Stats 1993 ch 219 §154 (AB 1500).

§ 6216. "Firearm"; "Firearm precursor part"
For the purposes of this division, "firearm" includes the frame or receiver of the weapon, including a completed frame or receiver or a firearm precursor part. "Firearm precursor part" has the same meaning as in subdivision (a) of Section 16531 of the Penal Code. **Leg.H.** Added Stats 2021 ch 682 §1 (AB 1057), effective January 1, 2022. Amended Stats 2022 ch 76 §2 (AB 1621), effective June 30, 2022.

§6218. "Protective order"
"Protective order" means an order that includes any of the following restraining orders, whether issued ex parte, after notice and hearing, or in a judgment:
(a) An order described in Section 6320 enjoining specific acts of abuse.
(b) An order described in Section 6321 excluding a person from a dwelling.
(c) An order described in Section 6322 enjoining other specified behavior. **Leg.H.** Added Stats 1993 ch 219 §154 (AB 1500).

§6219. Development of demonstration project to identify best practices in certain court cases; Report
Subject to adequate, discretionary funding from a city or a county, the superior courts in San Diego County and in Santa Clara County may develop a demonstration project to identify the best practices in civil, juvenile, and criminal court cases involving domestic violence. The superior courts in any other county that is able and willing may also participate in the demonstration project. The superior courts participating in this demonstration project shall report their findings and recommendations to the Judicial Council and the Legislature on or before May 1, 2004. The Judicial Council may make those recommendations available to any court or county. **Leg.H.** Added Stats 2002 ch 192 §1 (AB 1909).

recordings, if any, shall be made available during regular business hours to a victim or the victim's representative no later than five working days after being requested, unless the state or local law enforcement agency informs the victim or the victim's representative of the reasons why, for good cause, the items are not available, in which case the items shall be made available no later than 10 working days after the request is made.

(c) A person requesting copies under this section shall present state or local law enforcement with the person's identification, including a current, valid driver's license, a state-issued identification card, or a passport. If the person is a representative of the victim and the victim is deceased, the representative shall also present a certified copy of the death certificate or other satisfactory evidence of the death of the victim at the time a request is made. If the person is a representative of the victim and the victim is alive and not the subject of a conservatorship, the representative shall also present a written authorization, signed by the victim, making the person the victim's personal representative.

(d) This section shall apply to requests for domestic violence, sexual assault, stalking, human trafficking, or abuse of an elder or a dependent adult face sheets or incident reports, photographs, 911 recordings, and evidence made within five years from the date of completion of the incident report.

(e) This section shall be known and may be cited as the Access to Domestic Violence Reports Act of 1999.

(f) For purposes of this section, "victim" includes a minor who is 12 years of age or older.

(g)(1) For purposes of this section, if the victim is deceased, a "representative of the victim" means any of the following:

(A) The surviving spouse.
(B) A surviving child of the decedent who has attained 18 years of age.
(C) A domestic partner, as defined in subdivision (a) of Section 297.
(D) A surviving parent of the decedent.
(E) A surviving adult relative.
(F) The personal representative of the victim, as defined in Section 58 of the Probate Code, if one is appointed.
(G) The public administrator if one has been appointed.

(2) For purposes of this section, if the victim is not deceased, a "representative of the victim" means any of the following:

(A) A parent, guardian, or adult child of the victim, or an adult sibling of a victim 12 years of age or older, who shall present to law enforcement identification pursuant to subdivision (c). A guardian shall also present to law enforcement a copy of the letters of guardianship demonstrating that the person is the appointed guardian of the victim.

(B) An attorney for the victim, who shall present to law enforcement identification pursuant to subdivision (c) and written proof that the person is the attorney for the victim.

(C) A conservator of the victim who shall present to law enforcement identification pursuant to subdivision (c) and a copy of the letters of conservatorship demonstrating that the person is the appointed conservator of the victim.

(3) A representative of the victim does not include any person who has been convicted of murder in the first degree, as defined in Section 189 of the Penal Code, of the victim, or any person identified in the incident report face sheet as a suspect. **Leg.H.** Added Stats 1999 ch 1022 §1 (AB 403). Amended Stats 2002 ch 377 §1 (SB 1265); Stats 2010 ch 363 §1 (AB 1738), effective January 1, 2011; Stats 2011 ch 296 §93 (AB 1023), effective January 1, 2012; Stats 2016 ch 875 §1 (AB 1678), effective January 1, 2017; Stats 2018 ch 423 §24 (SB 1494), effective January 1, 2019; Stats 2019 ch 115 §59 (AB 1817), effective January 1, 2020; Stats 2023 ch 71 §1 (SB 290), effective January 1, 2024; Stats 2024 ch 495 §1 (SB 1518), effective January 1, 2025.

§6228. 2024 Deletes. [1] 262, 265, [2] 266

§6229. Minor allowed access to court for requesting or opposing request for temporary restraining order or injunction

A minor, under 12 years of age, accompanied by a duly appointed and acting guardian ad litem, shall be permitted to appear in court without counsel for the limited purpose of requesting or opposing a request for a temporary restraining order or injunction, or both, under this division as provided in Section 374 of the Code of Civil Procedure. **Leg.H.** Added Stats 2010 ch 572 §12 (AB 1596), effective January 1, 2011, operative January 1, 2012.

PART 3
EMERGENCY PROTECTIVE ORDERS

Chapter 1. General Provisions.
Chapter 2. Issuance and Effect of Emergency Protective Order.
Chapter 3. Duties of Law Enforcement Officer.

CHAPTER 1
GENERAL PROVISIONS

Definitions. §6240.
Designation of judicial officer to orally issue ex parte emergency protective orders. §6241.

§6240. Definitions

As used in this part:

(a) "Judicial officer" means a judge, commissioner, or referee designated under Section 6241.

(b) "Law enforcement officer" means one of the following officers who requests or enforces an emergency protective order under this part:

(1) A police officer.
(2) A sheriff's officer.
(3) A peace officer of the Department of the California Highway Patrol.
(4) A peace officer of the University of California Police Department.
(5) A peace officer of the California State University and College Police Departments.
(6) A peace officer of the Department of Parks and Recreation, as defined in subdivision (f) of Section 830.2 of the Penal Code.
(7) A peace officer of the Department of General Services of the City of Los Angeles, as defined in subdivision (c) of Section 830.31 of the Penal Code.
(8) A housing authority patrol officer, as defined in subdivision (d) of Section 830.31 of the Penal Code.
(9) A peace officer for a district attorney, as defined in Section 830.1 or 830.35 of the Penal Code.
(10) A parole officer, probation officer, or deputy probation officer, as defined in Section 830.5 of the Penal Code.
(11) A peace officer of a California Community College police department, as defined in subdivision (a) of Section 830.32.
(12) A peace officer employed by a police department of a school district, as defined in subdivision (b) of Section 830.32.

(c) "Abduct" means take, entice away, keep, withhold, or conceal. **Leg.H.** Added Stats 1993 ch 219 §154 (AB 1500). Amended Stats ch 1229 §1 (AB 224); Stats 1996 ch 305 §5 (AB 3103), Stats 1996 ch 988 §3 (AB 2936) (ch 988 prevails); Stats 1999 ch 659 §1 (SB 355); Stats 2004 ch 250 §1 (SB 1391).

§6241. Designation of judicial officer to orally issue ex parte emergency protective orders

The presiding judge of the superior court in each county shall designate at least one judge, commissioner, or referee to be reasonably available to issue orally, by telephone or otherwise, emergency protective orders at all times whether or not the court is in session. **Leg.H.** Added Stats 1993 ch 219 §154 (AB 1500).

CHAPTER 2
ISSUANCE AND EFFECT OF EMERGENCY PROTECTIVE ORDER

Grounds for issuance. §6250.
When emergency protective order is valid. §6250.3.
Issuance of ex parte emergency protective order for threat to campus safety. §6250.5.
Required findings. §6251.
Issuance of specific orders. §6252.
Court order prohibiting obtaining address or location of protected party or family member. §6252.5.
Contents of order. §6253.
Availability of emergency protective order. §6254.
Issuance without prejudice. §6255.
Expiration of order. §6256.
Application for restraining order under other law. §6257.

§6250. Grounds for issuance

A judicial officer may issue an ex parte emergency protective order where a law enforcement officer asserts reasonable grounds to believe any of the following:

(a) That a person is in immediate and present danger of domestic violence, based on the person's allegation of a recent incident of abuse or threat of abuse by the person against whom the order is sought.

(b) That a child is in immediate and present danger of abuse by a family or household member, based on an allegation of a recent incident of abuse or threat of abuse by the family or household member.

(c) That a child is in immediate and present danger of being abducted by a parent or relative, based on a reasonable belief that a person has an intent to abduct the child or flee with the child from the jurisdiction or based on an allegation of a recent threat to abduct the child or flee with the child from the jurisdiction.

(d) That an elder or dependent adult is in immediate and present danger of abuse as defined in Section 15610.07 of the Welfare and Institutions Code, based on an allegation of a recent incident of abuse or threat of abuse by the person against whom the order is sought, except that no emergency protective order shall be issued based solely on an allegation of financial abuse. **Leg.H.** Added Stats 1993 ch 219 §154 (AB 1500). Amended Stats 1996 ch 988 §4 (AB 2936); Stats 1999 ch 561 §1 (AB 59); Stats 2003 ch 468 §3 (SB 851).

§6250.3. When emergency protective order is valid

An emergency protective order is valid only if it is issued by a judicial officer after making the findings required by Section 6251 and pursuant to a specific request by a law enforcement officer. **Leg.H.** Added Stats 2006 ch 82 §1 (AB 1787), effective January 1, 2007.

§6250.5. Issuance of ex parte emergency protective order for threat to campus safety

A judicial officer may issue an ex parte emergency protective order to a peace officer defined in subdivisions (a) and (b) of Section 830.32 if the issuance of that order is consistent with an existing memorandum of understanding between the college or school police department where the peace officer is employed and the sheriff or police chief of the city in whose jurisdiction the peace officer's college or school is located and the peace officer asserts reasonable grounds to believe that there is a demonstrated threat to campus safety. **Leg.H.** Added Stats 1999 ch 659 §1.5 (SB 355).

§6251. Required findings

An emergency protective order may be issued only if the judicial officer finds both of the following:

(a) That reasonable grounds have been asserted to believe that an immediate and present danger of domestic violence exists, that a child is in immediate and present danger of abuse or abduction, or that an elder or dependent adult is in immediate and present danger of abuse as defined in Section 15610.07 of the Welfare and Institutions Code.

(b) That an emergency protective order is necessary to prevent the occurrence or recurrence of domestic violence, child abuse, child abduction, or abuse of an elder or dependent adult. **Leg.H.** Added Stats 1993 ch 219 §154 (AB 1500). Amended Stats 1996 ch 988 §5 (AB 2936); Stats 1999 ch 561 §2 (AB 59).

§6252. Issuance of specific orders

An emergency protective order may include any of the following specific orders, as appropriate:

(a) A protective order, as defined in Section 6218.

(b) An order determining the temporary care and control of any minor child of the endangered person and the person against whom the order is sought.

(c) An order authorized in Section 213.5 of the Welfare and Institutions Code, including provisions placing the temporary care and control of the endangered child and any other minor children in the family or household with the parent or guardian of the endangered child who is not a restrained party.

(d) An order determining the temporary care and control of any minor child who is in danger of being abducted.

(e) An order authorized by Section 15657.03 of the Welfare and Institutions Code. **Leg.H.** Added Stats 1993 ch 219 §154 (AB 1500). Amended Stats 1996 ch 988 §6 (AB 2936); Stats 1999 ch 561 §3 (AB 59).

§6252.5. Court order prohibiting obtaining address or location of protected party or family member

(a) The court shall order that any party enjoined pursuant to an order issued under this part be prohibited from taking any action to obtain the address or location of a protected party or a protected party's family members, caretakers, or guardian, unless there is good cause not to make that order.

(b) The Judicial Council shall promulgate forms necessary to effectuate this section. **Leg.H.** Added Stats 2005 ch 472 §2 (AB 978), effective January 1, 2006.

§6253. Contents of order

An emergency protective order shall include all of the following:

(a) A statement of the grounds asserted for the order.

(b) The date and time the order expires.

(c) The address of the superior court for the district or county in which the endangered person or child in danger of being abducted resides.

(d) The following statements, which shall be printed in English and Spanish:

(1) "To the Protected Person: This order will last only until the date and time noted above. If you wish to seek continuing protection, you will have to apply for an order from the court, at the address noted above. You may seek the advice of an attorney as to any matter connected with your application for any future court orders. The attorney should be consulted promptly so that the attorney may assist you in making your application."

(2) "To the Restrained Person: This order will last until the date and time noted above. The protected party may, however, obtain a more permanent restraining order from the court. You may seek the advice of an attorney as to any matter connected with the application. The attorney should be consulted promptly so that the attorney may assist you in responding to the application."

(e) In the case of an endangered child, the following statement, which shall be printed in English and Spanish: "This order will last only until the date and time noted above. You may apply for a more permanent restraining order under Section 213.5 of the Welfare and Institutions Code from the court at the address noted above. You may seek the advice of an attorney in connection with the application for a more permanent restraining order."

(f) In the case of a child in danger of being abducted, the following statement, which shall be printed in English and Spanish: "This order will last only until the date and time noted above. You may apply for a child custody order from the court, at the address noted above. You may seek the advice of an attorney as to any matter connected with the application. The attorney should be consulted promptly so that the attorney may assist you in responding to the application." **Leg.H.** Added Stats 1993 ch 219 §154 (AB 1500). Amended Stats 1996 ch 988 §7 (AB 2936).

§6254. Availability of emergency protective order

The fact that the endangered person has left the household to avoid abuse does not affect the availability of an emergency protective order. **Leg.H.** Added Stats 1993 ch 219 §154 (AB 1500).

§6255. Issuance without prejudice

An emergency protective order shall be issued without prejudice to any person. **Leg.H.** Added Stats 1993 ch 219 §154 (AB 1500).

§6256. Expiration of order

An emergency protective order expires at the earlier of the following times:

(a) The close of judicial business on the fifth court day following the day of its issuance.

(b) The seventh calendar day following the day of its issuance. **Leg.H.** Added Stats 1993 ch 219 §154 (AB 1500). Amended Stats 1993 ch 1229 §2 (AB 224).

§6257. Application for restraining order under other law

If an emergency protective order concerns an endangered child, the child's parent or guardian who is not a restrained person, or a person having temporary custody of the endangered child, may apply to the court for a restraining order under Section 213.5 of the Welfare and Institutions Code. **Leg.H.** Added Stats 1993 ch 219 §154 (AB 1500).

CHAPTER 3
DUTIES OF LAW ENFORCEMENT OFFICER

Reducing order to writing and signing order. §6270.
Service, filing, and delivery of order; Entry of order into Department of Justice computer database system. §6271.
Means of enforcement; Protection of officer from liability. §6272.
Emergency protective order for stalking. §6274.
Emergency protective orders. §6275.

§6270. Reducing order to writing and signing order

A law enforcement officer who requests an emergency protective order shall reduce the order to writing and sign it. **Leg.H.** Added Stats 1993 ch 219 §154 (AB 1500).

§6271. Service, filing, and delivery of order; Entry of order into Department of Justice computer database system

A law enforcement officer who requests an emergency protective order shall do all of the following:

(a) Serve the order on the restrained person, if the restrained person can reasonably be located.

(b) Give a copy of the order to the protected person or, if the protected person is a minor child, to a parent or guardian of the endangered child who is not a restrained person, if the parent or guardian can reasonably be located, or to a person having temporary custody of the endangered child.

(c) File a copy of the order with the court as soon as practicable after issuance.

(d) Have the order entered into the computer database system for protective and restraining orders maintained by the Department of Justice. **Leg.H.** Added Stats 1993 ch 219 §154 (AB 1500). Amended Stats 2013 ch 145 §1 (AB 238), effective January 1, 2014.

§6272. Means of enforcement; Protection of officer from liability

(a) A law enforcement officer shall use every reasonable means to enforce an emergency protective order.

(b) A law enforcement officer who acts in good faith to enforce an emergency protective order is not civilly or criminally liable. **Leg.H.** Added Stats 1993 ch 219 §154 (AB 1500).

§6273. [Section repealed 2014]

Leg.H. Added Stats 1993 ch 219 §154 (AB 1500). Repealed Stats 2013 ch 145 §2 (AB 238), effective January 1, 2014. The repealed section related to the requirement for an officer who requests an emergency protective order to carry copies of that order while on duty.

§6274. Emergency protective order for stalking

A peace officer, as defined in Section 830.1 or 830.2 of the Penal Code, may seek an emergency protective order relating to stalking under Section 646.91 of the Penal Code if the requirements of that section are complied with. **Leg.H.** Added Stats 1997 ch 169 §1 (AB 350).

§6275. Emergency protective orders

(a) A law enforcement officer who responds to a situation in which the officer believes that there may be grounds for the issuance of an emergency protective order pursuant to Section 6250 of this code or Section 646.91 of the Penal Code, shall inform the person for whom an emergency protective order may be sought, or, if that person is a minor, the minor's parent or guardian, provided that the parent or guardian is not the person against whom the emergency protective order may be obtained, that the person may request the officer to request an emergency protective order pursuant to this part.

(b) Notwithstanding Section 6250, and pursuant to this part, an officer shall request an emergency protective order if the officer believes that the person requesting an emergency protective order is in immediate and present danger. **Leg.H.** Added Stats 2006 ch 479 §1 (AB 2139), effective January 1, 2007. Amended Stats 2019 ch 115 §60 (AB 1817), effective January 1, 2020.

PART 4
PROTECTIVE ORDERS AND OTHER DOMESTIC VIOLENCE PREVENTION ORDERS

Chapter 1. General Provisions.
Chapter 2. Issuance of Orders.
Chapter 3. Registration and Enforcement of Orders.

CHAPTER 1
GENERAL PROVISIONS

Issuance on affidavit or testimony showing reasonable proof of past act or acts of abuse. §6300.
Persons who may be granted restraining order. §6301.
Information regarding a minor. §6301.5.
Notice of hearing. §6302.
Support person for victim of domestic violence. §6303.
Information to parties concerning terms and effect of order. §6304.
Conditions for issuance of mutual order. §6305.
Search of specific records and databases required prior to issuance or denial of order; Information to be obtained; Release of information to parties; Confidentiality. §6306.
Electronic submission of petitions seeking domestic violence restraining orders. § 6306.5.
Posting of information regarding domestic violence restraining order self-help services on superior court's website. § 6306.6.
Electronic submission of petitions for domestic violence restraining orders or domestic violence temporary restraining orders . § 6307.
Remote appearances by parties, support persons and witnesses . § 6308.
Domestic violence restraining order discovery. § 6309.

§6300. Issuance on affidavit or testimony showing reasonable proof of past act or acts of abuse

(a) An order may be issued under this part to restrain any person for the purpose specified in Section 6220, if an affidavit or testimony and any additional information provided to the court pursuant to Section 6306, shows, to the satisfaction of the court, reasonable proof of a past act or acts of abuse. The court may issue an order under this part based solely on the affidavit or testimony of the person requesting the restraining order.

(b) An ex parte restraining order issued pursuant to Article 1 (commencing with Section 6320) shall not be denied solely because the other party was not provided with notice.

(c) An ex parte request for a protective order, as defined in Section 6218, shall not be rejected for filing by the court clerk if it is submitted on mandatory Judicial Council forms, includes all of the forms required to issue an order, and identifies the party submitting the request and the party who is the subject of the requested order.
Leg.H. Added Stats 1993 ch 219 §154 (AB 1500). Amended Stats 2001 ch 572 §2 (SB 66); Stats 2014 ch 635 §4 (AB 2089), effective January 1, 2015; Stats 2018 ch 219 §1 (AB 2694), effective January 1, 2019; Stats 2024 ch 648 §1 (AB 2024), effective January 1, 2025.

§6301. Persons who may be granted restraining order

(a) An individual need not be a resident of the state to file a petition for an order under this part. A petition for an order under this part may be filed in any superior court in this state, consistent with Section 410.10 of the Code of Civil Procedure, which may include, but is not limited to:

(1) The county in which the petitioner resides or is temporarily located.

(2) The county in which the defendant resides.

(3) The county in which the offense occurred.

(4) Any other court that may have jurisdiction over the parties or the subject matter of the case.

[1] (b) An order under this part may be granted to any person described in Section 6211, including a minor pursuant to subdivision (b) of Section 372 of the Code of Civil Procedure.

[2] (c) The right to petition for relief shall not be denied because the petitioner has vacated the household to avoid abuse, and in the case of a marital relationship, notwithstanding that a petition for dissolution of marriage, for nullity of marriage, or for legal separation of the parties has not been filed.

[3] (d) The length of time since the most recent act of abuse is not, by itself, determinative. The court shall consider the totality of the circumstances in determining whether to grant or deny a petition for relief.
Leg.H. Added Stats 1993 ch 219 §154 (AB 1500). Amended Stats 1996 ch 727 §3 (AB 2155); Stats 2014 ch 635 §5 (AB 2089), effective January 1, 2015; Stats 2015 ch 303 §150 (AB 731), effective January 1, 2016; Stats 2024 ch 652 §2 (SB 554), effective January 1, 2025.

§6301. 2024 Deletes. [1] (a) **[2]** (b) **[3]** (c)

§6301.5. Information regarding a minor

(a) A minor or the minor's legal guardian may petition the court to have information regarding a minor that was obtained in connection with a request for a protective order pursuant to this division, including, but not limited to, the minor's name, address, and the circumstances surrounding the request for a protective order with respect to that minor, be kept confidential, except as provided in subdivision (d).

(b) The court may order the information specified in subdivision (a) be kept confidential if the court expressly finds all of the following:

(1) The minor's right to privacy overcomes the right of public access to the information.

(2) There is a substantial probability that the minor's interest will be prejudiced if the information is not kept confidential.

(3) The order to keep the information confidential is narrowly tailored.

(4) No less restrictive means exist to protect the minor's privacy.

(c)(1) If the request is granted, except as provided in subdivision (d), information regarding the minor shall be maintained in a confidential case file and shall not become part of the public file in the proceeding, any other proceeding initiated under the Family Code, or any other civil proceeding between the parties. Except as provided in paragraph (2), if the court determines that disclosure of confidential information has been made without a court order, the court may impose a sanction of up to one thousand dollars ($1,000). The minor who has alleged abuse as defined under this division shall not be sanctioned for disclosure of the confidential information. If the court imposes a sanction, the court shall first determine whether the person has, or is reasonably likely to have, the ability to pay.

(2) Confidential information may be disclosed without a court order pursuant to subdivision (d) only in the following circumstances:

(A) By the minor's legal guardian who petitioned to keep the information confidential pursuant to this section or the protected party in an order pursuant to this division, provided that the disclosure effectuates the purpose of this division specified in Section 6220 or is in the minor's best interest. A legal guardian or a protected party who makes a disclosure under this subparagraph is subject to the sanction in paragraph (1) only if the disclosure was malicious.

(B) By a person to whom confidential information is disclosed, provided that the disclosure effectuates the purpose of this division specified in Section 6220 or is in the best interest of the minor, no more information than necessary is disclosed, and a delay would be caused by first obtaining a court order to authorize the disclosure of the information. A person who makes a disclosure pursuant to this subparagraph is subject to the sanction in paragraph (1) if the person discloses the information in a manner that recklessly or maliciously disregards these requirements.

(d)(1) Confidential information shall be made available to both of the following:

(A) Law enforcement pursuant to Section 6380, to the extent necessary and only for the purpose of enforcing the protective order.

(B) The respondent to allow the respondent to comply with the order for confidentiality and to allow the respondent to comply with and respond to the protective order. A notice shall be provided to the respondent that identifies the specific information that has been made confidential and shall include a statement that disclosure is punishable by a monetary fine.

(2) At any time, the court on its own may authorize a disclosure of any portion of the confidential information to certain individuals or entities as necessary to effectuate the purpose of this division specified in Section 6220, including implementation of the protective order, or if it is in the best interest of the minor, including, but not limited to, disclosure to

educational institutions, childcare providers, medical or mental health providers, professional or nonprofessional supervisors for visitation, the Department of Child Support Services, attorneys for the parties or the minor, judicial officers, court employees, child custody evaluators, family court mediators, and court reporters.

(3) The court may authorize a disclosure of any portion of the confidential information to any person that files a petition if the court determines disclosure would effectuate the purpose of this division specified in Section 6220 or if the court determines that disclosure is in the best interest of the minor. The party who petitioned the court to keep the information confidential pursuant to this section shall be served personally or by first-class mail with a copy of the petition and afforded an opportunity to object to the disclosure. **Leg.H.** Added Stats 2017 ch 384 §2 (AB 953), effective January 1, 2018. Amended Stats 2019 ch 294 §2 (AB 925), effective January 1, 2020.

Editor's Notes— 2017 Note: The Legislature finds and declares that Sections 1 and 2 of this act, which amend Section 527.6 of the Code of Civil Procedure and add Section 6301.5 to the Family Code, respectively, impose a limitation on the public's right of access to the meetings of public bodies or the writings of public officials and agencies within the meaning of Section 3 of Article I of the California Constitution. Pursuant to that constitutional provision, the Legislature makes the following findings to demonstrate the interest protected by this limitation and the need for protecting that interest:

This limitation is required to protect the private information of vulnerable minors who are the victims of domestic abuse and human trafficking. Stats 2017 ch 384 (AB 953) §3.

§6302. Notice of hearing

A notice of hearing under this part shall notify the respondent that, if the respondent does not attend the hearing, the court may make orders against the respondent that could last up to five years. **Leg.H.** Added Stats 2010 ch 572 §14 (AB 1596), effective January 1, 2011, operative January 1, 2012. Amended Stats 2019 ch 115 §61 (AB 1817), effective January 1, 2020.

Prior Law: Former §6302, similar to present section, was added Stats 1993 ch 219 §154 and repealed Stats 2010 ch 572 §13.

Former Sections: Former Fam C §6302, similar to present section, was added Stats 1993 ch 219 §154 and repealed Stats 2010 ch 572 §13.

§6303. Support person for victim of domestic violence

(a) It is the function of a support person to provide moral and emotional support for a person who alleges to be a victim of domestic violence. The person who alleges to be a victim of domestic violence may select any individual to act as a support person. No certification, training, or other special qualification is required for an individual to act as a support person. The support person shall assist the person in feeling more confident that the person will not be injured or threatened by the other party during the proceedings where the person and the other party must be present in close proximity. The support person is not present as a legal adviser and shall not give legal advice.

(b) A support person shall be permitted to accompany either party to any proceeding to obtain a protective order, as defined in Section 6218. Where the party is not represented by an attorney, the support person may sit with the party at the table that is generally reserved for the party and the party's attorney.

(c) Notwithstanding any other law to the contrary, if a court has issued a protective order, a support person shall be permitted to accompany a party protected by the order during any mediation orientation or mediation session, including separate mediation sessions, held pursuant to a proceeding described in Section 3021. Family Court Services, and any agency charged with providing family court services, shall advise the party protected by the order of the right to have a support person during mediation. A mediator may exclude a support person from a mediation session if the support person participates in the mediation session, or acts as an advocate, or the presence of a particular support person is disruptive or disrupts the process of mediation. The presence of the support person does not waive the confidentiality of the mediation, and the support person is bound by the confidentiality of the mediation.

(d) In a proceeding subject to this section, a support person shall be permitted to accompany a party in court where there are allegations or threats of domestic violence and, where the party is not represented by an attorney, may sit with the party at the table that is generally reserved for the party and the party's attorney.

(e) This section does not preclude a court from exercising its discretion to remove a person from the courtroom when it would be in the interest of justice to do so, or when the court believes the person is prompting, swaying, or influencing the party protected by the order. **Leg.H.** Added Stats 1993 ch 219 §154 (AB 1500). Amended Stats 1996 ch 761 §7 (SB 1995); Stats 2012 ch 470 §21 (AB 1529), effective January 1, 2013; Stats 2019 ch 115 §62 (AB 1817), effective January 1, 2020.

§6304. Information to parties concerning terms and effect of order

When making a protective order, as defined in Section 6218, where both parties are present in court, the court shall inform both the petitioner and the respondent of the terms of the order, including notice that the respondent is prohibited from owning, possessing, purchasing, or receiving or attempting to own, possess, purchase, or receive a firearm or ammunition, and including notice of the penalty for violation. Information provided shall include how any firearms or ammunition still in the restrained party's possession are to be relinquished, according to local procedures, and the process for submitting a receipt to the court showing proof of relinquishment. **Leg.H.** Added Stats 1993 ch 219 §154 (AB 1500). Amended Stats 1999 ch 662 §2 (SB 218); Stats 2010 ch 572 §15 (AB 1596), effective January 1, 2011, operative January 1, 2012; Stats 2021 ch 685 §3 (SB 320), effective January 1, 2022.

§6305. Conditions for issuance of mutual order

(a) The court shall not issue a mutual order enjoining the parties from specific acts of abuse described in Section 6320 unless both of the following apply:

(1) Both parties personally appear and each party presents written evidence of abuse or domestic violence in an application for relief using a mandatory Judicial Council restraining order application form. For purposes of this paragraph, written evidence of abuse or domestic violence in a responsive pleading does not satisfy the party's obligation to present written evidence of abuse or domestic violence. By July 1, 2016, the Judicial Council shall modify forms as necessary to provide notice of this information.

(2) The court makes detailed findings of fact indicating that both parties acted as a primary aggressor and that neither party acted primarily in self-defense.

(b) For purposes of subdivision (a), in determining if both parties acted primarily as aggressors, the court shall consider the provisions concerning dominant aggressors set forth in paragraph (3) of subdivision (c) of Section 836 of the Penal Code. **Leg.H.** Added Stats 1993 ch 219 §154 (AB 1500). Amended Stats 1995 ch 246 §2 (SB 591); Stats 2014 ch 635 §6 (AB 2089), effective January 1, 2015; Stats 2015 ch 73 §1 (AB 536), effective January 1, 2016.

§6306. Search of specific records and databases required prior to issuance or denial of order; Information to be obtained; Release of information to parties; Confidentiality

(a)(1) [1] **Before** a hearing on the issuance or denial of an order under this part, the court shall ensure that a search is or has been conducted to determine if the subject of the proposed order has a prior criminal conviction for a violent felony specified in Section 667.5 of the Penal Code or a serious felony specified in Section 1192.7 of the Penal Code; has a misdemeanor conviction involving domestic violence, weapons, or other violence; has an outstanding warrant; is currently on parole or probation; [2] **owns or possesses a firearm as reflected in the Department of Justice Automated Firearms System**; or has a prior restraining order or a violation of a prior restraining order. The search shall be conducted of all records and databases readily available and reasonably accessible to the court, including, but not limited to, the following:

[3] **(A) The California Sex and Arson Registry (CSAR).**
[4] **(B) The Supervised Release File.**
[5] **(C)** State summary criminal history information maintained by the Department of Justice pursuant to Section 11105 of the Penal Code.
[6] **(D)** The Federal Bureau of Investigation's nationwide database.
[7] **(F)** Locally maintained criminal history records or databases.
(F) The Department of Justice Automated Firearms System.

(2) However, a record or database need not be searched if the information available in that record or database can be obtained as a result of a search conducted in another record or database.

(3) If a court does not have electronic or other access to the Department of Justice Automated Firearms System and if there is no

preexisting agreement between the court and a law enforcement agency that the law enforcement agency will conduct a search of the California Law Enforcement Telecommunications System in order to report to the court whether the subject of the proposed order owns or possesses a firearm, upon the request of the court, the sheriff shall access the California Law Enforcement Telecommunications System in order to search the Department of Justice Automated Firearms System for the purpose of determining whether the subject of the order owns or possesses firearms. The sheriff shall report the results of this search to the court.

(b)(1) [8] **Before** deciding whether to issue an order under this part or when determining appropriate temporary custody and visitation orders, the court shall consider the following information obtained pursuant to a search conducted under subdivision (a): a conviction for a violent felony specified in Section 667.5 of the Penal Code or a serious felony specified in Section 1192.7 of the Penal Code; a misdemeanor conviction involving domestic violence, weapons, or other violence; an outstanding warrant; parole or probation status; a prior restraining order; and a violation of a prior restraining order.

(2) Information obtained as a result of the search that does not involve a conviction described in this subdivision shall not be considered by the court in making a determination regarding the issuance of an order pursuant to this part. That information shall be destroyed and shall not become part of the public file in this or any other civil proceeding.

(c)(1) After issuing its ruling, the court shall advise the parties that they may request the information described in subdivision (b) upon which the court relied. The court shall admonish the party seeking the proposed order that it is unlawful, pursuant to Sections 11142 and 13303 of the Penal Code, to willfully release the information, except as authorized by law.

(2) Upon the request of either party to obtain the information described in subdivision (b) upon which the court relied, the court shall release the information to the parties or, upon either party's request, to the party's attorney in that proceeding.

(3) The party seeking the proposed order may release the information to the party's counsel, court personnel, and court-appointed mediators for the purpose of seeking judicial review of the court's order or for purposes of court proceedings under Section 213.5 of the Welfare and Institutions Code.

(d) Information obtained as a result of the search conducted pursuant to subdivision (a) and relied upon by the court shall be maintained in a confidential case file and shall not become part of the public file in the proceeding or any other civil proceeding. However, the contents of the confidential case file shall be disclosed to the court-appointed mediator assigned to the case or to a child custody evaluator appointed by the court pursuant to Section 3111 of this code or Section 730 of the Evidence Code. All court-appointed mediators and child custody evaluators appointed or contracted by the court pursuant to Section 3111 of this code or Section 730 of the Evidence Code who receive information from the search conducted pursuant to subdivision (a) shall be subject to, and shall comply with, the California Law Enforcement Telecommunications System policies, practices, and procedures adopted pursuant to Section 15160 of the Government Code.

(e) If the results of the search conducted pursuant to subdivision (a) indicate that an outstanding warrant exists against the subject of the order, the court shall order the clerk of the court to immediately notify, by the most effective means available, appropriate law enforcement officials of the issuance and contents of a protective order and of any other information obtained through the search that the court determines is appropriate. The law enforcement officials so notified shall take all actions necessary to execute any outstanding warrants or any other actions, with respect to the restrained person, as appropriate and as soon as practicable.

(f) If the results of the search conducted pursuant to subdivision (a) indicate that the subject of the order owns **or possesses** a [9] firearm or if the court receives evidence of the subject's possession of a firearm or ammunition, the court shall make a written record as to whether the subject has relinquished the firearm or ammunition and provided proof of the required storage, sale, or relinquishment of the firearm or ammunition. If evidence of compliance with firearms prohibitions is not provided pursuant to subdivision (c) of Section 6389, the court shall order the clerk of the court to immediately notify, by the most effective means available, appropriate law enforcement officials of the issuance and contents of a protective order, information about the firearm or ammunition, and of any other information obtained through the search that the court determines is appropriate. The law enforcement officials so notified shall take all actions necessary to obtain those and any other firearms or ammunition owned, possessed, or controlled by the restrained person and to address any violation of the order with respect to firearms or ammunition as appropriate and as soon as practicable.

(g) If the results of the search conducted pursuant to subdivision (a) indicate that the subject of the order is currently on parole or probation, the court shall order the clerk of the court to immediately notify, by the most effective means available, the appropriate parole or probation officer of the issuance and contents of a protective order issued by the court and of any other information obtained through the search that the court determines is appropriate. That officer shall take all actions necessary to revoke parole or probation, or any other actions, with respect to the restrained person, as appropriate and as soon as practicable.

(h) This section shall not delay the granting of an application for an order that may otherwise be granted without the information resulting from the database search. If the court finds that a protective order under this part should be granted on the basis of the affidavit presented with the petition, the court shall issue the protective order and shall then ensure that a search is conducted pursuant to subdivision (a) [10] **before** the hearing.

(i) It is the intent of the Legislature that, except with regard to a search whether the subject of a proposed order owns or possesses a firearm, this section shall be implemented in those courts identified by the Judicial Council as having resources currently available for these purposes. This act shall be implemented in other courts to the extent that funds are appropriated for purposes of the act in the annual Budget Act. Leg.H. Added Stats 2001 ch 572 §3 (SB 66). Amended Stats 2012 ch 765 §1 (SB 1433), effective January 1, 2013; Stats 2014 ch 54 §2 (SB 1461), effective January 1, 2015; Stats 2019 ch 115 §63 (AB 1817), effective January 1, 2020; Stats 2021 ch 685 §4 (SB 320), effective January 1, 2022; Stats 2024 ch 541 §2 (AB 3083), effective January 1, 2025.

§6306. 2024 Deletes. [1] Prior to [2] has a registered firearm [3] (1) [4] (2) [5] (3) [6] (4) [7] (5) [8] Prior to [9] registered [10] prior to

2012 Note: Section 1 of this act shall be implemented pursuant to the provisions of Section 7 of Chapter 572 of the Statutes of 2001. Stats 2012 ch 765 (SB 1433) §4.

2001 Note: This act shall be implemented in those courts identified by the Judicial Council as having resources currently available for these purposes. This act shall be implemented in other courts to the extent that funds are appropriated for purposes of the act in the annual Budget Act. Stats 2001 ch 572 §7.

§ 6306.5. Electronic submission of petitions seeking domestic violence restraining orders

(a)(1) Petitions seeking domestic violence restraining orders under Chapter 2 (commencing with Section 6320) and domestic violence temporary restraining orders under Part 4 (commencing with Section 240) of Division 2 may be submitted electronically in every trial court. Courts shall accept these filings consistent with the timeframe in Section 246.

(2) The notice of court date, copies of the request to mail on respondent, and the temporary restraining order, if granted, shall be remitted to the petitioner electronically.

(3) Notwithstanding paragraph (2), the petitioner may elect to receive documents by regular mail or to retrieve documents from the court.

(b) The Judicial Council shall develop or amend rules and forms as necessary to implement this section.

(c) There shall be no fee for any filings related to a petition submitted electronically in accordance with this section.

(d) This section shall become operative only upon an appropriation of funds for this purpose in the annual Budget Act or other statute. **Leg.H.** Added Stats 2021 ch 681 §1 (AB 887), effective January 1, 2022.

§ 6306.6. Posting of information regarding domestic violence restraining order self-help services on superior court's website

(a) Information about access to self-help services regarding domestic violence restraining orders shall be prominently visible on the superior court's internet website.

(b) The Judicial Council shall develop or amend rules as necessary to implement this section. **Leg.H.** Added Stats 2021 ch 681 §2 (AB 887), effective January 1, 2022.

§ 6307. Electronic submission of petitions for domestic violence restraining orders or domestic violence temporary restraining orders

(a)(1) A court or court facility that receives petitions for domestic violence restraining orders under this part or domestic violence temporary restraining orders under Part 4 (commencing with Section 240) of Division 2 shall permit those petitions and any filings related to those petitions to be submitted electronically. The court or court facility shall, based on the time of receipt, act on these filings consistent with Section 246.

(2) The request, notice of the court date, copies of the request to serve on the respondent, and the temporary restraining order, if granted, shall be provided to the petitioner electronically, unless the petitioner notes, at the time of electronic filing, that these documents will be picked up from the court or court facility.

(b)(1) Information regarding electronic filing and access to the court's self-help center shall be prominently displayed on each court's homepage.

(2) Each self-help center shall maintain and make available information related to domestic violence restraining orders pursuant to this section.

(c) The Judicial Council may adopt or amend rules and forms to implement this section.

(d) This section shall become operative on July 1, 2023. **Leg.H.** Added Stats 2022 ch 420 §17 (AB 2960), effective January 1, 2023, operative July 1, 2023.

Prior Law Former Fam C §6307, relating to electronic filing of petitions and related documents, was added Stats 2021 ch 686 §2 (SB 538), effective January 1, 2022 and repealed Stats 2022 ch 420 §16 (AB 2960), effective January 1, 2023.

§ 6308. Remote appearances by parties, support persons and witnesses

A party, support person as defined in Section 6303, or witness may appear remotely at the hearing on a petition for a domestic violence restraining order. The superior court of each county shall develop local rules and instructions for remote appearances permitted under this section, which shall be posted on its internet website. **Leg.H.** Added Stats 2021 ch 686 §3 (SB 538), effective January 1, 2022. Amended Stats 2022 ch 420 §18 (AB 2960), effective January 1, 2023.

§ 6309. Domestic violence restraining order discovery

(a)(1) The Legislature finds and declares all of the following:

(A) Domestic violence is an urgent public safety and public health crisis. More than one in three California women and one in seven men experience intimate partner physical violence, intimate partner sexual violence, or intimate partner stalking in their lifetimes. Sexual and gender minorities, including queer, gender nonbinary, intersex, and transgender persons, experience domestic violence at rates as high or higher than cisgender and heterosexual persons. Domestic violence accounts for more than 15 percent of all violent crimes in California and more than 10 percent of all California homicides.

(B) Domestic violence survivors are most at risk when attempting to leave an abusive relationship. Without effective intervention in domestic abuse, the violence often increases in frequency and severity over time. Research has established that the civil domestic violence restraining order is the most effective legal remedy for intervening in and preventing future abuse.

(C) Domestic violence survivors who enter the family or civil court systems seeking protection often face ongoing abuse in the form of litigation abuse. Litigation abuse is the use of legal or bureaucratic procedures by abusive partners to continue to attack, harass, intimidate, coercively control, or maintain contact with their former partners through the litigation system by exerting power over them, forcing them to have contact, financially burdening them with excessive discovery and litigation, degrading and insulting them in legal papers, unduly delaying the court process and final resolution of important issues, or dissuading them from pursuing legal protection. Studies show that litigation abuse causes severe consequences for survivors, including economic hardship and psychological harm, and foregoing legal relief in part or in whole. Research also shows that judicial officers and court evaluators often misunderstand or overlook litigation abuse and its effects on survivors.

(2) It is the intent of the Legislature to accomplish the following:

(A) To promote the health and safety of domestic violence survivors and their children.

(B) To ensure that domestic violence survivors can seek and receive, without delay, the protection offered by the domestic violence restraining orders, which are remedial injunctive orders intended to offer expedited separation and protection from abuse.

(C) To provide for separation and to prevent future acts of domestic violence by streamlining any domestic violence restraining order discovery to expedite the adjudication of requests for restraining orders and prevent abusive litigation tactics that interfere with legislative intent to protect domestic violence victims.

(b) Consistent with the findings and declarations and statements of legislative intent in subdivision (a), discovery pursuant to the Civil Discovery Act (Title 4 (commencing with Section 2016.010) of Part 4 of the Code of Civil Procedure), is not permitted pursuant to this part except as set forth in this section.

(c)(1) A court may grant a request for discovery only upon a showing of good cause for the discovery by the party making the request.

(2) A party may make an oral or written request for discovery to the court at an evidentiary hearing pursuant to this part.

(3) A person shall not be required to make a written objection or response to a request for discovery but may express any objection or response orally or in writing or at the hearing.

(d) In determining whether to permit discovery in a proceeding pursuant to this part, the court shall consider all of the following:

(1) The importance and relevance of, and need for, the information sought to be obtained.

(2) The likelihood that the information may be acquired by another permitted discovery method, or may be acquired by other methods including pleadings or examination at the hearing.

(3) The delay in completion of the hearing, which is entitled to calendar preference pursuant to Section 244, if the discovery is permitted.

(4) The potential, if any, that the discovery may induce trauma in any person involved in the proceeding.

(5) Whether one or more persons are subject to any restraining or protective orders.

(6) Any other factor that may affect the prompt and fair resolution of the proceeding.

(e) If a court finds good cause and grants a request for discovery pursuant to subdivision (c), the court may do either of the following:

(1)(A) Continue the commencement of hearing for a reasonable period to permit one or more methods of discovery.

(B) If the court continues the hearing to allow for discovery pursuant to subparagraph (A), the court shall extend, and may modify, any restraining order in place.

(2) Commence the hearing to receive evidence and then continue the hearing to permit one or more methods of discovery.

(f) The court shall limit and control any permitted discovery to the least intrusive methods as authorized pursuant to the Civil Discovery Act (Title 4 (commencing with Section 2016.010) of Part 4 of the Code of Civil Procedure) and the minimum number of items reasonably necessary to secure the requested information. The court shall specify the time for response to any permitted discovery after considering the items in subdivision (d).

(g) Nothing in this section is intended to take away rights afforded in the Domestic Violence Prevention Act. Nothing in this section is intended to infringe on the ability for abuse survivors to receive their police reports and evidence pursuant to Section 6228 or on parties' ability to discover their own business records without obtaining court permission, including medical records, phone records, or recordings of calls to 911, to provide corroborating proof. **Leg.H.** Added Stats 2023 ch 503 §1 (SB 741), effective January 1, 2024.

CHAPTER 2
ISSUANCE OF ORDERS

Article 1. Ex Parte Orders.
Article 2. Orders Issuable After Notice and Hearing.
Article 3. Orders Included in Judgment.

ARTICLE 1
Ex Parte Orders

Enjoining harassment, threats, and violence. §6320.
Reasons for denying petition for ex parte order required; Availability of hearing. §6320.5.
Exclusion from dwelling. §6321.

Enjoining additional specified behaviors. §6322.
Possession of firearm or ammunition in violation of Section 6389 of Cal Fam Code; Considerations when making determination; Review hearing. § 6322.5.
Court order prohibiting obtaining address or location of protected person. §6322.7.
Determining temporary custody and visitation. §6323.
Provision restraining access of records and information pertaining to minor child. § 6323.5.
Determining temporary use of property and payment of liens or encumbrances. §6324.
Restraints on property of married persons. §6325.
Restraining orders prohibiting fraudulent activities regarding insurance beneficiaries. §6325.5.
Time for issuance or denial of ex parte temporary restraining order. §6326.
Application of Part 4 to this Article. §6327.

§6320. Enjoining harassment, threats, and violence

(a) The court may issue an ex parte order enjoining a party from molesting, attacking, striking, stalking, threatening, sexually assaulting, battering, credibly impersonating as described in Section 528.5 of the Penal Code, falsely personating as described in Section 529 of the Penal Code, harassing, telephoning, including, but not limited to, making annoying telephone calls as described in Section 653m of the Penal Code, destroying personal property, contacting, either directly or indirectly, by mail or otherwise, coming within a specified distance of, or disturbing the peace of the other party, and, in the discretion of the court, on a showing of good cause, of other named family or household members.

(b) On a showing of good cause, the court may include in a protective order a grant to the petitioner of the exclusive care, possession, or control of any animal owned, possessed, leased, kept, or held by either the petitioner or the respondent or a minor child residing in the residence or household of either the petitioner or the respondent. The court may order the respondent to stay away from the animal and forbid the respondent from taking, transferring, encumbering, concealing, molesting, attacking, striking, threatening, harming, or otherwise disposing of the animal.

(c) As used in this subdivision (a), "disturbing the peace of the other party" refers to conduct that, based on the totality of the circumstances, destroys the mental or emotional calm of the other party. This conduct may be committed directly or indirectly, including through the use of a third party, and by any method or through any means including, but not limited to, telephone, online accounts, text messages, internet-connected devices, or other electronic technologies. This conduct includes, but is not limited to, coercive control, which is a pattern of behavior that in purpose or effect unreasonably interferes with a person's free will and personal liberty. Examples of coercive control include, but are not limited to, unreasonably engaging in any of the following:

(1) Isolating the other party from friends, relatives, or other sources of support.

(2) Depriving the other party of basic necessities.

(3) Controlling, regulating, or monitoring the other party's movements, communications, daily behavior, finances, economic resources, or access to services.

(4) Compelling the other party by force, threat of force, or intimidation, including threats based on actual or suspected immigration status, to engage in conduct from which the other party has a right to abstain or to abstain from conduct in which the other party has a right to engage.

(5) Engaging in reproductive coercion, which consists of control over the reproductive autonomy of another through force, threat of force, or intimidation, and may include, but is not limited to, unreasonably pressuring the other party to become pregnant, deliberately interfering with contraception use or access to reproductive health information, or using coercive tactics to control, or attempt to control, pregnancy outcomes.

(d) This section does not limit any remedies available under this act or any other provision of law. **Leg.H.** Added Stats 2013 ch 260 §2 (AB 157), effective January 1, 2014, operative July 1, 2014. Amended Stats 2020 ch 248 §2 (SB 1141), effective January 1, 2021; Stats 2021 ch 135 §1 (SB 374), effective January 1, 2022.

Prior Law: Former Fam C § 6320, relating to enjoining harassment, threats, and violence, was added Stats 1993 ch 219 §154 (AB 1500). Amended Stats 1995 ch 598 §1 (AB 878); Stats 1996 ch 904 §1 (AB 2224); Stats 2007 ch 205 §2 (SB 353), effective January 1, 2008; Stats 2010 ch 572 §16 (AB 1596), effective January 1, 2011, operative January 1, 2012 and repealed July 1, 2014, by Stats 2013 ch 260 §1 (AB 157), effective January 1, 2014.

Former Sections: Former Fam C §6320, relating to enjoining harassment, threats, and violence, was added Stats 1993 ch 219 §154 (AB 1500) and repealed operative July 1, 2014, by its own provisions. Stats 2013 ch 260 §1 (AB 157).

§6320.5. Reasons for denying petition for ex parte order required; Availability of hearing

(a) An order denying a petition for an ex parte order pursuant to Section 6320 shall include the reasons for denying the petition.

(b) An order denying a jurisdictionally adequate petition for an ex parte order, pursuant to Section 6320, shall provide the petitioner the right to a noticed hearing on the earliest date that the business of the court will permit, but not later than 21 days or, if good cause appears to the court, 25 days from the date of the order. The petitioner shall serve on the respondent, at least five days before the hearing, copies of all supporting papers filed with the court, including the application and affidavits.

(c) Notwithstanding subdivision (b), upon the denial of the ex parte order pursuant to Section 6320, the petitioner shall have the option of waiving the right to a noticed hearing. However, this section does not preclude a petitioner who waives the right to a noticed hearing from refiling a new petition, without prejudice, at a later time. **Leg.H.** Added Stats 2008 ch 263 §1 (AB 2553), effective January 1, 2009. Amended Stats 2010 ch 572 §17 (AB 1596), effective January 1, 2011, operative January 1, 2012; Stats 2019 ch 115 §64 (AB 1817), effective January 1, 2020.

§6321. Exclusion from dwelling

(a) The court may issue an ex parte order excluding a party from the family dwelling, the dwelling of the other party, the common dwelling of both parties, or the dwelling of the person who has care, custody, and control of a child to be protected from domestic violence for the period of time and on the conditions the court determines, regardless of which party holds legal or equitable title or is the lessee of the dwelling.

(b) The court may issue an order under subdivision (a) only on a showing of all of the following:

(1) Facts sufficient for the court to ascertain that the party who will stay in the dwelling has a right under color of law to possession of the premises.

(2) That the party to be excluded has assaulted or threatens to assault the other party or any other person under the care, custody, and control of the other party, or any minor child of the parties or of the other party.

(3) That physical or emotional harm would otherwise result to the other party, to any person under the care, custody, and control of the other party, or to any minor child of the parties or of the other party. **Leg.H.** Added Stats 1993 ch 219 §154 (AB 1500).

§6322. Enjoining additional specified behaviors

The court may issue an ex parte order enjoining a party from specified behavior that the court determines is necessary to effectuate orders under Section 6320 or 6321. **Leg.H.** Added Stats 1993 ch 219 §154 (AB 1500).

§ 6322.5. Possession of firearm or ammunition in violation of Section 6389 of Cal Fam Code; Considerations when making determination; Review hearing

(a) When relevant information is presented to the court at a noticed hearing that a restrained person has a firearm or ammunition, the court shall consider that information and determine, by a preponderance of the evidence, whether the person subject to a protective order has a firearm or ammunition in, or subject to, their immediate possession or control in violation of Section 6389.

(b)(1) In making the determination required pursuant to subdivision (a), the court may consider whether the restrained person filed a firearm relinquishment, storage, or sales receipt or if an exemption from the firearm prohibition was granted pursuant to subdivision (h) of Section 6389.

(2) The court may make the determination at a noticed hearing when a domestic violence protective order is issued, at a subsequent review hearing, or at any subsequent family or juvenile law hearing while the order remains in effect.

(3) If the court makes a determination that the restrained person has a firearm or ammunition in violation of Section 6389, the court shall make a written record of the determination and provide a copy to any party who is present at the hearing and, upon request, to any party not present at the hearing.

(c)(1) When presented with information pursuant to subdivision (a), the court may set a review hearing to determine whether there has been a violation of Section 6389.

(2) The review hearing shall be held within 10 court days after the noticed hearing at which the information was presented. If the restrained person is not present when the court sets the review hearing, the protected person shall provide notice of the review hearing to the restrained person at least two court days before the review hearing, in accordance with Section 414.10 of the Code of Civil Procedure, by personal service or by mail to the restrained person's last known address.

(3) The court may, for good cause, extend the date of the review hearing for a reasonable period or remove it from the calendar.

(4) The court shall order the restrained person to appear at the hearing.

(5) The court may conduct the review hearing in the absence of the protected person.

(6) This section does not prohibit the court from permitting a party or witness to appear through technology that enables remote appearances, as determined by the court.

(d) The determination made pursuant to this section may be considered by the court in issuing an order to show cause for contempt pursuant to paragraph (5) of subdivision (a) of Section 1209 of the Code of Civil Procedure or an order for monetary sanctions pursuant to Section 177.5 of the Code of Civil Procedure. **Leg.H.** Added Stats 2021 ch 685 §5 (SB 320), effective January 1, 2022.

Prior Law: Former Fam C §6322.5, relating to the issuance of an ex parte order prohibiting disclosure of address or identifying information, was added Stats 1998 ch 511 §5 (AB 1900), and repealed January 1, 2016, by Stats 2015 ch 493 §6 (SB 646).

§6322.7. Court order prohibiting obtaining address or location of protected person

(a) The court shall order that any party enjoined pursuant to an order issued under this part be prohibited from taking any action to obtain the address or location of any protected person, unless there is good cause not to make that order.

(b) The Judicial Council shall develop forms necessary to effectuate this section. **Leg.H.** Added Stats 2005 ch 472 §3 (AB 978), effective January 1, 2006. Amended Stats 2010 ch 572 §18 (AB 1596), effective January 1, 2011, operative January 1, 2012.

§6323. Determining temporary custody and visitation

(a) Subject to Section 3064:

(1) The court may issue an ex parte order determining the temporary custody and visitation of a minor child, on the conditions the court determines, to a party who has established a parent and child relationship pursuant to paragraph (2). The parties shall inform the court if a custody or visitation order has already been issued in any other proceeding.

(2)(A) In making a determination of the best interest of the child, in order to limit the child's exposure to potential domestic violence, and to ensure the safety of all family members, if the party who has obtained the restraining order has established a parent and child relationship and the other party has not established that relationship, the court may award temporary sole legal and physical custody to the party to whom the restraining order was issued and may make an order of no visitation to the other party pending the establishment of a parent and child relationship between the child and the other party.

(B) A party may establish a parent and child relationship for purposes of subparagraph (A) only by offering proof of any of the following:

(i) The party gave birth to the child.

(ii) The child is conclusively presumed to be a child of the marriage between the parties, pursuant to Section 7540, or the party has been determined by a court to be a parent of the child, pursuant to Section 7541.

(iii) Legal adoption or pending legal adoption of the child by the party.

(iv) The party has signed a valid voluntary declaration of paternity, which has been in effect more than 60 days prior to the issuance of the restraining order, and that declaration has not been rescinded or set aside.

(v) A determination made by the juvenile court that there is a parent and child relationship between the party offering the proof and the child.

(vi) A determination of parentage made in a proceeding to determine custody or visitation in a case brought by the local child support agency pursuant to Chapter 2 (commencing with Section 17400) of Division 17.

(vii) The party has been determined to be the parent of the child through a proceeding under the Uniform Parentage Act (Part 3 (commencing with Section 7600) of Division 12).

(viii) Both parties stipulate, in writing or on the record, for purposes of this proceeding, that they are the parents of the child.

(b)(1) Except as provided in paragraph (2), the court shall not make a finding of paternity in this proceeding, and an order issued pursuant to this section shall be without prejudice in any other action brought to establish a parent and child relationship.

(2) The court may accept a stipulation of paternity by the parties and, if paternity is uncontested, enter a judgment establishing paternity, subject to the set-aside provisions in Section 7646.

(c) When making an order for custody or visitation pursuant to this section, the court's order shall specify the time, day, place, and manner of transfer of the child for custody or visitation to limit the child's exposure to potential domestic conflict or violence and to ensure the safety of all family members. If the court finds a party is staying in a place designated as a shelter for victims of domestic violence or other confidential location, the court's order for time, day, place, and manner of transfer of the child for custody or visitation shall be designed to prevent disclosure of the location of the shelter or other confidential location.

(d) When making an order for custody or visitation pursuant to this section, the court shall consider whether the best interest of the child, based upon the circumstances of the case, requires that a visitation or custody arrangement shall be limited to situations in which a third person, specified by the court, is present, or whether visitation or custody shall be suspended or denied.

(e) When determining whether visitation should be suspended, denied, or limited to situations in which a third person is present pursuant to subdivision (d), the court shall consider a determination made pursuant to Section 6322.5 that the party is a restrained person in possession or control of a firearm or ammunition in violation of Section 6389. **Leg.H.** Added Stats 1993 ch 219 §154 (AB 1500). Amended Stats 1994 ch 320 §3 (AB 356); Stats 1997 ch 396 §2 (SB 564); Stats 2010 ch 352 §18 (AB 939), effective January 1, 2011; Stats 2019 ch 115 §65 (AB 1817), effective January 1, 2020; Stats 2019 ch 497 §111 (AB 991), effective January 1, 2020 (ch 115 prevails); Stats 2021 ch 685 §6 (SB 320), effective January 1, 2022.

§6323.5. Provision restraining access of records and information pertaining to minor child

(a) For purposes of this section, the following definitions apply:

(1) "Discretionary services organization" includes any organization that provides nonessential services to children, such as recreational activities, entertainment, and summer camps. "Discretionary services organization" also includes a place of employment of a minor described in subdivision (b).

(2) "Essential care provider" includes a public or private school, health care facility, daycare facility, dental facility, or other similar organization that frequently provides essential social, health, or care services to children.

(b)(1) Notwithstanding Section 3025, and in accordance with Section 6322, a court may include in an ex parte order a provision restraining a party from accessing records and information pertaining to the health care, education, daycare, recreational activities, or employment of a minor child of the parties.

(2) A parent or guardian may provide a copy of an order with a provision specified in paragraph (1) to an essential care provider or a discretionary services organization, or both.

(c)(1)(A) An essential care provider shall, on or before February 1, 2023, develop protocols relating to the provider's compliance with the order described in subdivision (b), including, at a minimum, designating the appropriate personnel responsible for receiving the protective order, establishing a means of ensuring that the restrained party is not able to access the records or information, and implementing a procedure for submission of a copy of an order and for providing the party that submits the copy of the order with documentation indicating when, and to whom, the copy of the order was submitted.

(B) A discretionary services organization that is provided an order described in subdivision (b), shall develop the protocols specified in paragraph (1) within 30 days of receipt of the first order.

(2) If an essential care provider or discretionary services organization is provided with a copy of an order described in subdivision (b), the essential care provider or discretionary services organization shall not release information or records pertaining to the child to the restrained

party. This requirement applies regardless of whether the essential care provider or discretionary services organization has finalized the protocols described in paragraph (1).

(d) The Judicial Council shall develop or update any forms or rules of court that are necessary to implement this section.

(e) This section shall become operative on January 1, 2023. **Leg.H.** Added Stats 2021 ch 129 §2 (SB 24), effective January 1, 2022, operative January 1, 2023.

§6324. Determining temporary use of property and payment of liens or encumbrances

The court may issue an ex parte order determining the temporary use, possession, and control of real or personal property of the parties and the payment of any liens or encumbrances coming due during the period the order is in effect. **Leg.H.** Added Stats 1993 ch 219 §154 (AB 1500).

§6325. Restraints on property of married persons

The court may issue an ex parte order restraining a married person from specified acts in relation to community, quasi-community, and separate property as provided in Section 2045. **Leg.H.** Added Stats 1993 ch 219 §154 (AB 1500).

§6325.5. Restraining orders prohibiting fraudulent activities regarding insurance beneficiaries

(a) The court may issue an ex parte order restraining any party from cashing, borrowing against, canceling, transferring, disposing of, or changing the beneficiaries of any insurance or other coverage held for the benefit of the parties, or their child or children, if any, for whom support may be ordered, or both.

(b) This section shall become operative on July 1, 2014. **Leg.H.** Added Stats 2013 ch 261 §1 (AB 161), effective January 1, 2014, operative July 1, 2014.

§6326. Time for issuance or denial of ex parte temporary restraining order

An ex parte order under this article shall be issued or denied on the same day that the application is submitted to the court, unless the application is filed too late in the day to permit effective review, in which case the order shall be issued or denied on the next day of judicial business in sufficient time for the order to be filed that day with the clerk of the court. A petition for an ex parte order pursuant to this article shall not be denied solely because the other party was not provided with notice. **Leg.H.** Added Stats 1993 ch 148 §2 (AB 1331). Amended Stats 2018 ch 219 §2 (AB 2694), effective January 1, 2019.

Prior Law: There was another section of this number, which was added Stats 1993 ch 219 §154, and renumbered §6327 by Stats 1993 ch 876 §27.2, effective October 6, 1993, operative January 1, 1994.

§6327. Application of Part 4 to this Article

Part 4 (commencing with Section 240) of Division 2 applies to the issuance of any ex parte order under this article, other than an order under Section 6322.5. **Leg.H.** Added Stats 1993 ch 219 §154 (AB 1500) as §6326. Renumbered by Stats 1993 ch 876 §27.2 (SB 1068), effective October 6, 1993, operative January 1, 1994. Amended Stats 1998 ch 511 §6 (AB 1900).

ARTICLE 2
Orders Issuable After Notice and Hearing

Ex parte orders; Reason given for denial; Order excluding party from dwelling. §6340.
Payment of child support by presumed father. §6341.
Payment of restitution for loss of earnings and out-of-pocket expenses. §6342.
Use, possession, and control of real or personal property of the parties. § 6342.5.
Participation in counseling. §6343.
Payment of attorney's fees and costs; Ability to pay. § 6344.
Duration of restraining order. §6345.
Custody and visitation orders when parenthood not established. §6346.
Transfer of billing responsibility and rights for wireless telephone service. §6347.

§6340. Ex parte orders; Reason given for denial; Order excluding party from dwelling

(a)(1) The court may issue any of the orders described in Article 1 (commencing with Section 6320) after notice and a hearing. When determining whether to make any orders under this subdivision, the court shall consider whether failure to make any of these orders may jeopardize the safety of the petitioner and the children for whom the custody or visitation orders are sought. If the court makes any order for custody, visitation, or support, that order shall survive the termination of any protective order. The Judicial Council shall provide notice of this provision on any Judicial Council forms related to this subdivision.

(2)(A) If at the time of a hearing with respect to an order issued pursuant to this part based on an ex parte temporary restraining order, the court determines that, after diligent effort, the petitioner has been unable to accomplish personal service, and that there is reason to believe that the restrained party is evading service, the court may permit an alternative method of service designed to give reasonable notice of the action to the respondent. Alternative methods of service include, but are not limited to, the following:

(i) Service by publication pursuant to the standards set forth in Section 415.50 of the Code of Civil Procedure.

(ii) Service by first-class mail sent to the respondent at the most current address for the respondent that is available to the court or delivering a copy of the pleadings and orders at the respondent's home or place of employment, pursuant to the standards set forth in Sections 415.20 to 415.40, inclusive, of the Code of Civil Procedure.

(B) If the court permits an alternative method of service under this paragraph, the court shall grant a continuance to allow for the alternative service pursuant to Section 245.

(b) The court shall, upon denying a petition under this part, provide a brief statement of the reasons for the decision in writing or on the record. A decision stating "denied" is insufficient.

(c) The court may issue an order described in Section 6321 excluding a person from a dwelling if the court finds that physical or emotional harm would otherwise result to the other party, to a person under the care, custody, and control of the other party, or to a minor child of the parties or of the other party. **Leg.H.** Added Stats 1993 ch 219 §154 (AB 1500). Amended Stats 2004 ch 472 §4 (AB 2148); Stats 2010 ch 352 §19 (AB 939), effective January 1, 2011; Stats 2014 ch 635 §7 (AB 2089), effective January 1, 2015; Stats 2018 ch 219 §3 (AB 2694), effective January 1, 2019.

§6341. Payment of child support by presumed father

(a) If the parties are married to each other and no other child support order exists or if there is a presumption under Section 7611 that the respondent is the natural father of a minor child and the child is in the custody of the petitioner, after notice and a hearing, the court may, if requested by the petitioner, order a party to pay an amount necessary for the support and maintenance of the child if the order would otherwise be authorized in an action brought pursuant to Division 9 (commencing with Section 3500) or the Uniform Parentage Act (Part 3 (commencing with Section 7600) of Division 12). When determining whether to make any orders under this subdivision, the court shall consider whether failure to make any of these orders may jeopardize the safety of the petitioner and the children for whom child support is requested, including safety concerns related to the financial needs of the petitioner and the children. The Judicial Council shall provide notice of this provision on any Judicial Council forms related to this subdivision.

(b) An order issued pursuant to subdivision (a) of this section shall be without prejudice in an action brought pursuant to the Uniform Parentage Act (Part 3 (commencing with Section 7600) of Division 12).

(c) If the parties are married to each other and no spousal support order exists, after notice and a hearing, the court may order the respondent to pay spousal support in an amount, if any, that would otherwise be authorized in an action pursuant to Part 1 (commencing with Section 3500) or Part 3 (commencing with Section 4300) of Division 9. When determining whether to make any orders under this subdivision, the court shall consider whether failure to make any of these orders may jeopardize the safety of the petitioner, including safety concerns related to the financial needs of the petitioner. The Judicial Council shall provide notice of this provision on any Judicial Council forms related to this subdivision.

(d) An order issued pursuant to subdivision (c) shall be without prejudice in a proceeding for dissolution of marriage, nullity of marriage, or legal separation of the parties. **Leg.H.** Added Stats 1993 ch 219 §154 (AB 1500). Amended Stats 1999 ch 980 §13 (AB 1671); Stats 2004 ch 472 §5 (AB 2148); Stats 2005 ch 22 §63 (SB 1108), effective January 1, 2006.

§6342. Payment of restitution for loss of earnings and out-of-pocket expenses

(a) After notice and a hearing, the court may issue any of the following orders:

(1) An order that restitution be paid to the petitioner for loss of earnings and out-of-pocket expenses, including, but not limited to, expenses for medical care and temporary housing, incurred as a direct result of the abuse inflicted by the respondent or any actual physical injuries sustained from the abuse.

(2) An order that restitution be paid by the petitioner for out-of-pocket expenses incurred by a party as a result of an ex parte order that is found by the court to have been issued on facts shown at a noticed hearing to be insufficient to support the order.

(3) An order that restitution be paid by the respondent to any public or private agency for the reasonable cost of providing services to the petitioner required as a direct result of the abuse inflicted by the respondent or any actual injuries sustained therefrom.

(b) An order for restitution under this section shall not include damages for pain and suffering. **Leg.H.** Added Stats 1993 ch 219 §154 (AB 1500).

§ 6342.5. Use, possession, and control of real or personal property of the parties

(a) After notice and a hearing, the court may issue an order determining the use, possession, and control of real or personal property of the parties during the period the order is in effect and the payment of any liens or encumbrances coming due during that period.

(b) The order described in subdivision (a) may include a finding that specific debts were incurred as the result of domestic violence and without the consent of a party. For purposes of this subdivision, the acts that may support this finding include, but are not limited to, the crimes proscribed by Section 530.5 of the Penal Code. This finding does not affect the priority of any lien or other security interest.

(c) The Judicial Council shall adopt appropriate forms and modify existing forms, as necessary, to effectuate this section.

(d) This section shall be operative on January 1, 2022. **Leg.H.** Added Stats 2020 ch 245 §1 (AB 2517), effective January 1, 2021, operative January 1, 2022.

§6343. Participation in counseling

(a) After notice and a hearing, the court may issue an order requiring the restrained party to participate in a batterer's program approved by the probation department as provided in Section 1203.097 of the Penal Code.

(b)(1) Commencing July 1, 2016, if the court orders a restrained party to participate in a batterer's program pursuant to subdivision (a), the restrained party shall do all of the following:

(A) Register for the program by the deadline ordered by the court. If no deadline is ordered by the court, the restrained party shall register no later than 30 days from the date the order was issued.

(B) At the time of enrollment, sign all necessary program consent forms for the program to release proof of enrollment, attendance records, and completion or termination reports to the court and the protected party, or the protected party's attorney. The court and the protected party may provide to the program a fax number or mailing address for purposes of receiving proof of enrollment, attendance records, and completion or termination reports.

(C) Provide the court and the protected party with the name, address, and telephone number of the program.

(2) By July 1, 2016, the Judicial Council shall revise or promulgate forms as necessary to effectuate this subdivision.

(c) The courts shall, in consultation with local domestic violence shelters and programs, develop a resource list of referrals to appropriate community domestic violence programs and services to be provided to each applicant for an order under this section. **Leg.H.** Added Stats 1993 ch 219 §154 (AB 1500). Amended Stats 1993 ch 876 §27.3 (SB 1068), effective October 6, 1993, operative January 1, 1994; Stats 1999 ch 662 §3 (SB 218); Stats 2015 ch 72 §1 (AB 439), effective January 1, 2016; Stats 2019 ch 115 §66 (AB 1817), effective January 1, 2020.

§ 6344. Payment of attorney's fees and costs; Ability to pay

(a) After notice and a hearing, a court, upon request, shall issue an order for the payment of attorney's fees and costs for a prevailing petitioner.

(b) After notice and a hearing, the court, upon request, may issue an order for the payment of attorney's fees and costs for a prevailing respondent only if the respondent establishes by a preponderance of the evidence that the petition or request is frivolous or solely intended to abuse, intimidate, or cause unnecessary delay.

(c) Before a court awards attorney's fees and costs pursuant to this section, the court shall first determine pursuant to Section 270 that the party ordered to pay has, or is reasonably likely to have, the ability to pay. **Leg.H.** Added Stats 2022 ch 591 §2 (AB 2369), effective January 1, 2023.

Prior Law Former Fam C §6344, similar to the present section, was added Stats 1993 ch 219 §154 (AB 1500), amended Stats 2004 ch 472 §6 (AB 2148), and repealed Stats 2022 ch 591 §1, effective January 1, 2023.

§6345. Duration of restraining order

(a) In the discretion of the court, the personal conduct, stay-away, and residence exclusion orders contained in a court order issued after notice and a hearing under this article may have a duration of not more than five years, subject to termination or modification by further order of the court either on written stipulation filed with the court or on the motion of a party. These orders may be renewed, upon the request of a party, either for five or more years, or permanently, at the discretion of the court, without a showing of further abuse since the issuance of the original order. Renewals and subsequent renewals shall be subject to termination, modification, or subsequent renewal by further order of the court either on written stipulation filed with the court or on the motion of a party. The request for renewal may be brought at any time within the three months before the expiration of the orders.

(b) Notwithstanding subdivision (a), the duration of any orders, other than the protective orders described in subdivision (a), that are also contained in a court order issued after notice and a hearing under this article, including, but not limited to, orders for custody, visitation, support, and disposition of property, shall be governed by the law relating to those specific subjects.

(c) The failure to state the expiration date on the face of the form creates an order with a duration of three years from the date of issuance.

(d) If an action is filed for the purpose of terminating or modifying a protective order prior to the expiration date specified in the order by a party other than the protected party, the party who is protected by the order shall be given notice, pursuant to subdivision (b) of Section 1005 of the Code of Civil Procedure, of the proceeding by personal service or, if the protected party has satisfied the requirements of Chapter 3.1 (commencing with Section 6205) of Division 7 of Title 1 of the Government Code, by service on the Secretary of State. If the party who is protected by the order cannot be notified prior to the hearing for modification or termination of the protective order, the court shall deny the motion to modify or terminate the order without prejudice or continue the hearing until the party who is protected can be properly noticed and may, upon a showing of good cause, specify another method for service of process that is reasonably designed to afford actual notice to the protected party. The protected party may waive the right to notice if the protected party is physically present in court and does not challenge the sufficiency of the notice.

(e) On or before January 1, 2025, the Judicial Council shall create one or more specific forms for the purpose of requesting a modification of an existing restraining order. **Leg.H.** Added Stats 1993 ch 219 §154 (AB 1500). Amended Stats 1995 ch 907 §2 (AB 935); Stats 2005 ch 125 §1 (AB 99), effective January 1, 2006; Stats 2010 ch 572 §19 (AB 1596), effective January 1, 2011, operative January 1, 2012; Stats 2011 ch 101 §4 (AB 454), effective January 1, 2012; Stats 2019 ch 115 §67 (AB 1817), effective January 1, 2020; Stats 2022 ch 88 §1 (SB 935), effective January 1, 2023; Stats 2023 ch 874 §2 (SB 459), effective January 1, 2024.

Prior Law Former Prob C §16345, relating to time of entitlement and time when asset subject to trust, was added Stats 1999 ch 145 §5 (AB 846), effective January 1, 2000, and repealed Stats 2023 ch 28 §1 (SB 522), effective January 1, 2024. Derivation: (a) Former Prob C §160. (b) Former Prob C §162, as amended Stats 1941 ch 336 §1, Stats 1953 ch 986 §1, Stats 1959 ch 1882 §1, amended 1982 ch 520 §1. (c) Former Prob C §661, as added Stats 1983 ch 842 §40. (d) Former Prob C §663, as added Stats 1983 ch 842 §40. (e) Former Prob C §16304, as enacted Stats 1990 ch 79 §14. (f) Former Prob C §16304, as added Stats 1986 ch 820 §40, amended Stats 1987 ch 923 §100, Stats 1988 ch 1199 §106. (g) Former CC §730.04, as added Stats 1967 ch 1508 §2, amended Stats 1968 ch 448 §1. (h) Former CC §730.06, as added Stats 1953 ch 37 §1. (i) Former CC §1366. (j) Former CC §§1368, 1369. (k) Stats 1941 ch 898 §4. (*l*) Field's Draft NY CC §623. (m) Uniform Principal and Income Act §4.

§6346. Custody and visitation orders when parenthood not established

The court may make appropriate custody and visitation orders pursuant to the Uniform Parentage Act (Part 3 (commencing with Section 7600) of

Division 12) after notice and a hearing under this section when the party who has requested custody or visitation has not established a parent and child relationship under subparagraph (B) of paragraph (2) of subdivision (a) of Section 6323, but has taken steps to establish that relationship by filing an action under the Uniform Parentage Act. **Leg.H.** Added Stats 1997 ch 396 §3 (SB 564).

§6347. Transfer of billing responsibility and rights for wireless telephone service

(a) Commencing July 1, 2016, in order to ensure that the requesting party can maintain an existing wireless telephone number, and the wireless numbers of any minor children in the care of the requesting party, the court may issue an order, after notice and a hearing, directing a wireless telephone service provider to transfer the billing responsibility for and rights to the wireless telephone number or numbers to the requesting party, if the requesting party is not the accountholder.

(b)(1) The order transferring billing responsibility for and rights to the wireless telephone number or numbers to a requesting party shall be a separate order that is directed to the wireless telephone service provider. The order shall list the name and billing telephone number of the accountholder, the name and contact information of the person to whom the telephone number or numbers will be transferred, and each telephone number to be transferred to that person. The court shall ensure that the contact information of the requesting party is not provided to the accountholder in proceedings held pursuant to Division 10 (commencing with Section 6200).

(2) The order shall be served on the wireless service provider's agent for service of process listed with the Secretary of State.

(3) Where the wireless service provider cannot operationally or technically effectuate the order due to certain circumstances, including, but not limited to, any of the following, the wireless service provider shall notify the requesting party within 72 hours of receipt of the order:

(A) When the accountholder has already terminated the account.

(B) When differences in network technology prevent the functionality of a device on the network.

(C) When there are geographic or other limitations on network or service availability.

(c)(1) Upon transfer of billing responsibility for and rights to a wireless telephone number or numbers to a requesting party pursuant to subdivision (b) by a wireless telephone service provider, the requesting party shall assume all financial responsibility for the transferred wireless telephone number or numbers, monthly service costs, and costs for any mobile device associated with the wireless telephone number or numbers.

(2) This section shall not preclude a wireless service provider from applying any routine and customary requirements for account establishment to the requesting party as part of this transfer of billing responsibility for a wireless telephone number or numbers and any devices attached to that number or numbers, including, but not limited to, identification, financial information, and customer preferences.

(d) This section shall not affect the ability of the court to apportion the assets and debts of the parties as provided for in law, or the ability to determine the temporary use, possession, and control of personal property pursuant to Sections 6324 and 6340.

(e) No cause of action shall lie against any wireless telephone service provider, its officers, employees, or agents, for actions taken in accordance with the terms of a court order issued pursuant to this section.

(f) The Judicial Council shall, on or before July 1, 2016, develop any forms or rules necessary to effectuate this section. **Leg.H.** Added Stats 2015 ch 415 §2 (AB 1407), effective January 1, 2016.

2015 Note: The Legislature finds and declares all of the following:

(a) For many victims of domestic violence, a wireless telephone is their lifeline to the community resources, life-saving services, and support network they need to leave their batterer and abusive environment. For the majority of victims, shelter in a confidential safe house is a last resort, and, in fact, unnecessary. Victims are going about their lives, working, and taking care of their children, as they are making plans and determining their next steps to safely leave their abuser. Many victims are able to access counseling services and obtain legal assistance, such as securing a restraining order, without entering into a safe house. For these victims, a wireless telephone serves as a critical tool for making appointments and communicating with their advocates.

(b) Allowing a victim of domestic violence to retain the use of an existing wireless telephone number and access to the contacts and other information that may be contained in an existing wireless telephone is important for both the safety and emotional support of the victim. This can be a problem if the domestic violence victim is not the accountholder for the wireless telephone, as only an accountholder has the authority to release the telephone number or numbers contained in the account.

(c) According to a Wall Street Journal article, in 2011 just under 71 percent of households had a landline in the home, down from a little more than 96 percent of households 15 years earlier. Cellular telephone ownership among adults reached 89 percent in 2011, up from approximately 36 percent in 1998.

(d) A 2014 National Public Radio Survey of 72 shelters in large cities and smaller towns across the nation found that 85 percent of the shelters worked directly with victims whose abusers tracked the victims using GPS. Seventy-five percent of the shelters worked with victims whose abusers eavesdropped on their conversations remotely by using hidden mobile applications. Stats 2015 ch 415 (AB 1407) §1.

ARTICLE 3
Orders Included in Judgment

Specified orders. §6360.
Required statement. §6361.

§6360. Specified orders

A judgment entered in a proceeding for dissolution of marriage, for nullity of marriage, for legal separation of the parties, in a proceeding brought pursuant to this division, or in an action brought pursuant to the Uniform Parentage Act (Part 3 (commencing with Section 7600) of Division 12) may include a protective order as defined in Section 6218. **Leg.H.** Added Stats 1993 ch 219 §154 (AB 1500).

§6361. Required statement

If an order is included in a judgment pursuant to this article, the judgment shall state on its face both of the following:

(a) Which provisions of the judgment are the orders.

(b) The date of expiration of the orders, which shall be not more than five years from the date the judgment is issued, unless extended by the court after notice and a hearing. **Leg.H.** Added Stats 1993 ch 219 §154 (AB 1500). Amended Stats 2005 ch 125 §2 (AB 99), effective January 1, 2006.

CHAPTER 3
REGISTRATION AND ENFORCEMENT OF ORDERS

Electronic transmission of data to Department of Justice; Domestic Violence Restraining Order System. §6380.
Enforcement of order. §6381.
Availability of information concerning order. §6382.
Service of restraining or protective order by law enforcement officer; Verbal notice of order; Immunity. §6383.
Personal service not required. §6384.
Notice to Department of Justice. §6385.
Appointment of counsel and payment of attorney's fees and costs. §6386.
Clerk to provide petitioner with copies of order. §6387.
Criminal penalty for violation of order. §6388.
Person subject to protective order prohibited from owning or possessing firearm; Relinquishment of firearm; Employment exemption [Repealed January 1, 2026]. §6389.
Relinquishment of firearms and ammunition upon issuance of protective order [Operative January 1, 2026]. § 6389.

§6380. Electronic transmission of data to Department of Justice; Domestic Violence Restraining Order System

(a) Each county, with the approval of the Department of Justice, shall, by July 1, 1996, develop a procedure, using existing systems, for the electronic transmission of data, as described in subdivision (b), to the Department of Justice. The data shall be electronically transmitted through the California Law Enforcement Telecommunications System (CLETS) of the Department of Justice by law enforcement personnel, or with the approval of the Department of Justice, court personnel, or another appropriate agency capable of maintaining and preserving the integrity of both the CLETS and the California Restraining and Protective Order System, as described in subdivision (e). Data entry is required to be entered only once under the requirements of this section, unless the order is served at a later time. A portion of all fees payable to the Department of Justice under subdivision (a) of Section 1203.097 of the Penal Code for the entry of the information required under this section, based upon the proportion of the costs incurred by the local agency and those incurred by the Department of Justice, shall be transferred to the local agency actually providing the data. All data with respect to criminal court protective orders issued, modified, extended, or terminated under Section 136.2 of the Penal Code, and all data filed with the court on the required Judicial Council forms with respect to protective orders, including their issuance, modification, extension, or termination, to which this division applies pursuant to Section 6221, shall be transmitted by the court or its designee within one business day to law enforcement personnel by either one of the following methods:

(1) Transmitting a physical copy of the order to a local law enforcement agency authorized by the Department of Justice to enter orders into CLETS.

(2) With the approval of the Department of Justice, entering the order into CLETS directly.

(b) Upon the issuance of a protective order to which this division applies pursuant to Section 6221, or the issuance of a temporary restraining order or injunction relating to harassment, unlawful violence, or the threat of violence pursuant to Section 527.6, 527.8, or 527.85 of the Code of Civil Procedure, or the issuance of a criminal court protective order under Section 136.2 of the Penal Code, or **a retail crime restraining order under Section 490.8 of the Penal Code, or** the issuance of a juvenile court restraining order related to domestic violence pursuant to Section 213.5, 304, or 362.4 of the Welfare and Institutions Code, or the issuance of a protective order pursuant to Section 15657.03 of the Welfare and Institutions Code, or upon registration with the court clerk of a domestic violence protective or restraining order issued by the tribunal of another state, as defined in Section 6401, and including any of the foregoing orders issued in connection with an order for modification of a custody or visitation order issued pursuant to a dissolution, legal separation, nullity, or paternity proceeding the Department of Justice shall be immediately notified of the contents of the order and the following information:

(1) The name, race, date of birth, and other personal descriptive information of the respondent as required by a form prescribed by the Department of Justice.

(2) The names of the protected persons.

(3) The date of issuance of the order.

(4) The duration or expiration date of the order.

(5) The terms and conditions of the protective order, including stay-away, no-contact, residency exclusion, custody, and visitation provisions of the order.

(6) The department or division number and the address of the court.

(7) Whether or not the order was served upon the respondent.

(8) The terms and conditions of any restrictions on the ownership or possession of firearms.

All available information shall be included; however, the inability to provide all categories of information shall not delay the entry of the information available.

(c) The information conveyed to the Department of Justice shall also indicate whether the respondent was present in court to be informed of the contents of the court order. The respondent's presence in court shall provide proof of service of notice of the terms of the protective order. The respondent's failure to appear shall also be included in the information provided to the Department of Justice.

(d)(1) Within one business day of service, a law enforcement officer who served a protective order shall submit the proof of service directly into the Department of Justice California Restraining and Protective Order System, including the officer's name and law enforcement agency, and shall transmit the original proof of service form to the issuing court.

(2) Within one business day of receipt of proof of service by a person other than a law enforcement officer, the clerk of the court shall submit the proof of service of a protective order directly into the Department of Justice California Restraining and Protective Order System, including the name of the person who served the order. If the court is unable to provide this notification to the Department of Justice by electronic transmission, the court shall, within one business day of receipt, transmit a copy of the proof of service to a local law enforcement agency. The local law enforcement agency shall submit the proof of service directly into the Department of Justice California Restraining and Protective Order System within one business day of receipt from the court.

(e) The Department of Justice shall maintain a California Restraining and Protective Order System and shall make available to court clerks and law enforcement personnel, through computer access, all information regarding the protective and restraining orders and injunctions described in subdivision (b), whether or not served upon the respondent.

(f) If a court issues a modification, extension, or termination of a protective order, it shall be on forms adopted by the Judicial Council of California and that have been approved by the Department of Justice, and the transmitting agency for the county shall immediately notify the Department of Justice, by electronic transmission, of the terms of the modification, extension, or termination.

(g) The Judicial Council shall assist local courts charged with the responsibility for issuing protective orders by developing informational packets describing the general procedures for obtaining a domestic violence restraining order and indicating the appropriate Judicial Council forms. The informational packets shall include a design, that local courts shall complete, that describes local court procedures and maps to enable applicants to locate filing windows and appropriate courts, and shall also include information on how to return proofs of service, including mailing addresses and fax numbers. The court clerk shall provide a fee waiver form to all applicants for domestic violence protective orders. The court clerk shall provide all Judicial Council forms required by this chapter to applicants free of charge. The informational packet shall also contain a statement that the protective order is enforceable in any state, as defined in Section 6401, and general information about agencies in other jurisdictions that may be contacted regarding enforcement of an order issued by a court of this state.

(h) For the purposes of this part, "electronic transmission" shall include computer access through the California Law Enforcement Telecommunications System (CLETS).

(i) Only protective and restraining orders issued on forms adopted by the Judicial Council of California and that have been approved by the Department of Justice shall be transmitted to the Department of Justice. However, this provision does not apply to a valid protective or restraining order related to domestic or family violence issued by a tribunal of another state, as defined in Section 6401. Those orders shall, upon request, be registered pursuant to Section 6404.

(j)(1) All protective orders subject to transmittal to CLETS pursuant to this section are required to be so transmitted.

(2) This subdivision does not constitute a change in, but is declaratory of, existing law. **Leg.H.** Added Stats 1994 ch 872 §2 (AB 3034). Amended Stats 1995 ch 731 §1 (AB 233); Stats 1996 ch 1139 §1 (AB 2647), ch 1140 §1.5 (AB 2231); Stats 1998 ch 187 §1 (AB 1531), ch 581 §17 (AB 2801), ch 702 §1 (AB 2177), ch 707 §2.7 (SB 1682); Stats 1999 ch 83 §52 (SB 966) (ch 661 prevails), ch 561 §4 (AB 59), ch 661 §5.5 (AB 825); Stats 2001ch 698 §2 (AB 160), (ch 816 prevails), ch 816 §1.5 (AB 731); Stats 2002 ch 265 §1 (SB 1627); Stats 2005 ch 631 §2 (SB 720), effective January 1, 2006; Stats 2010 ch 572 §20 (AB 1596), effective January 1, 2011, operative January 1, 2012; Stats 2018 ch 89 §2 (SB 1089), effective January 1, 2019; Stats 2019 ch 115 §68 (AB 1817), effective January 1, 2020; Stats 2019 ch 497 §112 (AB 991), effective January 1, 2020 (ch 115 prevails); Stats 2024 ch 169 §1 (AB 3209), effective January 1, 2025.

Prior Law: Former Fam C §6380, similar to the present section, was added Stats 1993 ch 219 §154 and repealed Stats 1994 ch 872 §1.

Editor's Notes— 2018 Note: It is the intent of the Legislature in enacting this measure to clarify that all protective orders subject to transmittal to CLETS are required to be so transmitted. Stats 2018 ch 89 §1(a) (SB 1089).

§6380.5. [Section repealed 2001]

Leg.H. Added Stats 1996 ch 1140 §2 (AB 2231). Amended Stats 1998 ch 702 §2 (AB 2177); Stats 1999 ch 661 §6 (AB 825), ch 662 §4.5 (SB 218). Repealed Stats 2001 ch 816 §2 (AB 731). The repealed section related to valid order concerning to domestic or family violence.

§6381. Enforcement of order

(a) Notwithstanding Section 6380 and subject to subdivision (b), an order issued under this part is enforceable in any place in this state.

(b) An order issued under this part is not enforceable by a law enforcement agency of a political subdivision unless that law enforcement agency has received a copy of the order, or the officer enforcing the order has been shown a copy of the order or has obtained information, through the California Restraining and Protective Order System maintained by the Department of Justice, of the contents of the order, as described in subdivision (b).

(c) The data contained in the California Restraining and Protective Order System shall be deemed to be original, self-authenticating, documentary evidence of the court orders. Oral notification of the terms of the orders shall be sufficient notice for enforcement under subdivision (g) of

Section 136.2 and Section 273.6 of the Penal Code. **Leg.H.** Added Stats 1993 ch 219 §154 (AB 1500). Amended Stats 1994 ch 872 §3 (AB 3034); Stats 1999 ch 661 §7 (AB 825); Stats 2019 ch 115 §69 (AB 1817), effective January 1, 2020.

§6382. Availability of information concerning order

Each appropriate law enforcement agency shall make available to any law enforcement officer responding to the scene of reported domestic violence, through an existing system for verification, information as to the existence, terms, and current status of an order issued under this part. **Leg.H.** Added Stats 1993 ch 219 §154 (AB 1500).

§6383. Service of restraining or protective order by law enforcement officer; Verbal notice of order; Immunity

(a) A temporary restraining order, emergency protective order, or an order issued after hearing pursuant to this part shall, on request of the petitioner, be served on the respondent, whether or not the respondent has been taken into custody, either by a law enforcement officer, excluding those defined in subdivision (a) of Section 830.5 of the Penal Code, who is present at the scene of reported domestic violence involving the parties to the proceeding or who receives a request from the petitioner to provide service of the order.

(b)(1) The petitioner shall provide the officer with an endorsed copy of the order and a proof of service that the officer shall complete and transmit to the issuing court.

(2) Service shall be provided pursuant to Section 6389 of the Family Code.

(3) Notwithstanding any other law, a fee shall not be charged to the petitioner for service of an order described in subdivision (a).

(4) If a firearm is obtained at the scene of a domestic violence incident or during service as provided in this section, law enforcement shall enter, or cause to be entered, the firearm into the Department of Justice Automated Firearms System pursuant to Section 11108.2 of the Penal Code.

(c) It is a rebuttable presumption that the proof of service was signed on the date of service.

(d) Upon receiving information at the scene of a domestic violence incident that a protective order has been issued under this part, or that a person who has been taken into custody is the respondent to that order, if the protected person cannot produce an endorsed copy of the order, a law enforcement officer shall immediately inquire of the California Restraining and Protective Order System to verify the existence of the order.

(e) If the law enforcement officer determines that a protective order has been issued but not served, the officer shall immediately notify the respondent of the terms of the order and where a written copy of the order can be obtained, and the officer shall, at that time, also enforce the order. The law enforcement officer's verbal notice of the terms of the order shall constitute service of the order and is sufficient notice for the purposes of this section and for the purposes of Sections 273.6 and 29825 of the Penal Code.

(f) If a report is required under Section 13730 of the Penal Code, or if no report is required, then in the daily incident log, the officer shall provide the name and assignment of the officer notifying the respondent pursuant to subdivision (e) and the case number of the order.

(g) Upon service of the order outside of the court, a law enforcement officer shall advise the respondent to go to the local court to obtain a copy of the order containing the full terms and conditions of the order.

(h)(1) There shall be no civil liability on the part of, and no cause of action for false arrest or false imprisonment against, a peace officer who makes an arrest pursuant to a protective or restraining order that is regular upon its face, if the peace officer, in making the arrest, acts in good faith and has reasonable cause to believe that the person against whom the order is issued has notice of the order and has committed an act in violation of the order.

(2) If there is more than one order issued and one of the orders is an emergency protective order that has precedence in enforcement pursuant to paragraph (1) of subdivision (c) of Section 136.2 of the Penal Code, the peace officer shall enforce the emergency protective order. If there is more than one order issued, none of the orders issued is an emergency protective order that has precedence in enforcement, and one of the orders issued is a no-contact order, as described in Section 6320, the peace officer shall enforce the no-contact order. If there is more than one civil order regarding the same parties and neither an emergency protective order that has precedence in enforcement nor a no-contact order has been issued, the peace officer shall enforce the order that was issued last. If there are both civil and criminal orders regarding the same parties and neither an emergency protective order that has precedence in enforcement nor a no-contact order has been issued, the peace officer shall enforce the criminal order issued last, subject to the provisions of subdivisions (h) and (i) of Section 136.2 of the Penal Code. This section does not exonerate a peace officer from liability for the unreasonable use of force in the enforcement of the order. The immunities afforded by this section shall not affect the availability of any other immunity that may apply, including, but not limited to, Sections 820.2 and 820.4 of the Government Code.

(i) A peace officer listed in Section 18250 of the Penal Code shall take temporary custody of any firearm or other deadly weapon in plain sight or discovered pursuant to a consensual or otherwise lawful search as necessary for the protection of the peace officer or other persons present in any of the following circumstances:

(1) The peace officer is at the scene of a domestic violence incident involving a threat to human life or a physical assault.

(2) The peace officer is serving a protective order issued pursuant to this part.

(3) The peace officer is serving a gun violence restraining order issued pursuant to Division 3.2 (commencing with Section 18100) of Title 2 of Part 6 of the Penal Code. **Leg.H.** Added Stats 1993 ch 219 §154 (AB 1500). Amended Stats 1994 ch 872 §4 (AB 3034); Stats 1997 ch 347 §1 (AB 356); Stats 1999 ch 661 §8 (AB 825); Stats 2001 ch 698 §3 (AB 160); Stats 2005 ch 467 §2 (AB 429), effective January 1, 2006; Stats 2010 ch 178 §24 (SB 1115), effective January 1, 2011, operative January 1, 2012; Stats 2013 ch 263 §2 (AB 176), effective January 1, 2014, operative July 1, 2014; Stats 2014 ch 71 §54 (SB 1304), effective January 1, 2015; Stats 2019 ch 115 §70 (AB 1817), effective January 1, 2020; Stats 2023 ch 242 §1 (AB 818), effective January 1, 2024.

2001 Note: The provisions of this act shall be implemented on January 1, 2003. Stats 2001 ch 698 §5.

§6384. Personal service not required

(a) If a respondent named in an order issued under this part after a hearing has not been served personally with the order but has received actual notice of the existence and substance of the order through personal appearance in court to hear the terms of the order from the court, no additional proof of service is required for enforcement of the order.

If a respondent named in a temporary restraining order or emergency protective order is personally served with the order and notice of hearing with respect to a restraining order or protective order based on the temporary restraining order or emergency protective order, but the respondent does not appear at the hearing either in person or by counsel, and the terms and conditions of the restraining order or protective order issued at the hearing are identical to the temporary restraining or emergency protective order, except for the duration of the order, the restraining order or protective order issued at the hearing may be served on the respondent by first-class mail sent to the respondent at the most current address for the respondent that is available to the court.

(b) The Judicial Council forms for orders issued under this part shall contain a statement in substantially the following form:

"If you have been personally served with a temporary restraining order and notice of hearing, but you do not appear at the hearing either in person or by a lawyer, and a restraining order that is the same as this temporary restraining order except for the expiration date is issued at the hearing, a copy of the order will be served on you by mail at the following address:

_____

If that address is not correct or you wish to verify that the temporary restraining order was converted to a restraining order at the hearing without substantive change and to find out the duration of that order, contact the clerk of the court." **Leg.H.** Added Stats 1993 ch 219 §154 (AB 1500). Amended Stats 1997 ch 347 §2 (AB 356); Stats 2010 ch 572 §21 (AB 1596), effective January 1, 2011, operative January 1, 2012.

§6385. Notice to Department of Justice

(a) Proof of service of the protective order is not required for the purposes of Section 6380 if the order indicates on its face that both parties were personally present at the hearing at which the order was issued and that, for the purpose of Section 6384, no proof of service is required, or if the order was served by a law enforcement officer pursuant to Section 6383.

(b) The failure of the petitioner to provide the Department of Justice with the personal descriptive information regarding the person restrained does not invalidate the protective order.

(c) There is no civil liability on the part of, and no cause of action arises against, an employee of a local law enforcement agency, a court, or the Department of Justice, acting within the scope of employment, if a person described in Section 29825 of the Penal Code unlawfully purchases or receives or attempts to purchase or receive a firearm and a person is injured by that firearm or a person who is otherwise entitled to receive a firearm is denied a firearm and either wrongful action is due to a failure of a court to provide the notification provided for in this chapter. **Leg.H.** Added Stats 1993 ch 219 §154 (AB 1500). Amended Stats 1994 ch 872 §5 (AB 3034); Stats 1995 ch 731 §2 (AB 233); Stats 2002 ch 265 §2 (SB 1627); Stats 2010 ch 178 §25 (SB 1115), effective January 1, 2011, operative January 1, 2012.

§6386. Appointment of counsel and payment of attorney's fees and costs

(a) The court may, in its discretion, appoint counsel to represent the petitioner in a proceeding to enforce the terms of a protective order, as defined in Section 6218.

(b) In a proceeding in which private counsel was appointed by the court pursuant to subdivision (a), the court may order the respondent to pay reasonable attorney's fees and costs incurred by the petitioner. **Leg.H.** Added Stats 1993 ch 219 §154 (AB 1500).

§6387. Clerk to provide petitioner with copies of order

The court shall order the clerk of the court to provide to a petitioner, without cost, up to three certified, stamped, and endorsed copies of any order issued under this part, and of an extension, modification, or termination of the order. **Leg.H.** Added Stats 1993 ch 219 §154 (AB 1500). Amended Stats 2001 ch 176 §5 (SB 210); Stats 2010 ch 572 §22 (AB 1596), effective January 1, 2011, operative January 1, 2012.

§6388. Criminal penalty for violation of order

A willful and knowing violation of a protective order, as defined in Section 6218, is a crime punishable as provided by Section 273.6 of the Penal Code. **Leg.H.** Added Stats 1993 ch 219 §154 (AB 1500).

§6389. Person subject to protective order prohibited from owning or possessing firearm; Relinquishment of firearm; Employment exemption [Repealed January 1, 2026]

(a) A person subject to a protective order, as defined in Section 6218, shall not own, possess, purchase, or receive a firearm or ammunition while that protective order is in effect. A person who owns, possesses, purchases, or receives, or attempts to purchase or receive, a firearm or ammunition while the protective order is in effect is punishable pursuant to Section 29825 of the Penal Code.

(b) On all forms providing notice that a protective order has been requested or granted, the Judicial Council shall include a notice that, upon service of the order, the respondent shall be ordered to relinquish possession or control of any firearms or ammunition and not to purchase or receive or attempt to purchase or receive any firearms or ammunition for a period not to exceed the duration of the restraining order.

(c)(1) Upon issuance of a protective order, as defined in Section 6218, the court shall order the respondent to relinquish any firearm or ammunition in the respondent's immediate possession or control or subject to the respondent's immediate possession or control.

(2) The relinquishment ordered pursuant to paragraph (1) shall occur by immediately surrendering the firearm or ammunition in a safe manner, upon request of a law enforcement officer, to the control of the officer, after being served with the protective order. A law enforcement officer serving a protective order that indicates that the respondent possesses weapons or ammunition shall request that the firearm or ammunition be immediately surrendered. Alternatively, if a request is not made by a law enforcement officer, the relinquishment shall occur within 24 hours of being served with the order, by either surrendering the firearm or ammunition in a safe manner to the control of local law enforcement officials, or by selling, transferring, or relinquishing for storage pursuant to Section 29830 of the Penal Code, the firearm or ammunition to a licensed gun dealer, as specified in Article 1 (commencing with Section 26700) and Article 2 (commencing with Section 26800) of Chapter 2 of Division 6 of Title 4 of Part 6 of the Penal Code. The law enforcement officer or licensed gun dealer taking possession of the firearm or ammunition pursuant to this subdivision shall issue a receipt to the person relinquishing the firearm or ammunition at the time of relinquishment. A person ordered to relinquish a firearm or ammunition pursuant to this subdivision shall, within 48 hours after being served with the order, do both of the following:

(A) File, with the court that issued the protective order, the receipt showing the firearm or ammunition was surrendered to a local law enforcement agency or sold to a licensed gun dealer. Failure to timely file a receipt shall constitute a violation of the protective order.

(B) File a copy of the receipt described in subparagraph (A) with the law enforcement agency that served the protective order. Failure to timely file a copy of the receipt shall constitute a violation of the protective order.

(3) The forms for protective orders adopted by the Judicial Council and approved by the Department of Justice shall require the petitioner to describe the number, types, and locations of any firearms or ammunition presently known by the petitioner to be possessed or controlled by the respondent.

(4) A court holding a hearing on this matter shall review the file to determine whether the receipt has been filed and inquire of the respondent whether they have complied with the requirement. Violations of the firearms prohibition of any restraining order under this section shall be reported to the prosecuting attorney in the jurisdiction where the order has been issued within two business days of the court hearing unless the restrained party provides a receipt showing compliance at a subsequent hearing or by direct filing with the clerk of the court.

(5) Every law enforcement agency in the state shall develop, adopt, and implement written policies and standards for law enforcement officers who request immediate relinquishment of firearms or ammunition.

(d) If the respondent declines to relinquish possession of a firearm or ammunition based on the assertion of the right against self-incrimination, as provided by the Fifth Amendment to the United States Constitution and Section 15 of Article I of the California Constitution, the court may grant use immunity for the act of relinquishing the firearm or ammunition required under this section.

(e) A local law enforcement agency may charge the respondent a fee for the storage of a firearm or ammunition pursuant to this section. This fee shall not exceed the actual cost incurred by the local law enforcement agency for the storage of the firearm or ammunition. For purposes of this subdivision, "actual cost" means expenses directly related to taking possession of a firearm or ammunition, storing the firearm or ammunition, and surrendering possession of the firearm or ammunition to a licensed dealer as defined in Section 26700 of the Penal Code or to the respondent.

(f) The restraining order requiring a person to relinquish a firearm or ammunition pursuant to subdivision (c) shall state on its face that the respondent is prohibited from owning, possessing, purchasing, or receiving a firearm or ammunition while the protective order is in effect and that the firearm or ammunition shall be relinquished to the local law enforcement agency for that jurisdiction or sold to a licensed gun dealer, and that proof of surrender or sale shall be filed with the court within a specified period of receipt of the order. The order shall also state on its face the expiration date for relinquishment. This section does not limit a respondent's right under existing law to petition the court at a later date for modification of the order.

(g) The restraining order requiring a person to relinquish a firearm or ammunition pursuant to subdivision (c) shall prohibit the person from possessing or controlling a firearm or ammunition for the duration of the order. At the expiration of the order, the local law enforcement agency shall return possession of the surrendered firearm or ammunition to the respondent, within five days after the expiration of the relinquishment order, unless the local law enforcement agency determines that (1) the firearm or ammunition has been stolen, (2) the respondent is prohibited from possessing a firearm or ammunition because the respondent is in a prohibited class for the possession of firearms or ammunition, as defined in Chapter 2 (commencing with Section 29800) and Chapter 3 (commencing with Section 29900) of Division 9 of Title 4 of Part 6 of the Penal Code, Section 30305 of the Penal Code, and Sections 8100 and 8103 of the Welfare and Institutions Code, or (3) another successive restraining order is issued against the respondent under this section. If the local law enforcement agency determines that the respondent is the legal owner of a firearm or ammunition deposited with the local law enforcement agency and is prohibited from possessing a firearm or ammunition, the respondent shall be entitled to sell or transfer the firearm or ammunition to a licensed dealer as defined in Section 26700 of the Penal Code. If the firearm or ammunition has been stolen, the firearm or ammunition shall be restored to the lawful owner upon the owner identifying the firearm and ammunition and providing proof of ownership.

(h) The court may, as part of the relinquishment order, grant an exemption from the relinquishment requirements of this section for a particular firearm or ammunition if the respondent **is not otherwise prohibited from owning, possessing, controlling, or purchasing a firearm and ammunition under state or federal law and one of the following applies:**

(1)(A) The [1] **respondent is currently employed as a sworn peace officer who is required,** as a condition of continued [2] **employment, to carry a firearm, ammunition, or firearm and ammunition and** the current employer is unable to reassign the [3] **peace officer** to another position where **use of** a **specified** firearm or ammunition is unnecessary. [4] **In such a case,** a court may allow the peace officer to continue to carry a [5] **specified firearm, ammunition, or firearm and** ammunition, either on duty or off duty, if the court finds by a preponderance of the evidence [6], in writing or on the record, both of the following:

(i) The peace officer's personal safety depends on the ability to carry that specific firearm, ammunition, or firearm and ammunition outside of scheduled work hours.

(ii) The peace officer does not pose an additional threat of harm to a protected party or the public by having access to that specific firearm, ammunition, or firearm and ammunition, including whether the peace officer might use the firearm for a purpose other than as permitted under this paragraph.

(B) Prior to making this finding, the court shall require a mandatory psychological evaluation of the peace officer by a licensed mental health professional with domestic violence expertise. The court shall consider the results of an evaluation and may require the peace officer to enter into counseling or another remedial treatment program to deal with a propensity for domestic violence.

(2)(A) The respondent is not a peace officer but is required to carry a specific firearm, ammunition, or firearm and ammunition during scheduled work hours as a condition of continued employment, the current employer is unable to reassign the respondent to another position where the firearm, ammunition, or firearm and ammunition is unnecessary. In such a case, a court may grant an exemption to allow the respondent to possess a specific firearm, ammunition, or firearm and ammunition only during scheduled work hours if the court finds by a preponderance of the evidence, in writing or on the record, that the respondent does not pose an additional threat of harm to a protected party or the public by having access to the specific firearm, ammunition, or firearm and ammunition only during scheduled work hours, including whether the respondent might utilize the firearm, ammunition, or firearm and ammunition for a purpose other than as permitted under this paragraph.

(B) To assist the court in making this determination, the court may order a psychological evaluation of the respondent by a licensed mental health professional with domestic violence expertise.

(C) If the court grants an exemption pursuant to this paragraph, the order shall provide that the specific firearm, ammunition, or firearm and ammunition shall be in the physical possession of the respondent only during scheduled work hours and that the exemption does not authorize the respondent to possess any other firearm or ammunition, or to possess the specific firearm, ammunition, or firearm and ammunition outside of scheduled work hours.

(i)(1) If an exemption is granted under subdivision (h) during the pendency of a temporary restraining order and the court subsequently issues a restraining order after hearing on the same application, the court shall review and make a finding, in writing or on the record, as to whether the exemption remains appropriate, based upon the criteria set forth in paragraph (1) or (2) of subdivision (h), as applicable, in light of the issuance of the order after hearing. This review and finding shall occur at the time the restraining order after hearing is issued.

(2) If an exemption is granted and the court subsequently renews the restraining order pursuant to Section 6345 at the request of a party, the court shall review and make a finding, in writing or on the record, as to whether the exemption remains appropriate, based upon the criteria set forth in paragraph (1) or (2) of subdivision (h), as applicable, in light of the renewal. This finding shall be made at the time the restraining order after hearing is renewed.

(3) The court may terminate or modify an exemption granted pursuant to this paragraph at any time if the respondent demonstrates a need to modify the specific firearm, ammunition, or firearm and ammunition authorized by the court pursuant to subdivision (h) or if the respondent no longer meets the requirements in this section or otherwise violates the restraining order.

[7] **(j)** During the period of the relinquishment order, a respondent is entitled to make one sale of all firearms or ammunition that are in the possession of a local law enforcement agency pursuant to this section. A licensed gun dealer, who presents a local law enforcement agency with a bill of sale indicating that all firearms or ammunition owned by the respondent that are in the possession of the local law enforcement agency have been sold by the respondent to the licensed gun dealer, shall be given possession of those firearms or ammunition, at the location where a respondent's firearms or ammunition are stored, within five days of presenting the local law enforcement agency with a bill of sale.

[8] **(k)** The disposition of any unclaimed property under this section shall be made pursuant to Section 1413 of the Penal Code.

[9] **(*l*)** The relinquishment of a firearm to a law enforcement agency pursuant to subdivision (g) or the return of a firearm to a person pursuant to subdivision (g) shall not be subject to the requirements of Section 27545 of the Penal Code.

[10] **(m)** If the respondent notifies the court that the respondent owns a firearm or ammunition that is not in their immediate possession, the court may limit the order to exclude that firearm or ammunition if the judge is satisfied the respondent is unable to gain access to that firearm or ammunition while the protective order is in effect.

[11] **(n)** A respondent to a protective order who violates an order issued pursuant to this section shall be punished under the provisions of Section 29825 of the Penal Code.

(o) This section shall remain in effect only until January 1, 2026, and as of that date is repealed. Leg.H. Added Stats 1994 ch 871 §2 (SB 1278). Amended Stats 1999 ch 662 §5 (SB 218); Stats 2003 ch 498 §5 (SB 226); Stats 2004 ch 250 §2 (SB 1391); Stats 2006 ch 467 §1 (SB 585), effective January 1, 2007; Stats 2010 ch 178 §26 (SB 1115), effective January 1, 2011, operative January 1, 2012; Stats 2010 ch 572 §23 (AB 1596), effective January 1, 2011, operative January 1, 2012 (ch 572 prevails); Stats 2011 ch 285 §6 (AB 1402), effective January 1, 2012; Stats 2012 ch 765 §2 (SB 1433), effective January 1, 2013; Stats 2019 ch 115 §71 (AB 1817), effective January 1, 2020; Stats 2021 ch 685 §7 (SB 320), effective January 1, 2022; Stats 2024 ch 535 §1.2 (AB 2759), effective January 1, 2025; Stats 2024 ch 544 §8.5 (SB 899), effective January 1, 2025, repealed January 1, 2026 (ch 544 prevails).

§6389. 2024 Deletes. [1] can show that a particular firearm or ammunition is necessary [2] employment and that [3] respondent [4] If an exemption is granted pursuant to this subdivision, the order shall provide that the firearm or ammunition shall be in the physical possession of the respondent only during scheduled work hours and during travel to and from the place of employment. When a peace officer is required, as a condition of employment, to carry a firearm or ammunition and whose personal safety depends on the ability to carry a firearm or ammunition [5] firearm or [6] that the officer does not pose a threat of harm. Prior to making this finding, the court shall require a mandatory psychological evaluation of the peace officer and may require the peace officer to enter into counseling or other remedial treatment program to deal with any propensity for domestic violence. [7] (i) [8] (j) [9] (k) [10] (l) [11] (m)

§ 6389. Relinquishment of firearms and ammunition upon issuance of protective order [Operative January 1, 2026]

(a) A person subject to a protective order, as defined in Section 6218, shall not own, possess, purchase, or receive a firearm or ammunition while that protective order is in effect. A person who owns, possesses, purchases, or receives, or attempts to purchase or receive, a firearm or ammunition while the protective order is in effect is punishable pursuant to Section 29825 of the Penal Code.

(b) On all forms providing notice that a protective order has been requested or granted, the Judicial Council shall include a notice that, upon service of the order, the respondent shall be ordered to relinquish possession or control of any firearms or ammunition and not to purchase or receive or attempt to purchase or receive any firearms or ammunition for a period not to exceed the duration of the restraining order.

(c)(1) Upon issuance of a protective order, as defined in Section 6218, the court shall order the respondent to relinquish any firearm or ammunition in the respondent's immediate possession or control or subject to the respondent's immediate possession or control.

(2) The relinquishment ordered pursuant to paragraph (1) shall occur by immediately surrendering the firearm or ammunition in a safe manner, upon request of a law enforcement officer, to the control of the officer, after being served with the protective order. A law enforcement officer serving a protective order that indicates that the respondent possesses weapons or ammunition shall request that the firearm or ammunition be immediately surrendered. Alternatively, if a request is not made by a law enforcement officer, the relinquishment shall occur within 24 hours of being served with the order, by either surrendering the firearm or ammunition in a safe manner to the control of local law enforcement officials, or by selling, transferring, or relinquishing for storage pursuant to Section 29830 of the Penal Code, the firearm or ammunition to a licensed gun dealer, as specified in Article 1 (commencing with Section 26700) and Article 2 (commencing with Section 26800) of Chapter 2 of Division 6 of Title 4 of Part 6 of the Penal Code. The law enforcement officer or licensed gun dealer taking possession of the firearm or ammunition pursuant to this subdivision shall issue a receipt to the person relinquishing the firearm or ammunition at the time of relinquishment. A person ordered to relinquish a firearm or ammunition pursuant to this subdivision shall, within 48 hours after being served with the order, do both of the following:

(A) File, with the court that issued the protective order, the receipt showing the firearm or ammunition was surrendered to a local law enforcement agency or sold to a licensed gun dealer. Failure to timely file a receipt shall constitute a violation of the protective order.

(B) File a copy of the receipt described in subparagraph (A) with the law enforcement agency that served the protective order. Failure to timely file a copy of the receipt shall constitute a violation of the protective order.

(3) The forms for protective orders adopted by the Judicial Council and approved by the Department of Justice shall require the petitioner to describe the number, types, and locations of any firearms or ammunition presently known by the petitioner to be possessed or controlled by the respondent.

(4) A court holding a hearing on this matter shall review the file to determine whether the receipt has been filed and inquire of the respondent whether they have complied with the requirement. Violations of the firearms prohibition of any restraining order under this section shall be reported to the prosecuting attorney in the jurisdiction where the order has been issued within two business days of the court hearing unless the restrained party provides a receipt showing compliance at a subsequent hearing or by direct filing with the clerk of the court.

(5) Every law enforcement agency in the state shall develop, adopt, and implement written policies and standards for law enforcement officers who request immediate relinquishment of firearms or ammunition.

(d) If the respondent declines to relinquish possession of a firearm or ammunition based on the assertion of the right against self-incrimination, as provided by the Fifth Amendment to the United States Constitution and Section 15 of Article I of the California Constitution, the court may grant use immunity for the act of relinquishing the firearm or ammunition required under this section.

(e) A local law enforcement agency may charge the respondent a fee for the storage of a firearm or ammunition pursuant to this section. This fee shall not exceed the actual cost incurred by the local law enforcement agency for the storage of the firearm or ammunition. For purposes of this subdivision, "actual cost" means expenses directly related to taking possession of a firearm or ammunition, storing the firearm or ammunition, and surrendering possession of the firearm or ammunition to a licensed dealer as defined in Section 26700 of the Penal Code or to the respondent.

(f) The restraining order requiring a person to relinquish a firearm or ammunition pursuant to subdivision (c) shall state on its face that the respondent is prohibited from owning, possessing, purchasing, or receiving a firearm or ammunition while the protective order is in effect and that the firearm or ammunition shall be relinquished to the local law enforcement agency for that jurisdiction or sold to a licensed gun dealer, and that proof of surrender or sale shall be filed with the court within a specified period of receipt of the order. The order shall also state on its face the expiration date for relinquishment. This section does not limit a respondent's right under existing law to petition the court at a later date for modification of the order.

(g) The restraining order requiring a person to relinquish a firearm or ammunition pursuant to subdivision (c) shall prohibit the person from possessing or controlling a firearm or ammunition for the duration of the order. At the expiration of the order, the local law enforcement agency shall return possession of the surrendered firearm or ammunition to the respondent, within five days after the expiration of the relinquishment order, unless the local law enforcement agency determines that (1) the firearm or ammunition has been stolen, (2) the respondent is prohibited from possessing a firearm or ammunition because the respondent is in a prohibited class for the possession of firearms or ammunition, as defined in Chapter 2 (commencing with Section 29800) and Chapter 3 (commencing with Section 29900) of Division 9 of Title 4 of Part 6 of the Penal Code, Section 30305 of the Penal Code, and Sections 8100 and 8103 of the Welfare and Institutions Code, or (3) another successive restraining order is issued against the respondent under this section. If the local law enforcement agency determines that the respondent is the legal owner of a firearm or ammunition deposited with the local law enforcement agency and is prohibited from possessing a firearm or ammunition, the respondent shall be entitled to sell or transfer the firearm or ammunition to a licensed dealer as defined in Section 26700 of the Penal Code. If the firearm or ammunition has been stolen, the firearm or ammunition shall be restored to the lawful owner upon the owner identifying the firearm and ammunition and providing proof of ownership.

(h) The court may, as part of the relinquishment order, grant an exemption from the relinquishment requirements of this section for a particular firearm or ammunition if the respondent is not otherwise prohibited from owning, possessing, controlling, or purchasing a firearm and ammunition under state or federal law and one of the following applies:

(1)(A) The respondent is currently employed as a sworn peace officer who is required, as a condition of continued employment, to carry a firearm, ammunition, or firearm and ammunition and the current employer is unable to reassign the peace officer to another position where use of a specified firearm or ammunition is unnecessary. In such a case, a court may allow the peace officer to continue to carry a specified firearm, ammunition, or firearm and ammunition, either on duty or off duty, if the court finds by a preponderance of the evidence, in writing or on the record, both of the following:

(i) The peace officer's personal safety depends on the ability to carry that specific firearm, ammunition, or firearm and ammunition outside of scheduled work hours.

(ii) The peace officer does not pose an additional threat of harm to a protected party or the public by having access to that specific firearm, ammunition, or firearm and ammunition, including whether the peace officer might use the firearm for a purpose other than as permitted under this paragraph.

(B) Prior to making this finding, the court shall require a mandatory psychological evaluation of the peace officer by a licensed mental health professional with domestic violence expertise. The court shall consider the results of an evaluation and may require the peace officer to enter into counseling or another remedial treatment program to deal with a propensity for domestic violence.

(2)(A) The respondent is not a peace officer but is required to carry a specific firearm, ammunition, or firearm and ammunition during scheduled work hours as a condition of continued employment, the current employer is unable to reassign the respondent to another position where the firearm, ammunition, or firearm and ammunition is unnecessary. In such a case, a court may grant an exemption to allow the respondent to possess a specific firearm, ammunition, or firearm and ammunition only during scheduled work hours if the court finds by a preponderance of the evidence, in writing or on the record, that the respondent does not pose an additional threat of harm to a protected party or the public by having access to the specific firearm, ammunition, or firearm and ammunition only during scheduled work hours, including whether the respondent might utilize the firearm, ammunition, or firearm and ammunition for a purpose other than as permitted under this paragraph.

(B) To assist the court in making this determination, the court may order a psychological evaluation of the respondent by a licensed mental health professional with domestic violence expertise.

(C) If the court grants an exemption pursuant to this paragraph, the order shall provide that the specific firearm, ammunition, or firearm and ammunition shall be in the physical possession of the respondent only during scheduled work hours and that the exemption does not authorize the respondent to possess any other firearm or ammunition, or to possess the specific firearm, ammunition, or firearm and ammunition outside of scheduled work hours.

(i)(1) If an exemption is granted under subdivision (h) during the pendency of a temporary restraining order and the court subsequently issues a restraining order after hearing on the same application, the court shall review and make a finding, in writing or on the record, as to whether the exemption remains appropriate, based upon the criteria set forth in paragraph (1) or (2) of subdivision (h), as applicable, in light of the issuance of the order after hearing. This review and finding shall occur at the time the restraining order after hearing is issued.

(2) If an exemption is granted and the court subsequently renews the restraining order pursuant to Section 6345 at the request of a party, the court shall review and make a finding, in writing or on the record, as to whether the exemption remains appropriate, based upon the criteria set forth in paragraph (1) or (2) of subdivision (h), as applicable, in light of the renewal. This finding shall be made at the time the restraining order after hearing is renewed.

(3) The court may terminate or modify an exemption granted pursuant to this paragraph at any time if the respondent demonstrates a need to modify the specific firearm, ammunition, or firearm and ammunition authorized by the court pursuant to subdivision (h) or if the respondent no longer meets the requirements in this section or otherwise violates the restraining order.

(j) During the period of the relinquishment order, a respondent is entitled to make one sale of all firearms or ammunition that are in the possession of a local law enforcement agency pursuant to this section. A licensed gun dealer, who presents a local law enforcement agency with a bill of sale indicating that all firearms or ammunition owned by the respondent that are in the possession of the local law enforcement agency have been sold by the respondent to the licensed gun dealer, shall be given possession of those firearms or ammunition, at the location where a respondent's firearms or ammunition are stored, within five days of presenting the local law enforcement agency with a bill of sale.

(k) The disposition of any unclaimed property under this section shall be made pursuant to Section 1413 of the Penal Code.

(*l*)(1) The relinquishment of a firearm to a law enforcement agency pursuant to subdivision (g) shall not be subject to the requirements of Section 27545 of the Penal Code.

(2) The return of firearms and ammunition by a law enforcement agency pursuant to this section shall be governed by the applicable provisions of Chapter 2 (commencing with Section 33850) of Division 11 of Title 4 of Part 6 of the Penal Code.

(m) If the respondent notifies the court that the respondent owns a firearm or ammunition that is not in their immediate possession, the court may limit the order to exclude that firearm or ammunition if the judge is satisfied the respondent is unable to gain access to that firearm or ammunition while the protective order is in effect.

(n) A respondent to a protective order who violates an order issued pursuant to this section shall be punished under the provisions of Section 29825 of the Penal Code.

(o) This section shall become operative on January 1, 2026. **Leg.H.** Added Stats 2024 ch 535 §1.2 (AB 2759), effective January 1, 2025, operative January 1, 2026; Stats 2024 ch 544 §9.5 (SB 899), effective January 1, 2025, operative January 1, 2026 (ch 544 prevails).

§6390. [Section repealed 2002]

Leg.H. Added Stats 1998 ch 703 §2 (AB 2700). Repealed Stats 2002 ch 784 §106 (SB 1316). The repealed section related to descriptive study of domestic violence courts.

PART 5
UNIFORM INTERSTATE ENFORCEMENT OF DOMESTIC VIOLENCE PROTECTION ORDERS ACT

Citation of part. §6400.
Definitions. §6401.
Enforcement of valid foreign protection order in state tribunal. §6402.
Enforcement of foreign protection order by law enforcement officer. §6403.
Registration of foreign protection order. §6404.
Liability of peace officer acting on foreign protection order; Enforcement where there are multiple orders. §6405.
Legal and equitable remedies of protected person. §6406.
Uniformity of law in application and construction of part. §6407.
Severability. §6408.
Application of part. §6409.

§6400. Citation of part

This part may be cited as the Uniform Interstate Enforcement of Domestic Violence Protection Orders Act. **Leg.H.** Added Stats 2001 ch 816 §3 (AB 731).

§6401. Definitions

In this part:

(1) "Foreign protection order" means a protection order issued by a tribunal of another state.

(2) "Issuing state" means the state whose tribunal issues a protection order.

(3) "Mutual foreign protection order" means a foreign protection order that includes provisions in favor of both the protected individual seeking enforcement of the order and the respondent.

(4) "Protected individual" means an individual protected by a protection order.

(5) "Protection order" means an injunction or other order, issued by a tribunal under the domestic violence, family violence, or antistalking laws of the issuing state, to prevent an individual from engaging in violent or threatening acts against, harassment of, contact or communication with, or physical proximity to, another individual.

(6) "Respondent" means the individual against whom enforcement of a protection order is sought.

(7) "State" means a state of the United States, the District of Columbia, Puerto Rico, the United States Virgin Islands, or any territory or insular possession subject to the jurisdiction of the United States. The term includes an Indian tribe or band, or any branch of the United States military, that has jurisdiction to issue protection orders.

(8) "Tribunal" means a court, agency, or other entity authorized by law to issue or modify a protection order. **Leg.H.** Added Stats 2001 ch 816 §3 (AB 731). Amended Stats 2003 ch 134 §1 (SB 399).

§6402. Enforcement of valid foreign protection order in state tribunal

(a) A person authorized by the law of this state to seek enforcement of a protection order may seek enforcement of a valid foreign protection order in a tribunal of this state. The tribunal shall enforce the terms of the order, including terms that provide relief that a tribunal of this state would lack power to provide but for this section. The tribunal shall enforce the order, whether the order was obtained by independent action or in another proceeding, if it is an order issued in response to a complaint, petition, or motion filed by or on behalf of an individual seeking protection. In a proceeding to enforce a foreign protection order, the tribunal shall follow the procedures of this state for the enforcement of protection orders.

(b) A tribunal of this state may not enforce a foreign protection order issued by a tribunal of a state that does not recognize the standing of a protected individual to seek enforcement of the order.

(c) A tribunal of this state shall enforce the provisions of a valid foreign protection order which govern custody and visitation, if the order was issued in accordance with the jurisdictional requirements governing the issuance of custody and visitation orders in the issuing state.

(d) A foreign protection order is valid if it meets all of the following criteria:

(1) Identifies the protected individual and the respondent.

(2) Is currently in effect.

(3) Was issued by a tribunal that had jurisdiction over the parties and subject matter under the law of the issuing state.

(4) Was issued after the respondent was given reasonable notice and had an opportunity to be heard before the tribunal issued the order or, in the case of an order ex parte, the respondent was given notice and has had or will have an opportunity to be heard within a reasonable time after the order was issued, in a manner consistent with the rights of the respondent to due process.

(e) A foreign protection order valid on its face is prima facie evidence of its validity.

(f) Absence of any of the criteria for validity of a foreign protection order is an affirmative defense in an action seeking enforcement of the order.

(g) A tribunal of this state may enforce provisions of a mutual foreign protection order which favor a respondent only if both of the following are true:

(1) The respondent filed a written pleading seeking a protection order from the tribunal of the issuing state.

(2) The tribunal of the issuing state made specific findings in favor of the respondent. **Leg.H.** Added Stats 2001 ch 816 §3 (AB 731). Amended Stats 2003 ch 134 §2 (SB 399).

2003 Note: The Legislature finds and declares that the changes made by Ch. 134 (SB 399) that delete the current subdivision (d) of Section 6402 of the Family Code are not intended to make a change in, but are declaratory of, existing law. Under existing law, support orders are enforced pursuant to the Uniform Interstate Family Support Act (Chapter 6 (commencing with Section 4900) of Part 5 of Division 9 of the Family Code). Because Section 6402 of the Family Code relates to protection orders, the Legislature further finds and declares that the reference to support orders in subdivision (d) of that provision is inappropriate and does not comport with the intent of the Legislature. Stats 2003 ch 134 (SB 399) §3.

§6403. Enforcement of foreign protection order by law enforcement officer

(a) A law enforcement officer of this state, upon determining that there is probable cause to believe that a valid foreign protection order exists and that the order has been violated, shall enforce the order as if it were the order of a tribunal of this state. Presentation of a protection order that identifies both the protected individual and the respondent and, on its face, is currently in effect constitutes, in and of itself, probable cause to believe that a valid foreign protection order exists. For the purposes of this section, the protection order may be inscribed on a tangible medium or may have been stored in an electronic or other medium if it is retrievable in perceivable form. Presentation of a certified copy of a protection order is not required for enforcement.

(b) If a foreign protection order is not presented, a law enforcement officer of this state may consider other information in determining whether there is probable cause to believe that a valid foreign protection order exists.

(c) If a law enforcement officer of this state determines that an otherwise valid foreign protection order cannot be enforced because the respondent has not been notified or served with the order, the officer shall inform the respondent of the order, make a reasonable effort to serve the order upon the respondent, and allow the respondent a reasonable opportunity to comply with the order before enforcing the order. Verbal notice of the terms of the order is sufficient notice for the purposes of this section.

(d) Registration or filing of an order in this state is not required for the enforcement of a valid foreign protection order pursuant to this part. **Leg.H.** Added Stats 2001 ch 816 §3 (AB 731).

§6404. Registration of foreign protection order

(a) A foreign protection order shall, upon request of the person in possession of the order, be registered with a court of this state in order to be entered in the California Restraining and Protective Order System established under Section 6380. The Judicial Council shall adopt rules of court to do the following:

(1) Set forth the process whereby a person in possession of a foreign protection order may voluntarily register the order with a court of this state for entry into the California Restraining and Protective Order System.

(2) Require the sealing of foreign protection orders and provide access only to law enforcement, the person who registered the order upon written request with proof of identification, the defense after arraignment on criminal charges involving an alleged violation of the order, or upon further order of the court.

(b) A fee shall not be charged for the registration of a foreign protection order. The court clerk shall provide all Judicial Council forms required by this part to a person in possession of a foreign protection order free of charge. **Leg.H.** Added Stats 2001 ch 816 §3 (AB 731). Amended Stats 2019 ch 115 §72 (AB 1817), effective January 1, 2020.

§6405. Liability of peace officer acting on foreign protection order; Enforcement where there are multiple orders

(a) There shall be no civil liability on the part of, and no cause of action for false arrest or false imprisonment against, a peace officer who makes an arrest pursuant to a foreign protection order that is regular upon its face, if the peace officer, in making the arrest, acts in good faith and has reasonable cause to believe that the person against whom the order is issued has notice of the order and has committed an act in violation of the order.

(b) If there is more than one order issued and one of the orders is an emergency protective order that has precedence in enforcement pursuant to paragraph (1) of subdivision (c) of Section 136.2 of the Penal Code, the peace officer shall enforce the emergency protective order. If there is more than one order issued, none of the orders issued is an emergency protective order that has precedence in enforcement, and one of the orders issued is a no-contact order, as described in Section 6320, the peace officer shall enforce the no-contact order. If there is more than one civil order regarding the same parties and neither an emergency protective order that has precedence in enforcement nor a no-contact order has been issued, the peace officer shall enforce the order that was issued last. If there are both civil and criminal orders regarding the same parties and neither an emergency protective order that has precedence in enforcement nor a no-contact order has been issued, the peace officer shall enforce the criminal order issued last.

(c) Nothing in this section shall be deemed to exonerate a peace officer from liability for the unreasonable use of force in the enforcement of the order. The immunities afforded by this section shall not affect the availability of any other immunity that may apply, including, but not limited to, Sections 820.2 and 820.4 of the Government Code. **Leg.H.** Added Stats 2001 ch 816 §3 (AB 731). Amended Stats 2013 ch 263 §3 (AB 176), effective January 1, 2014, operative July 1, 2014.

§6406. Legal and equitable remedies of protected person

A protected individual who pursues remedies under this part is not precluded from pursuing other legal or equitable remedies against the respondent. **Leg.H.** Added Stats 2001 ch 816 §3 (AB 731).

§6407. Uniformity of law in application and construction of part

In applying and construing this part, consideration shall be given to the need to promote uniformity of the law with respect to its subject matter among states that also have adopted the act cited in Section 6400. **Leg.H.** Added Stats 2001 ch 816 §3 (AB 731).

§6408. Severability

If any provision of this part or its application to any person or circumstance is held invalid, the invalidity does not affect other provisions or applications of this part which can be given effect without the invalid provision or application, and to this end the provisions of this part are severable. **Leg.H.** Added Stats 2001 ch 816 §3 (AB 731).

§6409. Application of part

This part applies to protection orders issued before January 1, 2002, and to continuing actions for enforcement of foreign protection orders commenced before January 1, 2002. A request for enforcement of a foreign protection order made on or after January 1, 2002, for violations of a foreign protection order occurring before January 1, 2002, is governed by this part. **Leg.H.** Added Stats 2001 ch 816 §3 (AB 731).

PART 6
UNIFORM RECOGNITION AND ENFORCEMENT OF CANADIAN DOMESTIC VIOLENCE PROTECTION ORDERS ACT

Citation of part. §6450.
Definitions. §6451.
Enforcement of Canadian domestic violence protection order by law enforcement officer. §6452.
Enforcement of Canadian domestic violence protection order in state tribunal. §6453.
Registration of Canadian domestic violence protection order. §6454.
Liability of law enforcement officer enforcing Canadian domestic violence protection order. §6455.
Other legal and equitable remedies. §6456.
Enforcement if there are multiple orders. §6457.
Construction with federal Electronic Signatures in Global and National Commerce Act. §6458.
Applicability of part. §6459.
Severability. §6460.

§6450. Citation of part

This part may be cited as the Uniform Recognition and Enforcement of Canadian Domestic Violence Protection Orders Act. **Leg.H.** Added Stats 2017 ch 98 §1 (SB 204), effective January 1, 2018.

§6451. Definitions

In this part:

(a) "Canadian domestic violence protection order" means a judgment or part of a judgment or order issued in English in a civil proceeding by a court of Canada under law of the issuing jurisdiction that relates to domestic violence and prohibits a respondent from doing any of the following:

(1) Being in physical proximity to a protected individual or following a protected individual.

(2) Directly or indirectly contacting or communicating with a protected individual or other individual described in the order.

(3) Being within a certain distance of a specified place or location associated with a protected individual.

(4) Molesting, annoying, harassing, or engaging in threatening conduct directed at a protected individual.

(b) "Domestic protection order" means an injunction or other order issued by a tribunal that relates to domestic or family violence laws to prevent an individual from engaging in violent or threatening acts against, harassment of, direct or indirect contact or communication with, or being in physical proximity to, another individual.

(c) "Issuing court" means the court that issues a Canadian domestic violence protection order.

(d) "Law enforcement officer" means an individual authorized by law of this state to enforce a domestic protection order.

(e) "Person" means an individual, estate, business or nonprofit entity, public corporation, government or governmental subdivision, agency, or instrumentality, or other legal entity.

(f) "Protected individual" means an individual protected by a Canadian domestic violence protection order.

(g) "Record" means information that is inscribed on a tangible medium or that is stored in an electronic or other medium and is retrievable in perceivable form.

(h) "Respondent" means an individual against whom a Canadian domestic violence protection order is issued.

(i) "State" means a state of the United States, the District of Columbia, Puerto Rico, the United States Virgin Islands, or any territory or insular possession subject to the jurisdiction of the United States. The term includes a federally recognized Indian tribe.

(j) "Tribunal" means a court, agency, or other entity authorized by law to establish, enforce, or modify a domestic protection order. **Leg.H.** Added Stats 2017 ch 98 §1 (SB 204), effective January 1, 2018.

§6452. Enforcement of Canadian domestic violence protection order by law enforcement officer

(a) If a law enforcement officer determines under subdivision (b) or (c) that there is probable cause to believe a valid Canadian domestic violence protection order exists and the order has been violated, the officer shall enforce the terms of the Canadian domestic violence protection order as if the terms were in an order of a tribunal of this state. Presentation to a law enforcement officer of a certified copy of a Canadian domestic violence protection order is not required for enforcement.

(b) Presentation to a law enforcement officer of a record of a Canadian domestic violence protection order that identifies both a protected individual and a respondent and on its face is in effect constitutes probable cause to believe that a valid order exists.

(c) If a record of a Canadian domestic violence protection order is not presented as provided in subdivision (b), a law enforcement officer may consider other information in determining whether there is probable cause to believe that a valid Canadian domestic violence protection order exists.

(d) If a law enforcement officer determines that an otherwise valid Canadian domestic violence protection order cannot be enforced because the respondent has not been notified of or served with the order, the officer shall notify the protected individual that the officer will make reasonable efforts to contact the respondent, consistent with the safety of the protected individual. After notice to the protected individual and consistent with the safety of the individual, the officer shall make a reasonable effort to inform the respondent of the order, notify the respondent of the terms of the order, provide a record of the order, if available, to the respondent, and allow the respondent a reasonable opportunity to comply with the order before the officer enforces the order. Verbal notice of the terms of the order is sufficient for purposes of this subdivision.

(e) If a law enforcement officer determines that an individual is a protected individual, the officer shall inform the individual of available local victim services. **Leg.H.** Added Stats 2017 ch 98 §1 (SB 204), effective January 1, 2018.

§6453. Enforcement of Canadian domestic violence protection order in state tribunal

(a) A tribunal of this state may issue an order enforcing or refusing to enforce a Canadian domestic violence protection order on application of any of the following:

(1) A protected party or other person authorized by law of this state other than this part to seek enforcement of a domestic protection order.

(2) A respondent.

(b) In a proceeding under subdivision (a), the tribunal of this state shall follow the procedures of this state for enforcement of a domestic protection order. An order entered under this section is limited to the enforcement of the terms of the Canadian domestic violence protection order as described in subdivision (a) of Section 6451.

(c) A Canadian domestic violence protection order is enforceable under this section if all of the following apply:

(1) The order identifies a protected individual and a respondent.

(2) The order is valid and in effect.

(3) The issuing court had jurisdiction over the parties and the subject matter under law applicable in the issuing court.

(4) The order was issued after either of the following:

(A) The respondent was given reasonable notice and had an opportunity to be heard before the court issued the order.

(B) In the case of an ex parte order, the respondent was given reasonable notice and had or will have an opportunity to be heard within a reasonable time after the order was issued, in a manner consistent with the right of the respondent to due process.

(d) A Canadian domestic violence protection order valid on its face is prima facie evidence of its enforceability under this section.

(e) A claim that a Canadian domestic violence protection order does not comply with subdivision (c) is an affirmative defense in a proceeding seeking enforcement of the order. If the tribunal of this state determines that the order is not enforceable, the tribunal of this state shall issue an order that the Canadian domestic violence protection order is not enforceable under this section and Section 6452 and may not be registered under Section 6454.

(f) This section applies to enforcement of a provision of a Canadian domestic violence protection order against a party to the order in which each party is a protected individual and respondent only if both of the following apply:

(1) The party seeking enforcement of the order filed a pleading requesting the order from the issuing court.

(2) The court made detailed findings of fact indicating that both parties acted as a primary aggressor and that neither party acted primarily in self-defense. **Leg.H.** Added Stats 2017 ch 98 §1 (SB 204), effective January 1, 2018.

§6454. Registration of Canadian domestic violence protection order

(a) An individual may register a Canadian domestic violence protection order in this state. To register the order, the individual must present a certified copy of the order to a court of this state to be entered into the California Restraining and Protective Order System established under Section 6380, pursuant to procedures set forth in Section 6404.

(b) A fee shall not be charged for the registration of a Canadian domestic violence protection order under this section.

(c) Registration in this state or filing under law of this state other than this part of a Canadian domestic violence protection order is not required for its enforcement under this part. **Leg.H.** Added Stats 2017 ch 98 §1 (SB 204), effective January 1, 2018. Amended Stats 2019 ch 115 §73 (AB 1817), effective January 1, 2020.

§6455. Liability of law enforcement officer enforcing Canadian domestic violence protection order

(a) There shall be no civil liability on the part of, and no cause of action for false arrest or false imprisonment against, a law enforcement officer who makes an arrest pursuant to a Canadian domestic violence protection order that is regular upon its face, if the law enforcement officer, in making the arrest, acts in good faith and has reasonable cause to believe that the person against whom the order is issued has notice of the order and has committed an act in violation of the order.

(b) Nothing in this section shall be deemed to exonerate a law enforcement officer from liability for the unreasonable use of force in the enforcement of the order. The immunities afforded by this section shall not affect the availability of any other immunity that may apply, including, but not limited to, Sections 820.2 and 820.4 of the Government Code. **Leg.H.** Added Stats 2017 ch 98 §1 (SB 204), effective January 1, 2018.

§6456. Other legal and equitable remedies

An individual who seeks a remedy under this part may seek other legal or equitable remedies. **Leg.H.** Added Stats 2017 ch 98 §1 (SB 204), effective January 1, 2018.

§6457. Enforcement if there are multiple orders

If there is more than one order issued and one of the orders is an emergency protective order that has precedence in enforcement pursuant to paragraph (1) of subdivision (c) of Section 136.2 of the Penal Code, the law enforcement officer shall enforce the emergency protective order. If there is more than one order issued, none of the orders issued is an emergency protective order that has precedence in enforcement, and one of the orders issued is a no-contact order, as described in Section 6320, the law enforcement officer shall enforce the no-contact order. If there is more than one civil order regarding the same parties and neither an emergency protective order that has precedence in enforcement nor a no-contact order has been issued, the law enforcement officer shall enforce the order that was issued last. If there are both civil and criminal orders regarding the same parties and neither an emergency protective order that has precedence in enforcement nor a no-contact order has been issued, the law enforcement officer shall enforce the criminal order issued last. **Leg.H.** Added Stats 2017 ch 98 §1 (SB 204), effective January 1, 2018.

§6458. Construction with federal Electronic Signatures in Global and National Commerce Act

This part modifies, limits, or supersedes the federal Electronic Signatures in Global and National Commerce Act (15 U.S.C. Sec. 7001 et seq.), but does not modify, limit, or supersede Section 101(c) of that act (15 U.S.C. Sec. 7001(c)), or authorize electronic delivery of any of the notices described in Section 103(b) of that act (15 U.S.C. Sec. 7003(b)). **Leg.H.** Added Stats 2017 ch 98 §1 (SB 204), effective January 1, 2018.

§6459. Applicability of part

This part applies to a Canadian domestic violence protection order issued before, on, or after January 1, 2018, and to a continuing action for enforcement of a Canadian domestic violence protection order commenced before, on, or after January 1, 2018. A request for enforcement of a Canadian domestic violence protection order made on or after January 1, 2018, for a violation of the order occurring before, on, or after January 1, 2018, is governed by this part. **Leg.H.** Added Stats 2017 ch 98 §1 (SB 204), effective January 1, 2018.

§6460. Severability

If any provision of this part or its application to any person or circumstance is held invalid, the invalidity does not affect other provisions or applications of this part that can be given effect without the invalid provision or application, and to this end the provisions of this part are severable. **Leg.H.** Added Stats 2017 ch 98 §1 (SB 204), effective January 1, 2018.

DIVISION 11
MINORS

Part 1. Age of Majority.
Part 1.5. Caregivers.
Part 2. Rights and Liabilities; Civil Actions and Proceedings.
Part 2.5. ONLINE PLATFORMS.
Part 3. Contracts.
Part 4. Medical Treatment.
Part 5. Enlistment in Armed Forces.
Part 6. Emancipation of Minors Law.

PART 1
AGE OF MAJORITY

Minor. §6500.
Adult. §6501.
Transitional provision. §6502.

§6500. Minor
A minor is an individual who is under 18 years of age. The period of minority is calculated from the first minute of the day on which the individual is born to the same minute of the corresponding day completing the period of minority. **Leg.H.** Enacted Stats 1992 ch 162 §10 (AB 2650), operative January 1, 1994.

§6501. Adult
An adult is an individual who is 18 years of age or older. **Leg.H.** Enacted Stats 1992 ch 162 §10 (AB 2650), operative January 1, 1994.

§6502. Transitional provision
(a) The use of or reference to the words "age of majority," "age of minority," "adult," "minor," or words of similar intent in any instrument, order, transfer, or governmental communication made in this state:

(1) Before March 4, 1972, makes reference to individuals 21 years of age and older, or younger than 21 years of age.

(2) On or after March 4, 1972, makes reference to individuals 18 years of age and older, or younger than 18 years of age.

(b) Nothing in subdivision (a) or in Chapter 1748 of the Statutes of 1971 prevents amendment of any court order, will, trust, contract, transfer, or instrument to refer to the 18-year-old age of majority if the court order, will, trust, contract, transfer, or instrument satisfies all of the following conditions:

(1) It was in existence on March 4, 1972.

(2) It is subject to amendment by law, and amendment is allowable or not prohibited by its terms.

(3) It is otherwise subject to the laws of this state. **Leg.H.** Enacted Stats 1992 ch 162 §10 (AB 2650), operative January 1, 1994.

PART 1.5
CAREGIVERS

Caregiver's authorization affidavit to provide medical or dental care. §6550.
Form. §6552.

§6550. Caregiver's authorization affidavit to provide medical or dental care

(a) A caregiver's authorization affidavit that meets the requirements of this part authorizes a caregiver 18 years of age or older who completes items 1 to 4, inclusive, of the affidavit provided in Section 6552 and signs the affidavit to enroll a minor in school and consent to school-related medical care on behalf of the minor. A caregiver who is a relative and who completes items 1 to 8, inclusive, of the affidavit provided in Section 6552 and signs the affidavit shall have the same rights to authorize medical care and dental care for the minor that are given to guardians under Section 2353 of the Probate Code. The medical care authorized by this caregiver who is a relative may include mental health treatment subject to the limitations of Section 2356 of the Probate Code.

(b) The decision of a caregiver to consent to or to refuse medical or dental care for a minor shall be superseded by any contravening decision of the parent or other person having legal custody of the minor, provided the decision of the parent or other person having legal custody of the minor does not jeopardize the life, health, or safety of the minor.

(c) A person who acts in good faith reliance on a caregiver's authorization affidavit to provide medical or dental care, without actual knowledge of facts contrary to those stated on the affidavit, is not subject to criminal liability or to civil liability to any person, and is not subject to professional disciplinary action, for that reliance if the applicable portions of the affidavit are completed. This subdivision applies even if medical or dental care is provided to a minor in contravention of the wishes of the parent or other person having legal custody of the minor as long as the person providing the medical or dental care has no actual knowledge of the wishes of the parent or other person having legal custody of the minor.

(d) A person who relies on the affidavit has no obligation to make any further inquiry or investigation.

(e) Nothing in this section relieves any individual from liability for violations of other provisions of law.

(f) If the minor stops living with the caregiver, the caregiver shall notify any school, health care provider, or health care service plan that has been given the affidavit. The affidavit is invalid after the school, health care provider, or health care service plan receives notice that the minor is no longer living with the caregiver.

(g) A caregiver's authorization affidavit shall be invalid, unless it substantially contains, in not less than 10-point boldface type or a reasonable equivalent thereof, the warning statement beginning with the word "warning" specified in Section 6552. The warning statement shall be enclosed in a box with 3-point rule lines.

(h) For purposes of this part, the following terms have the following meanings:

(1) "Person" includes an individual, corporation, partnership, association, the state, or any city, county, city and county, or other public entity or governmental subdivision or agency, or any other legal entity.

(2) "Relative" means a spouse, parent, stepparent, brother, sister, stepbrother, stepsister, half brother, half sister, uncle, aunt, niece, nephew, first cousin, or any person denoted by the prefix "grand" or "great," or the spouse of any of the persons specified in this definition, even after the marriage has been terminated by death or dissolution.

(3) "School-related medical care" means medical care that is required by state or local governmental authority as a condition for school enrollment, including immunizations, physical examinations, and medical examinations conducted in schools for pupils. **Leg.H.** Added Stats 1994 ch 98 §4 (SB 592), effective June 6, 1994. Amended Stats 1996 ch 563 §1.5 (SB 392); Stats 2004 ch 895 §12 (AB 2855).

§6552. Form

The caregiver's authorization affidavit shall be in substantially the following form:

Caregiver's Authorization Affidavit

Use of this affidavit is authorized by Part 1.5 (commencing with Section 6550) of Division 11 of the California Family Code.

Instructions: Completion of items 1–4 and the signing of the affidavit is sufficient to authorize enrollment of a minor in school and authorize school-related medical care. Completion of items 5–8 is additionally required to authorize any other medical care. Print clearly.

The minor named below lives in my home and I am 18 years of age or older.

1. Name of minor: _____
2. Minor's birth date: _____
3. My name (adult giving authorization): _____
4. My home address: _____
5. ☐ I am a grandparent, aunt, uncle, or other qualified relative of the minor (see back of this form for a definition of "qualified relative").
6. Check one or both (for example, if one parent was advised and the other cannot be located):
☐ I have advised the parent(s) or other person(s) having legal custody of the minor of my intent to authorize medical care, and have received no objection.
☐ I am unable to contact the parent(s) or other person(s) having legal custody of the minor at this time, to notify them of my intended authorization.
7. My date of birth: _____
8. My California driver's license or identification card number: _____

Warning: Do not sign this form if any of the statements above are incorrect, or you will be committing a crime punishable by a fine, imprisonment, or both.

I declare under penalty of perjury under the laws of the State of California that the foregoing is true and correct.
Dated: _____ Signed: _____

Notices:
1. This declaration does not affect the rights of the minor's parents or legal guardian regarding the care, custody, and control of the minor, and does not mean that the caregiver has legal custody of the minor.

2. A person who relies on this affidavit has no obligation to make any further inquiry or investigation.

Additional Information:

TO CAREGIVERS:

1. "Qualified relative," for purposes of item 5, means a spouse, parent, stepparent, brother, sister, stepbrother, stepsister, half brother, half sister, uncle, aunt, niece, nephew, first cousin, or any person denoted by the prefix "grand" or "great," or the spouse of any of the persons specified in this definition, even after the marriage has been terminated by death or dissolution.

2. The law may require you, if you are not a relative or a currently licensed, certified, or approved foster parent, to obtain resource family approval pursuant to Section 1517 of the Health and Safety Code or Section 16519.5 of the Welfare and Institutions Code in order to care for a minor. If you have any questions, please contact your local department of social services.

3. If the minor stops living with you, you are required to notify any school, health care provider, or health care service plan to which you have given this affidavit. The affidavit is invalid after the school, health care provider, or health care service plan receives notice that the minor no longer lives with you.

4. If you do not have the information requested in item 8 (California driver's license or I.D.), provide another form of identification such as your social security number or Medi-Cal number.

TO SCHOOL OFFICIALS:

1. Section 48204 of the Education Code provides that this affidavit constitutes a sufficient basis for a determination of residency of the minor, without the requirement of a guardianship or other custody order, unless the school district determines from actual facts that the minor is not living with the caregiver.

2. The school district may require additional reasonable evidence that the caregiver lives at the address provided in item 4.

TO HEALTH CARE PROVIDERS AND HEALTH CARE SERVICE PLANS:

1. A person who acts in good faith reliance upon a caregiver's authorization affidavit to provide medical or dental care, without actual knowledge of facts contrary to those stated on the affidavit, is not subject to criminal liability or to civil liability to any person, and is not subject to professional disciplinary action, for that reliance if the applicable portions of the form are completed.

2. This affidavit does not confer dependency for health care coverage purposes.

Leg.H. Added Stats 1994 ch 98 §4 (SB 592), effective June 6, 1994. Amended Stats 1994 ch 1269 §50.6 (AB 2208); Stats 2004 ch 895 §13 (AB 2855); Stats 2016 ch 612 §6 (AB 1997), effective January 1, 2017.

2016 Note: (a) The State Department of Social Services and the State Department of Health Care Services shall adopt regulations as required to implement this act and Chapter 773 of the Statutes of 2015.

(b) Notwithstanding the rulemaking provisions of the Administrative Procedure Act (Chapter 3.5 (commencing with Section 11340) of Part 1 of Division 3 of Title 2 of the Government Code), the State Department of Social Services and the State Department of Health Care Services may implement and administer the changes made by this act through all-county letters or similar written instructions until regulations are adopted. Stats 2016 ch 612 (AB 1997) §131.

PART 2
RIGHTS AND LIABILITIES; CIVIL ACTIONS AND PROCEEDINGS

Civil liability of minor. §6600.
Enforcement of minor's rights by civil proceeding. §6601.
Minor's attorney's fees. §6602.

§6600. Civil liability of minor

A minor is civilly liable for a wrong done by the minor, but is not liable in exemplary damages unless at the time of the act the minor was capable of knowing that the act was wrongful. **Leg.H.** Enacted Stats 1992 ch 162 §10 (AB 2650), operative January 1, 1994.

§6601. Enforcement of minor's rights by civil proceeding

A minor may enforce the minor's rights by civil action or other legal proceedings in the same manner as an adult, except that a guardian must conduct the action or proceedings. **Leg.H.** Enacted Stats 1992 ch 162 §10 (AB 2650), operative January 1, 1994.

§6602. Minor's attorney's fees

A contract for attorney's fees for services in litigation, made by or on behalf of a minor, is void unless the contract is approved, on petition by an interested person, by the court in which the litigation is pending or by the court having jurisdiction of the guardianship estate of the minor. If the contract is not approved and a judgment is recovered by or on behalf of the minor, the attorney's fees chargeable against the minor shall be fixed by the court rendering the judgment. **Leg.H.** Enacted Stats 1992 ch 162 §10 (AB 2650), operative January 1, 1994.

PART 2.5
ONLINE PLATFORMS

Definitions. § 6650.
Criteria for minor engaged in vlogging work. § 6651.
Record keeping requirements for vloggers featuring minors. § 6652.
Trust account requirements for compensation of minors engaged in vlogging. § 6653.
Enforcement and damages for violations. § 6654.
No effect on right or remedy under other law and minor's own content. § 6655.
Court approval of contract between minor and parent or guardian. § 6656.

§ 6650. Definitions

For the purposes of this part, all of the following definitions apply:

(a) "Age of majority" means 18 years of age or older.

(b) "Content" has the same meaning as defined in subdivision (b) of Section 22675 of the Business and Professions Code.

(c) "Family" means a group of persons related by blood or marriage, including civil partnerships, or whose close relationship with each other is considered equivalent to a family relationship by the individuals.

(d) "Minor" means an individual who is under 18 years of age.

(e) "Online platform" means any public-facing internet website, web application, or digital application, including a mobile application. "Online platform" includes a social media platform, as defined in Section 22675 of the Business and Professions Code, advertising network, mobile operating system, search engine, email service, or internet access service.

(f) "Reporting period" means a given month for which a parent, legal guardian, or family must set aside compensation for a minor pursuant to subdivision (a) of Section 6651.

(g) "Vlog" means content shared on an online platform in exchange for compensation.

(h) "Vlogger" means a parent, legal guardian, or family residing in California that creates image or video content that is performed in California in exchange for compensation. "Vlogger" does not include any person under 18 years of age who produces their own content.

(i) "Vlogging" means the act of sharing content on an online platform in exchange for compensation. **Leg.H.** Added Stats 2024 ch 611 §1 (SB 764), effective January 1, 2025.

§ 6651. Criteria for minor engaged in vlogging work

A minor is considered engaged in the work of vlogging when the following are met at any time during a given month:

(a)(1) At least 30 percent of the vlogger's compensated video content or the vlogger's compensated image content includes the likeness, name, or photograph of the minor.

(2) The percentage pursuant to paragraph (1) is measured by the amount of time the likeness, name, or photograph of the minor visually appears or is the subject of an oral narrative in a video segment, as compared to the total length of the segment.

(b) The number of views received per image or video segment on any online platform met the online platform's threshold for compensation or the vlogger received actual compensation for image or video content equal to or greater than ten cents ($0.10) per view.

(c) The vlogger received actual compensation for image or video content of at least one thousand two hundred fifty dollars ($1,250) in the month. **Leg.H.** Added Stats 2024 ch 611 §1 (SB 764), effective January 1, 2025.

§ 6652. Record keeping requirements for vloggers featuring minors

All vloggers whose content features a minor engaged in the work of vlogging, as described in subdivision (a) of Section 6651, shall maintain, and make available to the minor upon request, all of the following records:

(a) Documentary proof of the minor's age when they started vlogging, as described in subdivision (a) of Section 6651.

(b) The number of vlogs that generated compensation, as described in Section 6651 during each reporting period.

(c) The total number of minutes of the vlogs that the vlogger received compensation for during each reporting period.

(d) The total number of minutes each minor was included in, as described in paragraph (1) of subdivision (a) of Section 6651, vlogs during each reporting period.

(e) The total compensation generated from vlogs featuring the minor during the reporting period.

(f) The amount deposited for the reporting period into the trust account for the benefit of the minor engaged in vlogging pursuant to Section 6653. This amount shall be calculated by multiplying the percentage of total minutes in subdivision (c) in which the minor is featured in subdivision (d) by the total compensation in subdivision (e) multiplied by .65. **Leg.H.** Added Stats 2024 ch 611 §1 (SB 764), effective January 1, 2025.

§ 6653. Trust account requirements for compensation of minors engaged in vlogging

(a) A minor satisfying the requirements of subdivision (a) of Section 6651 shall be compensated by the vlogger, pursuant to the terms of this section. The vlogger shall set aside gross earnings on the image or video content meeting the requirements of Section 6651 in a trust account to be preserved for the benefit of the minor upon reaching the age of majority according to the following distribution:

(1) When only one minor meets the content threshold described in Section 6651, the minor shall receive a percentage of total gross earnings on any image or video segment, meeting the requirements of Section 6651, that is in proportion to the minor's appearances in vlogging content during an applicable reporting period.

(2) When more than one minor meets the content threshold described in Section 6651 and an image or video segment includes more than one of those minors, the percentage described in paragraph (1) for all minors in any segment shall be equally divided between the minors, regardless of the differences in percentage of content provided by the individual minors. Each minor shall have their own trust account.

(b)(1) The vlogger shall establish the trust within 60 business days after the minor first meets the criteria in subdivision (a) of Section 6651. The vlogger shall establish a trust for each qualifying minor.

(2) The vlogger shall establish the trust in California either with a financial institution that is and remains insured at all times by the Federal Deposit Insurance Corporation, the Securities Investor Protection Corporation, or the National Credit Union Share Insurance Fund or their respective successors, or with a company that is and remains registered under the Investment Company Act of 1940. The trustee or trustees of the trust shall be the only individual, individuals, entity, or entities with the obligation or duty to ensure that the funds remain in trust, in an account or other savings plan insured in accordance with this section, or with a company that is and remains registered under the Investment Company Act of 1940 as authorized by this section.

(3) The vlogger shall, within 10 business days of establishing the trust, prepare a written statement, under penalty of perjury, that shall include the name, address, and telephone number of the financial institution, the name of the account, the number of the account, the name of the minor beneficiary, the name of the trustee or trustees of the account, and any additional information needed by the vlogger to deposit into the account the portion of the minor's gross earnings prescribed by subdivision (a). The trustee or trustees shall attach to the written statement a true and accurate photocopy of any information received from the financial institution confirming the creation of the account, such as an account agreement, account terms, passbook, or other similar writings.

(4) The funds in the account shall be available only to the beneficiary of the trust. The vlogger shall deposit the funds into the account no less than once every three months.

(5) Except as otherwise provided in this section, prior to the date on which the beneficiary of the trust attains the age of majority or the issuance of a declaration of emancipation of the minor pursuant to Section 7122, a withdrawal by the beneficiary or any other individual, individuals, entity, or entities shall not be made for the funds deposited in trust. Upon reaching the age of majority, the beneficiary may withdraw the funds on deposit in the trust only after providing a certified copy of the beneficiary's birth certificate to the financial institution where the trust is located.

(c) Upon application by the trustee or trustees, the trust funds shall be handled by the financial institution or company in which the trust is held in one or more of the following methods:

(1) The financial institution or company may transfer funds to another account or other savings plan at the same financial institution or company, provided that the funds transferred shall continue to be held in trust, and subject to this part.

(2) The financial institution or company may transfer funds to another financial institution or company, provided that the funds transferred shall continue to be held in trust, and subject to this part and that the transferring financial institution or company has provided written notice to the financial institution or company to which the funds will be transferred that the funds are subject to this section and written notice of the requirements of this part.

(3) The financial institution or company may use all or a part of the funds to purchase, in the name of and for the benefit of the minor, either of the following:

(A) Investment funds offered by a company registered under the Investment Company Act of 1940, provided that if the underlying investments are equity securities, the investment fund is a broad-based index fund or invests broadly across the domestic or a foreign regional economy, is not a sector fund, and has assets under management of at least two hundred fifty million dollars ($250,000,000).

(B) Government securities and bonds, certificates of deposit, money market instruments, money market accounts, or mutual funds investing solely in those government securities and bonds, certificates, instruments, and accounts that are available at the financial institution where the trust fund or other savings plan is held, provided that the funds shall continue to be held in trust and subject to this part, those purchases shall have a maturity date on or before the date upon which the minor will attain the age of majority, and any proceeds accruing from those purchases shall be redeposited into that account or accounts or used to further purchase any of those or similar securities, bonds, certificates, instruments, funds, or accounts. **Leg.H.** Added Stats 2024 ch 611 §1 (SB 764), effective January 1, 2025.

§ 6654. Enforcement and damages for violations

If a vlogger knowingly violates this part or should have known they were in violation of this part, a minor satisfying the criteria described in subdivision (a) of Section 6651 may commence an action to enforce the provisions of this part. The court may award, to a minor who prevails in any action brought in accordance with this part, any of the following damages:

(a) Actual damages.

(b) Punitive damages.

(c) Cost of the action, including attorney's fees and litigation costs. **Leg.H.** Added Stats 2024 ch 611 §1 (SB 764), effective January 1, 2025.

§ 6655. No effect on right or remedy under other law and minor's own content

(a) This part does not affect a right or remedy available under any other law of the state.

(b) This part does not have any effect on a minor who produces their own content. **Leg.H.** Added Stats 2024 ch 611 §1 (SB 764), effective January 1, 2025.

§ 6656. Court approval of contract between minor and parent or guardian

This part shall not apply to a contract for vlogging services between a minor and their parent or guardian only if a court approves the contract pursuant to subdivision (a) of Section 6751. In determining whether to approve such a contract, the court shall consider whether the terms of the contract are at least as beneficial to the minor as the compensation the minor would otherwise receive under this part. **Leg.H.** Added Stats 2024 ch 611 §1 (SB 764), effective January 1, 2025.

PART 3
CONTRACTS

Chapter 1. Capacity to Contract.
Chapter 2. Disaffirmance of Contracts.
Chapter 3. Contracts in Art, Entertainment, and Professional Sports.

CHAPTER 1
CAPACITY TO CONTRACT

Contractual capacity of minor. §6700.
Limitation on authority of minor. §6701.

§6700. Contractual capacity of minor

Except as provided in Section 6701, a minor may make a contract in the same manner as an adult, subject to the power of disaffirmance under Chapter 2 (commencing with Section 6710), and subject to Part 1 (commencing with Section 300) of Division 3 (validity of marriage). **Leg.H.** Enacted Stats 1992 ch 162 §10 (AB 2650), operative January 1, 1994.

§6701. Limitation on authority of minor

A minor cannot do any of the following:
(a) Give a delegation of power.
(b) Make a contract relating to real property or any interest therein.
(c) Make a contract relating to any personal property not in the immediate possession or control of the minor. **Leg.H.** Enacted Stats 1992 ch 162 §10 (AB 2650), operative January 1, 1994.

CHAPTER 2
DISAFFIRMANCE OF CONTRACTS

Right of disaffirmance. §6710.
Contract made under express statutory authority. §6711.
Contracts for necessaries. §6712.
Protection of good faith purchaser. §6713.

§6710. Right of disaffirmance

Except as otherwise provided by statute, a contract of a minor may be disaffirmed by the minor before majority or within a reasonable time afterwards or, in case of the minor's death within that period, by the minor's heirs or personal representative. **Leg.H.** Enacted Stats 1992 ch 162 §10 (AB 2650), operative January 1, 1994.

§6711. Contract made under express statutory authority

A minor cannot disaffirm an obligation, otherwise valid, entered into by the minor under the express authority or direction of a statute. **Leg.H.** Enacted Stats 1992 ch 162 §10 (AB 2650), operative January 1, 1994.

§6712. Contracts for necessaries

A contract, otherwise valid, entered into during minority, may not be disaffirmed on that ground either during the actual minority of the person entering into the contract, or at any time thereafter, if all of the following requirements are satisfied:
(a) The contract is to pay the reasonable value of things necessary for the support of the minor or the minor's family.
(b) These things have been actually furnished to the minor or to the minor's family.
(c) The contract is entered into by the minor when not under the care of a parent or guardian able to provide for the minor or the minor's family. **Leg.H.** Enacted Stats 1992 ch 162 §10 (AB 2650), operative January 1, 1994.

§6713. Protection of good faith purchaser

If, before the contract of a minor is disaffirmed, goods the minor has sold are transferred to another purchaser who bought them in good faith for value and without notice of the transferor's defect of title, the minor cannot recover the goods from an innocent purchaser. **Leg.H.** Enacted Stats 1992 ch 162 §10 (AB 2650), operative January 1, 1994.

CHAPTER 3
CONTRACTS IN ART, ENTERTAINMENT, AND PROFESSIONAL SPORTS

Types of contracts governed by chapter; Person or entity considered minor's employer; Minor's "gross earnings". §6750.
Contract approved by court not subject to disaffirmance. §6751.
Placement of percentage of minor's gross earnings in trust; Duties of trustee, parent or guardian, minor's employer, and Actors' Fund of America; Notice to beneficiary; Fiduciary relationship between parent or guardian and minor. §6752.
Establishment of Coogan Trust Account for minor; Requirements for withdrawal; Provision of information to minor's employer; Management of funds. §6753.

§6750. Types of contracts governed by chapter; Person or entity considered minor's employer; Minor's "gross earnings"

(a) This chapter applies to the following **types of** contracts entered into between an unemancipated minor and a third party on or after January 1, 2000:
(1) A contract pursuant to which a minor is employed or agrees to render artistic or creative services, either directly or through a third party, including, but not limited to, a personal services corporation (loan-out company), or through a casting agency. "Artistic or creative services" includes, but is not limited to, services as an actor, actress, dancer, musician, comedian, singer, stuntperson, voice-over artist, **content creator,** or other performer or entertainer, or as a songwriter, musical producer or arranger, writer, director, producer, production executive, choreographer, composer, conductor, or designer.
(2) A contract pursuant to which a minor agrees to purchase, or otherwise secure, sell, lease, license, or otherwise dispose of literary, musical, or dramatic properties, or use of a person's likeness, voice recording, performance, or story of or incidents in the person's life, either tangible or intangible, or any rights therein for use in motion pictures, television, the production of sound recordings in any format now known or hereafter devised, the legitimate or living stage, or otherwise in the entertainment field.
(3) A contract pursuant to which a minor is employed or agrees to render services as a participant or player in a sport.
(b)(1) If a minor is employed or agrees to render services directly for a person or entity, that person or entity shall be considered the minor's employer for purposes of this chapter.
(2) If a minor's services are being rendered through a third-party individual or personal services corporation (loan-out company), the person to whom or entity to which that third party is providing the minor's services shall be considered the minor's employer for purposes of this chapter.
(3) If a minor renders services as an extra, background performer, or in a similar capacity through an agency or service that provides one or more of those performers for a fee (casting agency), the agency or service shall be considered the minor's employer for the purposes of this chapter.
(c) For purposes of this chapter, the following definitions apply:
(1) "Content creator" means an individual who creates, posts, shares, or otherwise interacts with digital content on an online platform and engages in a direct contractual relationship with third parties. Content creators include, but are not limited to, vloggers, podcasters, social media influencers, and streamers.
(2) "Online platform" means any public-facing internet website, web application, or digital application, including, but not limited to, social media platforms as defined in Section 22675 of the Business and Professions Code, advertising networks, mobile applications, mobile operating systems, search engines, email services, and internet access services.
[1] **(d)**(1) For purposes of this chapter, the minor's "gross earnings" means the total compensation payable to the minor under the contract or, if the minor's services are being rendered through a third-party individual or personal services corporation (loan-out company), the total compensation payable to that third party for the services of the minor.
(2) Notwithstanding paragraph (1), with respect to contracts pursuant to which a minor is employed or agrees to render services as a musician, singer, songwriter, musical producer, or arranger only, for purposes of this chapter, the minor's "gross earnings" means the total amount paid to the minor pursuant to the contract, including the payment of any advances to the minor pursuant to the contract, but excluding deductions to offset those advances or other expenses incurred by the employer pursuant to the

contract, or, if the minor's services are being rendered through a third-party individual or personal services corporation (loan-out company), the total amount payable to that third party for the services of the minor. **Leg.H.** Enacted Stats 1992 ch 162 §10 (AB 2650), operative January 1, 1994. Amended Stats 1999 ch 940 §2 (SB 1162); Stats 2003 ch 667 §1 (SB 210); Stats 2019 ch 115 §74 (AB 1817), effective January 1, 2020; Stats 2024 ch 610 §1 (AB 1880), effective January 1, 2025.

§6750. 2024 Deletes. [1] (c)

§6751. Contract approved by court not subject to disaffirmance

(a) A contract, otherwise valid, of a type described in Section 6750, entered into during minority, cannot be disaffirmed on that ground either during the minority of the person entering into the contract, or at any time thereafter, if the contract has been approved by the superior court in any county in which the minor resides or is employed or in which any party to the contract has its principal office in this state for the transaction of business.

(b) Approval of the court may be given on petition of any party to the contract, after such reasonable notice to all other parties to the contract as is fixed by the court, with opportunity to such other parties to appear and be heard.

(c) Approval of the court given under this section extends to the whole of the contract and all of its terms and provisions, including, but not limited to, any optional or conditional provisions contained in the contract for extension, prolongation, or termination of the term of the contract.

(d) For the purposes of any proceeding under this chapter, a parent or legal guardian, as the case may be, entitled to the physical custody, care, and control of the minor at the time of the proceeding shall be considered the minor's guardian ad litem for the proceeding, unless the court shall determine that appointment of a different individual as guardian ad litem is required in the best interests of the minor. **Leg.H.** Enacted Stats 1992 ch 162 §10 (AB 2650), operative January 1, 1994. Amended Stats 1999 ch 940 §3 (SB 1162).

§6752. Placement of percentage of minor's gross earnings in trust; Duties of trustee, parent or guardian, minor's employer, and Actors' Fund of America; Notice to beneficiary; Fiduciary relationship between parent or guardian and minor

(a) A parent or guardian entitled to the physical custody, care, and control of a minor who enters into a contract of a type described in Section 6750 shall provide a certified copy of the minor's birth certificate indicating the minor's minority to the other party or parties to the contract and in addition, in the case of a guardian, a certified copy of the court document appointing the person as the minor's legal guardian.

(b)(1) Notwithstanding any other statute, in an order approving a minor's contract of a type described in Section 6750, the court shall require that 15 percent of the minor's gross earnings pursuant to the contract be set aside by the minor's employer, except an employer of a minor for services as an extra, background performer, or in a similar capacity, as described in paragraph (3) of subdivision (b) of Section 6750. These amounts shall be held in trust, in an account or other savings plan, and preserved for the benefit of the minor in accordance with Section 6753.

(2) The court shall require that at least one parent or legal guardian, as the case may be, entitled to the physical custody, care, and control of the minor at the time the order is issued be appointed as trustee of the funds ordered to be set aside in trust for the benefit of the minor, unless the court shall determine that appointment of a different individual, individuals, entity, or entities as trustee or trustees is required in the best interest of the minor.

(3) Within 10 business days after commencement of employment, the trustee or trustees of the funds ordered to be set aside in trust shall provide the minor's employer with a true and accurate photocopy of the trustee's statement pursuant to Section 6753. Upon presentation of the trustee's statement offered pursuant to this subdivision, the employer shall provide the parent or guardian with a written acknowledgment of receipt of the statement.

(4) The minor's employer shall deposit or disburse the 15 percent of the minor's gross earnings pursuant to the contract within 15 business days after receiving a true and accurate copy of the trustee's statement pursuant to subdivision (c) of Section 6753, a certified copy of the minor's birth certificate, and, in the case of a guardian, a certified copy of the court document appointing the person as the minor's guardian. Notwithstanding any other law, pending receipt of these documents, the minor's employer shall hold, for the benefit of the minor, the 15 percent of the minor's gross earnings pursuant to the contract. This paragraph does not apply to an employer of a minor for services as an extra, background performer, or in a similar capacity, as described in paragraph (3) of subdivision (b) of Section 6750.

(5) When making the initial deposit of funds, the minor's employer shall provide written notification to the financial institution or company that the funds are subject to Section 6753. Upon receipt of the court order, the minor's employer shall provide the financial institution with a copy of the order.

(6) Once the minor's employer deposits the set-aside funds pursuant to Section 6753, in trust, in an account or other savings plan, the minor's employer shall have no further obligation or duty to monitor or account for the funds. The trustee or trustees of the trust shall be the only individual, individuals, entity, or entities with the obligation or duty to monitor and account for those funds once they have been deposited by the minor's employer. The trustee or trustees shall do an annual accounting of the funds held in trust, in an account or other savings plan, in accordance with Sections 16062 and 16063 of the Probate Code.

(7) The court shall have continuing jurisdiction over the trust established pursuant to the order and may at any time, upon petition of the parent or legal guardian, the minor, through the minor's guardian ad litem, or the trustee or trustees, on good cause shown, order that the trust be amended or terminated, notwithstanding the provisions of the declaration of trust. An order amending or terminating a trust may be made only after reasonable notice to the beneficiary and, if the beneficiary is then a minor, to the parent or guardian, if any, and to the trustee or trustees of the funds with opportunity for all parties to appear and be heard.

(8) A parent or guardian entitled to the physical custody, care, and control of the minor shall promptly notify the minor's employer, in writing, of any change in facts that affect the employer's obligation or ability to set aside the funds in accordance with the order, including, but not limited to, a change of financial institution or account number, or the existence of a new or amended order issued pursuant to paragraph (7) amending or terminating the employer's obligations under this section. The written notification shall be accompanied by a true and accurate photocopy of the trustee's statement pursuant to Section 6753 and, if applicable, a true and accurate photocopy of the new or amended order.

(9)(A) If a parent, guardian, or trustee fails to provide the minor's employer with a true and accurate photocopy of the trustee's statement pursuant to Section 6753 within 180 days after the commencement of employment, the employer shall forward to The Actors' Fund of America 15 percent of the minor's gross earnings pursuant to the contract, together with the minor's name and, if known, the minor's social security number, birth date, last known address, telephone number, email address, dates of employment, and title of the project on which the minor was employed, and shall notify the parent, guardian, or trustee of that transfer by certified mail to the last known address. Upon receipt of those forwarded funds, The Actors' Fund of America shall become the trustee of those funds and the minor's employer shall have no further obligation or duty to monitor or account for the funds.

(B) The Actors' Fund of America shall make its best efforts to notify the parent, guardian, or trustee of their responsibilities to provide a true and accurate photocopy of the trustee's statement pursuant to Section 6753, and in the case of a guardian, a certified copy of the court document appointing the person as the minor's legal guardian. Within 15 business days after receiving those documents, The Actors' Fund of America shall deposit or disburse the funds as directed by the trustee's statement. When making that deposit or disbursal of the funds, The Actors' Fund of America shall provide to the financial institution notice that the funds are subject to Section 6753 and a copy of each applicable order, and shall thereafter have no further obligation or duty to monitor or account for the funds.

(C) The Actors' Fund of America shall notify each beneficiary of their entitlement to the funds that it holds for the beneficiary within 60 days after the date on which its records indicated that the beneficiary has attained 18 years of age or the date on which it received notice that the minor has been emancipated, by sending that notice to the last known address for the beneficiary or, if it has no specific separate address for the beneficiary, to the beneficiary's parent or guardian.

(c)(1) Notwithstanding any other statute, for any minor's contract of a type described in Section 6750 that is not being submitted for approval by the court pursuant to Section 6751, or for which the court has issued a final order denying approval, 15 percent of the minor's gross earnings pursuant to the contract shall be set aside by the minor's employer, except an employer of a minor for services as an extra, background performer, or in a similar capacity, as described in paragraph (3) of subdivision (b) of Section 6750. These amounts shall be held in trust, in an account or other savings plan, and preserved for the benefit of the minor in accordance with Section 6753. At least one parent or legal guardian, as the case may be, entitled to the physical custody, care, and control of the minor, shall be the trustee of the funds set aside for the benefit of the minor, unless the court, upon petition by the parent or legal guardian, the minor, through the minor's guardian ad litem, or the trustee or trustees of the trust, shall determine that appointment of a different individual, individuals, entity, or entities as trustee or trustees is required in the best interest of the minor.

(2) Within 10 business days of commencement after employment, a parent or guardian, as the case may be, entitled to the physical custody, care, and control of the minor shall provide the minor's employer with a true and accurate photocopy of the trustee's statement pursuant to Section 6753 and in addition, in the case of a guardian, a certified copy of the court document appointing the person as the minor's legal guardian. Upon presentation of the trustee's statement offered pursuant to this subdivision, the employer shall provide the parent or guardian with a written acknowledgment of receipt of the statement.

(3) The minor's employer shall deposit 15 percent of the minor's gross earnings pursuant to the contract within 15 business days of receiving the trustee's statement pursuant to Section 6753, or if the court denies approval of the contract, within 15 business days of receiving a final order denying approval of the contract. Notwithstanding any other statute, pending receipt of the trustee's statement or the final court order, the minor's employer shall hold for the benefit of the minor the 15 percent of the minor's gross earnings pursuant to the contract. When making the initial deposit of funds, the minor's employer shall provide written notification to the financial institution or company that the funds are subject to Section 6753. This paragraph does not apply to an employer of a minor for services as an extra, background performer, or in a similar capacity, as described in paragraph (3) of subdivision (b) of Section 6750.

(4) Once the minor's employer deposits the set-aside funds in trust, in an account or other savings plan pursuant to Section 6753, the minor's employer shall have no further obligation or duty to monitor or account for the funds. The trustee or trustees of the trust shall be the only individual, individuals, entity, or entities with the obligation or duty to monitor and account for those funds once they have been deposited by the minor's employer. The trustee or trustees shall do an annual accounting of the funds held in trust, in an account or other savings plan, in accordance with Sections 16062 and 16063 of the Probate Code.

(5) Upon petition of the parent or legal guardian, the minor, through the minor's guardian ad litem, or the trustee or trustees of the trust, to the superior court in a county in which the minor resides or in which the trust is established, the court may at any time, on good cause shown, order that the trust be amended or terminated, notwithstanding the provisions of the declaration of trust. An order amending or terminating a trust may be made only after reasonable notice to the beneficiary and, if the beneficiary is then a minor, to the parent or guardian, if any, and to the trustee or trustees of the funds with opportunity for all parties to appear and be heard.

(6) A parent or guardian entitled to the physical custody, care, and control of the minor shall promptly notify the minor's employer in writing of any change in facts that affect the employer's obligation or ability to set aside funds for the benefit of the minor in accordance with this section, including, but not limited to, a change of financial institution or account number, or the existence of a new or amended order issued pursuant to paragraph (5) amending or terminating the employer's obligations under this section. The written notification shall be accompanied by a true and accurate photocopy of the trustee's statement and attachments pursuant to Section 6753 and, if applicable, a true and accurate photocopy of the new or amended order.

(7)(A) If a parent, guardian, or trustee fails to provide the minor's employer with a true and accurate photocopy of the trustee's statement pursuant to Section 6753, within 180 days after commencement of employment, the employer shall forward to The Actors' Fund of America the 15 percent of the minor's gross earnings pursuant to the contract, together with the minor's name and, if known, the minor's social security number, birth date, last known address, telephone number, email address, dates of employment, and the title of the project on which the minor was employed, and shall notify the parent, guardian, or trustee of that transfer by certified mail to the last known address. Upon receipt of those forwarded funds, The Actors' Fund of America shall become the trustee of those funds and the minor's employer shall have no further obligation or duty to monitor or account for the funds.

(B) The Actors' Fund of America shall make best efforts to notify the parent, guardian, or trustee of their responsibilities to provide a true and accurate photocopy of the trustee's statement pursuant to Section 6753 and in the case of a guardian, a certified copy of the court document appointing the person as the minor's legal guardian. After receiving those documents, The Actors' Fund of America shall deposit or disburse the funds as directed by the trustee's statement, and in accordance with Section 6753, within 15 business days. When making that deposit or disbursal of the funds, The Actors' Fund of America shall provide notice to the financial institution that the funds are subject to Section 6753, and shall thereafter have no further obligation or duty to monitor or account for the funds.

(C) The Actors' Fund of America shall notify each beneficiary of their entitlement to the funds that it holds for the beneficiary, within 60 days after the date on which its records indicate that the beneficiary has attained 18 years of age or the date on which it received notice that the minor has been emancipated, by sending that notice to the last known address that it has for the beneficiary, or to the beneficiary's parent or guardian, where it has no specific separate address for the beneficiary.

(d) Where a parent or guardian is entitled to the physical custody, care, and control of a minor who enters into a contract of a type described in Section 6750, the relationship between the parent or guardian and the minor is a fiduciary relationship that is governed by the law of trusts, whether or not a court has issued a formal order to that effect. The parent or guardian acting in a fiduciary relationship, shall, with the earnings and accumulations of the minor under the contract, pay all liabilities incurred by the minor under the contract, including, but not limited to, payments for taxes on all earnings, including taxes on the amounts set aside under subdivisions (b) and (c) of this section, and payments for personal or professional services rendered to the minor or the business related to the contract. This subdivision does not alter any other existing responsibilities of a parent or legal guardian to provide for the support of a minor child.

(e)(1) Except as otherwise provided in this subdivision, The Actors' Fund of America, as trustee of unclaimed set-aside funds, shall manage and administer those funds in the same manner as a trustee under the Probate Code. Notwithstanding the foregoing, The Actors' Fund of America is not required to open separate, segregated individual trust accounts for each beneficiary but may hold the set-aside funds in a single, segregated master account for all beneficiaries, provided it maintains accounting records for each beneficiary's interest in the master account.

(2) The Actors' Fund of America shall have the right to transfer funds from the master account, or from a beneficiary's segregated account to its general account in an amount equal to the beneficiary's balance. The Actors' Fund of America shall have the right to use those funds transferred to its general account to provide programs and services for young performers. This use of the funds does not limit or alter The Actors' Fund of America's obligation to disburse the set-aside funds to the beneficiary, or the beneficiary's parent, guardian, trustee, or estate pursuant to this chapter.

(3)(A) Upon receiving a certified copy of the beneficiary's birth certificate, or United States passport, and a true and accurate photocopy of the trustee's statement pursuant to Section 6753, The Actors' Fund of America shall transfer the beneficiary's balance to the trust account established for the beneficiary.

(B) The Actors' Fund of America shall disburse the set-aside funds to a beneficiary who has attained 18 years of age, after receiving proof of the beneficiary's identity and a certified copy of the beneficiary's birth certificate or United States passport, or to a beneficiary who has been emancipated, after receiving proof of the beneficiary's identity and appropriate documentation evidencing the beneficiary's emancipation.

(C) The Actors' Fund of America shall disburse the set-aside funds to the estate of a deceased beneficiary after receiving appropriate documentation evidencing the death of the beneficiary and the claimant's authority to collect those funds on behalf of the beneficiary.

(f)(1) The beneficiary of an account held by The Actors' Fund of America pursuant to this section shall be entitled to receive imputed interest on the balance in the account for the entire period during which the account is held at a rate equal to the lesser of the federal reserve rate in effect on the last business day of the prior calendar quarter or the national average money market rate as published in the New York Times on the last Sunday of the prior calendar quarter, adjusted quarterly.

(2) The Actors' Fund of America may assess and deduct from the balance in the beneficiary's account reasonable management, administrative, and investment expenses, including beneficiary-specific fees for initial setup, account notifications and account disbursements, and a reasonably allocable share of management, administrative, and investment expenses of the master account. Fees may not be charged to a beneficiary's account during the first year that the account is held by The Actors' Fund of America.

(3) Notwithstanding paragraph (2), the amount paid on any claim made by a beneficiary or the beneficiary's parent or guardian after The Actors' Fund of America receives and holds funds pursuant to this section may not be less than the amount of the funds received plus the imputed interest.

(g) Notwithstanding any provision of this chapter to the contrary, a minor's employer holding set-aside funds under this chapter, which funds remain unclaimed 180 days after the effective date hereof, shall forward those unclaimed funds to The Actors' Fund of America, along with the minor's name and, if known, the minor's social security number, birth date, last known address, telephone number, email address, dates of employment, and the title of the project on which the minor was employed, and shall notify the parent, guardian, or trustee of that transfer by certified mail to the last known address. Upon receipt of those forwarded funds by The Actors' Fund of America, the minor's employer shall have no further obligation or duty to monitor or account for the funds.

(h) All funds received by The Actors' Fund of America pursuant to this section shall be exempt from the application of the Unclaimed Property Law (Title 10 (commencing with Section 1300) of Part 3 of the Code of Civil Procedure), including, but not limited to, Section 1510 of the Code of Civil Procedure. **Leg.H.** Added Stats 1999 ch 940 §5 (SB 1162). Amended Stats 2003 ch 667 §2 (SB 210); Stats 2013 ch 102 §1 (AB 533), effective January 1, 2014; Stats 2019 ch 115 §75 (AB 1817), effective January 1, 2020.

Prior Law: Former §6752, similar to the present section, was enacted Stats 1992 ch 162 §10, operative January 1, 1994, and repealed Stats 1999 ch 940 §4.

Former Sections: Former Fam C §6752, similar to the present section, was enacted Stats 1992 ch 162 §10, operative January 1, 1994, and repealed Stats 1999 ch 940 §4.

§6753. Establishment of Coogan Trust Account for minor; Requirements for withdrawal; Provision of information to minor's employer; Management of funds

(a) The trustee or trustees shall establish a trust account, that shall be known as a Coogan Trust Account, pursuant to this section at a bank, savings and loan institution, credit union, brokerage firm, or company registered under the Investment Company Act of 1940, that is located in the State of California, unless a similar trust has been previously established, for the purpose of preserving for the benefit of the minor the portion of the minor's gross earnings pursuant to paragraph (1) of subdivision (b) of Section 6752 or pursuant to paragraph (1) of subdivision (c) of Section 6752. The trustee or trustees shall establish the trust pursuant to this section within seven business days after the minor's contract is signed by the minor, the third-party individual or personal services corporation (loan-out company), and the employer.

(b) Except as otherwise provided in this section, prior to the date on which the beneficiary of the trust attains the age of 18 years or the issuance of a declaration of emancipation of the minor under Section 7122, no withdrawal by the beneficiary or any other individual, individuals, entity, or entities may be made of funds on deposit in trust without written order of the superior court pursuant to paragraph (7) of subdivision (b) or paragraph (5) of subdivision (c) of Section 6752. Upon reaching the age of 18 years, the beneficiary may withdraw the funds on deposit in trust only after providing a certified copy of the beneficiary's birth certificate to the financial institution where the trust is located.

(c) The trustee or trustees shall, within 10 business days after the minor's contract is signed by the minor, the third-party individual or personal services corporation (loan-out company), and the employer, prepare a written statement under penalty of perjury that shall include the name, address, and telephone number of the financial institution, the name of the account, the number of the account, the name of the minor beneficiary, the name of the trustee or trustees of the account, and any additional information needed by the minor's employer to deposit into the account the portion of the minor's gross earnings prescribed by paragraph (1) of subdivision (b) or paragraph (1) of subdivision (c) of Section 6752. The trustee or trustees shall attach to the written statement a true and accurate photocopy of any information received from the financial institution confirming the creation of the account, such as an account agreement, account terms, passbook, or other similar writings.

(d) The trust shall be established in California either with a financial institution that is and remains insured at all times by the Federal Deposit Insurance Corporation (FDIC), the Securities Investor Protection Corporation (SIPC), or the National Credit Union Share Insurance Fund (NCUSIF) or their respective successors, or with a company that is and remains registered under the Investment Company Act of 1940. The trustee or trustees of the trust shall be the only individual, individuals, entity, or entities with the obligation or duty to ensure that the funds remain in trust, in an account or other savings plan insured in accordance with this section, or with a company that is and remains registered under the Investment Company Act of 1940 as authorized by this section.

(e) Upon application by the trustee or trustees to the financial institution or company in which the trust is held, the trust funds shall be handled by the financial institution or company in one or more of the following methods:

(1) The financial institution or company may transfer funds to another account or other savings plan at the same financial institution or company, provided that the funds transferred shall continue to be held in trust, and subject to this chapter.

(2) The financial institution or company may transfer funds to another financial institution or company, provided that the funds transferred shall continue to be held in trust, and subject to this chapter and that the transferring financial institution or company has provided written notification to the financial institution or company to which the funds will be transferred that the funds are subject to this section and written notice of the requirements of this chapter.

(3) The financial institution or company may use all or a part of the funds to purchase, in the name of and for the benefit of the minor, (A) investment funds offered by a company registered under the Investment Company Act of 1940, provided that if the underlying investments are equity securities, the investment fund is a broad-based index fund or invests broadly across the domestic or a foreign regional economy, is not a sector fund, and has assets under management of at least two hundred fifty million dollars ($250,000,000); or (B) government securities and bonds, certificates of deposit, money market instruments, money market accounts, or mutual funds investing solely in those government securities and bonds, certificates, instruments, and accounts, that are available at the financial institution where the trust fund or other savings plan is held, provided that the funds shall continue to be held in trust and subject to this chapter, those purchases shall have a maturity date on or before the date upon which the minor will attain the age of 18 years, and any proceeds accruing from those purchases shall be redeposited into that account or accounts or used to further purchase any of those or similar securities, bonds, certificates, instruments, funds, or accounts. **Leg.H.** Added Stats 1999 ch 940 §7 (SB 1162). Amended Stats 2003 ch 667 §3 (SB 210).

Former Sections: Former Fam C §6753, similar to present Fam C §6752, was enacted Stats 1992 ch 162 §10, operative January 1, 1994, and repealed Stats 1999 ch 940 §6.

Prior Law: Former §6753, similar to present Fam C §6752, was enacted Stats 1992 ch 162 §10, operative January 1, 1994, and repealed Stats 1999 ch 940 §6.

PART 4
MEDICAL TREATMENT

Chapter 1. Definitions.
Chapter 2. Consent by Person Having Care of Minor or by Court.
Chapter 3. Consent by Minor.

CHAPTER 1
DEFINITIONS

Definitions to govern construction. §6900.
"Dental care". §6901.
"Medical care". §6902.
"Parent or guardian". §6903.
"Vision care". § 6904.

§6900. Definitions to govern construction

Unless the provision or context otherwise requires, the definitions in this chapter govern the construction of this part. **Leg.H.** Enacted Stats 1992 ch 162 §10 (AB 2650), operative January 1, 1994.

§6901. "Dental care"

"Dental care" means X-ray examination, anesthetic, dental or surgical diagnosis or treatment, and hospital care by a dentist licensed under the Dental Practice Act. **Leg.H.** Enacted Stats 1992 ch 162 §10 (AB 2650), operative January 1, 1994.

§6902. "Medical care"

"Medical care" means X-ray examination, anesthetic, medical or surgical diagnosis or treatment, and hospital care under the general or special supervision and upon the advice of or to be rendered by a physician and surgeon licensed under the Medical Practice Act. **Leg.H.** Enacted Stats 1992 ch 162 §10 (AB 2650), operative January 1, 1994.

§6903. "Parent or guardian"

"Parent or guardian" means either parent if both parents have legal custody, or the parent or person having legal custody, or the guardian, of a minor. **Leg.H.** Enacted Stats 1992 ch 162 §10 (AB 2650), operative January 1, 1994.

§ 6904. "Vision care"

"Vision care" means the diagnosis, prevention, treatment, and management of disorders, diseases, and dysfunctions of the visual system and the provision of habilitative or rehabilitative optometric services by an optometrist licensed pursuant to Article 1 (commencing with Section 3000) of Chapter 7 of Division 2 of the Business and Professions Code. **Leg.H.** Added Stats 2023 ch 152 §1 (SB 457), effective January 1, 2024.

CHAPTER 2
CONSENT BY PERSON HAVING CARE OF MINOR OR BY COURT

Parent or guardian may authorize care provider to consent. §6910.
Court consent. §6911.

§6910. Parent or guardian may authorize care provider to consent

The parent, guardian, or caregiver of a minor who is a relative of the minor and who may authorize medical care and dental care under Section 6550, may authorize in writing an adult into whose care a minor has been entrusted to consent to medical care or dental care, or both, for the minor. **Leg.H.** Enacted Stats 1992 ch 162 §10 (AB 2650), operative January 1, 1994. Amended Stats 1996 ch 563 §2 (SB 392).

§6911. Court consent

(a) Upon application by a minor, the court may summarily grant consent for medical care or dental care or both for the minor if the court determines all of the following:

(1) The minor is 16 years of age or older and resides in this state.

(2) The consent of a parent or guardian is necessary to permit the medical care or dental care or both, and the minor has no parent or guardian available to give the consent.

(b) No fee may be charged for proceedings under this section. **Leg.H.** Enacted Stats 1992 ch 162 §10 (AB 2650), operative January 1, 1994.

CHAPTER 3
CONSENT BY MINOR

Minor's capacity to consent to medical or dental care without consent of parent or guardian. §6920.
Minor's consent not subject to disaffirmance. §6921.
Consent by minor to medical care, vision care, or dental care. §6922.
Consent by minor to outpatient mental health treatment or counseling, or residential shelter services. § 6924.
Consent by minor to pregnancy treatment. §6925.
Consent by minor to treatment for communicable disease or prevention of sexually transmitted disease. §6926.
Consent by rape victim to treatment. §6927.
Consent by assault victim to treatment. §6928.
Consent by minor to drug or alcohol treatment; Involvement, liability and rights of parent or guardian. §6929.
Minor consent to opioid use disorder treatment. § 6929.1.
Consent to treatment by victim of intimate partner violence; Report; Attempt to notify parent or guardian. §6930.

§6920. Minor's capacity to consent to medical or dental care without consent of parent or guardian

Subject to the limitations provided in this chapter, notwithstanding any other provision of law, a minor may consent to the matters provided in this chapter, and the consent of the minor's parent or guardian is not necessary. **Leg.H.** Enacted Stats 1992 ch 162 §10 (AB 2650), operative January 1, 1994.

§6921. Minor's consent not subject to disaffirmance

A consent given by a minor under this chapter is not subject to disaffirmance because of minority. **Leg.H.** Enacted Stats 1992 ch 162 §10 (AB 2650), operative January 1, 1994.

§6922. Consent by minor to medical care, vision care, or dental care

(a) A minor may consent to the minor's medical care, vision care, or dental care if all of the following conditions are satisfied:

(1) The minor is 15 years of age or older.

(2) The minor is living separate and apart from the minor's parents or guardian, whether with or without the parent's or guardian's consent and regardless of the duration of the separate residence.

(3) The minor is managing the minor's own financial affairs, regardless of the source of the minor's income.

(b) The parents or guardian are not liable for medical care, vision care, or dental care provided pursuant to this section.

(c) A physician and surgeon, optometrist, or dentist may, with or without the consent of the minor patient, advise the minor's parent or guardian of the treatment given or needed if the physician and surgeon, optometrist, or dentist has reason to know, on the basis of the information given by the minor, the whereabouts of the parent or guardian. **Leg.H.** Enacted Stats 1992 ch 162 §10 (AB 2650), operative January 1, 1994. Amended Stats 2023 ch 152 §2 (SB 457), effective January 1, 2024.

§6924. Consent by minor to mental health treatment or counseling or residential shelter services [Repealed]

Leg.H. Enacted Stats 1992 ch 162 §10 (AB 2650), operative January 1, 1994. Amended Stats 1993 ch 219 §155 (AB 1500); Stats 2000 ch 519 §1 (AB 2161); Stats 2009 ch 26 §22 (SB 33), effective January 1, 2010; Stats 2011 ch 381 §25 (SB 146), effective January 1, 2012; Stats 2018 ch 703 §46 (SB 1491), effective January 1, 2019; Stats 2019 ch 115 §76 (AB 1817), effective January 1, 2020; Stats 2019 ch 497 §113 (AB 991), effective January 1, 2020 (ch 115 prevails); Stats 2023 ch 338 §2 (AB 665), effective January 1, 2024, inoperative July 1, 2024, repealed January 1, 2025.

§ 6924. Consent by minor to outpatient mental health treatment or counseling, or residential shelter services

(a) As used in this section:

(1) "Mental health treatment or counseling services" means the provision of mental health treatment or counseling on an outpatient basis by any of the following:

(A) A governmental agency.

(B) A person or agency having a contract with a governmental agency to provide the services.

(C) An agency that receives funding from community united funds.

(D) A runaway house or crisis resolution center.

(E) A professional person, as defined in paragraph (2).

(2) "Professional person" means either of the following:

(A) A professional person as defined in Section 124260 of the Health and Safety Code.

(B) The chief administrator of an agency referred to in paragraph (1) or (3).

(3) "Residential shelter services" means any of the following:

(A) The provision of residential and other support services to minors on a temporary or emergency basis in a facility that services only minors by a governmental agency, a person or agency having a contract with a governmental agency to provide these services, an agency that receives funding from community funds, or a licensed community care facility or crisis resolution center.

(B) The provision of other support services on a temporary or emergency basis by any professional person as defined in paragraph (2).

(b) A minor who is 12 years of age or older may consent to mental health treatment or counseling on an outpatient basis, or to residential shelter services, if the minor, in the opinion of the attending professional person, is mature enough to participate intelligently in the outpatient services or residential shelter services.

(c) A professional person offering residential shelter services, whether as an individual or as a representative of an entity specified in paragraph (3) of subdivision (a), shall make their best efforts to notify the parent or guardian of the provision of services.

(d) The mental health treatment or counseling of a minor authorized by this section shall include involvement of the minor's parent or guardian unless the professional person who is treating or counseling the minor, after consulting with the minor, determines that the involvement would be inappropriate. The professional person who is treating or counseling the minor shall state in the client record whether and when the person attempted to contact the minor's parent or guardian, and whether the attempt to contact was successful or unsuccessful, or the reason why, in the professional person's opinion, it would be inappropriate to contact the minor's parent or guardian.

(e) The minor's parents or guardian are not liable for payment for mental health treatment or counseling services provided pursuant to this section unless the parent or guardian participates in the mental health treatment or counseling, and then only for services rendered with the participation of the parent or guardian. The minor's parents or guardian are not liable for payment for any residential shelter services provided pursuant to this section unless the parent or guardian consented to the provision of those services.

(f) This section does not authorize a minor to receive convulsive therapy or psychosurgery as defined in subdivisions (f) and (g) of Section 5325 of the Welfare and Institutions Code, or psychotropic drugs without the consent of the minor's parent or guardian.

(g) This section shall become operative on July 1, 2024. **Leg.H.** Added Stats 2023 ch 338 §3 (AB 665), effective January 1, 2024, operative July 1, 2024.

§6925. Consent by minor to pregnancy treatment

(a) A minor may consent to medical care related to the prevention or treatment of pregnancy.

(b) This section does not authorize a minor:

(1) To be sterilized without the consent of the minor's parent or guardian.

(2) To receive an abortion without the consent of a parent or guardian other than as provided in Section 123450 of the Health and Safety Code. **Leg.H.** Enacted Stats 1992 ch 162 §10 (AB 2650), operative January 1, 1994. Amended Stats 1996 ch 1023 §46 (SB 1497), effective September 29, 1996.

§6926. Consent by minor to treatment for communicable disease or prevention of sexually transmitted disease

(a) A minor who is 12 years of age or older and who may have come into contact with an infectious, contagious, or communicable disease may consent to medical care related to the diagnosis or treatment of the disease, if the disease or condition is one that is required by law or regulation adopted pursuant to law to be reported to the local health officer, or is a related sexually transmitted disease, as may be determined by the State Public Health Officer.

(b) A minor who is 12 years of age or older may consent to medical care related to the prevention of a sexually transmitted disease.

(c) The minor's parents or guardian are not liable for payment for medical care provided pursuant to this section. **Leg.H.** Enacted Stats 1992 ch 162 §10 (AB 2650), operative January 1, 1994. Amended Stats 2011 ch 652 §1 (AB 499), effective January 1, 2012.

§6927. Consent by rape victim to treatment

A minor who is 12 years of age or older and who is alleged to have been raped may consent to medical care related to the diagnosis or treatment of the condition and the collection of medical evidence with regard to the alleged rape. **Leg.H.** Enacted Stats 1992 ch 162 §10 (AB 2650), operative January 1, 1994.

§6928. Consent by assault victim to treatment

(a) "Sexually assaulted" as used in this section includes, but is not limited to, conduct coming within Section 261, 286, or 287 of the Penal Code.

(b) A minor who is alleged to have been sexually assaulted may consent to medical care related to the diagnosis and treatment of the condition, and the collection of medical evidence with regard to the alleged sexual assault.

(c) The professional person providing medical treatment shall attempt to contact the minor's parent or guardian and shall note in the minor's treatment record the date and time the professional person attempted to contact the parent or guardian and whether the attempt was successful or unsuccessful. This subdivision does not apply if the professional person reasonably believes that the minor's parent or guardian committed the sexual assault on the minor. **Leg.H.** Enacted Stats 1992 ch 162 §10 (AB 2650), operative January 1, 1994. Amended Stats 2018 ch 423 §25 (SB 1494), effective January 1, 2019.

§6929. Consent by minor to drug or alcohol treatment; Involvement, liability and rights of parent or guardian

(a) As used in this section:

(1) "Counseling" means the provision of counseling services by a provider under a contract with the state or a county to provide alcohol or drug abuse counseling services pursuant to Part 2 (commencing with Section 5600) of Division 5 of the Welfare and Institutions Code or pursuant to Division 10.5 (commencing with Section 11750) of the Health and Safety Code.

(2) "Drug or alcohol" includes, but is not limited to, any substance listed in any of the following:

(A) Section 380 or 381 of the Penal Code.

(B) Division 10 (commencing with Section 11000) of the Health and Safety Code.

(C) Subdivision (f) of Section 647 of the Penal Code.

(3) "LAAM" means levoalphacetylmethadol as specified in paragraph (10) of subdivision (c) of Section 11055 of the Health and Safety Code.

(4) "Professional person" means a physician and surgeon, registered nurse, psychologist, clinical social worker, professional clinical counselor, marriage and family therapist, registered marriage and family therapist intern when appropriately employed and supervised pursuant to Section 4980.43 of the Business and Professions Code, psychological assistant when appropriately employed and supervised pursuant to Section 2913 of the Business and Professions Code, associate clinical social worker when appropriately employed and supervised pursuant to Section 4996.18 of the Business and Professions Code, or registered clinical counselor intern when appropriately employed and supervised pursuant to Section 4999.42 of the Business and Professions Code.

(b) A minor who is 12 years of age or older may consent to medical care and counseling relating to the diagnosis and treatment of a drug- or alcohol-related problem.

(c) The treatment plan of a minor authorized by this section shall include the involvement of the minor's parent or guardian, if appropriate, as determined by the professional person or treatment facility treating the minor. The professional person providing medical care or counseling to a minor shall state in the minor's treatment record whether and when the professional person attempted to contact the minor's parent or guardian, and whether the attempt to contact the parent or guardian was successful or unsuccessful, or the reason why, in the opinion of the professional person, it would not be appropriate to contact the minor's parent or guardian.

(d) The minor's parent or guardian is not liable for payment for care provided to a minor pursuant to this section, except that if the minor's parent or guardian participates in a counseling program pursuant to this section, the parent or guardian is liable for the cost of the services provided to the minor and the parent or guardian.

(e)(1) This section does not authorize a minor to receive replacement narcotic therapy, in a program licensed pursuant to Article 1 (commencing with Section 11839) of Chapter 10 of Part 2 of Division 10.5 of the Health and Safety Code, without the consent of the minor's parent or guardian.

(2) Notwithstanding paragraph (1), a minor 16 years of age or older may consent to receive medications for opioid use disorder from a licensed narcotic treatment program as replacement narcotic therapy without the consent of the minor's parent or guardian only if, and to the extent, expressly permitted by federal law.

(f) It is the intent of the Legislature that the state shall respect the right of a parent or legal guardian to seek medical care and counseling for a drug- or alcohol-related problem of a minor child when the child does not consent to the medical care and counseling, and nothing in this section shall be construed to restrict or eliminate this right.

(g) Notwithstanding any other law, when a parent or legal guardian has sought the medical care and counseling for a drug- or alcohol-related problem of a minor child, the physician and surgeon shall disclose medical information concerning the care to the minor's parent or legal guardian upon the parent's or guardian's request, even if the minor child does not consent to disclosure, without liability for the disclosure. **Leg.H.** Enacted Stats 1992 ch 162 §10 (AB 2650), operative January 1, 1994. Amended Stats 1995 ch 455 §1 (AB 1113), effective September 5, 1995; Stats 1996 ch 656 §1 (AB 2883); Stats 2002 ch 1013 §79 (SB 2026); Stats 2004 ch 59 §1 (AB 2182); Stats 2009 ch 26 §23 (SB 33), effective January 1, 2010; Stats 2011 ch 381 §26 (SB 146), effective January 1, 2012; Stats 2019 ch 115 §77 (AB 1817), effective January 1, 2020; Stats 2023 ch 456 §1 (AB 816), effective January 1, 2024.

§ 6929.1. Minor consent to opioid use disorder treatment

Notwithstanding any other law, a minor 16 years of age or older may consent to opioid use disorder treatment that uses buprenorphine at a physician's office, clinic, or health facility, by a licensed physician and surgeon or other health care provider acting within the scope of their practice, whether or not the minor also has the consent of their parent or guardian. **Leg.H.** Added Stats 2023 ch 456 §2 (AB 816), effective January 1, 2024.

§6930. Consent to treatment by victim of intimate partner violence; Report; Attempt to notify parent or guardian

(a) A minor who is 12 years of age or older and who states that the minor is injured as a result of intimate partner violence may consent to medical care related to the diagnosis or treatment of the injury and the collection of medical evidence with regard to the alleged intimate partner violence.

(b)(1) For purposes of this section, "intimate partner violence" means an intentional or reckless infliction of bodily harm that is perpetrated by a person with whom the minor has or has had a sexual, dating, or spousal relationship.

(2) This section does not apply when a minor is an alleged victim of rape, as defined in Section 261 of the Penal Code, in which case Section 6927 shall apply, and does not apply when a minor is alleged to have been sexually assaulted, as described in Section 6928, in which case that section shall apply.

(c) If the health practitioner providing treatment believes that the injuries described in subdivision (a) require a report pursuant to Section 11160 of the Penal Code, the health practitioner shall do both of the following:

(1) Inform the minor that the report will be made.

(2) Attempt to contact the minor's parent or guardian and inform them of the report. The health practitioner shall note in the minor's treatment record the date and time of the attempt to contact the parent or guardian and whether the attempt was successful or unsuccessful. This paragraph does not apply if the health practitioner reasonably believes that the minor's parent or guardian committed the intimate partner violence on the minor. **Leg.H.** Added Stats 2018 ch 1003 §1 (AB 3189), effective January 1, 2019. Amended Stats 2019 ch 115 §78 (AB 1817), effective January 1, 2020; Stats 2021 ch 626 §11 (AB 1171), effective January 1, 2022.

PART 5
ENLISTMENT IN ARMED FORCES

Court consent. §6950.

§6950. Court consent

(a) Upon application by a minor, the court may summarily grant consent for enlistment by the minor in the armed forces of the United States if the court determines all of the following:

(1) The minor is 16 years of age or older and resides in this state.

(2) The consent of a parent or guardian is necessary to permit the enlistment, and the minor has no parent or guardian available to give the consent.

(b) No fee may be charged for proceedings under this section. **Leg.H.** Enacted Stats 1992 ch 162 §10 (AB 2650), operative January 1, 1994.

PART 6
EMANCIPATION OF MINORS LAW

Chapter 1. General Provisions.
Chapter 2. Effect of Emancipation.
Chapter 3. Court Declaration of Emancipation.

CHAPTER 1
GENERAL PROVISIONS

Citation of part. §7000.
Purpose and intent of part. §7001.
Emancipated minor. §7002.

§7000. Citation of part

This part may be cited as the Emancipation of Minors Law. **Leg.H.** Enacted Stats 1992 ch 162 §10 (AB 2650), operative January 1, 1994.

§7001. Purpose and intent of part

It is the purpose of this part to provide a clear statement defining emancipation and its consequences and to permit an emancipated minor to obtain a court declaration of the minor's status. This part is not intended to affect the status of minors who may become emancipated under the decisional case law that was in effect before the enactment of Chapter 1059 of the Statutes of 1978. **Leg.H.** Enacted Stats 1992 ch 162 §10 (AB 2650), operative January 1, 1994.

§7002. Emancipated minor

A person under the age of 18 years is an emancipated minor if any of the following conditions is satisfied:

(a) The person has entered into a valid marriage, or has established a valid domestic partnership, regardless of whether the marriage or the domestic partnership has been dissolved.

(b) The person is on active duty with the Armed Forces of the United States.

(c) The person has received a declaration of emancipation pursuant to Section 7122. **Leg.H.** Enacted Stats 1992 ch 162 §10 (AB 2650), operative January 1, 1994. Amended Stats 2018 ch 660 §9 (SB 273), effective January 1, 2019.

CHAPTER 2
EFFECT OF EMANCIPATION

Emancipated minor considered an adult. §7050.
Insurance contracts. §7051.
Stock, memberships, and property. §7052.

§7050. Emancipated minor considered an adult

An emancipated minor shall be considered as being an adult for the following purposes:

(a) The minor's right to support by the minor's parents.

(b) The right of the minor's parents to the minor's earnings and to control the minor.

(c) The application of Sections 300 and 601 of the Welfare and Institutions Code.

(d) Ending all vicarious or imputed liability of the minor's parents or guardian for the minor's torts. Nothing in this section affects any liability of a parent, guardian, spouse, or employer imposed by the Vehicle Code, or any vicarious liability that arises from an agency relationship.

(e) The minor's capacity to do any of the following:

(1) Consent to medical, dental, or psychiatric care, without parental consent, knowledge, or liability.

(2) Enter into a binding contract or give a delegation of power.

(3) Buy, sell, lease, encumber, exchange, or transfer an interest in real or personal property, including, but not limited to, shares of stock in a domestic or foreign corporation or a membership in a nonprofit corporation.

(4) Sue or be sued in the minor's own name.

(5) Compromise, settle, arbitrate, or otherwise adjust a claim, action, or proceeding by or against the minor.

(6) Make or revoke a will.

(7) Make a gift, outright or in trust.

(8) Convey or release contingent or expectant interests in property, including marital property rights and any right of survivorship incident to joint tenancy, and consent to a transfer, encumbrance, or gift of marital property.

(9) Exercise or release the minor's powers as donee of a power of appointment unless the creating instrument otherwise provides.

(10) Create for the minor's own benefit or for the benefit of others a revocable or irrevocable trust.

(11) Revoke a revocable trust.

(12) Elect to take under or against a will.

(13) Renounce or disclaim any interest acquired by testate or intestate succession or by inter vivos transfer, including exercise of the right to surrender the right to revoke a revocable trust.

(14) Make an election referred to in Section 13502 of, or an election and agreement referred to in Section 13503 of, the Probate Code.

(15) Establish the minor's own residence.

(16) Apply for a work permit pursuant to Section 49110 of the Education Code without the request of the minor's parents.

(17) Enroll in a school or college. **Leg.H.** Enacted Stats 1992 ch 162 §10 (AB 2650), operative January 1, 1994.

§7051. Insurance contracts

An insurance contract entered into by an emancipated minor has the same effect as if it were entered into by an adult and, with respect to that contract, the minor has the same rights, duties, and liabilities as an adult. **Leg.H.** Enacted Stats 1992 ch 162 §10 (AB 2650), operative January 1, 1994.

§7052. Stock, memberships, and property

With respect to shares of stock in a domestic or foreign corporation held by an emancipated minor, a membership in a nonprofit corporation held by an emancipated minor, or other property held by an emancipated minor, the minor may do all of the following:

(a) Vote in person, and give proxies to exercise any voting rights, with respect to the shares, membership, or property.

(b) Waive notice of any meeting or give consent to the holding of any meeting.

(c) Authorize, ratify, approve, or confirm any action that could be taken by shareholders, members, or property owners. **Leg.H.** Enacted Stats 1992 ch 162 §10 (AB 2650), operative January 1, 1994.

CHAPTER 3
COURT DECLARATION OF EMANCIPATION

Article 1. General Provisions.
Article 2. Procedure for Declaration.
Article 3. Voiding or Rescinding Declaration.
Article 4. Identification Cards and Information.

ARTICLE 1
General Provisions

Legislative intent. §7110.
Effect of declaration on benefits. §7111.

§7110. Legislative intent

It is the intent of the Legislature that proceedings under this part be as simple and inexpensive as possible. To that end, the Judicial Council is requested to prepare and distribute to the clerks of the superior courts appropriate forms for the proceedings that are suitable for use by minors acting as their own counsel. **Leg.H.** Enacted Stats 1992 ch 162 §10 (AB 2650), operative January 1, 1994.

§7111. Effect of declaration on benefits

The issuance of a declaration of emancipation does not entitle the minor to any benefits under Division 9 (commencing with Section 10000) of the Welfare and Institutions Code which would not otherwise accrue to an emancipated minor. **Leg.H.** Enacted Stats 1992 ch 162 §10 (AB 2650), operative January 1, 1994.

ARTICLE 2
Procedure for Declaration

Petition. §7120.
Notice. §7121.
Issuance of declaration of emancipation. §7122.

Writ of mandate. §7123.

§7120. Petition
(a) A minor may petition the superior court of the county in which the minor resides or is temporarily domiciled for a declaration of emancipation.

(b) The petition shall set forth with specificity all of the following facts:

(1) The minor is at least 14 years of age.

(2) The minor willingly lives separate and apart from the minor's parents or guardian with the consent or acquiescence of the minor's parents or guardian.

(3) The minor is managing their own financial affairs. As evidence of this, the minor shall complete and attach a declaration of income and expenses as provided in Judicial Council form FL-150.

(4) The source of the minor's income is not derived from any activity declared to be a crime by the laws of this state or the laws of the United States. **Leg.H.** Enacted Stats 1992 ch 162 §10 (AB 2650), operative January 1, 1994. Amended Stats 1993 ch 219 §156 (AB 1500); Stats 2004 ch 811 §3 (AB 3079); Stats 2019 ch 115 §79 (AB 1817), effective January 1, 2020.

§7121. Notice
(a) Before the petition for a declaration of emancipation is heard, notice the court determines is reasonable shall be given to the minor's parents, guardian, or other person entitled to the custody of the minor, or proof shall be made to the court that their addresses are unknown or that for other reasons the notice cannot be given.

(b) The clerk of the court shall also notify the local child support agency of the county in which the matter is to be heard of the proceeding. If the minor is a ward of the court, notice shall be given to the probation department. If the child is a dependent child of the court, notice shall be given to the county welfare department.

(c) The notice shall include a form whereby the minor's parents, guardian, or other person entitled to the custody of the minor may give their written consent to the petitioner's emancipation. The notice shall include a warning that a court may void or rescind the declaration of emancipation and the parents may become liable for support and medical insurance coverage pursuant to Chapter 2 (commencing with Section 4000) of Part 2 of Division 9 and Sections 17400, 17402, 17404, and 17422. **Leg.H.** Enacted Stats 1992 ch 162 §10 (AB 2650), operative January 1, 1994. Amended Stats 1993 ch 219 §157 (AB 1500); Stats 2003 ch 365 §1 (AB 1710).

§7122. Issuance of declaration of emancipation
(a) The court shall sustain the petition if it finds that the minor is a person described by Section 7120 and that emancipation would not be contrary to the minor's best interest.

(b) If the petition is sustained, the court shall forthwith issue a declaration of emancipation, which shall be filed by the clerk of the court.

(c) A declaration is conclusive evidence that the minor is emancipated. **Leg.H.** Enacted Stats 1992 ch 162 §10 (AB 2650), operative January 1, 1994. Amended Stats 2002 ch 784 §107 (SB 1316).

§7123. Writ of mandate
(a) If the petition is denied, the minor has a right to file a petition for a writ of mandate.

(b) If the petition is sustained, the parents or guardian have a right to file a petition for a writ of mandate if they have appeared in the proceeding and opposed the granting of the petition. **Leg.H.** Enacted Stats 1992 ch 162 §10 (AB 2650), operative January 1, 1994.

ARTICLE 3
Voiding or Rescinding Declaration

Grounds for voiding or rescinding. §7130.
Petition to void declaration. §7131.
Petition to rescind declaration. §7132.
Notice. §7133.
Court order. §7134.
Effect of voiding or rescission on contract and property rights. §7135.

§7130. Grounds for voiding or rescinding
(a) A declaration of emancipation obtained by fraud or by the withholding of material information is voidable.

(b) A declaration of emancipation of a minor who is indigent and has no means of support is subject to rescission. **Leg.H.** Enacted Stats 1992 ch 162 §10 (AB 2650), operative January 1, 1994.

§7131. Petition to void declaration
A petition to void a declaration of emancipation on the ground that the declaration was obtained by fraud or by the withholding of material information may be filed by any person or by any public or private agency. The petition shall be filed in the court that made the declaration. **Leg.H.** Enacted Stats 1992 ch 162 §10 (AB 2650), operative January 1, 1994.

§7132. Petition to rescind declaration
(a) A petition to rescind a declaration of emancipation on the ground that the minor is indigent and has no means of support may be filed by the minor declared emancipated, by the minor's conservator, or by the district attorney of the county in which the minor resides. The petition shall be filed in the county in which the minor or the conservator resides.

(b) The minor may be considered indigent if the minor's only source of income is from public assistance benefits. The court shall consider the impact of the rescission of the declaration of emancipation on the minor and shall find the rescission of the declaration of emancipation will not be contrary to the best interest of the minor before granting the order to rescind. **Leg.H.** Enacted Stats 1992 ch 162 §10 (AB 2650), operative January 1, 1994. Amended Stats 1993 ch 219 §158 (AB 1500).

§7133. Notice
(a) Before a petition under this article is heard, notice the court determines is reasonable shall be given to the minor's parents or guardian, or proof shall be made to the court that their addresses are unknown or that for other reasons the notice cannot be given.

(b) The notice to parents shall state that if the declaration of emancipation is voided or rescinded, the parents may be liable to provide support and medical insurance coverage for the child pursuant to Chapter 2 (commencing with Section 4000) of Part 2 of Division 9 of this code and Sections 11350, 11350.1, 11475.1, and 11490 of the Welfare and Institutions Code.

(c) No liability accrues to a parent or guardian not given actual notice, as a result of voiding or rescinding the declaration of emancipation, until that parent or guardian is given actual notice. **Leg.H.** Enacted Stats 1992 ch 162 §10 (AB 2650), operative January 1, 1994. Amended Stats 1993 ch 219 §159 (AB 1500).

§7134. Court order
If the petition is sustained, the court shall forthwith issue an order voiding or rescinding the declaration of emancipation, which shall be filed by the clerk of the court. **Leg.H.** Enacted Stats 1992 ch 162 §10 (AB 2650), operative January 1, 1994. Amended Stats 2002 ch 784 §108 (SB 1316).

§7135. Effect of voiding or rescission on contract and property rights
Voiding or rescission of the declaration of emancipation does not alter any contractual obligation or right or any property right or interest that arose during the period that the declaration was in effect. **Leg.H.** Enacted Stats 1992 ch 162 §10 (AB 2650), operative January 1, 1994.

ARTICLE 4
Identification Cards and Information

Department of Motor Vehicles records system and identification cards. §7140.
Good faith reliance on identification card. §7141.
Protection of public entities and public employees. §7142.
Notice of Department of Motor Vehicles if declaration voided or rescinded. §7143.

§7140. Department of Motor Vehicles records system and identification cards
On application of a minor declared emancipated under this chapter, the Department of Motor Vehicles shall enter identifying information in its law enforcement computer network, and the fact of emancipation shall be stated on the department's identification card issued to the emancipated minor. **Leg.H.** Enacted Stats 1992 ch 162 §10 (AB 2650), operative January 1, 1994.

§7141. Good faith reliance on identification card
A person who, in good faith, has examined a minor's identification card and relies on a minor's representation that the minor is emancipated, has the same rights and obligations as if the minor were in fact emancipated at the time of the representation. **Leg.H.** Enacted Stats 1992 ch 162 §10 (AB 2650), operative January 1, 1994.

§7142. Protection of public entities and public employees
No public entity or employee is liable for any loss or injury resulting directly or indirectly from false or inaccurate information contained in the

Department of Motor Vehicles records system or identification cards as provided in this part. **Leg.H.** Enacted Stats 1992 ch 162 §10 (AB 2650), operative January 1, 1994.

§7143. Notice of Department of Motor Vehicles if declaration voided or rescinded

If a declaration of emancipation is voided or rescinded, notice shall be sent immediately to the Department of Motor Vehicles which shall remove the information relating to emancipation in its law enforcement computer network. Any identification card issued stating emancipation shall be invalidated. **Leg.H.** Enacted Stats 1992 ch 162 §10 (AB 2650), operative January 1, 1994.

DIVISION 12
PARENT AND CHILD RELATIONSHIP

Part 1. Rights of Parents.
Part 2. Presumption Concerning Child of Marriage and Genetic Testing to Determine Parentage.
Part 3. Uniform Parentage Act.
Part 4. Freedom From Parental Custody and Control.
Part 5. Interstate Compact on Placement of Children.
Part 6. Foster Care Placement Considerations.
Part 7. Surrogacy and Donor Facilitators, Assisted Reproduction Agreements for Gestational Carriers, and Oocyte Donations.

PART 1
RIGHTS OF PARENTS

Right of parent to services and earnings of unemancipated minor child. §7500.
Parent's right to determine residence of child. §7501.
Parent's control over property of child. §7502.
Earnings of minor. §7503.
Parent's relinquishment of control and earnings of child. §7504.
Cessation of parental authority. §7505.
Compensation and support of adult child. §7506.
Remedy for parental abuse. §7507.

§7500. Right of parent to services and earnings of unemancipated minor child

(a) The mother of an unemancipated minor child, and the father, if presumed to be the father under Section 7611, are equally entitled to the services and earnings of the child.

(b) If one parent is dead, is unable or refuses to take custody, or has abandoned the child, the other parent is entitled to the services and earnings of the child.

(c) This section shall not apply to any services or earnings of an unemancipated minor child related to a contract of a type described in Section 6750. **Leg.H.** Added Stats 1993 ch 219 §162 (AB 1500). Amended Stats 1999 ch 940 §8 (SB 1162).

Prior Law: There was another section of this number which was added Stats 1992 ch 162 §10, operative January 1, 1994, and renumbered to be §7540 by Stats 1993 ch 219 §161.

§7501. Parent's right to determine residence of child

(a) A parent entitled to the custody of a child has a right to change the residence of the child, subject to the power of the court to restrain a removal that would prejudice the rights or welfare of the child.

(b) It is the intent of the Legislature to affirm the decision in In re Marriage of Burgess (1996) 13 Cal.4th 25, and to declare that ruling to be the public policy and law of this state. **Leg.H.** Added Stats 1993 ch 219 §164 (AB 1500). Amended Stats 2003 ch 674 §1 (SB 156).

Prior Law: There was another section of this number which was added Stats 1992 ch 162 §10, operative January 1, 1994, and amended and renumbered §7541 by Stats 1993 ch 219 §163.

§7502. Parent's control over property of child

The parent, as such, has no control over the property of the child. **Leg.H.** Added Stats 1993 ch 219 §165 (AB 1500).

§7503. Earnings of minor

The employer of a minor shall pay the earnings of the minor to the minor until the parent or guardian entitled to the earnings gives the employer notice that the parent or guardian claims the earnings. **Leg.H.** Added Stats 1993 ch 219 §166 (AB 1500).

§7504. Parent's relinquishment of control and earnings of child

The parent, whether solvent or insolvent, may relinquish to the child the right of controlling the child and receiving the child's earnings. Abandonment by the parent is presumptive evidence of that relinquishment. **Leg.H.** Added Stats 1993 ch 219 §167 (AB 1500).

§7505. Cessation of parental authority

The authority of a parent ceases on any of the following:

(a) The appointment, by a court, of a guardian of the person of the child.

(b) The marriage of the child.

(c) The child attaining the age of majority. **Leg.H.** Added Stats 1993 ch 219 §168 (AB 1500).

§7506. Compensation and support of adult child

Where a child, after attaining the age of majority, continues to serve and to be supported by the parent, neither party is entitled to compensation, in the absence of an agreement for the compensation. **Leg.H.** Added Stats 1993 ch 219 §169 (AB 1500).

§7507. Remedy for parental abuse

The abuse of parental authority is the subject of judicial cognizance in a civil action brought by the child, or by the child's relative within the third degree, or by the supervisors of the county where the child resides; and when the abuse is established, the child may be freed from the dominion of the parent, and the duty of support and education enforced. **Leg.H.** Added Stats 1993 ch 219 §170 (AB 1500).

PART 2
PRESUMPTION CONCERNING CHILD OF MARRIAGE AND GENETIC TESTING TO DETERMINE PARENTAGE

Chapter 1. Child of Wife Cohabiting With Husband.
Chapter 2. Genetic Testing to Determine Parentage.
Chapter 3. Establishment of Parentage by Voluntary Declaration.

CHAPTER 1
CHILD OF WIFE COHABITING WITH HUSBAND

Presumption arising from birth of child during marriage. §7540.
Use of blood tests to determine paternity. §7541.

§7540. Presumption arising from birth of child during marriage

(a) Except as provided in Section 7541, the child of spouses who cohabited at the time of conception and birth is conclusively presumed to be a child of the marriage.

(b) The conclusive marital presumption in subdivision (a) does not apply if the court determines that the husband of the woman who gave birth was impotent or sterile at the time of conception and that the child was not conceived through assisted reproduction. **Leg.H.** Added Stats 2018 ch 876 §5 (AB 2684), effective January 1, 2019.

Prior Law: Former Fam C §7540, similar to the present section, was enacted Stats 1992 ch 162 §10 (AB 2650), effective January 1, 1993, operative January 1, 1994, as Fam C §7500, renumbered by Stats 1993 ch 219 §161 (AB 1500), effective January 1, 1994, and repealed Stats 2018 ch 876 §4 (AB 2684), effective January 1, 2019.

Editor's Notes— 2018 Notes: The provisions of this act should be interpreted to provide equal treatment to same-sex parents, transgender parents, and their children. Stats 2018 ch 876 §1(c).

It is not the intent of the Legislature to abrogate case law interpreting the laws amended in this act that is consistent with the purposes of this act, unless it is inconsistent with specific statutory language. Stats 2018 ch 876 §1(d).

Former Sections: Former Fam C §7540, similar to the present section, was enacted Stats 1992 ch 162 §10 (AB 2650), operative January 1, 1994, as Fam C §7500, renumbered by Stats 1993 ch 219 §161 (AB 1500), and repealed Stats 2018 ch 876 §4 (AB 2684).

§7541. Use of blood tests to determine paternity

(a) If the court finds that the spouse who is a presumed parent under Section 7540 is not a genetic parent of the child pursuant to Chapter 2 (commencing with Section 7550), the question of parentage shall be resolved in accordance with all other applicable provisions of this division, including, but not limited to, Section 7612.

(b) An action to challenge the parentage of the spouse who is a presumed parent under Section 7540 shall be filed and served not later than two years from the child's date of birth and may only be filed by any of the following:

(1) By either spouse.

(2) By a person who is a presumed parent under Section 7611 or by the child, through or by the child's guardian ad litem, to establish the parentage of the person who is a presumed parent under Section 7611.

(c) The petition or motion to challenge a presumption under Section 7540 pursuant to this section shall be supported by a declaration under oath submitted by the moving party stating the factual basis for placing the issue of parentage before the court.

(d) Genetic testing may not be used to challenge parentage, in either of the following cases:

(1) A case that reached final judgment of parentage on or before September 30, 1980.

(2) A case challenging the parentage of a spouse who is a parent pursuant to Section 7962 or subdivision (a) of Section 7613, except to resolve a dispute regarding whether the child was conceived through assisted reproduction. **Leg.H.** Enacted Stats 1992 ch 162 §10 (AB 2650), operative January 1, 1994 as §7501. Amended and renumbered by Stats 1993 ch 219 §163 (AB 1500). Amended Stats 1998 ch 581 §18 (AB 2801); Stats 2018 ch 876 §6 (AB 2684), effective January 1, 2019; Stats 2019 ch 115 §80 (AB 1817), effective January 1, 2020.

Editor's Notes— 2018 Note: For legislative intent, see the 2018 Notes following Fam C §7540.

CHAPTER 2
GENETIC TESTING TO DETERMINE PARENTAGE

Scope of chapter. §7550.
Definitions. §7550.5.
Order for genetic testing in civil action or proceeding involving parentage. §7551.
Facilitation of genetic tests. §7551.5.
Requirements for genetic testing; Rules if objection to testing laboratory's relationship index calculation. §7552.
Service of copies of results of genetic testing. §7552.5.
Compensation of experts. §7553.
Finding of parentage. §7554.
Identification as genetic parent; Challenge to genetic testing results. §7555.
Limitation on application in criminal matters. §7556.
Right to produce other expert evidence. §7557.
Administrative order requiring genetic testing; Costs; Motion for relief; Additional test. §7558.
Advance payment of initial genetic testing cost. §7559.
Order for additional genetic testing upon request of person contesting initial testing results. §7560.
Order for genetic testing of deceased person. §7562.

§7550. Scope of chapter

This chapter shall govern both of the following:

(a) The genetic testing of a person who either voluntarily submits to genetic testing or is ordered to submit to genetic testing pursuant to an order of a court or local child support agency.

(b) The use of genetic testing in a proceeding to determine parentage. **Leg.H.** Added Stats 2018 ch 876 §9 (AB 2684), effective January 1, 2019.

Prior Law: Former Fam C §7550, relating to citation of chapter as Uniform Act on Blood Tests to Determine Paternity, was enacted Stats 1992 ch 162 §10 (AB 2650), effective January 1, 1993, operative January 1, 1994, amended Stats 1993 ch 219 §174 (AB 1500), effective January 1, 1994, and repealed Stats 2018 ch 876 §8 (AB 2684), effective January 1, 2019. Historical derivation: (a) former CCP §1980.1, as added Stats 1953 ch 1426 §1; (b) former Ev C §890, as enacted 1965 ch 299 §2.

Editor's Notes— 2018 Note: For legislative intent, see the 2018 Notes following Fam C §7540.

Former Sections: Former Fam C §7550, relating to citation of chapter as Uniform Act on Blood Tests to Determine Paternity, was enacted Stats 1992 ch 162 §10 (AB 2650), operative January 1, 1994, and repealed Stats 2018 ch 876 §8 (AB 2684).

§7550.5. Definitions

The following definitions shall apply to this chapter:

(a) "Combined relationship index" means the product of all tested relationship indices.

(b) "Ethnic or racial group" means, for the purpose of genetic testing, a recognized group that a person identifies as the person's ancestry, or part of the ancestry, or that is identified by other information.

(c) "Genetic testing" means any genetic testing that complies with Section 7552.

(d) "Hypothesized genetic relationship" means an asserted genetic relationship between a person and a child.

(e) "Probability of parentage" means, for the ethnic or racial group to which a person alleged to be a parent belongs, the probability that a hypothesized genetic relationship is supported, compared to the probability that a genetic relationship is supported between the child and a random person of the ethnic or racial group used in the hypothesized genetic relationship, expressed as a percentage incorporating the combined relationship index and a prior probability.

(f) "Relationship index" means a likelihood ratio that compares the probability of a genetic marker given a hypothesized genetic relationship and the probability of the genetic marker given a genetic relationship between the child and a random person of the ethnic or racial group used in the hypothesized genetic relationship. **Leg.H.** Added Stats 2018 ch 876 §10 (AB 2684), effective January 1, 2019.

2018 Note: For legislative intent, see the 2018 Notes following Fam C §7540.

§7551. Order for genetic testing in civil action or proceeding involving parentage

(a) Except as provided in subdivisions (b) and (c), in a civil action or proceeding in which parentage is a relevant fact, the court may, upon its own initiative or upon suggestion made by or on behalf of any person who is involved, and shall upon motion of any party to the action or proceeding made at a time so as not to delay the proceedings unduly, order the woman who gave birth, the child, and the alleged genetic parent to submit to genetic testing.

(b)(1) Genetic testing shall not be used for any of the following purposes:

(A) To challenge the parentage of a person who is a parent pursuant to subdivision (a) of Section 7613, except to resolve a dispute whether the child was conceived through assisted reproduction.

(B) To challenge the parentage of a person who is a parent pursuant to Section 7962, except to resolve a dispute whether the gestational carrier surrogate is a genetic parent.

(C) To establish the parentage of a person who is a donor pursuant to Section 7613, except to resolve a dispute whether the child was conceived through assisted reproduction.

(2) If the child has a presumed parent pursuant to Section 7540, a motion for genetic testing is governed by Section 7541.

(3) If the child has a parent whose parentage has been previously established in a judgment, a request for genetic testing shall be governed by Section 7647.7.

(4) A court shall not order genetic testing if the genetic testing would be used to establish the parentage of a person who is prohibited under this division from establishing parentage based on evidence of genetic testing.

(c) A court shall not order in utero genetic testing.

(d) In any case under this division in which genetic testing is ordered, the following shall apply:

(1) If a party refuses to submit to genetic testing, the court may resolve the question of parentage against that party or enforce its order if the rights of others and the interests of justice so require.

(2) The refusal of a party to submit to genetic testing is admissible in evidence in any proceeding to determine parentage.

(3) If two or more persons are subject to court-ordered genetic testing, the court may order that the testing be completed concurrently or sequentially.

(4) Genetic testing of a woman who gave birth to a child is not a condition precedent to the testing of the child and a person whose genetic parentage of the child is being determined. If the woman is unavailable for genetic testing, the court may order genetic testing of the child and each person whose genetic parentage of the child is at issue.

(5) An order under this division for genetic testing is enforceable by contempt. **Leg.H.** Added Stats 2018 ch 876 §12 (AB 2684), effective January 1, 2019. Amended Stats 2023 ch 851 §3 (AB 1650), effective January 1, 2024.

Prior Law: Former Fam C §7551, similar to the present section, was enacted Stats 1992 ch 162 §10 (AB 2650), effective January 1, 1993, operative January 1, 1994, amended Stats 1997 ch 599 §36 (AB 573), effective January 1, 1998, and repealed Stats 2018 ch 876 §11 (AB 2684), effective January 1, 2019.

Editor's Notes—2018 Note: For legislative intent, see the 2018 Notes following Fam C §7540.

Former Sections: Former Fam C §7551, similar to the present section, was enacted Stats 1992 ch 162 §10 (AB 2650), operative January 1, 1994, and repealed Stats 2018 ch 876 §11 (AB 2684).

§7551.5. Facilitation of genetic tests

All hospitals, local child support agencies, welfare offices, and family courts shall facilitate genetic tests for purposes of enforcement of this chapter. This may include having a health care professional available for purposes of extracting samples to be used for genetic testing. **Leg.H.** §6.

§7552. Requirements for genetic testing; Rules if objection to testing laboratory's relationship index calculation

(a) Genetic testing shall be of a type reasonably relied on by experts in the field of genetic testing and performed in a testing laboratory accredited by either of the following:

(1) The AABB, formerly known as the American Association of Blood Banks, or a successor organization.

(2) An accrediting body designated by the Secretary of the United States Department of Health and Human Services.

(b) A specimen used in genetic testing may consist of a sample or a combination of samples of blood, buccal cells, bone, hair, or other body tissue or fluid. The specimen used in the testing need not be of the same kind for each person undergoing genetic testing.

(c) Based on the ethnic or racial group of a person undergoing genetic testing, a testing laboratory shall determine the databases from which to select frequencies for use in calculating a relationship index. If a person or a local child support agency objects to the laboratory's choice, the following rules shall apply:

(1) Not later than 30 days after receipt of the report of the test, the objecting person or local child support agency may request the court to require the laboratory to recalculate the relationship index using an ethnic or racial group different from that used by the laboratory.

(2) The person or local child support agency objecting to the choice of laboratories under this subdivision shall do either of the following:

(A) If the requested frequencies are not available to the laboratory for the ethnic or racial group requested, provide the requested frequencies compiled in a manner recognized by accrediting bodies.

(B) Engage another laboratory to perform the calculations.

(3) The laboratory may use its own statistical estimate if there is a question of which ethnic or racial group is appropriate. The laboratory shall calculate the frequencies using statistics, if available, for any other ethnic or racial group requested.

(d) If, after recalculation of the relationship index pursuant to subdivision (c) using a different ethnic or racial group, genetic testing does not identify a person as a genetic parent of the child, the court may require a person who has been tested to submit to additional genetic testing to identify a genetic parent. **Leg.H.** Added Stats 2018 ch 876 §14 (AB 2684), effective January 1, 2019.

Prior Law: Former Fam C §7552, similar to the present section, was enacted Stats 1992 ch 162 §10 (AB 2650), effective January 1, 1993, operative January 1, 1994, amended Stats 1994 ch 1266 §3.5 (AB 3804), effective January 1, 1995, Stats 1997 ch 599 §37 (AB 573), effective January 1, 1998, Stats 1998 ch 485 §66 (AB 2803), effective January 1, 1999, and repealed Stats 2018 ch 876 §13 (AB 2684), effective January 1, 2019.

2018 Note: For legislative intent, see the 2018 Notes following Fam C §7540.

Former Sections: Former Fam C §7552, similar to the present section, was enacted Stats 1992 ch 162 §10 (AB 2650), operative January 1, 1994, and repealed Stats 2018 ch 876 §13 (AB 2684).

§7552.5. Service of copies of results of genetic testing

(a) A copy of the results of all genetic testing performed under Section 7551 or 7558 shall be served upon all parties, by any method of service authorized under Chapter 5 (commencing with Section 1010) of Title 14 of Part 2 of the Code of Civil Procedure except personal service, no later than 20 days prior to a hearing in which the genetic test results may be admitted into evidence. The genetic test results shall be accompanied by a declaration under penalty of perjury of the custodian of records or other qualified employee of the laboratory that conducted the genetic tests, stating in substance each of the following:

(1) The declarant is the duly authorized custodian of the records or other qualified employee of the laboratory, and has authority to certify the records.

(2) A statement that establishes in detail the chain of custody of all genetic samples collected, including the date on which the genetic sample was collected, the identity of each person from whom a genetic sample was collected, the identity of the person who performed or witnessed the collecting of the genetic samples and packaged them for transmission to the laboratory, the date on which the genetic samples were received by the laboratory, the identity of the person who unpacked the samples and forwarded them to the person who performed the laboratory analysis of the genetic sample, and the identification and qualifications of all persons who performed the laboratory analysis and published the results.

(3) A statement that establishes that the procedures used by the laboratory to conduct the tests for which the test results are attached are used in the laboratory's ordinary course of business to ensure accuracy and proper identification of genetic samples.

(4) The genetic test results were prepared at or near the time of completion of the genetic tests by personnel of the business qualified to perform genetic tests in the ordinary course of business.

(b) The genetic test results shall be admitted into evidence at the hearing or trial to establish parentage, without the need for foundation testimony of authenticity and accuracy, unless a written objection to the genetic test results is filed with the court and served on all other parties, by a party no later than five days prior to the hearing or trial in which parentage is at issue.

(c) If a written objection is filed with the court and served on all parties within the time specified in subdivision (b), experts appointed by the court shall be called by the court as witnesses to testify to their findings and are subject to cross-examination by the parties. **Leg.H.** Added Stats 1994 ch 1266 §3.7 (AB 3804). Amended Stats 1997 ch 599 §38 (AB 573); Stats 1999 ch 652 §7 (SB 240); Stats 2018 ch 876 §15 (AB 2684), effective January 1, 2019.

2018 Note: For legislative intent, see the 2018 Notes following Fam C §7540.

§7553. Compensation of experts

(a) The compensation of each expert witness appointed by the court shall be fixed at a reasonable amount. It shall be paid as the court shall order. Except as provided in subdivision (b), the court may order that it be paid by the parties in the proportions and at the times the court prescribes, or that the proportion of any party be paid by the county, and that, after payment by the parties or the county or both, all or part or none of it be taxed as costs in the action or proceeding.

(b) If the expert witness is appointed for the court's needs, the compensation shall be paid by the court. **Leg.H.** Enacted Stats 1992 ch 162 §10 (AB 2650), operative January 1, 1994. Amended Stats 2012 ch 470 §22 (AB 1529), effective January 1, 2013.

§7554. Finding of parentage

(a) If the woman who gave birth to the child is the only other person who is a parent or has a claim to parentage of the child under this division, the court shall find the person who is the alleged father or genetic parent who is not a donor under Section 7613 to be a parent of the child if the person meets any of the following:

(1) Is identified pursuant to Section 7555 as a genetic parent of the child and the identification is not successfully challenged.

(2) Admits parentage in a pleading, when making an appearance, or during a hearing, the court accepts the admission, and the court determines that the person is a genetic parent of the child.

(3) Declines to submit to genetic testing ordered by the court or a local child support agency, in which case, the court may find that the person is a parent of the child even if the person denies a genetic relationship with the child.

(4) Is in default after service of process and the court determines the person to be a genetic parent of the child.

(5) Is neither identified nor excluded as a genetic parent by genetic testing and, based on other evidence, the court determines the person to be a genetic parent of the child.

(b) If more than one person other than the woman who gave birth asserts a claim under this division to be the child's parent, parentage shall be determined under provisions of this division. **Leg.H.** Added Stats 2018 ch 876 §17 (AB 2684), effective January 1, 2019. Amended Stats 2019 ch 115 §81 (AB 1817), effective January 1, 2020.

Prior Law: Former Fam C §7554, similar to the present section, was enacted Stats 1992 ch 162 §10 (AB 2650), effective January 1, 1993, operative January 1, 1994, and repealed Stats 2018 ch 876 §16 (AB 2684), effective January 1, 2019.

Editor's Notes—2018 Note: For legislative intent, see the 2018 Notes following Fam C §7540.

Former Sections: Former Fam C §7554, similar to the present section, was enacted Stats 1992 ch 162 §10 (AB 2650), operative January 1, 1994, and repealed Stats 2018 ch 876 §16 (AB 2684).

§7555. Identification as genetic parent; Challenge to genetic testing results

(a) Subject to a challenge under subdivision (b), a person is identified under this part as a genetic parent of a child if genetic testing complies with this part and the results of the testing disclose both of the following:

(1) The person has at least a 99 percent probability of parentage, using a prior probability of 0.50, as calculated by using the combined relationship index obtained in the testing.

(2) A combined relationship index of at least 100 to 1.

(b) A person identified pursuant to subdivision (a) as a genetic parent of the child may challenge the genetic testing results only by other genetic testing satisfying the requirements of this chapter that either excludes the person as a genetic parent of the child or identifies another person as a possible genetic parent of the child other than the woman who gave birth to the child or the person challenging parentage.

(c) If more than one person, other than the woman who gave birth to the child, is identified by genetic testing as a possible genetic parent of the child, the court shall order each person to submit to further genetic testing to identify a genetic parent. **Leg.H.** Added Stats 2018 ch 876 §19 (AB 2684), effective January 1, 2019.

Prior Law: Former Fam C §7555, relating to rebuttable presumption of paternity, similar to the present section, was enacted Stats 1992 ch 162 §10 (AB 2650), effective January 1, 1993, operative January 1, 1994, amended Stats 1993 ch 219 §175 (AB 1500), effective January 1, 1994, Stats 1997 ch 599 §39 (AB 573), effective January 1, 1998, and repealed Stats 2018 ch 876 §18 (AB 2684), effective January 1, 2019.

2018 Note: For legislative intent, see the 2018 Notes following Fam C §7540.

Former Sections: Former Fam C §7555, relating to rebuttable presumption of paternity, similar to the present section, was enacted Stats 1992 ch 162 §10 (AB 2650), operative January 1, 1994, and repealed Stats 2018 ch 876 §18 (AB 2684).

§7556. Limitation on application in criminal matters

This part applies to criminal actions subject to the following limitations and provisions:

(a) An order for genetic testing shall be made only upon application of a party or on the court's initiative.

(b) The compensation of the experts, other than an expert witness appointed by the court for the court's needs, shall be paid by the county under order of court. The compensation of an expert witness appointed for the court's needs shall be paid by the court.

(c) The court may direct a verdict of acquittal if the person is found not to be a genetic parent pursuant to Section 7555, otherwise the case shall be submitted for determination upon all the evidence. **Leg.H.** Enacted Stats 1992 ch 162 §10 (AB 2650), operative January 1, 1994. Amended Stats 2012 ch 470 §23 (AB 1529), effective January 1, 2013; Stats 2018 ch 876 §20 (AB 2684), effective January 1, 2019.

2018 Note: For legislative intent, see the 2018 Notes following Fam C §7540.

§7557. Right to produce other expert evidence

Nothing in this part prevents a party to an action or proceeding from producing other expert evidence on the matter covered by this part; but, where other expert witnesses are called by a party to the action or proceeding, their fees shall be paid by the party calling them and only ordinary witness fees shall be taxed as costs in the action or proceeding. **Leg.H.** Enacted Stats 1992 ch 162 §10 (AB 2650), operative January 1, 1994.

§7558. Administrative order requiring genetic testing; Costs; Motion for relief; Additional test

(a) This section applies only to cases where support enforcement services are being provided by the local child support agency pursuant to Section 17400.

(b) In any civil action or proceeding in which parentage is a relevant fact, and in which the issue of parentage is contested, the local child support agency may issue an administrative order requiring the mother, child, and the alleged father to submit to genetic testing if any of the following conditions exist:

(1) The person alleging parentage has signed a statement under penalty of perjury that sets forth facts that establish a reasonable possibility that the person is the child's genetic parent.

(2) The person denying parentage has signed a statement under penalty of perjury that sets forth facts that establish a reasonable possibility that the person is not a genetic parent of the child.

(3) The alleged father has filed an answer in the action or proceeding in which parentage is a relevant fact and has requested that genetic tests be performed.

(4) The woman who gave birth to the child and the alleged father agree in writing to submit to genetic tests.

(c) Notwithstanding subdivision (b), the local child support agency may not order a person to submit to genetic tests in any of the following instances:

(1) The person has been found to have good cause for failure to cooperate in the determination of parentage pursuant to Section 11477 of the Welfare and Institutions Code.

(2) A case in which more than one person other than the woman who gave birth asserts a claim under this division to be the child's parent.

(3) A case involving a child conceived through assisted reproduction.

(d) The local child support agency shall pay the costs of any genetic tests that are ordered under subdivision (b), subject to the county obtaining a court order for reimbursement from the alleged father if parentage is established pursuant to Section 7553.

(e) This section does not prohibit a person who has been ordered by the local child support agency to submit to genetic tests pursuant to this section from filing a notice of motion with the court in the action or proceeding in which parentage is a relevant fact seeking relief from the local child support agency's order to submit to genetic tests. In that event, the court shall resolve the issue of whether genetic tests should be ordered as provided in Section 7551. When a person refuses to submit to the tests after receipt of the administrative order pursuant to this section and fails to seek relief from the court from the administrative order either prior to the scheduled tests or within 10 days after the tests are scheduled, the court may resolve the question of parentage against that person or enforce the administrative order if the rights of others or the interest of justice so require. Except as provided in subdivision (c), a person's refusal to submit to tests ordered by the local child support agency is admissible in evidence in any proceeding to determine parentage if a notice of motion is not filed within the timeframes specified in this subdivision.

(f) If the original test result is contested, the local child support agency shall order an additional test only upon request and advance payment of the contestant.

(g) The local child support agency shall not order in utero genetic testing.

(h) The local child support agency shall administer this section consistent with federal law. **Leg.H.** Added Stats 1997 ch 599 §40 (AB 573). Amended Stats 2000 ch 808 §72 (AB 1358), effective September 28, 2000; Stats 2018 ch 876 §21 (AB 2684), effective January 1, 2019.

2018 Note: For legislative intent, see the 2018 Notes following Fam C §7540.

§7559. Advance payment of initial genetic testing cost

Payment of the cost of initial genetic testing shall be made in advance when agreed to by the parties or ordered by the court pursuant to Section 7640. **Leg.H.** Added Stats 2018 ch 876 §22 (AB 2684), effective January 1, 2019.

2018 Note: For legislative intent, see the 2018 Notes following Fam C §7540.

§7560. Order for additional genetic testing upon request of person contesting initial testing results

The court or local child support agency shall order additional genetic testing upon the request of a person who contests the results of the initial testing under Section 7555. **Leg.H.** Added Stats 2018 ch 876 §23 (AB 2684), effective January 1, 2019.

Editor's Notes—2018 Note: For legislative intent, see the 2018 Notes following Fam C §7540.

§7562. Order for genetic testing of deceased person

If a person seeking genetic testing demonstrates good cause, the court may order genetic testing of a deceased person. **Leg.H.** Added Stats 2018 ch 876 §24 (AB 2684), effective January 1, 2019.

2018 Note: For legislative intent, see the 2018 Notes following Fam C §7540.

CHAPTER 3
ESTABLISHMENT OF PARENTAGE BY VOLUNTARY DECLARATION

Legislative findings and declarations. §7570.
Voluntary declaration of parentage. §7571.
Informational and training materials; Regulations. §7572.
Persons who may sign declaration of parentage; Signature requirements; Effective date of declaration; Effect of declaration; Declaration effective in another state. §7573.
When voluntary declaration of parentage is void; Notice of action for determination that declaration is void. §7573.5.
Form for voluntary declaration of parentage. §7574.
Rescission of voluntary declaration of parentage. §7575.
Proceeding by signatory to challenge voluntary declaration of parentage on basis of fraud, duress, or mistake; Time limitations. §7576.
Action by nonsignatory to challenge voluntary declaration of parentage; Standing; Supporting declaration; Hearing; Time limitation; Notice; Burden of proof; Factors for setting aside declaration; Basis for denial; Requirements if petition to set aside granted. §7577.
Signatory as required party to proceeding to challenge voluntary declaration of parentage; Submission of signatory to personal jurisdiction; Legal responsibilities during pendency of proceeding to challenge; Burden of proof; Order for issuance of new birth certificate. §7578.
Effect of voluntary declaration of parentage signed by minor parent. §7580.
Presumption of parentage applicable to declarations signed on or before specified date. §7581.

§7570. Legislative findings and declarations

(a) The Legislature hereby finds and declares as follows:

(1) There is a compelling state interest in establishing parentage for all children. Establishing parentage is the first step toward a child support award, which, in turn, provides children with equal rights and access to benefits, including, but not limited to, social security, health insurance, survivors' benefits, military benefits, and inheritance rights.

(2) A simple administrative system allowing for establishment of voluntary parentage will result in a significant increase in the ease of establishing parentage, a significant increase in parentage establishment, an increase in the number of children who have greater access to child support and other benefits, and a significant decrease in the time and money required to establish parentage due to the removal of the need for a lengthy and expensive court process to determine and establish parentage and is in the public interest.

(b) This section shall become operative on January 1, 2020. **Leg.H.** Added Stats 2018 ch 876 §27 (AB 2684), effective January 1, 2019, operative January 1, 2020.

Prior Law: Former Fam C §7570, similar to the present section, was added Stats 1993 ch 1240 §1 (AB 1277), amended Stats 2018 ch 876 §26 (AB 2684), effective January 1, 2019, and repealed January 1, 2020, by its own terms.

§7571. Voluntary declaration of parentage

(a) On and after January 1, 1995, upon the event of a live birth, prior to an unmarried mother or a mother who gave birth to a child conceived through assisted reproduction leaving a hospital, the person responsible for registering live births under Section 102405 of the Health and Safety Code shall provide to the woman giving birth and shall attempt to provide, at the place of birth, to the person identified by the woman giving birth as either the only possible genetic parent other than the woman who gave birth or the intended parent of a child conceived through assisted reproduction, a voluntary declaration of parentage together with the written materials described in Section 7572. Staff in the hospital shall witness the signatures of parents signing a voluntary declaration of parentage and shall forward the signed declaration to the Department of Child Support Services within 20 days of the date the declaration was signed. A copy of the declaration shall be made available to each of the attesting parents.

(b) A health care provider shall not be subject to civil, criminal, or administrative liability for a negligent act or omission relative to the accuracy of the information provided or for filing the declaration with the appropriate state or local agencies.

(c) The local child support agency shall pay the sum of ten dollars ($10) to birthing hospitals and other entities that provide prenatal services for each completed declaration of parentage that is filed with the Department of Child Support Services, provided that the local child support agency and the hospital or other entity providing prenatal services has entered into a written agreement that specifies the terms and conditions for the payment as required by federal law.

(d) If the declaration is not registered by the person responsible for registering live births at the hospital, it may be completed by the attesting parents, notarized, and mailed to the Department of Child Support Services at any time after the child's birth.

(e) Prenatal clinics shall offer prospective parents the opportunity to sign a voluntary declaration of parentage. In order to be paid for their services as provided in subdivision (c), prenatal clinics must ensure that the form is witnessed and forwarded to the Department of Child Support Services within 20 days of the date the declaration was signed.

(f) Declarations shall be made available without charge at all local child support agency offices, offices of local registrars of births and deaths, courts, and county welfare departments within this state. Staff in these offices shall witness the signatures of parents wishing to sign a voluntary declaration of parentage and shall be responsible for forwarding the signed declaration to the Department of Child Support Services within 20 days of the date the declaration was signed.

(g) The Department of Child Support Services, at its option, may pay the sum of ten dollars ($10) to local registrars of births and deaths, county welfare departments, or courts for each completed declaration of parentage that is witnessed by staff in these offices and filed with the Department of Child Support Services. In order to receive payment, the Department of Child Support Services and the entity shall enter into a written agreement that specifies the terms and conditions for payment as required by federal law. The Department of Child Support Services shall study the effect of the ten dollar ($10) payment on obtaining completed voluntary declaration of parentage forms.

(h) The Department of Child Support Services and local child support agencies shall publicize the availability of the declarations. The local child support agency shall make the declaration, together with the written materials described in subdivision (a) of Section 7572, available upon request to any parent and any agency or organization that is required to offer parents the opportunity to sign a voluntary declaration of parentage. The local child support agency shall also provide qualified staff to answer parents' questions regarding the declaration and the process of establishing parentage.

(i) Copies of the declaration and any rescissions filed with the Department of Child Support Services shall be made available only to the parents, the child, the local child support agency, the county welfare department, the county counsel, the State Department of Public Health, and the courts.

(j) Publicly funded or licensed health clinics, pediatric offices, Head Start programs, child care centers, social services providers, prisons, and schools may offer parents the opportunity to sign a voluntary declaration of parentage. In order to be paid for their services as provided in subdivision (c), publicly funded or licensed health clinics, pediatric offices, Head Start programs, child care centers, social services providers, prisons, and schools shall ensure that the form is witnessed and forwarded to the Department of Child Support Services.

(k) An agency or organization required to offer parents the opportunity to sign a voluntary declaration of parentage shall also identify parents who are willing to sign but were unavailable when the child was born. The organization shall then contact these parents within 10 days and again offer the parent the opportunity to sign a voluntary declaration of parentage.

(*l*) This section shall become operative on January 1, 2020. **Leg.H.** Added Stats 2018 ch 876 §29 (AB 2684), effective January 1, 2019, operative January 1, 2020. Amended Stats 2023 ch 131 §59 (AB 1754), effective January 1, 2024.

2018 Note: For legislative intent, see the 2018 Notes following Fam C §7540.

Prior Law: Former Fam C §7571, similar to the present section, was added Stats 1993 ch 1240 §1 (AB 1277), amended Stats 1994 ch 1269 §51 (AB 2208), Stats 1996 ch 1023 §47 (SB 1497), effective September 29, 1996 (ch 1062 prevails), ch 1062 §4 (AB 1832), Stats 1997 ch 599 §41 (AB 573);, tats 1998 ch 485 §67 (AB 2803), ch 858 §3 (AB 2169) (ch 858 prevails), Stats 1999 ch 652 §8 (SB 240), Stats 2001 ch 745 §44 (SB 1191), effective October 12, 2001, Stats 2001 ch 755 §9 (SB 943), effective October 12, 2001, Stats 2012 ch 728 §37 (SB 71), effective January 1, 2013, Stats 2018 ch 876 §28 (AB 2684), effective January 1, 2019, and repealed January 1, 2020, by its own terms.

§7572. Informational and training materials; Regulations

(a) The Department of Child Support Services, in consultation with the State Department of Health Care Services, the California Association of Hospitals and Health Systems, and other affected health provider organizations, shall work cooperatively to develop written materials to assist providers and parents in complying with this chapter. These written materials shall be updated periodically by the Department of Child Support Services to reflect changes in law, procedures, or public need.

(b) The written materials for unmarried parents or parents of a child conceived through assisted reproduction that shall be attached to the form specified in Section 7574 and shall contain the following information:

(1) A signed voluntary declaration of parentage that is filed with the Department of Child Support Services legally establishes parentage.

(2) The legal rights and obligations of both parents and the child that result from the establishment of parentage.

(3) An alleged father's constitutional rights to have the issue of parentage decided by a court; to notice of any hearing on the issue of parentage; to have an opportunity to present the alleged father's case to the court, including the right to present and cross-examine witnesses; to be represented by an attorney; and to have an attorney appointed if the alleged father cannot afford one in a parentage action filed by a local child support agency.

(4) That by signing the voluntary declaration of parentage, the father is voluntarily waiving the father's constitutional rights.

(c) Parents shall also be given oral notice of the rights and responsibilities specified in subdivision (b). Oral notice may be accomplished through the use of audio- or video-recorded programs developed by the Department of Child Support Services to the extent permitted by federal law.

(d) The Department of Child Support Services shall, free of charge, make available to hospitals, clinics, and other places of birth all informational and training materials for the program under this chapter, as well as the declaration of parentage form. The Department of Child Support Services shall make training available to every participating hospital, clinic, local registrar of births and deaths, and other place of birth no later than June 30, 1999.

(e) The Department of Child Support Services may adopt regulations, including emergency regulations, necessary to implement this chapter. **Leg.H.** Added Stats 2018 ch 876 §31 (AB 2684), effective January 1, 2019, operative January 1, 2020. Amended Stats 2019 ch 115 §82 (AB 1817), effective January 1, 2020; Stats 2023 ch 131 §60 (AB 1754), effective January 1, 2024.

Editor's Notes—2018 Note: For legislative intent, see the 2018 Notes following Fam C §7540.

Prior Law: Former Fam C §7572, similar to the present section, was added Stats 1993 ch 1240 §1 (AB 1277), amended Stats 1994 ch 1269 §51.5 (AB 2208), Stats 1996 ch 1062 §5 (AB 1832), Stats 1997 ch 599 §42 (AB 573), Stats 1998 ch 485 §68 (AB 2803), ch 858 §4 (AB 2169) (ch 858 prevails), Stats 1999 ch 83 §53 (SB 966) (ch 652 prevails), ch 652 §10 (SB 240), Stats 2009 ch 88 §38 (AB 176), effective January 1, 2010, Stats 2010 ch 328 §65 (SB 1330), effective January 1, 2011, Stats 2018 ch 876 §30 (AB 2684), effective January 1, 2019, and repealed January 1, 2020, by its own terms.

§7573. Persons who may sign declaration of parentage; Signature requirements; Effective date of declaration; Effect of declaration; Declaration effective in another state

(a) The following persons may sign a voluntary declaration of parentage to establish the parentage of the child:

(1) An unmarried woman who gave birth to the child and another person who is a genetic parent.

(2) A married or unmarried woman who gave birth to the child and another person who is a parent under Section 7613 of a child conceived through assisted reproduction.

(b) A voluntary declaration of parentage shall be in a record signed by the woman who gave birth to the child and by either the only possible genetic parent other than the woman who gave birth or the intended parent of a child conceived through assisted reproduction, and the signatures shall be attested by a notary or witnessed.

(c) Except as provided by Section 7580, a voluntary declaration of parentage takes effect on the filing of the document with the Department of Child Support Services.

(d) Except as provided in Sections 7573.5, 7575, 7576, 7577, and 7580, a completed voluntary declaration of parentage that complies with this chapter and that has been filed with the Department of Child Support Services is equivalent to a judgment of parentage of the child and confers on the declarant all rights and duties of a parent.

(e) The court shall give full faith and credit to a voluntary declaration of parentage effective in another state if the declaration was in a signed record and otherwise complies with the law of the other state.

(f) This section shall become operative on January 1, 2020. **Leg.H.** Added Stats 2018 ch 876 §33 (AB 2684), effective January 1, 2019, operative January 1, 2020.

Editor's Notes—2018 Note: For legislative intent, see the 2018 Notes following Fam C §7540.

Prior Law: Former Fam C §7573, similar to the present section, was added Stats 1996 ch 1062 §6 (AB 1832), amended Stats 1998 ch 858 §5 (AB 2169), Stats 2000 ch 808 §73 (AB 1358), effective September 28, 2000, Stats 2011 ch 185 §1 (AB 1349), effective January 1, 2012, Stats 2018 ch 876 §32 (AB 2684), effective January 1, 2019, and repealed January 1, 2020, by its own terms.

§7573.5. When voluntary declaration of parentage is void; Notice of action for determination that declaration is void

(a) A voluntary declaration of parentage is void if, at the time of signing, any of the following are true:

(1) A person other than the woman who gave birth to the child or a person seeking to establish parentage through a voluntary declaration of

parentage is a presumed parent under Section 7540 or subdivision (a), (b), or (c) of Section 7611.

(2) A court has entered a judgment of parentage of the child.

(3) Another person has signed a valid voluntary declaration of parentage.

(4) The child has a parent under Section 7613 or 7962 other than the signatories.

(5) The person seeking to establish parentage is a donor pursuant to Section 7613.

(6) The person seeking to establish parentage asserts that the person is a parent under Section 7613 and the child was not conceived through assisted reproduction.

(b) In an action in which a party is seeking a determination that a voluntary declaration of parentage is void under this section, notice shall be provided pursuant to Section 7635. **Leg.H.** Added Stats 2018 ch 876 §34 (AB 2684), effective January 1, 2019, operative January 1, 2020. Amended Stats 2019 ch 115 §83 (AB 1817), effective January 1, 2020; Stats 2023 ch 851 §4 (AB 1650), effective January 1, 2024.

2018 Note: For legislative intent, see the 2018 Notes following Fam C §7540.

§7574. Form for voluntary declaration of parentage

(a) The voluntary declaration of parentage shall be executed on a form developed by the Department of Child Support Services in consultation with the State Department of Public Health and groups addressing child support, child custody, assisted reproduction issues, and lesbian, gay, bisexual, and transgender rights.

(b) The form described in subdivision (a) shall contain, at a minimum, all of the following:

(1) The name and the signature of the woman who gave birth to the child.

(2) The name and the signature of the person seeking to establish parentage.

(3) The name of the child.

(4) The date of birth of the child.

(5) For a voluntary declaration of parentage signed pursuant to paragraph (1) of subdivision (a) of Section 7573, all of the following:

(A) A statement by the woman who gave birth that the woman is unmarried and understands the written materials described in Section 7572, that the person who is signing the voluntary declaration of parentage is the only possible genetic parent other than the woman who gave birth, that the woman who gave birth consents to the establishment of parentage by the genetic parent signing the voluntary declaration of parentage, and that the woman who gave birth understands that a challenge by a signatory to a valid declaration of parentage is permitted only under limited circumstances and is barred two years after the effective date of the declaration.

(B) A statement by the person signing the voluntary declaration of parentage that the person has read and understands the written materials described in Section 7572, understands that by signing the voluntary declaration of parentage the person is waiving rights as described in the written materials, that the person is the genetic parent of the child, that the person consents to the establishment of parentage by signing the voluntary declaration of parentage, that the person is assuming all the rights and responsibilities of a parent and wishes to be named on the child's birth certificate, and that the person understands that a challenge by a signatory to a valid declaration of parentage is permitted only under limited circumstances and is barred two years after the effective date of the declaration.

(6) For a voluntary declaration of parentage signed pursuant to paragraph (2) of subdivision (a) of Section 7573, all of the following:

(A) A statement by the woman who gave birth that the woman has read and understands the written materials described in Section 7572, that the person who is signing the voluntary declaration of parentage is the intended parent of a child conceived through assisted reproduction, that the woman who gave birth consents to the establishment of parentage by the other person signing the voluntary declaration of parentage, and that the woman who gave birth understands that a challenge by a signatory to a valid declaration of parentage is permitted only under limited circumstances and is barred two years after the effective date of the declaration.

(B) A statement that the person seeking to establish parentage has read and understands the written materials described in Section 7572, understands that by signing the voluntary declaration of parentage the person is waiving rights as described in the written materials, that the person is the intended parent of the child conceived through assisted reproduction, that the person consents to the establishment of parentage by signing the voluntary declaration of parentage, that the person is assuming all the rights and responsibilities of a parent and wishes to be named on the child's birth certificate, and that the person understands that a challenge by a signatory to a valid declaration of parentage is permitted only under limited circumstances and is barred two years after the effective date of the declaration.

(7) The name and the signature of the person who witnesses the signing of the declaration. **Leg.H.** Added Stats 2018 ch 876 §36 (AB 2684), effective January 1, 2019, operative January 1, 2020. Amended Stats 2019 ch 115 §84 (AB 1817), effective January 1, 2020.

Prior Law: Former Fam C §7574, similar to the present section, was added Stats 1996 ch 1062 §8 (AB 1832), amended Stats 2000 ch 808 §74 (AB 1358), effective September 28, 2000, Stats 2018 ch 876 §35 (AB 2684), effective January 1, 2019, and repealed January 1, 2020, by its own terms.

Editor's Notes— 2018 Note: For legislative intent, see the 2018 Notes following Fam C §7540.

§7575. Rescission of voluntary declaration of parentage

(a) Either parent may rescind the voluntary declaration of parentage by filing a rescission form with the Department of Child Support Services within 60 days of the date of execution of the declaration by the attesting parents, whichever signature is later, unless a court order for custody, visitation, or child support has been entered in an action in which the signatory seeking to rescind was a party. The Department of Child Support Services shall develop a form to be used by parents to rescind the declaration of parentage and instructions on how to complete and file the rescission with the Department of Child Support Services. The form shall include a declaration under penalty of perjury completed by the person filing the rescission form that certifies that a copy of the rescission form was sent by any form of mail requiring a return receipt to the other person who signed the voluntary declaration of parentage. A copy of the return receipt shall be attached to the rescission form when filed with the Department of Child Support Services. The form and instructions shall be written in simple, easy to understand language and shall be made available at the local family support office and the office of local registrar of births and deaths. The department shall, upon written request, provide to a court or commissioner a copy of any rescission form filed with the department that is relevant to proceedings before the court or commissioner.

(b) This section shall become operative on January 1, 2020. **Leg.H.** Added Stats 2018 ch 876 §38 (AB 2684), effective January 1, 2019, operative January 1, 2020.

2018 Note: For legislative intent, see the 2018 Notes following Fam C §7540.

Prior Law: Former Fam C §7575, similar to the present section, was added Stats 1996 ch 1062 §10 (AB 1832), amended Stats 1997 ch 599 §43 (AB 573), Stats 1998 ch 485 §69 (AB 2803), ch 858 §6 (AB 2169) (ch 858 prevails), Stats 1999 ch 83 §54 (SB 966) (ch 653 prevails), ch 652 §11 (SB 240), ch 653 §10.5 (AB 380), Stats 2000 ch 808 §75 (AB 1358), effective September 28, 2000, Stats 2002 ch 927 §3.3 (AB 3032), Stats 2004 ch 849 §1 (AB 252), Stats 2018 ch 876 §37 (AB 2684), effective January 1, 2019, and repealed January 1, 2020, by its own terms.

§7576. Proceeding by signatory to challenge voluntary declaration of parentage on basis of fraud, duress, or mistake; Time limitations

(a) After the period for rescission provided in Section 7575 expires, but not later than two years after the effective date provided in subdivision (c) of Section 7573 of a voluntary declaration of parentage, a signatory of the voluntary declaration of parentage may commence a proceeding to challenge the declaration on the basis of fraud, duress, or material mistake of fact.

(b) The limitations period provided in subdivision (a) shall not apply if the voluntary declaration of parentage is void under Section 7573.5.

(c) This section shall become operative on January 1, 2020. **Leg.H.** Added Stats 2018 ch 876 §40 (AB 2684), effective January 1, 2019, operative January 1, 2020.

Editor's Notes—2018 Note: For legislative intent, see the 2018 Notes following Fam C §7540.

Prior Law: Former Fam C §7576, similar to the present section, was added Stats 1996 ch 1062 §12 (AB 1832), amended Stats 2011 ch 185 §2 (AB 1349), effective January 1, 2012, Stats 2018 ch 876 §39 (AB 2684), effective January 1, 2019, and repealed January 1, 2020, by its own terms.

§7577. Action by nonsignatory to challenge voluntary declaration of parentage; Standing; Supporting declaration; Hearing; Time limitation; Notice; Burden of proof; Factors for setting aside declaration; Basis for denial; Requirements if petition to set aside granted

The following rules apply in an action to challenge a valid voluntary declaration of parentage brought by a person who is not a signatory to the declaration. This section does not apply to a voluntary declaration of parentage that is void under Section 7573.5.

(a) A person has standing under this section if the person is an alleged genetic parent who is not a donor under Section 7613, is a presumed parent under Section 7611, or any person who has standing under Section 7630.

(b) The petition challenging a voluntary declaration of parentage pursuant to this section shall be supported by a declaration under oath alleging specific facts to support standing under this section.

(c) If the court holds a hearing to determine standing, the hearing shall be held on an expedited basis. If the person challenging the voluntary declaration of parentage is an alleged genetic parent, genetic testing shall be ordered on an expedited basis.

(d) The action shall be filed not later than two years after the effective date of the declaration. This limitations period does not apply if the voluntary declaration of parentage is void under Section 7573.5.

(e) Notice shall be provided to the signatories of the declaration and to any person entitled to notice under Section 7635. A person who asserts a claim to parentage under this division shall be joined in the action.

(f) With respect to whether the voluntary declaration of parentage should be set aside, the person petitioning to set aside the voluntary declaration of parentage shall have the burden of proof by a preponderance of the evidence.

(g) The court may grant the petition to set aside the voluntary declaration of parentage only if the court finds that setting aside the voluntary declaration of parentage is in the best interest of the child, based on consideration of all of the following factors:

(1) The age of the child.

(2) The length of time since the effective date of the voluntary declaration of parentage.

(3) The nature, duration, and quality of any relationship between the person who signed the voluntary declaration of parentage and the child, including the duration and frequency of any time periods during which the child and the person resided in the same household or enjoyed a parent and child relationship.

(4) The request of the person who signed the voluntary declaration of parentage that the parent and child relationship continue.

(5) If the person challenges a voluntary declaration of parentage signed pursuant to paragraph (1) of subdivision (a) of Section 7573, the court shall additionally consider all of the following:

(A) Notice by the genetic parent of the child that the genetic parent does not oppose preservation of the relationship between the person who signed the declaration of parentage and the child.

(B) Whether any conduct of the person who signed the voluntary declaration has impaired the ability to ascertain the identity of, or obtain support from, the genetic parent.

(6) Additional factors deemed by the court to be relevant to its determination of the best interest of the child.

(h) If the voluntary declaration of parentage is challenged by a person who is presumed to be a parent under subdivision (d) of Section 7611, the court's ruling on the petition to set aside the voluntary declaration of parentage shall, in addition to the factors under subdivision (g), also take into account the nature, duration, and quality of the relationship between the petitioning party and the child and the benefit or detriment to the child of continuing that relationship.

(i) If the court denies the petition to set aside the voluntary declaration of parentage, the court shall state on the record the basis for the denial of the action and any supporting facts.

(j)(1) If the court grants the petition to set aside the voluntary declaration of parentage, the court shall adjudicate parentage pursuant to Section 7612.

(2) An order for custody, visitation, or child support shall remain in effect until the court determines that the voluntary declaration of parentage should be set aside, subject to the court's power to modify the orders as otherwise provided by law.

(k) This section does not prejudice or bar the rights of a person who is not a signatory and has standing under subdivision (a) to file an action or motion to set aside the voluntary declaration of parentage on any of the grounds described in, and within the time limits specified in, Section 473 of the Code of Civil Procedure. If the action or motion to set aside a judgment is required to be filed within a specified time period under Section 473 of the Code of Civil Procedure, the period within which the action or motion to set aside the voluntary declaration of parentage must be filed shall commence on the date that the court makes an initial order for custody, visitation, or child support based upon a voluntary declaration of parentage.

(l) This section does not restrict a court from acting as a court of equity.

(m) The Judicial Council shall develop the forms and procedures necessary to effectuate this section. **Leg.H.** Added Stats 2018 ch 876 §42 (AB 2684), effective January 1, 2019, operative January 1, 2020. Amended Stats 2019 ch 115 §85 (AB 1817), effective January 1, 2020.

Editor's Notes—2018 Note: For legislative intent, see the 2018 Notes following Fam C §7540.

§7578. Signatory as required party to proceeding to challenge voluntary declaration of parentage; Submission of signatory to personal jurisdiction; Legal responsibilities during pendency of proceeding to challenge; Burden of proof; Order for issuance of new birth certificate

(a) Every signatory to a voluntary declaration of parentage shall be made a party to a proceeding to challenge the declaration.

(b) By signing a voluntary declaration, a signatory submits to personal jurisdiction in this state in a proceeding to challenge the declaration, effective on the filing of the declaration with the Department of Child Support Services.

(c) The court shall not suspend the legal responsibilities arising from a voluntary declaration of parentage, including the duty to pay child support, during the pendency of a proceeding to challenge the voluntary declaration of parentage, unless the party challenging the declaration shows good cause.

(d) A party challenging a voluntary declaration of parentage has the burden of proof by a preponderance of the evidence.

(e) If the judgment or order of the court is at variance with the child's birth certificate, the court shall order that a new birth certificate be issued as prescribed in Article 2 (commencing with Section 102725) of Chapter 5 of Part 1 of Division 102 of the Health and Safety Code.

(f) This section shall become operative on January 1, 2020. **Leg.H.** Added Stats 2018 ch 876 §43 (AB 2684), effective January 1, 2019, operative January 1, 2020.

Editor's Notes— 2018 Note: For legislative findings and declarations, see the 2018 Note following Fam C §7540.

§7580. Effect of voluntary declaration of parentage signed by minor parent

(a) Notwithstanding subdivision (c) of Section 7573, a voluntary declaration of parentage that is signed by a minor parent does not establish parentage until 60 days after both signatories have reached 18 years of age or are emancipated, whichever first occurs.

(b) A person who signs a voluntary declaration of parentage as a minor may rescind the voluntary declaration of parentage at any time up to 60 days after the signatory reaches 18 years of age or becomes emancipated, whichever first occurs.

(c) A voluntary declaration of parentage signed by a minor creates a rebuttable presumption for or against parentage until the date that it establishes parentage as specified in subdivision (a).

(d) A voluntary declaration of parentage signed by a minor shall be admissible as evidence in a civil action to establish parentage of the minor named in the voluntary declaration.

(e) A voluntary declaration of parentage that is signed by a minor shall not be admissible as evidence in a criminal prosecution for violation of Section 261.5 of the Penal Code. **Leg.H.** Added Stats 2018 ch 876 §44 (AB 2684), effective January 1, 2019, operative January 1, 2020. Amended Stats 2019 ch 115 §86 (AB 1817), effective January 1, 2020.

Editor's Notes— 2018 Note: For legislative findings and declarations, see the 2018 Note following Fam C §7540.

§7581. Presumption of parentage applicable to declarations signed on or before specified date

The following provisions shall apply for voluntary declarations signed on or before December 31, 1996.

(a) Except as provided in subdivision (d), the child of a woman and a man executing a declaration of paternity under this chapter is conclusively presumed to be the man's child. The presumption under this section has the same force and effect as the presumption under Section 7540.

(b) A voluntary declaration of paternity shall be recognized as the basis for the establishment of an order for child custody or support.

(c) In an action to rebut the presumption created by this section, a voluntary declaration of paternity shall be admissible as evidence to determine paternity of the child named in the voluntary declaration of paternity.

(d) The presumption established by this section may be rebutted by any person by requesting genetic testing pursuant to Chapter 2 (commencing with Section 7550). The notice of motion for genetic testing pursuant to this section shall be supported by a declaration under oath submitted by the moving party stating the factual basis for placing the issue of paternity before the court. The notice of motion for genetic testing shall be made within three years from the date of execution of the declaration by the attesting father, or by the attesting mother, whichever signature is later. The two-year statute of limitations specified in subdivision (b) of Section 7541 is inapplicable for purposes of this section.

(e) A presumption under this section shall override all statutory presumptions of paternity, except a presumption arising under Section 7540, a claim made pursuant to Section 7555, or as provided in Section 7612.

(f) This section shall become operative on January 1, 2020. **Leg.H.** Added Stats 2018 ch 876 §45 (AB 2684), effective January 1, 2019, operative January 1, 2020.

Editor's Notes— 2018 Note: For legislative findings and declarations, see the 2018 Note following Fam C §7540.

PART 3
UNIFORM PARENTAGE ACT

Chapter 1. General Provisions.
Chapter 2. Establishing Parent and Child Relationship.
Chapter 3. Jurisdiction and Venue.
Chapter 4. Determination of Parent and Child Relationship.
Chapter 5. Termination of Parental Rights in Adoption Proceedings.
Chapter 6. Protective and Restraining Orders.

CHAPTER 1
GENERAL PROVISIONS

Citation of part. §7600.
"Natural parent" and "parent and child relationship". §7601.
Relationship not dependent on marriage. §7602.
Check to determine if child is missing person. §7603.
Pendente lite relief of custody or grant of visitation rights. §7604.
Bills for pregnancy, childbirth, and genetic testing as evidence. §7604.5.
Access to legal representation in custody and visitation proceedings; Attorney's fees and costs. §7605.
Definitions. §7606.

§7600. Citation of part
This part may be cited as the Uniform Parentage Act. **Leg.H.** Enacted Stats 1992 ch 162 §10 (AB 2650), operative January 1, 1994.

§7601. "Natural parent" and "parent and child relationship"
(a) "Natural parent" as used in this code means a nonadoptive parent established under this part, whether biologically related to the child or not.

(b) "Parent and child relationship" as used in this part means the legal relationship existing between a child and the child's natural or adoptive parents incident to which the law confers or imposes rights, privileges, duties, and obligations. The term includes the mother and child relationship and the father and child relationship.

(c) This part does not preclude a finding that a child has a parent and child relationship with more than two parents.

(d) For purposes of state law, administrative regulations, court rules, government policies, common law, and any other provision or source of law governing the rights, protections, benefits, responsibilities, obligations, and duties of parents, any reference to two parents shall be interpreted to apply to every parent of a child where that child has been found to have more than two parents under this part. **Leg.H.** Enacted Stats 1992 ch 162 §10 (AB 2650), operative January 1, 1994. Amended Stats 2013 ch 510 §1 (AB 1403), effective January 1, 2014, ch 564 §5.5 (AB 1403), effective January 1, 2014.

§7602. Relationship not dependent on marriage
The parent and child relationship extends equally to every child and to every parent, regardless of the marital status of the parents. **Leg.H.** Enacted Stats 1992 ch 162 §10 (AB 2650), operative January 1, 1994.

§7603. Check to determine if child is missing person
Section 3140 is applicable to proceedings pursuant to this part. **Leg.H.** Enacted Stats 1992 ch 162 §10 (AB 2650), operative January 1, 1994.

§7604. Pendente lite relief of custody or grant of visitation rights
A court may order pendente lite relief consisting of a custody or visitation order pursuant to Part 2 (commencing with Section 3020) of Division 8, if the court finds both of the following:

(a) A parent and child relationship exists pursuant to Section 7540 or 7541.

(b) The custody or visitation order would be in the best interest of the child. **Leg.H.** Enacted Stats 1992 ch 162 §10 (AB 2650), operative January 1, 1994. Amended Stats 1993 ch 219 §175.5 (AB 1500); Stats 2018 ch 876 §46 (AB 2684), effective January 1, 2019.

2018 Note: For legislative intent, see the 2018 Notes following Fam C §7540.

§7604.5. Bills for pregnancy, childbirth, and genetic testing as evidence
Notwithstanding any other provision of law, bills for pregnancy, childbirth, and genetic testing shall be admissible as evidence without third-party foundation testimony and shall constitute prima facie evidence of costs incurred for those services. **Leg.H.** Added Stats 1997 ch 599 §44 (AB 573).

§7605. Access to legal representation in custody and visitation proceedings; Attorney's fees and costs
(a) In any proceeding to establish physical or legal custody of a child or a visitation order under this part, and in any proceeding subsequent to entry of a related judgment, the court shall ensure that each party has access to legal representation to preserve each party's rights by ordering, if necessary based on the income and needs assessments, one party, except a government entity, to pay to the other party, or to the other party's attorney, whatever amount is reasonably necessary for attorney's fees and for the cost of maintaining or defending the proceeding during the pendency of the proceeding.

(b) When a request for attorney's fees and costs is made under this section, the court shall make findings on whether an award of attorney's fees and costs is appropriate, whether there is a disparity in access to funds to retain counsel, and whether one party is able to pay for legal representation of both parties. If the findings demonstrate disparity in access and ability to pay, the court shall make an order awarding attorney's fees and costs. A party who lacks the financial ability to hire an attorney may request, as an in pro per litigant, that the court order the other party, if that other party has the financial ability, to pay a reasonable amount to allow the unrepresented party to retain an attorney in a timely manner before proceedings in the matter go forward.

(c) Attorney's fees and costs within this section may be awarded for legal services rendered or costs incurred before or after the commencement of the proceeding.

(d) The court shall augment or modify the original award for attorney's fees and costs as may be reasonably necessary for the prosecution or defense of a proceeding described in subdivision (a), or any proceeding related thereto, including after any appeal has been concluded.

(e) Except as provided in subdivision (f), an application for a temporary order making, augmenting, or modifying an award of attorney's fees, including a reasonable retainer to hire an attorney, or costs, or both, shall be made by motion on notice or by an order to show cause during the pendency of any proceeding described in subdivision (a).

(f) The court shall rule on an application for fees under this section within 15 days of the hearing on the motion or order to show cause. An order described in subdivision (a) may be made without notice by an oral motion in open court at either of the following times:

(1) At the time of the hearing of the cause on the merits.

(2) At any time before entry of judgment against a party whose default has been entered pursuant to Section 585 or 586 of the Code of Civil Procedure. The court shall rule on any motion made pursuant to this subdivision within 15 days and prior to the entry of any judgment. **Leg.H.** Added Stats 2004 ch 472 §7 (AB 2148). Amended Stats 2006 ch 538 §160 (SB 1852), effective January 1, 2007; Stats 2012 ch 107 §3 (AB 1406), effective January 1, 2013.

§7606. Definitions
As used in this part, the following definitions shall apply:

(a) "Assisted reproduction" means conception by any means other than sexual intercourse.

(b) "Assisted reproduction agreement" means a written contract that includes a person who intends to be the legal parent of a child or children born through assisted reproduction and that defines the terms of the relationship between the parties to the contract. **Leg.H.** Added Stats 2006 ch 806 §1 (SB 1325), effective January 1, 2007.

CHAPTER 2
ESTABLISHING PARENT AND CHILD RELATIONSHIP

Methods of establishing. §7610.
Presumption of parentage. §7611.
Prohibition on presumption of paternity. §7611.5.
Rebuttal of parentage presumption; Controlling presumption if conflict; Finding that more than two persons are parents. §7612.

Assisted reproduction; Provider of an embryo not a natural parent; Written agreements. §7613.
Optional statutory forms for assisted reproduction. §7613.5.
Promise to furnish support. §7614.

§7610. Methods of establishing

The parent and child relationship may be established as follows:

(a) Between a child and the natural parent, it may be established by proof of having given birth to the child, or under this part.

(b) Between a child and an adoptive parent, it may be established by proof of adoption. **Leg.H.** Enacted Stats 1992 ch 162 §10 (AB 2650), operative January 1, 1994. Amended Stats 2013 ch 510 §2 (AB 1403), effective January 1, 2014.

§7611. Presumption of parentage

A person is presumed to be the natural parent of a child if the person meets the conditions provided in Chapter 1 (commencing with Section 7540) or Chapter 3 (commencing with Section 7570) of Part 2 or in any of the following subdivisions:

(a) The presumed parent and the child's natural mother are, or have been, married to each other and the child is born during the marriage, or within 300 days after the marriage is terminated by death, annulment, declaration of invalidity, or divorce, or after a judgment of separation is entered by a court.

(b) Before the child's birth, the presumed parent and the child's natural mother have attempted to marry each other by a marriage solemnized in apparent compliance with law, although the attempted marriage is or could be declared invalid, and either of the following is true:

(1) If the attempted marriage could be declared invalid only by a court, the child is born during the attempted marriage, or within 300 days after its termination by death, annulment, declaration of invalidity, or divorce.

(2) If the attempted marriage is invalid without a court order, the child is born within 300 days after the termination of cohabitation.

(c) After the child's birth, the presumed parent and the child's natural mother have married, or attempted to marry, each other by a marriage solemnized in apparent compliance with law, although the attempted marriage is or could be declared invalid, and either of the following is true:

(1) With the presumed parent's consent, the presumed parent is named as the child's parent on the child's birth certificate.

(2) The presumed parent is obligated to support the child under a written voluntary promise or by court order.

(d) The presumed parent receives the child into their home and openly holds out the child as their natural child.

(e) The child is in utero after the death of the decedent and the conditions set forth in Section 249.5 of the Probate Code are satisfied. **Leg.H.** Enacted Stats 1992 ch 162 §10 (AB 2650), operative January 1, 1994. Amended Stats 1993 ch 219 §176 (AB 1500); Stats 1994 ch 1269 §53 (AB 2208); Stats 2004 ch 775 §1 (AB 1910); Stats 2013 ch 510 §3 (AB 1403), effective January 1, 2014; Stats 2019 ch 115 §87 (AB 1817), effective January 1, 2020.

§7611.5. Prohibition on presumption of paternity

Where Section 7611 does not apply, a man shall not be presumed to be the natural father of a child if either of the following is true:

(a) The child was conceived as a result of an act in violation of Section 261 of the Penal Code and the father was convicted of that violation.

(b) The child was conceived as a result of an act in violation of Section 261.5 of the Penal Code, the father was convicted of that violation, and the mother was under the age of 15 years and the father was 21 years of age or older at the time of conception. **Leg.H.** Added Stats 1993 ch 219 §177 (AB 1500).

§7612. Rebuttal of parentage presumption; Controlling presumption if conflict; Finding that more than two persons are parents

(a) Except as provided in Chapter 1 (commencing with Section 7540) and Chapter 3 (commencing with Section 7570) of Part 2, a presumption under Section 7611 is a rebuttable presumption affecting the burden of proof and may be rebutted in an appropriate action only by clear and convincing evidence.

(b) If two or more presumptions arise under Section 7611 that conflict with each other, or if one or more presumptions under Section 7611 conflict with a claim by a person identified as a genetic parent pursuant to Section 7555, the presumption that on the facts is founded on the weightier considerations of policy and logic controls. If one of the presumed parents is also a presumed parent under Section 7540, the presumption arising under Section 7540 may only be rebutted pursuant to Section 7541.

(c) In an appropriate action, a court may find that more than two persons with a claim to parentage under this division are parents if the court finds that recognizing only two parents would be detrimental to the child. In determining detriment to the child, the court shall consider all relevant factors, including, but not limited to, the harm of removing the child from a stable placement with a parent who has fulfilled the child's physical needs and the child's psychological needs for care and affection, and who has assumed that role for a substantial period of time. A finding of detriment to the child does not require a finding of unfitness of any of the parents or persons with a claim to parentage.

(d) Unless a court orders otherwise after making the determination specified in subdivision (c), a presumption under Section 7611 is rebutted by a judgment establishing parentage of the child by another person.

(e) A person's offer or refusal to sign a voluntary declaration of parentage may be considered as a factor, but shall not be determinative, as to the issue of legal parentage in a proceeding regarding the establishment or termination of parental rights.

(f) This section shall become operative on January 1, 2020. **Leg.H.** Added Stats 2018 ch 876 §48 (AB 2684), effective January 1, 2019, operative January 1, 2020.

2018 Note: For legislative intent, see the 2018 Notes following Fam C §7540.

Prior Law: Former Fam C §7612, similar to the present section, was enacted Stats 1992 ch 162 §10 (AB 2650), operative January 1, 1994, amended Stats 1993 ch 219 §178 (AB 1500), Stats 1994 ch 1269 §54 (AB 2208), Stats 2008 ch 534 §1 (SB 1726), effective January 1, 2009, Stats 2011 ch 185 §3 (AB 1349), effective January 1, 2012, Stats 2013 ch 510 §4 (AB 1403), effective January 1, 2014, ch 564 §6.5 (SB 274), effective January 1, 2014, Stats 2015 ch 91 §1 (AB 1049), effective January 1, 2016, Stats 2016 ch 86 §129 (SB 1171), effective January 1, 2017, Stats 2018 ch 876 §47 (AB 2684), effective January 1, 2019, and repealed January 1, 2020, by its own terms.

§7613. Assisted reproduction; Provider of an embryo not a natural parent; Written agreements

(a)(1) If a woman conceives through assisted reproduction with semen or ova or both donated by a donor who is not the woman's spouse, with the consent of another intended parent, that intended parent is treated in law as if that intended parent is the natural parent of a child thereby conceived. The other intended parent's consent shall be in writing and signed by the other intended parent and the woman conceiving through assisted reproduction.

(2) Failure to consent in writing, as required by paragraph (1), does not preclude the court from finding that the intended parent consented if the court finds by clear and convincing evidence that, prior to the conception of the child, the woman and the intended parent had an oral agreement that the woman and the intended parent would both be parents of the child.

(b)(1) The donor of semen provided to a licensed physician and surgeon or to a licensed sperm bank for use in assisted reproduction by a woman other than the donor's spouse is treated in law as if the donor is not the natural parent of a child thereby conceived, unless the donor and the woman signed a written agreement before the conception of the child, that the donor would be a parent.

(2) If the semen is not provided to a licensed physician and surgeon or a licensed sperm bank as specified in paragraph (1), the donor of semen for use in assisted reproduction by a woman other than the donor's spouse is treated in law as if the donor is not the natural parent of a child thereby conceived if either of the following are met:

(A) The donor and the woman signed a written agreement before conception that the donor would not be a parent.

(B) A court finds by clear and convincing evidence that the child was conceived through assisted reproduction and that, prior to the conception of the child, the woman and the donor had an oral agreement that the donor would not be a parent.

(c) A person providing ova for use in assisted reproduction by a person other than the provider's spouse or nonmarital partner is treated in law as if the provider is not the natural parent of a child thereby conceived unless the court finds satisfactory evidence that the provider of the ova, and each recipient, intended for that provider to have parental rights.

(d)(1) A provider of an embryo for use in assisted reproduction to an intended parent who is not the provider's spouse or nonmarital partner is treated in law as if the provider is not the natural parent of a child thereby conceived unless the court finds satisfactory evidence that the provider and the intended parent intended for the provider to be a parent.

(2) If the provider of ova, semen, or embryos is not the original source of the ova or sperm, each original provider's written consent to the donation is required unless that person has executed a writing to consent to the donation, or to waive or relinquish their right to the genetic material, or as otherwise ordered by a court of law.

(e)(1) Notwithstanding any other law, persons who are not married to one another and who share legal control over the disposition of embryos shall not be prevented from entering into a written agreement whereby one person renounces all legal interest in the embryos, with the specific intent that the person renouncing all legal interest shall not be a legal parent of any child conceived with use of the embryos, despite any prior oral or written agreements, or legal judgments to the contrary. After that interest has been renounced in a writing signed by all persons with legal interest in or control over disposition of the embryos, the renouncing person shall be treated in law as a donor, and not a legal parent. Upon execution of that agreement, the person who retains legal interest in and control over disposition of the embryos shall have the sole right to determine the use and disposition of the embryos, including the right to attempt conception of a child, subject to any limitation pursuant to paragraph (2) of subdivision (d). Either party may file the agreement with the court, and the court shall issue an order establishing the nonparentage of the donor.

(2) If persons who share legal control over and interest in one or more embryos are married to one another at the time of signing the agreement, the agreement shall only become legally binding upon the court's entry of a final decree of dissolution that incorporates the agreement, after which the presumptions pursuant to Section 7540 or subdivisions (a), (b), or (c) of Section 7611 shall not apply. **Leg.H.** Enacted Stats 1992 ch 162 §10 (AB 2650), operative January 1, 1994. Amended Stats 2008 ch 534 §2 (SB 1726), effective January 1, 2009; Stats 2011 ch 185 §4 (AB 1349), effective January 1, 2012; Stats 2013 ch 510 §5 (AB 1403), effective January 1, 2014; Stats 2015 ch 566 §1 (AB 960), effective January 1, 2016; Stats 2016 ch 385 §2 (AB 2349), effective January 1, 2017; Stats 2018 ch 876 §49 (AB 2684), effective January 1, 2019; Stats 2019 ch 115 §88 (AB 1817), effective January 1, 2020; Stats 2022 ch 159 §1 (AB 2495), effective January 1, 2023; Stats 2023 ch 851 §5 (AB 1650), effective January 1, 2024.

Editor's Notes—2018 Note: For legislative intent, see the 2018 Notes following Fam C §7540.

2016 Note: The Legislature finds and declares both of the following:

(a) California courts already have subject matter jurisdiction over actions involving an assisted reproduction agreement between a surrogate and an intended parent or parents under Section 7630 of the Family Code. However, current law does not explicitly provide that California courts have subject matter jurisdiction or clearly explain the circumstances under which subject matter jurisdiction exists.

(b) Many intended parents and surrogates enter into assisted reproduction agreements in California in which one or more of the parties end up living in another state. California court orders regarding the parentage of a child born through surrogacy must be given full faith and credit only if the issuing court had subject matter jurisdiction. For these reasons, California has an interest in clarifying that California courts have subject matter jurisdiction over assisted reproduction agreements between a surrogate and an intended parent or parents if one or more parties resides in California, any medical procedures leading to conception occurs in California, or the child is born in California. Stats 2016 ch 385 (AB 2349) §1.

§7613.5. Optional statutory forms for assisted reproduction

(a) An intended parent may, but is not required to, use the forms set forth in this section to demonstrate the intent to be a legal parent of a child conceived through assisted reproduction. These forms shall satisfy the writing requirement specified in Section 7613, and are designed to provide clarity regarding the intentions, at the time of conception, of intended parents using assisted reproduction. These forms do not affect any presumptions of parentage based on Section 7611, and do not preclude a court from considering any other claims to parentage under California statute or case law.

(b) These forms apply only in very limited circumstances. Please read the forms carefully to see if you qualify for use of the forms.

(c) These forms do not apply to assisted reproduction agreements for gestational carriers or surrogacy agreements.

(d) This section does not require the use of one of these forms to satisfy the writing requirement of Section 7613.

(e) The following are the optional California Statutory Forms for Assisted Reproduction:

California Statutory Forms for Assisted Reproduction, Form 1:

<u>Two Married or Unmarried People Using Assisted Reproduction to Conceive a Child</u>
Use this form if: You and another intended parent, who may be your spouse or registered domestic partner, are conceiving a child through assisted reproduction using sperm and/or egg donation; and one of you will be giving birth.

WARNING: Signing this form does not terminate the parentage claim of a sperm donor. A sperm donor's claim to parentage is terminated if the sperm is provided to a licensed physician and surgeon or to a licensed sperm bank prior to insemination, or if you conceive without having sexual intercourse and you have a written agreement signed by you and the donor that you will conceive using assisted reproduction and do not intend for the donor to be a parent, as required by Section 7613(b) of the Family Code.

The laws about parentage of a child are complicated. You are strongly encouraged to consult with an attorney about your rights. Even if you do not fill out this form, a spouse or domestic partner of the parent giving birth is presumed to be a legal parent of any child born during the marriage or domestic partnership.

_____

This form demonstrates your intent to be parents of the child you plan to conceive through assisted reproduction using sperm and/or egg donation.

I, _____ (print name of person not giving birth), intend to be a parent of a child that _____ (print name of person giving birth) will or has conceived through assisted reproduction using sperm and/or egg donation. I consent to the use of assisted reproduction by the person who will give birth. <u>I INTEND to be a parent of the child conceived</u>.

SIGNATURES

Intended parent who will give birth: _____ (print name)
_____(signature)_____(date)

Intended parent who will not give birth: _____ (print name)
_____(signature)_____(date)

NOTARY ACKNOWLEDGMENT

State of California
County of _____)

On _____ before me, _____ (insert name and title of the officer) personally appeared_____, who proved to me on the basis of satisfactory evidence to be the person(s) whose name(s) is/are subscribed to the within instrument and acknowledged to me that he/she/they executed the same in his/her/their authorized capacity, and that by his/her/their signature(s) on the instrument the person(s), or the entity upon behalf of which the person(s) acted, executed the instrument.

I certify under PENALTY OF PERJURY under the laws of the State of California that the foregoing paragraph is true and correct.

WITNESS my hand and official seal.

Signature _____ (Seal)

California Statutory Forms for Assisted Reproduction, Form 2:

Unmarried, Intended Parents Using Intended Parent's Sperm to Conceive a Child
Use this form if: (1) Neither you or the other person are married or in a registered domestic partnership (including a registered domestic partnership or civil union from another state); (2) one of you will give birth to a child conceived through assisted reproduction using the intended parent's sperm; and (3) you both intend to be parents of that child.

Do not use this form if you are conceiving using a surrogate.

WARNING: If you do not sign this form, or a similar agreement, you may be treated as a sperm donor if you conceive without having sexual intercourse according to Section 7613(b) of the Family Code.

The laws about parentage of a child are complicated. **You are strongly encouraged to consult with an attorney about your rights.**

_____
This form demonstrates your intent to be parents of the child you plan to conceive through assisted reproduction using sperm donation.

I, _____ (print name of parent giving birth), plan to use assisted reproduction with another intended parent who is providing sperm to conceive the child. I am not married and am not in a registered domestic partnership (including a registered domestic partnership or civil union from another jurisdiction), and I INTEND for the person providing sperm to be a parent of the child to be conceived.

I, _____ (print name of parent providing sperm), plan to use assisted reproduction to conceive a child using my sperm with the parent giving birth. I am not married and am not in a registered domestic partnership (including a registered domestic partnership or civil union from another jurisdiction), and I INTEND to be a parent of the child to be conceived.

SIGNATURES

Intended parent giving birth: _____ (print name)
_____(signature) _____(date)

Intended parent providing sperm: _____ (print name)
_____(signature) _____(date)
_____

NOTARY ACKNOWLEDGMENT

On _____ before me, _____ (insert name and title of the officer) personally appeared _____, who proved to me on the basis of satisfactory evidence to be the person(s) whose name(s)is/are subscribed to the within instrument and acknowledged to me that he/she/they executed the same in his/her/their authorized capacity, and that by his/her/their signature(s) on the instrument the person(s), or the entity upon behalf of which the person(s) acted, executed the instrument.
I certify under PENALTY OF PERJURY under the laws of the State of California that the foregoing paragraph is true and correct.
WITNESS my hand and official seal.
Signature _____(Seal)

California Statutory Forms for Assisted Reproduction, Form 3:

Intended Parents Conceiving a Child Using Eggs from One Parent and the Other Parent Will Give Birth
Use this form if: You are conceiving a child using the eggs from one of you and the other person will give birth to the child; (2) and you both intend to be parents to that child.

Do not use this form if you are conceiving using a surrogate.

WARNING: Signing this form does not terminate the parentage claim of a sperm donor. A sperm donor's claim to parentage is terminated if the sperm is provided to a licensed physician and surgeon or to a licensed sperm bank prior to insemination, or if you conceive without having sexual intercourse and you have a written agreement signed by you and the donor that you will conceive using assisted reproduction and do not intend for the donor to be a parent, as required by Section 7613(b) of the Family Code.

The laws about parentage of a child are complicated. **You are strongly encouraged to consult with an attorney about your rights.**

_____
This form demonstrates your intent to be parents of the child you plan to conceive through assisted reproduction using eggs from one parent and the other parent will give birth to the child.

I, _____ (print name of parent giving birth), plan to use assisted reproduction to conceive and give birth to a child with another person who will provide eggs to conceive the child. I INTEND for the person providing eggs to be a parent of the child to be conceived.

I, _____ (print name of parent providing eggs), plan to use assisted reproduction to conceive a child with another person who will give birth to the child conceived using my eggs. I INTEND to be a parent of the child to be conceived.

SIGNATURES

Intended parent giving birth: _____ (print name)
_____(signature) _____(date)

Intended parent providing eggs: _____ (print name)
_____(signature) _____(date)
_____

NOTARY ACKNOWLEDGMENT

On _____ before me, _____ (insert name and title of the officer) personally appeared _____, who proved to me on the basis of satisfactory evidence to be the person(s) whose name(s)is/are subscribed to the within instrument and acknowledged to me that he/she/they executed the same in his/her/their authorized capacity, and that by his/her/their signature(s) on the instrument the person(s), or the entity upon behalf of which the person(s) acted, executed the instrument. I certify under PENALTY OF PERJURY under the laws of the State of California that the foregoing paragraph is true and correct.
WITNESS my hand and official seal.
Signature _____(Seal)

California Statutory Forms for Assisted Reproduction, Form 4:

Intended Parent(s) Using a Known Sperm and/or Egg Donor(s) to Conceive a Child
Use this form if: You are using a known sperm and/or egg donor(s), or embryo donation, to conceive a child and you do not intend for the donor(s) to be a parent.

Do not use this form if you are conceiving using a surrogate.

If you do not sign this form or a similar agreement, your sperm donor may be treated as a parent unless the sperm is provided to a licensed physician and surgeon or to a licensed sperm bank prior to insemination, or a court finds by clear and convincing evidence that you planned to conceive through assisted reproduction and did not intend for the donor to be a parent, as required by Section 7613(b) of the Family Code. If you do not sign this form or a similar agreement, your egg donor may be treated as a parent unless a court finds that there is satisfactory evidence that you planned to conceive through assisted reproduction and did not intend for the donor to be a parent, as required by Section 7613(c) of the Family Code.

The laws about parentage of a child are complicated. **You are strongly encouraged to consult with an attorney about your rights.**

_____

This form demonstrates your intent that your sperm and/or egg or embryo donor(s) will not be a parent or parents of the child you plan to conceive through assisted reproduction.

I, _____ (print name of parent giving birth), plan to use assisted reproduction to conceive using a sperm and/or egg donor(s) or embryo donation, and I DO NOT INTEND for the sperm and/or egg or embryo donor(s) to be a parent of the child to be conceived.

(If applicable) I, _____ (print name of sperm donor), plan to donate my sperm to_____ (print name of parent giving birth and second parent if applicable). I am not married to and am not in a registered domestic partnership (including a registered domestic partnership or a civil union from another jurisdiction) with _____ (print name of parent giving birth), and I DO NOT INTEND to be a parent of the child to be conceived.

(If applicable) I, _____ (print name of egg donor), plan to donate my ova to_____ (print name of parent giving birth and second parent if applicable). I am not married to and am not in a registered domestic partnership (including a registered domestic partnership or a civil union from another jurisdiction) with _____ (print name of parent giving birth), or any intimate and nonmarital relationship with _____ (print name of parent giving birth) and I DO NOT INTEND to be a parent of the child to be conceived.

(If applicable) I, _____ (print name of intended parent not giving birth), INTEND to be a parent of the child that _____ (print name of parent giving birth) will conceive through assisted reproduction using sperm and/or egg donation and I DO NOT INTEND for the sperm and/or egg or embryo donor(s) to be a parent. I consent to the use of assisted reproduction by the person who will give birth.

SIGNATURES

Intended parent giving birth: _____ (print name)
_____ (signature) _____ (date)

(If applicable) Sperm Donor: _____ (print name)
_____ (signature) _____ (date)

(If applicable) Egg Donor: _____ (print name)
_____ (signature) _____ (date)

(If applicable) Intended parent not giving birth: _____ (print name)
_____ (signature) _____ (date)

_____
NOTARY ACKNOWLEDGMENT

On _____ before me, _____ (insert name and title of the officer) personally appeared _____, who proved to me on the basis of satisfactory evidence to be the person(s) whose name(s)is/are subscribed to the within instrument and acknowledged to me that he/she/they executed the same in his/her/their authorized capacity, and that by his/her/their signature(s) on the instrument the person(s), or the entity upon behalf of which the person(s) acted, executed the instrument.
I certify under PENALTY OF PERJURY under the laws of the State of California that the foregoing paragraph is true and correct.
WITNESS my hand and official seal.
Signature _____ (Seal)

Leg.H. Added Stats 2014 ch 636 §1 (AB 2344), effective January 1, 2015. Amended Stats 2015 ch 566 §2 (AB 960), effective January 1, 2016; Stats 2016 ch 86 §130 (SB 1171), effective January 1, 2017; Stats 2019 ch 115 §89 (AB 1817), effective January 1, 2020.

§7614. Promise to furnish support

(a) A promise in writing to furnish support for a child, growing out of a presumed parent or alleged father and child relationship, does not require consideration and, subject to Section 7632, is enforceable according to its terms.

(b) In the best interest of the child or the other parent, the court may, and upon the promisor's request shall, order the promise to be kept in confidence and designate a person or agency to receive and disburse on behalf of the child all amounts paid in performance of the promise. **Leg.H.** Enacted Stats 1992 ch 162 §10 (AB 2650), operative January 1, 1994. Amended Stats 2013 ch 510 §6 (AB 1403), effective January 1, 2014.

CHAPTER 3
JURISDICTION AND VENUE

Jurisdiction; Venue. §7620.

§7620. Jurisdiction; Venue

(a) A person who has sexual intercourse or causes conception with the intent to become a legal parent by assisted reproduction in this state, or who enters into an assisted reproduction agreement for gestational carriers in this state, thereby submits to the jurisdiction of the courts of this state as to an action brought under this part with respect to a child who may have been conceived by that act of intercourse or assisted reproduction, or who may have been conceived as a result of that assisted reproduction agreement.

(b) If a child is conceived pursuant to an assisted reproduction agreement for gestational carriers, as defined in Section 7960 and as described in Section 7962, the courts of this state shall have jurisdiction over a proceeding to determine parentage of the child if any of the following conditions is satisfied:

(1) One or more of the parties to the assisted reproduction agreement for gestational carriers resides in this state, or resided in this state at the time the assisted reproduction agreement for gestational carriers was executed.

(2) The medical procedures leading to conception, including in vitro fertilization or embryo transfer, or both, were carried out in this state.

(3) The child is born in this state.

(c) An action under this part shall be brought in one of the following:

(1) The county in which the child resides or is found.

(2) If the child is the subject of a pending or proposed adoption, any county in which a licensed California adoption agency to which the child has been relinquished or is proposed to be relinquished maintains an office.

(3) If the child is the subject of a pending or proposed adoption, the county in which an office of the department or a public adoption agency investigating the petition is located.

(4) If the parent is deceased, the county in which proceedings for probate of the estate of the parent of the child have been or could be commenced.

(5) If the child was conceived pursuant to an assisted reproduction agreement for gestational carriers, any county described in subdivision (e) of Section 7962. **Leg.H.** Enacted Stats 1992 ch 162 §10 (AB 2650), operative January 1, 1994. Amended Stats 2003 ch 251 §1 (SB 182); Stats 2005 ch 627 §1 (SB 302), effective January 1, 2006; Stats 2006 ch 806 §2 (SB 1325), effective January 1, 2007; Stats 2009 ch 492 §1 (AB 941), effective January 1, 2010; Stats 2013 ch 510 §7 (AB 1403), effective

January 1, 2014; Stats 2016 ch 385 §3 (AB 2349), effective January 1, 2017.

2016 Note: For legislative findings and declarations, see the 2016 Note following §7613.

CHAPTER 4
DETERMINATION OF PARENT AND CHILD RELATIONSHIP

Article 1. Determination of Parent and Child Relationship.
Article 1.5. Setting Aside or Vacating Judgment of Parentage.
Article 2. Determination of Mother and Child Relationship.

ARTICLE 1
Determination of Parent and Child Relationship

Who may bring action; When action may be brought; Consolidation of proceedings; Joinder of parties; Service; Notice of proceedings. §7630.
Agreement between alleged father or presumed parent and the other parent or child does not bar action. §7632.
Action, order or judgment before birth of child. §7633.
Action by local child support agency; Review of current practices of service of process. §7634.
Parties. §7635.
Right to genetic testing; Right to move to set aside or vacate judgment. §7635.5.
Effect of judgment determining existence or nonexistence of parent and child relationship. §7636.
Other provisions of judgment. §7637.
Change of name of child. §7638.
Issuance of new birth certificate. §7639.
Award of attorney's fees and other costs. §7640.
Enforcement of judgment. §7641.
Modification of judgment. §7642.
Confidentiality of hearings and records. §7643.
Hearing may be held in closed court; Inspecting or copying records pertaining to the action. § 7643.5.
Action based on voluntary declaration of parentage; Effect of declaration. §7644.

§7630. Who may bring action; When action may be brought; Consolidation of proceedings; Joinder of parties; Service; Notice of proceedings

(a) A child, the child's natural mother, a person presumed to be the child's parent under subdivision (a), (b), or (c) of Section 7611, a person seeking to be adjudicated as a parent or donor under Section 7613, an adoption agency to whom the child has been relinquished, or a prospective adoptive parent of the child may bring an action as follows:

(1) At any time for the purpose of declaring the existence of the parent and child relationship presumed under subdivision (a), (b), or (c) of Section 7611, or established pursuant to Section 7613.

(2) For the purpose of declaring the nonexistence of the parent and child relationship presumed under subdivision (a), (b), or (c) of Section 7611 only if the action is brought within a reasonable time after obtaining knowledge of relevant facts. After the presumption has been rebutted, parentage of the child by another person may be determined in the same action, if that person has been made a party.

(3) At any time for the purpose of declaring the nonexistence of the parent and child relationship of a donor under Section 7613.

(b) Any interested party may bring an action at any time for the purpose of determining the existence or nonexistence of the parent and child relationship presumed under subdivision (d) or (e) of Section 7611.

(c) Except as to cases coming within Chapter 1 (commencing with Section 7540) of Part 2 or when paragraph (2) of subdivision (a) applies, an action to determine parentage may be brought by the child, a personal representative of the child, the Department of Child Support Services, a presumed parent or the personal representative or a parent of that presumed parent if that parent has died or is a minor, or, when the natural mother is the only presumed parent or an action under Section 300 of the Welfare and Institutions Code or adoption is pending, a man alleged or claiming to be the father or the personal representative or a parent of the alleged father if the alleged father has died or is a minor.

(d)(1) If a proceeding has been filed under Chapter 2 (commencing with Section 7820) of Part 4, an action under subdivision (a) or (b) shall be consolidated with that proceeding. The parental rights of the presumed parent shall be determined as set forth in Sections 7820 to 7829, inclusive.

(2) If a proceeding pursuant to Section 7662 has been filed under Chapter 5 (commencing with Section 7660), an action under subdivision (c) shall be consolidated with that proceeding. The parental rights of the alleged father shall be determined as set forth in Section 7664.

(3) The consolidated action under paragraph (1) or (2) shall be heard in the court in which the proceeding under Section 7662 or Chapter 2 (commencing with Section 7820) of Part 4 is filed, unless the court finds, by clear and convincing evidence, that transferring the action to the other court poses a substantial hardship to the petitioner. Mere inconvenience does not constitute a sufficient basis for a finding of substantial hardship. If the court determines there is a substantial hardship, the consolidated action shall be heard in the court in which the parentage action is filed.

(e)(1) If a prospective adoptive parent who has physical custody of the child, a licensed California adoption agency that has legal custody of the child or to which the mother proposes to relinquish the child for adoption, or a person whom the mother has designated as the prospective adoptive parent in a written statement executed before a hospital social worker, an adoption service provider, an adoption agency representative, or a notary public, has not been joined as a party to an action to determine the existence of a parent and child relationship under subdivision (a), (b), or (c), or an action for custody by a person claiming to be a parent under this division, the court shall join the prospective adoptive parent or licensed California adoption agency as a party upon application or on its own motion, without the necessity of a motion for joinder. A joined party shall not be required to pay a fee in connection with this action.

(2) If a person brings an action to determine parentage and custody of a child who the person has reason to believe is in the physical or legal custody of an adoption agency, or of one or more persons other than the child's parent who are prospective adoptive parents, the person shall serve the entire pleading on, and give notice of all proceedings to, the adoption agency or the prospective adoptive parents, or both.

(f) A party to an assisted reproduction agreement may bring an action at any time to establish a parent and child relationship consistent with the intent expressed in that assisted reproduction agreement.

(g)(1) In an action to determine the existence of the parent and child relationship brought pursuant to subdivision (b), if the child's other parent has died and there are no existing court orders or pending court actions involving custody or guardianship of the child, then the persons having physical custody of the child shall be served with notice of the proceeding at least 15 days prior to the hearing, either by mail or in a manner authorized by the court. If a person identified as having physical custody of the child cannot be located, the court shall prescribe the manner of giving notice.

(2) If known to the person bringing the parentage action, relatives within the second degree of the child shall be given notice of the proceeding at least 15 days prior to the hearing, either by mail or in a manner authorized by the court. If a person identified as a relative of the second degree of the child cannot be located, or the relative's whereabouts are unknown or cannot be ascertained, the court shall prescribe the manner of giving notice, or shall dispense with giving notice to that person.

(3) Proof of notice pursuant to this subdivision shall be filed with the court before the proceeding to determine the existence of the parent and child relationship is heard. **Leg.H.** Enacted Stats 1992 ch 162 §10 (AB 2650), operative January 1, 1994. Amended Stats 2000 ch 808 §76 (AB 1358), effective September 28, 2000; Stats 2001 ch 353 §1 (AB 538); Stats 2003 ch 251 §2 (SB 182); Stats 2004 ch 775 §2 (AB 1910); Stats 2005 ch 627 §2 (SB 302), effective January 1, 2006; Stats 2006 ch 806 §3 (SB 1325), effective January 1, 2007; Stats 2007 ch 47 §1 (SB 313), effective January 1, 2008; Stats 2008 ch 534 §3 (SB 1726), effective January 1, 2009; Stats 2010 ch 588 §1 (AB 2020), effective January 1, 2011; Stats 2012 ch 155 §1 (AB 1337), effective January 1, 2013; Stats 2013 ch 510 §8 (AB 1403), effective January 1, 2014; Stats 2014 ch 763 §1 (AB 1701), effective January 1, 2015; Stats 2018 ch 876 §51 (AB 2684), effective January 1, 2019; Stats 2019 ch 115 §90 (AB 1817), effective January 1, 2020; Stats 2021 ch 124 §28 (AB 938), effective January 1, 2022.

Editor's Notes—2018 Note: For legislative intent, see the 2018 Notes following Fam C §7540.

2016 Note: The Legislature finds and declares both of the following:

(a) California courts already have subject matter jurisdiction over actions involving an assisted reproduction agreement between a surrogate and an intended parent or parents under Section 7630 of the Family Code. However, current law does not explicitly provide that California courts have subject matter jurisdiction or clearly explain the circumstances under which subject matter jurisdiction exists.

(b) Many intended parents and surrogates enter into assisted reproduction agreements in California in which one or more of the parties end up living in another state. California court orders regarding the parentage of a child born through surrogacy must be given full faith and credit only if the issuing court had subject matter jurisdiction. For these reasons, California has an interest in clarifying that California courts have subject matter jurisdiction over assisted reproduction agreements between a surrogate and an intended parent or parents if one or more parties resides in California, any medical procedures leading to conception occurs in California, or the child is born in California. Stats 2016 ch 385 (AB 2349) §1.

§7631. [Section repealed 2011]

Leg.H. Enacted Stats 1992 ch 162 §10 (AB 2650), operative January 1, 1994. Amended Stats 1993 ch 219 §178.5 (AB 1500). Repealed Stats 2010 ch 588 §2 (AB 2020), effective January 1, 2011. The repealed section related to action by man not presumed father to establish paternity.

§7632. Agreement between alleged father or presumed parent and the other parent or child does not bar action

Regardless of its terms, an agreement between an alleged father or a presumed parent and the other parent or child does not bar an action under this chapter. **Leg.H.** Enacted Stats 1992 ch 162 §10 (AB 2650), operative January 1, 1994. Amended Stats 2013 ch 510 §9 (AB 1403), effective January 1, 2014.

§7633. Action, order or judgment before birth of child

An action under this chapter may be brought, an order or judgment may be entered before the birth of the child, and enforcement of that order or judgment shall be stayed until the birth of the child. **Leg.H.** Enacted Stats 1992 ch 162 §10 (AB 2650), operative January 1, 1994. Amended Stats 2006 ch 806 §4 (SB 1325), effective January 1, 2007.

§7634. Action by local child support agency; Review of current practices of service of process

(a) The local child support agency may, in the local child support agency's discretion, bring an action under this chapter in any case in which the local child support agency believes it to be appropriate.

(b) The Department of Child Support Services may review the current practices of service of process used by the local child support agencies pursuant to subdivision (a), and may develop methods to increase the number of persons served using personal delivery. **Leg.H.** Enacted Stats 1992 ch 162 §10 (AB 2650), operative January 1, 1994. Amended Stats 2000 ch 808 §77 (AB 1358), effective September 28, 2000; Stats 2004 ch 849 §2 (AB 252).

§7635. Parties

(a) The child may, if under the age of 12 years, and shall, if 12 years of age or older, be made a party to the action. If the child is a minor and a party to the action, the child shall be represented by a guardian ad litem appointed by the court. The guardian ad litem need not be represented by counsel if the guardian ad litem is a relative of the child.

(b) A natural parent, each person presumed to be a parent under Section 7611 or 7540, each person who is a parent of the child under Section 7613 or 7962, and each person alleged to be the genetic parent unless precluded under this division from establishing parentage based on genetic testing, shall be given notice of the action in the manner prescribed in Section 7666 and an opportunity to be heard, and shall be made a party if they request to be joined. Appointment of a guardian ad litem shall not be required for a minor who is a parent of the child who is the subject of the petition to establish parental relationship, unless the minor parent is unable to understand the nature of the proceedings or to assist counsel in preparing the case.

(c) The court may align the parties.

(d) In any initial or subsequent proceeding under this chapter where custody of, or visitation with, a minor child is in issue, the court may, if it determines it would be in the best interest of the minor child, appoint private counsel to represent the interests of the minor child pursuant to Chapter 10 (commencing with Section 3150) of Part 2 of Division 8. **Leg.H.** Enacted Stats 1992 ch 162 §10 (AB 2650), operative January 1, 1994. Amended Stats 1994 ch 1269 §55 (AB 2208); Stats 2008 ch 181 §2 (SB 1612), effective January 1, 2009; Stats 2013 ch 510 §10 (AB 1403), effective January 1, 2014; Stats 2018 ch 876 §52 (AB 2684), effective January 1, 2019.

Editor's Notes— 2018 Note: For legislative intent, see the 2018 Notes following Fam C §7540.

§7635.5. Right to genetic testing; Right to move to set aside or vacate judgment

In any action brought pursuant to this article, if the alleged father is present in court for the action, the court shall inform the alleged father of the alleged father's right to have genetic testing performed to determine the biological parentage of the child. The court shall further inform the alleged father of the alleged father's right to move to set aside or vacate a judgment of parentage pursuant to Section 7646 within two years of the date notice of the action to establish parentage is received, and that after that time has expired the alleged father may not move to set aside or vacate the judgment of parentage, regardless of whether genetic testing shows the alleged father not to be the biological father of the child. **Leg.H.** Added Stats 2004 ch 849 §3 (AB 252). Amended Stats 2019 ch 115 §91 (AB 1817), effective January 1, 2020.

§7636. Effect of judgment determining existence or nonexistence of parent and child relationship

The judgment or order of the court determining the existence or nonexistence of the parent and child relationship is determinative for all purposes except for actions brought pursuant to Section 270 of the Penal Code. **Leg.H.** Enacted Stats 1992 ch 162 §10 (AB 2650), operative January 1, 1994.

§7637. Other provisions of judgment

The judgment or order may contain any other provision directed against the appropriate party to the proceeding, concerning the duty of support, the custody and guardianship of the child, visitation privileges with the child, the furnishing of bond or other security for the payment of the judgment, or any other matter in the best interest of the child. The judgment or order may direct the parent to pay the reasonable expenses of the mother's pregnancy and confinement. **Leg.H.** Enacted Stats 1992 ch 162 §10 (AB 2650), operative January 1, 1994. Amended Stats 1993 ch 219 §179 (AB 1500); Stats 2013 ch 510 §11 (AB 1403), effective January 1, 2014.

§7638. Change of name of child

The procedure in an action under this part to change the name of a minor or adult child for whom a parent and child relationship is established pursuant to Section 7636, upon application in accordance with Title 8 (commencing with Section 1275) of Part 3 of the Code of Civil Procedure shall conform to those provisions, except that the application for the change of name may be included with the petition filed under this part and except as provided in Sections 1277 and 1278 of the Code of Civil Procedure. **Leg.H.** Enacted Stats 1992 ch 162 §10 (AB 2650), operative January 1, 1994.

§7639. Issuance of new birth certificate

If the judgment or order of the court is at variance with the child's birth certificate, the court shall order that a new birth certificate be issued as prescribed in Article 2 (commencing with Section 102725) of Chapter 5 of Part 1 of Division 102 of the Health and Safety Code. **Leg.H.** Enacted Stats 1992 ch 162 §10 (AB 2650), operative January 1, 1994. Amended Stats 1996 ch 1023 §48 (SB 1497), effective September 29, 1996.

§7640. Award of attorney's fees and other costs

The court may order reasonable fees of counsel, experts, and the child's guardian ad litem, and other costs of the action and pretrial proceedings, including genetic testing, to be paid by the parties, excluding any governmental entity, in proportions and at times determined by the court. The court may apply the standards set forth in Sections 2032 and 7605 in making this determination. **Leg.H.** Enacted Stats 1992 ch 162 §10 (AB 2650), operative January 1, 1994. Amended Stats 1994 ch 1269 §55.2 (AB 2208); Stats 2018 ch 876 §53 (AB 2684), effective January 1, 2019.

2018 Note: For legislative intent, see the 2018 Notes following Fam C §7540.

§7641. Enforcement of judgment

(a) If there is a voluntary declaration of paternity in place, or parentage or a duty of support has been acknowledged or adjudicated under this part or under prior law, the obligation of the parent may be enforced in the same or other proceedings by any of the following:

(1) The other parent.

(2) The child.

(3) The public authority that has furnished or may furnish the reasonable expenses of pregnancy, confinement, education, support, or funeral.

(4) Any other person, including a private agency, to the extent the person has furnished or is furnishing these expenses.

(b) The court may order support payments to be made to any of the following:

(1) The other parent.

(2) The clerk of the court.

(3) A person, corporation, or agency designated to administer the payments for the benefit of the child under the supervision of the court.

(c) Willful failure to obey the judgment or order of the court is a civil contempt of the court. All remedies for the enforcement of judgments, including imprisonment for contempt, apply. **Leg.H.** Enacted Stats 1992 ch 162 §10 (AB 2650), operative January 1, 1994. Amended Stats 2013 ch 510 §12 (AB 1403), effective January 1, 2014.

§7642. Modification of judgment

The court has continuing jurisdiction to modify or set aside a judgment or order made under this part. A judgment or order relating to an adoption may only be modified or set aside in the same manner and under the same conditions as an order of adoption may be modified or set aside under Section 9100 or 9102. **Leg.H.** Enacted Stats 1992 ch 162 §10 (AB 2650), operative January 1, 1994. Amended Stats 1999 ch 653 §11 (AB 380).

§7643. Confidentiality of hearings and records

(a) Notwithstanding any other law concerning public hearings and records, a hearing or trial held under this part may be held in closed court without admittance of any person other than those necessary to the action or proceeding. Except as provided in subdivision (b), all papers and records, other than the final judgment, pertaining to the action or proceeding, whether part of the permanent record of the court or of a file in a public agency or elsewhere, are subject to inspection and copying only in exceptional cases upon an order of the court for good cause shown.

(b)(1) Papers and records pertaining to the action or proceeding that are part of the permanent record of the court are subject to inspection and copying by the parties to the action, their attorneys, and by agents acting pursuant to written authorization from the parties to the action or their attorneys. An attorney shall obtain the consent of the party to the action before authorizing an agent to inspect and copy the permanent record. An attorney shall also state on the written authorization that the attorney has obtained the consent of the party to authorize an agent to inspect and copy the permanent record.

(2) For purposes of establishing parentage and establishing and enforcing child support orders, papers and records pertaining to the action or proceeding that are part of the permanent record of the court are subject to inspection and copying by any local child support agency, as defined in subdivision (h) of Section 17000.

(c) This section applies only to actions filed before January 1, 2023. **Leg.H.** Enacted Stats 1992 ch 162 §10 (AB 2650), operative January 1, 1994. Amended Stats 2008 ch 50 §1 (AB 1679), effective January 1, 2009; Stats 2010 ch 212 §5 (AB 2767), effective January 1, 2011; Stats 2018 ch 504 §4 (AB 3248), effective January 1, 2019; Stats 2019 ch 115 §92 (AB 1817), effective January 1, 2020; Stats 2021 ch 52 §1 (AB 429), effective January 1, 2022; Stats 2022 ch 420 §19 (AB 2960), effective January 1, 2023.

§ 7643.5. Hearing may be held in closed court; Inspecting or copying records pertaining to the action

(a) Notwithstanding any other law concerning public hearings and records, a hearing or trial held under this part for an action filed on or after January 1, 2023, under Section 7613, subdivision (f) of Section 7630, or Part 7 (commencing with Section 7960), may be held in closed court without admittance of any person other than those necessary to the action or proceeding. Except as provided in subdivision (b), all papers and records, other than the final judgment, pertaining to the action or proceeding, whether part of the permanent record of the court or of a file in a public agency or elsewhere, are subject to inspection and copying only in exceptional cases upon an order of the court for good cause shown.

(b)(1) Papers and records pertaining to the action or proceeding that are part of the permanent record of the court are subject to inspection and copying by the parties to the action, their attorneys, and by agents acting pursuant to written authorization from the parties to the action or their attorneys. An attorney shall obtain the consent of the party to the action before authorizing an agent to inspect and copy the permanent record. An attorney shall also state on the written authorization that the attorney has obtained the consent of the party to authorize an agent to inspect and copy the permanent record.

(2) For purposes of establishing parentage and establishing and enforcing child support orders, papers and records pertaining to the action or proceeding that are part of the permanent record of the court are subject to inspection and copying by any local child support agency, as defined in subdivision (h) of Section 17000.

(c) On or before January 1, 2023, the Judicial Council shall create a new form or modify an existing form, as it deems appropriate, that requires a party initiating an action or proceeding filed under Section 7613, subdivision (f) of Section 7630, or Part 7 (commencing with Section 7960) to designate the action or proceeding as filed under the identified statutory provision.

(d) Notwithstanding Section 4, this section shall apply to all actions filed before January 1, 2023. **Leg.H.** Added Stats 2021 ch 52 §2 (AB 429), effective January 1, 2022. Amended Stats 2022 ch 420 §20 (AB 2960), effective January 1, 2023.

§7644. Action based on voluntary declaration of parentage; Effect of declaration

(a) Notwithstanding any other law, an action for child custody and support and for other relief as provided in Section 7637 may be filed based upon a voluntary declaration of parentage as provided in Chapter 3 (commencing with Section 7570) of Part 2.

(b) Except as provided in Section 7581, the voluntary declaration of parentage shall be given the same force and effect as a judgment of parentage entered by a court of competent jurisdiction. The court shall make appropriate orders as specified in Section 7637 based upon the voluntary declaration of parentage unless evidence is presented that the voluntary declaration of parentage has been rescinded by the parties, set aside as provided in Section 7575, 7576, or 7577, or is void under Section 7573.5.

(c) The Judicial Council shall develop the forms and procedures necessary to implement this section.

(d) This section shall become operative on January 1, 2020. **Leg.H.** Added Stats 2018 ch 876 §55 (AB 2684), effective January 1, 2019, operative January 1, 2020.

Prior Law: Former Fam C §7644, similar to the present section, was added Stats 1994 ch 1266 §7 (AB 3804), amended Stats 1996 ch 1062 §14 (AB 1832), Stats 2013 ch 510 §13 (AB 1403), effective January 1, 2014, Stats 2018 ch 876 §54 (AB 2684), effective January 1, 2019, and repealed January 1, 2020, by its own terms.

Editor's Notes— 2018 Note: For legislative intent, see the 2018 Notes following Fam C §7540.

ARTICLE 1.5
Setting Aside or Vacating Judgment of Parentage

Definitions. §7645.
Motion challenging paternity judgment upon genetic testing showing non-paternity; Time limitations; Request for reconsideration. §7646.
Conditions for granting motion; Proof of service on specified persons required. §7647.
Guardian ad litem. §7647.5.
Genetic testing. §7647.7.
Denial of motion in best interest of child; Factors of consideration. §7648.
Statement on record after denial of motion. §7648.1.
Applicability of section; Administrative order; Costs; Relief from order to submit to genetic tests. §7648.2.
Circumstances where setting aside or vacating judgment not allowed. §7648.3.
Vacating order of child support and arrearages. §7648.4.
Effect on adoption. §7648.8.
Child conceived by assisted reproduction or pursuant to surrogacy agreement. §7648.9.
No limitation on rights and remedies provided by other law. §7649.
Effect on distribution or payment made in good faith reliance on paternity judgment; Immunity from liability for such distribution or payment. §7649.5.

§7645. Definitions

For purposes of this article, the following definitions shall apply:

(a) "Child" means the child of a previously established father or mother, as determined by the superior court in a judgment that is the subject of a motion brought pursuant to this article, or as a matter of law.

(b) "Judgment" means a judgment, order, or decree entered in a court of this state that establishes parentage, including a determination of parentage made pursuant to a petition filed under Section 300, 601, or 602 of the Welfare and Institutions Code. For purposes of this article, "judgment" does not include a judgment in any action for marital dissolution, legal separation, or nullity.

(c) "Previously established father" means a person identified as the father of a child in a judgment that is the subject of a motion brought pursuant to this article.

(d) "Previously established mother" means a person identified as the mother of a child in a judgment that is the subject of a motion brought pursuant to this article. **Leg.H.** Added Stats 2004 ch 849 §4 (AB 252). Amended Stats 2018 ch 876 §57 (AB 2684), effective January 1, 2019.

Editor's Notes— 2018 Note: For legislative intent, see the 2018 Notes following Fam C §7540.

§7646. Motion challenging paternity judgment upon genetic testing showing non-paternity; Time limitations; Request for reconsideration

(a) Notwithstanding any other law, a judgment establishing parentage may be set aside or vacated upon a motion by a previously established parent, the child, or the legal representative of any of these persons if genetic testing indicates that the previously established father of a child is not the genetic father of the child. The motion shall be brought within one of the following time periods:

(1) Within a two-year period commencing with the date on which the previously established father knew or should have known of a judgment that established the father's parentage of the child or commencing with the date the previously established father knew or should have known of the existence of an action to adjudicate the issue of parentage, whichever is first, except as provided in paragraph (2).

(2) In the case of a previously established father who is the legal father as a result of a default judgment as of the effective date of this section, within a two-year period from January 1, 2005, to December 31, 2006, inclusive.

(b) Subdivision (a) does not apply if the child is presumed to be a child of a marriage pursuant to Section 7540, the previously established parent is a parent under Section 7613 or 7962, or the action is barred by paragraph (2) of subdivision (a) of Section 7630.

(c) Reconsideration of a motion brought under paragraph (3) of subdivision (a) may be requested and granted if the following requirements are met:

(1) The motion was filed with the court between September 24, 2006, and December 31, 2006, inclusive.

(2) The motion was denied solely on the basis that it was untimely.

(3) The request for reconsideration of the motion is filed on or before December 31, 2009. **Leg.H.** Added Stats 2004 ch 849 §4 (AB 252). Amended Stats 2008 ch 58 §1 (SB 1333), effective January 1, 2009; Stats 2018 ch 876 §58 (AB 2684), effective January 1, 2019; Stats 2019 ch 115 §93 (AB 1817), effective January 1, 2020.

2018 Note: For legislative intent, see the 2018 Notes following Fam C §7540.

§7647. Conditions for granting motion; Proof of service on specified persons required

(a) A court may grant a motion to set aside or vacate a judgment establishing parentage only if all of the following conditions are met:

(1) The motion is filed in a court of proper venue.

(2) The motion contains, at a minimum, all of the following information, if known:

(A) The legal name, age, county of residence, and residence address of the child.

(B) The names, mailing addresses, and counties of residence, or, if deceased, the date and place of death, of the following persons:

(i) The previously established parents and the alleged father of the child.

(ii) The guardian of the child, if any.

(iii) Any person who has physical custody of the child.

(iv) The guardian ad litem of the child, if any, as appointed pursuant to Section 7647.5.

(C) A declaration that the person filing the motion believes that the previously established father is not the genetic father of the child, the specific reasons for this belief, and a declaration that the person desires that the motion be granted. The moving party is not required to present evidence of genetic testing indicating that the previously established father is not the genetic father of the child in order to bring this motion pursuant to Section 7646.

(D) A declaration that the marital presumption set forth in Section 7540 does not apply and that an action is not barred under paragraph (2) of subdivision (a) of Section 7630.

(3) The court finds that the previously established father is not a genetic parent pursuant to Section 7555.

(b) The motion shall include a proof of service upon the following persons, excluding the person bringing the motion:

(1) The parties to the action resulting in the judgment of parentage.

(2) The local child support agency, if services are being provided to the child pursuant to Title IV-D or IV-E of the Social Security Act (42 U.S.C. Sec. 651 et seq. and 42 U.S.C. Sec. 670 et seq.).

(3) The child's guardian ad litem, if any. **Leg.H.** Added Stats 2004 ch 849 §4 (AB 252). Amended Stats 2018 ch 876 §59 (AB 2684), effective January 1, 2019.

Editor's Notes—2018 Note: For legislative intent, see the 2018 Notes following Fam C §7540.

§7647.5. Guardian ad litem

A guardian ad litem may be appointed for the child to represent the best interests of the child in an action brought pursuant to this article. **Leg.H.** Added Stats 2004 ch 849 §4 (AB 252).

§7647.7. Genetic testing

Any genetic testing used to support the motion to set aside or vacate shall be conducted in accordance with Section 7552. The court shall, at the request of any person authorized to make a motion pursuant to this article, or may upon its own motion, order genetic testing to assist the court in making a determination whether the previously established father is the genetic father of the child. **Leg.H.** Added Stats 2004 ch 849 §4 (AB 252). Amended Stats 2018 ch 876 §60 (AB 2684), effective January 1, 2019.

Editor's Notes—2018 Note: For legislative intent, see the 2018 Notes following Fam C §7540.

§7648. Denial of motion in best interest of child; Factors of consideration

The court may deny the motion to set aside or vacate a judgment establishing parentage if it determines that denial of the motion is in the best interest of the child, after consideration of the following factors:

(a) The age of the child.

(b) The length of time since the entry of the judgment establishing parentage.

(c) The nature, duration, and quality of any relationship between the previously established father and the child, including the duration and frequency of any time periods during which the child and the previously established father resided in the same household or enjoyed a parent and child relationship.

(d) The request of the previously established father that the parent and child relationship continue.

(e) Notice by the biological father of the child that the biological father does not oppose preservation of the relationship between the previously established father and the child.

(f) The benefit or detriment to the child in establishing the genetic father as the parent of the child.

(g) Whether the conduct of the previously established father has impaired the ability to ascertain the identity of, or get support from, the biological father.

(h) Additional factors deemed by the court to be relevant to its determination of the best interest of the child. **Leg.H.** Added Stats 2004 ch 849 §4 (AB 252). Amended Stats 2018 ch 876 §61 (AB 2684), effective January 1, 2019; Stats 2019 ch 115 §94 (AB 1817), effective January 1, 2020.

2018 Note: For legislative intent, see the 2018 Notes following Fam C §7540.

§7648.1. Statement on record after denial of motion

If the court denies a motion pursuant to Section 7648, the court shall state on the record the basis for the denial of that motion and any supporting facts. **Leg.H.** Added Stats 2004 ch 849 §4 (AB 252).

§7648.2. Applicability of section; Administrative order; Costs; Relief from order to submit to genetic tests

(a) This section applies only to cases where support enforcement services are being provided by a local child support agency pursuant to Section 17400.

(b) Upon receipt of any motion brought pursuant to Section 7646, the local child support agency may issue an administrative order requiring the mother, child, and the previously established father to submit to genetic testing if all of the conditions of paragraphs (1) and (2) of subdivision (a) of Section 7647 are satisfied.

(c) The local child support agency shall pay the costs of any genetic tests that are ordered under subdivision (b) or are ordered by a court for cases in which the local child support agency is providing services under Title IV–D of the Social Security Act (42 U.S.C. Sec. 651 et seq.).

(d) Nothing in this section prohibits any person who has been ordered by a local child support agency to submit to genetic tests pursuant to this section from filing a notice of motion with the court seeking relief from the local child support agency's order to submit to genetic tests. In that event, the court shall resolve the issue of whether genetic tests should be ordered as provided in Section 7647.7. If any person refuses to submit to the tests after receipt of the administrative order pursuant to this section and fails to seek relief from the court from the administrative order either prior to the scheduled tests or within 10 days after the tests are scheduled, the court may resolve the question of paternity against that person or enforce the administrative order if the rights of others or the interest of justice so require. **Leg.H.** Added Stats 2004 ch 849 §4 (AB 252).

§7648.3. Circumstances where setting aside or vacating judgment not allowed

A court may not issue an order setting aside or vacating a judgment establishing paternity pursuant to this article under any of the following circumstances:

(a) The judgment was made or entered by a tribunal of another state, even if the enforcement of that judgment is sought in this state.

(b) The judgment was made or entered in this state and genetic tests were conducted prior to the entry of the judgment which did not exclude the previously established father as the biological father of the child. **Leg.H.** Added Stats 2004 ch 849 §4 (AB 252).

§7648.4. Vacating order of child support and arrearages

Notwithstanding any other provision of law, if the court grants a motion to set aside or vacate a paternity judgment pursuant to this article, the court shall vacate any order for child support and arrearages issued on the basis of that previous judgment of paternity. The previously established father has no right of reimbursement for any amount of support paid prior to the granting of the motion. **Leg.H.** Added Stats 2004 ch 849 §4 (AB 252).

§7648.8. Effect on adoption

This article does not establish a basis for termination of any adoption, and does not affect any obligation of an adoptive parent to an adoptive child. **Leg.H.** Added Stats 2004 ch 849 §4 (AB 252).

§7648.9. Child conceived by assisted reproduction or pursuant to surrogacy agreement

This article does not establish a basis for setting aside or vacating a judgment establishing paternity with regard to a child conceived by assisted reproduction pursuant to Section 7613 or a child conceived pursuant to a surrogacy agreement. **Leg.H.** Added Stats 2004 ch 849 §4 (AB 252). Amended Stats 2013 ch 510 §14 (AB 1403), effective January 1, 2014.

§7649. No limitation on rights and remedies provided by other law

This article does not limit the rights and remedies available under any other law with regard to setting aside or vacating a judgment of parentage. **Leg.H.** Added Stats 2004 ch 849 §4 (AB 252). Amended Stats 2018 ch 876 §62 (AB 2684), effective January 1, 2019.

Editor's Notes— **2018 Note:** For legislative intent, see the 2018 Notes following Fam C §7540.

§7649.5. Effect on distribution or payment made in good faith reliance on paternity judgment; Immunity from liability for such distribution or payment

Notwithstanding any other provision of this article, a distribution from the estate of a decedent or payment made by a trustee, insurance company, pension fund, or any other person or entity that was made in good faith reliance on a judgment establishing paternity that is final for purposes of direct appeal, may not be set aside or subject to direct or collateral attack because of the entry of an order setting aside or vacating a judgment under this article. An estate, trust, personal representative, trustee, or any other person or entity that made that distribution or payment may not incur any liability to any person because of the distribution or payment or because of the entry of an order under this article. **Leg.H.** Added Stats 2004 ch 849 §4 (AB 252).

ARTICLE 2
Determination of Mother and Child Relationship

Action to determine mother and child relationship; Presumption. §7650.

§7650. Action to determine mother and child relationship; Presumption

(a) Any interested person may bring an action to determine the existence or nonexistence of a mother and child relationship. Insofar as practicable, the provisions of this division applicable to the father and child relationship apply.

(b) A woman is presumed to be the natural mother of a child if the child is in utero after the death of the decedent and the conditions set forth in Section 249.5 of the Probate Code are satisfied. **Leg.H.** Enacted Stats 1992 ch 162 §10 (AB 2650), operative January 1, 1994. Amended Stats 2004 ch 775 §2.3 (AB 1910); Stats 2018 ch 876 §63 (AB 2684), effective January 1, 2019.

Editor's Notes— **2018 Note:** For legislative intent, see the 2018 Notes following Fam C §7540.

CHAPTER 5
TERMINATION OF PARENTAL RIGHTS IN ADOPTION PROCEEDINGS

Relinquishment or consent by mother; Notice to and rights of presumed parent. §7660.
Voluntary waiver of father's right to notice of adoption proceedings; Rights of Indian tribes. §7660.5.
Relinquishment or consent by other parent; Notice to and rights of mother. §7661.
Proceeding to terminate parental rights of alleged father; Stay pending final determination; Domestic violence orders. §7662.
Effort to identify alleged father and presumed parent. §7663.
Notice to man identified as possible biological father; Determination and order concerning parental rights. §7664.
Order terminating parental rights of unknown biological father. §7665.
Manner of giving notice; Order dispensing with notice. §7666.
Setting for hearing; Preference for trial; Issuance of ex parte order terminating parental rights. §7667.
Continuance of hearing. §7668.
Order requiring or dispensing with alleged father's consent; Appeal; Binding effect. §7669.
No filing fee. §7670.
Petition to terminate parental rights of alleged father. §7671.

§7660. Relinquishment or consent by mother; Notice to and rights of presumed parent

If a mother relinquishes for or consents to, or proposes to relinquish for or consent to, the adoption of a child who has a presumed parent under Section 7611, the presumed parent shall be given notice of the adoption proceeding and have the rights provided under Part 2 (commencing with Section 8600) of Division 13, unless that parent's relationship to the child has been previously terminated or determined by a court not to exist or the presumed parent has voluntarily relinquished for or consented to the adoption of the child. **Leg.H.** Enacted Stats 1992 ch 162 §10 (AB 2650), operative January 1, 1994. Amended Stats 2000 ch 937 §1 (AB 2433); Stats 2013 ch 510 §15 (AB 1403), effective January 1, 2014.

§7660.5. Voluntary waiver of father's right to notice of adoption proceedings; Rights of Indian tribes

Notwithstanding any other provision of law, a presumed father may waive the right to notice of any adoption proceeding by executing a form developed by the department before an authorized representative of the department, an authorized representative of a licensed public or private adoption agency, or a notary public or other person authorized to perform notarial acts. The waiver of notice form may be validly executed before or after the birth of the child, and once signed no notice, relinquishment for, or consent to adoption of the child shall be required from the father for the adoption to proceed. This shall be a voluntary and informed waiver without undue influence. If the child is an Indian child as defined under the Indian Child Welfare Act (ICWA), any waiver of consent by an Indian presumed father shall be executed in accordance with the requirements for voluntary adoptions set forth in Section 1913 of Title 25 of the United States Code. The waiver shall not affect the rights of any known federally recognized Indian tribe or tribes from which the child or the presumed father may be descended to notification of, or participation in, adoption proceedings as provided by the ICWA. Notice that the waiver has been executed shall be given to any known federally recognized Indian tribe or tribes from which the child or the presumed father may be descended, as required by the ICWA. **Leg.H.** Added Stats 2004 ch 858 §1 (SB 1357). Amended Stats 2008 ch 534 §4 (SB 1726), effective January 1, 2009.

§7661. Relinquishment or consent by other parent; Notice to and rights of mother

If the other parent relinquishes for or consents to, or proposes to relinquish for or consent to, the adoption of a child, the mother shall be given notice of the adoption proceeding and have the rights provided under Part 2 (commencing with Section 8600) of Division 13, unless the mother's relationship to the child has been previously terminated by a court or the mother has voluntarily relinquished for or consented to the adoption of the child. **Leg.H.** Enacted Stats 1992 ch 162 §10 (AB 2650), operative January 1, 1994. Amended Stats 2013 ch 510 §16 (AB 1403), effective January 1, 2014.

§7662. Proceeding to terminate parental rights of alleged father; Stay pending final determination; Domestic violence orders

(a) If a mother relinquishes for or consents to, or proposes to relinquish for or consent to, the adoption of a child, or if a child otherwise becomes the subject of an adoption proceeding, the agency or person to whom the child has been or is to be relinquished, or the mother or the person having physical or legal custody of the child, or the prospective adoptive parent, shall file a petition to terminate the parental rights of the alleged father, unless one of the following occurs:

(1) The alleged father's relationship to the child has been previously terminated or determined not to exist by a court.

(2) The alleged father has been served as prescribed in Section 7666 with a written notice alleging that the alleged father is or could be the biological father of the child to be adopted or placed for adoption and has failed to bring an action for the purpose of declaring the existence of the father and child relationship pursuant to subdivision (c) of Section 7630 within 30 days of service of the notice or the birth of the child, whichever is later.

(3) The alleged father has executed a written form developed by the department to waive notice, to deny parentage, relinquish the child for adoption, or consent to the adoption of the child.

(b) The alleged father may validly execute a waiver or denial of parentage before or after the birth of the child, and, once signed, no notice of, relinquishment for, or consent to adoption of the child shall be required from the alleged father for the adoption to proceed.

(c) Except as provided in this subdivision and subdivision (d), all proceedings affecting a child, including proceedings under Divisions 8 (commencing with Section 3000) to 11 (commencing with Section 6500), inclusive, Part 1 (commencing with Section 7500) to Part 3 (commencing with Section 7600), inclusive, of this division, and Part 1 (commencing with Section 1400), Part 2 (commencing with Section 1500), and Part 4 (commencing with Section 2100) of Division 4 of the Probate Code, and any motion or petition for custody or visitation filed in a proceeding under this part, shall be stayed. The petition to terminate parental rights under this section is the only matter that may be heard during the stay until the court issues a final ruling on the petition.

(d) This section does not limit the jurisdiction of the court pursuant to Part 3 (commencing with Section 6240) and Part 4 (commencing with Section 6300) of Division 10 with respect to domestic violence orders, or pursuant to Article 6 (commencing with Section 300) of Chapter 2 of Part 1 of Division 2 of the Welfare and Institutions Code with respect to dependency proceedings. **Leg.H.** Enacted Stats 1992 ch 162 §10 (AB 2650), operative January 1, 1994. Amended Stats 2000 ch 937 §2 (AB 2433); Stats 2003 ch 251 §3 (SB 182); Stats 2008 ch 534 §5 (SB 1726), effective January 1, 2009; Stats 2010 ch 588 §3 (AB 2020), effective January 1, 2011; Stats 2013 ch 510 §17 (AB 1403), effective January 1, 2014; Stats 2014 ch 763 §2 (AB 1701), effective January 1, 2015; Stats 2019 ch 115 §95 (AB 1817), effective January 1, 2020.

§7663. Effort to identify alleged father and presumed parent

(a) In an effort to identify all alleged fathers and presumed parents, the court shall cause inquiry to be made of the mother and any other appropriate person by one of the following:

(1) The State Department of Social Services.

(2) A licensed county adoption agency.

(3) The licensed adoption agency to which the child is to be relinquished.

(4) In the case of a stepparent adoption, the licensed clinical social worker, licensed marriage and family therapist, or licensed professional clinical counselor who is performing the investigation pursuant to Section 9001, if applicable. In the case of a stepparent adoption in which a licensed clinical social worker, licensed marriage and family therapist, or licensed professional clinical counselor is not performing the investigation pursuant to Section 9001, the board of supervisors may assign those inquiries to a licensed county adoption agency, the county department designated by the board of supervisors to administer the public social services program, or the county probation department.

(b) The inquiry shall include all of the following:

(1) Whether the mother was married at the time of conception of the child or at any time thereafter.

(2) Whether the mother was cohabiting with a man at the time of conception or birth of the child.

(3) Whether the mother has received support payments or promises of support with respect to the child or in connection with the pregnancy.

(4) Whether any person has formally or informally acknowledged or declared possible parentage of the child.

(5) The names and whereabouts, if known, of every person presumed or alleged to be the parent of the child, and the efforts made to give notice of the proposed adoption to each person identified.

(c) The agency that completes the inquiry shall file a written report of the findings with the court. **Leg.H.** Enacted Stats 1992 ch 162 §10 (AB 2650), operative January 1, 1994. Amended Stats 2011 ch 462 §1 (AB 687), effective January 1, 2012; Stats 2012 ch 638 §1 (AB 1757), effective January 1, 2013; Stats 2013 ch 510 §18 (AB 1403), effective January 1, 2014; Stats 2018 ch 389 §12 (AB 2296), effective January 1, 2019; Stats 2019 ch 115 §96 (AB 1817), effective January 1, 2020.

§7664. Notice to man identified as possible biological father; Determination and order concerning parental rights

(a) If, after the inquiry, the biological father is identified to the satisfaction of the court, or if more than one man is identified as a possible biological father, notice of the proceeding shall be given in accordance with Section 7666. If an alleged biological father fails to appear or, if appearing, fails to claim parental rights, those parental rights with reference to the child shall be terminated.

(b) If the biological father or a man claiming to be the biological father claims parental rights, the court shall determine biological parentage. The court shall then determine if it is in the best interest of the child that the biological father retain parental rights, or that an adoption of the child be allowed to proceed. The court, in making that determination, may consider all relevant evidence, including the efforts made by the biological father to obtain custody, the age and prior placement of the child, and the effects of a change of placement on the child.

(c) If the court finds that it is in the best interest of the child that the biological father should be allowed to retain parental rights, the court shall order that the biological father's consent is necessary for an adoption. If the court finds that the man claiming parental rights is not the biological father, or that if the man is the biological father it is in the child's best interest that an adoption be allowed to proceed, the court shall order that the consent of that man is not required for an adoption. This finding terminates all parental rights and responsibilities with respect to the child. **Leg.H.** Enacted Stats 1992 ch 162 §10 (AB 2650), operative January 1, 1994. Amended Stats 2011 ch 462 §2 (AB 687), effective January 1, 2012; Stats 2013 ch 510 §19 (AB 1403), effective January 1, 2014; Stats 2019 ch 115 §97 (AB 1817), effective January 1, 2020.

§7665. Order terminating parental rights of unknown biological father

If, after the inquiry, the court is unable to identify the biological father or any possible biological father and no person has appeared claiming to be the biological father and claiming custodial rights, the court shall enter an order terminating the unknown biological father's parental rights with reference to the child. **Leg.H.** Enacted Stats 1992 ch 162 §10 (AB 2650), operative January 1, 1994. Amended Stats 2013 ch 510 §20 (AB 1403), effective January 1, 2014.

§7666. Manner of giving notice; Order dispensing with notice

(a) Except as provided in subdivision (b), notice of the proceeding shall be given to every person identified as the biological father or a possible biological father in accordance with the Code of Civil Procedure for the service of process in a civil action in this state at least 10 days before the date of the proceeding, except that publication or posting of the notice of the proceeding is not required, and service on the parent or guardian of a biological father or possible biological father who is a minor is not required unless the minor has previously provided written authorization to serve the minor's parent or guardian. Proof of giving the notice shall be filed with the court before the petition is heard.

(b) Notice to a man identified as or alleged to be the biological father is not required, and the court shall issue an order dispensing with that notice under any of the following circumstances:

(1) The relationship to the child has been previously terminated or determined not to exist by a court.

(2) The alleged father has executed a written form to waive notice, deny parentage, relinquish the child for adoption, or consent to the adoption of the child.

(3) The whereabouts or identity of the alleged father are unknown or cannot be ascertained.

(4) The alleged father has been served with written notice of alleged parentage and the proposed adoption, and has failed to bring an action pursuant to subdivision (c) of Section 7630 within 30 days of service of the notice or the birth of the child, whichever is later. **Leg.H.** Enacted Stats 1992 ch 162 §10 (AB 2650), operative January 1, 1994. Amended Stats 2002 ch 260 §1 (SB 1512); Stats 2011 ch 462 §3 (AB 687), effective January 1, 2012; Stats 2013 ch 510 §21 (AB 1403), effective January 1, 2014; Stats 2014 ch 763 §3 (AB 1701), effective January 1, 2015; Stats 2019 ch 115 §98 (AB 1817), effective January 1, 2020.

§7667. Setting for hearing; Preference for trial; Issuance of ex parte order terminating parental rights

(a) Notwithstanding any other law, an action to terminate the parental rights of an alleged father of a child as specified in this part shall be set for hearing not more than 45 days after filing of the petition, except as provided in subdivision (c).

(b) The matter so set shall have precedence over all other civil matters on the date set for trial, except an action to terminate parental rights pursuant to Part 4 (commencing with Section 7800).

(c) The court may dispense with a hearing and issue an ex parte order terminating parental rights if any of the following applies:

(1) The identity or whereabouts of the alleged father are unknown.

(2) The alleged father has validly executed a waiver of the right to notice or a denial of parentage.

(3) The alleged father has been served with written notice of alleged parentage and the proposed adoption, and has failed to bring an action pursuant to subdivision (c) of Section 7630 within 30 days of service of the notice or the birth of the child, whichever is later. **Leg.H.** Enacted Stats 1992 ch 162 §10 (AB 2650), operative January 1, 1994. Amended Stats 2010 ch 588 §4 (AB 2020), effective January 1, 2011; Stats 2011 ch 462 §4 (AB 687), effective January 1, 2012; Stats 2013 ch 510 §22 (AB 1403), effective January 1, 2014; Stats 2019 ch 115 §99 (AB 1817), effective January 1, 2020.

§7668. Continuance of hearing

(a) The court may continue the proceedings for not more than 30 days as necessary to appoint counsel and to enable counsel to prepare for the case adequately or for other good cause.

(b) In order to obtain an order for a continuance of the hearing, written notice shall be filed within two court days of the date set for the hearing, together with affidavits or declarations detailing specific facts showing that a continuance is necessary, unless the court for good cause entertains an oral motion for continuance.

(c) Continuances shall be granted only upon a showing of good cause. Neither a stipulation between counsel nor the convenience of the parties is in and of itself a good cause.

(d) A continuance shall be granted only for that period of time shown to be necessary by the evidence considered at the hearing on the motion. If a continuance is granted, the facts proven which require the continuance shall be entered upon the minutes of the court. **Leg.H.** Enacted Stats 1992 ch 162 §10 (AB 2650), operative January 1, 1994.

§7669. Order requiring or dispensing with alleged father's consent; Appeal; Binding effect

(a) An order requiring or dispensing with an alleged father's consent for the adoption of a child may be appealed from in the same manner as an order of the juvenile court declaring a person to be a ward of the juvenile court and is conclusive and binding upon the alleged father.

(b) After making the order, the court has no power to set aside, change, or modify that order.

(c) Nothing in this section limits the right to appeal from the order and judgment. **Leg.H.** Enacted Stats 1992 ch 162 §10 (AB 2650), operative January 1, 1994. Amended Stats 2002 ch 260 §2 (SB 1512); Stats 2003 ch 251 §4 (SB 182); Stats 2013 ch 510 §23 (AB 1403), effective January 1, 2014.

§7670. No filing fee

There shall be no filing fee charged for a petition filed pursuant to Section 7662. **Leg.H.** Enacted Stats 1992 ch 162 §10 (AB 2650), operative January 1, 1994.

§7671. Petition to terminate parental rights of alleged father

A single petition may be filed pursuant to Section 7662 to terminate the parental rights of the alleged father or fathers of two or more biological siblings or to terminate the parental rights of two or more alleged fathers of the same child. A petition filed in accordance with this section may be granted in whole or in part in accordance with the procedures set forth in this chapter. The court shall retain discretion to bifurcate any case in which the petition was filed in accordance with this section, and shall do so whenever it is necessary to protect the interests of a party or a child who is the subject of the proceeding. **Leg.H.** Added Stats 2014 ch 763 §4 (AB 1701), effective January 1, 2015.

CHAPTER 6
PROTECTIVE AND RESTRAINING ORDERS

Article 1. Orders in Summons.
Article 2. Ex Parte Orders.
Article 3. Orders After Notice and Hearing.
Article 4. Orders Included in Judgment.

ARTICLE 1
Orders in Summons

Temporary restraining order in summons. §7700.

§7700. Temporary restraining order in summons

In addition to the contents required by Section 412.20 of the Code of Civil Procedure, in a proceeding under this part the summons shall contain a temporary restraining order restraining all parties, without the prior written consent of the other party or an order of the court, from removing from the state any minor child for whom the proceeding seeks to establish a parent and child relationship. **Leg.H.** Added Stats 1993 ch 219 §179.6 (AB 1500).

Prior Law: Former §7700, similar to the present section, was enacted Stats 1992 ch 162 §10, operative January 1, 1994, and repealed Stats 1993 ch 219 §179.5.

ARTICLE 2
Ex Parte Orders

Protective and other restraining orders. §7710.

§7710. Protective and other restraining orders

During the pendency of a proceeding under this part, on application of a party in the manner provided by Part 4 (commencing with Section 240) of Division 2, the court may issue ex parte a protective order as defined in Section 6218 and any other order as provided in Article 1 (commencing with Section 6320) of Chapter 2 of Part 4 of Division 10. **Leg.H.** Added Stats 1993 ch 219 §179.6 (AB 1500).

Prior Law: Former §7710, similar to present Fam C §6320, was enacted Stats 1992 ch 162 §10, operative January 1, 1994, and repealed Stats 1993 ch 219 §179.5.

§7711. [Section repealed 1993]

Leg.H. Enacted Stats 1992 ch 162 §10 (AB 2650), operative January 1, 1994. Repealed Stats 1993 ch 219 §179.5 (AB 1500). See Fam C §6305.

§7712. [Section repealed 1993]

Leg.H. Added Stats 1993 ch 301 §3 (AB 197). Repealed Stats 1993 ch 876 §27.4 (SB 1068), effective October 6, 1993. The repealed section related to counseling for parties involved in domestic violence.

ARTICLE 3
Orders After Notice and Hearing

Issuable orders. §7720.

§7720. Issuable orders

(a) After notice and a hearing, the court may issue a protective order as defined in Section 6218 and any other restraining order as provided in Article 2 (commencing with Section 6340) of Chapter 2 of Part 4 of Division 10.

(b) The court may not issue a mutual protective order pursuant to subdivision (a) unless it meets the requirements of Section 6305. **Leg.H.** Added Stats 1993 ch 219 §179.6 (AB 1500). Amended Stats 1995 ch 246 §3 (SB 591).

Prior Law: Former §7720, similar to present Fam C §6340, was enacted Stats 1992 ch 162 §10, operative January 1, 1994, and repealed Stats 1993 ch 219 §179.5.

§7721. [Section repealed 1993]

Leg.H. Enacted Stats 1992 ch 162 §10 (AB 2650), operative January 1, 1994. Repealed Stats 1993 ch 219 §179.5 (AB 1500). See Fam C §6340.

§7722. [Section repealed 1993]

Leg.H. Enacted Stats 1992 ch 162 §10 (AB 2650), operative January 1, 1994. Repealed Stats 1993 ch 219 §179.5 (AB 1500). See Fam C §6345.

ARTICLE 4
Orders Included in Judgment

Specified orders. §7730.

§7730. Specified orders

A judgment entered in a proceeding under this part may include a protective order as defined in Section 6218 and any other restraining order as provided in Article 3 (commencing with Section 6360) of Chapter 2 of Part 4 of Division 10. **Leg.H.** Added Stats 1993 ch 219 §179.6 (AB 1500).

Prior Law: Former §7730, similar to present Fam C §6224, was added Stats 1992 ch 162 §10, operative January 1, 1994, and repealed Stats 1993 ch 219 §179.5.

§7731. [Section repealed 1993]

Leg.H. Enacted Stats 1992 ch 162 §10 (AB 2650), operative January 1, 1994. Repealed Stats 1993 ch 219 §179.5 (AB 1500). See Fam C §6302.

§7740. [Section repealed 1993]

Leg.H. Enacted Stats 1992 ch 162 §10 (AB 2650), operative January 1, 1994. Repealed Stats 1993 ch 219 §179.5 (AB 1500). See Fam C §6380.

§7741. [Section repealed 1993]

Leg.H. Enacted Stats 1992 ch 162 §10 (AB 2650), operative January 1, 1994. Repealed Stats 1993 ch 219 §179.5 (AB 1500). See Fam C §6382.

§7742. [Section repealed 1993]

Leg.H. Enacted Stats 1992 ch 162 §10 (AB 2650), operative January 1, 1994. Repealed Stats 1993 ch 219 §179.5 (AB 1500). See Fam C §6383.

§7743. [Section repealed 1993]

Leg.H. Enacted Stats 1992 ch 162 §10 (AB 2650), operative January 1, 1994. Repealed Stats 1993 ch 219 §179.5 (AB 1500). See Fam C §6388.

§7750. [Section repealed 1993]

Leg.H. Enacted Stats 1992 ch 162 §10 (AB 2650), operative January 1, 1994. Repealed Stats 1993 ch 219 §179.5 (AB 1500). See Fam C §6360.

PART 4
FREEDOM FROM PARENTAL CUSTODY AND CONTROL

Chapter 1. General Provisions.
Chapter 2. Circumstances Where Proceeding May Be Brought.
Chapter 3. Procedure.

CHAPTER 1
GENERAL PROVISIONS

Purpose of part. §7800.
Liberal construction. §7801.
Proceeding to declare minor free from parental custody and control. §7802.
Effect of declaration. §7803.
Appointment of person to act on child's behalf. §7804.
Persons entitled to inspect petitions, reports, and records. §7805.
No filing fee. §7806.
Inapplicability of certain statutory provisions in proceeding under this part. §7807.
Child adjudged to be dependent child after January 1, 1989. §7808.

§7800. Purpose of part
The purpose of this part is to serve the welfare and best interest of a child by providing the stability and security of an adoptive home when those conditions are otherwise missing from the child's life. **Leg.H.** Enacted Stats 1992 ch 162 §10 (AB 2650), operative January 1, 1994.

§7801. Liberal construction
This part shall be liberally construed to serve and protect the interests and welfare of the child. **Leg.H.** Enacted Stats 1992 ch 162 §10 (AB 2650), operative January 1, 1994.

§7802. Proceeding to declare minor free from parental custody and control
A proceeding may be brought under this part for the purpose of having a minor child declared free from the custody and control of either or both parents. **Leg.H.** Enacted Stats 1992 ch 162 §10 (AB 2650), operative January 1, 1994.

§7803. Effect of declaration
A declaration of freedom from parental custody and control pursuant to this part terminates all parental rights and responsibilities with regard to the child. **Leg.H.** Enacted Stats 1992 ch 162 §10 (AB 2650), operative January 1, 1994.

§7804. Appointment of person to act on child's behalf
In a proceeding under this part, the court may appoint a suitable party to act in behalf of the child and may order such further notice of the proceedings to be given as the court deems proper. **Leg.H.** Enacted Stats 1992 ch 162 §10 (AB 2650), operative January 1, 1994.

§7805. Persons entitled to inspect petitions, reports, and records
(a) A petition filed in a proceeding under this part, or a report of the probation officer or county department designated by the board of supervisors to administer the public social services program filed in a proceeding under this part, may be inspected only by the following persons:
(1) Court personnel.
(2) The child who is the subject of the proceeding.
(3) The parents or guardian of the child.
(4) The attorneys for the parties.
(5) Any other person designated by the judge.
(b) In a proceeding before the court of appeal or Supreme Court to review a judgment or order entered in a proceeding under this part, the court record and briefs filed by the parties may be inspected only by the following persons:
(1) Court personnel.
(2) A party to the proceeding.
(3) The attorneys for the parties.
(4) Any other person designated by the presiding judge of the court before which the matter is pending.
(c) Notwithstanding any other provision of law, if it is believed that the welfare of the child will be promoted thereby, the court and the probation officer may furnish information, pertaining to a petition under this part, to any of the following:
(1) The State Department of Social Services.
(2) A county welfare department.
(3) A public welfare agency.
(4) A private welfare agency licensed by the State Department of Social Services. **Leg.H.** Enacted Stats 1992 ch 162 §10 (AB 2650), operative January 1, 1994.

§7806. No filing fee
There shall be no filing fee charged for a proceeding brought under this part. **Leg.H.** Enacted Stats 1992 ch 162 §10 (AB 2650), operative January 1, 1994.

§7807. Inapplicability of certain statutory provisions in proceeding under this part
(a) Sections 3020, 3022, 3040 to 3043, inclusive, and 3409 do not apply in a proceeding under this part.
(b) Except as provided in this subdivision and subdivision (c), all proceedings affecting a child, including proceedings under Divisions 8 (commencing with Section 3000) to 11 (commencing with Section 6500), inclusive, Part 1 (commencing with Section 7500) to Part 3 (commencing with Section 7600), inclusive, of this division, and Part 1 (commencing with Section 1400), Part 2 (commencing with Section 1500), and Part 4 (commencing with Section 2100) of Division 4 of the Probate Code, and any motion or petition for custody or visitation filed in a proceeding under this part, shall be stayed. The petition to free the minor from parental custody and control under this section is the only matter that may be heard during the stay until the court issues a final ruling on the petition.
(c) This section does not limit the jurisdiction of the court pursuant to Part 3 (commencing with Section 6240) and Part 4 (commencing with Section 6300) of Division 10 with respect to domestic violence orders, or pursuant to Article 6 (commencing with Section 300) of Chapter 2 of Part 1 of Division 2 of the Welfare and Institutions Code with respect to dependency proceedings. **Leg.H.** Enacted Stats 1992 ch 162 §10 (AB 2650), operative January 1, 1994. Amended Stats 1993 ch 219 §179.9 (AB 1500); Stats 2002 ch 260 §3 (SB 1512); Stats 2014 ch 763 §5 (AB 1701), effective January 1, 2015.

§7808. Child adjudged to be dependent child after January 1, 1989
This part does not apply to a minor adjudged a dependent child of the juvenile court pursuant to subdivision (c) of Section 360 of the Welfare and Institutions Code on and after January 1, 1989, during the period in which the minor is a dependent child of the court. For those minors, the exclusive means for the termination of parental rights are provided in the following statutes:
(a) Section 366.26 of the Welfare and Institutions Code.
(b) Sections 8604 to 8606, inclusive, and 8700 of this code.
(c) Chapter 5 (commencing with Section 7660) of Part 3 of this division of this code. **Leg.H.** Enacted Stats 1992 ch 162 §10 (AB 2650), operative January 1, 1994. Amended Stats 1994 ch 1269 §55.4 (AB 2208).

§7810. [Section repealed 2007]
Leg.H. Added Stats 1999 ch 275 §1 (AB 65), effective September 1, 1999. Amended Stats 2003 ch 469 §2 (SB 947). Repealed Stats 2006 ch 838 §3 (SB 678), effective January 1, 2007. The repealed section related to a child's connection to a tribal community.

CHAPTER 2
CIRCUMSTANCES WHERE PROCEEDING MAY BE BROUGHT

Proceeding to declare minor free from parental custody and control. §7820.
Clear and convincing evidence. §7821.
Abandoned child. §7822.
Neglected or cruelly treated child. §7823.
Parent under disability due to alcohol or controlled substance or moral depravity. §7824.
Parent convicted of felony. §7825.
Parent declared developmentally disabled or mentally ill. §7826.
Parent mentally disabled. §7827.

§7820. Proceeding to declare minor free from parental custody and control
A proceeding may be brought under this part for the purpose of having

a child under the age of 18 years declared free from the custody and control of either or both parents if the child comes within any of the descriptions set out in this chapter. **Leg.H.** Enacted Stats 1992 ch 162 §10 (AB 2650), operative January 1, 1994.

§7821. Clear and convincing evidence

A finding pursuant to this chapter shall be supported by clear and convincing evidence, except as otherwise provided. **Leg.H.** Enacted Stats 1992 ch 162 §10 (AB 2650), operative January 1, 1994. Amended Stats 2006 ch 838 §4 (SB 678), effective January 1, 2007.

§7822. Abandoned child

(a) A proceeding under this part may be brought if any of the following occur:

(1) The child has been left without provision for the child's identification by the child's parent or parents.

(2) The child has been left by both parents or the sole parent in the care and custody of another person for a period of six months without any provision for the child's support, or without communication from the parent or parents, with the intent on the part of the parent or parents to abandon the child.

(3) One parent has left the child in the care and custody of the other parent for a period of one year without any provision for the child's support, or without communication from the parent, with the intent on the part of the parent to abandon the child.

(b) The failure to provide identification, failure to provide support, or failure to communicate is presumptive evidence of the intent to abandon. If the parent or parents have made only token efforts to support or communicate with the child, the court may declare the child abandoned by the parent or parents. In the event that a guardian has been appointed for the child, the court may still declare the child abandoned if the parent or parents have failed to communicate with or support the child within the meaning of this section.

(c) If the child has been left without provision for the child's identification and the whereabouts of the parents are unknown, a petition may be filed after the 120th day following the discovery of the child and citation by publication may be commenced. The petition may not be heard until after the 180th day following the discovery of the child.

(d) If the parent has agreed for the child to be in the physical custody of another person or persons for adoption and has not signed an adoption placement agreement pursuant to Section 8801.3, a consent to adoption pursuant to Section 8814, or a relinquishment to a licensed adoption agency pursuant to Section 8700, evidence of the adoptive placement shall not in itself preclude the court from finding an intent on the part of that parent to abandon the child. If the parent has placed the child for adoption pursuant to Section 8801.3, consented to adoption pursuant to Section 8814, or relinquished the child to a licensed adoption agency pursuant to Section 8700, and has then either revoked the consent or rescinded the relinquishment, but has not taken reasonable action to obtain custody of the child, evidence of the adoptive placement shall not in itself preclude the court from finding an intent on the part of that parent to abandon the child.

(e) Notwithstanding subdivisions (a), (b), (c), and (d), if the parent of an Indian child has transferred physical care, custody, and control of the child to an Indian custodian, that action shall not be deemed to constitute an abandonment of the child, unless the parent manifests the intent to abandon the child by either of the following:

(1) Failing to resume physical care, custody, and control of the child upon the request of the Indian custodian provided that, if the Indian custodian is unable to make a request because the parent has failed to keep the Indian custodian apprised of the parent's whereabouts and the Indian custodian has made reasonable efforts to determine the whereabouts of the parent without success, there may be evidence of intent to abandon.

(2) Failing to substantially comply with any obligations assumed by the parent in the agreement with the Indian custodian despite the Indian custodian's objection to the noncompliance. **Leg.H.** Enacted Stats 1992 ch 162 §10 (AB 2650), operative January 1, 1994. Amended Stats 2006 ch 838 §5 (SB 678), effective January 1, 2007; Stats 2007 ch 47 §2 (SB 313), effective January 1, 2008; Stats 2019 ch 115 §100 (AB 1817), effective January 1, 2020.

§7823. Neglected or cruelly treated child

(a) A proceeding under this part may be brought if all of the following requirements are satisfied:

(1) The child has been neglected or cruelly treated by either or both parents. A finding that a parent committed severe sexual abuse, as described in paragraph (6) of subdivision (b) of Section 361.5 of the Welfare and Institutions Code, against the child shall be prima facie evidence that the parent has neglected or cruelly treated the child within the meaning of this subdivision.

(2) The child has been a dependent child of the juvenile court under any subdivision of Section 300 of the Welfare and Institutions Code and the parent or parents have been deprived of the child's custody for one year before the filing of a petition pursuant to this part.

(b) Physical custody by the parent or parents for insubstantial periods of time does not interrupt the running of the one-year period. **Leg.H.** Enacted Stats 1992 ch 162 §10 (AB 2650), operative January 1, 1994. Amended Stats 2018 ch 83 §1 (AB 2792), effective January 1, 2019.

§7824. Parent under disability due to alcohol or controlled substance or moral depravity

(a) "Disability" as used in this section means any physical or mental incapacity which renders the parent or parents unable to care for and control the child adequately.

(b) A proceeding under this part may be brought where all of the following requirements are satisfied:

(1) The child is one whose parent or parents (A) suffer a disability because of the habitual use of alcohol, or any of the controlled substances specified in Schedules I to V, inclusive, of Division 10 (commencing with Section 11000) of the Health and Safety Code, except when these controlled substances are used as part of a medically prescribed plan, or (B) are morally depraved.

(2) The child has been a dependent child of the juvenile court, and the parent or parents have been deprived of the child's custody continuously for one year immediately before the filing of a petition pursuant to this part.

(c) Physical custody by the parent or parents for insubstantial periods of time does not interrupt the running of the one-year period. **Leg.H.** Enacted Stats 1992 ch 162 §10 (AB 2650), operative January 1, 1994.

§7825. Parent convicted of felony

(a) A proceeding under this part may be brought where both of the following requirements are satisfied:

(1) The child is one whose parent or parents are convicted of a felony.

(2) The facts of the crime of which the parent or parents were convicted are of such a nature so as to prove the unfitness of the parent or parents to have the future custody and control of the child. In making a determination pursuant to this section, the court may consider the parent's criminal record prior to the felony conviction to the extent that the criminal record demonstrates a pattern of behavior substantially related to the welfare of the child or the parent's ability to exercise custody and control regarding the child.

(b) The mother of a child may bring a proceeding under this part against the father of the child, where the child was conceived as a result of an act in violation of Section 261 of the Penal Code, and where the father was convicted of that violation. For purposes of this subdivision, there is a conclusive presumption that the father is unfit to have custody or control of the child. **Leg.H.** Enacted Stats 1992 ch 162 §10 (AB 2650), operative January 1, 1994. Amended Stats 1997 ch 594 §2 (AB 1222); Stats 2006 ch 806 §5 (SB 1325), effective January 1, 2007; Stats 2019 ch 115 §101 (AB 1817), effective January 1, 2020.

§7826. Parent declared developmentally disabled or mentally ill

A proceeding under this part may be brought where both of the following requirements are satisfied:

(a) The child is one whose parent or parents have been declared by a court of competent jurisdiction, wherever situated, to be developmentally disabled or mentally ill.

(b) In the state or country in which the parent or parents reside or are hospitalized, the Director of State Hospitals or the Director of Developmental Services, or their equivalent, if any, and the executive director of the hospital, if any, of which the parent or parents are inmates or patients, certify that the parent or parents so declared to be developmentally disabled or mentally ill will not be capable of supporting or controlling the child in a proper manner. **Leg.H.** Enacted Stats 1992 ch 162 §10 (AB 2650), operative January 1, 1994. Amended Stats 2012 ch 440 §6 (AB 1488), effective September 22, 2012.

§7827. Parent mentally disabled

(a) "Mentally disabled" as used in this section means that a parent or parents suffer a mental incapacity or disorder that renders the parent or parents unable to care for and control the child adequately.

(b) A proceeding under this part may be brought if the child is one whose parent or parents are mentally disabled and are likely to remain so in the foreseeable future.

(c) Except as provided in subdivision (d), the evidence of any two experts, each of whom shall be a physician and surgeon, certified either by the American Board of Psychiatry and Neurology or under Section 6750 of the Welfare and Institutions Code, a licensed psychologist who has a doctoral degree in psychology and at least five years of postgraduate experience in the diagnosis and treatment of emotional and mental disorders, is required to support a finding under this section. In addition to this requirement, the court shall have the discretion to call a licensed marriage and family therapist, a licensed professional clinical counselor, or a licensed clinical social worker, either of whom shall have at least five years of relevant postlicensure experience, in circumstances in which the court determines that this testimony is in the best interest of the child and is warranted by the circumstances of the particular family or parenting issues involved. However, the court may not call a licensed marriage and family therapist, licensed professional clinical counselor, or licensed clinical social worker pursuant to this section who is the adoption service provider, as defined in Section 8502, of the child who is the subject of the petition to terminate parental rights.

(d) If the parent or parents reside in another state or in a foreign country, the evidence required by this section may be supplied by the affidavits of two experts, each of whom shall be either of the following:

(1) A physician and surgeon who is a resident of that state or foreign country, and who has been certified by a medical organization or society of that state or foreign country to practice psychiatric or neurological medicine.

(2) A licensed psychologist who has a doctoral degree in psychology and at least five years of postgraduate experience in the diagnosis and treatment of emotional and mental disorders and who is licensed in that state or authorized to practice in that country.

(e) If the rights of a parent are sought to be terminated pursuant to this section, and the parent does not have an attorney, the court shall appoint an attorney for the parent pursuant to Article 4 (commencing with Section 7860) of Chapter 3, whether or not a request for the appointment is made by the parent. **Leg.H.** Enacted Stats 1992 ch 162 §10 (AB 2650), operative January 1, 1994. Amended Stats 1996 ch 288 §1 (SB 2027); Stats 2002 ch 1013 §80 (SB 2026); Stats 2018 ch 389 §13 (AB 2296), effective January 1, 2019.

§7828. [Section repealed 2013]

Leg.H. Enacted Stats 1992 ch 162 §10 (AB 2650), operative January 1, 1994. Repealed Stats 2012 ch 638 §2 (AB 1757), effective January 1, 2013. The repealed section related to proceedings when child has been in out-of-home placement under the supervision of the juvenile court.

§7829. [Section repealed 2013]

Leg.H. Enacted Stats 1992 ch 162 §10 (AB 2650), operative January 1, 1994. Repealed Stats 2012 ch 638 §3 (AB 1757), effective January 1, 2013. The repealed section related to proceedings when a child has been found to be a dependent child of the juvenile court and reunification services.

CHAPTER 3
PROCEDURE

Article 1. Authorized Petitioners.
Article 2. Venue.
Article 3. Investigation and Report.
Article 4. Appointment of Counsel.
Article 5. Time for Hearing; Continuance.
Article 6. Notice of Proceeding and Attendance at Hearing.
Article 7. Hearing and Subsequent Proceedings.

ARTICLE 1
Authorized Petitioners

Petition by private or public adoption agency or state or county agency. §7840.
Right of interested person to file petition. §7841.
Petition to free a child from custody and control of both parents. §7842.

§7840. Petition by private or public adoption agency or state or county agency

(a) A petition may be filed under this part for an order or judgment declaring a child free from the custody and control of either or both parents by any of the following:

(1) The State Department of Social Services, a county welfare department, a licensed private or public adoption agency, a county adoption department, or a county probation department which is planning adoptive placement of the child with a licensed adoption agency.

(2) The State Department of Social Services acting as an adoption agency in counties which are not served by a county adoption agency.

(b) The fact that a child is in a foster care home subject to the requirements of Chapter 3 (commencing with Section 1500) of Division 2 of the Health and Safety Code does not prevent the filing of a petition under subdivision (a).

(c) The county counsel or, if there is no county counsel, the district attorney of the county specified in Section 7845 shall, in a proper case, institute the proceeding upon the request of any of the state or county agencies mentioned in subdivision (a). The proceeding shall be instituted pursuant to this part within 30 days of the request.

(d) If, at the time of the filing of a petition by a department or agency specified in subdivision (a), the child is in the custody of the petitioner, the petitioner may continue to have custody of the child pending the hearing on the petition unless the court, in its discretion, makes such other order regarding custody pending the hearing as it finds will best serve and protect the interest and welfare of the child. **Leg.H.** Enacted Stats 1992 ch 162 §10 (AB 2650), operative January 1, 1994.

§7841. Right of interested person to file petition

(a) An interested person may file a petition under this part for an order or judgment declaring a child free from the custody and control of either or both parents.

(b) For purposes of this section, an "interested person" is one who has a direct interest in the action, and includes, but is not limited to, a person who has filed, or who intends to file within a period of 6 months, an adoption petition under Section 8714, 8802, or 9000, or a licensed adoption agency to whom the child has been relinquished by the other parent. **Leg.H.** Enacted Stats 1992 ch 162 §10 (AB 2650), operative January 1, 1994. Amended Stats 2007 ch 47 §3 (SB 313), effective January 1, 2008.

§7842. Petition to free a child from custody and control of both parents

A single petition may be filed under this part to free a child, or more than one child if the children are biological siblings, from the custody and control of both parents. A petition filed in accordance with this section may be granted in whole or in part in accordance with the procedures set forth in this chapter. The court shall retain discretion to bifurcate any case in which the petition was filed in accordance with this section, and shall do so whenever it is necessary to protect the interests of a party or a child who is the subject of the proceeding. **Leg.H.** Added Stats 2014 ch 763 §6 (AB 1701), effective January 1, 2015.

ARTICLE 2
Venue

Venue. §7845.

§7845. Venue

The petition shall be filed in any of the following:

(a) The county in which a minor described in Chapter 2 (commencing with Section 7820) resides or is found.

(b) The county in which any of the acts which are set forth in Chapter 2 (commencing with Section 7820) are alleged to have occurred.

(c) The county in which a petition for the adoption of the child has been filed or the adoption agency to which the child has been relinquished or proposed to be relinquished has an office. **Leg.H.** Enacted Stats 1992 ch 162 §10 (AB 2650), operative January 1, 1994. Amended Stats 2009 ch 492 §2 (AB 941), effective January 1, 2010.

ARTICLE 3
Investigation and Report

Investigation of circumstances of child. §7850.
Report and recommendations to court. §7851.
Petitioner liable for costs incurred in investigation; Exemptions. §7851.5.

"Qualified court investigator". §7852.

§7850. Investigation of circumstances of child

Upon the filing of a petition under Section 7841, the clerk of the court shall, in accordance with the direction of the court, immediately notify the juvenile probation officer, qualified court investigator, licensed clinical social worker, licensed marriage and family therapist, licensed professional clinical counselor, or the county department designated by the board of supervisors to administer the public social services program, who shall immediately investigate the circumstances of the child and the circumstances which are alleged to bring the child within any provision of Chapter 2 (commencing with Section 7820). **Leg.H.** Enacted Stats 1992 ch 162 §10 (AB 2650), operative January 1, 1994. Amended Stats 1993 ch 219 §180 (AB 1500); Stats 2002 ch 260 §4 (SB 1512); Stats 2018 ch 389 §14 (AB 2296), effective January 1, 2019.

§7851. Report and recommendations to court

(a) The juvenile probation officer, qualified court investigator, licensed clinical social worker, licensed marriage and family therapist, licensed professional clinical counselor, or the county department shall render to the court a written report of the investigation with a recommendation of the proper disposition to be made in the proceeding in the best interest of the child.

(b) The report shall include all of the following:

(1) A statement that the person making the report explained to the child the nature of the proceeding to end parental custody and control.

(2) A statement of the child's feelings and thoughts concerning the pending proceeding.

(3) A statement of the child's attitude towards the child's parent or parents and particularly whether or not the child would prefer living with the parent or parents.

(4) A statement that the child was informed of the child's right to attend the hearing on the petition and the child's feelings concerning attending the hearing.

(c) If the age, or the physical, emotional, or other condition of the child precludes the child's meaningful response to the explanations, inquiries, and information required by subdivision (b), a description of the condition shall satisfy the requirement of that subdivision.

(d) The court shall receive the report in evidence and shall read and consider its contents in rendering the court's judgment. **Leg.H.** Enacted Stats 1992 ch 162 §10 (AB 2650), operative January 1, 1994. Amended Stats 1993 ch 219 §181 (AB 1500); Stats 2002 ch 260 §5 (SB 1512); Stats 2018 ch 389 §15 (AB 2296), effective January 1, 2019; Stats 2019 ch 115 §102 (AB 1817), effective January 1, 2020.

§7851.5. Petitioner liable for costs incurred in investigation; Exemptions

The petitioner shall be liable for all reasonable costs incurred in connection with the termination of parental rights, including, but not limited to, costs incurred for the investigation required by this article. However, public agencies and nonprofit organizations are exempt from payment of the costs of the investigation. The liability of a petitioner for costs under this section shall not exceed nine hundred dollars ($900). The court may defer, waive, or reduce the costs when the payment would cause an economic hardship which would be detrimental to the welfare of the child. **Leg.H.** Added Stats 1994 ch 1286 §1 (AB 2902).

§7852. "Qualified court investigator"

"Qualified court investigator," as used in this article, has the meaning provided by Section 8543. **Leg.H.** Added Stats 1993 ch 219 §182 (AB 1500).

ARTICLE 4
Appointment of Counsel

Procedure for appointment of counsel. §7860.
Appointment to protect interests of child. §7861.
Appointment of counsel for parent. §7862.
Compensation and expenses of private appointed counsel. §7863.
Continuance. §7864.

§7860. Procedure for appointment of counsel

At the beginning of the proceeding on a petition filed pursuant to this part, counsel shall be appointed as provided in this article. The public defender or private counsel may be appointed as counsel pursuant to this article. The same counsel shall not be appointed to represent both the child and the child's parent. **Leg.H.** Enacted Stats 1992 ch 162 §10 (AB 2650), operative January 1, 1994.

§7861. Appointment to protect interests of child

The court shall consider whether the interests of the child require the appointment of counsel. If the court finds that the interests of the child require representation by counsel, the court shall appoint counsel to represent the child, whether or not the child is able to afford counsel. The child shall not be present in court unless the child so requests or the court so orders. **Leg.H.** Enacted Stats 1992 ch 162 §10 (AB 2650), operative January 1, 1994.

§7862. Appointment of counsel for parent

If a parent appears without counsel and is unable to afford counsel, the court shall appoint counsel for the parent, unless that representation is knowingly and intelligently waived. **Leg.H.** Enacted Stats 1992 ch 162 §10 (AB 2650), operative January 1, 1994.

§7863. Compensation and expenses of private appointed counsel

Private counsel appointed under this article shall receive a reasonable sum for compensation and expenses, the amount of which shall be determined by the court. The amount so determined shall be paid by the real parties in interest, other than the child, in proportions the court deems just. However, if the court finds that any of the real parties in interest are unable to afford counsel, the amount shall be paid out of the general fund of the county. **Leg.H.** Enacted Stats 1992 ch 162 §10 (AB 2650), operative January 1, 1994.

§7864. Continuance

The court may continue the proceeding for not to exceed 30 days as necessary to appoint counsel and to enable counsel to become acquainted with the case. **Leg.H.** Enacted Stats 1992 ch 162 §10 (AB 2650), operative January 1, 1994.

ARTICLE 5
Time for Hearing; Continuance

Time for hearing; Precedence over other matters; Continuance. §7870.
Continuance of hearing. §7871.

§7870. Time for hearing; Precedence over other matters; Continuance

(a) It is the public policy of this state that judicial proceedings to declare a child free from parental custody and control shall be fully determined as expeditiously as possible.

(b) Notwithstanding any other provision of law, a proceeding to declare a child free from parental custody and control pursuant to this part shall be set for hearing not more than 45 days after the filing of the petition. If, at the time set for hearing, or at any continuance thereof, service has been completed and no interested person appears to contest, the court may issue an order based on the verified pleadings and any other evidence as may be submitted. If any interested person appears to contest the matter, the court shall set the matter for trial. The matter so set has precedence over all other civil matters on the date set for trial.

(c) The court may continue the proceeding as provided in Section 7864 or Section 7871. **Leg.H.** Enacted Stats 1992 ch 162 §10 (AB 2650), operative January 1, 1994. Amended Stats 2012 ch 638 §4 (AB 1757), effective January 1, 2013.

§7871. Continuance of hearing

(a) A continuance may be granted only upon a showing of good cause. Neither a stipulation between counsel nor the convenience of the parties is in and of itself a good cause.

(b) Unless the court for good cause entertains an oral motion for continuance, written notice of a motion for a continuance of the hearing shall be filed within two court days of the date set for the hearing, together with affidavits or declarations detailing specific facts showing that a continuance is necessary.

(c) A continuance shall be granted only for that period of time shown to be necessary by the evidence considered at the hearing on the motion. Whenever a continuance is granted, the facts proven which require the continuance shall be entered upon the minutes of the court. **Leg.H.** Enacted Stats 1992 ch 162 §10 (AB 2650), operative January 1, 1994.

ARTICLE 6
Notice of Proceeding and Attendance at Hearing

Citation requiring attendance at hearing. §7880.
Service of citation on parents or relatives. §7881.

Service on parent who cannot be found or whose residence is unknown. §7882.
Failure to comply with citation as contempt. §7883.
Admission of public to proceeding. §7884.

§7880. Citation requiring attendance at hearing

(a) Upon the filing of the petition, a citation shall issue requiring any person having the custody or control of the child, or the person with whom the child is, to appear at a time and place stated in the citation.

(b) The citation shall also require the person to appear with the child except that, if the child is under the age of 10 years, appearance with the child is required only upon order of the court after necessity has been shown.

(c) Service of the citation shall be made in the manner prescribed by law for service of civil process at least 10 days before the time stated in the citation for the appearance. The party or attorney responsible for serving the citation shall do so in a timely manner in order to maximize the response time available to the party being served. **Leg.H.** Enacted Stats 1992 ch 162 §10 (AB 2650), operative January 1, 1994. Amended Stats 2012 ch 638 §5 (AB 1757), effective January 1, 2013.

§7881. Service of citation on parents or relatives

(a) Notice of the proceeding shall be given by service of a citation on the father or mother of the child, if the place of residence of the father or mother is known to the petitioner. If the place of residence of the father or mother is not known to the petitioner, then the citation shall be served on the grandparents and adult brothers, sisters, uncles, aunts, and first cousins of the child, if there are any and if their residences and relationships to the child are known to the petitioner.

(b) The citation shall advise the person or persons that they may appear at the time and place stated in the citation. The citation shall also advise the person or persons of the rights and procedures set forth in Article 4 (commencing with Section 7860). If the petition is filed for the purpose of freeing the child for placement for adoption, the citation shall so state.

(c) The citation shall be served in the manner provided by law for the service of a summons in a civil action, other than by publication. If one parent has relinquished the child for the purpose of adoption, or has signed a consent for adoption as provided in Sections 8700, 8814, or 9003, notice as provided in this section need not be given to the parent who has signed the relinquishment or consent.

(d) Service of the citations required by this section shall be made at least 10 days before the time stated in the citation for the appearance. **Leg.H.** Enacted Stats 1992 ch 162 §10 (AB 2650), operative January 1, 1994.

§7882. Service on parent who cannot be found or whose residence is unknown

(a) If the parent of the child or a person alleged to be or claiming to be the parent cannot, with reasonable diligence, be served as provided for in Section 7881, or if the parent's place of residence is not known to the petitioner, the petitioner or the petitioner's agent or attorney shall make and file an affidavit stating the name of the parent or alleged parent and their place of residence, if known to the petitioner, and the name of the parent or alleged parent whose place of residence is unknown to the petitioner.

(b) Upon the filing of the affidavit, the court shall make an order that (1) the service shall be made by the publication of a citation requiring the parent or alleged parent to appear at the time and place stated in the citation and (2) the citation shall be published pursuant to Section 6064 of the Government Code in a newspaper to be named and designated in the order as most likely to give notice to the parent or alleged parent to be served.

(c) In case of publication where the residence of a parent or alleged parent is known, the court shall also direct a copy of the citation to be forthwith served upon that parent or alleged parent by mail by deposit in the post office properly addressed and with the postage thereon fully prepaid, directed to that parent or alleged parent at the place of residence. When publication is ordered, service of a copy of the citation in the manner provided for in Section 7881 is equivalent to publication and deposit in the post office.

(d) If one or both of the parents of the child are unknown or if the names of one or both of the child's parents are uncertain, that fact shall be set forth in the affidavit and the court shall order the citation to be directed to either or both of the child's parents, naming and otherwise describing the child, and to all persons claiming to be a parent of the child.

(e) Service is complete at the expiration of the time prescribed by the order for publication or when service is made as provided for in Section 7881, whichever event first occurs. **Leg.H.** Enacted Stats 1992 ch 162 §10 (AB 2650), operative January 1, 1994. Amended Stats 2019 ch 115 §103 (AB 1817), effective January 1, 2020.

§7883. Failure to comply with citation as contempt

If a person personally served with a citation within this state as provided in Section 7880 fails without reasonable cause to appear and abide by the order of the court, or to bring the child before the court if so required in the citation, the failure constitutes a contempt of court. **Leg.H.** Enacted Stats 1992 ch 162 §10 (AB 2650), operative January 1, 1994.

§7884. Admission of public to proceeding

(a) Unless requested by the child concerning whom the petition has been filed and any parent or guardian present, the public shall not be admitted to a proceeding under this part.

(b) Notwithstanding subdivision (a), the judge may admit those persons the judge determines have a direct and legitimate interest in the particular case or in the work of the court. **Leg.H.** Enacted Stats 1992 ch 162 §10 (AB 2650), operative January 1, 1994.

ARTICLE 7
Hearing and Subsequent Proceedings

Wishes and best interest of child. §7890.
Hearing in chambers to determine wishes of child. §7891.
Testimony of child in chambers. §7892.
Declaration of freedom for Indian child from custody or control of parent. §7892.5.
Appointment of guardian or referral for adoption. §7893.
Conclusiveness of order or judgment. §7894.
Appointment of counsel for indigent appellant; Free copy of transcripts. §7895.

§7890. Wishes and best interest of child

In a proceeding under this part, the court shall consider the wishes of the child, bearing in mind the age of the child, and shall act in the best interest of the child. **Leg.H.** Enacted Stats 1992 ch 162 §10 (AB 2650), operative January 1, 1994.

§7891. Hearing in chambers to determine wishes of child

(a) Except as otherwise provided in this section, if the child who is the subject of the petition is 10 years of age or older, the child shall be heard by the court in chambers on at least the following matters:

(1) The feelings and thoughts of the child concerning the custody proceeding about to take place.

(2) The feelings and thoughts of the child about the child's parent or parents.

(3) The child's preference as to custody, according to Section 3042.

(b) The court shall inform the child of the child's right to attend the hearing. However, counsel for the child may waive the hearing in chambers by the court.

(c) This section does not apply if the child is confined because of illness or other incapacity to an institution or residence and is therefore unable to attend. **Leg.H.** Enacted Stats 1992 ch 162 §10 (AB 2650), operative January 1, 1994. Amended Stats 1993 ch 219 §182.5 (AB 1500).

§7892. Testimony of child in chambers

(a) The testimony of the child may be taken in chambers and outside the presence of the child's parent or parents if the child's parent or parents are represented by counsel, the counsel is present, and any of the following circumstances exist:

(1) The court determines that testimony in chambers is necessary to ensure truthful testimony.

(2) The child is likely to be intimidated by a formal courtroom setting.

(3) The child is afraid to testify in front of the child's parent or parents.

(b) The testimony of a child also may be taken in chambers and outside the presence of the guardian or guardians of a child under the circumstances specified in subdivision (a).

(c) A finding pursuant to this section shall be supported by clear and convincing evidence.

(d) After testimony in chambers, the parent or parents of the child may elect to have the court reporter read back the testimony or have the testimony summarized by counsel for the parent or parents. **Leg.H.** Enacted Stats 1992 ch 162 §10 (AB 2650), operative January 1, 1994.

§7892.5. Declaration of freedom for Indian child from custody or control of parent

The court shall not declare an Indian child free from the custody or control of a parent, unless both of the following apply:

(a) The court finds, supported by clear and convincing evidence, that active efforts were made in accordance with Section 361.7 of the Welfare and Institutions Code.

(b) The court finds, supported by evidence beyond a reasonable doubt, including testimony of one or more "qualified expert witnesses" as described in Section 224.5 of the Welfare and Institutions Code, that the continued custody of the child by the parent is likely to result in serious emotional or physical damage to the child.

(c) This section shall only apply to proceedings involving an Indian child. **Leg.H.** Added Stats 2006 ch 838 §6 (SB 678), effective January 1, 2007.

§7893. Appointment of guardian or referral for adoption

(a) If the court, by order or judgment, declares a child free from the custody and control of both parents under this part, or one parent if the other no longer has custody and control, the court shall at the same time take one of the following actions:

(1) Appoint a guardian for the child.

(2) At the request of the State Department of Social Services or a licensed adoption agency, or where the court finds it is in the child's best interest, refer the child to a licensed adoption agency for adoptive placement by the agency.

(b) When the court refers the child to a licensed adoption agency for adoptive placement by the agency:

(1) The agency is responsible for the care of the child and is entitled to the exclusive custody and control of the child at all times until a petition for adoption has been granted.

(2) After the referral, no petition for guardianship may be filed without the consent of the agency.

(3) No petition for adoption may be heard until the appellate rights of the natural parents have been exhausted. **Leg.H.** Enacted Stats 1992 ch 162 §10 (AB 2650), operative January 1, 1994.

§7894. Conclusiveness of order or judgment

(a) An order and judgment of the court declaring a child free from the custody and control of a parent or parents under this part is conclusive and binding upon the child, upon the parent or parents, and upon all other persons who have been served with citations by publication or otherwise as provided in this part.

(b) After making the order and judgment, the court has no power to set aside, change, or modify it.

(c) Nothing in this section limits the right to appeal from the order and judgment. **Leg.H.** Enacted Stats 1992 ch 162 §10 (AB 2650), operative January 1, 1994.

§7895. Appointment of counsel for indigent appellant; Free copy of transcripts

(a) Upon appeal from a judgment freeing a child who is a dependent child of the juvenile court from parental custody and control, the appellate court shall appoint counsel for the appellant as provided by this section.

(b) Upon motion by the appellant and a finding that the appellant is unable to afford counsel, the appellate court shall appoint counsel for the indigent appellant, and appellant's counsel shall be provided a free copy of the reporter's and clerk's transcript. All of those costs are a charge against the court.

(c) The reporter's and clerk's transcripts shall be prepared and transmitted immediately after filing of the notice of appeal, at court expense and without advance payment of fees. If the appellant is able to afford counsel, the court may seek reimbursement from the appellant for the cost of the transcripts under subdivision (c) of Section 68511.3 of the Government Code as though the appellant had been granted permission to proceed in forma pauperis. **Leg.H.** Enacted Stats 1992 ch 162 §10 (AB 2650), operative January 1, 1994. Amended Stats 2000 ch 447 §4 (SB 1533); Stats 2001 ch 754 §3 (AB 1697).

PART 5
INTERSTATE COMPACT ON PLACEMENT OF CHILDREN

Adoption of compact. §7900.
Provisions of compact. §7901.
Study of home environment on request from another state; Time requirements. §7901.1.
Financial responsibility for child placed pursuant to compact. §7902.
"Appropriate public authorities". §7903.
"Appropriate authority in receiving state". §7904.
Agreements with party states; Approval of financial obligations. §7905.
Requirements for visitation, inspection, or supervision in another state. §7906.
Study of home environment on request from another state where child is in custody of requesting state; Time requirements. §7906.5.
Application of law restricting out-of-state placements. §7907.
Application to Indian child. §7907.3.
Children subject to compact. §7907.5.
Placement of children adjudged wards of court in out-of-state facility. §7908.
"Jurisdiction". §7908.5.
"Executive head"; Appointment of compact administrator. §7909.
Refusal to grant approval of placement in violation of state law. §7910.
Legislative findings and declarations; Authority of State Department of Social Services with placement of children in out-of-state residential facilities; Limitations on foster care placement; Decertification of out-of-state residential facilities for placement on January 1, 2023. § 7911.
Investigations of threats to health or safety of children in out-of-state residential facilities; Review of placement request; Certification of facilities; Licensing standards; Exception for placement of certain emotionally disturbed children and Indian children. § 7911.1.
Legislative findings, declarations, and intent relating to rights of children in out-of-state residential facilities; Reports on number of children placed in out-of-state facilities and capacity to serve all foster children in state or in home-based settings out-of-state. §7912.
Determination of placement by full service licensed private adoption agencies; Required documentation and notifications; Application of section. §7913.

§7900. Adoption of compact

The Interstate Compact on Placement of Children as set forth in Section 7901 is hereby adopted and entered into with all other jurisdictions joining therein. **Leg.H.** Enacted Stats 1992 ch 162 §10 (AB 2650), operative January 1, 1994.

§7901. Provisions of compact

The provisions of the interstate compact referred to in Section 7900 are as follows:

INTERSTATE COMPACT ON THE PLACEMENT OF CHILDREN

Article 1. Purpose and Policy

It is the purpose and policy of the party states to cooperate with each other in the interstate placement of children to the end that:

(a) Each child requiring placement shall receive the maximum opportunity to be placed in a suitable environment and with persons or institutions having appropriate qualifications and facilities to provide a necessary and desirable degree and type of care.

(b) The appropriate authorities in a state where a child is to be placed may have full opportunity to ascertain the circumstances of the proposed placement, thereby promoting full compliance with applicable requirements for the protection of the child.

(c) The proper authorities of the state from which the placement is made may obtain the most complete information on the basis on which to evaluate a projected placement before it is made.

(d) Appropriate jurisdictional arrangements for the care of children will be promoted.

Article 2. Definitions

As used in this compact:

(a) "Child" means a person who, by reason of minority, is legally subject to parental, guardianship, or similar control.

(b) "Sending agency" means a party state, or officer or employee thereof; subdivision of a party state, or officer or employee thereof; a court of a party state; a person, corporation, association, charitable agency, or other entity that sends, brings, or causes to be sent or brought any child to another party state.

(c) "Receiving state" means the state to which a child is sent, brought, or caused to be sent or brought, whether by public authorities or private persons or agencies, and whether for placement with state or local public authorities or for placement with private agencies or persons.

(d) "Placement" means the arrangement for the care of a child in a family free or boarding home or in a child-caring agency or institution, but does not include any institution caring for persons with developmental disabilities or mental health disorders or any institution primarily educational in character, and any hospital or other medical facility.

Article 3. Conditions for Placement

(a) A sending agency shall not send, bring, or cause to be sent or brought into any other party state any child for placement in foster care or as a preliminary to a possible adoption unless the sending agency complies with each and every requirement set forth in this article and with the applicable laws of the receiving state governing the placement of children therein.

(b) Before sending, bringing, or causing any child to be sent or brought into a receiving state for placement in foster care or as a preliminary to a possible adoption, the sending agency shall furnish the appropriate public authorities in the receiving state written notice of the intention to send, bring, or place the child in the receiving state. The notice shall contain:

(1) The name, date, and place of birth of the child.

(2) The identity and address or addresses of the parents or legal guardian.

(3) The name and address of the person, agency, or institution to or with which the sending agency proposes to send, bring, or place the child.

(4) A full statement of the reasons for the proposed action and evidence of the authority pursuant to which the placement is proposed to be made.

(c) Any public officer or agency in a receiving state that receives notice pursuant to paragraph (b) of this article may request of the sending agency, or any other appropriate officer or agency of or in the sending agency's state, and shall be entitled to receive therefrom, supporting or additional information it deems necessary under the circumstances to carry out the purpose and policy of this compact.

(d) The child shall not be sent, brought, or caused to be sent or brought into the receiving state until the appropriate public authorities in the receiving state notify the sending agency, in writing, to the effect that the proposed placement does not appear to be contrary to the interest of the child.

Article 4. Penalty for Illegal Placement

The sending, bringing, or causing to be sent or brought into any receiving state of a child in violation of the terms of this compact shall constitute a violation of the laws respecting the placement of children of both the state in which the sending agency is located or from which it sends or brings the child and of the receiving state. A violation may be punished or subjected to penalty in either jurisdiction in accordance with its laws. In addition to liability for any punishment or penalty, any violation shall constitute full and sufficient grounds for the suspension or revocation of any license, permit, or other legal authorization held by the sending agency that empowers or allows it to place or care for children.

Article 5. Continuing Jurisdiction

(a) The sending agency shall retain jurisdiction over the child sufficient to determine all matters in relation to the custody, supervision, care, treatment, and disposition of the child that it would have had if the child had remained in the sending agency's state, until the child is adopted, reaches majority, becomes self-supporting, or is discharged with the concurrence of the appropriate authority in the receiving state. That jurisdiction shall also include the power to effect or cause the return of the child or the child's transfer to another location and custody pursuant to law. The sending agency shall continue to have financial responsibility for support and maintenance of the child during the period of the placement. Nothing contained herein shall defeat a claim of jurisdiction by a receiving state sufficient to deal with an act of delinquency or crime committed therein.

(b) When the sending agency is a public agency, it may enter into an agreement with an authorized public or private agency in the receiving state providing for the performance of one or more services in respect of that case by the latter as agent for the sending agency.

(c) This compact shall not be construed to prevent a private charitable agency authorized to place children in the receiving state from performing services or acting as agent in that state for a private charitable agency of the sending stateor to prevent the agency in the receiving state from discharging financial responsibility for the support and maintenance of a child who has been placed on behalf of the sending agency without relieving the responsibility set forth in paragraph (a) of this article.

Article 6. Institutional Care of Delinquent Children

A child adjudicated delinquent may be placed in an institution in another party jurisdiction pursuant to this compact but that placement shall not be made unless the child is given a court hearing on notice to the parent or guardian with opportunity to be heard, before being sent to the other party jurisdiction for institutional care and the court finds that both of the following exist:

(a) Equivalent facilities for the child are not available in the sending agency's jurisdiction.

(b) Institutional care in the other jurisdiction is in the best interest of the child and will not produce undue hardship.

Article 7. Compact Administrator

The executive head of each jurisdiction party to this compact shall designate an officer who shall be general coordinator of activities under this compact in that jurisdiction and who, acting jointly with like officers of other party jurisdictions, shall have power to promulgate rules and regulations to carry out more effectively the terms and provisions of this compact.

Article 8. Limitations

This compact shall not apply to:

(a) The sending or bringing of a child into a receiving state by the child's parent, stepparent, grandparent, adult brother or sister, adult uncle or aunt, or the child's guardian and leaving the child with any such relative or nonagency guardian in the receiving state.

(b) Any placement, sending, or bringing of a child into a receiving state pursuant to any other interstate compact to which both the state from which the child is sent or brought and the receiving state are party, or to any other agreement between those states that has the force of law.

Article 9. Enactment and Withdrawal

This compact shall be open to joinder by any state, territory, or possession of the United States, the District of Columbia, the Commonwealth of Puerto Rico, and, with the consent of Congress, the government of Canada or any province thereof. It shall become effective with respect to any of these jurisdictions when that jurisdiction has enacted the same into law. Withdrawal from this compact shall be by the enactment of a statute repealing the same, but shall not take effect until two years after the effective date of the statute and until written notice of the withdrawal has been given by the withdrawing state to the Governor of each other party jurisdiction. Withdrawal of a party state shall not affect the rights, duties, and obligations under this compact of any sending agency therein with respect to a placement made before the effective date of withdrawal.

Article 10. Construction and Severability

The provisions of this compact shall be liberally construed to effectuate the purposes thereof. The provisions of this compact shall be severable and if any phrase, clause, sentence, or provision of this compact is declared to be contrary to the constitution of any party state or of the United States or the applicability thereof to any government, agency, person, or circumstance is held invalid, the validity of the remainder of this compact and the applicability thereof to any government, agency, person, or circumstance shall not be affected thereby. If this compact shall be held contrary to the constitution of any state party thereto, the compact shall remain in full force and effect as to the remaining states and in full force and effect as to the state affected as to all severable matters. **Leg.H.** Enacted Stats 1992 ch 162 §10 (AB 2650), operative January 1, 1994. Amended Stats 2002 ch 260 §6 (SB 1512); Stats 2014 ch 144 §13 (AB 1847), effective January 1, 2015; Stats 2019 ch 115 §104 (AB 1817), effective January 1, 2020.

§7901.1. Study of home environment on request from another state; Time requirements

(a) Within 60 days of receipt of a request from another state to conduct a study of a home environment for purposes of assessing the safety and suitability of placing a child in the home, a county child welfare agency shall, directly or by contract, do both of the following:

(1) Conduct and complete the study.

(2) Return a report to the requesting state on the results of the study. The report shall address the extent to which placement in the home would meet the needs of the child.

(b) Except as provided in subdivision (c), in the case of a home study commenced on or before September 30, 2008, if the agency fails to comply with subdivision (a) within the 60-day period as a result of circumstances beyond the control of the agency, the agency shall have 75 days to comply with subdivision (a). The agency shall document the circumstances involved and certify that completing the home study is in the best interests of the child. For purposes of this subdivision, "circumstances beyond the control of the agency" include, but are not limited to, the failure of a federal agency to provide the results of a background check or the failure of any entity to provide completed medical forms, if the background check or records were requested by the agency at least 45 days before the end of the 60-day period.

(c) Subdivision (b) shall not be construed to require the agency to have completed, within the applicable period, the parts of the home study involving the education and training of the prospective foster or adoptive parents.

(d) The agency shall treat any report described in subdivision (a) that is received from another state, an Indian tribe, or a private agency under contract with another state, as meeting any requirements imposed by the state for the completion of a home study before placing a child in the home, unless, within 14 days after receipt of the report, the agency determines, based on grounds that are specific to the content of the report, that making a decision in reliance on the report would be contrary to the welfare of the child.

(e) A county is not restricted from contracting with a private agency for the conduct of a home study described in subdivision (a).

(f) The department shall work with counties to identify barriers to meeting the timeframes specified in this section and to develop recommendations to reduce or eliminate those barriers. **Leg.H.** Added Stats 2007 ch 583 §1 (SB 703), effective January 1, 2008.

§7902. Financial responsibility for child placed pursuant to compact

Financial responsibility for a child placed pursuant to the Interstate Compact on the Placement of Children shall be determined in accordance with Article 5 of the compact in the first instance. However, in the event of partial or complete default of performance thereunder, the provisions of other state laws also may be invoked. **Leg.H.** Enacted Stats 1992 ch 162 §10 (AB 2650), operative January 1, 1994.

§7903. "Appropriate public authorities"

The phrase "appropriate public authorities" as used in Article 3 of the Interstate Compact on the Placement of Children means, with reference to this state, the State Department of Social Services, and that department shall receive and act with reference to notices required by Article 3 of the compact. **Leg.H.** Enacted Stats 1992 ch 162 §10 (AB 2650), operative January 1, 1994.

§7904. "Appropriate authority in receiving state"

The phrase "appropriate authority in receiving state" as used in paragraph (a) of Article 5 of the Interstate Compact on the Placement of Children, with reference to this state, means the State Department of Social Services. **Leg.H.** Enacted Stats 1992 ch 162 §10 (AB 2650), operative January 1, 1994.

§7905. Agreements with party states; Approval of financial obligations

The officers and agencies of this state and its subdivisions having authority to place children are hereby empowered to enter into agreements with appropriate officers or agencies of or in other party states pursuant to paragraph (b) of Article 5 of the Interstate Compact on the Placement of Children. Any such agreement which contains a financial commitment or imposes a financial obligation on this state or subdivision or agency thereof is not binding unless it has the approval in writing of the Controller in the case of the state and of the chief local fiscal officer in the case of a subdivision of the state. **Leg.H.** Enacted Stats 1992 ch 162 §10 (AB 2650), operative January 1, 1994.

§7906. Requirements for visitation, inspection, or supervision in another state

Any requirements for visitation, inspection, or supervision of children, homes, institutions, or other agencies in another party state which may apply under the law of this state shall be deemed to be met if performed pursuant to an agreement entered into by appropriate officers or agencies of this state or a subdivision thereof as contemplated by paragraph (b) of Article 5 of the Interstate Compact on the Placement of Children. **Leg.H.** Enacted Stats 1992 ch 162 §10 (AB 2650), operative January 1, 1994.

§7906.5. Study of home environment on request from another state where child is in custody of requesting state; Time requirements

(a) Within 60 days after an officer or agency of this state, or its political subdivision, receives a request from another state to conduct a study of a home environment for purposes of assessing the safety and suitability of placing a child, who is in the custody of the requesting state, in the home, the county child welfare agency shall, directly or indirectly, do both of the following:

(1) Conduct and complete the home study.

(2) Return to the requesting state a report on the results of the home study, which shall address the extent to which placement in the home would meet the needs of the child.

(b) A licensed private adoption agency may agree to provide the services listed in subdivision (a), and upon that agreement, shall comply with the requirements of paragraphs (1) and (2) of subdivision (a).

(c) Notwithstanding subdivision (a), in the case of a home study commenced on or before September 30, 2008, if the county fails to comply with subdivision (a) within the 60-day period as a result of circumstances beyond the control of the state, including, but not limited to, failure by a federal agency to provide the results of a background check or failure of any entity to provide completed medical forms requested by the state at least 45 days before the end of the 60-day period, the county shall have 75 days to comply with subdivision (a) if the county documents the circumstances involved and certifies that completing the home study is in the best interest of the child.

(d) Nothing in this section shall be construed to require the county to have completed, within the applicable period, those portions of the home study concerning the education and training of the prospective foster parent or adoptive parent.

(e) The county shall treat any report described in subdivision (a) that is received from another state, an Indian tribe, or a private agency under contract with another state, as meeting any requirements imposed by the state for the completion of a home study before placing a child in the home, unless, within 14 days after receipt of the report, the county determines, based on grounds that are specific to the content of the report, that making a decision in reliance on the report would be contrary to the welfare of the child.

(f) A county is not restricted from contracting with a private agency for the conduct of a home study described in subdivision (a). **Leg.H.** Added Stats 2007 ch 583 §2 (SB 703), effective January 1, 2008.

§7907. Application of law restricting out-of-state placements

No provision of law restricting out-of-state placement of children for adoption shall apply to placements made pursuant to the Interstate Compact on the Placement of Children. **Leg.H.** Enacted Stats 1992 ch 162 §10 (AB 2650), operative January 1, 1994.

§7907.3. Application to Indian child

The Interstate Compact on the Placement of Children shall not apply to any placement, sending, or bringing of an Indian child into another state pursuant to a transfer of jurisdiction to a tribal court under Section 1911 of the Indian Child Welfare Act (25 U.S.C. Sec. 1901 et seq.). **Leg.H.** Added Stats 2006 ch 838 §7 (SB 678), effective January 1, 2007.

§7907.5. Children subject to compact

(a) A child who is born in this state and placed for adoption in this state with a resident of this state is not subject to the provisions of the Interstate Compact on the Placement of Children.

(b) A child who is born in this state and placed for adoption with a person who is not a resident of this state is subject to the provisions of the Interstate Compact on the Placement of Children, regardless of whether the adoption petition is filed in this state. In interstate placements, this state shall be deemed the sending state for any child born in the state. **Leg.H.** Added Stats 2004 ch 858 §2 (SB 1357).

§7908. Placement of children adjudged wards of court in out-of-state facility

A court having jurisdiction to place children adjudged wards of the court may place a ward in an out-of-state facility, as defined in subdivision (b) of Section 7910, pursuant to Section 727.1 of the Welfare and Institutions Code and Article 6 of the Interstate Compact on the Placement of Children and shall retain jurisdiction as provided in Article 5 of the compact. **Leg.H.** Enacted Stats 1992 ch 162 §10 (AB 2650), operative January 1, 1994. Amended Stats 2021 ch 86 §3 (AB 153), effective July 16, 2021.

§7908.5. "Jurisdiction"

For the purposes of an interstate adoption placement, the term "jurisdiction" as used in Article 5 of the Interstate Compact on the Placement of Children means "jurisdiction over or legal responsibility for the child." It is the intent of the Legislature that this section make a technical clarification to the Interstate Compact on the Placement of Children and not a substantive change. **Leg.H.** Added Stats 2002 ch 260 §7 (SB 1512).

§7909. "Executive head"; Appointment of compact administrator

"Executive head" as used in Article 7 of the Interstate Compact on the Placement of Children means the Governor. The Governor shall appoint a compact administrator in accordance with the terms of Article 7 of the compact. **Leg.H.** Enacted Stats 1992 ch 162 §10 (AB 2650), operative January 1, 1994.

§7910. Refusal to grant approval of placement in violation of state law

(a) Approval of an interstate placement of a child for adoption shall not be granted by the Compact Administrator if the placement is in violation of either Section 8801 of this code or Section 273 of the Penal Code.

(b)(1) The Compact Administrator shall not submit to a receiving state a request to place a dependent or ward for whom a county child welfare agency or county probation department has placement and care responsibility in an out-of-state residential facility, unless the requirements of Section 7911.1 of this code and Section 361.21 of, or subdivision (b) of Section 727.1 of, the Welfare and Institutions Code are met.

(2) For the purpose of this section, an "out-of-state residential facility" is a facility that is located in a state outside of California, is licensed or otherwise approved by the applicable state or tribal authority, and provides an integrated program of specialized and intensive care and supervision, services and supports, treatment, and short-term, 24-hour, trauma-informed care and supervision to children. An out-of-state residential facility may be called another name, including a group home, a residential treatment facility, or a residential care treatment facility. **Leg.H.** Enacted Stats 1992 ch 162 §10 (AB 2650), operative January 1, 1994. Amended Stats 2021 ch 86 §4 (AB 153), effective July 16, 2021.

§7911. Legislative findings and declarations; Authority of State Department of Social Services with placement of children in out-of-state residential facilities; Limitations on foster care placement; Decertification of out-of-state residential facilities for placement on January 1, 2023

(a) The Legislature finds and declares all of the following:

(1) The health and safety of California children placed by a county child welfare agency or probation department out of state pursuant to the provisions of the Interstate Compact on the Placement of Children are a matter of statewide concern.

(2) The State Department of Social Services has full authority to require any placement of a child in an out-of-state residential facility by a county child welfare agency or county probation department be approved on a child-specific basis after the county has exhausted in-state placement and services options that meet the needs of the child and participated in the department's technical assistance program. Before the juvenile court approves the placement pursuant to Section 361.21 of, or subdivision (b) of Section 727.1 of, the Welfare and Institutions Code, the State Department of Social Services shall certify the out-of-state residential facility pursuant to Section 7911.1. Before processing an application for out-of-state placement in a residential facility pursuant to the Interstate Compact on the Placement of Children, the Compact Administrator shall

verify that the placement was approved by the juvenile court and that it has been certified by the department.

(3) The Legislature further finds and declares that certification of facilities licensed under a separate state's licensing standards has not been sufficient to ensure that the stringent California short-term residential therapeutic programs requirements are maintained to safeguard the health, safety, and well-being of California's foster children and youth. Further research demonstrates that dependents and wards in foster care placements are generally better served when they are able to maintain and develop local community supports closer to their families and communities.

(b)(1) On and after July 1, 2021, foster care placements by county child welfare agencies or probation departments into out-of-state residential facilities shall not be made, except in the limited circumstances authorized by Section 361.21 of, or subdivision (b) of Section 727.1 of, the Welfare and Institutions Code, as applicable. Unless placement of a child in an out-of-state residential facility does not require certification pursuant to subdivision (h) of Section 7911.1, the Compact Administrator shall not seek approval of placement in an out-of-state residential facility from the receiving state unless all of the following criteria are met:

(A) The Compact Administrator has received from the county placing agency documentation that it has complied with the requirements of Section 16010.9 of the Welfare and Institutions Code.

(B) The Compact Administrator has received documentation that the out-of-state residential facility has been certified by the State Department of Social Services, including documentation that the director of the State Department of Social Services has approved the certification.

(C) The Compact Administrator has received a copy of the juvenile court order authorizing placement of the child in the out-of-state residential facility pursuant to Section 361.21 or 727.1 of the Welfare and Institutions Code.

(2) On and after July 1, 2022, county child welfare agencies or probation departments shall not make new placements in out-of-state residential facilities, except for placements described in subdivision (h) of Section 7911.1.

(c) Notwithstanding any other law, on and after July 1, 2022, the State Department of Social Services shall not certify any new out-of-state residential facilities for placement by county child welfare agencies or probation departments. On and after July 1, 2022, the Compact Administrator shall not seek approval of any new placements by county child welfare agencies or probation departments in out-of-state residential facilities.

(d) The state shall decertify all out-of-state residential facilities for placement by county child welfare agencies or probation departments on January 1, 2023, and ensure that all children and youth placed in out of state residential facilities have been returned to California by that date.

(e) This section is declaratory of existing law with respect to the Governor's designation of the State Department of Social Services to act as the Compact Administrator and of that department to act as the single state agency charged with supervision of public social services under Section 10600 of the Welfare and Institutions Code. **Leg.H.** Added Stats 2021 ch 86 §6 (AB 153), effective July 16, 2021.

Prior Law: Former Fam C §7911, similar to the present section, was added Stats 1998 ch 311 §9 (SB 933), effective August 19, 1998, amended Stats 1999 ch 881 §1 (AB 1659), effective October 10, 1999, Stats 2015 ch 773 §2 (AB 403), effective January 1, 2016, Stats 2016 ch 612 §7 (AB 1997), effective January 1, 2017, and repealed Stats 2021 ch 86 §5 (AB 153), effective July 16, 2021.

§7911.1. Investigations of threats to health or safety of children in out-of-state residential facilities; Review of placement request; Certification of facilities; Licensing standards; Exception for placement of certain emotionally disturbed children and Indian children

(a) Notwithstanding any other law, the State Department of Social Services or its designee shall investigate any threat to the health and safety of children placed by a California county child welfare agency or probation department in an out-of-state residential facility, as defined in subdivision (b) of Section 7910, pursuant to the provisions of the Interstate Compact on the Placement of Children. This authority shall include the authority to interview children or staff in private or review their file at the out-of-state residential facility or wherever the child or files may be at the time of the investigation. Notwithstanding any other law, the State Department of Social Services or its designee shall require certified out-of-state residential facilities to comply with the reporting requirements applicable to short-term residential therapeutic programs licensed in California for each child in care, regardless of whether or not the child is a California placement, by submitting a copy of the required reports to the Compact Administrator within regulatory timeframes. The Compact Administrator, within one business day of receiving a serious incident report from a certified out-of-state residential facility, shall verbally notify any county child welfare agency or probation department with a child placed at the certified out-of-state residential facility of the serious incident report. The Compact Administrator, within five business days of receiving a written serious incident report from a certified out-of-state residential facility, shall forward a copy of the written serious incident report to any county child welfare agency or probation department with a child placed at the certified out-of-state residential facility.

(b) Any contract, memorandum of understanding, or agreement entered into pursuant to paragraph (b) of Article 5 of the Interstate Compact on the Placement of Children regarding the placement of a child out of state by a California county social services agency or probation department shall include the language set forth in subdivision (a).

(c) Upon receipt of a request from a county child welfare agency or probation department for a child-specific certification of a placement in an out-of-state residential facility, the State Department of Social Services or its designee shall expedite the review of the request in order to determine any additional information needed, shall communicate with the requesting county agency regarding its review including regular status updates, and shall, in a timely manner, determine whether it will issue a child-specific certification to the out-of-state residential facility pursuant to this section.

(1) The licensing standards applicable to an out-of-state residential facility certified by the department shall be those required of short-term residential therapeutic programs operated in this state.

(2) Before issuing a child-specific certification to the out-of-state residential facility, the department shall do all of the following:

(A) Review documentation provided by the county placing agency pursuant to subdivision (e) of Section 16010.9 of the Welfare and Institutions Code.

(B) Perform an on-site inspection of the out-of-state residential facility's physical site.

(C) At a minimum, review all of the following sections of the out-of-state residential facility's program statement:

(i) Core Services and Supports.

(ii) Trauma Informed Interventions and Treatment Practices.

(iii) Personal Rights.

(iv) House Rules.

(v) Discipline Policies and Procedures.

(vi) Emergency Intervention Plan (Including Runaway Plan).

(D) Review the out-of-state residential facility's serious incident reports.

(E) Review the out-of-state residential facility's current license. In order for the out-of-state residential facility to receive a certification, the out-of-state residential facility shall have a current license, or an equivalent approval, in good standing issued by the appropriate authority or authorities of the state in which it is operating.

(F) Review the out-of-state residential facility's licensing history, including any substantiated complaints.

(G) Review the documentation provided by the State Department of Health Care Services pursuant to subdivision (d).

(H) Obtain approval from the director of the department of the child-specific certification for the out-of-state residential facility. Director approval may be given after all of the requirements of subparagraphs (A) to (G), inclusive, have been satisfied.

(3) The department shall not issue a child-specific certification to the out-of-state residential facility if the out-of-state residential facility fails to cooperate during the certification process, including failing to provide any of the documentation listed in paragraph (2).

(4) If all the requirements of paragraph (2) have been satisfied, the department shall certify the out-of-state residential facility pursuant to this section. The department shall provide written documentation of this certification to the county placing agency.

(5) The child-specific certification is discontinued, effective immediately, upon the child transitioning out of the out-of-state residential facility's program.

(d) The licensing standards applicable to out-of-state residential facilities certified by the department, as described in subdivision (c), shall include the licensing standards for mental health program approval described in Section 1562.01 of the Health and Safety Code. These standards shall be satisfied if the State Department of Health Care Services determines that the out-of-state residential facility has an equivalent mental health program approval in the state in which it is operating. Upon receipt of a request for the State Department of Health Care Services to determine whether an out-of-state residential facility has an equivalent mental health program approval in the state in which it is operation, the State Department of Health Care Services shall expedite the review of the request in order to determine any additional information needed, shall communicate with the requesting county agency regarding its review including regular status updates, and shall, in a timely manner, make its determination. If an out-of-state residential facility cannot satisfy the licensing standards for an equivalent mental health program approval, the department shall not certify the facility.

(e) Failure by an out-of-state residential facility to make children or staff available as required by subdivision (a) for a private interview or make files available for review shall be grounds to deny or discontinue the certification.

(f) Certifications made pursuant to this section shall be reviewed as often as necessary to ensure the health and safety of children in care. At a minimum, certifications made pursuant to this section shall be reviewed semiannually. The department shall complete a full review of the facility's program statement semiannually.

(g)(1) The department may deny or discontinue the certification of the out-of-state residential facility if the department makes a finding that the out-of-state residential facility is not operating in compliance with the requirements of this section. The department shall engage with counties that have one or more youth at a facility proposed for decertification to allow for a transition to occur, to the extent possible while ensuring the youths' safety and well-being.

(2) If the out-of-state residential facility disagrees with any decision by the department to deny or discontinue the certification, the out-of-state residential facility may appeal the decision immediately upon receipt of the notice of decertification. If the out-of-state residential facility decides to appeal the decision, the appeal shall be submitted to the department not later than 30 calendar days after the out-of-state residential facility receives the decision. The out-of-state residential facility's appeal shall be in writing and include all information, including supporting documents, that forms the basis of the appeal. The department shall issue a final determination not later than 30 calendar days after receipt of the appeal. If the out-of-state residential facility disagrees with the department's determination, the out-of-state residential facility may file a writ pursuant to paragraph (3). If the out-of-state residential facility decides to file a writ, the writ shall be filed not later than 30 calendar days after the out-of-state residential facility receives the final determination.

(3) Any judicial proceeding to contest the department's determination as to the status of the out-of-state residential facility's certificate shall be held in California pursuant to Section 1085 of the Code of Civil Procedure.

(h) The certification requirements of this section shall not impact any of the following:

(1) Placement of emotionally disturbed children made pursuant to an individualized education program developed pursuant to the federal Individuals with Disabilities Education Act (20 U.S.C. Sec. 1400 et seq.) if the placement is not funded with federal or state foster care funds.

(2) Placement of Indian children, as defined by the Indian Child Welfare Act of 1978 (25 U.S.C. Sec. 1901 et. seq.) and Section 224.1 of the Welfare and Institutions Code.

(i) Failure by an out-of-state residential facility to obtain or maintain its certification, as required by this section, shall preclude the use of any public funds, whether county, state, or federal, in the payment for the placement of any child in that out-of-state residential facility pursuant to the Interstate Compact on the Placement of Children.

(j) Notwithstanding the rulemaking provisions of the Administrative Procedure Act (Chapter 3.5 (commencing with Section 11340) of Part 1 of Division 3 of Title 2 of the Government Code), the State Department of Social Services and the State Department of Health Care Services may implement, interpret, or make specific this section by means of all-county letters, written directives, interim licensing standards, or similar written instructions from the department until regulations are adopted. These all-county letters, written directives, interim licensing standards, or similar written instructions shall have the same force and effect as regulations until the adoption of regulations. **Leg.H.** Added Stats 2021 ch 86 §8 (AB 153), effective July 16, 2021.

Prior Law: Former Fam C §7911.1, similar to the present section, was added Stats 1998 ch 311 §10 (SB 933), effective August 19, 1998, amended Stats 1999 ch 881 §2 (AB 1659), effective October 10, 1999, Stats 2011 ch 43 §31 (AB 114), effective June 30, 2011, Stats 2015 ch 773 §3 (AB 403), effective January 1, 2016, Stats 2016 ch 612 §8 (AB 1997), effective January 1, 2017, Stats 2018 ch 910 §1 (AB 1930), effective January 1, 2019, Stats 2020 ch 104 §1 (AB 2944), effective September 18, 2020, and repealed Stats 2021 ch 86 §7 (AB 153), effective July 16, 2021.

§7912. Legislative findings, declarations, and intent relating to rights of children in out-of-state residential facilities; Reports on number of children placed in out-of-state facilities and capacity to serve all foster children in state or in home-based settings out-of-state

(a) The Legislature finds and declares that the health and safety of children placed in out-of-state residential facilities pursuant to the Interstate Compact on the Placement of Children is a matter of statewide concern. The Legislature therefore affirms its intention that children placed by a county child welfare agency or probation department in out-of-state residential facilities be accorded the same personal rights and safeguards of a child placed in a California licensed short-term residential therapeutic program. This section is in clarification of existing law.

(b)(1) On or before September 1, 2021, and each month thereafter, the department shall report to the relevant policy and fiscal committees of the Legislature the number of children placed by a county child welfare agency or probation department in out-of-state residential facilities pursuant to the Interstate Compact on the Placement of Children.

(2) On On or before January 1, 2022, and every six months thereafter until facilities are decertified and all children returned to California on or before January 1, 2023, the department, in consultation with the counties, shall report to the relevant policy and fiscal committees of the Legislature on the capacity for serving all child welfare and probation-supervised foster children within California or in home-based settings outside of the state. The report shall also include all of the following data, as applicable:

(A) The number of children served by out-of-state residential facilities, disaggregated by child welfare services agency and probation department supervision.

(B) Data measures related to ongoing transition planning efforts, including child and family team meetings, child-specific recruitment and family finding activities, and multiagency care coordination efforts that occurred for each child before and during placement in the out-of-state residential facility.

(C) The lengths of stay of each child placed in an out-of-state residential facility by a California child welfare agency or probation department.

(D) The total number of all serious incident reports received regarding out-of-state residential facilities, and descriptions of the types of incidents reported.

(E) The total number of serious incident reports received regarding California children placed in out-of-state residential facilities, and descriptions of the types of incidents reported.

(3) Reports made pursuant to this subdivision shall not include any demographic data that would permit identification of any child or nonminor dependent. **Leg.H.** Added Stats 1998 ch 311 §11 (SB 933), effective August 19, 1998. Amended Stats 2015 ch 773 §4 (AB 403), effective January 1, 2016; Stats 2016 ch 612 §9 (AB 1997), effective January 1, 2017; Stats 2021 ch 86 §9 (AB 153), effective July 16, 2021.

2016 Note: For adoption of regulations, see the 2016 Note following §6552.
2015 Note: For legislative intent, see the 2015 Note following §7911.

§7913. Determination of placement by full service licensed private adoption agencies; Required documentation and notifications; Application of section

(a) When a full service licensed private adoption agency has provided adoption-related services to a birth parent or prospective adoptive parent, that agency is delegated the authority to determine whether the placement shall or shall not be made pursuant to the Interstate Compact on the

Placement of Children, and to sign the compact forms documenting that determination and date of placement.

(b) For children entering California in independent adoptions, prior to making a determination regarding placement and as soon as feasible, the private adoption agency shall notify the appropriate district office or delegated county adoption agency of the matter and verify that the preplacement interview of the prospective adoptive parent or parents has been completed.

(c) This section shall not apply to a child who is a dependent of the court or a child subject to a petition filed under Section 300 of the Welfare and Institutions Code. **Leg.H.** Added Stats 2011 ch 462 §5 (AB 687), effective January 1, 2012.

PART 6
FOSTER CARE PLACEMENT CONSIDERATIONS

Order of placement preference; Consideration of race, color, or national origin; Application of Indian Child Welfare Act. §7950.
Placement of child for period not intended to exceed 30 days. §7951.
Minor's right to make statement. §7952.

§7950. Order of placement preference; Consideration of race, color, or national origin; Application of Indian Child Welfare Act

(a) With full consideration for the proximity of the natural parents to the placement so as to facilitate visitation and family reunification, when a placement in foster care is being made, the following considerations shall be used:

(1) Placement shall, if possible, be made in the home of a relative, unless the placement would not be in the best interest of the child. Diligent efforts shall be made by an agency or entity to which this subdivision applies, to locate an appropriate relative [1] as defined in paragraph (2) of subdivision [2] (h) of Section 319 of the Welfare and Institutions Code. At [3] a permanency hearing in which the court terminates reunification services, or at [4] a postpermanency hearing for a child not placed for adoption, the court shall find that the agency or entity to which this subdivision applies has made diligent efforts to locate an appropriate relative and that each relative whose name has been submitted to the agency or entity as a possible caretaker, either by the relative or by other persons, has been evaluated as an appropriate placement resource.

(2) An agency or entity that receives [5] state assistance and is involved in foster care placements shall not do either of the following:

(A) Deny [6] a person the opportunity to become a foster parent on the basis of the race, color, or national origin of the person or the child involved.

(B) Delay or deny the placement of a child into foster care on the basis of the race, color, or national origin of the foster parent or the child involved.

(b) Subdivision (a) does not affect the application of the Indian Child Welfare Act of 1978 (25 U.S.C. Sec. 1901 et seq.).

(c) This section does not preclude a search for an appropriate relative being conducted simultaneously with a search for a foster family. **Leg.H.** Added Stats 1995 ch 884 §2 (AB 1743). Amended Stats 2003 ch 323 §1 (SB 984), ch 469 §3 (SB 947); Stats 2015 ch 425 §1 (SB 794), effective January 1, 2016; Stats 2019 ch 115 §106 (AB 1817), effective January 1, 2020; Stats 2024 ch 845 §1 (AB 2929), effective January 1, 2025.

§7950. 2024 Deletes. [1] , [2] (f) [3] any [4] any [5] any [6] to any

Prior Law: Former §7950, similar to the present section, was enacted Stats 1992 ch 162 §10, operative January 1, 1994, and repealed Stats 1995 ch 884 §1.

§7951. Placement of child for period not intended to exceed 30 days

This part does not apply in determining the foster care setting in which the child may be placed for a period not intended to exceed 30 days. **Leg.H.** Added Stats 1995 ch 884 §2 (AB 1743).

Prior Law: Former §7951, relating to considerations constituting good cause not to follow rules, was enacted Stats 1992 ch 162 §10, operative January 1, 1994, and repealed Stats 1995 ch 884 §1.

§7952. Minor's right to make statement

A minor 10 years of age or older being considered for placement in a foster home has the right to make a brief statement to the court making a decision on placement. The court may disregard any preferences expressed by the minor. The minor's right to make a statement is not limited to the initial placement, but continues for any proceedings concerning continued placement or a decision to return to parental custody. **Leg.H.** Added Stats 1995 ch 884 §2 (AB 1743).

Prior Law: Former §7952, relating to records showing diligent search, was enacted Stats 1992 ch 162 §10, operative January 1, 1994, and repealed Stats 1995 ch 884 §1.

§7953. [Section repealed 1995]

Leg.H. Enacted Stats 1992 ch 162 §10 (AB 2650), operative January 1, 1994. Repealed Stats 1995 ch 884 §1 (AB 1743). See Fam C §7951.

§7954. [Section repealed 1995]

Leg.H. Enacted Stats 1992 ch 162 §10 (AB 2650), operative January 1, 1994. Repealed Stats 1995 ch 884 §1 (AB 1743). See Fam C §7952.

PART 7
SURROGACY AND DONOR FACILITATORS, ASSISTED REPRODUCTION AGREEMENTS FOR GESTATIONAL CARRIERS, AND OOCYTE DONATIONS

Definitions. §7960.
Surrogacy or donor facilitators; Client funds; Financial interests; Exceptions. §7961.
Assisted reproduction agreement. §7962.

§7960. Definitions

For purposes of this part, the following terms have the following meanings:

(a) "Assisted reproduction agreement" has the same meaning as defined in subdivision (b) of Section 7606.

(b) "Fund management agreement" means the agreement between the intended parents and the surrogacy or donor facilitator relating to the fee or other valuable consideration for services rendered or that will be rendered by the surrogacy or donor facilitator.

(c) "Intended parent" means an individual, married or unmarried, who manifests the intent to be legally bound as the parent of a child resulting from assisted reproduction.

(d) "Nonattorney surrogacy or donor facilitator" means a surrogacy or donor practitioner who is not an attorney in good standing licensed to practice law in this state.

(e) "Surrogacy or donor facilitator" means a person or organization that engages in either of the following activities:

(1) Advertising for the purpose of soliciting parties to an assisted reproduction agreement or for the donation of oocytes for use by a person other than the provider of the oocytes, or acting as an intermediary between the parties to an assisted reproduction agreement or oocyte donation.

(2) Charging a fee or other valuable consideration for services rendered relating to an assisted reproduction agreement or oocyte donation.

(f) "Surrogate" means a woman who bears and carries a child for another through medically assisted reproduction and pursuant to a written agreement, as set forth in Sections 7606 and 7962. Within the definition of surrogate are two different and distinct types:

(1) "Traditional surrogate" means a woman who agrees to gestate an embryo, in which the woman is the gamete donor and the embryo was created using the sperm of the intended father or a donor arranged by the intended parent or parents.

(2) "Gestational carrier" means a woman who is not an intended parent and who agrees to gestate a genetically unrelated embryo pursuant to an assisted reproduction agreement.

(g) "Donor" means a woman who provides oocytes for use by another for the purpose of assisting the recipient of the oocytes in having a child or children. **Leg.H.** Added Stats 2010 ch 138 §1 (AB 2426), effective January 1, 2011. Amended Stats 2012 ch 466 §2 (AB 1217), effective January 1, 2013; Stats 2015 ch 91 §3 (AB 1049), effective January 1, 2016; Stats 2019 ch 115 §107 (AB 1817), effective January 1, 2020.

§7961. Surrogacy or donor facilitators; Client funds; Financial interests; Exceptions

(a) A nonattorney surrogacy or donor facilitator shall direct the client to deposit all client funds into either of the following:

(1) An independent, bonded escrow depository maintained by a licensed, independent, bonded escrow company.

(2) A trust account maintained by an attorney.

(b) For purposes of this section, a nonattorney surrogacy or donor facilitator may not have a financial interest in any escrow company holding client funds. A nonattorney surrogacy or donor facilitator and any of its directors or employees shall not be an agent of any escrow company holding client funds.

(c) Client funds may only be disbursed by the attorney or escrow agent as set forth in the assisted reproduction agreement and fund management agreement.

(d) This section shall not apply to funds that are both of the following:

(1) Not provided for in the fund management agreement.

(2) Paid directly to a medical doctor for medical services or a psychologist for psychological services. **Leg.H.** Added Stats 2010 ch 138 §1 (AB 2426), effective January 1, 2011. Amended Stats 2015 ch 91 §4 (AB 1049), effective January 1, 2016.

§7962. Assisted reproduction agreement

(a) An assisted reproduction agreement for gestational carriers shall contain, but shall not be limited to, all of the following information:

(1) The date on which the assisted reproduction agreement for gestational carriers was executed.

(2) The persons from which the gametes originated, unless donated gametes were used, in which case the assisted reproduction agreement does not need to specify the name of the donor but shall specify whether the donated gamete or gametes were eggs, sperm, or embryos, or all.

(3) The identity of the intended parent or parents.

(4) Disclosure of how the intended parents will cover the medical expenses of the gestational carrier and of the newborn or newborns. If health care coverage is used to cover those medical expenses, the disclosure shall include a review of the health care policy provisions related to coverage for surrogate pregnancy, including any possible liability of the gestational carrier, third-party liability liens or other insurance coverage, and any notice requirements that could affect coverage or liability of the gestational carrier. The review and disclosure do not constitute legal advice. If coverage of liability is uncertain, a statement of that fact shall be sufficient to meet the requirements of this section.

(b) Prior to executing the written assisted reproduction agreement for gestational carriers, a surrogate and the intended parent or intended parents shall be represented by separate independent licensed attorneys of their choosing.

(c) The assisted reproduction agreement for gestational carriers shall be executed by the parties and the signatures on the assisted reproduction agreement for gestational carriers shall be notarized or witnessed by an equivalent method of affirmation as required in the jurisdiction where the assisted reproduction agreement for gestational carriers is executed.

(d) The parties to an assisted reproduction agreement for gestational carriers shall not undergo an embryo transfer procedure, or commence injectable medication in preparation for an embryo transfer for assisted reproduction purposes, until the assisted reproduction agreement for gestational carriers has been fully executed as required by subdivisions (b) and (c) of this section.

(e) An action to establish the parent and child relationship between the intended parent or parents and the child as to a child conceived pursuant to an assisted reproduction agreement for gestational carriers may be filed before the child's birth and may be filed in the county where the child is anticipated to be born, the county where the intended parent or intended parents reside, the county where the surrogate resides, the county where the assisted reproduction agreement for gestational carriers is executed, or the county where medical procedures pursuant to the agreement are to be performed. A copy of the assisted reproduction agreement for gestational carriers shall be lodged in the court action filed for the purpose of establishing the parent and child relationship. The parties to the assisted reproduction agreement for gestational carriers shall attest, under penalty of perjury, and to the best of their knowledge and belief, as to the parties' compliance with this section in entering into the assisted reproduction agreement for gestational carriers. Submitting those declarations shall not constitute a waiver, under Section 912 of the Evidence Code, of the lawyer-client privilege described in Article 3 (commencing with Section 950) of Chapter 4 of Division 8 of the Evidence Code.

(f)(1) A notarized assisted reproduction agreement for gestational carriers signed by all the parties, with the attached declarations of independent attorneys, and lodged with the superior court in accordance with this section, shall rebut any presumptions contained within Part 2 (commencing with Section 7540), subdivision (a) of Section 7610, and Sections 7611 and 7613, as to the gestational carrier surrogate, or the gestational carrier surrogate's spouse or partner, being a parent of the child or children.

(2) Upon petition of any party to a properly executed assisted reproduction agreement for gestational carriers, the court shall issue a judgment or order establishing a parent and child relationship, whether pursuant to Section 7630 or otherwise. The judgment or order may be issued before or after the child's or children's birth subject to the limitations of Section 7633. Subject to proof of compliance with this section, the judgment or order shall establish the parent and child relationship of the intended parent or intended parents identified in the surrogacy agreement and shall establish that the surrogate, and the surrogate's spouse or partner, is not a parent of, and has no parental rights or duties with respect to, the child or children. The judgment or order shall be issued forthwith and without further hearing or evidence, unless the court or a party to the assisted reproduction agreement for gestational carriers has a good faith, reasonable belief that the assisted reproduction agreement for gestational carriers or attorney declarations were not executed in accordance with this section. Upon motion by a party to the assisted reproduction agreement for gestational carriers, the matter shall be scheduled for hearing before a judgment or order is issued. This section does not prevent a court from finding and declaring that the intended parent is, or intended parents are, the parent or parents of the child where compliance with this section has not been met; however, the court shall require sufficient proof entitling the parties to the relief sought.

(g) The petition, relinquishment or consent, agreement, order, report to the court from any investigating agency, and any power of attorney and deposition filed in the office of the clerk of the court pursuant to this part shall not be open to inspection by any person other than the parties to the proceeding and their attorneys and the State Department of Social Services, except upon the written authority of a judge of the superior court. A judge of the superior court shall not authorize anyone to inspect the petition, relinquishment or consent, agreement, order, report to the court from any investigating agency, or power of attorney or deposition, or any portion of those documents, except in exceptional circumstances and where necessary. The petitioner may be required to pay the expense of preparing the copies of the documents to be inspected.

(h) Upon the written request of any party to the proceeding and the order of any judge of the superior court, the clerk of the court shall not provide any documents referred to in subdivision (g) for inspection or copying to any other person, unless the name of the gestational carrier or any information tending to identify the gestational carrier is deleted from the documents or copies thereof.

(i) An assisted reproduction agreement for gestational carriers executed in accordance with this section is presumptively valid and shall not be rescinded or revoked without a court order. For purposes of this part, any failure to comply with the requirements of this section shall rebut the presumption of the validity of the assisted reproduction agreement for gestational carriers. **Leg.H.** Added Stats 2012 ch 466 §3 (AB 1217), effective January 1, 2013. Amended Stats 2014 ch 636 §2 (AB 2344), effective January 1, 2015; Stats 2016 ch 385 §4 (AB 2349), effective January 1, 2017; Stats 2017 ch 326 §1 (AB 1396), effective January 1, 2018; Stats 2019 ch 115 §108 (AB 1817), effective January 1, 2020.

2016 Note: For legislative findings and declarations, see the 2016 Note following §7613.

DIVISION 13
ADOPTION

Part 1. Definitions.
Part 2. Adoption of Unmarried Minors.
Part 3. Adoption of Adults and Married Minors.

PART 1
DEFINITIONS

Definitions to govern construction. §8500.
"Adoption service provider". §8502.
"Adoptive parent". §8503.
"Agency adoption". §8506.
"Applicant". §8509.
"Birth parent". §8512.
"County adoption agency". §8513.
"Days". §8514.
"Delegated county adoption agency". §8515.
"Department". §8518.
"Full-service adoption agency"; Private full-service adoption agencies. §8521.
"Independent adoption". §8524.
"Intercountry adoption". §8527.
"Licensed adoption agency". §8530.
"Noncustodial adoption agency"; Private noncustodial adoption agencies. §8533.
"Place for adoption". §8539.
"Prospective adoptive parent". §8542.
"Qualified court investigator". §8543.
"Special needs child". §8545.
"Stepparent adoption". §8548.

§8500. Definitions to govern construction

Unless the provision or context otherwise requires, the definitions in this part govern the construction of this division. **Leg.H.** Enacted Stats 1992 ch 162 §10 (AB 2650), operative January 1, 1994.

§8502. "Adoption service provider"

(a) "Adoption service provider" means any of the following:

(1) A licensed private adoption agency.

(2) An individual who has presented satisfactory evidence to the department that the individual is a licensed clinical social worker who also has a minimum of five years of experience providing professional social work services while employed by a licensed California adoption agency or the department.

(3) In a state other than California, or a country other than the United States, an adoption agency licensed or otherwise approved under the laws of that state or country, or an individual who is licensed or otherwise certified as a clinical social worker under the laws of that state or country.

(4) An individual who has presented satisfactory evidence to the department that the individual is a licensed marriage and family therapist who has a minimum of five years of experience providing professional adoption casework services while employed by a licensed California adoption agency or the department. The department shall review the qualifications of each individual to determine if the individual has performed professional adoption casework services for five years as required by this section while employed by a licensed California adoption agency or the department.

(5) An individual who has presented satisfactory evidence to the department that the individual is a licensed professional clinical counselor who has a minimum of five years' experience providing professional adoption casework services while employed by a licensed California adoption agency or the department. The department shall review the credentials of each individual to determine if the individual has performed professional adoption casework services as required by this paragraph.

(b) If, in the case of a birth parent located in California, at least three adoption service providers are not reasonably available, or, in the case of a birth parent located outside of California or outside of the United States who has contacted at least three potential adoption service providers and been unsuccessful in obtaining the services of an adoption service provider who is reasonably available and willing to provide services, independent legal counsel for the birth parent may serve as an adoption service provider pursuant to subdivision (e) of Section 8801.5. "Reasonably available" means that an adoption service provider is all of the following:

(1) Available within five days for an advisement of rights pursuant to Section 8801.5, or within 24 hours for the signing of the placement agreement pursuant to paragraph (3) of subdivision (b) of Section 8801.3.

(2) Within 100 miles of the birth mother.

(3) Available for a cost not exceeding five hundred dollars ($500) to make an advisement of rights and to witness the signing of the placement agreement.

(c) If an attorney acts as an adoption service provider, the fee to make an advisement of rights and to witness the signing of the placement agreement shall not exceed five hundred dollars ($500). **Leg.H.** Added Stats 1993 ch 758 §3 (SB 792), operative January 1, 1995. Amended Stats 1994 ch 585 §1 (AB 3336), operative January 1, 1995; Stats 1997 ch 559 §1 (SB 1121); Stats 2002 ch 1013 §81 (SB 2026); Stats 2004 ch 858 §3 (SB 1357); Stats 2018 ch 389 §16 (AB 2296), effective January 1, 2019; Stats 2019 ch 115 §109 (AB 1817), effective January 1, 2020.

Prior Law: There was another section of this number, similar to the present section, which was added Stats 1993 ch 219 §183, and repealed Stats 1993 ch 758 §2.5.

1993 Note: Section 8502 applies to all petitions for independent adoption filed on or after January 1, 1995. Petitions filed prior to, and pending on, that date shall be governed by the law in effect on December 31, 1994. Stats 1993 ch 758 §17(b).

§8503. "Adoptive parent"

"Adoptive parent" means a person who has obtained an order of adoption of a minor child or, in the case of an adult adoption, an adult. **Leg.H.** Enacted Stats 1992 ch 162 §10 (AB 2650), operative January 1, 1994.

§8506. "Agency adoption"

"Agency adoption" means the adoption of a minor, other than an intercountry adoption, in which the department, county adoption agency, or licensed adoption agency is a party to, or joins in, the adoption petition. **Leg.H.** Enacted Stats 1992 ch 162 §10 (AB 2650), operative January 1, 1994. Amended Stats 2012 ch 35 §2 (SB 1013), effective June 27, 2012.

2012 Note: This act is titled and may be cited as the 2011 Realignment Legislation addressing public safety. Stats 2012 ch 35 (SB 1013) §1.

§8509. "Applicant"

"Applicant" means a person who has submitted a written application to adopt a child from the department, county adoption agency, or licensed adoption agency and who is being considered by the adoption agency for the adoptive placement of a child. **Leg.H.** Enacted Stats 1992 ch 162 §10 (AB 2650), operative January 1, 1994. Amended Stats 2012 ch 35 §3 (SB 1013), effective June 27, 2012.

2012 Note: For title and citation of Stats 2012 ch 35 (SB 1013), see 2012 Note following §8506.

§8512. "Birth parent"

"Birth parent" means the biological parent or, in the case of a person previously adopted, the adoptive parent. **Leg.H.** Enacted Stats 1992 ch 162 §10 (AB 2650), operative January 1, 1994.

§8513. "County adoption agency"

"County adoption agency" means an adoption agency operated by a county or consortium of counties. **Leg.H.** Added Stats 2012 ch 35 §4 (SB 1013), effective June 27, 2012.

2012 Note: For title and citation of Stats 2012 ch 35 (SB 1013), see 2012 Note following §8506.

§8514. "Days"

"Days" means calendar days, unless otherwise specified. **Leg.H.** Added Stats 1994 ch 585 §2 (AB 3336).

§8515. "Delegated county adoption agency"

"Delegated county adoption agency" means a county adoption agency that has agreed to provide the services described in Chapter 3 (commencing with Section 8800) of Part 2. **Leg.H.** Enacted Stats 1992 ch 162 §10 (AB 2650), operative January 1, 1994. Amended Stats 2012 ch 35 §5 (SB 1013), effective June 27, 2012.

2012 Note: For title and citation of Stats 2012 ch 35 (SB 1013), see 2012 Note following §8506.

§8518. "Department"

"Department" means the State Department of Social Services. **Leg.H.** Enacted Stats 1992 ch 162 §10 (AB 2650), operative January 1, 1994.

§8521. "Full-service adoption agency"; Private full-service adoption agencies

(a) "Full-service adoption agency" means a licensed or authorized entity engaged in the business of providing adoption services, that does all of the following:

(1) Assumes care, custody, and control of a child through relinquishment of the child to the agency or involuntary termination of parental rights to the child.

(2) Assesses the birth parents, prospective adoptive parents, or child.

(3) Places children for adoption.

(4) Supervises adoptive placements.

(5) Recruits prospective adoptive parents, locates children for adoption, or acts as an intermediary between the parties to an adoption.

(b) Private full-service adoption agencies shall be organized and operated on a nonprofit basis. As a condition of licensure to provide intercountry adoption services, a private full-service adoption agency shall be accredited by the Council on Accreditation, or supervised by an accredited primary provider, or acting as an exempted provider, in compliance with Subpart F (commencing with Section 96.29) of Part 96 of Title 22 of the Code of Federal Regulations. **Leg.H.** Enacted Stats 1992 ch 162 §10 (AB 2650), operative January 1, 1994. Amended Stats 2007 ch 583 §3 (SB 703), effective January 1, 2008; Stats 2012 ch 35 §6 (SB 1013), effective June 27, 2012; Stats 2023 ch 43 §2 (AB 120), effective July 10, 2023.

2012 Note: For title and citation of Stats 2012 ch 35 (SB 1013), see 2012 Note following §8506.

§8524. "Independent adoption"

"Independent adoption" means the adoption of a child in which neither the department, county adoption agency, nor agency licensed by the department is a party to, or joins in, the adoption petition. **Leg.H.** Enacted Stats 1992 ch 162 §10 (AB 2650), operative January 1, 1994. Amended Stats 2012 ch 35 §7 (SB 1013), effective June 27, 2012.

2012 Note: For title and citation of Stats 2012 ch 35 (SB 1013), see 2012 Note following §8506.

§8527. "Intercountry adoption"

"Intercountry adoption" means the adoption of a foreign-born child for whom federal law makes a special immigration visa available. Intercountry adoption includes completion of the adoption in the child's native country or completion of the adoption in this state. **Leg.H.** Enacted Stats 1992 ch 162 §10 (AB 2650), operative January 1, 1994.

§8530. "Licensed adoption agency"

"Licensed adoption agency" means any agency licensed by the department to provide the adoption services specified in paragraphs (9) and (10) of subdivision (a) of Section 1502 of the Health and Safety Code. **Leg.H.** Enacted Stats 1992 ch 162 §10 (AB 2650), operative January 1, 1994. Amended Stats 2012 ch 35 §8 (SB 1013), effective June 27, 2012; Stats 2023 ch 43 §3 (AB 120), effective July 10, 2023.

2012 Note: For title and citation of Stats 2012 ch 35 (SB 1013), see 2012 Note following §8506.

§8533. "Noncustodial adoption agency"; Private noncustodial adoption agencies

(a) "Noncustodial adoption agency" means any licensed entity engaged in the business of providing adoption services, which does all of the following:

(1) Assesses the prospective adoptive parents.

(2) Cooperatively matches children freed for adoption, who are under the care, custody, and control of a licensed adoption agency, for adoption, with assessed and approved prospective adoptive parents.

(3) Cooperatively supervises adoptive placements with a full-service adoption agency, but does not disrupt a placement or remove a child from a placement.

(4) Recruits prospective adoptive parents, locates children for an adoption, or acts as an intermediary between the parties to an adoption.

(b) Private noncustodial adoption agencies shall be organized and operated on a nonprofit basis. As a condition of licensure to provide intercountry adoption services, a noncustodial adoption agency shall be accredited by the Council on Accreditation, or supervised by an accredited primary provider, or acting as an exempted provider, in compliance with Subpart F (commencing with Section 96.29) of Part 96 of Title 22 of the Code of Federal Regulations. **Leg.H.** Enacted Stats 1992 ch 162 §10 (AB 2650), operative January 1, 1994. Amended Stats 2007 ch 583 §4 (SB 703), effective January 1, 2008; Stats 2023 ch 43 §4 (AB 120), effective July 10, 2023.

§8539. "Place for adoption"

"Place for adoption" means, in the case of an independent adoption, the selection of a prospective adoptive parent or parents for a child by the birth parent or parents and the completion of an adoptive placement agreement on a form prescribed by the department by the birth parent or parents placing the child with prospective adoptive parents.

This section shall become operative on January 1, 1995. **Leg.H.** Added Stats 1993 ch 758 §4 (SB 792), operative January 1, 1995.

Prior Law: There was another section of this number, similar to the present section, which was added Stats 1993 ch 219 §184, and repealed Stats 1993 ch 758 §3.5.

1993 Note: Section 8539 applies to all petitions for independent adoption filed on or after January 1, 1995. Petitions filed prior to, and pending on, that date shall be governed by the law in effect on December 31, 1994. Stats 1993 ch 758 §17(b).

§8542. "Prospective adoptive parent"

"Prospective adoptive parent" means a person who has filed or intends to file a petition under Part 2 (commencing with Section 8600) to adopt a child who has been or who is to be placed in the person's physical care or a petition under Part 3 (commencing with Section 9300) to adopt an adult. **Leg.H.** Enacted Stats 1992 ch 162 §10 (AB 2650), operative January 1, 1994.

§8543. "Qualified court investigator"

"Qualified court investigator" means a superior court investigator with the same minimum qualifications as a probation officer or county welfare worker designated to conduct stepparent adoption investigations in stepparent adoption proceedings and proceedings to declare a minor free from parental custody and control. **Leg.H.** Added Stats 1993 ch 219 §185 (AB 1500).

§8545. "Special needs child"

"Special needs child" means a child for whom all of the following are true:

(a) It has been determined that the child cannot or should not be returned to the parent's home, as evidenced by a petition for termination of parental rights, a court order terminating parental rights, or a signed relinquishment.

(b) The child has at least one of the following characteristics that is a barrier to adoption:

(1) Adoptive placement without financial assistance is unlikely because of membership in a sibling group that should remain intact, or by virtue of race, ethnicity, color, language, age of three years or older, or parental background of a medical or behavioral nature that can be determined to adversely affect the development of the child.

(2) Adoptive placement without financial assistance is unlikely because the child has a mental, physical, emotional, or medical disability that has been certified by a licensed professional competent to make an assessment and operating within the scope of that person's profession. This paragraph shall also apply to children with a developmental disability as defined in subdivision (a) of Section 4512 of the Welfare and Institutions Code, including those determined to require out-of-home nonmedical care as described in Section 11464 of the Welfare and Institutions Code.

(c) The need for adoption subsidy is evidenced by an unsuccessful search for an adoptive home to take the child without financial assistance, as documented in the case file of the prospective adoptive child. The requirement for this search shall be waived when it would be against the best interest of the child because of the existence of significant emotional ties with prospective adoptive parents while in the care of these persons as a foster child. **Leg.H.** Enacted Stats 1992 ch 162 §10 (AB 2650), operative January 1, 1994. Amended Stats 2009 ch 339 §1 (SB 597), effective January 1, 2010; Stats 2019 ch 115 §110 (AB 1817), effective January 1, 2020.

§8548. "Stepparent adoption"

"Stepparent adoption" means an adoption of a child by a stepparent where one birth parent retains custody and control of the child. **Leg.H.** Enacted Stats 1992 ch 162 §10 (AB 2650), operative January 1, 1994.

PART 2
ADOPTION OF UNMARRIED MINORS

Chapter 1. General Provisions.
Chapter 2. Agency Adoptions.
Chapter 2.5. Adoptions by Relative Caregivers or Foster Parents.
Chapter 3. Independent Adoptions.
Chapter 4. Intercountry Adoptions.
Chapter 5. Stepparent Adoptions.
Chapter 6. Vacation of Adoption.
Chapter 7. Disclosure of Information.
Chapter 8. Adoption Proceedings: Conflict of Laws.

CHAPTER 1
GENERAL PROVISIONS

Minors eligible for adoption. §8600.
Application of tribal customary adoption to part. §8600.5.
Required age difference between adoptive parents and child. §8601.
Court order of adoption entered nunc pro tunc; Eligibility for publicly funded benefit program. §8601.5.
Consent of child over 12. §8602.
Consent of spouse of married adoptive parent; Establishing parental rights or responsibilities; Dispense with attaining consent of spouse. §8603.
Consent of parents; Applying for temporary custody order by approved prospective parent or licensed private adoption agency. §8604.
Consent of mother. §8605.
Exception to requirement of parental consent. §8606.
Consent to adoption by Indian child's parents. §8606.5.
Required provisions in forms. §8607.
Regulations concerning medical reports. §8608.
Advertising by unlicensed person prohibited. §8609.
Locations for filing request for adoption or readoption of nondependent minor. §8609.5.
Accounting report. §8610.
Closed hearings. §8611.
Examination by court; Agreement; Order of adoption. §8612.
Appearance by counsel for adoptive parent in military, charitable, or religious service. §8613.
Waiver of personal appearance of prospective adoptive parent; Appearance of prospective adoptive parent by remote electronic means; Appearance by counsel. §8613.5.
Notice of eligibility for reduced-cost coverage through California Health Benefit Exchange or no-cost coverage through Medi-Cal. §8613.7.
Certificate of adoption. §8614.
New birth certificate naming deceased spouse. §8615.
Relationship between adopted child and adoptive parents. §8616.
Postadoption contact agreements; Legislative findings; Terms; Postadoption privileges; Child as party to agreement; Modifications; Warnings; Enforcement; Costs and fees; Required forms. §8616.5.
Termination of existing parents' duties; Waiver of termination. §8617.
Name of child. §8618.
Children of Indian ancestry. §8619.
Petition for return of custody where adoption decree vacated or set aside. §8619.5.
Inquiry into tribal status of child when relinquishing for adoption or executing adoption placement agreement. §8620.
Adoption of regulations and monitoring of services provided; Department authority to implement and interpret changes to chapter. §8621.
Duty to inform parents of service limitations to particular target population. §8622.
Cessation of adoption facilitator operations. § 8623.
Remedies for violations of Section 8609. § 8624.
Creation of website educating the public on unlicensed adoption agencies. § 8625.

§8600. Minors eligible for adoption

An unmarried minor may be adopted by an adult as provided in this part. **Leg.H.** Enacted Stats 1992 ch 162 §10 (AB 2650), operative January 1, 1994.

§8600.5. Application of tribal customary adoption to part

Tribal customary adoption as defined in Section 366.24 of the Welfare and Institutions Code and as applied to Indian Children who are dependents of the court, does not apply to this part. **Leg.H.** Added Stats 2009 ch 287 §1 (AB 1325), effective January 1, 2010, operative July 1, 2010, repealed January 1, 2014. Amended Stats 2012 ch 35 §9 (SB 1013), effective June 27, 2012.

2012 Note: For title and citation of Stats 2012 ch 35 (SB 1013), see 2012 Note following §8506.

§8601. Required age difference between adoptive parents and child

(a) Except as otherwise provided in subdivision (b), a prospective adoptive parent or parents shall be at least 10 years older than the child.

(b) If the court is satisfied that the adoption of a child by a stepparent, or by a sister, brother, aunt, uncle, or first cousin and, if that person is married, by that person and that person's spouse, is in the best interest of the parties and is in the public interest, it may approve the adoption without regard to the ages of the child and the prospective adoptive parent or parents. **Leg.H.** Enacted Stats 1992 ch 162 §10 (AB 2650), operative January 1, 1994.

§8601.5. Court order of adoption entered nunc pro tunc; Eligibility for publicly funded benefit program

(a) A court may issue an order of adoption and declare that it shall be entered nunc pro tunc when it will serve public policy and the best interests of the child, such as cases where adoption finalization has been delayed beyond the child's 18th birthday due to factors beyond the control of the prospective adoptive family and the proposed adoptee.

(b) The request for nunc pro tunc entry of the order shall be stated in the adoption request or an amendment thereto, and shall set forth specific facts in support thereof.

(c) To the extent that a child's eligibility for any publicly funded benefit program is or could be altered by the entry of an order of adoption, the change in eligibility shall not be determined as of the nunc pro tunc date, but shall be determined as of the date of the adoption finalization hearing.

(d) The nunc pro tunc date shall not precede the date upon which the parental rights of the birth parent or parents were initially terminated, whether voluntarily or involuntarily. **Leg.H.** Added Stats 2011 ch 462 §6 (AB 687), effective January 1, 2012.

§8602. Consent of child over 12

The consent of a child, if over the age of 12 years, is necessary to the child's adoption. **Leg.H.** Enacted Stats 1992 ch 162 §10 (AB 2650), operative January 1, 1994.

§8603. Consent of spouse of married adoptive parent; Establishing parental rights or responsibilities; Dispense with attaining consent of spouse

(a) A married person, not lawfully separated from the person's spouse, shall not adopt a child without the consent of the spouse, provided that the spouse is capable of giving that consent.

(b) The consent of the spouse shall not establish any parental rights or responsibilities on the part of the consenting spouse unless that person has consented to adopt the child in a writing filed with the court and is named in the final decree as an adoptive parent. The court shall not name the consenting spouse as an adoptive parent in the final decree unless the consenting spouse has filed a written consent to adopt the child with the court and has an approved adoption home study.

(c) The court may dispense with the consent of a spouse who cannot be located after diligent search, or a spouse determined by the court to lack the capacity to consent. A spouse for whom consent was dispensed shall not be named as an adoptive parent in the final decree. **Leg.H.** Enacted Stats 1992 ch 162 §10 (AB 2650), operative January 1, 1994. Amended Stats 2014 ch 763 §7 (AB 1701), effective January 1, 2015; Stats 2019 ch 115 §111 (AB 1817), effective January 1, 2020.

§8604. Consent of parents; Applying for temporary custody order by approved prospective parent or licensed private adoption agency

(a) Except as provided in subdivision (b), a child having a presumed father under Section 7611 shall not be adopted without the consent of the child's birth parents, if living. The consent of a presumed father is not required for the child's adoption unless the person became a presumed father as described in Chapter 1 (commencing with Section 7540) or Chapter 3 (commencing with Section 7570) of Part 2 of Division 12, or subdivision (a), (b), or (c) of Section 7611 before the mother's relinquishment or consent becomes irrevocable or before the mother's parental rights have been terminated.

(b) If one birth parent has been awarded custody by judicial order, or has custody by agreement of both parents, and the other birth parent for a period of one year willfully fails to communicate with, and to pay for, the care, support, and education of the child when able to do so, then the birth parent having sole custody may consent to the adoption, but only after the birth parent not having custody has been served with a copy of a citation in the manner provided by law for the service of a summons in a civil action that requires the birth parent not having custody to appear at the time and place set for the appearance in court under Section 8718, 8823, 8913, or 9007.

(c) Failure of a birth parent to pay for the care, support, and education of the child for the period of one year or failure of a birth parent to communicate with the child for the period of one year is prima facie evidence that the failure was willful and without lawful excuse. If the birth parent or parents have made only token efforts to support or communicate with the child, the court may disregard those token efforts.

(d)(1) If the birth mother of a child for whom there is not a presumed father leaves the child in the physical care of a licensed private adoption agency, in the physical care of a prospective adoptive parent who has an approved preplacement evaluation or private agency adoption home study, or in the hospital after designating a licensed private adoption agency or an approved prospective adoptive parent in a signed document, completed with a hospital social worker, adoption service provider, licensed private adoption agency worker, notary, or attorney, but fails to sign a placement agreement, consent, or relinquishment for adoption, the approved prospective adoptive parent or the licensed private adoption agency may apply for, and the court may issue, a temporary custody order placing the child in the care and custody of the applicant.

(2) A temporary custody order issued pursuant to this subdivision shall include all of the following:

(A) A requirement that the applicant keep the court informed of the child's residence at all times.

(B) A requirement that the child shall not be removed from the state or concealed within the state.

(C) The expiration date of the order, which shall not be more than six months after the order is issued.

(3) A temporary custody order issued pursuant to this subdivision may be voided upon the birth mother's request to have the child returned to the birth mother's care and custody. **Leg.H.** Enacted Stats 1992 ch 162 §10 (AB 2650), operative January 1, 1994. Amended Stats 2005 ch 627 §3 (SB 302), effective January 1, 2006; Stats 2007 ch 47 §4 (SB 313), effective January 1, 2008; Stats 2014 ch 763 §8 (AB 1701), effective January 1, 2015; Stats 2019 ch 115 §112 (AB 1817), effective January 1, 2020.

§8605. Consent of mother

A child not having a presumed father under Section 7611 may not be adopted without the consent of the child's mother, if living. **Leg.H.** Enacted Stats 1992 ch 162 §10 (AB 2650), operative January 1, 1994.

§8606. Exception to requirement of parental consent

Notwithstanding Sections 8604 and 8605, the consent of a birth parent is not necessary in the following cases:

(a) Where the birth parent has been judicially deprived of the custody and control of the child (1) by a court order declaring the child to be free from the custody and control of either or both birth parents pursuant to Part 4 (commencing with Section 7800) of Division 12 of this code, or Section 366.25 or 366.26 of the Welfare and Institutions Code, or (2) by a similar order of a court of another jurisdiction, pursuant to a law of that jurisdiction authorizing the order.

(b) Where the birth parent has, in a judicial proceeding in another jurisdiction, voluntarily surrendered the right to the custody and control of the child pursuant to a law of that jurisdiction providing for the surrender.

(c) Where the birth parent has deserted the child without provision for identification of the child.

(d) Where the birth parent has relinquished the child for adoption as provided in Section 8700.

(e) Where the birth parent has relinquished the child for adoption to a licensed or authorized child-placing agency in another jurisdiction pursuant to the law of that jurisdiction. **Leg.H.** Enacted Stats 1992 ch 162 §10 (AB 2650), operative January 1, 1994.

§8606.5. Consent to adoption by Indian child's parents

(a) Notwithstanding any other section in this part, and in accordance with Section 1913 of the Indian Child Welfare Act (25 U.S.C. Sec. 1901 et seq.), consent to adoption given by an Indian child's parent is not valid unless both of the following occur:

(1) The consent is executed in writing at least 10 days after the child's birth and recorded before a judge.

(2) The judge certifies that the terms and consequences of the consent were fully explained in detail in English and were fully understood by the parent or that they were interpreted into a language that the parent understood.

(b) The parent of an Indian child may withdraw consent to adoption for any reason at any time prior to the entry of a final decree of adoption and the child shall be returned to the parent.

(c) After the entry of a final decree of adoption of an Indian child, the Indian child's parent may withdraw consent to the adoption upon the grounds that consent was obtained through fraud or duress and may petition the court to vacate the decree. Upon a finding that consent was obtained through fraud or duress, the court shall vacate the decree and return the child to the parent, provided that no adoption that has been effective for at least two years may be invalidated unless otherwise permitted under state law. **Leg.H.** Added Stats 2006 ch 838 §8 (SB 678), effective January 1, 2007. Amended Stats 2019 ch 115 §113 (AB 1817), effective January 1, 2020.

§8607. Required provisions in forms

All forms adopted by the department authorizing the release of an infant from a health facility to the custody of persons other than the person entitled to custody of the child pursuant to Section 3010 and authorizing these other persons to obtain medical care for the infant shall contain a statement in boldface type delineating the various types of adoptions available, the birth parents' rights with regard thereto, including, but not limited to, rights with regard to revocation of consent to adoption, and a statement regarding the authority of the court under Part 4 (commencing with Section 7800) of Division 12 to declare the child abandoned by the birth parent or parents. **Leg.H.** Enacted Stats 1992 ch 162 §10 (AB 2650), operative January 1, 1994.

§8608. Regulations concerning medical reports

(a) The department shall adopt regulations specifying the form and content of the reports required by Sections 8706, 8817, and 8909. In addition to any other material that may be required by the department, the form shall include inquiries designed to elicit information on any illness, disease, or defect of a genetic or hereditary nature.

(b) All county adoption agencies and licensed adoption agencies shall cooperate with and assist the department in devising a plan that will effectuate the effective and discreet transmission to adoptees or prospective adoptive parents of pertinent medical information reported to the department, county adoption agency, or licensed adoption agency, upon the request of the person reporting the medical information. **Leg.H.** Enacted Stats 1992 ch 162 §10 (AB 2650), operative January 1, 1994. Amended Stats 2012 ch 35 §10 (SB 1013), effective June 27, 2012.

2012 Note: For title and citation of Stats 2012 ch 35 (SB 1013), see 2012 Note following §8506.

§8609. Advertising by unlicensed person prohibited

(a) Any person or organization that advertises in any periodical or newspaper, by radio, or other public medium, that the person or organization will place children for adoption, or accept, supply, provide, or obtain children for adoption, or that causes any advertisement to be published in or by any public medium soliciting, requesting, or asking for any child or children for adoption, is guilty of a misdemeanor, unless one of the following conditions apply:

(1) The person or organization holds a valid and unrevoked license to operate as a licensed adoption agency, as defined in Section 8530, and is authorized to place children for adoption.

(2) The person or organization is exempt from licensure pursuant to subdivision (w) or (x) of Section 1505 of the Health and Safety Code.

(b) Any person, organization, association, or corporation that seeks to place any child for adoption is guilty of a misdemeanor, unless one of the following conditions applies:

(1) The person, organization, or corporation holds a valid and unrevoked license to operate as a licensed adoption agency, as defined in Section 8530, and is authorized to place children for adoption.

(2) The person, organization, or corporation is exempt from licensure pursuant to subdivision (w) or (x) of Section 1505 of the Health and Safety Code.

(3) The person is the legal parent.

(c) Any person or organization that performs any of the functions of an adoption agency or holds itself out as performing any of the functions of an adoption agency, as described in paragraphs (9) and (10) of subdivision (a) of Section 1502 of the Health and Safety Code, without a valid and unrevoked license issued by the department shall be deemed an unlicensed adoption agency, as referenced in paragraph (6) of subdivision (a) of Section 1503.5 of Health and Safety Code, unless otherwise permitted under California law. **Leg.H.** Enacted Stats 1992 ch 162 §10 (AB 2650), operative January 1, 1994. Amended Stats 2023 ch 43 §5 (AB 120), effective July 10, 2023; Stats 2023 ch 192 §1 (SB 138), effective September 13, 2023.

§8609.5. Locations for filing request for adoption or readoption of nondependent minor

An adoption request for the adoption or readoption of a nondependent minor may be filed with the court in the county in which one of the following applies:

(a) The petitioner resides.

(b) The child was born or resides at the time of filing.

(c) An office of the agency that placed the child or is filing the petition for adoption is located.

(d) An office of the department or a public adoption agency that is investigating the petition is located.

(e) The county in which a placing birth parent or parents resided when the adoptive placement agreement, consent, or relinquishment was signed.

(f) The county in which a placing birth parent or parents resided when the petition was filed.

(g) The county in which the child was freed for adoption. **Leg.H.** Added Stats 2012 ch 638 §6 (AB 1757), effective January 1, 2013. Amended Stats 2022 ch 159 §2 (AB 2495), effective January 1, 2023.

§8610. Accounting report

(a) The petitioners in a proceeding for adoption of a child shall file with the court a full accounting report of all disbursements of anything of value made or agreed to be made by them or on their behalf in connection with the birth of the child, the placement of the child with the petitioners, any medical or hospital care received by the child's birth mother or by the child in connection with the child's birth, any other expenses of either birth parent, or the adoption. The accounting report shall be made under penalty of perjury and shall be submitted to the court on or before the date set for the hearing on the adoption petition, unless the court grants an extension of time.

(b) The accounting report shall be itemized in detail and shall show the services relating to the adoption or to the placement of the child for adoption that were received by the petitioners, by either birth parent, or by the child. The report shall also include the dates of each payment, the names and addresses of each attorney, physician and surgeon, hospital, licensed adoption agency, or any other person or organization that received payment.

(c) This section does not apply to an adoption by a stepparent if at least one legal parent retains custody and control of the child. **Leg.H.** Enacted Stats 1992 ch 162 §10 (AB 2650), operative January 1, 1994. Amended Stats 2023 ch 43 §6 (AB 120), effective July 10, 2023; Stats 2023 ch 192 §2 (SB 138), effective September 13, 2023.

§8611. Closed hearings

All court hearings in an adoption proceeding shall be held in private, and the court shall exclude all persons except the officers of the court, the parties, their witnesses, counsel, and representatives of the agencies present to perform their official duties under the law governing adoptions. **Leg.H.** Enacted Stats 1992 ch 162 §10 (AB 2650), operative January 1, 1994.

§8612. Examination by court; Agreement; Order of adoption

(a) The court shall examine all persons appearing before it pursuant to this part. The examination of each person shall be conducted separately but within the physical presence of every other person unless the court, in its discretion, orders otherwise.

(b) The prospective adoptive parent or parents shall execute and acknowledge an agreement in writing that the child will be treated in all respects as their lawful child.

(c) If satisfied that the interest of the child will be promoted by the adoption, the court may make and enter an order of adoption of the child by the prospective adoptive parent or parents. **Leg.H.** Enacted Stats 1992 ch 162 §10 (AB 2650), operative January 1, 1994.

§8613. Appearance by counsel for adoptive parent in military, charitable, or religious service

(a) If the prospective adoptive parent is commissioned or enlisted in the military service, or auxiliary thereof, of the United States, or of any of its allies, or is engaged in service on behalf of any governmental entity of the United States, or in the American Red Cross, or in any other recognized charitable or religious organization, so that it is impossible or impracticable, because of the prospective adoptive parent's absence from this state, or otherwise, to make an appearance in person, and the circumstances are established by satisfactory evidence, the appearance may be made for the prospective adoptive parent by counsel, commissioned and empowered in writing for that purpose. The power of attorney may be incorporated in the adoption petition.

(b) Where the prospective adoptive parent is permitted to appear by counsel, the agreement may be executed and acknowledged by the counsel, or may be executed by the absent party before a notary public, or any other person authorized to take acknowledgments including the persons authorized by Sections 1183 and 1183.5 of the Civil Code.

(c) Where the prospective adoptive parent is permitted to appear by counsel, or otherwise, the court may, in its discretion, cause an examination of the prospective adoptive parent, other interested person, or witness to be made upon deposition, as it deems necessary. The deposition shall be taken upon commission, as prescribed by the Code of Civil Procedure, and the expense thereof shall be borne by the petitioner.

(d) The petition, relinquishment or consent, agreement, order, report to the court from any investigating agency, and any power of attorney and deposition shall be filed in the office of the clerk of the court.

(e) The provisions of this section permitting an appearance through counsel are equally applicable to the spouse of a prospective adoptive parent who resides with the prospective adoptive parent outside this state.

(f) Where, pursuant to this section, neither prospective adoptive parent need appear before the court, the child proposed to be adopted need not appear. If the law otherwise requires that the child execute any document during the course of the hearing, the child may do so through counsel.

(g) Where none of the parties appears, the court may not make an order of adoption until after a report has been filed with the court pursuant to Section 8715, 8807, 8914, or 9001. **Leg.H.** Enacted Stats 1992 ch 162 §10 (AB 2650), operative January 1, 1994. Amended Stats 1993 ch 1158 §1 (SB 1152); Stats 2002 ch 784 §109 (SB 1316).

§8613.5. Waiver of personal appearance of prospective adoptive parent; Appearance of prospective adoptive parent by remote electronic means; Appearance by counsel

(a)(1) If it is impossible or impracticable for either prospective adoptive parent to make an appearance in person, and the circumstances are established by clear and convincing documentary evidence, the court may, in its discretion, do either of the following:

(A) Waive the personal appearance of the prospective adoptive parent. The appearance may be made for the prospective adoptive parent by counsel, commissioned and empowered in writing for that purpose. The power of attorney may be incorporated in the adoption petition.

(B) Authorize the prospective adoptive parent to appear by telephone, videoconference, or other remote electronic means that the court deems reasonable, prudent, and reliable.

(2) For purposes of this section, if the circumstances that make an appearance in person by a prospective adoptive parent impossible or impracticable are temporary in nature or of a short duration, the court shall not waive the personal appearance of that prospective adoptive parent.

(b) If the prospective adoptive parent is permitted to appear by counsel, the agreement may be executed and acknowledged by the counsel, or may be executed by the absent party before a notary public, or any other person authorized to take acknowledgments including the persons authorized by Sections 1183 and 1183.5 of the Civil Code.

(c) If the prospective adoptive parent is permitted to appear by counsel, or otherwise, the court may, in its discretion, cause an examination of the prospective adoptive parent, other interested person, or witness to be made upon deposition, as it deems necessary. The deposition shall be taken upon commission, as prescribed by the Code of Civil Procedure, and the expense thereof shall be borne by the petitioner.

(d) The petition, relinquishment or consent, agreement, order, report to the court from any investigating agency, and any power of attorney and deposition shall be filed in the office of the clerk of the court.

(e) The provisions of this section permitting an appearance by counsel or electronically pursuant to subparagraph (B) of paragraph (1) of subdivision (a) are equally applicable to the spouse of a prospective adoptive parent who resides with the prospective adoptive parent outside this state.

(f) If, pursuant to this section, neither prospective adoptive parent need appear before the court, the child proposed to be adopted need not appear. If the law otherwise requires that the child execute any document during the course of the hearing, the child may do so through counsel.

(g) If none of the parties appear, the court may not make an order of adoption until after a report has been filed with the court pursuant to Section 8715, 8807, 8914, or 9001. **Leg.H.** Added Stats 2006 ch 806 §6 (SB 1325), effective January 1, 2007. Amended Stats 2014 ch 763 §9 (AB 1701), effective January 1, 2015.

§8613.7. Notice of eligibility for reduced-cost coverage through California Health Benefit Exchange or no-cost coverage through Medi-Cal

On and after January 1, 2014, the court shall provide to any petitioner for adoption pursuant to this part a notice informing the petitioner that they may be eligible for reduced-cost coverage through the California Health Benefit Exchange established under Title 22 (commencing with Section 100500) of the Government Code or no-cost coverage through Medi-Cal. The notice shall include information on obtaining coverage pursuant to those programs, and shall be developed by the California Health Benefit Exchange. **Leg.H.** Added Stats 2012 ch 851 §2 (AB 792), effective January 1, 2013. Amended Stats 2019 ch 115 §114 (AB 1817), effective January 1, 2020.

§8614. Certificate of adoption

Upon the request of the adoptive parents or the adopted child, a clerk of the superior court may issue a certificate of adoption that states the date and place of adoption, the birthday of the child, the names of the adoptive parents, and the name the child has taken. Unless the child has been adopted by a stepparent or by a relative, as defined in subdivision (c) of Section 8616.5, the certificate shall not state the name of the birth parents of the child. **Leg.H.** Enacted Stats 1992 ch 162 §10 (AB 2650), operative January 1, 1994. Amended Stats 1997 ch 793 §2 (AB 1544); Stats 2002 ch 784 §110 (SB 1316); Stats 2003 ch 251 §5 (SB 182).

§8615. New birth certificate naming deceased spouse

(a) Notwithstanding any other law, an action may be brought in the county in which the petitioner resides for the purpose of obtaining for a child adopted by the petitioner a new birth certificate specifying that a deceased spouse of the petitioner who was in the home at the time of the initial placement of the child is a parent of the child.

(b) In an adoption proceeding, the petitioner may request that the new birth certificate specify that a deceased spouse of the petitioner who was in the home at the time of the initial placement of the child is a parent of the child.

(c) The inclusion of the name of a deceased person in a birth certificate issued pursuant to a court order under this section does not affect any matter of testate or intestate succession, and is not competent evidence on the issue of the relationship between the adopted child and the deceased person in any action or proceeding. **Leg.H.** Enacted Stats 1992 ch 162 §10 (AB 2650), operative January 1, 1994.

§8616. Relationship between adopted child and adoptive parents

After adoption, the adopted child and the adoptive parents shall sustain towards each other the legal relationship of parent and child and have all the rights and are subject to all the duties of that relationship. **Leg.H.** Enacted Stats 1992 ch 162 §10 (AB 2650), operative January 1, 1994.

§8616.5. Postadoption contact agreements; Legislative findings; Terms; Postadoption privileges; Child as party to agreement; Modifications; Warnings; Enforcement; Costs and fees; Required forms

(a) The Legislature finds and declares that some adoptive children may benefit from either direct or indirect contact with birth relatives, including the birth parent or parents or any siblings, or an Indian tribe, after being adopted. Postadoption contact agreements are intended to ensure children of an achievable level of continuing contact when contact is beneficial to the children and the agreements are voluntarily executed by birth relatives, including the birth parent or parents or any siblings, or an Indian tribe, and adoptive parents. Nothing in this section requires all of the listed parties to participate in the development of a postadoption contact agreement in order for the agreement to be executed.

(b)(1) Nothing in the adoption laws of this state shall be construed to prevent the adopting parent or parents, the birth relatives, including the birth parent or parents or any siblings, or an Indian tribe, and the child from voluntarily executing a written agreement to permit continuing contact between the birth relatives, including the birth parent or parents or any siblings, or an Indian tribe, and the child if the agreement is found by the court to have been executed voluntarily and to be in the best interests of the child at the time the adoption petition is granted.

(2) The terms of [1] **a** postadoption contact agreement executed under this section shall be limited to, but need not include, all of the following:

(A) Provisions for visitation between the child and a birth parent or parents and other birth relatives, including siblings, and the child's Indian tribe if the case is governed by the **federal** Indian Child Welfare Act **of 1978** (25 U.S.C. Sec. 1901 et seq.).

(B) Provisions for future contact between a birth parent or parents or other birth relatives, including siblings, or both, and the child or an adoptive parent, or both, and in cases governed by the Indian Child Welfare Act, the child's Indian tribe.

(C) Provisions for the sharing of information about the child in the future.

(3) The terms of [2] **a** postadoption contact agreement with birth relatives, including siblings, other than the child's birth parent or parents shall be limited to the sharing of information about the child, unless the child has a preexisting relationship with the birth relative.

(c) At the time an adoption decree is entered pursuant to a petition filed pursuant to Section 8714, 8714.5, 8802, 8912, or 9000, the court entering the decree may grant postadoption privileges if an agreement for those privileges has been executed, including agreements executed pursuant to subdivision (f) of Section 8620. The hearing to grant the adoption petition and issue an order of adoption may be continued as necessary to permit parties who are in the process of negotiating a postadoption agreement to reach a final agreement.

(d) The child who is the subject of the adoption petition shall be considered a party to the postadoption contact agreement. The written consent to the terms and conditions of the postadoption contact agreement and any subsequent modifications of the agreement by a child who is 12 years of age or older is a necessary condition to the granting of privileges regarding visitation, contact, or sharing of information about the child, unless the court finds by a preponderance of the evidence that the agreement, as written, is in the best interests of the child. [3] **A** child who has been found to come within Section 300 of the Welfare and Institutions Code or who is the subject of a petition for jurisdiction of the juvenile court under Section 300 of the Welfare and Institutions Code shall be represented by an attorney for purposes of consent to the postadoption contact agreement.

(e) A postadoption contact agreement shall contain the following warnings in bold type:

(1) After the adoption petition has been granted by the court, the adoption cannot be set aside due to the failure of an adopting parent, a birth parent, a birth relative, including a sibling, an Indian tribe, or the child to follow the terms of this agreement or a later change to this agreement.

(2) A disagreement between the parties or litigation brought to enforce or modify the agreement shall not affect the validity of the adoption and shall not serve as a basis for orders affecting the custody of the child.

(3) A court will not act on a petition to change or enforce this agreement unless the petitioner has participated, or attempted to participate, in good faith in mediation or other appropriate dispute resolution proceedings to resolve the dispute.

(f) Upon the granting of the adoption petition and the issuing of the order of adoption of a child who is a dependent of the juvenile court, juvenile court dependency jurisdiction shall be terminated. Enforcement of the postadoption contact agreement shall be under the continuing jurisdiction of the court granting the petition of adoption. The court may not order compliance with the agreement absent a finding that the party seeking the enforcement participated, or attempted to participate, in good faith in mediation or other appropriate dispute resolution proceedings regarding the conflict, prior to the filing of the enforcement action, and that the enforcement is in the best interests of the child. Documentary evidence or offers of proof may serve as the basis for the court's decision regarding enforcement. No testimony or evidentiary hearing shall be required. The court shall not order further investigation or evaluation by [4] a public or private agency or individual absent a finding by clear and convincing evidence that the best interests of the child may be protected or advanced only by that inquiry and that the inquiry will not disturb the stability of the child's home to the detriment of the child.

(g) The court may not award monetary damages as a result of the filing of the civil action pursuant to subdivision (e).

(h) A postadoption contact agreement may be modified or terminated only if either of the following occurs:

(1) All parties, including the child if the child is 12 years of age or older at the time of the requested termination or modification, have signed a modified postadoption contact agreement and the agreement is filed with the court that granted the petition of adoption.

(2) The court finds all of the following:

(A) The termination or modification is necessary to serve the best interests of the child.

(B) There has been a substantial change of circumstances since the original agreement was executed and approved by the court.

(C) The party seeking the termination or modification has participated, or attempted to participate, in good faith in mediation or other appropriate dispute resolution proceedings prior to seeking court approval of the proposed termination or modification.

Documentary evidence or offers of proof may serve as the basis for the court's decision. No testimony or evidentiary hearing shall be required. The court shall not order further investigation or evaluation by [5] a public or private agency or individual absent a finding by clear and convincing evidence that the best interests of the child may be protected or advanced only by that inquiry and that the inquiry will not disturb the stability of the child's home to the detriment of the child.

(i) All costs and fees of mediation or other appropriate dispute resolution proceedings shall be borne by each party, excluding the child. All costs and fees of litigation shall be borne by the party filing the action to modify or enforce the agreement when no party has been found by the court as failing to comply with an existing postadoption contact agreement. Otherwise, a party, other than the child, found by the court as failing to comply without good cause with an existing agreement shall bear all the costs and fees of litigation.

(j) The Judicial Council shall adopt rules of court and forms for motions to enforce, terminate, or modify postadoption contact agreements.

(k) The court shall not set aside a decree of adoption, rescind a relinquishment, or modify an order to terminate parental rights or any other prior court order because of the failure of a birth parent, adoptive parent, birth relative, including a sibling, an Indian tribe, or the child to comply with any [6] of the original terms of, or subsequent modifications to, the postadoption contact agreement, except as follows:

(1) Prior to issuing the order of adoption, in an adoption involving an Indian child, the court may, upon a petition of the birth parent, birth relative, including a sibling, or an Indian tribe, order the parties to engage in family mediation services for the purpose of reaching a postadoption contact agreement if the prospective adoptive parent fails to negotiate in good faith to execute a postadoption contact agreement, after having agreed to enter into negotiations, provided that the failure of the parties to reach an agreement is not in and of itself proof of bad faith.

(2) Prior to issuing the order of adoption, if the parties fail to negotiate in good faith to execute a postadoption contact agreement during the negotiations entered into pursuant to, and in accordance with, paragraph (1), the court may modify prior orders or issue new orders as necessary to ensure the best interest of the Indian child is met, including, but not limited to, requiring parties to engage in further family mediation services for the purpose of reaching a postadoption contact agreement, initiating guardianship proceeding in lieu of adoption, or authorizing a change of adoptive placement for the child.

(*l*) As used in this section, "sibling" means a person related to the identified child by blood, adoption, or affinity through a common legal or biological parent.

(m)(1) In every adoption, each petitioner shall inform the court in writing, on ADOPT-200, whether that petitioner has entered, or has agreed to enter into a postadoption contact agreement with any person or persons.

(2)(A) If a postadoption contact agreement has been entered into, the terms of the agreement shall be set forth on or attached to ADOPT-310 and that form shall be signed by all adult parties to the agreement, and if applicable pursuant to subdivision (d), by the child who is the subject of the adoption.

(B) Prior to finalization of the adoption, the petitioner shall file this form and any attachments with the court. The petitioner shall provide a file-marked copy of the form to all signatories to the agreement, and to any licensed adoption agency that placed the child for adoption or consented to the adoption, within 30 days of the petitioner's receipt of the file-marked copy. **Leg.H.** Added Stats 1997 ch 793 §5 (AB 1544), as Fam C §8714.7. Amended Stats 2000 ch 910 §4 (AB 2921), ch 930 §3 (SB 2157). Amended and renumbered by Stats 2003 ch 251 §8 (SB 182). Amended Stats 2004 ch 858 §4 (SB 1357); Stats 2006 ch 838 §9 (SB 678), effective January 1, 2007; Stats 2009 ch 492 §3 (AB 941), effective January 1, 2010; Stats 2016 ch 719 §1 (SB 1060), effective January 1, 2017; Stats 2023 ch 851 §6 (AB 1650), effective January 1, 2024; Stats 2024 ch 80 §43 (SB 1525), effective January 1, 2025.

§8616.5. 2024 Deletes. [1] any [2] any [3] Any [4] any [5] any [6] or all

§8617. Termination of existing parents' duties; Waiver of termination

(a) Except as provided in subdivision (b), the existing parent or parents of an adopted child are, from the time of the adoption, relieved of all parental duties towards, and all responsibility for, the adopted child, and have no right over the child.

(b) The termination of the parental duties and responsibilities of the existing parent or parents under subdivision (a) may be waived if both the existing parent or parents and the prospective adoptive parent or parents sign a waiver at any time prior to the finalization of the adoption. The waiver shall be filed with the court.

(c) This section applies to all adoptions except intercountry adoptions governed by Chapter 4 (commencing with Section 8900). **Leg.H.** Enacted Stats 1992 ch 162 §10 (AB 2650), operative January 1, 1994. Amended Stats 2013 ch 564 §7 (SB 274), effective January 1, 2014; Stats 2019 ch 192 §1 (AB 1373), effective January 1, 2020.

§8618. Name of child

A child adopted pursuant to this part may take the family name of the adoptive parent. **Leg.H.** Enacted Stats 1992 ch 162 §10 (AB 2650), operative January 1, 1994.

§8619. Children of Indian ancestry

The department shall adopt rules and regulations it determines are reasonably necessary to ensure that the birth parent or parents of Indian ancestry, seeking to relinquish a child for adoption, provide sufficient information to the department, county adoption agency, or licensed adoption agency so that a certificate of degree of Indian blood can be obtained from the Bureau of Indian Affairs. The department shall immediately request a certificate of degree of Indian blood from the Bureau of Indian Affairs upon obtaining the information. A copy of all documents pertaining to the degree of Indian blood and tribal enrollment, including a copy of the certificate of degree of Indian blood, shall become a permanent record in the adoption files and shall be housed in a central location and made available to authorized personnel from the Bureau of Indian Affairs when required to determine the adopted person's eligibility to receive services or benefits because of the adopted person's status as an Indian. This information shall be made available to the adopted person upon reaching the age of majority. **Leg.H.** Enacted Stats 1992 ch 162 §10 (AB 2650), operative January 1, 1994. Amended Stats 2012 ch 35 §11 (SB 1013), effective June 27, 2012.

2012 Note: For title and citation of Stats 2012 ch 35 (SB 1013), see 2012 Note following §8506.

§8619.5. Petition for return of custody where adoption decree vacated or set aside

Whenever a final decree of adoption of an Indian child has been vacated or set aside or the adoptive parent voluntary consents to termination of parental rights to the child, a biological parent or prior Indian custodian may petition for return of custody and the court shall grant that petition unless there is a showing, in a proceeding subject to the provisions of Section 1912 of the Indian Child Welfare Act (25 U.S.C. Sec. 1901 et seq.), that the return of custody is not in the best interest of the child. **Leg.H.** Added Stats 2006 ch 838 §10 (SB 678), effective January 1, 2007. Amended Stats 2019 ch 115 §115 (AB 1817), effective January 1, 2020.

§8620. Inquiry into tribal status of child when relinquishing for adoption or executing adoption placement agreement

(a)(1) If a parent is seeking to relinquish a child pursuant to Section 8700 or execute an adoption placement agreement pursuant to Section 8801.3, the department, county adoption agency, licensed adoption agency, or adoption service provider, as applicable, shall ask the child and the child's parent or custodian whether the child is, or may be, a member of, or eligible for membership in an Indian tribe or whether the child has been identified as a member of an Indian organization. The department, county adoption agency, licensed adoption agency, or adoption service provider, as applicable, shall complete the forms provided for this purpose by the department and shall make this completed form a part of the file.

(2) If there is any oral or written information that indicates that the child is, or may be, an Indian child, the department, county adoption agency, licensed adoption agency, or adoption service provider, as applicable, shall obtain the following information:

(A) The name of the child involved, and the actual date and place of birth of the child.

(B) The name, address, date of birth, and tribal affiliation of the birth parents, maternal and paternal grandparents, and maternal and paternal great-grandparents of the child.

(C) The name and address of extended family members of the child who have a tribal affiliation.

(D) The name and address of the Indian tribes or Indian organizations of which the child is, or may be, a member.

(E) A statement of the reasons why the child is, or may be, an Indian.

(3)(A) The department, county adoption agency, licensed adoption agency, attorney for the prospective adoptive parents, or adoption service provider shall send a notice, which shall include information obtained pursuant to paragraph (2) and a request for confirmation of the child's Indian status, to any parent and any custodian of the child, and to any Indian tribe of which the child is, or may be, a member or eligible for membership. If any of the information required under paragraph (2) cannot be obtained, the notice shall indicate that fact.

(B) The notice sent pursuant to subparagraph (A) shall describe the nature of the proceeding and advise the recipient of the Indian tribe's right to intervene in the proceeding on its own behalf or on behalf of a tribal member relative of the child.

(b) The department shall adopt regulations to ensure that if a child who is being voluntarily relinquished for adoption, pursuant to Section 8700, is an Indian child, the parent of the child shall be advised of the right to withdraw consent and thereby rescind the relinquishment of an Indian child for any reason at any time prior to entry of a final decree of termination of parental rights or adoption, pursuant to Section 1913 of Title 25 of the United States Code.

(c) If a child who is the subject of an adoption proceeding after being relinquished for adoption pursuant to Section 8700, is an Indian child, the child's Indian tribe may intervene in that proceeding on behalf of a tribal member relative of the child.

(d) Any notice sent under this section shall comply with Section 180.

(e) If all prior notices required by this section have been provided to an Indian tribe, the Indian tribe receiving those prior notices is encouraged to provide notice to the department and to the licensed adoption agency, county adoption agency, or adoption service provider, not later than five calendar days prior to the date of the hearing to determine whether or not the final adoption order is to be granted, indicating whether or not it intends to intervene in the proceeding required by this section, either on its own behalf or on behalf of a tribal member who is a relative of the child.

(f) The Legislature finds and declares that some adoptive children may benefit from either direct or indirect contact with an Indian tribe. The adoption laws of this state shall not be construed to prevent the adopting parent or parents, the birth relatives, including the birth parent or parents, an Indian tribe, and the child, from voluntarily entering into a written agreement to permit continuing contact between the Indian tribe and the child, if the agreement is found by the court to have been entered into voluntarily and to be in the best interest of the child at the time the adoption petition is granted.

(g) With respect to giving notice to Indian tribes in the case of voluntary placements of Indian children pursuant to this section, a person, other than a birth parent of the child, shall be subject to a civil penalty if that person knowingly and willfully:

(1) Falsifies, conceals, or covers up by trick, scheme, or device, a material fact concerning whether the child is an Indian child or the parent is an Indian.

(2) Makes a false, fictitious, or fraudulent statement, omission, or representation.

(3) Falsifies a written document knowing that the document contains a false, fictitious, or fraudulent statement or entry relating to a material fact.

(4) Assists a person in physically removing a child from the State of California in order to obstruct the application of notification.

(h) Civil penalties for a violation of subdivision (g) by a person other than a birth parent of the child are as follows:

(1) For the initial violation, a person shall be fined not more than ten thousand dollars ($10,000).

(2) For any subsequent violation, a person shall be fined not more than twenty thousand dollars ($20,000). **Leg.H.** Added Stats 2003 ch 469 §4 (SB 947). Amended Stats 2006 ch 838 §11 (SB 678), effective January 1, 2007; Stats 2010 ch 588 §5 (AB 2020), effective January 1, 2011; Stats 2012 ch 35 §12 (SB 1013), effective June 27, 2012; Stats 2019 ch 115 §116 (AB 1817), effective January 1, 2020.

2012 Note: For title and citation of Stats 2012 ch 35 (SB 1013), see 2012 Note following §8506.

Prior Law: Former §8620, relating to the purpose of adoption, was added Stats 1993 ch 219 §186 and repealed Stats 1993 ch 758 §5. The repealed section related to the purpose of adoption.

§8621. Adoption of regulations and monitoring of services provided; Department authority to implement and interpret changes to chapter

(a) The department shall adopt regulations regarding the provision of adoption services by the department, county adoption agencies, licensed adoption agencies, and other adoption service providers authorized pursuant to this division and shall monitor the provision of those services by county adoption agencies, licensed adoption agencies, and other adoption service providers as provided by law. The department shall report any violations of these regulations to the appropriate licensing authority.

(b) Notwithstanding the rulemaking provisions of the Administrative Procedure Act (Chapter 3.5 (commencing with Section 11340) of Part 1 of Division 3 of Title 2 of the Government Code), the State Department of Social Services may implement, interpret, or make specific the changes made to this chapter by the act adding this subdivision by means of all-county letters, written directives, interim licensing standards, or similar written instructions from the department until regulations are adopted. These all-county letters, written directives, interim licensing standards, or similar written instructions shall have the same force and effect as regulations until the adoption of regulations. **Leg.H.** Added Stats 1993 ch 758 §6 (SB 792), operative January 1, 1995. Amended Stats 2012 ch 35 §13 (SB 1013), effective June 27, 2012; Stats 2023 ch 43 §7 (AB 120), effective July 10, 2023.

2012 Note: For title and citation of Stats 2012 ch 35 (SB 1013), see 2012 Note following §8506.

1993 Note: Section 8621 applies to all petitions for independent adoption filed on or after January 1, 1995. Petitions filed prior to, and pending on, that date shall be governed by the law in effect on December 31, 1994. Stats 1993 ch 758 §17(b).

Prior Law: There was another section of this number, similar to this section, which was added Stats 1993 ch 219 §187, but failed to become operative as it was repealed by Stats 1993 ch 758 §5.5.

§8622. Duty to inform parents of service limitations to particular target population

A licensed private adoption agency whose services are limited to a particular target population shall inform all birth parents and prospective adoptive parents of its service limitations before commencing any services, signing any documents or agreements, or accepting any fees.

This section shall become operative on January 1, 1995. **Leg.H.** Added Stats 1993 ch 758 §6.2 (SB 792), operative January 1, 1995.

Prior Law: There was another section of this number, similar to the present section, which was added Stats 1993 ch 219 §188, but failed to become operative as it was repealed by Stats 1993 ch 758 §6.1.

1993 Note: Section 8622 applies to all petitions for independent adoption filed on or after January 1, 1995. Petitions filed prior to, and pending on, that date shall be governed by the law in effect on December 31, 1994. Stats 1993 ch 758 §17(b).

Former Sections: Former Fam C §8622, similar to the present section, was added by Stats 1993 ch 219 §188, operative January 1, 2994, and repealed by Stats 1993 ch 758 §6.1.

§ 8623. Cessation of adoption facilitator operations

Notwithstanding any other law, all adoption facilitators registered with the department on its statewide registry as of July 1, 2023, shall cease operation in this state on or before December 31, 2023. An adoption facilitator that continues to operate on or after January 1, 2024, shall be deemed an unlicensed adoption agency as referenced in paragraph (6) of subdivision (a) of Section 1503.5 of the Health and Safety Code. **Leg.H.** Added Stats 2023 ch 43 §9 (AB 120), effective July 10, 2023.

Prior Law Former Fam C §8623, relating to who or what constitutes an adoption facilitator, was added Stats 1996 ch 1135 §1 (SB 2035), amended Stats 2007 ch 130 §90 (AB 299), effective January 1, 2008, and repealed Stats 2023 ch 43 §8 (AB 120), effective July 10, 2023.

§ 8624. Remedies for violations of Section 8609

(a) A person aggrieved by a violation of Section 8609 may bring a civil action for damages, rescission, injunctive relief, or any other civil or equitable remedy. Operation of an unlicensed adoption agency, as referenced in paragraph (6) of subdivision (a) of Section 1503.5 of the Health and Safety Code, shall be an act of unfair competition and an unfair business practice within the meaning of Chapter 5 (commencing with Section 17200) of Part 2 of Division 7 of the Business and Professions Code.

(b) If the court finds that a person has violated Section 8609, it shall award actual damages plus an amount equal to treble the amount of the actual damages or two thousand five hundred dollars ($2,500) per violation, whichever is greater.

(c) In a civil action under this section, a prevailing party may recover reasonable attorney's fees and costs.

(d) The Attorney General, a district attorney, or a city attorney may bring a civil action for injunctive relief, restitution, or other equitable relief against an unlicensed adoption agency as referenced in paragraph (6) of subdivision (a) of Section 1503.5 of the Health and Safety Code pursuant to this section in the name of the people of the State of California.

(e) Any other interested person who, based upon information or belief, claims a violation of Section 8609 has been committed may bring a civil action for injunctive relief on behalf of the general public. This section authorizes a referral by the department to the appropriate law enforcement entities consistent with these provisions. **Leg.H.** Added Stats 2023 ch 43 §10 (AB 120), effective July 10, 2023.

Prior Law Former Fam C §8624, relating to advertising, was added Stats 1996 ch 1135 §1 (SB 2035) and repealed Stats 2023 ch 43 §8 (AB 120), effective July 10, 2023.

§ 8625. Creation of website educating the public on unlicensed adoption agencies

(a) The department shall create a section on its internet website dedicated to educating the public on unlicensed adoption agencies. The section shall include both of the following:

(1) A statement informing the public that, as of January 1, 2024, operating as an "adoption facilitator" in the state is prohibited. The statement shall include common practices and services undertaken by adoption facilitators. The statement shall also inform the public that only the authorized persons or organizations specified in Section 8609 may engage in the practices described in that section.

(2) A listing of all persons or organizations on the department's adoption facilitator registry as of December 31, 2023.

(b) The department shall individually notify each adoption facilitator on the registry as July 1, 2023, that operations must cease pursuant to Section 8623. The notice shall also require each adoption facilitator to comply with both of the following:

(1) Publish the statement described in subdivision (a) on any internet website operated by the adoption facilitator.

(2) Provide written notice to any individuals under contract indicating that the adoption facilitator must cease operation on or before December 31, 2023. This written notice must also include information on licensed entities that can provide adoption services and any additional information the department deems necessary. **Leg.H.** Added Stats 2023 ch 43 §11 (AB 120), effective July 10, 2023.

Prior Law Former Fam C §8625, relating to representations concerning status or services, was added Stats 1996 ch 1135 §1 (SB 2035), amended Stats 2006 ch 754 §2 (SB 1758), effective January 1, 2007, Stats 2019 ch 115 §117 (AB 1817), effective January 1, 2020, and repealed Stats 2023 ch 43 §8 (AB 120), effective July 10, 2023.

CHAPTER 1.5
ADOPTION FACILITATORS [REPEALED]

§8623. Who or what constitutes an adoption facilitator [Repealed]

Leg.H. Added Stats 1996 ch 1135 §1 (SB 2035). Amended Stats 2007 ch 130 §90 (AB 299), effective January 1, 2008. Repealed Stats 2023 ch 43 §8 (AB 120), effective July 10, 2023.

Prior Law Former Fam C §8623, relating to who or what constitutes an adoption facilitator, was added Stats 1996 ch 1135 §1 (SB 2035), amended Stats 2007 ch 130 §90 (AB 299), effective January 1, 2008, and repealed Stats 2023 ch 43 §8 (AB 120), effective July 10, 2023.

§8624. Advertising [Repealed]

Leg.H. Added Stats 1996 ch 1135 §1 (SB 2035). Repealed Stats 2023 ch 43 §8 (AB 120), effective July 10, 2023.

Prior Law Former Fam C §8624, relating to advertising, was added Stats 1996 ch 1135 §1 (SB 2035) and repealed Stats 2023 ch 43 §8 (AB 120), effective July 10, 2023.

§8625. Representations concerning status or services [Repealed]

Leg.H. Added Stats 1996 ch 1135 §1 (SB 2035). Amended Stats 2006 ch 754 §2 (SB 1758), effective January 1, 2007; Stats 2019 ch 115 §117 (AB 1817), effective January 1, 2020. Repealed Stats 2023 ch 43 §8 (AB 120), effective July 10, 2023.

Prior Law Former Fam C §8625, relating to representations concerning status or services, was added Stats 1996 ch 1135 §1 (SB 2035), amended Stats 2006 ch 754 §2 (SB 1758), effective January 1, 2007, Stats 2019 ch 115 §117 (AB 1817), effective January 1, 2020, and repealed Stats 2023 ch 43 §8 (AB 120), effective July 10, 2023.

§8626. Disclosure that facilitator is not licensed agency [Repealed]

Leg.H. Added Stats 1996 ch 1135 §1 (SB 2035). Repealed Stats 2023 ch 43 §8 (AB 120), effective July 10, 2023.

Prior Law Former Fam C § 8626, relating to disclosure that facilitator is not licensed agency, was added Stats 1996 ch 1135 §1 (SB 2035).

§8627. Agreement by parties represented [Repealed]

Leg.H. Added Stats 1996 ch 1135 §1 (SB 2035). Repealed Stats 2023 ch 43 §8 (AB 120), effective July 10, 2023.

Prior Law Former Fam C §8627, relating to agreement by parties represented, was added Stats 1996 ch 1135 §1 (SB 2035).

§8628. Transmission of information from birthparents [Repealed]

Leg.H. Added Stats 1996 ch 1135 §1 (SB 2035). Repealed Stats 2023 ch 43 §8 (AB 120), effective July 10, 2023.

Prior Law Former Fam C §8628, relating to transmission of information from birthparents, was added Stats 1996 ch 1135 §1 (SB 2035).

§8629. Period for revocation of contract or request for return of fees [Repealed]

Leg.H. Added Stats 1996 ch 1135 §1 (SB 2035). Repealed Stats 2023 ch 43 §8 (AB 120), effective July 10, 2023.

Prior Law Former Fam C §8629, relating to period for revocation of contract or request for return of fees, was added Stats 1996 ch 1135 §1 (SB 2035).

§8630. Report of fees paid to or by facilitator [Repealed]

Leg.H. Added Stats 1996 ch 1135 §1 (SB 2035). Repealed Stats 2023 ch 43 §8 (AB 120), effective July 10, 2023.

Prior Law Former Fam C §8630, relating to report of fees paid to or by facilitator, was added Stats 1996 ch 1135 §1 (SB 2035).

§8631. Requirements for contract [Repealed]

Leg.H. Added Stats 1996 ch 1135 §1 (SB 2035). Repealed Stats 2023 ch 43 §8 (AB 120), effective July 10, 2023.

Prior Law Former Fam C §8631, relating to requirements for contract, was added Stats 1996 ch 1135 §1 (SB 2035).

§8632. Explanation of contract to parties [Repealed]

Leg.H. Added Stats 1996 ch 1135 §1 (SB 2035). Repealed Stats 2023 ch 43 §8 (AB 120), effective July 10, 2023.

Prior Law Former Fam C §8632, relating to explanation of contract to parties, was added Stats 1996 ch 1135 §1 (SB 2035).

§8632.5. Registration and enforcement process for adoption facilitators [Repealed]

Leg.H. Added Stats 2006 ch 754 §3 (SB 1758), effective January 1, 2007. Amended Stats 2007 ch 130 §91 (AB 299), effective January 1, 2008; Stats 2008 ch 534 §6 (SB 1726), effective January 1, 2009; Stats 2019 ch 27 §3 (SB 80); Stats 2019 ch 115 §118 (AB 1817), effective January 1, 2020 (ch 27 prevails). Repealed Stats 2023 ch 43 §8 (AB 120), effective July 10, 2023.

Prior Law Former Fam C §8632.5, relating to registration and enforcement process for adoption facilitators, was added Stats 2006 ch 754 §3 (SB 1758), effective January 1, 2007, amended Stats 2007 ch 130 §91 (AB 299), effective January 1, 2008, Stats 2008 ch 534 §6 (SB 1726), effective January 1, 2009.

§8633. Penalty for violations [Repealed]

Leg.H. Added Stats 1996 ch 1135 §1 (SB 2035). Repealed Stats 2023 ch 43 §8 (AB 120), effective July 10, 2023.

Prior Law Former Fam C §8633, relating to penalty for violations, was added Stats 1996 ch 1135 §1 (SB 2035).

§8634. Applicability of general contract law [Repealed]

Leg.H. Added Stats 1996 ch 1135 §1 (SB 2035). Repealed Stats 2023 ch 43 §8 (AB 120), effective July 10, 2023.

Prior Law Former Fam C §8634, relating to applicability of general contract law, was added Stats 1996 ch 1135 §1 (SB 2035).

§8635. [Section repealed 2007]

Leg.H. Added Stats 1996 ch 1135 §1 (SB 2035). Repealed Stats 2006 ch 754 §4 (SB 1758), effective January 1, 2007. The repealed section related to recovering attorneys fees and costs.

2006 Note: The repeal of Section 8635 of the Family Code by this act is not retroactive and does not apply to actions that are pending before January 1, 2007. Stats 2006 ch 754 (SB 1758) §7.

§8636. Business license; Surety bond [Repealed]

Leg.H. Added Stats 1996 ch 1135 §1 (SB 2035). Amended Stats 2006 ch 754 §5 (SB 1758), effective January 1, 2007. Repealed Stats 2023 ch 43 §8 (AB 120), effective July 10, 2023.

Prior Law Former Fam C §8636, relating to business license; surety bond, was added Stats 1996 ch 1135 §1 (SB 2035).

§8637. Attorney as facilitator [Repealed]

Leg.H. Added Stats 1996 ch 1135 §1 (SB 2035). Repealed Stats 2023 ch 43 §8 (AB 120), effective July 10, 2023.

Prior Law Former Fam C §8637, relating to attorney as facilitator, was added Stats 2007 ch 583 §7 (SB 703), effective January 1, 2008.

§8638. Civil remedies for violations [Repealed]

Leg.H. Added Stats 1996 ch 1135 §1 (SB 2035). Amended Stats 2006 ch 754 §6 (SB 1758), effective January 1, 2007. Repealed Stats 2023 ch 43 §8 (AB 120), effective July 10, 2023.

Prior Law Former Fam C §8638, relating to civil remedies for violations, was added Stats 1996 ch 1135 §1 (SB 2035).

§8639. Civil penalty; Appeal process [Repealed]

Leg.H. Added Stats 2008 ch 534 §7 (SB 1726), effective January 1, 2009. Repealed Stats 2023 ch 43 §8 (AB 120), effective July 10, 2023.

Prior Law Former Fam C §8639, relating to civil penalty; appeal process, was added Stats 1996 ch 1135 §1 (SB 2035).

CHAPTER 2
AGENCY ADOPTIONS

Relinquishment of child to department, county adoption agency, or licensed adoption agency. §8700.
Waiver of right to revoke relinquishment; Form; Submission. §8700.5.
Information to birth parents on status of adoption. §8701.
Statement to birth parents at time of relinquishment. §8702.
Notice to birth parent on termination of parental rights. §8703.
Custody by department, county adoption agency, or licensed adoption agency; Petition only by prospective adoptive parents; Removal of child from prospective adoptive parents. §8704.
When foster care license or certification not required; Placement exceeding or within 30 days; In-home supervisory visits. §8704.5.
Consent to adoption of child of deceased parents. §8705.
Medical report on child and biological parents; Parents' blood sample. §8706.
Photo-listing service. §8707.
Diversity of potential adoptive parents: Construction with Indian Child Welfare Act. §8707.1.
Discrimination in adoption or placement; Effect on application of federal Indian Child Welfare Act. §8708.
Consideration of child's religious background; Applicability of federal Indian Child Welfare Act. §8709.
Order of placement preference. §8710.
Exchange system where no placement plan in jurisdiction. §8710.1.
Statewide exchange system. §8710.2.
Registration with exchange system. §8710.3.
Access to information. §8710.4.
Applicability of racial or ethnic criteria. §8711.
Adoption of regulations. §8711.5.
Investigation of prospective adoptive parents. §8712.
Concealment or removal of child from county. §8713.
Adoption petition and order; Notice; Filing of postadoption contract agreement; Consolidation of guardianship proceeding. §8714.
Adoption by relative; Legislative findings; Petition; Notice; Filing of postadoption contact agreement; Consolidation of guardianship proceeding. §8714.5.
[Section renumbered 2003]. §8714.7.
Report of department or agency. §8715.
Fee. §8716.
Copy of report or findings to petitioner or attorney. §8717.
Appearance of prospective adoptive parents and child. §8718.
Notice to department of motion to withdraw or dismiss petition. §8719.
Unfavorable recommendation by department or agency. §8720.

§8700. Relinquishment of child to department, county adoption agency, or licensed adoption agency

(a) Either birth parent may relinquish a child to the department, county adoption agency, or licensed adoption agency for adoption by a written statement signed before two subscribing witnesses and acknowledged before an authorized official of the department, county adoption agency, or licensed adoption agency. The relinquishment, when reciting that the person making it is entitled to the sole custody of the child and acknowledged before the officer, is prima facie evidence of the right of the person making it to the sole custody of the child and the person's sole right to relinquish.

(b) A relinquishing parent who is a minor has the right to relinquish a child for adoption to the department, county adoption agency, or licensed adoption agency, and the relinquishment is not subject to revocation by the relinquishing parent by reason of the minority, or because the parent or guardian of the relinquishing minor parent was not served with notice that the relinquishing minor parent relinquished the child for adoption, unless the relinquishing minor parent has previously provided written authorization to serve the relinquishing minor's parent or guardian with that notice.

(c) If a parent resides outside this state and the other parent has relinquished the child for adoption pursuant to subdivision (a) or (d), the parent residing out of state may relinquish the child by a written statement signed before a notary on a form prescribed by the department, and previously signed by an authorized official of the department, county adoption agency, or licensed adoption agency that signifies the willingness of the department, county adoption agency, or licensed adoption agency to accept the relinquishment.

(d) If a parent and child reside outside this state and the other parent has not relinquished the child for adoption to the department, county adoption agency, or licensed adoption agency, the parent residing out of state may relinquish the child to the department, county adoption agency, or licensed adoption agency by a written statement signed by the relinquishing parent, after the following requirements have been satisfied:

(1) Prior to signing the relinquishment, the relinquishing parent shall have received, from a representative of an agency licensed or otherwise approved to provide adoption services under the laws of the relinquishing parent's state of residence, the same counseling and advisement services as if the relinquishing parent resided in this state.

(2) The relinquishment shall be signed before a representative of an agency licensed or otherwise approved to provide adoption services under the laws of the relinquishing parent's state of residence whenever possible or before a licensed social worker on a form prescribed by the department, and previously signed by an authorized official of the department, county adoption agency, or licensed adoption agency, that signifies the willingness of the department, county adoption agency, or licensed adoption agency to accept the relinquishment.

(e)(1) The relinquishment authorized by this section has no effect until a certified copy is sent to, and filed with, the department. The county adoption agency or licensed adoption agency shall send that copy by certified mail, return receipt requested, or by overnight courier or messenger, with proof of delivery, to the department no earlier than the end of the business day following the signing thereof. The agency shall inform the birth parent that during this time period the birth parent may request that the relinquishment be withdrawn and that, if the birth parent makes the request, the relinquishment shall be withdrawn. The relinquishment shall be final 10 business days after receipt of the filing by the department, unless any of the following applies:

(A) The department sends written acknowledgment of receipt of the relinquishment prior to the expiration of that 10-day period, at which time the relinquishment shall be final.

(B) A longer period of time is necessary due to a pending court action or some other cause beyond control of the department.

(C) The birth parent signs a waiver of right to revoke relinquishment pursuant to Section 8700.5, in which case the relinquishment shall become final as provided in that section.

(2) After the relinquishment is final, it may be rescinded only by the mutual consent of the department, county adoption agency, or licensed adoption agency to which the child was relinquished and the birth parent or parents relinquishing the child.

(f) The relinquishing parent may name in the relinquishment the person or persons with whom the relinquishing parent intends that placement of the child for adoption be made by the department, county adoption agency, or licensed adoption agency.

(g) Notwithstanding subdivision (e), if the relinquishment names the person or persons with whom placement by the department, county adoption agency, or licensed adoption agency is intended and the child is not placed in the home of the named person or persons or the child is removed from the home prior to the granting of the adoption, the department, county adoption agency, or licensed adoption agency shall mail a notice by certified mail, return receipt requested, to the birth parent signing the relinquishment within 72 hours of the decision not to place the child for adoption or the decision to remove the child from the home.

(h) The relinquishing parent has 30 days from the date on which the notice described in subdivision (g) was mailed to rescind the relinquishment.

(1) If the relinquishing parent requests rescission during the 30-day period, the department, county adoption agency, or licensed adoption agency shall rescind the relinquishment.

(2) If the relinquishing parent does not request rescission during the 30-day period, the department, county adoption agency, or licensed adoption agency shall select adoptive parents for the child.

(3) If the relinquishing parent and the department, county adoption agency, or licensed adoption agency wish to identify a different person or persons during the 30-day period with whom the child is intended to be placed, the initial relinquishment shall be rescinded and a new relinquishment identifying the person or persons completed.

(i) Subject to the requirements of subdivision (b) of Section 361 of the Welfare and Institutions Code, a parent may sign a relinquishment of a child described in paragraph (1) of subdivision (b) of Section 361 of the Welfare and Institutions Code. If the relinquishment is to a licensed private adoption agency, the parent shall be advised, in writing, that the relinquishment shall have no effect and will be not be filed with, or acknowledged by, the department, unless the court approves the relinquishment pursuant to paragraph (3) of subdivision (b) of Section 361 of the Welfare and Institutions Code. If the court issues an order approving the relinquishment, the licensed private adoption agency shall file the relinquishment and the order with the department. If the court denies the relinquishment, the licensed private adoption agency shall void the relinquishment and inform the parent of that fact.

(j) The filing of the relinquishment with the department terminates all parental rights and responsibilities with regard to the child, except as provided in subdivisions (g) and (h).

(k) The department shall adopt regulations to administer the provisions of this section. **Leg.H.** Enacted Stats 1992 ch 162 §10 (AB 2650), operative January 1, 1994. Amended Stats 1993 ch 219 §189 (AB 1500); Stats 1994 ch 1269 §56 (AB 2208); Stats 1997 ch 793 §3 (AB 1544); Stats 1998 ch 1056 §1 (AB 2773); Stats 2004 ch 306 §1 (AB 2674); Stats 2006 ch 806 §7 (SB 1325), effective January 1, 2007; Stats 2008 ch 534 §8 (SB 1726), effective January 1, 2009; Stats 2012 ch 35 §14 (SB 1013), effective June 27, 2012, ch 638 §7 (AB 1757), effective January 1, 2013; Stats 2014 ch 763 §10 (AB 1701), effective January 1, 2015; Stats 2019 ch 115 §119 (AB 1817), effective January 1, 2020.

2012 Note: For title and citation of Stats 2012 ch 35 (SB 1013), see 2012 Note following §8506.

2004 Note: It is the Legislature's intent, in enacting Stats 2004 ch 306 (AB 2674), to ensure that the process for the relinquishment for adoption of a child to the State Department of Social Services or a licensed adoption agency is expedited to the greatest extent possible while also ensuring that the interests of all parties are considered, especially the interests of the child. Stats 2004 ch 306 §2.

§8700.5. Waiver of right to revoke relinquishment; Form; Submission

(a) A relinquishing birth parent may elect to sign a waiver of the right to revoke relinquishment in the presence of any of the following:

(1) A representative of the department or the delegated county adoption agency, or any public adoption agency of another state.

(2) A judicial officer of a court of record, within or outside of California, if the birth parent is represented by independent legal counsel.

(3) An authorized representative of a licensed private adoption agency within or outside of California, including a representative of the adoption agency that witnessed or accepted the relinquishment, if the birth parent is represented by independent legal counsel.

(b) The waiver of the right to revoke relinquishment may not be signed until the department, delegated county adoption agency, or public adoption agency of another state has completed an interview, unless the waiver is signed in the presence of a judicial officer of a court of record of any state or an authorized representative of a private adoption agency licensed within or outside of California. If the waiver is signed in the presence of a judicial officer, the interview and witnessing of the signing of the waiver shall be conducted by the judicial officer. If the waiver is signed in the presence of an authorized representative of a licensed adoption agency, the interview shall be conducted by the independent legal counsel for the birth parent or parents, who shall:

(1) Review the waiver with the birth parent or parents.

(2) Counsel the birth parent or parents about the nature of the intended waiver.

(3) Sign and deliver to the birth parent or parents and the licensed adoption agency a certificate in substantially the following form:

"I, (name of attorney), have counseled my client, (name of client), about the nature and legal effect of the waiver of the right to revoke the relinquishment for adoption. I am so disassociated from the interest of the prospective adoptive parent(s) and the licensed adoption agency as to be in a position to advise my client impartially and confidentially as to the consequences of the waiver. My client is aware that California law provides an indeterminate period, usually 2 to 10 business days, during which a birth parent may revoke a relinquishment for adoption. On the basis of this counsel, I conclude that it is the intent of my client to waive the right to revoke, and to make a permanent and irrevocable relinquishment for adoption. My client understands that upon signing this waiver, my client will not be able to regain custody of the child unless the prospective adoptive parent or parents agree to withdraw the petition for adoption or the court denies the adoption petition."

(c) If the placing birth parent signs the waiver in front of a judicial officer or the department, the relinquishment shall become final and irrevocable at the time the waiver is signed. If the waiver is signed in the presence of an authorized representative of a private licensed adoption agency, the relinquishment shall become final and irrevocable at the close of the next business day after the relinquishment was signed, or at the close of the next business day after expiration of any holding period specified in writing, whichever is later.

(d) The licensed adoption agency shall submit the waiver and certificate to the department with the relinquishment, unless the relinquishment was submitted to the department before the waiver was signed, in which case the waiver and certificate shall be submitted to the department no later than two business days after signing.

(e) A waiver executed pursuant to this section shall be void if any of the following occur:

(1) The relinquishment is determined to be invalid.

(2) The relinquishment is revoked during any holding period specified in writing.

(3) The relinquishment is rescinded pursuant to Section 8700.

(f) This section does not limit the birth parent's right to rescind the relinquishment pursuant to Section 8700. **Leg.H.** Added Stats 2012 ch 638 §8 (AB 1757), effective January 1, 2013. Amended Stats 2013 ch 743 §1 (AB 848), effective January 1, 2014; Stats 2019 ch 115 §120 (AB 1817), effective January 1, 2020.

§8701. Information to birth parents on status of adoption

At or before the time a relinquishment is signed, the department, county adoption agency, or licensed adoption agency shall advise the birth parent signing the relinquishment, verbally and in writing, that the birth parent may, at any time in the future, request from the department, county adoption agency, or licensed adoption agency all known information about the status of the child's adoption, except for personal, identifying information about the adoptive family. The birth parent shall be advised that this information includes, but is not limited to, all of the following:

(a) Whether the child has been placed for adoption.

(b) The approximate date that an adoption was completed.

(c) If the adoption was not completed or was vacated, for any reason, whether adoptive placement of the child is again being considered. **Leg.H.** Enacted Stats 1992 ch 162 §10 (AB 2650), operative January 1, 1994. Amended Stats 2012 ch 35 §15 (SB 1013), effective June 27, 2012.

2012 Note: For title and citation of Stats 2012 ch 35 (SB 1013), see 2012 Note following §8506.

§8702. Statement to birth parents at time of relinquishment

(a) The department shall adopt a statement to be presented to the birth parents at the time a relinquishment is signed and to prospective adoptive parents at the time of the home study. The statement shall, in a clear and concise manner and in words calculated to ensure the confidence of the birth parents in the integrity of the adoption process, communicate to the birth parents of a child who is the subject of an adoption petition all of the following facts:

(1) It is in the child's best interest that the birth parent keep the department, county adoption agency, or licensed adoption agency to whom the child was relinquished for adoption informed of any health problems that the parent develops that could affect the child.

(2) It is extremely important that the birth parent keep an address current with the department, county adoption agency, or licensed adoption agency to whom the child was relinquished for adoption in order to permit a response to inquiries concerning medical or social history.

(3) Section 9203 of the Family Code authorizes a person who has been adopted and who attains the age of 21 years to request the department, county adoption agency, or the licensed adoption agency to disclose the name and address of the adoptee's birth parents. Consequently, it is of the utmost importance that the birth parent indicate whether to allow this disclosure by checking the appropriate box provided on the form.

(4) The birth parent may change the decision whether to permit disclosure of the birth parent's name and address, at any time, by sending a notarized letter to that effect, by certified mail, return receipt requested, to the department, county adoption agency, or to the licensed adoption agency that joined in the adoption petition.

(5) The relinquishment will be filed in the office of the clerk of the court in which the adoption takes place. The file is not open to inspection by any persons other than the parties to the adoption proceeding, their attorneys, and the department, except upon order of a judge of the superior court.

(b) The department shall adopt a form to be signed by the birth parents at the time the relinquishment is signed, which shall provide as follows:

"Section 9203 of the Family Code authorizes a person who has been adopted and who attains the age of 21 years to make a request to the State Department of Social Services, county adoption agency, or licensed adoption agency that joined in the adoption petition, for the name and address of the adoptee's birth parents. Indicate by checking one of the boxes below whether or not you wish your name and address to be disclosed:

☐ YES

☐ NO

☐ UNCERTAIN AT THIS TIME; WILL NOTIFY AGENCY AT LATER DATE." **Leg.H.** Enacted Stats 1992 ch 162 §10 (AB 2650), operative January 1, 1994. Amended Stats 2002 ch 784 §111 (SB 1316); Stats 2012 ch 35 §16 (SB 1013), effective June 27, 2012.

2012 Note: For title and citation of Stats 2012 ch 35 (SB 1013), see 2012 Note following §8506.

§8703. Notice to birth parent on termination of parental rights

When the parental rights of a birth parent are terminated pursuant to Chapter 5 (commencing with Section 7660) of Part 3 of Division 12 or Part 4 (commencing with Section 7800) of Division 12, or pursuant to Section 366.25 or 366.26 of the Welfare and Institutions Code, the department, county adoption agency, or licensed adoption agency responsible for the adoptive placement of the child shall send a written notice to the birth parent, if the birth parent's address is known, that contains the following statement:

(a) "You are encouraged to keep the department or this agency informed of your current address in order to permit a response to any inquiry concerning medical or social history made by or on behalf of the child who was the subject of the court action terminating parental rights.

(b) Section 9203 of the Family Code authorizes a person who has been adopted and who attains the age of 21 years to make a request to the State Department of Social Services, county adoption agency, or licensed adoption agency, that joined in the adoption petition, for the name and address of the adoptee's birth parents. Indicate by checking one of the boxes below whether or not you wish your name and address to be disclosed:

( ) YES

( ) NO

( ) UNCERTAIN AT THIS TIME; WILL NOTIFY AGENCY AT LATER DATE" **Leg.H.** Enacted Stats 1992 ch 162 §10 (AB 2650), operative January 1, 1994. Amended Stats 2000 ch 910 §1 (AB 2921); Stats 2012 ch 35 §17 (SB 1013), effective June 27, 2012.

2012 Note: For title and citation of Stats 2012 ch 35 (SB 1013), see 2012 Note following §8506.

§8704. Custody by department, county adoption agency, or licensed adoption agency; Petition only by prospective adoptive parents; Removal of child from prospective adoptive parents

(a) The department, county adoption agency, or licensed adoption agency to which a child has been freed for adoption by either relinquishment or termination of parental rights is responsible for the care of the child, and is entitled to the exclusive custody and control of the child until an order of adoption is granted. Any placement for temporary care, or for adoption, made by the department, county adoption agency, or licensed adoption agency may be terminated in its discretion at any time before the granting of an order of adoption. In the event of termination of any placement for temporary care or for adoption, the child shall be returned promptly to the physical custody of the department, county adoption agency, or licensed adoption agency.

(b) No petition may be filed to adopt a child relinquished to the department, county adoption agency, or licensed adoption agency or a child declared free from the custody and control of either or both birth parents and referred to the department, county adoption agency, or licensed adoption agency for adoptive placement, except by the prospective adoptive parents with whom the child has been placed for adoption by the department, county adoption agency, or licensed adoption agency.

After the adoption petition has been filed, the department, county adoption agency, or licensed adoption agency may remove the child from the prospective adoptive parents only with the approval of the court, upon motion by the department, county adoption agency, or licensed adoption agency after notice to the prospective adoptive parents, supported by an affidavit or affidavits stating the grounds on which removal is sought. If the department, county adoption agency, or licensed adoption agency refuses to consent to the adoption of a child by the person or persons with whom the department, county adoption agency, or licensed adoption agency placed the child for adoption, the court may nevertheless order the adoption if it finds that the refusal to consent is not in the child's best interest. **Leg.H.** Enacted Stats 1992 ch 162 §10 (AB 2650), operative January 1, 1994. Amended Stats 1995 ch 884 §3 (AB 1743); Stats 2012 ch 35 §18 (SB 1013), effective June 27, 2012.

2012 Note: For title and citation of Stats 2012 ch 35 (SB 1013), see 2012 Note following §8506.

§8704.5. When foster care license or certification not required; Placement exceeding or within 30 days; In-home supervisory visits

(a) A foster care license or certification or resource family approval shall not be required for placement of a nondependent child who is relinquished for adoption to a licensed private adoption agency, if the child is placed in the care of prospective adoptive parents who have an approved adoption home study that meets the criteria established by the department for home studies conducted within the state.

(b) During a preadoptive placement made pursuant to subdivision (a), the licensed private adoption agency shall conduct in-home supervisory visits no less than once every 30 days, until the child has been legally freed and formally placed for adoption. **Leg.H.** Added Stats 2011 ch 462 §7 (AB 687), effective January 1, 2012. Amended Stats 2017 ch 732 §2 (AB 404), effective January 1, 2018.

§8705. Consent to adoption of child of deceased parents

(a) Where a child is in the custody of a public agency or licensed adoption agency, if it is established that the persons whose consent to the adoption is required by law are deceased, an action may be brought by the department, county adoption agency, or licensed adoption agency requesting the court to make an order establishing that the requesting agency has the right to custody and control of the child and the authority to place the child for adoption. The department, county adoption agency, or licensed adoption agency bringing the action shall give notice in the form prescribed by the court to all known relatives of the child up to and including the third degree of lineal or collateral consanguinity.

(b) This section does not apply where a guardian of the person of the child has been appointed pursuant to nomination by a will. **Leg.H.** Enacted Stats 1992 ch 162 §10 (AB 2650), operative January 1, 1994. Amended Stats 2012 ch 35 §19 (SB 1013), effective June 27, 2012.

2012 Note: For title and citation of Stats 2012 ch 35 (SB 1013), see 2012 Note following §8506.

§8706. Medical report on child and biological parents; Parents' blood sample

(a) An agency may not place a child for adoption unless a written report on the child's medical background and, if available, the medical background of the child's biological parents so far as ascertainable, has been submitted to the prospective adoptive parents and they have acknowledged in writing the receipt of the report.

(b) The report on the child's background shall contain all known diagnostic information, including current medical reports on the child, psychological evaluations, and scholastic information, as well as all known information regarding the child's developmental history and family life.

(c)(1) The biological parents may provide a blood sample at a clinic or hospital approved by the State Department of Health Services. The biological parents' failure to provide a blood sample shall not affect the adoption of the child.

(2) The blood sample shall be stored at a laboratory under contract with the State Department of Health Services for a period of 30 years following the adoption of the child.

(3) The purpose of the stored sample of blood is to provide a blood sample from which DNA testing can be done at a later date after entry of the order of adoption at the request of the adoptive parents or the adopted child. The cost of drawing and storing the blood samples shall be paid for by a separate fee in addition to the fee required under Section 8716. The amount of this additional fee shall be based on the cost of drawing and storing the blood samples but at no time shall the additional fee be more than one hundred dollars ($100).

(d)(1) The blood sample shall be stored and released in such a manner as to not identify any party to the adoption.

(2) Any results of the DNA testing shall be stored and released in such a manner as to not identify any party to the adoption. **Leg.H.** Enacted Stats 1992 ch 162 §10 (AB 2650), operative January 1, 1994. Amended Stats 1996 ch 1053 §1 (AB 3241).

§8707. Photo-listing service

(a) The department shall establish a statewide photo-listing service to serve all county adoption agencies and licensed adoption agencies in the state as a means of recruiting adoptive families. The department shall adopt regulations governing the operations of the photo-listing service and shall establish procedures for monitoring compliance with this section.

(b) The photo-listing service shall maintain child specific information that, except as provided in this section, contains a photograph and description of each child who has been legally freed for adoption and whose case plan goal is adoption. Registration of children with the photo-listing service and notification by the licensed adoption agency of changes in a child's photo-listing status shall be reflected in the photo-listing service within 30 working days of receipt of the registration or notification.

(c) The photo-listing service shall be provided to all county adoption agencies, licensed adoption agencies, adoption support groups, and state, regional, and national photo-listings and exchanges requesting copies of the photo-listing service.

(d) All children legally freed for adoption whose case plan goal is adoption shall be photo-listed, unless deferred as provided in subdivision (e) or (f). Adoption agencies shall send a recent photograph and description of each legally freed child to the photo-listing service within 15 working days of the time a child is legally freed for adoption. When adoption has become the case plan goal for a particular child, the adoption agency may photo-list that child before the child becomes legally freed for adoption.

(e) A child shall be deferred from the photo-listing service when the child's foster parents or other identified individuals who have applied to adopt the child are meeting the county adoption agency's or licensed adoption agency's requests for required documentation and are cooperating in the completion of a home study being conducted by the agency.

(f) A child who is 12 years old or older may be deferred from the photo-listing service if the child does not consent to being adopted.

(g) Within 15 working days following a one-year period in which a child is listed in the photo-listing service, the county adoption agency or licensed adoption agency shall submit a revised description and photograph of the child.

(h) County adoption agencies and licensed adoption agencies shall notify the photo-listing service, by telephone, of any adoptive placements or of significant changes in a child's photo-listing status within two working days of the change.

(i) The department shall establish procedures for semiannual review of the photo-listing status of all legally freed children whose case plan goal is adoption, including those who are registered with the photo-listing service and those whose registration has been deferred. **Leg.H.** Enacted Stats 1992 ch 162 §10 (AB 2650), operative January 1, 1994. Amended Stats 1998 ch 1056 §2 (AB 2773); Stats 2012 ch 35 §20 (SB 1013), effective June 27, 2012.

2012 Note: For title and citation of Stats 2012 ch 35 (SB 1013), see 2012 Note following §8506.

§8707.1. Diversity of potential adoptive parents; Construction with Indian Child Welfare Act

(a) The agency responsible for recruitment of potential adoptive parents shall make diligent efforts to recruit individuals who reflect the ethnic, racial, and cultural diversity of children for whom adoptive homes are needed.

(b) This section shall not be construed to affect the application of the federal Indian Child Welfare Act. **Leg.H.** Added Stats 2014 ch 772 §1 (SB 1460), effective January 1, 2015.

§8708. Discrimination in adoption or placement; Effect on application of federal Indian Child Welfare Act

(a) The adoption agency to which a child has been freed for adoption by either relinquishment or termination of parental rights shall not do any of the following:

(1) Deny to any person the opportunity to become an adoptive parent on the basis of the race, color, or national origin of the person or the child involved.

(2) Delay or deny the placement of a child for adoption on the basis of the race, color, or national origin of the adoptive parent or the child involved.

(3) Delay or deny the placement of a child for adoption solely because the prospective, approved adoptive family resides outside the jurisdiction of the department, county adoption agency, or licensed adoption agency. For purposes of this paragraph, an approved adoptive family means a family approved pursuant to the California adoptive applicant assessment standards or approved as a resource family pursuant to Section 1517 of the Health and Safety Code or Section 16519.5 of the Welfare and Institutions Code. If the adoptive applicant assessment was conducted in another state according to that state's standards, the California placing agency shall determine whether the standards of the other state substantially meet the standards and criteria established in California adoption regulations.

(b) This section shall not be construed to affect the application of the federal Indian Child Welfare Act (25 U.S.C. Sec. 1901 and following). **Leg.H.** Added Stats 1995 ch 884 §4 (AB 1743). Amended Stats 1998 ch 1056 §3 (AB 2773); Stats 2003 ch 323 §2 (SB 984); Stats 2012 ch 35 §21 (SB 1013), effective June 27, 2012; Stats 2017 ch 732 §3 (AB 404), effective January 1, 2018.

2012 Note: For title and citation of Stats 2012 ch 35 (SB 1013), see 2012 Note following §8506.

Prior Law: Former §8708, relating to placement preferences regarding racial, ethnic, and religious background, was enacted Stats 1992 ch 162 §10, operative January 1, 1994, and repealed Stats 1995 ch 884 §3.5.

§8709. Consideration of child's religious background; Applicability of federal Indian Child Welfare Act

(a) The department, county adoption agency, or licensed adoption agency to which a child has been freed for adoption by either relinquishment or termination of parental rights may consider the child's religious background in determining an appropriate placement.

(b) This section shall not be construed to affect the application of the federal Indian Child Welfare Act (25 U.S.C. Sec. 1901 and following). **Leg.H.** Added Stats 1995 ch 884 §6 (AB 1743). Amended Stats 2003 ch 323 §3 (SB 984); Stats 2012 ch 35 §22 (SB 1013), effective June 27, 2012.

2012 Note: For title and citation of Stats 2012 ch 35 (SB 1013), see 2012 Note following §8506.

Prior Law: Former §8709, relating to good cause not to follow rules regarding placement preferences in racial, ethnic, and religious background, was enacted Stats 1992 ch 162 §10, operative January 1, 1994, and repealed Stats 1995 ch 884 §5.

§8710. Order of placement preference

(a) If a child is being considered for adoption, the department, county adoption agency, or licensed adoption agency shall first consider adoptive placement in the home of a relative or, in the case of an Indian child, according to the placement preferences and standards set out in subdivisions (c), (d), (e), (f), (g), (h), and (i) of Section 361.31 of the Welfare and Institutions Code. However, if the birth parent refuses to consider a relative or sibling placement, if a relative is not available, if placement with an available relative is not in the child's best interest, or if placement would permanently separate the child from other siblings who are being considered for adoption or who are in foster care and an alternative placement would not require the permanent separation, the foster parent or parents of the child shall be considered with respect to the child along with all other prospective adoptive parents where all of the following conditions are present:

(1) The child has been in foster care with the foster parent or parents for a period of more than four months.

(2) The child has substantial emotional ties to the foster parent or parents.

(3) The child's removal from the foster home would be seriously detrimental to the child's well-being.

(4) The foster parent or parents have made a written request to be considered to adopt the child.

(b) In the case of an Indian child whose foster parent or parents or other prospective adoptive parents do not fall within the placement preferences established in subdivision (c) or (d) of Section 361.31 of the Welfare and Institutions Code, the foster parent or parents or other prospective adoptive parents shall only be considered if the court finds, supported by clear and convincing evidence, that good cause exists to deviate from these placement preferences.

(c) This section does not apply to a child who has been adjudged a dependent of the juvenile court pursuant to Section 300 of the Welfare and Institutions Code.

(d) Upon a request to move a child from a prospective adoptive home for the purpose of placement with siblings or other relatives, the court shall consider the best interests of the child. **Leg.H.** Added Stats 1995 ch 884 §8 (AB 1743). Amended Stats 2006 ch 838 §12 (SB 678), effective January 1, 2007; Stats 2010 ch 588 §6 (AB 2020), effective January 1, 2011; Stats 2012 ch 35 §23 (SB 1013), effective June 27, 2012.

2012 Note: For title and citation of Stats 2012 ch 35 (SB 1013), see 2012 Note following §8506.

Prior Law: Former §8710, relating to search for families meeting racial or ethnic criteria, was enacted Stats 1992 ch 162 §10, operative January 1, 1994, and repealed Stats 1995 ch 884 §7.

§8710.1. Exchange system where no placement plan in jurisdiction

If there is not an adoptive placement plan for a child with an approved adoptive family, as defined in subdivision (c) of Section 8708, within the department's, county adoption agency's, or licensed adoption agency's jurisdiction, then the department, county adoption agency, or licensed adoption agency shall register the child with the exchange system described in Section 8710.2. **Leg.H.** Added Stats 1998 ch 1056 §4 (AB 2773). Amended Stats 2012 ch 35 §24 (SB 1013), effective June 27, 2012.

2012 Note: For title and citation of Stats 2012 ch 35 (SB 1013), see 2012 Note following §8506.

§8710.2. Statewide exchange system

In order to preclude the delays or denials described in paragraph (3) of subdivision (a) of Section 8708, the department shall establish a statewide exchange system that interjurisdictionally matches waiting children and approved adoptive families. The department may create a new statewide exchange system, modify an existing statewide exchange system, such as the photo-listing service described in Section 8707, or designate an existing exchange system, such as the Adoption Exchange Enhancement Program, as the statewide exchange system for purposes of this section. **Leg.H.** Added Stats 1998 ch 1056 §5 (AB 2773). Amended Stats 2019 §114 (AB 991), effective January 1, 2020.

§8710.3. Registration with exchange system

If the department, county adoption agency, or licensed adoption agency has approved a family for adoption pursuant to subdivision (c) of Section 8708 and that family may be appropriate for placement of a child who has been adjudged a dependent child of the juvenile court, the department, county adoption agency, or licensed adoption agency shall register the family with the statewide exchange system established pursuant to Section 8710.2, except in either of the following circumstances:

(a) The family refuses to consent to the registration.

(b) A specific child or children have already been identified for adoptive placement with the family. **Leg.H.** Added Stats 1998 ch 1056 §6 (AB 2773). Amended Stats 2012 ch 35 §25 (SB 1013), effective June 27, 2012.

2012 Note: For title and citation of Stats 2012 ch 35 (SB 1013), see 2012 Note following §8506.

§8710.4. Access to information

(a) The department shall ensure that information regarding families and children registered with the statewide exchange system described in Section 8710.2 is accessible by licensed adoption agency personnel throughout the state. Provision shall be made for secure Internet, telephone, and facsimile access by authorized licensed adoption agency personnel.

(b) Information regarding children maintained by the statewide exchange system described in Section 8710.2 shall be confidential and shall not be disclosed to any parties other than authorized adoption agency personnel, except when consent to disclosure has been received in writing from the birth parents or the court that has jurisdiction. **Leg.H.** Added Stats 1998 ch 1056 §7 (AB 2773).

§8711. Applicability of racial or ethnic criteria

Sections 8708 to 8710.4, inclusive, apply only in determining the placement of a child who has been relinquished for adoption or has been declared free from the custody and control of the birth parents. **Leg.H.** Enacted Stats 1992 ch 162 §10 (AB 2650), operative January 1, 1994. Amended Stats 1998 ch 1056 §8 (AB 2773).

§8711.5. Adoption of regulations

The department shall adopt regulations to administer the provisions of Sections 8708 to 8711, inclusive. **Leg.H.** Added Stats 1995 ch 884 §9 (AB 1743).

§8712. Investigation of prospective adoptive parents

(a)(1) The department, county adoption agency, or licensed adoption agency shall require each person who files an application for adoption to be fingerprinted and shall secure from an appropriate law enforcement agency any criminal record of that person to determine whether the person has ever been convicted of a crime other than a minor traffic violation. The department, county adoption agency, or licensed adoption agency may also secure the person's full criminal record, if any, with the exception of any convictions for which relief has been granted pursuant to Section 1203.49 of the Penal Code. A federal-level criminal offender record request to the Department of Justice shall be submitted with fingerprint images and related information required by the Department of Justice for the purposes of obtaining information as to the existence and content of a record of an out-of-state or federal conviction or arrest of a person or information regarding any out-of-state or federal crimes or arrests for which the Department of Justice establishes that the person is free on bail, or on their own recognizance pending trial or appeal. The Department of Justice shall forward to the Federal Bureau of Investigation any requests for federal summary criminal history information received pursuant to this section. The Department of Justice shall review the information returned from the Federal Bureau of Investigation and shall compile and disseminate a response to the department, county adoption agency, or licensed adoption agency.

(2) The department, county adoption agency, or licensed adoption agency may obtain arrest or conviction records or reports from any law enforcement agency as necessary to the performance of its duties, as provided in this section.

(b) Notwithstanding subdivision (c), the criminal record, if any, shall be taken into consideration when evaluating the prospective adoptive parent, and an assessment of the effects of any criminal history on the ability of the prospective adoptive parent to provide adequate and proper care and guidance to the child shall be included in the report to the court.

(c) The department, county adoption agency, or licensed adoption agency shall not give final approval for an adoptive placement in any home in which the prospective adoptive parent or any adult living in the prospective adoptive home has been convicted of an offense for which an exemption cannot be granted pursuant to subparagraph (A) of paragraph (2) of subdivision (g) of Section 1522 of the Health and Safety Code.

(d) Any fee charged by a law enforcement agency for fingerprinting or for checking or obtaining the criminal record of the applicant shall be paid by the applicant. The department, county adoption agency, or licensed adoption agency may defer, waive, or reduce the fee when its payment would cause economic hardship to prospective adoptive parents detrimental to the welfare of the adopted child, when the child has been in the foster care of the prospective adoptive parents for at least one year, or if necessary for the placement of a special-needs child. **Leg.H.** Enacted Stats 1992 ch 162 §10 (AB 2650), operative January 1, 1994. Amended Stats 2007 ch 464 §1 (AB 340), effective January 1, 2008; Stats 2008 ch 701 §1 (AB 2651), effective September 30, 2008; Stats 2012 ch 35 §26 (SB 1013), effective June 27, 2012; Stats 2014 ch 708 §1 (AB 1585), effective January 1, 2015; Stats 2015 ch 303 §151 (AB 731), effective January 1, 2016; Stats 2016 ch 612 §10 (AB 1997), effective January 1, 2017; Stats 2017 ch 733 §1 (SB 213), effective January 1, 2018; Stats 2019 ch 115 §121 (AB 1817), effective January 1, 2020.

2016 Note: For adoption of regulations, see the 2016 Note following §6552.
2012 Note: For title and citation of Stats 2012 ch 35 (SB 1013), see 2012 Note following §8506.

§8713. Concealment or removal of child from county

(a) In no event may a child who has been freed for adoption be removed from the county in which the child was placed, by any person who has not petitioned to adopt the child, without first obtaining the written consent of the department, county adoption agency, or licensed adoption agency responsible for the child.

(b) During the pendency of an adoption proceeding:

(1) The child proposed to be adopted shall not be concealed from the agency that is investigating the adoption or from the court with jurisdiction over the adoption proceeding.

(2) The child shall not be removed from the county of the petitioner's residence at the time of placement, unless the petitioners or other interested persons first obtain permission for the removal from the court, after giving advance written notice of intent to obtain the court's permission to the department, county adoption agency, or licensed adoption agency responsible for the child. Upon proof of giving notice, permission may be granted by the court if, within a period of 15 days after the date of giving notice, no objections are filed with the court by the department, county adoption agency, or licensed adoption agency responsible for the child. If the department, county adoption agency, or licensed adoption agency files objections within the 15-day period, upon the request of the petitioners the court shall immediately set the matter for hearing and give to the objector, the petitioners, and the party or parties requesting permission for the removal reasonable notice of the hearing by certified mail, return receipt requested, to the address of each as shown in the records of the adoption proceeding. Upon a finding that the objections are without good cause, the court may grant the requested permission for removal of the child, subject to any limitations that appear to be in the child's best interest.

(c) This section does not apply in any of the following situations:

(1) When the child is absent for a period of not more than 30 days from the county of the petitioner's residence at the time of placement, unless a notice of recommendation of denial of petition has been personally served on the petitioners or the court has issued an order prohibiting the child's removal from the county of the petitioner's residence at the time of placement, pending consideration of any of the following:

(A) The suitability of the petitioners.

(B) The care provided the child.

(C) The availability of the legally required agency consents to the adoption.

(2) Where the child has been returned to and remains in the custody and control of the child's birth parent or parents.

(3) Where written consent for the removal of the child is obtained from the department, county adoption agency, or licensed adoption agency responsible for the child.

(d) A violation of this section is a violation of Section 280 of the Penal Code.

(e) Neither this section nor Section 280 of the Penal Code may be construed to render lawful any act that is unlawful under any other applicable law. **Leg.H.** Enacted Stats 1992 ch 162 §10 (AB 2650), operative January 1, 1994. Amended Stats 2012 ch 35 §27 (SB 1013), effective June 27, 2012; Stats 2022 ch 159 §3 (AB 2495), effective January 1, 2023.

2012 Note: For title and citation of Stats 2012 ch 35 (SB 1013), see 2012 Note following §8506.

§8714. Adoption petition and order; Notice; Filing of postadoption contract agreement; Consolidation of guardianship proceeding

(a) A person desiring to adopt a nondependent child may for that purpose file an adoption request in a county authorized by Section 8609.5. A person desiring to adopt a child who has been adjudged to be a dependent of the juvenile court pursuant to Section 300 of the Welfare and Institutions Code, freed for adoption by the juvenile court, and placed for adoption with the petitioner, may file the adoption request either in the county where the petitioner resides or in the county where the child was freed for adoption.

(b) The court clerk shall immediately notify the department at Sacramento in writing of the pendency of the proceeding and of any subsequent action taken.

(c) If the petitioner has entered into a postadoption contact agreement as set forth in Section 8616.5, the petitioner shall file the agreement, signed by the participating parties, with the court before the adoption is finalized.

(d) The caption of the adoption petition shall contain the names of the petitioners, but not the child's name. The petition shall state the child's sex and date of birth. The name the child had before adoption shall appear in the joinder signed by the licensed adoption agency.

(e) If the child is the subject of a guardianship petition, the adoption petition shall so state and shall include the caption and docket number or have attached a copy of the letters of the guardianship or temporary guardianship. The petitioners shall notify the court of any petition for guardianship or temporary guardianship filed after the adoption petition. The guardianship proceeding shall be consolidated with the adoption proceeding.

(f) The order of adoption shall contain the child's adopted name and the name the child had before adoption. **Leg.H.** Enacted Stats 1992 ch 162 §10 (AB 2650), operative January 1, 1994. Amended Stats 1993 ch 219 §190 (AB 1500); Stats 2000 ch 910 §2 (AB 2921), ch 930 §1 (SB 2157); Stats 2002 ch 1112 §1 (AB 746); Stats 2003 ch 251 §6 (SB 182); Stats 2012 ch 638 §9 (AB 1757), effective January 1, 2013; Stats 2016 ch 474 §10 (AB 2882), effective January 1, 2017; Stats 2022 ch 159 §4 (AB 2495), effective January 1, 2023; Stats 2023 ch 851 §7 (AB 1650), effective January 1, 2024.

§8714.5. Adoption by relative; Legislative findings; Petition; Notice; Filing of postadoption contact agreement; Consolidation of guardianship proceeding

(a) The Legislature finds and declares the following:

(1) It is the intent of the Legislature to expedite legal permanency for children who cannot return to their parents and to remove barriers to adoption by relatives of children who are already in the dependency system or who are at risk of entering the dependency system.

(2) This goal will be achieved by empowering families, including extended families, to care for their own children safely and permanently whenever possible, by preserving existing family relationships, thereby causing the least amount of disruption to the child and the family, and by recognizing the importance of sibling and half-sibling relationships.

(b) A relative desiring to adopt a child may for that purpose file a petition in the county in which the petitioner resides. Where a child has been adjudged to be a dependent of the juvenile court pursuant to Section 300 of the Welfare and Institutions Code, and thereafter has been freed for adoption by the juvenile court, the petition may be filed either in the county where the petitioner resides or in the county where the child was freed for adoption.

(c) Upon the filing of a petition for adoption by a relative, the clerk of the court shall immediately notify the State Department of Social Services in Sacramento in writing of the pendency of the proceeding and of any subsequent action taken.

(d) If the adopting relative has entered into a postadoption contact agreement with the birth parent as set forth in Section 8616.5 and the agreement, signed by the participating parties, shall be attached to and filed with the petition for adoption under subdivision (b).

(e) The caption of the adoption petition shall contain the name of the relative petitioner. The petition shall state the child's name, sex, and date of birth.

(f) If the child is the subject of a guardianship petition, the adoption petition shall so state and shall include the caption and docket number or have attached a copy of the letters of the guardianship or temporary guardianship. The petitioner shall notify the court of any petition for adoption. The guardianship proceeding shall be consolidated with the adoption proceeding, and the consolidated case shall be heard and decided in the court in which the adoption is pending.

(g) The order of adoption shall contain the child's adopted name and, if requested by the adopting relative, or if requested by the child who is 12 years of age or older, the name the child had before adoption.

(h) For purposes of this section, "relative" means an adult who is related to the child or the child's half-sibling by blood or affinity, including all relatives whose status is preceded by the words "step," "great," "great-great," or "grand," or the spouse of any of these persons, even if the marriage was terminated by death or dissolution. **Leg.H.** Added Stats 1997 ch 793 §4 (AB 1544). Amended Stats 2000 ch 910 §3 (AB 2921), ch 930 §2 (SB 2157); Stats 2002 ch 784 §112 (SB 1316); Stats 2003 ch 251 §7 (SB 182); Stats 2008 ch 534 §9 (SB 1726), effective January 1, 2009.

§8714.7. [Section renumbered 2003]

Leg.H. Added Stats 1997 ch 793 §5 (AB 1544). Amended Stats 2000 ch 910 §4 (AB 2921), ch 930 §3 (SB 2157). Amended and renumbered Fam C §8616.5 by Stats 2003 ch 251 §8 (SB 182).

§8715. Report of department or agency

(a) The department, county adoption agency, or licensed adoption agency, whichever is a party to, or joins in, the petition, shall submit a full report of the facts of the case to the court.

(b) If the child has been adjudged to be a dependent of the juvenile court pursuant to Section 300 of the Welfare and Institutions Code, and has thereafter been freed for adoption by the juvenile court, the report required by this section shall describe whether the requirements of subdivision (e) of Section 16002 of the Welfare and Institutions Code have been completed and what, if any, plan exists for facilitation of postadoptive contact between the child who is the subject of the adoption petition and the child's siblings and half siblings.

(c) If a petition for adoption has been filed with a postadoption contact agreement pursuant to Section 8616.5, the report shall address whether the postadoption contact agreement has been entered into voluntarily, and whether it is in the best interest of the child who is the subject of the petition.

(d) The department may also submit a report in those cases in which a county adoption agency, or licensed adoption agency is a party or joins in the adoption petition.

(e) If a petitioner is a resident of a state other than California, an updated and current home study report, conducted and approved by a licensed adoption agency or other authorized resource in the state in which the petitioner resides, shall be reviewed and endorsed by the department, county adoption agency, or licensed adoption agency, if the standards and criteria established for a home study report in the other state are substantially commensurate with the home study standards and criteria established in California adoption regulations. **Leg.H.** Enacted Stats 1992 ch 162 §10 (AB 2650), operative January 1, 1994. Amended Stats 1997 ch 793 §6 (AB 1544); Stats 1998 ch 1072 §1 (AB 2196); Stats 2000 ch 910 §4.5 (AB 2921), ch 930 §4 (SB 2157); Stats 2002 ch 1112 §2 (AB 746); Stats 2003 ch 251 §9 (SB 182); Stats 2012 ch 35 §28 (SB 1013), effective June 27, 2012; Stats 2019 ch 115 §122 (AB 1817), effective January 1, 2020.

2012 Note: For title and citation of Stats 2012 ch 35 (SB 1013), see 2012 Note following §8506.

§8716. Fee

Where a petition is filed for the adoption of a child who has been placed for adoption by a county adoption agency, licensed county adoption agency, or the department, the county adoption agency, licensed adoption agency, or department may, at the time of filing a favorable report with the court, require the petitioners to pay to the agency, as agent of the state, or to the department, a fee of five hundred dollars ($500). The county adoption agency, licensed adoption agency, or department may defer, waive, or reduce the fee if its payment would cause economic hardship to the prospective adoptive parents detrimental to the welfare of the adopted child, if the child has been in the foster care of the prospective adoptive parents for at least one year, or if necessary for the placement of a special-needs child. **Leg.H.** Enacted Stats 1992 ch 162 §10 (AB 2650), operative January 1, 1994. Amended Stats 2012 ch 35 §29 (SB 1013), effective June 27, 2012.

2012 Note: For title and citation of Stats 2012 ch 35 (SB 1013), see 2012 Note following §8506.

§8717. Copy of report or findings to petitioner or attorney

When any report or findings are submitted to the court by the department, county adoption agency, or licensed adoption agency, a copy of the report or findings, whether favorable or unfavorable, shall be given to the petitioner's attorney in the proceeding, if the petitioner has an attorney of record, or to the petitioner. **Leg.H.** Enacted Stats 1992 ch 162 §10 (AB 2650), operative January 1, 1994. Amended Stats 2012 ch 35 §30 (SB 1013), effective June 27, 2012.

2012 Note: For title and citation of Stats 2012 ch 35 (SB 1013), see 2012 Note following §8506.

§8718. Appearance of prospective adoptive parents and child

The prospective adoptive parents and the child proposed to be adopted shall appear before the court pursuant to Sections 8612 and 8613. **Leg.H.** Enacted Stats 1992 ch 162 §10 (AB 2650), operative January 1, 1994.

§8719. Notice to department of motion to withdraw or dismiss petition

If the petitioners move to withdraw the adoption petition or to dismiss the proceeding, the court clerk shall immediately notify the department at Sacramento of the action. **Leg.H.** Enacted Stats 1992 ch 162 §10 (AB 2650), operative January 1, 1994.

§8720. Unfavorable recommendation by department or agency

(a) If the department, county adoption agency, or licensed adoption agency finds that the home of the petitioners is not suitable for the child or that the required agency consents are not available and the department, county adoption agency, or licensed adoption agency recommends that the petition be denied, or if the petitioners desire to withdraw the petition and the department, county adoption agency, or licensed adoption agency recommends that the petition be denied, the clerk upon receipt of the report of the department, county adoption agency, or licensed adoption agency shall immediately refer it to the court for review.

(b) Upon receipt of the report, the court shall set a date for a hearing of the petition and shall give reasonable notice of the hearing to the department, county adoption agency, or licensed adoption agency, the petitioners, and, if necessary, the birth parents, by certified mail, return receipt requested, to the address of each as shown in the proceeding.

(c) The department, county adoption agency, or licensed adoption agency shall appear to represent the child. **Leg.H.** Enacted Stats 1992 ch 162 §10 (AB 2650), operative January 1, 1994. Amended Stats 2012 ch 35 §31 (SB 1013), effective June 27, 2012.

2012 Note: For title and citation of Stats 2012 ch 35 (SB 1013), see 2012 Note following §8506.

CHAPTER 2.5
ADOPTIONS BY RELATIVE CAREGIVERS OR FOSTER PARENTS

Abbreviated home study assessment; Applicability. §8730.
Timing of assessment. §8731.
Report of medical examination. §8732.
Information to be provided. §8733.
Training programs. §8734.
Denial of approval. §8735.
Use of requirements of chapter. §8736.

§8730. Abbreviated home study assessment; Applicability

(a) Subject to the requirements of subdivision (b), the department, county adoption agency, or licensed adoption agency may provide an abbreviated home study assessment for any of the following:

(1) A licensed or certified foster parent with whom the child has lived for a minimum of six months.

(2) An approved relative caregiver or nonrelated extended family member with whom the child has had an ongoing and significant relationship.

(3) A court-appointed relative guardian of the child who has been investigated and approved pursuant to the guardianship investigation process and has had physical custody of the child for at least one year.

(4) A prospective adoptive parent who has completed an agency-supervised adoption within the last two years.

(b) Unless otherwise ordered by a court with jurisdiction over the child, home study assessments completed pursuant to subdivision (a) shall include, at minimum, all of the following:

(1) A criminal records check, as required by all applicable state and federal statutes and regulations.

(2) A determination that the applicant has sufficient financial stability to support the child and ensure that an adoption assistance program payment or other government assistance to which the child is entitled is used exclusively to meet the child's needs. In making this determination, the experience of the applicant only while the child was in the applicant's care shall be considered. For purposes of this section, the applicant shall be required to provide verification of employment records or income or both.

(3) A determination that the applicant has not abused or neglected the child while the child has been in the applicant's care and has fostered the healthy growth and development of the child. This determination shall include a review of the disciplinary practices of the applicant to ensure that the practices are age appropriate and do not physically or emotionally endanger the child.

(4) A determination that the applicant is not likely to abuse or neglect the child in the future and that the applicant can protect the child, ensure necessary care and supervision, and foster the child's healthy growth and development.

(5) A determination that the applicant can address issues that may affect the child's well-being, including, but not limited to, the child's physical health, mental health, and educational needs.

(6) An interview with the applicant, an interview with each individual residing in the home, and an interview with the child to be adopted.

(7) A review by the department, county adoption agency, or licensed adoption agency of all previous guardianship investigation reports, home study assessments, and preplacement evaluations of each applicant. Notwithstanding any other law regarding the confidential nature of these reports, upon the written request of the department, county adoption agency, or licensed adoption agency that is accompanied by a signed release from the applicant, the department, county adoption agency, or licensed adoption agency may receive a copy of any of these reports from a court, investigating agency, or other person or entity in possession of the report. The department, county adoption agency, or licensed adoption agency shall document attempts to obtain the report and, if applicable, the reason the report is unavailable.

(c) The department may promulgate regulations as necessary or appropriate to implement this section.

(d) This section does not apply to independent adoptions filed pursuant to Chapter 3 (commencing with Section 8800). **Leg.H.** Added Stats 1998 ch 983 §3 (AB 2286). Amended Stats 2012 ch 35 §32 (SB 1013), effective June 27, 2012; Stats 2013 ch 743 §2 (AB 848), effective January 1, 2014; Stats 2014 ch 71 §55 (SB 1304), effective January 1, 2015; Stats 2019 ch 115 §123 (AB 1817), effective January 1, 2020.

2012 Note: For title and citation of Stats 2012 ch 35 (SB 1013), see 2012 Note following §8506.

§8731. Timing of assessment

If the prospective adoptive parent of a child is a foster parent, the assessment or home study described in Section 8730 shall not be initiated until the child to be adopted has resided in the home of the foster parent for at least six months. **Leg.H.** Added Stats 1998 ch 983 §3 (AB 2286).

§8732. Report of medical examination

A report of a medical examination of the foster parent with whom the child has lived for a minimum of six months or the relative caregiver who has had an ongoing and significant relationship with the child shall be included in the assessment of each applicant unless the department, county adoption agency, or licensed adoption agency determines that, based on other available information, this report is unnecessary. **Leg.H.** Added Stats 1998 ch 983 §3 (AB 2286). Amended Stats 2012 ch 35 §33 (SB 1013), effective June 27, 2012; Stats 2020 ch 104 §2 (AB 2944), effective September 18, 2020.

2012 Note: For title and citation of Stats 2012 ch 35 (SB 1013), see 2012 Note following §8506.

§8733. Information to be provided

The department, county adoption agency, or licensed adoption agency shall require the adoptive parent to be provided with information related to the specific needs of the child to be adopted, that, as determined by the licensed adoption agency, may include information regarding the following: issues surrounding birth parents, the effects of abuse and neglect on children, cultural and racial issues, sexuality, contingency planning for children in the event of the parents' death or disability, financial assistance for adopted children, common childhood disabilities, including, but not limited to, emotional disturbances, attention deficit disorder, learning disabilities, speech and hearing impairment, and dyslexia, the importance of sibling and half-sibling relationships, and other issues related to adoption and child development and the availability of counseling to deal with these issues. **Leg.H.** Added Stats 1998 ch 983 §3 (AB 2286). Amended Stats 2012 ch 35 §34 (SB 1013), effective June 27, 2012.

2012 Note: For title and citation of Stats 2012 ch 35 (SB 1013), see 2012 Note following §8506.

§8734. Training programs

The department shall encourage adoption agencies to make adoption training programs available to prospective adoptive families. **Leg.H.** Added Stats 1998 ch 983 §3 (AB 2286).

§8735. Denial of approval

The department shall adopt regulations requiring county adoption agencies and licensed adoption agencies to inform the agency responsible for the foster care placement when a relative caregiver or foster parent has been denied approval to adopt based on an inability of the relative caregiver or foster parent to provide for the mental and emotional health, safety, and security of the child and to recommend either that the relative caregiver or foster parent be provided with additional support and supervision or that the child be removed from the home of the relative caregiver or foster parent. **Leg.H.** Added Stats 1998 ch 983 §3 (AB 2286). Amended Stats 2012 ch 35 §35 (SB 1013), effective June 27, 2012.

2012 Note: For title and citation of Stats 2012 ch 35 (SB 1013), see 2012 Note following §8506.

§8736. Use of requirements of chapter

The requirements of this chapter shall not be used as basis for removing a child who has been placed with a relative caregiver or foster parent prior to January 1, 1999, unless the noncompliance with the standards described therein present a danger to the health, safety, or emotional well-being of the child. **Leg.H.** Added Stats 1998 ch 983 §3 (AB 2286).

CHAPTER 3
INDEPENDENT ADOPTIONS

Legislative declaration concerning attorney-client relationship. §8800.
Selection of adoptive parents. §8801.
Placement for adoption. §8801.3.
Duties of adoption service provider. §8801.5.
Witnessing signature of adoption placement agreement; Interview; Concerns of birth parent concerning placement. §8801.7.
Who may file petition; Contents; Child's name; Order. §8802.
Concealment or removal of child from county. §8803.
Notice to department of motion to withdraw or dismiss petition. §8804.
Removal of child from home of petitioners. §8805.
Duty of department or agency. §8806.
Investigation of proposed independent adoption; Report. §8807.
Interview by department or agency. §8808.
Fees. §8810.
Investigation of prospective adoptive parents. §8811.
Certification of prospective adoptive parents; Preplacement evaluation; Cost for renewal. §8811.5.
Payment by prospective adoptive parents of specified fees and expenses; Receipts. §8812.
Request for information on status of adoption. §8813.
Consent of birth parents to adoption. §8814.
Revocation of consent; Reinstatement of original consent; Waiver of right to revoke; Time limits. §8814.5.
Irrevocability of consent. §8815.
Consent of agency or department. §8816.
Medical report on child and biological parents; Parents' blood sample. §8817.
Statement to birth parents at time of consent. §8818.
Notice to birth parent on termination of parental rights. §8819.
Appeal from department or agency disapproval. §8820.
Copy of report or findings to petitioner or attorney. §8821.
Unfavorable recommendation by department or agency. §8822.
Appearance of prospective adoptive parents and child. §8823.

§8800. Legislative declaration concerning attorney-client relationship

(a) The Legislature finds and declares that an attorney's ability to effectively represent a client may be seriously impaired when conflict of interest deprives the client of the attorney's undivided loyalty and effort. The Legislature further finds and declares that the relation between attorney and client is a fiduciary relation of the very highest character, and binds the attorney to the most conscientious fidelity.

(b) The Legislature finds that Rule 2-111(A)(2) of the State Bar Rules of Professional Conduct provides that an attorney shall not withdraw from employment until the attorney has taken reasonable steps to avoid foreseeable prejudice to the rights of the client, including giving due notice to the client, allowing time for employment of other counsel, delivering to the client all papers and property to which the client is entitled, and complying with applicable laws and rules.

(c) The Legislature declares that in an independent adoption proceeding, whether or not written consent is obtained, multiple representation by an attorney should be avoided whenever a birth parent displays the slightest reason for the attorney to believe any controversy might arise. The Legislature finds and declares that it is the duty of the attorney, when a conflict of interest occurs, to withdraw promptly from any case, advise the parties to retain independent counsel, refrain from taking positions in opposition to any of these former clients, and thereafter maintain an impartial, fair, and open attitude toward the new attorneys.

(d) Notwithstanding any other law, it is unethical for an attorney to undertake the representation of both the prospective adoptive parents and the birth parents of a child in any negotiations or proceedings in connection with an adoption unless a written consent is obtained from both parties. The written consent shall include all of the following:

(1) A notice to the birth parents, in the form specified in this section, of their right to have an independent attorney advise and represent them in the adoption proceeding and that the prospective adoptive parents may be required to pay the reasonable attorney's fees up to a maximum of five hundred dollars ($500) for that representation, unless a higher fee is agreed to by the parties.

(2) A notice to the birth parents that they may waive their right to an independent attorney and may be represented by the attorney representing the prospective adoptive parents.

(3) A waiver by the birth parents of representation by an independent attorney.

(4) An agreement that the attorney representing the prospective adoptive parents shall represent the birth parents.

(e) Upon the petition or motion of any party, or upon motion of the court, the court may appoint an attorney to represent a child's birth parent or parents in negotiations or proceedings in connection with the child's adoption.

(f) The birth parent or parents may have an attorney, other than the attorney representing the interests of the prospective adoptive parents, to advise them fully of the adoption procedures and of their legal rights. The birth parent or parents also may retain an attorney to represent them in negotiations or proceedings in connection with the child's adoption. The court may award attorney's fees and costs for just cause and based upon the ability of the parties to pay those fees and costs.

(g) In the initial communication between the attorney retained by or representing the prospective adoptive parents and the birth parents, or as soon thereafter as reasonable, but before any written consent for dual representation, the attorney shall advise the birth parents of their rights regarding an independent attorney and that it is possible to waive the independent attorney.

(h) The attorney retained by or representing the prospective adoptive parents shall inform the prospective adoptive parents in writing that the birth parent or parents can revoke consent to the adoption pursuant to Section 8814.5 and that any moneys expended in negotiations or proceedings in connection with the child's adoption are not reimbursable. The prospective adoptive parents shall sign a statement to indicate their understanding of this information.

(i) Written consent to dual representation shall be filed with the court before the filing of the birth parent's consent to adoption. **Leg.H.** Enacted Stats 1992 ch 162 §10 (AB 2650), operative January 1, 1994. Amended Stats 1993 ch 450 §1 (SB 255), operative until January 1, 1995, ch 450 §2 (SB 255), operative January 1, 1995; Stats 2019 ch 115 §124 (AB 1817), effective January 1, 2020.

§8801. Selection of adoptive parents

(a) The selection of a prospective adoptive parent or parents shall be personally made by the child's birth parent or parents and may not be delegated to an agent. The act of selection by the birth parent or parents shall be based upon personal knowledge of the prospective adoptive parent or parents.

(b) "Personal knowledge" as used in this section includes, but is not limited to, substantially correct knowledge of all of the following regarding the prospective adoptive parents: their full legal names, ages, religion, race or ethnicity, length of current marriage and number of previous marriages, employment, whether other children or adults reside in their home, whether there are other children who do not reside in their home and the child support obligation for these children and any failure to meet these obligations, any health conditions curtailing their normal daily activities or reducing their normal life expectancies, any convictions for crimes other than minor traffic violations, any removals of children from their care due to child abuse or neglect, and their general area of residence or, upon request, their address. **Leg.H.** Added Stats 1993 ch 758 §6.4 (SB 792), operative January 1, 1995. Amended Stats 2019 ch 115 §125 (AB 1817), effective January 1, 2020.

Prior Law: Former §8801, similar to the present section, was enacted Stats 1992 ch 162 §10, operative January 1, 1994, amended Stats 1993 ch 219 §191, ch 758 §6.3, operative until January 1, 1995, and repealed, operative January 1, 1995, by its own terms.

1993 Note: Section 8801, as added by ch 758 §6.4, applies to all petitions for independent adoption filed on or after January 1, 1995. Petitions filed prior to, and pending on, that date shall be governed by the law in effect on December 31, 1994. Stats 1993 ch 758 §17(b).

§8801.3. Placement for adoption

A child shall not be considered to have been placed for adoption unless each of the following is true:

(a) Each birth parent placing the child for adoption has been advised of their rights, and if desired, has been counseled pursuant to Section 8801.5.

(b) The adoption service provider, each prospective adoptive parent, and each birth parent placing the child have signed an adoption placement agreement on a form prescribed by the department. The signing of the agreement shall satisfy all of the following requirements:

(1) Each birth parent shall have been advised of their rights pursuant to Section 8801.5 at least 10 days before signing the agreement, unless the adoption service provider finds exigent circumstances that shall be set forth in the adoption placement agreement.

(2) The agreement may not be signed by either the birth parents or the prospective adoptive parents until the time of discharge of the birth mother from the hospital. However, if the birth mother remains hospitalized for a period longer than the hospitalization of the child, the agreement may be signed by all parties at the time of or after the child's discharge from the hospital but prior to the birth mother's discharge from the hospital if the birth mother's competency to sign is verified by the attending physician and surgeon before signing the agreement.

(3) The birth parents and prospective adoptive parents shall sign the agreement in the presence of an adoption service provider.

(4) The adoption service provider who witnesses the signatures shall keep the original of the adoption placement agreement and immediately forward it and supporting documentation as required by the department to the department or delegated county adoption agency.

(5) The child is not deemed to be placed for adoption with the prospective adoptive parents until the adoption placement agreement has been signed and witnessed.

(6) If the birth parent is not located in this state or country, the adoption placement agreement shall be signed before an adoption service provider or, for purposes of identification of the birth parent only, before a notary or other person authorized to perform notarial acts in the state or country in which the birth parent is located. This paragraph is not applicable to intercountry adoptions, as defined in Section 8527, which shall be governed by Chapter 4 (commencing with Section 8900).

(c) The adoption placement agreement form shall include all of the following:

(1) A statement that the birth parent received the advisement of rights and the date upon which it was received.

(2) A statement that the birth parent understands that the placement is for the purpose of adoption and that if the birth parent takes no further action, on the 31st day after signing the adoption placement agreement, the agreement shall become a permanent and irrevocable consent to the adoption.

(3) A statement that the birth parent signs the agreement having personal knowledge of certain facts regarding the prospective adoptive parents as provided in Section 8801.

(4) A statement that the adoptive parents have been informed of the basic health and social history of the birth parents.

(5) A consent to the adoption that may be revoked as provided by Section 8814.5.

(d) The adoption placement agreement shall also meet the requirements of the Interstate Compact on the Placement of Children in Section 7901. **Leg.H.** Added Stats 1993 ch 758 §7 (SB 792), operative January 1, 1995. Amended Stats 1994 ch 585 §3 (AB 3336), operative January 1, 1995; Stats 2000 ch 937 §3 (AB 2433); Stats 2001 ch 688 §1 (SB 104); Stats 2019 ch 115 §126 (AB 1817), effective January 1, 2020.

Prior Law: There was another section of this number, similar to the present section, which was added Stats 1993 ch 219 §192, but failed to become operative as it was repealed Stats 1993 ch 758 §6.5.

§8801.5. Duties of adoption service provider

(a) Each birth parent placing a child for adoption shall be advised of their rights by an adoption service provider.

(b) The birth parent shall be advised of their rights in a face-to-face meeting in which the birth parent may ask questions and have questions answered, as provided by Section 8801.3.

(c) The department shall prescribe the format and process for advising birth parents of their rights, the content of which shall include, but not be limited to, the following:

(1) The alternatives to adoption.

(2) The alternative types of adoption, including a description of the full procedures and timeframes involved in each type.

(3) The full rights and responsibilities of the birth parent with respect to adoption, including the need to keep the department informed of the birth parent's current address in case of a medical emergency requiring contact and of providing a full health history.

(4) The right to separate legal counsel paid for by the prospective adoptive parents upon the request of the birth parent, as provided for by Section 8800.

(5) The right to a minimum of three separate counseling sessions, each to be held on different days, to be paid for by the prospective adoptive parents upon the request of the birth parents, as provided for by subdivision (d).

(d) Each person advised pursuant to this section shall be offered at least three separate counseling sessions, to be held on different days. Each counseling session shall be not less than 50 minutes in duration. The counseling may be provided by the adoption service provider who informs the birth parent of their rights, or by another adoption service provider, or by a licensed psychotherapist, as defined by Section 1010 of the Evidence Code, as elected by the person, and after having been informed of these choices.

(e) The counselor owes a duty of care to the birth parent being counseled, similar to the duty of care established by a psychotherapist-patient relationship, regardless of who pays the fees of the counselor. A counselor shall not have a contractual relationship with the adoptive parents, an attorney for the adoptive parents, or any other individual or an organization performing any type of services for the adoptive parents and for which the adoptive parents are paying a fee, except as relates to payment of the birth parents' fee.

(f) The advisement and counseling fees shall be paid by the prospective adoptive parents at the request of the birth parent.

(g) Failure to fulfill the duties specified in this section shall not be construed as a basis for setting aside the consent or the adoption, but may give rise to a cause of action for malpractice or negligence against those professionals or agencies serving as adoption service providers that are responsible for fulfilling the duties. **Leg.H.** Added Stats 1993 ch 758 §8 (SB 792), operative January 1, 1995. Amended Stats 1994 ch 585 §4 (AB 3336), operative January 1, 1995; Stats 1997 ch 559 §2 (SB 1121); Stats 2019 ch 115 §127 (AB 1817), effective January 1, 2020.

Prior Law: There was another section of this number, similar to the present section, which was added Stats 1993 ch 219 §193, but failed to become operative as it was repealed Stats 1993 ch 758 §7.5.

1993 Note: Section 8801.5 applies to all petitions for independent adoption filed on or after January 1, 1995. Petitions filed prior to, and pending on, that date shall be governed by the law in effect on December 31, 1994. Stats 1993 ch 758 §17(b).

§8801.7. Witnessing signature of adoption placement agreement; Interview; Concerns of birth parent concerning placement

(a) An adoption service provider shall also witness the signature of the adoption placement agreement and offer to interview the birth parent after the placement of the child with prospective adoptive parents. The interview shall occur within 10 working days after the placement of the child for adoption and shall include a consideration of any concerns or problems the birth parent has with the placement, a readvisement of the rights of the birth parent, and the taking of the health and social history of the birth parent, if not taken previously.

(b) The adoption service provider shall immediately notify the department or delegated county adoption agency if the birth parent is not interviewed as provided in subdivision (a) or if there are any concerns regarding the placement. If the birth parent wishes to revoke the consent, the adoption service provider shall assist the birth parent in obtaining the return of the child.

(c) The adoption service provider owes a very high duty of care to the birth parent being advised, regardless of who pays the provider's fees. The duty of care specifically does not include a duty to investigate information provided by the birth parents, prospective adoptive parents, or their attorneys or agents. No adoption service provider shall have a contractual relationship with prospective adoptive parents, an attorney or representative for prospective adoptive parents, or any individual or organization providing services of any type to prospective adoptive parents for which the adoptive parents are paying a fee, except as relates to the payment of the fees for the advising and counseling of the birth parents.

(d) This section shall become operative on January 1, 1995. **Leg.H.** Added Stats 1993 ch 758 §9 (SB 792), operative January 1, 1995.

Prior Law: There was another section of this number, similar to the present section, which was added Stats 1993 ch 219 §194, but failed to become operative as it was repealed Stats 1993 ch 758 §8.5.

1993 Note: Section 8801.7 applies to all petitions for independent adoption filed on or after January 1, 1995. Petitions filed prior to, and pending on, that date shall be governed by the law in effect on December 31, 1994. Stats 1993 ch 758 §17(b).

§8802. Who may file petition; Contents; Child's name; Order

(a) Any of the following adult persons who desire to adopt a child may, for that purpose, file an adoption request in a county authorized by Section 8609.5:

(1) A person who is related to the child or the child's half sibling by blood or affinity, including all relatives whose status is preceded by the words "step," "great," "great-great," or "grand," or the spouse of any of these persons, even if the marriage was terminated by death or dissolution.

(2) A person named in the will of a deceased parent as an intended adoptive parent where the child has no other parent.

(3) A person with whom a child has been placed for adoption, in which case a copy of the independent adoption placement agreement shall be attached to the petition.

(4) A person who has been the child's legal guardian for more than one year. However, if the guardian was nominated by a parent for a purpose other than adoption and for a specified time period, or if the guardianship was established pursuant to Section 360 of the Welfare and Institutions Code, the guardianship shall have been in existence for at least three years, unless parental rights have already been terminated.

(5) If the child is alleged to have been abandoned pursuant to Section 7822, a person who has been the child's legal guardian for more than six months. The legal guardian may file a petition pursuant to Section 7822 in the same court and concurrently with the adoption request.

(6) A person named in a court order terminating parental rights as the child's legal guardian or prospective adoptive parent.

(b) The court clerk shall immediately notify the department in Sacramento in writing of the pendency of the proceeding and of any subsequent action taken.

(c) The adoption request shall contain an allegation that the petitioners will file promptly with the department or delegated county adoption agency information required by the department in the investigation of the proposed adoption. The omission of the allegation from the adoption request does not affect the jurisdiction of the court to proceed or the validity of an adoption order or other order based on the adoption request.

(d) The caption of the adoption request shall contain the names of the petitioners, but not the child's name. The body of the adoption request shall state the child's sex and date of birth and the name the child had before adoption.

(e) If the child is the subject of a guardianship petition, the adoption request shall so state and shall include the caption and docket number or have attached a copy of the letters of the guardianship or temporary guardianship. The petitioners shall notify the court of any petition for guardianship or temporary guardianship filed after the adoption request. The guardianship proceeding shall be consolidated with the adoption proceeding, and the consolidated case shall be heard and decided in the court in which the adoption is pending.

(f) If the petitioner has entered into a postadoption contact agreement as set forth in Section 8616.5, the petitioner shall file the agreement, signed by the participating parties, with the court before the adoption is finalized.

(g) The order of adoption shall contain the child's adopted name and the name the child had before adoption. **Leg.H.** Added Stats 1993 ch 758 §9.2 (SB 792), operative January 1, 1995. Amended Stats 1996 ch 510 §1 (AB 2165); Stats 2000 ch 937 §4 (AB 2433); Stats 2002 ch 1112 §3 (AB 746); Stats 2003 ch 62 §88 (SB 600), ch. 81 §1 (AB 416) (ch. 81 prevails); Stats 2004 ch 858 §5 (SB 1357); Stats 2007 ch 47 §5 (SB 313), effective January 1, 2008; Stats 2008 ch 534 §10 (SB 1726), effective January 1, 2009; Stats 2012 ch 638 §10 (AB 1757), effective January 1, 2013; Stats 2022 ch 159 §5 (AB 2495), effective January 1, 2023; Stats 2023 ch 851 §8 (AB 1650), effective January 1, 2024.

Prior Law: Former Fam C §8802, similar to the present section, was enacted Stats 1992 ch 162 §10, operative January 1, 1994, amended Stats 1993 ch 219 §195, ch 758 §9.1, operative until January 1, 1995, and repealed, operative January 1, 1995, by its own terms.

1993 Note: Section 8802, as added by ch 758 §9.2, applies to all petitions for independent adoption filed on or after January 1, 1995. Petitions filed prior to, and pending on, that date shall be governed by the law in effect on December 31, 1994. Stats 1993 ch 758 §17(b).

§8803. Concealment or removal of child from county

(a) During the pendency of an adoption proceeding:

(1) The child proposed to be adopted shall not be concealed from the agency that is investigating the adoption, or from the court with jurisdiction over the adoption proceeding.

(2) The child shall not be removed from the county of the petitioner's residence at the time of placement, unless the petitioners or other interested persons first obtain permission for the removal from the court, after giving advance written notice of intent to obtain the court's permission to the department or delegated county adoption agency responsible for the investigation of the proposed adoption. Upon proof of giving notice, permission may be granted by the court if, within a period of 15 days after the date of giving notice, no objections are filed with the court by the department or delegated county adoption agency. If the department or delegated county adoption agency files objections within the 15-day period, upon the request of the petitioners the court shall immediately set the matter for hearing and give to the objector, the petitioners, and the party or parties requesting permission for the removal reasonable notice of the hearing by certified mail, return receipt requested, to the address of each as shown in the records of the adoption proceeding. Upon a finding that the objections are without good cause, the court may grant the requested permission for removal of the child, subject to any limitations that appear to be in the child's best interest.

(b) This section does not apply in any of the following situations:

(1) When the child is absent for a period of not more than 30 days from the county of the petitioner's residence at the time of placement, unless a notice of recommendation of denial of petition has been personally served on the petitioners or the court has issued an order prohibiting the child's removal from the county of the petitioner's residence at the time of placement, pending consideration of any of the following:

(A) The suitability of the petitioners.

(B) The care provided the child.

(C) The availability of the legally required consents to the adoption.

(2) Where the child has been returned to and remains in the custody and control of the child's birth parent or parents.

(c) A violation of this section is a violation of Section 280 of the Penal Code.

(d) Neither this section nor Section 280 of the Penal Code may be construed to render lawful any act that is unlawful under any other applicable law. **Leg.H.** Enacted Stats 1992 ch 162 §10 (AB 2650), operative January 1, 1994. Amended Stats 2022 ch 159 §6 (AB 2495), effective January 1, 2023.

§8804. Notice to department of motion to withdraw or dismiss petition

(a) Whenever the petitioners move to withdraw the petition for the adoption or to dismiss the proceeding, the clerk of the court in which the proceeding is pending shall immediately notify the department at Sacramento of the action. The department or the delegated county adoption agency shall file a full report with the court recommending a suitable plan for the child in every case where the petitioners move to withdraw the petition for the adoption or where the department or delegated county adoption agency recommends that the petition for adoption be denied and shall appear before the court for the purpose of representing the child.

(b) Notwithstanding the withdrawal or dismissal of the petition, the court may retain jurisdiction over the child for the purposes of making any order for the child's custody that the court deems to be in the child's best interest.

(c) If a birth parent who did not place a child for adoption as specified in Section 8801.3 has refused to give the required consent, or a birth parent revokes consent as specified in Section 8814.5, the child shall be restored to the care and custody of the birth parent or parents, unless the court orders otherwise, subject to Section 3041. **Leg.H.** Added Stats 1993 ch 758 §10 (SB 792), operative January 1, 1995. Amended Stats 2002 ch 1118 §4 (AB 1938); Stats 2014 ch 763 §11 (AB 1701), effective January 1, 2015.

Prior Law: Former §8804, similar to the present section, was enacted Stats 1992 ch 162 §10, operative January 1, 1994, amended Stats 1993 ch 219 §196, ch 758 §9.5, operative until January 1, 1995, and repealed, operative January 1, 1995, by its own terms.

1993 Note: Section 8804, as added by ch 758 §10, applies to all petitions for independent adoption filed on or after January 1, 1995. Petitions filed prior to, and pending on, that date shall be governed by the law in effect on December 31, 1994. Stats 1993 ch 758 §17(b).

§8805. Removal of child from home of petitioners

At the hearing, if the court sustains the recommendation of the department or delegated county adoption agency that the child be removed from the home of the petitioners because the department or agency recommends denial or if the petitioners move to withdraw the petition or if the court dismisses the petition and does not return the child to the birth parents, the court shall commit the child to the care of the department or delegated county adoption agency, whichever made the recommendation, for the department or agency to arrange adoptive placement or to make a suitable plan. In those counties not served by a delegated county adoption agency, the county welfare department shall act as the agent of the department and shall provide care for the child in accordance with rules and regulations established by the department. **Leg.H.** Enacted Stats 1992 ch 162 §10 (AB 2650), operative January 1, 1994.

§8806. Duty of department or agency

The department or delegated county adoption agency shall accept the consent of the birth parents to the adoption of the child by the petitioners and, before filing its report with the court, shall ascertain whether the child is a proper subject for adoption and whether the proposed home is suitable for the child. **Leg.H.** Enacted Stats 1992 ch 162 §10 (AB 2650), operative January 1, 1994.

§8807. Investigation of proposed independent adoption; Report

(a) Except as provided in subdivisions (b) and (c), within 180 days after receiving 50 percent of the fee, the department or delegated county adoption agency shall investigate the proposed independent adoption and, after the remaining balance of the fee is paid, submit to the court a full report of the facts disclosed by its inquiry with a recommendation regarding the granting of the petition. If the petitioners have a valid preplacement evaluation or a valid private agency adoption home study, as described in paragraph (2) of subdivision (a) of Section 8810, and no new information has been discovered and no new event has occurred subsequent to the approval of the evaluation or home study that creates a reasonable belief that further investigation is necessary, the department or delegated county adoption agency may elect not to reinvestigate any matters covered in the evaluation or home study, except that the department shall complete all background clearances required by law.

(b) If the investigation establishes that there is a serious question concerning the suitability of the petitioners, the care provided to the child, or the availability of the consent to adoption, the report shall be filed immediately.

(c) In its discretion, the court may allow additional time for the filing of the report, after at least five days' notice to the petitioner or petitioners and an opportunity for the petitioner or petitioners to be heard with respect to the request for additional time.

(d) If a petitioner is a resident of a state other than California, an updated and current home study report, conducted and approved by a licensed adoption agency or other authorized resource in the state in which the petitioner resides, shall be reviewed and endorsed by the department or delegated county adoption agency, if the standards and criteria established for a home study report in the other state are substantially commensurate with the home study standards and criteria established in California adoption regulations. **Leg.H.** Added Stats 2008 ch 759 §8 (AB 1279), effective September 30, 2008, operative October 1, 2008. Amended Stats 2014 ch 763 §12 (AB 1701), effective January 1, 2015.

Former Sections: Former Fam C §8807, similar to the present section, was enacted Stats 1992 ch 162 §10, operative January 1, 1994, and repealed operative October 1, 2008, by its own provisions.

Prior Law: Former §8807, similar to the present section, was enacted Stats 1992 ch 162 §10, operative January 1, 1994, amended Stats 2002 ch 1112 §4, Stats 2008 ch 759 § 7, effective September 30, 2008, and repealed, operative October 1, 2008, by its own terms.

§8808. Interview by department or agency

(a) The department or delegated county adoption agency shall interview the petitioners within 45 working days, excluding legal holidays, after the department or delegated county adoption agency receives 50 percent of the investigation fee together with a stamped file copy of the adoption petition.

(b) The department or delegated county adoption agency shall interview all persons from whom consent is required and whose addresses are known. The interview with the placing parent or parents shall include, but not be limited to, discussion of any concerns or problems that the parent has with the placement and, if the placing parent was not interviewed as provided in Section 8801.7, the content required in that interview. At the interview, the agency shall give the parent an opportunity to sign either a statement revoking the consent, or a waiver of the right to revoke consent, as provided in Section 8814.5, unless the parent has already signed a waiver or the time period allowed to revoke consent has expired.

(c) In order to facilitate the interview described in this section, within five business days of filing the petition, the petitioners shall provide the department or delegated county adoption agency a stamped file copy of the petition together with 50 percent of the fee, a copy of any valid preplacement evaluation or any valid private agency adoption home study, as described in paragraph (2) of subdivision (a) of Section 8810, and the names, addresses, and telephone numbers of all parties to be interviewed, if known. **Leg.H.** Added Stats 2008 ch 759 §10 (AB 1279), effective September 30, 2008, operative October 1, 2008. Amended Stats 2014 ch 763 §13 (AB 1701), effective January 1, 2015.

Former Sections: Former Fam C §8808, similar to the present section, was added Stats 1993 ch 758 §11, operative January 1, 1995, and repealed operative October 1, 2008, by its own provisions.

Prior Law: Former § 8808, similar to the present section, was added Stats 1993 ch 758 §11, operative January 1, 1995, amended Stats 2008 ch 759 §9, effective September 30, 2008, and repealed, October 1, 2008, by its own terms.

Former §8808, similar to the present section, was enacted Stats 1992 ch 162 §10, operative January 1, 1994, amended Stats 1993 ch 219 §197, ch 758 §10.5, operative until January 1, 1995, and repealed, operative January 1, 1995.

§8809. [Section repealed 1993]

Leg.H. Enacted Stats 1992 ch 162 §10 (AB 2650), operative January 1, 1994. Repealed, operative January 1, 1993, by its own terms. The repealed section related to request to sign consent in presence of court.

§8810. Fees

(a) Except as otherwise provided in this section, whenever a petition is filed under this chapter for the adoption of a child, the petitioner shall pay a nonrefundable fee to the department or to the delegated county adoption agency for the cost of investigating the adoption petition. Fifty percent of the payment shall be made to the department or delegated county adoption agency at the time the adoption petition is filed, and the remaining balance shall be paid no later than the date determined by the department or the delegated county adoption agency in an amount as follows:

(1) For petitions filed on and after October 1, 2008, four thousand five hundred dollars ($4,500).

(2) For petitioners who have a valid preplacement evaluation less than one year old pursuant to Section 8811.5, or a valid private agency adoption home study less than two years old at the time of filing a petition, one thousand five hundred fifty dollars ($1,550) for a postplacement evaluation pursuant to Sections 8806 and 8807.

(b) Revenues produced by fees collected by the department pursuant to subdivision (a) shall be used, when appropriated by the Legislature, to fund only the direct costs associated with the state program for independent adoptions. Revenues produced by fees collected by the delegated county adoption agency pursuant to subdivision (a) shall be used by the county to fund the county program for independent adoptions.

(c) The department or delegated county adoption agency may reduce the fee to no less than five hundred dollars ($500) when the prospective adoptive parents are lower income, according to the income limits published by the Department of Housing and Community Development, and when making the required payment would be detrimental to the welfare of an adopted child. The department shall develop additional guidelines regarding income and assets to determine the financial criteria for reduction of the fee under this subdivision. **Leg.H.** Added Stats 2008 ch 759 §12 (AB 1279), effective September 30, 2008, operative October 1, 2008. Amended Stats 2012 ch 638 §11 (AB 1757), effective January 1, 2013; Stats 2013 ch 743 §3 (AB 848), effective January 1, 2014.

Former Sections: Former Fam C §8810, similar to the present section, was added Stats 1993 ch 1158 §2 and repealed operative October 1, 2008, by its own provisions.

Former Fam C §8810, similar to the present section, was enacted Stats 1992 ch 162 §10 and repealed operative January 1, 1993, by its own provisions.

Prior Law: Former §8810, similar to the present section, was added Stats 1993 ch 1158 §2, operative until January 1, 1999, amended Stats 1996 ch 510 §2, Stats 2003 ch 225 §2, effective August 11, 2003, Stats 2008 ch 759 § 11, effective September 30, 2008, and repealed, October 1, 2008, by its own terms.

Former §8810, similar to the present section, was enacted Stats 1992 ch 162 §10, to become operative January 1, 1994, and repealed, operative January 1, 1993, by its own terms.

§8811. Investigation of prospective adoptive parents

(a) The department or delegated county adoption agency shall require each person who files an adoption petition to be fingerprinted and shall secure from an appropriate law enforcement agency any criminal record of that person to determine if the person has ever been convicted of a crime other than a minor traffic violation. The department or delegated county adoption agency may also secure the person's full criminal record, if any, with the exception of any convictions for which relief has been granted pursuant to Section 1203.49 of the Penal Code. Any federal-level criminal offender record requests to the Department of Justice shall be submitted with fingerprint images and related information required by the Department of Justice for the purposes of obtaining information as to the existence and content of a record of an out-of-state or federal conviction or arrest of a person or information regarding any out-of-state or federal crimes or arrests for which the Department of Justice establishes that the person is free on bail, or on their own recognizance pending trial or appeal. The Department of Justice shall forward to the Federal Bureau of Investigation any requests for federal summary criminal history information received pursuant to this section. The Department of Justice shall review the information returned from the Federal Bureau of Investigation and shall compile and disseminate a response to the department or delegated county adoption agency.

(b) Notwithstanding subdivision (c), the criminal record, if any, shall be taken into consideration when evaluating the prospective adoptive parent, and an assessment of the effects of any criminal history on the ability of the prospective adoptive parent to provide adequate and proper care and guidance to the child shall be included in the report to the court.

(c)(1) The department or a delegated county adoption agency shall not give final approval for an adoptive placement in any home in which the prospective adoptive parent or any adult living in the prospective adoptive home has either of the following:

(A) A felony conviction for child abuse or neglect, spousal abuse, crimes against a child, including child pornography, or for a crime involving violence, including rape, sexual assault, or homicide, but not including other physical assault and battery. For purposes of this subdivision, crimes involving violence means those violent crimes contained in clause (i) of subparagraph (A), and subparagraph (B), of paragraph (1) of subdivision (g) of Section 1522 of the Health and Safety Code.

(B) A felony conviction that occurred within the last five years for physical assault, battery, or a drug- or alcohol-related offense.

(2) This subdivision shall become operative on October 1, 2008, and shall remain operative only to the extent that compliance with its provisions is required by federal law as a condition of receiving funding under Title IV-E of the federal Social Security Act (42 U.S.C. Sec. 670 et seq.).

(d) A fee charged by a law enforcement agency for fingerprinting or for checking or obtaining the criminal record of the petitioner shall be paid by the petitioner. The department or delegated county adoption agency may defer, waive, or reduce the fee if its payment would cause economic hardship to the prospective adoptive parents detrimental to the welfare of the adopted child, if the child has been in the foster care of the prospective adoptive parents for at least one year, or if necessary for the placement of a special-needs child. **Leg.H.** Enacted Stats 1992 ch 162 §10 (AB 2650), operative January 1, 1994. Amended Stats 2008 ch 701 §2 (AB 2651), effective September 30, 2008; Stats 2014 ch 708 §2 (AB 1585), effective January 1, 2015; Stats 2015 ch 303 §152 (AB 731), effective January 1, 2016; Stats 2016 ch 86 §131 (SB 1171), effective January 1, 2017; Stats 2019 ch 115 §128 (AB 1817), effective January 1, 2020.

§8811.5. Certification of prospective adoptive parents; Preplacement evaluation; Cost for renewal

(a) A licensed private or public adoption agency of the state of the petitioners' residency may certify prospective adoptive parents by a preplacement evaluation that contains a finding that an individual is suited to be an adoptive parent.

(b) The preplacement evaluation shall include an investigation pursuant to standards included in the regulations governing independent adoption investigations established by the department. Fees for the investigation shall be commensurate with those fees charged for a comparable investigation conducted by the department or by a delegated licensed county adoption agency.

(c) The preplacement evaluation, whether it is conducted for the purpose of initially certifying prospective adoptive parents or for renewing that certification, shall be completed no more than one year prior to the signing of an adoption placement agreement. The cost for renewal of that certification shall be in proportion to the extent of the work required to prepare the renewal that is attributable to changes in family circumstances. **Leg.H.** Added Stats 1996 ch 510 §3 (AB 2165). Amended Stats 2004 ch 128 §1 (AB 2492).

§8812. Payment by prospective adoptive parents of specified fees and expenses; Receipts

Any request by a birth parent or birth parents for payment by the prospective adoptive parents of attorney's fees, medical fees and expenses, counseling fees, or living expenses of the birth mother shall be in writing. The birth parent or parents shall, by first-class mail or other agreed upon means to ensure receipt, provide the prospective adoptive parents written receipts for any money provided to the birth parent or birth parents. The prospective adoptive parents shall provide the receipts to the court when the accounting report required pursuant to Section 8610 is filed. **Leg.H.** Added Stats 1993 ch 450 §3 (SB 255).

§8813. Request for information on status of adoption

At or before the time a consent to adoption is signed, the department or delegated county adoption agency shall advise the birth parent signing the consent, verbally and in writing, that the birth parent may, at any time in the future, request from the department or agency, all known information about the status of the child's adoption, except for personal, identifying information about the adoptive family. The birth parent shall be advised that this information includes, but is not limited to, all of the following:

(a) Whether the child has been placed for adoption.

(b) The approximate date that an adoption was completed.

(c) If the adoption was not completed or was vacated, for any reason, whether adoptive placement of the child is again being considered. **Leg.H.** Enacted Stats 1992 ch 162 §10 (AB 2650), operative January 1, 1994.

§8814. Consent of birth parents to adoption

(a) Except as provided in Section 7662, the consent of the birth parent or parents who did not place the child for adoption, as described in Section 8801.3, to the adoption shall be signed in the presence of an agent of the department or of a delegated county adoption agency on a form prescribed by the department. The consent shall be filed with the clerk of the appropriate superior court.

(b) The consent described in subdivision (a), when reciting that the person giving it is entitled to the sole custody of the child and when acknowledged before that agent, is prima facie evidence of the right of the person making it to the sole custody of the child and that person's sole right to consent.

(c) If the birth parent described in subdivision (a) is located outside this state for an extended period of time unrelated to the adoption at the time of signing the consent, the consent may be signed before a notary or other person authorized to perform notarial acts, and in that case the consent of the department or of the delegated county adoption agency is also necessary.

(d) A birth parent who is a minor has the right to sign a consent for the adoption of the birth parent's child and the consent is not subject to revocation by the birth parent by reason of minority, or because the parent or guardian of the consenting minor parent was not served with notice that the minor parent consented to the adoption, unless the minor parent has previously provided written authorization to serve the minor parent's parent or guardian with that notice. **Leg.H.** Added Stats 1993 ch 758 §12 (SB 792), operative January 1, 1995. Amended Stats 1994 ch 585 §5 (AB 3336), operative January 1, 1995; Stats 1996 ch 510 §4 (AB 2165); Stats 2014 ch 763 §14 (AB 1701), effective January 1, 2015; Stats 2019 ch 115 §129 (AB 1817), effective January 1, 2020.

Prior Law: Former §8814, similar to the present section, was enacted Stats 1992 ch 162 §10, operative January 1, 1994, amended Stats 1993 ch 219 §198, ch 758 §11.5, operative until January 1, 1995, and repealed, operative January 1, 1995, by its own term.

1993 Note: Section 8814, as added by ch 758 §12, applies to all petitions for independent adoption filed on or after January 1, 1995. Petitions filed prior to, and pending on, that date shall be governed by the law in effect on December 31, 1994. Stats 1993 ch 758 §17(b).

§8814.5. Revocation of consent; Reinstatement of original consent; Waiver of right to revoke; Time limits

(a) After a consent to the adoption is signed by the birth parent or parents pursuant to Section 8801.3 or 8814, the birth parent or parents signing the consent shall have 30 days to take one of the following actions:

(1) Sign and deliver to the department or delegated county adoption agency a written statement revoking the consent and requesting the child to be returned to the birth parent or parents. After revoking consent, in cases where the birth parent or parents have not regained custody, or the birth parent or parents have failed to make efforts to exercise their rights under subdivision (b) of Section 8815, a written notarized statement reinstating the original consent may be signed and delivered to the department or delegated county adoption agency, in which case the revocation of consent shall be void and the remainder of the original 30-day period shall commence. After revoking consent, in cases in which the birth parent or parents have regained custody or made efforts to exercise their rights under subdivision (b) of Section 8815 by requesting the return of the child, upon the delivery of a written notarized statement reinstating the original consent to the department or delegated county adoption agency, the revocation of consent shall be void and a new 30-day period shall commence. The birth mother shall be informed of the operational timelines associated with this section at the time of signing of the statement reinstating the original consent.

(2)(A) Sign a waiver of the right to revoke consent on a form prescribed by the department in the presence of any of the following:

(i) A representative of the department or delegated county adoption agency.

(ii) A judicial officer of a court of record if the birth parent is represented by independent legal counsel.

(iii) An adoption service provider, including, but not limited to, the adoption service provider who advised the birth mother and witnessed the signing of the consent, if the birth parent or parents are represented by independent legal counsel. The adoption service provider shall ensure that the waiver is delivered to the department, the petitioners, or their counsel no earlier than the end of the business day following the signing of the waiver. The adoption service provider shall inform the birth parent that during this time period the birth parent may request that the waiver be withdrawn and that, if that request is made, the waiver shall be withdrawn.

(B) An adoption service provider may assist the birth parent or parents in any activity where the primary purpose of that activity is to facilitate the signing of the waiver with the department, a delegated county agency, or a judicial officer. The adoption service provider or another person designated by the birth parent or parents may also be present at any interview conducted pursuant to this section to provide support to the birth parent or parents, except when the interview is conducted by independent legal counsel for the birth parent or parents.

(C) The waiver of the right to revoke consent may not be signed until an interview has been completed by the department or delegated county adoption agency unless the waiver of the right to revoke consent is signed in the presence of a judicial officer of a court of record or an adoption service provider as specified in this section. If the waiver is signed in the presence of a judicial officer, the interview and the witnessing of the signing of the waiver shall be conducted by the judicial officer. If the waiver is signed in the presence of an adoption service provider, the interview shall be conducted by the independent legal counsel for the birth parent or parents. If the waiver is to be signed in the presence of an adoption service provider, prior to the waiver being signed the waiver shall be reviewed by the independent legal counsel who (i) counsels the birth parent or parents about the nature of the intended waiver and (ii) signs and delivers to the birth parent or parents and the department a certificate in substantially the following form:

I, (name of attorney), have counseled my client, (name of client), on the nature and legal effect of the waiver of right to revoke consent to adoption. I am so disassociated from the interest of the petitioner(s)/prospective adoptive parent(s) as to be in a position to advise my client impartially and confidentially as to the consequences of the waiver. (Name of client) is aware that California law provides for a 30-day period during which a birth parent may revoke consent to adoption. On the basis of this counsel, I conclude that it is the intent of (name of client) to waive the right to revoke, and make a permanent and irrevocable consent to adoption. (Name of client) understands that they will not be able to regain custody of the child unless the petitioner(s)/prospective adoptive parent(s) agree(s) to withdraw their petition for adoption or the court denies the adoption petition.

(D) Within 10 working days of a request made after the department or the delegated county adoption agency has received a copy of the petition for the adoption and the names and addresses of the persons to be interviewed, the department or the delegated county adoption agency shall interview, at the department or agency office, any birth parent requesting to be interviewed.

(E) Notwithstanding subparagraphs (A) and (C), the interview, and the witnessing of the signing of a waiver of the right to revoke consent of a birth parent residing outside of California or located outside of California for an extended period of time unrelated to the adoption may be conducted in the state where the birth parent is located, by any of the following:

(i) A representative of a public adoption agency in that state.

(ii) A judicial officer in that state where the birth parent is represented by independent legal counsel.

(iii) An adoption service provider.

(3) Allow the consent to become a permanent consent on the 31st day after signing.

(b) The consent may not be revoked after a waiver of the right to revoke consent has been signed or after 30 days, beginning on the date the consent was signed or as provided in paragraph (1) of subdivision (a), whichever occurs first. **Leg.H.** Added Stats 1993 ch 758 §13 (SB 792), operative January 1, 1995. Amended Stats 1994 ch 585 §6 (AB 3336), operative January 1, 1995; Stats 1996 ch 510 §5 (AB 2165); Stats 2000 ch 937 §5 (AB 2433); Stats 2001 ch 688 §2 (SB 104); Stats 2002 ch 664 §79 (AB 3034); Stats 2003 ch 251 §10 (SB 182); Stats 2008 ch 534 §11 (SB 1726), effective January 1, 2009; Stats 2009 ch 492 §4 (AB 941), effective January 1, 2010; Stats 2010 ch 588 §7 (AB 2020), effective January 1, 2011; Stats 2019 ch 115 §130 (AB 1817), effective January 1, 2020.

Prior Law: There was another section of this number, similar to the present section, which was added Stats 1993 ch 219 §199, but failed to become operative as it was repealed Stats 1993 ch 758 §12.5.

§8815. Irrevocability of consent

(a) Once the revocable consent to adoption has become permanent as provided in Section 8814.5, the consent to the adoption by the prospective adoptive parents may not be withdrawn.

(b) Before the time when the revocable consent becomes permanent as provided in Section 8814.5, the birth parent or parents may request return of the child. In that case the child shall immediately be returned to the requesting birth parent or parents, unless a court orders otherwise.

(c) If the person or persons with whom the child has been placed have concerns that the birth parent or parents requesting return of the child are unfit or present a danger of harm to the child, that person or those persons may report their concerns to the appropriate child welfare agency. These concerns shall not be a basis for failure to immediately return the child, unless a court orders otherwise. **Leg.H.** Added Stats 1993 ch 758 §16 (SB 792), operative January 1, 1995. Amended Stats 2014 ch 763 §15 (AB 1701), effective January 1, 2015.

Prior Law: Former §8815, relating to motion or petition for withdrawal of consent, was added Stats 1993 ch 758 §15 and repealed, operative January 1, 1995, by its own terms.

Former §8815, relating to motion or petition for withdrawal of consent, was enacted Stats 1992 ch 162 §10, operative January 1, 1994, but failed to become operative since it was repealed Stats 1993 ch 219 §200.

There was another section of this number, similar to the present section, which was added Stats 1993 ch 219 §201, but failed to become operative as it was repealed Stats 1993 ch 758 §14.

1993 Note: Section 8815, as added by ch 758 §16, applies to all petitions for independent adoption filed on or after January 1, 1995. Petitions filed prior to, and pending on, that date shall be governed by the law in effect on December 31, 1994. Stats 1993 ch 758 §17(b).

§8816. Consent of agency or department

In an independent adoption where the consent of the birth parent or parents is not necessary, the department or delegated county adoption agency shall, before the hearing of the petition, file its consent to the adoption with the clerk of the court in which the petition is filed. The consent may not be given unless the child's welfare will be promoted by the adoption. **Leg.H.** Enacted Stats 1992 ch 162 §10 (AB 2650), operative January 1, 1994.

§8817. Medical report on child and biological parents; Parents' blood sample

(a) A written report on the child's medical background, and if available, the medical background of the child's biological parents so far as ascertainable, shall be made by the department or delegated county adoption agency as part of the study required by Section 8806.

(b) The report on the child's background shall contain all known diagnostic information, including current medical reports on the child, psychological evaluations, and scholastic information, as well as all known information regarding the child's developmental history and family life.

(c) The report shall be submitted to the prospective adoptive parents who shall acknowledge its receipt in writing.

(d)(1) The biological parents may provide a blood sample at a clinic or hospital approved by the State Department of Health Services. The biological parents' failure to provide a blood sample shall not affect the adoption of the child.

(2) The blood sample shall be stored at a laboratory under contract with the State Department of Health Services for a period of 30 years following the adoption of the child.

(3) The purpose of the stored sample of blood is to provide a blood sample from which DNA testing can be done at a later date after entry of the order of adoption at the request of the adoptive parents or the adopted child. The cost of drawing and storing the blood samples shall be paid for by a separate fee in addition to the fee required under Section 8810. The amount of this additional fee shall be based on the cost of drawing and storing the blood samples but at no time shall the additional fee be more than one hundred dollars ($100).

(e)(1) The blood sample shall be stored and released in such a manner as to not identify any party to the adoption.

(2) Any results of the DNA testing shall be stored and released in such a manner as to not identify any party to the adoption. **Leg.H.** Enacted Stats 1992 ch 162 §10 (AB 2650), operative January 1, 1994. Amended Stats 1996 ch 1053 §2 (AB 3241).

§8818. Statement to birth parents at time of consent

(a) The department shall adopt a statement to be presented to the birth parents at the time the consent to adoption is signed and to prospective adoptive parents at the time of the home study. The statement shall, in a clear and concise manner and in words calculated to ensure the confidence of the birth parents in the integrity of the adoption process, communicate to the birth parent of a child who is the subject of an adoption petition all of the following facts:

(1) It is in the child's best interest that the birth parents keep the department informed of any health problems that the parent develops that could affect the child.

(2) It is extremely important that the birth parent keep an address current with the department in order to permit a response to inquiries concerning medical or social history.

(3) Section 9203 of the Family Code authorizes a person who has been adopted and who attains the age of 21 years to request the department to disclose the name and address of the adoptee's birth parents. Consequently, it is of the utmost importance that the birth parent indicate whether to allow this disclosure by checking the appropriate box provided on the form.

(4) The birth parent may change the decision whether to permit disclosure of the birth parent's name and address, at any time, by sending a notarized letter to that effect, by certified mail, return receipt requested, to the department.

(5) The consent will be filed in the office of the clerk of the court in which the adoption takes place. The file is not open to inspection by any persons other than the parties to the adoption proceeding, their attorneys, and the department, except upon order of a judge of the superior court.

(b) The department shall adopt a form to be signed by the birth parents at the time the consent to adoption is signed, which shall provide as follows:

"Section 9203 of the Family Code authorizes a person who has been adopted and who attains the age of 21 years to make a request to the State Department of Social Services, or the licensed adoption agency that joined in the adoption petition, for the name and address of the adoptee's birth parents. Indicate by checking one of the boxes below whether or not you wish your name and address to be disclosed:

☐ YES

☐ NO

☐ UNCERTAIN AT THIS TIME; WILL NOTIFY AGENCY AT LATER DATE." **Leg.H.** Enacted Stats 1992 ch 162 §10 (AB 2650), operative January 1, 1994. Amended Stats 2002 ch 784 §113 (SB 1316).

§8819. Notice to birth parent on termination of parental rights

When the parental rights of a birth parent are terminated pursuant to Chapter 5 (commencing with Section 7660) of Part 3 of Division 12 or Part 4 (commencing with Section 7800) of Division 12, the department or delegated county adoption agency shall send a written notice to the birth parent, if the birth parent's address is known, that contains the following statement:

"You are encouraged to keep the department or this agency informed of your current address in order to permit a response to any inquiry concerning medical or social history made by or on behalf of the child who was the subject of the court action terminating parental rights." **Leg.H.** Enacted Stats 1992 ch 162 §10 (AB 2650), operative January 1, 1994.

§8820. Appeal from department or agency disapproval

(a) The birth parent or parents or the petitioner may appeal in either of the following cases:

(1) If for a period of 180 days from the date of paying 50 percent of the fee, or upon the expiration of any extension of the period granted by the court, the department or delegated county adoption agency fails or refuses to accept the consent of the birth parent or parents to the adoption.

(2) In a case where the consent of the department or delegated county adoption agency is required by this chapter, if the department or agency fails or refuses to file or give its consent to the adoption after full payment has been received.

(b) The appeal shall be filed in the court in which the adoption petition is filed. The court clerk shall immediately notify the department or delegated county adoption agency of the appeal and the department or agency shall, within 10 days, file a report of its findings and the reasons for its failure or refusal to consent to the adoption or to accept the consent of the birth parent or parents.

(c) After the filing of the report by the department or delegated county adoption agency, the court may, if it deems that the welfare of the child will be promoted by that adoption, allow the signing of the consent by the birth parent or parents in open court or, if the appeal is from the refusal of the department or delegated county adoption agency to consent thereto, grant the petition without the consent.

(d) This section shall become operative on October 1, 2008. **Leg.H.** Added Stats 2008 ch 759 §14 (AB 1279), effective September 30, 2008, operative October 1, 2008.

Former Sections: Former Fam C §8820, similar to the present section, was enacted Stats 1992 ch 162 §10, operative January 1, 1994, and repealed operative October 1, 2008, by its own provisions.

Prior Law: Former §8820, similar to the present section, was enacted Stats 1992 ch 162 §10, operative January 1, 1994, amended Stats 2008 ch 759 § 13, effective September 30, 2008, and repealed, October 1, 2008, by its own terms.

§8821. Copy of report or findings to petitioner or attorney

When any report or findings are submitted to the court by the department or a delegated county adoption agency, a copy of the report or findings, whether favorable or unfavorable, shall be given to the petitioner's attorney in the proceeding, if the petitioner has an attorney of record, or to the petitioner. **Leg.H.** Enacted Stats 1992 ch 162 §10 (AB 2650), operative January 1, 1994.

§8822. Unfavorable recommendation by department or agency

(a) If the findings of the department or delegated county adoption agency are that the home of the petitioners is not suitable for the child or that the required consents are not available and the department or agency recommends that the petition be denied, or if the petitioners desire to withdraw the petition and the department or agency recommends that the petition be denied, the clerk upon receipt of the report of the department or agency shall immediately refer it to the court for review.

(b) Upon receipt of the report, the court shall set a date for a hearing of the petition and shall give reasonable notice of the hearing to the department or delegated county adoption agency, the petitioners, and the birth parents by certified mail, return receipt requested, to the address of each as shown in the proceeding.

(c) The department or delegated county adoption agency shall appear to represent the child. **Leg.H.** Enacted Stats 1992 ch 162 §10 (AB 2650), operative January 1, 1994.

§8823. Appearance of prospective adoptive parents and child

The prospective adoptive parents and the child proposed to be adopted shall appear before the court pursuant to Sections 8612 and 8613. **Leg.H.** Enacted Stats 1992 ch 162 §10 (AB 2650), operative January 1, 1994.

CHAPTER 4
INTERCOUNTRY ADOPTIONS

Who may provide intercountry adoption services; Accreditation; Supervised providers. §8900.
Definitions. §8900.5.
Department regulations. §8901.
Agency services. §8902.
Care, custody, and control of child; Medi-Cal eligibility. §8903.
Agency services for adoptions finalized in foreign country. §8904.
Agreements of licensed adoption agencies with other agencies. §8905.
Agreement to share or transfer financial responsibility. §8906.
Funding by fees. §8907.
Investigation of prospective adoptive parents. §8908.
Medical report on child and biological parents; Parents' blood sample. §8909.
Concealment or removal of child from county. §8910.
Petition to adopt within 30 days of placement. §8911.
International adoption or readoption request. §8912.
Appearance of prospective adoptive parents and child. §8913.
Report to court. §8914.
Copy of report or findings to petitioner or attorney. §8915.
Notice to department of motion to withdraw or dismiss. §8916.
Unfavorable recommendation by licensed adoption agency. §8917.
Transfer of child to care of agency. §8918.
Readoption of children adopted through intercountry adoption. §8919.
Report of arrival. §8919.5.
Readoption of children adopted through intercountry adoption; Visitation agreement following readoption of sibling. §8920.
Complaints in connection with convention adoption; Notice to department; Revocation of license. §8923.
Duties of agency or person providing adoption service for child emigrating to convention country. §8924.
Recognition of Hague adoption certificate or custody declaration. §8925.

§8900. Who may provide intercountry adoption services; Accreditation; Supervised providers

(a) Intercountry adoption services described in this chapter shall be exclusively provided by private adoption agencies licensed by the department specifically to provide these services. As a condition of licensure to provide intercountry adoption services, any private full-service adoption agency and any noncustodial adoption agency shall be accredited by the Council on Accreditation, or supervised by an accredited primary provider, or acting as an exempted provider, in compliance with Subpart F (commencing with Section 96.29) of Part 96 of Title 22 of the Code of Federal Regulations.

(b) A private full-service adoption agency or a noncustodial adoption agency, when acting as the primary provider and using a supervised provider, shall ensure that each supervised provider operates under a written agreement with the primary provider pursuant to subdivision (b) of Section 96.45 of Title 22 of the Code of Federal Regulations.

(c) The primary provider shall provide to the department a copy of the written agreement with each supervised provider containing all provisions required pursuant to subdivision (b) of Section 96.45 of Title 22 of the Code of Federal Regulations. **Leg.H.** Enacted Stats 1992 ch 162 §10 (AB 2650), operative January 1, 1994. Amended Stats 2007 ch 583 §5 (SB 703), effective January 1, 2008.

§8900.5. Definitions

As used in this chapter:

(a) "Accredited agency" means an agency that has been accredited by an accrediting entity, in accordance with the standards in Subpart F (commencing with Section 96.29) of Part 96 of Title 22 of the Code of Federal Regulations, to provide adoption services in the United States in cases subject to the convention. Accredited agency does not include a temporarily accredited agency.

(b) "Adoption service" means any of the following services:

(1) Identifying a child for adoption and arranging an adoption.

(2) Securing the necessary consent to termination of parental rights and to adoption.

(3) Performing a background study on a child or a home study on any prospective adoptive parent, and reporting on the study.

(4) Making nonjudicial determinations of the best interests of a child and the appropriateness of an adoptive placement for the child.

(5) Monitoring a case after a child has been placed with any prospective adoptive parent until final adoption.

(6) If necessary because of a disruption before final adoption, assuming custody and providing or facilitating child care or any other social service pending an alternative placement.

(c) "Central authority" means the entity designated under paragraph (1) of Article 6 of the convention by a convention country. The United States Department of State is designated as the United States Central Authority pursuant to the federal Intercountry Adoption Act of 2000 (42 U.S.C. Sec. 14911).

(d) "Convention" means the Hague Convention on Protection of Children and Co-operation in Respect of Intercountry Adoption, May 29, 1993.

(e) "Convention adoption" means the adoption of a child resident in a convention country by a United States citizen, or an adoption of a child resident in the United States by an individual or individuals residing in a convention country, if, in connection with the adoption, the child has moved or will move between the United States and the convention country.

(f) "Convention country" means a country that is party to the convention and with which the convention is in force for the United States.

(g) "Exempted provider" means a social work professional or organization that performs a home study on any prospective adoptive parent, or a child background study, or both, in the United States in connection with a convention adoption, and who is not currently providing and has not previously provided any other adoption service in the case.

(h) "Hague adoption certificate" means a certificate issued by the secretary in an outgoing case (where the child is emigrating from the United States to another convention country) certifying that a child has been adopted in the United States in accordance with the convention and, except as provided in subdivision (b) of Section 97.4 of Title 22 of the Code of Federal Regulations, the Intercountry Adoption Act of 2000 (42 U.S.C. Sec. 14901 et seq.; the IAA).

(i) "Hague custody declaration" means a declaration issued by the secretary in an outgoing case (where the child is emigrating from the United States to another convention country) declaring that custody of a child for purposes of adoption has been granted in the United States in accordance with the convention and, except as provided in subdivision (b) of Section 97.4 of Title 22 of the Code of Federal Regulations, the IAA.

(j) "Legal service" means any service, other than those defined in this section as an adoption service, that relates to the provision of legal advice and information or to the drafting of legal instruments. Legal service includes, but is not limited to, any of the following services:

(1) Drafting contracts, powers of attorney, and other legal instruments.

(2) Providing advice and counsel to an adoptive parent on completing forms for the State Department of Health Care Services or the United States Department of State.

(3) Providing advice and counsel to accredited agencies, temporarily accredited agencies, approved persons, or prospective adoptive parents on how to comply with the convention, the IAA, and any regulations implementing the IAA.

(k) "Primary provider" means the accredited agency that is identified pursuant to Section 96.14 of Title 22 of the Code of Federal Regulations as responsible for ensuring that all adoption services are provided and responsible for supervising any supervised providers when used.

(*l*) "Public domestic authority" means an authority operated by a state, local, or tribal government.

(m) "Secretary" means the United States Secretary of State, and includes any official of the United States Department of State exercising the authority of the Secretary of State under the convention, the IAA, or any regulations implementing the IAA, pursuant to a delegation of authority.

(n) "Supervised provider" means any agency, person, or other nongovernmental entity that is providing any adoption service in a convention adoption under the supervision and responsibility of an accredited agency that is acting as the primary provider in the case. **Leg.H.** Added Stats 2007 ch 583 §6 (SB 703), effective January 1, 2008.

§8901. Department regulations

The department shall adopt regulations to administer the intercountry adoption program. **Leg.H.** Enacted Stats 1992 ch 162 §10 (AB 2650), operative January 1, 1994.

§8902. Agency services

For intercountry adoptions that will be finalized in this state, the licensed adoption agency shall provide all of the following services:

(a) Assessment of the suitability of the applicant's home.

(b) Placement of the foreign-born child in an approved home.

(c) Postplacement supervision.

(d) Submission to the court of a report on the intercountry adoptive placement with a recommendation regarding the granting of the petition.

(e) Services to applicants seeking to adopt related children living in foreign countries. The Legislature recognizes that these children have an impelling need for adoptive placement with their relatives. **Leg.H.** Enacted Stats 1992 ch 162 §10 (AB 2650), operative January 1, 1994.

§8903. Care, custody, and control of child; Medi-Cal eligibility

(a) For each intercountry adoption finalized in this state, the licensed adoption agency shall assume all responsibilities for the child including care, custody, and control as if the child had been relinquished for adoption in this state from the time the child left the child's native country.

(b) Notwithstanding subdivision (a), if the child's native country requires and has given full guardianship to the prospective adoptive parents, the prospective adoptive parents shall assume all responsibilities for the child including care, custody, control, and financial support.

(c) If the licensed adoption agency or prospective adoptive parents fail to meet the responsibilities under subdivision (a) or (b) and the child becomes a dependent of the court pursuant to Section 300 of the Welfare and Institutions Code, the state shall assume responsibility for the cost of care for the child. When the child becomes a dependent of the court and if, for any reason, is ineligible for AFDC under Section 14005.1 of the Welfare and Institutions Code and loses Medi-Cal eligibility, the child shall be deemed eligible for Medi-Cal under Section 14005.4 of the Welfare and Institutions Code and the State Director of Health Services has authority to provide payment for the medical services to the child that are necessary to meet the child's needs. **Leg.H.** Enacted Stats 1992 ch 162 §10 (AB 2650), operative January 1, 1994.

§8904. Agency services for adoptions finalized in foreign country

For an intercountry adoption that will be finalized in a foreign country, the licensed adoption agency shall provide all of the following services:

(a) Assessment of the suitability of the applicant's home.

(b) Certification to the United States Citizenship and Immigration Services that this state's intercountry adoption requirements have been met.

(c) Readoption services as required by the United States Citizenship and Immigration Services.

(d) Postadoption services pursuant to any written agreement between the licensed adoption agency and any other person or entity for which the postadoption services have been paid. **Leg.H.** Enacted Stats 1992 ch 162 §10 (AB 2650), operative January 1, 1994. Amended Stats 1993 ch 219 §202 (AB 1500); Stats 2019 ch 805 §1 (AB 677), effective January 1, 2020.

§8905. Agreements of licensed adoption agencies with other agencies

Licensed adoption agencies may work only with domestic and foreign adoption agencies with whom they have written agreements that specify the responsibilities of each. The agreements may not violate any statute or regulation of the United States or of this state. **Leg.H.** Enacted Stats 1992 ch 162 §10 (AB 2650), operative January 1, 1994.

§8906. Agreement to share or transfer financial responsibility

Nothing in this chapter may be construed to prohibit the licensed adoption agency from entering into an agreement with the prospective adoptive parents to share or transfer financial responsibility for the child. **Leg.H.** Enacted Stats 1992 ch 162 §10 (AB 2650), operative January 1, 1994.

§8907. Funding by fees

The costs incurred by a licensed adoption agency pursuant to programs established by this chapter shall be funded by fees charged by the agency for services required by this chapter. The agency's fee schedule is required to be approved by the department initially and whenever it is altered. **Leg.H.** Enacted Stats 1992 ch 162 §10 (AB 2650), operative January 1, 1994.

§8908. Investigation of prospective adoptive parents

(a) A licensed adoption agency shall require each person filing an application for adoption to be fingerprinted and shall secure from an appropriate law enforcement agency any criminal record of that person to determine if the person has ever been convicted of a crime other than a minor traffic violation. The licensed adoption agency may also secure the person's full criminal record, if any, with the exception of any convictions for which relief has been granted pursuant to Section 1203.49 of the Penal Code. Any federal-level criminal offender record requests to the Department of Justice shall be submitted with fingerprint images and related information required by the Department of Justice for the purposes of obtaining information as to the existence and content of a record of an out-of-state or federal conviction or arrest of a person or information regarding any out-of-state or federal crimes or arrests for which the Department of Justice establishes that the person is free on bail, or on their own recognizance pending trial or appeal. The Department of Justice shall forward to the Federal Bureau of Investigation any requests for federal summary criminal history information received pursuant to this section. The Department of Justice shall review the information returned from the Federal Bureau of Investigation and shall compile and disseminate a fitness determination to the licensed adoption agency.

(b) Notwithstanding subdivision (c), the criminal record, if any, shall be taken into consideration when evaluating the prospective adoptive parent, and an assessment of the effects of any criminal history on the ability of the prospective adoptive parent to provide adequate and proper care and guidance to the child shall be included in the report to the court.

(c)(1) A licensed adoption agency shall not give final approval for an adoptive placement in any home in which the prospective adoptive parent, or any adult living in the prospective adoptive home, has a felony conviction for either of the following:

(A) A felony conviction for child abuse or neglect, spousal abuse, crimes against a child, including child pornography, or for a crime involving violence, including rape, sexual assault, or homicide, but not including other physical assault and battery. For purposes of this subdivision, crimes involving violence means those violent crimes contained in clause (i) of subparagraph (A), and subparagraph (B), of paragraph (1) of subdivision (g) of Section 1522 of the Health and Safety Code.

(B) A felony conviction that occurred within the last five years for physical assault, battery, or a drug- or alcohol-related offense.

(2) This subdivision shall become operative on October 1, 2008, and shall remain operative only to the extent that compliance with its

provisions is required by federal law as a condition of receiving funding under Title IV-E of the federal Social Security Act (42 U.S.C. Sec. 670 et seq.).

(d) Any fee charged by a law enforcement agency for fingerprinting or for checking or obtaining the criminal record of the applicant shall be paid by the applicant. The licensed adoption agency may defer, waive, or reduce the fee if its payment would cause economic hardship to the prospective adoptive parents detrimental to the welfare of the adopted child. **Leg.H.** Enacted Stats 1992 ch 162 §10 (AB 2650), operative January 1, 1994. Amended Stats 2008 ch 701 §3 (AB 2651), effective September 30, 2008; Stats 2014 ch 708 §3 (AB 1585), effective January 1, 2015; Stats 2015 ch 303 §153 (AB 731), effective January 1, 2016; Stats 2016 ch 86 §132 (SB 1171), effective January 1, 2017; Stats 2019 ch 115 §131 (AB 1817), effective January 1, 2020.

§8909. Medical report on child and biological parents; Parents' blood sample

(a) An agency may not place a child for adoption unless a written report on the child's medical background and, if available, the medical background of the child's biological parents so far as ascertainable, has been submitted to the prospective adoptive parents and they have acknowledged in writing the receipt of the report.

(b) The report on the child's background shall contain all known diagnostic information, including current medical reports on the child, psychological evaluations, and scholastic information, as well as all known information regarding the child's developmental history and family life.

(c)(1) The biological parents may provide a blood sample at a clinic or hospital approved by the State Department of Health Services. The biological parents' failure to provide a blood sample shall not affect the adoption of the child.

(2) The blood sample shall be stored at a laboratory under contract with the State Department of Health Services for a period of 30 years following the adoption of the child.

(3) The purpose of the stored sample of blood is to provide a blood sample from which DNA testing can be done at a later date after entry of the order of adoption at the request of the adoptive parents or the adopted child. The cost of drawing and storing the blood samples shall be paid for by a separate fee in addition to any fee required under Section 8907. The amount of this additional fee shall be based on the cost of drawing and storing the blood samples but at no time shall the additional fee be more than one hundred dollars ($100).

(d)(1) The blood sample shall be stored and released in such a manner as to not identify any party to the adoption.

(2) Any results of the DNA testing shall be stored and released in such a manner as to not identify any party to the adoption. **Leg.H.** Enacted Stats 1992 ch 162 §10 (AB 2650), operative January 1, 1994. Amended Stats 1996 ch 1053 §3 (AB 3241).

§8910. Concealment or removal of child from county

(a) In no event may a child who has been placed for adoption be removed from the county in which the child was placed, by any person who has not petitioned to adopt the child, without first obtaining the written consent of the licensed adoption agency responsible for the child.

(b) During the pendency of an adoption proceeding:

(1) The child proposed to be adopted shall not be concealed from the agency that is investigating the adoption or from the court with jurisdiction over the adoption proceeding.

(2) The child shall not be removed from the county of the petitioner's residence at the time of placement, unless the petitioners or other interested persons first obtain permission for the removal from the court, after giving advance written notice of intent to obtain the court's permission to the licensed adoption agency responsible for the child. Upon proof of giving notice, permission may be granted by the court if, within a period of 15 days after the date of giving notice, no objections are filed with the court by the licensed adoption agency responsible for the child. If the licensed adoption agency files objections within the 15-day period, upon the request of the petitioners the court shall immediately set the matter for hearing and give to the objector, the petitioners, and the party or parties requesting permission for the removal reasonable notice of the hearing by certified mail, return receipt requested, to the address of each as shown in the records of the adoption proceeding. Upon a finding that the objections are without good cause, the court may grant the requested permission for removal of the child, subject to any limitations that appear to be in the child's best interest.

(c) This section does not apply in any of the following situations:

(1) When the child is absent for a period of not more than 30 days from the county of the petitioner's residence at the time of placement, unless a notice of recommendation of denial of petition has been personally served on the petitioners or the court has issued an order prohibiting the removal of the child from the county of the petitioner's residence at the time of placement, pending consideration of any of the following:

(A) The suitability of the petitioners.

(B) The care provided the child.

(C) The availability of the legally required agency consents to the adoption.

(2) Where the child has been returned to and remains in the custody and control of the child's birth parent or parents.

(3) Where written consent for the removal of the child is obtained from the licensed adoption agency responsible for the child.

(d) A violation of this section is a violation of Section 280 of the Penal Code.

(e) Neither this section nor Section 280 of the Penal Code may be construed to render lawful any act that is unlawful under any other applicable law. **Leg.H.** Enacted Stats 1992 ch 162 §10 (AB 2650), operative January 1, 1994. Amended Stats 2022 ch 159 §7 (AB 2495), effective January 1, 2023.

§8911. Petition to adopt within 30 days of placement

As a condition of placement, the prospective adoptive parents shall file a petition to adopt the child under Section 8912 within 30 days of placement. **Leg.H.** Enacted Stats 1992 ch 162 §10 (AB 2650), operative January 1, 1994.

§8912. International adoption or readoption request

(a) An international adoption or readoption request may be filed by a resident of this state in a county authorized by Section 8609.5. The court clerk shall immediately notify the department at Sacramento in writing of the pendency of the proceeding and of any subsequent action taken.

(b) The caption of the adoption request shall contain the names of the petitioners, but not the child's name. The request shall state the child's sex, date of birth, and the name the child had before adoption.

(c) If the child is the subject of a guardianship petition, the adoption request shall so state and shall include the caption and docket number or have attached a copy of the letters of the guardianship or temporary guardianship. The petitioners shall notify the court of any petition for guardianship or temporary guardianship filed after the adoption petition. The guardianship proceeding shall be consolidated with the adoption proceeding.

(d) The order of adoption shall contain the child's adopted name and the name the child had before adoption.

(e) If the petitioner has entered into a postadoption contact agreement as set forth in Section 8616.5, the petitioner shall file the agreement, signed by the participating parties, with the court before the adoption is finalized. **Leg.H.** Enacted Stats 1992 ch 162 §10 (AB 2650), operative January 1, 1994. Amended Stats 2004 ch 858 §6 (SB 1357); Stats 2012 ch 638 §12 (AB 1757), effective January 1, 2013; Stats 2022 ch 159 §8 (AB 2495), effective January 1, 2023; Stats 2023 ch 851 §9 (AB 1650), effective January 1, 2024.

§8913. Appearance of prospective adoptive parents and child

The prospective adoptive parents and the child proposed to be adopted shall appear before the court pursuant to Sections 8612 and 8613. **Leg.H.** Enacted Stats 1992 ch 162 §10 (AB 2650), operative January 1, 1994.

§8914. Report to court

If the licensed adoption agency is a party to or joins in the adoption petition, it shall submit a full report of the facts of the case to the court. The department may also submit a report. **Leg.H.** Enacted Stats 1992 ch 162 §10 (AB 2650), operative January 1, 1994.

§8915. Copy of report or findings to petitioner or attorney

When any report or findings are submitted to the court by a licensed adoption agency, a copy of the report or findings, whether favorable or unfavorable, shall be given to the petitioner's attorney in the proceeding, if the petitioner has an attorney of record, or to the petitioner. **Leg.H.** Enacted Stats 1992 ch 162 §10 (AB 2650), operative January 1, 1994.

§8916. Notice to department of motion to withdraw or dismiss

(a) If the petitioners move to withdraw the adoption petition or to dismiss the proceeding, the court clerk shall immediately notify the department at Sacramento of the action. The licensed adoption agency shall file a full report with the court recommending a suitable plan for the child in every case where the petitioners desire to withdraw the adoption petition or where the licensed adoption agency recommends that the adoption petition be denied and shall appear before the court for the purpose of representing the child.

(b) Notwithstanding the petitioners' withdrawal or dismissal, the court may retain jurisdiction over the child for the purpose of making any order for the child's custody that the court deems to be in the child's best interest. **Leg.H.** Enacted Stats 1992 ch 162 §10 (AB 2650), operative January 1, 1994.

§8917. Unfavorable recommendation by licensed adoption agency

(a) If the licensed adoption agency finds that the home of the petitioners is not suitable for the child or that the required agency consents are not available and the agency recommends that the petition be denied, or if the petitioners desire to withdraw the petition and the agency recommends that the petition be denied, the clerk upon receipt of the report of the licensed adoption agency shall immediately refer it to the court for review.

(b) Upon receipt of the report, the court shall set a date for a hearing of the petition and shall give reasonable notice of the hearing to the licensed adoption agency and the petitioners by certified mail, return receipt requested, to the address of each as shown in the proceeding.

(c) The licensed adoption agency shall appear to represent the child. **Leg.H.** Enacted Stats 1992 ch 162 §10 (AB 2650), operative January 1, 1994.

§8918. Transfer of child to care of agency

At the hearing, if the court sustains the recommendation that the child be removed from the home of the petitioners because the licensed adoption agency has recommended denial or the petitioners desire to withdraw the petition or the court dismisses the petition and does not return the child to the child's parents, the court shall commit the child to the care of the licensed adoption agency for the agency to arrange adoptive placement or to make a suitable plan. **Leg.H.** Enacted Stats 1992 ch 162 §10 (AB 2650), operative January 1, 1994.

§ 8919. Readoption of children adopted through intercountry adoption

(a) In order to establish a record by which an adoptee can prove the facts of the foreign adoption, a state resident who has finalized an intercountry adoption in a foreign country shall file the petition to readopt within the earlier of 60 days of the adoptee's entry into the United States or the adoptee's 16th birthday. The petition shall include all of the following:

(1) A certified or otherwise official copy of the foreign decree, order, or certification of adoption that reflects finalization of the adoption in the foreign country.

(2) A certified or otherwise official copy of the child's foreign birth certificate.

(3) A certified translation of all documents described in this subdivision that are not written in English. The court shall accept the certified translation, if any, that was completed abroad for purposes of obtaining the child's visa or passport.

(4) Proof that the child was granted lawful entry into the United States as an immediate relative of the adoptive parent or parents.

(5) A report from at least one postplacement home visit by an intercountry adoption agency or a contractor of that agency licensed to provide intercountry adoption services in the State of California.

(6) A copy of the home study report previously completed for the international finalized adoption by an adoption agency authorized to provide intercountry adoption services pursuant to Section 8900.

(b) A readoption order shall not be granted unless the court receives a copy of the reports listed in paragraphs (5) and (6) of subdivision (a). The court shall consider the postplacement visit or visits and the previously completed home study when deciding whether to grant or deny the petition for readoption.

(c) If an adoptive parent who has adopted a child through an intercountry adoption that is finalized in a foreign country fails to file a petition pursuant to this section by the earlier of 60 days of the child's entry into the United States or the child's 16th birthday or fails to provide a copy of the petition to each adoption agency that provided the adoption services to the adoptive parent, then the adoption agency that facilitated the adoption shall file a petition within 90 days of the child's entry into the United States, and shall provide a file-marked copy of the petition to the adoptive parent and to any other adoption agency that provided services to the adoptive parent within five business days of filing. An adoptive parent shall be liable to the adoption agency for all costs and fees incurred as a result of good faith actions taken by the adoption agency to fulfill its requirement pursuant to this subdivision. If the adoption agency fails to file a petition as required by this subdivision, the department may take appropriate disciplinary action against the adoption agency if it is licensed in the State of California and the department has actual or constructive knowledge that the petition was not filed.

(d) If the court finds that the child may be the subject of human trafficking or may be a child who is described in Section 300 of the Welfare and Institutions Code, the court shall, in accordance with existing law, notify all appropriate authorities.

(e) Within 10 business days, the clerk of the court shall submit to the State Registrar the order granting the petition to readopt. Upon receipt, the State Registrar shall issue a delayed registration of birth in accordance with Section 102695 of the Health and Safety Code that lists the adoptive parent or parents as the child's legal parent or parents.

(f) A state resident who has adopted a child through an intercountry adoption that is finalized in a foreign country may obtain a birth certificate for that child pursuant to Section 102635 or 103450 of the Health and Safety Code. **Leg.H.** Added Stats 2019 ch 805 §3 (AB 677), effective January 1, 2020.

Prior Law: Former Fam C §8919, relating to readoption of children adopted through intercounty adoption, postplacement in-home visit and final adoption order, and obtaining birth certificate, was added Stats 1993 ch 219 §203 (AB 1500), amended Stats 2001 ch 353 §2 (AB 538), Stats 2006 ch 809 §1 (SB 1393), effective January 1, 2007, Stats 2007 ch 130 §92 (AB 299), effective January 1, 2008, and repealed Stats 2019 ch 805 §2 (AB 677), effective January 1, 2020.

§ 8919.5. Report of arrival

(a) An intercountry adoption agency shall report the arrival of an adoptee whose adoption was finalized in a foreign country to the department within 14 calendar days of the adoptee's arrival in California.

(b) If the adoption agency fails to report to the department pursuant to subdivision (a), the department may take appropriate disciplinary action against the adoption agency if it is licensed in the State of California. **Leg.H.** Added Stats 2019 ch 805 §4 (AB 677), effective January 1, 2020.

§8920. Readoption of children adopted through intercountry adoption; Visitation agreement following readoption of sibling

(a) A child who was adopted as part of a sibling group and who has been separated from the child's sibling or siblings through readoption by a resident of this state may petition the court to enforce any agreement for visitation to which the separate adoptive families of the siblings subscribed prior to the child's readoption or to order visitation if such agreement does not exist. The court may order that the agreement be enforced or grant visitation rights upon a finding that visitation is in the best interest of the child.

(b) In making a finding that enforcement of an existing agreement or the granting of visitation rights is in the best interest of the child under subdivision (a), the court shall take into consideration the nature and extent of the child's sibling relationship, including, but not limited to, whether the child was raised with a sibling in the same home, whether the child shares significant common experiences or has close and strong bonds with a sibling, and whether ongoing contact with a sibling is in the child's best interest, including the child's long-term interest.

(c) As used in this section, "sibling" means full-siblings or half-siblings.

(d) As used in this section, "readoption" means the process by which a child who belongs to a foreign-born sibling group that was adopted together through an intercountry adoption is subsequently adopted by a different set of adoptive parents who are residents of the state. **Leg.H.**

Added Stats 2003 ch 19 §1 (SB 169). Amended Stats 2019 ch 115 §132 (AB 1817), effective January 1, 2020.

§8921. Bond as prerequisite to facilitating convention adoption [Repealed]

Leg.H. Added Stats 2007 ch 583 §7 (SB 703), effective January 1, 2008. Repealed Stats 2023 ch 43 §12 (AB 120), effective July 10, 2023.

Prior Law Former Fam C §8921, relating to bond as prerequisite to facilitating convention adoption, was added Stats 2007 ch 583 §7 (SB 703), effective January 1, 2008.

§8923. Complaints in connection with convention adoption; Notice to department; Revocation of license

(a) A complaint against an accredited agency or approved person in connection with a convention adoption shall be filed according to the procedures set forth in Subpart J (commencing with Section 96.68) of Part 96 of Title 22 of the Code of Federal Regulations.

(b) Each private full-service adoption agency and noncustodial adoption agency licensed by the department under this chapter shall notify the department of any complaint filed against it pursuant to Subpart J (commencing with Section 96.68) of Part 96 of Title 22 of the Code of Federal Regulations.

(c) The department may revoke the license of any agency that fails to comply with the provisions of this chapter and Part 96 of Title 22 of the Code of Federal Regulations. **Leg.H.** Added Stats 2007 ch 583 §8 (SB 703), effective January 1, 2008.

§8924. Duties of agency or person providing adoption service for child emigrating to convention country

(a) For cases in which a child is emigrating from California to a convention country, an accredited agency or approved person providing any adoption service described in this chapter, shall perform all of the following:

(1) A background study on the child prepared in accordance with all requirements set forth in subdivisions (a) and (b) of Section 96.53 of Title 22 of the Code of Federal Regulations, Section 8706, and applicable state law.

(2) Consents are obtained in accordance with subdivision (c) of Section 96.53 of Title 22 of the Code of Federal Regulations and applicable state law.

(3) If the child is 12 years of age or older, the agency or person has given due consideration to the child's wishes or opinions before determining that an intercountry adoption is in the child's best interests and in accordance with applicable state law.

(4) Transmission to the United States Department of State or other competent authority, or accredited bodies of the convention country, of the child background study, proof that the necessary consents have been obtained, and the reasons for the determination that the placement is in the child's best interests.

(b) The accredited agency shall comply with all placement standards set forth in Section 96.54 of Title 22 of the Code of Federal Regulations for children emigrating from California to a convention country.

(c) The accredited agency shall keep the central authority of the convention country and the Secretary informed as necessary about the adoption process and the measures taken to complete it for children emigrating from California to a convention country, in accordance with all communication and coordination functions set forth in Section 96.55 of Title 22 of the Code of Federal Regulations.

(d) For all convention and nonconvention adoption cases involving children emigrating from California to a convention country, the agency, person, or public domestic authority providing adoption services shall report information to the Secretary in accordance with Part 99 of Title 22 of the Code of Federal Regulations. **Leg.H.** Added Stats 2007 ch 583 §9 (SB 703), effective January 1, 2008.

§8925. Recognition of Hague adoption certificate or custody declaration

A Hague adoption certificate or, in outgoing cases, a Hague custody declaration, obtained pursuant to Part 97 of Title 22 of the Code of Federal Regulations shall be recognized as a final valid adoption for purposes of all state and local laws. **Leg.H.** Added Stats 2007 ch 583 §10 (SB 703), effective January 1, 2008.

CHAPTER 5
STEPPARENT ADOPTIONS

Adoption petition; Order. §9000.
Stepparent adoption for a child born during a marriage, domestic partnership or civil union. §9000.5.
Investigation; Written investigative report; Fees. §9001.
Cost of investigation. §9002.
Consent of birth parents to adoption. §9003.
Consent form. §9004.
Motion or petition to withdraw consent. §9005.
Notice of withdrawal or dismissal; Dismissal where consent refused. §9006.
Appearance of prospective adoptive parent and child. §9007.

§9000. Adoption petition; Order

(a) A stepparent desiring to adopt a child of the stepparent's spouse may for that purpose file a petition in any county authorized by Section 8609.5.

(b) A domestic partner, as defined in Section 297, desiring to adopt a child of the other domestic partner may, for that purpose, file a petition in any county authorized pursuant to Section 8609.5.

(c) The caption of the adoption petition shall contain the names of the petitioners, but not the child's name. The petition shall state the child's sex and date of birth and the name the child had before adoption.

(d) If the child is the subject of a guardianship petition, the adoption petition shall so state and shall include the caption and docket number or have attached a copy of the letters of the guardianship or temporary guardianship. The petitioners shall notify the court of any petition for guardianship or temporary guardianship filed after the adoption petition. The guardianship proceeding shall be consolidated with the adoption proceeding.

(e) The order of adoption shall contain the child's adopted name and the name the child had before adoption.

(f) If the petitioner has entered into a postadoption contact agreement pursuant to Section 8616.5, the petitioner shall file the agreement, signed by the participating parties, with the court before the adoption is finalized.

(g) For the purposes of this chapter, stepparent adoption includes adoption by a domestic partner, as defined in Section 297. **Leg.H.** Enacted Stats 1992 ch 162 §10 (AB 2650), operative January 1, 1994. Amended Stats 2001 ch 893 §5 (AB 25); Stats 2004 ch 858 §7 (SB 1357); Stats 2019 ch 115 §133 (AB 1817), effective January 1, 2020; Stats 2022 ch 159 §9 (AB 2495), effective January 1, 2023; Stats 2023 ch 851 §10 (AB 1650), effective January 1, 2024.

§9000.5. Stepparent adoption for a child born during a marriage, domestic partnership or civil union

(a) The procedures provided in this section apply to a stepparent adoption where the child was born during the marriage or domestic partnership, including a registered domestic partnership or civil union from another jurisdiction, and either of the following circumstances applies:

(1) One of the spouses or partners gave birth to the child.

(2) The child was born through a gestational surrogacy process brought about by one or both of the spouses or partners, and the parentage of only one spouse or partner was established pursuant to the Uniform Parentage Act (Part 3 (commencing with Section 7600) of Division 12) or another parentage proceeding related to the surrogacy.

(b)(1) The following are not required in stepparent adoptions under this section unless otherwise ordered by the court for good cause:

(A) A home investigation pursuant to Section 9001 or a home study.

(B) Costs incurred pursuant to Section 9002.

(C) A hearing pursuant to Section 9007.

(2) In stepparent adoptions under this section, the parties shall not be required to have been married or in a domestic partnership, including a registered domestic partnership or civil union from another jurisdiction, for a minimum period of time prior to the adoption being granted or to provide verification of their income or education.

(c) For stepparent adoptions filed under this section, the following shall be filed with the petition for adoption:

(1) A copy of the parties' marriage certificate, registered domestic partner certificate, or civil union from another jurisdiction.

(2) A copy of the child's birth certificate.

(3) Declarations by the parent who gave birth, or who caused the birth through gestational surrogacy, and the spouse or partner who is adopting

explaining the circumstances of the child's conception in detail sufficient to identify whether there may be other persons with a claim to parentage of the child who are required to be provided notice of, or who must consent to, the adoption.

(d) The court may order a hearing to ascertain whether there are additional persons who must be provided notice of, or who must consent to, the adoption if it appears from the face of the pleadings and the evidence that proper notice or consent have not been provided.

(e) The court shall grant the stepparent adoption under this section upon finding both of the following:

(1) That the parent who gave birth, or who caused the birth through gestational surrogacy, and the spouse or partner who is adopting were married or in a domestic partnership, including a registered domestic partnership or civil union from another jurisdiction, at the time of the child's birth.

(2) Any other person with a claim to parentage of the child who is required to be provided notice of, or who must consent to, the adoption has been noticed or provided consent to the adoption. **Leg.H.** Added Stats 2014 ch 636 §3 (AB 2344), effective January 1, 2015. Amended Stats 2019 ch 192 §2 (AB 1373), effective January 1, 2020; Stats 2021 ch 199 §1 (AB 746), effective January 1, 2022.

§9001. Investigation; Written investigative report; Fees

(a) Except as provided in Section 9000.5, before granting or denying a stepparent adoption request, the court shall review and consider a written investigative report. The report in a stepparent adoption case shall not require a home study unless so ordered by the court upon request of an investigator or interested person, or on the court's own motion. "Home study" as used in this section means a physical investigation of the premises where the child is residing.

(b) At the time of filing the adoption request, the petitioner shall inform the court in writing if the petitioner is electing to have the investigation and written report completed by a licensed clinical social worker, a licensed marriage and family therapist, a licensed professional clinical counselor, or a private licensed adoption agency, in which cases the petitioner shall not be required to pay an investigation fee pursuant to Section 9002 at the time of filing, but shall pay these fees directly to the investigator. Absent that notification, the court may, at the time of filing, collect an investigation fee pursuant to Section 9002, and may assign one of the following to complete the investigation: a probation officer, a qualified court investigator, or the county welfare department, if so authorized by the board of supervisors of the county where the action is pending.

(c) If a private licensed adoption agency conducts the investigation, it shall assign the investigation to a licensed clinical social worker, licensed professional clinical counselor, or licensed marriage and family therapist associated with the agency. A grievance regarding the investigation shall be directed to the licensing authority of the clinical social worker, licensed professional clinical counselor, or marriage and family therapist, as applicable.

(d) This section does not require the State Department of Social Services to issue regulations for stepparent adoptions. **Leg.H.** Enacted Stats 1992 ch 162 §10 (AB 2650), operative January 1, 1994. Amended Stats 1993 ch 219 §204 (AB 1500); Stats 2001 ch 353 §3 (AB 538); Stats 2010 ch 588 §8 (AB 2020), effective January 1, 2011; Stats 2014 ch 636 §4 (AB 2344), effective January 1, 2015; Stats 2016 ch 702 §1 (AB 2872), effective January 1, 2017; Stats 2018 ch 389 §17 (AB 2296), effective January 1, 2019.

§9002. Cost of investigation

Except as provided in Section 9000.5, in a stepparent adoption, the prospective adoptive parent is liable for all reasonable costs incurred in connection with the stepparent adoption, including, but not limited to, costs incurred for the investigation required by Section 9001, up to a maximum of seven hundred dollars ($700). The court, probation officer, qualified court investigator, or county welfare department may defer, waive, or reduce the fee if its payment would cause economic hardship to the prospective adoptive parent detrimental to the welfare of the adopted child. **Leg.H.** Enacted Stats 1992 ch 162 §10 (AB 2650), operative January 1, 1994. Amended Stats 1993 ch 219 §205 (AB 1500), ch 494 §1 (AB 1430); Stats 2001 ch 893 §6 (AB 25); Stats 2014 ch 636 §5 (AB 2344), effective January 1, 2015.

§9003. Consent of birth parents to adoption

(a) In a stepparent adoption, the consent of either or both birth parents shall be signed in the presence of a notary public, court clerk, probation officer, qualified court investigator, authorized representative of a licensed adoption agency, or county welfare department staff member of any county of this state. The petitioner, petitioner's counsel, or person before whom the consent is signed shall immediately file the consent with the clerk of the court where the adoption request is filed. If the request has not been filed at the time the consent has been signed, the consent shall be filed simultaneously with the adoption request. Upon filing of the adoption request, the clerk shall immediately notify the probation officer or, at the option of the board of supervisors, the county welfare department of that county.

(b) If the birth parent of a child to be adopted is outside this state at the time of signing the consent, the consent may be signed before an authorized representative of an adoption agency licensed in the state or country where the consent is being signed, a notary, or other person authorized to perform notarial acts.

(c) The consent, when reciting that the person giving it is entitled to sole custody of the child and when acknowledged before any authorized witness specified in subdivision (a), is prima facie evidence of the right of the person signing the consent to the sole custody of the child and that person's sole right to consent.

(d) A birth parent who is a minor has the right to sign a consent for the adoption of the birth parent's child and the consent is not subject to revocation by reason of the minority. **Leg.H.** Enacted Stats 1992 ch 162 §10 (AB 2650), operative January 1, 1994. Amended Stats 1993 ch 219 §206 (AB 1500); Stats 2005 ch 627 §4 (SB 302), effective January 1, 2006; Stats 2011 ch 462 §8 (AB 687), effective January 1, 2012.

§9004. Consent form

In a stepparent adoption, the form prescribed by the department for the consent of the birth parent shall contain substantially the following notice:

"Notice to the parent who gives the child for adoption: If you and your child lived together at any time as parent and child, the adoption of your child through a stepparent adoption does not affect the child's right to inherit your property or the property of other blood relatives." **Leg.H.** Enacted Stats 1992 ch 162 §10 (AB 2650), operative January 1, 1994. Amended Stats 2001 ch 893 §7 (AB 25).

§9005. Motion or petition to withdraw consent

(a) Consent of the birth parent to the adoption of the child through a stepparent adoption may not be withdrawn except with court approval. Request for that approval may be made by motion, or a birth parent seeking to withdraw consent may file with the clerk of the court where the adoption petition is pending, a petition for approval of withdrawal of consent, without the necessity of paying a fee for filing the petition. The petition or motion shall be in writing, and shall set forth the reasons for withdrawal of consent, but otherwise may be in any form.

(b) The court clerk shall set the matter for hearing and shall give notice thereof to the probation officer, qualified court investigator, or county welfare department, to the prospective adoptive parent, and to the birth parent or parents by certified mail, return receipt requested, to the address of each as shown in the proceeding, at least 10 days before the time set for hearing.

(c) The probation officer, qualified court investigator, or county welfare department shall, before the hearing of the motion or petition for withdrawal, file a full report with the court and shall appear at the hearing to represent the interests of the child.

(d) At the hearing, the parties may appear in person or with counsel. The hearing shall be held in chambers, but the court reporter shall report the proceedings and, on court order, the fee therefor shall be paid from the county treasury. If the court finds that withdrawal of the consent to adoption is reasonable in view of all the circumstances and that withdrawal of the consent is in the child's best interest, the court shall approve the withdrawal of the consent. Otherwise the court shall withhold its approval. Consideration of the child's best interest shall include, but is not limited to, an assessment of the child's age, the extent of bonding with the prospective adoptive parent, the extent of bonding or the potential to bond with the birth parent, and the ability of the birth parent to provide adequate and proper care and guidance to the child. If the court approves the withdrawal of consent, the adoption proceeding shall be dismissed.

(e) A court order granting or withholding approval of a withdrawal of consent to an adoption may be appealed in the same manner as an order of the juvenile court declaring a person to be a ward of the juvenile court. **Leg.H.** Enacted Stats 1992 ch 162 §10 (AB 2650), operative January 1, 1994. Amended Stats 1993 ch 219 §207 (AB 1500); Stats 2001 ch 893 §8 (AB 25).

§9006. Notice of withdrawal or dismissal; Dismissal where consent refused

(a) If the petitioner moves to withdraw the adoption petition or to dismiss the proceeding, the court clerk shall immediately notify the probation officer, qualified court investigator, or county welfare department of the action, unless a home investigation was not required pursuant to Section 9000.5.

(b) If a birth parent has refused to give the required consent, the adoption petition shall be dismissed. **Leg.H.** Enacted Stats 1992 ch 162 §10 (AB 2650), operative January 1, 1994. Amended Stats 1993 ch 219 §208 (AB 1500); Stats 2014 ch 636 §6 (AB 2344), effective January 1, 2015.

§9007. Appearance of prospective adoptive parent and child

Except as provided in Section 9000.5, the prospective adoptive parent and the child proposed to be adopted shall appear before the court pursuant to Sections 8612, 8613, and 8613.5. **Leg.H.** Enacted Stats 1992 ch 162 §10 (AB 2650), operative January 1, 1994. Amended Stats 2009 ch 492 §5 (AB 941), effective January 1, 2010; Stats 2014 ch 636 §7 (AB 2344), effective January 1, 2015.

CHAPTER 6
VACATION OF ADOPTION

Petition to set aside adoption. §9100.
Court order to county officer. §9101.
Limitation of actions. §9102.

§9100. Petition to set aside adoption

(a) If a child adopted pursuant to the law of this state shows evidence of a developmental disability or mental illness as a result of conditions existing before the adoption to an extent that the child cannot be relinquished to an adoption agency on the grounds that a plan of adoption is not currently suitable, and of which conditions the adoptive parents or parent had no knowledge or notice before the entry of the order of adoption, a petition setting forth those facts may be filed by the adoptive parents or parent with the court that granted the adoption petition. If these facts are proved to the satisfaction of the court, it may make an order setting aside the order of adoption.

(b) The petition shall be filed within five years after the entry of the order of adoption.

(c)(1) The court clerk shall immediately notify the department at Sacramento of the petition. Within 60 days after the notice, the department shall file a full report with the court and shall appear before the court for the purpose of representing the adopted child.

(2) Notwithstanding any other law, an adoption case file, including a juvenile case file, as defined in subdivision (e) of Section 827 of the Welfare and Institutions Code, may be inspected and copied by the department for the purpose of completing the duties pursuant to this subdivision. **Leg.H.** Enacted Stats 1992 ch 162 §10 (AB 2650), operative January 1, 1994. Amended Stats 2022 ch 870 §1 (AB 2711), effective January 1, 2023.

§9101. Court order to county officer

(a) If an order of adoption is set aside as provided in Section 9100, the court making the order shall direct the district attorney, the county counsel, or the county welfare department to take appropriate action under the Welfare and Institutions Code. The court may also make any order relative to the care, custody, or confinement of the child pending the proceeding the court sees fit.

(b) The county in which the proceeding for adoption was had is liable for the child's support until the child is able to be self-supporting. **Leg.H.** Enacted Stats 1992 ch 162 §10 (AB 2650), operative January 1, 1994. Amended Stats 2019 ch 115 §134 (AB 1817), effective January 1, 2020.

§9102. Limitation of actions

(a) Except as provided in Section 9100, an action or proceeding of any kind to vacate, set aside, or otherwise nullify an order of adoption on any ground, except fraud, shall be commenced within one year after entry of the order.

(b) Except as provided in Section 9100, an action or proceeding of any kind to vacate, set aside, or nullify an order of adoption, based on fraud, shall be commenced within three years after entry of the order, or within 90 days of discovery of the fraud, whichever is earlier.

(c) In any action to set aside an order of adoption pursuant to this section or Section 9100, the court shall first determine whether the facts presented are legally sufficient to set aside the order of adoption. If the facts are not legally sufficient, the petition shall be denied. If the facts are legally sufficient, the court's final ruling on the matter shall take into consideration the best interests of the child, in conjunction with all other factors required by law.

(d) The department shall not be required under any circumstances to investigate a petition filed pursuant to this section or to represent a child who is the subject of a proceeding under this section. **Leg.H.** Enacted Stats 1992 ch 162 §10 (AB 2650), operative January 1, 1994. Amended Stats 1995 ch 567 §1 (AB 898); Stats 2000 ch 937 §6 (AB 2433); Stats 2011 ch 462 §9 (AB 687), effective January 1, 2012.

CHAPTER 7
DISCLOSURE OF INFORMATION

Confidentiality of records; Certificate of adoption. §9200.
Information to public agencies and licensed adoption agencies. §9201.
Medical report. §9202.
Access to blood samples. §9202.5.
Disclosure of identity of birth parents. §9203.
Request for disclosure of adoption homestudy. §9203.1.
Waiver of confidentiality of adoption records. §9204.
Request for contact with sibling; Confidential intermediary; Implementation of 2006 amendments; Funding and expenditures for programs and activities. §9205.
Release of letters, photographs, or other items of personal property. §9206.
Copy of final order of adoption of Indian child to Secretary of Interior. §9208.
Information as to tribal affiliation. §9209.

§9200. Confidentiality of records; Certificate of adoption

(a) The petition, relinquishment or consent, agreement, order, report to the court from any investigating agency, and any power of attorney and deposition filed in the office of the clerk of the court pursuant to this part is not open to inspection by any person other than the parties to the proceeding and their attorneys and the department, except upon the written authority of the judge of the superior court. A judge of the superior court may not authorize anyone to inspect the petition, relinquishment or consent, agreement, order, report to the court from any investigating agency, or power of attorney or deposition or any portion of any of these documents, except in exceptional circumstances and for good cause approaching the necessitous. The petitioner may be required to pay the expenses for preparing the copies of the documents to be inspected.

(b) Upon written request of any party to the proceeding and upon the order of any judge of the superior court, the clerk of the court shall not provide any documents referred to in this section for inspection or copying to any other person, unless the name of the child's birth parents or any information tending to identify the child's birth parents is deleted from the documents or copies thereof.

(c) Upon the request of the adoptive parents or the child, a clerk of the court may issue a certificate of adoption that states the date and place of adoption, the child's birth date, the names of the adoptive parents, and the name the child has taken. Unless the child has been adopted by a stepparent, the certificate shall not state the name of the child's birth parents. **Leg.H.** Enacted Stats 1992 ch 162 §10 (AB 2650), operative January 1, 1994. Amended Stats 2002 ch 784 §114 (SB 1316).

§9201. Information to public agencies and licensed adoption agencies

(a) Except as otherwise permitted or required by statute, neither the department nor a licensed adoption agency shall release information that would identify persons who receive, or have received, adoption services.

(b) Employees of the department and licensed adoption agencies shall release to the department at Sacramento any requested information, including identifying information, for the purposes of recordkeeping and monitoring, evaluation, and regulation of the provision of adoption services.

(c) Prior to the placement of a child for adoption, the department or licensed adoption agency may, upon the written request of both a birth and a prospective adoptive parent, arrange for contact between these birth and prospective adoptive parents that may include the sharing of identifying information regarding these parents.

(d) The department and any licensed adoption agency may, upon written authorization for the release of specified information by the subject of that information, share information regarding a prospective adoptive parent or birth parent with other social service agencies, including the department, other licensed adoption agencies, counties or licensed foster family agencies for purposes of approving a resource family pursuant to subparagraph (A) of paragraph (4) of subdivision (p) of Section 16519.5 of the Welfare and Institutions Code, or providers of health care as defined in Section 56.05 of the Civil Code.

(e) Notwithstanding any other law, the department and any licensed adoption agency may furnish information relating to an adoption petition or to a child in the custody of the department or any licensed adoption agency to the juvenile court, county welfare department, public welfare agency, private welfare agency licensed by the department, provider of foster care services, potential adoptive parent, or provider of health care as defined in Section 56.05 of the Civil Code, if it is believed the child's welfare will be promoted thereby.

(f) The department and any licensed adoption agency may make adoption case records, including identifying information, available for research purposes, provided that the research will not result in the disclosure of the identity of the child or the parties to the adoption to anyone other than the entity conducting the research. **Leg.H.** Enacted Stats 1992 ch 162 §10 (AB 2650), operative January 1, 1994. Amended Stats 2000 ch 910 §5 (AB 2921); Stats 2006 ch 538 §161 (SB 1852), effective January 1, 2007; Stats 2016 ch 612 §11 (AB 1997), effective January 1, 2017.

2016 Note: For adoption of regulations, see the 2016 Note following §6552.

§9202. Medical report

(a) Notwithstanding any other law, the department or licensed adoption agency that made a medical report required by Section 8706, 8817, or 8909 shall provide a copy of the medical report, in the manner the department prescribes by regulation, to any of the following persons upon the person's request:

(1) A person who has been adopted pursuant to this part and who has attained the age of 18 years or who presents a certified copy of the person's marriage certificate.

(2) The adoptive parent of a person under the age of 18 years who has been adopted pursuant to this part.

(b) A person who is denied access to a medical report pursuant to regulations adopted pursuant to this section may petition the court for review of the reasonableness of the department's or licensed adoption agency's decision.

(c) The names and addresses of any persons contained in the report shall be removed unless the person requesting the report has previously received the information. **Leg.H.** Enacted Stats 1992 ch 162 §10 (AB 2650), operative January 1, 1994. Amended Stats 2000 ch 910 §6 (AB 2921).

§9202.5. Access to blood samples

(a) Notwithstanding any other law, the laboratory that is storing a blood sample pursuant to Section 8706, 8817, or 8909 shall provide access to the blood sample to only the following persons upon the person's request:

(1) A person who has been adopted pursuant to this part.

(2) The adoptive parent of a person under the age of 18 years who has been adopted pursuant to this part. The adoptive parent may receive access to the blood sample only after entry of the order of adoption.

(b) The birth parent or parents shall be given access to any DNA test results related to the blood sample on request.

(c) Except as provided in subdivision (b), no person other than the adoptive parent and the adopted child shall have access to the blood sample or any DNA test results related to the blood sample, unless the adoptive parent or the child authorizes another person or entity to have that access. **Leg.H.** Added Stats 1996 ch 1053 §4 (AB 3241).

§9203. Disclosure of identity of birth parents

(a) The department or a licensed adoption agency shall do the following:

(1) Upon the request of a person who has been adopted pursuant to this part and who has attained 21 years of age, disclose the identity of the person's birth parent or parents and their most current address shown in the records of the department or licensed adoption agency, if the birth parent or parents have indicated consent to the disclosure in writing.

(2) Upon the request of the birth parent of a person who has been adopted pursuant to this part and who has attained 21 years of age, disclose the adopted name of the adoptee and the adoptee's most current address shown in the records of the department or licensed adoption agency, if the adult adoptee has indicated in writing, pursuant to the registration program developed by the department, that the adult adoptee wishes the adult adoptee's name and address to be disclosed.

(3) Upon the request of the adoptive parent of a person under 21 years of age who has been adopted pursuant to this part, disclose the identity of a birth parent and the birth parent's most current address shown in the records of the department or licensed adoption agency if the department or licensed adoption agency finds that a medical necessity or other extraordinary circumstances justify the disclosure.

(b) The department shall prescribe the form of the request required by this section. The form shall provide for an affidavit to be executed by the requester that to the best of the requester's knowledge the requester is an adoptee, the adoptee's birth parent, or the adoptee's adoptive parent. The department may adopt regulations requiring any additional means of identification from a requester that it deems necessary. The request shall advise an adoptee that if the adoptee consents, the adoptee's adoptive parents will be notified of the filing of the request before the release of the name and address of the adoptee's birth parent.

(c) Subdivision (a) is not applicable if a birth parent or an adoptee has indicated a desire that the name or address of the birth parent or adoptee not be disclosed.

(d) Within 20 working days of receipt of a request for information pursuant to this section, the department shall either respond to the request or forward the request to a licensed adoption agency that was a party to the adoption.

(e) Notwithstanding any other law, the department shall announce the availability of the present method of arranging contact among an adult adoptee, the adult adoptee's birth parents, and adoptive parents authorized by Section 9204 utilizing a means of communication appropriate to inform the public effectively.

(f) The department or licensed adoption agency may charge a reasonable fee in an amount the department establishes by regulation to cover the costs of processing requests for information made pursuant to subdivision (a). The department or licensed adoption agency shall waive fees authorized by this section for a person who is receiving public assistance pursuant to Part 3 (commencing with Section 11000) of Division 9 of the Welfare and Institutions Code. The revenue resulting from the fees so charged shall be utilized by the department or licensed adoption agency to increase existing staff as needed to process these requests. Fees received by the department shall be deposited in the Adoption Information Fund. This revenue shall be in addition to any other funds appropriated in support of the state adoption program.

(g) This section applies only to adoptions in which the relinquishment for or consent to adoption was signed or the birth parent's rights were involuntarily terminated by court action on or after January 1, 1984. **Leg.H.** Enacted Stats 1992 ch 162 §10 (AB 2650), operative January 1, 1994. Amended Stats 2000 ch 910 §7 (AB 2921); Stats 2019 ch 115 §135 (AB 1817), effective January 1, 2020.

§9203.1. Request for disclosure of adoption homestudy

(a) The department or a licensed adoption agency shall, upon the request of a prospective adoptive parent, disclose an adoption homestudy and any updates to an adoption homestudy to a county or licensed foster family agency for the purpose of approving the prospective adoptive parent as a resource family pursuant to subparagraph (A) of paragraph (4) of subdivision (p) of Section 16519.5 of the Welfare and Institutions Code.

(b) The department shall prescribe the form of the request described in subdivision (a).

(c) The department or a licensed adoption agency shall respond to a request made pursuant to subdivision (a) within 20 working days of receiving it.

(d) The department or a licensed adoption agency may charge a fee to cover the reasonable costs of processing requests made pursuant to subdivision (a). The department or a licensed adoption agency shall waive fees authorized by this subdivision for any person who is receiving public assistance pursuant to Part 3 (commencing with Section 11000) of Division 9 of the Welfare and Institutions Code. **Leg.H.** Added Stats 2016 ch 612 §12 (AB 1997), effective January 1, 2017.

2016 Note: For adoption of regulations, see the 2016 Note following §6552.

§9204. Waiver of confidentiality of adoption records

(a) Notwithstanding any other law, if an adult adoptee and the adult adoptee's birth parents have each filed a written consent with the department or licensed adoption agency, the department or licensed adoption agency may arrange for contact between those persons. Neither the department nor a licensed adoption agency may solicit, directly or indirectly, the execution of a written consent.

(b) The written consent authorized by this section shall be in a form prescribed by the department. **Leg.H.** Enacted Stats 1992 ch 162 §10 (AB 2650), operative January 1, 1994.

§9205. Request for contact with sibling; Confidential intermediary; Implementation of 2006 amendments; Funding and expenditures for programs and activities

(a) Notwithstanding any other law, the department, county adoption agency, or licensed adoption agency that joined in the adoption petition shall release the names and addresses of siblings to one another if both of the siblings have attained 18 years of age and have filed the following with the department or agency:

(1) A current address.

(2) A written request for contact with any sibling whose existence is known to the person making the request.

(3) A written waiver of the person's rights with respect to the disclosure of the person's name and address to the sibling, if the person is an adoptee.

(b) Upon inquiry and proof that a person is the sibling of an adoptee who has filed a waiver pursuant to this section, the department, county adoption agency, or licensed adoption agency may advise the sibling that a waiver has been filed by the adoptee. The department, county adoption agency, or licensed adoption agency may charge a reasonable fee, not to exceed fifty dollars ($50), for providing the service required by this section.

(c) An adoptee may revoke a waiver filed pursuant to this section by giving written notice of revocation to the department or agency.

(d) The department shall adopt a form for the request authorized by this section. The form shall provide for an affidavit to be executed by a person seeking to employ the procedure provided by this section that, to the best of the person's knowledge, the person is an adoptee or sibling of an adoptee. The form also shall contain a notice of an adoptee's rights pursuant to subdivision (c) and a statement that information will be disclosed only if there is a currently valid waiver on file with the department or agency. The department may adopt regulations requiring any additional means of identification from a person making a request pursuant to this section as it deems necessary.

(e) The department, county adoption agency, or licensed adoption agency may not solicit the execution of a waiver authorized by this section. However, the department shall announce the availability of the procedure authorized by this section, utilizing a means of communication appropriate to inform the public effectively.

(f) Notwithstanding the age requirement described in subdivision (a), an adoptee or sibling who is under 18 years of age may file a written waiver of confidentiality for the release of the person's name, address, and telephone number pursuant to this section provided that, if an adoptee, the adoptive parent consents, and, if a sibling, the sibling's legal parent or guardian consents. If the sibling is under the jurisdiction of the dependency court and has no legal parent or guardian able or available to provide consent, the dependency court may provide that consent.

(g) Notwithstanding subdivisions (a) and (e), an adoptee or sibling who seeks contact with the other for whom no waiver is on file may petition the court to appoint a confidential intermediary. If the sibling being sought is the adoptee, the intermediary shall be the department, county adoption agency, or licensed adoption agency that provided adoption services as described in Section 8521 or 8533. If the sibling being sought was formerly under the jurisdiction of the juvenile court, but is not an adoptee, the intermediary shall be the department, the county child welfare agency that provided services to the dependent child, or the licensed adoption agency that provided adoption services to the sibling seeking contact, as appropriate. If the court finds that the agency that conducted the adoptee's adoption is unable, due to economic hardship, to serve as the intermediary, then the agency shall provide all records related to the adoptee or the sibling to the court and the court shall appoint an alternate confidential intermediary. The court shall grant the petition unless it finds that it would be detrimental to the adoptee or sibling with whom contact is sought. The intermediary shall have access to all records of the adoptee or the sibling and shall make all reasonable efforts to locate and attempt to obtain the consent of the adoptee, sibling, or adoptive or birth parent, as required to make the disclosure authorized by this section. The confidential intermediary shall notify any located adoptee, sibling, or adoptive or birth parent that consent is optional, not required by law, and does not affect the status of the adoption. If that individual denies the request for consent, the confidential intermediary shall not make any further attempts to obtain consent. The confidential intermediary shall use information found in the records of the adoptee or the sibling for authorized purposes only, and may not disclose that information without authorization. If contact is sought with an adoptee or sibling who is under 18 years of age, the confidential intermediary shall contact and obtain the consent of that child's legal parent before contacting the child. If the sibling is under 18 years of age, under the jurisdiction of the dependency court, and has no legal parent or guardian able or available to provide consent, the intermediary shall obtain that consent from the dependency court. If the adoptee is seeking information regarding a sibling who is known to be a dependent child of the juvenile court, the procedures set forth in subdivision (b) of Section 388 of the Welfare and Institutions Code shall be utilized. If the adoptee is foreign born and was the subject of an intercountry adoption as defined in Section 8527, the adoption agency may fulfill the reasonable efforts requirement by utilizing all information in the agency's case file, and any information received upon request from the foreign adoption agency that conducted the adoption, if any, to locate and attempt to obtain the consent of the adoptee, sibling, or adoptive or birth parent. If that information is neither in the agency's case file, nor received from the foreign adoption agency, or if the attempts to locate are unsuccessful, then the agency shall be relieved of any further obligation to search for the adoptee or the sibling.

(h) For purposes of this section, "sibling" means a biological sibling, half-sibling, or step-sibling of the adoptee.

(i) It is the intent of the Legislature that implementation of some or all of the changes made to this section by Chapter 386 of the Statutes of 2006 shall continue, to the extent possible.

(j) Beginning in the 2011–12 fiscal year, and each fiscal year thereafter, funding and expenditures for programs and activities under this section shall be in accordance with the requirements provided in Sections 30025 and 30026.5 of the Government Code. **Leg.H.** Enacted Stats 1992 ch 162 §10 (AB 2650), operative January 1, 1994. Amended Stats 2006 ch 386 §1 (AB 2488), effective January 1, 2007; Stats 2007 ch 130 §93 (AB 299), effective January 1, 2008; Stats 2008 ch 759 §15 (AB 1279), effective September 30, 2008; Stats 2010 ch 725 §2 (AB 1612), effective October 19, 2010; Stats 2011 ch 8 §1 (SB 72), effective March 24, 2011; Stats 2012 ch 35 §36 (SB 1013), effective June 27, 2012; Stats 2019 ch 115 §136 (AB 1817), effective January 1, 2020.

2012 Note: For title and citation of Stats 2012 ch 35 (SB 1013), see 2012 Note following §8506.

§9206. Release of letters, photographs, or other items of personal property

(a) Notwithstanding any other law, the department or licensed adoption agency shall release any letters, photographs, or other items of personal property in its possession to an adoptee, birth parent, or adoptive parent, upon written request. The material may be requested by any of the following persons:

(1) The adoptee, if the adoptee has attained the age of 18 years.

(2) The adoptive parent or parents, on behalf of an adoptee under the age of 18 years, as long as instructions to the contrary have not been made by the depositor.

(3) The birth parent or parents.

(b) Notwithstanding any other law, all identifying names and addresses shall be deleted from the letters, photographs, or items of personal property before delivery to the requester.

(c) Letters, photographs, and other items of personal property deposited on or after January 1, 1985, shall be accompanied by a release form or similar document signed by the person depositing the material, specifying to whom the material may be released. At its discretion, the department or licensed adoption agency may refuse for deposit items of personal property that, because of value or bulk, would pose storage problems.

(d) Notwithstanding subdivisions (a) and (b), only the following photographs deposited before January 1, 1985, shall be released:

(1) Photographs of the adoptee that have been requested by the adoptee.

(2) Photographs that have been deposited by the adoptee, the adoptive parent or parents, or the birth parent or parents, and for which there is a letter or other document on file indicating that person's consent to the release of the photographs.

(e) The department and licensed adoption agencies may charge a fee to cover the actual costs of any services required by this section in excess of normal postadoptive services provided by the department or agency. The department shall develop a fee schedule that shall be implemented by the department and licensed adoption agencies in assessing charges to the person who deposits the material or the person to whom the material is released. The fee may be waived by the department or licensed adoption agencies in cases in which it is established that a financial hardship exists.

(f) "Photograph" as used in this section means a photograph of the person depositing the photograph or the person making the request for the release. **Leg.H.** Enacted Stats 1992 ch 162 §10 (AB 2650), operative January 1, 1994.

§9208. Copy of final order of adoption of Indian child to Secretary of Interior

(a) The clerk of the superior court entering a final order of adoption concerning an Indian child shall provide the United States Secretary of the Interior or a designee with a copy of the order within 30 days of the date of the order, together with any information necessary to show the following:

(1) The name and tribal affiliation of the child.

(2) The names and addresses of the biological parents.

(3) The names and addresses of the adoptive parents.

(4) The identity of any agency having files or information relating to that adoptive placement.

(b) If the court records contain an affidavit of the biological parent or parents that their identity remain confidential, the court shall include that affidavit with the other information. **Leg.H.** Added Stats 2006 ch 838 §13 (SB 678), effective January 1, 2007. Amended Stats 2019 ch 115 §137 (AB 1817), effective January 1, 2020.

§9209. Information as to tribal affiliation

(a) Upon application by an Indian individual who has reached the age of 18 years and who was the subject of an adoptive placement, the court which entered the final decree of adoption shall inform that individual of the tribal affiliation, if any, of the individual's biological parents and provide any other information as may be necessary to protect any rights flowing from the individual's tribal relationship, including, but not limited to, tribal membership rights or eligibility for federal or tribal programs or services available to Indians.

(b) If the court records contain an affidavit of the biological parent or parents that their identity remain confidential, the court shall inform the individual that the Secretary of the Interior may, upon request, certify to the individual's tribe that the individual's parentage and other circumstances of birth entitle the individual to membership under the criteria established by the tribe. **Leg.H.** Added Stats 2006 ch 838 §14 (SB 678), effective January 1, 2007.

CHAPTER 8
ADOPTION PROCEEDINGS: CONFLICT OF LAWS

Jurisdiction. §9210.
Applicability of Sections 9210 and 9211. §9212.
[Section renumbered 2013]. §9213.

§9210. Jurisdiction

(a) Except as otherwise provided in subdivisions (b) and (c), a court of this state has jurisdiction over a proceeding for the adoption of a minor commenced under this part if any of the following applies:

(1) Immediately before commencement of the proceeding, the minor lived in this state with a parent, a guardian, a prospective adoptive parent, or another person acting as parent, for at least six consecutive months, excluding periods of temporary absence, or, in the case of a minor under six months of age, lived in this state with any of those individuals from soon after birth and there is available in this state substantial evidence concerning the minor's present or future care.

(2) Immediately before commencement of the proceeding, the prospective adoptive parent lived in this state for at least six consecutive months, excluding periods of temporary absence, and there is available in this state substantial evidence concerning the minor's present or future care.

(3) The agency that placed the minor for adoption is located in this state and both of the following apply:

(A) The minor and the minor's parents, or the minor and the prospective adoptive parent, have a significant connection with this state.

(B) There is available in this state substantial evidence concerning the minor's present or future care.

(4) The minor and the prospective adoptive parent are physically present in this state and the minor has been abandoned or it is necessary in an emergency to protect the minor because the minor has been subjected to or threatened with mistreatment or abuse or is otherwise neglected.

(5) It appears that no other state would have jurisdiction under requirements substantially in accordance with paragraphs (1) to (4), inclusive, or another state has declined to exercise jurisdiction on the ground that this state is the more appropriate forum to hear a petition for adoption of the minor, and there is available in this state substantial evidence concerning the minor's present or future care.

(b) A court of this state may not exercise jurisdiction over a proceeding for adoption of a minor if at the time the petition for adoption is filed a proceeding concerning the custody or adoption of the minor is pending in a court of another state exercising jurisdiction substantially in conformity with this part, unless the proceeding is stayed by the court of the other state because this state is a more appropriate forum or for another reason.

(c) If a court of another state has issued a decree or order concerning the custody of a minor who may be the subject of a proceeding for adoption in this state, a court of this state may not exercise jurisdiction over a proceeding for adoption of the minor, unless both of the following apply:

(1) The requirements for modifying an order of a court of another state under this part are met, the court of another state does not have jurisdiction over a proceeding for adoption substantially in conformity with paragraphs (1) to (4), inclusive, of subdivision (a), or the court of another state has declined to assume jurisdiction over a proceeding for adoption.

(2) The court of this state has jurisdiction under this section over the proceeding for adoption.

(d) For purposes of subdivisions (b) and (c), "a court of another state" includes, in the case of an Indian child, a tribal court having and exercising jurisdiction over a custody proceeding involving the Indian child. **Leg.H.** Added Stats 2002 ch 260 §8 (SB 1512). Amended Stats 2003 ch 62 §89 (SB 600); Stats 2006 ch 838 §15 (SB 678), effective January 1, 2007.

§9211. [Section repealed 2013]

Leg.H. Added Stats 2002 ch 260 §8 (SB 1512). Amended Stats 2009 ch 492 §6 (AB 941), effective January 1, 2010. Repealed Stats 2012 ch 638 §13 (AB 1757), effective January 1, 2013. The repealed section related to locations for filing a petition for the adoption of a child.

§9212. Applicability of Sections 9210 and 9211

(a) Sections 9210 and 9211 apply to interstate adoptions if the prospective adoptive parents reside outside of the state.

(b) This section shall become operative only if Assembly Bill 746 of the 2001–02 Regular Session is enacted. If Assembly Bill 746 is not enacted, the application of Sections 9210 and 9211 is not intended to expand jurisdiction to apply to interstate adoptions if the prospective adoptive parents reside outside of the state. **Leg.H.** Added Stats 2002 ch 260 §8 (SB 1512). Amended Stats 2003 ch 62 §90 (SB 600).

2012 Note: Stats 2012 ch 638 (AB 1757) repealed Fam C §9211, operative January 1, 2013. The cross reference in this section was not corrected by the Legislature.

2002 Note: Assembly Bill 746 of the 2001–02 Regular Session was enacted as Stats 2002 ch 1112.

§9213. [Section renumbered 2013]

Leg.H. Added Stats 2011 ch 462 §10 (AB 687), effective January 1, 2012. Renumbered Fam C §9321.5 by Stats 2012 ch 162 §48 (SB 1171), effective January 1, 2013.

PART 3
ADOPTION OF ADULTS AND MARRIED MINORS

Chapter 1. General Provisions.
Chapter 2. Procedure for Adult Adoption.
Chapter 3. Procedure for Terminating Adult Adoption.

CHAPTER 1
GENERAL PROVISIONS

Adoption of adult or married minor. §9300.
Consent of spouse of prospective adoptive parent. §9301.
Consent of spouse of proposed adoptee. §9302.
Adoption of more than one unrelated adult within one year. §9303.
Name of adopted person. §9304.
Relationship of parent and child. §9305.
Relief from parental duties of birth parents. §9306.
Hearing open and public. §9307.

§9300. Adoption of adult or married minor

(a) An adult may be adopted by another adult, including a stepparent, as provided in this part.

(b) A married minor may be adopted in the same manner as an adult under this part. **Leg.H.** Enacted Stats 1992 ch 162 §10 (AB 2650), operative January 1, 1994. Amended Stats 1993 ch 266 §1 (SB 970).

§9301. Consent of spouse of prospective adoptive parent

A married person who is not lawfully separated from the person's spouse may not adopt an adult without the consent of the spouse, provided that the spouse is capable of giving that consent. **Leg.H.** Enacted Stats 1992 ch 162 §10 (AB 2650), operative January 1, 1994.

§9302. Consent of spouse of proposed adoptee

(a) A married person who is not lawfully separated from the person's spouse may not be adopted without the consent of the spouse, provided that the spouse is capable of giving that consent.

(b) The consent of the parents of the proposed adoptee, of the department, or of any other person is not required. **Leg.H.** Enacted Stats 1992 ch 162 §10 (AB 2650), operative January 1, 1994.

§9303. Adoption of more than one unrelated adult within one year

(a) Except as permitted by the court, upon a finding of good cause, a person shall not adopt more than one unrelated adult pursuant to this part within one year of the person's adoption of an unrelated adult unless the proposed adoptee is the biological sibling of a person previously adopted pursuant to this part or unless the proposed adoptee is disabled or physically handicapped. An order finding good cause shall be in writing or stated on the record.

(b) Except as permitted by the court, upon a finding of good cause, a person shall not adopt an unrelated adult pursuant to this part within one year of an adoption of another person pursuant to this part by the prospective adoptive parent's spouse unless the proposed adoptee is a biological sibling of a person previously adopted pursuant to this part. An order finding good cause shall be in writing or stated on the record. **Leg.H.** Enacted Stats 1992 ch 162 §10 (AB 2650), operative January 1, 1994. Amended Stats 2023 ch 478 §22 (AB 1756), effective January 1, 2024.

§9304. Name of adopted person

A person adopted pursuant to this part may take the family name of the adoptive parent. **Leg.H.** Enacted Stats 1992 ch 162 §10 (AB 2650), operative January 1, 1994.

§9305. Relationship of parent and child

After adoption, the adoptee and the adoptive parent or parents shall sustain towards each other the legal relationship of parent and child and have all the rights and are subject to all the duties of that relationship. **Leg.H.** Enacted Stats 1992 ch 162 §10 (AB 2650), operative January 1, 1994.

§9306. Relief from parental duties of birth parents

(a) Except as provided in subdivisions (b) and (c), the birth parents of a person adopted pursuant to this part are, from the time of the adoption, relieved of all parental duties towards, and all responsibility for, the adopted person, and have no right over the adopted person.

(b) If an adult is adopted by the spouse of a birth parent, the parental rights and responsibilities of that birth parent are not affected by the adoption.

(c) An adult being adopted pursuant to this part may waive the termination of the parental duties and responsibilities of an existing parent or parents under subdivision (a) by signing a waiver at any time prior to the finalization of the adoption. The waiver may be included in the adoption agreement or in a separate writing filed with the court. **Leg.H.** Enacted Stats 1992 ch 162 §10 (AB 2650), operative January 1, 1994. Amended Stats 1993 ch 266 §2 (SB 970); Stats 2019 ch 192 §3 (AB 1373), effective January 1, 2020.

§9307. Hearing open and public

A hearing with regard to adoption under Chapter 2 (commencing with Section 9320) or termination of a parent and child relationship under Chapter 3 (commencing with Section 9340) may, in the discretion of the court, be open and public. **Leg.H.** Enacted Stats 1992 ch 162 §10 (AB 2650), operative January 1, 1994.

CHAPTER 2
PROCEDURE FOR ADULT ADOPTION

Adoption agreement. §9320.
Petition for approval of adoption. §9321.
Petition for adult adoption. §9321.5.
Setting matter for hearing. §9322.
Notice to and appearance by interested persons. §9323.
Appearance by prospective adoptive parent and proposed adoptee. §9324.
Court's discretion to require report. §9325.
Notice of hearing for developmentally disabled adult. §9326.
Report concerning person with developmental disability. §9327.
Hearing and order. §9328.

§9320. Adoption agreement

(a) An adult may adopt another adult who is younger, except the spouse of the prospective adoptive parent, by an adoption agreement approved by the court, as provided in this chapter.

(b) The adoption agreement shall be in writing, executed by the prospective adoptive parent and the proposed adoptee, and shall state that the parties agree to assume toward each other the legal relationship of parent and child and to have all of the rights and be subject to all of the duties and responsibilities of that relationship. **Leg.H.** Enacted Stats 1992 ch 162 §10 (AB 2650), operative January 1, 1994.

§9321. Petition for approval of adoption

(a) The prospective adoptive parent and the proposed adoptee may file in the county in which either person resides a petition for approval of the adoption agreement.

(b) The petition for approval of the adoption agreement shall state all of the following:

(1) The length and nature of the relationship between the prospective adoptive parent and the proposed adoptee.

(2) The degree of kinship, if any.

(3) The reason the adoption is sought.

(4) A statement as to why the adoption would be in the best interest of the prospective adoptive parent, the proposed adoptee, and the public.

(5) The names and addresses of any living birth parents or adult children of the proposed adoptee.

(6) Whether the prospective adoptive parent or the prospective adoptive parent's spouse has previously adopted any other adult and, if so, the name of the adult, together with the date and place of the adoption. **Leg.H.** Enacted Stats 1992 ch 162 §10 (AB 2650), operative January 1, 1994.

§9321.5. Petition for adult adoption

(a) Notwithstanding Section 9321, a person who is a resident of this state may file a petition for adult adoption with the court in any of the following:

(1) The county in which the prospective adoptive parent resides.

(2) The county in which the proposed adoptee was born or resides at the time the petition was filed.

(3) The county in which an office of the public or private agency that placed the proposed adoptee for foster care or adoption as a minor or dependent child is located.

(b) A petitioner who is not a resident of this state may file a petition for adult adoption with the court in a county specified in paragraph (3) of subdivision (a). **Leg.H.** Added Stats 2011 ch 462 §10 (AB 687), as Fam C §9213, effective January 1, 2012. Renumbered by Stats 2012 ch 162 §48 (SB 1171), effective January 1, 2013.

§9322. Setting matter for hearing

When the petition for approval of the adoption agreement is filed, the court clerk shall set the matter for hearing. **Leg.H.** Enacted Stats 1992 ch 162 §10 (AB 2650), operative January 1, 1994.

§9323. Notice to and appearance by interested persons

The court may require notice of the time and place of the hearing to be served on any other interested person and any interested person may appear and object to the proposed adoption. **Leg.H.** Enacted Stats 1992 ch 162 §10 (AB 2650), operative January 1, 1994.

§9324. Appearance by prospective adoptive parent and proposed adoptee

Both the prospective adoptive parent and the proposed adoptee shall appear at the hearing in person, unless the court allows otherwise pursuant to Section 8613.5. **Leg.H.** Enacted Stats 1992 ch 162 §10 (AB 2650), operative January 1, 1994. Amended Stats 2022 ch 159 §10 (AB 2495), effective January 1, 2023.

§9325. Court's discretion to require report

No investigation or report to the court by any public officer or agency is required, but the court may require the county probation officer or the department to investigate the circumstances of the proposed adoption and report thereon with recommendations, to the court before the hearing. **Leg.H.** Enacted Stats 1992 ch 162 §10 (AB 2650), operative January 1, 1994.

§9326. Notice of hearing for developmentally disabled adult

The prospective adoptive parent shall mail or personally serve notice of the hearing and a copy of the petition to the director of the regional center for the developmentally disabled, established pursuant to Chapter 5 (commencing with Section 4620) of Division 4.5 of the Welfare and Institutions Code, and to any living birth parents or adult children of the proposed adoptee, at least 30 days before the day of the hearing on an adoption petition in any case in which both of the following conditions exist:

(a) The proposed adoptee is an adult with developmental disabilities.

(b) The prospective adoptive parent is a provider of board and care, treatment, habilitation, or other services to persons with developmental disabilities or is a spouse or employee of a provider. **Leg.H.** Enacted Stats 1992 ch 162 §10 (AB 2650), operative January 1, 1994.

§9327. Report concerning person with developmental disability

If the prospective adoptive parent is a provider of board and care, treatment, habilitation, or other services to persons with developmental disabilities, or is a spouse or employee of a provider, and seeks to adopt an unrelated adult with developmental disabilities, the regional center for the developmentally disabled notified pursuant to Section 9326 shall file a written report with the court regarding the suitability of the proposed adoption in meeting the needs of the proposed adoptee and regarding any known previous adoption by the prospective adoptive parent. **Leg.H.** Enacted Stats 1992 ch 162 §10 (AB 2650), operative January 1, 1994.

§9328. Hearing and order

(a) At the hearing the court shall examine the parties, or the counsel of any party not present in person.

(b) If the court is satisfied that the adoption will be in the best interests of the persons seeking the adoption and in the public interest and that there is no reason why the petition should not be granted, the court shall approve the adoption agreement and make an order of adoption declaring that the person adopted is the child of the adoptive parent. Otherwise, the court shall withhold approval of the agreement and deny the petition.

(c) In determining whether or not the adoption of any person pursuant to this part is in the best interests of the persons seeking the adoption or the public interest, the court may consider evidence, oral or written, whether or not it is in conformity with the Evidence Code. **Leg.H.** Enacted Stats 1992 ch 162 §10 (AB 2650), operative January 1, 1994.

CHAPTER 3
PROCEDURE FOR TERMINATING ADULT ADOPTION

Petition to terminate relationship of parent and child. §9340.

§9340. Petition to terminate relationship of parent and child

(a) Any person who has been adopted under this part may, upon written notice to the adoptive parent, file a petition to terminate the relationship of parent and child. The petition shall state the name and address of the petitioner, the name and address of the adoptive parent, the date and place of the adoption, and the circumstances upon which the petition is based.

(b) If the adoptive parent consents in writing to the termination, an order terminating the relationship of parent and child may be issued by the court without further notice.

(c) If the adoptive parent does not consent in writing to the termination, a written response shall be filed within 30 days of the date of mailing of the notice, and the matter shall be set for hearing. The court may require an investigation by the county probation officer or the department. **Leg.H.** Enacted Stats 1992 ch 162 §10 (AB 2650), operative January 1, 1994.

DIVISION 14
FAMILY LAW FACILITATOR ACT

Citation of division. §10000.
Legislative findings and declarations. §10001.
Office; Staffing; Appointment. §10002.
Applicability of division. §10003.
Facilitator services. §10004.
Additional duties of facilitator. §10005.
Protocol. §10006.
Costs. §10007.
Services provided as required by Code. §10008.
Standards for office. §10010.
Funding; Federal approval. §10011.
History of domestic violence; mediation. §10012.
Relationship between facilitator and party. §10013.
Public comments by employee or supervisee of facilitator; Signed acknowledgment of Code of Judicial Ethics. §10014.
Creation of forms by Judicial Council. §10015.

§10000. Citation of division

This division shall be known and may be cited as the Family Law Facilitator Act. **Leg.H.** Added Stats 1996 ch 957 §9 (AB 1058).

§10001. Legislative findings and declarations

(a) The Legislature finds and declares the following:

(1) Child and spousal support are serious legal obligations. The entry of a child support order is frequently delayed while parents engage in protracted litigation concerning custody and visitation. The current system for obtaining child and spousal support orders is suffering because the family courts are unduly burdened with heavy case loads and do not have sufficient personnel to meet increased demands on the courts.

(2) Reports to the Legislature regarding the family law pilot projects in the Superior Courts of the Counties of Santa Clara and San Mateo indicate that the pilot projects have provided a cost-effective and efficient method for the courts to process family law cases that involve unrepresented litigants with issues concerning child support, spousal support, and health insurance.

(3) The reports to the Legislature further indicate that the pilot projects in both counties have been successful in making the process of obtaining court orders concerning child support, spousal support, and health insurance more accessible to unrepresented parties. Surveys conducted by both counties indicate a high degree of satisfaction with the services provided by the pilot projects.

(4) There is a compelling state interest in having a speedy, conflict-reducing system for resolving issues of child support, spousal support, and health insurance that is cost-effective and accessible to families that cannot afford legal representation.

(b) Therefore, it is the intent of the Legislature to make the services provided in the family law pilot projects in the Counties of Santa Clara and San Mateo available to unrepresented parties in the superior courts of all California counties. **Leg.H.** Added Stats 1996 ch 957 §9 (AB 1058).

§10002. Office; Staffing; Appointment

Each superior court shall maintain an office of the family law facilitator. The office of the family law facilitator shall be staffed by an attorney licensed to practice law in this state who has mediation or litigation experience, or both, in the field of family law. The family law facilitator shall be appointed by the superior court. **Leg.H.** Added Stats 1996 ch 957 §9 (AB 1058).

§10003. Applicability of division

This division shall apply to all actions or proceedings for temporary or permanent child support, spousal support, health insurance, child custody, or visitation in a proceeding for dissolution of marriage, nullity of marriage, legal separation, or exclusive child custody, or pursuant to the Uniform Parentage Act (Part 3 (commencing with Section 7600) of Division 12) or the Domestic Violence Prevention Act (Division 10 (commencing with Section 6200)). **Leg.H.** Added Stats 1996 ch 957 §9 (AB 1058). Amended Stats 1999 ch 652 §12 (SB 240).

§10004. Facilitator services

Services provided by the family law facilitator shall include, but are not limited to, the following: providing educational materials to parents concerning the process of establishing parentage and establishing, modifying, and enforcing child support and spousal support in the courts; distributing necessary court forms and voluntary declarations of paternity; providing assistance in completing forms; preparing support schedules based upon statutory guidelines; and providing referrals to the local child support agency, family court services, and other community agencies and resources that provide services for parents and children. In counties where a family law information center exists, the family law facilitator shall provide assistance on child support issues. **Leg.H.** Added Stats 1996 ch 957 §9 (AB 1058). Amended Stats 1999 ch 652 §13 (SB 240).

§10005. Additional duties of facilitator

(a) By local rule, the superior court may designate additional duties of the family law facilitator, which may include, but are not limited to, the following:

(1) Meeting with litigants to mediate issues of child support, spousal support, and maintenance of health insurance, subject to Section 10012. Actions in which one or both of the parties are unrepresented by counsel shall have priority.

(2) Drafting stipulations to include all issues agreed to by the parties, which may include issues other than those specified in Section 10003.

(3) If the parties are unable to resolve issues with the assistance of the family law facilitator, prior to or at the hearing, and at the request of the court, the family law facilitator shall review the paperwork, examine documents, prepare support schedules, and advise the judge whether or not the matter is ready to proceed.

(4) Assisting the clerk in maintaining records.

(5) Preparing formal orders consistent with the court's announced order in cases where both parties are unrepresented.

(6) Serving as a special master in proceedings and making findings to the court unless the family law facilitator has served as a mediator in that case.

(7) Providing the services specified in Section 10004 concerning the issues of child custody and visitation as they relate to calculating child support, if funding is provided for that purpose.

(b) If staff and other resources are available and the duties listed in subdivision (a) have been accomplished, the duties of the family law facilitator may also include the following:

(1) Assisting the court with research and any other responsibilities that will enable the court to be responsive to the litigants' needs.

(2) Developing programs for bar and community outreach through day and evening programs, video recordings, and other innovative means that will assist unrepresented and financially disadvantaged litigants in gaining meaningful access to family court. These programs shall specifically include information concerning underutilized legislation, such as expedited child support orders (Chapter 5 (commencing with Section 3620) of Part 1 of Division 9), and preexisting, court-sponsored programs, such as supervised visitation and appointment of attorneys for children. **Leg.H.** Added Stats 1996 ch 957 §9 (AB 1058). Amended Stats 1997 ch 599 §45 (AB 573); Stats 1999 ch 652 §13.5 (SB 240); Stats 2009 ch 88 §39 (AB 176), effective January 1, 2010; Stats 2019 ch 115 §138 (AB 1817), effective January 1, 2020.

§10006. Protocol

The court shall adopt a protocol wherein all litigants, both unrepresented by counsel and represented by counsel, have ultimate access to a hearing before the court. **Leg.H.** Added Stats 1996 ch 957 §9 (AB 1058).

§10007. Costs

The court shall provide the family law facilitator at no cost to the parties. **Leg.H.** Added Stats 1996 ch 957 §9 (AB 1058).

§10008. Services provided as required by Code

(a) Except as provided in subdivision (b), nothing in this chapter shall be construed to apply to a child for whom services are provided or required to be provided by a local child support agency pursuant to Section 17400.

(b) In cases in which the services of the local child support agency are provided pursuant to Section 17400, either parent may utilize the services of the family law facilitator that are specified in Section 10004. In order for a custodial parent who is receiving the services of the local child support agency pursuant to Section 17400 to utilize the services specified in Section 10005 relating to support, the custodial parent must obtain written authorization from the local child support agency. It is not the intent of the Legislature in enacting this section to limit the duties of local child support agencies with respect to seeking child support payments or to in any way limit or supersede other provisions of this code respecting temporary child support. **Leg.H.** Added Stats 1996 ch 957 §9 (AB 1058). Amended Stats 2000 ch 808 §78 (AB 1358), effective September 28, 2000.

§10010. Standards for office

The Judicial Council shall adopt minimum standards for the office of the family law facilitator and any forms or rules of court that are necessary to implement this division. **Leg.H.** Added Stats 1996 ch 957 §9 (AB 1058).

§10011. Funding; Federal approval

The Director of the State Department of Social Services shall seek approval from the United States Department of Health and Human Services, Office of Child Support Enforcement, to utilize funding under Title IV-D of the Social Security Act for the services provided pursuant to this division. **Leg.H.** Added Stats 1996 ch 957 §9 (AB 1058).

§10012. History of domestic violence; mediation

(a) In a proceeding in which mediation is required pursuant to paragraph (1) of subdivision (a) of Section 10005, where there has been a history of domestic violence between the parties or where a protective order as defined in Section 6218 is in effect, at the request of the party alleging domestic violence in a written declaration under penalty of perjury or protected by the order, the family law facilitator shall meet with the parties separately and at separate times.

(b) Any intake form that the office of the family law facilitator requires the parties to complete before the commencement of mediation shall state that, if a party alleging domestic violence in a written declaration under penalty of perjury or a party protected by a protective order so requests, the mediator will meet with the parties separately and at separate times. **Leg.H.** Added Stats 1996 ch 957 §9 (AB 1058).

§10013. Relationship between facilitator and party

The family law facilitator shall not represent any party. No attorney-client relationship is created between a party and the family law facilitator as a result of any information or services provided to the party by the family law facilitator. The family law facilitator shall give conspicuous notice that no attorney-client relationship exists between the facilitator, its staff, and the family law litigant. The notice shall include the advice that the absence of an attorney-client relationship means that communications between the party and the family law facilitator are not privileged and that the family law facilitator may provide services to the other party. **Leg.H.** Added Stats 1999 ch 652 §14 (SB 240).

§10014. Public comments by employee or supervisee of facilitator; Signed acknowledgment of Code of Judicial Ethics

A person employed by, or directly supervised by, the family law facilitator shall not make any public comment about a pending or impending proceeding in the court as provided by paragraph (9) of subdivision (B) of Canon 3 of the Code of Judicial Ethics. All persons employed by or directly supervised by the family law facilitator shall be provided a copy of paragraph (9) of subdivision (B) of Canon 3 of the Code of Judicial Ethics, and shall be required to sign an acknowledgment that the person is aware of its provisions. **Leg.H.** Added Stats 1999 ch 652 §15 (SB 240). Amended Stats 2019 ch 115 §139 (AB 1817), effective January 1, 2020.

§10015. Creation of forms by Judicial Council

The Judicial Council shall create any necessary forms to advise the parties of the types of services provided, that there is no attorney-client relationship, that the family law facilitator is not responsible for the outcome of any case, that the family law facilitator does not represent any party and will not appear in court on the party's behalf, and that the other party may also be receiving information and services from the family law facilitator. **Leg.H.** Added Stats 1999 ch 652 §15.5 (SB 240).

DIVISION 15
FRIEND OF THE COURT ACT [REPEALED]

§10100. [Section repealed 1999]

Leg.H. Added Stats 1996 ch 958 §1 (SB 506). Repealed Stats 1999 ch 1004 §6 (AB 673). The repealed section related to citation of Friend of the Court Act.

§10101. [Section repealed 1999]

Leg.H. Added Stats 1996 ch 958 §1 (SB 506). Repealed Stats 1999 ch 1004 §6 (AB 673). The repealed section related to legislative intent as regards Friend of the Court Act.

§10102. [Section repealed 1999]

Leg.H. Added Stats 1996 ch 958 §1 (SB 506). Repealed Stats 1999 ch 1004 §6 (AB 673). The repealed section related to federal funding for Friend of the Court Act.

DIVISION 16
FAMILY LAW INFORMATION CENTERS [REPEALED]

§15000. [Section repealed 2004]

Leg.H. Added Stats 1998 ch 721 §1 (AB 2207). Repealed by the terms of Fam C §15012, effective January 1, 2004. The repealed section related to legislative findings and declarations.

§15010. [Section repealed 2004]

Leg.H. Added Stats 1998 ch 721 §1 (AB 2207). Amended Stats 1999 ch 886 §1 (SB 874). Repealed by the terms of Fam C §15012. The repealed section related to pilot project to provide information.

§15012. [Section repealed 2004]

Leg.H. Added Stats 1998 ch 721 §1 (AB 2207). Amended Stats 1999 ch 886 §2 (SB 874), operative until January 1, 2004. Repealed by its own terms, effective January 1, 2004. The repealed section related to repeal of division.

DIVISION 17
SUPPORT SERVICES

Chapter 1. Department of Child Support Services.
Chapter 2. Child Support Enforcement.
Chapter 5. Complaint Resolution.

CHAPTER 1
DEPARTMENT OF CHILD SUPPORT SERVICES

Article 1. General.
Article 2. Organization.
Article 3. Director of Child Support Services.
Article 4. Statewide Registry for Child Support.

ARTICLE 1
General

Definitions. §17000.

§17000. Definitions

The definitions contained in this section, and definitions applicable to Division 9 (commencing with Section 3500), shall govern the construction of this division, unless the context requires otherwise.

(a) "Child support debt" means the amount of money owed as child support pursuant to a court order.

(b) "Child support order" means a court order for the payment of a set or determinable amount of support by a parent or a court order requiring a parent to provide for health insurance coverage. "Child support order" includes any court order for spousal support or for medical support to the extent these obligations are to be enforced by a single state agency for child support under Title IV-D.

(c) "Court" means any superior court of this state and any court or tribunal of another state that has jurisdiction to determine the liability of persons for the support of another person.

(d) "Court order" means a judgment, decree, or order of any court of this state that orders the payment of a set or determinable amount of support by a parent. It does not include any order or decree of any proceeding in which a court did not order support.

(e) "Department" means the Department of Child Support Services.

(f) "Dependent child" means any of the following:

(1) Any person under 18 years of age who is not emancipated, self-supporting, married, or a member of the Armed Forces of the United States.

(2) Any unmarried person who is at least 18 years of age but who has not reached 19 years of age, is not emancipated, and is a student regularly attending high school or a program of vocational or technical training designed to train that person for gainful employment.

(g) "Director" means the Director of Child Support Services or an authorized representative.

(h) "Local child support agency" means the county department of child support services created pursuant to this chapter and with which the department has entered into a cooperative agreement, to secure child and spousal support, medical support, and determine paternity. Local child support agency includes county programs in multiple counties that have been consolidated into a single agency pursuant to subdivision (a) of Section 17304.

(i) "Parent" means the natural or adoptive father or mother of a dependent child, and includes any person who has an enforceable obligation to support a dependent child.

(j) "Public assistance" means any amount paid under the California Work Opportunity and Responsibility to Kids Act (Chapter 2 (commencing with Section 11200) of Part 3 of Division 9 of the Welfare and Institutions Code), or any Medi-Cal benefit, for the benefit of any dependent child or the caretaker of a child.

(k) "Public assistance debt" means any amount paid under the California Work Opportunity and Responsibility to Kids Act, contained in Chapter 2 (commencing with Section 11200) of Part 3 of Division 9 of the Welfare and Institutions Code, for the benefit of a dependent child or the caretaker of a child for whom the department is authorized to seek recoupment under this division, subject to applicable federal law.

(*l*) "Title IV-D" or "IV-D" means Part D of Title IV of the federal Social Security Act (42 U.S.C. Sec. 651 et seq.). **Leg.H.** Added Stats 1999 ch 478 §1 (AB 196). Amended Stats 1999 ch 480 §5 (SB 542); Stats 2000 ch 808 §78.3 (AB 1358), effective September 28, 2000; Stats 2003 ch 308 §3 (AB 738); Stats 2019 ch 115 §140 (AB 1817), effective January 1, 2020.

ARTICLE 2
Organization

Creation of administrative entity. §17200.
Duty of organizational unit. §17202.
Director and administrative units. §17204.
Sufficient staff to perform functions. §17206.
Responsibility of administrative unit; Administrative service fee. §17208.
Accessibility of local offices. §17210.
Administration of Child Support Assurance Demonstration Project to provide employment and training services. §17211.
Legislative intent; Disclosure of information and files. §17212.

§17200. Creation of administrative entity

The Department of Child Support Services is hereby created within the California Health and Human Services Agency. The department shall administer all services and perform all functions necessary to establish, collect, and distribute child support. **Leg.H.** Added Stats 1999 ch 478 §1 (AB 196).

§17202. Duty of organizational unit

(a) The department is hereby designated the single organizational unit whose duty it shall be to administer the Title IV-D state plan for securing child and spousal support, medical support, and determining paternity. State plan functions shall be performed by other agencies as required by law, by delegation of the department, or by cooperative agreements.

(b) The department shall appoint the local child support agency, as defined in Section 17304, or any other entity receiving federal tax information in performance of its child support duties as its designee for purposes of paragraph (26) of subdivision (b) of Section 11105 of the Penal Code.

(c) For purposes of this section, "federal tax information" is as defined in Section 1044 of the Government Code. **Leg.H.** Added Stats 1999 ch 478 §1 (AB 196). Amended Stats 2017 ch 19 §7 (AB 111), effective June 27, 2017.

§17204. Director and administrative units

The department consists of the director and such division or other administrative units as the director may find necessary. **Leg.H.** Added Stats 1999 ch 478 §1 (AB 196).

§17206. Sufficient staff to perform functions

The department shall ensure that there is an adequate organizational structure and sufficient staff to perform functions delegated to any governmental unit relating to Part D (commencing with Section 651) of Subchapter 4 of Chapter 7 of Title 42 of the United States Code, including a sufficient number of attorneys to ensure that all requirements of due process are satisfied in the establishment and enforcement of child support orders. **Leg.H.** Added Stats 1999 ch 478 §1 (AB 196).

§17208. Responsibility of administrative unit; Administrative service fee

(a) The department shall reduce the cost of, and increase the speed and efficiency of, child support enforcement operations. It is the intent of the Legislature to operate the child support enforcement program through local child support agencies without a net increase in state General Fund or county general fund costs, considering all increases to the General Fund as a result of increased collections and welfare recoupment.

(b) The department shall maximize the use of federal funds available for the costs of administering a child support services department, and to the maximum extent feasible, obtain funds from federal financial incentives for the efficient collection of child support, to defray the remaining costs of administration of the department consistent with effective and efficient support enforcement.

(c) Effective October 1, 2019, the Department of Child Support Services shall impose an administrative service fee in the amount of thirty-five dollars ($35) on a never-assisted custodial party receiving services from the California child support program for order establishment, enforcement, and collection services provided. The annual amount of child support payments collected on behalf of the custodial party must be fifty dollars ($550) or more before an administrative service fee is imposed pursuant to this subdivision. The fee shall be deducted from the custodial party's collection payment at the time the collection payments for that year have reached levels specified by the department. **Leg.H.** Added Stats 1999 ch 478 §1 (AB 196). Amended Stats 2009 4th Ex Sess 2009–2010 ch 4 §1 (ABX4-4), effective July 28, 2009; Stats 2019 ch 27 §4 (SB 80), effective June 27, 2019.

§17210. Accessibility of local offices

The department shall ensure that the local child support agency offices and services are reasonably accessible throughout the counties, and shall establish systems for informing the public, including custodial and noncustodial parents of dependent children, of its services and operations. **Leg.H.** Added Stats 1999 ch 478 §1 (AB 196).

§17211. Administration of Child Support Assurance Demonstration Project to provide employment and training services

The department shall administer the Child Support Assurance Demonstration Project established by Article 5 (commencing with Section 18241) of Chapter 3.3 of Part 6 of the Welfare and Institutions Code, and the county demonstration projects to provide employment and training services to nonsupporting noncustodial parents authorized by Section 18205.5 of the Welfare and Institutions Code. However, the department may contract with the State Department of Social Services to continue development and implementation of these demonstration projects until they have been fully implemented. After the demonstration projects have been fully implemented, the department shall consult with the State Department of Social Services on the administration of the projects. The contracts for evaluation of the demonstration projects shall continue to be maintained by the State Department of Social Services. The department shall be responsible for the final evaluation of the projects. **Leg.H.** Added Stats 1999 ch 478 §1 (AB 196). Amended Stats 1999 ch 480 §6 (SB 542).

§17212. Legislative intent; Disclosure of information and files

(a) It is the intent of the Legislature to protect individual rights of privacy, and to facilitate and enhance the effectiveness of the child and spousal support enforcement program, by ensuring the confidentiality of support enforcement and child abduction records, and to thereby encourage the full and frank disclosure of information relevant to all of the following:

(1) The establishment or maintenance of parent and child relationships and support obligations.

(2) The enforcement of the child support liability of absent parents.

(3) The enforcement of spousal support liability of the spouse or former spouse to the extent required by the state plan under Section 17604 and Part 6 (commencing with Section 5700.101) of Division 9.

(4) The location of absent parents.

(5) The location of parents and children abducted, concealed, or detained by them.

(b)(1)(A) Except as provided in subdivision (c), all files, applications, papers, documents, and records established or maintained by a public entity pursuant to the administration and implementation of the child and spousal support enforcement program established pursuant to Part D (commencing with Section 651) of Subchapter IV of Chapter 7 of Title 42 of the United States Code and this division, shall be confidential, and shall not be open to examination or released for disclosure for any purpose not directly connected with the administration of the child and spousal support enforcement program. A public entity shall not disclose any file, application, paper, document, or record, or the information contained therein, except as expressly authorized by this section.

(B) For purposes of this section, "public entity" does not include the court. This subparagraph is declaratory of existing law.

(2) Information shall not be released or the whereabouts of one party or the child disclosed to another party, or to the attorney of any other party, if a protective order has been issued by a court or administrative agency with respect to the party, a good cause claim under Section 11477.04 of the Welfare and Institutions Code has been approved or is pending, or the public agency responsible for establishing paternity or enforcing support has reason to believe that the release of the information may result in physical or emotional harm to the party or the child. When a local child support agency is prohibited from releasing information pursuant to this subdivision, the information shall be omitted from any pleading or document to be submitted to the court and this subdivision shall be cited in the pleading or other document as the authority for the omission. The information shall be released only upon an order of the court pursuant to paragraph (6) of subdivision (c).

(3) Notwithstanding any other law, a proof of service filed by the local child support agency shall not disclose the address where service of process was accomplished. Instead, the local child support agency shall keep the address in its own records. The proof of service shall specify that the address is on record at the local child support agency and that the address may be released only upon an order from the court pursuant to paragraph (6) of subdivision (c). The local child support agency shall, upon request by a party served, release to that person the address where service was effected.

(c) Disclosure of the information described in subdivision (b) is authorized as follows:

(1) All files, applications, papers, documents, and records as described in subdivision (b) shall be available and may be used by a public entity for all administrative, civil, or criminal investigations, actions, proceedings, or prosecutions conducted in connection with the administration of the child and spousal support enforcement program approved under Part D (commencing with Section 651) of Subchapter IV of Chapter 7 of Title 42 of the United States Code and to the county welfare department responsible for administering a program operated under a state plan pursuant to Part A, Subpart 1 or 2 of Part B, or Part E of Subchapter IV of Chapter 7 of Title 42 of the United States Code.

(2) A document requested by a person who wrote, prepared, or furnished the document may be examined by or disclosed to that person or a designee.

(3) The payment history of an obligor pursuant to a support order may be examined by or released to the court, the obligor, or the person on whose behalf enforcement actions are being taken or that person's designee.

(4) An income and expense declaration of either parent may be released to the other parent for the purpose of establishing or modifying a support order.

(5) Public records subject to disclosure under the California Public Records Act (Division 10 (commencing with Section 7920.000) of Title 1 of the Government Code) may be released.

(6) After a noticed motion and a finding by the court, in a case in which establishment or enforcement actions are being taken, that release or disclosure to the obligor or obligee is required by due process of law, the court may order a public entity that possesses an application, paper, document, or record as described in subdivision (b) to make that item available to the obligor or obligee for examination or copying, or to disclose to the obligor or obligee the contents of that item. Article 9 (commencing with Section 1040) of Chapter 4 of Division 8 of the Evidence Code shall not be applicable to proceedings under this part. At any hearing of a motion filed pursuant to this section, the court shall inquire of the local child support agency and the parties appearing at the hearing if there is reason to believe that release of the requested information may result in physical or emotional harm to a party. If the court determines that harm may occur, the court shall issue any protective orders or injunctive orders restricting the use and disclosure of the information as are necessary to protect the individuals.

(7) To the extent not prohibited by federal law or regulation, information indicating the existence or imminent threat of a crime against a child, or location of a concealed, detained, or abducted child, or the location of the concealing, detaining, or abducting person, may be disclosed to a district attorney, an appropriate law enforcement agency, or to a state or county child protective agency, or may be used in any judicial proceedings to prosecute that crime or to protect the child.

(8) The social security number, most recent address, and the place of employment of the absent parent may be released to an authorized person as defined in Section 653(c) of Title 42 of the United States Code, only if the authorized person has filed a request for the information, and only if the information has been provided to the California Parent Locator Service by the federal Parent Locator Service pursuant to Section 653 of Title 42 of the United States Code.

(9) A parent's or relative's name, social security number, most recent address, telephone number, place of employment, or other contact information may be released to a county child welfare agency or county probation department pursuant to subdivision (c) of Section 17506.

(d)(1) "Administration and implementation of the child and spousal support enforcement program," as used in this division, means the carrying out of the state and local plans for establishing, modifying, and enforcing child support obligations, enforcing spousal support orders, and determining paternity pursuant to Part D (commencing with Section 651) of Subchapter IV of Chapter 7 of Title 42 of the United States Code and this article.

(2) For purposes of this division, "obligor" means a person owing a duty of support.

(3) As used in this division, "putative parent" shall refer to any person reasonably believed to be the parent of a child for whom the local child support agency is attempting to establish paternity or establish, modify, or enforce support pursuant to Section 17400.

(e) A person who willfully, knowingly, and intentionally violates this section is guilty of a misdemeanor.

(f) This section does not compel the disclosure of information relating to a deserting parent who is a recipient of aid under a public assistance program for which federal aid is paid to this state, if that information is required to be kept confidential by the federal law or regulations relating to the program. **Leg.H.** Added Stats 1999 ch 478 §1 (AB 196). Amended Stats 1999 ch 653 §12 (AB 380); Stats 2000 ch 808 §79 (AB 1358), effective September 28, 2000; Stats 2001 ch 755 §10 (SB 943), effective October 12, 2001; Stats 2012 ch 637 §2 (AB 1751), effective January 1, 2013; Stats 2014 ch 772 §2 (SB 1460), effective January 1, 2015; Stats 2015 ch 493 §7 (SB 646), effective January 1, 2016; Stats 2016 ch 474 §11 (AB 2882), effective January 1, 2017; Stats 2019 ch 115 §141 (AB 1817), effective January 1, 2020; Stats 2020 ch 36 §30 (AB 3364), effective January 1, 2021; Stats 2021 ch 615 §106 (AB 474), effective January 1, 2022.

ARTICLE 3
Director of Child Support Services

Appointment of executive officer to be director of department. §17300.
Responsibilities of director. §17302.
Legislative findings. §17303.
Establishment of new county departments of child support services; Local child support agencies; Supervision of Title IV-D operations. §17304.
Deadline for beginning transition to new system; Order in which counties transferred. §17305.
Development of uniform policies and procedures for local child support agencies. §17306.
Local child support agency funding methodology. § 17306.1.
Authority to remedy effects of changes in timing of child support payments. §17307.
Delegation of responsibility. §17308.
State Disbursement Unit. §17309.
Employer to make child support payments by electronic fund transfer. §17309.5.
Regulations and policies relating to responsibilities and jurisdiction of department. §17310.
Child Support Payment Trust Fund; Creation and purpose; Revolving account; Startup funds; Loans from and to General Fund authorized. §17311.
Trust agreement to receive or disburse child support collections. §17311.5.
Payments; State disbursement unit. §17311.7.
Regulations, orders, or standards governing law enforced by department. §17312.
Assistants and regional administrators. §17314.
Conflict of interest. §17316.
Applicability of other code sections. §17318.
Avoidance of federal penalties. §17320.
Qualifying account for direct deposit of child support payments. §17325.

§17300. Appointment of executive officer to be director of department

(a) With the consent of the Senate, the Governor shall appoint, to serve at the Governor's pleasure, an executive officer who shall be director of the department. In making the appointment the Governor shall consider training, demonstrated ability, experience, and leadership in organized child support enforcement administration. The director shall receive the salary provided for by Chapter 6 (commencing with Section 11550) of Part 1 of Division 3 of Title 2 of the Government Code.

(b) The Governor also may appoint, to serve at the Governor's pleasure, not to exceed two chief deputy directors of the department, and one deputy director of the department. The salaries of the chief deputy directors and the deputy director shall be fixed in accordance with law. **Leg.H.** Added Stats 1999 ch 478 §1 (AB 196). Amended Stats 1999 ch 480 §6.5 (SB 542); Stats 2019 ch 115 §142 (AB 1817), effective January 1, 2020.

§17302. Responsibilities of director

The director shall do all of the following:
(a) Be responsible for the management of the department.
(b) Administer all federal and state laws and regulations pertaining to the administration of child support enforcement obligations.
(c) Perform all duties as may be prescribed by law, and any other administrative and executive duties imposed by law.
(d) Observe, and report to the Governor, the Legislature, and the public on, the conditions of child support enforcement activities throughout the state pursuant to subdivision (e) of Section 17602. **Leg.H.** Added Stats 1999 ch 478 §1 (AB 196). Amended Stats 1999 ch 480 §7 (SB 542).

§17303. Legislative findings

The Legislature finds and declares all of the following:
(a) Title IV-D of the federal Social Security Act, contained in Part D (commencing with Section 651) of Subchapter 4 of Chapter 7 of Title 42 of the United States Code, requires that there be a single state agency for child support enforcement. California's child support enforcement system is extremely complex, involving numerous state and local agencies. The state's system was divided between the State Department of Social Services, the Attorney General's office, the Franchise Tax Board, the Employment Development Department, the Department of Motor Vehicles, and the 58 county district attorneys' offices.
(b) The lack of coordination and integration between state and local child support agencies has been a major impediment to getting support to the children of this state. An effective child support enforcement program must have strong leadership and effective state oversight and management to best serve the needs of the children of the state.
(c) The state would benefit by centralizing its obligation to hold counties responsible for collecting support. Oversight would be best accomplished by direct management by the state.
(d) A single state agency for child support enforcement with strong leadership and direct accountability for local child support agencies will benefit the taxpayers of the state by reducing the inefficiencies introduced by involving multiple layers of government in child support enforcement operations. **Leg.H.** Added Stats 1999 ch 478 §1 (AB 196).

§17304. Establishment of new county departments of child support services; Local child support agencies; Supervision of Title IV-D operations

To address the concerns stated by the Legislature in Section 17303, each county shall establish a new county department of child support services. Each department is also referred to in this division as the local child support agency. The local child support agency shall be separate and independent from any other county department and shall be responsible for promptly and effectively establishing, modifying, and enforcing child support obligations, including medical support, enforcing spousal support orders established by a court of competent jurisdiction, and determining paternity in the case of a child born out of wedlock. The local child support agency shall refer all cases requiring criminal enforcement services to the district attorney and the district attorney shall prosecute those cases, as appropriate. If a district attorney fails to comply with this section, the director shall notify the Attorney General and the Attorney General shall take appropriate action to secure compliance. The director shall be responsible for implementing and administering all aspects of the state plan that direct the functions to be performed by the local child support agencies relating to their Title IV-D operations. In developing the new system, all of the following shall apply:

(a) The director shall negotiate and enter into cooperative agreements with county and state agencies to carry out the requirements of the state plan and provide services relating to the establishment of paternity or the establishment, modification, or enforcement of child support obligations as required pursuant to Section 654 of Title 42 of the United States Code. The cooperative agreements shall require that the local child support agencies are reasonably accessible to the citizens of each county and are visible and accountable to the public for their activities. The director, in consultation with the impacted counties, may consolidate the local child support agencies, or any function of the agencies, in more than one county into a single local child support agency, if the director determines that the consolidation will increase the efficiency of the state Title IV-D program and each county has at least one local child support office accessible to the public.

(b) The director shall have direct oversight and supervision of the Title IV-D operations of the local child support agency, and no other local or state agency shall have any authority over the local child support agency as to any function relating to its Title IV-D operations. The local child support agency shall be responsible for the performance of child support enforcement activities required by law and regulation in a manner prescribed by the department. The administrator of the local child support agency shall be responsible for reporting to and responding to the director on all aspects of the child support program.

(c) Nothing in this section prohibits the local child support agency, with the prior approval of the director, from entering into cooperative arrangements with other county departments, as necessary to carry out the responsibilities imposed by this section pursuant to plans of cooperation submitted to the department and approved by the director. The local child support agency may not enter into a cooperative agreement or contract with any county department or independently elected official, including the office of the district attorney, to run, supervise, manage, or oversee the Title IV-D functions of the local child support agency. Until September 1, 2004, the local child support agency may enter into a cooperative agreement or contract of restricted scope and duration with a district attorney to utilize individual attorneys as necessary to carry out limited attorney services. Any cooperative agreement or contract for the attorney services shall be subject to approval by the department and contingent upon a written finding by the department that either the relatively small size of the local child support agency program, or other serious programmatic needs, arising as a result of the transition make it most efficient and cost-effective to contract for limited attorney services. The department shall ensure that any cooperative agreement or contract for attorney services provides that all attorneys be supervised by, and report directly to, the local child support agency, and comply with all state and federal child support laws and regulations. The office of the Legislative Analyst shall review and assess the efficiency and effectiveness of that cooperative agreement or contract, and shall report its findings to the Legislature by January 1, 2004. Within 60 days of receipt of a plan of cooperation or contract from the local child support agency, the department shall either approve the plan of cooperation or contract or notify the agency that the plan is denied. If an agency is notified that the plan is denied, the agency shall have the opportunity to resubmit a revised plan of cooperation or contract. If the director fails to respond in writing within 60 days of receipt, the plan shall otherwise be deemed approved. Nothing in this section shall be deemed an approval of program costs relative to the cooperative arrangements entered into by the counties with other county departments.

(d) In order to minimize the disruption of services provided and to capitalize on the expertise of employees, the director shall create a program that builds on existing staff and facilities to the fullest extent possible. All assets of the family support division in the district attorney's office shall become assets of the local child support agency.

(e)(1)(A) Except as provided in subparagraph (B), all employees and other personnel who serve the office of the district attorney and perform child support collection and enforcement activities shall become the employees and other personnel of the county child support agency at their existing or equivalent classifications, and at their existing salaries and benefits that include, but are not limited to, accrued and unused vacation, sick leave, personal leave, and health and pension plans.

(B) The Title IV-D director is entitled to become an employee of the local child support agency or may be selected as the administrator pursuant to the provisions of subdivision (f).

(2) Permanent employees of the office of the district attorney on the effective date of this chapter shall be deemed qualified, and no other qualifications shall be required for employment or retention in the county child support agency. Probationary employees on the effective date of this chapter shall retain their probationary status and rights, and shall not be deemed to have transferred, so as to require serving a new probationary period.

(3) Employment seniority of an employee of the office of the district attorney on the effective date of this chapter shall be counted toward seniority in the county child support agency and all time spent in the same, equivalent, or higher classification shall be counted toward classification seniority.

(4) An employee organization that has been recognized as the representative or exclusive representative of an established appropriate bargaining unit of employees who perform child support collection and enforcement activities shall continue to be recognized as the representative or exclusive representative of the same employees of the county.

(5) An existing memorandum of understanding or agreement between the county or the office of the district attorney and the employee organization shall remain in effect and be fully binding on the parties involved for the term of the agreement.

(6) Nothing in this section shall be construed to limit the rights of employees or employee organizations to bargain in good faith on matters of wages, hours, or other terms and conditions of employment, including the negotiation of workplace standards within the scope of bargaining as authorized by state and federal law.

(7)(A) Except as provided in subparagraph (B), a public agency shall, in implementing programs affected by the act of addition or amendment of this chapter to this code, perform program functions exclusively through the use of merit civil service employees of the public agency.

(B) Prior to transition from the district attorney to the local child support agency under Section 17305, the district attorney may continue existing contracts and their renewals, as appropriate. After the transition under Section 17305, any contracting out of program functions shall be approved by the director consistent with Section 31000 and following of the Government Code, except as otherwise provided in subdivision (c) with regard to attorney services. The director shall approve or disapprove a proposal to contract out within 60 days. Failure of the director to respond to a request to contract out within 60 days after receipt of the request shall be deemed approval, unless the director submits an extension to respond, which in no event shall be longer than 30 days.

(f) The administrator of the local child support agency shall be an employee of the county selected by the board of supervisors, or in the case of a city and county, selected by the mayor, pursuant to the qualifications established by the department. The administrator may hire staff, including attorneys, to fulfill the functions required by the agency and in conformity with any staffing requirements adopted by the department, including all those set forth in Section 17306. All staff shall be employees of the county and shall comply with all local, state, and federal child support laws, regulations, and directives. **Leg.H.** Added Stats 1999 ch 478 §1 (AB 196). Amended Stats 1999 ch 480 §8 (SB 542); Stats 2000 ch 808 §80 (AB 1358), effective September 28, 2000; Stats 2001 ch 755 §11 (SB 943), effective October 12, 2001.

§17305. Deadline for beginning transition to new system; Order in which counties transferred

(a) In order to achieve an orderly and timely transition to the new system with minimal disruption of services, the director shall begin the transition from the office of the district attorney to the local child support agencies pursuant to Section 17304, commencing January 1, 2001. The director shall transfer the appropriate number of counties, equaling at least 50 percent of the statewide caseload into the new system by January 1, 2002. The transition shall be completed by January 1, 2003. A county that has appointed an administrator for the local child support agency and has complied with the requirements of subdivision (b) may transition prior to January 1, 2001, subject to the approval of the director. In determining the order in which counties will be transferred from the office of the district attorney to the local child support agencies, the director shall do all of the following:

(1) Consider the performance of the counties in establishing and collecting child support.

(2) Minimize the disruption of the services provided by the counties.

(3) Optimize the chances of a successful transition.

(b) In order to achieve an orderly transition with minimal disruption of services, a county shall submit a plan of transition which shall be approved by the department prior to transition.

(c) The director shall consult with the district attorney to achieve an orderly transition and to minimize the disruption of services. Each district attorney shall cooperate in the transition as requested by the director.

(d) To minimize any disruption of services provided under the child support enforcement program during the transition, each district attorney shall:

(1) Continue to be designated the single organizational unit whose duty it shall be to administer the Title IV-D state plan for securing child and spousal support, medical support, and determining paternity for that county until such time as the county is notified by the director that the county has been transferred pursuant to subdivision (a) or sooner under Section 17602.

(2) At a minimum, maintain all levels of funding, staffing, and services as of January 1, 1999, to administer the Title IV-D state plan for securing child and spousal support, medical support, and determining paternity. If the director determines that a district attorney has lowered the funding, staffing, or services of the child support enforcement program, the director may withhold part or all state and federal funds, including incentive funds, from the district attorney. Before the director withholds part of or all state and federal funds, including incentive funds, the district attorney shall have the opportunity to demonstrate good cause for any reductions in funding, staffing, or services. Good cause exceptions for reductions shall include, but not be limited to, natural staff attrition and caseload changes. **Leg.H.** Added Stats 1999 ch 478 §1 (AB 196). Amended Stats 1999 ch 480 §9 (SB 542).

§17306. Development of uniform policies and procedures for local child support agencies

(a) The Department of Child Support Services shall develop uniform forms, policies, and procedures to be employed statewide by all local child support agencies. Pursuant to this subdivision, the department shall:

(1) Adopt uniform procedures and forms.

(2) Establish standard caseload-to-staffing ratios, adjusted as appropriate to meet the varying needs of local programs.

(3) Institute a consistent statewide policy on the appropriateness of closing cases to ensure that, without relying solely on federal minimum requirements, all cases are fully and pragmatically pursued for collections prior to closing.

(4) Evaluate the best practices for the establishment, enforcement, and collection of child support, for the purpose of determining which practices should be implemented statewide in an effort to improve performance by local child support agencies. In evaluating the best practices, the director shall review existing practices in better performing counties within California, as well as practices implemented by other state Title IV-D programs nationwide.

(5) Evaluate the best practices for the management of effective child support enforcement operations for the purpose of determining what management structure should be implemented statewide in an effort to improve the establishment, enforcement, and collection of child support by local child support agencies, including an examination of the need for attorneys in management level positions. In evaluating the best practices, the director shall review existing practices in better performing counties within California, as well as practices implemented by other state Title IV-D programs nationwide.

(6) Set priorities for the use of specific enforcement mechanisms for use by local child support agencies. As part of establishing these priorities, the director shall set forth caseload processing priorities to target enforcement efforts and services in a way that will maximize collections.

(7) Develop uniform training protocols, require periodic training of all child support staff, and conduct training sessions as appropriate.

(8) Review and approve annual budgets submitted by the local child support agencies to ensure each local child support agency operates an effective and efficient program that complies with all federal and state laws, regulations, and directives, including the directive to hire sufficient staff.

(b) The director shall submit any forms intended for use in court proceedings to the Judicial Council for approval at least six months prior to the implementation of the use of the forms.

(c) In adopting the forms, policies, and procedures, the director shall consult with appropriate organizations representing stakeholders in California, such as the California State Association of Counties, the Child Support Directors Association of California, labor organizations, parent advocates, child support commissioners, family law facilitators, and the appropriate committees of the Legislature. **Leg.H.** Added Stats 1999 ch 478 §1 (AB 196). Amended Stats 1999 ch 480 §10 (SB 542); Stats 2001 ch 111 §2 (AB 429), effective July 30, 2001; Stats 2002 ch 927 §3.5 (AB 3032); Stats 2004 ch 806 §2 (AB 2358); Stats 2016 ch 474 §12 (AB 2882), effective January 1, 2017; Stats 2019 ch 27 §5 (SB 80), effective June 27, 2019.

§ 17306.1. Local child support agency funding methodology

(a) Commencing with the 2019-20 fiscal year, the department shall implement a revised local child support agency funding methodology that was developed in consultation with the California Child Support Directors Association. The methodology shall consist of both of the following components in the 2019-20 fiscal year:

(1) Casework operations, which consists of a statewide standard case-to-staff ratio, the respective labor costs for each local child support agency, and an operating expense and equipment complement based on a percentage of staffing costs. The department shall propose a specific ratio informed by the working sessions described in subdivision (c) and as part of the required update to the Legislature required by subdivision (d).

(2) Call center operations, which consists of a standard statewide ratio of calls to call center agents, the respective labor costs for each local child support agency, and an operating expense and equipment complement based on a percentage of staffing costs.

(b) Any increased state costs that result, either directly or indirectly, from implementation of the funding methodology described in subdivision (a) shall be implemented to the extent of an appropriation of funds in the annual Budget Act.

(c)(1) The Department of Child Support Services shall convene a series of stakeholder working sessions to develop the ongoing methodology, which shall take effect in the 2020-21 fiscal year. There shall be at least three working sessions during the summer and fall of 2019, beginning as early as possible after July 1, 2019.

(2) The working sessions shall include, but not be limited to, representatives from the Child Support Directors Association, the Legislative Analyst's Office, the Department of Finance, consultants from the Assembly and Senate Health and Human Services budget subcommittees, any other interested Legislative consultants, antipoverty advocates, advocacy organizations representing custodial and noncustodial parents, including fathers' rights advocates, impacted families, and any other interested advocates or stakeholders for the child support program.

(3) The working sessions shall do all of the following:

(A) Further refine or change the local child support agency funding methodology defined in subdivision (a), including accounting for performance incentives to be provided in future years.

(B) Discuss additional strategies that might improve the customer service, pragmatic collectability, and cost efficiency of the child support program and assess fiscal impact to operations and collections.

(C) Consider any policy changes that may affect the workload and associated funding needs of the local child support agencies and assess fiscal impact to operations and collections.

(D) Consider the ways that child support collection improves outcomes for children, impacts the well-being of children in relationship to their parents who are ordered to pay support, particularly their fathers, and impacts the racial wealth gap and further analyze the impact that child support has on parents ordered to pay support who do not have the capacity to pay.

(d) The department shall provide a written update describing recommended changes to the funding methodology described in subdivision (a) to the relevant policy committees and budget subcommittee of the Legislature on February 1, 2020. The written update shall include, but not be limited to, a description of the programmatic and policy changes discussed in the working sessions, the feasibility of implementing the discussed programmatic and policy changes, the impact that the discussed programmatic and policy changes would have on operations, collections, and families served, and additional required statutory changes. **Leg.H.** Added Stats 2019 ch 27 §6 (SB 80), effective June 27, 2019. Amended Stats 2020 ch 370 §116 (SB 1371), effective January 1, 2021.

§17307. Authority to remedy effects of changes in timing of child support payments

(a) The Legislature hereby finds and declares that the Department of Child Support Services has the authority and discretion to prevent, correct, or remedy the effects of changes in the timing of the receipt of child support payments resulting solely from the initial implementation of the federally required State Disbursement Unit. This authority shall not be construed to supplant existing statutory appropriation and technology project approval processes, limits, and requirements.

(b) The Legislature hereby finds and declares that this section is declaratory of existing law. **Leg.H.** Added Stats 2006 ch 75 §6 (AB 1808), effective July 12, 2006.

§17308. Delegation of responsibility

The director shall assume responsibility for implementing and managing all aspects of a single statewide automated child support system that will comply with state and federal requirements. The director may delegate responsibility to, or enter into an agreement with, any agency or entity that it deems necessary to satisfy this requirement. **Leg.H.** Added Stats 1999 ch 478 §1 (AB 196).

§17309. State Disbursement Unit

Effective October 1, 1998, the state shall operate a State Disbursement Unit as required by federal law (42 U.S.C. Secs. 654 (27), 654a(g), and 654b). **Leg.H.** Added Stats 1999 ch 478 §1 (AB 196). Amended Stats 2003 ch 387 §10 (AB 739).

§17309.5. Employer to make child support payments by electronic fund transfer

(a) An employer who is required to withhold and, by electronic fund transfer, pay tax pursuant to Section 19011 of the Revenue and Taxation Code or Section 13021 of the Unemployment Insurance Code, shall make child support payments to the State Disbursement Unit by electronic fund transfer. All child support payments required to be made to the State Disbursement Unit shall be remitted to the State Disbursement Unit by electronic fund transfer pursuant to Division 11 (commencing with Section 11101) of the Commercial Code.

(b) An employer not required to make payment to the State Disbursement Unit pursuant to paragraph (a), may elect to make payment by electronic fund transfer under the following conditions:

(1) The election shall be made in a form, and shall contain information, as prescribed by the Director of the Department of Child Support Services, and shall be subject to approval of the department.

(2) The election may be terminated upon written request to the Department of Child Support Services.

(c) For the purposes of this section:

(1) "Electronic fund transfer" means any transfer of funds, other than a transaction originated by check, draft, or similar paper instrument, that is initiated through an electronic terminal, telephonic instrument, or computer or magnetic tape, so as to order, instruct, or authorize a financial institution to debit or credit an account. Electronic fund transfers shall be accomplished by an automated clearinghouse debit, an automated clearinghouse credit, or by Federal Reserve Wire Transfer (Fedwire).

(2) "Automated clearinghouse" means any federal reserve bank, or an organization established in agreement with the National Automated Clearinghouse Association, that operates as a clearinghouse for transmitting or receiving entries between banks or bank accounts and that authorizes an electronic transfer of funds between these banks or bank accounts.

(3) "Automated clearinghouse debit" means a transaction in which the state, through its designated depository bank, originates an automated clearinghouse transaction debiting the person's bank account and crediting the state's bank account for the amount of tax. Banking costs incurred for the automated clearinghouse debit transaction shall be paid by the state.

(4) "Automated clearinghouse credit" means an automated clearinghouse transaction in which the person, through their own bank, originates an entry crediting the state's bank account and debiting the person's own bank account. Banking costs incurred for the automated clearinghouse credit transaction charged to the state shall be paid by the person originating the credit.

(5) "Fedwire transfer" means a transaction originated by a person and utilizing the national electronic payment system to transfer funds through the federal reserve banks, when that person debits their own bank account and credits the state's bank account. Electronic fund transfers pursuant to this section may be made by Fedwire only if payment cannot, for good cause, be made according to subdivision (a), and the use of Fedwire is preapproved by the department. Banking costs incurred for the Fedwire transaction charged to the person and to the state shall be paid by the person originating the transaction. **Leg.H.** Added Stats 2004 ch 806 §3 (AB 2358). Amended Stats 2019 ch 115 §143 (AB 1817), effective January 1, 2020.

§17310. Regulations and policies relating to responsibilities and jurisdiction of department

(a) The director shall formulate, adopt, amend, or repeal regulations and general policies affecting the purposes, responsibilities, and jurisdiction of the department that are consistent with law and necessary for the administration of the state plan for securing child support and enforcing spousal support orders and determining paternity.

(b) Notwithstanding any other provision of law, all regulations, including, but not limited to, regulations of the State Department of Social Services and the State Department of Health Services, relating to child support enforcement shall remain in effect and shall be fully enforceable by the department. The department may readopt, amend, or repeal the regulations in accordance with Section 17312 as necessary and appropriate. **Leg.H.** Added Stats 1999 ch 478 §1 (AB 196). Amended Stats 1999 ch 480 §11 (SB 542).

§17311. Child Support Payment Trust Fund; Creation and purpose; Revolving account; Startup funds; Loans from and to General Fund authorized

(a) The Child Support Payment Trust Fund is hereby created in the State Treasury. The department shall administer the fund.

(b)(1) The state may deposit child support payments received by the State Disbursement Unit, including those amounts that result in overpayment of child support, into the Child Support Payment Trust Fund, for the purpose of processing and providing child support payments. Notwithstanding Section 13340 of the Government Code, the fund is continuously appropriated for the purposes of disbursing child support payments from the State Disbursement Unit.

(2) The state share of the interest and other earnings that accrue on the fund shall be available to the department and used to offset the following General Fund costs in this order:

(A) Any transfers made to the Child Support Payment Trust Fund from the General Fund.

(B) The cost of administering the State Disbursement Unit, subject to appropriation by the Legislature.

(C) Other child support program activities, subject to appropriation by the Legislature.

(c) The department may establish and administer a revolving account in the Child Support Payment Trust Fund in an amount not to exceed six hundred million dollars ($600,000,000) to ensure the timely disbursement of child support. This amount may be adjusted by the Director of Finance upon notification of the Legislature as required, to meet payment timeframes required under federal law.

(d) It is the intent of the Legislature to provide transfers from the General Fund to provide startup funds for the Child Support Payment Trust Fund so that, together with the balances transferred pursuant to Section 17311.7, the Child Support Payment Trust Fund will have sufficient cash on hand to make all child support payments within the required timeframes.

(e) Notwithstanding any other law, an ongoing loan shall be made available from the General Fund, from funds not otherwise appropriated, to the Child Support Payment Trust Fund, not to exceed one hundred fifty million dollars ($150,000,000) to ensure the timely disbursement of child support payments when funds have not been recorded to the Child Support Payment Trust Fund or due to other fund liabilities, including, but not limited to, Internal Revenue Service negative adjustments to tax intercept payments. Whenever an adjustment of this amount is required to meet payment timeframes under federal law, the amount shall be adjusted after approval of the Director of Finance. In conjunction with the Department of Finance and the Controller's office, the department shall establish repayment procedures to ensure the outstanding loan balance does not exceed the average daily cash needs. The ongoing evaluation of the fund as detailed in these procedures shall occur no less frequently than monthly.

(f) Notwithstanding any other law, the Controller may use the moneys in the Child Support Payment Trust Fund for loans to the General Fund as provided in Sections 16310 and 16381 of the Government Code. However, interest shall be paid on all moneys loaned to the General Fund from the Child Support Payment Trust Fund. Interest payable shall be computed at a rate determined by the Pooled Money Investment Board to be the current earning rate of the fund from which loaned. This subdivision does not authorize any transfer that will interfere with the carrying out of the object for which the Child Support Payment Trust Fund was created. **Leg.H.** Added Stats 2003 ch 387 §11 (AB 739). Amended Stats 2005 ch 78 §6 (SB 68), effective July 19, 2005; Stats 2009–2010 3rd Ex sess ch 9 §4 (ABX3-13), effective February 20, 2009.

§17311.5. Trust agreement to receive or disburse child support collections

(a) The department may enter into a trust agreement with a trustee or fiscal intermediary to receive or disburse child support collections. The trust agreement may contain provisions the department deems reasonable and proper for the security of the child support payments. Any trust accounts created by the trust agreements may be held outside the State Treasury.

(b) For the 2012–13 fiscal year only, trust account moneys may be invested in any of the types of securities listed in Section 16430 of the Government Code or alternatives offering comparable security, including, but not limited to, mutual funds and money market funds. This subdivision does not authorize investments or transfers that would interfere with carrying out the objective for which the Child Support Payment Trust Fund was created. **Leg.H.** Added Stats 2003 ch 387 §12 (AB 739). Amended Stats 2012 ch 47 §1 (SB 1041), effective June 27, 2012.

§17311.7. Payments; State disbursement unit

(a) Any payment required to be made to a family through the State Disbursement Unit shall be made directly to the obligee parent in the child support order requiring the payment, the conservator or guardian of the obligee parent, a special needs trust for the benefit of the obligee parent, the guardian of the person and the estate of the child subject to the order, any caregiver relative having custody or responsibility for the child, pursuant to a written record, or an alternate caregiver to whom the obligee under the child support order directs, in a written record, that payments be made.

(b) For purposes of this section, "alternate caregiver" means a non-relative caregiver who is designated in writing by the obligee parent to take care of the child for a limited time. **Leg.H.** Added Stats 2018 ch 504 §6 (AB 3248), effective January 1, 2019.

Prior Law: Former Fam C §17311.7, relating to closeout activities, guidelines, and audit, was added Stats 2003 ch 387 §13 (AB 739), effective January 1, 2004, and repealed Stats 2018 ch 504 §5 (AB 3248), effective January 1, 2019.

Former Sections: Former Fam C §17311.7, relating to closeout activities, guidelines, and audit, was added Stats 2003 ch 387 §13 (AB 739) and repealed Stats 2018 ch 504 §5 (AB 3248).

§17312. Regulations, orders, or standards governing law enforced by department

(a) The department shall adopt regulations, orders, or standards of general application to implement, interpret, or make specific the law enforced by the department. Regulations, orders, and standards shall be adopted, amended, or repealed by the director only in accordance with Chapter 3.5 (commencing with Section 11340) of Part 1 of Division 3 of Title 2 of the Government Code.

(b) In adopting regulations, the department shall strive for clarity of language that may be readily understood by those administering public social services or subject to those regulations.

(c) The rules of the department need not specify or include the detail of forms, reports, or records, but shall include the essential authority by which any person, agency, organization, association, or institution subject to the supervision or investigation of the department is required to use, submit, or maintain the forms, reports, or records.

(d) The department's regulations and other materials shall be made available pursuant to the California Code of Regulations and in the same manner as are materials of the State Department of Social Services under the provisions of Section 205.70 of Title 45 of the Code of Federal Regulations. **Leg.H.** Added Stats 1999 ch 478 §1 (AB 196). Amended Stats 1999 ch 480 §12 (SB 542).

§17314. Assistants and regional administrators

(a) Subject to the State Civil Service Act (Part 2 (commencing with Section 18500) of Division 5 of Title 2 of the Government Code), the director shall appoint any assistants and other employees that are necessary for the administration of the affairs of the department and shall prescribe their duties and, subject to the approval of the Department of Finance, fix their salaries.

(b) As the director adopts a plan for a local child support agency to assume responsibility for child support enforcement activities in any county served by a district attorney pursuant to Section 17304, the director shall hire a sufficient number of regional state administrators to oversee the local child support agencies to ensure compliance with all state and federal laws and regulations. The regions shall be divided based on the total caseload of each local child support agency. The responsibilities of the regional state administrators shall include all of the following:

(1) Conducting regular and comprehensive site visits to the local child support agencies assigned to their region and preparing quarterly reports to be submitted to the department. The local child support agencies shall fully cooperate with all reasonable requests made by the regional state administrators, including providing all requested data on the local child support agency's program.

(2) Notifying a local child support agency of any potential or actual noncompliance with any state or federal law or regulation by the agency and working with the local child support agency to develop an immediate plan to ensure compliance.

(3) Participating in program monitoring teams as set forth in subdivision (c) of Section 17602.

(4) Participating in meetings with all regional state administrators and the director on at least a monthly basis to promote statewide uniformity as to the functions and structure of the local child support agencies. The regional state administrators may recommend proposals for approval and adoption by the director to achieve this goal.

(5) Responding to requests for management or technical assistance regarding program operations by local child support agencies. **Leg.H.** Added Stats 1999 ch 478 §1 (AB 196).

§17316. Conflict of interest

No person, while holding the office of director, shall be a trustee, manager, director, or other officer or employee of any agency performing any function supervised by the department or any institution that is subject to examination, inspection, or supervision by the department. **Leg.H.** Added Stats 1999 ch 478 §1 (AB 196).

§17318. Applicability of other code sections

Except as otherwise expressly provided, Part 1 (commencing with Section 11000) of Division 3 of Title 2 of the Government Code, as it may be added to or amended from time to time, shall apply to the conduct of the department. **Leg.H.** Added Stats 1999 ch 478 §1 (AB 196).

§17320. Avoidance of federal penalties

The department shall coordinate with the State Department of Social Services to avoid the imposition of any federal penalties that cause a reduction in the state's Temporary Assistance to Needy Families grant, payable pursuant to Section 603(a)(1) of Title 42 of the United States Code. **Leg.H.** Added Stats 1999 ch 478 §1 (AB 196).

§17325. Qualifying account for direct deposit of child support payments

(a)(1) Notwithstanding any other law, if child support payments are directly deposited to an account of the recipient's choice, as authorized under the federal Electronic Fund Transfer Act (EFTA) (15 U.S.C. Sec. 1693 et seq.), the payments may only be deposited to an account that meets the requirements of a qualifying account, as defined in paragraph (2), for deposit of child support payments.

(2) For purposes of this section, a "qualifying account" is one of the following:

(A) A demand deposit or savings account at an insured depository financial institution that is offered directly by the insured depository financial institution on its internet website or through its branches and that is in the name of the person entitled to the receipt of child support payments.

(B) A prepaid account, or a demand deposit or savings account offered by, or through, an entity other than an insured depository financial institution, that meets all of the following:

(i) The account is held at an insured depository financial institution.

(ii) The account is set up to meet the requirements for direct or passthrough deposit or share insurance payable to the person entitled to the receipt of child support payments by the Federal Deposit Insurance Corporation in accordance with Part 330 of Title 12 of the Code of Federal Regulations, or the National Credit Union Share Insurance Fund in accordance with Part 745 of Title 12 of the Code of Federal Regulations.

(iii) The account is not attached to a credit or overdraft feature that is automatically repaid from the account unless the credit or overdraft feature has no fee, charge, or cost, whether direct, required, voluntary, or involuntary, or the credit or overdraft feature complies with the requirements for credit offered in connection with a prepaid account under the federal Truth in Lending Act (15 U.S.C. Sec. 1601 et seq.) and its implementing regulations.

(iv) The account complies with all of the requirements, and provides the holder of the account with all of the consumer protections, that apply to an account under the rules implementing the EFTA.

(3) A person or entity that is not an insured depository financial institution that offers, maintains, or manages an account that does not comply with paragraph (2) shall not solicit, accept, or facilitate the direct deposit of child support payments to the account.

(b) For purposes of this section, the department shall not be held liable for authorizing a direct deposit of child support payments into an account designated by the recipient that does not comply with paragraph (2) of subdivision (a). The department has no obligation to determine whether an account at the insured depository financial institution of the recipient's choice is a qualifying account as described in subdivision (a).

(c) For the purposes of this section, the following definitions shall apply:

(1) "Insured depository financial institution" means a state or national bank, a state or federal savings and loan association, a mutual savings bank, or a state or federal credit union that holds deposits insured by the Federal Deposit Insurance Corporation or the National Credit Union Administration.

(2) "Prepaid account" has the same meaning as that term is defined in regulations under the EFTA. **Leg.H.** Added Stats 2014 ch 180 §1 (AB 2252), effective July 23, 2014. Amended Stats 2014 ch 720 §1 (AB 1614), effective January 1, 2015; Stats 2015 ch 416 §2 (AB 1519), effective January 1, 2016; Stats 2021 ch 546 §1 (SB 497), effective January 1, 2022.

ARTICLE 4
Statewide Registry for Child Support

Legislative finding and declaration; Utilization of California Child Support Enforcement System. §17390.
Statewide Child Support Registry; Implementation plan; Operation; Provision of information by clerks of court; Duties of department. §17391.
Development of forms for implementation of Statewide Child Support Registry; Information transmitted from clerks of court. §17392.
Development of forms by Judicial Council. §17393.

§17390. Legislative finding and declaration; Utilization of California Child Support Enforcement System

(a) The Legislature finds and declares that there is no single statewide database containing statistical data regarding child support orders.

(b) The California Child Support Enforcement System or its replacement may be utilized to provide a single statewide registry of all child support orders in California, including orders for cases under Title IV-D of the Social Security Act and all cases with child support orders. **Leg.H.** Added Stats 2016 ch 474 §13 (AB 2882), effective January 1, 2017.

§17391. Statewide Child Support Registry; Implementation plan; Operation; Provision of information by clerks of court; Duties of department

(a) The department shall develop an implementation plan for the Statewide Child Support Registry. The Statewide Child Support Registry shall be operated by the agency responsible for operation of the California Child Support Enforcement System or its replacement. The Statewide Child Support Registry shall include storage and data retrieval of the data elements specified in Section 17392 for all California child support orders. The Statewide Child Support Registry will operate to ensure that all data in the Statewide Child Support Registry can be accessed and integrated for statistical analysis and reporting purposes with all child support order data contained in the California Child Support Enforcement System.

(b) Each clerk of the court shall provide the information specified in Section 17392 within 20 days to the department or the Statewide Child Support Registry from each new or modified child support order, including child support arrearage orders.

(c) The department shall maintain a system for compiling the child support data received from the clerks of the court, ensure that all child support data received from the clerks of the court are entered into the Statewide Child Support Registry within five business days of receipt in the Statewide Child Support Registry, and ensure that the Statewide Child Support Registry is fully implemented statewide.

(d) The department shall provide aggregate data on a periodic basis on the data maintained by the Statewide Child Support Registry to the Judicial Council, the appropriate agencies of the executive branch, and the Legislature for statistical analysis and review. The data shall not include individual identifying information for specific cases.

(e) Any information maintained by the Statewide Child Support Registry received from clerks of the court shall be provided to local child support agencies, the courts, and others as provided by law. **Leg.H.** Added Stats 2016 ch 474 §13 (AB 2882), effective January 1, 2017.

§17392. Development of forms for implementation of Statewide Child Support Registry; Information transmitted from clerks of court

(a) The Judicial Council shall develop any forms that may be necessary to implement the Statewide Child Support Registry. The forms may be in electronic form or in hardcopy, as appropriate. The forms shall be developed so as not to delay implementation, and shall be available no later than 30 days prior to the implementation, of the Statewide Child Support Registry.

(b) The information transmitted from the clerks of the court to the Statewide Child Support Registry shall include all of the following:

(1) Any information required under federal law.

(2) Any other information the department and the Judicial Council find appropriate. **Leg.H.** Added Stats 2016 ch 474 §13 (AB 2882), effective January 1, 2017.

§17393. Development of forms by Judicial Council

The Judicial Council shall develop the forms necessary to implement this article. **Leg.H.** Added Stats 2016 ch 474 §13 (AB 2882), effective January 1, 2017.

CHAPTER 2
CHILD SUPPORT ENFORCEMENT

Article 1. Support Obligations.
Article 1.5. Delinquent Child Support Obligations and Financial Institution Data Match.
Article 2. Collections and Enforcement.
Article 3. Program Compliance.
Article 4. Program Costs.

ARTICLE 1
Support Obligations

Obligation of county to maintain local child support agency; Actions brought by agency; Summons, complaint, and answer forms; Outreach program; Order for temporary support; "Enforcing obligations"; Intervention by agency [Repealed January 1, 2027]. § 17400.
Obligation of county to maintain local child support agency; Actions brought by agency; Summons, complaint, and answer forms; Outreach program; Order for temporary support; "Enforcing obligations"; Intervention by agency [Operative January 1, 2026]. § 17400.
Modification of support obligation when obligor receiving federal assistance. §17400.5.
Requirements upon receipt of obligor's address. §17401.
Notice and information about child support service hearings. §17401.5.
Obligation of noncustodial parent. §17402.
Remittance of public assistance child support payments. §17402.1.
Parties to actions; Hearing and judgment; Pleadings; Actions under other code provisions; Independent action to modify support order. §17404.
Summons or order to show cause [Repealed January 1, 2027]. §17404.1.
Summons or order to show cause [Operative January 1, 2026]. § 17404.1.
Transfers of actions. §17404.2.
Hearings by telephone, audiovisual means, or other electronic means. §17404.3.
Administrative change of payee. §17404.4.
Interview of custodial parent. §17405.
Actions involving paternity or support; Notice of hearing. §17406.
Appeal by Attorney General. §17407.
Declaration of state reciprocity. §17407.5.
Consolidation of orders. §17408.
Voluntary acknowledgment of paternity. §17410.
Effect of voluntary declaration of parentage. §17412.
Filing of written stipulation. §17414.
Referral from county welfare department. §17415.
Judgment based on agreement. §17416.
Inquiry of parents. §17418.
Earnings assignment order. §17420.
State medical insurance form. §17422.
Time for completion of medical insurance form. §17424.
Supplemental complaint. §17428.

Failure to answer or appear; Additional information and amended proposed judgment [Repealed January 1, 2027]. §17430.
Failure to answer or appear; Additional information and amended proposed judgment [Operative January 1, 2026]. § 17430.
Relief from, and setting aside orders [Repealed January 1, 2027]. §17432.
Relief from and setting aside orders [Operative January 1, 2026]. § 17432.
Adoption of necessary forms. § 17432.5.
Judgment or order after default. §17433.
When interest on support obligation accrues. §17433.5.
Booklet of procedures and processes; Information hotline. §17434.
Modification of support orders of activated service members; Form. §17440.

§ 17400. Obligation of county to maintain local child support agency; Actions brought by agency; Summons, complaint, and answer forms; Outreach program; Order for temporary support; "Enforcing obligations"; Intervention by agency [Repealed January 1, 2027]

(a)(1) Each county shall maintain a local child support agency, as specified in Section 17304, that shall have the responsibility for promptly and effectively establishing, modifying, and enforcing child support obligations, including medical support, enforcing spousal support orders established by a court of competent jurisdiction, and determining paternity in the case of a child born out of wedlock. The local child support agency shall take appropriate action, including criminal action in cooperation with the district attorneys, to establish, modify, and enforce child support and, if appropriate, enforce spousal support orders if the child is receiving public assistance, including Medi-Cal, and, if requested, shall take the same actions on behalf of a child who is not receiving public assistance, including Medi-Cal.

(2)(A) Provided that no reduction in aid or payment to a custodial parent would result, the local child support agency shall cease enforcement of child support arrearages assigned to the state and other fees and costs owed to the state that the department or the local child support agency has determined to be uncollectible. If enforcement is ceased pursuant to this paragraph, cases shall be closed to the maximum extent permitted under Section 303.11 of Title 45 of the Code of Federal Regulations, as adopted under Section 118203 of Title 22 of the California Code of Regulations.

(B) In determining the meaning of uncollectible for purposes of arrearages assigned to the state and other fees and costs owed to the state, the department and the local child support agency shall consider, but not be limited to, the following factors:

(i) Income and assets available to pay the arrearage or other fees and costs.
(ii) Source of income.
(iii) Age of the arrearage or other fees and costs.
(iv) The number of support orders.
(v) Employment history.
(vi) Payment history.
(vii) Incarceration history.
(viii) Whether the order was based on imputed income.
(ix) Other readily ascertainable debts.

(C) Notwithstanding subparagraph (B), the department and a local child support agency shall deem an arrearage assigned to the state or fees and costs owed to the state as uncollectible if the noncustodial parent's sole income is from any of the following:

(i) Supplemental Security Income/State Supplementary Program for the Aged, Blind, and Disabled (SSI/SSP) benefits.
(ii) A combination of SSI/SSP benefits and Social Security Disability Insurance (SSDI) benefits.
(iii) Cash Assistance Program for Aged, Blind, and Disabled Legal Immigrants (CAPI) benefits.
(iv) Veterans Administration Disability Compensation Benefits in an amount equal to or less than the amount the noncustodial parent would receive in SSI/SSP benefits.

(D) Notwithstanding the Administrative Procedure Act (Chapter 3.5 (commencing with Section 11340) of Part 1 of Division 3 of Title 2 of the Government Code), the department may implement and administer this subdivision through a child support services letter or similar instruction until regulations are adopted. Thereafter, the department shall adopt regulations to implement this subdivision by July 1, 2024.

(b)(1) Notwithstanding Sections 25203 and 26529 of the Government Code, attorneys employed within the local child support agency may direct, control, and prosecute civil actions and proceedings in the name of the county in support of child support activities of the Department of Child Support Services and the local child support agency.

(2) Notwithstanding any other law, and except for pleadings or documents required to be signed under penalty of perjury, a local child support agency may substitute original signatures of the agent of the local child support agency with any form of electronic signatures, including, but not limited to, typed, digital, or facsimile images of signatures, digital signatures, or other computer-generated signatures, on pleadings filed for the purpose of establishing, modifying, or enforcing paternity, child support, or medical support. A substituted signature used by a local child support agency shall have the same effect as an original signature, including, but not limited to, the requirements of Section 128.7 of the Code of Civil Procedure.

(3) Notwithstanding any other law, effective July 1, 2016, a local child support agency may electronically file pleadings signed by an agent of the local child support agency under penalty of perjury. An original signed pleading shall be executed prior to, or on the same day as, the day of electronic filing. Original signed pleadings shall be maintained by the local child support agency for the period of time prescribed by subdivision (a) of Section 68152 of the Government Code. A local child support agency may maintain the original signed pleading by way of an electronic copy in the Statewide Automated Child Support System. The Judicial Council, by July 1, 2016, shall develop rules to implement this subdivision.

(4)(A) Notwithstanding any other law, a local child support agency may substitute any original signatures, including, but not limited to, signatures of agents of the local child support agencies, support obligors, support obligees, other parents, witnesses, and the attorneys for the parties to the action, with a printed copy or electronic image of an electronic signature obtained in compliance with the rules of court adopted pursuant to paragraph (2) of subdivision (e) of Section 1010.6 of the Code of Civil Procedure, on pleadings or documents filed for the purpose of establishing, modifying, or enforcing paternity, child support, or medical support. If the pleading or document is signed under the penalty of perjury or the signature does not belong to an agent of the local child support agency, the local child support agency represents, by the act of filing, that the declarant electronically signed the pleading or document before, or on the same day as, the date of filing.

(B) The local child support agency shall maintain the electronic form of the pleading or document bearing the original electronic signature for the period of time prescribed by subdivision (a) of Section 68152 of the Government Code, and shall make it available for review upon the request of the court or any party to the action or proceeding in which it is filed. Printed copies or electronic images of electronic signatures used by a local child support agency in this manner shall have the same effect as an original signature, including, but not limited to, the requirements of Section 128.7 of the Code of Civil Procedure.

(c) Actions brought by the local child support agency to establish paternity or child support or to enforce child support obligations shall be completed within the time limits set forth by federal law. The local child support agency's responsibility applies to spousal support only if the spousal support obligation has been reduced to an order of a court of competent jurisdiction. In any action brought for modification or revocation of an order that is being enforced under Title IV-D of the Social Security Act (42 U.S.C. Sec. 651 et seq.), the effective date of the modification or revocation shall be as prescribed by federal law (42 U.S.C. Sec. 666(a)(9)), or any subsequent date.

(d)(1) The Judicial Council, in consultation with the department, the Senate Committee on Judiciary, the Assembly Committee on Judiciary, and a legal services organization providing representation on child support matters, shall develop simplified summons, complaint, and answer forms for any action for support brought pursuant to this section or Section 17404. The Judicial Council may combine the summons and complaint in a single form.

(2) The simplified complaint form shall provide notice of the amount of child support that is sought pursuant to the guidelines set forth in Article 2 (commencing with Section 4050) of Chapter 2 of Part 2 of Division 9 based upon the income or income history of the support obligor as known to the local child support agency. If the support obligor's income or income history is unknown to the local child support agency, the complaint shall inform the support obligor that income shall be

presumed to be the amount of the minimum wage, at 40 hours per week, established by the Industrial Welfare Commission pursuant to Section 1182.11 of the Labor Code unless information concerning the support obligor's income is provided to the court. The complaint form shall be accompanied by a proposed judgment. The complaint form shall include a notice to the support obligor that the proposed judgment will become effective if the obligor fails to file an answer with the court within 30 days of service. Except as provided in paragraph (2) of subdivision (a) of Section 17402, if the proposed judgment is entered by the court, the support order in the proposed judgment shall be effective as of the first day of the month following the filing of the complaint.

(3)(A) The simplified answer form shall be written in simple English and shall permit a defendant to answer and raise defenses by checking applicable boxes. The answer form shall include instructions for completion of the form and instructions for proper filing of the answer.

(B) The answer form shall be accompanied by a blank income and expense declaration or simplified financial statement and instructions on how to complete the financial forms. The answer form shall direct the defendant to file the completed income and expense declaration or simplified financial statement with the answer, but shall state that the answer will be accepted by a court without the income and expense declaration or simplified financial statement.

(C) The clerk of the court shall accept and file answers, income and expense declarations, and simplified financial statements that are completed by hand provided they are legible.

(4)(A) The simplified complaint form prepared pursuant to this subdivision shall be used by the local child support agency or the Attorney General in all cases brought under this section or Section 17404.

(B) The simplified answer form prepared pursuant to this subdivision shall be served on all defendants with the simplified complaint. Failure to serve the simplified answer form on all defendants shall not invalidate any judgment obtained. However, failure to serve the answer form may be used as evidence in any proceeding under Section 17432 of this code or Section 473 of the Code of Civil Procedure.

(C) The Judicial Council shall add language to the governmental summons, for use by the local child support agency with the governmental complaint to establish parental relationship and child support, informing defendants that a blank answer form should have been received with the summons and additional copies may be obtained from either the local child support agency or the superior court clerk.

(e) In any action brought or enforcement proceedings instituted by the local child support agency pursuant to this section for payment of child or spousal support, an action to recover an arrearage in support payments may be maintained by the local child support agency at any time within the period otherwise specified for the enforcement of a support judgment, notwithstanding the fact that the child has attained the age of majority.

(f) The county shall undertake an outreach program to inform the public that the services described in subdivisions (a) to (c), inclusive, are available to persons not receiving public assistance. There shall be prominently displayed in every public area of every office of the agencies established by this section a notice, in clear and simple language prescribed by the Director of Child Support Services, that the services provided in subdivisions (a) to (c), inclusive, are provided to all individuals, whether or not they are recipients of public assistance.

(g)(1) In any action to establish a child support order brought by the local child support agency in the performance of duties under this section, the local child support agency may make a motion for an order effective during the pendency of that action, for the support, maintenance, and education of the child or children that are the subject of the action. This order shall be referred to as an order for temporary support. This order has the same force and effect as a like or similar order under this code.

(2) The local child support agency shall file a motion for an order for temporary support within the following time limits:

(A) If the defendant is the mother, a presumed father under Section 7611, or any father if the child is at least six months old when the defendant files the answer, the time limit is 90 days after the defendant files an answer.

(B) In any other case in which the defendant has filed an answer prior to the birth of the child or not more than six months after the birth of the child, then the time limit is nine months after the birth of the child.

(3) If more than one child is the subject of the action, the limitation on reimbursement shall apply only as to those children whose parental relationship and age would bar recovery were a separate action brought for support of that child or those children.

(4) If the local child support agency fails to file a motion for an order for temporary support within the time limits specified in this section, the local child support agency shall be barred from obtaining a judgment of reimbursement for any support provided for that child during the period between the date the time limit expired and the date the motion was filed, or, if no motion is filed, when a final judgment is entered.

(5) Except as provided in Section 17304, this section does not prohibit the local child support agency from entering into cooperative arrangements with other county departments as necessary to carry out the responsibilities imposed by this section pursuant to plans of cooperation with the departments approved by the Department of Child Support Services.

(6) This section does not otherwise limit the ability of the local child support agency from securing and enforcing orders for support of a spouse or former spouse as authorized under any other law.

(h) As used in this article, "enforcing obligations" includes, but is not limited to, all of the following:

(1) The use of all interception and notification systems operated by the department for the purpose of aiding in the enforcement of support obligations.

(2) The obtaining by the local child support agency of an initial order for child support that may include medical support or that is for medical support only, by civil or criminal process.

(3) The initiation of a motion or order to show cause to increase an existing child support order, and the response to a motion or order to show cause brought by an obligor parent to decrease an existing child support order, or the initiation of a motion or order to show cause to obtain an order for medical support, and the response to a motion or order to show cause brought by an obligor parent to decrease or terminate an existing medical support order, without regard to whether the child is receiving public assistance.

(4) The response to a notice of motion or order to show cause brought by an obligor parent to decrease an existing spousal support order if the child or children are residing with the obligee parent and the local child support agency is also enforcing a related child support obligation owed to the obligee parent by the same obligor.

(5) The referral of child support delinquencies to the department under subdivision (c) of Section 17500 in support of the local child support agency.

(i) As used in this section, "out of wedlock" means that the biological parents of the child were not married to each other at the time of the child's conception.

(j)(1) The local child support agency is the public agency responsible for administering wage withholding for current support for the purposes of Title IV-D of the Social Security Act (42 U.S.C. Sec. 651 et seq.).

(2) This section does not limit the authority of the local child support agency granted by other sections of this code or otherwise granted by law.

(k) In the exercise of the authority granted under this article, the local child support agency may intervene, pursuant to subdivision (b) of Section 387 of the Code of Civil Procedure, by ex parte application, in any action under this code, or other proceeding in which child support is an issue or a reduction in spousal support is sought. By notice of motion, order to show cause, or responsive pleading served upon all parties to the action, the local child support agency may request any relief that is appropriate that the local child support agency is authorized to seek.

(*l*) The local child support agency shall comply with all regulations and directives established by the department that set time standards for responding to requests for assistance in locating noncustodial parents, establishing paternity, establishing child support awards, and collecting child support payments.

(m) As used in this article, medical support activities that the local child support agency is authorized to perform are limited to the following:

(1) The obtaining and enforcing of court orders for health insurance coverage.

(2) Any other medical support activity mandated by federal law or regulation.

(n)(1) Notwithstanding any other law, venue for an action or proceeding under this division shall be determined as follows:

(A) Venue shall be in the superior court in the county that is currently expending public assistance.

(B) If public assistance is not currently being expended, venue shall be in the superior court in the county where the child who is entitled to current support resides or is domiciled.

(C) If current support is no longer payable through, or enforceable by, the local child support agency, venue shall be in the superior court in the county that last provided public assistance for actions to enforce arrearages assigned pursuant to Section 11477 of the Welfare and Institutions Code.

(D) If subparagraphs (A), (B), and (C) do not apply, venue shall be in the superior court in the county of residence of the support obligee.

(E) If the support obligee does not reside in California, and subparagraphs (A), (B), (C), and (D) do not apply, venue shall be in the superior court of the county of residence of the obligor.

(2) Notwithstanding paragraph (1), if the child becomes a resident of another county after an action under this part has been filed, venue may remain in the county where the action was filed until the action is completed.

(o) The local child support agency of one county may appear on behalf of the local child support agency of any other county in an action or proceeding under this part.

(p) This section shall become inoperative on January 1, 2026, and, as of January 1, 2027, is repealed. **Leg.H.** Added Stats 2021 ch 85 §4 (AB 135), effective July 16, 2021, operative January 1, 2023. Amended Stats 2021 ch 696 §3 (AB 172), effective October 8, 2021, operative January 1, 2023; Stats 2022 ch 215 §3 (AB 2961), effective January 1, 2023, operative January 1, 2023; Stats 2023 ch 213 §14 (SB 343), effective January 1, 2024, inoperative January 1, 2026, repealed January 1, 2027; Stats 2024 ch 853 §21 (AB 3281), effective January 1, 2025, inoperative January 1, 2026, repealed January 1, 2027.

Prior Law Former Fam C §17400, similar to the present section, was added Stats 1999 ch 478 §1 (AB 196), amended Stats 1999 ch 480 §13 (SB 542), ch 980 §14.2 (AB 1671), Stats 2000 ch 808 §81 (AB 1358), effective September 28, 2000, Stats 2001 ch 111 §3 (AB 429), effective July 30, 2001, Stats 2002 ch 927 §3.7 (AB 3032), Stats 2003 ch 225 §3 (AB 1752), effective August 11, 2003, Stats 2004 ch 339 §6 (AB 1704), Stats2 007 ch 249 §3 (SB 523), effective January 1, 2008, Stats 2015 ch 416 §3 (AB 1519), effective January 1, 2016, Stats 2016 ch 474 §14 (AB 2882), effective January 1, 2017, Stats 2019 ch 115 §144 (AB 1817), effective January 1, 2020, Stats 2021 ch 85 §3 (AB 135), effective July 16, 2021, and repealed by its own terms January 1, 2023.

§ 17400. Obligation of county to maintain local child support agency; Actions brought by agency; Summons, complaint, and answer forms; Outreach program; Order for temporary support; "Enforcing obligations"; Intervention by agency [Operative January 1, 2026]

(a)(1) Each county shall maintain a local child support agency, as specified in Section 17304, that shall have the responsibility for promptly and effectively establishing, modifying, and enforcing child support obligations, including medical support, enforcing spousal support orders established by a court of competent jurisdiction, and determining paternity in the case of a child born out of wedlock. The local child support agency shall take appropriate action, including criminal action in cooperation with the district attorneys, to establish, modify, and enforce child support and, if appropriate, enforce spousal support orders if the child is receiving public assistance, including Medi-Cal, and, if requested, shall take the same actions on behalf of a child who is not receiving public assistance, including Medi-Cal.

(2)(A) Provided that no reduction in aid or payment to a custodial parent would result, the local child support agency shall cease enforcement of child support arrearages assigned to the state and other fees and costs owed to the state that the department or the local child support agency has determined to be uncollectible. If enforcement is ceased pursuant to this paragraph, cases shall be closed to the maximum extent permitted under Section 303.11 of Title 45 of the Code of Federal Regulations, as adopted under Section 118203 of Title 22 of the California Code of Regulations.

(B) In determining the meaning of uncollectible for purposes of arrearages assigned to the state and other fees and costs owed to the state, the department and the local child support agency shall consider, but not be limited to, the following factors:

(i) Income and assets available to pay the arrearage or other fees and costs.

(ii) Source of income.

(iii) Age of the arrearage or other fees and costs.

(iv) The number of support orders.

(v) Employment history.

(vi) Payment history.

(vii) Incarceration history.

(viii) Whether the order was based on imputed income.

(ix) Other readily ascertainable debts.

(C) Notwithstanding subparagraph (B), the department and a local child support agency shall deem an arrearage assigned to the state or fees and costs owed to the state as uncollectible if the noncustodial parent's sole income is from any of the following:

(i) Supplemental Security Income/State Supplementary Program for the Aged, Blind, and Disabled (SSI/SSP) benefits.

(ii) A combination of SSI/SSP benefits and Social Security Disability Insurance (SSDI) benefits.

(iii) Cash Assistance Program for Aged, Blind, and Disabled Legal Immigrants (CAPI) benefits.

(iv) Veterans Administration Disability Compensation Benefits in an amount equal to or less than the amount the noncustodial parent would receive in SSI/SSP benefits.

(D) Notwithstanding the Administrative Procedure Act (Chapter 3.5 (commencing with Section 11340) of Part 1 of Division 3 of Title 2 of the Government Code), the department may implement and administer this subdivision through a child support services letter or similar instruction until regulations are adopted. Thereafter, the department shall adopt regulations to implement this subdivision by July 1, 2024.

(b)(1) Notwithstanding Sections 25203 and 26529 of the Government Code, attorneys employed within the local child support agency may direct, control, and prosecute civil actions and proceedings in the name of the county in support of child support activities of the Department of Child Support Services and the local child support agency.

(2) Notwithstanding any other law, and except for pleadings or documents required to be signed under penalty of perjury, a local child support agency may substitute original signatures of the agent of the local child support agency with any form of electronic signatures, including, but not limited to, typed, digital, or facsimile images of signatures, digital signatures, or other computer-generated signatures, on pleadings filed for the purpose of establishing, modifying, or enforcing paternity, child support, or medical support. A substituted signature used by a local child support agency shall have the same effect as an original signature, including, but not limited to, the requirements of Section 128.7 of the Code of Civil Procedure.

(3) Notwithstanding any other law, a local child support agency may electronically file pleadings signed by an agent of the local child support agency under penalty of perjury. An original signed pleading shall be executed prior to, or on the same day as, the day of electronic filing. Original signed pleadings shall be maintained by the local child support agency for the period of time prescribed by subdivision (a) of Section 68152 of the Government Code. A local child support agency may maintain the original signed pleading by way of an electronic copy in the Statewide Automated Child Support System. The Judicial Council shall develop rules to implement this subdivision.

(4)(A) Notwithstanding any other law, a local child support agency may substitute any original signatures, including, but not limited to, signatures of agents of the local child support agencies, support obligors, support obligees, other parents, witnesses, and the attorneys for the parties to the action, with a printed copy or electronic image of an electronic signature obtained in compliance with the rules of court adopted pursuant to paragraph (2) of subdivision (e) of Section 1010.6 of the Code of Civil Procedure, on pleadings or documents filed for the purpose of establishing, modifying, or enforcing paternity, child support, or medical support. If the pleading or document is signed under the penalty of perjury or the signature does not belong to an agent of the local child support agency, the local child support agency represents, by the act of filing, that the declarant electronically signed the pleading or document before, or on the same day as, the date of filing.

(B) The local child support agency shall maintain the electronic form of the pleading or document bearing the original electronic signature for the period of time prescribed by subdivision (a) of Section 68152 of the Government Code, and shall make it available for review upon the request of the court or any party to the action or proceeding in which it is filed. Printed copies or electronic images of electronic signatures used by a local child support agency in this manner shall have the same effect as an original signature, including, but not limited to, the requirements of Section 128.7 of the Code of Civil Procedure.

(c) Actions brought by the local child support agency to establish paternity or child support or to enforce child support obligations shall be completed within the time limits set forth by federal law. The local child support agency's responsibility applies to spousal support only if the spousal support obligation has been reduced to an order of a court of competent jurisdiction. In any action brought for modification or revocation of an order that is being enforced under Title IV-D of the Social Security Act (42 U.S.C. Sec. 651 et seq.), the effective date of the modification or revocation shall be as prescribed by federal law (42 U.S.C. Sec. 666(a)(9)), or any subsequent date.

(d)(1) The Judicial Council, in consultation with the department, the Senate Committee on Judiciary, the Assembly Committee on Judiciary, and a legal services organization providing representation on child support matters, shall develop simplified summons, complaint, and answer forms for any action for support brought pursuant to this section or Section 17404. The Judicial Council may combine the summons and complaint in a single form.

(2)(A) The simplified complaint form shall provide notice of the amount of child support that is sought pursuant to the guidelines set forth in Article 2 (commencing with Section 4050) of Chapter 2 of Part 2 of Division 9 based upon one of the following methods used to determine income:

(i) If sufficient information is available to determine actual income, pursuant to subdivision (a) of Section 4058 and Section 4060, the local child support agency shall use actual income as the basis of the proposed support obligation, unless the local child support agency has sufficient information to proceed under clause (ii).

(ii) If the local child support agency has sufficient information that the earning capacity is greater than the actual income, and sufficient evidence is available to establish earning capacity pursuant to subdivision (b) of Section 4058, the local child support agency may use earning capacity as the basis of the proposed support obligation.

(iii) If the actual income of the support obligor is unknown to the local child support agency, and sufficient evidence is available to establish earning capacity pursuant to subdivision (b) of Section 4058, the local child support agency shall use earning capacity as the basis of the proposed support obligation. A complaint seeking child support under this clause shall set forth the steps first taken by the local child support agency to establish the support obligor's actual income prior to considering earning capacity, which must include, but are not limited to:

(I) Attempting to contact the support obligor through telephonic, electronic, and postal means, to the extent contact information is known or can be discovered through reasonably available means. At least three attempts to contact the support obligor shall be made.

(II) Seeking information about the support obligor's expenses and work history from the party seeking support.

(III) Searching in available databases for information relating to the support obligor's employment, income, or both.

(B) The complaint shall inform the support obligor of the basis for the proposed support amount. If the basis of the proposed support amount is the support obligor's earning capacity rather than actual income, the complaint shall inform the obligor of the factors considered by the local child support agency and used to determine the obligor's earning capacity.

(C) The complaint form shall be accompanied by a proposed judgment. The complaint form shall include a notice to the support obligor that the proposed judgment may become effective if the obligor fails to file an answer with the court within 30 days of the service. If the proposed judgment is entered by the court, the support order in the proposed judgment shall be effective as of the first day of the month following the filing of the complaint.

(D) If the proposed judgment is based on the support obligor's earning capacity pursuant to clause (ii) or (iii) of subparagraph (A), the local child support agency shall file a motion for judgment, as provided in subdivision (b) of Section 17404. The motion for judgment filed pursuant to this subparagraph shall be served on the defendant in compliance with Section 1013 of the Code of Civil Procedure or otherwise as provided by law. If the hearing on the motion for judgment under this subdivision is continued, the court may make a temporary order as authorized by Section 17404.

(E) Notwithstanding the Administrative Procedure Act (Chapter 3.5 (commencing with Section 11340) of Part 1 of Division 3 of Title 2 of the Government Code), the department may implement and administer this subdivision through a child support services letter or similar instruction until permanent regulations are adopted. The department shall adopt regulations to implement this subdivision by January 1, 2028.

(3)(A) The simplified answer form shall be written in simple English and shall permit a defendant to answer and raise defenses by checking applicable boxes. The answer form shall include instructions for completion of the form and instructions for proper filing of the answer.

(B) The answer form shall be accompanied by a blank income and expense declaration or simplified financial statement and instructions on how to complete the financial forms. The answer form shall direct the defendant to file the completed income and expense declaration or simplified financial statement with the answer, but shall state that the answer will be accepted by a court without the income and expense declaration or simplified financial statement.

(C) The clerk of the court shall accept and file answers, income and expense declarations, and simplified financial statements that are completed by hand provided they are legible.

(4)(A) The simplified complaint form prepared pursuant to this subdivision shall be used by the local child support agency or the Attorney General in all cases brought under this section or Section 17404.

(B) The simplified answer form prepared pursuant to this subdivision shall be served on all defendants with the simplified complaint. Failure to serve the simplified answer form on all defendants shall not invalidate any judgment obtained. However, failure to serve the answer form may be used as evidence in any proceeding under Section 17432 of this code or Section 473 of the Code of Civil Procedure.

(C) The Judicial Council shall add language to the governmental summons, for use by the local child support agency with the governmental complaint to establish parental relationship and child support, informing defendants that a blank answer form should have been received with the summons and additional copies may be obtained from either the local child support agency or the superior court clerk.

(e) In any action brought or enforcement proceedings instituted by the local child support agency pursuant to this section for payment of child or spousal support, an action to recover an arrearage in support payments may be maintained by the local child support agency at any time within the period otherwise specified for the enforcement of a support judgment, notwithstanding the fact that the child has attained the age of majority.

(f) The county shall undertake an outreach program to inform the public that the services described in subdivisions (a) to (c), inclusive, are available to persons not receiving public assistance. There shall be prominently displayed in every public area of every office of the agencies established by this section a notice, in clear and simple language prescribed by the Director of Child Support Services, that the services provided in subdivisions (a) to (c), inclusive, are provided to all individuals, whether or not they are recipients of public assistance.

(g)(1) In any action to establish a child support order brought by the local child support agency in the performance of duties under this section, the local child support agency may make a motion for an order effective during the pendency of that action, for the support, maintenance, and education of the child or children that are the subject of the action. This order shall be referred to as an order for temporary support. This order has the same force and effect as a like or similar order under this code.

(2) The local child support agency shall file a motion for an order for temporary support within the following time limits:

(A) If the defendant is the mother, a presumed father under Section 7611, or any father if the child is at least six months old when the defendant files the answer, the time limit is 90 days after the defendant files an answer.

(B) In any other case in which the defendant has filed an answer prior to the birth of the child or not more than six months after the birth of the child, then the time limit is nine months after the birth of the child.

(3) If more than one child is the subject of the action, the limitation on reimbursement shall apply only as to those children whose parental relationship and age would bar recovery were a separate action brought for support of that child or those children.

(4) If the local child support agency fails to file a motion for an order for temporary support within the time limits specified in this section, the local child support agency shall be barred from obtaining a judgment of

reimbursement for any support provided for that child during the period between the date the time limit expired and the date the motion was filed, or, if no motion is filed, when a final judgment is entered.

(5) Except as provided in Section 17304, this section does not prohibit the local child support agency from entering into cooperative arrangements with other county departments as necessary to carry out the responsibilities imposed by this section pursuant to plans of cooperation with the departments approved by the Department of Child Support Services.

(6) This section does not otherwise limit the ability of the local child support agency from securing and enforcing orders for support of a spouse or former spouse as authorized under any other law.

(h) As used in this article, "enforcing obligations" includes, but is not limited to, all of the following:

(1) The use of all interception and notification systems operated by the department for the purpose of aiding in the enforcement of support obligations.

(2) The obtaining by the local child support agency of an initial order for child support that may include medical support or that is for medical support only, by civil or criminal process.

(3) The initiation of a motion or order to show cause to increase an existing child support order, and the response to a motion or order to show cause brought by an obligor parent to decrease an existing child support order, or the initiation of a motion or order to show cause to obtain an order for medical support, and the response to a motion or order to show cause brought by an obligor parent to decrease or terminate an existing medical support order, without regard to whether the child is receiving public assistance.

(4) The response to a notice of motion or order to show cause brought by an obligor parent to decrease an existing spousal support order if the child or children are residing with the obligee parent and the local child support agency is also enforcing a related child support obligation owed to the obligee parent by the same obligor.

(5) The referral of child support delinquencies to the department under subdivision (c) of Section 17500 in support of the local child support agency.

(i) As used in this section, "out of wedlock" means that the biological parents of the child were not married to each other at the time of the child's conception.

(j)(1) The local child support agency is the public agency responsible for administering wage withholding for current support for the purposes of Title IV-D of the Social Security Act (42 U.S.C. Sec. 651 et seq.).

(2) This section does not limit the authority of the local child support agency granted by other sections of this code or otherwise granted by law.

(k) In the exercise of the authority granted under this article, the local child support agency may intervene, pursuant to subdivision (b) of Section 387 of the Code of Civil Procedure, by ex parte application, in any action under this code, or other proceeding in which child support is an issue or a reduction in spousal support is sought. By notice of motion, order to show cause, or responsive pleading served upon all parties to the action, the local child support agency may request any relief that is appropriate that the local child support agency is authorized to seek.

(l) The local child support agency shall comply with all regulations and directives established by the department that set time standards for responding to requests for assistance in locating noncustodial parents, establishing paternity, establishing child support awards, and collecting child support payments.

(m) As used in this article, medical support activities that the local child support agency is authorized to perform are limited to the following:

(1) The obtaining and enforcing of court orders for health insurance coverage.

(2) Any other medical support activity mandated by federal law or regulation.

(n)(1) Notwithstanding any other law, except when a court of competent jurisdiction under Section 4251 hearing the action or proceeding under this division transfers the action or proceeding pursuant to Section 397.5 of the Code of Civil Procedure pursuant to a directly filed motion, a redirected motion, or on the court's own motion under Section 397.5 of the Code of Civil Procedure, venue for an action or proceeding under this division shall be determined as follows:

(A) Venue shall be in the superior court in the county that is currently expending public assistance.

(B) If public assistance is not currently being expended, venue shall be in the superior court in the county where the child who is entitled to current support resides or is domiciled.

(C) If current support is no longer payable through, or enforceable by, the local child support agency, venue shall be in the superior court in the county that last provided public assistance for actions to enforce arrearages assigned pursuant to Section 11477 of the Welfare and Institutions Code.

(D) If subparagraphs (A), (B), and (C) do not apply, venue shall be in the superior court in the county of residence of the support obligee.

(E) If the support obligee does not reside in California, and subparagraphs (A), (B), (C), and (D) do not apply, venue shall be in the superior court of the county of residence of the obligor.

(2) Notwithstanding paragraph (1), if the child becomes a resident of another county after an action under this part has been filed, venue may remain in the county where the action was filed until the action is completed. Nothing in this paragraph shall be construed to limit the court hearing the action or proceeding under this division from exercising its discretion under Section 397.5 of the Code of Civil Procedure.

(o) The local child support agency of one county may appear on behalf of the local child support agency of any other county in an action or proceeding under this part.

(p) This section shall become operative January 1, 2026. **Leg.H.** Added Stats 2023 ch 213 §15 (SB 343), effective January 1, 2024, operative January 1, 2026.

§17400.5. Modification of support obligation when obligor receiving federal assistance

If an obligor has an ongoing child support order being enforced by a local child support agency pursuant to Title IV-D of the Social Security Act and the obligor is disabled, meets the SSI resource test, and is receiving Supplemental Security Income/State Supplemental Payments (SSI/SSP) or, but for excess income as described in Section 416.1100 et seq. of Part 416 of Title 20 of the Code of Federal Regulations, would be eligible to receive as SSI/SSP, pursuant to Section 12200 of the Welfare and Institutions Code, and the obligor has supplied the local child support agency with proof of eligibility for, and, if applicable, receipt of, SSI/SSP or Social Security Disability Insurance benefits, then the local child support agency shall prepare and file a motion to modify the support obligation within 30 days of receipt of verification from the noncustodial parent or any other source of the receipt of SSI/SSP or Social Security Disability Insurance benefits. The local child support agency shall serve the motion on both the noncustodial parent and custodial person and any modification of the support order entered pursuant to the motion shall be effective as provided in Section 3653 of the Family Code. **Leg.H.** Added Stats 2001 ch 651 §3 (AB 891). Amended Stats 2002 ch 787 §1 (SB 1798); Stats 2019 ch 115 §145 (AB 1817), effective January 1, 2020.

Former Sections: Former §17400.5, relating to effective date of support order in proposed judgment, was added Stats 1999 ch 653 §13, and repealed Stats 2000 ch 808 §82, effective September 28, 2000.

Former Sections: Former Fam C §17400.5, relating to effective date of support order in proposed judgment, was added Stats 1999 ch 653 §13 and repealed Stats 2000 ch 808 §82, effective September 28, 2000.

§17401. Requirements upon receipt of obligor's address

If the parent who is receiving support enforcement services provides to the local child support agency substantial, credible, information regarding the residence or work address of the support obligor, the agency shall initiate an establishment or enforcement action and serve the defendant, if service is required, within 60 days and inform the parent in writing when those actions have been taken. If the address or any other information provided by the support obligee is determined by the local child support agency to be inaccurate and if, after reasonable diligence, the agency is unable to locate and serve the support obligor within that 60-day period, the local child support agency shall inform the support obligee in writing of those facts. The requirements of this section shall be in addition to the time standards established by the Department of Child Support Services pursuant to subdivision (l) of Section 17400. **Leg.H.** Added Stats 1999 ch 653 §14 (AB 380). Amended Stats 2000 ch 808 §83 (AB 1358), effective September 28, 2000; Stats 2001 ch 755 §12 (SB 943), effective October 12, 2001.

Former Sections: There was another section of this number which was added Stats 1999 ch 803 §1 and renumbered Fam C §17401.5 by Stats 2000 ch 808 §84.

Former Sections: Former Fam C §17401 was added Stats 1999 ch 803 §1 and renumbered Fam C §17401.5 by Stats 2000 ch 808 §84.

§17401.5. Notice and information about child support service hearings

(a) All of the following shall include notice of, and information about, the child support service hearings available pursuant to Section 17801, provided that there is federal financial participation available as set forth in subdivision (j) of Section 17801:

(1) The booklet required by subdivision (a) of Section 17434.

(2) Any notice required by subdivision (c) or (h) of Section 17406.

(b) To the extent not otherwise required by law, the local child support agency shall provide notice of, and information about, the child support services hearings available pursuant to Section 17801 in any regularly issued notices to custodial and noncustodial parents subject to Section 17400, provided that there is federal financial participation available as set forth in subdivision (e) of Section 17801.

Notice of and information about the child support service hearings and the child support complaint resolution process required under Section 17800 shall be easily accessible and shall be provided in a single section of the booklet. **Leg.H.** Added Stats 1999 ch 803 §1 (AB 472), as Fam C §17401. Renumbered by Stats 2000 ch 808 §84 (AB 1358).

§17402. Obligation of noncustodial parent

(a) In any case of separation or desertion of a parent or parents from a child or children that results in aid under Chapter 2 (commencing with Section 11200) of Part 3 of Division 9 of the Welfare and Institutions Code being granted to that family, the noncustodial parent or parents shall be obligated to the county for an amount equal to the amount specified in an order for the support and maintenance of the family issued by a court of competent jurisdiction.

(b) The local child support agency shall take appropriate action pursuant to this section as provided in subdivision (l) of Section 17400. The local child support agency may establish liability for child support as provided in subdivision (a) when public assistance was provided by another county or by other counties.

(c) The amount of the obligation established for each parent with a liability under subdivision (a) shall be determined by using the appropriate child support guideline currently in effect and shall be computed as follows:

(1) If one parent remains as a custodial parent, the support shall be computed according to the guideline.

(2) If the parents reside together and neither father nor mother remains as a custodial parent, the guideline support shall be computed by combining the noncustodial parents' incomes. The combined incomes shall be used as the high earner's net monthly disposable income in the guideline formula. Income shall not be attributed to the caretaker or governmental agency. The amount of guideline support resulting shall be proportionately shared between the noncustodial parents based upon their net monthly disposable incomes.

(3) If the parents reside apart and neither father nor mother remains as a custodial parent, the guideline support shall be computed separately for each parent by treating each parent as a noncustodial parent. Income shall not be attributed to the caretaker or government agency.

(d) A parent shall pay the amount of support specified in the support order to the local child support agency. **Leg.H.** Added Stats 1999 ch 478 §1 (AB 196). Amended Stats 1999 ch 653 §15 (AB 380); Stats 2000 ch 808 §84.3 (AB 1358), effective September 28, 2000; Stats 2004 ch 305 §5 (AB 2669).

§17402.1. Remittance of public assistance child support payments

(a) Each local child support agency shall, on a monthly basis, remit to the department both the federal and state public assistance child support payments received pursuant to Section 17402.

(b) The department shall promulgate regulations to implement this section. **Leg.H.** Added Stats 2001 ch 111 §4 (AB 429), effective July 30, 2001.

§17404. Parties to actions; Hearing and judgment; Pleadings; Actions under other code provisions; Independent action to modify support order

(a) Notwithstanding any other statute, in any action brought by the local child support agency for the support of a minor child or children, the action may be prosecuted in the name of the county on behalf of the child, children, or a parent of the child or children. The parent who has requested or is receiving support enforcement services of the local child support agency shall not be a necessary party to the action but may be subpoenaed as a witness. Except as provided in subdivision (e), in an action under this section there shall be no joinder of actions, or coordination of actions, or cross-complaints, and the issues shall be limited strictly to the question of parentage, if applicable, and child support, including an order for medical support. A final determination of parentage may be made in any action under this section as an incident to obtaining an order for support. An action for support or parentage pursuant to this section shall not be delayed or stayed because of the pendency of any other action between the parties.

(b)(1) Judgment in an action brought pursuant to this section, and in an action brought pursuant to Section 17402, if at issue, may be rendered pursuant to a noticed motion, that shall inform the defendant that in order to exercise the right to trial, the defendant shall appear at the hearing on the motion.

(2) If the defendant appears at the hearing on the motion, the court shall inquire of the defendant if the defendant desires to subpoena evidence and witnesses, if parentage is at issue and genetic tests have not already been conducted whether the defendant desires genetic tests, and if the defendant desires a trial. If the defendant's answer is in the affirmative, a continuance shall be granted to allow the defendant to exercise those rights. A continuance shall not postpone the hearing to more than 90 days from the date of service of the motion. If a continuance is granted, the court may make an order for temporary support without prejudice to the right of the court to make an order for temporary support as otherwise allowed by law.

(c) In any action to enforce a spousal support order the action may be pled in the name of the county in the same manner as an action to establish a child support obligation. The same restrictions on joinder of actions, coordination of actions, cross-complaints, and delay because of the pendency of any other action as relates to actions to establish a child support obligation shall also apply to actions to enforce a spousal support order.

(d) This section does not prevent the parties from bringing an independent action under other provisions of this code and litigating the issues of support, custody, visitation, or protective orders. In that event, any support, custody, visitation, or protective order issued by the court in an action pursuant to this section shall be filed in the action commenced under the other provisions of this code and shall continue in effect until modified by a subsequent order of the court. To the extent that the orders conflict, the court order last issued shall supersede all other orders and be binding upon all parties in that action.

(e)(1) After a support order, including a temporary support order and an order for medical support only, has been entered in an action brought pursuant to this section, the parent who has requested or is receiving support enforcement services of the local child support agency shall become a party to the action brought pursuant to this section, only in the manner and to the extent provided by this section, and only for the purposes allowed by this section.

(2) Notice of the parent's status as a party shall be given to the parent by the local child support agency in conjunction with the notice required by subdivision (e) of Section 17406. The complaint shall contain this notice. Service of the complaint on the parent in compliance with Section 1013 of the Code of Civil Procedure, or as otherwise provided by law, shall constitute compliance with this section. In all actions commenced under the procedures and forms in effect on or before December 31, 1996, the parent who has requested or is receiving support enforcement services of the local child support agency shall not become a party to the action until joined as a party pursuant to an ex parte application or noticed motion for joinder filed by the local child support agency or a noticed motion filed by either parent. The local child support agency shall serve a copy of any order for joinder of a parent obtained by the local child support agency's application on both parents in compliance with Section 1013 of the Code of Civil Procedure.

(3) Once both parents are parties to an action brought pursuant to this section in cases where Title IV-D services are currently being provided, the local child support agency shall be required, within five days of receipt, to mail the nonmoving party in the action all pleadings relating solely to the support issue in the action that have been served on the local

child support agency by the moving party in the action, as provided in subdivision (f) of Section 17406. There shall be a rebuttable presumption that service on the local child support agency consistent with the provisions of this paragraph constitutes valid service on the nonmoving party. Where this procedure is used to effectuate service on the nonmoving party, the pleadings shall be served on the local child support agency not less than 30 days prior to the hearing.

(4) The parent who has requested or is receiving support enforcement services of the local child support agency is a party to an action brought under this section for issues relating to the support, custody, and visitation of a child, and for restraining orders, and for no other purpose. The local child support agency shall not be required to serve or receive service of papers, pleadings, or documents, or participate in, or attend any hearing or proceeding relating to issues of custody or visitation, except as otherwise required by law. Orders concerning custody and visitation may be made in an action pursuant to this subdivision only if orders concerning custody and visitation have not been previously made by a court of competent jurisdiction in this state or another state and the court has jurisdiction and is the proper venue for custody and visitation determinations. All issues regarding custody and visitation shall be heard and resolved in the manner provided by this code. Except as otherwise provided by law, the local child support agency shall control support and parentage litigation brought pursuant to this section, and the manner, method, and procedures used in establishing parentage and in establishing and enforcing support obligations unless and until the parent who requested or is receiving support enforcement services has requested in writing that the local child support agency close the case and the case has been closed in accordance with state and federal regulation or policy.

(f)(1) A parent who has requested or is receiving support enforcement services of the local child support agency may take independent action to modify a support order made pursuant to this section while support enforcement services are being provided by the local child support agency. The parent shall serve the local child support agency with notice of any action filed to modify the support order and provide the local child support agency with a copy of the modified order within 15 calendar days after the date the order is issued.

(2) A parent who has requested or is receiving support enforcement services of the local child support agency may take independent action to enforce a support order made pursuant to this section while support enforcement services are being provided by the local child support agency with the written consent of the local child support agency. At least 30 days prior to filing an independent enforcement action, the parent shall provide the local child support agency with written notice of the parent's intent to file an enforcement action that includes a description of the type of enforcement action the parent intends to file. Within 30 days of receiving the notice, the local child support agency shall either provide written consent for the parent to proceed with the independent enforcement action or notify the parent that the local child support agency objects to the parent filing the proposed independent enforcement action. The local child support agency may object only if the local child support agency is currently using an administrative or judicial method to enforce the support obligation or if the proposed independent enforcement action would interfere with an investigation being conducted by the local child support agency. If the local child support agency does not respond to the parent's written notice within 30 days, the local child support agency shall be deemed to have given consent.

(3) The court shall order that all payments of support shall be made to the local child support agency in any action filed under this section by the parent who has requested, or is receiving, support enforcement services of the local child support agency unless support enforcement services have been terminated by the local child support agency by case closure as provided by state and federal law. Any order obtained by a parent prior to support enforcement services being terminated in which the local child support agency did not receive proper notice pursuant to this section shall be voidable upon the motion of the local child support agency.

(g) Any notice from the local child support agency requesting a meeting with the support obligor for any purpose authorized under this section shall contain a statement advising the support obligor of the right to have an attorney present at the meeting.

(h) For the purpose of this section, "a parent who is receiving support enforcement services" includes a parent who has assigned their rights to support pursuant to Section 11477 of the Welfare and Institutions Code.

(i) The Judicial Council shall develop forms to implement this section. **Leg.H.** Added Stats 1999 ch 478 §1 (AB 196). Amended Stats 1999 ch 480 §14 (SB 542); Stats 2000 ch 808 §84.5 (AB 1358), effective September 28, 2000; Stats 2001 ch 755 §13 (SB 943), effective October 12, 2001; Stats 2019 ch 115 §146 (AB 1817), effective January 1, 2020.

§17404.1. Summons or order to show cause [Repealed January 1, 2027]

(a) Upon receipt of a petition or comparable pleading pursuant to Part 6 (commencing with Section 5700.101) of Division 9, the local child support agency or petitioner may either (1) request the issuance of a summons or (2) request the court to issue an order requiring the respondent to appear personally at a specified time and place to show cause why an order should not be issued as prayed in the petition or comparable pleading on file.

(b) The respondent may also be served with a proposed judgment consistent with the relief sought in the petition or other comparable pleading. If the respondent's income or income history is unknown to the local child support agency, the local child support agency may serve a form of proposed judgment with the petition and other documents on the respondent that shall inform the respondent that income shall be presumed to be the amount of the state minimum wage, at 40 hours per week, unless information concerning the respondent's income is provided to the court. The respondent shall also receive notice that the proposed judgment will become effective if the respondent fails to file a response with the court within 30 days after service.

(c) If a summons is issued for a petition or comparable pleading pursuant to Part 6 (commencing with Section 5700.101) of Division 9, the local child support agency or petitioner shall cause a copy of the summons, petition, and other documents to be served upon the respondent according to law.

(d) If an order to show cause is issued on a petition or comparable pleading pursuant to Part 6 (commencing with Section 5700.101) of Division 9 requiring the respondent to appear at a specified time and place to respond to the petition, a copy of the order to show cause, the petition, and other documents shall be served upon the respondent at least 15 days prior to the hearing.

(e) A petition or comparable pleading served upon a respondent in accordance with this section shall be accompanied by a blank responsive form that shall permit the respondent to answer the petition and raise any defenses by checking applicable boxes and by a blank income and expense declaration or simplified financial statement together with instructions for completion of the forms.

(f) In any action pursuant to Part 6 (commencing with Section 5700.101) of Division 9 in which the judgment was obtained pursuant to presumed income, as set forth in this section, the court may set aside that part of the judgment or order concerning the amount of child support to be paid on the grounds specified and in the manner set forth in Section 17432.

(g) This section shall become inoperative on January 1, 2026, and, as of January 1, 2027, is repealed. **Leg.H.** Added Stats 2015 ch 493 §8 (SB 646), effective January 1, 2016. Amended Stats 2019 ch 115 §147 (AB 1817), effective January 1, 2020; Stats 2023 ch 213 §16 (SB 343), effective January 1, 2024, inoperative January 1, 2026, repealed January 1, 2027.

§ 17404.1. Summons or order to show cause [Operative January 1, 2026]

(a) Upon receipt of a petition or comparable pleading pursuant to Part 6 (commencing with Section 5700.101) of Division 9, the local child support agency or petitioner may either (1) request the issuance of a summons or (2) request the court to issue an order requiring the respondent to appear personally at a specified time and place to show cause why an order should not be issued as prayed in the petition or comparable pleading on file.

(b) The respondent may also be served with a proposed judgment consistent with the relief sought in the petition or other comparable pleading. The petition or other comparable pleading shall provide notice to the obligor of the amount of child support that is being sought pursuant to the guidelines set forth in Article 2 (commencing with Section 4050) of Chapter 2 of Part 2 of Division 9 based upon the methodology for determining the obligor's income for purposes of a simplified complaint as required by subparagraph (A) of paragraph (2) of subdivision (d) of Section 17400.

(c) If the proposed judgment is based on the support obligor's earning capacity pursuant to clause (ii) or (iii) of subparagraph (A) of paragraph (2) of subdivision (d) of Section 17400, the local child support agency shall file a motion for judgment, as provided in subdivision (b) of Section 17404.

(d) If a summons is issued for a petition or comparable pleading pursuant to Part 6 (commencing with Section 5700.101) of Division 9, the local child support agency or petitioner shall cause a copy of the summons, petition, and other documents to be served upon the respondent according to law.

(e) If an order to show cause is issued on a petition or comparable pleading pursuant to Part 6 (commencing with Section 5700.101) of Division 9 requiring the respondent to appear at a specified time and place to respond to the petition, a copy of the order to show cause, the petition, and other documents shall be served upon the respondent at least 15 days prior to the hearing.

(f) A petition or comparable pleading served upon a respondent in accordance with this section shall be accompanied by a blank responsive form that shall permit the respondent to answer the petition and raise any defenses by checking applicable boxes and by a blank income and expense declaration or simplified financial statement together with instructions for completion of the forms.

(g) This section shall become operative January 1, 2026. **Leg.H.** Added Stats 2023 ch 213 §17 (SB 343), effective January 1, 2024, operative January 1, 2026.

§17404.2. Transfers of actions

(a) If, prior to filing, a petition or comparable pleading pursuant to Part 6 (commencing with Section 5700.101) of Division 9 is received by the local child support agency or the superior court and the county in which the pleadings are received is not the appropriate jurisdiction for trial of the action, the court or the local child support agency shall forward the pleadings and any accompanying documents to the appropriate court of this state or to the jurisdiction of another state without filing the pleadings or order of the court, and shall notify the petitioner, the California Central Registry, and the local child support agency of the receiving county where and when the pleading was sent.

(b) If, after a petition or comparable pleading has been filed with the superior court of a county pursuant to Part 6 (commencing with Section 5700.101) of Division 9, it appears that the respondent is not or is no longer a resident of the county in which the action has been filed, upon ex parte application by the local child support agency or petitioner, the court shall transfer the action to the appropriate court of this state or to the appropriate jurisdiction of another state and shall notify the petitioner, the respondent, the California Central Registry, and the local child support agency of the receiving county where and when the pleading was sent.

(c) If, after entry of an order by a court of this state or an order of another state registered in a court of this state for enforcement or modification pursuant to Part 6 (commencing with Section 5700.101) of Division 9, it appears that the respondent is not or is no longer a resident of the county in which the foreign order has been registered, upon ex parte application by the local child support agency of the transferring or receiving county or the petitioner, the court shall transfer the registered order and all documents subsequently filed in that action to the appropriate court of this state and shall notify the petitioner, the respondent, the California Central Registry, and the local child support agency of the transferring and receiving county where and when the registered order and all other appropriate documents were sent. Transfer of certified copies of documents shall meet the requirements of this section.

(d) If, in an action initiated in a court of this state pursuant to Part 6 (commencing with Section 5700.101) of Division 9 or a predecessor law for interstate enforcement of support, the petitioner is no longer a resident of the county in which the action has been filed, upon ex parte application by the petitioner or the local child support agency, the court shall transfer the action to the appropriate court of this state and shall notify the responding jurisdiction where and when the action was transferred.

(e) Notwithstanding subdivisions (b) and (c), if the respondent becomes a resident of another county or jurisdiction after an action or registered order has been filed pursuant to Part 6 (commencing with Section 5700.101) of Division 9, the action may remain in the county where the action was filed until the action is completed. **Leg.H.** Added Stats 2015 ch 493 §9 (SB 646), effective January 1, 2016.

§17404.3. Hearings by telephone, audiovisual means, or other electronic means

Hearings by telephone, audiovisual means, or other electronic means shall be permitted in child support cases in which the local child support agency is providing child support services. The Judicial Council shall adopt court rules implementing this provision and subdivision (f) of Section 5700.316 on or before July 1, 2016. **Leg.H.** Added Stats 2015 ch 493 §10 (SB 646), effective January 1, 2016.

§17404.4. Administrative change of payee

In exercising the jurisdiction under Section 5700.319, either the department or the local child support agency shall issue a notice to change payee on a support order issued in this state, upon request from the support enforcement agency of another state where a custodial party has either assigned the right to receive support or has requested support enforcement services. Notice of the administrative change of payee shall be filed with the court in which the order was issued or last registered. **Leg.H.** Added Stats 2015 ch 493 §11 (SB 646), effective January 1, 2016. Amended Stats 2022 ch 420 §21 (AB 2960), effective January 1, 2023.

§17405. Interview of custodial parent

In carrying out duties under this article, the local child support agency shall interview the custodial parent within 10 business days of opening a child support case. This interview shall solicit financial and all other information about the noncustodial parent. This information shall be acted upon immediately. The local child support agency shall reinterview the custodial parent as needed. **Leg.H.** Added Stats 1999 ch 652 §16 (SB 240).

§17406. Actions involving paternity or support; Notice of hearing

(a) In all actions involving paternity or support, including, but not limited to, other proceedings under this code, and under Division 9 (commencing with Section 10000) of the Welfare and Institutions Code, the local child support agency and the Attorney General represent the public interest in establishing, modifying, and enforcing support obligations. No attorney-client relationship shall be deemed to have been created between the local child support agency or Attorney General and any person by virtue of the action of the local child support agency or the Attorney General in carrying out these statutory duties.

(b) Subdivision (a) is declaratory of existing law.

(c) In all requests for services of the local child support agency or Attorney General pursuant to Section 17400 relating to actions involving paternity or support, not later than the same day an individual makes a request for these services in person, and not later than five working days after either (1) a case is referred for services from the county welfare department, (2) receipt of a request by mail for an application for services, or (3) an individual makes a request for services by telephone, the local child support agency or Attorney General shall give notice to the individual requesting services or on whose behalf services have been requested that the local child support agency or Attorney General does not represent the individual or the children who are the subject of the case, that no attorney-client relationship exists between the local child support agency or Attorney General and those persons, and that no such representation or relationship shall arise if the local child support agency or Attorney General provides the services requested. Notice shall be in bold print and in plain English and shall be translated into the language understandable by the recipient when reasonable. The notice shall include the advice that the absence of an attorney-client relationship means that communications from the recipient are not privileged and that the local child support agency or Attorney General may provide support enforcement services to the other parent in the future.

(d) The local child support agency or Attorney General shall give the notice required pursuant to subdivision (c) to all recipients of services under Section 17400 who have not otherwise been provided that notice, not later than the date of the next annual notice required under Section 11476.2 of the Welfare and Institutions Code. This notice shall include notification to the recipient of services under Section 17400 that the recipient may inspect the clerk's file at the office of the clerk of the court, and that, upon request, the local child support agency, or, if appropriate, the Attorney General, will furnish a copy of the most recent order entered in the case.

(e) The local child support agency or, if appropriate, the Attorney General shall serve a copy of the complaint for paternity or support, or both, on recipients of support services under Section 17400, as specified in paragraph (2) of subdivision (e) of Section 17404. A notice shall accompany the complaint that informs the recipient that the local child support agency or Attorney General may enter into a stipulated order resolving the complaint, and that the recipient shall assist the prosecuting attorney, by sending all information on the noncustodial parent's earnings and assets to the prosecuting attorney.

(f)(1)(A) The local child support agency or Attorney General shall provide written notice to recipients of services under Section 17400 of the initial date and time, and purpose of every hearing in a civil action for paternity or support.

(B) Once the parent who has requested or is receiving support enforcement services becomes a party to the action pursuant to subdivision (e) of Section 17404, in lieu of the above, the local child support agency or Attorney General shall serve on a parent all pleadings relating to paternity or support that have been served on the local child support agency by the other parent. The pleading shall be accompanied by a notice.

(C) The notice provided subject to subparagraphs (A) and (B) shall include the following language:

IMPORTANT NOTICE

It may be important that you attend the hearing. The local child support agency does not represent you or your children. You may have information about the other parent, such as information about that parent's income or assets that will not be presented to the court unless you attend the hearing. You have the right to attend the hearing and to be heard in court and tell the court what you think the court should do with the child support order. This hearing could change your rights or your children's rights to support.

(2) The notice shall state the purpose of the hearing or be attached to the motion or other pleading which caused the hearing to be scheduled.

(3) The notice shall be provided separate from all other material and shall be in at least 14-point type. The failure of the local child support agency or Attorney General to provide the notice required pursuant to subparagraph (A) of paragraph (1) does not affect the validity of any order.

(4)(A) The notice required pursuant to subparagraph (A) of paragraph (1) shall be provided not later than seven calendar days prior to the hearing, or, if the local child support agency or Attorney General receives notice of the hearing less than seven days prior to the hearing, within two days of the receipt by the local child support agency or Attorney General of the notice of the hearing.

(B) Service of the notice and the pleadings required pursuant to subparagraph (B) of paragraph (1) shall be completed not later than five days after receipt of the pleadings served on the local child support agency by the parent.

(5) The local child support agency or Attorney General shall, in order to implement this subdivision, make reasonable efforts to ensure that the local child support agency or Attorney General has current addresses for all parties to the child support action.

(g) The local child support agency or Attorney General shall give notice to recipients of services under Section 17400 of every order obtained by the local child support agency or Attorney General that establishes or modifies the support obligation for the recipient or the children who are the subject of the order, by sending a copy of the order to the recipient. The notice shall be made within the time specified by federal law after the order has been filed. The local child support agency or Attorney General shall also give notice to these recipients of every order obtained in any other jurisdiction that establishes or modifies the support obligation for the recipient or the children who are the subject of the order, and which is received by the local child support agency or Attorney General, by sending a copy of the order to the recipient within the timeframe specified by federal law after the local child support agency or Attorney General has received a copy of the order. In any action enforced under Part 6 (commencing with Section 5700.101) of Division 9, the notice shall be made in compliance with the requirements of that chapter. The failure of the local child support agency or Attorney General to comply with this subdivision does not affect the validity of any order.

(h) The local child support agency or Attorney General shall give notice to the noncustodial parent against whom a civil action is filed that the local child support agency or Attorney General is not the attorney representing any individual, including, but not limited to, the custodial parent, the child, or the noncustodial parent.

(i) This section does not preclude a person who is receiving services under Section 17400 from filing and prosecuting an independent action to establish, modify, and enforce an order for current support on behalf of that person or a child if that person is not receiving public assistance.

(j) A person who is receiving services under Section 17400 but who is not currently receiving public assistance on their own behalf or on behalf of a child shall be asked to execute, or consent to, any stipulation establishing or modifying a support order in any action in which that person is named as a party, before the stipulation is filed. The local child support agency or Attorney General may not submit to the court for approval a stipulation to establish or modify a support order in the action without first obtaining the signatures of all parties to the action, their attorneys of record, or persons authorized to act on their behalf. Any stipulation approved by the court in violation of this subdivision shall be void.

(k) The local child support agency or Attorney General may not enter into a stipulation that reduces the amount of past due support, including interest and penalties accrued pursuant to an order of current support, on behalf of a person who is receiving support enforcement services under Section 17400 and who is owed support arrearages that exceed unreimbursed public assistance paid to the recipient of the support enforcement services, without first obtaining the consent of the person who is receiving services under Section 17400 on their own behalf or on behalf of the child.

(l) The notices required in this section shall be provided in the following manner:

(1) In all cases in which the person receiving services under Section 17400 resides in California, notice shall be provided by mailing the item by first-class mail to the last known address of, or personally delivering the item to, that person.

(2) In all actions enforced under Part 6 (commencing with Section 5700.101) of Division 9, unless otherwise specified, notice shall be provided by mailing the item by first-class mail to the initiating court.

(m) Notwithstanding any other provision of this section, the notices provided for pursuant to subdivisions (c) to (g), inclusive, are not required in foster care cases. **Leg.H.** Added Stats 1999 ch 478 §1 (AB 196). Amended Stats 1999 ch 480 §15 (SB 542); Stats 2000 ch 808 §84.7 (AB 1358), effective September 28, 2000; Stats 2001 ch 176 §6 (SB 210); Stats 2004 ch 339 §7 (AB 1704); Stats 2015 ch 493 §12 (SB 646), effective January 1, 2016; Stats 2019 ch 115 §148 (AB 1817), effective January 1, 2020.

§17407. Appeal by Attorney General

(a) If the Attorney General is of the opinion that a support order or support-related order is erroneous and presents a question of law warranting an appeal, or that an order is sound and should be defended on appeal, in the public interest the Attorney General may:

(1) Perfect or oppose an appeal to the proper appellate court if the order was issued by a court of this state.

(2) If the order was issued in another state, cause an appeal to be taken or opposed in the other state.

(b) In either case, expenses of the appeal may be paid on order of the Attorney General from funds appropriated for the Office of the Attorney General. **Leg.H.** Added Stats 1999 ch 652 §17 (SB 240).

§17407.5. Declaration of state reciprocity

A declaration of state reciprocity issued by the Attorney General on or before December 31, 2015, and a declaration issued pursuant to subdivision (b) of Section 5700.308, shall remain in full force and effect unless one of the following occurs:

(a) The declaration is revoked or declared invalid by the Attorney General, in consultation with the department, or by the other party to the reciprocity agreement.

(b) The declaration is superseded by a subsequent federal bilateral agreement with the other party.

(c) The declaration is superseded by the other party's ratification of or accession to the Hague Convention on the International Recovery of Child Support and Other Forms of Family Maintenance. **Leg.H.** Added Stats 2015 ch 493 §13 (SB 646), effective January 1, 2016.

§17408. Consolidation of orders

(a) Notwithstanding Section 17404, upon noticed motion of the local child support agency, the superior court may consolidate or combine support or reimbursement arrearages owed by one obligor to one obligee in two or more court files into a single court file, or combine or consolidate two or more orders for current child support into a single court file. A motion to consolidate may be made by a local child support agency only if it is seeking to enforce the orders being consolidated. The motion shall be filed only in the court file the local child support agency is seeking to have designated as the primary file.

(b) Orders may be consolidated regardless of the nature of the underlying action, whether initiated under the Welfare and Institutions Code, this code, or another law. Orders for support shall not be consolidated unless the children involved have the same mother and father and venue is proper pursuant to Section 17400.

(c) Upon consolidation of orders, the court shall designate which court file the support orders are being consolidated into the primary file, and which court files are subordinate. Upon consolidation, the court shall order the local child support agency to file a notice in the subordinate court actions indicating the support orders in those actions were consolidated into the primary file. The notice shall state the date of the consolidation, the name of the court, and the primary file number.

(d) Upon consolidation of orders, the superior court shall not issue further orders pertaining to support in a subordinate court file; and all enforcement and modification of support orders shall occur in the primary court action.

(e) After consolidation of court orders, a single wage assignment for current support and arrearages may be issued when possible. **Leg.H.** Added Stats 1999 ch 478 §1 (AB 196).

§17410. Voluntary acknowledgment of paternity

In any action filed by the local child support agency pursuant to Section 17402 or 17404, the local child support agency shall provide the mother and the alleged father the opportunity to voluntarily acknowledge paternity by signing a paternity declaration as described in Section 7574 prior to a hearing or trial where the paternity of a minor child is at issue. The opportunity to voluntarily acknowledge paternity may be provided either before or after an action pursuant to Section 17402 or 17404 is filed and served upon the alleged father. For the purpose of meeting the requirements of this section, the local child support agency may afford the defendant an opportunity to enter into a stipulation for judgment of paternity after an action for paternity has been filed in lieu of the voluntary declaration of paternity. **Leg.H.** Added Stats 1999 ch 478 §1 (AB 196).

§17412. Effect of voluntary declaration of parentage

(a) Notwithstanding any other law, an action for child support may be brought by the local child support agency on behalf of a minor child or caretaker parent based upon a voluntary declaration of parentage as provided in Chapter 3 (commencing with Section 7570) of Part 2 of Division 12.

(b) Except as provided in Sections 7580 and 7581, the voluntary declaration of parentage shall be given the same force and effect as a judgment for parentage entered by a court of competent jurisdiction. The court shall make appropriate orders for support of the minor child based upon the voluntary declaration of parentage unless evidence is presented that the voluntary declaration of parentage has been rescinded by the parties or set aside by a court as provided in Section 7575, 7576, or 7577.

(c) The Judicial Council shall develop the forms and procedures necessary to implement this section.

(d) This section shall become operative on January 1, 2020. **Leg.H.** Added Stats 2018 ch 876 §65 (AB 2684), effective January 1, 2019, operative January 1, 2020.

2018 Note: For legislative intent, see the 2018 Notes following Fam C §7540.

§17414. Filing of written stipulation

In any action or proceeding brought by the local child support agency to establish parentage pursuant to Section 17400, the court shall enter a judgment establishing parentage upon the filing of a written stipulation between the parties provided that the stipulation is accompanied by a written advisement and waiver of rights which is signed by the defendant. The written advisement and waiver of rights shall be developed by the Judicial Council. **Leg.H.** Added Stats 1999 ch 478 §1 (AB 196).

§17415. Referral from county welfare department

(a) It shall be the duty of the county welfare department to refer all cases in which a parent is absent from the home, or in which the parents are unmarried and parentage has not been established by the completion and filing of a voluntary declaration of paternity pursuant to Section 7573 or a court of competent jurisdiction, to the local child support agency immediately at the time the application for public assistance, including Medi-Cal benefits, or certificate of eligibility, is signed by the applicant or recipient, except as provided in Section 17552 and Sections 11477 and 11477.04 of the Welfare and Institutions Code. If an applicant is found to be ineligible, the applicant shall be notified in writing that the referral of the case to the local child support agency may be terminated at the applicant's request. The county welfare department shall cooperate with the local child support agency and shall make available all pertinent information pursuant to Section 17505.

(b) Upon referral from the county welfare department, the local child support agency shall investigate the question of nonsupport or paternity and shall take all steps necessary to obtain child support for the needy child, enforce spousal support as part of the state plan under Section 17604, and determine paternity in the case of a child born out of wedlock. Upon the advice of the county welfare department that a child is being considered for adoption, the local child support agency shall delay the investigation and other actions with respect to the case until advised that the adoption is no longer under consideration. The granting of public assistance or Medi-Cal benefits to an applicant shall not be delayed or contingent upon investigation by the local child support agency.

(c) In cases where Medi-Cal benefits are the only assistance provided, the local child support agency shall provide child and spousal support services unless the recipient of the services notifies the local child support agency that only services related to securing health insurance benefits are requested.

(d) Whenever a court order has been obtained, any contractual agreement for support between the local child support agency or the county welfare department and the noncustodial parent shall be deemed null and void to the extent that it is not consistent with the court order.

(e) Whenever a family that has been receiving public assistance, including Medi-Cal, ceases to receive assistance, including Medi-Cal, the local child support agency shall, to the extent required by federal regulations, continue to enforce support payments from the noncustodial parent until the individual on whose behalf the enforcement efforts are made sends written notice to the local child support agency requesting that enforcement services be discontinued.

(f) The local child support agency shall, when appropriate, utilize reciprocal arrangements adopted with other states in securing support from an absent parent. In individual cases where utilization of reciprocal arrangements has proven ineffective, the local child support agency may forward to the Attorney General a request to utilize federal courts in order to obtain or enforce orders for child or spousal support. If reasonable efforts to collect amounts assigned pursuant to Section 11477 of the Welfare and Institutions Code have failed, the local child support agency may request that the case be forwarded to the United States Treasury Department for collection in accordance with federal regulations. The Attorney General, when appropriate, shall forward these requests to the Secretary of Health and Human Services, or a designated representative. **Leg.H.** Added Stats 1999 ch 478 §1 (AB 196). Amended Stats 1999 ch 480 §16 (SB 542); Stats 2001 ch 463 §1 (AB 1449); Stats 2014 ch 29 §1 (SB 855), effective June 20, 2014.

2001 Note: The provisions of Section 17415 of the Family Code, as amended by this act, shall be implemented only to the extent that federal financial participation is not reduced for the AFDC-FC program and the CalWORKs program. Stats 2001 ch 463 §6.

§17416. Judgment based on agreement

(a) When the local child support agency has undertaken enforcement of support, the local child support agency may enter into an agreement with the noncustodial parent, on behalf of a minor child or children, a spouse, or former spouse for the entry of a judgment without action determining paternity, if applicable, and for periodic child and spousal support payments based on the noncustodial parent's reasonable ability to pay or, if for spousal support, an amount previously ordered by a court of competent jurisdiction. An agreement for entry of a judgment under this section may be executed prior to the birth of the child and may include a provision that the judgment is not to be entered until after the birth of the child.

(b) A judgment based on the agreement shall be entered only if one of the following requirements is satisfied:

(1) The noncustodial parent is represented by legal counsel and the attorney signs a certificate stating: "I have examined the proposed judgment and have advised my client concerning their rights in connection with this matter and the consequences of signing or not signing the agreement for the entry of the judgment and my client, after being so advised, has agreed to the entry of the judgment."

(2) A judge of the court in which the judgment is to be entered, after advising the noncustodial parent concerning their rights in connection with the matter and the consequences of agreeing or not agreeing to the entry of the judgment, makes a finding that the noncustodial parent has appeared before the judge and the judge has determined that under the circumstances of the particular case the noncustodial parent has willingly, knowingly, and intelligently waived due process rights in agreeing to the entry of the judgment.

(c) The clerk shall file the agreement, together with any certificate of the attorney or finding of the court, without the payment of any fees or charges. If the requirements of this section are satisfied, the court shall enter judgment thereon without action. The provisions of Article 4 (commencing with Section 4200) of Chapter 2 of Part 2 of Division 9 or Chapter 4 (commencing with Section 4350) of Part 3 of Division 9 shall apply to the judgment. A judgment for support so entered may be enforced by any means by which any other judgment for support may be enforced.

(d) Upon request of the local child support agency in any case under this section, the clerk shall set the matter for hearing by the court. The hearing shall be held within 10 days after the clerk receives the request. The local child support agency may require the person who signed the agreement for the entry of judgment to attend the hearing by process of subpoena in the same manner as the attendance of a witness in a civil action may be required. The presence of the person who signed the agreement for entry of judgment at the hearing shall constitute the presence of the person in court at the time the order is pronounced for the purposes of Section 1209.5 of the Code of Civil Procedure if the court makes the findings required by paragraph (2) of subdivision (b).

(e) The local child support agency shall cause the following to be served, in the manner specified in Section 415.10, 415.20, 415.30, or 415.40 of the Code of Civil Procedure, upon the person who signed the agreement for entry of the judgment and shall file proof of service thereof with the court:

(1) A copy of the judgment as entered.

(2) If the judgment includes an order for child or spousal support payments, a notice stating the substance of the following: "The court has continuing authority to make an order increasing or decreasing the amount of the child or spousal support payments. You have the right to request that the court order the child and spousal support payments be decreased or eliminated entirely."

(f) An order for child and spousal support included in a judgment entered under this section may be modified or revoked as provided in Article 1 (commencing with Section 3650) of Chapter 6 of Part 1 of Division 9 and in (1) Article 1 (commencing with Section 4000) of Chapter 2 of Part 2 of Division 9 or (2) Chapter 2 (commencing with Section 4320) and Chapter 3 (commencing with Section 4330) of Part 3 of Division 9. The court may modify the order to make the support payments payable to a different person.

(g) For the purposes of this section, in making a determination of the noncustodial parent's reasonable ability to pay, any relevant circumstances set out in Section 4005 shall be considered.

(h) After arrest and before plea or trial, or after conviction or plea of guilty, under Section 270 of the Penal Code, if the defendant appears before the court in which the criminal action is pending and the requirements of paragraph (1) or (2) of subdivision (b) have been satisfied, the court may suspend proceedings or sentence in the criminal action, but this does not limit the later institution of a civil or criminal action or limit the use of any other procedures available to enforce the judgment entered pursuant to this section.

(i) Nothing in this section applies to a case where a civil action has been commenced. **Leg.H.** Added Stats 1999 ch 478 §1 (AB 196). Amended Stats 2019 ch 115 §149 (AB 1817), effective January 1, 2020.

§17418. Inquiry of parents

In enforcing the provisions of this division, the local child support agency shall inquire of both the custodial and noncustodial parent as to the number of minor children each is legally obligated to support. The local child support agency shall consider the needs of all of these children in computing the level of support requested to be ordered by the court. **Leg.H.** Added Stats 1999 ch 478 §1 (AB 196).

§17420. Earnings assignment order

After judgment in any court action brought to enforce the support obligation of a noncustodial parent pursuant to the provisions of this division, the court shall issue an earnings assignment order for support pursuant to Chapter 8 (commencing with Section 5200) of Part 5 of Division 9. **Leg.H.** Added Stats 1999 ch 478 §1 (AB 196).

§17422. State medical insurance form

(a) The state medical insurance form required in Article 1 (commencing with Section 3750) of Chapter 7 of Part 1 of Division 9 shall include, but shall not be limited to, all of the following:

(1) The parent or parents' names, addresses, and social security numbers.

(2) The name and address of each parent's place of employment.

(3) The name or names, addresses, policy number or numbers, and coverage type of the medical insurance policy or policies of the parents, if any.

(4) The name, CalWORKs case number, social security number, and Title IV-E foster care case number or Medi-Cal case numbers of the parents and children covered by the medical insurance policy or policies.

(b)(1) In an action brought or enforcement proceeding instituted by the local child support agency under this division for payment of child or spousal support, a completed state medical insurance form shall be obtained and sent by the local child support agency to the State Department of Health Care Services in the manner prescribed by the State Department of Health Care Services.

(2) Where it has been determined under Section 3751 that health insurance coverage is not available at no or reasonable cost, the local child support agency shall seek a provision in the support order that provides for health insurance coverage should it become available at no or reasonable cost.

(3) Health insurance coverage shall be considered reasonable in cost if the cost to the responsible parent providing medical support does not exceed 5 percent of the parent's gross income. In applying the 5 percent for the cost of health insurance, the cost is the difference between self-only and family coverage. If the obligor is entitled to a low-income adjustment as provided in paragraph (7) of subdivision (b) of Section 4055, health insurance shall not be enforced, unless the court determines that not requiring medical support would be unjust and inappropriate in the particular case. As used in this section, "health insurance coverage" also includes providing for the delivery of health care services by a fee for service, health maintenance organization, preferred provider organization, or any other type of health care delivery system under which medical services could be provided to the dependent child or children of an absent parent.

(c)(1) The local child support agency shall request employers and other groups offering health insurance coverage that is being enforced under this division to notify the local child support agency if there has been a lapse in insurance coverage. The local child support agency shall be responsible for forwarding information pertaining to the health insurance policy secured for the dependent children for whom the local child support agency is enforcing the court-ordered medical support to the custodial parent.

(2) The local child support agency shall periodically communicate with the State Department of Health Care Services to determine if there have been lapses in health insurance coverage for public assistance applicants and recipients. The State Department of Health Care Services shall notify the local child support agency when there has been a lapse in court-ordered insurance coverage.

(3) The local child support agency shall take appropriate action, civil or criminal, to enforce the obligation to obtain health insurance when there has been a lapse in insurance coverage or failure by the responsible parent to obtain insurance as ordered by the court.

(4) The local child support agency shall inform all individuals upon their application for child support enforcement services that medical support enforcement services are available. **Leg.H.** Added Stats 1999 ch 478 §1 (AB 196). Amended Stats 2000 ch 119 §3 (SB 2045); Stats 2002 ch 927 §4 (AB 3032); Stats 2010 ch 103 §4 (SB 580), effective January 1, 2011; Stats 2019 ch 115 §150 (AB 1817), effective January 1, 2020.

§17424. Time for completion of medical insurance form

(a) A parent who has been served with a medical insurance form shall complete and return the form to the local child support agency's office within 20 calendar days of the date the form was served.

(b) The local child support agency shall send the completed medical insurance form to the department in the manner prescribed by the department. **Leg.H.** Added Stats 1999 ch 478 §1 (AB 196).

§17428. Supplemental complaint

In any action or judgment brought or obtained pursuant to Section 17400, 17402, 17404, or 17416, a supplemental complaint may be filed, pursuant to Section 464 of the Code of Civil Procedure and Section 2330.1, either before or after a final judgment, seeking a judgment or order of paternity or support for a child of the mother and father of the child whose paternity and support are already in issue before the court. A supplemental judgment entered in the proceedings shall include, when appropriate and requested in the supplemental complaint, an order establishing or modifying support for all children named in the original or supplemental actions in conformity with the statewide uniform guideline for child support. A supplemental complaint for paternity or support of children may be filed without leave of court either before or after final judgment in the underlying action. Service of the supplemental summons and complaint shall be made in the manner provided for the initial service of a summons by the Code of Civil Procedure. **Leg.H.** Added Stats 1999 ch 478 §1 (AB 196).

§17430. Failure to answer or appear; Additional information and amended proposed judgment [Repealed January 1, 2027]

(a) Notwithstanding any other law, in an action filed by the local child support agency pursuant to Section 17400, 17402, or 17404, a judgment shall be entered without hearing, without the presentation of any other evidence or further notice to the defendant, upon the filing of proof of service by the local child support agency evidencing that more than 30 days have passed since the simplified summons and complaint, proposed judgment, blank answer, blank income and expense declaration, and all notices required by this division were served on the defendant.

(b) If the defendant fails to file an answer with the court within 30 days of having been served as specified in subdivision (d) of Section 17400, or at any time before the default judgment is entered, the proposed judgment filed with the original summons and complaint shall be conformed by the court as the final judgment and a copy provided to the local child support agency, unless the local child support agency has filed a declaration and amended proposed judgment pursuant to subdivision (c).

(c) If the local child support agency receives additional financial information within 30 days of service of the complaint and proposed judgment on the defendant and the additional information would result in a support order that is different from the amount in the proposed judgment, the local child support agency shall file a declaration setting forth the additional information and an amended proposed judgment. The declaration and amended proposed judgment shall be served on the defendant in compliance with Section 1013 of the Code of Civil Procedure or otherwise as provided by law. The defendant's time to answer or otherwise appear shall be extended to 30 days from the date of service of the declaration and amended proposed judgment.

(d) Upon entry of the judgment, the clerk of the court shall provide a conformed copy of the judgment to the local child support agency. The local child support agency shall mail by first-class mail, postage prepaid, a notice of entry of judgment by default and a copy of the judgment to the defendant to the address where the summons and complaint were served and last known address if different from that address.

(e) This section shall become inoperative on January 1, 2026, and, as of January 1, 2027, is repealed. **Leg.H.** Added Stats 1999 ch 478 §1 (AB 196). Amended Stats 1999 ch 480 §17 (SB 542), ch 652 §17.5 (SB 240); Stats 2000 ch 808 §85 (AB 1358), effective September 28, 2000; Stats 2002 ch 927 §5 (AB 3032); Stats 2019 ch 115 §151 (AB 1817), effective January 1, 2020; Stats 2023 ch 213 §18 (SB 343), effective January 1, 2024, inoperative January 1, 2026, repealed January 1, 2027.

§ 17430. Failure to answer or appear; Additional information and amended proposed judgment [Operative January 1, 2026]

(a)(1) Notwithstanding any other law, in an action filed by the local child support agency pursuant to Section 17400, 17402, 17404, or 17404.1, in which the proposed child support amount is based on actual income, a judgment shall be entered without hearing, without the presentation of any other evidence or further notice to the defendant, upon the filing of proof of service by the local child support agency evidencing that more than 30 days have passed since the simplified summons and complaint, proposed judgment, blank answer, blank income and expense declaration, and all notices required by this division were served on the defendant.

(2) If the defendant fails to file an answer with the court within 30 days of having been served as specified in subdivision (d) of Section 17400 in an action in which the proposed child support amount is based on actual income, or at any time before the default judgment is entered, the proposed judgment filed with the original summons and complaint shall be conformed by the court as the final judgment and a copy provided to the local child support agency, unless the local child support agency has filed a declaration and amended proposed judgment pursuant to subdivision (c).

(b)(1) If the proposed judgment is based on the support obligor's earning capacity pursuant to clause (ii) or (iii) of subparagraph (A) of paragraph (2) of subdivision (d) of Section 17400, the local child support agency shall file a motion for judgment, as provided in subdivision (b) of Section 17404. The motion for judgment filed pursuant to this paragraph shall be served on the defendant in compliance with Section 1013 of the Code of Civil Procedure or otherwise as provided by law.

(2) At the motion for judgment hearing, the court shall permit the appearance and participation of the defendant and the other parent in the hearing, including, but not limited to, sworn testimony and the introduction of evidence, regardless of whether the defendant has filed an answer to the complaint.

(3) If the defendant fails to file an answer with the court and does not appear at the motion for judgment hearing, the judgment shall be entered by way of default after the court considers the factors set forth in subdivision (b) of Section 4058 and states its findings on the record. When considering those factors or any other relevant matter, the court may inquire of the local child support agency regarding the factors set forth in subdivision (b) of Section 4058 or any other relevant matter. If after consideration of the factors set forth in subdivision (b) of Section 4058 and the evidence presented by the local child support agency or the other parent the court determines that child support pursuant to the guidelines set forth in Article 2 (commencing with Section 4050) of Chapter 2 of Part 2 of Division 9 would be lower than the proposed support obligation listed in the proposed judgment, the court shall enter an order for guideline child support. This paragraph does not limit the court's discretion to order an amount higher than, lower than, or equal to the proposed support obligation listed in the proposed judgment based on the evidence presented if the defendant files an answer or appears at the motion for judgment hearing.

(c) If the local child support agency receives additional information before the answer is filed and the additional information would result in a support order that is different from the amount in the proposed judgment, the local child support agency shall file a declaration setting forth the additional information and an amended proposed judgment. The local child support agency shall be permitted to file the amended proposed judgment at any time after the filing of the initial summons and complaint and before the answer is filed. The declaration and amended proposed judgment shall be served on the defendant in compliance with Section 1013 of the Code of Civil Procedure or otherwise as provided by law. The defendant's time to answer or otherwise appear shall be extended to 30 days from the date of service of the declaration and amended proposed judgment.

(d) Upon entry of the judgment, the clerk of the court shall provide a conformed copy of the judgment to the local child support agency. The local child support agency shall mail by first-class mail, postage prepaid, a notice of entry of judgment by default and a copy of the judgment to the defendant to the address where the summons and complaint were served and last known address if different from that address.

(e)(1)(A) Notwithstanding any other law, if the judgment is entered by way of default from a proposed support order that is based on earning capacity pursuant to clause (iii) of subparagraph (A) of paragraph (2) of subdivision (d) of Section 17400, within one year after entry of judgment and then annually thereafter, until a modified order is entered, the local child support agency shall conduct a review of the case to determine if there is sufficient additional evidence of income or earning capacity as described by Section 4058 available to establish actual income of the defendant or a different earning capacity, as described by subdivision (b) of Section 4058, from that which was the basis of the initial support order.

(B) If after any review pursuant to subparagraph (A), the local child support agency determines sufficient additional evidence exists, the local child support agency shall file a motion to modify the support order prospectively with the court within 60 days of its determination, and additional evidence shall constitute a change in circumstances to obtain a modification of the support order. This subdivision does not prohibit the local child support agency from filing the motion to modify pursuant to this subdivision prior to the expiration of any annual review period if additional evidence is discovered sooner.

(2)(A) Notwithstanding any other law, if the judgment is entered by way of default from a proposed support order that is based on earning capacity pursuant to clause (iii) of subparagraph (A) of paragraph (2) of subdivision (d) of Section 17400, the defendant or the other parent may file a motion to modify the initial support order prospectively if sufficient additional evidence becomes available to establish actual income of the defendant or a different earning capacity.

(B) Additional evidence available pursuant to subparagraph (A) shall constitute a change in circumstances to obtain a modification of the initial support order.

(f) This section shall become operative January 1, 2026. **Leg.H.** Added Stats 2023 ch 213 §19 (SB 343), effective January 1, 2024, operative January 1, 2026.

§17432. Relief from, and setting aside orders [Repealed January 1, 2027]

(a) In any action filed by the local child support agency pursuant to Section 17400, 17402, or 17404, the court may, on any terms that may be just, set aside that part of the judgment or order concerning the amount of child support to be paid. This relief may be granted after the six-month time limit of Section 473 of the Code of Civil Procedure has elapsed, based on the grounds, and within the time limits, specified in this section.

(b) This section shall apply only to judgments or orders for support that were based upon presumed income as specified in subdivision (d) of Section 17400 and that were entered after the entry of the default of the defendant under Section 17430. This section shall apply only to the amount of support ordered and not that portion of the judgment or order concerning the determination of parentage.

(c) The court may set aside the child support order contained in a judgment described in subdivision (b) if the defendant's income was substantially different for the period of time during which judgment was effective compared with the income the defendant was presumed to have. A "substantial difference" means that amount of income that would result in an order for support that deviates from the order entered by default by 10 percent or more.

(d) Application for relief under this section shall be filed together with an income and expense declaration or simplified financial statement or other information concerning income for any relevant years. The Judicial Council may combine the application for relief under this section and the proposed answer into a single form.

(e) The burden of proving that the actual income of the defendant deviated substantially from the presumed income shall be on the party seeking to set aside the order.

(f) A motion for relief under this section shall be filed within one year of the first collection of money by the local child support agency or the obligee. The one-year time period shall run from the date that the local child support agency receives the first collection.

(g) Within three months from the date the local child support agency receives the first collection for any order established using presumed income, the local child support agency shall check all appropriate sources for income information, and if income information exists, the local child support agency shall make a determination whether the order qualifies for set aside under this section. If the order qualifies for set aside, the local child support agency shall bring a motion for relief under this section.

(h) In all proceedings under this section, before granting relief, the court shall consider the amount of time that has passed since the entry of the order, the circumstances surrounding the defendant's default, the relative hardship on the child or children to whom the duty of support is owed, the caretaker parent, and the defendant, and other equitable factors that the court deems appropriate.

(i) If the court grants the relief requested, the court shall issue a new child support order using the appropriate child support guidelines currently in effect. The new order shall have the same commencement date as the order set aside.

(j) The Judicial Council shall review and modify any relevant forms for purposes of this section. Any modifications to the forms shall be effective July 1, 2005. Prior to the implementation of any modified Judicial Council forms, the local child support agency or custodial parent may file any request to set aside a default judgment under this section using Judicial Council Form FL-680 entitled "Notice of Motion (Governmental)" and Form FL-684 entitled "Request for Order and Supporting Declaration (Governmental)."

(k) This section shall become inoperative on January 1, 2026, and, as of January 1, 2027, is repealed. **Leg.H.** Added Stats 1999 ch 478 §1 (AB 196). Amended Stats 2002 ch 927 §6 (AB 3032); Stats 2003 ch 225 §4 (AB 1752), effective August 11, 2003; Stats 2004 ch 339 §8 (AB 1704); Stats 2023 ch 213 §20 (SB 343), effective January 1, 2024, inoperative January 1, 2026, repealed January 1, 2027.

§ 17432. Relief from and setting aside orders [Operative January 1, 2026]

(a) In any action filed by the local child support agency pursuant to Section 17400, 17402, 17404, or 17404.1, the court may, on any terms that may be just, set aside that part of the judgment or order concerning the amount of child support to be paid. This relief may be granted after the six-month time limit of Section 473 of the Code of Civil Procedure has elapsed, based on the grounds, and within the time limits, specified in this section.

(b) This section shall apply only to judgments or orders for support that were based upon presumed income or earning capacity and that were entered after the entry of the default of the support obligor as specified in Sections 17400, 17404.1, and 17430 or any predecessors of those sections in the Family Code or the Welfare and Institutions Code. This section shall apply only to the amount of support ordered and not that portion of the judgment or order concerning the determination of parentage or the obligation of medical support or health insurance.

(c)(1) The court may set aside the child support order contained in a judgment described in subdivision (b) if the support obligor's income or earning capacity was substantially different for the period of time during which judgment was effective compared with the income or earning capacity the support obligor was presumed to have.

(2) For purposes of this section, "substantially different" means that amount of income that would result in an order for support that deviates from the order entered by default by 10 percent or more.

(d) The court, in its discretion, may set aside and reinstate child support for all or partial relevant periods of time depending on the income or earning capacity information available at the time the motion is filed. Relief setting aside the child support order for less than the full period of time that the judgment was effective shall not preclude a subsequent review within the timeframe provided pursuant to subdivision (g).

(e) Application for relief under this section shall be filed together with an income and expense declaration or simplified financial statement or other information concerning income or earning capacity for any relevant years. The Judicial Council may combine the application for relief under this section and the proposed answer into a single form.

(f) The party seeking to set aside the order has the burden of proving that the actual income or earning capacity of the support obligor was substantially different from the presumed income or earning capacity.

(g)(1) A party to the action described in subdivision (a), including the local child support agency, may file a motion for relief pursuant to this section within two years of the local child support agency's first collection of money through an earnings assignment order or an order or notice to withhold income for child support. The two-year time period shall run from the date that the local child support agency receives the first collection of money from one of the sources listed in this subdivision. Immediately upon receipt of the first collection of money from an earnings assignment order or order or notice to withhold income for child support, the local child support agency shall notify the support obligor and the support obligee in writing of the first collection, including the source of the collection, and the commencement of the two-year time period to file a motion for relief under this section.

(2) This subdivision does not prohibit any party to the action, including the local child support agency, from filing a motion for relief under this section prior to the commencement of the two-year time period.

(h) Within three months from the date the local child support agency receives the first collection for an order established using presumed income or earning capacity when the order was entered by default, the local child support agency shall check all appropriate sources for income information, and, if income information exists, the local child support agency shall determine whether the order qualifies for set aside under this section. If the order qualifies for set aside, the local child support agency shall bring a motion for relief under this section. When a party to the action, including the local child support agency, has taken subsequent legal action to modify the support prospectively, but did not address a possible set aside under this section, the subsequent modification shall not preclude the filing of a potential set aside at a later date.

(i) In all proceedings under this section, before granting relief, the court shall consider the amount of time that has passed since the entry of the order, the circumstances surrounding the support obligor's default, the relative hardship on the child or children to whom the duty of support is owed, the caretaker parent, and the support obligor, and other equitable factors that the court deems appropriate.

(j) If the court grants the relief requested, the court shall issue a new child support order using the appropriate child support guidelines currently in effect. The new order shall have the same commencement date as the order set aside.

(k) This section shall become operative on January 1, 2026. **Leg.H.** Added Stats 2023 ch 213 §21 (SB 343), effective January 1, 2024, operative January 1, 2026.

§ 17432.5. Adoption of necessary forms

No later than September 1, 2024, the Judicial Council shall adopt and approve any forms necessary to implement Sections 17400, 17404.1, 17430, and 17432 as added by the act that added this section. Forms adopted pursuant to this section shall have an effective date of January 1, 2026. **Leg.H.** Added Stats 2023 ch 213 §22 (SB 343), effective January 1, 2024.

§17433. Judgment or order after default

In an action in which a judgment or order for support was entered after the entry of the default of the defendant under Section 17430, the court shall relieve the defendant from that judgment or order if the defendant establishes that the defendant was mistakenly identified in the order or in any subsequent documents or proceedings as the person having an obligation to provide support. The defendant shall also be entitled to the remedies specified in subdivisions (d) and (e) of Section 17530 with respect to any actions taken to enforce that judgment or order. This section is only intended to apply where an order has been entered against a person who is not the support obligor named in the judgment or order. **Leg.H.** Added Stats 1999 ch 653 §16 (AB 380). Amended Stats 2000 ch 808 §85.3 (AB 1358), effective September 28, 2000; Stats 2019 ch 115 §152 (AB 1817), effective January 1, 2020.

§17433.5. When interest on support obligation accrues

In any action enforced pursuant to this article, no interest shall accrue on an obligation for current child, spousal, family, or medical support due in a given month until the first day of the following month. **Leg.H.** Added Stats 2006 ch 75 §7 (AB 1808), effective July 12, 2006.

§17434. Booklet of procedures and processes; Information hotline

(a) The department shall publish a booklet describing the proper procedures and processes for the collection and payment of child and spousal support. The booklet shall be written in language understandable to the lay person and shall direct the reader to obtain the assistance of the local child support agency, the family law facilitator, or legal counsel where appropriate. The department may contract on a competitive basis with an organization or individual to write the booklet.

(b) The department shall have primary responsibility for the design and development of the contents of the booklet. The department shall solicit comment regarding the content of the booklet from the Director of the Administrative Office of the Courts. The department shall verify the appropriateness and accuracy of the contents of the booklet with at least one representative of each of the following organizations:

(1) A local child support agency.

(2) The State Attorney General's office.

(3) A community organization that advocates for the rights of custodial parents.

(4) A community organization that advocates for the rights of supporting parents.

(c) Upon receipt of booklets on support collection, each county welfare department shall provide a copy to each head of household whose application for public assistance under Division 9 (commencing with Section 10000) of the Welfare and Institutions Code has been approved and for whom support rights have been assigned pursuant to Section 11477 of the Welfare and Institutions Code. The department shall provide copies of the booklet to local child support agencies for distribution, and to any person upon request. The department shall also distribute the booklets to all superior courts. Upon receipt of those booklets, each clerk of the court shall provide two copies of the booklet to the petitioner or plaintiff in any action involving the support of a minor child. The moving party shall serve a copy of the booklet on the responding party.

(d) The department shall expand the information provided under its toll-free information hotline in response to inquiries regarding the process and procedures for collection and payment of child and spousal support. This toll-free number shall be advertised as providing information on child and spousal support. The hotline personnel shall not provide legal consultation or advice, but shall provide only referral services.

(e) The department shall maintain a file of referral sources to provide callers to the telephone hotline with the following information specific to the county in which the caller resides:

(1) The location and telephone number of the local child support agency, the county welfare office, the family law facilitator, and any other government agency that handles child and spousal support matters.

(2) The telephone number of the local bar association for referral to attorneys in family law practice.

(3) The name and telephone number of at least one organization that advocates the payment of child and spousal support or the name and telephone number of at least one organization that advocates the rights of supporting parents, if these organizations exist in the county. **Leg.H.** Added Stats 1999 ch 478 §1 (AB 196). Amended Stats 2000 ch 808 §86 (AB 1358), effective September 28, 2000; Stats 2016 ch 474 §15 (AB 2882), effective January 1, 2017.

§17440. Modification of support orders of activated service members; Form

(a) The Department of Child Support Services shall work with all branches of the United States military and the National Guard to ensure that information is made available regarding the rights and abilities of activated service members to have their support orders modified based on a change in income resulting from their activation, or other change of circumstance affecting the child support calculation, or to have a portion of their child support arrearages compromised pursuant to Section 17560.

(b) No later than 90 days after the effective date of this section, the department shall develop a form for completion by the service member that will allow the local child support agency to proceed with a motion for modification without the service member being required to appear. The form shall contain only the information necessary for the local child support agency to proceed with the motion.

(c) Within five business days of receipt of a properly completed form, the local child support agency shall bring a motion to modify the support order. The local child support agency shall bring the motion if the change in circumstances would result in any change in the dollar amount of the support order.

(d) The department shall work with the United States military to have this form and the form developed pursuant to Section 3651 distributed at all mobilization stations or other appropriate locations to ensure timely notification to all activated personnel of their rights and responsibilities. **Leg.H.** Added Stats 2005 ch 154 §4 (SB 1082), effective August 30, 2005.

§17441. [Section repealed 2010]

Leg.H. Added Stats 2006 ch 876 §1 (SB 1483), effective January 1, 2007. Repealed January 1, 2010, by its own terms. The repealed section related to modification of a child support order when a local child support agency submits an application for modification of support.

ARTICLE 1.5
Delinquent Child Support Obligations and Financial Institution Data Match

Collection of delinquency; Costs; Return or retention; Disabled obligor; Transfer of functions to Franchise Tax Board. §17450.

Availability of tax return information for purposes of collecting child support delinquencies. §17452.
Financial Institution Data Match System; Implementation and maintenance guidelines; County responsibilities until implementation; Financial institutions' duties to effectuate system. §17453.
Notice to withhold, §17454.
Court action not required for withholding and transmittal of delinquency amounts; Liability; Notice to persons named in deposit accounts. §17456.
Reciprocal agreements with other states authorized. §17460.

§17450. Collection of delinquency; Costs; Return or retention; Disabled obligor; Transfer of functions to Franchise Tax Board

(a) For purposes of this article:

(1) "Child support delinquency" means a delinquency defined in subdivision (c) of Section 17500.

(2) "Earnings" shall include the items described in Section 5206.

(b)(1) When a delinquency is submitted to the department pursuant to subdivision (c) of Section 17500, the amount of the child support delinquency shall be collected by the department in any manner authorized under state or federal law.

(2) Any compensation, fee, commission, expense, or other fee for service incurred by the department in the collection of a child support delinquency authorized under this article shall not be an obligation of, or collected from, the obligated parent.

(c)(1) The department may return or allow a local child support agency to retain a child support delinquency for a specified purpose for collection where the department determines that the return or retention of the delinquency for the purpose so specified will enhance the collectibility of the delinquency. The department shall establish a process whereby a local child support agency may request and shall be allowed to withdraw, rescind, or otherwise recall the submittal of an account that has been submitted.

(2) If an obligor is disabled, meets the federal Supplemental Security Income resource test, and is receiving Supplemental Security Income/State Supplementary Payments (SSI/SSP), or, but for excess income as described in Section 416.1100 and following of Part 416 of Title 20 of the Code of Federal Regulations, would be eligible to receive as SSI/SSP, pursuant to Section 12200 of the Welfare and Institutions Code, and the obligor has supplied the local child support agency with proof of eligibility for, and, if applicable, receipt of, SSI/SSP or Social Security Disability Insurance benefits, then the child support delinquency shall not be referred to the department for collection, and, if referred, shall be withdrawn, rescinded, or otherwise recalled from the department by the local child support agency. The department shall not take any collection action, or if the local child support agency has already taken collection action, shall cease collection actions in the case of a disabled obligor when the delinquency is withdrawn, rescinded, or otherwise recalled by the local child support agency in accordance with the process established as described in paragraph (1).

(d) It is the intent of the Legislature that when the California Child Support Enforcement System (CSE) is fully operational, any statutes that should be modified based upon the status of the system shall be revised. During the development and implementation of CSE, the department, as the Title IV-D agency, may, through appropriate interagency agreement, delegate any and all of the functions or procedures specified in this article to the Franchise Tax Board. The Franchise Tax Board shall perform those functions or procedures as specified in Sections 19271 to 19275, inclusive, of the Revenue and Taxation Code until the director, by letter to the executive officer of the Franchise Tax Board, revokes the delegation of Title IV-D functions. Sections 19271 to 19275, inclusive, of the Revenue and Taxation Code shall be effective for these purposes until the revocation of delegation to the Franchise Tax Board.

(e) Consistent with the development and implementation of the California Child Support Enforcement System, the Franchise Tax Board and the department shall enter into a letter of agreement and an interagency agreement whereby the department shall assume responsibility for collection of child support delinquencies and the Financial Institution Data Match System as set forth in this article. The letter of agreement and interagency agreement shall, at a minimum, set forth all of the following:

(1) Contingent upon the enactment of the Budget Act, and staffing authorization from the Department of Finance and the Department of Human Resources, the department shall assume responsibility for leadership and staffing of the collection of child support delinquencies and the Financial Institution Data Match System.

(2) All employees and other personnel who staff or provide support for the collection of child support delinquencies and the Financial Institution Data Match System at the Franchise Tax Board shall become the employees of the department at their existing or equivalent classification, salaries, and benefits.

(3) Any other provisions necessary to ensure continuity of function and meet or exceed existing levels of service, including, but not limited to, agreements for continued use of automated systems used by the Franchise Tax Board to locate child support obligors and their assets. **Leg.H.** Added Stats 2004 ch 806 §6 (AB 2358). See this section as modified in 2011 Governor's Reorganization Plan No. 1 §31. Amended Stats 2012 ch 665 §13 (SB 1308), effective January 1, 2013; Stats 2016 ch 474 §16 (AB 2882), effective January 1, 2017; Stats 2019 ch 115 §153 (AB 1817), effective January 1, 2020.

2012 Note: Stats 2012 ch 665 (SB 1308) enacts the statutory changes necessary to reflect the changes made by the Governor's Reorganization Plan No. 1 of 2011.

2011 Note: 2011 Governor's Reorganization Plan No. 1 was submitted to the Legislature on June 9, 2011, and became effective September 9, 2011, pursuant to Gov C §12080.5, and substantively operative July 1, 2012.

§17452. Availability of tax return information for purposes of collecting child support delinquencies

(a) Subject to state and federal privacy and information security laws, the Franchise Tax Board shall make tax return information available to the department, upon request, for the purpose of collecting child support delinquencies referred to the department.

(b) For purposes of this article, the Franchise Tax Board shall incur no obligation or liability to any person arising from any of the following:

(1) Furnishing information to the department as required by this section.

(2) Failing to disclose to a taxpayer or accountholder that the name, address, social security number, or other taxpayer identification number or other identifying information of that person was included in the data exchange with the department required by this section.

(3) Any other action taken in good faith to comply with the requirements of this section.

(c) It is the intent of the Legislature that any provision of income tax return information by the Franchise Tax Board to the department pursuant to this article shall be done in accordance with the privacy and confidential information laws of this state and of the United States, and to the satisfaction of the Franchise Tax Board. **Leg.H.** Added Stats 2004 ch 806 §6 (AB 2358).

§17453. Financial Institution Data Match System; Implementation and maintenance guidelines; County responsibilities until implementation; Financial institutions' duties to effectuate system

(a) The department, in coordination with financial institutions doing business in this state, shall operate a Financial Institution Data Match System utilizing automated data exchanges to the maximum extent feasible. The Financial Institution Data Match System shall be implemented and maintained pursuant to guidelines prescribed by the department. These guidelines shall include a structure by which financial institutions, or their designated data-processing agents, shall receive from the department the file or files of past-due support obligors compiled in accordance with subdivision (c), so that the institution shall match with its own list of accountholders to identify past-due support obligor accountholders at the institution. To the extent allowed by the federal Personal Responsibility and Work Opportunity Reconciliation Act of 1996 (P.L. 104-193), the guidelines shall include an option by which financial institutions without the technical ability to process the data exchange, or without the ability to employ a third-party data processor to process the data exchange, may forward to the department a list of all accountholders and their social security numbers, so that the department shall match that list with the file or files of past-due support obligors compiled in accordance with subdivision (c).

(b) The Financial Institution Data Match System shall not be subject to any limitation set forth in Chapter 20 (commencing with Section 7460) of Division 7 of Title 1 of the Government Code. However, any use of the information provided pursuant to this section for any purpose other than the enforcement and collection of a child support delinquency, as set forth in Section 17450, shall be a violation of Section 17212.

(c)(1) Until implementation of the California Child Support Automation System, each county shall compile a file of support obligors with judgments and orders that are being enforced by local child support agencies pursuant to Section 17400, and who are past due in the payment of their support obligations. The file shall be compiled, updated, and forwarded to the department, in accordance with the guidelines prescribed by the department.

(2) The department shall compile a file of obligors with support arrearages from requests made by other states for administrative enforcement in interstate cases, in accordance with federal requirements pursuant to paragraph 14 of subsection (a) of Section 666 of Title 42 of the United States Code. The file shall include, to the extent possible, the obligor's address.

(d) To effectuate the Financial Institution Data Match System, financial institutions subject to this section shall do all of the following:

(1) Provide to the department on a quarterly basis, the name, record address and other addresses, social security number or other taxpayer identification number, and other identifying information for each noncustodial parent who maintains an account at the institution and who owes past-due support, as identified by the department by name and social security number or other taxpayer identification number.

(2) Except as provided in subdivision (j), in response to a notice or order to withhold issued by the department, withhold from any accounts of the obligor the amount of any past-due support stated on the notice or order and transmit the amount to the department in accordance with Section 17454.

(e) Unless otherwise required by applicable law, a financial institution furnishing a report or providing information to the department pursuant to this section shall not disclose to a depositor, accountholder, codepositor, or coaccountholder, that the name, address, social security number, or other taxpayer identification number or other identifying information of that person has been received from, or furnished to, the department.

(f) A financial institution shall incur no obligation or liability to any person arising from any of the following:

(1) Furnishing information to the department as required by this section.

(2) Failing to disclose to a depositor, accountholder, codepositor, or coaccountholder, that the name, address, social security number, or other taxpayer identification number or other identifying information of that person was included in the data exchange with the department required by this section.

(3) Withholding or transmitting any assets in response to a notice or order to withhold issued by the department as a result of the data exchange. This paragraph shall not preclude any liability that may result if the financial institution does not comply with subdivision (b) of Section 17456.

(4) Any other action taken in good faith to comply with the requirements of this section.

(g)(1) With respect to files compiled under paragraph (1) of subdivision (c), the department shall forward to the counties, in accordance with guidelines prescribed by the department, information obtained from the financial institutions pursuant to this section. No county shall use this information for directly levying on any account. Each county shall keep the information confidential as provided by Section 17212.

(2) With respect to files compiled under paragraph (2) of subdivision (c), the amount collected by the department shall be deposited and distributed to the referring state in accordance with Section 17458.

(h) For those noncustodial parents owing past-due support for which there is a match under paragraph (1) of subdivision (d), the amount past due as indicated on the file or files compiled pursuant to subdivision (c) at the time of the match shall be a delinquency under this article for the purposes of the department taking any collection action pursuant to Section 17454.

(i) A child support delinquency need not be referred to the department for collection if a jurisdiction outside this state is enforcing the support order.

(j)(1) Each county shall notify the department upon the occurrence of the circumstances described in the following subparagraphs with respect to an obligor of past-due support:

(A) A court has ordered an obligor to make scheduled payments on a child support arrearages obligation and the obligor is in compliance with that order.

(B) An earnings assignment order or an order/notice to withhold income that includes an amount for past-due support has been served on the obligated parent's employer and earnings are being withheld pursuant to the earnings assignment order or an order/notice to withhold income.

(C) At least 50 percent of the obligated parent's earnings are being withheld for support.

(2) Notwithstanding Section 704.070 of the Code of Civil Procedure, if any of the conditions set forth in paragraph (1) exist, the assets of an obligor held by a financial institution are subject to levy as provided by paragraph (2) of subdivision (d). However, the first three thousand five hundred dollars ($3,500) of an obligor's assets are exempt from collection under this subdivision without the obligor having to file a claim of exemption.

(3) If any of the conditions set forth in paragraph (1) exist, an obligor may apply for a claim of exemption pursuant to Article 2 (commencing with Section 703.510) of Chapter 4 of Division 2 of Title 9 of Part 2 of the Code of Civil Procedure for an amount that is less than or equal to the total amount levied. The sole basis for a claim of exemption under this subdivision shall be the financial hardship for the obligor and the obligor's dependents.

(4) For the purposes of a claim of exemption made pursuant to paragraph (3), Section 688.030 of the Code of Civil Procedure shall not apply.

(5) For claims of exemption made pursuant to paragraph (3), the local child support agency responsible for enforcement of the obligor's child support order shall be the levying officer for the purpose of compliance with the provisions set forth in Article 2 (commencing with Section 703.510) of Chapter 4 of Division 2 of Title 9 of Part 2 of the Code of Civil Procedure except for the release of property required by subdivision (e) of Section 703.580 of the Code of Civil Procedure.

(6) The local child support agency shall notify the department within two business days of the receipt of a claim of exemption from an obligor. The department shall direct the financial institution subject to the order to withhold to hold any funds subject to the order pending notification by the department to remit or release the amounts held.

(7) The superior court in the county in which the local child support agency enforcing the support obligation is located shall have jurisdiction to determine the amount of exemption to be allowed. The court shall consider the needs of the obligor, the obligee, and all persons the obligor is required to support, and all other relevant circumstances in determining whether to allow any exemption pursuant to this subdivision. The court shall give effect to its determination by an order specifying the extent to which the amount levied is exempt.

(8) Within two business days of receipt of an endorsed copy of a court order issued pursuant to subdivision (e) of Section 703.580 of the Code of Civil Procedure, the local child support agency shall provide the department with a copy of the order. The department shall instruct the financial institution to remit or release the obligor's funds in accordance with the court's order.

(k) Out of any money received from the federal government for the purpose of reimbursing financial institutions for their actual and reasonable costs incurred in complying with this section, the state shall reimburse those institutions. To the extent that money is not provided by the federal government for that purpose, the state shall not reimburse financial institutions for their costs in complying with this section.

(*l*) For purposes of this section:

(1) "Account" means any demand deposit account, share or share draft account, checking or negotiable withdrawal order account, savings account, time deposit account, or a money market mutual fund account, whether or not the account bears interest.

(2) "Financial institution" has the same meaning as defined in paragraph (1) of subsection (d) of Section 669A of Title 42 of the United States Code. **Leg.H.** Added Stats 2004 ch 806 §6 (AB 2358).

§17454. Notice to withhold

(a) At least 45 days before sending a notice to withhold, the department shall request that a depository institution provide the department with a designated address for receiving notices to withhold.

(b) Once the depository institution has specified a designated address pursuant to subdivision (a), the department shall send all notices to that address unless the depository institution provides notification of another address. The department shall send all notices to withhold to a new designated address 30 days after notification.

(c) If a notice to withhold is mailed to the branch where the account is located or principal banking office, the depository institution shall be liable for a failure to withhold only to the extent that the accounts can be identified in information normally maintained at that location in the ordinary course of business.

(d) The department may by notice, served by magnetic media, electronic transmission, or other electronic technology, require any depository institution, as defined in the Federal Reserve Act (12 U.S.C.A. Sec. 461(b)(1)(A)), that the department, in its sole discretion, has reason to believe may have in its possession, or under its control, any credits or other personal property or other things of value, belonging to a child support obligor, to withhold, from the credits or other personal property or other things of value, the amount of any child support delinquency, and interest, due from an obligor and transmit that amount withheld to the department at the times that it may designate, but not less than 10 business days from receipt of the notice. The notice shall state the amount due from the obligor and shall be delivered or transmitted to the branch or office reported pursuant to subdivision (a), or other address designated by that depository institution for purposes of the department serving notice by magnetic media, electronic transmission, or other electronic technology.

(e) For purposes of this section, the term "address" shall include telephone or modem number, facsimile number, or any other number designated by the depository institution to receive data by electronic means. **Leg.H.** Added Stats 2004 ch 806 §6 (AB 2358).

§17456. Court action not required for withholding and transmittal of delinquency amounts; Liability; Notice to persons named in deposit accounts

(a) Any person required to withhold and transmit any amount pursuant to this article shall comply with the requirement without resort to any legal or equitable action in a court of law or equity. Any person paying to the department any amount required by it to be withheld is not liable therefore to the person from whom withheld unless the amount withheld is refunded to the withholding agent. However, if a depository institution, as defined in the Federal Reserve Act (12 U.S.C.A. Sec. 461(b)(1)(A)) withholds and pays to the department pursuant to this article any moneys held in a deposit account in which the delinquent obligor and another person or persons have an interest, or in an account held in the name of a third party or parties in which the delinquent obligor is ultimately determined to have no interest, the depository institution paying those moneys to the department is not liable therefore to any of the persons who have an interest in the account, unless the amount withheld is refunded to the withholding agent.

(b) In the case of a deposit account or accounts for which this notice to withhold applies, the depository institution shall send a notice by first-class mail to each person named on the account or accounts included in the notice from the department, provided that a current address for each person is available to the institution. This notice shall inform each person as to the reason for the hold placed on the account or accounts, the amount subject to being withheld, and the date by which this amount is to be remitted to the department. An institution may assess the account or accounts of each person receiving this notice a reasonable service charge not to exceed three dollars ($3). **Leg.H.** Added Stats 2004 ch 806 §6 (AB 2358).

§17458. Deposit of collected amounts to State Special Deposit Fund; Distribution [Repealed]

Leg.H. Added Stats 2004 ch 806 §6 (AB 2358). Repealed Stats 2016 ch 474 §17 (AB 2882), effective January 1, 2017.

Prior Law Former Fam C §17458, relating to Deposit of collected amounts to State Special Deposit Fund; Distribution, was added Stats 2004 ch 806 §6 (AB 2358).

§17460. Reciprocal agreements with other states authorized

(a) As necessary, the department shall seek reciprocal agreements with other states to improve its ability to collect child support payments from out-of-state obligated parents on behalf of custodial parents residing in California. The department may pursue agreements with the Internal Revenue Service, as permitted by federal law, to improve collections of child support delinquencies from out-of-state obligated parents through cooperative agreements with the service.

(b) The California Child Support Enforcement System shall, for purposes of this article, include the capacity to interface and exchange information, if feasible, with the Internal Revenue Service, to enable the immediate reporting and tracking of obligated parent information.

(c) The department shall enter into any interagency agreements that are necessary for the implementation of this article. State departments and boards shall cooperate with the department to the extent necessary for the implementation of this article. Out of any money received from the federal government for the purpose of reimbursing state departments and boards for their actual and reasonable costs incurred in complying with this section, the department shall reimburse those departments and boards. To the extent that money is not provided by the federal government for that purpose, and subject to the annual Budget Act, the state shall fund departments and boards for their costs in complying with this section. **Leg.H.** Added Stats 2004 ch 806 §6 (AB 2358). Amended Stats 2016 ch 474 §18 (AB 2882), effective January 1, 2017.

ARTICLE 2
Collections and Enforcement

Obligations of department and local child support agency under Title IV-D of Social Security Act. §17500.
Return of undeliverable payments. §17502.
Amounts not considered income [Operative date contingent]. § 17504.
Notice of assigned support payments made on behalf of CalWORKs recipient [Renumbered]. §17504.1.
Passthrough payments of assigned support obligation to former recipient of aid [Operative date contingent]. § 17504.2.
Notice of assigned support payments made on behalf of CalWORKs recipient. § 17504.4.
Agency cooperation; Information exchange. §17505.
California Parent Locator Service and Central Registry. §17506.
Access to information collected pursuant to law. §17508.
Identification of cases where employed obligor has no earning withholding order. §17509.
Workers' compensation notification project. §17510.
Employer and labor organization cooperation. §17512.
Confidentiality of child abduction records; Release of information. §17514.
Benefits that may not satisfy support obligations. §17516.
Actions to enforce support obligations. §17518.
Consolidated lists of persons; License renewals; Review procedures; Report to Legislature; Rules and regulations; Forms; Use of information; Suspension or revocation of driver's license; Severability. §17520.
Use of support compliance information to deny, withhold, or suspend driver's license. § 17520.5.
Court where proceedings will take place. §17521.
Levies. §17522.
Liquidation of assets; Transfer of liquidation funds; Instructions from obligor. §17522.5.
Lien for child support. §17523.
Lien record in digital form permitted. §17523.5.
Statement of arrearages. §17524.
Notice of support delinquency. §17525.
Review and judicial determination of arrearages. §17526.
Actions to enforce obligations; Retirement systems. §17528.
Enforcement actions taken in error. §17530.
Case containing summary criminal history. §17531.
Time for filing claims. §17540.
Establishing regulations for compromising obligor parent's liability for public assistance debt in certain cases; Conditions to be met. §17550.
Promulgation of regulations for determining if in best interest of child or nonminor to have case referred to local child support agency. §17552.
Appropriations augmenting funding for local child support agencies subject to specified requirements. §17555.
Annual status report to Legislature; Required information. §17556.
Program establishing arrears collection enhancement process; Acceptance of compromise offers; Rescission of offers; Conditions; Finality; Compliance with federal law; Uniform application. §17560.

§17500. Obligations of department and local child support agency under Title IV-D of Social Security Act

(a) In carrying out its obligations under Title IV-D of the Social Security Act (42 U.S.C. Sec. 651 et seq.), the department and the local child support agency shall have the responsibility for promptly and effectively collecting and enforcing child support obligations.

(b) The department and the local child support agency are the public agencies responsible for administering wage withholding for the purposes of Title IV-D of the Social Security Act (42 U.S.C. Sec. 651 et seq.)

(c) Except as provided in Section 17450, the local child support agency shall submit child support delinquencies to the department for purposes of supplementing the collection efforts of the local child support agencies. Submissions shall be in the form and manner and at the time prescribed by the department. Collection shall be made by the department in accordance with Section 17450. For purposes of this subdivision, "child support delinquency" means an arrearage or otherwise past due amount that accrues when an obligor fails to make any court-ordered support payment when due, which is more than 60 days past due, and the aggregate amount of which exceeds one hundred dollars ($100).

(d) If a child support delinquency exists at the time a case is opened by the local child support agency, the responsibility for the collection of the child support delinquency shall be submitted to the department no later than 30 days after receipt of the case by the local child support agency. **Leg.H.** Added Stats 1999 ch 478 §1 (AB 196). Amended Stats 1999 ch 480 §18 (SB 542); Stats 2001 ch 111 §5 (AB 429), effective July 30, 2001, ch 651 §4 (AB 891); Stats 2004 ch 339 §9 (AB 1704), ch 806 §4 (AB 2358).

§17501. [Section repealed 2001]

Leg.H. Added Stats 1999 ch 480 §19 (SB 542). Repealed Stats 2001 ch 111 §6 (AB 429), effective July 30, 2001. The repealed section related to Franchise Tax Board's responsibility for accounts receivable management of child support delinquencies.

§17502. Return of undeliverable payments

A local child support agency that is collecting child support payments on behalf of a child and who is unable to deliver the payments to the obligee because the local child support agency is unable to locate the obligee shall make all reasonable efforts to locate the obligee for a period of six months. If the local child support agency is unable to locate the obligee within the six-month period, it shall return the undeliverable payments to the obligor, with written notice advising the obligor that (a) the return of the funds does not relieve the obligor of the support order, and (b) the obligor should consider placing the funds aside for purposes of child support in case the obligee appears and seeks collection of the undistributed amounts. No interest shall accrue on any past-due child support amount for which the obligor made payment to the local child support agency for six consecutive months, or on any amounts due thereafter until the obligee is located, provided that the local child support agency returned the funds to the obligor because the local child support agency was unable to locate the obligee and, when the obligee was located, the obligor made full payment for all past-due child support amounts. **Leg.H.** Added Stats 1999 ch 478 §1 (AB 196). Amended Stats 2004 ch 806 §5 (AB 2358).

§17504. Amounts not considered income [Operative date contingent]

(a) The first one hundred dollars ($100) of any amount of child support collected in a month for a family with one child, or the first two hundred dollars ($200) for a family with two or more children, in payment of the required support obligation for that month shall be paid to a recipient of aid under Article 2 (commencing with Section 11250) of Chapter 2 of Part 3 of Division 9 of the Welfare and Institutions Code, except recipients of foster care payments under Article 5 (commencing with Section 11400) of Chapter 2 of Part 3 of Division 9 of the Welfare and Institutions Code, and shall not be considered income or resources of the recipient family, and shall not be deducted from the amount of aid to which the family would otherwise be eligible. The local child support agency in each county shall ensure that payments are made to recipients as required by this section.

(b) Notwithstanding the rulemaking provisions of the Administrative Procedure Act (Chapter 3.5 (commencing with Section 11340) of Part 1 of Division 3 of Title 2 of the Government Code), the State Department of Social Services and the Department of Child Support Services may implement, interpret, or make specific this section by means of all-county letters or similar instructions from the department until regulations are adopted. These all-county letters or similar written instructions shall have the same force and effect as regulations until the adoption of regulations.

(c) This section shall become operative on January 1, 2022, or when the State Department of Social Services and the Department of Child Support Services notify the Legislature that the Statewide Automated Welfare System and Child Support Enforcement System can perform the necessary automation to implement this section, whichever date is later.

Leg.H. Added Stats 2020 ch 11 §2 (AB 79), effective June 29, 2020, operative January 1, 2022.

Prior Law Former Fam C §17504, similar to the present section, was added Stats 1999 ch 478 §1 (AB 196), amended Stats 2000 ch 808 §86.3 (AB 1358), effective September 28, 2000, Stats 2001 ch 159 §90 (SB 662), Stats 2020 ch 11 §1 (AB 79), effective June 29, 2020, operative January 1, 2022, inoperative January 1, 2022, and repealed by its own terms January 1, 2022.

§17504.1. Notice of assigned support payments made on behalf of CalWORKs recipient [Renumbered]

Leg.H. Added Stats 2016 ch 474 §19 (AB 2882), effective January 1, 2017. Amended and renumbered to Cal Fam Code §17504.4 by Stats 2022 ch 573 §6 (AB 207), effective September 27, 2022.

§ 17504.2. Passthrough payments of assigned support obligation to former recipient of aid [Operative date contingent]

(a)(1) Any amount of support collected in a month in payment of an assigned support obligation shall be passed through to a former recipient of aid under Article 2 (commencing with Section 11250) of Chapter 2 of Part 3 of Division 9 of the Welfare and Institutions Code, except recipients of foster care payments under Article 5 (commencing with Section 11400) of Chapter 2 of Part 3 of Division 9 of the Welfare and Institutions Code.

(2) The local child support agency in each county shall ensure that payments are made to former recipients of aid when required by this section.

(3) The Department of Child Support Services and the local child support agencies shall provide written or electronic informational materials, which shall be developed by the Department of Child Support Services in collaboration with the Department of Social Services, to child support case participants, who are former recipients of aid, to notify them of the potential impacts of passthrough collections pursuant to this section on eligibility for public benefit programs.

(b) Notwithstanding Section 17502 of the Family Code, any passthrough payments under this section that cannot be delivered to a former recipient of aid pursuant to paragraph (2) of subdivision (a) for a period of six months shall not be returned to the obligor and shall be sent to recoup aid paid on behalf of the recipient pursuant to Section 11477 of the Welfare and Institutions Code. If the former recipient of aid makes a claim for the passthrough payment within 12 months of the payment being sent to recoupment, the payment shall be removed from recoupment and sent to the former recipient of aid. The Department of Child Support Services shall monitor the number of claims made after payments are sent for recoupment. The department shall provide that information to the Legislature no later than April 1, 2025, or two years and three months after the operative date of this section as established by subdivision (e), whichever date is later.

(c) Nothing in this section shall be construed to discontinue assignments under Section 11477 of the Welfare and Institutions Code.

(d) Notwithstanding the rulemaking provisions of the Administrative Procedure Act (Chapter 3.5 (commencing with Section 11340) of Part 1 of Division 3 of Title 2 of the Government Code), the State Department of Social Services and the Department of Child Support Services may implement, interpret, or make specific this section by means of all-county letters or similar instructions from the department until regulations are adopted. These all-county letters or similar written instructions shall have the same force and effect as regulations until the adoption of regulations.

(e) This section shall become operative on July 1, 2023, or on the date the department notifies the Legislature that the Child Support Enforcement System can perform the necessary automation to implement this section, and the Department of Child Support Services has developed and provided the written materials pursuant to subdivision (a), whichever date is later. **Leg.H.** Added Stats 2022 ch 573 §7 (AB 207), effective September 27, 2022, operative July 1, 2023, operative date contingent.

§ 17504.4. Notice of assigned support payments made on behalf of CalWORKs recipient

On a monthly basis, the local child support agency shall provide to any CalWORKs recipient or former recipient for whom an assignment pursuant to subdivision (a) of Section 11477 of the Welfare and Institutions Code is currently effective, a notice of the amount of assigned support payments made on behalf of the recipient or former recipient or any other family member for whom public assistance is received. **Leg.H.**

Added Stats 2016 ch 474 §19 (AB 2882), effective January 1, 2017. Amended and renumbered from Cal Fam Code §17504.1 by Stats 2022 ch 573 §6 (AB 207), effective September 27, 2022.

§ 17504.6. Report to legislative committees on impact of passthrough payments on eligibility determination for other need-based assistance programs [Repealed]

Leg.H. Added Stats 2022 ch 573 §8 (AB 207), effective September 27, 2022, repealed January 1, 2025.

Prior Law Former Fam C §17504.6, realated to report to legislative committees on impact of passthrough payments on eligibility determination for other need-based assistance programs, was added Stats 2022 ch 573 §8 (AB 207), effective September 27, 2022, repealed January 1, 2025.

§17505. Agency cooperation; Information exchange

(a) All state, county, and local agencies shall cooperate with the local child support agency (1) in the enforcement of any child support obligation or to the extent required under the state plan under Part 6 (commencing with Section 5700.101) of Division 9, Section 270 of the Penal Code, and Section 17604, and (2) the enforcement of spousal support orders and in the location of parents or putative parents. The local child support agency may enter into an agreement with and shall secure from a municipal, county, or state law enforcement agency, pursuant to that agreement, state summary criminal record information through the California Law Enforcement Telecommunications System. This subdivision applies irrespective of whether the children are or are not receiving aid to families with dependent children. All state, county, and local agencies shall cooperate with the district attorney in implementing Chapter 8 (commencing with Section 3130) of Part 2 of Division 8 concerning the location, seizure, and recovery of abducted, concealed, or detained minor children.

(b) On request, all state, county, and local agencies shall supply the local child support agency of any county in this state or the California Parent Locator Service with all information on hand relative to the location, income, or property of any parents, putative parents, spouses, or former spouses, notwithstanding any other provision of law making the information confidential, and with all information on hand relative to the location and prosecution of any person who has, by means of false statement or representation or by impersonation or other fraudulent device, obtained aid for a child under this chapter.

(c) The California Child Support Automation System, or its replacement, shall be entitled to the same cooperation and information provided to the California Parent Locator Service, to the extent allowed by law. The California Child Support Automation System, or its replacement, shall be allowed access to criminal offender record information only to the extent that access is allowed by law.

(d) Information exchanged between the California Parent Locator Service or the California Child Support Automation System, or its replacement, and state, county, or local agencies as specified in Sections 653(c)(4) and 666(c)(1)(D) of Title 42 of the United State Code shall be through automated processes to the maximum extent feasible. **Leg.H.** Added Stats 1999 ch 478 §1 (AB 196). Amended Stats 2000 ch 808 §87 (AB 1358), effective September 28, 2000; Stats 2012 ch 637 §3 (AB 1751), effective January 1, 2013; Stats 2015 ch 493 §14 (SB 646), effective January 1, 2016.

§17506. California Parent Locator Service and Central Registry

(a) There is in the department a California Parent Locator Service and Central Registry that shall collect and disseminate all of the following, with respect to any parent, putative parent, spouse, or former spouse:

(1) The full and true name of the parent together with any known aliases.

(2) Date and place of birth.

(3) Physical description.

(4) Social security number, individual taxpayer identification number, or other uniform identification number.

(5) Employment history and earnings.

(6) Military status and Veterans Administration or military service serial number.

(7) Last known address, telephone number, and date thereof.

(8) Driver's license number or identification card number issued by the Department of Motor Vehicles, driving record, and vehicle registration information.

(9) Criminal, licensing, and applicant records and information.

(10)(A) Any additional location, asset, and income information, including income tax return information obtained pursuant to Section 19548 of the Revenue and Taxation Code, and to the extent permitted by federal law, the address, telephone number, and social security number obtained from a public utility, cable television corporation, a provider of electronic digital pager communication, or a provider of mobile telephony services that may be of assistance in locating the parent, putative parent, abducting, concealing, or detaining parent, spouse, or former spouse, in establishing a parent and child relationship, in enforcing the child support liability of the absent parent, or enforcing the spousal support liability of the spouse or former spouse to the extent required by the state plan pursuant to Section 17604.

(B) For purposes of this subdivision, "income tax return information" means all of the following regarding the taxpayer:

(i) Assets.
(ii) Credits.
(iii) Deductions.
(iv) Exemptions.
(v) Identity.
(vi) Liabilities.
(vii) Nature, source, and amount of income.
(viii) Net worth.
(ix) Payments.
(x) Receipts.
(xi) Address.
(xii) Social security number, individual taxpayer identification number, or other uniform identification number.

(b) Pursuant to a letter of agreement entered into between the Department of Child Support Services and the Department of Justice, the Department of Child Support Services shall assume responsibility for the California Parent Locator Service and Central Registry. The letter of agreement shall, at a minimum, set forth all of the following:

(1) Contingent upon funding in the Budget Act, the Department of Child Support Services shall assume responsibility for leadership and staff of the California Parent Locator Service and Central Registry commencing July 1, 2003.

(2) All employees and other personnel who staff or provide support for the California Parent Locator Service and Central Registry shall, at the time of the transition, at their option, become the employees of the Department of Child Support Services at their existing or equivalent classification, salaries, and benefits.

(3) Until the department's automation system for the California Parent Locator Service and Central Registry functions is fully operational, the department shall use the automation system operated by the Department of Justice.

(4) Any other provisions necessary to ensure continuity of function and meet or exceed existing levels of service.

(c) To effectuate the purposes of this section, the California Child Support Enforcement System and the California Parent Locator Service and Central Registry shall utilize the federal Parent Locator Service to the extent necessary, and may request and shall receive from all departments, boards, bureaus, or other agencies of the state, or any of its political subdivisions, and those entities shall provide, that assistance and data that will enable the Department of Child Support Services and other public agencies to carry out their powers and duties to locate parents, spouses, and former spouses, and to identify their assets, to establish parent-child relationships, and to enforce liability for child or spousal support, and for any other obligations incurred on behalf of children, and shall also provide that information to any local child support agency in fulfilling the duties prescribed in Section 270 of the Penal Code, and in Chapter 8 (commencing with Section 3130) of Part 2 of Division 8 of this code, relating to abducted, concealed, or detained children and to any county child welfare agency or county probation department in fulfilling the duties prescribed in Article 5.5 (commencing with Section 290.1) of Chapter 2 of Part 1 of Division 2 of the Welfare and Institutions Code, and prescribed in Article 6 (commencing with Section 300) of Chapter 2 of Part 1 of Division 2 of the Welfare and Institutions Code to identify, locate, and notify parents or relatives of children who are the subject of juvenile court proceedings, to establish parent and child relationships pursuant to Section 316.2 of the Welfare and Institutions Code, and to assess the appropriateness of placement of a child with a noncustodial parent pursuant to Section 361.2

of the Welfare and Institutions Code. Consistent with paragraph (1) of subdivision (e) of Section 309 of, and paragraph (2) of subdivision (d) of Section 628 of, the Welfare and Institutions Code, in order for county child welfare and probation departments to carry out their duties to identify and locate all grandparents, adult siblings, and other adult relatives of the child as defined in paragraph (2) of subdivision (f) of Section 319 of the Welfare and Institutions Code, including any other adult relatives suggested by the parents, county personnel are permitted to request and receive information from the California Parent Locator Service and Federal Parent Locator Service. County child welfare agencies and probation departments shall be entitled to the information described in this subdivision regardless of whether an all-county letter or similar instruction is issued pursuant to subparagraph (C) of paragraph (8) of subdivision (c) of Section 11478.1 of the Welfare and Institutions Code. The California Child Support Enforcement System shall be entitled to the same cooperation and information as the California Parent Locator Service and Central Registry to the extent allowed by law. The California Child Support Enforcement System shall be allowed access to criminal record information only to the extent that access is allowed by state and federal law.

(d)(1) To effectuate the purposes of this section, and notwithstanding any other law, regulation, or tariff, and to the extent permitted by federal law, the California Parent Locator Service and Central Registry and the California Child Support Enforcement System may request and shall receive from public utilities, as defined in Section 216 of the Public Utilities Code, customer service information, including the full name, address, telephone number, date of birth, employer name and address, and social security number of customers of the public utility, to the extent that this information is stored within the computer database of the public utility.

(2) To effectuate the purposes of this section, and notwithstanding any other law, regulation, or tariff, and to the extent permitted by federal law, the California Parent Locator Service and Central Registry and the California Child Support Enforcement System may request and shall receive from cable television corporations, as defined in Section 216.4 of the Public Utilities Code, the providers of electronic digital pager communication, as defined in Section 629.51 of the Penal Code, and the providers of mobile telephony services, as defined in Section 224.4 of the Public Utilities Code, customer service information, including the full name, address, telephone number, date of birth, employer name and address, and social security number of customers of the cable television corporation, customers of the providers of electronic digital pager communication, and customers of the providers of mobile telephony services.

(3) In order to protect the privacy of utility, cable television, electronic digital pager communication, and mobile telephony service customers, a request to a public utility, cable television corporation, provider of electronic digital pager communication, or provider of mobile telephony services for customer service information pursuant to this section shall meet the following requirements:

(A) Be submitted to the public utility, cable television corporation, provider of electronic digital pager communication, or provider of mobile telephony services in writing, on a transmittal document prepared by the California Parent Locator Service and Central Registry or the California Child Support Enforcement System and approved by all of the public utilities, cable television corporations, providers of electronic digital pager communication, and providers of mobile telephony services. The transmittal shall be deemed to be an administrative subpoena for customer service information.

(B) Have the signature of a representative authorized by the California Parent Locator Service and Central Registry or the California Child Support Enforcement System.

(C) Contain at least three of the following data elements regarding the person sought:

(i) First and last name, and middle initial, if known.
(ii) Social security number.
(iii) Driver's license number or identification card number issued by the Department of Motor Vehicles.
(iv) Birth date.
(v) Last known address.
(vi) Spouse's name.

(D) The California Parent Locator Service and Central Registry and the California Child Support Enforcement System shall ensure that each public utility, cable television corporation, provider of electronic digital pager communication services, and provider of mobile telephony services has at all times a current list of the names of persons authorized to request customer service information.

(E) The California Child Support Enforcement System and the California Parent Locator Service and Central Registry shall ensure that customer service information supplied by a public utility, cable television corporation, provider of electronic digital pager communication, or provider of mobile telephony services is applicable to the person who is being sought before releasing the information pursuant to subdivision (d).

(4) During the development of the California Child Support Enforcement System, the department shall determine the necessity of additional locate sources, including those specified in this section, based upon the cost-effectiveness of those sources.

(5) The public utility, cable television corporation, electronic digital pager communication provider, or mobile telephony service provider may charge a fee to the California Parent Locator Service and Central Registry or the California Child Support Enforcement System for each search performed pursuant to this subdivision to cover the actual costs to the public utility, cable television corporation, electronic digital pager communication provider, or mobile telephony service provider for providing this information.

(6) No public utility, cable television corporation, electronic digital pager communication provider, or mobile telephony service provider or official or employee thereof, shall be subject to criminal or civil liability for the release of customer service information as authorized by this subdivision.

(e) Notwithstanding Section 14203 of the Penal Code, any records established pursuant to this section shall be disseminated only to the Department of Child Support Services, the California Child Support Enforcement System, the California Parent Locator Service and Central Registry, the parent locator services and central registries of other states as defined by federal statutes and regulations, a local child support agency of any county in this state, and the federal Parent Locator Service. The California Child Support Enforcement System shall be allowed access to criminal offender record information only to the extent that access is allowed by law.

(f)(1) At no time shall any information received by the California Parent Locator Service and Central Registry or by the California Child Support Enforcement System be disclosed to any person, agency, or other entity, other than those persons, agencies, and entities specified pursuant to Section 17505, this section, or any other provision.

(2) This subdivision shall not otherwise affect discovery between parties in any action to establish, modify, or enforce child, family, or spousal support, that relates to custody or visitation.

(g)(1) The Department of Justice, in consultation with the Department of Child Support Services, shall promulgate rules and regulations to facilitate maximum and efficient use of the California Parent Locator Service and Central Registry. Upon implementation of the California Child Support Enforcement System, the Department of Child Support Services shall assume all responsibility for promulgating rules and regulations for use of the California Parent Locator Service and Central Registry.

(2) The Department of Child Support Services, the Public Utilities Commission, the cable television corporations, providers of electronic digital pager communication, and the providers of mobile telephony services shall develop procedures for obtaining the information described in subdivision (c) from public utilities, cable television corporations, providers of electronic digital pager communication, and providers of mobile telephony services and for compensating the public utilities, cable television corporations, providers of electronic digital pager communication, and providers of mobile telephony services for providing that information.

(h) The California Parent Locator Service and Central Registry may charge a fee not to exceed eighteen dollars ($18) for any service it provides pursuant to this section that is not performed or funded pursuant to Section 651 and following of Title 42 of the United States Code.

(i) This section shall be construed in a manner consistent with the other provisions of this article. **Leg.H.** Added Stats 1999 ch 478 §1 (AB 196). Amended Stats 1999 ch 652 §18 (SB 240); Stats 2002 ch 759 §2 (AB

3033); Stats 2003 ch 62 §91 (SB 600); Stats 2004 ch 806 §7 (AB 2358); Stats 2006 ch 198 §1 (AB 3073), effective January 1, 2007; Stats 2012 ch 637 §4 (AB 1751), effective January 1, 2013; Stats 2014 ch 437 §3 (SB 1066), effective January 1, 2015, ch 772 §3.5 (SB 1460), effective January 1, 2015; Stats 2016 ch 474 §20 (AB 2882), effective January 1, 2017; Stats 2018 ch 838 §6 (SB 695), effective January 1, 2019.

§17508. Access to information collected pursuant to law

(a) The Employment Development Department shall, when requested by the Department of Child Support Services local child support agency, the federal Parent Locator Service, or the California Parent Locator Service, provide access to information collected pursuant to Division 1 (commencing with Section 100) of the Unemployment Insurance Code to the requesting department or agency for purposes of administering the child support enforcement program, and for purposes of verifying employment of applicants and recipients of aid under this chapter or CalFresh under Chapter 10 (commencing with Section 18900) of Part 6 of Division 9 of the Welfare and Institutions Code.

(b)(1) To the extent possible, the Employment Development Department shall share information collected under Sections 1088.5 and 1088.8 of the Unemployment Insurance Code immediately upon receipt. This sharing of information may include electronic means.

(2) This subdivision shall not authorize the Employment Development Department to share confidential information with any individuals not otherwise permitted by law to receive the information or preclude batch runs or comparisons of data. **Leg.H.** Added Stats 1999 ch 478 §1 (AB 196). Amended Stats 1999 ch 652 §19 (SB 240); Stats 2000 ch 808 §88 (AB 1358), effective September 28, 2000; Stats 2011 ch 227 §4 (AB 1400), effective January 1, 2012; Stats 2016 ch 474 §21 (AB 2882), effective January 1, 2017.

§17509. Identification of cases where employed obligor has no earning withholding order

Once the statewide automated system is fully implemented, the Department of Child Support Services shall periodically compare Employment Development Department information collected under Division 1 (commencing with Section 100) of the Unemployment Insurance Code to child support obligor records and identify cases where the obligor is employed but there is no earning withholding order in effect. The department shall immediately notify local child support agencies in those cases. **Leg.H.** Added Stats 1999 ch 652 §20 (SB 240).

§17510. Workers' compensation notification project

To assist local agencies in child support enforcement activities, the department shall operate a workers' compensation notification project based on information received pursuant to Section 138.5 of the Labor Code or any other source of information. **Leg.H.** Added Stats 1999 ch 478 §1 (AB 196).

§17512. Employer and labor organization cooperation

(a) Upon receipt of a written request from a local child support agency enforcing the obligation of parents to support their children pursuant to Section 17400, or from an agency of another state enforcing support obligations pursuant to Section 654 of Title 42 of the United States Code, every employer, as specified in Section 5210, and every labor organization shall cooperate with and provide relevant employment and income information that they have in their possession to the local child support agency or other requesting agency for the purpose of establishing, modifying, or enforcing the support obligation. No employer or labor organization shall incur any liability for providing this information to the local child support agency or other requesting agency.

(b) Relevant employment and income information shall include, but not be limited to, all of the following:

(1) Whether a named person has or has not been employed by an employer or whether a named person has or has not been employed to the knowledge of the labor organization.

(2) The full name of the employee or member or the first and middle initial and last name of the employee or member.

(3) The employee's or member's last known residence address.

(4) The employee's or member's date of birth.

(5) The employee's or member's social security number.

(6) The dates of employment.

(7) All earnings paid to the employee or member and reported as W-2 compensation in the prior tax year and the employee's or member's current basic rate of pay.

(8) Other earnings, as specified in Section 5206, paid to the employee or member.

(9) Whether dependent health insurance coverage is available to the employee through employment or membership in the labor organization.

(c) The local child support agency or other agency shall notify the employer and labor organization of the local child support agency case file number in making a request pursuant to this section. The written request shall include at least three of the following elements regarding the person who is the subject of the inquiry: (A) first and last name and middle initial, if known; (B) social security number; (C) driver's license number; (D) birth date; (E) last known address; or (F) spouse's name.

(d) The local child support agency or other requesting agency shall send a notice that a request for this information has been made to the last known address of the person who is the subject of the inquiry.

(e) An employer or labor organization that fails to provide relevant employment information to the local child support agency or other requesting agency within 30 days of receiving a request pursuant to subdivision (a) may be assessed a civil penalty of a maximum of one thousand dollars ($1,000), plus attorneys' fees and costs. Proceedings to impose the civil penalty shall be commenced by the filing and service of an order to show cause.

(f) "Labor organization," for the purposes of this section means a labor organization as defined in Section 1117 of the Labor Code or any related benefit trust fund covered under the federal Employee Retirement Income Security Act of 1974 (Chapter 18 (commencing with Section 1001) of Title 29 of the United States Code).

(g) Any reference to the local child support agency in this section shall apply only when the local child support agency is otherwise ordered or required to act pursuant to existing law. Nothing in this section shall be deemed to mandate additional enforcement or collection duties upon the local child support agency beyond those imposed under existing law on the effective date of this section. **Leg.H.** Added Stats 1999 ch 478 §1 (AB 196).

§17514. Confidentiality of child abduction records; Release of information

(a) It is the intent of the Legislature to protect individual rights of privacy, and to facilitate and enhance the effectiveness of the child abduction and recovery programs, by ensuring the confidentiality of child abduction records, and to thereby encourage the full and frank disclosure of information relevant to all of the following:

(1) The establishment or maintenance of parent and child relationships and support obligations.

(2) The enforcement of the child support liability of absent parents.

(3) The enforcement of spousal support liability of the spouse or former spouse to the extent required by the state plan under Section 17400, and Chapter 6 (commencing with Section 4800) of Part 5 of Division 9.

(4) The location of absent parents.

(5) The location of parents and children abducted, concealed, or detained by them.

(b)(1) Except as provided in this subdivision, all files, applications, papers, documents, and records, established or maintained by a public entity for the purpose of locating an abducted child, locating a person who has abducted a child, or prosecution of a person who has abducted a child shall be confidential, and shall not be open to examination or released for disclosure for any purpose not directly connected with locating or recovering the abducted child or abducting person or prosecution of the abducting person.

(2) Except as provided in subdivision (c), a public entity shall not disclose any file, application, paper, document, or record described in this section, or the information contained therein.

(c)(1) All files, applications, papers, documents, and records as described in subdivision (b) shall be available and may be used by a public entity for all administrative, civil, or criminal investigations, actions, proceedings, or prosecution conducted in connection with the child abduction or prosecution of the abducting person.

(2) A document requested by a person who wrote, prepared, or furnished the document may be examined by or disclosed to that person or a designee.

(3) Public records subject to disclosure under Division 10 (commencing with Section 7920.000) of Title 1 of the Government Code may be released.

(4) After a noticed motion and a finding by the court, in a case in which child recovery or abduction prosecution actions are being taken, that release or disclosure is required by due process of law, the court may order a public entity that possesses an application, paper, document, or record described in this subdivision to make that item available to the defendant or other party for examination or copying, or to disclose to an appropriate person the contents of that item. Article 9 (commencing with Section 1040) of Chapter 4 of Division 8 of the Evidence Code shall not be applicable to proceedings under this part.

(5) To the extent not prohibited by federal law or regulation, information indicating the existence or imminent threat of a crime against a minor child, or location of a concealed or abducted child, or the location of the concealing or abducting person, may be disclosed to any appropriate law enforcement agency, or to any state or county child protective agency, or may be used in any judicial proceedings to prosecute that crime or to protect the child.

(6) Information may be released to any state or local agency for the purposes connected with establishing, modifying, and enforcing child support obligations, enforcing spousal support orders, and determining paternity as required by Part D (commencing with Section 651) of Subchapter IV of Chapter 7 of Title 42 of the United States Code and this article. **Leg.H.** Added Stats 1999 ch 478 §1 (AB 196). Amended Stats 2019 ch 115 §154 (AB 1817), effective January 1, 2020; Stats 2021 ch 615 §107 (AB 474), effective January 1, 2022.

Editor's Note: Family Code §§4800 et seq., referred to in subdivision (a)(3) of this section, has been repealed. See Family Code §§5700.101 et seq.

§17516. Benefits that may not satisfy support obligations

In no event shall public social service benefits, as defined in Section 10051 of the Welfare and Institutions Code, or benefits paid pursuant to Title XVI of the Social Security Act be employed to satisfy a support obligation. **Leg.H.** Added Stats 1999 ch 478 §1 (AB 196).

§17518. Actions to enforce support obligations

(a) As authorized by subdivision (d) of Section 704.120 of the Code of Civil Procedure, the following actions shall be taken in order to enforce support obligations that are not being met. Whenever a support judgment or order has been rendered by a court of this state against an individual who is entitled to unemployment compensation benefits or unemployment compensation disability benefits, the local child support agency may file a certification of support judgment or support order with the Department of Child Support Services, verifying under penalty of perjury that there is or has been a judgment or an order for support with sums overdue thereunder. The department shall periodically present and keep current, by deletions and additions, a list of the certified support judgments and orders and shall periodically notify the Employment Development Department of individuals certified as owing support obligations.

(b) If the Employment Development Department determines that an individual who owes support may have a claim for unemployment compensation disability insurance benefits under a voluntary plan approved by the Employment Development Department in accordance with Chapter 6 (commencing with Section 3251) of Part 2 of Division 1 of the Unemployment Insurance Code, the Employment Development Department shall immediately notify the voluntary plan payer. When the department notifies the Employment Development Department of changes in an individual's support obligations, the Employment Development Department shall promptly notify the voluntary plan payer of these changes. The Employment Development Department shall maintain and keep current a record of individuals who owe support obligations who may have claims for unemployment compensation or unemployment compensation disability benefits.

(c) Notwithstanding any other law, the Employment Development Department shall withhold the amounts specified below from the unemployment compensation benefits or unemployment compensation disability benefits of individuals with unmet support obligations. The Employment Development Department shall forward the amounts to the Department of Child Support Services for distribution to the appropriate certifying county.

(d) Notwithstanding any other law, during the payment of unemployment compensation disability benefits to an individual, with respect to whom the Employment Development Department has notified a voluntary plan payer that the individual has a support obligation, the voluntary plan payer shall withhold the amounts specified below from the individual's unemployment compensation disability benefits and shall forward the amounts to the appropriate certifying county.

(e) The amounts withheld in subdivisions (c) and (d) shall be equal to 25 percent of each weekly unemployment compensation benefit payment or periodic unemployment compensation disability benefit payment, rounded down to the nearest whole dollar, which is due the individual identified on the certified list. However, the amount withheld may be reduced to a lower whole dollar amount through a written agreement between the individual and the local child support agency or through an order of the court.

(f) The department shall ensure that the appropriate certifying county shall resolve any claims for refunds in the amounts overwithheld by the Employment Development Department or voluntary plan payer.

(g) No later than the time of the first withholding, the individuals who are subject to the withholding shall be notified by the payer of benefits of all of the following:

(1) That the individual's unemployment compensation benefits or unemployment compensation disability benefits have been reduced by a court-ordered support judgment or order pursuant to this section.

(2) The address and telephone number of the local child support agency that submitted the certificate of support judgment or order.

(3) That the support order remains in effect even though the individual is unemployed or disabled unless it is modified by court order, and that if the amount withheld is less than the monthly support obligation, an arrearage will accrue.

(h) The individual may ask the appropriate court for an equitable division of the individual's unemployment compensation or unemployment compensation disability amounts withheld to take into account the needs of all the persons the individual is required to support.

(i) The Department of Child Support Services and the Employment Development Department shall enter into any agreements necessary to carry out this section.

(j) For purposes of this section, "support obligations" means the child and related spousal support obligations that are being enforced pursuant to a plan described in Section 454 of the Social Security Act and as that section may hereafter be amended. However, to the extent "related spousal support obligation" may not be collected from unemployment compensation under federal law, those obligations shall not be included in the definition of support obligations under this section. **Leg.H.** Added Stats 1999 ch 478 §1 (AB 196). Amended Stats 2000 ch 808 §89 (AB 1358), effective September 28, 2000; Stats 2019 ch 115 §155 (AB 1817), effective January 1, 2020.

§17520. Consolidated lists of persons; License renewals; Review procedures; Report to Legislature; Rules and regulations; Forms; Use of information; Suspension or revocation of driver's license; Severability

(a) As used in this section:

(1) "Applicant" means a person applying for issuance or renewal of a license.

(2) "Board" means an entity specified in Section 101 of the Business and Professions Code, the entities referred to in Sections 1000 and 3600 of the Business and Professions Code, the State Bar of California, the Department of Real Estate, the Department of Motor Vehicles, the Secretary of State, the Department of Fish and Wildlife, and any other state commission, department, committee, examiner, or agency that issues a license, certificate, credential, permit, registration, or any other authorization to engage in a business, occupation, or profession, or to the extent required by federal law or regulations, for recreational purposes. This term includes all boards, commissions, departments, committees, examiners, entities, and agencies that issue a license, certificate, credential, permit, registration, or any other authorization to engage in a business, occupation, or profession. The failure to specifically name a particular board, commission, department, committee, examiner, entity, or agency that issues a license, certificate, credential, permit, registration, or any other authorization to engage in a business, occupation, or profession does not exclude that board, commission, department, committee, examiner, entity, or agency from this term.

(3) "Certified list" means a list provided by the local child support agency to the Department of Child Support Services in which the local child support agency verifies, under penalty of perjury, that the names contained therein are support obligors found to be out of compliance with

a judgment or order for support in a case being enforced under Title IV-D of the federal Social Security Act.

(4) "Compliance with a judgment or order for support" means that, as set forth in a judgment or order for child or family support, the obligor is no more than 30 calendar days in arrears in making payments in full for current support, in making periodic payments in full, whether court ordered or by agreement with the local child support agency, on a support arrearage, or in making periodic payments in full, whether court ordered or by agreement with the local child support agency, on a judgment for reimbursement for public assistance, or has obtained a judicial finding that equitable estoppel as provided in statute or case law precludes enforcement of the order. The local child support agency is authorized to use this section to enforce orders for spousal support only when the local child support agency is also enforcing a related child support obligation owed to the obligee parent by the same obligor, pursuant to Sections 17400 and 17604.

(5) "License" includes membership in the State Bar of California, and a certificate, credential, permit, registration, or any other authorization issued by a board that allows a person to engage in a business, occupation, or profession, or to operate a commercial motor vehicle, including appointment and commission by the Secretary of State as a notary public. "License" also includes any driver's license issued by the Department of Motor Vehicles, any commercial fishing license issued by the Department of Fish and Wildlife, and to the extent required by federal law or regulations, any license used for recreational purposes. This term includes all licenses, certificates, credentials, permits, registrations, or any other authorization issued by a board that allows a person to engage in a business, occupation, or profession. The failure to specifically name a particular type of license, certificate, credential, permit, registration, or other authorization issued by a board that allows a person to engage in a business, occupation, or profession, does not exclude that license, certificate, credential, permit, registration, or other authorization from this term.

(6) "Licensee" means a person holding a license, certificate, credential, permit, registration, or other authorization issued by a board, to engage in a business, occupation, or profession, or a commercial driver's license as defined in Section 15210 of the Vehicle Code, including an appointment and commission by the Secretary of State as a notary public. "Licensee" also means a person holding a driver's license issued by the Department of Motor Vehicles, a person holding a commercial fishing license issued by the Department of Fish and Wildlife, and to the extent required by federal law or regulations, a person holding a license used for recreational purposes. This term includes all persons holding a license, certificate, credential, permit, registration, or any other authorization to engage in a business, occupation, or profession, and the failure to specifically name a particular type of license, certificate, credential, permit, registration, or other authorization issued by a board does not exclude that person from this term. For licenses issued to an entity that is not an individual person, "licensee" includes an individual who is either listed on the license or who qualifies for the license.

(b) The local child support agency shall maintain a list of those persons included in a case being enforced under Title IV-D of the federal Social Security Act against whom a support order or judgment has been rendered by, or registered in, a court of this state, and who are not in compliance with that order or judgment. The local child support agency shall submit a certified list with the names, social security numbers, individual taxpayer identification numbers, or other uniform identification numbers, and last known addresses of these persons and the name, address, and telephone number of the local child support agency who certified the list to the department. The local child support agency shall verify, under penalty of perjury, that the persons listed are subject to an order or judgment for the payment of support and that these persons are not in compliance with the order or judgment. The local child support agency shall submit to the department an updated certified list on a monthly basis.

(c) The department shall consolidate the certified lists received from the local child support agencies and, within 30 calendar days of receipt, shall provide a copy of the consolidated list to each board that is responsible for the regulation of licenses, as specified in this section.

(d) On or before November 1, 1992, or as soon thereafter as economically feasible, as determined by the department, all boards subject to this section shall implement procedures to accept and process the list provided by the department, in accordance with this section. Notwithstanding any other law, all boards shall collect social security numbers or individual taxpayer identification numbers from all applicants for the purposes of matching the names of the certified list provided by the department to applicants and licensees and of responding to requests for this information made by child support agencies.

(e)(1) Promptly after receiving the certified consolidated list from the department, and prior to the issuance or renewal of a license, each board shall determine whether the applicant is on the most recent certified consolidated list provided by the department. The board shall have the authority to withhold issuance or renewal of the license of an applicant on the list.

(2) If an applicant is on the list, the board shall immediately serve notice as specified in subdivision (f) on the applicant of the board's intent to withhold issuance or renewal of the license. The notice shall be made personally or by mail to the applicant's last known mailing address on file with the board. Service by mail shall be complete in accordance with Section 1013 of the Code of Civil Procedure.

(A) The board shall issue a temporary license valid for a period of 150 days to any applicant whose name is on the certified list if the applicant is otherwise eligible for a license.

(B) Except as provided in subparagraph (D), the 150-day time period for a temporary license shall not be extended. Except as provided in subparagraph (D), only one temporary license shall be issued during a regular license term and it shall coincide with the first 150 days of that license term. As this paragraph applies to commercial driver's licenses, "license term" shall be deemed to be 12 months from the date the application fee is received by the Department of Motor Vehicles. A license for the full or remainder of the license term shall be issued or renewed only upon compliance with this section.

(C) In the event that a license or application for a license or the renewal of a license is denied pursuant to this section, any funds paid by the applicant or licensee shall not be refunded by the board.

(D) This paragraph shall apply only in the case of a driver's license, other than a commercial driver's license. Upon the request of the local child support agency or by order of the court upon a showing of good cause, the board shall extend a 150-day temporary license for a period not to exceed 150 extra days.

(3)(A) The department may, when it is economically feasible for the department and the boards to do so as determined by the department, in cases where the department is aware that certain child support obligors listed on the certified lists have been out of compliance with a judgment or order for support for more than four months, provide a supplemental list of these obligors to each board with which the department has an interagency agreement to implement this paragraph. Upon request by the department, the licenses of these obligors shall be subject to suspension, provided that the licenses would not otherwise be eligible for renewal within six months from the date of the request by the department. The board shall have the authority to suspend the license of any licensee on this supplemental list.

(B) If a licensee is on a supplemental list, the board shall immediately serve notice as specified in subdivision (f) on the licensee that the license will be automatically suspended 150 days after notice is served, unless compliance with this section is achieved. The notice shall be made personally or by mail to the licensee's last known mailing address on file with the board. Service by mail shall be complete in accordance with Section 1013 of the Code of Civil Procedure.

(C) The 150-day notice period shall not be extended.

(D) In the event that any license is suspended pursuant to this section, any funds paid by the licensee shall not be refunded by the board.

(E) This paragraph shall not apply to licenses subject to annual renewal or annual fee.

(f) Notices shall be developed by each board in accordance with guidelines provided by the department and subject to approval by the department. The notice shall include the address and telephone number of the local child support agency that submitted the name on the certified list, and shall emphasize the necessity of obtaining a release from that local child support agency as a condition for the issuance, renewal, or continued valid status of a license or licenses.

(1) In the case of applicants not subject to paragraph (3) of subdivision (e), the notice shall inform the applicant that the board shall issue a temporary license, as provided in subparagraph (A) of paragraph (2) of subdivision (e), for 150 calendar days if the applicant is otherwise eligible

and that upon expiration of that time period the license will be denied unless the board has received a release from the local child support agency that submitted the name on the certified list.

(2) In the case of licensees named on a supplemental list, the notice shall inform the licensee that the license will continue in its existing status for no more than 150 calendar days from the date of mailing or service of the notice and thereafter will be suspended indefinitely unless, during the 150-day notice period, the board has received a release from the local child support agency that submitted the name on the certified list. Additionally, the notice shall inform the licensee that any license suspended under this section will remain so until the expiration of the remaining license term, unless the board receives a release along with applications and fees, if applicable, to reinstate the license during the license term.

(3) The notice shall also inform the applicant or licensee that if an application is denied or a license is suspended pursuant to this section, any funds paid by the applicant or licensee shall not be refunded by the board. The Department of Child Support Services shall also develop a form that the applicant shall use to request a review by the local child support agency. A copy of this form shall be included with every notice sent pursuant to this subdivision.

(g)(1) Each local child support agency shall maintain review procedures consistent with this section to allow an applicant to have the underlying arrearage and any relevant defenses investigated, to provide an applicant information on the process of obtaining a modification of a support order, or to provide an applicant assistance in the establishment of a payment schedule on arrearages if the circumstances so warrant.

(2) It is the intent of the Legislature that a court or local child support agency, when determining an appropriate payment schedule for arrearages, base its decision on the facts of the particular case and the priority of payment of child support over other debts. The payment schedule shall also recognize that certain expenses may be essential to enable an obligor to be employed. Therefore, in reaching its decision, the court or the local child support agency shall consider both of these goals in setting a payment schedule for arrearages.

(h) If the applicant wishes to challenge the submission of their name on the certified list, the applicant shall make a timely written request for review to the local child support agency who certified the applicant's name. A request for review pursuant to this section shall be resolved in the same manner and timeframe provided for resolution of a complaint pursuant to Section 17800. The local child support agency shall immediately send a release to the appropriate board and the applicant, if any of the following conditions are met:

(1) The applicant is found to be in compliance or negotiates an agreement with the local child support agency for a payment schedule on arrearages or reimbursement.

(2) The applicant has submitted a request for review, but the local child support agency will be unable to complete the review and send notice of its findings to the applicant within the time specified in Section 17800.

(3) The applicant has filed and served a request for judicial review pursuant to this section, but a resolution of that review will not be made within 150 days of the date of service of notice pursuant to subdivision (f). This paragraph applies only if the delay in completing the judicial review process is not the result of the applicant's failure to act in a reasonable, timely, and diligent manner upon receiving the local child support agency's notice of findings.

(4) The applicant has obtained a judicial finding of compliance as defined in this section.

(i) An applicant is required to act with diligence in responding to notices from the board and the local child support agency with the recognition that the temporary license will lapse or the license suspension will go into effect after 150 days and that the local child support agency and, where appropriate, the court must have time to act within that period. An applicant's delay in acting, without good cause, which directly results in the inability of the local child support agency to complete a review of the applicant's request or the court to hear the request for judicial review within the 150-day period shall not constitute the diligence required under this section which would justify the issuance of a release.

(j) Except as otherwise provided in this section, the local child support agency shall not issue a release if the applicant is not in compliance with the judgment or order for support. The local child support agency shall notify the applicant, in writing, that the applicant may, by filing an order to show cause or notice of motion, request any or all of the following:

(1) Judicial review of the local child support agency's decision not to issue a release.

(2) A judicial determination of compliance.

(3) A modification of the support judgment or order.

The notice shall also contain the name and address of the court in which the applicant shall file the order to show cause or notice of motion and inform the applicant that their name shall remain on the certified list if the applicant does not timely request judicial review. The applicant shall comply with all statutes and rules of court regarding orders to show cause and notices of motion.

This section does not limit an applicant from filing an order to show cause or notice of motion to modify a support judgment or order or to fix a payment schedule on arrearages accruing under a support judgment or order or to obtain a court finding of compliance with a judgment or order for support.

(k) The request for judicial review of the local child support agency's decision shall state the grounds for which review is requested and judicial review shall be limited to those stated grounds. The court shall hold an evidentiary hearing within 20 calendar days of the filing of the request for review. Judicial review of the local child support agency's decision shall be limited to a determination of each of the following issues:

(1) Whether there is a support judgment, order, or payment schedule on arrearages or reimbursement.

(2) Whether the petitioner is the obligor covered by the support judgment or order.

(3) Whether the support obligor is or is not in compliance with the judgment or order of support.

(4)(A) The extent to which the needs of the obligor, taking into account the obligor's payment history and the current circumstances of both the obligor and the obligee, warrant a conditional release as described in this subdivision.

(B) The request for judicial review shall be served by the applicant upon the local child support agency that submitted the applicant's name on the certified list within seven calendar days of the filing of the petition. The court has the authority to uphold the action, unconditionally release the license, or conditionally release the license.

(C) If the judicial review results in a finding by the court that the obligor is in compliance with the judgment or order for support, the local child support agency shall immediately send a release in accordance with subdivision (*l*) to the appropriate board and the applicant. If the judicial review results in a finding by the court that the needs of the obligor warrant a conditional release, the court shall make findings of fact stating the basis for the release and the payment necessary to satisfy the unrestricted issuance or renewal of the license without prejudice to a later judicial determination of the amount of support arrearages, including interest, and shall specify payment terms, compliance with which are necessary to allow the release to remain in effect.

(*l*)(1) The department shall prescribe release forms for use by local child support agencies. When the obligor is in compliance, the local child support agency shall mail to the applicant and the appropriate board a release stating that the applicant is in compliance. The receipt of a release shall serve to notify the applicant and the board that, for the purposes of this section, the applicant is in compliance with the judgment or order for support. A board that has received a release from the local child support agency pursuant to this subdivision shall process the release within five business days of its receipt.

(2) When the local child support agency determines, subsequent to the issuance of a release, that the applicant is once again not in compliance with a judgment or order for support, or with the terms of repayment as described in this subdivision, the local child support agency may notify the board, the obligor, and the department in a format prescribed by the department that the obligor is not in compliance.

(3) The department may, when it is economically feasible for the department and the boards to develop an automated process for complying with this subdivision, notify the boards in a manner prescribed by the department, that the obligor is once again not in compliance. Upon receipt of this notice, the board shall immediately notify the obligor on a form prescribed by the department that the obligor's license will be suspended on a specific date, and this date shall be no longer than 30 days from the date the form is mailed. The obligor shall be further notified that the

license will remain suspended until a new release is issued in accordance with subdivision (h). This section does not limit the obligor from seeking judicial review of suspension pursuant to the procedures described in subdivision (k).

(m) The department may enter into interagency agreements with the state agencies that have responsibility for the administration of boards necessary to implement this section, to the extent that it is cost effective to implement this section. These agreements shall provide for the receipt by the other state agencies and boards of federal funds to cover that portion of costs allowable in federal law and regulation and incurred by the state agencies and boards in implementing this section. Notwithstanding any other law, revenue generated by a board or state agency shall be used to fund the nonfederal share of costs incurred pursuant to this section. These agreements shall provide that boards shall reimburse the department for the nonfederal share of costs incurred by the department in implementing this section. The boards shall reimburse the department for the nonfederal share of costs incurred pursuant to this section from moneys collected from applicants and licensees.

(n) Notwithstanding any other law, in order for the boards subject to this section to be reimbursed for the costs incurred in administering its provisions, the boards may, with the approval of the appropriate department director, levy on all licensees and applicants a surcharge on any fee or fees collected pursuant to law, or, alternatively, with the approval of the appropriate department director, levy on the applicants or licensees named on a certified list or supplemental list, a special fee.

(o) The process described in subdivision (h) shall constitute the sole administrative remedy for contesting the issuance of a temporary license or the denial or suspension of a license under this section. The procedures specified in the administrative adjudication provisions of the Administrative Procedure Act (Chapter 4.5 (commencing with Section 11400) and Chapter 5 (commencing with Section 11500) of Part 1 of Division 3 of Title 2 of the Government Code) shall not apply to the denial, suspension, or failure to issue or renew a license or the issuance of a temporary license pursuant to this section.

(p) In furtherance of the public policy of increasing child support enforcement and collections, on or before November 1, 1995, the State Department of Social Services shall make a report to the Legislature and the Governor based on data collected by the boards and the district attorneys in a format prescribed by the State Department of Social Services. The report shall contain all of the following:

(1) The number of delinquent obligors certified by district attorneys under this section.

(2) The number of support obligors who also were applicants or licensees subject to this section.

(3) The number of new licenses and renewals that were delayed, temporary licenses issued, and licenses suspended subject to this section and the number of new licenses and renewals granted and licenses reinstated following board receipt of releases as provided by subdivision (h) by May 1, 1995.

(4) The costs incurred in the implementation and enforcement of this section.

(q) A board receiving an inquiry as to the licensed status of an applicant or licensee who has had a license denied or suspended under this section or has been granted a temporary license under this section shall respond only that the license was denied or suspended or the temporary license was issued pursuant to this section. Information collected pursuant to this section by a state agency, board, or department shall be subject to the Information Practices Act of 1977 (Chapter 1 (commencing with Section 1798) of Title 1.8 of Part 4 of Division 3 of the Civil Code).

(r) Any rules and regulations issued pursuant to this section by a state agency, board, or department may be adopted as emergency regulations in accordance with the rulemaking provisions of the Administrative Procedure Act (Chapter 3.5 (commencing with Section 11340) of Part 1 of Division 3 of Title 2 of the Government Code). The adoption of these regulations shall be deemed an emergency and necessary for the immediate preservation of the public peace, health, and safety, or general welfare. The regulations shall become effective immediately upon filing with the Secretary of State.

(s) The department and boards, as appropriate, shall adopt regulations necessary to implement this section.

(t) The Judicial Council shall develop the forms necessary to implement this section, except as provided in subdivisions (f) and (l).

(u) The release or other use of information received by a board pursuant to this section, except as authorized by this section, is punishable as a misdemeanor.

(v) The State Board of Equalization shall enter into interagency agreements with the department and the Franchise Tax Board that will require the department and the Franchise Tax Board to maximize the use of information collected by the State Board of Equalization, for child support enforcement purposes, to the extent it is cost effective and permitted by the Revenue and Taxation Code.

(w)(1) The suspension or revocation of a driver's license, including a commercial driver's license, under this section shall not subject the licensee to vehicle impoundment pursuant to Section 14602.6 of the Vehicle Code.

(2) Notwithstanding any other law, the suspension or revocation of a driver's license, including a commercial driver's license, under this section shall not subject the licensee to increased costs for vehicle liability insurance.

(x) If any provision of this section or the application thereof to any person or circumstance is held invalid, that invalidity shall not affect other provisions or applications of this section which can be given effect without the invalid provision or application, and to this end the provisions of this section are severable.

(y) All rights to administrative and judicial review afforded by this section to an applicant shall also be afforded to a licensee. **Leg.H.** Added Stats 1999 ch 654 §3.5 (AB 370). Amended Stats 2001 ch 755 §14 (SB 943), effective October 12, 2001; Stats 2013 ch 352 §79 (AB 1317), effective September 26, 2013, operative July 1, 2013; Stats 2014 ch 752 §10 (SB 1159), effective January 1, 2015; Stats 2018 ch 838 §7 (SB 695), effective January 1, 2019; Stats 2019 ch 115 §156 (AB 1817), effective January 1, 2020.

§ 17520.5. Use of support compliance information to deny, withhold, or suspend driver's license

(a)(1) Notwithstanding any other law, the department shall not include in the list sent to the Department of Motor Vehicles pursuant to Section 17520, for the purpose of denying, withholding, or suspending a driver's license, the information of a support obligor found to be out of compliance with a judgment or order for support in a case being enforced under Title IV-D of the federal Social Security Act, if the annual household income of the support obligor is at or below 70 percent of the median income for the county in which the department or the local child support agency believes the support obligor resides, based on the most recent available data published by the Department of Housing and Community Development pursuant to Section 6932 of Title 25 of the California Code of Regulations or successor regulation thereto.

(2) Commencing January 1, 2027, this subdivision shall apply only with respect to noncommercial driver's licenses.

(b) This section shall be implemented to the extent allowed under federal law.

(c) This section shall become operative on January 1, 2025. **Leg.H.** Added Stats 2022 ch 830 §1 (SB 1055), effective January 1, 2023, operative January 1, 2025.

§17521. Court where proceedings will take place

The order to show cause or notice of motion described in subdivision (j) of Section 17520 shall be filed and heard in the superior court. **Leg.H.** Added Stats 1999 ch 653 §17 (AB 380). Amended Stats 2002 ch 784 §115 (SB 1316).

§17522. Levies

(a) Notwithstanding any other law, if a support obligor is delinquent in the payment of support for at least 30 days and the local child support agency is enforcing the support obligation pursuant to Section 17400, the local child support agency may collect the delinquency or enforce a lien by levy served on all persons having in their possession, or who will have in their possession or under their control, credits or personal property belonging to the delinquent support obligor, or who owe any debt to the obligor at the time they receive the notice of levy.

(b) A levy may be issued by a local child support agency for a support obligation that accrued under a court order or judgment if the obligor had notice of the accrued support arrearage as provided in this section, and did not make a timely request for review.

(c) The notice requirement shall be satisfied by the local child support agency sending a statement of support arrearages to the obligor at the obligor's last known address by first-class mail, postage prepaid. The notice shall advise the obligor of the amount of the support arrearage. The notice shall advise the obligor that the obligor may have the arrearage determination reviewed by administrative procedures and state how the review may be obtained. The local child support agency shall conduct the review pursuant to this section in the same manner and timeframe provided for resolution of a complaint pursuant to Section 17800. The notice shall also advise the obligor of the right to seek a judicial determination of arrearages pursuant to Section 17526 and shall include a form to be filed with the court to request a judicial determination of arrearages. If the obligor requests an administrative review of the arrearage determination within 20 days from the date the notice was mailed to the obligor, the local child support agency may not issue the levy for a disputed amount of support until the administrative review procedure is completed.

(d) If the obligor requests a judicial determination of the arrearages within 20 days from the date the notice was mailed to the obligor, the local child support agency shall not issue the levy for a disputed amount of support until the judicial determination is complete.

(e) A person upon whom a levy has been served who possesses or controls any credits or personal property belonging to the delinquent support obligor or owing any debts to the delinquent support obligor at the time of receipt of the levy or coming into the person's possession or control within one year of receipt of the notice of levy, shall surrender the credits or personal property to the local child support agency or pay to the local child support agency the amount of any debt owing the delinquent support obligor within 10 days of service of the levy, and shall surrender the credits or personal property, or the amount of any debt owing to the delinquent support obligor coming into the person's possession or control within one year of receipt of the notice of levy, within 10 days of the date of coming into possession or control of the credits or personal property or the amount of any debt owing to the delinquent support obligor.

(f) A person who surrenders any credits or personal property or pays the debts owing the delinquent support obligor to the local child support agency pursuant to this section shall be discharged from any obligation or liability to the delinquent support obligor to the extent of the amount paid to the local child support agency as a result of the levy.

(g) When the levy is made on a deposit or credits or personal property in the possession or under the control of a bank, savings and loan association, or other financial institution as defined by Section 669A(d)(1) of Title 42 of the United States Code, the notice of levy may be delivered or mailed to a centralized location designated by the bank, savings and loan association, or other financial institution pursuant to Section 689.040 of the Code of Civil Procedure.

(h) A person who is served with a levy pursuant to this section and who fails or refuses to surrender any credits or other personal property or pay any debts owing to the delinquent support obligor shall be liable in their own person or estate to the local child support agency in an amount equal to the value of the credits or other personal property or in the amount of the levy, up to the amount specified in the levy.

(i) If an amount required to be paid pursuant to a levy under this section is not paid when due, the local child support agency may issue a warrant for enforcement of a lien and for the collection of any amount required to be paid to the local child support agency under this section. The warrant shall be directed to any sheriff, marshal, or the Department of the California Highway Patrol and shall have the same force and effect as a writ of execution. The warrant shall be levied and sale made pursuant to it in the manner and with the same force and effect as a levy and sale pursuant to a writ of execution. The local child support agency may pay or advance to the levying officer the same fees, commissions, and expenses for services under this section as are provided by law for similar services pursuant to a writ of execution, except for those fees and expenses for which a district attorney is exempt by law from paying. The local child support agency, and not the court, shall approve the fees for publication in a newspaper.

(j) The fees, commissions, expenses, and the reasonable costs associated with the sale of property levied upon by warrant or levy pursuant to this section, including, but not limited to, appraisers' fees, auctioneers' fees, and advertising fees are an obligation of the support obligor and may be collected from the obligor by virtue of the warrant or levy or in any other manner as though these items were support payments delinquent for at least 30 days. **Leg.H.** Added Stats 1999 ch 478 §1 (AB 196). Amended Stats 2001 ch 755 §15 (SB 943), effective October 12, 2001; Stats 2019 ch 115 §157 (AB 1817), effective January 1, 2020.

§17522.5. Liquidation of assets; Transfer of liquidation funds; Instructions from obligor

(a) Notwithstanding Section 8112 of the Commercial Code and Section 700.130 of the Code of Civil Procedure, when a local child support agency pursuant to Section 17522, or the department pursuant to Section 17454 or 17500, issues a levy upon, or requires by notice any employer, person, political officer or entity, or depository institution to withhold the amount of, as applicable, a financial asset for the purpose of collecting a delinquent child support obligation, the person, financial institution, or securities intermediary (as defined in Section 8102 of the Commercial Code) in possession or control of the financial asset shall liquidate the financial asset in a commercially reasonable manner within 20 days of the issuance of the levy or the notice to withhold. Within five days of liquidation, the person, financial institution, or securities intermediary shall transfer to the State Disbursement Unit, established under Section 17309, the proceeds of the liquidation, less any reasonable commissions or fees, or both, which are charged in the normal course of business.

(b) If the value of the financial assets exceed the total amount of support due, the obligor may, within 10 days after the service of the levy or notice to withhold upon the person, financial institution, or securities intermediary, instruct the person, financial institution, or securities intermediary who possesses or controls the financial assets as to which financial assets are to be sold to satisfy the obligation for delinquent support. If the obligor does not provide instructions for liquidation, the person, financial institution, or securities intermediary who possesses or controls the financial assets shall liquidate the financial assets in a commercially reasonable manner and in an amount sufficient to cover the obligation for delinquent child support, and any reasonable commissions or fees, or both, which are charged in the normal course of business, beginning with the financial assets purchased most recently.

(c) For the purposes of this section, a financial asset shall include, but not be limited to, an uncertificated security, certificated security, or security entitlement (as defined in Section 8102 of the Commercial Code), security (as defined in Section 8103 of the Commercial Code), or a securities account (as defined in Section 8501 of the Commercial Code). **Leg.H.** Added Stats 2003 ch 225 §5 (AB 1752), effective August 11, 2003. Amended Stats 2004 ch 806 §8 (AB 2358); Stats 2016 ch 474 §22 (AB 2882), effective January 1, 2017.

§17523. Lien for child support

(a) Notwithstanding any other provision of law, if a support obligor is delinquent in the payment of support and the local child support agency is enforcing the support obligation pursuant to Section 17400 or 17402, a lien for child support shall arise against the personal property of the support obligor in either of the following circumstances:

(1) By operation of law for all amounts of overdue support, regardless of whether the amounts have been adjudicated or otherwise determined.

(2) When either a court having continuing jurisdiction or the local child support agency determines a specific amount of arrearages is owed by the support obligor.

(b) The lien for child support shall be perfected by filing a notice of child support lien with the Secretary of State pursuant to Section 697.510 of the Code of Civil Procedure. Once filed, the child support lien shall have the same priority, force, and effect as a judgment lien on personal property pursuant to Article 3 (commencing with Section 697.510) of Chapter 2 of Division 2 of Article 9 of the Code of Civil Procedure.

(c) For purposes of this section, the following definitions shall apply:

(1) "Notice of child support lien" means a document filed with the Secretary of State that substantially complies with the requirements of Section 697.530 of the Code of Civil Procedure.

(2) "Support obligor is delinquent in payment of support" means that the support obligor has failed to make payment equal to one month's support obligation.

(3) "Personal property" means that property that is subject to attachment by a judgment lien pursuant to Section 697.530 of the Code of Civil Procedure.

(d) Nothing in this section shall affect the priority of any of the following interests:

(1) State tax liens as set forth in Article 2 (commencing with Section 7170) of Division 7 of Title 1 of the Government Code.

(2) Liens or security interests as set forth in Article 3 (commencing with Section 697.510) of Chapter 2 of Division 2 of Article 9 of the Code of Civil Procedure.

(e) As between competing child support liens and state tax liens, a child support lien arising under this section shall have priority over a state tax lien if (1) the child support lien is filed with the Secretary of State, (2) the notice of child support lien is filed in an action or proceeding in which the obligor may become entitled to property or money judgment, or (3) the levy for child support on personal property is made, before a notice of state tax lien is filed with the Secretary of State pursuant to Section 7171 of the Government Code or filed in an action or proceeding in accordance with Section 7173 of the Government Code.

(f) A personal property lien for child support arising in another state may be enforced in the same manner and to the same extent as a personal property lien arising in this state. **Leg.H.** Added Stats 1999 ch 980 §15 (AB 1671).

§17523.5. Lien record in digital form permitted

(a)(1) Notwithstanding any other law, in connection with the duty of the department and the local child support agency to promptly and effectively collect and enforce child support obligations under Title IV-D, the transmission, filing, and recording of a lien record by departmental and local child support agency staff that arises pursuant to subdivision (a) of Section 4506 of this code or Section 697.320 of the Code of Civil Procedure against the real property of a support obligor in the form of a digital or a digitized electronic record shall be permitted and governed only by this section.

(2) A facsimile signature that complies with the requirements of paragraph (2) of subdivision (b) of Section 27201 of the Government Code shall be accepted on any document relating to a lien that is filed or recorded pursuant to this section.

(3) The department and the local child support agency may use the California Child Support Enforcement System to transmit, file, and record a lien record under this section.

(b) Nothing in this section shall be construed to require a county recorder to establish an electronic recording delivery system or to enter into a contract with an entity to implement this section.

(c) For purposes of this section, the following terms have the following meanings:

(1) "Digital electronic record" means a record containing information that is created, generated, sent, communicated, received, or stored by electronic means, but not created in original paper form.

(2) "Digitized electronic record" means a scanned image of the original paper document. **Leg.H.** Added Stats 2007 ch 441 §2 (SB 892), effective January 1, 2008. Amended Stats 2016 ch 474 §23 (AB 2882), effective January 1, 2017.

§17524. Statement of arrearages

(a) Upon making application to the local child support agency for child support enforcement services pursuant to Section 17400, every applicant shall be requested to give the local child support agency a statement of arrearages stating whether any support arrearages are owed. If the applicant alleges arrearages are owed, the statement shall be signed under penalty of perjury.

(b) For all cases opened by the district attorney or local child support agency after December 31, 1995, the local child support agency shall enforce only arrearages declared under penalty of perjury pursuant to subdivision (a), arrearages accrued after the case was opened, or arrearages determined by the court in the child support action. Arrearages may be determined by judgment, noticed motion, renewal of judgment, or registration of the support order.

(c) For all cases opened by the district attorney on or before December 31, 1995, the local child support agency shall enforce only arrearages that have been based upon a statement of arrearages signed under penalty of perjury or where the local child support agency has some other reasonable basis for believing the amount of claimed arrearages to be correct. **Leg.H.** Added Stats 1999 ch 478 §1 (AB 196).

§17525. Notice of support delinquency

(a) Whenever a state or local governmental agency issues a notice of support delinquency, the notice shall state the date upon which the amount of the delinquency was calculated, and shall notify the obligor that the amount calculated may, or may not, include accrued interest. This requirement shall not be imposed until the local child support agency has instituted the California Child Support Enforcement System implemented and maintained by the Department of Child Support Services pursuant to Section 17308. The notice shall further notify the obligor of the right to an administrative determination of arrears by requesting that the local child support agency review the arrears, but that payments on arrears continue to be due and payable unless and until the local child support agency notifies the obligor otherwise. A state agency shall not be required to suspend enforcement of any arrearages as a result of the obligor's request for an administrative determination of arrears, unless the agency receives notification of a suspension pursuant to subdivision (b) of Section 17526.

(b) For purposes of this section, "notice of support delinquency" means a notice issued to a support obligor that includes a specific statement of the amount of delinquent support due and payable.

(c) This section does not require a state or local entity to calculate the amount of a support delinquency, except as otherwise required by law. **Leg.H.** Added Stats 1999 ch 654 §4 (AB 370). Amended Stats 2000 ch 808 §90 (AB 1358), effective September 28, 2000; Stats 2001 ch 755 §16 (SB 943), effective October 12, 2001; Stats 2016 ch 474 §24 (AB 2882), effective January 1, 2017; Stats 2019 ch 115 §158 (AB 1817), effective January 1, 2020.

§17526. Review and judicial determination of arrearages

(a) Upon request of an obligor or obligee, the local child support agency shall review the amount of arrearages alleged in a statement of arrearages that may be submitted to the local child support agency by an applicant for child support enforcement services. The local child support agency shall complete the review in the same manner and pursuant to the same timeframes as a complaint submitted pursuant to Section 17800. In the review, the local child support agency shall consider all evidence and defenses submitted by either parent on the issues of the amount of support paid or owed.

(b) The local child support agency may, in its discretion, suspend enforcement or distribution of arrearages if it believes there is a substantial probability that the result of the administrative review will result in a finding that there are no arrearages.

(c) Any party to an action involving child support enforcement services of the local child support agency may request a judicial determination of arrearages. The party may request an administrative review of the alleged arrearages prior to requesting a judicial determination of arrearages. The local child support agency shall complete the review in the same manner and pursuant to the same timeframes specified in subdivision (a). Any motion to determine arrearages filed with the court shall include a monthly breakdown showing amounts ordered and amounts paid, in addition to any other relevant information.

(d) A county that submits a claim for reimbursement as a state-mandated local program of costs incurred with respect to the administrative review of alleged child support arrearages under this section shall be ineligible for state subventions or, to the extent permitted by federal law, state-administered federal subventions, for child support in the amount of any local costs under this section. **Leg.H.** Added Stats 1999 ch 478 §1 (AB 196). Amended Stats 2001 ch 755 §17 (SB 943), effective October 12, 2001; Stats 2002 ch 927 §6.5 (AB 3032).

§17528. Actions to enforce obligations; Retirement systems

(a) As authorized by subdivision (c) of Section 704.110 of the Code of Civil Procedure, the following actions shall be taken in order to enforce support obligations that are not being met:

(1) Within 18 months of implementation of the California Child Support Enforcement System (CSE), or its replacement as prescribed by former Section 10815 of the Welfare and Institutions Code, and certification of CSE or its replacement by the United States Department of Health and Human Services, the department shall compile a file of all support judgments and orders that are being enforced by local child support agencies pursuant to Section 17400 that have sums overdue by at least 60 days or by an amount equal to 60 days of support.

(2) The file shall contain the name and social security number of the person who owes overdue support, the amount of overdue support as of the date the file is created, the name of the county in which the support obligation is being enforced by the local child support agency, and any other information that is deemed necessary by the department and the Public Employees' Retirement System.

(3) The department shall provide the certified file to the Public Employees' Retirement System for the purpose of matching the names in

the file with members and beneficiaries of the Public Employees' Retirement System that are entitled to receive Public Employees' Retirement System benefits. The department and the Public Employees' Retirement System shall work cooperatively to develop an interface in order to match the names in their respective electronic data processing systems. The interface required to intercept benefits that are payable periodically shall be done as soon as it is technically feasible.

(4) The department shall update the certified file no less than on a monthly basis to add new cases within the local child support agencies or existing cases that become delinquent and to delete persons who are no longer delinquent. The department shall provide the updated file no less than on a monthly basis to the Public Employees' Retirement System.

(5) Information contained in the certified file provided to the Public Employees' Retirement System by the department and the local child support agencies and information provided by the Public Employees' Retirement System to the department shall be used exclusively for child support enforcement purposes and may not be used for any other purpose.

(b) Notwithstanding any other law, the Public Employees' Retirement System shall withhold the amount certified from the benefits and refunds to be distributed to members with overdue support obligations or from benefits to be distributed to beneficiaries with overdue support obligations. If the benefits are payable periodically, the amount withheld pursuant to this section shall not exceed the amount permitted to be withheld for an earnings withholding order for support under Section 706.052 of the Code of Civil Procedure.

(c) The Public Employees' Retirement System shall forward the amounts withheld pursuant to subdivision (b) within 10 days of withholding to the department for distribution to the appropriate county.

(d) On an annual basis, the department shall notify individuals with overdue support obligations that PERS benefits or PERS contribution refunds may be intercepted for the purpose of enforcing family support obligations.

(e) No later than the time of the first withholding, the Public Employees' Retirement System shall send those persons subject to withholding the following:

(1) Notice that the person's benefits or retirement contribution refund have been reduced by payment on a support judgment pursuant to this section.

(2) A form developed by the department that the applicant shall use to request either a review by the local child support agency or a court hearing, as appropriate.

(f) The notice shall include the address and telephone number of the local child support agency that is enforcing the support obligation pursuant to Section 17400, and shall specify that the form requesting either a review by the local child support agency or a court hearing must be received by the local child support agency within 20 days of the date of the notice.

(g) The form shall include instructions that are designed to enable the member or beneficiary to obtain a review or a court hearing as appropriate on their own behalf. The form shall specify that if the member or beneficiary disputes the amount of support arrearages certified by the local child support agency pursuant to this section, the member or beneficiary may request a review by the local child support agency.

(h) The department shall develop procedures that are consistent with this section to be used by each local child support agency in conducting the requested review. The local child support agency shall complete the review in accordance with the procedures developed by the department and shall notify the member or beneficiary of the result of the review within 20 days of receiving the request for review. The notification of review results shall include a request for hearing form and shall inform the member or beneficiary that if the member or beneficiary returns the completed request for hearing form within 20 days of the date of the notice of review results, the local child support agency shall calendar the matter for court review. If the local child support agency cannot complete the review within 20 days, the local child support agency shall calendar the matter for hearing as specified in subdivision (k).

(i) The form specified in subdivision (g) shall also notify the member or beneficiary that the member or beneficiary may request a court hearing to claim an exemption of any benefit not payable periodically by returning the completed form to the local child support agency within 20 days. If the local child support agency receives a timely request for a hearing for a claim of exemption, the local child support agency shall calendar a court hearing. The amount of the exemption, if any, shall be determined by the court in accordance with the procedures set forth in Section 703.070 of the Code of Civil Procedure.

(j) If the local child support agency receives the form requesting either a review by the local child support agency or a court hearing within the 20 days specified in subdivision (f), the local child support agency shall not distribute the amount intercepted until the review by the local child support agency or the court hearing is completed. If the local child support agency determines that all or a portion of the member's or beneficiary's benefits were intercepted in error, or if the court determines that any amount of the benefits are exempt, the local child support agency shall refund any amount determined to be exempt or intercepted in excess of the correct amount to the member or beneficiary within 10 days of determination that a refund is due.

(k) A hearing properly requested pursuant to this section shall be calendared by the local child support agency. The hearing shall be held within 20 days from the date that the local child support agency receives the request for hearing. The local child support agency shall provide notice of the time and place for hearing by first-class mail no later than five days prior to the hearing.

(*l*) This section does not limit any existing rights of the member or beneficiary, including, but not limited to, the right to seek a determination of arrearages or other appropriate relief directly from the court. However, if the procedures of this section are not utilized by the member or beneficiary, the court may not require the local child support agency to refund any money that was distributed to the child support obligee prior to the local child support agency receiving notice of a court determination that a refund is due to the member or beneficiary.

(m) The Department of Child Support Services and the Public Employees' Retirement System shall enter into any agreement necessary to implement this section, which shall include provisions for the department to provide funding to the Public Employees' Retirement System to develop, implement, and maintain the intercept process described in this section.

(n) The Public Employees' Retirement System shall not assess service charges on members or beneficiaries in order to recover any administrative costs resulting from complying with this section. **Leg.H.** Added Stats 1999 ch 478 §1 (AB 196). Amended Stats 2016 ch 474 §25 (AB 2882), effective January 1, 2017; Stats 2019 ch 115 §159 (AB 1817), effective January 1, 2020.

§17530. Enforcement actions taken in error

(a) Notwithstanding any other law, this section applies to any actions taken to enforce a judgment or order for support entered as a result of action filed by the local child support agency pursuant to Section 17400, 17402, or 17404, where it is alleged that the enforcement actions have been taken in error against a person who is not the support obligor named in the judgment or order.

(b) A person claiming that a support enforcement action has been taken against that person, or the person's wages or assets, in error, shall file a claim of mistaken identity with the local child support agency. The claim shall include verifiable information or documentation to establish that the person against whom the enforcement actions have been taken is not the person named in the support order or judgment. The local child support agency shall resolve a claim of mistaken identity submitted pursuant to this section in the same manner and timeframes provided for resolution of a complaint pursuant to Section 17800.

(c) If the local child support agency determines that a claim filed pursuant to this section is meritorious, or if the court enters an order pursuant to Section 17433, the agency shall immediately take the steps necessary to terminate all enforcement activities with respect to the claimant, to return to the claimant any assets seized, to terminate any levying activities or attachment or assignment orders, to release any license renewal or application being withheld pursuant to Section 17520, to return any sums paid by the claimant pursuant to the judgment or order, including sums paid to any federal, state, or local government, but excluding sums paid directly to the support obligee, and to ensure that all other enforcement agencies and entities cease further actions against the claimant. With respect to a claim filed under this section, the local child support agency shall also provide the claimant with a statement certifying that the claimant is not the support obligor named in the support order or judgment, which statement shall be prima facie evidence of the claimant's identity in any subsequent enforcement proceedings or actions with respect to that support order or judgment.

(d) If the local child support agency rejects a claim pursuant to this section, or if the agency, after finding a claim to be meritorious, fails to take any of the remedial steps provided in subdivision (c), the claimant may file an action with the superior court to establish the mistaken identity or to obtain the remedies described in subdivision (c), or both.

(e) Filing a false claim pursuant to this section shall be a misdemeanor. **Leg.H.** Added Stats 1999 ch 653 §18 (AB 380), operative April 1, 2000. Amended Stats 2001 ch 755 §18 (SB 943), effective October 12, 2001; Stats 2019 ch 115 §160 (AB 1817), effective January 1, 2020.

§17531. Case containing summary criminal history

When a local child support agency closes a child support case containing summary criminal history information, the local child support agency shall delete or purge from the file and destroy any documents or information concerning or arising from offenses for or of which the parent has been arrested, charged, or convicted, other than offenses related to the parent's having failed to provide support for minor children, no later than four years and four months, or any other timeframe that is consistent with federal regulations controlling child support records retention, after the date the local child support agency closes the case. **Leg.H.** Added Stats 2000 ch 808 §91 (AB 1358), effective September 28, 2000.

§17540. Time for filing claims

(a)(1) Commencing July 1, 2000, the department shall pay only those county claims for federal or state reimbursement under this division which are filed with the department within nine months of the end of the calendar quarter in which the costs are paid. A claim filed after that time may only be paid if the claim falls within the exceptions set forth in federal law.

(2) The department may change the nine-month limitation specified in paragraph (1), as deemed necessary by the department to comply with federal changes which affect time limits for filing a claim.

(b)(1) The department may waive the time limit imposed by subdivision (a) if the department determines there was good cause for a county's failure to file a claim or claims within the time limit.

(2)(A) For purposes of this subdivision, "good cause" means circumstances which are beyond the county's control, including acts of God and documented action or inaction by the state or federal government.

(B) "Circumstances beyond the county's control" do not include neglect or failure on the part of the county or any of its offices, officers, or employees.

(C) A county shall request a waiver of the time limit imposed by this section for good cause in accordance with regulations adopted and promulgated by the department.

(3) The department's authority to waive the time limit under this subdivision shall be subject to the availability of funds and shall not apply to claims submitted more than 18 months after the end of the calendar quarter in which costs were paid. **Leg.H.** Added Stats 2000 ch 808 §92 (AB 1358), effective September 28, 2000.

§17550. Establishing regulations for compromising obligor parent's liability for public assistance debt in certain cases; Conditions to be met

(a) The Department of Child Support Services, in consultation with the State Department of Social Services, shall establish regulations by which the local child support agency, in any case of separation or desertion of a parent from a child that results in aid under Chapter 2 (commencing with Section 11200) of Part 3 of Division 9 of the Welfare and Institutions Code being granted to the child, may compromise the obligor parent or parents' liability for public assistance debt, including interest thereon, owed to the state where the child for whom public assistance was paid is residing with the obligor parent, and all of the following conditions are met:

(1) The obligor parent establishes one of the following:

(A) The child has been adjudged a dependent of the court under Section 300 of the Welfare and Institutions Code and the child has been reunified with the obligor parent pursuant to a court order.

(B) The child received public assistance while living with a guardian or relative caregiver and the child has been returned to the custody of the obligor parent, provided that the obligor parent for whom the debt compromise is being considered was the parent with whom the child resided prior to the child's placement with the guardian or relative caregiver.

(2) The obligor parent, for whom the debt compromise is being considered, has an income less than 250 percent of the current federal poverty level.

(3) The local child support agency, pursuant to regulations set forth by the department, has determined that the compromise is necessary for the child's support.

(b) Prior to compromising an obligor parent's liability for debt incurred for either AFDC-FC payments provided to a child pursuant to Section 11400 of the Welfare and Institutions Code, or incurred for CalWORKs payments provided on behalf of a child, the local child support agency shall consult with the county child welfare department.

(c) This section does not relieve an obligor, who has not been reunified with their child, of any liability for public assistance debt.

(d) For the purposes of this section, the following definitions apply:

(1) "Guardian" means the legal guardian of the child, who assumed care and control of the child while the child was in the guardian's control, and who is not a biological or adoptive parent.

(2) "Relative caregiver" means a relative as defined in subdivision (c) of Section 11362 of the Welfare and Institutions Code, who assumed primary responsibility for the child while the child was in the relative's care and control, and who is not a biological or adoptive parent.

(e) The department shall promulgate all necessary regulations pursuant to this section on or before October 1, 2002, including regulations that set forth guidelines to be used by the local child support agency when compromising public assistance debt. **Leg.H.** Added Stats 2001 ch 463 §2 (AB 1449). Amended Stats 2019 ch 115 §161 (AB 1817), effective January 1, 2020.

2001 Note: The provisions of Section 17550 of the Family Code, as added by this act, shall be implemented only to the extent that federal financial participation is not reduced for the AFDC-FC program and the CalWORKs program. Stats 2001 ch 463 §6.

§17552. Promulgation of regulations for determining if in best interest of child or nonminor to have case referred to local child support agency

(a)(1) The State Department of Social Services, in consultation with the Department of Child Support Services, shall promulgate regulations by which the county child welfare department, in any case of separation or desertion of a parent or parents from a child that results in foster care assistance payments under Section 11400 of, or a voluntary placement under Section 11401.1 of, or the payments for a minor child placed in the same home as a minor or nonminor dependent parent under Section 11401.4 of, the Welfare and Institutions Code, or CalWORKs payments to a caretaker relative of a child who comes within the jurisdiction of the juvenile court under Section 300, 601, or 602 of the Welfare and Institutions Code, who has been removed from the parental home and placed with the caretaker relative by court order, and who is under the supervision of the county child welfare agency or probation department under Section 11250 of, or Kin-GAP payments under Article 4.5 (commencing with Section 11360) or Article 4.7 (commencing with Section 11385) of, or aid under subdivision (b) of Section 10101 of, the Welfare and Institutions Code, shall determine whether it is in the best interests of the child or nonminor to have the case referred to the local child support agency for child support services. If reunification services are not offered or are terminated, the case may be referred to the local child support agency, unless the child's permanent plan is legal guardianship with a relative who is receiving Kin-GAP and the payment of support by the parent may compromise the stability of the current placement with the related guardian, or the permanent plan is transitional foster care for the nonminor under Section 11403 of the Welfare and Institutions Code. In making the determination, the department regulations shall provide the factors the county child welfare department shall consider, including:

(A) Whether the payment of support by the parent will pose a barrier to the proposed reunification, in that the payment of support will compromise the parent's ability to meet the requirements of the parent's reunification plan.

(B) Whether the payment of support by the parent will pose a barrier to the proposed reunification in that the payment of support will compromise the parent's current or future ability to meet the financial needs of the child.

(2) The department's regulations shall require the county welfare department, in making the determination pursuant to paragraph (1), to

presume that the payment of support by the parent is likely to pose a barrier to the proposed reunification.

(b) The department regulations shall provide that, when the county child welfare department determines that it is not in the best interest of the child to seek a support order against the parent, the county child welfare department shall refrain from referring the case to the local child support agency. The regulations shall define those circumstances in which it is not in the best interest of the child to refer the case to the local child support agency. The regulations shall include the presumption described in paragraph (2) of subdivision (a) that the payment of support by the parent is likely to pose a barrier to the proposed reunification.

(c) The department regulations shall provide, when the county child welfare department determines that it is not in the child's best interest to have the case referred to the local child support agency, the county child welfare department shall review that determination periodically to coincide with the redetermination of AFDC-FC eligibility under Section 11401.5 of, or the CalWORKs eligibility under Section 11265 of, or Kin-GAP eligibility under Article 4.5 (commencing with Section 11360) or Article 4.7 (commencing with Section 11385) of Chapter 2 of Part 3 of Division 9 of, the Welfare and Institutions Code, and shall refer the child's case to the local child support agency upon a determination that, due to a change in the child's circumstances, it is no longer contrary to the child's best interest to have the case referred to the local child support agency.

(d) Notwithstanding any other law, a nonminor dependent, as described in subdivision (v) of Section 11400 of the Welfare and Institutions Code, who is over 19 years of age, is not a child for purposes of referral to the local child support agency for collection or enforcement of child support.

(e) Notwithstanding any other law, a minor or a nonminor dependent, as defined in subdivision (v) of Section 11400 of the Welfare and Institutions Code, who has a minor child placed in the same licensed or approved facility pursuant to Section 11401.4 of the Welfare and Institutions Code is not a parent for purposes of referral to the local child support agency for collection or enforcement of child support.

(f) The State Department of Social Services shall revise its regulations to implement the changes made by the act that added this subdivision on or before October 1, 2023. **Leg.H.** Added Stats 2001 ch 463 §3 (AB 1449). Amended Stats 2005 ch 198 §1 (AB 1743), effective January 1, 2006; Stats 2010 ch 559 §2 (AB 12), effective January 1, 2011; Stats 2011 ch 459 §1 (AB 212), effective October 4, 2011; Stats 2012 ch 846 §2 (AB 1712), effective January 1, 2013; Stats 2019 ch 115 §162 (AB 1817), effective January 1, 2020; Stats 2022 ch 755 §2 (AB 1686), effective January 1, 2023; Stats 2023 ch 131 §61 (AB 1754), effective January 1, 2024.

2012 Note: This act is titled and may be cited as 2011 Realignment Legislation. Stats 2012 ch 846 (AB 1712) §1.

2010 Note: This act shall be known, and may be cited, as the "California Fostering Connections to Success Act." Stats 2010 ch 559 (AB 12) §1.

2001 Note: The provisions of Section 17552 of the Family Code, as added by this act, shall be implemented only to the extent that federal financial participation is not reduced for the AFDC-FC program and the CalWORKs program. Stats 2001 ch 463 §6.

§17555. Appropriations augmenting funding for local child support agencies subject to specified requirements

(a) Any appropriation made available in the annual Budget Act for the purposes of augmenting funding for local child support agencies in the furtherance of their revenue collection responsibilities shall be subject to all of the following requirements:

(1) Each local child support agency shall submit to the department an early intervention plan with all components to take effect upon receipt of their additional allocation as a result of this proposal.

(2) Funds shall be distributed to counties based on their performance on the following two federal performance measures:

(A) Measure 3: Collections on Current Support.

(B) Measure 4: Cases with Collections on Arrears.

(3) A local child support agency shall be required to use and ensure that 100 percent of the new funds allocated are dedicated to maintaining caseworker staffing levels in order to stabilize child support collections.

(4) At the end of each fiscal year that this augmentation is in effect, the department shall provide a report on the cost-effectiveness of this augmentation, including an assessment of caseload changes over time.

(b) It is the intent of the Legislature to review the results of this augmentation and the level of related appropriation during the legislative budget review process. **Leg.H.** Added Stats 2009 4th Ex Sess 2009–2010 ch 4 §2 (ABX4-4), effective July 28, 2009. Amended Stats 2010 ch 725 §3 (AB 1612), effective October 19, 2010; Stats 2012 ch 728 §38 (SB 71), effective January 1, 2013.

§17556. Annual status report to Legislature; Required information

On or before March 1, 2019, and annually thereafter, the department shall submit a report to the Legislature providing information on the status of all of the following:

(a) Case-to-staff ratios for each local child support agency.

(b) Collections to families and recoupment collections to county, state, and federal governmental agencies.

(c) Cost avoidance benefits.

(d) The number of families served by the child support program. **Leg.H.** Added Stats 2018 ch 35 §2 (AB 1811), effective June 27, 2018.

§17560. Program establishing arrears collection enhancement process; Acceptance of compromise offers; Rescission of offers; Conditions; Finality; Compliance with federal law; Uniform application

(a) The department shall establish and operate a statewide compromise of arrears program pursuant to which the department may accept offers in compromise of child support arrears and interest accrued thereon owed to the state for reimbursement of aid paid pursuant to Chapter 2 (commencing with Section 11200) of Part 3 of Division 9 of the Welfare and Institutions Code. The program shall operate uniformly across California and shall take into consideration the needs of the children subject to the child support order and the obligor's ability to pay.

(b) If the obligor owes current child support, the offer in compromise shall require the obligor to be in compliance with the current support order for a set period of time before any arrears and interest accrued thereon may be compromised.

(c) Absent a finding of good cause, or a determination by the director that it is in the best interest of the state to do otherwise, any offer in compromise entered into pursuant to this section shall be rescinded, all compromised liabilities shall be reestablished notwithstanding any statute of limitations that otherwise may be applicable, and no portion of the amount offered in compromise may be refunded, if either of the following occurs:

(1) The department or local child support agency determines that the obligor did any of the following acts regarding the offer in compromise:

(A) Concealed from the department or local child support agency any income, assets, or other property belonging to the obligor or any reasonably anticipated receipt of income, assets, or other property.

(B) Intentionally received, withheld, destroyed, mutilated, or falsified any information, document, or record, or intentionally made any false statement, relating to the financial conditions of the obligor.

(2) The obligor fails to comply with any of the terms and conditions of the offer in compromise.

(d) Pursuant to subdivision (k) of Section 17406, in no event may the administrator, director, or director's designee within the department, accept an offer in compromise of any child support arrears owed directly to the custodial party unless that party consents to the offer in compromise in writing and participates in the agreement. Prior to giving consent, the custodial party shall be provided with a clear written explanation of the rights with respect to child support arrears owed to the custodial party and the compromise thereof.

(e) Subject to the requirements of this section, the director shall delegate to the administrator of a local child support agency the authority to compromise an amount of child support arrears up to five thousand dollars ($5,000), and may delegate additional authority to compromise up to an amount determined by the director to support the effective administration of the offers in compromise program.

(f) For an amount to be compromised under this section, the following conditions shall exist:

(1)(A) The administrator, director or director's designee within the department determines that acceptance of an offer in compromise is in the best interest of the state and that the compromise amount equals or exceeds what the state can expect to collect for reimbursement of aid paid pursuant to Chapter 2 (commencing with Section 11200) of Part 3 of

Division 9 of the Welfare and Institutions Code in the absence of the compromise, based on the obligor's ability to pay.

(B) Acceptance of an offer in compromise shall be deemed to be in the best interest of the state, absent a finding of good cause to the contrary, with regard to arrears that accrued as a result of a decrease in income when an obligor was a reservist or member of the National Guard, was activated to United States military service, and failed to modify the support order to reflect the reduction in income. Good cause to find that the compromise is not in the best interest of the state shall include circumstances in which the service member's failure to seek, or delay in seeking, the modification were not reasonable under the circumstances faced by the service member. The director, no later than 90 days after the effective date of the act adding this subparagraph, shall establish rules that compromise, at a minimum, the amount of support that would not have accrued had the order been modified to reflect the reduced income earned during the period of active military service.

(2) Any other terms and conditions that the director establishes that may include, but may not be limited to, paying current support in a timely manner, making lump-sum payments, and paying arrears in exchange for compromise of interest owed.

(3) The obligor shall provide evidence of income and assets, including, but not limited to, wage stubs, tax returns, and bank statements as necessary to establish all of the following:

(A) That the amount set forth in the offer in compromise of arrears owed is the most that can be expected to be paid or collected from the obligor's present assets or income.

(B) That the obligor does not have reasonable prospects of acquiring increased income or assets that would enable the obligor to satisfy a greater amount of the child support arrears than the amount offered, within a reasonable period of time.

(C) That the obligor has not withheld payment of child support in anticipation of the offers in compromise program.

(g) A determination by the administrator, director or the director's designee within the department that it would not be in the best interest of the state to accept or rescind an offer in compromise in satisfaction of child support arrears shall be final and not subject to the provisions of Chapter 5 (commencing with Section 17800) of Division 17, or subject to judicial review.

(h) Any offer in compromise entered into pursuant to this section shall be filed with the appropriate court. The local child support agency shall notify the court if the compromise is rescinded pursuant to subdivision (c).

(i) Any compromise of child support arrears pursuant to this section shall maximize to the greatest extent possible the state's share of the federal performance incentives paid pursuant to the Child Support Performance and Incentive Act of 1998 and shall comply with federal law.

(j) The department shall ensure uniform application of this section across the state. **Leg.H.** Added Stats 2003 ch 225 §6 (AB 1752), effective August 11, 2003. Amended Stats 2005 ch 154 §5 (SB 1082), effective August 30, 2005; Stats 2006 ch 75 §8 (AB 1808), effective July 12, 2006; Stats 2008 ch 759 §16 (AB 1279), effective September 30, 2008.

2008 Note: Stats 2008 ch 759 (AB 1279) §16 purported to amend this section. However, it was repealed by its own provisions on July 1, 2008. Therefore, this section was not in effect from July 1, 2008 until September 30, 2008. On the advice of Legislative Counsel, the Publisher has treated the legislative amendment as an enactment.

§17561. Joint report by Office of Chief Information Officer and Department of Child Support Services regarding implementation of California Child Support Automation System [Repealed]

Leg.H. Added Stats 2009 4th Ex Sess 2009–2010 ch 4 §3 (ABX4-4), effective July 28, 2009. Repealed Stats 2024 ch 46 §1 (AB 161), effective July 2, 2024.

Prior Law Former Fam C §17561, related to joint report by office of chief information officer and department of child support services regarding implementation of California child support automation system, was added Stats 2009 4th Ex Sess 2009–2010 ch 4 §3 (ABX4-4), effective July 28, 2009.

ARTICLE 3
Program Compliance

Legislative findings and declarations; County compilation of data; Regulations; Reports [Operative term contingent]. §17600.
Provision of data; Display of data on Web site. §17601.

Performance standards; Phases in statewide process; Reports. §17602.
Sanctions for agency's failure to comply. §17604.

§17600. Legislative findings and declarations; County compilation of data; Regulations; Reports [Operative term contingent]

(a) The Legislature finds and declares all of the following:

(1) The Legislative Analyst has found that county child support enforcement programs provide a net increase in revenues to the state.

(2) The state has a fiscal interest in ensuring that county child support enforcement programs perform efficiently.

(3) The state does not provide information to counties on child support enforcement programs, based on common denominators that would facilitate comparison of program performance.

(4) Providing this information would allow county officials to monitor program performance and to make appropriate modifications to improve program efficiency.

(5) This information is required for effective management of the child support program.

(b) Except as provided in this subdivision commencing with the 1998-99 fiscal year, and for each fiscal year thereafter, each county that is participating in the state incentive program described in Section 17704 shall provide to the department, and the department shall compile from this county child support information, monthly and annually, all of the following performance-based data, as established by the federal incentive funding system, provided that the department may revise the data required by this paragraph in order to conform to the final federal incentive system data definitions:

(1) One of the following data relating to paternity establishment, as required by the department, provided that the department shall require all counties to report on the same measurement:

(A) The total number of children in the caseload governed by Part D (commencing with Section 451) of Title IV of the federal Social Security Act (42 U.S.C. Sec. 651 et seq.), as of the end of the federal fiscal year, who were born to unmarried parents for whom paternity was established or acknowledged, and the total number of children in that caseload, as of the end of the preceding federal fiscal year, who were born to unmarried parents.

(B) The total number of minor children who were born in the state to unmarried parents for whom paternity was established or acknowledged during a federal fiscal year, and the total number of children in the state born to unmarried parents during the preceding calendar year.

(2) The number of cases governed by Part D (commencing with Section 451) of Title IV of the federal Social Security Act (42 U.S.C. Sec. 651 et seq.) during the federal fiscal year and the total number of those cases with support orders.

(3) The total dollars collected during the federal fiscal year for current support in cases governed by Part D (commencing with Section 451) of Title IV of the federal Social Security Act (42 U.S.C. Sec. 651 et seq.) and the total number of dollars owing for current support during that federal fiscal year in cases governed by those provisions.

(4) The total number of cases for the federal fiscal year governed by Part D (commencing with Section 451) of Title IV of the federal Social Security Act (42 U.S.C. Sec. 651 et seq.) in which payment was being made toward child support arrearages and the total number of cases for that fiscal year governed by these federal provisions that had child support arrearages.

(5) The total number of dollars collected and expended during a federal fiscal year in cases governed by Part D (commencing with Section 451) of Title IV of the federal Social Security Act (42 U.S.C. Sec. 651 et seq.).

(6) The total amount of child support dollars collected during a federal fiscal year, and, if and when required by federal law, the amount of these collections broken down by collections distributed on behalf of current recipients of federal Temporary Assistance for Needy Families block grant funds or federal foster care funds, on behalf of former recipients of federal Temporary Assistance for Needy Families block grant funds or federal foster care funds, or on behalf of persons who have never been recipients of these federal funds.

(c) In addition to the information required by subdivision (b), the department shall collect, on a monthly basis, from each county that is participating in the state incentive program described in Section 17704, information on the local child support agency for each federal fiscal year, and shall report semiannually on all of the following performance measurements:

(1) The percentage of cases with collections of current support. This percentage shall be calculated by dividing the number of cases with an order for current support by the number of those cases with collections of current support. The number of cases with support collected shall include only the number of cases actually receiving a collection, not the number of payments received. Cases with a medical support order that do not have an order for current support may not be counted.

(2) The average amount collected per case for all cases with collections.

(3) The percentage of cases that had a support order established during the period. A support order shall be counted as established only when the appropriate court has issued an order for child support, including an order for temporary child support, or an order for medical support.

(4) The total cost of administering the local child support agency, including the federal, state, and county share of the costs, and the federal and state incentives received by each county. The total cost of administering the program shall be broken down by the following:

(A) The direct costs of the program, broken down further by total employee salaries and benefits, a list of the number of employees broken down into at least the following categories: attorneys, administrators, caseworkers, investigators, and clerical support; contractor costs; space charges; and payments to other county agencies. Employee salaries and numbers need only be reported in the annual report.

(B) The indirect costs, showing all overhead charges.

(5) In addition, the local child support agency shall report monthly on measurements developed by the department that provide data on the following:

(A) Locating obligors.

(B) Obtaining and enforcing medical support.

(C) Providing customer service.

(D) Any other measurements that the director determines to be an appropriate determination of a local child support agency's performance.

(6) A county may apply for an exemption from any or all of the reporting requirements of this subdivision for a fiscal year by submitting an application for the exemption to the department at least three months prior to the commencement of the fiscal year or quarter for which the exemption is sought. A county shall provide a separate justification for each data element under this subdivision for which the county is seeking an exemption and the cost to the county of providing the data. The department may not grant an exemption for more than one year. The department may grant a single exemption only if both of the following conditions are met:

(A) The county cannot compile the data being sought through its existing automated system or systems.

(B) The county cannot compile the data being sought through manual means or through an enhanced automated system or systems without significantly harming the child support collection efforts of the county.

(d) After implementation of the statewide automated system, in addition to the information required by subdivision (b), the Department of Child Support Services shall collect, on a monthly basis, from each county that is participating in the state incentive program described in Section 17704, information on the county child support enforcement program beginning with the 1998-99 fiscal year or a later fiscal year, as appropriate, and for each subsequent fiscal year, and shall report semiannually on all of the following measurements:

(1) For each of the following support collection categories, the number of cases with support collected shall include only the number of cases actually receiving a collection, not the number of payments received.

(A)(i) The number of cases with collections for current support.

(ii) The number of cases with arrears collections only.

(iii) The number of cases with both current support and arrears collections.

(B) For cases with current support only due:

(i) The number of cases in which the full amount of current support owed was collected.

(ii) The number of cases in which some amount of current support, but less than the full amount of support owed, was collected.

(iii) The number of cases in which no amount of support owed was collected.

(C) For cases in which arrears only were owed:

(i) The number of cases in which all arrears owed were collected.

(ii) The number of cases in which some amount of arrears, but less than the full amount of arrears owed, was collected.

(iii) The number of cases in which no amount of arrears owed was collected.

(D) For cases in which both current support and arrears are owed:

(i) The number of cases in which the full amount of current support and arrears owed was collected.

(ii) The number of cases in which some amount of current support and arrears, but less than the full amount of support owed, was collected.

(iii) The number of cases in which no amount of support owed was collected.

(E) The total number of cases in which an amount was due for current support only.

(F) The total number of cases in which an amount was due for both current support and arrears.

(G) The total number of cases in which an amount was due for arrears only.

(H) For cases with current support due, the number of cases without orders for medical support and the number of cases with an order for medical support.

(2) The number of alleged fathers or obligors who were served with a summons and complaint to establish paternity or a support order, and the number of alleged fathers or obligors for whom it is required that paternity or a support order be established. In order to be counted under this paragraph, the alleged father or obligor shall be successfully served with process. An alleged father shall be counted under this paragraph only once if served with process simultaneously for both a paternity and a support order proceeding for the same child or children. For purposes of this paragraph, a support order shall include a medical support order.

(3) The number of new asset seizures or successful initial collections on a wage assignment for purposes of child support collection. For purposes of this paragraph, a collection made on a wage assignment shall be counted only once for each wage assignment issued.

(4) The number of children requiring paternity establishment and the number of children for whom paternity has been established during the period. Paternity may only be established once for each child. A child for whom paternity is not at issue shall not be counted in the number of children for whom paternity has been established. For this purpose, paternity is not at issue if the parents were married and neither parent challenges paternity or a voluntary paternity declaration has been executed by the parents prior to the local child support agency obtaining the case and neither parent challenges paternity.

(5) The number of cases requiring that a support order be established and the number of cases that had a support order established during the period. A support order shall be counted as established only when the appropriate court has issued an order for child support, including an order for temporary child support, or an order for medical support.

(6) The total cost of administering the local child support agency, including the federal, state, and county share of the costs and the federal and state incentives received by each county. The total cost of administering the program shall be broken down by the following:

(A) The direct costs of the program, broken down further by total employee salaries and benefits, a list of the number of employees broken down into at least the following categories: attorneys, administrators, caseworkers, investigators, and clerical support; contractor costs; space charges; and payments to other county agencies. Employee salaries and numbers need only be reported in the annual report.

(B) The indirect costs, showing all overhead charges.

(7) The total child support collections due, broken down by current support, interest on arrears, and principal, and the total child support collections that have been collected, broken down by current support, interest on arrears, and principal.

(8) The actual case status for all cases in the county child support enforcement program. Each case shall be reported in one case status only. If a case falls within more than one status category, it shall be counted in the first status category of the list set forth below in which it qualifies. The following shall be the case status choices:

(A) No support order, location of obligor parent required.

(B) No support order, alleged obligor parent located and paternity required.

(C) No support order, location and paternity not at issue but support order must be established.

(D) Support order established with current support obligation and obligor is in compliance with support obligation.

(E) Support order established with current support obligation, obligor is in arrears, and location of obligor is necessary.

(F) Support order established with current support obligation, obligor is in arrears, and location of obligor's assets is necessary.

(G) Support order established with current support obligation, obligor is in arrears, and no location of obligor or obligor's assets is necessary.

(H) Support order established with current support obligation, obligor is in arrears, the obligor is located, but the local child support agency has established satisfactorily that the obligor has no income or assets and no ability to earn.

(I) Support order established with current support obligation and arrears, obligor is paying the current support and is paying some or all of the interest on the arrears, but is paying no principal.

(J) Support order established for arrears only and obligor is current in repayment obligation.

(K) Support order established for arrears only, obligor is not current in arrears repayment schedule, and location of obligor is required.

(L) Support order established for arrears only, obligor is not current in arrears repayment schedule, and location of obligor's assets is required.

(M) Support order established for arrears only, obligor is not current in arrears repayment schedule, and no location of obligor or obligor's assets is required.

(N) Support order established for arrears only, obligor is not current in arrears repayment, and the obligor is located, but the local child support agency has established satisfactorily that the obligor has no income or assets and no ability to earn.

(O) Support order established for arrears only and obligor is repaying some or all of the interest, but no principal.

(P) Other, if necessary, to be defined in the regulations promulgated under subdivision (e).

(e) Upon implementation of the statewide automated system, or at the time that the department determines that compliance with this subdivision is possible, whichever is earlier, each county that is participating in the state incentive program described in Section 17704 shall collect and report, and the department shall compile for each participating county, information on the county child support program in each fiscal year, all of the following data, in a manner that facilitates comparison of counties and the entire state, except that the department may eliminate or modify the requirement to report any data mandated to be reported pursuant to this subdivision if the department determines that the local child support agencies are unable to accurately collect and report the information or that collecting and reporting of the data by the local child support agencies will be onerous:

(1) The number of alleged obligors or fathers who receive CalWORKs benefits, CalFresh benefits, and Medi-Cal benefits.

(2) The number of obligors or alleged fathers who are in state prison or county jail.

(3) The number of obligors or alleged fathers who do not have a social security number.

(4) The number of obligors or alleged fathers whose address is unknown.

(5) The number of obligors or alleged fathers whose complete name, consisting of at least a first and last name, is not known by the local child support agency.

(6) The number of obligors or alleged fathers who filed a tax return with the Franchise Tax Board in the last year for which a data match is available.

(7) The number of obligors or alleged fathers who have no income reported to the Employment Development Department during the third quarter of the fiscal year.

(8) The number of obligors or alleged fathers who have income between one dollar ($1) and five hundred dollars ($500) reported to the Employment Development Department during the third quarter of the fiscal year.

(9) The number of obligors or alleged fathers who have income between five hundred one dollars ($501) and one thousand five hundred dollars ($1,500) reported to the Employment Development Department during the third quarter of the fiscal year.

(10) The number of obligors or alleged fathers who have income between one thousand five hundred one dollars ($1,501) and two thousand five hundred dollars ($2,500) reported to the Employment Development Department during the third quarter of the fiscal year.

(11) The number of obligors or alleged fathers who have income between two thousand five hundred one dollars ($2,501) and three thousand five hundred dollars ($3,500) reported to the Employment Development Department during the third quarter of the fiscal year.

(12) The number of obligors or alleged fathers who have income between three thousand five hundred one dollars ($3,501) and four thousand five hundred dollars ($4,500) reported to the Employment Development Department during the third quarter of the fiscal year.

(13) The number of obligors or alleged fathers who have income between four thousand five hundred one dollars ($4,501) and five thousand five hundred dollars ($5,500) reported to the Employment Development Department during the third quarter of the fiscal year.

(14) The number of obligors or alleged fathers who have income between five thousand five hundred one dollars ($5,501) and six thousand five hundred dollars ($6,500) reported to the Employment Development Department during the third quarter of the fiscal year.

(15) The number of obligors or alleged fathers who have income between six thousand five hundred one dollars ($6,501) and seven thousand five hundred dollars ($7,500) reported to the Employment Development Department during the third quarter of the fiscal year.

(16) The number of obligors or alleged fathers who have income between seven thousand five hundred one dollars ($7,501) and nine thousand dollars ($9,000) reported to the Employment Development Department during the third quarter of the fiscal year.

(17) The number of obligors or alleged fathers who have income exceeding nine thousand dollars ($9,000) reported to the Employment Development Department during the third quarter of the fiscal year.

(18) The number of obligors or alleged fathers who have two or more employers reporting earned income to the Employment Development Department during the third quarter of the fiscal year.

(19) The number of obligors or alleged fathers who receive unemployment benefits during the third quarter of the fiscal year.

(20) The number of obligors or alleged fathers who receive state disability benefits during the third quarter of the fiscal year.

(21) The number of obligors or alleged fathers who receive workers' compensation benefits during the third quarter of the fiscal year.

(22) The number of obligors or alleged fathers who receive Social Security Disability Insurance benefits during the third quarter of the fiscal year.

(23) The number of obligors or alleged fathers who receive Supplemental Security Income/State Supplementary Program for the Aged, Blind and Disabled benefits during the third quarter of the fiscal year.

(f) The department, in consultation with the Legislative Analyst's Office, the Judicial Council, the California Family Support Council, and child support advocates, shall develop regulations to ensure that all local child support agencies report the data required by this section uniformly and consistently throughout California.

(g) For each federal fiscal year, the department shall provide the information for all participating counties to each member of a county board of supervisors, county executive officer, local child support agency, and the appropriate policy committees and fiscal committees of the Legislature on or before June 30, of each fiscal year. The department shall provide data semiannually, based on the federal fiscal year, on or before December 31, of each year. The department shall present the information in a manner that facilitates comparison of county performance.

(h) For purposes of this section, "case" means a noncustodial parent, whether mother, father, or putative father, who is, or eventually may be, obligated under law for support of a child or children. For purposes of this definition, a noncustodial parent shall be counted once for each family that has a dependent child they may be obligated to support.

(i) This section shall be operative only for as long as Section 17704 requires participating counties to report data to the department. **Leg.H.** Added Stats 1999 ch 478 §1 (AB 196). Amended Stats 1999 ch 480 §20 (SB 542); Stats 2002 ch 927 §7 (AB 3032); Stats 2003 ch 308 §4 (AB 738); Stats 2004 ch 183 §96 (AB 3082); Stats 2011 ch 227 §5 (AB 1400), effective January 1, 2012; Stats 2019 ch 115 §163 (AB 1817), effective January 1, 2020.

§17601. Provision of data; Display of data on Web site

The department shall provide to the Legislature actual performance data on child support collections within 60 days of the end of each quarter. This data shall include all comparative data for managing program performance currently provided to local child support agencies, including national, state, and local performance data, as available. The department shall prominently post the data on its Web site, and shall require all local child support agency Web sites to prominently post a link to the state Web site. The department shall update the Legislature during the annual budget subcommittee hearing process, commencing in 2008, on the state and local progress on child support federal performance measures and collections. **Leg.H.** Added Stats 2007 ch 177 §1 (SB 84), effective August 24, 2007.

§17602. Performance standards; Phases in statewide process; Reports

(a) The department shall adopt the federal minimum standards as the baseline standard of performance for the local child support agencies and work in consultation with the local child support agencies to develop program performance targets on an annual federal fiscal year basis. The performance measures shall include, at a minimum, the federal performance measures and the state performance measures, as described in subdivision (c) of Section 17600. The program performance targets shall represent ongoing improvement in the performance measures for each local child support agency, as well as the department's statewide performance level.

(b) In determining the performance measures in subdivision (a), the department shall consider the total amount of uncollected child support arrearages that are realistically collectible. The director shall analyze, in consultation with local child support agencies and child support advocates, the current amount of uncollected child support arrearages statewide and in each county to determine the amount of child support that may realistically be collected. The director shall consider, in conducting the analysis, factors that may influence collections, including demographic factors such as welfare caseload, levels of poverty and unemployment, rates of incarceration of obligors, and age of delinquencies. The director shall use this analysis to establish program priorities as provided in paragraph (7) of subdivision (b) of Section 17306.

(c) The department shall use the performance-based data, and the criteria for that data, as set forth in Section 17600 to determine a local child support agency's performance measures for the quarter.

(d) The director shall adopt a three phase process to be used statewide when a local child support agency is out of compliance with the performance standards adopted pursuant to subdivision (a), or the director determines that the local child support agency is failing in a substantial manner to comply with any provision of the state plan, the provisions of this code, the requirements of federal law, the regulations of the department, or the cooperative agreement. The director shall adopt policies as to the implementation of each phase, including requirements for measurement of progress and improvement, which shall be met as part of the performance improvement plan specified in paragraphs (1) and (2), in order to avoid implementation of the next phase of compliance. The director shall not implement any of these phases until July 1, 2001, or until six months after a local child support agency has completed its transition from the office of the district attorney to the new county department of child support services, whichever is later. The phases shall include the following:

(1) Phase I: Development of a performance improvement plan that is prepared jointly by the local child support agency and the department, subject to the department's final approval. The plan shall provide performance expectations and goals for achieving compliance with the state plan and other state and federal laws and regulations that must be reviewed and assessed within specific timeframes in order to avoid execution of Phase II.

(2) Phase II: Onsite investigation, evaluation, and oversight of the local child support agency by the department. The director shall appoint program monitoring teams to make site visits, conduct educational and training sessions, and help the local child support agency identify and attack problem areas. The program monitoring teams shall evaluate all aspects of the functions and performance of the local child support agency, including compliance with state and federal laws and regulations. Based on these investigations and evaluations, the program monitoring team shall develop a final performance improvement plan and shall oversee implementation of all recommendations made in the plan. The local child support agency shall adhere to all recommendations made by the program monitoring team. The plan shall provide performance expectations and compliance goals that must be reviewed and assessed within specific timeframes in order to avoid execution of Phase III.

(3) Phase III: The director shall assume, either directly or through agreement with another entity, responsibility for the management of the child and spousal support enforcement program in the county, until the local child support agency provides reasonable assurances to the director of its intention and ability to comply. During the period of state management responsibility, the director or an authorized representative shall have all of the powers and responsibilities of the local child support agency concerning the administration of the program. The local child support agency shall be responsible for providing any funds necessary for the continued operation of the program. If the local child support agency fails or refuses to provide these funds, including a sufficient amount to reimburse any and all costs incurred by the department in managing the program, the Controller may deduct an amount certified by the director as necessary for the continued operation of the program by the department from any state or federal funds payable to the county for any purpose.

(e) The director shall report in writing to the Legislature semiannually, beginning July 1, 2001, on the status of the state child support enforcement program. The director shall submit data semiannually to the Legislature, the Governor, and the public, on the progress of all local child support agencies in each performance measure, including identification of the local child support agencies that are out of compliance, the performance measures that they have failed to satisfy, and the performance improvement plan that is being taken for each. **Leg.H.** Added Stats 1999 ch 478 §1 (AB 196). Amended Stats 1999 ch 480 §21 (SB 542); Stats 2002 ch 927 §8 (AB 3032); Stats 2003 ch 308 §5 (AB 738); Stats 2019 ch 115 §164 (AB 1817), effective January 1, 2020.

§17604. Sanctions for agency's failure to comply

(a)(1) If at any time the director considers any public agency, that is required by law, by delegation of the department, or by cooperative agreement to perform functions relating to the state plan for securing child and spousal support and determining paternity, to be failing in a substantial manner to comply with any provision of the state plan, the director shall put that agency on written notice to that effect.

(2) The state plan concerning spousal support shall apply only to spousal support included in a child support order.

(3) In this chapter the term spousal support shall include support for a former spouse.

(b) After receiving notice, the public agency shall have 45 days to make a showing to the director of full compliance or set forth a compliance plan that the director finds to be satisfactory.

(c) If the director determines that there is a failure on the part of that public agency to comply with the provisions of the state plan, or to set forth a compliance plan that the director finds to be satisfactory, or if the state certifies to the director that the public agency is not in conformity with applicable merit system standards under Part 2.5 (commencing with Section 19800) of Division 5 of Title 2 of the Government Code, and that sanctions are necessary to secure compliance, the director shall withhold part or all of state and federal funds, including incentive funds, from that public agency until the public agency shall make a showing to the director of full compliance.

(d) After sanctions have been invoked pursuant to subdivision (c), if the director determines that there remains a failure on the part of the public agency to comply with the provisions of the state plan, the director may remove that public agency from performing any part or all of the functions relating to the state plan.

(e) In the event of any other audit or review that results in the reduction or modification of federal funding for the program under Part D (commencing with Section 652) of Subchapter IV of Title 42 of the United States Code, the sanction shall be assessed against those counties specifically cited in the federal findings in the amount cited in those findings.

(f) The department shall establish a process whereby any county assessed a portion of any sanction may appeal the department's decision.

(g) Nothing in this section shall be construed as relieving the board of supervisors of the responsibility to provide funds necessary for the continued operation of the state plan as required by law. **Leg.H.** Added

Stats 1999 ch 478 §1 (AB 196). Amended Stats 1999 ch 480 §21.5 (SB 542); Stats 2000 ch 808 §93 (AB 1358), effective September 28, 2000; Stats 2013 ch 427 §1 (AB 1062), effective January 1, 2014.

ARTICLE 4
Program Costs

Quality assurance and performance improvement program established; Minimum requirements. §17701.
Assessment of county's compliance. §17702.
Child Support Collections Recovery Fund created. §17702.5.
Child Support Services Advance Fund. §17703.
State child support incentive. §17704.
Requirements for participants in incentive program. §17708.
Administrative costs. §17710.
Costs of child support commissioners. §17712.
Excess funds accumulated. §17714.

§17700. [Section repealed 2002]

Leg.H. Added Stats 1999 ch 480 §22 (SB 542). Repealed Stats 2002 ch 927 §9 (AB 3032). The repealed section related to legislative intent with respect to allocating funds to counties, the use of funds, and methods for counties to obtain funds.

§17701. Quality assurance and performance improvement program established; Minimum requirements

(a) There is established within California's child support program a quality assurance and performance improvement program, pursuant to which local child support agencies, in partnership with the Department of Child Support Services, shall monitor and measure program performance and compliance, and ensure the implementation of actions necessary to meet state and federal requirements and to continuously improve the quality of child support program services.

(b) Under the direction and oversight of the department, each local child support agency shall implement a quality assurance and performance improvement program that shall include, at a minimum, all of the following:

(1) An annual planning process that incorporates statewide standards and requirements, and establishes local performance goals that the department and local agency agree are appropriate.

(2) The inclusion of local performance goals and other performance-related measures in the local child support agency's Plan of Cooperation agreement with the department.

(3) Implementation of actions necessary to promote the delivery of enhanced program services and improved performance.

(4) An ongoing self-assessment process that evaluates progress in achieving performance improvement and compliance with program requirements.

(5) Regular and ongoing oversight by the department, including onsite reviews and the provision of technical assistance.

(c) The department shall promulgate regulations to implement this section. **Leg.H.** Added Stats 2003 ch 308 §6 (AB 738).

§17702. Assessment of county's compliance

(a) The department shall assess, at least once every three years, each county's compliance with federal and state child support laws and regulations in effect for the time period being reviewed, using a statistically valid sample of cases. Counties found to be out of compliance shall be assessed annually, until they are found to be in compliance. The information for the assessment shall be based on reviews conducted and reports produced by either state or county staff, as determined by the department.

In addition, in order to meet federal self-assessment requirements, the department shall conduct an annual assessment of the state's compliance, using a statistically valid statewide sample of cases.

(b) A county shall be eligible for the state incentives under Section 17704 only if the department determines that the county is in compliance with all federal and state laws and regulations or if the county has a corrective action plan in place that has been certified by the department pursuant to this subdivision. If a county is determined not to be in compliance the county shall develop and submit a corrective action plan to the department. The department shall certify a corrective action plan if the department determines that the plan will put the county into compliance with federal and state laws and regulations. A county shall be eligible for state incentives under Section 17704 only for any quarter the county remains in compliance with a corrective action plan that has been certified by the department.

(c) Counties under a corrective action plan shall be assessed on a quarterly basis until the department determines that they are in compliance with federal and state child support program requirements. **Leg.H.** Added Stats 1999 ch 478 §1 (AB 196). Amended Stats 2003 ch 308 §7 (AB 738).

§17702.5. Child Support Collections Recovery Fund created

(a) The Child Support Collections Recovery Fund is hereby created in the State Treasury, and shall be administered by the department for the purposes specified in subdivision (c).

(b) Except as otherwise provided in this section, the fund shall consist of both of the following:

(1) All public moneys transferred by public agencies to the department for deposit into the fund, as permitted under Section 304.30 of Title 45 of the Code of Federal Regulations or any other applicable federal statutes.

(2) Any interest that accrues on amounts in the fund.

(c) Upon appropriation by the Legislature, all moneys in the fund shall be used to make payments or advances to local child support agencies of the federal share of administrative payments for costs incurred pursuant to this article.

(d) Upon repeal of this section, the Legislature intends that any moneys remaining in the fund shall be returned to the federal agency that provides federal financial participation to the department. **Leg.H.** Added Stats 2001 ch 111 §7 (AB 429), effective July 30, 2001.

§17703. Child Support Services Advance Fund

(a) A revolving fund in the State Treasury is hereby created to be known as the Child Support Services Advance Fund. All moneys deposited into the fund are for the purpose of making a consolidated payment or advance to counties, state agencies, or other governmental entities, comprised of the state and federal share of costs associated with the programs administered by the Department of Child Support Services, inclusive of the payment of refunds. In addition, the fund may be used for the purpose of making a consolidated payment to a payee, comprised of the state and federal shares of local assistance costs associated with the programs administered by the Department of Child Support Services.

(b) Payments or advances of funds to counties, state agencies, or other governmental agencies and other payees doing business with the state that are properly chargeable to appropriations or other funds in the State Treasury, may be made by a Controller's warrant drawn against the Child Support Services Advance Fund. For every warrant so issued, a remittance advice shall be issued by the Department of Child Support Services to identify the purposes and amounts for which it was drawn.

(c) The amounts to be transferred to the Child Support Services Advance Fund at any time shall be determined by the department, and, upon order of the Controller, shall be transferred from the funds and appropriations otherwise properly chargeable.

(d) Refunds of amounts disbursed from the Child Support Services Advance Fund shall, on order of the Controller, be deposited in the Child Support Services Advance Fund, and, on order of the Controller, shall be transferred therefrom to the funds and appropriations from which those amounts were originally derived. Claims for amounts erroneously deposited into the Child Support Services Advance Fund shall be submitted by the department to the Controller who, if the claims are approved, shall draw a warrant in payment thereof against the Child Support Services Advance Fund.

(e) All amounts increasing the cash balance in the Child Support Services Advance Fund, that were derived from the cancellation of warrants issued therefrom, shall, on order of the Controller, be transferred to the appropriations from which the amounts were originally derived. **Leg.H.** Added Stats 2000 ch 108 §2 (AB 2876), effective July 10, 2000. Amended Stats 2019 ch 115 §165 (AB 1817), effective January 1, 2020.

§17704. State child support incentive

(a) For the 1998–99 fiscal year the department shall pay to each county a child support incentive payment. Every county shall receive the federal child support incentive. A county shall receive the state child support incentive if it elects to do both of the following:

(1) Comply with the reporting requirements of Section 17600 while federal financial participation is available for collecting and reporting data.

(2) Comply with federal and state child support laws and regulations, or has a corrective action plan certified by the department pursuant to Section 17702. The combined federal and state incentive payment shall be 13.6 percent of distributed collections. If the amount appropriated by the Legislature for the state incentives is less than the amount necessary to satisfy each county's actual incentives pursuant to this section, each county shall receive its proportional share of incentives.

(b)(1) Beginning July 1, 1999, the department shall pay to each county a child support incentive for child support collections. Every county shall receive the federal child support incentive. The combined federal and state incentive payments shall be 13.6 percent of distributed collections. In addition to the federal child support incentive, each county may also receive a state child support incentive. A county shall receive the state child support incentive if it elects to do both of the following:

(A) Comply with the reporting requirements of Section 17600 while federal financial participation is available for collecting and reporting data.

(B) Be in compliance with federal and state child support laws and regulations, or have a performance improvement plan certified by the department pursuant to Section 17702.

(2)(A) For purposes of paragraph (1), the federal incentive component shall be each county's share of the child support incentive payments that the state receives from the federal government, based on the county's collections.

(B)(i) Effective July 1, 1999, and annually thereafter, state funds appropriated for child support incentives shall first be used to fund the administrative costs incurred by local child support agencies in administering the child support program, excluding automation costs as set forth in Section 10085 of the Welfare and Institutions Code, after subtracting all federal financial participation for administrative costs and all federal child support incentives received by the state and passed on to the local child support agencies. The department shall allocate sufficient resources to each local child support agency to fully fund the remaining administrative costs of its budget as approved by the director pursuant to paragraph (9) of subdivision (b) of Section 17306, subject to the appropriation of funding in the annual Budget Act. No later than January 1, 2000, the department shall identify allowable administrative costs that may be claimed for reimbursement from the state, which shall be limited to reasonable amounts in relation to the scope of services and the total funds available. If the total amount of administrative costs claimed in any year exceeds the amount appropriated in the Budget Act, the amount provided to local child support agencies shall be reduced by the percentage necessary to ensure that projected General Fund expenditures do not exceed the amount authorized in the Budget Act.

(ii) Effective July 1, 2001, and annually thereafter, after allowable administrative costs are funded under clause (i), the department shall use any remaining unallocated incentive funds appropriated from the prior fiscal year which are hereby reappropriated to implement an incentive program that rewards up to 10 local child support agencies in each year, based on their performance or increase in performance on one or more of the federal performance standards set forth in Section 458 of the federal Social Security Act (42 U.S.C. Sec. 658), or state performance standards set forth in subdivision (a) of Section 17602, as determined by the department. The department shall determine the number of local agencies that receive state incentive funds under this program, subject to a maximum of 10 agencies and shall determine the amount received by each local agency based on the availability of funds and each local child support agency's proportional share based on the performance standard or standards used.

(iii) Any funds received pursuant to this subdivision shall be used only for child support enforcement activities.

(c) Each county shall continue to receive its federal child support incentive funding whether or not it elects to participate in the state child support incentive funding program.

(d) The department shall provide incentive funds pursuant to this section only during any fiscal year in which funding is provided for that purpose in the Budget Act. **Leg.H.** Added Stats 1999 ch 478 §1 (AB 196). Amended Stats 1999 ch 480 §23 (SB 542); Stats 2001 ch 111 §8 (AB 429), effective July 30, 2001; Stats 2002 ch 927 §10 (AB 3032); Stats 2003 ch 308 §8 (AB 738).

§17705. Jointly-led discussions to identify programwide operational efficiencies and budget methodology refinements for child support program; Report to legislative budget committees [Repealed]

Leg.H. Added Stats 2018 ch 35 §3 (AB 1811), effective June 27, 2018, repealed January 1, 2021. Amended Stats 2019 ch 497 §115 (AB 991), effective January 1, 2020, repealed January 1, 2021.

Prior Law Former Fam C §17705, related to jointly-led discussions to identify program wide operational efficiencies and budget methodology refinements for child support program; report to legislative budget committees, was added Stats 2018 ch 35 §3 (AB 1811), effective June 27, 2018, repealed January 1, 2021, amended Stats 2019 ch 497 §115 (AB 991),effective January 1, 2020, repealed January 1, 2021.

§17706. Increased recoupment to counties with 10 best performance standards; Suspension of operation for specified fiscal years [Repealed]

Leg.H. Added Stats 1999 ch 478 §1 (AB 196). Amended Stats 1999 ch 480 §24 (SB 542); Stats 2001 ch 111 §9 (AB 429), effective July 30, 2001; Stats 2002 ch 1022 §1 (AB 444), effective September 28, 2002; Stats 2003 1st Ex Sess 2003–2004 ch 7 §1 (SBX1-24), effective May 5, 2003; Stats 2006 ch 75 §9 (AB 1808), effective July 12, 2006; Stats 2007 ch 177 §2 (SB 84), effective August 24, 2007; Stats 2008 ch 759 §17 (AB 1279), effective September 30, 2008; Stats 2009 ch 140 §67 (AB 1164), effective January 1, 2010; Stats 2012 ch 47 §2 (SB 1041), effective June 27, 2012; Stats 2015 ch 20 §2 (SB 79), effective June 24, 2015; Stats 2017 ch 24 §4 (SB 89), effective June 27, 2017; Stats 2019 ch 27 §7 (SB 80), effective June 27, 2019; Stats 2021 ch 85 §5 (AB 135), effective July 16, 2021. Repealed Stats 2024 ch 46 §2 (AB 161), effective July 2, 2024.

Prior Law Former Fam C §17706, related to increased recoupment to counties with 10 best performance standards; suspension of operation for specified fiscal years, was added Stats 1999 ch 478 §1 (AB 196), amended Stats 1999 ch 480 §24 (SB 542); Stats 2001 ch 111 §9 (AB 429), effective July 30,2001; Stats 2002 ch 1022 §1 (AB 444), effective September 28, 2002; Stats 2003 1st Ex Sess 2003–2004 ch 7 §1 (SBX1-24), effective May 5,2003; Stats 2006 ch 75 §9 (AB 1808), effective July 12, 2006; Stats 2007 ch 177 §2 (SB 84),effective August 24, 2007; Stats 2008 ch 759 §17 (AB 1279), effective September 30, 2008; Stats 2009 ch 140 §67 (AB 1164), effective January 1, 2010; Stats 2012 ch 47 §2 (SB 1041), effective June 27, 2012; Stats 2015 ch 20§2 (SB 79), effective June 24, 2015; Stats 2017 ch 24 §4 (SB 89), effective June 27, 2017; Stats 2019 ch 27 §7 (SB 80), effective June 27, 2019; Stats 2021 ch 85 §5 (AB 135), effective July 16,2021. Repealed Stats 2024 ch 46 §2 (AB 161), effective July 2, 2024.

§17708. Requirements for participants in incentive program

(a) This section shall apply to any county that elects to participate in the state incentive program described in Section 17704.

(b) Each participating county child support enforcement program shall provide the data required by Section 17600 to the department on a quarterly basis. The data shall be provided no later than 15 days after the end of each quarter.

(c) On and after July 1, 1998, a county shall be required to comply with the provisions of this section only during fiscal years in which funding is provided for that purpose in the Budget Act. **Leg.H.** Added Stats 1999 ch 478 §1 (AB 196). Amended Stats 2001 ch 755 §19 (SB 943), effective October 12, 2001.

§17710. Administrative costs

(a) Each county shall be responsible for any administrative expenditures for administering the child support program not covered by federal and state funds.

(b) Notwithstanding subdivision (a), effective July 1, 1991, to June 30, 1992, inclusive, counties shall pay the nonfederal share of the administrative costs of conducting the reviews required under former Section 15200.8 of the Welfare and Institutions Code from the savings counties will obtain as a result of the reduction in the maximum aid payments specified in Section 11450. Effective July 1, 1992, to June 30, 1993, inclusive, the state shall pay the nonfederal share of administrative costs of conducting the reviews required under former Section 15200.8 of the Welfare and Institutions Code. Funding for county costs after June 30, 1993, shall be subject to the availability of funds in the annual Budget Act. **Leg.H.** Added Stats 1999 ch 478 §1 (AB 196), effective January 1, 2000. Amended Stats 1999 ch 479 §1 (AB 150), effective September 27, 1999, operative January 1, 2000, ch 480 §24.5 (SB 542), effective January 1, 2000; Stats 2016 ch 474 §26 (AB 2882), effective January 1, 2017.

§17712. Costs of child support commissioners

Notwithstanding subdivision (a) of Section 17708, and to the extent funds are appropriated by the annual Budget Act, funds shall be provided to the Judicial Council for the nonfederal share of costs for the costs of child support commissioners pursuant to Section 4251 and family law facilitators pursuant to Division 14 (commencing with Section 10000). The Judicial Council shall distribute the funds to the counties for the purpose of matching federal funds for the costs of child support commissioners and family law facilitators and related costs. Funds distributed pursuant to this section may also be used to offset the nonfederal share of costs incurred by the Judicial Council for performing the duties specified in Sections 4252 and 10010. **Leg.H.** Added Stats 1999 ch 478 §1 (AB 196).

§17714. Excess funds accumulated

(a)(1) Any funds paid to a county pursuant to this chapter prior to June 30, 1999, which exceed the county's cost of administering the child support program of the local child support agency pursuant to Section 17400 to that date, hereafter referred to as "excess funds," shall be expended by the county only upon that program. All these excess funds shall be deposited by the county into a special fund established by the county for this purpose.

(2) Performance incentive funds shall include, but not be limited to, incentive funds paid pursuant to Section 17704, and performance incentive funds paid pursuant to Section 14124.93 of the Welfare and Institutions Code and all interest earned on deposits in the special fund. Performance incentive funds shall not include funds paid pursuant to Section 17706. Performance incentive funds shall be expended by the county only upon that program. All performance incentive funds shall be deposited by the county into a special fund established by the county for this purpose.

(b) All excess funds and performance incentive funds shall be expended by the county on the support enforcement program of the local child support agency within two fiscal years following the fiscal year of receipt of the funds by the county. Except as provided in subdivision (c), any excess funds or performance incentive funds paid pursuant to this chapter since July 1, 1992, that the department determines have not been spent within the required two-year period shall revert to the state General Fund, and shall be distributed by the department only to counties that have complied with this section. The formula for distribution shall be based on the number of CalWORKs cases within each county.

(c) A county that submits to the department a written plan approved by that county's local child support agency for the expenditure of excess funds or performance incentive funds shall be exempted from the requirements of subdivision (b), if the department determines that the expenditure will be cost-effective, will maximize federal funds, and the expenditure plan will require more than the time provided for in subdivision (b) to expend the funds. Once the department approves a plan pursuant to this subdivision, funds received by a county and designated for an expenditure in the plan shall not be expended by the county for any other purpose.

(d) Nothing in this section shall be construed to nullify the recovery and reversion to the General Fund of unspent incentive funds as provided in Section 6 of Chapter 479 of the Statutes of 1999. **Leg.H.** Added Stats 1999 ch 478 §1 (AB 196). Amended Stats 2000 ch 808 §94 (AB 1358), effective September 28, 2000; Stats 2001 ch 755 §20 (SB 943), effective October 12, 2001.

CHAPTER 5
COMPLAINT RESOLUTION

Complaint resolution process. §17800.
Request for hearing. §17801.
Petition for review. §17803.
Time for establishment of complaint resolution process. §17804.

§17800. Complaint resolution process

Each local child support agency shall maintain a complaint resolution process. The department shall specify by regulation, no later than July 1, 2001, uniform forms and procedures that each local child support agency shall use in resolving all complaints received from custodial and noncustodial parents. A complaint shall be made within 90 days after the custodial or noncustodial parent affected knew or should have known of the child support action complained of. The local child support agency shall provide a written resolution of the complaint within 30 days of the receipt of the complaint. The director of the local child support agency may extend the period for resolution of the complaint an additional 30 days in accordance with the regulations adopted pursuant to Section 17804. **Leg.H.** Added Stats 1999 ch 803 §2 (AB 472). Amended Stats 2001 ch 755 §21 (SB 943), effective October 12, 2001.

§17801. Request for hearing

(a) A custodial or noncustodial parent who is dissatisfied with the local child support agency's resolution of a complaint shall be accorded an opportunity for a state hearing when one or more of the following actions or failures to take action by the department or the local child support agency is claimed by the parent:

(1) An application for child support services has been denied or has not been acted upon within the required timeframe.

(2) The child support services case has been acted upon in violation of state or federal law or regulation or department letter ruling, or has not yet been acted upon within the required timeframe, including services for the establishment, modification, and enforcement of child support orders and child support accountings.

(3) Child support collections have not been distributed or have been distributed or disbursed incorrectly, or the amount of child support arrears, as calculated by the department or the local child support agency is inaccurate. The amount of the court order for support, including current support and arrears, is not subject to a state hearing under this section.

(4) The child support agency's decision to close a child support case.

(b) Prior to requesting a hearing pursuant to subdivision (a), the custodial or noncustodial parent shall exhaust the complaint resolution process required in Section 17800, unless the local child support agency has not, within the 30-day period required by that section, submitted a written resolution of the complaint. If the custodial or noncustodial parent does not receive that timely written resolution, the custodial parent may request a hearing pursuant to subdivision (a).

(c) A hearing shall be provided under subdivision (a) when the request for a hearing is made within 90 days after receiving the written notice of resolution required in Section 17800 or, if no written notice of resolution is provided within 30 days from the date the complaint was made, within 90 days after making the complaint.

(d)(1) A hearing under subdivision (a) shall be set to commence within 45 days after the request is received by the state hearing office, and at least 10 days prior to the hearing, all parties shall be given written notice of the time and place of the hearing. Unless the time period is waived by the complainant, the proposed hearing decision shall be rendered by the state hearing office within 75 days after the request for a state hearing is received by the state hearing office. The department shall have 15 days from the date the proposed decision is rendered to act upon the decision. When a hearing is postponed, continued, or reopened with the consent of the complainant, the time for issuance of the decision, and action on the decision by the department, shall be extended for a period of time consistent with the postponement, continuance, or reopening.

(2) For purposes of this subdivision, the "state hearing office" refers to the division of the office or agency designated by the department to carry out state hearings, that conducts those state hearings.

(e) To the extent not inconsistent with this section, hearings under subdivision (a) shall be provided in the same manner in which hearings are provided in Sections 10950 to 10967 of the Welfare and Institutions Code and the State Department of Social Services' regulations implementing and interpreting those sections.

(f) Pendency of a state hearing shall not affect the obligation to comply with an existing child support order.

(g) A child support determination that is subject to the jurisdiction of the superior court and that is required by law to be addressed by motion, order to show cause, or appeal under this code shall not be subject to a state hearing under this section. The director shall, by regulation, specify and exclude from the subject matter jurisdiction of state hearings provided under subdivision (a), grievances arising from a child support case in the superior court that must, by law, be addressed by motion, order to show cause, or appeal under this code.

(h) The local child support agency shall comply with, and execute, every decision of the director rendered pursuant to this section.

(i) The director shall contract with the State Department of Social Services or the Office of Administrative Hearings for the provision of state hearings in accordance with this section.

(j) This section shall be implemented only to the extent that there is federal financial participation available at the child support funding rate set forth in Section 655(a)(2) of Title 42 of the United States Code. **Leg.H.** Added Stats 1999 ch 803 §2 (AB 472). Amended Stats 2002 ch 927 §10.5 (AB 3032); Stats 2016 ch 474 §27 (AB 2882), effective January 1, 2017; Stats 2019 ch 115 §166 (AB 1817), effective January 1, 2020.

§17802. Resolution of complaint [Repealed]

Leg.H. Added Stats 1999 ch 803 §2 (AB 472). Repealed Stats 2016 ch 474 §28 (AB 2882), effective January 1, 2017.

Prior Law Former Fam C §17802, related to resolution of complaint, was added Stats 1999 ch 803 §2 (AB 472), repealed Stats 2016 ch 474 §28 (AB 2882), effective January 1, 2017.

§17803. Petition for review

The custodial or noncustodial parent, within one year after receiving notice of the director's final decision, may file a petition with the superior court, under Section 1094.5 of the Code of Civil Procedure, praying for a review of the entire proceedings in the matter, upon questions of law involved in the case. The review, if granted, shall be the exclusive remedy available to the custodial or noncustodial parent for review of the director's decision. The director shall be the sole respondent in the proceedings. A filing fee shall not be required for the filing of a petition pursuant to this section. Any such petition to the superior court shall be entitled to a preference in setting a date for hearing on the petition. A bond shall not be required in the case of any petition for review, nor in any appeal therefrom. The custodial or noncustodial parent shall be entitled to reasonable attorney's fees and costs, if the parent obtains a decision in their favor. **Leg.H.** Added Stats 1999 ch 803 §2 (AB 472). Amended Stats 2019 ch 115 §167 (AB 1817), effective January 1, 2020.

§17804. Time for establishment of complaint resolution process

Each local child support agency shall establish the complaint resolution process specified in Section 17800. The department shall implement the state hearing requirements specified in Section 17801 no later than July 1, 2001. **Leg.H.** Added Stats 1999 ch 803 §2 (AB 472). Amended Stats 2001 ch 755 §22 (SB 943), effective October 12, 2001.

DIVISION 20
PILOT PROJECTS

Part 1. Family Law Pilot Projects.
Part 2. Paternity Pilot Projects [Repealed].

PART 1
FAMILY LAW PILOT PROJECTS

Chapter 1. General Provisions.
Chapter 2. San Mateo County Pilot Project.
Chapter 3. Santa Clara County Pilot Project.

CHAPTER 1
GENERAL PROVISIONS

Legislative findings, declarations, and intent. §20000.
Pilot projects in Santa Clara and San Mateo Counties. §20001.
Duration of projects. §20002.

§20000. Legislative findings, declarations, and intent

(a) The Legislature finds and declares the following:

(1) Child and spousal support are serious legal obligations. In addition, children are frequently left in limbo while their parents engage in protracted litigation concerning custody and visitation. The current system for obtaining child and spousal support orders is suffering because the family courts are unduly burdened with heavy case loads and personnel insufficient to meet the needs of increased demands on the courts.

(2) There is a compelling state interest in the development of a child and spousal support system that is cost-effective and accessible to families with middle or low incomes.

(3) There is a compelling state interest in first implementing such a system on a small scale.

(4) There is a compelling state interest in the development of a speedy, conflict-reducing method of resolving custody and visitation disputes.

(b) Therefore, it is the intent of the Legislature in enacting this part to provide a means for experimenting with and evaluating procedural innovations with significant potential to improve the California child and spousal support systems, and the system for mediation, evaluation, and litigation of custody and visitation disputes. **Leg.H.** Added Stats 1993 ch 219 §210 (AB 1500).

Prior Law: Former §20000, similar to the present section, was enacted Stats 1992 ch 162 §10, operative January 1, 1994, but failed to become operative since it was repealed Stats 1993 ch 219 §209.

§20001. Pilot projects in Santa Clara and San Mateo Counties

The Superior Courts of the Counties of Santa Clara and San Mateo may conduct pilot projects pursuant to this part. Chapter 2 (commencing with Section 20010) shall govern the San Mateo County Pilot Project, and Chapter 3 (commencing with Section 20030) shall govern the Santa Clara County Pilot Project. **Leg.H.** Added Stats 1993 ch 219 §210 (AB 1500).

Prior Law: Former §20001, similar to the present section, was enacted Stats 1992 ch 162 §10, operative January 1, 1994, but failed to become operative since it was repealed Stats 1993 ch 219 §209.

§20002. Duration of projects

The duration of the pilot projects shall be two years. **Leg.H.** Added Stats 1993 ch 219 §210 (AB 1500).

Prior Law: Former §20002, similar to the present section, was enacted Stats 1992 ch 162 §10, operative January 1, 1994, but failed to become operative since it was repealed Stats 1993 ch 219 §210.

§20003. [Section repealed 1993]

Leg.H. Enacted Stats 1992 ch 162 §10 (AB 2650), operative January 1, 1994. Repealed Stats 1993 ch 219 §209 (AB 1500). See Fam C §20010.

§20004. [Section repealed 1993]

Leg.H. Enacted Stats 1992 ch 162 §10 (AB 2650), operative January 1, 1994. Repealed Stats 1993 ch 219 §209 (AB 1500). See Fam C §§20023, 20037.

§20005. [Section repealed 1993]

Leg.H. Enacted Stats 1992 ch 162 §10 (AB 2650), operative January 1, 1994. Repealed Stats 1993 ch 219 §209 (AB 1500). See Fam C §20011.

§20006. [Section repealed 1993]

Leg.H. Enacted Stats 1992 ch 162 §10 (AB 2650), operative January 1, 1994. Repealed Stats 1993 ch 219 §209 (AB 1500). See Fam C §20023.

§20007. [Section repealed 1993]

Leg.H. Enacted Stats 1992 ch 162 §10 (AB 2650), operative January 1, 1994. Repealed Stats 1993 ch 219 §209 (AB 1500). See Fam C §20012.

§20008. [Section repealed 1993]

Leg.H. Enacted Stats 1992 ch 162 §10 (AB 2650), operative January 1, 1994. Repealed Stats 1993 ch 219 §209 (AB 1500). See Fam C §§20018, 20035.

§20009. [Section repealed 1993]

Leg.H. Enacted Stats 1992 ch 162 §10 (AB 2650), operative January 1, 1994. Repealed Stats 1993 ch 219 §209 (AB 1500). See Fam C §§20016, 20040.

CHAPTER 2
SAN MATEO COUNTY PILOT PROJECT

Motions to which project applies. §20010.
Hearings. §20011.
Family Law Evaluator. §20012.
Cost of providing Family Law Evaluator. §20013.
Stamping papers. §20014.
Protocol for access to hearing before court. §20015.
Publication of booklet describing program. §20016.
Qualifications of family law evaluator. §20017.
Compliance with statewide uniform guideline. §20018.
Mediation. §20019.
Submission of documents. §20020.
Failure to submit documents. §20021.
Review and examination of tax return. §20022.
Services provided by district attorney. §20023.
Estimated service and savings. §20026.

§20010. Motions to which project applies

The San Mateo County Pilot Project shall apply to hearings on motions for temporary child support, temporary spousal support, and temporary health insurance issuable in proceedings under this code, where at least one party is unrepresented by counsel. **Leg.H.** Added Stats 1993 ch 219 §210 (AB 1500).

Prior Law: Former §20010, similar to present Fam C §20019, was enacted Stats 1992 ch 162 §10, operative January 1, 1994, but failed to become operative since it was repealed Stats 1993 ch 219 §209.

§20011. Hearings

Motions for temporary orders under this chapter shall be heard as soon as practicable, consistent with the rules governing other civil actions. **Leg.H.** Added Stats 1993 ch 219 §210 (AB 1500).

Prior Law: Former §20011, similar to §§20020, 20021, 20022, 20032, was enacted Stats 1992 ch 162 §10, operative January 1, 1994, but failed to become operative since it was repealed Stats 1993 ch 219 §209.

§20012. Family Law Evaluator

The court shall appoint a Family Law Evaluator, who shall be available to assist parties. By local rule the superior court may designate the duties of the Family Law Evaluator, which may include, but are not limited to, the following:

(a) Requiring litigants in actions which involve temporary child support, temporary spousal support, and temporary maintenance of health insurance in which at least one litigant is unrepresented, to meet with the Family Law Evaluator prior to the support hearing.

(b) Preparing support schedules based on standardized formulae accessed through existing up-to-date computer technology.

(c) Drafting stipulations to include all issues agreed to by the parties.

(d) Prior to, or at, any hearing pursuant to this chapter, reviewing the paperwork by the court, advising the judge whether or not the matter is ready to proceed, and making a recommendation to the court regarding child support, spousal support, and health insurance.

(e) Assisting the clerk in maintaining records.

(f) Preparing a formal order consistent with the court's announced oral order, unless one of the parties is represented by an attorney.

(g) Assisting the court with research and any other responsibilities which will enable the court to be responsive to the litigants' needs. **Leg.H.** Added Stats 1993 ch 219 §210 (AB 1500).

Prior Law: Former §20012, similar to Fam C §§20025, 20042, was enacted Stats 1992 ch 162 §10, operative January 1, 1994, but failed to become operative since it was repealed Stats 1993 ch 219 §209.

§20013. Cost of providing Family Law Evaluator

The court shall provide the Family Law Evaluator at no cost to the parties. **Leg.H.** Added Stats 1993 ch 219 §210 (AB 1500).

§20014. Stamping papers

The clerk shall stamp all moving papers in which a party is not represented by counsel with a notice of a requirement to see the Family Law Evaluator. The unrepresented party shall serve the stamped pleadings on the other party. **Leg.H.** Added Stats 1993 ch 219 §210 (AB 1500).

§20015. Protocol for access to hearing before court

The court shall adopt a protocol wherein all litigants, both unrepresented by counsel and represented by counsel, have ultimate access to a hearing before the court. **Leg.H.** Added Stats 1993 ch 219 §210 (AB 1500).

§20016. Publication of booklet describing program

The court may elect to publish a low-cost booklet describing this program. **Leg.H.** Added Stats 1993 ch 219 §210 (AB 1500).

§20017. Qualifications of family law evaluator

The Family Law Evaluator shall be an attorney, licensed to practice in this state. **Leg.H.** Added Stats 1993 ch 219 §210 (AB 1500).

§20018. Compliance with statewide uniform guideline

Orders for temporary support issued pursuant to this chapter shall comply with the statewide uniform guideline set forth in Article 2 (commencing with Section 4050) of Chapter 2 of Part 2 of Division 9 and shall be based on the economic evidence supplied by the parties or otherwise available to the court. **Leg.H.** Added Stats 1993 ch 219 §210 (AB 1500).

§20019. Mediation

Where it appears from a party's application for an order under this chapter or otherwise in the proceedings that the custody of, or visitation with, a minor child is contested, the court shall set those issues for mediation pursuant to Section 3170. The pendency of the mediation proceedings shall not delay a hearing on any other matter for which a temporary order is required, including child support, and a separate hearing, if required, shall be scheduled respecting the custody and visitation issues following mediation in accordance with Section 3170. However, the court may grant a continuance for good cause shown. **Leg.H.** Added Stats 1993 ch 219 §210 (AB 1500).

§20020. Submission of documents

In a contested proceeding for temporary child or spousal support under this chapter, both the moving party and the responding party shall provide all of the following documents to the Family Law Evaluator, and to the court at the time of the hearing:

(a) Copies of the last two federal and state income tax returns filed.

(b) Paycheck stubs for all paychecks received in the four months immediately prior to the hearing. **Leg.H.** Added Stats 1993 ch 219 §210 (AB 1500).

§20021. Failure to submit documents

A party who fails to submit documents to the court as required by Section 20020 may, in the court's discretion, not be granted the relief requested, or the court may impose evidentiary sanctions. **Leg.H.** Added Stats 1993 ch 219 §210 (AB 1500).

§20022. Review and examination of tax return

The tax return submitted pursuant to Section 20020 may be reviewed by the other party. A party may be examined by the other party as to the contents of the tax return. **Leg.H.** Added Stats 1993 ch 219 §210 (AB 1500).

§20023. Services provided by district attorney

(a) Except as provided in subdivision (c):

(1) Nothing in this chapter shall be construed to apply to a child for whom services are provided or required to be provided by a district attorney pursuant to Section 11475.5 of the Welfare and Institutions Code.

(2) The court shall not hear or enter any order under this chapter in a matter involving such a child.

(b) Any order entered contrary to the provisions of subdivision (a) is void and without legal effect.

(c) For purposes of enabling a custodial parent receiving assistance under Chapter 2 (commencing with Section 11200) of Part 3 of Division 9 of the Welfare and Institutions Code to participate in a pilot project authorized by this chapter, the district attorney, upon the request of the custodial parent, may execute a limited waiver of the obligation or representation under Section 11475.1 of the Welfare and Institutions Code. These limited waivers shall be signed by both the district attorney and custodial parent and shall only permit the custodial parent to participate in the proceedings under this chapter. It is not the intent of the Legislature in enacting this section to limit the duties of district attorneys with respect to seeking child support payments or to in any way limit or supersede other provisions of this code respecting temporary child support. **Leg.H.** Added Stats 1993 ch 219 §210 (AB 1500).

§20024. [Section repealed 2017]

Leg.H. Added Stats 1993 ch 219 §210 (AB 1500), ch 876 §27.5 (SB 1068), effective January 1, 1994. Repealed Stats 2016 ch 86 §133 (SB 1171), effective January 1, 2017. The repealed section related to costs of the San Mateo County Pilot Project Family Law Evaluator and program booklet, and solicitation of donations from existing hardware and software providers.

Prior Law: Former Fam C §20024, relating to costs of the San Mateo County Pilot Project Family Law Evaluator and program booklet, and solicitation of donations from existing hardware and software providers, was added Stats 1993 ch 876 §27.5 (SB 1068), effective October 6, 1993, and repealed July 1, 1994, by its own terms.

§20025. [Section repealed 2004]

Leg.H. Added Stats 1993 ch 219 §210 (AB 1500). Repealed Stats 2004 ch 193 §18 (SB 111). The repealed section related to the study and report of the San Mateo County Pilot Project.

§20026. Estimated service and savings

(a) It is estimated that under the pilot project authorized by this chapter, approximately 2,200 litigants will be served annually and that the following savings will occur:

(1) The program would save 520 hours, or 65 days, of court time per year.

(2) There would be a concomitant saving of time by litigants due to the expedited proceedings and, in addition, there would be a saving to litigants of wages that would otherwise be lost due to time off from work.

(b) The estimated costs of the pilot project are as follows:

(1) The salaries of the Family Law Evaluator and any staff necessary for the evaluator to carry out the evaluator's functions.

(2) The cost of a booklet, if any, describing the program.

(c) There would be no cost for the following:

(1) Computers, printers, or other equipment. This equipment is already available in the family law department.

(2) Training for the Family Law Evaluator or the evaluator's staff. They will be trained by already existing judicial personnel. **Leg.H.** Added Stats 1993 ch 219 §210 (AB 1500). Amended Stats 2019 ch 115 §168 (AB 1817), effective January 1, 2020.

CHAPTER 3
SANTA CLARA COUNTY PILOT PROJECT

Authorization to conduct project. §20030.
Application of project. §20031.

Hearing and procedure; Required documents. §20032.
Local rule. §20033.
Attorney-Mediator. §20034.
Compliance with statewide uniform guideline. §20035.
Exemption from project. §20036.
Services provided by district attorney. §20037.
Mediation. §20038.
Booklet describing program. §20040.
Centralization of programs. §20041.
Estimated services and savings. §20043.

§20030. Authorization to conduct project

The Superior Court of the County of Santa Clara may conduct a pilot project pursuant to this chapter. **Leg.H.** Added Stats 1993 ch 219 §210 (AB 1500).

§20031. Application of project

The pilot project applies to all hearings, for temporary or permanent child or spousal support, modifications thereof, health insurance, custody, or visitation in a proceeding for dissolution of marriage, nullity of marriage, legal separation of the parties, exclusive custody, or pursuant to the Uniform Parentage Act (Part 3 (commencing with Section 7600) of Division 12). **Leg.H.** Added Stats 1993 ch 219 §210 (AB 1500).

§20032. Hearing and procedure; Required documents

(a) Each and every hearing in a proceeding described in Section 20031 in which child or spousal support is at issue, including related contempt matters, shall be set by the clerk of the court for hearing within 30 days of filing.

(b) At any hearing in which child or spousal support is at issue, each party, both moving and responding, shall bring to the hearing, copies of the last two federal and state income tax returns filed by the party and pay stubs from the last four full months immediately preceding the hearing received by the party, and shall serve those documents on the opposing party at least five days in advance of the hearing date. Willful failure to comply with these requirements or any of the requirements of this pilot project may result in a citation for contempt under Title 5 (commencing with Section 1209) of Part 3 of the Code of Civil Procedure, or in the court's discretion, the court may refuse to grant relief requested or may impose evidentiary sanctions on a party who fails to submit these documents. The clerk shall cause to be placed on the face sheet of any moving papers for child or spousal support at the time of filing, a notice informing the parties of the requirements of this section. The notice shall also inform the parties that prior to the hearing, they must meet with the Attorney-Mediator pursuant to Section 20034. That meeting may occur in advance of the hearing dates by agreement of the parties, or on the day of the hearing.

(c) No continuance of any hearing involving child or spousal support shall be granted by a court without an order setting an interim support level unless the parties stipulate otherwise or the court finds good cause therefor. **Leg.H.** Added Stats 1993 ch 219 §210 (AB 1500).

§20033. Local rule

The court may pass a local rule that suspends the use of the Income and Expense Declaration mandated by California Rule of Court 1285.50 in some or all proceedings during the pendency of the pilot project, provided that substitute forms are developed and adopted to solicit substantially the same information in a simplified format. The court may, notwithstanding the adoption of a local form, require the use of the Income and Expense Declaration mandated by California Rule of Court 1285.50 in appropriate cases on the motion of either party or on the court's own motion. **Leg.H.** Added Stats 1993 ch 219 §210 (AB 1500).

§20034. Attorney-Mediator

(a) An attorney, known as an Attorney-Mediator, shall be hired to assist the court in resolving child and spousal support disputes, to develop community outreach programs, and to undertake other duties as assigned by the court.

(b) The Attorney-Mediator shall be an attorney, licensed to practice in this state, with mediation or litigation experience, or both, in the field of family law.

(c) By local rule, the superior court may designate the duties of the Attorney-Mediator, which may include, but are not limited to, the following:

(1) Meeting with litigants to mediate issues of child support, spousal support, and maintenance of health insurance. Actions in which one or both of the parties are unrepresented by counsel shall have priority.

(2) Preparing support schedules based on statutory guidelines accessed through existing up-to-date computer technology.

(3) Drafting stipulations to include all issues agreed to by the parties, which may include issues other than those specified in Section 20031.

(4) If the parties are unable to resolve issues with the assistance of the Attorney-Mediator, prior to or at the hearing, and at the request of the court, the Attorney-Mediator shall review the paperwork, examine documents, prepare support schedules, and advise the judge whether or not the matter is ready to proceed.

(5) Assisting the clerk in maintaining records.

(6) Preparing formal orders consistent with the court's announced order in cases where both parties are unrepresented.

(7) Serving as a special master to hearing proceedings and making findings to the court unless the individual has served as a mediator in that case.

(8) Assisting the court with research and any other responsibilities that will enable the court to be responsive to the litigants' needs.

(9) Developing programs for bar and community outreach through day and evening programs, video recordings, and other innovative means that will assist unrepresented and financially disadvantaged litigants in gaining meaningful access to family court. These programs shall specifically include information concerning underutilized legislation, such as expedited temporary support orders (Chapter 5 (commencing with Section 3620) of Part 1 of Division 9), modification of support orders (Article 3 (commencing with Section 3680) of Chapter 6 of Part 1 of Division 9), and preexisting, court-sponsored programs, such as supervised visitation and appointment of attorneys for children.

(d) The court shall develop a protocol wherein all litigants, both unrepresented by counsel and represented by counsel, have ultimate access to a hearing before the court. **Leg.H.** Added Stats 1993 ch 219 §210 (AB 1500). Amended Stats 2009 ch 88 §40 (AB 176), effective January 1, 2010; Stats 2019 ch 115 §169 (AB 1817), effective January 1, 2020.

§20035. Compliance with statewide uniform guideline

Orders for temporary support issued pursuant to this chapter shall comply with the statewide uniform guideline set forth in Article 2 (commencing with Section 4050) of Chapter 2 of Part 2 of Division 9 and shall be based on the economic evidence supplied by the parties or otherwise available to the court. **Leg.H.** Added Stats 1993 ch 219 §210 (AB 1500).

§20036. Exemption from project

Upon motion by either party or on the court's own motion, any proceeding that would otherwise fall within this pilot project may by judicial order be exempted from its requirements. **Leg.H.** Added Stats 1993 ch 219 §210 (AB 1500).

§20037. Services provided by district attorney

(a) Except as provided in subdivision (c):

(1) Nothing in this chapter shall be construed to apply to a child for whom services are provided or required to be provided by a district attorney pursuant to Section 11475.1 of the Welfare and Institutions Code.

(2) The court shall not hear or enter any order under this chapter in a matter involving such a child.

(b) Any order entered contrary to subdivision (a) is void and without legal effect.

(c) For purposes of enabling a custodial parent receiving assistance under Chapter 2 (commencing with Section 11200) of Part 3 of Division 9 of the Welfare and Institutions Code to participate in a pilot project authorized by this chapter, the district attorney, upon the request of the custodial parent, may execute a limited waiver of the obligation of representation under Section 11475.1 of the Welfare and Institutions Code. These limited waivers shall be signed by both the district attorney and custodial parent and shall only permit the custodial parent to participate in the proceedings under this chapter. It is not the intent of the Legislature in enacting this section to limit the duties of district attorneys with respect to seeking child support payments or to in any way limit or supersede other provisions of this code respecting temporary child support. **Leg.H.** Added Stats 1993 ch 219 §210 (AB 1500).

§20038. Mediation

(a) In any case where either party has filed a motion regarding a custody or visitation dispute and has not yet scheduled an appointment for the mediation orientation class by the time of the hearing on the order to show cause, the court shall order all parties to go to Family Court Services that day to schedule an appointment. The mediation orientation shall be scheduled within 14 days. Mediation orientation shall be conducted by Family Court Services and shall include general information on the effect of separation and dissolution on children and parents, the developmental and emotional needs of children in those circumstances, time-sharing considerations and various options concerning legal and physical custody of children, the effect of exposure to domestic violence and extreme conflict on children and parents, the nature of the mediation process and other Family Court Services procedures, and related community resources.

(b) After the mediation orientation, the parties may elect to utilize private mental health professionals, in which case the parties or the court may modify the fast track time guidelines provided for in this section.

(c) If, after orientation, either party requests mediation, and both parties complete Family Court Services mediation petitions, an appointment shall be scheduled within four weeks after both petitions are submitted and both parties shall attend the mediation as scheduled.

(d) At the mediation, if the parties agree to all of the issues regarding custody or visitation, the mediator shall memorialize the agreement in writing, and shall mail copies of the document to the attorneys and parents. Unless written objections to the agreement are sent to Family Court Services within 20 days of mailing the agreement, it will be submitted to the court and become a court order. A copy of the order shall be sent with proof of service to the parties and attorneys by the Family Court.

(e) If mediation is completed and there are remaining disputes, the mediator shall write a memorandum of any partial agreement and shall outline the remaining disputes which shall be sent to the attorneys and parties acting in propria persona. The mediator shall refer the parties to the Early Resolution Project. The parties shall meet and confer within 14 days of the referral to determine if a solution can be formulated. If there are remaining issues to be settled after the meeting, an early resolution judicial conference shall be scheduled within 30 days of the request of either party.

(f) At the early resolution conference, the judge may take stipulations resolving the issues of custody or visitation. The judge may also request the staff of Family Court Services to provide assessments and expedited evaluations to be held on the same day as the conference, in which case the judge, upon stipulation of the parties, may also order a hearing as soon as the same day on the issues. The judge may also order counseling, a mental health special master, psychological testing, or an extended evaluation by Family Court Services or a private evaluator on some or all issues.

(g) When the court at the early resolution judicial conference orders an extended evaluation, the parties shall complete all paperwork, submit deposits to Family Court Services, or both, within five days of the early resolution judicial conference. An evaluator shall be assigned to the case within 10 days thereafter.

(h) Evaluation shall be completed within 60 days of assignment to the evaluator, and the evaluator shall submit a report and recommendations which include a proposed order resolving all disputed issues. This report shall be served by certified mail on the attorneys of record, or on the parties if they are appearing in propria persona. If there are objections to the proposed order, the parties shall file written objections, meet with the evaluator within 30 days of service of the report, and serve a copy of the order on Family Court Services within the 30-day period. If a stipulation is reached, it shall be filed with the court. If a dispute remains, a judicial settlement conference shall be scheduled within 14 days of the meeting with the evaluator. Parties, counsel, and the evaluator shall be present at this judicial settlement conference. If there is no resolution at this settlement conference, a trial shall be set within 30 days from the settlement conference by the settlement conference judge. If no objections are filed, Family Court Services shall file the proposed order with the court, and it shall become the court's order.

(i) For good cause shown, all deadlines in this section may be altered by the court. **Leg.H.** Added Stats 1993 ch 219 §210 (AB 1500).

§20039. [Section repealed 2017]

Leg.H. Added Stats 1993 ch 219 §210 (AB 1500), effective January 1, 1994. Repealed Stats 2016 ch 86 §134 (SB 1171), effective January 1, 2017. The repealed section related to costs of the Santa Clara County Pilot Project, solicitation of donations from existing hardware and software providers, and administration of funds.

Prior Law: Former Fam C §20039, relating to costs of the Santa Clara County Pilot Project, solicitation of donations from existing hardware and software providers, and administration of funds, was added Stats 1993 ch 876 §27.6 (SB 1068), effective October 6, 1993, and repealed July 1, 1994, by its own terms.

§20040. Booklet describing program

The court may elect to publish a low-cost booklet describing the program. **Leg.H.** Added Stats 1993 ch 219 §210 (AB 1500).

§20041. Centralization of programs

The court shall centralize, augment, and coordinate all presently existing programs under the court's supervision that relate to children, including, but not limited to, mental health special masters, appointment of attorneys for children, supervised visitation, and other supporting personnel. **Leg.H.** Added Stats 1993 ch 219 §210 (AB 1500).

§20042. [Section repealed 2004]

Leg.H. Added Stats 1993 ch 219 §210 (AB 1500). Repealed Stats 2004 ch 193 §19 (SB 111). The repealed section related to the study and report of the Santa Clara County Pilot Project.

§20043. Estimated services and savings

(a) It is estimated for Santa Clara County's participation in the pilot project authorized by this chapter, that 4,000 litigants will be served annually, and that the following savings will occur:

(1) With an estimated 20 percent reduction in the use of court time over the current system, the county would save approximately 178 hours per year of court time, or approximately 22 workdays per year.

(2) With an estimated cost savings in incomes of judges, court reporters, clerks, bailiffs, and sheriffs, the project is expected to save approximately twenty thousand dollars ($20,000) per year. Cases involving child support obligations which the district attorney's office was required to handle in one participating county, for the 1989–90 fiscal year, number 2,461. The average time spent on a typical child support order is approximately five hours. There is a potential of 12,500 man-hours per year that could be saved, resulting in a savings of three hundred sixty-seven thousand eight hundred seventy-five dollars ($367,875) per year in attorney salaries alone. This does not take into consideration costs for documents, filing, and other district attorney personnel.

(3) The average savings personally to litigants who otherwise would require private representation would be from fifty dollars ($50) to two hundred fifty dollars ($250) per hour of court time and other preparation work.

(b) The satisfaction of participating parties will be determined by requiring the litigants using the pilot project to fill out a simple exit poll. The response of at least 70 percent of those questionnaires will be analyzed to decide whether the program has been deemed satisfactory by the participants.

(c) The estimated cost of the program is as follows:

(1) The estimated salary for an Attorney-Mediator is sixty thousand dollars ($60,000) to sixty-five thousand dollars ($65,000) per year, plus an additional 25 percent of salary to cover the costs of benefits for that position. In addition, there may be other costs connected with this position for support staff at the court.

(2) The costs of exit polling and any informational materials to be handed out to the public by the Attorney-Mediator is undetermined and cannot be estimated.

(d) The estimated income to cover the costs of this program will be as follows:

(1) There are approximately 10,000 dissolution of marriage petitions filed in Santa Clara County each year. Of those cases, approximately one-third of them have responses filed. At the present time, it costs one hundred sixty-five dollars ($165) to have a petition for dissolution of marriage filed and one hundred twenty-seven dollars ($127) to have a response filed, for a cost differential of thirty-eight dollars ($38). By equalizing the response fee with the petition fee, income generated would be approximately one hundred twenty-five thousand four hundred dollars ($125,400) per year. This does not include the cost of fourteen dollars ($14) for each responsive declaration filed to a motion or order to show cause, the annual number of which is significantly greater than 3,300. It is estimated that an additional fifty thousand dollars ($50,000) per year

could be generated by equalizing the responsive fees to a motion or order to show cause with the filing of those motions. These fees generated would more than offset the costs of the program.

(2) It is also anticipated that the Attorney-Mediator will develop public information and outreach programs which will be paid for by any excess revenue generated from the pilot project and ultimately will result in savings to the public and the court. The public will save by not having to pay attorneys for certain information regarding child support matters, and the court will save by not having to educate the public from the bench, thus expediting the handling of support and custody cases.

(e) The cost of computers, printers, and other equipment will be defrayed by contributions. **Leg.H.** Added Stats 1993 ch 219 §210 (AB 1500).

PART 2
PATERNITY PILOT PROJECTS [REPEALED]

§20100. [Section repealed 1993]

Leg.H. Added Stats 1993 ch 219 §211 (AB 1500), never becoming operative. Repealed Stats 1993 ch 1240 §2 (AB 1277). The repealed section related to establishment of pilot project.

§20101. [Section repealed 1993]

Leg.H. Added Stats 1993 ch 219 §211 (AB 1500), never becoming operative. Repealed Stats 1993 ch 1240 §2 (AB 1277). The repealed section related to duties of Department of Social Services.

§20102. [Section repealed 1993]

Leg.H. Added Stats 1993 ch 219 §211 (AB 1500), never becoming operative. Repealed Stats 1993 ch 1240 §2 (AB 1277). See Fam C §§7571, 7574, 7575.

§20103. [Section repealed 1993]

Leg.H. Added Stats 1993 ch 219 §211 (AB 1500), never becoming operative. Repealed Stats 1993 ch 1240 §2 (AB 1277). See Fam C §§7571, 7576.

§20104. [Section repealed 1993]

Leg.H. Added Stats 1993 ch 219 §211 (AB 1500), never becoming operative. Repealed Stats 1993 ch 1240 §2 (AB 1277). See Fam C §7577.

The STANDARD PROBATE CODE

of the

STATE OF CALIFORNIA

2025 EDITION

The Re-Enacted Probate Code
Effective January 1, 1991—Operative July 1, 1991
With All Subsequent Legislative Enactments

Table Showing 2024 Changes in the Probate Code

Effective January 1, 2025, unless otherwise noted at end of section.

Section	Effect	Chapter	Section	Effect	Chapter
871	Amended	799	2700	Amended	455
872	Amended	799	13100	Amended	331
879.1	Added	799	13101	Amended	331
879.2	Added	799	13150	Amended	331
879.3	Added	799	13151	Amended	331
880	Amended	799	13152	Amended	331
881	Amended	799	13154	Amended	331
1209	Amended	853	13158	Repealed	331
1510.1	Amended	955	15408	Amended	76
1514	Amended	955	21621	Amended	80
2352	Amended	455			
2361	Amended	455			

CONTENTS

Sections

DIVISION 1. PRELIMINARY PROVISIONS AND DEFINITIONS
- Part 1. Preliminary Provisions — 1 – 13
- Part 2. Definitions — 20 – 88

DIVISION 2. GENERAL PROVISIONS
- Part 1. Effect of Death of Married Person on Community and Quasi-Community Property — 100 – 105
- Part 2. Right in California Real Property of Nondomiciliary Decedent — 120
- Part 3. Contractual Arrangements Relating to Rights at Death — 140 – 147
- Part 4. Establishing and Reporting Fact of Death — 200 – 217
- Part 5. Simultaneous Death — 220 – 234
- Part 6. Distribution Among Heirs or Beneficiaries — 240 – 249.8
- Part 7. Effect of Homicide or Abuse of an Elder or Dependent Adult — 250 – 259
- Part 8. Disclaimer of Testamentary and Other Interests — 260 – 295
- Part 9. Trust Company as Fiduciary — 300 – 301
- Part 10. Immediate Steps Concerning Decedent's Tangible Personal Property and Safe Deposit Box — 330 – 331
- Part 11. Fiduciaries' Wartime Substitution Law — 350 – 388
- Part 12. Probate Referees — 400 – 453
- Part 13. Litigation Involving Decedent — 550 – 555
- Part 14. Powers of Appointment — 600 – 695
- Part 15. Deposit of Estate Planning Documents With Attorney — 700 – 735
- Part 16. Jurisdiction — 800 – 801
- Part 17. Legal Mental Capacity — 810 – 813
- Part 18. Right to Trial — 825
- Part 19. Conveyance or Transfer of Property Claimed to Belong to Decedent or Other Person — 850 – 859
- Part 20. Revised Uniform Fiduciary Access to Digital Assets Act — 870 – 884
- Part 21. Periodic Adjustment of Dollar Amounts — 890

DIVISION 3. GENERAL PROVISIONS OF A PROCEDURAL NATURE
- Part 1. General Provisions — 1000 – 1064
- Part 2. Notices and Citations — 1200 – 1266
- Part 3. Appeals — 1300 – 1312

DIVISION 4. GUARDIANSHIP, CONSERVATORSHIP, AND OTHER PROTECTIVE PROCEEDINGS
- Part 1. Definitions and General Provisions — 1400 – 1490
- Part 2. Guardianship — 1500 – 1611
- Part 3. Conservatorship — 1800 – 2033
- Part 4. Provisions Common to Guardianship and Conservatorship — 2100 – 2893
- Part 5. Public Guardian — 2900 – 2955
- Part 6. Management or Disposition of Community Property Where Spouse Lacks Legal Capacity — 3000 – 3154
- Part 7. Capacity Determinations and Health Care Decisions for Adult Without Conservator — 3200 – 3212
- Part 8. Other Protective Proceedings — 3300 – 3803
- Part 9. California Uniform Transfers to Minors Act — 3900 – 3925

DIVISION 4.5. POWERS OF ATTORNEY
- Part 1. Definitions and General Provisions — 4000 – 4054
- Part 2. Powers of Attorney Generally — 4100 – 4310
- Part 3. Uniform Statutory Form Power of Attorney — 4400 – 4465
- Part 4. Judicial Proceedings Concerning Powers of Attorney — 4500 – 4545

DIVISION 4.7. HEALTH CARE DECISIONS
- Part 1. Definitions and General — 4600 – 4665
- Part 2. Uniform Health Care Decisions Act — 4670 – 4743

Part 3.	Judicial Proceedings	4750 – 4771
Part 4.	Request Regarding Resuscitative Measures	4780 – 4786
Part 5.	Advance Health Care Directive Registry	4800 – 4806

DIVISION 5. NONPROBATE TRANSFERS

Part 1.	Provisions Relating to Effect of Death	5000 – 5048
Part 2.	Multiple-Party Accounts	5100 – 5407
Part 3.	Uniform TOD Security Registration Act	5500 – 5512
Part 4.	Revocable Transfer on Death Deed [Repealed January 1, 2032]	5600 – 5698
Part 5.	Gifts in View of Impending Death	5700 – 5705

DIVISION 6. WILLS AND INTESTATE SUCCESSION

Part 1.	Wills	6100 – 6391–6399
Part 2.	Intestate Succession	6400 – 6455
Part 3.	Family Protection	6500 – 6615
Part 4.	Escheat of Decedent's Property	6800 – 6806

DIVISION 7. ADMINISTRATION OF ESTATES OF DECEDENTS

Part 1.	General Provisions	7000 – 7666
Part 2.	Opening Estate Administration	8000 – 8577
Part 3.	Inventory and Appraisal	8800 – 8980
Part 4.	Creditor Claims	9000 – 9400–9599
Part 5.	Estate Management	9600 – 10382
Part 6.	Independent Administration of Estates	10400 – 10592
Part 7.	Compensation of Personal Representative and Attorney for the Personal Representative	10800 – 10850
Part 8.	Accounts	10900 – 11052
Part 9.	Payment of Debts	11400 – 11467
Part 10.	Distribution of Estate	11600 – 12008–12199
Part 11.	Closing Estate Administration	12200 – 12252
Part 12.	Administration of Estates of Missing Persons Presumed Dead	12400 – 12408
Part 13.	Nondomiciliary Decedents	12500 – 12591

DIVISION 8. DISPOSITION OF ESTATE WITHOUT ADMINISTRATION

Part 1.	Collection or Transfer of Small Estate Without Administration	13000 – 13211
Part 2.	Passage of Property to Surviving Spouse Without Administration	13500 – 13660

DIVISION 9. TRUST LAW

Part 1.	General Provisions	15000 – 15004
Part 2.	Creation, Validity, Modification, and Termination of Trusts	15200 – 15414
Part 3.	Trustees and Beneficiaries	15600 – 15805
Part 4.	Trust Administration	16000 – 16632
Part 5.	Judicial Proceedings Concerning Trusts	17000 – 17457
Part 6.	Rights of Third Persons	18000 – 18201
Part 7.	Uniform Prudent Management of Institutional Funds Act	18501 – 18510
Part 8.	Payment of Claims, Debts, and Expenses from Revocable Trust of Deceased Settlor	19000 – 19403
Part 9.	Uniform Trust Decanting Act	19501 – 19530

DIVISION 10. PRORATION OF TAXES

Chapter 1.	Proration of Estate Taxes	20100 – 20125
Chapter 2.	Proration of Taxes on Generation-Skipping Transfer	20200 – 20225

DIVISION 11. CONSTRUCTION OF WILLS, TRUSTS, AND OTHER INSTRUMENTS

Part 1.	Rules for Interpretation of Instruments	21101 – 21140
Part 2.	Perpetuities	21200 – 21231
Part 3.	No Contest Clause	21310 – 21315
Part 3.7.	Presumption of Fraud or Undue Influence	21360 – 21392
Part 4.	Abatement	21400 – 21406
Part 5.	Compliance with Internal Revenue Code	21500 – 21541
Part 6.	Family Protection: Omitted Spouses and Children	21600 – 21630
Part 7.	Contracts Regarding Testamentary or Intestate Succession	21700

PROBATE CODE

An Act to amend Sections 683 and 954 of the Civil Code, to amend Sections 852, 952, 6661, 6800, 6804, 6855, 14854, 14860, and 18318.5 of the Financial Code, to amend Section 8751.1 of the Health and Safety Code, and to repeal and reenact the Probate Code, relating to probate.

[Former Code: approved May 11, 1931; effective August 14, 1931; repealed operative July 1, 1991.]

DIVISION 1
PRELIMINARY PROVISIONS AND DEFINITIONS

Part 1. Preliminary Provisions.

Part 2. Definitions.

PART 1
PRELIMINARY PROVISIONS

Title of code. §1.
Continuation of existing law; Construction of provisions drawn from uniform acts. §2.
General transitional provision. §3.
Effect of headings in code. §4.
Certified mail sufficient compliance with requirement of use of registered mail. §5.
Construction of code. §6.
Reference to statute includes amendments and additions. §7.
Reference to division, part, chapter, article, section, or part of section. §8.
Construction of tenses. §9.
Construction of singular and plural. §10.
Severability of provisions. §11.
Meaning of "shall" and "may". §12.
Determination of degree of kinship or consanguinity. §13.

§1. Title of code

This code shall be known as the Probate Code. **Leg.H.** Enacted Stats 1990 ch 79 §14 (AB 759), operative July 1, 1991.

Prior Law: Former Prob C §1, similar to the present section, was added Stats 1983 ch 842 §21, operative January 1, 1985, and repealed Stats 1990 ch 79 §13, operative July 1, 1991.

Former Prob C §1, similar to the present section, was enacted Stats 1931, amended Stats 1979 ch 730 §95, operative January 1, 1981, and repealed Stats 1983 ch 842 §17, operative January 1, 1985.

§2. Continuation of existing law; Construction of provisions drawn from uniform acts

(a) A provision of this code, insofar as it is substantially the same as a previously existing provision relating to the same subject matter, shall be construed as a restatement and continuation thereof and not as a new enactment.

(b) A provision of this code, insofar as it is the same in substance as a provision of a uniform act, shall be so construed as to effectuate the general purpose to make uniform the law in those states which enact that provision. **Leg.H.** Enacted Stats 1990 ch 79 §14 (AB 759), operative July 1, 1991.

Prior Law: Former Prob C §2, similar to the present section, was added Stats 1983 ch 842 §21, operative January 1, 1985, and repealed Stats 1990 ch 79 §13, operative July 1, 1991.

Former Prob C §2, similar to the present section, was enacted Stats 1931 and repealed Stats 1983 ch 842 §17, operative January 1, 1985.

§3. General transitional provision

(a) As used in this section:

(1) "New law" means either of the following, as the case may be:

(A) The act that enacted this code.

(B) The act that makes a change in this code, whether effectuated by amendment, addition, or repeal of any provision of this code.

(2) "Old law" means the applicable law in effect before the operative date of the new law.

(3) "Operative date" means the operative date of the new law.

(b) This section governs the application of a new law except to the extent otherwise expressly provided in the new law.

(c) Subject to the limitations provided in this section, a new law applies on the operative date to all matters governed by the new law, regardless of whether an event occurred or circumstance existed before, on, or after the operative date, including, but not limited to, creation of a fiduciary relationship, death of a person, commencement of a proceeding, making of an order, or taking of an action.

(d) If a petition, account, report, inventory, appraisal, or other document or paper is filed before the operative date, the contents, execution, and notice thereof are governed by the old law and not by the new law; but any subsequent proceedings taken after the operative date concerning the petition, account, report, inventory, appraisal, or other document or paper, including an objection or response, a hearing, an order, or other matter relating thereto is governed by the new law and not by the old law.

(e) If an order is made before the operative date, including an order appointing a personal representative, guardian, conservator, trustee, probate referee, or any other fiduciary or officer, or any action on an order is taken before the operative date, the validity of the order or action is governed by the old law and not by the new law. Nothing in this subdivision precludes proceedings after the operative date to modify an order made, or alter a course of action commenced, before the operative date to the extent proceedings for modification of an order or alteration of a course of action of that type are otherwise provided by statute.

(f) No personal representative, guardian, conservator, trustee, probate referee, or any other fiduciary, officer, or person is liable for any action taken before the operative date that was proper at the time the action was taken, even though the action would be improper if taken on or after the operative date, and such a person has no duty, as a result of the enactment of the new law, to take any step to alter the course of action or its consequences.

(g) If the new law does not apply to a matter that occurred before the operative date, the old law continues to govern the matter notwithstanding its amendment or repeal by the new law.

(h) If a party shows, and the court determines, that application of a particular provision of the new law or of the old law in the manner required by this section or by the new law would substantially interfere with the effective conduct of the proceedings or the rights of the parties or other interested persons in connection with an event that occurred or circumstance that existed before the operative date, the court may, notwithstanding this section or the new law, apply either the new law or the old law to the extent reasonably necessary to mitigate the substantial interference. **Leg.H.** Enacted Stats 1990 ch 79 §14 (AB 759), operative July 1, 1991.

Prior Law: Former Prob C §3, similar to the present section, was added Stats 1988 ch 1199 §24.5, operative July 1, 1989, amended Stats 1989 ch 21 §1, effective May 25, 1989, operative July 1, 1989, and repealed Stats 1990 ch 79 §13, operative July 1, 1991.

Former Prob C §3, relating to transitional provision for former statute, was added Stats 1983 ch 842 §21, operative January 1, 1985, and repealed Stats 1984 ch 892 §3.

Former Prob C §3, relating to actions, etc., not affected by code, was enacted Stats 1931 and repealed Stats 1983 ch 842 §17, operative January 1, 1985.

§4. Effect of headings in code

Division, part, chapter, article, and section headings do not in any manner affect the scope, meaning, or intent of the provisions of this code. **Leg.H.** Enacted Stats 1990 ch 79 §14 (AB 759), operative July 1, 1991.

Prior Law: Former Prob C §4, similar to the present section, was added Stats 1983 ch 842 §21, operative January 1, 1985, and repealed Stats 1990 ch 79 §13, operative July 1, 1991.

Former Prob C §4, similar to the present section, was added Stats 1943 ch 523 §1 and repealed Stats 1983 ch 482 §17, operative January 1, 1985.

§5. Certified mail sufficient compliance with requirement of use of registered mail

If a notice or other communication is required by this code to be mailed by registered mail, the mailing of the notice or other communication by certified mail is deemed to be sufficient compliance with the requirement. **Leg.H.** Enacted Stats 1990 ch 79 §14 (AB 759), operative July 1, 1991.

Prior Law: Former Prob C 5, similar to the present section, was added Stats 1983 ch 842 §21, operative January 1, 1985, and repealed Stats 1990 ch 79 §13, operative July 1, 1991.

Former Prob C 5, similar to the present section, was added Stats 1959 ch 426 §7 and repealed Stats 1983 ch 482 §17, operative January 1, 1985.

§6. Construction of code

Unless the provision or context otherwise requires, the general provisions and rules of construction in this part govern the construction of this code. **Leg.H.** Enacted Stats 1990 ch 79 §14 (AB 759), operative July 1, 1991.

Prior Law: Former Prob C 6, similar to the present section, was added Stats 1983 ch 842 §21, operative January 1, 1985, and repealed Stats 1990 ch 79 §13, operative July 1, 1991.

Former Prob C 6, similar to the present section, was added Stats 1979 ch 165 §1 and repealed Stats 1983 ch 482 §17, operative January 1, 1985.

§7. Reference to statute includes amendments and additions

Whenever a reference is made to any portion of this code or to any other law, the reference applies to all amendments and additions heretofore or hereafter made. **Leg.H.** Enacted Stats 1990 ch 79 §14 (AB 759), operative July 1, 1991.

Prior Law: Former Prob C 7, similar to the present section, was added Stats 1983 ch 842 §21, operative January 1, 1985, and repealed Stats 1990 ch 79 §13, operative July 1, 1991.

Former Prob C 7, similar to the present section, was added Stats 1979 ch 165 §2 and repealed Stats 1983 ch 482 §17, operative January 1, 1985.

§8. Reference to division, part, chapter, article, section, or part of section

Unless otherwise expressly stated:

(a) "Division" means a division of this code.

(b) "Part" means a part of the division in which that term occurs.

(c) "Chapter" means a chapter of the division or part, as the case may be, in which that term occurs.

(d) "Article" means an article of the chapter in which that term occurs.

(e) "Section" means a section of this code.

(f) "Subdivision" means a subdivision of the section in which that term occurs.

(g) "Paragraph" means a paragraph of the subdivision in which that term occurs.

(h) "Subparagraph" means a subparagraph of the paragraph in which that term occurs. **Leg.H.** Enacted Stats 1990 ch 79 §14 (AB 759), operative July 1, 1991.

Prior Law: Former Prob C §8, similar to the present section, was added Stats 1983 ch 842 §21, operative January 1, 1985, amended Stats 1987 ch 923 §4, operative January 1, 1988, and repealed Stats 1990 ch 79 §13, operative July 1, 1991.

Former Prob C §8, similar to the present section, was added Stats 1979 ch 165 §3 and repealed Stats 1983 ch 482 §17, operative January 1, 1985.

§9. Construction of tenses

The present tense includes the past and future tenses, and the future, the present. **Leg.H.** Enacted Stats 1990 ch 79 §14 (AB 759), operative July 1, 1991.

Prior Law: Former Prob C 9, similar to the present section, was added Stats 1983 ch 842 §21, operative January 1, 1985, and repealed Stats 1990 ch 79 §13, operative July 1, 1991.

Former Prob C 9, similar to the present section, was added Stats 1979 ch 165 §4 and repealed Stats 1983 ch 482 §17, operative January 1, 1985.

§10. Construction of singular and plural

The singular number includes the plural, and the plural, the singular. **Leg.H.** Enacted Stats 1990 ch 79 §14 (AB 759), operative July 1, 1991.

Prior Law: Former Prob C 10, similar to the present section, was added Stats 1983 ch 842 §21, operative January 1, 1985, and repealed Stats 1990 ch 79 §13, operative July 1, 1991.

Former Prob C 10, similar to the present section, was added Stats 1979 ch 165 §5 and repealed Stats 1983 ch 482 §17, operative January 1, 1985.

§11. Severability of provisions

If any provision or clause of this code or application thereof to any person or circumstances is held invalid, the invalidity does not affect other provisions or applications of the code which can be given effect without the invalid provision or application, and to this end the provisions of this code are severable. **Leg.H.** Enacted Stats 1990 ch 79 §14 (AB 759), operative July 1, 1991.

Prior Law: Former Prob C 11, similar to the present section, was added Stats 1983 ch 842 §21, operative January 1, 1985, and repealed Stats 1990 ch 79 §13, operative July 1, 1991.

Former Prob C 11, similar to the present section, was added Stats 1979 ch 165 §6 and repealed Stats 1983 ch 482 §17, operative January 1, 1985.

§12. Meaning of "shall" and "may"

"Shall" is mandatory and "may" is permissive. **Leg.H.** Enacted Stats 1990 ch 79 §14 (AB 759), operative July 1, 1991.

Prior Law: Former Prob C 12, similar to the present section, was added Stats 1983 ch 842 §21, operative January 1, 1985, and repealed Stats 1990 ch 79 §13, operative July 1, 1991.

§13. Determination of degree of kinship or consanguinity

(a) The degree of kinship or consanguinity between two persons is determined by counting the number of generations separating those persons, pursuant to subdivision (b) or (c). Each generation is called a degree.

(b) Lineal kinship or consanguinity is the relationship between two persons, one of whom is a direct descendant of the other. The degree of kinship between those persons is determined by counting the generations separating the first person from the second person. In counting the generations, the first person is excluded and the second person is included. For example, parent and child are related in the first degree of lineal kinship or consanguinity, grandchild and grandparent are related in the second degree, and great-grandchild and great-grandparent are related in the third degree.

(c) Collateral kinship or consanguinity is the relationship between two people who spring from a common ancestor, but neither person is the direct descendent of the other. The degree of kinship is determined by counting the generations from the first person up to the common ancestor and from the common ancestor down to the second person. In counting the generations, the first person is excluded, the second person is included, and the common ancestor is counted only once. For example, siblings are related in the second degree of collateral kinship or consanguinity, an aunt or uncle and a niece or nephew are related in the third degree, and first cousins are related in the fourth degree. **Leg.H.** Added Stats 2009 ch 348 §4 (SB 308), effective January 1, 2010.

PART 2
DEFINITIONS

Application of definitions. §20.
"Account". §21.
"Account in an insured credit union". §22.
"Account in an insured savings and loan association". §23.
"Beneficiary". §24.
"Child". §26.
"Community property". §28.
"Conservatee". §29.
"Conservator". §30.
"Devise". §32.
"Devisee". §34.
"Dissolution of marriage". §36.
"Domestic partner"; Rights of surviving domestic partner. §37.
"Family allowance". §38.
"Fiduciary". §39.
"Financial institution". §40.
"General personal representative". §42.
"Heir". §44.
"Instrument". §45.
"Insured account in a financial institution". §46.
"Interested person". §48.
"Issue". §50.
"Letters". §52.
"Parent". §54.
"Pay-on-death account" or "P.O.D. account". §55.
"Person". §56.
"Personal representative"; "General personal representative". §58.
"Predeceased spouse". §59.
"Probate homestead". §60.
"Professional fiduciary". §60.1.
"Property". §62.
"Quasi-community property". §66.
"Real property". §68.
"Revocable transfer on death deed" or "revocable TOD deed". §69.
"Security". §70.
"Spouse" to include registered domestic partner. §72.
"State". §74.
"Subscribing witness". §76.
"Surviving spouse". §78.
"Totten trust account". §80.
"Transferor". §81.
"Transferee". §81.5.
"Trust". §82.
"Trust company". §83.
"Trustee". §84.
Undue influence. §86.
"Will". §88.

§20. Application of definitions

Unless the provision or context otherwise requires, the definitions in this part govern the construction of this code. **Leg.H.** Enacted Stats 1990 ch 79 §14 (AB 759), operative July 1, 1991. Amended Stats 1991 ch 82 §1, effective June 30, 1991, operative July 1, 1991.

Prior Law: Former Prob C §20, similar to the present section, was added Stats 1983 ch 842 §21, operative January 1, 1985, amended Stats 1986 ch 783 §2, operative July 1, 1987, ch 820 §27.5, operative July 1, 1987, Stats 1987 ch 923 §6, operative January 1, 1988, Stats 1988 ch 1199 §25, operative July 1, 1989, Stats 1989 ch 397 §21, operative July 1, 1989, and repealed Stats 1990 ch 79 §13, operative July 1, 1991.

Former Prob C §20, similar to present Prob C §§6100, 6101 and H & S C §7150.5, was enacted Stats 1931, amended Stats 1947 ch 126 §1, Stats 1957 ch 1950 §1, and repealed Stats 1983 ch 842 §18, operative January 1, 1985.

§21. "Account"

"Account," when used to mean a contract of deposit of funds between a depositor and a financial institution, includes a checking account, savings account, certificate of deposit, share account, mutual capital certificate, and other like arrangements. **Leg.H.** Enacted Stats 1990 ch 79 §14 (AB 759), operative July 1, 1991.

Prior Law: Former Prob C §21, similar to the present section, was added Stats 1983 ch 842 §21, operative January 1, 1985, amended Stats 1987 ch 923 §7, operative January 1, 1988, and repealed Stats 1990 ch 79 §13 (AB 759), operative July 1, 1991.

Former Prob C §21, similar to present Prob C §§6100 and 6101, was enacted Stats 1931, amended Stats 1933 ch 969 §1, and repealed Stats 1983 ch 842 §18, operative January 1, 1985.

§22. "Account in an insured credit union"

"Account in an insured credit union" means a share account in a credit union, either federally chartered or state licensed, that is insured under Title II of the Federal Credit Union Act (12 U.S.C. Sec. 1781, et seq.). **Leg.H.** Enacted Stats 1990 ch 79 §14 (AB 759), operative July 1, 1991.

Prior Law: Former Prob C §22, similar to the present section, was added Stats 1987 ch 923 §9, operative January 1, 1988, and repealed Stats 1990 ch 79 §13, operative July 1, 1991.

Former Prob C §22, defining "annulment of marriage", was added Stats 1983 ch 842 §21, operative January 1, 1985, and repealed Stats 1987 ch 923 §81, operative January 1, 1988.

Former Prob C §22, similar to present Prob C §6104, was enacted Stats 1931 and repealed Stats 1983 ch 842 §18, operative January 1, 1985.

§23. "Account in an insured savings and loan association"

(a) "Account in an insured savings and loan association" means a savings account or mutual capital certificate of either of the following:

(1) A federal association.

(2) A savings association doing business in this state which is an "insured institution" as defined in Title IV of the National Housing Act (12 U.S.C. Sec. 1724, et seq.).

(b) As used in this section:

(1) "Federal association" has the meaning given that term in subdivision (b) of Section 5102 of the Financial Code.

(2) "Mutual capital certificate" has the meaning given that term in Section 5111 of the Financial Code.

(3) "Savings account" has the meaning given that term in Section 5116 of the Financial Code.

(4) "Savings association" has the meaning given that term in subdivision (a) of Section 5102 of the Financial Code. **Leg.H.** Enacted Stats 1990 ch 79 §14 (AB 759), operative July 1, 1991.

Prior Law: Former Prob C §23, similar to the present section, was added Stats 1987 ch 923 §10, operative January 1, 1988, and repealed Stats 1990 ch 79 §13, operative July 1, 1991.

Former Prob C §23, similar to present Prob C §21700, was enacted Stats 1931 and repealed Stats 1983 ch 842 §18, operative January 1, 1985.

§24. "Beneficiary"

"Beneficiary" means a person to whom a donative transfer of property is made or that person's successor in interest, and:

(a) As it relates to the intestate estate of a decedent, means an heir.

(b) As it relates to the testate estate of a decedent, means a devisee.

(c) As it relates to a trust, means a person who has any present or future interest, vested or contingent.

(d) As it relates to a charitable trust, includes any person entitled to enforce the trust. **Leg.H.** Enacted Stats 1990 ch 79 §14 (AB 759), operative July 1, 1991.

Prior Law: Former Prob C §24, similar to the present section, was added Stats 1983 ch 842 §21, operative January 1, 1985, amended Stats 1986 ch 783 §2, operative July 1, 1987, ch 820 §27.5, operative July 1, 1987, Stats 1987 ch 923 §§6, 11, operative January 1, 1988, Stats 1988 ch 1199 §25, operative July 1, 1989, and repealed Stats 1990 ch 79 §13, operative July 1, 1991.

Former Prob C §24, similar to present Prob C §6105, was enacted Stats 1931 and repealed Stats 1983 ch 842 §18, operative January 1, 1985.

§26. "Child"

"Child" means any individual entitled to take as a child under this code by intestate succession from the parent whose relationship is involved. **Leg.H.** Enacted Stats 1990 ch 79 §14 (AB 759), operative July 1, 1991.

Prior Law: Former Prob C §26, similar to the present section, was added Stats 1983 ch 842 §21, operative January 1, 1985, amended Stats 1984 ch 892 §4, Stats 1987 ch 923 §12, operative January 1, 1988, and repealed Stats 1990 ch 79 §13, operative July 1, 1991.

Former Prob C §26, similar to present Prob C §6113, was enacted Stats 1931, amended Stats 1972 ch 713 §1, and repealed Stats 1983 ch 842 §18, operative January 1, 1985.

§28. "Community property"

"Community property" means:

(a) Community property heretofore or hereafter acquired during marriage by a married person while domiciled in this state.

(b) All personal property wherever situated, and all real property situated in this state, heretofore or hereafter acquired during the marriage by a married person while domiciled elsewhere, that is community property, or a substantially equivalent type of marital property, under the laws of the place where the acquiring spouse was domiciled at the time of its acquisition.

(c) All personal property wherever situated, and all real property situated in this state, heretofore or hereafter acquired during the marriage by a married person in exchange for real or personal property, wherever situated, that is community property, or a substantially equivalent type of marital property, under the laws of the place where the acquiring spouse was domiciled at the time the property so exchanged was acquired. **Leg.H.** Enacted Stats 1990 ch 79 §14 (AB 759), operative July 1, 1991.

Prior Law: Former Prob C §28, similar to the present section, was added Stats 1983 ch 842 §21, operative January 1, 1985, and repealed Stats 1990 ch 79 §13, operative July 1, 1991.

Former Prob C §28, relating to vesting of dispositions at death of testator, was enacted Stats 1931 and repealed Stats 1983 ch 842 §18, operative January 1, 1985.

§29. "Conservatee"

"Conservatee" includes a limited conservatee. **Leg.H.** Enacted Stats 1990 ch 79 §14 (AB 759), operative July 1, 1991.

Prior Law: Former Prob C §29, relating to transferee as owners in common, was enacted Stats 1931 and repealed Stats 1983 ch 842 §18, operative January 1, 1985.

§30. "Conservator"

"Conservator" includes a limited conservator. **Leg.H.** Enacted Stats 1990 ch 79 §14 (AB 759), operative July 1, 1991.

§32. "Devise"

"Devise," when used as a noun, means a disposition of real or personal property by will, and, when used as a verb, means to dispose of real or personal property by will. **Leg.H.** Enacted Stats 1990 ch 79 §14 (AB 759), operative July 1, 1991.

Prior Law: Former Prob C §32, similar to the present section, was added Stats 1983 ch 842 §21, operative January 1, 1985, and repealed Stats 1990 ch 79 §13, operative July 1, 1991.

§34. "Devisee"

(a) "Devisee" means any person designated in a will to receive a devise.

(b) In the case of a devise to an existing trust or trustee, or to a trustee on trust described by will, the trust or trustee is the devisee and the beneficiaries are not devisees. **Leg.H.** Enacted Stats 1990 ch 79 §14 (AB 759), operative July 1, 1991.

Prior Law: Former Prob C §34, similar to the present section, was added Stats 1983 ch 842 §21, operative January 1, 1985, and repealed Stats 1990 ch 79 §13, operative July 1, 1991.

§36. "Dissolution of marriage"

"Dissolution of marriage" includes divorce. **Leg.H.** Enacted Stats 1990 ch 79 §14 (AB 759), operative July 1, 1991.

Prior Law: Former Prob C §36, similar to the present section, was added Stats 1983 ch 842 §21, operative January 1, 1985, and repealed Stats 1990 ch 79 §13, operative July 1, 1991.

§37. "Domestic partner"; Rights of surviving domestic partner

(a) "Domestic partner" means one of two persons who have filed a Declaration of Domestic Partnership with the Secretary of State pursuant to Division 2.5 (commencing with Section 297) of the Family Code, provided that the domestic partnership has not been terminated pursuant to Section 299 of the Family Code.

(b) Notwithstanding Section 299 of the Family Code, if a domestic partnership is terminated by the death of one of the parties and Notice of Termination was not filed by either party prior to the date of death of the decedent, the domestic partner who survives the deceased is a surviving domestic partner, and shall be entitled to the rights of a surviving domestic partner as provided in this code. **Leg.H.** Added Stats 2001 ch 893 §13 (AB 25).

§38. "Family allowance"

"Family allowance" means an allowance provided for in Chapter 4 (commencing with Section 6540) of Part 3 of Division 6. **Leg.H.** Enacted Stats 1990 ch 79 §14 (AB 759), operative July 1, 1991.

Prior Law: Former Prob C §38, similar to the present section, was added Stats 1983 ch 842 §21, operative January 1, 1985, and repealed Stats 1990 ch 79 §13, operative July 1, 1991.

§39. "Fiduciary"

"Fiduciary" means personal representative, trustee, guardian, conservator, attorney-in-fact under a power of attorney, custodian under the California Uniform Transfer To Minors Act (Part 9 (commencing with Section 3900) of Division 4), or other legal representative subject to this code. **Leg.H.** Enacted Stats 1990 ch 79 §14 (AB 759), operative July 1, 1991. Amended Stats 1997 ch 724 §2 (AB 1172).

Prior Law: Former Prob C §39, similar to the present section, was added Stats 1988 ch 1199 §25.2, operative July 1, 1989, and repealed Stats 1990 ch 79 §13, operative July 1, 1991.

§40. "Financial institution"

"Financial institution" means a state or national bank, state or federal savings and loan association or credit union, or like organization. **Leg.H.** Enacted Stats 1990 ch 79 §14 (AB 759), operative July 1, 1991.

Prior Law: Former Prob C §40, similar to the present section, was added Stats 1983 ch 842 §21, operative January 1, 1985, and repealed Stats 1990 ch 79 §13, operative July 1, 1991.

Former Prob C §40, relating to charitable dispositions subject to code limitations, was enacted Stats 1931 and repealed Stats 1971 ch 1395 §1.

§42. "General personal representative"

"General personal representative" is defined in subdivision (b) of Section 58. **Leg.H.** Enacted Stats 1990 ch 79 §14 (AB 759), operative July 1, 1991.

Prior Law: Former Prob C §42, relating to exceptions from restrictions for gifts to the State, municipalities, etc., was enacted Stats 1931, amended Stats 1937 ch 479 §1, Stats 1939 ch 334 §1, and repealed Stats 1971 ch 1395 §1.

§44. "Heir"

"Heir" means any person, including the surviving spouse, who is entitled to take property of the decedent by intestate succession under this code. **Leg.H.** Enacted Stats 1990 ch 79 §14 (AB 759), operative July 1, 1991.

Prior Law: Former Prob C §44, similar to the present section, was added Stats 1983 ch 842 §21, operative January 1, 1985, and repealed Stats 1990 ch 79 §13, operative July 1, 1991.

§45. "Instrument"

"Instrument" means a will, a document establishing or modifying a trust, a deed, or any other writing that designates a beneficiary or makes a donative transfer of property. **Leg.H.** Enacted Stats 1990 ch 79 §14 (AB 759), operative July 1, 1991. Amended Stats 2019 ch 56 §1 (SB 308), effective January 1, 2020.

Prior Law: Former Prob C §45, similar to the present section, was added Stats 1988 ch 1199 §25.4, operative July 1, 1989, and repealed Stats 1990 ch 79 §13, operative July 1, 1991.

§46. "Insured account in a financial institution"

"Insured account in a financial institution" means an account in a bank, an account in an insured credit union, and an account in an insured savings and loan association, to the extent that the account is insured. **Leg.H.** Enacted Stats 1990 ch 79 §14 (AB 759), operative July 1, 1991.

Prior Law: Former Prob C §46, similar to the present section, was added Stats 1987 ch 923 §13, operative January 1, 1988, and repealed Stats 1990 ch 79 §13, operative July 1, 1991.

§48. "Interested person"

(a) Subject to subdivision (b), "interested person" includes any of the following:

(1) An heir, devisee, child, spouse, creditor, beneficiary, and any other person having a property right in or claim against a trust estate or the estate of a decedent which may be affected by the proceeding.

(2) Any person having priority for appointment as personal representative.

(3) A fiduciary representing an interested person.

(b) The meaning of "interested person" as it relates to particular persons may vary from time to time and shall be determined according to the particular purposes of, and matter involved in, any proceeding. **Leg.H.** Enacted Stats 1990 ch 79 §14 (AB 759), operative July 1, 1991.

Prior Law: Former Prob C §48, similar to the present section, was added Stats 1983 ch 842 §21, operative January 1, 1985, and repealed Stats 1990 ch 79 §13, operative July 1, 1991.

§50. "Issue"

"Issue" of a person means all his or her lineal descendants of all generations, with the relationship of parent and child at each generation being determined by the definitions of child and parent. **Leg.H.** Enacted Stats 1990 ch 79 §14 (AB 759), operative July 1, 1991.

Prior Law: Former Prob C §50, similar to the present section, was added Stats 1983 ch 842 §21, operative January 1, 1985, and repealed Stats 1990 ch 79 §13, operative July 1, 1991.

Former Prob C §50, similar to present Prob C §6110, was enacted Stats 1931, amended Stats 1982 ch 187 §1, and repealed Stats 1983 ch 842 §18, operative January 1, 1985.

§52. "Letters"

"Letters":

(a) As it relates to a personal representative, means letters testamentary, letters of administration, letters of administration with the will annexed, or letters of special administration.

(b) As it relates to a guardian or conservator, means letters of guardianship or conservatorship or temporary guardianship or conservatorship. **Leg.H.** Enacted Stats 1990 ch 79 §14 (AB 759), operative July 1, 1991.

Prior Law: Former Prob C §52, similar to the present section, was added Stats 1987 ch 923 §14, amended Stats 1988 ch 1199 §26, operative July 1, 1989, and repealed Stats 1990 ch 79 §13, operative July 1, 1991.

Former Prob C §52, similar to present Prob C §6112, was enacted Stats 1931 and repealed Stats 1983 ch 842 §18, operative January 1, 1985.

§54. "Parent"

"Parent" means any individual entitled to take as a parent under this code by intestate succession from the child whose relationship is involved. **Leg.H.** Enacted Stats 1990 ch 79 §14 (AB 759), operative July 1, 1991.

Prior Law: Former Prob C §54, similar to the present section, was added Stats 1983 ch 842 §21, operative January 1, 1985, amended Stats 1984 ch 892 §5, Stats 1987 ch 923 §15, operative January 1, 1988, and repealed Stats 1990 ch 79 §13, operative July 1, 1991.

Former Prob C §54, relating to nuncupative wills, was enacted Stats 1931 and repealed Stats 1982 ch 187 §4.

§55. "Pay-on-death account" or "P.O.D. account"

"Pay-on-death account" or "P.O.D. account" is defined in Section 5140. **Leg.H.** Enacted Stats 1990 ch 79 §14 (AB 759), operative July 1, 1991.

Prior Law: Former Prob C §55, relating to property disposable by nuncupative will, was enacted Stats 1931 and repealed Stats 1982 ch 187 §5.

§56. "Person"

"Person" means an individual, corporation, government or governmental subdivision or agency, business trust, estate, trust, partnership, limited liability company, association, or other entity. **Leg.H.** Enacted Stats 1990 ch 79 §14 (AB 759), operative July 1, 1991. Amended Stats 1994 ch 1010 §202 (SB 2053).

Prior Law: Former Prob C §56, similar to the present section, was added Stats 1983 ch 842 §21, operative January 1, 1985, and repealed Stats 1990 ch 79 §13, operative July 1, 1991.

Former Prob C §56, similar to present Prob C §§6200–6210, was added Stats 1982 ch 1401 §1, and repealed Stats 1983 ch 842 §18, operative January 1, 1985.

§58. "Personal representative"; "General personal representative"

(a) "Personal representative" means executor, administrator, administrator with the will annexed, special administrator, successor personal representative, public administrator acting pursuant to Section 7660, or a person who performs substantially the same function under the law of another jurisdiction governing the person's status.

(b) "General personal representative" excludes a special administrator unless the special administrator has the powers, duties, and obligations of a general personal representative under Section 8545. **Leg.H.** Enacted Stats 1990 ch 79 §14 (AB 759), operative July 1, 1991. Amended Stats 2004 ch 888 §1 (AB 2687).

Prior Law: Former Prob C §58, similar to the present section, was added Stats 1987 ch 923 §17, operative January 1, 1988, amended Stats 1988 ch 1199 §27, operative July 1, 1989, and repealed Stats 1990 ch 79 §13, operative July 1, 1991.

Former Prob C §58, defining "personal property", was added Stats 1983 ch 842 §21, operative January 1, 1985, and repealed Stats 1987 ch 923 §16, operative January 1, 1988.

§59. "Predeceased spouse"

"Predeceased spouse" means a person who died before the decedent while married to the decedent, except that the term does not include any of the following:

(a) A person who obtains or consents to a final decree or judgment of dissolution of marriage from the decedent or a final decree or judgment of annulment of their marriage, which decree or judgment is not recognized as valid in this state, unless they (1) subsequently participate in a marriage ceremony purporting to marry each to the other or (2) subsequently live together as spouses.

(b) A person who, following a decree or judgment of dissolution or annulment of marriage obtained by the decedent, participates in a marriage ceremony to a third person.

(c) A person who was a party to a valid proceeding concluded by an order purporting to terminate all marital property rights. **Leg.H.** Enacted Stats 1990 ch 79 §14 (AB 759), operative July 1, 1991. Amended Stats 2016 ch 50 §76 (SB 1005), effective January 1, 2017.

2016 Note: It is the intent of the Legislature that the changes made by this act have only technical and nonsubstantive effect. Hence, no change made by this act shall create any new right, duty, or other obligation that did not exist immediately preceding the effective date of this act, or result in the limitation or termination of any right, duty, or other obligation that existed immediately preceding the effective date of this act. Stats 2016 ch 50 (SB 1005) §125.

Prior Law: Former Prob C §59, similar to the present section, was added Stats 1984 ch 892 §6 and repealed Stats 1990 ch 79 §13, operative July 1, 1991.

§60. "Probate homestead"

"Probate homestead" means a homestead provided for in Chapter 3 (commencing with Section 6520) of Part 3 of Division 6. **Leg.H.** Enacted Stats 1990 ch 79 §14 (AB 759), operative July 1, 1991.

Prior Law: Former Prob C §60, similar to the present section, was added Stats 1983 ch 842 §21, operative January 1, 1985, and repealed Stats 1990 ch 79 §13, operative July 1, 1991.

Former Prob C §60, similar to present Prob C §6380, was added Stats 1979 ch 632 §1 and repealed Stats 1983 ch 842 §18, operative January 1, 1985.

§60.1. "Professional fiduciary"

(a) "Professional fiduciary" means a person who is a professional fiduciary as defined under subdivision (f) of Section 6501 of the Business and Professions Code.

(b) On and after January 1, 2009, no person shall act or hold himself or herself out to the public as a professional fiduciary unless he or she is licensed as a professional fiduciary under Chapter 6 (commencing with Section 6500) of Division 3 of the Business and Professions Code. **Leg.H.** Added Stats 2006 ch 491 §4 (SB 1550), effective January 1, 2007. Amended Stats 2007 ch 354 §70 (SB 1047), effective January 1, 2008.

2006 Note: This act, together with Senate Bill 1116, Senate Bill 1716, and Assembly Bill 1363, shall be known and may be cited as the Omnibus Conservatorship and Guardianship Reform Act of 2006. Stats 2006 ch 491 (SB 1550) §1.

Prior Law: Former Prob C §60.1, similar to present Prob C §6381, was added Stats 1979 ch 632 §1 and repealed Stats 1990 ch 79 §13, operative July 1, 1991.

§62. "Property"

"Property" means anything that may be the subject of ownership and includes both real and personal property and any interest therein. **Leg.H.** Enacted Stats 1990 ch 79 §14 (AB 759), operative July 1, 1991.

Prior Law: Former Prob C §62, similar to the present section, was added Stats 1983 ch 842 §21, operative January 1, 1985, amended Stats 1987 ch 923 §18, operative January 1, 1988, and repealed Stats 1990 ch 79 §13, operative July 1, 1991.

§66. "Quasi-community property"

"Quasi-community property" means the following property, other than community property as defined in Section 28:

(a) All personal property wherever situated, and all real property situated in this state, heretofore or hereafter acquired by a decedent while domiciled elsewhere that would have been the community property of the decedent and the surviving spouse if the decedent had been domiciled in this state at the time of its acquisition.

(b) All personal property wherever situated, and all real property situated in this state, heretofore or hereafter acquired in exchange for real or personal property, wherever situated, that would have been the community property of the decedent and the surviving spouse if the decedent had been domiciled in this state at the time the property so exchanged was acquired. **Leg.H.** Enacted Stats 1990 ch 79 §14 (AB 759), operative July 1, 1991.

Prior Law: Former Prob C §66, similar to the present section, was added Stats 1983 ch 842 §21, operative January 1, 1985, and repealed Stats 1990 ch 79 §13, operative July 1, 1991.

§68. "Real property"

"Real property" includes a leasehold interest in real property. Leg.H. Enacted Stats 1990 ch 79 §14 (AB 759), operative July 1, 1991.

Prior Law: Former Prob C §68, similar to the present section, was added Stats 1983 ch 842 §21 and repealed Stats 1990 ch 79 §13, operative July 1, 1991.

§69. "Revocable transfer on death deed" or "revocable TOD deed"

"Revocable transfer on death deed" or "revocable TOD deed" means a revocable transfer on death deed as described in Section 5614. Leg.H. Added Stats 2015 ch 293 §3 (AB 139), effective January 1, 2016.

§70. "Security"

"Security" includes any note, stock, treasury stock, bond, debenture, evidence of indebtedness, certificate of interest or participation in an oil, gas, or mining title or lease or in payments out of production under such a title or lease, collateral trust certificate, transferable share, voting trust certificate or, in general, any interest or instrument commonly known as a security, or any certificate of interest or participation, any temporary or interim certificate, receipt, or certificate of deposit for, or any warrant or right to subscribe to or purchase, any of the foregoing. Leg.H. Enacted Stats 1990 ch 79 §14 (AB 759), operative July 1, 1991.

Prior Law: Former Prob C §70, similar to the present section, was added Stats 1983 ch 842 §21, operative January 1, 1985, and repealed Stats 1990 ch 79 §13, operative July 1, 1991.

Former Prob C §70, similar to present Prob C §§21610–21612, was enacted Stats 1931 and repealed Stats 1983 ch 842 §18, operative January 1, 1985.

§72. "Spouse" to include registered domestic partner

"Spouse" includes domestic partner, as defined in Section 37 of this code, as required by Section 297.5 of the Family Code. Leg.H. Added Stats 2016 ch 50 §77 (SB 1005), effective January 1, 2017.

2016 Note: For legislative intent, see the 2016 Note following Prob C §59.

§74. "State"

"State" includes any state of the United States, the District of Columbia, the Commonwealth of Puerto Rico, and any territory or possession subject to the legislative authority of the United States. Leg.H. Enacted Stats 1990 ch 79 §14 (AB 759), operative July 1, 1991.

Prior Law: Former Prob C §74, similar to the present section, was added Stats 1983 ch §21, operative January 1, 1985, and repealed Stats 1990 ch 79 §13, operative July 1, 1991.

Former Prob C §74, similar to present Prob C §6120, was enacted Stats 1931 and repealed Stats 1983 ch 842 §18, operative January 1, 1985.

§76. "Subscribing witness"

A "subscribing witness" to a will means a witness who signs the will as provided in Section 6110. Leg.H. Enacted Stats 1990 ch 79 §14 (AB 759), operative July 1, 1991.

Prior Law: Former Prob C §76, similar to present Prob C §6121, was enacted Stats 1931 and repealed Stats 1983 ch 842 §18, operative January 1, 1985.

§78. "Surviving spouse"

"Surviving spouse" does not include any of the following:

(a) A person whose marriage to, or registered domestic partnership with, the decedent has been dissolved or annulled, unless, by virtue of a subsequent marriage or registered domestic partnership, the person is married to, or in a registered domestic partnership with, the decedent at the time of death.

(b) A person who obtains or consents to a final decree or judgment of dissolution of marriage or termination of registered domestic partnership from the decedent or a final decree or judgment of annulment of their marriage or termination of registered domestic partnership, which decree or judgment is not recognized as valid in this state, unless they (1) subsequently participate in a marriage ceremony purporting to marry each to the other or (2) subsequently live together as spouses.

(c) A person who, following a decree or judgment of dissolution or annulment of marriage or registered domestic partnership obtained by the decedent, participates in a marriage ceremony with a third person.

(d) A person who was a party to a valid proceeding concluded by an order purporting to terminate all marital or registered domestic partnership property rights. Leg.H. Enacted Stats 1990 ch 79 §14 (AB 759), operative July 1, 1991. Amended Stats 2016 ch 50 §78 (SB 1005), effective January 1, 2017.

2016 Note: For legislative intent, see the 2016 Note following Prob C §59.

Prior Law: Former Prob C §78, similar to the present section, was added Stats 1983 ch 842 §21, operative January 1, 1985, and repealed Stats 1990 ch 79 §13, operative July 1, 1991.

Former Prob C §78, relating to rights of beneficiary of specific encumbered gifts, was enacted Stats 1931 and repealed Stats 1983 ch 842 §18, operative January 1, 1985.

§80. "Totten trust account"

"Totten trust account" means an account in the name of one or more parties as trustee for one or more beneficiaries where the relationship is established by the form of the account and the deposit agreement with the financial institution and there is no subject of the trust other than the sums on deposit in the account. In a Totten trust account, it is not essential that payment to the beneficiary be mentioned in the deposit agreement. A Totten trust account does not include (1) a regular trust account under a testamentary trust or a trust agreement which has significance apart from the account or (2) a fiduciary account arising from a fiduciary relation such as attorney-client. Leg.H. Enacted Stats 1990 ch 79 §14 (AB 759), operative July 1, 1991.

Prior Law: Former Prob C §80, similar to the present section, was added Stats 1983 ch 842 §21, operative January 1, 1985, and repealed Stats 1990 ch 79 §13, operative July 1, 1991.

Former Prob C §80, similar to present Prob C §§140–147, was added Stats 1980 ch 1188 §2 and repealed Stats 1983 ch 842 §18, operative January 1, 1985.

§81. "Transferor"

"Transferor" means the testator, settlor, grantor, owner, or other person who executes an instrument. Leg.H. Enacted Stats 1990 ch 79 §14 (AB 759), operative July 1, 1991.

Prior Law: Former Prob C §81, similar to the present section, was added Stats 1988 ch 1199 §27.5, operative July 1, 1989, and repealed Stats 1990 ch 79 §13, operative July 1, 1991.

§81.5. "Transferee"

"Transferee" means the beneficiary, donee, or other recipient of an interest transferred by an instrument. Leg.H. Added Stats 1994 ch 806 §2 (AB 3686).

§82. "Trust"

(a) "Trust" includes the following:

(1) An express trust, private or charitable, with additions thereto, wherever and however created.

(2) A trust created or determined by a judgment or decree under which the trust is to be administered in the manner of an express trust.

(b) "Trust" excludes the following:

(1) Constructive trusts, other than those described in paragraph (2) of subdivision (a), and resulting trusts.

(2) Guardianships and conservatorships.

(3) Personal representatives.

(4) Totten trust accounts.

(5) Custodial arrangements pursuant to the Uniform Gifts to Minors Act or the Uniform Transfers to Minors Act of any state.

(6) Business trusts that are taxed as partnerships or corporations.

(7) Investment trusts subject to regulation under the laws of this state or any other jurisdiction.

(8) Common trust funds.

(9) Voting trusts.

(10) Security arrangements.

(11) Transfers in trust for purpose of suit or enforcement of a claim or right.

(12) Liquidation trusts.

(13) Trusts for the primary purpose of paying debts, dividends, interest, salaries, wages, profits, pensions, or employee benefits of any kind.

(14) Any arrangement under which a person is nominee or escrowee for another. Leg.H. Enacted Stats 1990 ch 79 §14 (AB 759), operative July 1, 1991.

Prior Law: Former Prob C §82, similar to the present section, was added Stats 1987 ch 128 §5, effective July 6, 1987, operative July 1, 1987, and repealed Stats 1990 ch 79 §13, operative July 1, 1991.

Former Prob C §82, similar to the present section, was added Stats 1983 ch 842 §21, operative January 1, 1985, amended Stats 1984 ch 892 §7, Stats 1986 ch 820

§28, operative July 1, 1987, and repealed Stats 1987 ch 128 §4, effective July 6, 1987, operative July 1, 1987.

§83. "Trust company"

"Trust company" means an entity that has qualified to engage in and conduct a trust business in this state. **Leg.H.** Enacted Stats 1990 ch 79 §14 (AB 759), operative July 1, 1991.

Prior Law: Former Prob C §83, similar to the present section, was added Stats 1986 ch 820 §29, operative July 1, 1987, and repealed Stats 1990 ch 79 §13, operative July 1, 1991.

§84. "Trustee"

"Trustee" includes an original, additional, or successor trustee, whether or not appointed or confirmed by a court. **Leg.H.** Enacted Stats 1990 ch 79 §14 (AB 759), operative July 1, 1991.

Prior Law: Former Prob C §84, similar to the present section, was added Stats 1983 ch 842 §21, operative January 1, 1985, and repealed Stats 1990 ch 79 §13, operative July 1, 1991.

§86. Undue influence

"Undue influence" has the same meaning as defined in Section 15610.70 of the Welfare and Institutions Code. It is the intent of the Legislature that this section supplement the common law meaning of undue influence without superseding or interfering with the operation of that law. **Leg.H.** Added Stats 2013 ch 668 §1 (AB 140), effective January 1, 2014.

§88. "Will"

"Will" includes codicil and any testamentary instrument which merely appoints an executor or revokes or revises another will. **Leg.H.** Enacted Stats 1990 ch 79 §14 (AB 759), operative July 1, 1991.

Prior Law: Former Prob C §88, similar to the present section, was added Stats 1983 ch 842 §21, operative January 1, 1985, and repealed Stats 1990 ch 79 §13, operative July 1, 1991.

DIVISION 2
GENERAL PROVISIONS

Part 1. Effect of Death of Married Person on Community and Quasi-Community Property.
Part 2. Right in California Real Property of Nondomiciliary Decedent.
Part 3. Contractual Arrangements Relating to Rights at Death.
Part 4. Establishing and Reporting Fact of Death.
Part 5. Simultaneous Death.
Part 6. Distribution Among Heirs or Beneficiaries.
Part 7. Effect of Homicide or Abuse of an Elder or Dependent Adult.
Part 8. Disclaimer of Testamentary and Other Interests.
Part 9. Trust Company as Fiduciary.
Part 10. Immediate Steps Concerning Decedent's Tangible Personal Property and Safe Deposit Box.
Part 11. Fiduciaries' Wartime Substitution Law.
Part 12. Probate Referees.
Part 13. Litigation Involving Decedent.
Part 14. Powers of Appointment.
Part 15. Deposit of Estate Planning Documents With Attorney.
Part 16. Jurisdiction.
Part 17. Legal Mental Capacity.
Part 18. Right to Trial.
Part 19. Conveyance or Transfer of Property Claimed to Belong to Decedent or Other Person.
Part 20. Revised Uniform Fiduciary Access to Digital Assets Act.
Part 21. Periodic Adjustment of Dollar Amounts.

PART 1
EFFECT OF DEATH OF MARRIED PERSON ON COMMUNITY AND QUASI-COMMUNITY PROPERTY

Community property. §100.
Quasi-community property. §101.
Recapture by surviving spouse of certain quasi-community property. §102.
Effect on community and quasi-community property where not clear one spouse survived the other. §103.
Community property held in certain revocable trusts. §104.
Transfers to revocable trust. §104.5.
Applicability of part. §105.

§100. Community property

(a) Upon the death of a person who is married or in a registered domestic partnership, one-half of the community property belongs to the surviving spouse and the other one-half belongs to the decedent.

(b) Notwithstanding subdivision (a), spouses may agree in writing to divide their community property on the basis of a non pro rata division of the aggregate value of the community property or on the basis of a division of each individual item or asset of community property, or partly on each basis. Nothing in this subdivision shall be construed to require this written agreement in order to permit or recognize a non pro rata division of community property. **Leg.H.** Enacted Stats 1990 ch 79 §14 (AB 759), operative July 1, 1991. Amended Stats 1998 ch 682 §2 (AB 2069); Stats 2016 ch 50 §79 (SB 1005), effective January 1, 2017.

2016 Note: For legislative intent, see the 2016 Note following Prob C §59.

Prior Law: Former Prob C §100, similar to the present section, was added Stats 1983 ch 842 §22, operative January 1, 1985, and repealed Stats 1990 ch 79 §13, operative July 1, 1991.

Former Prob C §100, similar to present Prob C §21103, was enacted Stats 1931 and repealed Stats 1983 ch 842 §18, operative January 1, 1985.

§101. Quasi-community property

(a) Upon the death of a person who is married or in a registered domestic partnership, and is domiciled in this state, one-half of the decedent's quasi-community property belongs to the surviving spouse and the other one-half belongs to the decedent.

(b) Notwithstanding subdivision (a), spouses may agree in writing to divide their quasi-community property on the basis of a non pro rata division of the aggregate value of the quasi-community property, or on the basis of a division of each individual item or asset of quasi-community property, or partly on each basis. Nothing in this subdivision shall be construed to require this written agreement in order to permit or recognize a non pro rata division of quasi-community property. **Leg.H.** Enacted Stats 1990 ch 79 §14 (AB 759), operative July 1, 1991. Amended Stats 1998 ch 682 §3 (AB 2069); Stats 2016 ch 50 §80 (SB 1005), effective January 1, 2017.

2016 Note: For legislative intent, see the 2016 Note following Prob C §59.

Prior Law: Former Prob C §101, similar to the present section, was added Stats 1983 ch 842 §22, operative January 1, 1985, and repealed Stats 1990 ch 79 §13, operative July 1, 1991.

Former Prob C §101, similar to present Prob C §21102, was enacted Stats 1931 and repealed Stats 1983 ch 842 §18, operative January 1, 1985.

§102. Recapture by surviving spouse of certain quasi-community property

(a) The decedent's surviving spouse may require the transferee of property in which the surviving spouse had an expectancy under Section 101 at the time of the transfer to restore to the decedent's estate one-half of the property if the transferee retains the property or, if not, one-half of its proceeds or, if none, one-half of its value at the time of transfer, if all of the following requirements are satisfied:

(1) The decedent died domiciled in this state.

(2) The decedent made a transfer of the property to a person other than the surviving spouse without receiving in exchange a consideration of substantial value and without the written consent or joinder of the surviving spouse.

(3) The transfer is any of the following types:

(A) A transfer under which the decedent retained at the time of death the possession or enjoyment of, or the right to income from, the property.

(B) A transfer to the extent that the decedent retained at the time of death a power, either alone or in conjunction with any other person, to revoke or to consume, invade, or dispose of the principal for the decedent's own benefit.

(C) A transfer whereby property is held at the time of the decedent's death by the decedent and another with right of survivorship.

(b) Nothing in this section requires a transferee to restore to the decedent's estate any life insurance, accident insurance, joint annuity, or pension payable to a person other than the surviving spouse.

(c) All property restored to the decedent's estate under this section belongs to the surviving spouse pursuant to Section 101 as though the transfer had not been made. **Leg.H.** Enacted Stats 1990 ch 79 §14 (AB 759), operative July 1, 1991.

Prior Law: Former Prob C §102, similar to the present section, was added Stats 1983 ch 842 §22, operative January 1, 1985, and repealed Stats 1990 ch 79 §13, operative July 1, 1991.

Former Prob C §102, similar to present Prob C §21120, was enacted Stats 1931 and repealed Stats 1983 ch 842 §18, operative January 1, 1985.

§103. Effect on community and quasi-community property where not clear one spouse survived the other

Except as provided by Section 224, if spouses die leaving community or quasi-community property and it cannot be established by clear and convincing evidence that one spouse survived the other:

(a) One-half of the community property and one-half of the quasi-community property shall be administered or distributed, or otherwise dealt with, as if one spouse had survived and as if that one-half belonged to that spouse.

(b) The other one-half of the community property and the other one-half of the quasi-community property shall be administered or distributed, or otherwise dealt with, as if the other spouse had survived and as if that one-half belonged to that spouse. **Leg.H.** Enacted Stats 1990 ch 79 §14 (AB 759), operative July 1, 1991. Amended Stats 2016 ch 50 §81 (SB 1005), effective January 1, 2017.

2016 Note: For legislative intent, see the 2016 Note following Prob C §59.

Prior Law: Former Prob C §103, similar to the present section, was added Stats 1983 ch 842 §22, operative January 1, 1985, and repealed Stats 1990 ch 79 §13, operative July 1, 1991.

Former Prob C §103, similar to present Prob C §21121, was enacted Sats 1931 and repealed Stats 1983 ch 842 §18, operative January 1, 1985.

§104. Community property held in certain revocable trusts

Notwithstanding Section 100, community property held in a revocable trust described in Section 761 of the Family Code is governed by the provisions, if any, in the trust for disposition in the event of death. **Leg.H.** Enacted Stats 1990 ch 79 §14 (AB 759), operative July 1, 1991. Amended Stats 1992 ch 163 §119 (AB 2641), operative January 1, 1994.

Prior Law: Former Prob C §104, similar to the present section, was added Stats 1983 ch 842 §22, operative January 1, 1985, amended Stats 1987 ch 128 §6, effective July 6, 1987, operative July 1, 1987, and repealed Stats 1990 ch 79 §13, operative July 1, 1991.

Former Prob C §104, similar to present Prob C §§21120, 21121, was enacted Stats 1931 and repealed Stats 1983 ch 842 §18, operative January 1, 1985.

§104.5. Transfers to revocable trust

Transfer of community and quasi-community property to a revocable trust shall be presumed to be an agreement, pursuant to Sections 100 and 101, that those assets retain their character in the aggregate for purposes of any division provided by the trust. This section shall apply to all transfers prior to, on, or after January 1, 2000. **Leg.H.** Added Stats 1999 ch 263 §1 (AB 1051).

§105. Applicability of part

This part does not apply where the decedent died before January 1, 1985, and the law applicable prior to January 1, 1985, continues to apply where the decedent died before January 1, 1985. **Leg.H.** Enacted Stats 1990 ch 79 §14 (AB 759), operative July 1, 1991.

Prior Law: Former Prob C §105, similar to the present section, was added Stats 1984 ch 892 §7.5 and repealed Stats 1990 ch 79 §13, operative July 1, 1991.

Former Prob C §105, relating to exclusion of oral declarations of testator, was enacted Stats 1931 and repealed Stats 1983 ch 842 §18, operative January 1, 1985.

PART 2
RIGHT IN CALIFORNIA REAL PROPERTY OF NONDOMICILIARY DECEDENT

Surviving spouse's right in California real property of nondomiciliary decedent. §120.

§120. Surviving spouse's right in California real property of nondomiciliary decedent

If a married person dies not domiciled in this state and leaves a valid will disposing of real property in this state which is not the community property of the decedent and the surviving spouse, the surviving spouse has the same right to elect to take a portion of or interest in such property against the will of the decedent as though the property were located in the decedent's domicile at death. **Leg.H.** Enacted Stats 1990 ch 79 §14 (AB 759), operative July 1, 1991.

Prior Law: Former Prob C §120, similar to the present section, was added Stats 1983 ch 842 §22, operative January 1, 1985, and repealed Stats 1990 ch 79 §13, operative July 1, 1991.

Former Prob C §120, similar to present Prob C §21105, was enacted Stats 1931 and repealed Stats 1983 ch 842 §18, operative January 1, 1985.

PART 3
CONTRACTUAL ARRANGEMENTS RELATING TO RIGHTS AT DEATH

Chapter 1. Surviving Spouse's Waiver of Rights.

CHAPTER 1
SURVIVING SPOUSE'S WAIVER OF RIGHTS

"Waiver" defined. §140.
Rights that may be waived. §141.
Requirement of writing and signature; Enforceability; Defenses. §142.
Enforceability of Waiver; Exceptions. §143.
Waiver enforceable in discretion of court. §144.
Effect of waiver of "all rights" or complete property settlement. §145.
Alteration, amendment, or revocation of waiver. §146.
Validity of waivers and agreements under prior law; Validity or effect of premarital property agreements; Revocation of consent or election to dispose of property under will of other spouse. §147.

§140. "Waiver" defined

As used in this chapter, "waiver" means a waiver by the surviving spouse of any of the rights listed in subdivision (a) of Section 141, whether signed before or during marriage. **Leg.H.** Enacted Stats 1990 ch 79 §14 (AB 759), operative July 1, 1991.

Prior Law: Former Prob C §140, similar to the present section, was added Stats 1983 ch 842 §22, operative January 1, 1985, amended Stats 1984 ch 892 §8, and repealed Stats 1990 ch 79 §13, operative July 1, 1991.

Former Prob C §140, relating to the death of a devisee or legatee of a limited interest before the testator's death did not defeat the interest of persons in remainder who survived the testator, was enacted Stats 1931 and repealed Stats 1983 ch 842 §18, operative January 1, 1985.

§141. Rights that may be waived

(a) The right of a surviving spouse to any of the following may be waived in whole or in part by a waiver under this chapter:

(1) Property that would pass from the decedent by intestate succession.

(2) Property that would pass from the decedent by testamentary disposition in a will executed before the waiver.

(3) A probate homestead.

(4) The right to have exempt property set aside.

(5) Family allowance.

(6) The right to have an estate set aside under Chapter 6 (commencing with Section 6600) of Part 3 of Division 6.

(7) The right to elect to take community or quasi-community property against the decedent's will.

(8) The right to take the statutory share of an omitted spouse.

(9) The right to be appointed as the personal representative of the decedent's estate.

(10) An interest in property that is the subject of a nonprobate transfer on death under Part 1 (commencing with Section 5000) of Division 5.

(b) Nothing in this chapter affects or limits the waiver or manner of waiver of rights other than those referred to in subdivision (a), including, but not limited to, the right to property that would pass from the decedent to the surviving spouse by nonprobate transfer upon the death of the decedent, such as the survivorship interest under a joint tenancy, a Totten trust account, or a pay-on-death account. **Leg.H.** Enacted Stats 1990 ch 79 §14 (AB 759), operative July 1, 1991. Amended Stats 1992 ch 51 §2 (AB 1719).

Prior Law: Former Prob C §141, similar to the present section, was added Stats 1983 ch 842 §22, operative January 1, 1985, amended Stats 1987 ch 923 §19, operative January 1, 1988, and repealed Stats 1990 ch 79 §13, operative July 1, 1991.

Former Prob C §141, defining conditional disposition as one which depends on occurrence of some uncertain event by which it is either to take effect or be defeated, was enacted Stats 1931 and repealed Stats 1983 ch 842 §18, operative January 1, 1985.

§142. Requirement of writing and signature; Enforceability; Defenses

(a) A waiver under this chapter shall be in writing and shall be signed by the surviving spouse.

(b) Subject to subdivision (c), a waiver under this chapter is enforceable only if it satisfies the requirements of subdivision (a) and is enforceable under either Section 143 or Section 144.

(c) Enforcement of the waiver against the surviving spouse is subject to the same defenses as enforcement of a contract, except that:

(1) Lack of consideration is not a defense to enforcement of the waiver.

(2) A minor intending to marry may make a waiver under this chapter as if married, but the waiver becomes effective only upon the marriage. **Leg.H.** Enacted Stats 1990 ch 79 §14 (AB 759), operative July 1, 1991.

Prior Law: Former Prob C §142, similar to the present section, was added Stats 1983 ch 842 §22, operative January 1, 1985, amended Stats 1984 ch 892 §9, and repealed Stats 1990 ch 79 §13 (AB 759), operative July 1, 1991.

Former Prob C §142, defining conditions precedent in wills, was enacted Stats 1931 and repealed Stats 1983 ch 842 §18, operative January 1, 1985.

§143. Enforceability of Waiver; Exceptions

(a) Subject to Section 142, a waiver is enforceable under this section unless the surviving spouse proves either of the following:

(1) A fair and reasonable disclosure of the property or financial obligations of the decedent was not provided to the surviving spouse prior to the signing of the waiver unless the surviving spouse waived such a fair and reasonable disclosure after advice by independent legal counsel.

(2) The surviving spouse was not represented by independent legal counsel at the time of signing of the waiver.

(b) Subdivision (b) of Section 721 of the Family Code does not apply if the waiver is enforceable under this section. **Leg.H.** Enacted Stats 1990 ch 79 §14 (AB 759), operative July 1, 1991. Amended Stats 1992 ch 163 §120 (AB 2641), operative January 1, 1994.

Prior Law: Former Prob C §143, similar to the present section, was added Stats 1983 ch 842 §22, operative January 1, 1985, amended Stats 1984 ch 892 §10, and repealed Stats 1990 ch 79 §13, operative July 1, 1991.

Former Prob C §143, defining conditions subsequent in wills, was enacted Stats 1931 and repealed Stats 1983 ch 842 §18, operative January 1, 1985.

§144. Waiver enforceable in discretion of court

(a) Except as provided in subdivision (b), subject to Section 142, a waiver is enforceable under this section if the court determines either of the following:

(1) The waiver at the time of signing made a fair and reasonable disposition of the rights of the surviving spouse.

(2) The surviving spouse had, or reasonably should have had, an adequate knowledge of the property and financial obligations of the decedent and the decedent did not violate the duty imposed by subdivision (b) of Section 721 of the Family Code.

(b) If, after considering all relevant facts and circumstances, the court finds that enforcement of the waiver pursuant to subdivision (a) would be unconscionable under the circumstances existing at the time enforcement is sought, the court may refuse to enforce the waiver, enforce the remainder of the waiver without the unconscionable provisions, or limit the application of the unconscionable provisions to avoid an unconscionable result.

(c) Except as provided in paragraph (2) of subdivision (a), subdivision (b) of Section 721 of the Family Code does not apply if the waiver is enforceable under this section. **Leg.H.** Enacted Stats 1990 ch 79 §14 (AB 759), operative July 1, 1991. Amended Stats 1992 ch 163 §121 (AB 2641), operative January 1, 1994.

Prior Law: Former Prob C §144, similar to the present section, was added Stats 1983 ch 842 §22, operative January 1, 1985, amended Stats 1984 ch 892 §11, and repealed Stats 1990 ch 79 §13 (AB 759), operative July 1, 1991.

§145. Effect of waiver of "all rights" or complete property settlement

Unless the waiver or property settlement provides to the contrary, a waiver under this chapter of "all rights" (or equivalent language) in the property or estate of a present or prospective spouse, or a complete property settlement entered into after or in anticipation of separation or dissolution or annulment of marriage, is a waiver by the spouse of the rights described in subdivision (a) of Section 141. **Leg.H.** Enacted Stats 1990 ch 79 §14 (AB 759), operative July 1, 1991.

Prior Law: Former Prob C §145, similar to the present section, was added Stats 1983 ch 842 §22, operative January 1, 1985 and repealed Stats 1990 ch 79 §13, operative July 1, 1991.

§146. Alteration, amendment, or revocation of waiver

(a) As used in this section, "agreement" means a written agreement signed by each spouse or prospective spouse altering, amending, or revoking a waiver under this chapter.

(b) Except as provided in subdivisions (c) and (d) of Section 147, unless the waiver specifically otherwise provides, a waiver under this chapter may not be altered, amended, or revoked except by a subsequent written agreement signed by each spouse or prospective spouse.

(c) Subject to subdivision (d), the agreement is enforceable only if it satisfies the requirements of subdivision (b) and is enforceable under either subdivision (e) or subdivision (f).

(d) Enforcement of the agreement against a party to the agreement is subject to the same defenses as enforcement of any other contract, except that:

(1) Lack of consideration is not a defense to enforcement of the agreement.

(2) A minor intending to marry may enter into the agreement as if married, but the agreement becomes effective only upon the marriage.

(e) Subject to subdivision (d), an agreement is enforceable under this subdivision unless the party to the agreement against whom enforcement is sought proves either of the following:

(1) A fair and reasonable disclosure of the property or financial obligations of the other spouse was not provided to the spouse against whom enforcement is sought prior to the signing of the agreement unless the spouse against whom enforcement is sought waived such a fair and reasonable disclosure after advice by independent legal counsel.

(2) The spouse against whom enforcement is sought was not represented by independent legal counsel at the time of signing of the agreement.

(f) Subject to subdivisions (d) and (g), an agreement is enforceable under this subdivision if the court determines that the agreement at the time of signing made a fair and reasonable disposition of the rights of the spouses.

(g) If, after considering all relevant facts and circumstances, the court finds that enforcement of the agreement pursuant to subdivision (f) would be unconscionable under the circumstances existing at the time enforcement is sought, the court may refuse to enforce the agreement, enforce the remainder of the agreement without the unconscionable provisions, or limit the application of the unconscionable provisions to avoid an unconscionable result.

(h) Subdivision (b) of Section 721 of the Family Code does not apply if the agreement is enforceable under this section. **Leg.H.** Enacted Stats 1990 ch 79 §14 (AB 759), operative July 1, 1991. Amended Stats 1992 ch 163 §122 (AB 2641), operative January 1, 1994.

Prior Law: Former Prob C §146, similar to the present section, was added Stats 1983 ch 842 §22, operative January 1, 1985, amended Stats 1984 ch 892 §12, and repealed Stats 1990 ch 79 §13, operative July 1, 1991.

§147. Validity of waivers and agreements under prior law; Validity or effect of premarital property agreements; Revocation of consent or election to dispose of property under will of other spouse

(a) Subject to subdivisions (c) and (d), a waiver, agreement, or property settlement made after December 31, 1984, is invalid insofar as it affects the rights listed in subdivision (a) of Section 141 unless it satisfies the requirements of this chapter.

(b) Nothing in this chapter affects the validity or effect of any waiver, agreement, or property settlement made prior to January 1, 1985, and the validity and effect of such waiver, agreement, or property settlement shall continue to be determined by the law applicable to the waiver, agreement, or settlement prior to January 1, 1985.

(c) Nothing in this chapter affects the validity or effect of any premarital property agreement, whether made prior to, on, or after January 1, 1985, insofar as the premarital property agreement affects the rights listed in subdivision (a) of Section 141, and the validity and effect of such premarital property agreement shall be determined by the law otherwise applicable to the premarital property agreement. Nothing in this subdivision limits the enforceability under this chapter of a waiver made under this chapter by a person intending to marry that is otherwise enforceable under this chapter.

(d) Nothing in this chapter limits any right one spouse otherwise has to revoke a consent or election to disposition of his or her half of the community or quasi-community property under the will of the other spouse. **Leg.H.** Enacted Stats 1990 ch 79 §14 (AB 759), operative July 1, 1991.

Prior Law: Former Prob C §147, similar to the present section, was added Stats 1983 ch 842 §22, operative January 1, 1985, amended Stats 1984 ch 892 §13, and repealed Stats 1990 ch 79 §13, operative July 1, 1991.

CHAPTER 2
CONTRACTS CONCERNING WILL OR SUCCESSION [REPEALED]

§150. [Section repealed 2001.]

Leg.H. Enacted Stats 1990 ch 79 §14 (AB 759), operative July 1, 1991. Repealed Stats 2000 ch 17 §2 (AB 1491). See Prob C §21700.

Prior Law: Former Prob C §150, similar to present Prob C Prob C §21700, was added Stats 1983 ch 842 §22, operative January 1, 1985, amended Stats 1984 ch 892 §14, and repealed Stats 1990 ch 79 §13, operative July 1, 1991.

PART 4
ESTABLISHING AND REPORTING FACT OF DEATH

Chapter 1. Proceedings to Establish Death.
Chapter 2. Recording Evidence of Death.
Chapter 3. Reporting Fact of Death.

CHAPTER 1
PROCEEDINGS TO ESTABLISH DEATH

Commencement of proceedings. §200.
Venue; Contents of petition. §201.
Pendency of administration proceedings; Combined proceedings. §202.
Notice of hearing. §203.
Admission of petition and affidavits in evidence; Judgment as prima facie evidence. §204.

§200. Commencement of proceedings

If title to or an interest in real or personal property is affected by the death of a person, another person who claims an interest in the property may commence proceedings pursuant to this chapter to establish the fact of the death. **Leg.H.** Enacted Stats 1990 ch 79 §14 (AB 759), operative July 1, 1991.

Prior Law: Former Prob C §200, similar to the present section, was added Stats 1984 ch 527 §2 and repealed Stats 1990 ch 79 §13, operative July 1, 1991.

Former Prob C §200, similar to present Prob C §6400, was enacted Stats 1931 and repealed Stats 1983 ch 842 §19, operative January 1, 1985.

§201. Venue; Contents of petition

(a) Proceedings under this chapter shall be commenced in the superior court of the county of which the decedent was a resident at the time of death or in the superior court of any county in which the property is located.

(b) Proceedings under this chapter shall be commenced by filing a petition that sets forth all of the following information:

(1) The jurisdictional facts.

(2) A particular description of the affected property and of the interest of the petitioner in the property. **Leg.H.** Enacted Stats 1990 ch 79 §14 (AB 759), operative July 1, 1991.

Prior Law: Former Prob C §201, similar to the present section, was added Stats 1984 ch 527 §2 and repealed Stats 1990 ch 79 §13, operative July 1, 1991.

Former Prob C §201, similar to present Prob C §§100, 6101, 6401, was enacted Stats 1931, amended Stats 1935 ch 831 §2, and repealed Stats 1983 ch 842 §19, operative January 1, 1985.

§202. Pendency of administration proceedings; Combined proceedings

If proceedings for the administration of the decedent's estate are pending, proceedings under this chapter may be combined with the administration proceedings in the following manner:

(a) The petition shall be filed in the administration proceedings by the person affected or by the personal representative.

(b) The petition shall be filed at any time before the filing of a petition for final distribution. The petition may be included in a petition for probate of the will of the decedent or for letters.

(c) The petition shall be filed without any additional fee. **Leg.H.** Enacted Stats 1990 ch 79 §14 (AB 759), operative July 1, 1991.

Prior Law: Former Prob C §202, similar to the present section, was added Stats 1984 ch 527 §2 and repealed Stats 1990 ch 79 §13, operative July 1, 1991.

Former Prob C §202, similar to present Prob C §§13500, 13503, was added Stats 1974 ch 11 §2, operative January 1, 1975, amended Stats 1974 ch 752 §5, Stats 1975 ch 173 §2, effective June 30, 1975, Stats 1979 ch 730 §98, operative January 1, 1981, ch 731 §1, ch 731 §1.1, operative January 1, 1981, Stats 1980 ch 955 §2, and repealed Stats 1983 ch 842 §19, operative January 1, 1985.

Former Prob C §202, similar to present Prob C §§13501, 13550–13554, was enacted Stats 1931 and repealed Stats 1974 ch 11 §1, operative January 1, 1975.

§203. Notice of hearing

(a) Except as provided in subdivision (b), notice of the hearing shall be given as provided in Section 1220.

(b) If the person who commenced the proceedings files an affidavit with the petition stating that the person has no reason to believe there is any opposition to, or contest of, the petition, the court may act ex parte. **Leg.H.** Enacted Stats 1990 ch 79 §14 (AB 759), operative July 1, 1991.

Prior Law: Former Prob C §203, similar to the present section, was added Stats 1984 ch 527 §2, amended Stats 1987 ch 923 §21, operative July 1, 1988, and repealed Stats 1990 ch 79 §13, operative July 1, 1991.

Former Prob C §203, similar to present Prob C §§13540, 13541, was enacted Stats 1931, amended Stats 1945 ch 1028 §1, Stats 1974 ch 11 §3, operative January 1, 1975, ch 752 §6, Stats 1975 ch 173 §3, effective June 30, 1975, Stats 1980 ch 955 §3, and repealed Stats 1983 ch 842 §19, operative January 1, 1985.

§204. Admission of petition and affidavits in evidence; Judgment as prima facie evidence

(a) The petition and supporting affidavits may be received in evidence and acted upon by the court with the same force and effect as if the petitioner and affiants were personally present and testified to the facts set forth.

(b) The court may render judgment establishing the fact of the death. The judgment is prima facie evidence of the fact of the death. The presumption established by this subdivision is a presumption affecting the burden of producing evidence. **Leg.H.** Enacted Stats 1990 ch 79 §14 (AB 759), operative July 1, 1991.

Prior Law: Former Prob C §204, similar to the present section, was added Stats 1984 ch 527 §2 and repealed Stats 1990 ch 79 §13, operative July 1, 1991.

Former Prob C §204, relating to disposal by deceased spouse to someone other than surviving spouse, was added Stats 1974 ch 11 §5, operative January 1, 1975, amended Stats 1974 ch 752 §7, Stats 1975 ch 173 §4, effective June 30, 1975, Stats 1977 ch 334 §1, Stats 1980 ch 955 §4, and repealed Stats 1983 ch 842 §19, operative January 1, 1985.

Former Prob C §204, similar to present Prob C §§104, 13504, was added Stats 1969 ch 647 §4, amended Stats 1970 ch 517 §3, and repealed Stats 1974 ch 11 §4, operative January 1, 1975.

CHAPTER 2
RECORDING EVIDENCE OF DEATH

Documents which may be recorded. §210.
Documents subject to statutory requirements; Index entry. §211.
Recorded document as prima facie evidence of death. §212.

§210. Documents which may be recorded

If title to real property is affected by the death of a person, any person may record in the county in which the property is located any of the following documents establishing the fact of the death:

(a) An affidavit of death executed by a person having knowledge of the facts. The affidavit shall include a particular description of the real property and an attested or certified copy of a record of the death made and filed in a designated public office as required by law. For purposes of this subdivision, a certified copy issued in this state shall include any copy issued pursuant to Section 103525 of, subdivision (a) of Section 103526 of, or paragraph (1) of subdivision (b) of Section 103526 of, the Health and Safety Code.

(b) A certified copy of a court order that determines the fact of death made pursuant to Chapter 1 (commencing with Section 200) or pursuant to another statute that provides for a determination of the fact of death. **Leg.H.** Enacted Stats 1990 ch 79 §14 (AB 759), operative July 1, 1991. Amended Stats 2013 ch 78 §4 (AB 464), effective January 1, 2014.

Prior Law: Former Prob C §210, similar to the present section, was added Stats 1984 ch 527 §2 and repealed Stats 1990 ch 79 §13, operative July 1, 1991.

§211. Documents subject to statutory requirements; Index entry

(a) A document establishing the fact of death recorded pursuant to this chapter is subject to all statutory requirements for recorded documents.

(b) The county recorder shall index a document establishing the fact of death recorded pursuant to this chapter in the index of grantors and grantees. The index entry shall be for the grantor, and for the purpose of this index, the person whose death is established shall be deemed to be the grantor. **Leg.H.** Enacted Stats 1990 ch 79 §14 (AB 759), operative July 1, 1991.

Prior Law: Former Prob C §211, similar to the present section, was added Stats 1984 ch 527 §2 and repealed Stats 1990 ch 79 §13, operative July 1, 1991.

§212. Recorded document as prima facie evidence of death

A document establishing the fact of the death of a person recorded pursuant to this chapter is prima facie evidence of the death insofar as the document identifies real property located in the county, title to which is affected by the death. The presumption established by this section is a presumption affecting the burden of producing evidence. **Leg.H.** Enacted Stats 1990 ch 79 §14 (AB 759), operative July 1, 1991.

Prior Law: Former Prob C §212, similar to the present section, was added Stats 1984 ch 527 §2 and repealed Stats 1990 ch 79 §13, operative July 1, 1991.

CHAPTER 3
REPORTING FACT OF DEATH

Notice to Director of Health Care Services. §215.
Notice of death of person who has heir or beneficiary confined in prison or correctional facility; Contents. §216.
In-person cancellation of services not required for deceased person. §217.

§215. Notice to Director of Health Care Services

Where a deceased person has received or may have received health care under Chapter 7 (commencing with Section 14000) or Chapter 8 (commencing with Section 14200) of Part 3 of Division 9 of the Welfare and Institutions Code, or was the surviving spouse of a person who received that health care, the estate attorney, or if there is no estate attorney, the beneficiary, the personal representative, or the person in possession of property of the decedent shall give the Director of Health Care Services notice of the decedent's death not later than 90 days after the date of death. The notice shall include a copy of the decedent's death certificate. The notice shall be given as provided in Section 1215, addressed to the director at the Sacramento office of the director. **Leg.H.** Added Stats 1990 ch 79 §14 (AB 759), operative July 1, 1991. Amended Stats 1993 ch 69 §4 (SB 35), effective June 30, 1993; Stats 2014 ch 71 §135 (SB 1304), effective January 1, 2015.

Prior Law: Former Prob C §215, similar to the present section, was added Stats 1987 ch 923 §22, operative July 1, 1988, amended Stats 1988 ch 830 §1, ch 1051 §1, and repealed Stats 1990 ch 79 §13, operative July 1, 1991.

§216. Notice of death of person who has heir or beneficiary confined in prison or correctional facility; Contents

(a) For the purposes of this section "confined" means to be confined in a prison or facility under the jurisdiction of the Department of Corrections and Rehabilitation, or its Division of Juvenile Facilities, or confined in any county or city jail, road camp, industrial farm, or other local correctional facility.

(b) The estate attorney, or if there is no estate attorney, the beneficiary, the personal representative, or the person in possession of property of the decedent shall give the Director of the California Victim Compensation Board notice of a decedent's death not later than 90 days after the date of death in either of the following circumstances:

(1) The deceased person has an heir or beneficiary who is confined.

(2) The estate attorney, or if there is no estate attorney, the beneficiary, the personal representative, or the person in possession of property of the decedent, knows that an heir or beneficiary has previously been confined.

(c) The notice shall be given as provided in Section 1215 and shall include all of the following:

(1) The name, date of birth, and location of incarceration, or current address if no longer incarcerated, of the decedent's heir or beneficiary.

(2) The heir's or beneficiary's CDCR number if incarcerated in a Department of Corrections and Rehabilitation facility or booking number if incarcerated in a county facility.

(3) A copy of the decedent's death certificate.

(4) The probate case number, and the name of the superior court hearing the case.

(d) Nothing in this section shall be interpreted as requiring the estate attorney, the beneficiary, the personal representative, or the person in possession of property of the decedent to conduct an additional investigation to determine whether a decedent has an heir or beneficiary who has been confined in a prison or facility under the jurisdiction of the Department of Corrections and Rehabilitation, or its Division of Juvenile Facilities, or confined in any county or city jail, road camp, industrial farm, or other local correctional facility. **Leg.H.** Added Stats 2005 ch 238 §3 (SB 972), effective January 1, 2006. Amended Stats 2008 ch 582 §3 (AB 717), effective January 1, 2009; Stats 2014 ch 508 §3 (AB 2685), effective January 1, 2015; Stats 2016 ch 31 §260 (SB 836), effective June 27, 2016.

§217. In-person cancellation of services not required for deceased person

(a) A business that receives an oral or written request from a family member, attorney, or personal representative of a deceased person to cancel that person's services may not require an in-person cancellation.

(b) For purposes of this section, "services" include, but are not limited to, gas, electrical, water, sewage, cable, satellite, telephone, or cellular telephone service. **Leg.H.** Added Stats 2007 ch 14 §1 (AB 604), effective January 1, 2008.

PART 5
SIMULTANEOUS DEATH

Chapter 1. General Provisions.
Chapter 2. Proceedings to Determine Survival.

CHAPTER 1
GENERAL PROVISIONS

Proof of survival by clear and convincing evidence. §220.
Exceptions to applicability of chapter. §221.
Survival of beneficiaries. §222.
Joint tenants. §223.
Life or accident insurance. §224.
Chapter not applicable if death prior to January 1, 1985. §226.

§220. Proof of survival by clear and convincing evidence

Except as otherwise provided in this chapter, if the title to property or the devolution of property depends upon priority of death and it cannot be established by clear and convincing evidence that one of the persons survived the other, the property of each person shall be administered or distributed, or otherwise dealt with, as if that person had survived the other. **Leg.H.** Enacted Stats 1990 ch 79 §14 (AB 759), operative July 1, 1991.

Prior Law: Former Prob C §220, similar to the present section, was added Stats 1983 ch 842 §22, operative January 1, 1985, and repealed Stats 1990 ch 79 §13, operative July 1, 1991.

Former Prob C §220, similar to present Prob C §§101, 102, 140–147, 6400, was enacted Stats 1931, amended Stats 1935 ch 831 §3, and repealed Stats 1983 ch 842 §19, operative January 1, 1985.

§221. Exceptions to applicability of chapter

(a) This chapter does not apply in any case where Section 103, 6211, or 6403 applies.

(b) This chapter does not apply in the case of a trust, deed, or contract of insurance, or any other situation, where (1) provision is made dealing explicitly with simultaneous deaths or deaths in a common disaster or otherwise providing for distribution of property different from the provisions of this chapter or (2) provision is made requiring one person to survive another for a stated period in order to take property or providing for a presumption as to survivorship that results in a distribution of property different from that provided by this chapter. **Leg.H.** Enacted Stats 1990 ch 79 §14 (AB 759), operative July 1, 1991. Amended Stats 1990 ch 710 §1 (SB 1775), operative July 1, 1991; Stats 2002 ch 138 §3 (AB 1784).

Prior Law: Former Prob C §221, similar to the present section, was added Stats 1983 ch 842 §22, operative January 1, 1985, repealed Stats 1990 ch 79 §13, operative July 1, 1991.

Former Prob C §221, similar to present Prob C §§240, 6401, 6402, was enacted Stats 1931 and repealed Stats 1983 ch 842 §19, operative January 1, 1985.

§222. Survival of beneficiaries

(a) If property is so disposed of that the right of a beneficiary to succeed to any interest in the property is conditional upon surviving another person and it cannot be established by clear and convincing evidence that the beneficiary survived the other person, the beneficiary is deemed not to have survived the other person.

(b) If property is so disposed of that one of two or more beneficiaries would have been entitled to the property if he or she had survived the others, and it cannot be established by clear and convincing evidence that any beneficiary survived any other beneficiary, the property shall be divided into as many equal portions as there are beneficiaries and the portion of each beneficiary shall be administered or distributed, or otherwise dealt with, as if that beneficiary had survived the other beneficiaries. **Leg.H.** Enacted Stats 1990 ch 79 §14 (AB 759), operative July 1, 1991.

Prior Law: Former Prob C §222, similar to the present section, was added Stats 1983 ch 842 §22, operative January 1, 1985, and repealed Stats 1990 ch 79 §13, operative July 1, 1991.

Former Prob C §222, similar to present Prob C §§240 and 6402, was enacted Stats 1931 and repealed Stats 1983 ch 842 §19, operative January 1, 1985.

§223. Joint tenants

(a) As used in this section, "joint tenants" includes owners of property held under circumstances that entitled one or more to the whole of the property on the death of the other or others.

(b) If property is held by two joint tenants and both of them have died and it cannot be established by clear and convincing evidence that one survived the other, the property held in joint tenancy shall be administered or distributed, or otherwise dealt with, one-half as if one joint tenant had survived and one-half as if the other joint tenant had survived.

(c) If property is held by more than two joint tenants and all of them have died and it cannot be established by clear and convincing evidence that any of them survived the others, the property held in joint tenancy shall be divided into as many portions as there are joint tenants and the share of each joint tenant shall be administered or distributed, or otherwise dealt with, as if that joint tenant had survived the other joint tenants. **Leg.H.** Enacted Stats 1990 ch 79 §14 (AB 759), operative July 1, 1991.

Prior Law: Former Prob C §223, similar to the present section, was added Stats 1983 ch 842 §22, operative January 1, 1985, and repealed Stats 1990 ch 79 §13, operative July 1, 1991.

Former Prob C §223, similar to present Prob C §§240, 6401, and 6402, was enacted Stats 1931 and repealed Stats 1983 ch 842 §19, operative January 1, 1985.

§224. Life or accident insurance

If the insured and a beneficiary under a policy of life or accident insurance have died and it cannot be established by clear and convincing evidence that the beneficiary survived the insured, the proceeds of the policy shall be administered or distributed, or otherwise dealt with, as if the insured had survived the beneficiary, except if the policy is community or quasi-community property of the insured and the spouse of the insured and there is no alternative beneficiary except the estate or personal representative of the insured, the proceeds shall be distributed as community property under Section 103. **Leg.H.** Enacted Stats 1990 ch 79 §14 (AB 759), operative July 1, 1991.

Prior Law: Former Prob C §224, similar to the present section, was added Stats 1983 ch 842 §22, operative January 1, 1985, amended Stats 1984 ch 892 §15, and repealed Stats 1990 ch 79 §13, operative July 1, 1991.

Former Prob C §224, similar to present Prob C §6401, was enacted Stats 1931 and repealed Stats 1983 ch 842 §19, operative January 1, 1985.

§226. Chapter not applicable if death prior to January 1, 1985

This chapter does not apply where a person the priority of whose death is in issue died before January 1, 1985, and the law applicable prior to January 1, 1985, continues to apply where none of the persons the priority of whose death is in issue died on or after January 1, 1985. **Leg.H.** Enacted Stats 1990 ch 79 §14 (AB 759), operative July 1, 1991.

Prior Law: Former Prob C §226, similar to the present section, was added Stats 1984 ch 892 §15.2 and repealed Stats 1990 ch 79 §13, operative July 1, 1991.

Former Prob C §226, similar to present Prob C §§240 and 6402, was enacted Stats 1931 and repealed Stats 1983 ch 842 §19, operative January 1, 1985.

CHAPTER 2
PROCEEDINGS TO DETERMINE SURVIVAL

Petition for purpose of determining survival. §230.
Persons authorized to file petition. §231.
Court where petition is to be filed. §232.
Notice of hearing. §233.
Determination and order. §234.

§230. Petition for purpose of determining survival

A petition may be filed under this chapter for any one or more of the following purposes:

(a) To determine for the purposes of Section 103, 220, 222, 223, 224, 6211, 6242, 6243, 6403, 21109, 21110 or other provision of this code whether one person survived another.

(b) To determine for the purposes of Section 673 whether issue of an appointee survived the donee.

(c) To determine for the purposes of Section 24611 of the Education Code whether a person has survived in order to receive benefits payable under the system.

(d) To determine for the purposes of Section 21509 of the Government Code whether a person has survived in order to receive money payable under the system. **Leg.H.** Enacted Stats 1990 ch 79 §14 (AB 759), operative July 1, 1991. Amended Stats 1990 ch 710 §2 (SB 1775), operative July 1, 1991; Stats 2002 ch 138 §4 (AB 1784).

Prior Law: Former Prob C §230, similar to the present section, was added Stats 1983 ch 842 §22, operative January 1, 1985, and repealed Stats 1990 ch 79 §13, operative July 1, 1991.

Former Prob C §230, similar to present Prob C §§240 and 6402, was enacted Stats 1931 and repealed Stats 1983 ch 842 §19, operative January 1, 1985.

§231. Persons authorized to file petition

A petition may be filed under this chapter by any of the following:

(a) The personal representative of any person the priority of whose death is in issue under the applicable provision referred to in Section 230.

(b) Any other person interested in the estate of any such person. **Leg.H.** Enacted Stats 1990 ch 79 §14 (AB 759), operative July 1, 1991.

Prior Law: Former Prob C §231, similar to the present section, was added Stats 1983 ch 842 §22, operative January 1, 1985, and repealed Stats 1990 ch 79 §13, operative July 1, 1991.

Former Prob C §231, similar to present Prob C §§6404, 6800, 6806, was enacted Stats 1931, amended Stats 1951 ch 1708 §35.1, Stats 1965 ch 2066 §1, Stats 1968 ch 247 §3, Stats 1972 ch 856 §5, operative January 1, 1973, Stats 1982 ch 182 §1, and repealed Stats 1983 ch 842 §19, operative January 1, 1985.

§232. Court where petition is to be filed

(a) The petition shall be filed in the estate proceeding in which the person filing the petition received his or her appointment or in the estate proceeding for the estate in which the person filing the petition claims an interest.

(b) The court that first acquires jurisdiction under this section has exclusive jurisdiction for the purposes of this chapter. **Leg.H.** Enacted Stats 1990 ch 79 §14 (AB 759), operative July 1, 1991.

Prior Law: Former Prob C §232, similar to the present section, was added Stats 1983 ch 842 §22, operative January 1, 1985, and repealed Stats 1990 ch 79 §13, operative July 1, 1991.

Former Prob C §232, similar to present Prob C §6801, was added Stats 1968 ch 247 §4 and repealed Stats 1983 ch 842 §19, operative January 1, 1985.

§233. Notice of hearing

Notice of the hearing on the petition shall be given as provided in Section 1220 to all of the following persons:

(a) The personal representative of each person the priority of whose death is in issue if there is a personal representative for the person.

(b) Each known devisee of each person the priority of whose death is in issue.

(c) Each known heir of each person the priority of whose death is in issue.

(d) All persons (or their attorneys if they have appeared by attorneys) who have requested special notice as provided in Section 1250 in the proceeding in which the petition is filed or who have given notice of appearance in person or by attorney in that proceeding. **Leg.H.** Enacted Stats 1990 ch 79 §14 (AB 759), operative July 1, 1991.

Prior Law: Former Prob C §233, similar to the present section, was added Stats 1983 ch 842 §22, operative January 1, 1985, amended Stats 1987 ch 923 §23, operative July 1, 1988, and repealed Stats 1990 ch 79 §13, operative July 1, 1991.

Former Prob C §233, similar to present Prob C §6802, was added Stats 1968 ch 247 §5 and repealed Stats 1983 ch 842 §19, operative January 1, 1985.

§234. Determination and order

If the court determines that the named persons are dead and that it has not been established by clear and convincing evidence that one person survived another, the court shall make an order to that effect. If the court determines that the named persons are dead and that there is clear and convincing evidence that one person survived another, the court shall make an order setting forth the order in which the persons died. The order, when it becomes final, is a binding determination of the facts set forth in the order and is conclusive as against the personal representatives of the deceased persons named in the order and against all persons claiming by, through, or under any of the deceased persons. **Leg.H.** Enacted Stats 1990 ch 79 §14 (AB 759), operative July 1, 1991.

Prior Law: Former Prob C §234, similar to the present section, was added Stats 1983 ch 842 §22, operative January 1, 1985, and repealed Stats 1990 ch 79 §13, operative July 1, 1991.

Former Prob C §234, similar to present Prob C §6803, was added Stats 1968 ch 247 §6 and repealed Stats 1983 ch 842 §19, operative January 1, 1985.

PART 6
DISTRIBUTION AMONG HEIRS OR BENEFICIARIES

Chapter 1. Intestate Distribution System.
Chapter 2. Distribution Under a Will, Trust, or Other Instrument.
Chapter 3. Identity of Heirs.

CHAPTER 1
INTESTATE DISTRIBUTION SYSTEM

Method of intestate distribution of shares. §240.
Section 240 not applicable where death occurs before January 1, 1985. §241.

§240. Method of intestate distribution of shares

If a statute calls for property to be distributed or taken in the manner provided in this section, the property shall be divided into as many equal shares as there are living members of the nearest generation of issue then living and deceased members of that generation who leave issue then living, each living member of the nearest generation of issue then living receiving one share and the share of each deceased member of that generation who leaves issue then living being divided in the same manner among his or her then living issue. **Leg.H.** Enacted Stats 1990 ch 79 §14 (AB 759), operative July 1, 1991.

Prior Law: Former Prob C §240, similar to the present section, was added Stats 1983 ch 842 §22, operative January 1, 1985, amended Stats 1984 ch 892 §16, Stats 1985 ch 982 §6, and repealed Stats 1990 ch 79 §13, operative July 1, 1991.

§241. Section 240 not applicable where death occurs before January 1, 1985

Section 240 does not apply where the death of the decedent in the case of intestate succession or of the testator, settlor, or other transferor occurred before January 1, 1985, and the law applicable prior to January 1, 1985, shall continue to apply where the death occurred before January 1, 1985. **Leg.H.** Enacted Stats 1990 ch 79 §14 (AB 759), operative July 1, 1991.

Prior Law: Former Prob C §241, similar to the present section, was added Stats 1984 ch 892 §16.1 and repealed Stats 1990 ch 79 §13, operative July 1, 1991.

CHAPTER 2
DISTRIBUTION UNDER A WILL, TRUST, OR OTHER INSTRUMENT

Distribution of shares where instrument does not specify manner. §245.
Distribution of shares where instrument specifies division by representation or per stirpes. §246.
Distribution of shares where instrument specifies division per capita at each generation. §247.

§245. Distribution of shares where instrument does not specify manner

(a) Where a will, trust, or other instrument calls for property to be distributed or taken "in the manner provided in Section 240 of the Probate Code," or where a will, trust, or other instrument that expresses no contrary intention provides for issue or descendants to take without specifying the manner, the property to be distributed shall be distributed in the manner provided in Section 240.

(b) Use of the following words without more, as applied to issue or descendants, is not an expression of contrary intention:
(1) "Per capita" when living members of the designated class are not all of the same generation.
(2) Contradictory wording, such as "per capita and per stirpes" or "equally and by right of representation." **Leg.H.** Enacted Stats 1990 ch 79 §14 (AB 759), operative July 1, 1991.

Prior Law: Former Prob C §245, similar to the present section, was added Stats 1985 ch 982 §7 and repealed Stats 1990 ch 79 §13, operative July 1, 1991.

§246. Distribution of shares where instrument specifies division by representation or per stirpes

(a) Where a will, trust, or other instrument calls for property to be distributed or taken "in the manner provided in Section 246 of the Probate Code," the property to be distributed shall be divided into as many equal shares as there are living children of the designated ancestor, if any, and deceased children who leave issue then living. Each living child of the designated ancestor is allocated one share, and the share of each deceased child who leaves issue then living is divided in the same manner.

(b) Unless the will, trust, or other instrument expressly provides otherwise, if an instrument executed on or after January 1, 1986, calls for property to be distributed or taken "per stirpes," "by representation," or "by right of representation," the property shall be distributed in the manner provided in subdivision (a).

(c) If a will, trust, or other instrument executed before January 1, 1986, calls for property to be distributed or taken "per stirpes," "by representation," or by "right of representation," the property shall be distributed in the manner provided in subdivision (a), absent a contrary intent of the transferor. **Leg.H.** Enacted Stats 1990 ch 79 §14 (AB 759), operative July 1, 1991.

Prior Law: Former Prob C §246, similar to the present section, was added Stats 1985 ch 982 §7 and repealed Stats 1990 ch 79 §13, operative July 1, 1991.

§247. Distribution of shares where instrument specifies division per capita at each generation

(a) Where a will, trust, or other instrument calls for property to be distributed or taken "in the manner provided in Section 247 of the Probate Code," the property to be distributed shall be divided into as many equal shares as there are living members of the nearest generation of issue then living and deceased members of that generation who leave issue then living. Each living member of the nearest generation of issue then living is allocated one share, and the remaining shares, if any, are combined and then divided and allocated in the same manner among the remaining issue as if the issue already allocated a share and their descendants were then deceased.

(b) Unless the will, trust, or other instrument expressly provides otherwise, if an instrument executed on or after January 1, 1986, calls for property to be distributed or taken "per capita at each generation," the property shall be distributed in the manner provided in subdivision (a).

(c) If a will, trust, or other instrument executed before January 1, 1986, calls for property to be distributed or taken "per capita at each generation," the property shall be distributed in the manner provided in subdivision (a), absent a contrary intent of the transferor. **Leg.H.** Enacted Stats 1990 ch 79 §14 (AB 759), operative July 1, 1991.

Prior Law: Former Prob C §247, similar to the present section, was added Stats 1985 ch 982 §7 and repealed Stats 1990 ch 79 §13, operative July 1, 1991.

CHAPTER 3
IDENTITY OF HEIRS

Determination of heirship; Filing of verified petition. §248.
Notice and hearing. §248.5.
Contesting petition. §249.
Conditions requisite for determination that child was born in the lifetime of decedent; Notice of availability of genetic material for posthumous conception. §249.5.
Receipt of notice; Effect of determination whether child was born in decedent's lifetime on distribution of decedent's property or benefits. §249.6.
Failure to give timely notice. §249.7.
Petition for early distribution. §249.8.

§248. Determination of heirship; Filing of verified petition

When title to real or personal property, or any interest therein, vests, other than by laws of succession, on the heirs, heirs of the body, issue, or children of any person, without other description, or means of identification of the persons embraced in the description, any person interested in the property as the heir, heir of the body, issue, or child, or his or her successor in interest, or the personal representative of any interested person or of his or her successor in interest, may file a verified petition in the superior court of the county in which the property or any part thereof is situated, setting forth briefly the deraignment of title of petitioner, a description of the property affected, and so far as known to the petitioner, the names, ages, and residences of the heirs, heirs of the body, issue or children whose identity is sought to be determined, and if any is dead or if the residence of any is unknown, stating the facts, and requesting that a decree be entered determining and establishing the identity of the persons embraced in the general description. **Leg.H.** Added Stats 1992 ch 871 §1 (AB 2975).

§248.5. Notice and hearing

The clerk shall set the petition for hearing by the court and give notice thereof in the manner provided in Sections 1230 and 1260. The petitioner shall cause notice of the hearing to be given in the manner specified in Sections 1220 and 1260. **Leg.H.** Added Stats 1992 ch 871 §1 (AB 2975).

§249. Contesting petition

At any time before the hearing any person interested in the property may answer the petition and deny any of the matters contained therein. The court shall hear the proofs offered by the petitioner and by any person contesting and shall make a decree conformable to the proofs. The decree shall be prima facie evidence of the facts determined thereby, and shall be conclusive in favor of anyone acting thereon in good faith without notice of any conflicting interest. **Leg.H.** Added Stats 1992 ch 871 §1 (AB 2975).

§249.5. Conditions requisite for determination that child was born in the lifetime of decedent; Notice of availability of genetic material for posthumous conception

For purposes of determining rights to property to be distributed upon the death of a decedent, a child of the decedent conceived and born after the death of the decedent shall be deemed to have been born in the lifetime of the decedent, and after the execution of all of the decedent's testamentary instruments, if the child or his or her representative proves by clear and convincing evidence that all of the following conditions are satisfied:

(a) The decedent, in writing, specifies that his or her genetic material shall be used for the posthumous conception of a child of the decedent, subject to the following:

(1) The specification shall be signed by the decedent and dated.

(2) The specification may be revoked or amended only by a writing, signed by the decedent and dated.

(3) A person is designated by the decedent to control the use of the genetic material.

(b) The person designated by the decedent to control the use of the genetic material has given written notice by certified mail, return receipt requested, that the decedent's genetic material was available for the purpose of posthumous conception. The notice shall have been given to a person who has the power to control the distribution of either the decedent's property or death benefits payable by reason of the decedent's death, within four months of the date of issuance of a certificate of the decedent's death or entry of a judgment determining the fact of the decedent's death, whichever event occurs first.

(c) The child was in utero using the decedent's genetic material and was in utero within two years of the date of issuance of a certificate of the decedent's death or entry of a judgment determining the fact of the decedent's death, whichever event occurs first. This subdivision does not apply to a child who shares all of his or her nuclear genes with the person donating the implanted nucleus as a result of the application of somatic nuclear transfer technology commonly known as human cloning. **Leg.H.** Added Stats 2004 ch 775 §5 (AB 1910). Amended Stats 2005 ch 285 §1 (AB 204), effective January 1, 2006.

§249.6. Receipt of notice; Effect of determination whether child was born in decedent's lifetime on distribution of decedent's property or benefits

(a) Upon timely receipt of the notice required by Section 249.5 or actual knowledge by a person who has the power to control the distribution of either the decedent's property or death benefits payable by reason of the decedent's death, that person may not make a distribution of property or pay death benefits payable by reason of the decedent's death before two years following the date of issuance of a certificate of the decedent's death or entry of a judgment determining the fact of decedent's death, whichever event occurs first.

(b) Subdivision (a) does not apply to, and the distribution of property or the payment of benefits may proceed in a timely manner as provided by law with respect to, any property if the birth of a child or children of the decedent conceived after the death of the decedent will not have an effect on any of the following:

(1) The proposed distribution of the decedent's property.

(2) The payment of death benefits payable by reason of the decedent's death.

(3) The determination of rights to property to be distributed upon the death of the decedent.

(4) The right of any person to claim a probate homestead or probate family allowance.

(c) Subdivision (a) does not apply to, and the distribution of property or the payment of benefits may proceed in a timely manner as provided by law with respect to, any property if the person named in subdivision (a) of Section 249.5 sends written notice by certified mail, return receipt requested, that the person does not intend to use the genetic material for the posthumous conception of a child of a decedent. This notice shall be signed by the person named in paragraph (3) of subdivision (a) of Section 249.5 and at least one competent witness, and dated.

(d) A person who has the power to control the distribution of either the decedent's property or death benefits payable by reason of the decedent's death, shall incur no liability for making a distribution of property or paying death benefits if that person made a distribution of property or paid death benefits prior to receiving notice or acquiring actual knowledge of the existence of genetic material available for posthumous conception purposes or the written notice required by subdivision (b) of Section 249.5.

(e) Each person to whom payment, delivery, or transfer of the decedent's property is made is personally liable to a person who, pursuant to Section 249.5, has a superior right to the payment, delivery, or transfer of the decedent's property. The aggregate of the personal liability of a person shall not exceed the fair market value, valued as of the time of the transfer, of the property paid, delivered, or transferred to the person under this section, less the amount of any liens and encumbrances on that property at that time.

(f) In addition to any other liability a person may have pursuant to this section, any person who fraudulently secures the payment, delivery, or transfer of the decedent's property pursuant to this section shall be liable to the person having a superior right for three times the fair market value of the property.

(g) An action to impose liability under this section shall be barred three years after the distribution to the holder of the decedent's property, or three years after the discovery of fraud, whichever is later. The three-year period specified in this subdivision may not be tolled for any reason. **Leg.H.** Added Stats 2004 ch 775 §6 (AB 1910). Amended Stats 2005 ch 285 §2 (AB 204), effective January 1, 2006.

§249.7. Failure to give timely notice

If the written notice required pursuant to Section 249.5 is not given in a timely manner to any person who has the power to control the distribution of either the decedent's property or death benefits payable by reason of the decedent's death, that person may make the distribution in the manner provided by law as if any child of the decedent conceived after the death of the decedent had predeceased the decedent without heirs. Any child of a decedent conceived after the death of the decedent, or that child's representative, shall be barred from making a claim against either the person making the distribution or the recipient of the distribution when the claim is based on wrongful distribution and written notice has not been given in a timely manner pursuant to Section 249.5 to the person making that distribution. **Leg.H.** Added Stats 2004 ch 775 §7 (AB 1910).

§249.8. Petition for early distribution

Notwithstanding Section 249.6, any interested person may file a petition in the manner prescribed in Section 248 or 17200 requesting a distribution of property of the decedent or death benefits payable by reason of decedent's death that are subject to the delayed distribution provisions of Section 249.6. The court may order distribution of all, or a portion of, the property or death benefits, if at the hearing it appears that distribution can be made without any loss to any interested person, including any loss, either actual or contingent, to a decedent's child who is conceived after the death of the decedent. The order for distribution shall be stayed until any bond required by the court is filed. **Leg.H.** Added Stats 2004 ch 775 §8 (AB 1910). Amended Stats 2005 ch 285 §3 (AB 204), effective January 1, 2006.

PART 7
EFFECT OF HOMICIDE OR ABUSE OF AN ELDER OR DEPENDENT ADULT

Wills, intestate succession, and family protection. §250.
Joint tenancies. §251.
Life insurance and other beneficiary designations. §252.
Cases not controlled by other provisions. §253.
Determination whether killing was felonious and intentional. §254.
Good faith purchasers. §255.
Protection of obligors. §256.
Applicability of part. §257.
Wrongful death action by felonious intentional killer of decedent. §258.
Restrictions on receipt of certain estate property and on service as fiduciary by person liable for abuse of elder or dependent adult decedent. §259.

§250. Wills, intestate succession, and family protection

(a) A person who feloniously and intentionally kills the decedent is not entitled to any of the following:

(1) Any property, interest, or benefit under a will of the decedent, or a trust created by or for the benefit of the decedent or in which the decedent has an interest, including any general or special power of appointment conferred by the will or trust on the killer and any nomination of the killer as executor, trustee, guardian, or conservator or custodian made by the will or trust.

(2) Any property of the decedent by intestate succession.

(3) Any of the decedent's quasi-community property the killer would otherwise acquire under Section 101 or 102 upon the death of the decedent.

(4) Any property of the decedent under Division 5 (commencing with Section 5000).

(5) Any property of the decedent under Part 3 (commencing with Section 6500) of Division 6.

(b) In the cases covered by subdivision (a):

(1) The property interest or benefit referred to in paragraph (1) of subdivision (a) passes as if the killer had predeceased the decedent and Section 21110 does not apply.

(2) Any property interest or benefit referred to in paragraph (1) of subdivision (a) which passes under a power of appointment and by reason of the death of the decedent passes as if the killer had predeceased the decedent, and Section 673 does not apply.

(3) Any nomination in a will or trust of the killer as executor, trustee, guardian, conservator, or custodian which becomes effective as a result of the death of the decedent shall be interpreted as if the killer had predeceased the decedent. **Leg.H.** Enacted Stats 1990 ch 79 §14 (AB 759), operative July 1, 1991. Amended Stats 1991 ch 1055 §13 (SB 271); Stats 1992 ch 871 §2 (AB 2975); Stats 1997 ch 724 §3 (AB 1172); Stats 2002 ch 138 §5 (AB 1784); Stats 2015 ch 293 §4 (AB 139), effective January 1, 2016.

Prior Law: Former Prob C §250, similar to the present section, was added Stats 1984 ch 527 §3 and repealed Stats 1990 ch 79 §13, operative July 1, 1991.

Former Prob C §250, similar to present Prob C §§240, 6407, was enacted Stats 1931 and repealed Stats 1983 ch 842 §19, operative January 1, 1985.

§251. Joint tenancies

A joint tenant who feloniously and intentionally kills another joint tenant thereby effects a severance of the interest of the decedent so that the share of the decedent passes as the decedent's property and the killer has no rights by survivorship. This section applies to joint tenancies in real and personal property, joint and multiple-party accounts in financial institutions, and any other form of coownership with survivorship incidents. **Leg.H.** Enacted Stats 1990 ch 79 §14 (AB 759), operative July 1, 1991.

Prior Law: Former Prob C §251, similar to the present section, was added Stats 1984 ch 527 §3 and repealed Stats 1990 ch 79 §13, operative July 1, 1991.

Former Prob C §251, similar to present Prob C §§6402, 6402.5, was enacted Stats 1931 and repealed Stats 1983 ch 842 §19, operative January 1, 1985.

§252. Life insurance and other beneficiary designations

A named beneficiary of a bond, life insurance policy, or other contractual arrangement who feloniously and intentionally kills the principal obligee or the person upon whose life the policy is issued is not entitled to any benefit under the bond, policy, or other contractual arrangement, and it becomes payable as though the killer had predeceased the decedent. **Leg.H.** Enacted Stats 1990 ch 79 §14 (AB 759), operative July 1, 1991.

Prior Law: Former Prob C §252, similar to the present section, was added Stats 1984 ch 527 §3 and repealed Stats 1990 ch 79 §13, operative July 1, 1991.

Former Prob C §252, relating to lineal consanguinity, was enacted Stats 1931 and repealed Stats 1983 ch 842 §19, operative January 1, 1985.

§253. Cases not controlled by other provisions

In any case not described in Section 250, 251, or 252 in which one person feloniously and intentionally kills another, any acquisition of property, interest, or benefit by the killer as a result of the killing of the decedent shall be treated in accordance with the principles of this part. **Leg.H.** Enacted Stats 1990 ch 79 §14 (AB 759), operative July 1, 1991.

Prior Law: Former Prob C §253, similar to the present section, was added Stats 1984 ch 527 §3 and repealed Stats 1990 ch 79 §13, operative July 1, 1991.

Former Prob C §253, relating to collateral consanguinity, was enacted Stats 1931 and repealed Stats 1983 ch 842 §19, operative January 1, 1985.

§254. Determination whether killing was felonious and intentional

(a) A final judgment of conviction of felonious and intentional killing is conclusive for purposes of this part.

(b) In the absence of a final judgment of conviction of felonious and intentional killing, the court may determine by a preponderance of evidence whether the killing was felonious and intentional for purposes of this part. The burden of proof is on the party seeking to establish that the killing was felonious and intentional for the purposes of this part. **Leg.H.** Enacted Stats 1990 ch 79 §14 (AB 759), operative July 1, 1991.

Prior Law: Former Prob C §254, similar to the present section, was added Stats 1984 ch 527 §3, amended Stats 1989 ch 21 §2, effective May 25, 1989, operative July 1, 1989, and repealed Stats 1990 ch 79 §13, operative July 1, 1991.

Former Prob C §254, similar to present Prob C §6406, was enacted Stats 1931 and repealed Stats 1983 ch 842 §19, operative January 1, 1985.

§255. Good faith purchasers

This part does not affect the rights of any person who, before rights under this part have been adjudicated, purchases from the killer for value and without notice property which the killer would have acquired except for this part, but the killer is liable for the amount of the proceeds or the value of the property. **Leg.H.** Enacted Stats 1990 ch 79 §14 (AB 759), operative July 1, 1991.

Prior Law: Former Prob C §255, similar to the present section, was added Stats 1984 ch 527 §3 and repealed Stats 1990 ch 79 §13, operative July 1, 1991.

Former Prob C §255, similar to present Prob C §6408, was added Stats 1975 ch 1244 §25 and repealed Stats 1983 ch 842 §19, operative January 1, 1985.

Former Prob C §255, similar to present Prob C §6408, was enacted Stats 1931, amended Stats 1943 ch 998 §1, Stats 1961 ch 581 §1, Stats 1975 ch 718 §2, and repealed Stats 1975 ch 1144 §24.

§256. Protection of obligors

An insurance company, financial institution, or other obligor making payment according to the terms of its policy or obligation is not liable by reason of this part, unless prior to payment it has received at its home office or principal address written notice of a claim under this part. **Leg.H.** Enacted Stats 1990 ch 79 §14 (AB 759), operative July 1, 1991.

Prior Law: Former Prob C §256, similar to the present section, was added Stats 1984 ch 527 §3 and repealed Stats 1990 ch 79 §13, operative July 1, 1991.

Former Prob C §256, relating to estate of illegitimate child, was enacted Stats 1931, amended Stats 1975 ch 718 §3, and repealed Stats 1975 ch 1244 §26.

§257. Applicability of part

This part does not apply where the decedent was killed before January 1, 1985; and the law applicable prior to January 1, 1985, continues to apply where the decedent was killed before January 1, 1985. **Leg.H.** Enacted Stats 1990 ch 79 §14 (AB 759), operative July 1, 1991.

Prior Law: Former Prob C §257, similar to the present section, was added Stats 1984 ch 892 §16.5 and repealed Stats 1990 ch 79 §13, operative July 1, 1991.

Former Prob C §257, similar to present Prob C §6408, was enacted Stats 1931, amended Stats 1955 ch 1478 §1, and repealed Stats 1983 ch 842 §19, operative January 1, 1985.

§258. Wrongful death action by felonious intentional killer of decedent

A person who feloniously and intentionally kills the decedent is not entitled to bring an action for wrongful death of the decedent or to benefit from the action brought by the decedent's personal representative. The persons who may bring an action for wrongful death of the decedent and to benefit from the action are determined as if the killer had predeceased the decedent. **Leg.H.** Added Stats 1992 ch 178 §29.5 (SB 1496).

§259. Restrictions on receipt of certain estate property and on service as fiduciary by person liable for abuse of elder or dependent adult decedent

(a) Any person shall be deemed to have predeceased a decedent to the extent provided in subdivision (c) where all of the following apply:

(1) It has been proven by clear and convincing evidence that the person is liable for physical abuse, neglect, or financial abuse of the decedent, who was an elder or dependent adult.

(2) The person is found to have acted in bad faith.

(3) The person has been found to have been reckless, oppressive, fraudulent, or malicious in the commission of any of these acts upon the decedent.

(4) The decedent, at the time those acts occurred and thereafter until the time of his or her death, has been found to have been substantially unable to manage his or her financial resources or to resist fraud or undue influence.

(b) Any person shall be deemed to have predeceased a decedent to the extent provided in subdivision (c) if that person has been convicted of a violation of Section 236 of the Penal Code or any offense described in Section 368 of the Penal Code.

(c) Any person found liable under subdivision (a) or convicted under subdivision (b) shall not (1) receive any property, damages, or costs that are awarded to the decedent's estate in an action described in subdivision (a) or (b), whether that person's entitlement is under a will, a trust, or the laws of intestacy; or (2) serve as a fiduciary as defined in Section 39, if the instrument nominating or appointing that person was executed during the period when the decedent was substantially unable to manage his or her financial resources or resist fraud or undue influence. This section shall not apply to a decedent who, at any time following the act or acts described in paragraph (1) of subdivision (a), or the act or acts described in subdivision (b), was substantially able to manage his or her financial resources and to resist fraud or undue influence within the meaning of subdivision (b) of Section 1801 of the Probate Code and subdivision (b) of Section 39 of the Civil Code.

(d) For purposes of this section, the following definitions shall apply:

(1) "Physical abuse" as defined in Section 15610.63 of the Welfare and Institutions Code.

(2) "Neglect" as defined in Section 15610.57 of the Welfare and Institutions Code.

(3) "False imprisonment" as defined in Section 368 of the Penal Code.

(4) "Financial abuse" as defined in Section 15610.30 of the Welfare and Institutions Code.

(e) Nothing in this section shall be construed to prohibit the severance and transfer of an action or proceeding to a separate civil action pursuant to Section 801. **Leg.H.** Added Stats 1998 ch 935 §4 (SB 1715). Amended Stats 2011 ch 308 §9 (SB 647), effective January 1, 2012.

PART 8
DISCLAIMER OF TESTAMENTARY AND OTHER INTERESTS

Chapter 1. Definitions.
Chapter 2. General Provisions.
Chapter 3. Disclaimers Effective Under Federal Law.

CHAPTER 1
DEFINITIONS

Definitions govern construction of this part. §260.
"Beneficiary". §262.
"Creator of the interest". §263.
"Disclaimant". §264.
"Disclaimer". §265.
"Employee benefit plan". §266.
"Interest". §267.

§260. Definitions govern construction of this part

Unless the provision or context otherwise requires, the definitions in this chapter govern the construction of this part. **Leg.H.** Enacted Stats 1990 ch 79 §14, operative July 1, 1991.

Prior Law: Former Prob C §260, similar to the present section, was added Stats 1983 ch 17 §2, amended Stats 1988 ch 1199 §29, operative July 1, 1989, and repealed Stats 1990 ch 79 §13 (AB 759), operative July 1, 1991.

Former Prob C §260, similar to present Prob C §§1804, 1846, was added Stats 1935 ch 712 §2, amended Stats 1968 ch 475 §1, and repealed Stats 1983 ch 201 §3.

§262. "Beneficiary"

"Beneficiary" means the person entitled, but for the person's disclaimer, to take an interest. **Leg.H.** Enacted Stats 1990 ch 79 §14 (AB 759), operative July 1, 1991.

Prior Law: Former Prob C §262, similar to the present section, was added Stats 1983 ch 17 §2 and repealed Stats 1990 ch 79 §13, operative July 1, 1991.

Former Prob C §262, similar to present Prob C §§1845, 1849, was added Stats 1935 ch 712 §2 and repealed Stats 1983 ch 201 §3.

§263. "Creator of the interest"

(a) "Creator of the interest" means a person who establishes, declares, creates, or otherwise brings into existence an interest.

(b) "Creator of the interest" includes, but is not limited to, the following:

(1) With respect to an interest created by intestate succession, the person dying intestate.

(2) With respect to an interest created under a will, the testator.

(3) With respect to an interest created under a trust, the settlor.

(4) With respect to an interest created by succession to a disclaimed interest, the disclaimant of the disclaimed interest.

(5) With respect to an interest created by virtue of an election to take against a will, the testator.

(6) With respect to an interest created by creation of a power of appointment, the donor.

(7) With respect to an interest created by exercise or nonexercise of a power of appointment, the donee.

(8) With respect to an interest created by an inter vivos gift, the donor.

(9) With respect to an interest created by surviving the death of a depositor of a Totten trust account or P.O.D. account, the deceased depositor.

(10) With respect to an interest created under an insurance or annuity contract, the owner, the insured, or the annuitant.

(11) With respect to an interest created by surviving the death of another joint tenant, the deceased joint tenant.

(12) With respect to an interest created under an employee benefit plan, the employee or other owner of an interest in the plan.

(13) With respect to an interest created under an individual retirement account, annuity, or bond, the owner. **Leg.H.** Enacted Stats 1990 ch 79 §14 (AB 759), operative July 1, 1991.

Prior Law: Former Prob C §263, similar to the present section, was added Stats 1983 ch 17 §2 and repealed Stats 1990 ch 79 §13, operative July 1, 1991.

Former Prob C §263, relating to who may be trustees, was added Stats 1935 ch 712 §2, amended Stats 1968 ch 475 §2, and repealed Stats 1983 ch 201 §3.

§264. "Disclaimant"

"Disclaimant" means a beneficiary who executes a disclaimer on his or her own behalf or a person who executes a disclaimer on behalf of a beneficiary. **Leg.H.** Enacted Stats 1990 ch 79 §14 (AB 759), operative July 1, 1991.

Prior Law: Former Prob C §264, similar to the present section, was added Stats 1983 ch 17 §2 and repealed Stats 1990 ch 79 §13, operative July 1, 1991.

Former Prob C §264, relating to surety bond of trustee, was added Stats 1935 ch 712 §2 and repealed Stats 1983 ch 201 §3.

§265. "Disclaimer"

"Disclaimer" means any writing which declines, refuses, renounces, or disclaims any interest that would otherwise be taken by a beneficiary. **Leg.H.** Enacted Stats 1990 ch 79 §14 (AB 759), operative July 1, 1991.

Prior Law: Former Prob C §265, similar to the present section, was added Stats 1983 ch 17 §2 and repealed Stats 1990 ch 79 §13, operative July 1, 1991.

Former Prob C §265, relating to powers and duties of trustee, was added Stats 1935 ch 712 §2, amended Stats 1951 ch 1272 §1, and repealed Stats 1983 ch 201 §3.

§266. "Employee benefit plan"

"Employee benefit plan" includes, but is not limited to, any pension, retirement, death benefit, stock bonus, or profit-sharing plan, system, or trust. **Leg.H.** Enacted Stats 1990 ch 79 §14 (AB 759), operative July 1, 1991.

Prior Law: Former Prob C §266, similar to the present section, was added Stats 1983 ch 17 §2 and repealed Stats 1990 ch 79 §13, operative July 1, 1991.

Former Prob C §266, relating to accounting by trustee, was added Stats 1935 ch 712 §2 and repealed Stats 1983 ch 201 §3.

§267. "Interest"

(a) "Interest" includes the whole of any property, real or personal, legal or equitable, or any fractional part, share, or particular portion or specific assets thereof, or any estate in any such property, or any power to appoint, consume, apply, or expend property, or any other right, power, privilege, or immunity relating to property.

(b) "Interest" includes, but is not limited to, an interest created in any of the following manners:

(1) By intestate succession.
(2) Under a will.
(3) Under a trust.
(4) By succession to a disclaimed interest.
(5) By virtue of an election to take against a will.
(6) By creation of a power of appointment.
(7) By exercise or nonexercise of a power of appointment.
(8) By an inter vivos gift, whether outright or in trust.
(9) By surviving the death of a depositor of a Totten trust account or P.O.D. account.
(10) Under an insurance or annuity contract.
(11) By surviving the death of another joint tenant.
(12) Under an employee benefit plan.
(13) Under an individual retirement account, annuity, or bond.
(14) Under a transfer on death beneficiary designation in a deed or other instrument.
(15) Any other interest created by a testamentary or inter vivos instrument or by operation of law. **Leg.H.** Enacted Stats 1990 ch 79 §14 (AB 759), operative July 1, 1991. Amended Stats 2015 ch 293 §5 (AB 139), effective January 1, 2016.

Prior Law: Former Prob C §267, similar to the present section, was added Stats 1983 ch 17 §2 and repealed Stats 1990 ch 79 §13, operative July 1, 1991.

Former Prob C §267, relating to sale or mortgage of property, was added Stats 1935 ch 712 §2 and repealed Stats 1983 ch 201 §3.

CHAPTER 2
GENERAL PROVISIONS

Right of beneficiary to disclaim interest. §275.
Disclaimer on behalf of conservatee. §276.
Disclaimer on behalf of minor or decedent. §277.
Contents of disclaimer. §278.
Time limits for filing disclaimer. §279.
Filing of disclaimer; Recording of disclaimers affecting real property. §280.
Disclaimer irrevocable and binding. §281.
Effect of disclaimer. §282.

Disclaimer not a voidable transfer. §283.
Waiver of right to disclaim. §284.
Disclaimer not permitted after interest accepted. §285.
Right to disclaim not affected by spendthrift or similar restriction. §286.
Application of part to interest created before January 1, 1984. §287.
Exclusive means of disclaimer. §288.

§275. Right of beneficiary to disclaim interest

A beneficiary may disclaim any interest, in whole or in part, by filing a disclaimer as provided in this part. **Leg.H.** Enacted Stats 1990 ch 79 §14 (AB 759), operative July 1, 1991.

Prior Law: Former Prob C §275, similar to the present section, was added Stats 1983 ch 17 §2, amended Stats 1988 ch 1199 §33, operative July 1, 1989, and repealed Stats 1990 ch 79 §13, operative July 1, 1991.

§276. Disclaimer on behalf of conservatee

A disclaimer on behalf of a conservatee shall be made by the conservator of the estate of the conservatee pursuant to a court order obtained under Article 10 (commencing with Section 2580) of Chapter 6 of Part 4 of Division 4 authorizing or requiring the conservator to execute and file the disclaimer. **Leg.H.** Enacted Stats 1990 ch 79 §14 (AB 759), operative July 1, 1991.

Prior Law: Former Prob C §276, similar to the present section, was added Stats 1983 ch 17 §2 and repealed Stats 1990 ch 79 §13, operative July 1, 1991.

§277. Disclaimer on behalf of minor or decedent

(a) A disclaimer on behalf of a minor shall be made by the guardian of the estate of the minor if one has been appointed or, if none has been appointed, by a guardian ad litem of the minor. A disclaimer by a guardian is not effective unless made pursuant to a court order obtained under this section.

(b) A disclaimer on behalf of a decedent shall be made by the personal representative of the decedent. Except as provided in Part 6 (commencing with Section 10400) of Division 7, a disclaimer by a guardian or personal representative is not effective unless made pursuant to a court order obtained under this section.

(c) A petition for an order authorizing or requiring a guardian or personal representative to execute and file a disclaimer shall be filed in the superior court in the county in which the estate of the minor or decedent is administered or, if there is no administration, the superior court in any county in which administration would be proper. The petition may be filed by the guardian, personal representative, or other interested person.

(d) The petition shall:
(1) Identify the creator of the interest.
(2) Describe the interest to be disclaimed.
(3) State the extent of the disclaimer.
(4) Identify the person or persons the petitioner believes would take the interest in the event of the disclaimer.

(e) Notice of the hearing on the petition shall be given as follows:
(1) If the petition is for an order authorizing or requiring the guardian of the estate of a minor to execute and file the disclaimer, notice of the hearing on the petition shall be given for the period and in the manner provided in Chapter 3 (commencing with Section 1460) of Part 1 of Division 4 to all of the persons required to be given notice under that chapter.
(2) If the petition is for an order authorizing or requiring the personal representative of a decedent to execute and file the disclaimer, notice of the hearing on the petition shall be given as provided in Section 1220.
(3) If the petition is for an order authorizing or requiring a guardian ad litem of a minor to execute and file the disclaimer, notice of the hearing on the petition shall be given to the persons and in the manner that the court shall by order direct.

(f) After hearing, the court in its discretion may make an order authorizing or requiring the guardian or personal representative to execute and file the disclaimer if the court determines, taking into consideration all of the relevant circumstances, that the minor or decedent as a prudent person would disclaim the interest if he or she had the capacity to do so. **Leg.H.** Enacted Stats 1990 ch 79 §14 (AB 759), operative July 1, 1991.

Prior Law: Former Prob C §277, similar to the present section, was added Stats 1983 ch 17 §2, amended Stats 1987 ch 923 §24, operative July 1, 1988, and repealed Stats 1990 ch 79 §13, operative July 1, 1991.

§278. Contents of disclaimer

The disclaimer shall be in writing, shall be signed by the disclaimant, and shall:

(a) Identify the creator of the interest.
(b) Describe the interest to be disclaimed.
(c) State the disclaimer and the extent of the disclaimer. **Leg.H.** Enacted Stats 1990 ch 79 §14 (AB 759), operative July 1, 1991.

Prior Law: Former Prob C §278, similar to the present section, was added Stats 1983 ch 17 §2 and repealed Stats 1990 ch 79 §13, operative July 1, 1991.

§279. Time limits for filing disclaimer

(a) A disclaimer to be effective shall be filed within a reasonable time after the person able to disclaim acquires knowledge of the interest.

(b) In the case of any of the following interests, a disclaimer is conclusively presumed to have been filed within a reasonable time if it is filed within nine months after the death of the creator of the interest or within nine months after the interest becomes indefeasibly vested, whichever occurs later:
(1) An interest created under a will.
(2) An interest created by intestate succession.
(3) An interest created pursuant to the exercise or nonexercise of a testamentary power of appointment.
(4) An interest created by surviving the death of a depositor of a Totten trust account or P.O.D. account.
(5) An interest created under a life insurance or annuity contract.
(6) An interest created by surviving the death of another joint tenant.
(7) An interest created under an employee benefit plan.
(8) An interest created under an individual retirement account, annuity, or bond.
(9) An interest created under a transfer on death beneficiary designation in a deed or other instrument.

(c) In the case of an interest created by a living trust, an interest created by the exercise of a presently exercisable power of appointment, an outright inter vivos gift, a power of appointment, or an interest created or increased by succession to a disclaimed interest, a disclaimer is conclusively presumed to have been filed within a reasonable time if it is filed within nine months after whichever of the following times occurs latest:
(1) The time of the creation of the trust, the exercise of the power of appointment, the making of the gift, the creation of the power of appointment, or the disclaimer of the disclaimed property.
(2) The time the first knowledge of the interest is acquired by the person able to disclaim.
(3) The time the interest becomes indefeasibly vested.

(d) In case of an interest not described in subdivision (b) or (c), a disclaimer is conclusively presumed to have been filed within a reasonable time if it is filed within nine months after whichever of the following times occurs later:
(1) The time the first knowledge of the interest is acquired by the person able to disclaim.
(2) The time the interest becomes indefeasibly vested.

(e) In the case of a future estate, a disclaimer is conclusively presumed to have been filed within a reasonable time if it is filed within whichever of the following times occurs later:
(1) Nine months after the time the interest becomes an estate in possession.
(2) The time specified in subdivision (b), (c), or (d), whichever is applicable.

(f) If the disclaimer is not filed within the time provided in subdivision (b), (c), (d), or (e), the disclaimant has the burden of establishing that the disclaimer was filed within a reasonable time after the disclaimant acquired knowledge of the interest. **Leg.H.** Enacted Stats 1990 ch 79 §14 (AB 759), operative July 1, 1991. Amended Stats 2015 ch 293 §6 (AB 139), effective January 1, 2016.

Prior Law: Former Prob C §279, similar to the present section, was added Stats 1983 ch 17 §2 and repealed Stats 1990 ch 79 §13, operative July 1, 1991.

§280. Filing of disclaimer; Recording of disclaimers affecting real property

(a) A disclaimer shall be filed with any of the following:
(1) The superior court in the county in which the estate of the decedent is administered or, if there is no administration of the decedent's estate, the superior court in any county in which administration of the estate of the decedent would be proper.
(2) The trustee, personal representative, other fiduciary, or person responsible for distributing the interest to the beneficiary.

(3) Any other person having custody or possession of or legal title to the interest.

(4) The creator of the interest.

(b) If a disclaimer made pursuant to this part affects real property or an obligation secured by real property and the disclaimer is acknowledged and proved in like manner as a grant of real property, the disclaimer may be recorded in like manner and with like effect as a grant of real property, and all statutory provisions relating to the recordation or nonrecordation of conveyances of real property and to the effect thereof apply to the disclaimer with like effect, without regard to the date when the disclaimer was filed pursuant to subdivision (a). Failure to file a disclaimer pursuant to subdivision (a) which is recorded pursuant to this subdivision does not affect the validity of any transaction with respect to the real property or the obligation secured thereby, and the general laws on recording and its effect govern any such transaction. **Leg.H.** Enacted Stats 1990 ch 79 §14 (AB 759), operative July 1, 1991.

Prior Law: Former Prob C §280, similar to the present section, was added Stats 1983 ch 17 §2, amended Stats 1988 ch 1199 §34, operative July 1, 1989, and repealed Stats 1990 ch 79 §13, operative July 1, 1991.

Former Prob C §280, similar to present Prob C §§12401, 12402, was added Stats 1935 ch 712 §2 and repealed Stats 1983 ch 201 §3.

§281. Disclaimer irrevocable and binding

A disclaimer, when effective, is irrevocable and binding upon the beneficiary and all persons claiming by, through, or under the beneficiary, including creditors of the beneficiary. **Leg.H.** Enacted Stats 1990 ch 79 §14 (AB 759), operative July 1, 1991.

Prior Law: Former Prob C §281, similar to the present section, was added Stats 1983 ch 17 §2 and repealed Stats 1990 ch 79 §13, operative July 1, 1991.

Former Prob C §281, similar to present Prob C §12403, was added Stats 1935 ch 712 §2 and repealed Stats 1983 ch 201 §3.

§282. Effect of disclaimer

(a) Unless the creator of the interest provides for a specific disposition of the interest in the event of a disclaimer, the interest disclaimed shall descend, go, be distributed, or continue to be held (1) as to a present interest, as if the disclaimant had predeceased the creator of the interest or (2) as to a future interest, as if the disclaimant had died before the event determining that the taker of the interest had become finally ascertained and the taker's interest indefeasibly vested. A disclaimer relates back for all purposes to the date of the death of the creator of the disclaimed interest or the determinative event, as the case may be.

(b) Notwithstanding subdivision (a), where the disclaimer is filed on or after January 1, 1985:

(1) The beneficiary is not treated as having predeceased the decedent for the purpose of determining the generation at which the division of the estate is to be made under Part 6 (commencing with Section 240) or other provision of a will, trust, or other instrument.

(2) The beneficiary of a disclaimed interest is not treated as having predeceased the decedent for the purpose of applying subdivision (d) of Section 6409 or subdivision (b) of Section 6410. **Leg.H.** Enacted Stats 1990 ch 79 §14 (AB 759), operative July 1, 1991.

Prior Law: Former Prob C §282, similar to the present section, was added Stats 1983 ch 17 §2, amended Stats 1983 ch 842 §23, operative January 1, 1985, Stats 1984 ch 892 §17, Stats 1987 ch 923 §25, operative January 1, 1988, and repealed Stats 1990 ch 79 §13, operative July 1, 1991.

Former Prob C §282, similar to present Prob C §12404, was added Stats 1935 ch 712 §2 and repealed Stats 1983 ch 201 §3.

§283. Disclaimer not a voidable transfer

A disclaimer is not a voidable transfer by the beneficiary under the Uniform Voidable Transactions Act (Chapter 1 (commencing with Section 3439) of Title 2 of Part 2 of Division 4 of the Civil Code). **Leg.H.** Enacted Stats 1990 ch 79 §14 (AB 759), operative July 1, 1991. Amended Stats 2015 ch 44 §26 (SB 161), effective January 1, 2016.

Prior Law: Former Prob C §283, similar to the present section, was added Stats 1983 ch 17 §2, amended Stats 1987 ch 40 §6, effective June 8, 1987, and repealed Stats 1990 ch 79 §13, operative July 1, 1991.

Former Prob C §283, similar to present Prob C §12405, was added Stats 1935 ch 712 §2, amended Stats 1951 ch 49 §1, Stats 1963 ch 809 §1, and repealed Stats 1983 ch 201 §3.

§284. Waiver of right to disclaim

A person who could file a disclaimer under this part may instead file a written waiver of the right to disclaim. The waiver shall specify the interest to which the waiver applies. Upon being filed as provided in Section 280, the waiver is irrevocable and is binding upon the beneficiary and all persons claiming by, through, or under the beneficiary. **Leg.H.** Enacted Stats 1990 ch 79 §14 (AB 759), operative July 1, 1991.

Prior Law: Former Prob C §284, similar to the present section, was added Stats 1983 ch 17 §2, amended Stats 1988 ch 1199 §35, operative July 1, 1989, and repealed Stats 1990 ch 79 §13, operative July 1, 1991.

Former Prob C §284, similar to present Prob C §§12406, 12407, was added Stats 1935 ch 712 §2 and repealed Stats 1983 ch 201 §3.

§285. Disclaimer not permitted after interest accepted

(a) A disclaimer may not be made after the beneficiary has accepted the interest sought to be disclaimed.

(b) For the purpose of this section, a beneficiary has accepted an interest if any of the following occurs before a disclaimer is filed with respect to that interest:

(1) The beneficiary, or someone acting on behalf of the beneficiary, makes a voluntary assignment, conveyance, encumbrance, pledge, or transfer of the interest or part thereof, or contracts to do so; provided, however, that a beneficiary will not have accepted an interest if the beneficiary makes a gratuitous conveyance or transfer of the beneficiary's entire interest in property to the person or persons who would have received the property had the beneficiary made an otherwise qualified disclaimer pursuant to this part.

(2) The beneficiary, or someone acting on behalf of the beneficiary, executes a written waiver under Section 284 of the right to disclaim the interest.

(3) The beneficiary, or someone acting on behalf of the beneficiary, accepts the interest or part thereof or benefit thereunder.

(4) The interest or part thereof is sold at a judicial sale.

(c) An acceptance does not preclude a beneficiary from thereafter disclaiming all or part of an interest if both of the following requirements are met:

(1) The beneficiary became entitled to the interest because another person disclaimed an interest.

(2) The beneficiary or other person acting on behalf of the beneficiary at the time of the acceptance had no knowledge of the interest to which the beneficiary so became entitled.

(d) The acceptance by a joint tenant of the joint tenancy interest created when the joint tenancy is created is not an acceptance by the joint tenant of the interest created when the joint tenant survives the death of another joint tenant. **Leg.H.** Enacted Stats 1990 ch 79 §14 (AB 759), operative July 1, 1991. Amended Stats 1994 ch 806 §3 (AB 3686).

Prior Law: Former Prob C §285, similar to the present section, was added Stats 1983 ch 17 §2 and repealed Stats 1990 ch 79 §13, operative July 1, 1991.

Former Prob C §285, similar to present Prob C §12402, was added Stats 1935 ch 712 §2 and repealed Stats 1983 ch 201 §3.

§286. Right to disclaim not affected by spendthrift or similar restriction

The right to disclaim exists regardless of any limitation imposed on the interest of a beneficiary in the nature of an expressed or implied spendthrift provision or similar restriction. **Leg.H.** Enacted Stats 1990 ch 79 §14 (AB 759), operative July 1, 1991.

Prior Law: Former Prob C §286, similar to the present section, was added Stats 1983 ch 17 §2 and repealed Stats 1990 ch 79 §13, operative July 1, 1991.

Former Prob C §286, similar to present Prob C §12402, was added Stats 1935 ch 712 §2 and repealed Stats 1983 ch 201 §3.

§287. Application of part to interest created before January 1, 1984

An interest created before January 1, 1984, that has not been accepted may be disclaimed after December 31, 1983, in the manner provided in this part, but no interest that arose before January 1, 1984, in a person other than the beneficiary may be destroyed or diminished by any action of the disclaimant taken pursuant to this part. **Leg.H.** Enacted Stats 1990 ch 79 §14 (AB 759), operative July 1, 1991.

Prior Law: Former Prob C §287, similar to the present section, was added Stats 1983 ch 17 §2, amended Stats 1988 ch 1199 §36, operative July 1, 1989, and repealed Stats 1990 ch 79 §13, operative July 1, 1991.

Former Prob C §287, similar to present Prob C §12408, was added Stats 1935 ch 712 §2, amended Stats 1982 ch 517 §323, and repealed Stats 1983 ch 201 §3.

§288. Exclusive means of disclaimer

This part does not limit or abridge any right a person may have under any other law to assign, convey, or release any property or interest, but after December 31, 1983, an interest that would otherwise be taken by a beneficiary may be declined, refused, renounced, or disclaimed only as provided in this part. **Leg.H.** Enacted Stats 1990 ch 79 §14 (AB 759), operative July 1, 1991.

Prior Law: Former Prob C §288, similar to the present section, was added Stats 1983 ch 17 §2, amended Stats 1988 ch 1199 §37, operative July 1, 1989, and repealed Stats 1990 ch 79 §13, operative July 1, 1991.

Former Prob C §288, similar to present Prob C §12408, was added Stats 1935 ch 712 §2 and repealed Stats 1983 ch 201 §3.

CHAPTER 3
DISCLAIMERS EFFECTIVE UNDER FEDERAL LAW

Disclaimer effective under federal law effective under this part. §295.

§295. Disclaimer effective under federal law effective under this part

Notwithstanding any other provision of this part, if as a result of a disclaimer or transfer the disclaimed or transferred interest is treated pursuant to the provisions of Title 26 of the United States Code, as now or hereafter amended, or any successor statute thereto, and the regulations promulgated thereunder, as never having been transferred to the beneficiary, then the disclaimer or transfer is effective as a disclaimer under this part. **Leg.H.** Enacted Stats 1990 ch 79 §14 (AB 759), operative July 1, 1991.

Prior Law: Former Prob C §295, similar to the present section, was added Stats 1983 ch 17 §2, amended Stats 1988 ch 1199 §38, operative July 1, 1989, and repealed Stats 1990 ch 79 §13, operative July 1, 1991.

Former Prob C §295, similar to present Prob C §3700 was added Stats 1972 ch 632 §1, effective August 9, 1972, and repealed Stats 1983 ch 201 §3.

PART 9
TRUST COMPANY AS FIDUCIARY

Appointment of trust company. §300.
Oath and bond of trust company. §301.

§300. Appointment of trust company

A trust company may be appointed to act as a personal representative, guardian or conservator of an estate, trust director, or trustee, in the same manner as an individual. A trust company may not be appointed guardian or conservator of the person of a ward or conservatee. **Leg.H.** Enacted Stats 1990 ch 79 §14 (AB 759), operative July 1, 1991. Amended Stats 2023 ch 721 §1 (SB 801), effective January 1, 2024.

Prior Law: Former Prob C §300, similar to the present section, was added Stats 1988 ch 1199 §41, operative July 1, 1989, and repealed Stats 1990 ch 79 §13, operative July 1, 1991.

Former Prob C §300, similar to present Prob C §§7000, 7001, was enacted Stats 1931, amended Stats 1983 ch 842 §24, operative January 1, 1985, Stats 1987 ch 923 §26, operative January 1, 1988, and repealed Stats 1988 ch 1199 §40, operative July 1, 1989.

§301. Oath and bond of trust company

(a) A trust company appointed to act as a personal representative, or guardian or conservator of an estate, may not be required to give a bond.

(b) The liability of a trust company and the manner of its making of oaths and affidavits are governed by Article 3 (commencing with Section 1540) of Chapter 12 of Division 1 of, and Section 1587 of, the Financial Code. **Leg.H.** Enacted Stats 1990 ch 79 §14 (AB 759), operative July 1, 1991.

Prior Law: Former Prob C §301, similar to the present section, was added Stats 1988 ch 1199 §41, operative July 1, 1989, and repealed Stats 1990 ch 79 §13, operative July 1, 1991.

Former Prob C §301, similar to present Prob C §§7050–7052, was enacted Stats 1931 and repealed Stats 1988 ch 1199 §40, operative July 1, 1989.

PART 10
IMMEDIATE STEPS CONCERNING DECEDENT'S TANGIBLE PERSONAL PROPERTY AND SAFE DEPOSIT BOX

Delivery of decedent's tangible personal property. §330.
Access to decedent's safe deposit box. §331.

§330. Delivery of decedent's tangible personal property

(a) Except as provided in subdivision (b), a public administrator, government official, law enforcement agency, the hospital or institution in which decedent died, or the decedent's employer, may, without the need to wait 40 days after death, deliver the tangible personal property of the decedent in its possession, including keys to the decedent's residence, to the decedent's surviving spouse, relative, or conservator or guardian of the estate acting in that capacity at the time of death.

(b) A person shall not deliver property pursuant to this section if the person knows or has reason to believe that there is a dispute over the right to possession of the property.

(c) A person that delivers property pursuant to this section shall require reasonable proof of the status and identity of the person to whom the property is delivered, and may rely on any document described in subdivision (d) of Section 13104 as proof of identity.

(d) A person that delivers property pursuant to this section shall, for a period of three years after the date of delivery of the property, keep a record of the property delivered and the status and identity of the person to whom the property is delivered.

(e) Delivery of property pursuant to this section does not determine ownership of the property or confer any greater rights in the property than the recipient would otherwise have and does not preclude later proceedings for administration of the decedent's estate. If proceedings for administration of the decedent's estate are commenced, the person holding the property shall deliver it to the personal representative on request by the personal representative.

(f) A person that delivers property pursuant to this section is not liable for loss or damage to the property caused by the person to whom the property is delivered. **Leg.H.** Enacted Stats 1990 ch 79 §14 (AB 759), operative July 1, 1991.

Prior Law: Former Prob C §330, similar to the present section, was added Stats 1989 ch 21 §3, effective May 25, 1989, operative July 1, 1989, and repealed and Stats 1990 ch 79 §13, operative July 1, 1991.

Former Prob C §330, similar to present Prob C §§8202, 8220, was enacted Stats 1931 and repealed Stats 1988 ch 1199 §40, operative July 1, 1989.

§331. Access to decedent's safe deposit box

(a) This section applies only to a safe deposit box in a financial institution held by the decedent in the decedent's sole name, or held by the decedent and others where all are deceased. Nothing in this section affects the rights of a surviving coholder.

(b) A person who has a key to the safe deposit box may, before letters have been issued, obtain access to the safe deposit box only for the purposes specified in this section by providing the financial institution with both of the following:

(1) Proof of the decedent's death. Proof shall be provided by a certified copy of the decedent's death certificate or by a written statement of death from the coroner, treating physician, or hospital or institution where the decedent died.

(2) Reasonable proof of the identity of the person seeking access. Reasonable proof of identity is provided for the purpose of this paragraph if the requirements of Section 13104 are satisfied.

(c) The financial institution has no duty to inquire into the truth of any statement, declaration, certificate, affidavit, or document offered as proof of the decedent's death or proof of identity of the person seeking access.

(d) If the person seeking access has satisfied the requirements of subdivision (b), the financial institution shall do all of the following:

(1) Keep a record of the identity of the person.

(2) Permit the person to open the safe deposit box under the supervision of an officer or employee of the financial institution, and to make an inventory of its contents.

(3) Make a photocopy of all wills and trust instruments removed from the safe deposit box, and keep the photocopy in the safe deposit box until the contents of the box are removed by the personal representative of the estate or other legally authorized person. The financial institution may charge the person given access a reasonable fee for photocopying.

(4) Permit the person given access to remove instructions for the disposition of the decedent's remains, and, after a photocopy is made, to remove the wills and trust instruments.

(e) The person given access shall deliver all wills found in the safe deposit box to the clerk of the superior court and deliver a copy pursuant to Section 1215 to the person named in the will as executor or beneficiary as provided in Section 8200.

(f) Except as provided in subdivision (d), the person given access shall not remove any of the contents of the decedent's safe deposit box. **Leg.H.** Added Stats 1991 ch 1055 §15 (SB 271). Amended Stats 2017 ch 319 §6 (AB 976), effective January 1, 2018.

PART 11
FIDUCIARIES' WARTIME SUBSTITUTION LAW

Chapter 1. General Provisions.
Chapter 2. Appointment of Substitute Fiduciary.
Chapter 3. Delegation of Powers.

CHAPTER 1
GENERAL PROVISIONS

Article 1. Short Title and Definitions.
Article 2. Scope of Part.
Article 3. Procedural Provisions.

ARTICLE 1
Short Title and Definitions

Short title. §350.
Definitions govern construction of this part. §351.
"Consultant". §352.
"Estate". §353.
"Interested person". §354.
"Original fiduciary". §355.
"War service". §356.

§350. Short title
This part may be cited as the Fiduciaries' Wartime Substitution Law. **Leg.H.** Enacted Stats 1990 ch 79 §14 (AB 759), operative July 1, 1991.

Prior Law: Former Prob C §350, similar to the present section, was added Stats 1988 ch 1199 §41.5, operative July 1, 1989, and repealed Stats 1990 ch 79 §13, operative July 1, 1991.

Former Prob C §350, relating to requisites of proof, was enacted Stats 1931, amended Stats 1957 ch 1964 §1, and repealed Stats 1983 ch 842 §28, operative January 1, 1985.

§351. Definitions govern construction of this part
Unless the provision or context otherwise requires, the definitions in this article govern the construction of this part. **Leg.H.** Enacted Stats 1990 ch 79 §14 (AB 759), operative July 1, 1991.

Prior Law: Former Prob C §351, similar to the present section, was added Stats 1988 ch 1199 §41.5, operative July 1, 1989, and repealed Stats 1990 ch 79 §13, operative July 1, 1991.

Former Prob C §351, similar to present Prob C §§8223, 8224, was enacted Stats 1931, amended Stats 1983 ch 842 §29, operative January 1, 1985, and repealed Stats 1988 ch 1199 §40, operative July 1, 1989.

§352. "Consultant"
"Consultant" means a person, other than a trustee, designated in a trust to advise or direct the trustee concerning the trust, or whose consent or approval is required for a purchase, sale, exchange, or other transaction by the trustee, and includes a settlor who reserves the power of a consultant. **Leg.H.** Enacted Stats 1990 ch 79 §14 (AB 759), operative July 1, 1991.

Prior Law: Former Prob C §352, similar to the present section, was added Stats 1988 ch 1199 §41.5, operative July 1, 1989, and repealed Stats 1990 ch 79 §13, operative July 1, 1991.

Former Prob C §352, similar to present Prob C §9614, was enacted Stats 1931 and repealed Stats 1988 ch 1199 §40, operative July 1, 1989.

§353. "Estate"
"Estate" means a trust estate, a decedent's estate, a guardianship or conservatorship estate, or other property that is the subject of a donative transfer. **Leg.H.** Enacted Stats 1990 ch 79 §14 (AB 759), operative July 1, 1991.

Prior Law: Former Prob C §353, similar to the present section, was added Stats 1988 ch 1199 §41.5, operative July 1, 1989, and repealed Stats 1990 ch 79 §13, operative July 1, 1991.

§354. "Interested person"
"Interested person" means, in addition to the meaning given that term in Section 48, a person having a property right in or claim against a guardianship or conservatorship estate or other estate that may be affected by the proceeding. **Leg.H.** Enacted Stats 1990 ch 79 §14 (AB 759), operative July 1, 1991.

Prior Law: Former Prob C §354, similar to the present section, was added Stats 1988 ch 1199 §41.5, operative July 1, 1989, and repealed Stats 1990 ch 79 §13, operative July 1, 1991.

§355. "Original fiduciary"
"Original fiduciary" means a fiduciary who is replaced by a substitute fiduciary or who makes a delegation of power under this part. **Leg.H.** Enacted Stats 1990 ch 79 §14 (AB 759), operative July 1, 1991.

Prior Law: Former Prob C §355, similar to the present section, was added Stats 1988 ch 1199 §41.5, operative July 1, 1989, and repealed Stats 1990 ch 79 §13, operative July 1, 1991.

§356. "War service"
A fiduciary or consultant is engaged in war service for the purpose of this part in each of the following cases:

(a) Where the person is a member of the armed forces of the United States or like forces of any nation with which the United States is allied or associated in time of war, including all of the following:

(1) Members of the Army, Navy, Marine Corps, Air Force, and Coast Guard.

(2) Members of the Public Health Service detailed by proper authority for duty with the armed forces.

(3) Members of all other organizations or services recognized by the laws of the United States as a part of or auxiliary to the armed forces of the United States.

(b) Where the person has been accepted for and is awaiting induction into the armed forces, or is receiving training or education under government supervision preliminary to induction into any of these forces, in time of war.

(c) Where the person is engaged, outside the 50 states of the United States, in any work in connection with a governmental agency of the United States or with the American Red Cross or any other body with similar objects operating with the approval and sanction of the government of the United States or of any nation with which the United States is allied or associated in time of war.

(d) Where the person is engaged in time of war in service on any ship of United States registry.

(e) Where the person is interned or a prisoner of war in a foreign country or in the United States or any possession or dependency of the United States.

(f) Where the person is absent from the 50 states of the United States and, due to war conditions, is unable to return freely at his or her own volition.

(g) Where the person is engaged in any service in the United States or abroad arising out of or connected with a state of war that the court having jurisdiction of the estate finds prevents the person from giving proper attention to his or her duties. **Leg.H.** Enacted Stats 1990 ch 79 §14 (AB 759), operative July 1, 1991.

Prior Law: Former Prob C §356, similar to the present section, was added Stats 1988 ch 1199 §41.5, operative July 1, 1989, and repealed Stats 1990 ch 79 §13, operative July 1, 1991.

ARTICLE 2
Scope of Part

Part applies to all fiduciaries. §360.
Provision in instrument controls. §361.

§360. Part applies to all fiduciaries
This part applies to all fiduciaries and consultants, whether appointed or acting before, on, or after July 1, 1989. **Leg.H.** Enacted Stats 1990 ch 79 §14 (AB 759), operative July 1, 1991.

Prior Law: Former Prob C §360, similar to the present section, was added Stats 1988 ch 1199 §41.5, operative July 1, 1989, and repealed Stats 1990 ch 79 §13, operative July 1, 1991.

Former Prob C §360, similar to present Prob C §§7050, 12510, 12511, was enacted Stats 1931, amended Stats 1953 ch 418 §1, and repealed Stats 1988 ch 1199 §40, operative July 1, 1989.

§361. Provision in instrument controls
This part does not apply to the extent an otherwise valid provision in an instrument provides a different or contrary rule or is otherwise inconsistent with this part. **Leg.H.** Enacted Stats 1990 ch 79 §14 (AB 759), operative July 1, 1991.

Prior Law: Former Prob C §361, similar to the present section, was added Stats 1988 ch 1199 §41.5, operative July 1, 1989, and repealed Stats 1990 ch 79 §13, operative July 1, 1991.

Former Prob C §361, similar to present Prob C §§12510, 12512, 12520, 12521, 12522, was enacted Stats 1931, amended Stats 1953 ch 418 §2, Stats 1969 ch 46 §1, Stats 1972 ch 713 §2, and repealed Stats 1988 ch 1199 §40, operative July 1, 1989.

ARTICLE 3
Procedural Provisions

Jurisdiction of proceedings. §365.
Notice of hearing. §366.

§365. Jurisdiction of proceedings

Proceedings under this part are in the court having jurisdiction over the estate or, if none, any court in which jurisdiction of the estate is proper. **Leg.H.** Enacted Stats 1990 ch 79 §14 (AB 759), operative July 1, 1991.

Prior Law: Former Prob C §365, similar to the present section, was added Stats 1988 ch 1199 §41.5, operative July 1, 1989, and repealed Stats 1990 ch 79 §13, operative July 1, 1991.

§366. Notice of hearing

Notice of a hearing under this part shall be delivered pursuant to Section 1215 at least 15 days before the hearing to each fiduciary and consultant, and to the following persons:

(a) In the case of a trust, to each known beneficiary, subject to the provisions of Chapter 2 (commencing with Section 15800) of Part 3 of Division 9.

(b) In the case of a decedent's estate, as provided in Section 1220, to both of the following:

(1) Each known heir whose interest in the estate would be affected by the proceedings.

(2) Each known devisee whose interest in the estate would be affected by the proceedings.

(c) In the case of a guardianship or conservatorship estate, as provided in Section 1460.

(d) In other cases, to any additional interested persons required by the court to receive notice. **Leg.H.** Enacted Stats 1990 ch 79 §14 (AB 759), operative July 1, 1991. Amended Stats 2017 ch 319 §7 (AB 976), effective January 1, 2018.

Prior Law: Former Prob C §366, similar to the present section, was added Stats 1988 ch 1199 §41.5, operative July 1, 1989, and repealed Stats 1990 ch 79 §13, operative July 1, 1991.

CHAPTER 2
APPOINTMENT OF SUBSTITUTE FIDUCIARY

Petition for appointment of substitute, suspension of powers, or account. §370.
Powers and duties of substitute fiduciary. §371.
Bond of substitute fiduciary. §372.
Reinstatement of original fiduciary. §373.
Fiduciary's immunity for predecessor's acts. §374.

§370. Petition for appointment of substitute, suspension of powers, or account

If a fiduciary is engaged in war service, on petition of the fiduciary, a cofiduciary, or an interested person, the court may do any one or more of the following:

(a) Appoint a substitute fiduciary. If there is a qualified and acting cofiduciary, the court is not required to appoint a substitute fiduciary but may vest in the cofiduciary the powers of the original fiduciary engaged in war service.

(b) Order a suspension of the powers and duties of the original fiduciary for the period the original fiduciary is engaged in war service and until further order of the court.

(c) Order an account by the original fiduciary. **Leg.H.** Enacted Stats 1990 ch 79 §14 (AB 759), operative July 1, 1991.

Prior Law: Former Prob C §370, similar to the present section, was added Stats 1988 ch 1199 §41.5, operative July 1, 1989, and repealed Stats 1990 ch 79 §13, operative July 1, 1991.

Former Prob C §370, similar to present Prob C §§1043, 8004, 8250, 8251, was enacted Stats 1931, amended Stats 1969 ch 1611 §34, Stats 1986 ch 14 §1, and repealed Stats 1988 ch 1199 §42, operative July 1, 1989.

§371. Powers and duties of substitute fiduciary

A substitute fiduciary has all the powers, including discretionary powers, that the original fiduciary had, except powers that the court determines are purely personal to the original fiduciary, and is subject to the same duties as the original fiduciary. **Leg.H.** Enacted Stats 1990 ch 79 §14 (AB 759), operative July 1, 1991.

Prior Law: Former Prob C §371, similar to the present section, was added Stats 1988 ch 1199 §41.5, operative July 1, 1989, and repealed Stats 1990 ch 79 §13, operative July 1, 1991.

Former Prob C §371, similar to present Prob C §8252, was enacted Stats 1931 and repealed Stats 1988 ch 1199 §42, operative July 1, 1989.

§372. Bond of substitute fiduciary

Except as otherwise ordered by the court, a substitute fiduciary shall give a bond in the manner and to the extent provided by law for the original fiduciary. **Leg.H.** Enacted Stats 1990 ch 79 §14 (AB 759), operative July 1, 1991.

Prior Law: Former Prob C §372, similar to the present section, was added Stats 1988 ch 1199 §41.5, operative July 1, 1989, and repealed Stats 1990 ch 79 §13, operative July 1, 1991.

Former Prob C §372, similar to present Prob C §8253, was enacted Stats 1931 and repealed Stats 1988 ch 1199 42, operative July 1, 1989.

§373. Reinstatement of original fiduciary

After the expiration of an original fiduciary's war service, if the estate has not been closed, the original fiduciary, on petition, is entitled to reinstatement as fiduciary. On reinstatement, the substitute fiduciary may, in the discretion of the court, be removed and may be discharged on conditions prescribed by the court. **Leg.H.** Enacted Stats 1990 ch 79 §14 (AB 759), operative July 1, 1991.

Prior Law: Former Prob C §373, similar to the present section, was added Stats 1988 ch 1199 §41.5, operative July 1, 1989, and repealed Stats 1990 ch 79 §13, operative July 1, 1991.

Former Prob C §373, similar to present Prob C §8254, was enacted Stats 1931 and repealed Stats 1988 ch 1199 42, operative July 1, 1989.

§374. Fiduciary's immunity for predecessor's acts

A substitute fiduciary or an original fiduciary reinstated under Section 373 is not liable for the acts or omissions of the predecessor fiduciary. **Leg.H.** Enacted Stats 1990 ch 79 §14 (AB 759), operative July 1, 1991.

Prior Law: Former Prob C §374, similar to the present section, was added Stats 1988 ch 1199 §41.5, operative July 1, 1989, and repealed Stats 1990 ch 79 §13, operative July 1, 1991.

Former Prob C §374, similar to present Prob C §8224, was enacted Stats 1931 and repealed Stats 1988 ch 1199 §42, operative July 1, 1989.

CHAPTER 3
DELEGATION OF POWERS

Article 1. Delegation by Fiduciary.
Article 2. Delegation by Consultant.

ARTICLE 1
Delegation by Fiduciary

Delegation of fiduciary's powers. §380.
Limitations on delegation. §381.
Resumption of fiduciary's powers. §382.
Fiduciary's immunity for delegate's acts. §383.

§380. Delegation of fiduciary's powers

(a) A fiduciary who is or will be engaged in war service may delegate the fiduciary's powers, including discretionary powers, to a fiduciary who is not engaged in war service. Delegation may be made for the period during which the original fiduciary is engaged in war service and not to exceed six months following the expiration of that period.

(b) Approval of the court, on petition of the original fiduciary, the delegate, or an interested person, is required for delegation. **Leg.H.** Enacted Stats 1990 ch 79 §14 (AB 759), operative July 1, 1991.

Prior Law: Former Prob C §380, similar to the present section, was added Stats 1988 ch 1199 §41.5, operative July 1, 1989, and repealed Stats 1990 ch 79 §13, operative July 1, 1991.

Former Prob C §380, similar to present Prob C §8270, was enacted Stats 1931, amended Stats 1969 ch 124 §1, Stats 1977 ch 217 §1, and repealed Stats 1988 ch 1199 §42, operative July 1, 1989.

§381. Limitations on delegation

The right of delegation does not exist to the extent the court determines that powers to be delegated are purely personal to the original fiduciary. **Leg.H.** Enacted Stats 1990 ch 79 §14 (AB 759), operative July 1, 1991.

Prior Law: Former Prob C §381, similar to the present section, was added Stats 1988 ch 1199 §41.5, operative July 1, 1989, and repealed Stats 1990 ch 79 §13, operative July 1, 1991.

Former Prob C §381, similar to present Prob C §8271, was enacted Stats 1931 and repealed Stats 1988 ch 1199 §42, operative July 1, 1989.

§382. Resumption of fiduciary's powers

After the expiration of the original fiduciary's war service, the court may, on petition of the original fiduciary, authorize the original fiduciary to resume the exercise of the fiduciary functions, and the delegated powers cease. **Leg.H.** Enacted Stats 1990 ch 79 §14 (AB 759), operative July 1, 1991.

Prior Law: Former Prob C §382, similar to the present section, was added Stats 1988 ch 1199 §41.5, operative July 1, 1989, and repealed Stats 1990 ch 79 §13, operative July 1, 1991.

Former Prob C §382, similar to present Prob C §§8271, 8272, was enacted Stats 1931 and repealed Stats 1988 ch 1199 §42, operative July 1, 1989.

§383. Fiduciary's immunity for delegate's acts

The original fiduciary is not liable for the acts or omissions of the delegate. **Leg.H.** Enacted Stats 1990 ch 79 §14 (AB 759), operative July 1, 1991.

Prior Law: Former Prob C §383, similar to the present section, was added Stats 1988 ch 1199 §41.5, operative July 1, 1989, and repealed Stats 1990 ch 79 §13, operative July 1, 1991.

Former Prob C §383, similar to present Prob C §1002, was enacted Stats 1931 and repealed Stats 1988 ch 1199 §42, operative July 1, 1989.

ARTICLE 2
Delegation by Consultant

Delegation of consultant's powers. §385.
Suspension of consultant's powers. §386.
Resumption of consultant's powers. §387.
Consultant's immunity for delegate's acts. §388.

§385. Delegation of consultant's powers

(a) A consultant who is or will be engaged in war service may delegate the powers of the consultant, including discretionary powers, to a coconsultant who is not engaged in war service, or to the trustee administering the trust. The procedure for delegation by a fiduciary governs delegation by a consultant.

(b) The right of delegation does not exist to the extent the court determines that powers to be delegated are purely personal to the consultant. These powers are suspended until their exercise is resumed pursuant to this article. **Leg.H.** Enacted Stats 1990 ch 79 §14 (AB 759), operative July 1, 1991.

Prior Law: Former Prob C §385, similar to the present section, was added Stats 1988 ch 1199 §41.5, operative July 1, 1989, and repealed Stats 1990 ch 79 §13, operative July 1, 1991.

Former Prob C §385, similar to present Prob C §8226, was enacted Stats 1931 and repealed Stats 1988 ch 1199 §42, operative July 1, 1989

§386. Suspension of consultant's powers

If a consultant who is engaged in war service does not delegate the consultant's powers, the court, on petition of the trustee or an interested person, may do either of the following:

(a) Suspend the consultant's powers for the period of the consultant's war service and not to exceed six months following the expiration of that period.

(b) Confer the powers, except discretionary powers that the court determines are purely personal to the consultant, on a coconsultant designated in the trust, the trustee, or any other qualified person. **Leg.H.** Enacted Stats 1990 ch 79 §14 (AB 759), operative July 1, 1991.

Prior Law: Former Prob C §386, similar to the present section, was added Stats 1988 ch 1199 §41.5, operative July 1, 1989, and repealed Stats 1990 ch 79 §13, operative July 1, 1991.

§387. Resumption of consultant's powers

If a consultant has delegated or the court has suspended the powers of the consultant, the court may, on petition by the consultant within six months following the expiration of the period of the consultant's war service, authorize the consultant to resume the exercise of the consultant's functions. All powers delegated to or conferred on other persons thereupon cease. **Leg.H.** Enacted Stats 1990 ch 79 §14 (AB 759), operative July 1, 1991.

Prior Law: Former Prob C §387, similar to the present section, was added Stats 1988 ch 1199 §41.5, operative July 1, 1989, and repealed Stats 1990 ch 79 §13, operative July 1, 1991.

§388. Consultant's immunity for delegate's acts

A consultant who delegates powers under this article is not liable for the acts or omissions of the delegate. **Leg.H.** Enacted Stats 1990 ch 79 §14 (AB 759), operative July 1, 1991.

Prior Law: Former Prob C §388, similar to the present section, was added Stats 1988 ch 1199 §41.5, operative July 1, 1989, and repealed Stats 1990 ch 79 §13, operative July 1, 1991.

PART 12
PROBATE REFEREES

Chapter 1. Appointment and Revocation.
Chapter 2. Powers of Probate Referee.

CHAPTER 1
APPOINTMENT AND REVOCATION

Appointment by Controller. §400.
Qualifications for appointment. §401.
Qualification examination. §402.
Term of office of probate referee. §403.
Standards for probate referee. §404.
Revocation of appointment of probate referee. §405.
Termination of authority. §406.
Political activities of probate referees. §407.
Appointment of probate referee before operative date. §408.

§400. Appointment by Controller

(a) The Controller shall appoint at least one person in each county to act as a probate referee for the county.

(b) If there are fewer than three qualified applicants to serve in a county, the Controller may designate a probate referee from another county or make an interim appointment, to serve until the vacancy has been filled by a qualified applicant. **Leg.H.** Enacted Stats 1990 ch 79 §14 (AB 759), operative July 1, 1991.

Prior Law: Former Prob C §400, similar to the present section, was added Stats 1988 ch 1199 §44, operative July 1, 1989, and repealed Stats 1990 ch 79 §13, operative July 1, 1991.

Former Prob C §400, similar to present Prob C §8400, was enacted Stats 1931 and repealed Stats 1988 ch 1199 §43, operative July 1, 1989.

§401. Qualifications for appointment

(a) Appointment shall be from among persons passing a qualification examination. A person who passes the examination is eligible for appointment for a period of five years from the date of the examination.

(b) Appointment shall be on the basis of merit without regard to sex, race, religious creed, color, national origin, ancestry, marital status, or political affiliation. **Leg.H.** Enacted Stats 1990 ch 79 §14 (AB 759), operative July 1, 1991.

Prior Law: Former Prob C §401, similar to the present section, was added Stats 1988 ch 1199 §44, operative July 1, 1989, and repealed Stats 1990 ch 79 §13, operative July 1, 1991.

Former Prob C §401, similar to present Prob C §8402, was enacted Stats 1931, amended Stats 1975 ch 718 §4, and repealed Stats 1988 ch 1199 §43, operative July 1, 1989.

§402. Qualification examination

(a) The qualification examination for applicants for appointment to act as a probate referee shall be held at times and places within the state determined by the Controller.

(b) The Controller may contract with another agency to administer the qualification examination. Administration of the examination shall include:

(1) Development of standards for passage of the examination.
(2) Preparation of examination questions.
(3) Giving the examination.
(4) Scoring the examination.

(c) Each applicant shall pay a fee for taking the qualification examination. The agency administering the examination shall transmit to the Controller a list of candidates who have received a passing score in the examination. The list is a public record. **Leg.H.** Enacted Stats 1990 ch 79 §14 (AB 759), operative July 1, 1991.

Prior Law: Former Prob C §402, similar to the present section, was added Stats 1988 ch 1199 §44, operative July 1, 1989, and repealed Stats 1990 ch 79 §13, operative July 1, 1991.

Former Prob C §402, similar to present Prob C §8421, was enacted Stats 1931 and repealed Stats 1988 ch 1199 §43, operative July 1, 1989.

§403. Term of office of probate referee

(a) The term of office of a probate referee is four years, expiring June 30. A person may be appointed to complete the unexpired term of office of a probate referee whose appointment is revoked or is otherwise terminated. For a period of five years from the date of expiration of the term of office, a person who had been appointed to act as a probate referee is eligible for reappointment.

(b) If the Controller increases the number of probate referees in a county, the Controller shall stagger the terms of the new appointees so that one-quarter, or as close to one-quarter as possible, of the terms of the probate referees in that county expire on June 30 of each succeeding year. **Leg.H.** Enacted Stats 1990 ch 79 §14 (AB 759), operative July 1, 1991.

Prior Law: Former Prob C §403, similar to the present section, was added Stats 1988 ch 1199 §44, operative July 1, 1989, and repealed Stats 1990 ch 79 §13, operative July 1, 1991.

Former Prob C §403, similar to present Prob C §8422, was added Stats 1972 ch 407 §2 and repealed Stats 1988 ch 1199 §43, operative July 1, 1989.

Former Prob C §403, relating to executor's authority to appoint an executor, was enacted Stats 1931 and repealed Stats 1972 ch 407 §1.

§404. Standards for probate referee

(a) The Controller shall establish and may amend standards of training, performance, and ethics of probate referees. The standards are a public record.

(b) The Controller may revoke the appointment of a person to act as a probate referee for noncompliance with any standard of training, performance, or ethics established under subdivision (a). The Controller may revoke an appointment under this subdivision without notice or a hearing, but the revocation is subject to review by writ of mandate in a court of competent jurisdiction. **Leg.H.** Enacted Stats 1990 ch 79 §14 (AB 759), operative July 1, 1991.

Prior Law: Former Prob C §404, similar to the present section, was added Stats 1988 ch 1199 §44, operative July 1, 1989, and repealed Stats 1990 ch 79 §13, operative July 1, 1991.

Former Prob C §404, similar to present Prob C §8423, was enacted Stats 1931 and repealed Stats 1988 ch 1199 §43, operative July 1, 1989.

§405. Revocation of appointment of probate referee

Notwithstanding Section 404, the Controller may, at the Controller's pleasure, revoke the appointment of a person to act as a probate referee. Under this section, the Controller may revoke the appointment of not more than 10 percent of the probate referees in each county in any one calendar year, but may revoke the appointment of at least one probate referee in each county in any one calendar year. **Leg.H.** Enacted Stats 1990 ch 79 §14 (AB 759), operative July 1, 1991.

Prior Law: Former Prob C §405, similar to the present section, was added Stats 1988 ch 1199 §44, operative July 1, 1989, and repealed Stats 1990 ch 79 §13, operative July 1, 1991.

Former Prob C §405, similar to present Prob C §8424, was enacted Stats 1931 and repealed Stats 1988 ch 1199 §43, operative July 1, 1989.

§406. Termination of authority

(a) The authority of a person to act as a probate referee ceases immediately upon expiration of the person's term of office, revocation of the person's appointment, or other termination pursuant to law.

(b) Upon cessation of authority of a person to act as a probate referee, the Controller shall notify the superior court of the county for which the probate referee was appointed. Upon receipt of notice, or if it otherwise comes to the attention of the court that the authority of a person to act as a probate referee has ceased, the court shall reassign any estate for which the person had been designated as probate referee to another probate referee. **Leg.H.** Enacted Stats 1990 ch 79 §14 (AB 759), operative July 1, 1991.

Prior Law: Former Prob C §406, similar to the present section, was added Stats 1988 ch 1199 §44, operative July 1, 1989, and repealed Stats 1990 ch 79 §13, operative July 1, 1991.

Former Prob C §406, similar to present Prob C §§8440, 8522, was enacted Stats 1931 and repealed Stats 1988 ch 1199 §43, operative July 1, 1989.

§407. Political activities of probate referees

(a) As used in this section, "prohibited political activity" means directly or indirectly soliciting, receiving, or contributing, or being in any manner involved in soliciting, receiving, or contributing, any of the following:

(1) An assessment, subscription, or contribution to any party, incumbent, committee, or candidate exceeding two hundred dollars ($200) in any one calendar year for any partisan public office of this state.

(2) An assessment, subscription, contribution, or political service in any amount for any campaign for the office of Controller.

(b) Upon a person's appointment and thereafter in January of each year during the person's tenure as a probate referee, the person shall file with the Controller a verified statement indicating whether the person has engaged in prohibited political activity during the preceding two calendar years.

(c) The Controller may not appoint or reappoint as a probate referee a person who within the preceding two calendar years has engaged in prohibited political activity, and any such appointment or reappointment is void and shall be revoked. The Controller shall revoke the appointment of a person who, during the person's tenure as a probate referee, engages in prohibited political activity. However, all acts not otherwise invalid, performed by the person before revocation of the person's appointment, are valid.

(d) A person shall not engage in prohibited political activity during the time the person is an applicant for appointment or reappointment, or during the person's tenure as a probate referee. A violation of this subdivision is a misdemeanor.

(e) Subdivisions (a), (c), and (d) do not apply to any prohibited political activity that occurred before July 1, 1989, and the applicable law in effect before July 1, 1989, continues to apply. Subdivision (b) applies on July 1, 1989, to persons who apply for appointment on or after July 1, 1989. A person who applied for appointment or who was appointed before July 1, 1989, shall file the first statement required by subdivision (b) on or before July 1, 1989, and thereafter as prescribed in subdivision (b). **Leg.H.** Enacted Stats 1990 ch 79 §14 (AB 759), operative July 1, 1991.

Prior Law: Former Prob C §407, similar to the present section, was added Stats 1988 ch 1199 §44, operative July 1, 1989, and repealed Stats 1990 ch 79 §13, operative July 1, 1991.

Former Prob C §407, similar to present Prob C §§1043, 1046, 8004, 8005, 8420, was enacted Stats 1931 and repealed Stats 1988 ch 1199 §43, operative July 1, 1989.

§408. Appointment of probate referee before operative date

The appointment of a probate referee by the Controller before July 1, 1989, is not invalidated by the repeal of the law under which the appointment was made. Appointment of a probate referee before July 1, 1989, may be revoked under this chapter only if revocation would otherwise be proper under this chapter. **Leg.H.** Enacted Stats 1990 ch 79 §14 (AB 759), operative July 1, 1991.

Prior Law: Former Prob C §408, similar to the present section, was added Stats 1988 ch 1199 §44, operative July 1, 1989, and repealed Stats 1990 ch 79 §13, operative July 1, 1991.

Former Prob C §408, similar to present Prob C §8425, was enacted Stats 1931 and repealed Stats 1988 ch 1199 §43, operative July 1, 1989.

§409. [Section repealed 1989]

Leg.H. Enacted Stats 1931 ch 281. Amended Stats 1963 ch 232 §1; Stats 1974 ch 511 §1. Repealed Stats 1988 ch 1199 §43, operative July 1, 1989. See Prob C §§8441, 8442.

§410. [Section repealed 1989]

Leg.H. Added Stats 1963 ch 337 §1. Repealed Stats 1988 ch 1199 §43, operative July 1, 1989. See Prob C §8480.

§420. [Section repealed 1989]

Leg.H. Enacted Stats 1931 ch 281. Amended Stats 1975 ch 718 §5; Stats 1980 ch 955 §12. Repealed Stats 1988 ch 1199 §43, operative July 1, 1989. See Prob C §8402.

§421. [Section repealed 1989]

Leg.H. Enacted Stats 1931 ch 281. Repealed Stats 1988 ch 1199 §43, operative July 1, 1989. See Prob C §8402.

§422. [Section repealed 1989]

Leg.H. Enacted Stats 1931 ch 281. Amended Stats 1943 ch 522 §1; Stats 1974 ch 511 §2; Stats 1984 ch 192 §1; Stats 1987 ch 923 §31. Repealed Stats 1988 ch 1199 §43, operative July 1, 1989. See Prob C §§8460–8463.

§423. [Section repealed 1989]

Leg.H. Enacted Stats 1931 ch 281. Amended Stats 1943 ch 941 §1; Stats 1967 ch 269 §1; Stats 1976 ch 475 §1; Stats 1979 ch 731 §8; Stats 1980 ch 955 §13. Repealed Stats 1988 ch 1199 §43, operative July 1, 1989. See Prob C §8465.

§424. [Section repealed 1989]

Leg.H. Enacted Stats 1931 ch 281. Repealed Stats 1988 ch 1199 §43, operative July 1, 1989. The repealed section related to preference for whole-blood relatives as entitled to administration over those of half-blood.

§425. [Section repealed 1989]

Leg.H. Enacted Stats 1931 ch 281. Repealed Stats 1988 ch 1199 §43, operative July 1, 1989. See Prob C §§8466, 8467.

§426. [Section repealed 1989]

Leg.H. Enacted Stats 1931 ch 281. Amended Stats 1967 ch 719 §1. Repealed Stats 1988 ch 1199 §43, operative July 1, 1989. See Prob C §8464.

§427. [Section repealed 1989]

Leg.H. Enacted Stats 1931 ch 281. Repealed Stats 1988 ch 1199 §43, operative July 1, 1989. See Prob C §8468.

§440. [Section repealed 1989]

Leg.H. Enacted Stats 1931 ch 281. Amended Stats 1933 ch 969 §2; Stats 1961 ch 508 §1; Stats 1963 ch 328 §1; Stats 1979 ch 731 §9; Stats 1980 ch 539 §5. Repealed Stats 1988 ch 1199 §43, operative July 1, 1989. See Prob C §§1020, 8002, 8006.

§441. [Section repealed 1989]

Leg.H. Enacted Stats 1931 ch 281. Amended Stats 1979 ch 731 §10; Stats 1980 ch 955 §13.1; Stats 1982 ch 520 §4; Stats 1987 ch 923 §32. Repealed Stats 1988 ch 1199 §43, operative July 1, 1989. See Prob C §§1041, 8003, 8110.

§442. [Section repealed 1989]

Leg.H. Enacted Stats 1931 ch 281. Amended Stats 1941 ch 769 §1. Repealed Stats 1988 ch 1199 §43, operative July 1, 1989. See Prob C §§1043, 8004.

§443. [Section repealed 1989]

Leg.H. Enacted Stats 1931 ch 281. Repealed Stats 1988 ch 1199 §43, operative July 1, 1989. See Prob C §8005.

CHAPTER 2
POWERS OF PROBATE REFEREE

General powers. §450.
Compelling appearance. §451.
Examination, testimony, and production of documents. §452.
Protective orders and enforcement. §453.

§450. General powers

Upon designation by the court, the probate referee has all the powers of a referee of the superior court and all other powers provided in this chapter. **Leg.H.** Enacted Stats 1990 ch 79 §14 (AB 759), operative July 1, 1991.

Prior Law: Former Prob C §450, similar to the present section, was added Stats 1988 ch 1199 §44, operative July 1, 1989, and repealed Stats 1990 ch 79 §13, operative July 1, 1991.

Former Prob C §450, similar to present Prob C §§8503, 8520, was enacted Stats 1931, amended Stats 1943 ch 941 §2, and repealed Stats 1988 ch 1199 §45, operative July 1, 1989.

§451. Compelling appearance

(a) For the purpose of appraisal of property in the estate, the probate referee may require, and may issue a subpoena to compel, the appearance before the referee of the personal representative, guardian, conservator, or other fiduciary, an interested person, or any other person the referee has reason to believe has knowledge of the property.

(b) A subpoena issued under subdivision (a) is subject to the provisions of Chapter 6 (commencing with Section 2020.010) of Title 4 of Part 4 of the Code of Civil Procedure governing deposition subpoenas. **Leg.H.** Enacted Stats 1990 ch 79 §14 (AB 759), operative July 1, 1991. Amended Stats 2004 ch 182 §52 (AB 3081), operative July 1, 2005.

Prior Law: Former Prob C §451, similar to the present section, was added Stats 1988 ch 1199 §44, operative July 1, 1989, and repealed Stats 1990 ch 79 §13, operative July 1, 1991.

Former Prob C §451, similar to present Prob C §§8500, 8520 et seq., was enacted Stats 1931, amended Stats 1979 ch 731 §11, and repealed Stats 1988 ch 1199 §45, operative July 1, 1989.

§452. Examination, testimony, and production of documents

(a) The probate referee may:

(1) Examine and take the testimony under oath of a person appearing before the referee.

(2) Require, and issue a subpoena to compel, the person to produce any document in the person's possession or control, concerning the value of any property in the estate.

(b) A subpoena issued under subdivision (a) is subject to the provisions of Chapter 6 (commencing with Section 2020.010) of Title 4 of Part 4 of the Code of Civil Procedure governing deposition subpoenas. **Leg.H.** Enacted Stats 1990 ch 79 §14 (AB 759), operative July 1, 1991. Amended Stats 2004 ch 182 §53 (AB 3081), operative July 1, 2005.

Prior Law: Former Prob C §452, similar to the present section, was added Stats 1988 ch 1199 §44, operative July 1, 1989, and repealed Stats 1990 ch 79 §13, operative July 1, 1991.

Former Prob C §452, similar to present Prob C §8503, was enacted Stats 1931, amended Stats 1943 ch 941 §3, Stats 1965 ch 1905 §1, and repealed Stats 1988 ch 1199 §45, operative July 1, 1989.

§453. Protective orders and enforcement

(a) On petition of a person required to appear before the probate referee pursuant to this chapter, the court may make a protective order to protect the person from annoyance, embarrassment, or oppression. The petitioner shall deliver pursuant to Section 1215 notice of the hearing on the petition to the probate referee and to the personal representative, guardian, conservator, or other fiduciary at least 15 days before the date set for the hearing. Any subpoena issued by the probate referee is stayed during the pendency of the petition.

(b) On petition of the probate referee, the court may make an order to show cause why a person who is required, but fails, to appear before the probate referee pursuant to this chapter, should not be compelled to do so. The probate referee shall deliver pursuant to Section 1215 notice of the hearing on the petition to the person at least 15 days before the date set for the hearing. **Leg.H.** Enacted Stats 1990 ch 79 §14 (AB 759), operative July 1, 1991. Amended Stats 2017 ch 319 §8 (AB 976), effective January 1, 2018.

Prior Law: Former Prob C §453, similar to the present section, was added Stats 1988 ch 1199 §44, operative July 1, 1989, and repealed Stats 1990 ch 79 §13, operative July 1, 1991.

Former Prob C §453, similar to present Prob C §8503, was enacted Stats 1931 and repealed Stats 1988 ch 1199 §45, operative July 1, 1989.

PART 13
LITIGATION INVOLVING DECEDENT

Chapter 1. Liability of Decedent Covered by Insurance.

CHAPTER 1
LIABILITY OF DECEDENT COVERED BY INSURANCE

Action authorized. §550.
Statute of limitations. §551.
Procedure. §552.
Defenses. §553.
Damages. §554.
Application of chapter. §555.

§550. Action authorized

(a) Subject to the provisions of this chapter, an action to establish the decedent's liability for which the decedent was protected by insurance may be commenced or continued against the decedent's estate without the need to join as a party the decedent's personal representative or successor in interest.

(b) The remedy provided in this chapter is cumulative and may be pursued concurrently with other remedies. **Leg.H.** Enacted Stats 1990 ch 79 §14 (AB 759), operative July 1, 1991.

Prior Law: Former Prob C §550, similar to the present section, was added Stats 1988 ch 1199 §49, operative July 1, 1989, and repealed Stats 1990 ch 79 §13, operative July 1, 1991.

Former Prob C §550, similar to present Prob C §9614, was enacted Stats 1931, amended Stats 1971 ch 527 §3, Stats 1982 ch 517 §331, and repealed Stats 1988 ch 1199 §48, operative July 1, 1989.

§551. Statute of limitations

Notwithstanding Section 366.2 of the Code of Civil Procedure, if the limitations period otherwise applicable to the action has not expired at the time of the decedent's death, an action under this chapter may be commenced within one year after the expiration of the limitations period otherwise applicable. **Leg.H.** Enacted Stats 1990 ch 79 §14 (AB 759), operative July 1, 1991. Amended Stats 1990 ch 140 §3.1 (SB 1855), operative July 1, 1991; Stats 1992 ch 178 §30 (SB 1496).

Prior Law: Former Prob C §551, similar to the present section, was added Stats 1988 ch 1199 §49, operative July 1, 1989, repealed Stats 1990 ch 79 §13, operative July 1, 1991 (ch 140 prevails), amended Stats 1990 ch 140 §3, operative until July 1, 1991, and repealed Stats 1990 ch 140 §19, operative July 1, 1991.

Former Prob C §551, similar to present CCP §996.110, was enacted Stats 1931, amended Stats 1939 ch 804 §1, and repealed Stats 1982 ch 517 §332.

§552. Procedure

(a) An action under this chapter shall name as the defendant, "Estate of (name of decedent), Deceased." Summons shall be served on a person designated in writing by the insurer or, if none, on the insurer. Further proceedings shall be in the name of the estate, but otherwise shall be conducted in the same manner as if the action were against the personal representative.

(b) On motion of an interested person, or on its own motion, the court in which the action is pending may, for good cause, order the appointment and substitution of a personal representative as the defendant.

(c) An action against the estate of the decedent under this chapter may be consolidated with an action against the personal representative. **Leg.H.** Enacted Stats 1990 ch 79 §14 (AB 759), operative July 1, 1991.

Prior Law: Former Prob C §552, similar to the present section, was added Stats 1988 ch 1199 §49, operative July 1, 1989, and repealed Stats 1990 ch 79 §13, operative July 1, 1991.

Former Prob C §552, similar to present CCP §996.140, was enacted Stats 1931 and repealed Stats 1982 ch 517 §333.

§553. Defenses

The insurer may deny or otherwise contest its liability in an action under this chapter or by an independent action. Unless the personal representative is joined as a party, a judgment in the action under this chapter or in the independent action does not adjudicate rights by or against the estate. **Leg.H.** Enacted Stats 1990 ch 79 §14 (AB 759), operative July 1, 1991.

Prior Law: Former Prob C §553, similar to the present section, was added Stats 1988 ch 1199 §49, operative July 1, 1989, and repealed Stats 1990 ch 79 §13, operative July 1, 1991.

Former Prob C §553, similar to present CCP §996.130, was enacted Stats 1931 and repealed Stats 1982 ch 517 §334.

§554. Damages

(a) Except as provided in subdivision (b), either the damages sought in an action under this chapter shall be within the limits and coverage of the insurance, or recovery of damages outside the limits or coverage of the insurance shall be waived. A judgment in favor of the plaintiff in the action is enforceable only from the insurance coverage and not against property in the estate.

(b) Where the amount of damages sought in the action exceeds the coverage of the insurance, subdivision (a) does not apply if both of the following conditions are satisfied:

(1) The personal representative is joined as a party to the action.

(2) The plaintiff files a claim in compliance with Section 9390. **Leg.H.** Enacted Stats 1990 ch 79 §14 (AB 759), operative July 1, 1991.

Prior Law: Former Prob C §554, similar to the present section, was added Stats 1988 ch 1199 §49, operative July 1, 1989, and repealed Stats 1990 ch 79 §13, operative July 1, 1991.

Former Prob C §554, similar to present CCP §§996.460, 996.480, was enacted Stats 1931, amended Stats 1971 ch 527 §4, and repealed Stats 1982 ch 517 §338.

§555. Application of chapter

(a) This chapter does not apply to an action commenced before July 1, 1989.

(b) The applicable law in effect before July 1, 1989, continues to apply to an action commenced before July 1, 1989, notwithstanding its repeal by Chapter 1199 of the Statutes of 1988. **Leg.H.** Enacted Stats 1990 ch 79 §14 (AB 759), operative July 1, 1991.

Prior Law: Former Prob C §555, similar to the present section, was added Stats 1988 ch 1199 §49, operative July 1, 1989, and repealed Stats 1990 ch 79 §13, operative July 1, 1991.

CHAPTER 2
SURVIVAL OF ACTIONS [REPEALED]

§573. [Section repealed 1992]

Leg.H. Enacted Stats 1990 ch 79 §14 (AB 759), operative July 1, 1991. Amended Stats 1991 ch 1055 §16 (SB 271). Repealed Stats 1992 ch 178 §31 (SB 1496). See CCP §§377.20, 377.22, 377.30, 377.34, 377.40, 377.42.

PART 14
POWERS OF APPOINTMENT

Chapter 1. General Provisions.
Chapter 2. Definitions; Classification of Powers of Appointment.
Chapter 3. Creation of Powers of Appointment.
Chapter 4. Exercise of Powers of Appointment.
Chapter 5. Effect of Failure to Make Effective Appointment.
Chapter 6. Rights of Creditors.
Chapter 7. Rule Against Perpetuities.
Chapter 8. Revocability of Creation, Exercise, or Release of Power of Appointment.

CHAPTER 1
GENERAL PROVISIONS

Common law as law of state. §600.
Controlling law. §601.

§600. Common law as law of state

Except to the extent that the common law rules governing powers of appointment are modified by statute, the common law as to powers of appointment is the law of this state. **Leg.H.** Added Stats 1992 ch 30 §2 (AB 1722).

§601. Controlling law

If the law existing at the time of the creation of a power of appointment and the law existing at the time of the release or exercise of the power of appointment or at the time of the assertion of a right given by this part differ, the law existing at the time of the release, exercise, or assertion of a right controls. Nothing in this section makes invalid a power of appointment created before July 1, 1970, that was valid under the law in existence at the time it was created. **Leg.H.** Added Stats 1992 ch 30 §2 (AB 1722).

CHAPTER 2
DEFINITIONS; CLASSIFICATION OF POWERS OF APPOINTMENT

Definitions. §610.
"General" and "special" powers; Power exercisable by powerholder. §611.
"Testamentary" and "presently exercisable" powers. §612.
"Imperative" and "discretionary" powers. §613.

§610. Definitions

As used in this part:

(a) "Appointee" means the person in whose favor a power of appointment is exercised.

(b) "Appointive property" means the property or interest in property that is the subject of the power of appointment.

(c) "Creating instrument" means the deed, will, trust, or other writing or document that creates or reserves the power of appointment.

(d) "Donor" means the person who creates or reserves a power of appointment.

(e) "Permissible appointee" means a person in whose favor a power of appointment can be exercised.

(f) "Power of appointment" means a power that enables a powerholder acting in a nonfiduciary capacity to designate a recipient of an ownership interest in or another power of appointment over the appointive property. The term does not include a power of attorney.

(g) "Powerholder" means the person to whom a power of appointment is given or in whose favor a power of appointment is reserved. **Leg.H.** Added Stats 1992 ch 30 §2 (AB 1722). Amended Stats 2016 ch 81 §1 (AB 2846), effective January 1, 2017.

§611. "General" and "special" powers; Power exercisable by powerholder

(a) A power of appointment is "general" only to the extent that it is exercisable in favor of the powerholder, the powerholder's estate, the powerholder's creditors, or creditors of the powerholder's estate, whether or not it is exercisable in favor of others.

(b) A power to consume, invade, or appropriate property for the benefit of a person in discharge of the powerholder's obligation of support that is limited by an ascertainable standard relating to the person's health, education, support, or maintenance is not a general power of appointment.

(c) A power exercisable by the powerholder only in conjunction with a person having a substantial interest in the appointive property that is adverse to the exercise of the power in favor of the powerholder, the powerholder's estate, the powerholder's creditors, or creditors of the powerholder's estate is not a general power of appointment.

(d) A power of appointment that is not "general" is "special."

(e) A power of appointment may be general as to some appointive property, or an interest in or a specific portion of appointive property, and be special as to other appointive property. **Leg.H.** Added Stats 1992 ch 30 §2 (AB 1722). Amended Stats 2016 ch 81 §2 (AB 2846), effective January 1, 2017.

§612. "Testamentary" and "presently exercisable" powers

(a) A power of appointment is "testamentary" if it is exercisable only by a will.

(b) A power of appointment is "presently exercisable" at the time in question to the extent that an irrevocable appointment can be made.

(c) A power of appointment is "not presently exercisable" if it is "postponed." A power of appointment is "postponed" in either of the following circumstances:

(1) The creating instrument provides that the power of appointment may be exercised only after a specified act or event occurs or a specified condition is met, and the act or event has not occurred or the condition has not been met.

(2) The creating instrument provides that an exercise of the power of appointment is revocable until a specified act or event occurs or a specified condition is met, and the act or event has not occurred or the condition has not been met. **Leg.H.** Added Stats 1992 ch 30 §2 (AB 1722).

§613. "Imperative" and "discretionary" powers

A power of appointment is "imperative" where the creating instrument manifests an intent that the permissible appointees be benefited even if the powerholder fails to exercise the power. An imperative power can exist even though the powerholder has the privilege of selecting some and excluding others of the designated permissible appointees. All other powers of appointment are "discretionary." The powerholder of a discretionary power is privileged to exercise, or not to exercise, the power as the powerholder chooses. **Leg.H.** Added Stats 1992 ch 30 §2 (AB 1722). Amended Stats 2016 ch 81 §3 (AB 2846), effective January 1, 2017.

CHAPTER 3
CREATION OF POWERS OF APPOINTMENT

Creation. §620.
Requirements on creation. §621.

§620. Creation

A power of appointment can be created only by a donor having the capacity to transfer the interest in property to which the power relates. **Leg.H.** Added Stats 1992 ch 30 §2 (AB 1722).

§621. Requirements on creation

(a) A power of appointment is created only if all of the following are satisfied:

(1) There is a creating instrument.

(2) The creating instrument is valid under applicable law.

(3) Except as provided in subdivision (b), the creating instrument transfers the appointive property.

(4) The terms of the creating instrument manifest the donor's intent to create in a powerholder a power of appointment over the appointive property exercisable in favor of a permissible appointee.

(b) Paragraph (3) of subdivision (a) does not apply to the creation of a power of appointment by the exercise of a power of appointment. **Leg.H.** Added Stats 2016 ch 81 §4 (AB 2846), effective January 1, 2017.

CHAPTER 4
EXERCISE OF POWERS OF APPOINTMENT

Article 1. Donee's Capacity.
Article 2. Scope of Donee's Authority.
Article 3. Donee's Required Intent.

Article 4. Types of Appointments.
Article 5. Contracts to Appoint; Releases.

ARTICLE 1
Donee's Capacity

Exercise. §625.

§625. Exercise

(a) A power of appointment can be exercised only by a powerholder having the capacity to transfer the interest in property to which the power relates.

(b) Unless the creating instrument otherwise provides, a powerholder who is a minor may not exercise a power of appointment during minority. **Leg.H.** Added Stats 1992 ch 30 §2 (AB 1722). Amended Stats 2016 ch 81 §5 (AB 2846), effective January 1, 2017.

ARTICLE 2
Scope of Donee's Authority

Compliance with requirements of creating instrument. §630.
Excuse from compliance. §631.
Direction that power be exercised by instrument making specific reference to power. §632.
Consent of donor. §633.
Power created in favor of two or more powerholders. §634.
Remedy of defective exercise of imperative power. §635.

§630. Compliance with requirements of creating instrument

(a) Except as otherwise provided in this part, if the creating instrument specifies requirements as to the manner, time, and conditions of the exercise of a power of appointment, the power can be exercised only by complying with those requirements.

(b) Unless expressly prohibited by the creating instrument, a power stated to be exercisable by an inter vivos instrument is also exercisable by a written will. **Leg.H.** Added Stats 1992 ch 30 §2 (AB 1722).

§631. Excuse from compliance

(a) Where an appointment does not satisfy the formal requirements specified in the creating instrument as provided in subdivision (a) of Section 630, the court may excuse compliance with the formal requirements and determine that exercise of the appointment was effective if both of the following requirements are satisfied:

(1) The appointment approximates the manner of appointment prescribed by the donor.

(2) The failure to satisfy the formal requirements does not defeat the accomplishment of a significant purpose of the donor.

(b) This section does not permit a court to excuse compliance with a specific reference requirement under Section 632. **Leg.H.** Added Stats 1992 ch 30 §2 (AB 1722).

§632. Direction that power be exercised by instrument making specific reference to power

If the creating instrument expressly directs that a power of appointment be exercised by an instrument that makes a specific reference to the power or to the instrument that created the power, the power can be exercised only by an instrument containing the required reference. **Leg.H.** Added Stats 1992 ch 30 §2 (AB 1722).

§633. Consent of donor

(a) If the creating instrument requires the consent of the donor or other person to exercise a power of appointment, the power can only be exercised when the required consent is contained in the instrument of exercise or in a separate written instrument, signed in each case by the person whose consent is required.

(b) Unless expressly prohibited by the creating instrument:

(1) If a person whose consent is required dies, the power may be exercised by the powerholder without the consent of that person.

(2) If a person whose consent is required becomes legally incapable of consenting, the person's guardian or conservator may consent to an exercise of the power.

(3) A consent may be given before or after the exercise of the power by the powerholder. **Leg.H.** Added Stats 1992 ch 30 §2 (AB 1722). Amended Stats 2016 ch 81 §6 (AB 2846), effective January 1, 2017.

§634. Power created in favor of two or more powerholders

A power of appointment created in favor of two or more powerholders can only be exercised when all of the powerholders unite in its exercise. If one or more of the powerholders dies, becomes legally incapable of exercising the power, or releases the power, the power may be exercised by the others, unless expressly prohibited by the creating instrument. **Leg.H.** Added Stats 1992 ch 30 §2 (AB 1722). Amended Stats 2016 ch 81 §7 (AB 2846), effective January 1, 2017.

§635. Remedy of defective exercise of imperative power

Nothing in this chapter affects the power of a court of competent jurisdiction to remedy a defective exercise of an imperative power of appointment. **Leg.H.** Added Stats 1992 ch 30 §2 (AB 1722).

ARTICLE 3
Donee's Required Intent

Manifestation of powerholder required intent. §640.
Effect of general residuary clause in will. §641.
Effect of power existing at powerholder's death but created after execution of will. §642.

§640. Manifestation of powerholder required intent

(a) The exercise of a power of appointment requires a manifestation of the powerholder's intent to exercise the power.

(b) A manifestation of the powerholder's intent to exercise a power of appointment exists in any of the following circumstances:

(1) The powerholder declares, in substance, that the powerholder exercises specific powers or all the powers the powerholder has.

(2) The powerholder purports to transfer an interest in the appointive property that the powerholder would have no power to transfer except by virtue of the power.

(3) The powerholder makes a disposition that, when considered with reference to the property owned and the circumstances existing at the time of the disposition, manifests the powerholder's understanding that the powerholder was disposing of the appointive property.

(c) The circumstances described in subdivision (b) are illustrative, not exclusive. **Leg.H.** Added Stats 1992 ch 30 §2 (AB 1722). Amended Stats 2016 ch 81 §8 (AB 2846), effective January 1, 2017.

§641. Effect of general residuary clause in will

(a) A general residuary clause in a will, or a will making general disposition of all the testator's property, does not exercise a power of appointment held by the testator unless specific reference is made to the power or there is some other indication of intent to exercise the power.

(b) This section applies in a case where the powerholder dies on or after July 1, 1982. **Leg.H.** Added Stats 1992 ch 30 §2 (AB 1722). Amended Stats 2016 ch 81 §9 (AB 2846), effective January 1, 2017.

§642. Effect of power existing at powerholder's death but created after execution of will

If a power of appointment existing at the powerholder's death, but created after the execution of the powerholder's will, is exercised by the will, the appointment is effective except in either of the following cases:

(a) The creating instrument manifests an intent that the power may not be exercised by a will previously executed.

(b) The will manifests an intent not to exercise a power subsequently acquired. **Leg.H.** Added Stats 1992 ch 30 §2 (AB 1722). Amended Stats 2016 ch 81 §10 (AB 2846), effective January 1, 2017.

ARTICLE 4
Types of Appointments

Appointments by powerholder of general power. §650.
Appointments by powerholder of special power. §651.
Appointment of whole or part of property to one or more appointees. §652.

§650. Appointments by powerholder of general power

(a) The powerholder of a general power of appointment may make an appointment:

(1) Of all of the appointive property at one time, or several partial appointments at different times, where the power is exercisable inter vivos.

(2) Of present or future interests or both.

(3) Subject to conditions or charges.

(4) Subject to otherwise lawful restraints on the alienation of the appointed interest.

(5) In trust.

(6) Creating a new power of appointment.

(b) The listing in subdivision (a) is illustrative, not exclusive. **Leg.H.** Added Stats 1992 ch 30 §2 (AB 1722). Amended Stats 2016 ch 81 §11 (AB 2846), effective January 1, 2017.

§651. Appointments by powerholder of special power

Subject to the limitations imposed by the creating instrument, the powerholder of a special power may make any of the types of appointment permissible for the powerholder of a general power under Section 650. **Leg.H.** Added Stats 1992 ch 30 §2 (AB 1722). Amended Stats 2016 ch 81 §12 (AB 2846), effective January 1, 2017.

§652. Appointment of whole or part of property to one or more appointees

(a) Except as provided in subdivision (b), the powerholder of a special power of appointment may appoint the whole or any part of the appointive property to any one or more of the permissible appointees and exclude others.

(b) If the donor specifies either a minimum or maximum share or amount to be appointed to one or more of the permissible appointees, the exercise of the power must conform to the specification. **Leg.H.** Added Stats 1992 ch 30 §2 (AB 1722). Amended Stats 2016 ch 81 §13 (AB 2846), effective January 1, 2017.

ARTICLE 5
Contracts to Appoint; Releases

When contract to appoint may be made. §660.
Release of power; Delivery. §661.
Release on behalf of minor powerholder. §662.

§660. When contract to appoint may be made

(a) The powerholder of a power of appointment that is presently exercisable, whether general or special, can contract to make an appointment to the same extent that the powerholder could make an effective appointment.

(b) The powerholder of a power of appointment cannot contract to make an appointment while the power of appointment is not presently exercisable. If a promise to make an appointment under such a power is not performed, the promisee cannot obtain either specific performance or damages, but the promisee is not prevented from obtaining restitution of the value given by the promisee for the promise.

(c) Unless the creating instrument expressly provides that the powerholder may not contract to make an appointment while the power of appointment is not presently exercisable, subdivision (b) does not apply to the case where the donor and the powerholder are the same person. In this case, the powerholder can contract to make an appointment to the same extent that the powerholder could make an effective appointment if the power of appointment were presently exercisable. **Leg.H.** Added Stats 1992 ch 30 §2 (AB 1722). Amended Stats 2016 ch 81 §14 (AB 2846), effective January 1, 2017.

§661. Release of power; Delivery

(a) Unless the creating instrument otherwise provides, a general or special power of appointment that is a discretionary power, whether testamentary or otherwise, may be released, either with or without consideration, by a written instrument signed by the powerholder and delivered as provided in subdivision (c).

(b) A releasable power may be released with respect to the whole or any part of the appointive property and may also be released in such manner as to reduce or limit the permissible appointees. No partial release of a power shall be deemed to make imperative the remaining power that was not imperative before the release unless the instrument of release expressly so provides. No release of a power that is not presently exercisable is permissible where the donor designated persons or a class to take in default of the powerholder's exercise of the power unless the release serves to benefit all persons designated as provided by the donor.

(c) A release shall be delivered as follows:

(1) If the creating instrument specifies a person to whom a release is to be delivered, the release shall be delivered to that person, but delivery need not be made as provided in this paragraph if the person cannot with due diligence be found.

(2) In a case where the property to which the power relates is held by a trustee, the release shall be delivered to the trustee.

(3) In a case not covered by paragraph (1) or (2), the release may be delivered to any of the following:

(A) A person, other than the powerholder, who could be adversely affected by the exercise of the power.

(B) The county recorder of the county in which the powerholder resides or in which the deed, will, or other instrument creating the power is filed.

(d) A release of a power of appointment that affects real property or obligations secured by real property shall be acknowledged and proved, and may be certified and recorded, in like manner and with like effect as grants of real property, and all statutory provisions relating to the recordation or nonrecordation of conveyances of real property and to the effect thereof apply to a release with like effect, without regard to the date when the release was delivered, if at all, pursuant to subdivision (c). Failure to deliver, pursuant to subdivision (c), a release that is recorded pursuant to this subdivision does not affect the validity of any transaction with respect to the real property or obligation secured thereby, and the general laws of this state on recording and its effect govern the transaction.

(e) This section does not impair the validity of a release made before July 1, 1970. **Leg.H.** Added Stats 1992 ch 30 §2 (AB 1722). Amended Stats 2016 ch 81 §15 (AB 2846), effective January 1, 2017.

§662. Release on behalf of minor powerholder

(a) A release on behalf of a minor powerholder shall be made by the guardian of the estate of the minor pursuant to an order of court obtained under this section.

(b) The guardian or other interested person may file a petition with the court in which the guardianship of the estate proceeding is pending for an order of the court authorizing or requiring the guardian to release the ward's powers as a powerholder or a power of appointment in whole or in part.

(c) Notice of the hearing on the petition shall be given for the period and in the manner provided in Chapter 3 (commencing with Section 1460) of Part 1 of Division 4 to all of the following (other than the petitioner or persons joining in the petition):

(1) The persons required to be given notice under Chapter 3 (commencing with Section 1460) of Part 1 of Division 4.

(2) The donor of the power, if alive.

(3) The trustee, if the property to which the power relates is held by a trustee.

(4) Other persons as ordered by the court.

(d) After hearing, the court in its discretion may make an order authorizing or requiring the guardian to release on behalf of the ward a general or special power of appointment as permitted under Section 661, if the court determines, taking into consideration all the relevant circumstances, that the ward as a prudent person would make the release of the power of appointment if the ward had the capacity to do so.

(e) Nothing in this section imposes any duty on the guardian to file a petition under this section, and the guardian is not liable for failure to file a petition under this section. **Leg.H.** Added Stats 1992 ch 30 §2 (AB 1722). Amended Stats 2016 ch 81 §16 (AB 2846), effective January 1, 2017.

CHAPTER 5
EFFECT OF FAILURE TO MAKE EFFECTIVE APPOINTMENT

Validity of exercise of power more extensive than authorized. §670.
Death of powerholder prior to exercise of imperative power; Defective exercise; Compelling proper exercise of power. §671.
Effect of failure to appoint property, release of entire power, or ineffective appointment. §672.
Effect of ineffective appointment by will or instrument effective only at death of powerholder. §673.
Effect of death of permissible appointee prior to exercise of special power. §674.
Effect of exercise of power of appointment in disposition that also disposes of property owned by powerholder. §675.
Effect of valid partial appointment to taker in default. §676.

§670. Validity of exercise of power more extensive than authorized

An exercise of a power of appointment is not void solely because it is more extensive than authorized by the power, but is valid to the extent that the exercise was permissible under the terms of the power. **Leg.H.** Added Stats 1992 ch 30 §2 (AB 1722).

§671. Death of powerholder prior to exercise of imperative power; Defective exercise; Compelling proper exercise of power

(a) Unless the creating instrument or the powerholder, in writing, manifests a contrary intent, where the powerholder dies without having exercised an imperative power of appointment either in whole or in part, the persons designated as permissible appointees take equally of the property not already appointed. Where the creating instrument establishes a minimum distribution requirement that is not satisfied by an equal division of the property not already appointed, the appointees who have received a partial appointment are required to return a pro rata portion of the property they would otherwise be entitled to receive in an amount sufficient to meet the minimum distribution requirement.

(b) Where an imperative power of appointment has been exercised defectively, either in whole or in part, its proper execution may be adjudged in favor of the person intended to be benefited by the defective exercise.

(c) Where an imperative power of appointment has been created so that it confers on a person a right to have the power exercised in the person's favor, the proper exercise of the power can be compelled in favor of the person, or the person's assigns, creditors, guardian, or conservator. **Leg.H.** Added Stats 1992 ch 30 §2 (AB 1722). Amended Stats 2016 ch 81 §17 (AB 2846), effective January 1, 2017.

§672. Effect of failure to appoint property, release of entire power, or ineffective appointment

(a) Except as provided in subdivision (b), if the powerholder of a discretionary power of appointment fails to appoint the property, releases the entire power, or makes an ineffective appointment, in whole or in part, the appointive property not effectively appointed passes to the person named by the donor as taker in default or, if there is none, reverts to the donor.

(b) If the powerholder of a general power of appointment makes an ineffective appointment, an implied alternative appointment to the powerholder's estate may be found if the powerholder has manifested an intent that the appointive property be disposed of as property of the powerholder rather than as in default of appointment. **Leg.H.** Added Stats 1992 ch 30 §2 (AB 1722). Amended Stats 2016 ch 81 §18 (AB 2846), effective January 1, 2017.

§673. Effect of ineffective appointment by will or instrument effective only at death of powerholder

(a) Except as provided in subdivision (b), if an appointment by will or by instrument effective only at the death of the powerholder is ineffective because of the death of an appointee before the appointment becomes effective and the appointee leaves issue surviving the powerholder, the surviving issue of the appointee take the appointed property in the same manner as the appointee would have taken had the appointee survived the powerholder, except that the property passes only to persons who are permissible appointees, including appointees permitted under Section 674. If the surviving issue are all of the same degree of kinship to the deceased appointee, they take equally, but if of unequal degree, then those of more remote degree take in the manner provided in Section 240.

(b) This section does not apply if either the donor or powerholder manifests an intent that some other disposition of the appointive property shall be made. **Leg.H.** Added Stats 1992 ch 30 §2 (AB 1722). Amended Stats 2016 ch 81 §19 (AB 2846), effective January 1, 2017.

§674. Effect of death of permissible appointee prior to exercise of special power

(a) Unless the creating instrument expressly provides otherwise, if a permissible appointee dies before the exercise of a special power of appointment, the powerholder has the power to appoint to the issue of the deceased permissible appointee, whether or not the issue was included within the description of the permissible appointees, if the deceased permissible appointee was alive at the time of the execution of the creating instrument or was born thereafter.

(b) This section applies whether the special power of appointment is exercisable by inter vivos instrument, by will, or otherwise.

(c) This section applies to a case where the power of appointment is exercised on or after July 1, 1982, but does not affect the validity of any exercise of a power of appointment made before July 1, 1982. **Leg.H.** Added Stats 1992 ch 30 §2 (AB 1722). Amended Stats 2016 ch 81 §20 (AB 2846), effective January 1, 2017.

§675. Effect of exercise of power of appointment in disposition that also disposes of property owned by powerholder

If a powerholder exercises a power of appointment in a disposition that also disposes of property the powerholder owns, the owned property and the appointive property shall be allocated in the permissible manner in accordance with the terms of the creating instrument and that best carries out the powerholder's intent. **Leg.H.** Added Stats 2016 ch 81 §21 (AB 2846), effective January 1, 2017.

§676. Effect of valid partial appointment to taker in default

Unless the terms of the instrument creating or exercising a power of appointment manifest a contrary intent, if the powerholder makes a valid partial appointment to a taker in default of appointment, the taker in default of appointment may share fully in unappointed property. **Leg.H.** Added Stats 2016 ch 81 §22 (AB 2846), effective January 1, 2017.

CHAPTER 6
RIGHTS OF CREDITORS

Alteration by language in instrument creating power. §680.
Property covered by special power. §681.
Property covered by general power. §682.
Property subject to general power of appointment created by donor. §683.
Person to whom powerholder owes duty of support as creditor. §684.

§680. Alteration by language in instrument creating power

The donor of a power of appointment cannot nullify or alter the rights given creditors of the powerholder by Sections 682, 683, and 684 by any language in the instrument creating the power. **Leg.H.** Added Stats 1992 ch 30 §2 (AB 1722). Amended Stats 2016 ch 81 §23 (AB 2846), effective January 1, 2017.

§681. Property covered by special power

(a) Except as provided in subdivision (b), property covered by a special power of appointment is not subject to the claims of creditors of the powerholder or of the powerholder's estate or to the expenses of the administration of the powerholder's estate.

(b) Property subject to a special power of appointment shall be subject to the claims of creditors of the powerholder or of the powerholder's estate or the expenses of administration of the powerholder's estate under either of the following circumstances:

(1) To the extent that the powerholder owned the property and, reserving the special power, transferred the property in violation of the Uniform Voidable Transactions Act (Chapter 1 (commencing with Section 3439) of Title 2 of Part 2 of Division 4 of the Civil Code).

(2) If the initial gift in default of the exercise of the power is to the powerholder or the powerholder's estate. **Leg.H.** Added Stats 1992 ch 30 §2 (AB 1722). Amended Stats 2016 ch 81 §24 (AB 2846), effective January 1, 2017.

§682. Property covered by general power

(a) To the extent that the property owned by the powerholder is inadequate to satisfy the claims of the powerholder's creditors, property subject to a general power of appointment that is presently exercisable is subject to the claims to the same extent that it would be subject to the claims if the property were owned by the powerholder.

(b) Upon the death of the powerholder, to the extent that the powerholder's estate is inadequate to satisfy the claims of creditors of the estate and the expenses of administration of the estate, property subject to a general testamentary power of appointment or to a general power of appointment that was presently exercisable at the time of the powerholder's death is subject to the claims and expenses to the same extent that it would be subject to the claims and expenses if the property had been owned by the powerholder.

(c) This section applies whether or not the power of appointment has been exercised. **Leg.H.** Added Stats 1992 ch 30 §2 (AB 1722). Amended Stats 2016 ch 81 §25 (AB 2846), effective January 1, 2017.

§683. Property subject to general power of appointment created by donor

Property subject to a general power of appointment created by the donor in the donor's favor, whether or not presently exercisable, is subject to the claims of the donor's creditors or the donor's estate and to the expenses of the administration of the donor's estate, except to the extent the donor effectively irrevocably appointed the property subject to the general power of appointment in favor of a person other than the donor or the donor's estate. **Leg.H.** Added Stats 1992 ch 30 §2 (AB 1722). Amended Stats 2016 ch 81 §26 (AB 2846), effective January 1, 2017.

§684. Person to whom powerholder owes duty of support as creditor

For the purposes of Sections 682 and 683, a person to whom the powerholder owes an obligation of support shall be considered a creditor of the powerholder to the extent that a legal obligation exists for the powerholder to provide the support. **Leg.H.** Added Stats 1992 ch 30 §2 (AB 1722). Amended Stats 2016 ch 81 §27 (AB 2846), effective January 1, 2017.

CHAPTER 7
RULE AGAINST PERPETUITIES

Application of rule against perpetuities. §690.

§690. Application of rule against perpetuities

The statutory rule against perpetuities provided by Part 2 (commencing with Section 21200) of Division 11 applies to powers of appointment governed by this part. **Leg.H.** Added Stats 1992 ch 30 §2 (AB 1722).

CHAPTER 8
REVOCABILITY OF CREATION, EXERCISE, OR RELEASE OF POWER OF APPOINTMENT

Creation of power as irrevocable; Exceptions. §695.

§695. Creation of power as irrevocable; Exceptions

(a) Unless the power to revoke is in the creating instrument or exists pursuant to Section 15400, the creation of a power of appointment is irrevocable.

(b) Unless made expressly irrevocable by the creating instrument or the instrument of exercise, an exercise of a power of appointment is revocable if the power to revoke exists pursuant to Section 15400 or so long as the interest in the appointive property, whether present or future, has not been transferred or become distributable pursuant to the appointment.

(c) Unless the power to revoke is reserved in the instrument releasing the power, a release of a power of appointment is irrevocable. **Leg.H.** Added Stats 1992 ch 30 §2 (AB 1722).

PART 15
DEPOSIT OF ESTATE PLANNING DOCUMENTS WITH ATTORNEY

Chapter 1. Definitions.
Chapter 2. Duties and Liabilities of Attorney.
Chapter 3. Termination of Deposit.

CHAPTER 1
DEFINITIONS

Definitions governing construction of part. §700.
"Attorney". §701.
"Deposit". §702.
"Depositor". §703.
"Document". §704.

§700. Definitions governing construction of part

Unless the provision or context otherwise requires, the definitions in this chapter govern the construction of this part. **Leg.H.** Added Stats 1993 ch 519 §4 (AB 209).

§701. "Attorney"

"Attorney" means an individual licensed to practice law in this state. **Leg.H.** Added Stats 1993 ch 519 §4 (AB 209).

§702. "Deposit"

"Deposit" means delivery of a document by a depositor to an attorney for safekeeping or authorization by a depositor for an attorney to retain a document for safekeeping. **Leg.H.** Added Stats 1993 ch 519 §4 (AB 209).

§703. "Depositor"

"Depositor" means a natural person who deposits the person's document with an attorney. **Leg.H.** Added Stats 1993 ch 519 §4 (AB 209).

§704. "Document"

"Document" means any of the following:

(a) A signed original will, declaration of trust, trust amendment, or other document modifying a will or trust.

(b) A signed original power of attorney.

(c) A signed original nomination of conservator.

(d) Any other signed original instrument that the attorney and depositor agree in writing to make subject to this part. **Leg.H.** Added Stats 1993 ch 519 §4 (AB 209).

CHAPTER 2
DUTIES AND LIABILITIES OF ATTORNEY

Care to be used in preservation. §710.
Notice of loss or destruction of document deposited with attorney. §711.
Liability of attorney for loss or destruction of document. §712.
Duties not imposed on attorney by acceptance of document for deposit. §713.
Compensation of attorney for safekeeping or delivery of deposited document; Lien. §714.
Notice and acknowledgment form. §715.
Care to be used in preservation of deposited document after notice and acknowledgment. §716.

§710. Care to be used in preservation

If a document is deposited with an attorney, the attorney, and a successor attorney that accepts transfer of the document, shall use ordinary care for preservation of the document on and after July 1, 1994, whether or not consideration is given, and shall hold the document in a safe, vault, safe deposit box, or other secure place where it will be reasonably protected against loss or destruction. **Leg.H.** Added Stats 1993 ch 519 §4 (AB 209).

§711. Notice of loss or destruction of document deposited with attorney

If a document deposited with an attorney is lost or destroyed, the attorney shall give notice of the loss or destruction to the depositor by one of the following methods:

(a) By delivering pursuant to Section 1215 the notice to the depositor's last known address.

(b) By the method most likely to give the depositor actual notice. **Leg.H.** Added Stats 1993 ch 519 §4 (AB 209). Amended Stats 2017 ch 319 §9 (AB 976), effective January 1, 2018.

§712. Liability of attorney for loss or destruction of document

Notwithstanding failure of an attorney to satisfy the standard of care required by Section 710 or 716, the attorney is not liable for loss or destruction of the document if the depositor has actual notice of the loss or destruction and a reasonable opportunity to replace the document, and the attorney offers without charge either to assist the depositor in replacing the document, or to prepare a substantially similar document and assist in its execution. **Leg.H.** Added Stats 1993 ch 519 §4 (AB 209).

§713. Duties not imposed on attorney by acceptance of document for deposit

The acceptance by an attorney of a document for deposit imposes no duty on the attorney to do either of the following:

(a) Inquire into the content, validity, invalidity, or completeness of the document, or the correctness of any information in the document.

(b) Provide continuing legal services to the depositor or to any beneficiary under the document. This subdivision does not affect the duty, if any, of the drafter of the document to provide continuing legal services to any person. **Leg.H.** Added Stats 1993 ch 519 §4 (AB 209).

§714. Compensation of attorney for safekeeping or delivery of deposited document; Lien

(a) If so provided in a written agreement signed by the depositor, an attorney may charge the depositor for compensation and expenses incurred in safekeeping or delivery of a document deposited with the attorney.

(b) No lien arises for the benefit of an attorney on a document deposited with the attorney, whether before or after its transfer, even if provided by agreement. **Leg.H.** Added Stats 1993 ch 519 §4 (AB 209).

§715. Notice and acknowledgment form

An attorney may give written notice to a depositor, and obtain written acknowledgment from the depositor, in the following form:

NOTICE AND ACKNOWLEDGMENT

To: _____
(Name of depositor)

_____
(Address)

_____
(City, state, and ZIP)

_____
(Electronic address)

I have accepted your will or other estate planning document for safekeeping. I must use ordinary care for preservation of the document. You must keep me advised of any change in your addresses shown above. If you do not and I cannot return this document to you when necessary, I will no longer be required to use ordinary care for preservation of the document, and I may transfer it to another attorney, or I may transfer it to the clerk of the superior court of the county of your last known domicile, and give notice of the transfer to the State Bar of California.

_____
(Signature of attorney)

_____
(Address of attorney)

_____
(City, state, and ZIP)

_____
(Electronic address)

My addresses shown above are correct. I understand that I must keep you advised of any change in these addresses.

Dated: _____

_____
(Signature of depositor)

Leg.H. Added Stats 1993 ch 519 §4 (AB 209). Amended Stats 2017 ch 319 §10 (AB 976), effective January 1, 2018.

§716. Care to be used in preservation of deposited document after notice and acknowledgment

Notwithstanding Section 710, ff an attorney has given written notice to the depositor, and has obtained written acknowledgment from the depositor, in substantially the form provided in Section 715, and the requirements of subdivision (a) of Section 732 are satisfied, the attorney, and a successor attorney that accepts transfer of a document, shall use at least slight care for preservation of a document deposited with the attorney. **Leg.H.** Added Stats 1993 ch 519 §4 (AB 209).

CHAPTER 3
TERMINATION OF DEPOSIT

Article 1. Termination by Depositor.
Article 2. Termination by Attorney.

ARTICLE 1
Termination by Depositor

Delivery on demand. §720.

§720. Delivery on demand

A depositor may terminate a deposit on demand, in which case the attorney shall deliver the document to the depositor. **Leg.H.** Added Stats 1993 ch 519 §4 (AB 209).

ARTICLE 2
Termination by Attorney

Requirements. §730.
Methods. §731.
Transfer to other attorney or court clerk after depositor's failure to reclaim after notice; Death of depositor. §732.
Notice of transfer to State Bar. §733.
Death of depositor. §734.
Death of attorney or lack of legal capacity. §735.

§730. Requirements

An attorney with whom a document has been deposited, or to whom a document has been transferred pursuant to this article, may terminate the deposit only as provided in this article. **Leg.H.** Added Stats 1993 ch 519 §4 (AB 209).

§731. Methods

An attorney may terminate the deposit by one of the following methods:

(a) Personal delivery of the document to the depositor.

(b) Mailing the document to the depositor's last known address, by registered or certified mail with return receipt requested, and receiving a signed receipt.

(c) The method agreed on by the depositor and attorney. **Leg.H.** Added Stats 1993 ch 519 §4 (AB 209).

§732. Transfer to other attorney or court clerk after depositor's failure to reclaim after notice; Death of depositor

(a) An attorney may terminate a deposit under this section if the attorney has delivered notice pursuant to Section 1215 to reclaim the document to the depositor's last known address and the depositor has failed to reclaim the document within 90 days after delivery.

(b) Subject to subdivision (f), an attorney may terminate a deposit under this section by transferring the document to another attorney. All documents transferred under this subdivision shall be transferred to the same attorney.

(c) Subject to subdivision (f), if an attorney is deceased, lacks legal capacity, or is no longer an active member of the State Bar, a deposit may be terminated under this section by transferring the document to the clerk of the superior court of the county of the depositor's last known domicile. The attorney shall advise the clerk that the document is being transferred pursuant to this section.

(d) An attorney may not accept a fee or compensation from a transferee for transferring a document under this section. An attorney may charge a fee for receiving a document under this section.

(e) Transfer of a document by an attorney under this section is not a waiver or breach of any privilege or confidentiality associated with the document, and is not a violation of the rules of professional conduct. If the document is privileged under Article 3 (commencing with Section 950) of Chapter 4 of Division 8 of the Evidence Code, the document remains privileged after the transfer.

(f) If the document is a will and the attorney has actual notice that the depositor has died, the attorney may terminate a deposit only as provided in Section 734. **Leg.H.** Added Stats 1993 ch 519 §4 (AB 209). Amended Stats 2017 ch 319 §11 (AB 976), effective January 1, 2018.

§733. Notice of transfer to State Bar

(a) An attorney transferring one or more documents under Section 732 shall deliver notice pursuant to Section 1215 of the transfer to the State Bar of California. The notice shall contain all of the following information:

(1) The name of the depositor.

(2) The date of the transfer.

(3) The name, address, and State Bar number of the transferring attorney.

(4) Whether any documents are transferred to an attorney, and the name, address, and State Bar number of the attorney to whom the documents are transferred.

(5) Whether any documents are transferred to a superior court clerk.

(b) The State Bar shall record only one notice of transfer for each transferring attorney. The State Bar shall prescribe the form for the notice of transfer. On request by any person, the State Bar shall give that person information in the notice of transfer. At its sole election, the State Bar may give the information orally or in writing. **Leg.H.** Added Stats 1993 ch 519 §4 (AB 209). Amended Stats 2017 ch 319 §12 (AB 976), effective January 1, 2018.

§734. Death of depositor

(a) In cases not governed by subdivision (b) or (c), after the death of the depositor an attorney may terminate a deposit by personal delivery of the document to the depositor's personal representative.

(b) If the document is a will and the attorney has actual notice that the depositor has died but does not have actual notice that a personal representative has been appointed for the depositor, an attorney may terminate a deposit only as provided in Section 8200.

(c) If the document is a trust, after the death of the depositor an attorney may terminate a deposit by personal delivery of the document either to the depositor's personal representative or to the trustee named in the document. **Leg.H.** Added Stats 1993 ch 519 §4 (AB 209).

§735. Death of attorney or lack of legal capacity

(a) If the attorney is deceased or lacks legal capacity, a deposit may be terminated as provided in this article by the attorney's law partner, by a shareholder of the attorney's law corporation, or by a lawyer or nonlawyer employee of the attorney's firm, partnership, or corporation.

(b) If the attorney lacks legal capacity and there is no person to act under subdivision (a), a deposit may be terminated by the conservator of the attorney's estate or by an attorney in fact acting under a durable power of attorney. A conservator of the attorney's estate may act without court approval.

(c) If the attorney is deceased and there is no person to act under subdivision (a), a deposit may be terminated by the attorney's personal representative.

(d) If a person authorized under this section terminates a deposit as provided in Section 732, the person shall give the notice required by Section 733. **Leg.H.** Added Stats 1993 ch 519 §4 (AB 209).

§760.5. [Section repealed 1987.]

Leg.H. Added Stats 1969 ch 462 §2. Repealed Stats 1987 ch 923 §39, operative July 1, 1988. See Prob C §10151; CCP §873.140.

§770. [Section repealed 1987.]

Leg.H. Enacted Stats 1931 ch 281 §770. Repealed Stats 1987 ch 923 §39, operative July 1, 1988. See Prob C §§10252, 10259; CCP §873.660.

§771. [Section repealed 1987.]

Leg.H. Enacted Stats 1931 ch 281 §771. Amended Stats 1937 ch 276 §1; Stats 1941 ch 678 §1; Stats 1945 ch 484 §1; Stats 1951 ch 647 §1; Stats 1961 ch 93 §2; Stats 1980 ch 955 §18.7; Stats 1985 ch 983 §26. Repealed Stats 1987 ch 923 §39, operative July 1, 1988. See Prob C §§10200, 10201; CCP §873.660.

PART 16
JURISDICTION

Court of general jurisdiction. §800.
Order for severance of action or proceeding. §801.

§800. Court of general jurisdiction

The court in proceedings under this code is a court of general jurisdiction and the court, or a judge of the court, has the same power and authority with respect to the proceedings as otherwise provided by law for a superior court, or a judge of the superior court, including, but not limited to, the matters authorized by Section 128 of the Code of Civil Procedure. **Leg.H.** Added Stats 1994 ch 806 §4 (AB 3686).

§801. Order for severance of action or proceeding

The court, on its own motion or on the motion of any interested party, may order that an action or proceeding not specifically provided in this code be determined in a separate civil action. Upon the payment of the appropriate filing fees, the court may order transfer of the severed action or proceeding to the separate civil action. **Leg.H.** Added Stats 1996 ch 862 §2 (AB 2751).

PART 17
LEGAL MENTAL CAPACITY

Legislative findings and declarations regarding legal capacity. §810.
Unsound mind or incapacity. §811.
Capacity to make decision. §812.
Capacity to give informed consent to medical treatment. §813.

§810. Legislative findings and declarations regarding legal capacity

The Legislature finds and declares the following:

(a) For purposes of this part, there shall exist a rebuttable presumption affecting the burden of proof that all persons have the capacity to make decisions and to be responsible for their acts or decisions.

(b) A person who has a mental or physical disorder may still be capable of contracting, conveying, marrying, making medical decisions, executing wills or trusts, and performing other actions.

(c) A judicial determination that a person is totally without understanding, or is of unsound mind, or suffers from one or more mental deficits so substantial that, under the circumstances, the person should be deemed to lack the legal capacity to perform a specific act, should be based on evidence of a deficit in one or more of the person's mental functions rather than on a diagnosis of a person's mental or physical disorder. **Leg.H.** Added Stats 1995 ch 842 §2 (SB 730). Amended Stats 1998 ch 581 §19 (AB 2801).

1995 Notes: This act shall be known and may be cited as the Due Process in Competence Determinations Act. Stats 1995 ch 842 §12.

This act shall not apply to proceedings under the Welfare and Institutions Code. Stats 1995 ch 842 §13.

§811. Unsound mind or incapacity

(a) A determination that a person is of unsound mind or lacks the capacity to make a decision or do a certain act, including, but not limited to, the incapacity to contract, to make a conveyance, to marry, to make medical decisions, to execute wills, or to execute trusts, shall be supported by evidence of a deficit in at least one of the following mental functions, subject to subdivision (b), and evidence of a correlation between the deficit or deficits and the decision or acts in question:

(1) Alertness and attention, including, but not limited to, the following:
(A) Level of arousal or consciousness.
(B) Orientation to time, place, person, and situation.
(C) Ability to attend and concentrate.
(2) Information processing, including, but not limited to, the following:
(A) Short- and long-term memory, including immediate recall.
(B) Ability to understand or communicate with others, either verbally or otherwise.
(C) Recognition of familiar objects and familiar persons.
(D) Ability to understand and appreciate quantities.
(E) Ability to reason using abstract concepts.
(F) Ability to plan, organize, and carry out actions in one's own rational self-interest.
(G) Ability to reason logically.
(3) Thought processes. Deficits in these functions may be demonstrated by the presence of the following:
(A) Severely disorganized thinking.
(B) Hallucinations.
(C) Delusions.
(D) Uncontrollable, repetitive, or intrusive thoughts.
(4) Ability to modulate mood and affect. Deficits in this ability may be demonstrated by the presence of a pervasive and persistent or recurrent state of euphoria, anger, anxiety, fear, panic, depression, hopelessness or despair, helplessness, apathy or indifference, that is inappropriate in degree to the individual's circumstances.

(b) A deficit in the mental functions listed above may be considered only if the deficit, by itself or in combination with one or more other mental function deficits, significantly impairs the person's ability to understand and appreciate the consequences of his or her actions with regard to the type of act or decision in question.

(c) In determining whether a person suffers from a deficit in mental function so substantial that the person lacks the capacity to do a certain act, the court may take into consideration the frequency, severity, and duration of periods of impairment.

(d) The mere diagnosis of a mental or physical disorder shall not be sufficient in and of itself to support a determination that a person is of unsound mind or lacks the capacity to do a certain act.

(e) This part applies only to the evidence that is presented to, and the findings that are made by, a court determining the capacity of a person to do a certain act or make a decision, including, but not limited to, making medical decisions. Nothing in this part shall affect the decisionmaking process set forth in Section 1418.8 of the Health and Safety Code, nor increase or decrease the burdens of documentation on, or potential liability of, health care providers who, outside the judicial context, determine the capacity of patients to make a medical decision. **Leg.H.** Added Stats 1996 ch 178 §3 (SB 1650). Amended Stats 1998 ch 581 §20 (AB 2801).

Prior Law: Former Prob C §811, similar to Prob C §812, was added Stats 1995 ch 842 §3, and repealed Stats 1996 ch 178 §2.

§812. Capacity to make decision

Except where otherwise provided by law, including, but not limited to, Section 813 and the statutory and decisional law of testamentary capacity, a person lacks the capacity to make a decision unless the person has the ability to communicate verbally, or by any other means, the decision, and to understand and appreciate, to the extent relevant, all of the following:

(a) The rights, duties, and responsibilities created by, or affected by the decision.

(b) The probable consequences for the decisionmaker and, where appropriate, the persons affected by the decision.

(c) The significant risks, benefits, and reasonable alternatives involved in the decision. **Leg.H.** Added Stats 1996 ch 178 §5 (SB 1650).

Prior Law: Former Prob C §812, similar to Prob C §811, was added Stats 1995 ch 842 §4 and repealed Stats 1996 ch 178 §4.

§813. Capacity to give informed consent to medical treatment

(a) For purposes of a judicial determination, a person has the capacity to give informed consent to a proposed medical treatment if the person is able to do all of the following:

(1) Respond knowingly and intelligently to queries about that medical treatment.

(2) Participate in that treatment decision by means of a rational thought process.

(3) Understand all of the following items of minimum basic medical treatment information with respect to that treatment:

(A) The nature and seriousness of the illness, disorder, or defect that the person has.

(B) The nature of the medical treatment that is being recommended by the person's health care providers.

(C) The probable degree and duration of any benefits and risks of any medical intervention that is being recommended by the person's health care providers, and the consequences of lack of treatment.

(D) The nature, risks, and benefits of any reasonable alternatives.

(b) A person who has the capacity to give informed consent to a proposed medical treatment also has the capacity to refuse consent to that treatment. **Leg.H.** Added Stats 1995 ch 842 §5 (SB 730). Amended Stats 1996 ch 178 §6 (SB 1650).

1995 Notes: This act shall be known and may be cited as the Due Process in Competence Determinations Act. Stats 1995 ch 842 §12.

This act shall not apply to proceedings under the Welfare and Institutions Code. Stats 1995 ch 842 §13.

§814. [Section repealed 1996]

Leg.H. Added Stats 1995 ch 842 §6 (SB 730). Repealed Stats 1996 ch 178 §7 (SB 1650). See Prob C §813.

§900. [Section repealed 1991]

Leg.H. Enacted Stats 1990 ch 79 §14 (AB 759), operative July 1, 1991. Amended Stats 1990 ch 710 §3.5 (SB 1775), operative July 1, 1991. Repealed Stats 1991 ch 82 §2 (SB 896), effective June 30, 1991, operative July 1, 1991. See Prob C §10850.

Prior Law: Former Prob C §900, similar to the present §10802, was enacted Stats 1931, amended Stats 1988 ch 1199 §54.3, operative July 1, 1989, and repealed Stats 1990 ch 79 §13, operative July 1, 1991.

PART 18
RIGHT TO TRIAL

Jury trial under Probate Code. §825.

§825. Jury trial under Probate Code

Except as otherwise expressly provided in this code, there is no right to a jury trial in proceedings under this code. **Leg.H.** Added Stats 1999 ch 175 §1 (AB 239).

PART 19
CONVEYANCE OR TRANSFER OF PROPERTY CLAIMED TO BELONG TO DECEDENT OR OTHER PERSON

Petition for order. §850.
Notice of hearing; Contents. §851.
Commencement of discovery. §851.1.
Response; Continuance for preparation for hearing. §852.
Denial of petition if objection based on venue. §853.
Abatement of petition if civil action pending. §854.
Allowable actions. §855.
Order granting property transfer. §856.
No petition where civil action appropriate. §856.5.
Execution of conveyance or transfer; Effect of order. §857.
Death of conservatee or minor. §858.
Remedies for wrongful taking, concealment, or disposition of property belonging to conservatee, minor, elder, dependent adult, trust, or estate of a decedent; Attorney's fees and costs. §859.

§850. Petition for order

(a) The following persons may file a petition requesting that the court make an order under this part:

(1) A guardian, conservator, or any claimant, in the following cases:

(A) Where the conservatee is bound by a contract in writing to convey real property or to transfer personal property, executed by the conservatee while competent or executed by the conservatee's predecessor in interest, and the contract is one that can be specifically enforced.

(B) Where the minor has succeeded to the interest of a person bound by a contract in writing to convey real property or to transfer personal property, and the contract is one that can be specifically enforced.

(C) Where the guardian or conservator or the minor or conservatee is in possession of, or holds title to, real or personal property, and the property or some interest therein is claimed to belong to another.

(D) Where the minor or conservatee has a claim to real or personal property title to or possession of which is held by another.

(2) The personal representative or any interested person in any of the following cases:

(A) Where the decedent while living is bound by a contract in writing to convey real property or to transfer personal property and dies before making the conveyance or transfer and the decedent, if living, could have been compelled to make the conveyance or transfer.

(B) Where the decedent while living binds himself or herself or his or her personal representative by a contract in writing to convey real property or to transfer personal property upon or after his or her death and the contract is one which can be specifically enforced.

(C) Where the decedent died in possession of, or holding title to, real or personal property, and the property or some interest therein is claimed to belong to another.

(D) Where the decedent died having a claim to real or personal property, title to or possession of which is held by another.

(3) The trustee or any interested person in any of the following cases:

(A) Where the trustee is in possession of, or holds title to, real or personal property, and the property, or some interest, is claimed to belong to another.

(B) Where the trustee has a claim to real or personal property, title to or possession of which is held by another.

(C) Where the property of the trust is claimed to be subject to a creditor of the settlor of the trust.

(b) The petition shall set forth facts upon which the claim is based. **Leg.H.** Added Stats 2001 ch 49 §1 (SB 669).

§851. Notice of hearing; Contents

(a) At least 30 days prior to the day of the hearing, the petitioner shall cause notice of the hearing and a copy of the petition to be served in the manner provided in Chapter 4 (commencing with Section 413.10) of Title 5 of Part 2 of the Code of Civil Procedure on all of the following persons where applicable:

(1) The personal representative, conservator, guardian, or trustee as appropriate.

(2) Each person claiming an interest in, or having title to or possession of, the property.

(b) Except for those persons given notice pursuant to subdivision (a), notice of the hearing, together with a copy of the petition, shall be given as provided in Section 1220 if the matter concerns a decedent estate, as provided in Section 1460 if the matter concerns a conservatorship or guardianship, or as provided in Section 17203 if the matter concerns a trust to all of the following persons:

(1) Each person listed in Section 1220 along with any heir or devisee whose interest in the property may be affected by the petition if the matter concerns a decedent estate.

(2) Each person listed in Section 1460 if the matter concerns a conservatorship or guardianship.

(3) Each person listed in Section 17203 if the matter concerns a trust.

(c) A notice of hearing shall contain all of the following:

(1) A description of the subject property sufficient to provide adequate notice to any party who may have an interest in the property. For real property, the notice shall state the street address or, if none, a description of the property's location and assessor's parcel number.

(2) If the petition seeks relief pursuant to Section 859, a description of the relief sought sufficient to provide adequate notice to the party against whom that relief is requested.

(3) A statement advising any person interested in the property that he or she may file a response to the petition.

(d) The court may not shorten the time for giving the notice of hearing under this section. **Leg.H.** Added Stats 2001 ch 49 §1 (SB 669). Amended Stats 2017 ch 32 §1 (AB 308), effective January 1, 2018.

§851.1. Commencement of discovery

A petitioner in a proceeding under Section 850 may commence discovery upon any person who receives notice of the hearing pursuant to subdivision (a) of Section 851 in accordance with the same time periods set forth in the Civil Discovery Act (Title 4 (commencing with Section 2016.010) of Part 4 of the Code of Civil Procedure), except that the time periods shall commence to run upon service of the petition and notice of hearing. Nothing in this section shall alter when a respondent in such a proceeding may commence discovery. **Leg.H.** Added Stats 2017 ch 32 §2 (AB 308), effective January 1, 2018.

§852. Response; Continuance for preparation for hearing

An interested person may request time for filing a response to the petition for discovery proceedings, or for other preparation for the hearing, and the court shall grant a continuance for a reasonable time for any of these purposes. **Leg.H.** Added Stats 2001 ch 49 §1 (SB 669).

§853. Denial of petition if objection based on venue

A person having or claiming title to or an interest in the property which is the subject of the petition may, at or prior to the hearing, object to the hearing of the petition if the petition is filed in a court which is not the proper court under any other provision of law for the trial of a civil action seeking the same relief and, if the objection is established, the court shall not grant the petition. **Leg.H.** Added Stats 2001 ch 49 §1 (SB 669).

§854. Abatement of petition if civil action pending

If a civil action is pending with respect to the subject matter of a petition filed pursuant to this chapter this part and jurisdiction has been obtained in the court where the civil action is pending prior to the filing of the petition, upon request of any party to the civil action, the court shall abate the petition until the conclusion of the civil action. This section shall not apply if the court finds that the civil action was filed for the purpose of delay. **Leg.H.** Added Stats 2001 ch 49 §1 (SB 669). Amended Stats 2023 ch 131 §166 (AB 1754), effective January 1, 2024.

§855. Allowable actions

An action brought under this part may include claims, causes of action, or matters that are normally raised in a civil action to the extent that the matters are related factually to the subject matter of a petition filed under this part. **Leg.H.** Added Stats 2001 ch 49 §1 (SB 669).

§856. Order granting property transfer

Except as provided in Sections 853 and 854, if the court is satisfied that a conveyance, transfer, or other order should be made, the court shall make an order authorizing and directing the personal representative or other fiduciary, or the person having title to or possession of the property, to execute a conveyance or transfer to the person entitled thereto, or granting other appropriate relief. **Leg.H.** Added Stats 2001 ch 49 §1 (SB 669).

§856.5. No petition where civil action appropriate

The court may not grant a petition under this chapter if the court determines that the matter should be determined by a civil action. **Leg.H.** Added Stats 2001 ch 417 §3 (AB 873).

§857. Execution of conveyance or transfer; Effect of order

(a) The order is prima facie evidence of the correctness of the proceedings and of the authority of the personal representative or other fiduciary or other person to make the conveyance or transfer.

(b) After entry of an order that the personal representative, other fiduciary, or other person execute a conveyance or transfer, the person entitled thereunder has the right to the possession of the property, and the right to hold the property, according to the terms of the order as if the property had been conveyed or transferred in accordance with the terms of the order. **Leg.H.** Added Stats 2001 ch 49 §1 (SB 669).

§858. Death of conservatee or minor

If a proceeding has been brought under this part by a conservator on behalf of a conservatee, or by a guardian on behalf of a minor, and the conservatee or minor dies during the pendency of the proceeding, the personal representative of the conservatee or minor's estate or other successor in interest may proceed with the matter and the existing proceeding shall not be dismissed on account of the death of the conservatee or minor. **Leg.H.** Added Stats 2001 ch 49 §1 (SB 669). Amended Stats 2004 ch 183 §278 (AB 3082).

§859. Remedies for wrongful taking, concealment, or disposition of property belonging to conservatee, minor, elder, dependent adult, trust, or estate of a decedent; Attorney's fees and costs

If a court finds that a person has in bad faith wrongfully taken, concealed, or disposed of property belonging to a conservatee, a minor, an elder, a dependent adult, a trust, or the estate of a decedent, or has taken, concealed, or disposed of the property by the use of undue influence in bad faith or through the commission of elder or dependent adult financial abuse, as defined in Section 15610.30 of the Welfare and Institutions Code, the person shall be liable for twice the value of the property recovered by an action under this part. In addition, except as otherwise required by law, including Section 15657.5 of the Welfare and Institutions Code, the person may, in the court's discretion, be liable for reasonable attorney's fees and costs. The remedies provided in this section shall be in addition to any other remedies available in law to a person authorized to bring an action pursuant to this part. **Leg.H.** Added Stats 2001 ch 49 §1 (SB 669). Amended Stats 2011 ch 55 §1 (AB 354), effective January 1, 2012; Stats 2013 ch 99 §1 (AB 381), effective January 1, 2014.

PART 20
REVISED UNIFORM FIDUCIARY ACCESS TO DIGITAL ASSETS ACT

Citation of part. §870.
Definitions. §871.
Applicability of part. §872.
Use of online tool to direct custodian regarding disclosure of user's digital assets. §873.
Effect of part on rights to access and use digital assets. §874.
Authority of custodian when disclosing digital assets of user. §875.
Disclosure of content of electronic communication of deceased user to personal representative of estate. §876.
Disclosure of catalogue of electronic communications and digital assets to personal representative of estate of deceased user. §877.
Disclosure of content of electronic communication to trustee that is not original user of account. §878.
Disclosure of catalogue of electronic communications and digital assets to trustee that is not original user of account. §879.
Agent authority over the content of electronic communications. § 879.1.
Power of attorney, over digital assets or general authority. § 879.2.
Conservator access to the digital assets of a conservatee. § 879.3.
Legal duties and rights of fiduciary managing digital assets; Limitations on fiduciary's or designated recipient's authority with respect to digital assets. §880.
Compliance with request to disclose digital assets or terminate account. §881.
Effect on federal Electronic Signatures in Global and National Commerce Act. §882.
Disclosure of contents of deceased user's or settlor's account to fiduciary of deceased user or settlor. §883.
Severability. §884.

§870. Citation of part

This part shall be known, and may be cited, as the Revised Uniform Fiduciary Access to Digital Assets Act. **Leg.H.** Added Stats 2016 ch 551 §1 (AB 691), effective January 1, 2017.

§871. Definitions

As used in this part, the following terms [1] have the following meanings:

(a) "Account" means an arrangement under a terms-of-service agreement in which the custodian carries, maintains, processes, receives, or stores a digital asset of the user or provides goods or services to the user.

(b) "Carries" means engages in the transmission of electronic communications.

(c) "Catalogue of electronic communications" means information that identifies each person with which a user has had an electronic communication, the time and date of the communication, and the electronic address of the person.

(d) "Content of an electronic communication" means information concerning the substance or meaning of the communication, which meets all of the following requirements:

(1) Has been sent or received by a user.

(2) Is in electronic storage by a custodian providing an electronic communication service to the public or is carried or maintained by a custodian providing a remote-computing service to the public.

(3) Is not readily accessible to the public.

(e)(1) "Court" means the superior court presiding over the judicial proceedings [2] **that** have been initiated under this code to administer the estate of the deceased user [3] or, if none, the superior court sitting in the exercise of jurisdiction under this code in the county of the user's domicile [4].

(2) The court, as defined in this section, shall have exclusive jurisdiction over proceedings brought under this part.

(f) "Custodian" means a person [5] **who** carries, maintains, processes, receives, or stores a digital asset of a user.

(g) "Designated recipient" means a person chosen by a user using an online tool to administer digital assets of the user.

(h)(1) "Digital asset" means an electronic record in which an individual has a right or interest.

(2) The term "digital asset" does not include an underlying asset or liability [6] unless the asset or liability is itself an electronic record.

(i) "Electronic" means relating to technology having electrical, digital, magnetic, wireless, optical, electromagnetic, or similar capabilities.

(j) "Electronic communication" has the same meaning as the definition in Section 2510(12) of Title 18 of the United States Code.

(k) "Electronic communication service" means a custodian [7] **who** provides to a user the ability to send or receive an electronic communication.

(l) "Fiduciary" means an original, additional, or successor personal representative, **conservator, agent,** or trustee.

(m) "Information" means data, text, images, videos, sounds, codes, computer programs, software, databases, or other items with like characteristics.

(n) "Online tool" means an electronic service provided by a custodian that allows the user, in an agreement distinct from the terms-of-service agreement between the custodian and user, to provide directions for disclosure or nondisclosure of digital assets to a third person.

(o) "Person" means an individual, estate, business or nonprofit entity, public corporation, government or governmental subdivision, agency, or instrumentality, or other legal entity.

(p) "Personal representative" means an executor, administrator, special administrator, or person [8] **who** performs substantially the same function under any other law.

(q) "Power of attorney" means a record that grants an agent authority to act in the place of the principal.

(r) "Record" means information that is inscribed on a tangible medium or that is stored in an electronic or other medium and is retrievable in a perceivable form.

(s) "Remote-computing service" means a custodian [9] **who** provides to a user computer processing services or the storage of digital assets by means of an electronic communications system [10] as defined in Section 2510(14) of Title 18 of the United States Code.

(t) "Terms-of-service agreement" means an agreement that controls the relationship between a user and a custodian.

(u)(1) "Trustee" means a fiduciary with legal title to property under an agreement or declaration that creates a beneficial interest in another.

(2) The term "trustee" includes a successor trustee.

(v) "User" means a person [11] **who** has an account with a custodian.

(w) "Will" includes a codicil, a testamentary instrument that only appoints an executor, or an instrument that revokes or revises a testamentary instrument.

(x) "Agent" means an attorney-in-fact granted authority over financial matters under a durable or nondurable power of attorney.

(y)(1) "Conservator" means a person appointed by a court to manage the estate of a living individual.

(2) The term "conservator" includes a limited conservator.

(z) "Conservatee" means an individual for whom a conservator has been appointed.

(aa) "Principal" means an individual who grants authority to an agent in a power of attorney. **Leg.H.** Added Stats 2016 ch 551 §1 (AB 691), effective January 1, 2017. Amended Stats 2024 ch 799 §1 (SB 1458), effective January 1, 2025.

§871. 2024 Deletes. [1] shall [2] which [3] , [4] , and the court, as defined in this section, shall have exclusive jurisdiction over proceedings brought under this part [5] that [6] , [7] that [8] that [9] that [10] , [11] that

§872. Applicability of part

(a) This part shall apply to [1] **all** of the following:

(1) A fiduciary acting under a will executed before, on, or after January 1, 2017.

(2) A personal representative acting for a decedent who died before, on, or after January 1, 2017.

(3) A trustee acting under a trust created before, on, or after January 1, 2017.

(4) A custodian of digital assets for a user if the user resides in this state or resided in this state at the time of the user's death.

(5) A conservator appointed before, on, or after January 1, 2025.

(6) A fiduciary acting under a power of attorney executed before, on, or after January 1, 2025.

(b) This part [2] **does** not apply to a digital asset of an employer used by an employee in the ordinary course of the employer's business. **Leg.H.** Added Stats 2016 ch 551 §1 (AB 691), effective January 1, 2017. Amended Stats 2024 ch 799 §2 (SB 1458), effective January 1, 2025.

§872. 2024 Deletes. [1] any [2] shall

§873. Use of online tool to direct custodian regarding disclosure of user's digital assets

(a) A user may use an online tool to direct the custodian to disclose to a designated recipient or not disclose some or all of the user's digital assets, including the content of electronic communications. If the online tool allows the user to modify or delete a direction at all times, a direction regarding disclosure using an online tool overrides a contrary direction by the user in a will, trust, power of attorney, or other record.

(b) If a user has not used an online tool to give direction under subdivision (a) or if a custodian has not provided an online tool, a user may allow or prohibit in a will, trust, power of attorney, or other record the disclosure to a fiduciary of some or all of the user's digital assets, including the contents of electronic communications sent or received by the user.

(c) A user's direction under subdivision (a) or (b) overrides a contrary provision in a terms-of-service agreement. **Leg.H.** Added Stats 2016 ch 551 §1 (AB 691), effective January 1, 2017.

§874. Effect of part on rights to access and use digital assets

(a) This part does not change or impair a right of a custodian or a user under a terms-of-service agreement to access and use digital assets of a user.

(b) This part does not give a fiduciary or designated recipient any new or expanded rights other than those held by the user for whom, or for whose estate or trust, the fiduciary or designated recipient acts or represents.

(c) A fiduciary's or designated recipient's access to digital assets may be modified or eliminated by a user, by federal law, or by a terms-of-service agreement when the user has not provided any direction that is recognized in Section 873. **Leg.H.** Added Stats 2016 ch 551 §1 (AB 691), effective January 1, 2017.

§875. Authority of custodian when disclosing digital assets of user

(a) When disclosing the digital assets of a user under this part, the custodian may, in its sole discretion, do any of the following:

(1) Grant the fiduciary or designated recipient full access to the user's account.

(2) Grant the fiduciary or designated recipient partial access to the user's account sufficient to perform the tasks with which the fiduciary or designated recipient is charged.

(3) Provide the fiduciary or designated recipient with a copy in a record of any digital asset that, on the date the custodian received the request for disclosure, the user could have accessed if the user were alive and had full capacity and access to the account.

(b) A custodian may assess a reasonable administrative charge for the cost of disclosing digital assets under this part.

(c) A custodian need not disclose under this part a digital asset deleted by a user.

(d) If a user directs or a fiduciary or designated recipient requests a custodian to disclose under this part some, but not all, of the user's digital assets, the custodian need not disclose the assets if segregation of the assets would impose an undue burden on the custodian. If the custodian believes the direction or request imposes an undue burden, the custodian, fiduciary, or designated recipient may petition the court for an order to do any of the following:

(1) Disclose a subset limited by date of the user's digital assets.

(2) Disclose all of the user's digital assets to the fiduciary or designated recipient.

(3) Disclose none of the user's digital assets.

(4) Disclose all of the user's digital assets to the court for review in camera. **Leg.H.** Added Stats 2016 ch 551 §1 (AB 691), effective January 1, 2017.

§876. Disclosure of content of electronic communication of deceased user to personal representative of estate

If a deceased user consented to or a court directs disclosure of the content of electronic communications of the user, the custodian shall disclose to the personal representative of the estate of the user the content of an electronic communication sent or received by the user if the personal representative gives to the custodian all of the following:

(a) A written request for disclosure in physical or electronic form.

(b) A certified copy of the death certificate of the user.

(c) A certified copy of the letter of appointment of the representative, a small-estate affidavit under Section 13101, or court order.

(d) Unless the user provided direction using an online tool, a copy of the user's will, trust, power of attorney, or other record evidencing the user's consent to disclosure of the content of electronic communications.

(e) If requested by the custodian, any of the following:

(1) A number, username, address, or other unique subscriber or account identifier assigned by the custodian to identify the user's account.

(2) Evidence linking the account to the user.

(3) An order of the court finding any of the following:

(A) That the user had a specific account with the custodian, identifiable by the information specified in paragraph (1).

(B) That disclosure of the content of the user's electronic communications would not violate Chapter 121 (commencing with Section 2701) of Part 1 of Title 18 of, and Section 222 of Title 47 of, the United States Code, or other applicable law.

(C) Unless the user provided direction using an online tool, that the user consented to disclosure of the content of electronic communications.

(D) That disclosure of the content of electronic communications of a user is reasonably necessary for estate administration. **Leg.H.** Added Stats 2016 ch 551 §1 (AB 691), effective January 1, 2017.

§877. Disclosure of catalogue of electronic communications and digital assets to personal representative of estate of deceased user

Unless the user prohibited disclosure of digital assets or the court directs otherwise, a custodian shall disclose to the personal representative of the estate of a deceased user a catalogue of electronic communications sent or received by the user and digital assets, other than the content of electronic communications, of the user, if the personal representative gives to the custodian all of the following:

(a) A written request for disclosure in physical or electronic form.

(b) A certified copy of the death certificate of the user.

(c) A certified copy of the letter of appointment of the representative, a small-estate affidavit under Section 13101, or court order.

(d) If requested by the custodian, any of the following:

(1) A number, username, address, or other unique subscriber or account identifier assigned by the custodian to identify the user's account.

(2) Evidence linking the account to the user.

(3) An affidavit stating that disclosure of the user's digital assets is reasonably necessary for estate administration.

(4) An order of the court finding either of the following:

(A) That the user had a specific account with the custodian, identifiable by the information specified in paragraph (1).

(B) That disclosure of the user's digital assets is reasonably necessary for estate administration. **Leg.H.** Added Stats 2016 ch 551 §1 (AB 691), effective January 1, 2017.

§878. Disclosure of content of electronic communication to trustee that is not original user of account

Unless otherwise ordered by the court, directed by the user, or provided in a trust, a custodian shall disclose to a trustee that is not an original user of an account the content of an electronic communication sent or received by an original or successor user and carried, maintained, processed, received, or stored by the custodian in the account of the trust if the trustee gives to the custodian all of the following:

(a) A written request for disclosure in physical or electronic form.

(b) A certified copy of the death certificate of the settlor.

(c) A certified copy of the trust instrument, or a certification of trust under Section 18100.5, evidencing the settlor's consent to disclosure of the content of electronic communications to the trustee.

(d) A certification by the trustee, under penalty of perjury, that the trust exists and that the trustee is a currently acting trustee of the trust.

(e) If requested by the custodian, any of the following:

(1) A number, username, address, or other unique subscriber or account identifier assigned by the custodian to identify the trust's account.

(2) Evidence linking the account to the trust. **Leg.H.** Added Stats 2016 ch 551 §1 (AB 691), effective January 1, 2017.

§879. Disclosure of catalogue of electronic communications and digital assets to trustee that is not original user of account

Unless otherwise ordered by the court, directed by the user, or provided in a trust, a custodian shall disclose, to a trustee that is not an original user of an account, the catalogue of electronic communications sent or received by an original or successor user and stored, carried, or maintained by the custodian in an account of the trust and any digital assets, other than the content of electronic communications, in which the trust has a right or interest if the settlor of the trust is deceased and the trustee gives the custodian all of the following:

(a) A written request for disclosure in physical or electronic form.

(b) A certified copy of the death certificate of the settlor.

(c) A certified copy of the trust instrument or a certification of trust under Section 18100.5.

(d) A certification by the trustee, under penalty of perjury, that the trust exists and that the trustee is a currently acting trustee of the trust.

(e) If requested by the custodian, any of the following:

(1) A number, username, address, or other unique subscriber or account identifier assigned by the custodian to identify the trust's account.

(2) Evidence linking the account to the trust. **Leg.H.** Added Stats 2016 ch 551 §1 (AB 691), effective January 1, 2017.

§ 879.1. Agent authority over the content of electronic communications

To the extent a power of attorney expressly grants an agent authority over the content of electronic communications sent or received by the principal, and unless directed otherwise by the principal or the court, a custodian shall disclose the content of electronic communications to the agent if the agent gives the custodian all of the following:

(a) A written request for disclosure in physical or electronic form.

(b) An original or copy of the power of attorney expressly granting the agent authority over the content of electronic communications of the principal.

(c) A certification by the agent, under penalty of perjury, that the power of attorney is in effect.

(d) If requested by the custodian, either of the following:

(1) A number, username, address, or other unique subscriber or account identifier assigned by the custodian to identify the principal's account.

(2) Evidence linking the account to the principal. **Leg.H.** Added Stats 2024 ch 799 §3 (SB 1458), effective January 1, 2025.

§ 879.2. Power of attorney, over digital assets or general authority

Unless otherwise ordered by the court, directed by the principal, or provided by a power of attorney, a custodian shall disclose to an agent with specific authority over digital assets or general authority to act on behalf of a principal a catalogue of electronic communications sent or received by the principal and digital assets, other than the content of electronic communications, of the principal if the agent gives the custodian all of the following:

(a) A written request for disclosure in physical or electronic form.

(b) An original or copy of the power of attorney that gives the agent specific authority over digital assets or general authority to act on behalf of the principal.

(c) A certification by the agent, under penalty of perjury, that the power of attorney is in effect.

(d) If requested by the custodian, either of the following:

(1) A number, username, address, or other unique subscriber or account identifier assigned by the custodian to identify the principal's account.

(2) Evidence linking the account to the principal. **Leg.H.** Added Stats 2024 ch 799 §4 (SB 1458), effective January 1, 2025.

§ 879.3. Conservator access to the digital assets of a conservatee

(a) After a noticed hearing, the court may grant a conservator access to the digital assets of a conservatee.

(b) Unless otherwise ordered by the court or directed by the user, a custodian shall disclose to a conservator the catalogue of electronic communications sent or received by a conservatee and digital assets, other than the content of electronic communications, in which the conservatee has a right or interest if the conservator gives the custodian all of the following:

(1) A written request for disclosure in physical or electronic form.

(2) A certified copy of the court order that gives the conservator authority over the digital assets of the conservatee.

(3) If requested by the custodian, either of the following:

(A) A number, username, address, or other unique subscriber or account identifier assigned by the custodian to identify the account of the conservatee.

(B) Evidence linking the account to the conservatee.

(c) The provisions of this part are subject to Sections 2351 and 2351.5.

Leg.H. Added Stats 2024 ch 799 §5 (SB 1458), effective January 1, 2025.

§880. Legal duties and rights of fiduciary managing digital assets; Limitations on fiduciary's or designated recipient's authority with respect to digital assets

(a) The legal duties imposed on a fiduciary charged with managing tangible property apply to the management of digital assets, including all of the following:

(1) The duty of care.

(2) The duty of loyalty.

(3) The duty of confidentiality.

(b) All of the following shall apply to a fiduciary's or designated recipient's authority with respect to a digital asset of a user:

(1) Except as otherwise provided in Section 873, a fiduciary's or designated recipient's authority is subject to the applicable terms-of-service agreement.

(2) A fiduciary's or designated recipient's authority is subject to other applicable law, including copyright law.

(3) [1] **A** fiduciary's authority is limited by the scope of the fiduciary's duties.

(4) A fiduciary's or designated recipient's authority may not be used to impersonate the user.

(c)(1) A fiduciary with authority over the property of a decedent or settlor has the right of access to any digital asset in which the decedent or settlor had a right or interest [2] that is not held by a custodian or subject to a terms-of-service agreement. [3]

(2) This subdivision does not require a custodian to share passwords or decrypt protected devices.

(d) A fiduciary acting within the scope of the fiduciary's duties is an authorized user of the property of the decedent, **conservatee, principal,** or settlor for the purpose of applicable computer-fraud and unauthorized-computer-access laws.

(e) The following shall apply to a fiduciary with authority over the tangible, personal property of a decedent, **conservatee, principal,** or settlor:

(1)(A) The fiduciary has the right to access the property and any digital asset stored in it. [4]

(B) This subdivision does not require a custodian to share passwords or decrypt protected devices.

(2) The fiduciary is an authorized user for purposes of any applicable computer-fraud and unauthorized-computer-access laws.

(f) A custodian may disclose information in an account to a fiduciary of the [5] **user if** the information is required to terminate an account used to access digital assets licensed to the user.

(g) A fiduciary of a [6] **user, or an affiant acting under Section 13101 with respect to a deceased user,** may request a custodian to terminate the user's account. A request for termination shall be in writing, in either physical or electronic form, and accompanied by all of the following:

(1)(A) If the user is deceased, a certified copy of the death certificate of the user.

(B) If the user is a conservatee, a court order authorizing the conservator to request termination of the user's account.

(2) A certified copy of the letter of appointment of the representative, a small-estate affidavit under Section 13101, a court order, a **power of attorney, a** certified copy of the trust instrument, or a certification of trust under Section 18100.5 giving the fiduciary authority over the account.

(3) If requested by the custodian, any of the following:

(A) A number, username, address, or other unique subscriber or account identifier assigned by the custodian to identify the user's account.

(B) Evidence linking the account to the user.

(C) A finding by the court that the user had a specific account with the custodian, identifiable by the information specified in subparagraph (A). **Leg.H.** Added Stats 2016 ch 551 §1 (AB 691), effective January 1, 2017. Amended Stats 2024 ch 799 §6 (SB 1458), effective January 1, 2025.

§880. 2024 Deletes. [1] In the case of a fiduciary, a [2] and [3] Nothing in this subdivision requires a custodian to share passwords or decrypt protected devices. [4] Nothing in this subdivision requires a custodian to share passwords or decrypt protected devices. [5] decedent or settlor when [6] decedent or settlor

§881. Compliance with request to disclose digital assets or terminate account

(a) Not later than 60 days after receipt of the information required under Sections 876 to [1] **879.3**, inclusive, a custodian shall comply with a request under this part from a fiduciary or designated recipient to disclose digital assets or terminate an account. If the custodian fails to comply with a request, the fiduciary or designated recipient may apply to the court for an order directing compliance.

(b) An order under subdivision (a) directing compliance shall contain a finding that compliance is not in violation of Section 2702 of Title 18 of the United States Code.

(c) A custodian may notify a user that a request for disclosure of digital assets or to terminate an account was made pursuant to this part.

(d) A custodian may deny a request under this part from a fiduciary or designated recipient for disclosure of digital assets or to terminate an account if the custodian is aware of any lawful access to the account following the date of death of the user.

(e) This part does not limit a custodian's ability to obtain, or to require a fiduciary or designated recipient requesting disclosure or account termination under this part to obtain, a court order that makes all of the following findings:

(1) The account belongs to the decedent, principal, **conservatee,** or trustee.

(2) There is sufficient consent from the decedent, principal, **conservatee,** or settlor to support the requested disclosure.

(3) [2] **A** specific factual finding required by any other applicable law in effect at that time, including, but not limited to, a finding that disclosure is not in violation of Section 2702 of Title 18 of the United States Code.

(f)(1) A custodian and its officers, employees, and agents are immune from liability for an act or omission done in good faith and in compliance with this part.

(2) The protections specified in paragraph (1) [3] **do** not apply in a case of gross negligence or willful or wanton misconduct of the custodian or its officers, employees, or agents. **Leg.H.** Added Stats 2016 ch 551 §1 (AB 691), effective January 1, 2017. Amended Stats 2016 ch 585 §2 (SB 873), effective January 1, 2017; Stats 2024 ch 799 §7 (SB 1458), effective January 1, 2025.

§881. 2024 Deletes. [1] 879 [2] Any [3] shall

§882. Effect on federal Electronic Signatures in Global and National Commerce Act

This part modifies, limits, or supersedes the federal Electronic Signatures in Global and National Commerce Act (15 U.S.C. Sec. 7001 et seq.), but does not modify, limit, or supersede Section 101(c) of that act (15 U.S.C. Sec. 7001(c)) or authorize electronic delivery of any of the notices described in Section 103(b) of that act (15 U.S.C. Sec. 7003(b)). **Leg.H.** Added Stats 2016 ch 551 §1 (AB 691), effective January 1, 2017.

§883. Disclosure of contents of deceased user's or settlor's account to fiduciary of deceased user or settlor

Disclosure of the contents of the deceased user's or settlor's account to a fiduciary of the deceased user or settlor is subject to the same license, restrictions, terms of service, and legal obligations, including copyright law, that applied to the deceased user or settlor. **Leg.H.** Added Stats 2016 ch 551 §1 (AB 691), effective January 1, 2017.

§884. Severability

If any provision of this part or its application to any person or circumstance is held invalid, the invalidity does not affect other provisions or applications of this part that can be given effect without the invalid provision or application, and, to this end, the provisions of this part are severable. **Leg.H.** Added Stats 2016 ch 551 §1 (AB 691), effective January 1, 2017.

PART 21
PERIODIC ADJUSTMENT OF DOLLAR AMOUNTS

Periodic adjustment of dollar amounts for small estate set-asides. § 890.

§ 890. Periodic adjustment of dollar amounts for small estate set-asides

(a) On April 1, 2022, and at each three-year interval ending on April 1 thereafter, the dollar amounts specified in Chapter 6 (commencing with Section 6600) of Part 3 of Division 6 and in Division 8 (commencing with Section 13000) in effect immediately before that date shall be adjusted as provided in subdivision (b).

(b) The Judicial Council shall determine the amount of the adjustment based on the change in the United States city average of the "Consumer Price Index for All Urban Consumers," as published by the United States Bureau of Labor Statistics, from the December that is 40 months prior to the adjustment to the December immediately preceding the adjustment, with each adjusted amount rounded to the nearest twenty-five dollars ($25).

(c) Beginning April 1, 2022, the Judicial Council shall, after adjusting the amounts as directed in subdivision (b), publish a list of the current dollar amounts for the provisions identified in subdivision (a), together with the date of the next scheduled adjustment.

(d) Adjustments made under subdivision (a) do not apply when the decedent's death preceded the date of adjustment. **Leg.H.** Added Stats 2019 ch 122 §1 (AB 473), effective January 1, 2020.

DIVISION 3
GENERAL PROVISIONS OF A PROCEDURAL NATURE

Part 1. General Provisions.
Part 2. Notices and Citations.
Part 3. Appeals.

PART 1
GENERAL PROVISIONS

Chapter 1. Rules of Practice.
Chapter 2. Petitions and Other Papers.
Chapter 3. Hearings and Orders.
Chapter 4. Accounts.

CHAPTER 1
RULES OF PRACTICE

General rules of practice; Commencement of discovery as to nonparties. §1000.
Judicial Council and local court rules; forms. §1001.
Costs. §1002.
Appointment of guardian ad litem; Disclosures. §1003.
Reasonable notice and inquiry prior to appointment. §1003.5.
Lis pendens. §1004.

§1000. General rules of practice; Commencement of discovery as to nonparties

(a) Except to the extent that this code provides applicable rules, the rules of practice applicable to civil actions, including discovery proceedings and proceedings under Title 3a (commencing with Section 391) of Part 2 of the Code of Civil Procedure, apply to, and constitute the rules of practice in, proceedings under this code. All issues of fact joined in probate proceedings shall be tried in conformity with the rules of practice in civil actions.

(b) For purposes of determining when a petitioner in a proceeding under this code may commence discovery as to nonparties, the time periods set forth in the Civil Discovery Act (Title 4 (commencing with Section 2016.010) of Part 4 of the Code of Civil Procedure) shall apply, except that the time periods shall commence to run upon service of the petition and notice of hearing upon all parties entitled to notice. Nothing in this subdivision shall either alter when a respondent in such a proceeding may commence discovery or increase the extent to which nonparties may be subject to discovery. **Leg.H.** Enacted Stats 1990 ch 79 §14 (AB 759), operative July 1, 1991. Amended Stats 1994 ch 806 §5 (AB 3686); Stats 1997 ch 724 §4 (AB 1172); Stats 2002 ch 1118 §5 (AB 1938); Stats 2017 ch 32 §3 (AB 308), effective January 1, 2018.

Prior Law: Former Prob C §1000, similar to the present section, was added Stats 1988 ch 1199 §56, operative July 1, 1989, and repealed Stats 1990 ch 79 §13, operative July 1, 1991.

Former Prob C §1000, similar to present Prob C §§11600–11602, 11620–11622, 12540, was added Stats 1953 ch 417 §2, amended Stats 1963 ch 179 §1, Stats 1969 ch 604 §1, Stats 1970 ch 775 §1, Stats 1980 ch 955 §23, Stats 1982 ch 41 §1.3, ch 520 §9, Stats 1987 ch 923 §49, operative July 1, 1988, and repealed Stats 1988 ch 1199 §55.5, operative July 1, 1989.

Former Prob C §1000, similar to present Prob C §§11600–11602, 11620–11622, 12540, was enacted Stats 1931, amended Stats 1937 ch 91 §1, and repealed Stats 1953 ch 417 §1.

§1001. Judicial Council and local court rules; forms

(a) The Judicial Council may provide by rule for the practice and procedure under this code. Unless disapproved by the Judicial Council, a court may provide by local rule for the practice and procedure under this code. Judicial Council and local court rules shall be consistent with the applicable statutes.

(b) The Judicial Council may prescribe the form of the applications, notices, orders, and other documents required by this code. Any form prescribed by the Judicial Council is deemed to comply with this code. **Leg.H.** Enacted Stats 1990 ch 79 §14 (AB 759), operative July 1, 1991.

Prior Law: Former Prob C §1001, similar to present section, was added Stats 1988 ch 1199 §56, operative July 1, 1989, and repealed Stats 1990 ch 79 §13, operative July 1, 1991.

Former Prob C §1001, similar to present Prob C §§11603, 11621, 11622, was added Stats 1953 ch 417 §2, amended Stats 1980 ch 634 §1.3, effective July 20, 1980, and repealed Stats 1988 ch 1199 §55.5, operative July 1, 1989.

Former Prob C §1001, similar to present Prob C §§11603, 11621, 11622, was enacted Stats 1931, amended Stats 1937 ch 91 §2, Stats 1939 ch 777 §1, and repealed Stats 1953 ch 417 §1.

§1002. Costs

Unless it is otherwise provided by this code or by rules adopted by the Judicial Council, either the superior court or the court on appeal may, in its discretion, order costs to be paid by any party to the proceedings, or out of the assets of the estate, as justice may require. **Leg.H.** Enacted Stats 1990 ch 79 §14 (AB 759), operative July 1, 1991.

Prior Law: Former Prob C §1002, similar to present section, was added Stats 1988 ch 1199 §56, operative July 1, 1989, and repealed Stats 1990 ch 79 §13, operative July 1, 1991.

Former Prob C §1002, similar to present Prob C §11624, was added Stats 1953 ch 417 §2 and repealed Stats 1988 ch 1199 §55.5, operative July 1, 1989.

Former Prob C §1002, relating to order of repayment, was enacted Stats 1931 and repealed Stats 1953 ch 417 §1.

§1003. Appointment of guardian ad litem; Disclosures

(a) The court may, on its own motion or on request of a personal representative, guardian, conservator, trustee, or other interested person, appoint a guardian ad litem at any stage of a proceeding under this code to represent the interest of any of the following persons, if the court determines that representation of the interest otherwise would be inadequate:

(1) A minor.
(2) A person who lacks legal capacity to make decisions.
(3) An unborn beneficiary.
(4) An unascertained person.
(5) A person whose identity or address is unknown.
(6) A designated class of persons who are not ascertained or are not in being.

(b) If not precluded by a conflict of interest, a guardian ad litem may be appointed to represent several persons or interests.

(c) The reasonable expenses of the guardian ad litem, including compensation and attorney's fees, shall be determined by the court and paid as the court orders, either out of the property of the estate involved or by the petitioner or from any other source as the court orders.

(d) Before a court appoints a guardian ad litem pursuant to this chapter, a proposed guardian ad litem shall disclose both of the following to the court and all parties to the action or proceeding:

(1) Any known actual or potential conflicts of interest that would or might arise from the appointment.
(2) Any familial or affiliate relationship the proposed guardian ad litem has with any of the parties.

(e) If a guardian ad litem becomes aware that a potential conflict of interest has become an actual conflict of interest or that a new potential or actual conflict of interest exists, the guardian ad litem shall promptly disclose the conflict of interest to the court. **Leg.H.** Enacted Stats 1990 ch 79 §14 (AB 759), operative July 1, 1991. Amended Stats 2022 ch 843 §2 (SB 1279), effective January 1, 2023; Stats 2023 ch 260 §20 (SB 345), effective January 1, 2024.

Prior Law: Former Prob C §1003, similar to the present section, was added ch 1199 §56, operative July 1, 1989, and repealed Stats 1990 ch 79 §13, operative July 1, 1991.

Former Prob C §1003, similar to present Prob C §§11605, 11753, was added Stats 1953 ch 417 §2 and repealed Stats 1988 ch 1199 §55.5, operative July 1, 1989.

Former Prob C §1003, similar to present Prob C §11624, was enacted Stats 1931 and repealed Stats 1953 ch 417 §1.

§1003.5. Reasonable notice and inquiry prior to appointment

The public guardian shall not be appointed as a guardian ad litem pursuant to Section 1003 unless the court, after reasonable notice and inquiry, finds that no other qualified person is willing to act as a guardian ad litem. **Leg.H.** Added Stats 1994 ch 472 §1 (AB 2725).

§1004. Lis pendens

If a proceeding under this code affects the title to or the right of possession of real property, notice of the pendency of the proceeding may be filed pursuant to Title 4.5 (commencing with Section 405) of Part 2 of the Code of Civil Procedure. **Leg.H.** Enacted Stats 1990 ch 79 §14 (AB 759), operative July 1, 1991. Amended Stats 2003 ch 32 §1 (AB 167).

Prior Law: Former Prob C §1004, similar to present section, was added 1988 ch 1199 §56, operative July 1, 1989, and repealed Stats 1990 ch 79 §13, operative July 1, 1991.

Former Prob C §1004, similar to present Prob C §§1041, 11621, 11623, was added Stats 1974 ch 961 §3, operative July 1, 1975, amended Stats 1980 ch 634 §1.4, effective July 20, 1980, Stats 1982 ch 1543 §8, Stats 1983 ch 29 §1, effective May 11, 1983, Stats 1987 ch 923 §50, operative July 1, 1988, and repealed Stats 1988 ch 1199 §55.5, operative July 1, 1989.

CHAPTER 2
PETITIONS AND OTHER PAPERS

General requirements for petitions, objections, responses, reports, and accounts. §1020.
Verification required. §1021.
Affidavit or verified petition as evidence. §1022.
Signing and verification by attorney. §1023.

§1020. General requirements for petitions, objections, responses, reports, and accounts

Except as provided in Section 1023, a petition, objection, response, report, or account filed pursuant to this code shall be in writing, signed by all of the petitioners, objectors, or respondents or by all of the persons making the report or account, and filed with the court clerk. Verification of a document shall constitute signature of that document, unless expressly provided to the contrary. **Leg.H.** Enacted Stats 1990 ch 79 §14 (AB 759), operative July 1, 1991. Amended Stats 1992 ch 871 §3 (AB 2975).

Prior Law: Former Prob C §1020, similar to the present section, was added Stats 1988 ch 1199 §56, operative July 1, 1989, and repealed Stats 1990 ch 79 §13, operative July 1, 1991.

Former Prob C §1020, similar to present Prob C §§9630, 11600–11602, 11640, was enacted Stats 1931, amended Stats 1933 ch 969 §11, Stats 1980 ch 955 §24, Stats 1987 ch 923 §51, operative July 1, 1988, and repealed Stats 1988 ch 1199 §55.5, operative July 1, 1989.

§1021. Verification required

(a) All of the following shall be verified:

(1) A petition, report, or account filed pursuant to this code.

(2) An objection or response filed pursuant to this code to a petition, report, or account.

(b) Except as provided in Section 1023, the verification shall be made as follows:

(1) A petition shall be verified by the petitioner or, if there are two or more parties joining in the petition, by any of them.

(2) A report or account shall be verified by the person who has the duty to make the report or account or, if there are two or more persons having a duty to make the report or account, by any of them.

(3) An objection or response shall be verified by the objector or respondent or, if there are two or more parties joining in the objection or response, by any of them. **Leg.H.** Enacted Stats 1990 ch 79 §14 (AB 759), operative July 1, 1991. Amended Stats 1992 ch 871 §4 (AB 2975); Stats 1996 ch 862 §3 (AB 2751).

Prior Law: Former Prob C §1021, similar to the present section, was added Stats 1988 ch 1199 §56, operative July 1, 1989, and repealed Stats 1990 ch 79 §13, operative July 1, 1991.

Former Prob C §1021, similar to present Prob C §§11603, 11605, was enacted Stats 1931, and repealed Stats 1988 ch 1199 §55.5, operative July 1, 1989.

§1022. Affidavit or verified petition as evidence

An affidavit or verified petition shall be received as evidence when offered in an uncontested proceeding under this code. **Leg.H.** Enacted Stats 1990 ch 79 §14 (AB 759), operative July 1, 1991.

Prior Law: Former Prob C §1022, similar to the present section, was added Stats 1988 ch 1199 §56, operative July 1, 1989, and repealed Stats 1990 ch 79 §13, operative July 1, 1991.

Former Prob C §1022, similar to present Prob C §§11801, 11802, was enacted Stats 1931 and repealed Stats 1988 ch 1199 §55.5, operative July 1, 1989.

§1023. Signing and verification by attorney

If a petitioner, objector, or respondent is absent from the county or for some other cause is unable to sign or verify a petition, objection, or response filed pursuant to this code, the person's attorney may sign or verify the petition, objection, or response unless the person is a fiduciary appointed in the proceeding. **Leg.H.** Enacted Stats 1990 ch 79 §14 (AB 759), operative July 1, 1991.

Prior Law: Former Prob C §1023, similar to the present section, was added Stats 1988 ch 1199 §56, operative July 1, 1989, amended Stats 1989 ch 21 §4, effective May 25, 1989, operative July 1, 1989, and repealed Stats 1990 ch 79 §13 (AB 759), operative July 1, 1991.

Former Prob C §1023, similar to present Prob C §§11801, 11802, was enacted Stats 1931, amended Stats 1943 ch 884 §1, Stats 1955 ch 679 §1, and repealed Stats 1988 ch 1199 §55.5, operative July 1, 1989.

CHAPTER 3
HEARINGS AND ORDERS

General hearing procedure. §1040.
Clerk to set matters for hearing. §1041.
Notice of hearing. §1042.
Response or objection. §1043.
Plaintiff and defendant. §1044.
Continuance or postponement. §1045.
Hearing and order. §1046.
Recital of jurisdictional facts unnecessary. §1047.
Entry and filing. §1048.
Enforcement of order. §1049.
Judgment roll. §1050.
Ex parte communication. §1051.

§1040. General hearing procedure

This chapter governs the hearing of all matters under this code, except where the statute that provides for the hearing of the matter prescribes a different procedure. **Leg.H.** Enacted Stats 1990 ch 79 §14 (AB 759), operative July 1, 1991.

Prior Law: Former Prob C §1040, similar to the present section, was added Stats 1988 ch 1199 §56, operative July 1, 1989, and repealed Stats 1990 ch 79 §13, operative July 1, 1991.

Former Prob C §1040, similar to present Prob C §§12540, 12541, was enacted Stats 1931, amended Stats 1970 ch 775 §2, and repealed Stats 1988 ch 1199 §55.5, operative July 1, 1989.

§1041. Clerk to set matters for hearing

When a petition, report, account, or other matter that requires a hearing is filed with the court clerk, the clerk shall set the matter for hearing. **Leg.H.** Enacted Stats 1990 ch 79 §14 (AB 759), operative July 1, 1991.

Prior Law: Former Prob C §1041, similar to the present section, was added Stats 1988 ch 1199 §56, operative July 1, 1989, and repealed Stats 1990 ch 79 §13, operative July 1, 1991.

Former Prob C §1041, similar to present section and Prob C §§1043, 12540, was enacted Stats 1931, amended Stats 1980 ch 955 §25.1, Stats 1987 ch 923 §55, operative July 1, 1988, and repealed Stats 1988 ch 1199 §55.5, operative July 1, 1989.

§1042. Notice of hearing

A hearing under this code shall be on notice unless the statute that provides for the hearing dispenses with notice. **Leg.H.** Enacted Stats 1990 ch 79 §14 (AB 759), operative July 1, 1991.

Prior Law: Former Prob C §1042, similar to the present section, was added Stats 1988 ch 1199 §56, operative July 1, 1989, and repealed Stats 1990 ch 79 §13, operative July 1, 1991.

Former Prob C §1042, similar to present Prob C §12540, was enacted Stats 1931, and repealed Stats 1988 ch 1199 §55.5, operative July 1, 1989.

§1043. Response or objection

(a) An interested person may appear and make a response or objection in writing at or before the hearing.

(b) An interested person may appear and make a response or objection orally at the hearing. The court in its discretion shall either hear and determine the response or objection at the hearing, or grant a continuance for the purpose of allowing a response or objection to be made in writing.

(c) A request for a continuance for the purpose of making a written response or objection shall not itself be considered as a response or objection, nor shall the failure to make a response or objection during the time allowed be considered as a response or objection. **Leg.H.** Enacted Stats 1990 ch 79 §14 (AB 759), operative July 1, 1991.

Prior Law: Former Prob C §1043, similar to the present section, was added Stats 1988 ch 1199 §56, operative July 1, 1989, and repealed Stats 1990 ch 79 §13, operative July 1, 1991.

Former Prob C §1043, similar to present Prob C §§12570–12572, was added Stats 1957 ch 563 §1, amended Stats 1968 ch 594 §1, Stats 1987 ch 894 §1, Stats 1988 ch 160 §144 (ch 1199) prevails), and repealed Stats 1988 ch 1199 §55.5, operative July 1, 1989.

§1044. Plaintiff and defendant

The petitioner or other party affirming is the plaintiff and the party objecting or responding is the defendant. **Leg.H.** Enacted Stats 1990 ch 79 §14 (AB 759), operative July 1, 1991.

Prior Law: Former Prob C §1044, similar to the present section, was added Stats 1988 ch 1199 §56, operative July 1, 1989, and repealed Stats 1990 ch 79 §13), operative July 1, 1991.

§1045. Continuance or postponement

The court may continue or postpone any hearing, from time to time, in the interest of justice. **Leg.H.** Enacted Stats 1990 ch 79 §14 (AB 759), operative July 1, 1991.

Prior Law: Former Prob C §1045, similar to the present section, was added Stats 1988 ch 1199 §56, operative July 1, 1989, and repealed Stats 1990 ch 79 §13, operative July 1, 1991.

§1046. Hearing and order

The court shall hear and determine any matter at issue and any response or objection presented, consider evidence presented, and make appropriate orders. **Leg.H.** Enacted Stats 1990 ch 79 §14 (AB 759), operative July 1, 1991.

Prior Law: Former Prob C §1046, similar to the present section, was added Stats 1988 ch 1199 §56, operative July 1, 1989, and repealed Stats 1990 ch 79 §13, operative July 1, 1991.

§1047. Recital of jurisdictional facts unnecessary

Except as otherwise provided in this code, an order made in a proceeding under this code need not recite the existence of facts, or the performance of acts, upon which jurisdiction depends, but need only contain the matters ordered. **Leg.H.** Enacted Stats 1990 ch 79 §14 (AB 759), operative July 1, 1991.

Prior Law: Former Prob C §1047, similar to the present section, was added Stats 1988 ch 1199 §56, operative July 1, 1989, and repealed Stats 1990 ch 79 §13, operative July 1, 1991.

§1048. Entry and filing

(a) Except as provided in subdivision (b), orders shall be either entered at length in the minute book of the court or signed by the judge and filed.

(b) An order for distribution shall be entered at length in a judgment book or other permanent record of the court. **Leg.H.** Enacted Stats 1990 ch 79 §14 (AB 759), operative July 1, 1991.

Prior Law: Former Prob C §1048, similar to the present section, was added Stats 1988 ch 1199 §56, operative July 1, 1989, and repealed Stats 1990 ch 79 §13, operative July 1, 1991.

§1049. Enforcement of order

An order may be enforced as provided in Title 9 (commencing with Section 680.010) of Part 2 of the Code of Civil Procedure. **Leg.H.** Enacted Stats 1990 ch 79 §14 (AB 759), operative July 1, 1991.

Prior Law: Former Prob C §1049, similar to the present section, was added Stats 1988 ch 1199 §56, operative July 1, 1989, and repealed Stats 1990 ch 79 §13, operative July 1, 1991.

§1050. Judgment roll

The judgment roll in a proceeding under this code consists of the following papers, where applicable:

(a) In all cases:

(1) The petition, application, report, or account that initiates a particular proceeding.

(2) Any order directing notice of the hearing to be given.

(3) Any notice of the hearing, and any order to show cause made in the proceeding, with the affidavits showing publication, posting, or delivery pursuant to Section 1215 of the notice or order as may be required by law or court order.

(4) Any citation, in case no answer or written opposition is filed by a party entitled, by law or court order, to notice of the proceeding by citation, with the affidavit or proof of service and, if service of the citation is made by publication, the affidavit of publication and the order directing publication.

(5) Any finding of the court or referee in the proceeding.

(6) The order or statement of decision made in the proceeding.

(7) Any letters, as defined in Section 52.

(b) If an answer, demurrer, written opposition, or counter petition is filed in a proceeding:

(1) Pleadings and papers in the nature of pleadings.

(2) Any orders striking out a pleading in whole or in part.

(3) Any order made on demurrer, or relating to a change of parties, in the proceeding.

(4) The verdict of the jury, if any.

(c) If the proceeding is for the probate of a will, the will.

(d) If the proceeding is a contest of a will, for the revocation of the probate of a will, or for a preliminary or final distribution of the estate under a will:

(1) The will.

(2) The order admitting the will to probate.

(e) If the proceeding is for the settlement of the final account of a personal representative or for the final distribution of an estate, the affidavit showing publication of notice to creditors. **Leg.H.** Enacted Stats 1990 ch 79 §14 (AB 759), operative July 1, 1991. Amended Stats 2017 ch 319 §13 (AB 976), effective January 1, 2018.

Prior Law: Former Prob C §1050, similar to the present section, was added Stats 1988 ch 1199 §56, operative July 1, 1989, and repealed Stats 1990 ch 79 §13, operative July 1, 1991.

Former Prob C §1050, similar to present Prob C §§6409, 21135 was enacted Stats 1931 and repealed Stats 1983 ch 842 §44, operative January 1, 1985.

§1051. Ex parte communication

(a) In the absence of a stipulation to the contrary between parties who have filed pleadings in a proceeding under this code, there shall be no ex parte communications between any party, or attorney for the party, and the court concerning a subject raised in those pleadings, except as permitted or required by law.

(b) Notwithstanding subdivision (a), in any case upon which the court has exercised its jurisdiction, the court may refer to the court investigator or take other appropriate action in response to an ex parte communication regarding either or both of the following:

(1) A fiduciary, as defined in Section 39, about the fiduciary's performance of their duties and responsibilities.

(2) A person who is the subject of a conservatorship or guardianship proceeding under Division 4 (commencing with Section 1400).

(c) An action by the court pursuant to subdivision (b) shall be consistent with due process and the requirements of this code. The court shall disclose the ex parte communication to all parties and counsel. The court may, for good cause, dispense with the disclosure if necessary to protect the ward or conservatee from harm.

(d) If the court imposes a penalty, including, but not limited to, a surcharge, punishment for contempt, suspension, or removal, on a professional fiduciary, the court shall report that action to the Professional Fiduciaries Bureau. If the court reports an action taken under this section, the court shall provide the bureau, at no charge, with access to the information, including confidential information, regarding its investigation of the professional fiduciary contained in the court records. The bureau shall maintain the confidentiality of the information, as required by paragraph (4) of subdivision (a) of Section 6580 of the Business and Professions Code or any other applicable state or federal law.

(e) A superior court shall not be required to perform any duties imposed by this section until the Legislature makes an appropriation identified for this purpose. **Leg.H.** Added Stats 2006 ch 492 §2 (SB 1716), effective January 1, 2007. Amended Stats 2011 ch 10 §11 (SB 78), effective March 24, 2011; Stats 2021 ch 417 §3 (AB 1194), effective January 1, 2022.

2006 Note: This act, together with AB 1363 (Jones), SB 1116 (Scott), and SB 1550 (Figueroa), shall be known and may be cited as the Omnibus Conservatorship and Guardianship Reform Act of 2006. Stats 2006 ch 492 (SB 1716) §1.

CHAPTER 4
ACCOUNTS

Application of chapter. §1060.
Operation of chapter. §1060.5.
Contents and format of accounts. §1061.
Schedules to accompany summary. §1062.
Additional schedules. §1063.

Contents of petition for approval of account or of report accompanying petition. §1064.

§1060. Application of chapter

This chapter governs all accounts to be filed with the court. Except as specifically provided elsewhere in this code, or unless good cause is shown therefore, no information in addition to that required in this chapter need be in an account. **Leg.H.** Added Stats 1996 ch 862 §4 (AB 2751), operative July 1, 1997. Amended Stats 1997 ch 724 §5 (AB 1172).

§1060.5. Operation of chapter

This chapter shall be operative on and after July 1, 1997. **Leg.H.** Added Stats 1996 ch 862 §4 (AB 2751), operative July 1, 1997.

§1061. Contents and format of accounts

(a) All accounts shall state the period covered by the account and contain a summary showing all of the following, to the extent applicable:

(1) The property on hand at the beginning of the period covered by the account, which shall be the value of the property initially received by the fiduciary if this is the first account, and shall be the property on hand at the end of the prior account if this is a subsequent account.

(2) The value of any assets received during the period of the accounting which are not assets on hand as of the commencement of the administration of an estate.

(3) The amount of any receipts of income or principal, excluding items listed under paragraphs (1) and (2) or receipts from a trade or business.

(4) Net income from a trade or business.

(5) Gains on sales.

(6) The amount of disbursements, excluding disbursements for a trade or business or distributions.

(7) Loss on sales.

(8) Net loss from trade or business.

(9) Distributions to beneficiaries, the ward or conservatee.

(10) Property on hand at the end of the accounting period, stated at its carry value.

(b) The summary shall be in a format substantially the same as the following, except that inapplicable categories need not be shown:

SUMMARY OF ACCOUNT

CHARGES:
Property on hand at beginning of account (or Inventories) $ _____
Additional property received (or Supplemental Inventories)   _____
Receipts (Schedule _____)   _____
Gains on Sale or Other Disposition (Schedule _____)   _____
Net income from trade or business (Schedule _____)   _____
  Total Charges: $ _____
CREDITS:
Disbursements (Schedule _____) $ _____
Losses on Sale or Other Disposition (Schedule _____)   _____
Net loss from trade or business (Schedule _____)   _____
Distributions (Schedule _____)   _____
Property on hand at close of account (Schedule _____)   _____
  Total Credits: $ _____

(c) Total charges shall equal total credits.

(d) For purposes of this section, the terms "net income" and "net loss" shall be utilized in accordance with general accounting principles. Nothing in this section is intended to require that the preparation of the summary must include "net income" and "net loss" as reflected in the tax returns governing the period of the account. **Leg.H.** Added Stats 1996 ch 862 §4 (AB 2751), operative July 1, 1997. Amended Stats 1997 ch 724 §6 (AB 1172).

§1062. Schedules to accompany summary

The summary shall be supported by detailed schedules showing the following:

(a) Receipts, showing the nature or purpose of each item, the source of the receipt, and the date thereof.

(b) Disbursement, including the nature or purpose of each item, the name of the payee, and the date thereof.

(c) Net income or loss from a trade or business, which shall be sufficient if it provides the information disclosed on Schedule C or F of the federal income tax return.

(d) Calculation of gains or losses on sale or other disposition.

(e) Distributions of cash or property to beneficiaries, ward or conservatee, showing the date and amount of each, with the distribution of property shown at its carry value.

(f) Itemized list of property on hand, describing each item at its carry value. **Leg.H.** Added Stats 1996 ch 862 §4 (AB 2751), operative July 1, 1997.

§1063. Additional schedules

(a) In all accounts, there shall be an additional schedule showing the estimated market value of the assets on hand as of the end of the accounting period, and a schedule of the estimated market value of the assets on hand as of the beginning of the accounting period for all accounts subsequent to the initial account. The requirement of an estimated value of real estate, a closely held business, or other assets without a ready market, may be satisfied by a good faith estimate by the fiduciary.

(b) If there were purchases or other changes in the form of assets occurring during the period of the account, there shall be a schedule showing these transactions. However, no reporting is required for transfers between cash or accounts in a financial institution or money market mutual funds as defined in subdivision (d) of Section 8901.

(c) If an estate of a decedent or a trust will be distributed to an income beneficiary, there shall be a schedule showing an allocation of receipts and disbursements between principal and income.

(d) If there is specifically devised property, there shall be an additional schedule accounting for income, disbursements, and proceeds of sale pursuant to Section 12002 and subdivision (a) of Section 16340.

(e) If any interest has been paid or is to be paid under Section 12003, 12004, or 12005, or subdivision (b) of Section 16340, there shall be a schedule showing the calculation of the interest.

(f) If the accounting contemplates a proposed distribution, there shall be a schedule setting forth the proposed distribution, including the allocation of income required under Section 12006. If the distribution requires an allocation between trusts, the allocation shall be set forth on the schedule, unless the allocation is to be made by a trustee after receipt of the assets. If the distribution requires valuation of assets as of the date of distribution, the schedule shall set forth the fair market value of those assets.

(g) If, at the end of the accounting period, there are liabilities of the estate or trust, except current or future periodic payments, including rent, salaries, utilities, or other recurring expenses, there shall be a schedule showing all of the following:

(1) All liabilities which are a lien on estate or trust assets.

(2) Taxes due but unpaid as shown on filed returns or assessments received subsequent to filing of returns.

(3) All notes payable.

(4) Any judgments for which the estate or trust is liable.

(5) Any other material liability.

(h) If the guardian or conservator has knowledge of any real property of the conservatee or ward located in a foreign jurisdiction, the guardian or conservator shall include an additional schedule that identifies the real property, provides a good faith estimate of the fair market value of the real property, and states what action, if any, will or has been taken to preserve and protect the real property, including a recommendation whether an ancillary proceeding is necessary to preserve and protect the real property. **Leg.H.** Added Stats 1996 ch 862 §4 (AB 2751), operative July 1, 1997. Amended Stats 1997 ch 724 §7 (AB 1172); Stats 1999 ch 145 §2 (AB 846); Stats 2008 ch 52 §1 (AB 2014), effective January 1, 2009.

§1064. Contents of petition for approval of account or of report accompanying petition

(a) The petition for approval of the account or a report accompanying the petition shall contain all of the following:

(1) A description of all sales, purchases, changes in the form of assets, or other transactions occurring during the period of the account that are not otherwise readily understandable from the schedule.

(2) An explanation of any unusual items appearing in the account.

(3) A statement of all compensation paid from the assets subject to the account to the fiduciary or to the attorneys for the fiduciary other than pursuant to a prior court order.

(4) A statement disclosing any family or affiliate relationship between the fiduciary and any agent hired by the fiduciary during the accounting period.

(5) An allegation disclosing whether all of the cash has been invested and maintained in interest bearing accounts or in investments authorized

by law or the governing instrument, except for an amount of cash that is reasonably necessary for the orderly administration of the estate.

(b) The filing of an account shall be deemed to include a petition requesting its approval, and may include additional petitions for authorization, instruction or confirmation authorized by the code, including, but not limited to, a request for an order for compensation of the fiduciary and the attorney for the fiduciary.

(c) For purposes of this section, "family" means a relationship created by blood or marriage. For purposes of this section, "affiliate" means an entity that directly or indirectly through one or more intermediaries controls, is controlled by, or is under common control with, the fiduciary.
Leg.H. Added Stats 1996 ch 862 §4 (AB 2751), operative July 1, 1997. Amended Stats 1997 ch 724 §8 (AB 1172).

PART 2
NOTICES AND CITATIONS

Chapter 1. General Notice Provisions.
Chapter 2. Mailing in General.
Chapter 3. Mailing Notice of Hearing.
Chapter 4. Posting Notice of Hearing.
Chapter 5. Citations.
Chapter 6. Request for Special Notice.
Chapter 7. Proof of Giving Notice.

CHAPTER 1
GENERAL NOTICE PROVISIONS

Application of part. §1200.
Notice not required to be given to oneself or persons joining in petition. §1201.
Additional notice on court order. §1202.
Order shortening time. §1203.
Waiver of notice. §1204.
Notice of continued or postponed hearing. §1205.
Notice to known heirs or devisees. §1206.
Exceptions to notice requirement involving parent-child relationship. §1207.
Notice to trust beneficiaries where personal representative and trustee are same person. §1208.
Notice to State of California or to Attorney General. §1209.
Guardian or conservator acting for ward or conservatee. §1210.
Form of notice when form not otherwise prescribed. §1211.
Manner of mailing notice of hearing. §1212.
Notice to surety who has filed court bond. §1213.
Notice to be mailed to attorney. §1214.

§1200. Application of part

(a) Except as otherwise provided in this code, this part governs notice required or permitted under this code.

(b) This part does not apply to notice under a particular provision to the extent that the particular provision is inconsistent with this part.

(c) This part does not apply to the giving of a particular notice where the notice was delivered, mailed, posted, or first published before July 1, 1991. The applicable law in effect before July 1, 1991, continues to apply to the giving of that notice, notwithstanding its repeal. **Leg.H.** Enacted Stats 1990 ch 79 §14 (AB 759), operative July 1, 1991.

Prior Law: Former Prob C §1200, similar to the present section, was added Stats 1987 ch 923 §60, operative July 1, 1988, amended Stats 1989 ch 21 §5, effective May 25, 1989, operative July 1, 1989, and repealed Stats 1990 ch 79 §13, operative July 1, 1991.

Former Prob C §1200, similar to the present section and §§1230 and 1260, was enacted Stats 1931, amended by Stats 1933 ch 969 §18, Stats 1939 ch 434 §1, Stats 1953 ch 841 §1, Stats 1955 ch 1183 §9, Stats 1977 ch 243 §4, Stats 1979 ch 730 §106, operative January 1, 1981, Stats 1980 ch 119 §18, ch 955 §29, Stats 1982 ch 1543 §13, Stats 1986 ch 820 §32, operative July 1, 1987, and repealed Stats 1987 ch 923 §59, operative July 1, 1988.

§1201. Notice not required to be given to oneself or persons joining in petition

If a person is required to give notice, the person required to give the notice need not give the notice to himself or herself or to any other person who joins in the petition. **Leg.H.** Enacted Stats 1990 ch 79 §14 (AB 759), operative July 1, 1991.

Prior Law: Former Prob C §1201, similar to the present section, was added Stats 1987 ch 923 §60, operative July 1, 1988, and repealed Stats 1990 ch 79 §13, operative July 1, 1991.

Former Prob C §1201, similar to present Prob C §1207, was added Stats 1985 ch 982 §15.3, amended by Stats 1987 ch 128 §6.5, effective July 6, 1987, operative July 1, 1987, and repealed by Stats 1987 ch 923 §59, operative July 1, 1988.

Former Prob C §1201, similar to the present Prob C §1207, was added Stats 1985 ch 359 §3, effective July 30, 1985, and repealed Stats 1985 ch 982 §15.2.

Former Prob C §1201, relating to publication of notice required in certain instances, was enacted Stats 1931, amended Stats 1933 ch 969 §19, Stats 1935 ch 724 §4, Stats 1951 ch 51 §1, Stats 1957 ch 1671 §3, and repealed Stats 1979 ch 731 §26.

§1202. Additional notice on court order

Where the court determines that the notice otherwise required is insufficient in the particular circumstances, the court may require that further or additional notice, including a longer period of notice, be given. **Leg.H.** Enacted Stats 1990 ch 79 §14 (AB 759), operative July 1, 1991.

Prior Law: Former Prob C §1202, similar to the present section, was added Stats 1987 ch 923 §60, operative July 1, 1988, and repealed Stats 1990 ch 79 §13, operative July 1, 1991.

Former Prob C §1202, similar to present Prob C §§1250, 1252, was enacted Stats 1931, amended Stats 1967 ch 381 §1, Stats 1980 ch 119 §19, Stats 1986 ch 820 §34, operative July 1, 1987, Stats 1987 ch 56 §145 (ch 923 prevails), and repealed Stats 1987 ch 923 §59, operative July 1, 1988.

§1203. Order shortening time

(a) Subject to subdivision (b), unless the particular provision governing the notice of hearing provides that the time for giving notice may not be shortened, the court may, for good cause, shorten the time for giving a notice of hearing.

(b) Unless the particular provision governing the publication of notice of hearing otherwise provides, the court may not shorten the time for publication of notice of hearing. **Leg.H.** Enacted Stats 1990 ch 79 §14 (AB 759), operative July 1, 1991. Amended Stats 1991 ch 82 §2.5, effective June 30, 1991, operative July 1, 1991.

Prior Law: Former Prob C §1203, similar to the present section, was added Stats 1987 ch 923 §60, operative July 1, 1988, amended Stats 1988 ch 1199 §59.5, operative July 1, 1989, and repealed Stats 1990 ch 79 §13, operative July 1, 1991.

Former Prob C §1203, similar to present Prob C §7280, was enacted Stats 1931 and repealed Stats 1987 ch 923 §59, operative July 1, 1988.

§1204. Waiver of notice

A person, including a guardian ad litem, guardian, conservator, trustee, or other fiduciary, may waive notice by a writing signed by the person or the person's attorney and filed in the proceeding. **Leg.H.** Enacted Stats 1990 ch 79 §14 (AB 759), operative July 1, 1991.

Prior Law: Former Prob C §1204, similar to the present section, was added Stats 1987 ch 923 §60, operative July 1, 1988, and repealed Stats 1990 ch 79 §13, operative July 1, 1991.

Former Prob C §1204, similar to present Prob C §1202, was enacted Stats 1931 and repealed Stats 1987 ch 923 §59, operative July 1, 1988.

§1205. Notice of continued or postponed hearing

If a hearing is continued or postponed, no further notice of the continued or postponed hearing is required unless ordered by the court. **Leg.H.** Enacted Stats 1990 ch 79 §14 (AB 759), operative July 1, 1991.

Prior Law: Former Prob C §1205, similar to the present section, was added Stats 1987 ch 923 §60, operative July 1, 1988, and repealed Stats 1990 ch 79 §13, operative July 1, 1991.

Former Prob C §1205, similar to the present section and Prob C §1045, was enacted Stats 1931 and repealed Stats 1987 ch 923 §59, operative July 1, 1988.

§1206. Notice to known heirs or devisees

(a) Subject to subdivision (b), where notice is required to be given to known heirs or known devisees, notice shall be given to the following persons:

(1) If the estate is an intestate estate, to the heirs named in the petition for letters of administration and to any additional heirs who become known to the person giving the notice prior to the giving of the notice.

(2) If the estate is a testate estate, to the devisees named in the petition for probate of the will and to any additional devisees who become known to the person giving the notice prior to the giving of the notice.

(b) Notice need not be given to a person under subdivision (a) if the person's interest has been satisfied pursuant to court order or as evidenced by the person's written receipt. **Leg.H.** Enacted Stats 1990 ch 79 §14 (AB 759), operative July 1, 1991.

Prior Law: Former Prob C §1206, similar to the present section, was added Stats 1987 ch 923 §60, operative July 1, 1988, and repealed Stats 1990 ch 79 §13, operative July 1, 1991.

Former Prob C §1206, similar to present Prob C §1241 was enacted Stats 1931 and repealed Stats 1987 ch 923 §59, operative July 1, 1988.

§1207. Exceptions to notice requirement involving parent-child relationship

(a) Subject to subdivision (b), where notice is required to be given to a decedent's beneficiaries, devisees, or heirs, notice need not be given to a person who, because of a possible parent-child relationship between a stepchild and a stepparent or between a foster child and a foster parent, may be (1) an heir of the decedent or (2) a member of a class to which a devise is made.

(b) Subdivision (a) does not apply where the person required to give the notice has actual knowledge of facts that a person would reasonably believe give rise under Section 6454 to the parent-child relationship between the stepchild and the stepparent or between the foster child and the foster parent. **Leg.H.** Enacted Stats 1990 ch 79 §14 (AB 759), operative July 1, 1991. Amended Stats 1993 ch 529 §1 (AB 1137).

Prior Law: Former Prob C §1207, similar to the present section, was added Stats 1987 ch 923 §60, operative July 1, 1988, and repealed Stats 1990 ch 79 §13, operative July 1, 1991.

Former Prob C §1207, similar to present Prob C §§1240, 1242, was enacted Stats 1931 and repealed Stats 1987 ch 923 §59, operative July 1, 1988.

§1208. Notice to trust beneficiaries where personal representative and trustee are same person

(a) Except as provided in subdivision (b), if notice is required to be given to a trust or trustee, notice to trust beneficiaries is not required.

(b) Subject to subdivision (c), where the personal representative and the trustee are the same person, or where no trustee has been appointed, notice shall be given to (1) each person to whom income or principal would be required or authorized in the trustee's discretion to be currently distributed if the trust were in effect, or (2) if there are no such persons, to each person who, under the terms of the trust, would be entitled to any distribution if the trust were terminated at the time the notice is required to be given.

(c) Notice to trust beneficiaries is not required under subdivision (b) where the trust has more than one trustee and notice is given to a cotrustee who is not a personal representative. **Leg.H.** Enacted Stats 1990 ch 79 §14 (AB 759), operative July 1, 1991. Amended Stats 1992 ch 871 §5 (AB 2975); Stats 1995 ch 730 §2 (AB 1466).

Prior Law: Former Prob C §1208, similar to the present section, was added Stats 1987 ch 923 §60, operative July 1, 1988, and repealed Stats 1990 ch 79 §13, operative July 1, 1991.

Former Prob C §1208, similar to present Prob C §1210 was enacted Stats 1931, amended Stats 1967 ch 719 §6, and repealed Stats 1987 ch 923 §59, operative July 1, 1988.

§1209. Notice to State of California or to Attorney General

(a) If notice is required to be given to the State of California, the notice shall be given to the Attorney General.

(b) If notice is required to be given to the Attorney General, the notice shall be delivered pursuant to Section 1215 to the Attorney General at the office of the Attorney General [1] **in** Sacramento, California.

(c) **The Attorney General does not waive the right to object to a proposed settlement that adversely impacts a charitable gift by failing to appear at a mediation, a mandatory settlement conference, or other court-ordered alternative dispute resolution proceeding related to the settlement.** **Leg.H.** Enacted Stats 1990 ch 79 §14 (AB 759), operative July 1, 1991. Amended Stats 2017 ch 319 §14 (AB 976), effective January 1, 2018; Stats 2024 ch 853 §29 (AB 3281), effective January 1, 2025.

§1209. 2024 Deletes. [1] at

Prior Law: Former Prob C §1209, similar to the present section, was added Stats 1987 ch 923 §60, operative July 1, 1988, and repealed Stats 1990 ch 79 §13, operative July 1, 1991.

Former Prob C §1209, relating to publication, was enacted Stats 1931 and repealed Stats 1987 ch 923 §59, operative July 1, 1988.

§1210. Guardian or conservator acting for ward or conservatee

If an interested person has a guardian or conservator of the estate who resides in this state, personal service on the guardian or conservator of any process, notice, or court order concerning a decedent's estate is equivalent to service on the ward or conservatee, and it is the duty of the guardian or conservator to attend to the interests of the ward or conservatee in the matter. The guardian or conservator may appear for the ward or conservatee and waive any process, notice, or order to show cause that a person not under legal disability might waive. **Leg.H.** Enacted Stats 1990 ch 79 §14 (AB 759), operative July 1, 1991.

Prior Law: Former Prob C §1210, similar to the present section, was added Stats 1988 ch 1199 §60, operative July 1, 1989, and repealed Stats 1990 ch 79 §13, operative July 1, 1991.

Former Prob C §1210, similar to present Prob C §1230, was enacted Stats 1931 and repealed Stats 1987 ch 923 §59, operative July 1, 1988.

§1211. Form of notice when form not otherwise prescribed

If a notice is required by this code and no other type of notice is prescribed by law, by the Judicial Council, or by the court or judge, the notice shall be in substantially the following form:

SUPERIOR COURT
OF THE STATE OF CALIFORNIA
FOR THE (CITY AND) COUNTY OF _____
Estate of _____ No. _____

NOTICE OF HEARING

(If to be published, describe purport or character of the notice to be given.) Notice is hereby given that (name of petitioner and representative capacity, if any) has filed herein a (nature of petition, application, report, or account), reference to which is made for further particulars, and that the time and place of hearing the same has been set for _____ (date), at ____.m., in the courtroom (of Department No. ____, if any) of said court, at (the courthouse, or state other location of the court), in the City of _____, California.

Dated _____
_____, Clerk
By _____, Deputy Clerk

Leg.H. Enacted Stats 1990 ch 79 §14 (AB 759), operative July 1, 1991.

Prior Law: Former Prob C §1211, similar to the present section, was added Stats 1988 ch 113 §13.3, effective May 25, 1988, operative July 1, 1988; and repealed Stats 1990 ch 79 §13, operative July 1, 1991.

§1212. Manner of mailing notice of hearing

Unless the court dispenses with the notice, if the address of the person to whom a notice or other paper is required to be delivered pursuant to Section 1215 is not known, notice shall be given as the court may require in the manner provided in Section 413.30 of the Code of Civil Procedure. **Leg.H.** Added Stats 1990 ch 710 §4 (SB 1775), operative July 1, 1991. Amended Stats 2017 ch 319 §15 (AB 976), effective January 1, 2018.

§1213. Notice to surety who has filed court bond

(a) The following persons shall deliver pursuant to Section 1215 a notice, as described in Section 1211, to a surety who has filed a court bond in a proceeding:

(1) A person who files a petition to surcharge.

(2) A person who files an objection to an account.

(3) A person who files a petition to suspend or remove a guardian, conservator, or personal representative.

(4) An attorney who files a motion to withdraw from representation of a guardian, conservator, or personal representative.

(b) Within five days after entry of an order to suspend or remove a guardian, conservator, or personal representative, the person who filed a petition to suspend or remove a guardian or, if the order to suspend or remove a guardian, conservator, or personal representative was issued upon a motion by the court, the court, shall notify pursuant to Section 1215 the surety who has filed a court bond of the order.

(c) The notice required by this section shall be delivered pursuant to Section 1215 to the addressee listed on the surety bond.

(d) Notwithstanding subdivisions (a) and (b), notice is not required to a surety pursuant to this section if the surety bond is for a guardian, conservator, or personal representative who is not the subject of the petition, motion, or order described in this section. **Leg.H.** Added Stats 1997 ch 198 §1 (SB 792). Amended Stats 2017 ch 319 §16 (AB 976), effective January 1, 2018.

§1214. Notice to be mailed to attorney

If a notice or other paper is required or permitted to be served or delivered pursuant to Section 1215 to a person who is represented by an attorney of record, the notice or other paper shall also be delivered pursuant to Section 1215 to this attorney, unless otherwise specified in a request for special notice. **Leg.H.** Added Stats 1999 ch 263 §2 (AB 1051). Amended Stats 2017 ch 319 §17 (AB 976), effective January 1, 2018.

CHAPTER 2
MAILING IN GENERAL

Manner of service; When service complete. §1215.
Delivered notice where no other manner of giving notice specified. §1217.

§1215. Manner of service; When service complete

Unless otherwise expressly provided, a notice or other paper that is required or permitted to be delivered to a person shall be delivered pursuant to one of the following methods:

(a) Delivery by mail.

(1) A notice or other paper shall be delivered by mail as follows:

(A) By first-class mail if the person's address is within the United States. First-class mail includes certified, registered, and express mail.

(B) By international mail if the person's address is not within the United States. International mail includes first-class mail international, priority mail international, priority mail express international, and global express guaranteed.

(2) The notice or other paper shall be deposited for collection in the United States mail, in a sealed envelope, with postage paid, addressed to the person to whom it is mailed.

(3) Subject to Section 1212, the notice or other paper shall be addressed to the person at the person's place of business or place of residence.

(4) Delivery by mail is complete when the notice or other paper is deposited in the mail. The period of notice is not extended.

(b) Personal delivery.

(1) A notice or other paper may be delivered personally to that person.

(2) Personal delivery is complete when the notice or other paper is delivered personally to the person who is to receive it.

(c) Electronic delivery.

(1) A notice or other paper shall not be delivered by electronic means unless the person to receive notice has expressly consented on the appropriate Judicial Council form to receive electronic delivery in the proceeding before the court and has provided an electronic address for that express purpose.

(2) Electronic delivery is complete when the notice or other paper is sent. The period of notice is not extended.

(3) Electronic delivery is not permitted for a notice or other paper that requires delivery by certified or registered mail. **Leg.H.** Enacted Stats 1990 ch 79 §14 (AB 759), operative July 1, 1991. Amended Stats 1990 ch 710 §5 (SB 1775), operative July 1, 1991; Stats 2017 ch 319 §18 (AB 976), effective January 1, 2018.

Prior Law: Former Prob C §1215, similar to the present section, was added Stats 1987 ch 923 §60, operative July 1, 1988, amended Stats 1988 ch 1199 §60.7, operative July 1, 1989, and repealed Stats 1990 ch 79 §13, operative July 1, 1991.

Former Prob C§1215, similar to present Prob C §17100, was added Stats 1974 ch 171 §1, amended Stats 1983 ch 842 §51, operative January 1, 1985, and repealed Stats 1986 ch 820 §35, operative July 1, 1987.

§1216. Personal delivery instead of mailing [Repealed]

Leg.H. Enacted Stats 1990 ch 79 §14 (AB 759), operative July 1, 1991. Repealed Stats 2017 ch 319 §19 (AB 976), effective January 1, 2018. The repealed section related to personal delivery instead of mailing.

Prior Law: Former Prob C §1216, similar to the present section, was added Stats 1987 ch 923 §60, operative July 1, 1988, and repealed Stats 1990 ch 79 §13, operative July 1, 1991.

§1217. Delivered notice where no other manner of giving notice specified

If a notice or other paper is required to be served or otherwise given and no other manner of giving the notice or other paper is specified by statute, the notice or other paper shall be delivered pursuant to Section 1215. **Leg.H.** Enacted Stats 1990 ch 79 §14 (AB 759), operative July 1, 1991. Amended Stats 2017 ch 319 §20 (AB 976), effective January 1, 2018.

Prior Law: Former Prob C §1217, similar to the present section, was added Stats 1987 ch 923 §60, operative July 1, 1988, amended Stats 1989 ch 21 §6, effective May 25, 1989, operative July 1, 1989, and repealed Stats 1990 ch 79 §13, operative July 1, 1991.

§1218. [Section repealed 2000]

Leg.H. Added Stats 1994 ch 806 §6 (AB 3686). Repealed Stats 1999 ch 263 §3 (AB 1051). See Prob C §1214.

CHAPTER 3
MAILING NOTICE OF HEARING

General manner of delivering notice of hearing. §1220.
Period and manner of giving notice of hearing where not otherwise prescribed by statute. §1221.

§1220. General manner of delivering notice of hearing

(a) If notice of hearing is required to be given as provided in this section:

(1) At least 15 days before the time set for the hearing, the petitioner or the person filing the report, account, or other paper shall cause notice of the time and place of the hearing to be delivered pursuant to Section 1215 to the persons required to be given notice.

(2) Unless the statute requiring notice specifies the persons to be given notice, notice shall be delivered pursuant to Section 1215 to all of the following:

(A) The personal representative.

(B) All persons who have requested special notice in the estate proceeding pursuant to Section 1250.

(3) Subject to Section 1212, the notice shall be delivered pursuant to Section 1215 to the person required to be given notice at the person's place of business, place of residence, or electronic address.

(b) Subject to subdivision (c), this section does not excuse compliance with the requirements for notice to a person who has requested special notice pursuant to Chapter 6 (commencing with Section 1250).

(c) The court for good cause may dispense with the notice otherwise required to be given to a person as provided in this section. **Leg.H.** Enacted Stats 1990 ch 79 §14 (AB 759), operative July 1, 1991. Amended Stats 1990 ch 710 §6 (SB 1775), operative July 1, 1991; Stats 1994 ch 806 §7 (AB 3686); Stats 2017 ch 319 §21 (AB 976), effective January 1, 2018.

Prior Law: Former Prob C §1220, similar to the present section, was added Stats 1987 ch 923 §60, operative July 1, 1988, amended Stats 1988 ch 1199 §61.3, operative July 1, 1989, Stats 1989 ch 21 §7, effective May 25, 1989, operative July 1, 1989, and repealed Stats 1990 ch 79 §13 (AB 759), operative July 1, 1991.

Former Prob C §1220, similar to present Prob C §1047, was enacted Stats 1931 and repealed Stats 1987 ch 923 §59, operative July 1, 1988.

§1221. Period and manner of giving notice of hearing where not otherwise prescribed by statute

Where notice of hearing is required but no other period or manner is prescribed by statute, unless the period or manner of giving the notice is ordered by the court or judge, the notice of hearing shall be given for the period and in the manner provided in Section 1220. **Leg.H.** Enacted Stats 1990 ch 79 §14 (AB 759), operative July 1, 1991.

CHAPTER 4
POSTING NOTICE OF HEARING

Manner of posting notice of hearing. §1230.

§1230. Manner of posting notice of hearing

Where notice of hearing is required to be posted as provided in this section:

(a) At least 15 days before the time set for the hearing, the court clerk shall cause a notice of the time and place of the hearing to be posted at the courthouse of the county where the proceedings are pending. If court is held at a place other than the county seat, the notice may be posted either at the courthouse of the county where the proceedings are pending or at the building where the court is held.

(b) The posted notice of hearing shall state all of the following:

(1) The name of the estate.

(2) The name of the petitioner.

(3) The nature of the petition, referring to the petition for further particulars.

(4) The time and place of the hearing of the petition. **Leg.H.** Enacted Stats 1990 ch 79 §14 (AB 759), operative July 1, 1991.

Prior Law: Former Prob C §1230, similar to the present section, was added Stats 1987 ch 923 §60, operative July 1, 1988, and repealed Stats 1990 ch 79 §13, operative July 1, 1991.

Former Prob C §1230, similar to present Prob C §§1000, 1044, 1048, 1049, 1452, 7200, 17006, was enacted Stats 1931 and repealed Stats 1987 ch 923 §59, operative July 1, 1988.

CHAPTER 5
CITATIONS

Issuance of citation. §1240.
Contents of citation. §1241.
Service of citation. §1242.

§1240. Issuance of citation

Where use of a citation is authorized or required by statute, a citation may be issued by the court clerk on the application of any party, without a court order, except in cases where an order is expressly required by law. **Leg.H.** Enacted Stats 1990 ch 79 §14 (AB 759), operative July 1, 1991.

Prior Law: Former Prob C §1240, similar to the present section, was added Stats 1987 ch 923 §60, operative July 1, 1988, and repealed Stats 1990 ch 79 §13, operative July 1, 1991.

Former Prob C §1240, similar to present Prob C §7240, was enacted Stats 1931, amended Stats 1935 ch 724 §5, Stats 1967 ch 17 §118, Stats 1968 ch 287 §3, Stats 1969 ch 272 §5, Stats 1972 ch 641 §4, Stats 1974 ch 752 §10, Stats 1975 ch 173 §13, effective June 30, 1975, Stats 1976 ch 1028 §6, Stats 1977 ch 243 §5, Stats 1980 ch 119 §20, Stats 1980 ch 119 §20, Stats 1986 ch 820 §36, operative July 1, 1987, and repealed Stats 1987 ch 923 §59, operative July 1, 1988.

§1241. Contents of citation

The citation shall be directed to the person to be cited, signed by the court clerk, and issued under the seal of the court. The citation shall contain the title of the proceeding, a brief statement of the nature of the proceeding, and a direction that the person cited appear at a time and place specified. **Leg.H.** Enacted Stats 1990 ch 79 §14 (AB 759), operative July 1, 1991.

Prior Law: Former Prob C §1241, similar to the present section, was added Stats 1987 ch 923 §60, operative July 1, 1988, and repealed Stats 1990 ch 79 §13, operative July 1, 1991.

Former Prob C §1241, related to effect of reversal of appointment of personal representative, was added Stats 1933 ch 969 §20 and repealed Stats 1987 ch 923 §59, operative July 1, 1988.

§1242. Service of citation

The citation shall be served on the person cited in the manner provided in Chapter 4 (commencing with Section 413.10) of Title 5 of Part 2 of the Code of Civil Procedure. Except as otherwise provided by statute, the citation shall be served at least five days before its return day. **Leg.H.** Enacted Stats 1990 ch 79 §14 (AB 759), operative July 1, 1991.

Prior Law: Former Prob C §1242, similar to the present section, was added Stats 1987 ch 923 §60, operative July 1, 1988, and repealed Stats 1990 ch 79 §13, operative July 1, 1991.

Former Prob C §1242, similar to present Prob C §1050, was added Stats 1933 ch 194 §1 and repealed Stats 1987 ch 923 §59, operative July 1, 1988.

CHAPTER 6
REQUEST FOR SPECIAL NOTICE

Request for special notice. §1250.
Modification or withdrawal of request for special notice. §1251.
Notice to be given to person requesting special notice. §1252.

§1250. Request for special notice

(a) At any time after the issuance of letters in a proceeding under this code for the administration of a decedent's estate, any person interested in the estate, whether as devisee, heir, creditor, beneficiary under a trust, or as otherwise interested, may, in person or by attorney, file with the court clerk a written request for special notice.

(b) The request for special notice shall be so entitled and shall set forth the name of the person and the address to which notices shall be delivered pursuant to Section 1215.

(c) Special notice may be requested of one or more of the following matters:

(1) Petitions filed in the administration proceeding.
(2) Inventories and appraisals of property in the estate, including any supplemental inventories and appraisals.
(3) Objections to an appraisal.
(4) Accounts of a personal representative.
(5) Reports of status of administration.

(d) Special notice may be requested of any matter in subdivision (c) by describing it, or of all the matters in subdivision (c) by referring generally to "the matters described in subdivision (c) of Section 1250 of the Probate Code" or by using words of similar meaning.

(e) A copy of the request shall be delivered pursuant to Section 1215 to the personal representative or to the attorney for the personal representative. If personally delivered, the request is effective when it is delivered. If mailed or electronically delivered, the request is effective when it is received.

(f) If the original of the request is filed with the court clerk, it shall be accompanied by a written admission or proof of service. **Leg.H.** Enacted Stats 1990 ch 79 §14 (AB 759), operative July 1, 1991. Amended Stats 2017 ch 319 §22 (AB 976), effective January 1, 2018.

Prior Law: Former Prob C §1250, similar to the present section, was added Stats 1987 ch 923 §60, operative July 1, 1988, amended Stats 1988 ch 1199 §63, operative July 1, 1989, and repealed Stats 1990 ch 79 §13, operative July 1, 1991.

§1251. Modification or withdrawal of request for special notice

A request for special notice under this chapter may be modified or withdrawn in the same manner as provided for the making of the initial request. **Leg.H.** Enacted Stats 1990 ch 79 §14 (AB 759), operative July 1, 1991.

Prior Law: Former Prob C §1251, similar to the present section, was added Stats 1987 ch 923 §60, operative July 1, 1988, and repealed Stats 1990 ch 79 §13, operative July 1, 1991.

§1252. Notice to be given to person requesting special notice

(a) Unless the court makes an order dispensing with the notice, if a request has been made pursuant to Section 1250 for special notice of a hearing, the person filing the petition, report, account, or other paper shall give written notice of the filing, together with a copy of the petition, report, account, or other paper, and the time and place set for the hearing, by delivering the documents pursuant to Section 1215 to the person named in the request at the address set forth in the request, at least 15 days before the time set for the hearing.

(b) If a request has been made pursuant to Section 1250 for special notice of the filing of an inventory and appraisal of the estate or of the filing of any other paper that does not require a hearing, the inventory and appraisal or other paper shall be delivered pursuant to Section 1215 not later than 15 days after the inventory and appraisal or other paper is filed with the court. **Leg.H.** Enacted Stats 1990 ch 79 §14 (AB 759), operative July 1, 1991. Amended Stats 2017 ch 319 §23 (AB 976), effective January 1, 2018.

Prior Law: Former Prob C §1252, similar to the present section, was added Stats 1987 ch 923 §60, operative July 1, 1988, amended Stats 1988 ch 1199 §63.5, operative July 1, 1989, and repealed Stats 1990 ch 79 §13, operative July 1, 1991.

CHAPTER 7
PROOF OF GIVING NOTICE

Proof of giving notice of hearing required; Conclusiveness of order. §1260.
Proof of mailing. §1261.
Proof of publication. §1262.
Proof of posting. §1263.
Proof of personal delivery. §1264.
Proof of electronic delivery. §1265.
Proof by testimony at hearing. §1266.

§1260. Proof of giving notice of hearing required; Conclusiveness of order

(a) If notice of a hearing is required, proof of giving notice of the hearing shall be made to the satisfaction of the court at or before the hearing.

(b) If it appears to the satisfaction of the court that notice has been regularly given or that the party entitled to notice has waived it, the court shall so find in its order.

(c) The finding described in subdivision (b), when the order becomes final, is conclusive on all persons. **Leg.H.** Enacted Stats 1990 ch 79 §14 (AB 759), operative July 1, 1991.

Prior Law: Former Prob C §1260, similar to the present section, was added Stats 1987 ch 923 §60, operative July 1, 1988, and repealed Stats 1990 ch 79 §13, operative July 1, 1991.

§1261. Proof of mailing

Proof of mailing may be made in the manner prescribed in Section 1013a of the Code of Civil Procedure. **Leg.H.** Enacted Stats 1990 ch 79 §14 (AB 759), operative July 1, 1991.

Prior Law: Former Prob C §1261, similar to the present section, was added Stats 1987 ch 923 §60, operative July 1, 1988, and repealed Stats 1990 ch 79 §13, operative July 1, 1991.

§1262. Proof of publication

Proof of publication may be made by the affidavit of the publisher or printer, or the foreman or principal clerk of the publisher or printer, showing the time and place of publication. **Leg.H.** Enacted Stats 1990 ch 79 §14 (AB 759), operative July 1, 1991.

Prior Law: Former Prob C §1262, similar to the present section, was added Stats 1987 ch 923 §60, operative July 1, 1988, and repealed Stats 1990 ch 79 §13, operative July 1, 1991.

§1263. Proof of posting

Proof of posting may be made by the affidavit of the person who posted the notice. **Leg.H.** Enacted Stats 1990 ch 79 §14 (AB 759), operative July 1, 1991.

Prior Law: Former Prob C §1263, similar to the present section, was added Stats 1987 ch 923 §60, operative July 1, 1988, and repealed Stats 1990 ch 79 §13, operative July 1, 1991.

§1264. Proof of personal delivery

Proof of notice by personal delivery may be made by the affidavit of the person making the delivery showing the time and place of delivery and the name of the person to whom delivery was made. **Leg.H.** Enacted Stats 1990 ch 79 §14 (AB 759), operative July 1, 1991.

Prior Law: Former Prob C §1264, similar to the present section, was added Stats 1987 ch 923 §60, operative July 1, 1988, and repealed Stats 1990 ch 79 §13, operative July 1, 1991.

§1265. Proof of electronic delivery

Proof of electronic delivery may be made in the manner prescribed in Section 1013b of the Code of Civil Procedure. **Leg.H.** Added Stats 2017 ch 319 §25 (AB 976), effective January 1, 2018.

Former Sections: Former Prob C §1265 was enacted Stats 1990 ch 79 §14 (AB 759), operative July 1, 1991, and amended and renumbered Prob C §1266 by Stats 2017 ch 319 §24 (AB 976).

Former Prob C §1265, similar to present Prob C §1266, was added Stats 1987 ch 923 §60, effective January 1, 1988, operative July 1, 1988, and repealed Stats 1990 ch 79 §13 (AB 759), effective January 1, 1991, operative July 1, 1991.

Prior Law: Former Prob C §1265 was enacted Stats 1990 ch 79 §14 (AB 759), effective January 1, 1991, operative July 1, 1991, and amended and renumbered Prob C §1266 by Stats 2017 ch 319 §24 (AB 976), effective January 1, 2018.

Former Prob C §1265, similar to present Prob C §1266, was added Stats 1987 ch 923 §60, effective January 1, 1988, operative July 1, 1988, and repealed Stats 1990 ch 79 §13 (AB 759), effective January 1, 1991, operative July 1, 1991.

§1266. Proof by testimony at hearing

Proof of notice, however given, may be made by evidence presented at the hearing. **Leg.H.** Enacted Stats 1990 ch 79 §14 (AB 759), operative July 1, 1991, as Prob C § 1265. Renumbered by Stats 2017 ch 319 §24 (AB 976), effective January 1, 2018.

PART 3
APPEALS

Chapter 1. General.
Chapter 2. Effect of an Appeal.

CHAPTER 1
GENERAL

Appealable orders, generally. §1300.
Appealable orders relating to guardianships, conservatorships, and other protective proceedings. §1301.
Appealable orders under California Conservatorship Jurisdiction Act. §1301.5.
Appeals respecting power of attorney. §1302.
Appeal respecting advance health care directive. §1302.5.
Appealable orders relating to decedent's estate. §1303.
Appealable orders relating to trust. §1304.

§1300. Appealable orders, generally

In all proceedings governed by this code, an appeal may be taken from the making of, or the refusal to make, any of the following orders:

(a) Directing, authorizing, approving, or confirming the sale, lease, encumbrance, grant of an option, purchase, conveyance, or exchange of property.

(b) Settling an account of a fiduciary.

(c) Authorizing, instructing, or directing a fiduciary, or approving or confirming the acts of a fiduciary.

(d) Directing or allowing payment of a debt, claim, or cost.

(e) Fixing, authorizing, allowing, or directing payment of compensation or expenses of an attorney.

(f) Fixing, directing, authorizing, or allowing payment of the compensation or expenses of a fiduciary.

(g) Surcharging, removing, or discharging a fiduciary.

(h) Transferring the property of the estate to a fiduciary in another jurisdiction.

(i) Allowing or denying a petition of the fiduciary to resign.

(j) Discharging a surety on the bond of a fiduciary.

(k) Adjudicating the merits of a claim made under Part 19 (commencing with Section 850) of Division 2. **Leg.H.** Added Stats 1997 ch 724 §11 (AB 1172). Amended Stats 2001 ch 417 §4 (AB 873).

§1301. Appealable orders relating to guardianships, conservatorships, and other protective proceedings

With respect to guardianships, conservatorships, and other protective proceedings, the grant or refusal to grant the following orders is appealable:

(a) Granting or revoking of letters of guardianship or conservatorship, except letters of temporary guardianship or temporary conservatorship.

(b) Granting permission to the guardian or conservator to fix the residence of the ward or conservatee at a place not within this state.

(c) Directing, authorizing, approving, or modifying payments, whether for support, maintenance, or education of the ward or conservatee or for a person legally entitled to support, maintenance, or education from the ward or conservatee.

(d) Granting or denying a petition under Section 2423 or under Article 10 (commencing with Section 2580) of Chapter 6 of Part 4 of Division 4.

(e) Affecting the legal capacity of the conservatee pursuant to Chapter 4 (commencing with Section 1870) of Part 3 of Division 4.

(f) Adjudicating the merits of a claim under Article 5 (commencing with Section 2500) of Chapter 6 of Part 4 of Division 4.

(g) Granting or denying a petition under Chapter 3 (commencing with Section 3100) of Part 6 of Division 4. **Leg.H.** Added Stats 1997 ch 724 §11 (AB 1172). Amended Stats 2001 ch 417 §5 (AB 873).

§1301.5. Appealable orders under California Conservatorship Jurisdiction Act

The following rules apply with respect to the California Conservatorship Jurisdiction Act (Chapter 8 (commencing with Section 1980) of Part 3 of Division 4):

(a)(1) An appeal may be taken from an order assessing expenses against a party under Section 1997 if the amount exceeds five thousand dollars ($5,000).

(2) An order under Section 1997 assessing expenses of five thousand dollars ($5,000) or less against a party may be reviewed on an appeal by that party after entry of a final judgment or an appealable order in the conservatorship proceeding. At the discretion of the court of appeal, that type of order may also be reviewed upon petition for an extraordinary writ.

(b) An appeal may be taken from an order under Section 2001 denying a petition to transfer a conservatorship to another state.

(c) An appeal may be taken from a final order under Section 2002 accepting a transfer and appointing a conservator in this state.

(d) Notwithstanding any other law, an appeal may not be taken from either of the following until the court enters a final order under Section 2002 accepting the proposed transfer and appointing a conservator in this state:

(1) An order under Section 2002 determining whether or how to conform a conservatorship to the law of this state.

(2) An order that is made pursuant to a court review under Sections 1851.1 and 2002. **Leg.H.** Added Stats 2014 ch 553 §3 (SB 940), effective January 1, 2015, operative January 1, 2016.

§1302. Appeals respecting power of attorney

With respect to a power of attorney governed by the Power of Attorney Law (Division 4.5 (commencing with Section 4000)), an appeal may be taken from any of the following:

(a) Any final order under Section 4541, except an order pursuant to subdivision (c) of Section 4541.

(b) An order dismissing the petition or denying a motion to dismiss under Section 4543. **Leg.H.** Added Stats 1997 ch 724 §11 (AB 1172). Amended Stats 1999 ch 658 §9 (AB 891), operative July 1, 2000.

§1302.5. Appeal respecting advance health care directive

With respect to an advance health care directive governed by the Health Care Decisions Law (Division 4.7 (commencing with Section 4600)), an appeal may be taken from any of the following:

(a) Any final order under Section 4766.

(b) An order dismissing the petition or denying a motion to dismiss under Section 4768. **Leg.H.** Added Stats 1999 ch 658 §10 (AB 891), operative July 1, 2000.

§1303. Appealable orders relating to decedent's estate

With respect to a decedent's estate, the grant or refusal to grant the following orders is appealable:

(a) Granting or revoking letters to a personal representative, except letters of special administration or letters of special administration with general powers.

(b) Admitting a will to probate or revoking the probate of a will.

(c) Setting aside a small estate under Section 6609.

(d) Setting apart a probate homestead or property claimed to be exempt from enforcement of a money judgment.

(e) Granting, modifying, or terminating a family allowance.

(f) Determining heirship, succession, entitlement, or the persons to whom distribution should be made.

(g) Directing distribution of property.

(h) Determining that property passes to, or confirming that property belongs to, the surviving spouse under Section 13656.

(i) Authorizing a personal representative to invest or reinvest surplus money under Section 9732.

(j) Determining whether an action constitutes a contest under former Chapter 2 (commencing with Section 21320) of Part 3 of Division 11, as that chapter read prior to its repeal by Chapter 174 of the Statutes of 2008.

(k) Determining the priority of debts under Chapter 3 (commencing with Section 11440) of Part 9 of Division 7.

(*l*) Any final order under Chapter 1 (commencing with Section 20100) or Chapter 2 (commencing with Section 20200) of Division 10. **Leg.H.** Added Stats 1997 ch 724 §11 (AB 1172). Amended Stats 2001 ch 417 §6 (AB 873), ch 699 §1 (AB 232); Stats 2009 ch 348 §5 (SB 308), effective January 1, 2010.

§1304. Appealable orders relating to trust

With respect to a trust, the grant or denial of the following orders is appealable:

(a) Any final order under Chapter 3 (commencing with Section 17200) of Part 5 of Division 9, except the following:

(1) Compelling the trustee or trust director to submit an account or report acts as trustee or trust director, respectively.

(2) Accepting the resignation of the trustee or trust director.

(b) Any final order under Chapter 2 (commencing with Section 19020) of Part 8 of Division 9.

(c) Any final order under Chapter 1 (commencing with Section 20100) and Chapter 2 (commencing with Section 20200) of Division 10.

(d) Determining whether an action constitutes a contest under former Chapter 2 (commencing with Section 21320) of Part 3 of Division 11, as that chapter read prior to its repeal by Chapter 174 of the Statutes of 2008. **Leg.H.** Added Stats 1997 ch 724 §11 (AB 1172). Amended Stats 2009 ch 348 §6 (SB 308), effective January 1, 2010; Stats 2019 ch 497 §210 (AB 991), effective January 1, 2020; Stats 2023 ch 721 §2 (SB 801), effective January 1, 2024.

CHAPTER 2
EFFECT OF AN APPEAL

Stay of operation and effect of order; Trial court's power. §1310.
Reversal of order appointing fiduciary. §1311.
Appealability of order or refusal relating to inheritance tax. §1312.

§1310. Stay of operation and effect of order; Trial court's power

(a) Except as provided in subdivisions (b), (c), (d), and (e), an appeal pursuant to Chapter 1 (commencing with Section 1300) stays the operation and effect of the judgment or order.

(b) Notwithstanding that an appeal is taken from the judgment or order, for the purpose of preventing injury or loss to a person or property, the trial court may direct the exercise of the powers of the fiduciary, or may appoint a temporary guardian or conservator of the person or estate, or both, or a special administrator or temporary trustee, to exercise the powers, from time to time, as if no appeal were pending. All acts of the fiduciary pursuant to the directions of the court made under this subdivision are valid, irrespective of the result of the appeal. An appeal of the directions made by the court under this subdivision shall not stay these directions.

(c) In proceedings for guardianship of the person, Section 917.7 of the Code of Civil Procedure shall apply.

(d) An appeal shall not stay the operation and effect of the judgment or order if the court requires an undertaking, as provided in Section 917.9 of the Code of Civil Procedure, and the undertaking is not given.

(e) An appeal shall not stay the operation and effect of a judgment for money or an order directing payment of money, unless one of the following applies:

(1) A bond is posted as provided in Section 917.1 of the Code of Civil Procedure.

(2) The payment is to be made from a decedent's estate being administered under Division 7 (commencing with Section 7000) or from the estate of a person who is subject to a guardianship or conservatorship of the estate under Division 4 (commencing with Section 1400). However, a court may require a bond as provided in subdivision (d). **Leg.H.** Added Stats 1997 ch 724 §11 (AB 1172). Amended Stats 2000 ch 688 §20 (AB 1669); Stats 2010 ch 94 §1 (AB 2271), effective January 1, 2011.

§1311. Reversal of order appointing fiduciary

If an order appointing a fiduciary is reversed on appeal for error, all acts of the fiduciary performed after issuance of letters and prior to the reversal are as valid as though the order were affirmed and the person appointed is not liable for any otherwise proper act done in good faith before the reversal, nor is any transaction void by reason of the reversal if entered into with a third person dealing in good faith and for value. **Leg.H.** Added Stats 1997 ch 724 §11 (AB 1172).

§1312. Appealability of order or refusal relating to inheritance tax

Notwithstanding the repeal of former Section 1297 by Chapter 1199 of the Statutes of 1988, an appeal may be taken from an order or the refusal to make an order fixing an inheritance tax or determining that none is due. **Leg.H.** Added Stats 1997 ch 724 §11 (AB 1172).

DIVISION 4
GUARDIANSHIP, CONSERVATORSHIP, AND OTHER PROTECTIVE PROCEEDINGS

Part 1. Definitions and General Provisions.
Part 2. Guardianship.
Part 3. Conservatorship.
Part 4. Provisions Common to Guardianship and Conservatorship.
Part 5. Public Guardian.
Part 6. Management or Disposition of Community Property Where Spouse Lacks Legal Capacity.
Part 7. Capacity Determinations and Health Care Decisions for Adult Without Conservator.
Part 8. Other Protective Proceedings.
Part 9. California Uniform Transfers to Minors Act.

PART 1
DEFINITIONS AND GENERAL PROVISIONS

Chapter 1. Short Title and Definitions.
Chapter 2. General Provisions.
Chapter 3. Notices.
Chapter 4. Appointment of Legal Counsel.
Chapter 5. Transitional Provisions.

CHAPTER 1
SHORT TITLE AND DEFINITIONS

Short title. §1400.
Application of definitions. §1401.
"Absentee". §1403.
"Court". §1418.
"Court investigator". §1419.
"Custodial parent". §1419.5.
"Developmental disability". §1420.
"Interested person". §1424.
"Petition". §1430.
"Proceedings to establish a limited conservatorship". §1431.
"Secretary concerned". §1440.
"Single-premium deferred annuity". §1446.
Definitions; Determination as to Indian tribe. §1449.

§1400. Short title
The portion of this division consisting of Part 1 (commencing with Section 1400), Part 2 (commencing with Section 1500), Part 3 (commencing with Section 1800), and Part 4 (commencing with Section 2100) may be cited as the Guardianship-Conservatorship Law. **Leg.H.** Enacted Stats 1990 ch 79 §14 (AB 759), operative July 1, 1991.

Prior Law: Former Prob C §1400, similar to present Prob C §1401, was added Stats 1979 ch 726 §3, operative January 1, 1981, and repealed Stats 1990 ch 79 §13 (AB 759), operative July 1, 1991.

Former Prob C §1400, similar to present Prob C §§2101, 2102, 2104, was enacted Stats 1931, amended Stats 1974 ch 1060 §2, and repealed Stats 1979 ch 726 §1, operative January 1, 1981.

§1401. Application of definitions
Unless the provision or context otherwise requires, the definitions in this chapter govern the construction of this division. **Leg.H.** Enacted Stats 1990 ch 79 §14 (AB 759), operative July 1, 1991.

Prior Law: Former Prob C §1401, relating to general and special guardians was enacted Stats 1931, and repealed Stats 1979 ch 726 §1, operative January 1, 1981.

§1403. "Absentee"
"Absentee" means either of the following:
(a) A member of a uniformed service covered by United States Code, Title 37, Chapter 10, who is determined thereunder by the secretary concerned, or by the authorized delegate thereof, to be in missing status as missing status is defined therein.
(b) An employee of the United States government or an agency thereof covered by United States Code, Title 5, Chapter 55, Subchapter VII, who is determined thereunder by the head of the department or agency concerned, or by the authorized delegate thereof, to be in missing status as missing status is defined therein. **Leg.H.** Enacted Stats 1990 ch 79 §14 (AB 759), operative July 1, 1991.

Prior Law: Former Prob C §1403, similar to the present section, was added Stats 1979 ch 726 §3, operative January 1, 1981, and repealed Stats 1990 ch 79 §13, operative July 1, 1991.

Former Prob C §1403, similar to present Prob C §§1489, 1500, 1502, was enacted Stats 1931, amended Stats 1975 ch 718 §7, ch 1244 §27, and repealed Stats 1979 ch 726 §1, operative January 1, 1981.

§1418. "Court"
"Court," when used in connection with matters in the guardianship or conservatorship proceeding, means the court in which such proceeding is pending. **Leg.H.** Enacted Stats 1990 ch 79 §14 (AB 759), operative July 1, 1991.

Prior Law: Former Prob C §1418, similar to the present section, was added Stats 1979 ch 726 §3, operative January 1, 1981, and repealed Stats 1990 ch 79 §13, operative July 1, 1991.

§1419. "Court investigator"
"Court investigator" means the person referred to in Section 1454. **Leg.H.** Enacted Stats 1990 ch 79 §14 (AB 759), operative July 1, 1991.

Prior Law: Former Prob C §1419, similar to the present section, was added Stats 1979 ch 726 §3, operative January 1, 1981, and repealed Stats 1990 ch 79 §13, operative July 1, 1991.

§1419.5. "Custodial parent"
"Custodial parent" means the parent who either (a) has been awarded sole legal and physical custody of the child in another proceeding, or (b) with whom the child resides if there is currently no operative custody order. If the child resides with both parents, then they are jointly the custodial parent. **Leg.H.** Added Stats 1993 ch 978 §1 (SB 305).

§1420. "Developmental disability"
"Developmental disability" means a disability that originates before an individual attains 18 years of age, continues, or can be expected to continue, indefinitely, and constitutes a substantial handicap for the individual. As defined by the Director of Developmental Services, in consultation with the Superintendent of Public Instruction, this term includes intellectual disability, cerebral palsy, epilepsy, and autism. This term also includes handicapping conditions found to be closely related to intellectual disability or to require treatment similar to that required for individuals with an intellectual disability, but does not include other handicapping conditions that are solely physical in nature. **Leg.H.** Enacted Stats 1990 ch 79 §14 (AB 759), operative July 1, 1991. Amended Stats 2012 ch 448 §44 (AB 2370), effective January 1, 2013, ch 457 §44 (SB 1381), effective January 1, 2013 (ch 457 prevails).

Prior Law: Former Prob C §1420, similar to the present section, was added Stats 1980 ch 1304 §3 and repealed Stats 1990 ch 79 §13, operative July 1, 1991.

§1424. "Interested person"
"Interested person" includes, but is not limited to:
(a) Any interested state, local, or federal entity or agency.
(b) Any interested public officer or employee of this state or of a local public entity of this state or of the federal government. **Leg.H.** Enacted Stats 1990 ch 79 §14 (AB 759), operative July 1, 1991.

Prior Law: Former Prob C §1424, similar to the present section, was added Stats 1979 ch 726 §3, operative January 1, 1981, and repealed Stats 1990 ch 79 §13, operative July 1, 1991.

§1430. "Petition"
"Petition" includes an application or request in the nature of a petition. **Leg.H.** Enacted Stats 1990 ch 79 §14 (AB 759), operative July 1, 1991.

Prior Law: Former Prob C §1430, similar to the present section, was added Stats 1979 ch 726 §3, operative January 1, 1981, and repealed Stats 1990 ch 79 §13, operative July 1, 1991.

Former Prob C §1430, similar to present Prob C §§3400–3402, was enacted Stats 1931, amended Stats 1939 ch 346 §1, Stats 1953 ch 1237 §1, Stats 1965 ch 1611 §1, Stats 1967 ch 878 §1, Stats 1973 ch 400 §1, and repealed Stats 1979 ch 726 §1, operative January 1, 1981.

§1431. "Proceedings to establish a limited conservatorship"

"Proceedings to establish a limited conservatorship" include proceedings to modify or revoke the powers or duties of a limited conservator. **Leg.H.** Enacted Stats 1990 ch 79 §14 (AB 759), operative July 1, 1991.

Prior Law: Former Prob C §1431, similar to the present section, was added Stats 1980 ch 1304 §4 and repealed Stats 1990 ch 79 §13, operative July 1, 1991.

Former Prob C §1431, similar to present Prob C §§1021, 3500, was enacted Stats 1931, amended Stats 1939 ch 300 §1, Stats 1951 ch 204 §1, Stats 1959 ch 684 §1, Stats 1961 ch 721 §2, Stats 1963 ch 127 §1, Stats 1st Ex Sess 1966 ch 120 §1, Stats 1973 ch 400 §3, Stats 1975 ch 500 §1, ch 718 §8, Stats 1976 ch 875 §2, and repealed Stats 1979 ch 726 §1, operative January 1, 1981.

§1440. "Secretary concerned"

"Secretary concerned" has the same meaning as provided in United States Code, Title 37, Section 101. **Leg.H.** Enacted Stats 1990 ch 79 §14 (AB 759), operative July 1, 1991.

Prior Law: Former Prob C §1440, similar to the present section, was added Stats 1979 ch 726 §3, operative January 1, 1981, and repealed Stats 1990 ch 79 §13, operative July 1, 1991.

Former Prob C §1440, similar to present Prob C §§1510, 1512, 1514, 1540–1543, 2106, 2200–2202, 2327, was enacted Stats 1931, amended Stats 1937 ch 528 §1, Stats 1975 ch 1181 §1, Stats 1979 ch 1142 §2, and repealed Stats 1979 ch 726 §1, operative January 1, 1981.

§1446. "Single-premium deferred annuity"

"Single-premium deferred annuity" means an annuity offered by an admitted life insurer for the payment of a one-time lump-sum premium and for which the insurer neither assesses any initial charges or administrative fees against the premium paid nor exacts or assesses any penalty for withdrawal of any funds by the annuitant after a period of five years. **Leg.H.** Enacted Stats 1990 ch 79 §14 (AB 759), operative July 1, 1991.

Prior Law: Former Prob C §1446, similar to the present section, was added Stats 1979 ch 726 §3, operative January 1, 1981, and repealed Stats 1990 ch 79 §13, operative July 1, 1991.

§1449. Definitions; Determination as to Indian tribe

(a) As used in this division, unless the context otherwise requires, the terms "Indian," "Indian child," "Indian child's tribe," "Indian custodian," "Indian tribe," "reservation," and "tribal court" shall be defined as provided in Section 1903 of the Indian Child Welfare Act (25 U.S.C. Sec. 1901 et seq.).

(b) When used in connection with an Indian child custody proceeding, the terms "extended family member" and "parent" shall be defined as provided in Section 1903 of the Indian Child Welfare Act (25 U.S.C. Sec. 1901 et seq.).

(c) "Indian child custody proceeding" means a "child custody proceeding" within the meaning of Section 1903 of the Indian Child Welfare Act (25 U.S.C. Sec. 1901 et seq.), including a voluntary or involuntary proceeding that may result in an Indian child's temporary or long-term foster care or guardianship placement if the parent or Indian custodian cannot have the child returned upon demand, termination of parental rights or adoptive placement.

(d) When an Indian child is a member of more than one tribe or is eligible for membership in more than one tribe, the court shall make a determination, in writing together with the reasons for it, as to which tribe is the Indian child's tribe for purposes of the Indian child custody proceeding. The court shall make that determination as follows:

(1) If the Indian child is or becomes a member of only one tribe, that tribe shall be designated as the Indian child's tribe, even though the child is eligible for membership in another tribe.

(2) If an Indian child is or becomes a member of more than one tribe, or is not a member of any tribe but is eligible for membership in more than one tribe, the tribe with which the child has the more significant contacts shall be designated as the Indian child's tribe. In determining which tribe the child has the more significant contacts with, the court shall consider, among other things, the following factors:

(A) The length of residence on or near the reservation of each tribe and frequency of contact with each tribe.

(B) The child's participation in activities of each tribe.

(C) The child's fluency in the language of each tribe.

(D) Whether there has been a previous adjudication with respect to the child by a court of one of the tribes.

(E) The residence on or near one of the tribes' reservations by the child parents, Indian custodian, or extended family members.

(F) Tribal membership of custodial parent or Indian custodian.

(G) Interest asserted by each tribe in response to the notice specified in Section 1460.2.

(H) The child's self-identification.

(3) If an Indian child becomes a member of a tribe other than the one designated by the court as the Indian child's tribe under paragraph (2), actions taken based on the court's determination prior to the child's becoming a tribal member shall continue to be valid. **Leg.H.** Added Stats 2006 ch 838 §16 (SB 678), effective January 1, 2007.

CHAPTER 2
GENERAL PROVISIONS

Trial by jury. §1452.
Motion for new trial. §1453.
Appointment of court investigator. §1454.
Filing petition for instructions or grant of power or authority. §1455.
Judicial Council to adopt specified rules of court relating to conservatorships and guardianships. §1456.
Public conservator, continuing education requirements. §1456.2.
Compliance with the requirements of filing inventory and appraisal and accountings. §1456.5.
Development of educational program for non-professional conservators or guardians. §1457.
Court effectiveness in conservatorship cases [Repealed January 1, 2028]. § 1458.
Legislative findings and declarations. §1459.
Application of Indian Child Welfare Act. §1459.5.

§1452. Trial by jury

Except as otherwise specifically provided in this division, there is no right to trial by jury in proceedings under this division. **Leg.H.** Enacted Stats 1990 ch 79 §14 (AB 759), operative July 1, 1991.

Prior Law: Former Prob C §1452, similar to the present section, was added Stats 1979 ch 726 §3, operative January 1, 1981, and repealed Stats 1990 ch 79 §13, operative July 1, 1991.

§1453. Motion for new trial

A motion for a new trial may be made only in cases in which, under the provisions of this division, a right to jury trial is expressly granted, whether or not the case was tried by a jury. **Leg.H.** Enacted Stats 1990 ch 79 §14 (AB 759), operative July 1, 1991.

Prior Law: Former Prob C §1453, similar to the present section, was added Stats 1979 ch 726 §3, operative January 1, 1981, and repealed Stats 1990 ch 79 §13, operative July 1, 1991.

§1454. Appointment of court investigator

(a) The court shall appoint a court investigator when one is required for the purposes of a proceeding under this division. The person appointed as the court investigator shall be an officer or special appointee of the court with no personal or other beneficial interest in the proceeding.

(b) The person appointed as the court investigator shall have the following qualifications:

(1) The training or experience, or both, necessary (i) to make the investigations required under this division, (ii) to communicate with, assess, and deal with persons who are or may be the subject of proceedings under this division, and (iii) to perform the other duties required of a court investigator.

(2) A demonstrated sufficient knowledge of law so as to be able to inform conservatees and proposed conservatees of the nature and effect of a conservatorship proceeding and of their rights, to answer their questions, and to inform conservators concerning their powers and duties. **Leg.H.** Enacted Stats 1990 ch 79 §14 (AB 759), operative July 1, 1991.

Prior Law: Former Prob C §1454, similar to the present section, was added Stats 1979 ch 726 §3, operative January 1, 1981, and repealed Stats 1990 ch 79 §13, operative July 1, 1991.

§1455. Filing petition for instructions or grant of power or authority

Any petition for instructions or to grant a guardian or a conservator any power or authority under this division, which may be filed by a guardian or conservator, may also be filed by a person who petitions for the appointment of a guardian or conservator, including, but not limited to, a person who petitions under Section 2002 for transfer of conservatorship. **Leg.H.** Added Stats 1996 ch 563 §5 (SB 392). Amended Stats 2014 ch 553 §4 (SB 940), effective January 1, 2015, operative January 1, 2016.

§1456. Judicial Council to adopt specified rules of court relating to conservatorships and guardianships

(a) In addition to any other requirements that are part of the judicial branch education program, on or before January 1, 2008, the Judicial Council shall adopt a rule of court that shall do all of the following:

(1) Specifies the qualifications of a court-employed staff attorney, examiner, and investigator, and any attorney appointed pursuant to Sections 1470 and 1471.

(2) Specifies the number of hours of education in classes related to conservatorships or guardianships that a judge who is regularly assigned to hear probate matters shall complete, upon assuming the probate assignment, and then over a three-year period on an ongoing basis.

(3) Specifies the number of hours of education in classes related to conservatorships or guardianships that a court-employed staff attorney, examiner, and investigator, and any attorney appointed pursuant to Sections 1470 and 1471 shall complete each year.

(4) Specifies the particular subject matter that shall be included in the education required each year. The subject matter shall, at a minimum, include the less restrictive alternatives to conservatorship set forth in Section 1800.3.

(5) Specifies reporting requirements to ensure compliance with this section.

(b) In formulating the rule required by this section, the Judicial Council shall consult with interested parties, including, but not limited to, the California Judges Association, the California Association of Superior Court Investigators, the California Public Defenders Association, the County Counsels' Association of California, the State Bar of California, the National Guardianship Association, the Professional Fiduciary Association of California, the California Association of Public Administrators, Public Guardians and Public Conservators, a disability rights organization, the State Council on Developmental Disabilities, the State Department of Developmental Services, the California Department of Aging, and the Association of Professional Geriatric Care Managers. **Leg.H.** Added Stats 2006 ch 493 §3 (AB 1363), effective January 1, 2007. Amended Stats 2007 ch 553 §2 (AB 1727), effective January 1, 2008; Stats 2022 ch 894 §3 (AB 1663), effective January 1, 2023.

2006 Note: This act, together with Senate Bill 1116 (Scott), Senate Bill 1550 (Figueroa), and Senate Bill 1716 (Bowen), shall be known and may be cited as the Omnibus Conservatorship and Guardianship Reform Act of 2006. Stats 2006 ch 493 (AB 1363) §1.

§1456.2. Public conservator, continuing education requirements

On or before January 1, 2010, the public conservator shall comply with the continuing education requirements that are established by the California State Association of Public Administrators, Public Guardians, and Public Conservators. **Leg.H.** Added Stats 2008 ch 237 §2 (AB 2343), effective January 1, 2009.

§1456.5. Compliance with the requirements of filing inventory and appraisal and accountings

Each court shall ensure compliance with the requirements of filing the inventory and appraisal and the accountings required by this division. Courts may comply with this section in either of the following ways:

(a) By placing on the court's calendar, at the time of the appointment of the guardian or conservator and at the time of approval of each accounting, a future hearing date to enable the court to confirm timely compliance with these requirements.

(b) By establishing and maintaining internal procedures to generate an order for appearance and consideration of appropriate sanctions or other actions if the guardian or conservator fails to comply with the requirements of this section. **Leg.H.** Added Stats 2007 ch 553 §3 (AB 1727), effective January 1, 2008.

§1457. Development of educational program for nonprofessional conservators or guardians

In order to assist relatives and friends who may seek appointment as a nonprofessional conservator or guardian the Judicial Council shall, on or before January 1, 2008, develop a short educational program of no more than three hours that is user-friendly and shall make that program available free of charge to each proposed conservator and guardian and each court-appointed conservator and guardian who is not required to be licensed as a professional conservator or guardian pursuant to Chapter 6 (commencing with Section 6500) of Division 3 of the Business and Professions Code. The program may be available by video presentation or Internet access. **Leg.H.** Added Stats 2006 ch 493 §4 (AB 1363), effective January 1, 2007. Amended Stats 2007 ch 553 §4 (AB 1727), effective January 1, 2008.

2006 Note: This act, together with Senate Bill 1116 (Scott), Senate Bill 1550 (Figueroa), and Senate Bill 1716 (Bowen), shall be known and may be cited as the Omnibus Conservatorship and Guardianship Reform Act of 2006. Stats 2006 ch 493 (AB 1363) §1.

§1458. [Section repealed 2009]

Leg.H. Added Stats 2006 ch 493 §5 (AB 1363), effective January 1, 2007. Amended Stats 2007 ch 130 §194 (AB 299), effective January 1, 2008, ch 553 §5 (AB 1727) (ch 553 prevails), effective January 1, 2007. Repealed January 1, 2009, by its own terms. The repealed section related to report on study measuring court effectiveness in conservatorship cases.

§ 1458. Court effectiveness in conservatorship cases [Repealed January 1, 2028]

(a) On or before January 1, 2027, the Judicial Council shall report to the Legislature the findings of a study measuring court effectiveness in conservatorship cases, including the effectiveness of protecting the legal rights and best interests of a conservatee. The report shall include all of the following, with respect to the courts chosen for evaluation pursuant to subdivision (b):

(1) Caseload statistics from the 2018-19 fiscal year, for both temporary and general probate conservatorships, including, at a minimum, all of the following:

(A) The number of petitions filed requesting appointment of a conservator, the number of those petitions granted, and the number denied, with cases in which a professional fiduciary was appointed presented separately from cases in which a nonprofessional conservator was appointed.

(B) The number of conservatorships under court supervision at the end of the fiscal year in which a court investigation was conducted, with cases in which a professional fiduciary was appointed presented separately from cases in which a nonprofessional conservator was appointed.

(C) The number of conservatorships under court supervision at the end of the fiscal year in which a court review hearing was held, with cases in which a professional fiduciary was appointed presented separately from cases in which a nonprofessional conservator was appointed.

(D) The number of petitions or objections filed by or on behalf of a conservatee challenging a conservator's action, failure to act, accounting, or compensation; the number of those petitions that were granted; and the number of petitions that were denied, with cases in which a professional fiduciary was appointed presented separately from cases in which a nonprofessional conservator was appointed.

(E) The number of conservatorships under court supervision in which accountings due, and the number of accountings received after they were due, or not received at all, with cases in which a professional fiduciary was appointed presented separately from cases in which a nonprofessional conservator was appointed.

(F) The number of conservatorships of the estate, or of the person and the estate, under court supervision in which bond was not required of the conservator, with cases in which a professional fiduciary was appointed presented separately from cases in which a nonprofessional conservator was appointed.

(2) An analysis of compliance with statutory timeframes in the 2018-19 fiscal year.

(3) A description of any operational differences between courts that affect the processing of conservatorship cases, including timeframes and steps taken to protect the legal rights and best interests of conservatees.

(b) The Judicial Council shall select at least three courts for the evaluation required by this section, including one small court, one medium-sized court, and one large court.

(c) The report shall include recommendations for statewide performance measures to be collected, best practices that serve to protect the legal rights of conservatees, and staffing needs to meet case processing requirements.

(d) The report shall be submitted pursuant to Section 9795 of the Government Code.

(e) This section shall remain in effect only until January 1, 2028, and as of that date is repealed. **Leg.H.** Added Stats 2021 ch 417 §4 (AB 1194), effective January 1, 2022, repealed January 1, 2026. Amended Stats 2023 ch 478 §57 (AB 1756), effective January 1, 2024, repealed January 1, 2028.

Prior Law: Former Prob C §1458, relating to court effectiveness in conservatorship cases, was added Stats 2006 ch 493 §5 (AB 1363), effective January 1, 2007, amended Stats 2007 ch 130 §194 (AB 299), effective January 1, 2008, ch 553 §5 (AB 1727) (ch 553 prevails), effective January 1, 2007, and repealed January 1, 2009, by its own terms.

§1459. Legislative findings and declarations

(a) The Legislature finds and declares the following:

(1) There is no resource that is more vital to the continued existence and integrity of recognized Indian tribes than their children, and the State of California has an interest in protecting Indian children who are members of, or are eligible for membership in, an Indian tribe. The state is committed to protecting the essential tribal relations and best interest of an Indian child by promoting practices, in accordance with the Indian Child Welfare Act (25 U.S.C. Sec. 1901 et seq.) and other applicable law, designed to prevent the child's involuntary out-of-home placement and, whenever such placement is necessary or ordered, by placing the child, whenever possible, in a placement that reflects the unique values of the child's tribal culture and is best able to assist the child in establishing, developing, and maintaining a political, cultural, and social relationship with the child's tribe and tribal community.

(2) It is in the interest of an Indian child that the child's membership in the child's Indian tribe and connection to the tribal community be encouraged and protected, regardless of whether or not the child is in the physical custody of an Indian parent or Indian custodian at the commencement of a child custody proceeding, the parental rights of the child's parents have been terminated, or where the child has resided or been domiciled.

(b) In all Indian child custody proceedings, as defined in the federal Indian Child Welfare Act, the court shall consider all of the findings contained in subdivision (a), strive to promote the stability and security of Indian tribes and families, comply with the federal Indian Child Welfare Act, and seek to protect the best interest of the child. Whenever an Indian child is removed from a foster care home or institution, guardianship, or adoptive placement for the purpose of further foster care, guardianship, or adoptive placement, placement of the child shall be in accordance with the Indian Child Welfare Act.

(c) A determination by an Indian tribe that an unmarried person, who is under the age of 18 years, is either (1) a member of an Indian tribe or (2) eligible for membership in an Indian tribe and a biological child of a member of an Indian tribe shall constitute a significant political affiliation with the tribe and shall require the application of the federal Indian Child Welfare Act to the proceedings.

(d) In any case in which this code or other applicable state or federal law provides a higher standard of protection to the rights of the parent or Indian custodian of an Indian child, or the Indian child's tribe, than the rights provided under the Indian Child Welfare Act, the court shall apply the higher state or federal standard.

(e) Any Indian child, the Indian child's tribe, or the parent or Indian custodian from whose custody the child has been removed, may petition the court to invalidate an action in an Indian child custody proceeding for foster care or guardianship placement or termination of parental rights if the action violated Sections 1911, 1912, and 1913 of the Indian Child Welfare Act. **Leg.H.** Added Stats 2006 ch 838 §17 (SB 678), effective January 1, 2007.

§1459.5. Application of Indian Child Welfare Act

(a) The Indian Child Welfare Act (25 U.S.C. Sec. 1901 et seq.) shall apply to the following guardianship or conservatorship proceedings under this division when the proposed ward or conservatee is an Indian child:

(1) In any case in which the petition is a petition for guardianship of the person and the proposed guardian is not the natural parent or Indian custodian of the proposed ward, unless the proposed guardian has been nominated by the natural parents pursuant to Section 1500 and the parents retain the right to have custody of the child returned to them upon demand.

(2) To a proceeding to have an Indian child declared free from the custody and control of one or both parents brought in a guardianship proceeding.

(3) In any case in which the petition is a petition for conservatorship of the person of a minor whose marriage has been dissolved, the proposed conservator is seeking physical custody of the minor, the proposed conservator is not the natural parent or Indian custodian of the proposed conservatee and the natural parent or Indian custodian does not retain the right to have custody of the child returned to them upon demand.

(b) When the Indian Child Welfare Act applies to a proceeding under this division, the court shall apply Sections 224.3 to 224.6, inclusive, and Sections 305.5, 361.31, and 361.7 of the Welfare and Institutions Code, and the following rules from the California Rules of Court, as they read on January 1, 2005:

(1) Paragraph (7) of subdivision (b) of Rule 1410.

(2) Subdivision (i) of Rule 1412.

(c) In the provisions cited in subdivision (b), references to social workers, probation officers, county welfare department, or probation department shall be construed as meaning the party seeking a foster care placement, guardianship, or adoption. **Leg.H.** Added Stats 2006 ch 838 §18 (SB 678), effective January 1, 2007.

CHAPTER 3
NOTICES

Notice of hearings generally. §1460.
Notice to child under 12. §1460.1.
Notice. §1460.2.
Notice to Director of State Hospitals or Director of Developmental Services. §1461.
Notice to director of regional center. §1461.4.
Notice to Veterans Administration. §1461.5.
Notice of time and place of hearing on petition, report, or account where conservatee is a missing person. §1461.7.
When service by mail deemed complete. §1467.
Reference to section governing mailing of notice of hearing as reference to this chapter. §1469.

§1460. Notice of hearings generally

(a) Subject to Sections 1202 and 1203, if notice of hearing is required under this division but the applicable provision does not fix the manner of giving notice of hearing, the notice of the time and place of the hearing shall be given at least 15 days before the day of the hearing as provided in this section.

(b) Subject to subdivision (e), the petitioner, who includes, for purposes of this section, a person filing a petition, report, or account, shall cause the notice of hearing to be delivered pursuant to Section 1215, to each of the following persons:

(1) The guardian or conservator.

(2) The ward or the conservatee.

(3) The spouse of the ward or conservatee, if the ward or conservatee has a spouse, or the domestic partner of the conservatee, if the conservatee has a domestic partner.

(4) Any person who has requested special notice of the matter, as provided in Section 2700.

(5) For any hearing on a petition to terminate a guardianship, to accept the resignation of a guardian, or to remove a guardian, the persons described in subdivision (c) of Section 1510.

(6) For any hearing to consider terminating a conservatorship, to accept the resignation of a conservator, or to remove a conservator, the persons described in subdivision (b) of Section 1821.

(c) The clerk of the court shall cause the notice of the hearing to be posted as provided in Section 1230 if the posting is required by subdivision (c) of Section 2543.

(d) Except as provided in subdivision (e), this section does not excuse compliance with the requirements for notice to a person who has requested special notice pursuant to Chapter 10 (commencing with Section 2700) of Part 4.

(e) The court, for good cause, may dispense with the notice otherwise required to be given to a person as provided in this section. **Leg.H.** Enacted Stats 1990 ch 79 §14 (AB 759), operative July 1, 1991. Amended Stats 1994 ch 806 §8 (AB 3686); Stats 1996 ch 862 §5 (AB 2751); Stats 2001 ch 893 §14 (AB 25); Stats 2017 ch 319 §26 (AB 976), effective January 1, 2018; Stats 2021 ch 417 §5 (AB 1194), effective January 1, 2022.

Prior Law: Former Prob C §1460, similar to the present section, was added Stats 1979 ch 726 §3, operative January 1, 1981, and repealed Stats 1990 ch 79 §13, operative July 1, 1991.

Former Prob C §1460, relating to power to appoint guardian, was enacted Stats 1931, amended Stats 1959 ch 500 §1, Stats 1976 ch 1357 §5, operative July 1, 1977, and repealed Stats 1979 ch 726 §1, operative January 1, 1981.

§1460.1. Notice to child under 12

Notwithstanding any other provision of this division, no notice is required to be given to any child under the age of 12 years if the court determines either of the following:

(a) Notice was properly given to a parent, guardian, or other person having legal custody of the minor, with whom the minor resides.

(b) The petition is brought by a parent, guardian, or other person having legal custody of the minor, with whom the minor resides. **Leg.H.** Added Stats 1997 ch 724 §9 (AB 1172).

§1460.2. Notice

(a) If the court or petitioner knows or has reason to know that the proposed ward or conservatee may be an Indian child, notice shall comply with subdivision (b) in any case in which the Indian Child Welfare Act (25 U.S.C. Sec. 1901 et seq.) applies, as specified in Section 1459.5.

(b) Any notice sent under this section shall be sent to the minor's parent or legal guardian, Indian custodian, if any, and the Indian child's tribe, and shall comply with all of the following requirements:

(1) Notice shall be sent by registered or certified mail with return receipt requested. Additional notice by first-class mail is recommended, but not required.

(2) Notice to the tribe shall be to the tribal chairperson, unless the tribe has designated another agent for service.

(3) Notice shall be sent to all tribes of which the child may be a member or eligible for membership until the court makes a determination as to which tribe is the Indian child's tribe in accordance with subdivision (d) of Section 1449, after which notice need only be sent to the tribe determined to be the Indian child's tribe.

(4) Notice, to the extent required by federal law, shall be sent to the Secretary of the Interior's designated agent, the Sacramento Area Director, Bureau of Indian Affairs. If the identity or location of the Indian child's tribe is known, a copy of the notice shall also be sent directly to the Secretary of the Interior, unless the Secretary of the Interior has waived the notice in writing and the person responsible for giving notice under this section has filed proof of the waiver with the court.

(5) The notice shall include all of the following information:

(A) The name, birthdate, and birthplace of the Indian child, if known.

(B) The name of any Indian tribe in which the child is a member or may be eligible for membership, if known.

(C) All names known of the Indian child's biological parents, grandparents and great-grandparents or Indian custodians, including maiden, married, and former names or aliases, as well as their current and former addresses, birthdates, places of birth and death, tribal enrollment numbers, and any other identifying information, if known.

(D) A copy of the petition.

(E) A copy of the child's birth certificate, if available.

(F) The location, mailing address, and telephone number of the court and all parties notified pursuant to this section.

(G) A statement of the following:

(i) The absolute right of the child's parents, Indian custodians, and tribe to intervene in the proceeding.

(ii) The right of the child's parents, Indian custodians, and tribe to petition the court to transfer the proceeding to the tribal court of the Indian child's tribe, absent objection by either parent and subject to declination by the tribal court.

(iii) The right of the child's parents, Indian custodians, and tribe to, upon request, be granted up to an additional 20 days from the receipt of the notice to prepare for the proceeding.

(iv) The potential legal consequences of the proceedings on the future custodial rights of the child's parents or Indian custodians.

(v) That if the parents or Indian custodians are unable to afford counsel, counsel shall be appointed to represent the parents or Indian custodians pursuant to Section 1912 of the Indian Child Welfare Act (25 U.S.C. Sec. 1901 et seq.).

(vi) That the information contained in the notice, petition, pleading, and other court documents is confidential, so any person or entity notified shall maintain the confidentiality of the information contained in the notice concerning the particular proceeding and not reveal it to anyone who does not need the information in order to exercise the tribe's rights under the Indian Child Welfare Act (25 U.S.C. Sec. 1901 et seq.).

(c) Notice shall be sent whenever it is known or there is reason to know that an Indian child is involved, and for every hearing thereafter, including, but not limited to, the hearing at which a final adoption order is to be granted. After a tribe acknowledges that the child is a member or eligible for membership in the tribe, or after the Indian child's tribe intervenes in a proceeding, the information set out in subparagraphs (C), (D), (E), and (G) of paragraph (5) of subdivision (b) need not be included with the notice.

(d) Proof of the notice, including copies of notices sent and all return receipts and responses received, shall be filed with the court in advance of the hearing except as permitted under subdivision (e).

(e) No proceeding shall be held until at least 10 days after receipt of notice by the parent, Indian custodian, the tribe or the Bureau of Indian Affairs. The parent, Indian custodian, or the tribe shall, upon request, be granted up to 20 additional days to prepare for the proceeding. Nothing herein shall be construed as limiting the rights of the parent, Indian custodian, or tribe to 10 days' notice when a lengthier notice period is required by statute.

(f) With respect to giving notice to Indian tribes, a party shall be subject to court sanctions if that person knowingly and willfully falsifies or conceals a material fact concerning whether the child is an Indian child, or counsels a party to do so.

(g) The inclusion of contact information of any adult or child that would otherwise be required to be included in the notification pursuant to this section, shall not be required if that person is at risk of harm as a result of domestic violence, child abuse, sexual abuse, or stalking. **Leg.H.** Added Stats 2006 ch 838 §19 (SB 678), effective January 1, 2007.

§1461. Notice to Director of State Hospitals or Director of Developmental Services

(a) As used in this section, "director" means:

(1) The Director of State Hospitals when the state hospital referred to in subdivision (b) is under the jurisdiction of the State Department of State Hospitals.

(2) The Director of Developmental Services when the state hospital referred to in subdivision (b) is under the jurisdiction of the State Department of Developmental Services.

(b) Notice of the time and place of hearing on the petition, report, or account, and a copy of the petition, report, or account, shall be delivered pursuant to Section 1215 to the director at the director's office in Sacramento or to the electronic address designated by the director for receipt of notice pursuant to this code, at least 15 days before the hearing if both of the following conditions exist:

(1) The ward or conservatee is or has been during the guardianship or conservatorship proceeding a patient in, or on leave from, a state hospital under the jurisdiction of the State Department of State Hospitals or the State Department of Developmental Services.

(2) The petition, report, or account is filed under any one or more of the following provisions: Section 1510, 1820, 1861, 2212, 2403, 2421, 2422, or 2423; Article 7 (commencing with Section 2540) of Chapter 6 of Part 4; Section 2580, 2592, or 2620; Chapter 9.5 (commencing with Section 2670) of Part 4; Section 3080 or 3088; or Chapter 3 (commencing with Section 3100) of Part 6. Notice under this section is not required in the case of an account pursuant to Section 2620 if the total guardianship or conservatorship assets are less than one thousand five hundred dollars ($1,500) and the gross annual income, exclusive of any public assistance income, is less than six thousand dollars ($6,000), and the ward or conservatee is not a patient in, or on leave or on outpatient status from, a state hospital at the time of the filing of the petition.

(c) If the ward or conservatee has been discharged from the state hospital, the director, upon ascertaining the facts, may file with the court a certificate stating that the ward or conservatee is not indebted to the state and waive the giving of further notices under this section. Upon the filing of the certificate of the director, compliance with this section thereafter is not required unless the certificate is revoked by the director and notice of the revocation is filed with the court.

(d) The statute of limitations does not run against any claim of the State Department of State Hospitals or the State Department of Developmental Services against the estate of the ward or conservatee for board, care, maintenance, or transportation with respect to an account that is settled without giving the notice required by this section. **Leg.H.** Enacted Stats 1990 ch 79 §14, operative July 1, 1991. Amended Stats 2012 ch 440 §39 (AB 1488), effective September 22, 2012; Stats 2017 ch 319 §27 (AB 976), effective January 1, 2018.

Prior Law: Former Prob C §1461, similar to the present section, was added Stats 1979 ch 726 §3, operative January 1, 1981, amended Stats 1981 ch 9 §1, Stats 1984 ch 797 §2, and repealed Stats 1990 ch 79 §13, operative July 1, 1991.

Former Prob C §1461, relating to petition for guardian for incompetent person, was enacted Stats 1931, amended Stats 1935 ch 668 §1, Stats 1943 ch 473 §1, Stats 1949 ch 821 §1, Stats 1953 ch 90 §1, Stats 1959 ch 500 §2, ch 1369 §1, Stats 1961 ch 497 §1, Stats 1976 ch 1357 §6, operative July 1, 1977, Stats 1978 ch 1363 §5, and repealed Stats 1979 ch 726 §1, operative January 1, 1981.

§1461.4. Notice to director of regional center

(a) The petitioner shall deliver pursuant to Section 1215 a notice of the hearing and a copy of the petition to the director of the regional center for the developmentally disabled at least 30 days before the day of the hearing on a petition for appointment in any case in which all of the following conditions exist:

(1) The proposed ward or conservatee has developmental disabilities.

(2) The proposed guardian or conservator is not the natural parent of the proposed ward or conservatee.

(3) The proposed guardian or conservator is a provider of board and care, treatment, habilitation, or other services to persons with developmental disabilities or is a spouse or employee of a provider.

(4) The proposed guardian or conservator is not a public entity.

(b) The regional center shall file a written report and recommendation with the court regarding the suitability of the petitioners to meet the needs of the proposed ward or conservatee in any case described in subdivision (a). **Leg.H.** Enacted Stats 1990 ch 79 §14 (AB 759), operative July 1, 1991. Amended Stats 2017 ch 319 §28 (AB 976), effective January 1, 2018.

Prior Law: Former Prob C §1461.4, similar to the present section, was added Stats 1985 ch 356 §2 and repealed Stats 1990 ch 79 §13, operative July 1, 1991.

§1461.5. Notice to Veterans Administration

Notice of the time and place of hearing on a petition, report, or account, and a notice of the filing of an inventory, together with a copy of the petition, report, inventory, or account, shall be delivered pursuant to Section 1215 to the office of the Veterans Administration having jurisdiction over the area in which the court is located at least 15 days before the hearing, or within 15 days after the inventory is filed, if both of the following conditions exist:

(a) The guardianship or conservatorship estate consists or will consist wholly or in part of any of the following:

(1) Money received from the Veterans Administration.

(2) Revenue or profit from such money or from property acquired wholly or in part from such money.

(3) Property acquired wholly or in part with such money or from such property.

(b) The petition, report, inventory, or account is filed under any one or more of the following provisions: Section 1510, 1601, 1820, 1861, 1874, 2422, or 2423; Article 7 (commencing with Section 2540) of Chapter 6 of Part 4; Section 2570, 2571, 2580, 2592, 2610, 2613, or 2620; Chapter 8 (commencing with Section 2640) of Part 4; Chapter 9.5 (commencing with Section 2670) of Part 4; Section 3080 or 3088; or Chapter 3 (commencing with Section 3100) of Part 6. **Leg.H.** Enacted Stats 1990 ch 79 §14 (AB 759), operative July 1, 1991. Amended Stats 2017 ch 319 §29 (AB 976), effective January 1, 2018.

Prior Law: Former Prob C §1461.5, similar to the present section, was added Stats 1980 ch 89 §2, amended Stats 1 981 ch 9 §2, and repealed Stats 1990 ch 79 §13, operative July 1, 1991.

Former Prob C §1461.5, relating to alleged incompetent, was added Stats 1973 ch 546 §54.5, effective September 17, 1973, amended Stats 1975 ch 694 §25, Stats 1976 ch 13576 §9, operative July 1, 1977, Stats 1978 ch 1363 §7, and repealed Stats 1979 ch 726 §1, operative January 1, 1981.

§1461.7. Notice of time and place of hearing on petition, report, or account where conservatee is a missing person

Unless the court for good cause dispenses with such notice, notice of the time and place of the hearing on a petition, report, or account, together with a copy of the petition, report, or account, shall be given to the same persons who are required to be given notice under Section 2581 for the period and in the manner provided in this chapter if both of the following conditions exist:

(a) A conservator of the estate has been appointed under Article 5 (commencing with Section 1845) of Chapter 1 of Part 3 for a person who is missing and whose whereabouts is unknown.

(b) The petition, report, or account is filed in the conservatorship proceeding under any one or more of the following provisions:

(1) Section 1861 or 2423.

(2) Article 7 (commencing with Section 2540) of Chapter 6 of Part 4.

(3) Section 2570, 2571, 2580, 2592, or 2620.

(4) Chapter 8 (commencing with Section 2640) of Part 4.

(5) Chapter 9.5 (commencing with Section 2670) of Part 4.

(6) Chapter 3 (commencing with Section 3100) of Part 6. **Leg.H.** Enacted Stats 1990 ch 79 §14 (AB 759), operative July 1, 1991.

Prior Law: Former Prob C §1461.7, similar to the present section, was added Stats 1983 ch 201 §5 and repealed Stats 1990 ch 79 §13, operative July 1, 1991.

§1467. When service by mail deemed complete

If service is made by mail pursuant to this division in the manner authorized in Section 415.30 of the Code of Civil Procedure, the service is complete on the date a written acknowledgment of receipt is executed. **Leg.H.** Enacted Stats 1990 ch 79 §14 (AB 759), operative July 1, 1991.

Prior Law: Former Prob C §1467, similar to the present section, was added Stats 1979 ch 726 §3, operative January 1, 1981, and repealed Stats 1990 ch 79 §13, operative July 1, 1991.

§1469. Reference to section governing mailing of notice of hearing as reference to this chapter

Where a provision of this division applies the provisions of this code applicable to personal representatives to proceedings under this division, a reference to Section 1220 in the provisions applicable to personal representatives shall be deemed to be a reference to this chapter. **Leg.H.** Enacted Stats 1990 ch 79 §14 (AB 759), operative July 1, 1991.

Prior Law: Former Prob C §1469, similar to the present section, was added Stats 1979 ch 726 §3, operative January 1, 1981, amended Stats 1980 ch 246 §4, Stats 1986 ch 783 §22, operative July 1, 1987, Stats 1987 ch 923 §62, operative July 1, 1988, and repealed Stats 1990 ch 79 §13, operative July 1, 1991.

CHAPTER 4
APPOINTMENT OF LEGAL COUNSEL

Discretionary appointment of legal counsel. §1470.
Mandatory appointment of legal counsel. §1471.
Compensation of mandatory court-appointed counsel. §1472.
Inability to afford counsel. §1474.

§1470. Discretionary appointment of legal counsel

(a) The court may appoint private legal counsel for a ward, a proposed ward, a conservatee, or a proposed conservatee in any proceeding under this division if the court determines the person is not otherwise represented by legal counsel and that the appointment would be helpful to the resolution of the matter or is necessary to protect the person's interests.

(b) If a person is furnished legal counsel under this section, the court shall, upon conclusion of the matter, fix a reasonable sum for compensation and expenses of counsel. The sum may, in the discretion of the court, include compensation for services rendered, and expenses incurred, before the date of the order appointing counsel.

(c) The court shall order the sum fixed under subdivision (b) to be paid:

(1) If the person for whom legal counsel is appointed is an adult, from the estate of that person.

(2) If the person for whom legal counsel is appointed is a minor, by a parent or the parents of the minor or from the minor's estate, or any combination thereof, in any proportions the court deems just.

(3) If a ward or proposed ward is furnished legal counsel for a guardianship proceeding, upon its own motion or that of a party, the court shall determine whether a parent or parents of the ward or proposed ward or the estate of the ward or proposed ward is financially unable to pay all or a portion of the cost of counsel appointed pursuant to this section. Any portion of the cost of that counsel that the court finds the parent or parents or the estate of the ward or proposed ward is unable to pay shall be paid by the county. The Judicial Council shall adopt guidelines to assist in determining financial eligibility for county payment of counsel appointed by the court pursuant to this chapter.

(d) The court may make an order under subdivision (c) requiring payment by a parent or parents of the minor only after the parent or parents, as the case may be, have been given notice and the opportunity to be heard on whether the order would be just under the circumstances of the particular case. **Leg.H.** Enacted Stats 1990 ch 79 §14 (AB 759), operative July 1, 1991. Amended Stats 1992 ch 572 §1.5 (SB 1455); Stats 2007 ch 719 §1 (SB 241), effective January 1, 2008.

Prior Law: Former Prob C §1470, similar to the present section, was added Stats 1979 ch 726 §3, operative January 1, 1981, and repealed Stats 1990 ch 79 §13, operative July 1, 1991.

Former Prob C §1470, relating to petition as to restoration to capacity, was enacted Stats 1931, amended Stats 1949 ch 1413 §1, Stats 1976 ch 1357 §11, operative July 1, 1977, and repealed Stats 1979 ch 726 §1, operative January 1, 1981.

§1471. Mandatory appointment of legal counsel

(a) If a conservatee, proposed conservatee, or person alleged to lack legal capacity is not represented by legal counsel and does not plan to retain counsel, whether or not that person lacks or appears to lack legal capacity, the court shall, at or before the time of the hearing, appoint the public defender or private counsel to represent the person in the following proceedings under this division:

(1) A proceeding to establish or transfer a conservatorship or to appoint a proposed conservator.

(2) A proceeding to terminate the conservatorship.

(3) A proceeding to remove the conservator.

(4) A proceeding for a court order affecting the legal capacity of the conservatee.

(5) A proceeding to obtain an order authorizing removal of a temporary conservatee from the temporary conservatee's place of residence.

(b) In a proceeding to establish a limited conservatorship, if the proposed limited conservatee has not retained legal counsel and does not plan to retain legal counsel, the court shall immediately appoint the public defender or private counsel to represent the proposed limited conservatee. The proposed limited conservatee shall pay the cost for that legal service if they are able. This subdivision applies irrespective of any medical or psychological inability to attend the hearing on the part of the proposed limited conservatee as allowed in Section 1825.

(c) If a conservatee, proposed conservatee, or person alleged to lack legal capacity expresses a preference for a particular attorney to represent them, the court shall allow representation by the preferred attorney, even if the attorney is not on the court's list of a court-appointed attorneys, and the attorney shall provide zealous representation as provided in subdivision (d). However, an attorney who cannot provide zealous advocacy or who has a conflict of interest with respect to the representation of the conservatee, proposed conservatee, or person alleged to lack legal capacity shall be disqualified.

(d) The role of legal counsel of a conservatee, proposed conservatee, or a person alleged to lack legal capacity is that of a zealous, independent advocate representing the wishes of their client, consistent with the duties set forth in Section 6068 of the Business and Professions Code and the California Rules of Professional Conduct.

(e) In an appeal or writ proceeding arising out of a proceeding described in this section, if a conservatee or proposed conservatee is not represented by legal counsel, the reviewing court shall appoint legal counsel to represent the conservatee or proposed conservatee before the court. **Leg.H.** Added Stats 1990 ch 79 §14 (AB 759), operative July 1, 1991. Amended Stats 2014 ch 553 §5 (SB 940), effective January 1, 2015, operative January 1, 2016; Stats 2021 ch 417 §6 (AB 1194), effective January 1, 2022; Stats 2022 ch 420 §32 (AB 2960), effective January 1, 2023.

Prior Law: Former Prob C §1471, similar to the present section, was added Stats 1979 ch 726 §3, operative January 1, 1981, amended Stats 1980 ch 1304 §5, and repealed Stats 1990 ch 79 §13, operative July 1, 1991.

Former Prob C §1471, relating to setting hearing as to restoration to capacity, was enacted Stats 1931, amended Stats 1949 ch 1413 §2, Stats 1976 ch 1357 §12, operative July 1, 1977, and repealed Stats 1979 ch 726 §1, operative January 1, 1981.

§1472. Compensation of mandatory court-appointed counsel

(a) If a person is furnished legal counsel under Section 1471:

(1) The court shall, upon conclusion of the matter, fix a reasonable sum for compensation and expenses of counsel and shall make a determination of the person's ability to pay all or a portion of that sum. The sum may, in the discretion of the court, include compensation for services rendered, and expenses incurred, before the date of the order appointing counsel.

(2) If the court determines that the person has the ability to pay all or a portion of the sum, the court shall order the conservator of the estate or, if none, the person, to pay in any installments and in any manner the court determines to be reasonable and compatible with the person's financial ability.

(3) In a proceeding under Chapter 3 (commencing with Section 3100) of Part 6 for court authorization of a proposed transaction involving community property, the court may order payment out of the proceeds of the transaction.

(4) If a conservator is not appointed for the person furnished legal counsel, the order for payment may be enforced in the same manner as a money judgment.

(b) If the court determines that a person furnished private counsel under Section 1471 lacks the ability to pay all or a portion of the sum determined under paragraph (1) of subdivision (a), the county shall pay the sum to the private counsel to the extent the court determines the person is unable to pay.

(c) The payment ordered by the court under subdivision (a) shall be made to the county if the public defender has been appointed or if private counsel has been appointed to perform the duties of the public defender and the county has compensated that counsel. In the case of other court-appointed counsel, the payment shall be made to that counsel. **Leg.H.** Enacted Stats 1990 ch 79 §14 (AB 759), operative July 1, 1991. Amended Stats 1992 ch 572 §2 (SB 1455).

Prior Law: Former Prob C §1472, similar to the present section, was added Stats 1979 ch 726 §3, operative January 1, 1981, and repealed Stats 1990 ch 79 §13, operative July 1, 1991.

Former Prob C §1472, relating to right to contest relief regarding incompetency, was enacted Stats 1931, amended Stats 1949 ch 1413 §3, Stats 1976 ch 1357 §13, operative July 1, 1977, Stats 1978 ch 1363 §9, and repealed Stats 1979 ch 726 §1, operative January 1, 1981.

§1474. Inability to afford counsel

If an Indian custodian or biological parent of an Indian child lacks the financial ability to retain counsel and requests the appointment of counsel in proceedings described in Section 1459.5, the provisions of subsection (b) of Section 1912 of the Indian Child Welfare Act (25 U.S.C. Sec. 1901 et seq.) and Section 23.13 of Title 25 of the Code of Federal Regulations are applicable. **Leg.H.** Added Stats 2006 ch 838 §20 (SB 678), effective January 1, 2007.

CHAPTER 5
TRANSITIONAL PROVISIONS

Effect of nomination by adult of guardian for such adult. §1488.
Effect of appointment of guardian by parent or other person for a minor. §1489.
References in statutes. §1490.

§1488. Effect of nomination by adult of guardian for such adult

If before January 1, 1981, an adult has in a signed writing nominated a person to serve as guardian if a guardian is in the future appointed for such adult, such nomination shall be deemed to be a nomination of a conservator. This section applies whether or not the signed writing was executed in the same manner as a witnessed will so long as the person signing the writing had at the time the writing was signed sufficient capacity to form an intelligent preference. **Leg.H.** Enacted Stats 1990 ch 79 §14 (AB 759), operative July 1, 1991.

Prior Law: Former Prob C §1488, similar to the present section, was added Stats 1979 ch 726 §3, operative January 1, 1981, and repealed Stats 1990 ch 79 §13, operative July 1, 1991.

Former Prob C §1488, similar to present CCP §§996.110– 996.150, was added Stats 1955 ch 775 §1, and repealed Stats 1979 ch 726 §1, operative January 1, 1981.

§1489. Effect of appointment of guardian by parent or other person for a minor

If, before January 1, 1981, a parent or other person has in a signed writing appointed a person to serve as the guardian of the person or estate or both of a minor, or as the guardian of the property the minor receives from or by designation of the person making the appointment, such appointment shall be deemed to be a nomination of a guardian if the requirements of Section 1500 or 1501 are satisfied and, in such case, shall be given the same effect it would have under Section 1500 or 1501, as the case may be, if made on or after January 1, 1981. This section applies whether or not the signed writing is a will or deed so long as the person signing the writing had at the time the writing was signed sufficient capacity to form an intelligent preference. **Leg.H.** Enacted Stats 1990 ch 79 §14 (AB 759), operative July 1, 1991.

Prior Law: Former Prob C §1489, similar to the present section, was added Stats 1979 ch 726 §3, operative January 1, 1981, and repealed Stats 1990 ch 79 §13, operative July 1, 1991.

Former Prob C §1489, similar to present CCP §§996.110–996.150, was added Stats 1955 ch 775 §1, and repealed Stats 1979 ch 726 §1, operative January 1, 1981.

§1490. References in statutes

Except as set forth in Section 1510.1, when used in any statute of this state with reference to an adult or to the person of a married minor, "guardian" means the conservator of that adult or the conservator of the person in the case of the married minor. **Leg.H.** Enacted Stats 1990 ch 79 §14 (AB 759), operative July 1, 1991. Amended Stats 2015 ch 694 §2 (AB 900), effective January 1, 2016; Stats 2016 ch 86 §244 (SB 1171), effective January 1, 2017.

2015 Note: (a) The Legislature finds and declares all of the following:

(1) California law grants the superior courts jurisdiction to make judicial determinations regarding the custody and care of children within the meaning of the federal Immigration and Nationality Act, including the juvenile, probate, and family court divisions of the superior court. These courts are empowered to make the findings necessary for a child to petition the United States Citizenship and Immigration Services for classification as a special immigrant juvenile under federal law.

(2) Special immigrant juvenile status, under the federal Immigration and Nationality Act, offers interim relief from deportation to undocumented immigrant children under 21 years of age, if a state juvenile court has made specific findings.

(3) The findings necessary for a child to petition for classification as a special immigrant juvenile include, among others, a finding that reunification with one or both parents is not viable due to abuse, neglect, abandonment, or a similar basis under state law, and a finding that it is not in the child's best interest to be returned to his or her country of origin.

(4) Despite recent changes to law that eliminate ambiguity regarding the jurisdiction of superior courts to make the findings necessary to petition for special immigrant juvenile status, misalignment between state and federal law continues to exist.

(5) Federal law allows a person under 21 years of age, who otherwise meets the requirements for special immigrant juvenile status, to file for relief as a special immigrant juvenile. In California, however, individuals who are between 18 and 21 years of age have largely been unable to obtain the findings from the superior court necessary to seek special immigrant juvenile status and the relief that it was intended to afford them, solely because probate courts cannot take jurisdiction of individuals 18 years of age or older by establishing a guardianship of the person. This is true despite the fact that many unaccompanied immigrant youth between 18 and 21 years of age face circumstances identical to those faced by their younger counterparts.

(6) Given the recent influx of unaccompanied immigrant children arriving to the United States, many of whom have been released to family members and other adults in California and have experienced parental abuse, neglect, or abandonment, it is necessary to provide an avenue for these unaccompanied children to petition the probate courts to have a guardian of the person appointed beyond reaching 18 years of age. This is particularly necessary in light of the vulnerability of this class of unaccompanied youth, and their need for a custodial relationship with a responsible adult as they adjust to a new cultural context, language, and education system, and recover from the trauma of abuse, neglect, or abandonment. These custodial arrangements promote permanency and the long-term well-being of immigrant children present in the United States who have experienced abuse, neglect, or abandonment.

(7) Guardianships of the person may be necessary and convenient for these individuals between 18 and 21 years of age, although a youth for whom a guardian has been appointed retains the rights that an adult may have under California law.

(b) It is the intent of the Legislature to give the probate court jurisdiction to appoint a guardian for a person between 18 and 21 years of age in connection with a special immigrant juvenile status petition. It is further the intent of the Legislature to provide an avenue for a person between 18 and 21 years of age to have a guardian of the person appointed beyond 18 years of age in conjunction with a request for the findings necessary to enable the person to petition the United States Citizenship and Immigration Services for classification as a special immigrant juvenile. Stats 2015 ch 694 (AB 900) §1.

Prior Law: Former Prob C §1490, similar to the present section, was added Stats 1979 ch 726 §3, operative January 1, 1981, and repealed Stats 1990 ch 79 §13, operative July 1, 1991.

Former Prob C §1490, similar to present CCP §§996.110–996.150, was added Stats 1955 ch 775 §1, and repealed Stats 1979 ch 726 §1, operative January 1, 1981.

PART 2
GUARDIANSHIP

Chapter 1. Establishment of Guardianship.
Chapter 2. Termination.
Chapter 3. Permanent and Stable Home.

CHAPTER 1
ESTABLISHMENT OF GUARDIANSHIP

Article 1. Nomination of Guardian.
Article 2. Appointment of Guardian Generally.
Article 3. Nonrelative Guardianships.

ARTICLE 1
Nomination of Guardian

Nomination of guardian of person or estate or both by parent. §1500.
Consent to nomination of guardian. §1500.1.
Nomination of guardian as to particular property. §1501.
Manner of making nomination; When effective; Effect of subsequent legal incapacity or death of nominator. §1502.

§1500. Nomination of guardian of person or estate or both by parent

Subject to Section 1502, a parent may nominate a guardian of the person or estate, or both, of a minor child in either of the following cases:

(a) Where the other parent nominates, or consents in writing to the nomination of, the same guardian for the same child.

(b) Where, at the time the petition for appointment of the guardian is filed, either (1) the other parent is dead or lacks legal capacity to consent to the nomination or (2) the consent of the other parent would not be required for an adoption of the child. **Leg.H.** Enacted Stats 1990 ch 79 §14 (AB 759), operative July 1, 1991.

Prior Law: Former Prob C §1500, similar to the present section, was added Stats 1979 ch 726 §3, operative January 1, 1981, and repealed Stats 1990 ch 79 §13 (AB 759), operative July 1, 1991.

Former Prob C §1500, similar to present Prob C §§1600, 1601, 2351, 2352, 2356, 2401, was enacted Stats 1931, amended Stats 1959 ch 1983 §1, Stats 1961 ch 608 §2, Stats 1976 ch 1357 §14, operative July 1, 1977, Stats 1978 ch 1315 §1, and repealed Stats 1979 ch 726 §1, operative January 1, 1981.

§1500.1. Consent to nomination of guardian

(a) Notwithstanding any other section in this part, and in accordance with Section 1913 of the Indian Child Welfare Act (25 U.S.C. Sec. 1901 et seq.), consent to nomination of a guardian of the person or of a guardian of the person and the estate given by an Indian child's parent is not valid unless both of the following occur:

(1) The consent is executed in writing at least 10 days after the child's birth and recorded before a judge.

(2) The judge certifies that the terms and consequences of the consent were fully explained in detail in English and were fully understood by the parent or that they were interpreted into a language that the parent understood.

(b) The parent of an Indian child may withdraw his or her consent to guardianship for any reason at any time prior to the issuance of letters of guardianship and the child shall be returned to the parent. **Leg.H.** Added Stats 2006 ch 838 §21 (SB 678), effective January 1, 2007.

§1501. Nomination of guardian as to particular property

Subject to Section 1502, a parent or any other person may nominate a guardian for property that a minor receives from or by designation of the nominator (whether before, at the time of, or after the nomination) including, but not limited to, property received by the minor by virtue of a gift, deed, trust, will, succession, insurance, or benefits of any kind. **Leg.H.** Enacted Stats 1990 ch 79 §14 (AB 759), operative July 1, 1991.

Prior Law: Former Prob C §1501, similar to the present section, was added Stats 1979 ch 726 §3, operative January 1, 1981, and repealed Stats 1990 ch 79 §13, operative July 1, 1991.

Former Prob C §1501, similar to present Prob C §§2430, 2451, 2462, 2500–2507, was enacted Stats 1931, amended Stats 1935 ch 724 §6, and repealed Stats 1979 ch 726 §1, operative January 1, 1981.

§1502. Manner of making nomination; When effective; Effect of subsequent legal incapacity or death of nominator

(a) A nomination of a guardian under this article may be made in the petition for the appointment of the guardian or at the hearing on the petition or in a writing signed either before or after the petition for the appointment of the guardian is filed.

(b) The nomination of a guardian under this article is effective when made except that a writing nominating a guardian under this article may provide that the nomination becomes effective only upon the occurrence of such specified condition or conditions as are stated in the writing, including but not limited to such conditions as the subsequent legal incapacity or death of the person making the nomination.

(c) Unless the writing making the nomination expressly otherwise provides, a nomination made under this article remains effective notwithstanding the subsequent legal incapacity or death of the person making the nomination. **Leg.H.** Enacted Stats 1990 ch 79 §14 (AB 759), operative July 1, 1991.

Prior Law: Former Prob C §1502, similar to the present section, was added Stats 1979 ch 726 §3, operative January 1, 1981, and repealed Stats 1990 ch 79 §13, operative July 1, 1991.

Former Prob C §1502, similar to present Prob C §§2401, 2420, was enacted Stats 1931, and repealed Stats 1979 ch 726 §1, operative January 1, 1981.

§1503. [Section repealed 1981]

Leg.H. Enacted Stats 1931 ch 281 §1503. Repealed Stats 1979 ch 726 §1, operative January 1, 1981. See Prob C §2404.

§§1504, 1505. [Sections repealed 1981]

Leg.H. Enacted Stats 1931 ch 281. Amended Stats 1975 ch 718 §§9, 10. Repealed Stats 1979 ch 726 §1, operative January 1, 1981. See Prob C §2422.

§§1506, 1507. [Sections repealed 1981]

Leg.H. Enacted Stats 1931 ch 281. Amended Stats 1971 ch 248 §§1, 2. Repealed Stats 1979 ch 726 §1, operative January 1, 1981. See Prob C §§2463, 2506.

§§1508, 1509. [Sections repealed 1981]

Leg.H. Enacted Stats 1931 ch 281. Repealed Stats 1979 ch 726 §1, operative January 1, 1981. See Prob C §2463; Fam C §6602.

ARTICLE 2
Appointment of Guardian Generally

Petition for appointment. §1510.
Appointment of guardian for unmarried individual who is at least 18 years of age, but less than 21 years of age. §1510.1.
Notice of hearing. §1511.
Amendment of petition to disclose newly discovered proceeding affecting custody. §1512.
Investigation and report by court-designated officer; Referrals to child welfare services agency; Examinations; Confidentiality. §1513.
Assessment for expense of county investigation and review. §1513.1.
Annual status report by guardian; Form and contents; Confidentiality. §1513.2.
Appointment of guardian. §1514.
Family court to provide available information. §1514.5.
No guardian of person for married minor. §1515.
Notice to local agency designated to investigate guardianships. §1516.
When proceeding to have child declared free from parental custody and control may be brought in guardianship proceeding, in adoption action, or separate action filed for that purpose; Appointment of investigator and written report; Rights of parent. §1516.5.
Application of part; Administration of funds for the benefit of the child. §1517.

§1510. Petition for appointment

(a) A relative or other person on behalf of the minor, or the minor if 12 years of age or older, may file a petition for the appointment of a guardian of the minor. A relative may file a petition for the appointment of a guardian under this section regardless of the relative's immigration status.

(b) The petition shall request that a guardian of the person or estate of the minor, or both, be appointed, shall specify the name and address of the proposed guardian and the name and date of birth of the proposed ward, and shall state that the appointment is necessary or convenient.

(c) The petition shall set forth, so far as is known to the petitioner, the names and addresses of all of the following:

(1) The parents of the proposed ward.

(2) The person having legal custody of the proposed ward and, if that person does not have the care of the proposed ward, the person having the care of the proposed ward.

(3) The relatives of the proposed ward within the second degree.

(4) In the case of a guardianship of the estate, the spouse of the proposed ward.

(5) Any person nominated as guardian for the proposed ward under Section 1500 or 1501.

(6) In the case of a guardianship of the person involving an Indian child, any Indian custodian and the Indian child's tribe.

(d) If the petitioner or proposed guardian is a professional fiduciary, as described in Section 2340, who is required to be licensed under the Professional Fiduciaries Act (Chapter 6 (commencing with Section 6500) of Division 3 of the Business and Professions Code), the petition shall include the following:

(1) The petitioner's or proposed guardian's proposed hourly fee schedule or another statement of his or her proposed compensation from the estate of the proposed ward for services performed as a guardian. The petitioner's or proposed guardian's provision of a proposed hourly fee schedule or another statement of his or her proposed compensation, as required by this paragraph, shall not preclude a court from later reducing the petitioner's or proposed guardian's fees or other compensation.

(2) Unless a petition for appointment of a temporary guardian that contains the statements required by this paragraph is filed together with a petition for appointment of a guardian, both of the following:

(A) A statement of the petitioner's or proposed guardian's license information.

(B) A statement explaining who engaged the petitioner or proposed guardian or how the petitioner or proposed guardian was engaged to file the petition for appointment of a guardian or to agree to accept the appointment as guardian and what prior relationship the petitioner or proposed guardian had with the proposed ward or the proposed ward's family or friends.

(e) If the proposed ward is a patient in or on leave of absence from a state institution under the jurisdiction of the State Department of State Hospitals or the State Department of Developmental Services and that fact is known to the petitioner or proposed guardian, the petition shall state that fact and name the institution.

(f) The petition shall state, so far as is known to the petitioner or proposed guardian, whether or not the proposed ward is receiving or is entitled to receive benefits from the Veterans Administration and the estimated amount of the monthly benefit payable by the Veterans Administration for the proposed ward.

(g) If the petitioner or proposed guardian has knowledge of any pending adoption, juvenile court, marriage dissolution, domestic relations, custody, or other similar proceeding affecting the proposed ward, the petition shall disclose the pending proceeding.

(h) If the petitioners or proposed guardians have accepted or intend to accept physical care or custody of the child with intent to adopt, whether formed at the time of placement or formed subsequent to placement, the petitioners or proposed guardians shall so state in the guardianship petition, whether or not an adoption petition has been filed.

(i) If the proposed ward is or becomes the subject of an adoption petition, the court shall order the guardianship petition consolidated with the adoption petition, and the consolidated case shall be heard and decided in the court in which the adoption is pending.

(j) If the proposed ward is or may be an Indian child, the petition shall state that fact. **Leg.H.** Enacted Stats 1990 ch 79 §14 (AB 759), operative July 1, 1991. Amended Stats 1992 ch 1064 §1 (SB 1445); Stats 2006 ch 838 §22 (SB 678), effective January 1, 2007; Stats 2008 ch 534 §12 (SB 1726), effective January 1, 2009; Stats 2012 ch 440 §40 (AB 1488), effective September 22, 2012, ch 845 §2 (SB 1064), effective January 1, 2013 (ch 845 prevails); Stats 2013 ch 248 §1 (AB 1339), effective January 1, 2014.

Prior Law: Former Prob C §1510, similar to the present section, was added Stats 1979 ch 726 §3, operative January 1, 1981, amended Stats 1980 ch 89 §3, Stats 1988 ch 1382 §3, and repealed Stats 1990 ch 79 §13, operative July 1, 1991.

Former Prob C §1510, similar to present Prob C §§23, 1446, 1490, 3600– 3603, 3610, 3611, 3612, was added Stats 1963 ch 127 §3, amended Stats 1970 ch 293 §1, Stats 1972 ch 579 §41.2, Stats 1973 ch 233 §1, Stats 1976 ch 875 §3, ch 1357 §17.5, operative July 1, 1977, and repealed Stats 1979 ch 726 §1, operative January 1, 1981.

§1510.1. Appointment of guardian for unmarried individual who is at least 18 years of age, but less than 21 years of age

(a)(1) With the consent of the proposed ward, the court may appoint a guardian of the person for an unmarried individual who is 18 years of age or older, but who has not yet attained 21 years of age, in connection with a petition to make the necessary findings regarding special immigrant juvenile status pursuant to subdivision (b) of Section 155 of the Code of Civil Procedure. **The court may appoint a parent as the guardian of the person of their unmarried child who is 18 years of age or older, but who has not yet attained 21 years of age.**

(2) A petition for guardianship of the person of a proposed ward who is 18 years of age or older, but who has not yet attained 21 years of age, may be filed by a parent, relative, or any other person on behalf of the proposed ward, or the proposed ward.

(b)(1) At the request of, or with the consent of, the ward, the court may extend an existing guardianship of the person for a ward past 18 years of age, for purposes of allowing the ward to complete the application process with the United States Citizenship and Immigration Services for classification as a special immigrant juvenile pursuant to Section 1101(a)(27)(J) of Title 8 of the United States Code.

(2) A relative or any other person on behalf of a ward, or the ward, may file a petition to extend the guardianship of the person for a period of time not to extend beyond the ward reaching 21 years of age.

(c) This section does not authorize the guardian to abrogate any of the rights that a person who has attained 18 years of age may have as an adult under state law, including, but not limited to, decisions regarding the ward's medical treatment, education, or residence, without the ward's express consent.

(d) For purposes of this division, the terms "child," "minor," and "ward" include an unmarried individual who is younger than 21 years of age and who, pursuant to this section, consents to the appointment of a guardian or extension of a guardianship after [1] **they attain** 18 years of age.

(e) The Judicial Council shall, by July 1, 2016, adopt any rules and forms needed to implement this section. **Leg.H.** Added Stats 2015 ch 694 §3 (AB 900), effective January 1, 2016. Amended Stats 2016 ch 86 §245 (SB 1171), effective January 1, 2017; Stats 2018 ch 209 §1 (AB 2090), effective January 1, 2019; Stats 2024 ch 955 §2 (AB 2224), effective January 1, 2025.

§1510.1. 2024 Deletes. [1] he or she attains

2015 Note: For legislative findings and declarations, see the 2015 Note following Prob C §1490.

§1511. Notice of hearing

(a) Except as provided in subdivisions (f) and (g), at least 15 days before the hearing on the petition for the appointment of a guardian, notice of the time and place of the hearing shall be given as provided in subdivisions (b), (c), (d), and (e) of this section. The notice shall be accompanied by a copy of the petition and shall include a copy of the form required by Section 68511.1 of the Government Code. The court shall not shorten the time for giving the notice of hearing under this section.

(b) Notice shall be served in the manner provided in Section 415.10 or 415.30 of the Code of Civil Procedure, or in any manner authorized by the court, on all of the following persons:

(1) The proposed ward if 12 years of age or older.

(2) Any person having legal custody of the proposed ward, or serving as guardian of the estate of the proposed ward.

(3) The parents of the proposed ward.

(4) Any person nominated as a guardian for the proposed ward under Section 1500 or 1501.

(c) Notice shall be delivered pursuant to Section 1215 to the addresses stated in the petition, or in any manner authorized by the court, to all of the following:

(1) The spouse named in the petition.

(2) The relatives named in the petition, except that if the petition is for the appointment of a guardian of the estate only the court may dispense with the giving of notice to any one or more or all of the relatives.

(3) The person having the care of the proposed ward if other than the person having legal custody of the proposed ward.

(d) If notice is required by Section 1461 or 1542 to be given to the Director of State Hospitals or the Director of Developmental Services or the Director of Social Services, notice shall be delivered pursuant to Section 1215 as required.

(e) If the petition states that the proposed ward is receiving or is entitled to receive benefits from the Veterans Administration, notice shall be delivered pursuant to Section 1215 to the office of the Veterans Administration referred to in Section 1461.5.

(f) Unless the court orders otherwise, notice shall not be given to any of the following:

(1) The parents or other relatives of a proposed ward who has been relinquished to a licensed adoption agency.

(2) The parents of a proposed ward who has been judicially declared free from their custody and control.

(g) Notice need not be given to any person if the court so orders upon a determination of either of the following:

(1) The person cannot with reasonable diligence be given the notice.

(2) The giving of the notice would be contrary to the interest of justice.

(h) Before the appointment of a guardian is made, proof shall be made to the court that each person entitled to notice under this section either:

(1) Has been given notice as required by this section.

(2) Has not been given notice as required by this section because the person cannot with reasonable diligence be given the notice or because the giving of notice to that person would be contrary to the interest of justice.

(i) If notice is required by Section 1460.2 to be given to an Indian custodian or tribe, notice shall be mailed as required. **Leg.H.** Enacted Stats 1990 ch 79 §14 (AB 759), operative July 1, 1991. Amended Stats 1992 ch 1064 §2 (SB 1445); Stats 1996 ch 563 §6 (SB 392); Stats 2006 ch 838 §23 (SB 678), effective January 1, 2007; Stats 2012 ch 440 §41 (AB 1488), effective September 22, 2012; Stats 2017 ch 319 §30 (AB 976), effective January 1, 2018; Stats 2021 ch 578 §2 (AB 260), effective January 1, 2022.

Prior Law: Former Prob C §1511, similar to the present section, was added Stats 1979 ch 726 §3, operative January 1, 1981, amended Stats 1980 ch 89 §4, and repealed Stats 1990 ch 79 §13, operative July 1, 1991.

Former Prob C §1511, similar to present Prob C §3601, was enacted Stats 1931, and repealed Stats 1979 ch 726 §§1, 2, operative January 1, 1981.

§1512. Amendment of petition to disclose newly discovered proceeding affecting custody

Within 10 days after the petitioner in the guardianship proceeding becomes aware of any proceeding not disclosed in the guardianship petition affecting the custody of the proposed ward (including any adoption, juvenile court, marriage dissolution, domestic relations, or other similar proceeding affecting the proposed ward), the petitioner shall amend the guardianship petition to disclose the other proceeding. **Leg.H.** Enacted Stats 1990 ch 79 §14 (AB 759), operative July 1, 1991.

Prior Law: Former Prob C §1512, similar to the present section, was added Stats 1979 ch 726 §3, operative January 1, 1981, and repealed Stats 1990 ch 79 §13, operative July 1, 1991.

Former Prob C §1512, similar to present Prob C §§2358, 2402, was enacted Stats 1931, and repealed Stats 1979 ch 726 §§1, 2, operative January 1, 1981.

§1513. Investigation and report by court-designated officer; Referrals to child welfare services agency; Examinations; Confidentiality

(a) Unless waived by the court for good cause, a court investigator, probation officer, or domestic relations investigator shall make an investigation and file with the court a report and recommendation concerning each proposed guardianship of the person or guardianship of the estate. Investigations where the proposed guardian is a relative shall be made by a court investigator. Investigations where the proposed guardian is a nonrelative shall be made by the county agency designated to investigate potential dependency. The report of the investigation for a guardianship of the person shall include, but need not be limited to, a discussion of all of the following:

(1) A social history of the proposed guardian.

(2) A social history of the proposed ward, including, to the extent feasible, an assessment of any identified developmental, emotional, psychological, or educational needs of the proposed ward and the capability of the proposed guardian to meet those needs.

(3) The relationship of the proposed ward to the proposed guardian, including the duration and character of the relationship, the circumstances under which the proposed guardian took physical custody of the proposed ward, and a statement of the proposed ward's wishes concerning the proposed guardianship, unless the proposed ward's developmental, physical, or emotional condition prevents the proposed ward from forming or stating their wishes concerning the proposed guardianship.

(4) The duration of the guardianship anticipated by the parents and the proposed guardian and the plans of each parent and the proposed guardian to provide a stable and permanent home for the child. The court may waive this requirement when no parent is available.

(b) If the proposed ward is or may be described by Section 300 of the Welfare and Institutions Code, the court may refer the matter, in writing, to the local child welfare agency to initiate an investigation pursuant to Section 329 of the Welfare and Institutions Code. The referral shall include a summary of the reasons for the referral and may include a copy of the petition under Section 1510, the investigator's report filed pursuant to subdivision (a), and any other material information.

(1) Pursuant to the timeline in Section 329 of the Welfare and Institutions Code, the child welfare agency shall report the findings and conclusions of its investigation, any decision made as a result, and the reasons for the decision to the probate court.

(2) The probate court shall not hear and determine the petition to appoint a guardian of the minor until the child welfare agency has completed its investigation and has submitted the report to the probate court.

(3) Notwithstanding paragraph (2), pending completion of the child welfare investigation, the probate court may take any reasonable steps it deems appropriate to protect the child's safety, including, but not limited to, appointing a temporary guardian or issuing a temporary restraining order.

(4) If the child welfare agency has not, within three weeks of the referral, notified the probate court that it has commenced juvenile dependency proceedings, the probate court or counsel appointed pursuant to Section 1470 to represent the minor may apply to the juvenile court, pursuant to Section 331 of the Welfare and Institutions Code, for an order directing the agency to commence juvenile dependency proceedings.

(5) If the juvenile court commences dependency proceedings, the guardianship proceedings shall be stayed in accordance with Section 304 of the Welfare and Institutions Code. This section does not affect the applicability of Section 16504 or 16506 of the Welfare and Institutions Code. If the juvenile court does not commence dependency proceedings, the probate court shall retain jurisdiction to hear and determine the guardianship petition.

(c) Before ruling on the petition for guardianship, the court shall read and consider all reports submitted pursuant to this section and shall affirm that it has done so in the minutes or on the record. A person who reports to the court pursuant to this section may be called and examined by any party to the proceeding.

(d) All reports authorized by this section are confidential and shall only be made available to persons who have been served in the proceedings or their attorneys. The clerk of the court shall make provisions to limit access to the reports exclusively to persons entitled to receipt. The reports shall be made available to all parties entitled to receipt no less than three court days before the hearing on the guardianship petition.

(e) For the purpose of writing either report authorized by this section, the person making the investigation and report shall have access to the proposed ward's school records, probation records, and public and private social services records, and to an oral or written summary of the proposed ward's medical records and psychological records prepared by any physician, psychologist, or psychiatrist who made or who is maintaining those records. The physician, psychologist, or psychiatrist shall be available to clarify information regarding these records pursuant to the investigator's responsibility to gather and provide information for the court.

(f) This section does not apply to guardianships resulting from a permanency plan for a dependent child pursuant to Section 366.26 of the Welfare and Institutions Code.

(g) For purposes of this section, a "relative" means a person who is a spouse, parent, stepparent, brother, sister, stepbrother, stepsister, half-brother, half-sister, uncle, aunt, niece, nephew, first cousin, or any person denoted by the prefix "grand" or "great," or the spouse of any of these persons, even after the marriage has been terminated by death or dissolution.

(h) In an Indian child custody proceeding, any person making an investigation and report shall consult with the Indian child's tribe and include in the report information provided by the tribe.

(i) It is the intent of the Legislature that the guardianship laws in this code and the juvenile court laws in the Welfare and Institutions Code operate together as a cohesive statutory structure that ensures all cases referred by the probate court for a child welfare investigation are subject to review by the juvenile court without limiting the probate court's ability to take immediate action to protect the child while the child welfare investigation and juvenile court review are pending. The purpose of this statutory structure is to ensure the protection of every child's health, safety, and welfare and to provide due process to every child, parent, and family.

(j) On or before January 1, 2023, the Judicial Council shall adopt, amend, or revise any rules or forms necessary to implement this section. **Leg.H.** Enacted Stats 1990 ch 79 §14 (AB 759), operative July 1, 1991. Amended Stats 1992 ch 572 §3 (SB 1455); Stats 1993 ch 59 §16 (SB 443), effective June 30, 1993; Stats 1996 ch 563 §7 (SB 392); Stats 2002 ch 784 §576 (SB 1316); Stats 2006 ch 838 §24 (SB 678), effective January 1, 2007; Stats 2012 ch 638 §14 (AB 1757), effective January 1, 2013; Stats 2021 ch 578 §3 (AB 260), effective January 1, 2022.

Prior Law: Former Prob C §1513, similar to the present section, was added Stats 1986 ch 107 §2 and repealed Stats 1990 ch 79 §13, operative July 1, 1991.

Former Prob C §1513, similar to the present section, was added Stats 1979 ch 726 §3, operative January 1, 1981, and repealed Stats 1986 ch 1017 §1.

Former Prob C §1513, similar to present Prob C §§23, 2453, 2456, was enacted Stats 1931, amended Stats 1959 ch 308 §4, Stats 1973 ch 233 §2, and repealed Stats 1979 ch 726 §§1, 2, operative January 1, 1981.

§1513.1. Assessment for expense of county investigation and review

(a) Each court or county shall assess (1) the parent, parents, or other person charged with the support and maintenance of the ward or proposed ward, and (2) the guardian, proposed guardian, or the estate of the ward or proposed ward, for court or county expenses incurred for any investigation or review conducted by the court investigator, probation officer, or domestic relations investigator. Subject to Section 68631 of the Government Code, the court may order reimbursement to the court or to the county in the amount of the assessment, unless the court finds that all or any part of the assessment would impose a hardship on the ward or the ward's estate. A county may waive any or all of an assessment against the guardianship on the basis of hardship. There shall be a rebuttable presumption that the assessment would impose a hardship if the ward is receiving Medi-Cal benefits.

(b) Any amount chargeable as state-mandated local costs incurred by a county for the cost of the investigation or review shall be reduced by any assessments actually collected by the county pursuant to subdivision (a) during that fiscal year. **Leg.H.** Added Stats 1990 ch 79 §14 (AB 759), operative July 1, 1991. Amended Stats 1991 ch 82 §4 (SB 896), effective June 30, 1991, operative July 1, 1991; Stats 1996 ch 563 §8 (SB 392); Stats 2002 ch 1008 §27 (AB 3028); Stats 2003 ch 62 §242 (SB 600); Stats 2014 ch 913 §27.5 (AB 2747), effective January 1, 2015.

2003 Note: No change was made to the text of the statute by Stats 2003 ch 62 (SB 600).

Prior Law: Former Prob C §1513.1, similar to the present section, was added Stats 1986 ch 1017 §3, repealed Stats 1990 ch 79 §13, operative July 1, 1991, amended Stats 1990 ch 1208 §1, effective September 24, 1990, and repealed Stats 1991 ch 82 §4, effective June 30, 1991, operative July 1, 1991.

§1513.2. Annual status report by guardian; Form and contents; Confidentiality

(a) To the extent resources are available, the court shall implement procedures, as described in this section, to ensure that every guardian annually completes and returns to the court a status report, including the statement described in subdivision (b). A guardian who willfully submits any material information required by the form which he or she knows to be false shall be guilty of a misdemeanor. Not later than one month before the date the status report is required to be returned, the clerk of the court shall deliver a notice pursuant to Section 1215 to the guardian informing the guardian that he or she is required to complete and return the status report to the court. The clerk shall enclose with the letter a blank status report form for the guardian to complete and return. If the status report is not completed and returned as required, or if the court finds, after a status report has been completed and returned, that further information is needed, the court shall attempt to obtain the information required in the report from the guardian or other sources. If the court is unable to obtain this information within 30 days after the date the status report is due, the court shall either order the guardian to make himself or herself available to the investigator for purposes of investigation of the guardianship, or to show cause why the guardian should not be removed.

(b) The Judicial Council shall develop a form for the status report. The form shall include the following statement: "A guardian who willfully submits any material information required by this form which he or she knows to be false is guilty of a misdemeanor." The form shall request information the Judicial Council deems necessary to determine the status of the guardianship, including, but not limited to, the following:

(1) The guardian's present address and electronic address.

(2) The name and birth date of the child under guardianship.

(3) The name of the school in which the child is enrolled, if any.

(4) If the child is not in the guardian's home, the name, relationship, address, electronic address, and telephone number of the person or persons with whom the child resides.

(5) If the child is not in the guardian's home, why the child was moved.

(c) The report authorized by this section is confidential and shall only be made available to persons who have been served in the proceedings or their attorneys. The clerk of the court shall implement procedures for the limitation of the report exclusively to persons entitled to its receipt. **Leg.H.** Added Stats 2002 ch 1115 §2 (AB 3036). Amended Stats 2017 ch 319 §31 (AB 976), effective January 1, 2018.

§1514. Appointment of guardian

(a) Upon hearing of the petition, if it appears necessary or convenient, the court may appoint a guardian of the person or estate of the proposed ward or both.

(b)(1) In appointing a guardian of the person, the court is governed by Chapter 1 (commencing with Section 3020) and Chapter 2 (commencing with Section 3040) of Part 2 of Division 8 of the Family Code, relating to custody of a minor.

(2) Except as provided in Section **1510.1 or** 2105, a minor's parent may not be appointed as a guardian of the person of the minor.

(c) The court shall appoint a guardian nominated under Section 1500 insofar as the nomination relates to the guardianship of the estate unless the court determines that the nominee is unsuitable. If the nominee is a relative, the nominee's immigration status alone shall not constitute unsuitability.

(d) The court shall appoint the person nominated under Section 1501 as guardian of the property covered by the nomination unless the court determines that the nominee is unsuitable. If the person so appointed is appointed only as guardian of the property covered by the nomination, the letters of guardianship shall so indicate.

(e) Subject to subdivisions (c) and (d), in appointing a guardian of the estate:

(1) The court is to be guided by what appears to be in the best interest of the proposed ward, taking into account the proposed guardian's ability to manage and to preserve the estate as well as the proposed guardian's concern for and interest in the welfare of the proposed ward.

(2) If the proposed ward is of sufficient age to form an intelligent preference as to the person to be appointed as guardian, the court shall give consideration to that preference in determining the person to be so appointed. **Leg.H.** Enacted Stats 1990 ch 79 §14 (AB 759), operative July 1, 1991. Amended Stats 1992 ch 163 §123 (AB 2641), operative January 1, 1994; Stats 2011 ch 102 §1 (AB 458), effective January 1, 2012; Stats 2012 ch 845 §3 (SB 1064), effective January 1, 2013; Stats 2024 ch 955 §3 (AB 2224), effective January 1, 2025.

Prior Law: Former Prob C §1514, similar to the present section, was added Stats 1979 ch 726 §3, operative January 1, 1981, and repealed Stats 1990 ch 79 §13, operative July 1, 1991.

Former Prob C §1514, similar to present Prob C §2454, was enacted Stats 1931, and repealed Stats 1979 ch 726 §§1, 2, operative January 1, 1981.

§1514.5. Family court to provide available information

Notwithstanding any other provision of law, except provisions of law governing the retention and storage of data, a family law court shall, upon request from the court in any county hearing a probate guardianship matter proceeding before the court pursuant to this part, provide to the court all available information the court deems necessary to make a determination regarding the best interest of a child, as described in Section 3011 of the Family Code, who is the subject of the proceeding. The information shall also be released to a guardianship investigator, as provided in subdivision (a) of Section 1513, acting within the scope of his or her duties in that proceeding. Any information released pursuant to this section that is confidential pursuant to any other provision of law shall remain confidential and may not be released, except to the extent necessary to comply with this section. No records shared pursuant to this section may be disclosed to any party in a case unless the party requests the agency or court that originates the record to release these records and the request is granted. In counties that provide confidential family law mediation, or confidential dependency mediation, those mediations are not covered by this section. **Leg.H.** Added Stats 2004 ch 574 §2 (AB 2228).

§1515. No guardian of person for married minor

Notwithstanding any other provision of this part, no guardian of the person may be appointed for a minor who is married or whose marriage has been dissolved. This section does not apply in the case of a minor whose marriage has been adjudged a nullity. **Leg.H.** Enacted Stats 1990 ch 79 §14 (AB 759), operative July 1, 1991.

Prior Law: Former Prob C §1515, similar to the present section, was added Stats 1979 ch 726 §3, operative January 1, 1981, and repealed Stats 1990 ch 79 §13, operative July 1, 1991.

Former Prob C §1515, similar to present Prob C §2556, was added Stats 1931 ch 1046 §2, amended Stats 1933 ch 365 §2, Stats 1935 ch 724 §7, Stats 1941 ch 471 §2, Stats 1951 ch 192 §2, Stats 1955 ch 1426 §2, Stats 1965 ch 632 §2, and repealed Stats 1979 ch 726 §§1, 2, operative January 1, 1981.

§1516. Notice to local agency designated to investigate guardianships

(a) In each case involving a petition for guardianship of the person, the petitioner shall deliver pursuant to Section 1215 a notice of the hearing and a copy of the petition, at least 15 days before the hearing, to the local agency designated by the board of supervisors to investigate guardianships for the court. The local social services agency providing child protection services shall screen the name of the guardian for prior referrals of neglect or abuse of minors. The results of this screening shall be provided to the court.

(b) This section does not apply to guardianships resulting from a permanency plan for a dependent child pursuant to Section 366.25 of the Welfare and Institutions Code. **Leg.H.** Enacted Stats 1990 ch 79 §14 (AB 759), operative July 1, 1991. Amended Stats 2017 ch 319 §32 (AB 976), effective January 1, 2018.

Prior Law: Former Prob C §1516, similar to the present section, was added Stats 1986 ch 1017 §4, amended Stats 1987 ch 229 §1, and repealed Stats 1990 ch 79 §13, operative July 1, 1991.

Former Prob C §1516, similar to present Prob C §§1461, 2359, 2403, was added Stats 1935 ch 724 §11, amended Stats 1943 ch 1053 §1, Stats 1953 ch 65 §1, Stats 1973 ch 142 §58, effective June 30, 1973, operative July 1, 1973, and repealed Stats 1979 ch 726 §1, operative January 1, 1981.

§1516.5. When proceeding to have child declared free from parental custody and control may be brought in guardianship proceeding, in adoption action, or separate action filed for that purpose; Appointment of investigator and written report; Rights of parent

(a) A proceeding to have a child declared free from the custody and control of one or both parents may be brought in accordance with the procedures specified in Part 4 (commencing with Section 7800) of Division 12 of the Family Code within an existing guardianship proceeding, in an adoption action, or in a separate action filed for that purpose, if all of the following requirements are satisfied:

(1) One or both parents do not have the legal custody of the child.

(2) The child has been in the physical custody of the guardian for a period of not less than two years.

(3) The court finds that the child would benefit from being adopted by his or her guardian. In making this determination, the court shall consider all factors relating to the best interest of the child, including, but not limited to, the nature and extent of the relationship between all of the following:

(A) The child and the birth parent.

(B) The child and the guardian, including family members of the guardian.

(C) The child and any siblings or half siblings.

(b) The court shall appoint a court investigator or other qualified professional to investigate all factors enumerated in subdivision (a). The findings of the investigator or professional regarding those issues shall be included in the written report required pursuant to Section 7851 of the Family Code.

(c) The rights of the parent, including the rights to notice and counsel provided in Part 4 (commencing with Section 7800) of Division 12 of the Family Code, shall apply to actions brought pursuant to this section.

(d) This section does not apply to any child who is a dependent of the juvenile court or to any Indian child. **Leg.H.** Added Stats 2003 ch 251 §11 (SB 182). Amended Stats 2006 ch 838 §25 (SB 678), effective January 1, 2007; Stats 2010 ch 588 §9 (AB 2020), effective January 1, 2011.

§1517. Application of part; Administration of funds for the benefit of the child

(a) This part does not apply to guardianships resulting from the selection and implementation of a permanent plan pursuant to Section 366.26 of the Welfare and Institutions Code. For those minors, Section 366.26 of the Welfare and Institutions Code and Division 3 (commencing with Rule 5.500) of Title Five of the California Rules of Court specify the exclusive procedures for establishing, modifying, and terminating legal guardianships. If no specific provision of the Welfare and Institutions Code or the California Rules of Court is applicable, the provisions applicable to the administration of estates under Part 4 (commencing with Section 2100) govern so far as they are applicable to like situations.

(b) This chapter shall not be construed to prevent a court that assumes jurisdiction of a minor child pursuant to Section 300 of the Welfare and Institutions Code, or a probate court, as appropriate, from issuing orders or making appointments, on motion of the child's counsel, consistent with Division 2 of the Welfare and Institutions Code or Divisions 4 to 6, inclusive, of the Probate Code necessary to ensure the appropriate administration of funds for the benefit of the child. Orders or appointments regarding those funds may continue after the court's jurisdiction is terminated pursuant to Section 391 of the Welfare and Institutions Code. **Leg.H.** Added Stats 1991 ch 82 §6 (SB 896), effective June 30, 1991, operative July 1, 1991. Amended Stats 2008 ch 166 §2 (AB 3051), effective January 1, 2009.

Prior Law: Former Prob C §1517, similar to the present section, was added Stats 1990 ch 1530 §1 and repealed Stats 1991 ch 82 §5, effective June 30, operative July 1, 1991.

Former Prob C §1517, similar to present Prob C §2458, was added Stats 1939 ch 538 §2, and repealed Stats 1979 ch 726 §1, operative January 1, 1981.

2008 Note: It is the intent of the Legislature that all children who want to attend their juvenile court hearings be given the means and the opportunity to attend, that these hearings be set to accommodate children's schedules, and that courtrooms and waiting areas help facilitate their attendance and participation. It is also the intent of the Legislature that juvenile courts promote communication with, and the participation of, children in attendance at hearings of which they are the subject, and that children attending these hearings leave the hearing with a clear understanding of what decisions the court made and why, and that the Administrative Office of the Courts help promote these objectives. Stats 2008 ch 166 (AB 3051) §1.

ARTICLE 3
Nonrelative Guardianships

Application of article. §1540.
Additional contents of petition for guardianship. §1541.
Notice to Director of Social Services and to local agency designated to investigate guardianships. §1542.
Report on suitability of guardian. §1543.

§1540. Application of article

This article does not apply in any of the following cases:

(a) Where the petition is for guardianship of the estate exclusively.

(b) Where the proposed guardian is a relative of the proposed ward.

(c) Where the Director of Developmental Services is appointed guardian pursuant to Article 7.5 (commencing with Section 416) of Chapter 2 of Part 1 of Division 1 of the Health and Safety Code.

(d) Where the director of the department designated by the board of supervisors to provide social services is appointed guardian.

(e) Where the public guardian is appointed guardian.

(f) Where the guardianship results from a permanency plan for a dependent child pursuant to Section 366.25 of the Welfare and Institutions Code. **Leg.H.** Enacted Stats 1990 ch 79 §14 (AB 759), operative July 1, 1991.

Prior Law: Former Prob C §1540, similar to the present section, was added Stats 1979 ch 726 §3, operative January 1, 1981, amended Stats 1980 ch 246 §4.1, Stats 1986 ch 1017 §5, and repealed Stats 1990 ch 79 §13, operative July 1, 1991.

Former Prob C §1540, similar to present Prob C §2557, was added Stats 1933 ch 133 §2, amended Stats 1935 ch 724 §8, and repealed Stats 1979 ch 726 §§1, 2, operative January 1, 1981.

§1541. Additional contents of petition for guardianship

In addition to the other required contents of the petition for appointment of a guardian, the petition shall include both of the following:

(a) A statement by the proposed guardian that, upon request by an agency referred to in Section 1543 for information relating to the investigation referred to in that section, the proposed guardian will promptly submit the information required.

(b) A disclosure of any petition for adoption by the proposed guardian of the minor who is the subject of the guardianship petition regardless of when or where filed.

(c) A statement whether or not the home of the proposed guardian is a licensed foster family home, a certified family home of a licensed foster family agency, or a resource family home approved by a county or a licensed foster family agency. **Leg.H.** Enacted Stats 1990 ch 79 §14 (AB 759), operative July 1, 1991. Amended Stats 2016 ch 612 §58 (AB 1997), effective January 1, 2017.

Prior Law: Former Prob C §1541, similar to the present section, was added Stats 1979 ch 726 §3, operative January 1, 1981, amended Stats 1980 ch 246 §4.2, and repealed Stats 1990 ch 79 §13, operative July 1, 1991.

2016 Note: (a) The State Department of Social Services and the State Department of Health Care Services shall adopt regulations as required to implement this act and Chapter 773 of the Statutes of 2015.

(b) Notwithstanding the rulemaking provisions of the Administrative Procedure Act (Chapter 3.5 (commencing with Section 11340) of Part 1 of Division 3 of Title 2 of the Government Code), the State Department of Social Services and the State Department of Health Care Services may implement and administer the changes made by this act through all-county letters or similar written instructions until regulations are adopted. Stats 2016 ch 612 (AB 1997) §131.

§1542. Notice to Director of Social Services and to local agency designated to investigate guardianships

In each case involving a petition for guardianship of the person, the petitioner shall deliver pursuant to Section 1215 a notice of the hearing and a copy of the petition, at least 15 days before the hearing, to the Director of Social Services at the director's office in Sacramento and to the local agency designated by the board of supervisors to investigate guardianships for the court. **Leg.H.** Enacted Stats 1990 ch 79 §14 (AB 759), operative July 1, 1991. Amended Stats 2017 ch 319 §33 (AB 976), effective January 1, 2018.

Prior Law: Former Prob C §1542, similar to the present section, was added Stats 1979 ch 726 §3, operative January 1, 1981, and repealed Stats 1990 ch 79 §13, operative July 1, 1991.

§1543. Report on suitability of guardian

(a) If the petition as filed or as amended states that an adoption petition has been filed, a report with respect to the suitability of the proposed guardian for guardianship shall be filed with the court by the agency investigating the adoption. In other cases, the local agency designated by the board of supervisors to provide public social services shall file a report with the court with respect to the proposed guardian of the same character required to be made with regard to an applicant for foster family home licensure, or, on and after January 1, 2020, resource family approval, as described in Section 16519.5 of the Welfare and Institutions Code.

(b) The report filed with the court pursuant to this section is confidential. The report may be considered by the court and shall be made available only to the persons who have been served in the proceeding and the persons who have appeared in the proceeding or their attorneys. The report may be received in evidence upon stipulation of counsel for all of those persons who are present at the hearing or, if a person is present at the hearing but is not represented by counsel, upon consent of that person. **Leg.H.** Enacted Stats 1990 ch 79 §14 (AB 759), operative July 1, 1991. Amended Stats 2016 ch 612 §59 (AB 1997), effective January 1, 2017.

Prior Law: Former Prob C §1543, similar to the present section, was added Stats 1979 ch 726 §3, operative January 1, 1981, amended Stats 1980 ch 246 §4.3, and repealed Stats 1990 ch 79 §13, operative July 1, 1991.

2016 Note: For adoption of regulations, see the 2016 Note following Prob C §1541.

CHAPTER 2
TERMINATION

Majority, death, adoption, or emancipation. §1600.
Termination by court order. §1601.
Visitation rights of former guardian. §1602.

§1600. Majority, death, adoption, or emancipation

(a) A guardianship of the person or estate or both terminates when the ward attains majority unless, pursuant to Section 1510.1, the ward requests the extension of, or consents to the extension of, the guardianship of the person until the ward attains 21 years of age.

(b) A guardianship of the person terminates upon the death of the ward, the adoption of the ward, or upon the emancipation of the ward under Section 7002 of the Family Code.

(c) A guardianship of the estate terminates upon the death of the ward, except as provided by Section 2467 and Article 4 (commencing with Section 2630) of Chapter 7 of Part 4, and except as otherwise provided by law. **Leg.H.** Enacted Stats 1990 ch 79 §14 (AB 759), operative July 1, 1991. Amended Stats 1996 ch 862 §6 (AB 2751); Stats 2015 ch 694 §4 (AB 900), effective January 1, 2016; Stats 2018 ch 73 §1 (AB 2113), effective January 1, 2019.

2015 Note: For legislative findings and declarations, see 2015 Note following Prob C §1490.

Prior Law: Former Prob C §1600, similar to the present section, was added Stats 1979 ch 726 §3, operative January 1, 1981, amended Stats 1986 ch 1017 §6, and repealed Stats 1990 ch 79 §13, operative July 1, 1991.

Former Prob C §1600, similar to present Prob C §2700, was enacted Stats 1931, amended Stats 1941 ch 89 §1, Stats 1953 ch 329 §1, and repealed Stats 1979 ch 726 §§1, 2, operative January 1, 1981.

§1601. Termination by court order

Upon petition of the guardian, a parent, the minor ward, or, in the case of an Indian child custody proceeding, an Indian custodian or the ward's tribe, the court may make an order terminating the guardianship if the court determines that it is in the ward's best interest to terminate the guardianship. Upon petition of a ward who is 18 years of age or older, the court shall make an order terminating the guardianship. Notice of the hearing on the petition shall be given for the period and in the manner provided in Chapter 3 (commencing with Section 1460) of Part 1. **Leg.H.** Enacted Stats 1990 ch 79 §14 (AB 759), operative July 1, 1991. Amended Stats 2002 ch 1118 §6 (AB 1938); Stats 2006 ch 838 §26 (SB 678), effective January 1, 2007; Stats 2015 ch 694 §5 (AB 900), effective January 1, 2016.

2015 Note: For legislative findings and declarations, see 2015 Note following Prob C §1490.

Prior Law: Former Prob C §1601, similar to the present section, was added Stats 1979 ch 726 §3, operative January 1, 1981, and repealed Stats 1990 ch 79 §13, operative July 1, 1991.

Former Prob C §1601, similar to present Prob C §§2700, 2702, was enacted Stats 1931, amended Stats 1949 ch 1336 §1, and repealed Stats 1979 ch 726 §§1, 2, operative January 1, 1981.

§1602. Visitation rights of former guardian

(a) The Legislature hereby finds and declares that guardians perform a critical and important role in the lives of minors, frequently assuming a parental role and caring for a child when the child's parent or parents are unable or unwilling to do so.

(b) Upon making a determination that a guardianship should be terminated pursuant to Section 1601, the court may consider whether continued visitation between the ward and the guardian is in the ward's best interest. As part of the order of termination, the court shall have jurisdiction to issue an order providing for ongoing visitation between a former guardian and his or her former minor ward after the termination of the guardianship. The order granting or denying visitation may not be modified unless the court determines, based upon evidence presented, that there has been a significant change of circumstances since the court issued the order and that modification of the order is in the best interest of the child.

(c) A copy of the visitation order shall be filed in any court proceeding relating to custody of the minor. If a prior order has not been filed, and a proceeding is not pending relating to the custody of the minor in the court of any county, the visitation order may be used as the sole basis for opening a file in the court of the county in which the custodial parent resides. While a parent of the child has custody of the child, proceedings for modification of the visitation order shall be determined in a proceeding under the Family Code. **Leg.H.** Added Stats 2004 ch 301 §2 (AB 2292).

CHAPTER 3
PERMANENT AND STABLE HOME

Legislative findings and declarations. §1610.

Vexatious litigant. §1611.

§1610. Legislative findings and declarations

(a) The Legislature finds and declares that it is in the best interests of children to be raised in a permanent, safe, stable, and loving environment.

(b) Unwarranted petitions, applications, or motions other than discovery motions after the guardianship has been established create an environment that can be harmful to children and are inconsistent with the goals of permanency, safety, and stability. **Leg.H.** Added Stats 2002 ch 1118 §7 (AB 1938). Amended Stats 2006 ch 493 §6 (AB 1363), effective January 1, 2007.

2006 Note: This act, together with Senate Bill 1116 (Scott), Senate Bill 1550 (Figueroa), and Senate Bill 1716 (Bowen), shall be known and may be cited as the Omnibus Conservatorship and Guardianship Reform Act of 2006. Stats 2006 ch 493 (AB 1363) §1.

§1611. Vexatious litigant

If a person files a petition for visitation, termination of the guardianship, or instruction to the guardian that is unmeritorious, or intended to harass or annoy the guardian, and the person has previously filed pleadings in the guardianship proceedings that were unmeritorious, or intended to harass or annoy the guardian, this petition shall be grounds for the court to determine that the person is a vexatious litigant for the purposes of Title 3a (commencing with Section 391) of Part 2 of the Code of Civil Procedure. For these purposes, the term "new litigation" shall include petitions for visitation, termination of the guardianship, or instruction to the guardian. **Leg.H.** Added Stats 2002 ch 1118 §7 (AB 1938).

PART 3
CONSERVATORSHIP

Chapter 1. Establishment of Conservatorship.
Chapter 2. Periodic Review of Conservatorship.
Chapter 3. Termination.
Chapter 4. Legal Capacity of Conservatee.
Chapter 5. Disqualification From Voting.
Chapter 6. Sterilization.
Chapter 7. Unwarranted Petitions.
Chapter 8. Interstate Jurisdiction, Transfer, and Recognition: California Conservatorship Jurisdiction Act.

CHAPTER 1
ESTABLISHMENT OF CONSERVATORSHIP

Article 1. Persons for Whom Conservator May Be Appointed.
Article 2. Order of Preference for Appointment of Conservator.
Article 3. Establishment of Conservatorship.
Article 4. Special Provisions Applicable Where Proposed Conservatee Is an Absentee.
Article 5. Special Provisions Applicable Where Proposed Conservatee Is a Missing Person.

ARTICLE 1
Persons for Whom Conservator May Be Appointed

Legislative intent. §1800.
Appointment of conservators and conservatorship of nonresident; Least restrictive alternative; Limited conservatorship. §1800.3.
Showing required for appointment. §1801.
Appointment upon request of proposed conservatee. §1802.
Conservator of estate of "absentee". §1803.
Conservator of estate of missing person. §1804.

§1800. Legislative intent

It is the intent of the Legislature in enacting this chapter to do the following:

(a) Protect the rights of persons who are placed under conservatorship.

(b) Provide that an assessment of the needs of the person is performed in order to determine the appropriateness and extent of a conservatorship and to set goals for increasing the conservatee's functional abilities to whatever extent possible.

(c) Provide that the health and psychosocial needs of the proposed conservatee are met.

(d) Provide that community-based services are used to the greatest extent in order to allow the conservatee to remain as independent and in the least restrictive setting as possible.

(e) Provide that the periodic review of the conservatorship by the court investigator shall consider the best interests and expressed wishes of the conservatee; whether the conservatee has regained or could regain abilities and capacity with or without supports; and whether the conservatee continues to need a conservatorship.

(f) Ensure that the conservatee's basic needs for physical health, food, clothing, and shelter are met.

(g) Provide for the proper management and protection of the conservatee's real and personal property.

(h) Ensure, to the greatest possible extent, that the conservatee is able to understand, make, and communicate their own, informed, choices while under conservatorship. **Leg.H.** Enacted Stats 1990 ch 79 §14 (AB 759), operative July 1, 1991. Amended Stats 2022 ch 894 §4 (AB 1663), effective January 1, 2023.

Prior Law: Former Prob C §1800, similar to the present section, was added Stats 1989 ch 1080 §2 and repealed Stats 1990 ch 79 §13, operative July 1, 1991.

Former Prob C §1800 was added Stats 1979 ch 726 §3, operative January 1, 1981, and renumbered §1800.3 by Stats 1989 ch 1080 §1.

§1800.3. Appointment of conservators and conservatorship of nonresident; Least restrictive alternative; Limited conservatorship

(a) If the need therefor is established to the satisfaction of the court and the other requirements of this chapter are satisfied, the court may appoint:

(1) A conservator of the person or estate of an adult, or both.

(2) A conservator of the person of a minor who is married or whose marriage has been dissolved.

(b) A conservatorship of the person or of the estate shall not be granted by the court unless the court makes an express finding that the granting of the conservatorship is the least restrictive alternative needed for the protection of the conservatee.

(c) In determining whether a conservatorship is the least restrictive alternative available, and whether to grant or deny a conservatorship petition, the court shall consider the person's abilities and capacities with current and possible supports, including, but not limited to, supported decisionmaking agreements, as defined in Section 21001 of the Welfare and Institutions Code, powers of attorney, designation of a health care surrogate as set forth in Section 4711, and advance health care directives.

(d) If the court becomes aware that the proposed conservatee has a developmental disability, and the proposed conservator is not seeking authority to act under Section 2356.5, the court shall deem the proceeding to be seeking a limited conservatorship. **Leg.H.** Enacted Stats 1990 ch 79 §14 (AB 759), operative July 1, 1991. Amended Stats 1997 ch 663 §1 (SB 628); Stats 2007 ch 553 §6 (AB 1727), effective January 1, 2008; Stats 2022 ch 894 §5 (AB 1663), effective January 1, 2023.

Prior Law: Former Prob C §1800.3, similar to the present section, was added Stats 1979 ch 726 §3 operative January 1, 1981, as Prob C §1800, renumbered by Stats 1989 ch 1080 §1, and repealed Stats 1990 ch 79 §13, operative July 1, 1991.

§1801. Showing required for appointment

Subject to Section 1800.3:

(a) A conservator of the person may be appointed for a person who is unable to provide properly for his or her personal needs for physical health, food, clothing, or shelter, except as provided for the person as described in subdivision (b) or (c) of Section 1828.5.

(b) A conservator of the estate may be appointed for a person who is substantially unable to manage his or her own financial resources or resist fraud or undue influence, except as provided for that person as described in subdivision (b) or (c) of Section 1828.5. Substantial inability may not be proved solely by isolated incidents of negligence or improvidence.

(c) A conservator of the person and estate may be appointed for a person described in subdivisions (a) and (b).

(d) A limited conservator of the person or of the estate, or both, may be appointed for a developmentally disabled adult. A limited conservatorship may be utilized only as necessary to promote and protect the well-being of the individual, shall be designed to encourage the development of maximum self-reliance and independence of the individual, and shall be ordered only to the extent necessitated by the individual's proven mental and adaptive limitations. The conservatee of the limited conservator shall not be presumed to be incompetent and shall retain all legal and civil rights except those which by court order have been designated as legal disabilities and have been specifically granted to the limited conservator. The intent of the Legislature, as expressed in Section 4501 of the Welfare and Institutions Code, that developmentally disabled citizens of this state receive services resulting in more independent, productive, and normal lives is the underlying mandate of this division in its application to adults alleged to be developmentally disabled.

(e) The standard of proof for the appointment of a conservator pursuant to this section shall be clear and convincing evidence. **Leg.H.** Enacted Stats 1990 ch 79 §14 (AB 759), operative July 1, 1991. Amended Stats 1995 ch 842 §7 (SB 730).

1995 Notes: This act shall be known and may be cited as the Due Process in Competence Determinations Act. Stats 1995 ch 842 §12.

This act shall not apply to proceedings under the Welfare and Institutions Code. Stats 1995 ch 842 §13.

Prior Law: Former Prob C §1801, similar to the present section, was added Stats 1979 ch 726 §3, operative January 1, 1981, amended Stats 1980 ch 1304 §6, amended Stats 1984 ch 183 §1, and repealed Stats 1990 ch 79 §13, operative July 1, 1991.

Former Prob C §1801, related to notice to ward or conservatee, was added Stats 1957 ch 1902 §1, amended Stats 1976 ch 1357 §28, operative July 1, 1977, and repealed Stats 1979 ch 726 §2, operative January 1, 1981.

§1802. Appointment upon request of proposed conservatee

Subject to Section 1800.3, a conservator of the person or estate, or both, may be appointed for a person who voluntarily requests the appointment and who, to the satisfaction of the court, establishes good cause for the appointment. **Leg.H.** Enacted Stats 1990 ch 79 §14 (AB 759), operative July 1, 1991.

Prior Law: Former Prob C §1802, similar to the present section, was added Stats 1979 ch 726 §3, operative January 1, 1981, and repealed Stats 1990 ch 79 §13, operative July 1, 1991.

Former Prob C §1802, similar to present Prob C §§2320–2322, 2326, was added Stats 1957 ch 1902 §1, amended Stats Stats 1959 ch 391 §2, and repealed Stats 1979 ch 726 §2, operative January 1, 1981.

§1803. Conservator of estate of "absentee"

A conservator of the estate may be appointed for a person who is an absentee as defined in Section 1403. **Leg.H.** Enacted Stats 1990 ch 79 §14 (AB 759), operative July 1, 1991.

Prior Law: Former Prob C §1803, similar to the present section, was added Stats 1979 ch 726 §3, operative January 1, 1981, and repealed Stats 1990 ch 79 §13, operative July 1, 1991.

Former Prob C §1803, similar to present Prob C §2329, was added Stats 1957 ch 1902 §1, and repealed Stats 1979 ch 726 §2, operative January 1, 1981.

§1804. Conservator of estate of missing person

Subject to Section 1800.3, a conservator of the estate may be appointed for a person who is missing and whose whereabouts is unknown. **Leg.H.** Enacted Stats 1990 ch 79 §14 (AB 759), operative July 1, 1991.

Prior Law: Former Prob C §1804, similar to the present section, was added Stats 1983 ch 201 §6 and repealed Stats 1990 ch 79 §13, operative July 1, 1991.

Former Prob C §1804, similar to present Prob C §2328, was added Stats 1957 ch 1902 §1 and repealed Stats 1979 ch 726 §2, operative January 1, 1981.

ARTICLE 2
Order of Preference for Appointment of Conservator

Nomination by proposed conservatee. §1810.
Nomination by spouse or relative of proposed conservatee. §1811.
Order of preference for appointment as conservator. §1812.
Condition for appointment of conservatee's spouse. §1813.
Petitioning for appointment of conservatorship by domestic partner; Notification of domestic partner's relationship to ward or conservatee when petitioning, as conservator, for approval of certain property transactions. §1813.1.

§1810. Nomination by proposed conservatee

If the proposed conservatee has sufficient capacity at the time to form an intelligent preference, the proposed conservatee may nominate a conservator in the petition or in a writing signed either before or after the petition is filed. The court shall appoint the nominee as conservator unless the court finds that the appointment of the nominee is not in the best interests of the proposed conservatee. **Leg.H.** Enacted Stats 1990 ch 79 §14 (AB 759), operative July 1, 1991.

Prior Law: Former Prob C §1810, similar to the present section, was added Stats 1979 ch 726 §3, operative January 1, 1981, and repealed Stats 1990 ch 79 §13, operative July 1, 1991.

§1811. Nomination by spouse or relative of proposed conservatee

(a) Subject to Sections 1813 and 1813.1, the spouse, domestic partner, or an adult child, parent, brother, or sister of the proposed conservatee may nominate a conservator in the petition or at the hearing on the petition.

(b) Subject to Sections 1813 and 1813.1, the spouse, domestic partner, or a parent of the proposed conservatee may nominate a conservator in a writing signed either before or after the petition is filed and that nomination remains effective notwithstanding the subsequent legal incapacity or death of the spouse, domestic partner, or parent. **Leg.H.** Added Stats 1990 ch 79 §14 (AB 759), operative July 1, 1991. Amended Stats 2000 ch 17 §3 (AB 1491); Stats 2001 ch 893 §15 (AB 25); Stats 2014 ch 913 §28 (AB 2747), effective January 1, 2015.

Prior Law: Former Prob C §1811, similar to the present section, was added Stats 1979 ch 726 §3, operative January 1, 1981, and repealed Stats 1990 ch 79 §13, operative July 1, 1991.

§1812. Order of preference for appointment as conservator

(a) Subject to Sections 1810, 1813, and 1813.1, the selection of a conservator of the person or estate, or both, is solely in the discretion of the court and, in making the selection, the court is to be guided by what appears to be for the best interests of the proposed conservatee.

(b) Subject to Sections 1810, 1813, and 1813.1, of persons equally qualified in the opinion of the court to appointment as conservator of the person or estate or both, preference is to be given in the following order:

(1) The conservatee or proposed conservatee's stated preference, including preferences expressed by speech, sign language, alternative or augmentative communication, actions, facial expressions, and other spoken and nonspoken methods of communication.

(2) The prior conservator's preference, if known, if the selection of a successor conservator is being made pursuant to the provisions of Article 2 (commencing with Section 2680) of Chapter 9.5 of Part 4 and the prior conservator is a person described in paragraphs (3) to (6), inclusive, unless either of the following apply:

(A) The reason for the appointment of a successor conservator is due to the prior conservator's removal pursuant to the provisions of Article 1 (commencing with Section 2650) of Chapter 9 of Part 4.

(B) The prior conservator or prior conservator's preference for a successor conservator has been found criminally, civilly, or administratively liable for abuse, neglect, mistreatment, coercion, or fraud with respect to the conservatee or any elder or dependent adult.

(3) The spouse or domestic partner of the proposed conservatee or the person nominated by the spouse or domestic partner pursuant to Section 1811.

(4) An adult child of the proposed conservatee or the person nominated by the child pursuant to Section 1811.

(5) A parent of the proposed conservatee or the person nominated by the parent pursuant to Section 1811.

(6) A sibling of the proposed conservatee or the person nominated by the brother or sister pursuant to Section 1811.

(7) Any other person or entity eligible for appointment as a conservator under this code or, if there is no person or entity willing to act as a conservator, under the Welfare and Institutions Code.

(c) The preference for any nominee for appointment under paragraphs (4), (5), and (6) of subdivision (b) is subordinate to the preference for any other parent, child, or sibling in that class.

(d) For any conservatorship petition filed on or after January 1, 2023, a regional center, as provided in Chapter 5 (commencing with Section 4620) of Division 4.5 of the Welfare and Institutions Code, or any employee or agent acting on a regional center's behalf, shall not act as a conservator, but may act as the designee of the Director of Developmental Services, subject to Section 416.19 of the Health and Safety Code. **Leg.H.** Added Stats 1990 ch 79 §14 (AB 759), operative July 1, 1991. Amended Stats 2001 ch 893 §16 (AB 25); Stats 2014 ch 913 §29 (AB 2747), effective January 1, 2015; Stats 2022 ch 894 §6 (AB 1663), effective January 1, 2023.

Prior Law: Former Prob C §1812, similar to the present section, was added Stats 1979 ch 726 §3, operative January 1, 1981, and repealed Stats 1990 ch 79 §13, operative July 1, 1991.

§1813. Condition for appointment of conservatee's spouse

(a)(1) The spouse of a proposed conservatee may not petition for the appointment of a conservator for a spouse or be appointed as conservator of the person or estate of the proposed conservatee unless the petitioner alleges in the petition for appointment as conservator, and the court finds, that the spouse is not a party to any action or proceeding against the proposed conservatee for legal separation of the parties, dissolution of marriage, or adjudication of nullity of their marriage. However, if the court finds by clear and convincing evidence that the appointment of the spouse, who is a party to an action or proceeding against the proposed conservatee for legal separation of the parties, dissolution of marriage, or adjudication of nullity of their marriage, or has obtained a judgment in any of these proceedings, is in the best interests of the proposed conservatee, the court may appoint the spouse.

(2) Prior to making this appointment, the court shall appoint counsel to consult with and advise the conservatee, and to report to the court his or her findings concerning the suitability of appointing the spouse as conservator.

(b) The spouse of a conservatee shall disclose to the conservator, or if the spouse is the conservator, shall disclose to the court, the filing of any action or proceeding against the conservatee for legal separation of the parties, dissolution of marriage, or adjudication of nullity of the marriage, within 10 days of the filing of the action or proceeding by filing a notice with the court and serving the notice according to the notice procedures under this title. The court may, upon receipt of the notice, set the matter for hearing on an order to show cause why the appointment of the spouse as conservator, if the spouse is the conservator, should not be terminated and a new conservator appointed by the court. **Leg.H.** Added Stats 1990 ch 79 §14 (AB 759), operative July 1, 1991. Amended Stats 2000 ch 17 §4 (AB 1491); Stats 2001 ch 159 §165 (SB 662); Stats 2014 ch 913 §30 (AB 2747), effective January 1, 2015.

Prior Law: Former Prob C §1813, similar to the present section, was added Stats 1979 ch 726 §3, operative January 1, 1981, and repealed Stats 1990 ch 79 §13, operative July 1, 1991.

§1813.1. Petitioning for appointment of conservatorship by domestic partner; Notification of domestic partner's relationship to ward or conservatee when petitioning, as conservator, for approval of certain property transactions

(a)(1) The domestic partner of a proposed conservatee may not petition for the appointment of a conservator for a domestic partner or be appointed as conservator of the person or estate of the proposed conservatee unless the petitioner alleges in the petition for appointment as conservator, and the court finds, that the domestic partner has not terminated and is not intending to terminate the domestic partnership as provided in Section 299 of the Family Code. However, if the court finds by clear and convincing evidence that the appointment of a domestic partner who has terminated or is intending to terminate the domestic partnership is in the best interests of the proposed conservatee, the court may appoint the domestic partner.

(2) Prior to making this appointment, the court shall appoint counsel to consult with and advise the conservatee, and to report to the court his or her findings concerning the suitability of appointing the domestic partner as conservator.

(b) The domestic partner of a conservatee shall disclose to the conservator, or if the domestic partner is the conservator, shall notify the court, of the termination of a domestic partnership as provided in Section 299 of the Family Code within 10 days of its occurrence. The court may, upon receipt of the notice, set the matter for hearing on an order to show cause why the appointment of the domestic partner as conservator, if the domestic partner is the conservator, should not be terminated and a new conservator appointed by the court. **Leg.H.** Added Stats 2001 ch 893 §16.5 (AB 25).

ARTICLE 3
Establishment of Conservatorship

Filing of petition. §1820.
Contents of petition. §1821.
Notice of hearing. §1822.
Citation to proposed conservatee; Completing affidavit of voter registration. §1823.
Service on proposed conservatee of citation and petition. §1824.
Attendance of proposed conservatee at hearing. §1825.
Investigation and report by court investigator if proposed conservatee will not attend hearing. §1826.
Law and procedure applicable to hearing. §1827.
Assessment of proposed limited conservatee at regional center. §1827.5.
Information to proposed conservatee by court. §1828.
Inquiry and information by court in limited conservatorship proceeding. §1828.5.
Persons who may support or oppose petition. §1829.
Contents of order appointing conservator. §1830.
Acknowledgment of receipt. §1834.
Informational package for conservator . §1835.
Informational package for conservatee. § 1835.5.
Conservatorship alternatives program. § 1836.

§1820. Filing of petition

(a) A petition for the appointment of a conservator may be filed by any of the following:
(1) The proposed conservatee.
(2) The spouse or domestic partner of the proposed conservatee.
(3) A relative of the proposed conservatee.
(4) Any interested state or local entity or agency of this state or any interested public officer or employee of this state or of a local public entity of this state.
(5) Any other interested person or friend of the proposed conservatee.

(b) If the proposed conservatee is a minor, the petition may be filed during his or her minority so that the appointment of a conservator may be made effective immediately upon the minor's attaining the age of majority. An existing guardian of the minor may be appointed as conservator under this part upon the minor's attaining the age of majority, whether or not the guardian's accounts have been settled.

(c) A creditor of the proposed conservatee may not file a petition for appointment of a conservator unless the creditor is a person described in paragraph (2), (3), or (4) of subdivision (a). **Leg.H.** Enacted Stats 1990 ch 79 §14 (AB 759), operative July 1, 1991. Amended Stats 2001 ch 893 §17 (AB 25).

Prior Law: Former Prob C §1820, similar to the present section, was added Stats 1979 ch 726 §3, operative January 1, 1981, and repealed Stats 1990 ch 79 §13, operative July 1, 1991.

§1821. Contents of petition

(a)(1) The petition shall request that a conservator be appointed for the person or estate, or both, shall specify the name, address, and telephone number of the proposed conservator and the name, address, and telephone number of the proposed conservatee, and state the reasons why a conservatorship is necessary. Unless the petitioner or proposed conservator is a bank or other entity authorized to conduct the business of a trust company, the petitioner or proposed conservator shall also file supplemental information as to why the appointment of a conservator is required. The supplemental information to be submitted shall include a brief statement of facts addressed to each of the following categories:

(A) The inability of the proposed conservatee to properly provide for their own their own needs for physical health, food, clothing, or shelter.

(B) The location and nature of the proposed conservatee's residence and the ability of the proposed conservatee to live in the residence while under conservatorship.

(C) Alternatives to conservatorship considered by the petitioner or proposed conservator and reasons why those alternatives are not suitable, alternatives tried by the petitioner or proposed conservators, if any, including details as to the length and duration of attempted alternatives and the reasons why those alternatives do not meet the conservatee's needs. Those alternatives include, but are not limited to, all of the following:

(i) Supported decisionmaking agreements, as defined in Section 21001 of the Welfare and Institutions Code.

(ii) Powers of Attorney set forth in Division 4.5 (commencing with Section 4000).

(iii) Advanced Health Care Directives set forth in Chapter 1 (commencing with Section 4670) of Part 2 of Division 4.7.

(iv) Designations of a health care surrogate as set forth in Section 4711.

(D) Health or social services provided to the proposed conservatee during the year immediately preceding the filing of the petition, when the petitioner or proposed conservator has information as to those services.

(E) The substantial inability of the proposed conservatee to manage their own financial resources, or to resist fraud or undue influence.

(2) The facts required to address the categories set forth in subparagraphs (A) to (E), inclusive, of paragraph (1) shall be set forth by the petitioner or proposed conservator if the proposed conservator has knowledge of the facts or by the declarations or affidavits of other persons having knowledge of those facts.

(3) If any of the categories set forth in subparagraphs (A) to (E), inclusive, of paragraph (1) are not applicable to the proposed conservatorship, the petitioner or proposed conservator shall so indicate and state on the supplemental information form the reasons therefor.

(4) The Judicial Council shall develop a supplemental information form for the information required pursuant to subparagraphs (A) to (E), inclusive, of paragraph (1) after consultation with individuals or organizations approved by the Judicial Council, who represent public conservators, court investigators, the State Bar, specialists with experience in performing assessments and coordinating community-based services, and legal services for the elderly and disabled.

(5) The supplemental information form shall be separate and distinct from the form for the petition. The supplemental information shall be confidential and shall be made available only to parties, persons given notice of the petition who have requested this supplemental information or who have appeared in the proceedings, their attorneys, and the court. The court shall have discretion at any other time to release the supplemental information to other persons if it would serve the interests of the conservatee. The clerk of the court shall make provision for limiting disclosure of the supplemental information exclusively to persons entitled thereto under this section.

(b) The petition shall set forth, so far as they are known to the petitioner or proposed conservator, the names and addresses of the spouse or domestic partner, and of the relatives of the proposed conservatee within the second degree. If no spouse or domestic partner of the proposed conservatee or relatives of the proposed conservatee within the second degree are known to the petitioner or proposed conservator, the petition shall set forth, so far as they are known to the petitioner or proposed conservator, the names and addresses of the following persons who, for the purposes of Section 1822, shall all be deemed to be relatives:

(1) A spouse or domestic partner of a predeceased parent of a proposed conservatee.

(2) The children of a predeceased spouse or domestic partner of a proposed conservatee.

(3) The siblings of the proposed conservatee's parents, if any, but if none, then the natural and adoptive children of the proposed conservatee's parents' siblings.

(4) The natural and adoptive children of the proposed conservatee's siblings.

(c) If the petitioner or proposed conservator is a professional fiduciary, as described in Section 2340, who is required to be licensed under the Professional Fiduciaries Act (Chapter 6 (commencing with Section 6500) of Division 3 of the Business and Professions Code), the petition shall include the following:

(1) The petitioner's or proposed conservator's proposed hourly fee schedule or another statement of their proposed compensation from the estate of the proposed conservatee for services performed as a conservator. The petitioner's or proposed conservator's provision of a proposed hourly fee schedule or another statement of their proposed compensation, as required by this paragraph, shall not preclude a court from later reducing the petitioner's or proposed conservator's fees or other compensation.

(2) Unless a petition for appointment of a temporary conservator that contains the statements required by this paragraph is filed together with a petition for appointment of a conservator, both of the following:

(A) A statement of the petitioner's or proposed conservator's license information.

(B) A statement explaining who engaged the petitioner or proposed conservator or how the petitioner or proposed conservator was engaged to file the petition for appointment of a conservator or to agree to accept the appointment as conservator and what prior relationship the petitioner or proposed conservator had with the proposed conservatee or the proposed conservatee's family or friends.

(d) If the petition is filed by a person other than the proposed conservatee, the petition shall include a declaration of due diligence showing both of the following:

(1) Either the efforts to find the proposed conservatee's relatives or why it was not feasible to contact any of them.

(2) Either the preferences of the proposed conservatee concerning the appointment of a conservator and the appointment of the proposed conservator or why it was not feasible to ascertain those preferences.

(e) If the petition is filed by a person other than the proposed conservatee, the petition shall state whether or not the petitioner is a creditor or debtor, or the agent of a creditor or debtor, of the proposed conservatee.

(f) If the proposed conservatee is a patient in, or on leave of absence from, a state institution under the jurisdiction of the State Department of State Hospitals or the State Department of Developmental Services and that fact is known to the petitioner or proposed conservator, the petition shall state that fact and name the institution.

(g) The petition shall state, so far as is known to the petitioner or proposed conservator, whether or not the proposed conservatee is receiving, or is entitled to receive, benefits from the Veterans Administration and the estimated amount of the monthly benefit payable by the Veterans Administration for the proposed conservatee.

(h) The petition may include an application for any order or orders authorized under this division, including, but not limited to, orders under Chapter 4 (commencing with Section 1870).

(i) The petition may include a further statement that the proposed conservatee is not willing to attend the hearing on the petition, does not wish to contest the establishment of the conservatorship, and does not object to the proposed conservator or prefer that another person act as conservator.

(j)(1) In the case of an allegedly developmentally disabled adult, the petition shall set forth the following:

(A) The nature and degree of the alleged disability, the specific duties and powers requested by or for the limited conservator, and the limitations of civil and legal rights requested to be included in the court's order of appointment.

(B) Whether or not the proposed limited conservatee is, or is alleged to be, developmentally disabled.

(2) Reports submitted pursuant to Section 416.8 of the Health and Safety Code meet the requirements of this section, and conservatorships filed pursuant to Article 7.5 (commencing with Section 416) of Chapter 2 of Part 1 of Division 1 of the Health and Safety Code are exempt from providing the supplemental information required by this section, as long as the guidelines adopted by the State Department of Developmental Services for regional centers are publicly accessible via the department's internet website and require the same information that is required pursuant to this section.

(k) The petition shall state, so far as is known to the petitioner, whether or not the proposed conservatee is a member of a federally recognized Indian tribe. If so, the petition shall state the name of the tribe, the state in which the tribe is located, whether the proposed conservatee resides on tribal land, and whether the proposed conservatee is known to own property on tribal land. For the purposes of this subdivision, "tribal land" means land that is, with respect to a specific Indian tribe and the members of that tribe, "Indian country" as defined in Section 1151 of Title 18 of the United States Code. **Leg.H.** Added Stats 1990 ch 79 §14 (AB 759), operative July 1, 1991. Amended Stats 1991 ch 82 §8 (SB 896), effective June 30, 1991, operative July 1, 1991; Stats 2001 ch 893 §18 (AB 25); Stats 2002 ch 784 §577 (SB 1316); Stats 2008 ch 293 §1 (AB 1340), effective January 1, 2009; Stats 2012 ch 440 §42 (AB 1488), effective September 22, 2012; Stats 2013 ch 248 §2 (AB 1339), effective January 1, 2014; Stats 2014 ch 553 §6 (SB 940), effective January 1, 2015, operative January 1, 2016; Stats 2022 ch 420 §33 (AB 2960), effective January 1, 2023; Stats 2022 ch 894 §7 (AB 1663), effective January 1, 2023 (ch 894 prevails).

Prior Law: Former Prob C §1821, similar to the present section, was added Stats 1989 ch 1080 §4, operative July 1, 1990, repealed Stats 1990 ch 79 §13, operative July 1, 1991, amended Stats 1990 ch 1208 §2, effective September 24, 1990, and repealed Stats 1991 ch 82 §7, effective June 30, operative July

Former Prob C §1821, similar to the present section, was added Stats 1979 ch 726 §3, operative January 1, 1981, and repealed Stats 1989 ch 1080 §5, operative July 1, 1990. 1, 1991.

§1822. Notice of hearing

(a) At least 15 days before the hearing on the petition for appointment of a conservator, notice of the time and place of the hearing shall be given as provided in this section. The notice shall be accompanied by a copy of the petition. The court shall not shorten the time for giving the notice of hearing under this section.

(b) Notice shall be delivered pursuant to Section 1215 to the following persons:

(1) The spouse, if any, or registered domestic partner, if any, of the proposed conservatee at the address stated in the petition.

(2) The relatives named in the petition at their addresses stated in the petition.

(c) If notice is required by Section 1461 to be given to the Director of State Hospitals or the Director of Developmental Services, notice shall be delivered pursuant to Section 1215 as required.

(d) If the petition states that the proposed conservatee is receiving or is entitled to receive benefits from the Veterans Administration, notice shall be mailed to the Office of the Veterans Administration referred to in Section 1461.5.

(e) If the proposed conservatee is a person with developmental disabilities, at least 30 days before the day of the hearing on the petition, the petitioner shall deliver pursuant to Section 1215 a notice of the hearing and a copy of the petition to the regional center identified in Section 1827.5.

(f) If the petition states that the petitioner and the proposed conservator have no prior relationship with the proposed conservatee and are not nominated by a family member, friend, or other person with a relationship to the proposed conservatee, notice shall be delivered pursuant to Section 1215 to the public guardian of the county in which the petition is filed. **Leg.H.** Enacted Stats 1990 ch 79 §14 (AB 759), operative July 1, 1991. Amended Stats 1991 ch 82 §10 (SB 896), effective June 30, 1991, operative July 1, 1991; Stats 2001 ch 893 §19 (AB 25); Stats 2006 ch 493 §7 (AB 1363), effective January 1, 2007; Stats 2008 ch 293 §2 (AB 1340), effective January 1, 2009; Stats 2012 ch 440 §43 (AB 1488), effective

September 22, 2012; Stats 2017 ch 319 §34 (AB 976), effective January 1, 2018.

2006 Note: This act, together with Senate Bill 1116 (Scott), Senate Bill 1550 (Figueroa), and Senate Bill 1716 (Bowen), shall be known and may be cited as the Omnibus Conservatorship and Guardianship Reform Act of 2006. Stats 2006 ch 493 (AB 1363) §1.

Prior Law: Former Prob C §1822, similar to the present section, was added Stats 1979 ch 726 §3, operative January 1, 1981, amended Stats 1980 ch 89 §6, ch 1304 §8.5, Stats 1985 ch 356 §3, repealed Stats 1990 ch 79 §13, operative July 1, 1991, amended Stats 1990 ch 1598 §1, and repealed Stats 1991 ch 82 §9, effective June 30, operative July 1, 1991.

§1823. Citation to proposed conservatee; Completing affidavit of voter registration

(a) If the petition is filed by a person other than the proposed conservatee, the clerk shall issue a citation directed to the proposed conservatee setting forth the time and place of hearing.

(b) The citation shall state the legal standards by which the need for a conservatorship is adjudged as stated in Section 1801 and shall state the substance of all of the following:

(1) The proposed conservatee may be adjudged unable to provide for personal needs or to manage financial resources and, by reason thereof, a conservator may be appointed for the person or estate, or both.

(2) Such adjudication may affect or transfer to the conservator the proposed conservatee's right to contract, in whole or in part, to manage and control property, to give informed consent for medical treatment, and to fix a residence.

(3)(A) The proposed conservatee may be disqualified from voting pursuant to Section 2208 of the Elections Code if the proposed conservatee is incapable of communicating, with or without reasonable accommodations, a desire to participate in the voting process.

(B) The proposed conservatee shall not be disqualified from voting on the basis that the proposed conservatee does, or would need to do, any of the following to complete an affidavit of voter registration:

(i) Signs the affidavit of voter registration with a mark or a cross pursuant to subdivision (b) of Section 2150 of the Elections Code.

(ii) Signs the affidavit of voter registration by means of a signature stamp pursuant to Section 354.5 of the Elections Code.

(iii) Completes the affidavit of voter registration with the assistance of another person pursuant to subdivision (d) of Section 2150 of the Elections Code.

(iv) Completes the affidavit of voter registration with reasonable accommodations.

(4) The court or a court investigator shall explain the nature, purpose, and effect of the proceeding to the proposed conservatee and shall answer questions concerning the explanation.

(5) The proposed conservatee has the right to appear at the hearing and to oppose the petition, and in the case of an alleged developmentally disabled adult, to oppose the petition in part, by objecting to any or all of the requested duties or powers of the limited conservator.

(6) The proposed conservatee has the right to choose and be represented by legal counsel and has the right to have legal counsel appointed by the court if not otherwise represented by legal counsel.

(7) The proposed conservatee has the right to a jury trial, if desired.
Leg.H. Added Stats 1990 ch 79 §14 (AB 759), operative July 1, 1991. Amended Stats 2014 ch 591 §4 (AB 1311), effective January 1, 2015; Stats 2015 ch 736 §8 (SB 589), effective January 1, 2016; Stats 2022 ch 420 §34 (AB 2960), effective January 1, 2023.

2015 Note: The Legislature finds and declares that federal disability nondiscrimination laws, including Title II of the federal Americans with Disabilities Act of 1990 (Public Law 101-336), entitle people with disabilities to reasonable accommodations, as needed, to participate in public activities such as voting. The Legislature further finds and declares that by explicitly adding the concept of reasonable accommodation to California laws on voter qualification, this act brings the state into compliance with federal standards. Stats 2015 ch 736 (SB 589) §1.

Prior Law: Former Prob C §1823, similar to the present section, was added Stats 1979 ch 726 §3, operative January 1, 1981, and repealed Stats 1990 ch 79 §13, operative July 1, 1991.

§1824. Service on proposed conservatee of citation and petition

The citation and a copy of the petition shall be served on the proposed conservatee at least 15 days before the hearing. Service shall be made in the manner provided in Section 415.10 or 415.30 of the Code of Civil Procedure or in such manner as may be authorized by the court. If the proposed conservatee is outside this state, service may also be made in the manner provided in Section 415.40 of the Code of Civil Procedure.
Leg.H. Enacted Stats 1990 ch 79 §14 (AB 759), operative July 1, 1991.

Prior Law: Former Prob C §1824, similar to the present section, was added Stats 1979 ch 726 §3, operative January 1, 1981, amended Stats 1980 ch 1304 §10, Stats 1981 ch 2 §1, effective February 13, 1981, and repealed Stats 1990 ch 79 §13, operative July 1, 1991.

§1825. Attendance of proposed conservatee at hearing

(a) The proposed conservatee shall be produced at the hearing except in the following cases:

(1) Where the proposed conservatee is out of the state when served and is not the petitioner.

(2) Where the proposed conservatee is unable to attend the hearing by reason of medical inability.

(3) Where the court investigator has reported to the court that the proposed conservatee has expressly communicated that the proposed conservatee (i) is not willing to attend the hearing, (ii) does not wish to contest the establishment of the conservatorship, and (iii) does not object to the proposed conservator or prefer that another person act as conservator, and the court makes an order that the proposed conservatee need not attend the hearing.

(b) If the proposed conservatee is unable to attend the hearing because of medical inability, such inability shall be established (1) by the affidavit or certificate of a licensed medical practitioner or (2) if the proposed conservatee is an adherent of a religion whose tenets and practices call for reliance on prayer alone for healing and is under treatment by an accredited practitioner of that religion, by the affidavit of the practitioner. The affidavit or certificate is evidence only of the proposed conservatee's inability to attend the hearing and shall not be considered in determining the issue of need for the establishment of a conservatorship.

(c) Emotional or psychological instability is not good cause for the absence of the proposed conservatee from the hearing unless, by reason of such instability, attendance at the hearing is likely to cause serious and immediate physiological damage to the proposed conservatee. **Leg.H.** Enacted Stats 1990 ch 79 §14 (AB 759), operative July 1, 1991.

Prior Law: Former Prob C §1825, similar to the present section, was added Stats 1979 ch 726 §3, operative January 1, 1981, and repealed Stats 1990 ch 79 §13, operative July 1, 1991.

§1826. Investigation and report by court investigator if proposed conservatee will not attend hearing

(a) Regardless of whether the proposed conservatee attends the hearing, the court investigator shall do all of the following:

(1) Conduct the following interviews:

(A) The proposed conservatee personally.

(B) All petitioners and all proposed conservators who are not petitioners.

(C) The proposed conservatee's spouse or registered domestic partner and relatives within the first degree. If the proposed conservatee does not have a spouse, registered domestic partner, or relatives within the first degree, to the greatest extent possible, the proposed conservatee's relatives within the second degree.

(D) To the greatest extent practical and taking into account the proposed conservatee's wishes, the proposed conservatee's relatives within the second degree not required to be interviewed under subparagraph (C), neighbors, and, if known, close friends.

(2) Inform the proposed conservatee of the contents of the petition and citation, of the nature, purpose, and effect of the proceeding, and of the right of the proposed conservatee to oppose the petition, to attend the hearing on the petition, to have the matter of the establishment of the conservatorship tried by jury, to be represented by legal counsel, and to have legal counsel appointed by the court if not otherwise represented by legal counsel.

(3) Determine if it appears that the proposed conservatee is unable to attend the hearing and, if able to attend, whether the proposed conservatee is willing to attend the hearing.

(4) Review the allegations of the petition as to why the appointment of the conservator is required and, in making the determination, do the following:

(A) Refer to the supplemental information form submitted by the petitioner and consider the facts set forth in the form that address each of the categories specified in subparagraphs (A) to (E), inclusive, of paragraph (1) of subdivision (a) of Section 1821, as well as the medical reports received pursuant to paragraph (9).

(B) Determine, to the extent practicable or possible, whether the court investigator believes the proposed conservatee suffers from any of the mental function deficits listed in subdivision (a) of Section 811 that significantly impairs the proposed conservatee's ability to understand and appreciate the consequences of the proposed conservatee's actions in connection with any of the functions described in subdivision (a) or (b) of Section 1801 and describe the observations that support that belief, including information in the medical reports received pursuant to paragraph (9).

(5) Determine if the proposed conservatee wishes to oppose the establishment of the conservatorship.

(6) Determine if the proposed conservatee objects to the proposed conservator or prefers another person to act as conservator.

(7) Determine if the proposed conservatee wishes to be represented by legal counsel and, if so, whether the proposed conservatee has retained legal counsel and, if not, whether the proposed conservatee plans to retain legal counsel.

(8)(A) Determine if the proposed conservatee is incapable of communicating, with or without reasonable accommodations, a desire to participate in the voting process, and may be disqualified from voting pursuant to Section 2208 of the Elections Code.

(B) The proposed conservatee shall not be disqualified from voting on the basis that the proposed conservatee does, or would need to do, any of the following to complete an affidavit of voter registration:

(i) Signs the affidavit of voter registration with a mark or a cross pursuant to subdivision (b) of Section 2150 of the Elections Code.

(ii) Signs the affidavit of voter registration by means of a signature stamp pursuant to Section 354.5 of the Elections Code.

(iii) Completes the affidavit of voter registration with the assistance of another person pursuant to subdivision (d) of Section 2150 of the Elections Code.

(iv) Completes the affidavit of voter registration with reasonable accommodations.

(9) Gather and review relevant medical reports regarding the proposed conservatee from the proposed conservatee's primary care physician and other relevant mental and physical health care providers.

(10) Report to the court in writing, at least five days before the hearing, concerning all of the foregoing, including the proposed conservatee's express communications concerning both of the following:

(A) Representation by legal counsel.

(B) If the proposed conservatee is not willing to attend the hearing, does not wish to contest the establishment of the conservatorship, and does not object to the proposed conservator or prefers that another person act as conservator.

(11) Deliver pursuant to Section 1215, at least five days before the hearing, a copy of the report referred to in paragraph (10) to all of the following:

(A) The attorney, if any, for the petitioner.

(B) The attorney, if any, for the proposed conservatee.

(C) The proposed conservatee.

(D) The spouse, registered domestic partner, and relatives within the first degree of the proposed conservatee who are required to be named in the petition for appointment of the conservator, unless the court determines that the delivery will harm the conservatee.

(E) Any other persons as the court orders.

(b) The court investigator has discretion to release the report required by this section to the public conservator, interested public agencies, and the long-term care ombudsperson.

(c)(1) The report required by this section is confidential and shall be made available only to parties, persons described in paragraph (11) of subdivision (a), persons given notice of the petition who have requested this report or who have appeared in the proceedings, their attorneys, and the court. The court has discretion at any other time to release the report, if it would serve the interests of the conservatee. The clerk of the court shall provide for the limitation of the report exclusively to persons entitled to its receipt.

(2) Notwithstanding paragraph (1), confidential medical information and confidential subinformation from the California Law Enforcement Telecommunications System (CLETS) shall be placed in a separate attachment to the report and shall be made available only to the proposed conservatee and the proposed conservatee's attorney.

(d) This section does not apply to a proposed conservatee who has personally executed the petition for conservatorship, or a proposed conservatee who has nominated their own conservator, if the proposed conservatee attends the hearing.

(e) If the court investigator has performed an investigation within the preceding six months and furnished a report thereon to the court, the court may order, upon good cause shown, that another investigation is not necessary or that a more limited investigation may be performed.

(f) An investigation by the court investigator related to a temporary conservatorship also may be a part of the investigation for the general petition for conservatorship, but the court investigator shall make a second visit to the proposed conservatee and the report required by this section shall include the effect of the temporary conservatorship on the proposed conservatee.

(g) The Judicial Council shall, on or before January 1, 2023, update the rules of court and Judicial Council forms as necessary to implement this section.

(h)(1) A superior court shall not be required to perform any duties imposed pursuant to the amendments to this section enacted by Chapter 493 of the Statutes of 2006 until the Legislature makes an appropriation identified for this purpose.

(2) A superior court shall not be required to perform any duties imposed pursuant to the amendments to this section enacted by the measure that added this paragraph until the Legislature makes an appropriation identified for this purpose. **Leg.H.** Added Stats 1990 ch 79 §14 (AB 759), operative July 1, 1991. Amended Stats 1998 ch 581 §21 (AB 2801); Stats 2002 ch 784 §578 (SB 1316); Stats 2006 ch 493 §8 (AB 1363), effective January 1, 2007, operative July 1, 2007; Stats 2007 ch 553 §7 (AB 1727), effective January 1, 2008; Stats 2011 ch 10 §12 (SB 78), effective March 24, 2011; Stats 2014 ch 591 §5 (AB 1311), effective January 1, 2015; Stats 2015 ch 736 §9 (SB 589), effective January 1, 2016; Stats 2017 ch 319 §35 (AB 976), effective January 1, 2018; Stats 2021 ch 417 §7 (AB 1194), effective January 1, 2022; Stats 2022 ch 420 §35 (AB 2960), effective January 1, 2023.

2015 Note: For legislative findings and declarations, see the 2015 Note following Prob C §1823.

2006 Note: This act, together with Senate Bill 1116 (Scott), Senate Bill 1550 (Figueroa), and Senate Bill 1716 (Bowen), shall be known and may be cited as the Omnibus Conservatorship and Guardianship Reform Act of 2006. Stats 2006 ch 493 (AB 1363) §1.

Prior Law: Former Prob C §1826, similar to the present section, was added Stats 1989 ch 1080 §6, operative July 1, 1990, and repealed Stats 1990 ch 79 §13, operative July 1, 1991.

Former Prob C §1826, similar to the present section, was added Stats 1979 ch 726 §3, operative January 1, 1981, and repealed Stats 1989 ch 1080 §5, operative July 1, 1990.

§1827. Law and procedure applicable to hearing

The court shall hear and determine the matter of the establishment of the conservatorship according to the law and procedure relating to the trial of civil actions, including trial by jury if demanded by the proposed conservatee. **Leg.H.** Enacted Stats 1990 ch 79 §14 (AB 759), operative July 1, 1991. Amended Stats 2000 ch 17 §4.2 (AB 1491).

Prior Law: Former Prob C §1827, similar to the present section, was added Stats 1979 ch 726 §3, operative January 1, 1981, and repealed Stats 1990 ch 79 §13, operative July 1, 1991.

§1827.5. Assessment of proposed limited conservatee at regional center

(a) In the case of any proceeding to establish a limited conservatorship for a person with developmental disabilities, within 30 days after the filing of a petition for limited conservatorship, a proposed limited conservatee, with his or her consent, shall be assessed at a regional center as provided in Chapter 5 (commencing with Section 4620) of Division 4.5 of the Welfare and Institutions Code. The regional center shall submit a written report of its findings and recommendations to the court.

(b) In the case of any proceeding to establish a general conservatorship for a person with developmental disabilities, the regional center, with the consent of the proposed conservatee, may prepare an assessment as provided in Chapter 5 (commencing with Section 4620) of Division 4.5 of the Welfare and Institutions Code. If an assessment is prepared, the regional center shall submit its findings and recommendations to the court.

(c)(1) A report prepared under subdivision (a) or (b) shall include a description of the specific areas, nature, and degree of disability of the proposed conservatee or proposed limited conservatee. The findings and recommendations of the regional center are not binding upon the court.

(2) In a proceeding where the petitioner is a provider of board and care, treatment, habilitation, or other services to persons with developmental disabilities or a spouse or employee of a provider, is not the natural parent of the proposed conservatee or proposed limited conservatee, and is not a public entity, the regional center shall include a recommendation in its report concerning the suitability of the petitioners to meet the needs of the proposed conservatee or proposed limited conservatee.

(d) At least five days before the hearing on the petition, the regional center shall deliver pursuant to Section 1215 a copy of the report described in subdivision (a) to all of the following:

(1) The proposed limited conservatee.

(2) The attorney, if any, for the proposed limited conservatee.

(3) If the petitioner is not the proposed limited conservatee, the attorney for the petitioner or the petitioner if the petitioner does not have an attorney.

(4) Any other persons as the court orders.

(e) The report referred to in subdivisions (a) and (b) shall be confidential and shall be made available only to parties listed in subdivision (d) unless the court, in its discretion, determines that the release of the report would serve the interests of the conservatee who is developmentally disabled. The clerk of the court shall limit disclosure of the report exclusively to persons entitled under this section. **Leg.H.** Enacted Stats 1990 ch 79 §14 (AB 759), operative July 1, 1991. Amended Stats 1991 ch 82 §12 (SB 896), effective June 30, 1991, operative July 1, 1991; Stats 2002 ch 784 §579 (SB 1316); Stats 2017 ch 319 §36 (AB 976), effective January 1, 2018.

Prior Law: Former Prob C §1827.5, similar to the present section, was added Stats 1980 ch 1304 §1, repealed Stats 1990 ch 79 §13, operative July 1, 1991, amended Stats 1990 ch 1208 §3, effective September 24, 1990, §3.5, effective September 24, 1990, operative January 1, 1991, ch 1598 §4, and repealed Stats 1991 ch 82 §9, effective June 30, 1991, operative July 1, 1991.

§1828. Information to proposed conservatee by court

(a) Except as provided in subdivision (c), before the establishment of a conservatorship of the person or estate, or both, the court shall inform the proposed conservatee of all of the following:

(1) The nature and purpose of the proceeding.

(2) The establishment of a conservatorship is a legal adjudication of the proposed conservatee's inability to properly provide for the proposed conservatee's personal needs or to manage the conservatee's own financial resources, or both, depending on the allegations made and the determinations requested in the petition, and the effect of such an adjudication on the proposed conservatee's basic rights.

(3)(A) The proposed conservatee may be disqualified from voting pursuant to Section 2208 of the Elections Code if the proposed conservatee is incapable of communicating, with or without reasonable accommodations, a desire to participate in the voting process.

(B) The proposed conservatee shall not be disqualified from voting on the basis that the proposed conservatee does, or would need to do, any of the following to complete an affidavit of voter registration:

(i) Signs the affidavit of voter registration with a mark or a cross pursuant to subdivision (b) of Section 2150 of the Elections Code.

(ii) Signs the affidavit of voter registration by means of a signature stamp pursuant to Section 354.5 of the Elections Code.

(iii) Completes the affidavit of voter registration with the assistance of another person pursuant to subdivision (d) of Section 2150 of the Elections Code.

(iv) Completes the affidavit of voter registration with reasonable accommodations.

(4) The identity of the proposed conservator.

(5) The nature and effect on the proposed conservatee's basic rights of any order requested under Chapter 4 (commencing with Section 1870), and in the case of an allegedly developmentally disabled adult, the specific effects of each limitation requested in such order.

(6) The proposed conservatee has the right to oppose the proceeding, to have the matter of the establishment of the conservatorship tried by jury, to be represented by legal counsel if the proposed conservatee so chooses, and to have legal counsel appointed by the court if not otherwise represented by legal counsel.

(b) After the court so informs the proposed conservatee and before the establishment of the conservatorship, the court shall consult the proposed conservatee to determine the proposed conservatee's opinion concerning all of the following:

(1) The establishment of the conservatorship.

(2) The appointment of the proposed conservator.

(3) Any order requested under Chapter 4 (commencing with Section 1870), and in the case of an allegedly developmentally disabled adult, of each limitation requested in that order.

(c) This section does not apply where both of the following conditions are satisfied:

(1) The proposed conservatee is absent from the hearing and is not required to attend the hearing under subdivision (a) of Section 1825.

(2) Any showing required by Section 1825 has been made. **Leg.H.** Enacted Stats 1990 ch 79 §14 (AB 759), operative July 1, 1991. Amended Stats 2014 ch 591 §6 (AB 1311), effective January 1, 2015; Stats 2015 ch 736 §10 (SB 589), effective January 1, 2016; Stats 2016 ch 86 §246 (SB 1171), effective January 1, 2017; Stats 2022 ch 420 §36 (AB 2960), effective January 1, 2023.

2015 Note: For legislative findings and declarations, see the 2015 Note following Prob C §1823.

Prior Law: Former Prob C §1828, similar to the present section, was added Stats 1979 ch 726 §3, operative January 1, 1981, amended Stats 1980 ch 1304 §12, and repealed Stats 1990 ch 79 §13, operative July 1, 1991.

§1828.5. Inquiry and information by court in limited conservatorship proceeding

(a) At the hearing on the petition for appointment of a limited conservator for an allegedly developmentally disabled adult, the court shall do each of the following:

(1) Inquire into the nature and extent of the general intellectual functioning of the individual alleged to be developmentally disabled.

(2) Evaluate the extent of the impairment of his or her adaptive behavior.

(3) Ascertain his or her capacity to care for himself or herself and his or her property.

(4) Inquire into the qualifications, abilities, and capabilities of the person seeking appointment as limited conservator.

(5) If a report by the regional center, in accordance with Section 1827.5, has not been filed in court because the proposed limited conservatee withheld his or her consent to assessment by the regional center, the court shall determine the reason for withholding such consent.

(b) If the court finds that the proposed limited conservatee possesses the capacity to care for himself or herself and to manage his or her property as a reasonably prudent person, the court shall dismiss the petition for appointment of a limited conservator.

(c) If the court finds that the proposed limited conservatee lacks the capacity to perform some, but not all, of the tasks necessary to provide properly for his or her own personal needs for physical health, food, clothing, or shelter, or to manage his or her own financial resources, the court shall appoint a limited conservator for the person or the estate or the person and the estate.

(d) If the court finds that the proposed limited conservatee lacks the capacity to perform all of the tasks necessary to provide properly for his or her own personal needs for physical health, food, clothing, or shelter, or to manage his or her own financial resources, the court shall appoint either a conservator or a limited conservator for the person or the estate, or the person and the estate.

(e) The court shall define the powers and duties of the limited conservator so as to permit the developmentally disabled adult to care for himself or herself or to manage his or her financial resources commensurate with his or her ability to do so.

(f) Prior to the appointment of a limited conservator for the person or estate or person and estate of a developmentally disabled adult, the court shall inform the proposed limited conservator of the nature and purpose of the limited conservatorship proceeding, that the appointment of a limited conservator for his or her person or estate or person and estate will result in the transfer of certain rights set forth in the petition and the effect of such transfer, the identity of the person who has been nominated as his or her limited conservator, that he or she has a right to oppose such proceeding, and that he or she has a right to have the matter tried by jury. After communicating such information to the person and prior to the appointment of a limited conservator, the court shall consult the person to determine his or her opinion concerning the appointment. **Leg.H.** Enacted Stats 1990 ch 79 §14 (AB 759), operative July 1, 1991.

Prior Law: Former Prob C §1828.5, similar to the present section, was added Stats 1980 ch 1304 §13, amended Stats 1984 ch 183 §2, and repealed Stats 1990 ch 79 §13, operative July 1, 1991.

§1829. Persons who may support or oppose petition

Any of the following persons may appear at the hearing to support or oppose the petition:

(a) The proposed conservatee.

(b) The spouse or registered domestic partner of the proposed conservatee.

(c) A relative of the proposed conservatee.

(d) Any interested person or friend of the proposed conservatee.

Leg.H. Enacted Stats 1990 ch 79 §14 (AB 759), operative July 1, 1991. Amended Stats 2001 ch 893 §20 (AB 25); Stats 2006 ch 493 §9 (AB 1363), effective January 1, 2007.

2006 Note: This act, together with Senate Bill 1116 (Scott), Senate Bill 1550 (Figueroa), and Senate Bill 1716 (Bowen), shall be known and may be cited as the Omnibus Conservatorship and Guardianship Reform Act of 2006. Stats 2006 ch 493 (AB 1363) §1.

Prior Law: Former Prob C §1829, similar to the present section, was added Stats 1979 ch 726 §3, operative January 1, 1981, amended Stats 1980 ch 1304 §14, and repealed Stats 1990 ch 79 §13, operative July 1, 1991.

§1830. Contents of order appointing conservator

(a) The order appointing the conservator shall contain, among other things, the names, addresses, and telephone numbers of:

(1) The conservator.

(2) The conservatee's attorney, if any.

(3) The court investigator, if any.

(b) In the case of a limited conservator for a developmentally disabled adult, any order the court issues shall include the findings of the court specified in Section 1828.5. The order shall specify the powers granted to and duties imposed upon the limited conservator, which powers and duties shall not exceed the powers and duties applicable to a conservator under this code. The order shall also specify all of the following:

(1) The properties of the limited conservatee to which the limited conservator is entitled to possession and management, giving a description of the properties that will be sufficient to identify them.

(2) The debts, rentals, wages, or other claims due to the limited conservatee which the limited conservator is entitled to collect, or file suit with respect to, if necessary, and thereafter to possess and manage.

(3) The contractual or other obligations which the limited conservator may incur on behalf of the limited conservatee.

(4) The claims against the limited conservatee which the limited conservator may pay, compromise, or defend, if necessary.

(5) Any other powers, limitations, or duties with respect to the care of the limited conservatee or the management of the property specified in this subdivision by the limited conservator which the court shall specifically and expressly grant.

(c) An information notice of the rights of conservatees shall be attached to the order. The conservator shall deliver pursuant to Section 1215 the order and the attached information notice to the conservatee and the conservatee's relatives, as set forth in subdivision (b) of Section 1821, within 30 days of the issuance of the order. By January 1, 2008, the Judicial Council shall develop the notice required by this subdivision.

Leg.H. Enacted Stats 1990 ch 79 §14 (AB 759), operative July 1, 1991. Amended Stats 2006 ch 493 §10 (AB 1363), effective January 1, 2007; Stats 2007 ch 553 §8 (AB 1727), effective January 1, 2008; Stats 2017 ch 319 §37 (AB 976), effective January 1, 2018.

2006 Note: This act, together with Senate Bill 1116 (Scott), Senate Bill 1550 (Figueroa), and Senate Bill 1716 (Bowen), shall be known and may be cited as the Omnibus Conservatorship and Guardianship Reform Act of 2006. Stats 2006 ch 493 (AB 1363) §1.

Prior Law: Former Prob C §1830, similar to the present section, was added Stats 1979 ch 726 §3, operative January 1, 1981, amended Stats 1980 ch 1304 §15, and repealed Stats 1990 ch 79 §13, operative July 1, 1991.

§1831. [Section repealed 1993]

Leg.H. Added Stats 1991 ch 82 §14 (SB 896), effective June 30, 1991, operative July 1, 1991. Repealed Stats 1993 ch 70 §9 (SB 86), effective June 30, 1993. The repealed section related to filing of general plan detailing how personal and financial needs of conservatee will be met and notice of plan.

Prior Law: Former Prob C §1831, similar to the repealed section, was added Stats 1990 ch 1208 §4, effective September 24, 1990, and repealed Stats 1991 ch 82 §13, effective June 30, operative July 1, 1991.

§1834. Acknowledgment of receipt

(a) Before letters are issued in a conservatorship that originates in this state or a conservatorship that is transferred to this state under Chapter 8 (commencing with Section 1980), the conservator (other than a trust company or a public conservator) shall file an acknowledgment of receipt of (1) a statement of duties and liabilities of the office of conservator, and (2) a copy of the conservatorship information required under Section 1835. The acknowledgment and the statement shall be in the form prescribed by the Judicial Council.

(b) The court may by local rules require the acknowledgment of receipt to include the conservator's birth date and driver's license number, if any, provided that the court ensures their confidentiality.

(c) The statement of duties and liabilities prescribed by the Judicial Council shall not supersede the law on which the statement is based.

Leg.H. Added Stats 1991 ch 1019 §1 (SB 1022). Amended Stats 1994 ch 806 §9 (AB 3686); Stats 2014 ch 553 §7 (SB 940), effective January 1, 2015, operative January 1, 2016.

§1835. Informational package for conservator

(a) Every superior court shall provide all conservators with written information concerning a conservator's rights, duties, limitations, and responsibilities under this division.

(b) The information to be provided shall include, but need not be limited to, the following:

(1) The rights, duties, limitations, and responsibilities of a conservator.

(2) The rights of a conservatee.

(3) How to assess the needs and preferences of the conservatee.

(4) How to use community-based services to meet the needs of the conservatee.

(5) How to ensure that the conservatee is provided with the least restrictive possible environment.

(6) The court procedures and processes relevant to conservatorships.

(7) The procedures for inventory and appraisal, and the filing of accounts.

(8) Procedures to petition to terminate or modify the conservatorship.

(9) The conservator's obligations pursuant to Section 2113.

(c) An information package shall be developed by the Judicial Council, after consultation with the following organizations or individuals:

(1) The California State Association of Public Administrators, Public Guardians, and Public Conservators, or other comparable organizations.

(2) The State Bar.

(3) Individuals or organizations, approved by the Judicial Council, who represent court investigators, specialists with experience in performing assessments and coordinating community-based services, and legal services programs for the elderly.

(d) The failure of any court or any employee or agent thereof, to provide information to a conservator as required by this section does not:

(1) Relieve the conservator of any of the conservator's duties as required by this division.

(2) Make the court or the employee or agent thereof, liable, in either a personal or official capacity, for damages to a conservatee, conservator, the conservatorship of a person or an estate, or any other person or entity.

(e) The information package shall be made available to individual courts. The Judicial Council shall periodically update the information package when changes in the law warrant revision. The revisions shall be provided to individual courts.

(f) To cover the costs of providing the written information required by this section, a court may charge each private conservator a fee of twenty dollars ($20) which shall be distributed to the court in which it was collected. **Leg.H.** Enacted Stats 1990 ch 79 §14 (AB 759), operative July 1, 1991. Amended Stats 1991 ch 1019 §2 (SB 1022); Stats 2005 ch 75 §147 (AB 145), effective July 19, 2005, operative January 1, 2006; Stats 2022 ch 894 §8 (AB 1663), effective January 1, 2023.

Prior Law: Former Prob C §1835, similar to the present section, was added Stats 1988 ch 742 §1, amended Stats 1989 ch 1360 §125, and repealed Stats 1990 ch 79 §13, operative July 1, 1991.

§ 1835.5. Informational package for conservatee

(a) Within 30 days of the establishment of a conservatorship under this division, and annually thereafter, the superior court shall provide information to a conservatee under its jurisdiction, written in plain language, with a list of the conservatee's rights within the conservatorship.

(b) The information to be provided shall include, but need not be limited to, all of the following:

(1) The name and contact information of the conservator.

(2) A description of the conservatorship, including the rights the conservatee retains under the conservatorship.

(3) The role, duties, and contact information, including name, telephone number, address, and email address, of the court investigator and the court alternatives program.

(4) The person to petition to end or change the conservatorship and contact information for the person to contact to begin that process.

(5) A personalized list of rights that the conservatee retains, even under the conservatorship, including the rights to do all of the following:

(A) Directly receive and control their own salary.

(B) Make or change their will.

(C) Get married.

(D) Receive mail.

(E) Have visits from family and friends.

(F) Have a lawyer.

(G) Ask a judge to change conservators.

(H) Ask a judge to end the conservatorship.

(I) Vote, unless expressly withheld by the court.

(J) Control personal spending money if a judge permits an allowance to be paid directly to the conservatee.

(K) Make their own health care decisions.

(L) Enter into business transactions to provide for the conservatee's basic needs and those of their children.

(M) Participate in other activities the court allows when the conservator is appointed, or when the court order later grants that right at the conservatee's request.

(6) The personalized list of rights in paragraph (5) shall state which rights, if any, were expressly withheld by the court. **Leg.H.** Added Stats 2022 ch 894 §9 (AB 1663), effective January 1, 2023.

§ 1836. Conservatorship alternatives program

(a) Upon appropriation by the Legislature, the Judicial Council shall establish a conservatorship alternatives program within each self-help center in every state Superior Court.

(b) The purposes of the conservatorship alternatives program are:

(1) To provide information relating to less restrictive alternatives to conservatorship, including, but not limited to, supported decisionmaking agreements, as defined in Section 21001 of the Welfare and Institutions Code, to interested individuals.

(2) To educate interested individuals on less restrictive alternatives to conservatorship that may be appropriate, and to provide assistance in considering and implementing those alternatives.

(c) Each court's conservatorship alternatives program shall include staff who provide information and resources to interested individuals about less restrictive alternatives to conservatorship.

(d) The conservatorship alternatives program shall operate as follows:

(1) Any interested individual who contacts a superior court self-help center to inquire about conservatorship proceedings or to request documents to petition for a conservatorship shall be advised of the conservatorship alternatives program.

(2) The conservatorship alternatives program shall be a component of each superior court's self-help center.

(3) Conservatorship alternatives program staff shall be trained in less restrictive alternatives to conservatorship and shall be available to meet, through in-person or remote means, with interested individuals to provide education and resources on supported decisionmaking agreements and other less restrictive alternatives to conservatorship, and to provide resources to assist people who wish to implement or establish those alternatives.

(4) Conservatorship alternatives program staff shall be able to provide the following to interested individuals:

(A) Practical resources, information, and documents to establish and implement alternatives to conservatorship, including powers of attorney, advance health care directives, and supported decisionmaking agreements.

(B) Technical support and education on these alternatives, including assistance in filling out any associated paperwork and in understanding these alternatives.

(5) Interactions or communication with the CAP Program shall not be used as evidence of incapacity or introduced for any other reason in a conservatorship proceeding under this division unless introduced by the conservatee or proposed conservatee. **Leg.H.** Added Stats 2022 ch 894 §10 (AB 1663), effective January 1, 2023.

ARTICLE 4
Special Provisions Applicable Where Proposed Conservatee Is an Absentee

Procedure for appointment of conservator for absentee. §1840.
Additional contents of petition. §1841.
Notice of hearing. §1842.
Citation to proposed conservatee not required. §1843.
Evidence of status of proposed conservatee; Inability to attend hearing. §1844.

§1840. Procedure for appointment of conservator for absentee

Except as otherwise provided in this article, a conservator for an absentee (Section 1403) shall be appointed as provided in Article 3 (commencing with Section 1820) of this chapter or Article 3 (commencing with Section 2001) of Chapter 8. **Leg.H.** Enacted Stats 1990 ch 79 §14 (AB 759), operative July 1, 1991. Amended Stats 2014 ch 553 §8 (SB 940), effective January 1, 2015, operative January 1, 2016.

Prior Law: Former Prob C §1840, similar to the present section, was added Stats 1979 ch 726 §3, operative January 1, 1981, and repealed Stats 1990 ch 79 §13, operative July 1, 1991.

§1841. Additional contents of petition

In addition to the other required contents of the petition, if the proposed conservatee is an absentee:

(a) The petition, and any notice required by Section 1822 or 2002, or any other law, shall set forth the last known military rank or grade and the social security account number of the proposed conservatee.

(b) The petition shall state whether the absentee's spouse has commenced any action or proceeding against the absentee for judicial or legal separation, dissolution of marriage, annulment, or adjudication of nullity of their marriage. **Leg.H.** Enacted Stats 1990 ch 79 §14 (AB 759), operative July 1, 1991. Amended Stats 2014 ch 553 §9 (SB 940), effective January 1, 2015, operative January 1, 2016.

Prior Law: Former Prob C §1841, similar to the present section, was added Stats 1979 ch 726 §3, operative January 1, 1981, and repealed Stats 1990 ch 79 §13, operative July 1, 1991.

§1842. Notice of hearing

In addition to the persons and entities to whom notice of hearing is required under Section 1822 or 2002, if the proposed conservatee is an absentee, a copy of the petition and notice of the time and place of the hearing shall be delivered pursuant to Section 1215 at least 15 days before the hearing to the secretary concerned or to the head of the United States department or agency concerned, as the case may be. In that case, notice shall also be published pursuant to Section 6061 of the Government Code in a newspaper of general circulation in the county in which the hearing will be held. **Leg.H.** Enacted Stats 1990 ch 79 §14 (AB 759), operative July 1, 1991. Amended Stats 2014 ch 553 §10 (SB 940), effective January 1, 2015, operative January 1, 2016; Stats 2017 ch 319 §38 (AB 976), effective January 1, 2018.

Prior Law: Former Prob C §1842, similar to the present section, was added Stats 1979 ch 726 §3, operative January 1, 1981, and repealed Stats 1990 ch 79 §13, operative July 1, 1991.

§1843. Citation to proposed conservatee not required

(a) No citation is required under Section 1823 to the proposed conservatee if the proposed conservatee is an absentee.

(b) No notice is required under Section 2002 to the proposed conservatee if the proposed conservatee is an absentee. **Leg.H.** Enacted Stats 1990 ch 79 §14 (AB 759), operative July 1, 1991. Amended Stats 2014 ch 553 §11 (SB 940), effective January 1, 2015, operative January 1, 2016.

Prior Law: Former Prob C §1843, similar to the present section, was added Stats 1979 ch 726 §3, operative January 1, 1981, and repealed Stats 1990 ch 79 §13, operative July 1, 1991.

§1844. Evidence of status of proposed conservatee; Inability to attend hearing

(a) In a proceeding to appoint a conservator for an absentee under

Article 3 (commencing with Section 1820) of this chapter or Article 3 (commencing with Section 2001) of Chapter 8, an official written report or record complying with Section 1283 of the Evidence Code that a proposed conservatee is an absentee shall be received as evidence of that fact and the court shall not determine the status of the proposed conservatee inconsistent with the status determined as shown by the written report or record.

(b) The inability of the proposed conservatee to attend the hearing is established by the official written report or record referred to in subdivision (a). **Leg.H.** Enacted Stats 1990 ch 79 §14 (AB 759), operative July 1, 1991. Amended Stats 2014 ch 553 §12 (SB 940), effective January 1, 2015, operative January 1, 2016.

Prior Law: Former Prob C §1844, similar to the present section, was added Stats 1979 ch 726 §3, operative January 1, 1981, and repealed Stats 1990 ch 79 §13, operative July 1, 1991.

ARTICLE 5
Special Provisions Applicable Where Proposed Conservatee Is a Missing Person

Appointment of conservator of estate of missing person. §1845.
Additional contents of petition. §1846.
Notice of hearing. §1847.
Acts not required in proceeding. §1848.
Findings prerequisite to appointment of conservator. §1849.
Application of article. §1849.5.

§1845. Appointment of conservator of estate of missing person

(a) Except as otherwise provided in this article, a conservator of the estate of a person who is missing and whose whereabouts is unknown shall be appointed as provided in Article 3 (commencing with Section 1820) of this chapter or Article 3 (commencing with Section 2001) of Chapter 8.

(b) This article does not apply where the proposed conservatee is an absentee as defined in Section 1403. **Leg.H.** Enacted Stats 1990 ch 79 §14 (AB 759), operative July 1, 1991. Amended Stats 2014 ch 553 §13 (SB 940), effective January 1, 2015, operative January 1, 2016.

Prior Law: Former Prob C §1845, similar to the present section, was added Stats 1983 ch 201 §7 and repealed Stats 1990 ch 79 §13, operative July 1, 1991.

§1846. Additional contents of petition

In addition to the other required contents of the petition, if the proposed conservatee is a person who is missing and whose whereabouts is unknown, the petition shall state all of the following:

(a) The proposed conservatee owns or is entitled to the possession of real or personal property located in this state. In a proceeding to transfer a conservatorship of a missing person to this state under Article 3 (commencing with Section 2001) of Chapter 8, this requirement is also satisfied if the petition states that the proposed conservatee owns or is entitled to the possession of personal property that is to be relocated to this state upon approval of the transfer.

(b) The time and circumstance of the person's disappearance and that the missing person has not been heard from by the persons most likely to hear (naming them and their relationship to the missing person) since the time of disappearance and that the whereabouts of the missing person is unknown to those persons and to the petitioner.

(c) The last known residence of the missing person.

(d) A description of any search or inquiry made concerning the whereabouts of the missing person.

(e) A description of the estate of the proposed conservatee which requires attention, supervision, and care. **Leg.H.** Enacted Stats 1990 ch 79 §14 (AB 759), operative July 1, 1991. Amended Stats 2014 ch 553 §14 (SB 940), effective January 1, 2015, operative January 1, 2016.

Prior Law: Former Prob C §1846, similar to the present section, was added Stats 1983 ch 201 §7 and repealed Stats 1990 ch 79 §13, operative July 1, 1991.

§1847. Notice of hearing

In addition to the persons and entities to whom notice of hearing is required under Section 1822 or 2002, if the proposed conservatee is a person who is missing and whose whereabouts is unknown:

(a) A copy of the petition for appointment of a conservator and notice of the time and place of the hearing on the petition shall be delivered pursuant to Section 1215 at least 15 days before the hearing to the proposed conservatee at the last known address of the proposed conservatee.

(b) Notice of the time and place of the hearing shall also be published pursuant to Section 6061 of the Government Code in a newspaper of general circulation in the county in which the proposed conservatee was last known to reside if the proposed conservatee's last known address is in this state.

(c) Pursuant to Section 1202, the court may require that further or additional notice of the hearing be given. **Leg.H.** Enacted Stats 1990 ch 79 §14 (AB 759), operative July 1, 1991. Amended Stats 2014 ch 553 §15 (SB 940), effective January 1, 2015, operative January 1, 2016; Stats 2017 ch 319 §39 (AB 976), effective January 1, 2018.

Prior Law: Former Prob C §1847, similar to the present section, was added Stats 1983 ch 201 §7 and repealed Stats 1990 ch 79 §13, operative July 1, 1991.

§1848. Acts not required in proceeding

(a) In a proceeding under Article 3 (commencing with Section 1820) to appoint a conservator of the estate of a person who is missing and whose whereabouts is unknown, the following acts are not required:

(1) Issuance of a citation to the proposed conservatee pursuant to Section 1823.

(2) Service of a citation and petition pursuant to Section 1824.

(3) Production of the proposed conservatee at the hearing pursuant to Section 1825.

(4) Performance of the duties of the court investigator pursuant to Section 1826.

(5) Performance of any other act that depends upon knowledge of the location of the proposed conservatee.

(b) In a proceeding to transfer a conservatorship of a missing person to this state under Article 3 (commencing with Section 2001) of Chapter 8, the following acts are not required:

(1) Notice to the proposed conservatee pursuant to Section 2002.

(2) Production of the proposed conservatee at the hearings pursuant to Section 2002.

(3) Performance of the duties of the court investigator pursuant to Section 1851.1.

(4) Performance of any other act that depends upon knowledge of the location of the proposed conservatee. **Leg.H.** Enacted Stats 1990 ch 79 §14 (AB 759), operative July 1, 1991. Amended Stats 2014 ch 553 §16 (SB 940), effective January 1, 2015, operative January 1, 2016.

Prior Law: Former Prob C §1848, similar to the present section, was added Stats 1983 ch 201 §7 and repealed Stats 1990 ch 79 §13, operative July 1, 1991.

§1849. Findings prerequisite to appointment of conservator

A conservator of the estate of a person who is missing and whose whereabouts is unknown may be appointed only if the court finds all of the following:

(a) The proposed conservatee owns or is entitled to the possession of real or personal property located in this state. In a proceeding to transfer a conservatorship of a missing person to this state under Article 3 (commencing with Section 2001) of Chapter 8, this requirement is also satisfied if the court finds that the proposed conservatee owns or is entitled to the possession of personal property that is to be relocated to this state upon approval of the transfer.

(b) The proposed conservatee remains missing and his or her whereabouts remains unknown.

(c) The estate of the proposed conservatee requires attention, supervision, and care. **Leg.H.** Enacted Stats 1990 ch 79 §14 (AB 759), operative July 1, 1991. Amended Stats 2014 ch 553 §17 (SB 940), effective January 1, 2015, operative January 1, 2016.

Prior Law: Former Prob C §1849, similar to the present section, was added Stats 1983 ch 201 §7 and repealed Stats 1990 ch 79 §13, operative July 1, 1991.

§1849.5. Application of article

(a) A petition may be filed under this article regardless of when the proposed conservatee became missing or how long the proposed conservatee has been missing.

(b) If a trustee was appointed pursuant to former Section 262, repealed by Chapter 201 of the Statutes of 1983, the provisions of former Sections 260 to 272, inclusive, repealed by Chapter 201 of the Statutes of 1983, continue to apply to the case after December 31, 1983, unless, upon a petition filed under this article after December 31, 1983, the trustee is replaced by a conservator. **Leg.H.** Enacted Stats 1990 ch 79 §14 (AB 759), operative July 1, 1991.

Prior Law: Former Prob C §1849.5, similar to the present section, was added Stats 1983 ch 201 §7 and repealed Stats 1990 ch 79 §13, operative July 1, 1991.

CHAPTER 2
PERIODIC REVIEW OF CONSERVATORSHIP

Court review of conservatorship. § 1850.
Review of limited conservatorship for developmentally disabled adult. §1850.5.
Visitation and findings by court investigator. §1851.
Investigation and report upon order provisionally granting petition to accept conservatorship transferred from another state. §1851.1.
Review of accountings. §1851.2.
Assessment of conservatee for investigation or review expense. §1851.5.
Persons who may petition the court to investigate an allegation of abuse. § 1851.6.
Notification of counsel; Representation of conservatee at hearing. §1852.
Failure to locate conservatee; Removal of conservator on failure to produce conservatee; Petition to appoint new conservator. §1853.

§ 1850. Court review of conservatorship

(a) Except as provided in subdivision (e), each conservatorship established pursuant to this part shall be reviewed by the court as follows:

(1) Six months after the initial appointment of the conservator, the court investigator shall visit the conservatee, conduct an investigation as provided in subdivision (a) of Section 1851, and report to the court regarding the appropriateness of the conservatorship and whether the conservator is acting in the best interests of the conservatee regarding the conservatee's placement, quality of care, including physical and mental health treatment, and finances. In response to the investigator's report, the court may take appropriate action including, but not limited to, ordering a hearing or ordering the conservator to submit an accounting pursuant to subdivision (a) of Section 2620.

(2) One year after the initial appointment of the conservator and annually thereafter, the court investigator shall, as provided in Section 1851, visit the conservatee, conduct an investigation, including, when possible, discussing with the conservatee less restrictive alternatives to conservatorship as set forth in Section 1800.3, and report the findings of the investigation to the court, including whether the conservator or conservatee wishes to modify or terminate the conservatorship and whether less restrictive alternatives could be tried. On receipt of the investigator's report, the court shall, if indicated by the report, consider promptly terminating or modifying the conservatorship at a hearing pursuant to Section 1860.5 or 1863 and take any other appropriate action.

(b) At any time, the court may, on its own motion or upon request by any interested person, take appropriate action including, but not limited to, ordering a review of the conservatorship at a noticed hearing or ordering the conservator to submit an accounting pursuant to Section 2620.

(c) Notice of a review hearing pursuant to this section shall be given to the persons, for the period and in the manner provided in Chapter 3 (commencing with Section 1460) of Part 1.

(d) This chapter does not apply to either of the following:

(1) A conservatorship for an absentee as defined in Section 1403.

(2) A conservatorship of the estate for a nonresident of this state where the conservatee is not present in this state.

(e)(1) A superior court shall not be required to perform any duties imposed pursuant to the amendments to this section enacted by Chapter 493 of the Statutes of 2006 until the Legislature makes an appropriation identified for this purpose.

(2) A superior court shall not be required to perform any duties imposed pursuant to the measure that added this paragraph until the Legislature makes an appropriation identified for this purpose. **Leg.H.** Enacted Stats 1990 ch 79 §14 (AB 759), operative July 1, 1991. Amended Stats 2006 ch 492 §3 (SB 1716), effective January 1, 2007, operative July 1, 2007, ch 493 §11.5 (AB 1363), effective January 1, 2007, operative July 1, 2007; Stats 2011 ch 10 §13 (SB 78), effective March 24, 2011; Stats 2021 ch 417 §8 (AB 1194), effective January 1, 2022; Stats 2022 ch 894 §11 (AB 1663), effective January 1, 2023.

2006 Note: This act, together with Senate Bill 1116 (Scott), Senate Bill 1550 (Figueroa), and Senate Bill 1716 (Bowen), shall be known and may be cited as the Omnibus Conservatorship and Guardianship Reform Act of 2006. Stats 2006 ch 493 (AB 1363) §1.

Prior Law: Former Prob C §1850, similar to the present section, was added Stats 1979 ch 726 §3, operative January 1, 1981, and repealed Stats 1990 ch 79 §13, operative July 1, 1991.

§1850.5. Review of limited conservatorship for developmentally disabled adult

(a) Notwithstanding Section 1850, each limited conservatorship for a developmentally disabled adult, as defined in subdivision (d) of Section 1801, shall be reviewed by the court one year after the appointment of the conservator and biennially thereafter.

(b) The court may, on its own motion or upon request by any interested person, take appropriate action, including, but not limited to, ordering a review of the limited conservatorship at a noticed hearing, at any time.

(c) At any review pursuant to this section, the court shall consider terminating the limited conservatorship, as provided in Section 1860.5.

(d) Notice of a review hearing pursuant to this section shall be given to the persons, for the period and in the manner provided in subdivision (d) of Section 1860.5.

(e)(1) A superior court shall not be required to perform any duties imposed by this section until the Legislature makes an appropriation identified for this purpose.

(2) A superior court shall not be required to perform any duties imposed pursuant to the amendments to this section enacted by the measure that added this paragraph until the Legislature makes an appropriation identified for this purpose. **Leg.H.** Added Stats 2006 ch 493 §11.7 (AB 1363), effective January 1, 2007, operative July 1, 2007. Amended Stats 2011 ch 10 §14 (SB 78), effective March 24, 2011; Stats 2021 ch 417 §9 (AB 1194), effective January 1, 2022.

2006 Note: This act, together with Senate Bill 1116 (Scott), Senate Bill 1550 (Figueroa), and Senate Bill 1716 (Bowen), shall be known and may be cited as the Omnibus Conservatorship and Guardianship Reform Act of 2006. Stats 2006 ch 493 (AB 1363) §1.

§1851. Visitation and findings by court investigator

(a)(1) If court review is required pursuant to Section 1850 or 1850.5, the court investigator shall, without prior notice to the conservator except as ordered by the court for necessity or to prevent harm to the conservatee, visit the conservatee. The court investigator shall inform the conservatee personally that the conservatee is under a conservatorship and shall give the name of the conservator to the conservatee. The court investigator shall determine all of the following:

(A) If the conservatee wishes the court to terminate the conservatorship.

(B) If the conservatee wishes the court to remove the conservator and appoint a successor conservator.

(C) If both of the following are true:

(i) The conservatee still meets the criteria for appointment of a conservator of the person under subdivision (a) of Section 1801, a conservator of the estate under subdivision (b) of Section 1801, or both.

(ii) The conservatorship remains the least restrictive alternative needed for the protection of the conservatee, as required by subdivision (b) of Section 1800.3.

(D) If the conservator is acting in the best interests of the conservatee. In determining if the conservator is acting in the best interests of the conservatee, the court investigator's evaluation shall include an examination of the conservatee's placement, the quality of care, including physical and mental health treatment, and the conservatee's finances. To the extent practicable, the investigator shall review the accounting with a conservatee who has sufficient capacity. To the greatest extent possible, the court investigator shall interview individuals set forth in paragraph (1) of subdivision (a) of Section 1826, in order to determine if the conservator is acting in the best interests of the conservatee.

(E)(i) If the conservatee is incapable of communicating, with or without reasonable accommodations, a desire to participate in the voting process and may be disqualified from voting pursuant to Section 2208 or 2209 of the Elections Code.

(ii) The conservatee shall not be disqualified from voting on the basis that the conservatee does, or would need to do, any of the following to complete an affidavit of voter registration:

(I) Signs the affidavit of voter registration with a mark or a cross pursuant to subdivision (b) of Section 2150 of the Elections Code.

(II) Signs the affidavit of voter registration by means of a signature stamp pursuant to Section 354.5 of the Elections Code.

(III) Completes the affidavit of voter registration with the assistance of another person pursuant to subdivision (d) of Section 2150 of the Elections Code.

(IV) Completes the affidavit of voter registration with reasonable accommodations.

(2) If the court investigator determines that the conservatee still meets the criteria for appointment of a conservator under Section 1801, the

investigator shall determine if the terms of the appointment order should be modified to reduce or expand the conservator's powers and duties to ensure that the conservatorship is the least restrictive alternative needed for the conservatee's protection.

(3) Upon request of the court investigator, the conservator shall make available to the court investigator during the investigation for inspection and copying all books and records, including receipts and any expenditures, of the conservatorship.

(b)(1) The findings of the court investigator, including the facts upon which the findings are based, shall be certified in writing to the court not less than 15 days before the date of review. A copy of the report shall be delivered pursuant to Section 1215 to the conservatee, the conservator, and the attorneys of record for the conservator and conservatee at the same time it is certified to the court. A copy of the report, modified as set forth in paragraph (2), also shall be delivered pursuant to Section 1215 to the conservatee's spouse or registered domestic partner and the conservatee's relatives in the first degree, or, if there are no such relatives, to the next closest relative, unless the court determines that the delivery will harm the conservatee.

(2) Confidential medical information and confidential information from the California Law Enforcement Telecommunications System shall be in a separate attachment to the report and shall not be provided in copies sent to the conservatee's spouse or registered domestic partner and the conservatee's relatives in the first degree, or, if there are no such relatives, to the next closest relative.

(c) In the case of a limited conservatee, the court investigator shall recommend whether to continue, modify, or terminate the limited conservatorship.

(d) The court investigator may personally visit the conservator and any other persons necessary to determine if the conservator is acting in the best interests of the conservatee.

(e) The report required by this section shall be confidential and shall be made available only to parties, persons described in subdivision (b), persons given notice of the petition who have requested the report or who have appeared in the proceeding, their attorneys, and the court. The court shall have discretion at any other time to release the report if it would serve the interests of the conservatee. The clerk of the court shall limit disclosure of the report exclusively to persons entitled to the report under this section.

(f)(1) A superior court is not required to perform any duties imposed pursuant to the amendments to this section enacted by Chapter 493 of the Statutes of 2006 until the Legislature makes an appropriation identified for this purpose.

(2) A superior court shall not be required to perform any duties imposed pursuant to the amendments to this section enacted by the measure that added this paragraph until the Legislature makes an appropriation identified for this purpose. **Leg.H.** Enacted Stats 1990 ch 79 §14 (AB 759), operative July 1, 1991. Amended Stats 1991 ch 82 §16 (SB 896), effective June 30, 1991, operative July 1, 1991; Stats 2002 ch 784 §580 (SB 1316), ch 1008 §28 (AB 3028) (ch 1008 prevails); Stats 2006 ch 492 §4 (SB 1716), effective January 1, 2007, operative July 1, 2007, ch 493 §12.5 (AB 1363), effective January 1, 2007, operative July 1, 2007; Stats 2007 ch 553 §9 (AB 1727), effective January 1, 2008; Stats 2011 ch 10 §15 (SB 78), effective March 24, 2011; Stats 2014 ch 591 §7 (AB 1311), effective January 1, 2015; Stats 2015 ch 736 §11 (SB 589), effective January 1, 2016; Stats 2016 ch 86 §247 (SB 1171), effective January 1, 2017; Stats 2017 ch 319 §40 (AB 976), effective January 1, 2018; Stats 2021 ch 417 §10 (AB 1194), effective January 1, 2022.

2015 Note: For legislative findings and declarations, see the 2015 Note following Prob C §1823.
2006 Note: This act, together with Senate Bill 1116 (Scott), Senate Bill 1550 (Figueroa), and Senate Bill 1716 (Bowen), shall be known and may be cited as the Omnibus Conservatorship and Guardianship Reform Act of 2006. Stats 2006 ch 493 (AB 1363) §1.

Prior Law: Former Prob C §1851, similar to present section, was added Stats 1989 ch 1080 §8, repealed Stats 1990 ch 79 §13, operative July 1, 1991, amended Stats 1990 ch 1208 §5, effective September 24, 1990, and repealed Stats 1991 ch 82 §15, effective June 30, operative July 1, 1991.

Former Prob C §1851, similar to the present section, was added Stats 1979 ch 726 §3, operative January 1, 1981, amended Stats 1980 ch 1304 §16, and repealed Stats 1989 ch 1080 §7.

Former Prob C §1851, similar to present Prob C §§2351, 2352, 2356, was added Stats 1957 ch 1902 §1, amended Stats 1976 ch 1357 §29, operative July 1, 1977, Stats 1978 ch 1315 §5, and repealed Stats 1979 ch 726 §2, operative January 1, 1981.

§1851.1. Investigation and report upon order provisionally granting petition to accept conservatorship transferred from another state

(a) When a court issues an order provisionally granting a petition under Section 2002, the investigator appointed under Section 2002 shall promptly commence an investigation under this section.

(b) In conducting an investigation and preparing a report under this section, the court investigator shall do all of the following:

(1) Comply with the requirements of Section 1851.

(2) Conduct an interview of the conservator.

(3) Conduct an interview of the conservatee's spouse or registered domestic partner, if any.

(4) Inform the conservatee of the nature, purpose, and effect of the conservatorship.

(5) Inform the conservatee and all other persons entitled to notice under subdivision (b) of Section 2002 of the right to seek termination of the conservatorship.

(6) Determine whether the conservatee objects to the conservator or prefers another person to act as conservator.

(7) Inform the conservatee of the right to attend the hearing under subdivision (c).

(8) Determine whether it appears that the conservatee is unable to attend the hearing and, if able to attend, whether the conservatee is willing to attend the hearing.

(9) Inform the conservatee of the right to be represented by legal counsel if the conservatee so chooses, and to have legal counsel appointed by the court if the conservatee is unable to retain legal counsel.

(10) Determine whether the conservatee wishes to be represented by legal counsel and, if so, whether the conservatee has retained legal counsel and, if not, the name of an attorney the conservatee wishes to retain.

(11) If the conservatee has not retained legal counsel, determine whether the conservatee desires the court to appoint legal counsel.

(12) Determine whether the appointment of legal counsel would be helpful to the resolution of the matter or is necessary to protect the interests of the conservatee when the conservatee does not plan to retain legal counsel and has not requested the appointment of legal counsel by the court.

(13) Consider each of the categories specified in paragraphs (1) to (5), inclusive, of subdivision (a) of Section 1821.

(14) Consider, to the extent practicable, whether the investigator believes the conservatee suffers from any of the mental function deficits listed in subdivision (a) of Section 811 that significantly impairs the conservatee's ability to understand and appreciate the consequences of the conservatee's actions in connection with any of the functions described in subdivision (a) or (b) of Section 1801 and identify the observations that support that belief.

(c) The court shall review the conservatorship as provided in Section 2002. The conservatee shall attend the hearing unless the conservatee's attendance is excused under Section 1825. The court may take appropriate action in response to the court investigator's report under this section.

(d) The court investigator's report under this section shall be confidential as provided in Section 1851.

(e) Except as provided in paragraph (2) of subdivision (a) of Section 1850, the court shall review the conservatorship again one year after the review conducted pursuant to subdivision (c), and annually thereafter, in the manner specified in Section 1850.

(f) The first time that the need for a conservatorship is challenged by any interested person or raised on the court's own motion after a transfer under Section 2002, whether in a review pursuant to this section or in a petition to terminate the conservatorship under Chapter 3 (commencing with Section 1860), the court shall presume that there is no need for a conservatorship. This presumption is rebuttable, but can only be overcome by clear and convincing evidence. The court shall make an express finding on whether continuation of the conservatorship is the least restrictive alternative needed for the protection of the conservatee.

(g)(1) If a duty described in this section is the same as a duty imposed pursuant to the amendments to Sections 1826, 1850, 1851, 2250, 2253, and 2620 and the addition of Sections 2250.4 and 2250.6 enacted by Chapter 493 of the Statutes of 2006, and the addition of Section 1051 enacted by Chapter 492 of the Statutes of 2006, a superior court shall not be required to perform that duty until the Legislature makes an appropriation identified for this purpose.

(2) If a duty described in this section is the same as a duty imposed pursuant to the amendments to Sections 1826, 1850, 1851, 2250, 2250.4, 2250.6, 2253, and 2620 enacted by the measure that added this paragraph, a superior court shall not be required to perform that duty until the Legislature makes an appropriation identified for this purpose. **Leg.H.** Added Stats 2014 ch 553 §18 (SB 940), effective January 1, 2015, operative January 1, 2016. Amended Stats 2021 ch 417 §11 (AB 1194), effective January 1, 2022.

§1851.2. Review of accountings

Each court shall coordinate investigations with the filing of accountings, so that investigators may review accountings before visiting conservatees, if feasible. **Leg.H.** Added Stats 2007 ch 553 §10 (AB 1727), effective January 1, 2008.

§1851.5. Assessment of conservatee for investigation or review expense

Each court shall assess each conservatee in the county for any investigation or review conducted by a court investigator with respect to that person. Subject to Section 68631 of the Government Code, the court may order reimbursement to the court for the amount of the assessment, unless the court finds that all or any part of the assessment would impose a hardship on conservatee or the conservatee's estate. There shall be a rebuttable presumption that the assessment would impose a hardship if the conservatee is receiving Medi-Cal benefits. **Leg.H.** Enacted Stats 1990 ch 79 §14 (AB 759), operative July 1, 1991. Amended Stats 1991 ch 82 §18 (SB 896), effective June 30, 1991, operative July 1, 1991; Stats 1996 ch 563 §9 (SB 392); Stats 2002 ch 1008 §29 (AB 3028); Stats 2014 ch 913 §30.5 (AB 2747), effective January 1, 2015.

Prior Law: Former Prob C §1851.5, similar to the present section, was added Stats 1982 ch 327 §130, effective June 30, 1982, amended Stats 1984 ch 268 §29, effective June 30, 1984, Stats 1989 ch 1080 §9, repealed Stats 1990 ch 79 §13, amended Stats 1990 ch 1208 §6, effective September 24, 1990, and repealed Stats 1991 ch 82 §17, effective June 30, operative July 1, 1991.

§ 1851.6. Persons who may petition the court to investigate an allegation of abuse

(a) Any interested person, as defined in Section 48 or any person entitled to receive notice pursuant to Section 1822, if they have personal knowledge of a conservatee, may petition the court to investigate an allegation of abuse, as defined by Section 15610.07 of the Welfare and Institutions Code, of the conservatee by a conservator. The court shall investigate all such allegations that establish a prima facie case of abuse. If the court investigator has performed an investigation within the preceding six months and reported the results of that investigation to the court, the court may order, upon good cause shown, that a new investigation is not necessary or that a more limited investigation is sufficient.

(b) A superior court shall not be required to perform any duties imposed pursuant to this section until the Legislature makes an appropriation identified for this purpose. **Leg.H.** Added Stats 2021 ch 417 §12 (AB 1194), effective January 1, 2022.

§1852. Notification of counsel; Representation of conservatee at hearing

If the conservatee wishes to petition the court for termination of the conservatorship or for removal of the existing conservator or for the making, modification, or revocation of a court order under Chapter 4 (commencing with Section 1870) or for restoration of the right to register to vote, or if, based on information contained in the court investigator's report or obtained from any other source, the court determines that a trial or hearing for termination of the conservatorship or removal of the existing conservator is in the best interests of the conservatee, the court shall notify the attorney of record for the conservatee, if any, or shall appoint the public defender or private counsel under Section 1471, to file the petition and represent the conservatee at the trial or hearing and, if such appointment is made, Section 1472 applies. **Leg.H.** Enacted Stats 1990 ch 79 §14 (AB 759), operative July 1, 1991.

Prior Law: Former Prob C §1852, similar to the present section, was added Stats 1979 ch 726 §3, operative January 1, 1981, and repealed Stats 1990 ch 79 §13, operative July 1, 1991.

Former Prob C §1852, relating to conservator powers, was added Stats 1976 ch 1357 §31, operative July 1, 1977, amended Stats Stats 1967 ch 555 §1, and repealed Stats 1979 ch 726 §2, operative January 1, 1981.

§1853. Failure to locate conservatee; Removal of conservator on failure to produce conservatee; Petition to appoint new conservator

(a) If the court investigator is unable to locate the conservatee, the court shall order the court investigator to serve notice upon the conservator of the person, or upon the conservator of the estate if there is no conservator of the person, in the manner provided in Section 415.10 or 415.30 of the Code of Civil Procedure or in such other manner as is ordered by the court, to make the conservatee available for the purposes of Section 1851 to the court investigator within 15 days of the receipt of such notice or to show cause why the conservatorship should not be terminated.

(b) If the conservatee is not made available within the time prescribed, unless good cause is shown for not doing so, the court shall make such a finding and shall enter judgment terminating the conservatorship and, in case of a conservatorship of the estate, shall order the conservator to file an account and to surrender the estate to the person legally entitled thereto. At the hearing, or thereafter on further notice and hearing, the conservator may be discharged and the bond given by the conservator may be exonerated upon the settlement and approval of the conservator's final account by the court.

(c) Termination of the conservatorship under this section does not preclude institution of new proceedings for the appointment of a conservator. Nothing in this section limits the power of a court to appoint a temporary conservator under Chapter 3 (commencing with Section 2250) of Part 4. **Leg.H.** Enacted Stats 1990 ch 79 §14 (AB 759), operative July 1, 1991.

Prior Law: Former Prob C §1853, similar to the present section, was added Stats 1979 ch 726 §3, operative January 1, 1981, and repealed Stats 1990 ch 79 §13, operative July 1, 1991.

Former Prob C §1853, similar to present Prob C §§2451, 2458– 2462, 2465, 2590– 2592, 2594, 2595, was added Stats 1957 ch 1902 §1, amended Stats 1959 ch 347 §1, Stats 1961 ch 932 §1, Stats 1969 ch 552 §2, Stats 1973 ch 142 §61, effective June 30, 1973, operative July 1, 1973, Stats 1976 ch 1357 §32, operative July 1, 1977, and repealed Stats 1979 ch 726 §2, operative January 1, 1981.

CHAPTER 3
TERMINATION

When conservatorship terminates. §1860.
When limited conservatorship terminates. § 1860.5.
Petition for termination of conservatorship. §1861.
Appointment of counsel for conservatee and setting hearing for conservatorship termination. § 1861.5.
Notice of hearing. §1862.
Hearing and judgment. §1863.
Termination of conservatorship of absentee. §1864.
Restoring right to vote. §1865.

§1860. When conservatorship terminates

(a) A conservatorship continues until terminated by the death of the conservatee or by order of the court pursuant to Section 1863, subject to Section 2467 and Article 4 (commencing with Section 2630) of Chapter 7 of Part 4, and except as otherwise provided by law.

(b) At a hearing under Section 1850 or a hearing on a petition to terminate a conservatorship under Section 1861, the court shall proceed as provided in Section 1863.

(c) If a conservatorship is established for the person of a married minor, the conservatorship does not terminate automatically if the marriage is dissolved or is adjudged a nullity.

(d) This section does not apply to limited conservatorships.

(e) A superior court shall not be required to perform any duties imposed pursuant to the amendments to this section enacted by the measure that added this subdivision until the Legislature makes an appropriation identified for this purpose. **Leg.H.** Enacted Stats 1990 ch 79 §14 (AB 759), operative July 1, 1991. Amended Stats 2018 ch 126 §1 (AB 2236), effective January 1, 2019; Stats 2021 ch 417 §13 (AB 1194), effective January 1, 2022.

Prior Law: Former Prob C §1860, similar to the present section, was added Stats 1979 ch 726 §3, operative January 1, 1981, amended Stats 1980 ch 1304 §17, and repealed Stats 1990 ch 79 §13, operative July 1, 1991.

Former Prob C §1860, similar to present Prob C §§2359, 2403, was added Stats 1957 ch 1902 §1, and repealed Stats 1979 ch 726 §2, operative January 1, 1981.

§ 1860.5. When limited conservatorship terminates

(a) A limited conservatorship continues until the authority of the conservator is terminated by one of the following:

(1) The death of the limited conservator.

(2) The death of the limited conservatee.

(3) An order appointing a conservator of the former limited conservatee.

(4) An order of the court terminating the limited conservatorship.

(b) A petition for the termination of a limited conservatorship may be filed by any of the following:

(1) The limited conservator.

(2) The limited conservatee.

(3) Any relative or friend of the limited conservatee.

(c) The petition shall state facts showing that the limited conservatorship is no longer required.

(d) Notice of a hearing pursuant to Section 1850.5 or on a petition filed pursuant to this section shall be given to the same persons and in the same manner as provided for a petition for the appointment of a limited conservator.

(1) If a petition is filed and the limited conservator is not the petitioner, or has not joined in the petition, the limited conservator shall be served with a notice of the time and place of the hearing accompanied by a copy of the petition at least five days prior to the hearing. This service shall be made in the same manner provided for in Section 415.10 or 415.30 of the Code of Civil Procedure or in another manner authorized by the court. If the limited conservator cannot, with reasonable diligence, be so served with notice, the court may dispense with notice.

(2) If the court sets a hearing pursuant to Section 1850.5 to consider termination of a limited conservatorship and no petition is filed, the court shall order the limited conservator to give notice of the hearing as provided in this subdivision and to appear at the hearing and show cause why the limited conservatorship should not be terminated.

(e)(1) The limited conservatee shall be produced at the hearing except in the following cases:

(A) When the limited conservatee is out of the state and is not the petitioner.

(B) When the limited conservatee is unable to attend the hearing by reason of medical inability.

(C) When the court investigator has reported to the court that the limited conservatee has expressly communicated that the limited conservatee (i) is not willing to attend the hearing, (ii) does not wish to contest the continuation of the limited conservatorship, and (iii) does not object to the current limited conservator or prefer that another person act as limited conservator, and the court makes an order that the limited conservatee need not attend the hearing.

(2) If the limited conservatee is unable to attend the hearing because of medical inability, that inability shall be established by the affidavit or certificate of a licensed medical practitioner or, if the conservatee is an adherent of a religion whose tenets and practices call for reliance on prayer alone for healing and is under treatment by an accredited practitioner of that religion, by the affidavit of the practitioner. The affidavit or certificate is evidence only of the limited conservatee's inability to attend the hearing and shall not be considered in determining the issue of need for the continuation of the limited conservatorship.

(3) Emotional or psychological instability is not good cause for the absence of the conservatee from the hearing unless, by reason of that instability, attendance at the hearing is likely to cause serious and immediate physiological damage to the conservatee.

(f) The limited conservator or any relative or friend of the limited conservatee may appear and support or oppose termination of the limited conservatorship. The court shall hear and determine the matter according to the laws and procedures relating to the trial of civil actions, including trial by jury if demanded. If the court terminates the limited conservatorship, the limited conservator may, either at the hearing or thereafter on further notice and hearing, be discharged and the bond exonerated upon the settlement and approval of the final account by the court.

(g)(1) The court shall order the termination of the limited conservatorship unless the court finds, on the record and on the record and by clear and convincing evidence, that the limited conservatee still meets the criteria for appointment of a limited conservator under Section 1801 and a limited conservatorship remains the least restrictive alternative needed for the limited conservatee's protection.

(2) If the petition for termination is uncontested and states facts showing that both the limited conservator and limited conservatee wish to terminate the limited conservatorship, and the conservatorship is no longer the least restrictive alternative for the limited conservatee's protection, the court may terminate the limited conservatorship without an evidentiary hearing.

(h) If the court determines, by clear and convincing evidence, that the limited conservatee meets the criteria for appointment of a limited conservator under Section 1801, the court shall determine whether to modify the powers granted to the limited conservator to ensure that the limited conservatorship remains the least restrictive alternative needed for the limited conservatee's protection. If the court modifies any powers granted to the limited conservator, new letters shall issue. **Leg.H.** Enacted Stats 1990 ch 79 §14 (AB 759), operative July 1, 1991. Amended Stats 2021 ch 417 §14 (AB 1194), effective January 1, 2022; Stats 2022 ch 894 §12 (AB 1663), effective January 1, 2023.

Prior Law: Former Prob C §1860.5, similar to the present section, was added Stats 1980 ch 1304 §18 and repealed Stats 1990 ch 79 §13, operative July 1, 1991.

§1861. Petition for termination of conservatorship

(a) A petition for the termination of the conservatorship may be filed by any of the following:

(1) The conservator.

(2) The conservatee.

(3) The spouse, or domestic partner, or any relative or friend of the conservatee or other interested person.

(b) The petition shall state facts showing that the conservatorship is no longer required. **Leg.H.** Enacted Stats 1990 ch 79 §14 (AB 759), operative July 1, 1991. Amended Stats 2001 ch 893 §21 (AB 25).

Prior Law: Former Prob C §1861, similar to the present section, was added Stats 1979 ch 726 §3, operative January 1, 1981, and repealed Stats 1990 ch 79 §13, operative July 1, 1991.

Former Prob C §1861, similar to present Prob C §2421, was added Stats 1957 ch 1902 §1, and repealed Stats 1979 ch 726 §2, operative January 1, 1981.

§ 1861.5. Appointment of counsel for conservatee and setting hearing for conservatorship termination

Upon the receipt of a communication from the conservatee that the conservatee wishes to terminate the conservatorship, a court shall appoint counsel for the conservatee and set a hearing for the termination of the conservatorship when either of the following conditions apply:

(a) There has not been a hearing for the termination of the conservatorship within the 12 months preceding the communication from the conservatee.

(b) The court believes there is good cause to set a hearing for the termination of the conservatorship. **Leg.H.** Added Stats 2022 ch 894 §13 (AB 1663), effective January 1, 2023.

§1862. Notice of hearing

(a) Notice of the hearing to consider the termination of the conservatorship shall be given for the period and in the manner provided in Chapter 3 (commencing with Section 1460) of Part 1.

(b) If the court sets a hearing pursuant to paragraph (2) of subdivision (a) of Section 1850 and no petition is filed, the court shall order the conservator to give notice of the hearing as provided in subdivision (a), and to appear at the hearing and show cause why the conservatorship should not be terminated. **Leg.H.** Enacted Stats 1990 ch 79 §14 (AB 759), operative July 1, 1991. Amended Stats 2021 ch 417 §15 (AB 1194), effective January 1, 2022.

Prior Law: Former Prob C §1862, similar to the present section, was added Stats 1987 ch 923 §64, operative July 1, 1988, and repealed Stats 1990 ch 79 §13 (AB 759), operative July 1, 1991.

Former Prob C §1862, similar to the present section, was added Stats 1979 ch 726 §3, operative January 1, 1981, and repealed Stats 1987 ch 923 §63, operative July 1, 1988.

Former Prob C §1862, similar to present Prob C §2625, was added Stats 1970 ch 376 §2, and repealed Stats 1979 ch 726 §2, operative January 1, 1981.

§1863. Hearing and judgment

(a) The court shall hear and determine the matter according to the law and procedure relating to the trial of civil actions, including trial by jury if demanded by the conservatee. The conservator, the conservatee, the spouse or domestic partner, or any relative or friend of the conservatee or other interested person may appear and support or oppose the termination of the conservatorship.

(b)(1) The conservatee shall be produced at the hearing except in the following cases:

(A) When the conservatee is out of the state and is not the petitioner.

(B) When the conservatee is unable to attend the hearing by reason of medical inability.

(C) When the court investigator has reported to the court that the conservatee has expressly communicated that the conservatee (i) is not willing to attend the hearing, (ii) does not wish to contest the continuation of the conservatorship, and (iii) does not object to the current conservator or prefer that another person act as conservator, and the court makes an order that the conservatee need not attend the hearing.

(2) If the conservatee is unable to attend the hearing because of medical inability, that inability shall be established by the affidavit or certificate of a licensed medical practitioner or, if the conservatee is an adherent of a religion whose tenets and practices call for reliance on prayer alone for healing and is under treatment by an accredited practitioner of that religion, by the affidavit of the practitioner. The affidavit or certificate is evidence only of the conservatee's inability to attend the hearing and shall not be considered in determining the issue of need for the continuation of the conservatorship.

(3) Emotional or psychological instability is not good cause for the absence of the conservatee from the hearing unless, by reason of that instability, attendance at the hearing is likely to cause serious and immediate physiological damage to the conservatee.

(c) Unless the court determines, on the record and by clear and convincing evidence, that (1) the conservatee still meets the criteria for appointment of a conservator of the person under subdivision (a) of Section 1801, a conservator of the estate under subdivision (b) of Section 1801, or both; and (2) a conservatorship remains the least restrictive alternative needed for the conservatee's protection, as required by subdivision (b) of Section 1800.3, the court shall enter judgment terminating the conservatorship.

(d) If the court determines, by clear and convincing evidence, that the conservatee meets the criteria for appointment of a conservator of the person under subdivision (a) of Section 1801, a conservator of the estate under subdivision (b) of Section 1801, or both, the court shall determine whether to modify the existing powers of the conservator to ensure that the conservatorship remains the least restrictive alternative needed for the conservatee's protection and shall order the conservatorship to continue accordingly. If the court modifies the existing powers of the conservator, new letters shall issue.

(e) At the hearing, or thereafter on further notice and hearing, the conservator may be discharged and the bond given by the conservator may be exonerated upon the settlement and approval of the conservator's final account by the court.

(f) This section does not apply to limited conservatorships.

(g) Termination of conservatorship does not preclude a new proceeding for appointment of a conservator on the same or other grounds.

(h) If a petition for termination pursuant to Section 1861 is uncontested and states facts showing that both the conservator and conservatee wish to terminate the conservatorship and the conservatorship is no longer the least restrictive alternative for the conservatee's protection, the court may terminate the conservatorship without an evidentiary hearing. **Leg.H.** Enacted Stats 1990 ch 79 §14 (AB 759), operative July 1, 1991. Amended Stats 2000 ch 17 §4.4 (AB 1491); Stats 2001 ch 893 §22 (AB 25); Stats 2021 ch 417 §16 (AB 1194), effective January 1, 2022; Stats 2022 ch 894 §14 (AB 1663), effective January 1, 2023.

Prior Law: Former Prob C §1863, similar to the present section, was added Stats 1979 ch 726 §3, operative January 1, 1981, and repealed Stats 1990 ch 79 §13, operative July 1, 1991.

§1864. Termination of conservatorship of absentee

(a) In the case of the conservatorship of an absentee as defined in Section 1403, the petition to terminate the conservatorship may also be filed by any officer or agency of this state or of the United States or the authorized delegate thereof.

(b) If the petition states and the court determines that the absentee has returned to the controllable jurisdiction of the military department or civilian department or agency concerned, or is deceased, as determined under 37 United States Code, Section 556, or 5 United States Code, Section 5566, as the case may be, the court shall order the conservatorship terminated. An official written report or record of such military department or civilian department or agency that the absentee has returned to such controllable jurisdiction or is deceased shall be received as evidence of such fact. **Leg.H.** Enacted Stats 1990 ch 79 §14 (AB 759), operative July 1, 1991.

Prior Law: Former Prob C §1864, similar to the present section, was added Stats 1979 ch 726 §3, operative January 1, 1981, and repealed Stats 1990 ch 79 §13, operative July 1, 1991.

§1865. Restoring right to vote

If the conservatee has been disqualified from voting pursuant to Section 2208 or 2209 of the Elections Code, upon termination of the conservatorship, the court shall notify the county elections official of the county of residence of the former conservatee that the former conservatee's right to register to vote is restored. **Leg.H.** Enacted Stats 1990 ch 79 §14 (AB 759), operative July 1, 1991. Amended Stats 1994 ch 923 §160 (SB 1546); Stats 2002 ch 221 §80 (SB 1019).

Prior Law: Former Prob C §1865, similar to the present section, was added Stats 1979 ch 726 §3, operative January 1, 1981, and repealed Stats 1990 ch 79 §13, operative July 1, 1991.

CHAPTER 4
LEGAL CAPACITY OF CONSERVATEE

Article 1. Capacity to Bind or Obligate Conservatorship Estate.
Article 2. Capacity to Give Informed Consent for Medical Treatment.
Article 3. Capacity of Conservatee to Marry.

ARTICLE 1
Capacity to Bind or Obligate Conservatorship Estate

"Transaction" defined. §1870.
Rights not affected by conservatorship. §1871.
Effect of conservatorship on legal capacity of conservatee. §1872.
Court order affecting legal capacity of conservatee. §1873.
Petition for order affecting legal capacity of conservatee. §1874.
Good faith purchaser or encumbrancer of real property. §1875.
Applicability of other governing law. §1876.

§1870. "Transaction" defined

As used in this article, unless the context otherwise requires, "transaction" includes, but is not limited to, making a contract, sale, transfer, or conveyance, incurring a debt or encumbering property, making a gift, delegating a power, and waiving a right. **Leg.H.** Enacted Stats 1990 ch 79 §14 (AB 759), operative July 1, 1991.

Prior Law: Former Prob C §1870, similar to the present section, was added Stats 1979 ch 726 §3, operative January 1, 1981, and repealed Stats 1990 ch 79 §13, operative July 1, 1991.

§1871. Rights not affected by conservatorship

Nothing in this article shall be construed to deny a conservatee any of the following:

(a) The right to control an allowance provided under Section 2421.

(b) The right to control wages or salary to the extent provided in Section 2601.

(c) The right to make a will.

(d) The right to enter into transactions to the extent reasonable to provide the necessaries of life to the conservatee and the spouse and minor children of the conservatee and to provide the basic living expenses, as defined in Section 297 of the Family Code, to the domestic partner of the conservatee. **Leg.H.** Enacted Stats 1990 ch 79 §14 (AB 759), operative July 1, 1991. Amended Stats 2001 ch 893 §23 (AB 25).

Prior Law: Former Prob C §1871, similar to the present section, was added Stats 1979 ch 726 §3, operative January 1, 1981, amended Stats 1983 ch 842 §52, operative January 1, 1985, and repealed Stats 1990 ch 79 §13, operative July 1, 1991.

§1872. Effect of conservatorship on legal capacity of conservatee

(a) Except as otherwise provided in this article, the appointment of a conservator of the estate is an adjudication that the conservatee lacks the legal capacity to enter into or make any transaction that binds or obligates the conservatorship estate.

(b) Except as otherwise provided in the order of the court appointing a limited conservator, the appointment does not limit the legal capacity of the limited conservatee to enter into transactions or types of transactions. **Leg.H.** Enacted Stats 1990 ch 79 §14 (AB 759), operative July 1, 1991.

Prior Law: Former Prob C §1872, similar to the present section, was added Stats 1979 ch 726 §3, operative January 1, 1981, amended Stats 1980 ch 1304 §19, and repealed Stats 1990 ch 79 §13, operative July 1, 1991.

§1873. Court order affecting legal capacity of conservatee

(a) In the order appointing the conservator or upon a petition filed under Section 1874, the court may, by order, authorize the conservatee, subject to Section 1876, to enter into transactions or types of transactions as may be appropriate in the circumstances of the particular conservatee and conservatorship estate. The court, by order, may modify the legal capacity a conservatee would otherwise have under Section 1872 by broadening or restricting the power of the conservatee to enter into transactions or types of transactions as may be appropriate in the circumstances of the particular conservatee and conservatorship estate.

(b) In an order made under this section, the court may include limitations or conditions on the exercise of the authority granted to the conservatee as the court determines to be appropriate including, but not limited to, the following:

(1) A requirement that for specific types of transactions or for all transactions authorized by the order, the conservatee obtain prior approval of the transaction by the court or conservator before exercising the authority granted by the order.

(2) A provision that the conservator has the right to avoid any transaction made by the conservatee pursuant to the authority of the order if the transaction is not one into which a reasonably prudent person might enter.

(c) The court, in its discretion, may provide in the order that, unless extended by subsequent order of the court, the order or specific provisions of the order terminate at a time specified in the order.

(d) An order under this section continues in effect until the earliest of the following times:

(1) The time specified in the order, if any.

(2) The time the order is modified or revoked.

(3) The time the conservatorship of the estate is terminated.

(e) An order under this section may be modified or revoked upon petition filed by the conservator, conservatee, the spouse or domestic partner of the conservatee, or any relative or friend of the conservatee, or any interested person. Notice of the hearing on the petition shall be given for the period and in the manner provided in Chapter 3 (commencing with Section 1460) of Part 1. **Leg.H.** Enacted Stats 1990 ch 79 §14 (AB 759), operative July 1, 1991. Amended Stats 2001 ch 893 §24 (AB 25).

Prior Law: Former Prob C §1873, similar to the present section, was added Stats 1979 ch 726 §3, operative January 1, 1981, amended Stats 1980 ch 1304 §20, and repealed Stats 1990 ch 79 §13, operative July 1, 1991.

§1874. Petition for order affecting legal capacity of conservatee

(a) After a conservator has been appointed, a petition requesting an order under Section 1873 may be filed by any of the following:

(1) The conservator.

(2) The conservatee.

(3) The spouse, domestic partner, or any relative or friend of the conservatee.

(b) Notice of the hearing on the petition shall be given for the period and in the manner provided in Chapter 3 (commencing with Section 1460) of Part 1. **Leg.H.** Enacted Stats 1990 ch 79 §14 (AB 759), operative July 1, 1991. Amended Stats 2001 ch 893 §25 (AB 25).

Prior Law: Former Prob C §1874, similar to the present section, was added Stats 1979 ch 726 §3, operative January 1, 1981, and repealed Stats 1990 ch 79 §13, operative July 1, 1991.

§1875. Good faith purchaser or encumbrancer of real property

A transaction that affects real property of the conservatorship estate, entered into by a person acting in good faith and for a valuable consideration and without knowledge of the establishment of the conservatorship, is not affected by any provision of this article or any order made under this article unless a notice of the establishment of the conservatorship or temporary conservatorship has been recorded prior to the transaction in the county in which the property is located. **Leg.H.** Enacted Stats 1990 ch 79 §14 (AB 759), operative July 1, 1991. Amended Stats 1991 ch 82 §20 (SB 896), effective June 30, 1991, operative July 1, 1991.

Prior Law: Former Prob C §1875, similar to the present section, was added Stats 1979 ch 726 §3, operative January 1, 1981, repealed Stats 1990 ch 79 §13 (AB 759), operative July 1, 1991, amended Stats 1990 ch 1208 §6 (SB 2427), effective September 24, 1990, and repealed Stats 1991 ch 82 §19 (SB 896), effective June 30, operative July 1, 1991.

§1876. Applicability of other governing law

The provisions of this article relating to the legal capacity of a conservatee to bind or obligate the conservatorship estate, and the provisions of any order of the court broadening such capacity, do not displace but are supplemented by general principles of law and equity relating to transactions including, but not limited to, capacity to contract, joinder or consent requirements, estoppel, fraud, misrepresentation, duress, coercion, mistake, or other validating or invalidating cause. **Leg.H.** Enacted Stats 1990 ch 79 §14 (AB 759), operative July 1, 1991.

Prior Law: Former Prob C §1876, similar to the present section, was added Stats 1979 ch 726 §3, operative January 1, 1981, and repealed Stats 1990 ch 79 §13 (AB 759), operative July 1, 1991.

ARTICLE 2
Capacity to Give Informed Consent for Medical Treatment

Order granting conservator exclusive authority to give consent for medical treatment. §1880.
Conservatee deemed unable to give informed consent to medical treatment. §1881.
Time for making order; Procedure. §1890.
Petition. §1891.
Notice of hearing. §1892.
Attendance of conservatee at hearing. §1893.
Investigation by court investigator if conservatee will not attend hearing. §1894.
Hearing. §1895.
Order. §1896.
Duration of order. §1897.
Modification or revocation of order. §1898.

§1880. Order granting conservator exclusive authority to give consent for medical treatment

If the court determines that there is no form of medical treatment for which the conservatee has the capacity to give an informed consent, the court shall (1) adjudge that the conservatee lacks the capacity to give informed consent for medical treatment and (2) by order give the conservator of the person the powers specified in Section 2355. If an order is made under this section, the letters shall include a statement that the conservator has the powers specified in Section 2355. **Leg.H.** Enacted Stats 1990 ch 79 §14 (AB 759), operative July 1, 1991.

Prior Law: Former Prob C §1880, similar to the present section, was added Stats 1979 ch 726 §3, operative January 1, 1981, and repealed Stats 1990 ch 79 §13, operative July 1, 1991.

§1881. Conservatee deemed unable to give informed consent to medical treatment

(a) A conservatee shall be deemed unable to give informed consent to any form of medical treatment pursuant to Section 1880 if, for all medical treatments, the conservatee is unable to respond knowingly and intelligently to queries about medical treatment or is unable to participate in a treatment decision by means of a rational thought process.

(b) In order for a court to determine that a conservatee is unable to respond knowingly and intelligently to queries about his or her medical treatment or is unable to participate in treatment decisions by means of a rational thought process, a court shall do both of the following:

(1) Determine that, for all medical treatments, the conservatee is unable to understand at least one of the following items of minimum basic medical treatment information:

(A) The nature and seriousness of any illness, disorder, or defect that the conservatee has or may develop.

(B) The nature of any medical treatment that is being or may be recommended by the conservatee's health care providers.

(C) The probable degree and duration of any benefits and risks of any medical intervention that is being or may be recommended by the conservatee's health care providers, and the consequences of lack of treatment.

(D) The nature, risks, and benefits of any reasonable alternatives.

(2) Determine that one or more of the mental functions of the conservatee described in subdivision (a) of Section 811 is impaired and that there is a link between the deficit or deficits and the conservatee's inability to give informed consent.

(c) A deficit in the mental functions listed in subdivision (a) of Section 811 may be considered only if the deficit by itself, or in combination with one or more other mental function deficits, significantly impairs the conservatee's ability to understand the consequences of his or her decisions regarding medical care.

(d) In determining whether a conservatee's mental functioning is so severely impaired that the conservatee lacks the capacity to give informed consent to any form of medical treatment, the court may take into consideration the frequency, severity, and duration of periods of impairment.

(e) In the interest of minimizing unnecessary expense to the parties to a proceeding, paragraph (2) of subdivision (b) shall not apply to a petition pursuant to Section 1880 wherein the conservatee, after notice by the court of his or her right to object which, at least, shall include an interview by a court investigator pursuant to Section 1826 prior to the hearing on the petition, does not object to the proposed finding of incapacity, or waives any objections. **Leg.H.** Added Stats 1995 ch 842 §8 (SB 730). Amended Stats 1996 ch 178 §8 (SB 1650).

1995 Notes: This act shall be known and may be cited as the Due Process in Competence Determinations Act. Stats 1995 ch 842 §12.

This act shall not apply to proceedings under the Welfare and Institutions Code. Stats 1995 ch 842 §13.

§1890. Time for making order; Procedure

(a) An order of the court under Section 1880 may be included in the order of appointment of the conservator if the order was requested in the petition for the appointment of the conservator or the transfer petition under Section 2002 or, except in the case of a limited conservator, may be made subsequently upon a petition made, noticed, and heard by the court in the manner provided in this article.

(b) In the case of a petition filed under this chapter requesting that the court make an order under this chapter or that the court modify or revoke an order made under this chapter, when the order applies to a limited conservatee, the order may only be made upon a petition made, noticed, and heard by the court in the manner provided by Article 3 (commencing with Section 1820) of Chapter 1.

(c) No court order under Section 1880, whether issued as part of an order granting the original petition for appointment of a conservator or issued subsequent thereto, may be granted unless supported by a declaration, filed at or before the hearing on the request, executed by a licensed physician, or a licensed psychologist within the scope of his or her licensure, and stating that the proposed conservatee or the conservatee, as the case may be, lacks the capacity to give an informed consent for any form of medical treatment and the reasons therefor. Nothing in this section shall be construed to expand the scope of practice of psychologists as set forth in the Business and Professions Code. **Leg.H.** Enacted Stats 1990 ch 79 §14 (AB 759), operative July 1, 1991. Amended Stats 1992 ch 572 §4 (SB 1455); Stats 1996 ch 563 §10 (SB 392); Stats 1997 ch 724 §10 (AB 1172); Stats 2014 ch 553 §19 (SB 940), effective January 1, 2015, operative January 1, 2016.

Prior Law: Former Prob C §1890, similar to the present section, was added Stats 1989 ch 1080 §11 and repealed Stats 1990 ch 79 §13, operative July 1, 1991.

Former Prob C §1890, similar to the present section, was added Stats 1979 ch 726 §3, operative January 1, 1981, amended Stats 1980 ch 1304 §21, and repealed Stats 1989 ch 1080 §10.

§1891. Petition

(a) A petition may be filed under this article requesting that the court make an order under Section 1880 or that the court modify or revoke an order made under Section 1880. The petition shall state facts showing that the order requested is appropriate.

(b) The petition may be filed by any of the following:

(1) The conservator.

(2) The conservatee.

(3) The spouse, domestic partner, or any relative or friend of the conservatee.

(c) The petition shall set forth, so far as they are known to the petitioner, the names and addresses of the spouse or domestic partner and of the relatives of the conservatee within the second degree. **Leg.H.** Enacted Stats 1990 ch 79 §14 (AB 759), operative July 1, 1991. Amended Stats 2001 ch 893 §26 (AB 25).

Prior Law: Former Prob C §1891, similar to the present section, was added Stats 1979 Ch 726 §3, operative January 1, 1981, and repealed Stats 1990 ch 79 §13, operative July 1, 1991.

§1892. Notice of hearing

Notice of the hearing on the petition shall be given for the period and in the manner provided in Chapter 3 (commencing with Section 1460) of Part 1. **Leg.H.** Enacted Stats 1990 ch 79 §14 (AB 759), operative July 1, 1991.

Prior Law: Former Prob C §1892, similar to the present section, was added Stats 1987 ch 923 §66, operative July 1, 1988, and repealed Stats 1990 ch 79 §13, operative July 1, 1991.

Former Prob C §1892, similar to the present section, was added Stats 1979 ch 726 §3, operative January 1, 1981, and repealed Stats 1987 ch 923 §65, operative July 1, 1988.

§1893. Attendance of conservatee at hearing

The conservatee shall be produced at the hearing except in the following cases:

(a) Where the conservatee is out of state when served and is not the petitioner.

(b) Where the conservatee is unable to attend the hearing by reason of medical inability established (1) by the affidavit or certificate of a licensed medical practitioner or (2) if the conservatee is an adherent of a religion whose tenets and practices call for reliance on prayer alone for healing and is under treatment by an accredited practitioner of that religion, by the affidavit of the practitioner. The affidavit or certificate is evidence only of the conservatee's inability to attend the hearing and shall not be considered in determining the issue of the legal capacity of the conservatee. Emotional or psychological instability is not good cause for the absence of the conservatee from the hearing unless, by reason of such instability, attendance at the hearing is likely to cause serious and immediate physiological damage to the conservatee.

(c) Where the court investigator has reported to the court that the conservatee has expressly communicated that the conservatee (1) is not willing to attend the hearing and (2) does not wish to contest the petition, and the court makes an order that the conservatee need not attend the hearing. **Leg.H.** Enacted Stats 1990 ch 79 §14 (AB 759), operative July 1, 1991.

Prior Law: Former Prob C §1893, similar to the present section, was added Stats 1979 ch 726 §3, operative January 1, 1981, and repealed Stats 1990 ch 79 §13, operative July 1, 1991.

§1894. Investigation by court investigator if conservatee will not attend hearing

If the petition alleges that the conservatee is not willing to attend the hearing or upon receipt of an affidavit or certificate attesting to the medical inability of the conservatee to attend the hearing, the court investigator shall do all of the following:

(a) Interview the conservatee personally.

(b) Inform the conservatee of the contents of the petition, of the nature, purpose, and effect of the proceeding, and of the right of the conservatee to oppose the petition, attend the hearing, be represented by legal counsel, and to have legal counsel appointed by the court if not otherwise represented by legal counsel.

(c) Determine whether it appears that the conservatee is unable to attend the hearing and, if able to attend, whether the conservatee is willing to attend the hearing.

(d) Determine whether the conservatee wishes to contest the petition.

(e) Determine whether the conservatee wishes to be represented by legal counsel and, if so, whether the conservatee has retained legal counsel and, if not, whether the conservatee plans to retain legal counsel.

(f) Report to the court in writing, at least five days before the hearing, concerning all of the foregoing, including the conservatee's express communications concerning both (1) representation by legal counsel and (2) whether the conservatee is not willing to attend the hearing and does not wish to contest the petition. **Leg.H.** Enacted Stats 1990 ch 79 §14 (AB 759), operative July 1, 1991. Amended Stats 2022 ch 420 §37 (AB 2960), effective January 1, 2023.

Prior Law: Former Prob C §1894, similar to the present section, was added Stats 1979 ch 726 §3, operative January 1, 1981, and repealed Stats 1990 ch 79 §13, operative July 1, 1991.

§1895. Hearing

(a) The conservatee, the spouse, the domestic partner, a relative, or a friend of the conservatee, the conservator, or any other interested person may appear at the hearing to support or oppose the petition.

(b) Except where the conservatee is absent from the hearing and is not required to attend the hearing under the provisions of Section 1893 and any showing required by Section 1893 has been made, the court shall inform, before granting the petition, the conservatee of all of the following:

(1) The nature and purpose of the proceeding.

(2) The nature and effect on the conservatee's basic rights of the order requested.

(3) The conservatee has the right to oppose the petition, to be represented by legal counsel if the conservatee so chooses, and to have legal counsel appointed by the court if not otherwise represented by legal counsel.

(c) After the court informs the conservatee of the matters listed in subdivision (b) and before granting the petition, the court shall consult the conservatee to determine the conservatee's opinion concerning the order requested in the petition. **Leg.H.** Enacted Stats 1990 ch 79 §14 (AB 759), operative July 1, 1991. Amended Stats 2001 ch 893 §27 (AB 25); Stats 2022 ch 420 §38 (AB 2960), effective January 1, 2023.

Prior Law: Former Prob C §1895, similar to the present section, was added Stats 1979 ch 726 §3, operative January 1, 1981, and repealed Stats 1990 ch 79 §13, operative July 1, 1991.

§1896. Order

(a) If the court determines that the order requested in the petition is proper, the court shall make the order.

(b) The court, in its discretion, may provide in the order that, unless extended by subsequent order of the court, the order or specific provisions of the order terminate at a time specified in the order. **Leg.H.** Enacted Stats 1990 ch 79 §14 (AB 759), operative July 1, 1991.

Prior Law: Former Prob C §1896, similar to the present section, was added Stats 1979 ch 726 §3, operative January 1, 1981, and repealed Stats 1990 ch 79 §13, operative July 1, 1991.

§1897. Duration of order

An order of the court under Section 1880 continues in effect until the earliest of the following times:

(1) The time specified in the order, if any.

(2) The time the order is modified or revoked.

(3) The time the conservatorship is terminated. **Leg.H.** Enacted Stats 1990 ch 79 §14 (AB 759), operative July 1, 1991.

Prior Law: Former Prob C §1897, similar to the present section, was added Stats 1979 ch 726 §3, operative January 1, 1981, and repealed Stats 1990 ch 79 §13, operative July 1, 1991.

§1898. Modification or revocation of order

An order of the court under Section 1880 may be modified or revoked upon a petition made, noticed, and heard by the court in the manner provided in this article. **Leg.H.** Enacted Stats 1990 ch 79 §14 (AB 759), operative July 1, 1991.

Prior Law: Former Prob C §1898, similar to the present section, was added Stats 1979 §726 §3, operative January 1, 1981, and repealed Stats 1990 ch 79 §13, operative July 1, 1991.

ARTICLE 3
Capacity of Conservatee to Marry

Capacity to marry or enter into registered domestic partnership not affected by conservatorship. §1900.

Court determination of capacity to marry or enter into registered domestic partnership. §1901.

§1900. Capacity to marry or enter into registered domestic partnership not affected by conservatorship

The appointment of a conservator of the person or estate or both does not affect the capacity of the conservatee to marry or to enter into a registered domestic partnership. **Leg.H.** Enacted Stats 1990 ch 79 §14 (AB 759), operative July 1, 1991. Amended Stats 2005 ch 418 §26 (SB 973), effective January 1, 2006.

Prior Law: Former Prob C §1900, similar to the present section, was added Stats 1979 ch 726 §3, operative January 1, 1981, and repealed Stats 1990 ch 79 §13, operative July 1, 1991.

§1901. Court determination of capacity to marry or enter into registered domestic partnership

(a) The court may by order determine whether the conservatee has the capacity to enter into a valid marriage, as provided in Part 1 (commencing with Section 300) of Division 3 of the Family Code, or to enter into a registered domestic partnership, as provided in Section 297 of the Family Code, at the time the order is made.

(b) A petition for an order under this section may be filed by the conservator of the person or estate or both, the conservatee, any relative or friend of the conservatee, or any interested person.

(c) Notice of the hearing on the petition shall be given for the period and in the manner provided in Chapter 3 (commencing with Section 1460) of Part 1. **Leg.H.** Enacted Stats 1990 ch 79 §14 (AB 759), operative July 1, 1991. Amended Stats 1992 ch 163 §124 (AB 2641), operative January 1, 1994; Stats 2005 ch 418 §27 (SB 973), effective January 1, 2006.

Prior Law: Former Prob C §1901, similar to the present section, was added Stats 1979 ch 726 §3, operative January 1, 1981, and repealed Stats 1990 ch 79 §13, operative July 1, 1991.

Former Prob C §1901, similar to present Prob C §§2610–2613, was added Stats 1957 ch 1902 §1, amended Stats 1959 ch 347 §2, Stats 1970 ch 1282 §22, operative July 1, 1971, Stats 1973 ch 142 §62, effective June 30, 1973, operative July 1, 1973, Stats 1976 ch 634 §4, and repealed Stats 1979 ch 726 §2, operative January 1, 1981.

CHAPTER 5
DISQUALIFICATION FROM VOTING

Disqualification from voting; Completing affidavit of voter registration. §1910.

§1910. Disqualification from voting; Completing affidavit of voter registration

(a) If the court determines the conservatee is incapable of communicating, with or without reasonable accommodations, a desire to participate in the voting process, the court shall by order disqualify the conservatee from voting pursuant to Section 2208 or 2209 of the Elections Code.

(b) The conservatee shall not be disqualified from voting on the basis that he or she does, or would need to do, any of the following to complete an affidavit of voter registration:

(1) Signs the affidavit of voter registration with a mark or a cross pursuant to subdivision (b) of Section 2150 of the Elections Code.

(2) Signs the affidavit of voter registration by means of a signature stamp pursuant to Section 354.5 of the Elections Code.

(3) Completes the affidavit of voter registration with the assistance of another person pursuant to subdivision (d) of Section 2150 of the Elections Code.

(4) Completes the affidavit of voter registration with reasonable accommodations. **Leg.H.** Enacted Stats 1990 ch 79 §14 (AB 759), operative July 1, 1991. Amended Stats 1994 ch 923 §161 (SB 1546); Stats 2014 ch 591 §8 (AB 1311), effective January 1, 2015; Stats 2015 ch 736 §12 (SB 589), effective January 1, 2016.

2015 Note: For legislative findings and declarations, see the 2015 Note following Prob C §1823.

Prior Law: Former Prob C §1910, similar to present Prob C §2601, was added Stats 1957 ch 1902 §1, amended Stats 1967 ch 638 §3, and repealed Stats 1979 ch 726 §2, operative January 1, 1981.

CHAPTER 6
STERILIZATION

Legislative intent. §1950.
Ability to consent; Definitions. §1951.
Petition for appointment of limited conservator. §1952.
Notice of hearing. §1953.
Appointment of counsel. §1954.
Appointment of facilitator; Duties. §1954.5.
Coordination of investigation by regional center; Examination by physicians; Reports. §1955.
Presence of conservatee at hearing. §1956.
Consideration of conservatee's views. §1957.
Factors to be established beyond a reasonable doubt before consent to sterilization may be authorized. §1958.
Vulnerability to unlawful sexual conduct by others. §1959.
Persons who already have conservator. §1960.
Sterilization procedure. §1961.
Statement of decision; automatic appeal. §1962.
Payment of court costs and fees. §1963.
Expiration of court order and termination of conservatorship; Reappointment. §1964.
Stay of order pending appeal. §1965.
Material change in circumstances prerequisite to new petition after petition denied. §1966.

Civil and criminal liability. §1967.
Sterilization resulting from other treatment or surgery. §1968.
Rights of developmentally disabled persons capable of giving consent. §1969.

§1950. Legislative intent

The Legislature recognizes that the right to exercise choice over matters of procreation is fundamental and may not be denied to an individual on the basis of disability. This chapter is enacted for the benefit of those persons with developmental disabilities who, despite those disabilities, are capable of engaging in sexual activity yet who, because of those disabilities, are unable to give the informed, voluntary consent necessary to their fully exercising the right to procreative choice, which includes the right to choose sterilization.

However, the Legislature further recognizes that the power to sterilize is subject to abuse and, historically, has been abused. It is the intent of the Legislature that no individual shall be sterilized solely by reason of a developmental disability and that no individual who knowingly opposes sterilization be sterilized involuntarily. It is further the intent of the Legislature that this chapter shall be applied in accord with the overall intent of Division 4.5 (commencing with Section 4500) of the Welfare and Institutions Code that persons with developmental disabilities be provided with those services needed to enable them to live more normal, independent, and productive lives, including assistance and training that might obviate the need for sterilization. **Leg.H.** Enacted Stats 1990 ch 79 §14 (AB 759), operative July 1, 1991.

Prior Law: Former Prob C §1950, similar to the present section, was added Stats 1986 ch 1012 §1 and repealed Stats 1990 ch 79 §13, operative July 1, 1991.

§1951. Ability to consent; Definitions

(a) No person who has the ability to consent to his or her sterilization shall be sterilized pursuant to this chapter.

(b) For the purposes of this chapter, the following terms have the meanings given:

(1) "Consent to sterilization" means making a voluntary decision to undergo sterilization after being fully informed about, and after fully understanding the nature and consequences of, sterilization.

(2) "Voluntary" means performed while competent to make the decision, and as a matter of free choice and will and not in response to coercion, duress, or undue influence.

(3) "Fully understanding the nature and consequences of sterilization," includes, but is not limited to, the ability to understand each of the following:

(A) That the individual is free to withhold or withdraw consent to the procedure at any time before the sterilization without affecting the right to future care or treatment and without loss or withdrawal of any publicly funded program benefits to which the individual might be otherwise entitled.

(B) Available alternative methods of family planning and birth control.

(C) That the sterilization procedure is considered to be irreversible.

(D) The specific sterilization procedure to be performed.

(E) The discomforts and risks that may accompany or follow the performing of the procedure, including an explanation of the type and possible effects of any anesthetic to be used.

(F) The benefits or advantages that may be expected as a result of the sterilization.

(G) The approximate length of the hospital stay.

(H) The approximate length of time for recovery.

(c) The court shall appoint a facilitator or interpreter if such a person's assistance would enable the person named in the petition to understand any of these factors. **Leg.H.** Enacted Stats 1990 ch 79 §14 (AB 759), operative July 1, 1991.

Prior Law: Former Prob C §1951, similar to the present section, was added Stats 1986 ch 1012 §1 and repealed Stats 1990 ch 79 §13, operative July 1, 1991.

Former Prob C §1951, similar to present Prob C §§2650–2654, was added Stats 1957 ch 1902 §1, amended Stats 1976 ch 1357 §33, operative July 1, 1977, and repealed Stats 1979 ch 726 §2, operative January 1, 1981.

§1952. Petition for appointment of limited conservator

The conservator of an adult, or any person authorized to file a petition for the appointment of a conservator under paragraphs (2) to (5), inclusive, of subdivision (a) of Section 1820, may file a petition under this chapter for appointment of a limited conservator authorized to consent to the sterilization of an adult with a developmental disability. The content of the petition under this chapter shall conform to the provisions of Section 1821 and in addition allege that the person for whom sterilization is proposed has a developmental disability as defined in Section 1420 and shall allege specific reasons why court-authorized sterilization is deemed necessary. A petition under this chapter shall be considered separately from any contemporaneous petition for appointment of a conservator under this division. **Leg.H.** Enacted Stats 1990 ch 79 §14 (AB 759), operative July 1, 1991.

Prior Law: Former Prob C §1952, similar to the present section, was added Stats 1986 ch 1012 §1 and repealed Stats 1990 ch 79 §13, operative July 1, 1991.

Former Prob C §1952, similar to present Prob C §2654, was added Stats 1957 ch 1902 §1, and repealed Stats 1979 ch 726 §2, operative January 1, 1981.

§1953. Notice of hearing

At least 90 days before the hearing on the petition under this chapter, notice of the time and place of the hearing and a copy of the petition shall be served on the person named in the petition and, if the petitioner is not the conservator of the person, on the conservator, if any. Service shall be made in the manner provided in Section 415.10 or Section 415.30 of the Code of Civil Procedure or in such manner as may be authorized by the court. **Leg.H.** Enacted Stats 1990 ch 79 §14 (AB 759), operative July 1, 1991.

Prior Law: Former Prob C §1953, similar to the present section, was added Stats 1986 ch 1012 §1 and repealed Stats 1990 ch 79 §13, operative July 1, 1991.

Former Prob C §1953, similar to present Prob C §2660, was added Stats 1957 ch 1902 §1, and repealed Stats 1979 ch 726 §2, operative January 1, 1981.

§1954. Appointment of counsel

In any proceeding under this chapter, if the person named in the petition for court authorization to consent to sterilization has not retained legal counsel and does not plan to retain legal counsel, the court shall immediately appoint the public defender or private counsel to represent the individual for whom sterilization is proposed. Counsel shall undertake the representation with the presumption that the individual opposes the petition. **Leg.H.** Enacted Stats 1990 ch 79 §14 (AB 759), operative July 1, 1991.

Prior Law: Former Prob C §1954, similar to the present section, was added Stats 1986 ch 1012 §1 and repealed Stats 1990 ch 79 §13, operative July 1, 1991.

Former Prob C §1954, similar to present Prob C §§2670 et seq., was added Stats 1957 ch 1902 §1, and repealed Stats 1979 ch 726 §2, operative January 1, 1981.

§1954.5. Appointment of facilitator; Duties

(a) The court shall appoint a facilitator for the person named in the petition, who shall assist the person named in the petition to do all of the following:

(1) Understand the nature of the proceedings.
(2) Understand the evaluation process required by Section 1955.
(3) Communicate his or her views.
(4) Participate as fully as possible in the proceedings.

(b) All of the following factors shall be considered by the court in appointing a facilitator:

(1) The preference of the person named in the petition.
(2) The proposed facilitator's personal knowledge of the person named in the petition.
(3) The proposed facilitator's ability to communicate with the person named in the petition, when that person is nonverbal, has limited verbal skills, or relies on alternative modes of communication.
(4) The proposed facilitator's knowledge of the developmental disabilities service system.

(c) The petitioner may not be appointed as the facilitator. **Leg.H.** Enacted Stats 1990 ch 79 §14 (AB 759), operative July 1, 1991.

Prior Law: Former Prob C §1954.5, similar to the present section, was added Stats 1986 ch 1012 §1 and repealed Stats 1990 ch 79 §13, operative July 1, 1991.

§1955. Coordination of investigation by regional center; Examination by physicians; Reports

(a) The court shall request the director of the appropriate regional center for the developmentally disabled to coordinate an investigation and prepare and file a written report thereon. The appropriate regional center for purposes of this section is (1) the regional center of which the person named in the petition is a client, (2) if the individual named in the petition is not a client of any regional center, the regional center responsible for the area in which the individual is then living, or (3) such other regional center as may be in the best interests of the individual. The report shall be based upon comprehensive medical, psychological, and sociosexual evaluations of the individual conducted pursuant to subdivisions (b) and (c), and shall address, but shall not be limited to, each of the factors listed in Section 1958. A copy of the report shall be provided to each of the parties at least 15 days prior to the hearing.

(b) Prior to the hearing on the issue of sterilization, the person who is proposed to be sterilized shall be personally examined by two physicians, one of whom shall be a surgeon competent to perform the procedure, and one psychologist or clinical social worker, each of whom has been mutually agreed to by the petitioner and counsel for the person named in the petition or, if agreement is not reached, appointed by the court from a panel of qualified professionals. At the request of counsel for the person named in the petition, the court shall appoint one additional psychologist, clinical social worker, or physician named by counsel. Any psychologist or clinical social worker and, to the extent feasible, any physicians conducting an examination shall have had experience with persons who have developmental disabilities. To the extent feasible, each of the examiners shall also have knowledge and experience relating to sociosexual skills and behavior. The examinations shall be at county expense subject to Section 1963.

(c) The examiners shall consider all available alternatives to sterilization and shall recommend sterilization only if no suitable alternative is available. Each examiner shall prepare a written, comprehensive report containing all relevant aspects of the person's medical, psychological, family, and sociosexual conditions. Each examiner shall address those factors specified in Section 1958 related to his or her particular area of expertise. In considering the factors in subdivision (a) of, and paragraph (1) of subdivision (d) of, Section 1958, each examiner shall include information regarding the intensity, extent, and recentness of the person's education and training, if any, regarding human sexuality, including birth control methods and parenting skills, and in addition, shall consider whether the individual would benefit from training provided by persons competent in education and training of persons with comparable intellectual impairments. If an examiner recommends against sterilization, the examiner shall set forth in his or her report available alternatives, including, as warranted, recommendations for sex education, parent training, or training in the use of alternative methods of contraception. Copies of each report shall be furnished at least 30 days prior to the hearing on the petition to the person or persons who filed the petition, the conservator, if any, and counsel for the person proposed to be sterilized, the regional center responsible for the investigation and report required under this section, and such other persons as the court may direct. The court may receive these reports in evidence.

(d) The contents of the reports prepared pursuant to this section shall be confidential. Upon judgment in the action or the proceeding becoming final, the court shall order the contents of the reports sealed.

(e) Regional centers for the developmentally disabled shall compile and maintain lists of persons competent to perform the examinations required by this section. These lists shall be provided to the court. If the person named in the petition resides at a state hospital or other residential care facility, no person conducting an examination pursuant to subdivision (b) shall be an employee of the facility.

(f) Any party to the proceedings has the right to submit additional reports from qualified experts.

(g) Any person who has written a report received in evidence may be subpoenaed and questioned by any party to the proceedings or by the court and when so called is subject to all rules of evidence including those of legal objections as to the qualification of expert witnesses.

(h) No regional center or person acting in his or her capacity as a regional center employee may file a petition under Section 1952. **Leg.H.** Enacted Stats 1990 ch 79 §14 (AB 759), operative July 1, 1991.

Prior Law: Former Prob C §1955, similar to the present section, was added Stats 1986 ch 1012 §1 and repealed Stats 1990 ch 79 §13, operative July 1, 1991.

Former Prob C §1955, similar to present Prob C §2105, was added Stats 1957 ch 1902 §1 and repealed Stats 1979 ch 726 §§1, 2, operative January 1, 1981.

§1956. Presence of conservatee at hearing

The person to whom the petition applies shall be present at the hearing except for reason of medical inability. Emotional or psychological instability is not good cause for the absence of the proposed conservatee from the hearing unless, by reason of the instability, attendance at the hearing is likely to cause serious and immediate physiological damage to the proposed conservatee. **Leg.H.** Enacted Stats 1990 ch 79 §14 (AB 759), operative July 1, 1991.

Prior Law: Former Prob C §1956, similar to the present section, was added Stats 1986 ch 1012 §1 and repealed Stats 1990 ch 79 §13, operative July 1, 1991.

Former Prob C §1956, similar to present Prob C §2105, was added Stats 1957 ch 1902 §1 and repealed Stats 1979 ch 726 §§1, 2, operative January 1, 1981.

§1957. Consideration of conservatee's views

To the greatest extent possible, the court shall elicit and take into account the views of the individual for whom sterilization is proposed in determining whether sterilization is to be authorized. **Leg.H.** Enacted Stats 1990 ch 79 §14 (AB 759), operative July 1, 1991.

Prior Law: Former Prob C §1957, similar to the present section, was added Stats 1986 ch 1012 §1 and repealed Stats 1990 ch 79 §13, operative July 1, 1991.

§1958. Factors to be established beyond a reasonable doubt before consent to sterilization may be authorized

The court may authorize the conservator of a person proposed to be sterilized to consent to the sterilization of that person only if the court finds that the petitioner has established all of the following beyond a reasonable doubt:

(a) The person named in the petition is incapable of giving consent to sterilization, as defined in Section 1951, and the incapacity is in all likelihood permanent.

(b) Based on reasonable medical evidence, the individual is fertile and capable of procreation.

(c) The individual is capable of engaging in, and is likely to engage in sexual activity at the present or in the near future under circumstances likely to result in pregnancy.

(d) Either of the following:

(1) The nature and extent of the individual's disability as determined by empirical evidence and not solely on the basis of any standardized test, renders him or her permanently incapable of caring for a child, even with appropriate training and reasonable assistance.

(2) Due to a medical condition, pregnancy or childbirth would pose a substantially elevated risk to the life of the individual to such a degree that, in the absence of other appropriate methods of contraception, sterilization would be deemed medically necessary for an otherwise nondisabled woman under similar circumstances.

(e) All less invasive contraceptive methods including supervision are unworkable even with training and assistance, inapplicable, or medically contraindicated. Isolation and segregation shall not be considered as less invasive means of contraception.

(f) The proposed method of sterilization entails the least invasion of the body of the individual.

(g) The current state of scientific and medical knowledge does not suggest either (1) that a reversible sterilization procedure or other less drastic contraceptive method will shortly be available, or (2) that science is on the threshold of an advance in the treatment of the individual's disability.

(h) The person named in the petition has not made a knowing objection to his or her sterilization. For purposes of this subdivision, an individual may be found to have knowingly objected to his or her sterilization notwithstanding his or her inability to give consent to sterilization as defined in Section 1951. In the case of persons who are nonverbal, have limited verbal ability to communicate, or who rely on alternative modes of communication, the court shall ensure that adequate effort has been made to elicit the actual views of the individual by the facilitator appointed pursuant to Section 1954.5, or by any other person with experience in communicating with developmentally disabled persons who communicate using similar means. **Leg.H.** Enacted Stats 1990 ch 79 §14 (AB 759), operative July 1, 1991.

Prior Law: Former Prob C §1958, similar to the present section, was added Stats 1986 ch 1012 §1 and repealed Stats 1990 ch 79 §13, operative July 1, 1991.

§1959. Vulnerability to unlawful sexual conduct by others

The fact that, due to the nature or severity of his or her disability, a person for whom an authorization to consent to sterilization is sought may be vulnerable to sexual conduct by others that would be deemed unlawful, shall not be considered by the court in determining whether sterilization is to be authorized under this chapter. **Leg.H.** Enacted Stats 1990 ch 79 §14 (AB 759), operative July 1, 1991.

Prior Law: Former Prob C §1959, similar to the present section, was added Stats 1986 ch 1012 §1 and repealed Stats 1990 ch 79 §13, operative July 1, 1991.

§1960. Persons who already have conservator

If the person named in the petition already has a conservator, the court may authorize that person to consent to sterilization or may appoint another person as limited conservator under the provisions of this chapter. The court shall ensure that the person or agency designated as conservator under this chapter is capable of adequately representing and safeguarding the interests of the conservatee. **Leg.H.** Enacted Stats 1990 ch 79 §14 (AB 759), operative July 1, 1991.

Prior Law: Former Prob C §1960, similar to the present section, was added Stats 1986 ch 1012 §1 and repealed Stats 1990 ch 79 §13, operative July 1, 1991.

§1961. Sterilization procedure

A sterilization procedure authorized under this chapter shall not include hysterectomy or castration. However, if the report prepared under Section 1955 indicates that hysterectomy or castration is a medically necessary treatment, regardless of the need for sterilization, the court shall proceed pursuant to Section 2357. **Leg.H.** Enacted Stats 1990 ch 79 §14 (AB 759), operative July 1, 1991.

Prior Law: Former Prob C §1961, similar to the present section, was added Stats 1986 ch 1012 §1 and repealed Stats 1990 ch 79 §13, operative July 1, 1991.

§1962. Statement of decision; automatic appeal

(a) Any court order granting a petition under this chapter shall be accompanied by a written statement of decision pursuant to Section 632 of the Code of Civil Procedure detailing the factual and legal bases for the court's determination on each of the findings required under Section 1958.

(b) When a judgment authorizing the conservator of a person to consent to the sterilization is rendered, an appeal is automatically taken by the person proposed to be sterilized without any action by that person, or by his or her counsel. The Judicial Council shall provide by rule for notice of and procedure for the appeal. The appeal shall have precedence over other cases in the court in which the appeal is pending. **Leg.H.** Enacted Stats 1990 ch 79 §14 (AB 759), operative July 1, 1991.

Prior Law: Former Prob C §1962, similar to the present section, was added Stats 1986 ch 1012 §1 and repealed Stats 1990 ch 79 §13, operative July 1, 1991.

§1963. Payment of court costs and fees

(a) At the conclusion of the hearing, the court, after inquiring into financial ability, may make an order based upon their ability that any one or more of the following persons pay court costs and fees in whole or in part as in the opinion of the court is proper and in any installments and manner which is both reasonable and compatible with ability to pay:

(1) The person to whom the petition applies.

(2) The petitioner.

(3) Any person liable for the support and maintenance of the person to whom the petition applies.

(b) An order under subdivision (a) may be enforced in the same manner as a money judgment.

(c) For the purposes of this section, court costs and fees include the costs of any examination or investigation ordered by the court, expert witnesses' fees, and the costs and fees of the court-appointed public defender or private counsel representing the person to whom the petition applies.

(d) Any fees and costs not ordered to be paid by persons under subdivision (a) are a charge against and paid out of the treasury of the county on order of the court. **Leg.H.** Enacted Stats 1990 ch 79 §14 (AB 759), operative July 1, 1991.

Prior Law: Former Prob C §1963, similar to the present section, was added Stats 1986 ch 1012 §1 and repealed Stats 1990 ch 79 §13, operative July 1, 1991.

§1964. Expiration of court order and termination of conservatorship; Reappointment

An order of the court authorizing a conservator to consent to sterilization which is upheld on appeal automatically expires in one year from the final determination on appeal unless earlier terminated by the court. A conservatorship established for the sole purpose of authorizing a conservator to consent to sterilization under this chapter shall automatically terminate upon completion of the sterilization procedure or upon expiration of the court's order authorizing the conservator to consent to sterilization, whichever occurs first. If, upon the expiration of the court's order under this chapter, the person named as conservator determines that the conservatorship is still required for the purpose of this chapter, he or she may petition the court for reappointment as conservator for a succeeding six-month period upon a showing of good cause as to why any sterilization authorized by the court has not been completed. **Leg.H.** Enacted Stats 1990 ch 79 §14 (AB 759), operative July 1, 1991.

Prior Law: Former Prob C §1964, similar to the present section, was added Stats 1986 ch 1012 §1 and repealed Stats 1990 ch 79 §13, operative July 1, 1991.

§1965. Stay of order pending appeal

Any court order made pursuant to this chapter granting authority to consent to sterilization shall be stayed pending a final determination on appeal. **Leg.H.** Enacted Stats 1990 ch 79 §14 (AB 759), operative July 1, 1991.

Prior Law: Former Prob C §1965, similar to the present section, was added Stats 1986 ch 1012 §1 and repealed Stats 1990 ch 79 §13, operative July 1, 1991.

§1966. Material change in circumstances prerequisite to new petition after petition denied

After the filing of a first petition for sterilization pursuant to this chapter and a determination by the court that any one or more of the conditions required in Section 1958 has not been proven beyond a reasonable doubt, and that therefore authorization for the proposed sterilization should not be given by the court, a subsequent petition may be filed only on the showing of a material change in circumstances. **Leg.H.** Enacted Stats 1990 ch 79 §14 (AB 759), operative July 1, 1991.

Prior Law: Former Prob C §1966, similar to the present section, was added Stats 1986 ch 1012 §1 and repealed Stats 1990 ch 79 §13, operative July 1, 1991.

§1967. Civil and criminal liability

(a) The sterilization of a person in accordance with this chapter does not render the petitioner or any person participating in the conservatorship proceedings or sterilization liable, either civilly or criminally, except for any injury caused by negligent or willful misconduct in the performance of the sterilization.

(b) Notwithstanding the provisions of subdivision (a), any individual who petitions for authorization to consent to sterilization knowing that the person to whom the petition relates is capable of giving consent to sterilization as defined in Section 1951 is guilty of a misdemeanor, and may be civilly liable to the person concerning whom sterilization was sought. **Leg.H.** Enacted Stats 1990 ch 79 §14 (AB 759), operative July 1, 1991.

Prior Law: Former Prob C §1967, similar to the present section, was added Stats 1986 ch 1012 §1 and repealed Stats 1990 ch 79 §13, operative July 1, 1991.

§1968. Sterilization resulting from other treatment or surgery

This chapter does not prohibit medical treatment or surgery required for other medical reasons and in which sterilization is an unavoidable or medically probable consequence, but is not the object of the treatment or surgery. **Leg.H.** Enacted Stats 1990 ch 79 §14 (AB 759), operative July 1, 1991.

Prior Law: Former Prob C §1968, similar to the present section, was added Stats 1986 ch 1012 §1 and repealed Stats 1990 ch 79 §13, operative July 1, 1991.

§1969. Rights of developmentally disabled persons capable of giving consent

Nothing in this chapter shall infringe on the right of persons with developmental disabilities who are capable of giving consent to sterilization to give that consent without the necessity of a court order or substitute decisionmaker. **Leg.H.** Enacted Stats 1990 ch 79 §14 (AB 759), operative July 1, 1991.

Prior Law: Former Prob C §1969, similar to the present section, was added Stats 1986 ch 1012 §1 and repealed Stats 1990 ch 79 §13, operative July 1, 1991.

CHAPTER 7
UNWARRANTED PETITIONS

Unmeritorious petition or petition intended to annoy or harass. §1970.

§1970. Unmeritorious petition or petition intended to annoy or harass

(a) The Legislature finds that unwarranted petitions, applications, or motions other than discovery motions after a conservatorship has been established create an environment that can be harmful to the conservatee and are inconsistent with the goal of protecting the conservatee.

(b) Notwithstanding Section 391 of the Code of Civil Procedure, if a person other than the conservatee files a petition for termination of the conservatorship, or instruction to the conservator, that is unmeritorious or intended to harass or annoy the conservator, and the person has previously filed pleadings in the conservatorship proceedings that were unmeritorious or intended to harass or annoy the conservator, the petition shall be grounds for the court to determine that the person is a vexatious litigant for the purposes of Title 3A (commencing with Section 391) of Part 2 of the Code of Civil Procedure. For these purposes, the term "new litigation" shall include petitions for visitation, termination of the conservatorship, or instruction to the conservator. **Leg.H.** Added Stats 2008 ch 293 §3 (AB 1340), effective January 1, 2009.

CHAPTER 8
INTERSTATE JURISDICTION, TRANSFER, AND RECOGNITION: CALIFORNIA CONSERVATORSHIP JURISDICTION ACT

Article 1. General Provisions.
Article 2. Jurisdiction.
Article 3. Transfer of Conservatorship.
Article 4. Registration and Recognition of Orders from Other States.
Article 5. Miscellaneous Provisions.
Article 6. Federally Recognized Indian Tribe.

ARTICLE 1
General Provisions

Legislative intent; Citation of chapter. §1980.
Applicability of chapter. §1981.
Definitions. §1982.
Treatment of foreign country as state. §1983.
Communication with court in another state. §1984.
Requests for assistance between courts; Travel expenses. §1985.
Taking testimony in another state. §1986.

§1980. Legislative intent; Citation of chapter

(a) By enacting this chapter, it is the Legislature's intent to enact a modified version of the Uniform Adult Guardianship and Protective Proceedings Jurisdiction Act.

(b) This chapter may be cited as the "California Conservatorship Jurisdiction Act." **Leg.H.** Added Stats 2014 ch 553 §20 (SB 940), effective January 1, 2015, operative January 1, 2016.

§1981. Applicability of chapter

(a)(1) This chapter does not apply to a minor, regardless of whether the minor is or was married.

(2) This chapter does not apply to any proceeding in which a person is appointed to provide personal care or property administration for a minor, including, but not limited to, a guardianship under Part 2 (commencing with Section 1500).

(b) This chapter does not apply to any proceeding in which a person is involuntarily committed to a mental health facility or subjected to other involuntary mental health care, including, but not limited to, any of the following proceedings or any proceeding that is similar in substance:

(1) A proceeding under Sections 1026 to 1027, inclusive, of the Penal Code.

(2) A proceeding under Chapter 6 (commencing with Section 1367) of Title 10 of Part 2 of the Penal Code.

(3) A proceeding under Article 4 (commencing with Section 2960) of Chapter 7 of Title 1 of Part 3 of the Penal Code.

(4) A proceeding under Article 6 (commencing with Section 1800) of Chapter 1 of Division 2.5 of the Welfare and Institutions Code.

(5) A proceeding under Part 1 (commencing with Section 5000) of Division 5 of the Welfare and Institutions Code, which is also known as the Lanterman-Petris-Short Act.

(6) A proceeding under Article 2 (commencing with Section 6500) of Chapter 2 of Part 2 of Division 6 of the Welfare and Institutions Code.

(7) A proceeding under Article 4 (commencing with Section 6600) of Chapter 2 of Part 2 of Division 6 of the Welfare and Institutions Code.

(c) Article 3 (commencing with Section 2001) does not apply to an adult with a developmental disability, or to any proceeding in which a person is appointed to provide personal care or property administration for an adult with a developmental disability, including, but not limited to, the following types of proceedings:

(1) A proceeding under Article 7.5 (commencing with Section 416) of Chapter 2 of Part 1 of Division 1 of the Health and Safety Code.

(2) A limited conservatorship under subdivision (d) of Section 1801.

(3) A proceeding under Section 4825 of the Welfare and Institutions Code.

(4) A proceeding under Article 2 (commencing with Section 6500) of Chapter 2 of Part 2 of Division 6 of the Welfare and Institutions Code.

(d) Application of this chapter to a conservatee with major neurocognitive disorder is subject to the express limitations of Sections 2002 and 2016, as well as the other requirements of this chapter. **Leg.H.** Added Stats 2014 ch 553 §20 (SB 940), effective January 1, 2015, operative January 1, 2016. Amended Stats 2017 ch 122 §4 (SB 413), effective January 1, 2018.

§1982. Definitions

In this chapter:

(a) "Adult" means an individual who has attained 18 years of age.

(b) "Conservatee" means an adult for whom a conservator of the estate, a conservator of the person, or a conservator of the person and estate has been appointed.

(c) "Conservator" means a person appointed by the court to serve as a conservator of the estate, a conservator of the person, or a conservator of the person and estate.

(d) "Conservator of the estate" means a person appointed by the court to administer the property of an adult, including, but not limited to, a person appointed for that purpose under subdivision (b) of Section 1801.

(e) "Conservator of the person" means a person appointed by the court to make decisions regarding the person of an adult, including, but not limited to, a person appointed for that purpose under subdivision (a) of Section 1801.

(f) "Conservator of the person and estate" means a person appointed by the court to make decisions regarding the person of an adult and to administer the property of that adult, including, but not limited to, a person appointed for those purposes under subdivision (c) of Section 1801.

(g) "Conservatorship order" means an order appointing a conservator of the estate, a conservator of the person, or a conservator of the person and estate in a conservatorship proceeding.

(h) "Conservatorship proceeding" means a judicial proceeding in which an order for the appointment of a conservator of the estate, a conservator of the person, or a conservator of the person and estate is sought or has been issued.

(i) "Party" means the conservatee, proposed conservatee, petitioner, conservator, proposed conservator, or any other person allowed by the court to participate in a conservatorship proceeding.

(j) "Person" means an individual, corporation, business trust, estate, trust, partnership, limited liability company, association, joint venture, public corporation, government or governmental subdivision, agency, or instrumentality, or any other legal or commercial entity.

(k) "Proposed conservatee" means an adult for whom a conservatorship order is sought.

(*l*) "Record" means information that is inscribed on a tangible medium or that is stored in an electronic or other medium and is retrievable in perceivable form.

(m) Notwithstanding Section 74, "state" means a state of the United States, the District of Columbia, Puerto Rico, the United States Virgin Islands, a federally recognized Indian tribe, or any territory or insular possession subject to the jurisdiction of the United States. **Leg.H.** Added Stats 2014 ch 553 §20 (SB 940), effective January 1, 2015, operative January 1, 2016.

§1983. Treatment of foreign country as state

A court of this state may treat a foreign country as if it were a state for the purpose of applying this article and Articles 2, 3, and 5. **Leg.H.** Added Stats 2014 ch 553 §20 (SB 940), effective January 1, 2015, operative January 1, 2016.

§1984. Communication with court in another state

(a) A court of this state may communicate with a court in another state concerning a proceeding arising under this chapter. The court may allow the parties to participate in the communication. Except as otherwise provided in subdivision (b), the court shall make a record of the communication. The record may be limited to the fact that the communication occurred.

(b) Courts may communicate concerning schedules, calendars, court records, and other administrative matters without making a record. **Leg.H.** Added Stats 2014 ch 553 §20 (SB 940), effective January 1, 2015, operative January 1, 2016.

§1985. Requests for assistance between courts; Travel expenses

(a) In a conservatorship proceeding in this state, a court of this state may request the appropriate court of another state to do any of the following:

(1) Hold an evidentiary hearing.

(2) Order a person in that state to produce evidence or give testimony pursuant to procedures of that state.

(3) Order that an evaluation or assessment be made of the proposed conservatee.

(4) Order any appropriate investigation of a person involved in a proceeding.

(5) Forward to the court of this state a certified copy of the transcript or other record of a hearing under paragraph (1) or any other proceeding, any evidence otherwise produced under paragraph (2), and any evaluation or assessment prepared in compliance with an order under paragraph (3) or (4).

(6) Issue any order necessary to ensure the appearance in the proceeding of a person whose presence is necessary for the court to make a determination, including the conservatee or the proposed conservatee.

(7) Issue an order authorizing the release of medical, financial, criminal, or other relevant information in that state, including protected health information as defined in Section 160.103 of Title 45 of the Code of Federal Regulations.

(b) If a court of another state in which a conservatorship proceeding is pending requests assistance of the kind provided in subdivision (a), a court of this state has jurisdiction for the limited purpose of granting the request or making reasonable efforts to comply with the request.

(c) Travel and other necessary and reasonable expenses incurred under subdivisions (a) and (b) may be assessed against the parties according to the law of this state. **Leg.H.** Added Stats 2014 ch 553 §20 (SB 940), effective January 1, 2015, operative January 1, 2016.

§1986. Taking testimony in another state

(a) In a conservatorship proceeding, in addition to other procedures that may be available, testimony of a witness who is located in another state may be offered by deposition or other means allowable in this state for testimony taken in another state. The court on its own motion may order that the testimony of a witness be taken in another state and may prescribe the manner in which and the terms upon which the testimony is to be taken.

(b) In a conservatorship proceeding, a court in this state may permit a witness located in another state to be deposed or to testify by telephone or audiovisual or other electronic means. A court of this state shall cooperate with the court of the other state in designating an appropriate location for the deposition or testimony. **Leg.H.** Added Stats 2014 ch 553 §20 (SB 940), effective January 1, 2015, operative January 1, 2016.

ARTICLE 2
Jurisdiction

Significant connection with state. §1991.
Exclusive basis. §1992.
Jurisdiction. §1993.
Special jurisdiction. §1994.
Exclusive and continuing jurisdiction. §1995.
Appropriate forum. §1996.
Jurisdiction declined by reason of conduct. §1997.
Notice of proceeding. §1998.
Proceedings in more than one state. §1999.

§1991. Significant connection with state

(a) In this article:

(1) "Emergency" means a circumstance that likely will result in substantial harm to a proposed conservatee's health, safety, or welfare, and for which the appointment of a conservator of the person is necessary because no other person has authority and is willing to act on behalf of the proposed conservatee.

(2) "Home state" means the state in which the proposed conservatee was physically present, including any period of temporary absence, for at least six consecutive months immediately before the filing of a petition for a conservatorship order, or, if none, the state in which the proposed conservatee was physically present, including any period of temporary absence, for at least six consecutive months ending within the six months prior to the filing of the petition.

(3) "Significant-connection state" means a state, other than the home state, with which a proposed conservatee has a significant connection other than mere physical presence and in which substantial evidence concerning the proposed conservatee is available.

(b) In determining under Section 1993 and subdivision (e) of Section 2001 whether a proposed conservatee has a significant connection with a particular state, the court shall consider all of the following:

(1) The location of the proposed conservatee's family and other persons required to be notified of the conservatorship proceeding.

(2) The length of time the proposed conservatee at any time was physically present in the state and the duration of any absence.

(3) The location of the proposed conservatee's property.

(4) The extent to which the proposed conservatee has ties to the state such as voting registration, state or local tax return filing, vehicle registration, driver's license, social relationship, and receipt of services. **Leg.H.** Added Stats 2014 ch 553 §20 (SB 940), effective January 1, 2015, operative January 1, 2016.

§1992. Exclusive basis

For a conservatorship proceeding governed by this article, this article provides the exclusive basis for determining whether the courts of this state, as opposed to the courts of another state, have jurisdiction to appoint a conservator of the person, a conservator of the estate, or a conservator of the person and estate. **Leg.H.** Added Stats 2014 ch 553 §20 (SB 940), effective January 1, 2015, operative January 1, 2016.

§1993. Jurisdiction

(a) A court of this state has jurisdiction to appoint a conservator for a proposed conservatee if this state is the proposed conservatee's home state.

(b) A court of this state has jurisdiction to appoint a conservator for a proposed conservatee if, on the date the petition is filed, this state is a significant-connection state and the proposed conservatee does not have a home state.

(c) A court of this state has jurisdiction to appoint a conservator for a proposed conservatee if, on the date the petition is filed, this state is a significant-connection state and a court of the proposed conservatee's home state has expressly declined to exercise jurisdiction because this state is a more appropriate forum.

(d) A court of this state has jurisdiction to appoint a conservator for a proposed conservatee if both of the following conditions are satisfied:

(1) On the date the petition is filed, this state is a significant-connection state, the proposed conservatee has a home state, and a conservatorship petition is not pending in a court of the home state or another significant-connection state.

(2) Before the court makes the appointment, no conservatorship petition is filed in the proposed conservatee's home state, no objection to the court's jurisdiction is filed by a person required to be notified of the proceeding, and the court in this state concludes that it is an appropriate forum under the factors set forth in Section 1996.

(e) A court of this state has jurisdiction to appoint a conservator for a proposed conservatee if all of the following conditions are satisfied:

(1) This state does not have jurisdiction under subdivision (a), (b), (c), or (d).

(2) The proposed conservatee's home state and all significant-connection states have expressly declined to exercise jurisdiction because this state is the more appropriate forum.

(3) Jurisdiction in this state is consistent with the constitutions of this state and the United States.

(f) A court of this state has jurisdiction to appoint a conservator for a proposed conservatee if the requirements for special jurisdiction under Section 1994 are met. **Leg.H.** Added Stats 2014 ch 553 §20 (SB 940), effective January 1, 2015, operative January 1, 2016. Amended Stats 2019 ch 497 §211 (AB 991), effective January 1, 2020.

§1994. Special jurisdiction

(a) A court of this state lacking jurisdiction under subdivisions (a) to (e), inclusive, of Section 1993 has special jurisdiction to do any of the following:

(1) Appoint a temporary conservator of the person in an emergency for a proposed conservatee who is physically present in this state. In making an appointment under this paragraph, a court shall follow the procedures specified in Chapter 3 (commencing with Section 2250) of Part 4. The temporary conservatorship shall terminate in accordance with Section 2257.

(2) Appoint a conservator of the estate with respect to real or tangible personal property located in this state.

(3) Appoint a conservator of the person, conservator of the estate, or conservator of the person and estate for a proposed conservatee for whom a provisional order to transfer a proceeding from another state has been issued under procedures similar to Section 2001. In making an appointment under this paragraph, a court shall follow the procedures specified in Chapter 3 (commencing with Section 2250) of Part 4. The temporary conservatorship shall terminate in accordance with Section 2257.

(b) If a petition for the appointment of a conservator of the person in an emergency is brought in this state and this state was not the home state of the proposed conservatee on the date the petition was filed, the court shall dismiss the proceeding at the request of the court of the home state, if any, whether dismissal is requested before or after the emergency appointment of a temporary conservator of the person. **Leg.H.** Added Stats 2014 ch 553 §20 (SB 940), effective January 1, 2015, operative January 1, 2016.

§1995. Exclusive and continuing jurisdiction

Except as otherwise provided in Section 1994, a court that has appointed a conservator consistent with this chapter has exclusive and continuing jurisdiction over the proceeding until it is terminated by the court or the appointment expires by its own terms. **Leg.H.** Added Stats 2014 ch 553 §20 (SB 940), effective January 1, 2015, operative January 1, 2016.

§1996. Appropriate forum

(a)(1) A court of this state having jurisdiction under Section 1993 to appoint a conservator may decline to exercise its jurisdiction if it determines at any time that a court of another state is a more appropriate forum.

(2) The issue of appropriate forum may be raised upon petition of any interested person, the court's own motion, or the request of another court.

(3) The petitioner, or, if there is no petitioner, the court in this state, shall give notice of the petition, motion, or request to the same persons and in the same manner as for a petition for a conservatorship under Section 1801. The notice shall state the basis for the petition, motion, or request, and shall inform the recipients of the date, time, and place of the hearing under paragraph (4). The notice shall also advise the recipients that they have a right to object to the petition, motion, or request. The notice to the potential conservatee shall inform the potential conservatee of the right to be represented by legal counsel if the potential conservatee so chooses, and to have legal counsel appointed by the court if the potential conservatee is unable to retain legal counsel.

(4) The court shall hold a hearing on the petition, motion, or request.

(b) If a court of this state declines to exercise its jurisdiction under subdivision (a), it shall grant the petition, motion, or request, and either dismiss or stay any conservatorship proceeding pending in this state. The court's order shall be based on evidence presented to the court. The order shall be in a record and shall expressly state that the court declines to exercise its jurisdiction because a court of another state is a more appropriate forum. The court may impose any condition the court considers just and proper, including the condition that a petition for the appointment of a conservator of the person, conservator of the estate, or conservator of the person and estate be filed promptly in another state.

(c) In determining whether it is an appropriate forum, the court shall consider all relevant factors, including all of the following:

(1) Any expressed preference of the proposed conservatee.

(2) Whether abuse, neglect, or exploitation of the proposed conservatee has occurred or is likely to occur and which state could best protect the proposed conservatee from the abuse, neglect, or exploitation.

(3) The length of time the proposed conservatee was physically present in or was a legal resident of this or another state.

(4) The location of the proposed conservatee's family, friends, and other persons required to be notified of the conservatorship proceeding.

(5) The distance of the proposed conservatee from the court in each state.

(6) The financial circumstances of the estate of the proposed conservatee.

(7) The nature and location of the evidence.

(8) The ability of the court in each state to decide the issue expeditiously and the procedures necessary to present evidence.

(9) The familiarity of the court of each state with the facts and issues in the proceeding.

(10) If an appointment were made, the court's ability to monitor the conduct of the conservator. **Leg.H.** Added Stats 2014 ch 553 §20 (SB 940), effective January 1, 2015, operative January 1, 2016.

§1997. Jurisdiction declined by reason of conduct

(a) If at any time a court of this state determines that it acquired jurisdiction to appoint a conservator because of unjustifiable conduct, the court may do any of the following:

(1) Decline to exercise jurisdiction.

(2) Exercise jurisdiction for the limited purpose of fashioning an appropriate remedy to ensure the health, safety, and welfare of the conservatee or proposed conservatee or the protection of the property of the conservatee or proposed conservatee or to prevent a repetition of the unjustifiable conduct, including staying the proceeding until a petition for the appointment of a conservator of the person, conservator of the estate, or conservator of the person and estate is filed in a court of another state having jurisdiction.

(3) Continue to exercise jurisdiction after considering all of the following:

(A) The extent to which the conservatee or proposed conservatee and all persons required to be notified of the proceedings have acquiesced in the exercise of the court's jurisdiction.

(B) Whether it is a more appropriate forum than the court of any other state under the factors set forth in subdivision (c) of Section 1996.

(C) Whether the court of any other state would have jurisdiction under factual circumstances in substantial conformity with the jurisdictional standards of Section 1993.

(b) If a court of this state determines that it acquired jurisdiction to appoint a conservator because a party seeking to invoke its jurisdiction engaged in unjustifiable conduct, it may assess against that party necessary and reasonable expenses, including attorney's fees, investigative fees, court costs, communication expenses, medical examination expenses, witness fees and expenses, and travel expenses. The court may not assess fees, costs, or expenses of any kind against this state or a governmental subdivision, agency, or instrumentality of this state unless authorized by law other than this chapter. **Leg.H.** Added Stats 2014 ch 553 §20 (SB 940), effective January 1, 2015, operative January 1, 2016.

§1998. Notice of proceeding

If a petition for the appointment of a conservator of the person, conservator of the estate, or conservator of the person and estate is brought in this state and this state was not the home state of the proposed conservatee on the date the petition was filed, in addition to complying with the notice requirements of this state, the petitioner shall give notice of the petition or of a hearing on the petition to those persons who would be entitled to notice of the petition or of a hearing on the petition if a proceeding were brought in the home state of the proposed conservatee. The notice shall be given in the same manner as notice is required to be given in this state. **Leg.H.** Added Stats 2014 ch 553 §20 (SB 940), effective January 1, 2015, operative January 1, 2016.

§1999. Proceedings in more than one state

Except for a petition for the appointment of a conservator under paragraph (1) or paragraph (2) of subdivision (a) of Section 1994, if a petition for the appointment of a conservator is filed in this state and in another state and neither petition has been dismissed or withdrawn, the following rules apply:

(a) If the court in this state has jurisdiction under Section 1993, it may proceed with the case unless a court in another state acquires jurisdiction under provisions similar to Section 1993 before the appointment.

(b) If the court in this state does not have jurisdiction under Section 1993, whether at the time the petition is filed or at any time before the appointment, the court shall stay the proceeding and communicate with the court in the other state. If the court in the other state has jurisdiction, the court in this state shall dismiss the petition unless the court in the other state determines that the court in this state is a more appropriate forum. **Leg.H.** Added Stats 2014 ch 553 §20 (SB 940), effective January 1, 2015, operative January 1, 2016.

ARTICLE 3
Transfer of Conservatorship

Transfer of conservatorship to another state. §2001.
Transfer of conservatorship from another state. §2002.

Transfer to or from court of California tribe. §2003.

§2001. Transfer of conservatorship to another state

(a) A conservator appointed in this state may petition the court to transfer the conservatorship to another state.

(b) The petitioner shall give notice of a hearing on a petition under subdivision (a) to the persons that would be entitled to notice of a hearing on a petition in this state for the appointment of a conservator.

(c) The court shall hold a hearing on a petition filed pursuant to subdivision (a).

(d) The court shall issue an order provisionally granting a petition to transfer a conservatorship of the person, and shall direct the conservator of the person to petition for acceptance of the conservatorship in the other state, if the court is satisfied that the conservatorship will be accepted by the court in the other state and the court finds all of the following:

(1) The conservatee is physically present in or is reasonably expected to move permanently to the other state.

(2) An objection to the transfer has not been made or, if an objection has been made, the court determines that the transfer would not be contrary to the interests of the conservatee.

(3) Plans for care and services for the conservatee in the other state are reasonable and sufficient.

(e) The court shall issue a provisional order granting a petition to transfer a conservatorship of the estate, and shall direct the conservator of the estate to petition for acceptance of the conservatorship in the other state, if the court is satisfied that the conservatorship will be accepted by the court of the other state and the court finds all of the following:

(1) The conservatee is physically present in or is reasonably expected to move permanently to the other state, or the conservatee has a significant connection to the other state considering the factors in subdivision (b) of Section 1991.

(2) An objection to the transfer has not been made or, if an objection has been made, the court determines that the transfer would not be contrary to the interests of the conservatee.

(3) Adequate arrangements will be made for management of the conservatee's property.

(f) The court shall issue a provisional order granting a petition to transfer a conservatorship of the person and estate, and shall direct the conservator to petition for acceptance of the conservatorship in the other state, if the requirements of subdivision (d) and the requirements of subdivision (e) are both satisfied.

(g) The court shall issue a final order confirming the transfer and terminating the conservatorship upon its receipt of both of the following:

(1) A provisional order accepting the proceeding from the court to which the proceeding is to be transferred which is issued under provisions similar to Section 2002.

(2) The documents required to terminate a conservatorship in this state, including, but not limited to, any required accounting. **Leg.H.** Added Stats 2014 ch 553 §20 (SB 940), effective January 1, 2015, operative January 1, 2016.

§2002. Transfer of conservatorship from another state

(a)(1) To confirm transfer of a conservatorship transferred to this state under provisions similar to Section 2001, the conservator shall petition the court in this state to accept the conservatorship.

(2) The petition shall include a certified copy of the other state's provisional order of transfer.

(3) On the first page of the petition, the petitioner shall state that the conservatorship does not fall within the limitations of Section 1981. The body of the petition shall allege facts showing that this chapter applies and the requirements for transfer of the conservatorship are satisfied.

(4) The petition shall specify any modifications necessary to conform the conservatorship to the law of this state, and the terms of a proposed final order accepting the conservatorship.

(5) A petition for the appointment of a temporary conservator under Section 1994 and Chapter 3 (commencing with Section 2250) of Part 4 may be filed while a petition under this section is pending. The petition for the appointment of a temporary conservator shall request the appointment of a temporary conservator eligible for appointment in this state, and shall be limited to powers authorized for a temporary conservator in this state. For purposes of Chapter 3 (commencing with Section 2250) of Part 4, the court shall treat a petition under this section as the equivalent of a petition for a general conservatorship.

(b) The petitioner shall give notice of a hearing on a petition under subdivision (a) to those persons that would be entitled to notice if the petition were a petition for the appointment of a conservator in both the transferring state and this state. The petitioner shall also give notice to any attorney of record for the conservatee in the transferring state and to any attorney appointed or appearing for the conservatee in this state. The petitioner shall give the notice in the same manner that notice of a petition for the appointment of a conservator is required to be given in this state, except that notice to the conservatee shall be given by mailing the petition instead of by personal service of a citation.

(c) Any person entitled to notice under subdivision (b) may object to the petition on one or more of the following grounds:

(1) Transfer of the proceeding would be contrary to the interests of the conservatee.

(2) Under the law of the transferring state, the conservator is ineligible for appointment in this state.

(3) Under the law of this state, the conservator is ineligible for appointment in this state, and the transfer petition does not identify a replacement who is willing and eligible to serve in this state.

(4) This chapter is inapplicable under Section 1981.

(d) Promptly after the filing of a petition under subdivision (a), the court shall appoint an investigator under Section 1454. The investigator shall promptly commence a preliminary investigation of the conservatorship, which focuses on the matters described in subdivision (f).

(e) The court shall hold a hearing on a petition filed pursuant to subdivision (a).

(f) The court shall issue an order provisionally granting a petition filed under subdivision (a) unless any of the following occurs:

(1) The court determines that transfer of the proceeding would be contrary to the interests of the conservatee.

(2) The court determines that, under the law of the transferring state, the conservator is ineligible for appointment in this state.

(3) The court determines that, under the law of this state, the conservator is ineligible for appointment in this state, and the transfer petition does not identify a replacement who is willing and eligible to serve in this state.

(4) The court determines that this chapter is inapplicable under Section 1981.

(g) If the court issues an order provisionally granting the petition, the investigator shall promptly commence an investigation under Section 1851.1.

(h)(1) Not later than 60 days after issuance of an order provisionally granting the petition, the court shall determine whether the conservatorship needs to be modified to conform to the law of this state. The court may take any action necessary to achieve compliance with the law of this state, including, but not limited to, striking or modifying any conservator powers that are not permitted under the law of this state.

(2) At the same time that it makes the determination required by paragraph (1), the court shall review the conservatorship as provided in Section 1851.1.

(3) The conformity determination and the review required by this subdivision shall occur at a hearing, which shall be noticed as provided in subdivision (b).

(i)(1) The court shall issue a final order accepting the proceeding and appointing the conservator in this state upon completion of the conformity determination and review required by subdivision (h), or upon its receipt from the court from which the proceeding is being transferred of a final order issued under provisions similar to Section 2001 transferring the proceeding to this state, whichever occurs later. In appointing a conservator under this paragraph, the court shall comply with Section 1830.

(2) A transfer to this state does not become effective unless and until the court issues a final order under paragraph (1). A conservator may not take action in this state pursuant to a transfer petition unless and until the transfer becomes effective and all of the following steps have occurred:

(A) The conservator has taken an oath in accordance with Section 2300.

(B) The conservator has filed the required bond, if any.

(C) The court has provided the information required by Section 1835 to the conservator.

(D) The conservator has filed an acknowledgment of receipt as required by Section 1834.

(E) The clerk of the court has issued the letters of conservatorship.

(3) Paragraph (2) does not preclude a person who has been appointed as a temporary conservator pursuant to Chapter 3 (commencing with Section 2250) from taking action in this state pursuant to the order establishing the temporary conservatorship.

(4) When a transfer to this state becomes effective, the conservatorship is subject to the law of this state and shall thereafter be treated as a conservatorship under the law of this state. If a law of this state, including, but not limited to, Section 2356.5, mandates compliance with special requirements to exercise a particular conservatorship power or take a particular step, the conservator of a transferred conservatorship may not exercise that power or take that step without first complying with those special requirements.

(j) Except as otherwise provided by Section 1851.1, Chapter 3 (commencing with Section 1860), Chapter 9 (commencing with Section 2650) of Part 4, and other law, when the court grants a petition under this section, the court shall recognize a conservatorship order from the other state, including the determination of the conservatee's incapacity and the appointment of the conservator.

(k) The denial by a court of this state of a petition to accept a conservatorship transferred from another state does not affect the ability of the conservator to seek appointment as conservator in this state under Chapter 1 (commencing with Section 1800) of Part 3 if the court has jurisdiction to make an appointment other than by reason of the provisional order of transfer. **Leg.H.** Added Stats 2014 ch 553 §20 (SB 940), effective January 1, 2015, operative January 1, 2016.

§2003. Transfer to or from court of California tribe

If a conservatorship is transferred under this article from a court of this state to the court of a California tribe or from the court of a California tribe to a court of this state, the order that provisionally grants the transfer may expressly provide that specified powers of the conservator will not be transferred. Jurisdiction over the specified powers will be retained by the transferring state and will not be included in the powers that are granted to the conservator in the state that accepts the transfer. **Leg.H.** Added Stats 2014 ch 553 §20 (SB 940), effective January 1, 2015, operative January 1, 2016.

ARTICLE 4
Registration and Recognition of Orders from Other States

Registration of conservatorship of the person. §2011.
Registration of conservatorship of the estate. §2012.
Registration of conservatorship of the person and estate. §2013.
Notice of intent to register. §2014.
Court to inform conservator of rights, duties, limitations, and responsibilities. §2015.
Authority of conservator. §2016.
Third-party immunity. §2017.
Recording of registration. §2018.
Applicability to California tribal court orders. §2019.

§2011. Registration of conservatorship of the person

If a conservator of the person has been appointed in another state and a petition for the appointment of a conservator of the person is not pending in this state, the conservator of the person appointed in the other state, after providing notice pursuant to Section 2014, may register the conservatorship order in this state by filing certified copies of the order and letters of office, and proof of notice as required herein, together with a cover sheet approved by the Judicial Council, in the superior court of any appropriate county of this state. **Leg.H.** Added Stats 2014 ch 553 §20 (SB 940), effective January 1, 2015, operative January 1, 2016.

§2012. Registration of conservatorship of the estate

If a conservator of the estate has been appointed in another state and a petition for the appointment of a conservator of the estate is not pending in this state, the conservator appointed in the other state, after providing notice pursuant to Section 2014, may register the conservatorship order in this state by filing certified copies of the order and letters of office and of any bond, and proof of notice as required herein, together with a cover sheet approved by the Judicial Council, in the superior court of any county of this state in which property belonging to the conservatee is located. **Leg.H.** Added Stats 2014 ch 553 §20 (SB 940), effective January 1, 2015, operative January 1, 2016.

§2013. Registration of conservatorship of the person and estate

If a conservator of the person and estate has been appointed in another state and a petition for a conservatorship of the person, conservatorship of the estate, or conservatorship of the person and estate is not pending in this state, the conservator appointed in the other state, after providing notice pursuant to Section 2014, may register the conservatorship order in this state by filing certified copies of the order and letters of office and of any bond, and proof of notice as required herein, together with a cover sheet approved by the Judicial Council, in the superior court of any appropriate county of this state. **Leg.H.** Added Stats 2014 ch 553 §20 (SB 940), effective January 1, 2015, operative January 1, 2016.

§2014. Notice of intent to register

(a) At least 15 days before registering a conservatorship in this state, the conservator shall provide notice of an intent to register to all of the following:

(1) The court supervising the conservatorship.

(2) Every person who would be entitled to notice of a petition for the appointment of a conservator in the state where the conservatorship is being supervised.

(3) Every person who would be entitled to notice of a petition for the appointment of a conservator in this state.

(b) Each notice provided pursuant to subdivision (a) shall comply with all of the following:

(1) The notice shall prominently state that when a conservator acts pursuant to this article, the conservator is subject to the law of this state governing the action, including, but not limited to, all applicable procedures, and is not authorized to take any action prohibited by the law of this state.

(2) The notice shall explain that if a conservatorship is registered pursuant to this article, and the conservator later proposes to take a specific action pursuant to this article, which, under the law of this state, requires court approval or other action in court, the conservator will be required to notify the recipient of the request for court approval or other court action, and the recipient will have an opportunity to object or otherwise participate at that time, in the same manner as other persons are entitled to object or otherwise participate under the law of this state.

(3) The notice shall advise the recipient that information about a conservator's rights, duties, limitations, and responsibilities under the law of this state is available, free of charge, on an Internet Web site maintained by the Judicial Council. The notice shall explain specifically how to locate that information on the Judicial Council's Internet Web site.

(c) Except as provided in subdivision (c) of Section 2023, each notice provided pursuant to subdivision (a) shall also prominently state that the registration is effective only while the conservatee resides in another jurisdiction and does not authorize the conservator to take any action while the conservatee is residing in this state. **Leg.H.** Added Stats 2014 ch 553 §20 (SB 940), effective January 1, 2015, operative January 1, 2016.

§2015. Court to inform conservator of rights, duties, limitations, and responsibilities

Upon registration of a conservatorship pursuant to this article, the court shall provide the conservator with written information concerning a conservator's rights, duties, limitations, and responsibilities in this state, as specified in Section 1835. To cover the costs of providing that information, a court may charge the conservator the fee specified in Section 1835, which shall be distributed as specified in that section. The conservator shall file an acknowledgment of receipt of the written information, on a form prescribed by the Judicial Council. **Leg.H.** Added Stats 2014 ch 553 §20 (SB 940), effective January 1, 2015, operative January 1, 2016.

§2016. Authority of conservator

(a) Upon registration of a conservatorship order from another state and the filing by the conservator of an acknowledgment of receipt of the written information required by Section 2015, the conservator may, while the conservatee resides out of this state, exercise in any county of this state all powers authorized in the order of appointment except as prohibited under the laws of this state, including maintaining actions and proceedings in this state and, if the conservator is not a resident of this state, subject to any conditions imposed upon nonresident parties. When acting pursuant to registration, the conservator is subject to the law of this state governing the action, including, but not limited to, all applicable procedures, and is not authorized to take any action prohibited by the law of this state. If a law of this state, including, but not limited to, Section 2352, 2352.5, 2355, 2356.5, 2540, 2543, 2545, or 2591.5, or Article 2 (commencing with Section 1880) of Chapter 4 of Part 4, mandates compliance with special requirements to exercise a particular conservatorship power or take a particular step, the conservator of a registered conservatorship may not exercise that power or take that step without first complying with those special requirements.

(b)(1) When subdivision (a) requires a conservator to comply with a law of this state that makes it necessary to obtain court approval or take other action in court, the conservator shall seek that approval or proceed as needed in an appropriate court of this state. In handling the matter, that court shall communicate and cooperate with the court that is supervising the conservatorship, in accordance with Sections 1984 and 1985.

(2) In addition to providing any other notice required by law, the conservator shall provide notice of a court proceeding under paragraph (1) to all of the following:

(A) The court supervising the conservatorship.

(B) Every person who would be entitled to notice of a petition for the appointment of a conservator in the state where the conservatorship is being supervised.

(C) Every person who would be entitled to notice of a petition for the appointment of a conservator in this state.

(3) Any person entitled to notice under paragraph (2) may raise an objection or otherwise participate in the proceeding in the same manner as other persons are allowed to do under the law of this state.

(c) Subdivision (a) applies only when the conservatee resides out of this state. When the conservatee resides in this state, a conservator may not exercise any powers pursuant to a registration under this article.

(d) A court of this state may grant any relief available under this chapter and other law of this state to enforce a registered order. **Leg.H.** Added Stats 2014 ch 553 §20 (SB 940), effective January 1, 2015, operative January 1, 2016.

§2017. Third-party immunity

(a) A third person who acts in good faith reliance on a conservatorship order registered under this article is not liable to any person for so acting if all of the following requirements are satisfied:

(1) The conservator presents to the third person a file-stamped copy of the registration documents required by Section 2011, 2012, or 2013, including, but not limited to, the certified copy of the conservatorship order.

(2) Each of the registration documents, including, but not limited to, the conservatorship order and the file-stamped cover sheet, appears on its face to be valid.

(3) The conservator presents to the third person a form approved by the Judicial Council, in which the conservator attests that the conservatee does not reside in this state and the conservator promises to promptly notify the third person if the conservatee becomes a resident of this state. The form shall also prominently state that the registration is effective only while the conservatee resides in another jurisdiction and does not authorize the conservator to take any action while the conservatee is residing in this state.

(4) The third person has not received any actual notice that the conservatee is residing in this state.

(b) Nothing in this section is intended to create an implication that a third person is liable for acting in reliance on a conservatorship order registered under this article under circumstances where the requirements of subdivision (a) are not satisfied. Nothing in this section affects any immunity that may otherwise exist apart from this section. **Leg.H.** Added Stats 2014 ch 553 §20 (SB 940), effective January 1, 2015, operative January 1, 2016.

§2018. Recording of registration

(a) A file-stamped copy of the registration documents required by Section 2011, 2012, or 2013 may be recorded in the office of any county recorder in this state.

(b) A county recorder may charge a reasonable fee for recordation under subdivision (a). **Leg.H.** Added Stats 2014 ch 553 §20 (SB 940), effective January 1, 2015, operative January 1, 2016.

§2019. Applicability to California tribal court orders

Notwithstanding any other provision of this article:

(a) A conservatorship order of a court of a California tribe can be registered under Section 2011, 2012, or 2013, regardless of whether the conservatee resides in California.

(b) The effect of a conservatorship order of a court of a California tribe that is registered under Section 2011, 2012, or 2013 is not contingent on whether the conservatee resides in California.

(c) Paragraphs (3) and (4) of subdivision (a) of Section 2017 do not apply to a conservatorship order of a court of a California tribe. **Leg.H.** Added Stats 2014 ch 553 §20 (SB 940), effective January 1, 2015, operative January 1, 2016.

ARTICLE 5
Miscellaneous Provisions

Uniformity of application and construction. §2021.
Relation to Electronic Signatures in Global and National Commerce Act. §2022.
Court rules and forms to be developed by Judicial Council. §2023.
Applicability. §2024.

§2021. Uniformity of application and construction

In applying and construing this uniform act, consideration shall be given to the need to promote uniformity of the law with respect to its subject matter among states that enact it, consistent with the need to protect individual civil rights and in accordance with due process. **Leg.H.** Added Stats 2014 ch 553 §20 (SB 940), effective January 1, 2015, operative January 1, 2016.

§2022. Relation to Electronic Signatures in Global and National Commerce Act

This chapter modifies, limits, and supersedes the federal Electronic Signatures in Global and National Commerce Act (Title 15 (commencing with Section 7001) of the United States Code), but does not modify, limit, or supersede subdivision (c) of Section 101 of that act, which is codified as subdivision (c) of Section 7001 of Title 15 of the United States Code, or authorize electronic delivery of any of the notices described in subdivision (b) of Section 103 of that act, which is codified as subdivision (b) of Section 7003 of Title 15 of the United States Code. **Leg.H.** Added Stats 2014 ch 553 §20 (SB 940), effective January 1, 2015, operative January 1, 2016.

§2023. Court rules and forms to be developed by Judicial Council

(a) On or before January 1, 2016, the Judicial Council shall develop court rules and forms as necessary for the implementation of this chapter.

(b) The materials developed pursuant to this section shall include, but not be limited to, all of the following:

(1) A cover sheet for registration of a conservatorship under Section 2011, 2012, or 2013. The cover sheet shall explain that a proceeding may not be registered under Section 2011, 2012, or 2013 if the proceeding relates to a minor. The cover sheet shall further explain that a proceeding in which a person is subjected to involuntary mental health care may not be registered under Section 2011, 2012, or 2013. The cover sheet shall require the conservator to initial each of these explanations. The cover sheet shall also prominently state that when a conservator acts pursuant to registration, the conservator is subject to the law of this state governing the action, including, but not limited to, all applicable procedures, and is not authorized to take any action prohibited by the law of this state. Except as provided in subdivision (c), the cover sheet shall also prominently state that the registration is effective only while the conservatee resides in another jurisdiction and does not authorize the conservator to take any action while the conservatee is residing in this state. Directly beneath these statements, the cover sheet shall include a signature box in which the conservator attests to these matters.

(2) The form required by paragraph (3) of subdivision (a) of Section 2017. If the Judicial Council deems it advisable, this form may be included in the civil cover sheet developed under paragraph (1).

(3) A form for providing notice of intent to register a proceeding under Section 2011, 2012, or 2013.

(4) A form for a conservator to acknowledge receipt of the written information required by Section 2015.

(c) The materials prepared pursuant to this section shall be consistent with Section 2019. **Leg.H.** Added Stats 2014 ch 553 §20 (SB 940), effective January 1, 2015, operative January 1, 2016.

§2024. Applicability

(a) This chapter applies to conservatorship proceedings begun on or after January 1, 2016.

(b) Articles 1, 3, and 4 and Sections 2021 and 2022 apply to proceedings begun before January 1, 2016, regardless of whether a conservatorship order has been issued. **Leg.H.** Added Stats 2014 ch 553 §20 (SB 940), effective January 1, 2015, operative January 1, 2016.

ARTICLE 6
Federally Recognized Indian Tribe

Definitions. §2031.
Applicability of article. §2032.
Dismissal on grounds that conservatee is member of Indian tribe with jurisdiction. §2033.

§2031. Definitions

For the purposes of this chapter:

(a) "California tribe" means an Indian tribe with jurisdiction that has tribal land located in California.

(b) "Indian tribe with jurisdiction" means a federally recognized Indian tribe that has a court system that exercises jurisdiction over proceedings that are substantially equivalent to conservatorship proceedings.

(c) "Tribal land" means land that is, with respect to a specific Indian tribe and the members of that tribe, "Indian country" as defined in Section 1151 of Title 18 of the United States Code. **Leg.H.** Added Stats 2014 ch 553 §20 (SB 940), effective January 1, 2015, operative January 1, 2016.

§2032. Applicability of article

Article 2 (commencing with Section 1991) does not apply to a proposed conservatee who is a member of an Indian tribe with jurisdiction. **Leg.H.** Added Stats 2014 ch 553 §20 (SB 940), effective January 1, 2015, operative January 1, 2016.

§2033. Dismissal on grounds that conservatee is member of Indian tribe with jurisdiction

(a) If a petition for the appointment of a conservator has been filed in a court of this state and a conservator has not yet been appointed, any person entitled to notice of a hearing on the petition may move to dismiss the petition on the grounds that the proposed conservatee is a member of an Indian tribe with jurisdiction. The petition shall state the name of the Indian tribe.

(b) If, after communicating with the named tribe, the court of this state finds that the proposed conservatee is a member of an Indian tribe with jurisdiction, it may grant the motion to dismiss if it finds that there is good cause to do so. If the motion is granted, the court may impose any condition the court considers just and proper, including the condition that a petition for the appointment of a conservator be filed promptly in the tribal court.

(c) In determining whether there is good cause to grant the motion, the court may consider all relevant factors, including, but not limited to, the following:

(1) Any expressed preference of the proposed conservatee.

(2) Whether abuse, neglect, or exploitation of the proposed conservatee has occurred or is likely to occur and which state could best protect the proposed conservatee from the abuse, neglect, or exploitation.

(3) The length of time the proposed conservatee was physically present in or was a legal resident of this or another state.

(4) The location of the proposed conservatee's family, friends, and other persons required to be notified of the conservatorship proceeding.

(5) The distance of the proposed conservatee from the court in each state.

(6) The financial circumstances of the estate of the proposed conservatee.

(7) The nature and location of the evidence.

(8) The ability of the court in each state to decide the issue expeditiously and the procedures necessary to present evidence.

(9) The familiarity of the court of each state with the facts and issues in the proceeding.

(10) If an appointment were made, the court's ability to monitor the conduct of the conservator.

(11) The timing of the motion, taking into account the parties' and court's expenditure of time and resources.

(d) Notwithstanding subdivision (b), the court shall not grant a motion to dismiss pursuant to this section if the tribal court expressly declines to exercise its jurisdiction with regard to the proposed conservatee. **Leg.H.** Added Stats 2014 ch 553 §20 (SB 940), effective January 1, 2015, operative January 1, 2016.

PART 4
PROVISIONS COMMON TO GUARDIANSHIP AND CONSERVATORSHIP

Chapter 1. General Provisions.
Chapter 2. Jurisdiction and Venue.
Chapter 3. Temporary Guardians and Conservators.
Chapter 4. Oath, Letters, and Bond.
Chapter 5. Powers and Duties of Guardian or Conservator of the Person.
Chapter 6. Powers and Duties of Guardian or Conservator of the Estate.
Chapter 7. Inventory and Accounts.
Chapter 8. Compensation of Guardian, Conservator, and Attorney.
Chapter 9. Removal or Resignation.
Chapter 9.5. Appointment of Successor Guardian or Conservator.
Chapter 10. Requests for Special Notice.
Chapter 12. Transfer of Personal Property Out of State.
Chapter 14. Notification to Court by Institutions.

CHAPTER 1
GENERAL PROVISIONS

Law governing guardianships and conservatorships. §2100.
Relationship as fiduciary relationship. §2101.
Court supervision. §2102.
Effect of court authorization, approval, or confirmation. §2103.
Nonprofit charitable corporation as guardian or conservator. §2104.
Appointment of nonprofit charitable corporation not incorporated in state as guardian of minor. §2104.1.
Joint guardians or conservators; Custodial parent with terminal condition. §2105.
Liability of joint guardian or conservator of estate for breach by other guardian or conservator. §2105.5.
One guardian or conservator for several wards or conservatees. §2106.
Powers and duties of guardian or conservator of nonresident. §2107.
Additional powers granted nominated guardian. §2108.
Powers and duties of guardian as to particular property; Allocation of duties between guardians. §2109.
Liability of guardian or conservator who signs instrument. §2110.
Transfer or conveyance of property pursuant to court order. §2111.
Certain persons prohibited from purchasing, renting or leasing property from estate. §2111.5.
Civil penalty for abuse of conservatee. § 2112.
Fiduciary status of conservatorship. §2113.

§2100. Law governing guardianships and conservatorships

Guardianships and conservatorships are governed by Division 3 (commencing with Section 1000), except to the extent otherwise expressly provided by statute, and by this division. If no specific provision of this division is applicable, the provisions applicable to administration of estates of decedents govern so far as they are applicable to like situations. **Leg.H.** Enacted Stats 1990 ch 79 §14 (AB 759), operative July 1, 1991.

Prior Law: Former Prob C §2100, similar to the present section, was added Stats 1979 ch 726 §3, operative January 1, 1981, amended Stats 1987 ch 923 §66.5, operative January 1, 1988, Stats 1988 ch 1199 §66, operative July 1, 1989, Stats 1989 ch 21 §8, effective May 25, 1989, operative July 1, 1989, and repealed Stats 1990 ch 79 §13, operative July 1, 1991.

§2101. Relationship as fiduciary relationship

The relationship of guardian and ward and of conservator and conservatee is a fiduciary relationship that is governed by the law of trusts, except as provided in this division. **Leg.H.** Enacted Stats 1990 ch 79 §14 (AB 759), operative July 1, 1991. Amended Stats 1993 ch 293 §2 (AB 21).

Prior Law: Former Prob C §2101, similar to the present section, was added Stats 1979 ch 726 §3, operative January 1, 1981, and repealed Stats 1990 ch 79 §13, operative July 1, 1991.

Former Prob C §2101, similar to present Prob C §§1300, 1301, was added Stats 1957 ch 1902 §1, amended Stats 1967 ch 17 §120, and repealed Stats 1979 ch 726 §2, operative January 1, 1981.

§2102. Court supervision

A guardian or conservator is subject to the regulation and control of the court in the performance of the duties of the office. **Leg.H.** Enacted Stats 1990 ch 79 §14 (AB 759), operative July 1, 1991.

Prior Law: Former Prob C §2102, similar to the present section, was added Stats 1979 ch 726 §3, operative January 1, 1981, and repealed Stats 1990 ch 79 §13, operative July 1, 1991.

Former Prob C §2102, similar to present Prob C §1310, was added Stats 1957 ch 1902 §1 and repealed Stats 1979 ch 726 §2, operative January 1, 1981.

§2103. Effect of court authorization, approval, or confirmation

(a) When a judgment or order made pursuant to this division becomes final, it releases the guardian or conservator and the sureties from all claims of the ward or conservatee and of any persons affected thereby based upon any act or omission directly authorized, approved, or confirmed in the judgment or order. For the purposes of this section, "order" includes an order settling an account of the guardian or conservator, whether an intermediate or final account.

(b) This section does not apply where the judgment or order is obtained by fraud or conspiracy or by misrepresentation contained in the petition or account or in the judgment or order as to any material fact. For the purposes of this subdivision, misrepresentation includes, but is not limited to, the omission of a material fact. **Leg.H.** Enacted Stats 1990 ch 79 §14 (AB 759), operative July 1, 1991.

Prior Law: Former Prob C §2103, similar to the present section, was added Stats 1979 ch 726 §3, operative January 1, 1981, and repealed Stats 1990 ch 79 §13, operative July 1, 1991.

Former Prob C §2103, similar to present Prob C §2103, was added Stats 1957 ch 1902 §1 and repealed Stats 1979 ch 726 §2, operative January 1, 1981.

§2104. Nonprofit charitable corporation as guardian or conservator

(a) A nonprofit charitable corporation may be appointed as a guardian or conservator of the person or estate, or both, if all of the following requirements are met:

(1) The corporation is incorporated in this state.

(2) The articles of incorporation specifically authorize the corporation to accept appointments as guardian or conservator, as the case may be.

(3) The corporation has been providing, at the time of appointment, care, counseling, or financial assistance to the proposed ward or conservatee under the supervision of a registered social worker certified by the Board of Behavioral Science Examiners of this state.

(b) The petition for appointment of a nonprofit charitable corporation described in this section as a guardian or conservator shall include in the caption the name of a responsible corporate officer who shall act for the corporation for the purposes of this division. If, for any reason, the officer so named ceases to act as the responsible corporate officer for the purposes of this division, the corporation shall file with the court a notice containing (1) the name of the successor responsible corporate officer and (2) the date the successor becomes the responsible corporate officer.

(c) If a nonprofit charitable corporation described in this section is appointed as a guardian or conservator:

(1) The corporation's compensation as guardian or conservator shall be allowed only for services actually rendered.

(2) Any fee allowed for an attorney for the corporation shall be for services actually rendered. **Leg.H.** Enacted Stats 1990 ch 79 §14 (AB 759), operative July 1, 1991. Amended Stats 2001 ch 351 §1 (AB 479).

Prior Law: Former Prob C §2104, similar to the present section, was added Stats 1979 ch 726 §3, operative January 1, 1981, and repealed Stats 1990 ch 79 §13, operative July 1, 1991.

§2104.1. Appointment of nonprofit charitable corporation not incorporated in state as guardian of minor

A nonprofit charitable corporation not incorporated in this state may be appointed as the guardian of a minor if all of the following requirements are met:

(a) The articles of incorporation specifically authorize the nonprofit charitable corporation to accept appointments as a guardian.

(b) The nonprofit charitable corporation is contracted by the federal Department of Health and Human Services, Office of Refugee Resettlement, or its successor federal government entity, to provide care and custody of the minor.

(c) The petition for guardianship is filed in connection with a petition to make the necessary findings regarding special immigrant juvenile status pursuant to subdivision (b) of Section 155 of the Code of Civil Procedure.

(d) The nonprofit charitable corporation is licensed by this state to provide care for minors.

(e) The nonprofit charitable corporation complies with all of the requirements of Section 2104, except for paragraphs (1) and (2) of subdivision (a) of Section 2104. **Leg.H.** Added Stats 2018 ch 103 §2 (AB 2642), effective January 1, 2019, repealed January 1, 2022. Amended Stats 2021 ch 528 §2 (AB 829), effective January 1, 2022.

§2105. Joint guardians or conservators; Custodial parent with terminal condition

(a) The court, in its discretion, may appoint for a ward or conservatee:

(1) Two or more joint guardians or conservators of the person.

(2) Two or more joint guardians or conservators of the estate.

(3) Two or more joint guardians or conservators of the person and estate.

(b) When joint guardians or conservators are appointed, each shall qualify in the same manner as a sole guardian or conservator.

(c) Subject to subdivisions (d) and (e):

(1) Where there are two guardians or conservators, both must concur to exercise a power.

(2) Where there are more than two guardians or conservators, a majority must concur to exercise a power.

(d) If one of the joint guardians or conservators dies or is removed or resigns, the powers and duties continue in the remaining joint guardians or conservators until further appointment is made by the court.

(e) Where joint guardians or conservators have been appointed and one or more are (1) absent from the state and unable to act, (2) otherwise unable to act, or (3) legally disqualified from serving, the court may, by order made with or without notice, authorize the remaining joint guardians or conservators to act as to all matters embraced within its order.

(f) If a custodial parent has been diagnosed as having a terminal condition, as evidenced by a declaration executed by a licensed physician, the court, in its discretion, may appoint the custodial parent and a person nominated by the custodial parent as joint guardians of the person of the minor. However, this appointment shall not be made over the objection of a noncustodial parent without a finding that the noncustodial parent's custody would be detrimental to the minor, as provided in Section 3041 of the Family Code. It is the intent of the Legislature in enacting the amendments to this subdivision adopted during the 1995–96 Regular Session for a parent with a terminal condition to be able to make arrangements for the joint care, custody, and control of his or her minor children so as to minimize the emotional stress of, and disruption for, the minor children whenever the parent is incapacitated or upon the parent's death, and to avoid the need to provide a temporary guardian or place the minor children in foster care, pending appointment of a guardian, as might otherwise be required.

"Terminal condition," for purposes of this subdivision, means an incurable and irreversible condition that, without the administration of life-sustaining treatment, will, within reasonable medical judgment, result in death. **Leg.H.** Enacted Stats 1990 ch 79 §14 (AB 759), operative July 1, 1991. Amended Stats 1993 ch 978 §2 (SB 305); Stats 1995 ch 278 §1 (AB 1104); Stats 1999 ch 658 §11 (AB 891), operative July 1, 2000.

Prior Law: Former Prob C §2105, similar to the present section, was added Stats 1979 ch 726 §3, operative January 1, 1981, amended Stats 1987 ch 923 §67, operative July 1, 1988, and repealed Stats 1990 ch 79 §13, operative July 1, 1991.

§2105.5. Liability of joint guardian or conservator of estate for breach by other guardian or conservator

(a) Except as provided in subdivision (b), where there is more than one guardian or conservator of the estate, one guardian or conservator is not liable for a breach of fiduciary duty committed by another guardian or conservator.

(b) Where there is more than one guardian or conservator of the estate, one guardian or conservator is liable for a breach of fiduciary duty committed by another guardian or conservator of the same estate under any of the following circumstances:

(1) Where the guardian or conservator participates in a breach of fiduciary duty committed by the other guardian or conservator.

(2) Where the guardian or conservator improperly delegates the administration of the estate to the other guardian or conservator.

(3) Where the guardian or conservator approves, knowingly acquiesces in, or conceals a breach of fiduciary duty committed by the other guardian or conservator.

(4) Where the guardian or conservator negligently enables the other guardian or conservator to commit a breach of fiduciary duty.

(5) Where the guardian or conservator knows or has information from which the guardian or conservator reasonably should have known of the breach of fiduciary duty by the other guardian or conservator and fails to take reasonable steps to compel the other guardian or conservator to redress the breach.

(c) The liability of a guardian or conservator for a breach of fiduciary duty committed by another guardian or conservator that occurred before July 1, 1988, is governed by prior law and not by this section. **Leg.H.** Enacted Stats 1990 ch 79 §14 (AB 759), operative July 1, 1991.

Prior Law: Former Prob C §2105.5, similar to the present section, was added Stats 1987 ch 923 §68, operative July 1, 1988, amended Stats 1989 ch 21 §9, effective May 25, 1989, operative July 1, 1989, and repealed Stats 1990 ch 79 §13, operative July 1, 1991.

§2106. One guardian or conservator for several wards or conservatees

(a) The court, in its discretion, may appoint one guardian or conservator for several wards or conservatees.

(b) The appointment of one guardian or conservator for several wards or conservatees may be requested in the initial petition filed in the proceeding or may be requested subsequently upon a petition filed in the same proceeding and noticed and heard with respect to the newly proposed ward or conservatee in the same manner as an initial petition for appointment of a guardian or conservator. **Leg.H.** Enacted Stats 1990 ch 79 §14 (AB 759), operative July 1, 1991.

Prior Law: Former Prob C §2106, similar to the present section, was added Stats 1979 ch 726 §3, operative January 1, 1981, and repealed Stats 1990 ch 79 §13, operative July 1, 1991.

§2107. Powers and duties of guardian or conservator of nonresident

(a) Unless limited by court order, when a court of this state appoints a guardian or conservator of the person of a nonresident, the appointee has the same powers and duties as a guardian or conservator of the person of a resident while the nonresident is in this state.

(b) When a court of this state appoints a guardian or conservator of the estate of a nonresident, the appointee has, with respect to the property of the nonresident within this state, the same powers and duties as a guardian or conservator of the estate of a resident. The responsibility of such a guardian or conservator with regard to inventory, accounting, and disposal of the estate is confined to the property that comes into the hands of the guardian or conservator in this state. **Leg.H.** Added Stats 1990 ch 79 §14 (AB 759), operative July 1, 1991. Amended Stats 2014 ch 553 §21 (SB 940), effective January 1, 2015, operative January 1, 2016.

Prior Law: Former Prob C §2107, similar to the present section, was added Stats 1979 ch 726 §3, operative January 1, 1981, and repealed Stats 1990 ch 79 §13, operative July 1, 1991.

§2108. Additional powers granted nominated guardian

(a) Except to the extent the court for good cause determines otherwise, if a guardian of the person is nominated as provided in Article 1 (commencing with Section 1500) of Chapter 1 of Part 2 and is appointed by the court, the guardian shall be granted in the order of appointment, to the extent provided in the nomination, the same authority with respect to the person of the ward as a parent having legal custody of a child and may exercise such authority without notice, hearing, or court authorization, instructions, approval, or confirmation in the same manner as if such authority were exercised by a parent having legal custody of a child.

(b) Except to the extent the court for good cause determines otherwise and subject to Sections 2593, 2594, and 2595, if a guardian of the estate is nominated under Section 1500 or a guardian for property is nominated under Section 1501 and the guardian is appointed by the court, the guardian shall be granted in the order of appointment, to the extent provided in the nomination, the right to exercise any one or more of the powers listed in Section 2591 without notice, hearing, or court authorization, instructions, approval, or confirmation in the same manner as if such authority were granted by order of the court under Section 2590. In the case of a guardian nominated under Section 1501, such additional authority shall be limited to the property covered by the nomination.

(c) The terms of any order made under this section shall be included in the letters. **Leg.H.** Enacted Stats 1990 ch 79 §14 (AB 759), operative July 1, 1991.

Prior Law: Former Prob C §2108, similar to the present section, was added Stats 1979 ch 726 §3, operative January 1, 1981, and repealed Stats 1990 ch 79 §13, operative July 1, 1991.

§2109. Powers and duties of guardian as to particular property; Allocation of duties between guardians

(a) Subject to Section 2108, a guardian appointed under subdivision (d) of Section 1514 for particular property upon a nomination made under Section 1501 has, with respect to that property, the same powers and duties as a guardian of the estate. The responsibility of such a guardian with regard to inventory, accounting, and disposal of the estate is confined to the property covered by the nomination.

(b) When a guardian is appointed under subdivision (d) of Section 1514 for particular property upon a nomination made under Section 1501 and there is a guardian of the estate appointed under any other provision of Part 2 (commencing with Section 1500):

(1) The guardian appointed for the property covered by the nomination manages and controls that property and the guardian of the estate manages and controls the balance of the guardianship estate.

(2) Either guardian may petition under Section 2403 to the court in which the guardianship of the estate proceeding is pending for instructions concerning how the duties that are imposed by law upon the guardian of the estate are to be allocated between the two guardians. **Leg.H.** Enacted Stats 1990 ch 79 §14 (AB 759), operative July 1, 1991.

Prior Law: Former Prob C §2109, similar to the present section, was added Stats 1979 ch 726 §3, operative January 1, 1981, and repealed Stats 1990 ch 79 §13, operative July 1, 1991.

§2110. Liability of guardian or conservator who signs instrument

Unless otherwise provided in the instrument or in this division, a guardian or conservator is not personally liable on an instrument, including but not limited to a note, mortgage, deed of trust, or other contract, properly entered into in the guardian's or conservator's fiduciary capacity in the course of the guardianship or conservatorship unless the guardian or conservator fails to reveal the guardian's or conservator's representative capacity or identify the guardianship or conservatorship estate in the instrument. **Leg.H.** Enacted Stats 1990 ch 79 §14 (AB 759), operative July 1, 1991.

Prior Law: Former Prob C §2110, similar to present Prob C §§2670, 2680, 2689, was added Stats 1979 ch 726 §3, operative January 1, 1981, and repealed Stats 1981 ch 9 §3.

§2111. Transfer or conveyance of property pursuant to court order

(a) As used in this section, "transaction" means any of the following:

(1) A conveyance or lease of real property of the guardianship or conservatorship estate.

(2) The creation of a mortgage or deed of trust on real property of the guardianship or conservatorship estate.

(3) A transfer of personal property of the guardianship or conservatorship estate.

(4) The creation of a security interest or other lien in personal property of the guardianship or conservatorship estate.

(b) Whenever the court authorizes or directs a transaction, the transaction shall be carried out by the guardian or conservator of the estate in accordance with the terms of the order.

(c) A conveyance, lease, or mortgage of, or deed of trust on, real property executed by a guardian or conservator shall set forth therein that it is made by authority of the order authorizing or directing the transaction and shall give the date of the order. A certified copy of the order shall be recorded in the office of the county recorder in each county in which any portion of the real property is located.

(d) A transaction carried out by a guardian or conservator in accordance with an order authorizing or directing the transaction has the same effect as if the ward or conservatee had carried out the transaction while having legal capacity to do so. **Leg.H.** Enacted Stats 1990 ch 79 §14 (AB 759), operative July 1, 1991.

Prior Law: Former Prob C §2111, similar to the present section, was added Stats 1979 ch 726 §3, operative January 1, 1981, and repealed Stats 1990 ch 79 §13, operative July 1, 1991.

§2111.5. Certain persons prohibited from purchasing, renting or leasing property from estate

(a) Except as provided in subdivision (b), every court official or employee who has duties or responsibilities related to the appointment of a guardian or conservator, or the processing of any document related to a guardian or conservator, and every person who is related by blood or marriage to a court official or employee who has these duties, is prohibited from purchasing, leasing, or renting any real or personal property from the estate of the ward or conservatee whom the guardian or conservator represents. For purposes of this subdivision, a "person related by blood or marriage" means any of the following:

(1) A person's spouse or domestic partner.

(2) Relatives within the second degree of lineal or collateral consanguinity of a person or a person's spouse.

(b) A person described in subdivision (a) is not prohibited from purchasing real or personal property from the estate of the ward or conservatee whom the guardian or conservator represents where the purchase is made under terms and conditions of a public sale of the property.

(c) A violation of this section shall result in the rescission of the purchase, lease, or rental of the property. Any losses incurred by the estate of the ward or conservatee because the property was sold or leased at less than fair market value shall be deemed as charges against the guardian or conservator under the provisions of Sections 2401.3 and 2401.5. The court shall assess a civil penalty equal to three times the charges against the guardian, conservator, or other person in violation of this section, and may assess punitive damages as it deems proper. If the estate does not incur losses as a result of the violation, the court shall order the guardian, conservator, or other person in violation of this section to pay a fine of up to five thousand dollars ($5,000) for each violation. The fines and penalties provided in this section are in addition to any other rights and remedies provided by law. **Leg.H.** Added Stats 2000 ch 565 §3 (AB 1950). Amended Stats 2001 ch 893 §28 (AB 25).

§2112. [Section repealed 2007]

Leg.H. Enacted Stats 1990 ch 79 §14 (AB 759), operative July 1, 1991. Repealed Stats 2006 ch 838 §27 (SB 678), effective January 1, 2007. The repealed section related to application of federal Indian law.

Prior Law: Former Prob C §2112, relating to application of federal Indian law, was added Stats 1979 ch 726 §3, operative January 1, 1981, and repealed Stats 1990 ch 79 §13, operative July 1, 1991.

§ 2112. Civil penalty for abuse of conservatee

(a)(1) In addition to other remedies available under statutory or common law, if the court finds that a conservator who is a professional fiduciary licensed by the Professional Fiduciaries Bureau has abused a conservatee, the conservator shall be liable for a civil penalty of up to ten thousand dollars ($10,000) for each separate act of abuse, payable to the estate of the conservatee.

(2) In addition to other remedies available under statutory or common law, if the court finds that a conservator who is not a professional fiduciary licensed by the Professional Fiduciaries Bureau has abused a conservatee, the conservator shall be liable for a civil penalty of up to one thousand dollars ($1,000) for each separate act of abuse, payable to the estate of the conservatee.

(b) If the court finds that a professional fiduciary has abused a conservatee, or if the court imposes a penalty on the professional fiduciary, including, but not limited to, surcharging, punishing for contempt, suspending, or removing the professional fiduciary as a conservator for cause, the court shall report that finding or penalty to the Professional Fiduciaries Bureau. If the court reports an action taken under this section, the court shall provide the bureau, at no charge, with access to the information, including confidential information, regarding its investigation of the professional fiduciary contained in court records. The bureau shall maintain the confidentiality of the information, as required by paragraph (4) of subdivision (a) of Section 6580 of the Business and Professions Code or any other applicable state or federal law.

(c) For purposes of this section, the following definitions apply:

(1) "Abused" means that the conservator engaged in an act described in Section 15610.07 of the Welfare and Institutions Code.

(2) "Professional fiduciary" has the same meaning as defined in Section 6501 of the Business and Professions Code.

(d) A superior court shall not be required to perform any duties imposed pursuant to this section until the Legislature makes an appropriation identified for this purpose. **Leg.H.** Added Stats 2021 ch 417 §17 (AB 1194), effective January 1, 2022.

Prior Law: Former Prob C §2112, relating to application of federal Indian law, enacted Stats 1990 ch 79 §14 (AB 759), operative July 1, 1991, and repealed by Stats 2006 ch 838 §27 (SB 678), effective January 1, 2007.

§2113. Fiduciary status of conservatorship

A conservator shall accommodate the desires of the conservatee, except to the extent that doing so would violate the conservator's fiduciary duties to the conservatee or impose an unreasonable expense on the conservatorship estate. To the greatest extent possible, the conservator shall support the conservatee to maximize their autonomy, support the conservatee in making decisions, and, on a regular basis, inform the conservatee of decisions made on their behalf. In determining the desires of the conservatee, the conservator shall consider stated or previously expressed preferences, including preferences expressed by speech, sign language, alternative or augmentative communication, actions, facial expressions, and other spoken and nonspoken methods of communication. **Leg.H.** Added Stats 2006 ch 493 §13 (AB 1363), effective January 1, 2007. Amended Stats 2022 ch 894 §15 (AB 1663), effective January 1, 2023.

2006 Note: This act, together with Senate Bill 1116 (Scott), Senate Bill 1550 (Figueroa), and Senate Bill 1716 (Bowen), shall be known and may be cited as the Omnibus Conservatorship and Guardianship Reform Act of 2006. Stats 2006 ch 493 (AB 1363) §1.

CHAPTER 2
JURISDICTION AND VENUE

Article 1. Jurisdiction and Venue.
Article 2. Change of Venue.

ARTICLE 1
Jurisdiction and Venue

Jurisdiction in superior court. §2200.
Venue for residents. §2201.
Venue for nonresidents. §2202.
Court having priority where proceedings commenced in several counties. §2203.
When proceeding concerning custody or visitation of minor child is pending in one or more counties at the time the petition for guardianship is filed; Transfer. §2204.
Exclusive jurisdiction to determine all issues of custody or visitation. §2205.

§2200. Jurisdiction in superior court

(a) The superior court has jurisdiction of guardianship and conservatorship proceedings.

(b) Chapter 8 (commencing with Section 1980) of Part 3 governs which state has jurisdiction of a conservatorship proceeding. **Leg.H.** Added Stats 1990 ch 79 §14 (AB 759), operative July 1, 1991. Amended Stats 2014 ch 553 §22 (SB 940), effective January 1, 2015, operative January 1, 2016.

Prior Law: Former Prob C §2200, similar to the present section, was added Stats 1979 ch 726 §3, operative January 1, 1981, and repealed Stats 1990 ch 79 §13, operative July 1, 1991.

§2201. Venue for residents

The proper county for the commencement of a guardianship or conservatorship proceeding for a resident of this state is either of the following:

(a) The county in which the proposed ward or proposed conservatee resides.

(b) Such other county as may be in the best interests of the proposed ward or proposed conservatee. **Leg.H.** Enacted Stats 1990 ch 79 §14 (AB 759), operative July 1, 1991.

Prior Law: Former Prob C §2201, similar to the present section, was added Stats 1979 ch 726 §3, operative January 1, 1981, and repealed Stats 1990 ch 79 §13, operative July 1, 1991.

Former Prob C §2201, similar to present Prob C §§1471, 2250, 2252, 2253, was added Stats 1957 ch 1902 §1, amended Stats 1977 ch 1237 §3, Stats 1978 ch 1268 §1, and repealed Stats 1979 ch 726 §2, operative January 1, 1981.

§2202. Venue for nonresidents

(a) The proper county for the commencement of a proceeding for the guardianship or conservatorship of the person of a nonresident of this state is either of the following:

(1) The county in which the proposed ward or conservatee is temporarily living.

(2) Such other county as may be in the best interests of the proposed ward or proposed conservatee.

(b) The proper county for the commencement of a proceeding for the guardianship or conservatorship of the estate for a nonresident of this state is any of the following:

(1) The county in which the proposed ward or proposed conservatee is temporarily living.

(2) Any county in which the proposed ward or proposed conservatee has property.

(3) Such other county as may be in the best interests of the proposed ward or proposed conservatee. **Leg.H.** Enacted Stats 1990 ch 79 §14 (AB 759), operative July 1, 1991.

Prior Law: Former Prob C §2202, similar to the present section, was added Stats 1979 ch 726 §3, operative January 1, 1981, and repealed Stats 1990 ch 79 §13, operative July 1, 1991.

Former Prob C §2202, similar to present Prob C §2251, was added Stats 1957 ch 1902 §1 and repealed Stats 1979 ch 726 §2, operative January 1, 1981.

§2203. Court having priority where proceedings commenced in several counties

(a) If proceedings for the guardianship or conservatorship of the estate are commenced in more than one county, the guardianship or conservatorship of the estate first granted, including a temporary guardianship or conservatorship of the estate, governs and extends to all the property of the ward or conservatee within this state and the other proceeding shall be dismissed.

(b) If proceedings for the guardianship or conservatorship of the person are commenced in more than one county, the guardianship or conservatorship of the person first granted, including a temporary guardianship or conservatorship of the person, governs and the other proceeding shall be dismissed.

(c) If a proceeding for the guardianship or conservatorship of the person is commenced in one county and a proceeding for the guardianship or conservatorship of the estate is commenced in a different county, the court first granting the guardianship or conservatorship, whether of the person or of the estate, may find that it is in the best interests of the ward or conservatee that the guardianship or conservatorship of both the person and the estate be maintained in that county or in such other county as the court shall determine. Thereupon, the guardianship or conservatorship proceeding in the court of the county found by the court to be in the best interests of the ward or conservatee shall govern and shall extend to all property of the ward or conservatee within this state, and the other proceeding shall be dismissed. **Leg.H.** Enacted Stats 1990 ch 79 §14 (AB 759), operative July 1, 1991.

Prior Law: Former Prob C §2203, similar to the present section, was added Stats 1979 ch 726 §3, operative January 1, 1981, amended Stats 1980 ch 246 §4.4 and repealed Stats 1990 ch 79 §13, operative July 1, 1991.

Former Prob C §2203, similar to present Prob C §2252, was added Stats 1957 ch 1902 §1 and repealed Stats 1979 ch 726 §2, operative January 1, 1981.

§2204. When proceeding concerning custody or visitation of minor child is pending in one or more counties at the time the petition for guardianship is filed; Transfer

(a) If a proceeding for the guardianship of the person of the minor is filed in one county and a custody or visitation proceeding has already been filed in one or more other counties, the following shall apply:

(1) If the guardianship proceeding is filed in a county where the proposed ward and the proposed guardian have resided for six or more consecutive months immediately prior to the commencement of the proceeding, or, in the case of a minor less than six months of age, since the minor's birth, the court in that county is the proper court to hear and determine the guardianship proceeding, unless that court determines that the best interests of the minor require that the proceeding be transferred to one of the other courts. A period of temporary absence no longer than 30 days from the county of the minor or the proposed guardian shall not be considered an interruption of the six-month period.

(2) If the guardianship proceeding is filed in a county where the proposed ward and the proposed guardian have resided for less than six consecutive months immediately prior to the commencement of the proceeding, or, in the case of a minor less than six months of age, a period less than the minor's life, the court shall transfer the case to one of the other courts, unless the court determines that the best interests of the minor require that the guardianship proceeding be maintained in the court where it was filed.

(3) If a petitioner or respondent in a custody or visitation proceeding who is an authorized petitioner under Section 2212 petitions the court where the guardianship proceeding is filed for transfer of the guardianship proceeding to the court where the custody or visitation proceeding is on file at any time before the appointment of a guardian, including a temporary guardian, the provisions of this subdivision shall apply to the court's determination of the petition for transfer. Except as provided in this paragraph, the petition for transfer shall be determined as provided in Sections 2212 to 2217, inclusive.

(b) The following shall apply concerning communications between the courts:

(1) The court where the guardianship proceeding is commenced shall communicate concerning the proceedings with each court where a custody or visitation proceeding is on file prior to making a determination authorized in subdivision (a), including a determination of a petition to transfer.

(2) If a petitioner or respondent, who is authorized to petition to transfer under Section 2212, petitions the court where the guardianship proceeding is filed for transfer of the guardianship after the appointment of a guardian, including a temporary guardian, the court in the guardianship proceeding may communicate with each court where a custody or visitation proceeding is on file before determining the petition for transfer.

(3) If the court in the guardianship proceeding appoints a guardian of the person of the minor, including a temporary guardian, the court shall transmit a copy of the order appointing a guardian to each court where a custody or visitation proceeding is on file, and each of those courts shall file the order in the case file for its custody or visitation proceeding.

(4) The provisions of subdivisions (b) to (e), inclusive, of Section 3410 of the Family Code shall apply to communications between courts under this subdivision.

(5) The Judicial Council shall, on or before January 1, 2013, adopt rules of court to implement the provisions of this subdivision.

(c) For purposes of this section, "custody or visitation proceeding" means a proceeding described in Section 3021 of the Family Code that relates to the rights to custody or visitation of the minor under Part 2 (commencing with Section 3020) of Division 8 of the Family Code. **Leg.H.** Added Stats 2011 ch 102 §2 (AB 458), effective January 1, 2012. Amended Stats 2012 ch 207 §1 (AB 2683), effective January 1, 2013.

§2205. Exclusive jurisdiction to determine all issues of custody or visitation

(a) Except as provided in Section 304 of the Welfare and Institutions Code, and subject to the provisions specified in subdivision (b), upon the filing of an order appointing a guardian of the person of a minor in a guardianship proceeding, including an order appointing a temporary guardian of the person of the minor, the court in the guardianship proceeding shall have exclusive jurisdiction to determine all issues of custody or visitation of the minor until the guardianship proceeding is terminated.

(b) This section is subject to the provisions of Sections 1510 of this code, and 8714, 8714.5, and 8802 of the Family Code, relating to consolidation of guardianship and adoption proceedings and the court where the consolidated case is to be heard and decided. **Leg.H.** Added Stats 2011 ch 102 §3 (AB 458), effective January 1, 2012.

ARTICLE 2
Change of Venue

Definitions. §2210.
Authority to transfer proceeding. §2211.
Who may petition for transfer. §2212.
Contents of petition. §2213.
Notice of hearing. §2214.
Hearing and order. §2215.
Transfer procedure. §2216.
Transfer of venue; Notification. §2217.

§2210. Definitions

As used in this article:

(a) "Guardian or conservator" includes a proposed guardian or proposed conservator.

(b) "Ward or conservatee" includes a proposed ward or proposed conservatee. **Leg.H.** Enacted Stats 1990 ch 79 §14 (AB 759), operative July 1, 1991.

Prior Law: Former Prob C §2210, similar to the present section, was added Stats 1979 ch 726 §3, operative January 1, 1981, and repealed Stats 1990 ch 79 §13, operative July 1, 1991.

§2211. Authority to transfer proceeding

The court in which a guardianship or conservatorship proceeding is pending may, upon petition therefor, transfer the proceeding to another county within this state. **Leg.H.** Enacted Stats 1990 ch 79 §14 (AB 759), operative July 1, 1991.

Prior Law: Former Prob C §2211, similar to the present section, was added Stats 1979 ch 726 §3, operative January 1, 1981, and repealed Stats 1990 ch 79 §13, operative July 1, 1991.

§2212. Who may petition for transfer

The petition for transfer may be filed only by one or more of the following:

(a) The guardian or conservator.

(b) The ward or conservatee.

(c) The spouse of the ward or the spouse or domestic partner of the conservatee.

(d) A relative or friend of the ward or conservatee.

(e) Any other interested person. **Leg.H.** Enacted Stats 1990 ch 79 §14 (AB 759), operative July 1, 1991. Amended Stats 2001 ch 893 §29 (AB 25).

Prior Law: Former Prob C §2212, similar to the present section, was added Stats 1979 ch 726 §3, operative January 1, 1981, and repealed Stats 1990 ch 79 §13, operative July 1, 1991.

§2213. Contents of petition

The petition for transfer shall set forth all of the following:

(a) The county to which the proceeding is to be transferred.

(b) The name and address of the ward or conservatee.

(c) A brief description of the character, value, and location of the property of the ward or conservatee.

(d) The reasons for the transfer.

(e) The names and addresses, so far as they are known to the petitioner, of the spouse and of the relatives of the ward within the second degree, or of the spouse or domestic partner and of the relatives of the conservatee within the second degree.

(f) The name and address of the guardian or conservator if other than the petitioner. **Leg.H.** Enacted Stats 1990 ch 79 §14 (AB 759), operative July 1, 1991. Amended Stats 2001 ch 893 §30 (AB 25).

Prior Law: Former Prob C §2213, similar to the present section, was added Stats 1979 ch 726 §3, operative January 1, 1981, and repealed Stats 1990 ch 79 §13, operative July 1, 1991.

§2214. Notice of hearing

Notice of the hearing shall be given for the period and in the manner provided in Chapter 3 (commencing with Section 1460) of Part 1. In addition, the petitioner shall deliver pursuant to Section 1215 a notice of the time and place of the hearing and a copy of the petition to all persons required to be listed in the petition at least 15 days before the date set for the hearing. **Leg.H.** Enacted Stats 1990 ch 79 §14 (AB 759), operative July 1, 1991. Amended Stats 2017 ch 319 §41 (AB 976), effective January 1, 2018.

Prior Law: Former Prob C §2214, similar to the present section, was added Stats 1979 ch 726 §3, operative January 1, 1981, and repealed Stats 1990 ch 79 §13, operative July 1, 1991.

§2215. Hearing and order

(a) Any of the following persons may appear at the hearing to support or oppose the petition and may file written objections to the petition:

(1) Any person required to be listed in the petition.

(2) Any creditor of the ward or conservatee or of the estate.

(3) Any other interested person.

(b)(1) If the court determines that the transfer requested in the petition will be for the best interests of the ward or conservatee, it shall make an order transferring the proceeding to the other county.

(2) In those cases in which the court has approved a change of residence of the conservatee, it shall be presumed to be in the best interests of the conservatee to transfer the proceedings if the ward or conservatee has moved his or her residence to another county within the state in which any person set forth in subdivision (b) of Section 1821 also resides. The presumption that the transfer is in the best interests of the ward or conservatee, may be rebutted by clear and convincing evidence

that the transfer will harm the ward or conservatee. **Leg.H.** Enacted Stats 1990 ch 79 §14 (AB 759), operative July 1, 1991. Amended Stats 2006 ch 493 §14 (AB 1363), effective January 1, 2007.

2006 Note: This act, together with Senate Bill 1116 (Scott), Senate Bill 1550 (Figueroa), and Senate Bill 1716 (Bowen), shall be known and may be cited as the Omnibus Conservatorship and Guardianship Reform Act of 2006. Stats 2006 ch 493 (AB 1363) §1.

Prior Law: Former Prob C §2215, similar to the present section, was added Stats 1979 ch 726 §3, operative January 1, 1981, and repealed Stats 1990 ch 79 §13, operative July 1, 1991.

§2216. Transfer procedure

(a) Upon the order of transfer, the clerk shall transmit to the clerk of the court to which the proceeding is transferred a certified or exemplified copy of the order, together with all papers in the proceeding on file with the clerk.

(b) The clerk of the court from which the removal is made shall receive no fee therefor but shall be paid out of the estate all expenses incurred by the clerk in the removal. The clerk of the court to which the proceeding is transferred is entitled to such fees as are payable on the filing of a like original proceeding. **Leg.H.** Enacted Stats 1990 ch 79 §14 (AB 759), operative July 1, 1991.

Prior Law: Former Prob C §2216, similar to the present section, was added Stats 1979 ch 726 §3, operative January 1, 1981, and repealed Stats 1990 ch 79 §13, operative July 1, 1991.

§2217. Transfer of venue; Notification

(a) When an order has been made transferring venue to another county, the court transferring the matter shall set a hearing within two months to confirm receipt of the notification described in subdivision (b). If the notification has not been made, the transferring court shall make reasonable inquiry into the status of the matter.

(b) When a court receives the file of a transferred guardianship or conservatorship, the court:

(1) Shall send written notification of the receipt to the court that transferred the matter.

(2) Shall take proper action pursuant to ensure compliance by the guardian or conservator with the matters provided in Section 1456.5.

(3) If the case is a conservatorship, may conduct a review, including an investigation, as described in Sections 1851 to 1853, inclusive. **Leg.H.** Added Stats 2007 ch 553 §11 (AB 1727), effective January 1, 2008.

CHAPTER 3
TEMPORARY GUARDIANS AND CONSERVATORS

Petition for temporary guardian or conservator; Notice and hearing. §2250.
Petition for temporary conservator; Limited application. §2250.2.
Attendance of proposed temporary conservator at hearing. §2250.4.
Duties of court investigator prior to hearing. §2250.6.
Application of Sections 2250, 2250.4 and 2250.6. §2250.8.
Issuance of letters. §2251.
Powers and duties. §2252.
Change of conservatee's residence generally. §2253.
Removal of conservatee from residence in case of emergency. §2254.
Inventory and appraisal of estate. §2255.
Accounts. §2256.
Termination. §2257.
Suspension, removal, resignation, and discharge. §2258.

§2250. Petition for temporary guardian or conservator; Notice and hearing

(a) On or after the filing of a petition for appointment of a guardian or conservator, any person entitled to petition for appointment of the guardian or conservator may file a petition for appointment of:

(1) A temporary guardian of the person or estate, or both.

(2) A temporary conservator of the person or estate, or both.

(b) The petition shall state facts that establish good cause for appointment of the temporary guardian or temporary conservator. The court, upon that petition or other showing as it may require, may appoint a temporary guardian of the person or estate, or both, or a temporary conservator of the person or estate, or both, to serve pending the final determination of the court upon the petition for the appointment of the guardian or conservator.

(c) If the petitioner, proposed guardian, or proposed conservator is a professional fiduciary, as described in Section 2340, who is required to be licensed under the Professional Fiduciaries Act (Chapter 6 (commencing with Section 6500) of Division 3 of the Business and Professions Code), the petition for appointment of a temporary guardian or temporary conservator shall include the following:

(1) The petitioner's, proposed guardian's, or proposed conservator's proposed hourly fee schedule or another statement of their proposed compensation from the estate of the proposed ward or proposed conservatee for services performed as a guardian or conservator. The petitioner's, proposed guardian's, or proposed conservator's provision of a proposed hourly fee schedule or another statement of their proposed compensation, as required by this paragraph, shall not preclude a court from later reducing the petitioner's, proposed guardian's, or proposed conservator's fees or other compensation.

(2) Unless a petition for appointment of a guardian or conservator that contains the statements required by this paragraph is filed together with a petition for appointment of a temporary guardian or temporary conservator, both of the following:

(A) A statement of the petitioner's, proposed guardian's, or proposed conservator's registration or license information.

(B) A statement explaining who engaged the petitioner, proposed guardian, or proposed conservator or how the petitioner, proposed guardian, or proposed conservator was engaged to file the petition for appointment of a temporary guardian or temporary conservator or to agree to accept the appointment as temporary guardian or temporary conservator and what prior relationship the petitioner, proposed guardian, or proposed conservator had with the proposed ward or proposed conservatee or the proposed ward's or proposed conservatee's family or friends.

(d) If the petition is filed by a party other than the proposed conservatee, the petition shall include a declaration of due diligence showing both of the following:

(1) Either the efforts to find the proposed conservatee's relatives named in the petition for appointment of a general conservator or why it was not feasible to contact any of them.

(2) Either the preferences of the proposed conservatee concerning the appointment of a temporary conservator and the appointment of the proposed temporary conservator or why it was not feasible to ascertain those preferences.

(e) Unless the court for good cause otherwise orders, at least five court days before the hearing on the petition, notice of the hearing shall be given as follows:

(1) Notice of the hearing shall be personally delivered to the proposed ward if the proposed ward is 12 years of age or older, to the parent or parents of the proposed ward, and to any person having a valid visitation order with the proposed ward that was effective at the time of the filing of the petition. Notice of the hearing shall not be delivered to the proposed ward if the proposed ward is under 12 years of age. In a proceeding for temporary guardianship of the person, evidence that a custodial parent has died or become incapacitated, and that the petitioner or proposed guardian is the nominee of the custodial parent, may constitute good cause for the court to order that this notice not be delivered.

(2) Notice of the hearing shall be personally delivered to the proposed conservatee, and notice of the hearing shall be delivered pursuant to Section 1215 on the persons required to be named in the petition for appointment of conservator. If the petition states that the petitioner and the proposed conservator have no prior relationship with the proposed conservatee and have not been nominated by a family member, friend, or other person with a relationship to the proposed conservatee, notice of hearing shall be delivered pursuant to Section 1215 on the public guardian of the county in which the petition is filed.

(3) A copy of the petition for temporary appointment shall be delivered pursuant to Section 1215 with the notice of hearing.

(f) If a temporary guardianship is granted ex parte and the hearing on the general guardianship petition is not to be held within 30 days of the granting of the temporary guardianship, the court shall set a hearing within 30 days to reconsider the temporary guardianship. Notice of the hearing for reconsideration of the temporary guardianship shall be provided pursuant to Section 1511, except that the court may for good cause shorten the time for the notice of the hearing.

(g) Visitation orders with the proposed ward granted before the filing of a petition for temporary guardianship shall remain in effect, unless for good cause the court orders otherwise.

(h)(1) If a temporary conservatorship is granted ex parte, and a petition to terminate the temporary conservatorship is filed more than 15 days before the first hearing on the general petition for appointment of conservator, the court shall set a hearing within 15 days of the filing of the petition for termination of the temporary conservatorship to reconsider the temporary conservatorship. Unless the court otherwise orders, notice of the hearing on the petition to terminate the temporary conservatorship shall be given at least 10 days before the hearing.

(2) If a petition to terminate the temporary conservatorship is filed within 15 days before the first hearing on the general petition for appointment of a conservator, the court shall set the hearing at the same time that the hearing on the general petition is set. Unless the court otherwise orders, notice of the hearing on the petition to terminate the temporary conservatorship pursuant to this section shall be given at least five court days before the hearing.

(i) If the court suspends powers of the guardian or conservator under Section 2334 or 2654 or under any other provision of this division, the court may appoint a temporary guardian or conservator to exercise those powers until the powers are restored to the guardian or conservator or a new guardian or conservator is appointed.

(j) If for any reason a vacancy occurs in the office of guardian or conservator, the court, on a petition filed under subdivision (a) or on its own motion, may appoint a temporary guardian or conservator to exercise the powers of the guardian or conservator until a new guardian or conservator is appointed.

(k) A superior court shall not be required to perform any duties imposed pursuant to the amendments to this section enacted by Chapter 493 of the Statutes of 2006 until the Legislature makes an appropriation identified for this purpose. **Leg.H.** Enacted Stats 1990 ch 79 §14 (AB 759), operative July 1, 1991. Amended Stats 1993 ch 978 §3 (SB 305); Stats 1995 ch 730 §3 (AB 1466); Stats 2006 ch 493 §15 (AB 1363), effective January 1, 2007, operative July 1, 2007; Stats 2007 ch 553 §12 (AB 1727), effective January 1, 2008; Stats 2008 ch 293 §4 (AB 1340), effective January 1, 2009; Stats 2011 ch 10 §16 (SB 78), effective March 24, 2011; Stats 2013 ch 248 §3 (AB 1339), effective January 1, 2014; Stats 2017 ch 319 §42 (AB 976), effective January 1, 2018; Stats 2021 ch 417 §18 (AB 1194), effective January 1, 2022.

2006 Note: This act, together with Senate Bill 1116 (Scott), Senate Bill 1550 (Figueroa), and Senate Bill 1716 (Bowen), shall be known and may be cited as the Omnibus Conservatorship and Guardianship Reform Act of 2006. Stats 2006 ch 493 (AB 1363) §1.

Prior Law: Former Prob C §2250, similar to the present section, was added Stats 1979 ch 726 §3, operative January 1, 1981, amended Stats 1988 ch 1199 §66.5, operative July 1, 1989, ch 1382 §4, ch 1447 §3, and repealed Stats 1990 ch 79 §13, operative July 1, 1991.

§2250.2. Petition for temporary conservator; Limited application

(a) On or after the filing of a petition for appointment of a conservator, any person entitled to petition for appointment of the conservator may file a petition for appointment of a temporary conservator of the person or estate or both.

(b) The petition shall state facts that establish good cause for appointment of the temporary conservator. The court, upon that petition or any other showing as it may require, may appoint a temporary conservator of the person or estate or both, to serve pending the final determination of the court upon the petition for the appointment of the conservator.

(c) Unless the court for good cause otherwise orders, not less than five days before the appointment of the temporary conservator, notice of the proposed appointment shall be personally delivered to the proposed conservatee.

(d) If the court suspends powers of the conservator under Section 2334 or 2654 or under any other provision of this division, the court may appoint a temporary conservator to exercise those powers until the powers are restored to the conservator or a new conservator is appointed.

(e) If for any reason a vacancy occurs in the office of conservator, the court, on a petition filed under subdivision (a) or on its own motion, may appoint a temporary conservator to exercise the powers of the conservator until a new conservator is appointed.

(f) This section shall only apply to proceedings under Chapter 3 (commencing with Section 5350) of Part 1 of Division 5 of the Welfare and Institutions Code. **Leg.H.** Added Stats 2006 ch 493 §15.5 (AB 1363), effective January 1, 2007, operative July 1, 2007. Amended Stats 2007 ch 553 §12.5 (AB 1727), effective January 1, 2008.

2006 Note: This act, together with Senate Bill 1116 (Scott), Senate Bill 1550 (Figueroa), and Senate Bill 1716 (Bowen), shall be known and may be cited as the Omnibus Conservatorship and Guardianship Reform Act of 2006. Stats 2006 ch 493 (AB 1363) §1.

§2250.4. Attendance of proposed temporary conservator at hearing

The proposed temporary conservatee shall attend the hearing except in the following cases:

(a) If the proposed temporary conservatee is out of the state when served and is not the petitioner.

(b) If the proposed temporary conservatee is unable to attend the hearing by reason of medical inability.

(c) If the court investigator has visited the proposed conservatee prior to the hearing and the court investigator has reported to the court that the proposed temporary conservatee has expressly communicated that all of the following apply:

(1) The proposed conservatee is not willing to attend the hearing.

(2) The proposed conservatee does not wish to contest the establishment of the temporary conservatorship.

(3) The proposed conservatee does not object to the proposed temporary conservator or prefer that another person act as temporary conservator.

(d) If the court determines that the proposed conservatee is unable or unwilling to attend the hearing, and holding the hearing in the absence of the proposed conservatee is necessary to protect the conservatee from substantial harm.

(e) A superior court shall not be required to perform any duties imposed by this section until the Legislature makes an appropriation identified for this purpose. **Leg.H.** Added Stats 2006 ch 493 §16 (AB 1363), effective January 1, 2007, operative July 1, 2007. Amended Stats 2011 ch 10 §17 (SB 78), effective March 24, 2011.

2006 Note: This act, together with Senate Bill 1116 (Scott), Senate Bill 1550 (Figueroa), and Senate Bill 1716 (Bowen), shall be known and may be cited as the Omnibus Conservatorship and Guardianship Reform Act of 2006. Stats 2006 ch 493 (AB 1363) §1.

§2250.6. Duties of court investigator prior to hearing

(a) Regardless of whether the proposed temporary conservatee attends the hearing, the court investigator shall do all of the following before the hearing, unless it is not feasible to do so, in which case the court investigator shall comply with the requirements set forth in subdivision (b):

(1) Interview the proposed conservatee personally. The court investigator also shall do all of the following:

(A) Interview the petitioner and the proposed conservator, if different from the petitioner.

(B) To the greatest extent possible, interview the proposed conservatee's spouse or registered domestic partner, relatives within the first degree, neighbors, and, if known, close friends.

(C) To the extent possible, interview the proposed conservatee's relatives within the second degree as set forth in subdivision (b) of Section 1821, before the hearing.

(2) Inform the proposed conservatee of the contents of the citation, of the nature, purpose, and effect of the temporary conservatorship, and of the right of the proposed conservatee to oppose the petition, to attend the hearing, to have the matter of the establishment of the conservatorship tried by jury, to be represented by legal counsel, and to have legal counsel appointed by the court.

(3) Determine whether it appears that the proposed conservatee is unable to attend the hearing and, if able to attend, whether the proposed conservatee is willing to attend the hearing.

(4) Determine whether the proposed conservatee wishes to oppose the establishment of the conservatorship.

(5) Determine whether the proposed conservatee objects to the proposed conservator or prefers another person to act as conservator.

(6) Report to the court, in writing, concerning all of the foregoing.

(b) If not feasible before the hearing, the court investigator shall do all of the following within two court days after the hearing:

(1) Interview the conservatee personally. The court investigator also shall do all of the following:

(A) Interview the petitioner and the proposed conservator, if different from the petitioner.

(B) To the greatest extent possible, interview the proposed conservatee's spouse or registered domestic partner, relatives within the first degree, neighbors, and, if known, close friends.

(C) To the extent possible, interview the proposed conservatee's relatives within the second degree as set forth in subdivision (b) of Section 1821.

(2) Inform the conservatee of the nature, purpose, and effect of the temporary conservatorship, as well as the right of the conservatee to oppose the petition to appoint a general conservator, to attend the hearing, to have the matter of the establishment of the conservatorship tried by jury, to be represented by legal counsel, and to have legal counsel appointed by the court if not otherwise represented by legal counsel.

(c) If the investigator does not visit the conservatee until after the hearing at which a temporary conservator was appointed, and the conservatee objects to the appointment of the temporary conservator, or requests appointment of legal counsel, the court investigator shall report this information promptly, and in no event more than three court days later, to the court. Upon receipt of that information, the court may proceed with appointment of legal counsel as provided in Chapter 4 (commencing with Section 1470) of Part 1.

(d) If it appears to the court investigator that the temporary conservatorship is inappropriate, the court investigator shall immediately, and in no event more than two court days later, provide a written report to the court so the court can consider taking appropriate action on its own motion.

(e) A superior court shall not be required to perform any duties imposed by this section until the Legislature makes an appropriation identified for this purpose. **Leg.H.** Added Stats 2006 ch 493 §17 (AB 1363), effective January 1, 2007, operative July 1, 2007. Amended Stats 2007 ch 553 §13 (AB 1727), effective January 1, 2008; Stats 2011 ch 10 §18 (SB 78), effective March 24, 2011; Stats 2021 ch 417 §19 (AB 1194), effective January 1, 2022; Stats 2022 ch 420 §39 (AB 2960), effective January 1, 2023.

2006 Note: This act, together with Senate Bill 1116 (Scott), Senate Bill 1550 (Figueroa), and Senate Bill 1716 (Bowen), shall be known and may be cited as the Omnibus Conservatorship and Guardianship Reform Act of 2006. Stats 2006 ch 493 (AB 1363) §1.

§2250.8. Application of Sections 2250, 2250.4 and 2250.6

Sections 2250, 2250.4, and 2250.6 shall not apply to proceedings under Chapter 3 (commencing with Section 5350) of Part 1 of Division 5 of the Welfare and Institutions Code. **Leg.H.** Added Stats 2006 ch 493 §17.5 (AB 1363), effective January 1, 2007.

2006 Note: This act, together with Senate Bill 1116 (Scott), Senate Bill 1550 (Figueroa), and Senate Bill 1716 (Bowen), shall be known and may be cited as the Omnibus Conservatorship and Guardianship Reform Act of 2006. Stats 2006 ch 493 (AB 1363) §1.

§2251. Issuance of letters

A temporary guardian or temporary conservator shall be issued letters of temporary guardianship or conservatorship upon taking the oath and filing the bond as in the case of a guardian or conservator. The letters shall indicate the termination date of the temporary appointment. **Leg.H.** Enacted Stats 1990 ch 79 §14 (AB 759), operative July 1, 1991.

Prior Law: Former Prob C §2251, similar to the present section, was added Stats 1979 ch 726 §3, operative January 1, 1981, and repealed Stats 1990 ch 79 §13, operative July 1, 1991.

§2252. Powers and duties

(a) Except as otherwise provided in subdivisions (b) and (c), a temporary guardian or temporary conservator has only those powers and duties of a guardian or conservator that are necessary to provide for the temporary care, maintenance, and support of the ward or conservatee and that are necessary to conserve and protect the property of the ward or conservatee from loss or injury.

(b) Unless the court otherwise orders:

(1) A temporary guardian of the person has the powers and duties specified in Section 2353 (medical treatment).

(2) A temporary conservator of the person has the powers and duties specified in Section 2354 (medical treatment).

(3) A temporary guardian of the estate or temporary conservator of the estate may marshal assets and establish accounts at financial institutions.

(c) The temporary guardian or temporary conservator has the additional powers and duties as may be ordered by the court (1) in the order of appointment or (2) by subsequent order made with or without notice as the court may require. Notwithstanding subdivision (e), those additional powers and duties may include relief granted pursuant to Article 10 (commencing with Section 2580) of Chapter 6 if this relief is not requested in a petition for the appointment of a temporary conservator but is requested in a separate petition.

(d) The terms of any order made under subdivision (b) or (c) shall be included in the letters of temporary guardianship or conservatorship.

(e) A temporary conservator is not permitted to sell or relinquish, on the conservatee's behalf, any lease or estate in real or personal property used as or within the conservatee's place of residence without the specific approval of the court. This approval may be granted only if the conservatee has been served with notice of the hearing, the notice to be personally delivered to the temporary conservatee unless the court for good cause otherwise orders, and only if the court finds that the conservatee will be unable to return to the residence and exercise dominion over it and that the action is necessary to avert irreparable harm to the conservatee. The temporary conservator is not permitted to sell or relinquish on the conservatee's behalf any estate or interest in other real or personal property without specific approval of the court, which may be granted only upon a finding that the action is necessary to avert irreparable harm to the conservatee. A finding of irreparable harm as to real property may be based upon a reasonable showing that the real property is vacant, that it cannot reasonably be rented, and that it is impossible or impractical to obtain fire or liability insurance on the property. **Leg.H.** Enacted Stats 1990 ch 79 §14 (AB 759), operative July 1, 1991. Amended Stats 1994 ch 806 §10 (AB 3686); Stats 1996 ch 563 §11 (SB 392).

Prior Law: Former Prob C §2252, similar to the present section, was added Stats 1979 ch 726 §3, operative January 1, 1981, and repealed Stats 1990 ch 79 §13, operative July 1, 1991.

§2253. Change of conservatee's residence generally

(a) If a temporary conservator of the person proposes to fix the residence of the conservatee at a place other than that where the conservatee resided before the commencement of the proceedings, that power shall be requested of the court in writing, unless the change of residence is required of the conservatee by a prior court order. The request shall be filed with the petition for temporary conservatorship or, if a temporary conservatorship has already been established, separately. The request shall specify in detail the place to which the temporary conservator proposes to move the conservatee, the precise reasons that the petitioner or temporary conservator has concluded that the conservatee will suffer irreparable harm if the change of residence is not permitted, and why no means less restrictive of the conservatee's liberty will suffice to prevent that harm.

(b) The court investigator shall do all of the following:

(1) Interview the conservatee personally.

(2) Inform the conservatee of the nature, purpose, and effect of the request made under subdivision (a), and of the right of the conservatee to oppose the request, attend the hearing, be represented by legal counsel, and to have legal counsel appointed by the court if not otherwise represented by legal counsel.

(3) Determine whether the conservatee is unable to attend the hearing because of medical inability and, if able to attend, whether the conservatee is willing to attend the hearing.

(4) Determine whether the conservatee wishes to oppose the request.

(5) Determine whether the conservatee wishes to be represented by legal counsel at the hearing and, if so, whether the conservatee has retained legal counsel and, if not, whether the conservatee plans to retain legal counsel.

(6) Determine, by considering, among other things, the medical information received pursuant to paragraph (7), whether the proposed change of place of residence is required to prevent irreparable harm to the conservatee and whether no means less restrictive of the conservatee's liberty will suffice to prevent that harm.

(7) Gather and review relevant medical reports regarding the proposed conservatee from the proposed conservatee's primary care physician and other relevant mental and physical health care providers.

(8) Report to the court in writing, at least two days before the hearing, concerning all of the foregoing, including the conservatee's express communications concerning representation by legal counsel and whether the conservatee is not willing to attend the hearing and does not wish to oppose the request.

(c) Within seven days of the date of filing of a temporary conservator's request to remove the conservatee from the conservatee's previous place of residence, the court shall hold a hearing on the request.

(d) The conservatee shall be present at the hearing except in the following cases:

(1) Where the conservatee is unable to attend the hearing by reason of medical inability. Emotional or psychological instability is not good cause for the absence of the conservatee from the hearing unless, by reason of that instability, attendance at the hearing is likely to cause serious and immediate physiological damage to the conservatee.

(2) Where the court investigator has reported to the court that the conservatee has expressly communicated that the conservatee is not willing to attend the hearing and does not wish to oppose the request, and the court makes an order that the conservatee need not attend the hearing.

(e) If the conservatee is unable to attend the hearing because of medical inability, that inability shall be established (1) by the affidavit or certificate of a licensed medical practitioner or (2) if the conservatee is an adherent of a religion whose tenets and practices call for reliance on prayer alone for healing and is under treatment by an accredited practitioner of that religion, by the affidavit of the practitioner. The affidavit or certificate is evidence only of the conservatee's inability to attend the hearing and shall not be considered in determining the issue of need for the establishment of a conservatorship.

(f) At the hearing, the conservatee has the right to be represented by counsel and the right to confront and cross-examine any witness presented by, or on behalf of, the temporary conservator and to present evidence on their own behalf.

(g) The court may approve the request to remove the conservatee from the previous place of residence only if the court finds (1) that change of residence is required to prevent irreparable harm to the conservatee and (2) that no means less restrictive of the conservatee's liberty will suffice to prevent that harm. If an order is made authorizing the temporary conservator to remove the conservatee from the previous place of residence, the order shall specify the specific place wherein the temporary conservator is authorized to place the conservatee. The temporary conservator may not be authorized to remove the conservatee from this state unless it is additionally shown that the removal is required to permit the performance of specified nonpsychiatric medical treatment, consented to by the conservatee, which is essential to the conservatee's physical survival. A temporary conservator who willfully removes a temporary conservatee from this state without authorization of the court is guilty of a felony.

(h) Subject to subdivision (e) of Section 2252, the court shall also order the temporary conservator to take all reasonable steps to preserve the status quo concerning the conservatee's previous place of residence.

(i)(1) The report required by this section shall be confidential and shall be made available only to parties, their attorneys, and the court. The clerk of the court shall limit disclosure of the report exclusively to persons entitled to the report pursuant to this section.

(2) Notwithstanding paragraph (1), confidential medical information and confidential information from the California Law Enforcement Telecommunications System (CLETS) shall be placed in a separate attachment to the report and shall not be made available to the petitioner or proposed temporary conservator if the request is filed with the petition, the temporary conservatee's spouse or registered domestic partner, and the conservatee's relatives in the first degree or, if there are no such relatives, to the next closest relative.

(j)(1) A superior court shall not be required to perform any duties imposed pursuant to the amendments to this section enacted by Chapter 493 of the Statutes of 2006 until the Legislature makes an appropriation identified for this purpose.

(2) A superior court shall not be required to perform any duties imposed pursuant to the amendments to this section enacted by the measure that added this paragraph until the Legislature makes an appropriation identified for this purpose. **Leg.H.** Enacted Stats 1990 ch 79 §14 (AB 759), operative July 1, 1991. Amended Stats 2006 ch 493 §18 (AB 1363), effective January 1, 2007, operative July 1, 2007; Stats 2011 ch 10 §19 (SB 78), effective March 24, 2011; Stats 2021 ch 417 §20 (AB 1194), effective January 1, 2022; Stats 2022 ch 420 §40 (AB 2960), effective January 1, 2023.

2006 Note: This act, together with Senate Bill 1116 (Scott), Senate Bill 1550 (Figueroa), and Senate Bill 1716 (Bowen), shall be known and may be cited as the Omnibus Conservatorship and Guardianship Reform Act of 2006. Stats 2006 ch 493 (AB 1363) §1.

Prior Law: Former Prob C §2253, similar to the present section, was added Stats 1979 ch 726 §3, operative January 1, 1981, and repealed Stats 1990 ch 79 §13, operative July 1, 1991.

§2254. Removal of conservatee from residence in case of emergency

(a) Notwithstanding Section 2253, a temporary conservator may remove a temporary conservatee from the temporary conservatee's place of residence without court authorization if an emergency exists. For the purposes of this section, an emergency exists if the temporary conservatee's place of residence is unfit for habitation or if the temporary conservator determines in good faith based upon medical advice that the case is an emergency case in which removal from the place of residence is required (1) to provide medical treatment needed to alleviate severe pain or (2) to diagnose or treat a medical condition which, if not immediately diagnosed and treated, will lead to serious disability or death.

(b) No later than one judicial day after the emergency removal of the temporary conservatee, the temporary conservator shall file a written request pursuant to Section 2253 for authorization to fix the residence of the temporary conservatee at a place other than the temporary conservatee's previous place of residence.

(c) Nothing in this chapter prevents a temporary conservator from removing a temporary conservatee from the place of residence to a health facility for treatment without court authorization when the temporary conservatee has given informed consent to the removal.

(d) Nothing in this chapter prevents a temporary conservator from removing a temporary conservatee without court authorization from one health facility where the conservatee is receiving medical care to another health facility where the conservatee will receive medical care. **Leg.H.** Enacted Stats 1990 ch 79 §14 (AB 759), operative July 1, 1991.

Prior Law: Former Prob C §2254, similar to the present section, was added Stats 1979 ch 726 §3, operative January 1, 1981, and repealed Stats 1990 ch 79 §13, operative July 1, 1991.

§2255. Inventory and appraisal of estate

(a) Except as provided in subdivision (b), an inventory and appraisal of the estate shall be filed by the temporary guardian or temporary conservator of the estate as required by Article 2 (commencing with Section 2610) of Chapter 7.

(b) A temporary guardian or temporary conservator of the estate may inventory the estate in the final account, without the necessity for an appraisal of the estate, if the final account is filed within 90 days after the appointment of the temporary guardian or temporary conservator. **Leg.H.** Enacted Stats 1990 ch 79 §14 (AB 759), operative July 1, 1991.

Prior Law: Former Prob C §2255, similar to the present section, was added Stats 1979 ch 726 §3, operative January 1, 1981, and repealed Stats 1990 ch 79 §13, operative July 1, 1991.

§2256. Accounts

(a) Except as provided in subdivision (b), the temporary guardian or temporary conservator of the estate shall present his or her account to the court for settlement and allowance within 90 days after the appointment of a guardian or conservator of the estate or within such other time as the court may fix.

(b) If the temporary guardian or temporary conservator of the estate is appointed guardian or conservator of the estate, the guardian or conservator may account for the administration as temporary guardian or temporary conservator in his or her first regular account.

(c) Accounts are subject to Sections 2621 to 2626, inclusive, Sections 2630 to 2633, inclusive, and Sections 2640 to 2642, inclusive. **Leg.H.** Enacted Stats 1990 ch 79 §14 (AB 759), operative July 1, 1991.

Prior Law: Former Prob C §2256, similar to the present section, was added Stats 1979 ch 726 §3, operative January 1, 1981, and repealed Stats 1990 ch 79 §13, operative July 1, 1991.

§2257. Termination

(a) Except as provided in subdivision (b), the powers of a temporary guardian or temporary conservator terminate except, for the rendering of the account, at the earliest of the following times:

(1) The time the temporary guardian or conservator acquires notice that a guardian or conservator is appointed and qualified.

(2) Thirty days after the appointment of the temporary guardian or temporary conservator or such earlier time as the court may specify in the order of appointment.

(b) With or without notice as the court may require, the court may for good cause order that the time for the termination of the powers of the temporary guardian or temporary conservator be extended or shortened pending final determination by the court of the petition for appointment of a guardian or conservator or pending the final decision on appeal therefrom or for other cause. The order which extends the time for termination shall fix the time when the powers of the temporary guardian or temporary conservator terminate except for the rendering of the account. **Leg.H.** Enacted Stats 1990 ch 79 §14 (AB 759), operative July 1, 1991. Amended Stats 2007 ch 553 §14 (AB 1727), effective January 1, 2008.

Prior Law: Former Prob C §2257, similar to the present section, was added Stats 1979 ch 726 §3, operative January 1, 1981, and repealed Stats 1990 ch 79 §13, operative July 1, 1991.

§2258. Suspension, removal, resignation, and discharge

A temporary guardian or temporary conservator is subject to the provisions of this division governing the suspension, removal, resignation, and discharge of a guardian or conservator. **Leg.H.** Enacted Stats 1990 ch 79 §14 (AB 759), operative July 1, 1991.

Prior Law: Former Prob C §2258, similar to the present section, was added Stats 1979 ch 726 §3, operative January 1, 1981, and repealed Stats 1990 ch 79 §13, operative July 1, 1991.

CHAPTER 4
OATH, LETTERS, AND BOND

Article 1. Requirement of Oath and Bond.
Article 2. Letters.
Article 3. Bonds of Guardians and Conservators.
Article 4. Professional Fiduciaries.

ARTICLE 1
Requirement of Oath and Bond

Oath and bond required before appointment effective. §2300.

§2300. Oath and bond required before appointment effective

Before the appointment of a guardian or conservator is effective, including, but not limited to, the appointment of a conservator under Section 2002, the guardian or conservator shall:

(a) Take an oath to perform the duties of the office according to law. The oath obligates the guardian or conservator to comply with the law of this state, as well as other applicable law, at all times, in any location within or without the state. If the conservator petitions for transfer of the conservatorship to another state pursuant to Section 2001, the conservator shall continue to comply with the law of this state until the court issues a final order confirming the transfer and terminating the conservatorship pursuant to Section 2001. The oath shall be attached to or endorsed upon the letters.

(b) File the required bond if a bond is required. **Leg.H.** Added Stats 1990 ch 79 §14 (AB 759), operative July 1, 1991. Amended Stats 2014 ch 553 §23 (SB 940), effective January 1, 2015, operative January 1, 2016.

Prior Law: Former Prob C §2300, similar to the present section, was added Stats 1979 ch 726 §3, operative January 1, 1981, and repealed Stats 1990 ch 79 §13, operative July 1, 1991.

ARTICLE 2
Letters

Issuance of letters; Warning. §2310.
Form of letters. §2311.
Recordation of letters. §2313.

§2310. Issuance of letters; Warning

(a) The appointment, the taking of the oath, and the filing of the bond, if required, shall thereafter be evidenced by the issuance of letters by the clerk of the court.

(b) The order appointing a guardian or conservator shall state in capital letters on the first page of the order, in at least 12-point type, the following: "WARNING: THIS APPOINTMENT IS NOT EFFECTIVE UNTIL LETTERS HAVE ISSUED." **Leg.H.** Enacted Stats 1990 ch 79 §14 (AB 759), operative July 1, 1991. Amended Stats 1996 ch 862 §7 (AB 2751).

Prior Law: Former Prob C §2310, similar to the present section, was added Stats 1979 ch 726 §3, operative January 1, 1981, and repealed Stats 1990 ch 79 §13, operative July 1, 1991.

§2311. Form of letters

Except as otherwise required by the order of appointment, the letters of guardianship or conservatorship shall be in substantially the same form as letters of administration. **Leg.H.** Enacted Stats 1990 ch 79 §14 (AB 759), operative July 1, 1991.

Prior Law: Former Prob C §2311, similar to the present section, was added Stats 1979 ch 726 §3, operative January 1, 1981, and repealed Stats 1990 ch 79 §13, operative July 1, 1991.

§2312. [Section repealed 1997]

Leg.H. Enacted Stats 1990 ch 79 §14 (AB 759), operative July 1, 1991. Repealed Stats 1997 ch 724 §12 (AB 1172). The repealed section related to notice to ward or conservatee.

Prior Law: Former Prob C §2312, relating to notice to ward or conservatee, was added Stats 1979 ch 726 §3, operative January 1, 1981, and repealed Stats 1990 ch 79 §13, operative July 1, 1991.

§2313. Recordation of letters

Except in temporary conservatorships, a conservator of the estate shall record a certified copy of the letters with the county recorder's office in each county in which the conservatee owns an interest in real property, including a security interest. The conservator shall record the letters as soon as practicable after they are issued, but no later than 90 days after the conservator is appointed. A temporary conservator of the estate may record the letters if the conservator deems it appropriate. **Leg.H.** Added Stats 1991 ch 1019 §3 (SB 1022).

ARTICLE 3
Bonds of Guardians and Conservators

General requirement of bond; Amount. §2320.
Ex parte application for increasing the bond. §2320.1.
Filing additional bond. §2320.2.
Waiver of bond by conservatee. §2321.
Guardian or conservator of person only. §2322.
Small estate. §2323.
Nominated guardian. §2324.
Bond of nonprofit charitable corporation. §2325.
Joint guardians or conservators. §2326.
Several wards or conservatees. §2327.
Deposit of money or other property subject to court control. §2328.
Reduction of amount of bond. §2329.
Additional bond on real property transactions. §2330.
Limitation period for suit against sureties on bond. §2333.
Suspension of powers upon filing of petition to require bond or objection to sufficiency of bond. §2334.
Substitution of surety. §2335.

§2320. General requirement of bond; Amount

(a) Except as otherwise provided by statute, every person appointed as guardian or conservator shall, before letters are issued, give a bond approved by the court.

(b) The bond shall be for the benefit of the ward or conservatee and all persons interested in the guardianship or conservatorship estate and shall be conditioned upon the faithful execution of the duties of the office, according to law, by the guardian or conservator.

(c) Except as otherwise provided by statute, unless the court increases or decreases the amount upon a showing of good cause, the amount of a bond given by an admitted surety insurer shall be the sum of all of the following:

(1) The value of the personal property of the estate.

(2) The probable annual gross income of all of the property of the estate.

(3) The sum of the probable annual gross payments from the following:

(A) Part 3 (commencing with Section 11000) of, Part 4 (commencing with Section 16000) of, or Part 5 (commencing with Section 17000) of, Division 9 of the Welfare and Institutions Code.

(B) Subchapter II (commencing with Section 401) of, or Part A of Subchapter XVI (commencing with Section 1382) of, Chapter 7 of Title 42 of the United States Code.

(C) Any other public entitlements of the ward or conservatee.

(4) On or after January 1, 2008, a reasonable amount for the cost of recovery to collect on the bond, including attorney's fees and costs. The attorney's fees and costs incurred in a successful action for surcharge against a conservator or guardian for breach of his or her duty under this code shall be a surcharge against the conservator or guardian and, if unpaid, shall be recovered against the surety on the bond. The Judicial Council shall, on or before January 1, 2008, adopt a rule of court to implement this paragraph.

(d) If the bond is given by personal sureties, the amount of the bond shall be twice the amount required for a bond given by an admitted surety insurer.

(e) The Bond and Undertaking Law (Chapter 2 (commencing with Section 995.010) of Title 14 of Part 2 of the Code of Civil Procedure) applies to a bond given under this article, except to the extent inconsistent with this article. **Leg.H.** Enacted Stats 1990 ch 79 §14 (AB 759), operative July 1, 1991. Amended Stats 2006 ch 493 §19 (AB 1363), effective January 1, 2007; Stats 2007 ch 553 §15 (AB 1727), effective January 1, 2008.

2006 Note: This act, together with Senate Bill 1116 (Scott), Senate Bill 1550 (Figueroa), and Senate Bill 1716 (Bowen), shall be known and may be cited as the Omnibus Conservatorship and Guardianship Reform Act of 2006. Stats 2006 ch 493 (AB 1363) §1.

Prior Law: Former Prob C §2320, similar to the present section, was added Stats 1979 ch 726 §3, operative January 1, 1981, amended Stats 1988 ch 1199 §67, operative July 1, 1989, Stats 1989 ch 544 §1, and repealed Stats 1990 ch 79 §13, operative July 1, 1991.

§2320.1. Ex parte application for increasing the bond

When the conservator or guardian has knowledge of facts from which the guardian or conservator knows or should know that the bond posted is less than the amount required under Section 2320, the conservator or guardian, and the attorney, if any, shall make an ex parte application for an order increasing the bond to the amount required under Section 2320. **Leg.H.** Added Stats 2001 ch 359 §1 (SB 140).

§2320.2. Filing additional bond

If additional bond is required by the court when the account is heard, the order approving the account and related matters, including fees, is not effective and the court shall not file the order until the additional bond is filed. **Leg.H.** Added Stats 2001 ch 359 §2 (SB 140).

§2321. Waiver of bond by conservatee

(a) Notwithstanding any other provision of law, the court in a conservatorship proceeding may not waive the filing of a bond or reduce the amount of bond required, without a good cause determination by the court which shall include a determination by the court that the conservatee will not suffer harm as a result of the waiver or reduction of the bond. Good cause may not be established merely by the conservator having filed a bond in another or prior proceeding.

(b) In a conservatorship proceeding, where the conservatee, having sufficient capacity to do so, has waived the filing of a bond, the court in its discretion may permit the filing of a bond in an amount less than would otherwise be required under Section 2320. **Leg.H.** Enacted Stats 1990 ch 79 §14 (AB 759), operative July 1, 1991. Amended Stats 2001 ch 563 §4 (AB 1286); Stats 2006 ch 493 §20 (AB 1363), effective January 1, 2007.

2006 Note: This act, together with Senate Bill 1116 (Scott), Senate Bill 1550 (Figueroa), and Senate Bill 1716 (Bowen), shall be known and may be cited as the Omnibus Conservatorship and Guardianship Reform Act of 2006. 2006 ch 493 (AB 1363) §1.

Prior Law: Former Prob C §2321, similar to the present section, was added Stats 1979 ch 726 §3, operative January 1, 1981, and repealed Stats 1990 ch 79 §13, operative July 1, 1991.

§2322. Guardian or conservator of person only

One appointed only as guardian of the person or conservator of the person need not file a bond unless required by the court. **Leg.H.** Enacted Stats 1990 ch 79 §14 (AB 759), operative July 1, 1991.

Prior Law: Former Prob C §2322, similar to the present section, was added Stats 1979 ch 726 §3, operative January 1, 1981, and repealed Stats 1990 ch 79 §13, operative July 1, 1991.

§2323. Small estate

(a) The court may dispense with the requirement of a bond if it appears likely that the estate will satisfy the conditions of subdivision (a) of Section 2628 for its duration.

(b) If at any time it appears that the estate does not satisfy the conditions of subdivision (a) of Section 2628, the court shall require the filing of a bond unless the court determines that good cause exists, as provided in Section 2321. **Leg.H.** Enacted Stats 1990 ch 79 §14 (AB 759), operative July 1, 1991. Amended Stats 2008 ch 293 §5 (AB 1340), effective January 1, 2009.

Prior Law: Former Prob C §2323, similar to the present section, was added Stats 1979 ch 726 §3, operative January 1, 1981, and repealed Stats 1990 ch 79 §13, operative July 1, 1991.

§2324. Nominated guardian

If the person making the nomination has waived the filing of the bond, a guardian nominated under Section 1500 or 1501 need not file a bond unless required by the court. **Leg.H.** Enacted Stats 1990 ch 79 §14 (AB 759), operative July 1, 1991.

Prior Law: Former Prob C §2324, similar to the present section, was added Stats 1979 ch 726 §3, operative January 1, 1981, and repealed Stats 1990 ch 79 §13, operative July 1, 1991.

§2325. Bond of nonprofit charitable corporation

The surety on the bond of a nonprofit charitable corporation described in Section 2104 shall be an admitted surety insurer. **Leg.H.** Enacted Stats 1990 ch 79 §14 (AB 759), operative July 1, 1991.

Prior Law: Former Prob C §2325, similar to the present section, was added Stats 1979 ch 726 §3, operative January 1, 1981, amended Stats 1988 ch 1199 §67.5, operative July 1, 1989, and repealed Stats 1990 ch 79 §13, operative July 1, 1991.

§2326. Joint guardians or conservators

(a) If joint guardians or conservators are appointed, the court may order that separate bonds or a joint bond or a combination thereof be furnished.

(b) If a joint bond is furnished, the liability on the bond is joint and several. **Leg.H.** Enacted Stats 1990 ch 79 §14 (AB 759), operative July 1, 1991.

Prior Law: Former Prob C §2326, similar to the present section, was added Stats 1979 ch 726 §3, operative January 1, 1981, and repealed Stats 1990 ch 79 §13, operative July 1, 1991.

§2327. Several wards or conservatees

(a) In a conservatorship proceeding, the court shall order a separate bond for each conservatee, except where the assets of the conservatees are commingled in which case a combined bond that covers all assets may be provided.

(b) If a guardianship proceeding involves more than one ward, the court may order separate bonds, or a single bond which is for the benefit of two or more wards in that proceeding, or a combination thereof. **Leg.H.** Enacted Stats 1990 ch 79 §14 (AB 759), operative July 1, 1991. Amended Stats 2001 ch 563 §5 (AB 1286).

Prior Law: Former Prob C §2327, similar to the present section, was added Stats 1979 ch 726 §3, operative January 1, 1981, and repealed Stats 1990 ch 79 §13, operative July 1, 1991.

§2328. Deposit of money or other property subject to court control

(a) In any proceeding to determine the amount of the bond of the guardian or conservator (whether at the time of appointment or subsequently), if the estate includes property which has been or will be deposited with a trust company or financial institution pursuant to Sections 2453 to 2456, inclusive, upon the condition that the property, including any earnings thereon, will not be withdrawn except on authorization of the court, the court, in its discretion, with or without notice, may so order and may do either of the following:

(1) Exclude the property deposited in determining the amount of the required bond or reduce the amount of the bond to be required in respect to the property deposited to such an amount as the court determines is reasonable.

(2) If a bond has already been furnished or the amount fixed, reduce the amount to such an amount as the court determines is reasonable.

(b) The petitioner for letters, or the proposed guardian or conservator in advance of appointment of a guardian or conservator, may do any one or more of the following:

(1) Deliver personal property in the person's possession to a trust company.

(2) Deliver money in the person's possession for deposit in an insured account in a financial institution in this state.

(3) Allow a trust company to retain personal property already in its possession.

(4) Allow a financial institution in this state to retain money already invested in an insured account in a financial institution.

(c) In the cases described in subdivision (b), the petitioner or proposed guardian or conservator shall obtain and file with the court a written receipt including the agreement of the trust company or financial institution that the property deposited, including any earnings thereon, shall not be allowed to be withdrawn except upon authorization of the court.

(d) In receiving and retaining property on deposit pursuant to subdivisions (b) and (c), the trust company or financial institution is protected to the same extent as though it received the property on deposit from a person to whom letters had been issued. **Leg.H.** Enacted Stats 1990 ch 79 §14 (AB 759), operative July 1, 1991.

Prior Law: Former Prob C §2328, similar to the present section, was added Stats 1979 ch 726 §3, operative January 1, 1981, and repealed Stats 1990 ch 79 §13, operative July 1, 1991.

§2329. Reduction of amount of bond

(a) If a guardian or conservator moves the court for reduction in the amount of the bond, the motion shall include an affidavit setting forth the condition of the estate.

(b) Except upon a showing of good cause, the amount of the bond shall not be reduced below the amount determined pursuant to Section 2320.

(c) Nothing in this section limits the authority of the court to reduce the amount of the bond with or without notice under Section 2328. **Leg.H.** Enacted Stats 1990 ch 79 §14 (AB 759), operative July 1, 1991.

Prior Law: Former Prob C §2329, similar to the present section, was added Stats 1979 ch 726 §3, operative January 1, 1981, amended Stats 1982 ch 517 §342, Stats 1983 ch 18 §27, effective April 21, 1983, and repealed Stats 1990 ch 79 §13, operative July 1, 1991.

§2330. Additional bond on real property transactions

Upon the confirmation of the sale of any real property of the estate, or upon the authorization of the borrowing of money secured by a mortgage or deed of trust on real property of the estate, the guardian or conservator shall furnish an additional bond as is required by the court in order to make the sum of the bonds furnished by the guardian or conservator equal to the amount determined pursuant to Section 2320, taking into account the proceeds of the sale or mortgage or deed of trust, unless the court makes an express finding stating the reason why the bond should not be increased. If a bond or additional bond is required under this section, the order confirming the sale of real property of the estate or authorizing the borrowing of money secured by a mortgage or deed of trust on real property of the estate is not effective and the court shall not file the order until the additional bond is filed. **Leg.H.** Enacted Stats 1990 ch 79 §14 (AB 759), operative July 1, 1991. Amended Stats 2001 ch 359 §3 (SB 140).

Prior Law: Former Prob C §2330, similar to the present section, was added Stats 1979 ch 726 §3, operative January 1, 1981, and repealed Stats 1990 ch 79 §13, operative July 1, 1991.

§2333. Limitation period for suit against sureties on bond

(a) In case of a breach of a condition of the bond, an action may be brought against the sureties on the bond for the use and benefit of the ward or conservatee or of any person interested in the estate.

(b) No action may be maintained against the sureties on the bond unless commenced within four years from the discharge or removal of the guardian or conservator or within four years from the date the order surcharging the guardian or conservator becomes final, whichever is later.

(c) In any case, and notwithstanding subdivision (b) of Section 2103, no action may be maintained against the sureties on the bond unless the action commences within six years from the date the judgment under Section 2103 or the later of the orders under subdivision (b) of this section becomes final. **Leg.H.** Enacted Stats 1990 ch 79 §14 (AB 759), operative July 1, 1991. Amended Stats 1990 ch 710 §7 (SB 1775), operative July 1, 1991; Stats 1993 ch 794 §1 (AB 516); Stats 1994 ch 806 §11 (AB 3686).

Prior Law: Former Prob C §2333, similar to the present section, was added Stats 1979 ch 726 §3, operative January 1, 1981, amended Stats 1988 ch 1199 §68, operative July 1, 1989, and repealed Stats 1990 ch 79 §13, operative July 1, 1991.

§2334. Suspension of powers upon filing of petition to require bond or objection to sufficiency of bond

Where a petition is filed requesting an order that a guardian or conservator be required to give a bond where no bond was originally required, or an objection is made to the sufficiency of the bond, and the petition or affidavit supporting the objection alleges facts showing that the guardian or conservator is failing to use ordinary care and diligence in the management of the estate, the court, by order, may suspend the powers of the guardian or conservator until the matter can be heard and determined. **Leg.H.** Enacted Stats 1990 ch 79 §14 (AB 759), operative July 1, 1991.

Prior Law: Former Prob C §2334, similar to the present section, was added Stats 1979 ch 726 §3, operative January 1, 1981, amended Stats 1982 ch 517 §345, Stats 1983 ch 18 §28, effective April 21, 1983, and repealed Stats 1990 ch 79 §13, operative July 1, 1991.

§2335. Substitution of surety

A guardian or conservator who applies for a substitution and release of a surety shall file an account with the application. The court shall not order a substitution unless the account is approved. **Leg.H.** Enacted Stats 1990 ch 79 §14 (AB 759), operative July 1, 1991.

Prior Law: Former Prob C §2335, similar to the present section, was added Stats 1979 ch 726 §3, operative January 1, 1981, amended Stats 1982 ch 517 §346, and repealed Stats 1990 ch 79 §13, operative July 1, 1991.

ARTICLE 4
Professional Fiduciaries

Requirements to carry out duties of professional fiduciary. §2340.
Operative date. §2341.

§2340. Requirements to carry out duties of professional fiduciary

A superior court may not appoint a person to carry out the duties of a professional fiduciary, or permit a person to continue those duties, unless he or she holds a valid, unexpired, unsuspended license as a professional fiduciary under Chapter 6 (commencing with Section 6500) of Division 3 of the Business and Professions Code, is exempt from the definition of "professional fiduciary" under Section 6501 of the Business and Professions Code, or is exempt from the licensing requirements of Section 6530 of the Business and Professions Code. **Leg.H.** Added Stats 2006 ch 491 §5 (SB 1550), effective January 1, 2007. Amended Stats 2008 ch 293 §6 (AB 1340), effective January 1, 2009.

2006 Note: This act, together with Senate Bill 1116, Senate Bill 1716, and Assembly Bill 1363, shall be known and may be cited as the Omnibus Conservatorship and Guardianship Reform Act of 2006. Stats 2006 ch 491 (SB 1550) §1.

Prior Law: Former Prob C §2340, relating to appointment or continuance of private professional conservator, trustee, or guardian, was enacted Stats 1990 ch 79 §14, operative July 1, 1991, amended Stats 1991 ch 1019 §4, Stats 1994 ch 806 §13, Stats 1999 ch 424 §2, Stats 2001 ch 176 §43, and repealed, January 1, 2009, by the terms of Prob C §2345.

Former Prob C §2340, relating to appointment of private professional conservator, was added Stats 1989 ch 781 §1, operative July 1, 1990, and repealed Stats 1990 ch 79 §13, operative July 1, 1991.

§2341. Operative date

This article shall become operative on July 1, 2008. **Leg.H.** Added Stats 2006 ch 491 §5 (SB 1550), effective January 1, 2007, operative July 1, 2008.

2006 Note: This act, together with Senate Bill 1116, Senate Bill 1716, and Assembly Bill 1363, shall be known and may be cited as the Omnibus Conservatorship and Guardianship Reform Act of 2006. Stats 2006 ch 491 (SB 1550) §1.

Prior Law: Former Prob C §2341, defining "private professional conservator", "private professional guardian", and "private professional trustee", was enacted Stats 1990 ch 79 §14, operative July 1, 1991, amended Stats 1994 ch 806 §14, Stats 1999 ch 424 §3, Stats 2002 ch 1115 §3, Stats 2005 ch 302 §2, effective January 1, 2006, and repealed, January 1, 2009, by the terms of Prob C §2345.

Former Prob C §2341, defining "private professional conservator", was added Stats 1989 ch 781 §1 and repealed Stats 1990 ch 79 §13, operative July 1, 1991.

§2342. [Section repealed 2009.]

Leg.H. Enacted Stats 1990 ch 79 §14 (AB 759), operative July 1, 1991. Amended Stats 1991 ch 1019 §5 (SB 1022); Stats 1994 ch 806 §15 (AB 3686); Stats 1999 ch 424 §4 (SB 1090); Stats 2001 ch 176 §44 (SB 210). Repealed operative January 1, 2009, by the terms of Prob C §2345. The repealed section related to statement and background check of private professional conservator, guardian, or trustee.

Prior Law: Former Prob C §2342, statement and background check of private professional conservator, was added Stats 1989 ch 781 §1 and repealed Stats 1990 ch 79 §13, operative July 1, 1991.

§2342.5. [Section repealed 2009]

Leg.H. Added Stats 1995 ch 165 §1 (SB 961). Amended Stats 2001 ch 176 §45 (SB 210); Stats 2004 ch 625 §2 (AB 1155). Repealed operative January 1, 2009, by the terms of Prob C §2345. The repealed section related to requirements for exempt conservators to file annual statement only in county of principal place of business.

§2343. [Section repealed 2009.]

Leg.H. Enacted Stats 1990 ch 79 §14 (AB 759), operative July 1, 1991. Amended Stats 1994 ch 806 §16 (AB 3686); Stats 2001 ch 176 §46 (SB 210); Stats 2005 ch 75 §148 (AB 145), effective July 19, 2005, operative January 1, 2006. Repealed January 1, 2009, by the terms of Prob C §2345. The repealed section related to annual filing fee.

Prior Law: Former Prob C §2343, relating to annual filing fee, was added Stats 1989 ch 781 §1, and repealed Stats 1990 ch 79 §13, operative July 1, 1991.

§2344. [Section repealed 2009]

Leg.H. Added Stats 2004 ch 625 §3 (AB 1155). Repealed operative January 1, 2009, by the terms of Prob C §2345. The repealed section related to education and experience required for private professional conservator or private professional guardian.

§2345. [Section repealed 2009]

Leg.H. Added Stats 2006 ch 491 §6 (SB 1550), effective January 1, 2007, inoperative July 1, 2008, repealed January 1, 2009. Repealed operative January 1, 2009, by its own terms. The repealed section related to repeal of article.

CHAPTER 5
POWERS AND DUTIES OF GUARDIAN OR CONSERVATOR OF THE PERSON

Definitions. §2350.
Care, custody, control, and education. §2351.
Care plan. § 2351.2.
Powers of limited conservator. §2351.5.
Residence of ward or conservatee; Change of residence; Applicability. §2352.
Presumption of least restrictive appropriate residence; Appropriate level of care; Applicability. §2352.5.
Medical treatment of ward. §2353.
Medical treatment of conservatee not adjudicated to lack capacity to give informed consent. §2354.
Health care decisions by conservator. §2355.
Involuntary civil placement; Experimental drugs; Convulsive treatment; Sterilization. §2356.
Conservatee with major neurocognitive disorder. §2356.5.
Court-authorized medical treatment for ward or conservatee. §2357.
Additional conditions in order of appointment. §2358.
Instructions from or confirmation by court. §2359.
Annual photograph of conservatee. §2360.
Notice of conservatee's death. §2361.
[No sections of these numbers.] §2362–2399.

§2350. Definitions

As used in this chapter:

(a) "Conservator" means the conservator of the person.

(b) "Guardian" means the guardian of the person.

(c) "Residence" does not include a regional center established pursuant to Chapter 5 (commencing with Section 4620) of Division 4.5 of the Welfare and Institutions Code. **Leg.H.** Enacted Stats 1990 ch 79 §14 (AB 759), operative July 1, 1991. Amended Stats 2008 ch 293 §7 (AB 1340), effective January 1, 2009.

Prior Law: Former Prob C §2350, similar to the present section, was added Stats 1979 ch 726 §3, operative January 1, 1981, and repealed Stats 1990 ch 79 §13, operative July 1, 1991.

§2351. Care, custody, control, and education

(a) Subject to subdivision (b), the guardian or conservator, but not a limited conservator, has the care, custody, and control of, and has charge of the education of, the ward or conservatee. This control shall not extend to personal rights retained by the conservatee, including, but not limited to, the right to receive visitors, telephone calls, and personal mail, unless specifically limited by court order. The court may issue an order that specifically grants the conservator the power to enforce the conservatee's rights to receive visitors, telephone calls, and personal mail, or that directs the conservator to allow those visitors, telephone calls, and personal mail.

(b) Where the court determines that it is appropriate in the circumstances of the particular conservatee, the court, in its discretion, may limit the powers and duties that the conservator would otherwise have under subdivision (a) by an order stating either of the following:

(1) The specific powers that the conservator does not have with respect to the conservatee's person and reserving the powers so specified to the conservatee.

(2) The specific powers and duties the conservator has with respect to the conservatee's person and reserving to the conservatee all other rights with respect to the conservatee's person that the conservator otherwise would have under subdivision (a).

(c) An order under this section (1) may be included in the order appointing a conservator of the person or (2) may be made, modified, or revoked upon a petition subsequently filed, notice of the hearing on the petition having been given for the period and in the manner provided in Chapter 3 (commencing with Section 1460) of Part 1.

(d) The guardian or conservator, in exercising his or her powers, may not hire or refer any business to an entity in which he or she has a financial interest except upon authorization of the court. Prior to authorization from the court, the guardian or conservator shall disclose to the court in writing his or her financial interest in the entity. For the purposes of this subdivision, "financial interest" shall mean (1) an ownership interest in a sole proprietorship, a partnership, or a closely held corporation, or (2) an ownership interest of greater than 1 percent of the outstanding shares in a publicly traded corporation, or (3) being an officer or a director of a corporation. This subdivision shall apply only to conservators and guardians required to register with the Statewide Registry under Chapter 13 (commencing with Section 2850). **Leg.H.** Enacted Stats 1990 ch 79 §14 (AB 759), operative July 1, 1991. Amended Stats 2000 ch 565 §4 (AB 1950); Stats 2013 ch 127 §1 (AB 937), effective January 1, 2014; Stats 2015 ch 92 §2 (AB 1085), effective January 1, 2016.

2015 Note: The Legislature finds and declares that every adult in this state has the right to visit with, and receive mail and telephone or electronic communication from, whomever he or she so chooses, unless a court has specifically ordered otherwise. Stats 2015 ch 92 (AB 1085) §1.

Prior Law: Former Prob C §2351, similar to the present section, was added Stats 1979 ch 726 §3, operative January 1, 1981, amended Stats 1980 ch 1304 §22, and repealed Stats 1990 ch 79 §13, operative July 1, 1991.

§ 2351.2. Care plan

(a)(1) Within 120 calendar days of appointment by the court and no later than 10 days before a hearing to determine the continuation or termination of an existing conservatorship, a conservator granted powers under this chapter shall file with the clerk of the court a care plan for the care, custody, and control of the conservatee as provided in this section. The court may require a conservator to update the care plan at any time. The court shall review the most recent care plan in determining the continuation or termination of the conservatorship.

(2)(A) The conservator shall deliver, pursuant to Section 1215, a copy of any care plan filed pursuant to paragraph (1) to the conservator of the estate, if a separate conservator is appointed, and that conservator's attorney, the attorney for the conservator, the attorney for the conservatee, and the conservatee. The conservator shall also deliver a copy of the care plan to the conservatee's spouse or registered domestic partner and relatives within the first degree unless the court determines that delivery of the care plan will result in harm to the conservatee. If the conservatee does not have a spouse, registered domestic partner, or relatives within the first degree, to the greatest extent possible, the conservator shall deliver the care plan to the conservatee's relatives within the second degree, unless the court determines that the delivery of the care plan will result in harm to the conservatee.

(B) Confidential medical information in a care plan shall be redacted in compliance with applicable state and federal medical privacy laws before transmission to a spouse, registered domestic partner, or relative, as described in paragraph (1).

(b) The care plan shall include, but not be limited to, all of the following:

(1) A description of the current living arrangement for the conservatee and any plans to modify this living arrangement within the next 12 months.

(2) A description of the conservatee's current level of care and any plans to modify the level of care within the next 12 months.

(3) A description of the status of the conservatee's health that lists medications currently prescribed for the conservatee, and any medical treatments, supports, or devices.

(4) A description of the conservator's schedule of visitation with the conservatee and actions to ensure the conservatee is able to exercise their rights to visitation and communications.

(5) A description of the normal activities of the conservatee, including outings and social and recreational activities.

(6) A description of any special problems raised by the court investigator, the court, or any other interested person, and a description of how the conservator has addressed or intends to address those problems.

(7) A description of the conservatee's financial needs, stating the conservatee's estimated monthly expenses, including food, entertainment, rent or mortgage, transportation, utilities, medication, clothing, and other relevant health care and living expenses, to the extent the conservator has that information.

(8) A list of all health care providers who provide care for the conservatee, including the provider's name, contact information, license type and number, and a description of the treatment provided by each provider.

(c) The Judicial Council shall, by January 1, 2025, develop and adopt a mandatory form to be used in preparing the care plan required by subdivision (a) with, at a minimum, all of the information required by subdivision (b). The form shall be combined with the information or form required to be submitted to the court by subdivision (c) of Section 2352.5.

(d)(1) If a conservator does not file a care plan as required by subdivision (a), the court may impose a civil penalty in any amount up to five hundred dollars ($500), payable to the estate of the conservatee.

(2) If the conservator is a professional fiduciary, in addition to the civil penalty imposed pursuant to paragraph (1), the court may find a failure to file a care plan is a separate and independent reason to refer the conservator to the Professional Fiduciaries Bureau for investigation.

(3) The court may remove the conservator for failure to file a care plan as required by this section.

(e) The care plan shall be confidential and shall be made available only as provided in this section. The court shall have discretion to release the care plan to other persons if it would serve the best interests of the conservatee. The clerk of the court shall make provision for limiting disclosure of the care plan exclusively to persons entitled thereto under this section.

(f) The court investigator shall review the most recent care plan when conducting an investigation pursuant to Section 1851.

(g) The requirement to file a care plan is effective January 1, 2025.

(h) This section does not apply to a limited conservator appointed for a developmentally disabled adult, as set forth in subdivision (d) of Section 1801, if the limited conservator is a relative within the first degree of the conservatee. **Leg.H.** Added Stats 2023 ch 705 §1 (SB 280), effective January 1, 2024.

§2351.5. Powers of limited conservator

(a) Subject to subdivision (b):

(1) The limited conservator has the care, custody, and control of the limited conservatee.

(2) The limited conservator shall secure for the limited conservatee those habilitation or treatment, training, education, medical and psychological services, and social and vocational opportunity as appropriate and as will assist the limited conservatee in the development of maximum self-reliance and independence.

(b) A limited conservator does not have any of the following powers or controls over the limited conservatee unless those powers or controls are specifically requested in the petition for appointment of a limited conservator and granted by the court in its order appointing the limited conservator:

(1) To fix the residence or specific dwelling of the limited conservatee.

(2) Access to the confidential records and papers of the limited conservatee.

(3) To consent or withhold consent to the marriage of, or the entrance into a registered domestic partnership by, the limited conservatee.

(4) The right of the limited conservatee to contract.

(5) The power of the limited conservatee to give or withhold medical consent.

(6) The limited conservatee's right to control his or her own social and sexual contacts and relationships.

(7) Decisions concerning the education of the limited conservatee.

(c) Any limited conservator, the limited conservatee, or any relative or friend of the limited conservatee may apply by petition to the superior court of the county in which the proceedings are pending to have the limited conservatorship modified by the elimination or addition of any of the powers which must be specifically granted to the limited conservator pursuant to subdivision (b). The petition shall state the facts alleged to establish that the limited conservatorship should be modified. The granting or elimination of those powers is discretionary with the court. Notice of the hearing on the petition shall be given for the period and in the manner provided in Chapter 3 (commencing with Section 1460) of Part 1.

(d) The limited conservator or any relative or friend of the limited conservatee may appear and oppose the petition. The court shall hear and determine the matter according to the laws and procedures relating to the trial of civil actions, including trial by jury if demanded. If any of the powers which must be specifically granted to the limited conservator pursuant to subdivision (b) are granted or eliminated, new letters of limited conservatorship shall be issued reflecting the change in the limited conservator's powers. **Leg.H.** Enacted Stats 1990 ch 79 §14 (AB 759), operative July 1, 1991. Amended Stats 2005 ch 418 §28 (SB 973), effective January 1, 2006.

Prior Law: Former Prob C §2351.5, similar to the present section, was added Stats 1980 ch 1304 §23, amended Stats 1987 ch 923 §69, operative July 1, 1988, and repealed Stats 1990 ch 79 §13, operative July 1, 1991.

§2352. Residence of ward or conservatee; Change of residence; Applicability

(a) The guardian may establish the residence of the ward at any place within this state without the permission of the court. The guardian shall select the least restrictive appropriate residence that is available and necessary to meet the needs of the ward, and that is in the best interests of the ward.

(b) The conservator may establish the residence of the conservatee at any place within this state without the permission of the court. The conservator shall select the least restrictive appropriate residence, as described in Section 2352.5, that is available and necessary to meet the needs of the conservatee, and that is in the best interests of the conservatee.

(c) If permission of the court is first obtained, a guardian or conservator may establish the residence of a ward or conservatee at a place not within this state. Notice of the hearing on the petition to establish the residence of the ward or conservatee out of state, together with a copy of the petition, shall be given in the manner required by subdivision (a) of Section 1460 to all persons entitled to notice under subdivision (b) of Section 1511 or subdivision (b) of Section 1822.

(d)(1) An order under subdivision (c) relating to a ward shall require the guardian either to return the ward to this state, or to cause a guardianship proceeding or its equivalent to be commenced in the place of the new residence, when the ward has resided in the place of new residence for a period of four months or a longer or shorter period specified in the order.

(2) An order under subdivision (c) relating to a conservatee shall require the conservator to do one of the following when the conservatee has resided in the other state for a period of four months or a longer or shorter period specified in the order:

(A) Return the conservatee to this state.

(B) Petition for transfer of the conservatorship to the other state under Article 3 (commencing with Section 2001) of Chapter 8 of Part 3 and corresponding law of the other state.

(C) Cause a conservatorship proceeding or its equivalent to be commenced in the other state.

(e)(1) The guardian or conservator shall file a notice of change of residence with the court within 30 days of the date of the change. The guardian or conservator shall include in the notice of change of residence a declaration stating that the ward's or conservatee's change of residence is consistent with the standard described in subdivision (b).

(2)(A) The guardian or conservator shall deliver pursuant to Section 1215 a copy of the notice to all persons entitled to notice under subdivision (b) of Section 1511 or subdivision (b) of Section 1822 and shall file proof of delivery of the notice with the court. The court may, for good cause, waive the delivery requirement pursuant to this paragraph in order to prevent harm to the conservatee or ward.

(B) A conservator also shall provide notice pursuant to subparagraph (A) to any person who has requested special notice of the matter pursuant to Section 2700.

(3) If the guardian or conservator proposes to remove the ward or conservatee from [1] **their current residence or** personal residence, except as provided by subdivision (c), the guardian or conservator shall deliver pursuant to Section 1215 a notice of [2] **their** intention to change the residence of the ward or conservatee to all persons entitled to notice under subdivision (b) of Section 1511 and subdivision (b) of Section 1822**, and any person who has requested special notice of the matter, pursuant to Section 2700**. In the absence of an emergency, that notice shall be delivered at least 15 days before the proposed removal of the ward [3]**, or at least 20 days of the conservatee, from their current residence or** personal residence. If the notice is delivered less than 15 **or 20** days before the proposed removal of the ward or conservatee, **as applicable,** the guardian or conservator shall set forth the basis for the emergency in the notice. The guardian or conservator shall file proof of delivery of that notice with the court.

(f) This section does not apply [4] **when** the court has made an order under Section 2351 pursuant to which the conservatee retains the right to establish [5] **their** own residence.

(g) As used in this section, "guardian" or "conservator" includes a proposed guardian or proposed conservator and "ward" or "conservatee" includes a proposed ward or proposed conservatee.

(h) This section does not apply to a person with developmental disabilities for whom the Director of Developmental Services or a regional center, established pursuant to Chapter 5 (commencing with Section 4620) of Division 4.5 of the Welfare and Institutions Code, acts as the conservator. **Leg.H.** Enacted Stats 1990 ch 79 §14 (AB 759), operative July 1, 1991. Amended Stats 2006 ch 490 §1 (SB 1116), effective January 1, 2007; Stats 2008 ch 293 §8 (AB 1340), effective January 1, 2009; Stats 2014 ch 553 §24 (SB 940), effective January 1, 2015, operative January 1, 2016; Stats 2017 ch 319 §43 (AB 976), effective January 1, 2018; Stats 2024 ch 455 §2 (SB 1106), effective January 1, 2025.

§2352. 2024 Deletes. [1] his or her [2] his or her [3] or conservatee from his or her [4] where [5] his or her

2006 Note: This act, together with Senate Bill 1550, Senate Bill 1716, and Assembly Bill 1363, shall be known and may be cited as the Omnibus Conservatorship and Guardianship Reform Act of 2006. Stats 2006 ch 490 (SB 1116) §9.

Prior Law: Former Prob C §2352, similar to the present section, was added Stats 1979 ch 726 §3, operative January 1, 1981, amended Stats 1986 ch 615 §1, and repealed Stats 1990 ch 79 §13, operative July 1, 1991.

§2352.5. Presumption of least restrictive appropriate residence; Appropriate level of care; Applicability

(a) It shall be presumed that the personal residence of the conservatee at the time of commencement of the proceeding is the least restrictive appropriate residence for the conservatee. In any hearing to determine if removal of the conservatee from the conservatee's personal residence is appropriate, that presumption may be overcome by clear and convincing evidence.

(b) Upon appointment, the conservator shall determine the appropriate level of care for the conservatee.

(1) That determination shall include an evaluation of the level of care existing at the time of commencement of the proceeding and the measures that would be necessary to keep the conservatee in their personal residence.

(2) If the conservatee is living at a location other than the conservatee's personal residence at the commencement of the proceeding, that determination shall either include a plan to return the conservatee to their personal residence or an explanation of the limitations or restrictions on a return of the conservatee to their personal residence in the foreseeable future.

(c) The determination made by the conservator pursuant to subdivision (b) shall be included in the care plan as required by Section 2351.2.

(d) The conservator shall evaluate the conservatee's placement and level of care if there is a material change in circumstances affecting the conservatee's needs for placement and care.

(e)(1) This section shall not apply to a conservatee with developmental disabilities for whom the Director of Developmental Services or a regional center for the developmentally disabled, established pursuant to Chapter 5 (commencing with Section 4620) of Division 4.5 of the Welfare and Institutions Code, acts as the conservator and who receives services from a regional center pursuant to the Lanterman Developmental Disabilities Act (Division 4.5 (commencing with Section 4500) of the Welfare and Institutions Code).

(2) Services, including residential placement, for a conservatee described in paragraph (1) who is a consumer, as defined in Section 4512 of the Welfare and Institutions Code, shall be identified, delivered, and evaluated consistent with the individual program plan process described in Article 2 (commencing with Section 4640) of Chapter 5 of Division 4.5 of the Welfare and Institutions Code. **Leg.H.** Added Stats 2006 ch 490 §2 (SB 1116), effective January 1, 2007. Amended Stats 2007 ch 130 §195 (AB 299), effective January 1, 2008; Stats 2019 ch 847 §1 (SB 303), effective January 1, 2020; Stats 2023 ch 705 §2 (SB 280), effective January 1, 2024.

Editor's Notes—2006 Note: This act, together with Senate Bill 1550, Senate Bill 1716, and Assembly Bill 1363, shall be known and may be cited as the Omnibus Conservatorship and Guardianship Reform Act of 2006. Stats 2006 ch 490 (SB 1116) §9.

§2353. Medical treatment of ward

(a) Subject to subdivision (b), the guardian has the same right as a parent having legal custody of a child to give consent to medical treatment performed upon the ward and to require the ward to receive medical treatment.

(b) Except as provided in subdivision (c), if the ward is 14 years of age or older, no surgery may be performed upon the ward without either (1) the consent of both the ward and the guardian or (2) a court order obtained pursuant to Section 2357 specifically authorizing such treatment.

(c) The guardian may consent to surgery to be performed upon the ward, and may require the ward to receive the surgery, in any case where the guardian determines in good faith based upon medical advice that the case is an emergency case in which the ward faces loss of life or serious bodily injury if the surgery is not performed. In such a case, the consent of the guardian alone is sufficient and no person is liable because the surgery is performed upon the ward without the ward's consent.

(d) Nothing in this section requires the consent of the guardian for medical or surgical treatment for the ward in any case where the ward alone may consent to such treatment under other provisions of law. **Leg.H.** Enacted Stats 1990 ch 79 §14 (AB 759), operative July 1, 1991.

Prior Law: Former Prob C §2353, similar to the present section, was added Stats 1979 ch 726 §3, operative January 1, 1981, and repealed Stats 1990 ch 79 §13, operative July 1, 1991.

§2354. Medical treatment of conservatee not adjudicated to lack capacity to give informed consent

(a) If the conservatee has not been adjudicated to lack the capacity to give informed consent for medical treatment, the conservatee may consent to his or her medical treatment. The conservator may also give consent to the medical treatment, but the consent of the conservator is not required if the conservatee has the capacity to give informed consent to the medical treatment, and the consent of the conservator alone is not sufficient under this subdivision if the conservatee objects to the medical treatment.

(b) The conservator may require the conservatee to receive medical treatment, whether or not the conservatee consents to the treatment, if a court order specifically authorizing the medical treatment has been obtained pursuant to Section 2357.

(c) The conservator may consent to medical treatment to be performed upon the conservatee, and may require the conservatee to receive the medical treatment, in any case where the conservator determines in good faith based upon medical advice that the case is an emergency case in which the medical treatment is required because (1) the treatment is required for the alleviation of severe pain or (2) the conservatee has a medical condition which, if not immediately diagnosed and treated, will lead to serious disability or death. In such a case, the consent of the conservator alone is sufficient and no person is liable because the medical treatment is performed upon the conservatee without the conservatee's consent. **Leg.H.** Enacted Stats 1990 ch 79 §14 (AB 759), operative July 1, 1991.

Prior Law: Former Prob C §2354, similar to the present section, was added Stats 1979 ch 726 §3, operative January 1, 1981, and repealed Stats 1990 ch 79 §13, operative July 1, 1991.

§2355. Health care decisions by conservator

(a) If the conservatee has been adjudicated to lack the capacity to make health care decisions, the conservator has the exclusive authority to make health care decisions for the conservatee that the conservator in good faith based on medical advice determines to be necessary. The conservator shall make health care decisions for the conservatee in accordance with the conservatee's individual health care instructions, if any, and other wishes to the extent known to the conservator. Otherwise, the conservator shall make the decision in accordance with the conservator's determination of the conservatee's best interest. In determining the conservatee's best interest, the conservator shall consider the conservatee's personal values to the extent known to the conservator. The conservator may require the conservatee to receive the health care, whether or not the conservatee objects. In this case, the health care decision of the conservator alone is sufficient and no person is liable because the health care is administered to the conservatee without the conservatee's consent. For the purposes of this subdivision, "health care" and "health care decision" have the meanings provided in Sections 4615 and 4617, respectively.

(b) If prior to the establishment of the conservatorship the conservatee was an adherent of a religion whose tenets and practices call for reliance on prayer alone for healing, the treatment required by the conservator under the provisions of this section shall be by an accredited practitioner of that religion. **Leg.H.** Enacted Stats 1990 ch 79 §14 (AB 759), operative July 1, 1991. Amended Stats 1999 ch 658 §12 (AB 891), operative July 1, 2000.

Prior Law: Former Prob C §2355, similar to the present section, was added Stats 1979 ch 726 §3, operative January 1, 1981, and repealed Stats 1990 ch 79 §13, operative July 1, 1991.

§2356. Involuntary civil placement; Experimental drugs; Convulsive treatment; Sterilization

(a) A ward or conservatee shall not be placed in a mental health treatment facility under this division against his or her will. Involuntary civil placement of a ward or conservatee in a mental health treatment facility may be obtained only pursuant to Chapter 2 (commencing with Section 5150) or Chapter 3 (commencing with Section 5350) of Part 1 of Division 5 of the Welfare and Institutions Code. Nothing in this subdivision precludes the placing of a ward in a state hospital under Section 6000 of the Welfare and Institutions Code upon application of the guardian as provided in that section.

(b) An experimental drug as defined in Section 111515 of the Health and Safety Code shall not be prescribed for or administered to a ward or conservatee under this division. An experimental drug may be prescribed for or administered to a ward or conservatee only as provided in Article 4 (commencing with Section 111515) of Chapter 6 of Part 5 of Division 104 of the Health and Safety Code.

(c) Convulsive treatment as defined in Section 5325 of the Welfare and Institutions Code shall not be performed on a ward or conservatee under this division. Convulsive treatment may be performed on a ward or conservatee only as provided in Article 7 (commencing with Section 5325) of Chapter 2 of Part 1 of Division 5 of the Welfare and Institutions Code.

(d) A minor shall not be sterilized under this division.

(e) This chapter is subject to a valid and effective advance health care directive under the Health Care Decisions Law (Division 4.7 (commencing with Section 4600)). **Leg.H.** Enacted Stats 1990 ch 79 §14 (AB 759), operative July 1, 1991. Amended Stats 1990 ch 710 §8 (SB 1775), operative July 1, 1991; Stats 1996 ch 1023 §398 (SB 1497), effective September 29, 1996; Stats 1999 ch 658 §13 (AB 891), operative July 1, 2000; Stats 2014 ch 442 §12 (SB 1465), effective September 18, 2014; Stats 2015 ch 117 §1 (AB 468), effective January 1, 2016.

Prior Law: Former Prob C §2356, similar to the present section, was added Stats 1979 ch 726 §3.01, operative January 1, 1981, amended Stats 1986 ch 1012 §2, and repealed Stats 1990 ch 79 §13, operative July 1, 1991.

§2356.5. Conservatee with major neurocognitive disorder

(a) The Legislature hereby finds and declares all of the following:

(1) That a person with a major neurocognitive disorder, as defined in the last published edition of the Diagnostic and Statistical Manual of Mental Disorders, should have a conservatorship to serve the person's unique and special needs.

(2) That, by adding powers to the probate conservatorship for people with major neurocognitive disorders, their unique and special needs can be met. This will reduce costs to the conservatee and the family of the conservatee, reduce costly administration by state and county government, and safeguard the basic dignity and rights of the conservatee.

(3) That it is the intent of the Legislature to recognize that the administration of psychotropic medications has been, and can be, abused by caregivers and, therefore, granting powers to a conservator to authorize these medications for the treatment of major neurocognitive disorders requires the protections specified in this section.

(b) Notwithstanding any other law, a conservator may authorize the placement of a conservatee in a secured perimeter residential care facility for the elderly operated pursuant to Section 1569.698 of the Health and Safety Code, and that has a care plan that meets the requirements of Section 87705 of Title 22 of the California Code of Regulations, upon a court's finding, by clear and convincing evidence, of all of the following:

(1) The conservatee has a major neurocognitive disorder, as defined in the last published edition of the Diagnostic and Statistical Manual of Mental Disorders.

(2) The conservatee lacks the capacity to give informed consent to this placement and has at least one mental function deficit pursuant to subdivision (a) of Section 811, and this deficit significantly impairs the person's ability to understand and appreciate the consequences of their actions pursuant to subdivision (b) of Section 811.

(3) The conservatee needs, or would benefit from, a restricted and secure environment, as demonstrated by evidence presented by the physician or psychologist referred to in paragraph (3) of subdivision (f).

(4) The court finds that the proposed placement in a locked facility is the least restrictive placement appropriate to the needs of the conservatee.

(c) Notwithstanding any other law, a conservator of a person may authorize the administration of medications appropriate for the care and treatment of a major neurocognitive disorder, upon a court's finding, by clear and convincing evidence, of all of the following:

(1) The conservatee has a major neurocognitive disorder, as defined in the last published edition of the Diagnostic and Statistical Manual of Mental Disorders.

(2) The conservatee lacks the capacity to give informed consent to the administration of medications appropriate to the care of a major neurocognitive disorder, has at least one mental function deficit pursuant to subdivision (a) of Section 811, and this deficit or deficits significantly impairs the person's ability to understand and appreciate the consequences of their actions pursuant to subdivision (b) of Section 811.

(3) The conservatee needs, or would benefit from, appropriate medication, as demonstrated by evidence presented by the physician or psychologist referred to in paragraph (3) of subdivision (f).

(d) Pursuant to subdivision (b) of Section 2355, in the case of a person who is an adherent of a religion whose tenets and practices call for a reliance on prayer alone for healing, the treatment required by the conservator under subdivision (c) shall be by an accredited practitioner of that religion in lieu of the administration of medications.

(e) A conservatee who is to be placed in a facility pursuant to this section shall not be placed in a mental health rehabilitation center as described in Section 5675 of the Welfare and Institutions Code, or in an institution for mental disease as described in Section 5900 of the Welfare and Institutions Code.

(f) A petition for authority to act under this section is governed by Section 2357, except as follows:

(1) The conservatee shall be represented by an attorney pursuant to Chapter 4 (commencing with Section 1470) of Part 1. Upon granting or denying authority to a conservator under this section, the court shall discharge the attorney or order the continuation of the legal representation, consistent with the standard set forth in subdivision (a) of Section 1470.

(2) The conservatee shall be produced at the hearing, unless excused pursuant to Section 1893.

(3) The petition shall be supported by a declaration of a licensed physician, or a licensed psychologist within the scope of their licensure, regarding each of the findings required to be made under this section for any power requested, except that the psychologist has at least two years of experience in diagnosing major neurocognitive disorders.

(4) The petition may be filed by any of the persons designated in Section 1891.

(g) The court investigator shall annually investigate and report to the court pursuant to Sections 1850 and 1851 if the conservator is authorized to act under this section. In addition to the other matters provided in Section 1851, the conservatee shall be specifically advised by the investigator that the conservatee has the right to object to the conservator's powers granted under this section, and the report shall also include whether powers granted under this section are warranted. If the conservatee objects to the conservator's powers granted under this section, or the investigator determines that some change in the powers granted under this section is warranted, the court shall provide a copy of the report to the attorney of record for the conservatee. If an attorney has not been appointed for the conservatee, one shall be appointed pursuant to Chapter 4 (commencing with Section 1470) of Part 1. The attorney shall, within 30 days after receiving this report, do either of the following:

(1) File a petition with the court regarding the status of the conservatee.

(2) File a written report with the court stating that the attorney has met with the conservatee and determined that the petition would be inappropriate.

(h) A petition to terminate authority granted under this section shall be governed by Section 2359.

(i) This section does not affect a conservatorship of the estate of a person who has a major neurocognitive disorder.

(j) This section does not affect the laws that would otherwise apply in emergency situations.

(k) This section does not affect current law regarding the power of a probate court to fix the residence of a conservatee or to authorize medical treatment for a conservatee who has not been determined to have a major neurocognitive disorder. **Leg.H.** Added Stats 1996 ch 910 §1 (SB 1481). Amended Stats 1997 ch 724 §13 (AB 1172); Stats 2003 ch 32 §2 (AB 167); Stats 2014 ch 913 §31 (AB 2747), effective January 1, 2015; Stats 2015 ch 197 §1 (AB 436), effective January 1, 2016; Stats 2017 ch 122 §5 (SB 413), effective January 1, 2018; Stats 2018 ch 92 §171 (SB 1289), effective January 1, 2019; Stats 2022 ch 420 §41 (AB 2960), effective January 1, 2023.

§2357. Court-authorized medical treatment for ward or conservatee

(a) As used in this section:

(1) "Guardian or conservator" includes a temporary guardian of the person or a temporary conservator of the person.

(2) "Ward or conservatee" includes a person for whom a temporary guardian of the person or temporary conservator of the person has been appointed.

(b) If the ward or conservatee requires medical treatment for an existing or continuing medical condition which is not authorized to be performed upon the ward or conservatee under Section 2252, 2353, 2354, or 2355, and the ward or conservatee is unable to give an informed consent to this medical treatment, the guardian or conservator may petition the court under this section for an order authorizing the medical treatment and authorizing the guardian or conservator to consent on behalf of the ward or conservatee to the medical treatment.

(c) The petition shall state, or set forth by medical affidavit attached thereto, all of the following so far as is known to the petitioner at the time the petition is filed:

(1) The nature of the medical condition of the ward or conservatee which requires treatment.

(2) The recommended course of medical treatment which is considered to be medically appropriate.

(3) The threat to the health of the ward or conservatee if authorization to consent to the recommended course of treatment is delayed or denied by the court.

(4) The predictable or probable outcome of the recommended course of treatment.

(5) The medically available alternatives, if any, to the course of treatment recommended.

(6) The efforts made to obtain an informed consent from the ward or conservatee.

(7) The name and addresses, so far as they are known to the petitioner, of the persons specified in subdivision (c) of Section 1510 in a guardianship proceeding or subdivision (b) of Section 1821 in a conservatorship proceeding.

(d) Upon the filing of the petition, unless an attorney is already appointed the court shall appoint the public defender or private counsel under Section 1471, to consult with and represent the ward or conservatee at the hearing on the petition and, if that appointment is made, Section 1472 applies.

(e) Notice of the petition shall be given as follows:

(1) Not less than 15 days before the hearing, notice of the time and place of the hearing, and a copy of the petition shall be personally served on the ward, if 12 years of age or older, or the conservatee, and on the attorney for the ward or conservatee.

(2) Not less than 15 days before the hearing, notice of the time and place of the hearing, and a copy of the petition shall be delivered pursuant to Section 1215 to the following persons:

(A) The spouse or domestic partner, if any, of the proposed conservatee at the address stated in the petition.

(B) The relatives named in the petition at their addresses stated in the petition.

(f) For good cause, the court may shorten or waive notice of the hearing as provided by this section. In determining the period of notice to be required, the court shall take into account both of the following:

(1) The existing medical facts and circumstances set forth in the petition or in a medical affidavit attached to the petition or in a medical affidavit presented to the court.

(2) The desirability, where the condition of the ward or conservatee permits, of giving adequate notice to all interested persons.

(g) Notwithstanding subdivisions (e) and (f), the matter may be submitted for the determination of the court upon proper and sufficient medical affidavits or declarations if the attorney for the petitioner and the attorney for the ward or conservatee so stipulate and further stipulate that there remains no issue of fact to be determined.

(h) The court may make an order authorizing the recommended course of medical treatment of the ward or conservatee and authorizing the guardian or conservator to consent on behalf of the ward or conservatee to the recommended course of medical treatment for the ward or conservatee if the court determines from the evidence all of the following:

(1) The existing or continuing medical condition of the ward or conservatee requires the recommended course of medical treatment.

(2) If untreated, there is a probability that the condition will become life-endangering or result in a serious threat to the physical or mental health of the ward or conservatee.

(3) The ward or conservatee is unable to give an informed consent to the recommended course of treatment.

(i) Upon petition of the ward or conservatee or other interested person, the court may order that the guardian or conservator obtain or consent to, or obtain and consent to, specified medical treatment to be performed upon the ward or conservatee. Notice of the hearing on the petition under this subdivision shall be given for the period and in the manner provided in Chapter 3 (commencing with Section 1460) of Part 1. **Leg.H.** Enacted Stats 1990 ch 79 §14 (AB 759), operative July 1, 1991. Amended Stats 1990 ch 710 §9 (SB 1775), operative July 1, 1991; Stats 1999 ch 175 §2 (AB 239); Stats 2000 ch 135 §143 (AB 2539); Stats 2001 ch 893 §31 (AB 25); Stats 2017 ch 319 §44 (AB 976), effective January 1, 2018.

Prior Law: Former Prob C §2357, similar to the present section, was added Stats 1979 ch 726 §3, operative January 1, 1981, and repealed Stats 1990 ch 79 §13, operative July 1, 1991.

§2358. Additional conditions in order of appointment

When a guardian or conservator is appointed, the court may, with the consent of the guardian or conservator, insert in the order of appointment conditions not otherwise obligatory providing for the care, treatment, education, and welfare of the ward or conservatee. Any such conditions shall be included in the letters. The performance of such conditions is a part of the duties of the guardian or conservator for the faithful performance of which the guardian or conservator and the sureties on the bond are responsible. **Leg.H.** Enacted Stats 1990 ch 79 §14 (AB 759), operative July 1, 1991.

Prior Law: Former Prob C §2358, similar to the present section, was added Stats 1979 ch 726 §3, operative January 1, 1981, and repealed Stats 1990 ch 79 §13, operative July 1, 1991.

§2359. Instructions from or confirmation by court

(a) Upon petition of the guardian or conservator or ward or conservatee or other interested person, the court may authorize and instruct the guardian or conservator or approve and confirm the acts of the guardian or conservator.

(b) Notice of the hearing on the petition shall be given for the period and in the manner provided in Chapter 3 (commencing with Section 1460) of Part 1.

(c)(1) When a guardian or conservator petitions for the approval of a purchase, lease, or rental of real or personal property from the estate of a ward or conservatee, the guardian or conservator shall provide a statement disclosing the family or affiliate relationship between the guardian or conservator and the purchaser, lessee, or renter of the property, and the family or affiliate relationship between the guardian or conservator and any agent hired by the guardian or conservator.

(2) For the purposes of this subdivision, "family" means a person's spouse, domestic partner, or relatives within the second degree of lineal or collateral consanguinity of a person or a person's spouse. For the purposes of this subdivision, "affiliate" means an entity that is under the direct control, indirect control, or common control of the guardian or conservator.

(3) A violation of this section shall result in the rescission of the purchase, lease, or rental of the property. Any losses incurred by the estate of the ward or conservatee because the property was sold or leased at less than fair market value shall be deemed as charges against the guardian or conservator under the provisions of Sections 2401.3 and 2401.5. The court shall assess a civil penalty equal to three times the charges against the guardian, conservator, or other person in violation of this section, and may assess punitive damages as it deems proper. If the estate does not incur losses as a result of the violation, the court shall order the guardian, conservator, or other person in violation of this section to pay a fine of up to five thousand dollars ($5,000) for each violation. The fines and penalties provided in this section are in addition to any other rights and remedies provided by law. **Leg.H.** Enacted Stats 1990 ch 79 §14 (AB 759), operative July 1, 1991, Amended Stats 2000 ch 565 §5 (AB 1950); Stats 2001 ch 893 §32 (AB 25).

Prior Law: Former Prob C §2359, similar to the present section, was added Stats 1979 ch 726 §3, operative January 1, 1981, and repealed Stats 1990 ch 79 §13, operative July 1, 1991.

§2360. Annual photograph of conservatee

Upon the establishment of a conservatorship by the court and annually thereafter, the conservator shall ensure that a clear photograph of the conservatee is taken and preserved for the purpose of identifying the conservatee if he or she becomes missing. **Leg.H.** Added Stats 2010 ch 97 §1 (AB 2493), effective January 1, 2011.

§2361. Notice of conservatee's death

(a) A conservator shall provide notice of a conservatee's death by delivering pursuant to Section 1215 a copy of the notice to all persons entitled to notice under Section 1460, **including, but not limited to, a person who has requested special notice of the matter, as provided in Section 2700,** and by filing a proof of delivery with the court, unless otherwise ordered by the court.

(b) A conservator also shall provide notice, as specified in subdivision (a), of the date, time, and location of any funeral, burial, or memorial arrangements for the conservatee, if the conservator makes those arrangements. Notice pursuant to this subdivision shall be delivered electronically whenever possible. Leg.H. Added Stats 2015 ch 92 §3 (AB 1085), effective January 1, 2016. Amended Stats 2017 ch 319 §45 (AB 976), effective January 1, 2018; Stats 2024 ch 455 §3 (SB 1106), effective January 1, 2025.

§§2362–2399. [No sections of these numbers.]

CHAPTER 6
POWERS AND DUTIES OF GUARDIAN OR CONSERVATOR OF THE ESTATE

Article 1. Definitions and General Provisions.
Article 2. Support and Maintenance of Ward or Conservatee and Dependents.
Article 3. Payment of Debts and Expenses.
Article 4. Estate Management Powers Generally.
Article 5. Compromise of Claims and Actions; Extension, Renewal, or Modification of Obligations.
Article 7. Sales.
Article 8. Notes, Mortgages, Leases, Conveyances, and Exchanges.
Article 9. Investments and Purchase of Property.
Article 10. Substituted Judgment.
Article 11. Independent Exercise of Powers.

ARTICLE 1
Definitions and General Provisions

Definitions. §2400.
Duty to manage estate using ordinary care and diligence. §2401.
Ordinary care and diligence in determining ownership of real property in foreign jurisdiction. §2401.1.
Measure of liability for breach of fiduciary duty. §2401.3.
Measure of liability for interest; Excuse. §2401.5.
Payment or offset of surcharges. §2401.6.
Other remedies not affected. §2401.7.
Additional conditions in order of appointment. §2402.
Instructions from or confirmation by court. §2403.
Order compelling guardian or conservator to pay support or debts. §2404.
Submitting disputed claim for summary determination. §2405.
Submitting dispute to arbitration. §2406.
Application of chapter to community property. §2407.
Independent administration. §2408.
Adoption of rule of court requiring uniform standards of conduct. §2410.

§2400. Definitions

As used in this chapter:

(a) "Conservator" means the conservator of the estate, or the limited conservator of the estate to the extent that the powers and duties of the limited conservator are specifically and expressly provided by the order appointing the limited conservator.

(b) "Estate" means all of the conservatee's or ward's personal property, wherever located, and real property located in this state.

(c) "Guardian" means the guardian of the estate. **Leg.H.** Enacted Stats 1990 ch 79 §14 (AB 759), operative July 1, 1991. Amended Stats 2008 ch 52 §2 (AB 2014), effective January 1, 2009.

Prior Law: Former Prob C §2400, similar to the present section, was added Stats 1979 ch 726 §3, operative January 1, 1981, amended Stats 1980 ch 1304 §24, and repealed Stats 1990 ch 79 §13, operative July 1, 1991.

§2401. Duty to manage estate using ordinary care and diligence

(a) The guardian or conservator, or limited conservator to the extent specifically and expressly provided in the appointing court's order, has the management and control of the estate and, in managing and controlling the estate, shall use ordinary care and diligence. What constitutes use of ordinary care and diligence is determined by all the circumstances of the particular estate.

(b) The guardian or conservator:

(1) Shall exercise a power to the extent that ordinary care and diligence requires that the power be exercised.

(2) Shall not exercise a power to the extent that ordinary care and diligence requires that the power not be exercised.

(c) Notwithstanding any other law, a guardian or conservator who is not a trust company, or an employee of that guardian or conservator, in exercising their powers, may not hire or refer any business to an entity in which the guardian or conservator or an employee has a financial interest. For the purposes of this subdivision, "financial interest" shall mean (1) an ownership interest in a sole proprietorship, a partnership, or a closely held corporation, or (2) an ownership interest of greater than 1 percent of the outstanding shares in a publicly held corporation, or (3) being an officer or a director of a corporation.

(d) Subdivision (c) does not prohibit a professional fiduciary appointed as a guardian or conservator from hiring and compensating individuals as employees, with court approval.

(e)(1) Notwithstanding any other law, a guardian or conservator who is a trust company, in exercising its powers may not, except upon authorization of the court, invest in securities of the trust company or an affiliate or subsidiary, or other securities from which the trust company or affiliate or subsidiary receives a financial benefit or in a mutual fund, other than a mutual fund authorized in paragraph (5) of subdivision (a) of Section 2574, registered under the Investment Company Act of 1940 (Subchapter 1 (commencing with Sec. 80a-1) of Chapter 2D of Title 15 of the United States Code), to which the trust company or its affiliate provides services, including, but not limited to, services as an investment adviser, sponsor, distributor, custodian, agent, registrar, administrator, servicer, or manager, and for which the trust company or its affiliate receives compensation.

(2) Before authorization from the court, the guardian or conservator shall disclose to the court in writing the trust company's financial interest. **Leg.H.** Enacted Stats 1990 ch 79 §14 (AB 759), operative July 1, 1991. Amended Stats 2000 ch 565 §6 (AB 1950); Stats 2006 ch 493 §21 (AB 1363), effective January 1, 2007; Stats 2021 ch 417 §21 (AB 1194), effective January 1, 2022.

2006 Note: This act, together with Senate Bill 1116 (Scott), Senate Bill 1550 (Figueroa), and Senate Bill 1716 (Bowen), shall be known and may be cited as the

Omnibus Conservatorship and Guardianship Reform Act of 2006. Stats 2006 ch 493 (AB 1363) §1.

Prior Law: Former Prob C §2401, similar to the present section, was added Stats 1979 ch 726 §3, operative January 1, 1981, amended Stats 1980 ch 1304 §25, and repealed Stats 1990 ch 79 §13, operative July 1, 1991.

§2401.1. Ordinary care and diligence in determining ownership of real property in foreign jurisdiction

The guardian or conservator shall use ordinary care and diligence to determine whether the ward or conservatee owns real property in a foreign jurisdiction and to preserve and protect that property. What constitutes use of ordinary care and diligence shall be determined by all the facts and circumstances known, or that become known, to the guardian or conservator, the value of the real property located in the foreign jurisdiction, and the needs of the ward or conservatee. The guardian or conservator, except as provided in subdivision (a) of Section 1061 and in Section 1062, is not charged with, and shall have no duty to inventory or account for the real property located in a foreign jurisdiction, but the guardian or conservator shall, when presenting the inventory and appraisal and accounting to the court, include the schedule set forth in subdivision (h) of Section 1063. **Leg.H.** Added Stats 2008 ch 52 §3 (AB 2014), effective January 1, 2009.

§2401.3. Measure of liability for breach of fiduciary duty

(a) If the guardian or conservator breaches a fiduciary duty, the guardian or conservator is chargeable with any of the following that is appropriate under the circumstances:

(1) Any loss or depreciation in value of the estate resulting from the breach of duty, with interest.

(2) Any profit made by the guardian or conservator through the breach of duty, with interest.

(3) Any profit that would have accrued to the estate if the loss of profit is the result of the breach of duty.

(b) If the guardian or conservator has acted reasonably and in good faith under the circumstances as known to the guardian or conservator, the court, in its discretion, may excuse the guardian or conservator in whole or in part from liability under subdivision (a) if it would be equitable to do so. **Leg.H.** Enacted Stats 1990 ch 79 §14 (AB 759), operative July 1, 1991.

§2401.5. Measure of liability for interest; Excuse

(a) If the guardian or conservator is liable for interest pursuant to Section 2401.3, the guardian or conservator is liable for the greater of the following amounts:

(1) The amount of interest that accrues at the legal rate on judgments.

(2) The amount of interest actually received.

(b) If the guardian or conservator has acted reasonably and in good faith under the circumstances as known to the guardian or conservator, the court, in its discretion, may excuse the guardian or conservator in whole or in part from liability under subdivision (a) if it would be equitable to do so. **Leg.H.** Enacted Stats 1990 ch 79 §14 (AB 759), operative July 1, 1991. Amended Stats 1998 ch 77 §2 (SB 1841).

§2401.6. Payment or offset of surcharges

Any surcharge that a guardian or conservator incurs under the provisions of Sections 2401.3 or 2401.5 may not be paid by or offset against future fees or wages to be provided by the estate to the guardian or conservator. **Leg.H.** Added Stats 2000 ch 565 §7 (AB 1950), effective January 1, 2001.

§2401.7. Other remedies not affected

The provisions of Sections 2401.3 and 2401.5 for liability of a guardian or conservator for breach of a fiduciary duty do not prevent resort to any other remedy available against the guardian or conservator under the statutory or common law. **Leg.H.** Enacted Stats 1990 ch 79 §14 (AB 759), operative July 1, 1991.

§2402. Additional conditions in order of appointment

When a guardian or conservator is appointed, the court may, with the consent of the guardian or conservator, insert in the order of appointment conditions not otherwise obligatory providing for the care and custody of the property of the ward or conservatee. Any such conditions shall be included in the letters. The performance of such conditions is a part of the duties of the guardian or conservator for the faithful performance of which the guardian or conservator and the sureties on the bond are responsible. **Leg.H.** Enacted Stats 1990 ch 79 §14 (AB 759), operative July 1, 1991.

Prior Law: Former Prob C §2402, similar to the present section, was added Stats 1979 ch 726 §3, operative January 1, 1981, and repealed Stats 1990 ch 79 §13, operative July 1, 1991.

§2403. Instructions from or confirmation by court

(a) Upon petition of the guardian or conservator, the ward or conservatee, a creditor, or other interested person, the court may authorize and instruct the guardian or conservator, or approve and confirm the acts of the guardian or conservator, in the administration, management, investment, disposition, care, protection, operation, or preservation of the estate, or the incurring or payment of costs, fees, or expenses in connection therewith.

(b) Notice of the hearing on the petition shall be given for the period and in the manner provided in Chapter 3 (commencing with Section 1460) of Part 1.

(c)(1) When a guardian or conservator petitions for the approval of a purchase, lease, or rental of real or personal property from the estate of a ward or conservatee, the guardian or conservator shall provide a statement disclosing the family or affiliate relationship between the guardian and conservator and the purchaser, lessee, or renter of the property, and the family or affiliate relationship between the guardian or conservator and any agent hired by the guardian or conservator.

(2) For the purposes of this subdivision, "family" means a person's spouse, domestic partner, or relatives within the second degree of lineal or collateral consanguinity of a person or a person's spouse. For the purposes of this subdivision, "affiliate" means an entity that is under the direct control, indirect control, or common control of the guardian or conservator.

(3) A violation of this section shall result in the rescission of the purchase, lease, or rental of the property. Any losses incurred by the estate of the ward or conservatee because the property was sold or leased at less than fair market value shall be deemed as charges against the guardian or conservator under the provisions of Sections 2401.3 and 2401.5. The court shall assess a civil penalty equal to three times the charges against the guardian, conservator, or other person in violation of this section, and may assess punitive damages as it deems proper. If the estate does not incur losses as a result of the violation, the court shall order the guardian, conservator, or other person in violation of this section to pay a fine of up to five thousand dollars ($5,000) for each violation. The fines and penalties provided in this section are in addition to any other rights and remedies provided by law. **Leg.H.** Enacted Stats 1990 ch 79 §14 (AB 759), operative July 1, 1991. Amended Stats 2000 ch 565 §8 (AB 1950); Stats 2001 ch 893 §33 (AB 25), effective January 1, 2002.

Prior Law: Former Prob C §2403, similar to the present section, was added Stats 1979 ch 726 §3, operative January 1, 1981, and repealed Stats 1990 ch 79 §13, operative July 1, 1991.

§2404. Order compelling guardian or conservator to pay support or debts

(a) If the guardian or conservator fails, neglects, or refuses to furnish comfortable and suitable support, maintenance, or education for the ward or conservatee as required by this division, or to pay a debt, expense, or charge lawfully due and payable by the ward or conservatee or the estate as provided in this division, the court shall, upon petition or upon its own motion, order the guardian or conservator to do so from the estate.

(b) The petition may be filed by the ward or conservatee or by the creditor or any other interested person. Notice of the hearing on the petition shall be given for the period and in the manner provided in Chapter 3 (commencing with Section 1460) of Part 1. **Leg.H.** Enacted Stats 1990 ch 79 §14 (AB 759), operative July 1, 1991.

Prior Law: Former Prob C §2404, similar to the present section, was added Stats 1979 ch 726 §3, operative January 1, 1981, and repealed Stats 1990 ch 79 §13, operative July 1, 1991.

§2405. Submitting disputed claim for summary determination

If there is a dispute relating to the estate between the guardian or conservator and a third person, the guardian or conservator, or the limited conservator to the extent specifically and expressly provided in the order appointing the limited conservator, may do either of the following:

(a) Enter into an agreement in writing with the third person to refer the dispute to a temporary judge designated in the agreement. The agreement shall be filed with the clerk, who shall thereupon, with the approval of the court, enter an order referring the matter to the designated person. The temporary judge shall proceed promptly to hear and determine the matter in controversy by summary procedure, without any pleadings, discovery, or jury trial. The decision of the temporary judge is subject to Section 632 of the Code of Civil Procedure. Judgment shall be entered on the decision and is as valid and effective as if rendered by a judge of the court in an action against the guardian or conservator or the third person commenced by ordinary process.

(b) Enter into an agreement in writing with the third person that a judge of the court, pursuant to the agreement and with the written consent of the judge, both filed with the clerk within the time for bringing an independent action on the matter in dispute, may hear and determine the dispute pursuant to the procedure provided in subdivision (a). **Leg.H.** Enacted Stats 1990 ch 79 §14 (AB 759), operative July 1, 1991.

Prior Law: Former Prob C §2405, similar to the present section, was added Stats 1979 ch 726 §3, operative January 1, 1981, amended Stats 1980 ch 1304 §26, Stats 1987 ch 923 §70, operative July 1, 1988, Stats 1989 ch 544 §2, and repealed Stats 1990 ch 79 §13, operative July 1, 1991.

§2406. Submitting dispute to arbitration

If there is a dispute relating to the estate between the guardian or conservator and a third person, the guardian or conservator may enter into an agreement in writing with the third person to submit the dispute to arbitration under Title 9 (commencing with Section 1280) of Part 3 of the Code of Civil Procedure. The agreement is not effective unless it has first been approved by the court and a copy of the approved agreement is filed with the court. **Leg.H.** Enacted Stats 1990 ch 79 §14 (AB 759), operative July 1, 1991.

Prior Law: Former Prob C §2406, similar to the present section, was added Stats 1979 ch 726 §3, operative January 1, 1981, amended Stats 1987 ch 923 §71, operative July 1, 1988, and repealed Stats 1990 ch 79 §13, operative July 1, 1991.

§2407. Application of chapter to community property

This chapter applies to property owned by spouses as community property only to the extent authorized by Part 6 (commencing with Section 3000). **Leg.H.** Enacted Stats 1990 ch 79 §14 (AB 759), operative July 1, 1991. Amended Stats 2016 ch 50 §82 (SB 1005), effective January 1, 2017.

2016 Note: For legislative intent, see the 2016 Note following Prob C §59.

Prior Law: Former Prob C §2407, similar to the present section, was added Stats 1979 ch 726 §3, operative January 1, 1981, amended Stats 1983 ch 155 §29, effective June 30, 1983, operative July 1, 1983, and repealed Stats 1990 ch 79 §13, operative July 1, 1991.

§2408. Independent administration

Nothing in this chapter limits or restricts any authority granted to a guardian or conservator pursuant to Article 11 (commencing with Section 2590) to administer the estate under that article. **Leg.H.** Enacted Stats 1990 ch 79 §14 (AB 759), operative July 1, 1991.

§2410. Adoption of rule of court requiring uniform standards of conduct

On or before January 1, 2008, the Judicial Council, in consultation with the California Judges Association, the California Association of Superior Court Investigators, the California State Association of Public Administrators, Public Guardians, and Public Conservators, the State Bar of California, the National Guardianship Association, and the Association of Professional Geriatric Care Managers, shall adopt a rule of court that shall require uniform standards of conduct for actions that conservators and guardians may take under this chapter on behalf of conservatees and wards to ensure that the estate of conservatees or wards are maintained and conserved as appropriate and to prevent risk of loss or harm to the conservatees or wards. This rule shall include at a minimum standards for determining the fees that may be charged to conservatees or wards and standards for asset management. **Leg.H.** Added Stats 2006 ch 493 §22 (AB 1363), effective January 1, 2007.

2006 Note: This act, together with Senate Bill 1116 (Scott), Senate Bill 1550 (Figueroa), and Senate Bill 1716 (Bowen), shall be known and may be cited as the Omnibus Conservatorship and Guardianship Reform Act of 2006. Stats 2006 ch 493 (AB 1363) §1.

ARTICLE 2
Support and Maintenance of Ward or Conservatee and Dependents

Support, maintenance, and education. §2420.
Personal allowance for ward or conservatee. §2421.
Order authorizing support notwithstanding third party liable. §2422.
Payment of surplus income to relatives of conservatee. §2423.

§2420. Support, maintenance, and education

(a) Subject to Section 2422, the guardian or conservator shall apply the income from the estate, so far as necessary, to the comfortable and suitable support, maintenance, and education of the ward or conservatee (including care, treatment, and support of a ward or conservatee who is a patient in a state hospital under the jurisdiction of the State Department of State Hospitals or the State Department of Developmental Services) and of those legally entitled to support, maintenance, or education from the ward or conservatee, taking into account the value of the estate and the condition of life of the persons required to be furnished such support, maintenance, or education.

(b) If the income from the estate is insufficient for the purpose described in subdivision (a), the guardian or conservator may sell or give a security interest in or other lien on any personal property of the estate, or sell or mortgage or give a deed of trust on any real property of the estate, as provided in this part.

(c) When the amount paid by the guardian or conservator for the purpose described in subdivision (a) satisfies the standard set out in that subdivision, and the payments are supported by proper vouchers or other proof satisfactory to the court, the guardian or conservator shall be allowed credit for such payments when the accounts of the guardian or conservator are settled.

(d) Nothing in this section requires the guardian or conservator to obtain court authorization before making the payments authorized by this section, but nothing in this section dispenses with the need to obtain any court authorization otherwise required for a particular transaction.

(e) Nothing in this section precludes the guardian or conservator from seeking court authorization or instructions or approval and confirmation pursuant to Section 2403. **Leg.H.** Enacted Stats 1990 ch 79 §14 (AB 759), operative July 1, 1991. Amended Stats 2012 ch 440 §44 (AB 1488), effective September 22, 2012.

Prior Law: Former Prob C §2420, similar to the present section, was added Stats 1979 ch 726 §3, operative January 1, 1981, and repealed Stats 1990 ch 79 §13, operative July 1, 1991.

§2421. Personal allowance for ward or conservatee

(a) Upon petition of the guardian or conservator or the ward or conservatee, the court may authorize the guardian or conservator to pay to the ward or conservatee out of the estate a reasonable allowance for the personal use of the ward or conservatee. The allowance shall be in such amount as the court may determine to be for the best interests of the ward or conservatee.

(b) Notice of the hearing on the petition shall be given for the period and in the manner provided in Chapter 3 (commencing with Section 1460) of Part 1.

(c) The guardian or conservator is not required to account for such allowance other than to establish that it has been paid to the ward or conservatee. The funds so paid are subject to the sole control of the ward or conservatee. **Leg.H.** Enacted Stats 1990 ch 79 §14 (AB 759), operative July 1, 1991.

Prior Law: Former Prob C §2421, similar to the present section, was added Stats 1979 ch 726 §3, operative January 1, 1981, and repealed Stats 1990 ch 79 §13, operative July 1, 1991.

§2422. Order authorizing support notwithstanding third party liable

(a) Upon petition of the guardian or conservator, the ward or conservatee, or any other interested person, the court may for good cause order the ward or conservatee to be wholly or partially supported, maintained, or educated out of the estate notwithstanding the existence of a third party legally obligated to provide such support, maintenance, or education. Such order may be made for a limited period of time. If not so limited, it continues in effect until modified or revoked.

(b) Notice of the hearing on the petition shall be given for the period and in the manner provided in Chapter 3 (commencing with Section 1460) of Part 1. **Leg.H.** Enacted Stats 1990 ch 79 §14 (AB 759), operative July 1, 1991.

Prior Law: Former Prob C §2422, similar to the present section, was added Stats 1979 ch 726 §3, operative January 1, 1981, and repealed Stats 1990 ch 79 §13, operative July 1, 1991.

§2423. Payment of surplus income to relatives of conservatee

(a) Upon petition of the conservator, the conservatee, the spouse or domestic partner of the conservatee, or a relative within the second degree of the conservatee, the court may by order authorize or direct the conservator to pay and distribute surplus income of the estate or any part of the surplus income (not used for the support, maintenance, and education of the conservatee and of those legally entitled to support, maintenance, or education from the conservatee) to the spouse or domestic partner of the conservatee and to relatives within the second degree of the conservatee whom the conservatee would, in the judgment of the court, have aided but for the existence of the conservatorship. The court in ordering payments under this section may impose conditions if the court determines that the conservatee would have imposed the conditions if the conservatee had the capacity to act.

(b) The granting of the order and the amounts and proportions of the payments are discretionary with the court, but the court shall consider all of the following:

(1) The amount of surplus income available after adequate provision has been made for the comfortable and suitable support, maintenance, and education of the conservatee and of those legally entitled to support, maintenance, or education from the conservatee.

(2) The circumstances and condition of life to which the conservatee and the spouse or domestic partner and relatives have been accustomed.

(3) The amount that the conservatee would in the judgment of the court have allowed the spouse or domestic partner and relatives but for the existence of the conservatorship.

(c) Notice of the hearing on the petition shall be given for the period and in the manner provided in Chapter 3 (commencing with Section 1460) of Part 1. **Leg.H.** Enacted Stats 1990 ch 79 §14 (AB 759), operative July 1, 1991. Amended Stats 2001 ch 893 §34 (AB 25), effective January 1, 2002.

Prior Law: Former Prob C §2423, similar to the present section, was added Stats 1979 ch 726 §3, operative January 1, 1981, and repealed Stats 1990 ch 79 §13, operative July 1, 1991.

ARTICLE 3
Payment of Debts and Expenses

Payment of debts and expenses generally. §2430.
Priority for wage claims. §2431.

§2430. Payment of debts and expenses generally

(a) Subject to subdivisions (b) and (c), the guardian or conservator shall pay the following from any principal and income of the estate:

(1) The debts incurred by the ward or conservatee before creation of the guardianship or conservatorship, giving priority to the debts described in Section 2431 to the extent required by that section.

(2) The debts incurred by the ward or conservatee during the guardianship or conservatorship to provide the necessaries of life to the ward or conservatee, and to the spouse and minor children of the ward or conservatee, to the extent the debt is reasonable. Also, the debts reasonably incurred by the conservatee during the conservatorship to provide the basic living expenses, as defined in Section 297 of the Family Code, to the domestic partner of the conservatee. The guardian or conservator may deduct the amount of any payments for these debts from any allowance otherwise payable to the ward or conservatee.

(3) In the case of a conservatorship, any other debt incurred by the conservatee during the conservatorship only if the debt satisfies the requirements of any order made under Chapter 4 (commencing with Section 1870) of Part 3.

(4) The reasonable expenses incurred in the collection, care, and administration of the estate, but court authorization is required for payment of compensation to any of the following:

(A) The guardian or conservator of the person or estate or both.

(B) An attorney for the guardian or conservator of the person or estate or both.

(C) An attorney for the ward or conservatee.

(D) An attorney for the estate.

(E) The public guardian for the costs and fee under Section 2902.

(b) The payments provided for by paragraph (3) of subdivision (a) are not required to be made to the extent the payments would impair the ability to provide the necessaries of life to the conservatee and the spouse and minor children of the conservatee and to provide the basic living expenses, as defined in Section 297 of the Family Code, of the domestic partner of the conservatee.

(c) The guardian or conservator may petition the court under Section 2403 for instructions when there is doubt whether a debt should be paid under this section. **Leg.H.** Enacted Stats 1990 ch 79 §14 (AB 759), operative July 1, 1991. Amended Stats 2001 ch 893 §35 (AB 25), effective January 1, 2002.

Prior Law: Former Prob C §2430, similar to the present section, was added Stats 1979 ch 726 §3, operative January 1, 1981, amended Stats 1988 ch 1199 §69, operative July 1, 1989, and repealed Stats 1990 ch 79 §13, operative July 1, 1991.

§2431. Priority for wage claims

(a) Subject to subdivision (d), the guardian or conservator may petition the court under Section 2403 for instructions when there is doubt whether a wage claim should be paid under this section.

(b) The guardian or conservator shall promptly pay wage claims for work done or services rendered for the ward or conservatee within 30 days prior to the date the petition for appointment of the guardian or conservator was filed. The payments made pursuant to this subdivision shall not exceed nine hundred dollars ($900) to each claimant. If there is insufficient money to pay all the claims described in this subdivision up to nine hundred dollars ($900), the money available shall be distributed among such claimants in proportion to the amount of their respective claims.

(c) After the payments referred to in subdivision (b) have been made, the guardian or conservator shall pay wage claims for work done or services rendered for the ward or conservatee within 90 days prior to the date the petition for appointment of the guardian or conservator was filed, excluding the claims described in subdivision (b). The payments made pursuant to this subdivision shall not exceed one thousand one hundred dollars ($1,100) to each claimant. If there is insufficient money to pay all the claims described in this subdivision up to one thousand one hundred dollars ($1,100), the money available shall be distributed among such claimants in proportion to the amounts of their respective claims.

(d) The guardian or conservator may require sworn claims to be presented. If there is reasonable cause to believe that the claim is not valid, the guardian or conservator may refuse to pay the claim in whole or in part but shall pay any part thereof that is not disputed without prejudice to the claimant's rights as to the balance of the claim. The guardian or conservator shall withhold sufficient money to cover the disputed portion until the claimant has had a reasonable opportunity to establish the validity of the claim by bringing an action, either in the claimant's own name or through an assignee, against the guardian or conservator.

(e) If the guardian or conservator neglects or refuses to pay all or any portion of a claim which is not in dispute, the court shall order the guardian or conservator to do so upon the informal application of any wage claimant or the assignee or legal representative of such claimant. **Leg.H.** Enacted Stats 1990 ch 79 §14 (AB 759), operative July 1, 1991.

Prior Law: Former Prob C §2431, similar to the present section, was added Stats 1979 ch 726 §3, operative January 1, 1981, and repealed Stats 1990 ch 79 §13, operative July 1, 1991.

ARTICLE 4
Estate Management Powers Generally

Extent of court supervision. §2450.
Collection of debts and benefits. §2451.
Powers of guardian or conservator. §2451.5.
Checks, warrants, and drafts. §2452.
Deposit in insured account in financial institution. §2453.
Interest on deposits by trust company. §2453.5.
Deposit of personal property with trust company. §2454.
Deposit of securities in securities depository. §2455.
Accounts and deposits withdrawable only on court order. §2456.
Maintaining home of ward or conservatee and dependents. §2457.
Voting rights with respect to corporate shares or memberships or property. §2458.
Life insurance, medical, retirement, and other plans and benefits. §2459.
Liability and casualty insurance. §2460.
Taxes and tax returns. §2461.
Representation in actions and proceedings. §2462.
Partition actions. §2463.
Acceptance of deed in lieu of foreclosure or trustee's sale. §2464.
Abandonment of valueless property. §2465.
Advances by guardian or conservator. §2466.
Care of estate after death of ward or conservatee. §2467.
Petition for practice administrator for disabled attorney. §2468.
Incapacitated professional fiduciary. §2469.

§2450. Extent of court supervision

(a) Unless this article specifically provides a proceeding to obtain court authorization or requires court authorization, the powers and duties set forth in this article may be exercised or performed by the guardian or conservator without court authorization, instruction, approval, or confirmation. Nothing in this subdivision precludes the guardian or conservator from seeking court authorization, instructions, approval, or confirmation pursuant to Section 2403.

(b) Upon petition of the ward or conservatee, a creditor, or any other interested person, or upon the court's own motion, the court may limit the authority of the guardian or conservator under subdivision (a) as to a particular power or duty or as to particular powers or duties. Notice of the hearing on a petition under this subdivision shall be given for the period and in the manner provided in Chapter 3 (commencing with Section 1460) of Part 1. **Leg.H.** Enacted Stats 1990 ch 79 §14 (AB 759), operative July 1, 1991.

Prior Law: Former Prob C §2450, similar to the present section, was added Stats 1979 ch 726 §3, operative January 1, 1981, and repealed Stats 1990 ch 79 §13, operative July 1, 1991.

§2451. Collection of debts and benefits

The guardian or conservator may collect debts and benefits due to the ward or conservatee and the estate. **Leg.H.** Enacted Stats 1990 ch 79 §14 (AB 759), operative July 1, 1991.

Prior Law: Former Prob C §2451, similar to the present section, was added Stats 1979 ch 726 §3, operative January 1, 1981, and repealed Stats 1990 ch 79 §13, operative July 1, 1991.

§2451.5. Powers of guardian or conservator

The guardian or conservator may do any of the following:

(a) Contract for the guardianship or conservatorship, perform outstanding contracts, and, thereby, bind the estate.

(b) Purchase tangible personal property.

(c) Subject to the provisions of Chapter 8 (commencing with Section 2640), employ an attorney to advise and represent the guardian or conservator in all matters, including the conservatorship proceeding and all other actions or proceedings.

(d) Employ and pay the expense of accountants, investment advisers, agents, depositaries, and employees.

(e) Operate for a period of 45 days after the issuance of the letters of guardianship or conservatorship, at the risk of the estate, a business, farm, or enterprise constituting an asset of the estate. **Leg.H.** Added Stats 2007 ch 553 §16 (AB 1727), effective January 1, 2008.

§2452. Checks, warrants, and drafts

(a) The guardian or conservator may endorse and cash or deposit any checks, warrants, or drafts payable to the ward or conservatee which constitute property of the estate.

(b) If it appears likely that the estate will satisfy the conditions of subdivision (b) of Section 2628, the court may order that the guardian or conservator be the designated payee for public assistance payments received pursuant to Part 3 (commencing with Section 11000) or Part 4 (commencing with Section 16000) of Division 9 of the Welfare and Institutions Code. **Leg.H.** Enacted Stats 1990 ch 79 §14 (AB 759), operative July 1, 1991.

Prior Law: Former Prob C §2452, similar to the present section, was added Stats 1980 ch 246 §4.6 and repealed Stats 1990 ch 79 §13 (AB 759), operative July 1, 1991.

Former Prob C §2452, similar to the present section, was added Stats 1979 ch 729, operative January 1, 1981, and repealed Stats 1980 ch 246 §4.5.

§2453. Deposit in insured account in financial institution

The guardian or conservator may deposit money belonging to the estate in an insured account in a financial institution in this state. Unless otherwise provided by court order, the money deposited under this section may be withdrawn without order of court. **Leg.H.** Enacted Stats 1990 ch 79 §14 (AB 759), operative July 1, 1991.

Prior Law: Former Prob C §2453, similar to the present section, was added Stats 1979 ch 726 §3, operative January 1, 1981, amended Stats 1987 ch 923 §72, operative July 1, 1988, and repealed Stats 1990 ch 79 §13, operative July 1, 1991.

§2453.5. Interest on deposits by trust company

(a) Subject to subdivision (b), where a trust company is a guardian or conservator and in the exercise of reasonable judgment deposits money of the estate in an account in any department of the corporation or association of which it is a part, it is chargeable with interest thereon at the rate of interest prevailing among banks of the locality on such deposits.

(b) Where it is to the advantage of the estate, the amount of cash that is reasonably necessary for orderly administration of the estate may be deposited in a checking account that does not bear interest which is maintained in a department of the corporation or association of which the trust company is a party. **Leg.H.** Enacted Stats 1990 ch 79 §14 (AB 759), operative July 1, 1991.

Prior Law: Former Prob C §2453.5, similar to the present section, was added Stats 1987 ch 923 §73, operative July 1, 1988, and repealed Stats 1990 ch 79 §13, operative July 1, 1991.

§2454. Deposit of personal property with trust company

The guardian or conservator may deposit personal property of the estate with a trust company for safekeeping. Unless otherwise provided by court order, the personal property may be withdrawn without order of court. **Leg.H.** Enacted Stats 1990 ch 79 §14 (AB 759), operative July 1, 1991.

Prior Law: Former Prob C §2454, similar to the present section, was added Stats 1979 ch 726 §3, operative January 1, 1981, and repealed Stats 1990 ch 79 §13, operative July 1, 1991.

§2455. Deposit of securities in securities depository

(a) A trust company serving as guardian or conservator may deposit securities that constitute all or part of the estate in a securities depository as provided in Section 775 of the Financial Code.

(b) If the securities have been deposited with a trust company pursuant to Section 2328 or Section 2454, the trust company may deposit the securities in a securities depository as provided in Section 775 of the Financial Code.

(c) The securities depository may hold securities deposited with it in the manner authorized by Section 775 of the Financial Code. **Leg.H.** Enacted Stats 1990 ch 79 §14 (AB 759), operative July 1, 1991.

Prior Law: Former Prob C §2455, similar to the present section, was added Stats 1979 ch 726 §3, operative July 1, 1981, amended Stats 1987 ch 923 §74, operative July 1, 1988, and repealed Stats 1990 ch 79 §13, operative July 1, 1991.

§2456. Accounts and deposits withdrawable only on court order

(a) Upon application of the guardian or conservator, the court may, with or without notice, order that money or other personal property be deposited pursuant to Section 2453 or 2454, and be subject to withdrawal only upon authorization of the court.

(b) The guardian or conservator shall deliver a copy of the court order to the financial institution or trust company at the time the deposit is made.

(c) No financial institution or trust company accepting a deposit pursuant to Section 2453 or 2454 is on notice of the existence of an order that the money or other property is subject to withdrawal only upon authorization of the court unless it has actual notice of the order. **Leg.H.** Enacted Stats 1990 ch 79 §14 (AB 759), operative July 1, 1991.

Prior Law: Former Prob C §2456, similar to the present section, was added Stats 1979 ch 726 §3, operative January 1, 1981, amended Stats 1987 ch 923 §75, operative July 1, 1988, and repealed Stats 1990 ch 79 §13, operative July 1, 1991.

§2457. Maintaining home of ward or conservatee and dependents

The guardian or conservator may maintain in good condition and repair the home or other dwelling of either or both of the following:

(a) The ward or conservatee.

(b) The persons legally entitled to such maintenance and repair from the ward or conservatee. **Leg.H.** Enacted Stats 1990 ch 79 §14 (AB 759), operative July 1, 1991.

Prior Law: Former Prob C §2457, similar to the present section, was added Stats 1979 ch 726 §3, operative January 1, 1981, and repealed Stats 1990 ch 79 §13, operative July 1, 1991.

§2458. Voting rights with respect to corporate shares or memberships or property

With respect to a share of stock of a domestic or foreign corporation held in the estate, a membership in a nonprofit corporation held in the estate, or other property held in the estate, a guardian or conservator may do any one or more of the following:

(a) Vote in person, and give proxies to exercise, any voting rights with respect to the share, membership, or other property.

(b) Waive notice of a meeting or give consent to the holding of a meeting.

(c) Authorize, ratify, approve, or confirm any action which could be taken by shareholders, members, or property owners. **Leg.H.** Enacted Stats 1990 ch 79 §14 (AB 759), operative July 1, 1991.

Prior Law: Former Prob C §2458, similar to the present section, was added Stats 1979 ch 726 §3, operative January 1, 1981, and repealed Stats 1990 ch 79 §13, operative July 1, 1991.

§2459. Life insurance, medical, retirement, and other plans and benefits

(a) The guardian or conservator may obtain, continue, renew, modify, terminate, or otherwise deal in any of the following for the purpose of providing protection to the ward or conservatee or a person legally entitled to support from the ward or conservatee:

(1) Medical, hospital, and other health care policies, plans, or benefits.
(2) Disability policies, plans, or benefits.

(b) The conservator may continue in force any of the following in which the conservatee, or a person legally entitled to support, maintenance, or education from the conservatee, has or will have an interest:

(1) Life insurance policies, plans, or benefits.
(2) Annuity policies, plans, or benefits.
(3) Mutual fund and other dividend reinvestment plans.
(4) Retirement, profit-sharing, and employee welfare plans or benefits.

(c) The right to elect benefit or payment options, to terminate, to change beneficiaries or ownership, to assign rights, to borrow, or to receive cash value in return for a surrender of rights, or to take similar actions under any of the policies, plans, or benefits described in subdivision (b) may be exercised by the conservator only after authorization or direction by order of the court, except as permitted in Section 2544.5. To obtain such an order, the conservator or other interested person shall petition under Article 10 (commencing with Section 2580).

(d) Notwithstanding subdivision (c), unless the court otherwise orders, the conservator without authorization of the court may borrow on the loan value of an insurance policy to pay the current premiums to keep the policy in force if the conservatee followed that practice prior to the establishment of the conservatorship.

(e) The guardian may give the consent provided in Section 10112 of the Insurance Code without authorization of the court, but the guardian may use funds of the guardianship estate to effect or maintain in force a contract entered into by the ward under Section 10112 of the Insurance Code only after authorization by order of the court. To obtain such an order, the guardian, the ward, or any other interested person shall file a petition showing that it is in the best interest of the ward or of the guardianship estate to do so. Notice of the hearing on the petition shall be given for the period and in the manner provided in Chapter 3 (commencing with Section 1460) of Part 1.

(f) Nothing in this section limits the power of the guardian or conservator to make investments as otherwise authorized by this division. **Leg.H.** Enacted Stats 1990 ch 79 §14 (AB 759), operative July 1, 1991. Amended Stats 1996 ch 86 §1 (AB 2146).

Prior Law: Former Prob C §2459, similar to the present section, was added Stats 1979 ch 726 §3, operative January 1, 1981, and repealed Stats 1990 ch 79 §13, operative July 1, 1991.

§2460. Liability and casualty insurance

The guardian or conservator may insure:

(a) Property of the estate against loss or damage.
(b) The ward or conservatee, the guardian or conservator, and all or any part of the estate against liability to third persons. **Leg.H.** Enacted Stats 1990 ch 79 §14 (AB 759), operative July 1, 1991.

Prior Law: Former Prob C §2460, similar to the present section, was added Stats 1979 ch 726 §3, operative January 1, 1981, and repealed Stats 1990 ch 79 §13, operative July 1, 1991.

§2461. Taxes and tax returns

(a) The guardian or conservator may prepare, execute, and file tax returns for the ward or conservatee and for the estate and may exercise options and elections and claim exemptions for the ward or conservatee and for the estate under the applicable tax laws.

(b) Notwithstanding Section 2502, the guardian or conservator may pay, contest, and compromise taxes, penalties, and assessments upon the property of the estate and income and other taxes payable or claimed to be payable by the ward or conservatee or the estate. **Leg.H.** Enacted Stats 1990 ch 79 §14 (AB 759), operative July 1, 1991.

Prior Law: Former Prob C §2461, similar to the present section, was added Stats 1979 ch 726 §3, operative January 1, 1981, and repealed Stats 1990 ch 79 §13, operative July 1, 1991.

§2462. Representation in actions and proceedings

Subject to Section 2463, unless another person is appointed for that purpose, the guardian or conservator may:

(a) Commence and maintain actions and proceedings for the benefit of the ward or conservatee or the estate.
(b) Defend actions and proceedings against the ward or conservatee, the guardian or conservator, or the estate.
(c) File a petition commencing a case under Title 11 of the United States Code (Bankruptcy) on behalf of the ward or conservatee. **Leg.H.** Enacted Stats 1990 ch 79 §14 (AB 759), operative July 1, 1991.

Prior Law: Former Prob C §2462, similar to the present section, was added Stats 1979 ch 726 §3, operative January 1, 1981, and repealed Stats 1990 ch 79 §13, operative July 1, 1991.

§2463. Partition actions

(a) The guardian or conservator may bring an action against the other cotenants for partition of any property in which the ward or conservatee has an undivided interest if the court has first made an order authorizing the guardian or conservator to do so. The court may make the order ex parte on a petition filed by the guardian or conservator.

(b) The guardian or conservator may consent and agree, without an action, to a partition of the property and to the part to be set off to the estate, and may execute deeds or conveyances to the owners of the remaining interests of the parts to which they may be respectively entitled, if the court has made an order under Article 5 (commencing with Section 2500) authorizing the guardian or conservator to do so.

(c) If the ward or conservatee, or the guardian or conservator in that capacity, is made a defendant in a partition action, the guardian or conservator may defend the action without authorization of the court.

(d) If the subject property is the conservatee's present or former personal residence, the powers granted pursuant to subdivisions (a) and (b) of this section are subject to the requirements of Sections 2352.5, 2540, 2541, and 2541.5, which govern the sale and partition of a conservatee's personal residence. **Leg.H.** Enacted Stats 1990 ch 79 §14 (AB 759), operative July 1, 1991. Amended Stats 2022 ch 91 §1 (SB 1005), effective January 1, 2023.

Prior Law: Former Prob C §2463, similar to the present section, was added Stats 1979 ch 726 §3, operative January 1, 1981, and repealed Stats 1990 ch 79 §13, operative July 1, 1991.

§2464. Acceptance of deed in lieu of foreclosure or trustee's sale

(a) If it is to the advantage of the estate to accept a deed to property which is subject to a mortgage or deed of trust in lieu of foreclosure of the mortgage or sale under the deed of trust, the guardian or conservator may, after authorization by order of the court and upon such terms and conditions as may be imposed by the court, accept a deed conveying the property to the ward or conservatee.

(b) To obtain an order under this section, the guardian or conservator shall file a petition showing the advantage to the estate of accepting the deed. Notice of the hearing on the petition shall be given for the period and in the manner provided in Chapter 3 (commencing with Section 1460) of Part 1.

(c) The court shall make an order under this section only if the advantage to the estate of accepting the deed is shown by clear and convincing evidence. **Leg.H.** Enacted Stats 1990 ch 79 §14 (AB 759), operative July 1, 1991.

Prior Law: Former Prob C §2464, similar to the present section, was added Stats 1979 ch 726 §3, operative January 1, 1981, and repealed Stats 1990 ch 79 §13, operative July 1, 1991.

§2465. Abandonment of valueless property

The guardian or conservator may dispose of or abandon valueless property. **Leg.H.** Enacted Stats 1990 ch 79 §14 (AB 759), operative July 1, 1991.

Prior Law: Former Prob C §2465, similar to the present section, was added Stats 1979 ch 726 §3, operative January 1, 1981, and repealed Stats 1990 ch 79 §13, operative July 1, 1991.

§2466. Advances by guardian or conservator

The guardian or conservator may advance the guardian's or conservator's own funds for the benefit of the ward or conservatee or the estate and may reimburse the advance out of the income and principal of the estate first available. With court authorization or approval, interest on the amount advanced may be allowed at the legal rate payable on judgments. **Leg.H.** Enacted Stats 1990 ch 79 §14 (AB 759), operative July 1, 1991.

Prior Law: Former Prob C §2466, similar to the present section, was added Stats 1979 ch 726 §3, operative January 1, 1981, and repealed Stats 1990 ch 79 §13, operative July 1, 1991.

§2467. Care of estate after death of ward or conservatee

(a) The guardian or conservator continues to have the duty of custody and conservation of the estate after the death of the ward or conservatee pending the delivery thereof to the personal representative of the ward's or conservatee's estate or other disposition according to law.

(b) The guardian or conservator has such powers as are granted to a guardian or conservator under this division as are necessary for the performance of the duty imposed by subdivision (a). **Leg.H.** Enacted Stats 1990 ch 79 §14 (AB 759), operative July 1, 1991.

Prior Law: Former Prob C §2467, similar to the present section, was added Stats 1979 ch 726 §3, operative January 1, 1981, and repealed Stats 1990 ch 79 §13, operative July 1, 1991.

§2468. Petition for practice administrator for disabled attorney

(a) The conservator of the estate of a disabled attorney who was engaged in the practice of law at the time of his or her disability, or other person interested in the estate, may bring a petition seeking the appointment of an active member of the State Bar of California to take control of the files and assets of the practice of the disabled member.

(b) The petition may be filed and heard on such notice that the court determines is in the best interests of the persons interested in the estate of the disabled member. If the petition alleges that the immediate appointment of a practice administrator is required to safeguard the interests of the estate, the court may dispense with notice provided that the conservator is the petitioner or has joined in the petition or has otherwise waived notice of hearing on the petition.

(c) The petition shall indicate the powers sought for the practice administrator from the list of powers set forth in Section 6185 of the Business and Professions Code. These powers shall be specifically listed in the order appointing the practice administrator.

(d) The petition shall allege the value of the assets that are to come under the control of the practice administrator, including but not limited by the amount of funds in all accounts used by the disabled member. The court shall require the filing of a surety bond in the amount of the value of the personal property to be filed with the court by the practice administrator. No action may be taken by the practice administrator unless a bond has been duly filed with the court.

(e) The practice administrator shall not be the attorney representing the conservator.

(f) The court shall appoint the attorney nominated by the disabled member in a writing, including but not limited to the disabled member's will, unless the court concludes that the appointment of the nominated person would be contrary to the best interests of the estate or would create a conflict of interest with any of the clients of the disabled member.

(g) The practice administrator shall be compensated only upon order of the court making the appointment for his or her reasonable and necessary services. The law practice shall be the source of the compensation for the practice administrator unless the assets are insufficient, in which case, the compensation of the practice administrator shall be charged against the assets of the estate as a cost of administration. The practice administrator shall also be entitled to reimbursement of his or her costs.

(h) Upon conclusion of the services of the practice administrator, the practice administrator shall render an accounting and petition for its approval by the superior court making the appointment. Upon settlement of the accounting, the practice administrator shall be discharged and the surety on his or her bond exonerated.

(i) If the court appointing the practice administrator determines upon petition that the disabled attorney has recovered his or her capacity to resume his or her law practice, the appointment of a practice administrator shall forthwith terminate and the disabled attorney shall be restored to his or her practice.

(j) For purposes of this section, the person appointed to take control of the practice of the disabled member shall be referred to as the "practice administrator" and the conservatee shall be referred to as the "disabled member." **Leg.H.** Added Stats 1998 ch 682 §4 (AB 2069).

§2469. Incapacitated professional fiduciary

(a) Commencing January 1, 2024, when a professional fiduciary becomes incapacitated and a vacancy exists, the incapacitated fiduciary's conservator, agent under a power of attorney for asset management, trustee, or interested person may petition for the appointment of one or more individuals qualified to act as a professional fiduciary under the Professional Fiduciaries Act (Chapter 6 (commencing with Section 6500) of Division 3 of the Business and Professions Code) as a professional fiduciary practice administrator to take control of the incapacitated professional fiduciary's files and to be appointed as temporary successor as to those matters for which a vacancy exists as a result of the professional fiduciary's incapacity.

(b) The petition shall request an order appointing a professional fiduciary practice administrator as temporary successor, with all of the powers and duties held by the incapacitated fiduciary, in each matter in which the incapacitated fiduciary was acting in a representative capacity, including guardianships of the estate, conservatorships of the person and the estate, decedent's estates, court-supervised trusts, and non-court-supervised trusts.

(c) The court shall require the professional fiduciary practice administrator to file a surety bond in each matter in which the professional fiduciary practice administrator is appointed temporary successor, in the amount currently required of the incapacitated fiduciary or in another amount as the court deems appropriate.

(d) The court may appoint as the professional fiduciary practice administrator the professional fiduciary nominated by the incapacitated fiduciary in a writing, including, but not limited to, the incapacitated fiduciary's will or trust, or in the absence thereof, the person nominated by the person having legal standing to act on behalf of the incapacitated professional fiduciary. The court shall not make the appointment if the court concludes that the appointment of the nominated person would be contrary to the best interests of, or would create a conflict of interest with, any interested party in a matter in which the incapacitated fiduciary was acting in a fiduciary capacity.

(e) The appointment of the professional fiduciary practice administrator as temporary successor shall terminate, in each of the matters in which the professional fiduciary practice administrator was appointed as temporary successor, 45 days after the entry of the order appointing the professional fiduciary practice administrator, or earlier if another person is appointed.

(f) Notice of the hearing on the petition for appointment of a professional fiduciary practice administrator as temporary successor shall be given to all persons entitled to notice in each of the matters which are the subject of the petition. The court may dispense with notice if the petition alleges that the immediate appointment of a professional fiduciary practice administrator is required to safeguard the interests of an individual or an asset in a matter in which the incapacitated fiduciary was acting in a representative capacity.

(g) The professional fiduciary practice administrator shall be compensated for services provided and reimbursement of costs incurred in each matter solely from the assets of that matter subject to the provisions of the applicable document or as determined by the court, and in no event more than the incapacitated fiduciary would have been paid.

(h) The professional fiduciary practice administrator appointed in a given matter shall do all of the following:

(1) File a copy of the order appointing the professional fiduciary practice administrator as temporary successor in each of the matters in which the court appoints the professional fiduciary practice administrator as temporary successor.

(2) Take control and review all files and writings maintained by the incapacitated fiduciary for matters in which the incapacitated fiduciary was acting in a representative capacity.

(3) Within 15 days after the entry of the order appointing the professional fiduciary practice administrator as temporary successor, provide written notice to all interested parties as to each matter in which the incapacitated fiduciary was acting in a representative capacity who can be reasonably ascertained and located to inform those parties of the appointment of the professional fiduciary practice administrator as temporary successor. The notice shall advise the interested parties of the

necessity and process for the appointment of a permanent successor, which shall include the following:

(A) The right of the parties to petition the court for the appointment of a permanent successor.

(B) The right of any interested party to nominate an individual to act as permanent successor, and then the obligation of the professional fiduciary practice administrator to petition for the appointment of the individual nominated, provided an interested party provides the professional fiduciary practice administrator with the name of their nominee within 15 days after the date notice was given.

(C) The ability of the professional fiduciary practice administrator, in the event none of the interested parties act within the time prescribed, under subparagraph (A) or (B), to petition the court for appointment of a permanent successor.

(4) Upon the court's appointment of a permanent successor, the professional fiduciary practice administrator shall file an account and report on behalf of the incapacitated fiduciary for any period of time the incapacitated fiduciary would have been required to account, as well as for the period of time the professional fiduciary practice administrator served as temporary successor. As part of that account and report, the professional fiduciary practice administrator may request compensation both on behalf of the incapacitated fiduciary, for services rendered prior to their incapacity, and on their own behalf for services rendered after the incapacitated fiduciary's incapacity, as temporary successor, subject to any limitation on fees and costs that existed for the incapacitated fiduciary, and may request discharge and exoneration of bond. The account filed for the period during which the matter was administered by the now incapacitated fiduciary may be verified on information and belief.

(5) Comply with any other obligations imposed by the court.

(i) Each of the time periods prescribed in this section may be extended by the court if the court determines that good cause exists, and if the court determines that the extension is in the best interest of the minor, the conservatee, the decedent's estate, or the current income beneficiaries under a trust, as applicable.

(j) For purposes of this section, the following definitions apply:

(1) "Incapacitated" means that the person is unable to fulfill their duties as a professional fiduciary because of either temporary or permanent disability, incapacity, or absence.

(2) "Professional fiduciary practice administrator" means the person or persons appointed pursuant to this section to take over the responsibilities from the incapacitated fiduciary.

(3) "Vacancy" means that the instrument under which the incapacitated fiduciary was acting does not name a successor to fill the vacancy, the instrument under which the incapacitated fiduciary was acting does not provide a nonjudicial method to fill the vacancy, or a cofiduciary, authorized to act solely, was not acting with the incapacitated fiduciary.

(k) This section does not limit the authority granted to the court under subdivision (j) of Section 2250, Section 8523, and subdivision (e) of Section 15642.

(*l*) The Judicial Council shall create or revise any forms or rules necessary to implement this section no later than January 1, 2024. **Leg.H.** Added Stats 2022 ch 612 §4 (SB 1024), effective January 1, 2023. Amended Stats 2023 ch 478 §58 (AB 1756), effective January 1, 2024.

ARTICLE 5
Compromise of Claims and Actions; Extension, Renewal, or Modification of Obligations

Authority to compromise claims and actions and to extend, renew, or modify obligations. §2500.
Matters relating to real property. §2501.
Compromise in excess of specified amounts. §2502.
Compromise of claim of ward or conservatee against guardian or conservator or attorney for guardian or conservator; Modification of terms of obligation of guardian or conservator or attorney owing to ward or conservatee or estate. §2503.
Support, wrongful death, and personal injury claims. §2504.
Court from which approval is to be obtained. §2505.
Petition for approval of court in guardianship or conservatorship proceeding. §2506.
When another statute controls. §2507.

§2500. Authority to compromise claims and actions and to extend, renew, or modify obligations

(a) Unless this article or some other applicable statute requires court authorization or approval, if it is to the advantage of the estate, the guardian or conservator may do any of the following without court authorization, instruction, approval, or confirmation:

(1) Compromise or settle a claim, action, or proceeding by or for the benefit of, or against, the ward or conservatee, the guardian or conservator, or the estate, including the giving of a covenant not to sue.

(2) Extend, renew, or in any manner modify the terms of an obligation owing to or running in favor of the ward or conservatee or the estate.

(b) Nothing in this section precludes the guardian or conservator from seeking court authorization, instructions, approval, or confirmation pursuant to Section 2403.

(c) Upon petition of the ward or conservatee, a creditor, or any interested person, or upon the court's own motion, the court may limit the authority of the guardian or conservator under subdivision (a). Notice of the hearing on the petition shall be given for the period and in the manner provided in Chapter 3 (commencing with Section 1460) of Part 1. **Leg.H.** Enacted Stats 1990 ch 79 §14 (AB 759), operative July 1, 1991.

Prior Law: Former Prob C §2500, similar to the present section, was added Stats 1979 ch 726 §3, operative January 1, 1981, and repealed Stats 1990 ch 79 §13, operative July 1, 1991.

§2501. Matters relating to real property

(a) Except as provided in subdivision (b), court approval is required for a compromise, settlement, extension, renewal, or modification which affects any of the following:

(1) Title to real property.

(2) An interest in real property or a lien or encumbrance on real property.

(3) An option to purchase real property or an interest in real property.

(b) If it is to the advantage of the estate, the guardian or conservator without prior court approval may extend, renew, or modify a lease of real property in either of the following cases:

(1) Where under the lease as extended, renewed, or modified the rental does not exceed five thousand dollars ($5,000) a month and the term does not exceed two years.

(2) Where the lease is from month to month, regardless of the amount of the rental.

(c) For the purposes of subdivision (b), if the lease as extended, renewed, or modified gives the lessee the right to extend the term of the lease, the length of the term shall be considered as though the right to extend had been exercised. **Leg.H.** Enacted Stats 1990 ch 79 §14 (AB 759), operative July 1, 1991. Amended Stats 1990 ch 710 §10 (SB 1775), operative July 1, 1991.

Prior Law: Former Prob C §2501, similar to the present section, was added Stats 1979 ch 726 §3, operative January 1, 1981, amended Stats 1989 ch 21 §10, effective May 25, 1989, operative July 1, 1989, and repealed Stats 1990 ch 79 §13, operative July 1, 1991.

§2502. Compromise in excess of specified amounts

Court approval is required for a compromise or settlement of a matter when the transaction requires the transfer or encumbrance of property of the estate, or the creation of an unsecured liability of the estate, or both, in an amount or value in excess of twenty-five thousand dollars ($25,000). **Leg.H.** Enacted Stats 1990 ch 79 §14 (AB 759), operative July 1, 1991.

Prior Law: Former Prob C §2502, similar to the present section, was added Stats 1979 ch 726 §3, operative January 1, 1981, and repealed Stats 1990 ch 79 §13, operative July 1, 1991.

§2503. Compromise of claim of ward or conservatee against guardian or conservator or attorney for guardian or conservator; Modification of terms of obligation of guardian or conservator or attorney owing to ward or conservatee or estate

Court approval is required for any of the following:

(a) A compromise or settlement of a claim by the ward or conservatee against the guardian or conservator or against the attorney for the guardian or conservator, whether or not the claim arises out of the administration of the estate.

(b) An extension, renewal, or modification of the terms of a debt or similar obligation of the guardian or conservator, or of the attorney for the guardian or conservator, owing to or running in favor of the ward or conservatee or the estate. **Leg.H.** Enacted Stats 1990 ch 79 §14 (AB 759), operative July 1, 1991.

Prior Law: Former Prob C §2503, similar to the present section, was added Stats 1979 ch 726 §3, operative January 1, 1981, and repealed Stats 1990 ch 79 §13, operative July 1, 1991.

§2504. Support, wrongful death, and personal injury claims

Court approval is required for the compromise or settlement of any of the following:

(a) A claim for the support, maintenance, or education of (1) the ward or conservatee, or (2) a person whom the ward or conservatee is legally obligated to support, maintain, or educate, against any other person (including, but not limited to, the spouse or parent of the ward or the spouse, domestic partner, parent, or adult child of the conservatee).

(b) A claim of the ward or conservatee for wrongful death.

(c) A claim of the ward or conservatee for physical or nonphysical harm to the person. **Leg.H.** Enacted Stats 1990 ch 79 §14 (AB 759), operative July 1, 1991. Amended Stats 2001 ch 893 §36 (AB 25), effective January 1, 2002.

Prior Law: Former Prob C §2504, similar to the present section, was added Stats 1979 ch 726 §3, operative January 1, 1981, and repealed Stats 1990 ch 79 §13, operative July 1, 1991.

§2505. Court from which approval is to be obtained

(a) Subject to subdivision (c), where the claim or matter is the subject of a pending action or proceeding, the court approval required by this article shall be obtained from the court in which the action or proceeding is pending.

(b) Where the claim or matter is not the subject of a pending action or proceeding, the court approval required by this article shall be obtained from one of the following:

(1) The court in which the guardianship or conservatorship proceeding is pending.

(2) The superior court of the county where the ward or conservatee or guardian or conservator resides at the time the petition for approval is filed.

(3) The superior court of any county where a suit on the claim or matter properly could be brought.

(c) Where the claim or matter is the subject of a pending action or proceeding that is not brought in a court of this state, court approval required by this article shall be obtained from either of the following:

(1) The court in which the action or proceeding is pending.

(2) The court in which the guardianship or conservatorship proceeding is pending.

(d)(1) Subdivisions (a), (b), and (c) do not apply to a conservatorship that is registered in this state pursuant to Article 4 (commencing with Section 2011) of Chapter 8 of Part 3.

(2) Except as provided in paragraph (3), when a conservatorship is registered in this state pursuant to Article 4 (commencing with Section 2011) of Chapter 8 of Part 3, the court approval required by this article shall be obtained in accordance with Section 2016.

(3) Notwithstanding Section 2016, when a conservatorship is registered in this state pursuant to Article 4 (commencing with Section 2011) of Chapter 8 of Part 3, and the claim or matter in question is the subject of a pending action or proceeding that is not brought in a court of this state, the court approval required by this article may be obtained from the court in which the action or proceeding is pending. **Leg.H.** Enacted Stats 1990 ch 79 §14 (AB 759), operative July 1, 1991. Amended Stats 2014 ch 553 §25 (SB 940), effective January 1, 2015, operative January 1, 2016.

Prior Law: Former Prob C §2505, similar to the present section, was added Stats 1979 ch 726 §3, operative January 1, 1981, and repealed Stats 1990 ch 79 §13, operative July 1, 1991.

§2506. Petition for approval of court in guardianship or conservatorship proceeding

Where approval of the court in which the guardianship or conservatorship proceeding is pending is required under this article, the guardian or conservator shall file a petition with the court showing the advantage of the compromise, settlement, extension, renewal, or modification to the ward or conservatee and the estate. Notice of the hearing on the petition shall be given for the period and in the manner provided in Chapter 3 (commencing with Section 1460) of Part 1. **Leg.H.** Enacted Stats 1990 ch 79 §14 (AB 759), operative July 1, 1991.

Prior Law: Former Prob C §2506, similar to the present section, was added Stats 1979 ch 726 §3, operative January 1, 1981, and repealed Stats 1990 ch 79 §13, operative July 1, 1991.

§2507. When another statute controls

Notwithstanding Sections 2500 to 2506, inclusive:

(a) Whenever another statute requires, provides a procedure for, or dispenses with court approval of a compromise, settlement, extension, renewal, or modification, the provisions of that statute govern any case to which that statute applies.

(b) Whenever another statute provides that a compromise or settlement of an administrative proceeding is not valid unless approved in such proceeding, the approval is governed by that statute, and approval in the guardianship or conservatorship proceeding is not required. **Leg.H.** Enacted Stats 1990 ch 79 §14 (AB 759), operative July 1, 1991.

Prior Law: Former Prob C §2507, similar to the present section, was added Stats 1979 ch 726 §3, operative January 1, 1981, and repealed Stats 1990 ch 79 §13, operative July 1, 1991.

ARTICLE 6
Conveyance or Transfer of Property Claimed to Belong to Ward or Conservatee or Other Person [Repealed]

§2520. [Section repealed 2002]

Leg.H. Enacted Stats 1990 ch 79 §14 (AB 759), operative July 1, 1991. Repealed Stats 2001 ch 49 §2 (SB 669). The repealed section related to petition for order.

Prior Law: Former Prob C §2520, similar to the repealed section, was added Stats 1979 ch 726 §3, operative January 1, 1981, and repealed Stats 1990 ch 79 §13, operative July 1, 1991.

§2521. [Section repealed 2002]

Leg.H. Enacted Stats 1990 ch 79 §14 (AB 759), operative July 1, 1991. Repealed Stats 2001 ch 49 §2 (SB 669). The repealed section related to notice of hearing.

Prior Law: Former Prob C §2521, similar to the repealed section, was added Stats 1979 ch 726 §3, operative January 1, 1981, and repealed Stats 1990 ch 79 §13, operative July 1, 1991.

§2522. [Section repealed 2002]

Leg.H. Enacted Stats 1990 ch 79 §14 (AB 759), operative July 1, 1991. Repealed Stats 2001 ch 49 §2 (SB 669). The repealed section related to continuance for preparation for hearing.

Prior Law: Former Prob C §2522, similar to the repealed section, was added Stats 1979 ch 726 §3, operative January 1, 1981, and repealed Stats 1990 ch 79 §13, operative July 1, 1991.

§2524. [Section repealed 2002]

Leg.H. Enacted Stats 1990 ch 79 §14 (AB 759), operative July 1, 1991. Repealed Stats 2001 ch 49 §2 (SB 669). The repealed section related to denial of petition if objection based on venue.

Prior Law: Former Prob C §2524, similar to the repealed section, was added Stats 1979 ch 726 §3, operative January 1, 1981, and repealed Stats 1990 ch 79 §13, operative July 1, 1991.

§2525. [Section repealed 2002]

Leg.H. Enacted Stats 1990 ch 79 §14 (AB 759), operative July 1, 1991. Repealed Stats 2001 ch 49 §2 (SB 669). The repealed section related to abatement of petition if civil action pending.

Prior Law: Former Prob C §2525, similar to the repealed section, was added Stats 1979 ch 726 §3, operative January 1, 1981, amended Stats 1987 ch 923 §76, operative July 1, 1988, and repealed Stats 1990 ch 79 §13, operative July 1, 1991.

§2526. [Section repealed 2002]

Leg.H. Enacted Stats 1990 ch 79 §14 (AB 759), operative July 1, 1991. Repealed Stats 2001 ch 49 §2 (SB 669). The repealed section related to denial of petition should matter be determined by civil action.

Prior Law: Former Prob C §2526, similar to the repealed section, was added Stats 1979 ch 726 §3, operative January 1, 1981, and repealed Stats 1990 ch 79 §13, operative July 1, 1991.

§2527. [Section repealed 2002]

Leg.H. Enacted Stats 1990 ch 79 §14 (AB 759), operative July 1, 1991. Repealed Stats 2001 ch 49 §2 (SB 669). The repealed section related to order.

Prior Law: Former Prob C §2527, similar to the repealed section, was added Stats 1979 ch 726 §3, operative January 1, 1981, and repealed Stats 1990 ch 79 §13, operative July 1, 1991.

§2528. [Section repealed 2002]

Leg.H. Enacted Stats 1990 ch 79 §14 (AB 759), operative July 1, 1991. Repealed Stats 2001 ch 49 §2 (SB 669). The repealed section related to execution of conveyance or transfer and effect of order.

Prior Law: Former Prob C §2528, similar to the repealed section, was added Stats 1979 ch 726 §3, operative January 1, 1981, and repealed Stats 1990 ch 79 §13, operative July 1, 1991.

§2529. [Section repealed 2002]

Leg.H. Added Stats 1994 ch 806 §17 (AB 3686). Repealed Stats 2001 ch 49 §2 (SB 669). The repealed section related to the disclosure to guardian or conservator by person in possession of personal property or document of title.

ARTICLE 7
Sales

Extent of court supervision. §2540.
Purposes for which sale or partition may be made. §2541.
Authorization of a conservator to sell or partition a conservatee's residence. § 2541.5.
Terms of sale. §2542.
Manner of sale. §2543.
Sales of securities not needing court supervision. §2544.
Mutual funds held without designation of beneficiary. §2544.5.
Sale or other disposition of tangible personal property not exceeding $5,000 in value. §2545.
Disposition of proceeds of sale. §2547.
Limitation of action to recover property sold. §2548.

§2540. Extent of court supervision

(a) Except as otherwise provided in Sections 2544 and 2545, and except for the sale of a conservatee's present or former personal residence as set forth in subdivision (b), sales of real or personal property of the estate under this article are subject to authorization, confirmation, or direction of the court, as provided in this article.

(b) In seeking authorization to sell a conservatee's present or former personal residence, consent and agree to partition of a conservatee's present or former personal residence, or bring an action for partition of a conservatee's present or former personal residence, the conservator shall notify the court that the present or former personal residence is proposed to be sold or partitioned and that the conservator has discussed the proposed sale or partition with the conservatee. The conservator shall inform the court whether the conservatee supports or is opposed to the proposed sale or partition and shall describe the circumstances that necessitate the proposed sale or partition, including whether the conservatee has the ability to live in the personal residence and why other alternatives, including, but not limited to, in-home care services, are not available. The court, in its discretion, may require the court investigator to discuss the proposed sale or partition with the conservatee.

(c) Notice under subdivision (b) shall be provided to the court before the conservator commits any significant resources to the proposed sale or partition of the residence, unless the conservator can establish that either the conservatee has the capacity to consent and unequivocally consents to the sale or partition, or there are exigent circumstances that require the conservator to commit resources to the sale or partition prior to court approval. **Leg.H.** Enacted Stats 1990 ch 79 §14 (AB 759), operative July 1, 1991. Amended Stats 2006 ch 490 §3 (SB 1116), effective January 1, 2007; Stats 2019 ch 847 §2 (SB 303), effective January 1, 2020; Stats 2022 ch 91 §2 (SB 1005), effective January 1, 2023.

Editor's Notes—2006 Note: This act, together with Senate Bill 1550, Senate Bill 1716, and Assembly Bill 1363, shall be known and may be cited as the Omnibus Conservatorship and Guardianship Reform Act of 2006. Stats 2006 ch 490 (SB 1116) §9.

Prior Law: Former Prob C §2540, similar to the present section, was added Stats 1979 ch 726 §3, operative January 1, 1981, amended Stats 1989 ch 1080 §11.5, and repealed Stats 1990 ch 79 §13, operative July 1, 1991.

§2541. Purposes for which sale or partition may be made

The guardian or conservator may sell real or personal property of the estate, consent and agree to partition of real or personal property of the estate, or bring an action for partition of real or personal property of the estate, in any of the following cases:

(a) If the income of the estate is insufficient for the comfortable and suitable support, maintenance, and education of the ward or conservatee (including care, treatment, and support of the ward or conservatee if a patient in a state hospital under the jurisdiction of the State Department of State Hospitals or the State Department of Developmental Services) or of those legally entitled to support, maintenance, or education from the ward or conservatee.

(b) If the sale or partition is necessary to pay the debts referred to in Sections 2430 and 2431.

(c) If the sale or partition is for the advantage, benefit, and best interest of (1) the ward or conservatee, (2) the estate, or (3) the ward or conservatee and those legally entitled to support, maintenance, or education from the ward or conservatee. **Leg.H.** Enacted Stats 1990 ch 79 §14 (AB 759), operative July 1, 1991. Amended Stats 2012 ch 440 §45 (AB 1488), effective September 22, 2012; Stats 2022 ch 91 §3 (SB 1005), effective January 1, 2023.

Prior Law: Former Prob C §2541, similar to the present section, was added Stats 1979 ch 726 §3, operative January 1, 1981, and repealed Stats 1990 ch 79 §13, operative July 1, 1991.

§ 2541.5. Authorization of a conservator to sell or partition a conservatee's residence

Notwithstanding Section 2541, the court may authorize a conservator to sell a conservatee's present or former personal residence, consent and agree to partition of a conservatee's present or former personal residence, or bring an action for partition of a conservatee's present or former personal residence, only if the court finds by clear and convincing evidence that the conservator demonstrated a compelling need to sell or partition the personal residence for the benefit of the conservatee. **Leg.H.** Added Stats 2019 ch 847 §3 (SB 303), effective January 1, 2020. Amended Stats 2022 ch 91 §4 (SB 1005), effective January 1, 2023.

§2542. Terms of sale

(a) All sales shall be for cash or for part cash and part deferred payments. Except as otherwise provided in Sections 2544 and 2545, the terms of sale are subject to the approval of the court.

(b) If real property is sold for part deferred payments, the guardian or conservator shall take the note of the purchaser for the unpaid portion of the purchase money, with a mortgage or deed of trust on the property to secure payment of the note. The mortgage or deed of trust shall be subject only to encumbrances existing at the date of sale and such other encumbrances as the court may approve.

(c) If real or personal property of the estate sold for part deferred payments consists of an undivided interest, a joint tenancy interest, or any other interest less than the entire ownership, and the owner or owners of the remaining interests in the property join in the sale, the note and deed of trust or mortgage may be made to the ward or conservatee and the other owner or owners. **Leg.H.** Enacted Stats 1990 ch 79 §14 (AB 759), operative July 1, 1991.

Prior Law: Former Prob C §2542, similar to the present section, was added Stats 1979 ch 726 §3, operative January 1, 1981, and repealed Stats 1990 ch 79 §13, operative July 1, 1991.

§2543. Manner of sale

(a) If estate property is required or permitted to be sold, the guardian or conservator may:

(1) Use discretion as to which property to sell first.

(2) Sell the entire interest of the estate in the property or any lesser interest therein.

(3) Sell the property either at public auction or private sale.

(b) Subject to Section 1469, unless otherwise specifically provided in this article, all proceedings concerning sales by guardians or conservators, publishing and posting notice of sale, reappraisal for sale, minimum offer price for the property, reselling the property, report of sale and petition for confirmation of sale, and notice and hearing of that petition, making orders authorizing sales, rejecting or confirming sales and reports of sales, ordering and making conveyances of property sold, and allowance of commissions, shall conform, as nearly as may be, to the provisions of this code concerning sales by a personal representative, including, but not limited to, Articles 6 (commencing with Section 10300), 7 (commencing with Section 10350), 8 (commencing with Section 10360), and 9 (commencing with Section 10380) of Chapter 18 of Part 5 of Division 7. The provisions concerning sales by a personal representative as described in the Independent Administration of Estates Act, Part 6 (commencing with Section 10400) of Division 7 shall not apply to this subdivision.

(c) Notwithstanding Section 10309, if the last appraisal of the conservatee's personal residence was conducted more than six months prior to the confirmation hearing, a new appraisal shall be required prior to the confirmation hearing, unless the court finds that it is in the best interests of the conservatee to rely on an appraisal of the personal residence that was conducted not more than one year prior to the confirmation hearing.

(d) The clerk of the court shall cause notice to be posted pursuant to subdivision (b) only in the following cases:

(1) If posting of notice of hearing is required on a petition for the confirmation of a sale of real or personal property of the estate.

(2) If posting of notice of a sale governed by Section 10250 (sales of personal property) is required or authorized.

(3) If posting of notice is ordered by the court. **Leg.H.** Enacted Stats 1990 ch 79 §14 (AB 759), operative July 1, 1991. Amended Stats 2006 ch 490 §4 (SB 1116), effective January 1, 2007; Stats 2007 ch 553 §17 (AB 1727), effective January 1, 2008.

2006 Note: This act, together with Senate Bill 1550, Senate Bill 1716, and Assembly Bill 1363, shall be known and may be cited as the Omnibus Conservatorship and Guardianship Reform Act of 2006. Stats 2006 ch 490 (SB 1116) §9.

Prior Law: Former Prob C §2543, similar to the present section, was added Stats 1979 ch 726 §3, operative January 1, 1981, amended Stats 1987 ch 923 §77, operative July 1, 1988, and repealed Stats 1990 ch 79 §13, operative July 1, 1991.

§2544. Sales of securities not needing court supervision

(a) Except as specifically limited by order of the court, subject to Section 2541, the guardian or conservator may sell securities without authorization, confirmation, or direction of the court if any of the following conditions is satisfied:

(1) The securities are to be sold on an established stock or bond exchange.

(2) The securities to be sold are securities designated as a national market system security on an interdealer quotation system or subsystem thereof, by the National Association of Securities Dealers, Inc., sold through a broker-dealer registered under the Securities Exchange Act of 1934 during the regular course of business of the broker-dealer.

(3) The securities are to be directly redeemed by the issuer thereof.

(b) Section 2543 does not apply to sales under this section. **Leg.H.** Enacted Stats 1990 ch 79 §14 (AB 759), operative July 1, 1991. Amended Stats 1996 ch 86 §2 (AB 2146).

Prior Law: Former Prob C §2544, similar to the present section, was added Stats 1979 ch 726 §3, operative January 1, 1981, and repealed Stats 1990 ch 79 §13, operative July 1, 1991.

§2544.5. Mutual funds held without designation of beneficiary

Except as specifically limited by the court, subject to Section 2541, the guardian or conservator may sell mutual funds held without designation of a beneficiary without authorization, confirmation, or direction of the court. Section 2543 does not apply to sales under this section. **Leg.H.** Added Stats 1996 ch 86 §2.5 (AB 2146).

§2545. Sale or other disposition of tangible personal property not exceeding $5,000 in value

(a) Subject to subdivisions (b) and (c) and to Section 2541, the guardian or conservator may sell or exchange tangible personal property of the estate without authorization, confirmation, or direction of the court.

(b) The aggregate of the sales or exchanges made during any calendar year under this section may not exceed five thousand dollars ($5,000).

(c) A sale or exchange of personal effects or of furniture or furnishings used for personal, family, or household purposes may be made under this section only if:

(1) In the case of a guardianship, the ward is under the age of 14 or, if 14 years of age or over, consents to the sale or exchange.

(2) In the case of a conservatorship, the conservatee either (i) consents to the sale or exchange or (ii) the conservatee does not have legal capacity to give such consent.

(d) Failure of the guardian or conservator to observe the limitations of subdivision (b) or (c) does not invalidate the title of, or impose any liability upon, a third person who acts in good faith and without actual notice of the lack of authority of the guardian or conservator.

(e) Subdivision (b) of Section 2543 does not apply to sales under this section. **Leg.H.** Enacted Stats 1990 ch 79 §14 (AB 759), operative July 1, 1991.

Prior Law: Former Prob C §2545, similar to the present section, was added Stats 1979 ch 726 §3, operative January 1, 1981, and repealed Stats 1990 ch 79 §13, operative July 1, 1991.

§2547. Disposition of proceeds of sale

The guardian or conservator shall apply the proceeds of the sale to the purposes for which it was made, as far as necessary, and the residue, if any, shall be managed as the other property of the estate. **Leg.H.** Enacted Stats 1990 ch 79 §14 (AB 759), operative July 1, 1991.

Prior Law: Former Prob C §2547, similar to the present section, was added Stats 1979 ch 726 §3, operative January 1, 1981, and repealed Stats 1990 ch 79 §13, operative July 1, 1991.

§2548. Limitation of action to recover property sold

No action for the recovery of any property sold by a guardian or conservator may be maintained by the ward or conservatee or by any person claiming under the ward or conservatee unless commenced within the later of the following times:

(a) Three years after the termination of the guardianship or conservatorship.

(b) When a legal disability to sue exists by reason of minority or otherwise at the time the cause of action accrues, within three years after the removal thereof. **Leg.H.** Enacted Stats 1990 ch 79 §14 (AB 759), operative July 1, 1991.

Prior Law: Former Prob C §2548, similar to the present section, was added Stats 1979 ch 726 §3, operative January 1, 1981, and repealed Stats 1990 ch 79 §13, operative July 1, 1991.

ARTICLE 8
Notes, Mortgages, Leases, Conveyances, and Exchanges

Extent of court supervision. §2550.
Borrowing money and giving security therefor. §2551.
Refinancing or improving or repairing property. §2552.
Lease term. §2552.5.
Order authorizing lease required. §2553.
Terms and conditions of leases. §2554.
Leases permitted without court authorization. §2555.
Dedication or conveyance of real property or easement with or without consideration. §2556.
Exchange of property. §2557.

§2550. Extent of court supervision

Except as otherwise provided by statute, a guardian or conservator may borrow money, lend money, give security, lease, convey, or exchange property of the estate, or engage in any other transaction under this article only after authorization by order of the court. Such an order may be obtained in the manner provided in this article. **Leg.H.** Enacted Stats 1990 ch 79 §14 (AB 759), operative July 1, 1991. Amended Stats 1992 ch 572 §5 (SB 1455).

Prior Law: Former Prob C §2550, similar to the present section, was added Stats 1979 ch 726 §3, operative January 1, 1981, and repealed Stats 1990 ch 79 §13, operative July 1, 1991.

§2551. Borrowing money and giving security therefor

(a) In any case described in Section 2541 or Section 2552, the guardian or conservator, after authorization by order of the court, may borrow money upon a note, either unsecured or to be secured by a security interest or other lien on the personal property of the estate or any part thereof or to be secured by a mortgage or deed of trust on the real property of the estate or any part thereof. The guardian or conservator shall apply the money to the purpose specified in the order.

(b) To obtain an order under this section, the guardian or conservator, the ward or conservatee, or any other interested person may file a petition with the court. The petition shall state the purpose for which the order is sought, the necessity for or advantage to accrue from the order, the amount of money proposed to be borrowed, the rate of interest to be paid, the length of time the note is to run, and a general description of the property proposed to be mortgaged or subjected to a deed of trust or other lien. Notice of the hearing on the petition shall be given for the period and in the manner provided in Chapter 3 (commencing with Section 1460) of Part 1.

(c) The court may require such additional proof of the fairness and feasibility of the transaction as the court determines is necessary. If the required showing is made, the court may make an order authorizing the transaction.

The court in its order may do any one or more of the following:

(1) Order that the amount specified in the petition, or a lesser amount, be borrowed.

(2) Prescribe the maximum rate of interest and the period of the loan.

(3) Require that the interest and the whole or any part of the principal be paid from time to time out of the estate or any part thereof.

(4) Require that the personal property used as security or any buildings on real property to be mortgaged or subjected to the deed of trust be insured for the further security of the lender and that the premiums be paid out of the estate.

(5) Specify the purpose for which the money to be borrowed is to be applied.

(6) Prescribe such other terms and conditions concerning the transaction as the court determines to be to the advantage of the estate.

(d) The note and the mortgage or deed of trust, if any, shall be signed by the guardian or conservator.

(e) Jurisdiction of the court to administer the estate of the ward or conservatee is effectual to vest the court with jurisdiction to make the order for the note and for the security interest, lien, mortgage, or deed of trust. This jurisdiction shall conclusively inure to the benefit of the owner of the security interest or lien, mortgagee named in the mortgage, or the trustee and beneficiary named in the deed of trust, and their heirs and assigns. No omission, error, or irregularity in the proceedings shall impair or invalidate the proceedings or the note, security interest, lien, mortgage, or deed of trust given pursuant to an order under this section.

(f) Upon any foreclosure or sale under a security interest, lien, mortgage, or deed of trust described in subdivision (a), if the proceeds of the sale of the encumbered property are insufficient to pay the note, the security interest, lien, mortgage, or deed of trust, and the costs or expenses of sale, no judgment or claim for any deficiency may be had or allowed against the ward or conservatee or the estate. **Leg.H.** Enacted Stats 1990 ch 79 §14 (AB 759), operative July 1, 1991.

Prior Law: Former Prob C §2551, similar to the present section and Prob C §2110, was added Stats 1979 ch 726 §3, operative January 1, 1981, and repealed Stats 1990 ch 79 §13, operative July 1, 1991.

§2552. Refinancing or improving or repairing property

(a) The guardian or conservator may give a security interest or other lien upon the personal property of the estate or any part thereof or a mortgage or deed of trust upon the real property of the estate or any part thereof, after authorization by order of the court as provided in Section 2551, for any of the following purposes:

(1) To pay, reduce, extend, or renew a security interest, lien, mortgage, or deed of trust already existing on property of the estate.

(2) To improve, use, operate, or preserve the property proposed to be mortgaged or subjected to a deed of trust, or some part thereof.

(b) If property of the estate consists of an undivided interest in real or personal property, or any other interest therein less than the entire ownership, upon a showing that it would be to the advantage of the estate to borrow money to improve, use, operate, or preserve the property jointly with the owners of the other interests therein, or to pay, reduce, extend, or renew a security interest, lien, mortgage, or deed of trust already existing on all of the property, the guardian or conservator, after authorization by order of the court as provided in Section 2551, may join with the owners of the other interests in the borrowing of money and the execution of a joint and several note and such security interest, lien, mortgage, or deed of trust as may be required to secure the payment of the note. The note may be for such sum as is required for the purpose.

(c) No omission, error, or irregularity in the proceedings under this section shall impair or invalidate the proceedings or the note, security interest, lien, mortgage, or deed of trust given pursuant to an order made under this section. **Leg.H.** Enacted Stats 1990 ch 79 §14 (AB 759), operative July 1, 1991.

Prior Law: Former Prob C §2552, similar to the present section, was added Stats 1979 ch 726 §3, operative January 1, 1981, and repealed Stats 1990 ch 79 §13, operative July 1, 1991.

§2552.5. Lease term

For the purpose of this article, if a lease gives the lessee the right to extend the term of the lease, the length of the term shall be considered as though the right to extend had been exercised. **Leg.H.** Enacted Stats 1990 ch 79 §14 (AB 759), operative July 1, 1991.

§2553. Order authorizing lease required

(a) Except as provided in Section 2555, leases may be executed by the guardian or conservator with respect to the property of the estate only after authorization by order of the court.

(b) To obtain an order under this section, the guardian or conservator or any interested person may file a petition with the court. The petition shall state (1) a general description of the property proposed to be leased, (2) the term, rental, and general conditions of the proposed lease, and (3) the advantage to the estate to accrue from giving the lease. If the lease is proposed to be for a term longer than 10 years, the petition shall also state facts showing the need for the longer lease and its advantage to the estate. Notice of the hearing on the petition shall be given for the period and in the manner provided in Chapter 3 (commencing with Section 1460) of Part 1.

(c) At the hearing, the court shall entertain and consider any other offer made in good faith at the hearing to lease the same property on more favorable terms. If the court is satisfied that it will be to the advantage of the estate, the court shall make an order authorizing the guardian or conservator to make the lease to the person and on the terms and conditions stated in the order. The court shall not make an order authorizing the guardian or conservator to make the lease to any person other than the lessee named in the petition unless the offer made at the hearing is acceptable to the guardian or conservator.

(d) Jurisdiction of the court to administer the estate of the ward or conservatee is effectual to vest the court with jurisdiction to make the order for the lease. This jurisdiction shall conclusively inure to the benefit of the lessee and the lessee's heirs and assigns. No omission, error, or irregularity in the proceedings shall impair or invalidate the proceedings or the lease made pursuant to an order made under this article. **Leg.H.** Enacted Stats 1990 ch 79 §14 (AB 759), operative July 1, 1991.

Prior Law: Former Prob C §2553, similar to the present section, was added Stats 1979 ch 726 §3, operative January 1, 1981, and repealed Stats 1990 ch 79 §13, operative July 1, 1991.

§2554. Terms and conditions of leases

(a) An order authorizing the execution of a lease shall set forth the minimum rental or royalty or both and the period of the lease, which shall be for such time as the court may authorize.

(b) The order may authorize other terms and conditions, including, with respect to a lease for the purpose of exploration for or production or removal of minerals, oil, gas, or other hydrocarbon substances, or geothermal energy, any one or more of the following:

(1) A provision for the payment of rental and royalty to a depositary.

(2) A provision for the appointment of a common agent to represent the interests of all the lessors.

(3) A provision for the payment of a compensatory royalty in lieu of rental and in lieu of drilling and producing operations on the land covered by the lease.

(4) A provision empowering the lessee to enter into any agreement authorized by Section 3301 of the Public Resources Code with respect to the land covered by the lease.

(5) A provision for a community oil lease or pooling or unitization by the lessee.

(c) If the lease covers additional property owned by other persons or an undivided or other interest of the ward or conservatee less than the entire ownership in the property, the order may authorize the lease to provide for division of rental and royalty in the proportion that the land or interest of each owner bears to the total area of the land or total interests covered by such lease.

(d) If the lease is for the purpose of exploration for or production or removal of minerals, oil, gas, or other hydrocarbon substances, or geothermal energy, the court may authorize that the lease be for a fixed period and any of the following:

(1) So long thereafter as minerals, oil, gas, or other hydrocarbon substances or geothermal energy are produced in paying quantities from the property leased or mining or drilling operations are conducted thereon.

(2) If the lease provides for the payment of a compensatory royalty, so long thereafter as such compensatory royalty is paid.

(3) If the land covered by the lease is included in an agreement authorized by Section 3301 of the Public Resources Code, so long thereafter as oil, gas, or other hydrocarbon substances are produced in paying quantities from any of the lands included in any such agreement or drilling operations are conducted thereon. **Leg.H.** Enacted Stats 1990 ch 79 §14 (AB 759), operative July 1, 1991.

§2555. Leases permitted without court authorization

If it is to the advantage of the estate, the guardian or conservator may lease, as lessor, real property of the estate without authorization of the court in either of the following cases:

(a) Where the rental does not exceed five thousand dollars ($5,000) a month and the term does not exceed two years.

(b) Where the lease is from month to month, regardless of the amount of the rental. **Leg.H.** Enacted Stats 1990 ch 79 §14 (AB 759), operative July 1, 1991. Amended Stats 1990 ch 710 §11 (SB 1775), operative July 1, 1991.

Prior Law: Former Prob C §2555, similar to the present section, was added Stats 1979 ch 726 §3, operative January 1, 1981, amended Stats 1987 ch 923 §79, operative July 1, 1988, and repealed Stats 1990 ch 79 §13, operative July 1, 1991.

§2556. Dedication or conveyance of real property or easement with or without consideration

(a) If it is for the advantage, benefit, and best interests of the estate and those interested therein, the guardian or conservator, after authorization by order of the court, may do any of the following either with or without consideration:

(1) Dedicate or convey real property of the estate for any purpose to any of the following:

(A) This state or any public entity in this state.

(B) The United States or any agency or instrumentality of the United States.

(2) Dedicate or convey an easement over any real property of the estate to any person for any purpose.

(3) Convey, release, or relinquish to this state or any public entity in this state any access rights to any street, highway, or freeway from any real property of the estate.

(4) Consent as a lienholder to a dedication, conveyance, release, or relinquishment under paragraph (1), (2), or (3) by the owner of property subject to the lien.

(b) To obtain an order under this section, the guardian or conservator or any other interested person shall file a petition with the court. Notice of the hearing on the petition shall be given for the period and in the manner provided in Chapter 3 (commencing with Section 1460) of Part 1. **Leg.H.** Enacted Stats 1990 ch 79 §14 (AB 759), operative July 1, 1991.

Prior Law: Former Prob C §2556, similar to the present section, was added Stats 1979 ch 726 §3, operative January 1, 1981, and repealed Stats 1990 ch 79 §13, operative July 1, 1991.

§2557. Exchange of property

(a) Whenever it is for the advantage, benefit, and best interests of the ward or conservatee and those legally entitled to support, maintenance, or education from the ward or conservatee, the guardian or conservator, after authorization by order of the court, may exchange any property of the estate for other property upon such terms and conditions as may be prescribed by the court. The terms and conditions prescribed by the court may include the payment or receipt of part cash by the guardian or conservator.

(b) To obtain an order under this section, the guardian or conservator or any interested person shall file a petition containing all of the following:

(1) A description of the property.

(2) The terms and conditions of the proposed exchange.

(3) A showing that the proposed exchange is for the advantage, benefit, and best interests of the ward or conservatee and those legally entitled to support, maintenance, or education from the ward or conservatee.

(c) Except as provided in subdivision (d), notice of the hearing on the petition shall be given for the period and in the manner provided in Chapter 3 (commencing with Section 1460) of Part 1.

(d) If the petition is for authorization to exchange stocks, bonds, or other securities as defined in Section 10200 for different stocks, bonds, or other securities, the court, upon a showing of good cause, may order that the notice be given for a shorter period or be dispensed with.

(e) After authorization by order of the court, the guardian or conservator may execute the conveyance or transfer to the person with whom the exchange is made to effectuate the exchange.

(f) No omission, error, or irregularity in the proceedings under this section shall impair or invalidate the proceedings or the exchange made pursuant to an order made under this section. **Leg.H.** Enacted Stats 1990 ch 79 §14 (AB 759), operative July 1, 1991.

Prior Law: Former Prob C §2557, similar to the present section, was added Stats 1979 ch 726 §3, operative January 1, 1981, amended Stats 1988 ch 113 §13.7, effective May 25, 1988, operative July 1, 1988. Stats 1989 ch 21 §11, effective May 25, 1989, operative July 1, 1989, and repealed Stats 1990 ch 79 §13, operative July 1, 1991.

ARTICLE 9
Investments and Purchase of Property

Authority to invest generally; Petition; Hearing; Order. §2570.
Purchase of home for ward or conservatee or dependents. §2571.
Order authorizing purchase of real property. §2572.
Order authorizing investment in government bonds. §2573.
United States and State of California obligations; Listed stocks, bonds, and other securities. §2574.

§2570. Authority to invest generally; Petition; Hearing; Order

(a) The guardian or conservator, after authorization by order of the court, may invest the proceeds of sales and any other money of the estate as provided in the order.

(b) To obtain an order of the court authorizing a transaction under subdivision (a) of this section, the guardian or conservator, the ward or conservatee, or any other interested person may file a petition with the court.

(c) Notice of the hearing on the petition shall be given for the period and in the manner provided in Chapter 3 (commencing with Section 1460) of Part 1. The court may order that the notice be dispensed with.

(d) The court may require such proof of the fairness and feasibility of the transaction as the court determines is necessary.

(e) If the required showing is made, the court may make an order authorizing the transaction and may prescribe in the order the terms and conditions upon which the transaction shall be made. **Leg.H.** Enacted Stats 1990 ch 79 §14 (AB 759), operative July 1, 1991.

Prior Law: Former Prob C §2570, similar to the present section, was added Stats 1979 ch 726 §3, operative January 1, 1981, and repealed Stats 1990 ch 79 §13, operative July 1, 1991.

§2571. Purchase of home for ward or conservatee or dependents

When authorized by order of the court under Section 2570, the guardian or conservator may purchase:

(a) Real property in this state as a home for the ward or conservatee if such purchase is for the advantage, benefit, and best interest of the ward or conservatee.

(b) Real property as a home for those legally entitled to support and maintenance from the ward or conservatee if such purchase is for the advantage, benefit, and best interest of the ward or conservatee and of those legally entitled to support and maintenance from the ward or conservatee. **Leg.H.** Enacted Stats 1990 ch 79 §14 (AB 759), operative July 1, 1991.

Prior Law: Former Prob C §2571, similar to the present section, was added Stats 1979 ch 726 §3, operative January 1, 1981, and repealed Stats 1990 ch 79 §13, operative July 1, 1991.

§2572. Order authorizing purchase of real property

An order authorizing the guardian or conservator to purchase real property may authorize the guardian or conservator to join with the spouse of the ward or the spouse or domestic partner of the conservatee or with any other person or persons in the purchase of the real property, or an interest, equity, or estate therein, in severalty, in common, in community, or in joint tenancy, for cash or upon a credit or for part cash and part credit. When the court authorizes the purchase of real property, the court may order the guardian or conservator to execute all necessary instruments and commitments to complete the transaction. **Leg.H.** Enacted Stats 1990 ch 79 §14 (AB 759), operative July 1, 1991. Amended Stats 2001 ch 893 §37 (AB 25).

Prior Law: Former Prob C §2572, similar to the present section, was added Stats 1979 ch 726 §3, operative January 1, 1981, and repealed Stats 1990 ch 79 §13, operative July 1, 1991.

§2573. Order authorizing investment in government bonds

An order authorizing investment in bonds issued by any state or of any city, county, city and county, political subdivision, public corporation, district, or special district of any state may authorize the guardian or conservator to select from among bonds issued by any such issuer, without specifying any particular issuer or issue of bonds, if the type of issuer is designated in general terms and the order specifies as to such bonds a minimum quality rating as shown in a recognized investment service, a minimum interest coupon rate, a minimum yield to maturity, and the date of maturity within a five-year range. **Leg.H.** Enacted Stats 1990 ch 79 §14 (AB 759), operative July 1, 1991.

Prior Law: Former Prob C §2573, similar to the present section, was added Stats 1979 ch 726 §3, operative January 1, 1981, and repealed Stats 1990 ch 79 §13, operative July 1, 1991.

§2574. United States and State of California obligations; Listed stocks, bonds, and other securities

(a) Subject to subdivision (b), the guardian or conservator, without authorization of the court, may invest funds of the estate pursuant to this section in:

(1) Direct obligations of the United States, or of the State of California, maturing not later than five years from the date of making the investment.

(2) United States Treasury bonds redeemable at par value on the death of the holder for payment of federal estate taxes, regardless of maturity date.

(3) Securities listed on an established stock or bond exchange in the United States which are purchased on such exchange.

(4) Eligible securities for the investment of surplus state moneys as provided for in Section 16430 of the Government Code.

(5) An interest in a money market mutual fund registered under the Investment Company Act of 1940 (15 U.S.C. Sec. 80a-1, et seq.) or an investment vehicle authorized for the collective investment of trust funds pursuant to Section 9.18 of Part 9 of Title 12 of the Code of Federal Regulations, the portfolios of which are limited to United States government obligations maturing not later than five years from the date of investment and to repurchase agreements fully collateralized by United States government obligations.

(6) Units of a common trust fund described in Section 1585 of the Financial Code. The common trust fund shall have as its objective investment primarily in short-term fixed income obligations and shall be permitted to value investments at cost pursuant to regulations of the appropriate regulatory authority.

(b) In making and retaining investments made under this section, the guardian or conservator shall take into consideration the circumstances of the estate, indicated cash needs, and, if reasonably ascertainable, the date of the prospective termination of the guardianship or conservatorship.

(c) This section shall not limit the authority of the guardian or conservator to seek court authorization for any investment, or to make other investments with court authorization, as provided in this division. **Leg.H.** Enacted Stats 1990 ch 79 §14 (AB 759), operative July 1, 1991. Amended Stats 2014 ch 71 §136 (SB 1304), effective January 1, 2015.

Prior Law: Former Prob C §2574, similar to the present section, was added Stats 1979 ch 726 §3, operative January 1, 1981, amended Stats 1982 ch 1521 §4, Stats 1983 ch 118 §2, Stats 1986 ch 820 §36.5, operative July 1, 1987, Stats 1987 ch 923 §80, operative July 1, 1988, and repealed Stats 1990 ch 79 §13, operative July 1, 1991.

ARTICLE 10
Substituted Judgment

Petition to authorize proposed action. §2580.
Notice of hearing. §2581.
Consent or lack of capacity of conservatee; Adequate provision for conservatee and dependents. §2582.
Circumstances considered in determining whether to authorize or require proposed action. §2583.
Order. §2584.
No duty to propose action. §2585.
Production of conservatee's will and other relevant estate plan documents. §2586.

§2580. Petition to authorize proposed action

(a) The conservator or other interested person may file a petition under this article for an order of the court authorizing or requiring the conservator to take a proposed action for any one or more of the following purposes:

(1) Benefiting the conservatee or the estate.

(2) Minimizing current or prospective taxes or expenses of administration of the conservatorship estate or of the estate upon the death of the conservatee.

(3) Providing gifts for any purposes, and to any charities, relatives (including the other spouse or domestic partner), friends, or other objects of bounty, as would be likely beneficiaries of gifts from the conservatee.

(b) The action proposed in the petition may include, but is not limited to, the following:

(1) Making gifts of principal or income, or both, of the estate, outright or in trust.

(2) Conveying or releasing the conservatee's contingent and expectant interests in property, including marital property rights and any right of survivorship incident to joint tenancy or tenancy by the entirety.

(3) Exercising or releasing the conservatee's powers as donee of a power of appointment.

(4) Entering into contracts.

(5) Creating for the benefit of the conservatee or others, revocable or irrevocable trusts of the property of the estate, which trusts may extend beyond the conservatee's disability or life. A special needs trust for money paid pursuant to a compromise or judgment for a conservatee may be established only under Chapter 4 (commencing with Section 3600) of Part 8, and not under this article.

(6) Transferring to a trust created by the conservator or conservatee any property unintentionally omitted from the trust.

(7) Exercising options of the conservatee to purchase or exchange securities or other property.

(8) Exercising the rights of the conservatee to elect benefit or payment options, to terminate, to change beneficiaries or ownership, to assign rights, to borrow, or to receive cash value in return for a surrender of rights under any of the following:

(A) Life insurance policies, plans, or benefits.

(B) Annuity policies, plans, or benefits.

(C) Mutual fund and other dividend investment plans.

(D) Retirement, profit sharing, and employee welfare plans and benefits.

(9) Exercising the right of the conservatee to elect to take under or against a will.

(10) Exercising the right of the conservatee to disclaim any interest that may be disclaimed under Part 8 (commencing with Section 260) of Division 2.

(11) Exercising the right of the conservatee (A) to revoke or modify a revocable trust or (B) to surrender the right to revoke or modify a revocable trust, but the court shall not authorize or require the conservator to exercise the right to revoke or modify a revocable trust if the instrument governing the trust (A) evidences an intent to reserve the right of revocation or modification exclusively to the conservatee, (B) provides expressly that a conservator may not revoke or modify the trust, or (C) otherwise evidences an intent that would be inconsistent with authorizing or requiring the conservator to exercise the right to revoke or modify the trust.

(12) Making an election referred to in Section 13502 or an election and agreement referred to in Section 13503.

(13) Making a will.

(14) Making or revoking a revocable transfer on death deed. **Leg.H.** Enacted Stats 1990 ch 79 §14 (AB 759), operative July 1, 1991. Amended Stats 1992 ch 355 §1 (AB 3328), ch 572 §6.5 (SB 1455); Stats 1995 ch 730 §4 (AB 1466); Stats 1999 ch 175 §3 (AB 239); Stats 2001 ch 893 §38 (AB 25); Stats 2015 ch 293 §7 (AB 139), effective January 1, 2016.

Prior Law: Former Prob C §2580, similar to the present section, was added Stats 1979 ch 726 §3, operative January 1, 1981, amended Stats 1980 ch 246 §5, Stats 1983 ch 17 §4, ch 842 §53, operative January 1, 1985, Stats 1987 ch 923 §81, operative January 1, 1988, Stats 1988 ch 1199 §70, operative July 1, 1989, and repealed Stats 1990 ch 79 §13, operative July 1, 1991.

§2581. Notice of hearing

Notice of the hearing of the petition shall be given, regardless of age, for the period and in the manner provided in Chapter 3 (commencing with Section 1460) or Part 1 to all of the following:

(a) The persons required to be given notice under Chapter 3 (commencing with Section 1460) of Part 1.

(b) The persons required to be named in a petition for the appointment of a conservator.

(c) So far as is known to the petitioner, beneficiaries under any document executed by the conservatee which may have testamentary effect unless the court for good cause dispenses with such notice.

(d) So far as is known to the petitioner, the persons who, if the conservatee were to die immediately, would be the conservatee's heirs under the laws of intestate succession unless the court for good cause dispenses with such notice.

(e) Such other persons as the court may order. **Leg.H.** Enacted Stats 1990 ch 79 §14 (AB 759), operative July 1, 1991. Amended Stats 1996 ch 862 §8 (AB 2751).

Prior Law: Former Prob C §2581, similar to the present section, was added Stats 1979 ch 726 §3, operative January 1, 1981, and repealed Stats 1990 ch 79 §13, operative July 1, 1991.

§2582. Consent or lack of capacity of conservatee; Adequate provision for conservatee and dependents

The court may make an order authorizing or requiring the proposed action under this article only if the court determines all of the following:

(a) The conservatee either (1) is not opposed to the proposed action or (2) if opposed to the proposed action, lacks legal capacity for the proposed action.

(b) Either the proposed action will have no adverse effect on the estate or the estate remaining after the proposed action is taken will be adequate to provide for the needs of the conservatee and for the support of those legally entitled to support, maintenance, and education from the conservatee, taking into account the age, physical condition, standards of living, and all other relevant circumstances of the conservatee and those legally entitled to support, maintenance, and education from the conservatee. **Leg.H.** Enacted Stats 1990 ch 79 §14 (AB 759), operative July 1, 1991.

Prior Law: Former Prob C §2582, similar to the present section, was added Stats 1979 ch 726 §3, operative January 1, 1981, and repealed Stats 1990 ch 79 §13, operative July 1, 1991.

§2583. Circumstances considered in determining whether to authorize or require proposed action

In determining whether to authorize or require a proposed action under this article, the court shall take into consideration all the relevant circumstances, which may include, but are not limited to, the following:

(a) Whether the conservatee has legal capacity for the proposed transaction and, if not, the probability of the conservatee's recovery of legal capacity.

(b) The past donative declarations, practices, and conduct of the conservatee.

(c) The traits of the conservatee.

(d) The relationship and intimacy of the prospective donees with the conservatee, their standards of living, and the extent to which they would be natural objects of the conservatee's bounty by any objective test based on such relationship, intimacy, and standards of living.

(e) The wishes of the conservatee.

(f) Any known estate plan of the conservatee (including, but not limited to, the conservatee's will, any trust of which the conservatee is the settlor or beneficiary, any power of appointment created by or exercisable by the conservatee, and any contract, transfer, or joint ownership arrangement with provisions for payment or transfer of benefits or interests at the conservatee's death to another or others which the conservatee may have originated).

(g) The manner in which the estate would devolve upon the conservatee's death, giving consideration to the age and the mental and physical condition of the conservatee, the prospective devisees or heirs of the conservatee, and the prospective donees.

(h) The value, liquidity, and productiveness of the estate.

(i) The minimization of current or prospective income, estate, inheritance, or other taxes or expenses of administration.

(j) Changes of tax laws and other laws which would likely have motivated the conservatee to alter the conservatee's estate plan.

(k) The likelihood from all the circumstances that the conservatee as a reasonably prudent person would take the proposed action if the conservatee had the capacity to do so.

(*l*) Whether any beneficiary is the spouse or domestic partner of the conservatee.

(m) Whether a beneficiary has committed physical abuse, neglect, false imprisonment, or financial abuse against the conservatee after the conservatee was substantially unable to manage his or her financial resources, or resist fraud or undue influence, and the conservatee's disability persisted throughout the time of the hearing on the proposed substituted judgment. **Leg.H.** Enacted Stats 1990 ch 79 §14 (AB 759), operative July 1, 1991. Amended Stats 1992 ch 871 §6 (AB 2975); Stats 1993 ch 293 §3 (AB 21); Stats 1998 ch 935 §5 (SB 1715); Stats 2010 ch 620 §2 (SB 105), effective January 1, 2011; Stats 2011 ch 308 §10 (SB 647), effective January 1, 2012.

Prior Law: Former Prob C §2583, similar to the present section, was added Stats 1979 ch 726 §3, operative January 1, 1981, and repealed Stats 1990 ch 79 §13, operative July 1, 1991.

§2584. Order

After hearing, the court, in its discretion, may approve, modify and approve, or disapprove the proposed action and may authorize or direct the conservator to transfer or dispose of assets or take other action as provided in the court's order. **Leg.H.** Enacted Stats 1990 ch 79 §14 (AB 759), operative July 1, 1991.

Prior Law: Former Prob C §2584, similar to the present section, was added Stats 1979 ch 726 §3, operative January 1, 1981, and repealed Stats 1990 ch 79 §13, operative July 1, 1991.

§2585. No duty to propose action

Nothing in this article imposes any duty on the conservator to propose any action under this article, and the conservator is not liable for failure to propose any action under this article. **Leg.H.** Enacted Stats 1990 ch 79 §14 (AB 759), operative July 1, 1991.

Prior Law: Former Prob C §2585, similar to the present section, was added Stats 1979 ch 726 §3, operative January 1, 1981, and repealed Stats 1990 ch 79 §13, operative July 1, 1991.

§2586. Production of conservatee's will and other relevant estate plan documents

(a) As used in this section, "estate plan of the conservatee" includes, but is not limited to, the conservatee's will, any trust of which the conservatee is the settlor or beneficiary, any power of appointment created by or exercisable by the conservatee, and any contract, transfer, or joint ownership arrangement with provisions for payment or transfer of benefits or interests at the conservatee's death to another or others which the conservatee may have originated.

(b) Notwithstanding Article 3 (commencing with Section 950) of Chapter 4 of Division 8 of the Evidence Code (lawyer-client privilege), the court, in its discretion, may order that any person having possession of any document constituting all or part of the estate plan of the conservatee shall deliver the document to the court for examination by the court, and, in the discretion of the court, by the attorneys for the persons who have appeared in the proceedings under this article, in connection with the petition filed under this article.

(c) Unless the court otherwise orders, no person who examines any document produced pursuant to an order under this section shall disclose the contents of the document to any other person. If that disclosure is made, the court may adjudge the person making the disclosure to be in contempt of court.

(d) For good cause, the court may order that a document constituting all or part of the estate plan of the conservatee, whether or not produced pursuant to an order under this section, shall be delivered for safekeeping to the custodian designated by the court. The court may impose those conditions it determines are appropriate for holding and safeguarding the document. The court may authorize the conservator to take any action a depositor may take under Part 15 (commencing with Section 700) of Division 2. **Leg.H.** Enacted Stats 1990 ch 79 §14 (AB 759), operative July 1, 1991. Amended Stats 1993 ch 519 §5 (AB 209), effective January 1, 1994.

Prior Law: Former Prob C §2586, similar to the present section, was added Stats 1979 ch 726 §3, operative January 1, 1981, amended Stats 1980 ch 246 §6, and repealed Stats 1990 ch 79 §13, operative July 1, 1991.

ARTICLE 11
Independent Exercise of Powers

Order granting authority for independent exercise of powers. §2590.
Powers that may be granted. §2591.
Terms of sale to be in best interest; Compliance with appraisal provisions; Service of final escrow settlement statement. §2591.5.
Petition. §2592.
Withdrawal or subsequent limitation of powers. §2593.
Contents of letters; When new letters required. §2594.
Use of other statutory authorizations or procedures not precluded. §2595.

§2590. Order granting authority for independent exercise of powers

(a) The court may, in its discretion, make an order granting the guardian or conservator any one or more or all of the powers specified in Section 2591 if the court determines that, under the circumstances of the particular guardianship or conservatorship, it would be to the advantage, benefit, and best interest of the estate to do so. Subject only to the requirements, conditions, or limitations as are specifically and expressly provided, either directly or by reference, in the order granting the power or powers, and if consistent with Section 2591, the guardian or conservator may exercise the granted power or powers without notice, hearing, or court authorization, instructions, approval, or confirmation in the same manner as the ward or conservatee could do if possessed of legal capacity.

(b) The guardian or conservator does not have a power specified in Section 2591 without authorization by a court under this article or other express provisions of this code. **Leg.H.** Enacted Stats 1990 ch 79 §14 (AB 759), operative July 1, 1991. Amended Stats 2006 ch 490 §5 (SB 1116), effective January 1, 2007; Stats 2007 ch 553 §18 (AB 1727), effective January 1, 2008.

2006 Note: This act, together with Senate Bill 1550, Senate Bill 1716, and Assembly Bill 1363, shall be known and may be cited as the Omnibus Conservatorship and Guardianship Reform Act of 2006. Stats 2006 ch 490 (SB 1116) §9.

Prior Law: Former Prob C §2590, similar to the present section, was added Stats 1979 ch 726 §3, operative January 1, 1981, and repealed Stats 1990 ch 79 §13, operative July 1, 1991.

§2591. Powers that may be granted

The powers referred to in Section 2590 are:

(a) The power to operate, for a period longer than 45 days, at the risk of the estate a business, farm, or enterprise constituting an asset of the estate.

(b) The power to grant and take options.

(c)(1) The power to sell at public or private sale real or personal property of the estate without confirmation of the court of the sale, other than the personal residence of a conservatee.

(2) The power to sell at public or private sale the personal residence of the conservatee as described in Section 2591.5 without confirmation of the court of the sale. The power granted pursuant to this paragraph is subject to the requirements of Sections 2352.5, 2540, 2541, and 2541.5.

(3) For purposes of this subdivision, authority to sell property includes authority to contract for the sale and fulfill the terms and conditions of the contract, including conveyance of the property.

(d) The power to create by grant or otherwise easements and servitudes.

(e) The power to borrow money.

(f) The power to give security for the repayment of a loan.

(g) The power to purchase real or personal property.

(h) The power to alter, improve, raze, replace, and rebuild property of the estate.

(i) The power to let or lease property of the estate, or extend, renew, or modify a lease of real property, for which the monthly rental or lease term exceeds the maximum specified in Sections 2501 and 2555 for any purpose (including exploration for and removal of gas, oil, and other minerals and natural resources) and for any period, including a term commencing at a future time.

(j) The power to lend money on adequate security.

(k) The power to exchange property of the estate.

(*l*) The power to sell property of the estate on credit if any unpaid portion of the selling price is adequately secured.

(m) The power to commence and maintain an action for partition. The power granted pursuant to this subdivision is subject to the requirements of Sections 2352.5, 2540, 2541, and 2541.5.

(n) The power to exercise stock rights and stock options.

(o) The power to participate in and become subject to and to consent to the provisions of a voting trust and of a reorganization, consolidation, merger, dissolution, liquidation, or other modification or adjustment affecting estate property.

(p) The power to pay, collect, compromise, or otherwise adjust claims, debts, or demands upon the guardianship or conservatorship described in subdivision (a) of Section 2501, Section 2502 or 2504, or to arbitrate any dispute described in Section 2406. **Leg.H.** Enacted Stats 1990 ch 79 §14 (AB 759), operative July 1, 1991. Amended Stats 2006 ch 490 §6 (SB 1116), effective January 1, 2007; Stats 2007 ch 553 §19 (AB 1727), effective January 1, 2008; Stats 2019 ch 847 §4 (SB 303), effective January 1, 2020; Stats 2022 ch 91 §5 (SB 1005), effective January 1, 2023.

Editor's Notes—2006 Note: This act, together with Senate Bill 1550, Senate Bill 1716, and Assembly Bill 1363, shall be known and may be cited as the Omnibus Conservatorship and Guardianship Reform Act of 2006. Stats 2006 ch 490 (SB 1116) §9.

Prior Law: Former Prob C §2591, similar to the present section, was added Stats 1979 ch 726 §3, operative January 1, 1981, and repealed Stats 1990 ch 79 §13, operative July 1, 1991.

§2591.5. Terms of sale to be in best interest; Compliance with appraisal provisions; Service of final escrow settlement statement

(a) Notwithstanding any other provisions of this article, a conservator seeking an order under Section 2590 authorizing a sale of the conservatee's personal residence shall demonstrate to the court that the terms of sale, including the price for which the property is to be sold, the commissions to be paid from the estate, estimated capital gains income and tax consequences, and impact on access to governmental benefits, are in all respects in the best interests of the conservatee.

(b) A conservator authorized to sell the conservatee's personal residence pursuant to Section 2590 shall comply with the provisions of Section 10309 concerning appraisal or new appraisal of the property for sale and sale at a minimum offer price. Notwithstanding Section 10309, if the last appraisal of the conservatee's personal residence was conducted more than six months prior to the proposed sale of the property, a new appraisal shall be required prior to the sale of the property, unless the court finds that it is in the best interests of the conservatee to rely on an appraisal of the personal residence that was conducted not more than one year prior to the proposed sale of the property. For purposes of this section, the date of sale is the date of the contract for sale of the property.

(c) Within 15 days of the close of escrow, the conservator shall serve a copy of the final escrow settlement statement on all persons entitled to notice of the petition for appointment for a conservator and all persons who have filed and served a request for special notice and shall file a copy of the final escrow statement along with a proof of service with the court. **Leg.H.** Added Stats 2006 ch 490 §7 (SB 1116), effective January 1, 2007. Amended Stats 2007 ch 553 §20 (AB 1727), effective January 1, 2008; Stats 2019 ch 847 §5 (SB 303), effective January 1, 2020.

Editor's Notes—2006 Note: This act, together with Senate Bill 1550, Senate Bill 1716, and Assembly Bill 1363, shall be known and may be cited as the Omnibus Conservatorship and Guardianship Reform Act of 2006. Stats 2006 ch 490 (SB 1116) §9.

§2592. Petition

(a) The guardian or conservator may apply by petition for an order under Section 2590.

(b) The application for the order may be included in the petition for the appointment of the guardian or conservator. In such case, the notice of hearing on the petition shall include a statement that the petition includes an application for the grant of one or more powers under this article and shall list the specific power or powers applied for.

(c) If the application for the order is made by petition filed after the filing of the petition for the appointment of the guardian or conservator, notice of the hearing on the petition shall be given for the period and in the manner provided in Chapter 3 (commencing with Section 1460) of Part 1. **Leg.H.** Enacted Stats 1990 ch 79 §14 (AB 759), operative July 1, 1991.

Prior Law: Former Prob C §2592, similar to the present section, was added Stats 1979 ch 726 §3, operative January 1, 1981, and repealed Stats 1990 ch 79 §13, operative July 1, 1991.

§2593. Withdrawal or subsequent limitation of powers

(a) The court, on its own motion or on petition of any interested person, when it appears to be for the best interests of the ward or conservatee or the estate, may withdraw any or all of the powers previously granted pursuant to this article or may impose restrictions, conditions, and limitations on the exercise of such powers by the guardian or conservator.

(b) Notice of the hearing on a petition under this section shall be given for the period and in the manner provided in Chapter 3 (commencing with Section 1460) of Part 1. **Leg.H.** Enacted Stats 1990 ch 79 §14 (AB 759), operative July 1, 1991.

Prior Law: Former Prob C §2593, similar to the present section, was added Stats 1979 ch 726 §3, operative January 1, 1981, and repealed Stats 1990 ch 79 §13, operative July 1, 1991.

§2594. Contents of letters; When new letters required

(a) When a power or powers are granted pursuant to this article, the letters of guardianship or conservatorship shall state the power or powers so granted and the restrictions, conditions, or limitations, if any, prescribed in the order and shall refer to this article.

(b) When a power or powers are granted by a subsequent order, new letters shall be issued in the form described in subdivision (a).

(c) If the powers are withdrawn, or if the powers are restricted, conditioned, or limited by a subsequent order after they are granted, new letters shall be issued accordingly. **Leg.H.** Enacted Stats 1990 ch 79 §14 (AB 759), operative July 1, 1991.

Prior Law: Former Prob C §2594, similar to the present section, was added Stats 1979 ch 726 §3, operative January 1, 1981, and repealed Stats 1990 ch 79 §13, operative July 1, 1991.

§2595. Use of other statutory authorizations or procedures not precluded

(a) The grant of a power or powers pursuant to this article does not affect the right of the guardian or conservator to petition the court as provided in Section 2403 or to petition the court under other provisions of this code, as to a particular transaction or matter, in the same manner as if the power or powers had not been granted pursuant to this article.

(b) Where authority exists under other provisions of law, either general or specific, for the guardian or conservator to do any act or to enter into any transaction described in Section 2591, the guardian or conservator may proceed under such other provisions of law and is not required to obtain authority under this article. **Leg.H.** Enacted Stats 1990 ch 79 §14 (AB 759), operative July 1, 1991.

Prior Law: Former Prob C §2595, similar to the present section, was added Stats 1979 ch 726 §3, operative January 1, 1981, and repealed Stats 1990 ch 79 §13, operative July 1, 1991.

CHAPTER 7
INVENTORY AND ACCOUNTS

Article 1. Definitions and General Provisions.
Article 2. Inventory and Appraisal of Estate.
Article 2.5. Examination Concerning Assets of Estate.
Article 3. Accounts.
Article 4. Accounts on Termination of Relationship.

ARTICLE 1
Definitions and General Provisions

Definitions. §2600.
Wages of ward or conservatee. §2601.

§2600. Definitions

As used in this chapter, unless the context otherwise requires:

(a) "Conservator" means (1) the conservator of the estate or (2) the limited conservator of the estate to the extent that the powers and duties of the limited conservator are specifically and expressly provided by the order appointing the limited conservator.

(b) "Estate" means all of the conservatee's or ward's personal property, wherever located, and real property located in this state.

(c) "Guardian" means the guardian of the estate. **Leg.H.** Enacted Stats 1990 ch 79 §14 (AB 759), operative July 1, 1991. Amended Stats 2008 ch 52 §4 (AB 2014), effective January 1, 2009.

Prior Law: Former Prob C §2600, similar to the present section, was added Stats 1979 ch 726 §3, operative January 1, 1981, amended Stats 1980 ch 1304 §27, and repealed Stats 1990 ch 79 §13, operative July 1, 1991.

§2601. Wages of ward or conservatee

(a) Unless otherwise ordered by the court, if the ward or conservatee is employed at any time during the continuance of the guardianship or conservatorship:

(1) The wages or salaries for such employment are not a part of the estate and the guardian or conservator is not accountable for such wages or salaries.

(2) The wages or salaries for such employment shall be paid to the ward or conservatee and are subject to his or her control to the same extent as if the guardianship or conservatorship did not exist.

(b) Any court order referred to in subdivision (a) is binding upon the employer only after notice of the order has been received by the employer. **Leg.H.** Enacted Stats 1990 ch 79 §14 (AB 759), operative July 1, 1991.

Prior Law: Former Prob C §2601, similar to the present section, was added Stats 1979 ch 726 §3, operative January 1, 1981, and repealed Stats 1990 ch 79 §13, operative July 1, 1991.

ARTICLE 2
Inventory and Appraisal of Estate

Filing inventory and appraisal. §2610.
Sending copy to Director of State Hospitals or Director of Developmental Services. §2611.
Sending copy to county assessor. §2612.
Subsequently discovered or acquired property; Supplemental inventory and appraisal. §2613.
Objections to appraisals. §2614.
Order to file inventory and appraisal. §2614.5.
Proposed hourly fee schedule required of professional fiduciary. §2614.7.
Subsequent submission of new hourly fee schedule. §2614.8.
Damages for failure to file inventory. §2615.

§2610. Filing inventory and appraisal

(a) Within 90 days after appointment, or within any further time as the court for reasonable cause upon ex parte petition of the guardian or conservator may allow, the guardian or conservator shall file with the clerk of the court and deliver pursuant to Section 1215 to the conservatee and to the attorneys of record for the ward or conservatee, along with notice of how to file an objection, an inventory and appraisal of the estate, made as of the date of the appointment of the guardian or conservator. A copy of this inventory and appraisal, along with notice of how to file an objection, also shall be delivered to the conservatee's spouse or registered domestic partner, the conservatee's relatives in the first degree, and, if there are no such relatives, to the next closest relative, unless the court determines that the delivery will result in harm to the conservatee.

(b) The guardian or conservator shall take and subscribe to an oath that the inventory contains a true statement of all of the estate of the ward or conservatee of which the guardian or conservator has possession or knowledge. The oath shall be endorsed upon or annexed to the inventory.

(c) The property described in the inventory shall be appraised in the manner provided for the inventory and appraisal of estates of decedents. The guardian or conservator may appraise the assets that a personal representative could appraise under Section 8901.

(d) If a conservatorship is initiated pursuant to the Lanterman-Petris-Short Act (Part 1 (commencing with Section 5000) of Division 5 of the Welfare and Institutions Code), and no sale of the estate will occur:

(1) The inventory and appraisal required by subdivision (a) shall be filed within 90 days after appointment of the conservator.

(2) The property described in the inventory may be appraised by the conservator and need not be appraised by a probate referee.

(e) By January 1, 2008, the Judicial Council shall develop a form to effectuate the notice required in subdivision (a). **Leg.H.** Enacted Stats 1990 ch 79 §14 (AB 759), operative July 1, 1991. Amended Stats 2006 ch 493 §23 (AB 1363), effective January 1, 2007; Stats 2017 ch 319 §46 (AB 976), effective January 1, 2018.

2006 Note: This act, together with Senate Bill 1116 (Scott), Senate Bill 1550 (Figueroa), and Senate Bill 1716 (Bowen), shall be known and may be cited as the Omnibus Conservatorship and Guardianship Reform Act of 2006. Stats 2006 ch 493 (AB 1363) §1.

Prior Law: Former Prob C §2610, similar to the present section, was added Stats 1979 ch 726 §3, operative January 1, 1981, amended Stats 1982 ch 1535 §11, Stats 1988 ch 1199 §70.5, operative July 1, 1989, and repealed Stats 1990 ch 79 §13, operative July 1, 1991.

§2611. Sending copy to Director of State Hospitals or Director of Developmental Services

If the ward or conservatee is or has been during the guardianship or conservatorship a patient in a state hospital under the jurisdiction of the State Department of State Hospitals or the State Department of Developmental Services, the guardian or conservator shall deliver pursuant to Section 1215 a copy of the inventory and appraisal filed under Section 2610 to the director of the appropriate department at the director's office in Sacramento not later than 15 days after the inventory and appraisal is filed with the court. Compliance with this section is not required if an unrevoked certificate described in subdivision (c) of Section 1461 is on file with the court with respect to the ward or conservatee. **Leg.H.** Enacted Stats 1990 ch 79 §14 (AB 759), operative July 1, 1991. Amended Stats 2012 ch 440 §46 (AB 1488), effective September 22, 2012; Stats 2017 ch 319 §47 (AB 976), effective January 1, 2018.

Prior Law: Former Prob C §2611, similar to the present section, was added Stats 1979 ch 726 §3, operative January 1, 1981, and repealed Stats 1990 ch 79 §13, operative July 1, 1991.

§2612. Sending copy to county assessor

If a timely request is made, the clerk of court shall deliver pursuant to Section 1215 a copy of the inventory and appraisal filed under Section 2610 to the county assessor. **Leg.H.** Enacted Stats 1990 ch 79 §14 (AB 759), operative July 1, 1991. Amended Stats 2017 ch 319 §48 (AB 976), effective January 1, 2018.

Prior Law: Former Prob C §2612, similar to the present section, was added Stats 1979 ch 726 §3, operative January 1, 1981, and repealed Stats 1990 ch 79 §13, operative July 1, 1991.

§2613. Subsequently discovered or acquired property; Supplemental inventory and appraisal

Whenever any property of the ward or conservatee is discovered that was not included in the inventory, or whenever any other property is received by the ward or conservatee or by the guardian or conservator on behalf of the ward or conservatee (other than by the actions of the guardian or conservator in the investment and management of the estate), the guardian or conservator shall file a supplemental inventory and appraisal for that property and like proceedings shall be followed with respect thereto as in the case of an original inventory, but the appraisal shall be made as of the date the property was so discovered or received. **Leg.H.** Enacted Stats 1990 ch 79 §14 (AB 759), operative July 1, 1991.

Prior Law: Former Prob C §2613, similar to the present section, was added Stats 1979 ch 726 §3, operative January 1, 1981, amended Stats 1986 ch 144 §1, and repealed Stats 1990 ch 79 §13, operative July 1, 1991.

§2614. Objections to appraisals

(a) Within 30 days after the inventory and appraisal is filed, the guardian or conservator or any creditor or other interested person may file written objections to any or all appraisals. The clerk shall set the objections for hearing not less than 15 days after their filing.

(b) Notice of the hearing, together with a copy of the objections, shall be given for the period and in the manner provided in Chapter 3 (commencing with Section 1460) of Part 1. If the appraisal was made by a probate referee, the person objecting shall also deliver pursuant to Section 1215 notice of the hearing and a copy of the objection to the probate referee at least 15 days before the time set for the hearing.

(c) The court shall determine the objections and may fix the true value of any asset to which objection has been filed. For the purpose of this subdivision, the court may cause an independent appraisal or appraisals to be made by at least one additional appraiser at the expense of the estate or, if the objecting party is not the guardian or conservator and the objection is rejected by the court, the court may assess the cost of any additional appraisal or appraisals against the objecting party. **Leg.H.** Enacted Stats 1990 ch 79 §14 (AB 759), operative July 1, 1991. Amended Stats 2017 ch 319 §49 (AB 976), effective January 1, 2018.

Prior Law: Former Prob C §2614, similar to the present section, was added Stats 1979 ch 726 §3, operative January 1, 1981, amended Stats 1982 ch 1535 §12, Stats 1987 ch 923 §82, operative July 1, 1988, and repealed Stats 1990 ch 79 §13, operative July 1, 1991.

§2614.5. Order to file inventory and appraisal

(a) If the guardian or conservator fails to file an inventory and appraisal within the time allowed by law or by court order, upon request of the ward or conservatee, the spouse of the ward or the spouse or domestic partner of the conservatee, any relative or friend of the ward or conservatee, or any interested person, the court shall order the guardian or conservator to file the inventory and appraisal within the time prescribed in the order or to show cause why the guardian or conservator should not be removed. The person who requested the order shall serve it upon the guardian or conservator in the manner provided in Section 415.10 or 415.30 of the Code of Civil Procedure or in a manner as is ordered by the court.

(b) If the guardian or conservator fails to file the inventory and appraisal as required by the order within the time prescribed in the order, unless good cause is shown for not doing so, the court, on its own motion or on petition, may remove the guardian or conservator, revoke the letters of guardianship or conservatorship, and enter judgment accordingly, and order the guardian or conservator to file an account and to surrender the estate to the person legally entitled thereto.

(c) The procedure provided in this section is optional and does not preclude the use of any other remedy or sanction when an inventory and appraisal is not timely filed. **Leg.H.** Enacted Stats 1990 ch 79 §14 (AB 759), operative July 1, 1991. Amended Stats 2001 ch 893 §39 (AB 25), effective January 1, 2002.

§2614.7. Proposed hourly fee schedule required of professional fiduciary

If a guardian or conservator of the person or estate, or both, is a professional fiduciary, as described in Section 2340, who is required to be licensed under the Professional Fiduciaries Act (Chapter 6 (commencing with Section 6500) of Division 3 of the Business and Professions Code), the guardian or conservator shall file, concurrently with the inventory and appraisal required by Section 2610, a proposed hourly fee schedule or another statement of his or her proposed compensation from the estate of the ward or conservatee for services performed as a guardian or conservator. The filing of a proposed hourly fee schedule or another statement of the guardian's or conservator's proposed compensation, as required by this section, shall not preclude a court from later reducing the guardian's, conservator's, or his or her attorney's fees or other compensation. **Leg.H.** Added Stats 2013 ch 248 §4 (AB 1339), effective January 1, 2014.

§2614.8. Subsequent submission of new hourly fee schedule

At any time on or after one year from the submission of an hourly fee schedule or another statement of proposed compensation under this section or under Section 1510, 1821, 2250, or 2614.7, a guardian or conservator who is a professional fiduciary may submit a new proposed hourly fee schedule or another statement of his or her proposed compensation from the estate of the proposed ward or proposed conservatee. The submittal of a new hourly fee schedule or another statement of the guardian's or conservator's proposed compensation, as authorized by this section, shall not preclude a court from later reducing the guardian's or conservator's hourly fees or other compensation, or his or her attorney's fees or other compensation. **Leg.H.** Added Stats 2013 ch 248 §5 (AB 1339), effective January 1, 2014.

§2615. Damages for failure to file inventory

If a guardian or conservator fails to file any inventory required by this article within the time prescribed by law or by court order, the guardian or conservator is liable for damages for any injury to the estate, or to any interested person, directly resulting from the failure timely to file the inventory. Damages awarded pursuant to this section are a personal liability of the guardian or conservator and a liability on the bond, if any. **Leg.H.** Enacted Stats 1990 ch 79 §14 (AB 759), operative July 1, 1991.

Prior Law: Former Prob C §2615, similar to the present section, was added Stats 1979 ch 726 §3, operative January 1, 1981, and repealed Stats 1990 ch 79 §13, operative July 1, 1991.

ARTICLE 2.5
Examination Concerning Assets of Estate

Filing of petition; Examination concerning assets of estate. §2616.
Written interrogatories. §2617.
Examination in court. §2618.
Citation to person controlling estate property. §2619.

§2616. Filing of petition; Examination concerning assets of estate

(a) A petition may be filed under this article by any one or more of the following:

(1) The guardian or conservator.

(2) The ward or conservatee.

(3) A creditor or other interested person, including persons having only an expectancy or prospective interest in the estate.

(b) Upon the filing of a petition under this article, the court may order that a citation be issued to a person to answer interrogatories, or to appear before the court and be examined under oath, or both, concerning any of the following allegations made in the petition:

(1) The person has wrongfully taken, concealed, or disposed of property of the ward or conservatee.

(2) The person has knowledge or possession of any of the following:

(A) A deed, conveyance, bond, contract, or other writing that contains evidence of or tends to disclose the right, title, interest, or claim of the ward or conservatee to property.

(B) An instrument in writing belonging to the ward or conservatee.

(3) The person asserts a claim against the ward or conservatee or the estate.

(4) The estate asserts a claim against the person.

(c) If the citation requires the person to appear before the court, the court and the petitioner may examine the person under oath upon the matters recited in the petition. The citation may include a requirement for this person to produce documents and other personal property specified in the citation.

(d) Disobedience of a citation issued pursuant to this section may be punished as a contempt of the court issuing the citation. **Leg.H.** Enacted Stats 1990 ch 79 §14 (AB 759), operative July 1, 1991. Amended Stats 1994 ch 806 §18 (AB 3686).

Prior Law: Former Prob C §2616, similar to the present section, was added Stats 1979 ch 726 §3, operative January 1, 1981, amended Stats 1988 ch 1199 §71, operative July 1, 1989, and repealed Stats 1990 ch 79 §13, operative July 1, 1991.

§2617. Written interrogatories

Interrogatories may be put to a person cited to answer interrogatories under Section 2616. The interrogatories and answers shall be in writing. The answers shall be signed under penalty of perjury by the person cited. The interrogatories and answers shall be filed with the court. **Leg.H.** Enacted Stats 1990 ch 79 §14 (AB 759), operative July 1, 1991.

§2618. Examination in court

(a) At an examination, witnesses may be produced and examined on either side.

(b) If upon the examination it appears that the allegations of the petition are true, the court may order the person to disclose the person's knowledge of the facts.

(c) If upon the examination it appears that the allegations of the petition are not true, the person's necessary expenses, including reasonable attorney's fees, shall be charged against the petitioner or allowed out of the estate, in the discretion of the court. **Leg.H.** Enacted Stats 1990 ch 79 §14 (AB 759), operative July 1, 1991.

§2619. Citation to person controlling estate property

(a) On petition of the guardian or conservator, the court may issue a citation to a person who has possession or control of property in the estate of the ward or conservatee to appear before the court and make an account under oath of the property and the person's actions with respect to the property.

(b) Disobedience of a citation issued pursuant to this section may be punished as a contempt of the court issuing the citation. **Leg.H.** Enacted Stats 1990 ch 79 §14 (AB 759), operative July 1, 1991.

§2619.5. [Section repealed 2002.]

Leg.H. Enacted Stats 1990 ch 79 §14 (AB 759), operative July 1, 1991. Repealed Stats 2001 ch 49 §3 (SB 669). The repealed section related to double damages.

ARTICLE 3
Accounts

Time for presentation of accounting; Final accounting following death of ward or conservatee; Account statements; Court review; Inspection and copying. §2620.
Review of accountings and detection of fraud. §2620.1.
Failure to file account. §2620.2.
Notice of hearing. §2621.
Objections to account. §2622.
Objections or opposition to objections made without reasonable cause and in bad faith; Costs and expenses. §2622.5.
Allowance for expenses, compensation, and disbursements. §2623.
Review of sales, purchases, and other transactions. §2625.
Termination of proceeding upon exhaustion of estate. §2626.
Settlement of accounts and release by ward; Discharge of guardian. §2627.
Exemption from accounting requirement for certain small estates. §2628.

§2620. Time for presentation of accounting; Final accounting following death of ward or conservatee; Account statements; Court review; Inspection and copying

(a) At the expiration of one year from the time of appointment and thereafter not less frequently than biennially, unless otherwise ordered by the court to be more frequent, the guardian or conservator shall present the accounting of the assets of the estate of the ward or conservatee to the court for settlement and allowance in the manner provided in Chapter 4 (commencing with Section 1060) of Part 1 of Division 3. By January 1, 2008, the Judicial Council, in consultation with the California Judges Association, the California Association of Superior Court Investigators, the California State Association of Public Administrators, Public Guardians, and Public Conservators, the State Bar of California, and the California Society of Certified Public Accountants, shall develop a standard accounting form, a simplified accounting form, and rules for when the simplified accounting form may be used. After January 1, 2008, all accountings submitted pursuant to this section shall be submitted on the Judicial Council form.

(b) The final court accounting of the guardian or conservator following the death of the ward or conservatee shall include a court accounting for the period that ended on the date of death and a separate accounting for the period subsequent to the date of death.

(c) Along with each court accounting, the guardian or conservator shall file supporting documents, as provided in this section.

(1) For purposes of this subdivision, the term "account statement" shall include any original account statement or verified electronic statement from any institution, as defined in Section 2890, or any financial institution, as defined in Section 2892, in which money or other assets of the estate are held or deposited. A court may also accept a computer-generated printout of an original verified electronic statement if the guardian or conservator verifies that the statement was received in electronic form and printed without alteration. A verification shall be executed by the guardian or conservator pursuant to Section 2015.5 of the Code of Civil Procedure.

(2) The filing shall include all account statements showing the account balance as of the closing date of the accounting period of the court accounting. If the court accounting is the first court accounting of the guardianship or conservatorship, the guardian or conservator shall provide to the court all account statements showing the account balance immediately preceding the date the conservator or guardian was appointed and all account statements showing the account balance as of the closing date of the first court accounting.

(3) The filing shall include the original closing escrow statement received showing the charges and credits for any sale of real property of the estate.

(4) If the ward or conservatee is in a residential care facility or a long-term care facility, the filing shall include the original bill statements for the facility.

(5) This subdivision shall not apply to the public guardian if the money belonging to the estate is pooled with money belonging to other estates pursuant to Section 2940 and Article 3 (commencing with Section 7640) of Chapter 4 of Part 1 of Division 7. Nothing in this section shall affect any other duty or responsibility of the public guardian with regard to managing money belonging to the estate or filing accountings with the court.

(6) If any document to be filed or lodged with the court under this section contains the ward's or conservatee's social security number or any other personal information regarding the ward or conservatee that would not ordinarily be disclosed in a court accounting, an inventory and appraisal, or other nonconfidential pleadings filed in the action, the account statement or other document shall be attached to a separate affidavit describing the character of the document, captioned "CONFIDENTIAL FINANCIAL STATEMENT" in capital letters. Except as otherwise ordered by the court, the clerk of the court shall keep the document confidential except to the court and subject to disclosure only upon an order of the court. The guardian or conservator may redact the ward's or conservatee's social security number from any document lodged with the court under this section.

(7) Courts may provide by local rule that the court shall retain all documents lodged with it under this subdivision until the court's determination of the guardian's or conservator's account has become final, at which time the supporting documents shall be returned to the depositing guardian or conservator or delivered to any successor appointed by the court.

(d) Each accounting is subject to random or discretionary, full or partial review by the court. The review may include consideration of any information necessary to determine the accuracy of the accounting. If the accounting has any material error, the court shall make an express finding as to the severity of the error and what further action is appropriate in response to the error, if any. Among the actions available to the court is immediate suspension of the guardian or conservator without further notice or proceedings and appointment of a temporary guardian or conservator or removal of the guardian or conservator pursuant to Section 2650 and appointment of a temporary guardian or conservator.

(e) The guardian or conservator shall make available for inspection and copying, upon reasonable notice, to any person designated by the court to verify the accuracy of the accounting, all books and records, including receipts for any expenditures, of the guardianship or conservatorship.

(f) A superior court shall not be required to perform any duties imposed pursuant to the amendments to this section enacted by Chapter 493 of the Statutes of 2006 until the Legislature makes an appropriation identified for this purpose. **Leg.H.** Added Stats 1996 ch 862 §10 (AB 2751), operative July 1, 1997. Amended Stats 1998 ch 581 §22 (AB 2801); Stats 2000 ch 565 §9 (AB 1950); Stats 2001 ch 232 §1 (AB 1517), ch 563 §6 (AB 1286); Stats 2006 ch 493 §24 (AB 1363), effective January 1, 2007, operative July 1, 2007; Stats 2008 ch 293 §9 (AB 1340), effective January 1, 2009; Stats 2009 ch 54 §8 (SB 544), effective January 1, 2010; Stats 2011 ch 10 §20 (SB 78), effective March 24, 2011; Stats 2020 ch 221 §1 (AB 2844), effective January 1, 2021; Stats 2021 ch 417 §22 (AB 1194), effective January 1, 2022.

2006 Note: This act, together with Senate Bill 1116 (Scott), Senate Bill 1550 (Figueroa), and Senate Bill 1716 (Bowen), shall be known and may be cited as the Omnibus Conservatorship and Guardianship Reform Act of 2006. Stats 2006 ch 493 (AB 1363) §1.

Prior Law: Former Prob C §2620, similar to the present section, was enacted Stats 1990 ch 79 §14, operative July 1, 1991, and repealed Stats 1996 ch 862 §9, operative July 1, 1997.

Former Prob C §2620, similar to the present section, was added Stats 1979 ch 726 §3, operative January 1, 1981, and repealed Stats 1990 ch 79 §13, operative July 1, 1991.

§2620.1. Review of accountings and detection of fraud

The Judicial Council shall, by January 1, 2009, develop guidelines to assist investigators and examiners in reviewing accountings and detecting fraud. **Leg.H.** Added Stats 2007 ch 553 §21 (AB 1727), effective January 1, 2008.

Former Sections: Former Prob C §2620.1, relating to conservator's report on status of conservatee, was enacted Stats 1990 ch 79 §14, operative July 1, 1991, and repealed Stats 1996 ch 862 §11.

Former Prob C §2620.1, relating to conservator's report on status of conservatee, was added Stats 1989 ch 1080 §12, and repealed Stats 1990 ch 79 §13, operative July 1, 1991.

Prior Law: Former Prob C §2620.1, relating to conservator's report on status of conservatee, was enacted Stats 1990 ch 79 §14, operative July 1, 1991, and repealed Stats 1996 ch 862 §11.

Former Prob C §2620.1, relating to conservator's report on status of conservatee, was added Stats 1989 ch 1080 §12, and repealed Stats 1990 ch 79 §13, operative July 1, 1991.

§2620.2. Failure to file account

(a) Whenever the conservator or guardian has failed to file an accounting as required by Section 2620, the court shall require that written notice be given to the conservator or guardian and the attorney of record for the conservatorship or guardianship directing the conservator or guardian to file an accounting and to set the accounting for hearing before the court within 30 days of the date of the notice or, if the conservator or guardian is a public agency, within 45 days of the date of the notice. The court may, upon cause shown, grant an additional 30 days to file the accounting.

(b) Failure to file the accounting within the time specified under subdivision (a), or within 45 days of actual receipt of the notice, whichever is later, shall constitute a contempt of the authority of the court as described in Section 1209 of the Code of Civil Procedure.

(c) If the conservator or guardian does not file an accounting with all appropriate supporting documentation and set the accounting for hearing as required by Section 2620, the court shall do one or more of the following and shall report that action to the bureau established pursuant to Section 6510 of the Business and Professions Code:

(1) Remove the conservator or guardian as provided under Article 1 (commencing with Section 2650) of Chapter 9 of Part 4 of Division 4.

(2) Issue and serve a citation requiring a guardian or conservator who does not file a required accounting to appear and show cause why the guardian or conservator should not be punished for contempt. If the guardian or conservator purposely evades personal service of the citation, the guardian or conservator shall be immediately removed from office.

(3) Suspend the powers of the conservator or guardian and appoint a temporary conservator or guardian, who shall take possession of the assets of the conservatorship or guardianship, investigate the actions of the conservator or guardian, and petition for surcharge if this is in the best interests of the ward or conservatee. Compensation for the temporary conservator or guardian, and counsel for the temporary conservator or guardian, shall be treated as a surcharge against the conservator or guardian, and if unpaid shall be considered a breach of condition of the bond.

(4)(A) Appoint legal counsel to represent the ward or conservatee if the court has not suspended the powers of the conservator or guardian and appoint a temporary conservator or guardian pursuant to paragraph (3). Compensation for the counsel appointed for the ward or conservatee shall be treated as a surcharge against the conservator or guardian, and if unpaid shall be considered a breach of a condition on the bond, unless for good cause shown the court finds that counsel for the ward or conservatee shall be compensated according to Section 1470. The court shall order the legal counsel to do one or more of the following:

(i) Investigate the actions of the conservator or guardian, and petition for surcharge if this is in the best interests of the ward or conservatee.

(ii) Recommend to the court whether the conservator or guardian should be removed.

(iii) Recommend to the court whether money or other property in the estate should be deposited pursuant to Section 2453, 2453.5, 2454, or 2455, to be subject to withdrawal only upon authorization of the court.

(B) After resolution of the matters for which legal counsel was appointed in subparagraph (A), the court shall terminate the appointment of legal counsel, unless the court determines that continued representation of the ward or conservatee and the estate is necessary and reasonable.

(5) If the conservator or guardian is exempt from the licensure requirements of Chapter 6 (commencing with Section 6500) of Division 3 of the Business and Professions Code, upon ex parte application or any notice as the court may require, extend the time to file the accounting, not to exceed an additional 30 days after the expiration of the deadline described in subdivision (a), where the court finds there is good cause and that the estate is adequately bonded. After expiration of any extensions, if the accounting has not been filed, the court shall take action as described in paragraphs (1) to (3), inclusive.

(d) Subdivision (c) does not preclude the court from additionally taking any other appropriate action in response to a failure to file a proper accounting in a timely manner. **Leg.H.** Enacted Stats 1990 ch 79 §14 (AB 759), operative July 1, 1991. Amended Stats 1991 ch 1019 §6 (SB 1022); Stats 1992 ch 572 §7 (SB 1455); Stats 2001 ch 359 §4 (SB 140); Stats 2002 ch 664 §178.5 (AB 3034); Stats 2006 ch 493 §25 (AB 1363), effective January 1, 2007; Stats 2007 ch 553 §22 (AB 1727), effective January 1, 2008.

2006 Note: This act, together with Senate Bill 1116 (Scott), Senate Bill 1550 (Figueroa), and Senate Bill 1716 (Bowen), shall be known and may be cited as the Omnibus Conservatorship and Guardianship Reform Act of 2006. Stats 2006 ch 493 (AB 1363) §1.

Prior Law: Former Prob C §2620.2, similar to the present section, was added Stats 1989 ch 1080 §13, and repealed Stats 1990 ch 79 §13, operative July 1, 1991.

§2621. Notice of hearing

Notice of the hearing on the account of the guardian or conservator shall be given for the period and in the manner provided in Chapter 3 (commencing with Section 1460) of Part 1. If notice is required to be given to the Director of State Hospitals or the Director of Developmental Services under Section 1461, the account shall not be settled or allowed unless notice has been given as provided in Section 1461. **Leg.H.** Enacted Stats 1990 ch 79 §14 (AB 759), operative July 1, 1991. Amended Stats 2012 ch 440 §47 (AB 1488), effective September 22, 2012.

Prior Law: Former Prob C §2621, similar to the present section, was added Stats 1979 ch 726 §3, operative January 1, 1981, and repealed Stats 1990 ch 79 §13, operative July 1, 1991.

§2622. Objections to account

The ward or conservatee, the spouse of the ward or the spouse or domestic partner of the conservatee, any relative or friend of the ward or conservatee, or any creditor or other interested person may file written objections to the account of the guardian or conservator, stating the items of the account to which objection is made and the basis for the objection. **Leg.H.** Enacted Stats 1990 ch 79 §14 (AB 759), operative July 1, 1991. Amended Stats 2001 ch 893 §40 (AB 25), effective January 1, 2002.

Prior Law: Former Prob C §2622, similar to the present section, was added Stats 1979 ch 726 §3, operative January 1, 1981, and repealed Stats 1990 ch 79 §13, operative July 1, 1991.

§2622.5. Objections or opposition to objections made without reasonable cause and in bad faith; Costs and expenses

(a) If the court determines that the objections were without reasonable cause and in bad faith, the court may order the objector to pay the compensation and costs of the conservator or guardian and other expenses and costs of litigation, including attorney's fees, incurred to defend the account. The objector shall be personally liable to the guardianship or conservatorship estate for the amount ordered.

(b) If the court determines that the opposition to the objections was without reasonable cause and in bad faith, the court may award the objector the costs of the objector and other expenses and costs of litigation, including attorney's fees, incurred to contest the account. The amount awarded is a charge against the compensation of the guardian or conservator, and the guardian or conservator is liable personally and on the bond, if any, for any amount that remains unsatisfied. **Leg.H.** Added Stats 1996 ch 563 §12 (SB 392).

§2623. Allowance for expenses, compensation, and disbursements

(a) Except as provided in subdivision (b), the guardian or conservator shall be allowed all of the following:

(1) The amount of the reasonable expenses incurred in the exercise of the powers and the performance of the duties of the guardian or conservator (including, but not limited to, the cost of any surety bond furnished, reasonable attorney's fees, and such compensation for services rendered by the guardian or conservator of the person as the court determines is just, reasonable, and in the best interest of the ward or conservatee).

(2) Such compensation for services rendered by the guardian or conservator as the court determines is just, reasonable, and in the best interest of the ward or conservatee.

(3) All reasonable disbursements made before appointment as guardian or conservator.

(4) In the case of termination other than by the death of the ward or conservatee, all reasonable disbursements made after the termination of the guardianship or conservatorship, but before the discharge of the guardian or conservator by the court.

(5) In the case of termination by the death of the ward or conservatee, all reasonable expenses incurred before the discharge of the guardian or conservator by the court for the custody and conservation of the estate and its delivery to the personal representative of the estate of the deceased ward or conservatee or in making other disposition of the estate as provided for by law.

(b)(1) The guardian or conservator shall not be compensated from the estate for any costs or fees that the guardian or conservator incurred in unsuccessfully defending their fee request petition, opposing a petition, or any other unsuccessful request or action made by, or behalf of, the ward or conservatee.

(2) If the court determines, by clear and convincing evidence, that the defense, opposition, or other action described in paragraph (1) was made in good faith, was based upon the best interest of the ward or conservatee, and did not harm the ward or conservatee, the court may reduce the compensation awarded for the costs or fees incurred instead of denying it completely. The court shall state the reasons for its determination in writing or on the record. **Leg.H.** Enacted Stats 1990 ch 79 §14 (AB 759), operative July 1, 1991. Amended Stats 2006 ch 493 §26 (AB 1363), effective January 1, 2007; Stats 2021 ch 417 §23 (AB 1194), effective January 1, 2022.

2006 Note: This act, together with Senate Bill 1116 (Scott), Senate Bill 1550 (Figueroa), and Senate Bill 1716 (Bowen), shall be known and may be cited as the Omnibus Conservatorship and Guardianship Reform Act of 2006. Stats 2006 ch 493 (AB 1363) §1.

Prior Law: Former Prob C §2623, similar to the present section, was added Stats 1979 ch 726 §3, operative January 1, 1981, and repealed Stats 1990 ch 79 §13, operative July 1, 1991.

§2624. [Section repealed 1997.]

Leg.H. Enacted Stats 1990 ch 79 §14 (AB 759), operative July 1, 1991. Repealed Stats 1996 ch 862 §12 (AB 2751). See Prob C §1064.

Prior Law: Former Prob C §2624, similar to the repealed section, was added Stats 1979 ch 726 §3, operative January 1, 1981, and repealed Stats 1990 ch 79 §13, operative July 1, 1991.

§2625. Review of sales, purchases, and other transactions

Any sale or purchase of property or other transaction not previously authorized, approved, or confirmed by the court is subject to review by the court upon the next succeeding account of the guardian or conservator occurring after the transaction. Upon such account and review, the court may hold the guardian or conservator liable for any violation of duties in connection with the sale, purchase, or other transaction. Nothing in this section shall be construed to affect the validity of any sale or purchase or other transaction. **Leg.H.** Enacted Stats 1990 ch 79 §14 (AB 759), operative July 1, 1991.

Prior Law: Former Prob C §2625, similar to the present section, was added Stats 1979 ch 726 §3, operative January 1, 1981, and repealed Stats 1990 ch 79 §13, operative July 1, 1991.

§2626. Termination of proceeding upon exhaustion of estate

If it appears upon the settlement of any account that the estate has been entirely exhausted through expenditures or disbursements which are approved by the court, the court, upon settlement of the account, shall order the proceeding terminated and the guardian or conservator forthwith discharged unless the court determines that there is reason to continue the proceeding. **Leg.H.** Enacted Stats 1990 ch 79 §14 (AB 759), operative July 1, 1991.

Prior Law: Former Prob C §2626, similar to the present section, was added Stats 1979 ch 726 §3, operative January 1, 1981, and repealed Stats 1990 ch 79 §13, operative July 1, 1991.

§2627. Settlement of accounts and release by ward; Discharge of guardian

(a) After a ward has reached majority, the ward may settle accounts with the guardian and give the guardian a release which is valid if obtained fairly and without undue influence.

(b) Except as otherwise provided by this code, a guardian is not entitled to a discharge until one year after the ward has attained majority. **Leg.H.** Enacted Stats 1990 ch 79 §14 (AB 759), operative July 1, 1991.

Prior Law: Former Prob C §2627, similar to the present section, was added Stats 1979 ch 726 §3, operative January 1, 1981, and repealed Stats 1990 ch 79 §13, operative July 1, 1991.

§2628. Exemption from accounting requirement for certain small estates

(a) The court may make an order that the guardian or conservator need not present the accounts otherwise required by this chapter so long as all of the following conditions are satisfied:

(1) The estate at the beginning and end of the accounting period for which an account is otherwise required consisted of property, exclusive of the residence of the ward or conservatee, of a total net value of less than fifteen thousand dollars ($15,000).

(2) The income of the estate for each month of the accounting period, exclusive of public benefit payments, was less than two thousand dollars ($2,000).

(3) All income of the estate during the accounting period, if not retained, was spent for the benefit of the ward or conservatee.

(b) Notwithstanding that the court has made an order under subdivision (a), the ward or conservatee or any interested person may petition the court for an order requiring the guardian or conservator to present an account as otherwise required by this chapter or the court on its own motion may make that an order. An order under this subdivision may be made ex parte or on such notice of hearing as the court in its discretion requires.

(c) For any accounting period during which all of the conditions of subdivision (a) are not satisfied, the guardian or conservator shall present the account as otherwise required by this chapter. **Leg.H.** Enacted Stats 1990 ch 79 §14 (AB 759), operative July 1, 1991. Amended Stats 1991 ch 1019 §7 (SB 1022); Stats 1998 ch 103 §1 (SB 1487); Stats 2007 ch 553 §23 (AB 1727), effective January 1, 2008.

Prior Law: Former Prob C §2628, similar to the present section, was added Stats 1980 ch 246 §6.2, amended Stats 1984 ch 451 §20.7, and repealed Stats 1990 ch 79 §13, operative July 1, 1991.

Former Prob C §2628, similar to the present section, was added Stats 1979 ch 726, operative January 1, 1981, and repealed Stats 1980 ch 246 §6.1.

§2629. [Section repealed 2002.]

Leg.H. Enacted Stats 1990 ch 79 §14 (AB 759), operative July 1, 1991. Amended Stats 1991 ch 82 §20.5 (SB 896), effective June 30, 1991, operative July 1, 1991. Repealed Stats 2001 ch 359 §5 (SB 140). The repealed section related to compelling filing of account.

ARTICLE 4
Accounts on Termination of Relationship

Continuing jurisdiction of court. §2630.
Death of ward or conservatee; Disposition of assets. §2631.
Account of dead, incapacitated, or absconding guardian or conservator. §2632.
Termination before inventory is filed. §2633.

§2630. Continuing jurisdiction of court

The termination of the relationship of guardian and ward or conservator and conservatee by the death of either, by the ward attaining majority, by the determination of the court that the guardianship or conservatorship is no longer necessary, by the removal or resignation of the guardian or conservator, or for any other reason, does not cause the court to lose jurisdiction of the proceeding for the purpose of settling the accounts of the guardian or conservator or for any other purpose incident to the enforcement of the judgments and orders of the court upon such accounts or upon the termination of the relationship. **Leg.H.** Enacted Stats 1990 ch 79 §14 (AB 759), operative July 1, 1991.

Prior Law: Former Prob C §2630, similar to the present section, was added Stats 1979 ch 726 §3, operative January 1, 1981, and repealed Stats 1990 ch 79 §13, operative July 1, 1991.

§2631. Death of ward or conservatee; Disposition of assets

(a) Upon the death of the ward or conservatee, the guardian or conservator may contract for and pay a reasonable sum for the expenses of the last illness and the disposition of the remains of the deceased ward or conservatee, and for unpaid court-approved attorney's fees, and may pay the unpaid expenses of the guardianship or conservatorship accruing before or after the death of the ward or conservatee, in full or in part, to the extent reasonable, from any personal property of the deceased ward or conservatee which is under the control of the guardian or conservator.

(b) If after payment of expenses under subdivision (a), the total market value of the remaining estate of the decedent does not exceed the amount determined under Section 13100, the guardian or conservator may petition the court for an order permitting the guardian or conservator to liquidate the decedent's estate. The guardian or conservator may petition even though there is a will of the decedent in existence if the will does not appoint an executor or if the named executor refuses to act. No notice of the petition need be given. If the order is granted, the guardian or conservator may sell personal property of the decedent, withdraw money of the decedent in an account in a financial institution, and collect a debt, claim, or insurance proceeds owed to the decedent or the decedent's estate, and a person having possession or control shall pay or deliver the money or property to the guardian or conservator.

(c) After payment of expenses, the guardian or conservator may transfer any remaining property as provided in Division 8 (commencing with Section 13000). For this purpose, the value of the property of the deceased ward or conservatee shall be determined after the deduction of the expenses so paid. **Leg.H.** Enacted Stats 1990 ch 79 §14 (AB 759), operative July 1, 1991. Amended Stats 1996 ch 563 §13 (SB 392).

Prior Law: Former Prob C §2631, similar to the present section, was added Stats 1979 ch 726 §3, operative January 1, 1981, amended Stats 1987 ch 923 §83, operative July 1, 1988, Stats 1988 ch 1199 §71.5, operative July 1, 1989, and repealed Stats 1990 ch 79 §13, operative July 1, 1991.

§2632. Account of dead, incapacitated, or absconding guardian or conservator

(a) As used in this section:

(1) "Incapacitated" means lack of capacity to serve as guardian or conservator.

(2) "Legal representative" means the personal representative of a deceased guardian or conservator or the conservator of the estate of an incapacitated guardian or conservator.

(b) If a guardian or conservator dies or becomes incapacitated and a legal representative is appointed for the deceased or incapacitated guardian or conservator, the legal representative shall, not later than 60 days after appointment unless the court extends the time, file an account of the administration of the deceased or incapacitated guardian or conservator.

(c) If a guardian or conservator dies or becomes incapacitated and no legal representative is appointed for the deceased or incapacitated guardian or conservator, or if the guardian or conservator absconds, the court may compel the attorney for the deceased, incapacitated, or absconding guardian or conservator or the attorney of record in the guardianship or conservatorship proceeding to file an account of the administration of the deceased, incapacitated, or absconding guardian or conservator.

(d) The legal representative or attorney shall exercise reasonable diligence in preparing an account under this section. Verification of the account may be made on information and belief. The court shall settle the account as in other cases. The court shall allow reasonable compensation to the legal representative or the attorney for preparing the account. The amount allowed shall be a charge against the estate that was being administered by the deceased, incapacitated, or absconding guardian or conservator. Legal services for which compensation shall be allowed to the attorney under this subdivision include those services rendered by any paralegal performing the services under the direction and supervision of an attorney. The petition or application for compensation shall set forth the hours spent and services performed by the paralegal. **Leg.H.** Enacted Stats 1990 ch 79 §14 (AB 759), operative July 1, 1991.

Prior Law: Former Prob C §2632, similar to the present section, was added Stats 1979 ch 726 §3, operative January 1, 1981, amended Stats 1987 ch 358 §4, and repealed Stats 1990 ch 79 §13, operative July 1, 1991.

§2633. Termination before inventory is filed

Subject to Section 2630, where the guardianship or conservatorship terminates before the inventory of the estate has been filed, the court, in its discretion and upon such notice as the court may require, may make an order that the guardian or conservator need not file the inventory and appraisal and that the guardian or conservator shall file an account covering only those assets of the estate of which the guardian or conservator has possession or control. **Leg.H.** Enacted Stats 1990 ch 79 §14 (AB 759), operative July 1, 1991.

Prior Law: Former Prob C §2633, similar to the present section, was added Stats 1979 ch 726 §3, operative January 1, 1981, and repealed Stats 1990 ch 79 §13, operative July 1, 1991.

CHAPTER 8
COMPENSATION OF GUARDIAN, CONSERVATOR, AND ATTORNEY

Petition by guardian or conservator of estate. §2640.
Compensation to person who petitioned for appointment of conservator but was not appointed. §2640.1.
Petition by guardian or conservator of person. §2641.
Petition by attorney. §2642.
Order authorizing periodic payments of compensation to guardian or conservator or attorney. §2643.
Petition required of professional fiduciary to authorize periodic payments; Notice and hearing. §2643.1.
Contingent fee contract with attorney. §2644.
Restrictions on compensation for legal services. §2645.
Restrictions on determination of fees. §2646.
Attorney fees. §2647.

§2640. Petition by guardian or conservator of estate

(a) At any time after the filing of the inventory and appraisal, but not before the expiration of 90 days from the issuance of letters or any other period of time as the court for good cause orders, the guardian or conservator of the estate may petition the court for an order fixing and allowing compensation to any one or more of the following:

(1) The guardian or conservator of the estate for services in the best interest of the ward or conservatee rendered to that time.

(2) The guardian or conservator of the person for services in the best interest of the ward or conservatee rendered to that time.

(3) The attorney for services in the best interest of the ward or conservatee rendered to that time by the attorney to the guardian or conservator of the person or estate or both.

(b) Notice of the hearing shall be given for the period and in the manner provided for in Chapter 3 (commencing with Section 1460) of Part 1.

(c) Upon the hearing, the court shall make an order allowing (1) any compensation requested in the petition the court determines is just and reasonable to the guardian or conservator of the estate for services rendered or to the guardian or conservator of the person for services rendered, or to both, and (2) any compensation requested in the petition the court determines is reasonable to the attorney for services rendered to the guardian or conservator of the person or estate or both. The compensation allowed to the guardian or conservator of the person, the guardian or conservator of the estate, and to the attorney may, in the discretion of the court, include compensation for services rendered before the date of the order appointing the guardian or conservator. The compensation allowed shall be charged to the estate. Legal services for which the attorney may be compensated include those services rendered by any paralegal performing legal services under the direction and supervision of an attorney. The petition or application for compensation shall set forth the hours spent and services performed by the paralegal.

(d)(1) Notwithstanding subdivision (c), the guardian or conservator shall not be compensated from the estate for any costs or fees that the guardian or conservator incurred in unsuccessfully defending their fee request petition, opposing a petition, or any other unsuccessful request or action made by, or behalf of, the ward or conservatee.

(2) If the court determines, by clear and convincing evidence, that the defense, opposition, or other action described in paragraph (1) was made in good faith, was based upon the best interest of the ward or conservatee, and did not harm the ward or conservatee, the court may reduce the compensation awarded for the costs or fees incurred instead of denying it completely. The court shall state the reasons for its determination in writing or on the record.

(e) Notwithstanding subdivision (c), the guardian, conservator, or attorney shall not be compensated with any government benefits program moneys unless deemed by the court as necessary to sustain the support and maintenance of the ward or conservatee, but in no event may this exceed the amount permitted by federal laws and regulations. **Leg.H.** Enacted Stats 1990 ch 79 §14 (AB 759), operative July 1, 1991. Amended Stats 1992 ch 572 §8 (SB 1455); Stats 1998 ch 581 §23 (AB 2801); Stats 2006 ch 493 §27 (AB 1363), effective January 1, 2007; Stats 2019 ch 847 §6 (SB 303), effective January 1, 2020; Stats 2021 ch 417 §24 (AB 1194), effective January 1, 2022.

Editor's Notes—2006 Note: This act, together with Senate Bill 1116 (Scott), Senate Bill 1550 (Figueroa), and Senate Bill 1716 (Bowen), shall be known and may be cited as the Omnibus Conservatorship and Guardianship Reform Act of 2006. Stats 2006 ch 493 (AB 1363) §1.

Prior Law: Former Prob C §2640, similar to the present section, was added Stats 1979 ch 726 §3, operative January 1, 1981, amended Stats 1987 ch 358 §5, and repealed Stats 1990 ch 79 §13, operative July 1, 1991.

§2640.1. Compensation to person who petitioned for appointment of conservator but was not appointed

(a) If a person has petitioned for the appointment of a particular conservator and another conservator was appointed while the petition was pending, but not before the expiration of 90 days from the issuance of letters, the person who petitioned for the appointment of a conservator but was not appointed and that person's attorney may petition the court for an order fixing and allowing compensation and reimbursement of costs, provided that the court determines that the petition was filed in the best interests of the conservatee.

(b) Notice of the hearing shall be given for the period and in the manner provided in Chapter 3 (commencing with Section 1460) of Part 1.

(c) Upon the hearing, the court shall make an order to allow both of the following:

(1) Any compensation or costs requested in the petition the court determines is just and reasonable to the person who petitioned for the appointment of a conservator but was not appointed, for his or her services rendered in connection with and to facilitate the appointment of a conservator, and costs incurred in connection therewith.

(2) Any compensation or costs requested in the petition the court determines is just and reasonable to the attorney for that person, for his or her services rendered in connection with and to facilitate the appointment of a conservator, and costs incurred in connection therewith.

Any compensation and costs allowed shall be charged to the estate of the conservatee. If a conservator of the estate is not appointed, but a conservator of the person is appointed, the compensation and costs allowed shall be ordered by the court to be paid from property belonging to the conservatee, whether held outright, in trust, or otherwise.

(d) It is the intent of the Legislature for this section to have retroactive effect. **Leg.H.** Added Stats 1995 ch 730 §5 (AB 1466). Amended Stats 2006 ch 493 §28 (AB 1363), effective January 1, 2007.

2006 Note: This act, together with Senate Bill 1116 (Scott), Senate Bill 1550 (Figueroa), and Senate Bill 1716 (Bowen), shall be known and may be cited as the Omnibus Conservatorship and Guardianship Reform Act of 2006. Stats 2006 ch 493 (AB 1363) §1.

§2641. Petition by guardian or conservator of person

(a) At any time permitted by Section 2640 and upon the notice therein prescribed, the guardian or conservator of the person may petition the court for an order fixing and allowing compensation for services in the best interest of the ward or conservatee rendered to that time.

(b) Upon the hearing, the court shall make an order allowing any compensation the court determines is just and reasonable to the guardian or conservator of the person for services rendered in the best interest of the ward or conservatee. The compensation allowed to the guardian or conservator of the person may, in the discretion of the court, include compensation for services rendered before the date of the order appointing the guardian or conservator. The compensation allowed shall thereupon be charged against the estate.

(c)(1) Notwithstanding subdivision (b), the guardian or conservator shall not be compensated from the estate for any costs or fees that the guardian or conservator incurred in unsuccessfully defending their fee request petition, opposing a petition, or any other unsuccessful request or action made by, or behalf of, the ward or conservatee.

(2) If the court determines, by clear and convincing evidence, that the defense, opposition, or other action described in paragraph (1) was made in good faith, was based upon the best interest of the ward or conservatee, and did not harm the ward or conservatee, the court may reduce the compensation awarded for the costs or fees incurred instead of denying it completely. The court shall state the reasons for its determination in writing or on the record.

(d) Notwithstanding subdivision (b), the guardian or conservator of the person shall not be compensated with any government benefits program moneys unless deemed by the court as necessary to sustain the support and maintenance of the ward or conservatee, but in no event may this exceed the amount permitted by federal laws and regulations. **Leg.H.** Enacted Stats 1990 ch 79 §14 (AB 759), operative July 1, 1991. Amended Stats 1992 ch 572 §9 (SB 1455); Stats 2006 ch 493 §29 (AB 1363), effective January 1, 2007; Stats 2019 ch 847 §7 (SB 303), effective January 1, 2020; Stats 2021 ch 417 §25 (AB 1194), effective January 1, 2022.

Editor's Notes—2006 Note: This act, together with Senate Bill 1116 (Scott), Senate Bill 1550 (Figueroa), and Senate Bill 1716 (Bowen), shall be known and may be cited as the Omnibus Conservatorship and Guardianship Reform Act of 2006. Stats 2006 ch 493 (AB 1363) §1.

Prior Law: Former Prob C §2641, similar to the present section, was added Stats 1979 ch 726 §3, operative January 1, 1981, and repealed Stats 1990 ch 79 §13, operative July 1, 1991.

§2642. Petition by attorney

(a) At any time permitted by Section 2640 and upon the notice therein prescribed, an attorney who has rendered legal services to the guardian or conservator of the person or estate or both, including services rendered under Section 2632, may petition the court for an order fixing and allowing compensation for such services rendered to that time. Legal services for which the attorney may petition the court for an order fixing and allowing compensation under this subdivision include those services rendered by any paralegal performing the legal services under the direction and supervision of an attorney. The petition or application for compensation shall set forth the hours spent and services performed by the paralegal.

(b) Upon the hearing, the court shall make an order allowing such compensation as the court determines reasonable to the attorney for services rendered to the guardian or conservator. The compensation so allowed shall thereupon be charged against the estate. **Leg.H.** Enacted Stats 1990 ch 79 §14 (AB 759), operative July 1, 1991.

Prior Law: Former Prob C §2642, similar to the present section, was added Stats 1979 ch 726 §3, operative January 1, 1981, amended Stats 1987 ch 358 §6, and repealed Stats 1990 ch 79 §13, operative July 1, 1991.

§2643. Order authorizing periodic payments of compensation to guardian or conservator or attorney

(a) Except as provided in Section 2643.1, on petition by the guardian or conservator of the person or estate, or both, the court may by order authorize periodic payments on account to any one or more of the following persons for the services rendered by that person during the period covered by each payment:

(1) The guardian of the person.

(2) The guardian of the estate.

(3) The conservator of the person.

(4) The conservator of the estate.

(5) The attorney for the guardian or conservator of the person or estate, or both.

(b) Notice of the hearing on the petition shall be given for the period and in the manner provided in Chapter 3 (commencing with Section 1460) of Part 1.

(c) The petition shall describe the services to be rendered on a periodic basis and the reason why authority to make periodic payments is requested. In fixing the amount of the periodic payment, the court shall take into account the services to be rendered on a periodic basis and the reasonable value of those services. The guardian or conservator of the estate may make the periodic payments authorized by the order only if the services described in the petition are actually rendered. The payments made pursuant to the order are subject to review by the court upon the next succeeding account of the guardian or conservator of the estate to determine that the services were actually rendered and that the amount paid on account was not unreasonable, and the court shall make an appropriate order if the court determines that the amount paid on account was either excessive or inadequate in view of the services actually rendered. **Leg.H.** Enacted Stats 1990 ch 79 §14 (AB 759), operative July 1, 1991. Amended Stats 2013 ch 248 §6 (AB 1339), effective January 1, 2014.

Prior Law: Former Prob C §2643, similar to the present section, was added Stats 1979 ch 726 §3, operative January 1, 1981, and repealed Stats 1990 ch 79 §13, operative July 1, 1991.

§2643.1. Petition required of professional fiduciary to authorize periodic payments; Notice and hearing

(a) On petition by a guardian or conservator of the person or estate, or both, who is a professional fiduciary, as described in Section 2340 and who is required to be licensed under the Professional Fiduciaries Act (Chapter 6 (commencing with Section 6500) of Division 3 of the Business and Professions Code), the court may by order authorize periodic payments on account to a person described in subdivision (a) of Section 2643 for the services rendered by that person during the period covered by each payment only if that person has filed a proposed hourly fee schedule or another statement of his or her proposed compensation from the estate of the ward or conservatee for services performed as a guardian or conservator, as required by Section 2614.7, and only after the court has addressed any objections filed pursuant to subdivision (d).

(b) The petition shall describe the services to be rendered on a periodic basis, the reason why authority to make periodic payments is requested, and a good faith estimate of the fees to be charged by the professional fiduciary from the date the petition is filed up to, and including, the date of the next succeeding account required by Section 2620 or, if the next succeeding account required by Section 2620 is due in less than one year, a good faith estimate of the fees to be charged by the professional fiduciary from the date the petition is filed through the next succeeding 12 months, inclusive. Prior to ordering periodic payments or fixing the amount of the periodic payment, the court shall determine whether making periodic payments is in the best interest of the ward or conservatee, taking into consideration the needs of the ward or conservatee and the need to preserve and protect the estate. If the court determines that making periodic payments is not in the best interest of the ward or conservatee, the court shall deny the petition to authorize periodic payments. If the court determines that making periodic payments is in the best interest of the ward or conservatee, the court shall fix the amount of the periodic payment. In fixing the amount of the periodic payment, the court shall take into account the services to be rendered on a periodic basis and the reasonable value of those services.

(c)(1) Notice of the hearing on the petition and notice of how to file an objection to the petition shall be given for the period and in the manner provided in Chapter 3 (commencing with Section 1460) of Part 1.

(2) The notices required by paragraph (1) shall be made to the court investigator for the period and in the manner provided in Chapter 3 (commencing with Section 1460) of Part 1.

(d)(1) Any person entitled to notice under paragraph (1) of subdivision (c) may file with the court a written objection to the authorization of periodic payments on account. The court clerk shall set any objections for a hearing no fewer than 15 days after the date the objections are filed.

(2) If an objection is filed pursuant to paragraph (1), the guardian or conservator shall have the burden of establishing the necessity for and amount, if any, of periodic payments.

(e) The guardian or conservator of the estate may make the periodic payments authorized by the order only if the services described in the petition are actually rendered. The payments made pursuant to the order shall be reviewed by the court upon the next succeeding account of the guardian or conservator of the estate to determine that the services were actually rendered and that the amount paid on account was reasonable and in the best interest of the ward or conservatee, taking into consideration the needs of the ward or conservatee and the need to preserve and protect the estate. The court shall make an appropriate order reducing the guardian or conservator's compensation if the court determines that the amount paid on account was either unreasonable or not in the best interest of the ward or conservatee in view of the services actually rendered.

(f) The authorization for periodic payments granted pursuant to this section shall terminate on a date determined by the court, but not later than the due date of the next succeeding account required by Section 2620. Nothing in this section shall preclude a guardian or conservator from filing a subsequent petition to receive periodic payments pursuant to this section. **Leg.H.** Added Stats 2013 ch 248 §7 (AB 1339), effective January 1, 2014.

§2644. Contingent fee contract with attorney

(a) Where it is to the advantage, benefit, and best interest of the ward or conservatee or the estate, the guardian or conservator of the estate may contract with an attorney for a contingent fee for the attorney's services in representing the ward or conservatee or the estate in connection with a matter that is of a type that is customarily the subject of a contingent fee contract, but such a contract is valid only if (1) the contract is made pursuant to an order of the court authorizing the guardian or conservator to execute the contract or (2) the contract is approved by order of the court.

(b) To obtain an order under this section, the guardian or conservator shall file a petition with the court showing the advantage, benefit, and best interest to the ward or conservatee or the estate of the contingent fee contract. A copy of the contingent fee contract shall be attached to the petition.

(c) Notice of the hearing on the petition shall be given for the period and in the manner provided in Chapter 3 (commencing with Section 1460) of Part 1.

(d) As used in this section, "court" includes either of the following:

(1) The court in which the guardianship or conservatorship proceeding is pending.

(2) Where the contract is in connection with a matter in litigation, the court in which the litigation is pending. **Leg.H.** Enacted Stats 1990 ch 79 §14 (AB 759), operative July 1, 1991.

Prior Law: Former Prob C §2644, similar to the present section, was added Stats 1979 ch 726 §3, operative January 1, 1981, and repealed Stats 1990 ch 79 §13, operative July 1, 1991.

§2645. Restrictions on compensation for legal services

(a) No attorney who is a guardian or conservator shall receive any compensation from the guardianship or conservatorship estate for legal services performed for the guardian or conservator unless the court specifically approves the right to the compensation and finds that it is to the advantage, benefit, and best interests of the ward or conservatee.

(b) No parent, child, sibling, or spouse of a person who is a guardian or conservator, and no law partnership or corporation whose partner, shareholder, or employee is serving as a guardian or conservator shall receive any compensation for legal services performed for the guardian or conservator unless the court specifically approves the right to the compensation and finds that it is to the advantage, benefit, and best interests of the ward or conservatee.

(c) This section shall not apply if the guardian or conservator is related by blood or marriage to, or is a cohabitant with, the ward or conservatee.

(d) After full disclosure of the relationships of all persons to receive compensation for legal services under this section, the court may, in its discretion and at any time, approve the right to that compensation, including any time during the pendency of any of the following orders:

(1) An order appointing the guardian or conservator.

(2) An order approving the general plan under Section 1831.

(3) An order settling any account of the guardian or conservator.

(4) An order approving a separate petition, with notice given under Section 2581. **Leg.H.** Added Stats 1993 ch 293 §4 (AB 21).

§2646. Restrictions on determination of fees

In proceedings under this chapter, the court shall only determine fees that are payable from the estate of the ward or conservatee and not limit fees payable from other sources. **Leg.H.** Added Stats 1995 ch 730 §6 (AB 1466).

§2647. Attorney fees

No attorney fees may be paid from the estate of the ward or conservatee without prior court order. The estate of the ward or conservatee is not obligated to pay attorney fees established by any engagement agreement or other contract until it has been approved by the court. This does not preclude an award of fees by the court pursuant to this chapter even if the contractual obligations are unenforceable pursuant to this section. **Leg.H.** Added Stats 2007 ch 553 §24 (AB 1727), effective January 1, 2008.

CHAPTER 9
REMOVAL OR RESIGNATION

Article 1. Removal of Guardian or Conservator.
Article 2. Resignation of Guardian or Conservator.

ARTICLE 1
Removal of Guardian or Conservator

Causes for removal. §2650.
Petition for removal. §2651.
Notice of hearing. §2652.
Hearing and judgment. §2653.
Surrender of estate and suspension of powers pending hearing. §2654.
Contempt. §2655.

§2650. Causes for removal

A guardian or conservator may be removed for any of the following causes:

(a) Failure to use ordinary care and diligence in the management of the estate.

(b) Failure to file an inventory or an account within the time allowed by law or by court order.

(c) Continued failure to perform duties or incapacity to perform duties suitably.

(d) Conviction of a felony, whether before or after appointment as guardian or conservator.

(e) Gross immorality.

(f) Having such an interest adverse to the faithful performance of duties that there is an unreasonable risk that the guardian or conservator will fail faithfully to perform duties.

(g) In the case of a guardian of the person or a conservator of the person, acting in violation of any provision of Section 2356.

(h) In the case of a guardian of the estate or a conservator of the estate, insolvency or bankruptcy of the guardian or conservator.

(i) In the case of a conservator appointed by a court in another jurisdiction, removal because that person would not have been appointed in this state despite being eligible to serve under the law of this state.

(j) In any other case in which the court in its discretion determines that removal is in the best interests of the ward or conservatee; but, in considering the best interests of the ward, if the guardian was nominated under Section 1500 or 1501, the court shall take that fact into consideration. **Leg.H.** Enacted Stats 1990 ch 79 §14 (AB 759), operative July 1, 1991. Amended Stats 2014 ch 553 §26 (SB 940), effective January 1, 2015, operative January 1, 2016.

Prior Law: Former Prob C §2650, similar to the present section, was added Stats 1979 ch 726 §3, operative January 1, 1981, and repealed Stats 1990 ch 79 §13, operative July 1, 1991.

§2651. Petition for removal

The ward or conservatee, the spouse of the ward or the spouse or domestic partner of the conservatee, any relative or friend of the ward or conservatee, or any interested person may apply by petition to the court to have the guardian or conservator removed. The petition shall state facts showing cause for removal. **Leg.H.** Enacted Stats 1990 ch 79 §14 (AB 759), operative July 1, 1991. Amended Stats 2001 ch 893 §41 (AB 25), effective January 1, 2002.

Prior Law: Former Prob C §2651, similar to the present section, was added Stats 1979 ch 726 §3, operative January 1, 1981, and repealed Stats 1990 ch 79 §13, operative July 1, 1991.

§2652. Notice of hearing

Notice of the hearing on the petition shall be given for the period and in the manner provided in Chapter 3 (commencing with Section 1460) of Part 1. **Leg.H.** Enacted Stats 1990 ch 79 §14 (AB 759), operative July 1, 1991.

Prior Law: Former Prob C §2652, similar to the present section, was added Stats 1987 ch 923 §85, operative July 1, 1988, and repealed Stats 1990 ch 79 §13, operative July 1, 1991.

Former Prob C §2652, similar to the present section, was added Stats 1979 ch 726 §3, operative January 1, 1981, and repealed Stats 1987 ch 923 §84, operative July 1, 1988.

§2653. Hearing and judgment

(a) The guardian or conservator, the ward or conservatee, the spouse of the ward or the spouse or registered domestic partner of the conservatee, a relative or friend of the ward or conservatee, and any interested person may appear at the hearing and support or oppose the petition.

(b) If the court determines that cause for removal of the guardian or conservator exists, the court may remove the guardian or conservator, revoke the letters of guardianship or conservatorship, and enter judgment accordingly and, in the case of a guardianship or conservatorship of the estate, order the guardian or conservator to file an accounting and to surrender the estate to the person legally entitled thereto. If the guardian or conservator fails to file the accounting as ordered, the court may compel the accounting pursuant to Section 2620.2.

(c) If the court removes the guardian or conservator for cause, as described in subdivisions (a) to (g), inclusive, of Section 2650 or Section 2655, both all of the following shall apply:

(1) The court shall award the petitioner the costs of the petition and other expenses and costs of litigation, including attorney's fees, incurred under this article.

(2) The guardian or conservator may not deduct from, or charge to, the estate the guardian's or conservator's costs of opposing the petition for removal, and is personally liable for those costs and expenses.

(3) If the court removes a professional fiduciary as guardian or conservator for cause, the court shall report that determination and the basis for removal to the Professional Fiduciaries Bureau. If the court reports an action taken under this section, the court shall provide the bureau, at no charge, with access to the information, including confidential information, regarding its investigation of the professional fiduciary contained in court records. The bureau shall maintain the confidentiality of the information, as required by paragraph (4) of subdivision (a) of Section 6580 of the Business and Professions Code or any other applicable state or federal law.

(d) A superior court shall not be required to perform any duties imposed pursuant to the amendments to this section enacted by the measure that added this subdivision until the Legislature makes an appropriation identified for this purpose. **Leg.H.** Enacted Stats 1990 ch 79 §14 (AB 759), operative July 1, 1991. Amended Stats 2001 ch 893 §42 (AB 25); Stats 2006 ch 493 §30 (AB 1363), effective January 1, 2007; Stats 2021 ch 417 §26 (AB 1194), effective January 1, 2022.

2006 Note: This act, together with Senate Bill 1116 (Scott), Senate Bill 1550 (Figueroa), and Senate Bill 1716 (Bowen), shall be known and may be cited as the Omnibus Conservatorship and Guardianship Reform Act of 2006. Stats 2006 ch 493 (AB 1363) §1.

Prior Law: Former Prob C §2653, similar to the present section, was added Stats 1979 ch 726 §3, operative January 1, 1981, and repealed Stats 1990 ch 79 §13, operative July 1, 1991.

§2654. Surrender of estate and suspension of powers pending hearing

Whenever it appears that the ward or conservatee or the estate may suffer loss or injury during the time required for notice and hearing under this article, the court, on its own motion or on petition, may do either or both of the following:

(a) Suspend the powers of the guardian or conservator pending notice and hearing to such extent as the court deems necessary.

(b) Compel the guardian or conservator to surrender the estate to a custodian designated by the court. **Leg.H.** Enacted Stats 1990 ch 79 §14 (AB 759), operative July 1, 1991.

Prior Law: Former Prob C §2654, similar to the present section, was added Stats 1979 ch 726 §3, operative January 1, 1981, and repealed Stats 1990 ch 79 §13, operative July 1, 1991.

§2655. Contempt

(a) A guardian or conservator may be removed from office if the guardian or conservator is found in contempt for disobeying an order of the court.

(b) Notwithstanding any other provision of this article, a guardian or conservator may be removed from office under subdivision (a) by a court order reciting the facts and without further showing or notice. **Leg.H.** Enacted Stats 1990 ch 79 §14 (AB 759), operative July 1, 1991.

ARTICLE 2
Resignation of Guardian or Conservator

Resignation of guardian or conservator. §2660.
Appointment of responsible adult to make educational decisions. §2662.

§2660. Resignation of guardian or conservator

A guardian or conservator may at any time file with the court a petition tendering the resignation of the guardian or conservator. Notice of the hearing on the petition shall be given for the period and in the manner provided in Chapter 3 (commencing with Section 1460) of Part 1. The court shall allow such resignation when it appears proper, to take effect at such time as the court shall fix, and may make any order as may be necessary to deal with the guardianship or conservatorship during the period prior to the appointment of a new guardian or conservator and the settlement of the accounts of the resigning guardian or conservator. **Leg.H.** Enacted Stats 1990 ch 79 §14 (AB 759), operative July 1, 1991.

Prior Law: Former Prob C §2660, similar to the present section, was added Stats 1979 ch 726 §3, operative January 1, 1981, and repealed Stats 1990 ch 79 §13, operative July 1, 1991.

§2662. Appointment of responsible adult to make educational decisions

Whenever the court grants a petition removing the guardian or conservator of a minor ward or conservatee or tendering the resignation of the guardian or conservator of a minor ward or conservatee, if the court does not immediately appoint a successor guardian or conservator, the court shall at the same time appoint a responsible adult to make educational decisions for the minor until a successor guardian or conservator is appointed. Whenever the court suspends or limits the powers of the guardian or conservator to make educational decisions for a minor ward or conservatee, the court shall at the same time appoint a responsible adult to make educational decisions for the minor ward or conservatee until the guardian or conservator is again authorized to make educational decisions for the minor ward or conservatee. An individual who would have a conflict of interest in representing the child may not be appointed to make educational decisions. For purposes of this section, "an individual who would have a conflict of interest," means a person having any interests that might restrict or bias his or her ability to make educational decisions, including, but not limited to, those conflicts of interest prohibited by Section 1126 of the Government Code, and the receipt of compensation or attorneys' fees for the provision of services pursuant to this section. A foster parent may not be deemed to have a conflict of interest solely because he or she receives compensation for the provision of services pursuant to this section. **Leg.H.** Added Stats 2002 ch 180 §1 (AB 886), effective January 1, 2003.

CHAPTER 9.5
APPOINTMENT OF SUCCESSOR GUARDIAN OR CONSERVATOR

Article 1. Appointment of Successor Guardian.
Article 2. Appointment of Successor Conservator.

ARTICLE 1
Appointment of Successor Guardian

Court authorized to appoint successor guardian. §2670.

§2670. Court authorized to appoint successor guardian

When for any reason a vacancy occurs in the office of guardian, the court may appoint a successor guardian, after notice and hearing as in the case of an original appointment of a guardian. **Leg.H.** Enacted Stats 1990 ch 79 §14 (AB 759), operative July 1, 1991.

Prior Law: Former Prob C §2670, similar to the present section, was added Stats 1981 ch 9 §4, and repealed Stats 1990 ch 79 §13, operative July 1, 1991.

ARTICLE 2
Appointment of Successor Conservator

Court authorized to appoint successor conservator. §2680.
Who may file petition. §2681.
Contents of petition. §2682.
Notice of hearing. §2683.
Interview and report by court investigator. §2684.
Information to conservatee by court. §2685.
Failure of conservatee to attend hearing. §2686.
Persons who may support or oppose petition. §2687.
Order appointing successor conservator. §2688.
Provisions applicable where conservatee is an "absentee". §2689.

§2680. Court authorized to appoint successor conservator

When for any reason a vacancy occurs in the office of conservator, the court may appoint a successor conservator in the manner provided in this article. **Leg.H.** Enacted Stats 1990 ch 79 §14 (AB 759), operative July 1, 1991.

Prior Law: Former Prob C §2680, similar to the present section, was added Stats 1981 ch 9 §4, and repealed Stats 1990 ch 79 §13, operative July 1, 1991.

§2681. Who may file petition

A petition for appointment of a successor conservator may be filed by any of the following:

(a) The conservatee.

(b) The spouse or domestic partner of the conservatee.

(c) A relative of the conservatee.

(d) Any interested state or local entity or agency of this state or any interested public officer or employee of this state or of a local public entity of this state.

(e) Any other interested person or friend of the conservatee. **Leg.H.** Enacted Stats 1990 ch 79 §14 (AB 759), operative July 1, 1991. Amended Stats 2001 ch 893 §43 (AB 25).

Prior Law: Former Prob C §2681, similar to the present section, was added Stats 1981 ch 9 §4, and repealed Stats 1990 ch 79 §13, operative July 1, 1991.

§2682. Contents of petition

(a) The petition shall request that a successor conservator be appointed for the person or estate, or both, and shall specify the name and address of the proposed successor conservator and the name and address of the conservatee.

(b) The petition shall set forth, so far as they are known to the petitioner, the names and addresses of the spouse or domestic partner and of the relatives of the conservatee within the second degree.

(c) If the petition is filed by one other than the conservatee, the petition shall state whether or not the petitioner is a creditor or debtor of the conservatee.

(d) If the conservatee is a patient in or on leave of absence from a state institution under the jurisdiction of the State Department of State Hospitals or the State Department of Developmental Services and that fact is known to the petitioner, the petition shall state that fact and name the institution.

(e) The petition shall state, so far as is known to the petitioner, whether or not the conservatee is receiving or is entitled to receive benefits from the Veterans Administration and the estimated amount of the monthly benefit payable by the Veterans Administration for the conservatee.

(f) The petition shall state whether or not the conservatee will be present at the hearing. **Leg.H.** Enacted Stats 1990 ch 79 §14 (AB 759), operative July 1, 1991. Amended Stats 2001 ch 893 §44 (AB 25); Stats 2012 ch 440 §48 (AB 1488), effective September 22, 2012.

Prior Law: Former Prob C §2682, similar to the present section, was added Stats 1981 ch 9 §4 and repealed Stats 1990 ch 79 §13, operative July 1, 1991.

§2683. Notice of hearing

(a) At least 15 days before the hearing on the petition for appointment of a successor conservator, notice of the time and place of the hearing shall be given as provided in this section. The notice shall be accompanied by a copy of the petition.

(b) Notice shall be delivered pursuant to Section 1215 to the persons designated in Section 1460 and to the relatives named in the petition.

(c) If notice is required by Section 1461 to be given to the Director of State Hospitals or the Director of Developmental Services, notice shall be delivered pursuant to Section 1215 as required.

(d) If notice is required by Section 1461.5 to be given to the Veterans Administration, notice shall be delivered pursuant to Section 1215 as required. **Leg.H.** Enacted Stats 1990 ch 79 §14 (AB 759), operative July 1, 1991. Amended Stats 1994 ch 806 §19 (AB 3686); Stats 2012 ch 440 §49 (AB 1488), effective September 22, 2012; Stats 2017 ch 319 §50 (AB 976), effective January 1, 2018.

Prior Law: Former Prob C §2683, similar to the present section, was added Stats 1981 ch 9 §4, and repealed Stats 1990 ch 79 §13, operative July 1, 1991.

§2684. Interview and report by court investigator

Unless the petition states that the conservatee will be present at the hearing, the court investigator shall do all of the following:

(a) Interview the conservatee personally.

(b) Inform the conservatee of the nature of the proceeding to appoint a successor conservator, the name of the person proposed as successor conservator, and the conservatee's right to appear personally at the hearing, to object to the person proposed as successor conservator, to nominate a person to be appointed as successor conservator, to be represented by legal counsel if the conservatee so chooses, and to have legal counsel appointed by the court if unable to retain legal counsel.

(c) Determine whether the conservatee objects to the person proposed as successor conservator or prefers another person to be appointed.

(d) If the conservatee is not represented by legal counsel, determine whether the conservatee wishes to be represented by legal counsel and, if so, determine the name of an attorney the conservatee wishes to retain or whether the conservatee desires the court to appoint legal counsel.

(e) Determine whether the appointment of legal counsel would be helpful to the resolution of the matter or is necessary to protect the interests of the conservatee in any case where the conservatee does not plan to retain legal counsel and has not requested the appointment of legal counsel by the court.

(f) Report to the court in writing, at least five days before the hearing, concerning all of the foregoing, including the conservatee's express communications concerning representation by legal counsel and whether the conservatee objects to the person proposed as successor conservator or prefers that some other person be appointed.

(g) Deliver pursuant to Section 1215, at least five days before the hearing, a copy of the report referred to in subdivision (f) to all of the following:

(1) The attorney, if any, for the petitioner.

(2) The attorney, if any, for the conservatee.

(3) Any other persons as the court orders. **Leg.H.** Enacted Stats 1990 ch 79 §14 (AB 759), operative July 1, 1991. Amended Stats 2017 ch 319 §51 (AB 976), effective January 1, 2018.

Prior Law: Former Prob C §2684, similar to the present section, was added Stats 1981 ch 9 §4, and repealed Stats 1990 ch 79 §13, operative July 1, 1991.

§2685. Information to conservatee by court

If the conservatee is present at the hearing, prior to making an order appointing a successor conservator the court shall do all of the following:

(a) Inform the conservatee of the nature and purpose of the proceeding.

(b) Inform the conservatee that the conservatee has the right to object to the person proposed as successor conservator, to nominate a person to be appointed as successor conservator, and, if not represented by legal counsel, to be represented by legal counsel if the conservatee so chooses and to have legal counsel appointed by the court if unable to retain legal counsel.

(c) After the court so informs the conservatee, the court shall consult the conservatee to determine the conservatee's opinion concerning the question of who should be appointed as successor conservator. **Leg.H.** Enacted Stats 1990 ch 79 §14 (AB 759), operative July 1, 1991.

Prior Law: Former Prob C §2685, similar to the present section, was added Stats 1981 ch 9 §4, and repealed Stats 1990 ch 79 §13, operative July 1, 1991.

§2686. Failure of conservatee to attend hearing

If the petition states that the conservatee will be present at the hearing and the conservatee fails to appear at the hearing, the court shall continue the hearing and direct the court investigator to perform the duties set forth in Section 2684. **Leg.H.** Enacted Stats 1990 ch 79 §14 (AB 759), operative July 1, 1991.

Prior Law: Former Prob C §2686, similar to the present section, was added Stats 1981 ch 9 §4, and repealed Stats 1990 ch 79 §13, operative July 1, 1991.

§2687. Persons who may support or oppose petition

The conservatee, the spouse, the domestic partner, or any relative or friend of the conservatee, or any other interested person may appear at the hearing to support or oppose the petition. **Leg.H.** Enacted Stats 1990 ch 79 §14 (AB 759), operative July 1, 1991. Amended Stats 2001 ch 893 §45 (AB 25), effective January 1, 2002.

Prior Law: Former Prob C §2687, similar to the present section, was added Stats 1981 ch 9 §4, and repealed Stats 1990 ch 79 §13, operative July 1, 1991.

§2688. Order appointing successor conservator

(a) The court shall determine the question of who should be appointed as successor conservator according to the provisions of Article 2 (commencing with Section 1810) of Chapter 1 of Part 3.

(b) The order appointing the successor conservator shall contain, among other things, the names, addresses and telephone numbers of the successor conservator, the conservatee's attorney, if any, and the court investigator, if any. **Leg.H.** Enacted Stats 1990 ch 79 §14 (AB 759), operative July 1, 1991.

Prior Law: Former Prob C §2688, similar to the present section, was added Stats 1981 ch 9 §4, and repealed Stats 1990 ch 79 §13, operative July 1, 1991.

§2689. Provisions applicable where conservatee is an "absentee"

If the conservatee is an "absentee" as defined in Section 1403:

(a) The petition for appointment of a successor conservator shall contain the matters required by Section 1841 in addition to the matters required by Section 2682.

(b) Notice of the hearing shall be given as provided by Section 1842 in addition to the requirements of Section 2683, except that notice need not be given to the conservatee.

(c) An interview and report by the court investigator is not required. **Leg.H.** Enacted Stats 1990 ch 79 §14 (AB 759), operative July 1, 1991.

Prior Law: Former Prob C §2689, similar to the present section, was added Stats 1981 ch 9 §4, and repealed Stats 1990 ch 79 §13, operative July 1, 1991.

CHAPTER 10
REQUESTS FOR SPECIAL NOTICE

Request for special notice. §2700.
Modification or withdrawal of request; New request. §2701.
Requirement that petitioner give requested special notice. §2702.

§2700. Request for special notice

(a)(1) At any time after the issuance of letters of guardianship or conservatorship, the ward, if over 14 years of age or the conservatee, the spouse of the ward or the spouse or domestic partner of the conservatee, any relative or creditor of the ward or conservatee, or any other interested person, in person or by attorney, may file with the court clerk a written request for special notice.

(2) An "interested person" may include, but is not limited to, a family member of the conservatee not included in Section 1460 or a friend of the conservatee.

(b) The request for special notice shall be so entitled and shall set forth the name of the person and the address to which notices shall be delivered pursuant to Section 1215.

(c) Special notice may be requested of any one or more of the following matters:

(1) Petitions filed in the guardianship or conservatorship proceeding.

(2) Inventories and appraisals of property in the estate, including any supplemental inventories and appraisals.

(3) Accounts of the guardian or conservator.

(4) Proceedings for the final termination of the guardianship or conservatorship proceeding.

(d) Special notice may be requested of:

(1) Any one or more of the matters in subdivision (c) by describing the matter or matters.

(2) All the matters in subdivision (c) by referring generally to "the matters described in subdivision (c) of Section 2700 of the Probate Code" or by using words of similar meaning.

(e) A copy of the request shall be delivered pursuant to Section 1215 to the guardian or conservator or to the attorney for the guardian or conservator. If personally delivered, the request is effective when it is delivered. If mailed or electronically delivered, the request is effective when it is received.

(f) If the original of the request is filed with the court clerk, it shall be accompanied by a written admission or proof of service. **Leg.H.** Enacted Stats 1990 ch 79 §14 (AB 759), operative July 1, 1991. Amended Stats 2001 ch 893 §46 (AB 25); Stats 2017 ch 319 §52 (AB 976), effective January 1, 2018; Stats 2024 ch 455 §4 (SB 1106), effective January 1, 2025.

Prior Law: Former Prob C §2700, similar to the present section, was added Stats 1979 ch 726 §3, operative January 1, 1981, amended Stats 1981 ch 9 §5, and repealed Stats 1990 ch 79 §13, operative July 1, 1991.

§2701. Modification or withdrawal of request; New request

(a) A request for special notice may be modified or withdrawn in the same manner as provided for the making of the initial request.

(b) A new request for special notice may be served and filed at any time as provided in the case of an initial request. **Leg.H.** Enacted Stats 1990 ch 79 §14 (AB 759), operative July 1, 1991. Amended Stats 2006 ch 493 §31 (AB 1363), effective January 1, 2007.

2006 Note: This act, together with Senate Bill 1116 (Scott), Senate Bill 1550 (Figueroa), and Senate Bill 1716 (Bowen), shall be known and may be cited as the Omnibus Conservatorship and Guardianship Reform Act of 2006. Stats 2006 ch 493 (AB 1363) §1.

Prior Law: Former Prob C §2701, similar to the present section, was added Stats 1979 ch 726 §3, operative January 1, 1981, and repealed Stats 1990 ch 79 §13, operative July 1, 1991.

§2702. Requirement that petitioner give requested special notice

(a) Unless the court makes an order dispensing with the notice, if a request has been made pursuant to this chapter for special notice of a hearing, the person filing the petition, account, or other paper shall give written notice pursuant to Section 1215 of the filing, together with a copy of the petition, account, or other paper, and the time and place set for the hearing, to the person named in the request at the address set forth in the request, at least 15 days before the time set for the hearing.

(b) If a request has been made pursuant to this chapter for special notice of the filing of an inventory and appraisal of the estate or of the filing of any other paper that does not require a hearing, the inventory and appraisal or other paper shall be delivered pursuant to Section 1215 not later than 15 days after the inventory and appraisal or other paper is filed with the court. **Leg.H.** Enacted Stats 1990 ch 79 §14 (AB 759), operative July 1, 1991. Amended Stats 2017 ch 319 §53 (AB 976), effective January 1, 2018.

Prior Law: Former Prob C §2702, similar to the present section, was added Stats 1979 ch 726 §3, operative January 1, 1981, and repealed Stats 1990 ch 79 §13, operative July 1, 1991.

CHAPTER 11
APPEALS [REPEALED]

§2750. [Section repealed 1998.]

Leg.H. Enacted Stats 1990 ch 79 §14 (AB 759), operative July 1, 1991. Repealed Stats 1997 ch 724 §15 (AB 1172). See Prob C §§1300, 1301.

Prior Law: Former Prob C §2750, similar to present Prob C §1301, was added Stats 1979 ch 726 §3, operative January 1, 1981, amended Stats 1981 ch 9 §6, and repealed Stats 1990 ch 79 §13, operative July 1, 1991.

§2751. [Section repealed 1998.]

Leg.H. Enacted Stats 1990 ch 79 §14 (AB 759), operative July 1, 1991. Amended Stats 1996 ch 563 §14 (SB 392). Repealed Stats 1997 ch 724 §15 (AB 1172). See Prob C §1310.

Prior Law: Former Prob C §2751, similar to present Prob C §1310, was added Stats 1979 ch 726 §3, operative January 1, 1981, and repealed Stats 1990 ch 79 §13, operative July 1, 1991.

§2752. [Section repealed 1998.]

Leg.H. Enacted Stats 1990 ch 79 §14 (AB 759), operative July 1, 1991. Repealed Stats 1997 ch 724 §15 (AB 1172). See Prob C §1311.

Prior Law: Former Prob C §2752, similar to present Prob C §1310, was added Stats 1979 ch 726 §3, operative January 1, 1981, and repealed Stats 1990 ch 79 §13, operative July 1, 1991.

CHAPTER 12
TRANSFER OF PERSONAL PROPERTY OUT OF STATE

"Foreign guardian or conservator" defined. §2800.
Order for transfer of assets out of state. §2801.
Who may petition for transfer. §2802.
Contents of petition. §2803.
Notice of hearing. §2804.
Objections to petition. §2805.
Order for transfer. §2806.
Manner of transfer; Conditions. §2807.
Termination of guardianship or conservatorship. §2808.

§2800. "Foreign guardian or conservator" defined

As used in this chapter, "foreign guardian or conservator" means a guardian, conservator, committee, or comparable fiduciary in another jurisdiction. **Leg.H.** Enacted Stats 1990 ch 79 §14 (AB 759), operative July 1, 1991.

Prior Law: Former Prob C §2800, similar to the present section, was added Stats 1979 ch 726 §3, operative January 1, 1981, and repealed Stats 1990 ch 79 §13, operative July 1, 1991.

§2801. Order for transfer of assets out of state

Subject to the limitations and requirements of this chapter, the court in which the guardianship of the estate or conservatorship of the estate is pending may order the transfer of some or all of the personal property of the estate to a foreign guardian or conservator in another jurisdiction outside this state where the ward or conservatee resides at the time the petition for the order authorizing the transfer is filed. **Leg.H.** Enacted Stats 1990 ch 79 §14 (AB 759), operative July 1, 1991.

Prior Law: Former Prob C §2801, similar to the present section, was added Stats 1979 ch 726 §3, operative January 1, 1981, and repealed Stats 1990 ch 79 §13, operative July 1, 1991.

§2802. Who may petition for transfer

A petition for an order authorizing a transfer may be filed by any of the following:

(a) The guardian of the estate or the conservator of the estate.

(b) The ward or conservatee.

(c) A foreign guardian or conservator. **Leg.H.** Enacted Stats 1990 ch 79 §14 (AB 759), operative July 1, 1991.

Prior Law: Former Prob C §2802, similar to the present section, was added Stats 1979 ch 726 §3, operative January 1, 1981, and repealed Stats 1990 ch 79 §13, operative July 1, 1991.

§2803. Contents of petition

The petition shall set forth all of the following:

(a) The name and address of:

(1) The foreign guardian or conservator, who may but need not be the guardian or conservator appointed in this state.

(2) The ward or conservatee.

(3) The guardian or conservator, so far as is known to the petitioner.

(b) The names, ages, and addresses, so far as they are known to the petitioner, of the spouse of the ward or the spouse or domestic partner of the conservatee and of relatives of the ward or conservatee within the second degree.

(c) A brief description of the character, condition, value, and location of the personal property sought to be transferred.

(d) A statement whether the foreign guardian or conservator has agreed to accept the transfer of the property. If the foreign guardian or conservator has so agreed, the acceptance shall be attached as an exhibit to the petition or otherwise filed with the court.

(e) A statement of the manner in which and by whom the foreign guardian or conservator was appointed.

(f) A general statement of the qualifications of the foreign guardian or conservator.

(g) The amount of bond, if any, of the foreign guardian or conservator.

(h) A general statement of the nature and value of the property of the ward or conservatee already under the management or control of the foreign guardian or conservator.

(i) The name of the court having jurisdiction of the foreign guardian or conservator or of the accounts of the foreign guardian or conservator or, if none, the court in which a proceeding may be had with respect to the guardianship or conservatorship if the property is transferred.

(j) Whether there is any pending civil action in this state against the guardian or conservator, the ward or conservatee, or the estate.

(k) A statement of the reasons for the transfer. **Leg.H.** Enacted Stats 1990 ch 79 §14 (AB 759), operative July 1, 1991. Amended Stats 2001 ch 893 §47 (AB 25), effective January 1, 2002.

§2804. Notice of hearing

At least 30 days before the hearing, the petitioner shall deliver pursuant to Section 1215 a notice of the time and place of the hearing and a copy of the petition to each person required to be listed in the petition at the address stated in the petition. **Leg.H.** Enacted Stats 1990 ch 79 §14 (AB 759), operative July 1, 1991. Amended Stats 2017 ch 319 §54 (AB 976), effective January 1, 2018.

Prior Law: Former Prob C §2804, similar to the present section, was added Stats 1979 ch 726 §3, operative January 1, 1981, and repealed Stats 1990 ch 79 §13, operative July 1, 1991.

§2805. Objections to petition

Any of the following may appear and file written objections to the petition:

(a) Any person required to be listed in the petition.
(b) Any creditor of the ward or conservatee or of the estate.
(c) The spouse of the ward or the spouse or domestic partner of the conservatee or any relative or friend of the ward or conservatee.
(d) Any other interested person. **Leg.H.** Enacted Stats 1990 ch 79 §14 (AB 759), operative July 1, 1991. Amended Stats 2001 ch 893 §48 (AB 25), effective January 1, 2002.

Prior Law: Former Prob C §2805, similar to the present section, was added Stats 1979 ch 726 §3, operative January 1, 1981, and repealed Stats 1990 ch 79 §13, operative July 1, 1991.

§2806. Order for transfer

The court may grant the petition and order the guardian or conservator to transfer some or all of the personal property of the estate to the foreign guardian or conservator if the court determines all of the following:

(a) The transfer will promote the best interests of the ward or conservatee and the estate.
(b) The substantial rights of creditors or claimants in this state will not be materially impaired by the transfer.
(c) The foreign guardian or conservator is qualified, willing, and able to administer the property to be transferred. **Leg.H.** Enacted Stats 1990 ch 79 §14 (AB 759), operative July 1, 1991.

Prior Law: Former Prob C §2806, similar to the present section, was added Stats 1979 ch 726 §3, operative January 1, 1981, and repealed Stats 1990 ch 79 §13, operative July 1, 1991.

§2807. Manner of transfer; Conditions

If a transfer is ordered, the court may direct the manner of transfer and impose such terms and conditions as may be just. **Leg.H.** Enacted Stats 1990 ch 79 §14 (AB 759), operative July 1, 1991.

Prior Law: Former Prob C §2807, similar to the present section, was added Stats 1979 ch 726 §3, operative January 1, 1981, and repealed Stats 1990 ch 79 §13, operative July 1, 1991.

§2808. Termination of guardianship or conservatorship

(a) If the court's order provides for the transfer of all of the property of the estate to the foreign guardian or conservator, the court, upon settlement of the final account, shall order the guardianship of the estate or the conservatorship of the estate terminated upon the filing with the clerk of the court of a receipt for the property executed by the foreign guardian or conservator.

(b) Unless notice is waived, a copy of the final account of the guardian or conservator and of the petition for discharge, together with a notice of the hearing, shall be delivered pursuant to Section 1215 at least 30 days before the date of the hearing to all persons required to be listed in the petition for transfer, including the foreign guardian or conservator. **Leg.H.** Enacted Stats 1990 ch 79 §14 (AB 759), operative July 1, 1991. Amended Stats 2017 ch 319 §55 (AB 976), effective January 1, 2018.

Prior Law: Former Prob C §2808, similar to the present section, was added Stats 1979 ch 726 §3, operative January 1, 1981, and repealed Stats 1990 ch 79 §13, operative July 1, 1991.

CHAPTER 13
STATEWIDE REGISTRY [REPEALED]

§2850. [Section repealed 2009]

Leg.H. Added Stats 1999 ch 409 §1 (AB 925). Amended Stats 2001 ch 176 §47 (SB 210); Stats 2003 ch 629 §1 (SB 294); Stats 2004 ch 548 §1 (SB 1248), ch 625 §4.5 (AB 1155). Repealed January 1, 2009, by the terms of Prob C §2856. The repealed section related to information in registry.

§2851. [Section repealed 2009]

Leg.H. Added Stats 1999 ch 409 §1 (AB 925). Amended Stats 2003 ch 629 §2 (SB 294); Stats 2004 ch 548 §2 (SB 1248). Repealed January 1, 2009, by the terms of Prob C §2856. The repealed section related to registration requirement.

§2852. [Section repealed 2009]

Leg.H. Added Stats 1999 ch 409 §1 (AB 925). Amended Stats 2003 ch 629 §3 (SB 294). Repealed January 1, 2009, by the terms of Prob C §2856. The repealed section related to violations and penalties.

§2853. [Section repealed 2009]

Leg.H. Added Stats 1999 ch 409 §1 (AB 925). Amended Stats 2003 ch 629 §4 (SB 294). Repealed January 1, 2009, by the terms of Prob C §2856. The repealed section related to cases of urgency.

§2854. [Section repealed 2009]

Leg.H. Added Stats 1999 ch 409 §1 (AB 925). Amended Stats 2002 ch 1115 §4 (AB 3036); Stats 2003 ch 296 §25.5 (SB 66), ch 629 §5 (SB 294); Stats 2004 ch 548 §3 (SB 1248); Stats 2005 ch 302 §3 (AB 541). Repealed January 1, 2009, by the terms of Prob C §2856. The repealed section related to application of chapter.

§2855. [Section repealed 2009]

Leg.H. Added Stats 1999 ch 409 §1 (AB 925). Amended Stats 2003 ch 629 §6 (SB 294). Repealed January 1, 2009, by the terms of Prob C §2856. The repealed section related to legislative intent.

§2856. [Section repealed 2009]

Leg.H. Added Stats 2006 ch 491 §7 (SB 1550), effective January 1, 2007, inoperative July 1, 2008, repealed January 1, 2009. Repealed January 1, 2009, by its own terms. The repealed section related to repeal of chapter.

Prior Law: Former Prob C §2856, similar to present Prob C §2850, was added Stats 1999 ch 409 §1 (AB 925) and repealed Stats 2003 ch 629 §7 (SB 294).

CHAPTER 14
NOTIFICATION TO COURT BY INSTITUTIONS

Information to be filed with court by institution upon guardian's or conservator's possession of asset of ward or conservatee held by institution. §2890.
Filing information in the form of affidavit; Confidentiality of information; Fee. §2891.
Change in name to an account or safe-deposit box by guardian or conservator; Statement by financial institution to the court. §2892.
Financial institution's statement concerning change in name to account or safe deposit box to be in the form of affidavit; Confidentiality. §2893.

§2890. Information to be filed with court by institution upon guardian's or conservator's possession of asset of ward or conservatee held by institution

(a) When a guardian or conservator, pursuant to letters of guardianship or conservatorship of the estate, takes possession or control of any asset of the ward or conservatee held by an institution, as defined in subdivision (c), the institution shall file with the court having jurisdiction of the guardianship or conservatorship a statement containing the following information:

(1) The name of the ward or conservatee.
(2) The name of the guardian or joint guardians or conservator or joint conservators.
(3) The court case number.
(4) The name of the institution.
(5) The address of the institution.
(6) The account number of the account, if any, in which the asset was held by the ward or conservatee.
(7) A description of the asset or assets held by the institution. If an asset is a life insurance policy or annuity, the description shall include the policy number, if available. If the asset is a security listed on a public exchange, the description shall include the name and reference number, if available.
(8) The value, if known, or the estimated value otherwise, of the asset on the date the letters were issued by the court to the guardian or

conservator, to the extent this value is routinely provided in the statements from the institution to the owner.

(b) Taking possession or control of an asset includes, for purposes of this chapter, changing title to the asset, withdrawing all or any portion of the asset, or transferring all or any portion of an asset from the institution.

(c) For purposes of this chapter, "institution" means an insurance company, insurance broker, insurance agent, investment company, investment bank, securities broker-dealer, investment adviser, financial planner, financial adviser, or any other person who takes, holds, or controls an asset subject to a conservatorship or guardianship that is not a "financial institution" as defined in Section 2892. **Leg.H.** Added Stats 2001 ch 563 §7 (AB 1286), effective January 1, 2002.

§2891. Filing information in the form of affidavit; Confidentiality of information; Fee

(a) The statement filed pursuant to Section 2890 shall be an affidavit by a person having authority to make the statement on behalf of the institution, as defined in Section 2890, and shall include that fact in the statement.

(b) If the affidavit and any accompanying information to be filed pursuant to this section also contains the ward or conservatee's social security number or any other personal information, including financial information regarding the ward or conservatee which would not be disclosed in an accounting, an inventory and appraisal, or any other nonconfidential pleading filed in the action, the information shall be kept confidential and subject to disclosure to any person only upon order of the court.

(c) This chapter does not apply to any trust arrangement described in subdivision (b) of Section 82 except paragraph (4) of that subdivision relating to assets held in Totten trust.

(d) No fee shall be charged by the court for the filing of the affidavit or related information as required by this section.

(e) The affidavit required by Section 2890 is not required to be filed in a proceeding more than once for each asset. However, all assets held by institutions may be listed in a single affidavit filed with the court.

(f) When a guardian or conservator takes possession or control of an asset in an institution, as defined in Section 2890, the institution may then file with the court the statement required by Section 2890 as to any or all other assets of the ward or conservatee held in the institution. **Leg.H.** Added Stats 2001 ch 563 §7 (AB 1286), effective January 1, 2002.

§2892. Change in name to an account or safe-deposit box by guardian or conservator; Statement by financial institution to the court

(a) When a guardian or conservator, pursuant to letters of guardianship or conservatorship of the estate, opens or changes the name to an account or safe-deposit box in a financial institution, as defined in subdivision (b), the financial institution shall send to the court identified in the letters of guardianship or conservatorship a statement containing the following information:

(1) The name of the person with whom the account or safe-deposit box is opened or changed.

(2) The account number or reference number.

(3) The date the account or safe-deposit box was opened or changed ownership pursuant to letters of guardianship or conservatorship.

(4) If the asset is held in an account in a financial institution, the balance as of the date the account was opened or changed.

(5) If the asset is held in a safe-deposit box, and the financial institution has been given access to the safe-deposit box, a list of the contents, including, for example, currency, coins, jewelry, tableware, insurance policies or certificates, stock certificates, bonds, deeds, and wills.

(6) The name and address of the financial institution in which the asset is maintained.

(b) For purposes of this chapter, "financial institution" means a bank, trust, savings and loan association, savings bank, industrial bank, or credit union. **Leg.H.** Added Stats 2001 ch 563 §7 (AB 1286). Amended Stats 2003 ch 888 §7 (AB 394), effective January 1, 2004.

§2893. Financial institution's statement concerning change in name to account or safe deposit box to be in the form of affidavit; Confidentiality

(a) The written statement provided pursuant to Section 2892 by the financial institution shall be in the form of an affidavit signed by an officer of the financial institution and the officer shall provide his or her name and title in the affidavit.

(b) The affidavit required by this section is subject to disclosure under the circumstances described in subdivision (*l*) of Section 7480 of the Government Code under the California Right to Financial Privacy Act (Chapter 20 (commencing with Section 7460) of Division 7 of Title 1 of the Government Code).

(c) This chapter does not apply to any trust arrangement described in subdivision (b) of Section 82 except paragraph (4) of that subdivision relating to assets held in a Totten trust.

(d) The affidavit described in Section 2892 is not required to be filed in a proceeding more than once for each asset. However, all assets held by the financial institution may be listed in a single affidavit filed with the court.

(e) If the affidavit and any accompanying information to be filed pursuant to this section also contains the ward or conservatee's social security number or any other personal information, including financial information regarding the ward or conservatee which would not be disclosed in an accounting, an inventory and appraisal, or other nonconfidential pleading filed in the action, the information shall be kept confidential and subject to disclosure to any person only upon order of the court. **Leg.H.** Added Stats 2001 ch 563 §7 (AB 1286), effective January 1, 2002.

PART 5
PUBLIC GUARDIAN

Chapter 1. Taking Temporary Possession or Control of Property.
Chapter 2. Prefiling Investigation by Public Guardian.
Chapter 3. Appointment of Public Guardian.
Chapter 4. Administration by Public Guardian.
Chapter 5. Financial Abuse of Mentally Impaired Elders.

CHAPTER 1
TAKING TEMPORARY POSSESSION OR CONTROL OF PROPERTY

Authority to take possession or control; Authority to restrain transfer, encumbrance, or disposal of property; Requirements. §2900.
Form of written certification; Effective term; Recording certificate with the county; Providing information and surrendering property to public guardian. §2901.
Certification entitling public guardian or conservator to restrain transfer, encumbrance, or disposal of property; Form of certification; Effective term; Recording. §2901.5.
Costs and compensation for taking possession or control. §2902.
Transitional provision. §2903.

§2900. Authority to take possession or control; Authority to restrain transfer, encumbrance, or disposal of property; Requirements

(a)(1) If the public guardian or public conservator determines that the requirements for appointment of a guardian or conservator of the estate are satisfied and the public guardian or public conservator intends to apply for appointment, the public guardian or public conservator may take possession or control of real or personal property of a person domiciled in the county that is subject to loss, injury, waste, or misappropriation, and, subject to subdivision (b), may deny use of, access to, or prohibit residency in, the real or personal property, by anyone who does not have a written rental agreement or other legal right to the use of, or access to, the property.

(2)(A) Except as provided in subparagraph (C), if the public guardian or public conservator determines that the requirements for appointment of a guardian or conservator of the estate are satisfied and the public guardian or public conservator intends to apply for appointment as the guardian or conservator of a person domiciled in the county, the public guardian or public conservator may restrain any person from transferring, encumbering, or in any way disposing of any real or personal property held in a trust, provided all of the following requirements are met:

(i) The real or personal property held in the trust is subject to loss, injury, waste, or misappropriation.

(ii) The proposed ward or conservatee is a settlor of the trust.

(iii) The proposed ward or conservatee has a beneficial interest in the trust to currently receive income or principal from the trust.

(iv) The proposed ward or conservatee holds a power to revoke the trust.

(B) During the period of any restraint under this paragraph, the property subject to the restraint shall continue to be retained as property of the trust pending termination of the restraint or further court order. The public guardian or public conservator shall provide notice of any action taken under this paragraph to all of the persons required to be noticed pursuant to Section 17203, to the extent the public guardian or public conservator has access to the trust documents or is otherwise able to determine the persons entitled to receive notice. Any settlor, trustee, or beneficiary may petition the court for relief from any action taken by the public guardian or public conservator under this paragraph.

(C) This paragraph shall not apply if a current trustee or cotrustee is a spouse of the proposed ward or conservatee and that spouse is also a settlor of the trust, unless the public guardian or public conservator determines that the real or personal property held in the trust is subject to substantial loss, injury, waste, or misappropriation.

(b) The authority provided to the public guardian and public conservator in subdivision (a) includes the authority to terminate immediately the occupancy of anyone living in the home of an intended ward or conservatee, other than the intended ward or conservatee, and the authority to remove any such occupant residing therein, subject to the following requirements:

(1) The public guardian or public conservator shall first determine that the person whose occupancy is to be terminated has no written rental agreement or other legal right to occupancy, and has caused, contributed to, enabled, or threatened loss, injury, waste, or misappropriation of the home or its contents. In making this determination, the public guardian or public conservator shall contact the intended ward or conservatee and the occupant, advise them of the proposed removal and the grounds therefor, and consider whatever information they provide.

(2) At the time of the removal, the public guardian or public conservator shall advise the intended ward or conservatee and the occupant that a hearing will be held as provided in paragraph (3).

(3) The public guardian or public conservator shall file a petition regarding removal, showing the grounds therefor, to be set for hearing within 10 days of the filing of the petition and within 15 days of the removal. The person removed and the intended ward or conservatee shall be personally served with a notice of hearing and a copy of the petition at least five days prior to the hearing, subject to Part 2 (commencing with Section 1200) of Division 3. The right of the public guardian or public conservator to deny occupancy by the removed person to the premises shall terminate 15 days after removal, unless extended by the court at the hearing on the petition. The court shall not grant an extension unless the public guardian or public conservator has filed a petition for appointment as guardian or conservator of the estate.

(c) If the public guardian or public conservator takes possession of the residence of an intended ward or conservatee under this section, then for purposes of Section 602.3 of the Penal Code, the public guardian or public conservator shall be the owner's representative. **Leg.H.** Added Stats 1992 ch 572 §11 (SB 1455). Amended Stats 2011 ch 370 §1 (AB 1288), effective January 1, 2012.

Prior Law: Former Prob C §2900, similar to the present section, was added Stats 1990 ch 79 §14, operative July 1, 1991, and repealed Stats 1992 ch 572 §10.

Former Prob C §2900, similar to the present section, was added Stats 1988 ch 1199 §72, operative July 1, 1989, and repealed Stats 1990 ch 79 §13, operative July 1, 1991.

§2901. Form of written certification; Effective term; Recording certificate with the county; Providing information and surrendering property to public guardian

(a) A public guardian who is authorized to take possession or control of property under this chapter may issue a written certification of that fact. The written certification is effective for 30 days after the date of issuance.

(b) The written recordable certification shall substantially comply with the following form:

"CERTIFICATE OF AUTHORITY

THIS IS AN OFFICIAL CERTIFICATE ENTITLING THE PUBLIC GUARDIAN TO TAKE POSSESSION OF ANY AND ALL PROPERTY BELONGING TO THE FOLLOWING INDIVIDUAL:

(Name of Individual) ____

This Certificate of Authority has been issued by the Public Guardian pursuant to and in compliance with Chapter 1 (commencing with Section 2900) of Part 5 of Division 4 of the California Probate Code. Under California law, this Certificate of Authority authorizes the Public Guardian to take possession or control of property belonging to the above-named individual.

SPECIAL NOTE TO FINANCIAL INSTITUTIONS:

State law requires that upon receiving a copy of this Certificate of Authority, financial institutions shall provide the public guardian with information concerning property held by the above-named individual and surrender the property to the Public Guardian if requested.

This Certificate of Authority shall only be valid when signed and dated by the Public Guardian or a deputy Public Guardian of the County of ____ and affixed with the official seal of the Public Guardian below.

This Certificate of Authority expires 30 days after the date of issuance.
Signature of Public Guardian:
Date:
Official Seal"

(c) The public guardian may record a copy of the written certification in any county in which is located real property of which the public guardian is authorized to take possession or control under this chapter.

(d) A financial institution or other person shall, without the necessity of inquiring into the truth of the written certification and without court order or letters being issued:

(1) Provide the public guardian information concerning property held in the sole name of the proposed ward or conservatee.

(2) Surrender to the public guardian property of the proposed ward or conservatee that is subject to loss, injury, waste, or misappropriation.

(e) Receipt of the written certification:

(1) Constitutes sufficient acquittance for providing information and for surrendering property of the proposed ward or conservatee.

(2) Fully discharges the financial institution or other person from any liability for any act or omission of the public guardian with respect to the property. **Leg.H.** Enacted Stats 1990 ch 79 §14 (AB 759), operative July 1, 1991. Amended Stats 2001 ch 232 §2 (AB 1517); Stats 2011 ch 370 §2 (AB 1288), effective January 1, 2012.

Prior Law: Former Prob C §2901, similar to the present section, was added Stats 1988 ch 1199 §72, operative July 1, 1989, and repealed Stats 1990 ch 79 §13, operative July 1, 1991.

§2901.5. Certification entitling public guardian or conservator to restrain transfer, encumbrance, or disposal of property; Form of certification; Effective term; Recording

(a) A public guardian or public conservator, who is authorized to restrain any person from transferring, encumbering, or in any way disposing of any real or personal property held in a trust in accordance with paragraph (2) of subdivision (a) of Section 2900, may issue a written certification of that fact. The written certification is effective for 30 days after the date of issuance.

(b) The written recordable certification shall substantially comply with the following form:

"CERTIFICATE OF AUTHORITY

THIS IS AN OFFICIAL CERTIFICATE ENTITLING THE PUBLIC GUARDIAN/PUBLIC CONSERVATOR TO RESTRAIN ANY PERSON FROM TRANSFERRING, ENCUMBERING, OR IN ANY WAY DISPOSING OF ANY REAL OR PERSONAL PROPERTY HELD IN THE FOLLOWING TRUST:

(Name of Trust) ____

THE PUBLIC GUARDIAN/PUBLIC CONSERVATOR HAS DETERMINED THAT IT HAS AUTHORITY TO ISSUE THIS CERTIFICATE WITH RESPECT TO THE ABOVE-NAMED TRUST AND IN CONNECTION WITH PROCEEDINGS THAT ARE OR WILL BE PENDING RELATED TO THE FOLLOWING INDIVIDUAL:

(Name of Individual) ____

This Certificate of Authority has been issued by the Public Guardian/Public Conservator pursuant to and in compliance with Chapter 1 (commencing with Section 2900) of Part 5 of Division 4 of the California Probate Code. Under California law, this Certificate of Authority authorizes the Public Guardian/Public Conservator to restrain any person from transferring, encumbering, or in any way disposing of any real or personal property held in the above-named trust.

SPECIAL NOTE TO FINANCIAL INSTITUTIONS:

State law requires that, upon receiving a copy of this Certificate of Authority, financial institutions shall provide the public guardian/public conservator with information concerning property held in the above-named trust and shall restrain any person from transferring, encumbering, or in any way disposing of any real or personal property held in the above-named trust.

This Certificate of Authority shall only be valid when signed and dated by the Public Guardian/Public Conservator or a deputy Public Guardian/Public Conservator of the County of ____ and affixed with the official seal of the Public Guardian/Public Conservator below.

This Certificate of Authority expires 30 days after the date of issuance.

Signature of Public Guardian/Public Conservator:

Date:

Official Seal"

(c) The public guardian or public conservator may record a copy of the written certification in any county in which is located real property held in a trust as to which the public guardian or public conservator has determined it has authority to issue the written certification.

(d) A financial institution or other person who is provided with the written certification by the public guardian or public conservator shall, without the necessity of inquiring into the truth of the written certification and without court order or letters being issued:

(1) Provide the public guardian or public conservator information concerning any real or personal property held in the trust identified in the written certification.

(2) Restrain any person from transferring, encumbering, or in any way disposing of any real or personal property, held in the trust identified in the written certification.

(e) Receipt of the written certification:

(1) Constitutes sufficient acquittance for providing information and for restraining any person from transferring, encumbering, or in any way disposing of any real or personal property held in the trust identified in the written certification.

(2) Fully discharges the financial institution or other person from any liability for any act or omission of the public guardian or public conservator with respect to the property. **Leg.H.** Added Stats 2011 ch 370 §3 (AB 1288), effective January 1, 2012.

§2902. Costs and compensation for taking possession or control

A public guardian who takes possession or control of property pursuant to this chapter is entitled to reasonable costs incurred for the preservation of the property, together with reasonable compensation for services, in case of the subsequent appointment of another person as guardian or conservator of the estate. The costs and compensation are a proper and legal charge against the estate of the ward or conservatee. **Leg.H.** Enacted Stats 1990 ch 79 §14 (AB 759), operative July 1, 1991.

Prior Law: Former Prob C §2902, similar to the present section, was added Stats 1988 ch 1199 §72, operative July 1, 1989, and repealed Stats 1990 ch 79 §13, operative July 1, 1991.

§2903. Transitional provision

This chapter applies only to possession or control of property by a public guardian on or after July 1, 1989. Possession or control of property by a public guardian before July 1, 1989, is governed by the applicable law in effect before July 1, 1989, notwithstanding its repeal by Chapter 1199 of the Statutes of 1988. **Leg.H.** Enacted Stats 1990 ch 79 §14 (AB 759), operative July 1, 1991.

Prior Law: Former Prob C §2903, similar to the present section, was added Stats 1988 ch 1199 §72, operative July 1, 1989, and repealed Stats 1990 ch 79 §13, operative July 1, 1991.

CHAPTER 2
PREFILING INVESTIGATION BY PUBLIC GUARDIAN

Petition for investigation to determine need for appointment of conservator where abuse or neglect suspected. §2910.

Contents of court order in response to public guardian's petition. §2911.

§2910. Petition for investigation to determine need for appointment of conservator where abuse or neglect suspected

(a) Upon a showing of probable cause to believe that a person is in substantial danger of abuse or neglect and needs a conservator of the person, the estate, or the person and estate for his or her own protection, the public guardian or the county's adult protective services agency may petition for either or both of the orders of the court provided in subdivision (b) in connection with his or her investigation to determine whether a petition for the appointment of the public guardian as conservator of the person, estate, or the person and estate of the person would be necessary or appropriate.

(b) The petition may request either or both of the following orders for the limited purposes of the investigation concerning a person:

(1) An order authorizing identified health care providers or organizations to provide private medical information about the person to the public guardian's authorized representatives.

(2) An order authorizing identified financial institutions or advisers, accountants, and others with financial information about the person to provide the information to the public guardian's authorized representatives.

(c) Notice of the hearing and a copy of the petition shall be served on the person who is the subject of the investigation in the manner and for the period required by Section 1460 or, on application of the public guardian contained in or accompanying the petition, on an expedited basis in the manner and for the period ordered by the court. The court may dispense with notice of the hearing only on a showing of facts demonstrating an immediate threat of substantial harm to the person if notice is given. **Leg.H.** Added Stats 2007 ch 553 §25 (AB 1727), effective January 1, 2008.

§2911. Contents of court order in response to public guardian's petition

A court order issued in response to a public guardian's petition pursuant to Section 2910 shall do all of the following:

(a) Authorize health care providers to disclose a person's confidential medical information as permitted under California law, and also authorize disclosure of the information under federal medical privacy regulations enacted pursuant to the Health Insurance Portability and Accountability Act of 1996.

(b) Direct the public guardian or the adult protective services agency to keep the information acquired under the order confidential, except as disclosed in a judicial proceeding or as required by law enforcement or an authorized regulatory agency.

(c) Direct the public guardian or the adult protective services agency to destroy all copies of written information obtained under the order or give them to the person who was the subject of the investigation if a conservatorship proceeding is not commenced within 60 days after the date of the order. The court may extend this time period as the court finds to be in the subject's best interest. **Leg.H.** Added Stats 2007 ch 553 §25 (AB 1727), effective January 1, 2008.

CHAPTER 3
APPOINTMENT OF PUBLIC GUARDIAN

Application for appointment. §2920.
Persons under jurisdiction of Departments of State Hospitals or Developmental Services. §2921.
Letters, oath, and bond. §2922.
Continuing education required for public guardian. §2923.

§2920. Application for appointment

(a) If any person domiciled in the county requires a guardian or conservator and there is no one else who is qualified and willing to act and whose appointment as guardian or conservator would be in the best interests of the person, then either of the following shall apply:

(1) The public guardian shall apply for appointment as guardian or conservator of the person, the estate, or the person and estate, if there is an imminent threat to the person's health or safety or the person's estate.

(2) The public guardian may apply for appointment as guardian or conservator of the person, the estate, or the person and estate in all other cases.

(b) The public guardian shall apply for appointment as guardian or conservator of the person, the estate, or the person and estate, if the court so orders. The court may make an order under this subdivision on motion of an interested person or on the court's own motion in a pending proceeding or in a proceeding commenced for that purpose. The court shall order the public guardian to apply for appointment as guardian or conservator of the person, the estate, or the person and estate, on behalf of any person domiciled in the county who appears to require a guardian or conservator, if it appears that there is no one else who is qualified and willing to act, and if that appointment as guardian or conservator appears to be in the best interests of the person. However, if prior to the filing of the petition for appointment it is discovered that there is someone else who is qualified and willing to act as guardian or conservator, the public guardian shall be relieved of the duty under the order. The court shall not make an order under this subdivision except after notice to the public guardian for the period and in the manner provided for in Chapter 3 (commencing with Section 1460) of Part 1, consideration of the alternatives, and a determination by the court that the appointment is necessary. The notice and hearing under this subdivision may be combined with the notice and hearing required for appointment of a guardian or conservator.

(c) The public guardian shall begin an investigation within two business days of receiving a referral for conservatorship or guardianship. **Leg.H.** Enacted Stats 1990 ch 79 §14 (AB 759), operative July 1, 1991. Amended Stats 2006 ch 493 §32 (AB 1363), effective January 1, 2007.

2006 Note: This act, together with Senate Bill 1116 (Scott), Senate Bill 1550 (Figueroa), and Senate Bill 1716 (Bowen), shall be known and may be cited as the Omnibus Conservatorship and Guardianship Reform Act of 2006. Stats 2006 ch 493 (AB 1363) § 1.

Prior Law: Former Prob C §2920, similar to the present section, was added Stats 1988 ch 1199 §72, operative July 1, 1989, and repealed Stats 1990 ch 79 §13, operative July 1, 1991.

§2920.5. [Section repealed 2007]

Leg.H. Added Stats 2002 ch 644 §1 (AB 1957). Repealed January 1, 2007, by its own terms. The repealed section related to fingerprinting of potential conservator.

§2921. Persons under jurisdiction of Departments of State Hospitals or Developmental Services

An application of the public guardian for guardianship or conservatorship of the person, the estate, or the person and estate, of a person who is under the jurisdiction of the State Department of State Hospitals or the State Department of Developmental Services shall not be granted without the written consent of the department having jurisdiction of the person. **Leg.H.** Enacted Stats 1990 ch 79 §14 (AB 759), operative July 1, 1991. Amended Stats 2012 ch 440 §50 (AB 1488), effective September 22, 2012.

Prior Law: Former Prob C §2921, similar to the present section, was added Stats 1988 ch 1199 §72, operative July 1, 1989, and repealed Stats 1990 ch 79 §13, operative July 1, 1991.

§2922. Letters, oath, and bond

If the public guardian is appointed as guardian or conservator:

(a) Letters shall be issued in the same manner and by the same proceedings as letters are issued to other persons. Letters may be issued to "the public guardian" of the county without naming the public guardian.

(b) The official bond and oath of the public guardian are in lieu of the guardian or conservator's bond and oath on the grant of letters. **Leg.H.** Enacted Stats 1990 ch 79 §14 (AB 759), operative July 1, 1991.

Prior Law: Former Prob C §2922, similar to the present section, was added Stats 1988 ch 1199 §72, operative July 1, 1989, and repealed Stats 1990 ch 79 §13, operative July 1, 1991.

§2923. Continuing education required for public guardian

On or before January 1, 2008, the public guardian shall comply with the continuing education requirements that are established by the California State Association of Public Administrators, Public Guardians, and Public Conservators. **Leg.H.** Added Stats 2006 ch 493 §33 (AB 1363), effective January 1, 2007.

2006 Note: This act, together with Senate Bill 1116 (Scott), Senate Bill 1550 (Figueroa), and Senate Bill 1716 (Bowen), shall be known and may be cited as the Omnibus Conservatorship and Guardianship Reform Act of 2006. Stats 2006 ch 493 (AB 1363) §1.

CHAPTER 4
ADMINISTRATION BY PUBLIC GUARDIAN

Deposit or investment of funds. §2940.
Employment of attorneys. §2941.
Compensation and expenses of public guardian; Bond fee. §2942.
Inventory and appraisal. §2943.
Immunity of public guardian. §2944.

§2940. Deposit or investment of funds

All funds coming into the custody of the public guardian shall be deposited or invested in the same manner and subject to the same terms and conditions as deposit or investment by the public administrator of money in an estate pursuant to Article 3 (commencing with Section 7640) of Chapter 4 of Part 1 of Division 7. **Leg.H.** Enacted Stats 1990 ch 79 §14 (AB 759), operative July 1, 1991.

Prior Law: Former Prob C §2940, similar to the present section, was added Stats 1988 ch 1199 §72, operative July 1, 1989, and repealed Stats 1990 ch 79 §13, operative July 1, 1991.

§2941. Employment of attorneys

The public guardian may, if necessary and in the public guardian's discretion, employ private attorneys where the cost of employment can be defrayed out of estate funds or where satisfactory pro bono or contingency fee arrangements can be made. **Leg.H.** Enacted Stats 1990 ch 79 §14 (AB 759), operative July 1, 1991.

Prior Law: Former Prob C §2941, similar to the present section, was added Stats 1988 ch 1199 §72, operative July 1, 1989, and repealed Stats 1990 ch 79 §13, operative July 1, 1991.

§2942. Compensation and expenses of public guardian; Bond fee

The public guardian shall be paid from the estate of the ward or conservatee for all of the following:

(a) Reasonable expenses incurred in the execution of the guardianship or conservatorship.

(b) Compensation for services of the public guardian and the attorney of the public guardian, and for the filing and processing services of the county clerk or the clerk of the superior court, in the amount the court determines is just and reasonable. In determining what constitutes just and reasonable compensation, the court shall, among other factors, take into consideration the actual costs of the services provided, the amount of the estate involved, the special value of services provided in relation to the estate, and whether the compensation requested might impose an economic hardship on the estate. Nothing in this section shall require a public guardian to base a request for compensation upon an hourly rate of service.

(c) An annual bond fee in the amount of twenty-five dollars ($25) plus one-fourth of 1 percent of the amount of an estate greater than ten thousand dollars ($10,000). The amount charged shall be deposited in the county treasury. This subdivision does not apply if the ward or conservatee is eligible for Social Security Supplemental Income benefits. **Leg.H.** Enacted Stats 1990 ch 79 §14 (AB 759), operative July 1, 1991. Amended Stats 1994 ch 472 §2 (AB 2725); Stats 1998 ch 103 §2 (SB 1487); Stats 1999 ch 866 §1 (AB 1152), effective January 1, 2000.

Prior Law: Former Prob C §2942, similar to the present section, was added Stats 1988 ch 1199 §72, operative July 1, 1989, and repealed Stats 1990 ch 79 §13, operative July 1, 1991.

§2943. Inventory and appraisal

(a) Notwithstanding subdivision (c) of Section 2610, the property described in the inventory may be appraised by the public guardian and need not be appraised by a probate referee if the public guardian files with the inventory an appraisal showing that the estimated value of the property in the estate does not exceed the amount prescribed in Section 13100.

(b) If the conservator seeks authority pursuant to subdivision (b) of Section 2540 to sell the conservatee's personal residence, whether or not it is real property, or if the conservator seeks authority pursuant to Section 2590 to sell the conservatee's real property, valued in excess of ten thousand dollars ($10,000), or an item of personal property valued in excess of ten thousand dollars ($10,000) that is not a security sold pursuant to subdivision (a) of Section 2544, that property shall be appraised by a probate referee. **Leg.H.** Enacted Stats 1990 ch 79 §14 (AB 759), operative July 1, 1991. Amended Stats 1996 ch 86 §3 (AB 2146), effective January 1, 1997.

Prior Law: Former Prob C §2943, similar to the present section, was added Stats 1988 ch 1199 §72, operative July 1, 1989, and repealed Stats 1990 ch 79 §13, operative July 1, 1991.

§2944. Immunity of public guardian

The public guardian is not liable for failing to take possession or control of property that is beyond the ability of the public guardian to possess or control. **Leg.H.** Enacted Stats 1990 ch 79 §14 (AB 759), operative July 1, 1991.

Prior Law: Former Prob C §2944, similar to the present section, was added Stats 1988 ch 1199 §72, operative July 1, 1989, and repealed Stats 1990 ch 79 §13, operative July 1, 1991.

CHAPTER 5
FINANCIAL ABUSE OF MENTALLY IMPAIRED ELDERS

Article 1. General.
Article 2. Estate Protection.

ARTICLE 1
General

Legislative intent; Authority of peace officer or public guardian; Coordination with existing programs. §2950.
Definitions. §2951.

§2950. Legislative intent; Authority of peace officer or public guardian; Coordination with existing programs

(a) It is the intent of the Legislature to do all of the following:

(1) Reduce the incidence of financial abuse perpetrated against mentally impaired elder adults.

(2) Minimize monetary losses to mentally impaired elder adults as a result of financial abuse.

(3) Facilitate timely intervention by law enforcement, in collaboration with the public guardian, to effectively protect mentally impaired elder adult victims of financial abuse, and to recover their assets.

(b) Any peace officer or public guardian of a county that has both of the following, as determined by the public guardian of that county, may take the actions authorized by this chapter:

(1) The existence of sufficient law enforcement personnel with expertise in the assessment of competence.

(2) The existence of a law enforcement unit devoted to investigating elder financial abuse and the enforcement of laws applicable to elder abuse.

(c) This chapter shall be coordinated with existing mandated programs affecting financial abuse of mentally impaired elders that are administered by the adult protective services agency of the county. **Leg.H.** Added Stats 2000 ch 813 §1 (SB 1742), effective January 1, 2001.

§2951. Definitions

The definitions contained in this section shall govern the construction of this chapter, unless the context requires otherwise.

(a) "Declaration" means a document that substantially complies with the requirements of Section 2954, and is signed by both a peace officer and a supervisor from the county's adult protective services agency and provided to the public guardian in accordance with subdivision (b) of Section 2952.

(b) "Elder person" means any person residing in this state, 65 years of age or older.

(c) "Financial abuse" means a situation described in Section 15610.30 of the Welfare and Institutions Code.

(d) "Financial abuse POST training" means an elder financial abuse training course certified by the Commission on Peace Officer Standards and Training.

(e) "Financial institution" means any bank, savings and loan, thrift, industrial loan company, credit union, or any branch of any of these institutions doing business in the state, as defined by provisions of the Financial Code.

(f) "Peace officer" means a sheriff, deputy sheriff, municipal police officer, or a peace officer authorized under subdivision (b) of Section 830.1 of the Penal Code, duly sworn under the requirements of state law, who satisfies any of the following requirements:

(1) The sheriff, deputy sheriff, municipal police officer, or peace officer authorized under subdivision (b) of Section 830.1 of the Penal Code has completed or participated as a lecturer in a financial abuse POST training program within the last 36 months. The completion of the course may be satisfied by telecourse, video training tape, or other instruction. The training shall, at a minimum, address relevant elder abuse laws, recognition of financial abuse and fraud, assessment of mental competence in accordance with the standards set forth in Part 17 (commencing with Section 810) of the Probate Code, reporting requirements and procedures for the investigation of financial abuse and related crimes, including neglect, and civil and criminal procedures for the protection of victims. The course may be presented as part of a training program that includes other subjects or courses.

(2) The sheriff, deputy sheriff, municipal police officer, or peace officer authorized under subdivision (b) of Section 830.1 of the Penal Code, has consulted with a sheriff, deputy sheriff, municipal police officer, or peace officer authorized under subdivision (b) of Section 830.1 of the Penal Code, who satisfies the requirements of paragraph (1) concerning the declaration defined in subdivision (a) and obtained the signature of that sheriff, deputy sheriff, municipal police officer, or peace officer authorized under subdivision (b) of Section 830.1 of the Penal Code on a declaration that substantially complies with the form described in Section 2954.

(g) "Property" means all personal property and real property of every kind belonging to, or alleged to belong to, the elder. **Leg.H.** Added Stats 2000 ch 813 §1 (SB 1742), effective January 1, 2001.

ARTICLE 2
Estate Protection

Conditions for issuing declaration; Signing; Transmission; Possession and control of property; Duties of public guardian; Written recordable certification; Notice requirements; Liability of public guardian. §2952.

Petition for costs and fees; Handling of expenses and debts of elder person; Petition to quash certification. §2953.

Form of declaration. §2954.

Effect of chapter on authority of public guardian. §2955.

§2952. Conditions for issuing declaration; Signing; Transmission; Possession and control of property; Duties of public guardian; Written recordable certification; Notice requirements; Liability of public guardian

(a) A peace officer may issue a declaration, as provided in Section 2954, concerning an elder person if all of the following conditions are satisfied:

(1) There is probable cause to believe that the elder person is substantially unable to manage his or her financial resources or to resist fraud or undue influence.

(2) There exists a significant danger that the elder person will lose all or a portion of his or her property as a result of fraud or misrepresentations or the mental incapacity of the elder person.

(3) There is probable cause to believe that a crime is being committed against the elder person.

(4) The crime is connected to the inability of the elder person to manage his or her financial resources or to resist fraud or undue influence, and that inability is the result of deficits in the elder person's mental functions.

(5) The peace officer has consulted with an individual qualified to perform a mental status examination.

(b) If the requirements of subdivision (a) are satisfied, the peace officer may provide a signed declaration to the public guardian of the county. The declaration provided by the peace officer under this subdivision shall be signed by both the peace officer and a supervisor from the county's adult protective services agency. The declaration shall be transmitted to the public guardian within 24 hours of its being signed, and may be transmitted by facsimile.

(c)(1) Upon receiving a signed declaration from a peace officer, the public guardian is authorized to rely on the information contained in the declaration to take immediate possession or control of any real or personal property belonging to the elder person referred to in the declaration, including any property that is held jointly between the elder person and a third party that is subject to loss, injury, waste, or misappropriation, and may issue a written recordable certification of that fact pursuant to this section. The written recordable certification shall substantially comply with the following form:

"CERTIFICATE OF AUTHORITY

THIS IS AN OFFICIAL CERTIFICATE ENTITLING THE PUBLIC GUARDIAN TO TAKE POSSESSION OF ANY AND ALL PROPERTY BELONGING TO THE FOLLOWING INDIVIDUAL:

(Name of Victim) ____

This Certificate of Authority has been issued by the Public Guardian pursuant to and in compliance with the Financial Abuse of Mentally Impaired Elders statute, Chapter 4 (commencing with Section 2950) of Part 5 of Division 4 of the California Probate Code. Under California law, this Certificate of Authority authorizes the Public Guardian to take possession or control of property belonging to the above-named individual.

SPECIAL NOTE TO FINANCIAL INSTITUTIONS:

State law requires that upon receiving a copy of this Certificate of Authority, financial institutions shall provide the public guardian with information concerning property held by the above-named individual and surrender the property to the Public Guardian if requested.

This Certificate of Authority shall only be valid when signed and dated by the Public Guardian or a deputy Public Guardian of the County of ____ and affixed with the official seal of the Public Guardian below.

Signature of Public Guardian:

Date:

Official Seal"

(2) The mere issuance of the declaration provided by this section shall not require the public guardian to take possession or control of property and shall not require the public guardian to make a determination that the requirements for the appointment of a conservator are satisfied.

(3) The authority provided to the public guardian in paragraph (1) includes the authority to deny use of, access to, or prohibit residency in the home of the elder, by anyone who does not have a written rental agreement or other legal right to the use of, or access to, the residence, and, subject to the requirements of subdivision (b) of Section 2900, the authority to terminate the occupancy of anyone living in the home of the elder person, and the authority to remove that occupant residing therein.

(4) The public guardian shall serve, or cause to be served, a copy of the certification issued pursuant to this section on the elder person by mail within 24 hours of the execution of the certification, or as soon thereafter as is practical, in the manner provided in Chapter 4 (commencing with Section 413.10) of Title 5 of Part 2 of the Code of Civil Procedure.

(5) Receipt of a certification issued under this section constitutes sufficient acquittance to financial institutions and others in possession of an elder person's property to provide information and surrender property of the elder person to the public guardian. Any financial institution or other person who provides information or surrenders property pursuant to this section shall be discharged from any liability for any act or omission of the public guardian with respect to the property.

(6) A public guardian acting in good faith is not liable when taking possession or control of property pursuant to this section.

(7) A certification issued pursuant to this section is valid for 15 days after the date of issuance. Upon ex parte petition to the superior court, the public guardian may seek additional 15-day certifications. The court shall grant that petition only if it determines that the additional certification is necessary to protect the elder from financial abuse and the elder's property from loss, injury, waste, or misappropriation.

(d)(1) If the public guardian takes possession of an elder person's property pursuant to this section, the public guardian shall attempt to find agents pursuant to the use of durable powers of attorney or successor trustees nominated in trust instruments, or other persons having legal authority under existing legal instruments, to manage the elder person's estate.

(2) If the public guardian is unable to find any appropriate person to manage the elder person's estate pursuant to paragraph (1), the public guardian shall attempt to find appropriate family members willing to manage the elder person's estate. If no documents exist appointing appropriate fiduciaries, the public guardian shall follow the priorities set forth in Article 2 (commencing with Section 1810) of Chapter 1 of Part 3.

(3) The public guardian shall take the steps described in paragraphs (1) and (2) within 15 days of taking possession of an elder person's property pursuant to this section.

(e) Nothing in this section prevents the county's adult protective services agency from conducting an investigation regarding the elder person named in the declaration and providing appropriate services, in coordination with any actions taken with the public guardian under this section or an investigation conducted by law enforcement regarding the elder person. **Leg.H.** Added Stats 2000 ch 813 §1 (SB 1742). Amended Stats 2001 ch 232 §3 (AB 1517), effective January 1, 2002.

§2953. Petition for costs and fees; Handling of expenses and debts of elder person; Petition to quash certification

(a)(1) A public guardian who has taken possession or control of the property of an elder person pursuant to this chapter is entitled to petition a court of competent jurisdiction for the reasonable costs incurred by the public guardian for the protection of the person or the property, together with reasonable fees for services, including, but not limited to, reasonable attorneys' fees. These fees shall be payable from the estate of the elder person if the person is not deemed competent by the court and if any of the following apply:

(A) The public guardian or someone else is appointed as the temporary or general conservator of the estate.

(B) An attorney-in-fact, under a durable power of attorney, or a trustee, takes steps, or is notified of the need to take steps, to protect the estate of the elder person.

(C) An action is brought against the alleged financial abuser by the elder person, his or her conservator, a trustee, a fiduciary, or a successor in interest of the elder person, arising from a harm that the public guardian taking charge was intended to prevent or minimize.

(2) Any costs incurred by the public guardian pursuant to paragraph (1) shall be compensable as provided in Section 2902. Fees collected by the

public guardian pursuant to this chapter shall be used for the activities described in this chapter.

(b) When a public guardian has taken possession or control of the property of an elder person pursuant to this chapter, the public guardian shall exercise reasonable care to ensure that the reasonable living expenses and legitimate debts of the elder person are addressed as well as is practical under the circumstances.

(c) Any person identified as a victim in a declaration described in Section 2954 may bring an ex parte petition in the superior court for an order quashing the certification issued by the public guardian as provided in subdivision (c) of Section 2952.

(1) Upon request by the petitioner, the court may defer filing fees related to the petition, and order the public guardian to authorize the release of funds from a financial institution to reimburse the petitioner the filing fees from assets belonging to the petitioner, but shall waive filing fees if the petitioner meets the standards of eligibility established by subparagraph (A) or (B) of paragraph (6) of subdivision (a) of Section 68511.3 of the Government Code for the waiver of a filing fee.

(2) The court shall quash the certification if the court determines that there is insufficient evidence to justify the imposition on the alleged victim's civil liberties caused by the certification.

(3) If the court determines that there is sufficient evidence to justify the imposition on the alleged victim's civil liberties caused by the certification, the court may, in its discretion, do one or more of the following:

(A) Order disbursements from the alleged victim's assets, as are reasonably needed to address the alleged victim's needs.

(B) Appoint a temporary conservator of the alleged victim's estate, where the facts before the court would be sufficient for the appointment of a temporary conservator under Section 2250.

(C) Deny the petition.

(D) Award reasonable attorney's fees to the respondent's attorney from the victim's estate. **Leg.H.** Added Stats 2000 ch 813 §1 (SB 1742). Amended Stats 2001 ch 232 §4 (AB 1517), effective January 1, 2002.

§2954. Form of declaration

A declaration issued by a peace officer under this chapter shall not be valid unless it substantially complies with the following form:

DECLARATION

PRINT OR TYPE
1. My name is: _____.
   My badge number is: _____.
   My office address and telephone number are:
   _____
   _____
   _____.
2. I am a duly sworn peace officer presently employed by _____
   _____, in the County of
   _____, in the State of California.
3. On ____ (date) I personally interviewed _____ (victim) at ____ a.m./p.m. at _____ (address). The victim resides at _____ (address, telephone number, and name of facility, if applicable).
4. There is probable cause to believe that:
   (a) _____ (Victim) is substantially unable to manage his or her financial resources or to resist fraud or undue influence, and
   (b) There exists a significant danger the victim will lose all or a portion of his or her property as a result of fraud or misrepresentations or the mental incapacity of the victim, and
   (c) There is probable cause to believe that a crime is being committed against the victim, and
   (d) The crime is connected to the victim's inability to manage his or her financial resources or to resist fraud or undue influence, and
   (e) The victim suffers from that inability as a result of deficits in one or more of the following mental functions:

INSTRUCTIONS TO PEACE OFFICER: CHECK ALL BLOCKS THAT APPLY:
[A] ALERTNESS AND ATTENTION
☐ 1. Levels of arousal. (Lethargic, responds only to vigorous and persistent stimulation, stupor.)
☐ 2. Orientation. Person ____ Time ____ (day, date, month, season, year), Place ____ (address, town, state), Situation _____ (why am I here?).
☐ 3. Ability to attend and concentrate. (Give detailed answers from memory, mental ability required to thread a needle.)

[B] INFORMATION PROCESSING
Ability to:
☐ 1. Remember, i.e., short- and long-term memory, immediate recall. (Deficits reflected by: forgets question before answering, cannot recall names, relatives, past presidents, events of past 24 hours.)
☐ 2. Understand and communicate either verbally or otherwise. (Deficits reflected by: inability to comprehend questions, follow instructions, use words correctly or name objects; nonsense words.)
☐ 3. Recognize familiar objects and persons. (Deficits reflected by: inability to recognize familiar faces, objects, etc.)
☐ 4. Understand and appreciate quantities. (Perform simple calculations.)
☐ 5. Reason using abstract concepts. (Grasp abstract aspects of his or her situation; interpret idiomatic expressions or proverbs.)
☐ 6. Plan, organize, and carry out actions (assuming physical ability) in one's own rational self-interest. (Break complex tasks down into simple steps and carry them out.)
☐ 7. Reason logically.

[C] THOUGHT DISORDERS
☐ 1. Severely disorganized thinking. (Rambling, nonsensical, incoherent, or nonlinear thinking.)
☐ 2. Hallucinations. (Auditory, visual, olfactory.)
☐ 3. Delusions. (Demonstrably false belief maintained without or against reason or evidence.)
☐ 4. Uncontrollable or intrusive thoughts. (Unwanted compulsive thoughts, compulsive behavior.)

[D] ABILITY TO MODULATE MOOD AND AFFECT
Pervasive and persistent or recurrent emotional state which appears severely inappropriate in degree to the patient's circumstances. Encircle the inappropriate mood(s):

Anger	Euphoria	Helplessness
Anxiety	Depression	Apathy
Fear	Hopelessness	Indifference
Panic	Despair	

5. The property at risk is identified as, but not limited to, the following:
   Bank account located at: _____
                              (name, telephone number, and address of the bank branch)
   Account number(s): _____
   Securities/other funds located at: _____
                              (name, telephone number, and address of financial institution)
   Account number(s): _____
   Real property located at: _____
                              (address)
   Automobile described as: _____
                              (make, model/color)
   _____
   (license plate number and state)
   Other property described as: _____
   Other property located at: _____
6. A criminal investigation will ☐ will not ☐ be commenced against _____
   (name, address, and telephone number) for alleged financial abuse.

BLOCKS 1, 2, AND 3 MUST BE CHECKED IN ORDER FOR THIS DECLARATION TO BE VALID:

☐ 1. I am a peace officer in the county identified above.

☐ 2. I have consulted concerning this case with a supervisor in the county's adult protective services agency who has signed below, indicating that he or she concurs that, based on the information I provided to him or her, or based on information he or she obtained independently, this declaration is warranted under the circumstances.

☐ 3. I have consulted concerning this case with an individual qualified to perform a mental status examination.

_____
Signature of Declarant Peace Officer

_____
Date

_____
Signature of Concurring Adult Protective Services Supervisor

Leg.H. Added Stats 2000 ch 813 §1 (SB 1742), effective January 1, 2001.

§2955. Effect of chapter on authority of public guardian

Nothing in this chapter shall prohibit or restrict a public guardian from undertaking any other proceeding authorized by law. **Leg.H.** Added Stats 2000 ch 813 §1 (SB 1742), effective January 1, 2001.

PART 6
MANAGEMENT OR DISPOSITION OF COMMUNITY PROPERTY WHERE SPOUSE LACKS LEGAL CAPACITY

Chapter 1. Definitions and General Provisions.
Chapter 2. Management, Control, and Disposition.
Chapter 3. Proceeding for Particular Transaction.

CHAPTER 1
DEFINITIONS AND GENERAL PROVISIONS

Article 1. Definitions.
Article 2. General Provisions.

ARTICLE 1
Definitions

Application of definitions. §3000.
"Community property". §3002.
"Conservator". §3004.
"Conservatorship estate". §3006.
"Conservatorship proceeding". §3008.
"Legal capacity" with respect to community property. §3012.

§3000. Application of definitions

Unless the provision or context otherwise requires, the definitions contained in this article govern the construction of this part. **Leg.H.** Enacted Stats 1990 ch 79 §14 (AB 759), operative July 1, 1991.

Prior Law: Former Prob C §3000, similar to the present section, was added Stats 1979 ch 726 §3, operative January 1, 1981, and repealed Stats 1990 ch 79 §13, operative July 1, 1991.

§3002. "Community property"

"Community property" means community real property and community personal property, including, but not limited to, a community property business that is or was under the primary management and control of one of the spouses. **Leg.H.** Enacted Stats 1990 ch 79 §14 (AB 759), operative July 1, 1991. Amended Stats 1992 ch 163 §125 (AB 2641), operative January 1, 1994; Stats 1996 ch 877 §1 (AB 1467).

Prior Law: Former Prob C §3002, similar to the present section, was added Stats 1979 ch 726 §3, operative January 1, 1981, amended Stats 1982 ch 497 §146, operative July 1, 1983, Stats 1988 ch 113 §14, effective May 25, 1988, operative July 1, 1988, and repealed Stats 1990 ch 79 §13, operative July 1, 1991.

§3004. "Conservator"

"Conservator" means conservator of the estate, or limited conservator of the estate to the extent that the powers and duties of the limited conservator are specifically and expressly provided by the order appointing the limited conservator, and includes the guardian of the estate of a married minor. **Leg.H.** Enacted Stats 1990 ch 79 §14 (AB 759), operative July 1, 1991.

Prior Law: Former Prob C §3004, similar to the present section, was added Stats 1979 ch 726 §3, operative January 1, 1981, amended Stats 1980 ch 1304 §28, and repealed Stats 1990 ch 79 §13, operative July 1, 1991.

§3006. "Conservatorship estate"

"Conservatorship estate" includes the guardianship estate of a married minor. **Leg.H.** Enacted Stats 1990 ch 79 §14 (AB 759), operative July 1, 1991.

Prior Law: Former Prob C §3006, similar to the present section, was added Stats 1979 ch 726 §3, operative January 1, 1981, and repealed Stats 1990 ch 79 §13, operative July 1, 1991.

§3008. "Conservatorship proceeding"

"Conservatorship proceeding" means conservatorship of the estate proceeding and includes a guardianship of the estate proceeding of a married minor. **Leg.H.** Enacted Stats 1990 ch 79 §14 (AB 759), operative July 1, 1991.

Prior Law: Former Prob C §3008, similar to the present section, was added Stats 1979 ch 726 §3, operative January 1, 1981, and repealed Stats 1990 ch 79 §13, operative July 1, 1991.

§3012. "Legal capacity" with respect to community property

(a) Unless the spouse lacks legal capacity under the applicable standard prescribed in subdivision (b), a spouse has legal capacity to:

(1) Manage and control community property, including legal capacity to dispose of community property.

(2) Join in or consent to a transaction involving community property.

(b) A spouse lacks legal capacity to:

(1) Manage and control, including legal capacity to dispose of, community property if the spouse is substantially unable to manage or control the community property.

(2) Join in or consent to a transaction involving community property if the spouse does not have legal capacity for the particular transaction measured by principles of law otherwise applicable to the particular transaction.

(3) Do any act, or engage in any activity, described in paragraph (1) or (2) if the spouse has a conservator.

(c) Nothing in this section shall be construed to deny a spouse, whether or not lacking legal capacity, any of the following:

(1) The right to control an allowance provided under Section 2421.

(2) The right to control wages or salary to the extent provided in Section 2601.

(3) The right to make a will.

(4) The right to enter into transactions to the extent reasonable to provide the necessities of life to the spouse, the other spouse, and the minor children of the spouses. **Leg.H.** Enacted Stats 1990 ch 79 §14 (AB 759), operative July 1, 1991.

Prior Law: Former Prob C §3012, similar to the present section, was added Stats 1979 ch 726 §3, operative January 1, 1981, amended Stats 1982 ch 497 §148, operative July 1, 1983, Stats 1983 ch 842, §54, operative January 1, 1985, and repealed Stats 1990 ch 79 §13, operative July 1, 1991.

ARTICLE 2
General Provisions

Rights of spouses in community property preserved. §3020.
Determination of character of property. §3023.

§3020. Rights of spouses in community property preserved

(a) The proceeds, rents, issues, and profits of community property dealt with or disposed of under this division, and any property taken in exchange for the community property or acquired with the proceeds, are community property.

(b) Except as provided in this part for the management, control, and disposition of community property, nothing in this division alters the rights of the spouses in community property or in the proceeds, rents, issues, or profits of community property. **Leg.H.** Enacted Stats 1990 ch 79 §14 (AB 759), operative July 1, 1991.

Prior Law: Former Prob C §3020, similar to the present section, was added Stats 1979 ch 726 §3, operative January 1, 1981, and repealed Stats 1990 ch 79 §13, operative July 1, 1991.

§3023. Determination of character of property

(a) Except as provided in subdivisions (b) and (c), where one or both of the spouses has a conservator, the court in which any of the conservatorship proceedings is pending may hear and determine whether property is community property or the separate property of either spouse when the issue is raised in any proceeding under this division.

(b) Any person having or claiming title to or an interest in the property, at or prior to the hearing on the issue, may object to the hearing if the court is not the proper court under any other provision of law for the trial of an action to determine the issue. If the objection is established, the court shall not hear and determine the issue.

(c) Except as provided in subdivision (d), if a civil action is pending with respect to the issue and jurisdiction has been obtained in the court in which the civil action is pending, upon request of any party to the civil action, the court shall abate the hearing until the conclusion of the civil action.

(d) The court need not abate the hearing if the court determines that the civil action was filed for the purpose of delay. **Leg.H.** Enacted Stats 1990 ch 79 §14 (AB 759), operative July 1, 1991.

§3024. [Section repealed 1998.]

Leg.H. Enacted Stats 1990 ch 79 §14 (AB 759), operative July 1, 1991. Repealed Stats 1997 ch 724 §14 (AB 1172). See Prob C §1301.

Prior Law: Former Prob C §3024, similar to present Prob C §1301, was added Stats 1981 ch 9 §7, and repealed Stats 1990 ch 79 §13, operative July 1, 1991.

CHAPTER 2
MANAGEMENT, CONTROL, AND DISPOSITION

Article 1. Management, Control, and Disposition Generally.
Article 2. Substitute for Joinder or Consent Requirements.
Article 3. Enforcement of Support of Spouse Who Has Conservator.

ARTICLE 1
Management, Control, and Disposition Generally

Community property. §3051.
Authority of court. §3054.
Effect on consent of death or subsequent lack of legal capacity. §3055.
Manner of management, control, and disposition of property as part of conservatorship estate. §3056.
Protection of rights of spouse who lacks legal capacity. §3057.

§3051. Community property

(a) Subject to Section 3071, the right of a spouse to manage and control community property, including the right to dispose of community property, is not affected by the lack or alleged lack of legal capacity of the other spouse.

(b) Except as provided in subdivision (c), if one spouse has legal capacity and the other has a conservator:

(1) The spouse who has legal capacity has the exclusive management and control of the community property including, subject to Section 3071, the exclusive power to dispose of the community property.

(2) The community property is not part of the conservatorship estate.

(c) If one spouse has legal capacity and the other has a conservator, the spouse having legal capacity may consent, by a writing filed in the proceeding, that all or part of the community property be included in and, subject to Section 3071, be managed, controlled, and disposed of as a part of the conservatorship estate.

(d) Except as provided in subdivision (e), if both spouses have conservators, an undivided one-half interest in the community property shall be included in and, subject to Section 3071, be managed, controlled, and disposed of as a part of the conservatorship estate of each spouse.

(e) If both spouses have conservators, when authorized by order of the court in which any of the conservatorship proceedings is pending, the conservators may agree in writing that all or specific parts of the community property shall be included in the conservatorship estate of one or the other of the spouses and, subject to Section 3071, be managed, controlled, and disposed of as a part of the conservatorship estate of that spouse. **Leg.H.** Enacted Stats 1990 ch 79 §14 (AB 759), operative July 1, 1991.

Prior Law: Former Prob C §3051, similar to the present section, was added Stats 1979 ch 726 §3, operative January 1, 1981, and repealed Stats 1990 ch 79 §13, operative July 1, 1991.

§3054. Authority of court

When community property is included or proposed to be included in the conservatorship estate of a spouse, the court in which the conservatorship proceeding is pending, upon its own motion or upon petition of a spouse having legal capacity or the conservator of either spouse and upon such notice to such persons as the court prescribes, may do any of the following:

(a) Determine that the inclusion of some or all of the community property that is proposed to be included in the conservatorship estate would not be in the best interest of the spouses or their estates and order that such property not be included.

(b) Permit revocation of a written consent for inclusion of property in the conservatorship estate, with or without terms or conditions.

(c) Determine that the continued inclusion of some or all of the community property in the conservatorship estate is not in the best interest of the spouses or their estates and order that the inclusion of such property in the conservatorship estate be terminated, with or without terms or conditions.

(d) Make such other orders as may be appropriate for the orderly administration of the conservatorship estate or to protect the interests of the spouses. **Leg.H.** Enacted Stats 1990 ch 79 §14 (AB 759), operative July 1, 1991.

Prior Law: Former Prob C §3054, similar to the present section, was added Stats 1979 ch 726 §3, operative January 1, 1981, amended Stats 1982 ch 497 §154, operative July 1, 1983, and repealed Stats 1990 ch 79 §13, operative July 1, 1991.

§3055. Effect on consent of death or subsequent lack of legal capacity

(a) If consent is given under this article that community property be included in the conservatorship estate of a spouse, the death of either spouse terminates the consent.

(b) If a spouse consents under this article that community property be included in the conservatorship estate of the other spouse:

(1) Subject to paragraph (2), the subsequent lack of legal capacity of the spouse giving the consent has no effect on the inclusion of the property in the conservatorship estate of the other spouse.

(2) The appointment of a conservator for the spouse giving the consent terminates the consent. **Leg.H.** Enacted Stats 1990 ch 79 §14 (AB 759), operative July 1, 1991.

Prior Law: Former Prob C §3055, similar to the present section, was added Stats 1979 ch 726 §3, operative January 1, 1981, amended Stats 1982 ch 497 §155, operative July 1, 1983, and repealed Stats 1990 ch 79 §13, operative July 1, 1991.

§3056. Manner of management, control, and disposition of property as part of conservatorship estate

Except as otherwise provided in this part and subject to Section 3071, when community property is included in a conservatorship estate under this article for the purpose of management, control, and disposition, the conservator has the same powers and duties with respect to such property as the conservator has with respect to other property of the conservatorship estate. **Leg.H.** Enacted Stats 1990 ch 79 §14 (AB 759), operative July 1, 1991.

Prior Law: Former Prob C §3056, similar to the present section, was added Stats 1979 ch 726 §3, operative January 1, 1981, amended Stats 1982 ch 497 §156, operative July 1, 1983, and repealed Stats 1990 ch 79 §13, operative July 1, 1991.

§3057. Protection of rights of spouse who lacks legal capacity

(a) Where a spouse lacks legal capacity and does not have a conservator, any interested person who has knowledge or reason to believe that the rights of such spouse in the community property are being prejudiced may bring an action on behalf of such spouse to enforce the duty imposed by Sections 721 and 1100 of the Family Code with respect to the management and control of the community property and to obtain such relief as may be appropriate.

(b) If one spouse has a conservator and the other spouse is managing or controlling community property, the conservator has the duty to keep reasonably informed concerning the management and control, including the disposition, of the community property. If the conservator has knowledge or reason to believe that the rights of the conservatee in the community property are being prejudiced, the conservator may bring an action on behalf of the conservatee to enforce the duty imposed by Sections 721 and 1100 of the Family Code with respect to the management and control of the community property and to obtain such relief as may be appropriate. **Leg.H.** Enacted Stats 1990 ch 79 §14 (AB 759), operative July 1, 1991. Amended Stats 1992 ch 163 §126 (AB 2641), operative January 1, 1994.

Prior Law: Former Prob C §3057, similar to the present section, was added Stats 1979 ch 726 §3, operative January 1, 1981, and repealed Stats 1990 ch 79 §13, operative July 1, 1991.

ARTICLE 2
Substitute for Joinder or Consent Requirements

Article provides substitute for joinder or consent requirements of other statutes. §3070.
Substitute for joinder or consent. §3071.
Court order authorizing joinder or consent by conservator. §3072.
Manner of joinder or consent. §3073.
Good faith purchaser or encumbrancer for value. §3074.

§3070. Article provides substitute for joinder or consent requirements of other statutes

If the requirements of this article are satisfied with respect to a transaction described in Section 3071, the transaction is deemed to satisfy the joinder or consent requirements of the statute referred to in that section. **Leg.H.** Enacted Stats 1990 ch 79 §14 (AB 759), operative July 1, 1991.

Prior Law: Former Prob C §3070, similar to the present section, was added Stats 1979 ch 726 §3, operative January 1, 1981, and repealed Stats 1990 ch 79 §13, operative July 1, 1991.

§3071. Substitute for joinder or consent

(a) In case of a transaction for which the joinder or consent of both spouses is required by Section 1100 or 1102 of the Family Code or by any other statute, if one or both spouses lacks legal capacity for the transaction, the requirement of joinder or consent shall be satisfied as provided in this section.

(b) Where one spouse has legal capacity for the transaction and the other spouse has a conservator, the requirement of joinder or consent is satisfied if both of the following are obtained:

(1) The joinder or consent of the spouse having legal capacity.

(2) The joinder or consent of the conservator of the other spouse given in compliance with Section 3072.

(c) Where both spouses have conservators, the joinder or consent requirement is satisfied by the joinder or consent of each such conservator given in compliance with Section 3072.

(d) In any case, the requirement of joinder or consent is satisfied if the transaction is authorized by an order of court obtained in a proceeding pursuant to Chapter 3 (commencing with Section 3100). **Leg.H.** Enacted Stats 1990 ch 79 §14 (AB 759), operative July 1, 1991. Amended Stats 1992 ch 163 §127 (AB 2641), operative January 1, 1994.

Prior Law: Former Prob C §3071, similar to the present section, was added Stats 1979 ch 726 §3, operative January 1, 1981, amended Stats 1982 ch 497 §157, operative July 1, 1983, and repealed Stats 1990 ch 79 §13, operative July 1, 1991.

§3072. Court order authorizing joinder or consent by conservator

(a) Except as provided in subdivision (b), a conservator may join in or consent to a transaction under Section 3071 only after authorization by either of the following:

(1) An order of the court obtained in the conservatorship proceeding upon a petition filed pursuant to Section 2403 or under Article 7 (commencing with Section 2540) or 10 (commencing with Section 2580) of Chapter 6 of Part 4.

(2) An order of the court made in a proceeding pursuant to Chapter 3 (commencing with Section 3100).

(b) A conservator may consent without court authorization to a sale, conveyance, or encumbrance of community personal property requiring consent under subdivision (c) of Section 1100 of the Family Code if the conservator could sell or transfer the property under Section 2545 without court authorization if the property were a part of the conservatorship estate. **Leg.H.** Enacted Stats 1990 ch 79 §14 (AB 759), operative July 1, 1991. Amended Stats 1992 ch 163 §128 (AB 2641), operative January 1, 1994; Stats 1993 ch 219 §223 (AB 1500).

Prior Law: Former Prob C §3072, similar to the present section, was added Stats 1979 ch 726 §3, operative January 1, 1981, and repealed Stats 1990 ch 79 §13, operative July 1, 1991.

§3073. Manner of joinder or consent

(a) The joinder or consent under Section 3071 of a spouse having legal capacity shall be in a manner that complies with Section 1100 or 1102 of the Family Code or other statute that applies to the transaction.

(b) The joinder or consent under Section 3071 of a conservator shall be in the same manner as a spouse would join in or consent to the transaction under the statute that applies to the transaction except that the joinder or consent shall be executed by the conservator and shall refer to the court order, if one is required, authorizing the conservator to join in or consent to the transaction. **Leg.H.** Enacted Stats 1990 ch 79 §14 (AB 759), operative July 1, 1991. Amended Stats 1992 ch 163 §129 (AB 2641), operative January 1, 1994; Stats 1993 ch 219 §224 (AB 1500).

Prior Law: Former Prob C §3073, similar to the present section, was added Stats 1979 ch 726 §3, operative January 1, 1981, amended Stats 1982 ch 497 §158, operative July 1, 1983, and repealed Stats 1990 ch 79 §13, operative July 1, 1991.

§3074. Good faith purchaser or encumbrancer for value

Notwithstanding any other provision of this article, a transaction that affects real property, entered into by a person acting in good faith and for a valuable consideration, is not affected by the fact that one or both spouses have conservators unless a notice of the establishment of the conservatorship or conservatorships, as the case may be, has been recorded prior to the transaction in the county in which the property is located. **Leg.H.** Enacted Stats 1990 ch 79 §14 (AB 759), operative July 1, 1991.

Prior Law: Former Prob C §3074, similar to the present section, was added Stats 1979 ch 726 §3, operative January 1, 1981, and repealed Stats 1990 ch 79 §13, operative July 1, 1991.

ARTICLE 3
Enforcement of Support of Spouse Who Has Conservator

Petition. §3080.
Notice of hearing. §3081.
Examination of spouse in control of property. §3082.
Order. §3083.
Income and expense declaration and property declaration. §3084.
Ex parte orders pending determination. §3085.
Continuance. §3086.
Determination of character of property. §3087.
Order for support and maintenance of conservatee. §3088.
Division of community property. §3089.
Enforcement of orders. §3090.
Judicial Council rules. §3091.
Other procedures not limited. §3092.

§3080. Petition

If one spouse has a conservator and the other spouse has the management or control of community property, the conservator or conservatee, a relative or friend of the conservatee, or any interested person may file a petition under this article in the court in which the conservatorship proceeding is pending for an order requiring the spouse who has the management or control of community property to apply the income or principal, or both, of the community property to the support and maintenance of the conservatee as ordered by the court. **Leg.H.** Enacted Stats 1990 ch 79 §14 (AB 759), operative July 1, 1991.

Prior Law: Former Prob C §3080, similar to the present section, was added Stats 1981 ch 9 §8 and repealed Stats 1990 ch 79 §13, operative July 1, 1991.

§3081. Notice of hearing

(a) Notice of the hearing on the petition shall be given for the period and in the manner provided in Chapter 3 (commencing with Section 1460) of Part 1.

(b) If the spouse who has the management or control of community property is not the conservator, the petitioner shall also cause notice of the hearing and a copy of the petition to be served on that spouse in accordance with Title 5 (commencing with Section 410.10) of Part 2 of the Code of Civil Procedure. **Leg.H.** Enacted Stats 1990 ch 79 §14 (AB 759), operative July 1, 1991.

Prior Law: Former Prob C §3081, similar to the present section, was added Stats 1981 ch 9 §8 and repealed Stats 1990 ch 79 §13, operative July 1, 1991.

§3082. Examination of spouse in control of property

Upon the filing of a petition under this article, the court may cite the spouse who has the management or control of community property to appear before the court, and the court and the petitioner may examine the spouse under oath concerning the community property and other matters relevant to the petition filed under this article. If the person so cited refuses to appear and submit to an examination, the court may proceed against the person as provided in Article 2 (commencing with Section 8870) of Chapter 2 of Part 3 of Division 7. Upon such examination, the court may make an order requiring the person cited to disclose his or her knowledge of the community property and other matters relevant to the petition filed under this article, and if the order is not complied with, the court may proceed against the person as provided in Article 2 (commencing with Section 8870) of Chapter 2 of Part 3 of Division 7. **Leg.H.** Enacted Stats 1990 ch 79 §14 (AB 759), operative July 1, 1991.

Prior Law: Former Prob C §3082, similar to the present section, was added Stats 1981 ch 9 §8, amended Stats 1988 ch 1199 §73, operative July 1, 1989, and repealed Stats 1990 ch 79 §13, operative July 1, 1991.

§3083. Order

In any proceeding under this article, the court may, after notice and hearing, order the spouse who has the management or control of community property to pay from the community property such amount as the court determines is necessary to the support and maintenance of the conservatee spouse pending the determination of the petition under this article. An order made pursuant to this section does not prejudice the rights of the spouses or other interested parties with respect to any subsequent order which may be made under this article. Any order made under this section may be modified or revoked at any time except as to any amount that may have accrued prior to the date of filing of the petition to modify or revoke the order. **Leg.H.** Enacted Stats 1990 ch 79 §14 (AB 759), operative July 1, 1991.

Prior Law: Former Prob C §3083, similar to the present section, was added Stats 1981 ch 9 §8 and repealed Stats 1990 ch 79 §13, operative July 1, 1991.

§3084. Income and expense declaration and property declaration

When a petition is filed under this article, the spouse having the management or control of community property shall serve and file a current income and expense declaration and a current property declaration on the forms prescribed by the Judicial Council for use in family law proceedings. **Leg.H.** Enacted Stats 1990 ch 79 §14 (AB 759), operative July 1, 1991.

Prior Law: Former Prob C §3084, similar to the present section, was added Stats 1981 ch 9 §8 and repealed Stats 1990 ch 79 §13, operative July 1, 1991.

§3085. Ex parte orders pending determination

During the pendency of any proceeding under this article, the court, upon the application of the petitioner, may issue ex parte orders:

(a) Restraining the spouse having the management or control of community property from transferring, encumbering, hypothecating, concealing, or in any way disposing of any property, real or personal, whether community, quasi-community, or separate, except in the usual course of business or for the necessities of life.

(b) Requiring the spouse having the management or control of the community property to notify the petitioner of any proposed extraordinary expenditures and to account to the court for all such extraordinary expenditures. **Leg.H.** Enacted Stats 1990 ch 79 §14 (AB 759), operative July 1, 1991.

Prior Law: Former Prob C §3085, similar to the present section, was added Stats 1981 ch 9 §8 and repealed Stats 1990 ch 79 §13, operative July 1, 1991.

§3086. Continuance

Any person interested in the proceeding under this article may request time for filing a response to the petition, for discovery proceedings, or for other preparation for the hearing, and the court shall grant a continuance for a reasonable time for any of such purposes. **Leg.H.** Enacted Stats 1990 ch 79 §14 (AB 759), operative July 1, 1991.

Prior Law: Former Prob C §3086, similar to the present section, was added Stats 1981 ch 9 §8 and repealed Stats 1990 ch 79 §13, operative July 1, 1991.

§3087. Determination of character of property

In a proceeding under this article, the court may hear and determine whether property is community property or the separate property of either spouse if that issue is raised in the proceeding. **Leg.H.** Enacted Stats 1990 ch 79 §14 (AB 759), operative July 1, 1991.

Prior Law: Former Prob C §3087, similar to the present section, was added Stats 1981 ch 9 §8 and repealed Stats 1990 ch 79 §13, operative July 1, 1991.

§3088. Order for support and maintenance of conservatee

(a) The court may order the spouse who has the management or control of community property to apply the income or principal, or both, of the community property to the support and maintenance of the conservatee, including care, treatment, and support of a conservatee who is a patient in a state hospital under the jurisdiction of the State Department of State Hospitals or the State Department of Developmental Services, as ordered by the court.

(b) In determining the amount ordered for support and maintenance, the court shall consider the following circumstances of the spouses:

(1) The earning capacity and needs of each spouse.

(2) The obligations and assets, including the separate property, of each spouse.

(3) The duration of the marriage.

(4) The age and health of the spouses.

(5) The standard of living of the spouses.

(6) Any other relevant factors which it considers just and equitable.

(c) At the request of any interested person, the court shall make appropriate findings with respect to the circumstances.

(d) The court may order the spouse who has the management or control of community property to make a specified monthly or other periodic payment to the conservator of the person of the conservatee or to any other person designated in the order. The court may order the spouse required to make the periodic payments to give reasonable security therefor.

(e)(1) The court may order the spouse required to make the periodic payments to assign, to the person designated in the order to receive the payments, that portion of the earnings of the spouse due or to be due in the future as will be sufficient to pay the amount ordered by the court for the support and maintenance of the conservatee. The order operates as an assignment and is binding upon any existing or future employer upon whom a copy of the order is served. The order shall be in the form of an earnings assignment order for support prescribed by the Judicial Council for use in family law proceedings. The employer may deduct the sum of one dollar and fifty cents ($1.50) for each payment made pursuant to the order. Any such assignment made pursuant to court order shall have priority as against any execution or other assignment unless otherwise ordered by the court or unless the other assignment is made pursuant to Chapter 8 (commencing with Section 5200) of Part 5 of Division 9 of the Family Code. An employer shall not use any assignment authorized by this subdivision as grounds for the dismissal of that employee.

(2) As used in this subdivision, "employer" includes the United States government and any public entity as defined in Section 811.2 of the Government Code. This subdivision applies to the money and benefits described in Sections 704.110 and 704.113 of the Code of Civil Procedure to the extent that those moneys and benefits are subject to a wage assignment for support under Chapter 4 (commencing with Section 703.010) of Division 2 of Title 9 of Part 2 of the Code of Civil Procedure.

(f) The court retains jurisdiction to modify or to vacate an order made under this section where justice requires, except as to any amount that may have accrued before the date of the filing of the petition to modify or revoke the order. At the request of any interested person, the order of modification or revocation shall include findings of fact and may be made retroactive to the date of the filing of the petition to revoke or modify, or to any date subsequent thereto. At least 15 days before the hearing on the petition to modify or vacate the order, the petitioner shall deliver pursuant to Section 1215 a notice of the time and place of the hearing on the petition, accompanied by a copy of the petition, to the spouse who has the management or control of the community property. Notice shall be given for the period and in the manner provided in Chapter 3 (commencing with Section 1460) of Part 1 to any other persons entitled to notice of the hearing under that chapter.

(g) In a proceeding for dissolution of the marriage or for legal separation, the court has jurisdiction to modify or vacate an order made under this section to the same extent as it may modify or vacate an order made in the proceeding for dissolution of the marriage or for legal separation. **Leg.H.** Enacted Stats 1990 ch 79 §14 (AB 759), operative July 1, 1991. Amended Stats 1992 ch 163 §130 (AB 2641), operative January 1, 1994; Stats 2004 ch 520 §7 (AB 2530); Stats 2012 ch 440 §51 (AB 1488), effective September 22, 2012; Stats 2017 ch 319 §56 (AB 976), effective January 1, 2018.

Prior Law: Former Prob C §3088, similar to the present section, was added Stats 1981 ch 9 §8, amended Stats 1982 ch 497 §158.5, operative July 1, 1983, and repealed Stats 1990 ch 79 §13 (AB 759), operative July 1, 1991.

§3089. Division of community property

If the spouse who has the management or control of the community property refuses to comply with any order made under this article or an order made in a separate action to provide support for the conservatee spouse, upon request of the petitioner or other interested person, the court may, in its discretion, divide the community property and the quasi-community property of the spouses, as it exists at the time of division, equally in the same manner as where a marriage is dissolved. If the property is so divided, the property awarded to each spouse is the separate property of that spouse and the court shall order that the property awarded to the conservatee spouse be transferred or paid over to the conservator of the estate of that spouse to be included in the conservatorship estate and be managed, controlled, and disposed of as a part of the conservatorship estate. The fact that property has been divided pursuant to this section has no effect on the nature of property thereafter acquired by the spouses, and the determination whether the thereafter-acquired property is community or separate property shall be made without regard to the fact that property has been divided pursuant to this section. **Leg.H.** Enacted Stats 1990 ch 79 §14 (AB 759), operative July 1, 1991.

Prior Law: Former Prob C §3089, similar to the present section, was added Stats 1981 ch 9 §8 and repealed Stats 1990 ch 79 §13, operative July 1, 1991.

§3090. Enforcement of orders

Any order of the court made under this article may be enforced by the court by execution, the appointment of a receiver, contempt, or by such other order or orders as the court in its discretion may from time to time deem necessary. **Leg.H.** Enacted Stats 1990 ch 79 §14 (AB 759), operative July 1, 1991.

Prior Law: Former Prob C §3090, similar to the present section, was added Stats 1981 ch 9 §8 and repealed Stats 1990 ch 79 §13, operative July 1, 1991.

§3091. Judicial Council rules

Notwithstanding any other provision of law, the Judicial Council may provide by rule for the practice and procedure in proceedings under this article. **Leg.H.** Enacted Stats 1990 ch 79 §14 (AB 759), operative July 1, 1991.

Prior Law: Former Prob C §3091, similar to the present section, was added Stats 1981 ch 9 §8 and repealed Stats 1990 ch 79 §13, operative July 1, 1991.

§3092. Other procedures not limited

Nothing in this article affects or limits the right of the conservator or any interested person to institute an action against any person to enforce the duty otherwise imposed by law to support the spouse having a conservator. This article is permissive and in addition to any other procedure otherwise available to enforce the obligation of support. **Leg.H.** Enacted Stats 1990 ch 79 §14 (AB 759), operative July 1, 1991.

Prior Law: Former Prob C §3092, similar to the present section, was added Stats 1981 ch 9 §8 and repealed Stats 1990 ch 79 §13, operative July 1, 1991.

CHAPTER 3
PROCEEDING FOR PARTICULAR TRANSACTION

Article 1. General Provisions.
Article 2. Commencement of Proceeding.
Article 3. Petition.
Article 4. Citation and Notice of Hearing.
Article 5. Hearing and Order.
Article 6. Consummation of Transaction.

ARTICLE 1
General Provisions

"Transaction"; Inclusion of separate property. §3100.
Nature of proceeding under this chapter. §3101.
Transactions that may be subject of the proceeding. §3102.

§3100. "Transaction"; Inclusion of separate property

(a) As used in this chapter, "transaction" means a transaction that involves community real or personal property, tangible or intangible, or an interest therein or a lien or encumbrance thereon, including, but not limited to, those transactions with respect thereto as are listed in Section 3102.

(b) However, if a proposed transaction involves property in which a spouse also has a separate property interest, for good cause the court may include that separate property in the transaction. **Leg.H.** Enacted Stats 1990 ch 79 §14 (AB 759), operative July 1, 1991. Amended Stats 1996 ch 877 §2 (AB 1467).

Prior Law: Former Prob C §3100, similar to the present section, was added Stats 1979 ch 726 §3, operative January 1, 1981, amended Stats 1982 ch 497 §159, operative July 1, 1983, and repealed Stats 1990 ch 79 §13, operative July 1, 1991.

§3101. Nature of proceeding under this chapter

(a) A proceeding may be brought under this chapter for a court order authorizing a proposed transaction, whether or not the proposed transaction is one that otherwise would require the joinder or consent of both spouses, if both of the following conditions are satisfied:

(1) One of the spouses is alleged to lack legal capacity for the proposed transaction, whether or not that spouse has a conservator.

(2) The other spouse either has legal capacity for the proposed transaction or has a conservator.

(b) A proceeding may be brought under this chapter for a court order declaring that one or both spouses has legal capacity for a proposed transaction.

(c) One proceeding may be brought under this chapter under both subdivision (a) and subdivision (b).

(d) In a proceeding under this chapter, the court may determine whether the property that is the subject of the proposed transaction is community property or the separate property of either spouse, but such determination shall not be made in the proceeding under this chapter if the court determines that the interest of justice requires that the determination be made in a civil action.

(e) This chapter is permissive and cumulative for the transactions to which it applies. **Leg.H.** Enacted Stats 1990 ch 79 §14 (AB 759), operative July 1, 1991.

Prior Law: Former Prob C §3101, similar to the present section, was added Stats 1979 ch 726 §3, operative January 1, 1981, amended Stats 1982 ch 497 §160, operative July 1, 1983, and repealed Stats 1990 ch 79 §13, operative July 1, 1991.

§3102. Transactions that may be subject of the proceeding

The transactions that may be the subject of a proceeding under this chapter include, but are not limited to:

(a) Sale, conveyance, assignment, transfer, exchange, conveyance pursuant to a preexisting contract, encumbrance by security interest, deed of trust, mortgage, or otherwise, lease, including but not limited to a lease for the exploration for and production of oil, gas, minerals, or other substances, or unitization or pooling with other property for or in connection with such exploration and production.

(b) Assignment, transfer, or conveyance, in whole or in part, in compromise or settlement of an indebtedness, demand, or proceeding to which the property may be subject.

(c) Dedication or conveyance, with or without consideration, of any of the following:

(1) The property to this state or any public entity in this state, or to the United States or any agency or instrumentality of the United States, for any purpose.

(2) An easement over the property to any person for any purpose.

(d) Conveyance, release, or relinquishment to this state or any public entity in this state, with or without consideration, of any access rights to a street, highway, or freeway from the property.

(e) Consent as a lienholder to a dedication, conveyance, release, or relinquishment under subdivision (c) or (d) by the owner of property subject to the lien.

(f) Conveyance or transfer, without consideration, to provide gifts for such purposes, and to such charities, relatives (including one of the spouses), friends, or other objects of bounty, as would be likely beneficiaries of gifts from the spouses. **Leg.H.** Enacted Stats 1990 ch 79 §14 (AB 759), operative July 1, 1991.

Prior Law: Former Prob C §3102, similar to the present section, was added Stats 1979 ch 726 §3, operative January 1, 1981, and repealed Stats 1990 ch 79 §13, operative July 1, 1991.

ARTICLE 2
Commencement of Proceeding

Jurisdiction and venue. §3110.
Who may file petition. §3111.
Representation of petitioning spouse. §3112.
Appointment of conservator not required. §3113.

§3110. Jurisdiction and venue

(a) A proceeding under this chapter shall be brought by a petition filed in the superior court.

(b) The proper county for commencement of the proceeding is the county in which a conservatorship proceeding of one of the spouses is pending. If a conservatorship proceeding is not pending, then in either of the following:

(1) The county in which one or both of the spouses resides.

(2) Any other county as may be in the best interests of the spouses.
Leg.H. Enacted Stats 1990 ch 79 §14 (AB 759), operative July 1, 1991. Amended Stats 1994 ch 806 §20 (AB 3686).

Prior Law: Former Prob C §3110, similar to the present section, was added Stats 1979 ch 762 §3, operative January 1, 1981 and repealed Stats 1990 ch 79 §13, operative July 1, 1991.

§3111. Who may file petition

(a) Except as provided in subdivision (b), any of the following persons may file, or join in, a petition under this chapter:

(1) Either spouse, whether or not the spouse has legal capacity.

(2) The conservator of either spouse.

(b) If the petition requests approval of a proposed transaction, at least one of the petitioners shall be either a conservator or a spouse having legal capacity for the transaction. **Leg.H.** Enacted Stats 1990 ch 79 §14 (AB 759), operative July 1, 1991.

Prior Law: Former Prob C §3111, similar to the present section, was added Stats 1979 ch 726 §3, operative January 1, 1981, and repealed Stats 1990 ch 79 §13, operative July 1, 1991.

§3112. Representation of petitioning spouse

(a) If a petitioning spouse is one whose legal capacity for the proposed transaction is to be determined in the proceeding, the court may do any of the following:

(1) Permit the spouse to appear without a representative.

(2) Appoint a guardian ad litem for the spouse.

(3) Take such other action as the circumstances warrant.

(b) If a petitioning spouse lacks legal capacity for the proposed transaction, the court may do either of the following:

(1) Require the spouse to be represented by the conservator of the spouse.

(2) Appoint a guardian ad litem for the spouse. **Leg.H.** Enacted Stats 1990 ch 79 §14 (AB 759), operative July 1, 1991.

Prior Law: Former Prob C §3112, similar to the present section, was added Stats 1979 ch 726 §3, operative January 1, 1981, and repealed Stats 1990 ch 79 §13, operative July 1, 1991.

§3113. Appointment of conservator not required

A proceeding may be brought under this chapter by the conservator of a spouse, or by a spouse having legal capacity for the proposed transaction, without the necessity of appointing a conservator for the other spouse. **Leg.H.** Enacted Stats 1990 ch 79 §14 (AB 759), operative July 1, 1991.

Prior Law: Former Prob C §3113, similar to the present section, was added Stats 1979 ch 726 §3, operative January 1, 1981, and repealed Stats 1990 ch 79 §13, operative July 1, 1991.

ARTICLE 3
Petition

Combining several transactions; Permissible allegations. §3120.
Required contents of petition. §3121.
Petition for court order authorizing transaction. §3122.
Petition for court order declaring legal capacity for transaction. §3123.

§3120. Combining several transactions; Permissible allegations

(a) Several proposed transactions may be included in one petition and proceeding under this chapter.

(b) The petition may contain inconsistent allegations and may request relief in the alternative. **Leg.H.** Enacted Stats 1990 ch 79 §14 (AB 759), operative July 1, 1991.

Prior Law: Former Prob C §3120, similar to the present section, was added Stats 1979 ch 726 §3, operative January 1, 1981, and repealed Stats 1990 ch 79 §13, operative July 1, 1991.

§3121. Required contents of petition

The petition shall set forth all of the following information:

(a) The name, age, and residence of each spouse.

(b) If one or both spouses is alleged to lack legal capacity for the proposed transaction, a statement that the spouse has a conservator or a statement of the facts upon which the allegation is based.

(c) If there is a conservator of a spouse, the name and address of the conservator, the county in which the conservatorship proceeding is pending, and the court number of the proceeding.

(d) If a spouse alleged to lack legal capacity for the proposed transaction is a patient in or on leave of absence from a state institution under the jurisdiction of the State Department of State Hospitals or the State Department of Developmental Services, the name and address of the institution.

(e) The names and addresses of all of the following persons:

(1) Relatives within the second degree of each spouse alleged to lack legal capacity for the proposed transaction.

(2) If the petition is to provide gifts or otherwise affect estate planning of the spouse who is alleged to lack capacity, as would be properly the subject of a petition under Article 10 (commencing with Section 2580) of Chapter 6 of Part 4 (substituted judgment) in the case of a conservatorship, the names and addresses of the persons identified in Section 2581.

(f) A sufficient description of the property that is the subject of the proposed transaction.

(g) An allegation that the property is community property, and, if the proposed transaction involves property in which a spouse also has a separate property interest, an allegation of good cause to include that separate property in the transaction.

(h) The estimated value of the property.

(i) The terms and conditions of the proposed transaction, including the names of all parties thereto.

(j) The relief requested. **Leg.H.** Enacted Stats 1990 ch 79 §14 (AB 759), operative July 1, 1991. Amended Stats 1996 ch 877 §3 (AB 1467); Stats 2003 ch 32 §3 (AB 167); Stats 2012 ch 440 §52 (AB 1488), effective September 22, 2012.

Prior Law: Former Prob C §3121, similar to the present section, was added Stats 1979 ch 726 §3, operative January 1, 1981, amended Stats 1982 ch 497 §161, operative July 1, 1983, and repealed Stats 1990 ch 79 §13, operative July 1, 1991.

§3122. Petition for court order authorizing transaction

If the proceeding is brought for a court order authorizing a proposed transaction, the petition shall set forth, in addition to the information required by Section 3121, all of the following:

(a) An allegation that one of the spouses has a conservator or facts establishing lack of legal capacity of the spouse for the proposed transaction.

(b) An allegation that the other spouse has legal capacity for the proposed transaction or has a conservator.

(c) An allegation that each spouse either: (1) joins in or consents to the proposed transaction, (2) has a conservator, or (3) is substantially unable to manage his or her financial resources or resist fraud or undue influence.

(d) Facts that may be relied upon to show that the authorization sought is for one or more of the following purposes:

(1) The advantage, benefit, or best interests of the spouses or their estates.

(2) The care and support of either spouse or of such persons as either spouse may be legally obligated to support.

(3) The payment of taxes, interest, or other encumbrances or charges for the protection and preservation of the community property.

(4) The providing of gifts for such purposes, and to such charities, relatives (including one of the spouses), friends, or other objects of bounty, as would be likely beneficiaries of gifts from the spouses. **Leg.H.** Enacted Stats 1990 ch 79 §14 (AB 759), operative July 1, 1991.

Prior Law: Former Prob C §3122, similar to the present section, was added Stats 1979 ch 726 §3, operative January 1, 1981, amended Stats 1982 ch 497 §162, operative July 1, 1983, and repealed Stats 1990 ch 79 §13, operative July 1, 1991.

§3123. Petition for court order declaring legal capacity for transaction

If the proceeding is brought for a court order declaring that one or both spouses has legal capacity for a proposed transaction, the petition shall set forth, in addition to the information required by Section 3121, an allegation of the legal capacity of such spouse or spouses for the proposed transaction. **Leg.H.** Enacted Stats 1990 ch 79 §14 (AB 759), operative July 1, 1991.

Prior Law: Former Prob C §3123, similar to the present section, was added Stats 1979 ch 726 §3, operative January 1, 1981, and repealed Stats 1990 ch 79 §13, operative July 1, 1991.

ARTICLE 4
Citation and Notice of Hearing

Citation to nonpetitioning spouse alleged to lack legal capacity; Notice to conservator in lieu of citation. §3130.
Service on nonpetitioning spouse having legal capacity. §3131.

§3130. Citation to nonpetitioning spouse alleged to lack legal capacity; Notice to conservator in lieu of citation

(a) Except as provided in subdivision (b), upon the filing of the petition, the clerk shall issue a citation to each nonpetitioning spouse alleged to lack legal capacity for the proposed transaction, setting forth the time and place of hearing. The citation and a copy of the petition shall be served upon the spouse at least 15 days before the hearing.

(b) Unless the court otherwise orders, if a spouse alleged to lack legal capacity for the proposed transaction has a conservator, no citation to the spouse need be issued, and the petitioner shall cause a notice of the time and place of the hearing on the petition, accompanied by a copy of the petition, to be served on the conservator at least 15 days before the hearing.

(c) Service under this section shall be made in the manner provided in Section 415.10 or 415.30 of the Code of Civil Procedure or in such other manner as may be authorized by the court. If the person to be served is outside this state, service may also be made in the manner provided in Section 415.40 of the Code of Civil Procedure. **Leg.H.** Enacted Stats 1990 ch 79 §14 (AB 759), operative July 1, 1991.

Prior Law: Former Prob C §3130, similar to the present section, was added Stats 1979 ch 726 §3, operative January 1, 1981, and repealed Stats 1990 ch 79 §13, operative July 1, 1991.

§3131. Service on nonpetitioning spouse having legal capacity

(a) At least 15 days before the hearing on the petition, the petitioner shall cause a notice of the time and place of the hearing and a copy of the petition to be served upon any nonpetitioning spouse not alleged to lack legal capacity for the proposed transaction.

(b) Service under subdivision (a) shall be made in the manner provided in Section 415.10 or 415.30 of the Code of Civil Procedure or in such other manner as may be authorized by the court. If the person to be served is outside this state, service may also be made in the manner provided in Section 415.40 of the Code of Civil Procedure.

(c) At least 15 days before the hearing on the petition, the petitioner shall deliver pursuant to Section 1215 a notice of the time and place of the hearing on the petition to those persons required to be named in the petition at the addresses set forth in the petition. **Leg.H.** Enacted Stats 1990 ch 79 §14 (AB 759), operative July 1, 1991. Amended Stats 1996 ch 877 §4 (AB 1467); Stats 2017 ch 319 §57 (AB 976), effective January 1, 2018.

Prior Law: Former Prob C §3131, similar to the present section, was added Stats 1979 ch 726 §3, operative January 1, 1981, and repealed Stats 1990 ch 79 §13, operative July 1, 1991.

ARTICLE 5
Hearing and Order

Representation of spouse alleged to lack legal capacity; Appointment of legal counsel; Costs and fees. §3140.
Presence of spouse at hearing. §3141.
Information to be given to spouse by court. §3142.
Order declaring legal capacity. §3143.
Court determinations before authorizing transaction; Order authorizing transaction. §3144.
Effect of determination of lack of legal capacity. §3145.

§3140. Representation of spouse alleged to lack legal capacity; Appointment of legal counsel; Costs and fees

(a) A conservator served pursuant to this article shall, and the Director of State Hospitals or the Director of Developmental Services given notice pursuant to Section 1461 may, appear at the hearing and represent a spouse alleged to lack legal capacity for the proposed transaction.

(b) The court may, in its discretion and if necessary, appoint an investigator to review the proposed transaction and report to the court regarding its advisability.

(c) If the court determines that a spouse alleged to lack legal capacity has not competently retained independent counsel, the court may in its discretion appoint the public guardian, public administrator, or a guardian ad litem to represent the interests of the spouse.

(d)(1) If a spouse alleged to lack legal capacity is unable to retain legal counsel, upon request of the spouse, the court shall appoint the public defender or private counsel under Section 1471 to represent the spouse and, if that appointment is made, Section 1472 applies.

(2) If the petition proposes a transfer of substantial assets to the petitioner from the other spouse and the court determines that the spouse has not competently retained independent counsel for the proceeding, the court may, in its discretion, appoint counsel for the other spouse if the court determines that appointment would be helpful to resolve the matter or necessary to protect the interests of the other spouse.

(e) Except as provided in paragraph (1) of subdivision (d), the court may fix a reasonable fee, to be paid out of the proceeds of the transaction or otherwise as the court may direct, for all services rendered by privately engaged counsel, the public guardian, public administrator, or guardian ad litem, and by counsel for such persons.

(f) The court may order the cost of the review and report by a court investigator pursuant to subdivision (b) to be paid out of the proceeds of the transaction or otherwise as the court may direct, if the court determines that its order would not cause a hardship. **Leg.H.** Enacted Stats 1990 ch 79 §14 (AB 759), operative July 1, 1991. Amended Stats 2008 ch 293 §10 (AB 1340), effective January 1, 2009; Stats 2009 ch 140 §153 (AB 1164), effective January 1, 2010, ch 596 §2 (SB 556) (ch 596 prevails), effective January 1, 2010; Stats 2012 ch 440 §53 (AB 1488), effective September 22, 2012.

Prior Law: Former Prob C §3140, similar to the present section, was added Stats 1979 ch 726 §3, operative January 1, 1981, and repealed Stats 1990 ch 79 §13, operative July 1, 1991.

§3141. Presence of spouse at hearing

(a) If a spouse is alleged to lack legal capacity for the proposed transaction and has no conservator, the spouse shall be produced at the hearing unless unable to attend the hearing.

(b) If the spouse is not able to attend the hearing because of medical inability, such inability shall be established (1) by the affidavit or certificate of a licensed medical practitioner or (2) if the spouse is an adherent of a religion whose tenets and practices call for reliance upon prayer alone for healing and is under treatment by an accredited practitioner of the religion, by the affidavit of the practitioner.

(c) Emotional or psychological instability is not good cause for absence of the spouse from the hearing unless, by reason of such instability, attendance at the hearing is likely to cause serious and immediate physiological damage. **Leg.H.** Enacted Stats 1990 ch 79 §14 (AB 759), operative July 1, 1991.

Prior Law: Former Prob C §3141, similar to the present section, was added Stats 1979 ch 726 §3, operative January 1, 1981, and repealed Stats 1990 ch 79 §13, operative July 1, 1991.

§3142. Information to be given to spouse by court

(a) If a spouse is alleged to lack legal capacity for the proposed transaction and has no conservator, the court, before commencement of the hearing on the merits, shall inform the spouse of all of the following:

(1) A determination of lack of legal capacity for the proposed transaction may result in approval of the proposed transaction.

(2) The spouse has the right to legal counsel of the spouse's own choosing, including the right to have legal counsel appointed by the court if unable to retain legal counsel.

(b) This section does not apply if the spouse is absent from the hearing and is not required to attend the hearing under the provisions of subdivision (a) of Section 3141 and any showing required by Section 3141 has been made. **Leg.H.** Enacted Stats 1990 ch 79 §14 (AB 759), operative July 1, 1991.

Prior Law: Former Prob C §3142, similar to the present section, was added Stats 1979 ch 726 §3, operative January 1, 1981, and repealed Stats 1990 ch 79 §13, operative July 1, 1991.

§3143. Order declaring legal capacity

(a) If the petition requests that the court make an order declaring a spouse to have legal capacity for the proposed transaction and the court determines that the spouse has legal capacity for the proposed transaction, the court shall so order.

(b) If the petition alleges that a spouse having no conservator lacks legal capacity for the proposed transaction and the court determines that the spouse has legal capacity for the transaction, the court shall make an order so declaring. **Leg.H.** Enacted Stats 1990 ch 79 §14 (AB 759), operative July 1, 1991.

Prior Law: Former Prob C §3143, similar to the present section, was added Stats 1979 ch 726 §3, operative January 1, 1981, and repealed Stats 1990 ch 79 §13, operative July 1, 1991.

§3144. Court determinations before authorizing transaction; Order authorizing transaction

(a) The court may authorize the proposed transaction if the court determines all of the following:

(1) The property that is the subject of the proposed transaction is community property of the spouses, and, if the proposed transaction involves property in which a spouse also has a separate property interest, that there is good cause to include that separate property in the transaction.

(2) One of the spouses then has a conservator or otherwise lacks legal capacity for the proposed transaction.

(3) The other spouse either has legal capacity for the proposed transaction or has a conservator.

(4) Each of the spouses either (i) joins in or consents to the proposed transaction, (ii) has a conservator, or (iii) is substantially unable to manage his or her own financial resources or resist fraud or undue influence. Substantial inability may not be proved by isolated incidents of negligence or improvidence.

(5) The proposed transaction is one that should be authorized under this chapter.

(b) If the proposed transaction is to provide gifts or otherwise affect estate planning of the spouse who is alleged to lack capacity, as would be properly the subject of a petition under Article 10 (commencing with Section 2580) of Chapter 6 of Part 4 (substituted judgment) in the case of a conservatorship, the court may authorize the transaction under this chapter only if the transaction is one that the court would authorize under that article.

(c) If the court determines under subdivision (a) that the transaction should be authorized, the court shall so order and may authorize the petitioner to do and perform all acts and to execute and deliver all papers, documents, and instruments necessary to effectuate the order.

(d) In an order authorizing a transaction, the court may prescribe any terms and conditions as the court in its discretion determines appropriate, including, but not limited to, requiring joinder or consent of another person. **Leg.H.** Enacted Stats 1990 ch 79 §14 (AB 759), operative July 1, 1991. Amended Stats 1996 ch 877 §5 (AB 1467); Stats 2003 ch 32 §4 (AB 167), effective January 1, 2004.

Prior Law: Former Prob C §3144, similar to the present section, was added Stats 1979 ch 726 §3, operative January 1, 1981, amended Stats 1982 ch 497 §163, operative July 1, 1983, and repealed Stats 1990 ch 79 §13, operative July 1, 1991.

§3145. Effect of determination of lack of legal capacity

A court determination pursuant to this chapter that a spouse lacks legal capacity for the proposed transaction affects the legal capacity of the spouse for that transaction alone and has no effect on the legal capacity of the spouse for any other purpose. **Leg.H.** Enacted Stats 1990 ch 79 §14 (AB 759), operative July 1, 1991.

Prior Law: Former Prob C §3145, similar to the present section, was added Stats 1979 ch 726 §3, operative January 1, 1981, and repealed Stats 1990 ch 79 §13, operative July 1, 1991.

ARTICLE 6
Consummation of Transaction

Bond. §3150.
Execution, delivery, and recording of documents; Credit sales. §3151.
Effect of action taken pursuant to court order. §3152.
Liability of conservator. §3153.
Further proceedings if transaction not consummated. §3154.

§3150. Bond

(a) Unless the court for good cause dispenses with the bond, the court shall require the petitioner to give a bond, in the amount fixed by the court, conditioned on the duty of the petitioner to account for and apply the proceeds of the transaction to be received by the petitioner only as the court may by order direct.

(b) Unless the court for good cause fixes the amount of the bond in a lesser amount, if given by an admitted surety insurer, the bond shall be in an amount not less than the value of the personal property (including cash and any notes) to be received by the petitioner, as determined by the court.

(c) If the sureties on the bond are personal sureties, the bond shall be approved by the court and shall be for twice the amount required for a bond given by an admitted surety insurer.

(d) Section 2328 is applicable to the bond of the petitioner under this chapter. **Leg.H.** Enacted Stats 1990 ch 79 §14 (AB 759), operative July 1, 1991.

Prior Law: Former Prob C §3150, similar to the present section, was added Stats 1979 ch 726 §3, operative January 1, 1981, amended Stats 1982 ch 517 §348, and repealed Stats 1990 ch 79 §13 (AB 759), operative July 1, 1991.

§3151. Execution, delivery, and recording of documents; Credit sales

(a) The petitioner shall, upon receipt of the consideration therefor, execute, acknowledge, and deliver any necessary instruments or documents as directed by the court, setting forth therein that they are made by authority of the order.

(b) The petitioner shall cause a certified copy of the order to be recorded in the office of the recorder of each county in which is located any real property affected by the order or any real property upon which there is a lien or encumbrance affected by the order.

(c) If a sale is made upon a credit pursuant to the order, the petitioner shall take the note of the person to whom the sale is made for the amount of the unpaid balance of the purchase money, with such security for the payment thereof as the court shall by order approve. The note shall be made payable to the petitioner or, if the petition was made by a conservator, to the petitioner as conservator. **Leg.H.** Enacted Stats 1990 ch 79 §14 (AB 759), operative July 1, 1991.

Prior Law: Former Prob C §3151, similar to the present section, was added Stats 1979 ch 726 §3, operative January 1, 1981, and repealed Stats 1990 ch 79 §13, operative July 1, 1991.

§3152. Effect of action taken pursuant to court order

A sale, conveyance, assignment, transfer, exchange, encumbrance, security interest, mortgage, deed of trust, lease, dedication, release, or relinquishment, and any instrument or document, made pursuant to the court's order, is as valid and effectual as if the property affected thereby were the sole and absolute property of the person making it. **Leg.H.** Enacted Stats 1990 ch 79 §14 (AB 759), operative July 1, 1991.

Prior Law: Former Prob C §3152, similar to the present section, was added Stats 1979 ch 726 §3, operative January 1, 1981, and repealed Stats 1990 ch 79 §13, operative July 1, 1991.

§3153. Liability of conservator

Notes, encumbrances, security interests, mortgages, leases, or deeds of trust, executed as provided in this chapter by a petitioning conservator create no personal liability against the conservator so executing, unless the conservator is one of the spouses and then only to the extent that personal liability would have resulted had both spouses had legal capacity for the transaction and joined in the execution. **Leg.H.** Enacted Stats 1990 ch 79 §14 (AB 759), operative July 1, 1991.

Prior Law: Former Prob C §3153, similar to the present section, was added Stats 1979 ch 726 §3, operative January 1, 1981, and repealed Stats 1990 ch 79 §13, operative July 1, 1991.

§3154. Further proceedings if transaction not consummated

(a) If any party to the transaction, other than the petitioner, does not consummate a transaction authorized by the court, the court, on application of the petitioner, after such notice to the parties to the transaction as the court directs, may vacate the order authorizing the transaction.

(b) If the order authorized the sale or encumbrance of property, the petitioner may by supplemental petition apply to the court for an order authorizing any other sale or encumbrance of the property to the advantage, benefit, or best interests of the spouses or their estates. The supplemental petition and a notice of the time and place of the hearing shall be served and mailed as provided in Article 4 (commencing with Section 3130) except that (1) no further citation shall be issued and (2) a copy of the supplemental petition and a notice of the time and place of the hearing shall be served upon any person who has appeared as representative of a nonpetitioning spouse or upon counsel of record for a nonpetitioning spouse or as the court may otherwise direct.

(c) If it appears to the court that the other sale or encumbrance is to the advantage, benefit, or best interests of the spouses or their estates and that the request in the supplemental petition that the transaction be authorized should be granted, the court may so order and may authorize the petitioner to do and perform acts and to execute and deliver all papers, documents, and instruments necessary to effectuate the order. **Leg.H.** Enacted Stats 1990 ch 79 §14 (AB 759), operative July 1, 1991.

Prior Law: Former Prob C §3154, similar to the present section, was added Stats 1979 ch 726 §3, operative January 1, 1981, and repealed Stats 1990 ch 79 §13, operative July 1, 1991.

PART 7
CAPACITY DETERMINATIONS AND HEALTH CARE DECISIONS FOR ADULT WITHOUT CONSERVATOR

Definitions. §3200.
Petition to determine capacity to make health care decision. §3201.
Jurisdiction and venue. §3202.
Persons who may file petition. §3203.
Contents of petition. §3204.
Appointment of legal counsel. §3205.
Notice of hearing. §3206.
Stipulation upon medical declarations. §3207.
Order authorizing recommended health care; Order authorizing artificial nutrition. §3208.
Patient with capacity to consent to recommended health care. §3208.5.
Continuing jurisdiction of court. §3209.
Construction of provisions in this part. §3210.
Prohibited placements and treatments. §3211.
Right to choose treatment by spiritual means. §3212.

§3200. Definitions
As used in this part:

(a) "Health care" means any care, treatment, service, or procedure to maintain, diagnose, or otherwise affect a patient's physical or mental condition.

(b) "Health care decision" means a decision regarding the patient's health care, including the following:

(1) Selection and discharge of health care providers and institutions.

(2) Approval or disapproval of diagnostic tests, surgical procedures, programs of medication.

(3) Directions to provide, withhold, or withdraw artificial nutrition and hydration and all other forms of health care, including cardiopulmonary resuscitation.

(c) "Health care institution" means an institution, facility, or agency licensed, certified, or otherwise authorized or permitted by law to provide health care in the ordinary course of business.

(d) "Patient" means an adult who does not have a conservator of the person and for whom a health care decision needs to be made. **Leg.H.** Enacted Stats 1990 ch 79 §14 (AB 759), operative July 1, 1991. Amended Stats 1999 ch 658 §15 (AB 891), operative July 1, 2000.

Prior Law: Former Prob C §3200, similar to the present section, was added Stats 1979 ch 726 §3, operative January 1, 1981, and repealed Stats 1990 ch 79 §13, operative July 1, 1991.

§3201. Petition to determine capacity to make health care decision

(a) A petition may be filed to determine that a patient has the capacity to make a health care decision concerning an existing or continuing condition.

(b) A petition may be filed to determine that a patient lacks the capacity to make a health care decision concerning specified treatment for an existing or continuing condition, and further for an order authorizing a designated person to make a health care decision on behalf of the patient.

(c) One proceeding may be brought under this part under both subdivisions (a) and (b). **Leg.H.** Enacted Stats 1990 ch 79 §14 (AB 759), operative July 1, 1991. Amended Stats 1995 ch 842 §9 (SB 730); Stats 1996 ch 178 §9 (SB 1650); Stats 1999 ch 658 §16 (AB 891), operative July 1, 2000.

1995 Notes: This act shall be known and may be cited as the Due Process in Competence Determinations Act. Stats 1995 ch 842 §12.

This act shall not apply to proceedings under the Welfare and Institutions Code. Stats 1995 ch 842 §13.

Prior Law: Former Prob C §3201, similar to the present section, was added Stats 1979 ch 726 §3, operative January 1, 1981, and repealed Stats 1990 ch 79 §13, operative July 1, 1991.

§3202. Jurisdiction and venue
The petition may be filed in the superior court of any of the following counties:

(a) The county in which the patient resides.

(b) The county in which the patient is temporarily living.

(c) Such other county as may be in the best interests of the patient. **Leg.H.** Enacted Stats 1990 ch 79 §14 (AB 759), operative July 1, 1991.

Prior Law: Former Prob C §3202, similar to the present section, was added Stats 1979 ch 726 §3, operative January 1, 1981, and repealed Stats 1990 ch 79 §13, operative July 1, 1991.

§3203. Persons who may file petition
A petition may be filed by any of the following:

(a) The patient.

(b) The patient's spouse.

(c) A relative or friend of the patient, or other interested person, including the patient's agent under a power of attorney for health care.

(d) The patient's physician.

(e) A person acting on behalf of the health care institution in which the patient is located if the patient is in a health care institution.

(f) The public guardian or other county officer designated by the board of supervisors of the county in which the patient is located or resides or is temporarily living. **Leg.H.** Enacted Stats 1990 ch 79 §14 (AB 759), operative July 1, 1991. Amended Stats 1999 ch 658 §17 (AB 891), operative July 1, 2000.

Prior Law: Former Prob C §3203, similar to the present section, was added Stats 1979 ch 726 §3, operative January 1, 1981, and repealed Stats 1990 ch 79 §13, operative July 1, 1991.

§3204. Contents of petition
The petition shall state, or set forth by a medical declaration attached to the petition, all of the following known to the petitioner at the time the petition is filed:

(a) The condition of the patient's health that requires treatment.

(b) The recommended health care that is considered to be medically appropriate.

(c) The threat to the patient's condition if authorization for the recommended health care is delayed or denied by the court.

(d) The predictable or probable outcome of the recommended health care.

(e) The medically available alternatives, if any, to the recommended health care.

(f) The efforts made to obtain consent from the patient.

(g) If the petition is filed by a person on behalf of a health care institution, the name of the person to be designated to give consent to the recommended health care on behalf of the patient.

(h) The deficit or deficits in the patient's mental functions listed in subdivision (a) of Section 811 that are impaired, and an identification of a link between the deficit or deficits and the patient's inability to respond knowingly and intelligently to queries about the recommended health care or inability to participate in a decision about the recommended health care by means of a rational thought process.

(i) The names and addresses, so far as they are known to the petitioner, of the persons specified in subdivision (b) of Section 1821. **Leg.H.** Enacted Stats 1990 ch 79 §14 (AB 759), operative July 1, 1991. Amended Stats 1995 ch 842 §10 (SB 730); Stats 1996 ch 178 §10 (SB 1650), ch 563 §15 (SB 392); Stats 1999 ch 658 §18 (AB 891), operative July 1, 2000.

Prior Law: Former Prob C §3204, similar to the present section, was added Stats 1979 ch 726 §3, operative January 1, 1981, and repealed Stats 1990 ch 79 §13, operative July 1, 1991.

1995 Notes: This act shall be known and may be cited as the Due Process in Competence Determinations Act. Stats 1995 ch 842 §12.

This act shall not apply to proceedings under the Welfare and Institutions Code. Stats 1995 ch 842 §13.

§3205. Appointment of legal counsel
Upon the filing of the petition, the court shall determine the name of the attorney the patient has retained to represent the patient in the proceeding under this part or the name of the attorney the patient plans to retain for that purpose. If the patient has not retained an attorney and does not plan to retain one, the court shall appoint the public defender or private counsel under Section 1471 to consult with and represent the patient at the hearing on the petition and, if such appointment is made, Section 1472 applies. **Leg.H.** Enacted Stats 1990 ch 79 §14 (AB 759), operative July 1, 1991.

Prior Law: Former Prob C §3205, similar to the present section, was added Stats 1979 ch 726 §3, operative January 1, 1981, and repealed Stats 1990 ch 79 §13, operative July 1, 1991.

§3206. Notice of hearing

(a) Not less than 15 days before the hearing, notice of the time and place of the hearing and a copy of the petition shall be personally served on the patient, the patient's attorney, and the agent under the patient's power of attorney for health care, if any.

(b) Not less than 15 days before the hearing, notice of the time and place of the hearing and a copy of the petition shall be delivered pursuant to Section 1215 to the following persons:

(1) The patient's spouse, if any, at the address stated in the petition.

(2) The patient's relatives named in the petition at their addresses stated in the petition.

(c) For good cause, the court may shorten or waive notice of the hearing as provided by this section. In determining the period of notice to be required, the court shall take into account both of the following:

(1) The existing medical facts and circumstances set forth in the petition or in a medical declaration attached to the petition or in a medical declaration presented to the court.

(2) The desirability, where the condition of the patient permits, of giving adequate notice to all interested persons. **Leg.H.** Added Stats 1996 ch 563 §17 (SB 392). Amended Stats 1999 ch 658 §19 (AB 891), operative July 1, 2000; Stats 2017 ch 319 §58 (AB 976), effective January 1, 2018.

Prior Law: Former Prob C §3206, similar to the present section, was enacted Stats 1990 ch 79 §14, operative July 1, 1991, and repealed Stats 1996 ch 563 §16.

Former Prob C §3206, similar to the present section, was added Stats 1979 ch 726 §3, operative January 1, 1981, and repealed Stats 1990 ch 79 §13, operative July 1, 1991.

§3207. Stipulation upon medical declarations

Notwithstanding Section 3206, the matter presented by the petition may be submitted for the determination of the court upon proper and sufficient medical declarations if the attorney for the petitioner and the attorney for the patient so stipulate and further stipulate that there remains no issue of fact to be determined. **Leg.H.** Enacted Stats 1990 ch 79 §14 (AB 759), operative July 1, 1991. Amended Stats 1999 ch 658 §20 (AB 891), operative July 1, 2000.

Prior Law: Former Prob C §3207, similar to the present section, was added Stats 1979 ch 726 §3, operative January 1, 1981, and repealed Stats 1990 ch 79 §13, operative July 1, 1991.

§3208. Order authorizing recommended health care; Order authorizing artificial nutrition

(a) Except as provided in subdivision (b), the court may make an order authorizing the recommended health care for the patient and designating a person to give consent to the recommended health care on behalf of the patient if the court determines from the evidence all of the following:

(1) The existing or continuing condition of the patient's health requires the recommended health care.

(2) If untreated, there is a probability that the condition will become life-endangering or result in a serious threat to the physical or mental health of the patient.

(3) The patient is unable to consent to the recommended health care.

(b) In determining whether the patient's mental functioning is so severely impaired that the patient lacks the capacity to make any health care decision, the court may take into consideration the frequency, severity, and duration of periods of impairment.

(c) The court may make an order authorizing withholding or withdrawing artificial nutrition and hydration and all other forms of health care and designating a person to give or withhold consent to the recommended health care on behalf of the patient if the court determines from the evidence all of the following:

(1) The recommended health care is in accordance with the patient's best interest, taking into consideration the patient's personal values to the extent known to the petitioner.

(2) The patient is unable to consent to the recommended health care. **Leg.H.** Enacted Stats 1990 ch 79 §14 (AB 759), operative July 1, 1991. Amended Stats 1990 ch 710 §12 (SB 1775), operative July 1, 1991; Stats 1995 ch 842 §11 (SB 730); Stats 1999 ch 658 §21 (AB 891), operative July 1, 2000.

Prior Law: Former Prob C §3208, similar to the present section, was added Stats 1979 ch 726 §3, operative January 1, 1981, and repealed Stats 1990 ch 79 §13, operative July 1, 1991.

1995 Notes: This act shall be known and may be cited as the Due Process in Competence Determinations Act. Stats 1995 ch 842 §12.

This act shall not apply to proceedings under the Welfare and Institutions Code. Stats 1995 ch 842 §13.

§3208.5. Patient with capacity to consent to recommended health care

In a proceeding under this part:

(a) Where the patient has the capacity to consent to the recommended health care, the court shall so find in its order.

(b) Where the court has determined that the patient has the capacity to consent to the recommended health care, the court shall, if requested, determine whether the patient has accepted or refused the recommended health care, and whether the patient's consent to the recommended health care is an informed consent.

(c) Where the court finds that the patient has the capacity to consent to the recommended health care, but that the patient refuses consent, the court shall not make an order authorizing the recommended health care or designating a person to give consent to the recommended health care. If an order has been made authorizing the recommended health care and designating a person to give consent to the recommended health care, the order shall be revoked if the court determines that the patient has recovered the capacity to consent to the recommended health care. Until revoked or modified, the order is effective authorization for the recommended health care. **Leg.H.** Added Stats 1999 ch 658 §22 (AB 891), operative July 1, 2000.

§3209. Continuing jurisdiction of court

The court in which the petition is filed has continuing jurisdiction to revoke or modify an order made under this part upon a petition filed, noticed, and heard in the same manner as an original petition filed under this part. **Leg.H.** Enacted Stats 1990 ch 79 §14 (AB 759), operative July 1, 1991.

Prior Law: Former Prob C §3209, similar to the present section, was added Stats 1979 ch 726 §3, operative January 1, 1981, and repealed Stats 1990 ch 79 §13, operative July 1, 1991.

§3210. Construction of provisions in this part

(a) This part is supplemental and alternative to other procedures or methods for obtaining consent to health care or making health care decisions, and is permissive and cumulative for the relief to which it applies.

(b) Nothing in this part limits the providing of health care in an emergency case in which the health care is required because (1) the health care is required for the alleviation of severe pain or (2) the patient has a medical condition that, if not immediately diagnosed and treated, will lead to serious disability or death.

(c) Nothing in this part supersedes the right that any person may have under existing law to make health care decisions on behalf of a patient, or affects the decisionmaking process of a health care institution. **Leg.H.** Enacted Stats 1990 ch 79 §14 (AB 759), operative July 1, 1991. Amended Stats 1999 ch 658 §23 (AB 891), operative July 1, 2000.

Prior Law: Former Prob C §3210, similar to the present section, was added Stats 1979 ch 726 §3, operative January 1, 1981, and repealed Stats 1990 ch 79 §13, operative July 1, 1991.

§3211. Prohibited placements and treatments

(a) No person may be placed in a mental health treatment facility under the provisions of this part.

(b) No experimental drug as defined in Section 111515 of the Health and Safety Code may be prescribed for or administered to any person under this part.

(c) No convulsive treatment as defined in Section 5325 of the Welfare and Institutions Code may be performed on any person under this part.

(d) No person may be sterilized under this part.

(e) The provisions of this part are subject to a valid advance health care directive under the Health Care Decisions Law, Division 4.7 (commencing with Section 4600). **Leg.H.** Enacted Stats 1990 ch 79 §14 (AB 759), operative July 1, 1991. Amended Stats 1996 ch 1023 §399 (SB 1497), effective September 29, 1996; Stats 1999 ch 658 §24 (AB 891), operative July 1, 2000.

Prior Law: Former Prob C §3211, similar to the present section, was added Stats 1979 ch 726 §3, operative January 1, 1981, and repealed Stats 1990 ch 79 §13, operative July 1, 1991.

§3212. Right to choose treatment by spiritual means

Nothing in this part shall be construed to supersede or impair the right of any individual to choose treatment by spiritual means in lieu of medical treatment, nor shall any individual choosing treatment by spiritual means, in accordance with the tenets and practices of that individual's established religious tradition, be required to submit to medical testing of any kind pursuant to a determination of capacity. **Leg.H.** Added Stats 1999 ch 658 §25 (AB 891), operative July 1, 2000.

PART 8
OTHER PROTECTIVE PROCEEDINGS

Chapter 1. General Provisions.
Chapter 2. Money or Property Belonging to Minor.
Chapter 3. Compromise by Parent of Minor's Disputed Claim.
Chapter 4. Money or Property Paid or Delivered Pursuant to Compromise or Judgment for Minor or Disabled Person.
Chapter 5. Property of Absent Federal Personnel.
Chapter 6. Removal of Property of Nonresident.

CHAPTER 1
GENERAL PROVISIONS

Accounting by parent to minor. §3300.
Effect on Uniform Transfers to Minors Act. §3303.

§3300. Accounting by parent to minor

A parent who receives any money or property belonging to a minor under any provision of this part shall account to the minor for the money or other property when the minor reaches the age of majority. **Leg.H.** Enacted Stats 1990 ch 79 §14 (AB 759), operative July 1, 1991.

Prior Law: Former Prob C §3300, similar to the present section, was added Stats 1979 ch 726 §3, operative January 1, 1981, and repealed Stats 1990 ch 79 §13, operative July 1, 1991.

§3301. [Section repealed 1992]

Leg.H. Enacted Stats 1990 ch 79 §14 (AB 759), operative July 1, 1991. Repealed Stats 1992 ch 162 §11 (AB 2650), operative January 1, 1994. See Fam C §§200, 6911, 6950.

Prior Law: Former Prob C §3301, similar to present Fam C §§200, 6911, 6950, was added Stats 1979 ch 726 §3, operative January 1, 1981, and repealed Stats 1990 ch 79 §13, operative July 1, 1991.

§3302. [Section repealed 1992]

Leg.H. Enacted Stats 1990 ch 79 §14 (AB 759), operative July 1, 1991. Repealed Stats 1992 ch 162 §12 (AB 2650), operative January 1, 1994. See Fam C §6602.

Prior Law: Former Prob C §3302, similar to present Fam C §6602, was added Stats 1979 ch 726 §3, operative January 1, 1981, and repealed Stats 1990 ch 79 §13, operative July 1, 1991.

§3303. Effect on Uniform Transfers to Minors Act

Nothing in this part limits the provisions of the California Uniform Transfers to Minors Act, Part 9 (commencing with Section 3900). **Leg.H.** Enacted Stats 1990 ch 79 §14 (AB 759), operative July 1, 1991.

Prior Law: Former Prob C §3303, similar to the present section, was added Stats 1984 ch 243 §2, and repealed Stats 1990 ch 79 §13, operative July 1, 1991.

CHAPTER 2
MONEY OR PROPERTY BELONGING TO MINOR

Article 1. Total Estate Not in Excess of $5,000.
Article 2. Property in the Form of Money.

ARTICLE 1
Total Estate Not in Excess of $5,000

"Total estate of the minor" defined. §3400.
Delivery of money or property to parent. §3401.
Effect of written receipt of parent. §3402.

§3400. "Total estate of the minor" defined

(a) As used in this article, "total estate of the minor" includes both the money and other property belonging to the minor and the money and other property belonging to the guardianship estate, if any, of the minor.

(b) In computing the "total estate of the minor" for the purposes of this article, all of the following shall be deducted:

(1) "Custodial property" held pursuant to the California Uniform Transfers to Minors Act, Part 9 (commencing with Section 3900).

(2) Any money or property subject to court order pursuant to subdivision (c) of Section 3602 or Article 2 (commencing with Section 3610) of Chapter 4. **Leg.H.** Enacted Stats 1990 ch 79 §14 (AB 759), operative July 1, 1991.

Prior Law: Former Prob C §3400, similar to the present section, was added Stats 1979 ch 726 §3, operative January 1, 1981, amended Stats 1984 ch 243 §3, and repealed Stats 1990 ch 79 §13 (AB 759), operative July 1, 1991.

§3401. Delivery of money or property to parent

(a) Where a minor does not have a guardian of the estate, money or other property belonging to the minor may be paid or delivered to a parent of the minor entitled to the custody of the minor to be held in trust for the minor until the minor reaches majority if the requirements of subdivision (c) are satisfied.

(b) Where the minor has a guardian of the estate, all the money and other property belonging to the guardianship estate may be paid or delivered to a parent entitled to the custody of the minor to be held in trust for the minor until the minor reaches majority if the requirements of subdivision (c) are satisfied.

(c) This section applies only if both of the following requirements are satisfied:

(1) The total estate of the minor, including the money and other property to be paid or delivered to the parent, does not exceed five thousand dollars ($5,000) in value.

(2) The parent to whom the money or other property is to be paid or delivered gives the person making the payment or delivery written assurance, verified by the oath of such parent, that the total estate of the minor, including the money or other property to be paid or delivered to the parent, does not exceed five thousand dollars ($5,000) in value. **Leg.H.** Enacted Stats 1990 ch 79 §14 (AB 759), operative July 1, 1991.

Prior Law: Former Prob C §3401, similar to the present section, was added Stats 1979 ch 726 §3, operative January 1, 1981, and repealed Stats 1990 ch 79 §13, operative July 1, 1991.

§3402. Effect of written receipt of parent

The written receipt of the parent giving the written assurance under Section 3401 shall be an acquittance of the person making the payment of money or delivery of other property pursuant to this article. **Leg.H.** Enacted Stats 1990 ch 79 §14 (AB 759), operative July 1, 1991.

Prior Law: Former Prob C §3402, similar to the present section, was added Stats 1979 ch 726 §3, operative January 1, 1981, and repealed Stats 1990 ch 79 §13, operative July 1, 1991.

ARTICLE 2
Property in the Form of Money

Application of article; Computing "money belonging to the minor". §3410.
Filing of petition. §3411.
Order of court when there is guardianship of estate. §3412.
Order of court when there is no guardianship of estate. §3413.

§3410. Application of article; Computing "money belonging to the minor"

(a) This article applies to both of the following cases:

(1) Where the minor has a guardian of the estate and the sole asset of the guardianship estate is money.

(2) Where the minor has no guardian of the estate and there is money belonging to the minor.

(b) This article does not apply to, and there shall be excluded in computing "money belonging to the minor" for the purpose of this article, all of the following:

(1) Money or property which is or will be held as "custodial property" pursuant to the California Uniform Transfers to Minors Act, Part 9 (commencing with Section 3900).

(2) Any money or property subject to court order pursuant to subdivision (c) of Section 3602 or Article 2 (commencing with Section 3610) of Chapter 4. **Leg.H.** Enacted Stats 1990 ch 79 §14 (AB 759), operative July 1, 1991.

Prior Law: Former Prob C §3410, similar to the present section, was added Stats 1979 ch 726 §3, operative January 1, 1981, amended Stats 1984 ch 243 §4, and repealed Stats 1990 ch 79 §13, operative July 1, 1991.

§3411. Filing of petition

(a) A parent of a minor entitled to custody of the minor, the guardian of the estate of the minor, or the person holding the money belonging to the minor may file a petition requesting that the court make an order under this article.

(b) The petition shall be filed in the superior court of:

(1) The county where the minor resides if the minor has no guardian of the estate.

(2) The county having jurisdiction of the guardianship estate if the minor has a guardian of the estate. **Leg.H.** Enacted Stats 1990 ch 79 §14 (AB 759), operative July 1, 1991.

Prior Law: Former Prob C §3411, similar to the present section, was added Stats 1979 ch 726 §3, operative January 1, 1981, and repealed Stats 1990 ch 79 §13, operative July 1, 1991.

§3412. Order of court when there is guardianship of estate

If the minor has a guardian of the estate and the sole asset of the guardianship estate is money, the court may order that the guardianship of the estate be terminated and, if the court so orders, the court in its discretion shall also order any one or more of the following:

(a) That the money be deposited in an insured account in a financial institution in this state, or in a single-premium deferred annuity, subject to withdrawal only upon authorization of the court.

(b) That all or any part of the money be transferred to a custodian for the benefit of the minor under the California Uniform Transfers to Minors Act, Part 9 (commencing with Section 3900).

(c) If the money of the guardianship estate does not exceed twenty thousand dollars ($20,000), that the money be held on any other condition that the court in its discretion determines to be in the best interests of the minor.

(d) If the money of the guardianship estate does not exceed five thousand dollars ($5,000), that all or any part of the money be paid to a parent of the minor, without bond, upon the terms and under the conditions specified in Article 1 (commencing with Section 3400).

(e) That the remaining balance of any money paid or to be paid be deposited with the county treasurer, if all of the following conditions are met:

(1) The county treasurer has been authorized by the county board of supervisors to handle the deposits.

(2) The county treasurer shall receive and safely keep all money deposited with the county treasurer pursuant to this subdivision, shall pay the money out only upon the order of the court, and shall credit each estate with the interest earned by the funds deposited less the county treasurer's actual cost authorized to be recovered under Section 27013 of the Government Code.

(3) The county treasurer and sureties on the official bond of the county treasurer are responsible for the safekeeping and payment of the money.

(4) The county treasurer shall ensure that the money deposited is to earn interest or dividends, or both, at the highest rate which the county can reasonably obtain as a prudent investor.

(5) Funds so deposited with the county treasurer shall only be invested or deposited in compliance with the provisions governing the investment or deposit of state funds set forth in Chapter 5 (commencing with Section 16640) of Part 2 of Division 4 of Title 2 of the Government Code, the investment or deposit of county funds set forth in Chapter 4 (commencing with Section 53600) of Part 1 of Division 2 of Title 5 of the Government Code, or as authorized under Chapter 6 (commencing with Section 2400) of Part 4. **Leg.H.** Enacted Stats 1990 ch 79 §14 (AB 759), operative July 1, 1991. Amended Stats 1991 ch 413 §1 (AB 934); Stats 2004 ch 67 §1 (AB 1851), effective January 1, 2005.

Prior Law: Former Prob C §3412, similar to the present section, was added Stats 1979 ch 726 §3, operative January 1, 1981, amended Stats 1984 ch 243 §5, and repealed Stats 1990 ch 79 §13, operative July 1, 1991.

§3413. Order of court when there is no guardianship of estate

If the minor has no guardian of the estate and there is money belonging to the minor, the court may order that a guardian of the estate be appointed and that the money be paid to the guardian or the court may order any one or more of the following:

(a) That the money be deposited in an insured account in a financial institution in this state, or in a single-premium deferred annuity, subject to withdrawal only upon authorization of the court.

(b) That all or any part of the money be transferred to a custodian for the benefit of the minor under the California Uniform Transfers to Minors Act, Part 9 (commencing with Section 3900).

(c) If the money belonging to the minor does not exceed twenty thousand dollars ($20,000), that the money be held on any other condition that the court in its discretion determines to be in the best interests of the minor.

(d) If the money belonging to the minor does not exceed five thousand dollars ($5,000), that all or any part of the money be paid to a parent of the minor, without bond, upon the terms and under the conditions specified in Article 1 (commencing with Section 3400).

(e) That the remaining balance of any money paid or to be paid be deposited with the county treasurer, if all of the following conditions are met:

(1) The county treasurer has been authorized by the county board of supervisors to handle the deposits.

(2) The county treasurer shall receive and safely keep all money deposited with the county treasurer pursuant to this subdivision, shall pay the money out only upon the order of the court, and shall credit each estate with the interest earned by the funds deposited less the county treasurer's actual cost authorized to be recovered under Section 27013 of the Government Code.

(3) The county treasurer and sureties on the official bond of the county treasurer are responsible for the safekeeping and payment of the money.

(4) The county treasurer shall ensure that the money deposited is to earn interest or dividends, or both, at the highest rate which the county can reasonably obtain as a prudent investor.

(5) Funds so deposited with the county treasurer shall only be invested or deposited in compliance with the provisions governing the investment or deposit of state funds set forth in Chapter 5 (commencing with Section 16640) of Part 2 of Division 4 of Title 2 of the Government Code, the investment or deposit of county funds set forth in Chapter 4 (commencing with Section 53600) of Part 1 of Division 2 of Title 5 of the Government Code, or as authorized under Chapter 6 (commencing with Section 2400) of Part 4. **Leg.H.** Enacted Stats 1990 ch 79 §14 (AB 759), operative July 1, 1991. Amended Stats 1991 ch 413 §2 (AB 934); Stats 2004 ch 67 §2 (AB 1851), effective January 1, 2005.

Prior Law: Former Prob C §3413, similar to the present section, was added Stats 1979 ch 726 §3, operative January 1, 1981, amended Stats 1984 ch 243 §6, and repealed Stats 1990 ch 79 §13, operative July 1, 1991.

CHAPTER 3
COMPROMISE BY PARENT OF MINOR'S DISPUTED CLAIM

Parent's right to compromise minor's claim. §3500.
Hearing. § 3505.

§3500. Parent's right to compromise minor's claim

(a) When a minor has a disputed claim for damages, money, or other property and does not have a guardian of the estate, the following persons have the right to compromise, or to execute a covenant not to sue on or a covenant not to enforce judgment on, the claim, unless the claim is against such person or persons:

(1) Either parent if the parents of the minor are not living separate and apart.

(2) The parent having the care, custody, or control of the minor if the parents of the minor are living separate and apart.

(b) The compromise or covenant is valid only after it has been approved, upon the filing of a petition, by the superior court of either of the following counties:

(1) The county where the minor resides when the petition is filed.

(2) Any county where suit on the claim or matter properly could be brought.

(c) Any money or other property to be paid or delivered for the benefit of the minor pursuant to the compromise or covenant shall be paid and delivered in the manner and upon the terms and conditions specified in Chapter 4 (commencing with Section 3600).

(d) A parent having the right to compromise the disputed claim of the minor under this section may execute a full release and satisfaction, or execute a covenant not to sue on or a covenant not to enforce judgment on the disputed claim, after the money or other property to be paid or delivered has been paid or delivered as provided in subdivision (c). If the court orders that all or any part of the money to be paid under the compromise or covenant be deposited in an insured account in a financial institution in this state, or in a single-premium deferred annuity, the release and satisfaction or covenant is not effective for any purpose until the money has been deposited as directed in the order of the court. **Leg.H.** Enacted Stats 1990 ch 79 §14 (AB 759), operative July 1, 1991.

Prior Law: Former Prob C §3500, similar to the present section, was added Stats 1979 ch 726 §3, operative January 1, 1981, and repealed Stats 1990 ch 79 §13, operative July 1, 1991.

§ 3505. Hearing

The court shall schedule a hearing on a petition for compromise of a minor's disputed claim pursuant to Section 3500 within 30 days from the date of filing. If the petition is unopposed, the court shall issue a decision on the petition at the conclusion of the hearing. **Leg.H.** Added Stats 2021 ch 214 §8 (SB 241), effective January 1, 2022.

CHAPTER 4
MONEY OR PROPERTY PAID OR DELIVERED PURSUANT TO COMPROMISE OR JUDGMENT FOR MINOR OR DISABLED PERSON

Article 1. General Provisions.
Article 2. Disposition of Money or Other Property Where No Guardianship or Conservatorship.

ARTICLE 1
General Provisions

Application of chapter. §3600.
Order directing payment of expenses, costs, and fees. §3601.
Disposition of remaining balance. §3602.
Reference to "person with a disability". §3603.
Payment to special needs trust; Petition for termination. §3604.
Tolling of statute of limitations during existence of special needs trust; Death of special needs trust beneficiary. §3605.

§3600. Application of chapter

This chapter applies whenever both of the following conditions exist:

(a) A court (1) approves a compromise of, or the execution of a covenant not to sue on or a covenant not to enforce judgment on, a minor's disputed claim, (2) approves a compromise of a pending action or proceeding to which a minor or person with a disability is a party, or (3) gives judgment for a minor or person with a disability.

(b) The compromise, covenant, or judgment provides for the payment or delivery of money or other property for the benefit of the minor or person with a disability. **Leg.H.** Enacted Stats 1990 ch 79 §14 (AB 759), operative July 1, 1991. Amended Stats 2004 ch 67 §3 (AB 1851), effective January 1, 2005.

Prior Law: Former Prob C §3600, similar to the present section, was added Stats 1979 ch 726 §3, operative January 1, 1981, and repealed Stats 1990 ch 79 §13, operative July 1, 1991.

§3601. Order directing payment of expenses, costs, and fees

(a) The court making the order or giving the judgment referred to in Section 3600, as a part thereof, shall make a further order authorizing and directing that reasonable expenses, medical or otherwise and including reimbursement to a parent, guardian, or conservator, costs, and attorney's fees, as the court shall approve and allow therein, shall be paid from the money or other property to be paid or delivered for the benefit of the minor or person with a disability.

(b) The order required by subdivision (a) may be directed to the following:

(1) A parent of the minor, the guardian ad litem, or the guardian of the estate of the minor or the conservator of the estate of the person with a disability.

(2) The payer of any money to be paid pursuant to the compromise, covenant, or judgment for the benefit of the minor or person with a disability. **Leg.H.** Enacted Stats 1990 ch 79 §14 (AB 759), operative July 1, 1991. Amended Stats 2004 ch 67 §4 (AB 1851), effective January 1, 2005.

Prior Law: Former Prob C §3601, similar to the present section, was added Stats 1979 ch 726 §3, operative January 1, 1981, and repealed Stats 1990 ch 79 §13, operative July 1, 1991.

§3602. Disposition of remaining balance

(a) If there is no guardianship of the estate of the minor or conservatorship of the estate of the person with a disability, the remaining balance of the money and other property, after payment of all expenses, costs, and fees as approved and allowed by the court under Section 3601, shall be paid, delivered, deposited, or invested as provided in Article 2 (commencing with Section 3610).

(b) Except as provided in subdivisions (c) and (d), if there is a guardianship of the estate of the minor or conservatorship of the estate of the person with a disability, the remaining balance of the money and other property, after payment of all expenses, costs, and fees as approved and allowed by the court under Section 3601, shall be paid or delivered to the guardian or conservator of the estate. Upon application of the guardian or conservator, the court making the order or giving the judgment referred to in Section 3600 or the court in which the guardianship or conservatorship proceeding is pending may, with or without notice, make an order that all or part of the money paid or to be paid to the guardian or conservator under this subdivision be deposited or invested as provided in Section 2456.

(c) Upon ex parte petition of the guardian or conservator or upon petition of any person interested in the guardianship or conservatorship estate, the court making the order or giving the judgment referred to in Section 3600 may for good cause shown order one or more of the following:

(1) That all or part of the remaining balance of money not become a part of the guardianship or conservatorship estate and instead be deposited in an insured account in a financial institution in this state, or in a single-premium deferred annuity, subject to withdrawal only upon authorization of the court.

(2) If there is a guardianship of the estate of the minor, that all or part of the remaining balance of money and other property not become a part of the guardianship estate and instead be transferred to a custodian for the benefit of the minor under the California Uniform Transfers to Minors Act, Part 9 (commencing with Section 3900).

(3) That all or part of the remaining balance of money and other property not become a part of the guardianship estate and, instead, be transferred to the trustee of a trust which is either created by, or approved of, in the order or judgment described in Section 3600. This trust shall be revocable by the minor upon attaining 18 years of age, and shall contain other terms and conditions, including, but not limited to, terms and conditions concerning trustee's accounts and trustee's bond, as the court determines to be necessary to protect the minor's interests.

(d) Upon petition of the guardian, conservator, or any person interested in the guardianship or conservatorship estate, the court making the order or giving the judgment referred to in Section 3600 may order that all or part of the remaining balance of money not become a part of the guardianship or conservatorship estate and instead be paid to a special needs trust established under Section 3604 for the benefit of the minor or person with a disability.

(e) If the petition is by a person other than the guardian or conservator, notice of hearing on a petition under subdivision (c) shall be given for the period and in the manner provided in Chapter 3 (commencing with Section 1460) of Part 1.

(f) Notice of the time and place of hearing on a petition under subdivision (d), and a copy of the petition, shall be delivered pursuant to Section 1215 to the State Director of Health Care Services, the Director of State Hospitals, and the Director of Developmental Services at the office of each director in Sacramento at least 15 days before the hearing. **Leg.H.** Enacted Stats 1990 ch 79 §14 (AB 759), operative July 1, 1991. Amended Stats 1992 ch 355 §2 (AB 3328); Stats 1996 ch 563 §18 (SB 392); Stats 2004 ch 67 §5 (AB 1851); Stats 2012 ch 440 §54 (AB 1488), effective September 22, 2012; Stats 2017 ch 319 §59 (AB 976), effective January 1, 2018.

Prior Law: Former Prob C §3602, similar to the present section, was added Stats 1979 ch 726 §3, operative January 1, 1981, amended Stats 1984 ch 243 §7, and repealed Stats 1990 ch 79 §13, operative July 1, 1991.

§3603. Reference to "person with a disability"

Where reference is made in this chapter to a "person with a disability," the reference shall be deemed to include the following:

(a) A person for whom a conservator may be appointed.

(b) Any of the following persons, subject to the provisions of Section 3613:

(1) A person who meets the definition of disability as defined in Section 1382c(a)(3) of Title 42 of the United States Code, or as defined in Section 416(i)(1) of Title II of the federal Social Security Act (42 U.S.C.

Sec. 401 et seq.) and regulations implementing that act, as set forth in Part 416.905 of Title 20 of the Federal Code of Regulations.

(2) A person who meets the definition of disability as defined in paragraphs (1), (2), and (3) of subsection (d) of Section 423 of Title II of the federal Social Security Act (42 U.S.C. Sec. 401 et seq.) and regulations implementing that act, as set forth in Part 404.1505 of Title 20 of the Federal Code of Regulations.

(3) A minor who meets the definition of disability, as set forth in Part 416.906 of Title 20 of the Federal Code of Regulations.

(4) A person with a developmental disability, as defined in Section 4512 of the Welfare and Institutions Code. **Leg.H.** Enacted Stats 1990 ch 79 §14 (AB 759), operative July 1, 1991. Amended Stats 2004 ch 67 §6 (AB 1851), effective January 1, 2005.

Prior Law: Former Prob C §3603, similar to the present section, was added Stats 1979 ch 726 §3, operative January 1, 1981, and repealed Stats 1990 ch 79 §13, operative July 1, 1991.

§3604. Payment to special needs trust; Petition for termination

(a)(1) If a court makes an order under Section 3602 or 3611 that money of a minor or person with a disability be paid to a special needs trust, the terms of the trust shall be reviewed and approved by the court and shall satisfy the requirements of this section. The trust is subject to continuing jurisdiction of the court, and is subject to court supervision to the extent determined by the court. The court may transfer jurisdiction to the court in the proper county for commencement of a proceeding as determined under Section 17005.

(2) If the court referred to in subdivision (a) could have made an order under Section 3602 or 3611 to place that money into a special needs trust, but that order was not requested, a parent, guardian, conservator, or other interested person may petition a court that exercises jurisdiction pursuant to Section 800 for that order. In doing so, notice shall be provided pursuant to subdivisions (e) and (f) of Section 3602, or subdivision (c) of Section 3611, and that notice shall be given at least 15 days before the hearing.

(b) A special needs trust may be established and continued under this section only if the court determines all of the following:

(1) That the minor or person with a disability has a disability that substantially impairs the individual's ability to provide for the individual's own care or custody and constitutes a substantial handicap.

(2) That the minor or person with a disability is likely to have special needs that will not be met without the trust.

(3) That money to be paid to the trust does not exceed the amount that appears reasonably necessary to meet the special needs of the minor or person with a disability.

(c) If at any time it appears (1) that any of the requirements of subdivision (b) are not satisfied or the trustee refuses without good cause to make payments from the trust for the special needs of the beneficiary, and (2) that the State Department of Health Care Services, the State Department of State Hospitals, the State Department of Developmental Services, or a county or city and county in this state has a claim against trust property, that department, county, or city and county may petition the court for an order terminating the trust.

(d) A court order under Section 3602 or 3611 for payment of money to a special needs trust shall include a provision that all statutory liens in favor of the State Department of Health Care Services, the State Department of State Hospitals, the State Department of Developmental Services, and any county or city and county in this state shall first be satisfied. **Leg.H.** Added Stats 1992 ch 355 §3 (AB 3328). Amended Stats 2004 ch 67 §7 (AB 1851); Stats 2012 ch 440 §55 (AB 1488), effective September 22, 2012.

§3605. Tolling of statute of limitations during existence of special needs trust; Death of special needs trust beneficiary

(a) This section applies only to a special needs trust established under Section 3604 on or after January 1, 1993.

(b) While the special needs trust is in existence, the statute of limitations otherwise applicable to claims of the State Department of Health Care Services, the State Department of State Hospitals, the State Department of Developmental Services, and any county or city and county in this state is tolled. Notwithstanding any provision in the trust instrument, at the death of the special needs trust beneficiary or on termination of the trust, the trust property is subject to claims of the State Department of Health Care Services, the State Department of State Hospitals, the State Department of Developmental Services, and any county or city and county in this state to the extent authorized by law as if the trust property is owned by the beneficiary or is part of the beneficiary's estate.

(c) At the death of the special needs trust beneficiary or on termination of the trust, the trustee shall give notice of the beneficiary's death or the trust termination, in the manner provided in Section 1215, to all of the following:

(1) The State Department of Health Care Services, the State Department of State Hospitals, and the State Department of Developmental Services, addressed to the director of that department at the Sacramento office of the director.

(2) Any county or city and county in this state that has made a written request to the trustee for notice, addressed to that county or city and county at the address specified in the request.

(d) Failure to give the notice required by subdivision (c) prevents the running of the statute of limitations against the claim of the department, county, or city and county not given the notice.

(e) The department, county, or city and county has four months after notice is given in which to make a claim with the trustee. If the trustee rejects the claim, the department, county, or city and county making the claim may petition the court for an order under Chapter 3 (commencing with Section 17200) of Part 5 of Division 9, directing the trustee to pay the claim. A claim made under this subdivision shall be paid as a preferred claim prior to any other distribution. If trust property is insufficient to pay all claims under this subdivision, the trustee shall petition the court for instructions and the claims shall be paid from trust property as the court deems just.

(f) If trust property is distributed before expiration of four months after notice is given without payment of the claim, the department, county, or city and county has a claim against the distributees to the full extent of the claim, or each distributee's share of trust property, whichever is less. The claim against distributees includes interest at a rate equal to that earned in the Pooled Money Investment Account, Article 4.5 (commencing with Section 16480) of Chapter 3 of Part 2 of Division 4 of Title 2 of the Government Code, from the date of distribution or the date of filing the claim, whichever is later, plus other accruing costs as in the case of enforcement of a money judgment. **Leg.H.** Added Stats 1992 ch 355 §4 (AB 3328). Amended Stats 2012 ch 440 §56 (AB 1488), effective September 22, 2012.

ARTICLE 2
Disposition of Money or Other Property Where No Guardianship or Conservatorship

Disposition of remaining balance. §3610.
Order of court. §3611.
Continuing jurisdiction. §3612.
Consent of adult with capacity to make decision to court order or judgment. §3613.

§3610. Disposition of remaining balance

When money or other property is to be paid or delivered for the benefit of a minor or person with a disability under a compromise, covenant, order or judgment, and there is no guardianship of the estate of the minor or conservatorship of the estate of the person with a disability, the remaining balance of the money and other property (after payment of all expenses, costs, and fees as approved and allowed by the court under Section 3601) shall be paid, delivered, deposited, or invested as provided in this article. **Leg.H.** Enacted Stats 1990 ch 79 §14 (AB 759), operative July 1, 1991. Amended Stats 2004 ch 67 §8 (AB 1851), effective January 1, 2005.

Prior Law: Former Prob C §3610, similar to the present section, was added Stats 1979 ch 726 §3, operative January 1, 1981, and repealed Stats 1990 ch 79 §13, operative July 1, 1991.

§3611. Order of court

In any case described in Section 3610, the court making the order or giving the judgment referred to in Section 3600 shall, upon application of counsel for the minor or person with a disability, order any one or more of the following:

(a) That a guardian of the estate or conservator of the estate be appointed and that the remaining balance of the money and other property be paid or delivered to the person so appointed.

(b) That the remaining balance of any money paid or to be paid be deposited in an insured account in a financial institution in this state, or in a single-premium deferred annuity, subject to withdrawal only upon the authorization of the court, and that the remaining balance of any other property delivered or to be delivered be held on conditions the court determines to be in the best interest of the minor or person with a disability.

(c) After a hearing by the court, that the remaining balance of any money and other property be paid to a special needs trust established under Section 3604 for the benefit of the minor or person with a disability. Notice of the time and place of the hearing and a copy of the petition shall be mailed to the State Director of Health Care Services, the Director of State Hospitals, and the Director of Developmental Services at the office of each director in Sacramento at least 15 days before the hearing.

(d) If the remaining balance of the money to be paid or delivered does not exceed twenty thousand dollars ($20,000), that all or any part of the money be held on any other conditions the court in its discretion determines to be in the best interest of the minor or person with a disability.

(e) If the remaining balance of the money and other property to be paid or delivered does not exceed five thousand dollars ($5,000) in value and is to be paid or delivered for the benefit of a minor, that all or any part of the money and the other property be paid or delivered to a parent of the minor, without bond, upon the terms and under the conditions specified in Article 1 (commencing with Section 3400) of Chapter 2.

(f) If the remaining balance of the money and other property to be paid or delivered is to be paid or delivered for the benefit of the minor, that all or any part of the money and other property be transferred to a custodian for the benefit of the minor under the California Uniform Transfers to Minors Act, Part 9 (commencing with Section 3900).

(g) That the remaining balance of the money and other property be paid or delivered to the trustee of a trust which is created by, or approved of, in the order or judgment referred to in Section 3600. This trust shall be revocable by the minor upon attaining the age of 18 years, and shall contain other terms and conditions, including, but not limited to, terms and conditions concerning trustee's accounts and trustee's bond, as the court determines to be necessary to protect the minor's interests.

(h) That the remaining balance of any money paid or to be paid be deposited with the county treasurer, if all of the following conditions are met:

(1) The county treasurer has been authorized by the county board of supervisors to handle the deposits.

(2) The county treasurer shall receive and safely keep all money deposited with the county treasurer pursuant to this subdivision, shall pay the money out only upon the order of the court, and shall credit each estate with the interest earned by the funds deposited less the county treasurer's actual cost authorized to be recovered under Section 27013 of the Government Code.

(3) The county treasurer and sureties on the official bond of the county treasurer are responsible for the safekeeping and payment of the money.

(4) The county treasurer shall ensure that the money deposited is to earn interest or dividends, or both, at the highest rate which the county can reasonably obtain as a prudent investor.

(5) Funds so deposited with the county treasurer shall only be invested or deposited in compliance with the provisions governing the investment or deposit of state funds set forth in Chapter 5 (commencing with Section 16640) of Part 2 of Division 4 of Title 2 of the Government Code, the investment or deposit of county funds set forth in Chapter 4 (commencing with Section 53600) of Part 1 of Division 2 of Title 5 of the Government Code, or as authorized under Chapter 6 (commencing with Section 2400) of Part 4.

(i) That the remaining balance of the money and other property be paid or delivered to the person with a disability. **Leg.H.** Enacted Stats 1990 ch 79 §14 (AB 759), operative July 1, 1991. Amended Stats 1991 ch 413 §3 (AB 934); Stats 1992 ch 355 §5 (AB 3328); Stats 1993 ch 978 §4 (SB 305); Stats 1996 ch 563 §19 (SB 392); Stats 2004 ch 67 §9 (AB 1851); Stats 2012 ch 440 §57 (AB 1488), effective September 22, 2012.

Prior Law: Former Prob C §3611, similar to the present section, was added Stats 1979 ch 726 §3, operative January 1, 1981, amended Stats 1984 ch 243 §8, and repealed Stats 1990 ch 79 §13, operative July 1, 1991.

§3612. Continuing jurisdiction

(a) Notwithstanding any other provision of law and except to the extent the court orders otherwise, the court making the order under Section 3611 shall have continuing jurisdiction of the money and other property paid, delivered, deposited, or invested under this article until the minor reaches 18 years of age.

(b) Notwithstanding subdivision (a), the trust of an individual who meets the definition of a person with a disability under paragraph (3) of subdivision (b) of Section 3603 and who reaches 18 years of age, shall continue and be under continuing court jurisdiction until terminated by the court. **Leg.H.** Enacted Stats 1990 ch 79 §14 (AB 759), operative July 1, 1991. Amended Stats 2004 ch 67 §10 (AB 1851), effective January 1, 2005.

Prior Law: Former Prob C §3612, similar to the present section, was added Stats 1979 ch 726 §3, operative January 1, 1981, and repealed Stats 1990 ch 79 §13, operative July 1, 1991.

§3613. Consent of adult with capacity to make decision to court order or judgment

Notwithstanding any other provision of this chapter, a court may not make an order or give a judgment pursuant to Section 3600, 3601, 3602, 3610, or 3611 with respect to an adult who has the capacity within the meaning of Section 812 to consent to the order and who has no conservator of the estate with authority to make that decision, without the express consent of that person. **Leg.H.** Added Stats 2004 ch 67 §11 (AB 1851), effective January 1, 2005.

CHAPTER 5
PROPERTY OF ABSENT FEDERAL PERSONNEL

Article 1. Definitions.
Article 2. Court Proceeding to Set Aside Personal Property of Absentee.
Article 3. Management and Disposition of Personal Property of Absentee Without Court Proceeding.
Article 4. Absentee's Power of Attorney.

ARTICLE 1
Definitions

Definitions. §3700.

§3700. Definitions

As used in this chapter:

(a) "Absentee" is defined in Section 1403.

(b) "Certificate of missing status" means the official written report complying with Section 1283 of the Evidence Code and showing the determination of the secretary of the military department or the head of the department or agency concerned or the delegate of the secretary or head that the absentee is in missing status.

(c) "Eligible spouse" means the spouse of an absentee who has not commenced an action or proceeding for judicial or legal separation, annulment, adjudication of nullity, or dissolution of the marriage of the spouse and the absentee.

(d) "Family of an absentee" means an eligible spouse, if any, or if no eligible spouse, the child or children of an absentee, equally, or if no child or children, the parent or parents of an absentee, equally, provided these persons are dependents of the absentee as defined in Section 401 of Title 37 of the United States Code, and the guardian of the estate or conservator of the estate of any person bearing such relationship to the absentee.

(e) "Secretary concerned" is defined in Section 1440. **Leg.H.** Enacted Stats 1990 ch 79 §14 (AB 759), operative July 1, 1991.

Prior Law: Former Prob C §3700, similar to the present section, was added Stats 1979 ch 726 §3, operative January 1, 1981, amended Stats 1983 ch 201 §10, and repealed Stats 1990 ch 79 §13, operative July 1, 1991.

ARTICLE 2
Court Proceeding to Set Aside Personal Property of Absentee

Setting aside personal property of absentee. §3701.
Who may petition. §3702.
Contents of petition. §3703.
Notice of hearing. §3704.
Hearing and order. §3705.
Jurisdiction of court not affected by size of absentee's estate. §3706.
Joint tenancy property. §3707.
Accounting. §3708.

§3701. Setting aside personal property of absentee

Upon petition as provided in this chapter, the court may set aside to the family of an absentee personal property of the absentee situated in this state for the purpose of managing, controlling, encumbering, selling, or conveying, or otherwise engaging in any transaction with respect to the property, if the court determines that to do so will be in the best interest of the absentee, including the interest of the absentee in providing for shelter, food, health care, education, transportation, or the maintenance of a reasonable and adequate standard of living for the family of the absentee. The absentee's interest in the property set aside shall not exceed twenty thousand dollars ($20,000). **Leg.H.** Enacted Stats 1990 ch 79 §14 (AB 759), operative July 1, 1991.

Prior Law: Former Prob C §3701, similar to the present section, was added Stats 1979 ch 726 §3, operative January 1, 1981, and repealed Stats 1990 ch 79 §13, operative July 1, 1991.

§3702. Who may petition

A petition that personal property of an absentee be set aside as provided in this chapter may be filed by any of the following persons:

(a) A person in whose favor the personal property of the absentee may be set aside.

(b) A person to whom the absentee has issued a general power of attorney while serving in the armed forces of the United States or while an employee of any agency or department of the United States, provided the power of attorney was valid and effective at the time issued, regardless whether it has expired or terminated. **Leg.H.** Enacted Stats 1990 ch 79 §14 (AB 759), operative July 1, 1991.

Prior Law: Former Prob C §3702, similar to the present section, was added Stats 1979 ch 726 §3, operative January 1, 1981, and repealed Stats 1990 ch 79 §13, operative July 1, 1991.

§3703. Contents of petition

(a) The petition shall contain all of the following:

(1) A statement that the petition is filed under this chapter.

(2) In its caption, the last known military rank or grade and the social security account number of the absentee.

(3) A specific description and estimate of the value of all of the absentee's property, wherever situated (including all sums due the absentee from the United States).

(4) A designation of the property to be set aside, and the facts establishing that setting aside the property is necessary and in the best interest of the absentee.

(5) If the property is to be set aside for the benefit of the spouse of the absentee, an allegation that the spouse is an eligible spouse.

(6) So far as known to the petitioner, the names and addresses of all persons comprising the family of the absentee, and an allegation whether a guardian of the estate or a conservator of the estate of any member of the family of the absentee has been appointed.

(b) There shall be attached to the petition a certificate of missing status. The certificate of missing status shall be received as evidence of that fact and the court shall not determine the status of the absentee inconsistent with the status shown in the certificate. **Leg.H.** Enacted Stats 1990 ch 79 §14 (AB 759), operative July 1, 1991.

Prior Law: Former Prob C §3703, similar to the present section, was added Stats 1979 ch 726 §3, operative January 1, 1981, amended Stats 1983 ch 201 §12, and repealed Stats 1990 ch 79 §13, operative July 1, 1991.

§3704. Notice of hearing

(a) Notice of the nature of the proceedings and the time and place of the hearing shall be given by the petitioner at least 15 days before the hearing date by all of the following means:

(1) By delivery pursuant to Section 1215, together with a copy of the petition, to all persons comprising the family of the absentee.

(2) By delivery by a method that would be sufficient for service of summons in a civil action, together with a copy of the petition, to the secretary concerned or to the head of the United States department or agency concerned.

(3) By publication pursuant to Section 6061 of the Government Code in a newspaper of general circulation in the county in which the proceedings will be held.

(b) If notice to an officer or agency of this state or of the United States is required under Section 1461 or 1822 upon petition for appointment of a conservator, notice shall be given of the petition under this chapter. **Leg.H.** Enacted Stats 1990 ch 79 §14 (AB 759), operative July 1, 1991. Amended Stats 2017 ch 319 §60 (AB 976), effective January 1, 2018.

Prior Law: Former Prob C §3704, similar to the present section, was added Stats 1979 ch 726 §3, operative January 1, 1981, and repealed Stats 1990 ch 79 §13, operative July 1, 1991.

§3705. Hearing and order

(a) Upon the hearing of the petition, any officer or agency of this state or the United States or the authorized delegate of the officer or agency, or any relative or friend of the absentee, may appear and support or oppose the petition.

(b) If the court determines that the allegations of the petition are true and correct, the court may order set aside to the family of the absentee personal property of the absentee situated in this state (excluding any sums due the absentee from the United States) in which the absentee's interest does not exceed twenty thousand dollars ($20,000). The property set aside shall be specified in the order.

(c) No bond shall be required of any person to whom property of the absentee has been set aside by order of the court pursuant to this chapter. **Leg.H.** Enacted Stats 1990 ch 79 §14 (AB 759), operative July 1, 1991.

Prior Law: Former Prob C §3705, similar to the present section, was added Stats 1979 ch 726 §3, operative January 1, 1981, and repealed Stats 1990 ch 79 §13, operative July 1, 1991.

§3706. Jurisdiction of court not affected by size of absentee's estate

A determination by the court that the value of all of the absentee's property, wherever situated, exceeds twenty thousand dollars ($20,000) or that the absentee owns or has an interest in real property, wherever situated, does not deprive the court of jurisdiction to set aside to the family of the absentee personal property of the absentee situated in this state in which the absentee's interest does not exceed twenty thousand dollars ($20,000), and the court shall order set aside such personal property to the family of the absentee if the court finds that all of the other provisions of this chapter have been complied with. The property set aside shall be specified in the order. **Leg.H.** Enacted Stats 1990 ch 79 §14 (AB 759), operative July 1, 1991.

Prior Law: Former Prob C §3706, similar to the present section, was added Stats 1979 ch 726 §3, operative January 1, 1981, and repealed Stats 1990 ch 79 §13, operative July 1, 1991.

§3707. Joint tenancy property

For the purposes of this chapter, any property or interest therein or lien thereon that the absentee holds as joint tenant shall be included in determining the property of the absentee and its value. The joint tenancy interest may be set aside to the family of the absentee as provided in this chapter but may only be set aside to a member of the absentee's family who was a joint tenant with the absentee in the property. **Leg.H.** Enacted Stats 1990 ch 79 §14 (AB 759), operative July 1, 1991.

Prior Law: Former Prob C §3707, similar to the present section, was added Stats 1979 ch 726 §3, operative January 1, 1981, and repealed Stats 1990 ch 79 §13, operative July 1, 1991.

§3708. Accounting

(a) Within six months after the absentee has returned to the controllable jurisdiction of the military department or civilian agency or department concerned, or within six months after the determination of death of the absentee by the secretary concerned or the head of the department or agency concerned or the delegate of the secretary or head, the former absentee or the personal representative of the deceased absentee may, by motion in the same proceeding, require the person or persons to whom the property of the absentee was set aside to account for the property and the proceeds, if any. The time of return to the controllable jurisdiction of the military department or civilian department or agency concerned or the determination of the time of death of the absentee shall be determined by the court under 37 United States Code, Section 556, or 5 United States Code, Section 5566. An official written report or record of the military department or civilian department or agency that the absentee has returned to its controllable jurisdiction or is deceased shall be received as evidence of that fact.

(b) This section does not in any manner derogate the finality and conclusiveness of any order, judgment, or decree previously entered in the proceeding. **Leg.H.** Enacted Stats 1990 ch 79 §14 (AB 759), operative July 1, 1991.

Prior Law: Former Prob C §3708, similar to the present section, was added Stats 1979 ch 726 §3, operative January 1, 1981, and repealed Stats 1990 ch 79 §13, operative July 1, 1991.

ARTICLE 3
Management and Disposition of Personal Property of Absentee Without Court Proceeding

Right of absentee's family to collect and dispose of property. §3710.

Transfer of evidences of interest, indebtedness, or right. §3711.
Commencement of time for action by absentee. §3712.

§3710. Right of absentee's family to collect and dispose of property

The family of an absentee may collect, receive, dispose of, or engage in any transaction relating to the absentee's personal property situated in this state without any judicial proceeding if all the following conditions are satisfied:

(a) The absentee owns no real property situated in this state.

(b) The aggregate value of all of the absentee's personal property situated in this state is five thousand dollars ($5,000) or less, excluding any money owed the absentee by the United States.

(c) The family of the absentee needs to dispose of such personal property to provide for shelter, food, health care, education, transportation, or the maintenance of a reasonable and adequate standard of living for the family of the absentee. **Leg.H.** Enacted Stats 1990 ch 79 §14 (AB 759), operative July 1, 1991.

Prior Law: Former Prob C §3710, similar to the present section, was added Stats 1983 ch 201 §13 and repealed Stats 1990 ch 79 §13, operative July 1, 1991.

§3711. Transfer of evidences of interest, indebtedness, or right

(a) If the conditions set forth in Section 3710 are satisfied, the family of the absentee may have any evidence of interest, indebtedness, or right attributable to the absentee's personal property transferred to the family of the absentee, or transferred to the person to whom the property is to be sold or transferred by the family of the absentee, upon furnishing the person (including any governmental body) having custody of the property both of the following:

(1) A certificate of missing status.

(2) An affidavit stating under oath that the provisions of this article are applicable and that the aggregate value of all property received pursuant to this affidavit, together with all other property previously received under this article, does not exceed five thousand dollars ($5,000).

(b) The receipt of a certificate of missing status and affidavit under subdivision (a) constitutes sufficient acquittance for any payment of money or delivery of property made pursuant to this article and fully discharges the recipient from any further liability concerning the money or property without the necessity of inquiring into the truth of any of the facts stated in the affidavit. **Leg.H.** Enacted Stats 1990 ch 79 §14 (AB 759), operative July 1, 1991.

Prior Law: Former Prob C §3711, similar to the present section, was added Stats 1983 ch 201 §13, and repealed Stats 1990 ch 79 §13, operative July 1, 1991.

§3712. Commencement of time for action by absentee

The time within which an absentee may commence an action against any person who executes an affidavit and receives property pursuant to this article commences to run on the earlier of the following dates:

(a) Ninety days after the absentee returns to the United States after the termination of the condition that caused the classification of an absentee.

(b) Two years after the termination of the condition that caused the classification of an absentee. **Leg.H.** Enacted Stats 1990 ch 79 §14 (AB 759), operative July 1, 1991.

Prior Law: Former Prob C §3712, similar to the present section, was added Stats 1983 ch 201 §13, and repealed Stats 1990 ch 79 §13, operative July 1, 1991.

ARTICLE 4
Absentee's Power of Attorney

Continuation of expired power of attorney. §3720.
Absentee principal. §3721.
Proceeding for dissolution or separation. §3722.

§3720. Continuation of expired power of attorney

If an absentee executed a power of attorney that expires during the period that occasions absentee status, the power of attorney continues in full force and effect until 30 days after the absentee status is terminated. Any person who acts in reliance upon the power of attorney when accompanied by a copy of a certificate of missing status is not liable for relying and acting upon the power of attorney. **Leg.H.** Enacted Stats 1990 ch 79 §14 (AB 759), operative July 1, 1991.

Prior Law: Former Prob C §3720, similar to the present section, was added Stats 1983 ch 201 §14 and repealed Stats 1990 ch 79 §13, operative July 1, 1991.

§3721. Absentee principal

For the purposes of Chapter 5 (commencing with Section 4300) of Part 2 of Division 4.5, in the case of a principal who is an absentee, an attorney-in-fact or third person shall be deemed to be without actual knowledge of the following:

(a) The principal's death or incapacity while the absentee continues in missing status and until the attorney-in-fact or third person receives notice of the determination of the absentee's death by the secretary concerned or the head of the department or agency concerned or the delegate of the secretary or head.

(b) Revocation by the principal during the period described in subdivision (a). **Leg.H.** Added Stats 1994 ch 307 §14 (SB 1907), effective January 1, 1995.

§3722. Proceeding for dissolution or separation

If after the absentee executes a power of attorney, the principal's spouse who is the attorney-in-fact commences a proceeding for dissolution, annulment, or legal separation, or a legal separation is ordered, the attorney-in-fact's authority is revoked. This section is in addition to the provisions of Sections 4154 and 4697. **Leg.H.** Added Stats 1994 ch 307 §15 (SB 1907). Amended Stats 1999 ch 658 §26 (AB 891), operative July 1, 2000.

CHAPTER 6
REMOVAL OF PROPERTY OF NONRESIDENT

Petition. §3800.
Notice. §3801.
Certificate of nonresident fiduciary. §3802.
Order for removal. §3803.

§3800. Petition

(a) If a nonresident has a duly appointed, qualified, and acting guardian, conservator, committee, or comparable fiduciary in the place of residence and if no proceeding for guardianship or conservatorship of the nonresident is pending or contemplated in this state, the nonresident fiduciary may petition to have property owned by the nonresident removed to the place of residence.

(b) The petition for removal of property of the nonresident shall be filed in the superior court of the county in which the nonresident is or has been temporarily present or in which the property of the nonresident, or the principal part thereof, is located.

(c) If a conservatorship was transferred from this state to another state pursuant to Article 3 (commencing with Section 2001) of Chapter 8 of Part 3, the foreign conservator may remove the conservatee's personal property from this state without seeking a petition under this chapter. **Leg.H.** Enacted Stats 1990 ch 79 §14 (AB 759), operative July 1, 1991. Amended Stats 2014 ch 553 §27 (SB 940), effective January 1, 2015, operative January 1, 2016.

Prior Law: Former Prob C §3800, similar to the present section, was added Stats 1979 ch 726 §3, operative January 1, 1981, and repealed Stats 1990 ch 79 §13, operative July 1, 1991.

§3801. Notice

(a) The petition shall be made upon 15 days' notice, by delivery pursuant to Section 1215, to all of the following persons:

(1) The personal representative or other person in whose possession the property may be.

(2) Persons in this state, known to the petitioner, who are obligated to pay a debt, perform an obligation, or issue a security to the nonresident or the estate of the nonresident.

(b) The petition shall be made upon additional notice, if any, as the court may order. **Leg.H.** Enacted Stats 1990 ch 79 §14 (AB 759), operative July 1, 1991. Amended Stats 2017 ch 319 §61 (AB 976), effective January 1, 2018.

Prior Law: Former Prob C §3801, similar to the present section, was added Stats 1979 ch 726 §3, operative January 1, 1981, and repealed Stats 1990 ch 79 §13, operative July 1, 1991.

§3802. Certificate of nonresident fiduciary

(a) The nonresident fiduciary shall produce and file one of the following certificates:

(1) A certificate that the fiduciary is entitled, by the laws of the place of appointment of the fiduciary, to the possession of the estate of the nonresident. The certificate shall be under the hand of the clerk and seal

of the court from which the appointment of the fiduciary was derived and shall show a transcript of the record of appointment and that the fiduciary has entered upon the discharge of the duties of the fiduciary.

(2) A certificate that the fiduciary is entitled, by the laws of the place of residence, to custody of the estate of the nonresident, without the appointment of any court. The certificate shall be under the hand of the clerk and seal of either (i) the court in the place of residence having jurisdiction of estates of persons that have a guardian, conservator, committee, or comparable fiduciary or (ii) the highest court in the place of residence.

(b) In the case of a foreign country, the certificate shall be accompanied by a final statement certifying the genuineness of the signature and official position of (1) the court clerk making the original certificate or (2) any foreign official who has certified either the genuineness of the signature and official position of the court clerk making the original certificate or the genuineness of the signature and official position of another foreign official who has executed a similar certificate in a chain of such certificates beginning with a certificate of the genuineness of the signature and official position of the clerk making the original certificate. The final statement may be made only by a secretary of an embassy or legation, consul general, consul, vice consul, or consular agent of the United States, or a diplomatic or consular official of the foreign country assigned or accredited to the United States. **Leg.H.** Enacted Stats 1990 ch 79 §14 (AB 759), operative July 1, 1991.

Prior Law: Former Prob C §3802, similar to the present section, was added Stats 1979 ch 726 §3, operative January 1, 1981, and repealed Stats 1990 ch 79 §13, operative July 1, 1991.

§3803. Order for removal

(a) Upon the petition, if the court determines that removal of the property will not conflict with any restriction or limitation on the property or impair the right of the nonresident to the property or the rights of creditors or claimants in this state, the court shall make an order granting to the nonresident fiduciary leave to remove the property of the nonresident to the place of residence unless good cause to the contrary is shown.

(b) The order is authority to the fiduciary to sue for and receive the property in his or her own name for the use and benefit of the nonresident.

(c) The order is a discharge of the personal representative or other person in whose possession the property may be at the time the order is made and of the person obligated to pay a debt, perform an obligation, or issue a security to the nonresident or the estate of the nonresident, upon filing with the clerk of the court the receipt of the nonresident fiduciary for the property and transmitting a duplicate receipt, or a certified copy of the receipt, to the court, if any, from which the nonresident fiduciary received his or her appointment. **Leg.H.** Enacted Stats 1990 ch 79 §14 (AB 759), operative July 1, 1991.

Prior Law: Former Prob C §3803, similar to the present section, was added Stats 1979 ch 726 §3, operative January 1, 1981, and repealed Stats 1990 ch 79 §13, operative July 1, 1991.

PART 9
CALIFORNIA UNIFORM TRANSFERS TO MINORS ACT

Short title. §3900.
Definitions. §3901.
Scope and jurisdiction. §3902.
Nomination of custodian. §3903.
Transfer by gift or exercise of power of appointment. §3904.
Transfer authorized by will or trust. §3905.
Other transfer by fiduciary. §3906.
Transfer by obligor. §3907.
Receipt for custodial property. §3908.
Methods of creation and transfer of custodial property. §3909.
Single custodianship. §3910.
Validity and effect of transfer. §3911.
Care of custodial property. §3912.
Powers of custodian. §3913.
Use of custodial property. §3914.
Custodian's expenses, compensation, and bond. §3915.
Protection of third person from liability. §3916.
Liability to third persons. §3917.
Renunciation, resignation, death, or removal of custodian; Designation of successor custodian. §3918.
Accounting; Determination of liability of custodian. §3919.
Termination of custodianship. §3920.
Delayed time for transfer to minor; Procedure. §3920.5.
Venue. §3921.
Transfers subject to part. §3922.
Transfers made before January 1, 1985. §3923.
Method of transfer provided by part not exclusive. §3925.

§3900. Short title

This part may be cited as the "California Uniform Transfers to Minors Act." **Leg.H.** Enacted Stats 1990 ch 79 §14 (AB 759), operative July 1, 1991.

Prior Law: Former Prob C §3900, similar to the present section, was added Stats 1984 ch 243 §9 and repealed Stats 1990 ch 79 §13, operative July 1, 1991.

§3901. Definitions

In this part:

(a) "Adult" means an individual who has attained the age of 18 years.

(b) "Benefit plan" means an employer's plan for the benefit of an employee or partner.

(c) "Broker" means a person lawfully engaged in the business of effecting transactions in securities or commodities for the person's own account or for the account of others.

(d) "Conservator" means a person appointed or qualified by a court to act as general, limited, or temporary guardian of a minor's property or a person legally authorized to perform substantially the same functions.

(e) "Court" means the superior court.

(f) "Custodial property" means (1) any interest in property transferred to a custodian under this part and (2) the income from and proceeds of that interest in property.

(g) "Custodian" means a person so designated under Section 3909 or a successor or substitute custodian designated under Section 3918.

(h) "Financial institution" means a bank, trust company, savings institution, or credit union, chartered and supervised under state or federal law or an industrial loan company licensed and supervised under the laws of this state.

(i) "Legal representative" means an individual's personal representative or conservator.

(j) "Member of the minor's family" means the minor's parent, stepparent, spouse, grandparent, brother, sister, uncle, or aunt, whether of the whole or half blood or by adoption.

(k) "Minor" means:

(1) Except as provided in paragraph (2), an individual who has not attained the age of 18 years.

(2) When used with reference to the beneficiary for whose benefit custodial property is held or is to be held, an individual who has not attained the age at which the custodian is required under Sections 3920 and 3920.5 to transfer the custodial property to the beneficiary.

(*l*) "Person" means an individual, corporation, organization, or other legal entity.

(m) "Personal representative" means an executor, administrator, successor personal representative, or special administrator of a decedent's estate or a person legally authorized to perform substantially the same functions.

(n) "State" includes any state of the United States, the District of Columbia, the Commonwealth of Puerto Rico, and any territory or possession subject to the legislative authority of the United States.

(o) "Transfer" means a transaction that creates custodial property under Section 3909.

(p) "Transferor" means a person who makes a transfer under this part.

(q) "Trust company" means a financial institution, corporation, or other legal entity, authorized to exercise general trust powers. **Leg.H.** Enacted Stats 1990 ch 79 §14 (AB 759), operative July 1, 1991.

Prior Law: Former Prob C §3901, similar to the present section, was added Stats 1984 ch 243 §9 and repealed Stats 1990 ch 79 §13, operative July 1, 1991.

§3902. Scope and jurisdiction

(a) This part applies to a transfer that refers to this part in the designation under subdivision (a) of Section 3909 by which the transfer is made if at the time of the transfer, the transferor, the minor, or the custodian is a resident of this state or the custodial property is located in this state. The custodianship so created remains subject to this part despite a subsequent change in residence of a transferor, the minor, or the custodian, or the removal of custodial property from this state.

(b) A person designated as custodian under this part is subject to personal jurisdiction in this state with respect to any matter relating to the custodianship.

(c) A transfer that purports to be made and which is valid under the Uniform Transfers to Minors Act, the Uniform Gifts to Minors Act, or a substantially similar act, of another state is governed by the law of the designated state and may be executed and is enforceable in this state if at the time of the transfer, the transferor, the minor, or the custodian is a resident of the designated state or the custodial property is located in the designated state. **Leg.H.** Enacted Stats 1990 ch 79 §14 (AB 759), operative July 1, 1991.

Prior Law: Former Prob C §3902, similar to the present section, was added Stats 1984 ch 243 §9 and repealed Stats 1990 ch 79 §13, operative July 1, 1991.

§3903. Nomination of custodian

(a) A person having the right to designate the recipient of property transferable upon the occurrence of a future event may revocably nominate a custodian to receive the property for a minor beneficiary upon the occurrence of the event by naming the custodian followed in substance by the words:

"as custodian for _____ (Name of Minor) under the California Uniform Transfers to Minors Act." The nomination may name one or more persons as substitute custodians to whom the property must be transferred, in the order named, if the first nominated custodian dies before the transfer or is unable, declines, or is ineligible to serve. The nomination may be made in a will, a trust, a deed, an instrument exercising a power of appointment, or in a writing designating a beneficiary of contractual rights which is registered with or delivered to the payor, issuer, or other obligor of the contractual rights.

(b) A custodian nominated under this section must be a person to whom a transfer of property of that kind may be made under subdivision (a) of Section 3909.

(c) The nomination of a custodian under this section does not create custodial property until the nominating instrument becomes irrevocable or a transfer to the nominated custodian is completed under Section 3909. Unless the nomination of a custodian has been revoked, upon the occurrence of the future event, the custodianship becomes effective, and the custodian shall enforce a transfer of the custodial property pursuant to Section 3909. **Leg.H.** Enacted Stats 1990 ch 79 §14 (AB 759), operative July 1, 1991.

Prior Law: Former Prob C §3903, similar to the present section, was added Stats 1984 ch 243 §9 and repealed Stats 1990 ch 79 §13, operative July 1, 1991.

§3904. Transfer by gift or exercise of power of appointment

A person may make a transfer by irrevocable gift to, or the irrevocable exercise of a power of appointment in favor of, a custodian for the benefit of a minor pursuant to Section 3909. **Leg.H.** Enacted Stats 1990 ch 79 §14 (AB 759), operative July 1, 1991.

Prior Law: Former Prob C §3904, similar to the present section, was added Stats 1984 ch 243 §9 and repealed Stats 1990 ch 79 §13, operative July 1, 1991.

§3905. Transfer authorized by will or trust

(a) A personal representative or trustee may make an irrevocable transfer pursuant to Section 3909 to a custodian for the benefit of a minor as authorized in the governing will or trust.

(b) If the testator or settlor has nominated a custodian under Section 3903 to receive the custodial property, the transfer shall be made to that person.

(c) If the testator or settlor has not nominated a custodian under Section 3903, or all persons so nominated as custodian die before the transfer or are unable, decline, or are ineligible to serve, the personal representative or the trustee, as the case may be, shall designate the custodian from among those eligible to serve as custodian for property of that kind under subdivision (a) of Section 3909. **Leg.H.** Enacted Stats 1990 ch 79 §14 (AB 759), operative July 1, 1991.

Prior Law: Former Prob C §3905, similar to the present section, was added Stats 1984 ch 243 §9 and repealed Stats 1990 ch 79 §13 (AB 759), operative July 1, 1991.

§3906. Other transfer by fiduciary

(a) Subject to subdivision (c), a personal representative or trustee may make an irrevocable transfer to another adult or trust company as custodian for the benefit of a minor pursuant to Section 3909, in the absence of a will or under a will or trust that does not contain an authorization to do so.

(b) Subject to subdivision (c), a conservator may make an irrevocable transfer to another adult or trust company as custodian for the benefit of the minor pursuant to Section 3909.

(c) A transfer under subdivision (a) or (b) may be made only if all of the following requirements are satisfied:

(1) The personal representative, trustee, or conservator considers the transfer to be in the best interest of the minor.

(2) The transfer is not prohibited by or inconsistent with provisions of the applicable will, trust agreement, or other governing instrument. For the purposes of this subdivision, a spendthrift provision (such as that described in Section 15300) shall not prohibit or be inconsistent with the transfer.

(3) The transfer is authorized by the court if it exceeds ten thousand dollars ($10,000) in value; provided, however, that such court authorization shall not be required when the transfer is to a custodian who is either (A) a trust company or (B) an individual designated as a trustee by the terms of a trust instrument which does not require a bond. **Leg.H.** Enacted Stats 1990 ch 79 §14 (AB 759), operative July 1, 1991. Amended Stats 1996 ch 862 §13 (AB 2751).

Prior Law: Former Prob C §3906, similar to the present section, was added Stats 1984 ch 243 §9, and repealed Stats 1990 ch 79 §13, operative July 1, 1991.

§3907. Transfer by obligor

(a) Subject to subdivisions (b) and (c), a person not subject to Section 3905 or 3906 who holds property of, or owes a liquidated debt to, a minor not having a conservator may make an irrevocable transfer to a custodian for the benefit of the minor pursuant to Section 3909.

(b) If a person having the right to do so under Section 3903 has nominated a custodian under that section to receive the custodial property, the transfer shall be made to that person.

(c) If no custodian has been nominated under Section 3903, or all persons so nominated as custodian die before the transfer or are unable, decline, or are ineligible to serve, a transfer under this section may be made to an adult member of the minor's family or to a trust company unless the property exceeds ten thousand dollars ($10,000) in value. **Leg.H.** Enacted Stats 1990 ch 79 §14 (AB 759), operative July 1, 1991.

Prior Law: Former Prob C §3907, similar to the present section, was added Stats 1984 ch 243 §9 and repealed Stats 1990 ch 79 §13, operative July 1, 1991.

§3908. Receipt for custodial property

A written acknowledgment of delivery by a custodian constitutes a sufficient receipt and discharge for custodial property transferred to the custodian pursuant to this part. **Leg.H.** Enacted Stats 1990 ch 79 §14 (AB 759), operative July 1, 1991.

Prior Law: Former Prob C §3908, similar to the present section, was added Stats 1984 ch 243 §9 and repealed Stats 1990 ch 79 §13, operative July 1, 1991.

§3909. Methods of creation and transfer of custodial property

(a) Custodial property is created and a transfer is made whenever any of the following occurs:

(1) An uncertificated security or a certificated security in registered form is either:

(A) Registered in the name of the transferor, an adult other than the transferor, or a trust company, followed in substance by the words: "as custodian for _____ (Name of Minor) under the California Uniform Transfers to Minors Act."

(B) Delivered if in certificated form, or any document necessary for the transfer of an uncertificated security is delivered, together with any necessary endorsement to an adult other than the transferor or to a trust company as custodian, accompanied by an instrument in substantially the form set forth in subdivision (b).

(2) Money is paid or delivered, or a security held in the name of a broker, financial institution, or its nominee is transferred, to a broker or financial institution for credit to an account in the name of the transferor, an adult other than the transferor, or a trust company, followed in substance by the words:

"as custodian for _____ (Name of Minor) under the California Uniform Transfers to Minors Act."

(3) The ownership of a life or endowment insurance policy or annuity contract is either:

(A) Registered with the issuer in the name of the transferor, an adult other than the transferor, or a trust company, followed in substance by the words:

"as custodian for _____ (Name of Minor) under the California Uniform Transfers to Minors Act."

(B) Assigned in a writing delivered to an adult other than the transferor or to a trust company whose name in the assignment is followed in substance by the words:

"as custodian for _____ (Name of Minor) under the California Uniform Transfers to Minors Act."

(4) An irrevocable exercise of a power of appointment or an irrevocable present right to future payment under a contract is the subject of a written notification delivered to the payor, issuer, or other obligor that the right is transferred to the transferor, an adult other than the transferor, or a trust company, whose name in the notification is followed in substance by the words:

"as custodian for _____ (Name of Minor) under the California Uniform Transfers to Minors Act."

(5) An interest in real property is recorded in the name of the transferor, an adult other than the transferor, or a trust company, followed in substance by the words:

"as custodian for _____ (Name of Minor) under the California Uniform Transfers to Minors Act."

(6) A certificate of title issued by a department or agency of a state or of the United States which evidences title to tangible personal property is either:

(A) Issued in the name of the transferor, an adult other than the transferor, or a trust company, followed in substance by the words:

"as custodian for _____ (Name of Minor) under the California Uniform Transfers to Minors Act."

(B) Delivered to an adult other than the transferor or to a trust company, endorsed to that person followed in substance by the words:

"as custodian for _____ (Name of Minor) under the California Uniform Transfers to Minors Act."

(7) An interest in any property not described in paragraphs (1) through (6) is transferred to an adult other than the transferor or to a trust company by a written instrument in substantially the form set forth in subdivision (b).

(b) An instrument in the following form satisfies the requirements of subparagraph (B) of paragraph (1) and paragraph (7) of subdivision (a):

"TRANSFER UNDER THE CALIFORNIA UNIFORM TRANSFERS TO MINORS ACT

I, _____ (Name of Transferor or Name and Representative Capacity if a Fiduciary) hereby transfer to _____ (Name of Custodian), as custodian for _____ (Name of Minor) under the California Uniform Transfers to Minors Act, the following:

(insert a description of the custodial property sufficient to identify it).

Dated: _____

_____
(Signature)

_____ (Name of Custodian) acknowledges receipt of the property described above as custodian for the minor named above under the California Uniform Transfers to Minors Act.

Dated: _____

_____"
(Signature of Custodian)

(c) A transferor shall place the custodian in control of the custodial property as soon as practicable. **Leg.H.** Enacted Stats 1990 ch 79 §14 (AB 759), operative July 1, 1991. Amended Stats 1991 ch 1055 §17 (SB 271).

Prior Law: Former Prob C §3909, similar to the present section, was added Stats 1984 ch 243 §9, amended Stats 1989 ch 544 §3, and repealed Stats 1990 ch 79 §13, operative July 1, 1991.

§3910. Single custodianship

A transfer may be made only for one minor, and only one person may be the custodian. All custodial property held under this part by the same custodian for the benefit of the same minor constitutes a single custodianship. **Leg.H.** Enacted Stats 1990 ch 79 §14 (AB 759), operative July 1, 1991.

Prior Law: Former Prob C §3910, similar to the present section, was added Stats 1984 ch 243 §9 and repealed Stats 1990 ch 79 §13, operative July 1, 1991.

§3911. Validity and effect of transfer

(a) The validity of a transfer made in a manner prescribed in this part is not affected by any of the following:

(1) Failure of the transferor to comply with subdivision (c) of Section 3909.

(2) Designation of an ineligible custodian, except designation of the transferor in the case of property for which the transferor is ineligible to serve as custodian under subdivision (a) of Section 3909.

(3) Death or incapacity of a person nominated under Section 3903 or designated under Section 3909 as custodian, or the disclaimer of the office by that person.

(b) A transfer made pursuant to Section 3909 is irrevocable, and the custodial property is indefeasibly vested in the minor, but the custodian has all the rights, powers, duties, and authority provided in this part, and neither the minor nor the minor's legal representative has any right, power, duty, or authority with respect to the custodial property except as provided in this part.

(c) By making a transfer, the transferor incorporates in the disposition all the provisions of this part and grants to the custodian, and to any third person dealing with a person designated as custodian, the respective powers, rights, and immunities provided in this part.

(d) A person is not precluded from being a custodian for a minor under this part with respect to some property because the person is a conservator of the minor with respect to other property.

(e) A person who is the conservator of the minor is not precluded from being a custodian for a minor under this part because the custodial property has or will be transferred to the custodian from the guardianship estate of the minor. In such case, for the purposes of Section 3909, the custodian shall be deemed to be "an adult other than the transferor."

(f) In the cases described in subdivisions (d) and (e), with respect to the property transferred to the custodian, this part applies to the extent it would apply if the person to whom the custodial property is transferred were not and had not been a conservator of the minor. **Leg.H.** Enacted Stats 1990 ch 79 §14 (AB 759), operative July 1, 1991.

Prior Law: Former Prob C §3911, similar to the present section, was added Stats 1984 ch 243 §9 and repealed Stats 1990 ch 79 §13, operative July 1, 1991.

§3912. Care of custodial property

(a) A custodian shall do all of the following:

(1) Take control of custodial property.

(2) Register or record title to custodial property if appropriate.

(3) Collect, hold, manage, invest, and reinvest custodial property.

(b) In dealing with custodial property, a custodian shall observe the standard of care that would be observed by a prudent person dealing with property of another and is not limited by any other statute restricting investments by fiduciaries except that:

(1) If a custodian is not compensated for his or her services, the custodian is not liable for losses to custodial property unless they result from the custodian's bad faith, intentional wrongdoing, or gross negligence, or from the custodian's failure to maintain the standard of prudence in investing the custodial property provided in this section.

(2) A custodian, in the custodian's discretion and without liability to the minor or the minor's estate, may retain any custodial property received from a transferor.

(c) A custodian may invest in or pay premiums on life insurance or endowment policies on (1) the life of the minor only if the minor or the minor's estate is the sole beneficiary or (2) the life of another person in whom the minor has an insurable interest only to the extent that the minor, the minor's estate, or the custodian in the capacity of custodian, is the irrevocable beneficiary.

(d) A custodian at all times shall keep custodial property separate and distinct from all other property in a manner sufficient to identify it clearly as custodial property of the minor. Custodial property consisting of an undivided interest is so identified if the minor's interest is held as a tenant in common and is fixed. Custodial property subject to recordation is so identified if it is recorded, and custodial property subject to registration is so identified if it is either registered, or held in an account designated, in the name of the custodian, followed in substance by the words:

"as a custodian for _____ (Name of Minor) under the California Uniform Transfers to Minors Act."

(e) A custodian shall keep records of all transactions with respect to custodial property, including information necessary for the preparation of the minor's tax returns, and shall make them available for inspection at reasonable intervals by a parent or legal representative of the minor or by the minor if the minor has attained the age of 14 years. **Leg.H.** Enacted Stats 1990 ch 79 §14 (AB 759), operative July 1, 1991.

Prior Law: Former Prob C §3912, similar to the present section, was added Stats 1984 ch 243 §9 and repealed Stats 1990 ch 79 §13, operative July 1, 1991.

§3913. Powers of custodian

(a) A custodian, acting in a custodial capacity, has all the rights, powers, and authority over custodial property that unmarried adult owners have over their own property, but a custodian may exercise those rights, powers, and authority in that capacity only.

(b) This section does not relieve a custodian from liability for breach of Section 3912. **Leg.H.** Enacted Stats 1990 ch 79 §14 (AB 759), operative July 1, 1991.

Prior Law: Former Prob C §3913, similar to the present section, was added Stats 1984 ch 243 §9 and repealed Stats 1990 ch 79 §13, operative July 1, 1991.

§3914. Use of custodial property

(a) A custodian may deliver or pay to the minor or expend for the minor's benefit as much of the custodial property as the custodian considers advisable for the use and benefit of the minor, without court order and without regard to (1) the duty or ability of the custodian personally, or of any other person, to support the minor or (2) any other income or property of the minor which may be applicable or available for that purpose.

(b) On petition of an interested person or the minor if the minor has attained the age of 14 years, the court may order the custodian to deliver or pay to the minor or expend for the minor's benefit so much of the custodial property as the court considers advisable for the use and benefit of the minor.

(c) A delivery, payment, or expenditure under this section is in addition to, not in substitution for, and does not affect, any obligation of a person to support the minor.

(d) In lieu of the powers and duties described in subdivision (a), a transferor who is also the custodian may elect to govern his or her custodial powers and duties under this subdivision. If such election is made, the custodian shall not pay over to the minor for expenditure by the minor, and shall not expend for the minor's use or benefit, any part of the custodial property for any purpose prior to the time specified in Section 3920, except by order of the court upon a showing that the expenditure is necessary for the support, maintenance, or education of the minor. When the powers and duties of the custodian are governed by this subdivision, the transferor-custodian shall file with the clerk of the court a declaration in substantially the following form:

Declaration Under the California Uniform Transfers to Minors Act

I, _____ (Name of Transferor-Custodian), as custodian for _____ (Name of Minor) under the California Uniform Transfers to Minors Act, hereby irrevocably elect to be governed under subdivision (d) of Section 3914 of the Probate Code in my custodial capacity over the following described property

_____
_____.

(Description of Custodial Property)

I declare under penalty of perjury that the foregoing is true and correct.

Dated: _____, 19___

_____
(Signature of Transferor-Custodian)

Leg.H. Enacted Stats 1990 ch 79 §14 (AB 759), operative July 1, 1991.

Prior Law: Former Prob C §3914, similar to the present section, was added Stats 1984 ch 243 §9 and repealed Stats 1990 ch 79 §13, operative July 1, 1991.

§3915. Custodian's expenses, compensation, and bond

(a) A custodian is entitled to reimbursement from custodial property for reasonable expenses incurred in the performance of the custodian's duties.

(b) Except for one who is a transferor under Section 3904, a custodian has a noncumulative election during each calendar year to charge reasonable compensation for services performed during that year.

(c) Except as provided in subdivision (f) of Section 3918, a custodian need not give a bond. **Leg.H.** Enacted Stats 1990 ch 79 §14 (AB 759), operative July 1, 1991.

Prior Law: Former Prob C §3915, similar to the present section, was added Stats 1984 ch 243 §9 and repealed Stats 1990 ch 79 §13, operative July 1, 1991.

§3916. Protection of third person from liability

A third person in good faith and without court order may act on the instructions of, or otherwise deal with, any person purporting to make a transfer or purporting to act in the capacity of a custodian and, in the absence of knowledge, is not responsible for determining any of the following:

(a) The validity of the purported custodian's designation.

(b) The propriety of, or the authority under this part for, any act of the purported custodian.

(c) The validity or propriety under this part of any instrument or instructions executed or given either by the person purporting to make a transfer or by the purported custodian.

(d) The propriety of the application of any property of the minor delivered to the purported custodian. **Leg.H.** Enacted Stats 1990 ch 79 §14 (AB 759), operative July 1, 1991.

Prior Law: Former Prob C §3916, similar to the present section, was added Stats 1984 ch 243 §9 and repealed Stats 1990 ch 79 §13, operative July 1, 1991.

§3917. Liability to third persons

(a) A claim based on (1) a contract entered into by a custodian acting in a custodial capacity, (2) an obligation arising from the ownership or control of custodial property, or (3) a tort committed during the custodianship, may be asserted against the custodial property by proceeding against the custodian in the custodial capacity, whether or not the custodian or the minor is personally liable therefor.

(b) A custodian is not personally liable for either of the following:

(1) On a contract properly entered into in the custodial capacity unless the custodian fails to reveal that capacity and to identify the custodianship in the contract.

(2) For an obligation arising from control of custodial property or for a tort committed during the custodianship unless the custodian is personally at fault.

(c) A minor is not personally liable for an obligation arising from ownership of custodial property or for a tort committed during the custodianship unless the minor is personally at fault. **Leg.H.** Enacted Stats 1990 ch 79 §14 (AB 759), operative July 1, 1991.

Prior Law: Former Prob C §3917, similar to the present section, was added Stats 1984 ch 243 §9 and repealed Stats 1990 ch 79 §1, operative July 1, 1991.

§3918. Renunciation, resignation, death, or removal of custodian; Designation of successor custodian

(a) A person nominated under Section 3903 or designated under Section 3909 as custodian may decline to serve by delivering a valid disclaimer under Part 8 (commencing with Section 260) of Division 2 to the person who made the nomination or to the transferor or the transferor's legal representative. If the event giving rise to a transfer has not occurred and no substitute custodian able, willing, and eligible to serve was nominated under Section 3903, the person who made the nomination may nominate a substitute custodian under Section 3903; otherwise the transferor or the transferor's legal representative shall designate a substitute custodian at the time of the transfer, in either case from among the persons eligible to serve as custodian for that kind of property under subdivision (a) of Section 3909. The custodian so designated has the rights of a successor custodian.

(b) A custodian at any time may designate a trust company or an adult other than a transferor under Section 3904 as successor custodian by executing and dating an instrument of designation before a subscribing witness other than the successor. If the instrument of designation does not contain or is not accompanied by the resignation of the custodian, the designation of the successor does not take effect until the custodian resigns, dies, becomes incapacitated, or is removed. The transferor may designate one or more persons as successor custodians to serve, in the designated order of priority, in case the custodian originally designated or a prior successor custodian is unable, declines, or is ineligible to serve or resigns, dies, becomes incapacitated, or is removed. The designation either (1) shall be made in the same transaction and by the same document by which the transfer is made or (2) shall be made by executing and dating a separate instrument of designation before a subscribing witness other than a successor as a part of the same transaction and contemporaneously with the execution of the document by which the transfer is made. The designation is made by setting forth the successor custodian's name, followed in substance by the words: "is designated [first, second, etc., where applicable] successor custodian." A successor custodian designated by the transferor may be a trust company or an adult other than a transferor under Section 3904. A successor custodian effectively designated by the transferor has priority over a successor custodian designated by a custodian.

(c) A custodian may resign at any time by delivering written notice to the minor if the minor has attained the age of 14 years and to the successor custodian and by delivering the custodial property to the successor custodian.

(d) If the transferor has not effectively designated a successor custodian, and a custodian is ineligible, dies, or becomes incapacitated without having effectively designated a successor and the minor has attained the age of 14 years, the minor may designate as successor custodian, in the manner prescribed in subdivision (b), an adult member of the minor's family, a conservator of the minor, or a trust company. If the minor has not attained the age of 14 years or fails to act within 60 days after the ineligibility, death, or incapacity, the conservator of the minor becomes successor custodian. If the minor has no conservator or the conservator declines to act, the transferor, the legal representative of the transferor or of the custodian, an adult member of the minor's family, or any other interested person may petition the court to designate a successor custodian.

(e) A custodian who declines to serve under subdivision (a) or resigns under subdivision (c), or the legal representative of a deceased or incapacitated custodian, as soon as practicable, shall put the custodial property and records in the possession and control of the successor custodian. The successor custodian by action may enforce the obligation to deliver custodial property and records and becomes responsible for each item as received.

(f) A transferor, the legal representative of a transferor, an adult member of the minor's family, a guardian of the person of the minor, the conservator of the minor, or the minor if the minor has attained the age of 14 years, may petition the court to remove the custodian for cause and to designate a successor custodian other than a transferor under Section 3904 or to require the custodian to give appropriate bond.

(g) At least 15 days before the hearing on a petition under subdivision (d) or (f), the petitioner shall deliver notice pursuant to Section 1215 to each of the following persons:

(1) The minor.

(2) The parent or parents of the minor.

(3) The transferor.

(h) Upon consideration of the petition under subdivision (d) or (f), the court may grant the relief that the court finds to be in the best interests of the minor. **Leg.H.** Enacted Stats 1990 ch 79 §14 (AB 759), operative July 1, 1991. Amended Stats 1992 ch 871 §7 (AB 2975); Stats 2017 ch 319 §62 (AB 976), effective January 1, 2018.

Prior Law: Former Prob C §3918, similar to the present section, was added Stats 1984 ch 243 §9, amended Stats 1985 ch 90 §1, Stats 1988 ch 1199 §73.5, operative July 1, 1989, and repealed Stats 1990 ch 79 §13, operative July 1, 1991.

§3919. Accounting; Determination of liability of custodian

(a) A minor who has attained the age of 14 years, the minor's guardian of the person or legal representative, an adult member of the minor's family, a transferor, or a transferor's legal representative may petition the court for any of the following:

(1) An accounting by the custodian or the custodian's legal representative.

(2) A determination of responsibility, as between the custodial property and the custodian personally, for claims against the custodial property unless the responsibility has been adjudicated in an action under Section 3917 to which the minor or the minor's legal representative was a party.

(b) A successor custodian may petition the court for an accounting by the predecessor custodian.

(c) The court, in a proceeding under this part or in any other proceeding, may require or permit the custodian or the custodian's legal representative to account.

(d) If a custodian is removed under subdivision (f) of Section 3918, the court shall require an accounting and order delivery of the custodial property and records to the successor custodian and the execution of all instruments required for transfer of the custodial property.

(e) The right to petition for an accounting shall continue for one year after the filing of a final accounting by the custodian or the custodian's legal representative and delivery of the custodial property to the minor or the minor's estate. **Leg.H.** Enacted Stats 1990 ch 79 §14 (AB 759), operative July 1, 1991.

Prior Law: Former Prob C §3919, similar to the present section, was added Stats 1984 ch 243 §9 and repealed Stats 1990 ch 79 §13, operative July 1, 1991.

§3920. Termination of custodianship

The custodian shall transfer in an appropriate manner the custodial property to the minor or to the minor's estate upon the earlier of the following:

(a) The minor's attainment of 18 years of age unless the time of transfer of the custodial property to the minor is delayed under Section 3920.5 to a time after the time the minor attains the age of 18 years.

(b) The time specified in the transfer pursuant to Section 3909 if the time of transfer of the custodial property to the minor is delayed under Section 3920.5 to a time after the time the minor attains the age of 18 years.

(c) The minor's death. **Leg.H.** Enacted Stats 1990 ch 79 §14 (AB 759), operative July 1, 1991.

Prior Law: Former Prob C §3920, similar to the present section, was added Stats 1984 ch 243 §9 and repealed Stats 1990 ch 79 §13, operative July 1, 1991.

§3920.5. Delayed time for transfer to minor; Procedure

(a) Subject to the requirements and limitations of this section, the time for transfer to the minor of custodial property transferred under or pursuant to Section 3903, 3904, 3905, or 3906, may be delayed until a specified time after the time the minor attains the age of 18 years, which time shall be specified in the transfer pursuant to Section 3909.

(b) To specify a delayed time for transfer to the minor of the custodial property, the words

"as custodian for _____
(Name of Minor)
until age _____
(Age for Delivery of Property to Minor)
under the California Uniform Transfers to Minors Act" shall be substituted in substance for the words
"as custodian for _____
(Name of Minor)
under the California Uniform Transfers to Minors Act" in making the transfer pursuant to Section 3909.

(c) The time for transfer to the minor of custodial property transferred under or pursuant to Section 3903 or 3905 may be delayed under this section only if the governing will or trust or nomination provides in substance that the custodianship is to continue until the time the minor attains a specified age, which time may not be later than the time the minor attains 25 years of age, and in that case the governing will or trust or nomination shall determine the time to be specified in the transfer pursuant to Section 3909.

(d) The time for transfer to the minor of custodial property transferred by the irrevocable exercise of a power of appointment under Section 3904 may be delayed under this section only if the transfer pursuant to Section 3909 provides in substance that the custodianship is to continue until the time the minor attains a specified age, which time may not be later than the time the minor attains 25 years of age.

(e) The time for transfer to the minor of custodial property transferred by irrevocable gift under Section 3904 may be delayed under this section only if the transfer pursuant to Section 3909 provides in substance that the custodianship is to continue until the time the minor attains a specified age, which time may not be later than the time the minor attains 21 years of age.

(f) The time for transfer to the minor of custodial property transferred by a trustee under Section 3906 may be delayed under this section only if the transfer pursuant to Section 3909 provides that the custodianship is to continue until a specified time not later than the time the minor attains 25 years of age or the time of termination of all present beneficial interests of the minor in the trust from which the custodial property was transferred, whichever is to occur first.

(g) If the transfer pursuant to Section 3909 does not specify any age, the time for the transfer of the custodial property to the minor under Section 3920 is the time when the minor attains 18 years of age.

(h) If the transfer pursuant to Section 3909 provides in substance that the duration of the custodianship is for a time longer than the maximum time permitted by this section for the duration of a custodianship created by that type of transfer, the custodianship shall be deemed to continue only until the time the minor attains the maximum age permitted by this section for the duration of a custodianship created by that type of transfer. **Leg.H.** Enacted Stats 1990 ch 79 §14 (AB 759), operative July 1, 1991. Amended Stats 1996 ch 862 §14 (AB 2751).

Prior Law: Former Prob C §3920.5, similar to the present section, was added Stats 1984 ch 243 §9 and repealed Stats 1990 ch 79 §13, operative July 1, 1991.

§3921. Venue

Subject to the power of the court to transfer actions and proceedings as provided in the Code of Civil Procedure, a petition filed under this part shall be heard and proceedings thereon held in the superior court in the proper county, which shall be determined as follows:

(a) If the minor resides in this state, in either of the following counties:

(1) Where the minor resides.

(2) Where the custodian resides.

(b) If the minor does not reside within this state, in any of the following counties:

(1) Where the transferor resides.

(2) Where the custodian resides.

(3) Where the estate of a deceased or legally incapacitated custodian is being administered.

(4) Where a parent of the minor resides.

(c) If neither the minor, nor the transferor, nor any parent resides within this state, and no estate of a deceased or legally incapacitated custodian is being administered within this state, in any county. **Leg.H.** Enacted Stats 1990 ch 79 §14 (AB 759), operative July 1, 1991.

Prior Law: Former Prob C §3921, similar to the present section, was added Stats 1984 ch 243 §9 and repealed Stats 1990 ch 79 §13, operative July 1, 1991.

§3922. Transfers subject to part

This part applies to a transfer within the scope of Section 3902 made on or after January 1, 1985, if either of the following requirements is satisfied:

(a) The transfer purports to have been made under the California Uniform Gifts to Minors Act.

(b) The instrument by which the transfer purports to have been made uses in substance the designation "as custodian under the Uniform Gifts to Minors Act" or "as custodian under the Uniform Transfers to Minors Act" of any other state, and the application of this part is necessary to validate the transfer. **Leg.H.** Enacted Stats 1990 ch 79 §14 (AB 759), operative July 1, 1991.

Prior Law: Former Prob C §3922, similar to the present section, was added Stats 1984 ch 243 §9 and repealed Stats 1990 ch 79 §13, operative July 1, 1991.

§3923. Transfers made before January 1, 1985

(a) As used in this section, "California Uniform Gifts to Minors Act" means former Article 4 (commencing with Section 1154) of Chapter 3 of Title 4 of Part 4 of Division 2 of the Civil Code.

(b) Any transfer of custodial property, as now defined in this part, made before January 1, 1985, is validated, notwithstanding that there was no specific authority in the California Uniform Gifts to Minors Act for the coverage of custodial property of that kind or for a transfer from that source at the time the transfer was made.

(c) This part applies to all transfers made before January 1, 1985, in a manner and form prescribed in the California Uniform Gifts to Minors Act, except insofar as the application impairs constitutionally vested rights.

(d) To the extent that this part, by virtue of subdivision (c), does not apply to transfers made in a manner prescribed in the California Uniform Gifts to Minors Act or to the powers, duties, and immunities conferred by transfers in that manner upon custodians and persons dealing with custodians, the repeal of the California Uniform Gifts to Minors Act does not affect those transfers or those powers, duties, and immunities. **Leg.H.** Enacted Stats 1990 ch 79 §14 (AB 759), operative July 1, 1991.

Prior Law: Former Prob C §3923, similar to the present section, was added Stats 1984 ch 243 §9 and repealed Stats 1990 ch 79 §13, operative July 1, 1991.

§3925. Method of transfer provided by part not exclusive

This part shall not be construed as providing an exclusive method for making gifts or other transfers to minors. **Leg.H.** Enacted Stats 1990 ch 79 §14 (AB 759), operative July 1, 1991.

Prior Law: Former Prob C §3925, similar to the present section, was added Stats 1984 ch 243 §9 and repealed Stats 1990 ch 79 §13, operative July 1, 1991.

DIVISION 4.5
POWERS OF ATTORNEY

Part 1. Definitions and General Provisions.
Part 2. Powers of Attorney Generally.
Part 3. Uniform Statutory Form Power of Attorney.
Part 4. Judicial Proceedings Concerning Powers of Attorney.
Part 5. Judicial Proceedings Concerning Powers of Attorney [Repealed].

PART 1
DEFINITIONS AND GENERAL PROVISIONS

Chapter 1. Short Title and Definitions.
Chapter 2. General Provisions.

CHAPTER 1
SHORT TITLE AND DEFINITIONS

Citation of division. §4000.
Citation of specified sections. §4001.
Definitions to govern chapter. §4010.
"Attorney-in-fact". §4014.
"Durable power of attorney". §4018.
"Power of attorney". §4022.
"Principal". §4026.
"Springing power of attorney". §4030.
"Third person". §4034.

§4000. Citation of division
This division may be cited as the Power of Attorney Law. **Leg.H.** Added Stats 1994 ch 307 §16 (SB 1907).

§4001. Citation of specified sections
Sections 4124, 4125, 4126, 4127, 4206, 4304, and 4305 may be cited as the Uniform Durable Power of Attorney Act. **Leg.H.** Added Stats 1994 ch 307 §16 (SB 1907).

§4010. Definitions to govern chapter
Unless the provision or context otherwise requires, the definitions in this chapter govern the construction of this division. **Leg.H.** Added Stats 1994 ch 307 §16 (SB 1907).

§4014. "Attorney-in-fact"
(a) "Attorney-in-fact" means a person granted authority to act for the principal in a power of attorney, regardless of whether the person is known as an attorney-in-fact or agent, or by some other term.
(b) "Attorney-in-fact" includes a successor or alternate attorney-in-fact and a person delegated authority by an attorney-in-fact. **Leg.H.** Added Stats 1994 ch 307 §16 (SB 1907).

§4018. "Durable power of attorney"
"Durable power of attorney" means a power of attorney that satisfies the requirements for durability provided in Section 4124. **Leg.H.** Added Stats 1994 ch 307 §16 (SB 1907).

§4022. "Power of attorney"
"Power of attorney" means a written instrument, however denominated, that is executed by a natural person having the capacity to contract and that grants authority to an attorney-in-fact. A power of attorney may be durable or nondurable. **Leg.H.** Added Stats 1994 ch 307 §16 (SB 1907).

§4026. "Principal"
"Principal" means a natural person who executes a power of attorney. **Leg.H.** Added Stats 1994 ch 307 §16 (SB 1907).

§4030. "Springing power of attorney"
"Springing power of attorney" means a power of attorney that by its terms becomes effective at a specified future time or on the occurrence of a specified future event or contingency, including, but not limited to, the subsequent incapacity of the principal. A springing power of attorney may be a durable power of attorney or a nondurable power of attorney. **Leg.H.** Added Stats 1994 ch 307 §16 (SB 1907).

§4034. "Third person"
"Third person" means any person other than the principal or attorney-in-fact. **Leg.H.** Added Stats 1994 ch 307 §16 (SB 1907).

CHAPTER 2
GENERAL PROVISIONS

Application of division. §4050.
Application of general law of agency. §4051.
Conditions for application of law to out-of-state acts and transmissions. §4052.
Validity of power of attorney executed out of state. §4053.
Application of division to powers of attorney executed prior to or after specified date. §4054.

§4050. Application of division
(a) This division applies to the following:
(1) Durable powers of attorney, other than powers of attorney for health care governed by Division 4.7 (commencing with Section 4600).
(2) Statutory form powers of attorney under Part 3 (commencing with Section 4400).
(3) Any other power of attorney that incorporates or refers to this division or the provisions of this division.
(b) This division does not apply to the following:
(1) A power of attorney to the extent that the authority of the attorney-in-fact is coupled with an interest in the subject of the power of attorney.
(2) Reciprocal or interinsurance exchanges and their contracts, subscribers, attorneys-in-fact, agents, and representatives.
(3) A proxy given by an attorney-in-fact to another person to exercise voting rights.
(c) This division is not intended to affect the validity of any instrument or arrangement that is not described in subdivision (a). **Leg.H.** Added Stats 1994 ch 307 §16 (SB 1907). Amended Stats 1999 ch 658 §27 (AB 891), operative July 1, 2000.

§4051. Application of general law of agency
Except where this division provides a specific rule, the general law of agency, including Article 2 (commencing with Section 2019) of Chapter 2 of Title 6 of, and Title 9 (commencing with Section 2295) of, Part 4 of Division 3 of the Civil Code, applies to powers of attorney. **Leg.H.** Added Stats 1994 ch 307 §16 (SB 1907).

§4052. Conditions for application of law to out-of-state acts and transmissions
(a) If a power of attorney provides that the Power of Attorney Law of this state governs the power of attorney or otherwise indicates the principal's intention that the Power of Attorney Law of this state governs the power of attorney, this division governs the power of attorney and applies to acts and transactions of the attorney-in-fact in this state or outside this state where any of the following conditions is satisfied:
(1) The principal or attorney-in-fact was domiciled in this state when the principal executed the power of attorney.
(2) The authority conferred on the attorney-in-fact relates to property, acts, or transactions in this state.
(3) The acts or transactions of the attorney-in-fact occurred or were intended to occur in this state.
(4) The principal executed the power of attorney in this state.
(5) There is otherwise a reasonable relationship between this state and the subject matter of the power of attorney.
(b) If subdivision (a) does not apply to the power of attorney, this division governs the power of attorney and applies to the acts and transactions of the attorney-in-fact in this state where either of the following conditions is satisfied:
(1) The principal was domiciled in this state when the principal executed the power of attorney.

(2) The principal executed the power of attorney in this state.

(c) A power of attorney described in this section remains subject to this division despite a change in domicile of the principal or the attorney-in-fact, or the removal from this state of property that was the subject of the power of attorney. **Leg.H.** Added Stats 1994 ch 307 §16 (SB 1907).

§4053. Validity of power of attorney executed out of state

A durable power of attorney executed in another state or jurisdiction in compliance with the law of that state or jurisdiction or the law of this state is valid and enforceable in this state to the same extent as a durable power of attorney executed in this state, regardless of whether the principal is a domiciliary of this state. **Leg.H.** Added Stats 1994 ch 307 §16 (SB 1907).

§4054. Application of division to powers of attorney executed prior to or after specified date

Except as otherwise provided by statute:

(a) On and after January 1, 1995, this division applies to all powers of attorney regardless of whether they were executed before, on, or after January 1, 1995.

(b) This division applies to all proceedings concerning powers of attorney commenced on or after January 1, 1995.

(c) This division applies to all proceedings concerning powers of attorney commenced before January 1, 1995, unless the court determines that application of a particular provision of this division would substantially interfere with the effective conduct of the proceedings or the rights of the parties and other interested persons, in which case the particular provision of this division does not apply and prior law applies.

(d) Nothing in this division affects the validity of a power of attorney executed before January 1, 1995, that was valid under prior law. **Leg.H.** Added Stats 1994 ch 307 §16 (SB 1907). Amended Stats 1995 ch 300 §3 (SB 984), effective August 3, 1995.

1995 Note: The amendment made by this act is declaratory of, and does not constitute a change in, existing law. Stats 1995 ch 300 §16.

PART 2
POWERS OF ATTORNEY GENERALLY

Chapter 1. General Provisions.
Chapter 2. Creation and Effect of Powers of Attorney.
Chapter 3. Modification and Revocation of Powers of Attorney.
Chapter 4. Attorneys-in-Fact.
Chapter 5. Relations With Third Persons.

CHAPTER 1
GENERAL PROVISIONS

Applicability of part. §4100.
Limitation of specified provisions of division. §4101.
Sale of printed forms. §4102.

§4100. Applicability of part

This part applies to all powers of attorney under this division, subject to any special rules applicable to statutory form powers of attorney under Part 3 (commencing with Section 4400). **Leg.H.** Added Stats 1994 ch 307 §16 (SB 1907). Amended Stats 1999 ch 658 §28 (AB 891), operative July 1, 2000.

§4101. Limitation of specified provisions of division

(a) Except as provided in subdivision (b), the principal may limit the application of any provision of this division by an express statement in the power of attorney or by providing an inconsistent rule in the power of attorney.

(b) A power of attorney may not limit either the application of a statute specifically providing that it is not subject to limitation in the power of attorney or a statute concerning any of the following:
 (1) Warnings or notices required to be included in a power of attorney.
 (2) Operative dates of statutory enactments or amendments.
 (3) Execution formalities.
 (4) Qualifications of witnesses.
 (5) Qualifications of attorneys-in-fact.
 (6) Protection of third persons from liability. **Leg.H.** Added Stats 1994 ch 307 §16 (SB 1907).

§4102. Sale of printed forms

Notwithstanding Section 4128:

(a) Except as provided in subdivision (b), on and after January 1, 1995, a printed form of a durable power of attorney may be sold or otherwise distributed if it satisfies the requirements of former Section 2510.5 of the Civil Code.

(b) A printed form of a durable power of attorney printed on or after January 1, 1986, that is sold or otherwise distributed in this state for use by a person who does not have the advice of legal counsel shall comply with former Section 2510 of the Civil Code or with Section 4128 of this code.

(c) A durable power of attorney executed on or after January 1, 1995, using a printed form that complies with subdivision (b) of former Section 2400 of the Civil Code, as enacted by Chapter 511 of the Statutes of 1981, or with former Section 2510 of the Civil Code, is as valid as if it had been executed using a printed form that complies with Section 4128 of this code. **Leg.H.** Added Stats 1994 ch 307 §16 (SB 1907).

CHAPTER 2
CREATION AND EFFECT OF POWERS OF ATTORNEY

Persons who may execute powers of attorney. §4120.
Requirements for legal sufficiency of power of attorney. §4121.
Witness signature requirements. §4122.
Grant of authority to act or make decisions. §4123.
Required statements. §4124.
Effect of acts of attorney-in-fact. §4125.
Effect of nomination of conservator or guardian. §4126.
Termination of authority. §4127.
Warning statement in printed durable power of attorney form; Notice to person executing durable power of attorney; Notice to person accepting appointment as Attorney-in-Fact. §4128.
Springing power of attorney; Effective date; Application of section. §4129.
Multiple powers of attorney. §4130.

§4120. Persons who may execute powers of attorney

A natural person having the capacity to contract may execute a power of attorney. **Leg.H.** Added Stats 1994 ch 307 §16 (SB 1907).

§4121. Requirements for legal sufficiency of power of attorney

A power of attorney is legally sufficient if all of the following requirements are satisfied:

(a) The power of attorney contains the date of its execution.

(b) The power of attorney is signed either (1) by the principal or (2) in the principal's name by another adult in the principal's presence and at the principal's direction.

(c) The power of attorney is either (1) acknowledged before a notary public or (2) signed by at least two witnesses who satisfy the requirements of Section 4122. **Leg.H.** Added Stats 1994 ch 307 §16 (SB 1907). Amended Stats 1999 ch 658 §29 (AB 891), operative July 1, 2000.

§4122. Witness signature requirements

If the power of attorney is signed by witnesses, as provided in Section 4121, the following requirements shall be satisfied:

(a) The witnesses shall be adults.

(b) The attorney-in-fact may not act as a witness.

(c) Each witness signing the power of attorney shall witness either the signing of the instrument by the principal or the principal's acknowledgment of the signature or the power of attorney. **Leg.H.** Added Stats 1994 ch 307 §16 (SB 1907). Amended Stats 1999 ch 658 §30 (AB 891), operative July 1, 2000.

§4123. Grant of authority to act or make decisions

(a) In a power of attorney under this division, a principal may grant authority to an attorney-in-fact to act on the principal's behalf with respect to all lawful subjects and purposes or with respect to one or more express subjects or purposes. The attorney-in-fact may be granted authority with regard to the principal's property, personal care, or any other matter.

(b) With regard to property matters, a power of attorney may grant authority to make decisions concerning all or part of the principal's real and personal property, whether owned by the principal at the time of the execution of the power of attorney or thereafter acquired or whether located in this state or elsewhere, without the need for a description of each item or parcel of property.

(c) With regard to personal care, a power of attorney may grant authority to make decisions relating to the personal care of the principal, including, but not limited to, determining where the principal will live, providing meals, hiring household employees, providing transportation, handling mail, and arranging recreation and entertainment. **Leg.H.** Added Stats 1994 ch 307 §16 (SB 1907). Amended Stats 1999 ch 658 §31 (AB 891), operative July 1, 2000; Stats 2001 ch 230 §2 (AB 1278), effective January 1, 2002.

§4124. Required statements

A durable power of attorney is a power of attorney by which a principal designates another person as attorney-in-fact in writing and the power of attorney contains any of the following statements:

(a) "This power of attorney shall not be affected by subsequent incapacity of the principal."

(b) "This power of attorney shall become effective upon the incapacity of the principal."

(c) Similar words showing the intent of the principal that the authority conferred shall be exercisable notwithstanding the principal's subsequent incapacity. **Leg.H.** Added Stats 1994 ch 307 §16.

§4125. Effect of acts of attorney-in-fact

All acts done by an attorney-in-fact pursuant to a durable power of attorney during any period of incapacity of the principal have the same effect and inure to the benefit of and bind the principal and the principal's successors in interest as if the principal had capacity. **Leg.H.** Added Stats 1994 ch 307 §16 (SB 1907).

§4126. Effect of nomination of conservator or guardian

(a) A principal may nominate, by a durable power of attorney, a conservator of the person or estate or both, or a guardian of the person or estate or both, for consideration by the court if protective proceedings for the principal's person or estate are thereafter commenced.

(b) If the protective proceedings are conservatorship proceedings in this state, the nomination has the effect provided in Section 1810 and the court shall give effect to the most recent writing executed in accordance with Section 1810, whether or not the writing is a durable power of attorney. **Leg.H.** Added Stats 1994 ch 307 §16 (SB 1907).

§4127. Termination of authority

Unless a power of attorney states a time of termination, the authority of the attorney-in-fact is exercisable notwithstanding any lapse of time since execution of the power of attorney. **Leg.H.** Added Stats 1994 ch 307 §16 (SB 1907).

§4128. Warning statement in printed durable power of attorney form; Notice to person executing durable power of attorney; Notice to person accepting appointment as Attorney-in-Fact

(a) Subject to subdivision (b), a printed form of a durable power of attorney that is sold or otherwise distributed in this state for use by a person who does not have the advice of legal counsel shall contain, in not less than 10-point boldface type or a reasonable equivalent thereof, the following warning statements:

Notice to Person Executing Durable Power of Attorney

A durable power of attorney is an important legal document. By signing the durable power of attorney, you are authorizing another person to act for you, the principal. Before you sign this durable power of attorney, you should know these important facts:

Your agent (attorney-in-fact) has no duty to act unless you and your agent agree otherwise in writing.

This document gives your agent the powers to manage, dispose of, sell, and convey your real and personal property, and to use your property as security if your agent borrows money on your behalf. This document does not give your agent the power to accept or receive any of your property, in trust or otherwise, as a gift, unless you specifically authorize the agent to accept or receive a gift.

Your agent will have the right to receive reasonable payment for services provided under this durable power of attorney unless you provide otherwise in this power of attorney.

The powers you give your agent will continue to exist for your entire lifetime, unless you state that the durable power of attorney will last for a shorter period of time or unless you otherwise terminate the durable power of attorney. The powers you give your agent in this durable power of attorney will continue to exist even if you can no longer make your own decisions respecting the management of your property.

You can amend or change this durable power of attorney only by executing a new durable power of attorney or by executing an amendment through the same formalities as an original. You have the right to revoke or terminate this durable power of attorney at any time, so long as you are competent.

This durable power of attorney must be dated and must be acknowledged before a notary public or signed by two witnesses. If it is signed by two witnesses, they must witness either (1) the signing of the power of attorney or (2) the principal's signing or acknowledgment of his or her signature. A durable power of attorney that may affect real property should be acknowledged before a notary public so that it may easily be recorded.

You should read this durable power of attorney carefully. When effective, this durable power of attorney will give your agent the right to deal with property that you now have or might acquire in the future. The durable power of attorney is important to you. If you do not understand the durable power of attorney, or any provision of it, then you should obtain the assistance of an attorney or other qualified person.

Notice to Person Accepting the Appointment as Attorney-in-Fact

By acting or agreeing to act as the agent (attorney-in-fact) under this power of attorney you assume the fiduciary and other legal responsibilities of an agent. These responsibilities include:

1. The legal duty to act solely in the interest of the principal and to avoid conflicts of interest.

2. The legal duty to keep the principal's property separate and distinct from any other property owned or controlled by you.

You may not transfer the principal's property to yourself without full and adequate consideration or accept a gift of the principal's property unless this power of attorney specifically authorizes you to transfer property to yourself or accept a gift of the principal's property. If you transfer the principal's property to yourself without specific authorization in the power of attorney, you may be prosecuted for fraud and/or embezzlement. If the principal is 65 years of age or older at the time that the property is transferred to you without authority, you may also be prosecuted for elder abuse under Penal Code Section 368. In addition to criminal prosecution, you may also be sued in civil court.

I have read the foregoing notice and I understand the legal and fiduciary duties that I assume by acting or agreeing to act as the agent (attorney-in-fact) under the terms of this power of attorney.

Date: _____

_____
(Signature of agent)

_____
(Print name of agent)

(b) Nothing in subdivision (a) invalidates any transaction in which a third person relied in good faith on the authority created by the durable power of attorney.

(c) This section does not apply to a statutory form power of attorney under Part 3 (commencing with Section 4400). **Leg.H.** Added Stats 1994 ch 307 §16 (SB 1907). Amended Stats 1999 ch 658 §32 (AB 891), operative July 1, 2000; Stats 2000 ch 999 §1 (SB 1869), effective January 1, 2001.

2000 Notes: The provisions of this bill shall not affect any legally sufficient power of attorney executed prior to January 1, 2001. Stats 2000 ch 999 §2.

The provisions of this bill shall not affect a durable power of attorney under Section 4128 of the Probate Code executed prior to March 1, 2001. Subsequent to March 1, 2001, all printed forms under Section 4128 of the Probate Code shall conform to the provisions of this bill. Stats 2000 ch 999 §3.

§4129. Springing power of attorney; Effective date; Application of section

(a) In a springing power of attorney, the principal may designate one or more persons who, by a written declaration under penalty of perjury, have the power to determine conclusively that the specified event or contingency has occurred. The principal may designate the attorney-in-fact or another person to perform this function, either alone or jointly with other persons.

(b) A springing power of attorney containing the designation described in subdivision (a) becomes effective when the person or persons designated in the power of attorney execute a written declaration under penalty of perjury that the specified event or contingency has occurred, and any person may act in reliance on the written declaration without liability to the principal or to any other person, regardless of whether the specified event or contingency has actually occurred.

(c) This section applies to a power of attorney whether executed before, on, or after January 1, 1991, if the power of attorney contains the designation described in subdivision (a).

(d) This section does not provide the exclusive method by which a power of attorney may be limited to take effect on the occurrence of a specified event or contingency. **Leg.H.** Added Stats 1994 ch 307 §16 (SB 1907).

§4130. Multiple powers of attorney

(a) If a principal grants inconsistent authority to one or more attorneys-in-fact in two or more powers of attorney, the authority granted last controls to the extent of the inconsistency.

(b) This section is not subject to limitation in the power of attorney. **Leg.H.** Added Stats 1994 ch 307 §16 (SB 1907).

CHAPTER 3
MODIFICATION AND REVOCATION OF POWERS OF ATTORNEY

Methods of modification of power of attorney. §4150.
Methods of revocation of power of attorney. §4151.
Events terminating power of attorney. §4152.
Methods of revoking authority of attorney-in-fact. §4153.
Revocation of designation of spouse of principal as attorney-in-fact. §4154.
Termination of authority of attorney in fact by incapacity of principal; Notice. §4155.

§4150. Methods of modification of power of attorney

(a) A principal may modify a power of attorney as follows:
(1) In accordance with the terms of the power of attorney.

(2) By an instrument executed in the same manner as a power of attorney may be executed.

(b) An attorney-in-fact or third person who does not have notice of the modification is protected from liability as provided in Chapter 5 (commencing with Section 4300). **Leg.H.** Added Stats 1994 ch 307 §16 (SB 1907). Amended Stats 1995 ch 300 §4 (SB 984), effective August 3, 1995.

§4151. Methods of revocation of power of attorney

(a) A principal may revoke a power of attorney as follows:

(1) In accordance with the terms of the power of attorney.

(2) By a writing. This paragraph is not subject to limitation in the power of attorney.

(b) An attorney-in-fact or third person who does not have notice of the revocation is protected from liability as provided in Chapter 5 (commencing with Section 4300). **Leg.H.** Added Stats 1994 ch 307 §16 (SB 1907). Amended Stats 1995 ch 300 §5 (SB 984), effective August 3, 1995.

§4152. Events terminating power of attorney

(a) Subject to subdivision (b), the authority of an attorney-in-fact under a power of attorney is terminated by any of the following events:

(1) In accordance with the terms of the power of attorney.

(2) Extinction of the subject or fulfillment of the purpose of the power of attorney.

(3) Revocation of the attorney-in-fact's authority, as provided in Section 4153.

(4) Death of the principal, except as to specific authority permitted by statute to be exercised after the principal's death.

(5) Removal of the attorney-in-fact.

(6) Resignation of the attorney-in-fact.

(7) Incapacity of the attorney-in-fact, except that a temporary incapacity suspends the attorney-in-fact's authority only during the period of the incapacity.

(8) Dissolution or annulment of the marriage of the attorney-in-fact and principal, as provided in Section 4154.

(9) Death of the attorney-in-fact.

(b) An attorney-in-fact or third person who does not have notice of an event that terminates the power of attorney or the authority of an attorney-in-fact is protected from liability as provided in Chapter 5 (commencing with Section 4300). **Leg.H.** Added Stats 1994 ch 307 §16 (SB 1907). Amended Stats 1995 ch 300 §6 (SB 984), effective August 3, 1995.

§4153. Methods of revoking authority of attorney-in-fact

(a) The authority of an attorney-in-fact under a power of attorney may be revoked as follows:

(1) In accordance with the terms of the power of attorney.

(2) Where the principal informs the attorney-in-fact orally or in writing that the attorney-in-fact's authority is revoked or when and under what circumstances it is revoked. This paragraph is not subject to limitation in the power of attorney.

(3) Where the principal's legal representative, with approval of the court as provided in Section 4206, informs the attorney-in-fact in writing that the attorney-in-fact's authority is revoked or when and under what circumstances it is revoked. This paragraph is not subject to limitation in the power of attorney.

(b) An attorney-in-fact or third person who does not have notice of the revocation is protected from liability as provided in Chapter 5 (commencing with Section 4300). **Leg.H.** Added Stats 1994 ch 307 §16 (SB 1907). Amended Stats 1995 ch 300 §7 (SB 984), effective August 3, 1995.

§4154. Revocation of designation of spouse of principal as attorney-in-fact

(a) If after executing a power of attorney the principal's marriage to the attorney-in-fact is dissolved or annulled, the principal's designation of the former spouse as an attorney-in-fact is revoked.

(b) If the attorney-in-fact's authority is revoked solely by subdivision (a), it is revived by the principal's remarriage to the attorney-in-fact. **Leg.H.** Added Stats 1994 ch 307 §16 (SB 1907).

§4155. Termination of authority of attorney in fact by incapacity of principal; Notice

(a) Subject to subdivision (b), the authority of an attorney-in-fact under a nondurable power of attorney is terminated by the incapacity of the principal to contract.

(b) An attorney-in-fact or third person who does not have notice of the incapacity of the principal is protected from liability as provided in Chapter 5 (commencing with Section 4300).

(c) This section is not subject to limitation in the power of attorney. **Leg.H.** Added Stats 1994 ch 307 §16 (SB 1907). Amended Stats 1995 ch 300 §8 (SB 984), effective August 3, 1995.

CHAPTER 4
ATTORNEYS-IN-FACT

Article 1. Qualifications and Authority of Attorneys-in-Fact.
Article 2. Duties of Attorneys-in-Fact.
Article 3. Authority of Attorneys-in-Fact.

ARTICLE 1
Qualifications and Authority of Attorneys-in-Fact

Qualification to act as attorney-in-fact. §4200.
Effect of designation of unqualified person. §4201.
Multiple attorneys-in-fact. §4202.
Successor attorneys-in-fact. §4203.
Compensation and reimbursement. §4204.
Revocable delegation of authority by attorney-in-fact. §4205.
Appointment of conservator or guardian of estate. §4206.
Methods of resignation of attorney-in-fact. §4207.

§4200. Qualification to act as attorney-in-fact

Only a person having the capacity to contract is qualified to act as an attorney-in-fact. **Leg.H.** Added Stats 1994 ch 307 §16 (SB 1907).

§4201. Effect of designation of unqualified person

Designating an unqualified person as an attorney-in-fact does not affect the immunities of third persons nor relieve the unqualified person of any applicable duties to the principal or the principal's successors. **Leg.H.** Added Stats 1994 ch 307 §16 (SB 1907).

§4202. Multiple attorneys-in-fact

(a) A principal may designate more than one attorney-in-fact in one or more powers of attorney.

(b) Authority granted to two or more attorneys-in-fact is exercisable only by their unanimous action.

(c) If a vacancy occurs, the remaining attorneys-in-fact may exercise the authority conferred as if they are the only attorneys-in-fact.

(d) If an attorney-in-fact is unavailable because of absence, illness, or other temporary incapacity, the other attorneys-in-fact may exercise the authority under the power of attorney as if they are the only attorneys-in-fact, where necessary to accomplish the purposes of the power of attorney or to avoid irreparable injury to the principal's interests.

(e) An attorney-in-fact is not liable for the actions of other attorneys-in-fact, unless the attorney-in-fact participates in, knowingly acquiesces in, or conceals a breach of fiduciary duty committed by another attorney-in-fact. **Leg.H.** Added Stats 1994 ch 307 §16 (SB 1907).

§4203. Successor attorneys-in-fact

(a) A principal may designate one or more successor attorneys-in-fact to act if the authority of a predecessor attorney-in-fact terminates.

(b) The principal may grant authority to another person, designated by name, by office, or by function, including the initial and any successor attorneys-in-fact, to designate at any time one or more successor attorneys-in-fact.

(c) A successor attorney-in-fact is not liable for the actions of the predecessor attorney-in-fact. **Leg.H.** Added Stats 1994 ch 307 §16 (SB 1907). Amended Stats 1999 ch 658 §33 (AB 891), operative July 1, 2000.

§4204. Compensation and reimbursement

An attorney-in-fact is entitled to reasonable compensation for services rendered to the principal as attorney-in-fact and to reimbursement for reasonable expenses incurred as a result of acting as attorney-in-fact. **Leg.H.** Added Stats 1994 ch 307 §16 (SB 1907).

§4205. Revocable delegation of authority by attorney-in-fact

(a) An attorney-in-fact may revocably delegate authority to perform mechanical acts to one or more persons qualified to exercise the authority delegated.

(b) The attorney-in-fact making a delegation remains responsible to the principal for the exercise or nonexercise of the delegated authority. **Leg.H.** Added Stats 1994 ch 307 §16 (SB 1907).

§4206. Appointment of conservator or guardian of estate

(a) If, following execution of a durable power of attorney, a court of the principal's domicile appoints a conservator of the estate, guardian of the estate, or other fiduciary charged with the management of all of the principal's property or all of the principal's property except specified exclusions, the attorney-in-fact is accountable to the fiduciary as well as to the principal. Except as provided in subdivision (b), the fiduciary has the same power to revoke or amend the durable power of attorney that the principal would have had if not incapacitated, subject to any required court approval.

(b) If a conservator of the estate is appointed by a court of this state, the conservator can revoke or amend the durable power of attorney only if the court in which the conservatorship proceeding is pending has first made an order authorizing or requiring the fiduciary to modify or revoke the durable power of attorney and the modification or revocation is in accord with the order.

(c) This section is not subject to limitation in the power of attorney. **Leg.H.** Added Stats 1994 ch 307 §16 (SB 1907). Amended Stats 1999 ch 658 §34 (AB 891), operative July 1, 2000.

§4207. Methods of resignation of attorney-in-fact

(a) An attorney-in-fact may resign by any of the following means:

(1) If the principal is competent, by giving notice to the principal.

(2) If a conservator has been appointed, by giving notice to the conservator.

(3) On written agreement of a successor who is designated in the power of attorney or pursuant to the terms of the power of attorney to serve as attorney-in-fact.

(4) Pursuant to a court order.

(b) This section is not subject to limitation in the power of attorney. **Leg.H.** Added Stats 1994 ch 307 §16 (SB 1907).

ARTICLE 2
Duties of Attorneys-in-Fact

Extent of duties. §4230.
Standard of care. §4231.
Breach of duty; Equitable excusal; Remedies for wrongful taking of property in bad faith, or by use of undue influence in bad faith or through commission of elder or dependent adult financial abuse; Attorney's fees and costs. §4231.5.
Conflicts of interests. §4232.
Commingling of property. §4233.
Communication with principal. §4234.
Incapacitation of principal. §4235.
Duty to keep records. §4236.
Duty of attorney-in-fact with special skills. §4237.
Duties upon termination of authority. §4238.

§4230. Extent of duties

(a) Except as provided in subdivisions (b) and (c), a person who is designated as an attorney-in-fact has no duty to exercise the authority granted in the power of attorney and is not subject to the other duties of an attorney-in-fact, regardless of whether the principal has become incapacitated, is missing, or is otherwise unable to act.

(b) Acting for the principal in one or more transactions does not obligate an attorney-in-fact to act for the principal in a subsequent transaction, but the attorney-in-fact has a duty to complete a transaction that the attorney-in-fact has commenced.

(c) If an attorney-in-fact has expressly agreed in writing to act for the principal, the attorney-in-fact has a duty to act pursuant to the terms of the agreement. The agreement to act on behalf of the principal is enforceable against the attorney-in-fact as a fiduciary regardless of whether there is any consideration to support a contractual obligation. **Leg.H.** Added Stats 1994 ch 307 §16 (SB 1907).

§4231. Standard of care

(a) Except as provided in subdivision (b), in dealing with property of the principal, an attorney-in-fact shall observe the standard of care that would be observed by a prudent person dealing with property of another and is not limited by any other statute restricting investments by fiduciaries.

(b) An attorney-in-fact who has special skills or expertise or was designated as an attorney-in-fact on the basis of representations of special skills or expertise shall observe the standard of care that would be observed by others with similar skills or expertise. **Leg.H.** Added Stats 1994 ch 307 §16 (SB 1907). Amended Stats 2010 ch 48 §1 (SB 1038), effective January 1, 2011.

§4231.5. Breach of duty; Equitable excusal; Remedies for wrongful taking of property in bad faith, or by use of undue influence in bad faith or through commission of elder or dependent adult financial abuse; Attorney's fees and costs

(a) If the attorney-in-fact breaches a duty pursuant to this division, the attorney-in-fact is chargeable with any of the following, as appropriate under the circumstances:

(1) Any loss or depreciation in value of the principal's property resulting from the breach of duty, with interest.

(2) Any profit made by the attorney-in-fact through the breach of duty, with interest.

(3) Any profit that would have accrued to the principal if the loss of profit is the result of the breach of duty.

(b) If the attorney-in-fact has acted reasonably and in good faith under the circumstances as known to the attorney-in-fact, the court, in its discretion, may excuse the attorney-in-fact in whole or in part from liability under subdivision (a) if it would be equitable to do so.

(c) If a court finds that a person has in bad faith wrongfully taken, concealed, or disposed of property that belongs to a principal under a power of attorney, or has taken, concealed, or disposed of property that belongs to a principal under a power of attorney by the use of undue influence in bad faith or through the commission of elder or dependent adult financial abuse, as defined in Section 15610.30 of the Welfare and Institutions Code, the person shall be liable for twice the value of the property recovered by an action to recover the property or for surcharge. In addition, except as otherwise required by law, including Section 15657.5 of the Welfare and Institutions Code, the person may, in the court's discretion, be liable for reasonable attorney's fees and costs to the prevailing party. The remedies provided in this section shall be in addition to any other remedies available in law to the principal or any successor in interest of the principal. **Leg.H.** Added Stats 2010 ch 48 §2 (SB 1038), effective January 1, 2011. Amended Stats 2013 ch 99 §2 (AB 381), effective January 1, 2014.

§4232. Conflicts of interests

(a) An attorney-in-fact has a duty to act solely in the interest of the principal and to avoid conflicts of interest.

(b) An attorney-in-fact is not in violation of the duty provided in subdivision (a) solely because the attorney-in-fact also benefits from acting for the principal, has conflicting interests in relation to the property, care, or affairs of the principal, or acts in an inconsistent manner regarding the respective interests of the principal and the attorney-in-fact. **Leg.H.** Added Stats 1994 ch 307 §16 (SB 1907).

§4233. Commingling of property

(a) The attorney-in-fact shall keep the principal's property separate and distinct from other property in a manner adequate to identify the property clearly as belonging to the principal.

(b) An attorney-in-fact holding property for a principal complies with subdivision (a) if the property is held in the name of the principal or in the name of the attorney-in-fact as attorney-in-fact for the principal. **Leg.H.** Added Stats 1994 ch 307 §16 (SB 1907).

§4234. Communication with principal

(a) To the extent reasonably practicable under the circumstances, an attorney-in-fact has a duty to keep in regular contact with the principal, to communicate with the principal, and to follow the instructions of the principal.

(b) With court approval, the attorney-in-fact may disobey instructions of the principal. **Leg.H.** Added Stats 1994 ch 307 §16 (SB 1907).

§4235. Incapacitation of principal

If the principal becomes wholly or partially incapacitated, or if there is a question concerning the capacity of the principal to give instructions to and supervise the attorney-in-fact, the attorney-in-fact may consult with a person previously designated by the principal for this purpose, and may also consult with and obtain information needed to carry out the attorney-in-fact's duties from the principal's spouse, physician, attorney, accountant, a member of the principal's family, or other person, business entity, or government agency with respect to matters to be undertaken on the principal's behalf and affecting the principal's personal affairs, welfare, family, property, and business interests. A person from whom information is requested shall disclose relevant information to the attorney-in-fact. Disclosure under this section is not a waiver of any privilege that may apply to the information disclosed. **Leg.H.** Added Stats 1994 ch 307 §16 (SB 1907).

§4236. Duty to keep records

(a) The attorney-in-fact shall keep records of all transactions entered into by the attorney-in-fact on behalf of the principal.

(b) The attorney-in-fact does not have a duty to make an account of transactions entered into on behalf of the principal, except in the following circumstances:

(1) At any time requested by the principal.

(2) Where the power of attorney requires the attorney-in-fact to account and specifies to whom the account is to be made.

(3) On request by the conservator of the estate of the principal while the principal is living.

(4) On request by the principal's personal representative or successor in interest after the death of the principal.

(5) Pursuant to court order.

(c) The following persons are entitled to examine and copy the records kept by the attorney-in-fact:

(1) The principal.

(2) The conservator of the estate of the principal while the principal is living.

(3) The principal's personal representative or successor in interest after the death of the principal.

(4) Any other person, pursuant to court order.

(d) This section is not subject to limitation in the power of attorney. **Leg.H.** Added Stats 1994 ch 307 §16 (SB 1907).

§4237. Duty of attorney-in-fact with special skills

An attorney-in-fact with special skills has a duty to apply the full extent of those skills. **Leg.H.** Added Stats 1994 ch 307 §16 (SB 1907).

§4238. Duties upon termination of authority

(a) On termination of an attorney-in-fact's authority, the attorney-in-fact shall promptly deliver possession or control of the principal's property as follows:

(1) If the principal is not incapacitated, to the principal or as directed by the principal.

(2) If the principal is incapacitated, to the following persons with the following priority:

(A) To a qualified successor attorney-in-fact.

(B) As to any community property, to the principal's spouse.

(C) To the principal's conservator of the estate or guardian of the estate.

(3) In the case of the death of the principal, to the principal's personal representative, if any, or the principal's successors.

(b) On termination of an attorney-in-fact's authority, the attorney-in-fact shall deliver copies of any records relating to transactions undertaken on the principal's behalf that are requested by the person to whom possession or control of the property is delivered.

(c) Termination of an attorney-in-fact's authority does not relieve the attorney-in-fact of any duty to render an account of actions taken as attorney-in-fact.

(d) The attorney-in-fact has the powers reasonably necessary under the circumstances to perform the duties provided by this section. **Leg.H.** Added Stats 1994 ch 307 §16 (SB 1907).

ARTICLE 3
Authority of Attorneys-in-Fact

Applicability of article to specified powers of attorney; Exceptions. §4260.
General authority. §4261.
Limitation on authority. §4262.
Incorporation by reference to statutes delineating authority. §4263.
Acts requiring express authorization. §4264.
Acts respecting wills. §4265.
Exercise of authority. §4266.

§4260. Applicability of article to specified powers of attorney; Exceptions

(a) Except as specified in subdivision (b), this article applies to all powers of attorney under this division.

(b) Sections 4261 and 4263 do not apply to the provisions of Part 3 (commencing with Section 4400). **Leg.H.** Added Stats 1994 ch 307 §16 (SB 1907). Amended Stats 1999 ch 658 §35 (AB 891), operative July 1, 2000; Stats 2011 ch 113 §1 (AB 1082), effective January 1, 2012.

§4261. General authority

If a power of attorney grants general authority to an attorney-in-fact and is not limited to one or more express actions, subjects, or purposes for which general authority is conferred, the attorney-in-fact has all the authority to act that a person having the capacity to contract may carry out through an attorney-in-fact specifically authorized to take the action. **Leg.H.** Added Stats 1994 ch 307 §16 (SB 1907).

§4262. Limitation on authority

Subject to this article, if a power of attorney grants limited authority to an attorney-in-fact, the attorney-in-fact has the following authority:

(a) The authority granted in the power of attorney, as limited with respect to permissible actions, subjects, or purposes.

(b) The authority incidental, necessary, or proper to carry out the granted authority. **Leg.H.** Added Stats 1994 ch 307 §16 (SB 1907).

§4263. Incorporation by reference to statutes delineating authority

(a) A power of attorney may grant authority to the attorney-in-fact by incorporating powers by reference to another statute, including, but not limited to, the following:

(1) Powers of attorneys-in-fact provided by the Uniform Statutory Form Power of Attorney Act (Part 3 (commencing with Section 4400)).

(2) Powers of guardians and conservators provided by Chapter 5 (commencing with Section 2350) and Chapter 6 (commencing with Section 2400) of Part 4 of Division 4.

(3) Powers of trustees provided by Chapter 2 (commencing with Section 16200) of Part 4 of Division 9.

(b) Incorporation by reference to another statute includes any amendments made to the incorporated provisions after the date of execution of the power of attorney. **Leg.H.** Added Stats 1994 ch 307 §16 (SB 1907).

§4264. Acts requiring express authorization

An attorney-in-fact under a power of attorney may perform any of the following acts on behalf of the principal or with the property of the principal only if the power of attorney expressly grants that authority to the attorney-in-fact:

(a) Create, modify, revoke, or terminate a trust, in whole or in part. If a power of attorney under this division empowers the attorney-in-fact to modify or revoke a trust created by the principal, the trust may be modified or revoked by the attorney-in-fact only as provided in the trust instrument.

(b) Fund with the principal's property a trust not created by the principal or a person authorized to create a trust on behalf of the principal.

(c) Make or revoke a gift of the principal's property in trust or otherwise.

(d) Exercise the right to reject, disclaim, release, or consent to a reduction in, or modification of, a share in, or payment from, an estate, trust, or other fund on behalf of the principal. This subdivision does not limit the attorney-in-fact's authority to disclaim a detrimental transfer to the principal with the approval of the court.

(e) Create or change survivorship interests in the principal's property or in property in which the principal may have an interest.

(f) Designate or change the designation of beneficiaries to receive any property, benefit, or contract right on the principal's death.

(g) Make a loan to the attorney-in-fact. **Leg.H.** Added Stats 1994 ch 307 §16 (SB 1907). Amended Stats 2011 ch 113 §2 (AB 1082), effective January 1, 2012.

§4265. Acts respecting wills

A power of attorney may not authorize an attorney-in-fact to make, publish, declare, amend, or revoke the principal's will. **Leg.H.** Added Stats 1994 ch 307 §16 (SB 1907). Amended Stats 1999 ch 658 §36 (AB 891), operative July 1, 2000.

§4266. Exercise of authority

The grant of authority to an attorney-in-fact, whether by the power of attorney, by statute, or by the court, does not in itself require or permit the exercise of the power. The exercise of authority by an attorney-in-fact is subject to the attorney-in-fact's fiduciary duties. **Leg.H.** Added Stats 1994 ch 307 §16 (SB 1907).

CHAPTER 5
RELATIONS WITH THIRD PERSONS

Rights and privileges of attorney-in-fact. §4300.
Scope of reliance by third person. §4301.
Requirement by third person of verification of power of attorney. §4302.
Liability of third person. §4303.
Effect of death or incapacity of principal. §4304.
Effect of lack of actual knowledge by attorney-in-fact of termination of power of attorney; Affidavit. §4305.
Rights and liabilities of third persons upon termination of power of attorney without actual knowledge of attorney-in-fact. §4306.
Certified copy of power of attorney. §4307.
Liability of third person conducting activities through employees. §4308.
Duties of third person when attorney-in-fact has breached agreement. §4309.
Duties of financial institution regarding deposit account. §4310.

§4300. Rights and privileges of attorney-in-fact

A third person shall accord an attorney-in-fact acting pursuant to the provisions of a power of attorney the same rights and privileges that would be accorded the principal if the principal were personally present and seeking to act. However, a third person is not required to honor the attorney-in-fact's authority or conduct business with the attorney-in-fact if the principal cannot require the third person to act or conduct business in the same circumstances. **Leg.H.** Added Stats 1994 ch 307 §16 (SB 1907).

§4301. Scope of reliance by third person

A third person may rely on, contract with, and deal with an attorney-in-fact with respect to the subjects and purposes encompassed or expressed in the power of attorney without regard to whether the power of attorney expressly authorizes the specific act, transaction, or decision by the attorney-in-fact. **Leg.H.** Added Stats 1994 ch 307 §16 (SB 1907).

§4302. Requirement by third person of verification of power of attorney

When requested to engage in transactions with an attorney-in-fact, a third person, before incurring any duty to comply with the power of attorney, may require the attorney-in-fact to provide identification, specimens of the signatures of the principal and the attorney-in-fact, and any other information reasonably necessary or appropriate to identify the principal and the attorney-in-fact and to facilitate the actions of the third person in transacting business with the attorney-in-fact. A third person may require an attorney-in-fact to provide the current and permanent residence addresses of the principal before agreeing to engage in a transaction with the attorney-in-fact. **Leg.H.** Added Stats 1994 ch 307 §16 (SB 1907).

§4303. Liability of third person

(a) A third person who acts in good faith reliance on a power of attorney is not liable to the principal or to any other person for so acting if all of the following requirements are satisfied:

(1) The power of attorney is presented to the third person by the attorney-in-fact designated in the power of attorney.

(2) The power of attorney appears on its face to be valid.

(3) The power of attorney includes a notary public's certificate of acknowledgment or is signed by two witnesses.

(b) Nothing in this section is intended to create an implication that a third person is liable for acting in reliance on a power of attorney under circumstances where the requirements of subdivision (a) are not satisfied. Nothing in this section affects any immunity that may otherwise exist apart from this section. **Leg.H.** Added Stats 1994 ch 307 §16 (SB 1907).

§4304. Effect of death or incapacity of principal

(a) The death of a principal who has executed a power of attorney, whether durable or nondurable, does not revoke or terminate the agency as to the attorney-in-fact or a third person who, without actual knowledge of the principal's death, acts in good faith under the power of attorney. Any action so taken, unless otherwise invalid or unenforceable, binds the principal's successors in interest.

(b) The incapacity of a principal who has previously executed a nondurable power of attorney does not revoke or terminate the agency as to the attorney-in-fact or a third person who, without actual knowledge of the incapacity of the principal, acts in good faith under the power of attorney. Any action so taken, unless otherwise invalid or unenforceable, binds the principal and the principal's successors in interest. **Leg.H.** Added Stats 1994 ch 307 §16 (SB 1907).

§4305. Effect of lack of actual knowledge by attorney-in-fact of termination of power of attorney; Affidavit

(a) As to acts undertaken in good faith reliance thereon, an affidavit executed by the attorney-in-fact under a power of attorney, whether durable or nondurable, stating that, at the time of the exercise of the power, the attorney-in-fact did not have actual knowledge of the termination of the power of attorney or the attorney-in-fact's authority by revocation or of the principal's death or incapacity is conclusive proof of the nonrevocation or nontermination of the power at that time. If the exercise of the power of attorney requires execution and delivery of any instrument that is recordable, the affidavit when authenticated for record is likewise recordable.

(b) This section does not affect any provision in a power of attorney for its termination by expiration of time or occurrence of an event other than express revocation or a change in the principal's capacity. **Leg.H.** Added Stats 1994 ch 307 §16 (SB 1907).

§4306. Rights and liabilities of third persons upon termination of power of attorney without actual knowledge of attorney-in-fact

(a) If an attorney-in-fact furnishes an affidavit pursuant to Section 4305, whether voluntarily or on demand, a third person dealing with the attorney-in-fact who refuses to accept the exercise of the attorney-in-fact's authority referred to in the affidavit is liable for attorney's fees incurred in an action or proceeding necessary to confirm the attorney-in-fact's qualifications or authority, unless the court determines that the third person believed in good faith that the attorney-in-fact was not qualified or was attempting to exceed or improperly exercise the attorney-in-fact's authority.

(b) The failure of a third person to demand an affidavit pursuant to Section 4305 does not affect the protection provided the third person by this chapter, and no inference as to whether a third person has acted in good faith may be drawn from the failure to demand an affidavit from the attorney-in-fact. **Leg.H.** Added Stats 1994 ch 307 §16 (SB 1907).

§4307. Certified copy of power of attorney

(a) A copy of a power of attorney certified under this section has the same force and effect as the original power of attorney.

(b) A copy of a power of attorney may be certified by any of the following:

(1) An attorney authorized to practice law in this state.

(2) A notary public in this state.

(3) An official of a state or of a political subdivision who is authorized to make certifications.

(c) The certification shall state that the certifying person has examined the original power of attorney and the copy and that the copy is a true and correct copy of the original power of attorney.

(d) Nothing in this section is intended to create an implication that a third person may be liable for acting in good faith reliance on a copy of a power of attorney that has not been certified under this section. **Leg.H.** Added Stats 1994 ch 307 §16 (SB 1907). Amended Stats 1995 ch 300 §9 (SB 984), effective August 3, 1995.

§4308. Liability of third person conducting activities through employees

(a) A third person who conducts activities through employees is not charged under this chapter with actual knowledge of any fact relating to a power of attorney, nor of a change in the authority of an attorney-in-fact, unless both of the following requirements are satisfied:

(1) The information is received at a home office or a place where there is an employee with responsibility to act on the information.

(2) The employee has a reasonable time in which to act on the information using the procedure and facilities that are available to the third person in the regular course of its operations.

(b) Knowledge of an employee in one branch or office of an entity that conducts business through branches or multiple offices is not attributable to an employee in another branch or office. **Leg.H.** Added Stats 1994 ch 307 §16 (SB 1907).

§4309. Duties of third person when attorney-in-fact has breached agreement

Nothing in this chapter requires a third person to engage in any transaction with an attorney-in-fact if the attorney-in-fact has previously breached any agreement with the third person. **Leg.H.** Added Stats 1994 ch 307 §16 (SB 1907).

§4310. Duties of financial institution regarding deposit account

Without limiting the generality of Section 4300, nothing in this chapter requires a financial institution to open a deposit account for a principal at the request of an attorney-in-fact if the principal is not currently a depositor of the financial institution or to make a loan to the attorney-in-fact on the principal's behalf if the principal is not currently a borrower of the financial institution. **Leg.H.** Added Stats 1994 ch 307 §16 (SB 1907).

PART 3
UNIFORM STATUTORY FORM POWER OF ATTORNEY

Chapter 1. General Provisions.
Chapter 2. Construction of Powers.

CHAPTER 1
GENERAL PROVISIONS

Citation of part. §4400.
Statutory form of power of attorney. §4401.
Requirements for legal sufficiency. §4402.
"All powers listed above". §4403.
Legally sufficient durable power of attorney. §4404.
Limitation to take effect on occurrence of event or contingency. §4405.
Action to require third person to honor authority of agent under power of attorney. §4406.
Application of division to statutory form of power of attorney. §4407.
Use of other forms. §4408.
Use of form complying with prior law. §4409.

§4400. Citation of part

This part may be cited as the Uniform Statutory Form Power of Attorney Act. **Leg.H.** Added Stats 1994 ch 307 §16 (SB 1907).

§4401. Statutory form of power of attorney

The following statutory form power of attorney is legally sufficient when the requirements of Section 4402 are satisfied:

UNIFORM STATUTORY FORM POWER OF ATTORNEY
(California Probate Code Section 4401)

NOTICE: THE POWERS GRANTED BY THIS DOCUMENT ARE BROAD AND SWEEPING. THEY ARE EXPLAINED IN THE UNIFORM STATUTORY FORM POWER OF ATTORNEY ACT (CALIFORNIA PROBATE CODE SECTIONS 4400–4465). THE POWERS LISTED IN THIS DOCUMENT DO NOT INCLUDE ALL POWERS THAT ARE AVAILABLE UNDER THE PROBATE CODE. ADDITIONAL POWERS AVAILABLE UNDER THE PROBATE CODE MAY BE ADDED BY SPECIFICALLY LISTING THEM UNDER THE SPECIAL INSTRUCTIONS SECTION OF THIS DOCUMENT. IF YOU HAVE ANY QUESTIONS ABOUT THESE POWERS, OBTAIN COMPETENT LEGAL ADVICE. THIS DOCUMENT DOES NOT AUTHORIZE ANYONE TO MAKE MEDICAL AND OTHER HEALTH-CARE DECISIONS FOR YOU. YOU MAY REVOKE THIS POWER OF ATTORNEY IF YOU LATER WISH TO DO SO.

I _____
(your name and address)
appoint _____
(name and address of the person appointed, or of each person appointed if you want to designate more than one)
as my agent (attorney-in-fact) to act for me in any lawful way with respect to the following initialed subjects:

TO GRANT ALL OF THE FOLLOWING POWERS, INITIAL THE LINE IN FRONT OF (N) AND IGNORE THE LINES IN FRONT OF THE OTHER POWERS.

TO GRANT ONE OR MORE, BUT FEWER THAN ALL, OF THE FOLLOWING POWERS, INITIAL THE LINE IN FRONT OF EACH POWER YOU ARE GRANTING.

TO WITHHOLD A POWER, DO NOT INITIAL THE LINE IN FRONT OF IT. YOU MAY, BUT NEED NOT, CROSS OUT EACH POWER WITHHELD.

INITIAL
____ (A) Real property transactions.
____ (B) Tangible personal property transactions.
____ (C) Stock and bond transactions.
____ (D) Commodity and option transactions.
____ (E) Banking and other financial institution transactions.
____ (F) Business operating transactions.
____ (G) Insurance and annuity transactions.
____ (H) Estate, trust, and other beneficiary transactions.
____ (I) Claims and litigation.
____ (J) Personal and family maintenance.
____ (K) Benefits from social security, medicare, medicaid, or other governmental programs, or civil or military service.
____ (L) Retirement plan transactions.
____ (M) Tax matters.
____ (N) ALL OF THE POWERS LISTED ABOVE.
YOU NEED NOT INITIAL ANY OTHER LINES IF YOU INITIAL LINE (N).

SPECIAL INSTRUCTIONS:
ON THE FOLLOWING LINES YOU MAY GIVE SPECIAL INSTRUCTIONS LIMITING OR EXTENDING THE POWERS GRANTED TO YOUR AGENT.
_____
_____
_____
_____
_____
_____
_____

UNLESS YOU DIRECT OTHERWISE ABOVE, THIS POWER OF ATTORNEY IS EFFECTIVE IMMEDIATELY AND WILL CONTINUE UNTIL IT IS REVOKED.

This power of attorney will continue to be effective even though I become incapacitated.

STRIKE THE PRECEDING SENTENCE IF YOU DO NOT WANT THIS POWER OF ATTORNEY TO CONTINUE IF YOU BECOME INCAPACITATED.

EXERCISE OF POWER OF ATTORNEY WHERE
MORE THAN ONE AGENT DESIGNATED

If I have designated more than one agent, the agents are to act _____

IF YOU APPOINTED MORE THAN ONE AGENT AND YOU WANT EACH AGENT TO BE ABLE TO ACT ALONE WITHOUT THE OTHER AGENT JOINING, WRITE THE WORD "SEPARATELY" IN THE BLANK SPACE ABOVE. IF YOU DO NOT INSERT ANY WORD IN THE BLANK SPACE, OR IF YOU INSERT THE WORD "JOINTLY", THEN ALL OF YOUR AGENTS MUST ACT OR SIGN TOGETHER.

I agree that any third party who receives a copy of this document may act under it. A third party may seek identification. Revocation of the power of attorney is not effective as to a third party until the third party has actual knowledge of the revocation. I agree to indemnify the third party for any claims that arise against the third party because of reliance on this power of attorney.

Signed this ____ day of _____, 20____
_____
(your signature)
State of _____ County of _____
BY ACCEPTING OR ACTING UNDER THE APPOINTMENT, THE AGENT ASSUMES THE FIDUCIARY AND OTHER LEGAL RESPONSIBILITIES OF AN AGENT.
[Include certificate of acknowledgment of notary public in compliance with Section 1189 of the Civil Code or other applicable law.]

Leg.H. Added Stats 1994 ch 307 §16 (SB 1907). Amended Stats 2005 ch 251 §1 (SB 158); Stats 2011 ch 113 §3 (AB 1082), effective January 1, 2012.

§4402. Requirements for legal sufficiency

A statutory form power of attorney under this part is legally sufficient if all of the following requirements are satisfied:

(a) The wording of the form complies substantially with Section 4401. A form does not fail to comply substantially with Section 4401 merely because the form does not include the provisions of Section 4401 relating to designation of co-agents. A form does not fail to comply substantially with Section 4401 merely because the form uses the sentence "Revocation of the power of attorney is not effective as to a third party until the third party learns of the revocation" in place of the sentence "Revocation of the power of attorney is not effective as to a third party until the third party has actual knowledge of the revocation," in which case the form shall be interpreted as if it contained the sentence "Revocation of the power of attorney is not effective as to a third party until the third party has actual knowledge of the revocation."

(b) The form is properly completed.

(c) The signature of the principal is acknowledged. **Leg.H.** Added Stats 1994 ch 307 §16 (SB 1907). Amended Stats 1995 ch 300 §10 (SB 984), effective August 3, 1995.

§4403. "All powers listed above"

If the line in front of (N) of the statutory form under Section 4401 is initialed, an initial on the line in front of any other power does not limit the powers granted by line (N). **Leg.H.** Added Stats 1994 ch 307 §16 (SB 1907).

§4404. Legally sufficient durable power of attorney

A statutory form power of attorney legally sufficient under this part is durable to the extent that the power of attorney contains language, such as "This power of attorney will continue to be effective even though I become incapacitated," showing the intent of the principal that the power granted may be exercised notwithstanding later incapacity. **Leg.H.** Added Stats 1994 ch 307 §16 (SB 1907).

§4405. Limitation to take effect on occurrence of event or contingency

(a) A statutory form power of attorney under this part that limits the power to take effect upon the occurrence of a specified event or contingency, including, but not limited to, the incapacity of the principal, may contain a provision designating one or more persons who, by a written declaration under penalty of perjury, have the power to determine conclusively that the specified event or contingency has occurred.

(b) A statutory form power of attorney that contains the provision described in subdivision (a) becomes effective when the person or persons designated in the power of attorney execute a written declaration under penalty of perjury that the specified event or contingency has occurred, and any person may act in reliance on the written declaration without liability to the principal or to any other person, regardless whether the specified event or contingency has actually occurred.

(c) The provision described in subdivision (a) may be included in the "Special Instructions" portion of the form set forth in Section 4401.

(d) Subdivisions (a) and (b) do not provide the exclusive method by which a statutory form power of attorney under this part may be limited to take effect upon the occurrence of a specified event or contingency. **Leg.H.** Added Stats 1994 ch 307 §16 (SB 1907).

§4406. Action to require third person to honor authority of agent under power of attorney

(a) If a third person to whom a properly executed statutory form power of attorney under this part is presented refuses to honor the agent's authority under the power of attorney within a reasonable time, the third person may be compelled to honor the agent's authority under the power of attorney in an action brought against the third person for this purpose, except that the third person may not be compelled to honor the agent's authority if the principal could not compel the third person to act in the same circumstances.

(b) If an action is brought under this section, the court shall award attorney's fees to the agent if the court finds that the third person acted unreasonably in refusing to accept the agent's authority under the statutory form power of attorney.

(c) For the purpose of subdivision (b), and without limiting any other grounds that may constitute a reasonable refusal to accept an agent's authority under a statutory form power of attorney, a third person shall not be deemed to have acted unreasonably in refusing to accept an agent's authority if the refusal is authorized or required by state or federal statute or regulation.

(d) Notwithstanding subdivision (c), a third person's refusal to accept an agent's authority under a statutory form power of attorney under this part shall be deemed unreasonable if the only reason for the refusal is that the power of attorney is not on a form prescribed by the third person to whom the power of attorney is presented.

(e) The remedy provided in this section is cumulative and nonexclusive. **Leg.H.** Added Stats 1994 ch 307 §16 (SB 1907).

§4407. Application of division to statutory form of power of attorney

The provisions of this division apply to a statutory form power of attorney except when there is a conflicting provision in this part, in which case the provision of this part governs, or when a provision of this division is expressly made inapplicable to a statutory form power of attorney. **Leg.H.** Added Stats 1994 ch 307 §16 (SB 1907). Amended Stats 2011 ch 113 §4 (AB 1082), effective January 1, 2012.

§4408. Use of other forms

Nothing in this part affects or limits the use of any other form for a power of attorney. A form that complies with the requirements of any law other than the provisions of this part may be used instead of the form set forth in Section 4401, and none of the provisions of this part apply if the other form is used. **Leg.H.** Added Stats 1994 ch 307 §16 (SB 1907).

§4409. Use of form complying with prior law

(a) A statutory short form power of attorney executed before, on, or after the repeal of Chapter 3 (commencing with Section 2450) of Title 9 of Part 4 of Division 3 of the Civil Code by Chapter 986 of the Statutes of 1990, using a form that complied with former Section 2450 of the Civil Code, as originally enacted by Chapter 602 of the Statutes of 1984, or as amended by Chapter 403 of the Statutes of 1985, is as valid as if Chapter 3 (commencing with Section 2450) of Title 9 of Part 4 of Division 3 of the Civil Code had not been repealed by, and former Section 2511 of the Civil Code amended by, Chapter 986 of the Statutes of 1990.

(b) A statutory form power of attorney executed before, on, or after the repeal of Chapter 3.5 (commencing with Section 2475) of Title 9 of Part 4 of Division 3 of the Civil Code by the act that enacted this section, using a form that complied with the repealed chapter of the Civil Code is as valid as if that chapter had not been repealed. **Leg.H.** Added Stats 1994 ch 307 §16 (SB 1907). Amended Stats 1995 ch 300 §11 (SB 984), effective August 3, 1995.

CHAPTER 2
CONSTRUCTION OF POWERS

Powers of agent. §4450.
"Real property transactions". §4451.
"Tangible personal property transactions". §4452.
"Stock and bond transactions". §4453.
"Commodity and option transactions". §4454.
"Banking transactions" and "Financial institution transactions". §4455.
"Business operating transactions". §4456.
"Insurance and annuity transactions". §4457.
"Estate transactions". §4458.
"Claims and litigation". §4459.
"Personal and family maintenance". §4460.
Benefits from governmental programs, civil or military service. §4461.
"Retirement plan transactions". §4462.
"Tax matters". §4463.
Application to present or later acquired interests. §4464.
Actions specified in Section 4264. §4465.

§4450. Powers of agent

By executing a statutory form power of attorney with respect to a subject listed in Section 4401, the principal, except as limited or extended by the principal in the power of attorney, empowers the agent, for that subject, to do all of the following:

(a) Demand, receive, and obtain by litigation or otherwise, money or other thing of value to which the principal is, may become, or claims to be entitled, and conserve, invest, disburse, or use anything so received for the purposes intended.

(b) Contract in any manner with any person, on terms agreeable to the agent, to accomplish a purpose of a transaction, and perform, rescind, reform, release, or modify the contract or another contract made by or on behalf of the principal.

(c) Execute, acknowledge, seal, and deliver a deed, revocation, mortgage, lease, notice, check, release, or other instrument the agent considers desirable to accomplish a purpose of a transaction.

(d) Prosecute, defend, submit to arbitration, settle, and propose or accept a compromise with respect to, a claim existing in favor of or against the principal or intervene in litigation relating to the claim.

(e) Seek on the principal's behalf the assistance of a court to carry out an act authorized by the power of attorney.

(f) Engage, compensate, and discharge an attorney, accountant, expert witness, or other assistant.

(g) Keep appropriate records of each transaction, including an accounting of receipts and disbursements.

(h) Prepare, execute, and file a record, report, or other document the agent considers desirable to safeguard or promote the principal's interest under a statute or governmental regulation.

(i) Reimburse the agent for expenditures properly made by the agent in exercising the powers granted by the power of attorney.

(j) In general, do any other lawful act with respect to the subject. **Leg.H.** Added Stats 1994 ch 307 §16 (SB 1907).

§4451. "Real property transactions"

In a statutory form power of attorney, the language granting power with respect to real property transactions empowers the agent to do all of the following:

(a) Accept as a gift or as security for a loan, reject, demand, buy, lease, receive, or otherwise acquire, an interest in real property or a right incident to real property.

(b) Sell, exchange, convey with or without covenants, quitclaim, release, surrender, mortgage, encumber, partition, consent to partitioning, subdivide, apply for zoning, rezoning, or other governmental permits, plat or consent to platting, develop, grant options concerning, lease, sublease, or otherwise dispose of, an interest in real property or a right incident to real property.

(c) Release, assign, satisfy, and enforce by litigation or otherwise, a mortgage, deed of trust, encumbrance, lien, or other claim to real property which exists or is asserted.

(d) Do any act of management or of conservation with respect to an interest in real property, or a right incident to real property, owned, or claimed to be owned, by the principal, including all of the following:

(1) Insuring against a casualty, liability, or loss.

(2) Obtaining or regaining possession, or protecting the interest or right, by litigation or otherwise.

(3) Paying, compromising, or contesting taxes or assessments, or applying for and receiving refunds in connection with them.

(4) Purchasing supplies, hiring assistance or labor, and making repairs or alterations in the real property.

(e) Use, develop, alter, replace, remove, erect, or install structures or other improvements upon real property in or incident to which the principal has, or claims to have, an interest or right.

(f) Participate in a reorganization with respect to real property or a legal entity that owns an interest in or right incident to real property and receive and hold shares of stock or obligations received in a plan of reorganization, and act with respect to them, including all of the following:

(1) Selling or otherwise disposing of them.

(2) Exercising or selling an option, conversion, or similar right with respect to them.

(3) Voting them in person or by proxy.

(g) Change the form of title of an interest in or right incident to real property.

(h) Dedicate to public use, with or without consideration, easements or other real property in which the principal has, or claims to have, an interest or right. **Leg.H.** Added Stats 1994 ch 307 §16 (SB 1907).

§4452. "Tangible personal property transactions"

In a statutory form power of attorney, the language granting power with respect to tangible personal property transactions empowers the agent to do all of the following:

(a) Accept as a gift or as security for a loan, reject, demand, buy, receive, or otherwise acquire ownership or possession of tangible personal property or an interest in tangible personal property.

(b) Sell, exchange, convey with or without covenants, release, surrender, mortgage, encumber, pledge, hypothecate, create a security interest in, pawn, grant options concerning, lease, sublease to others, or otherwise dispose of tangible personal property or an interest in tangible personal property.

(c) Release, assign, satisfy, or enforce by litigation or otherwise, a mortgage, security interest, encumbrance, lien, or other claim on behalf of the principal, with respect to tangible personal property or an interest in tangible personal property.

(d) Do an act of management or conservation with respect to tangible personal property or an interest in tangible personal property on behalf of the principal, including all of the following:

(1) Insuring against casualty, liability, or loss.

(2) Obtaining or regaining possession, or protecting the property or interest, by litigation or otherwise.

(3) Paying, compromising, or contesting taxes or assessments or applying for and receiving refunds in connection with taxes or assessments.

(4) Moving from place to place.

(5) Storing for hire or on a gratuitous bailment.

(6) Using, altering, and making repairs or alterations. **Leg.H.** Added Stats 1994 ch 307 §16 (SB 1907).

§4453. "Stock and bond transactions"

In a statutory form power of attorney, the language granting power with respect to stock and bond transactions empowers the agent to do all of the following:

(a) Buy, sell, and exchange stocks, bonds, mutual funds, and all other types of securities and financial instruments except commodity futures contracts and call and put options on stocks and stock indexes.

(b) Receive certificates and other evidences of ownership with respect to securities.

(c) Exercise voting rights with respect to securities in person or by proxy, enter into voting trusts, and consent to limitations on the right to vote. **Leg.H.** Added Stats 1994 ch 307 §16 (SB 1907).

§4454. "Commodity and option transactions"

In a statutory form power of attorney, the language granting power with respect to commodity and option transactions empowers the agent to do all of the following:

(a) Buy, sell, exchange, assign, settle, and exercise commodity futures contracts and call and put options on stocks and stock indexes traded on a regulated option exchange.

(b) Establish, continue, modify, and terminate option accounts with a broker. **Leg.H.** Added Stats 1994 ch 307 §16 (SB 1907).

§4455. "Banking transactions" and "Financial institution transactions"

In a statutory form power of attorney, the language granting power with respect to banking and other financial institution transactions empowers the agent to do all of the following:

(a) Continue, modify, and terminate an account or other banking arrangement made by or on behalf of the principal.

(b) Establish, modify, and terminate an account or other banking arrangement with a bank, trust company, savings and loan association, credit union, thrift company, industrial loan company, brokerage firm, or other financial institution selected by the agent.

(c) Hire or close a safe deposit box or space in a vault.

(d) Contract to procure other services available from a financial institution as the agent considers desirable.

(e) Withdraw by check, order, or otherwise money or property of the principal deposited with or left in the custody of a financial institution.

(f) Receive bank statements, vouchers, notices, and similar documents from a financial institution and act with respect to them.

(g) Enter a safe deposit box or vault and withdraw or add to the contents.

(h) Borrow money at an interest rate agreeable to the agent and pledge as security personal property of the principal necessary in order to borrow, pay, renew, or extend the time of payment of a debt of the principal.

(i) Make, assign, draw, endorse, discount, guarantee, and negotiate promissory notes, checks, drafts, and other negotiable or nonnegotiable paper of the principal, or payable to the principal or the principal's order, receive the cash or other proceeds of those transactions, and accept a draft drawn by a person upon the principal and pay it when due.

(j) Receive for the principal and act upon a sight draft, warehouse receipt, or other negotiable or nonnegotiable instrument.

(k) Apply for and receive letters of credit, credit cards, and traveler's checks from a financial institution, and give an indemnity or other agreement in connection with letters of credit.

(*l*) Consent to an extension of the time of payment with respect to commercial paper or a financial transaction with a financial institution. **Leg.H.** Added Stats 1994 ch 307 §16 (SB 1907).

§4456. "Business operating transactions"

In a statutory form power of attorney, the language granting power with respect to business operating transactions empowers the agent to do all of the following:

(a) Operate, buy, sell, enlarge, reduce, and terminate a business interest.

(b) To the extent that an agent is permitted by law to act for a principal and subject to the terms of the partnership agreement:

(1) Perform a duty or discharge a liability and exercise a right, power, privilege, or option that the principal has, may have, or claims to have, under a partnership agreement, whether or not the principal is a partner.

(2) Enforce the terms of a partnership agreement by litigation or otherwise.

(3) Defend, submit to arbitration, settle, or compromise litigation to which the principal is a party because of membership in the partnership.

(c) Exercise in person or by proxy, or enforce by litigation or otherwise, a right, power, privilege, or option the principal has or claims to have as the holder of a bond, share, or other instrument of similar character, and defend, submit to arbitration, settle, or compromise litigation to which the principal is a party because of a bond, share, or similar instrument.

(d) With respect to a business owned solely by the principal:

(1) Continue, modify, renegotiate, extend, and terminate a contract made with an individual or a legal entity, firm, association, or corporation by or on behalf of the principal with respect to the business before execution of the power of attorney.

(2) Determine the policy of the business as to (A) the location of its operation, (B) the nature and extent of its business, (C) the methods of manufacturing, selling, merchandising, financing, accounting, and advertising employed in its operation, (D) the amount and types of insurance carried, and (E) the mode of engaging, compensating, and dealing with its accountants, attorneys, and other agents and employees.

(3) Change the name or form of organization under which the business is operated and enter into a partnership agreement with other persons or organize a corporation to take over all or part of the operation of the business.

(4) Demand and receive money due or claimed by the principal or on the principal's behalf in the operation of the business, and control and disburse the money in the operation of the business.

(e) Put additional capital into a business in which the principal has an interest.

(f) Join in a plan of reorganization, consolidation, or merger of the business.

(g) Sell or liquidate a business or part of it at the time and upon the terms the agent considers desirable.

(h) Represent the principal in establishing the value of a business under a buy-out agreement to which the principal is a party.

(i) Prepare, sign, file, and deliver reports, compilations of information, returns, or other papers with respect to a business which are required by a governmental agency or instrumentality or which the agent considers desirable, and make related payments.

(j) Pay, compromise, or contest taxes or assessments and do any other act which the agent considers desirable to protect the principal from illegal or unnecessary taxation, fines, penalties, or assessments with respect to a business, including attempts to recover, in any manner permitted by law, money paid before or after the execution of the power of attorney. **Leg.H.** Added Stats 1994 ch 307 §16 (SB 1907).

§4457. "Insurance and annuity transactions"

In a statutory form power of attorney, the language granting power with respect to insurance and annuity transactions empowers the agent to do all of the following:

(a) Continue, pay the premium or assessment on, modify, rescind, release, or terminate a contract procured by or on behalf of the principal that insures or provides an annuity to either the principal or another person, whether or not the principal is a beneficiary under the contract.

(b) Procure new, different, and additional contracts of insurance and annuities for the principal and the principal's spouse, children, and other dependents, and select the amount, type of insurance or annuity, and mode of payment.

(c) Pay the premium or assessment on, modify, rescind, release, or terminate a contract of insurance or annuity procured by the agent.

(d) Apply for and receive a loan on the security of the contract of insurance or annuity.

(e) Surrender and receive the cash surrender value.

(f) Exercise an election.

(g) Change the manner of paying premiums.

(h) Change or convert the type of insurance contract or annuity as to any insurance contract or annuity with respect to which the principal has or claims to have a power described in this section.

(i) Apply for and procure government aid to guarantee or pay premiums of a contract of insurance on the life of the principal.

(j) Collect, sell, assign, hypothecate, borrow upon, or pledge the interest of the principal in a contract of insurance or annuity.

(k) Pay from proceeds or otherwise, compromise or contest, and apply for refunds in connection with, a tax or assessment levied by a taxing authority with respect to a contract of insurance or annuity or its proceeds or liability accruing by reason of the tax or assessment. **Leg.H.** Added Stats 1994 ch 307 §16 (SB 1907). Amended Stats 2011 ch 113 §5 (AB 1082), effective January 1, 2012.

§4458. "Estate transactions"

In a statutory form power of attorney, the language granting power with respect to estate, trust, and other beneficiary transactions, empowers the agent to act for the principal in all matters that affect a trust, probate estate, guardianship, conservatorship, escrow, custodianship, or other fund from which the principal is, may become, or claims to be entitled, as a beneficiary, to a share or payment, including the power to do all of the following:

(a) Accept, receive, receipt for, sell, assign, pledge, or exchange, a share in, or payment from, the fund.

(b) Demand or obtain by litigation or otherwise money or other thing of value to which the principal is, may become, or claims to be entitled by reason of the fund.

(c) Initiate, participate in, and oppose litigation to ascertain the meaning, validity, or effect of a deed, will, declaration of trust, or other instrument or transaction affecting the interest of the principal.

(d) Initiate, participate in, and oppose litigation to remove, substitute, or surcharge a fiduciary.

(e) Conserve, invest, disburse, and use anything received for an authorized purpose.

(f) Transfer an interest of the principal in real property, stocks, bonds, accounts with financial institutions, insurance, and other property, to the trustee of a revocable trust created by the principal as settlor.

(g) Disclaim a detrimental transfer to the principal with the approval of the court. **Leg.H.** Added Stats 1994 ch 307 §16 (SB 1907). Amended Stats 2011 ch 113 §6 (AB 1082), effective January 1, 2012.

§4459. "Claims and litigation"

In a statutory form power of attorney, the language with respect to claims and litigation empowers the agent to do all of the following:

(a) Assert and prosecute before a court or administrative agency a claim, claim for relief, cause of action, counterclaim, cross-complaint, or offset, and defend against an individual, a legal entity, or government, including suits to recover property or other thing of value, to recover damages sustained by the principal, to eliminate or modify tax liability, or to seek an injunction, specific performance, or other relief.

(b) Bring an action to determine adverse claims, intervene in litigation, and act as amicus curiae.

(c) In connection with litigation:

(1) Procure an attachment, garnishment, libel, order of arrest, or other preliminary, provisional, or intermediate relief and use any available procedure to effect, enforce, or satisfy a judgment, order, or decree.

(2) Perform any lawful act, including acceptance of tender, offer of judgment, admission of facts, submission of a controversy on an agreed statement of facts, consent to examination before trial, and binding the principal in litigation.

(d) Submit to arbitration, settle, and propose or accept a compromise with respect to a claim or litigation.

(e) Waive the issuance and service of process upon the principal, accept service of process, appear for the principal, designate persons upon whom process directed to the principal may be served, execute and file or deliver stipulations on the principal's behalf, verify pleadings, seek appellate review, procure and give surety and indemnity bonds, contract and pay for the preparation and printing of records and briefs, receive and execute and file or deliver a consent, waiver, release, satisfaction of judgment, notice, agreement, or other instrument in connection with the prosecution, settlement, or defense of a claim or litigation.

(f) Act for the principal with respect to bankruptcy or insolvency proceedings, whether voluntary or involuntary, concerning the principal or some other person, or with respect to a reorganization proceeding, or with respect to an assignment for the benefit of creditors, receivership, or application for the appointment of a receiver or trustee which affects an interest of the principal in property or other thing of value.

(g) Pay a judgment against the principal or a settlement made in connection with litigation and receive and conserve money or other thing of value paid in settlement of or as proceeds of a claim or litigation. **Leg.H.** Added Stats 1994 ch 307 §16 (SB 1907). Amended Stats 2022 ch 851 §7 (SB 688), effective January 1, 2023.

§4460. "Personal and family maintenance"

(a) In a statutory form power of attorney, the language granting power with respect to personal and family maintenance empowers the agent to do all of the following:

(1) Do the acts necessary to maintain the customary standard of living of the principal, the principal's spouse, children, and other individuals customarily or legally entitled to be supported by the principal, including providing living quarters by purchase, lease, or other contract, or paying the operating costs, including interest, amortization payments, repairs, and taxes on premises owned by the principal and occupied by those individuals.

(2) Provide for the individuals described in paragraph (1) all of the following:

(A) Normal domestic help.

(B) Usual vacations and travel expenses.

(C) Funds for shelter, clothing, food, appropriate education, and other current living costs.

(3) Pay for the individuals described in paragraph (1) necessary medical, dental, and surgical care, hospitalization, and custodial care.

(4) Continue any provision made by the principal, for the individuals described in paragraph (1), for automobiles or other means of transportation, including registering, licensing, insuring, and replacing them.

(5) Maintain or open charge accounts for the convenience of the individuals described in paragraph (1) and open new accounts the agent considers desirable to accomplish a lawful purpose.

(6) Continue payments incidental to the membership or affiliation of the principal in a church, club, society, order, or other organization and continue contributions to those organizations.

(b) The authority of an agent with respect to personal and family maintenance under this section is not dependent on any other grant of authority to the agent to make gifts on the principal's behalf and is not limited by any limitation that otherwise applies to the authority of the agent to make gifts on the principal's behalf. **Leg.H.** Added Stats 1994 ch 307 §16 (SB 1907). Amended Stats 2011 ch 113 §7 (AB 1082), effective January 1, 2012.

§4461. Benefits from governmental programs, civil or military service

In a statutory form power of attorney, the language granting power with respect to benefits from social security, Medicare, Medicaid, or other governmental programs, or civil or military service, empowers the agent to do all of the following:

(a) Execute vouchers in the name of the principal for allowances and reimbursements payable by the United States or a foreign government or by a state or subdivision of a state to the principal, including allowances and reimbursements for transportation of the individuals described in paragraph (1) of subdivision (a) of Section 4460, and for shipment of their household effects.

(b) Take possession and order the removal and shipment of property of the principal from a post, warehouse, depot, dock, or other place of storage or safekeeping, either governmental or private, and execute and deliver a release, voucher, receipt, bill of lading, shipping ticket, certificate, or other instrument for that purpose.

(c) Prepare, file, and prosecute a claim of the principal to a benefit or assistance, financial or otherwise, to which the principal claims to be entitled, under a statute or governmental regulation.

(d) Prosecute, defend, submit to arbitration, settle, and propose or accept a compromise with respect to any benefits the principal may be entitled to receive.

(e) Receive the financial proceeds of a claim of the type described in this section, conserve, invest, disburse, or use anything received for a lawful purpose. **Leg.H.** Added Stats 1994 ch 307 §16 (SB 1907). Amended Stats 2011 ch 113 §8 (AB 1082), effective January 1, 2012; Stats 2012 ch 162 §138 (SB 1171), effective January 1, 2013.

§4462. "Retirement plan transactions"

In a statutory form power of attorney, the language granting power with respect to retirement plan transactions empowers the agent to do all of the following:

(a) Select payment options under any retirement plan in which the principal participates, including plans for self-employed individuals.

(b) Make voluntary contributions to those plans.

(c) Exercise the investment powers available under any self-directed retirement plan.

(d) Make rollovers of plan benefits into other retirement plans.

(e) If authorized by the plan, borrow from, sell assets to, and purchase assets from the plan.

(f) Waive the right of the principal to be a beneficiary of a joint or survivor annuity if the principal is a spouse who is not employed. **Leg.H.** Added Stats 1994 ch 307 §16 (SB 1907). Amended Stats 2011 ch 113 §9 (AB 1082), effective January 1, 2012.

§4463. "Tax matters"

In a statutory form power of attorney, the language granting power with respect to tax matters empowers the agent to do all of the following:

(a) Prepare, sign, and file federal, state, local, and foreign income, gift, payroll, Federal Insurance Contributions Act returns, and other tax returns, claims for refunds, requests for extension of time, petitions regarding tax matters, and any other tax-related documents, including receipts, offers, waivers, consents (including consents and agreements under Internal Revenue Code Section 2032A or any successor section), closing agreements, and any power of attorney required by the Internal Revenue Service or other taxing authority with respect to a tax year upon which the statute of limitations has not run and to the tax year in which the power of attorney was executed and any subsequent tax year.

(b) Pay taxes due, collect refunds, post bonds, receive confidential information, and contest deficiencies determined by the Internal Revenue Service or other taxing authority.

(c) Exercise any election available to the principal under federal, state, local, or foreign tax law.

(d) Act for the principal in all tax matters for all periods before the Internal Revenue Service and any other taxing authority. **Leg.H.** Added Stats 1994 ch 307 §16 (SB 1907).

§4464. Application to present or later acquired interests

The powers described in this chapter are exercisable equally with respect to an interest the principal has when the statutory form power of attorney is executed or acquires later, whether or not the property is located in this state, and whether or not the powers are exercised or the power of attorney is executed in this state. **Leg.H.** Added Stats 1994 ch 307 §16 (SB 1907).

§4465. Actions specified in Section 4264

A statutory form power of attorney under this part does not empower the agent to take any of the actions specified in Section 4264 unless the statutory form power of attorney expressly grants that authority to the attorney-in-fact. **Leg.H.** Added Stats 2011 ch 113 §11 (AB 1082), effective January 1, 2012.

Former Sections: Former Prob C §4465, relating to modification or revocation of trust created by principal, was added Stats 1994 ch 307 §16 and repealed Stats 2011 ch 113 §10. Historical derivation: Former CC §2499.5, as added Stats 1990 ch 986 §3.

Prior Law: Former Prob C §4465, relating to modification or revocation of trust created by principal, was added Stats 1994 ch 307 §16 and repealed Stats 2011 ch 113 §10. Historical derivation: Former CC §2499.5, as added Stats 1990 ch 986 §3.

PART 4
JUDICIAL PROCEEDINGS CONCERNING POWERS OF ATTORNEY

Chapter 1. General Provisions.
Chapter 2. Jurisdiction and Venue.
Chapter 3. Petitions, Orders, Appeals.

CHAPTER 1
GENERAL PROVISIONS

Judicial intervention. §4500.
Remedies. §4501.
Limitation in power of attorney. §4502.
Express elimination of authority. §4503.
Right to jury trial. §4504.
General provisions applicable. §4505.

§4500. Judicial intervention

A power of attorney is exercisable free of judicial intervention, subject to this part. **Leg.H.** Added Stats 1999 ch 658 §37 (AB 891), operative July 1, 2000.

§4501. Remedies

The remedies provided in this part are cumulative and not exclusive of any other remedies provided by law. **Leg.H.** Added Stats 1999 ch 658 §37 (AB 891), operative July 1, 2000.

§4502. Limitation in power of attorney

Except as provided in Section 4503, this part is not subject to limitation in the power of attorney. **Leg.H.** Added Stats 1999 ch 658 §37 (AB 891), operative July 1, 2000.

§4503. Express elimination of authority

(a) Subject to subdivision (b), a power of attorney may expressly eliminate the authority of a person listed in Section 4540 to petition the court for any one or more of the purposes enumerated in Section 4541 if both of the following requirements are satisfied:

(1) The power of attorney is executed by the principal at a time when the principal has the advice of a lawyer authorized to practice law in the state where the power of attorney is executed.

(2) The principal's lawyer signs a certificate stating in substance: "I am a lawyer authorized to practice law in the state where this power of attorney was executed, and the principal was my client at the time this power of attorney was executed. I have advised my client concerning his or her rights in connection with this power of attorney and the applicable law and the consequences of signing or not signing this power of attorney, and my client, after being so advised, has executed this power of attorney."

(b) A power of attorney may not limit the authority of the attorney-in-fact, the principal, the conservator of the person or estate of the principal, or the public guardian to petition under this part. **Leg.H.** Added Stats 1999 ch 658 §37 (AB 891), operative July 1, 2000.

§4504. Right to jury trial

There is no right to a jury trial in proceedings under this division. **Leg.H.** Added Stats 1999 ch 658 §37 (AB 891), operative July 1, 2000.

§4505. General provisions applicable

Except as otherwise provided in this division, the general provisions in Division 3 (commencing with Section 1000) apply to proceedings under this division. **Leg.H.** Added Stats 1999 ch 658 §37 (AB 891), operative July 1, 2000.

CHAPTER 2
JURISDICTION AND VENUE

Court jurisdiction. §4520.
Basis of jurisdiction. §4521.
Personal jurisdiction. §4522.
Venue. §4523.

§4520. Court jurisdiction

(a) The superior court has jurisdiction in proceedings under this division.

(b) The court in proceedings under this division is a court of general jurisdiction and the court, or a judge of the court, has the same power and authority with respect to the proceedings as otherwise provided by law for a superior court, or a judge of the superior court, including, but not limited to, the matters authorized by Section 128 of the Code of Civil Procedure. **Leg.H.** Added Stats 1999 ch 658 §37 (AB 891), operative July 1, 2000.

§4521. Basis of jurisdiction

The court may exercise jurisdiction in proceedings under this division on any basis permitted by Section 410.10 of the Code of Civil Procedure. **Leg.H.** Added Stats 1999 ch 658 §37 (AB 891), operative July 1, 2000.

§4522. Personal jurisdiction

Without limiting Section 4521, a person who acts as an attorney-in-fact under a power of attorney governed by this division is subject to personal jurisdiction in this state with respect to matters relating to acts and transactions of the attorney-in-fact performed in this state or affecting property or a principal in this state. **Leg.H.** Added Stats 1999 ch 658 §37 (AB 891), operative July 1, 2000.

§4523. Venue

The proper county for commencement of a proceeding under this division shall be determined in the following order of priority:

(a) The county in which the principal resides.

(b) The county in which the attorney-in-fact resides.

(c) A county in which property subject to the power of attorney is located.

(d) Any other county that is in the principal's best interest. **Leg.H.** Added Stats 1999 ch 658 §37 (AB 891), operative July 1, 2000.

CHAPTER 3
PETITIONS, ORDERS, APPEALS

Persons who may file petition. §4540.
Purposes of petition. §4541.
Contents of petition. §4542.
Dismissal. §4543.
Notice of hearing. §4544.
Attorney fee award. §4545.

§4540. Persons who may file petition

Subject to Section 4503, a petition may be filed under this part by any of the following persons:

(a) The attorney-in-fact.

(b) The principal.

(c) The spouse of the principal.

(d) A relative of the principal.

(e) The conservator of the person or estate of the principal.

(f) The court investigator, described in Section 1454, of the county where the power of attorney was executed or where the principal resides.

(g) The public guardian of the county where the power of attorney was executed or where the principal resides.

(h) The personal representative or trustee of the principal's estate.

(i) The principal's successor in interest.

(j) A person who is requested in writing by an attorney-in-fact to take action.

(k) Any other interested person or friend of the principal. **Leg.H.** Added Stats 1999 ch 658 §37 (AB 891), operative July 1, 2000.

§4541. Purposes of petition

A petition may be filed under this part for any one or more of the following purposes:

(a) Determining whether the power of attorney is in effect or has terminated.

(b) Passing on the acts or proposed acts of the attorney-in-fact, including approval of authority to disobey the principal's instructions pursuant to subdivision (b) of Section 4234.

(c) Compelling the attorney-in-fact to submit the attorney-in-fact's accounts or report the attorney-in-fact's acts as attorney-in-fact to the principal, the spouse of the principal, the conservator of the person or estate of the principal, or to any other person required by the court in its discretion, if the attorney-in-fact has failed to submit an accounting or report within 60 days after written request from the person filing the petition.

(d) Declaring that the authority of the attorney-in-fact is revoked on a determination by the court of all of the following:

(1) The attorney-in-fact has violated or is unfit to perform the fiduciary duties under the power of attorney.

(2) At the time of the determination by the court, the principal lacks the capacity to give or to revoke a power of attorney.

(3) The revocation of the attorney-in-fact's authority is in the best interest of the principal or the principal's estate.

(e) Approving the resignation of the attorney-in-fact:

(1) If the attorney-in-fact is subject to a duty to act under Section 4230, the court may approve the resignation, subject to any orders the court determines are necessary to protect the principal's interests.

(2) If the attorney-in-fact is not subject to a duty to act under Section 4230, the court shall approve the resignation, subject to the court's discretion to require the attorney-in-fact to give notice to other interested persons.

(f) Compelling a third person to honor the authority of an attorney-in-fact. **Leg.H.** Added Stats 1999 ch 658 §37 (AB 891), operative July 1, 2000.

§4542. Contents of petition

A proceeding under this part is commenced by filing a petition stating facts showing that the petition is authorized under this part, the grounds of the petition, and, if known to the petitioner, the terms of the power of attorney. **Leg.H.** Added Stats 1999 ch 658 §37 (AB 891), operative July 1, 2000.

§4543. Dismissal

The court may dismiss a petition if it appears that the proceeding is not reasonably necessary for the protection of the interests of the principal or the principal's estate and shall stay or dismiss the proceeding in whole or in part when required by Section 410.30 of the Code of Civil Procedure. **Leg.H.** Added Stats 1999 ch 658 §37 (AB 891), operative July 1, 2000.

§4544. Notice of hearing

(a) Subject to subdivision (b), at least 15 days before the time set for hearing, the petitioner shall serve notice of the time and place of the hearing, together with a copy of the petition, on the following:

(1) The attorney-in-fact if not the petitioner.

(2) The principal if not the petitioner.

(b) In the case of a petition to compel a third person to honor the authority of an attorney-in-fact, notice of the time and place of the hearing, together with a copy of the petition, shall be served on the third person in the manner provided in Chapter 4 (commencing with Section 413.10) of Title 5 of Part 2 of the Code of Civil Procedure. **Leg.H.** Added Stats 1999 ch 658 §37 (AB 891), operative July 1, 2000.

§4545. Attorney fee award

In a proceeding under this part commenced by the filing of a petition by a person other than the attorney-in-fact, the court may in its discretion award reasonable attorney's fees to one of the following:

(a) The attorney-in-fact, if the court determines that the proceeding was commenced without any reasonable cause.

(b) The person commencing the proceeding, if the court determines that the attorney-in-fact has clearly violated the fiduciary duties under the power of attorney or has failed without any reasonable cause or justification to submit accounts or report acts to the principal or conservator of the estate or of the person, as the case may be, after written request from the principal or conservator. **Leg.H.** Added Stats 1999 ch 658 §37 (AB 891), operative July 1, 2000.

PART 5
JUDICIAL PROCEEDINGS CONCERNING POWERS OF ATTORNEY [REPEALED]

DIVISION 4.7
HEALTH CARE DECISIONS

Part 1. Definitions and General.
Part 2. Uniform Health Care Decisions Act.
Part 3. Judicial Proceedings.
Part 4. Request Regarding Resuscitative Measures.
Part 5. Advance Health Care Directive Registry.

PART 1
DEFINITIONS AND GENERAL

Chapter 1. Short Title and Definitions.
Chapter 2. General Provisions.
Chapter 3. Transitional Provisions.

CHAPTER 1
SHORT TITLE AND DEFINITIONS

Citation. §4600.
Definitions in general. §4603.
"Advance health care directive" or "advance directive". §4605.
"Agent". §4607.
"Capacity". §4609.
"Community care facility". §4611.
"Conservator". §4613.
"Health care". §4615.
"Health care decision". §4617.
"Health care institution". §4619.
"Health care provider". §4621.
"Individual health care instruction" or "individual instruction". §4623.
"Patient". §4625.
"Physician". §4627.
"Power of attorney for health care". §4629.
"Primary physician". §4631.
"Principal". §4633.
"Reasonably available". §4635.
"Residential care facility for the elderly". §4637.
"Skilled nursing facility". §4639.
"Supervising health care provider". §4641.
"Surrogate". §4643.

§4600. Citation

This division may be cited as the Health Care Decisions Law. **Leg.H.** Added Stats 1999 ch 658 §39 (AB 891), operative July 1, 2000.

Prior Law: Former Prob C §4600, similar to present Prob C §4603, was added Stats 1994 ch 307 §16 and repealed Stats 1999 ch 658 §38, operative July 1, 2000.

§4603. Definitions in general

Unless the provision or context otherwise requires, the definitions in this chapter govern the construction of this division. **Leg.H.** Added Stats 1999 ch 658 §39 (AB 891), operative July 1, 2000.

Prior Law: Former Prob C §4603, similar to present Prob C §4611, was added Stats 1994 ch 307 §16 and repealed Stats 1999 ch 658 §38, operative July 1, 2000.

§4605. "Advance health care directive" or "advance directive"

"Advance health care directive" or "advance directive" means either an individual health care instruction or a power of attorney for health care. **Leg.H.** Added Stats 1999 ch 658 §39 (AB 891), operative July 1, 2000.

§4606. [Section repealed 2000]

Leg.H. Added Stats 1994 ch 307 §16 (SB 1907). Repealed Stats 1999 ch 658 §38 (AB 891), operative July 1, 2000. See Prob C §4629.

§4607. "Agent"

(a) "Agent" means an individual designated in a power of attorney for health care to make a health care decision for the principal, regardless of whether the person is known as an agent or attorney-in-fact, or by some other term.

(b) "Agent" includes a successor or alternate agent. **Leg.H.** Added Stats 1999 ch 658 §39 (AB 891), operative July 1, 2000.

§4609. "Capacity"

"Capacity" means a person's ability to understand the nature and consequences of a decision and to make and communicate a decision, and includes in the case of proposed health care, the ability to understand its significant benefits, risks, and alternatives. **Leg.H.** Added Stats 1999 ch 658 §39 (AB 891), operative July 1, 2000. Amended Stats 2001 ch 230 §3 (AB 1278), effective January 1, 2002.

Prior Law: Former Prob C §4609, similar to present Prob C §4615, was added Stats 1994 ch 307 §16 and repealed Stats 1999 ch 658 §38, operative July 1, 2000.

§4611. "Community care facility"

"Community care facility" means a "community care facility" as defined in Section 1502 of the Health and Safety Code. **Leg.H.** Added Stats 1999 ch 658 §39 (AB 891), operative July 1, 2000.

§4612. [Section repealed 2000]

Leg.H. Added Stats 1994 ch 307 §16 (SB 1907). Repealed Stats 1999 ch 658 §38 (AB 891), operative July 1, 2000. See Prob C §4617.

§4613. "Conservator"

"Conservator" means a court-appointed conservator having authority to make a health care decision for a patient. **Leg.H.** Added Stats 1999 ch 658 §39 (AB 891), operative July 1, 2000.

§4615. "Health care"

"Health care" means any care, treatment, service, or procedure to maintain, diagnose, or otherwise affect a patient's physical or mental health condition. **Leg.H.** Added Stats 1999 ch 658 §39 (AB 891), operative July 1, 2000. Amended Stats 2022 ch 21 §1 (AB 2288), effective January 1, 2023.

Prior Law: Former Prob C §4615, similar to present Prob C §4621, was added Stats 1994 ch 307 §16 and repealed Stats 1999 ch 658 §38, operative July 1, 2000.

§4617. "Health care decision"

(a) "Health care decision" means a decision made by a patient or the patient's agent, conservator, or surrogate, regarding the patient's health care, including the following:

(1) Selection and discharge of health care providers and institutions.

(2) Approval or disapproval of diagnostic tests, surgical procedures, and programs of medication, including mental health conditions.

(3) Directions to provide, withhold, or withdraw artificial nutrition and hydration and all other forms of health care, including cardiopulmonary resuscitation.

(b) "Health care decision" does not include a decision made by a patient's agent, conservator, or surrogate to consent to treatments identified in Section 4652. **Leg.H.** Added Stats 1999 ch 658 §39 (AB 891), operative July 1, 2000. Amended Stats 2022 ch 21 §2 (AB 2288), effective January 1, 2023; Stats 2023 ch 171 §1 (AB 1029), effective January 1, 2024.

§4618. [Section repealed 2000]

Leg.H. Added Stats 1994 ch 307 §16 (SB 1907). Repealed Stats 1999 ch 658 §38 (AB 891), operative July 1, 2000. See Prob C §4637.

§4619. "Health care institution"

"Health care institution" means an institution, facility, or agency licensed, certified, or otherwise authorized or permitted by law to provide health care in the ordinary course of business. **Leg.H.** Added Stats 1999 ch 658 §39 (AB 891), operative July 1, 2000.

§4621. "Health care provider"

"Health care provider" means an individual licensed, certified, or otherwise authorized or permitted by the law of this state to provide health care in the ordinary course of business or practice of a profession. **Leg.H.** Added Stats 1999 ch 658 §39 (AB 891), operative July 1, 2000.

Prior Law: Former Prob C §4621, defining "statutory form durable power of attorney for health care", was added Stats 1994 ch 307 §16 and repealed Stats 1999 ch 658 §38, operative July 1, 2000.

§4623. "Individual health care instruction" or "individual instruction"

"Individual health care instruction" or "individual instruction" means a patient's written or oral direction concerning a health care decision for the patient. **Leg.H.** Added Stats 1999 ch 658 §39 (AB 891), operative July 1, 2000.

§4625. "Patient"

"Patient" means an adult whose health care is under consideration, and includes a principal under a power of attorney for health care and an adult who has given an individual health care instruction or designated a surrogate. **Leg.H.** Added Stats 1999 ch 658 §39 (AB 891), operative July 1, 2000.

§4627. "Physician"

"Physician" means a physician and surgeon licensed by the Medical Board of California or the Osteopathic Medical Board of California. **Leg.H.** Added Stats 1999 ch 658 §39 (AB 891), operative July 1, 2000.

§4629. "Power of attorney for health care"

"Power of attorney for health care" means a written instrument designating an agent to make health care decisions for the principal. **Leg.H.** Added Stats 1999 ch 658 §39 (AB 891), operative July 1, 2000.

§4631. "Primary physician"

"Primary physician" means a physician designated by a patient or the patient's agent, conservator, or surrogate, to have primary responsibility for the patient's health care or, in the absence of a designation or if the designated physician is not reasonably available or declines to act as primary physician, a physician who undertakes the responsibility. **Leg.H.** Added Stats 1999 ch 658 §39 (AB 891), operative July 1, 2000.

§4633. "Principal"

"Principal" means an adult who executes a power of attorney for health care. **Leg.H.** Added Stats 1999 ch 658 §39 (AB 891), operative July 1, 2000.

§4635. "Reasonably available"

"Reasonably available" means readily able to be contacted without undue effort and willing and able to act in a timely manner considering the urgency of the patient's health care needs. **Leg.H.** Added Stats 1999 ch 658 §39 (AB 891), operative July 1, 2000.

§4637. "Residential care facility for the elderly"

"Residential care facility for the elderly" means a "residential care facility for the elderly" as defined in Section 1569.2 of the Health and Safety Code. **Leg.H.** Added Stats 1999 ch 658 §39 (AB 891), operative July 1, 2000.

§4639. "Skilled nursing facility"

"Skilled nursing facility" means a "skilled nursing facility" as defined in Section 1250 of the Health and Safety Code. **Leg.H.** Added Stats 1999 ch 658 §39 (AB 891), operative July 1, 2000.

§4641. "Supervising health care provider"

"Supervising health care provider" means the primary physician or, if there is no primary physician or the primary physician is not reasonably available, the health care provider who has undertaken primary responsibility for a patient's health care. **Leg.H.** Added Stats 1999 ch 658 §39 (AB 891), operative July 1, 2000.

§4643. "Surrogate"

"Surrogate" means an adult, other than a patient's agent or conservator, authorized under this division to make a health care decision for the patient. **Leg.H.** Added Stats 1999 ch 658 §39 (AB 891), operative July 1, 2000.

CHAPTER 2
GENERAL PROVISIONS

Legislative findings. §4650.
Legislative findings. §4651.
Consent not authorized for some placements or treatments. §4652.
Mercy killing or euthanasia. §4653.
Care contrary to accepted standards. §4654.
Presumptions; Attempted suicide. §4655.
Death as suicide or homicide. §4656.
Presumed capacity. §4657.
Determination of capacity. §4658.
Prohibition as to certain persons as agents. §4659.
Copy of directive, revocation, or designation. §4660.

§4650. Legislative findings

The Legislature finds the following:

(a) In recognition of the dignity and privacy a person has a right to expect, the law recognizes that an adult has the fundamental right to control the decisions relating to his or her own health care, including the decision to have life-sustaining treatment withheld or withdrawn.

(b) Modern medical technology has made possible the artificial prolongation of human life beyond natural limits. In the interest of protecting individual autonomy, this prolongation of the process of dying for a person for whom continued health care does not improve the prognosis for recovery may violate patient dignity and cause unnecessary pain and suffering, while providing nothing medically necessary or beneficial to the person.

(c) In the absence of controversy, a court is normally not the proper forum in which to make health care decisions, including decisions regarding life-sustaining treatment. **Leg.H.** Added Stats 1999 ch 658 §39 (AB 891), effective January 1, 2000, operative July 1, 2000.

Prior Law: Former Prob C §4650, similar to present Prob C §4671, was added Stats 1994 ch 307 §16 and repealed Stats 1999 ch 658 §38, operative July 1, 2000.

§4651. Legislative findings

(a) Except as otherwise provided, this division applies to health care decisions for adults who lack capacity to make health care decisions for themselves.

(b) This division does not affect any of the following:

(1) The right of an individual to make health care decisions while having the capacity to do so.

(2) The law governing health care in an emergency.

(3) The law governing health care for unemancipated minors. **Leg.H.** Added Stats 1999 ch 658 §39 (AB 891), operative July 1, 2000.

Prior Law: Former Prob C §4651, relating to requirements for printed form of durable power of attorney for health care, was added Stats 1994 ch 307 §16 and repealed Stats 1999 ch 658 §38, operative July 1, 2000. Historical derivation: Former CC §2444, as added Stats 1985 ch 403 §6.5, amended Stats 1988 ch 1543 §4, Stats 1991 ch 896 §3.

§4652. Consent not authorized for some placements or treatments

This division does not authorize consent to any of the following on behalf of a patient:

(a) Commitment to or placement in a mental health treatment facility.

(b) Convulsive treatment (as defined in Section 5325 of the Welfare and Institutions Code).

(c) Psychosurgery (as defined in Section 5325 of the Welfare and Institutions Code).

(d) Sterilization.

(e) Abortion. **Leg.H.** Added Stats 1999 ch 658 §39 (AB 891), operative July 1, 2000.

Prior Law: Former Prob C §4652, similar to present Prob C §§4685 and 4687, was added Stats 1994 ch 307 §16 and repealed Stats 1999 ch 658 §38, operative July 1, 2000.

§4653. Mercy killing or euthanasia

Nothing in this division shall be construed to condone, authorize, or approve mercy killing, assisted suicide, or euthanasia. This division is not intended to permit any affirmative or deliberate act or omission to end life other than withholding or withdrawing health care pursuant to an advance health care directive, by a surrogate, or as otherwise provided, so as to permit the natural process of dying. **Leg.H.** Added Stats 1999 ch 658 §39 (AB 891), operative July 1, 2000.

Prior Law: Former Prob C §4653, similar to present Prob C §4676, was added Stats 1994 ch 307 §16 and repealed Stats 1999 ch 658 §38, operative July 1, 2000.

§4654. Care contrary to accepted standards

This division does not authorize or require a health care provider or health care institution to provide health care contrary to generally accepted health care standards applicable to the health care provider or health care institution. **Leg.H.** Added Stats 1999 ch 658 §39 (AB 891), operative July 1, 2000.

Prior Law: Former Prob C §4654, relating to expiration date and exception, was added Stats 1994 ch 307 §16 and repealed Stats 1999 ch 658 §38, operative July

1, 2000. Historical derivation: Former CC §2436.5, as added Stats 1983 ch 1204 §10, amended Stats 1991 ch 896 §2.

§4655. Presumptions; Attempted suicide

(a) This division does not create a presumption concerning the intention of a patient who has not made or who has revoked an advance health care directive.

(b) In making health care decisions under this division, a patient's attempted suicide shall not be construed to indicate a desire of the patient that health care be restricted or inhibited. **Leg.H.** Added Stats 1999 ch 658 §39 (AB 891), operative July 1, 2000.

§4656. Death as suicide or homicide

Death resulting from withholding or withdrawing health care in accordance with this division does not for any purpose constitute a suicide or homicide or legally impair or invalidate a policy of insurance or an annuity providing a death benefit, notwithstanding any term of the policy or annuity to the contrary. **Leg.H.** Added Stats 1999 ch 658 §39 (AB 891), operative July 1, 2000.

§4657. Presumed capacity

A patient is presumed to have the capacity to make a health care decision, to give or revoke an advance health care directive, and to designate or disqualify a surrogate. This presumption is a presumption affecting the burden of proof. **Leg.H.** Added Stats 1999 ch 658 §39 (AB 891), operative July 1, 2000.

§4658. Determination of capacity

Unless otherwise specified in a written advance health care directive, for the purposes of this division, a determination that a patient lacks or has recovered capacity, or that another condition exists that affects an individual health care instruction or the authority of an agent or surrogate, shall be made by the primary physician. **Leg.H.** Added Stats 1999 ch 658 §39 (AB 891), operative July 1, 2000.

§4659. Prohibition as to certain persons as agents

(a) Except as provided in subdivision (b), none of the following persons may make health care decisions as an agent under a power of attorney for health care or a surrogate under this division:

(1) The supervising health care provider or an employee of the health care institution where the patient is receiving care.

(2) An operator or employee of a community care facility or residential care facility where the patient is receiving care.

(b) The prohibition in subdivision (a) does not apply to the following persons:

(1) An employee, other than the supervising health care provider, who is related to the patient by blood, marriage, or adoption, or is a registered domestic partner of the patient.

(2) An employee, other than the supervising health care provider, who is employed by the same health care institution, community care facility, or residential care facility for the elderly as the patient.

(c) A conservator under the Lanterman-Petris-Short Act (Part 1 (commencing with Section 5000) of Division 5 of the Welfare and Institutions Code) may not be designated as an agent or surrogate to make health care decisions by the conservatee, unless all of the following are satisfied:

(1) The advance health care directive is otherwise valid.

(2) The conservatee is represented by legal counsel.

(3) The lawyer representing the conservatee signs a certificate stating in substance:

"I am a lawyer authorized to practice law in the state where this advance health care directive was executed, and the principal or patient was my client at the time this advance directive was executed. I have advised my client concerning his or her rights in connection with this advance directive and the applicable law and the consequences of signing or not signing this advance directive, and my client, after being so advised, has executed this advance directive." **Leg.H.** Added Stats 1999 ch 658 §39 (AB 891), operative July 1, 2000. Amended Stats 2001 ch 230 §4 (AB 1278), effective January 1, 2002.

§4660. Copy of directive, revocation, or designation

A copy of a written advance health care directive, revocation of an advance directive, or designation or disqualification of a surrogate has the same effect as the original. **Leg.H.** Added Stats 1999 ch 658 §39 (AB 891), operative July 1, 2000.

CHAPTER 3
TRANSITIONAL PROVISIONS

Transitional provisions. §4665.

§4665. Transitional provisions

Except as otherwise provided by statute:

(a) On and after July 1, 2000, this division applies to all advance health care directives, including, but not limited to, durable powers of attorney for health care and declarations under the Natural Death Act (former Chapter 3.9 (commencing with Section 7185) of Part 1 of Division 7 of the Health and Safety Code), regardless of whether they were given or executed before, on, or after July 1, 2000.

(b) This division applies to all proceedings concerning advance health care directives commenced on or after July 1, 2000.

(c) This division applies to all proceedings concerning written advance health care directives commenced before July 1, 2000, unless the court determines that application of a particular provision of this division would substantially interfere with the effective conduct of the proceedings or the rights of the parties and other interested persons, in which case the particular provision of this division does not apply and prior law applies.

(d) Nothing in this division affects the validity of an advance health care directive executed before July 1, 2000, that was valid under prior law.

(e) Nothing in this division affects the validity of a durable power of attorney for health care executed on a printed form that was valid under prior law, regardless of whether execution occurred before, on, or after July 1, 2000. **Leg.H.** Added Stats 1999 ch 658 §39 (AB 891), operative July 1, 2000.

PART 2
UNIFORM HEALTH CARE DECISIONS ACT

Chapter 1. Advance Health Care Directives.
Chapter 2. Advance Health Care Directive Forms.
Chapter 3. Health Care Surrogates.
Chapter 4. Duties of Health Care Providers.
Chapter 5. Immunities and Liabilities.

CHAPTER 1
ADVANCE HEALTH CARE DIRECTIVES

Article 1. General Provisions.
Article 2. Powers of Attorney for Health Care.
Article 3. Revocation of Advance Directives.

ARTICLE 1
General Provisions

Individual instruction. §4670.
Agent and principal. §4671.
Nomination of conservator or guardian. §4672.
Sufficiency of directive. §4673.
Witness requirements. §4674.
Patient advocate or ombudsman. §4675.
Document executed in another state or jurisdiction. §4676.
Condition for admission to facility or furnishing insurance. §4677.
Consent to disclosure. §4678.
Psychiatric advance directive. § 4679.

§4670. Individual instruction

An adult having capacity may give an individual health care instruction. The individual instruction may be oral or written. The individual instruction may be limited to take effect only if a specified condition arises. **Leg.H.** Added Stats 1999 ch 658 §39 (AB 891), operative July 1, 2000.

§4671. Agent and principal

(a) An adult having capacity may execute a power of attorney for health care, as provided in Article 2 (commencing with Section 4680). The power of attorney for health care may authorize the agent to make health care decisions and may also include individual health care instructions.

(b) The principal in a power of attorney for health care may grant authority to make decisions relating to the personal care of the principal, including, but not limited to, determining where the principal will live, providing meals, hiring household employees, providing transportation, handling mail, and arranging recreation and entertainment. **Leg.H.** Added Stats 1999 ch 658 §39 (AB 891), operative July 1, 2000.

§4672. Nomination of conservator or guardian

(a) A written advance health care directive may include the individual's nomination of a conservator of the person or estate or both, or a guardian of the person or estate or both, for consideration by the court if protective proceedings for the individual's person or estate are thereafter commenced.

(b) If the protective proceedings are conservatorship proceedings in this state, the nomination has the effect provided in Section 1810 and the court shall give effect to the most recent writing executed in accordance with Section 1810, whether or not the writing is a written advance health care directive. **Leg.H.** Added Stats 1999 ch 658 §39 (AB 891), operative July 1, 2000.

§4673. Sufficiency of directive

(a) A written advance health care directive is legally sufficient if all of the following requirements are satisfied:

(1) The advance directive contains the date of its execution.

(2) The advance directive is signed either by the patient or in the patient's name by another adult in the patient's presence and at the patient's direction.

(3) The advance directive is either acknowledged before a notary public or signed by at least two witnesses who satisfy the requirements of Sections 4674 and 4675.

(b) An electronic advance health care directive or power of attorney for health care is legally sufficient if the requirements in subdivision (a) are satisfied, except that for the purposes of paragraph (3) of subdivision (a), an acknowledgment before a notary public shall be required, and if a digital signature is used, it meets all of the following requirements:

(1) The digital signature either meets the requirements of Section 16.5 of the Government Code and Chapter 10 (commencing with Section 22000) of Division 7 of Title 2 of the California Code of Regulations or the digital signature uses an algorithm approved by the National Institute of Standards and Technology.

(2) The digital signature is unique to the person using it.

(3) The digital signature is capable of verification.

(4) The digital signature is under the sole control of the person using it.

(5) The digital signature is linked to data in such a manner that if the data are changed, the digital signature is invalidated.

(6) The digital signature persists with the document and not by association in separate files.

(7) The digital signature is bound to a digital certificate. **Leg.H.** Added Stats 1999 ch 658 §39 (AB 891), operative July 1, 2000. Amended Stats 2006 ch 579 §1 (AB 2805), effective September 28, 2006.

§4674. Witness requirements

If the written advance health care directive is signed by witnesses, as provided in Section 4673, the following requirements shall be satisfied:

(a) The witnesses shall be adults.

(b) Each witness signing the advance directive shall witness either the signing of the advance directive by the patient or the patient's acknowledgment of the signature or the advance directive.

(c) None of the following persons may act as a witness:

(1) The patient's health care provider or an employee of the patient's health care provider.

(2) The operator or an employee of a community care facility.

(3) The operator or an employee of a residential care facility for the elderly.

(4) The agent, where the advance directive is a power of attorney for health care.

(d) Each witness shall make the following declaration in substance:

"I declare under penalty of perjury under the laws of California (1) that the individual who signed or acknowledged this advance health care directive is personally known to me, or that the individual's identity was proven to me by convincing evidence, (2) that the individual signed or acknowledged this advance directive in my presence, (3) that the individual appears to be of sound mind and under no duress, fraud, or undue influence, (4) that I am not a person appointed as agent by this advance directive, and (5) that I am not the individual's health care provider, an employee of the individual's health care provider, the operator of a community care facility, an employee of an operator of a community care facility, the operator of a residential care facility for the elderly, nor an employee of an operator of a residential care facility for the elderly."

(e) At least one of the witnesses shall be an individual who is neither related to the patient by blood, marriage, or adoption, nor entitled to any portion of the patient's estate upon the patient's death under a will existing when the advance directive is executed or by operation of law then existing.

(f) The witness satisfying the requirement of subdivision (e) shall also sign the following declaration in substance:

"I further declare under penalty of perjury under the laws of California that I am not related to the individual executing this advance health care directive by blood, marriage, or adoption, and, to the best of my knowledge, I am not entitled to any part of the individual's estate upon his or her death under a will now existing or by operation of law."

(g) The provisions of this section applicable to witnesses do not apply to a notary public before whom an advance health care directive is acknowledged. **Leg.H.** Added Stats 1999 ch 658 §39 (AB 891), operative July 1, 2000.

§4675. Patient advocate or ombudsman

(a) If an individual is a patient in a skilled nursing facility when a written advance health care directive is executed, the advance directive is not effective unless a patient advocate or ombudsman, as may be designated by the Department of Aging for this purpose pursuant to any other applicable provision of law, signs the advance directive as a witness, either as one of two witnesses or in addition to notarization. The patient advocate or ombudsman shall declare that he or she is serving as a witness as required by this subdivision. It is the intent of this subdivision to recognize that some patients in skilled nursing facilities are insulated from a voluntary decisionmaking role, by virtue of the custodial nature of their care, so as to require special assurance that they are capable of willfully and voluntarily executing an advance directive.

(b) A witness who is a patient advocate or ombudsman may rely on the representations of the administrators or staff of the skilled nursing facility, or of family members, as convincing evidence of the identity of the patient if the patient advocate or ombudsman believes that the representations provide a reasonable basis for determining the identity of the patient. **Leg.H.** Added Stats 1999 ch 658 §39 (AB 891), operative July 1, 2000.

§4676. Document executed in another state or jurisdiction

(a) A written advance health care directive or similar instrument executed in another state or jurisdiction in compliance with the laws of that state or jurisdiction or of this state, is valid and enforceable in this state to the same extent as a written advance directive validly executed in this state.

(b) In the absence of knowledge to the contrary, a physician or other health care provider may presume that a written advance health care directive or similar instrument, whether executed in another state or jurisdiction or in this state, is valid. **Leg.H.** Added Stats 1999 ch 658 §39 (AB 891), operative July 1, 2000.

§4677. Condition for admission to facility or furnishing insurance

A health care provider, health care service plan, health care institution, disability insurer, self-insured employee welfare plan, or nonprofit hospital plan or a similar insurance plan may not require or prohibit the execution or revocation of an advance health care directive as a condition for providing health care, admission to a facility, or furnishing insurance. **Leg.H.** Added Stats 1999 ch 658 §39 (AB 891), operative July 1, 2000.

§4678. Consent to disclosure

Unless otherwise specified in an advance health care directive, a person then authorized to make health care decisions for a patient has the same rights as the patient to request, receive, examine, copy, and consent to the disclosure of medical or any other health care information. **Leg.H.** Added Stats 1999 ch 658 §39 (AB 891), operative July 1, 2000.

§ 4679. Psychiatric advance directive

(a)(1) This chapter does not prohibit the execution of a voluntary standalone psychiatric advance directive.

(2) As used in this chapter, "psychiatric advance directive" means a legal document, executed on a voluntary basis by a person who has the capacity to make medical decisions and in accordance with the requirements for an advance health care directive in this division, that allows a person with mental illness to protect their autonomy and ability to direct their own care by documenting their preferences for treatment in advance of a mental health crisis.

(b) It is the intent of the Legislature to promote the use of a psychiatric advance directive, subject to the requirements of this division, by a person who wants to make sure their health care providers know their treatment preferences in the event of a future mental health crisis.

(c) The Legislature finds and declares all of the following:

(1) Research has demonstrated that the use of psychiatric advance directives improves collaboration, which improves outcomes, increases empowerment, and improves medication adherence.

(2) A psychiatric advance directive is most helpful when it includes reasons for preferring or opposing specific types of treatment.

(3) Mental health preferences that do not constitute health care instructions or decisions as defined in this part may provide valuable information to improve an individual's mental health care. **Leg.H.** Added Stats 2023 ch 171 §2 (AB 1029), effective January 1, 2024.

ARTICLE 2
Powers of Attorney for Health Care

Legal sufficiency of power of attorney. §4680.
Limitation of application of provisions. §4681.
When authority becomes effective. §4682.
Agent's powers. §4683.
Agent's decisions. §4684.
Agent as having priority. §4685.
Lapses of time. §4686.
Effect on rights of agent. §4687.
Application of law of agency. §4688.
Objection by principal. §4689.
Incapacity of principal. §4690.
Death of principal. §4691.

§4680. Legal sufficiency of power of attorney

A power of attorney for health care is legally sufficient if it satisfies the requirements of Section 4673. **Leg.H.** Added Stats 1999 ch 658 §39 (AB 891), operative July 1, 2000.

§4681. Limitation of application of provisions

(a) Except as provided in subdivision (b), the principal may limit the application of any provision of this division by an express statement in the power of attorney for health care or by providing an inconsistent rule in the power of attorney.

(b) A power of attorney for health care may not limit either the application of a statute specifically providing that it is not subject to limitation in the power of attorney or a statute concerning any of the following:

(1) Statements required to be included in a power of attorney.
(2) Operative dates of statutory enactments or amendments.
(3) Formalities for execution of a power of attorney for health care.
(4) Qualifications of witnesses.
(5) Qualifications of agents.
(6) Protection of third persons from liability. **Leg.H.** Added Stats 1999 ch 658 §39 (AB 891), operative July 1, 2000.

§4682. When authority becomes effective

Unless otherwise provided in a power of attorney for health care, the authority of an agent becomes effective only on a determination that the principal lacks capacity, and ceases to be effective on a determination that the principal has recovered capacity. **Leg.H.** Added Stats 1999 ch 658 §39 (AB 891), operative July 1, 2000.

§4683. Agent's powers

Subject to any limitations in the power of attorney for health care:

(a) An agent designated in the power of attorney may make health care decisions for the principal to the same extent the principal could make health care decisions if the principal had the capacity to do so.

(b) The agent may also make decisions that may be effective after the principal's death, including the following:

(1) Making a disposition under the Uniform Anatomical Gift Act (Chapter 3.5 (commencing with Section 7150) of Part 1 of Division 7 of the Health and Safety Code).

(2) Authorizing an autopsy under Section 7113 of the Health and Safety Code.

(3) Directing the disposition of remains under Section 7100 of the Health and Safety Code.

(4) Authorizing the release of the records of the principal to the extent necessary for the agent to fulfill his or her duties as set forth in this division. **Leg.H.** Added Stats 1999 ch 658 §39 (AB 891), operative July 1, 2000. Amended Stats 2006 ch 249 §2 (SB 1307), effective January 1, 2007.

§4684. Agent's decisions

An agent shall make a health care decision in accordance with the principal's individual health care instructions, if any, and other wishes to the extent known to the agent. Otherwise, the agent shall make the decision in accordance with the agent's determination of the principal's best interest. In determining the principal's best interest, the agent shall consider the principal's personal values to the extent known to the agent. **Leg.H.** Added Stats 1999 ch 658 §39 (AB 891), operative July 1, 2000.

§4685. Agent as having priority

Unless the power of attorney for health care provides otherwise, the agent designated in the power of attorney who is known to the health care provider to be reasonably available and willing to make health care decisions has priority over any other person in making health care decisions for the principal. **Leg.H.** Added Stats 1999 ch 658 §39 (AB 891), operative July 1, 2000.

§4686. Lapses of time

Unless the power of attorney for health care provides a time of termination, the authority of the agent is exercisable notwithstanding any

§4687. Effect on rights of agent
Nothing in this division affects any right the person designated as an agent under a power of attorney for health care may have, apart from the power of attorney, to make or participate in making health care decisions for the principal. **Leg.H.** Added Stats 1999 ch 658 §39 (AB 891), operative July 1, 2000.

§4688. Application of law of agency
Where this division does not provide a rule governing agents under powers of attorney, the law of agency applies. **Leg.H.** Added Stats 1999 ch 658 §39 (AB 891), operative July 1, 2000.

§4689. Objection by principal
Nothing in this division authorizes an agent under a power of attorney for health care to make a health care decision if the principal objects to the decision. If the principal objects to the health care decision of the agent under a power of attorney, the matter shall be governed by the law that would apply if there were no power of attorney for health care. **Leg.H.** Added Stats 1999 ch 658 §39 (AB 891), operative July 1, 2000.

§4690. Incapacity of principal
(a) If the principal becomes wholly or partially incapacitated, or if there is a question concerning the capacity of the principal, the agent may consult with a person previously designated by the principal for this purpose, and may also consult with and obtain information needed to carry out the agent's duties from the principal's spouse, physician, supervising health care provider, attorney, a member of the principal's family, or other person, including a business entity or government agency, with respect to matters covered by the power of attorney for health care.

(b) A person described in subdivision (a) from whom information is requested shall disclose information that the agent requires to carry out his or her duties. Disclosure under this section is not a waiver of any privilege that may apply to the information disclosed. **Leg.H.** Added Stats 1999 ch 658 §39 (AB 891), operative July 1, 2000. Amended Stats 2006 ch 249 §3 (SB 1307), effective January 1, 2007; Stats 2007 ch 130 §196 (AB 299), effective January 1, 2008.

§4691. Death of principal
If directed by the principal in a power of attorney for health care, an attorney-in-fact shall, upon the death of the principal, inform those individuals whose names are provided by the principal to the attorney-in-fact for that purpose. **Leg.H.** Added Stats 2015 ch 92 §4 (AB 1085), effective January 1, 2016.

ARTICLE 3
Revocation of Advance Directives

Revocation of agent's designation. §4695.
Communication of revocation. §4696.
Dissolved marriage. §4697.
Conflicting directives. §4698.

§4695. Revocation of agent's designation
(a) A patient having capacity may revoke the designation of an agent only by a signed writing or by personally informing the supervising health care provider.

(b) A patient having capacity may revoke all or part of an advance health care directive, other than the designation of an agent, at any time and in any manner that communicates an intent to revoke. **Leg.H.** Added Stats 1999 ch 658 §39 (AB 891), operative July 1, 2000.

§4696. Communication of revocation
A health care provider, agent, conservator, or surrogate who is informed of a revocation of an advance health care directive shall promptly communicate the fact of the revocation to the supervising health care provider and to any health care institution where the patient is receiving care. **Leg.H.** Added Stats 1999 ch 658 §39 (AB 891), operative July 1, 2000.

§4697. Dissolved marriage
(a) If after executing a power of attorney for health care the principal's marriage to the agent is dissolved or annulled, the principal's designation of the former spouse as an agent to make health care decisions for the principal is revoked.

(b) If the agent's authority is revoked solely by subdivision (a), it is revived by the principal's remarriage to the agent. **Leg.H.** Added Stats 1999 ch 658 §39 (AB 891), operative July 1, 2000.

§4698. Conflicting directives
An advance health care directive that conflicts with an earlier advance directive revokes the earlier advance directive to the extent of the conflict. **Leg.H.** Added Stats 1999 ch 658 §39 (AB 891), operative July 1, 2000.

CHAPTER 2
ADVANCE HEALTH CARE DIRECTIVE FORMS

Form to create advance health care directive. §4700.
Statutory advance health care directive form. §4701.

§4700. Form to create advance health care directive
The form provided in Section 4701 may, but need not, be used to create an advance health care directive. The other sections of this division govern the effect of the form or any other writing used to create an advance health care directive. An individual may complete or modify all or any part of the form in Section 4701. **Leg.H.** Added Stats 1999 ch 658 §39 (AB 891), operative July 1, 2000.

Prior Law: Former Prob C §4700, similar to present Prob C §4671, was added Stats 1994 ch 307 §16 and repealed Stats 1999 ch 658 §38, operative July 1, 2000.

§4701. Statutory advance health care directive form
The statutory advance health care directive form is as follows:

ADVANCE HEALTH CARE DIRECTIVE

(California Probate Code Section 4701)

Explanation

You have the right to give instructions about your own physical and mental health care. You also have the right to name someone else to make those health care decisions for you. This form lets you do either or both of these things. It also lets you express your wishes regarding donation of organs and the designation of your primary physician. If you use this form, you may complete or modify all or any part of it. You are free to use a different form.

Part 1 of this form is a power of attorney for health care. Part 1 lets you name another individual as agent to make health care decisions for you if you become incapable of making your own decisions or if you want someone else to make those decisions for you now even though you are still capable. You may also name an alternate agent to act for you if your first choice is not willing, able, or reasonably available to make decisions for you. (Your agent may not be an operator or employee of a community care facility or a residential care facility where you are receiving care, or your supervising health care provider or employee of the health care institution where you are receiving care, unless your agent is related to you or is a coworker.)

Unless the form you sign limits the authority of your agent, your agent may make all health care decisions for you. This form has a place for you to limit the authority of your agent. You need not limit the authority of your agent if you wish to rely on your agent for all health care decisions that may have to be made. If you choose not to limit the authority of your agent, your agent will have the right to:

(a) Consent or refuse consent to any care, treatment, service, or procedure to maintain, diagnose, or otherwise affect a physical or mental condition.

(b) Select or discharge health care providers and institutions.

(c) For all physical and mental health care, approve or disapprove diagnostic tests, surgical procedures, and programs of medication.

(d) Direct the provision, withholding, or withdrawal of artificial nutrition and hydration and all other forms of health care, including cardiopulmonary resuscitation.

(e) Donate your organs, tissues, and parts, authorize an autopsy, and direct disposition of remains.

However, your agent will not be able to commit you to a mental health facility, or consent to convulsive treatment, psychosurgery, sterilization, or abortion for you.

Part 2 of this form lets you give specific instructions about any aspect of your health care, whether or not you appoint an agent. Choices are provided for you to express your wishes regarding the provision, withholding, or withdrawal of treatment to keep you alive, as well as the provision of pain relief. Space is also provided for you to add to the choices you have made or for you to write out any additional wishes. If you are satisfied to allow your agent to determine what is best for you in making end-of-life decisions, you need not fill out Part 2 of this form.

Part 3 of this form lets you express an intention to donate your bodily organs, tissues, and parts following your death.

Part 4 of this form lets you designate a physician to have primary responsibility for your health care.

After completing this form, sign and date the form at the end. The form shall be signed by two qualified witnesses or acknowledged before a notary public. Give a copy of the signed and completed form to your physician, to any other health care providers you may have, to any health care institution at which you are receiving care, and to any health care agents you have named. You should talk to the person you have named as agent to make sure that they understand your wishes and is willing to take the responsibility.

You have the right to revoke this advance health care directive or replace this form at any time.

****

PART 1
POWER OF ATTORNEY FOR HEALTH CARE

(1.1) DESIGNATION OF AGENT: I designate the following individual as my agent to make health care decisions for me:

_____
(name of individual you choose as agent)

_____
(address)   (city)   (state)   (ZIP Code)

_____
(home phone)   (work phone)

OPTIONAL: If I revoke my agent's authority or if my agent is not willing, able, or reasonably available to make a health care decision for me, I designate as my first alternate agent:

_____
(name of individual you choose as first alternate agent)

_____
(address)   (city)   (state)   (ZIP Code)

_____
(home phone)   (work phone)

OPTIONAL: If I revoke the authority of my agent and first alternate agent or if neither is willing, able, or reasonably available to make a health care decision for me, I designate as my second alternate agent:

_____
(name of individual you choose as second alternate agent)

_____
(address)   (city)   (state)   (ZIP Code)

_____
(home phone)   (work phone)

(1.2) AGENT'S AUTHORITY: My agent is authorized to make all physical and mental health care decisions for me, including decisions to provide, withhold, or withdraw artificial nutrition and hydration and all other forms of health care to keep me alive, except as I state here:

_____
_____
_____

(Add additional sheets if needed.)

(1.3) WHEN AGENT'S AUTHORITY BECOMES EFFECTIVE: My agent's authority becomes effective when my primary physician determines that I am unable to make my own health care decisions unless I mark the following box. If I mark this box ☐, my agent's authority to make health care decisions for me takes effect immediately.

(1.4) AGENT'S OBLIGATION: My agent shall make health care decisions for me in accordance with this power of attorney for health care, any instructions I give in Part 2 of this form, and my other wishes to the extent known to my agent. To the extent my wishes are unknown, my agent shall make health care decisions for me in accordance with what my agent determines to be in my best interest. In determining my best interest, my agent shall consider my personal values to the extent known to my agent.

(1.5) AGENT'S POSTDEATH AUTHORITY: My agent is authorized to donate my organs, tissues, and parts, authorize an autopsy, and direct disposition of my remains, except as I state here or in Part 3 of this form:

_____
_____
_____

(Add additional sheets if needed.)

(1.6) NOMINATION OF CONSERVATOR: If a conservator of my person needs to be appointed for me by a court, I nominate the agent designated in this form. If that agent is not willing, able, or reasonably available to act as conservator, I nominate the alternate agents whom I have named, in the order designated.

PART 2
INSTRUCTIONS FOR HEALTH CARE

If you fill out this part of the form, you may strike any wording you do not want.

(2.1) END-OF-LIFE DECISIONS: I direct that my health care providers and others involved in my care provide, withhold, or withdraw treatment in accordance with the choice I have marked below:

☐ (a) Choice Not To Prolong Life

I do not want my life to be prolonged if (1) I have an incurable and irreversible condition that will result in my death within a relatively short time, (2) I become unconscious and, to a reasonable degree of medical certainty, I will not regain consciousness, or (3) the likely risks and burdens of treatment would outweigh the expected benefits, OR

☐ (b) Choice To Prolong Life

I want my life to be prolonged as long as possible within the limits of generally accepted health care standards.

(2.2) RELIEF FROM PAIN: Except as I state in the following space, I direct that treatment for alleviation of pain or discomfort be provided at all times, even if it hastens my death:

_____
_____

(Add additional sheets if needed.)

WISHES FOR PHYSICAL AND MENTAL HEALTH CARE: (If you do not agree with any of the optional choices above and wish to write your own, or if you wish to add to the instructions you have given above, you may do so here.) I direct that:

_____
_____

(Add additional sheets if needed.)

PART 3
DONATION OF ORGANS, TISSUES, AND PARTS AT DEATH
(OPTIONAL)

(3.1) ☐ Upon my death, I give my organs, tissues, and parts (mark box to indicate yes). By checking the box above, and notwithstanding my choice in Part 2 of this form, I authorize my agent to consent to any temporary medical procedure necessary solely to evaluate and/or maintain my organs, tissues, and/or parts for purposes of donation.

My donation is for the following purposes (strike any of the following you do not want):

(a) Transplant
(b) Therapy
(c) Research
(d) Education

If you want to restrict your donation of an organ, tissue, or part in some way, please state your restriction on the following lines:

_____
_____

If I leave this part blank, it is not a refusal to make a donation. My state-authorized donor registration should be followed, or, if none, my agent may make a donation upon my death. If no agent is named above, I acknowledge that California law permits an authorized individual to make such a decision on my behalf. (To state any limitation, preference, or instruction regarding donation, please use the lines above or in Section 1.5 of this form).

PART 4
PRIMARY PHYSICIAN
(OPTIONAL)

(4.1) I designate the following physician as my primary physician:

_____
(name of physician)

_____
(address) (city) (state) (ZIP Code)

_____
(phone)

OPTIONAL: If the physician I have designated above is not willing, able, or reasonably available to act as my primary physician, I designate the following physician as my primary physician:

_____
(name of physician)

_____
(address) (city) (state) (ZIP Code)

_____
(phone)

* * * * * * * * * * * * * * *

PART 5

(5.1) EFFECT OF COPY: A copy of this form has the same effect as the original.

(5.2) SIGNATURE: Sign and date the form here:

_____
(date)   (sign your name)

_____
(address) (print your name)

_____
(city)   (state)

(5.3) STATEMENT OF WITNESSES: I declare under penalty of perjury under the laws of California (1) that the individual who signed or acknowledged this advance health care directive is personally known to me, or that the individual's identity was proven to me by convincing evidence, (2) that the individual signed or acknowledged this advance directive in my presence, (3) that the individual appears to be of sound mind and under no duress, fraud, or undue influence, (4) that I am not a person appointed as agent by this advance directive, and (5) that I am not the individual's health care provider, an employee of the individual's health care provider, the operator of a community care facility, an employee of an operator of a community care facility, the operator of a residential care facility for the elderly, nor an employee of an operator of a residential care facility for the elderly.

First witness   Second witness

_____   _____
(print name)   (print name)

_____   _____
(address)   (address)

_____   _____
(city)   (state)   (city)   (state)

_____   _____
(signature of witness)   (signature of witness)

_____   _____
(date)   (date)

(5.4) ADDITIONAL STATEMENT OF WITNESSES: At least one of the above witnesses must also sign the following declaration:
I further declare under penalty of perjury under the laws of California that I am not related to the individual executing this advance health care directive by blood, marriage, or adoption, and, to the best of my knowledge, I am not entitled to any part of the individual's estate upon their death under a will now existing or by operation of law.

_____   _____
(signature of witness)   (signature of witness)

PART 6
SPECIAL WITNESS REQUIREMENT

(6.1) The following statement is required only if you are a patient in a skilled nursing facility—a health care facility that provides the following basic services: skilled nursing care and supportive care to patients whose primary need is for availability of skilled nursing care on an extended basis. The patient advocate or ombudsman must sign the following statement:

STATEMENT OF PATIENT ADVOCATE OR OMBUDSMAN

I declare under penalty of perjury under the laws of California that I am a patient advocate or ombudsman as designated by the State Department of Aging and that I am serving as a witness as required by Section 4675 of the Probate Code.

_____   _____
(date)   (sign your name)

_____   _____
(address)   (print your name)

_____
(city)   (state)

Leg.H. Added Stats 1999 ch 658 §39 (AB 891), operative July 1, 2000. Amended Stats 2018 ch 287 §1 (AB 3211), effective January 1, 2019; Stats 2022 ch 21 §3 (AB 2288), effective January 1, 2023; Stats 2023 ch 171 §3 (AB 1029), effective January 1, 2024.

Prior Law: Former Prob C §4701, similar to present Prob C §4674, was added Stats 1994 ch 307 §16, amended Stats 1995 ch 417 §2 and repealed Stats 1999 ch 658 §38, operative July 1, 2000.

§4702. [Section repealed 2000]

Leg.H. Added Stats 1994 ch 307 §16 (SB 1907). Amended Stats 1995 ch 417 §3 (SB 1148). Repealed Stats 1999 ch 658 §38 (AB 891), operative July 1, 2000. See Prob C §4659.

§4703. [Section repealed 2000]

Leg.H. Added Stats 1994 ch 307 §16 (SB 1907). Amended Stats 1995 ch 300 §12 (SB 984), effective August 3, 1995. Repealed Stats 1999 ch 658 §38 (AB 891), operative July 1, 2000. See Prob C §4701.

§4704. [Section repealed 2000]

Leg.H. Added Stats 1994 ch 307 §16 (SB 1907). Repealed Stats 1999 ch 658 §38 (AB 891), operative July 1, 2000. See Prob C §4701.

CHAPTER 3
HEALTH CARE SURROGATES

Designation of surrogate; Effective term and expiration effects; Priority of surrogate versus agent. §4711.
Priority of legally recognized health care decisionmakers; Selection of surrogate for health care decisions. § 4712.
Decisions by surrogates. §4714.
Disqualification of surrogate. §4715.
Authority of domestic partner to make health care decision for incapacitated partner. §4716.
Hospital duty to attempt contact with person having authority for health care decisions for non-communicable patient; What constitutes reasonable effort. §4717.

§4711. Designation of surrogate; Effective term and expiration effects; Priority of surrogate versus agent

(a) A patient may designate an adult as a surrogate to make health care decisions by personally informing the supervising health care provider or a designee of the health care facility caring for the patient. The designation of a surrogate shall be promptly recorded in the patient's health care record.

(b) Unless the patient specifies a shorter period, a surrogate designation under subdivision (a) is effective only during the course of treatment or illness or during the stay in the health care institution when the surrogate designation is made, or for 60 days, whichever period is shorter.

(c) The expiration of a surrogate designation under subdivision (b) does not affect any role the person designated under subdivision (a) may have in making health care decisions for the patient under any other law or standards of practice.

(d) Notwithstanding Section 4685, if the patient has designated an agent under a power of attorney for health care, the surrogate designated under subdivision (a) has priority over the agent for the period provided in subdivision (b), but the designation of a surrogate does not revoke the designation of an agent unless the patient communicates the intention to revoke in compliance with subdivision (a) of Section 4695. **Leg.H.** Added Stats 1999 ch 658 §39 (AB 891), operative July 1, 2000. Amended Stats

2001 ch 230 §5 (AB 1278), effective January 1, 2002; Stats 2022 ch 782 §1 (AB 2338), effective January 1, 2023.

§ 4712. Priority of legally recognized health care decisionmakers; Selection of surrogate for health care decisions

(a) If a patient lacks the capacity to make a health care decision, the following legally recognized health care decisionmakers may make health care decisions on the patient's behalf, in the following descending order of priority:

(1) The patient's surrogate selected pursuant to Section 4711.

(2) The patient's agent pursuant to an advance health care directive or a power of attorney for health care.

(3) The conservator or guardian of the patient having the authority to make health care decisions for the patient.

(b) Except as set forth in Section 4715, if a patient lacks the capacity to make a health care decision, but does not have a legally recognized health care decisionmaker pursuant to subdivision (a), a health care provider or a designee of the health care facility caring for the patient may choose a surrogate to make health care decisions on the patient's behalf, as appropriate in the given situation. The patient's surrogate shall be an adult who has demonstrated special care and concern for the patient, is familiar with the patient's personal values and beliefs to the extent known, and is reasonably available and willing to serve. A surrogate may be chosen from any of the following persons:

(1) The spouse or domestic partner of the patient.

(2) An adult child of the patient.

(3) A parent of the patient.

(4) An adult sibling of the patient.

(5) An adult grandchild of the patient.

(6) An adult relative or close personal friend. **Leg.H.** Added Stats 2022 ch 782 §2 (AB 2338), effective January 1, 2023.

§4714. Decisions by surrogates

A surrogate, including a person acting as a surrogate, shall make a health care decision in accordance with the patient's individual health care instructions, if any, and other wishes to the extent known to the surrogate. Otherwise, the surrogate shall make the decision in accordance with the surrogate's determination of the patient's best interest. In determining the patient's best interest, the surrogate shall consider the patient's personal values to the extent known to the surrogate. **Leg.H.** Added Stats 1999 ch 658 §39 (AB 891), operative July 1, 2000.

§4715. Disqualification of surrogate

A patient having capacity at any time may disqualify another person, including a member of the patient's family, from acting as the patient's surrogate by a signed writing or by personally informing the supervising health care provider of the disqualification. **Leg.H.** Added Stats 1999 ch 658 §39 (AB 891), operative July 1, 2000.

§4716. Authority of domestic partner to make health care decision for incapacitated partner

(a) If a patient lacks the capacity to make a health care decision, the patient's domestic partner shall have the same authority as a spouse has to make a health care decision for his or her incapacitated spouse. This section may not be construed to expand or restrict the ability of a spouse to make a health care decision for an incapacitated spouse.

(b) For the purposes of this section, the following definitions shall apply:

(1) "Capacity" has the same meaning as defined in Section 4609.

(2) "Health care" has the same meaning as defined in Section 4615.

(3) "Health care decision" has the same meaning as defined in Section 4617.

(4) "Domestic partner" has the same meaning as that term is used in Section 297 of the Family Code. **Leg.H.** Added Stats 2001 ch 893 §49 (AB 25).

Former Sections: Former Prob C §4716, relating to hospital duty to attempt contact with person having authority for health care decisions for non-communicable patient and what constitutes reasonable effort, was added Stats 2001 ch 329 §1 (SB 751) and amended and renumbered to Prob C §4717 by Stats 2004 ch 882 §2 (AB 2445).

Prior Law: There was another section of this number, relating to hospital duty to attempt contact with person having authority for health care decisions for non-communicable patient and what constitutes reasonable effort, which was added Stats 2001 ch 329 §1 (SB 751) and amended and renumbered to be Prob C §4717 by Stats 2004 ch 882 §2 (AB 2445).

§4717. Hospital duty to attempt contact with person having authority for health care decisions for non-communicable patient; What constitutes reasonable effort

(a) Notwithstanding any other provision of law, within 24 hours of the arrival in the emergency department of a general acute care hospital of a patient who is unconscious or otherwise incapable of communication, the hospital shall make reasonable efforts to contact the patient's agent, surrogate, or a family member or other person the hospital reasonably believes has the authority to make health care decisions on behalf of the patient. A hospital shall be deemed to have made reasonable efforts, and to have discharged its duty under this section, if it does all of the following:

(1) Examines the personal effects, if any, accompanying the patient and any medical records regarding the patient in its possession, and reviews any verbal or written report made by emergency medical technicians or the police, to identify the name of any agent, surrogate, or a family member or other person the hospital reasonably believes has the authority to make health care decisions on behalf of the patient.

(2) Contacts or attempts to contact any agent, surrogate, or a family member or other person the hospital reasonably believes has the authority to make health care decisions on behalf of the patient, as identified in paragraph (1).

(3) Contacts the Secretary of State directly or indirectly, including by voice mail or facsimile, to inquire whether the patient has registered an advance health care directive with the Advance Health Care Directive Registry, if the hospital finds evidence of the patient's Advance Health Care Directive Registry identification card either from the patient or from the patient's family or authorized agent.

(b) The hospital shall document in the patient's medical record all efforts made to contact any agent, surrogate, or a family member or other person the hospital reasonably believes has the authority to make health care decisions on behalf of the patient.

(c) Application of this section shall be suspended during any period in which the hospital implements its disaster and mass casualty program, or its fire and internal disaster program. **Leg.H.** Added Stats 2001 ch 329 §1 (SB 751), as Prob C §4716. Amended and renumbered by Stats 2004 ch 882 §2 (AB 2445), effective January 1, 2005.

§4720. [Section repealed 2000]

Leg.H. Added Stats 1994 ch 307 §16 (SB 1907). Repealed Stats 1999 ch 658 §38 (AB 891), operative July 1, 2000. See Prob C §§4682–4685 and 4687.

§4721. [Section repealed 2000]

Leg.H. Added Stats 1994 ch 307 §16 (SB 1907). Repealed Stats 1999 ch 658 §38 (AB 891), operative July 1, 2000. See Prob C §4678.

§4722. [Section repealed 2000]

Leg.H. Added Stats 1994 ch 307 §16 (SB 1907). Repealed Stats 1999 ch 658 §38 (AB 891), operative July 1, 2000. See Prob C §4652.

§4723. [Section repealed 2000]

Leg.H. Added Stats 1994 ch 307 §16 (SB 1907). Repealed Stats 1999 ch 658 §38 (AB 891), operative July 1, 2000. See Prob C §§4653 and 4655.

§4724. [Section repealed 2000]

Leg.H. Added Stats 1994 ch 307 §16 (SB 1907). Repealed Stats 1999 ch 658 §38 (AB 891), operative July 1, 2000. See Prob C §4689.

§4725. [Section repealed 2000]

Leg.H. Added Stats 1994 ch 307 §16 (SB 1907). Repealed Stats 1999 ch 658 §38 (AB 891), operative July 1, 2000. See Prob C §4677.

§4726. [Section repealed 2000]

Leg.H. Added Stats 1994 ch 307 §16 (SB 1907). Repealed Stats 1999 ch 658 §38 (AB 891), operative July 1, 2000. See Prob C §4743.

§4727. [Section repealed 2000]

Leg.H. Added Stats 1994 ch 307 §16 (SB 1907). Repealed Stats 1999 ch 658 §38 (AB 891), operative July 1, 2000. See Prob C §§4657, 4695, 4697, 4698, 4731, and 4740.

CHAPTER 4
DUTIES OF HEALTH CARE PROVIDERS

Communication with patient. §4730.
Recording of documents. §4731.
Records of primary physician. §4732.
Compliance by institution or provider. §4733.
Permission to decline to comply. §4734.
Medically ineffective care. §4735.
Requirements after declining to comply. §4736.

§4730. Communication with patient

Before implementing a health care decision made for a patient, a supervising health care provider, if possible, shall promptly communicate to the patient the decision made and the identity of the person making the decision. **Leg.H.** Added Stats 1999 ch 658 §39 (AB 891), operative July 1, 2000.

§4731. Recording of documents

(a) A supervising health care provider who knows of the existence of an advance health care directive, a revocation of an advance health care directive, or a designation or disqualification of a surrogate, shall promptly record its existence in the patient's health care record and, if it is in writing, shall request a copy. If a copy is furnished, the supervising health care provider shall arrange for its maintenance in the patient's health care record.

(b) A supervising health care provider who knows of a revocation of a power of attorney for health care or a disqualification of a surrogate shall make a reasonable effort to notify the agent or surrogate of the revocation or disqualification. **Leg.H.** Added Stats 1999 ch 658 §39 (AB 891), operative July 1, 2000.

§4732. Records of primary physician

A primary physician who makes or is informed of a determination that a patient lacks or has recovered capacity, or that another condition exists affecting an individual health care instruction or the authority of an agent, conservator of the person, or surrogate, shall promptly record the determination in the patient's health care record and communicate the determination to the patient, if possible, and to a person then authorized to make health care decisions for the patient. **Leg.H.** Added Stats 1999 ch 658 §39 (AB 891), operative July 1, 2000.

§4733. Compliance by institution or provider

Except as provided in Sections 4734 and 4735, a health care provider or health care institution providing care to a patient shall do the following:

(a) Comply with an individual health care instruction of the patient and with a reasonable interpretation of that instruction made by a person then authorized to make health care decisions for the patient.

(b) Comply with a health care decision for the patient made by a person then authorized to make health care decisions for the patient to the same extent as if the decision had been made by the patient while having capacity. **Leg.H.** Added Stats 1999 ch 658 §39 (AB 891), operative July 1, 2000.

§4734. Permission to decline to comply

(a) A health care provider may decline to comply with an individual health care instruction or health care decision for reasons of conscience.

(b) A health care institution may decline to comply with an individual health care instruction or health care decision if the instruction or decision is contrary to a policy of the institution that is expressly based on reasons of conscience and if the policy was timely communicated to the patient or to a person then authorized to make health care decisions for the patient. **Leg.H.** Added Stats 1999 ch 658 §39 (AB 891), operative July 1, 2000.

§4735. Medically ineffective care

A health care provider or health care institution may decline to comply with an individual health care instruction or health care decision that requires medically ineffective health care or health care contrary to generally accepted health care standards applicable to the health care provider or institution. **Leg.H.** Added Stats 1999 ch 658 §39 (AB 891), operative July 1, 2000.

§4736. Requirements after declining to comply

A health care provider or health care institution that declines to comply with an individual health care instruction or health care decision shall do all of the following:

(a) Promptly so inform the patient, if possible, and any person then authorized to make health care decisions for the patient.

(b) Unless the patient or person then authorized to make health care decisions for the patient refuses assistance, immediately make all reasonable efforts to assist in the transfer of the patient to another health care provider or institution that is willing to comply with the instruction or decision.

(c) Provide continuing care to the patient until a transfer can be accomplished or until it appears that a transfer cannot be accomplished. In all cases, appropriate pain relief and other palliative care shall be continued. **Leg.H.** Added Stats 1999 ch 658 §39 (AB 891), operative July 1, 2000.

CHAPTER 5
IMMUNITIES AND LIABILITIES

Immunity as to specified conduct. §4740.
Agent or surrogate immunity. §4741.
Intentional violations. §4742.
Forgeries and concealments. §4743.

§4740. Immunity as to specified conduct

A health care provider or health care institution acting in good faith and in accordance with generally accepted health care standards applicable to the health care provider or institution is not subject to civil or criminal liability or to discipline for unprofessional conduct for any actions in compliance with this division, including, but not limited to, any of the following conduct:

(a) Complying with a health care decision of a person that the health care provider or health care institution believes in good faith has the authority to make a health care decision for a patient, including a decision to withhold or withdraw health care.

(b) Declining to comply with a health care decision of a person based on a belief that the person then lacked authority.

(c) Complying with an advance health care directive and assuming that the directive was valid when made and has not been revoked or terminated.

(d) Declining to comply with an individual health care instruction or health care decision, in accordance with Sections 4734 to 4736, inclusive. **Leg.H.** Added Stats 1999 ch 658 §39 (AB 891), operative July 1, 2000.

§4741. Agent or surrogate immunity

A person acting as agent or surrogate under this part is not subject to civil or criminal liability or to discipline for unprofessional conduct for health care decisions made in good faith. **Leg.H.** Added Stats 1999 ch 658 §39 (AB 891), operative July 1, 2000.

§4742. Intentional violations

(a) A health care provider or health care institution that intentionally violates this part is subject to liability to the aggrieved individual for damages of two thousand five hundred dollars ($2,500) or actual damages resulting from the violation, whichever is greater, plus reasonable attorney's fees.

(b) A person who intentionally falsifies, forges, conceals, defaces, or obliterates an individual's advance health care directive or a revocation of an advance health care directive without the individual's consent, or who coerces or fraudulently induces an individual to give, revoke, or not to give an advance health care directive, is subject to liability to that individual for damages of ten thousand dollars ($10,000) or actual damages resulting from the action, whichever is greater, plus reasonable attorney's fees.

(c) The damages provided in this section are cumulative and not exclusive of any other remedies provided by law. **Leg.H.** Added Stats 1999 ch 658 §39 (AB 891), operative July 1, 2000.

§4743. Forgeries and concealments

Any person who alters or forges a written advance health care directive of another, or willfully conceals or withholds personal knowledge of a revocation of an advance directive, with the intent to cause a withholding or withdrawal of health care necessary to keep the patient alive contrary to the desires of the patient, and thereby directly causes health care necessary to keep the patient alive to be withheld or withdrawn and the death of the patient thereby to be hastened, is subject to prosecution for unlawful homicide as provided in Chapter 1 (commencing with Section 187) of Title 8 of Part 1 of the Penal Code. **Leg.H.** Added Stats 1999 ch 658 §39 (AB 891), operative July 1, 2000.

PART 3
JUDICIAL PROCEEDINGS

Chapter 1. General Provisions.
Chapter 2. Jurisdiction and Venue.
Chapter 3. Petitions and Orders.

CHAPTER 1
GENERAL PROVISIONS

Nature of directive or decision. §4750.
Remedies as cumulative. §4751.
Provisions as subject to limitations in directives. §4752.
Elimination of authority. §4753.
Jury trial. §4754.
Applicable general provisions. §4755.

§4750. Nature of directive or decision
Subject to this division:

(a) An advance health care directive is effective and exercisable free of judicial intervention.

(b) A health care decision made by an agent for a principal is effective without judicial approval.

(c) A health care decision made by a surrogate for a patient is effective without judicial approval. **Leg.H.** Added Stats 1999 ch 658 §39 (AB 891), operative July 1, 2000.

Prior Law: Former Prob C §4750, similar to present Prob C §4740, was added Stats 1994 ch 307 §16 and repealed Stats 1999 ch 658 §38, operative July 1, 2000.

§4751. Remedies as cumulative
The remedies provided in this part are cumulative and not exclusive of any other remedies provided by law. **Leg.H.** Added Stats 1999 ch 658 §39 (AB 891), operative July 1, 2000.

Prior Law: Former Prob C §4751, defining "convincing evidence", was added Stats 1994 ch 307 §16 and repealed Stats 1999 ch 658 §38, operative July 1, 2000. Historical derivation: Former CC §2511, as added Stats 1985 ch 403 §12, amended Stats 1990 ch 331 §3, ch 986 §5.5.

§4752. Provisions as subject to limitations in directives
Except as provided in Section 4753, this part is not subject to limitation in an advance health care directive. **Leg.H.** Added Stats 1999 ch 658 §39 (AB 891), operative July 1, 2000.

Prior Law: Former Prob C §4752, similar to present Prob C §4676, was added Stats 1994 ch 307 §16 and repealed Stats 1999 ch 658 §38, operative July 1, 2000.

§4753. Elimination of authority
(a) Subject to subdivision (b), an advance health care directive may expressly eliminate the authority of a person listed in Section 4765 to petition the court for any one or more of the purposes enumerated in Section 4766, if both of the following requirements are satisfied:

(1) The advance directive is executed by an individual having the advice of a lawyer authorized to practice law in the state where the advance directive is executed.

(2) The individual's lawyer signs a certificate stating in substance: "I am a lawyer authorized to practice law in the state where this advance health care directive was executed, and _____ [insert name] was my client at the time this advance directive was executed. I have advised my client concerning his or her rights in connection with this advance directive and the applicable law and the consequences of signing or not signing this advance directive, and my client, after being so advised, has executed this advance directive."

(b) An advance health care directive may not limit the authority of the following persons to petition under this part:

(1) The conservator of the person, with respect to a petition relating to an advance directive, for a purpose specified in subdivision (b) or (d) of Section 4766.

(2) The agent, with respect to a petition relating to a power of attorney for health care, for a purpose specified in subdivision (b) or (c) of Section 4766. **Leg.H.** Added Stats 1999 ch 658 §39 (AB 891), operative July 1, 2000.

Prior Law: Former Prob C §4753, similar to present Prob C §§4780 et seq., was added Stats 1994 ch 307 §16 and repealed Stats 1999 ch 658 §38, operative July 1, 2000.

§4754. Jury trial
There is no right to a jury trial in proceedings under this division. **Leg.H.** Added Stats 1999 ch 658 §39 (AB 891), operative July 1, 2000.

§4755. Applicable general provisions
Except as otherwise provided in this division, the general provisions in Division 3 (commencing with Section 1000) apply to proceedings under this division. **Leg.H.** Added Stats 1999 ch 658 §39 (AB 891), operative July 1, 2000.

CHAPTER 2
JURISDICTION AND VENUE

Court jurisdiction. §4760.
Basis for jurisdiction. §4761.
Personal jurisdiction over agent or surrogate. §4762.
Venue. §4763.

§4760. Court jurisdiction
(a) The superior court has jurisdiction in proceedings under this division.

(b) The court in proceedings under this division is a court of general jurisdiction and the court, or a judge of the court, has the same power and authority with respect to the proceedings as otherwise provided by law for a superior court, or a judge of the superior court, including, but not limited to, the matters authorized by Section 128 of the Code of Civil Procedure. **Leg.H.** Added Stats 1999 ch 658 §39 (AB 891), operative July 1, 2000.

§4761. Basis for jurisdiction
The court may exercise jurisdiction in proceedings under this division on any basis permitted by Section 410.10 of the Code of Civil Procedure. **Leg.H.** Added Stats 1999 ch 658 §39 (AB 891), operative July 1, 2000.

§4762. Personal jurisdiction over agent or surrogate
Without limiting Section 4761, a person who acts as an agent under a power of attorney for health care or as a surrogate under this division is subject to personal jurisdiction in this state with respect to matters relating to acts and transactions of the agent or surrogate performed in this state or affecting a patient in this state. **Leg.H.** Added Stats 1999 ch 658 §39 (AB 891), operative July 1, 2000.

§4763. Venue
The proper county for commencement of a proceeding under this division shall be determined in the following order of priority:

(a) The county in which the patient resides.
(b) The county in which the agent or surrogate resides.
(c) Any other county that is in the patient's best interest. **Leg.H.** Added Stats 1999 ch 658 §39 (AB 891), operative July 1, 2000.

CHAPTER 3
PETITIONS AND ORDERS

Persons who may file petition. §4765.
Purposes of petition. §4766.
Contents of petition. §4767.
Dismissals. §4768.
Notice of hearing. §4769.
Temporary order prescribing care. §4770.
Award of fees. §4771.

§4765. Persons who may file petition
Subject to Section 4753, a petition may be filed under this part by any of the following persons:

(a) The patient.
(b) The patient's spouse, unless legally separated.
(c) A relative of the patient.
(d) The patient's agent or surrogate.
(e) The conservator of the person of the patient.
(f) The court investigator, described in Section 1454, of the county where the patient resides.
(g) The public guardian of the county where the patient resides.
(h) The supervising health care provider or health care institution involved with the patient's care.

(i) Any other interested person or friend of the patient. **Leg.H.** Added Stats 1999 ch 658 §39 (AB 891), operative July 1, 2000.

§4766. Purposes of petition

A petition may be filed under this part for any one or more of the following purposes:

(a) Determining whether or not the patient has capacity to make health care decisions.

(b) Determining whether an advance health care directive is in effect or has terminated.

(c) Determining whether the acts or proposed acts of an agent or surrogate are consistent with the patient's desires as expressed in an advance health care directive or otherwise made known to the court or, where the patient's desires are unknown or unclear, whether the acts or proposed acts of the agent or surrogate are in the patient's best interest.

(d) Declaring that the authority of an agent or surrogate is terminated, upon a determination by the court that the agent or surrogate has made a health care decision for the patient that authorized anything illegal or upon a determination by the court of both of the following:

(1) The agent or surrogate has violated, has failed to perform, or is unfit to perform, the duty under an advance health care directive to act consistent with the patient's desires or, where the patient's desires are unknown or unclear, is acting (by action or inaction) in a manner that is clearly contrary to the patient's best interest.

(2) At the time of the determination by the court, the patient lacks the capacity to execute or to revoke an advance health care directive or disqualify a surrogate.

(e) Compelling a third person to honor individual health care instructions or the authority of an agent or surrogate. **Leg.H.** Added Stats 1999 ch 658 §39 (AB 891), operative July 1, 2000. Amended Stats 2001 ch 230 §7 (AB 1278), effective January 1, 2002.

§4767. Contents of petition

A proceeding under this part is commenced by filing a petition stating facts showing that the petition is authorized under this part, the grounds of the petition, and, if known to the petitioner, the terms of any advance health care directive in question. **Leg.H.** Added Stats 1999 ch 658 §39 (AB 891), operative July 1, 2000.

§4768. Dismissals

The court may dismiss a petition if it appears that the proceeding is not reasonably necessary for the protection of the interests of the patient and shall stay or dismiss the proceeding in whole or in part when required by Section 410.30 of the Code of Civil Procedure. **Leg.H.** Added Stats 1999 ch 658 §39 (AB 891), operative July 1, 2000.

§4769. Notice of hearing

(a) Subject to subdivision (b), at least 15 days before the time set for hearing, the petitioner shall serve notice of the time and place of the hearing, together with a copy of the petition, on the following:

(1) The agent or surrogate, if not the petitioner.

(2) The patient, if not the petitioner.

(b) In the case of a petition to compel a third person to honor individual health care instructions or the authority of an agent or surrogate, notice of the time and place of the hearing, together with a copy of the petition, shall be served on the third person in the manner provided in Chapter 4 (commencing with Section 413.10) of Title 5 of Part 2 of the Code of Civil Procedure. **Leg.H.** Added Stats 1999 ch 658 §39 (AB 891), operative July 1, 2000. Amended Stats 2001 ch 230 §8 (AB 1278), effective January 1, 2002.

§4770. Temporary order prescribing care

The court in its discretion, on a showing of good cause, may issue a temporary order prescribing the health care of the patient until the disposition of the petition filed under Section 4766. If a power of attorney for health care is in effect and a conservator (including a temporary conservator) of the person is appointed for the principal, the court that appoints the conservator in its discretion, on a showing of good cause, may issue a temporary order prescribing the health care of the principal, the order to continue in effect for the period ordered by the court but in no case longer than the period necessary to permit the filing and determination of a petition filed under Section 4766. **Leg.H.** Added Stats 1999 ch 658 §39 (AB 891), operative July 1, 2000.

Prior Law: Former Prob C §4770, relating to citation of chapter, as added Stats 1994 ch 307 §16 and repealed Stats 1999 ch 658 §38, operative July 1, 2000. Historical derivation: Former CC §2508, as added Stats 1984 ch 312 §8.

§4771. Award of fees

In a proceeding under this part commenced by the filing of a petition by a person other than the agent or surrogate, the court may in its discretion award reasonable attorney's fees to one of the following:

(a) The agent or surrogate, if the court determines that the proceeding was commenced without any reasonable cause.

(b) The person commencing the proceeding, if the court determines that the agent or surrogate has clearly violated the duties under the advance health care directive. **Leg.H.** Added Stats 1999 ch 658 §39 (AB 891), operative July 1, 2000.

Prior Law: Former Prob C §4771, similar to present Prob C §4701, was added Stats 1994 ch 307 §16 and repealed Stats 1999 ch 658 §38, operative July 1, 2000.

§4772. [Section repealed 2000]

Leg.H. Added Stats 1994 ch 307 §16 (SB 1907). Repealed Stats 1999 ch 658 §38 (AB 891), operative July 1, 2000. The repealed section related to type size of warning statement, exception, and attorney's certificate.

§4773. [Section repealed 2000]

Leg.H. Added Stats 1994 ch 307 §16 (SB 1907). Repealed Stats 1999 ch 658 §38 (AB 891), operative July 1, 2000. The repealed section related to requirements for valid execution.

§4774. [Section repealed 2000]

Leg.H. Added Stats 1994 ch 307 §16 (SB 1907). Repealed Stats 1999 ch 658 §38 (AB 891), operative July 1, 2000. The repealed section related to power of attorney as valid under chapter.

§4775. [Section repealed 2000]

Leg.H. Added Stats 1994 ch 307 §16 (SB 1907). Repealed Stats 1999 ch 658 §38 (AB 891), operative July 1, 2000. The repealed section related to use of form complying with prior law.

§4776. [Section repealed 2000]

Leg.H. Added Stats 1994 ch 307 §16 (SB 1907). Repealed Stats 1999 ch 658 §38 (AB 891), operative July 1, 2000. The repealed section related to authority of attorney-in-fact to select and discharge health care professionals.

§4777. [Section repealed 2000]

Leg.H. Added Stats 1994 ch 307 §16 (SB 1907). Repealed Stats 1999 ch 658 §38 (AB 891), operative July 1, 2000. The repealed section related to validity of document when executed by attorney-in-fact.

§4778. [Section repealed 2000]

Leg.H. Added Stats 1994 ch 307 §16 (SB 1907). Repealed Stats 1999 ch 658 §38 (AB 891), operative July 1, 2000. The repealed section related to effect of judicial termination of authority and alternate agents.

§4779. [Section repealed 2000]

Leg.H. Added Stats 1994 ch 307 §16 (SB 1907). Repealed Stats 1999 ch 658 §38 (AB 891), operative July 1, 2000. See Prob C §4700.

PART 4
REQUEST REGARDING RESUSCITATIVE MEASURES

Execution of Physician Orders for Life Sustaining Treatment form; Revocation; Medallion. §4780.
"Health care provider". §4781.
Duty of health care provider; New or modified order. §4781.2.
Resolution of conflict between order and instruction. §4781.4.
Duty of health care decisionmaker. §4781.5.
Immunity of provider. §4782.
Forms for requests regarding resuscitative measures. §4783.
Presumed validity. §4784.
Location of individual executing request. §4785.
Construction of code provisions in part. §4786.

§4780. Execution of Physician Orders for Life Sustaining Treatment form; Revocation; Medallion

(a) As used in this part:

(1) "Request regarding resuscitative measures" means a written document, signed by (A) an individual with capacity, or a legally recognized health care decisionmaker, and (B) the individual's physician, that directs a health care provider regarding resuscitative measures. A request regarding resuscitative measures is not an advance health care directive.

(2) "Request regarding resuscitative measures" includes one, or both of, the following:

(A) A prehospital "do not resuscitate" form as developed by the Emergency Medical Services Authority or other substantially similar form.

(B) A Physician Orders for Life Sustaining Treatment form, as approved by the Emergency Medical Services Authority.

(3) "Physician Orders for Life Sustaining Treatment form" means a request regarding resuscitative measures that directs a health care provider regarding resuscitative and life-sustaining measures.

(b) A legally recognized health care decisionmaker may execute the Physician Orders for Life Sustaining Treatment form only if the individual lacks capacity, or the individual has designated that the decisionmaker's authority is effective pursuant to Section 4682.

(c) The Physician Orders for Life Sustaining Treatment form and medical intervention and procedures offered by the form shall be explained by a health care provider, as defined in Section 4621. The form shall be completed by a health care provider based on patient preferences and medical indications, and signed by a physician, or a nurse practitioner or a physician assistant acting under the supervision of the physician and within the scope of practice authorized by law, and the patient or his or her legally recognized health care decisionmaker. The health care provider, during the process of completing the Physician Orders for Life Sustaining Treatment form, should inform the patient about the difference between an advance health care directive and the Physician Orders for Life Sustaining Treatment form.

(d) An individual having capacity may revoke a Physician Orders for Life Sustaining Treatment form at any time and in any manner that communicates an intent to revoke, consistent with Section 4695.

(e) A request regarding resuscitative measures may also be evidenced by a medallion engraved with the words "do not resuscitate" or the letters "DNR," a patient identification number, and a 24-hour toll-free telephone number, issued by a person pursuant to an agreement with the Emergency Medical Services Authority. **Leg.H.** Added Stats 1999 ch 658 §39 (AB 891), operative July 1, 2000. Amended Stats 2008 ch 266 §3 (AB 3000), effective January 1, 2009; Stats 2015 ch 217 §1 (AB 637), effective January 1, 2016.

§4781. "Health care provider"

As used in this part, "health care provider" includes, but is not limited to, the following:

(a) Persons described in Section 4621.

(b) Emergency response employees, including, but not limited to, firefighters, law enforcement officers, emergency medical technicians I and II, paramedics, and employees and volunteer members of legally organized and recognized volunteer organizations, who are trained in accordance with standards adopted as regulations by the Emergency Medical Services Authority pursuant to Sections 1797.170, 1797.171, 1797.172, 1797.182, and 1797.183 of the Health and Safety Code to respond to medical emergencies in the course of performing their volunteer or employee duties with the organization. **Leg.H.** Added Stats 1999 ch 658 §39 (AB 891), operative July 1, 2000.

§4781.2. Duty of health care provider; New or modified order

(a) A health care provider shall treat an individual in accordance with a Physician Orders for Life Sustaining Treatment form.

(b) Subdivision (a) does not apply if the Physician Orders for Life Sustaining Treatment form requires medically ineffective health care or health care contrary to generally accepted health care standards applicable to the health care provider or institution.

(c) A physician may conduct an evaluation of the individual and, if possible, in consultation with the individual, or the individual's legally recognized health care decisionmaker, issue a new order consistent with the most current information available about the individual's health status and goals of care.

(d) The legally recognized health care decisionmaker of an individual without capacity shall consult with the physician who is, at that time, the individual's treating physician prior to making a request to modify that individual's Physician Orders for Life Sustaining Treatment form.

(e) An individual with capacity may, at any time, request alternative treatment to that treatment that was ordered on the form. **Leg.H.** Added Stats 2008 ch 266 §4 (AB 3000), effective January 1, 2009.

§4781.4. Resolution of conflict between order and instruction

If the orders in an individual's request regarding resuscitative measures directly conflict with his or her individual health care instruction, as defined in Section 4623, then, to the extent of the conflict, the most recent order or instruction is effective. **Leg.H.** Added Stats 2008 ch 266 §5 (AB 3000), effective January 1, 2009.

§4781.5. Duty of health care decisionmaker

The legally recognized health care decisionmaker shall make health care decisions pursuant to this part in accordance with Sections 4684 and 4714. **Leg.H.** Added Stats 2008 ch 266 §6 (AB 3000), effective January 1, 2009.

§4782. Immunity of provider

A health care provider who honors a request regarding resuscitative measures is not subject to criminal prosecution, civil liability, discipline for unprofessional conduct, administrative sanction, or any other sanction, as a result of his or her reliance on the request, if the health care provider (a) believes in good faith that the action or decision is consistent with this part, and (b) has no knowledge that the action or decision would be inconsistent with a health care decision that the individual signing the request would have made on his or her own behalf under like circumstances. **Leg.H.** Added Stats 1999 ch 658 §39 (AB 891), operative July 1, 2000. Amended Stats 2008 ch 266 §7 (AB 3000), effective January 1, 2009.

§4783. Forms for requests regarding resuscitative measures

(a) Forms for requests regarding resuscitative measures printed after January 1, 1995, shall contain the following:

"By signing this form, the legally recognized health care decisionmaker acknowledges that this request regarding resuscitative measures is consistent with the known desires of, and with the best interest of, the individual who is the subject of the form."

(b) A printed form substantially similar to that described in subparagraph (A) of paragraph (2) of subdivision (a) of Section 4780 is valid and enforceable if all of the following conditions are met:

(1) The form is signed by the individual, or the individual's legally recognized health care decisionmaker, and a physician.

(2) The form directs health care providers regarding resuscitative measures.

(3) The form contains all other information required by this section. **Leg.H.** Added Stats 1999 ch 658 §39 (AB 891), operative July 1, 2000. Amended Stats 2008 ch 266 §8 (AB 3000), effective January 1, 2009.

§4784. Presumed validity

In the absence of knowledge to the contrary, a health care provider may presume that a request regarding resuscitative measures is valid and unrevoked. **Leg.H.** Added Stats 1999 ch 658 §39 (AB 891), operative July 1, 2000. Amended Stats 2008 ch 266 §9 (AB 3000), effective January 1, 2009.

§4785. Location of individual executing request

This part applies regardless of whether the individual executing a request regarding resuscitative measures is within or outside a hospital or other health care institution. **Leg.H.** Added Stats 1999 ch 658 §39 (AB 891), operative July 1, 2000. Amended Stats 2008 ch 266 §10 (AB 3000), effective January 1, 2009.

§4786. Construction of code provisions in part

This part does not repeal or narrow laws relating to health care decisionmaking. **Leg.H.** Added Stats 1999 ch 658 §39 (AB 891), operative July 1, 2000.

§4788. California Physician Orders for Life Sustaining Treatment (POLST) eRegistry Pilot [Repealed January 1, 2020]

Leg.H. Added Stats 2015 ch 504 §2 (SB 19), effective January 1, 2016, repealed January 1, 2020. Amended Stats 2016 ch 86 §248 (SB 1171), effective January 1, 2017, repealed January 1, 2020.

PART 5
ADVANCE HEALTH CARE DIRECTIVE REGISTRY

Registry system. §4800.
Verification procedures. §4801.
Procedures to advise registrants. §4802.
Failure to register. §4803.
Effect on ability to revoke directive. §4804.
Construction as to request for information. §4805.
Advance Directives and Terminal Illness Decisions Program. §4806.

§4800. Registry system

(a) The Secretary of State shall establish a registry system through which a person who has executed a written advance health care directive may register in a central information center, information regarding the advance directive, making that information available upon request to any health care provider, the public guardian, or the legal representative of the registrant. A request for information pursuant to this section shall state the need for the information.

(b) The Secretary of State shall respond by the close of business on the next business day to a request for information made pursuant to Section 4717 by the emergency department of a general acute care hospital.

(c) Information that may be received is limited to the registrant's name, social security number, driver's license number, or other individual identifying number established by law, if any, address, date and place of birth, the registrant's advance health care directive, an intended place of deposit or safekeeping of a written advance health care directive, and the name and telephone number of the agent and any alternative agent. Information that may be released upon request may not include the registrant's social security number except when necessary to verify the identity of the registrant.

(d) When the Secretary of State receives information from a registrant, the secretary shall issue the registrant an Advance Health Care Directive Registry identification card indicating that an advance health care directive, or information regarding an advance health care directive, has been deposited with the registry. Costs associated with issuance of the card shall be offset by the fee charged by the Secretary of State to receive and register information at the registry.

(e) The Secretary of State, at the request of the registrant or his or her legal representative, shall transmit the information received regarding the written advance health care directive to the registry system of another jurisdiction as identified by the registrant, or his or her legal representative.

(f) The Secretary of State shall charge a fee to each registrant in an amount such that, when all fees charged to registrants are aggregated, the aggregated fees do not exceed the actual cost of establishing and maintaining the registry. **Leg.H.** Added Stats 1999 ch 658 §39 (AB 891), operative July 1, 2000. Amended Stats 2004 ch 882 §3 (AB 2445).

Prior Law: Former Prob C §4800, similar to the present section, was added Stats 1994 ch 1280 §2, amended Stats 1995 ch 91 §136 and repealed Stats 1999 ch 658 §38, operative July 1, 2000.

§4801. Verification procedures

The Secretary of State shall establish procedures to verify the identities of health care providers, the public guardian, and other authorized persons requesting information pursuant to Section 4800. No fee shall be charged to any health care provider, the public guardian, or other authorized person requesting information pursuant to Section 4800. **Leg.H.** Added Stats 1999 ch 658 §39 (AB 891), operative July 1, 2000.

Prior Law: Former Prob C §4801, similar to the present section, was added Stats 1994 ch 1280 §2 and repealed Stats 1999 ch 658 §38, operative July 1, 2000.

§4802. Procedures to advise registrants

The Secretary of State shall establish procedures to advise each registrant of the following:

(a) A health care provider may not honor a written advance health care directive until it receives a copy from the registrant.

(b) Each registrant must notify the registry upon revocation of the advance directive.

(c) Each registrant must reregister upon execution of a subsequent advance directive. **Leg.H.** Added Stats 1999 ch 658 §39 (AB 891), operative July 1, 2000.

Prior Law: Former Prob C §4802, similar to the present section, was added Stats 1994 ch 1280 §2 and repealed Stats 1999 ch 658 §38, operative July 1, 2000.

§4803. Failure to register

Failure to register with the Secretary of State does not affect the validity of any advance health care directive. **Leg.H.** Added Stats 1999 ch 658 §39 (AB 891), operative July 1, 2000.

§4804. Effect on ability to revoke directive

Registration with the Secretary of State does not affect the ability of the registrant to revoke the registrant's advance health care directive or a later executed advance directive, nor does registration raise any presumption of validity or superiority among any competing advance directives or revocations. **Leg.H.** Added Stats 1999 ch 658 §39 (AB 891), operative July 1, 2000.

Prior Law: Former Prob C §4804, similar to present Prob C §4803, was added Stats 1994 ch 1280 §2 and repealed Stats 1999 ch 658 §38, operative July 1, 2000.

§4805. Construction as to request for information

Nothing in this part shall be construed to affect the duty of a health care provider to provide information to a patient regarding advance health care directives pursuant to any provision of federal law. **Leg.H.** Added Stats 1999 ch 658 §39 (AB 891), operative July 1, 2000. Amended Stats 2004 ch 882 §4 (AB 2445).

Prior Law: Former Prob C §4805, similar to present Prob C §4804, was added Stats 1994 ch 1280 §2 and repealed Stats 1999 ch 658 §38, operative July 1, 2000.

§4806. Advance Directives and Terminal Illness Decisions Program

(a) The Secretary of State shall work with the State Department of Health Services and the office of the Attorney General to develop information about end of life care, advance health care directives, and registration of the advance health care directives at the registry established pursuant to subdivision (a) of Section 4800. This information shall be developed utilizing existing information developed by the office of the Attorney General.

(b) Links to the information specified in subdivision (a) and to the registry shall be available on the Web sites of the Secretary of State, the State Department of Health Services, the office of the Attorney General, the Department of Managed Health Care, the Department of Insurance, the Board of Registered Nursing, and the Medical Board of California. **Leg.H.** Added Stats 2005 ch 434 §3 (AB 1676).

2005 Note: This act shall be known, and may be cited, as the Advance Directives and Terminal Illness Decisions Program. Stats 2005 ch 434 (AB 1676) §1.

Prior Law: Former Prob C §4806, similar to present Prob C §4805, was added Stats 1994 ch 1280 §2, amended Stats 1995 ch 300 §14, effective August 3, 1995, and repealed Stats 1999 ch 658 §38, operative July 1, 2000.

§4900. [Section repealed 2000]

Leg.H. Added Stats 1994 ch 307 §16 (SB 1907). Repealed Stats 1999 ch 658 §41 (AB 891), operative July 1, 2000. See Prob C §§4500 and 4750.

§4901. [Section repealed 2000]

Leg.H. Added Stats 1994 ch 307 §16 (SB 1907). Repealed Stats 1999 ch 658 §41 (AB 891), operative July 1, 2000. See Prob C §§4501 and 4751.

§4902. [Section repealed 2000]

Leg.H. Added Stats 1994 ch 307 §16 (SB 1907). Repealed Stats 1999 ch 658 §41 (AB 891), operative July 1, 2000. See Prob C §§4502 and 4752.

§4903. [Section repealed 2000]

Leg.H. Added Stats 1994 ch 307 §16 (SB 1907). Repealed Stats 1999 ch 658 §41 (AB 891), operative July 1, 2000. See Prob C §§4503 and 4753.

§4904. [Section repealed 2000]

Leg.H. Added Stats 1994 ch 307 §16 (SB 1907). Repealed Stats 1999 ch 658 §41 (AB 891), operative July 1, 2000. See Prob C §§4504 and 4754.

§4905. [Section repealed 2000]

Leg.H. Added Stats 1994 ch 307 §16 (SB 1907). Repealed Stats 1999 ch 658 §41 (AB 891), operative July 1, 2000. See Prob C §§4505 and 4755.

§4920. [Section repealed 2000]

Leg.H. Added Stats 1994 ch 307 §16 (SB 1907). Repealed Stats 1999 ch 658 §41 (AB 891), operative July 1, 2000. See Prob C §§4520 and 4760.

§4921. [Section repealed 2000]

Leg.H. Added Stats 1994 ch 307 §16 (SB 1907). Repealed Stats 1999 ch 658 §41 (AB 891), operative July 1, 2000. See Prob C §§4521 and 4761.

§4922. [Section repealed 2000]

Leg.H. Added Stats 1994 ch 307 §16 (SB 1907). Repealed Stats 1999 ch 658 §41 (AB 891), operative July 1, 2000. See Prob C §§4522 and 4762.

§4923. [Section repealed 2000]

Leg.H. Added Stats 1994 ch 307 §16 (SB 1907). Repealed Stats 1999 ch 658 §41 (AB 891), operative July 1, 2000. See Prob C §§4523 and 4763.

§4940. [Section repealed 2000]

Leg.H. Added Stats 1994 ch 307 §16 (SB 1907). Repealed Stats 1999 ch 658 §41 (AB 891), operative July 1, 2000. See Prob C §§4540 and 4765.

§4941. [Section repealed 2000]

Leg.H. Added Stats 1994 ch 307 §16 (SB 1907). Repealed Stats 1999 ch 658 §41 (AB 891), operative July 1, 2000. See Prob C §4541.

§4942. [Section repealed 2000]

Leg.H. Added Stats 1994 ch 307 §16 (SB 1907). Repealed Stats 1999 ch 658 §41 (AB 891), operative July 1, 2000. See Prob C §4766.

§4943. [Section repealed 2000]

Leg.H. Added Stats 1994 ch 307 §16 (SB 1907). Repealed Stats 1999 ch 658 §41 (AB 891), operative July 1, 2000. See Prob C §§4542 and 4767.

§4944. [Section repealed 2000]

Leg.H. Added Stats 1994 ch 307 §16 (SB 1907). Repealed Stats 1999 ch 658 §41 (AB 891), operative July 1, 2000. See Prob C §§4543 and 4768.

§4945. [Section repealed 2000]

Leg.H. Added Stats 1994 ch 307 §16 (SB 1907). Repealed Stats 1999 ch 658 §41 (AB 891), operative July 1, 2000. See Prob C §§4544 and 4769.

§4946. [Section repealed 2000]

Leg.H. Added Stats 1994 ch 307 §16 (SB 1907). Repealed Stats 1999 ch 658 §41 (AB 891), operative July 1, 2000. See Prob C §4770.

§4947. [Section repealed 2000]

Leg.H. Added Stats 1994 ch 307 §16 (SB 1907). Repealed Stats 1999 ch 658 §41 (AB 891), operative July 1, 2000. See Prob C §§4545 and 4771. See Prob C §§4545 and 4771.

§4948. [Section repealed 1998]

Leg.H. Added Stats 1994 ch 307 §16 (SB 1907). Repealed Stats 1997 ch 724 §16 (AB 1172). See Prob C §1302.

DIVISION 5
NONPROBATE TRANSFERS

Part 1. Provisions Relating to Effect of Death.
Part 2. Multiple-Party Accounts.
Part 3. Uniform TOD Security Registration Act.
Part 4. Revocable Transfer on Death Deed [Repealed effective January 1, 2032].
Part 5. Gifts in View of Impending Death.

PART 1
PROVISIONS RELATING TO EFFECT OF DEATH

Chapter 1. General Provisions.
Chapter 2. Nonprobate Transfers of Community Property.
Chapter 3. Nonprobate Transfer to Former Spouse.

CHAPTER 1
GENERAL PROVISIONS

Nonprobate transfers at death. §5000.
When holder of property not required to comply with provision for nonprobate transfer on death. §5002.
Transfer of property in compliance with provision for nonprobate transfer on death. §5003.

§5000. Nonprobate transfers at death

(a) A provision for a nonprobate transfer on death in an insurance policy, contract of employment, bond, mortgage, promissory note, certificated or uncertificated security, account agreement, custodial agreement, deposit agreement, compensation plan, pension plan, individual retirement plan, employee benefit plan, trust, conveyance, deed of gift, revocable transfer on death deed, marital property agreement, or other written instrument of a similar nature is not invalid because the instrument does not comply with the requirements for execution of a will, and this code does not invalidate the instrument.

(b) Included within subdivision (a) are the following:

(1) A written provision that moneys or other benefits due to, controlled by, or owned by a decedent before death shall be paid after the decedent's death to a person whom the decedent designates either in the instrument or in a separate writing, including a will, executed either before or at the same time as the instrument, or later.

(2) A written provision that moneys due or to become due under the instrument shall cease to be payable in the event of the death of the promisee or the promisor before payment or demand.

(3) A written provision that any property controlled by or owned by the decedent before death that is the subject of the instrument shall pass to a person whom the decedent designates either in the instrument or in a separate writing, including a will, executed either before or at the same time as the instrument, or later.

(c) Nothing in this section limits the rights of creditors under any other law. **Leg.H.** Enacted Stats 1990 ch 79 §14 (AB 759), operative July 1, 1991. Amended Stats 2015 ch 293 §8 (AB 139), effective January 1, 2016.

§5002. When holder of property not required to comply with provision for nonprobate transfer on death

Notwithstanding any other provision of this part, a holder of property under an instrument of a type described in Section 5000 is not required to receive, hold, or transfer the property in compliance with a provision for a nonprobate transfer on death executed by a person who has an interest in the property if either (1) the person is not authorized by the terms of the instrument to execute a provision for transfer of the property, or (2) the provision for transfer of the property does not otherwise satisfy the terms of the instrument. **Leg.H.** Added Stats 1992 ch 51 §4 (AB 1719).

§5003. Transfer of property in compliance with provision for nonprobate transfer on death

(a) A holder of property under an instrument of a type described in Section 5000 may transfer the property in compliance with a provision for a nonprobate transfer on death that satisfies the terms of the instrument, whether or not the transfer is consistent with the beneficial ownership of the property as between the person who executed the provision for transfer of the property and other persons having an interest in the property or their successors, and whether or not the transfer is consistent with the rights of the person named as beneficiary.

(b) Except as provided in this subdivision, no notice or other information shown to have been available to the holder of the property affects the right of the holder to the protection provided by subdivision (a). The protection provided by subdivision (a) does not extend to a transfer made after either of the following events:

(1) The holder of the property has been served with a contrary court order.

(2) The holder of the property has been served with a written notice of a person claiming an adverse interest in the property. However, this paragraph does not apply to a pension plan to the extent the transfer is a periodic payment pursuant to the plan.

(c) The protection provided by this section does not affect the rights of the person who executed the provision for transfer of the property and other persons having an interest in the property or their successors in disputes among themselves concerning the beneficial ownership of the property.

(d) The protection provided by this section is not exclusive of any protection provided the holder of the property by any other provision of law.

(e) A person shall not serve notice under paragraph (2) of subdivision (b) in bad faith. If the court in an action or proceeding relating to the rights of the parties determines that a person has served notice under paragraph (2) of subdivision (b) in bad faith, the court shall award against the person the cost of the action or proceeding, including a reasonable attorney's fee, and the damages caused by the service. **Leg.H.** Added Stats 1992 ch 51 §5 (AB 1719). Amended Stats 2001 ch 417 §7 (AB 873), effective January 1, 2002.

CHAPTER 2
NONPROBATE TRANSFERS OF COMMUNITY PROPERTY

Article 1. General Provisions.
Article 2. Consent to Nonprobate Transfer.
Article 3. Revocation of Consent.

ARTICLE 1
General Provisions

"Written consent". §5010.
Rights of parties in nonprobate transfer of community property on death. §5011.
Relevance of specified provisions. §5012.
Effect of surviving spouse's waiver of rights in community property. §5013.
Application of chapter. §5014.
Application of other provisions. §5015.

§5010. "Written consent"

As used in this chapter, "written consent" to a provision for a nonprobate transfer of community property on death includes a written joinder in such a provision. **Leg.H.** Added Stats 1992 ch 51 §6 (AB 1719).

§5011. Rights of parties in nonprobate transfer of community property on death

Notwithstanding any other provision of this part, the rights of the parties in a nonprobate transfer of community property on death are subject to all of the following:

(a) The terms of the instrument under which the nonprobate transfer is made.

(b) A contrary state statute specifically applicable to the instrument under which the nonprobate transfer is made.

(c) A written expression of intent of a party in the provision for transfer of the property or in a written consent to the provision. **Leg.H.** Added Stats 1992 ch 51 §6 (AB 1719).

§5012. Relevance of specified provisions

A provision of this chapter concerning rights between a married person and the person's spouse in community property is relevant only to controversies between the person and spouse and their successors and does not affect the obligation of a holder of community property under an instrument of a type described in Section 5000 to hold, receive, or transfer the property in compliance with a provision for a nonprobate transfer on death, or the protection provided the holder by Section 5003. **Leg.H.** Added Stats 1992 ch 51 §6 (AB 1719).

§5013. Effect of surviving spouse's waiver of rights in community property

Nothing in this chapter limits the effect of a surviving spouse's waiver of rights in community property under Chapter 1 (commencing with Section 140) of Part 3 of Division 2 or other instrument or agreement that affects a married person's interest in community property. **Leg.H.** Added Stats 1992 ch 51 §6 (AB 1719).

§5014. Application of chapter

(a) Except as provided in subdivision (b), this chapter applies to a provision for a nonprobate transfer of community property on the death of a married person, regardless of whether the provision for transfer of the property was executed by the person, or written consent to the provision for transfer of the property was given by the person's spouse, before, on, or after January 1, 1993.

(b) Subdivision (c) of Section 5030 does not apply, and the applicable law in effect on the date of death does apply, to revocation of a written consent given by a spouse who died before January 1, 1993. **Leg.H.** Added Stats 1992 ch 51 §6 (AB 1719).

§5015. Application of other provisions

Nothing in this chapter limits the application of principles of fraud, undue influence, duress, mistake, or other invalidating cause to a written consent to a provision for a nonprobate transfer of community property on death. **Leg.H.** Added Stats 1992 ch 51 §6 (AB 1719).

ARTICLE 2
Consent to Nonprobate Transfer

Execution of provision for nonprobate transfer of community property on death by married person without written consent of spouse. §5020.
Proceeding to set aside nonprobate transfer of community property on death by married person without consent of spouse. §5021.
Effect of spouse's written consent to transfer of community property on death. §5022.
"Modification"; Effect on person's interest in community property. §5023.

§5020. Execution of provision for nonprobate transfer of community property on death by married person without written consent of spouse

A provision for a nonprobate transfer of community property on death executed by a married person without the written consent of the person's spouse (1) is not effective as to the nonconsenting spouse's interest in the property and (2) does not affect the nonconsenting spouse's disposition on death of the nonconsenting spouse's interest in the community property by will, intestate succession, or nonprobate transfer. **Leg.H.** Added Stats 1992 ch 51 §6 (AB 1719).

§5021. Proceeding to set aside nonprobate transfer of community property on death by married person without consent of spouse

(a) In a proceeding to set aside a nonprobate transfer of community property on death made pursuant to a provision for transfer of the property executed by a married person without the written consent of the person's spouse, the court shall set aside the transfer as to the nonconsenting spouse's interest in the property, subject to terms and conditions or other remedies that appear equitable under the circumstances of the case, taking into account the rights of all interested persons.

(b) Nothing in subdivision (a) affects any additional remedy the nonconsenting spouse may have against the person's estate for a nonprobate transfer of community property on death without the spouse's written consent. **Leg.H.** Added Stats 1992 ch 51 §6 (AB 1719).

§5022. Effect of spouse's written consent to transfer of community property on death

(a) Except as provided in subdivision (b), a spouse's written consent to a provision for a nonprobate transfer of community property on death is not a transmutation of the consenting spouse's interest in the property.

(b) This chapter does not apply to a spouse's written consent to a provision for a nonprobate transfer of community property on death that satisfies Section 852 of the Family Code. Such a consent is a transmutation and is governed by the law applicable to transmutations. **Leg.H.** Added Stats 1992 ch 51 §6 (AB 1719). Amended Stats 1993 ch 219 §224.3 (AB 1500).

§5023. "Modification"; Effect on person's interest in community property

(a) As used in this section "modification" means revocation of a provision for a nonprobate transfer on death in whole or part, designation of a different beneficiary, or election of a different benefit or payment option. As used in this section, "modification" does not mean, and this section does not apply to, the exercise of a power of appointment under a trust.

(b) If a married person executes a provision for a nonprobate transfer of community property on death with the written consent of the person's spouse and thereafter executes a modification of the provision for transfer of the property without written consent of the spouse, the modification is effective as to the person's interest in the community property and has the following effect on the spouse's interest in the community property:

(1) If the person executes the modification during the spouse's lifetime, the modification revokes the spouse's previous written consent to the provision for transfer of the property.

(2) If the person executes the modification after the spouse's death, the modification does not affect the spouse's previous written consent to the provision for transfer of the property, and the spouse's interest in the community property is subject to the nonprobate transfer on death as consented to by the spouse.

(3) If a written expression of intent of a party in the provision for transfer of the property or in the written consent to the provision for transfer of the property authorizes the person to execute a modification after the spouse's death, the spouse's interest in the community property is deemed transferred to the married person on the spouse's death, and the modification is effective as to both the person's and the spouse's interests in the community property. **Leg.H.** Added Stats 1992 ch 51 §6 (AB 1719). Amended Stats 1993 ch 527 §3 (AB 908).

ARTICLE 3
Revocation of Consent

Revocation; Irrevocability on death of either spouse. §5030.
Method of revoking consent; Effect on authority of holder to transfer property in compliance with other provisions. §5031.
Effect of revocation on how property passes. §5032.

§5030. Revocation; Irrevocability on death of either spouse

(a) A spouse's written consent to a provision for a nonprobate transfer of community property on death is revocable during the marriage.

(b) On termination of the marriage by dissolution or on legal separation, the written consent is revocable and the community property is subject to division under Division 7 (commencing with Section 2500) of the Family Code or other disposition on order within the jurisdiction of the court.

(c) On the death of either spouse, the written consent is irrevocable. **Leg.H.** Added Stats 1992 ch 51 §6 (AB 1719). Amended Stats 1993 ch 219 §224.5 (AB 1500).

§5031. Method of revoking consent; Effect on authority of holder to transfer property in compliance with other provisions

(a) If a married person executes a provision for a nonprobate transfer of community property on death with the written consent of the person's spouse, the consenting spouse may revoke the consent by a writing, including a will, that identifies the provision for transfer of the property being revoked, and that is served on the married person before the married person's death.

(b) Revocation of a spouse's written consent to a provision for a nonprobate transfer of community property on death does not affect the authority of the holder of the property to transfer the property in compliance with the provision for transfer of the property to the extent provided in Section 5003. **Leg.H.** Added Stats 1992 ch 51 §6 (AB 1719).

§5032. Effect of revocation on how property passes

On revocation of a spouse's written consent to a nonprobate transfer of community property on death, the property passes in the same manner as if the consent had not been given. **Leg.H.** Added Stats 1992 ch 51 §6 (AB 1719).

CHAPTER 3
NONPROBATE TRANSFER TO FORMER SPOUSE

Failure of nonprobate transfer; Exceptions. §5040.
Severance of joint tenancy. §5042.
Good faith reliance on affidavit or declaration. §5044.
Authority of court. §5046.
Operative date; Applicability. §5048.

§5040. Failure of nonprobate transfer; Exceptions

(a) Except as provided in subdivision (b), a nonprobate transfer to the transferor's former spouse, in an instrument executed by the transferor before or during the marriage or registered domestic partnership, fails if, at the time of the transferor's death, the former spouse is not the transferor's surviving spouse as defined in Section 78, as a result of the dissolution or annulment of the marriage or termination of registered domestic partnership. A judgment of legal separation that does not terminate the status of spouses is not a dissolution for purposes of this section.

(b) Subdivision (a) does not cause a nonprobate transfer to fail in any of the following cases:

(1) The nonprobate transfer is not subject to revocation by the transferor at the time of the transferor's death.

(2) There is clear and convincing evidence that the transferor intended to preserve the nonprobate transfer to the former spouse.

(3) A court order that the nonprobate transfer be maintained on behalf of the former spouse is in effect at the time of the transferor's death.

(c) Where a nonprobate transfer fails by operation of this section, the instrument making the nonprobate transfer shall be treated as it would if the former spouse failed to survive the transferor.

(d) Nothing in this section affects the rights of a subsequent purchaser or encumbrancer for value in good faith who relies on the apparent failure of a nonprobate transfer under this section or who lacks knowledge of the failure of a nonprobate transfer under this section.

(e) As used in this section, "nonprobate transfer" means a provision, other than a provision of a life insurance policy, of either of the following types:

(1) A provision of a type described in Section 5000.

(2) A provision in an instrument that operates on death, other than a will, conferring a power of appointment or naming a trustee. **Leg.H.** Added Stats 2001 ch 417 §9 (AB 873), as Prob C §5600. Renumbered from Prob C §5600 by Stats 2015 ch 293 §12 (AB 139), effective January 1, 2016; Stats 2016 ch 50 §83 (SB 1005), effective January 1, 2017.

2016 Note: For legislative intent, see the 2016 Note following Prob C §59.

§5042. Severance of joint tenancy

(a) Except as provided in subdivision (b), a joint tenancy between the decedent and the decedent's former spouse, created before or during the marriage or registered domestic partnership, is severed as to the decedent's interest if, at the time of the decedent's death, the former spouse is not the decedent's surviving spouse as defined in Section 78, as a result of the dissolution or annulment of the marriage or registered domestic partnership. A judgment of legal separation that does not terminate the status of spouses is not a dissolution for purposes of this section.

(b) Subdivision (a) does not sever a joint tenancy in either of the following cases:

(1) The joint tenancy is not subject to severance by the decedent at the time of the decedent's death.

(2) There is clear and convincing evidence that the decedent intended to preserve the joint tenancy in favor of the former spouse.

(c) Nothing in this section affects the rights of a subsequent purchaser or encumbrancer for value in good faith who relies on an apparent severance under this section or who lacks knowledge of a severance under this section.

(d) For purposes of this section, property held in "joint tenancy" includes property held as community property with right of survivorship, as described in Section 682.1 of the Civil Code. **Leg.H.** Added Stats 2001 ch 417 §9 (AB 873), as Prob C §5601. Renumbered from Prob C §5601 by Stats 2015 ch 293 §13 (AB 139), effective January 1, 2016; Stats 2016 ch 50 §84 (SB 1005), effective January 1, 2017.

2016 Note: For legislative intent, see the 2016 Note following Prob C §59.

§5044. Good faith reliance on affidavit or declaration

(a) Nothing in this chapter affects the rights of a purchaser or encumbrancer of real property for value who in good faith relies on an affidavit or a declaration under penalty of perjury under the laws of this state that states all of the following:

(1) The name of the decedent.

(2) The date and place of the decedent's death.

(3) A description of the real property transferred to the affiant or declarant by an instrument making a nonprobate transfer or by operation of joint tenancy survivorship.

(4) Either of the following, as appropriate:

(A) The affiant or declarant is the surviving spouse of the decedent.

(B) The affiant or declarant is not the surviving spouse of the decedent, but the rights of the affiant or declarant to the described property are not affected by Section 5040 or 5042.

(b) A person relying on an affidavit or declaration made pursuant to subdivision (a) has no duty to inquire into the truth of the matters stated in the affidavit or declaration.

(c) An affidavit or declaration made pursuant to subdivision (a) may be recorded. **Leg.H.** Added Stats 2001 ch 417 §9 (AB 873), as Prob C §5602. Amended and renumbered from Prob C §5602 by Stats 2015 ch 293 §14 (AB 139), effective January 1, 2016.

§5046. Authority of court

Nothing in this chapter is intended to limit the court's authority to order a party to a dissolution or annulment of marriage to maintain the former spouse as a beneficiary on any nonprobate transfer described in this chapter, or to preserve a joint tenancy in favor of the former spouse. **Leg.H.** Added Stats 2001 ch 417 §9 (AB 873), as Prob C §5603. Amended and renumbered from Prob C §5603 by Stats 2015 ch 293 §15 (AB 139), effective January 1, 2016.

§5048. Operative date; Applicability

(a) This chapter, formerly Part 4 (commencing with Section 5600), is operative on January 1, 2002.

(b) Except as provided in subdivision (c), this chapter applies to an instrument making a nonprobate transfer or creating a joint tenancy whether executed before, on, or after the operative date of this chapter.

(c) Sections 5040 and 5042 do not apply, and the applicable law in effect before the operative date of this chapter applies, to an instrument making a nonprobate transfer or creating a joint tenancy in either of the following circumstances:

(1) The person making the nonprobate transfer or creating the joint tenancy dies before the operative date of this chapter.

(2) The dissolution of marriage or other event that terminates the status of the nonprobate transfer beneficiary or joint tenant as a surviving spouse occurs before the operative date of this chapter. **Leg.H.** Added Stats 2001 ch 417 §9 (AB 873), as Prob C §5604. Amended and renumbered from Prob C §5604 by Stats 2015 ch 293 §16 (AB 139), effective January 1, 2016.

PART 2
MULTIPLE-PARTY ACCOUNTS

Chapter 1. Short Title and Definitions.
Chapter 2. General Provisions.
Chapter 3. Ownership Between Parties and Their Creditors and Successors.
Chapter 4. Protection of Financial Institution.

CHAPTER 1
SHORT TITLE AND DEFINITIONS

Article 1. Short Title.
Article 2. Definitions.

ARTICLE 1
Short Title

Citation of part. §5100.

§5100. Citation of part
This part may be cited as the California Multiple-Party Accounts Law. **Leg.H.** Enacted Stats 1990 ch 79 §14 (AB 759), operative July 1, 1991.

Prior Law: Former Prob C §5100, similar to the present section, was added Stats 1983 ch 92 §5, operative July 1, 1984, and repealed Stats 1990 ch 79 §13, operative July 1, 1991.

ARTICLE 2
Definitions

Application of definitions. §5120.
Account. §5122.
Agent. §5124.
Beneficiary. §5126.
Financial institution. §5128.
Joint account. §5130.
Multiple-party account. §5132.
Net contribution. §5134.
Party. §5136.
Payment. §5138.
"P.O.D." defined. §5139.
P.O.D. account. §5140.
P.O.D. payee. §5142.
Proof of death. §5144.
Receives. §5146.
Request. §5148.
Sums on deposit. §5150.
Withdrawal. §5152.

§5120. Application of definitions
Unless the provision or context otherwise requires, the definitions in this article govern the construction of this part. **Leg.H.** Enacted Stats 1990 ch 79 §14 (AB 759), operative July 1, 1991.

Prior Law: Former Prob C §5120, similar to the present section, was added Stats 1989 ch 397 §25, operative July 1, 1990, and repealed Stats 1990 ch 79 §13, operative July 1, 1991.

§5122. Account
(a) "Account" means a contract of deposit of funds between a depositor and a financial institution, and includes a checking account, savings account, certificate of deposit, share account, and other like arrangement.
(b) "Account" does not include:
(1) An account established for deposit of funds of a partnership, joint venture, or other association for business purposes.
(2) An account controlled by one or more persons as the duly authorized agent or trustee for a corporation, unincorporated association, or charitable or civic organization.
(3) A regular fiduciary or trust account where the relationship is established other than by deposit agreement.
(4) An account established for the deposit of funds of the estate of a ward, conservatee, or decedent. **Leg.H.** Enacted Stats 1990 ch 79 §14 (AB 759), operative July 1, 1991.

Prior Law: Former Prob C §5122, similar to the present section, was added Stats 1989 ch 397 §25, operative July 1, 1990, and repealed Stats 1990 ch 79 §13, operative July 1, 1991.

§5124. Agent
"Agent" means a person who has a present right, subject to request, to payment from an account as an attorney in fact under a power of attorney. **Leg.H.** Enacted Stats 1990 ch 79 §14 (AB 759), operative July 1, 1991.

Prior Law: Former Prob C §5124, similar to the present section, was added Stats 1989 ch 397 §25, operative July 1, 1990, and repealed Stats 1990 ch 79 §13, operative July 1, 1991.

§5126. Beneficiary
"Beneficiary" means a person named in a Totten trust account as one for whom a party to the account is named as trustee. **Leg.H.** Enacted Stats 1990 ch 79 §14 (AB 759), operative July 1, 1991.

Prior Law: Former Prob C §5126, similar to the present section, was added Stats 1989 ch 397 §25, operative July 1, 1990, and repealed Stats 1990 ch 79 §13, operative July 1, 1991.

§5128. Financial institution
"Financial institution" includes:
(a) A financial institution as defined in Section 40.
(b) An industrial loan company as defined in Section 18003 of the Financial Code. **Leg.H.** Enacted Stats 1990 ch 79 §14 (AB 759), operative July 1, 1991.

Prior Law: Former Prob C §5128, similar to the present section, was added Stats 1989 ch 397 §25, operative July 1, 1990, and repealed Stats 1990 ch 79 §13, operative July 1, 1991.

§5130. Joint account
"Joint account" means an account payable on request to one or more of two or more parties whether or not mention is made of any right of survivorship. **Leg.H.** Enacted Stats 1990 ch 79 §14 (AB 759), operative July 1, 1991.

Prior Law: Former Prob C §5130, similar to the present section, was added Stats 1989 ch 397 §25, operative July 1, 1990, and repealed Stats 1990 ch 79 §13, operative July 1, 1991.

§5132. Multiple-party account
A "multiple-party account" is any of the following types of account:
(a) A joint account.
(b) A P.O.D. account.
(c) A Totten trust account. **Leg.H.** Enacted Stats 1990 ch 79 §14 (AB 759), operative July 1, 1991.

Prior Law: Former Prob C §5132, similar to the present section, was added Stats 1989 ch 397 §25, operative July 1, 1990, and repealed Stats 1990 ch 79 §13, operative July 1, 1991.

§5134. Net contribution
(a) "Net contribution" of a party to an account as of any given time is the sum of all of the following:
(1) All deposits thereto made by or for the party, less all withdrawals made by or for the party that have not been paid to or applied to the use of any other party.
(2) A pro rata share of any interest or dividends earned, whether or not included in the current balance.
(3) Any proceeds of deposit life insurance added to the account by reason of the death of the party whose net contribution is in question.
(b) In the absence of proof otherwise:
(1) Only parties who have a present right of withdrawal shall be considered as having a net contribution.
(2) The net contribution of each of the parties having a present right of withdrawal is deemed to be an equal amount.
(c) It is the intent of the Legislature in enacting this section to provide a definition for the purpose of determining ownership interests in an account as between the parties to the account, and not as between the parties and the financial institution. **Leg.H.** Enacted Stats 1990 ch 79 §14 (AB 759), operative July 1, 1991.

Prior Law: Former Prob C §5134, similar to the present section, was added Stats 1989 ch 397 §25, operative July 1, 1990, and repealed Stats 1990 ch 79 §13, operative July 1, 1991.

§5136. Party
(a) "Party" means a person who, by the terms of the account, has a present right, subject to request, to payment from a multiple-party account other than as an agent.
(b) A P.O.D. payee is a party, by reason of being a P.O.D. payee, only after the account becomes payable to the payee by reason of surviving all persons named as original payees.

(c) A beneficiary of a Totten trust account is a party, by reason of being a beneficiary, only after the account becomes payable to the beneficiary by reason of surviving all persons named as trustees. **Leg.H.** Enacted Stats 1990 ch 79 §14 (AB 759), operative July 1, 1991.

Prior Law: Former Prob C §5136, similar to the present section, was added Stats 1989 ch 397 §25, operative July 1, 1990, and repealed Stats 1990 ch 79 §13, operative July 1, 1991.

§5138. Payment

"Payment" of sums on deposit includes all of the following:

(a) A withdrawal, including payment on check or other directive of a party.

(b) A pledge of sums of deposit.

(c) A setoff, reduction, or other disposition of all or part of an account pursuant to a pledge. **Leg.H.** Enacted Stats 1990 ch 79 §14 (AB 759), operative July 1, 1991.

Prior Law: Former Prob C §5138, similar to the present section, was added Stats 1989 ch 397 §25, operative July 1, 1990, and repealed Stats 1990 ch 79 §13, operative July 1, 1991.

§5139. "P.O.D." defined

"P.O.D." means pay on death. **Leg.H.** Enacted Stats 1990 ch 79 §14 (AB 759), operative July 1, 1991.

Prior Law: Former Prob C §5139, similar to the present section, was added Stats 1989 ch 397 §25, operative July 1, 1990, and repealed Stats 1990 ch 79 §13, operative July 1, 1991.

§5140. P.O.D. account

"P.O.D. account" means any of the following:

(a) An account payable on request to one person during the person's lifetime and on the person's death to one or more P.O.D. payees.

(b) An account payable on request to one or more persons during their lifetimes and on the death of all of them to one or more P.O.D. payees. **Leg.H.** Enacted Stats 1990 ch 79 §14 (AB 759), operative July 1, 1991.

Prior Law: Former Prob C §5140, similar to the present section, was added Stats 1989 ch 397 §25, operative July 1, 1990, and repealed Stats 1990 ch 79 §13, operative July 1, 1991.

§5142. P.O.D. payee

"P.O.D. payee" means a person designated on a P.O.D. account as one to whom the account is payable on request after the death of one or more persons. **Leg.H.** Enacted Stats 1990 ch 79 §14 (AB 759), operative July 1, 1991.

Prior Law: Former Prob C §5142, similar to the present section, was added Stats 1989 ch 397 §25, operative July 1, 1990, and repealed Stats 1990 ch 79 §13, operative July 1, 1991.

§5144. Proof of death

"Proof of death" includes any of the following:

(a) An original or attested or certified copy of a death certificate.

(b) A record or report that is prima facie evidence of death under Section 103550 of the Health and Safety Code, Sections 1530 to 1532, inclusive, of the Evidence Code, or another statute of this state. **Leg.H.** Enacted Stats 1990 ch 79 §14 (AB 759), operative July 1, 1991. Amended Stats 1996 ch 1023 §400 (SB 1497), effective September 29, 1996.

Prior Law: Former Prob C §5144, similar to the present section, was added Stats 1989 ch 397 §25, operative July 1, 1990, and repealed Stats 1990 ch 79 §13, operative July 1, 1991.

§5146. Receives

Except to the extent the terms of the account or deposit agreement expressly provide otherwise, a financial institution "receives" an order or notice under this part when it is received by the particular office or branch office of the financial institution where the account is carried. **Leg.H.** Enacted Stats 1990 ch 79 §14 (AB 759), operative July 1, 1991.

Prior Law: Former Prob C §5146, similar to the present section, was added Stats 1989 ch 397 §25, operative July 1, 1990, and repealed Stats 1990 ch 79 §13, operative July 1, 1991.

§5148. Request

"Request" means a proper request for withdrawal, including a check or order for payment, that complies with all conditions of the account (including special requirements concerning necessary signatures) and regulations of the financial institution; but, if the financial institution conditions withdrawal or payment on advance notice, for purposes of this part the request for withdrawal or payment is treated as immediately effective and a notice of intent to withdraw is treated as a request for withdrawal. **Leg.H.** Enacted Stats 1990 ch 79 §14 (AB 759), operative July 1, 1991.

Prior Law: Former Prob C §5148, similar to the present section, was added Stats 1989 ch 397 §25, operative July 1, 1990, and repealed Stats 1990 ch 79 §13, operative July 1, 1991.

§5150. Sums on deposit

"Sums on deposit" means both of the following:

(a) The balance payable on an account, including interest and dividends earned, whether or not included in the current balance.

(b) Any life insurance proceeds added to the account by reason of the death of a party. **Leg.H.** Enacted Stats 1990 ch 79 §14 (AB 759), operative July 1, 1991.

Prior Law: Former Prob C §5150, similar to the present section, was added Stats 1989 ch 397 §25, operative July 1, 1990, and repealed Stats 1990 ch 79 §13, operative July 1, 1991.

§5152. Withdrawal

"Withdrawal" includes payment to a third person pursuant to a check or other directive of a party or an agent. **Leg.H.** Enacted Stats 1990 ch 79 §14 (AB 759), operative July 1, 1991.

Prior Law: Former Prob C §5152, similar to the present section, was added Stats 1989 ch 397 §25, operative July 1, 1990, and repealed Stats 1990 ch 79 §13, operative July 1, 1991.

CHAPTER 2
GENERAL PROVISIONS

Governing provisions. §5201.
Transfer in fraud of creditors. §5202.
Creation of multiple-party relationship. §5203.
Special power of attorney for account transactions. §5204.
Application of part. §5205.

§5201. Governing provisions

(a) The provisions of Chapter 3 (commencing with Section 5301) concerning beneficial ownership as between parties, or as between parties and P.O.D. payees or beneficiaries of multiple-party accounts, are relevant only to controversies between these persons and their creditors and other successors, and have no bearing on the power of withdrawal of these persons as determined by the terms of account contracts.

(b) The provisions of Chapter 4 (commencing with Section 5401) govern the liability of financial institutions who make payments pursuant to that chapter. **Leg.H.** Enacted Stats 1990 ch 79 §14 (AB 759), operative July 1, 1991.

Prior Law: Former Prob C §5201, similar to the present section, was added Stats 1983 ch 92 §5, operative July 1, 1984, and repealed Stats 1990 ch 79 §13, operative July 1, 1991.

§5202. Transfer in fraud of creditors

Nothing in this part affects the law relating to transfers in fraud of creditors. **Leg.H.** Enacted Stats 1990 ch 79 §14 (AB 759), operative July 1, 1991.

Prior Law: Former Prob C §5202, similar to the present section, was added Stats 1983 ch 92 §5, operative July 1, 1984, and repealed Stats 1990 ch 79 §13, operative July 1, 1991.

§5203. Creation of multiple-party relationship

(a) Words in substantially the following form in a signature card, passbook, contract, or instrument evidencing an account, or words to the same effect, executed before, on, or after July 1, 1990, create the following accounts:

(1) Joint account: "This account or certificate is owned by the named parties. Upon the death of any of them, ownership passes to the survivor(s)."

(2) P.O.D. account with single party: "This account or certificate is owned by the named party. Upon the death of that party, ownership passes to the named pay-on-death payee(s)."

(3) P.O.D. account with multiple parties: "This account or certificate is owned by the named parties. Upon the death of any of them, ownership passes to the survivor(s). Upon the death of all of them, ownership passes to the named pay-on-death payee(s)."

(4) Joint account of spouses with right of survivorship: "This account or certificate is owned by the named parties, who are spouses, and is

presumed to be their community property. Upon the death of either of them, ownership passes to the survivor."

(5) Community property account of spouses: "This account or certificate is the community property of the named parties who are spouses. The ownership during lifetime and after the death of a spouse is determined by the law applicable to community property generally and may be affected by a will."

(6) Tenancy in common account: "This account or certificate is owned by the named parties as tenants in common. Upon the death of any party, the ownership interest of that party passes to the named pay-on-death payee(s) of that party or, if none, to the estate of that party."

(b) Use of the form language provided in this section is not necessary to create an account that is governed by this part. If the contract of deposit creates substantially the same relationship between the parties as an account created using the form language provided in this section, this part applies to the same extent as if the form language had been used. **Leg.H.** Enacted Stats 1990 ch 79 §14 (AB 759), operative July 1, 1991. Amended Stats 2016 ch 50 §85 (SB 1005), effective January 1, 2017; Stats 2016 ch 86 §249 (SB 1171), effective January 1, 2017 (ch 50 prevails; ch 86 not effective).

Editor's Notes—2016 Note: For legislative intent, see the 2016 Note following Prob C §59.

Prior Law: Former Prob C §5203, similar to the present section, was added Stats 1989 ch 397 §26, operative July 1, 1990, and repealed Stats 1990 ch 79 §13, operative July 1, 1991.

§5204. Special power of attorney for account transactions

(a) In addition to a power of attorney otherwise authorized by law, a special power of attorney is authorized under this section to apply to one or more accounts at a financial institution or to one or more contracts with a financial institution concerning safe deposit services. For the purposes of this section, "account" includes checking accounts, savings accounts, certificates of deposit, savings certificates, and any other depository relationship with the financial institution.

(b) The special power of attorney under this section shall:

(1) Be in writing.

(2) Be signed by the person or persons giving the power of attorney.

(3) Explicitly identify the attorney-in-fact or attorneys-in-fact, the financial institution, and the accounts or contracts subject to the power.

(c) The special power of attorney shall contain language in substantially the following form:

"WARNING TO PERSON EXECUTING THIS DOCUMENT: This is an important legal document. It creates a power of attorney that provides the person you designate as your attorney-in-fact with the broad powers it sets forth. You have the right to terminate this power of attorney. If there is anything about this form that you do not understand, you should ask a lawyer to explain it to you."

(d) In addition to the language required by subdivision (c), special powers of attorney that are or may be durable shall also contain substantially the following language:

"These powers of attorney shall continue even if you later become disabled or incapacitated."

(e) The power of attorney granted under this section shall endure as between the grantor and grantee of the power until the earliest of the following occurs:

(1) Revocation by the grantor of the power.

(2) Termination of the account.

(3) Death of the grantor of the power.

(4) In the case of a nondurable power of attorney, appointment of a guardian or conservator of the estate of the grantor of the power.

(f) A financial institution may rely in good faith upon the validity of the power of attorney granted under this section and is not liable to the principal or any other person for doing so if (1) the power of attorney is on file with the financial institution and the transaction is made by the attorney-in-fact named in the power of attorney, (2) the power of attorney appears on its face to be valid, and (3) the financial institution has convincing evidence of the identity of the person signing the power of attorney as principal.

(g) For the purposes of subdivision (f), "convincing evidence" requires both of the following:

(1) Reasonable reliance on a document that satisfies the requirement of Section 4751.

(2) The absence of any information, evidence, or other circumstances that would lead a reasonable person to believe that the person signing the power of attorney as principal is not the individual he or she claims to be.

(h) The protection provided by subdivision (f) does not extend to payments made after written notice is received by the financial institution as to any of the events of termination of the power under subdivision (e) if the financial institution has had a reasonable time to act on the notice. No other notice or any other information shown to have been available to the financial institution shall affect its right to the protection provided by this subdivision.

(i) The attorney-in-fact acting under the power of attorney granted under this section shall maintain books or records to permit an accounting of the acts of the attorney-in-fact if an accounting is requested by a legal representative of the grantor of the power.

(j) The attorney-in-fact acting under a power of attorney granted under this section is liable for any disbursement other than a disbursement to or for the benefit of the grantor of the power, unless the grantor has authorized the disbursement in writing.

(k) Nothing in this section limits the use or effect of any other form of power of attorney for transactions with a financial institution. Nothing in this section creates an implication that a financial institution is liable for acting in reliance upon a power of attorney under circumstances where the requirements of subdivision (f) are not satisfied. Nothing in this section affects any immunity that may otherwise exist apart from this section.

(*l*) Nothing in this section prevents the attorney-in-fact from also being designated as a P.O.D. payee.

(m) Except as otherwise provided in this section, the Power of Attorney Law, Division 4.5 (commencing with Section 4000) shall not apply to a special power of attorney under this section. Section 4130 and Part 5 (commencing with Section 4900) of Division 4.5 shall apply to a special power of attorney under this section. **Leg.H.** Enacted Stats 1990 ch 79 §14 (AB 759), operative July 1, 1991. Amended Stats 1994 ch 307 §17 (SB 1907); Stats 1995 ch 300 §15 (SB 984), effective August 3, 1995.

Prior Law: Former Prob C §5204, similar to the present section, was added Stats 1989 ch 397 §27, operative July 1, 1990, and repealed Stats 1990 ch 79 §13, operative July 1, 1991.

§5205. Application of part

This part applies to accounts in existence on July 1, 1990, and accounts thereafter established. **Leg.H.** Enacted Stats 1990 ch 79 §14 (AB 759), operative July 1, 1991.

CHAPTER 3
OWNERSHIP BETWEEN PARTIES AND THEIR CREDITORS AND SUCCESSORS

Ownership during lifetime. §5301.
Right of survivorship. §5302.
Rights of survivorship determined by form of account at time of death; Methods for change of terms of account. §5303.
Testamentary effect of statutory survivorship provisions. §5304.
Presumption that sums on deposit are community property. §5305.
Account expressly described as "tenancy in common" account. §5306.
Account expressly described as "community property" account. §5307.

§5301. Ownership during lifetime

(a) An account belongs, during the lifetime of all parties, to the parties in proportion to the net contributions by each, unless there is clear and convincing evidence of a different intent.

(b) If a party makes an excess withdrawal from an account, the other parties to the account shall have an ownership interest in the excess withdrawal in proportion to the net contributions of each to the amount on deposit in the account immediately following the excess withdrawal, unless there is clear and convincing evidence of a contrary agreement between the parties.

(c) Only a living party, or a conservator, guardian, or agent acting on behalf of a living party, shall be permitted to make a claim to recover the living party's ownership interest in an excess withdrawal, pursuant to subdivision (b). A court may, at its discretion, and in the interest of justice, reduce any recovery under this section to reflect funds withdrawn and applied for the benefit of the claiming party.

(d) In the case of a P.O.D. account, the P.O.D. payee has no rights to the sums on deposit during the lifetime of any party, unless there is clear and convincing evidence of a different intent.

(e) In the case of a Totten trust account, the beneficiary has no rights to the sums on deposit during the lifetime of any party, unless there is clear and convincing evidence of a different intent. If there is an irrevocable trust, the account belongs beneficially to the beneficiary.

(f) For purposes of this section, "excess withdrawal" means the amount of a party's withdrawal that exceeds that party's net contribution on deposit in the account immediately preceding the withdrawal. **Leg.H.** Enacted Stats 1990 ch 79 §14 (AB 759), operative July 1, 1991. Amended Stats 2012 ch 235 §1 (AB 1624), effective January 1, 2013.

Prior Law: Former Prob C §5301, similar to the present section, was added Stats 1983 ch 92 §5, operative July 1, 1984, amended Stats 1989 ch 397 §28, operative July 1, 1990, and repealed Stats 1990 ch 79 §13, operative July 1, 1991.

§5302. Right of survivorship

Subject to Section 5040:

(a) Sums remaining on deposit at the death of a party to a joint account belong to the surviving party or parties as against the estate of the decedent unless there is clear and convincing evidence of a different intent. If there are two or more surviving parties, their respective ownerships during lifetime are in proportion to their previous ownership interests under Section 5301 augmented by an equal share for each survivor of any interest the decedent may have owned in the account immediately before the decedent's death; and the right of survivorship continues between the surviving parties.

(b) If the account is a P.O.D. account:

(1) On death of one of two or more parties, the rights to any sums remaining on deposit are governed by subdivision (a).

(2) On death of the sole party or of the survivor of two or more parties, (A) any sums remaining on deposit belong to the P.O.D. payee or payees if surviving, or to the survivor of them if one or more die before the party, (B) if two or more P.O.D. payees survive, any sums remaining on deposit belong to them in equal and undivided shares unless the terms of the account or deposit agreement expressly provide for different shares, and (C) if two or more P.O.D. payees survive, there is no right of survivorship in the event of death of a P.O.D. payee thereafter unless the terms of the account or deposit agreement expressly provide for survivorship between them.

(c) If the account is a Totten trust account:

(1) On death of one of two or more trustees, the rights to any sums remaining on deposit are governed by subdivision (a).

(2) On death of the sole trustee or the survivor of two or more trustees, (A) any sums remaining on deposit belong to the person or persons named as beneficiaries, if surviving, or to the survivor of them if one or more die before the trustee, unless there is clear and convincing evidence of a different intent, (B) if two or more beneficiaries survive, any sums remaining on deposit belong to them in equal and undivided shares unless the terms of the account or deposit agreement expressly provide for different shares, and (C) if two or more beneficiaries survive, there is no right of survivorship in event of death of any beneficiary thereafter unless the terms of the account or deposit agreement expressly provide for survivorship between them.

(d) In other cases, the death of any party to a multiparty account has no effect on beneficial ownership of the account other than to transfer the rights of the decedent as part of the decedent's estate.

(e) A right of survivorship arising from the express terms of the account or under this section, a beneficiary designation in a Totten trust account, or a P.O.D. payee designation, cannot be changed by will. **Leg.H.** Enacted Stats 1990 ch 79 §14 (AB 759), operative July 1, 1991. Amended Stats 2001 ch 417 §8 (AB 873); Stats 2015 ch 293 §9 (AB 139), effective January 1, 2016.

Prior Law: Former Prob C §5302, similar to the present section, was added Stats 1983 ch 92 §5, operative July 1, 1984, amended Stats 1989 ch 397 §29, operative July 1, 1990, and repealed Stats 1990 ch 79 §13, operative July 1, 1991.

§5303. Rights of survivorship determined by form of account at time of death; Methods for change of terms of account

(a) The provisions of Section 5302 as to rights of survivorship are determined by the form of the account at the death of a party.

(b) Once established, the terms of a multiple-party account can be changed only by any of the following methods:

(1) Closing the account and reopening it under different terms.

(2) Presenting to the financial institution a modification agreement that is signed by all parties with a present right of withdrawal. If the financial institution has a form for this purpose, it may require use of the form.

(3) If the provisions of the terms of the account or deposit agreement provide a method of modification of the terms of the account, complying with those provisions.

(4) As provided in subdivision (c) of Section 5405.

(c) During the lifetime of a party, the terms of the account may be changed as provided in subdivision (b) to eliminate or to add rights of survivorship. Withdrawal of funds from the account by a party also eliminates rights of survivorship with respect to the funds withdrawn to the extent of the withdrawing party's net contribution to the account. **Leg.H.** Enacted Stats 1990 ch 79 §14 (AB 759), operative July 1, 1991. Amended Stats 2012 ch 235 §2 (AB 1624), effective January 1, 2013.

Prior Law: Former Prob C §5303, similar to the present section, was added Stats 1983 ch 92 §5, operative July 1, 1984, amended Stats 1984 ch 452 §7, Stats 1989 ch 397 §30, operative July 1, 1990, and repealed Stats 1990 ch 79 §13, operative July 1, 1991.

§5304. Testamentary effect of statutory survivorship provisions

Any transfers resulting from the application of Section 5302 are effective by reason of the account contracts involved and this part and are not to be considered as testamentary. The right under this part of a surviving party to a joint account, or of a beneficiary, or of a P.O.D. payee, to the sums on deposit on the death of a party to a multiple-party account shall not be denied, abridged, or affected because such right has not been created by a writing executed in accordance with the laws of this state prescribing the requirements to effect a valid testamentary disposition of property. **Leg.H.** Enacted Stats 1990 ch 79 §14 (AB 759), operative July 1, 1991.

Prior Law: Former Prob C §5304, similar to the present section, was added Stats 1983 ch 92 §5, operative July 1, 1984, and repealed Stats 1990 ch 79 §13, operative July 1, 1991.

§5305. Presumption that sums on deposit are community property

(a) Notwithstanding Sections 5301 to 5303, inclusive, if parties to an account are married to each other, whether or not they are so described in the deposit agreement, their net contribution to the account is presumed to be and remain their community property.

(b) Notwithstanding Sections 2581 and 2640 of the Family Code, the presumption established by this section is a presumption affecting the burden of proof and may be rebutted by proof of either of the following:

(1) The sums on deposit that are claimed to be separate property can be traced from separate property unless it is proved that the married persons made a written agreement that expressed their clear intent that the sums be their community property.

(2) The married persons made a written agreement, separate from the deposit agreement, that expressly provided that the sums on deposit, claimed not to be community property, were not to be community property.

(c) Except as provided in Section 5307, a right of survivorship arising from the express terms of the account or under Section 5302, a beneficiary designation in a Totten trust account, or a P.O.D. payee designation, may not be changed by will.

(d) Except as provided in subdivisions (b) and (c), a multiple-party account created with community property funds does not in any way alter community property rights. **Leg.H.** Enacted Stats 1990 ch 79 §14 (AB 759), operative July 1, 1991. Amended Stats 1992 ch 163 §131 (AB 2641), operative January 1, 1994; Stats 1993 ch 219 §224.7 (AB 1500).

Prior Law: Former Prob C §5305, similar to the present section, was added Stats 1983 ch 92 §5, operative July 1, 1984, amended Stats 1989 ch 397 §31, operative July 1, 1990, and repealed Stats 1990 ch 79 §13, operative July 1, 1991.

§5306. Account expressly described as "tenancy in common" account

For the purposes of this chapter, if an account is expressly described in the deposit agreement as a "tenancy in common" account, no right of survivorship arises from the terms of the account or under Section 5302 unless the terms of the account or deposit agreement expressly provide for survivorship. **Leg.H.** Enacted Stats 1990 ch 79 §14 (AB 759), operative July 1, 1991.

Prior Law: Former Prob C §5306, similar to the present section, was added Stats 1983 ch 92 §5, operative July 1, 1984, amended Stats 1989 ch 397 §32, operative July 1, 1990, and repealed Stats 1990 ch 79 §13, operative July 1, 1991.

§5307. Account expressly described as "community property" account

For the purposes of this chapter, except to the extent the terms of the account or deposit agreement expressly provide otherwise, if the parties to an account are married to each other and the account is expressly described in the account agreement as a "community property" account, the ownership of the account during lifetime and after the death of a spouse is governed by the law governing community property generally. **Leg.H.** Enacted Stats 1990 ch 79 §14 (AB 759), operative July 1, 1991.

Prior Law: Former Prob C §5307, similar to the present section, was added Stats 1989 ch 397 §33, operative July 1, 1990, and repealed Stats 1990 ch 79 §13, operative July 1, 1991.

CHAPTER 4
PROTECTION OF FINANCIAL INSTITUTION

Multiple-party accounts; Terms; Requirements. §5401.
Payment of joint account. §5402.
Payment of P.O.D. account. §5403.
Payment of Totten trust account. §5404.
Payment as discharge; refusal to pay upon receipt of notice. §5405.
Payment of account held in trust form where financial institution has no notice that account is not a "Totten trust account". §5406.
Payment to minor. §5407.

§5401. Multiple-party accounts; Terms; Requirements

(a) Financial institutions may enter into multiple-party accounts to the same extent that they may enter into single-party accounts. Any multiple-party account may be paid, on request and according to its terms, to any one or more of the parties or agents.

(b) The terms of the account or deposit agreement may require the signatures of more than one of the parties to a multiple-party account during their lifetimes or of more than one of the survivors after the death of any one of them on any check, check endorsement, receipt, notice of withdrawal, request for withdrawal, or withdrawal order. In such case, the financial institution shall pay the sums on deposit only in accordance with such terms, but those terms do not limit the right of the sole survivor or of all of the survivors to receive the sums on deposit.

(c) A financial institution is not required to do any of the following pursuant to Section 5301, 5303, or any other provision of this part:

(1) Inquire as to the source of funds received for deposit to a multiple-party account, or inquire as to the proposed application of any sum withdrawn from an account, for purposes of establishing net contributions.

(2) Determine any party's net contribution.

(3) Limit withdrawals or any other use of an account based on the net contribution of any party, whether or not the financial institution has actual knowledge of each party's contribution.

(d) All funds in an account, unless otherwise agreed in writing by the financial institution and the parties to the account, remain subject to liens, security interests, rights of setoff, and charges, notwithstanding the determination or allocation of net contributions with respect to the parties. **Leg.H.** Enacted Stats 1990 ch 79 §14 (AB 759), operative July 1, 1991. Amended Stats 2012 ch 235 §3 (AB 1624), effective January 1, 2013.

Prior Law: Former Prob C §5401, similar to the present section, was added Stats 1983 ch 92 §5, operative July 1, 1984, amended Stats 1989 ch 397 §34, operative July 1, 1990, and repealed Stats 1990 ch 79 §13, operative July 1, 1991.

§5402. Payment of joint account

Any sums in a joint account may be paid, on request and according to its terms, to any party without regard to whether any other party is incapacitated or deceased at the time the payment is demanded; but payment may not be made to the personal representative or heirs of a deceased party unless proof of death is presented to the financial institution showing that the decedent was the last surviving party or unless there is no right of survivorship under Section 5302. **Leg.H.** Enacted Stats 1990 ch 79 §14 (AB 759), operative July 1, 1991.

Prior Law: Former Prob C §5402, similar to the present section, was added Stats 1983 ch 92 §5, operative July 1, 1984, and repealed Stats 1990 ch 79 §13, operative July 1, 1991.

§5403. Payment of P.O.D. account

Any P.O.D. account may be paid, on request and according to its terms, to any original party to the account. Payment may be made, on request, to the P.O.D. payee or to the personal representative or heirs of a deceased P.O.D. payee upon presentation to the financial institution of proof of death showing that the P.O.D. payee survived all persons named as original payees. Payment may be made to the personal representative or heirs of a deceased original payee if proof of death is presented to the financial institution showing that the deceased original payee was the survivor of all other persons named on the account either as an original payee or as P.O.D. payee. **Leg.H.** Enacted Stats 1990 ch 79 §14 (AB 759), operative July 1, 1991.

Prior Law: Former Prob C §5403, similar to the present section, was added Stats 1983 ch 92 §5, operative July 1, 1984, and repealed Stats 1990 ch 79 §13, operative July 1, 1991.

§5404. Payment of Totten trust account

Any Totten trust account may be paid, on request and according to its terms, to any trustee. Unless the financial institution has received written notice that the beneficiary has a vested interest not dependent upon surviving the trustee, payment may be made to the personal representative or heirs of a deceased trustee if proof of death is presented to the financial institution showing that the deceased trustee was the survivor of all other persons named on the account either as trustee or beneficiary. A Totten trust account may be paid to a beneficiary or beneficiaries or the personal representative or heirs of a beneficiary or beneficiaries if proof of death is presented to the financial institution showing that the beneficiary or beneficiaries survived all persons named as trustees. **Leg.H.** Enacted Stats 1990 ch 79 §14 (AB 759), operative July 1, 1991.

Prior Law: Former Prob C §5404, similar to the present section, was added Stats 1983 ch 92 §5, operative July 1, 1984, amended Stats 1989 ch 397 §35, operative July 1, 1990, and repealed Stats 1990 ch 79 §13, operative July 1, 1991.

§5405. Payment as discharge; refusal to pay upon receipt of notice

(a) Payment made pursuant to Section 5401, 5402, 5403, or 5404 discharges the financial institution from all claims for amounts so paid whether or not the payment is consistent with the beneficial ownership of the account as between parties, P.O.D. payees, or beneficiaries, or their successors.

(b) The protection provided by subdivision (a) does not extend to payments made after the financial institution has been served with a court order restraining payment. No other notice or any other information shown to have been available to a financial institution shall affect its right to the protection provided by subdivision (a).

(c) Unless the notice is withdrawn by a subsequent writing, after receipt of a written notice from any party that withdrawals in accordance with the terms of the account, other than a checking account, share draft account, or other similar third-party payment instrument, should not be permitted, except with the signatures of more than one of the parties during their lifetimes or of more than one of the survivors after the death of any one of the parties, the financial institution may only pay the sums on deposit in accordance with the written instructions pending determination of the rights of the parties or their successors. No liability shall attach to the financial institution for complying with the terms of any written notice provided pursuant to this subdivision.

(d) The protection provided by this section has no bearing on the rights of parties in disputes between themselves or their successors concerning the beneficial ownership of funds in, or withdrawn from, multiple-party accounts and is in addition to, and not exclusive of, any protection provided the financial institution by any other provision of law. **Leg.H.** Enacted Stats 1990 ch 79 §14 (AB 759), operative July 1, 1991.

Prior Law: Former Prob C §5405, similar to the present section, was added Stats 1983 ch 92 §5, operative July 1, 1984, amended Stats 1984 ch 452 §8, and repealed Stats 1990 ch 79 §13, operative July 1, 1991.

§5406. Payment of account held in trust form where financial institution has no notice that account is not a "Totten trust account"

The provisions of this chapter that apply to the payment of a Totten trust account apply to an account in the name of one or more parties as trustee for one or more other persons if the financial institution has no other or further notice in writing that the account is not a Totten trust account as defined in Section 80. **Leg.H.** Enacted Stats 1990 ch 79 §14 (AB 759), operative July 1, 1991.

Prior Law: Former Prob C §5406, similar to the present section, was added Stats 1983 ch 92 §5, operative July 1, 1984, amended Stats 1989 ch 397 §36, operative July 1, 1990, and repealed Stats 1990 ch 79 §13, operative July 1, 1991.

§5407. Payment to minor

If a financial institution is required or permitted to make payment pursuant to this chapter to a person who is a minor:

(a) If the minor is a party to a multiple-party account, payment may be made to the minor or to the minor's order, and payment so made is a valid release and discharge of the financial institution, but this subdivision does not apply if the account is to be paid to the minor because the minor was designated as a P.O.D. payee or as a beneficiary of a Totten trust account.

(b) In cases where subdivision (a) does not apply, payment shall be made pursuant to the California Uniform Transfers to Minors Act (Part 9 (commencing with Section 3900) of Division 4), or as provided in Chapter 2 (commencing with Section 3400) of Part 8 of Division 4. **Leg.H.** Enacted Stats 1990 ch 79 §14 (AB 759), operative July 1, 1991.

Prior Law: Former Prob C §5407, similar to the present section, was added Stats 1983 ch 92 §5, operative July 1, 1984, amended Stats 1989 ch 397 §37, operative July 1, 1990, and repealed Stats 1990 ch 79 §13, operative July 1, 1991.

PART 3
UNIFORM TOD SECURITY REGISTRATION ACT

Citation, construction, and purposes of part. §5500.
Definitions. §5501.
Individuals who may obtain registration. §5502.
Authorization for registration. §5503.
When security registered in beneficiary form. §5504.
Words showing registration. §5505.
Effect on ownership. §5506.
Death of owner. §5507.
Protection for registering entity. §5508.
Transfer on death. §5509.
Terms and conditions. §5510.
Community property. §5511.
Applicability or part. §5512.

§5500. Citation, construction, and purposes of part

(a) This part shall be known as and may be cited as the Uniform TOD Security Registration Act.

(b) This part shall be liberally construed and applied to promote its underlying purposes and policy.

(c) The underlying purposes and policy of this act are to (1) encourage development of a title form for use by individuals that is effective, without probate and estate administration, for transferring property at death in accordance with directions of a deceased owner of a security as included in the title form in which the security is held and (2) protect issuers offering and implementing the new title form.

(d) Unless displaced by the particular provisions of this part, the principles of law and equity supplement its provisions. **Leg.H.** Added Stats 1998 ch 242 §2 (AB 1683).

§5501. Definitions

For purposes of this part:

(a) "Beneficiary form" means a registration of a security that indicates the present owner of the security and the intention of the owner regarding the person who will become the owner of the security upon the death of the owner.

(b) "Register," including its derivatives, means to issue a certificate showing the ownership of a certificated security or, in the case of an uncertificated security, to initiate or transfer an account showing ownership of securities.

(c) "Registering entity" means a person who originates or transfers a security title by registration, and includes a broker maintaining security accounts for customers and a transfer agent or other person acting for or as an issuer of securities.

(d) "Security" means a share, participation, or other interest in property, in a business, or in an obligation of an enterprise or other issuer, and includes a certificated security, an uncertificated security, and a security account.

(e)(1) "Security account" means any of the following:

(A) A reinvestment account associated with a security, a securities account with a broker, a cash balance in a brokerage account, cash, cash equivalents, interest, earnings, or dividends earned or declared on a security in an account, a reinvestment account, or a brokerage account, whether or not credited to the account before the owner's death.

(B) An investment management or custody account with a trust company or a trust department of a bank with trust powers, including the securities in the account, the cash balance in the account, and cash equivalents, and interest, earnings, or dividends earned or declared on a security in the account, whether or not credited to the account before the owner's death.

(C) A cash balance or other property held for or due to the owner of a security as a replacement for or product of an account security, whether or not credited to the account before the owner's death.

(2) For the purposes of this subdivision, "cash equivalent" means an investment that is easily converted into cash, including, treasury bills, treasury notes, money market funds, savings bonds, short-term instruments, and short-term obligations.

(f) This section may not be construed to govern cash equivalents in multiple-party accounts that are governed by the California Multiple-Party Accounts Law, Part 2 (commencing with Section 5100). **Leg.H.** Added Stats 1998 ch 242 §2 (AB 1683). Amended Stats 2002 ch 67 §1 (SB 1271), ch 809 §3 (SB 1504), effective January 1, 2003.

§5502. Individuals who may obtain registration

Only individuals whose registration of a security shows sole ownership by one individual or multiple ownership by two or more individuals with right of survivorship, rather than as tenants in common, may obtain registration in beneficiary form. Multiple owners of a security registered in beneficiary form hold as joint tenants with right of survivorship, as tenants by the entireties, or as owners of community property held in survivorship form, and not as tenants in common. **Leg.H.** Added Stats 1998 ch 242 §2 (AB 1683).

§5503. Authorization for registration

A security may be registered in beneficiary form if the form is authorized by this or a similar statute of the state of organization of the issuer or registering entity, the location of the registering entity's principal office, the office of its transfer agent or its office making the registration, or by this or a similar statute of the law of the state listed as the owner's address at the time of registration. A registration governed by the law of a jurisdiction in which this or similar legislation is not in force or was not in force when a registration in beneficiary form was made is nevertheless presumed to be valid and authorized as a matter of contract law. **Leg.H.** Added Stats 1998 ch 242 §2 (AB 1683).

§5504. When security registered in beneficiary form

A security, whether evidenced by certificate or account, is registered in beneficiary form when the registration includes a designation of a beneficiary to take the ownership at the death of the owner or the deaths of all multiple owners. **Leg.H.** Added Stats 1998 ch 242 §2 (AB 1683).

§5505. Words showing registration

Registration in beneficiary form may be shown by the words "transfer on death" or the abbreviation "TOD," or by the words "pay on death" or the abbreviation "POD," after the name of the registered owner and before the name of a beneficiary. **Leg.H.** Added Stats 1998 ch 242 §2 (AB 1683).

§5506. Effect on ownership

The designation of a TOD beneficiary on a registration in beneficiary form has no effect on ownership until the owner's death. A registration of a security in beneficiary form may be canceled or changed at any time by the sole owner or all then surviving owners without the consent of the beneficiary. **Leg.H.** Added Stats 1998 ch 242 §2 (AB 1683).

§5507. Death of owner

On death of a sole owner or the last to die of all multiple owners, ownership of securities registered in beneficiary form passes to the beneficiary or beneficiaries who survive all owners. On proof of death of all owners and compliance with any applicable requirements of the registering entity, a security registered in beneficiary form may be reregistered in the name of the beneficiary or beneficiaries who survive the death of all owners. Until division of the security after the death of all owners, multiple beneficiaries surviving the death of all owners hold their interests as tenants in common. If no beneficiary survives the death of all owners, the security belongs to the estate of the deceased sole owner or the estate of the last to die of all multiple owners. **Leg.H.** Added Stats 1998 ch 242 §2 (AB 1683).

§5508. Protection for registering entity

(a) A registering entity is not required to offer or to accept requests for security registration in beneficiary form. If a registration in beneficiary form is offered by a registering entity, the owner requesting registration in beneficiary form assents to the protections given to the registering entity by this part.

(b) By accepting a request for registration of a security in beneficiary form, the registering entity agrees that the registration will be implemented as provided in this part.

(c) A registering entity is discharged from all claims to a security by the estate, creditors, heirs, or devisees of a deceased owner if it registers a transfer of the security in accordance with Section 5507 and does so in good faith reliance (1) on the registration, (2) on this part, and (3) on information provided to it by affidavit of the personal representative of the deceased owner, or by the surviving beneficiary or the surviving beneficiary's representatives, or other information available to the registering entity. The protections of this part do not extend to a reregistration or payment made after a registering entity has received written notice from any claimant to any interest in the security objecting to implementation of a registration in beneficiary form. No other notice or other information available to the registering entity shall affect its right to protection under this part.

(d) The protection provided by this part to the registering entity of a security does not affect the rights of beneficiaries in disputes between themselves and other claimants to ownership of the security transferred or its value or proceeds. **Leg.H.** Added Stats 1998 ch 242 §2 (AB 1683).

§5509. Transfer on death

(a) Any transfer on death resulting from a registration in beneficiary form is effective by reason of the contract regarding the registration between the owner and the registering entity and this part and is not testamentary.

(b) This part does not limit the rights of a surviving spouse or creditors of security owners against beneficiaries and other transferees under other laws of this state. **Leg.H.** Added Stats 1998 ch 242 §2 (AB 1683).

§5510. Terms and conditions

(a) A registering entity offering to accept registrations in beneficiary form may establish the terms and conditions under which it will receive requests for (1) registrations in beneficiary form, and (2) implementation of registrations in beneficiary form, including requests for cancellation of previously registered TOD beneficiary designations and requests for reregistration to effect a change of beneficiary.

(b) The terms and conditions established pursuant to subdivision (a) may provide for (1) proving death, (2) avoiding or resolving any problems concerning fractional shares, (3) designating primary and contingent beneficiaries, and (4) substituting a named beneficiary's descendants to take in the place of the named beneficiary in the event of the beneficiary's death. Substitution may be indicated by appending to the name of the primary beneficiary the letters LDPS, standing for "lineal descendants per stirpes." This designation substitutes a deceased beneficiary's descendants who survive the owner for a beneficiary who fails to so survive, the descendants to be identified and to share in accordance with the law of the beneficiary's domicile at the owner's death governing inheritance by descendants of an intestate. Other forms of identifying beneficiaries who are to take on one or more contingencies, and rules for providing proofs and assurances needed to satisfy reasonable concerns by registering entities regarding conditions and identities relevant to accurate implementation of registrations in beneficiary form, may be contained in a registering entity's terms and conditions.

(c) The following are illustrations of registrations in beneficiary form that a registering entity may authorize:

(1) Sole owner-sole beneficiary: John S. Brown TOD (or POD) John S. Brown, Jr.

(2) Multiple owners-sole beneficiary: John S. Brown Mary B. Brown, JT TEN TOD John S. Brown, Jr.

(3) Multiple owners-primary and secondary (substituted) beneficiaries: John S. Brown Mary B. Brown, JT TEN TOD John S. Brown, Jr. SUB BENE Peter Q. Brown , or John S. Brown Mary B. Brown JT TEN TOD John S. Brown Jr. LDPS. **Leg.H.** Added Stats 1998 ch 242 §2 (AB 1683).

1998 Note: It appears the Legislature inadvertently added a space preceding the comma following "Peter Q. Brown" in subsection (c)(3).

§5511. Community property

Nothing in this part alters the community character of community property or community rights in community property. This part is subject to Chapter 2 (commencing with Section 5010) of Part 1 of Division 5. **Leg.H.** Added Stats 1998 ch 242 §2 (AB 1683).

§5512. Applicability or part

This part applies to registrations of securities in beneficiary form made before, on, or after January 1, 1999, by decedents dying on or after January 1, 1999. **Leg.H.** Added Stats 1998 ch 242 §2 (AB 1683).

PART 4
REVOCABLE TRANSFER ON DEATH DEED [REPEALED EFFECTIVE JANUARY 1, 2032]

Chapter 1. General Provisions [Repealed effective January 1, 2032].
Chapter 2. Execution and Revocation [Repealed effective January 1, 2032].
Chapter 3. Effect [Repealed effective January 1, 2032].
Chapter 4. Effectuation of Transfer [Repealed effective January 1, 2032].
Chapter 5. Contest [Repealed effective January 1, 2032].

CHAPTER 1
GENERAL PROVISIONS [REPEALED EFFECTIVE JANUARY 1, 2032]

Article 1. Preliminary Provisions [Repealed effective January 1, 2032].
Article 2. Definitions [Repealed effective January 1, 2032].

ARTICLE 1
Preliminary Provisions [Repealed effective January 1, 2032]

Applicability of part; Repeal of part [Repealed January 1, 2032]. § 5600.
Severance of Joint tenancy [Section renumbered 2016]. §5601.
Effect of part on use of other methods of conveyance of real property [Repealed January 1, 2032]. §5602.
Authority of court [Section renumbered 2016]. §5603.
Effect of part on applicability of other statutes [Repealed January 1, 2032]. §5604.
Study and report on effect of California's revocable transfer on death deed [Repealed January 1, 2032]. § 5605.

§ 5600. Applicability of part; Repeal of part [Repealed January 1, 2032]

(a) This part applies to a revocable transfer on death deed made by a transferor who dies on or after January 1, 2016, whether the deed was executed or recorded before, on, or after January 1, 2016.

(b) Nothing in this part invalidates an otherwise valid transfer under Section 5602.

(c) This part shall remain in effect only until January 1, 2032, and as of that date is repealed, unless a later enacted statute, that is enacted before January 1, 2032, deletes or extends that date. The repeal of this part pursuant to this subdivision shall not affect the validity or effect of a revocable transfer on death deed that is executed before January 1, 2032, and shall not affect the authority of the transferor to revoke a transfer on death deed by recording a signed and notarized instrument that is substantially in the form specified in Section 5644.

(d) The revisions made by the act that added this subdivision do not apply to a revocable transfer on death deed or revocation form that was signed before January 1, 2022. **Leg.H.** Added Stats 2015 ch 293 §17 (AB 139), effective January 1, 2016, repealed January 1, 2021. Amended Stats 2020 ch 238 §1 (SB 1305), effective January 1, 2021, repealed January 1, 2022; Stats 2021 ch 215 §2 (SB 315), effective January 1, 2022, repealed January 1, 2032 (repealer amended).

2016 Note: (a) The California Law Revision Commission shall study the effect of California's revocable transfer on death deed set forth in Part 4 (commencing with Section 5600) of Division 5 of the Probate Code and make recommendations in this regard. The commission shall report all of its findings to the Legislature on or before January 1, 2020.

(b) In the study required by subdivision (a), the commission shall address all of the following:

(1) Whether the revocable transfer on death deed is working effectively.
(2) Whether the revocable transfer on death deed should be continued.
(3) Whether the revocable transfer on death deed is subject to misuse or misunderstanding.
(4) What changes should be made to the revocable transfer on death deed or the law associated with the deed to improve its effectiveness and to avoid misuse or misunderstanding.
(5) Whether the revocable transfer on death deed has been used to perpetuate financial abuse on property owners and, if so, how the law associated with the deed should be changed to minimize this abuse.
(6) Whether it is feasible and appropriate to expand the revocable transfer on death deed to include the following:
  (A) The transfer of stock cooperatives or other common interest developments.
  (B) Transfers to a trust or other legal entity.

(c) (1) The report required by subdivision (a) shall comply with Section 9795 of the Government Code.

(2) Pursuant to Section 10231.5 of the Government Code, this section is repealed on January 1, 2024. Stats 2016 ch 179 (AB 1779) §1.

Prior Law: Former Prob C §5600 was added Stats 2001 ch 417 §9 and renumbered Prob C §5040 by Stats 2015 ch 293 §12, effective January 1, 2016.

§5601. Severance of Joint tenancy [Section renumbered 2016]

Leg.H. Added Stats 2001 ch 417 §9 (AB 873). Amended and renumbered Prob C §5042 by Stats 2015 ch 293 §13 (AB 139), effective January 1, 2016.

§5602. Effect of part on use of other methods of conveyance of real property [Repealed January 1, 2032]

This part does not preclude use of any other method of conveying real property that is permitted by law and that has the effect of postponing enjoyment of the property until the death of the owner. **Leg.H.** Added Stats 2015 ch 293 §17 (AB 139), effective January 1, 2016, repealed January 1, 2020. Amended Stats 2020 ch 238 §1 (SB 1305), effective January 1, 2021, repealed January 1, 2022 (repealer amended); Stats 2021 ch 215 §2 (SB 315), effective January 1, 2022, repealed January 1, 2032 (repealer amended).

2015 Note: For repeal of part, see Prob C §5600.

Prior Law: Former Prob C §5602 was added Stats 2001 ch 417 §9 and amended and renumbered Prob C §5044 by Stats 2015 ch 293 §14, effective January 1, 2016.

§5603. Authority of court [Section renumbered 2016]

Leg.H. Added Stats 2001 ch 417 §9 (AB 873). Amended and renumbered Prob C §5046 by Stats 2015 ch 293 §15 (AB 139), effective January 1, 2016.

§5604. Effect of part on applicability of other statutes [Repealed January 1, 2032]

(a) Except as provided in subdivision (b), nothing in this part affects the application to a revocable transfer on death deed of any other statute governing a nonprobate transfer on death, including, but not limited to, any of the following provisions that by its terms or intent would apply to a nonprobate transfer on death:

(1) Division 2 (commencing with Section 100).
(2) Part 1 (commencing with Section 5000) of this division.
(3) Division 10 (commencing with Section 20100).
(4) Division 11 (commencing with Section 21101).

(b) Notwithstanding subdivision (a), a provision of another statute governing a nonprobate transfer on death does not apply to a revocable transfer on death deed to the extent this part provides a contrary rule. **Leg.H.** Added Stats 2015 ch 293 §17 (AB 139), effective January 1, 2016, repealed January 1, 2021. Amended Stats 2020 ch 238 §1 (SB 1305), effective January 1, 2021, repealed January 1, 2022 (repealer amended); Stats 2021 ch 215 §2 (SB 315), effective January 1, 2022, repealed January 1, 2032 (repealer amended).

2015 Note: For repeal of part, see Prob C §5600.

Prior Law: Former Prob C §5604 was added Stats 2001 ch 417 §9 and amended and renumbered Prob C §5048 by Stats 2015 ch 293 §16, effective January 1, 2016.

§ 5605. Study and report on effect of California's revocable transfer on death deed [Repealed January 1, 2032]

(a) The California Law Revision Commission shall study the effect of California's revocable transfer on death deed and make recommendations for improvement of this part. The commission shall report all of its findings and recommendations to the Legislature on or before January 1, 2031.

(b) In the study required by subdivision (a), the commission shall address all of the following:

(1) Whether the revocable transfer on death deed is working effectively.
(2) Whether the revocable transfer on death deed should be continued.
(3) Whether the revocable transfer on death deed is subject to misuse or misunderstanding.

(4) What changes should be made to the revocable transfer on death deed or the law associated with the deed to improve its effectiveness and to avoid misuse or misunderstanding.

(5) Whether the revocable transfer on death deed has been used to perpetuate financial abuse on property owners and, if so, how the law associated with the deed should be changed to minimize this abuse.

(6) Whether there should be any change to the types of property that can be transferred by revocable transfer on death deed.

(7) Whether there should be any change to the types of persons or entities that can be named as the beneficiary of a revocable transfer on death deed.

(c) The report required by subdivision (a) shall comply with Section 9795 of the Government Code. **Leg.H.** Added Stats 2021 ch 215 §3 (SB 315), effective January 1, 2022, repealed January 1, 2032.

ARTICLE 2
Definitions [Repealed effective January 1, 2032]

Governance of definitions in construction of part [Repealed January 1, 2032]. §5606.
"Beneficiary" [Repealed January 1, 2032]. § 5608.
"Real property" [Repealed January 1, 2032]. § 5610.
"Recorded" [Repealed January 1, 2032]. §5612.
"Revocable transfer on death deed" [Repealed January 1, 2032]. §5614.
"Stock cooperative" [Repealed January 1, 2032]. § 5614.5.
"Subscribing witness" [Repealed January 1, 2032]. § 5615.
"Transferor" [Repealed January 1, 2032]. §5616.
"Unsecured debts" [Repealed January 1, 2032]. § 5618.

§5606. Governance of definitions in construction of part [Repealed January 1, 2032]

Unless the provision or context otherwise requires, the definitions in this article govern the construction of this part. **Leg.H.** Added Stats 2015 ch 293 §17 (AB 139), effective January 1, 2016, repealed January 1, 2021. Amended Stats 2020 ch 238 §1 (SB 1305), effective January 1, 2021, repealed January 1, 2022 (repealer amended); Stats 2021 ch 215 §2 (SB 315), effective January 1, 2022, repealed January 1, 2032 (repealer amended).

2015 Note: For repeal of part, see Prob C §5600.

§ 5608. "Beneficiary" [Repealed January 1, 2032]

"Beneficiary" means a person named in a revocable transfer on death deed as transferee of the property. A natural person, trust, or legal entity may be named as a beneficiary. **Leg.H.** Added Stats 2015 ch 293 §17 (AB 139), effective January 1, 2016, repealed January 1, 2021. Amended Stats 2021 ch 215 §4 (SB 315), effective January 1, 2022; Stats 2021 ch 215 §2 (SB 315), effective January 1, 2022, repealed January 1, 2032 (repealer amended).

2015 Note: For repeal of part, see Prob C §5600.

§ 5610. "Real property" [Repealed January 1, 2032]

(a) Except as provided in subdivision (b), "real property" means either of the following:

(1) A parcel of land that is improved with one to four residential dwelling units.

(2) A residential separate interest and its appurtenant common area in a common interest development, regardless of the number of separate interests in the common interest development.

(b) "Real property" does not include a parcel of agricultural land that is greater than 40 acres in size. For the purposes of this subdivision, "agricultural land" means land that is designated for agricultural use by law or by a document that is recorded in the county in which the land is located.

(c) The definition of "real property" shall be construed pursuant to the circumstances that existed on the execution date shown on the revocable transfer on death deed. **Leg.H.** Added Stats 2021 ch 215 §6 (SB 315), effective January 1, 2022, repealed January 1, 2032. Amended Stats 2023 ch 62 §1 (AB 288), effective January 1, 2024, repealed January 1, 2032.

Prior Law Former Prob C §5610, relating to "real property" definition, was added Stats 2015 ch 293 §17 (AB 139), effective January 1, 2016, and repealed Stats 2021 ch 215 §5 (SB 315), effective January 1, 2022.

§5612. "Recorded" [Repealed January 1, 2032]

"Recorded" has the meaning provided in Section 1170 of the Civil Code. **Leg.H.** Added Stats 2015 ch 293 §17 (AB 139), effective January 1, 2016, repealed January 1, 2021. Amended Stats 2020 ch 238 §1 (SB 1305), effective January 1, 2021, repealed January 1, 2022 (repealer amended); Stats 2021 ch 215 §2 (SB 315), effective January 1, 2022, repealed January 1, 2032 (repealer amended).

2015 Note: For repeal of part, see Prob C §5600.

§5614. "Revocable transfer on death deed" [Repealed January 1, 2032]

(a) "Revocable transfer on death deed" means an instrument created pursuant to this part that does all of the following:

(1) Makes a donative transfer of real property to a named beneficiary.
(2) Operates on the transferor's death.
(3) Remains revocable until the transferor's death.

(b) A revocable transfer on death deed may also be known as a "revocable TOD deed."

(c) A revocable transfer on death deed may be used to transfer real property even if ownership of the property is not typically evidenced or transferred by use of a deed. **Leg.H.** Added Stats 2015 ch 293 §17 (AB 139), effective January 1, 2016, repealed January 1, 2021. Amended Stats 2020 ch 238 §1 (SB 1305), effective January 1, 2021, repealed January 1, 2022 (repealer amended); Stats 2021 ch 215 §2 (SB 315), effective January 1, 2022, repealed January 1, 2032 (repealer amended); Stats 2023 ch 62 §2 (AB 288), effective January 1, 2024, repealed January 1, 2032.

2015 Note: For repeal of part, see Prob C §5600.

§ 5614.5. "Stock cooperative" [Repealed January 1, 2032]

"Stock cooperative" has the same meaning as in Section 4190 of the Civil Code. **Leg.H.** Added Stats 2023 ch 62 §3 (AB 288), effective January 1, 2024.

§ 5615. "Subscribing witness" [Repealed January 1, 2032]

"Subscribing witness" means a person who signs a revocable transfer on death deed as a witness, as provided in Section 5624. **Leg.H.** Added Stats 2021 ch 215 §7 (SB 315), effective January 1, 2022, repealed January 1, 2032.

§5616. "Transferor" [Repealed January 1, 2032]

"Transferor" means an owner of real property who makes a revocable transfer on death deed of the property. **Leg.H.** Added Stats 2015 ch 293 §17 (AB 139), effective January 1, 2016, repealed January 1, 2021. Amended Stats 2020 ch 238 §1 (SB 1305), effective January 1, 2021, repealed January 1, 2022 (repealer amended); Stats 2021 ch 215 §2 (SB 315), effective January 1, 2022, repealed January 1, 2032 (repealer amended).

2015 Note: For repeal of part, see Prob C §5600.

§ 5618. "Unsecured debts" [Repealed January 1, 2032]

"Unsecured debts" includes, but is not limited to, a transferor's funeral expenses, expenses of a transferor's last illness, and wage claims. **Leg.H.** Added Stats 2021 ch 215 §8 (SB 315), effective January 1, 2022, repealed January 1, 2032.

CHAPTER 2
EXECUTION AND REVOCATION [REPEALED EFFECTIVE JANUARY 1, 2032]

Article 1. Execution [Repealed effective January 1, 2032].
Article 2. Revocation [Repealed effective January 1, 2032].
Article 3. Statutory Forms [Repealed effective January 1, 2032].

ARTICLE 1
Execution [Repealed effective January 1, 2032]

Capacity [Repealed January 1, 2032]. §5620.
Identification of beneficiary [Repealed January 1, 2032]. §5622.
Execution; Signature, date, witnesses and notarization [Repealed January 1, 2032]. § 5624.
Witnesses [Repealed January 1, 2032]. § 5625.
Recordation of deed [Repealed January 1, 2032]. §5626.
Recordation as revocation of earlier executed deed [Repealed January 1, 2032]. §5628.

§5620. Capacity [Repealed January 1, 2032]

An owner of real property who has the capacity to contract may make a revocable transfer on death deed of the property. **Leg.H.** Added Stats 2015 ch 293 §17 (AB 139), effective January 1, 2016, repealed January 1, 2021. Amended Stats 2020 ch 238 §1 (SB 1305), effective January 1, 2021, repealed January 1, 2022 (repealer amended); Stats 2021 ch 215 §2

(SB 315), effective January 1, 2022, repealed January 1, 2032 (repealer amended).

2015 Note: For repeal of part, see Prob C §5600.

§5622. Identification of beneficiary [Repealed January 1, 2032]

The transferor shall identify the beneficiary by name in a revocable transfer on death deed. **Leg.H.** Added Stats 2015 ch 293 §17 (AB 139), effective January 1, 2016, repealed January 1, 2021. Amended Stats 2021 ch 215 §2 (SB 315), effective January 1, 2022, repealed January 1, 2032 (repealer amended).

2015 Note: For repeal of part, see Prob C §5600.

§ 5624. Execution; Signature, date, witnesses and notarization [Repealed January 1, 2032]

A revocable transfer on death deed is not effective unless all of the following conditions are satisfied:

(a) The deed is signed by the transferor and dated.

(b) The deed is signed by two witnesses who were present at the same time and who witnessed either the signing of the deed or the transferor's acknowledgment that the transferor had signed the deed.

(c) The deed is acknowledged before a notary public. **Leg.H.** Added Stats 2015 ch 293 §17 (AB 139), effective January 1, 2016, repealed January 1, 2021. Amended Stats 2021 ch 215 §9 (SB 315), effective January 1, 2022; Stats 2021 ch 215 §2 (SB 315), effective January 1, 2022, repealed January 1, 2032 (repealer amended).

2015 Note: For repeal of part, see Prob C §5600.

§ 5625. Witnesses [Repealed January 1, 2032]

(a) Any person generally competent to be a witness may act as a witness to a revocable transfer on death deed.

(b) A revocable transfer on death deed is not invalid because it is signed by an interested witness.

(c) If a beneficiary of a revocable transfer on death deed is also a subscribing witness, there is a presumption that the witness procured the revocable transfer on death deed by duress, menace, fraud, or undue influence. This presumption is a presumption affecting the burden of proof. This presumption does not apply where the witness is named as beneficiary solely in a fiduciary capacity. **Leg.H.** Added Stats 2021 ch 215 §10 (SB 315), effective January 1, 2022, repealed January 1, 2032.

§5626. Recordation of deed [Repealed January 1, 2032]

(a) A revocable transfer on death deed is not effective unless the deed is recorded on or before 60 days after the date it was acknowledged before a notary.

(b) The transferor is not required to deliver a revocable transfer on death deed to the beneficiary during the transferor's life.

(c) The beneficiary is not required to accept a revocable transfer on death deed from the transferor during the transferor's life.

(d)(1) Subdivision (a) does not require the recordation of the "Common Questions" language that is specified in subdivision (b) of Section 5642. The failure to record that part of the statutory form has no effect on the effectiveness of a revocable transfer on death deed.

(2)(A) This subdivision applies to a revocable transfer on death deed executed on or after July 9, 2018.

(B) This subdivision applies to a revocable transfer on death deed executed before July 9, 2018, only if the transferor was alive on July 9, 2018. **Leg.H.** Added Stats 2015 ch 293 §17 (AB 139), effective January 1, 2016, repealed January 1, 2021. Amended Stats 2018 ch 65 §1 (AB 1739), effective July 9, 2018, repealed January 1, 2021; Stats 2020 ch 238 §1 (SB 1305), effective January 1, 2021, repealed January 1, 2022 (repealer amended); Stats 2021 ch 215 §2 (SB 315), effective January 1, 2032 (repealer amended); Stats 2021 ch 215 §11 (SB 315), effective January 1, 2022; Stats 2021 ch 215 §2 (SB 315), effective January 1, 2022, repealed January 1, 2032 (repealer amended).

2015 Note: For repeal of part, see Prob C §5600.

§5628. Recordation as revocation of earlier executed deed [Repealed January 1, 2032]

(a) If a revocable transfer on death deed is recorded for the same property for which another revocable transfer on death deed is recorded, the later executed deed is the operative instrument and its recordation revokes the earlier executed deed.

(b) Revocation of a revocable transfer on death deed does not revive an instrument earlier revoked by recordation of that deed. **Leg.H.** Added Stats 2015 ch 293 §17 (AB 139), effective January 1, 2016, repealed January 1, 2021. Amended Stats 2020 ch 238 §1 (SB 1305), effective January 1, 2021, repealed January 1, 2022 (repealer amended); Stats 2021 ch 215 §2 (SB 315), effective January 1, 2022, repealed January 1, 2032 (repealer amended).

2015 Note: For repeal of part, see Prob C §5600.

ARTICLE 2
Revocation [Repealed effective January 1, 2032]

Capacity [Repealed January 1, 2032]. §5630.
Execution and recordation; Consent of beneficiary [Repealed January 1, 2032]. § 5632.

§5630. Capacity [Repealed January 1, 2032]

A transferor who has the capacity to contract may revoke a revocable transfer on death deed at any time. **Leg.H.** Added Stats 2015 ch 293 §17 (AB 139), effective January 1, 2016, repealed January 1, 2021. Amended Stats 2020 ch 238 §1 (SB 1305), effective January 1, 2021, repealed January 1, 2022 (repealer amended); Stats 2021 ch 215 §2 (SB 315), effective January 1, 2022, repealed January 1, 2032 (repealer amended).

2015 Note: For repeal of part, see Prob C §5600.

§ 5632. Execution and recordation; Consent of beneficiary [Repealed January 1, 2032]

(a) An instrument revoking a revocable transfer on death deed shall be executed and recorded in the same manner as execution and recordation of a revocable transfer on death deed.

(b) Joinder, consent, or agreement of, or notice to, the beneficiary is not required for revocation of a revocable transfer on death deed. **Leg.H.** Added Stats 2015 ch 293 §17 (AB 139), effective January 1, 2016, repealed January 1, 2021. Amended Stats 2021 ch 215 §12 (SB 315), effective January 1, 2022; Stats 2021 ch 215 §2 (SB 315), effective January 1, 2022, repealed January 1, 2032 (repealer amended).

2015 Note: For repeal of part, see Prob C §5600.

ARTICLE 3
Statutory Forms [Repealed effective January 1, 2032]

Revocable transfer on death (TOD) deed [Repealed January 1, 2032]. § 5642.
Revocation of revocable transfer on death (TOD) deed [Repealed January 1, 2032]. § 5644.

§ 5642. Revocable transfer on death (TOD) deed [Repealed January 1, 2032]

A revocable transfer on death deed shall be substantially in the following form.

(a) The first page of the form shall be substantially the following:

REVOCABLE TRANSFER ON DEATH (TOD) DEED

(California Probate Code Section 5642)

Recording Requested By:
When Recorded Mail This Deed To
Name:
Address:
Assessor's Parcel Number: Space Above For Recorder's Use

This document is exempt from documentary transfer tax under Rev. & Tax. Code § 11930. This document is exempt from preliminary change of ownership report under Rev. & Tax. Code § 480.3.

IMPORTANT NOTICE: THIS DEED MUST BE RECORDED ON OR BEFORE 60 DAYS AFTER THE DATE IT IS NOTARIZED

Use this deed to transfer the residential property described below directly to your named beneficiaries when you die. YOU SHOULD CAREFULLY READ ALL OF THE INFORMATION ON THE OTHER PAGES OF THIS FORM. You may wish to consult an attorney before using this deed. It may have results that you do not want. Provide only the information asked for in the form. DO NOT INSERT ANY OTHER INFORMATION OR INSTRUCTIONS. This form MUST be RECORDED on or before 60 days after the date it is notarized or it will not be effective.

PROPERTY DESCRIPTION

Print the legal description of the residential property affected by this deed:

BENEFICIARY(IES)

Name the person(s) or entity(ies) who will receive the described property on your death.

IF YOU ARE NAMING A PERSON, state the person's FULL NAME (DO NOT use general terms like "my children"). You may also wish to state the RELATIONSHIP that the person has to you (spouse, son, daughter, friend, etc.), but this is not required.

IF YOU ARE NAMING A TRUST, state the full name of the trust, the name of the trustee(s), and the date shown on the signature page of the trust.IF YOU ARE NAMING A PRIVATE OR PUBLIC ENTITY, state the name of the entity as precisely as you can.

_____

_____

TRANSFER ON DEATH

I transfer all of my interest in the described property to the named beneficiary(ies) on my death. I may revoke this deed. When recorded, this deed revokes any TOD deed that I made before signing this deed.

Sign and print your name below (your name should exactly match the name shown on your title documents):

_____ Date _____

NOTE: This deed only transfers MY ownership share of the property. The deed does NOT transfer the share of any co-owner of the property. Any co-owner who wants to name a TOD beneficiary must execute and RECORD a SEPARATE deed.

WITNESSES

To be valid, this deed must be signed by two persons, both present at the same time, who witness your signing of the deed or your acknowledgment that it is your deed. The signatures of the witnesses do not need to be acknowledged by a notary public.

Witness #1   Witness #2
Print and sign your name: Print and sign your name:
-------------------------   -------------------------

ACKNOWLEDGMENT OF NOTARY

A notary public or other officer completing this certificate verifies only the identity of the individual who signed the document to which this certificate is attached, and not the truthfulness, accuracy, or validity of that document.

State of California }
County of _____

On _____ before me, (here insert name and title of the officer), personally appeared _____, who proved to me on the basis of satisfactory evidence to be the person(s) whose name(s) is/are subscribed to the within instrument and acknowledged to me that they executed the same in their authorized capacity(ies), and that by their signature(s) on the instrument the person(s), or the entity upon behalf of which the person(s) acted, executed the instrument.

I certify under PENALTY OF PERJURY under the laws of the State of California that the foregoing paragraph is true and correct.

WITNESS my hand and official seal.

Signature _____ (Seal)

(b) Subsequent pages of a form executed under this section shall be in substantially the following form:

COMMON QUESTIONS ABOUT THE USE OF THIS FORM

WHAT DOES THE TOD DEED DO? When you die, the identified property will transfer to your named beneficiary without probate. The TOD deed has no effect until you die. You can revoke it at any time.

CAN I USE THIS DEED TO TRANSFER NONRESIDENTIAL PROPERTY? This deed can only be used to transfer residential property. Also, the deed cannot be used to transfer a parcel of agricultural land that is over 40 acres in size. CAN I USE THIS DEED TO TRANSFER A MOBILEHOME? The deed can only be used to transfer a mobilehome if it is a "fixture" or improvement under Section 18551 of the Health and Safety Code. If you are unsure whether your mobilehome is a fixture, you may wish to consult an attorney. An error on this point could cause the transfer of your mobilehome to fail.

HOW DO I USE THE TOD DEED? Complete this form. Have it signed by two persons who are both present at the same time and who witness you either signing the form or acknowledging the form. Then NOTARIZE your signature (witness signatures do not need to be notarized). RECORD the form in the county where the property is located. The form MUST be recorded on or before 60 days after the date you notarize it or the deed has no effect.

IF I AM UNABLE TO SIGN THE DEED, MAY I ASK SOMEONE ELSE TO SIGN MY NAME FOR ME? Yes. However, if the person who signs for you would benefit from the transfer of your property, there is a chance that the transfer under this deed will fail. You may wish to consult an attorney before taking that step. CAN A PERSON WHO SIGNS THE DEED AS A WITNESS ALSO BE A BENEFICIARY? Yes, but this can cause serious legal problems, including the possible invalidation of the deed. You should avoid using a beneficiary as a witness.

IS THE "LEGAL DESCRIPTION" OF THE PROPERTY NECESSARY? Yes.

HOW DO I FIND THE "LEGAL DESCRIPTION" OF THE PROPERTY? This information may be on the deed you received when you became an owner of the property. This information may also be available in the office of the county recorder for the county where the property is located. If you are not absolutely sure, consult an attorney.

HOW DO I "RECORD" THE FORM? Take the completed and notarized form to the county recorder for the county in which the property is located. Follow the instructions given by the county recorder to make the form part of the official property records.

WHAT IF I SHARE OWNERSHIP OF THE PROPERTY? This form only transfers YOUR share of the property. If a co-owner also wants to name a TOD beneficiary, that co-owner must complete and RECORD a separate form.

CAN I REVOKE THE TOD DEED IF I CHANGE MY MIND? Yes. You may revoke the TOD deed at any time. No one, including your beneficiary, can prevent you from revoking the deed.

HOW DO I REVOKE THE TOD DEED? There are three ways to revoke a recorded TOD deed: (1) Complete, have witnessed and notarized, and RECORD a revocation form. (2) Create, have witnessed and notarized, and RECORD a new TOD deed. (3) Sell or give away the property, or transfer it to a trust, before your death and RECORD the deed. A TOD deed can only affect property that you own when you die. A TOD deed cannot be revoked by will.

CAN I REVOKE A TOD DEED BY CREATING A NEW DOCUMENT THAT DISPOSES OF THE PROPERTY (FOR EXAMPLE, BY CREATING A NEW TOD DEED OR BY ASSIGNING THE PROPERTY TO A TRUST)? Yes, but only if the new document is RECORDED. To avoid any doubt, you may wish to RECORD a TOD deed revocation form before creating the new instrument. A TOD deed cannot be revoked by will, or by purporting to leave the subject property to anyone via will.

IF I SELL OR GIVE AWAY THE PROPERTY DESCRIBED IN A TOD DEED, WHAT HAPPENS WHEN I DIE? If the deed or other document used to transfer your property is RECORDED within 120 days after the TOD deed would otherwise operate, the TOD deed will have no effect. If the transfer document is not RECORDED within that time period, the TOD deed will take effect.

I AM BEING PRESSURED TO COMPLETE THIS FORM. WHAT SHOULD I DO? Do NOT complete this form unless you freely choose to do so. If you are being pressured to dispose of your property in a way that you do not want, you may want to alert a family member, friend, the district attorney, or a senior service agency.

DO I NEED TO TELL MY BENEFICIARY ABOUT THE TOD DEED? No. But secrecy can cause later complications and might make it easier for others to commit fraud.

WHAT DOES MY BENEFICIARY NEED TO DO WHEN I DIE? Your beneficiary must do all of the following: (1) RECORD evidence of your death (Prob. Code §210). (2) File a change in ownership notice (Rev. & Tax. Code §480). (3) Provide notice to your heirs that includes a copy of this deed and your death certificate (Prob. Code §5681). Determining who is an "heir" can be complicated. Your beneficiary should consider seeking professional advice to make that determination. (4) RECORD an affidavit affirming that notice was sent to your heirs (Prob. Code §5682(c). (5) If you received Medi-Cal benefits, your beneficiary must notify the State Department of Health Care Services of your death and provide a copy of your death certificate (Prob. Code §215). Your beneficiary may wish to consult a professional for assistance with these requirements.

WHAT IF I NAME MORE THAN ONE BENEFICIARY? Your beneficiaries will become co-owners in equal shares as tenants in common. If you want a different result, you should not use this form.

HOW DO I NAME BENEFICIARIES? (1) If the beneficiary is a person, you MUST state the person's FULL name. You MAY NOT use general terms to describe beneficiaries, such as "my children." You may also briefly state that person's relationship to you (for example, my spouse, my son, my daughter, my friend, etc.), but this is not required. (2) If the beneficiary is a trust, you MUST name the trust, name the trustee(s), and state the date shown on the trust's signature page. (3) If the beneficiary is a public or private entity, name the entity as precisely as you can.

WHAT IF A BENEFICIARY DIES BEFORE I DO? If all beneficiaries die before you, the TOD deed has no effect. If a beneficiary dies before you, but other beneficiaries survive you, the share of the deceased beneficiary will be divided equally between the surviving beneficiaries. If that is not the result you want, you should not use the TOD deed.

WHAT IS THE EFFECT OF A TOD DEED ON PROPERTY THAT I OWN AS JOINT TENANCY OR COMMUNITY PROPERTY WITH RIGHT OF SURVIVORSHIP? If you are the first joint tenant or spouse to die, the deed is VOID and has no effect. The property transfers to your joint tenant or surviving spouse and not according to this deed. If you are the last joint tenant or spouse to die, the deed takes effect and controls the ownership of your property when you die. If you do not want these results, do not use this form. The deed does NOT transfer the share of a co-owner of the property. Any co-owner who wants to name a TOD beneficiary must complete and RECORD a SEPARATE deed.

CAN I ADD OTHER CONDITIONS ON THE FORM? No. If you do, your beneficiary may need to go to court to clear title.

IS PROPERTY TRANSFERRED BY THE TOD DEED SUBJECT TO MY DEBTS? Yes.

DOES THE TOD DEED HELP ME TO AVOID GIFT AND ESTATE TAXES? No.

HOW DOES THE TOD DEED AFFECT PROPERTY TAXES? The TOD deed has no effect on your property taxes until your death. At that time, property tax law applies as it would to any other change of ownership.

DOES THE TOD DEED AFFECT MY ELIGIBILITY FOR MEDI-CAL? No.

Leg.H. Added Stats 2015 ch 293 §17 (AB 139), effective January 1, 2016, repealed January 1, 2021. Amended Stats 2020 ch 238 §1 (SB 1305), effective January 1, 2021, repealed January 1, 2022 (repealer amended); Stats 2021 ch 215 §13 (SB 315), effective January 1, 2022; Stats 2021 ch 215 §2 (SB 315), effective January 1, 2022, repealed January 1, 2032 (repealer amended); Stats 2023 ch 62 §4 (AB 288), effective January 1, 2024, repealed January 1, 2032.

2015 Note: For repeal of part, see Prob C §5600.

§ 5644. Revocation of revocable transfer on death (TOD) deed [Repealed January 1, 2032]

A transferor may revoke a revocable transfer on death deed by an instrument in substantially the following form:

Revocation of Revocable Transfer on Death (TOD) Deed

(California Probate Code Section 5600)

Recording Requested By:
When Recorded Mail This Deed To
Name:
Address:
Assessor's Parcel Number: Space Above For Recorder's Use

This deed revocation is exempt from documentary transfer tax under Rev. & Tax. Code § 11930. This deed revocation is exempt from preliminary change of ownership report under Rev. & Tax. Code § 480.3.

IMPORTANT NOTICE: THIS FORM MUST BE RECORDED TO BE EFFECTIVE

This revocation form MUST be RECORDED on or before 60 days after the date it is notarized or it will not be effective. This revocation form only affects a transfer on death deed that YOU made. A transfer on death deed made by a co-owner of your property is not affected by this revocation form. A co-owner who wants to revoke a transfer on death deed that they made must complete and RECORD a SEPARATE revocation form.

PROPERTY DESCRIPTION

Print the legal description of the property affected by this revocation:
_____

REVOCATION

I revoke any TOD deed to transfer the described property that I executed before executing this form.

SIGNATURE AND DATE

Sign and print your name below (your name should exactly match the name shown on your title documents):
_____ Date _____

WITNESSES

To be valid, this form must be signed by two persons, both present at the same time, who witness your signing of the form or your acknowledgment that it is your form. The signatures of the witnesses do not need to be acknowledged by a notary public.

Witness #1 Witness #2
Print and sign your name: Print and sign your name:

ACKNOWLEDGMENT OF NOTARY

A notary public or other officer completing this certificate verifies only the identity of the individual who signed the document to which this certificate is attached, and not the truthfulness, accuracy, or validity of that document.

State of California
County of _____

On _____ before me, (here insert name and title of the officer), personally appeared _____, who proved to me on the basis of satisfactory evidence to be the person(s) whose name(s) is/are subscribed to the within instrument and acknowledged to me that he/she/they executed the same in his/her/their authorized capacity(ies), and that by his/her/their signature(s) on the instrument the person(s), or the entity upon behalf of which the person(s) acted, executed the instrument.

I certify under PENALTY OF PERJURY under the laws of the State of California that the foregoing paragraph is true and correct.

WITNESS my hand and official seal.
Signature _____ (Seal)

Leg.H. Added Stats 2015 ch 293 §17 (AB 139), effective January 1, 2016, repealed January 1, 2021. Amended Stats 2021 ch 215 §14 (SB 315), effective January 1, 2022; Stats 2021 ch 215 §2 (SB 315), effective January 1, 2022, repealed January 1, 2032 (repealer amended).

2015 Note: For repeal of part, see Prob C §5600.

CHAPTER 3
EFFECT [REPEALED EFFECTIVE JANUARY 1, 2032]

Article 1. General Provisions [Repealed effective January 1, 2032].
Article 2. Other Instruments and Forms of Tenure [Repealed effective January 1, 2032].
Article 3. Creditors [Repealed effective January 1, 2032].

ARTICLE 1
General Provisions [Repealed effective January 1, 2032]

During transferor's life [Repealed January 1, 2032]. §5650.
Rules of transfer upon death [Repealed January 1, 2032]. § 5652.
"Lifetime transfer of property" for purposes of health care eligibility; Property subject to Department of Health Care Services claims [Repealed January 1, 2032]. §5654.
"Change in ownership" for purposes of tax provisions of Revenue and Taxation Code [Repealed January 1, 2032]. §5656.
Application of cy pres doctrine [Repealed January 1, 2032]. § 5658.
Effect of error or ambiguity [Repealed January 1, 2032]. § 5659.

§5650. During transferor's life [Repealed January 1, 2032]

During the transferor's life, execution and recordation of a revocable transfer on death deed:

(a) Does not affect the ownership rights of the transferor, and the transferor or the transferor's agent or other fiduciary may convey, assign, contract, encumber, or otherwise deal with the property, and the property is subject to process of the transferor's creditors, as if no revocable transfer on death deed were executed or recorded.

(b) Does not create any legal or equitable right in the beneficiary, and the property is not subject to process of the beneficiary's creditors.

(c) Does not transfer or convey any right, title, or interest in the property. **Leg.H.** Added Stats 2015 ch 293 §17 (AB 139), effective January 1, 2016, repealed January 1, 2021. Amended Stats 2020 ch 238 §1 (SB 1305), effective January 1, 2021, repealed January 1, 2022 (repealer amended); Stats 2021 ch 215 §2 (SB 315), effective January 1, 2022, repealed January 1, 2032 (repealer amended).

2015 Note: For repeal of part, see Prob C §5600.

§ 5652. Rules of transfer upon death [Repealed January 1, 2032]

(a) A revocable transfer on death deed transfers all of the transferor's interest in the property on the transferor's death according to the following rules:

(1) Subject to the beneficiary's right to disclaim the transfer, the interest in the property is transferred to the beneficiary in accordance with the deed.

(2) The interest of a beneficiary is contingent on the beneficiary surviving the transferor. Notwithstanding Section 21110, the interest of a beneficiary that fails to survive the transferor lapses.

(3) Except as provided in paragraph (4), if there is more than one beneficiary, they take the property as tenants in common, in equal shares.

(4) If there is more than one beneficiary, the share of a beneficiary that lapses or fails for any reason is transferred to the others in equal shares.

(b) Property is transferred by a revocable transfer on death deed subject to any limitation on the transferor's interest that is of record at the transferor's death or that is recorded no later than 120 days after the affidavit required by subdivision (c) of Section 5682 is recorded, including, but not limited to, a lien, encumbrance, easement, lease, or other instrument affecting the transferor's interest, whether recorded before or after recordation of the revocable transfer on death deed. The holder of rights under that instrument may enforce those rights against the property notwithstanding its transfer by the revocable transfer on death deed. An enforceable restriction on the use of the transferred property does not affect the transfer of title to the property by a revocable transfer on death deed.

(c) Notwithstanding subdivision (b), an interest in a stock cooperative is transferred by a revocable transfer on death deed subject to any limitation on the transferor's interest that is expressed in the governing documents of the stock cooperative or in a written agreement between the stock cooperative and the transferor, without regard for whether or not those instruments are recorded.

(d) If a stock cooperative exercises an option to purchase property transferred by a revocable transfer on death deed on the transferor's death, the result is as follows:

(1) The property is transferred to the stock cooperative rather than the beneficiary.

(2) The purchase price is paid to the beneficiary. Unless the law or the governing documents of the stock cooperative provide otherwise, the purchase price is the fair market value of the property, less the amount of any liens or encumbrances on the property at the time of the owner's death and less any amount that the decedent owed to the stock cooperative.

(e) A revocable transfer on death deed transfers the property without covenant or warranty of title. **Leg.H.** Added Stats 2015 ch 293 §17 (AB 139), effective January 1, 2016, repealed January 1, 2021. Amended Stats 2021 ch 215 §15 (SB 315), effective January 1, 2022; Stats 2021 ch 215 §2 (SB 315), effective January 1, 2022, repealed January 1, 2032 (repealer amended); Stats 2023 ch 62 §5 (AB 288), effective January 1, 2024, repealed January 1, 2032.

2015 Note: For repeal of part, see Prob C §5600.

§5654. "Lifetime transfer of property" for purposes of health care eligibility; Property subject to Department of Health Care Services claims [Repealed January 1, 2032]

(a) For the purpose of determination of eligibility for health care under Chapter 7 (commencing with Section 14000) or Chapter 8 (commencing with Section 14200) of Part 3 of Division 9 of the Welfare and Institutions Code, execution and recordation of a revocable transfer on death deed is not a lifetime transfer of the property.

(b) Property transferred by a revocable transfer on death deed is subject to claims of the State Department of Health Care Services to the extent authorized by law. **Leg.H.** Added Stats 2015 ch 293 §17 (AB 139), effective January 1, 2016, repealed January 1, 2021. Amended Stats 2020 ch 238 §1 (SB 1305), effective January 1, 2021, repealed January 1, 2022 (repealer amended); Stats 2021 ch 215 §2 (SB 315), effective January 1, 2022, repealed January 1, 2032 (repealer amended).

2015 Note: For repeal of part, see Prob C §5600.

§5656. "Change in ownership" for purposes of tax provisions of Revenue and Taxation Code [Repealed January 1, 2032]

For the purpose of application of the property taxation and documentary transfer tax provisions of the Revenue and Taxation Code:

(a) Execution and recordation of, or revocation of, a revocable transfer on death deed of real property is not a change in ownership of the property and does not require declaration or payment of a documentary transfer tax or filing of a preliminary change of ownership report.

(b) Transfer of real property on the death of the transferor by a revocable transfer on death deed is a change in ownership of the property. **Leg.H.** Added Stats 2015 ch 293 §17 (AB 139), effective January 1, 2016, repealed January 1, 2021. Amended Stats 2020 ch 238 §1 (SB 1305), effective January 1, 2021, repealed January 1, 2022 (repealer amended); Stats 2021 ch 215 §2 (SB 315), effective January 1, 2022, repealed January 1, 2032 (repealer amended).

2015 Note: For repeal of part, see Prob C §5600.

§ 5658. Application of cy pres doctrine [Repealed January 1, 2032]

A court in which the transferor's estate is being administered may, on the petition of the personal representative or interested person, or on its own motion, apply the doctrine of cy pres to reform a revocable transfer on death deed that was made by the transferor for a charitable purpose, in either of the following circumstances:

(a) The beneficiary does not accept the gift.

(b) The beneficiary is a legal entity that dissolved or was merged into another entity before the transferor's death. **Leg.H.** Added Stats 2021 ch 215 §16 (SB 315), effective January 1, 2022, repealed January 1, 2032.

§ 5659. Effect of error or ambiguity [Repealed January 1, 2032]

An error or ambiguity in describing property or designating a beneficiary does not invalidate a revocable transfer on death deed if the transferor's intention can be determined by a court. The general law that governs judicial construction or reformation of an error or ambiguity in a deed applies to a revocable transfer on death deed. **Leg.H.** Added Stats 2021 ch 215 §17 (SB 315), effective January 1, 2022, repealed January 1, 2032.

ARTICLE 2
Other Instruments and Forms of Tenure [Repealed effective January 1, 2032]

Another instrument disposing of same property [Repealed January 1, 2032]. § 5660.
Property held in joint tenancy or community property with right of survivorship at time of death [Repealed January 1, 2032]. §5664.
Community property; Applicability of Chapter 2; Written consent, revocation, or modification to deed [Repealed January 1, 2032]. §5666.
Deed of community property with right of survivorship subject to Section 5666 [Repealed January 1, 2032]. §5668.

§ 5660. Another instrument disposing of same property [Repealed January 1, 2032]

(a) If a revocable transfer on death deed recorded on or before 60 days after the date it was acknowledged before a notary public and another instrument both purport to dispose of the same property:

(1) If the other instrument makes a revocable disposition of the property, the later executed of the revocable transfer on death deed or the other instrument is the operative instrument.

(2) If the other instrument makes an irrevocable disposition of the property, the other instrument and not the revocable transfer on death deed is the operative instrument.

(b) A claim that a revocable transfer on death deed is inoperative pursuant to this section shall be brought as a contest under Chapter 5 (commencing with Section 5690). **Leg.H.** Added Stats 2015 ch 293 §17 (AB 139), effective January 1, 2016, repealed January 1, 2021. Amended Stats 2020 ch 238 §1 (SB 1305), effective January 1, 2021, repealed January 1, 2022 (repealer amended); Stats 2021 ch 215 §18 (SB 315), effective January 1, 2022; Stats 2021 ch 215 §2 (SB 315), effective January 1, 2022, repealed January 1, 2032 (repealer amended); Stats 2023 ch 62 §6 (AB 288), effective January 1, 2024, repealed January 1, 2032.

2015 Note: For repeal of part, see Prob C §5600.

§5664. Property held in joint tenancy or community property with right of survivorship at time of death [Repealed January 1, 2032]

If, at the time of the transferor's death, title to the property described in the revocable transfer on death deed is held in joint tenancy or as community property with right of survivorship, the revocable transfer on death deed is void. The transferor's interest in the property is governed by the right of survivorship and not by the revocable transfer on death deed. **Leg.H.** Added Stats 2015 ch 293 §17 (AB 139), effective January 1, 2016, repealed January 1, 2021. Amended Stats 2020 ch 238 §1 (SB 1305), effective January 1, 2021, repealed January 1, 2022 (repealer amended); Stats 2021 ch 215 §2 (SB 315), effective January 1, 2022, repealed January 1, 2032 (repealer amended).

2015 Note: For repeal of part, see Prob C §5600.

§5666. Community property; Applicability of Chapter 2; Written consent, revocation, or modification to deed [Repealed January 1, 2032]

(a) Chapter 2 (commencing with Section 5010) of Part 1 applies to a revocable transfer on death deed of community property.

(b) For the purpose of application of Chapter 2 (commencing with Section 5010) of Part 1 to a revocable transfer on death deed of community property, written consent to the deed, revocation of written consent to the deed, or modification of the deed, is ineffective unless recorded within the time required by that chapter for execution or service of the written consent, revocation, or modification. **Leg.H.** Added Stats 2015 ch 293 §17 (AB 139), effective January 1, 2016, repealed January 1, 2021. Amended Stats 2020 ch 238 §1 (SB 1305), effective January 1, 2021, repealed January 1, 2022 (repealer amended); Stats 2021 ch 215 §2 (SB 315), effective January 1, 2022, repealed January 1, 2032 (repealer amended).

2015 Note: For repeal of part, see Prob C §5600.

§5668. Deed of community property with right of survivorship subject to Section 5666 [Repealed January 1, 2032]

A revocable transfer on death deed of community property with right of survivorship is subject to Section 5666, relating to a revocable transfer on death deed of community property. **Leg.H.** Added Stats 2015 ch 293 §17 (AB 139), effective January 1, 2016, repealed January 1, 2021. Amended Stats 2020 ch 238 §1 (SB 1305), effective January 1, 2021, repealed January 1, 2022 (repealer amended); Stats 2021 ch 215 §2 (SB 315), effective January 1, 2022, repealed January 1, 2032 (repealer amended).

2015 Note: For repeal of part, see Prob C §5600.

ARTICLE 3
Creditors [Repealed effective January 1, 2032]

Priority of transferor's creditor [Repealed January 1, 2032]. §5670.
Liability of beneficiary for transferor's unsecured debt [Repealed January 1, 2032]. §5672.
Limitations on liability of beneficiary [Repealed January 1, 2032]. § 5674.
Personal liability of beneficiary; Calculation [Repealed January 1, 2032]. § 5677.
Voluntary return of property to estate [Repealed January 1, 2032]. § 5678.

§5670. Priority of transferor's creditor [Repealed January 1, 2032]

Notwithstanding any other statute governing priorities among creditors, a creditor of the transferor whose right is evidenced at the time of the transferor's death by an encumbrance or lien of record on property transferred by a revocable transfer on death deed has priority against the property over a creditor of the beneficiary, regardless of whether the beneficiary's obligation was created before or after the transferor's death and regardless of whether the obligation is secured or unsecured, voluntary or involuntary, recorded or unrecorded. **Leg.H.** Added Stats 2015 ch 293 §17 (AB 139), effective January 1, 2016, repealed January 1, 2021. Amended Stats 2020 ch 238 §1 (SB 1305), effective January 1, 2021, repealed January 1, 2022 (repealer amended); Stats 2021 ch 215 §2 (SB 315), effective January 1, 2022, repealed January 1, 2032 (repealer amended).

2015 Note: For repeal of part, see Prob C §5600.

§5672. Liability of beneficiary for transferor's unsecured debt [Repealed January 1, 2032]

Each beneficiary is personally liable to the extent provided in Section 5674 for the unsecured debts of the transferor. Any such debt may be enforced against the beneficiary in the same manner as it could have been enforced against the transferor if the transferor had not died. In any action based on the debt, the beneficiary may assert any defense, cross-complaint, or setoff that would have been available to the transferor if the transferor had not died. Nothing in this section permits enforcement of a claim that is barred under Part 4 (commencing with Section 9000) of Division 7. Section 366.2 of the Code of Civil Procedure applies in an action under this section. **Leg.H.** Added Stats 2015 ch 293 §17 (AB 139), effective January 1, 2016, repealed January 1, 2021. Amended Stats 2020 ch 238 §1 (SB 1305), effective January 1, 2021, repealed January 1, 2022 (repealer amended); Stats 2021 ch 215 §2 (SB 315), effective January 1, 2022, repealed January 1, 2032 (repealer amended).

2015 Note: For repeal of part, see Prob C §5600.

§ 5674. Limitations on liability of beneficiary [Repealed January 1, 2032]

(a) A beneficiary is not liable under Section 5672 if proceedings for the administration of the transferor's estate are commenced and the beneficiary satisfies the requirements of Section 5677 or 5678.

(b) The personal liability of a beneficiary under Section 5672 shall not exceed the fair market value at the time of the transferor's death of the property received by the beneficiary pursuant to the revocable transfer on death deed, less the amount of any liens and encumbrances on the property at that time. **Leg.H.** Added Stats 2015 ch 293 §17 (AB 139), effective January 1, 2016, repealed January 1, 2021. Amended Stats 2021 ch 215 §19 (SB 315), effective January 1, 2022; Stats 2021 ch 215 §2 (SB 315), effective January 1, 2022, repealed January 1, 2032 (repealer amended).

2015 Note: For repeal of part, see Prob C §5600.

§5676. Liability of beneficiary after commencement of estate proceedings; Significant improvements to property; Action to enforce liability [Repealed]

Leg.H. Added Stats 2015 ch 293 §17 (AB 139), effective January 1, 2016. Repealed Stats 2021 ch 215 §20 (SB 315), effective January 1, 2022.

§ 5677. Personal liability of beneficiary; Calculation [Repealed January 1, 2032]

(a) If proceedings for the administration of the transferor's estate are commenced, a beneficiary of a revocable transfer on death deed is personally liable to the estate for a share of the transferor's unsecured debts.

(b) In calculating the beneficiary's share of liability under subdivision (a), the abatement rules provided in Part 4 (commencing with Section 21400) of Division 11 shall be applied, using all of the following assumptions:

(1) The property that was transferred to the beneficiary by revocable transfer on death deed shall be treated as if it were a specific gift made by the decedent's will.

(2) The value of the property received by the beneficiary pursuant to the revocable transfer on death deed shall be deemed to be the fair market value of the property at the time of the transferor's death, less the amount of any liens and encumbrances on the property at that time.

(3) Any unsecured debts of the transferor that were paid by the beneficiary pursuant to Section 5672 shall be treated as if they were claims made against the transferor's estate.

(c) The personal representative shall provide a written statement of liability to the beneficiary, which specifies the amount that must be paid to the estate.

(d) The beneficiary is personally liable to the estate for the amount specified in the statement of liability. Any amount that the beneficiary paid toward the unsecured debts of the transferor pursuant to Section 5672 shall be credited against the amount that the beneficiary owes the estate under this subdivision. If the amount that the beneficiary paid pursuant to Section 5672 exceeds the amount specified in the written statement of liability, the estate shall reimburse the difference to the beneficiary. For the purposes of Section 11420, this reimbursement shall be deemed an expense of administration.

(e) In the event that the beneficiary and the personal representative cannot agree on the reimbursement or liability due under this section, the beneficiary or personal representative may petition the court for an order determining the amount of the reimbursement or liability.

(f) The reasonable cost of proceeding under this section shall be reimbursed as an extraordinary service under Sections 10801 and 10811. The beneficiary is liable for the payment of that cost, which shall be separately identified in the statement of liability. **Leg.H.** Added Stats 2021 ch 215 §21 (SB 315), effective January 1, 2022, repealed January 1, 2032.

§ 5678. Voluntary return of property to estate [Repealed January 1, 2032]

(a) If proceedings for the administration of the transferor's estate are commenced, a beneficiary who receives property from the transferor under a revocable transfer on death deed may voluntarily return that property to the transferor's estate for administration.

(b) Property returned to the transferor's estate under this section shall be treated as if it had been specifically devised to the beneficiary by the transferor.

(c) If the beneficiary's action or inaction increased the value of property returned to the estate or decreased the estate's obligations, the estate shall reimburse the beneficiary by the same amount. Actions or inaction that increase the value of returned property or decrease the estate's obligations include, but are not necessarily limited to, the following actions:

(1) A payment toward an unsecured debt of the decedent.

(2) A payment toward a debt secured against the returned property.

(3) A significant improvement of the returned property that increased the fair market value of the property.

(d) If the beneficiary's action or inaction decreased the value of property returned to the estate or increased the estate's obligations, the beneficiary is personally liable to the estate for that amount. Actions or inaction that decrease the value of the returned property or increase the estate's obligations include, but are not necessarily limited to, the following actions or inaction:

(1) An action or inaction that resulted in a lien or encumbrance being recorded against the property.

(2) The receipt of income from the property, if that income would have accrued to the estate had the property not been transferred to the beneficiary.

(e) The personal representative shall provide the beneficiary a written statement of any reimbursement or liability under this section, along with a statement of the reasons for the reimbursement or liability. For the purposes of Section 11420, any reimbursement under this section shall be deemed an expense of administration.

(f) In the event that the beneficiary and the personal representative cannot agree on the reimbursement or liability due under this section, the beneficiary or personal representative may petition the court for an order determining the amount of the reimbursement or liability. In making a decision under this subdivision, the court should consider the surrounding circumstances, including whether the parties acted in good faith and whether a particular result would impose an unfair burden on the beneficiary or the estate. **Leg.H.** Added Stats 2021 ch 215 §22 (SB 315), effective January 1, 2022, repealed January 1, 2032.

CHAPTER 4
EFFECTUATION OF TRANSFER [REPEALED EFFECTIVE JANUARY 1, 2032]

Beneficiary's status for purposes of specified laws [Repealed January 1, 2032]. §5680.
Notice of revocable transfer on death deed [Repealed January 1, 2032]. § 5681.
Rights and protections of person dealing with beneficiary [Repealed January 1, 2032]. § 5682.

§5680. Beneficiary's status for purposes of specified laws [Repealed January 1, 2032]

(a) The beneficiary may establish the fact of the transferor's death under the procedure provided in Chapter 2 (commencing with Section 210) of Part 4 of Division 2. For the purpose of this subdivision, the beneficiary is a person empowered by statute to act on behalf of the transferor or the transferor's estate within the meaning of Section 103526 of the Health and Safety Code.

(b) For the purpose of filing the change in ownership statement required by Section 480 of the Revenue and Taxation Code, the beneficiary is a transferee of real property by reason of death.

(c) For the purpose of giving the notice to the Director of Health Care Services provided for in Section 215, the beneficiary is a beneficiary of the transferor.

(d) The beneficiary is liable to the transferor's estate for prorated estate and generation-skipping transfer taxes to the extent provided in Division 10 (commencing with Section 20100). **Leg.H.** Added Stats 2015 ch 293 §17 (AB 139), effective January 1, 2016, repealed January 1, 2021. Amended Stats 2020 ch 238 §1 (SB 1305), effective January 1, 2021, repealed January 1, 2022 (repealer amended); Stats 2021 ch 215 §2 (SB 315), effective January 1, 2022, repealed January 1, 2032 (repealer amended).

2015 Note: For repeal of part, see Prob C §5600.

§ 5681. Notice of revocable transfer on death deed [Repealed January 1, 2032]

(a) After the death of the transferor, the beneficiary of a revocable transfer on death deed shall serve notice on the transferor's heirs, along with a copy of the revocable transfer on death deed and a copy of the transferor's death certificate.

(b) The notice required by subdivision (a) shall be in substantially the following form:

NOTICE OF REVOCABLE TRANSFER ON DEATH DEED

The enclosed revocable transfer on death deed was created by: [name of deceased transferor].

It affects the following property: [description of property used on revocable transfer on death deed].

It names the following beneficiaries: [beneficiary(ies) named on the revocable transfer on death deed].

As a result of the death of [name of deceased transferor], the deed will transfer the described property to the named beneficiaries, without probate administration.

If you believe that the revocable transfer on death deed is invalid and you wish to stop it from taking effect, you have only 120 days from the date of this notice to file a fully effective challenge. You should act promptly and may wish to consult an attorney.

(c) For the purposes of this section, if the beneficiary has actual knowledge of a final judicial determination of heirship for the deceased transferor, the beneficiary shall rely on that determination. Otherwise, the beneficiary shall have discretion to make a good faith determination, by any reasonable means, of the heirs of the transferor.

(d) The beneficiary need not provide a copy of the notice to an heir who is either of the following:

(1) Known to the beneficiary but who cannot be located by the beneficiary after reasonable diligence.

(2) Unknown to the beneficiary.

(e) The notice shall be served by any of the methods described in Section 1215 to the last known address.

(f) If a revocable transfer on death deed names more than one beneficiary, only one of the beneficiaries is required to comply with this section.

(g)(1) A beneficiary who fails to serve the notification required by this section on an heir who is not a beneficiary and whose identity is known to the beneficiary shall be responsible for all damages caused to the heir by the failure, unless the beneficiary shows that they made a reasonably diligent effort to comply. For purposes of this subdivision, "reasonably diligent effort" means that the beneficiary has delivered notice pursuant to Section 1215 to the heir at the heir's last address actually known to the beneficiary.

(2) A beneficiary is not liable under this subdivision if that beneficiary reasonably relied, in good faith, on another beneficiary's statement that the other beneficiary would satisfy the requirements of this section.

(3) A beneficiary is not to be held to the same standard as a fiduciary. **Leg.H.** Added Stats 2021 ch 215 §23 (SB 315), effective January 1, 2022, repealed January 1, 2032.

§ 5682. Rights and protections of person dealing with beneficiary [Repealed January 1, 2032]

If all of the following conditions are satisfied, a person dealing with a beneficiary of a revocable transfer on death deed of real property shall have the same rights and protections as the person would have if the beneficiary had been named as a distributee of the property in an order for distribution of the transferor's estate that had become final:

(a) The person acted in good faith and for a valuable consideration.

(b) An affidavit of death was recorded for the property under Chapter 2 (commencing with Section 210) of Part 4 of Division 2.

(c)(1) An affidavit was recorded for the property, which contains a statement in substantially the following form: "I, [name of beneficiary], served the notice required by Probate Code Section 5681."

(2) If a revocable transfer on death deed names more than one beneficiary, only one beneficiary is required to comply with this subdivision. **Leg.H.** Added Stats 2015 ch 293 §17 (AB 139), effective January 1, 2016, repealed January 1, 2021. Amended Stats 2020 ch 238 §1 (SB 1305), effective January 1, 2021, repealed January 1, 2022 (repealer amended); Stats 2021 ch 215 §24 (SB 315), effective January 1, 2022; Stats 2021 ch 215 §2 (SB 315), effective January 1, 2022, repealed January 1, 2032 (repealer amended).

2015 Note: For repeal of part, see Prob C §5600.

CHAPTER 5
CONTEST [REPEALED EFFECTIVE JANUARY 1, 2032]

Action to contest validity of transfer of property [Repealed January 1, 2032]. § 5690.
Commencement and time limitations [Repealed January 1, 2032]. §5692.
Remedies [Repealed January 1, 2032]. § 5694.
Applicability of principles of fraud, undue influence, duress, mistake, or other invalidating cause; Petition by transferor's guardian or conservator [Repealed January 1, 2032]. §5696.
Application of other law with penalties or remedies for creation of revocable transfer on death deed by means of fraud, undue influence, menace, or duress [Repealed January 1, 2032]. § 5698.

§ 5690. Action to contest validity of transfer of property [Repealed January 1, 2032]

(a)(1) An action for the disqualification of a beneficiary under Part 3.7 (commencing with Section 21360) of Division 11 may be brought to contest the validity of a transfer of property by a revocable transfer on death deed.

(2) An action to contest the validity of a transfer of property by a revocable transfer on death deed may be filed by the transferor's personal representative or an interested person under Part 19 (commencing with Section 850) of Division 2.

(3) An action to contest the validity of a revocation of a revocable transfer on death deed may be filed by the transferor's personal representative or a beneficiary of the revoked deed under Part 19 (commencing with Section 850) of Division 2. If the contest is successful, the court shall determine the appropriate remedy, which may include revival of the revoked deed. In deciding the remedy, the court shall attempt to effectuate the intentions of the transferor.

(b) The proper county for a contest proceeding is the proper county for proceedings concerning administration of the transferor's estate, whether or not proceedings concerning administration of the transferor's estate have been commenced at the time of the contest.

(c) On commencement of a contest proceeding, the contestant may record a lis pendens in the county in which the revocable transfer on death deed is recorded.

(d) In a contest proceeding, each subscribing witness of the revocable transfer on death deed shall be produced and examined. If no subscribing witness is available as a witness within the meaning of Section 240 of the Evidence Code, the court may admit the evidence of other witnesses to prove the due execution of the deed. **Leg.H.** Added Stats 2015 ch 293 §17 (AB 139), effective January 1, 2016, repealed January 1, 2021. Amended Stats 2021 ch 215 §25 (SB 315), effective January 1, 2022; Stats 2021 ch 215 §2 (SB 315), effective January 1, 2022, repealed January 1, 2032 (repealer amended).

2015 Note: For repeal of part, see Prob C §5600.

§5692. Commencement and time limitations [Repealed January 1, 2032]

(a) A contest proceeding pursuant to Section 5690 shall not be commenced before the transferor's death.

(b) For the purposes of the applicable limitations period, a contest proceeding accrues on the date of the transferor's death. **Leg.H.** Added Stats 2015 ch 293 §17 (AB 139), effective January 1, 2016, repealed January 1, 2021. Amended Stats 2020 ch 238 §1 (SB 1305), effective January 1, 2021, repealed January 1, 2022 (repealer amended); Stats 2021 ch 215 §2 (SB 315), effective January 1, 2022, repealed January 1, 2032 (repealer amended).

2015 Note: For repeal of part, see Prob C §5600.

§ 5694. Remedies [Repealed January 1, 2032]

If the court in a contest proceeding determines that a transfer of property by a revocable transfer on death deed is invalid, the court shall order the following relief:

(a) If the proceeding was commenced and a lis pendens was recorded no later than within 120 days after the affidavit required by subdivision (c) of Section 5682 was recorded, the court shall void the deed and order transfer of the property to the person entitled to it.

(b) If the proceeding was not commenced and a lis pendens was not recorded within 120 days after the affidavit required by subdivision (c) of Section 5682 was recorded, the court shall grant appropriate relief but the court order shall not affect the rights in the property of a purchaser or encumbrancer for value and in good faith acquired before commencement of the proceeding and recordation of a lis pendens. **Leg.H.** Added Stats 2015 ch 293 §17 (AB 139), effective January 1, 2016, repealed January 1, 2021. Amended Stats 2021 ch 215 §26 (SB 315), effective January 1, 2022; Stats 2021 ch 215 §2 (SB 315), effective January 1, 2022, repealed January 1, 2032 (repealer amended).

2015 Note: For repeal of part, see Prob C §5600.

§5696. Applicability of principles of fraud, undue influence, duress, mistake, or other invalidating cause; Petition by transferor's guardian or conservator [Repealed January 1, 2032]

(a) Nothing in this chapter limits the application of principles of fraud, undue influence, duress, mistake, or other invalidating cause to a transfer of property by a revocable transfer on death deed.

(b) Notwithstanding subdivision (a) of Section 5692, the conservator or guardian of a transferor may, before the transferor's death, petition the court for invalidation of a revocable transfer on death deed executed by the transferor. **Leg.H.** Added Stats 2015 ch 293 §17 (AB 139), effective January 1, 2016, repealed January 1, 2021. Amended Stats 2020 ch 238 §1 (SB 1305), effective January 1, 2021, repealed January 1, 2022 (repealer amended); Stats 2021 ch 215 §2 (SB 315), effective January 1, 2022, repealed January 1, 2032 (repealer amended).

2015 Note: For repeal of part, see Prob C §5600.

§ 5698. Application of other law with penalties or remedies for creation of revocable transfer on death deed by means of fraud, undue influence, menace, or duress [Repealed January 1, 2032]

Nothing in this chapter limits the application of other law that imposes a penalty or provides a remedy for the creation of a revocable transfer on death deed by means of fraud, undue influence, menace, or duress, including, but not limited to, Section 368 of the Penal Code and Sections 15656 and 15657.5 of the Welfare and Institutions Code. **Leg.H.** Added Stats 2021 ch 215 §27 (SB 315), effective January 1, 2022, repealed January 1, 2032.

PART 5
GIFTS IN VIEW OF IMPENDING DEATH

"Gift". §5700.
Rules applicable to gifts in view of impending death. §5701.
"Gift in view of impending death". §5702.
Presumption regarding gifts made during final illness of giver. §5703.
Revocation of gift in view of impending death. §5704.
Applicability of rule that personal representative has duty to recover property transferred in fraud of creditors. §5705.

§5700. "Gift"

As used in this part, "gift" means a transfer of personal property made voluntarily and without consideration. **Leg.H.** Added Stats 1991 ch 1055 §18 (SB 271).

§5701. Rules applicable to gifts in view of impending death

Except as provided in this part, a gift in view of impending death is subject to the general law relating to gifts of personal property. **Leg.H.** Added Stats 1991 ch 1055 §18 (SB 271).

§5702. "Gift in view of impending death"

(a) A gift in view of impending death is one which is made in contemplation, fear, or peril of impending death, whether from illness or other cause, and with intent that it shall be revoked if the giver recovers from the illness or escapes from the peril.

(b) A reference in a statute to a gift in view of death means a gift in view of impending death. **Leg.H.** Added Stats 1991 ch 1055 §18 (SB 271).

§5703. Presumption regarding gifts made during final illness of giver

A gift made during the last illness of the giver, or under circumstances which would naturally impress the giver with an expectation of speedy death, is presumed to be a gift in view of impending death. **Leg.H.** Added Stats 1991 ch 1055 §18 (SB 271).

§5704. Revocation of gift in view of impending death

(a) A gift in view of impending death is revoked by:

(1) The giver's recovery from the illness, or escape from the peril, under the presence of which it was made.

(2) The death of the donee before the death of the giver.

(b) A gift in view of impending death may be revoked by:

(1) The giver at any time.

(2) The giver's will if the will expresses an intention to revoke the gift.

(c) A gift in view of impending death is not affected by a previous will of the giver.

(d) Notwithstanding subdivisions (a) and (b), when the gift has been delivered to the donee, the rights of a purchaser or encumbrancer, acting before the revocation in good faith, for a valuable consideration, and without knowledge of the conditional nature of the gift, are not affected by the revocation. **Leg.H.** Added Stats 1991 ch 1055 §18 (SB 271).

§5705. Applicability of rule that personal representative has duty to recover property transferred in fraud of creditors

A gift in view of impending death is subject to Section 9653. **Leg.H.** Added Stats 1991 ch 1055 §18 (SB 271).

DIVISION 6
WILLS AND INTESTATE SUCCESSION

Part 1. Wills.
Part 2. Intestate Succession.
Part 3. Family Protection.
Part 4. Escheat of Decedent's Property.

PART 1
WILLS

Chapter 1. General Provisions.
Chapter 2. Execution of Wills.
Chapter 3. Revocation and Revival.
Chapter 4. Reference to Matters Outside the Will.
Chapter 6. California Statutory Will.
Chapter 7. Uniform Testamentary Additions to Trusts Act.
Chapter 8. Nonprobate Transfer to Trustee Named in Decedent's Will.
Chapter 9. Devise Subject to California Uniform Transfers to Minors Act.
Chapter 11. Uniform International Wills Act.

CHAPTER 1
GENERAL PROVISIONS

Persons who may make will. §6100.
Persons not mentally competent to make a will. §6100.5.
Property which may be disposed of by will. §6101.
Persons to whom will may dispose of property. §6102.
Application of certain chapters where testator died before January 1, 1985. §6103.
Effect of duress, menace, fraud, or undue influence. §6104.
Conditional will. §6105.

§6100. Persons who may make will

(a) An individual 18 or more years of age who is of sound mind may make a will.

(b) A conservator may make a will for the conservatee if the conservator has been so authorized by a court order pursuant to Section 2580. Nothing in this section shall impair the right of a conservatee who is mentally competent to make a will from revoking or amending a will made by the conservator or making a new and inconsistent will. **Leg.H.** Enacted Stats 1990 ch 79 §14 (AB 759), operative July 1, 1991. Amended Stats 1995 ch 730 §7 (AB 1466).

Prior Law: Former Prob C §6100, similar to the present section, was added Stats 1983 ch 842 §55, operative January 1, 1985, and repealed Stats 1990 ch 79 §13, operative July 1, 1991.

§6100.5. Persons not mentally competent to make a will

(a) An individual is not mentally competent to make a will if, at the time of making the will, either of the following is true:

(1) The individual does not have sufficient mental capacity to be able to do any of the following:

(A) Understand the nature of the testamentary act.

(B) Understand and recollect the nature and situation of the individual's property.

(C) Remember and understand the individual's relations to living descendants, spouse, and parents, and those whose interests are affected by the will.

(2) The individual suffers from a mental health disorder with symptoms including delusions or hallucinations, which delusions or hallucinations result in the individual's devising property in a way that, except for the existence of the delusions or hallucinations, the individual would not have done.

(b) This section does not supersede existing law relating to the admissibility of evidence to prove the existence of mental incompetence or mental health disorders.

(c) Notwithstanding subdivision (a), a conservator may make a will on behalf of a conservatee if the conservator has been authorized to do so by a court order pursuant to Section 2580. **Leg.H.** Enacted Stats 1990 ch 79 §14 (AB 759), operative July 1, 1991. Amended Stats 1995 ch 730 §8 (AB 1466); Stats 2019 ch 9 §18 (AB 46), effective January 1, 2020.

Prior Law: Former Prob C §6100.5, similar to the present section, was added Stats 1985 ch 940 §1, and repealed Stats 1990 ch 79 §13 (AB 759), operative July 1, 1991.

§6101. Property which may be disposed of by will

A will may dispose of the following property:

(a) The testator's separate property.

(b) The one-half of the community property that belongs to the testator under Section 100.

(c) The one-half of the testator's quasi-community property that belongs to the testator under Section 101. **Leg.H.** Enacted Stats 1990 ch 79 §14 (AB 759), operative July 1, 1991.

Prior Law: Former Prob C §6101, similar to the present section, was added Stats 1983 ch 842 §55, operative January 1, 1985, and repealed Stats 1990 ch 79 §13, operative July 1, 1991.

§6102. Persons to whom will may dispose of property

A will may make a disposition of property to any person, including but not limited to any of the following:

(a) An individual.

(b) A corporation.

(c) An unincorporated association, society, lodge, or any branch thereof.

(d) A county, city, city and county, or any municipal corporation.

(e) Any state, including this state.

(f) The United States or any instrumentality thereof.

(g) A foreign country or a governmental entity therein. **Leg.H.** Enacted Stats 1990 ch 79 §14 (AB 759), operative July 1, 1991.

Prior Law: Former Prob C §6102, similar to the present section, was added Stats 1983 ch 842 §55, operative January 1, 1985, and repealed Stats 1990 ch 79 §13, operative July 1, 1991.

§6103. Application of certain chapters where testator died before January 1, 1985

Except as otherwise specifically provided, Chapter 1 (commencing with Section 6100), Chapter 2 (commencing with Section 6110), Chapter 3 (commencing with Section 6120), Chapter 4 (commencing with Section 6130), Chapter 6 (commencing with Section 6200), and Chapter 7 (commencing with Section 6300) of this division, and Part 1 (commencing with Section 21101) of Division 11, do not apply where the testator died before January 1, 1985, and the law applicable prior to January 1, 1985, continues to apply where the testator died before January 1, 1985. **Leg.H.** Enacted Stats 1990 ch 79 §14 (AB 759), operative July 1, 1991. Amended Stats 2002 ch 138 §6 (AB 1784).

Prior Law: Former Prob C §6103, similar to the present section, was added Stats 1984 ch 892 §21.7, and repealed Stats 1990 ch 79 §13, operative July 1, 1991.

§6104. Effect of duress, menace, fraud, or undue influence

The execution or revocation of a will or a part of a will is ineffective to the extent the execution or revocation was procured by duress, menace, fraud, or undue influence. **Leg.H.** Enacted Stats 1990 ch 79 §14 (AB 759), operative July 1, 1991.

Prior Law: Former Prob C §6104, similar to the present section, was added Stats 1988 ch 1199 §74, operative July 1, 1989, and repealed Stats 1990 ch 79 §13, operative July 1, 1991.

§6105. Conditional will

A will, the validity of which is made conditional by its own terms, shall be admitted to probate or rejected, or denied effect after admission to probate, in conformity with the condition. **Leg.H.** Enacted Stats 1990 ch 79 §14 (AB 759), operative July 1, 1991.

Prior Law: Former Prob C §6105, similar to the present section, was added Stats 1988 ch 1199 §74.5, operative July 1, 1989, and repealed Stats 1990 ch 79 §13 (AB 759), operative July 1, 1991.

CHAPTER 2
EXECUTION OF WILLS

Witnessed will. §6110.
Holographic will. §6111.
Admissibility of extrinsic evidence. §6111.5.
Witnesses; Interested witnesses. §6112.
Choice of law as to validity of execution of will. §6113.

§6110. Witnessed will

(a) Except as provided in this part, a will shall be in writing and satisfy the requirements of this section.

(b) The will shall be signed by one of the following:

(1) By the testator.

(2) In the testator's name by some other person in the testator's presence and by the testator's direction.

(3) By a conservator pursuant to a court order to make a will under Section 2580.

(c)(1) Except as provided in paragraph (2), the will shall be witnessed by being signed, during the testator's lifetime, by at least two persons each of whom (A) being present at the same time, witnessed either the signing of the will or the testator's acknowledgment of the signature or of the will and (B) understand that the instrument they sign is the testator's will.

(2) If a will was not executed in compliance with paragraph (1), the will shall be treated as if it was executed in compliance with that paragraph if the proponent of the will establishes by clear and convincing evidence that, at the time the testator signed the will, the testator intended the will to constitute the testator's will. **Leg.H.** Enacted Stats 1990 ch 79 §14 (AB 759), operative July 1, 1991. Amended Stats 1996 ch 563 §20 (SB 392); Stats 2008 ch 53 §1 (AB 2248), effective January 1, 2009.

Prior Law: Former Prob C 6110, similar to the present section, was added Stats 1983 ch 842 §55, operative January 1, 1985, and repealed Stats 1990 ch 79 §13, operative July 1, 1991.

§6111. Holographic will

(a) A will that does not comply with Section 6110 is valid as a holographic will, whether or not witnessed, if the signature and the material provisions are in the handwriting of the testator.

(b) If a holographic will does not contain a statement as to the date of its execution and:

(1) If the omission results in doubt as to whether its provisions or the inconsistent provisions of another will are controlling, the holographic will is invalid to the extent of the inconsistency unless the time of its execution is established to be after the date of execution of the other will.

(2) If it is established that the testator lacked testamentary capacity at any time during which the will might have been executed, the will is invalid unless it is established that it was executed at a time when the testator had testamentary capacity.

(c) Any statement of testamentary intent contained in a holographic will may be set forth either in the testator's own handwriting or as part of a commercially printed form will. **Leg.H.** Enacted Stats 1990 ch 79 §14 (AB 759), operative July 1, 1991. Amended Stats 1990 ch 710 §13 (SB 1775), operative July 1, 1991.

Prior Law: Former Prob C §6111, similar to the present section, was added Stats 1983 ch 842 §55, operative January 1, 1985, repealed Stats 1990 ch 79 §13, operative July 1, 1991, and amended Stats 1990 ch 263 §1.

§6111.5. Admissibility of extrinsic evidence

Extrinsic evidence is admissible to determine whether a document constitutes a will pursuant to Section 6110 or 6111, or to determine the meaning of a will or a portion of a will if the meaning is unclear. **Leg.H.** Added Stats 1990 ch 710 §14 (SB 1775), operative July 1, 1991.

Prior Law: Former Prob C §6111.5, similar to the present section, was added Stats 1990 ch 263 §2 and repealed Stats 1990 ch 79 §13, operative July 1, 1991.

§6112. Witnesses; Interested witnesses

(a) Any person generally competent to be a witness may act as a witness to a will.

(b) A will or any provision thereof is not invalid because the will is signed by an interested witness.

(c) Unless there are at least two other subscribing witnesses to the will who are disinterested witnesses, the fact that the will makes a devise to a subscribing witness creates a presumption that the witness procured the devise by duress, menace, fraud, or undue influence. This presumption is a presumption affecting the burden of proof. This presumption does not apply where the witness is a person to whom the devise is made solely in a fiduciary capacity.

(d) If a devise made by the will to an interested witness fails because the presumption established by subdivision (c) applies to the devise and the witness fails to rebut the presumption, the interested witness shall take such proportion of the devise made to the witness in the will as does not exceed the share of the estate which would be distributed to the witness if the will were not established. Nothing in this subdivision affects the law that applies where it is established that the witness procured a devise by duress, menace, fraud, or undue influence. **Leg.H.** Enacted Stats 1990 ch 79 §14 (AB 759), operative July 1, 1991.

Prior Law: Former Prob C §6112, similar to the present section, was added Stats 1983 ch 842 §55, operative January 1, 1985, amended Stats 1984 ch 892 §22, Stats 1988 ch 1199 §75, operative July 1, 1989, Stats 1989 ch 544 §4, and repealed Stats 1990 ch 79 §13, operative July 1, 1991.

§6113. Choice of law as to validity of execution of will

A written will is validly executed if its execution complies with any of the following:

(a) The will is executed in compliance with Section 6110 or 6111 or Chapter 6 (commencing with Section 6200) (California statutory will) or Chapter 11 (commencing with Section 6380) (Uniform International Wills Act).

(b) The execution of the will complies with the law at the time of execution of the place where the will is executed.

(c) The execution of the will complies with the law of the place where at the time of execution or at the time of death the testator is domiciled, has a place of abode, or is a national. **Leg.H.** Enacted Stats 1990 ch 79 §14 (AB 759), operative July 1, 1991.

Prior Law: Former Prob C §6113, similar to the present section, was added Stats 1983 ch 842 §55, operative January 1, 1985, and repealed Stats 1990 ch 79 §13, operative July 1, 1991.

CHAPTER 3
REVOCATION AND REVIVAL

Revocation by subsequent will or by act. §6120.
Revocation of will executed in duplicate. §6121.
Dissolution or annulment of marriage; Provisions revoked; No revocation by other change in circumstances. §6122.
Effect of termination of domestic partnership after execution of will. §6122.1.
Second will revoking first will; Effect of revocation of second will. §6123.
Presumption that will destroyed with intent to revoke. §6124.

§6120. Revocation by subsequent will or by act

A will or any part thereof is revoked by any of the following:

(a) A subsequent will which revokes the prior will or part expressly or by inconsistency.

(b) Being burned, torn, canceled, obliterated, or destroyed, with the intent and for the purpose of revoking it, by either (1) the testator or (2) another person in the testator's presence and by the testator's direction. **Leg.H.** Enacted Stats 1990 ch 79 §14 (AB 759), operative July 1, 1991.

Prior Law: Former Prob C §6120, similar to the present section, was added Stats 1983 ch 842 §55, operative January 1, 1985, and repealed Stats 1990 ch 79 §13, operative July 1, 1991.

§6121. Revocation of will executed in duplicate

A will executed in duplicate or any part thereof is revoked if one of the duplicates is burned, torn, canceled, obliterated, or destroyed, with the intent and for the purpose of revoking it, by either (1) the testator or (2) another person in the testator's presence and by the testator's direction. **Leg.H.** Enacted Stats 1990 ch 79 §14 (AB 759), operative July 1, 1991.

Prior Law: Former Prob C §6121, similar to the present section, was added Stats 1983 ch 842 §55, operative January 1, 1985, and repealed Stats 1990 ch 79 §13, operative July 1, 1991.

§6122. Dissolution or annulment of marriage; Provisions revoked; No revocation by other change in circumstances

(a) Unless the will expressly provides otherwise, if after executing a will the testator's marriage is dissolved or annulled, the dissolution or annulment revokes all of the following:

(1) Any disposition or appointment of property made by the will to the former spouse.

(2) Any provision of the will conferring a general or special power of appointment on the former spouse.

(3) Any provision of the will nominating the former spouse as executor, trustee, conservator, or guardian.

(b) If any disposition or other provision of a will is revoked solely by this section, it is revived by the testator's remarriage to the former spouse.

(c) In case of revocation by dissolution or annulment:

(1) Property prevented from passing to a former spouse because of the revocation passes as if the former spouse failed to survive the testator.

(2) Other provisions of the will conferring some power or office on the former spouse shall be interpreted as if the former spouse failed to survive the testator.

(d) For purposes of this section, dissolution or annulment means any dissolution or annulment which would exclude the spouse as a surviving spouse within the meaning of Section 78. A decree of legal separation which does not terminate the status of spouses is not a dissolution for purposes of this section.

(e) Except as provided in Section 6122.1, no change of circumstances other than as described in this section revokes a will.

(f) Subdivisions (a) to (d), inclusive, do not apply to any case where the final judgment of dissolution or annulment of marriage occurs before January 1, 1985. That case is governed by the law in effect prior to January 1, 1985. **Leg.H.** Enacted Stats 1990 ch 79 §14 (AB 759), operative July 1, 1991. Amended Stats 2001 ch 893 §50 (AB 25); Stats 2002 ch 664 §179 (AB 3034); Stats 2016 ch 50 §86 (SB 1005), effective January 1, 2017.

2016 Note: For legislative intent, see the 2016 Note following Prob C §59.

Prior Law: Former Prob C §6122, similar to the present section, was added Stats 1983 ch 842 §55, operative January 1, 1985, amended Stats 1984 ch 892 §23, and repealed Stats 1990 ch 79 §13, operative July 1, 1991.

§6122.1. Effect of termination of domestic partnership after execution of will

(a) Unless the will expressly provides otherwise, if after executing a will the testator's domestic partnership is terminated, the termination revokes all of the following:

(1) Any disposition or appointment of property made by the will to the former domestic partner.

(2) Any provision of the will conferring a general or special power of appointment on the former domestic partner.

(3) Any provision of the will nominating the former domestic partner as executor, trustee, conservator, or guardian.

(b) If any disposition or other provision of a will is revoked solely by this section, it is revived by the testator establishing another domestic partnership with the former domestic partner.

(c) In case of revocation by termination of a domestic partnership:

(1) Property prevented from passing to a former domestic partner because of the revocation passes as if the former domestic partner failed to survive the testator.

(2) Other provisions of the will conferring some power or office on the former domestic partner shall be interpreted as if the former domestic partner failed to survive the testator.

(d) This section shall apply only to wills executed on or after January 1, 2002. **Leg.H.** Added Stats 2001 ch 893 §51 (AB 25), effective January 1, 2002.

§6123. Second will revoking first will; Effect of revocation of second will

(a) If a second will which, had it remained effective at death, would have revoked the first will in whole or in part, is thereafter revoked by acts under Section 6120 or 6121, the first will is revoked in whole or in part unless it is evident from the circumstances of the revocation of the second will or from the testator's contemporary or subsequent declarations that the testator intended the first will to take effect as executed.

(b) If a second will which, had it remained effective at death, would have revoked the first will in whole or in part, is thereafter revoked by a third will, the first will is revoked in whole or in part, except to the extent it appears from the terms of the third will that the testator intended the first will to take effect. **Leg.H.** Enacted Stats 1990 ch 79 §14 (AB 759), operative July 1, 1991.

Prior Law: Former Prob C §6123, similar to the present section, was added Stats 1983 ch 842 §55, operative January 1, 1985, and repealed Stats 1990 ch 79 §13, operative July 1, 1991.

§6124. Presumption that will destroyed with intent to revoke

If the testator's will was last in the testator's possession, the testator was competent until death, and neither the will nor a duplicate original of the will can be found after the testator's death, it is presumed that the testator destroyed the will with intent to revoke it. This presumption is a presumption affecting the burden of producing evidence. **Leg.H.** Enacted Stats 1990 ch 79 §14 (AB 759), operative July 1, 1991.

Prior Law: Former Prob C §6124, similar to the present section, was added Stats 1985 ch 982 §15.5, and repealed Stats 1990 ch 79 §13, operative July 1, 1991.

CHAPTER 4
REFERENCE TO MATTERS OUTSIDE THE WILL

Incorporation by reference. §6130.
References to acts and events of independent significance. §6131.
Writing disposing of tangible personal property. §6132.

§6130. Incorporation by reference

A writing in existence when a will is executed may be incorporated by reference if the language of the will manifests this intent and describes the writing sufficiently to permit its identification. **Leg.H.** Enacted Stats 1990 ch 79 §14 (AB 759), operative July 1, 1991.

Prior Law: Former Prob C §6130, similar to the present section, was added Stats 1983 ch 842 §55, operative January 1, 1985, and repealed Stats 1990 ch 79 §13, operative July 1, 1991.

§6131. References to acts and events of independent significance

A will may dispose of property by reference to acts and events that have significance apart from their effect upon the dispositions made by the will, whether the acts and events occur before or after the execution of the will or before or after the testator's death. The execution or revocation of a will of another person is such an event. **Leg.H.** Enacted Stats 1990 ch 79 §14 (AB 759), operative July 1, 1991.

Prior Law: Former Prob C §6131, similar to the present section, was added Stats 1983 ch 842 §55, operative January 1, 1985, and repealed Stats 1990 ch 79 §13, operative July 1, 1991.

§6132. Writing disposing of tangible personal property

(a) Notwithstanding any other provision, a will may refer to a writing that directs disposition of tangible personal property not otherwise specifically disposed of by the will, except for money that is common coin or currency and property used primarily in a trade or business. A writing directing disposition of a testator's tangible personal property is effective if all of the following conditions are satisfied:

(1) An unrevoked will refers to the writing.

(2) The writing is dated and is either in the handwriting of, or signed by, the testator.

(3) The writing describes the items and the recipients of the property with reasonable certainty.

(b) The failure of a writing to conform to the conditions described in paragraph (2) of subdivision (a) does not preclude the introduction of evidence of the existence of the testator's intent regarding the disposition of tangible personal property as authorized by this section.

(c) The writing may be written or signed before or after the execution of the will and need not have significance apart from its effect upon the dispositions of property made by the will. A writing that meets the requirements of this section shall be given effect as if it were actually contained in the will itself, except that if any person designated to receive property in the writing dies before the testator, the property shall pass as further directed in the writing and, in the absence of any further directions, the disposition shall lapse.

(d) The testator may make subsequent handwritten or signed changes to any writing. If there is an inconsistent disposition of tangible personal property as between writings, the most recent writing controls.

(e)(1) If the writing directing disposition of tangible personal property omits a statement as to the date of its execution, and if the omission results in doubt whether its provisions or the provisions of another writing inconsistent with it are controlling, then the writing omitting the statement is invalid to the extent of its inconsistency unless the time of its execution is established to be after the date of execution of the other writing.

(2) If the writing directing disposition of tangible personal property omits a statement as to the date of its execution, and it is established that the testator lacked testamentary capacity at any time during which the writing may have been executed, the writing is invalid unless it is

established that it was executed at a time when the testator had testamentary capacity.

(f)(1) Concurrent with the filing of the inventory and appraisal required by Section 8800, the personal representative shall also file the writing that directs disposition of the testator's tangible personal property.

(2) Notwithstanding paragraph (1), if the writing has not been found or is not available at the time of the filing of the inventory and appraisal, the personal representative shall file the writing no later than 60 days prior to filing the petition for final distribution pursuant to Section 11640.

(g) The total value of tangible personal property identified and disposed of in the writing shall not exceed twenty-five thousand dollars ($25,000). If the value of an item of tangible personal property described in the writing exceeds five thousand dollars ($5,000), that item shall not be subject to this section and that item shall be disposed of pursuant to the remainder clause of the will. The value of an item of tangible personal property that is disposed of pursuant to the remainder clause of the will shall not be counted towards the twenty-five thousand dollar ($25,000) limit described in this subdivision.

(h) As used in this section, the following definitions shall apply:

(1) "Tangible personal property" means articles of personal or household use or ornament, including, but not limited to, furniture, furnishings, automobiles, boats, and jewelry, as well as precious metals in any tangible form, such as bullion or coins and articles held for investment purposes. The term "tangible personal property" does not mean real property, a mobilehome as defined in Section 798.3 of the Civil Code, intangible property, such as evidences of indebtedness, bank accounts and other monetary deposits, documents of title, or securities.

(2) "Common coin or currency" means the coins and currency of the United States that are legal tender for the payment of public and private debts, but does not include coins or currency kept or acquired for their historical, artistic, collectable, or investment value apart from their normal use as legal tender for payment. **Leg.H.** Added Stats 2006 ch 280 §1 (AB 2568), effective January 1, 2007.

CHAPTER 5
RULES OF CONSTRUCTION OF WILLS
[REPEALED]

§6140. [Section repealed 1995.]

Leg.H. Enacted Stats 1990 ch 79 §14 (AB 759), operative July 1, 1991. Repealed Stats 1994 ch 806 §21 (AB 3686). See Prob C §21102.

Prior Law: Former Prob C §6140, similar to the present section, was added Stats 1983 ch 842 §55, operative January 1, 1985, amended Stats 1984 ch 892 §24, and repealed Stats 1990 ch 79 §13, operative July 1, 1991.

§6141. [Section repealed 1995.]

Leg.H. Enacted Stats 1990 ch 79 §14 (AB 759), operative July 1, 1991. Repealed Stats 1994 ch 806 §21 (AB 3686). See Prob C §21103.

Prior Law: Former Prob C §6141, similar to the present section, was added Stats 1983 ch 842 §55, operative January 1, 1985, and repealed Stats 1990 ch 79 §13, operative July 1, 1991.

§6142. [Section repealed 1995.]

Leg.H. Enacted Stats 1990 ch 79 §14 (AB 759), operative July 1, 1991. Repealed Stats 1994 ch 806 §21 (AB 3686). See Prob C §21105.

Prior Law: Former Prob C §6142, similar to the present section, was added Stats 1983 ch 842 §55, operative January 1, 1985, amended Stats 1984 ch 892 §25, and repealed Stats 1990 ch 79 §13, operative July 1, 1991.

§6143. [Section repealed 1995.]

Leg.H. Enacted Stats 1990 ch 79 §14 (AB 759), operative July 1, 1991. Repealed Stats 1994 ch 806 §21 (AB 3686). The repealed section related to devisees as owners in common.

Prior Law: Former Prob C §6143, similar to the present section, was added Stats 1983 ch 842 §55, operative January 1, 1985, amended Stats 1984 ch 892 §26, and repealed Stats 1990 ch 79 §13, operative July 1, 1991.

§6144. [Section repealed 1995.]

Leg.H. Enacted Stats 1990 ch 79 §14 (AB 759), operative July 1, 1991. Repealed Stats 1994 ch 806 §21 (AB 3686). See Prob C §21107.

Prior Law: Former Prob C §6144, similar to the present section, was added Stats 1983 ch 842 §55, operative January 1, 1985, amended Stats 1984 ch 892 §27, and repealed Stats 1990 ch 79 §13, operative July 1, 1991.

§6145. [Section repealed 1995.]

Leg.H. Enacted Stats 1990 ch 79 §14 (AB 759), operative July 1, 1991. Repealed Stats 1994 ch 806 §21 (AB 3686). See Prob C §21108.

Prior Law: Former Prob C §6145, similar to the present section, was added Stats 1983 ch 842 §55, operative January 1, 1985, and repealed Stats 1990 ch 79 §13, operative July 1, 1991.

§6146. [Section repealed 1995.]

Leg.H. Enacted Stats 1990 ch 79 §14 (AB 759), operative July 1, 1991. Repealed Stats 1994 ch 806 §21 (AB 3686). See Prob C §21109.

Prior Law: Former Prob C §6146, similar to the present section, was added Stats 1983 ch 842 §55, operative January 1, 1985, amended Stats 1984 ch 892 §28, and repealed Stats 1990 ch 79 §13, operative July 1, 1991.

§6147. [Section repealed 1995.]

Leg.H. Enacted Stats 1990 ch 79 §14 (AB 759), operative July 1, 1991. Repealed Stats 1994 ch 806 §21 (AB 3686). See Prob C §21110.

Prior Law: Former Prob C §6147, similar to the present section, was added Stats 1983 ch 842 §55, operative January 1, 1985, amended Stats 1984 ch 892 §29, Stats 1985 ch 359 §4, effective July 30, 1985, ch 982 §16, and repealed Stats 1990 ch 79 §13, operative July 1, 1991.

§6148. [Section repealed 1995.]

Leg.H. Enacted Stats 1990 ch 79 §14 (AB 759), operative July 1, 1991. Repealed Stats 1994 ch 806 §21 (AB 3686). See Prob C §21111.

Prior Law: Former Prob C §6148, similar to the present section, was added Stats 1983 ch 842 §55, operative January 1, 1985, and repealed Stats 1990 ch 79 §13, operative July 1, 1991.

§6149. [Section repealed 1995.]

Leg.H. Enacted Stats 1990 ch 79 §14 (AB 759), operative July 1, 1991. Repealed Stats 1994 ch 806 §21 (AB 3686). See Prob C §21112.

Prior Law: Former Prob C §6149, similar to the present section, was added Stats 1983 ch 842 §55, operative January 1, 1985, and repealed Stats 1990 ch 79 §13, operative July 1, 1991.

§6150. [Section repealed 1995.]

Leg.H. Enacted Stats 1990 ch 79 §14 (AB 759), operative July 1, 1991. Repealed Stats 1994 ch 806 §21 (AB 3686). The repealed section related to devises to a class, time of vesting and afterborn members.

Prior Law: Former Prob C §6150, similar to the present section, was added Stats 1983 ch 842 §55, operative January 1, 1985, and repealed Stats 1990 ch 79 §13, operative July 1, 1991.

§6151. [Section repealed 1995.]

Leg.H. Enacted Stats 1990 ch 79 §14 (AB 759), operative July 1, 1991. Amended Stats 1992 ch 871 §8 (AB 2975). Repealed Stats 1994 ch 806 §21 (AB 3686). See Prob C §21114.

Prior Law: Former Prob C §6151, similar to the present section, was added Stats 1983 ch 842 §55, operative January 1, 1985, and repealed Stats 1990 ch 79 §13, operative July 1, 1991.

§6152. [Section repealed 1995.]

Leg.H. Enacted Stats 1990 ch 79 §14 (AB 759), operative July 1, 1991. Repealed Stats 1994 ch 806 §21 (AB 3686). See Prob C §21115.

Prior Law: Former Prob C §6152, similar to the present section, was added Stats 1983 ch 842 §55, operative January 1, 1985, amended Stats 1984 ch 892 §30, Stats 1985 ch 982 §17, and repealed Stats 1990 ch 79 §13, operative July 1, 1991.

§6153. [Section repealed 1995.]

Leg.H. Enacted Stats 1990 ch 79 §14 (AB 759), operative July 1, 1991. Repealed Stats 1994 ch 806 §21 (AB 3686). The repealed section related to the presumption that testamentary dispositions vest at testator's death.

Prior Law: Former Prob C §6153, similar to the present section, was added Stats 1984 ch 892 §31, and repealed Stats 1990 ch 79 §13, operative July 1, 1991.

§6154. [Section repealed 1995.]

Leg.H. Enacted Stats 1990 ch 79 §14 (AB 759), operative July 1, 1991. Repealed Stats 1994 ch 806 §21 (AB 3686). See Prob C §21117.

Prior Law: Former Prob C §6154, similar to the present section, was added Stats 1988 ch 1199 §75.5, operative July 1, 1989, and repealed Stats 1990 ch 79 §13, operative July 1, 1991.

§6160. [Section repealed 1995.]

§6161. [Section repealed 1995.]

Leg.H. Enacted Stats 1990 ch 79 §14 (AB 759), operative July 1, 1991. Repealed Stats 1994 ch 806 §21 (AB 3686). See Prob C §21121.

Prior Law: Former Prob C §6161, similar to present Prob C §21121, was added Stats 1983 ch 842 §55, operative January 1, 1985, and repealed Stats 1990 ch 79 §13, operative July 1, 1991.

§6162. [Section repealed 1995.]

Leg.H. Enacted Stats 1990 ch 79 §14 (AB 759), operative July 1, 1991. Repealed Stats 1994 ch 806 §21 (AB 3686). See Prob C §21122.

Prior Law: Former Prob C §6162, similar to present Prob C §21121, was added Stats 1983 ch 842 §55, operative January 1, 1985, and repealed Stats 1990 ch 79 §13, operative July 1, 1991.

§6165. [Section repealed 1995.]

Leg.H. Enacted Stats 1990 ch 79 §14 (AB 759), operative July 1, 1991. Repealed Stats 1994 ch 806 §21 (AB 3686). See Prob C §21102.

Prior Law: Former Prob C §6165, similar to present Prob C §21121, was added Stats 1983 ch 842 §55, operative January 1, 1985, amended Stats 1984 ch 892 §32, and repealed Stats 1990 ch 79 §13, operative July 1, 1991.

§6170. [Section repealed 1995.]

Leg.H. Enacted Stats 1990 ch 79 §14 (AB 759), operative July 1, 1991. Repealed Stats 1994 ch 806 §21 (AB 3686). See Prob C §21131.

Prior Law: Former Prob C §6170, similar to present Prob C §21121, was added Stats 1983 ch 842 §55, operative January 1, 1985, and repealed Stats 1990 ch 79 §13, operative July 1, 1991.

§6171. [Section repealed 1995.]

Leg.H. Enacted Stats 1990 ch 79 §14 (AB 759), operative July 1, 1991. Repealed Stats 1994 ch 806 §21 (AB 3686). See Prob C §21132.

Prior Law: Former Prob C §6171, similar to present Prob C §21121, was added Stats 1983 ch 842 §55, operative January 1, 1985, and repealed Stats 1990 ch 79 §13, operative July 1, 1991.

§6172. [Section repealed 1995.]

Leg.H. Enacted Stats 1990 ch 79 §14 (AB 759), operative July 1, 1991. Repealed Stats 1994 ch 806 §21 (AB 3686). See Prob C §21133.

Prior Law: Former Prob C §6172, similar to present Prob C §21121, was added Stats 1983 ch 842 §55, operative January 1, 1985, and repealed Stats 1990 ch 79 §13, operative July 1, 1991.

§6173. [Section repealed 1995.]

Leg.H. Enacted Stats 1990 ch 79 §14 (AB 759), operative July 1, 1991. Repealed Stats 1994 ch 806 §21 (AB 3686). See Prob C §21134.

Prior Law: Former Prob C §6173, similar to present Prob C §21121, was added Stats 1983 ch 842 §55, operative January 1, 1985, and repealed Stats 1990 ch 79 §13, operative July 1, 1991.

§6174. [Section repealed 1995.]

Leg.H. Enacted Stats 1990 ch 79 §14 (AB 759), operative July 1, 1991. Repealed Stats 1994 ch 806 §21 (AB 3686). See Prob C §21135.

Prior Law: Former Prob C §6174, similar to present Prob C §21121, was added Stats 1983 ch 842 §55, operative January 1, 1985, and repealed Stats 1990 ch 79 §13, operative July 1, 1991.

§6175. [Section repealed 1995.]

Leg.H. Enacted Stats 1990 ch 79 §14 (AB 759), operative July 1, 1991. Repealed Stats 1994 ch 806 §21 (AB 3686). The repealed section related to the rights of a beneficiary of a specific gift when the transferor enters into an agreement for sale or transfer of the specifically given property.

Prior Law: Former Prob C §6175, similar to present Prob C §21121, was added Stats 1983 ch 842 §55, operative January 1, 1985, and repealed Stats 1990 ch 79 §13, operative July 1, 1991.

§6176. [Section repealed 1995.]

Leg.H. Enacted Stats 1990 ch 79 §14 (AB 759), operative July 1, 1991. Repealed Stats 1994 ch 806 §21 (AB 3686). The repealed section related to the rights of a beneficiary of a specific gift when the transferor encumbers such gift.

Prior Law: Former Prob C §6176, similar to present Prob C §21121, was added Stats 1983 ch 842 §55, operative January 1, 1985, and repealed Stats 1990 ch 79 §13, operative July 1, 1991.

§6177. [Section repealed 1995.]

Leg.H. Enacted Stats 1990 ch 79 §14 (AB 759), operative July 1, 1991. Repealed Stats 1994 ch 806 §21 (AB 3686). The repealed section related to the rights of a beneficiary of a specific gift when the transferor alters his or her interest in the property.

Prior Law: Former Prob C §6177, similar to to present Prob C §21121, was added Stats 1983 ch 842 §55, operative January 1, 1985, and repealed Stats 1990 ch 79 §13, operative July 1, 1991.

§6178. [Section repealed 1995.]

Leg.H. Enacted Stats 1990 ch 79 §14 (AB 759), operative July 1, 1991. Repealed Stats 1994 ch 806 §21 (AB 3686). See Prob C §21139.

Prior Law: Former Prob C §6178, similar to present Prob C §21121, was added Stats 1983 ch 842 §55, operative January 1, 1985, and repealed Stats 1990 ch 79 §13, operative July 1, 1991.

§6179. [Section repealed 1995.]

Leg.H. Enacted Stats 1990 ch 79 §14 (AB 759), operative July 1, 1991. Repealed Stats 1994 ch 806 §21 (AB 3686). See Prob C §21140.

Prior Law: Former Prob C §6179, similar to Prob C §21140, was added Stats 1988 ch 1199 §76, operative July 1, 1989, and repealed Stats 1990 ch 79 §13, operative July 1, 1991.

CHAPTER 6
CALIFORNIA STATUTORY WILL

Article 1. Definitions and Rules of Construction.
Article 2. General Provisions.
Article 3. Form and Full Text of Clauses.

ARTICLE 1
Definitions and Rules of Construction

Applicability of definitions and rules of construction. §6200.
"Testator". §6201.
"Executor". §6203.
"Trustee". §6204.
"Descendants". §6205.
Acts included in particular references in statutory wills. §6206.
Construction of gender and number. §6207.
Use of "shall" or "may". §6208.
Manner of distribution to "descendants". §6209.
"Person". §6210.
Requirement that beneficiaries must survive decedent. §6211.

§6200. Applicability of definitions and rules of construction

Unless the provision or context clearly requires otherwise, these definitions and rules of construction govern the construction of this chapter. **Leg.H.** Added Stats 1991 ch 1055 §20 (SB 271).

Prior Law: Former Prob C §6200, similar to the present section, was enacted Stats 1990 ch 79 §14, operative July 1, 1991, and repealed Stats 1991 ch 1055 §19.
Former Prob C §6200, similar to the present section, was added Stats 1983 ch 842 §55, operative January 1, 1985, and repealed Stats 1990 ch 79 §13, operative July 1, 1991.

§6201. "Testator"

"Testator" means a person choosing to adopt a California statutory will. **Leg.H.** Added Stats 1991 ch 1055 §20 (SB 271).

Prior Law: Former Prob C §6201, similar to the present section, was enacted Stats 1990 ch 79 §14, operative July 1, 1991, and repealed Stats 1991 ch 1055 §19.
Former Prob C §6201, similar to the present section, was added Stats 1983 ch 842 §55, operative January 1, 1985, and repealed Stats 1990 ch 79 §13, operative July 1, 1991.

§6202. [Section repealed 2002]

Leg.H. Added Stats 1991 ch 1055 §20 (SB 271). Repealed Stats 2001 ch 417 §10 (AB 873). The repealed section related to the definition of spouse.

Prior Law: Former Prob C §6202, relating to the definition of spouse, was enacted Stats 1990 ch 79 §14, operative July 1, 1991, and repealed Stats 1991 ch 1055 §19.
Former Prob C §6202, relating to the definition of spouse, was added Stats 1983 ch 842 §55, operative January 1, 1985, and repealed Stats 1990 ch 79 §13, operative July 1, 1991.

§6203. "Executor"

"Executor" means both the person so designated in a California statutory will and any other person acting at any time as the executor or administrator under a California statutory will. **Leg.H.** Added Stats 1991 ch 1055 §20 (SB 271).

Prior Law: Former Prob C §6203, similar to the present section, was enacted Stats 1990 ch 79 §14, operative July 1, 1991, and repealed Stats 1991 ch 1055 §19.

Former Prob C §6203, similar to the present section, was added Stats 1983 ch 842 §55, operative January 1, 1985, and repealed Stats 1990 ch 79 §13, operative July 1, 1991.

§6204. "Trustee"

"Trustee" means both the person so designated in a California statutory will and any other person acting at any time as the trustee under a California statutory will. **Leg.H.** Added Stats 1991 ch 1055 §20 (SB 271).

Prior Law: Former Prob C §6204, similar to the present section, was enacted Stats 1990 ch 79 §14, operative July 1, 1991, and repealed Stats 1991 ch 1055 §19.

Former Prob C §6204, similar to the present section, was added Stats 1983 ch 842 §55, operative January 1, 1985, and repealed Stats 1990 ch 79 §13, operative July 1, 1991.

§6205. "Descendants"

"Descendants" mean children, grandchildren, and their lineal descendants of all generations, with the relationship of parent and child at each generation being determined as provided in Section 21115. A reference to "descendants" in the plural includes a single descendant where the context so requires. **Leg.H.** Added Stats 1991 ch 1055 §20 (SB 271). Amended Stats 2002 ch 138 §7 (AB 1784).

Prior Law: Former Prob C §6205, similar to the present section, was enacted Stats 1990 ch 79 §14, operative July 1, 1991, and repealed Stats 1991 ch 1055 §19.

Former Prob C §6205, similar to the present section, was added Stats 1983 ch 842 §55, operative January 1, 1985, amended Stats 1984 ch 892 §33, Stats 1985 ch 359 §5, effective July 30, 1985, ch 982 §18, and repealed Stats 1990 ch 79 §13, operative July 1, 1991.

§6206. Acts included in particular references in statutory wills

A reference in a California statutory will to the "Uniform Gifts to Minors Act of any state" or the "Uniform Transfers to Minors Act of any state" includes both the Uniform Gifts to Minors Act of any state and the Uniform Transfers to Minors Act of any state. A reference to a "custodian" means the person so designated in a California statutory will or any other person acting at any time as a custodian under a Uniform Gifts to Minors Act or Uniform Transfers to Minors Act. **Leg.H.** Added Stats 1991 ch 1055 §20 (SB 271).

Prior Law: Former Prob C §6206, similar to the present section, was enacted Stats 1990 ch 79 §14, operative July 1, 1991, and repealed Stats 1991 ch 1055 §19.

Former Prob C §6206, similar to the present section, was added Stats 1984 ch 892 §35 and repealed Stats 1990 ch 79 §13, operative July 1, 1991.

Former Prob C §6206, was added Stats 1983 ch 842 §55, to become operative January 1, 1985, and repealed Stats 1984 ch 892 §34.

§6207. Construction of gender and number

Masculine pronouns include the feminine, and plural and singular words include each other, where appropriate. **Leg.H.** Added Stats 1991 ch 1055 §20 (SB 271).

Prior Law: Former Prob C §6207, similar to the present section, was enacted Stats 1990 ch 79 §14, operative July 1, 1991, and repealed Stats 1991 ch 1055 §19.

Former Prob C §6207, similar to the present section, was added Stats 1983 ch 842 §55, operative January 1, 1985, and repealed Stats 1990 ch 79 §13, operative July 1, 1991.

§6208. Use of "shall" or "may"

(a) If a California statutory will states that a person shall perform an act, the person is required to perform that act.

(b) If a California statutory will states that a person may do an act, the person's decision to do or not to do the act shall be made in the exercise of the person's fiduciary powers. **Leg.H.** Added Stats 1991 ch 1055 §20 (SB 271).

Prior Law: Former Prob C §6208, similar to the present section, was enacted Stats 1990 ch 79 §14, operative July 1, 1991, and repealed Stats 1991 ch 1055 §19.

Former Prob C §6208, similar to the present section, was added Stats 1983 ch 842 §55, operative January 1, 1985, and repealed Stats 1990 ch 79 §13, operative July 1, 1991.

§6209. Manner of distribution to "descendants"

Whenever a distribution under a California statutory will is to be made to a person's descendants, the property shall be divided into as many equal shares as there are then living descendants of the nearest degree of living descendants and deceased descendants of that same degree who leave descendants then living; and each living descendant of the nearest degree shall receive one share and the share of each deceased descendant of that same degree shall be divided among his or her descendants in the same manner. **Leg.H.** Added Stats 1991 ch 1055 §20 (SB 271).

Prior Law: Former Prob C §6209, similar to the present section, was enacted Stats 1990 ch 79 §14, operative July 1, 1991, and repealed Stats 1991 ch 1055 §19.

Former Prob C §6209, similar to the present section, was added Stats 1983 ch 842 §55, operative January 1, 1985, and repealed Stats 1990 ch 79 §13, operative July 1, 1991.

§6210. "Person"

"Person" includes individuals and institutions. **Leg.H.** Added Stats 1991 ch 1055 §20 (SB 271).

Prior Law: Former Prob C §6210, similar to the present section, was enacted Stats 1990 ch 79 §14, operative July 1, 1991, and repealed Stats 1991 ch 1055 §19.

Former Prob C §6210, similar to the present section, was added Stats 1983 ch 842 §55, operative January 1, 1985, and repealed Stats 1990 ch 79 §13, operative July 1, 1991.

§6211. Requirement that beneficiaries must survive decedent

Reference to a person "if living" or who "survives me" means a person who survives the decedent by 120 hours. A person who fails to survive the decedent by 120 hours is deemed to have predeceased the decedent for the purpose of a California statutory will, and the beneficiaries are determined accordingly. If it cannot be established by clear and convincing evidence that a person who would otherwise be a beneficiary has survived the decedent by 120 hours, it is deemed that the person failed to survive for the required period. The requirement of this section that a person who survives the decedent must survive the decedent by 120 hours does not apply if the application of the 120-hour survival requirement would result in the escheat of property to the state. **Leg.H.** Added Stats 1991 ch 1055 §20 (SB 271).

Prior Law: Former Prob C §6211, similar to the present section, was added Stats 1990 ch 710 §15, operative July 1, 1991, and repealed Stats 1991 ch 1055 §19.

ARTICLE 2
General Provisions

Persons who may execute. §6220.
Method of executing. §6221.
Execution of attestation clause. §6222.
Contents of California statutory will. §6223.
Selection of property disposition clauses. §6224.
Text of property disposition clause as controlling. §6225.
Revocation; Amendment; Additions; Deletions; Requirements for valid will. §6226.
Revocation by dissolution, termination, or annulment. §6227.

§6220. Persons who may execute

Any individual of sound mind and over the age of 18 may execute a California statutory will under the provisions of this chapter. **Leg.H.** Added Stats 1991 ch 1055 §20 (SB 271).

Prior Law: Former Prob C §6220, similar to the present section, was enacted Stats 1990 ch 79 §14, operative July 1, 1991, and repealed Stats 1991 ch 1055 §19.

Former Prob C §6220, similar to the present section, was added Stats 1983 ch 842 §55, operative January 1, 1985, and repealed Stats 1990 ch 79 §13, operative July 1, 1991.

§6221. Method of executing

A California statutory will shall be executed only as follows:

(a) The testator shall complete the appropriate blanks and shall sign the will.

(b) Each witness shall observe the testator's signing and each witness shall sign his or her name in the presence of the testator. **Leg.H.** Added Stats 1991 ch 1055 §20 (SB 271).

Prior Law: Former Prob C §6221, similar to the present section, was enacted Stats 1990 ch 79 §14, operative July 1, 1991, and repealed Stats 1991 ch 1055 §19.

Former Prob C §6221, similar to the present section, was added Stats 1983 ch 842 §55, operative January 1, 1985, and repealed Stats 1990 ch 79 §13, operative July 1, 1991.

§6221.5. [Section repealed 1992]

Leg.H. Enacted Stats 1990 ch 79 §14 (AB 759), operative July 1, 1991. Repealed Stats 1991 ch 1055 §19 (SB 271). See Prob C §6222.

Prior Law: Former Prob C §6221.5, similar to Prob C §6222, was added Stats 1983 ch 842 §55, operative January 1, 1985, amended Stats 1988 ch 1199 76.5, operative July 1, 1989, and repealed Stats 1990 ch 79 §13, operative July 1, 1991.

§6222. Execution of attestation clause

The execution of the attestation clause provided in the California statutory will by two or more witnesses satisfies Section 8220. **Leg.H.** Added Stats 1991 ch 1055 §20 (SB 271).

Prior Law: Former Prob C §6222, relating to two types of statutory wills and contents, was enacted Stats 1990 ch 79 §14, operative July 1, 1991, and repealed Stats 1991 ch 1055 §19.

Former Prob C §6222, relating to statutory wills and contents, was added Stats 1983 ch 842 §55, operative January 1, 1985, and repealed Stats 1990 ch 79 §13, operative July 1, 1991.

§6223. Contents of California statutory will

(a) There is only one California statutory will.

(b) The California statutory will includes all of the following:

(1) The contents of the California statutory will form set out in Section 6240, excluding the questions and answers at the beginning of the California statutory will.

(2) By reference, the full texts of each of the following:

(A) The definitions and rules of construction set forth in Article 1 (commencing with Section 6200).

(B) The property disposition clauses adopted by the testator. If no property disposition clause is adopted, Section 6224 shall apply.

(C) The mandatory clauses set forth in Section 6241.

(c) Notwithstanding this section, any California statutory will or California statutory will with trust executed on a form allowed under prior law shall be governed by the law that applied prior to January 1, 1992. **Leg.H.** Added Stats 1991 ch 1055 §20 (SB 271).

Prior Law: Former Prob C §6223, similar to present Prob C §6224, was enacted Stats 1990 ch 79 §14, operative July 1, 1991, and repealed Stats 1991 ch 1055 §19.

Former Prob C §6223, similar to present Prob C §6224, was added Stats 1983 ch 842 §55, operative January 1, 1985, and repealed Stats 1990 ch 79 §13, operative July 1, 1991.

§6224. Selection of property disposition clauses

If more than one property disposition clause appearing in paragraphs 2 or 3 of a California statutory will is selected, no gift is made. If more than one property disposition clause in paragraph 5 of a California statutory will form is selected, or if none is selected, the residuary estate of a testator who signs a California statutory will shall be distributed to the testator's heirs as if the testator did not make a will. **Leg.H.** Added Stats 1991 ch 1055 §20 (SB 271).

Prior Law: Former Prob C §6224, similar to present Prob C §6225, was enacted Stats 1990 ch 79 §14, operative July 1, 1991, and repealed Stats 1991 ch 1055 §19.

Former Prob C §6224, similar to present Prob C §6225, was added Stats 1983 ch 842 §55, operative January 1, 1985, and repealed Stats 1990 ch 79 §13, operative July 1, 1991.

§6225. Text of property disposition clause as controlling

Only the texts of property disposition clauses and the mandatory clauses shall be considered in determining their meaning. Their titles shall be disregarded. **Leg.H.** Added Stats 1991 ch 1055 §20 (SB 271).

Prior Law: Former Prob C §6225, similar to present Prob C §6226, was enacted Stats 1990 ch 79 §14, operative July 1, 1991, and repealed Stats 1991 ch 1055 §19.

Former Prob C §6225, similar to present Prob C §6226, was added Stats 1983 ch 842 §55, operative January 1, 1985, and repealed Stats 1990 ch 79 §13, operative July 1, 1991.

§6226. Revocation; Amendment; Additions; Deletions; Requirements for valid will

(a) A California statutory will may be revoked and may be amended by codicil in the same manner as other wills.

(b) Any additions to or deletions from the California statutory will on the face of the California statutory will form, other than in accordance with the instructions, shall be given effect only where clear and convincing evidence shows that they would effectuate the clear intent of the testator. In the absence of such a showing, the court either may determine that the addition or deletion is ineffective and shall be disregarded, or may determine that all or a portion of the California statutory will is invalid, whichever is more likely to be consistent with the intent of the testator.

(c) Notwithstanding Section 6110, a document executed on a California statutory will form is valid as a will if all of the following requirements are shown to be satisfied by clear and convincing evidence:

(1) The form is signed by the testator.

(2) The court is satisfied that the testator knew and approved of the contents of the will and intended it to have testamentary effect.

(3) The testamentary intent of the maker as reflected in the document is clear. **Leg.H.** Added Stats 1991 ch 1055 §20 (SB 271).

Prior Law: Former Prob C §6226, similar to present Prob C §6227, was enacted Stats 1990 ch 79 §14, operative July 1, 1991, and repealed Stats 1991 ch 1055 §19.

Former Prob C §6226, similar to present Prob C §6227, was added Stats 1983 ch 842 §55, operative January 1, 1985, amended Stats 1984 ch 892 §36, and repealed Stats 1990 ch 79 §13, operative July 1, 1991.

§6227. Revocation by dissolution, termination, or annulment

(a) If after executing a California statutory will the testator's marriage is dissolved or annulled, or the testator's registered domestic partnership is terminated, the dissolution, annulment, or termination revokes any disposition of property made by the will to the former spouse and any nomination of the former spouse as executor, trustee, guardian, or custodian made by the will. If any disposition or nomination is revoked solely by this section, it is revived by the testator's remarriage to, or entry into a subsequent registered domestic partnership with, the former spouse.

(b) In case of revocation by dissolution or annulment:

(1) Property prevented from passing to a former spouse because of the revocation passes as if the former spouse failed to survive the testator.

(2) Provisions nominating the former spouse as executor, trustee, guardian, or custodian shall be interpreted as if the former spouse failed to survive the testator.

(c) For purposes of this section, dissolution or annulment means any dissolution or annulment that would exclude the spouse as a surviving spouse within the meaning of Section 78. A decree of legal separation which does not terminate the status of spouses is not a dissolution or annulment for purposes of this section.

(d) This section applies to any California statutory will, without regard to the time when the will was executed, but this section does not apply to any case where the final judgment of dissolution or annulment of marriage occurs before January 1, 1985; and, if the final judgment of dissolution or annulment of marriage occurs before January 1, 1985, the case is governed by the law that applied prior to January 1, 1985. **Leg.H.** Added Stats 1991 ch 1055 §20 (SB 271). Amended Stats 2016 ch 50 §87 (SB 1005), effective January 1, 2017.

Editor's Notes—2016 Note: For legislative intent, see the 2016 Note following Prob C §59.

ARTICLE 3
Form and Full Text of Clauses

California Statutory Will form. §6240.
Mandatory clauses. §6241.
Inclusion of clauses as existing on date of execution; Governing law. §6242.
Applicability of general California law. §6243.

§6240. California Statutory Will form

The following is the California Statutory Will form:

QUESTIONS AND ANSWERS ABOUT THIS CALIFORNIA STATUTORY WILL

The following information, in question and answer form, is not a part of the California Statutory Will. It is designed to help you understand about Wills and to decide if this Will meets your needs. This Will is in a simple form. The complete text of each paragraph of this Will is printed at the end of the Will.

1. *What happens if I die without a Will?* If you die without a Will, what you own (your "assets") in your name alone will be divided among your spouse, domestic partner, children, or other relatives according to state law. The court will appoint a relative to collect and distribute your assets.

2. *What can a Will do for me?* In a Will you may designate who will receive your assets at your death. You may designate someone (called an "executor") to appear before the court, collect your assets, pay your debts and taxes, and distribute your assets as you specify. You may nominate someone (called a "guardian") to raise your children who are under age 18. You may designate someone (called a "custodian") to manage assets for your children until they reach any age from 18 to 25.

3. *Does a Will avoid probate?* No. With or without a Will, assets in your name alone usually go through the court probate process. The court's first job is to determine if your Will is valid.

4. *What is community property?* Can I give away my share in my Will? If you are married or in a domestic partnership and you or your spouse earned money during your marriage or domestic partnership from work and wages, that money (and the assets bought with it) is community property. Your Will can only give away your one-half of community property. Your Will cannot give away your spouse's one-half of community property.

5. *Does my Will give away all of my assets?* Do all assets go through probate? No. Money in a joint tenancy bank account automatically belongs to the other named owner without probate. If your spouse, domestic partner, or child is on the deed to your house as a joint tenant, the house automatically passes to him or her. Life insurance and retirement plan benefits may pass directly to the named beneficiary. A Will does not necessarily control how these types of "nonprobate" assets pass at your death.

6. *Are there different kinds of Wills?* Yes. There are handwritten Wills, typewritten Wills, attorney-prepared Wills, and statutory Wills. All are valid if done precisely as the law requires. You should see a lawyer if you do not want to use this Statutory Will or if you do not understand this form.

7. *Who may use this Will?* This Will is based on California law. It is designed only for California residents. You may use this form if you are single, married, a member of a domestic partnership, or divorced. You must be age 18 or older and of sound mind.

8. *Are there any reasons why I should NOT use this Statutory Will?* Yes. This is a simple Will. It is not designed to reduce death taxes or other taxes. Talk to a lawyer to do tax planning, especially if (i) your assets will be worth more than $600,000 or the current amount excluded from estate tax under federal law at your death, (ii) you own business-related assets, (iii) you want to create a trust fund for your children's education or other purposes, (iv) you own assets in some other state, (v) you want to disinherit your spouse, domestic partner, or descendants, or (vi) you have valuable interests in pension or profit-sharing plans. You should talk to a lawyer who knows about estate planning if this Will does not meet your needs. This Will treats most adopted children like natural children. You should talk to a lawyer if you have stepchildren or foster children whom you have not adopted.

9. *May I add or cross out any words on this Will?* No. If you do, the Will may be invalid or the court may ignore the crossed out or added words. You may only fill in the blanks. You may amend this Will by a separate document (called a codicil). Talk to a lawyer if you want to do something with your assets which is not allowed in this form.

10. *May I change my Will?* Yes. A Will is not effective until you die. You may make and sign a new Will. You may change your Will at any time, but only by an amendment (called a codicil). You can give away or sell your assets before your death. Your Will only acts on what you own at death.

11. *Where should I keep my Will?* After you and the witnesses sign the Will, keep your Will in your safe deposit box or other safe place. You should tell trusted family members where your Will is kept.

12. *When should I change my Will?* You should make and sign a new Will if you marry, divorce, or terminate your domestic partnership after you sign this Will. Divorce, annulment, or termination of a domestic partnership automatically cancels all property stated to pass to a former spouse or domestic partner under this Will, and revokes the designation of a former spouse or domestic partner as executor, custodian, or guardian. You should sign a new Will when you have more children, or if your spouse or a child dies, or a domestic partner dies or marries. You may want to change your Will if there is a large change in the value of your assets. You may also want to change your Will if you enter a domestic partnership or your domestic partnership has been terminated after you sign this Will.

13. *What can I do if I do not understand something in this Will?* If there is anything in this Will you do not understand, ask a lawyer to explain it to you.

14. *What is an executor?* An "executor" is the person you name to collect your assets, pay your debts and taxes, and distribute your assets as the court directs. It may be a person or it may be a qualified bank or trust company.

15. *Should I require a bond?* You may require that an executor post a "bond." A bond is a form of insurance to replace assets that may be mismanaged or stolen by the executor. The cost of the bond is paid from the estate's assets.

16. *What is a guardian?* Do I need to designate one? If you have children under age 18, you should designate a guardian of their "persons" to raise them.

17. *What is a custodian?* Do I need to designate one? A "custodian" is a person you may designate to manage assets for someone (including a child) who is under the age of 25 and who receives assets under your Will. The custodian manages the assets and pays as much as the custodian determines is proper for health, support, maintenance, and education. The custodian delivers what is left to the person when the person reaches the age you choose (from 18 to 25). No bond is required of a custodian.

18. *Should I ask people if they are willing to serve before I designate them as executor, guardian, or custodian?* Probably yes. Some people and banks and trust companies may not consent to serve or may not be qualified to act.

19. *What happens if I make a gift in this Will to someone and that person dies before I do?* A person must survive you by 120 hours to take a gift under this Will. If that person does not, then the gift fails and goes with the rest of your assets. If the person who does not survive you is a relative of yours or your spouse, then certain assets may go to the relative's descendants.

20. *What is a trust?* There are many kinds of trusts, including trusts created by Wills (called "testamentary trusts") and trusts created during your lifetime (called "revocable living trusts"). Both kinds of trusts are long-term arrangements in which a manager (called a "trustee") invests and manages assets for someone (called a "beneficiary") on the terms you specify. Trusts are too complicated to be used in this Statutory Will. You should see a lawyer if you want to create a trust.

21. *What is a domestic partner?* You have a domestic partner if you have met certain legal requirements and filed a form entitled "Declaration of Domestic Partnership" with the Secretary of State. Notwithstanding Section 299.6 of the Family Code, if you have not filed a Declaration of Domestic Partnership with the Secretary of State, you do not meet the required definition and should not use the section of the Statutory Will form that refers to domestic partners even if you have registered your domestic partnership with another governmental entity. If you are unsure if you have a domestic partner or if your domestic partnership meets the required definition, please contact the Secretary of State's office.

INSTRUCTIONS

1. READ THE WILL. Read the whole Will first. If you do not understand something, ask a lawyer to explain it to you.
2. FILL IN THE BLANKS. Fill in the blanks. Follow the instructions in the form carefully. Do not add any words to the Will (except for filling in blanks) or cross out any words.
3. DATE AND SIGN THE WILL AND HAVE TWO WITNESSES SIGN IT. Date and sign the Will and have two witnesses sign it. You and the witnesses should read and follow the Notice to Witnesses found at the end of this Will.

*You do not need to have this document notarized. Notarization will not fulfill the witness requirement.

CALIFORNIA STATUTORY WILL OF

Print Your Full Name

1. <u>Will.</u> This is my Will. I revoke all prior Wills and codicils.
2. <u>Specific Gift of Personal Residence.</u> (Optional—use only if you want to give your personal residence to a different person or persons than you give the balance of your assets to under paragraph 5 below.) I give my interest in my principal personal residence at the time of my death (subject to mortgages and liens) as follows:(Select one choice only and sign in the box after your choice.)

a. <u>Choice One:</u> All to my spouse or domestic partner, registered with the California Secretary of State, if my spouse, domestic partner, registered with the California

Secretary of State, survives me; otherwise to my descendants (my children and the descendants of my children) who survive me.

   b. Choice Two: Nothing to my spouse or domestic partner, registered with the California Secretary of State; all to my descendants (my children and the descendants of my children) who survive me.

   c. Choice Three: All to the following person if he or she survives me (Insert the name of the person.):
   _____

   d. Choice Four: Equally among the following persons who survive me (Insert the names of two or more persons.):
   _____
   _____
   _____

3. Specific Gift of Automobiles, Household and Personal Effects. (Optional—use only if you want to give automobiles and household and personal effects to a different person or persons than you give the balance of your assets to under paragraph 5 below.) I give all of my automobiles (subject to loans), furniture, furnishings, household items, clothing, jewelry, and other tangible articles of a personal nature at the time of my death as follows:(Select one choice only and sign in the box after your choice.)

   a. Choice One: All to my spouse or domestic partner, registered with the California Secretary of State, if my spouse, domestic partner, registered with the California Secretary of State, survives me; otherwise to my descendants (my children and the descendants of my children) who survive me.

   b. Choice Two: Nothing to my spouse or domestic partner, registered with the California Secretary of State; all to my descendants (my children and the descendants of my children) who survive me.

   c. Choice Three: All to the following person if he or she survives me (Insert the name of the person.):
   _____

   d. Choice Four: Equally among the following persons who survive me (Insert the names of two or more persons.):
   _____

_____
_____

4. Specific Gifts of Cash. (Optional) I make the following cash gifts to the persons named below who survive me, or to the named charity, and I sign my name in the box after each gift. If I do not sign in the box, I do not make a gift. (Sign in the box after each gift you make.)

Name of Person or Charity to receive gift (name one only—please print)	Amount of Cash Gift
	Sign your name in this box to make this gift

Name of Person or Charity to receive gift (name one only—please print)	Amount of Cash Gift
	Sign your name in this box to make this gift

Name of Person or Charity to receive gift (name one only—please print)	Amount of Cash Gift
	Sign your name in this box to make this gift

Name of Person or Charity to receive gift (name one only—please print)	Amount of Cash Gift
	Sign your name in this box to make this gift

Name of Person or Charity to receive gift (name one only—please print)	Amount of Cash Gift
	Sign your name in this box to make this gift

5. Balance of My Assets. Except for the specific gifts made in paragraphs 2, 3 and 4 above, I give the balance of my assets as follows:(Select one choice only and sign in the box after your choice. If I sign in more than one box or if I do not sign in any box, the court will distribute my assets as if I did not make a Will.)

   a. Choice One: All to my spouse or domestic partner, registered with the California Secretary of State, if my spouse or domestic partner, registered with the California Secretary of State, survives me; otherwise to my descendants (my children and the descendants of my children) who survive me.

   b. Choice Two: Nothing to my spouse or domestic partner, registered with the California Secretary of State; all to my descendants (my children and the descendants of my children) who survive me.

   c. Choice Three: All to the following person if he or she survives me (Insert the name of the person.):
   _____

   d. Choice Four: Equally among the following persons who survive me (Insert the

names of two or more persons.):
_____
_____
_____

6. Guardian of the Child's Person. If, at my death, I have a child under age 18, whether the child is alive at the time this will is executed or born after the date this will is executed, and the child does not have a living parent, I nominate the individual named below as First Choice as guardian of the person of that child (to raise the child). If the First Choice does not serve, then I nominate the Second Choice, and then the Third Choice, to serve. Only an individual (not a bank or trust company) may serve.

| Name of First Choice for Guardian of the Person |
| Name of Second Choice for Guardian of the Person |
| Name of Third Choice for Guardian of the Person |

7. Special Provision for Property of Persons Under Age 25. (Optional—unless you use this paragraph, assets that go to a child or other person who is under age 18 may be given to the parent of the person, or to the Guardian named in paragraph 6 above as guardian of the person until age 18, and the court will require a bond, and assets that go to a child or other person who is age 18 or older will be given outright to the person. By using this paragraph you may provide that a custodian will hold the assets for the person until the person reaches any age from 18 to 25 which you choose.) If a beneficiary of this Will is under the age chosen below, I nominate the individual or bank or trust company named below as First Choice as custodian of the property. If the First Choice does not serve, then I nominate the Second Choice, and then the Third Choice, to serve.

| Name of First Choice for Custodian of Assets |
| Name of Second Choice for Custodian of Assets |
| Name of Third Choice for Custodian of Assets |

Insert any age from 18 to 25 as the age for the person to receive the property: _____

(If you do not choose an age, age 18 will apply.)

8. Executor. I nominate the individual or bank or trust company named below as First Choice as executor. If the First Choice does not serve, then I nominate the Second Choice, and then the Third Choice, to serve.

| Name of First Choice for Executor |
| Name of Second Choice for Executor |
| Name of Third Choice for Executor |

9. Bond. My signature in this box means a bond is not required for any person named as executor. A bond may be required if I do not sign in this box:
No bond shall be required.

(Notice: You must sign this Will in the presence of two (2) adult witnesses. The witnesses must sign their names in your presence. You must first read to them the following sentence.)

This is my Will: I ask the persons who sign below to be my witnesses. Signed on _____ at _____, California.
(date)   (city)

_____
Signature of Maker of Will

(Notice to Witnesses: Two (2) adults must sign as witnesses. Each witness must read the following clause before signing. The witnesses should not receive assets under this Will.)

Each of us declares under penalty of perjury under the laws of the State of California that the following is true and correct:

a. On the date written below the maker of this Will declared to us that this instrument was the maker's Will and requested us to act as witnesses to it;

b. We understand this is the maker's Will;

c. The maker signed this Will in our presence, all of us being present at the same time;

d. We now, at the maker's request, and in the maker's presence, sign below as witnesses;

e. We believe the maker is of sound mind and memory;

f. We believe that this Will was not procured by duress, menace, fraud or undue influence;

g. The maker is age 18 or older; and

h. Each of us is now age 18 or older, is a competent witness, and resides at the address set forth after his or her name.

Dated: _____, ____

Signature of witness	Signature of witness
Print name here:	Print name here:
_____	_____
Residence Address:	Residence Address:
_____	_____
_____	_____

AT LEAST TWO WITNESSES MUST SIGN

Leg.H. Added Stats 1991 ch 1055 §20 (SB 271). Amended Stats 2001 ch 893 §52 (AB 25); Stats 2003 ch 32 §5 (AB 167); Stats 2010 ch 88 §1 (AB 1986), effective January 1, 2011; Stats 2016 ch 50 §88 (SB 1005), effective January 1, 2017.

2016 Note: For legislative intent, see the 2016 Note following Prob C §59.

Prior Law: Former Prob C §6240, similar to the present section, was enacted Stats 1990 ch 79 §14, operative July 1, 1991, and repealed Stats 1991 ch 1055 §19. Former Prob C §6240, similar to the present section, was added Stats 1983 ch 842 §55, operative January 1, 1985, and repealed Stats 1990 ch 79 §13, operative July 1, 1991.

§6241. Mandatory clauses

The mandatory clauses of the California statutory will form are as follows:

(a) *Intestate Disposition.* If the testator has not made an effective disposition of the residuary estate, the executor shall distribute it to the testator's heirs at law, their identities and respective shares to be determined according to the laws of the State of California in effect on the date of the testator's death relating to intestate succession of property not acquired from a predeceased spouse.

(b) *Powers of Executor.*

(1) In addition to any powers now or hereafter conferred upon executors by law, including all powers granted under the Independent Administration of Estates Act, the executor shall have the power to:

(A) Sell estate assets at public or private sale, for cash or on credit terms.

(B) Lease estate assets without restriction as to duration.

(C) Invest any surplus moneys of the estate in real or personal property, as the executor deems advisable.

(2) The executor may distribute estate assets otherwise distributable to a minor beneficiary to one of the following:

(A) The guardian of the minor's person or estate.

(B) Any adult person with whom the minor resides and who has the care, custody, or control of the minor.

(C) A custodian of the minor under the Uniform Transfers to Minors Act as designated in the California statutory will form.

The executor is free of liability and is discharged from any further accountability for distributing assets in compliance with the provisions of this paragraph.

(3) On any distribution of assets from the estate, the executor shall have the discretion to partition, allot, and distribute the assets in the following manner:

(A) In kind, including undivided interest in an asset or in any part of it.

(B) Partly in cash and partly in kind.

(C) Entirely in cash.

If a distribution is being made to more than one beneficiary, the executor shall have the discretion to distribute assets among them on a pro rata or non pro rata basis, with the assets valued as of the date of distribution.

(c) *Powers of Guardian.* A guardian of the person nominated in the California statutory will shall have the same authority with respect to the person of the ward as a parent having legal custody of a child would have. All powers granted to guardians in this paragraph may be exercised without court authorization. **Leg.H.** Added Stats 1991 ch 1055 §20 (SB 271).

Prior Law: Former Prob C §6241, relating to California statutory will with trust form, was enacted Stats 1990 ch 79 §14, operative July 1, 1991, and repealed Stats 1991 ch 1055 §19.

Former Prob C §6241, relating to California statutory will with trust form, was added Stats 1983 ch 842 §55, operative January 1, 1985, and repealed Stats 1990 ch 79 §13, operative July 1, 1991.

§6242. Inclusion of clauses as existing on date of execution; Governing law

(a) Except as specifically provided in this chapter, a California statutory will shall include only the texts of the property disposition clauses and the mandatory clauses as they exist on the day the California statutory will is executed.

(b) Sections 6205, 6206, and 6227 apply to every California statutory will, including those executed before January 1, 1985. Section 6211 applies only to California statutory wills executed after July 1, 1991.

(c) Notwithstanding Section 6222, and except as provided in subdivision (b), a California statutory will is governed by the law that applied prior to January 1, 1992, if the California statutory will is executed on a form that (1) was prepared for use under former Sections 56 to 56.14, inclusive, or former Sections 6200 to 6248, inclusive, of the Probate Code, and (2) satisfied the requirements of law that applied prior to January 1, 1992.

(d) A California statutory will does not fail to satisfy the requirements of subdivision (a) merely because the will is executed on a form that incorporates the mandatory clauses of Section 6241 that refer to former Section 1120.2. If the will incorporates the mandatory clauses with a reference to former Section 1120.2, the trustee has the powers listed in Article 2 (commencing with Section 16220) of Chapter 2 of Part 4 of Division 9. **Leg.H.** Added Stats 1991 ch 1055 §20 (SB 271). Amended Stats 2004 ch 183 §279 (AB 3082), effective January 1, 2005.

Prior Law: Former Prob C §6242, relating to full text of paragraph 2.1 of statutory wills, was enacted Stats 1990 ch 79 §14, operative July 1, 1991, and repealed Stats 1991 ch 1055 §19.

Former Prob C §6242, relating to statutory wills, was added Stats 1983 ch 842 §55, operative January 1, 1985, and repealed Stats 1990 ch 79 §13, operative July 1, 1991.

§6243. Applicability of general California law

Except as specifically provided in this chapter, the general law of California applies to a California statutory will. **Leg.H.** Added Stats 1991 ch 1055 §20 (SB 271).

Prior Law: Former Prob C §6243, relating to full text of property disposition clauses of statutory will form, was enacted Stats 1990 ch 79 §14, operative July 1, 1991, and repealed Stats 1991 ch 1055 §19. Historical derivation: (a) Former Prob C §56.10, as added Stats 1982 ch 1401 §1. (b) Former Prob C §6243, as added Stats 1983 ch 842 §55.

Former Prob C §6243, relating to property disposition clauses of statutory will form, was added Stats 1983 ch 842 §55, operative January 1, 1985, and repealed Stats 1990 ch 79 §13, operative July 1, 1991.

§6244. [Section repealed 1992]

Leg.H. Enacted Stats 1990 ch 79 §14 (AB 759), operative July 1, 1991. Repealed Stats 1991 ch 1055 §19 (SB 271). The repealed section related to full text of property disposition clauses of statutory will with trust form.

Prior Law: Former Prob C §6244, relating to full text of property disposition clauses of statutory will with trust form, was added Stats 1983 ch 842 §55, operative January 1, 1985, and repealed Stats 1990 ch 79 §13, operative July 1, 1991.

§6245. [Section repealed 1992]

Leg.H. Enacted Stats 1990 ch 79 §14 (AB 759), operative July 1, 1991. Repealed Stats 1991 ch 1055 §19 (SB 271). See Prob C §6241.

Prior Law: Former Prob C §6245, similar to present Prob C §6241, was added Stats 1983 ch 842 §55, operative January 1, 1985, amended Stats 1984 ch 243 §9.2, and repealed Stats 1990 ch 79 §13, operative July 1, 1991.

§6246. [Section repealed 1992]

Leg.H. Enacted Stats 1990 ch 79 §14 (AB 759), operative July 1, 1991. Repealed Stats 1991 ch 1055 §19 (SB 271). See Prob C §6241.

Prior Law: Former Prob C §6246, similar to Prob C §6241, was added Stats 1983 ch 842 §55, operative January 1, 1985, amended Stats 1984 ch 243 §9.3, Stats 1987 ch 923 §85.3, operative January 1, 1988, and repealed Stats 1990 ch 79 §13, operative July 1, 1991.

§6247. [Section repealed 1992]

Leg.H. Enacted Stats 1990 ch 79 §14 (AB 759), operative July 1, 1991. Amended Stats 1990 ch 710 §16 (SB 1775), operative July 1, 1991; Stats 1991 ch 82 §21 (SB 896), effective June 30, 1991, operative July 1, 1991. Repealed Stats 1991 ch 1055 §19 (SB 271). See Prob C §6242.

Prior Law: Former Prob C §6247, similar to present Prob C §6242, was added Stats 1983 ch 842 §55, operative January 1, 1985, amended Stats 1984 ch 892 §37, Stats 1987 ch 923 §85.7, operative January 1, 1988, and repealed Stats 1990 ch 79 §13, operative July 1, 1991.

§6248. [Section repealed 1992]

Leg.H. Enacted Stats 1990 ch 79 §14 (AB 759), operative July 1, 1991. Repealed Stats 1991 ch 1055 §19 (SB 271). See Prob C §6243.

Prior Law: Former Prob C §6248, similar to present Prob C §6243, was added Stats 1983 ch 842 §55, operative January 1, 1985, amended Stats 1984 ch 892 §38, and repealed Stats 1990 ch 79 §13, operative July 1, 1991.

CHAPTER 7
UNIFORM TESTAMENTARY ADDITIONS TO TRUSTS ACT

Testamentary additions to trusts. §6300.
Validity of devise made by will executed before September 17, 1965. §6301.
Chapter citation. §6303.

§6300. Testamentary additions to trusts

(a) A devise, the validity of which is determinable by the law of this state, may be made by a will to the trustee of a trust established or to be established by the testator, by the testator and some other person, or by some other person (including a funded or unfunded life insurance trust, although the settlor has reserved any or all rights of ownership of the insurance contracts) if the trust is identified in the testator's will and its terms are set forth in a written instrument (other than a will) executed before, concurrently with, or within 60 days after the execution of the testator's will or in the valid last will of a person who has predeceased the testator (regardless of the existence, size, or character of the trust property). The devise is not invalid because the trust is amendable or revocable, or both, or because the trust was amended after the execution of the will or after the death of the testator.

(b) Unless the testator's will provides otherwise, the property so devised (1) is not deemed to be held under a testamentary trust of the testator but becomes a part of the trust to which it is given and (2) shall be administered and disposed of in accordance with the provisions of the instrument or will setting forth the terms of the trust, including any amendments thereto made before or after the death of the testator (regardless of whether made before or after the execution of the testator's will).

(c) Unless otherwise provided in the will, a revocation or termination of the trust before the death of the testator causes the devise to lapse.

Leg.H. Enacted Stats 1990 ch 79 §14 (AB 759), operative July 1, 1991. Amended Stats 2017 ch 33 §1 (AB 309), effective January 1, 2018.

Prior Law: Former Prob C §6300, similar to the present section, was added Stats 1983 ch 842 §55, operative January 1, 1985, amended Stats 1984 ch 892 §39, and repealed Stats 1990 ch 79 §13, operative July 1, 1991.

§6301. Validity of devise made by will executed before September 17, 1965

This chapter does not invalidate any devise made by a will executed prior to September 17, 1965. **Leg.H.** Enacted Stats 1990 ch 79 §14 (AB 759), operative July 1, 1991.

Prior Law: Former Prob C §6301, similar to the present section, was added Stats 1983 ch 842 §55, operative January 1, 1985, and repealed Stats 1990 ch 79 §13, operative July 1, 1991.

§6303. Chapter citation

This chapter may be cited as the Uniform Testamentary Additions to Trusts Act. **Leg.H.** Enacted Stats 1990 ch 79 §14 (AB 759), operative July 1, 1991.

Prior Law: Former Prob C §6303, similar to the present section, was added Stats 1983 ch 842 §55, operative January 1, 1985, and repealed Stats 1990 ch 79 §13, operative July 1, 1991.

CHAPTER 8
NONPROBATE TRANSFER TO TRUSTEE NAMED IN DECEDENT'S WILL

Definitions. §6320.
Designation of trustee as beneficiary, payee, or owner. §6321.
Required provision in designator's will. §6322.
Payment or transfer to trustee without administration. §6323.
Effect of designator's debts. §6324.
Jurisdiction of court. §6325.
Applicability of Division 9. §6326.
Appealable orders. §6327.
Absence of qualified trustee. §6328.
No effect on other trusts. §6329.
Chapter as restatement and continuation of former law. §6330.

§6320. Definitions

As used in this chapter, unless the context otherwise requires:

(a) "Designation" means a designation made pursuant to Section 6321.

(b) "Instrument" includes all of the following:

(1) An insurance, annuity, or endowment contract (including any agreement issued or entered into by the insurer in connection therewith, supplemental thereto, or in settlement thereof).

(2) A pension, retirement benefit, death benefit, stock bonus, profit-sharing or employees' saving plan, employee benefit plan, or contract created or entered into by an employer for the benefit of some or all of his or her employees.

(3) A self-employed retirement plan, or an individual retirement annuity or account, established or held pursuant to the Internal Revenue Code.

(4) A multiple-party account, as defined in Section 5132.

(5) Any other written instrument of a type described in Section 5000.
Leg.H. Enacted Stats 1990 ch 79 §14 (AB 759), operative July 1, 1991. Amended Stats 1992 ch 178 §31.4 (SB 1496).

Prior Law: Former Prob C §6320, similar to the present section, was added Stats 1983 ch 842 §55, operative January 1, 1985, and repealed Stats 1990 ch 79 §13, operative July 1, 1991.

§6321. Designation of trustee as beneficiary, payee, or owner

An instrument may designate as a primary or contingent beneficiary, payee, or owner a trustee named or to be named in the will of the person entitled to designate the beneficiary, payee, or owner. The designation shall be made in accordance with the provisions of the contract or plan or, in the absence of such provisions, in a manner approved by the insurer if an insurance, annuity, or endowment contract is involved, and by the trustee, custodian, or person or entity administering the contract or plan, if any. The designation may be made before or after the execution of the designator's will and is not required to comply with the formalities for execution of a will. **Leg.H.** Enacted Stats 1990 ch 79 §14 (AB 759), operative July 1, 1991. Amended Stats 1992 ch 178 §31.6 (SB 1496).

Prior Law: Former Prob C §6321, similar to the present section, was added Stats 1983 ch 842 §55, operative January 1, 1985, and repealed Stats 1990 ch 79 §13, operative July 1, 1991.

§6322. Required provision in designator's will

The designation is ineffective unless the designator's will contains provisions creating the trust or makes a disposition valid under Section 6300. **Leg.H.** Enacted Stats 1990 ch 79 §14 (AB 759), operative July 1, 1991.

Prior Law: Former Prob C §6322, similar to the present section, was added Stats 1983 ch 842 §55, operative January 1, 1985, and repealed Stats 1990 ch 79 §13, operative July 1, 1991.

§6323. Payment or transfer to trustee without administration

Subject to the provisions of Section 6325, the benefits or rights resulting from the designation are payable or transferable directly to the trustee, without becoming subject to administration, upon or at any time after admission of the designator's will to probate. A designation pursuant to this chapter does not have the effect of naming a trustee of a separate inter vivos trust but the rights and benefits or the proceeds thereof when paid to the trustee are, or become a part of, the testamentary trust or trusts established pursuant to the designator's will or shall be added to an inter vivos trust or trusts if the disposition is governed by Section 6300. **Leg.H.** Enacted Stats 1990 ch 79 §14 (AB 759), operative July 1, 1991.

Prior Law: Former Prob C §6323, similar to the present section, was added Stats 1983 ch 842 §55, operative January 1, 1985, and repealed Stats 1990 ch 79 §13, operative July 1, 1991.

§6324. Effect of designator's debts

Except as otherwise provided in the designator's will, the rights and benefits and their proceeds paid or transferred to the trustee are not subject to the debts of the designator to any greater extent than if they were paid or transferred to a named beneficiary, payee, or owner other than the estate of the designator. **Leg.H.** Enacted Stats 1990 ch 79 §14 (AB 759), operative July 1, 1991.

Prior Law: Former Prob C §6324, similar to the present section, was added Stats 1983 ch 842 §55, operative January 1, 1985, and repealed Stats 1990 ch 79 §13, operative July 1, 1991.

§6325. Jurisdiction of court

(a) The court in which the proceedings are pending for administration of the estate of the decedent has jurisdiction, before or after payment or transfer of benefits and rights or their proceeds to the trustee, to:

(1) Determine the validity of the trust.

(2) Determine the terms of the trust.

(3) Fill vacancies in the office of trustee.

(4) Require a bond of a trustee in its discretion and in such amount as the court may determine for the faithful performance of duties as trustee, subject to the provisions of Article 3 (commencing with Section 1570) of Chapter 16 of Division 1.1 of the Financial Code and Section 15602 of this code.

(5) Grant additional powers to the trustee, as provided in Section 16201.

(6) Instruct the trustee.

(7) Fix or allow payment of compensation of a trustee as provided in Sections 15680 to 15683, inclusive.

(8) Hear and determine adverse claims to the trust property by the personal representative, surviving spouse, or other third person.

(9) Determine the identity of the trustee and the trustee's acceptance or rejection of the office and, upon request, furnish evidence of trusteeship to a trustee.

(10) Order postponement of the payment or transfer of the benefits and rights or their proceeds.

(11) Authorize or direct removal of the trust or trust property to another jurisdiction pursuant to the procedure provided in Chapter 5 (commencing with Section 17400) of Part 5 of Division 9.

(12) Make any order incident to the foregoing or to the accomplishment of the purposes of this chapter.

(b) The personal representative of the designator's estate, any trustee named in the will or designation or successor to such trustee, or any person interested in the estate or trust may petition the court for an order under this section. Notice of hearing of the petition shall be given in the manner provided in Section 17203, except as the court may otherwise order. **Leg.H.** Enacted Stats 1990 ch 79 §14 (AB 759), operative July 1, 1991. Amended Stats 2014 ch 71 §138 (SB 1304), effective January 1, 2015.

Prior Law: Former Prob C §6325, similar to the present section, was added Stats 1983 ch 842 §55, operative January 1, 1985, amended Stats 1986 ch 820 §37, operative July 1, 1987, and repealed Stats 1990 ch 79 §13, operative July 1, 1991.

§6326. Applicability of Division 9
As to matters not specifically provided in Section 6325, the provisions of Division 9 (commencing with Section 15000) apply to the trust. **Leg.H.** Enacted Stats 1990 ch 79 §14 (AB 759), operative July 1, 1991.

Prior Law: Former Prob C §6326, similar to the present section, was added Stats 1983 ch 842 §55, operative January 1, 1985, amended Stats 1986 ch 820 §38, operative July 1, 1987, and repealed Stats 1990 ch 79 §13, operative July 1, 1991.

§6327. Appealable orders
An appeal may be taken from any of the following:

(a) Any order described in Part 3 (commencing with Section 1300) of Division 3 made pursuant to this chapter.

(b) An order making or refusing to make a determination specified in paragraph (1), (2), or (8) of subdivision (a) of Section 6325.

(c) As provided in Section 1304 for an order made pursuant to Section 6326. **Leg.H.** Enacted Stats 1990 ch 79 §14 (AB 759), operative July 1, 1991. Amended Stats 2003 ch 32 §6 (AB 167), effective January 1, 2004.

Prior Law: Former Prob C §6327, similar to the present section, was added Stats 1983 ch 842 §55, operative January 1, 1985, amended Stats 1986 ch 820 §39, operative July 1, 1987, Stats 1987 ch 923 §86, operative July 1, 1988, Stats 1988 ch 1199 §77, operative July 1, 1989, and repealed Stats 1990 ch 79 §13, operative July 1, 1991.

§6328. Absence of qualified trustee
If no qualified trustee makes claim to the benefits or rights or proceeds within one year after the death of the designator, or if satisfactory evidence is furnished within such one-year period showing that no trustee can qualify to receive them, payment or transfer may be made, unless the designator has otherwise provided, by the obligor to the personal representative of the designator or to those thereafter entitled, and the obligor is discharged from liability. **Leg.H.** Enacted Stats 1990 ch 79 §14 (AB 759), operative July 1, 1991.

Prior Law: Former Prob C §6328, similar to the present section, was added Stats 1983 ch 842 §55, operative January 1, 1985, and repealed Stats 1990 ch 79 §13, operative July 1, 1991.

§6329. No effect on other trusts
Enactment of this chapter does not invalidate trusts, otherwise valid, not made pursuant to the provisions of this chapter. **Leg.H.** Enacted Stats 1990 ch 79 §14 (AB 759), operative July 1, 1991.

Prior Law: Former Prob C §6329, similar to the present section, was added Stats 1983 ch 842 §55, operative January 1, 1985, and repealed Stats 1990 ch 79 §13, operative July 1, 1991.

§6330. Chapter as restatement and continuation of former law
This chapter, insofar as it is substantially the same as former Chapter 10 (commencing with Section 175) of former Division 1, repealed by Section 18 of Chapter 842 of the Statutes of 1983, shall be construed as a restatement and continuation thereof and not as a new enactment. After December 31, 1984, a reference in a written instrument to the previously existing provisions relating to the subject matter of this chapter shall be deemed to be a reference to the corresponding provisions of this chapter. **Leg.H.** Enacted Stats 1990 ch 79 §14 (AB 759), operative July 1, 1991.

Prior Law: Former Prob C §6330, similar to the present section, was added Stats 1984 ch 892 §39.3 and repealed Stats 1990 ch 79 §13, operative July 1, 1991.

CHAPTER 9
DEVISE SUBJECT TO CALIFORNIA UNIFORM TRANSFERS TO MINORS ACT

Devised property paid, delivered, or transferred to custodian subject to Uniform Gifts to Minors Act or Uniform Transfers to Minors Act. §6341.
Successor or substitute custodians; Compensation. §6345.
Notice to and participation of custodian. §6347.
Jurisdiction of court. §6348.
Construction of chapter. §6349.

§6341. Devised property paid, delivered, or transferred to custodian subject to Uniform Gifts to Minors Act or Uniform Transfers to Minors Act
If a testator's will provides that devised property shall be paid or delivered or transferred to a custodian subject to the California Uniform Gifts to Minors Act or the California Uniform Transfers to Minors Act:

(a) All of the provisions of the California Uniform Transfers to Minors Act, Part 9 (commencing with Section 3900) of Division 4, including, but not limited to, the definitions and the provisions concerning powers, rights, and immunities contained in that act, are applicable to the devise during the period prior to distribution of the property.

(b) Unless the will clearly requires otherwise, if the person named as the beneficiary for whose benefit the custodial property is to be held attains the age at which the custodianship was to terminate prior to the order of distribution, the devise shall be deemed to be a direct devise to the person named as the beneficiary for whose benefit the custodial property was to be held.

(c) The personal representative of the testator's estate, upon entry of an order for distribution, shall make distribution pursuant to the order for distribution by transferring the devised property in the form and manner provided by the California Uniform Transfers to Minors Act.

(d) If a vacancy in the custodianship exists prior to full distribution of the devised property by the personal representative, a successor custodian shall be appointed for any undistributed property in the manner provided by the California Uniform Transfers to Minors Act. **Leg.H.** Enacted Stats 1990 ch 79 §14 (AB 759), operative July 1, 1991.

Prior Law: Former Prob C §6341, similar to the present section, was added Stats 1983 ch 842 §55, operative January 1, 1985, amended Stats 1984 ch 243 §11, and repealed Stats 1990 ch 79 §13, operative July 1, 1991.

§6345. Successor or substitute custodians; Compensation
The will may provide for successor or substitute custodians and may specify the standard of compensation of the custodian. **Leg.H.** Enacted Stats 1990 ch 79 §14 (AB 759), operative July 1, 1991.

Prior Law: Former Prob C §6345, similar to the present section, was added Stats 1983 ch 842 §55, operative January 1, 1985, amended Stats 1985 ch 90 §2, and repealed Stats 1990 ch 79 §13, operative July 1, 1991.

§6347. Notice to and participation of custodian
(a) Except as otherwise provided in the will or ordered by a court, each custodian designated in the will and the person for whom the property is to be held shall be deemed a devisee for the purpose of receiving notices which may be required or permitted to be sent to a devisee in the estate of the testator.

(b) Unless required by the will or ordered by the court, a custodian does not have a duty to participate in the proceedings in the estate on behalf of the minor, and in no event does the custodian have a duty to so participate until the custodian has filed a written notice of acceptance of the office of custodian with the clerk of the court in which administration of the estate of the testator is pending. **Leg.H.** Enacted Stats 1990 ch 79 §14 (AB 759), operative July 1, 1991.

Prior Law: Former Prob C §6347, similar to the present section, was added Stats 1983 ch 842 §55, operative January 1, 1985, and repealed Stats 1990 ch 79 §13, operative July 1, 1991.

§6348. Jurisdiction of court
Until distribution of the property pursuant to an order for distribution is completed, the court in which administration of the estate of the testator is pending has exclusive jurisdiction over all proceedings and matters concerning undistributed property, including, but not limited to, the appointment, declination, resignation, removal, bonding, and compensation of, and the delivery or transfer of the undistributed property to, a custodian. After distribution of any property is completed, the court has no further jurisdiction over the distributed property and the property shall be held subject to the California Uniform Transfers to Minors Act. **Leg.H.** Enacted Stats 1990 ch 79 §14 (AB 759), operative July 1, 1991.

Prior Law: Former Prob C §6348, similar to the present section, was added Stats 1983 ch 842 §55, amended Stats 1984 ch 243 §16, and repealed Stats 1990 ch 79 §13, operative July 1, 1991.

§6349. Construction of chapter
(a) This chapter shall not be construed as providing an exclusive method for making devises to or for the benefit of minors.

(b) Nothing in this chapter limits any provision of the California Uniform Transfers to Minors Act, Part 9 (commencing with Section 3900) of Division 4. **Leg.H.** Enacted Stats 1990 ch 79 §14 (AB 759), operative July 1, 1991.

Prior Law: Former Prob C §6349, similar to the present section, was added Stats 1983 ch 842 §55, operative January 1, 1985, amended Stats 1984 ch 243 §17, and repealed Stats 1990 ch 79 §13, operative July 1, 1991.

CHAPTER 11
UNIFORM INTERNATIONAL WILLS ACT

Definitions. §6380.
Validity of international will; Application of chapter. §6381.
Requirements for international will. §6382.
Additional provisions concerning form of will. §6383.
Certificate of authorized person. §6384.
Effect of certificate. §6385.
Revocation. §6386.
Source and construction of this chapter. §6387.
"Authorized person". §6388.
Registry system. §6389.
Chapter as restatement and continuation of former law. §6390.
[No sections of these numbers]. §6391–6399.

§6380. Definitions

In this chapter:

(a) "International will" means a will executed in conformity with Sections 6381 to 6384, inclusive.

(b) "Authorized person" and "person authorized to act in connection with international wills" means a person who by Section 6388, or by the laws of the United States including members of the diplomatic and consular service of the United States designated by Foreign Service Regulations, is empowered to supervise the execution of international wills. **Leg.H.** Enacted Stats 1990 ch 79 §14 (AB 759), operative July 1, 1991.

Prior Law: Former Prob C §6380, similar to the present section, was added Stats 1983 ch 842 §55, operative January 1, 1985, and repealed Stats 1990 ch 79 §13, operative July 1, 1991.

§6381. Validity of international will; Application of chapter

(a) A will is valid as regards form, irrespective particularly of the place where it is made, of the location of the assets and of the nationality, domicile, or residence of the testator, if it is made in the form of an international will complying with the requirements of this chapter.

(b) The invalidity of the will as an international will does not affect its formal validity as a will of another kind.

(c) This chapter does not apply to the form of testamentary dispositions made by two or more persons in one instrument. **Leg.H.** Enacted Stats 1990 ch 79 §14 (AB 759), operative July 1, 1991.

Prior Law: Former Prob C §6381, similar to the present section, was added Stats 1983 ch 842 §55, operative January 1, 1985, and repealed Stats 1990 ch 79 §13, operative July 1, 1991.

§6382. Requirements for international will

(a) The will shall be made in writing. It need not be written by the testator himself or herself. It may be written in any language, by hand or by any other means.

(b) The testator shall declare in the presence of two witnesses and of a person authorized to act in connection with international wills that the document is the testator's will and that the testator knows the contents thereof. The testator need not inform the witnesses, or the authorized person, of the contents of the will.

(c) In the presence of the witnesses, and of the authorized person, the testator shall sign the will or, if the testator has previously signed it, shall acknowledge his or her signature.

(d) If the testator is unable to sign, the absence of the testator's signature does not affect the validity of the international will if the testator indicates the reason for his or her inability to sign and the authorized person makes note thereof on the will. In that case, it is permissible for any other person present, including the authorized person or one of the witnesses, at the direction of the testator, to sign the testator's name for the testator if the authorized person makes note of this also on the will, but it is not required that any person sign the testator's name for the testator.

(e) The witnesses and the authorized person shall there and then attest the will by signing in the presence of the testator. **Leg.H.** Enacted Stats 1990 ch 79 §14 (AB 759), operative July 1, 1991.

Prior Law: Former Prob C §6382, similar to the present section, was added Stats 1983 ch 842 §55, operative January 1, 1985, and repealed Stats 1990 ch 79 §13, operative July 1, 1991.

§6383. Additional provisions concerning form of will

(a) The signatures shall be placed at the end of the will. If the will consists of several sheets, each sheet shall be signed by the testator or, if the testator is unable to sign, by the person signing on his or her behalf or, if there is no such person, by the authorized person. In addition, each sheet shall be numbered.

(b) The date of the will shall be the date of its signature by the authorized person. That date shall be noted at the end of the will by the authorized person.

(c) The authorized person shall ask the testator whether the testator wishes to make a declaration concerning the safekeeping of the will. If so and at the express request of the testator, the place where the testator intends to have the will kept shall be mentioned in the certificate provided for in Section 6384.

(d) A will executed in compliance with Section 6382 is not invalid merely because it does not comply with this section. **Leg.H.** Enacted Stats 1990 ch 79 §14 (AB 759), operative July 1, 1991.

Prior Law: Former Prob C §6383, similar to the present section, was added Stats 1983 ch 842 §55, operative January 1, 1985, and repealed Stats 1990 ch 79 §13, operative July 1, 1991.

§6384. Certificate of authorized person

The authorized person shall attach to the will a certificate to be signed by the authorized person establishing that the requirements of this chapter for valid execution of an international will have been fulfilled. The authorized person shall keep a copy of the certificate and deliver another to the testator. The certificate shall be substantially in the following form:

CERTIFICATE
(Convention of October 26, 1973)

1. I, _____ (name, address, and capacity) a person authorized to act in connection with international wills,
2. certify that on ____ (date) at ____ (place)
3. ____ (testator) _____ (name, address, date and place of birth) in my presence and that of the witnesses
4. (a) _____ (name, address, date and place of birth)
   (b) _____ (name, address, date and place of birth) has declared that the attached document is his will and that he knows the contents thereof.
5. I furthermore certify that:
6. (a) in my presence and in that of the witnesses
    (1) the testator has signed the will or has acknowledged his signature previously affixed.
    (2) following a declaration of the testator stating that he was unable to sign his will for the following reason ____, I have mentioned this declaration on the will,* and the signature has been affixed by _____ (name and address)*
7. (b) the witnesses and I have signed the will;
8. (c) each page of the will has been signed by ____ and numbered;*
9. (d) I have satisfied myself as to the identity of the testator and of the witnesses as designated above;
10. (e) the witnesses met the conditions requisite to act as such according to the law under which I am acting;
11. (f) the testator has requested me to include the following statement concerning the safekeeping of his will:*
    _____
12. PLACE OF EXECUTION
13. DATE
14. SIGNATURE and, if necessary, SEAL

_____
* to be completed if appropriate

Leg.H. Enacted Stats 1990 ch 79 §14 (AB 759), operative July 1, 1991.

Prior Law: Former Prob C §6384, similar to the present section, was added Stats 1983 ch 842 §55, operative January 1, 1985, and repealed Stats 1990 ch 79 §13, operative July 1, 1991.

§6385. Effect of certificate

In the absence of evidence to the contrary, the certificate of the authorized person is conclusive of the formal validity of the instrument as a will under this chapter. The absence or irregularity of a certificate does not affect the formal validity of a will under this chapter. **Leg.H.** Enacted Stats 1990 ch 79 §14 (AB 759), operative July 1, 1991.

Prior Law: Former Prob C §6385, similar to the present section, was added Stats 1983 ch 842 §55, operative January 1, 1985, and repealed Stats 1990 ch 79 §13, operative July 1, 1991.

§6386. Revocation

The international will is subject to the ordinary rules of revocation of wills. **Leg.H.** Enacted Stats 1990 ch 79 §14 (AB 759), operative July 1, 1991.

§6387. Source and construction of this chapter

Sections 6380 to 6386, inclusive, derive from Annex to Convention of October 26, 1973, Providing a Uniform Law on the Form of an International Will. In interpreting and applying this chapter, regard shall be had to its international origin and to the need for uniformity in its interpretation. **Leg.H.** Enacted Stats 1990 ch 79 §14 (AB 759), operative July 1, 1991.

Prior Law: Former Prob C §6387, similar to the present section, was added Stats 1983 ch 842 §55, operative January 1, 1985, and repealed Stats 1990 ch 79 §13, operative July 1, 1991.

§6388. "Authorized person"

Individuals who have been admitted to practice law before the courts of this state and who are in good standing as active law practitioners of this state are authorized persons in relation to international wills. **Leg.H.** Enacted Stats 1990 ch 79 §14 (AB 759), operative July 1, 1991.

Prior Law: Former Prob C §6388, similar to the present section, was added Stats 1983 ch 842 §55, operative January 1, 1985, and repealed Stats 1990 ch 79 §13, operative July 1, 1991.

§6389. Registry system

The Secretary of State shall establish a registry system by which authorized persons may register in a central information center information regarding the execution of international wills, keeping that information in strictest confidence until the death of the maker and then making it available to any person desiring information about any will who presents a death certificate or other satisfactory evidence of the testator's death to the center. Information that may be received, preserved in confidence until death, and reported as indicated is limited to the name, social security or other individual identifying number established by law, if any, address, date and place of birth of the testator, and the intended place of deposit or safekeeping of the instrument pending the death of the maker. The Secretary of State, at the request of the authorized person, may cause the information it receives about execution of any international will to be transmitted to the registry system of another jurisdiction as identified by the testator, if that other system adheres to rules protecting the confidentiality of the information similar to those established in this state. **Leg.H.** Enacted Stats 1990 ch 79 §14 (AB 759), operative July 1, 1991.

Prior Law: Former Prob C §6389, similar to the present section, was added Stats 1983 ch 842 §55, operative January 1, 1985, and repealed Stats 1990 ch 79 §13, operative July 1, 1991.

§6390. Chapter as restatement and continuation of former law

After December 31, 1984, a reference in a written instrument, including a will, to the former law (repealed by Chapter 892 of the Statutes of 1984) shall be deemed to be a reference to the corresponding provision of this chapter. **Leg.H.** Enacted Stats 1990 ch 79 §14 (AB 759), operative July 1, 1991.

Prior Law: Former Prob C §6390, similar to the present section, was added Stats 1984 ch 892 §39.7 and repealed Stats 1990 ch 79 §13, operative July 1, 1991.

§§6391–6399. [No sections of these numbers]

PART 2
INTESTATE SUCCESSION

Chapter 1. Intestate Succession Generally.
Chapter 2. Parent and Child Relationship.

CHAPTER 1
INTESTATE SUCCESSION GENERALLY

Property subject to intestacy provisions. §6400.
Intestate share of surviving spouse. §6401.
Intestate share of heirs other than surviving spouse. §6402.
Portion of decedent's estate attributable to decedent's predeceased spouse. §6402.5.
Requirement that heir survive decedent. §6403.
Escheat if no taker. §6404.
Relatives of halfblood. §6406.
Unborn relatives of decedent. §6407.
Advancements. §6409.
Debt owed to decedent. §6410.
Non-citizens or non-nationals. §6411.
Dower and curtesy not recognized. §6412.
Person related to decedent through two lines of relationships. §6413.
Testator's death before January 1, 1985. §6414.

§6400. Property subject to intestacy provisions

Any part of the estate of a decedent not effectively disposed of by will passes to the decedent's heirs as prescribed in this part. **Leg.H.** Enacted Stats 1990 ch 79 §14 (AB 759), operative July 1, 1991.

Prior Law: Former Prob C §6400, similar to the present section, was added Stats 1983 ch 842 §55, operative January 1, 1985, and repealed Stats 1990 ch 79 §13, operative July 1, 1991.

§6401. Intestate share of surviving spouse

(a) As to community property, the intestate share of the surviving spouse is the one-half of the community property that belongs to the decedent under Section 100.

(b) As to quasi-community property, the intestate share of the surviving spouse is the one-half of the quasi-community property that belongs to the decedent under Section 101.

(c) As to separate property, the intestate share of the surviving spouse is as follows:

(1) The entire intestate estate if the decedent did not leave any surviving issue, parent, brother, sister, or issue of a deceased brother or sister.

(2) One-half of the intestate estate in the following cases:

(A) Where the decedent leaves only one child or the issue of one deceased child.

(B) Where the decedent leaves no issue, but leaves a parent or parents or their issue or the issue of either of them.

(3) One-third of the intestate estate in the following cases:

(A) Where the decedent leaves more than one child.

(B) Where the decedent leaves one child and the issue of one or more deceased children.

(C) Where the decedent leaves issue of two or more deceased children.

Leg.H. Enacted Stats 1990 ch 79 §14 (AB 759), operative July 1, 1991. Amended Stats 2002 ch 447 §1 (AB 2216), operative July 1, 2003; Stats 2014 ch 913 §32 (AB 2747), effective January 1, 2015.

2003 Note: On or before March 1, 2003, the Secretary of State shall send the following letter to the mailing address on file of each registered domestic partner who registered prior to January 1, 2003:

"Dear Registered Domestic Partner:

This letter is being sent to all persons who have registered with the Secretary of State as a domestic partner.

As of July 1, 2003, California's law of intestate succession will change. The intestate succession law specifies what happens to a person's property when that person dies without a will, trust, or other estate plan.

Under existing law, if a domestic partner dies without a will, trust, or other estate plan, a surviving domestic partner cannot inherit any of the deceased partner's separate property. Instead, surviving relatives, including, for example, children, brothers, sisters, nieces, nephews, or parents may inherit the deceased partner's separate property.

Under the law to take effect July 1, 2003, if a domestic partner dies without a will, trust, or other estate plan, the surviving domestic partner will inherit the deceased partner's separate property in the same manner as a surviving spouse. This change will mean that the surviving domestic partner would inherit a third, a half, or all of the deceased partner's separate property, depending on whether the deceased domestic partner has surviving children or other relatives. This change does not affect any community or quasi-community property that the deceased partner may have had.

This change in the intestate succession law will not affect you if you have a will, trust, or other estate plan.

If you do not have a will, trust, or other estate plan and you do not wish to have your domestic partner inherit your separate property in the manner provided by the revised law, you may prepare a will, trust, or other estate plan, or terminate your domestic partnership.

Under existing law, your domestic partnership is automatically terminated if you or your partner married or died while you were registered as domestic partners. It is also terminated by you sending your partner or your partner sending to you by certified mail a notice terminating the domestic partnership, or by you and your partner no longer sharing a common residence. In all cases, you are required to file a Notice of Termination of Domestic Partnership with the Secretary of State in order to establish the actual date of termination of the domestic partnership. You can obtain a Notice of Termination of Domestic Partnership from the Secretary of State's office.

If your domestic partnership has terminated because you sent your partner or your partner sent to you a notice of termination of your domestic partnership, you must immediately file a Notice of Termination of Domestic Partnership. If you do not file that notice, your former domestic partner may inherit under the new law. However, if your domestic partnership has terminated because you or your partner married or you and your partner no longer share a common residence, neither you nor your former partner may inherit from the other under this new law.

If you have any questions about this change, please consult an estate planning attorney. If you cannot find an estate planning attorney in your locale, please contact your county bar association for a referral.

Sincerely,
The Secretary of State"

Stats 2002 ch 447 §3 (AB 2216); 2003 ch 421 §13 (AB 205).

Prior Law: Former Prob C §6401, similar to the present section, was added Stats 1983 ch 842 §55, operative January 1, 1985, amended Stats 1984 ch 892 §40, and repealed Stats 1990 ch 79 §13, operative July 1, 1991.

§6402. Intestate share of heirs other than surviving spouse

Except as provided in Section 6402.5, the part of the intestate estate not passing to the surviving spouse, under Section 6401, or the entire intestate estate if there is no surviving spouse, passes as follows:

(a) To the issue of the decedent, the issue taking equally if they are all of the same degree of kinship to the decedent, but if of unequal degree those of more remote degree take in the manner provided in Section 240.

(b) If there is no surviving issue, to the decedent's parent or parents equally.

(c) If there is no surviving issue or parent, to the issue of the parents or either of them, the issue taking equally if they are all of the same degree of kinship to the decedent, but if of unequal degree those of more remote degree take in the manner provided in Section 240.

(d) If there is no surviving issue, parent or issue of a parent, but the decedent is survived by one or more grandparents or issue of grandparents, to the grandparent or grandparents equally, or to the issue of those grandparents if there is no surviving grandparent, the issue taking equally if they are all of the same degree of kinship to the decedent, but if of unequal degree those of more remote degree take in the manner provided in Section 240.

(e) If there is no surviving issue, parent or issue of a parent, grandparent or issue of a grandparent, but the decedent is survived by the issue of a predeceased spouse, to that issue, the issue taking equally if they are all of the same degree of kinship to the predeceased spouse, but if of unequal degree those of more remote degree take in the manner provided in Section 240.

(f) If there is no surviving issue, parent or issue of a parent, grandparent or issue of a grandparent, or issue of a predeceased spouse, but the decedent is survived by next of kin, to the next of kin in equal degree, but where there are two or more collateral kindred in equal degree who claim through different ancestors, those who claim through the nearest ancestor are preferred to those claiming through an ancestor more remote.

(g) If there is no surviving next of kin of the decedent and no surviving issue of a predeceased spouse of the decedent, but the decedent is survived by the parents of a predeceased spouse or the issue of those parents, to the parent or parents equally, or to the issue of those parents if both are deceased, the issue taking equally if they are all of the same degree of kinship to the predeceased spouse, but if of unequal degree those of more remote degree take in the manner provided in Section 240. **Leg.H.** Enacted Stats 1990 ch 79 §14 (AB 759), operative July 1, 1991. Amended Stats 2002 ch 447 §2 (AB 2216), operative July 1, 2003; Stats 2014 ch 913 §32.5 (AB 2747), effective January 1, 2015.

Prior Law: Former Prob C §6402, similar to the present section, was added Stats 1983 ch 842 §55, operative January 1, 1985, amended Stats 1984 ch 892 §41, Stats 1985 ch 982 §19, and repealed Stats 1990 ch 79 §13, operative July 1, 1991.

§6402.5. Portion of decedent's estate attributable to decedent's predeceased spouse

(a) For purposes of distributing real property under this section if the decedent had a predeceased spouse who died not more than 15 years before the decedent and there is no surviving spouse or issue of the decedent, the portion of the decedent's estate attributable to the decedent's predeceased spouse passes as follows:

(1) If the decedent is survived by issue of the predeceased spouse, to the surviving issue of the predeceased spouse; if they are all of the same degree of kinship to the predeceased spouse they take equally, but if of unequal degree those of more remote degree take in the manner provided in Section 240.

(2) If there is no surviving issue of the predeceased spouse but the decedent is survived by a parent or parents of the predeceased spouse, to the predeceased spouse's surviving parent or parents equally.

(3) If there is no surviving issue or parent of the predeceased spouse but the decedent is survived by issue of a parent of the predeceased spouse, to the surviving issue of the parents of the predeceased spouse or either of them, the issue taking equally if they are all of the same degree of kinship to the predeceased spouse, but if of unequal degree those of more remote degree take in the manner provided in Section 240.

(4) If the decedent is not survived by issue, parent, or issue of a parent of the predeceased spouse, to the next of kin of the decedent in the manner provided in Section 6402.

(5) If the portion of the decedent's estate attributable to the decedent's predeceased spouse would otherwise escheat to the state because there is no kin of the decedent to take under Section 6402, the portion of the decedent's estate attributable to the predeceased spouse passes to the next of kin of the predeceased spouse who shall take in the same manner as the next of kin of the decedent take under Section 6402.

(b) For purposes of distributing personal property under this section if the decedent had a predeceased spouse who died not more than five years before the decedent, and there is no surviving spouse or issue of the decedent, the portion of the decedent's estate attributable to the decedent's predeceased spouse passes as follows:

(1) If the decedent is survived by issue of the predeceased spouse, to the surviving issue of the predeceased spouse; if they are all of the same degree of kinship to the predeceased spouse they take equally, but if of unequal degree those of more remote degree take in the manner provided in Section 240.

(2) If there is no surviving issue of the predeceased spouse but the decedent is survived by a parent or parents of the predeceased spouse, to the predeceased spouse's surviving parent or parents equally.

(3) If there is no surviving issue or parent of the predeceased spouse but the decedent is survived by issue of a parent of the predeceased spouse, to the surviving issue of the parents of the predeceased spouse or either of them, the issue taking equally if they are all of the same degree of kinship to the predeceased spouse, but if of unequal degree those of more remote degree take in the manner provided in Section 240.

(4) If the decedent is not survived by issue, parent, or issue of a parent of the predeceased spouse, to the next of kin of the decedent in the manner provided in Section 6402.

(5) If the portion of the decedent's estate attributable to the decedent's predeceased spouse would otherwise escheat to the state because there is no kin of the decedent to take under Section 6402, the portion of the decedent's estate attributable to the predeceased spouse passes to the next of kin of the predeceased spouse who shall take in the same manner as the next of kin of the decedent take under Section 6402.

(c) For purposes of disposing of personal property under subdivision (b), the claimant heir bears the burden of proof to show the exact personal property to be disposed of to the heir.

(d) For purposes of providing notice under any provision of this code with respect to an estate that may include personal property subject to distribution under subdivision (b), if the aggregate fair market value of tangible and intangible personal property with a written record of title or ownership in the estate is believed in good faith by the petitioning party to be less than ten thousand dollars ($10,000), the petitioning party need not give notice to the issue or next of kin of the predeceased spouse. If the personal property is subsequently determined to have an aggregate fair market value in excess of ten thousand dollars ($10,000), notice shall be given to the issue or next of kin of the predeceased spouse as provided by law.

(e) For the purposes of disposing of property pursuant to subdivision (b), "personal property" means that personal property in which there is a written record of title or ownership and the value of which in the aggregate is ten thousand dollars ($10,000) or more.

(f) For the purposes of this section, the "portion of the decedent's estate attributable to the decedent's predeceased spouse" means all of the following property in the decedent's estate:

(1) One-half of the community property in existence at the time of the death of the predeceased spouse.

(2) One-half of any community property, in existence at the time of death of the predeceased spouse, which was given to the decedent by the predeceased spouse by way of gift, descent, or devise.

(3) That portion of any community property in which the predeceased spouse had any incident of ownership and which vested in the decedent upon the death of the predeceased spouse by right of survivorship.

(4) Any separate property of the predeceased spouse which came to the decedent by gift, descent, or devise of the predeceased spouse or which vested in the decedent upon the death of the predeceased spouse by right of survivorship.

(g) For the purposes of this section, quasi-community property shall be treated the same as community property.

(h) For the purposes of this section:

(1) Relatives of the predeceased spouse conceived before the decedent's death but born thereafter inherit as if they had been born in the lifetime of the decedent.

(2) A person who is related to the predeceased spouse through two lines of relationship is entitled to only a single share based on the relationship which would entitle the person to the larger share. **Leg.H.** Enacted Stats 1990 ch 79 §14 (AB 759), operative July 1, 1991.

Prior Law: Former Prob C §6402.5, similar to the present section, was added Stats 1983 ch 842 §55, operative January 1, 1985, amended Stats 1985 ch 982 §20, Stats 1986 ch 873 §1, and repealed Stats 1990 ch 79 §13, operative July 1, 1991.

§6403. Requirement that heir survive decedent

(a) A person who fails to survive the decedent by 120 hours is deemed to have predeceased the decedent for the purpose of intestate succession, and the heirs are determined accordingly. If it cannot be established by clear and convincing evidence that a person who would otherwise be an heir has survived the decedent by 120 hours, it is deemed that the person failed to survive for the required period. The requirement of this section that a person who survives the decedent must survive the decedent by 120 hours does not apply if the application of the 120-hour survival requirement would result in the escheat of property to the state.

(b) This section does not apply to the case where any of the persons upon whose time of death the disposition of property depends died before January 1, 1990, and such case continues to be governed by the law applicable before January 1, 1990. **Leg.H.** Enacted Stats 1990 ch 79 §14 (AB 759), operative July 1, 1991.

Prior Law: Former Prob C §6403, similar to the present section, was added Stats 1983 ch 842 §55, operative January 1, 1985, amended Stats 1989 ch 544 §5, and repealed Stats 1990 ch 79 §13, operative July 1, 1991.

§6404. Escheat if no taker

Part 4 (commencing with Section 6800) (escheat) applies if there is no taker of the intestate estate under the provisions of this part. **Leg.H.** Enacted Stats 1990 ch 79 §14 (AB 759), operative July 1, 1991.

Prior Law: Former Prob C §6404, similar to the present section, was added Stats 1983 ch 842 §55, operative January 1, 1985, and repealed Stats 1990 ch 79 §13, operative July 1, 1991.

§6406. Relatives of halfblood

Except as provided in Section 6451, relatives of the halfblood inherit the same share they would inherit if they were of the whole blood. **Leg.H.**

Enacted Stats 1990 ch 79 §14 (AB 759), operative July 1, 1991. Amended Stats 1993 ch 529 §3 (AB 1137).

Prior Law: Former Prob C §6406, similar to the present section, was added Stats 1983 ch 842 §55, operative January 1, 1985, and repealed Stats 1990 ch 79 §13, operative July 1, 1991.

§6407. Unborn relatives of decedent

Relatives of the decedent conceived before the decedent's death but born thereafter inherit as if they had been born in the lifetime of the decedent. **Leg.H.** Enacted Stats 1990 ch 79 §14 (AB 759), operative July 1, 1991.

Prior Law: Former Prob C 6407, similar to the present section, was added Stats 1983 ch 842 §55, operative January 1, 1985, and repealed Stats 1990 ch 79 §13, operative July 1, 1991.

§6408. [Section repealed 1993]

Leg.H. Enacted Stats 1990 ch 79 §14 (AB 759), operative July 1, 1991. Amended Stats 1992 ch 163 §132 (AB 2641), operative January 1, 1994. Repealed Stats 1993 ch 529 §4 (AB 1137). See Prob C §§6450 et seq.

Prior Law: Former Prob C §6408, similar to present Prob C §§6450 et seq., was added Stats 1983 ch 842 §55, operative January 1, 1985, amended Stats 1984 ch 892 §41.5, Stats 1985 ch 982 §21, and repealed Stats 1990 ch 79 §13, operative July 1, 1991.

§6409. Advancements

(a) If a person dies intestate as to all or part of his or her estate, property the decedent gave during lifetime to an heir is treated as an advancement against that heir's share of the intestate estate only if one of the following conditions is satisfied:

(1) The decedent declares in a contemporaneous writing that the gift is an advancement against the heir's share of the estate or that its value is to be deducted from the value of the heir's share of the estate.

(2) The heir acknowledges in writing that the gift is to be so deducted or is an advancement or that its value is to be deducted from the value of the heir's share of the estate.

(b) Subject to subdivision (c), the property advanced is to be valued as of the time the heir came into possession or enjoyment of the property or as of the time of death of the decedent, whichever occurs first.

(c) If the value of the property advanced is expressed in the contemporaneous writing of the decedent, or in an acknowledgment of the heir made contemporaneously with the advancement, that value is conclusive in the division and distribution of the intestate estate.

(d) If the recipient of the property advanced fails to survive the decedent, the property is not taken into account in computing the intestate share to be received by the recipient's issue unless the declaration or acknowledgment provides otherwise. **Leg.H.** Enacted Stats 1990 ch 79 §14 (AB 759), operative July 1, 1991. Amended Stats 2002 ch 138 §8 (AB 1784), effective January 1, 2003.

Prior Law: Former Prob C §6409, similar to the present section, was added Stats 1983 ch 842 §55, operative January 1, 1985, amended Stats 1984 ch 892 §43, and repealed Stats 1990 ch 79 §13, operative July 1, 1991.

§6410. Debt owed to decedent

(a) A debt owed to the decedent is not charged against the intestate share of any person except the debtor.

(b) If the debtor fails to survive the decedent, the debt is not taken into account in computing the intestate share of the debtor's issue. **Leg.H.** Enacted Stats 1990 ch 79 §14 (AB 759), operative July 1, 1991.

Prior Law: Former Prob C §6410, similar to the present section, was added Stats 1983 ch 842 §55, operative January 1, 1985, and repealed Stats 1990 ch 79 §13, operative July 1, 1991.

§6411. Non-citizens or non-nationals

No person is disqualified to take as an heir because that person or a person through whom the person claims is or has been a person who is not a citizen or national of the United States. **Leg.H.** Enacted Stats 1990 ch 79 §14 (AB 759), operative July 1, 1991. Amended Stats 2021 ch 296 §54 (AB 1096), effective January 1, 2022.

Prior Law: Former Prob C §6411, similar to the present section, was added Stats 1983 ch 842 §55, operative January 1, 1985, and repealed Stats 1990 ch 79 §13, operative July 1, 1991.

§6412. Dower and curtesy not recognized

Except to the extent provided in Section 120, the estates of dower and curtesy are not recognized. **Leg.H.** Enacted Stats 1990 ch 79 §14 (AB 759), operative July 1, 1991.

Prior Law: Former Prob C §6412, similar to the present section, was added Stats 1983 ch 842 §55, operative January 1, 1985, amended Stats 1984 ch 892 §44, and repealed Stats 1990 ch 79 §13, operative July 1, 1991.

§6413. Person related to decedent through two lines of relationships

A person who is related to the decedent through two lines of relationship is entitled to only a single share based on the relationship which would entitle the person to the larger share. **Leg.H.** Enacted Stats 1990 ch 79 §14 (AB 759), operative July 1, 1991.

Prior Law: Former Prob C §6413, similar to the present section, was added Stats 1983 ch 842 §55, operative January 1, 1985, and repealed Stats 1990 ch 79 §13, operative July 1, 1991.

§6414. Testator's death before January 1, 1985

(a) Except as provided in subdivision (b), this part does not apply where the decedent died before January 1, 1985, and the law applicable prior to January 1, 1985, continues to apply where the decedent died before January 1, 1985.

(b) Section 6412 applies whether the decedent died before, on, or after January 1, 1985.

(c) Where any of the following provisions is applied in a case where the decedent died before January 1, 1985, any reference in that provision to this part shall be deemed to be a reference to former Division 2 (commencing with Section 200) which was repealed by Section 19 of Chapter 842 of the Statutes of 1983:

(1) Section 377 of the Code of Civil Procedure.

(2) Section 3524 of the Penal Code. **Leg.H.** Enacted Stats 1990 ch 79 §14 (AB 759), operative July 1, 1991.

Prior Law: Former Prob C §6414, similar to the present section, was added Stats 1984 ch 892 §44.5, amended Stats 1989 ch 21 §12, effective May 25, 1989, operative July 1, 1989, and repealed Stats 1990 ch 79 §13, operative July 1, 1991.

CHAPTER 2
PARENT AND CHILD RELATIONSHIP

Circumstances for existence of relationship. §6450.
Effect of adoption. §6451.
Inheritance from or through child on basis of relationship; When parent deemed to predecease child. §6452.
"Natural parent". §6453.
Foster parent or stepparent. §6454.
Equitable adoption. §6455.

§6450. Circumstances for existence of relationship

Subject to the provisions of this chapter, a relationship of parent and child exists for the purpose of determining intestate succession by, through, or from a person in the following circumstances:

(a) The relationship of parent and child exists between a person and the person's natural parents, regardless of the marital status of the natural parents.

(b) The relationship of parent and child exists between an adopted person and the person's adopting parent or parents. **Leg.H.** Added Stats 1993 ch 529 §5 (AB 1137).

§6451. Effect of adoption

(a) An adoption severs the relationship of parent and child between an adopted person and a natural parent of the adopted person unless both of the following requirements are satisfied:

(1) The natural parent and the adopted person lived together at any time as parent and child, or the natural parent was married to or cohabiting with the other natural parent at the time the person was conceived and died before the person's birth.

(2) The adoption was by the spouse of either of the natural parents or after the death of either of the natural parents.

(b) Neither a natural parent nor a relative of a natural parent, except for a wholeblood brother or sister of the adopted person or the issue of that brother or sister, inherits from or through the adopted person on the basis of a parent and child relationship between the adopted person and the natural parent that satisfies the requirements of paragraphs (1) and (2) of subdivision (a), unless the adoption is by the spouse or surviving spouse of that parent.

(c) For the purpose of this section, a prior adoptive parent and child relationship is treated as a natural parent and child relationship. **Leg.H.** Added Stats 1993 ch 529 §5 (AB 1137).

§6452. Inheritance from or through child on basis of relationship; When parent deemed to predecease child

(a) A parent does not inherit from or through a child on the basis of the parent and child relationship if any of the following apply:

(1) The parent's parental rights were terminated and the parent-child relationship was not judicially reestablished.

(2) The parent did not acknowledge the child.

(3) The parent left the child during the child's minority without an effort to provide for the child's support or without communication from the parent, for at least seven consecutive years that continued until the end of the child's minority, with the intent on the part of the parent to abandon the child. The failure to provide support or to communicate for the prescribed period is presumptive evidence of an intent to abandon.

(b) A parent who does not inherit from or through the child as provided in subdivision (a) shall be deemed to have predeceased the child, and the intestate estate shall pass as otherwise required under Section 6402. **Leg.H.** Added Stats 2013 ch 39 §2 (AB 490), effective January 1, 2014.

Former Sections: Former Prob C §6452, relating to inheritance from or through child born out of wedlock, was added Stats 1993 ch 529 §5 (AB 1137), amended Stats 1996 ch 862 §15 (AB 2751) and repealed Stats 2013 ch 39 §1 (AB 490), effective January 1, 2014.

Prior Law: Former Prob C §6452, relating to inheritance from or through child born out of wedlock, was added Stats 1993 ch 529 §5 (AB 1137), amended Stats 1996 ch 862 §15 (AB 2751), and repealed Stats 2013 ch 39 §1 (AB 490), effective January 1, 2014.

§6453. "Natural parent"

For the purpose of determining whether a person is a "natural parent" as that term is used in this chapter:

(a) A natural parent and child relationship is established where that relationship is presumed and not rebutted pursuant to the Uniform Parentage Act (Part 3 (commencing with Section 7600) of Division 12 of the Family Code).

(b) A natural parent and child relationship may be established pursuant to any other provisions of the Uniform Parentage Act, except that the relationship may not be established by an action under subdivision (c) of Section 7630 of the Family Code unless any of the following conditions exist:

(1) A court order was entered during the parent's lifetime declaring parentage.

(2) Parentage is established by clear and convincing evidence that the parent has openly held out the child as that parent's own.

(3) It was impossible for the parent to hold out the child as that parent's own and parentage is established by clear and convincing evidence, which may include genetic DNA evidence acquired during the parent's lifetime.

(c) A natural parent and child relationship may be established pursuant to Section 249.5. **Leg.H.** Added Stats 1993 ch 529 §5 (AB 1137). Amended Stats 2004 ch 775 §9 (AB 1910); Stats 2018 ch 116 §1 (SB 1436), effective January 1, 2019.

§6454. Foster parent or stepparent

For the purpose of determining intestate succession by a person or the person's issue from or through a foster parent or stepparent, the relationship of parent and child exists between that person and the person's foster parent or stepparent if both of the following requirements are satisfied:

(a) The relationship began during the person's minority and continued throughout the joint lifetimes of the person and the person's foster parent or stepparent.

(b) It is established by clear and convincing evidence that the foster parent or stepparent would have adopted the person but for a legal barrier. **Leg.H.** Added Stats 1993 ch 529 §5 (AB 1137).

§6455. Equitable adoption

Nothing in this chapter affects or limits application of the judicial doctrine of equitable adoption for the benefit of the child or the child's issue. **Leg.H.** Added Stats 1993 ch 529 §5 (AB 1137).

PART 3
FAMILY PROTECTION

Chapter 1. Temporary Possession of Family Dwelling and Exempt Property.
Chapter 2. Setting Aside Exempt Property Other Than Family Dwelling.
Chapter 3. Setting Aside Probate Homestead.
Chapter 4. Family Allowance.
Chapter 6. Small Estate Set-Aside.

CHAPTER 1
TEMPORARY POSSESSION OF FAMILY DWELLING AND EXEMPT PROPERTY

Temporary right to remain in possession. §6500.
Petition for order; Notice of hearing. §6501.

§6500. Temporary right to remain in possession
Until the inventory is filed and for a period of 60 days thereafter, or for such other period as may be ordered by the court for good cause on petition therefor, the decedent's surviving spouse and minor children are entitled to remain in possession of the family dwelling, the wearing apparel of the family, the household furniture, and the other property of the decedent exempt from enforcement of a money judgment. **Leg.H.** Enacted Stats 1990 ch 79 §14 (AB 759), operative July 1, 1991.

Prior Law: Former Prob C §6500, similar to the present section, was added Stats 1983 ch 842 §55, operative January 1, 1985, and repealed Stats 1990 ch 79 §13, operative July 1, 1991.

§6501. Petition for order; Notice of hearing
A petition for an order under Section 6500 may be filed by any interested person. Notice of the hearing on the petition shall be given as provided in Section 1220. **Leg.H.** Enacted Stats 1990 ch 79 §14 (AB 759), operative July 1, 1991.

Prior Law: Former Prob C §6501, similar to the present section, was added Stats 1983 ch 842 §55, operative January 1, 1985, amended Stats 1987 ch 923 §87, operative July 1, 1988, and repealed Stats 1990 ch 79 §13, operative July 1, 1991.

CHAPTER 2
SETTING ASIDE EXEMPT PROPERTY OTHER THAN FAMILY DWELLING

Setting aside exempt property. §6510.
Petition for order; Notice of hearing. §6511.

§6510. Setting aside exempt property
Upon the filing of the inventory or at any subsequent time during the administration of the estate, the court in its discretion may on petition therefor set apart all or any part of the property of the decedent exempt from enforcement of a money judgment, other than the family dwelling, to any one or more of the following:
(a) The surviving spouse.
(b) The minor children of the decedent. **Leg.H.** Enacted Stats 1990 ch 79 §14 (AB 759), operative July 1, 1991.

Prior Law: Former Prob C §6510, similar to the present section, was added Stats 1983 ch 842 §55, operative January 1, 1985, and repealed Stats 1990 ch 79 §13, operative July 1, 1991.

§6511. Petition for order; Notice of hearing
A petition for an order under Section 6510 may be filed by any interested person. Notice of the hearing on the petition shall be given as provided in Section 1220. **Leg.H.** Enacted Stats 1990 ch 79 §14 (AB 759), operative July 1, 1991.

Prior Law: Former Prob C §6511, similar to the present section, was added Stats 1983 ch 842 §55, operative January 1, 1985, amended Stats 1987 ch 923 §88, operative July 1, 1988, and repealed Stats 1990 ch 79 §13, operative July 1, 1991.

CHAPTER 3
SETTING ASIDE PROBATE HOMESTEAD

Court may select and set aside probate homestead. §6520.
Persons for whose use homestead to be set apart. §6521.
Property out of which homestead selected. §6522.
Factors to be considered in setting apart homestead. §6523.
Duration of homestead; Rights of parties. §6524.
Petition; Notice of hearing. §6525.
Liability of property set apart as homestead for claims against estate. §6526.
Modification or termination of homestead right. §6527.
Declared homestead not affected. §6528.

§6520. Court may select and set aside probate homestead
Upon the filing of the inventory or at any subsequent time during the administration of the estate, the court in its discretion may on petition therefor select and set apart one probate homestead in the manner provided in this chapter. **Leg.H.** Enacted Stats 1990 ch 79 §14 (AB 759), operative July 1, 1991.

Prior Law: Former Prob C §6520, similar to the present section, was added Stats 1983 ch 842 §55, operative January 1, 1985, and repealed Stats 1990 ch 79 §13, operative July 1, 1991.

§6521. Persons for whose use homestead to be set apart
The probate homestead shall be set apart for the use of one or more of the following persons:
(a) The surviving spouse.
(b) The minor children of the decedent. **Leg.H.** Enacted Stats 1990 ch 79 §14 (AB 759), operative July 1, 1991.

Prior Law: Former Prob C §6521, similar to the present section, was added Stats 1983 ch 842 §55, operative January 1, 1985, and repealed Stats 1990 ch 79 §13, operative July 1, 1991.

§6522. Property out of which homestead selected
(a) The probate homestead shall be selected out of the following property, giving first preference to the community and quasi-community property of, or property owned in common by, the decedent and the person entitled to have the homestead set apart:
(1) If the homestead is set apart for the use of the surviving spouse or for the use of the surviving spouse and minor children, out of community property or quasi-community property.
(2) If the homestead is set apart for the use of the surviving spouse or for the use of the minor children or for the use of the surviving spouse and minor children, out of property owned in common by the decedent and the persons entitled to have the homestead set apart, or out of the separate property of the decedent or, if the decedent was not married at the time of death, out of property owned by the decedent.
(b) The probate homestead shall not be selected out of property the right to possession of which is vested in a third person unless the third person consents thereto. As used in this subdivision, "third person" means a person whose right to possession of the property (1) existed at the time of the death of the decedent or came into existence upon the death of the decedent and (2) was not created by testate or intestate succession from the decedent. **Leg.H.** Enacted Stats 1990 ch 79 §14 (AB 759), operative July 1, 1991. Amended Stats 1990 ch 710 §17 (SB 1775), operative July 1, 1991.

Prior Law: Former Prob C §6522, similar to the present section, was added Stats 1983 ch 842 §55, operative January 1, 1985, and repealed Stats 1990 ch 79 §13, operative July 1, 1991.

§6523. Factors to be considered in setting apart homestead
(a) In selecting and setting apart the probate homestead, the court shall consider the needs of the surviving spouse and minor children, the liens and encumbrances on the property, the claims of creditors, the needs of the heirs or devisees of the decedent, and the intent of the decedent with respect to the property in the estate and the estate plan of the decedent as expressed in inter vivos and testamentary transfers or by other means.
(b) The court, in light of subdivision (a) and other relevant considerations as determined by the court in its discretion, shall:
(1) Select as a probate homestead the most appropriate property available that is suitable for that use, including in addition to the dwelling itself such adjoining property as appears reasonable.
(2) Set the probate homestead so selected apart for such a term and upon such conditions (including, but not limited to, assignment by the homestead recipient of other property to the heirs or devisees of the property set apart as a homestead) as appear proper. **Leg.H.** Enacted Stats 1990 ch 79 §14 (AB 759), operative July 1, 1991.

Prior Law: Former Prob C §6523, similar to the present section, was added Stats 1983 ch 842 §55, operative January 1, 1985, and repealed Stats 1990 ch 79 §13, operative July 1, 1991.

§6524. Duration of homestead; Rights of parties

The property set apart as a probate homestead shall be set apart only for a limited period, to be designated in the order, and in no case beyond the lifetime of the surviving spouse, or, as to a child, beyond its minority. Subject to the probate homestead right, the property of the decedent remains subject to administration including testate and intestate succession. The rights of the parties during the period for which the probate homestead is set apart are governed, to the extent applicable, by the Legal Estates Principal and Income Law, Chapter 2.6 (commencing with Section 731) of Title 2 of Part 1 of Division 2 of the Civil Code. **Leg.H.** Enacted Stats 1990 ch 79 §14 (AB 759), operative July 1, 1991.

Prior Law: Former Prob C §6524, similar to the present section, was added Stats 1983 ch 842 §55, operative January 1, 1985, and repealed Stats 1990 ch 79 §13, operative July 1, 1991.

§6525. Petition; Notice of hearing

(a) A petition to select and set apart a probate homestead may be filed by any interested person.

(b) Notice of the hearing on the petition shall be given as provided in Section 1220 to all of the following persons:

(1) Each person listed in Section 1220.

(2) Each known heir whose interest in the estate would be affected by the petition.

(3) Each known devisee whose interest in the estate would be affected by the petition. **Leg.H.** Enacted Stats 1990 ch 79 §14 (AB 759), operative July 1, 1991.

Prior Law: Former Prob C §6525, similar to the present section, was added Stats 1983 ch 842 §55, operative January 1, 1985, amended Stats 1987 ch 923 §89, operative July 1, 1988, and repealed Stats 1990 ch 79 §13, operative July 1, 1991.

§6526. Liability of property set apart as homestead for claims against estate

(a) Property of the decedent set apart as a probate homestead is liable for claims against the estate of the decedent, subject to the probate homestead right. The probate homestead right in property of the decedent is liable for claims that are secured by liens and encumbrances on the property at the time of the decedent's death but is exempt to the extent of the homestead exemption as to any claim that would have been subject to a homestead exemption at the time of the decedent's death under Article 4 (commencing with Section 704.710) of Chapter 4 of Division 2 of Title 9 of Part 2 of the Code of Civil Procedure.

(b) The probate homestead right in the property of the decedent is not liable for claims against the person for whose use the probate homestead is set apart.

(c) Property of the decedent set apart as a probate homestead is liable for claims against the testate or intestate successors of the decedent or other successors to the property after administration, subject to the probate homestead right. **Leg.H.** Enacted Stats 1990 ch 79 §14 (AB 759), operative July 1, 1991.

Prior Law: Former Prob C §6526, similar to the present section, was added Stats 1983 ch 842 §55, operative January 1, 1985, and repealed Stats 1990 ch 79 §13, operative July 1, 1991.

§6527. Modification or termination of homestead right

(a) The court may by order modify the term or conditions of the probate homestead right or terminate the probate homestead right at any time prior to entry of an order for final distribution of the decedent's estate if in the court's discretion to do so appears appropriate under the circumstances of the case.

(b) A petition for an order under this section may be filed by any of the following:

(1) The person for whose use the probate homestead is set apart.

(2) The testate or intestate successors of the decedent or other successors to the property set apart as a probate homestead.

(3) Persons having claims secured by liens or encumbrances on the property set apart as a probate homestead.

(c) Notice of the hearing on the petition shall be given to all the persons listed in subdivision (b) as provided in Section 1220. **Leg.H.** Enacted Stats 1990 ch 79 §14 (AB 759), operative July 1, 1991.

Prior Law: Former Prob C §6527, similar to the present section, was added Stats 1983 ch 842 §55, operative January 1, 1985, amended Stats 1987 ch 923 §90, operative July 1, 1988, Stats 1988 ch 1199 §77.5, operative July 1, 1989, and repealed Stats 1990 ch 79 §13, operative July 1, 1991.

§6528. Declared homestead not affected

Nothing in this chapter terminates or otherwise affects a declaration of homestead by, or for the benefit of, a surviving spouse or minor child of the decedent with respect to the community, quasi-community, or common interest of the surviving spouse or minor child in property in the decedent's estate. This section is declaratory of, and does not constitute a change in, existing law. **Leg.H.** Enacted Stats 1990 ch 79 §14 (AB 759), operative July 1, 1991.

Prior Law: Former Prob C §6528, similar to the present section, was added Stats 1983 ch 842 §55, operative January 1, 1985, and repealed Stats 1990 ch 79 §13, operative July 1, 1991.

CHAPTER 4
FAMILY ALLOWANCE

Persons for whom family allowance may be made. §6540.
Grant or modification; Petition; Notice of hearing. §6541.
Time of commencement of allowance. §6542.
Termination of allowance. §6543.
Cost of proceeding paid as expense of administration. §6544.
No stay on appeal if undertaking furnished. §6545.

§6540. Persons for whom family allowance may be made

(a) The following are entitled to such reasonable family allowance out of the estate as is necessary for their maintenance according to their circumstances during administration of the estate:

(1) The surviving spouse of the decedent.

(2) Minor children of the decedent.

(3) Adult children of the decedent who are physically or mentally incapacitated from earning a living and were actually dependent in whole or in part upon the decedent for support.

(b) The following may be given such reasonable family allowance out of the estate as the court in its discretion determines is necessary for their maintenance according to their circumstances during administration of the estate:

(1) Other adult children of the decedent who were actually dependent in whole or in part upon the decedent for support.

(2) A parent of the decedent who was actually dependent in whole or in part upon the decedent for support.

(c) If a person otherwise eligible for family allowance has a reasonable maintenance from other sources and there are one or more other persons entitled to a family allowance, the family allowance shall be granted only to those who do not have a reasonable maintenance from other sources. **Leg.H.** Enacted Stats 1990 ch 79 §14 (AB 759), operative July 1, 1991.

Prior Law: Former Prob C §6540, similar to the present section, was added Stats 1983 ch 842 §55, operative January 1, 1985, and repealed Stats 1990 ch 79 §13, operative July 1, 1991.

§6541. Grant or modification; Petition; Notice of hearing

(a) The court may grant or modify a family allowance on petition of any interested person.

(b) With respect to an order for the family allowance provided for in subdivision (a) of Section 6540:

(1) Before the inventory is filed, the order may be made or modified either (A) ex parte or (B) after notice of the hearing on the petition has been given as provided in Section 1220.

(2) After the inventory is filed, the order may be made or modified only after notice of the hearing on the petition has been given as provided in Section 1220.

(c) An order for the family allowance provided in subdivision (b) of Section 6540 may be made only after notice of the hearing on the petition has been given as provided in Section 1220 to all of the following persons:

(1) Each person listed in Section 1220.

(2) Each known heir whose interest in the estate would be affected by the petition.

(3) Each known devisee whose interest in the estate would be affected by the petition. **Leg.H.** Enacted Stats 1990 ch 79 §14 (AB 759), operative July 1, 1991.

Prior Law: Former Prob C §6541, similar to the present section, was added Stats 1983 ch 842 §55, operative January 1, 1985, amended Stats 1987 ch 923 §91, operative July 1, 1988, and repealed Stats 1990 ch 79 §13, operative July 1, 1991.

§6542. Time of commencement of allowance

A family allowance commences on the date of the court's order or such other time as may be provided in the court's order, whether before or after the date of the order, as the court in its discretion determines, but the allowance may not be made retroactive to a date earlier than the date of the decedent's death. **Leg.H.** Enacted Stats 1990 ch 79 §14 (AB 759), operative July 1, 1991.

Prior Law: Former Prob C §6542, similar to the present section, was added Stats 1983 ch 842 §55, operative January 1, 1985, and repealed Stats 1990 ch 79 §13, operative July 1, 1991.

§6543. Termination of allowance

(a) A family allowance shall terminate no later than the entry of the order for final distribution of the estate or, if the estate is insolvent, no later than one year after the granting of letters.

(b) Subject to subdivision (a), a family allowance shall continue until modified or terminated by the court or until such time as the court may provide in its order. **Leg.H.** Enacted Stats 1990 ch 79 §14 (AB 759), operative July 1, 1991.

Prior Law: Former Prob C §6543, similar to the present section, was added Stats 1983 ch 842 §55, operative January 1, 1985, and repealed Stats 1990 ch 79 §13, operative July 1, 1991.

§6544. Cost of proceeding paid as expense of administration

The costs of proceedings under this chapter shall be paid by the estate as expenses of administration. **Leg.H.** Enacted Stats 1990 ch 79 §14 (AB 759), operative July 1, 1991.

Prior Law: Former Prob C §6544, similar to the present section, was added Stats 1983 ch 842 §55, operative January 1, 1985, and repealed Stats 1990 ch 79 §13, operative July 1, 1991.

§6545. No stay on appeal if undertaking furnished

Notwithstanding Chapter 2 (commencing with Section 916) of Title 13 of Part 2 of the Code of Civil Procedure, the perfecting of an appeal from an order made under this chapter does not stay proceedings under this chapter or the enforcement of the order appealed from if the person in whose favor the order is made gives an undertaking in double the amount of the payment or payments to be made to that person. The undertaking shall be conditioned that if the order appealed from is modified or reversed so that the payment or any part thereof to the person proves to have been unwarranted, the payment or part thereof shall, unless deducted from any preliminary or final distribution ordered in favor of the person, be repaid and refunded into the estate within 30 days after the court so orders following the modification or reversal, together with interest and costs. **Leg.H.** Enacted Stats 1990 ch 79 §14 (AB 759), operative July 1, 1991.

Prior Law: Former Prob C §6545, similar to the present section, was added Stats 1983 ch 842 §55, operative January 1, 1985, and repealed Stats 1990 ch 79 §13, operative July 1, 1991.

CHAPTER 5
SPOUSE OR CHILD OMITTED FROM WILL [REPEALED]

§6560. [Section repealed 1997]

Leg.H. Enacted Stats 1990 ch 79 §14 (AB 759), operative July 1, 1991. Repealed Stats 1997 ch 724 §17 (AB 1172). See Prob C §21610.

Prior Law: Former Prob C §6560, similar to present Prob C §21610, was added Stats 1983 ch 842 §55, operative January 1, 1985, amended Stats 1984 ch 892 §45, and repealed Stats 1990 ch 79 §13, operative July 1, 1991.

§6561. [Section repealed 1997]

Leg.H. Enacted Stats 1990 ch 79 §14 (AB 759), operative July 1, 1991. Repealed Stats 1997 ch 724 §17 (AB 1172). See Prob C §21611.

Prior Law: Former Prob C §6561, similar to present Prob C §21611, was added Stats 1983 ch 842 §55, operative January 1, 1985, and repealed Stats 1990 ch 79 §13.

§6562. [Section repealed 1997]

Leg.H. Enacted Stats 1990 ch 79 §14 (AB 759), operative July 1, 1991. Repealed Stats 1997 ch 724 §17 (AB 1172). See Prob C §21612.

Prior Law: Former Prob C §6562, similar to present Prob C §21612, was added Stats 1983 ch 842 §55, operative January 1, 1985, amended Stats 1984 ch 892 §46, and repealed Stats 1990 ch 79 §13, operative July 1, 1991.

§6570. [Section repealed 1997]

Leg.H. Enacted Stats 1990 ch 79 §14 (AB 759), operative July 1, 1991. Repealed Stats 1997 ch 724 §17 (AB 1172). See Prob C §21620.

Prior Law: Former Prob C §6570, similar to present Prob C §21620, was added Stats 1983 ch 842 §55, operative January 1, 1985, and repealed Stats 1990 ch 79 §13, operative July 1, 1991.

§6571. [Section repealed 1997]

Leg.H. Enacted Stats 1990 ch 79 §14 (AB 759), operative July 1, 1991. Repealed Stats 1997 ch 724 §17 (AB 1172). See Prob C §21621.

Prior Law: Former Prob C §6571, similar to present Prob C §21621, was added Stats 1983 ch 842 §55, operative January 1, 1985, and repealed Stats 1990 ch 79 §13, operative July 1, 1991.

§6572. [Section repealed 1997]

Leg.H. Enacted Stats 1990 ch 79 §14 (AB 759), operative July 1, 1991. Repealed Stats 1997 ch 724 §17 (AB 1172). See Prob C §21622.

Prior Law: Former Prob C §6572, similar to present Prob C §21622, was added Stats 1983 ch 842 §55, operative January 1, 1985, and repealed Stats 1990 ch 79 §13, operative July 1, 1991.

§6573. [Section repealed 1997]

Leg.H. Enacted Stats 1990 ch 79 §14 (AB 759), operative July 1, 1991. Repealed Stats 1997 ch 724 §17 (AB 1172). See Prob C §21623.

Prior Law: Former Prob C §6573, similar to present Prob C §21623, was added Stats 1983 ch 842 §55, operative January 1, 1985, amended Stats 1984 ch 892 §47, and repealed Stats 1990 ch 79 §13, operative July 1, 1991.

§6580. [Section repealed 1997]

Leg.H. Enacted Stats 1990 ch 79 §14 (AB 759), operative July 1, 1991. Repealed Stats 1997 ch 724 §17 (AB 1142). See Prob C §21610.

Prior Law: Former Prob C §6580, similar to present Prob C §21610, was added Stats 1984 ch 892 §48, and repealed Stats 1990 ch 79 §13, operative July 1, 1991.

CHAPTER 6
SMALL ESTATE SET-ASIDE

"Decedent's estate" defined; Exclusions in determining estate of the decedent or its value. §6600.
"Minor child" defined. §6601.
Petition to set aside estate; Maximum value. §6602.
Venue. §6603.
Contents of petition. §6604.
Filing of petition. §6605.
Who may file. §6606.
Notice of hearing. §6607.
Inventory and appraisal. §6608.
Court order. §6609.
Effect of court order. §6610.
Liability for unsecured debts of decedent. §6611.
Order where estate not set aside. §6612.
Attorney's fee. §6613.
Chapter not applicable where decedent died before July 1, 1987. §6614.
Reference to provision of former law deemed reference to provision of this chapter. §6615.

§6600. "Decedent's estate" defined; Exclusions in determining estate of the decedent or its value

(a) Subject to subdivision (b), for the purposes of this chapter, "decedent's estate" means all the decedent's personal property, wherever located, and all the decedent's real property located in this state.

(b) For the purposes of this chapter:

(1) Any property or interest or lien thereon which, at the time of the decedent's death, was held by the decedent as a joint tenant, or in which the decedent had a life or other interest terminable upon the decedent's death, shall be excluded in determining the estate of the decedent or its value.

(2) A multiple-party account to which the decedent was a party at the time of the decedent's death shall be excluded in determining the estate of the decedent or its value, whether or not all or a portion of the sums on deposit are community property, to the extent that the sums on deposit belong after the death of the decedent to a surviving party, P.O.D. payee, or beneficiary. As used in this paragraph, the terms "multiple-party account," "party," "P.O.D. payee," and "beneficiary" have the meanings given those terms in Article 2 (commencing with Section 5120) of Chapter 1 of Part 2 of Division 5. **Leg.H.** Enacted Stats 1990 ch 79 §14 (AB 759), operative July 1, 1991.

Prior Law: Former Prob C §6600, similar to the present section, was added Stats 1986 ch 783 §23, operative July 1, 1987, amended Stats 1989 ch 397 §38, operative July 1, 1990, and repealed Stats 1990 ch 79 §13, operative July 1, 1991.

§6601. "Minor child" defined

As used in this chapter, "minor child" means a child of the decedent who was under the age of 18 at the time of the decedent's death and who survived the decedent. **Leg.H.** Enacted Stats 1990 ch 79 §14 (AB 759), operative July 1, 1991.

Prior Law: Former Prob C §6601, similar to the present section, was added Stats 1986 ch 783 §23, operative July 1, 1987, and repealed Stats 1990 ch 79 §13, operative July 1, 1991.

§6602. Petition to set aside estate; Maximum value

A petition may be filed under this chapter requesting an order setting aside the decedent's estate to the decedent's surviving spouse and minor children, or one or more of them, as provided in this chapter, if the net value of the decedent's estate, over and above all liens and encumbrances at the date of death and over and above the value of any probate homestead interest set apart out of the decedent's estate under Section 6520, does not exceed eighty-five thousand nine hundred dollars ($85,900), as adjusted periodically in accordance with Section 890. **Leg.H.** Enacted Stats 1990 ch 79 §14 (AB 759), operative July 1, 1991. Amended Stats 2019 ch 122 §2 (AB 473), effective January 1, 2020.

Prior Law: Former Prob C §6602, similar to the present section, was added Stats 1986 ch 783 §23, operative July 1, 1987, and repealed Stats 1990 ch 79 §13, operative July 1, 1991.

§6603. Venue

The petition shall be filed in the superior court of a county in which the estate of the decedent may be administered. **Leg.H.** Enacted Stats 1990 ch 79 §14 (AB 759), operative July 1, 1991.

Prior Law: Former Prob C §6603, similar to the present section, was added Stats 1986 ch 783 §23, operative July 1, 1987, and repealed Stats 1990 ch 79 §13, operative July 1, 1991.

§6604. Contents of petition

(a) The petition shall allege that this chapter applies and request that an order be made setting aside the estate of the decedent as provided in this chapter.

(b) The petition shall include the following:

(1) If proceedings for administration of the estate are not pending, the facts necessary to determine the county in which the estate of the decedent may be administered.

(2) The name, age, address, and relation to the decedent of each heir and devisee of the decedent, so far as known to the petitioner.

(3) A specific description and estimate of the value of the decedent's estate and a list of all liens and encumbrances at the date of death.

(4) A specific description and estimate of the value of any of the decedent's real property located outside this state that passed to the surviving spouse and minor children of the decedent, or any one or more of them, under the will of the decedent or by intestate succession.

(5) A specific description and estimate of the value of any of the decedent's property described in subdivision (b) of Section 6600 that passed to the surviving spouse and minor children of the decedent, or any one or more of them, upon the death of the decedent.

(6) A designation of any property as to which a probate homestead is set apart out of the decedent's estate under Section 6520.

(7) A statement of any unpaid liabilities for expenses of the last illness, funeral charges, and expenses of administration.

(8) The requested disposition of the estate of the decedent under this chapter and the considerations that justify the requested disposition. **Leg.H.** Enacted Stats 1990 ch 79 §14 (AB 759), operative July 1, 1991.

Prior Law: Former Prob C §6604, similar to the present section, was added Stats 1986 ch 783 §23, operative July 1, 1987, and repealed Stats 1990 ch 79 §13, operative July 1, 1991.

§6605. Filing of petition

(a) If proceedings for the administration of the estate of the decedent are pending, a petition under this chapter shall be filed in those proceedings without the payment of an additional fee.

(b) If proceedings for the administration of the estate of the decedent have not yet been commenced, a petition under this chapter may be filed concurrently with a petition for the probate of the decedent's will or for administration of the estate of the decedent, or, if no petition for probate or for administration is being filed, a petition under this chapter may be filed independently.

(c) A petition may be filed under this chapter at any time prior to the entry of the order for final distribution of the estate. **Leg.H.** Enacted Stats 1990 ch 79 §14 (AB 759), operative July 1, 1991.

Prior Law: Former Prob C §6605, similar to the present section, was added Stats 1986 ch 783 §23, operative July 1, 1987, and repealed Stats 1990 ch 79 §13, operative July 1, 1991.

§6606. Who may file

(a) A petition may be filed under this chapter by any of the following:

(1) The person named in the will of the decedent as executor.

(2) The surviving spouse of the decedent.

(3) The guardian of a minor child of the decedent.

(4) A child of the decedent who was a minor at the time the decedent died.

(5) The personal representative if a personal representative has been appointed for the decedent's estate.

(b) The guardian of a minor child of the decedent may file the petition without authorization or approval of the court in which the guardianship proceeding is pending. **Leg.H.** Enacted Stats 1990 ch 79 §14 (AB 759), operative July 1, 1991.

Prior Law: Former Prob C §6606, similar to the present section, was added Stats 1986 ch 783 §23, operative July 1, 1987, and repealed Stats 1990 ch 79 §13, operative July 1, 1991.

§6607. Notice of hearing

(a) Where proceedings for the administration of the estate of the decedent are not pending when the petition is filed under this chapter and the petition under this chapter is not joined with a petition for the probate of the decedent's will or for administration of the estate of the decedent, the petitioner shall give notice of the hearing on the petition as provided in Section 1220 to (1) each person named as executor in the decedent's will and to (2) each heir or devisee of the decedent, if known to the petitioner. A copy of the petition shall be sent with the notice of hearing to the surviving spouse, each child, and each devisee who is not petitioning.

(b) If the petition under this chapter is filed with a petition for the probate of the decedent's will or with a petition for administration of the estate of the deceased spouse, notice of the hearing on the petition shall be given to the persons and in the manner prescribed by Section 8003 and shall be included in the notice required by that section.

(c) If proceedings for the administration of the estate of the decedent are pending when the petition is filed under this chapter and the hearing of the petition for probate of the will or administration of the estate of the decedent is set for a day more than 15 days after the filing of the petition filed under this chapter, the petition under this chapter shall be set for hearing at the same time as the petition for probate of the will or for administration of the estate, and notice of hearing on the petition filed under this chapter shall be given by the petitioner as provided in Section 1220. If the hearing of the petition for probate of the will or for administration of the estate is not set for hearing for a day more than 15 days after the filing of the petition under this chapter, (1) the petition filed under this chapter shall be set for hearing at least 15 days after the date on which it is filed, (2) notice of the hearing on the petition filed under this chapter shall be given by the petitioner as provided in Section 1220, and (3) if the petition for probate of the will or for administration of the estate has not already been heard, that petition shall be continued until that date and heard at the same time unless the court otherwise orders. **Leg.H.** Enacted Stats 1990 ch 79 §14 (AB 759), operative July 1, 1991.

Prior Law: Former Prob C §6607, similar to the present section, was added Stats 1986 ch 783 §23, operative July 1, 1987, amended Stats 1987 ch 923 §92, operative July 1, 1988, Stats 1988 ch 1199 §78, operative July 1, 1989, and repealed Stats 1990 ch 79 §13, operative July 1, 1991.

§6608. Inventory and appraisal

If a petition is filed under this chapter, the personal representative, or the petitioner if no personal representative has been appointed, shall file with the clerk of the court, prior to the hearing of the petition, an inventory and appraisal made as provided in Part 3 (commencing with Section 8800) of Division 7. The personal representative or the petitioner, as the case may be, may appraise the assets which a personal representative could appraise under Section 8901. **Leg.H.** Enacted Stats 1990 ch 79 §14 (AB 759), operative July 1, 1991.

Prior Law: Former Prob C §6608, similar to the present section, was added Stats 1986 ch 783 §23, operative July 1, 1987, amended Stats 1988 ch 1199 §78.5, operative July 1, 1989, and repealed Stats 1990 ch 79 §13, operative July 1, 1991.

§6609. Court order

(a) If the court determines that the net value of the decedent's estate, over and above all liens and encumbrances at the date of death of the decedent and over and above the value of any probate homestead interest set apart out of the decedent's estate under Section 6520, does not exceed eighty-five thousand nine hundred dollars ($85,900), as adjusted periodically in accordance with Section 890, as of the date of the decedent's death, the court shall make an order under this section unless the court determines that making an order under this section would be inequitable under the circumstances of the particular case.

(b) In determining whether to make an order under this section, the court shall consider the needs of the surviving spouse and minor children, the liens and encumbrances on the property of the decedent's estate, the claims of creditors, the needs of the heirs or devisees of the decedent, the intent of the decedent with respect to the property in the estate and the estate plan of the decedent as expressed in inter vivos and testamentary transfers or by other means, and any other relevant considerations. If the surviving spouse has remarried at the time the petition is heard, it shall be presumed that the needs of the surviving spouse do not justify the setting aside of the small estate, or any portion thereof, to the surviving spouse. This presumption is a presumption affecting the burden of proof.

(c) Subject to subdivision (d), if the court makes an order under this section, the court shall assign the whole of the decedent's estate, subject to all liens and encumbrances on property in the estate at the date of the decedent's death, to the surviving spouse and the minor children of the decedent, or any one or more of them.

(d) If there are any liabilities for expenses of the last illness, funeral charges, or expenses of administration that are unpaid at the time the court makes an order under this section, the court shall make the necessary orders for payment of those unpaid liabilities.

(e) Title to property in the decedent's estate vests absolutely in the surviving spouse, minor children, or any or all of them, as provided in the order, subject to all liens and encumbrances on property in the estate at the date of the decedent's death, and there shall be no further proceedings in the administration of the decedent's estate unless additional property in the decedent's estate is discovered. **Leg.H.** Enacted Stats 1990 ch 79 §14 (AB 759), operative July 1, 1991. Amended Stats 2019 ch 122 §3 (AB 473), effective January 1, 2020.

Prior Law: Former Prob C §6609, similar to the present section, was added Stats 1986 ch 783 §23, operative July 1, 1987, and repealed Stats 1990 ch 79 §13, operative July 1, 1991.

§6610. Effect of court order

Upon becoming final, an order under Section 6609 shall be conclusive on all persons, whether or not they are then in being. **Leg.H.** Enacted Stats 1990 ch 79 §14 (AB 759), operative July 1, 1991.

Prior Law: Former Prob C §6610, similar to the present section, was added Stats 1986 ch 783 §23, operative July 1, 1987, and repealed Stats 1990 ch 79 §13, operative July 1, 1991.

§6611. Liability for unsecured debts of decedent

(a) Subject to the limitations and conditions specified in this section, the person or persons in whom title vested pursuant to Section 6609 are personally liable for the unsecured debts of the decedent.

(b) The personal liability of a person under this section does not exceed the fair market value at the date of the decedent's death of the property title to which vested in that person pursuant to Section 6609, less the total of all of the following:

(1) The amount of any liens and encumbrances on that property.

(2) The value of any probate homestead interest set apart under Section 6520 out of that property.

(3) The value of any other property set aside under Section 6510 out of that property.

(c) In any action or proceeding based upon an unsecured debt of the decedent, the surviving spouse of the decedent, the child or children of the decedent, or the guardian of the minor child or children of the decedent, may assert any defense, cross-complaint, or setoff which would have been available to the decedent if the decedent had not died.

(d) If proceedings are commenced in this state for the administration of the estate of the decedent and the time for filing claims has commenced, any action upon the personal liability of a person under this section is barred to the same extent as provided for claims under Part 4 (commencing with Section 9000) of Division 7, except as to the following:

(1) Creditors who commence judicial proceedings for the enforcement of the debt and serve the person liable under this section with the complaint therein prior to the expiration of the time for filing claims.

(2) Creditors who have or who secure an acknowledgment in writing of the person liable under this section that that person is liable for the debts.

(3) Creditors who file a timely claim in the proceedings for the administration of the estate of the decedent.

(e) Section 366.2 of the Code of Civil Procedure applies in an action under this section. **Leg.H.** Enacted Stats 1990 ch 79 §14 (AB 759), operative July 1, 1991. Amended Stats 1990 ch 140 §4.1 (SB 1855), operative July 1, 1991; Stats 1992 ch 178 §32 (SB 1496).

Prior Law: Former Prob C §6611, similar to the present section, was added Stats 1986 ch 783 §23, operative July 1, 1987, amended Stats 1987 ch 923 §92.5, operative July 1, 1988, repealed Stats 1990 ch 79 §13, operative July 1, 1991, and amended Stats 1990 ch 140 §4, operative until July 1, 1991, and repealed Stats 1990 ch 140 §20, operative July 1, 1991.

§6612. Order where estate not set aside

If a petition filed under this chapter is filed with a petition for the probate of the decedent's will or for administration of the estate of the decedent and the court determines not to make an order under Section 6609, the court shall act on the petition for probate of the decedent's will or for administration of the estate of the decedent in the same manner as if no petition had been filed under this chapter, and the estate shall then be administered in the same manner as if no petition had been filed under this chapter. **Leg.H.** Enacted Stats 1990 ch 79 §14 (AB 759), operative July 1, 1991.

Prior Law: Former Prob C §6612, similar to the present section, was added Stats 1986 ch 783 §23, operative July 1, 1987, and repealed Stats 1990 ch 79 §13, operative July 1, 1991.

§6613. Attorney's fee

The attorney's fees for services performed in connection with the filing of a petition and the obtaining of a court order under this chapter shall be determined by private agreement between the attorney and the client and are not subject to approval by the court. If there is no agreement between the attorney and the client concerning the attorney's fees for services performed in connection with the filing of a petition and obtaining of a court order under this chapter and there is a dispute concerning the reasonableness of the attorney's fees for those services, a petition may be filed with the court in the same proceeding requesting that the court determine the reasonableness of the attorney's fees for those services. If there is an agreement between the attorney and the client concerning the attorney's fees for services performed in connection with the filing of a petition and obtaining a court order under this chapter and there is a dispute concerning the meaning of the agreement, a petition may be filed with the court in the same proceeding requesting that the court determine the dispute. **Leg.H.** Enacted Stats 1990 ch 79 §14 (AB 759), operative July 1, 1991.

Prior Law: Former Prob C §6613, similar to the present section, was added Stats 1986 ch 783 §23, operative July 1, 1987, and repealed Stats 1990 ch 79 §13, operative July 1, 1991.

§6614. Chapter not applicable where decedent died before July 1, 1987

Sections 6600 to 6613, inclusive, do not apply if the decedent died before July 1, 1987. If the decedent died before July 1, 1987, the case continues to be governed by the law applicable to the case prior to July 1, 1987. **Leg.H.** Enacted Stats 1990 ch 79 §14 (AB 759), operative July 1, 1991.

Prior Law: Former Prob C §6614, similar to the present section, was added Stats 1986 ch 783 §23, operative July 1, 1987, and repealed Stats 1990 ch 79 §13, operative July 1, 1991.

§6615. Reference to provision of former law deemed reference to provision of this chapter

A reference in any statute of this state or in a written instrument, including a will or trust, to a provision of former Sections 640 to 647.5, inclusive, repealed by Chapter 783 of the Statutes of 1986, shall be

Sec. 6615 PROBATE CODE 264

deemed to be a reference to the comparable provisions of this chapter.
Leg.H. Enacted Stats 1990 ch 79 §14 (AB 759), operative July 1, 1991.

Prior Law: Former Prob C §6615, similar to the present section, was added Stats 1986 ch 783 §23, operative July 1, 1987, and repealed Stats 1990 ch 79 §13, operative July 1, 1991.

PART 4
ESCHEAT OF DECEDENT'S PROPERTY

Escheat of property of decedent. §6800.
Real property in this state. §6801.
Tangible personal property customarily kept in this state. §6802.
Tangible personal property subject to control of superior court in this state. §6803.
Intangible personal property of decedent domiciled in this state. §6804.
Intangible personal property subject to control of superior court in this state. §6805.
Benefits distributable from certain trusts. §6806.

§6800. Escheat of property of decedent

(a) If a decedent, whether or not the decedent was domiciled in this state, leaves no one to take the decedent's estate or any portion thereof by testate succession, and no one other than a government or governmental subdivision or agency to take the estate or a portion thereof by intestate succession, under the laws of this state or of any other jurisdiction, the same escheats at the time of the decedent's death in accordance with this part.

(b) Property that escheats to the state under this part, whether held by the state or its officers, is subject to the same charges and trusts to which it would have been subject if it had passed by succession and is also subject to the provisions of Title 10 (commencing with Section 1300) of Part 3 of the Code of Civil Procedure relating to escheated estates. **Leg.H.** Enacted Stats 1990 ch 79 §14 (AB 759), operative July 1, 1991.

Prior Law: Former Prob C §6800, similar to the present section, was added Stats 1983 ch 842 §55, operative January 1, 1985, and repealed Stats 1990 ch 79 §13, operative July 1, 1991.

§6801. Real property in this state

Real property in this state escheats to this state in accordance with Section 6800. **Leg.H.** Enacted Stats 1990 ch 79 §14 (AB 759), operative July 1, 1991.

Prior Law: Former Prob C §6801, similar to the present section, was added Stats 1983 ch 842 §55, operative January 1, 1985, and repealed Stats 1990 ch 79 §13, operative July 1, 1991.

§6802. Tangible personal property customarily kept in this state

All tangible personal property owned by the decedent, wherever located at the decedent's death, that was customarily kept in this state prior to the decedent's death, escheats to this state in accordance with Section 6800. **Leg.H.** Enacted Stats 1990 ch 79 §14 (AB 759), operative July 1, 1991.

Prior Law: Former Prob C §6802, similar to the present section, was added Stats 1983 ch 842 §55, operative January 1, 1985, and repealed Stats 1990 ch 79 §13, operative July 1, 1991.

§6803. Tangible personal property subject to control of superior court in this state

(a) Subject to subdivision (b), all tangible personal property owned by the decedent that is subject to the control of a superior court of this state for purposes of administration under this code escheats to this state in accordance with Section 6800.

(b) The property described in subdivision (a) does not escheat to this state but goes to another jurisdiction if the other jurisdiction claims the property and establishes all of the following:

(1) The other jurisdiction is entitled to the property under its law.

(2) The decedent customarily kept the property in that jurisdiction prior to the decedent's death.

(3) This state has the right to escheat and take tangible personal property being administered as part of a decedent's estate in that jurisdiction if the decedent customarily kept the property in this state prior to the decedent's death. **Leg.H.** Enacted Stats 1990 ch 79 §14 (AB 759), operative July 1, 1991.

Prior Law: Former Prob C §6803, similar to the present section, was added Stats 1983 ch 842 §55, operative January 1, 1985, amended Stats 1988 ch 1199 §79, operative July 1, 1989, and repealed Stats 1990 ch 79 §13, operative July 1, 1991.

§6804. Intangible personal property of decedent domiciled in this state

All intangible property owned by the decedent escheats to this state in accordance with Section 6800 if the decedent was domiciled in this state at the time of the decedent's death. **Leg.H.** Enacted Stats 1990 ch 79 §14 (AB 759), operative July 1, 1991.

Prior Law: Former Prob C §6804, similar to the present section, was added Stats 1983 ch 842 §55, operative January 1, 1985, and repealed Stats 1990 ch 79 §13, operative July 1, 1991.

§6805. Intangible personal property subject to control of superior court in this state

(a) Subject to subdivision (b), all intangible property owned by the decedent that is subject to the control of a superior court of this state for purposes of administration under this code escheats to this state in accordance with Section 6800 whether or not the decedent was domiciled in this state at the time of the decedent's death.

(b) The property described in subdivision (a) does not escheat to this state but goes to another jurisdiction if the other jurisdiction claims the property and establishes all of the following:

(1) The other jurisdiction is entitled to the property under its laws.

(2) The decedent was domiciled in that jurisdiction at the time of the decedent's death.

(3) This state has the right to escheat and take intangible property being administered as part of a decedent's estate in that jurisdiction if the decedent was domiciled in this state at the time of the decedent's death. **Leg.H.** Enacted Stats 1990 ch 79 §14 (AB 759), operative July 1, 1991.

Prior Law: Former Prob C §6805, similar to the present section, was added Stats 1983 ch 842 §55, operative January 1, 1985, amended Stats 1988 ch 1199 §79.5, operative July 1, 1989, and repealed Stats 1990 ch 79 §13, operative July 1, 1991.

§6806. Benefits distributable from certain trusts

Notwithstanding any other provision of law, a benefit consisting of money or other property distributable from a trust established under a plan providing health and welfare, pension, vacation, severance, retirement benefit, death benefit, unemployment insurance or similar benefits does not pass to or escheat to the state under this part but goes to the trust or fund from which it is distributable, subject to the provisions of Section 1521 of the Code of Civil Procedure. However, if such plan has terminated and the trust or fund has been distributed to the beneficiaries thereof prior to distribution of such benefit from the estate, such benefit passes to the state and escheats to the state under this part. **Leg.H.** Enacted Stats 1990 ch 79 §14 (AB 759), operative July 1, 1991.

Prior Law: Former Prob C §6806, similar to the present section, was added Stats 1983 ch 842 §55, operative January 1, 1985, and repealed Stats 1990 ch 79 §13, operative July 1, 1991.

DIVISION 7
ADMINISTRATION OF ESTATES OF DECEDENTS

Part 1. General Provisions.
Part 2. Opening Estate Administration.
Part 3. Inventory and Appraisal.
Part 4. Creditor Claims.
Part 5. Estate Management.
Part 6. Independent Administration of Estates.
Part 7. Compensation of Personal Representative and Attorney for the Personal Representative.
Part 8. Accounts.
Part 9. Payment of Debts.
Part 10. Distribution of Estate.
Part 11. Closing Estate Administration.
Part 12. Administration of Estates of Missing Persons Presumed Dead.
Part 13. Nondomiciliary Decedents.

PART 1
GENERAL PROVISIONS

Chapter 1. Passage of Decedent's Property.
Chapter 2. Jurisdiction and Courts.
Chapter 3. Rules of Procedure.
Chapter 4. Public Administrators.

CHAPTER 1
PASSAGE OF DECEDENT'S PROPERTY

Passage of decedent's property. §7000.
Limitations on passage of decedent's property. §7001.

§7000. Passage of decedent's property

Subject to Section 7001, title to a decedent's property passes on the decedent's death to the person to whom it is devised in the decedent's last will or, in the absence of such a devise, to the decedent's heirs as prescribed in the laws governing intestate succession. **Leg.H.** Enacted Stats 1990 ch 79 §14 (AB 759), operative July 1, 1991.

Prior Law: Former Prob C §7000, similar to the present section, was added Stats 1987 ch 923 §93, operative July 1, 1988, and repealed Stats 1990 ch 79 §13, operative July 1, 1991.

§7001. Limitations on passage of decedent's property

The decedent's property is subject to administration under this code, except as otherwise provided by law, and is subject to the rights of beneficiaries, creditors, and other persons as provided by law. **Leg.H.** Enacted Stats 1990 ch 79 §14 (AB 759), operative July 1, 1991.

Prior Law: Former Prob C §7001, similar to the present section, was added Stats 1988 ch 1199 §80.5, operative July 1, 1989, and repealed Stats 1990 ch 79 §13, operative July 1, 1991.

CHAPTER 2
JURISDICTION AND COURTS

Article 1. Jurisdiction and Venue.
Article 2. Disqualification of Judge.
Article 3. Transfer of Proceedings.

ARTICLE 1
Jurisdiction and Venue

Jurisdiction of superior court. §7050.
Venue where decedent domiciled in this state. §7051.
Venue where decedent not domiciled in this state. §7052.

§7050. Jurisdiction of superior court

The superior court has jurisdiction of proceedings under this code concerning the administration of the decedent's estate. **Leg.H.** Enacted Stats 1990 ch 79 §14 (AB 759), operative July 1, 1991. Amended Stats 1994 ch 806 §22 (AB 3686).

Prior Law: Former Prob C §7050, similar to the present section, was added Stats 1988 ch 1199 §80.5, operative July 1, 1989, amended Stats 1989 ch 21 §13, effective May 25, 1989, operative July 1, 1989, and repealed Stats 1990 ch 79 §13, operative July 1, 1991.

§7051. Venue where decedent domiciled in this state

If the decedent was domiciled in this state at the time of death, the proper county for proceedings concerning administration of the decedent's estate is the county in which the decedent was domiciled, regardless of where the decedent died. **Leg.H.** Enacted Stats 1990 ch 79 §14 (AB 759), operative July 1, 1991.

Prior Law: Former Prob C §7051, similar to the present section, was added Stats 1988 ch 1199 §80.5, operative July 1, 1989, and repealed Stats 1990 ch 79 §13, operative July 1, 1991.

§7052. Venue where decedent not domiciled in this state

If the decedent was not domiciled in this state at the time of death, the proper county for proceedings under this code concerning the administration of the decedent's estate is one of the following:

(a) If property of the nondomiciliary decedent is located in the county in which the nondomiciliary decedent died, the county in which the nondomiciliary decedent died.

(b) If no property of the nondomiciliary decedent is located in the county in which the nondomiciliary decedent died or if the nondomiciliary decedent did not die in this state, any county in which property of the nondomiciliary decedent is located, regardless of where the nondomiciliary decedent died. If property of the nondomiciliary decedent is located in more than one county, the proper county is the county in which a petition for ancillary administration is first filed, and the court in that county has jurisdiction of the administration of the estate. **Leg.H.** Enacted Stats 1990 ch 79 §14 (AB 759), operative July 1, 1991.

Prior Law: Former Prob C §7052, similar to the present section, was added Stats 1988 ch 1199 §80.5, operative July 1, 1989, and repealed Stats 1990 ch 79 §13, operative July 1, 1991.

ARTICLE 2
Disqualification of Judge

Disqualification of judge. §7060.

§7060. Disqualification of judge

(a) In addition to any other ground provided by law for disqualification of a judge, a judge is disqualified from acting in proceedings under this code concerning the administration of the decedent's estate, except to order the transfer of a proceeding as provided in Article 3 (commencing with Section 7070), if any of the following circumstances exist:

(1) The judge is interested as a beneficiary or creditor.
(2) The judge is named as executor or trustee in the will.
(3) The judge is otherwise interested.

(b) A judge who participates in any manner in the drafting or execution of a will, including acting as a witness to the will, is disqualified from acting in any proceeding prior to and including the admission of the will to probate or in any proceeding involving its validity or interpretation.

(c) The amendments made to former Section 303 by Section 27 of Chapter 923 of the Statutes of 1987 do not apply in any proceeding commenced prior to July 1, 1988. **Leg.H.** Enacted Stats 1990 ch 79 §14 (AB 759), operative July 1, 1991.

Prior Law: Former Prob C §7060, similar to the present section, was added Stats 1988 ch 1199 §80.5, operative July 1, 1989, amended Stats 1989 ch 21 §14, effective May 25, 1989, operative July 1, 1989, and repealed Stats 1990 ch 79 §13, operative July 1, 1991.

ARTICLE 3
Transfer of Proceedings

Grounds for transfer. §7070.
Place of transfer. §7071.
Retransfer. §7072.

§7070. Grounds for transfer

The court or judge shall order a proceedings under this code concerning the administration of the decedent's estate transferred to another county if there is no judge of the court in which the proceeding is pending who is qualified to act. This section does not apply if a judge qualified to act is assigned by the chairman of the Judicial Council to sit in the county and hear the proceeding. **Leg.H.** Enacted Stats 1990 ch 79 §14 (AB 759), operative July 1, 1991.

Prior Law: Former Prob C §7070, similar to the present section, was added Stats 1988 ch 1199 §80.5, operative July 1, 1989, and repealed Stats 1990 ch 79 §13, operative July 1, 1991.

§7071. Place of transfer

Transfer of a proceeding under this article shall be to another county in which property of the decedent is located or, if there is no other county in which property of the decedent is located, to an adjoining county. **Leg.H.** Enacted Stats 1990 ch 79 §14 (AB 759), operative July 1, 1991.

§7072. Retransfer

Upon petition of the personal representative or other interested person before entry of the order for final distribution of the estate, a proceeding transferred under this article may be retransferred to the court in which the proceeding was originally commenced if the court determines that both of the following conditions are satisfied:

(a) Another person has become judge of the court where the proceeding was originally commenced who is not disqualified to act in the administration of the estate.

(b) The convenience of the parties interested would be promoted by the retransfer. **Leg.H.** Enacted Stats 1990 ch 79 §14 (AB 759), operative July 1, 1991.

Prior Law: Former Prob C §7072, similar to the present section, was added Stats 1988 ch 1199 §80.5, operative July 1, 1989, and repealed Stats 1990 ch 79 §13, operative July 1, 1991.

CHAPTER 3
RULES OF PROCEDURE

Article 2. New Trials.
Article 3.5. Judgments and Orders.
Article 4. Orders and Transactions Affecting Property.
Article 5. United States as Interested Person.

ARTICLE 1
Trial by Jury [Repealed]

§7200. [Section repealed 1999]

Leg.H. Enacted Stats 1990 ch 79 §14 (AB 759), operative July 1, 1991. Repealed Stats 1999 ch 175 §4 (AB 239). See Prob C §825.

Prior Law: Former Prob C §7200, similar to the present section, was added Stats 1988 ch 1199 §80.5, operative July 1, 1989, amended Stats 1989 ch 21 §15, effective May 25, 1989, operative July 1, 1989, and repealed Stats 1990 ch 79 §13, operative July 1, 1991.

ARTICLE 2
New Trials

New trial. §7220.

§7220. New trial

In proceedings under this code concerning the administration of the decedent's estate, a motion for a new trial may be made only in the following cases:

(a) Contest of a will or revocation of probate of a will.

(b) Cases in which a right to jury trial is expressly granted, whether or not the case was tried by a jury. **Leg.H.** Enacted Stats 1990 ch 79 §14 (AB 759), operative July 1, 1991.

Prior Law: Former Prob C §7220, similar to the present section, was added Stats 1988 ch 1199 §80.5, operative July 1, 1989, and repealed Stats 1990 ch 79 §13, operative July 1, 1991.

ARTICLE 3
Appeals [Repealed]

§7240. [Section repealed 1997]

Leg.H. Enacted Stats 1990 ch 79 §14 (AB 759), operative July 1, 1991. Amended Stats 1991 ch 1055 §21 (SB 271); Stats 1992 ch 871 §9 (AB 2975); Stats 1994 ch 806 §23 (AB 3686). Repealed Stats 1997 ch 724 §18 (AB 1172). See Prob C §1303.

Prior Law: Former Prob C §7240, similar to present Prob C §1303, was added Stats 1988 ch 1199 §80.5, operative July 1, 1989, and repealed Stats 1990 ch 79 §13, operative July 1, 1991.

§7241. [Section repealed 1997]

Leg.H. Enacted Stats 1990 ch 79 §14 (AB 759), operative July 1, 1991. Amended Stats 1996 ch 563 §21 (SB 392). Repealed Stats 1997 ch 724 §18 (AB 1172). See Prob C §1310.

Prior Law: Former Prob C §7241, similar to present Prob C §1310, was added Stats 1988 ch 1199 §80.5, operative July 1, 1989, and repealed Stats 1990 ch 79 §13, operative July 1, 1991.

§7242. [Section repealed 1997]

Leg.H. Enacted Stats 1990 ch 79 §14 (AB 759), operative July 1, 1991. Repealed Stats 1997 ch 724 §18 (AB 1172). See Prob C §1312.

Prior Law: Former Prob C §7242, similar to present Prob C §1312, was added Stats 1988 ch 1199 §80.5, operative July 1, 1989, and repealed Stats 1990 ch 79 §13, operative July 1, 1991.

ARTICLE 3.5
Judgments and Orders

Effect of court authorization or approval. §7250.

§7250. Effect of court authorization or approval

(a) When a judgment or order made pursuant to the provisions of this code concerning the administration of the decedent's estate becomes final, it releases the personal representative and the sureties from all claims of the heirs or devisees and of any persons affected thereby based upon any act or omission directly authorized, approved, or confirmed in the judgment or order. For the purposes of this section, "order" includes an order settling an account of the personal representative, whether an interim or final account.

(b) Nothing in this section affects any order, judgment, or decree made, or any action taken, before July 1, 1988. The validity of any action taken before July 1, 1988, is determined by the applicable law in effect before July 1, 1988, and not by this section.

(c) This section shall not apply where the judgment or order is obtained by fraud or conspiracy or by misrepresentation contained in the petition or account or in the judgment as to any material fact. For purposes of this subdivision, misrepresentation includes, but shall not be limited to, the omission of a material fact. **Leg.H.** Enacted Stats 1990 ch 79 §14 (AB 759), operative July 1, 1991. Amended Stats 1993 ch 794 §2 (AB 516).

ARTICLE 4
Orders and Transactions Affecting Property

"Transaction" defined. §7260.
Court-ordered real property transaction; Statement in instrument. §7261.
Effect of court-ordered transaction. §7262.
Recording of order affecting title to real property. §7263.

§7260. "Transaction" defined

As used in this article, "transaction" means a transaction affecting title to property in the estate, including, but not limited to, the following:

(a) In the case of real property, a conveyance (including a sale, option, or order confirming a sale or option), a lease, the creation of a mortgage, deed of trust, or other lien or encumbrance, the setting apart of a probate homestead, or the distribution of property.

(b) In the case of personal property, a transfer of the property or the creation of a security interest or other lien on the property. **Leg.H.** Enacted Stats 1990 ch 79 §14 (AB 759), operative July 1, 1991.

Prior Law: Former Prob C §7260, similar to the present section, was added Stats 1988 ch 1199 §80.5, operative July 1, 1989, and repealed Stats 1990 ch 79 §13, operative July 1, 1991.

§7261. Court-ordered real property transaction; Statement in instrument

If a transaction affecting real property in the estate is executed by the personal representative in accordance with the terms of a court order, the instrument shall include a statement that the transaction is made by authority of the order authorizing or directing the transaction and shall give the date of the order. **Leg.H.** Enacted Stats 1990 ch 79 §14 (AB 759), operative July 1, 1991.

Prior Law: Former Prob C §7261, similar to the present section, was added Stats 1988 ch 1199 §80.5, operative July 1, 1989, and repealed Stats 1990 ch 79 §13, operative July 1, 1991.

§7262. Effect of court-ordered transaction

A transaction executed by the personal representative in accordance with an order authorizing or directing the transaction has the same effect as if the decedent were living at the time of the transaction and had carried it out in person while having legal capacity to do so. **Leg.H.** Enacted Stats 1990 ch 79 §14 (AB 759), operative July 1, 1991.

Prior Law: Former Prob C §7262, similar to the present section, was added Stats 1988 ch 1199 §80.5, operative July 1, 1989, and repealed Stats 1990 ch 79 §13, operative July 1, 1991.

§7263. Recording of order affecting title to real property

If an order is made setting apart a probate homestead, confirming a sale or making a distribution of real property, or determining any other matter affecting title to real property in the estate, the personal representative shall record a certified copy of the order in the office of the county recorder in each county in which any portion of the real property is located. **Leg.H.** Enacted Stats 1990 ch 79 §14 (AB 759), operative July 1, 1991.

Prior Law: Former Prob C §7263, similar to the present section, was added Stats 1988 ch 1199 §80.5, operative July 1, 1989, and repealed Stats 1990 ch 79 §13, operative July 1, 1991.

ARTICLE 5
United States as Interested Person

Rights of United States where federal allowance made to decedent's estate. §7280.

§7280. Rights of United States where federal allowance made to decedent's estate

Where compensation, pension, insurance, or other allowance is made or awarded by a department or bureau of the United States government to a decedent's estate, the department or bureau has the same right as an interested person to do any of the following:

(a) Request special notice.

(b) Commence and prosecute an action on the bond of a personal representative.

(c) Contest an account of a personal representative. **Leg.H.** Enacted Stats 1990 ch 79 §14 (AB 759), operative July 1, 1991.

Prior Law: Former Prob C §7280, similar to the present section, was added Stats 1988 ch 1199 §80.5, operative July 1, 1989, and repealed Stats 1990 ch 79 §13, operative July 1, 1991.

CHAPTER 4
PUBLIC ADMINISTRATORS

Article 1. Taking Temporary Possession or Control of Property.
Article 2. Appointment as Personal Representative.
Article 3. Deposit of Money of Estate.
Article 4. Summary Disposition of Small Estates.

ARTICLE 1
Taking Temporary Possession or Control of Property

Report of public employee to inform public administrator. §7600.
Giving notice of death of patient to public administrator. §7600.5.
Notification of public administrator if persons entitled to control decedent's remains cannot be found. §7600.6.
Duty of public administrator to take control of property. §7601.
Search for property, will, and instructions for disposition of remains. §7602.
Providing information and access to public administrator. §7603.
Costs and compensation when public administrator or subsequently appointed representative takes control. §7604.
Public administrator, continuing education requirements. §7605.

§7600. Report of public employee to inform public administrator

If a public officer or employee knows of property of a decedent that is subject to loss, injury, waste, or misappropriation and that ought to be in the possession or control of the public administrator, the officer or employee shall inform the public administrator. **Leg.H.** Enacted Stats 1990 ch 79 §14 (AB 759), operative July 1, 1991.

Prior Law: Former Prob C §7600, similar to the present section, was added Stats 1988 ch 1199 §80.5, operative July 1, 1989, and repealed Stats 1990 ch 79 §13, operative July 1, 1991.

§7600.5. Giving notice of death of patient to public administrator

If a person dies in a hospital, convalescent hospital, or board and care facility without known next of kin, the person in charge of the hospital or facility shall give immediate notice of that fact to the public administrator of the county in which the hospital or facility is located. If the notice required by this section is not given, the hospital or facility is liable for (1) any cost of interment incurred by the estate or the county as a result of the failure and (2) any loss to the estate or beneficiaries caused by loss, injury, waste, or misappropriation of property of the decedent as a result of the failure. **Leg.H.** Enacted Stats 1990 ch 79 §14 (AB 759), operative July 1, 1991.

Prior Law: Former Prob C §7600.5, similar to the present section, was added Stats 1988 ch 1199 §80.5, operative July 1, 1989, and repealed Stats 1990 ch 79 §13, operative July 1, 1991.

§7600.6. Notification of public administrator if persons entitled to control decedent's remains cannot be found

A funeral director in control of the decedent's remains pursuant to subdivision (c) of Section 7100 of the Health and Safety Code shall notify the public administrator if none of the persons described in paragraphs (2) to (6), inclusive, of subdivision (a) of Section 7100 of the Health and Safety Code exist, can be found after reasonable inquiry, or can be contacted by reasonable means. **Leg.H.** Added Stats 1997 ch 93 §1 (SB 696). Amended Stats 1998 ch 253 §3 (SB 1360).

§7601. Duty of public administrator to take control of property

(a) If no personal representative has been appointed, the public administrator of a county shall take prompt possession or control of property of a decedent in the county that is deemed by the public administrator to be subject to loss, injury, waste, or misappropriation, or that the court orders into the possession or control of the public administrator after notice to the public administrator as provided in Section 1220.

(b) If property described in subdivision (a) is beyond the ability of the public administrator to take possession or control, the public administrator is not liable for failing to take possession or control of the property. **Leg.H.** Enacted Stats 1990 ch 79 §14 (AB 759), operative July 1, 1991. Amended Stats 2004 ch 888 §2 (AB 2687), effective January 1, 2005.

Prior Law: Former Prob C §7601, similar to the present section, was added Stats 1988 ch 1199 §80.5, operative July 1, 1989, and repealed Stats 1990 ch 79 §13, operative July 1, 1991.

§7602. Search for property, will, and instructions for disposition of remains

(a) A public administrator who is authorized to take possession or control of property of a decedent under this article shall make a prompt search for other property, a will, and instructions for disposition of the decedent's remains.

(b) If a will is found, the public administrator or custodian of the will shall deliver the will as provided in Section 8200.

(c) If instructions for disposition of the decedent's remains are found, the public administrator shall promptly deliver the instructions to the person upon whom the right to control disposition of the decedent's remains devolves as provided in Section 7100 of the Health and Safety Code.

(d) If other property is located, the public administrator shall take possession or control of any property that, in the sole discretion of the public administrator, is deemed to be subject to loss, injury, waste, or misappropriation and that is located anywhere in this state or that is subject to the laws of this state. The public administrator does not have any liability for loss, injury, waste, or misappropriation of property of which he or she is unable to take possession or control. **Leg.H.** Enacted Stats 1990 ch 79 §14 (AB 759), operative July 1, 1991. Amended Stats 2004 ch 888 §3 (AB 2687), effective January 1, 2005.

Prior Law: Former Prob C §7602, similar to the present section, was added Stats 1988 ch 1199 §80.5, operative July 1, 1989, and repealed Stats 1990 ch 79 §13, operative July 1, 1991.

§7603. Providing information and access to public administrator

(a) A public administrator who is authorized to take possession or control of property of a decedent pursuant to this article may issue a written certification of that fact. The written certification is effective for 30 days after the date of issuance.

(b) The public administrator may record a copy of the written certification in any county in which is located real property of which the public administrator is authorized to take possession or control under this article.

(c) A financial institution, government or private agency, retirement fund administrator, insurance company, licensed securities dealer, or other person shall, without the necessity of inquiring into the truth of the written certification, without requiring a death certificate, without charge, and without court order or letters being issued:

(1) Provide the public administrator complete information concerning property held in the sole name of the decedent, including the names and addresses of any beneficiaries.

(2) Grant the public administrator access to a safe-deposit box rented in the sole name of the decedent for the purpose of inspection and removal of any will or instructions for disposition of the decedent's remains. Costs and expenses incurred in drilling or forcing a safe-deposit box shall be borne by the estate of the decedent.

(3) Surrender to the public administrator any property of the decedent that, in the sole discretion of the public administrator, is deemed to be subject to loss, injury, waste, or misappropriation.

(d) Receipt of the written certification provided by this section:

(1) Constitutes sufficient acquittance for providing information or granting access to the safe-deposit box, for removal of the decedent's will and instructions for disposition of the decedent's remains, and for surrendering property of the decedent.

(2) Fully discharges the financial institution, government or private agency, retirement fund administrator, insurance company, licensed securities dealer, or other person from any liability for any act or omission of the public administrator with respect to the property or the safe-deposit box. **Leg.H.** Enacted Stats 1990 ch 79 §14 (AB 759), operative July 1, 1991. Amended Stats 2004 ch 888 §4 (AB 2687), effective January 1, 2005.

Prior Law: Former Prob C §7603, similar to the present section, was added Stats 1988 ch 1199 §80.5, operative July 1, 1989, and repealed Stats 1990 ch 79 §13, operative July 1, 1991.

§7604. Costs and compensation when public administrator or subsequently appointed representative takes control

If the public administrator takes possession or control of property of a decedent under this article, but another person is subsequently appointed personal representative or subsequently takes control or possession, the public administrator is entitled to reasonable costs incurred for the preservation of the estate, together with reasonable compensation for services. The costs and compensation are a proper expense of administration. **Leg.H.** Enacted Stats 1990 ch 79 §14 (AB 759), operative July 1, 1991. Amended Stats 1994 ch 806 §24 (AB 3686).

Prior Law: Former Prob C §7604, similar to the present section, was added Stats 1988 ch 1199 §80.5, operative July 1, 1989, and repealed Stats 1990 ch 79 §13, operative July 1, 1991.

§7605. Public administrator, continuing education requirements

On or before January 1, 2010, the public administrator shall comply with the continuing education requirements that are established by the California State Association of Public Administrators, Public Guardians, and Public Conservators. **Leg.H.** Added Stats 2008 ch 237 §3 (AB 2343), effective January 1, 2009.

ARTICLE 2
Appointment as Personal Representative

Petition for appointment; Court-ordered appointment. §7620.
Procedure for appointment; Bond fee. §7621.
Manner of administration; Compensation of public administrator. §7622.
Additional compensation. §7623.
Money remaining after final distribution of estate. §7624.

§7620. Petition for appointment; Court-ordered appointment

The public administrator of the county in which the estate of a decedent may be administered shall promptly:

(a) Petition for appointment as personal representative of the estate if no person having higher priority has petitioned for appointment and the total value of the property in the decedent's estate exceeds one hundred fifty thousand dollars ($150,000).

(b) Petition for appointment as personal representative of any other estate the public administrator determines is proper.

(c) Accept appointment as personal representative of an estate when so ordered by the court, whether or not on petition of the public administrator, after notice to the public administrator as provided in Section 7621.

(d) Proceed with summary disposition of the estate as authorized by Article 4 (commencing with Section 7660), if the total value of the property in the decedent's estate does not exceed the amount prescribed in Section 13100 and a person having higher priority has not assumed responsibility for administration of the estate. **Leg.H.** Enacted Stats 1990 ch 79 §14 (AB 759), operative July 1, 1991. Amended Stats 2004 ch 888 §5 (AB 2687); Stats 2011 ch 117 §1 (AB 1305), effective January 1, 2012.

Prior Law: Former Prob C §7620, similar to the present section, was added Stats 1988 ch 1199 §80.5, operative July 1, 1989, and repealed Stats 1990 ch 79 §13, operative July 1, 1991.

§7621. Procedure for appointment; Bond fee

(a) Except as otherwise provided in this section, appointment of the public administrator as personal representative shall be made, and letters issued, in the same manner and pursuant to the same procedure as for appointment of and issuance of letters to personal representatives generally.

(b) Appointment of the public administrator may be made on the court's own motion, after notice to the public administrator as provided in Section 1220.

(c) Letters may be issued to "the public administrator" of the county without naming the public administrator.

(d) The public administrator's oath and official bond are in lieu of the personal representative's oath and bond. Every estate administered under this chapter shall be charged an annual bond fee in the amount of twenty-five dollars ($25) plus one-fourth of one percent of the amount of an estate greater than ten thousand dollars ($10,000). The amount charged is an expense of administration and that amount shall be deposited in the county treasury. If a successor personal representative is appointed, the amount of the bond fee shall be prorated over the period of months during which the public administrator acted as personal representative. Upon final distribution by the public administrator, any amount of bond charges in excess of one year shall be a prorated charge to the estate. **Leg.H.** Enacted Stats 1990 ch 79 §14 (AB 759), operative July 1, 1991. Amended Stats 1995 ch 160 §1 (AB 128).

Prior Law: Former Prob C §7621, similar to the present section, was added Stats 1988 ch 1199 §80.5, operative July 1, 1989, and repealed Stats 1990 ch 79 §13, operative July 1, 1991.

§7622. Manner of administration; Compensation of public administrator

Except as otherwise provided in this chapter:

(a) The public administrator shall administer the estate in the same manner as a personal representative generally, and the provisions of this code concerning the administration of the decedent's estate apply to administration by the public administrator.

(b) The public administrator is entitled to receive the same compensation as is granted by this division to a personal representative generally. The attorney for the public administrator is entitled to receive the same compensation as is granted by this division to an attorney for a personal representative generally. However, the compensation of the public administrator and the public administrator's attorney may not be less than the compensation in effect at the time of appointment of the public administrator or the minimum amount provided in subdivision (b) of Section 7666, whichever is greater. **Leg.H.** Enacted Stats 1990 ch 79 §14 (AB 759), operative July 1, 1991. Amended Stats 1991 ch 82 §22 (SB 896), effective June 30, 1991, operative July 1, 1991; Stats 2004 ch 888 §6 (AB 2687), effective January 1, 2005.

Prior Law: Former Prob C §7622, similar to the present section, was added Stats 1988 ch 1199 §80.5, operative July 1, 1989, amended Stats 1989 ch 21 §16, effective May 25, 1989, operative July 1, 1989, and repealed Stats 1990 ch 79 §13, operative July 1, 1991.

§7623. Additional compensation

(a) As used in this section, "additional compensation" means the difference between the reasonable compensation of the public administrator in administering the estate and the compensation awarded the public administrator under Chapter 1 (commencing with Section 10800) of Part 7.

(b) The public administrator may be awarded additional compensation if any of the following conditions are satisfied:

(1) A person having priority for appointment as personal representative has been given notice under Section 8110 of the public administrator's

petition for appointment, and the person has not petitioned for appointment in preference to the public administrator.

(2) The public administrator has been appointed after the resignation or removal of a personal representative. **Leg.H.** Enacted Stats 1990 ch 79 §14 (AB 759), operative July 1, 1991.

Prior Law: Former Prob C §7623, similar to the present section, was added Stats 1988 ch 1199 §80.5, operative July 1, 1989, and repealed Stats 1990 ch 79 §13, operative July 1, 1991.

§7624. Money remaining after final distribution of estate

(a) If after final distribution of an estate any money remains in the possession of the public administrator that should be paid over to the county treasurer pursuant to Chapter 5 (commencing with Section 11850) of Part 10, the court shall order payment to be made within 60 days.

(b) Upon failure of the public administrator to comply with an order made pursuant to subdivision (a), the district attorney of the county shall promptly institute proceedings against the public administrator and the sureties on the official bond for the amount ordered to be paid, plus costs. **Leg.H.** Enacted Stats 1990 ch 79 §14 (AB 759), operative July 1, 1991.

Prior Law: Former Prob C §7624, similar to the present section, was added Stats 1988 ch 1199 §80.5, operative July 1, 1989, and repealed Stats 1990 ch 79 §13, operative July 1, 1991.

ARTICLE 3
Deposit of Money of Estate

Deposit with financial institution or county treasurer. §7640.
Withdrawals. §7641.
Interest or dividends. §7642.
County treasurer's duties with reference to deposit. §7643.
Abandoned deposit in financial institution. §7644.

§7640. Deposit with financial institution or county treasurer

(a) The public administrator shall, upon receipt, deposit all money of the estate in an insured account in a financial institution or with the county treasurer of the county in which the proceedings are pending.

(b) Upon deposit under this section the public administrator is discharged from further responsibility for the money deposited until the public administrator withdraws the money. **Leg.H.** Enacted Stats 1990 ch 79 §14 (AB 759), operative July 1, 1991.

Prior Law: Former Prob C §7640, similar to the present section, was added Stats 1988 ch 1199 §80.5, operative July 1, 1989, and repealed Stats 1990 ch 79 §13, operative July 1, 1991.

§7641. Withdrawals

Money deposited in a financial institution or with the county treasurer under this article may be withdrawn upon the order of the public administrator when required for the purposes of administration. **Leg.H.** Enacted Stats 1990 ch 79 §14 (AB 759), operative July 1, 1991.

Prior Law: Former Prob C §7641, similar to the present section, was added Stats 1988 ch 1199 §80.5, operative July 1, 1989, and repealed Stats 1990 ch 79 §13, operative July 1, 1991.

§7642. Interest or dividends

(a) The public administrator shall credit each estate with the highest rate of interest or dividends that the estate would have received if the funds available for deposit had been individually and separately deposited.

(b) Interest or dividends credited to the account of the public administrator in excess of the amount credited to the estates pursuant to subdivision (a) shall be deposited in the county general fund. **Leg.H.** Enacted Stats 1990 ch 79 §14 (AB 759), operative July 1, 1991.

Prior Law: Former Prob C §7642, similar to the present section, was added Stats 1988 ch 1199 §80.5, operative July 1, 1989, and repealed Stats 1990 ch 79 §13, operative July 1, 1991.

§7643. County treasurer's duties with reference to deposit

(a) The county treasurer shall receive and safely keep all money deposited with the county treasurer under this chapter and pay the money out on the order of the public administrator when required for the purposes of administration. The county treasurer and sureties on the official bond of the county treasurer are responsible for the safekeeping and payment of the money.

(b) The county treasurer shall deliver to the State Treasurer or the Controller all money in the possession of the county treasurer belonging to the estate, if there are no beneficiaries or other persons entitled to the money, or the beneficiaries or other persons entitled to the money do not appear and claim it. Delivery shall be made under the provisions of Article 1 (commencing with Section 1440) of Chapter 6 of Title 10 of Part 3 of the Code of Civil Procedure. **Leg.H.** Enacted Stats 1990 ch 79 §14 (AB 759), operative July 1, 1991.

Prior Law: Former Prob C §7643, similar to the present section, was added Stats 1988 ch 1199 §80.5, operative July 1, 1989, and repealed Stats 1990 ch 79 §13, operative July 1, 1991.

§7644. Abandoned deposit in financial institution

(a) If a deposit in a financial institution is made under this article, money remaining unclaimed at the expiration of five years after the date of the deposit, together with the increase and proceeds of the deposit, shall be presumed abandoned in any of the following circumstances:

(1) The deposit belongs to the estate of a known decedent for which a personal representative has never been appointed.

(2) The deposit belongs to the estate of a known decedent for which a personal representative has been appointed but no order of distribution has been made due to the absence of interested persons or the failure of interested persons diligently to protect their interests by taking reasonable steps for the purpose of securing a distribution of the estate.

(b) The Controller may, at any time after the expiration of the five-year period, file a petition with the court setting forth the fact that the money has remained on deposit in a financial institution under the circumstances described in subdivision (a) for the five-year period, and requesting an order declaring that the money is presumptively abandoned and directing the holder of the money to pay the money to the State Treasurer.

(c) Upon presentation of a certified copy of a court order made under subdivision (b), the financial institution shall forthwith transmit the money to the State Treasurer for deposit in the State Treasury. The deposit shall be made as provided in Section 1310 of the Code of Civil Procedure. All money deposited in the State Treasury under the provisions of this section shall be deemed to be deposited in the State Treasury under the provisions of Article 1 (commencing with Section 1440) of Chapter 6 of Title 10 of Part 3 of the Code of Civil Procedure. The deposit shall be transmitted, received, accounted for, and disposed of as provided by Title 10 (commencing with Section 1300) of Part 3 of the Code of Civil Procedure. **Leg.H.** Enacted Stats 1990 ch 79 §14 (AB 759), operative July 1, 1991.

Prior Law: Former Prob C §7644, similar to the present section, was added Stats 1988 ch 1199 §80.5, operative July 1, 1989, and repealed Stats 1990 ch 79 §13, operative July 1, 1991.

ARTICLE 4
Summary Disposition of Small Estates

Estates subject to summary disposition; Fee. §7660.
Collection and sale of property. §7661.
Priority for payments from estate. §7662.
Distribution of property. §7663.
Liability for decedent's unsecured debts. §7664.
Statement showing property and disposition; Receipts and records of expenditures. §7665.
Compensation of public administrator and attorney for public administrator. §7666.

§7660. Estates subject to summary disposition; Fee

(a) If a public administrator takes possession or control of an estate pursuant to this chapter, the public administrator may, acting as personal representative of the estate, summarily dispose of the estate in the manner provided in this article in either of the following circumstances:

(1) The total value of the property in the decedent's estate does not exceed the amount prescribed in Section 13100. The authority provided by this paragraph may be exercised only upon order of the court. The order may be made upon ex parte application. The fee to be allowed to the clerk for the filing of the application is two hundred five dollars ($205). The authority for this summary administration of the estate shall be evidenced by a court order for summary disposition.

(2) The total value of the property in the decedent's estate does not exceed fifty thousand dollars ($50,000). The authority provided by this paragraph may be exercised without court authorization.

(A) A public administrator who is authorized to summarily dispose of property of a decedent pursuant to this paragraph may issue a written certification of Authority for Summary Administration. The written certification is effective for 30 days after the date of issuance.

(B) A financial institution, government or private agency, retirement fund administrator, insurance company, licensed securities dealer, or other person shall, without the necessity of inquiring into the truth of the written certification of Authority for Summary Administration and without court order or letters being issued, do all of the following:

(i) Provide the public administrator complete information concerning any property held in the name of the decedent, including the names and addresses of any beneficiaries or joint owners.

(ii) Grant the public administrator access to a safe-deposit box or storage facility rented in the name of the decedent for the purpose of inspection and removal of property of the decedent. Costs and expenses incurred in accessing a safe-deposit box or storage facility shall be borne by the estate of the decedent.

(iii) Surrender to the public administrator any property of the decedent that is held or controlled by the financial institution, agency, retirement fund administrator, insurance company, licensed securities dealer, or other person.

(C) Receipt by a financial institution, government or private agency, retirement fund administrator, insurance company, licensed securities dealer, or other person of the written certification provided by this article shall do both of the following:

(i) Constitute sufficient acquittance for providing information or granting access to a safe-deposit box or a storage facility and for surrendering any property of the decedent.

(ii) Fully discharge the financial institution, government or private agency, retirement fund administrator, insurance company, licensed securities dealer, or other person from liability for any act or omission of the public administrator with respect to the property, a safe-deposit box, or a storage facility.

(b) Summary disposition may be made notwithstanding the existence of the decedent's will, if the will does not name an executor or if the named executor refuses to act.

(c) Nothing in this article precludes the public administrator from filing a petition with the court under any other provision of this code concerning the administration of the decedent's estate.

(d) Petitions filed pursuant to this article shall contain the information required by Section 8002.

(e) If a public administrator takes possession or control of an estate pursuant to this chapter, this article conveys the authority of a personal representative as described in Section 9650 to the public administrator to summarily dispose of the estates pursuant to the procedures described in paragraphs (1) and (2) of subdivision (a).

(f) The fee charged under paragraph (1) of subdivision (a) shall be distributed as provided in Section 68085.4 of the Government Code. When an application is filed under that paragraph, no other fees shall be charged in addition to the uniform filing fee provided for in Section 68085.4 of the Government Code. **Leg.H.** Enacted Stats 1990 ch 79 §14 (AB 759), operative July 1, 1991. Amended Stats 1997 ch 63 §1 (AB 1165), ch 93 §2.5 (SB 696); Stats 2004 ch 888 §7 (AB 2687); Stats 2005 ch 75 §149 (AB 145), effective July 19, 2005, operative January 1, 2006; Stats 2008 ch 311 §29 (SB 1407), effective January 1, 2009; Stats 2009 4th Ex Sess 2009–2010 ch 22 §32 (SBX4-13), effective July 28, 2009; Stats 2011 ch 117 §2 (AB 1305), effective January 1, 2012; Stats 2012 ch 162 §139 (SB 1171), effective January 1, 2013.

Prior Law: Former Prob C §7660, similar to the present section, was added Stats 1988 ch 1199 §80.5, operative July 1, 1989, and repealed Stats 1990 ch 79 §13, operative July 1, 1991.

§7661. Collection and sale of property

A public administrator acting under authority of this article may:

(a) Withdraw money or take possession of any other property of the decedent that is in the possession or control of a financial institution, government or private agency, retirement fund administrator, insurance company, licensed securities dealer, or other person.

(b) Collect any debts owed to the decedent, including, but not limited to, any rents, issues, or profits from the real and personal property in the estate until the estate is distributed.

(c) Sell any personal property of the decedent, including, but not limited to, stocks, bonds, mutual funds and other types of securities. Sales may be made with or without notice, as the public administrator elects. Title to the property sold passes without the need for confirmation by the court.

(d) Sell any real property of the decedent. The sale shall be accomplished through one of the following procedures:

(1) The sale may be conducted subject to Article 6 (commencing with Section 10300) of Chapter 18 of Part 5.

(2) With approval specified in the original court order for summary disposition of the estate, the sale of real property may be accomplished using a Notice of Proposed Action according to the following requirements:

(A) The publication of the sale shall be accomplished according to Sections 10300 to 10307, inclusive.

(B) The appraisal of the property and determination of the minimum sale price of 90 percent of the appraised value shall be accomplished according to Section 10309.

(C) If an offer meets the approval of the public administrator and the offered price is at least 90 percent of the appraised value, a notice of proposed action shall be made according to Sections 10581 to 10588, inclusive. If objection is not made to the notice of proposed action, the sale may be completed without a court confirmation of the sale. The sale may be consummated by recording a public administrator's deed and a copy of the court order for summary disposition that authorized the use of the notice of proposed action.

(D) If an objection to the notice of proposed action is made pursuant to Section 10587, the sale shall be confirmed in court according to Sections 10308 to 10316, inclusive. The sale may be consummated by recording an administrator's deed and a copy of the court order confirming the sale.

(E) If objection to the notice of proposed action is not made under Section 10587, the public administrator may still elect to have the sale confirmed in court according to Sections 10308 to 10316, inclusive, if the public administrator deems that is in the best interest of the estate. Title to the property sold passes with the public administrator's deed. **Leg.H.** Enacted Stats 1990 ch 79 §14 (AB 759), operative July 1, 1991. Amended Stats 2004 ch 888 §8 (AB 2687), effective January 1, 2005.

Prior Law: Former Prob C §7661, similar to the present section, was added Stats 1988 ch 1199 §80.5, operative July 1, 1989, and repealed Stats 1990 ch 79 §13, operative July 1, 1991.

§7662. Priority for payments from estate

The public administrator acting under authority of this article shall pay out the money of the estate in the order prescribed in Section 11420, for expenses of administration, charges against the estate, and claims presented to the public administrator before distribution of the decedent's property pursuant to Section 7663. A creditor whose claim is paid under this section is not liable for contribution to a creditor whose claim is presented after the payment. **Leg.H.** Enacted Stats 1990 ch 79 §14 (AB 759), operative July 1, 1991. Amended Stats 1990 ch 710 §18 (SB 1775), operative July 1, 1991; Stats 1991 ch 82 §23 (SB 896), effective June 30, 1991, operative July 1, 1991.

Prior Law: Former Prob C §7662, similar to the present section, was added Stats 1988 ch 1199 §80.5, operative July 1, 1989, and repealed Stats 1990 ch 79 §13, operative July 1, 1991.

§7663. Distribution of property

(a) After payment of debts pursuant to Section 7662, but in no case before four months after court authorization of the public administrator to act under this article or after the public administrator takes possession or control of the estate, the public administrator shall distribute to the decedent's beneficiaries any money or other property of the decedent remaining in the possession of the public administrator.

(b) If there are no beneficiaries, the public administrator shall deposit the balance with the county treasurer for use in the general fund of the county, subject to Article 3 (commencing with Section 50050) of Chapter 1 of Part 1 of Division 1 of Title 5 of the Government Code. If the amount deposited exceeds five thousand dollars ($5,000), the public administrator shall at the time of the deposit give the Controller written notice of the information specified in Section 1311 of the Code of Civil Procedure. **Leg.H.** Enacted Stats 1990 ch 79 §14 (AB 759), operative July 1, 1991. Amended Stats 1990 ch 324 §2 (SB 1774), effective July 16, 1990, operative July 1, 1991; Stats 1996 ch 401 §2 (SB 1582).

Prior Law: Former Prob C §7663, similar to the present section, was added Stats 1988 ch 1199 §80.5, operative July 1, 1989, repealed Stats 1990 ch 79 §13, operative July 1, 1991, amended Stats 1990 ch 324 §1, effective July 16, 1990, operative until July 1, 1991, and repealed Stats 1990 ch 324 Former Prob C §4, effective July 16, 1990, operative July 1, 1991.

§7664. Liability for decedent's unsecured debts

A person to whom property is distributed under this article is personally liable for the unsecured debts of the decedent. Such a debt may be enforced against the person in the same manner as it could have been enforced against the decedent if the decedent had not died. In an action based on the debt, the person may assert any defenses available to the decedent if the decedent had not died. The aggregate personal liability of a person under this section shall not exceed the fair market value of the property distributed to the person, valued as of the date of the distribution, less the amount of any liens and encumbrances on the property on that date. Section 366.2 of the Code of Civil Procedure applies in an action under this section. **Leg.H.** Enacted Stats 1990 ch 79 §14 (AB 759), operative July 1, 1991. Amended Stats 1990 ch 140 §5.1 (SB 1855), operative July 1, 1991; Stats 1992 ch 178 §33 (SB 1496).

Prior Law: Former Prob C§7664, similar to the present section, was added Stats 1988 ch 1199 §80.5, operative July 1, 1989, repealed Stats 1990 ch 79 §13, operative July 1, 1991, amended Stats 1990 ch 140 §5, operative until July 1, 1991, and repealed Stats 1990 ch 140 §21, operative July 1, 1991.

§7665. Statement showing property and disposition; Receipts and records of expenditures

(a) The public administrator shall file with the clerk a statement showing the property of the decedent that came into possession of the public administrator and the disposition made of the property, together with receipts for all distributions. This subdivision does not apply to proceedings under paragraph (2) of subdivision (a) of Section 7660.

(b) The public administrator shall maintain a file of all receipts and records of expenditures for a period of three years after disposition of the property pursuant to Section 7663. **Leg.H.** Enacted Stats 1990 ch 79 §14 (AB 759), operative July 1, 1991.

Prior Law: Former Prob C §7665, similar to the present section, was added Stats 1988 ch 1199 §80.5, operative July 1, 1989, and repealed Stats 1990 ch 79 §13, operative July 1, 1991.

§7666. Compensation of public administrator and attorney for public administrator

(a) Except as provided in Section 7623 and in subdivision (b), the compensation payable to the public administrator and the attorney, if any, for the public administrator for the filing of an application pursuant to this chapter and for performance of any duty or service connected with that filing is as set forth in Part 7 (commencing with Section 10800).

(b) The public administrator is entitled to a minimum compensation of three thousand dollars ($3,000). **Leg.H.** Enacted Stats 1990 ch 79 §14 (AB 759), operative July 1, 1991. Amended Stats 1990 ch 710 §19 (SB 1775), operative July 1, 1991; Stats 1991 ch 1019 §8 (SB 1022); Stats 1998 ch 103 §3 (SB 1487); Stats 2004 ch 888 §9 (AB 2687); Stats 2022 ch 151 §1 (SB 928), effective January 1, 2023.

Prior Law: Former Prob C §7666, similar to the present section, was added Stats 1988 ch 1199 §80.5, operative July 1, 1989, and repealed Stats 1990 ch 79 §13, operative July 1, 1991.

PART 2
OPENING ESTATE ADMINISTRATION

Chapter 1. Commencement of Proceedings.
Chapter 2. Notice of Hearing.
Chapter 3. Probate of Will.
Chapter 4. Appointment of Personal Representative.

CHAPTER 1
COMMENCEMENT OF PROCEEDINGS

Petition. §8000.
Failure of person named executor to petition. §8001.
Contents of petition. §8002.
Setting and notice of hearing. §8003.
Opposition. §8004.
Hearing; Examination and compelling attendance of witnesses; Matters to be established. §8005.
Court order. §8006.
Determination of jurisdiction conclusive. §8007.

§8000. Petition

(a) At any time after a decedent's death, any interested person may commence proceedings for administration of the estate of the decedent by a petition to the court for an order determining the date and place of the decedent's death and for either or both of the following:

(1) Appointment of a personal representative.

(2) Probate of the decedent's will.

(b) A petition for probate of the decedent's will may be made, regardless of whether the will is in the petitioner's possession or is lost, destroyed, or beyond the jurisdiction of the state. **Leg.H.** Enacted Stats 1990 ch 79 §14 (AB 759), operative July 1, 1991.

Prior Law: Former Prob C §8000, similar to the present section, was added Stats 1988 ch 1199 §81.5, operative July 1, 1989, and repealed Stats 1990 ch 79 §13, operative July 1, 1991.

§8001. Failure of person named executor to petition

Unless good cause for delay is shown, if a person named in a will as executor fails to petition the court for administration of the estate within 30 days after the person has knowledge of the death of the decedent and that the person is named as executor, the person may be held to have waived the right to appointment as personal representative. **Leg.H.** Enacted Stats 1990 ch 79 §14 (AB 759), operative July 1, 1991.

Prior Law: Former Prob C §8001, similar to the present section, was added Stats 1988 ch 1199 §81.5, operative July 1, 1989, and repealed Stats 1990 ch 79 §13, operative July 1, 1991.

§8002. Contents of petition

(a) The petition shall contain all of the following information:

(1) The date and place of the decedent's death.

(2) The street number, street, and city, or other address, and the county, of the decedent's residence at the time of death.

(3) The name, age, address, and relation to the decedent of each heir and devisee of the decedent, so far as known to or reasonably ascertainable by the petitioner.

(4) The character and estimated value of the property in the estate.

(5) The name of the person for whom appointment as personal representative is petitioned.

(b) If the decedent left a will:

(1) The petitioner shall attach to the petition a photographic copy of the will. In the case of a holographic will or other will of which material provisions are handwritten, the petitioner shall also attach a typed copy of the will.

(2) If the will is in a foreign language, the petitioner shall attach an English language translation. On admission of the will to probate, the court shall certify to a correct translation into English, and the certified translation shall be filed with the will.

(3) The petition shall state whether the person named as executor in the will consents to act or waives the right to appointment. **Leg.H.** Enacted Stats 1990 ch 79 §14 (AB 759), operative July 1, 1991.

Prior Law: Former Prob C §8002, similar to the present section, was added Stats 1988 ch 1199 §81.5, operative July 1, 1989, and repealed Stats 1990 ch 79 §13, operative July 1, 1991.

§8003. Setting and notice of hearing

(a) The hearing on the petition shall be set for a day not less than 15 nor more than 30 days after the petition is filed. At the request of the petitioner made at the time the petition is filed, the hearing on the petition shall be set for a day not less than 30 nor more than 45 days after the petition is filed. The court may not shorten the time for giving the notice of hearing under this section.

(b) The petitioner shall serve and publish notice of the hearing in the manner prescribed in Chapter 2 (commencing with Section 8100). **Leg.H.** Enacted Stats 1990 ch 79 §14 (AB 759), operative July 1, 1991.

Prior Law: Former Prob C §8003, similar to the present section, was added Stats 1988 ch 1199 §81.5, operative July 1, 1989, and repealed Stats 1990 ch 79 §13, operative July 1, 1991.

§8004. Opposition

(a) If appointment of the personal representative is contested, the grounds of opposition may include a challenge to the competency of the personal representative or the right to appointment. If the contest asserts the right of another person to appointment as personal representative, the contestant shall also file a petition and serve notice in the manner provided in Article 2 (commencing with Section 8110) of Chapter 2, and the court shall hear the two petitions together.

(b) If a will is contested, the applicable procedure is that provided in Article 3 (commencing with Section 8250) of Chapter 3. **Leg.H.** Enacted Stats 1990 ch 79 §14 (AB 759), operative July 1, 1991.

Prior Law: Former Prob C §8004, similar to the present section, was added Stats 1988 ch 1199 §81.5, operative July 1, 1989, and repealed Stats 1990 ch 79 §13, operative July 1, 1991.

§8005. Hearing; Examination and compelling attendance of witnesses; Matters to be established

(a) At the hearing on the petition, the court may examine and compel any person to attend as a witness concerning any of the following matters:

(1) The time, place, and manner of the decedent's death.

(2) The place of the decedent's domicile and residence at the time of death.

(3) The character and value of the decedent's property.

(4) Whether or not the decedent left a will.

(b) The following matters shall be established:

(1) The jurisdictional facts, including:

(A) The date and place of the decedent's death.

(B) That the decedent was domiciled in this state or left property in this state at the time of death.

(C) The publication of notice under Article 3 (commencing with Section 8120) of Chapter 2.

(2) The existence or nonexistence of the decedent's will.

(3) That notice of the hearing was served as provided in Article 2 (commencing with Section 8110) of Chapter 2. **Leg.H.** Enacted Stats 1990 ch 79 §14 (AB 759), operative July 1, 1991.

Prior Law: Former Prob C §8005, similar to the present section, was added Stats 1988 ch 1199 §81.5, operative July 1, 1989, and repealed Stats 1990 ch 79 §13, operative July 1, 1991.

§8006. Court order

(a) If the court finds that the matters referred to in paragraph (1) of subdivision (b) of Section 8005 are established, the court shall make an order determining the time and place of the decedent's death and the jurisdiction of the court. Where appropriate and on satisfactory proof, the order shall admit the decedent's will to probate and appoint a personal representative. The date the will is admitted to probate shall be included in the order.

(b) If through defect of form or error the matters referred to in paragraph (1) of subdivision (b) of Section 8005 are incorrectly stated in the petition but actually are established, the court has and retains jurisdiction to correct the defect or error at any time. No such defect or error makes void an order admitting the will to probate or appointing a personal representative or an order made in any subsequent proceeding. **Leg.H.** Enacted Stats 1990 ch 79 §14 (AB 759), operative July 1, 1991.

Prior Law: Former Prob C §8006, similar to the present section, was added Stats 1988 ch 1199 §81.5, operative July 1, 1989, and repealed Stats 1990 ch 79 §13, operative July 1, 1991.

§8007. Determination of jurisdiction conclusive

(a) Except as provided in subdivision (b), an order admitting a will to probate or appointing a personal representative, when it becomes final, is a conclusive determination of the jurisdiction of the court and cannot be collaterally attacked.

(b) Subdivision (a) does not apply in either of the following cases:

(1) The presence of extrinsic fraud in the procurement of the court order.

(2) The court order is based on the erroneous determination of the decedent's death. **Leg.H.** Enacted Stats 1990 ch 79 §14 (AB 759), operative July 1, 1991.

Prior Law: Former Prob C §8007, similar to the present section, was added Stats 1988 ch 1199 §81.5, operative July 1, 1989, and repealed Stats 1990 ch 79 §13, operative July 1, 1991.

CHAPTER 2
NOTICE OF HEARING

Article 1. Contents.
Article 2. Service of Notice of Hearing.
Article 3. Publication.

ARTICLE 1
Contents

Form of notice of hearing. §8100.

§8100. Form of notice of hearing

The notice of hearing of a petition for administration of a decedent's estate, whether delivered under Article 2 (commencing with Section 8110) or published under Article 3 (commencing with Section 8120), shall state substantially as follows:

NOTICE OF PETITION TO ADMINISTER
ESTATE OF _____, ESTATE NO. _____

To all heirs, beneficiaries, creditors, and contingent creditors of _____ and persons who may be otherwise interested in the will or estate, or both:

A petition has been filed by _____ in the Superior Court of California, County of _____, requesting that _____ be appointed as personal representative to administer the estate of _____ [and for probate of the decedent's will, which is available for examination in the court file].

[The petition requests authority to administer the estate under the Independent Administration of Estates Act. This will avoid the need to obtain court approval for many actions taken in connection with the estate. However, before taking certain actions, the personal representative will be required to give notice to interested persons unless they have waived notice or have consented to the proposed action. The petition will be granted unless good cause is shown why it should not be.]

The petition is set for hearing in Dept. No. ____
at _____ on _____
(Address)   (Date of hearing)
at _____.
(Time of hearing)

IF YOU OBJECT to the granting of the petition, you should appear at the hearing and state your objections or file written objections with the court before the hearing. Your appearance may be in person or by your attorney.

IF YOU ARE A CREDITOR or a contingent creditor of the deceased, you must file your claim with the court and mail a copy to the personal representative appointed by the court within the later of either (1) four months from the date of first issuance of letters to a general personal representative, as defined in subdivision (b) of Section 58 of the California Probate Code, or (2) 60 days from the date of delivery of the notice to you under Section 9052 of the California Probate Code.

YOU MAY EXAMINE the file kept by the court. If you are interested in the estate, you may request special notice of the filing of an inventory and appraisal of estate assets or of any petition or account as provided in Section 1250 of the California Probate Code.

_____
(Name and address of petitioner or petitioner's attorney)

Leg.H. Enacted Stats 1990 ch 79 §14 (AB 759), operative July 1, 1991. Amended Stats 2012 ch 207 §2 (AB 2683), effective January 1, 2012; Stats 2017 ch 319 §63 (AB 976), effective January 1, 2018.

Prior Law: Former Prob C §8100, similar to the present section, was added Stats 1988 ch 1199 §81.5, operative July 1, 1989, and repealed Stats 1990 ch 79 §13, operative July 1, 1991.

ARTICLE 2
Service of Notice of Hearing

Time for delivery of notice; Manner; Persons to be served. §8110.
Delivery to Attorney General. §8111.
Notice to creditors and public entity claimants. §8112.
Notice involving foreign citizen. §8113.

§8110. Time for delivery of notice; Manner; Persons to be served

At least 15 days before the hearing of a petition for administration of a decedent's estate, the petitioner shall deliver notice of the hearing pursuant to Section 1215 on all of the following persons:

(a) Each heir of the decedent, so far as known to or reasonably ascertainable by the petitioner.

(b) Each devisee, executor, and alternative executor named in any will being offered for probate, regardless of whether the devise or appointment is purportedly revoked in a subsequent instrument. **Leg.H.** Enacted Stats 1990 ch 79 §14 (AB 759), operative July 1, 1991. Amended Stats 1996 ch 563 §22 (SB 392); Stats 2017 ch 319 §64 (AB 976), effective January 1, 2018.

Prior Law: Former Prob C §8110, similar to the present section, was added Stats 1988 ch 1199 §81.5, operative July 1, 1989, and repealed Stats 1990 ch 79 §13, operative July 1, 1991.

§8111. Delivery to Attorney General

If the decedent's will involves or may involve a testamentary trust of property for charitable purposes other than a charitable trust with a designated trustee resident in this state, or involves or may involve a devise for charitable purposes without an identified devisee, notice of hearing accompanied by a copy of the petition and of the will shall be delivered pursuant to Section 1215 to the Attorney General as provided in Section 1209. **Leg.H.** Enacted Stats 1990 ch 79 §14 (AB 759), operative July 1, 1991. Amended Stats 2017 ch 319 §65 (AB 976), effective January 1, 2018.

Prior Law: Former Prob C §8111, similar to the present section, was added Stats 1988 ch 1199 §81.5, operative July 1, 1989, and repealed Stats 1990 ch 79 §13, operative July 1, 1991.

§8112. Notice to creditors and public entity claimants

A general personal representative shall give notice of administration of the estate of the decedent to creditors under Chapter 2 (commencing with Section 9050), and to public entities under Chapter 5 (commencing with Section 9200), of Part 4. **Leg.H.** Enacted Stats 1990 ch 79 §14 (AB 759), operative July 1, 1991.

Prior Law: Former Prob C §8112, similar to the present section, was added Stats 1988 ch 1199 §81.5, operative July 1, 1989, and repealed Stats 1990 ch 79 §13, operative July 1, 1991.

§8113. Notice involving foreign citizen

If a citizen of a foreign country dies without leaving a will or leaves a will without naming an executor, or if it appears that property will pass to a citizen of a foreign country, notice shall be given to a recognized diplomatic or consular official of the foreign country maintaining an office in the United States. **Leg.H.** Enacted Stats 1990 ch 79 §14 (AB 759), operative July 1, 1991.

Prior Law: Former Prob C §8113, similar to the present section, was added Stats 1988 ch 1199 §81.5, operative July 1, 1989, and repealed Stats 1990 ch 79 §13, operative July 1, 1991.

ARTICLE 3
Publication

Publication required. §8120.
Time and manner of publication. §8121.
Good faith compliance with publication requirement. §8122.
Type size. §8123.
Affidavit of publication. §8124.
Contents of subsequent published notice. §8125.

§8120. Publication required

In addition to service of the notice of hearing as provided in Article 2 (commencing with Section 8110), notice of hearing of a petition for administration of a decedent's estate shall also be published before the hearing in the manner provided in this article. **Leg.H.** Enacted Stats 1990 ch 79 §14 (AB 759), operative July 1, 1991.

Prior Law: Former Prob C §8120, similar to the present section, was added Stats 1988 ch 1199 §81.5, operative July 1, 1989, and repealed Stats 1990 ch 79 §13, operative July 1, 1991.

§8121. Time and manner of publication

(a) The first publication date of the notice shall be at least 15 days before the hearing. Three publications in a newspaper published once a week or more often, with at least five days intervening between the first and last publication dates, not counting the publication dates, are sufficient.

(b) Notice shall be published in a newspaper of general circulation in the city where the decedent resided at the time of death, or where the decedent's property is located if the court has jurisdiction under Section 7052. If there is no such newspaper, or if the decedent did not reside in a city, or if the property is not located in a city, then notice shall be published in a newspaper of general circulation in the county which is circulated within the area of the county in which the decedent resided or the property is located. If there is no such newspaper, notice shall be published in a newspaper of general circulation published in this state nearest to the county seat of the county in which the decedent resided or the property is located, and which is circulated within the area of the county in which the decedent resided or the property is located.

(c) For purposes of this section, "city" means a charter city as defined in Section 34101 of the Government Code or a general law city as defined in Section 34102 of the Government Code. **Leg.H.** Enacted Stats 1990 ch 79 §14 (AB 759), operative July 1, 1991.

Prior Law: Former Prob C §8121, similar to the present section, was added Stats 1988 ch 1199 §81.5, operative July 1, 1989, and repealed Stats 1990 ch 79 §13, operative July 1, 1991.

§8122. Good faith compliance with publication requirement

The Legislature finds and declares that, to be most effective, notice of hearing should be published in compliance with Section 8121. However, the Legislature recognizes the possibility that in unusual cases due to confusion over jurisdictional boundaries or oversight such notice may inadvertently be published in a newspaper that does not satisfy Section 8121. Therefore, to prevent a minor error in publication from invalidating what would otherwise be a proper proceeding, the Legislature further finds and declares that notice published in a good faith attempt to comply with Section 8121 is sufficient to provide notice of hearing and to establish jurisdiction if the court expressly finds that the notice was published in a newspaper of general circulation published within the county and widely circulated within a true cross-section of the area of the county in which the decedent resided or the property was located in substantial compliance with Section 8121. **Leg.H.** Enacted Stats 1990 ch 79 §14 (AB 759), operative July 1, 1991.

Prior Law: Former Prob C §8122, similar to the present section, was added Stats 1988 ch 1199 §81.5, operative July 1, 1989, and repealed Stats 1990 ch 79 §13, operative July 1, 1991.

§8123. Type size

The caption of a notice under this article shall be in 8-point type or larger and the text shall be in 7-point type or larger. **Leg.H.** Enacted Stats 1990 ch 79 §14 (AB 759), operative July 1, 1991.

Prior Law: Former Prob C §8123, similar to the present section, was added Stats 1988 ch 1199 §81.5, operative July 1, 1989, and repealed Stats 1990 ch 79 §13, operative July 1, 1991.

§8124. Affidavit of publication

A petition for administration of a decedent's estate shall not be heard by the court unless an affidavit showing due publication of the notice of hearing has been filed with the court. The affidavit shall contain a copy of the notice and state the date of its publication. **Leg.H.** Enacted Stats 1990 ch 79 §14 (AB 759), operative July 1, 1991.

Prior Law: Former Prob C §8124, similar to the present section, was added Stats 1988 ch 1199 §81.5, operative July 1, 1989, and repealed Stats 1990 ch 79 §13, operative July 1, 1991.

§8125. Contents of subsequent published notice

Notwithstanding Section 8100, after the notice of hearing is published and an affidavit filed, any subsequent publication of the notice ordered by the court may omit the information for creditors and contingent creditors. **Leg.H.** Enacted Stats 1990 ch 79 §14 (AB 759), operative July 1, 1991.

Prior Law: Former Prob C §8125, similar to the present section, was added Stats 1988 ch 1199 §81.5, operative July 1, 1989, and repealed Stats 1990 ch 79 §13, operative July 1, 1991.

CHAPTER 3
PROBATE OF WILL

Article 1. Production of Will.
Article 2. Proof of Will.
Article 3. Contest of Will.
Article 4. Revocation of Probate.

ARTICLE 1
Production of Will

Delivery of will. §8200.
Order to produce will. §8201.
Will detained outside California. §8202.
Transfer of will. §8203.

§8200. Delivery of will

(a) Unless a petition for probate of the will is earlier filed, the custodian of a will shall, within 30 days after having knowledge of the death of the testator, do both of the following:

(1) Deliver the will, personally or by registered or certified mail, to the clerk of the superior court of the county in which the estate of the decedent may be administered.

(2) Deliver a copy of the will pursuant to Section 1215 to the person named in the will as executor, if the person's whereabouts is known to the custodian, or if not, to a person named in the will as a beneficiary, if the person's whereabouts is known to the custodian.

(b) A custodian of a will who fails to comply with the requirements of this section shall be liable for all damages sustained by any person injured by the failure.

(c) The clerk shall release a copy of a will delivered under this section for attachment to a petition for probate of the will or otherwise on receipt of payment of the required fee and either a court order for production of the will or a certified copy of a death certificate of the decedent.

(d) The fee for delivering a will to the clerk of the superior court pursuant to paragraph (1) of subdivision (a) shall be as provided in Section 70626 of the Government Code. If an estate is commenced for the decedent named in the will, the fee for any will delivered pursuant to paragraph (1) of subdivision (a) shall be reimbursable from the estate as an expense of administration. **Leg.H.** Enacted Stats 1990 ch 79 §14 (AB 759), operative July 1, 1991. Amended Stats 1994 ch 806 §25 (AB 3686); Stats 2012 ch 41 §86 (SB 1021), effective June 27, 2012; Stats 2013 ch 61 §2 (SB 826), effective January 1, 2014; Stats 2017 ch 319 §66 (AB 976), effective January 1, 2018.

Prior Law: Former Prob C §8200, similar to the present section, was added Stats 1988 ch 1199 §81.5, operative July 1, 1989, and repealed Stats 1990 ch 79 §13, operative July 1, 1991.

§8201. Order to produce will

If, on petition to the superior court of the county in which the estate of the decedent is being or may be administered alleging that a person has possession of a decedent's will, the court is satisfied that the allegation is true, the court shall order the person to produce the will. **Leg.H.** Enacted Stats 1990 ch 79 §14 (AB 759), operative July 1, 1991.

Prior Law: Former Prob C §8201, similar to the present section, was added Stats 1988 ch 1199 §81.5, operative July 1, 1989, and repealed Stats 1990 ch 79 §13, operative July 1, 1991.

§8202. Will detained outside California

If the will of a person who was domiciled in this state at the time of death is detained in a court of any other state or country and cannot be produced for probate in this state, a certified photographic copy of the will may be admitted to probate in this state with the same force and effect as the original will. The same proof shall be required as if the original will were produced. **Leg.H.** Enacted Stats 1990 ch 79 §14 (AB 759), operative July 1, 1991.

Prior Law: Former Prob C §8202, similar to the present section, was added Stats 1988 ch 1199 §81.5, operative July 1, 1989, and repealed Stats 1990 ch 79 §13, operative July 1, 1991.

§8203. Transfer of will

If a will has been delivered to the clerk of the superior court in a county in which no proceeding is pending to administer the testator's estate, that court may order the will transferred to the clerk of the superior court in a county in which such a proceeding is pending. A petition for the transfer may be presented and heard without notice, but shall not be granted without proof that a copy of the petition has been delivered pursuant to Section 1215 to the petitioner and any persons who have requested special notice in the proceeding in the court to which the will is to be transferred. The petition and order shall include the case number of the proceeding in the court to which transfer is prayed. Certified copies of the petition, any supporting documents, and the order shall be transmitted by the clerk along with the original will, and these copies shall be filed in the proceeding by the clerk of the recipient court. **Leg.H.** Added Stats 1992 ch 871 §10 (AB 2975). Amended Stats 2017 ch 319 §67 (AB 976), effective January 1, 2018.

ARTICLE 2
Proof of Will

Evidence of subscribing witness. §8220.
Proof where no subscribing witness available. §8221.
Holographic will. §8222.
Lost or destroyed will. §8223.
Preserving testimony; Admissibility in subsequent proceeding. §8224.
Admission of will to probate. §8225.
Effect of admission of will to probate. §8226.

§8220. Evidence of subscribing witness

Unless there is a contest of a will:

(a) The will may be proved on the evidence of one of the subscribing witnesses only, if the evidence shows that the will was executed in all particulars as prescribed by law.

(b) Evidence of execution of a will may be received by an affidavit of a subscribing witness to which there is attached a photographic copy of the will, or by an affidavit in the original will that includes or incorporates the attestation clause.

(c) If no subscribing witness resides in the county, but the deposition of a witness can be taken elsewhere, the court may direct the deposition to be taken. On the examination, the court may authorize a photographic copy of the will to be made and presented to the witness, and the witness may be asked the same questions with respect to the photographic copy as if the original will were present. **Leg.H.** Enacted Stats 1990 ch 79 §14 (AB 759), operative July 1, 1991.

Prior Law: Former Prob C §8220, similar to the present section, was added Stats 1988 ch 1199 §81.5, operative July 1, 1989, and repealed Stats 1990 ch 79 §13, operative July 1, 1991.

§8221. Proof where no subscribing witness available

If no subscribing witness is available as a witness within the meaning of Section 240 of the Evidence Code, the court may, if the will on its face conforms to all requirements of law, permit proof of the will by proof of the handwriting of the testator and one of the following:

(a) Proof of the handwriting of any one subscribing witness.

(b) Receipt in evidence of one of the following documents reciting facts showing due execution of the will:

(1) A writing in the will bearing the signatures of all subscribing witnesses.

(2) An affidavit of a person with personal knowledge of the circumstances of the execution. **Leg.H.** Enacted Stats 1990 ch 79 §14 (AB 759), operative July 1, 1991.

Prior Law: Former Prob C §8221, similar to the present section, was added Stats 1988 ch 1199 §81.5, operative July 1, 1989, and repealed Stats 1990 ch 79 §13, operative July 1, 1991.

§8222. Holographic will

A holographic will may be proved in the same manner as other writings. **Leg.H.** Enacted Stats 1990 ch 79 §14 (AB 759), operative July 1, 1991.

Prior Law: Former Prob C §8222, similar to the present section, was added Stats 1988 ch 1199 §81.5, operative July 1, 1989, and repealed Stats 1990 ch 79 §13, operative July 1, 1991.

§8223. Lost or destroyed will

The petition for probate of a lost or destroyed will shall include a written statement of the testamentary words or their substance. If the will is proved, the provisions of the will shall be set forth in the order admitting the will to probate. **Leg.H.** Enacted Stats 1990 ch 79 §14 (AB 759), operative July 1, 1991.

Prior Law: Former Prob C §8223, similar to the present section, was added Stats 1988 ch 1199 §81.5, operative July 1, 1989, and repealed Stats 1990 ch 79 §13, operative July 1, 1991.

§8224. Preserving testimony; Admissibility in subsequent proceeding

The testimony of each witness in a proceeding concerning the execution or provisions of a will, the testamentary capacity of the decedent, and other issues of fact, may be reduced to writing, signed by the witness, and filed, whether or not the will is contested. The testimony so preserved, or an official reporter's transcript of the testimony, is admissible in evidence in any subsequent proceeding concerning the will if the witness has become unavailable as a witness within the meaning of Section 240 of the Evidence Code. **Leg.H.** Enacted Stats 1990 ch 79 §14 (AB 759), operative July 1, 1991.

Prior Law: Former Prob C §8224, similar to the present section, was added Stats 1988 ch 1199 §81.5, operative July 1, 1989, and repealed Stats 1990 ch 79 §13, operative July 1, 1991.

§8225. Admission of will to probate

When the court admits a will to probate, that fact shall be recorded in the minutes by the clerk and the will shall be filed. **Leg.H.** Enacted Stats 1990 ch 79 §14 (AB 759), operative July 1, 1991.

Prior Law: Former Prob C §8225, similar to the present section, was added Stats 1988 ch 1199 §81.5, operative July 1, 1989, and repealed Stats 1990 ch 789 §13, operative July 1, 1991.

§8226. Effect of admission of will to probate

(a) If no person contests the validity of a will or petitions for revocation of probate of the will within the time provided in this chapter, admission of the will to probate is conclusive, subject to Section 8007.

(b) Subject to subdivision (c), a will may be admitted to probate notwithstanding prior admission to probate of another will or prior distribution of property in the proceeding. The will may not affect property previously distributed, but the court may determine how any provision of the will affects property not yet distributed and how any provision of the will affects provisions of another will.

(c) If the proponent of a will has received notice of a petition for probate or a petition for letters of administration for a general personal representative, the proponent of the will may petition for probate of the will only within the later of either of the following time periods:

(1) One hundred twenty days after issuance of the order admitting the first will to probate or determining the decedent to be intestate.

(2) Sixty days after the proponent of the will first obtains knowledge of the will. **Leg.H.** Enacted Stats 1990 ch 79 §14 (AB 759), operative July 1, 1991. Amended Stats 1997 ch 724 §19 (AB 1172).

Prior Law: Former Prob C §8226, similar to the present section, was added Stats 1988 ch 1199 §81.5, operative July 1, 1989, and repealed Stats 1990 ch 79 §13, operative July 1, 1991.

ARTICLE 3
Contest of Will

Summons; Persons to be served; Time for responsive pleading; Executor's duty to defend will. §8250.
Responsive pleading. §8251.
Trial. §8252.
Evidence of execution. §8253.
Judgment. §8254.

§8250. Summons; Persons to be served; Time for responsive pleading; Executor's duty to defend will

(a) When a will is contested under Section 8004, the contestant shall file with the court an objection to probate of the will. Thereafter, a summons shall be issued and served, with a copy of the objection, on the persons required by Section 8110 to be served with notice of hearing of a petition for administration of the decedent's estate. The summons shall be issued and served as provided in Chapter 3 (commencing with Section 412.10) and Chapter 4 (commencing with Section 413.10) of Title 5 of Part 2 of the Code of Civil Procedure. The summons shall contain a direction that the persons summoned file with the court a written pleading in response to the contest within 30 days after service of the summons.

(b) A person named as executor in the will is under no duty to defend a contest until the person is appointed personal representative. **Leg.H.** Enacted Stats 1990 ch 79 §14 (AB 759), operative July 1, 1991. Amended

Stats 1998 ch 581 §24 (AB 2801); Stats 2011 ch 308 §11 (SB 647), effective January 1, 2012.

Prior Law: Former Prob C §8250, similar to the present section, was added Stats 1988 ch 1199 §81.5, operative July 1, 1989, and repealed Stats 1990 ch 79 §13, operative July 1, 1991.

§8251. Responsive pleading

(a) The petitioner and any other interested person may jointly or separately answer the objection or demur to the objection within the time prescribed in the summons.

(b) Demurrer may be made on any of the grounds of demurrer available in a civil action. If the demurrer is sustained, the court may allow the contestant a reasonable time, not exceeding 15 days, within which to amend the objection. If the demurrer is overruled, the petitioner and other interested persons may, within 15 days thereafter, answer the objection.

(c) If a person fails timely to respond to the summons:

(1) The case is at issue notwithstanding the failure and the case may proceed on the petition and other documents filed by the time of the hearing, and no further pleadings by other persons are necessary.

(2) The person may not participate further in the contest, but the person's interest in the estate is not otherwise affected. Nothing in this paragraph precludes further participation by the petitioner.

(3) The person is bound by the decision in the proceeding. **Leg.H.** Enacted Stats 1990 ch 79 §14 (AB 759), operative July 1, 1991.

Prior Law: Former Prob C §8251, similar to the present section, was added Stats 1988 ch 1199 §81.5, operative July 1, 1989, and repealed Stats 1990 ch 79 §13, operative July 1, 1991.

§8252. Trial

(a) At the trial, the proponents of the will have the burden of proof of due execution. The contestants of the will have the burden of proof of lack of testamentary intent or capacity, undue influence, fraud, duress, mistake, or revocation. If the will is opposed by the petition for probate of a later will revoking the former, it shall be determined first whether the later will is entitled to probate.

(b) The court shall try and determine any contested issue of fact that affects the validity of the will. **Leg.H.** Enacted Stats 1990 ch 79 §14 (AB 759), operative July 1, 1991.

Prior Law: Former Prob C §8252, similar to the present section, was added Stats 1988 ch 1199 §81.5, operative July 1, 1989, and repealed Stats 1990 ch 79 §13, operative July 1, 1991.

§8253. Evidence of execution

At the trial, each subscribing witness shall be produced and examined. If no subscribing witness is available as a witness within the meaning of Section 240 of the Evidence Code, the court may admit the evidence of other witnesses to prove the due execution of the will. **Leg.H.** Enacted Stats 1990 ch 79 §14 (AB 759), operative July 1, 1991.

Prior Law: Former Prob C §8253, similar to the present section, was added Stats 1988 ch 1199 §81.5, operative July 1, 1989, and repealed Stats 1990 ch 79 §13, operative July 1, 1991.

§8254. Judgment

The court may make appropriate orders, including orders sustaining or denying objections, and shall render judgment either admitting the will to probate or rejecting it, in whole or in part, and appointing a personal representative. **Leg.H.** Enacted Stats 1990 ch 79 §14 (AB 759), operative July 1, 1991.

Prior Law: Former Prob C §8254, similar to the present section, was added Stats 1988 ch 1199 §81.5, operative July 1, 1989, and repealed Stats 1990 ch 79 §13, operative July 1, 1991.

ARTICLE 4
Revocation of Probate

Time to petition for revocation; Eligible petitioners; Contents of petition. §8270.
Summons; Service; Time for responsive pleading; Failure to respond timely. §8271.
Revocation; Effect of revocation. §8272.

§8270. Time to petition for revocation; Eligible petitioners; Contents of petition

(a) Within 120 days after a will is admitted to probate, any interested person, other than a party to a will contest and other than a person who had actual notice of a will contest in time to have joined in the contest, may petition the court to revoke the probate of the will. The petition shall include objections setting forth written grounds of opposition.

(b) Notwithstanding subdivision (a), a person who was a minor or who was incompetent and had no guardian or conservator at the time a will was admitted to probate may petition the court to revoke the probate of the will at any time before entry of an order for final distribution. **Leg.H.** Enacted Stats 1990 ch 79 §14 (AB 759), operative July 1, 1991.

Prior Law: Former Prob C §8270, similar to the present section, was added Stats 1988 ch 1199 §81.5, operative July 1, 1989, and repealed Stats 1990 ch 79 §13, operative July 1, 1991.

§8271. Summons; Service; Time for responsive pleading; Failure to respond timely

(a) On the filing of the petition, a summons shall be directed to the personal representative and to the heirs and devisees of the decedent, so far as known to the petitioner. The summons shall contain a direction that the persons summoned file with the court a written pleading in response to the petition within 30 days after service of the summons. Failure of a person timely to respond to the summons precludes the person from further participation in the revocation proceeding, but does not otherwise affect the person's interest in the estate.

(b) The summons shall be issued and served with a copy of the petition and proceedings had as in the case of a contest of the will.

(c) If a person fails timely to respond to the summons:

(1) The case is at issue notwithstanding the failure and the case may proceed on the petition and other documents filed by the time of the hearing, and no further pleadings by other persons are necessary.

(2) The person may not participate further in the contest, but the person's interest in the estate is not otherwise affected.

(3) The person is bound by the decision in the proceeding. **Leg.H.** Enacted Stats 1990 ch 79 §14 (AB 759), operative July 1, 1991. Amended Stats 1998 ch 581 §25 (AB 2801).

Prior Law: Former Prob C §8271, similar to the present section, was added Stats 1988 ch 1199 §81.5, operative July 1, 1989, and repealed Stats 1990 ch 79 §13, operative July 1, 1991.

§8272. Revocation; Effect of revocation

(a) If it appears on satisfactory proof that the will should be denied probate, the court shall revoke the probate of the will.

(b) Revocation of probate of a will terminates the powers of the personal representative. The personal representative is not liable for any otherwise proper act done in good faith before the revocation, nor is any transaction void by reason of the revocation if entered into with a third person dealing in good faith and for value. **Leg.H.** Enacted Stats 1990 ch 79 §14 (AB 759), operative July 1, 1991.

Prior Law: Former Prob C §8272, similar to the present section, was added Stats 1988 ch 1199 §81.5, operative July 1, 1989, and repealed Stats 1990 ch 79 §13, operative July 1, 1991.

CHAPTER 4
APPOINTMENT OF PERSONAL REPRESENTATIVE

Article 1. General Provisions.
Article 2. Executors.
Article 3. Administrators With the Will Annexed.
Article 4. Administrators.
Article 5. Bond.
Article 6. Removal From Office.
Article 7. Changes in Administration.
Article 8. Special Administrators.
Article 9. Nonresident Personal Representative.

ARTICLE 1
General Provisions

Appointment necessary. §8400.
Deposit of money or other property subject to withdrawal by court order only. §8401.
Persons ineligible for appointment. §8402.
Oath. §8403.
Statement of duties and liabilities. §8404.
Form of letters. §8405.

§8400. Appointment necessary

(a) A person has no power to administer the estate until the person is appointed personal representative and the appointment becomes effective.

Appointment of a personal representative becomes effective when the person appointed is issued letters.

(b) Subdivision (a) applies whether or not the person is named executor in the decedent's will, except that a person named executor in the decedent's will may, before the appointment is made or becomes effective, pay funeral expenses and take necessary measures for the maintenance and preservation of the estate.

(c) The order appointing a personal representative shall state in capital letters on the first page of the order, in at least 12-point type, the following: "WARNING: THIS APPOINTMENT IS NOT EFFECTIVE UNTIL LETTERS HAVE ISSUED." **Leg.H.** Enacted Stats 1990 ch 79 §14 (AB 759), operative July 1, 1991. Amended Stats 1996 ch 862 §16 (AB 2751).

Prior Law: Former Prob C §8400, similar to the present section, was added Stats 1988 ch 1199 §81.5, operative July 1, 1989, and repealed Stats 1990 ch 79 §13, operative July 1, 1991.

§8401. Deposit of money or other property subject to withdrawal by court order only

(a) Notwithstanding Section 8400, a petitioner for appointment as personal representative may deliver property in the petitioner's possession to a trust company or financial institution for deposit, or allow a trust company or financial institution to retain on deposit property already in its possession, as provided in Chapter 3 (commencing with Section 9700) of Part 5.

(b) The petitioner shall obtain and file with the court a written receipt including the agreement of the trust company or financial institution that the property on deposit, including any earnings thereon, shall not be allowed to be withdrawn except on order of the court.

(c) In receiving and retaining property under this section, the trust company or financial institution is protected to the same extent as though it had received the property from a person who had been appointed personal representative. **Leg.H.** Enacted Stats 1990 ch 79 §14 (AB 759), operative July 1, 1991.

Prior Law: Former Prob C §8401, similar to the present section, was added Stats 1988 ch 1199 §81.5, operative July 1, 1989, amended Stats 1989 ch 544 §6, and repealed Stats 1990 ch 79 §13, operative July 1, 1991.

§8402. Persons ineligible for appointment

(a) Notwithstanding any other provision of this chapter, a person is not competent to act as personal representative in any of the following circumstances:

(1) The person is under the age of majority.

(2) The person is subject to a conservatorship of the estate or is otherwise incapable of executing, or is otherwise unfit to execute, the duties of the office.

(3) There are grounds for removal of the person from office under Section 8502.

(4) The person is not a resident of the United States.

(5) The person is a surviving business partner of the decedent and an interested person objects to the appointment.

(b) Paragraphs (4) and (5) of subdivision (a) do not apply to a person named as executor or successor executor in the decedent's will. **Leg.H.** Enacted Stats 1990 ch 79 §14 (AB 759), operative July 1, 1991. Amended Stats 2016 ch 703 §19 (AB 2881), effective January 1, 2017.

Prior Law: Former Prob C §8402, similar to the present section, was added Stats 1988 ch 1199 §81.5, operative July 1, 1989, and repealed Stats 1990 ch 79 §13, operative July 1, 1991.

§8403. Oath

(a) Before letters are issued, the personal representative shall take and subscribe an oath to perform, according to law, the duties of the office. The oath may be taken and dated on or after the time the petition for appointment as personal representative is signed, and may be filed with the clerk at any time after the petition is granted.

(b) The oath constitutes an acceptance of the office and shall be attached to or endorsed on the letters. **Leg.H.** Enacted Stats 1990 ch 79 §14 (AB 759), operative July 1, 1991.

Prior Law: Former Prob C §8403, similar to the present section, was added Stats 1988 ch 1199 §81.5, operative July 1, 1989, and repealed Stats 1990 ch 79 §13, operative July 1, 1991.

§8404. Statement of duties and liabilities

(a) Before letters are issued, the personal representative (other than a trust company or a public administrator) shall file an acknowledgment of receipt of a statement of duties and liabilities of the office of personal representative. The statement shall be in the form prescribed by the Judicial Council.

(b) The court may by local rule require the acknowledgment of receipt to include the personal representative's birth date and driver's license number, if any, provided that the court ensures their confidentiality.

(c) The statement of duties and liabilities prescribed by the Judicial Council does not supersede the law on which the statement is based. **Leg.H.** Enacted Stats 1990 ch 79 §14 (AB 759), operative July 1, 1991. Amended Stats 1994 ch 806 §26 (AB 3686).

Prior Law: Former Prob C §8404, similar to the present section, was added Stats 1988 ch 1199 §81.5, operative July 1, 1989, amended Stats 1989 ch 21 §17, effective May 25, 1989, operative July 1, 1989, and repealed Stats 1990 ch 79 §13, operative July 1, 1991.

§8405. Form of letters

Letters shall be signed by the clerk under the seal of the court and shall include:

(a) The county from which the letters are issued.

(b) The name of the person appointed as personal representative and whether the personal representative is an executor, administrator, administrator with the will annexed, or special administrator.

(c) A notation whether the personal representative is authorized to act under the Independent Administration of Estates Act (Part 6 (commencing with Section 10400) of Division 7), and if so authorized whether the independent administration authority includes or excludes the power to do any of the following:

(1) Sell real property.

(2) Exchange real property.

(3) Grant an option to purchase real property.

(4) Borrow money with the loan secured by an encumbrance upon real property. **Leg.H.** Enacted Stats 1990 ch 79 §14 (AB 759), operative July 1, 1991.

Prior Law: Former Prob C §8405, similar to the present section, was added Stats 1988 ch 1199 §81.5, operative July 1, 1989, amended Stats 1989 ch 21 §18, effective May 25, 1989, operative July 1, 1989, and repealed Stats 1990 ch 79 §13, operative July 1, 1991.

§8406. [Section repealed 1997]

Leg.H. Enacted Stats 1990 ch 79 §14 (AB 759), operative July 1, 1991. Repealed Stats 1997 ch 724 §20 (AB 1172). The repealed section related to effect of reversal of appointment of personal representative.

Prior Law: Former Prob C §8406, relating to effect of reversal of appointment of personal representative, was added Stats 1988 ch 1199 §81.5, operative July 1, 1989, amended Stats 1989 ch 544 §7, and repealed Stats 1990 ch 79 §13, operative July 1, 1991.

ARTICLE 2
Executors

Person named in will as executor. §8420.
Person not named in will but apparently intended by will to be executor. §8421.
Power conferred by will to designate executor. §8422.
Successor trust company as executor. §8423.
Minor named as executor. §8424.
Court appointment of fewer than all persons named in will as executors. §8425.

§8420. Person named in will as executor

The person named as executor in the decedent's will has the right to appointment as personal representative. **Leg.H.** Enacted Stats 1990 ch 79 §14 (AB 759), operative July 1, 1991.

Prior Law: Former Prob C §8420, similar to the present section, was added Stats 1988 ch 1199 §81.5, operative July 1, 1989, and repealed Stats 1990 ch 79 §13, operative July 1, 1991.

§8421. Person not named in will but apparently intended by will to be executor

If a person is not named as executor in a will but it appears by the terms of the will that the testator intended to commit the execution of the will and the administration of the estate to the person, the person is entitled to appointment as personal representative in the same manner as if named as executor. **Leg.H.** Enacted Stats 1990 ch 79 §14 (AB 759), operative July 1, 1991.

Prior Law: Former Prob C §8421, similar to the present section, was added Stats 1988 ch 1199 §81.5, operative July 1, 1989, and repealed Stats 1990 ch 79 §13, operative July 1, 1991.

§8422. Power conferred by will to designate executor

(a) The testator may by will confer on a person the power to designate an executor or coexecutor, or successor executor or coexecutor. The will may provide that the persons so designated may serve without bond.

(b) A designation shall be in writing and filed with the court. Unless the will provides otherwise, if there are two or more holders of the power to designate, the designation shall be unanimous, unless one of the holders of the power is unable or unwilling to act, in which case the remaining holder or holders may exercise the power.

(c) Except as provided in this section, an executor does not have authority to name a coexecutor, or a successor executor or coexecutor. **Leg.H.** Enacted Stats 1990 ch 79 §14 (AB 759), operative July 1, 1991.

Prior Law: Former Prob C §8422, similar to the present section, was added Stats 1988 ch 1199 §81.5, operative July 1, 1989, and repealed Stats 1990 ch 79 §13, operative July 1, 1991.

§8423. Successor trust company as executor

If the executor named in the will is a trust company that has sold its business and assets to, has consolidated or merged with, or is in any manner provided by law succeeded by, another trust company, the court may, and to the extent required by the Banking Law (Division 1 (commencing with Section 99) of the Financial Code) shall, appoint the successor trust company as executor. **Leg.H.** Enacted Stats 1990 ch 79 §14 (AB 759), operative July 1, 1991.

Prior Law: Former Prob C §8423, similar to the present section, was added Stats 1988 ch 1199 §81.5, operative July 1, 1989, and repealed Stats 1990 ch 79 §13, operative July 1, 1991.

§8424. Minor named as executor

(a) If a person named as executor is under the age of majority and there is another person named as executor, the other person may be appointed and may administer the estate until the majority of the minor, who may then be appointed as coexecutor.

(b) If a person named as executor is under the age of majority and there is no other person named as executor, another person may be appointed as personal representative, but the court may revoke the appointment on the majority of the minor, who may then be appointed as executor. **Leg.H.** Enacted Stats 1990 ch 79 §14 (AB 759), operative July 1, 1991.

Prior Law: Former Prob C §8424, similar to the present section, was added Stats 1988 ch 1199 §81.5, operative July 1, 1989, and repealed Stats 1990 ch 79 §13, operative July 1, 1991.

§8425. Court appointment of fewer than all persons named in will as executors

If the court does not appoint all the persons named in the will as executors, those appointed have the same authority to act in every respect as all would have if appointed. **Leg.H.** Enacted Stats 1990 ch 79 §14 (AB 759), operative July 1, 1991.

Prior Law: Former Prob C §8425, similar to the present section, was added Stats 1988 ch 1199 §81.5, operative July 1, 1989, and repealed Stats 1990 ch 79 §13, operative July 1, 1991.

ARTICLE 3
Administrators With the Will Annexed

When appointment required. §8440.
Priority for appointment. §8441.
Authority of administrator with the will annexed. §8442.

§8440. When appointment required

An administrator with the will annexed shall be appointed as personal representative if no executor is named in the will or if the sole executor or all the executors named in the will have waived the right to appointment or are for any reason unwilling or unable to act. **Leg.H.** Enacted Stats 1990 ch 79 §14 (AB 759), operative July 1, 1991.

Prior Law: Former Prob C §8440, similar to the present section, was added Stats 1988 ch 1199 §81.5, operative July 1, 1989, and repealed Stats 1990 ch 79 §13, operative July 1, 1991.

§8441. Priority for appointment

(a) Except as provided in subdivision (b), persons and their nominees are entitled to appointment as administrator with the will annexed in the same order of priority as for appointment of an administrator.

(b) A person who takes under the will has priority over a person who does not, but the court in its discretion may give priority to a person who does not take under the will if the person is entitled to a statutory interest that is a substantially greater portion of the estate than the devise to the person who takes under the will and the priority appears appropriate under the circumstances. A person who takes more than 50 percent of the value of the estate under the will or the person's nominee, or the nominee of several persons who together take more than 50 percent of the value of the estate under the will, has priority over other persons who take under the will. **Leg.H.** Enacted Stats 1990 ch 79 §14 (AB 759), operative July 1, 1991.

Prior Law: Former Prob C §8441, similar to the present section, was added Stats 1988 ch 1199 §81.5, operative July 1, 1989, and repealed Stats 1990 ch 79 §13, operative July 1, 1991.

§8442. Authority of administrator with the will annexed

(a) Subject to subdivision (b), an administrator with the will annexed has the same authority over the decedent's estate as an executor named in the will would have.

(b) If the will confers a discretionary power or authority on an executor that is not conferred by law and the will does not extend the power or authority to other personal representatives, the power or authority shall not be deemed to be conferred on an administrator with the will annexed, but the court in its discretion may authorize the exercise of the power or authority. **Leg.H.** Enacted Stats 1990 ch 79 §14 (AB 759), operative July 1, 1991.

Prior Law: Former Prob C §8442, similar to the present section, was added Stats 1988 ch 1199 §81.5, operative July 1, 1989, and repealed Stats 1990 ch 79 §13, operative July 1, 1991.

ARTICLE 4
Administrators

Appointment of administrator. §8460.
Priority for appointment. §8461.
Priority of relatives. §8462.
Surviving spouse. §8463.
Minors and incompetent persons. §8464.
Appointment of administrator; Nominations; Considerations; Resignation. §8465.
Priority of creditor. §8466.
Equal priority. §8467.
Failure of persons having priority to claim appointment. §8468.
Conservator or guardian who does not meet requirements of Section 8461. §8469.

§8460. Appointment of administrator

(a) If the decedent dies intestate, the court shall appoint an administrator as personal representative.

(b) The court may appoint one or more persons as administrator. **Leg.H.** Enacted Stats 1990 ch 79 §14 (AB 759), operative July 1, 1991.

Prior Law: Former Prob C §8460, similar to the present section, was added Stats 1988 ch 1199 §81.5, operative July 1, 1989, and repealed Stats 1990 ch 79 §13, operative July 1, 1991.

§8461. Priority for appointment

Subject to the provisions of this article, a person in the following relation to the decedent is entitled to appointment as administrator in the following order of priority:

(a) Surviving spouse or domestic partner as defined in Section 37.
(b) Children.
(c) Grandchildren.
(d) Other issue.
(e) Parents.
(f) Brothers and sisters.
(g) Issue of brothers and sisters.
(h) Grandparents.
(i) Issue of grandparents.
(j) Children of a predeceased spouse or domestic partner.
(k) Other issue of a predeceased spouse or domestic partner.
(*l*) Other next of kin.
(m) Parents of a predeceased spouse or domestic partner.
(n) Issue of parents of a predeceased spouse or domestic partner.
(o) Conservator or guardian of the estate acting in that capacity at the time of death who has filed a first account and is not acting as conservator or guardian for any other person.
(p) Public administrator.
(q) Creditors.
(r) Any other person. **Leg.H.** Enacted Stats 1990 ch 79 §14 (AB 759), operative July 1, 1991. Amended Stats 1990 ch 710 §20 (SB 1775), operative July 1, 1991; Stats 2001 ch 893 §53 (AB 25).

Prior Law: Former Prob C §8461, similar to the present section, was added Stats 1988 ch 1199 §81.5, operative July 1, 1989, amended Stats 1989 ch 544 §8, and repealed Stats 1990 ch 79 §13, operative July 1, 1991.

§8462. Priority of relatives

The surviving spouse or domestic partner of the decedent, a relative of the decedent, or a relative of a predeceased spouse or domestic partner of the decedent, has priority under Section 8461 only if one of the following conditions is satisfied:

(a) The surviving spouse, domestic partner, or relative is entitled to succeed to all or part of the estate.

(b) The surviving spouse, domestic partner, or relative either takes under the will of, or is entitled to succeed to all or part of the estate of, another deceased person who is entitled to succeed to all or part of the estate of the decedent. **Leg.H.** Enacted Stats 1990 ch 79 §14 (AB 759), operative July 1, 1991. Amended Stats 2001 ch 893 §54 (AB 25), effective January 1, 2002.

Prior Law: Former Prob C §8462, similar to the present section, was added Stats 1988 ch 1199 §81.5, operative July 1, 1989, and repealed Stats 1990 ch 79 §13, operative July 1, 1991.

§8463. Surviving spouse

If the surviving spouse is a party to an action for separate maintenance, annulment, or dissolution of the marriage of the decedent and the surviving spouse, and was living apart from the decedent on the date of the decedent's death, the surviving spouse has priority next after brothers and sisters and not the priority prescribed in Section 8461. **Leg.H.** Enacted Stats 1990 ch 79 §14 (AB 759), operative July 1, 1991.

Prior Law: Former Prob C §8463, similar to the present section, was added Stats 1988 ch 1199 §81.5, operative July 1, 1989, and repealed Stats 1990 ch 79 §13, operative July 1, 1991.

§8464. Minors and incompetent persons

If a person otherwise entitled to appointment as administrator is a person under the age of majority or a person for whom a guardian or conservator of the estate has been appointed, the court in its discretion may appoint the guardian or conservator or another person entitled to appointment. **Leg.H.** Enacted Stats 1990 ch 79 §14 (AB 759), operative July 1, 1991.

Prior Law: Former Prob C §8464, similar to the present section, was added Stats 1988 ch 1199 §81.5, operative July 1, 1989, and repealed Stats 1990 ch 79 §13, operative July 1, 1991.

§8465. Appointment of administrator; Nominations; Considerations; Resignation

(a) The court may appoint as administrator a person nominated by any of the following persons:

(1) A person otherwise entitled to appointment.

(2) A person who would otherwise be entitled for appointment but who is ineligible for appointment under paragraph (4) of subdivision (a) of Section 8402 because he or she is not a resident of the United States.

(3) The guardian or conservator of the estate of a person otherwise entitled to appointment. The nomination shall be made in writing and filed with the court.

(b) If a person making a nomination for appointment of an administrator is the surviving spouse or domestic partner, child, grandchild, other issue, parent, brother or sister, or grandparent of the decedent, the nominee has priority next after those in the class of the person making the nomination.

(c) If a person making a nomination for appointment of an administrator is other than a person described in subdivision (b), the court in its discretion may appoint either the nominee or a person of a class lower in priority to that of the person making the nomination, but other persons of the class of the person making the nomination have priority over the nominee.

(d) If a person making a nomination for appointment of an administrator is a person described in paragraph (2) of subdivision (a), the court shall not appoint a nominee who is not a California resident to act as administrator. For California residents nominated under paragraph (2) of subdivision (a), the court shall consider whether the nominee is capable of faithfully executing the duties of the office. The court may in its discretion deny the appointment and appoint another person. In determining whether to appoint the nominee, the factors the court may consider include, but are not limited to, the following:

(1) Whether the nominee has a conflict of interest with the heirs or any other interested party.

(2) Whether the nominee had a business or personal relationship with the decedent or decedent's family before the decedent's death.

(3) Whether the nominee is engaged in or acting on behalf of an individual, a business, or other entity that solicits heirs to obtain the person's nomination for appointment as administrator.

(4) Whether the nominee has been appointed as a personal representative in any other estate.

(e) If the court decides to appoint a nominee under the circumstances described in subdivision (d), the court shall require the nominee to obtain bond, unless the court orders otherwise for good cause. Any order for good cause must be supported by specific findings of fact, and shall consider the need for the protection of creditors, heirs, and any other interested parties. Before waiving a bond, the court shall consider all other alternatives, including, but not limited to, the deposit of property in the estate pursuant to Chapter 3 (commencing with Section 9700) of Part 5 on the condition that the property, including any earnings thereon, will not be withdrawn except on authorization of the court. The waiver of all of the heirs of the requirement of a bond shall not constitute good cause.

(f) If the appointed nominee ceases to be a California resident following his or her appointment, he or she shall be deemed to have resigned as administrator for the purposes of Article 7 (commencing with Section 8520). The court shall not lose jurisdiction of the proceeding by any resignation under this subdivision.

(g) By accepting appointment as personal representative, the nominee shall submit personally to the jurisdiction of the court. **Leg.H.** Enacted Stats 1990 ch 79 §14 (AB 759), operative July 1, 1991. Amended Stats 2001 ch 893 §55 (AB 25); Stats 2012 ch 635 §1 (AB 1670), effective January 1, 2013, repealed January 1, 2016; Stats 2015 ch 54 §1 (AB 548), effective January 1, 2016.

Former Sections: Former Prob C §8465, similar to the present section, was added Stats 2012 ch 635 §2, operative date contingent, and repealed Stats 2015 ch 54 §2, effective January 1, 2016.

Former Prob C §8465, similar to the present section, was added Stats 1988 ch 1199 §81.5, operative July 1, 1989, and repealed Stats 1990 ch 79 §13, operative July 1, 1991.

Prior Law: Former Prob C §8465, similar to the present section, was added Stats 1988 ch 1199 §81.5, operative July 1, 1989, and repealed Stats 1990 ch 79 §13, operative July 1, 1991.

Former Prob C §8465, similar to the present section, was added Stats 2012 ch 635 §2, effective January 1, 2013, operative date contingent, and repealed Stats 2015 ch 54 §2, effective January 1, 2016.

§8466. Priority of creditor

If a person whose only priority is that of a creditor claims appointment as administrator, the court in its discretion may deny the appointment and appoint another person. **Leg.H.** Enacted Stats 1990 ch 79 §14 (AB 759), operative July 1, 1991.

Prior Law: Former Prob C §8466, similar to the present section, was added Stats 1988 ch 1199 §81.5, operative July 1, 1989, and repealed Stats 1990 ch 79 §13, operative July 1, 1991.

§8467. Equal priority

If several persons have equal priority for appointment as administrator, the court may appoint one or more of them, or if such persons are unable to agree, the court may appoint the public administrator or a disinterested person in the same or the next lower class of priority as the persons who are unable to agree. **Leg.H.** Enacted Stats 1990 ch 79 §14 (AB 759), operative July 1, 1991.

Prior Law: Former Prob C §8467, similar to the present section, was added Stats 1988 ch 1199 §81.5, operative July 1, 1989, and repealed Stats 1990 ch 79 §13, operative July 1, 1991.

§8468. Failure of persons having priority to claim appointment

If persons having priority fail to claim appointment as administrator, the court may appoint any person who claims appointment. **Leg.H.** Enacted Stats 1990 ch 79 §14 (AB 759), operative July 1, 1991.

Prior Law: Former Prob C §8468, similar to the present section, was added Stats 1988 ch 1199 §81.5, operative July 1, 1989, and repealed Stats 1990 ch 79 §13, operative July 1, 1991.

§8469. Conservator or guardian who does not meet requirements of Section 8461

(a) For good cause, the court may allow the priority given by Section 8461 to a conservator or guardian of the estate of the decedent serving in that capacity at the time of death that has not filed a first account, or that is acting as guardian or conservator for another person, or both.

(b) If the petition for appointment as administrator requests the court to allow the priority permitted by subdivision (a), the petitioner shall, in addition to the notice otherwise required by statute, deliver notice of the hearing pursuant to Section 1215 to the public administrator. **Leg.H.** Added Stats 1990 ch 710 §21 (SB 1775), operative July 1, 1991. Amended Stats 2017 ch 319 §68 (AB 976), effective January 1, 2018.

ARTICLE 5
Bond

When bond is required; Failure to give bond. §8480.
Waiver of bond. §8481.
Amount of bond. §8482.
Reduction of bond by deposit of assets. §8483.
Petition to reduce amount of bond. §8484.
Substitution or release of sureties. §8485.
Cost of bond. §8486.
Law governing bond. §8487.
Statute of limitation for action against sureties on bond. §8488.

§8480. When bond is required; Failure to give bond

(a) Except as otherwise provided by statute, every person appointed as personal representative shall, before letters are issued, give a bond approved by the court. If two or more persons are appointed, the court may require either a separate bond from each or a joint and several bond. If a joint bond is furnished, the liability on the bond is joint and several.

(b) The bond shall be for the benefit of interested persons and shall be conditioned on the personal representative's faithful execution of the duties of the office according to law.

(c) If the person appointed as personal representative fails to give the required bond, letters shall not be issued. If the person appointed as personal representative fails to give a new, additional, or supplemental bond, or to substitute a sufficient surety, under court order, the person may be removed from office. **Leg.H.** Enacted Stats 1990 ch 79 §14 (AB 759), operative July 1, 1991. Amended Stats 1998 ch 77 §3 (SB 1841).

Prior Law: Former Prob C §8480, similar to the present section, was added Stats 1988 ch 1199 §81.5, operative July 1, 1989, and repealed Stats 1990 ch 79 §13, operative July 1, 1991.

§8481. Waiver of bond

(a) A bond is not required in either of the following cases:
(1) The will waives the requirement of a bond.
(2) All beneficiaries waive in writing the requirement of a bond and the written waivers are attached to the petition for appointment of a personal representative. This paragraph does not apply if the will requires a bond.

(b) Notwithstanding the waiver of a bond by a will or by all the beneficiaries, on petition of any interested person or on its own motion, the court may for good cause require that a bond be given, either before or after issuance of letters. **Leg.H.** Enacted Stats 1990 ch 79 §14 (AB 759), operative July 1, 1991.

Prior Law: Former Prob C §8481, similar to the present section, was added Stats 1988 ch 1199 §81.5, operative July 1, 1989, and repealed Stats 1990 ch 79 §13, operative July 1, 1991.

§8482. Amount of bond

(a) The court in its discretion may fix the amount of the bond, but the amount of the bond shall be not more than the sum of:
(1) The estimated value of the personal property.
(2) The probable annual gross income of the estate.
(3) If independent administration is granted as to real property, the estimated value of the decedent's interest in the real property.

(b) Notwithstanding subdivision (a), if the bond is given by an admitted surety insurer, the court may establish a fixed minimum amount for the bond, based on the minimum premium required by the admitted surety insurer.

(c) If the bond is given by personal sureties, the amount of the bond shall be twice the amount fixed by the court under subdivision (a).

(d) Before confirming a sale of real property the court shall require such additional bond as may be proper, not exceeding the maximum requirements of this section, treating the expected proceeds of the sale as personal property. **Leg.H.** Enacted Stats 1990 ch 79 §14 (AB 759), operative July 1, 1991.

Prior Law: Former Prob C §8482, similar to the present section, was added Stats 1988 ch 1199 §81.5, operative July 1, 1989, amended Stats 1989 ch 21 §19, effective May 25, 1989, operative July 1, 1989, repealed Stats 1990 ch 79 §13, operative July 1, 1991.

§8483. Reduction of bond by deposit of assets

(a) This section applies where property in the estate has been deposited pursuant to Chapter 3 (commencing with Section 9700) of Part 5 on condition that the property, including any earnings thereon, will not be withdrawn except on authorization of the court.

(b) In a proceeding to determine the amount of the bond of the personal representative (whether at the time of appointment or subsequently), on production of a receipt showing the deposit of property of the estate in the manner described in subdivision (a), the court may order that the property shall not be withdrawn except on authorization of the court and may, in its discretion, do either of the following:

(1) Exclude the property in determining the amount of the required bond or reduce the amount of the bond to an amount the court determines is reasonable.

(2) If a bond has already been given or the amount fixed, reduce the amount to an amount the court determines is reasonable. **Leg.H.** Enacted Stats 1990 ch 79 §14 (AB 759), operative July 1, 1991.

Prior Law: Former Prob C §8483, similar to the present section, was added Stats 1988 ch 1199 §81.5, operative July 1, 1989, amended Stats 1989 ch 544 §9, and repealed Stats 1990 ch 79 §13, operative July 1, 1991.

§8484. Petition to reduce amount of bond

If a personal representative petitions to have the amount of the bond reduced, the petition shall include an affidavit setting forth the condition of the estate and notice of hearing shall be given as provided in Section 1220. **Leg.H.** Enacted Stats 1990 ch 79 §14 (AB 759), operative July 1, 1991.

Prior Law: Former Prob C §8484, similar to the present section, was added Stats 1988 ch 1199 §81.5, operative July 1, 1989, and repealed Stats 1990 ch 79 §13, operative July 1, 1991.

§8485. Substitution or release of sureties

A personal representative who petitions for substitution or release of a surety shall file with the petition an account in the form provided in Section 10900. The court shall not order a substitution or release unless the account is approved. **Leg.H.** Enacted Stats 1990 ch 79 §14 (AB 759), operative July 1, 1991.

Prior Law: Former Prob C §8485, similar to the present section, was added Stats 1988 ch 1199 §81.5, operative July 1, 1989, and repealed Stats 1990 ch 79 §13, operative July 1, 1991.

§8486. Cost of bond

The personal representative shall be allowed the reasonable cost of the bond for every year it remains in force. **Leg.H.** Enacted Stats 1990 ch 79 §14 (AB 759), operative July 1, 1991.

Prior Law: Former Prob C §8486, similar to the present section, was added Stats 1988 ch 1199 §81.5, operative July 1, 1989, and repealed Stats 1990 ch 79 §13, operative July 1, 1991.

§8487. Law governing bond

The provisions of the Bond and Undertaking Law (Chapter 2 (commencing with Section 995.010) of Title 14 of Part 2 of the Code of Civil Procedure) apply to a bond given under this division, except to the extent this division is inconsistent. **Leg.H.** Enacted Stats 1990 ch 79 §14 (AB 759), operative July 1, 1991.

Prior Law: Former Prob C §8487, similar to the present section, was added Stats 1988 ch 1199 §81.5, operative July 1, 1989, and repealed Stats 1990 ch 79 §13, operative July 1, 1991.

§8488. Statute of limitation for action against sureties on bond

(a) In case of a breach of a condition of the bond, an action may be brought against the sureties on the bond for the use and benefit of the decedent's estate or of any person interested in the estate.

(b) No action may be maintained against the sureties on the bond of the personal representative unless commenced within four years from the discharge or removal of the personal representative or within four years from the date the order surcharging the personal representative becomes final, whichever is later.

(c) In any case, and notwithstanding subdivision (c) of Section 7250, no action may be maintained against the sureties on the bond unless commenced within six years from the date the judgment under Section 7250 or the later of the orders under subdivision (b) of this section becomes final. **Leg.H.** Enacted Stats 1990 ch 79 §14 (AB 759), operative July 1, 1991; Stats 1993 ch 794 §3 (AB 516); Stats 1994 ch 806 §27 (AB 3686).

Prior Law: Former Prob C §8488, similar to the present section, was added Stats 1988 ch 1199 §81.5, operative July 1, 1989, and repealed Stats 1990 ch 79 §13, operative July 1, 1991.

ARTICLE 6
Removal From Office

Procedure for removal. §8500.
Revocation of letters. §8501.
Grounds for removal. §8502.
Removal at request of person with higher priority. §8503.
Subsequent probate of will. §8504.
Contempt for disobeying court order. §8505.

§8500. Procedure for removal

(a) Any interested person may petition for removal of the personal representative from office. A petition for removal may be combined with a petition for appointment of a successor personal representative under Article 7 (commencing with Section 8520). The petition shall state facts showing cause for removal.

(b) On a petition for removal, or if the court otherwise has reason to believe from the court's own knowledge or from other credible information, whether on the settlement of an account or otherwise, that there are grounds for removal, the court shall issue a citation to the personal representative to appear and show cause why the personal representative should not be removed. The court may suspend the powers of the personal representative and may make such orders as are necessary to deal with the property pending the hearing.

(c) Any interested person may appear at the hearing and file a written declaration showing that the personal representative should be removed or retained. The personal representative may demur to or answer the declaration. The court may compel the attendance of the personal representative and may compel the personal representative to answer questions, on oath, concerning the administration of the estate. Failure to attend or answer is cause for removal of the personal representative from office.

(d) The issues shall be heard and determined by the court. If the court is satisfied from the evidence that the citation has been duly served and cause for removal exists, the court shall remove the personal representative from office. **Leg.H.** Enacted Stats 1990 ch 79 §14 (AB 759), operative July 1, 1991.

Prior Law: Former Prob C §8500, similar to the present section, was added Stats 1988 ch 1199 §81.5, operative July 1, 1989, and repealed Stats 1990 ch 79 §13, operative July 1, 1991.

§8501. Revocation of letters

On removal of a personal representative from office, the court shall revoke any letters issued to the personal representative, and the authority of the personal representative ceases. **Leg.H.** Enacted Stats 1990 ch 79 §14 (AB 759), operative July 1, 1991.

Prior Law: Former Prob C §8501, similar to the present section, was added Stats 1988 ch 1199 §81.5, operative July 1, 1989, and repealed Stats 1990 ch 79 §13, operative July 1, 1991.

§8502. Grounds for removal

A personal representative may be removed from office for any of the following causes:

(a) The personal representative has wasted, embezzled, mismanaged, or committed a fraud on the estate, or is about to do so.

(b) The personal representative is incapable of properly executing the duties of the office or is otherwise not qualified for appointment as personal representative.

(c) The personal representative has wrongfully neglected the estate, or has long neglected to perform any act as personal representative.

(d) Removal is otherwise necessary for protection of the estate or interested persons.

(e) Any other cause provided by statute. **Leg.H.** Enacted Stats 1990 ch 79 §14 (AB 759), operative July 1, 1991.

Prior Law: Former Prob C §8502, similar to the present section, was added Stats 1988 ch 1199 §81.5, operative July 1, 1989, and repealed Stats 1990 ch 79 §13, operative July 1, 1991.

§8503. Removal at request of person with higher priority

(a) Subject to subdivision (b), an administrator may be removed from office on the petition of the surviving spouse or a relative of the decedent entitled to succeed to all or part of the estate, or the nominee of the surviving spouse or relative, if such person is higher in priority than the administrator.

(b) The court in its discretion may refuse to grant the petition:

(1) Where the petition is by a person or the nominee of a person who had actual notice of the proceeding in which the administrator was appointed and an opportunity to contest the appointment.

(2) Where to do so would be contrary to the sound administration of the estate. **Leg.H.** Enacted Stats 1990 ch 79 §14 (AB 759), operative July 1, 1991.

Prior Law: Former Prob C §8503, similar to the present section, was added Stats 1988 ch 1199 §81.5, operative July 1, 1989, and repealed Stats 1990 ch 79 §13, operative July 1, 1991.

§8504. Subsequent probate of will

(a) After appointment of an administrator on the ground of intestacy, the personal representative shall be removed from office on the later admission to probate of a will.

(b) After appointment of an executor or administrator with the will annexed, the personal representative shall be removed from office on admission to probate of a later will. **Leg.H.** Enacted Stats 1990 ch 79 §14 (AB 759), operative July 1, 1991.

Prior Law: Former Prob C §8504, similar to the present section, was added Stats 1988 ch 1199 §81.5, operative July 1, 1989, and repealed Stats 1990 ch 79 §13, operative July 1, 1991.

§8505. Contempt for disobeying court order

(a) A personal representative may be removed from office if the personal representative is found in contempt for disobeying an order of the court.

(b) Notwithstanding any other provision of this article, a personal representative may be removed from office under this section by a court order reciting the facts and without further showing or notice. **Leg.H.** Enacted Stats 1990 ch 79 §14 (AB 759), operative July 1, 1991.

Prior Law: Former Prob C §8505, similar to the present section, was added Stats 1988 ch 1199 §81.5, operative July 1, 1989, and repealed Stats 1990 ch 79 §13, operative July 1, 1991.

ARTICLE 7
Changes in Administration

Vacancy in office of personal representative. §8520.
Vacancy where other personal representatives remain. §8521.
Vacancy where no personal representatives remain. §8522.
Interim protection of estate. §8523.
Powers and duties of successor personal representative. §8524.
Effect of vacancy. §8525.

§8520. Vacancy in office of personal representative

A vacancy occurs in the office of a personal representative who resigns, dies, or is removed from office under Article 6 (commencing with Section 8500), or whose authority is otherwise terminated. **Leg.H.** Enacted Stats 1990 ch 79 §14 (AB 759), operative July 1, 1991.

Prior Law: Former Prob C §8520, similar to the present section, was added Stats 1988 ch 1199 §81.5, operative July 1, 1989, and repealed Stats 1990 ch 79 §13, operative July 1, 1991.

§8521. Vacancy where other personal representatives remain

(a) Unless the will provides otherwise or the court in its discretion orders otherwise, if a vacancy occurs in the office of fewer than all personal representatives, the remaining personal representatives shall complete the administration of the estate.

(b) The court, on the filing of a petition alleging that a vacancy has occurred in the office of fewer than all personal representatives, may order the clerk to issue appropriate amended letters to the remaining personal representatives. **Leg.H.** Enacted Stats 1990 ch 79 §14 (AB 759), operative July 1, 1991.

Prior Law: Former Prob C §8521, similar to the present section, was added Stats 1988 ch 1199 §81.5, operative July 1, 1989, and repealed Stats 1990 ch 79 §13, operative July 1, 1991.

§8522. Vacancy where no personal representatives remain

(a) If a vacancy occurs in the office of a personal representative and there are no other personal representatives, the court shall appoint a successor personal representative.

(b) Appointment of a successor personal representative shall be made on petition and notice shall be delivered to interested persons in the manner provided in Article 2 (commencing with Section 8110) of Chapter 2, and shall be subject to the same priority as for an original appointment of a personal representative. The personal representative of a deceased personal representative is not, as such, entitled to appointment as successor personal representative. **Leg.H.** Enacted Stats 1990 ch 79 §14 (AB 759), operative July 1, 1991. Amended Stats 2017 ch 319 §69 (AB 976), effective January 1, 2018.

Prior Law: Former Prob C §522, similar to the present section, was added Stats 1988 ch 1199 §81.5, operative July 1, 1989, and repealed Stats 1990 ch 79 §13, operative July 1, 1991.

§8523. Interim protection of estate

The court may make orders that are necessary to deal with the estate of the decedent between the time a vacancy occurs in the office of personal representative and appointment of a successor. Those orders may include appointment of a special administrator. **Leg.H.** Enacted Stats 1990 ch 79 §14 (AB 759), operative July 1, 1991.

Prior Law: Former Prob C §523, similar to the present section, was added Stats 1988 ch 1199 §81.5, operative July 1, 1989, and repealed Stats 1990 ch 79 §13, operative July 1, 1991.

§8524. Powers and duties of successor personal representative

(a) A successor personal representative is entitled to demand, sue for, recover and collect all the estate of the decedent remaining unadministered, and may prosecute to final judgment any suit commenced by the former personal representative before the vacancy.

(b) No notice, process, or claim given to or served on the former personal representative need be given to or served on the successor in order to preserve any position or right the person giving the notice or filing the claim may thereby have obtained or preserved with reference to the former personal representative.

(c) Except as provided in subdivision (b) of Section 8442 (authority of administrator with will annexed) or as otherwise ordered by the court, the successor personal representative has the powers and duties in respect to the continued administration that the former personal representative would have had. **Leg.H.** Enacted Stats 1990 ch 79 §14 (AB 759), operative July 1, 1991.

Prior Law: Former Prob C §524, similar to the present section, was added Stats 1988 ch 1199 §81.5, operative July 1, 1989, and repealed Stats 1990 ch 79 §13, operative July 1, 1991.

§8525. Effect of vacancy

(a) The acts of the personal representative before a vacancy occurs are valid to the same extent as if no vacancy had later occurred.

(b) The liability of a personal representative whose office is vacant, or of the surety on the bond, is not discharged, released, or affected by the vacancy or by appointment of a successor, but continues until settlement of the accounts of the personal representative and delivery of all the estate of the decedent to the successor personal representative or other person appointed by the court to receive it. The personal representative shall render an account of the administration within the time that the court directs. **Leg.H.** Enacted Stats 1990 ch 79 §14 (AB 759), operative July 1, 1991.

Prior Law: Former Prob C §525, similar to the present section, was added Stats 1988 ch 1199 §81.5, operative July 1, 1989, and repealed Stats 1990 ch 79 §13, operative July 1, 1991.

ARTICLE 8
Special Administrators

Grounds for appointment; Term of office. §8540.
Procedure for appointment. §8541.
Issuance of letters. §8542.
Waiver of bond. §8543.
Special powers, duties, and obligations. §8544.
Special administrator with powers and duties of a general personal representative. §8545.
Termination of authority. §8546.
Compensation of special administrator and attorney for special administrator. §8547.

§8540. Grounds for appointment; Term of office

(a) If the circumstances of the estate require the immediate appointment of a personal representative, the court may appoint a special administrator to exercise any powers that may be appropriate under the circumstances for the preservation of the estate.

(b) The appointment may be for a specified term, to perform particular acts, or on any other terms specified in the court order. **Leg.H.** Enacted Stats 1990 ch 79 §14 (AB 759), operative July 1, 1991.

Prior Law: Former Prob C §540, similar to the present section, was added Stats 1988 ch 1199 §81.5, operative July 1, 1989, and repealed Stats 1990 ch 79 §13, operative July 1, 1991.

§8541. Procedure for appointment

(a) Appointment of a special administrator may be made at any time without notice or on such notice to interested persons as the court deems reasonable.

(b) In making the appointment, the court shall ordinarily give preference to the person entitled to appointment as personal representative. The court may appoint the public administrator.

(c) In the case of an appointment to perform a particular act, request for approval of the act may be included in the petition for appointment, and approval may be made on the same notice and at the same time as the appointment.

(d) The court may act, if necessary, to remedy any errors made in the appointment. **Leg.H.** Enacted Stats 1990 ch 79 §14 (AB 759), operative July 1, 1991.

Prior Law: Former Prob C §541, similar to the present section, was added Stats 1988 ch 1199 §81.5, operative July 1, 1989, and repealed Stats 1990 ch 79 §13, operative July 1, 1991.

§8542. Issuance of letters

(a) The clerk shall issue letters to the special administrator after both of the following conditions are satisfied:

(1) The special administrator gives any bond that may be required by the court under Section 8480.

(2) The special administrator takes the usual oath attached to or endorsed on the letters.

(b) Subdivision (a) does not apply to the public administrator.

(c) The letters of a special administrator appointed to perform a particular act shall include a notation of the particular act the special administrator was appointed to perform. **Leg.H.** Enacted Stats 1990 ch 79 §14 (AB 759), operative July 1, 1991.

Prior Law: Former Prob C §542, similar to the present section, was added Stats 1988 ch 1199 §81.5, operative July 1, 1989, and repealed Stats 1990 ch 79 §13, operative July 1, 1991.

§8543. Waiver of bond

Subject to subdivision (b) of Section 8481, the court shall direct that no bond be given in either of the following cases:

(a) The will waives the requirement of a bond and the person named as executor in the will is appointed special administrator.

(b) All beneficiaries waive in writing the requirement of a bond and the written waivers are attached to the petition for appointment of the special administrator. This paragraph does not apply if the will requires a bond. **Leg.H.** Enacted Stats 1990 ch 79 §14 (AB 759), operative July 1, 1991.

Prior Law: Former Prob C §543, similar to the present section, was added Stats 1988 ch 1199 §81.5, operative July 1, 1989, and repealed Stats 1990 ch 79 §13, operative July 1, 1991.

§8544. Special powers, duties, and obligations

(a) Except to the extent the order appointing a special administrator prescribes terms, the special administrator has the power to do all of the following without further order of the court:

(1) Take possession of all of the real and personal property of the estate of the decedent and preserve it from damage, waste, and injury.

(2) Collect all claims, rents, and other income belonging to the estate.

(3) Commence and maintain or defend suits and other legal proceedings.

(4) Sell perishable property.

(b) Except to the extent the order prescribes terms, the special administrator has the power to do all of the following on order of the court:

(1) Borrow money, or lease, mortgage, or execute a deed of trust on real property, in the same manner as an administrator.

(2) Pay the interest due or all or any part of an obligation secured by a mortgage, lien, or deed of trust on property in the estate, where there is danger that the holder of the security may enforce or foreclose on the

obligation and the property exceeds in value the amount of the obligation. This power may be ordered only on petition of the special administrator or any interested person, with any notice that the court deems proper, and shall remain in effect until appointment of a successor personal representative. The order may also direct that interest not yet accrued be paid as it becomes due, and the order shall remain in effect and cover the future interest unless and until for good cause set aside or modified by the court in the same manner as for the original order.

(3) Exercise other powers that are conferred by order of the court.

(c) Except where the powers, duties, and obligations of a general personal representative are granted under Section 8545, the special administrator is not a proper party to an action on a claim against the decedent.

(d) A special administrator appointed to perform a particular act has no duty to take any other action to protect the estate. **Leg.H.** Enacted Stats 1990 ch 79 §14 (AB 759), operative July 1, 1991.

Prior Law: Former Prob C §8544, similar to the present section, was added Stats 1988 ch 1199 §81.5, operative July 1, 1989, and repealed Stats 1990 ch 79 §13, operative July 1, 1991.

§8545. Special administrator with powers and duties of a general personal representative

(a) Notwithstanding Section 8544, the court may grant a special administrator the same powers, duties, and obligations as a general personal representative where to do so appears proper. Notwithstanding Section 8541, if letters have not previously been issued to a general personal representative, the grant shall be on the same notice required under Section 8003 for appointment of a personal representative, unless the appointment is made at a hearing on a petition for appointment of a general personal representative and the notice of that petition required under Section 8003 has been given.

(b) Subject to Section 8543, the court may require as a condition of the grant that the special administrator give any additional bond that the court deems proper. From the time of approving and filing any required additional bond, the special administrator shall have the powers, duties, and obligations of a general personal representative.

(c) If a grant is made under this section, the letters shall recite that the special administrator has the powers, duties, and obligations of a general personal representative. **Leg.H.** Enacted Stats 1990 ch 79 §14 (AB 759), operative July 1, 1991. Amended Stats 1994 ch 806 §28 (AB 3686).

Prior Law: Former Prob C §8545, similar to the present section, was added Stats 1988 ch 1199 §81.5, operative July 1, 1989, and repealed Stats 1990 ch 79 §13, operative July 1, 1991.

§8546. Termination of authority

(a) The powers of a special administrator cease on issuance of letters to a general personal representative or as otherwise directed by the court.

(b) The special administrator shall promptly deliver to the general personal representative:

(1) All property of the estate in the possession of the special administrator. The court may authorize the special administrator to complete a sale or other transaction affecting property in the possession of the special administrator.

(2) A list of all creditor claims of which the special administrator has knowledge. The list shall show the name and address of each creditor, the amount of the claim, and what action has been taken with respect to the claim. A copy of the list shall be filed in the court.

(c) The special administrator shall account in the same manner as a general personal representative is required to account. If the same person acts as both special administrator and general personal representative, the account of the special administrator may be combined with the first account of the general personal representative. **Leg.H.** Enacted Stats 1990 ch 79 §14 (AB 759), operative July 1, 1991.

Prior Law: Former Prob C §8546, similar to the present section, was added Stats 1988 ch 1199 §81.5, operative July 1, 1989, and repealed Stats 1990 ch 79 §13, operative July 1, 1991.

§8547. Compensation of special administrator and attorney for special administrator

(a) Subject to the limitations of this section, the court shall fix the compensation of the special administrator and the compensation of the attorney of the special administrator.

(b) The compensation of the special administrator shall not be allowed until the close of administration, unless the general personal representative joins in the petition for allowance of the special administrator's compensation or the court in its discretion so allows. Compensation for extraordinary services of a special administrator may be allowed on settlement of the final account of the special administrator. The total compensation paid to the special administrator and general personal representative shall not, together, exceed the sums provided in Part 7 (commencing with Section 10800) for compensation for the ordinary and extraordinary services of a personal representative. If the same person does not act as both special administrator and general personal representative, the compensation shall be divided in such proportions as the court determines to be just or as may be agreed to by the special administrator and general personal representative.

(c) The total compensation paid to the attorneys both of the special administrator and the general personal representative shall not, together, exceed the sums provided in Part 7 (commencing with Section 10800) as compensation for the ordinary and extraordinary services of attorneys for personal representatives. When the same attorney does not act for both the special administrator and general personal representative, the compensation shall be divided between the attorneys in such proportions as the court determines to be just or as agreed to by the attorneys.

(d) Compensation of an attorney for extraordinary services to a special administrator may be awarded in the same manner and subject to the same standards as for extraordinary services to a general personal representative, except that the award of compensation to the attorney may be made on settlement of the final account of the special administrator. **Leg.H.** Enacted Stats 1990 ch 79 §14 (AB 759), operative July 1, 1991. Amended Stats 1990 ch 710 §22 (SB 1775), operative July 1, 1991.

Prior Law: Former Prob C §8547, similar to the present section, was added Stats 1988 ch 1199 §81.5, operative July 1, 1989, amended Stats 1989 ch 21 §20, effective May 25, 1989, operative July 1, 1989, and repealed Stats 1990 ch 79 §13, operative July 1, 1991.

ARTICLE 9
Nonresident Personal Representative

"Nonresident personal representative". §8570.
Bond of nonresident personal representative. §8571.
Secretary of State as attorney for service. §8572.
Statement of address. §8573.
Manner of service. §8574.
Proof of service. §8575.
Effect of service; Time limits for answer or hearing of motion. §8576.
Removal from office for failure to file statement of address. §8577.

§8570. "Nonresident personal representative"

As used in this article, "nonresident personal representative" means a nonresident of this state appointed as personal representative, or a resident of this state appointed as personal representative who later removes from and resides without this state. **Leg.H.** Enacted Stats 1990 ch 79 §14 (AB 759), operative July 1, 1991. Amended Stats 1991 ch 1055 §22 (SB 271).

Prior Law: Former Prob C §8570, similar to the present section, was added Stats 1988 ch 1199 §81.5, operative July 1, 1989, and repealed Stats 1990 ch 79 §13, operative July 1, 1991.

§8571. Bond of nonresident personal representative

Notwithstanding any other provision of this chapter and notwithstanding a waiver of a bond, the court in its discretion may require a nonresident personal representative to give a bond in an amount determined by the court. **Leg.H.** Enacted Stats 1990 ch 79 §14 (AB 759), operative July 1, 1991.

Prior Law: Former Prob C §8571, similar to the present section, was added Stats 1988 ch 1199 §81.5, operative July 1, 1989, and repealed Stats 1990 ch 79 §13, operative July 1, 1991.

§8572. Secretary of State as attorney for service

(a) Acceptance of appointment by a nonresident personal representative is equivalent to and constitutes an irrevocable and binding appointment by the nonresident personal representative of the Secretary of State to be the attorney of the personal representative for the purpose of this article. The appointment of the nonresident personal representative also applies to any personal representative of a deceased nonresident personal representative.

(b) All lawful processes, and notices of motion under Section 377.41 of the Code of Civil Procedure, in an action or proceeding against the nonresident personal representative with respect to the estate or founded on or arising out of the acts or omissions of the nonresident personal representative in that capacity may be served on the Secretary of State as the attorney for service of the nonresident personal representative. **Leg.H.** Enacted Stats 1990 ch 79 §14 (AB 759), operative July 1, 1991. Amended Stats 1993 ch 589 §129 (AB 2211).

Prior Law: Former Prob C §8572, similar to the present section, was added Stats 1988 ch 1199 §81.5, operative July 1, 1989, and repealed Stats 1990 ch 79 §13, operative July 1, 1991.

§8573. Statement of address

A nonresident personal representative shall sign and file with the court a statement of the permanent address of the nonresident personal representative. If the permanent address is changed, the nonresident personal representative shall promptly file in the same manner a statement of the change of address. **Leg.H.** Enacted Stats 1990 ch 79 §14 (AB 759), operative July 1, 1991.

Prior Law: Former Prob C §8573, similar to the present section, was added Stats 1988 ch 1199 §81.5, operative July 1, 1989, and repealed Stats 1990 ch 79 §13, operative July 1, 1991.

§8574. Manner of service

(a) Service of process or notice of a motion under Section 377.41 of the Code of Civil Procedure in any action or proceeding against the nonresident personal representative shall be made by delivering to and leaving with the Secretary of State two copies of the summons and complaint or notice of motion and either of the following:

(1) A copy of the statement by the nonresident personal representative under Section 8573.

(2) If the nonresident personal representative has not filed a statement under Section 8573, a copy of the letters issued to the nonresident personal representative together with a written statement signed by the party or attorney of the party seeking service that sets forth an address for use by the Secretary of State.

(b) The Secretary of State shall promptly mail by registered mail one copy of the summons and complaint or notice of motion to the nonresident personal representative at the address shown on the statement delivered to the Secretary of State.

(c) Personal service of process, or notice of motion, on the nonresident personal representative wherever found shall be the equivalent of service as provided in this section. **Leg.H.** Enacted Stats 1990 ch 79 §14 (AB 759), operative July 1, 1991. Amended Stats 1993 ch 589 §130 (AB 2211).

Prior Law: Former Prob C §8574, similar to the present section, was added Stats 1988 ch 1199 §81.5, operative July 1, 1989, and repealed Stats 1990 ch 79 §13, operative July 1, 1991.

§8575. Proof of service

Proof of compliance with Section 8574 shall be made in the following manner:

(a) In the event of service by mail, by certificate of the Secretary of State, under official seal, showing the mailing. The certificate shall be filed with the court from which process issued.

(b) In the event of personal service outside this state, by the return of any duly constituted public officer qualified to serve like process, or notice of motion, of and in the jurisdiction where the nonresident personal representative is found, showing the service to have been made. The return shall be attached to the original summons, or notice of motion, and filed with the court from which process issued. **Leg.H.** Enacted Stats 1990 ch 79 §14 (AB 759), operative July 1, 1991. Amended Stats 1991 ch 1055 §23 (SB 271).

Prior Law: Former Prob C §8575, similar to the present section, was added Stats 1988 ch 1199 §81.5, operative July 1, 1989, and repealed Stats 1990 ch 79 §13, operative July 1, 1991.

§8576. Effect of service; Time limits for answer or hearing of motion

(a) Except as provided in this section, service made under Section 8574 has the same legal force and validity as if made personally in this state.

(b) A nonresident personal representative served under Section 8574 may appear and answer the complaint within 30 days from the date of service.

(c) Notice of motion shall be served on a nonresident personal representative under Section 8574 not less than 30 days before the date of the hearing on the motion. **Leg.H.** Enacted Stats 1990 ch 79 §14 (AB 759), operative July 1, 1991.

Prior Law: Former Prob C §8576, similar to the present section, was added Stats 1988 ch 1199 §81.5, operative July 1, 1989, and repealed Stats 1990 ch 79 §13, operative July 1, 1991.

§8577. Removal from office for failure to file statement of address

(a) Failure of a nonresident personal representative to comply with Section 8573 is cause for removal from office.

(b) Nothing in this section limits the liability of, or the availability of any other remedy against, a nonresident personal representative who is removed from office under this section. **Leg.H.** Enacted Stats 1990 ch 79 §14 (AB 759), operative July 1, 1991.

Prior Law: Former Prob C §8577, similar to the present section, was added Stats 1988 ch 1199 §81.5, operative July 1, 1989, and repealed Stats 1990 ch 79 §13, operative July 1, 1991.

PART 3
INVENTORY AND APPRAISAL

Chapter 1. General Provisions.
Chapter 2. Inventory.
Chapter 3. Appraisal.

CHAPTER 1
GENERAL PROVISIONS

Inventory and appraisal; Certification that tax requirements have been satisfied or are inapplicable. §8800.
Supplemental inventory and appraisal. §8801.
Form of inventory and appraisal. §8802.
Notice of filing of inventory and appraisal. §8803.
Failure to timely file inventory and appraisal. §8804.

§8800. Inventory and appraisal; Certification that tax requirements have been satisfied or are inapplicable

(a) The personal representative shall file with the court clerk an inventory of property to be administered in the decedent's estate together with an appraisal of property in the inventory. An inventory and appraisal shall be combined in a single document.

(b) The inventory and appraisal shall be filed within four months after letters are first issued to a general personal representative. The court may allow such further time for filing an inventory and appraisal as is reasonable under the circumstances of the particular case.

(c) The personal representative may file partial inventories and appraisals where appropriate under the circumstances of the particular case, but all inventories and appraisals shall be filed before expiration of the time allowed under subdivision (b).

(d) Concurrent with the filing of the inventory and appraisal pursuant to this section, the personal representative shall also file a certification that the requirements of Section 480 of the Revenue and Taxation Code either:

(1) Are not applicable because the decedent owned no real property in California at the time of death.

(2) Have been satisfied by the filing of a change in ownership statement with the county recorder or assessor of each county in California in which the decedent owned property at the time of death. **Leg.H.** Enacted Stats 1990 ch 79 §14 (AB 759), operative July 1, 1991. Amended Stats 1992 ch 1180 §1 (SB 1639).

Prior Law: Former Prob C §8800, similar to the present section, was added Stats 1988 ch 1199 §82.5, operative July 1, 1989, and repealed Stats 1990 ch 79 §13, operative July 1, 1991.

§8801. Supplemental inventory and appraisal

If the personal representative acquires knowledge of property to be administered in the decedent's estate that is not included in a prior inventory and appraisal, the personal representative shall file a supplemental inventory and appraisal of the property in the manner prescribed for an original inventory and appraisal. The supplemental inventory and appraisal shall be filed within four months after the personal representative acquires knowledge of the property. The court may allow such further time for filing a supplemental inventory and appraisal as is reasonable under the circumstances of the particular case. **Leg.H.** Enacted Stats 1990 ch 79 §14 (AB 759), operative July 1, 1991.

Prior Law: Former Prob C §8801, similar to the present section, was added Stats 1988 ch 1199 §82.5, operative July 1, 1989, and repealed Stats 1990 ch 79 §13, operative July 1, 1991.

§8802. Form of inventory and appraisal

The inventory and appraisal shall separately list each item and shall state the fair market value of the item at the time of the decedent's death in monetary terms opposite the item. **Leg.H.** Enacted Stats 1990 ch 79 §14 (AB 759), operative July 1, 1991.

Prior Law: Former Prob C §8802, similar to the present section, was added Stats 1988 ch 1199 §82.5, operative July 1, 1989, and repealed Stats 1990 ch 79 §13, operative July 1, 1991.

§8803. Notice of filing of inventory and appraisal

On the filing of an inventory and appraisal or a supplemental inventory and appraisal, the personal representative shall, pursuant to Section 1252, deliver a copy to each person who has requested special notice. **Leg.H.** Enacted Stats 1990 ch 79 §14 (AB 759), operative July 1, 1991. Amended Stats 2017 ch 319 §70 (AB 976), effective January 1, 2018.

Prior Law: Former Prob C §8803, similar to the present section, was added Stats 1988 ch 1199 §82.5, operative July 1, 1989, and repealed Stats 1990 ch 79 §13, operative July 1, 1991.

§8804. Failure to timely file inventory and appraisal

If the personal representative refuses or negligently fails to file an inventory and appraisal within the time allowed under this chapter, upon petition of an interested person:

(a) The court may compel the personal representative to file an inventory and appraisal pursuant to the procedure prescribed in Chapter 4 (commencing with Section 11050) of Part 8.

(b) The court may remove the personal representative from office.

(c) The court may impose on the personal representative personal liability for injury to the estate or to an interested person that directly results from the refusal or failure. The liability may include attorney's fees, in the court's discretion. Damages awarded pursuant to this subdivision are a liability on the bond of the personal representative, if any. **Leg.H.** Enacted Stats 1990 ch 79 §14 (AB 759), operative July 1, 1991.

Prior Law: Former Prob C §8804, similar to the present section, was added Stats 1988 ch 1199 §82.5, operative July 1, 1989, and repealed Stats 1990 ch 79 §13, operative July 1, 1991.

CHAPTER 2
INVENTORY

Article 1. General Provisions.
Article 2. Discovery of Property of Decedent.

ARTICLE 1
General Provisions

Contents of inventory. §8850.
Discharge or devise of claims. §8851.
Oath of personal representative; Determination of property to be administered. §8852.

§8850. Contents of inventory

(a) The inventory, including partial and supplemental inventories, shall include all property to be administered in the decedent's estate.

(b) The inventory shall particularly specify the following property:

(1) Money owed to the decedent, including debts, bonds, and notes, with the name of each debtor, the date, the sum originally payable, and the endorsements, if any, with their dates. The inventory shall also specify security for the payment of money to the decedent, including mortgages and deeds of trust. If security for the payment of money is real property, the inventory shall include the recording reference or, if not recorded, a legal description of the real property.

(2) A statement of the interest of the decedent in a partnership, appraised as a single item.

(3) All money and other cash items, as defined in Section 8901, of the decedent.

(c) The inventory shall show, to the extent ascertainable by the personal representative, the portions of the property that are community, quasi-community, and separate property of the decedent. **Leg.H.** Enacted Stats 1990 ch 79 §14 (AB 759), operative July 1, 1991.

Prior Law: Former Prob C §8850, similar to the present section, was added Stats 1988 ch 1199 §82.5, operative July 1, 1989, and repealed Stats 1990 ch 79 §13, operative July 1, 1991.

§8851. Discharge or devise of claims

The discharge or devise in a will of any debt or demand of the testator against the executor or any other person is not valid against creditors of the testator, but is a specific devise of the debt or demand. The debt or demand shall be included in the inventory. If necessary, the debt or demand shall be applied in the payment of the debts of the testator. If not necessary for that purpose, the debt or demand shall be distributed in the same manner and proportion as other specific devises. **Leg.H.** Enacted Stats 1990 ch 79 §14 (AB 759), operative July 1, 1991.

Prior Law: Former Prob C §8851, similar to the present section, was added Stats 1988 ch 1199 §82.5, operative July 1, 1989, and repealed Stats 1990 ch 79 §13, operative July 1, 1991.

§8852. Oath of personal representative; Determination of property to be administered

(a) The personal representative shall take and subscribe an oath that the inventory contains a true statement of the property to be administered in the decedent's estate of which the personal representative has knowledge, and particularly of money of the decedent and debts or demands of the decedent against the personal representative. The oath shall be endorsed upon or attached to the inventory.

(b) If there is more than one personal representative, each shall take and subscribe the oath. If the personal representatives are unable to agree as to property to be included in the inventory, any personal representative may petition for a court order determining whether the property is to be administered in the decedent's estate. The determination shall be made pursuant to the procedure provided in Part 19 (commencing with Section 850) of Division 2 or, if there is an issue of property belonging or passing to the surviving spouse, pursuant to Chapter 5 (commencing with Section 13650) of Part 2 of Division 8. **Leg.H.** Enacted Stats 1990 ch 79 §14 (AB 759), operative July 1, 1991. Amended Stats 2003 ch 32 §7 (AB 167), effective January 1, 2004.

Prior Law: Former Prob C §8852, similar to the present section, was added Stats 1988 ch 1199 §82.5, operative July 1, 1989, and repealed Stats 1990 ch 79 §13, operative July 1, 1991.

ARTICLE 2
Discovery of Property of Decedent

Citation to appear and be examined concerning decedent's property. §8870.
Interrogatories. §8871.
Examination. §8872.
Citation to appear and account. §8873.

§8870. Citation to appear and be examined concerning decedent's property

(a) On petition by the personal representative or an interested person, the court may order that a citation be issued to a person to answer interrogatories, or to appear before the court and be examined under oath, or both, concerning any of the following allegations:

(1) The person has wrongfully taken, concealed, or disposed of property in the estate of the decedent.

(2) The person has knowledge or possession of any of the following:

(A) A deed, conveyance, bond, contract, or other writing that contains evidence of or tends to disclose the right, title, interest, or claim of the decedent to property.

(B) A claim of the decedent.

(C) A lost will of the decedent.

(b) If the person does not reside in the county in which the estate is being administered, the superior court either of the county in which the person resides or of the county in which the estate is being administered may issue a citation under this section.

(c) Disobedience of a citation issued pursuant to this section may be punished as a contempt of the court issuing the citation.

(d) Notice to the personal representative of a proceeding under subdivision (a) shall be given for the period and in the manner provided in Section 1220. Other persons requesting notice of the hearing pursuant to Section 1250 shall be notified by the person filing the petition as set forth in Section 1252. **Leg.H.** Enacted Stats 1990 ch 79 §14 (AB 759), operative July 1, 1991. Amended Stats 1996 ch 563 §23 (SB 392).

Prior Law: Former Prob C §8870, similar to the present section, was added Stats 1988 ch 1199 §82.5, operative July 1, 1989, and repealed Stats 1990 ch 79 §13, operative July 1, 1991.

§8871. Interrogatories

Interrogatories may be put to a person cited to answer interrogatories pursuant to Section 8870. The interrogatories and answers shall be in writing. The answers shall be signed under penalty of perjury by the person cited. The interrogatories and answers shall be filed with the court. **Leg.H.** Enacted Stats 1990 ch 79 §14 (AB 759), operative July 1, 1991.

Prior Law: Former Prob C §8871, similar to the present section, was added Stats 1988 ch 1199 §82.5, operative July 1, 1989, and repealed Stats 1990 ch 79 §13, operative July 1, 1991.

§8872. Examination

(a) At an examination witnesses may be produced and examined on either side.

(b) If upon the examination it appears that the allegations of the petition are true, the court may order the person to disclose the person's knowledge of the facts to the personal representative.

(c) If upon the examination it appears that the allegations of the petition are not true, the person's necessary expenses, including a reasonable attorney's fee, shall be charged against the petitioner or allowed out of the estate, in the discretion of the court. **Leg.H.** Enacted Stats 1990 ch 79 §14 (AB 759), operative July 1, 1991.

Prior Law: Former Prob C §8872, similar to the present section, was added Stats 1988 ch 1199 §82.5, operative July 1, 1989, and repealed Stats 1990 ch 79 §13, operative July 1, 1991.

§8873. Citation to appear and account

(a) On petition by the personal representative, the court may issue a citation to a person who has possession or control of property in the decedent's estate to appear before the court and make an account under oath of the property and the person's actions with respect to the property.

(b) Disobedience of a citation issued pursuant to this section may be punished as a contempt of the court issuing the citation. **Leg.H.** Enacted Stats 1990 ch 79 §14 (AB 759), operative July 1, 1991.

Prior Law: Former Prob C §8873, similar to the present section, was added Stats 1988 ch 1199 §82.5, operative July 1, 1989, and repealed Stats 1990 ch 79 §13, operative July 1, 1991.

§8874. [Section repealed 1994]

Leg.H. Enacted Stats 1990 ch 79 §14 (AB 759), operative July 1, 1991. Repealed Stats 1994 ch 806 §29 (AB 3686). See Prob C §859.

Prior Law: Former Prob C §8874, similar to present Prob C §859, was added Stats 1988 ch 1199 §82.5, operative July 1, 1989, and repealed Stats 1990 ch 79 §13, operative July 1, 1991.

CHAPTER 3
APPRAISAL

Article 1. Procedure.
Article 2. Designation and Removal of Probate Referee.
Article 3. Time for Probate Referee Appraisal.
Article 4. Commission and Expenses of Probate Referee.
Article 5. Transitional Provision.

ARTICLE 1
Procedure

Appraisal by personal representative, probate referee, and independent expert. §8900.
Appraisal by personal representative. §8901.
Appraisal by probate referee. §8902.
Waiver of appraisal by probate referee. §8903.
Appraisal by independent expert. §8904.
Verification of appraisal. §8905.
Objection to appraisal. §8906.
Fee for appraisal by personal representative or attorney. §8907.
Appraisal report, backup data, and justification of appraisal. §8908.
Retention of records by probate referee. §8909.

§8900. Appraisal by personal representative, probate referee, and independent expert

The appraisal of property in the inventory shall be made by the personal representative, probate referee, or independent expert as provided in this chapter. **Leg.H.** Enacted Stats 1990 ch 79 §14 (AB 759), operative July 1, 1991.

Prior Law: Former Prob C §8900, similar to the present section, was added Stats 1988 ch 1199 §82.5, operative July 1, 1989, and repealed Stats 1990 ch 79 §13, operative July 1, 1991.

§8901. Appraisal by personal representative

The personal representative shall appraise the following property, excluding items whose fair market value is, in the opinion of the personal representative, an amount different from the face value of the property:

(a) Money and other cash items. As used in this subdivision, a "cash item" is a check, draft, money order, or similar instrument issued on or before the date of the decedent's death that can be immediately converted to cash.

(b) The following checks issued after the date of the decedent's death:

(1) Checks for wages earned before death.

(2) Refund checks, including tax and utility refunds, and Medicare, medical insurance, and other health care reimbursements and payments.

(c) Accounts (as defined in Section 21) in financial institutions.

(d) Cash deposits and money market mutual funds, as defined in subdivision (b) of Section 9730, whether in a financial institution or otherwise, including a brokerage cash account. All other mutual funds, stocks, bonds, and other securities shall be appraised pursuant to Sections 8902 to 8909, inclusive.

(e) Proceeds of life and accident insurance policies and retirement plans and annuities payable on death in lump sum amounts. **Leg.H.** Enacted Stats 1990 ch 79 §14 (AB 759), operative July 1, 1991. Amended Stats 1994 ch 806 §30 (AB 3686).

Prior Law: Former Prob C §8901, similar to the present section, was added Stats 1988 ch 1199 §82.5, operative July 1, 1989, and repealed Stats 1990 ch 79 §13, operative July 1, 1991.

§8902. Appraisal by probate referee

Except as otherwise provided by statute:

(a) The personal representative shall deliver the inventory to the probate referee designated by the court, together with necessary supporting data to enable the probate referee to make an appraisal of the property in the inventory to be appraised by the probate referee.

(b) The probate referee shall appraise all property other than that appraised by the personal representative. **Leg.H.** Enacted Stats 1990 ch 79 §14 (AB 759), operative July 1, 1991.

Prior Law: Former Prob C §8902, similar to the present section, was added Stats 1988 ch 1199 §82.5, operative July 1, 1989, and repealed Stats 1990 ch 79 §13, operative July 1, 1991.

§8903. Waiver of appraisal by probate referee

(a) The court may, for good cause, waive appraisal by a probate referee in the manner provided in this section.

(b) The personal representative may apply for a waiver together with the petition for appointment of the personal representative or together with another petition, or may apply for a waiver in a separate petition filed in the administration proceedings, but the application shall not be made later than the time the personal representative delivers the inventory to the probate referee, if a probate referee has been designated. A copy of the proposed inventory and appraisal and a statement that sets forth the good cause that justifies the waiver shall be attached to the petition.

(c) The hearing on the waiver shall be not sooner than 15 days after the petition is filed. Notice of the hearing on the petition, together with a copy of the petition and a copy of the proposed inventory and appraisal, shall be given as provided in Sections 1215 and 1220 to all of the following persons:

(1) Each person listed in Section 1220.

(2) Each known heir whose interest in the estate would be affected by the waiver.

(3) Each known devisee whose interest in the estate would be affected by the waiver.

(4) The Attorney General, at the office of the Attorney General in Sacramento, if any portion of the estate is to escheat to the state and its interest in the estate would be affected by the waiver.

(5) The probate referee, if a probate referee has been designated.

(d) A probate referee to whom notice is given under this section may oppose the waiver. If the opposition fails and the court determines the opposition was made without substantial justification, the court shall award litigation expenses, including reasonable attorney's fees, against the probate referee. If the opposition succeeds, the court may designate a different probate referee to appraise property in the estate.

(e) If the petition is granted, the inventory and appraisal attached to the petition shall be filed pursuant to Section 8800. **Leg.H.** Enacted Stats 1990 ch 79 §14 (AB 759), operative July 1, 1991. Amended Stats 2017 ch 319 §71 (AB 976), effective January 1, 2018.

Prior Law: Former Prob C §8903, similar to the present section, was added Stats 1988 ch 1199 §82.5, operative July 1, 1989, and repealed Stats 1990 ch 79 §13, operative July 1, 1991.

§8904. Appraisal by independent expert

(a) A unique, artistic, unusual, or special item of tangible personal property that would otherwise be appraised by the probate referee may, at the election of the personal representative, be appraised by an independent expert qualified to appraise the item.

(b) The personal representative shall make the election provided in subdivision (a) by a notation on the inventory delivered to the probate referee indicating the property to be appraised by an independent expert. The probate referee may, within five days after delivery of the inventory, petition for a court determination whether the property to be appraised by an independent expert is a unique, artistic, unusual, or special item of tangible personal property. If the petition fails and the court determines that the petition was made without substantial justification, the court shall award litigation expenses, including reasonable attorney's fees, against the probate referee. **Leg.H.** Enacted Stats 1990 ch 79 §14 (AB 759), operative July 1, 1991.

Prior Law: Former Prob C §8904, similar to the present section, was added Stats 1988 ch 1199 §82.5, operative July 1, 1989, and repealed Stats 1990 ch 79 §13, operative July 1, 1991.

§8905. Verification of appraisal

A person who appraises property, whether a personal representative, probate referee, or independent expert, shall sign the appraisal as to property appraised by that person, and shall take and subscribe an oath that the person has truly, honestly, and impartially appraised the property to the best of the person's ability. **Leg.H.** Enacted Stats 1990 ch 79 §14 (AB 759), operative July 1, 1991.

Prior Law: Former Prob C §8905, similar to the present section, was added Stats 1988 ch 1199 §82.5, operative July 1, 1989, and repealed Stats 1990 ch 79 §13, operative July 1, 1991.

§8906. Objection to appraisal

(a) At any time before the hearing on the petition for final distribution of the estate, the personal representative or an interested person may file with the court a written objection to the appraisal.

(b) The clerk shall fix a time, not less than 15 days after the filing, for a hearing on the objection.

(c) The person objecting shall give notice of the hearing, together with a copy of the objection, as provided in Section 1220. If the appraisal was made by a probate referee, the person objecting shall also deliver notice of the hearing and a copy of the objection to the probate referee at least 15 days before the date set for the hearing.

(d) The person objecting to the appraisal has the burden of proof.

(e) Upon completion of the hearing, the court may make any orders that appear appropriate. If the court determines the objection was filed without reasonable cause or good faith, the court may order that the fees of the personal representative and attorney and any costs incurred for defending the appraisal be made a charge against the person filing the objection. **Leg.H.** Enacted Stats 1990 ch 79 §14 (AB 759), operative July 1, 1991. Amended Stats 2017 ch 319 §72 (AB 976), effective January 1, 2018.

Prior Law: Former Prob C §8906, similar to the present section, was added Stats 1988 ch 1199 §82.5, operative July 1, 1989, and repealed Stats 1990 ch 79 §13, operative July 1, 1991.

§8907. Fee for appraisal by personal representative or attorney

Neither the personal representative nor the attorney for the personal representative is entitled to receive compensation for extraordinary services by reason of appraising any property in the estate. **Leg.H.** Enacted Stats 1990 ch 79 §14 (AB 759), operative July 1, 1991. Amended Stats 1991 ch 82 §24 (SB 896), effective June 30, 1991, operative July 1, 1991.

Prior Law: Former Prob C §8907, similar to the present section, was added Stats 1988 ch 1199 §82.5, operative July 1, 1989, and repealed Stats 1990 ch 79 §13, operative July 1, 1991.

§8908. Appraisal report, backup data, and justification of appraisal

A probate referee who appraises property in the estate shall, upon demand by the personal representative or by a beneficiary:

(a) Provide any appraisal report or backup data in the possession of the probate referee used by the referee to appraise an item of property. The probate referee shall not disclose any information that is required by law to be confidential. The probate referee shall provide the appraisal report or backup data without charge. The cost of providing the appraisal report or backup data shall not be allowed as an expense of appraisal but is included in the commission for services of the probate referee.

(b) Justify the appraisal of an item of property if the appraisal is contested, whether by objection pursuant to Section 8906, by tax audit, or otherwise. The probate referee may be entitled to an additional fee for services provided to justify the appraisal, to be agreed upon by the personal representative or beneficiary and referee. If the personal representative or beneficiary and the probate referee are unable to agree, the court shall determine what fee, if any, is appropriate. **Leg.H.** Enacted Stats 1990 ch 79 §14 (AB 759), operative July 1, 1991.

Prior Law: Former Prob C §8908, similar to the present section, was added Stats 1988 ch 1199 §82.5, operative July 1, 1989, and repealed Stats 1990 ch 79 §13, operative July 1, 1991.

§8909. Retention of records by probate referee

A probate referee who appraises property in an estate shall retain possession of all appraisal reports and backup data used by the referee to appraise the property for a period of three years after the appraisal is filed. The probate referee shall, during the three-year period, offer the personal representative the reports and data used by the referee to appraise the property and deliver the reports and data to the personal representative on request. Any reports and data not requested by the personal representative may be destroyed at the end of the three-year period without further notice. **Leg.H.** Enacted Stats 1990 ch 79 §14 (AB 759), operative July 1, 1991.

Prior Law: Former Prob C §8909, similar to the present section, was added Stats 1988 ch 1199 §82.5, operative July 1, 1989, and repealed Stats 1990 ch 79 §13, operative July 1, 1991.

ARTICLE 2
Designation and Removal of Probate Referee

Designation by court. §8920.
Designation at request of personal representative. §8921.
Discretion not to designate person as probate referee. §8922.
Disqualification of probate referee. §8923.
Removal of probate referee. §8924.

§8920. Designation by court

The probate referee, when designated by the court, shall be among the persons appointed by the Controller to act as a probate referee for the county. If there is no person available who is able to act or if, pursuant to authority of Section 8922 or otherwise, the court does not designate a person appointed for the county, the court may designate a probate referee from another county. **Leg.H.** Enacted Stats 1990 ch 79 §14 (AB 759), operative July 1, 1991.

Prior Law: Former Prob C §8920, similar to the present section, was added Stats 1988 ch 1199 §82.5, operative July 1, 1989, and repealed Stats 1990 ch 79 §13, operative July 1, 1991.

§8921. Designation at request of personal representative

The court may designate a person requested by the personal representative as probate referee, on a showing by the personal representative of good cause for the designation. The following circumstances are included within the meaning of good cause, as used in this section:

(a) The probate referee has recently appraised the same property that will be appraised in the administration proceeding.

(b) The probate referee will be making related appraisals in another proceeding.

(c) The probate referee has recently appraised similar property in another proceeding. **Leg.H.** Enacted Stats 1990 ch 79 §14 (AB 759), operative July 1, 1991.

Prior Law: Former Prob C §8921, similar to the present section, was added Stats 1988 ch 1199 §82.5, operative July 1, 1989, and repealed Stats 1990 ch 79 §13, operative July 1, 1991.

§8922. Discretion not to designate person as probate referee

The court has authority and discretion not to designate a particular person as probate referee even though appointed by the Controller to act as a probate referee for the county. **Leg.H.** Enacted Stats 1990 ch 79 §14 (AB 759), operative July 1, 1991.

Prior Law: Former Prob C §8922, similar to the present section, was added Stats 1988 ch 1199 §82.5, operative July 1, 1989, and repealed Stats 1990 ch 79 §13, operative July 1, 1991.

§8923. Disqualification of probate referee

The court may not designate as probate referee any of the following persons:

(a) The court clerk.

(b) A partner or employee of the judge or commissioner who orders the designation.

(c) The spouse of the judge or commissioner who orders the designation.

(d) A person, or the spouse of a person, who is related within the third degree either (1) to the judge or commissioner who orders the designation or (2) to the spouse of the judge or commissioner who orders the designation. **Leg.H.** Enacted Stats 1990 ch 79 §14 (AB 759), operative July 1, 1991.

Prior Law: Former Prob C §8923, similar to the present section, was added Stats 1988 ch 1199 §82.5, operative July 1, 1989, and repealed Stats 1990 ch 79 §13, operative July 1, 1991.

§8924. Removal of probate referee

(a) The court shall remove the designated probate referee in any of the following circumstances:

(1) The personal representative shows cause, including incompetence or undue delay in making the appraisal, that in the opinion of the court warrants removal of the probate referee. The showing shall be made at a hearing on petition of the personal representative. The personal representative shall deliver pursuant to Section 1215 notice of the hearing on the petition to the probate referee at least 15 days before the date set for the hearing.

(2) The personal representative has the right to remove the first probate referee who is designated by the court. Cause need not be shown for removal under this paragraph. The personal representative may exercise the right at any time before the personal representative delivers the inventory to the probate referee. The personal representative shall exercise the right by filing an affidavit or declaration under penalty of perjury with the court and delivering a copy to the probate referee pursuant to Section 1215. Thereupon, the court shall remove the probate referee without any further act or proof.

(3) Any other cause provided by statute.

(b) Upon removal of the probate referee, the court shall designate another probate referee in the manner prescribed in Section 8920. **Leg.H.** Enacted Stats 1990 ch 79 §14 (AB 759), operative July 1, 1991. Amended Stats 2017 ch 319 §73 (AB 976), effective January 1, 2018.

Prior Law: Former Prob C §8924, similar to the present section, was added Stats 1988 ch 1199 §82.5, operative July 1, 1989, and repealed Stats 1990 ch 79 §13, operative July 1, 1991.

ARTICLE 3
Time for Probate Referee Appraisal

Time required for appraisal or status report. §8940.
Hearing and order. §8941.

§8940. Time required for appraisal or status report

(a) The probate referee shall promptly and with reasonable diligence appraise the property scheduled for appraisal by the probate referee in the inventory that the personal representative delivers to the referee.

(b) The probate referee shall, not later than 60 days after delivery of the inventory, do one of the following:

(1) Return the completed appraisal to the personal representative.

(2) Make a report of the status of the appraisal. The report shall show the reason why the property has not been appraised and an estimate of the time needed to complete the appraisal. The report shall be delivered to the personal representative and filed with the court. **Leg.H.** Enacted Stats 1990 ch 79 §14 (AB 759), operative July 1, 1991.

Prior Law: Former Prob C §8940, similar to the present section, was added Stats 1988 ch 1199 §82.5, operative July 1, 1989, and repealed Stats 1990 ch 79 §13, operative July 1, 1991.

§8941. Hearing and order

(a) The court shall, on petition of the personal representative or probate referee, or may, on the court's own motion, hear the report of the status of the appraisal. The court may issue a citation to compel the personal representative or the probate referee to attend the hearing.

(b) If the probate referee does not make the report of the status of the appraisal within the time required by this article or prescribed by the court, the court shall, on petition of the personal representative or may, on its own motion, cite the probate referee to appear before the court and show the reason why the property has not been appraised.

(c) Upon the hearing, the court may order any of the following:

(1) That the appraisal be completed within a time that appears reasonable.

(2) That the probate referee be removed. Upon removal of the probate referee the court shall designate another probate referee in the manner prescribed in Section 8920.

(3) That the commission of the probate referee be reduced by an amount the court deems appropriate, regardless of whether the commission otherwise allowable under the provisions of Sections 8960 to 8964 would be reasonable compensation for the services rendered.

(4) That the personal representative deliver to the probate referee all information necessary to allow the probate referee to complete the appraisal. Failure to comply with such an order is grounds for removal of the personal representative.

(5) Such other orders as may be appropriate. **Leg.H.** Enacted Stats 1990 ch 79 §14 (AB 759), operative July 1, 1991.

Prior Law: Former Prob C §8941, similar to the present section, was added Stats 1988 ch 1199 §82.5, operative July 1, 1989, and repealed Stats 1990 ch 79 §13, operative July 1, 1991.

ARTICLE 4
Commission and Expenses of Probate Referee

Payment of commission and expenses. §8960.
Amount of commission and expenses. §8961.
Maximum and minimum commissions. §8963.
Division of commission between referees. §8964.

§8960. Payment of commission and expenses

(a) The commission and expenses provided by this article as compensation for the services of the probate referee shall be paid from the estate.

(b) The probate referee may not withhold the appraisal until the commission and expenses are paid, but shall deliver the appraisal to the personal representative promptly upon completion.

(c) The commission and expenses of the probate referee are an expense of administration, entitled to the priority for payment provided by Section 11420, and shall be paid in the course of administration. **Leg.H.** Enacted Stats 1990 ch 79 §14 (AB 759), operative July 1, 1991.

Prior Law: Former Prob C §8960, similar to the present section, was added Stats 1988 ch 1199 §82.5, operative July 1, 1989, and repealed Stats 1990 ch 79 §13, operative July 1, 1991.

§8961. Amount of commission and expenses

As compensation for services the probate referee shall receive all of the following:

(a) A commission of one-tenth of one percent of the total value of the property for each estate appraised, subject to Section 8963. The commission shall be computed excluding property appraised by the personal representative pursuant to Section 8901 or by an independent expert pursuant to Section 8904.

(b) Actual and necessary expenses for each estate appraised. The referee shall file with, or list on, the inventory and appraisal a verified account of the referee's expenses. **Leg.H.** Enacted Stats 1990 ch 79 §14 (AB 759), operative July 1, 1991.

Prior Law: Former Prob C §8961, similar to the present section, was added Stats 1988 ch 1199 §82.5, operative July 1, 1989, and repealed Stats 1990 ch 79 §13, operative July 1, 1991.

§8963. Maximum and minimum commissions

(a) Notwithstanding Section 8961 and subject to subdivision (b), the commission of the probate referee shall in no event be less than seventy-five dollars ($75) nor more than ten thousand dollars ($10,000) for any estate appraised.

(b) Upon application of the probate referee, the court may allow a commission in excess of ten thousand dollars ($10,000) if the court determines that the reasonable value of the referee's services exceeds that amount. Notice of the hearing under this subdivision shall be given as provided in Section 1220 to all of the following persons:

(1) Each person listed in Section 1220.

(2) Each known heir whose interest in the estate would be affected by the petition.

(3) Each known devisee whose interest in the estate would be affected by the petition.

(4) The Attorney General, at the office of the Attorney General in Sacramento, if any portion of the estate is to escheat to the state and its interest in the estate would be affected by the petition.

(5) Each person who has requested special notice of petitions filed in the proceeding. **Leg.H.** Enacted Stats 1990 ch 79 §14 (AB 759), operative July 1, 1991.

Prior Law: Former Prob C §8963, similar to the present section, was added Stats 1988 ch 1199 §82.5, operative July 1, 1989, and repealed Stats 1990 ch 79 §13, operative July 1, 1991.

§8964. Division of commission between referees

If more than one probate referee appraises or participates in the appraisal of property in the estate, each is entitled to the share of the commission agreed upon by the referees or, absent an agreement, that the court allows. In no case shall the total commission for all referees exceed the maximum commission that would be allowable for a single referee. **Leg.H.** Enacted Stats 1990 ch 79 §14 (AB 759), operative July 1, 1991.

Prior Law: Former Prob C §8964, similar to the present section, was added Stats 1988 ch 1199 §82.5, operative July 1, 1989, and repealed Stats 1990 ch 79 §13, operative July 1, 1991.

ARTICLE 5
Transitional Provision

Transitional provision. §8980.

§8980. Transitional provision

If an inventory is delivered to a probate referee for appraisal before July 1, 1989, all matters relating to the appraisal by the referee, including the property to be included in the appraisal, waiver of the appraisal, and compensation of the referee, are governed by the applicable law in effect before July 1, 1989, and are not governed by this chapter. **Leg.H.** Enacted Stats 1990 ch 79 §14 (AB 759), operative July 1, 1991.

Prior Law: Former Prob C §8980, similar to the present section, was added Stats 1988 ch 1199 §82.5, operative July 1, 1989, and repealed Stats 1990 ch 79 §13, operative July 1, 1991.

PART 4
CREDITOR CLAIMS

Chapter 1. General Provisions.
Chapter 2. Notice to Creditors.
Chapter 3. Time for Filing Claims.
Chapter 4. Filing of Claims.
Chapter 5. Claims by Public Entities.
Chapter 6. Allowance and Rejection of Claims.
Chapter 7. Claims Established by Judgment.
Chapter 8. Claims in Litigation.

CHAPTER 1
GENERAL PROVISIONS

"Claim". §9000.
Notice to creditors. §9001.
Claim requirement. §9002.
Payment of claims. §9003.
Application of part. §9004.

§9000. "Claim"

As used in this division:

(a) "Claim" means a demand for payment for any of the following, whether due, not due, accrued or not accrued, or contingent, and whether liquidated or unliquidated:

(1) Liability of the decedent, whether arising in contract, tort, or otherwise.

(2) Liability for taxes incurred before the decedent's death, whether assessed before or after the decedent's death, other than property taxes and assessments secured by real property liens.

(3) Liability of the estate for funeral expenses of the decedent.

(b) "Claim" does not include a dispute regarding title of a decedent to specific property alleged to be included in the decedent's estate.

(c) "Creditor" means a person who may have a claim against estate property. **Leg.H.** Enacted Stats 1990 ch 79 §14 (AB 759), operative July 1, 1991. Amended Stats 1996 ch 862 §17 (AB 2751); Stats 2007 ch 159 §1 (AB 341), effective January 1, 2008.

Prior Law: Former Prob C §9000, similar to the present section, was added Stats 1987 ch 923 §93, operative July 1, 1988, and repealed Stats 1990 ch 79 §13, operative July 1, 1991.

§9001. Notice to creditors

(a) The publication of notice under Section 8120 and the giving of notice of administration of the estate of the decedent under Chapter 2 (commencing with Section 9050) constitute notice to creditors of the requirements of this part.

(b) Nothing in subdivision (a) affects a notice or request to a public entity required by Chapter 5 (commencing with Section 9200). **Leg.H.** Enacted Stats 1990 ch 79 §14 (AB 759), operative July 1, 1991.

Prior Law: Former Prob C §9001, similar to the present section, was added Stats 1987 ch 923 §93, operative July 1, 1988, amended Stats 1988 ch 1199 §83, operative July 1, 1989, and repealed Stats 1990 ch 79 §13, operative July 1, 1991.

§9002. Claim requirement

Except as otherwise provided by statute:

(a) All claims shall be filed in the manner and within the time provided in this part.

(b) A claim that is not filed as provided in this part is barred. **Leg.H.** Enacted Stats 1990 ch 79 §14 (AB 759), operative July 1, 1991.

Prior Law: Former Prob C §9002, similar to the present section, was added Stats 1987 ch 923 §93, operative July 1, 1988, amended Stats 1988 ch 1199 §83.5, operative July 1, 1989, and repealed Stats 1990 ch 79 §13, operative July 1, 1991.

§9003. Payment of claims

A claim that is established under this part shall be included among the debts to be paid in the course of administration. **Leg.H.** Enacted Stats 1990 ch 79 §14 (AB 759), operative July 1, 1991.

Prior Law: Former Prob C §9003, similar to the present section, was added Stats 1987 ch 923 §93, operative July 1, 1988, and repealed Stats 1990 ch 79 §13, operative July 1, 1991.

§9004. Application of part

(a) This part does not apply in any proceeding for administration of a decedent's estate commenced before July 1, 1988.

(b) The applicable law in effect before July 1, 1988, governing the subject matter of this part continues to apply in any proceeding for administration of a decedent's estate commenced before July 1, 1988, notwithstanding its repeal by Chapter 923 of the Statutes of 1987. **Leg.H.** Enacted Stats 1990 ch 79 §14 (AB 759), operative July 1, 1991.

Prior Law: Former Prob C §9004, similar to the present section, was added Stats 1987 ch 923 §93, operative July 1, 1988, and repealed Stats 1990 ch 79 §13, operative July 1, 1991.

CHAPTER 2
NOTICE TO CREDITORS

Notice required. §9050.
Time of notice. §9051.
Form of notice. §9052.
Immunity of personal representative. §9053.
When notice not required. §9054.

§9050. Notice required

(a) Subject to Section 9054, the personal representative shall give notice of administration of the estate to the known or reasonably ascertainable creditors of the decedent. The notice shall be given as provided in Section 1215. For the purpose of this subdivision, a personal representative has knowledge of a creditor of the decedent if the personal representative is aware that the creditor has demanded payment from the decedent or the estate.

(b) The giving of notice under this chapter is in addition to the publication of the notice under Section 8120. **Leg.H.** Enacted Stats 1990 ch 79 §14 (AB 759), operative July 1, 1991. Amended Stats 1990 ch 140 §6.1 (SB 1855), operative July 1, 1991; Stats 1991 ch 82 §25 (SB 896), effective June 30, 1991, operative July 1, 1991; Stats 1996 ch 862 §18 (AB 2751).

Prior Law: Former Prob C §9050, similar to the present section, was added Stats 1987 ch 923 §93, operative July 1, 1988, amended Stats 1988 ch 1199 §84, operative July 1, 1989, repealed Stats 1990 ch 79 §13, operative July 1, 1991, amended Stats 1990 ch 140 §6, and repealed Stats 1990 ch 140 §22, operative July 1, 1991.

§9051. Time of notice

The notice shall be given within the later of:

(a) Four months after the date letters are first issued.

(b) Thirty days after the personal representative first has knowledge of the creditor. **Leg.H.** Enacted Stats 1990 ch 79 §14 (AB 759), operative July 1, 1991. Amended Stats 1990 ch 140 §7.1 (SB 1855), operative July 1, 1991; Stats 1996 ch 862 §19 (AB 2751).

Prior Law: Former Prob C §9051, similar to the present section, was added Stats 1987 ch 923 §93, operative July 1, 1988, repealed Stats 1990 ch 79 §13, operative July 1, 1991, amended Stats 1990 ch 140 §7, and repealed Stats 1990 ch 140 §23, operative July 1, 1991.

§9052. Form of notice

The notice shall be in substantially the following form:

NOTICE OF ADMINISTRATION OF
ESTATE OF _____, DECEDENT

Notice to creditors:
Administration of the estate of _____ (deceased) has been commenced by _____ (personal representative) in Estate No. ____ in the Superior Court of California, County of _____. You must file your claim with the court and deliver a copy pursuant to Section 1215 of the California Probate Code to the personal representative within the last to occur of four months after _____ (the date letters were first issued to a general personal representative, as defined in subdivision (b) of Section 58 of the California Probate Code), or 60 days after the date this notice was mailed to you or, in the case of personal delivery, 60 days after the date this notice was delivered to you, or you must petition to file a late claim as provided in Section 9103 of the California Probate Code. Failure to file a claim with the court and serve a copy of the claim on the personal representative will, in most instances, invalidate your claim. A claim form may be obtained

from the court clerk. For your protection, you are encouraged to file your claim by certified mail, with return receipt requested.

_____   _____
(Date of mailing   (Name and address of personal
this notice)   representative or attorney)

Leg.H. Enacted Stats 1990 ch 79 §14 (AB 759), operative July 1, 1991. Amended Stats 1990 ch 140 §8.1 (SB 1855), operative July 1, 1991; Stats 1996 ch 862 §20 (AB 2751); Stats 2012 ch 207 §3 (AB 2683), effective January 1, 2013; Stats 2017 ch 319 §74 (AB 976), effective January 1, 2018.

Prior Law: Former Prob C §9052, similar to the present section, was added Stats 1987 ch 923 §93, operative July 1, 1988, amended Stats 1988 ch 113 §15, effective May 25, 1988, operative July 1, 1988, repealed Stats 1990 ch 79 §13, operative July 1, 1991, amended Stats 1990 ch 140 §8, and repealed Stats 1990 ch 140 §24, operative July 1, 1991.

§9053. Immunity of personal representative

(a) If the personal representative believes that notice to a particular creditor is or may be required by this chapter and gives notice based on that belief, the personal representative is not liable to any person for giving the notice, whether or not required by this chapter.

(b) If the personal representative fails to give notice required by this chapter, the personal representative is not liable to any person for the failure, unless a creditor establishes all of the following:

(1) The failure was in bad faith.

(2) The creditor had no actual knowledge of the administration of the estate before expiration of the time for filing a claim, and payment would have been made on the creditor's claim in the course of administration if the claim had been properly filed.

(3) Within 16 months after letters were first issued to a general personal representative, the creditor did both of the following:

(A) Filed a petition requesting that the court in which the estate was administered make an order determining the liability of the personal representative under this subdivision.

(B) At least 30 days before the hearing on the petition, caused notice of the hearing and a copy of the petition to be served on the personal representative in the manner provided in Chapter 4 (commencing with Section 413.10) of Title 5 of Part 2 of the Code of Civil Procedure.

(c) Nothing in this section affects the liability of the estate, if any, for the claim of a creditor, and the personal representative is not liable for the claim to the extent it is paid out of the estate or could be paid out of the estate pursuant to Section 9103.

(d) A personal representative has a duty to make reasonably diligent efforts to identify reasonably ascertainable creditors of the decedent. **Leg.H.** Enacted Stats 1990 ch 79 §14 (AB 759), operative July 1, 1991. Amended Stats 1991 ch 1055 §24 (SB 271); Stats 1996 ch 862 §21 (AB 2751); Stats 1999 ch 263 §4 (AB 1051).

Prior Law: Former Prob C §9053, similar to the present section, was added Stats 1987 ch 923 §93, operative July 1, 1988, amended Stats 1989 ch 544 §9.5, and repealed Stats 1990 ch 79 §13, operative July 1, 1991.

§9054. When notice not required

Notwithstanding Section 9050, the personal representative need not give notice to a creditor even though the personal representative has knowledge of the creditor if any of the following conditions is satisfied:

(a) The creditor has filed a claim as provided in this part.

(b) The creditor has demanded payment and the personal representative elects to treat the demand as a claim under Section 9154. **Leg.H.** Enacted Stats 1990 ch 79 §14 (AB 759), operative July 1, 1991.

Prior Law: Former Prob C §9054, similar to the present section, was added Stats 1987 ch 923 §93, operative July 1, 1988, and repealed Stats 1990 ch 79 §13, operative July 1, 1991.

CHAPTER 3
TIME FOR FILING CLAIMS

Claim period. §9100.
Time not extended by vacancy in office. §9101.
Where personal representative acts on claim after expiration of time. §9102.
Late claims. §9103.
Amended or revised claim. §9104.

§9100. Claim period

(a) A creditor shall file a claim before expiration of the later of the following times:

(1) Four months after the date letters are first issued to a general personal representative.

(2) Sixty days after the date notice of administration is mailed or personally delivered to the creditor. Nothing in this paragraph extends the time provided in Section 366.2 of the Code of Civil Procedure.

(b) A reference in another statute to the time for filing a claim means the time provided in paragraph (1) of subdivision (a).

(c) Nothing in this section shall be interpreted to extend or toll any other statute of limitations or to revive a claim that is barred by any statute of limitations. The reference in this subdivision to a "statute of limitations" includes Section 366.2 of the Code of Civil Procedure. **Leg.H.** Enacted Stats 1990 ch 79 §14 (AB 759), operative July 1, 1991. Amended Stats 1990 ch 140 §9.1 (SB 1855), operative July 1, 1991; Stats 1996 ch 862 §22 (AB 2751); Stats 1999 ch 263 §5 (AB 1051); Stats 2007 ch 159 §2 (AB 341), effective January 1, 2008.

Prior Law: Former Prob C §9100, similar to the present section, was added Stats 1987 ch 923 §93, operative July 1, 1988, repealed Stats 1990 ch 79 §13, operative July 1, 1991, amended Stats 1990 ch 140 §9, and repealed Stats 1990 ch 140 §25, operative July 1, 1991.

§9101. Time not extended by vacancy in office

A vacancy in the office of the personal representative that occurs before expiration of the time for filing a claim does not extend the time. **Leg.H.** Enacted Stats 1990 ch 79 §14 (AB 759), operative July 1, 1991.

Prior Law: Former Prob C §9101, similar to the present section, was added Stats 1987 ch 923 §93, operative July 1, 1988, and repealed Stats 1990 ch 79 §13, operative July 1, 1991.

§9102. Where personal representative acts on claim after expiration of time

A claim that is filed before expiration of the time for filing the claim is timely even if acted on by the personal representative or by the court after expiration of the time for filing claims. **Leg.H.** Enacted Stats 1990 ch 79 §14 (AB 759), operative July 1, 1991. Amended Stats 2007 ch 159 §3 (AB 341), effective January 1, 2008.

Prior Law: Former Prob C §9102, similar to the present section, was added Stats 1987 ch 923 §93, operative July 1, 1988, and repealed Stats 1990 ch 79 §13, operative July 1, 1991.

§9103. Late claims

(a) Upon petition by a creditor or the personal representative, the court may allow a claim to be filed after expiration of the time for filing a claim provided in Section 9100 if either of the following conditions is satisfied:

(1) The personal representative failed to send proper and timely notice of administration of the estate to the creditor, and that petition is filed within 60 days after the creditor has actual knowledge of the administration of the estate.

(2) The creditor had no knowledge of the facts reasonably giving rise to the existence of the claim more than 30 days prior to the time for filing a claim as provided in Section 9100, and the petition is filed within 60 days after the creditor has actual knowledge of both of the following:

(A) The existence of the facts reasonably giving rise to the existence of the claim.

(B) The administration of the estate.

(b) Notwithstanding subdivision (a), the court shall not allow a claim to be filed under this section after the court makes an order for final distribution of the estate.

(c) The court may condition the claim on terms that are just and equitable, and may require the appointment or reappointment of a personal representative if necessary. The court may deny the creditor's petition if a payment to general creditors has been made and it appears that the filing or establishment of the claim would cause or tend to cause unequal treatment among creditors.

(d) Regardless of whether the claim is later established in whole or in part, payments otherwise properly made before a claim is filed under this section are not subject to the claim. Except to the extent provided in Section 9392 and subject to Section 9053, the personal representative or payee is not liable on account of the prior payment. Nothing in this subdivision limits the liability of a person who receives a preliminary distribution of property to restore to the estate an amount sufficient for payment of the distributee's proper share of the claim, not exceeding the amount distributed.

(e) Notice of hearing on the petition shall be given as provided in Section 1220.

(f) Nothing in this section authorizes allowance or approval of a claim barred by, or extends the time provided in, Section 366.2 of the Code of Civil Procedure. **Leg.H.** Enacted Stats 1990 ch 79 §14 (AB 759), operative July 1, 1991. Amended Stats 1990 ch 140 §10.1 (SB 1855), operative July 1, 1991; Stats 1991 ch 1055 §25 (SB 271); Stats 1992 ch 178 §34 (SB 1496); Stats 1996 ch 862 §23 (AB 2751); Stats 2007 ch 159 §4 (AB 341), effective January 1, 2008.

Prior Law: Former Prob C §9103, similar to the present section, was added Stats 1987 ch 923 §93, operative July 1, 1988, amended Stats 1988 ch 113 §15.1, effective May 25, 1988, operative July 1, 1988, ch 1199 §84.5, operative July 1, 1989, repealed Stats 1990 ch 79 §13, operative July 1, 1991, amended Stats 1990 ch 140 §10, and repealed Stats 1990 ch 140 §26, operative July 1, 1991.

§9104. Amended or revised claim

(a) Subject to subdivision (b), if a claim is filed within the time provided in this chapter, the creditor may later amend or revise the claim. The amendment or revision shall be filed in the same manner as the claim.

(b) An amendment or revision may not be made to increase the amount of the claim after the time for filing a claim has expired. An amendment or revision to specify the amount of a claim that, at the time of filing, was not due, was contingent, or was not yet ascertainable, is not an increase in the amount of the claim within the meaning of this subdivision.

(c) An amendment or revision may not be made for any purpose after the earlier of the following times:

(1) The time the court makes an order for final distribution of the estate.

(2) One year after letters are first issued to a general personal representative. This paragraph does not extend the time provided by Section 366.2 of the Code of Civil Procedure or authorize allowance or approval of a claim barred by that section. **Leg.H.** Enacted Stats 1990 ch 79 §14 (AB 759), operative July 1, 1991. Amended Stats 2007 ch 159 §5 (AB 341), effective January 1, 2008.

Prior Law: Former Prob C §9104, similar to the present section, was added Stats 1987 ch 923 §93, operative July 1, 1988, and repealed Stats 1990 ch 79 §13, operative July 1, 1991.

CHAPTER 4
FILING OF CLAIMS

How claim is filed. §9150.
Documentary support of claim. §9151.
Claim based on written instrument. §9152.
Form for claim. §9153.
Waiver of formal defects. §9154.

§9150. How claim is filed

(a) A claim may be filed by the creditor or a person acting on behalf of the creditor.

(b) A claim shall be filed with the court and a copy shall be served on the personal representative, or on a person who is later appointed and qualified as personal representative.

(c) Service of the claim on the personal representative shall be made within the later of 30 days of the filing of the claim or four months after letters issue to a personal representative with general powers. Service shall not be required after the claim has been allowed or rejected.

(d) If the creditor does not file the claim with the court and serve the claim on the personal representative as provided in this section, the claim shall be invalid. **Leg.H.** Enacted Stats 1990 ch 79 §14 (AB 759), operative July 1, 1991. Amended Stats 1996 ch 862 §24 (AB 2751).

Prior Law: Former Prob C §9150, similar to the present section, was added Stats 1987 ch 923 §93, operative July 1, 1988, and repealed Stats 1990 ch 79 §13, operative July 1, 1991.

§9151. Documentary support of claim

(a) A claim shall be supported by the affidavit of the creditor or the person acting on behalf of the creditor stating:

(1) The claim is a just claim.

(2) If the claim is due, the facts supporting the claim, the amount of the claim, and that all payments on and offsets to the claim have been credited.

(3) If the claim is not due or contingent, or the amount is not yet ascertainable, the facts supporting the claim.

(4) If the affidavit is made by a person other than the creditor, the reason it is not made by the creditor.

(b) The personal representative may require satisfactory vouchers or proof to be produced to support the claim. An original voucher may be withdrawn after a copy is provided. If a copy is provided, the copy shall be attached to the claim. **Leg.H.** Enacted Stats 1990 ch 79 §14 (AB 759), operative July 1, 1991.

Prior Law: Former Prob C §9151, similar to the present section, was added Stats 1987 ch 923 §93, operative July 1, 1988, and repealed Stats 1990 ch 79 §13, operative July 1, 1991.

§9152. Claim based on written instrument

(a) If a claim is based on a written instrument, either the original or a copy of the original with all endorsements shall be attached to the claim. If a copy is attached, the original instrument shall be exhibited to the personal representative or court or judge on demand unless it is lost or destroyed, in which case the fact that it is lost or destroyed shall be stated in the claim.

(b) If the claim or a part of the claim is secured by a mortgage, deed of trust, or other lien that is recorded in the office of the recorder of the county in which the property subject to the lien is located, it is sufficient to describe the mortgage, deed of trust, or lien and the recording reference for the instrument that created the mortgage, deed of trust, or other lien. **Leg.H.** Enacted Stats 1990 ch 79 §14 (AB 759), operative July 1, 1991.

Prior Law: Former Prob C §9152, similar to the present section, was added Stats 1987 ch 923 §93, operative July 1, 1988, and repealed Stats 1990 ch 79 §13, operative July 1, 1991.

§9153. Form for claim

A claim form adopted by the Judicial Council shall inform the creditor that the claim must be filed with the court and a copy delivered pursuant to Section 1215 to the personal representative. The claim form shall include a proof of delivery of a copy of the claim to the personal representative, which may be completed by the creditor. **Leg.H.** Enacted Stats 1990 ch 79 §14 (AB 759), operative July 1, 1991. Amended Stats 2017 ch 319 §75 (AB 976), effective January 1, 2018.

Prior Law: Former Prob C §9153, similar to the present section, was added Stats 1987 ch 923 §93, operative July 1, 1988, and repealed Stats 1990 ch 79 §13, operative July 1, 1991.

§9154. Waiver of formal defects

(a) Notwithstanding any other provision of this part, if a creditor makes a written demand for payment within four months after the date letters are first issued to a general personal representative, the personal representative may waive formal defects and elect to treat the demand as a claim that is filed and established under this part by paying the amount demanded before the expiration of 30 days after the four-month period if all of the following conditions are satisfied:

(1) The debt was justly due.

(2) The debt was paid in good faith.

(3) The amount paid was the true amount of the indebtedness over and above all payments and offsets.

(4) The estate is solvent.

(b) Nothing in this section limits application of (1) the doctrines of waiver, estoppel, laches, or detrimental reliance or (2) any other equitable principle. **Leg.H.** Enacted Stats 1990 ch 79 §14 (AB 759), operative July 1, 1991.

Prior Law: Former Prob C §9154, similar to the present section, was added Stats 1987 ch 923 §93, operative July 1, 1988, amended Stats 1989 ch 21 §21, effective May 25, 1989, operative July 1, 1989, and repealed Stats 1990 ch 79 §13, operative July 1, 1991.

CHAPTER 5
CLAIMS BY PUBLIC ENTITIES

Claim by public entity required. §9200.
Claims governed by special statutes. §9201.
Notice to Director of Health Care Services, Director of California Victim Compensation Board, and Franchise Tax Board; Time for filing claim or pursuing collection. §9202.
Effect of failure to give notice or request; Distribution before claim. §9203.
Priority of claims not affected by chapter. §9204.
Limitation on application of chapter. §9205.

§9200. Claim by public entity required

(a) Except as provided in this chapter, a claim by a public entity shall be filed within the time otherwise provided in this part. A claim not so filed is barred, including any lien imposed for the claim.

(b) As used in this chapter, "public entity" has the meaning provided in Section 811.2 of the Government Code, and includes an officer authorized to act on behalf of the public entity. **Leg.H.** Enacted Stats 1990 ch 79 §14 (AB 759), operative July 1, 1991.

Prior Law: Former Prob C §9200, similar to the present section, was added Stats 1987 ch 923 §93, operative July 1, 1988, and repealed Stats 1990 ch 79 §13, operative July 1, 1991.

§9201. Claims governed by special statutes

(a) Notwithstanding any other statute, if a claim of a public entity arises under a law, act, or code listed in subdivision (b):

(1) The public entity may provide a form to be used for the written notice or request to the public entity required by this chapter. Where appropriate, the form may require the decedent's social security number, if known.

(2) The claim is barred only after written notice or request to the public entity and expiration of the period provided in the applicable section. If no written notice or request is made, the claim is enforceable by the remedies, and is barred at the time, otherwise provided in the law, act, or code.

(b)

Law, Act, or Code	Applicable Section
Sales and Use Tax Law (commencing with Section 6001 of the Revenue and Taxation Code)	Section 6487.1 of the Revenue and Taxation Code
Bradley-Burns Uniform Local Sales and Use Tax Law (commencing with Section 7200 of the Revenue and Taxation Code)	Section 6487.1 of the Revenue and Taxation Code
Transactions and Use Tax Law (commencing with Section 7251 of the Revenue and Taxation Code)	Section 6487.1 of the Revenue and Taxation Code
Motor Vehicle Fuel License Tax Law (commencing with Section 7301 of the Revenue and Taxation Code)	Section 7675.1 of the Revenue and Taxation Code
Use Fuel Tax Law (commencing with Section 8601 of the Revenue and Taxation Code)	Section 8782.1 of the Revenue and Taxation Code
Administration of Franchise and Income Tax Law (commencing with Section 18401 of the Revenue and Taxation Code)	Section 19517 of the Revenue and Taxation Code
Cigarette Tax Law (commencing with Section 30001 of the Revenue and Taxation Code)	Section 30207.1 of the Revenue and Taxation Code
Alcoholic Beverage Tax Law (commencing with Section 32001 of the Revenue and Taxation Code)	Section 32272.1 of the Revenue and Taxation Code
Unemployment Insurance Code	Section 1090 of the Unemployment Insurance Code
State Hospitals (commencing with Section 7200 of the Welfare and Institutions Code)	Section 7277.1 of the Welfare and Institutions Code
Medi-Cal Act (commencing with Section 14000 of the Welfare and Institutions Code)	Section 9202 of the Probate Code
Waxman-Duffy Prepaid Health Plan Act (commencing with Section 14200 of the Welfare and Institutions Code)	Section 9202 of the Probate Code

Leg.H. Enacted Stats 1990 ch 79 §14 (AB 759), operative July 1, 1991. Amended Stats 1990 ch 140 §11.1 (SB 1855), operative July 1, 1991; Stats 1999 ch 987 §2 (SB 1229), effective October 10, 1999; Stats 2014 ch 144 §49 (AB 1847), effective January 1, 2015.

Prior Law: Former Prob C §9201, similar to the present section, was added Stats 1987 ch 923 §93, operative July 1, 1988, repealed Stats 1990 ch 79 §13, operative July 1, 1991, amended Stats 1990 ch 140 §11, and repealed Stats 1990 ch 140 §27, operative July 1, 1991.

§9202. Notice to Director of Health Care Services, Director of California Victim Compensation Board, and Franchise Tax Board; Time for filing claim or pursuing collection

(a) Not later than 90 days after the date letters are first issued to a general personal representative, the general personal representative or estate attorney shall give the Director of Health Care Services notice of the decedent's death in the manner provided in Section 215 if the general personal representative knows or has reason to believe that the decedent received health care under Chapter 7 (commencing with Section 14000) or Chapter 8 (commencing with Section 14200) of Part 3 of Division 9 of the Welfare and Institutions Code, or was the surviving spouse of a person who received that health care. The director has four months after notice is given in which to file a claim.

(b) Not later than 90 days after the date letters are first issued to a general personal representative, the general personal representative or estate attorney shall give the Director of the California Victim Compensation Board notice of the decedent's death in the manner provided in Section 216 if the general personal representative or estate attorney knows that an heir or beneficiary is or has previously been confined in a prison or facility under the jurisdiction of the Department of Corrections and Rehabilitation or confined in any county or city jail, road camp, industrial farm, or other local correctional facility. The director of the board shall have four months after that notice is received in which to pursue collection of any outstanding restitution fines or orders.

(c)(1) Not later than 90 days after the date letters are first issued to a general personal representative, the general personal representative or estate attorney shall give the Franchise Tax Board notice of the administration of the estate. The notice shall be given as provided in Section 1215.

(2) The provisions of this subdivision shall apply to estates for which letters are first issued on or after July 1, 2008.

(d) Nothing in this section shall be interpreted as requiring the estate attorney, the beneficiary, the personal representative, or the person in possession of property of the decedent to conduct an additional investigation to determine whether a decedent has an heir or beneficiary who has been confined in a prison or facility under the jurisdiction of the Department of Corrections and Rehabilitation, or its Division of Juvenile Facilities, or confined in any county or city jail, road camp, industrial farm, or other local correctional facility. **Leg.H.** Enacted Stats 1990 ch 79 §14 (AB 759), operative July 1, 1991. Amended Stats 1993 ch 69 §5 (SB 35), effective June 30, 1993; Stats 2005 ch 238 §4 (SB 972), effective January 1, 2006; Stats 2007 ch 105 §1 (AB 361), effective January 1, 2008; Stats 2014 ch 508 §4 (AB 2685), effective January 1, 2015; Stats 2016 ch 31 §261 (SB 836), effective June 27, 2016.

Prior Law: Former Prob C §9202, similar to the present section, was added Stats 1987 ch 923 §93, operative July 1, 1988, amended Stats 1988 ch 830 §2, ch 1051 §2, and repealed Stats 1990 ch 79 §13, operative July 1, 1991.

§9203. Effect of failure to give notice or request; Distribution before claim

(a) Failure of a person to give the written notice or request required by this chapter does not affect the validity of any proceeding under this code concerning the administration of the decedent's estate.

(b) If property in the estate is distributed before expiration of the time allowed a public entity to file a claim, the public entity has a claim against the distributees to the full extent of the public entity's claim, or each distributee's share of the distributed property, whichever is less. The public entity's claim against distributees includes interest at a rate equal to that specified in Section 19521 of the Revenue and Taxation Code, from the date of distribution or the date of filing the claim by the public entity, whichever is later, plus other accruing costs as in the case of enforcement of a money judgment. **Leg.H.** Enacted Stats 1990 ch 79 §14 (AB 759), operative July 1, 1991. Amended Stats 1993 ch 69 §6 (SB 35), effective June 30, 1993; Stats 1999 ch 987 §3 (SB 1229), effective October 10, 1999.

Prior Law: Former Prob C §9203, similar to the present section, was added Stats 1987 ch 923 §93, operative July 1, 1988, and repealed Stats 1990 ch 79 §13, operative July 1, 1991.

§9204. Priority of claims not affected by chapter

Nothing in this chapter shall be construed to affect the order of priority of claims provided for under other provisions of law. **Leg.H.** Enacted Stats 1990 ch 79 §14 (AB 759), operative July 1, 1991.

Prior Law: Former Prob C §9204, similar to the present section, was added Stats 1987 ch 923 §93, operative July 1, 1988, and repealed Stats 1990 ch 79 §13, operative July 1, 1991.

§9205. Limitation on application of chapter

This chapter does not apply to liability for the restitution of amounts illegally acquired through the means of a fraudulent, false, or incorrect representation, or a forged or unauthorized endorsement. **Leg.H.** Enacted Stats 1990 ch 79 §14 (AB 759), operative July 1, 1991.

Prior Law: Former Prob C §9205, similar to the present section, was added Stats 1987 ch 923 §93, operative July 1, 1988, and repealed Stats 1990 ch 79 §13, operative July 1, 1991.

CHAPTER 6
ALLOWANCE AND REJECTION OF CLAIMS

Procedure by personal representative. §9250.
Procedure by court. §9251.
Where personal representative is creditor. §9252.
Effect of statute of limitations. §9253.
Contest of allowed and approved claims. §9254.
Partial allowance. §9255.
Failure of personal representative or court to act. §9256.

§9250. Procedure by personal representative

(a) When a claim is filed, the personal representative shall allow or reject the claim in whole or in part.

(b) The allowance or rejection shall be in writing. The personal representative shall file the allowance or rejection with the court clerk and give notice to the creditor as provided in Part 2 (commencing with Section 1200) of Division 3, together with a copy of the allowance or rejection.

(c) The allowance or rejection shall contain the following information:
(1) The name of the creditor.
(2) The total amount of the claim.
(3) The date of issuance of letters.
(4) The date of the decedent's death.
(5) The estimated value of the decedent's estate.
(6) The amount allowed or rejected by the personal representative.
(7) Whether the personal representative is authorized to act under the Independent Administration of Estates Act (Part 6 (commencing with Section 10400)).
(8) A statement that the creditor has 90 days in which to act on a rejected claim.

(d) The Judicial Council may prescribe an allowance or rejection form, which may be part of the claim form. Use of a form prescribed by the Judicial Council is deemed to satisfy the requirements of this section.

(e) This section does not apply to a demand the personal representative elects to treat as a claim under Section 9154. **Leg.H.** Enacted Stats 1990 ch 79 §14 (AB 759), operative July 1, 1991. Amended Stats 1999 ch 263 §6 (AB 1051); Stats 2007 ch 159 §6 (AB 341), effective January 1, 2008.

Prior Law: Former Prob C §9250, similar to the present section, was added Stats 1987 ch 923 §93, operative July 1, 1988, amended Stats 1989 ch 21 §22, effective May 25, 1989, operative July 1, 1989, and repealed Stats 1990 ch 79 §13, operative July 1, 1991.

§9251. Procedure by court

If the personal representative is not authorized to act under the Independent Administration of Estates Act (Part 6 (commencing with Section 10400)):

(a) Immediately on the filing of the allowance of a claim, the clerk shall present the claim and allowance to the court or judge for approval or rejection.

(b) On presentation of a claim and allowance, the court or judge may, in its discretion, examine the creditor and others on oath and receive any evidence relevant to the validity of the claim. The court or judge shall endorse on the claim whether the claim is approved or rejected and the date. **Leg.H.** Enacted Stats 1990 ch 79 §14 (AB 759), operative July 1, 1991.

Prior Law: Former Prob C §9251, similar to the present section, was added Stats 1987 ch 923 §93, operative July 1, 1988, and repealed Stats 1990 ch 79 §13, operative July 1, 1991.

§9252. Where personal representative is creditor

(a) If the personal representative or the attorney for the personal representative is a creditor of the decedent, the clerk shall present the claim to the court or judge for approval or rejection. The court or judge may in its discretion require the creditor to file a petition and give notice of hearing.

(b) If the court or judge approves the claim, the claim is established and shall be included with other established claims to be paid in the course of administration.

(c) If the court or judge rejects the claim, the personal representative or attorney may bring an action against the estate. Summons shall be served on the judge, who shall appoint an attorney at the expense of the estate to defend the action. **Leg.H.** Enacted Stats 1990 ch 79 §14 (AB 759), operative July 1, 1991.

Prior Law: Former Prob C §9252, similar to the present section, was added Stats 1987 ch 923 §93, operative July 1, 1988, and repealed Stats 1990 ch 79 §13, operative July 1, 1991.

§9253. Effect of statute of limitations

A claim barred by the statute of limitations may not be allowed by the personal representative or approved by the court or judge. **Leg.H.** Enacted Stats 1990 ch 79 §14 (AB 759), operative July 1, 1991.

Prior Law: Former Prob C §9253, similar to the present section, was added Stats 1987 ch 923 §93, operative July 1, 1988, amended Stats 1988 ch 1199 §85, operative July 1, 1989, and repealed Stats 1990 ch 79 §13, operative July 1, 1991.

§9254. Contest of allowed and approved claims

(a) The validity of an allowed or approved claim may be contested by any interested person at any time before settlement of the report or account of the personal representative in which it is first reported as an allowed or approved claim. The burden of proof is on the contestant, except where the personal representative has acted under the Independent Administration of Estates Act (Part 6 (commencing Section 10400)), in which case the burden of proof is on the personal representative.

(b) Subdivision (a) does not apply to a claim established by a judgment. **Leg.H.** Enacted Stats 1990 ch 79 §14 (AB 759), operative July 1, 1991.

Prior Law: Former Prob C §9254, similar to the present section, was added Stats 1987 ch 923 §93, operative July 1, 1988, and repealed Stats 1990 ch 79 §13, operative July 1, 1991.

§9255. Partial allowance

(a) The personal representative may allow a claim, or the court or judge may approve a claim, in part. The allowance or approval shall state the amount for which the claim is allowed or approved.

(b) A creditor who refuses to accept the amount allowed or approved in satisfaction of the claim may bring an action on the claim in the manner provided in Chapter 8 (commencing with Section 9350). The creditor may not recover costs in the action unless the creditor recovers an amount greater than that allowed or approved. **Leg.H.** Enacted Stats 1990 ch 79 §14 (AB 759), operative July 1, 1991.

Prior Law: Former Prob C §9255, similar to the present section, was added Stats 1987 ch 923 §93, operative July 1, 1988, amended Stats 1988 ch 1199 §85.3, operative July 1, 1989, and repealed Stats 1990 ch 79 §13, operative July 1, 1991.

§9256. Failure of personal representative or court to act

If within 30 days after a claim is filed the personal representative or the court or judge has refused or neglected to act on the claim, the refusal or neglect may, at the option of the creditor, be deemed equivalent to giving a notice of rejection on the 30th day. **Leg.H.** Enacted Stats 1990 ch 79 §14 (AB 759), operative July 1, 1991.

Prior Law: Former Prob C §9256, similar to the present section, was added Stats 1987 ch 923 §93, operative July 1, 1988, and repealed Stats 1990 ch 79 §13, operative July 1, 1991.

CHAPTER 7
CLAIMS ESTABLISHED BY JUDGMENT

Money judgment against decedent. §9300.
Money judgment against personal representative. §9301.
Enforcement of nonmoney judgment. §9302.
Property subject to execution lien. §9303.
Converting attachment lien to judgment lien. §9304.

§9300. Money judgment against decedent

(a) Except as provided in Section 9303, after the death of the decedent all money judgments against the decedent or against the personal representative on a claim against the decedent or estate are payable in the course of administration and are not enforceable against property in the estate of the decedent under the Enforcement of Judgments Law (Title 9 (commencing with Section 680.010) of Part 2 of the Code of Civil Procedure).

(b) Subject to Section 9301, a judgment referred to in subdivision (a) shall be filed in the same manner as other claims. **Leg.H.** Enacted Stats 1990 ch 79 §14 (AB 759), operative July 1, 1991.

Prior Law: Former Prob C §9300, similar to the present section, was added Stats 1987 ch 923 §93, operative July 1, 1988, and repealed Stats 1990 ch 79 §13, operative July 1, 1991.

§9301. Money judgment against personal representative

When a money judgment against a personal representative in a representative capacity becomes final, it conclusively establishes the validity of the claim for the amount of the judgment. The judgment shall provide that it is payable out of property in the decedent's estate in the course of administration. An abstract of the judgment shall be filed in the administration proceedings. **Leg.H.** Enacted Stats 1990 ch 79 §14 (AB 759), operative July 1, 1991.

Prior Law: Former Prob C §9301, similar to the present section, was added Stats 1987 ch 923 §93, operative July 1, 1988, and repealed Stats 1990 ch 79 §13, operative July 1, 1991.

§9302. Enforcement of nonmoney judgment

(a) Notwithstanding the death of the decedent, a judgment for possession of property or a judgment for sale of property may be enforced under the Enforcement of Judgments Law (Title 9 (commencing with Section 680.010) of Part 2 of the Code of Civil Procedure). Nothing in this subdivision authorizes enforcement under the Enforcement of Judgments Law against any property in the estate of the decedent other than the property described in the judgment for possession or sale.

(b) After the death of the decedent, a demand for money that is not satisfied from the property described in a judgment for sale of property shall be filed as a claim in the same manner as other claims and is payable in the course of administration. **Leg.H.** Enacted Stats 1990 ch 79 §14 (AB 759), operative July 1, 1991.

Prior Law: Former Prob C §9302, similar to the present section, was added Stats 1987 ch 923 §93, operative July 1, 1988, and repealed Stats 1990 ch 79 §13, operative July 1, 1991.

§9303. Property subject to execution lien

If property of the decedent is subject to an execution lien at the time of the decedent's death, enforcement against the property may proceed under the Enforcement of Judgments Law (Title 9 (commencing with Section 680.010) of Part 2 of the Code of Civil Procedure) to satisfy the judgment. The levying officer shall account to the personal representative for any surplus. If the judgment is not satisfied, the balance of the judgment remaining unsatisfied is payable in the course of administration. **Leg.H.** Enacted Stats 1990 ch 79 §14 (AB 759), operative July 1, 1991.

Prior Law: Former Prob C §9303, similar to the present section, was added Stats 1987 ch 923 §93, operative July 1, 1988, and repealed Stats 1990 ch 79 §13, operative July 1, 1991.

§9304. Converting attachment lien to judgment lien

(a) An attachment lien may be converted into a judgment lien on property in the estate subject to the attachment lien, with the same priority as the attachment lien, in either of the following cases:

(1) Where the judgment debtor dies after entry of judgment in an action in which the property was attached.

(2) Where a judgment is entered after the death of the defendant in an action in which the property was attached.

(b) To convert the attachment lien into a judgment lien, the levying officer shall, after entry of judgment in the action in which the property was attached and before the expiration of the attachment lien, do one of the following:

(1) Serve an abstract of the judgment, and a notice that the attachment lien has become a judgment lien, on the person holding property subject to the attachment lien.

(2) Record or file, in any office where the writ of attachment and notice of attachment are recorded or filed, an abstract of the judgment and a notice that the attachment lien has become a judgment lien. If the attached property is real property, the plaintiff or the plaintiff's attorney may record the required abstract and notice with the same effect as if recorded by the levying officer.

(c) After the death of the decedent, any members of the decedent's family who were supported in whole or in part by the decedent may claim an exemption provided in Section 487.020 of the Code of Civil Procedure for property levied on under the writ of attachment if the right to the exemption exists at the time the exemption is claimed. The personal representative may claim the exemption on behalf of members of the decedent's family. The claim of exemption may be made at any time before the time the abstract and notice are served, recorded, or filed under subdivision (b) with respect to the property claimed to be exempt. The claim of exemption shall be made in the same manner as an exemption is claimed under Section 482.100 of the Code of Civil Procedure. **Leg.H.** Enacted Stats 1990 ch 79 §14 (AB 759), operative July 1, 1991.

Prior Law: Former Prob C §9304, similar to the present section, was added Stats 1987 ch 923 §93, operative July 1, 1988, and repealed Stats 1990 ch 79 §13, operative July 1, 1991.

CHAPTER 8
CLAIMS IN LITIGATION

Article 1. Claim Where No Pending Action or Proceeding.
Article 2. Claim Where Action or Proceeding Pending.
Article 3. Litigation Where No Claim Required.
Article 4. Transitional Provision.

ARTICLE 1
Claim Where No Pending Action or Proceeding

Application of article. §9350.
Claim prerequisite to bringing action. §9351.
Tolling of statute of limitations. §9352.
Bar of rejected claims. §9353.
Venue and procedure for action on claim. §9354.

§9350. Application of article

This article applies to any claim other than a claim on an action or proceeding pending against the decedent at the time of death. **Leg.H.** Enacted Stats 1990 ch 79 §14 (AB 759), operative July 1, 1991.

Prior Law: Former Prob C §9350, similar to the present section, was added Stats 1988 ch 1199 §86, operative July 1, 1989, and repealed Stats 1990 ch 79 §13, operative July 1, 1991.

§9351. Claim prerequisite to bringing action

An action may not be commenced against a decedent's personal representative on a cause of action against the decedent unless a claim is first filed as provided in this part and the claim is rejected in whole or in part. **Leg.H.** Enacted Stats 1990 ch 79 §14 (AB 759), operative July 1, 1991.

Prior Law: Former Prob C §9351, similar to the present section, was added Stats 1988 ch 1199 §86, operative July 1, 1989, and repealed Stats 1990 ch 79 §13, operative July 1, 1991.

§9352. Tolling of statute of limitations

(a) The filing of a claim or a petition under Section 9103 to file a claim tolls the statute of limitations otherwise applicable to the claim until allowance, approval, or rejection.

(b) The allowance or approval of a claim in whole or in part further tolls the statute of limitations during the administration of the estate as to the part allowed or approved. **Leg.H.** Enacted Stats 1990 ch 79 §14 (AB 759), operative July 1, 1991. Amended Stats 1991 ch 1055 §26 (SB 271).

Prior Law: Former Prob C §9352, similar to the present section, was added Stats 1988 ch 1199 §86, operative July 1, 1989, and repealed Stats 1990 ch 79 §13, operative July 1, 1991.

§9353. Bar of rejected claims

(a) Regardless of whether the statute of limitations otherwise applicable to a claim will expire before or after the following times, a claim rejected in whole or in part is barred as to the part rejected unless, within the following times, the creditor commences an action on the claim or the matter is referred to a referee or to arbitration:

(1) If the claim is due at the time the notice of rejection is given, 90 days after the notice is given.

(2) If the claim is not due at the time the notice of rejection is given, 90 days after the claim becomes due.

(b) The time during which there is a vacancy in the office of the personal representative shall be excluded from the period determined under subdivision (a). **Leg.H.** Enacted Stats 1990 ch 79 §14 (AB 759), operative July 1, 1991. Amended Stats 2007 ch 159 §7 (AB 341), effective January 1, 2008.

Prior Law: Former Prob C §9353, similar to the present section, was added Stats 1988 ch 1199 §86, operative July 1, 1989, and repealed Stats 1990 ch 79 §13, operative July 1, 1991.

§9354. Venue and procedure for action on claim

(a) In addition to any other county in which an action may be commenced, an action on the claim may be commenced in the county in which the proceeding for administration of the decedent's estate is pending.

(b) The plaintiff shall file a notice of the pendency of the action with the court clerk in the estate proceeding, together with proof of giving a copy of the notice to the personal representative as provided in Section 1215. Personal service of a copy of the summons and complaint on the personal representative is equivalent to the filing and giving of the notice. Any property distributed under court order, or any payment properly made, before the notice is filed and given is not subject to the claim. The personal representative, distributee, or payee is not liable on account of the prior distribution or payment.

(c) The prevailing party in the action shall be awarded court costs and, if the court determines that the prosecution or defense of the action against the prevailing party was unreasonable, the prevailing party shall be awarded reasonable litigation expenses, including attorney's fees. **Leg.H.** Enacted Stats 1990 ch 79 §14 (AB 759), operative July 1, 1991.

Prior Law: Former Prob C §9354, similar to the present section, was added Stats 1988 ch 1199 §86, operative July 1, 1989, and repealed Stats 1990 ch 79 §13, operative July 1, 1991.

ARTICLE 2
Claim Where Action or Proceeding Pending

Claim prerequisite to continuing action. §9370.

§9370. Claim prerequisite to continuing action

(a) An action or proceeding pending against the decedent at the time of death may not be continued against the decedent's personal representative unless all of the following conditions are satisfied:

(1) A claim is first filed as provided in this part.
(2) The claim is rejected in whole or in part.
(3) Within three months after the notice of rejection is given, the plaintiff applies to the court in which the action or proceeding is pending for an order to substitute the personal representative in the action or proceeding. This paragraph applies only if the notice of rejection contains a statement that the plaintiff has three months within which to apply for an order for substitution.

(b) No recovery shall be allowed in the action against property in the decedent's estate unless proof is made of compliance with this section. **Leg.H.** Enacted Stats 1990 ch 79 §14 (AB 759), operative July 1, 1991.

Prior Law: Former Prob C §9370, similar to the present section, was added Stats 1988 ch 1199 §86, operative July 1, 1989, and repealed Stats 1990 ch 79 §13, operative July 1, 1991.

ARTICLE 3
Litigation Where No Claim Required

Claim covered by insurance. §9390.
Enforcement of lien. §9391.
Liability of distributee. §9392.

§9390. Claim covered by insurance

(a) An action to establish the decedent's liability for which the decedent was protected by insurance may be commenced or continued under Section 550, and a judgment in the action may be enforced against the insurer, without first filing a claim as provided in this part.

(b) Unless a claim is first made as provided in this part, an action to establish the decedent's liability for damages outside the limits or coverage of the insurance may not be commenced or continued under Section 550.

(c) If the insurer seeks reimbursement under the insurance contract for any liability of the decedent, including, but not limited to, deductible amounts in the insurance coverage and costs and attorney's fees for which the decedent is liable under the contract, an insurer defending an action under Section 550 shall file a claim as provided in this part. Failure to file a claim is a waiver of reimbursement under the insurance contract for any liability of the decedent. **Leg.H.** Enacted Stats 1990 ch 79 §14 (AB 759), operative July 1, 1991. Amended Stats 1990 ch 710 §23 (SB 1775), operative July 1, 1991.

Prior Law: Former Prob C §9390, similar to the present section, was added Stats 1988 ch 1199 §86, operative July 1, 1989, and repealed Stats 1990 ch 79 §13, operative July 1, 1991.

§9391. Enforcement of lien

Except as provided in Section 10361, the holder of a mortgage or other lien on property in the decedent's estate, including, but not limited to, a judgment lien, may commence an action to enforce the lien against the property that is subject to the lien, without first filing a claim as provided in this part, if in the complaint the holder of the lien expressly waives all recourse against other property in the estate. Section 366.2 of the Code of Civil Procedure does not apply to an action under this section. The personal representative shall have the authority to seek to enjoin any action of the lienholder to enforce a lien against property that is subject to the lien. **Leg.H.** Enacted Stats 1990 ch 79 §14 (AB 759), operative July 1, 1991. Amended Stats 1990 ch 140 §12.1 (SB 1855), operative July 1, 1991; Stats 1992 ch 178 §35 (SB 1496); Stats 1996 ch 563 §24 (SB 392), ch 862 §25 (AB 2751).

Prior Law: Former Prob C §9391, similar to the present section, was added Stats 1988 ch 1199 §86, operative July 1, 1989, repealed Stats 1990 ch 79 §13, operative July 1, 1991, amended Stats 1990 ch 140 §12, operative until July 1, 1991, and repealed Stats 1990 ch 140 §28, operative July 1, 1991.

§9392. Liability of distributee

(a) Subject to subdivision (b), a person to whom property is distributed is personally liable for the claim of a creditor, without a claim first having been filed, if all of the following conditions are satisfied:

(1) The identity of the creditor was known to, or reasonably ascertainable by, a general personal representative within four months after the date letters were first issued to the personal representative, and the claim of the creditor was not merely conjectural.

(2) Notice of administration of the estate was not given to the creditor under Chapter 2 (commencing with Section 9050) and neither the creditor nor the attorney representing the creditor in the matter has actual knowledge of the administration of the estate before the time the court made an order for final distribution of the property.

(3) The statute of limitations applicable to the claim under Section 366.2 of the Code of Civil Procedure has not expired at the time of commencement of an action under this section.

(b) Personal liability under this section is applicable only to the extent the claim of the creditor cannot be satisfied out of the estate of the decedent and is limited to a pro rata portion of the claim of the creditor, based on the proportion that the value of the property distributed to the person out of the estate bears to the total value of all property distributed to all persons out of the estate. Personal liability under this section for all claims of all creditors shall not exceed the value of the property distributed to the person out of the estate. As used in this section, the value of property is the fair market value of the property on the date of the order for distribution, less the amount of any liens and encumbrances on the property at that time.

(c) Nothing in this section affects the rights of a purchaser or encumbrancer of property in good faith and for value from a person who is personally liable under this section. **Leg.H.** Added Stats 1990 ch 140 §13.1 (SB 1855), operative July 1, 1991. Amended Stats 1992 ch 178 §36 (SB 1496).

Prior Law: Former Prob C §9392, similar to the present section, was added Stats 1990 ch 140 §13 and repealed Stats 1990 ch 140 §2, operative July 1, 1991.

ARTICLE 4
Transitional Provision

Transitional provision for claims in litigation. §9399.
[No sections of these numbers] . §9400–9599.

§9399. Transitional provision for claims in litigation

(a) This chapter does not apply to an action commenced before July 1, 1989.

(b) The applicable law in effect before July 1, 1989, continues to apply to an action commenced before July 1, 1989, notwithstanding its repeal by Chapter 1199 of the Statutes of 1988. **Leg.H.** Enacted Stats 1990 ch 79 §14 (AB 759), operative July 1, 1991.

Prior Law: Former Prob C §9399, similar to the present section, was added Stats 1988 ch 1199 §86, operative July 1, 1989, and repealed Stats 1990 ch 79 §13, operative July 1, 1991.

§§9400–9599. [No sections of these numbers]

PART 5
ESTATE MANAGEMENT

Chapter 1. General Provisions.
Chapter 2. Estate Management Generally.
Chapter 3. Deposit of Money and Personal Property With Financial Institutions.
Chapter 4. Investments and Purchase of Property.
Chapter 5. Operation of Decedent's Business.
Chapter 6. Abandonment of Tangible Personal Property.
Chapter 7. Borrowing, Refinancing, and Encumbering Property.
Chapter 8. Actions and Proceedings by or Against Personal Representative.
Chapter 9. Compromise of Claims and Actions; Extension, Renewal, or Modification of Obligations.
Chapter 10. Acceptance of Deed In Lieu of Foreclosure or Trustee's Sale; Grant of Partial Satisfaction or Partial Reconveyance.
Chapter 12. Purchase of Claims or Estate Property by Personal Representative or Personal Representative's Attorney.
Chapter 13. Dedication or Conveyance to Governmental Entity; Easements and Access Rights.
Chapter 14. Exchange of Property.
Chapter 15. Leases.
Chapter 16. Granting Option to Purchase Real Property.
Chapter 17. Option to Purchase Given in Will.
Chapter 18. Sales.

CHAPTER 1
GENERAL PROVISIONS

Article 1. Duties and Liabilities of Personal Representative.
Article 2. Court Supervision.
Article 3. Summary Determination of Disputes.
Article 4. Joint Personal Representatives.
Article 5. Independent Administration.
Article 6. Transitional Provision.

ARTICLE 1
Duties and Liabilities of Personal Representative

Duty to manage estate using ordinary care and diligence. §9600.
Measure of liability for breach of fiduciary duty. §9601.
Measure of liability for interest. §9602.
Other remedies not affected. §9603.
Enforceability of promise of personal representative personally to answer in damages or to pay debts of decedent. §9604.
Claims against personal representative. §9605.
Liability of personal representative who signs instrument. §9606.

§9600. Duty to manage estate using ordinary care and diligence

(a) The personal representative has the management and control of the estate and, in managing and controlling the estate, shall use ordinary care and diligence. What constitutes ordinary care and diligence is determined by all the circumstances of the particular estate.

(b) The personal representative:

(1) Shall exercise a power to the extent that ordinary care and diligence require that the power be exercised.

(2) Shall not exercise a power to the extent that ordinary care and diligence require that the power not be exercised. **Leg.H.** Enacted Stats 1990 ch 79 §14 (AB 759), operative July 1, 1991.

Prior Law: Former Prob C §9600, similar to the present section, was added Stats 1987 ch 923 §93, operative July 1, 1988, and repealed Stats 1990 ch 79 §13, operative July 1, 1991.

§9601. Measure of liability for breach of fiduciary duty

(a) If a personal representative breaches a fiduciary duty, the personal representative is chargeable with any of the following that is appropriate under the circumstances:

(1) Any loss or depreciation in value of the decedent's estate resulting from the breach of duty, with interest.

(2) Any profit made by the personal representative through the breach of duty, with interest.

(3) Any profit that would have accrued to the decedent's estate if the loss of profit is the result of the breach of duty.

(b) If the personal representative has acted reasonably and in good faith under the circumstances as known to the personal representative, the court, in its discretion, may excuse the personal representative in whole or in part from liability under subdivision (a) if it would be equitable to do so. **Leg.H.** Enacted Stats 1990 ch 79 §14 (AB 759), operative July 1, 1991.

Prior Law: Former Prob C §9601, similar to the present section, was added Stats 1987 ch 923 §93, operative July 1, 1988, and repealed Stats 1990 ch 79 §13, operative July 1, 1991.

§9602. Measure of liability for interest

(a) If the personal representative is liable for interest pursuant to Section 9601, the personal representative is liable for the greater of the following amounts:

(1) The amount of interest that accrues at the legal rate on judgments.

(2) The amount of interest actually received.

(b) If the personal representative has acted reasonably and in good faith under the circumstances as known to the personal representative, the court, in its discretion, may excuse the personal representative in whole or in part from liability under subdivision (a) if it would be equitable to do so. **Leg.H.** Enacted Stats 1990 ch 79 §14 (AB 759), operative July 1, 1991. Amended Stats 1998 ch 77 §4 (SB 1841).

Prior Law: Former Prob C §9602, similar to the present section, was added Stats 1987 ch 923 §93, operative July 1, 1988, and repealed Stats 1990 ch 79 §13, operative July 1, 1991.

§9603. Other remedies not affected

The provisions of Sections 9601 and 9602 for liability of a personal representative for breach of a fiduciary duty do not prevent resort to any other remedy available against the personal representative under the statutory or common law. **Leg.H.** Enacted Stats 1990 ch 79 §14 (AB 759), operative July 1, 1991.

Prior Law: Former Prob C §9603, similar to the present section, was added Stats 1987 ch 923 §93, operative July 1, 1988, and repealed Stats 1990 ch 79 §13, operative July 1, 1991.

§9604. Enforceability of promise of personal representative personally to answer in damages or to pay debts of decedent

No personal representative is chargeable upon a special promise to answer in damages for a liability of the decedent or to pay a debt of the decedent out of the personal representative's own estate unless the agreement for that purpose, or some memorandum or note thereof, is in writing and is signed by one of the following:

(a) The personal representative.

(b) Some other person specifically authorized by the personal representative in writing to sign the agreement or the memorandum or note. **Leg.H.** Enacted Stats 1990 ch 79 §14 (AB 759), operative July 1, 1991.

Prior Law: Former Prob C §9604, similar to the present section, was added Stats 1987 ch 923 §93, operative July 1, 1988, and repealed Stats 1990 ch 79 §13, operative July 1, 1991.

§9605. Claims against personal representative

Appointment of a person as personal representative does not discharge any claim the decedent has against the person. **Leg.H.** Enacted Stats 1990 ch 79 §14 (AB 759), operative July 1, 1991.

Prior Law: Former Prob C §9605, similar to the present section, was added Stats 1988 ch 1199 §86.5, operative July 1, 1989, and repealed Stats 1990 ch 79 §13, operative July 1, 1991.

§9606. Liability of personal representative who signs instrument

Unless otherwise provided in the instrument or in this division, a personal representative is not personally liable on an instrument, including but not limited to a note, mortgage, deed of trust, or other contract, properly entered into in the personal representative's fiduciary capacity in the course of administration of the estate unless the personal representative fails to reveal the personal representative's representative capacity or identify the estate in the instrument. **Leg.H.** Enacted Stats 1990 ch 79 §14 (AB 759), operative July 1, 1991.

ARTICLE 2
Court Supervision

Extent of court supervision. §9610.
Instructions from or confirmation by court. §9611.

Order compelling personal representative to act or not to act. §9613.
Suspension of powers of personal representative. §9614.

§9610. Extent of court supervision

Unless this part specifically provides a proceeding to obtain court authorization or requires court authorization, the powers and duties set forth in this part may be exercised by the personal representative without court authorization, instruction, approval, or confirmation. Nothing in this section precludes the personal representative from seeking court authorization, instructions, approval, or confirmation. **Leg.H.** Enacted Stats 1990 ch 79 §14 (AB 759), operative July 1, 1991.

Prior Law: Former Prob C §9610, similar to the present section, was added Stats 1987 ch 923 §93, operative July 1, 1988, and repealed Stats 1990 ch 79 §13, operative July 1, 1991.

§9611. Instructions from or confirmation by court

(a) In all cases where no other procedure is provided by statute, upon petition of the personal representative, the court may authorize and instruct the personal representative, or approve and confirm the acts of the personal representative, in the administration, management, investment, disposition, care, protection, operation, or preservation of the estate, or the incurring or payment of costs, fees, or expenses in connection therewith. Section 9613 does not preclude a petition for instructions under this section.

(b) Notice of the hearing on the petition shall be given as provided in Section 1220. **Leg.H.** Enacted Stats 1990 ch 79 §14 (AB 759), operative July 1, 1991.

Prior Law: Former Prob C §9611, similar to the present section, was added Stats 1987 ch 923 §93, operative July 1, 1988, and repealed Stats 1990 ch 79 §13, operative July 1, 1991.

§9613. Order compelling personal representative to act or not to act

(a) On petition of any interested person, and upon a showing that if the petition is not granted the estate will suffer great or irreparable injury, the court may direct the personal representative to act or not to act concerning the estate. The order may include terms and conditions the court determines are appropriate under the circumstances.

(b) Notice of the hearing on the petition shall be given as provided in Section 1220. **Leg.H.** Enacted Stats 1990 ch 79 §14 (AB 759), operative July 1, 1991.

Prior Law: Former Prob C §9613, similar to the present section, was added Stats 1987 ch 923 §93, operative July 1, 1988, and repealed Stats 1990 ch 79 §13, operative July 1, 1991.

§9614. Suspension of powers of personal representative

(a) On petition of an interested person, the court may suspend the powers of the personal representative in whole or in part, for a time, as to specific property or circumstances or as to specific duties of the office, or may make any other order to secure proper performance of the duties of the personal representative, if it appears to the court that the personal representative otherwise may take some action that would jeopardize unreasonably the interest of the petitioner. Persons with whom the personal representative may transact business may be made parties.

(b) The matter shall be set for hearing within 10 days unless the parties agree otherwise. Notice as the court directs shall be given to the personal representative and attorney of record, if any, and to any other parties named in the petition.

(c) The court may, in its discretion, if it determines that the petition was brought unreasonably and for the purpose of hindering the personal representative in the performance of the duties of the office, assess attorney's fees against the petitioner and make the assessment a charge against the interest of the petitioner. **Leg.H.** Enacted Stats 1990 ch 79 §14 (AB 759), operative July 1, 1991.

Prior Law: Former Prob C §9614, similar to the present section, was added Stats 1988 ch 1199 §87, operative July 1, 1989, and repealed Stats 1990 ch 79 §13, operative July 1, 1991.

ARTICLE 3
Summary Determination of Disputes

Submission of dispute to temporary judge. §9620.
Submission of dispute to arbitration. §9621.

§9620. Submission of dispute to temporary judge

If there is a dispute relating to the estate between the personal representative and a third person, the personal representative may do either of the following:

(a) Enter into an agreement in writing with the third person to refer the dispute to a temporary judge designated in the agreement. The agreement shall be filed with the clerk, who shall thereupon, with the approval of the court, enter an order referring the matter to the designated person. The temporary judge shall proceed promptly to hear and determine the matter in controversy by summary procedure, without pleadings or discovery. The decision of the designated person is subject to Section 632 of the Code of Civil Procedure. Judgment shall be entered on the decision and shall be as valid and effective as if rendered by a judge of the court in an action against the personal representative or the third person commenced by ordinary process.

(b) Enter into an agreement in writing with the third person that a judge, pursuant to the agreement and with the written consent of the judge, both filed with the clerk within the time specified in Section 9353 for bringing an independent suit on the matter in dispute, may hear and determine the dispute pursuant to the procedure provided in subdivision (a). **Leg.H.** Enacted Stats 1990 ch 79 §14 (AB 759), operative July 1, 1991.

Prior Law: Former Prob C §9620, similar to the present section, was added Stats 1987 ch 923 §11, operative July 1, 1988, amended Stats 1988 ch 1199 §87.5, operative July 1, 1989, Stats 1989 ch 21 §24, effective May 25, 1989, operative July 1, 1989, and repealed Stats 1990 ch 79 §13, operative July 1, 1991.

§9621. Submission of dispute to arbitration

If there is a dispute relating to the estate between the personal representative and a third person, the personal representative may enter into an agreement in writing with the third person to submit the dispute to arbitration under Title 9 (commencing with Section 1280) of Part 3 of the Code of Civil Procedure. The agreement is not effective unless it is first approved by the court and a copy of the approved agreement is filed with the court. Notice of the hearing on the petition for approval of the agreement shall be given as provided in Section 1220. The order approving the agreement may be made ex parte. **Leg.H.** Enacted Stats 1990 ch 79 §14 (AB 759), operative July 1, 1991.

Prior Law: Former Prob C §9621, similar to the present section, was added Stats 1987 ch 923 §93, operative July 1, 1988, and repealed Stats 1990 ch 79 §13, operative July 1, 1991.

ARTICLE 4
Joint Personal Representatives

Authority of joint personal representatives to act. §9630.
Liability of joint personal representative for breach of duty by another personal representative. §9631.

§9630. Authority of joint personal representatives to act

(a) Subject to subdivisions (b), (c), and (d):

(1) Where there are two personal representatives, both must concur to exercise a power.

(2) Where there are more than two personal representatives, a majority must concur to exercise a power.

(b) If one of the joint personal representatives dies or is removed or resigns, the powers and duties continue in the remaining joint personal representatives as if they were the only personal representatives until further appointment is made by the court.

(c) Where joint personal representatives have been appointed and one or more are (1) absent from the state and unable to act, or (2) otherwise unable to act, or (3) legally disqualified from serving, the court may, by order made with or without notice, authorize the remaining joint personal representatives to act as to all matters embraced within its order.

(d) Where there are two or more personal representatives, any of them may:

(1) Oppose a petition made by one or more of the other personal representatives or by any other person.

(2) Petition the court for an order requiring the personal representatives to take a specific action for the benefit of the estate or directing the personal representatives not to take a specific action. If a procedure is provided by statute for a petition to authorize the specific action by the personal representatives, the petitioner shall file the petition under the provision relating to that procedure. Otherwise, the petitioner shall file the petition under Section 9611. **Leg.H.** Enacted Stats 1990 ch 79 §14 (AB 759), operative July 1, 1991.

Prior Law: Former Prob C §9630, similar to the present section, was added Stats 1987 ch 923 §93, operative July 1, 1988, and repealed Stats 1990 ch 79 §13, operative July 1, 1991.

§9631. Liability of joint personal representative for breach of duty by another personal representative

(a) Except as provided in subdivision (b), where there is more than one personal representative, one personal representative is not liable for a breach of fiduciary duty committed by another of the personal representatives.

(b) Where there is more than one personal representative, one personal representative is liable for a breach of fiduciary duty committed by another of the personal representatives under any of the following circumstances:

(1) Where the personal representative participates in a breach of fiduciary duty committed by the other personal representative.

(2) Where the personal representative improperly delegates the administration of the estate to the other personal representative.

(3) Where the personal representative approves, knowingly acquiesces in, or conceals a breach of fiduciary duty committed by the other personal representative.

(4) Where the personal representative's negligence enables the other personal representative to commit a breach of fiduciary duty.

(5) Where the personal representative knows or has information from which the personal representative reasonably should have known of the breach of fiduciary duty by the other personal representative and fails to take reasonable steps to compel the other personal representative to redress the breach.

(c) The liability of a personal representative for a breach of fiduciary duty committed by another of the personal representatives that occurred before July 1, 1988, is governed by prior law and not by this section. **Leg.H.** Enacted Stats 1990 ch 79 §14 (AB 759), operative July 1, 1991.

Prior Law: Former Prob C §9631, similar to the present section, was added Stats 1987 ch 923 §93, operative July 1, 1988, and repealed Stats 1990 ch 79 §13, operative July 1, 1991.

ARTICLE 5
Independent Administration

Independent administration authority not limited. §9640.

§9640. Independent administration authority not limited

Nothing in this part limits or restricts any authority granted to a personal representative under the Independent Administration of Estates Act (Part 6 (commencing with Section 10400)) to administer the estate under that part. **Leg.H.** Enacted Stats 1990 ch 79 §14 (AB 759), operative July 1, 1991.

Prior Law: Former Prob C §9640, similar to the present section, was added Stats 1987 ch 923 §93, operative July 1, 1988, and repealed Stats 1990 ch 79 §13, operative July 1, 1991.

ARTICLE 6
Transitional Provision

Matters pending on July 1, 1988; orders made or actions taken before July 1, 1988. §9645.

§9645. Matters pending on July 1, 1988; orders made or actions taken before July 1, 1988

(a) Subject to subdivisions (b) and (c), any petition or other matter filed or commenced before July 1, 1988, shall be continued under this part, so far as applicable, except where the court determines that application of a particular provision of this part would substantially interfere with the rights of the parties or other interested persons, in which case the particular provision of this part does not apply and the applicable law in effect before July 1, 1988, applies.

(b) Nothing in this part affects any order, judgment, or decree made, or any action taken, before July 1, 1988.

(c) Notwithstanding the enactment of this part:

(1) An order, judgment, or decree made before July 1, 1988, shall continue in full force and effect in accordance with its terms or until modified or terminated by the court.

(2) The validity of an order, judgment, or decree made before July 1, 1988, is determined by the applicable law in effect before July 1, 1988, and not by this part.

(3) The validity of any action taken before July 1, 1988, is determined by the applicable law in effect before July 1, 1988, and not by this part. **Leg.H.** Enacted Stats 1990 ch 79 §14 (AB 759), operative July 1, 1991.

Prior Law: Former Prob C §9645, similar to the present section, was added Stats 1987 ch 923 §93, operative July 1, 1988, and repealed Stats 1990 ch 79 §13, operative July 1, 1991.

CHAPTER 2
ESTATE MANAGEMENT GENERALLY

Possession and management of decedent's estate. §9650.
Taking possession of property in good faith. §9651.
Duty to keep cash invested. §9652.
Duty to recover transferred property, voidable to creditors. §9653.
Action by heirs or devisees for possession of or to quiet title to property. §9654.
Voting rights with respect to corporate shares or memberships or property. §9655.
Insuring estate property; Insuring personal representative against liability. §9656.
Profit or loss to the estate. §9657.

§9650. Possession and management of decedent's estate

(a) Except as provided by statute and subject to subdivision (c):

(1) The personal representative has the right to, and shall take possession or control of, all the property of the decedent to be administered in the decedent's estate and shall collect all debts due to the decedent or the estate. The personal representative is not accountable for any debts that remain uncollected without his or her fault.

(2) The personal representative is entitled to receive the rents, issues, and profits from the real and personal property in the estate until the estate is distributed.

(b) The personal representative shall pay taxes on, and take all steps reasonably necessary for the management, protection, and preservation of, the estate in his or her possession.

(c) Real property or tangible personal property may be left with or surrendered to the person presumptively entitled to it unless or until, in the judgment of the personal representative, possession of the property by the personal representative will be necessary for purposes of administration. The person holding the property shall surrender it to the personal representative on request by the personal representative. **Leg.H.** Enacted Stats 1990 ch 79 §14 (AB 759), operative July 1, 1991.

Prior Law: Former Prob C §9650, similar to the present section, was added Stats 1987 ch 923 §93, operative July 1, 1988, and repealed Stats 1990 ch 79 §13, operative July 1, 1991.

§9651. Taking possession of property in good faith

(a) A personal representative who in good faith takes into possession real or personal property, and reasonably believes that the property is part of the estate of the decedent, is not:

(1) Criminally liable for so doing.

(2) Civilly liable to any person for so doing.

(b) The personal representative shall make reasonable efforts to determine the true nature of, and title to, the property so taken into possession.

(c) During his or her possession, the personal representative is entitled to receive all rents, issues, and profits of the property. If the property is later determined not to be part of the estate of the decedent, the personal representative shall deliver the property, or cause it to be delivered, to the person legally entitled to it, together with all rents, issues, and profits of the property received by the personal representative, less any expenses incurred in protecting and maintaining the property and in collecting rents, issues, and profits. The personal representative may request court approval before delivering the property pursuant to this subdivision.

(d) The court may allow the personal representative reasonable compensation for services rendered in connection with the duties specified in this section as to property later determined not to be part of the estate of the decedent, if the court makes one of the following findings:

(1) The services were of benefit to the estate. If the court makes this finding, the compensation and the expenses and costs of litigation, including attorney's fees of the attorney hired by the personal representative to handle the matter, are a proper expense of administration.

(2) The services were essential to preserve, protect, and maintain the property. If the court makes this finding, the court shall award compensation and the expenses and costs of litigation, including attorney's fees of the attorney hired by the personal representative to handle the matter, as an expense deductible from the rents, issues, and profits received by the personal representative, or, if these are insufficient, as a lien against the property. **Leg.H.** Enacted Stats 1990 ch 79 §14 (AB 759), operative July 1, 1991.

Prior Law: Former Prob C §9651, similar to the present section, was added Stats 1987 ch 923 §93, operative July 1, 1988, and repealed Stats 1990 ch 79 §13, operative July 1, 1991.

§9652. Duty to keep cash invested

(a) Except as provided in subdivisions (b) and (c), the personal representative shall keep all cash in his or her possession invested in interest-bearing accounts or other investments authorized by law.

(b) The requirement of subdivision (a) does not apply to the amount of cash that is reasonably necessary for orderly administration of the estate.

(c) The requirement of subdivision (a) does not apply to the extent that the testator's will otherwise provides. **Leg.H.** Enacted Stats 1990 ch 79 §14 (AB 759), operative July 1, 1991.

Prior Law: Former Prob C §9652, similar to the present section, was added Stats 1987 ch 923 §93, operative July 1, 1988, and repealed Stats 1990 ch 79 §13, operative July 1, 1991.

§9653. Duty to recover transferred property voidable to creditors

(a) On application of a creditor of the decedent or the estate, the personal representative shall commence and prosecute an action for the recovery of real or personal property of the decedent for the benefit of creditors if the personal representative has insufficient assets to pay creditors and the decedent during lifetime did any of the following with respect to the property:

(1) Made a conveyance of the property, or any right or interest in the property, that is voidable as to creditors under the Uniform Voidable Transactions Act (Chapter 1 (commencing with Section 3439) of Title 2 of Part 2 of Division 4 of the Civil Code).

(2) Made a gift of the property in view of impending death.

(3) Made a direction to transfer a vehicle, undocumented vessel, manufactured home, mobilehome, commercial coach, truck camper, or floating home to a designated beneficiary on the decedent's death pursuant to Section 18102.2 of the Health and Safety Code, or Section 5910.5 or 9916.5 of the Vehicle Code, and the property has been transferred as directed.

(b) A creditor making application under this section shall pay such part of the costs and expenses of the suit and attorney's fees, or give an undertaking to the personal representative for that purpose, as the personal representative and the creditor agree, or, absent an agreement, as the court or judge orders.

(c) The property recovered under this section shall be sold for the payment of debts in the same manner as if the decedent had died seized or possessed of the property. The proceeds of the sale shall be applied first to payment of the costs and expenses of suit, including attorney's fees, and then to payment of the debts of the decedent in the same manner as other property in possession of the personal representative. After all the debts of the decedent have been paid, the remainder of the proceeds shall be paid to the person from whom the property was recovered. The property may be sold in its entirety or in such portion as necessary to pay the debts. **Leg.H.** Enacted Stats 1990 ch 79 §14 (AB 759), operative July 1, 1991. Amended Stats 1991 ch 1055 §27 (SB 271), operative January 1, 1993; Stats 2015 ch 44 §27 (SB 161), effective January 1, 2016.

Prior Law: Former Prob C §9653, similar to the present section, was added Stats 1987 ch 923 §93, operative July 1, 1988, and repealed Stats 1990 ch 79 §13, operative July 1, 1991.

§9654. Action by heirs or devisees for possession of or to quiet title to property

The heirs or devisees may themselves, or jointly with the personal representative, maintain an action for possession of property or to quiet title to property against any person except the personal representative. **Leg.H.** Enacted Stats 1990 ch 79 §14 (AB 759), operative July 1, 1991.

Prior Law: Former Prob C §9654, similar to the present section, was added Stats 1987 ch 923 §93, operative July 1, 1988, and repealed Stats 1990 ch 79 §13, operative July 1, 1991.

§9655. Voting rights with respect to corporate shares or memberships or property

With respect to a share of stock of a domestic or foreign corporation held in the estate, a membership in a nonprofit corporation held in the estate, or other property held in the estate, a personal representative may do any one or more of the following:

(a) Vote in person, and give proxies to exercise, any voting rights with respect to the share, membership, or other property.

(b) Waive notice of a meeting or give consent to the holding of a meeting.

(c) Authorize, ratify, approve, or confirm any action which could be taken by shareholders, members, or property owners. **Leg.H.** Enacted Stats 1990 ch 79 §14 (AB 759), operative July 1, 1991.

Prior Law: Former Prob C §9655, similar to the present section, was added Stats 1987 ch 923 §93, operative July 1, 1988, and repealed Stats 1990 ch 79 §13, operative July 1, 1991.

§9656. Insuring estate property; Insuring personal representative against liability

The personal representative may insure the property of the estate against damage or loss and may insure himself or herself against liability to third persons. **Leg.H.** Enacted Stats 1990 ch 79 §14 (AB 759), operative July 1, 1991.

Prior Law: Former Prob C §9656, similar to the present section, was added Stats 1987 ch 923 §93, operative July 1, 1988, and repealed Stats 1990 ch 79 §13, operative July 1, 1991.

§9657. Profit or loss to the estate

The personal representative shall not make profit by the increase, nor suffer loss by the decrease or destruction without his or her fault, of any part of the estate. **Leg.H.** Enacted Stats 1990 ch 79 §14 (AB 759), operative July 1, 1991.

Prior Law: Former Prob C §9657, similar to the present section, was added Stats 1987 ch 923 §93, operative July 1, 1988, and repealed Stats 1990 ch 79 §13, operative July 1, 1991.

CHAPTER 2.5
HIRING AND PAYING ATTORNEYS, ADVISERS, AND OTHERS [REPEALED]

CHAPTER 3
DEPOSIT OF MONEY AND PERSONAL PROPERTY WITH FINANCIAL INSTITUTIONS

Deposit in insured account. §9700.
Deposit of personal property with trust company. §9701.
Deposit of securities in securities depository. §9702.
Accounts and deposits withdrawable only upon court order. §9703.
Direct distribution by depository. §9704.
Interest on deposits by trust company. §9705.

§9700. Deposit in insured account

The personal representative may deposit money of the estate in an insured account in a financial institution in this state. Unless otherwise provided by court order, the money may be withdrawn without order of the court. **Leg.H.** Enacted Stats 1990 ch 79 §14 (AB 759), operative July 1, 1991.

Prior Law: Former Prob C §9700, similar to the present section, was added Stats 1987 ch 923 §93, operative July 1, 1988, and repealed Stats 1990 ch 79 §13, operative July 1, 1991.

§9701. Deposit of personal property with trust company

The personal representative may deposit personal property of the estate with a trust company for safekeeping. Unless otherwise provided by court order, the personal property may be withdrawn without order of the court. **Leg.H.** Enacted Stats 1990 ch 79 §14, operative July 1, 1991.

Prior Law: Former Prob C §9701, similar to the present section, was added Stats 1987 ch 923 §93, operative July 1, 1988, and repealed Stats 1990 ch 79 §13, operative July 1, 1991.

§9702. Deposit of securities in securities depository

(a) A trust company serving as personal representative may deposit securities that constitute all or part of the estate in a securities depository, as provided in Section 1612 of the Financial Code.

(b) If securities have been deposited with a trust company by a personal representative pursuant to Section 9701, the trust company may deposit the securities in a securities depository, as provided in Section 1612 of the Financial Code.

(c) The securities depository may hold securities deposited with it in the manner authorized by Section 1612 of the Financial Code. **Leg.H.** Enacted Stats 1990 ch 79 §14 (AB 759), operative July 1, 1991. Amended Stats 2014 ch 71 §139 (SB 1304), effective January 1, 2015.

Prior Law: Former Prob C §9702, similar to the present section, was added Stats 1987 ch 923 §93, operative July 1, 1988, and repealed Stats 1990 ch 79 §13, operative July 1, 1991.

§9703. Accounts and deposits withdrawable only upon court order

(a) Upon application of the personal representative, the court may, with or without notice, order that money or other personal property be deposited pursuant to Section 9700 or 9701 and be subject to withdrawal only upon authorization of the court.

(b) The personal representative shall deliver a copy of the court order to the financial institution or trust company at the time the deposit is made.

(c) No financial institution or trust company accepting a deposit pursuant to Section 9700 or 9701 shall be on notice of the existence of an order that the money or other property is subject to withdrawal only upon authorization of the court unless it has actual notice of the order. **Leg.H.** Enacted Stats 1990 ch 79 §14 (AB 759), operative July 1, 1991.

Prior Law: Former Prob C §9703, similar to the present section, was added Stats 1987 ch 923 §93, operative July 1, 1988, and repealed Stats 1990 ch 79 §13, operative July 1, 1991.

§9704. Direct distribution by depository

When an order for distribution of money or personal property deposited pursuant to this chapter is made, the financial institution, trust company, or securities depository may deliver the property directly to the distributees and shall file receipts therefor with the clerk. **Leg.H.** Enacted Stats 1990 ch 79 §14 (AB 759), operative July 1, 1991.

Prior Law: Former Prob C §9704, similar to the present section, was added Stats 1987 ch 923 §93, operative July 1, 1988, amended Stats 1988 ch 1199 §88, operative July 1, 1989, and repealed Stats 1990 ch 79 §13, operative July 1, 1991.

§9705. Interest on deposits by trust company

(a) Subject to subdivision (b), where a trust company is a personal representative and in the exercise of reasonable judgment deposits money of the estate in an account in any department of the corporation or association of which it is a part, it is chargeable with interest thereon at the rate of interest prevailing among banks of the locality on such deposits.

(b) Where it is to the advantage of the estate, the amount of cash that is reasonably necessary for orderly administration of the estate may be deposited in a checking account that does not earn interest which is maintained in a department of the corporation or association of which the trust company is a part. **Leg.H.** Enacted Stats 1990 ch 79 §14 (AB 759), operative July 1, 1991.

Prior Law: Former Prob C §9705, similar to the present section, was added Stats 1987 ch 923 §93, operative July 1, 1988, and repealed Stats 1990 ch 79 §13, operative July 1, 1991.

CHAPTER 4
INVESTMENTS AND PURCHASE OF PROPERTY

Investments permitted without prior court authorization. §9730.
Investment in federal or state securities with court authorization. §9731.
Investment of money as provided in will. §9732.
Purchase of annuity granted in will. §9733.
Exercise of option right. §9734.
Purchase of securities or commodities sold short. §9735.
Holding securities in name of nominee or in other form. §9736.
Exercise of subscription rights. §9737.

§9730. Investments permitted without prior court authorization

Pending distribution of the estate, the personal representative may invest money of the estate in possession of the personal representative in any one or more of the following:

(a) Direct obligations of the United States, or of the State of California, maturing not later than one year from the date of making the investment.

(b) An interest in a money market mutual fund registered under the Investment Company Act of 1940 (15 U.S.C. Sec. 80a-1, et seq.) or an investment vehicle authorized for the collective investment of trust funds pursuant to Section 9.18 of Part 9 of Title 12 of the Code of Federal Regulations, the portfolios of which are limited to United States government obligations maturing not later than five years from the date of investment and to repurchase agreements fully collateralized by United States government obligations.

(c) Units of a common trust fund described in Section 1585 of the Financial Code. The common trust fund shall have as its objective investment primarily in short term fixed income obligations and shall be permitted to value investments at cost pursuant to regulations of the appropriate regulatory authority. **Leg.H.** Enacted Stats 1990 ch 79 §14 (AB 759), operative July 1, 1991. Amended Stats 2014 ch 71 §140 (SB 1304), effective January 1, 2015.

Prior Law: Former Prob C §9730, similar to the present section, was added Stats 1987 ch 923 §93, operative July 1, 1988, and repealed Stats 1990 ch 79 §13, operative July 1, 1991.

§9731. Investment in federal or state securities with court authorization

(a) Pending distribution of the estate, upon a showing that it is to the advantage of the estate, the court may order that money of the estate in possession of the personal representative be invested in securities of the United States or of this state.

(b) To obtain an order under this section, the personal representative or any interested person shall file a petition stating the types of securities that are proposed to be purchased and the advantage to the estate of the purchase.

(c) Notice of the hearing on the petition shall be given as provided in Section 1220. **Leg.H.** Enacted Stats 1990 ch 79 §14 (AB 759), operative July 1, 1991.

Prior Law: Former Prob C §9731, similar to the present section, was added Stats 1987 ch 923 §93, operative July 1, 1988, and repealed Stats 1990 ch 79 §13, operative July 1, 1991.

§9732. Investment of money as provided in will

(a) The court may order that money of the estate in possession of the personal representative be invested in any manner provided by the will if all of the following conditions are satisfied:

(1) The time for filing claims has expired.

(2) All debts, as defined in Section 11401, have been paid or are sufficiently secured by mortgage or otherwise, or there is sufficient cash in the estate aside from the money to be invested to pay all the debts, or the court is otherwise satisfied that all the debts will be paid.

(3) The estate is not in a condition to be finally distributed.

(b) To obtain an order under this section, the personal representative or any interested person shall file a petition showing the general condition of the estate and the types of investments that are proposed to be made.

(c) Notice of the hearing on the petition shall be delivered as provided in Section 1220. In addition, the petitioner shall cause notice of the hearing and a copy of the petition to be delivered pursuant to Section 1215 to all known devisees of property which is proposed to be invested. Where the property proposed to be invested is devised to a trust or trustee, notice of the hearing and a copy of the petition shall be delivered pursuant to Section 1215 to the trustee or, if the trustee has not yet accepted the trust, to the person named in the will as trustee. Delivery pursuant to this subdivision shall be to the person's last known address as provided in Section 1220.

(d) If no objection has been filed by an interested person, the court may make an order authorizing or directing the personal representative to invest such portion of the money of the estate as the court deems advisable in the types of investments proposed in the petition and authorized by the will. If there is no objection by an interested person and no substantial reason why some or all of the investment powers given by the will should not be exercised, the court shall make the order. The order may be for a limited period or until the administration of the estate is completed. Upon petition of the personal representative or any interested person, the order may be renewed, modified, or terminated at any time. **Leg.H.** Enacted Stats 1990 ch 79 §14 (AB 759), operative July 1, 1991. Amended Stats 2017 ch 319 §76 (AB 976), effective January 1, 2018.

Prior Law: Former Prob C §9732, similar to the present section, was added Stats 1987 ch 923 §93, operative July 1, 1988, and repealed Stats 1990 ch 79 §13, operative July 1, 1991.

§9733. Purchase of annuity granted in will

(a) Pending distribution of the estate or at the time the court makes an order for final distribution of the estate, on petition of the personal representative or any interested person, the court may, upon good cause shown, order that the personal representative purchase an annuity from an insurer admitted to do business in this state to satisfy a devise of an annuity or other direction in the will for periodic payments to a devisee.

(b) Notice of the hearing on the petition shall be given as provided in Section 1220. **Leg.H.** Enacted Stats 1990 ch 79 §14 (AB 759), operative July 1, 1991.

Prior Law: Former Prob C §9733, similar to the present section, was added Stats 1987 ch 923 §93, operative July 1, 1988, and repealed Stats 1990 ch 79 §13, operative July 1, 1991.

§9734. Exercise of option right

(a) If an asset of the estate consists of an option right, the personal representative may exercise the option after authorization by order of court upon a showing that the exercise would be to the advantage of the estate and would be in the best interest of the interested persons. The personal representative may use any funds or property in the estate to acquire the property covered by the option.

(b) A petition under this section may be filed by the personal representative or any interested person.

(c) Notice of the hearing on the petition shall be given as provided in Section 1220. **Leg.H.** Enacted Stats 1990 ch 79 §14 (AB 759), operative July 1, 1991.

Prior Law: Former Prob C §9734, similar to the present section, was added Stats 1987 ch 923 §93, operative July 1, 1988, and repealed Stats 1990 ch 79 §13, operative July 1, 1991.

§9735. Purchase of securities or commodities sold short

(a) After authorization by order of court, the personal representative may purchase securities or commodities required to perform an incomplete contract of sale where the decedent died having sold but not delivered securities or commodities not owned by the decedent. The court's order shall fix the terms and conditions of purchase.

(b) A petition under this section may be filed by the personal representative or by any party to the contract. Notice of the hearing on the petition shall be given as provided in Section 1220.

(c) No notice of hearing need be given where the maximum purchase price is fixed or where the securities or commodities are to be purchased on an established stock, bond, or commodity exchange. **Leg.H.** Enacted Stats 1990 ch 79 §14 (AB 759), operative July 1, 1991.

Prior Law: Former Prob C §9735, similar to the present section, was added Stats 1987 ch 923 §93, operative July 1, 1988, and repealed Stats 1990 ch 79 §13, operative July 1, 1991.

§9736. Holding securities in name of nominee or in other form

The personal representative may hold a security in the name of a nominee or in any other form without disclosure of the estate so that title to the security may pass by delivery. **Leg.H.** Enacted Stats 1990 ch 79 §14 (AB 759), operative July 1, 1991.

Prior Law: Former Prob C §9736, similar to the present section, was added Stats 1987 ch 923 §93, operative July 1, 1988, and repealed Stats 1990 ch 79 §13, operative July 1, 1991.

§9737. Exercise of subscription rights

(a) If an estate by reason of owning securities also owns or receives subscription rights for the purchase of additional securities, the personal representative may exercise the subscription rights after authorization by order of court upon a showing that it is to the advantage of the estate.

(b) To obtain an order under this section, the personal representative or any interested person shall file a petition stating the nature of the subscription rights and the advantage to the estate of exercising them.

(c) Notice of the hearing on the petition shall be given as provided in Section 1220. **Leg.H.** Enacted Stats 1990 ch 79 §14 (AB 759), operative July 1, 1991.

Prior Law: Former Prob C §9737, similar to the present section, was added Stats 1987 ch 923 §93, operative July 1, 1988, and repealed Stats 1990 ch 79 §13, operative July 1, 1991.

CHAPTER 5
OPERATION OF DECEDENT'S BUSINESS

Operation of decedent's business other than partnership. §9760.
Account by decedent's surviving partner. §9761.
Personal representative continuing as partner in decedent's general partnership. §9762.
Exercise of decedent's partnership rights by personal representative. §9763.
Practice administrator for deceased bar member. §9764.
Deceased professional fiduciary. § 9765.

§9760. Operation of decedent's business other than partnership

(a) As used in this section, "decedent's business" means an unincorporated business or venture in which the decedent was engaged or which was wholly or partly owned by the decedent at the time of the decedent's death, but does not include a business operated by a partnership in which the decedent was a partner.

(b) If it is to the advantage of the estate and in the best interest of the interested persons, the personal representative, with or without court authorization, may continue the operation of the decedent's business; but the personal representative may not continue the operation of the decedent's business for a period of more than six months from the date letters are first issued to a personal representative unless a court order has been obtained under this section authorizing the personal representative to continue the operation of the business.

(c) The personal representative or any interested person may file a petition requesting an order (1) authorizing the personal representative to continue the operation of the decedent's business or (2) directing the personal representative to discontinue the operation of the decedent's business. The petition shall show the advantage to the estate and the benefit to the interested persons of the order requested. Notice of the hearing on the petition shall be given as provided in Section 1220.

(d) If a petition is filed under this section, the court may make an order that either:

(1) Authorizes the personal representative to continue the operation of the decedent's business to such an extent and subject to such restrictions as the court determines to be to the advantage of the estate and in the best interest of the interested persons.

(2) Directs the personal representative to discontinue the operation of the decedent's business within the time specified in, and in accordance with the provisions of, the order. **Leg.H.** Enacted Stats 1990 ch 79 §14 (AB 759), operative July 1, 1991.

Prior Law: Former Prob C §9760, similar to the present section, was added Stats 1987 ch 923 §93, operative July 1, 1988, and repealed Stats 1990 ch 79 §13, operative July 1, 1991.

§9761. Account by decedent's surviving partner

If a partnership existed between the decedent and another person at the time of the decedent's death, on application of the personal representative, the court may order any surviving partner to render an account pursuant to Section 15510, 15634, or 16807 of the Corporations Code. An order under this section may be enforced by the court's power to punish for contempt. **Leg.H.** Enacted Stats 1990 ch 79 §14 (AB 759), operative July 1, 1991. Amended Stats 2003 ch 32 §8 (AB 167), effective January 1, 2004.

Prior Law: Former Prob C §9761, similar to the present section, was added Stats 1987 ch 923 §93, operative July 1, 1988, and repealed Stats 1990 ch 79 §13, operative July 1, 1991.

§9762. Personal representative continuing as partner in decedent's general partnership

(a) After authorization by order of court upon a showing that it would be to the advantage of the estate and in the best interest of the interested persons, the personal representative may continue as a general or a limited partner in any partnership in which the decedent was a general partner at the time of death. In its order, the court may specify any terms and conditions of the personal representative's participation as a partner that the court determines are to the advantage of the estate and in the best interest of the interested persons, but any terms and conditions that are inconsistent with the terms of any written partnership agreement are subject to the written consent of all of the surviving partners.

(b) If there is a written partnership agreement permitting the decedent's personal representative to participate as a partner, the personal representative has all the rights, powers, duties, and obligations provided in the written partnership agreement, except as otherwise ordered by the court pursuant to subdivision (a).

(c) If there is not a written partnership agreement, the personal representative has the rights, powers, duties, and obligations that the court specifies in its order pursuant to subdivision (a).

(d) To obtain an order under this section, the personal representative or any interested person shall file a petition showing that the order requested would be to the advantage of the estate and in the best interest of the interested persons. Notice of the hearing on the petition shall be given as provided in Section 1220. In addition, unless the court otherwise orders, the petitioner, not less than 15 days before the hearing, shall cause notice of hearing and a copy of the petition to be delivered pursuant to Section 1215 to each of the surviving general partners at his or her last known address. **Leg.H.** Enacted Stats 1990 ch 79 §14 (AB 759), operative July 1, 1991. Amended Stats 2017 ch 319 §77 (AB 976), effective January 1, 2018.

Prior Law: Former Prob C §9762, similar to the present section, was added Stats 1987 ch 923 §93, operative July 1, 1988, and repealed Stats 1990 ch 79 §13, operative July 1, 1991.

§9763. Exercise of decedent's partnership rights by personal representative

(a) If the decedent was a general partner, the personal representative may commence and maintain any action against the surviving partner that the decedent could have commenced and maintained.

(b) The personal representative may exercise the decedent's rights as a limited partner as provided in Section 15675 of the Corporations Code.
Leg.H. Enacted Stats 1990 ch 79 §14 (AB 759), operative July 1, 1991.

Prior Law: Former Prob C §9763, similar to the present section, was added Stats 1987 ch 923 §93, operative July 1, 1988, and repealed Stats 1990 ch 79 §13, operative July 1, 1991.

§9764. Practice administrator for deceased bar member

(a) The personal representative of the estate of a deceased attorney who was engaged in a practice of law at the time of his or her death or other person interested in the estate may bring a petition for appointment of an active member of the State Bar of California to take control of the files and assets of the practice of the deceased member.

(b) The petition may be filed and heard on such notice that the court determines is in the best interests of the estate of the deceased member. If the petition alleges that the immediate appointment of a practice administrator is required to safeguard the interests of the estate, the court may dispense with notice only if the personal representative is the petitioner or has joined in the petition or has otherwise waived notice of hearing on the petition.

(c) The petition shall indicate the powers sought for the practice administrator from the list of powers set forth in Section 6185 of the Business and Professions Code. These powers shall be specifically listed in the order appointing the practice administrator.

(d) The petition shall allege the value of the assets that are to come under the control of the practice administrator, including, but not limited by the amount of funds in all accounts used by the deceased member. The court shall require the filing of a surety bond in the amount of the value of the personal property to be filed with the court by the practice administrator. No action may be taken by the practice administrator unless a bond has been fully filed with the court.

(e) The practice administrator shall not be the attorney representing the personal representative.

(f) The court shall appoint the attorney nominated by the deceased member in a writing, including, but not limited to, the deceased member's will, unless the court concludes that the appointment of the nominated person would be contrary to the best interests of the estate or would create a conflict of interest with any of the clients of the deceased member.

(g) The practice administrator shall be compensated only upon order of the court making the appointment for his or her reasonable and necessary services. The law practice shall be the source of the compensation for the practice administrator unless the assets are insufficient in which case, the compensation of the practice administrator shall be charged against the assets of the estate as a cost of administration. The practice administrator shall also be entitled to reimbursement of his or her costs.

(h) Upon conclusion of the services of the practice administrator, the practice administrator shall render an accounting and petition for its approval by the superior court making the appointment. Upon settlement of the accounting, the practice administrator shall be discharged and the surety on his or her bond exonerated.

(i) For the purposes of this section, the person appointed to take control of the practice of the deceased member shall be referred to as the "practice administrator" and the decedent shall be referred to as the "deceased member." **Leg.H.** Added Stats 1998 ch 682 §5 (AB 2069).

§ 9765. Deceased professional fiduciary

(a) Commencing January 1, 2024, when a professional fiduciary is deceased and a vacancy exists, the deceased fiduciary's personal representative, trustee, or interested person may petition for the appointment of one or more individuals, qualified to act as a professional fiduciary under the Professional Fiduciaries Act (Chapter 6 (commencing with Section 6500) of Division 3 of the Business and Professions Code), as a professional fiduciary practice administrator, to take control of the deceased professional fiduciary's files and to be appointed as temporary successor as to those matters for which a vacancy exists as a result of the professional fiduciary's death.

(b) The petition shall request an order appointing a professional fiduciary practice administrator as temporary successor, with all of the powers and duties held by the deceased fiduciary, in each matter in which the deceased fiduciary was acting in a representative capacity, including guardianships of the estate, conservatorships of the person and estate, decedent's estates, court-supervised trusts, and non-court-supervised trusts.

(c) The court shall require the professional fiduciary practice administrator to file a surety bond in each matter in which the professional fiduciary practice administrator is appointed temporary successor, in the amount currently required of the deceased fiduciary or in another amount as the court deems appropriate.

(d) The court may appoint as the professional fiduciary practice administrator the professional fiduciary nominated by the deceased professional fiduciary in a writing, including, but not limited to, the decedent's will or trust, or in the absence thereof, the person nominated by the person having legal standing to act on behalf of the deceased professional fiduciary. The court shall not make the appointment if the court concludes that the appointment of the nominated person would be contrary to the best interests of, or would create a conflict of interest with, any interested party in a matter in which the deceased fiduciary was acting in a fiduciary capacity.

(e) The appointment of the professional fiduciary practice administrator as temporary successor shall terminate, in each of the matters in which the professional fiduciary practice administrator was appointed as temporary successor, 45 days after the entry of the order appointing the professional fiduciary practice administrator, or earlier if another person is appointed.

(f) Notice of the hearing on the petition for appointment of a professional fiduciary practice administrator as temporary successor shall be given to all persons entitled to notice in each of the matters that are the subject of the petition. The court may dispense with notice if the court determines that the immediate appointment of a professional fiduciary practice administrator is required to safeguard the interests of an individual or an asset in a matter in which the deceased fiduciary was acting in a representative capacity.

(g) The professional fiduciary practice administrator shall be compensated for services provided and reimbursement of costs incurred in each matter solely from the assets of that matter subject to the provisions of the applicable document or as determined by the court, and in no event more than the incapacitated fiduciary would have been paid.

(h) The professional fiduciary practice administrator shall do all of the following:

(1) File a copy of the order appointing the professional fiduciary practice administrator as temporary successor in each of the matters in which the court appoints the professional fiduciary practice administrator as temporary successor.

(2) Take control and review all files and writings maintained by the deceased fiduciary for matters in which the deceased fiduciary was acting in a representative capacity.

(3) Within 15 days after the entry of the order appointing the professional fiduciary practice administrator as temporary successor, provide written notice to all interested parties as to each matter in which the deceased fiduciary was acting in a representative capacity who can be reasonably ascertained and located to inform those parties of the appointment of the professional fiduciary practice administrator as temporary successor. The notice shall advise the parties of the need for the appointment for a permanent successor, which shall include the following:

(A) The right of the parties to petition the court for the appointment of a permanent successor.

(B) The right of any interested party to nominate an individual to act as permanent successor, and then the obligation of the professional fiduciary practice administrator to petition for the appointment of the individual nominated, provided an interested party provides the professional fiduciary practice administrator with the name of their nominee within 15 days after the date notice was given.

(C) The ability of the professional fiduciary practice administrator, in the event that none of the interested parties act within the time prescribed above, under subparagraph (A) or (B), to petition the court for appointment of a permanent successor.

(4) Upon the court's appointment of a permanent successor, the professional fiduciary practice administrator shall file an account and report on behalf of the deceased fiduciary for any period of time the deceased fiduciary would have been required to account, as well as for the period of time the professional fiduciary practice administrator served as temporary successor. As part of that account and report, the professional fiduciary practice administrator may request compensation both on behalf of the deceased fiduciary, for services rendered prior to their death, and on their own behalf for services rendered after the deceased fiduciary's death as temporary successor, subject to any limitation on fees and costs that existed for the deceased fiduciary, and may request discharge and exoneration of bond. The account filed for the period during which the matter was administered by the now deceased fiduciary may be verified on information and belief.

(5) Comply with any other obligations imposed by the court.

(i) Each of the time periods prescribed in this section may be extended by the court if the court determines that good cause exists, and if the court determines that the extension is in the best interest of the minor, the conservatee, the decedent's estate, or the current income beneficiaries under a trust, as applicable.

(j) For purposes of this section, the following definitions apply:

(1) "Professional fiduciary practice administrator" means the person appointed pursuant to this section to take over the responsibilities from the deceased fiduciary.

(2) "Vacancy" means that the instrument under which the deceased fiduciary was acting does not name a successor to fill the vacancy, the instrument under which the deceased fiduciary was acting does not provide a nonjudicial method to fill the vacancy, or a cofiduciary, authorized to act solely, was not acting with the deceased fiduciary.

(k) This section does not limit the authority granted to the court under subdivision (j) of Section 2250, Section 8523, and subdivision (e) of Section 15642.

(*l*) The Judicial Council shall create or revise any forms or rules necessary to implement this section no later than January 1, 2024. **Leg.H.** Added Stats 2022 ch 612 §5 (SB 1024), effective January 1, 2023. Amended Stats 2023 ch 478 §59 (AB 1756), effective January 1, 2024.

CHAPTER 6
ABANDONMENT OF TANGIBLE PERSONAL PROPERTY

Abandonment of tangible personal property. §9780.
Court authorization or approval not required unless will otherwise provides. §9781.
Notice of proposed disposition or abandonment. §9782.
Objection to proposed disposition or abandonment. §9783.
Restraining order. §9784.
Notice not required where consent or waiver. §9785.
Notice of hearing of petition for court authorization. §9786.
Waiver of right to court review. §9787.
Tender of possession of property to person objecting. §9788.

§9780. Abandonment of tangible personal property

Unless the property is specifically devised, subject to the requirements of this chapter, the personal representative may dispose of or abandon tangible personal property where the cost of collecting, maintaining, and safeguarding the property would exceed its fair market value. **Leg.H.** Enacted Stats 1990 ch 79 §14 (AB 759), operative July 1, 1991.

Prior Law: Former Prob C §9780, similar to the present section, was added Stats 1987 ch 923 §93, operative July 1, 1988, and repealed Stats 1990 ch 79 §13, operative July 1, 1991.

§9781. Court authorization or approval not required unless will otherwise provides

Unless otherwise provided in the will, subject to the requirements of this chapter, the personal representative may exercise the power provided in Section 9780 without court authorization or approval. **Leg.H.** Enacted Stats 1990 ch 79 §14 (AB 759), operative July 1, 1991.

Prior Law: Former Prob C §9781, similar to the present section, was added Stats 1987 ch 923 §93, operative July 1, 1988, and repealed Stats 1990 ch 79 §13, operative July 1, 1991.

§9782. Notice of proposed disposition or abandonment

(a) Except as provided in Section 9785, before disposing of or abandoning property under Section 9780, the personal representative shall give notice of the proposed disposition or abandonment as provided in subdivision (c) to all of the following:

(1) Each known devisee whose interest in the estate would be affected by the proposed action.

(2) Each known heir whose interest in the estate would be affected by the proposed action.

(3) Each person who has filed a request for special notice pursuant to Section 1250.

(4) The Attorney General, at the office of the Attorney General in Sacramento, if any portion of the estate is to escheat to the state and its interest in the estate would be affected by the proposed action.

(b) The notice of the proposed disposition or abandonment shall describe the property to be disposed of or abandoned, indicate the manner in which the property is to be disposed of or abandoned, and specify the date on or after which the property will be disposed of or abandoned.

(c) The notice shall be delivered personally to each person required to be given notice or shall be sent by mail to the person at the person's last known address. If the notice is delivered personally, it shall be delivered to the person not less than five days before the date specified in the notice as the date on or after which the property will be disposed of or abandoned. If the notice is sent by mail, it shall be deposited in the mail not less than 10 days before the date specified in the notice as the date on or after which the property will be disposed of or abandoned. **Leg.H.** Enacted Stats 1990 ch 79 §14 (AB 759), operative July 1, 1991.

Prior Law: Former Prob C §9782, similar to the present section, was added Stats 1987 ch 923 §93, operative July 1, 1988, and repealed Stats 1990 ch 79 §13, operative July 1, 1991.

§9783. Objection to proposed disposition or abandonment

A person described in Section 9782 may personally deliver or mail a written objection to the disposition or abandonment to the personal representative on or before the date specified in the notice as the date on or after which the property will be disposed of or abandoned. Subject to Section 9788, after receipt of the written objection, the personal representative shall not dispose of or abandon the property without authorization by order of the court obtained under Section 9611. **Leg.H.** Enacted Stats 1990 ch 79 §14 (AB 759), operative July 1, 1991. Amended Stats 2017 ch 319 §78 (AB 976), effective January 1, 2018.

Prior Law: Former Prob C §9783, similar to the present section, was added Stats 1987 ch 923 §93, operative July 1, 1988, and repealed Stats 1990 ch 79 §13, operative July 1, 1991.

§9784. Restraining order

(a) A person described in Section 9782 who objects to the disposition or abandonment of property by the personal representative under Section 9780 may apply to the court in which proceedings for administration of the estate are pending for an order restraining the personal representative from disposing of or abandoning the property without prior court authorization.

(b) The court shall grant the requested order without requiring notice to the personal representative and without cause being shown for the order if the court is satisfied that the estate will not suffer any loss or unreasonable expense if the order is granted. As a condition of granting the order, the court may require the person applying for the order (1) to pay the costs of storing and protecting the property or (2) to provide security by bond or cash deposit that the costs will be paid.

(c) The personal representative is deemed to have notice of the restraining order if it is served upon the personal representative in the manner provided in Section 415.10 or 415.30 of the Code of Civil Procedure, or in the manner authorized by the court, before the date specified in the notice as the date on or after which the property will be disposed of or abandoned. **Leg.H.** Enacted Stats 1990 ch 79 §14 (AB 759), operative July 1, 1991.

Prior Law: Former Prob C §9784, similar to the present section, was added Stats 1987 ch 923 §93, operative July 1, 1988, and repealed Stats 1990 ch 79 §13, operative July 1, 1991.

§9785. Notice not required where consent or waiver

Notice of the proposed disposition or abandonment need not be given to any of the following:

(a) A person who consents in writing to the proposed disposition or abandonment.

(b) A person who, in writing, waives the right to notice of the proposed disposition or abandonment. **Leg.H.** Enacted Stats 1990 ch 79 §14 (AB 759), operative July 1, 1991.

§9786. Notice of hearing of petition for court authorization

A person who objects to the disposition or abandonment as provided in Section 9783, or who serves a restraining order issued under Section 9784 in the manner provided in that section, shall be given notice of any court hearing on a petition for court authorization of the disposition or abandonment of the property. **Leg.H.** Enacted Stats 1990 ch 79 §14 (AB 759), operative July 1, 1991.

Prior Law: Former Prob C §9786, similar to the present section, was added Stats 1987 ch 923 §93, operative July 1, 1988, and repealed Stats 1990 ch 79 §13, operative July 1, 1991.

§9787. Waiver of right to court review

(a) Except as provided in subdivision (b), a person described in Section 9782 who receives notice of the proposed disposition or abandonment as provided in Section 9782, waives the right to have the court later review the disposition or abandonment of the property unless the person does one of the following:

(1) Personally delivers or mails a written objection as provided in Section 9783.

(2) Serves a restraining order obtained under Section 9784 before whichever of the following is the later time:

(A) The date specified in the notice of proposed disposition or abandonment as the date on or after which the property will be disposed of or abandoned.

(B) The date the property has actually been disposed of or abandoned.

(b) Subject to Section 9785, the court may review the disposition or abandonment of the property upon the motion of a person described in subdivision (a) of Section 9782 who establishes that he or she did not actually receive notice of the proposed disposition or abandonment before the time to object expired. **Leg.H.** Enacted Stats 1990 ch 79 §14 (AB 759), operative July 1, 1991. Amended Stats 2017 ch 319 §79 (AB 976), effective January 1, 2018.

Prior Law: Former Prob C §9787, similar to the present section, was added Stats 1987 ch 923 §93, operative July 1, 1988, and repealed Stats 1990 ch 79 §13, operative July 1, 1991.

§9788. Tender of possession of property to person objecting

(a) Notwithstanding Sections 9783 and 9784, the personal representative may abandon or dispose of the property without court authorization if the person who made the objection or obtained the restraining order fails to take possession of the property at his or her expense within 10 days after the personal representative requests that the person do so.

(b) A person who takes possession of estate property pursuant to this section is liable for the safekeeping of the property until a court order is made relieving the person of this obligation. **Leg.H.** Enacted Stats 1990 ch 79 §14 (AB 759), operative July 1, 1991.

Prior Law: Former Prob C §9788, similar to the present section, was added Stats 1987 ch 923 §93, operative July 1, 1988, and repealed Stats 1990 ch 79 §13, operative July 1, 1991.

CHAPTER 7
BORROWING, REFINANCING, AND ENCUMBERING PROPERTY

Borrowing money, refinancing, and encumbering property. §9800.
Acting jointly with other owners of interests in estate property. §9801.
Petition. §9802.
Notice of hearing. §9803.
Court order. §9804.
Execution of instrument. §9805.
Effectiveness of encumbrance. §9806.
Deficiency in case of foreclosure or sale under security interest or deed of trust. §9807.

§9800. Borrowing money, refinancing, and encumbering property

(a) Subject to subdivision (c), after authorization by order of court obtained under this chapter upon a showing that it would be to the advantage of the estate, the personal representative may borrow money on a note, either unsecured or to be secured by a security interest or other lien on the personal property of the estate, or any part thereof, or to be secured by a mortgage or deed of trust on the real property of the estate, or any part thereof, and may give a security interest or other lien on the personal property of the estate, or any part thereof, or a mortgage or deed of trust on the real property of the estate, or any part thereof, in order to do any one or more of the following:

(1) Pay the debts of the decedent or the estate, devises, expenses of administration, and charges against the estate.

(2) Pay, reduce, extend, or renew a security interest or lien or mortgage or deed of trust already existing on property of the estate.

(3) Improve, use, operate, or preserve property in the estate.

(b) The personal representative shall apply the money to the purpose specified in the order.

(c) Where the surviving spouse has elected to have his or her share of the community real property administered in the decedent's estate, the personal representative is authorized to borrow money to be secured by a mortgage or deed of trust on the community real property of the estate, or any part thereof, only with the written consent of the surviving spouse. **Leg.H.** Enacted Stats 1990 ch 79 §14 (AB 759), operative July 1, 1991.

Prior Law: Former Prob C §9800, similar to the present section, was added Stats 1987 ch 923 §93, operative July 1, 1988, and repealed Stats 1990 ch 79 §13, operative July 1, 1991.

§9801. Acting jointly with other owners of interests in estate property

If property of the estate consists of an undivided interest in real or personal property, or any other interest therein less than the entire ownership, upon a showing that it would be to the advantage of the estate to borrow money to improve, use, operate, or preserve the property jointly with the owners of the other interests therein, or to pay, reduce, extend, or renew a security interest, lien, mortgage, or deed of trust already existing on all of the property, the personal representative, after authorization by order of the court obtained under this chapter, may join with the owners of the other interests in borrowing money and the execution of a joint and several note and such security interest, lien, mortgage, or deed of trust as may be required to secure the payment of the note. The note may be for such sum as is required for the purpose. **Leg.H.** Enacted Stats 1990 ch 79 §14 (AB 759), operative July 1, 1991.

Prior Law: Former Prob C §9801, similar to the present section, was added Stats 1987 ch 923 §93, operative July 1, 1988, and repealed Stats 1990 ch 79 §13, operative July 1, 1991.

§9802. Petition

(a) The personal representative or any interested person may file a petition for an order under this chapter.

(b) The petition shall state the purpose for which the order is sought and the necessity for or the advantage to accrue from the order. If applicable, the petition shall also show the amount of money proposed to be borrowed, the rate of interest to be paid, the length of time the note is to run, and a general description of the property proposed to be mortgaged or subjected to the deed of trust, security interest, or other lien. **Leg.H.** Enacted Stats 1990 ch 79 §14 (AB 759), operative July 1, 1991.

Prior Law: Former Prob C §9802, similar to the present section, was added Stats 1987 ch 923 §93, operative July 1, 1988, and repealed Stats 1990 ch 79 §13, operative July 1, 1991.

§9803. Notice of hearing

Notice of the hearing on the petition shall be given as provided in Section 1220. **Leg.H.** Enacted Stats 1990 ch 79 §14 (AB 759), operative July 1, 1991.

Prior Law: Former Prob C §9803, similar to the present section, was added Stats 1987 ch 923 §93, operative July 1, 1988, and repealed Stats 1990 ch 79 §13, operative July 1, 1991.

§9804. Court order

(a) Subject to subdivision (c), if the court is satisfied that it will be to the advantage of the estate, the court shall make an order that authorizes or requires that the personal representative do any one or more of the following:

(1) Borrow money and execute a note.

(2) Execute a mortgage or deed of trust or give other security by security interest or other lien.

(3) Pay, reduce, extend, or renew a security interest or lien or mortgage or deed of trust already existing upon property of the estate.

(b) The court in its order may do any one or more of the following:

(1) Order that the amount specified in the petition, or a lesser amount, be borrowed.

(2) Prescribe the maximum rate of interest and the period of the loan.

(3) Require that the interest and the whole or any part of the principal be paid from time to time out of the whole estate or any part thereof.

(4) Require that the personal property used as security, or any buildings on real property to be mortgaged or subjected to the deed of trust, be insured for the further security of the lender and that the premiums be paid out of the estate.

(5) Specify the purpose for which the money to be borrowed is to be applied.

(6) Specify the terms and conditions of any extension or renewal agreement.

(7) Prescribe such other terms and conditions concerning the transaction as the court determines to be to the advantage of the estate.

(c) Where the surviving spouse has elected to have his or her share of the community real property administered in the decedent's estate, an order authorizing or requiring the personal representative to borrow money to be secured by a mortgage or deed of trust upon the community real property of the estate, or any part thereof, may be made only if the written consent of the surviving spouse has been filed with the court. **Leg.H.** Enacted Stats 1990 ch 79 §14 (AB 759), operative July 1, 1991.

Prior Law: Former Prob C §9804, similar to the present section, was added Stats 1987 ch 923 §93, operative July 1, 1988, and repealed Stats 1990 ch 79 §13, operative July 1, 1991.

§9805. Execution of instrument

(a) The personal representative shall execute and deliver the mortgage or deed of trust, or execute and deliver the instrument creating the security interest, setting forth therein that it is made by authority of the order, giving the date of the order.

(b) The note and the mortgage or deed of trust or other instrument creating the security interest, if any, shall be signed by the personal representative and shall be acknowledged by the personal representative if the instrument creates a lien on real property. **Leg.H.** Enacted Stats 1990 ch 79 §14 (AB 759), operative July 1, 1991.

Prior Law: Former Prob C §9805, similar to the present section, was added Stats 1987 ch 923 §93, operative July 1, 1988, and repealed Stats 1990 ch 79 §13, operative July 1, 1991.

§9806. Effectiveness of encumbrance

(a) Every mortgage, deed of trust, or security interest made pursuant to a court order obtained under this chapter is effectual to mortgage, or to subject to the deed of trust or security interest, all of the following:

(1) All right, title, and interest which the decedent had to the property described therein at the time of the decedent's death.

(2) Any right, title, or interest in the property acquired by the estate of the decedent, by operation of law or otherwise, since the time of the decedent's death.

(3) Any right, title, or interest in the community real property belonging to the decedent's surviving spouse whose written consent has been filed with the court and which is referred to in the court order obtained under this chapter.

(b) Jurisdiction of the court to administer the estate of the decedent vests the court with jurisdiction to make the order for the note and for the security interest, lien, mortgage, or deed of trust. This jurisdiction shall conclusively inure to the benefit of the owner of the security interest or lien, mortgagee named in the mortgage, or the trustee and beneficiary named in the deed of trust, and their heirs and assigns.

(c) No omission, error, or irregularity in the proceedings under this chapter shall impair or invalidate the proceedings or the note, security interest, lien, mortgage, or deed of trust given pursuant to an order under this chapter. Subject to Section 9807, the owner of the security interest or lien, the mortgagee named in the mortgage, or the trustee and beneficiary named in the deed of trust, and their heirs and assigns, have and possess the same rights and remedies on the note and the security interest or lien or mortgage or deed of trust as if it had been made by the decedent prior to his or her death. **Leg.H.** Enacted Stats 1990 ch 79 §14 (AB 759), operative July 1, 1991.

Prior Law: Former Prob C §9806, similar to the present section, was added Stats 1987 ch 923 §93, operative July 1, 1988, and repealed Stats 1990 ch 79 §13, operative July 1, 1991.

§9807. Deficiency in case of foreclosure or sale under security interest or deed of trust

(a) Except as provided in subdivision (b), no judgment or claim for any deficiency shall be had or allowed against the personal representative or the estate if (1) there is a foreclosure or sale under a security interest, lien, mortgage, or deed of trust and (2) the proceeds of sale of the encumbered property are insufficient to pay the note, the security interest, lien, mortgage, or deed of trust, and the costs or expenses of sale.

(b) If the note, security interest, mortgage, or deed of trust was given to pay, reduce, extend, or renew a lien, security interest, mortgage, or deed of trust existing on property of the estate at the time of death of the decedent and the indebtedness secured thereby was a claim established under Part 4 (commencing with Section 9000), the part of the indebtedness remaining unsatisfied shall be classed with other established claims. **Leg.H.** Enacted Stats 1990 ch 79 §14 (AB 759), operative July 1, 1991.

Prior Law: Former Prob C §9807, similar to the present section, was added Stats 1987 ch 923 §93, operative July 1, 1988, and repealed Stats 1990 ch 79 §13, operative July 1, 1991.

CHAPTER 8
ACTIONS AND PROCEEDINGS BY OR AGAINST PERSONAL REPRESENTATIVE

Authority to sue and defend. §9820.
Action on bond of former personal representative. §9822.
Partition actions. §9823.

§9820. Authority to sue and defend

The personal representative may:

(a) Commence and maintain actions and proceedings for the benefit of the estate.

(b) Defend actions and proceedings against the decedent, the personal representative, or the estate. **Leg.H.** Enacted Stats 1990 ch 79 §14 (AB 759), operative July 1, 1991.

Prior Law: Former Prob C §9820, similar to the present section, was added Stats 1987 ch 923 §93, operative July 1, 1988, and repealed Stats 1990 ch 79 §13, operative July 1, 1991.

§9822. Action on bond of former personal representative

The personal representative may bring an action on the bond of any former personal representative of the same estate, for the use and benefit of all interested persons. **Leg.H.** Enacted Stats 1990 ch 79 §14 (AB 759), operative July 1, 1991.

Prior Law: Former Prob C §9822, similar to the present section, was added Stats 1987 ch 923 §93, operative July 1, 1988, and repealed Stats 1990 ch 79 §13, operative July 1, 1991.

§9823. Partition actions

(a) If the decedent leaves an undivided interest in any property, an action for partition of the property may be brought against the personal representative.

(b) The personal representative may bring an action against the other cotenants for partition of any property in which the decedent left an undivided interest. **Leg.H.** Enacted Stats 1990 ch 79 §14 (AB 759), operative July 1, 1991.

Prior Law: Former Prob C §9823, similar to the present section, was added Stats 1987 ch 923 §93, operative July 1, 1988, and repealed Stats 1990 ch 79 §13, operative July 1, 1991.

CHAPTER 9
COMPROMISE OF CLAIMS AND ACTIONS; EXTENSION, RENEWAL, OR MODIFICATION OF OBLIGATIONS

Authority to compromise claims and actions and to extend, renew, or modify obligations. §9830.
Compromise before time for filing creditors' claims has expired. §9831.
Matters relating to real property. §9832.
Compromise in excess of specified amount. §9833.
Claim of estate against personal representative or estate attorney; Debt or obligation of personal representative or estate attorney to estate. §9834.
Wrongful death and personal injury claims. §9835.
Court having authority to give authorization. §9836.
Petition for court authorization; Notice of hearing. §9837.
Transfer of property to effectuate court approved compromise or settlement. §9838.
Claim paid for less than full amount. §9839.

§9830. Authority to compromise claims and actions and to extend, renew, or modify obligations

(a) Unless this chapter or some other applicable statute requires court authorization or approval, if it is to the advantage of the estate, the personal representative may do any of the following without court authorization, instruction, approval, or confirmation:

(1) Compromise or settle a claim, action, or proceeding by or for the benefit of, or against, the decedent, the personal representative, or the estate, including the giving of a covenant not to sue.

(2) Extend, renew, or in any manner modify the terms of an obligation owing to or in favor of the decedent or the estate.

(3) Release, in whole or in part, any claim belonging to the estate to the extent that the claim is uncollectible.

(b) Nothing in this section precludes the personal representative from seeking court authorization pursuant to the provisions of this chapter.

(c) Upon petition of an interested person or upon the court's own motion, the court may limit the authority of the personal representative under subdivision (a). Notice of the hearing on the petition shall be given as provided in Section 1220. **Leg.H.** Enacted Stats 1990 ch 79 §14 (AB 759), operative July 1, 1991.

Prior Law: Former Prob C §9830, similar to the present section, was added Stats 1987 ch 923 §93, operative July 1, 1988, and repealed Stats 1990 ch 79 §13, operative July 1, 1991.

§9831. Compromise before time for filing creditors' claims has expired

Unless the time for filing creditor claims has expired, authorization by order of court is required for a compromise or settlement of a claim, action, or proceeding by or for the benefit of, or against, the decedent, the personal representative, or the estate. **Leg.H.** Enacted Stats 1990 ch 79 §14 (AB 759), operative July 1, 1991.

Prior Law: Former Prob C §9831, similar to the present section, was added Stats 1987 ch 923 §93, operative July 1, 1988, and repealed Stats 1990 ch 79 §13, operative July 1, 1991.

§9832. Matters relating to real property

(a) Except as provided in subdivision (b), authorization by order of court is required for a compromise, settlement, extension, renewal, or modification which affects any of the following:

(1) Title to real property.

(2) An interest in real property or a lien or encumbrance on real property.

(3) An option to purchase real property or an interest in real property.

(b) If it is to the advantage of the estate, the personal representative without prior court authorization may extend, renew, or modify a lease of real property in either of the following cases:

(1) Where under the lease as extended, renewed, or modified the rental does not exceed five thousand dollars ($5,000) a month and the term does not exceed one year.

(2) Where the lease is from month to month, regardless of the amount of the rental.

(c) For the purposes of subdivision (b), if the lease as extended, renewed, or modified gives the lessee the right to extend the term of the lease, the length of the term shall be considered as though the right to extend had been exercised. **Leg.H.** Enacted Stats 1990 ch 79 §14 (AB 759), operative July 1, 1991. Amended Stats 1990 ch 710 §24 (SB 1775), operative July 1, 1991.

Prior Law: Former Prob C §9832, similar to the present section, was added Stats 1987 ch 923 §93, operative July 1, 1988, and repealed Stats 1990 ch 79 §13, operative July 1, 1991.

§9833. Compromise in excess of specified amount

Authorization by order of court is required for a compromise or settlement of a matter when the transaction requires the transfer or encumbrance of property of the estate, or the creation of an unsecured liability of the estate, or both, in an amount or value in excess of twenty-five thousand dollars ($25,000). **Leg.H.** Enacted Stats 1990 ch 79 §14 (AB 759), operative July 1, 1991.

Prior Law: Former Prob C §9833, similar to the present section, was added Stats 1987 ch 923 §93, operative July 1, 1988, and repealed Stats 1990 ch 79 §13, operative July 1, 1991.

§9834. Claim of estate against personal representative or estate attorney; Debt or obligation of personal representative or estate attorney to estate

Authorization by order of court is required for any of the following:

(a) A compromise or settlement of a claim by the estate against the personal representative or the personal representative's attorney, whether or not the claim arises out of the administration of the estate.

(b) An extension, renewal, or modification of the terms of a debt or similar obligation of the personal representative, or the personal representative's attorney, owing to, or in favor of, the estate. **Leg.H.** Enacted Stats 1990 ch 79 §14 (AB 759), operative July 1, 1991.

Prior Law: Former Prob C §9834, similar to the present section, was added Stats 1987 ch 923 §93, operative July 1, 1988, and repealed Stats 1990 ch 79 §13, operative July 1, 1991.

§9835. Wrongful death and personal injury claims

Authorization by order of court is required for the compromise or settlement of a claim or right of action given to the personal representative by any law for the wrongful death or injury of the decedent, including any action brought by the personal representative in attempting enforcement of the claim or right of action. Authorization to compromise or settle the claim or right of action includes authorization to give a covenant not to sue. **Leg.H.** Enacted Stats 1990 ch 79 §14 (AB 759), operative July 1, 1991.

Prior Law: Former Prob C §9835, similar to the present section, was added Stats 1987 ch 923 §93, operative July 1, 1988, and repealed Stats 1990 ch 79 §13, operative July 1, 1991.

§9836. Court having authority to give authorization

The court authorization required by this chapter shall be obtained from the court in which the estate is being administered. **Leg.H.** Enacted Stats 1990 ch 79 §14 (AB 759), operative July 1, 1991.

Prior Law: Former Prob C §9836, similar to the present section, was added Stats 1987 ch 923 §93, operative July 1, 1988, and repealed Stats 1990 ch 79 §13, operative July 1, 1991.

§9837. Petition for court authorization; Notice of hearing

(a) A petition for an order authorizing a compromise, settlement, extension, renewal, or modification under this chapter may be filed by any of the following:

(1) The personal representative.

(2) Any interested person who has obtained the written approval of the personal representative to file the petition.

(b) The petition shall show the terms of the compromise, settlement, extension, renewal, or modification and its advantage to the estate.

(c) Notice of the hearing on the petition shall be given as provided in Section 1220. **Leg.H.** Enacted Stats 1990 ch 79 §14 (AB 759), operative July 1, 1991.

Prior Law: Former Prob C §9837, similar to the present section, was added Stats 1987 ch 923 §93, operative July 1, 1988, and repealed Stats 1990 ch 79 §13, operative July 1, 1991.

§9838. Transfer of property to effectuate court approved compromise or settlement

(a) If an order made under Section 9837 authorizes a compromise or settlement that requires the transfer of real property of the estate, the personal representative shall execute a conveyance of the real property to the person entitled thereto under the compromise or settlement. The conveyance shall refer to the order authorizing the compromise or settlement and directing that the conveyance be executed. A certified copy of the order shall be recorded in the office of the county recorder in each county in which any portion of the real property is located.

(b) A conveyance made in compliance with the court order authorizing the compromise or settlement and directing the conveyance to be executed vests in the person to whom the property is transferred both of the following:

(1) All the right, title, and interest which the decedent had in the property at the time of the decedent's death.

(2) Any other or additional right, title, or interest in the property acquired by the estate of the decedent, by operation of law or otherwise, prior to the transfer. **Leg.H.** Enacted Stats 1990 ch 79 §14 (AB 759), operative July 1, 1991.

Prior Law: Former Prob C §9838, similar to the present section, was added Stats 1987 ch 923 §93, operative July 1, 1988, and repealed Stats 1990 ch 79 §13, operative July 1, 1991.

§9839. Claim paid for less than full amount

If the personal representative pays a claim for less than its full amount, the personal representative's accounts may be credited only for the amount actually paid. **Leg.H.** Enacted Stats 1990 ch 79 §14 (AB 759), operative July 1, 1991.

Prior Law: Former Prob C §9839, similar to the present section, was added Stats 1987 ch 923 §93, operative July 1, 1988, and repealed Stats 1990 ch 79 §13, operative July 1, 1991.

CHAPTER 10
ACCEPTANCE OF DEED IN LIEU OF FORECLOSURE OR TRUSTEE'S SALE; GRANT OF PARTIAL SATISFACTION OR PARTIAL RECONVEYANCE

Acceptance of deed in lieu of foreclosure or trustee's sale. §9850.
Grant of partial satisfaction or partial reconveyance. §9851.

§9850. Acceptance of deed in lieu of foreclosure or trustee's sale

(a) If it is to the advantage of the estate to accept a deed to property which is subject to a mortgage or deed of trust in lieu of foreclosure of the mortgage or sale under the deed of trust, the personal representative may, after authorization by order of the court and upon such terms and conditions as may be imposed by the court, accept a deed conveying the property to the heirs or devisees of the decedent, subject to administration.

(b) To obtain an order under this section, the personal representative or any interested person shall file a petition showing the advantage to the estate of accepting the deed. Notice of the hearing on the petition shall be given as provided in Section 1220.

(c) The court shall make an order under this section only if the advantage to the estate of accepting the deed is shown by clear and convincing evidence. **Leg.H.** Enacted Stats 1990 ch 79 §14 (AB 759), operative July 1, 1991.

Prior Law: Former Prob C §9850, similar to the present section, was added Stats 1987 ch 923 §93, operative July 1, 1988, and repealed Stats 1990 ch 79 §13, operative July 1, 1991.

§9851. Grant of partial satisfaction or partial reconveyance

(a) Except as provided in subdivision (c), if it is to the advantage of the estate for the personal representative to give a partial satisfaction of a mortgage or to cause a partial reconveyance to be executed by a trustee under a trust deed held by the estate, the personal representative may, after authorization by order of the court and upon such terms and conditions as may be imposed by the court, give the partial satisfaction or cause the partial reconveyance to be executed by the trustee.

(b) To obtain an order under this section, the personal representative or any interested person shall file a petition showing the advantage to the estate of giving the partial satisfaction or causing the partial reconveyance. Notice of the hearing on the petition shall be given as provided in Section 1220.

(c) No authorization by the court is necessary for the personal representative to give a partial satisfaction of a mortgage or to cause a partial reconveyance to be executed by a trustee under a deed of trust held by the estate if the partial satisfaction or partial reconveyance is executed pursuant to the terms of the mortgage or deed of trust held by the estate. **Leg.H.** Enacted Stats 1990 ch 79 §14 (AB 759), operative July 1, 1991.

Prior Law: Former Prob C §9851, similar to the present section, was added Stats 1987 ch 923 §93, operative July 1, 1988, and repealed Stats 1990 ch 79 §13, operative July 1, 1991.
(a) Former Prob C §718.7, as added Stats 1939 ch 119 §1.
(b) Former Prob C §9851, as added Stats 1987 ch 923 §93.

CHAPTER 11
CONVEYANCE OR TRANSFER OF PROPERTY CLAIMED TO BELONG TO DECEDENT OR OTHER PERSON [REPEALED]

§9860. [Section repealed 2002]

Leg.H. Enacted Stats 1990 ch 79 §14 (AB 759), operative July 1, 1991. Repealed Stats 2001 ch 49 §4 (SB 669). See Prob C §850.

Prior Law: Former Prob C §9860, similar to present Prob C §850, was added Stats 1987 ch 923 §93, operative July 1, 1988, and repealed Stats 1990 ch 79 §13, operative July 1, 1991.

§9861. [Section repealed 2002]

Leg.H. Enacted Stats 1990 ch 79 §14 (AB 759), operative July 1, 1991. Amended Stats 1994 ch 806 §31 (AB 3686). Repealed Stats 2001 ch 49 §4 (SB 669). See Prob C §851.

Prior Law: Former Prob C §9861, similar to present Prob C §851, was added Stats 1987 ch 923 §93, operative July 1, 1988, and repealed Stats 1990 ch 79 §13, operative July 1, 1991.

§9862. [Section repealed 2002]

Leg.H. Enacted Stats 1990 ch 79 §14 (AB 759), operative July 1, 1991. Repealed Stats 2001 ch 49 §4 (SB 669). See Prob C §852.

Prior Law: Former Prob C §9862, similar to present Prob C §852, was added Stats 1987 ch 923 §93, operative July 1, 1988, and repealed Stats 1990 ch 79 §13, operative July 1, 1991.

§9864. [Section repealed 2002]

Leg.H. Enacted Stats 1990 ch 79 §14 (AB 759), operative July 1, 1991. Repealed Stats 2001 ch 49 §4 (SB 669). See Prob C §853.

Prior Law: Former Prob C §9864, similar to present Prob C §853, was added Stats 1987 ch 923 §93, operative July 1, 1988, and repealed Stats 1990 ch 79 §13, operative July 1, 1991.

§9865. [Section repealed 2002]

Leg.H. Enacted Stats 1990 ch 79 §14 (AB 759), operative July 1, 1991. Repealed Stats 2001 ch 49 §4 (SB 669). See Prob C §854.

Prior Law: Former Prob C §9865, similar to present Prob C §854, was added Stats 1987 ch 923 §93, operative July 1, 1988, and repealed Stats 1990 ch 79 §13, operative July 1, 1991.

§9866. [Section repealed 2002]

Leg.H. Enacted Stats 1990 ch 79 §14 (AB 759), operative July 1, 1991. Repealed Stats 2001 ch 49 §4 (SB 669). The repealed section related to denial of petition if matter should be determined by civil action.

Prior Law: Former Prob C §9866, similar to the repealed section, was added Stats 1987 ch 923 §93, operative July 1, 1988, and repealed Stats 1990 ch 79 §13, operative July 1, 1991.

§9867. [Section repealed 2002]

Leg.H. Enacted Stats 1990 ch 79 §14 (AB 759), operative July 1, 1991. Repealed Stats 2001 ch 49 §4 (SB 669). See Prob C §856.

Prior Law: Former Prob C §9867, similar to present Prob C §856, was added Stats 1987 ch 923 §93, operative July 1, 1988, and repealed Stats 1990 ch 79 §13, operative July 1, 1991.

§9868. [Section repealed 2002]

Leg.H. Enacted Stats 1990 ch 79 §14 (AB 759), operative July 1, 1991. Repealed Stats 2001 ch 49 §4 (SB 669). See Prob C §857.

Prior Law: Former Prob C §9868, similar to present Prob C §857, was added Stats 1987 ch 923 §93, operative July 1, 1988, and repealed Stats 1990 ch 79 §13, operative July 1, 1991.

§9869. [Section repealed 2002]

Leg.H. Added Stats 1994 ch 806 §32 (AB 3686). Repealed Stats 2001 ch 49 §4 (SB 669). See Prob C §859.

CHAPTER 12
PURCHASE OF CLAIMS OR ESTATE PROPERTY BY PERSONAL REPRESENTATIVE OR PERSONAL REPRESENTATIVE'S ATTORNEY

Prohibition against purchase of estate property or claim against estate. §9880.
Purchase with consent of heirs or devisees. §9881.
Purchase where authorized by will. §9882.
Petition for order under Section 9881 or 9882. §9883.
Purchase pursuant to contract of decedent to sell. §9884.
Option to purchase given in will. §9885.

§9880. Prohibition against purchase of estate property or claim against estate

Except as provided in this chapter, neither the personal representative nor the personal representative's attorney may do any of the following:

(a) Purchase any property of the estate or any claim against the estate, directly or indirectly.

(b) Be interested in any such purchase. **Leg.H.** Enacted Stats 1990 ch 79 §14 (AB 759), operative July 1, 1991.

§9881. Purchase with consent of heirs or devisees

Upon a petition filed under Section 9883, the court may make an order under this section authorizing the personal representative or the personal representative's attorney to purchase property of the estate if all of the following requirements are satisfied:

(a) Written consent to the purchase is signed by (1) each known heir whose interest in the estate would be affected by the proposed purchase and (2) each known devisee whose interest in the estate would be affected by the proposed purchase.

(b) The written consents are filed with the court.

(c) The purchase is shown to be to the advantage of the estate. **Leg.H.** Enacted Stats 1990 ch 79 §14 (AB 759), operative July 1, 1991.

Prior Law: Former Prob C §9881, similar to the present section, was added Stats 1987 ch 923 §93, operative July 1, 1988, and repealed Stats 1990 ch 79 §13, operative July 1, 1991.

§9882. Purchase where authorized by will

Upon a petition filed under Section 9883, the court may make an order under this section authorizing the personal representative or the personal representative's attorney to purchase property of the estate if the will of the decedent authorizes the personal representative or the personal representative's attorney to purchase the property. **Leg.H.** Enacted Stats 1990 ch 79 §14 (AB 759), operative July 1, 1991.

Prior Law: Former Prob C §9882, similar to the present section, was added Stats 1987 ch 923 §93, operative July 1, 1988, and repealed Stats 1990 ch 79 §13, operative July 1, 1991.

(a) Former Prob C §583, as amended Stats 1961 ch 821 §1, Stats 1963 ch 338 §1.

(b) Former Prob C §9882, as added Stats 1987 ch 923 §93.

(c) Former CCP §§1576, 1617.

(d) Probate Act of 1851 §§193, 220 (Stats 1851 ch 124 §§193, 220.).

(e) Stats 1850 ch 129 §§194, 221.

§9883. Petition for order under Section 9881 or 9882

(a) The personal representative may file a petition requesting that the court make an order under Section 9881 or 9882. The petition shall set forth the facts upon which the request for the order is based.

(b) If court confirmation of the sale is required, the court may make its order under Section 9881 or 9882 at the time of the confirmation.

(c) Notice of the hearing on the petition shall be given as provided in Section 1220 to all of the following persons:

(1) Each person listed in Section 1220.

(2) Each known heir whose interest in the estate would be affected by the proposed purchase.

(3) Each known devisee whose interest in the estate would be affected by the proposed purchase.

(d) If the court is satisfied that the purchase should be authorized, the court shall make an order authorizing the purchase upon the terms and conditions specified in the order, and the personal representative may execute a conveyance or transfer according to the terms of the order. Unless otherwise provided in the will or in the order of the court, the sale of the property shall be made in the same manner as the sale of other estate property of the same nature. **Leg.H.** Enacted Stats 1990 ch 79 §14 (AB 759), operative July 1, 1991.

Prior Law: Former Prob C §9883, similar to the present section, was added Stats 1987 ch 923 §93, operative July 1, 1988, and repealed Stats 1990 ch 79 §13, operative July 1, 1991.

§9884. Purchase pursuant to contract of decedent to sell

This chapter does not prohibit the purchase of property of the estate by the personal representative or the personal representative's attorney pursuant to a contract in writing made during the lifetime of the decedent if the contract is one that can be specifically enforced and the requirements of Part 19 (commencing with Section 850) of Division 2 are satisfied. **Leg.H.** Enacted Stats 1990 ch 79 §14 (AB 759), operative July 1, 1991. Amended Stats 2003 ch 32 §9 (AB 167).

Prior Law: Former Prob C §9884, similar to the present section, was added Stats 1987 ch 923 §93, operative July 1, 1988, and repealed Stats 1990 ch 79 §13, operative July 1, 1991.

§9885. Option to purchase given in will

This chapter does not prevent the exercise by the personal representative or the personal representative's attorney of an option to purchase property of the estate given in the will of the decedent if the requirements of Chapter 17 (commencing with Section 9980) are satisfied. **Leg.H.** Enacted Stats 1990 ch 79 §14 (AB 759), operative July 1, 1991.

Prior Law: Former Prob C §9885, similar to the present section, was added Stats 1987 ch 923 §93, operative July 1, 1988, and repealed Stats 1990 ch 79 §13, operative July 1, 1991.

CHAPTER 13
DEDICATION OR CONVEYANCE TO GOVERNMENTAL ENTITY; EASEMENTS AND ACCESS RIGHTS

Dedication or conveyance of real property to governmental entity; Dedication or conveyance of easement; Conveyance or release of access rights. §9900.
Petition; Notice of hearing. §9901.

§9900. Dedication or conveyance of real property to governmental entity; Dedication or conveyance of easement; Conveyance or release of access rights

If it is to the advantage of the estate and in the best interest of the interested persons, the personal representative, after authorization by order of the court obtained under this chapter and upon such terms and conditions as the court may prescribe, may do any of the following either with or without consideration:

(a) Dedicate or convey real property of the estate for any purpose to any of the following:

(1) This state or any public entity in this state.

(2) The United States or any agency or instrumentality of the United States.

(b) Dedicate or convey an easement over real property of the estate to any person for any purpose.

(c) Convey, release, or relinquish to this state or any public entity in this state any access rights to any street, highway, or freeway from any real property of the estate.

(d) Consent as a lienholder to a dedication, conveyance, release, or relinquishment under subdivision (a), (b), or (c) by the owner of property subject to the lien. **Leg.H.** Enacted Stats 1990 ch 79 §14 (AB 759), operative July 1, 1991.

Prior Law: Former Prob C §9900, similar to the present section, was added Stats 1987 ch 923 §93, operative July 1, 1988, and repealed Stats 1990 ch 79 §13, operative July 1, 1991.

§9901. Petition; Notice of hearing

(a) The personal representative or any interested person may file a petition for an order under this chapter.

(b) Notice of the hearing on the petition shall be given as provided in Section 1220. **Leg.H.** Enacted Stats 1990 ch 79 §14 (AB 759), operative July 1, 1991.

Prior Law: Former Prob C §9901, similar to the present section, was added Stats 1987 ch 923 §93, operative July 1, 1988, and repealed Stats 1990 ch 79 §13, operative July 1, 1991.

CHAPTER 14
EXCHANGE OF PROPERTY

Court authorization for exchange. §9920.
Petition. §9921.
Notice of hearing. §9922.
Error does not invalidate proceedings. §9923.

§9920. Court authorization for exchange

If it is to the advantage of the estate to exchange property of the estate for other property, the personal representative may, after authorization by order of court obtained under this chapter and upon such terms and conditions as may be prescribed by the court, exchange the property for the other property. The terms and conditions prescribed by the court may include the payment or receipt of part cash by the personal representative. **Leg.H.** Enacted Stats 1990 ch 79 §14 (AB 759), operative July 1, 1991.

Prior Law: Former Prob C §9920, similar to the present section, was added Stats 1987 ch 923 §93, operative July 1, 1988, and repealed Stats 1990 ch 79 §13, operative July 1, 1991.

§9921. Petition

To obtain an order under this chapter, the personal representative or any interested person shall file a petition containing all of the following:

(a) A description of the property.

(b) The terms and conditions of the proposed exchange.

(c) A showing that the proposed exchange is to the advantage of the estate. **Leg.H.** Enacted Stats 1990 ch 79 §14 (AB 759), operative July 1, 1991.

Prior Law: Former Prob C §9921, similar to the present section, was added Stats 1987 ch 923 §93, operative July 1, 1988, and repealed Stats 1990 ch 79 §13, operative July 1, 1991.

§9922. Notice of hearing

(a) Except as provided in subdivision (b), notice of the hearing on the petition shall be given as provided in Section 1220.

(b) If the petition is for authorization to exchange securities as defined in Section 10200 for different securities, the court, upon a showing of good cause, may order that the notice be given for a shorter period or that the notice be dispensed with. The order provided by this subdivision may be made ex parte. **Leg.H.** Enacted Stats 1990 ch 79 §14 (AB 759), operative July 1, 1991.

Prior Law: Former Prob C §9922, similar to the present section, was added Stats 1987 ch 923 §93, operative July 1, 1988, and repealed Stats 1990 ch 79 §13, operative July 1, 1991.

§9923. Error does not invalidate proceedings

No omission, error, or irregularity in the proceedings under this chapter shall impair or invalidate the proceedings or the exchange made pursuant to an order made under this chapter. **Leg.H.** Enacted Stats 1990 ch 79 §14 (AB 759), operative July 1, 1991.

Prior Law: Former Prob C §9923, similar to the present section, was added Stats 1987 ch 923 §93, operative July 1, 1988, and repealed Stats 1990 ch 79 §13, operative July 1, 1991.

CHAPTER 15
LEASES

Effect of including option to purchase in lease. §9940.
Leases permitted without court authorization. §9941.
Court authorization for lease; Proposed lease that includes option to purchase. §9942.
Petition for order. §9943.
Notice of hearing. §9944.
Hearing and order. §9945.
Terms and conditions of leases. §9946.
Maximum term of lease. §9947.
Execution and effectiveness of lease. §9948.

§9940. Effect of including option to purchase in lease

For the purpose of this chapter:

(a) "Lease" includes, without limitation, a lease that includes an option to purchase real property of the estate.

(b) If a lease gives the lessee the right to extend the term of the lease, the length of the term shall be considered as though the right to extend had been exercised. **Leg.H.** Enacted Stats 1990 ch 79 §14 (AB 759), operative July 1, 1991.

Prior Law: Former Prob C §9940, similar to the present section, was added Stats 1987 ch 923 §93, operative July 1, 1988, and repealed Stats 1990 ch 79 §13 (AB 759), operative July 1, 1991.

§9941. Leases permitted without court authorization

If it is to the advantage of the estate, the personal representative may lease, as lessor, real property of the estate without authorization of the court in either of the following cases:

(a) Where the rental does not exceed five thousand dollars ($5,000) a month and the term does not exceed one year.

(b) Where the lease is from month to month, regardless of the amount of the rental. **Leg.H.** Enacted Stats 1990 ch 79 §14 (AB 759), operative July 1, 1991. Amended Stats 1990 ch 710 §25 (SB 1775), operative July 1, 1991.

Prior Law: Former Prob C §9941, similar to the present section, was added Stats 1987 ch 923 §93, operative July 1, 1988, and repealed Stats 1990 ch 79 §13 (AB 759), operative July 1, 1991.

§9942. Court authorization for lease; Proposed lease that includes option to purchase

(a) The personal representative may lease, as lessor, real property of the estate after authorization by order of court obtained under this chapter upon a showing that the proposed lease is to the advantage of the estate.

(b) If the proposed lease includes an option to purchase real property of the estate, a petition for an order authorizing the lease shall be filed under this chapter but the applicable provisions for court approval both in this chapter and in Chapter 16 (commencing with Section 9960) apply to the execution of the lease. **Leg.H.** Enacted Stats 1990 ch 79 §14 (AB 759), operative July 1, 1991.

Prior Law: Former Prob C §9942, similar to the present section, was added Stats 1987 ch 923 §93, operative July 1, 1988, and repealed Stats 1990 ch 79 §13 (AB 759), operative July 1, 1991.

§9943. Petition for order

(a) To obtain an order under this chapter, the personal representative or any interested person shall file a petition containing all of the following:

(1) A general description of the real property proposed to be leased.

(2) The term, rental, and general conditions of the proposed lease.

(3) A showing that the proposed lease is to the advantage of the estate.

(b) If the lease is proposed to be for a term longer than 10 years, the petition shall also state facts showing the need for the longer lease and its advantage to the estate and its benefit to the interested persons. **Leg.H.** Enacted Stats 1990 ch 79 §14 (AB 759), operative July 1, 1991.

Prior Law: Former Prob C §9943, similar to the present section, was added Stats 1987 ch 923 §93, operative July 1, 1988, and repealed Stats 1990 ch 79 §13 (AB 759), operative July 1, 1991.

§9944. Notice of hearing

(a) Notice of the hearing on the petition shall be given as provided in Section 1220 and posted as provided in Section 1230.

(b) Notice of the hearing on the petition also shall be given as provided in Section 10300, but this notice is not required if the will authorizes or directs the personal representative to lease or sell property.

(c) If the lease is proposed to be for a term longer than 10 years, in addition to the notice required by subdivision (a), notice of the hearing shall be given as provided in Section 1220 to all of the following persons:

(1) Each known heir whose interest in the estate would be affected by the proposed lease.

(2) Each known devisee whose interest in the estate would be affected by the proposed lease. **Leg.H.** Enacted Stats 1990 ch 79 §14 (AB 759), operative July 1, 1991.

Prior Law: Former Prob C §9944, similar to the present section, was added Stats 1987 ch 923 §93, operative July 1, 1988, and repealed Stats 1990 ch 79 §13 (AB 759), operative July 1, 1991.

§9945. Hearing and order

(a) At the hearing, the court shall entertain and consider any other offer made in good faith at the hearing to lease the same property on more favorable terms.

(b) If the court is satisfied that it will be to the advantage of the estate, and, if the lease is for more than 10 years, that it is to the benefit of interested persons, the court shall make an order authorizing the personal representative to make the lease to the person on the terms and conditions stated in the order. The court shall not make an order authorizing the personal representative to make the lease to any person other than the lessee named in the petition unless the offer made at the hearing is acceptable to the personal representative. **Leg.H.** Enacted Stats 1990 ch 79 §14 (AB 759), operative July 1, 1991.

Prior Law: Former Prob C §9945, similar to the present section, was added Stats 1987 ch 923 §93, operative July 1, 1988, and repealed Stats 1990 ch 79 §13 (AB 759), operative July 1, 1991.

§9946. Terms and conditions of leases

(a) Subject to Section 9947, an order authorizing the execution of a lease shall set forth the minimum rental or royalty or both and the period of the lease.

(b) The order may authorize other terms and conditions of the lease, including, with respect to a lease for the purpose of exploration for or production or removal of minerals, oil, gas, or other hydrocarbon substances, or geothermal energy, any one or more of the following provisions:

(1) A provision for the payment of rental and royalty to a depositary.

(2) A provision for the appointment of a common agent to represent the interests of all the lessors.

(3) A provision for the payment of a compensatory royalty in lieu of rental and in lieu of drilling and producing operations on the land covered by the lease.

(4) A provision empowering the lessee to enter into any agreement authorized by Section 3301 of the Public Resources Code with respect to the land covered by the lease.

(5) A provision for a community oil lease or a pooling or unitization by the lessee.

(c) If the lease covers additional property owned by other persons or an undivided or other interest of the decedent less than the entire ownership in the property, the order may authorize the lease to provide for division of rental and royalty in the proportion that the land or interest of each owner bears to the total area of the land or total interests covered by the lease. **Leg.H.** Enacted Stats 1990 ch 79 §14 (AB 759), operative July 1, 1991.

Prior Law: Former Prob C §9946, similar to the present section, was added Stats 1987 ch 923 §93, operative July 1, 1988, and repealed Stats 1990 ch 79 §13 (AB 759), operative July 1, 1991.

§9947. Maximum term of lease

(a) Except as provided in this section, the term of the lease shall be for such period as the court may authorize.

(b) Except as provided in subdivision (c), the court shall not authorize a lease for longer than 10 years if any heir or devisee who has an interest in the property to be leased objects at the hearing.

(c) If the lease is for the purpose of exploration for or production or removal of minerals, oil, gas, or other hydrocarbon substances, or geothermal energy, the court may authorize that the lease be for a fixed period and any of the following:

(1) So long thereafter as minerals, oil, gas, or other hydrocarbon substances or geothermal energy are produced in paying quantities from the property leased or mining or drilling operations are conducted thereon.

(2) If the lease provides for the payment of a compensatory royalty, so long thereafter as such compensatory royalty is paid.

(3) If the land covered by the lease is included in an agreement authorized by Section 3301 of the Public Resources Code, so long thereafter as oil, gas, or other hydrocarbon substances are produced in paying quantities from any of the lands included in any such agreement or drilling operations are conducted thereon. **Leg.H.** Enacted Stats 1990 ch 79 §14 (AB 759), operative July 1, 1991.

Prior Law: Former Prob C §9947, similar to the present section, was added Stats 1987 ch 923 §93, operative July 1, 1988, and repealed Stats 1990 ch 79 §13 (AB 759), operative July 1, 1991.

§9948. Execution and effectiveness of lease

(a) The personal representative shall execute, acknowledge, and deliver the lease as directed, setting forth therein that it is made by authority of the order, giving the date of the order.

(b) A lease made pursuant to an order obtained under this chapter is effectual to lease the premises described in the order at the rent, for the term, and upon the terms and conditions prescribed in the order.

(c) Jurisdiction of the court in proceedings under this code concerning the administration of the estate of the decedent vests the court with jurisdiction to make the order for the lease. This jurisdiction shall conclusively inure to the benefit of the lessee and the lessee's heirs and assigns.

(d) No omission, error, or irregularity in the proceedings under this chapter shall impair or invalidate the proceedings or the lease made pursuant to an order made under this chapter. **Leg.H.** Enacted Stats 1990 ch 79 §14 (AB 759), operative July 1, 1991.

Prior Law: Former Prob C §9948, similar to the present section, was added Stats 1987 ch 923 §93, operative July 1, 1988, and repealed Stats 1990 ch 79 §13 (AB 759), operative July 1, 1991.

CHAPTER 16
GRANTING OPTION TO PURCHASE REAL PROPERTY

Authority to grant option. §9960.
Petition. §9961.
Minimum purchase price. §9962.
Notice of hearing. §9963.
Order. §9964.
Expiration of record of recorded option. §9965.
Error does not invalidate proceedings. §9966.

§9960. Authority to grant option

After authorization by order of court obtained under this chapter, the personal representative may grant an option to purchase real property of the estate for a period within or beyond the period of administration. **Leg.H.** Enacted Stats 1990 ch 79 §14 (AB 759), operative July 1, 1991.

Prior Law: Former Prob C §9960, similar to the present section, was added Stats 1987 ch 923 §93, operative July 1, 1988, and repealed Stats 1990 ch 79 §13, operative July 1, 1991.

§9961. Petition

To obtain an order under this chapter, the personal representative shall file a petition containing all of the following:

(a) A description of the real property.
(b) The terms and conditions of the proposed option.
(c) A showing that granting the option is to the advantage of the estate. **Leg.H.** Enacted Stats 1990 ch 79 §14 (AB 759), operative July 1, 1991.

Prior Law: Former Prob C §9961, similar to the present section, was added Stats 1987 ch 923 §93, operative July 1, 1988, and repealed Stats 1990 ch 79 §13, operative July 1, 1991.

§9962. Minimum purchase price

The purchase price of the real property subject to the option shall be at least 90 percent of the appraised value of the real property. The appraisal shall be made in the manner provided in subdivision (c) of Section 10309 within one year prior to the hearing of the petition. **Leg.H.** Enacted Stats 1990 ch 79 §14 (AB 759), operative July 1, 1991.

Prior Law: Former Prob C §9962, similar to the present section, was added Stats 1987 ch 923 §93, operative July 1, 1988, and repealed Stats 1990 ch 79 §13, operative July 1, 1991.

§9963. Notice of hearing

Notice of the hearing on the petition shall be posted as provided in Section 1230 and given as provided in Section 1220 to all of the following persons:

(a) Each person listed in Section 1220.
(b) Each known heir whose interest in the estate would be affected by the granting of the option.
(c) Each known devisee whose interest in the estate would be affected by the granting of the option. **Leg.H.** Enacted Stats 1990 ch 79 §14 (AB 759), operative July 1, 1991.

Prior Law: Former Prob C §9963, similar to the present section, was added Stats 1987 ch 923 §93, operative July 1, 1988, and repealed Stats 1990 ch 79 §13, operative July 1, 1991.

§9964. Order

(a) The court shall make an order authorizing the personal representative to grant the option upon the terms and conditions stated in the order if the court is satisfied as to all of the following:

(1) Good reason exists to grant the option and granting the option will be to the advantage of the estate.

(2) It does not appear that a higher offer with respect to the purchase price of the real property subject to the option may be obtained. An offer is a higher offer with respect to purchase price only if the offer satisfies the requirements of Section 10311 governing increased bids in real property sales.

(3) It does not appear that a better offer with respect to the terms of the option may be obtained. An offer is a better offer with respect to the terms of the option only if the offer is materially more advantageous to the estate.

(b) A higher offer made either for cash or on credit, whether on the same or different credit terms, or a better offer, shall be considered only if the personal representative informs the court in person or by counsel, before the court makes its order authorizing the granting of the option, that the offer is acceptable. **Leg.H.** Enacted Stats 1990 ch 79 §14 (AB 759), operative July 1, 1991.

Prior Law: Former Prob C §9964, similar to the present section, was added Stats 1987 ch 923 §93, operative July 1, 1988, and repealed Stats 1990 ch 79 §13, operative July 1, 1991.

§9965. Expiration of record of recorded option

An option granted pursuant to an order made under this chapter, whether within or beyond the administration of the estate, is subject to Chapter 4 (commencing with Section 884.010) of Title 5 of Part 2 of Division 2 of the Civil Code. **Leg.H.** Enacted Stats 1990 ch 79 §14 (AB 759), operative July 1, 1991.

Prior Law: Former Prob C §9965, similar to the present section, was added Stats 1987 ch 923 §93, operative July 1, 1988, and repealed Stats 1990 ch 79 §13, operative July 1, 1991.

§9966. Error does not invalidate proceedings

No omission, error, or irregularity in the proceedings under this chapter shall impair or invalidate the proceedings or the granting of an option

CHAPTER 17
OPTION TO PURCHASE GIVEN IN WILL

Option to purchase given in will. §9980.
Order; Petition; Notice of hearing. §9981.
Protection of rights of creditors. §9982.
Error does not invalidate proceedings. §9983.

§9980. Option to purchase given in will

(a) Where an option to purchase real or personal property is given in a will, the person given the option has the right to exercise the option at any time within the time limits provided by the will. For the purposes of this section, if a time limitation in the will is measured from the death of the testator, that time shall be extended by the period between the testator's death and the issuance of letters testamentary or of administration with the will annexed or by six months, whichever is the shorter period.

(b) If the will does not provide a time limit for exercise of the option, the time limit is one year from the death of the decedent.

(c) Subject to subdivision (b), if the option given in the will is exercisable under the terms of the will after the time that the estate would otherwise be closed, the property subject to the option shall be distributed subject to the option. **Leg.H.** Enacted Stats 1990 ch 79 §14 (AB 759), operative July 1, 1991.

Prior Law: Former Prob C §9980, similar to the present section, was added Stats 1987 ch 923 §93, operative July 1, 1988, and repealed Stats 1990 ch 79 §13, operative July 1, 1991.

§9981. Order; Petition; Notice of hearing

(a) Where an option to purchase real or personal property is given in a will admitted to probate, the court may make an order under this chapter directing the personal representative to transfer or convey the property to the person given the option upon compliance with the terms and conditions stated in the will.

(b) The personal representative or the person given the option to purchase the property may file a petition for an order pursuant to this chapter.

(c) Notice of the hearing on the petition shall be given as provided in Section 1220. **Leg.H.** Enacted Stats 1990 ch 79 §14 (AB 759), operative July 1, 1991.

Prior Law: Former Prob C §9981, similar to the present section, was added Stats 1987 ch 923 §93, operative July 1, 1988, and repealed Stats 1990 ch 79 §13, operative July 1, 1991.

§9982. Protection of rights of creditors

The court shall not make an order under this chapter unless one of the following requirements is satisfied:

(a) The court determines that the rights of creditors will not be impaired by the making of the order.

(b) The court requires a bond in an amount and with such surety as the court shall direct or approve. **Leg.H.** Enacted Stats 1990 ch 79 §14 (AB 759), operative July 1, 1991.

Prior Law: Former Prob C §9982, similar to the present section, was added Stats 1987 ch 923 §93, operative July 1, 1988, and repealed Stats 1990 ch 79 §13, operative July 1, 1991.

§9983. Error does not invalidate proceedings

No omission, error, or irregularity in the proceedings under this chapter shall impair or invalidate the proceedings or the transfer or conveyance made pursuant to an order made under this chapter. **Leg.H.** Enacted Stats 1990 ch 79 §14 (AB 759), operative July 1, 1991.

Prior Law: Former Prob C §9983, similar to the present section, was added Stats 1987 ch 923 §93, operative July 1, 1988, and repealed Stats 1990 ch 79 §13, operative July 1, 1991.

CHAPTER 18
SALES

Article 1. General Provisions.
Article 2. Contract With Agent, Broker, or Auctioneer.
Article 3. Compensation of Agent, Broker, or Auctioneer.
Article 4. Special Provisions Applicable to Particular Types of Property.
Article 5. Sale of Personal Property.
Article 6. Sale of Real Property.
Article 7. Vacating Sale for Purchaser's Default; Liability of Defaulting Purchaser for Damages.
Article 8. Application of Sale Proceeds of Encumbered Property; Sale to Lienholder.
Article 9. Damages and Recovery of Property.

ARTICLE 1
General Provisions

When estate property may be sold. §10000.
Court order requiring sale of property. §10001.
Directions in will as to mode of selling or property to be sold. §10002.
Discretion of personal representative as to property to be sold and mode of selling. §10003.
Sale of assets, whether real or personal, as a unit. §10004.
Sale for more or less than appraised value. §10005.
Cotenant's consent to sale. §10006.

§10000. When estate property may be sold

Subject to the limitations, conditions, and requirements of this chapter, the personal representative may sell real or personal property of the estate in any of the following cases:

(a) Where the sale is necessary to pay debts, devises, family allowance, expenses of administration, or taxes.

(b) Where the sale is to the advantage of the estate and in the best interest of the interested persons.

(c) Where the property is directed by the will to be sold.

(d) Where authority is given in the will to sell the property. **Leg.H.** Enacted Stats 1990 ch 79 §14 (AB 759), operative July 1, 1991.

Prior Law: Former Prob C §10000, similar to the present section, was added Stats 1987 ch 923 §93, operative July 1, 1988, and repealed Stats 1990 ch 79 §13, operative July 1, 1991.

§10001. Court order requiring sale of property

(a) If the personal representative neglects or refuses to sell the property, any interested person may petition the court for an order requiring the personal representative to sell real or personal property of the estate in any of the following cases:

(1) Where the sale is necessary to pay debts, devises, family allowance, expenses of administration, or taxes.

(2) Where the sale is to the advantage of the estate and in the best interest of the interested persons.

(3) Where the property is directed by the will to be sold.

(b) Notice of the hearing on the petition shall be given as provided in Section 1220.

(c) Notice of the hearing on the petition also shall be given to the personal representative by citation served at least five days before the hearing. **Leg.H.** Enacted Stats 1990 ch 79 §14 (AB 759), operative July 1, 1991.

Prior Law: Former Prob C §10001, similar to the present section, was added Stats 1987 ch 923 §93, operative July 1, 1988, and repealed Stats 1990 ch 79 §13, operative July 1, 1991.

§10002. Directions in will as to mode of selling or property to be sold

(a) Subject to subdivision (b), if directions are given in the will as to the mode of selling or the particular property to be sold, the personal representative shall comply with those directions.

(b) If the court determines that it would be to the advantage of the estate and in the best interest of the interested persons, the court may make an order relieving the personal representative of the duty to comply with the directions in the will. The order shall specify the mode and the terms and conditions of selling or the particular property to be sold, or both. The personal representative or any interested person may file a petition for an order under this subdivision. Notice of the hearing on the petition shall be given as provided in Section 1220. **Leg.H.** Enacted Stats 1990 ch 79 §14 (AB 759), operative July 1, 1991.

Prior Law: Former Prob C §10002, similar to the present section, was added Stats 1987 ch 923 §93, operative July 1, 1988, and repealed Stats 1990 ch 79 §13, operative July 1, 1991.

§10003. Discretion of personal representative as to property to be sold and mode of selling

Subject to Part 4 (commencing with Section 21400) of Division 11 and to Sections 10001 and 10002, if estate property is required or permitted to be sold, the personal representative may:

(a) Use discretion as to which property to sell first.

(b) Sell the entire interest of the estate in the property or any lesser interest therein.

(c) Sell the property either at public auction or private sale. **Leg.H.** Enacted Stats 1990 ch 79 §14 (AB 759), operative July 1, 1991.

Prior Law: Former Prob C §10003, similar to the present section, was added Stats 1987 ch 923 §93, operative July 1, 1988, amended Stats 1988 ch 1199 §89, operative July 1, 1989, and repealed Stats 1990 ch 79 §13, operative July 1, 1991.

§10004. Sale of assets, whether real or personal, as a unit

(a) Where the personal representative determines in his or her discretion that, by use or relationship, any assets of the estate, whether real or personal, constitute a unit for purposes of sale, the personal representative may cause the property to be appraised as a unit.

(b) Whether or not the property is appraised as a unit, the personal representative may sell all the assets described in subdivision (a) as a unit and under one bid if the court finds the sale of the assets as a unit to be to the advantage of the estate.

(c) No private sale of the assets as a unit may be made for less than 90 percent of the sum of the appraised values of the personal property and the sum of the appraised values of the real property, appraised separately, or for less than 90 percent of the appraised value if appraised as a unit.

(d) If the assets to be sold as a unit include any real property, the sale shall be made in the manner provided for the sale of real property, and the bid and sale are subject to the limitations and restrictions established for the sale of real property. If the assets to be sold as a unit are entirely personal property, the property shall be sold in the manner provided for the sale of personal property. **Leg.H.** Enacted Stats 1990 ch 79 §14 (AB 759), operative July 1, 1991.

Prior Law: Former Prob C §10004, similar to the present section, was added Stats 1987 ch 923 §93, operative July 1, 1988, and repealed Stats 1990 ch 79 §13, operative July 1, 1991.

§10005. Sale for more or less than appraised value

(a) If any property in the estate is sold for more than the appraised value, the personal representative shall account for the proceeds of sale, including the excess over the appraised value.

(b) If any property in the estate is sold for less than the appraised value and the sale has been made in accordance with law, the personal representative is not responsible for the loss. **Leg.H.** Enacted Stats 1990 ch 79 §14 (AB 759), operative July 1, 1991.

Prior Law: Former Prob C §10005, similar to the present section, was added Stats 1987 ch 923 §93, operative July 1, 1988, amended Stats 1988 ch 1199 §89.5, operative July 1, 1989, and repealed Stats 1990 ch 79 §13, operative July 1, 1991.

§10006. Cotenant's consent to sale

If property in the estate is to be sold as an undivided interest in a cotenancy, the other cotenants may file in the estate proceeding written consent to have their interests sold pursuant to this chapter. Thereafter, the court's orders made pursuant to this chapter are as binding on the consenting cotenants as on the personal representative. **Leg.H.** Enacted Stats 1990 ch 79 §14 (AB 759), operative July 1, 1991.

ARTICLE 2
Contract With Agent, Broker, or Auctioneer

Contract with agent or broker. §10150.
Contract with auctioneer. §10151.

§10150. Contract with agent or broker

(a) The personal representative may enter into a written contract with either or both of the following:

(1) A licensed real estate broker to secure a purchaser for any real property of the estate. The broker may associate other licensed real estate brokers for this purpose, including use of a multiple listing service as defined in Section 1087 of the Civil Code.

(2) One or more agents or brokers to secure a purchaser for any personal property of the estate. If the particular property to be sold or the particular manner of sale requires that the agent or broker be licensed, the contract may be made only with an agent or broker that is so licensed.

(b) The contract may provide for payment of a fee, commission, or other compensation out of the proceeds of sale, but the contract is binding and valid as against the estate only for such amount as the court allows pursuant to Article 3 (commencing with Section 10160). No liability of any kind is incurred by the estate under the contract or a sale unless the sale is confirmed by the court, except for the obligations of the estate to the purchaser of personal property as to which title passes pursuant to Section 10259 without court confirmation or approval. The personal representative is not personally liable on the contract by reason of execution of the contract.

(c) The contract may grant an exclusive right to sell property for a period not in excess of 90 days if, prior to execution of the contract granting an exclusive right to sell, the personal representative obtains permission of the court to enter into the contract upon a showing of necessity and advantage to the estate. The court may grant the permission when the personal representative is appointed or at any subsequent time upon ex parte application. The personal representative may execute one or more extensions of the contract granting an exclusive right to sell property, each extension being for a period not to exceed 90 days, if for each extension the personal representative obtains permission of the court upon ex parte application to extend the contract upon a showing of necessity and advantage to the estate of the extension. **Leg.H.** Enacted Stats 1990 ch 79 §14 (AB 759), operative July 1, 1991.

Prior Law: Former Prob C §10150, similar to the present section, was added Stats 1987 ch 923 §93, operative July 1, 1988, and repealed Stats 1990 ch 79 §13, operative July 1, 1991.

§10151. Contract with auctioneer

(a) The personal representative may enter into a written contract with any of the following:

(1) Where the public auction sale will be held in this state, an auctioneer who is qualified to conduct business under Title 2.95 (commencing with Section 1812.600) of Part 4 of Division 3 of the Civil Code.

(2) Where the public auction sale will be held outside this state pursuant to an order made under Section 10254, an auctioneer who is legally permitted in the jurisdiction where the sale will be held to conduct a public auction sale and to secure purchasers by that method for the personal property authorized to be sold by public auction sale in that jurisdiction under the court order.

(b) The contract shall be one that is legally enforceable under the law of the jurisdiction where made.

(c) The contract may provide for payment to the auctioneer of a fee, commission, or other compensation out of the proceeds of sale and for reimbursement of expenses, but the contract is binding and valid as against the estate only for such amounts as the court allows pursuant to Section 10167. No liability of any kind is incurred by the estate under the contract or a sale unless the sale is approved by the court, except for the obligations of the estate to the purchaser of personal property as to which title passes pursuant to Section 10259 without court confirmation or approval. The personal representative is not personally liable on the contract by reason of execution of the contract.

(d) The contract may provide that personal property of two or more estates being administered by the same personal representative may be sold at the same public auction sale. Items of personal property may be sold separately or in a lot with other items from the same estate. A sale pursuant to the contract shall be with reserve. The auctioneer shall comply with the instructions of the personal representative with respect to withdrawal of items, risk of loss, place of delivery, warranties, and other matters. **Leg.H.** Enacted Stats 1990 ch 79 §14 (AB 759), operative July 1, 1991. Amended Stats 2003 ch 32 §10 (AB 167), effective January 1, 2004.

Prior Law: Former Prob C §10151, similar to the present section, was added Stats 1987 ch 923 §93, operative July 1, 1988, and repealed Stats 1990 ch 79 §13, operative July 1, 1991.

ARTICLE 3
Compensation of Agent, Broker, or Auctioneer

Limitation on liability of estate. §10160.
No commission where broker is purchaser. §10160.5.
Compensation and fees to be in reasonable amount determined by court. §10161.
Limitation on compensation of agent or broker producing successful overbidder. §10162.
Compensation where there is no exclusive contract and sale is made to purchaser produced by agent or broker on bid returned to court or on overbid. §10162.3.
Compensation where there is an exclusive contract and no other broker or agent is involved in sale. §10162.5.
Exclusive contract providing that no compensation payable if sale confirmed to particular purchaser named in contract. §10162.6.
Compensation where there is an exclusive contract and sale is made to purchaser produced by another agent or broker on bid returned to court or on overbid. §10162.7.

Compensation where original bid made by purchaser not produced by agent or broker and sale made to overbidder produced by agent or broker. §10163.

Compensation where sale made on increased bid by purchaser not produced by agent or broker. §10164.

Sale made on increased bid by purchaser produced by agent or broker; Compensation where original bid returned to court made by a purchaser produced by another agent or broker; Compensation where another agent or broker holds exclusive right to sell contract. §10165.

Condition of bid that certain amount of bid be paid to agent or broker. §10166.

Compensation and expenses of auctioneer. §10167.

Agreement dividing compensation between cooperating agents and brokers. §10168.

§10160. Limitation on liability of estate

The estate is not liable to an agent, broker, or auctioneer under a contract for the sale of property or for any fee, commission, or other compensation or expenses in connection with a sale of property unless the following requirements are satisfied:

(a) An actual sale is made.

(b) If court confirmation or approval is required, the sale is confirmed or approved by the court as required.

(c) The sale is consummated. **Leg.H.** Enacted Stats 1990 ch 79 §14 (AB 759), operative July 1, 1991.

Prior Law: Former Prob C §10160, similar to the present section, was added Stats 1987 ch 923 §93, operative July 1, 1988, and repealed Stats 1990 ch 79 §13, operative July 1, 1991.

§10160.5. No commission where broker is purchaser

The estate is not liable to an agent or broker under a contract for the sale of property or for any fee, commission, or other compensation or expenses in connection with sale of the property in either of the following cases:

(a) Where the agent or broker, directly or indirectly, is the purchaser of the property.

(b) Where the agent or broker representing the purchaser to whom the sale is confirmed has any interest in the purchaser. **Leg.H.** Enacted Stats 1990 ch 79 §14 (AB 759), operative July 1, 1991.

Prior Law: Former Prob C §10160.5, similar to the present section, was added Stats 1989 ch 544 §10, and repealed Stats 1990 ch 79 §13, operative July 1, 1991.

§10161. Compensation and fees to be in reasonable amount determined by court

(a) Subject to the provisions of this article, whether or not the agent or broker has a contract with the personal representative, the fee, commission, or other compensation of an agent or broker in connection with a sale of property shall be the amount the court, in its discretion, determines to be a reasonable compensation for the services of the agent or broker to the estate.

(b) Unless the agent or broker holds a contract granting an exclusive right to sell the property, an agent or broker is not entitled to any fee, commission, or other compensation for services to the estate in connection with a sale except in the following cases:

(1) Where the agent or broker produces the original bid which is returned to the court for confirmation.

(2) Where the property is sold on an increased bid, made at the time of the hearing on the petition for confirmation, to a purchaser procured by the agent or broker.

(c) If the agent or broker has a contract with the personal representative, the amount of the compensation of the agent or broker in connection with the sale of property shall not exceed the amount provided for in the contract. **Leg.H.** Enacted Stats 1990 ch 79 §14 (AB 759), operative July 1, 1991.

Prior Law: Former Prob C §10161, similar to the present section, was added Stats 1987 ch 923 §93, operative July 1, 1988, and repealed Stats 1990 ch 79 §13, operative July 1, 1991.

§10162. Limitation on compensation of agent or broker producing successful overbidder

(a) Subject to subdivision (b), where the bid returned to the court for confirmation is made by a person who is not represented by an agent or broker and the successful bidder is represented by an agent or broker, the compensation of the agent or broker who procured the purchaser to whom the sale is confirmed shall not exceed one-half of the difference between the amount of the bid in the original return and the amount of the successful bid.

(b) This section does not limit the compensation of the agent or broker who holds a contract under Section 10150 granting him or her the exclusive right to sell the property. **Leg.H.** Enacted Stats 1990 ch 79 §14 (AB 759), operative July 1, 1991.

Prior Law: Former Prob C §10162, similar to the present section, was added Stats 1987 ch 923 §93, operative July 1, 1988, and repealed Stats 1990 ch 79 §13, operative July 1, 1991.

§10162.3. Compensation where there is no exclusive contract and sale is made to purchaser produced by agent or broker on bid returned to court or on overbid

(a) This section applies if all of the following circumstances exist:

(1) There is no agent or broker holding a contract under Section 10150 granting the exclusive right to sell the property.

(2) The bid returned to court for confirmation is made by a purchaser represented by an agent or broker.

(3) The court confirms the sale to that purchaser either on the bid returned to court for confirmation or on an increased bid made at the time of the hearing on the petition for confirmation.

(b) If all the circumstances described in subdivision (a) exist, the court shall allow the agent or broker who procured the purchaser to whom the sale is confirmed the compensation determined under Section 10161 on the full amount for which the sale is confirmed. **Leg.H.** Enacted Stats 1990 ch 79 §14 (AB 759), operative July 1, 1991.

Prior Law: Former Prob C §10162.3, similar to the present section, was added Stats 1987 ch 923 §93, operative July 1, 1988, amended Stats 1989 ch 544 §11, and repealed Stats 1990 ch 79 §13, operative July 1, 1991.

§10162.5. Compensation where there is an exclusive contract and no other broker or agent is involved in sale

Subject to Section 10162.6, where an agent or broker holds a contract under Section 10150 granting the exclusive right to sell the property, the court shall allow to the agent or broker holding the contract the compensation determined under Section 10161 on:

(a) The full amount for which the sale is confirmed in either of the following circumstances:

(1) The bid returned to the court for confirmation is made by a purchaser who is not represented by an agent or broker and the court confirms the sale to that purchaser on that bid.

(2) The bid returned to the court for confirmation is made by a purchaser who is represented by the agent or broker holding the contract and the court confirms the sale to that purchaser on an increased bid made at the time of the hearing on the petition for confirmation.

(b) The amount of the original bid if both of the following circumstances exist:

(1) The bid returned to court for confirmation is made by a purchaser who is not represented by an agent or broker or who is represented by the agent or broker holding a contract under Section 10150 granting the exclusive right to sell the property.

(2) The court confirms the sale on an increased bid, made at the time of the hearing on the petition for confirmation, to a purchaser who was not procured by a bona fide agent or broker. **Leg.H.** Enacted Stats 1990 ch 79 §14 (AB 759), operative July 1, 1991.

Prior Law: Former Prob C §10162.5, similar to the present section, was added Stats 1987 ch 923 §93, operative July 1, 1988, amended Stats 1989 ch 544 §12, and repealed Stats 1990 ch 79 §13, operative July 1, 1991.

§10162.6. Exclusive contract providing that no compensation payable if sale confirmed to particular purchaser named in contract

(a) This section applies if both of the following circumstances exist:

(1) An agent or broker holds a contract under Section 10150 granting the exclusive right to sell the property.

(2) The contract provides that no compensation is payable to the agent or broker holding the contract if sale is confirmed to a particular purchaser named in the contract.

(b) If the court confirms the sale to the purchaser named in the contract, whether on an original bid returned to the court or on an increased bid made at the time of the hearing on the petition for confirmation, the compensation of any agents or brokers involved in the sale is determined as provided in this article, except that no compensation is payable to the agent or broker holding the contract.

(c) If the court confirms the sale to a purchaser other than the person named in the contract, whether on an original bid returned to the court or on an increased bid made at the time of the hearing on the petition for confirmation, the compensation of the agent or broker holding the contract, and of any other agents or brokers involved in the sale, is determined under this article as if the limitation in the contract did not exist. **Leg.H.** Enacted Stats 1990 ch 79 §14 (AB 759), operative July 1, 1991.

§10162.7. Compensation where there is an exclusive contract and sale is made to purchaser produced by another agent or broker on bid returned to court or on overbid

(a) Subject to Section 10162.6, this section applies if all of the following circumstances exist:

(1) There is an agent or broker holding a contract under Section 10150 granting the exclusive right to sell the property.

(2) The bid returned to court for confirmation is made by a purchaser procured by another agent or broker.

(3) The court confirms the sale to that purchaser either on the bid returned to court for confirmation or on an increased bid made at the time of the hearing on the petition for confirmation.

(b) If all the circumstances described in subdivision (a) exist, the court shall allow the compensation determined under Section 10161 on the full amount for which the sale is confirmed. The compensation allowed by the court shall be divided between the agent or broker holding the contract and the other agent or broker as is provided in any agreement between the agent or broker holding the contract and the other agent or broker. If there is no agreement, the compensation on the amount of the original bid returned to the court shall be divided equally between the agent or broker holding the contract and the other agent or broker and, if the sale is confirmed on an increased bid, the other agent or broker shall be paid all of the compensation on the difference between the original bid and the amount for which the sale is confirmed. **Leg.H.** Enacted Stats 1990 ch 79 §14 (AB 759), operative July 1, 1991.

Prior Law: Former Prob C §10162.7, similar to the present section, was added Stats 1987 ch 923 §93, operative July 1, 1988, amended Stats 1989 ch 544 §13, and repealed Stats 1990 ch 79 §13, operative July 1, 1991.

§10163. Compensation where original bid made by purchaser not produced by agent or broker and sale made to overbidder produced by agent or broker

Subject to Sections 10162 and 10162.6, where the original bid returned to the court for confirmation was made by a purchaser who was not procured by an agent or broker, the court shall allow the compensation determined under Section 10161 on the full amount for which the sale is confirmed to the agent or broker who procured the purchaser to whom the sale is confirmed if either of the following conditions is satisfied:

(a) The court confirms a sale on an increased bid, made at the time of the hearing on the petition for confirmation, to a purchaser procured by an agent or broker holding a contract under Section 10150 granting the exclusive right to sell the property.

(b) There is no agent or broker holding a contract under Section 10150 granting the exclusive right to sell the property and the court confirms a sale on an increased bid, made at the time of the hearing on the petition for confirmation, to a purchaser procured by a bona fide agent or broker. **Leg.H.** Enacted Stats 1990 ch 79 §14 (AB 759), operative July 1, 1991.

Prior Law: Former Prob C §10163, similar to the present section, was added Stats 1987 ch 923 §93, operative July 1, 1988, amended Stats 1989 ch 544 §14, and repealed Stats 1990 ch 79 §13, operative July 1, 1991.

§10164. Compensation where sale made on increased bid by purchaser not produced by agent or broker

(a) This section applies only where the court confirms a sale on an increased bid, made at the time of the hearing on the petition for confirmation, to a purchaser who was not procured by a bona fide agent or broker.

(b) Except as provided in subdivision (c), the court shall allow the compensation determined under Section 10161 on the amount of the original bid to the agent or broker whose original bid was returned to the court.

(c) If an agent or broker holds a contract under Section 10150 granting the exclusive right to sell the property and the original bid returned to the court is made by a purchaser who was procured by another agent or broker, the compensation determined under Section 10161 on the amount of the original bid shall be divided between the agent or broker holding the contract and the other agent or broker as is provided in any agreement between the agent or broker holding the contract and the other agent or broker. If there is no agreement, the compensation shall be divided equally between the agent or broker holding the contract and the other agent or broker. **Leg.H.** Enacted Stats 1990 ch 79 §14 (AB 759), operative July 1, 1991.

Prior Law: Former Prob C §10164, similar to the present section, was added Stats 1987 ch 923 §93, operative July 1, 1988, and repealed Stats 1990 ch 79 §13, operative July 1, 1991.

§10165. Sale made on increased bid by purchaser produced by agent or broker; Compensation where original bid returned to court made by a purchaser produced by another agent or broker; Compensation where another agent or broker holds exclusive right to sell contract

(a) Subject to Section 10162.6, where the court confirms a sale on an increased bid, made at the time of the hearing on the petition for confirmation, to a purchaser procured by a bona fide agent or broker, the court shall allow the compensation determined under Section 10161 on the full amount for which the sale is confirmed, as provided in this section, if either of the following conditions is satisfied:

(1) The original bid returned to the court for confirmation was made by a purchaser who was procured by another agent or broker.

(2) The original bid returned to the court for confirmation was made by a purchaser who was not represented by an agent or broker, and another agent or broker holds a contract under Section 10150 granting the exclusive right to sell the property.

(b) The agent or broker who procured the purchaser to whom the sale is confirmed shall be paid one-half of the compensation on the amount of the original bid and all of the compensation on the difference between the original bid and the amount for which the sale is confirmed.

(c) The other one-half of the compensation on the amount of the original bid shall be paid as follows:

(1) If the original bid returned to the court is made by a purchaser who was procured by the agent or broker holding a contract under Section 10150 granting the exclusive right to sell the property, the entire one-half of the compensation on the original bid shall be paid to that agent or broker.

(2) If the original bid returned to the court is made by a purchaser who was procured by a bona fide agent or broker and there is no agent or broker holding a contract under Section 10150 granting the exclusive right to sell the property, the entire one-half of the compensation on the original bid shall be paid to that agent or broker.

(3) If there is an agent or broker who holds a contract under Section 10150 granting the exclusive right to sell the property and the original bid returned to the court is made by a purchaser who was procured by another agent or broker, the one-half of the compensation on the amount of the original bid shall be divided between the agent or broker holding the contract granting the exclusive right to sell the property and the other agent or broker whose original bid was returned to the court for confirmation as is provided in any agreement between the agent or broker holding the contract and the other agent or broker. If there is no agreement, the one-half of the compensation on the amount of the original bid shall be divided equally between the agent or broker holding the contract and the other agent or broker whose original bid was returned to the court for confirmation.

(4) If there is an agent or broker who holds a contract under Section 10150 granting the exclusive right to sell the property and the original bid returned to the court is made by a purchaser who is not represented by an agent or broker and the court confirms the sale on an increased bid, made at the time of the hearing on the petition for confirmation, to a purchaser procured by another agent or broker, the entire one-half of the compensation on the original bid shall be paid to the agent or broker holding the contract.

(5) If the agent or broker compensated under subdivision (b) holds a contract under Section 10150 granting the exclusive right to sell the property, the entire one-half of the compensation on the original bid shall be paid to the other agent or broker who procured the original bid returned to the court. **Leg.H.** Enacted Stats 1990 ch 79 §14 (AB 759), operative July 1, 1991.

Prior Law: Former Prob C §10165, similar to the present section, was added Stats 1987 ch 923 §93, operative July 1, 1988, amended Stats 1989 ch 544 §15, and repealed Stats 1990 ch 79 §13, operative July 1, 1991.

§10166. Condition of bid that certain amount of bid be paid to agent or broker

Notwithstanding that a bid contains a condition that a certain amount of the bid shall be paid to an agent or broker by the personal representative, only such compensation as is proper under this article shall be allowed. Acceptance of the bid by the court binds the bidder even though the compensation allowed by the court is less than that specified by the condition. **Leg.H.** Enacted Stats 1990 ch 79 §14 (AB 759), operative July 1, 1991.

Prior Law: Former Prob C §10166, similar to the present section, was added Stats 1987 ch 923 §93, operative July 1, 1988, and repealed Stats 1990 ch 79 §13, operative July 1, 1991.

§10167. Compensation and expenses of auctioneer

(a) Subject to subdivision (b), whether or not the auctioneer has a contract with the personal representative, the fees, compensation, and expenses of an auctioneer in connection with a sale of property shall be the amount the court, in its discretion, determines to be a reasonable compensation for the services of the auctioneer to the estate.

(b) If the auctioneer has a contract with the personal representative, the amount of the compensation of the auctioneer in connection with the sale of property shall not exceed the amount provided for in the contract. **Leg.H.** Enacted Stats 1990 ch 79 §14 (AB 759), operative July 1, 1991.

Prior Law: Former Prob C §10167, similar to the present section, was added Stats 1987 ch 923 §93, operative July 1, 1988, and repealed Stats 1990 ch 79 §13, operative July 1, 1991.

§10168. Agreement dividing compensation between cooperating agents and brokers

This article does not supersede any agreement cooperating agents or brokers may have among themselves to divide the compensation payable under this article. **Leg.H.** Added Stats 1990 ch 710 §26 (SB 1775), operative July 1, 1991.

ARTICLE 4
Special Provisions Applicable to Particular Types of Property

Sale or surrender for redemption or conversion of securities. §10200.
Sale or withdrawal of savings accounts and mutual capital certificates. §10201.
Sale of subscription rights. §10202.
Sale of decedent's leasehold interest. §10203.
Sale of decedent's partnership interest. §10204.
Sale of decedent's chose in action. §10205.
Sale of decedent's contract right to purchase real property. §10206.
Sale to grazing or pasture association in conformity with the federal Consolidated Farm and Rural Development Act. §10207.

§10200. Sale or surrender for redemption or conversion of securities

(a) As used in this section, "securities" means "security" as defined in Section 70, land trust certificates, certificates of beneficial interest in trusts, investment trust certificates, mortgage participation certificates, or certificates of deposit for any of the foregoing, but does not include notes secured by a mortgage or deed of trust unless the note or notes have been authorized or permitted to be issued by the Commissioner of Financial Protection and Innovation or have been made by a public utility subject to the Public Utilities Act (Part 1 (commencing with Section 201) of Division 1 of the Public Utilities Code).

(b) After authorization by order of court, securities may be sold or may be surrendered for redemption or conversion. Title to the securities sold or surrendered as authorized by an order obtained under this section passes without the need for subsequent court confirmation.

(c) To obtain an order under this section, the personal representative or any interested person shall file a petition stating the terms and conditions and the advantage to the estate of the proposed sale or redemption or conversion. If the court authorizes the sale, redemption, or conversion, the court's order shall fix the terms and conditions of sale, redemption, or conversion.

(d) Notice of the hearing on the petition shall be given as provided in Section 1220 and posted as provided in Section 1230, but the court may order that the notice be given for a shorter period or dispensed with.

(e) No notice of sale or of the redemption or conversion need be given if any of the following conditions are satisfied:

(1) The minimum selling price is fixed by the court.

(2) The securities are to be sold on an established stock or bond exchange.

(3) The securities to be sold are securities designated as a national market system security on an interdealer quotation system, or subsystem thereof, by the National Association of Securities Dealers, Inc., sold through a broker-dealer registered under the Securities Exchange Act of 1934 during the regular course of business of the broker-dealer.

(4) The securities are to be surrendered for redemption or conversion. **Leg.H.** Enacted Stats 1990 ch 79 §14 (AB 759), operative July 1, 1991. Amended Stats 2019 ch 143 §77 (SB 251), effective January 1, 2020; Stats 2022 ch 452 §207 (SB 1498), effective January 1, 2023.

Prior Law: Former Prob C §10200, similar to the present section, was added Stats 1987 ch 923 §93, operative July 1, 1988, and repealed Stats 1990 ch 79 §13, operative July 1, 1991.

§10201. Sale or withdrawal of savings accounts and mutual capital certificates

(a) For purposes of this section:

(1) "Federal association" is defined in Section 5102 of the Financial Code.

(2) "Mutual capital certificate" is defined in Section 5111 of the Financial Code.

(3) "Savings account" is defined in Section 5116 of the Financial Code.

(4) "Savings association" is defined in Section 5102 of the Financial Code.

(5) "Withdrawal value" is defined in Section 5124 of the Financial Code.

(b) Notwithstanding Section 10200, savings accounts and mutual capital certificates of a savings association or federal association may be sold or surrendered for withdrawal by the personal representative, and title thereto passed, without notice of sale, prior order of court, or subsequent confirmation by the court, if an amount of money is obtained upon the sale or withdrawal not less than the withdrawal value of the savings account or the value of the mutual capital certificate.

(c) Notwithstanding Section 10200, credit union share accounts and certificates for funds may be sold or withdrawn by the personal representative, and title thereto passed, without notice of sale, prior order of court, or subsequent confirmation by the court, if an amount of money is obtained upon the sale or withdrawal not less than the withdrawal value of the share account or the value of the certificate for funds. **Leg.H.** Enacted Stats 1990 ch 79 §14 (AB 759), operative July 1, 1991.

Prior Law: Former Prob C §10201, similar to the present section, was added Stats 1987 ch 923 §93, operative July 1, 1988, and repealed Stats 1990 ch 79 §13, operative July 1, 1991.

§10202. Sale of subscription rights

Notwithstanding Section 10200, if an estate by reason of owning securities, also owns or receives subscription rights for the purchase of additional securities, the personal representative may sell all or part of the subscription rights without notice of sale, prior order of court, or subsequent confirmation by the court. **Leg.H.** Enacted Stats 1990 ch 79 §14 (AB 759), operative July 1, 1991.

Prior Law: Former Prob C §10202, similar to the present section, was added Stats 1987 ch 923 §93, operative July 1, 1988, and repealed Stats 1990 ch 79 §13, operative July 1, 1991.

§10203. Sale of decedent's leasehold interest

(a) Except as provided in subdivision (b), where property to be sold consists of a leasehold interest, the sale shall be made as in the case of the sale of personal property of the estate.

(b) The sale of a leasehold interest shall be made as in the case of the sale of real property of the estate if the interest to be sold consists of any of the following:

(1) A leasehold interest in real property with an unexpired term of 10 years or longer. For this purpose, the leasehold interest shall be considered to have an unexpired term of 10 years or longer if the lessee has the right to extend the term and the term, if extended, would exceed 10 years.

(2) A leasehold interest in real property together with an option to purchase the leased property or some part thereof.

(3) A lease for the purpose of production of minerals, oil, gas, or other hydrocarbon substances, or geothermal energy. **Leg.H.** Enacted Stats 1990 ch 79 §14 (AB 759), operative July 1, 1991.

Prior Law: Former Prob C §10203, similar to the present section, was added Stats 1987 ch 923 §93, operative July 1, 1988, and repealed Stats 1990 ch 79 §13, operative July 1, 1991.

§10204. Sale of decedent's partnership interest

Property of the estate that consists of a partnership interest or an interest belonging to an estate by virtue of a partnership formerly existing may be sold in the same manner as other personal property. **Leg.H.** Enacted Stats 1990 ch 79 §14 (AB 759), operative July 1, 1991.

Prior Law: Former Prob C §10204, similar to the present section, was added Stats 1987 ch 923 §93, operative July 1, 1988, and repealed Stats 1990 ch 79 §13, operative July 1, 1991.

§10205. Sale of decedent's chose in action

A chose in action belonging to the estate may be sold in the same manner as other personal property. **Leg.H.** Enacted Stats 1990 ch 79 §14 (AB 759), operative July 1, 1991.

Prior Law: Former Prob C §10205, similar to the present section, was added Stats 1987 ch 923 §93, operative July 1, 1988, and repealed Stats 1990 ch 79 §13, operative July 1, 1991.

§10206. Sale of decedent's contract right to purchase real property

(a) Except as otherwise provided in this section, if the decedent at the time of death was possessed of a contract for the purchase of real property and the decedent's interest in the property and under the contract is to be sold, the sale shall be made as in the case of the sale of real property of the estate.

(b) If the decedent's interest in the property and under the contract is sold, the sale shall be made subject to all payments which are due at the time of sale or which may thereafter become due on the contract. Except as provided in subdivision (d), if there are any payments due or to become due, the court shall not confirm the sale until the purchaser executes a bond to the personal representative that satisfies the requirements of subdivision (c).

(c) The bond shall be for the benefit and indemnity of the personal representative and the persons entitled to the interest of the decedent in the real property contracted for. The amount of the bond shall be equal to the amount of payments then due and thereafter to become due on the contract, with such sureties as the court may approve. The bond shall be conditioned that the purchaser will (1) make all payments for the property which are then due or which become due after the date of the sale and (2) fully indemnify the personal representative and the person entitled to the interest of the decedent against all demands, costs, charges, and expenses, by reason of any covenant or agreement contained in the contract.

(d) The bond need not be given in either of the following cases:

(1) Where no claim has been made against the estate on the contract and the time for filing claims has expired.

(2) Where the person entitled to payment under the contract waives all recourse to the assets of the estate for payment and releases the estate and the personal representative from liability for payment. **Leg.H.** Enacted Stats 1990 ch 79 §14 (AB 759), operative July 1, 1991.

Prior Law: Former Prob C §10206, similar to the present section, was added Stats 1987 ch 923 §93, operative July 1, 1988, and repealed Stats 1990 ch 79 §13, operative July 1, 1991.

§10207. Sale to grazing or pasture association in conformity with the federal Consolidated Farm and Rural Development Act

(a) Real property suitable for a shift-in-land-use loan to develop grazing or pasture facilities may be sold under this section by the personal representative to a grazing or pasture association in conformity with the federal Consolidated Farm and Rural Development Act (7 U.S.C. Sec. 1921, et seq.) after authorization by order of the court.

(b) The personal representative or any interested person may file a petition for an order under this section. Notice of the hearing on the petition shall be given as provided in Section 1220.

(c) An order for sale of property under this section may be made only if the court determines both of the following:

(1) Either the sale is made pursuant to the will of the decedent or all of the following have consented to the sale:

(A) Each known heir whose interest in the estate would be affected by the sale.

(B) Each known devisee who has an interest in the property under the decedent's will.

(2) The sale will not jeopardize the rights of creditors of the estate.

(d) If the court makes an order authorizing sale of the property, the personal representative may make the sale in accord with the terms and conditions set out in the order, subject to the following requirements:

(1) Except as provided in Sections 10002, 10301, 10303, and 10503, notice of the time and place of the sale shall be published pursuant to Section 10300.

(2) The price of the sale made shall be not less than the value of the property as established by an independent and competent appraiser mutually acceptable to the federal government, the grazing or pasture association, and the personal representative.

(3) Except as provided in Sections 10002 and 10503, the sale shall be reported to and confirmed by the court as provided in Article 6 (commencing with Section 10300) before title to the property passes, but the sale may be made irrespective of whether a higher bid is made to the court at the hearing on the petition to confirm the sale. **Leg.H.** Enacted Stats 1990 ch 79 §14 (AB 759), operative July 1, 1991.

Prior Law: Former Prob C §10207, similar to the present section, was added Stats 1987 ch 923 §93, operative July 1, 1988, and repealed Stats 1990 ch 79 §13, operative July 1, 1991.

ARTICLE 5
Sale of Personal Property

Notice of sale. §10250.
Shortening time of notice of sale. §10251.
Sale without notice. §10252.
Contents of notice of sale. §10253.
Sale at public auction. §10254.
Private sale. §10255.
Bids to comply with notice of sale. §10256.
Sale for cash or on credit. §10257.
Court order relaxing requirements for credit sale. §10258.
Passage of title without court confirmation. §10259.
Report of sale and petition for confirmation of sale. §10260.
Hearing on petition for confirmation of sale. §10261.
Overbid. §10262.
Proof that notice of sale was given. §10263.
Error does not invalidate proceedings. §10264.

§10250. Notice of sale

Subject to Sections 10251 and 10252 and except as otherwise provided by statute, personal property of the estate may be sold only after notice of sale is given by one or both of the following methods, as the personal representative may determine:

(a) Posting at the county courthouse of the county in which the proceedings are pending at least 15 days before:

(1) In the case of a private sale, the day specified in the notice of sale as the day on or after which the sale is to be made.

(2) In the case of a public auction sale, the day of the auction.

(b) Publication pursuant to Section 6063a of the Government Code in a newspaper in the county in which the proceedings are pending, such publication to be completed before:

(1) In the case of a private sale, the day specified in the notice of sale as the day on or after which the sale is to be made.

(2) In the case of a public auction sale, the day of the auction. **Leg.H.** Enacted Stats 1990 ch 79 §14 (AB 759), operative July 1, 1991.

Prior Law: Former Prob C §10250, similar to the present section, was added Stats 1987 ch 923 §93, operative July 1, 1988, and repealed Stats 1990 ch 79 §13, operative July 1, 1991.

§10251. Shortening time of notice of sale

(a) If it is shown that it will be to the advantage of the estate, the court or judge may by order shorten the time of notice of sale to not less than five days.

(b) If the court or judge makes an order under subdivision (a), notice of sale shall be given by one or both of the following methods, as the personal representative may determine:

(1) By posting as provided in Section 10250 except that the posting shall be for at least five days instead of 15 days as required by Section 10250.

(2) By publication as provided in Section 10250 except that the publication shall be pursuant to Section 6061 of the Government Code. **Leg.H.** Enacted Stats 1990 ch 79 §14 (AB 759), operative July 1, 1991.

Prior Law: Former Prob C §10251, similar to the present section, was added Stats 1987 ch 923 §93, operative July 1, 1988, and repealed Stats 1990 ch 79 §13, operative July 1, 1991.

§10252. Sale without notice

Personal property may be sold with or without notice, as the personal representative may determine, in any of the following cases:

(a) Where the property is directed by the will to be sold.

(b) Where authority is given in the will to sell the property.

(c) Where the property is perishable, will depreciate in value if not disposed of promptly, or will incur loss or expense by being kept.

(d) Where sale of the property is necessary to provide for the payment of a family allowance pending receipt of other sufficient funds. **Leg.H.** Enacted Stats 1990 ch 79 §14 (AB 759), operative July 1, 1991.

Prior Law: Former Prob C §10252, similar to the present section, was added Stats 1987 ch 923 §93, operative July 1, 1988, and repealed Stats 1990 ch 79 §13, operative July 1, 1991.

§10253. Contents of notice of sale

(a) The notice of sale given pursuant to Section 10250 shall state all of the following:

(1) Whether the sale is to be a private sale or a public auction sale.

(2) In the case of a private sale, the place at which bids or offers will be received and a day on or after which the sale will be made or, in the case of a public auction sale, the time and place of sale.

(3) A brief description of the personal property to be sold.

(b) The notice of sale may state other matters in addition to those required by subdivision (a), including terms and conditions of sale. **Leg.H.** Enacted Stats 1990 ch 79 §14 (AB 759), operative July 1, 1991.

Prior Law: Former Prob C §10253, similar to the present section, was added Stats 1987 ch 923 §93, operative July 1, 1988, and repealed Stats 1990 ch 79 §13, operative July 1, 1991.

§10254. Sale at public auction

(a) Unless the court orders otherwise pursuant to subdivision (b):

(1) A sale of personal property at a public auction sale shall be made within this state at the courthouse door, at the auction house, at some other public place, or at the residence of the decedent.

(2) No public auction sale shall be made of any tangible personal property that is not present at the time of sale.

(b) Upon petition of the personal representative or any interested person, the court may order either or both of the following:

(1) That a sale of personal property at public auction be made at any place within or without the United States.

(2) That tangible personal property need not be present at the time of sale.

(c) The personal representative may postpone a public auction sale of personal property from time to time if all of the following conditions are satisfied:

(1) The personal representative believes that the postponement is to the advantage of the estate.

(2) Notice of the postponement is given by public declaration at the time and place appointed for the sale.

(3) The postponement, together with previous postponements of sale of the property, does not exceed three months. **Leg.H.** Enacted Stats 1990 ch 79 §14 (AB 759), operative July 1, 1991.

Prior Law: Former Prob C §10254, similar to the present section, was added Stats 1987 ch 923 §93, operative July 1, 1988, and repealed Stats 1990 ch 79 §13, operative July 1, 1991.

§10255. Private sale

(a) A private sale of personal property may not be made before the day stated in the notice of sale as the day on or after which the sale will be made, nor later than one year after that day.

(b) In the case of a private sale of personal property, the bids or offers shall be in writing and shall be left at the place designated in the notice of sale, or be delivered to the personal representative personally or to the person specified in the notice of sale, at any time after the first publication or posting of notice of sale and before the making of the sale. **Leg.H.** Enacted Stats 1990 ch 79 §14 (AB 759), operative July 1, 1991.

Prior Law: Former Prob C §10255, similar to the present section, was added Stats 1987 ch 923 §93, operative July 1, 1988, and repealed Stats 1990 ch 79 §13, operative July 1, 1991.

§10256. Bids to comply with notice of sale

Whether a sale of personal property is private or at public auction, bids shall substantially comply with any terms specified in the notice of sale. **Leg.H.** Enacted Stats 1990 ch 79 §14 (AB 759), operative July 1, 1991.

Prior Law: Former Prob C §10256, similar to the present section, was added Stats 1987 ch 923 §93, operative July 1, 1988, and repealed Stats 1990 ch 79 §13, operative July 1, 1991.

§10257. Sale for cash or on credit

(a) Personal property may be sold for cash or on credit.

(b) Except as may otherwise be ordered by the court pursuant to Section 10258, if a sale is made on credit, not less than 25 percent of the purchase price shall be paid in cash at the time of sale, and the personal representative shall do one of the following:

(1) Take the note of the purchaser for the balance of the purchase money, with a security interest in the personal property sold, to secure the payment of the balance.

(2) Enter into a conditional sale contract under which title is retained until the balance is paid.

(c) The terms of the note and security interest or conditional sale contract shall be approved by the court at the time of confirmation of sale.

(d) Where property sold by the personal representative for part cash and part deferred payments consists of an undivided interest in personal property or any other interest therein less than the entire ownership and the owner or owners of the remaining interests therein join in the sale, the note and security interest may be made to the personal representative and such others having an interest in the property. The interest of the personal representative in the note and security interest shall be in the same interest and in the same proportions as the estate's interest in the property prior to the sale. **Leg.H.** Enacted Stats 1990 ch 79 §14 (AB 759), operative July 1, 1991.

Prior Law: Former Prob C §10257, similar to the present section, was added Stats 1987 ch 923 §93, operative July 1, 1988, and repealed Stats 1990 ch 79 §13, operative July 1, 1991.

§10258. Court order relaxing requirements for credit sale

(a) On petition of the personal representative, the court may by order authorize a sale of personal property on credit on terms providing for less than 25 percent of the purchase price to be paid in cash at the time of sale, or may waive or modify the requirement that a security interest or other lien shall be retained or taken to secure payment of the balance of the purchase price, where it is shown that the terms are to the advantage of the estate and the property to be sold is of such a nature that it is impracticable to sell the property for a larger cash payment at the time of sale or to retain a security interest or other lien in the property. The order of the court shall fix the terms and conditions of the sale.

(b) Notice of the hearing on the petition shall be posted as provided in Section 1230 and given as provided in Section 1220 to all of the following persons:

(1) Each person listed in Section 1220.

(2) Each known heir whose interest in the estate would be affected by the sale.

(3) Each known devisee whose interest in the estate would be affected by the sale. **Leg.H.** Enacted Stats 1990 ch 79 §14 (AB 759), operative July 1, 1991.

Prior Law: Former Prob C §10258, similar to the present section, was added Stats 1987 ch 923 §93, operative July 1, 1988, and repealed Stats 1990 ch 79 §13, operative July 1, 1991.

§10259. Passage of title without court confirmation

(a) Title to the following personal property passes upon sale without the need for court confirmation or approval:

(1) Personal property which is perishable, which will depreciate in value if not disposed of promptly, or which will incur loss or expense by being kept.

(2) Personal property the sale of which is necessary to provide for the payment of a family allowance pending receipt of other sufficient funds.

(b) Title to personal property sold at public auction passes without the need for court confirmation or approval upon receipt of the purchase price and:

(1) In the case of tangible personal property, the delivery of the property to the purchaser.

(2) In the case of intangible personal property, the delivery to the purchaser of the instrument that transfers the title to the property to the purchaser.

(c) The personal representative is responsible for the actual value of the property described in subdivision (a) or (b) unless the sale is reported to and approved by the court. **Leg.H.** Enacted Stats 1990 ch 79 §14 (AB 759), operative July 1, 1991.

Prior Law: Former Prob C §10259, similar to the present section, was added Stats 1987 ch 923 §93, operative July 1, 1988, and repealed Stats 1990 ch 79 §13, operative July 1, 1991.

§10260. Report of sale and petition for confirmation of sale

(a) Except as provided in Sections 10200, 10201, 10202, 10259, and 10503, all sales of personal property shall be reported to and be confirmed by the court before title to the property passes to the purchaser, notwithstanding that the property is directed by the will to be sold or authority is given in the will to sell the property.

(b) If the personal representative fails to file the report and a petition for confirmation of the sale within 30 days after the sale, the purchaser at the sale may file the report and petition for confirmation of the sale.

(c) Notice of the hearing on the petition for confirmation filed under subdivision (a) or (b) shall be given as provided in Section 1220 and posted as provided in Section 1230. **Leg.H.** Enacted Stats 1990 ch 79 §14 (AB 759), operative July 1, 1991.

Prior Law: Former Prob C §10260, similar to the present section, was added Stats 1987 ch 923 §93, operative July 1, 1988, and repealed Stats 1990 ch 79 §13, operative July 1, 1991.

§10261. Hearing on petition for confirmation of sale

(a) Except as provided in this subdivision, at the hearing on the petition for confirmation of the sale, the court shall examine into the necessity for the sale or the advantage to the estate and the benefit to the interested persons in making the sale. If the decedent's will authorizes or directs the property to be sold, there need be no showing of the necessity of the sale or the advantage to the estate and the benefit to the interested persons in making the sale.

(b) Any interested person may file written objections to the confirmation of the sale at or before the hearing and may testify and produce witnesses in support of the objections.

(c) Before confirming the sale of a partnership interest, whether made to the surviving partner or to any other person, the court shall do both of the following:

(1) Inquire into the condition of the partnership affairs.

(2) Examine any surviving partner if that surviving partner is a resident within the state at the time of the hearing and able to be present in court. The court may issue a citation to compel the surviving partner to attend the hearing.

(d) Upon its own motion or upon the request of the personal representative, the agent or broker, or any other interested person, made at the time of the confirmation hearing or at another time, the court shall fix the compensation of the agent or broker as provided in Article 3 (commencing with Section 10160). **Leg.H.** Enacted Stats 1990 ch 79 §14 (AB 759), operative July 1, 1991.

Prior Law: Former Prob C §10261, similar to the present section, was added Stats 1987 ch 923 §93, operative July 1, 1988, and repealed Stats 1990 ch 79 §13, operative July 1, 1991.

§10262. Overbid

(a) Except as provided in subdivision (b), if a written offer to purchase the property is made to the court at the hearing on the petition for confirmation of the sale and the new bid is at least 10 percent more than the amount stated in the report made to the court, the court in its discretion may accept the new bid and confirm the sale to the offeror, or may order a new sale, if all of the following conditions are satisfied:

(1) The original bid as stated in the report to the court is more than one hundred dollars ($100) or, if the original bid is less than one hundred dollars ($100), the new bid is at least one hundred dollars ($100) more than the original bid.

(2) The new bid is made by a responsible person.

(3) The new bid complies with all provisions of law.

(b) If there is more than one offer that satisfies the requirements of subdivision (a), the court shall do one of the following:

(1) Accept the highest such offer and confirm the sale to the offeror.

(2) Order a new sale.

(c) This section does not apply to a sale of property described in Section 10259. **Leg.H.** Enacted Stats 1990 ch 79 §14 (AB 759), operative July 1, 1991.

Prior Law: Former Prob C §10262, similar to the present section, was added Stats 1987 ch 923 §93, operative July 1, 1988, and repealed Stats 1990 ch 79 §13, operative July 1, 1991.

§10263. Proof that notice of sale was given

If notice of the sale was required, before an order is made confirming the sale, it shall be proved to the satisfaction of the court that notice of the sale was given as required by this article, and the order of confirmation shall show that such proof was made. **Leg.H.** Enacted Stats 1990 ch 79 §14 (AB 759), operative July 1, 1991.

Prior Law: Former Prob C §10263, similar to the present section, was added Stats 1987 ch 923 §93, operative July 1, 1988, and repealed Stats 1990 ch 79 §13, operative July 1, 1991.

§10264. Error does not invalidate proceedings

No omission, error, or irregularity in the proceedings under this article shall impair or invalidate the proceedings or the sale pursuant to an order made under this article. **Leg.H.** Enacted Stats 1990 ch 79 §14 (AB 759), operative July 1, 1991.

Prior Law: Former Prob C §10264, similar to the present section, was added Stats 1987 ch 923 §93, operative July 1, 1988, and repealed Stats 1990 ch 79 §13, operative July 1, 1991.

ARTICLE 6
Sale of Real Property

Publication of notice of sale. §10300.
Notice of sale where property appraised at not more than $5,000. §10301.
Shortening time of notice of sale. §10302.
Sale without notice where will directs or authorizes sale. §10303.
Contents of notice of sale. §10304.
Sale at public auction. §10305.
Private sale. §10306.
Bids to comply with notice of sale. §10307.
Report of sale and petition for confirmation of sale. §10308.
Minimum price for private sale of real property. §10309.
Hearing on petition for confirmation of sale. §10310.
Overbid. §10311.
Proof that notice of sale was given. §10312.
Order confirming or vacating sale. §10313.
Conveyance or assignment after confirmation. §10314.
Sale on credit. §10315.
Error does not invalidate proceedings. §10316.

§10300. Publication of notice of sale

(a) Except as provided in Sections 10301 to 10303, inclusive, and in Section 10503, real property of the estate may be sold only after notice of sale has been published pursuant to Section 6063a of the Government Code (1) in a newspaper published in the county in which the real property or some portion thereof is located or (2) if there is no such newspaper, in such newspaper as the court or judge may direct.

(b) The publication of notice of sale shall be completed before:

(1) In the case of a private sale, the day specified in the notice as the day on or after which the sale is to be made.

(2) In the case of a public auction sale, the day of the auction. **Leg.H.** Enacted Stats 1990 ch 79 §14 (AB 759), operative July 1, 1991.

Prior Law: Former Prob C §10300, similar to the present section, was added Stats 1987 ch 923 §93, operative July 1, 1988, and repealed Stats 1990 ch 79 §13, operative July 1, 1991.

§10301. Notice of sale where property appraised at not more than $5,000

(a) If it appears from the inventory and appraisal that the value of the real property to be sold does not exceed five thousand dollars ($5,000), the personal representative may in his or her discretion dispense with publication of notice of sale and, in lieu of publication, post the notice of sale at the courthouse of the county in which the real property or some portion thereof is located.

(b) Except as provided in Section 10302, posting pursuant to this section shall be for at least 15 days before:

(1) In the case of a private sale, the day specified in the notice of sale as the day on or after which the sale is to be made.

(2) In the case of a public auction sale, the day of the auction. **Leg.H.** Enacted Stats 1990 ch 79 §14 (AB 759), operative July 1, 1991.

Prior Law: Former Prob C §10301, similar to the present section, was added Stats 1987 ch 923 §93, operative July 1, 1988, amended Stats 1988 ch 1199 §90, operative July 1, 1989, and repealed Stats 1990 ch 79 §13, operative July 1, 1991.

§10302. Shortening time of notice of sale

(a) If it is shown that it will be to the advantage of the estate, the court or judge may by order shorten the time of notice of sale to not less than five days.

(b) Except as provided in subdivision (c), if the court or judge makes an order under subdivision (a), notice of sale shall be published as provided in Section 10300 except that the publication shall be pursuant to Section 6061 of the Government Code.

(c) In a case described in Section 10301, if the court makes an order under subdivision (a), notice of sale shall be posted as provided in Section 10301 except that the notice of sale shall be posted at least five days before the sale instead of 15 days as required by Section 10301. **Leg.H.** Enacted Stats 1990 ch 79 §14 (AB 759), operative July 1, 1991.

Prior Law: Former Prob C §10302, similar to the present section, was added Stats 1987 ch 923 §93, operative July 1, 1988, and repealed Stats 1990 ch 79 §13, operative July 1, 1991.

§10303. Sale without notice where will directs or authorizes sale

Real property may be sold with or without notice, as the personal representative may determine, in either of the following cases:

(a) Where the property is directed by the will to be sold.

(b) Where authority is given in the will to sell the property. **Leg.H.** Enacted Stats 1990 ch 79 §14 (AB 759), operative July 1, 1991.

Prior Law: Former Prob C §10303, similar to the present section, was added Stats 1987 ch 923 §93, operative July 1, 1988, and repealed Stats 1990 ch 79 §13, operative July 1, 1991.

§10304. Contents of notice of sale

(a) The notice of sale given pursuant to this article shall state all of the following:

(1) Whether the sale is to be a private sale or a public auction sale.

(2) In the case of a private sale, the place at which bids or offers will be received and a day on or after which the sale will be made or, in the case of a public auction sale, the time and place of sale.

(3) The street address or other common designation or, if none, a legal description of the real property to be sold.

(b) The notice of sale may state other matters in addition to those required by subdivision (a), including terms and conditions of sale. **Leg.H.** Enacted Stats 1990 ch 79 §14 (AB 759), operative July 1, 1991.

Prior Law: Former Prob C §10304, similar to the present section, was added Stats 1987 ch 923 §93, operative July 1, 1988, and repealed Stats 1990 ch 79 §13, operative July 1, 1991.

§10305. Sale at public auction

(a) A sale of real property at public auction shall be made in the county in which the property is located. If the property is located in two or more counties, it may be sold in any one of them.

(b) A sale of real property at public auction shall be made between 9 a.m. and 9 p.m., and the sale shall be made on the day specified in the notice of sale unless the sale is postponed.

(c) The personal representative may postpone a public auction sale of real property from time to time if all of the following conditions are satisfied:

(1) The personal representative believes that the postponement is to the advantage of the estate.

(2) Notice of the postponement is given by public declaration at the time and place appointed for the sale.

(3) The postponement, together with previous postponements of sale of the property, does not exceed three months in all. **Leg.H.** Enacted Stats 1990 ch 79 §14 (AB 759), operative July 1, 1991.

Prior Law: Former Prob C §10305, similar to the present section, was added Stats 1987 ch 923 §93, operative July 1, 1988, and repealed Stats 1990 ch 79 §13, operative July 1, 1991.

§10306. Private sale

(a) A private sale of real property may not be made before the day stated in the notice of sale as the day on or after which the sale will be made, nor later than one year after that day.

(b) In the case of a private sale of real property, the bids or offers shall be in writing and shall be left at the place designated in the notice of sale, or be delivered to the personal representative personally or to the person specified in the notice of sale, at any time after the first publication or posting of notice of sale and before the making of the sale. **Leg.H.** Enacted Stats 1990 ch 79 §14 (AB 759), operative July 1, 1991.

Prior Law: Former Prob C §10306, similar to the present section, was added Stats 1987 ch 923 §93, operative July 1, 1988, and repealed Stats 1990 ch 79 §13, operative July 1, 1991.

§10307. Bids to comply with notice of sale

Whether a sale of real property is private or at public auction, bids shall substantially comply with any terms specified in the notice of sale. **Leg.H.** Enacted Stats 1990 ch 79 §14 (AB 759), operative July 1, 1991.

Prior Law: Former Prob C §10307, similar to the present section, was added Stats 1987 ch 923 §93, operative July 1, 1988, and repealed Stats 1990 ch 79 §13, operative July 1, 1991.

§10308. Report of sale and petition for confirmation of sale

(a) Except as provided in Section 10503, all sales of real property shall be reported to and be confirmed by the court before title to the property passes to the purchaser, whether the sale is a private sale or a public auction sale and notwithstanding that the property is directed by the will to be sold or authority is given in the will to sell the property.

(b) If the personal representative fails to file the report and a petition for confirmation of the sale within 30 days after the sale, the purchaser at the sale may file the report and petition for confirmation of the sale.

(c) Notice of the hearing on the petition for confirmation filed under subdivision (a) or (b) shall be given as provided in Section 1220 to the persons designated by that section and to the purchasers named in the petition, and posted as provided in Section 1230. **Leg.H.** Enacted Stats 1990 ch 79 §14 (AB 759), operative July 1, 1991. Amended Stats 1992 ch 871 §11 (AB 2975).

Prior Law: Former Prob C §10308, similar to the present section, was added Stats 1987 ch 923 §93, operative July 1, 1988, and repealed Stats 1990 ch 79 §13, operative July 1, 1991.

§10309. Minimum price for private sale of real property

(a) Except as provided in Section 10207, no sale of real property at private sale shall be confirmed by the court unless all of the following conditions are satisfied:

(1) The real property has been appraised within one year prior to the date of the confirmation hearing.

(2) The valuation date used in the appraisal described in paragraph (1) is within one year prior to the date of the confirmation hearing.

(3) The sum offered for the property is at least 90 percent of the appraised value of the property as determined by the appraisal described in paragraph (1).

(b) An appraisal of the property may be had at any time before the sale or the confirmation of sale in any of the following cases:

(1) Where the property has not been previously appraised.

(2) Where the property has not been appraised within one year before the date of the confirmation hearing.

(3) Where the valuation date used in the latest appraisal is more than one year before the date of the confirmation hearing.

(4) Where the court is satisfied that the latest appraisal is too high or too low.

(c) A new appraisal made pursuant to subdivision (b) need not be made by a probate referee if the original appraisal of the property was made by a person other than a probate referee. If the original appraisal of the property was made by a probate referee, the new appraisal may be made by the probate referee who made the original appraisal without further order of the court or further request for the appointment of a new probate referee. If appraisal by a probate referee is required, a new probate referee shall be appointed, using the same procedure as for the appointment of an original referee, to make the new appraisal if the original probate referee is dead, has been removed, or is otherwise unable to act, or if there is other reason to appoint another probate referee. **Leg.H.** Enacted Stats 1990 ch 79 §14 (AB 759), operative July 1, 1991.

Prior Law: Former Prob C §10309, similar to the present section, was added Stats 1987 ch 923 §93, operative July 1, 1988, and repealed Stats 1990 ch 79 §13, operative July 1, 1991.

§10310. Hearing on petition for confirmation of sale

(a) Except as provided in this subdivision, at the hearing on the petition for confirmation of the sale of the real property, the court shall examine into the necessity for the sale or the advantage to the estate and the benefit to the interested persons in making the sale. If the decedent's will authorizes or directs the property to be sold, there need be no showing of the necessity of the sale or the advantage to the estate and benefit to the interested persons in making the sale.

(b) The court shall examine into the efforts of the personal representative to obtain the highest and best price for the property reasonably attainable.

(c) Any interested person may file written objections to the confirmation of the sale at or before the hearing and may testify and produce witnesses in support of the objections. **Leg.H.** Enacted Stats 1990 ch 79 §14 (AB 759), operative July 1, 1991.

Prior Law: Former Prob C §10310, similar to the present section, was added Stats 1987 ch 923 §93, operative July 1, 1988, and repealed Stats 1990 ch 79 §13, operative July 1, 1991.

§10311. Overbid

(a) Subject to subdivisions (b), (c), (d), and (e), and except as provided in Section 10207, if a written offer to purchase the real property is made to the court at the hearing on the petition for confirmation of the sale, the court shall accept the offer and confirm the sale to the offeror if all of the following conditions are satisfied:

(1) The offer is for an amount at least 10 percent more on the first ten thousand dollars ($10,000) of the original bid and 5 percent more on the amount of the original bid in excess of ten thousand dollars ($10,000).

(2) The offer is made by a responsible person.

(3) The offer complies with all provisions of law.

(b) Subject to subdivisions (c), (d), and (e), if there is more than one offer that satisfies the requirements of subdivision (a), the court shall accept the highest such offer and confirm the sale to the person making that offer.

(c) The court may, in its discretion, decline to accept the offer that satisfies the requirements of subdivisions (a) and (b); and, in such case, the court shall order a new sale.

(d) If the sale returned for confirmation is on credit and the higher offer is for cash or on credit, whether on the same or different credit terms, or the sale returned for confirmation is for cash and the higher offer is on credit, the court may not consider the higher offer unless the personal representative informs the court in person or by counsel prior to confirmation of sale that the higher offer is acceptable.

(e) For the purpose of this section, the amount of the original bid and any higher offer shall be determined by the court without regard to any of the following:

(1) Any commission on the amount of the bid to which an agent or broker may be entitled under a contract with the personal representative.

(2) Any condition of the bid that a certain amount of the bid be paid to an agent or broker by the personal representative. **Leg.H.** Enacted Stats 1990 ch 79 §14 (AB 759), operative July 1, 1991.

Prior Law: Former Prob C §10311, similar to the present section, was added Stats 1987 ch 923 §93, operative July 1, 1988, and repealed Stats 1990 ch 79 §13, operative July 1, 1991.

§10312. Proof that notice of sale was given

If notice of the sale was required, before an order is made confirming the sale it shall be proved to the satisfaction of the court that notice of the sale was given as required by this article, and the order of confirmation shall show that the proof was made. **Leg.H.** Enacted Stats 1990 ch 79 §14 (AB 759), operative July 1, 1991.

Prior Law: Former Prob C §10312, similar to the present section, was added Stats 1987 ch 923 §93, operative July 1, 1988, and repealed Stats 1990 ch 79 §13, operative July 1, 1991.

§10313. Order confirming or vacating sale

(a) The court shall make an order confirming the sale to the person making the highest offer that satisfies the requirements of this article, and directing conveyances or assignments or both to be executed, if it appears to the court that all of the following requirements are satisfied:

(1) Either the sale was authorized or directed to be made by the decedent's will or good reason existed for the sale.

(2) If notice of the sale was required, the proof required by Section 10312 has been made.

(3) The sale was legally made and fairly conducted.

(4) The amount for which the sale is to be confirmed is not disproportionate to the value of the property.

(5) In the case of a private sale, the sale complied with the requirements of Section 10309.

(6) If the sale is confirmed to the original bidder, it does not appear that a sum exceeding the original bid by at least 10 percent more on the first ten thousand dollars ($10,000) of the original bid and 5 percent more on the amount of the original bid in excess of ten thousand dollars ($10,000), exclusive of the expenses of a new sale, may be obtained.

(b) Upon its own motion or upon the request of the personal representative, the agent or broker, or any other interested person, made at the time of the confirmation hearing or at another time, the court shall fix the compensation of the agent or broker as provided in Article 3 (commencing with Section 10160).

(c) If it appears to the court that the requirements of subdivision (a) are not satisfied, the court shall vacate the sale and order a new sale.

(d) If the court orders a new sale under subdivision (c) of this section or under subdivision (c) of Section 10311, notice of the new sale shall be given and the new sale shall in all respects be conducted as if no previous sale had taken place. **Leg.H.** Enacted Stats 1990 ch 79 §14 (AB 759), operative July 1, 1991.

Prior Law: Former Prob C §10313, similar to the present section, was added Stats 1987 ch 923 §93, operative July 1, 1988, and repealed Stats 1990 ch 79 §13, operative July 1, 1991.

§10314. Conveyance or assignment after confirmation

(a) Except as provided in subdivision (b), upon confirmation of the sale, the personal representative shall execute a conveyance to the purchaser which shall refer to the order confirming the sale and directing the conveyance to be executed. A certified copy of the order shall be recorded in the office of the recorder of the county in which the real property or some portion thereof is located.

(b) Upon confirmation of a sale of the decedent's interest under a contract for the purchase of real property by the decedent and after the purchaser has given a bond if one is required under Section 10206, the personal representative shall execute an assignment of the contract to the purchaser.

(c) A conveyance made in compliance with the court order confirming the sale and directing the conveyance to be executed vests in the purchaser both of the following:

(1) All the right, title, and interest which the decedent had in the property at the time of the decedent's death.

(2) Any other or additional right, title, or interest in the property acquired by the estate of the decedent, by operation of law or otherwise, prior to the sale.

(d) An assignment made in compliance with the court order confirming the sale of the decedent's interest under a contract for the purchase of real property by the decedent vests in the purchaser all the right, title, and interest of the estate, or of the persons entitled to the interest of the decedent, at the time of sale in the property assigned. The purchaser of the decedent's interest under the contract for the purchase of the real property by the decedent has the same rights and remedies against the vendor of the property as the decedent would have had if living. **Leg.H.** Enacted Stats 1990 ch 79 §14 (AB 759), operative July 1, 1991.

Prior Law: Former Prob C §10314, similar to the present section, was added Stats 1987 ch 923 §93, operative July 1, 1988, and repealed Stats 1990 ch 79 §13, operative July 1, 1991.

§10315. Sale on credit

(a) If a sale is made on credit, the personal representative shall take the note of the purchaser for the unpaid portion of the purchase money, with a mortgage or deed of trust on the property to secure payment of the note. The mortgage or deed of trust shall be subject only to encumbrances existing at the date of sale and such other encumbrances as the court may approve.

(b) Where property sold by the personal representative for part cash and part deferred payments consists of an undivided interest in real property or any other interest therein less than the entire ownership and the owner or owners of the remaining interests therein join in the sale, the note and deed of trust or mortgage may be made to the personal representative and such others having an interest in the property. The interest of the personal representative in the note and deed of trust or mortgage shall be in the same interest and in the same proportions as the estate's interest in the property prior to the sale. **Leg.H.** Enacted Stats 1990 ch 79 §14 (AB 759), operative July 1, 1991.

Prior Law: Former Prob C §10315, similar to the present section, was added Stats 1987 ch 923 §93, operative July 1, 1988, and repealed Stats 1990 ch 79 §13, operative July 1, 1991.

§10316. Error does not invalidate proceedings

No omission, error, or irregularity in the proceedings under this article shall impair or invalidate the proceedings or the sale pursuant to an order made under this article. **Leg.H.** Enacted Stats 1990 ch 79 §14 (AB 759), operative July 1, 1991.

Prior Law: Former Prob C §10316, similar to the present section, was added Stats 1987 ch 923 §93, operative July 1, 1988, and repealed Stats 1990 ch 79 §13, operative July 1, 1991.

ARTICLE 7
Vacating Sale for Purchaser's Default; Liability of Defaulting Purchaser for Damages

Order vacating sale, and directing resale, and awarding damages; Liability of defaulting purchaser. §10350.
Order vacating sale and confirming sale to new high bidder. §10351.

§10350. Order vacating sale, and directing resale, and awarding damages; Liability of defaulting purchaser

(a) If after court confirmation of sale of real or personal property the purchaser fails to comply with the terms of sale, the court may, on petition of the personal representative, vacate the order of confirmation, order a resale of the property, and award damages to the estate against the purchaser.

(b) Notice of the hearing on the petition shall be given as provided in Section 1220 to the persons designated by that section and the notice and a copy of the petition shall be given to the buyers and brokers named in the order confirming sale, except that notice need not be given to a defaulting purchaser whose written consent to the petition is filed with the court before the hearing.

(c) Notice of the resale of the property shall be given as provided in this chapter for a sale of the property in the first instance.

(d) Proceedings after notice of the resale shall be as provided in this chapter for a sale of the property in the first instance.

(e) If the property is resold, the defaulting purchaser is liable to the estate for damages equal to the sum of the following:

(1) The difference between the contract price of the first sale and the amount paid by the purchaser at the resale.

(2) Expenses made necessary by the purchaser's breach.

(3) Other consequential damages. **Leg.H.** Enacted Stats 1990 ch 79 §14 (AB 759), operative July 1, 1991. Amended Stats 1992 ch 871 §12 (AB 2975).

Prior Law: Former Prob C §10350, similar to the present section, was added Stats 1987 ch 923 §93, operative July 1, 1988, and repealed Stats 1990 ch 79 §13, operative July 1, 1991.

§10351. Order vacating sale and confirming sale to new high bidder

(a) The court may vacate the order of confirmation of a sale of real or personal property and make an order confirming the sale to the new high bidder if both of the following requirements are satisfied:

(1) A petition is filed within 60 days after confirmation of the sale showing that (A) the purchaser at the sale has failed to complete the purchase and (B) a bid has been made for the property in the same or a higher amount, on the same or better terms, and in the manner prescribed in the original notice of sale.

(2) The sale has not been vacated pursuant to Section 10350.

(b) Notice of the hearing on the petition shall be given as provided in Section 1220 to the persons designated by that section and the notice and a copy of the petition shall be given to the buyers and brokers named in the order confirming sale, except that notice need not be given to a defaulting purchaser whose written consent to the vacation of the order confirming the sale is filed with the court prior to the hearing.

(c) If the report and petition for confirmation of the second sale are not filed within 60 days of the confirmation of the first sale, the property may be resold only in the manner provided in Section 10350. **Leg.H.** Enacted Stats 1990 ch 79 §14 (AB 759), operative July 1, 1991. Amended Stats 1992 ch 871 §13 (AB 2975), effective January 1, 1993.

Prior Law: Former Prob C §10351, similar to the present section, was added Stats 1987 ch 923 §93, operative July 1, 1988, and repealed Stats 1990 ch 79 §13, operative July 1, 1991.

ARTICLE 8
Application of Sale Proceeds of Encumbered Property; Sale to Lienholder

Definitions. §10360.
Application of purchase money on sale of encumbered property. §10361.
Petition for order determining expenses of administration for encumbered property. §10361.5.
Service of notice of hearing and copy of petition. §10361.6.
Payment to clerk of court. §10362.
Sale to lienholder. §10363.

§10360. Definitions

As used in this article:

(a) "Amount secured by the lien" includes interest and any costs and charges secured by the lien.

(b) "Encumbered property" means real or personal property that is subject to a lien for a secured debt which is a valid claim against the estate and which has been allowed or approved.

(c) "Lien" means a mortgage, deed of trust, or other lien. **Leg.H.** Enacted Stats 1990 ch 79 §14 (AB 759), operative July 1, 1991.

Prior Law: Former Prob C §10360, similar to the present section, was added Stats 1987 ch 923 §93, operative July 1, 1988, and repealed Stats 1990 ch 79 §13, operative July 1, 1991.

§10361. Application of purchase money on sale of encumbered property

(a) If encumbered property is sold, the purchase money shall be applied in the following order:

(1) Expenses of administration which are reasonably related to the administration of the property sold as provided in paragraph (1) of subdivision (a) of Section 11420.

(2) The payment of the expenses of the sale.

(3) The payment and satisfaction of the amount secured by the lien on the property sold if payment and satisfaction of the lien is required under the terms of the sale.

(4) Application in the course of administration.

(b) The application of the purchase money, after the payment of those expenses set forth in paragraphs (1) and (2) of subdivision (a), to the payment and satisfaction of the amount secured by the lien on the property sold shall be made without delay; and, subject to Section 10362, the property sold remains subject to the lien until the purchase money has been actually so applied. **Leg.H.** Enacted Stats 1990 ch 79 §14 (AB 759), operative July 1, 1991. Amended Stats 1996 ch 862 §26 (AB 2751), effective January 1, 1997.

Prior Law: Former Prob C §10361, similar to the present section, was added Stats 1987 ch 923 §93, operative July 1, 1988, and repealed Stats 1990 ch 79 §13, operative July 1, 1991.

§10361.5. Petition for order determining expenses of administration for encumbered property

The personal representative or any interested party may, at any time before payment is made to satisfy all liens on the encumbered property sold, petition for an order determining the amount of expenses of administration that are reasonably related to the administration of that encumbered property as provided in paragraph (1) of subdivision (a) of Section 11420. The petition may be heard as part of a petition for confirmation of sale of personal or real property as provided in Section 10260 or 10308, respectively or may be heard separately. If the petition is presented as part of a petition for confirmation of sale of real or personal property, the notice of hearing otherwise required by this code for a petition for confirmation of sale shall be given in addition to the notice requirements under Section 10361.6. **Leg.H.** Added Stats 1996 ch 862 §27 (AB 2751), effective January 1, 1997.

§10361.6. Service of notice of hearing and copy of petition

(a) At least 30 days prior to the day of the hearing, the petitioner shall cause notice of the hearing and a copy of the petition to be served in the manner provided in Chapter 4 (commencing with Section 413.10) of Title 5 of Part 3 of the Code of Civil Procedure on all of the following persons:

(1) The personal representative, if the personal representative is not the petitioner.

(2) The holder of any mortgage or other lien secured by the property that is sold.

(3) All agents or brokers entitled to compensation from the proceeds of the property that is sold.

(b) Except for those persons given notice pursuant to subdivision (a), notice of the hearing, together with a copy of the petition, shall be given as provided in Section 1220 to all of the following persons:

(1) Each person listed in Section 1220.

(2) Each known heir whose interest in the estate would be affected by the petition.

(3) Each known devisee whose interest in the estate would be affected by the petition.

(4) The Attorney General, at the office of the Attorney General in Sacramento, if any portion of the estate is to escheat to the state and its interest in the estate would be affected by the petition.

(c) The court may not shorten the time for giving the notice of hearing under this section. **Leg.H.** Added Stats 1996 ch 862 §28 (AB 2751), effective January 1, 1997.

§10362. Payment to clerk of court

(a) If encumbered property is sold, the purchase money, or so much of the purchase money as is sufficient to pay the amount secured by the lien on the property sold and the expenses of the sale, may be paid to the clerk of the court. Upon the payment being so made, the lien on the property sold ceases.

(b) The clerk of court without delay shall use the money paid to the clerk under this section to pay the expenses of the sale and to pay and satisfy the amount secured by the lien on the property sold. The clerk shall at once return the surplus, if any, to the personal representative unless the court, for good cause shown and after notice to the personal representative, otherwise orders. **Leg.H.** Enacted Stats 1990 ch 79 §14 (AB 759), operative July 1, 1991.

Prior Law: Former Prob C §10362, similar to the present section, was added Stats 1987 ch 923 §93, operative July 1, 1988, and repealed Stats 1990 ch 79 §13, operative July 1, 1991.

§10363. Sale to lienholder

(a) At a sale of real or personal property subject to a lien, the lienholder may become the purchaser of the property, even though no claim for the amount secured by the lien on the property sold has been, or could have been, filed, allowed, or approved.

(b) Unless the property is sold subject to the lien:

(1) If the lienholder becomes the purchaser of the property and the amount secured by the lien on the property is a valid claim against the estate and has been allowed or approved, the receipt of the lienholder for the amount due the lienholder from the proceeds of the sale is a payment pro tanto.

(2) If the lienholder becomes the purchaser of the property and no claim for the amount secured by the lien on the property has been filed, allowed, or approved, the court may at the hearing on the petition for confirmation of the sale examine into the validity and enforceability of the lien and the amount secured by the lien, and the court may authorize the personal representative to accept the receipt of the lienholder for the amount secured by the lien as payment pro tanto.

(3) If the lienholder becomes the purchaser of the property and the amount for which the property is purchased is insufficient to pay the expenses of the sale and to discharge the lienholder's lien, whether or not a claim has been filed, allowed, or approved, the lienholder shall pay to the clerk of the court an amount sufficient to cover the expenses of the sale.

(c) Nothing permitted under this section shall be deemed to be an allowance or approval of a claim based upon the lien or the amount secured by the lien. **Leg.H.** Enacted Stats 1990 ch 79 §14 (AB 759), operative July 1, 1991.

Prior Law: Former Prob C §10363, similar to the present section, was added Stats 1987 ch 923 §93, operative July 1, 1988, and repealed Stats 1990 ch 79 §13, operative July 1, 1991.

ARTICLE 9
Damages and Recovery of Property

Damages for neglect or misconduct of personal representative. §10380.
Liquidated damages for fraudulent sale of real property. §10381.
Statute of limitation for action for recovery of property. §10382.

§10380. Damages for neglect or misconduct of personal representative

The personal representative is liable to an interested person for damages suffered by the interested person by reason of the neglect or misconduct of the personal representative in the proceedings in relation to a sale. **Leg.H.** Enacted Stats 1990 ch 79 §14 (AB 759), operative July 1, 1991.

Prior Law: Former Prob C §10380, similar to the present section, was added Stats 1987 ch 923 §93, operative July 1, 1988, and repealed Stats 1990 ch 79 §13, operative July 1, 1991.

§10381. Liquidated damages for fraudulent sale of real property

In addition to any other damages for which the personal representative is liable, if the personal representative fraudulently sells real property of the estate contrary to or otherwise than under the provisions of this chapter, the person having an estate of inheritance in the real property may recover from the personal representative, as liquidated damages, an amount equal to double the fair market value of the real property sold on the date of sale. **Leg.H.** Enacted Stats 1990 ch 79 §14 (AB 759), operative July 1, 1991.

Prior Law: Former Prob C §10381, similar to the present section, was added Stats 1987 ch 923 §93, operative July 1, 1988, and repealed Stats 1990 ch 79 §13, operative July 1, 1991.

§10382. Statute of limitation for action for recovery of property

(a) No action for the recovery of property sold by a personal representative on the claim that the sale is void may be maintained by an heir or other person claiming under the decedent unless the action is commenced within whichever of the following is the later time:

(1) Three years after the settlement of the final account of the personal representative.

(2) Three years after the discovery of any fraud upon which the action is based.

(b) The limitation established by subdivision (a) is not tolled for any reason. **Leg.H.** Enacted Stats 1990 ch 79 §14 (AB 759), operative July 1, 1991.

Prior Law: Former Prob C §10382, similar to the present section, was added Stats 1987 ch 923 §93, operative July 1, 1988, and repealed Stats 1990 ch 79 §13, operative July 1, 1991.

PART 6
INDEPENDENT ADMINISTRATION OF ESTATES

Chapter 1. General Provisions.
Chapter 2. Granting or Revoking Independent Administration Authority.
Chapter 3. Administration Under Independent Administration Authority.
Chapter 4. Notice of Proposed Action Procedure.

CHAPTER 1
GENERAL PROVISIONS

Citation of this part. §10400.
"Court supervision" defined. §10401.
"Full authority" defined. §10402.
"Limited authority" defined. §10403.
This part not applicable if will so provides. §10404.
Special administrator. §10405.
Application of part where independent administration authority granted under repealed Probate Code. §10406.

§10400. Citation of this part

This part shall be known and may be cited as the Independent Administration of Estates Act. **Leg.H.** Enacted Stats 1990 ch 79 §14 (AB 759), operative July 1, 1991.

Prior Law: Former Prob C §10400, similar to the present section, was added Stats 1987 ch 923 §93, operative July 1, 1988, and repealed Stats 1990 ch 79 §13, operative July 1, 1991.

§10401. "Court supervision" defined

As used in this part, "court supervision" means the judicial order, authorization, approval, confirmation, or instructions that would be required if authority to administer the estate had not been granted under this part. **Leg.H.** Enacted Stats 1990 ch 79 §14 (AB 759), operative July 1, 1991.

Prior Law: Former Prob C §10401, similar to the present section, was added Stats 1987 ch 923 §93, operative July 1, 1988, and repealed Stats 1990 ch 79 §13, operative July 1, 1991.

§10402. "Full authority" defined

As used in this part, "full authority" means authority to administer the estate under this part that includes all the powers granted under this part. **Leg.H.** Enacted Stats 1990 ch 79 §14 (AB 759), operative July 1, 1991.

Prior Law: Former Prob C §10402, similar to the present section, was added Stats 1987 ch 923 §93, operative July 1, 1988, and repealed Stats 1990 ch 79 §13, operative July 1, 1991.

§10403. "Limited authority" defined

As used in this part, "limited authority" means authority to administer the estate under this part that includes all the powers granted under this part except the power to do any of the following:
(a) Sell real property.
(b) Exchange real property.
(c) Grant an option to purchase real property.
(d) Borrow money with the loan secured by an encumbrance upon real property. **Leg.H.** Enacted Stats 1990 ch 79 §14 (AB 759), operative July 1, 1991.

Prior Law: Former Prob C §10403, similar to the present section, was added Stats 1987 ch 923 §93, operative July 1, 1988, and repealed Stats 1990 ch 79 §13, operative July 1, 1991.

§10404. This part not applicable if will so provides

The personal representative may not be granted authority to administer the estate under this part if the decedent's will provides that the estate shall not be administered under this part. **Leg.H.** Enacted Stats 1990 ch 79 §14 (AB 759), operative July 1, 1991.

Prior Law: Former Prob C §10404, similar to the present section, was added Stats 1987 ch 923 §93, operative July 1, 1988, and repealed Stats 1990 ch 79 §13, operative July 1, 1991.

§10404.5. [Section repealed 1991]

Leg.H. Enacted Stats 1990 ch 79 §14 (AB 759), operative July 1, 1991. Repealed Stats 1990 ch 710 §27 (SB 1775), operative July 1, 1991. The repealed section related to power of personal representative to hire persons to assist with administration of estate.

§10405. Special administrator

A special administrator may be granted authority to administer the estate under this part if the special administrator is appointed with, or has been granted, the powers of a general personal representative. **Leg.H.** Enacted Stats 1990 ch 79 §14 (AB 759), operative July 1, 1991.

Prior Law: Former Prob C §10405, similar to the present section, was added Stats 1987 ch 923 §93, operative July 1, 1988, amended Stats 1988 ch 1199 §90.5, operative July 1, 1989, and repealed Stats 1990 ch 79 §13, operative July 1, 1991.

§10406. Application of part where independent administration authority granted under repealed Probate Code

(a) Subject to subdivision (b), this part applies in any case where authority to administer the estate is granted under this part or where independent administration authority was granted under prior law.
(b) If the personal representative was granted independent administration authority prior to July 1, 1988, the personal representative may use that existing authority on and after July 1, 1988, to borrow money on a loan secured by an encumbrance upon real property, whether or not that existing authority includes the authority to sell real property. **Leg.H.** Enacted Stats 1990 ch 79 §14 (AB 759), operative July 1, 1991. Amended Stats 1990 ch 710 §28 (SB 1775), operative July 1, 1991.

Prior Law: Former Prob C §10406, similar to the present section, was added Stats 1987 ch 923 §93, operative July 1, 1988, and repealed Stats 1990 ch 79 §13, operative July 1, 1991.

CHAPTER 2
GRANTING OR REVOKING INDEPENDENT ADMINISTRATION AUTHORITY

Petition for order granting independent administration authority. §10450.
Notice of hearing. §10451.
Hearing and order. §10452.
Amount of bond. §10453.
Revoking or limiting independent administration authority. §10454.

§10450. Petition for order granting independent administration authority

(a) To obtain authority to administer the estate under this part, the personal representative shall petition the court for that authority either in the petition for appointment of the personal representative or in a separate petition filed in the estate proceedings.
(b) The petition may request either of the following:
(1) Full authority to administer the estate under this part.
(2) Limited authority to administer the estate under this part. **Leg.H.** Enacted Stats 1990 ch 79 §14 (AB 759), operative July 1, 1991.

Prior Law: Former Prob C §10450, similar to the present section, was added Stats 1987 ch 923 §93, operative July 1, 1988, and repealed Stats 1990 ch 79 §13, operative July 1, 1991.

§10451. Notice of hearing

(a) If the authority to administer the estate under this part is requested in the petition for appointment of the personal representative, notice of the hearing on the petition shall be given for the period and in the manner applicable to the petition for appointment.
(b) Where proceedings for the administration of the estate are pending at the time a petition is filed under Section 10450, notice of the hearing on the petition shall be given as provided in Section 1220 to all of the following persons:
(1) Each person listed in Section 1220.
(2) Each known heir whose interest in the estate would be affected by the petition.
(3) Each known devisee whose interest in the estate would be affected by the petition.
(4) Each person named as executor in the will of the decedent.
(c) The notice of hearing of the petition for authority to administer the estate under this part, whether included in the petition for appointment or in a separate petition, shall include the substance of the following statement: "The petition requests authority to administer the estate under the Independent Administration of Estates Act. This will avoid the need to obtain court approval for many actions taken in connection with the estate. However, before taking certain actions, the personal representative will be required to give notice to interested persons unless they have waived

notice or have consented to the proposed action. Independent administration authority will be granted unless good cause is shown why it should not be." **Leg.H.** Enacted Stats 1990 ch 79 §14 (AB 759), operative July 1, 1991.

Prior Law: Former Prob C §10451, similar to the present section, was added Stats 1987 ch 923 §93, operative July 1, 1988, and repealed Stats 1990 ch 79 §13, operative July 1, 1991.

§10452. Hearing and order

Unless an interested person objects as provided in Section 1043 to the granting of authority to administer the estate under this part and the court determines that the objecting party has shown good cause why the authority to administer the estate under this part should not be granted, the court shall grant the requested authority. If the objecting party has shown good cause why only limited authority should be granted, the court shall grant only limited authority. **Leg.H.** Enacted Stats 1990 ch 79 §14 (AB 759), operative July 1, 1991.

Prior Law: Former Prob C §10452, similar to the present section, was added Stats 1987 ch 923 §93, operative July 1, 1988, amended Stats 1989 ch 21 §25, effective May 25, 1989, operative July 1, 1989, and repealed Stats 1990 ch 79 §13, operative July 1, 1991.

§10453. Amount of bond

(a) If the personal representative is otherwise required to file a bond and has full authority, the court, in its discretion, shall fix the amount of the bond at not more than the estimated value of the personal property, the estimated value of the decedent's interest in the real property authorized to be sold under this part, and the probable annual gross income of the estate, or, if the bond is to be given by personal sureties, at not less than twice that amount.

(b) If the personal representative is otherwise required to file a bond and has limited authority, the court, in its discretion, shall fix the amount of the bond at not more than the estimated value of the personal property and the probable annual gross income of the estate, or, if the bond is to be given by personal sureties, at not less than twice that amount. **Leg.H.** Enacted Stats 1990 ch 79 §14 (AB 759), operative July 1, 1991.

Prior Law: Former Prob C §10453, similar to the present section, was added Stats 1987 ch 923 §93, operative July 1, 1988, and repealed Stats 1990 ch 79 §13, operative July 1, 1991.

§10454. Revoking or limiting independent administration authority

(a) Any interested person may file a petition requesting that the court make either of the following orders:

(1) An order revoking the authority of the personal representative to continue administration of the estate under this part.

(2) An order revoking the full authority of the personal representative to administer the estate under this part and granting the personal representative limited authority to administer the estate under this part.

(b) The petition shall set forth the basis for the requested order.

(c) Notice of the hearing on the petition shall be given as provided in Section 1220. In addition, the personal representative shall be served with a copy of the petition and a notice of the time and place of the hearing at least 15 days prior to the hearing. Service on the personal representative shall be made in the manner provided in Section 415.10 or 415.30 of the Code of Civil Procedure or in such manner as may be authorized by the court.

(d) If the court determines that good cause has been shown, the court shall make an order revoking the authority of the personal representative to continue administration of the estate under this part. Upon the making of the order, new letters shall be issued without the notation described in subdivision (c) of Section 8405.

(e) If the personal representative was granted full authority and the court determines that good cause has been shown, the court shall make an order revoking the full authority and granting the personal representative limited authority. Upon the making of the order, new letters shall be issued with the notation described in subdivision (c) of Section 8405 that is required where the authority granted is limited authority. **Leg.H.** Enacted Stats 1990 ch 79 §14 (AB 759), operative July 1, 1991.

Prior Law: Former Prob C §10454, similar to the present section, was added Stats 1987 ch 923 §93, operative July 1, 1988, amended Stats 1989 ch 544 §16, and repealed Stats 1990 ch 79 §13, operative July 1, 1991.

CHAPTER 3
ADMINISTRATION UNDER INDEPENDENT ADMINISTRATION AUTHORITY

Article 1. General Provisions.
Article 2. Powers Exercisable Only After Giving Notice of Proposed Action.
Article 3. Powers the Exercise of Which Requires Giving of Notice of Proposed Action Under Some Circumstances.
Article 4. Powers Exercisable Without Giving Notice of Proposed Action.

ARTICLE 1
General Provisions

Administration without court supervision. §10500.
Matters requiring court supervision. §10501.
Powers exercisable under independent administration authority. §10502.
Manner of sale of property under independent administration authority. §10503.

§10500. Administration without court supervision

(a) Subject to the limitations and conditions of this part, a personal representative who has been granted authority to administer the estate under this part may administer the estate as provided in this part without court supervision, but in all other respects the personal representative shall administer the estate in the same manner as a personal representative who has not been granted authority to administer the estate under this part.

(b) Notwithstanding subdivision (a), the personal representative may obtain court supervision as provided in this code of any action to be taken by the personal representative during administration of the estate. **Leg.H.** Enacted Stats 1990 ch 79 §14 (AB 759), operative July 1, 1991.

Prior Law: Former Prob C §10500, similar to the present section, was added Stats 1987 ch 923 §93, operative July 1, 1988, and repealed Stats 1990 ch 79 §13, operative July 1, 1991.

§10501. Matters requiring court supervision

(a) Notwithstanding any other provision of this part, whether the personal representative has been granted full authority or limited authority, a personal representative who has obtained authority to administer the estate under this part is required to obtain court supervision, in the manner provided in this code, for any of the following actions:

(1) Allowance of the personal representative's compensation.

(2) Allowance of compensation of the attorney for the personal representative.

(3) Settlement of accounts.

(4) Subject to Section 10520, preliminary and final distributions and discharge.

(5) Sale of property of the estate to the personal representative or to the attorney for the personal representative.

(6) Exchange of property of the estate for property of the personal representative or for property of the attorney for the personal representative.

(7) Grant of an option to purchase property of the estate to the personal representative or to the attorney for the personal representative.

(8) Allowance, payment, or compromise of a claim of the personal representative, or the attorney for the personal representative, against the estate.

(9) Compromise or settlement of a claim, action, or proceeding by the estate against the personal representative or against the attorney for the personal representative.

(10) Extension, renewal, or modification of the terms of a debt or other obligation of the personal representative, or the attorney for the personal representative, owing to or in favor of the decedent or the estate.

(b) Notwithstanding any other provision of this part, a personal representative who has obtained only limited authority to administer the estate under this part is required to obtain court supervision, in the manner provided in this code, for any of the following actions:

(1) Sale of real property.

(2) Exchange of real property.

(3) Grant of an option to purchase real property.

(4) Borrowing money with the loan secured by an encumbrance upon real property.

(c) Paragraphs (5) to (10), inclusive, of subdivision (a) do not apply to a transaction between the personal representative as such and the personal representative as an individual where all of the following requirements are satisfied:

(1) Either (A) the personal representative is the sole beneficiary of the estate or (B) all the known heirs or devisees have consented to the transaction.

(2) The period for filing creditor claims has expired.

(3) No request for special notice is on file or all persons who filed a request for special notice have consented to the transaction.

(4) The claim of each creditor who filed a claim has been paid, settled, or withdrawn, or the creditor has consented to the transaction. **Leg.H.** Enacted Stats 1990 ch 79 §14 (AB 759), operative July 1, 1991. Amended Stats 1990 ch 710 §29 (SB 1775), operative July 1, 1991; Stats 1992 ch 178 §37 (SB 1496), effective January 1, 1993.

Prior Law: Former Prob C §10501, similar to the present section, was added Stats 1987 ch 923 §93, operative July 1, 1988, and repealed Stats 1990 ch 79 §13, operative July 1, 1991.

§10502. Powers exercisable under independent administration authority

(a) Subject to the conditions and limitations of this part and to Section 9600, a personal representative who has been granted authority to administer the estate under this part has the powers described in Article 2 (commencing with Section 10510), Article 3 (commencing with Section 10530), and Article 4 (commencing with Section 10550).

(b) The will may restrict the powers that the personal representative may exercise under this part. **Leg.H.** Enacted Stats 1990 ch 79 §14 (AB 759), operative July 1, 1991.

Prior Law: Former Prob C §10502, similar to the present section, was added Stats 1987 ch 923 §93, operative July 1, 1988, and repealed Stats 1990 ch 79 §13, operative July 1, 1991.

§10503. Manner of sale of property under independent administration authority

Subject to the limitations and requirements of this part, when the personal representative exercises the authority to sell property of the estate under this part, the personal representative may sell the property either at public auction or private sale, and with or without notice, for such price, for cash or on credit, and upon such terms and conditions as the personal representative may determine, and the requirements applicable to court confirmation of sales of real property (including, but not limited to, publication of notice of sale, court approval of agents' and brokers' commissions, sale at not less than 90 percent of appraised value, and court examination into the necessity for the sale, advantage to the estate and benefit to interested persons, and efforts of the personal representative to obtain the highest and best price for the property reasonably attainable), and the requirements applicable to court confirmation of sales of personal property, do not apply to the sale. **Leg.H.** Enacted Stats 1990 ch 79 §14 (AB 759), operative July 1, 1991.

Prior Law: Former Prob C §10503, similar to the present section, was added Stats 1987 ch 923 §93, operative July 1, 1988, and repealed Stats 1990 ch 79 §13, operative July 1, 1991.

ARTICLE 2
Powers Exercisable Only After Giving Notice of Proposed Action

Article describes powers that may be exercised only after giving notice of proposed action. §10510.
Selling or exchanging real property. §10511.
Selling or incorporating decedent's business. §10512.
Abandoning tangible personal property. §10513.
Borrowing; Encumbering estate property. §10514.
Granting option to purchase real property. §10515.
Transferring to person given option to purchase in will. §10516.
Completing contract of decedent to convey or transfer property. §10517.
Determining claims to property claimed to belong to decedent or other person. §10518.
Making a disclaimer. §10519.
Preliminary distributions. §10520.

§10510. Article describes powers that may be exercised only after giving notice of proposed action

The personal representative may exercise the powers described in this article only if the requirements of Chapter 4 (commencing with Section 10580) (notice of proposed action procedure) are satisfied. **Leg.H.** Enacted Stats 1990 ch 79 §14 (AB 759), operative July 1, 1991.

Prior Law: Former Prob C §10510, similar to the present section, was added Stats 1987 ch 923 §93, operative July 1, 1988, and repealed Stats 1990 ch 79 §13, operative July 1, 1991.

§10511. Selling or exchanging real property

The personal representative who has full authority has the power to sell or exchange real property of the estate. **Leg.H.** Enacted Stats 1990 ch 79 §14 (AB 759), operative July 1, 1991.

Prior Law: Former Prob C§10511, similar to the present section, was added Stats 1987 ch 923 §93, operative July 1, 1988, and repealed Stats 1990 ch 79 §13, operative July 1, 1991.

§10512. Selling or incorporating decedent's business

The personal representative has the power to sell or incorporate any of the following:

(a) An unincorporated business or venture in which the decedent was engaged at the time of the decedent's death.

(b) An unincorporated business or venture which was wholly or partly owned by the decedent at the time of the decedent's death. **Leg.H.** Enacted Stats 1990 ch 79 §14 (AB 759), operative July 1, 1991.

Prior Law: Former Prob C §10512, similar to the present section, was added Stats 1987 ch 923 §93, operative July 1, 1988, and repealed Stats 1990 ch 79 §13, operative July 1, 1991.

§10513. Abandoning tangible personal property

The personal representative has the power to abandon tangible personal property where the cost of collecting, maintaining, and safeguarding the property would exceed its fair market value. **Leg.H.** Enacted Stats 1990 ch 79 §14 (AB 759), operative July 1, 1991.

Prior Law: Former Prob C §10513, similar to the present section, was added Stats 1987 ch 923 §93, operative July 1, 1988, and repealed Stats 1990 ch 79 §13, operative July 1, 1991.

§10514. Borrowing; Encumbering estate property

(a) Subject to subdivision (b), the personal representative has the following powers:

(1) The power to borrow.

(2) The power to place, replace, renew, or extend any encumbrance upon any property of the estate.

(b) Only a personal representative who has full authority has the power to borrow money with the loan secured by an encumbrance upon real property. **Leg.H.** Enacted Stats 1990 ch 79 §14 (AB 759), operative July 1, 1991.

Prior Law: Former Prob C §10514, similar to the present section, was added Stats 1987 ch 923 §93, operative July 1, 1988, and repealed Stats 1990 ch 79 §13, operative July 1, 1991.

§10515. Granting option to purchase real property

The personal representative who has full authority has the power to grant an option to purchase real property of the estate for a period within or beyond the period of administration. **Leg.H.** Enacted Stats 1990 ch 79 §14 (AB 759), operative July 1, 1991.

Prior Law: Former Prob C §10515, similar to the present section, was added Stats 1987 ch 923 §93, operative July 1, 1988, and repealed Stats 1990 ch 79 §13, operative July 1, 1991.

§10516. Transferring to person given option to purchase in will

If the will gives a person the option to purchase real or personal property and the person has complied with the terms and conditions stated in the will, the personal representative has the power to convey or transfer the property to the person. **Leg.H.** Enacted Stats 1990 ch 79 §14 (AB 759), operative July 1, 1991.

Prior Law: Former Prob C §10516, similar to the present section, was added Stats 1987 ch 923 §93, operative July 1, 1988, and repealed Stats 1990 ch 79 §13, operative July 1, 1991.

§10517. Completing contract of decedent to convey or transfer property

The personal representative has the power to convey or transfer real or personal property to complete a contract entered into by the decedent to convey or transfer the property. **Leg.H.** Enacted Stats 1990 ch 79 §14 (AB 759), operative July 1, 1991.

Prior Law: Former Prob C §10517, similar to the present section, was added Stats 1987 ch 923 §93, operative July 1, 1988, and repealed Stats 1990 ch 79 §13, operative July 1, 1991.

§10518. Determining claims to property claimed to belong to decedent or other person

The personal representative has the power to allow, compromise, or settle any of the following:

(a) A third-party claim to real or personal property if the decedent died in possession of, or holding title to, the property.

(b) The decedent's claim to real or personal property title to or possession of which is held by another. **Leg.H.** Enacted Stats 1990 ch 79 §14 (AB 759), operative July 1, 1991.

Prior Law: Former Prob C §10518, similar to the present section, was added Stats 1987 ch 923 §93, operative July 1, 1988, and repealed Stats 1990 ch 79 §13, operative July 1, 1991.

§10519. Making a disclaimer

The personal representative has the power to make a disclaimer. **Leg.H.** Enacted Stats 1990 ch 79 §14 (AB 759), operative July 1, 1991.

Prior Law: Former Prob C §10519, similar to the present section, was added Stats 1987 ch 923 §93, operative July 1, 1988, and repealed Stats 1990 ch 79 §13, operative July 1, 1991.

§10520. Preliminary distributions

If the time for filing claims has expired and it appears that the distribution may be made without loss to creditors or injury to the estate or any interested person, the personal representative has the power to make preliminary distributions of the following:

(a) Income received during administration to the persons entitled under Chapter 8 (commencing with Section 12000) of Part 10.

(b) Household furniture and furnishings, motor vehicles, clothing, jewelry, and other tangible articles of a personal nature to the persons entitled to the property under the decedent's will, not to exceed an aggregate fair market value to all persons of fifty thousand dollars ($50,000) computed cumulatively through the date of distribution. Fair market value shall be determined on the basis of the inventory and appraisal.

(c) Cash to general pecuniary devisees entitled to it under the decedent's will, not to exceed ten thousand dollars ($10,000) to any one person. **Leg.H.** Added Stats 1992 ch 178 §38 (SB 1496), effective January 1, 1993.

ARTICLE 3
Powers the Exercise of Which Requires Giving of Notice of Proposed Action Under Some Circumstances

Article describes powers that may in some circumstances be exercised only after giving notice of proposed action. §10530.
Managing and controlling estate property generally. §10531.
Entering into contracts. §10532.
Investing money of the estate. §10533.
Continuing operation of decedent's business. §10534.
Paying family allowance. §10535.
Leasing real and personal property. §10536.
Selling or exchanging personal property. §10537.
Granting or extending exclusive right to sell property. §10538.

§10530. Article describes powers that may in some circumstances be exercised only after giving notice of proposed action

Except to the extent that this article otherwise provides, the personal representative may exercise the powers described in this article without giving notice of proposed action under Chapter 4 (commencing with Section 10580). **Leg.H.** Enacted Stats 1990 ch 79 §14 (AB 759), operative July 1, 1991.

Prior Law: Former Prob C §10530, similar to the present section, was added Stats 1987 ch 923 §93, operative July 1, 1988, and repealed Stats 1990 ch 79 §13, operative July 1, 1991.

§10531. Managing and controlling estate property generally

(a) The personal representative has the power to manage and control property of the estate, including making allocations and determinations under the Uniform Principal and Income Act, Chapter 3 (commencing with Section 16320) of Part 4 of Division 9. Except as provided in subdivision (b), the personal representative may exercise this power without giving notice of proposed action under Chapter 4 (commencing with Section 10580).

(b) The personal representative shall comply with the requirements of Chapter 4 (commencing with Section 10580) in any case where a provision of Chapter 3 (commencing with Section 10500) governing the exercise of a specific power so requires. **Leg.H.** Enacted Stats 1990 ch 79 §14 (AB 759), operative July 1, 1991. Amended Stats 1999 ch 145 §3 (AB 846), effective January 1, 2000.

Prior Law: Former Prob C §10531, similar to the present section, was added Stats 1987 ch 923 §93, operative July 1, 1988, and repealed Stats 1990 ch 79 §13, operative July 1, 1991.

§10532. Entering into contracts

(a) The personal representative has the power to enter into a contract in order to carry out the exercise of a specific power granted by this part, including, but not limited to, the powers granted by Sections 10531 and 10551. Except as provided in subdivision (b), the personal representative may exercise this power without giving notice of proposed action under Chapter 4 (commencing with Section 10580).

(b) The personal representative shall comply with the requirements of Chapter 4 (commencing with Section 10580) where the contract is one that by its provisions is not to be fully performed within two years, except that the personal representative is not required to comply with those requirements if the personal representative has the unrestricted right under the contract to terminate the contract within two years.

(c) Nothing in this section excuses compliance with the requirements of Chapter 4 (commencing with Section 10580) when the contract is made to carry out the exercise of a specific power and the provision that grants that power requires compliance with Chapter 4 (commencing with Section 10580) for the exercise of the power. **Leg.H.** Enacted Stats 1990 ch 79 §14 (AB 759), operative July 1, 1991.

Prior Law: Former Prob C §10532, similar to the present section, was added Stats 1987 ch 923 §93, operative July 1, 1988, and repealed Stats 1990 ch 79 §13, operative July 1, 1991.

§10533. Investing money of the estate

(a) The personal representative has the power to do all of the following:

(1) Deposit money belonging to the estate in an insured account in a financial institution in this state.

(2) Invest money of the estate in any one or more of the following:

(A) Direct obligations of the United States, or of the State of California, maturing not later than one year from the date of making the investment.

(B) An interest in a money market mutual fund registered under the Investment Company Act of 1940 (15 U.S.C. Sec. 80a-1, et seq.) or an investment vehicle authorized for the collective investment of trust funds pursuant to Section 9.18 of Part 9 of Title 12 of the Code of Federal Regulations, the portfolios of which are limited to United States government obligations maturing not later than five years from the date of investment and to repurchase agreements fully collateralized by United States government obligations.

(C) Units of a common trust fund described in Section 1564 of the Financial Code. The common trust fund shall have as its objective investment primarily in short term fixed income obligations and shall be permitted to value investments at cost pursuant to regulations of the appropriate regulatory authority.

(D) Eligible securities for the investment of surplus state moneys as provided for in Section 16430 of the Government Code.

(3) Invest money of the estate in any manner provided by the will.

(b) Except as provided in subdivision (c), the personal representative may exercise the powers described in subdivision (a) without giving notice of proposed action under Chapter 4 (commencing with Section 10580).

(c) The personal representative shall comply with the requirements of Chapter 4 (commencing with Section 10580) where the personal representative exercises the power to make any investment pursuant to the power granted by subparagraph (D) of paragraph (2) of subdivision (a) or paragraph (3) of subdivision (a), except that the personal representative may invest in direct obligations of the United States, or of the State of California, maturing not later than one year from the date of making the investment without complying with the requirements of Chapter 4 (commencing with Section 10580). **Leg.H.** Enacted Stats 1990 ch 79 §14 (AB 759), operative July 1, 1991.

Prior Law: Former Prob C §10533, similar to the present section, was added Stats 1987 ch 923 §93, operative July 1, 1988, and repealed Stats 1990 ch 79 §13, operative July 1, 1991.

§10534. Continuing operation of decedent's business

(a) Subject to the partnership agreement and the provisions of the Uniform Partnership Act of 1994 (Chapter 5 (commencing with Section

16100) of Title 2 of the Corporations Code), the personal representative has the power to continue as a general partner in any partnership in which the decedent was a general partner at the time of death.

(b) The personal representative has the power to continue operation of any of the following:

(1) An unincorporated business or venture in which the decedent was engaged at the time of the decedent's death.

(2) An unincorporated business or venture which was wholly or partly owned by the decedent at the time of the decedent's death.

(c) Except as provided in subdivision (d), the personal representative may exercise the powers described in subdivisions (a) and (b) without giving notice of proposed action under Chapter 4 (commencing with Section 10580).

(d) The personal representative shall comply with the requirements of Chapter 4 (commencing with Section 10580) if the personal representative continues as a general partner under subdivision (a), or continues the operation of any unincorporated business or venture under subdivision (b), for a period of more than six months from the date letters are first issued to a personal representative. **Leg.H.** Enacted Stats 1990 ch 79 §14 (AB 759), operative July 1, 1991. Amended Stats 2003 ch 32 §11 (AB 167), effective January 1, 2004.

Prior Law: Former Prob C §10534, similar to the present section, was added Stats 1987 ch 923 §93, operative July 1, 1988, and repealed Stats 1990 ch 79 §13, operative July 1, 1991.

§10535. Paying family allowance

(a) The personal representative has the power to pay a reasonable family allowance. Except as provided in subdivision (b), the personal representative may exercise this power without giving notice of proposed action under Chapter 4 (commencing with Section 10580).

(b) The personal representative shall comply with the requirements of Chapter 4 (commencing with Section 10580) for all of the following:

(1) Making the first payment of a family allowance.

(2) Making the first payment of a family allowance for a period commencing more than 12 months after the death of the decedent.

(3) Making any increase in the amount of the payment of a family allowance. **Leg.H.** Enacted Stats 1990 ch 79 §14 (AB 759), operative July 1, 1991.

Prior Law: Former Prob C §10535, similar to the present section, was added Stats 1987 ch 923 §93, operative July 1, 1988, and repealed Stats 1990 ch 79 §13, operative July 1, 1991.

§10536. Leasing real and personal property

(a) The personal representative has the power to enter as lessor into a lease of property of the estate for any purpose (including, but not limited to, exploration for and production or removal of minerals, oil, gas, or other hydrocarbon substances or geothermal energy, including a community oil lease or a pooling or unitization agreement) for such period, within or beyond the period of administration, and for such rental or royalty or both, and upon such other terms and conditions as the personal representative may determine. Except as provided in subdivisions (b) and (c), the personal representative may exercise this power without giving notice of proposed action under Chapter 4 (commencing with Section 10580).

(b) The personal representative shall comply with the requirements of Chapter 4 (commencing with Section 10580) where the personal representative enters into a lease of real property for a term in excess of one year. If the lease gives the lessee the right to extend the term of the lease, the lease shall be considered as if the right to extend has been exercised.

(c) The personal representative shall comply with the requirements of Chapter 4 (commencing with Section 10580) where the personal representative enters into a lease of personal property and the lease is one described in subdivision (b) of Section 10532. **Leg.H.** Enacted Stats 1990 ch 79 §14 (AB 759), operative July 1, 1991.

Prior Law: Former Prob C §10536, similar to the present section, was added Stats 1987 ch 923 §93, operative July 1, 1988, and repealed Stats 1990 ch 79 §13, operative July 1, 1991.

§10537. Selling or exchanging personal property

(a) The personal representative has the power to sell personal property of the estate or to exchange personal property of the estate for other property upon such terms and conditions as the personal representative may determine. Except as provided in subdivision (b), the personal representative shall comply with the requirements of Chapter 4 (commencing with Section 10580) in exercising this power.

(b) The personal representative may exercise the power granted by subdivision (a) without giving notice of proposed action under Chapter 4 (commencing with Section 10580) in case of the sale or exchange of any of the following:

(1) A security sold on an established stock or bond exchange.

(2) A security designated as a national market system security on an interdealer quotation system, or subsystem thereof, by the National Association of Securities Dealers, Inc., sold through a broker-dealer registered under the Securities Exchange Act of 1934 during the regular course of business of the broker-dealer.

(3) Personal property referred to in Section 10202 or 10259 when sold for cash.

(4) A security described in Section 10200 surrendered for redemption or conversion. **Leg.H.** Enacted Stats 1990 ch 79 §14 (AB 759), operative July 1, 1991.

Prior Law: Former Prob C §10537, similar to the present section, was added Stats 1987 ch 923 §93, operative July 1, 1988, and repealed Stats 1990 ch 79 §13, operative July 1, 1991.

§10538. Granting or extending exclusive right to sell property

(a) The personal representative has the following powers:

(1) The power to grant an exclusive right to sell property for a period not to exceed 90 days.

(2) The power to grant to the same broker one or more extensions of an exclusive right to sell property, each extension being for a period not to exceed 90 days.

(b) Except as provided in subdivision (c), the personal representative may exercise the powers described in subdivision (a) without giving notice of proposed action under Chapter 4 (commencing with Section 10580).

(c) The personal representative shall comply with the requirements of Chapter 4 (commencing with Section 10580) where the personal representative grants to the same broker an extension of an exclusive right to sell property and the period of the extension, together with the periods of the original exclusive right to sell the property and any previous extensions of that right, is more than 270 days. **Leg.H.** Enacted Stats 1990 ch 79 §14 (AB 759), operative July 1, 1991.

Prior Law: Former Prob C §10538, similar to the present section, was added Stats 1987 ch 923 §93, operative July 1, 1988, and repealed Stats 1990 ch 79 §13, operative July 1, 1991.

ARTICLE 4
Powers Exercisable Without Giving Notice of Proposed Action

Article describes powers that may be exercised without giving notice of proposed action. §10550.
Powers that any personal representative may exercise without court supervision. §10551.
Acting on claims against estate. §10552.
Commencing and defending actions and proceedings. §10553.
Modifying terms of obligation. §10554.
Conveying property to effectuate a specific power. §10555.
Paying taxes, assessments, and expenses. §10556.
Purchasing annuity granted in will. §10557.
Exercising option. §10558.
Purchasing securities or commodities sold short. §10559.
Holding securities in name of nominee or in other form. §10560.
Exercising security subscription or conversion rights. §10561.
Making repairs and improvements. §10562.
Accepting deed in lieu of foreclosure or trustee's sale. §10563.
Giving partial satisfaction of mortgage or partial reconveyance under trust deed. §10564.

§10550. Article describes powers that may be exercised without giving notice of proposed action

The personal representative may exercise the powers described in this article without giving notice of proposed action under Chapter 4 (commencing with Section 10580). **Leg.H.** Enacted Stats 1990 ch 79 §14 (AB 759), operative July 1, 1991.

Prior Law: Former Prob C §10550, similar to the present section, was added Stats 1987 ch 923 §93, operative July 1, 1988, and repealed Stats 1990 ch 79 §13, operative July 1, 1991.

§10551. Powers that any personal representative may exercise without court supervision

In addition to the powers granted to the personal representative by other sections of this chapter, the personal representative has all the powers that the personal representative could exercise without court supervision under this code if the personal representative had not been granted authority to administer the estate under this part. **Leg.H.** Enacted Stats 1990 ch 79 §14 (AB 759), operative July 1, 1991.

Prior Law: Former Prob C §10551, similar to the present section, was added Stats 1987 ch 923 §93, operative July 1, 1988, and repealed Stats 1990 ch 79 §13, operative July 1, 1991.

§10552. Acting on claims against estate

The personal representative has the power to do all of the following:
(a) Allow, pay, reject, or contest any claim by or against the estate.
(b) Compromise or settle a claim, action, or proceeding by or for the benefit of, or against, the decedent, the personal representative, or the estate.
(c) Release, in whole or in part, any claim belonging to the estate to the extent that the claim is uncollectible.
(d) Allow a claim to be filed after the expiration of the time for filing the claim. **Leg.H.** Enacted Stats 1990 ch 79 §14 (AB 759), operative July 1, 1991. Amended Stats 1996 ch 862 §29 (AB 2751), effective January 1, 1997.

Prior Law: Former Prob C §10552, similar to the present section, was added Stats 1987 ch 923 §93, operative July 1, 1988, and repealed Stats 1990 ch 79 §13, operative July 1, 1991.

§10553. Commencing and defending actions and proceedings

The personal representative has the power to do all of the following:
(a) Commence and maintain actions and proceedings for the benefit of the estate.
(b) Defend actions and proceedings against the decedent, the personal representative, or the estate. **Leg.H.** Enacted Stats 1990 ch 79 §14 (AB 759), operative July 1, 1991.

Prior Law: Former Prob C §10553, similar to the present section, was added Stats 1987 ch 923 §93, operative July 1, 1988, and repealed Stats 1990 ch 79 §13, operative July 1, 1991.

§10554. Modifying terms of obligation

The personal representative has the power to extend, renew, or in any manner modify the terms of an obligation owing to or in favor of the decedent or the estate. **Leg.H.** Enacted Stats 1990 ch 79 §14 (AB 759), operative July 1, 1991.

Prior Law: Former Prob C §10554, similar to the present section, was added Stats 1987 ch 923 §93, operative July 1, 1988, and repealed Stats 1990 ch 79 §13, operative July 1, 1991.

§10555. Conveying property to effectuate a specific power

The personal representative has the power to convey or transfer property in order to carry out the exercise of a specific power granted by this part. **Leg.H.** Enacted Stats 1990 ch 79 §14 (AB 759), operative July 1, 1991.

Prior Law: Former Prob C §10555, similar to the present section, was added Stats 1987 ch 923 §93, operative July 1, 1988, and repealed Stats 1990 ch 79 §13, operative July 1, 1991.

§10556. Paying taxes, assessments, and expenses

The personal representative has the power to pay all of the following:
(a) Taxes and assessments.
(b) Expenses incurred in the collection, care, and administration of the estate. **Leg.H.** Enacted Stats 1990 ch 79 §14 (AB 759), operative July 1, 1991.

Prior Law: Former Prob C §10556, similar to the present section, was added Stats 1987 ch 923 §93, operative July 1, 1988, and repealed Stats 1990 ch 79 §13, operative July 1, 1991.

§10557. Purchasing annuity granted in will

The personal representative has the power to purchase an annuity from an insurer admitted to do business in this state to satisfy a devise of an annuity or other direction in the will for periodic payments to a devisee. **Leg.H.** Enacted Stats 1990 ch 79 §14 (AB 759), operative July 1, 1991.

Prior Law: Former Prob C §10557, similar to the present section, was added Stats 1987 ch 923 §93, operative July 1, 1988, and repealed Stats 1990 ch 79 §13, operative July 1, 1991.

§10558. Exercising option

The personal representative has the power to exercise an option right that is property of the estate. **Leg.H.** Enacted Stats 1990 ch 79 §14 (AB 759), operative July 1, 1991.

Prior Law: Former Prob C §10558, similar to the present section, was added Stats 1987 ch 923 §93, operative July 1, 1988, and repealed Stats 1990 ch 79 §13, operative July 1, 1991.

§10559. Purchasing securities or commodities sold short

The personal representative has the power to purchase securities or commodities required to perform an incomplete contract of sale where the decedent died having sold but not delivered securities or commodities not owned by the decedent. **Leg.H.** Enacted Stats 1990 ch 79 §14 (AB 759), operative July 1, 1991.

Prior Law: Former Prob C §10559, similar to the present section, was added Stats 1987 ch 923 §93, operative July 1, 1988, and repealed Stats 1990 ch 79 §13, operative July 1, 1991.

§10560. Holding securities in name of nominee or in other form

The personal representative has the power to hold a security in the name of a nominee or in any other form without disclosure of the estate, so that title to the security may pass by delivery. **Leg.H.** Enacted Stats 1990 ch 79 §14 (AB 759), operative July 1, 1991.

Prior Law: Former Prob C §10560, similar to the present section, was added Stats 1987 ch 923 §93, operative July 1, 1988, and repealed Stats 1990 ch 79 §13, operative July 1, 1991.

§10561. Exercising security subscription or conversion rights

The personal representative has the power to exercise security subscription or conversion rights. **Leg.H.** Enacted Stats 1990 ch 79 §14 (AB 759), operative July 1, 1991.

Prior Law: Former Prob C §10561, similar to the present section, was added Stats 1987 ch 923 §93, operative July 1, 1988, and repealed Stats 1990 ch 79 §13, operative July 1, 1991.

§10562. Making repairs and improvements

The personal representative has the power to make repairs and improvements to real and personal property of the estate. **Leg.H.** Enacted Stats 1990 ch 79 §14 (AB 759), operative July 1, 1991.

Prior Law: Former Prob C §10562, similar to the present section, was added Stats 1987 ch 923 §93, operative July 1, 1988, and repealed Stats 1990 ch 79 §13, operative July 1, 1991.

§10563. Accepting deed in lieu of foreclosure or trustee's sale

The personal representative has the power to accept a deed to property which is subject to a mortgage or deed of trust in lieu of foreclosure of the mortgage or sale under the deed of trust. **Leg.H.** Enacted Stats 1990 ch 79 §14 (AB 759), operative July 1, 1991.

Prior Law: Former Prob C §10563, similar to the present section, was added Stats 1987 ch 923 §93, operative July 1, 1988, and repealed Stats 1990 ch 79 §13, operative July 1, 1991.

§10564. Giving partial satisfaction of mortgage or partial reconveyance under trust deed

The personal representative has the power to give a partial satisfaction of a mortgage or to cause a partial reconveyance to be executed by a trustee under a deed of trust held by the estate. **Leg.H.** Enacted Stats 1990 ch 79 §14 (AB 759), operative July 1, 1991.

Prior Law: Former Prob C §10564, similar to the present section, was added Stats 1987 ch 923 §93, operative July 1, 1988, and repealed Stats 1990 ch 79 §13, operative July 1, 1991.

§10565. [Section repealed 1991]

Leg.H. Enacted Stats 1990 ch 79 §14 (AB 759), operative July 1, 1991. Repealed Stats 1990 ch 710 §30 (SB 1775), operative July 1, 1991. The repealed section related to power of personal representative to hire persons to assist with administration of estate.

CHAPTER 4
NOTICE OF PROPOSED ACTION PROCEDURE

When notice of proposed action required or permitted. §10580.
Persons to whom notice must be given. §10581.
Consent to proposed action. §10582.
Waiver of notice. §10583.
Revocation of consent or waiver. §10584.
Form and contents of notice of proposed action. §10585.
Delivery of notice. §10586.

Delivery of objection to proposed action. §10587.
Restraining order. §10588.
Court supervision and notice of hearing required if personal representative has notice of objection. §10589.
Effect of failure to object to proposed action. §10590.
Protection of persons dealing in good faith with personal representative. §10591.
Failure of personal representative to satisfy statutory requirements grounds for removal from office. §10592.

§10580. When notice of proposed action required or permitted

(a) A personal representative who has been granted authority to administer the estate under this part shall give notice of proposed action as provided in this chapter prior to the taking of the proposed action without court supervision if the provision of Chapter 3 (commencing with Section 10500) giving the personal representative the power to take the action so requires. Nothing in this subdivision authorizes a personal representative to take an action under this part if the personal representative does not have the power to take the action under this part.

(b) A personal representative who has been granted authority to administer the estate under this part may give notice of proposed action as provided in this chapter even if the provision of Chapter 3 (commencing with Section 10500) giving the personal representative the power to take the action permits the personal representative to take the action without giving notice of proposed action. Nothing in this subdivision requires the personal representative to give notice of proposed action where not required under subdivision (a) or authorizes a personal representative to take any action that the personal representative is not otherwise authorized to take. **Leg.H.** Enacted Stats 1990 ch 79 §14 (AB 759), operative July 1, 1991.

Prior Law: Former Prob C §10580, similar to the present section, was added Stats 1987 ch 923 §93, operative July 1, 1988, and repealed Stats 1990 ch 79 §13, operative July 1, 1991.

§10581. Persons to whom notice must be given

Except as provided in Sections 10582 and 10583, notice of proposed action shall be given to all of the following:

(a) Each known devisee whose interest in the estate would be affected by the proposed action.

(b) Each known heir whose interest in the estate would be affected by the proposed action.

(c) Each person who has filed a request under Chapter 6 (commencing with Section 1250) of Part 2, of Division 3 for special notice of petitions filed in the administration proceeding.

(d) The Attorney General, at the office of the Attorney General in Sacramento, if any portion of the estate is to escheat to the state and its interest in the estate would be affected by the proposed action. **Leg.H.** Enacted Stats 1990 ch 79 §14 (AB 759), operative July 1, 1991.

Prior Law: Former Prob C §10581, similar to the present section, was added Stats 1987 ch 923 §93, operative July 1, 1988, and repealed Stats 1990 ch 79 §13, operative July 1, 1991.

§10582. Consent to proposed action

Notice of proposed action need not be given to any person who consents in writing to the proposed action. The consent may be executed at any time before or after the proposed action is taken. **Leg.H.** Enacted Stats 1990 ch 79 §14 (AB 759), operative July 1, 1991.

Prior Law: Former Prob C §10582, similar to the present section, was added Stats 1987 ch 923 §93, operative July 1, 1988, and repealed Stats 1990 ch 79 §13, operative July 1, 1991.

§10583. Waiver of notice

(a) Notice of proposed action need not be given to any person who, in writing, waives the right to notice of proposed action with respect to the particular proposed action. The waiver may be executed at any time before or after the proposed action is taken. The waiver shall describe the particular proposed action and may waive particular aspects of the notice, such as the delivery, mailing, or time requirements of Section 10586, or the giving of the notice in its entirety for the particular proposed action.

(b) Notice of proposed action need not be given to any person who has executed the Statutory Waiver of Notice of Proposed Action Form prescribed by the Judicial Council and in that form has made either of the following:

(1) A general waiver of the right to notice of proposed action.

(2) A waiver of the right to notice of proposed action for all transactions of a type which includes the particular proposed action. **Leg.H.** Enacted Stats 1990 ch 79 §14 (AB 759), operative July 1, 1991.

Prior Law: Former Prob C §10583, similar to the present section, was added Stats 1987 ch 923 §93, operative July 1, 1988, and repealed Stats 1990 ch 79 §13, operative July 1, 1991.

§10584. Revocation of consent or waiver

(a) A waiver or consent may be revoked only in writing and is effective only when the writing is received by the personal representative.

(b) A copy of the revocation may be filed with the court, but the effectiveness of the revocation is not dependent upon a copy being filed with the court. **Leg.H.** Enacted Stats 1990 ch 79 §14 (AB 759), operative July 1, 1991.

Prior Law: Former Prob C §10584, similar to the present section, was added Stats 1987 ch 923 §93, operative July 1, 1988, and repealed Stats 1990 ch 79 §13, operative July 1, 1991.

§10585. Form and contents of notice of proposed action

(a) The notice of proposed action shall state all of the following:

(1) The name, mailing address, and electronic address of the personal representative.

(2) The name, telephone number, and electronic address of a person who may be contacted for additional information.

(3) The action proposed to be taken, with a reasonably specific description of the action. If the proposed action involves the sale or exchange of real property, or the granting of an option to purchase real property, the notice of proposed action shall state the material terms of the transaction, including, if applicable, the sale price and the amount of, or method of calculating, any commission or compensation paid or to be paid to an agent or broker in connection with the transaction.

(4) The date on or after which the proposed action is to be taken.

(b) The notice of proposed action may be given using the most current Notice of Proposed Action form prescribed by the Judicial Council.

(c) If the most current form prescribed by the Judicial Council is not used to give notice of proposed action, the notice of proposed action shall satisfy all of the following requirements:

(1) The notice of proposed action shall be in substantially the same form as the form prescribed by the Judicial Council.

(2) The notice of proposed action shall contain the statements described in subdivision (a).

(3) The notice of proposed action shall contain a form for objecting to the proposed action in substantially the form set out in the Judicial Council form. **Leg.H.** Enacted Stats 1990 ch 79 §14 (AB 759), operative July 1, 1991. Amended Stats 2017 ch 319 §80 (AB 976), effective January 1, 2018.

Prior Law: Former Prob C §10585, similar to the present section, was added Stats 1987 ch 923 §93, operative July 1, 1988, and repealed Stats 1990 ch 79 §13, operative July 1, 1991.

§10585.5. [Section repealed 1991]

Leg.H. Enacted Stats 1990 ch 79 §14 (AB 759), operative July 1, 1991. Repealed Stats 1990 ch 710 §31 (SB 1775), operative July 1, 1991. The repealed section related to notice of proposed action to hire persons to assist with administration of estate.

§10586. Delivery of notice

The notice of proposed action shall be delivered pursuant to Section 1215 to each person required to be given notice of proposed action not less than 15 days before the date specified in the notice of proposed action on or after which the proposed action is to be taken. If mailed, the notice of proposed action shall be addressed to the person at the person's last known address. **Leg.H.** Enacted Stats 1990 ch 79 §14 (AB 759), operative July 1, 1991. Amended Stats 2017 ch 319 §81 (AB 976), effective January 1, 2018.

Prior Law: Former Prob C §10586, similar to the present section, was added Stats 1987 ch 923 §93, operative July 1, 1988, and repealed Stats 1990 ch 79 §13, operative July 1, 1991.

§10587. Delivery of objection to proposed action

(a) Any person entitled to notice of proposed action under Section 10581 may object to the proposed action as provided in this section.

(b) The objection to the proposed action is made by delivering pursuant to Section 1215 a written objection to the proposed action to the personal representative at the address stated in the notice of proposed action. The person objecting to the proposed action either may use the Judicial Council form or may make the objection in any other writing that identifies the proposed action with reasonable certainty and indicates that the person objects to the taking of the proposed action.

(c) The personal representative is deemed to have notice of the objection to the proposed action if it is delivered or received at the address stated in the notice of proposed action before whichever of the following times is the later:

(1) The date specified in the notice of proposed action on or after which the proposed action is to be taken.

(2) The date the proposed action is actually taken. **Leg.H.** Enacted Stats 1990 ch 79 §14 (AB 759), operative July 1, 1991. Amended Stats 2017 ch 319 §82 (AB 976), effective January 1, 2018.

Prior Law: Former Prob C §10587, similar to the present section, was added Stats 1987 ch 923 §93, operative July 1, 1988, and repealed Stats 1990 ch 79 §13, operative July 1, 1991.

§10588. Restraining order

(a) Any person who is entitled to notice of proposed action for a proposed action described in subdivision (a) of Section 10580, or any person who is given notice of a proposed action described in subdivision (b) of Section 10580, may apply to the court having jurisdiction over the proceeding for an order restraining the personal representative from taking the proposed action without court supervision. The court shall grant the requested order without requiring notice to the personal representative and without cause being shown for the order.

(b) The personal representative is deemed to have notice of the restraining order if it is served upon the personal representative in the same manner as is provided for in Section 415.10 or 415.30 of the Code of Civil Procedure, or in the manner authorized by the court, before whichever of the following times is the later:

(1) The date specified in a notice of proposed action on or after which the proposed action is to be taken.

(2) The date the proposed action is actually taken. **Leg.H.** Enacted Stats 1990 ch 79 §14 (AB 759), operative July 1, 1991.

Prior Law: Former Prob C §10588, similar to the present section, was added Stats 1987 ch 923 §93, operative July 1, 1988, and repealed Stats 1990 ch 79 §13, operative July 1, 1991.

§10589. Court supervision and notice of hearing required if personal representative has notice of objection

(a) If the proposed action is one that would require court supervision if the personal representative had not been granted authority to administer the estate under this part and the personal representative has notice of a written objection made under Section 10587 to the proposed action or a restraining order issued under Section 10588, the personal representative shall, if the personal representative desires to take the proposed action, take the proposed action under the provisions of this code dealing with court supervision of that kind of action.

(b) If the proposed action is one that would not require court supervision even if the personal representative had not been granted authority to administer the estate under this part but the personal representative has given notice of the proposed action and has notice of a written objection made under Section 10587 to the proposed action or a restraining order issued under Section 10588, the personal representative shall, if he or she desires to take the proposed action, request instructions from the court concerning the proposed action. The personal representative may take the proposed action only under such order as may be entered by the court.

(c) A person who objects to a proposed action as provided in Section 10587 or serves a restraining order issued under Section 10588 in the manner provided in that section shall be given notice of any hearing on a petition for court authorization or confirmation of the proposed action. **Leg.H.** Enacted Stats 1990 ch 79 §14 (AB 759), operative July 1, 1991. Amended Stats 1991 ch 82 §26 (SB 896), effective June 30, 1991, operative July 1, 1991.

Prior Law: Former Prob C §10589, similar to the present section, was added Stats 1987 ch 923 §93, operative July 1, 1988, and repealed Stats 1990 ch 79 §13, operative July 1, 1991.

§10590. Effect of failure to object to proposed action

(a) Except as provided in subdivision (c), only a person described in Section 10581 has a right to have the court review the proposed action after it has been taken or otherwise to object to the proposed action after it has been taken. Except as provided in subdivisions (b) and (c), a person described in Section 10581 waives the right to have the court review the proposed action after it has been taken, or otherwise to object to the proposed action after it has been taken, if either of the following circumstances exists:

(1) The person has been given notice of a proposed action, as provided in Sections 10580 to 10586, inclusive, and fails to object as provided in subdivision (d).

(2) The person has waived notice of or consented to the proposed action as provided in Sections 10582 to 10584, inclusive.

(b) Unless the person has waived notice of or consented to the proposed action as provided in Sections 10582 to 10584, inclusive, the court may review the action taken upon motion of a person described in Section 10581 who establishes that he or she did not actually receive the notice of proposed action before the time to object under subdivision (d) expires.

(c) The court may review the action of the personal representative upon motion of an heir or devisee who establishes all of the following:

(1) At the time the notice was given, the heir or devisee lacked capacity to object to the proposed action or was a minor.

(2) No notice of proposed action was actually received by the guardian, conservator, or other legal representative of the heir or devisee.

(3) The guardian, conservator, or other legal representative did not waive notice of proposed action.

(4) The guardian, conservator, or other legal representative did not consent to the proposed action.

(d) For the purposes of this section, an objection to a proposed action is made only by one or both of the following methods:

(1) Delivering or mailing a written objection as provided in Section 10587 within the time specified in subdivision (c) of that section.

(2) Serving a restraining order obtained under Section 10588 in the manner prescribed and within the time specified in subdivision (b) of that section. **Leg.H.** Enacted Stats 1990 ch 79 §14 (AB 759), operative July 1, 1991.

Prior Law: Former Prob C §10590, similar to the present section, was added Stats 1987 ch 923 §93, operative July 1, 1988, and repealed Stats 1990 ch 79 §13, operative July 1, 1991.

§10591. Protection of persons dealing in good faith with personal representative

(a) The failure of the personal representative to comply with subdivision (a) of Section 10580 and with Sections 10581, 10585, 10586, and 10589, and the taking of the action by the personal representative without such compliance, does not affect the validity of the action so taken or the title to any property conveyed or transferred to bona fide purchasers or the rights of third persons who, dealing in good faith with the personal representative, changed their position in reliance upon the action, conveyance, or transfer without actual notice of the failure of the personal representative to comply with those provisions.

(b) No person dealing with the personal representative has any duty to inquire or investigate whether or not the personal representative has complied with the provisions listed in subdivision (a). **Leg.H.** Enacted Stats 1990 ch 79 §14 (AB 759), operative July 1, 1991.

Prior Law: Former Prob C §10591, similar to the present section, was added Stats 1987 ch 923 §93, operative July 1, 1988, and repealed Stats 1990 ch 79 §13, operative July 1, 1991.

§10592. Failure of personal representative to satisfy statutory requirements grounds for removal from office

(a) In a case where notice of proposed action is required by this chapter, the court in its discretion may remove the personal representative from office unless the personal representative does one of the following:

(1) Gives notice of proposed action as provided in this chapter.

(2) Obtains a waiver of notice of proposed action as provided in this chapter.

(3) Obtains a consent to the proposed action as provided in this chapter.

(b) The court in its discretion may remove the personal representative from office if the personal representative takes a proposed action in violation of Section 10589. **Leg.H.** Enacted Stats 1990 ch 79 §14 (AB 759), operative July 1, 1991.

Prior Law: Former Prob C §10592, similar to the present section, was added Stats 1987 ch 923 §93, operative July 1, 1988, and repealed Stats 1990 ch 79 §13, operative July 1, 1991.

PART 7
COMPENSATION OF PERSONAL REPRESENTATIVE AND ATTORNEY FOR THE PERSONAL REPRESENTATIVE

Chapter 1. Amount of Compensation.
Chapter 2. Allowance of Compensation by Court.
Chapter 3. Application of Part.

CHAPTER 1
AMOUNT OF COMPENSATION

Article 1. Compensation of Personal Representative.
Article 2. Compensation of Attorney for the Personal Representative.

ARTICLE 1
Compensation of Personal Representative

Compensation for ordinary services. §10800.
Additional compensation for extraordinary services. §10801.
Compensation provided by decedent's will. §10802.
Agreement for higher compensation void. §10803.
No compensation as estate attorney unless authorized by will or court order. §10804.
Apportionment of compensation. §10805.

§10800. Compensation for ordinary services

(a) Subject to the provisions of this part, for ordinary services the personal representative shall receive compensation based on the value of the estate accounted for by the personal representative, as follows:

(1) Four percent on the first one hundred thousand dollars ($100,000).
(2) Three percent on the next one hundred thousand dollars ($100,000).
(3) Two percent on the next eight hundred thousand dollars ($800,000).
(4) One percent on the next nine million dollars ($9,000,000).
(5) One-half of one percent on the next fifteen million dollars ($15,000,000).
(6) For all amounts above twenty-five million dollars ($25,000,000), a reasonable amount to be determined by the court.

(b) For the purposes of this section, the value of the estate accounted for by the personal representative is the total amount of the appraisal value of property in the inventory, plus gains over the appraisal value on sales, plus receipts, less losses from the appraisal value on sales, without reference to encumbrances or other obligations on estate property. **Leg.H.** Enacted Stats 1990 ch 79 §14 (AB 759), operative July 1, 1991. Amended Stats 1991 ch 82 §27 (SB 896), effective June 30, 1991, operative July 1, 1991; Stats 2001 ch 699 §2 (AB 232), effective January 1, 2002.

§10801. Additional compensation for extraordinary services

(a) Subject to the provisions of this part, in addition to the compensation provided by Section 10800, the court may allow additional compensation for extraordinary services by the personal representative in an amount the court determines is just and reasonable.

(b) The personal representative may also employ or retain tax counsel, tax auditors, accountants, or other tax experts for the performance of any action which such persons, respectively, may lawfully perform in the computation, reporting, or making of tax returns, or in negotiations or litigation which may be necessary for the final determination and payment of taxes, and pay from the funds of the estate for such services. **Leg.H.** Enacted Stats 1990 ch 79 §14 (AB 759), operative July 1, 1991. Amended Stats 1991 ch 82 §28, effective June 30, 1991, operative July 1, 1991.

§10802. Compensation provided by decedent's will

(a) Except as otherwise provided in this section, if the decedent's will makes provision for the compensation of the personal representative, the compensation provided by the will shall be the full and only compensation for the services of the personal representative.

(b) The personal representative may petition the court to be relieved from a provision of the will that provides for the compensation of the personal representative.

(c) Notice of the hearing on the petition shall be given as provided in Section 1220 to all of the following persons:

(1) Each person listed in Section 1220.
(2) Each known heir whose interest in the estate would be affected by the petition.
(3) Each known devisee whose interest in the estate would be affected by the petition.
(4) The Attorney General, at the office of the Attorney General in Sacramento, if any portion of the estate is to escheat to the state and its interest in the estate would be affected by the petition.

(d) If the court determines that it is to the advantage of the estate and in the best interest of the persons interested in the estate, the court may make an order authorizing compensation for the personal representative in an amount greater than provided in the will. **Leg.H.** Enacted Stats 1990 ch 79 §14 (AB 759), operative July 1, 1991.

§10803. Agreement for higher compensation void

An agreement between the personal representative and an heir or devisee for higher compensation than that provided by this part is void. **Leg.H.** Enacted Stats 1990 ch 79 §14 (AB 759), operative July 1, 1991.

§10804. No compensation as estate attorney unless authorized by will or court order

Notwithstanding any provision in the decedent's will, a personal representative who is an attorney shall be entitled to receive the personal representative's compensation as provided in this part, but shall not receive compensation for services as the attorney for the personal representative unless the court specifically approves the right to the compensation in advance and finds that the arrangement is to the advantage, benefit, and best interests of the decedent's estate. **Leg.H.** Enacted Stats 1990 ch 79 §14 (AB 759), operative July 1, 1991. Amended Stats 1993 ch 293 §5 (AB 21); Stats 1996 ch 563 §26 (SB 392); Stats 2001 ch 699 §3 (AB 232), effective January 1, 2002.

§10805. Apportionment of compensation

If there are two or more personal representatives, the personal representative's compensation shall be apportioned among the personal representatives by the court according to the services actually rendered by each personal representative or as agreed to by the personal representatives. **Leg.H.** Enacted Stats 1990 ch 79 §14 (AB 759), operative July 1, 1991.

ARTICLE 2
Compensation of Attorney for the Personal Representative

Compensation of estate attorney. §10810.
Additional compensation for extraordinary services. §10811.
Compensation provided by decedent's will. §10812.
Agreement for higher compensation void. §10813.
Apportionment of compensation. §10814.

§10810. Compensation of estate attorney

(a) Subject to the provisions of this part, for ordinary services the attorney for the personal representative shall receive compensation based on the value of the estate accounted for by the personal representative, as follows:

(1) Four percent on the first one hundred thousand dollars ($100,000).
(2) Three percent on the next one hundred thousand dollars ($100,000).
(3) Two percent on the next eight hundred thousand dollars ($800,000).
(4) One percent on the next nine million dollars ($9,000,000).
(5) One-half of 1 percent on the next fifteen million dollars ($15,000,000).
(6) For all amounts above twenty-five million dollars ($25,000,000), a reasonable amount to be determined by the court.

(b) For the purposes of this section, the value of the estate accounted for by the personal representative is the total amount of the appraisal of property in the inventory, plus gains over the appraisal value on sales, plus receipts, less losses from the appraisal value on sales, without reference to encumbrances or other obligations on estate property. **Leg.H.** Added Stats 1991 ch 82 §30 (SB 896), effective June 30, 1991, operative July 1, 1991. Amended Stats 2001 ch 699 §4 (AB 232), effective January 1, 2002.

Prior Law: Former Prob C §10810, similar to the present Prob C §§10810–10814, was added Stats 1990 ch 710 §34, operative July 1, 1991, and repealed Stats 1991 ch 82 §29, effective June 30, 1991, operative July 1, 1991.

§10811. Additional compensation for extraordinary services

(a) Subject to the provisions of this part, in addition to the compensation provided by Section 10810, the court may allow additional compensation for extraordinary services by the attorney for the personal representative in an amount the court determines is just and reasonable.

(b) Extraordinary services by the attorney for which the court may allow compensation include services by a paralegal performing the extraordinary services under the direction and supervision of an attorney. The petition for compensation shall set forth the hours spent and services performed by the paralegal.

(c) An attorney for the personal representative may agree to perform extraordinary service on a contingent fee basis subject to the following conditions:

(1) The agreement is written and complies with all the requirements of Section 6147 of the Business and Professions Code.

(2) The agreement is approved by the court following a hearing noticed as provided in Section 10812.

(3) The court determines that the compensation provided in the agreement is just and reasonable and the agreement is to the advantage of the estate and in the best interests of the persons who are interested in the estate. **Leg.H.** Added Stats 1991 ch 82 §30 (SB 896), effective June 30, 1991, operative July 1, 1991. Amended Stats 1993 ch 527 §4 (AB 908), effective January 1, 1994.

§10812. Compensation provided by decedent's will

(a) Except as otherwise provided in this section, if the decedent's will makes provision for the compensation of the attorney for the personal representative, the compensation provided by the will shall be the full and only compensation for the services of the attorney for the personal representative.

(b) The personal representative or the attorney for the personal representative may petition the court to be relieved from a provision of the will that provides for the compensation of the attorney for the personal representative.

(c) Notice of the hearing on the petition shall be given as provided in Section 1220 to all of the following persons:

(1) Each person listed in Section 1220.

(2) Each known heir whose interest in the estate would be affected by the petition.

(3) Each known devisee whose interest in the estate would be affected by the petition.

(4) The Attorney General, at the office of the Attorney General in Sacramento, if any portion of the estate is to escheat to the state and its interest in the estate would be affected by the petition.

(5) If the court determines that it is to the advantage of the estate and in the best interest of the persons interested in the estate, the court may make an order authorizing compensation of the attorney for the personal representative in an amount greater than provided in the will. **Leg.H.** Added Stats 1991 ch 82 §30 (SB 896), effective June 30, 1991, operative July 1, 1991.

§10813. Agreement for higher compensation void

An agreement between the personal representative and the attorney for higher compensation for the attorney than that provided by this part is void. **Leg.H.** Added Stats 1991 ch 82 §30 (SB 896), effective June 30, 1991, operative July 1, 1991.

§10814. Apportionment of compensation

If there are two or more attorneys for the personal representative, the attorney's compensation shall be apportioned among the attorneys by the court according to the services actually rendered by each attorney or as agreed to by the attorneys. **Leg.H.** Added Stats 1991 ch 82 §30, effective June 30, 1991, operative July 1, 1991.

CHAPTER 2
ALLOWANCE OF COMPENSATION BY COURT

Partial allowance of compensation. §10830.
Final compensation. §10831.
Limitation on allowance of compensation for extraordinary services. §10832.

§10830. Partial allowance of compensation

(a) At any time after four months from the issuance of letters:

(1) The personal representative may file a petition requesting an allowance on the compensation of the personal representative.

(2) The personal representative or the attorney for the personal representative may file a petition requesting an allowance on the compensation of the attorney for the personal representative.

(b) Notice of the hearing on the petition shall be given as provided in Section 1220 to all of the following:

(1) Each person listed in Section 1220.

(2) Each known heir whose interest in the estate would be affected by the payment of the compensation.

(3) Each known devisee whose interest in the estate would be affected by the payment of the compensation.

(4) The Attorney General, at the office of the Attorney General in Sacramento, if any portion of the estate is to escheat to the state and its interest in the estate would be affected by the petition.

(c) On the hearing, the court may make an order allowing the portion of the compensation of the personal representative or the attorney for the personal representative, as the case may be, on account of services rendered up to that time, that the court determines is proper. The order shall authorize the personal representative to charge against the estate the amount allowed. **Leg.H.** Enacted Stats 1990 ch 79 §14 (AB 759), operative July 1, 1991. Amended Stats 1990 ch 710 §35 (SB 1775), operative July 1, 1991.

§10831. Final compensation

(a) At the time of the filing of the final account and petition for an order for final distribution:

(1) The personal representative may petition the court for an order fixing and allowing the personal representative's compensation for all services rendered in the estate proceeding.

(2) The personal representative or the attorney for the personal representative may petition the court for an order fixing and allowing the compensation, of the attorney for all services rendered in the estate proceeding.

(b) The request for compensation may be included in the final account or the petition for final distribution or may be made in a separate petition.

(c) Notice of the hearing on the petition shall be given as provided in Section 1220 to all of the following:

(1) Each person listed in Section 1220.

(2) Each known heir whose interest in the estate would be affected by the payment of the compensation.

(3) Each known devisee whose interest in the estate would be affected by the payment of the compensation.

(4) The Attorney General, at the office of the Attorney General in Sacramento, if any portion of the estate is to escheat to the state and its interest in the estate would be affected by the petition.

(d) On the hearing, the court shall make an order fixing and allowing the compensation for all services rendered in the estate proceeding. In the case of an allowance to the personal representative, the order shall authorize the personal representative to charge against the estate the amount allowed, less any amount previously charged against the estate pursuant to Section 10830. In the case of the attorney's compensation the order shall require the personal representative to pay the attorney out of the estate the amount allowed, less any amount paid to the attorney out of the estate pursuant to Section 10830. **Leg.H.** Enacted Stats 1990 ch 79 §14 (AB 759), operative July 1, 1991. Amended Stats 1990 ch 710 §36 (SB 1775), operative July 1, 1991.

§10832. Limitation on allowance of compensation for extraordinary services

Notwithstanding Sections 10830 and 10831, the court may allow compensation to the personal representative or to the attorney for the personal representative for extraordinary services before final distribution when any of the following requirements is satisfied:

(a) It appears likely that administration of the estate will continue, whether due to litigation or otherwise, for an unusually long time.

(b) Present payment will benefit the estate or the beneficiaries of the estate.

(c) Other good cause is shown. **Leg.H.** Enacted Stats 1990 ch 79 §14 (AB 759), operative July 1, 1991. Amended Stats 1994 ch 806 §33 (AB 3686), effective January 1, 1995.

CHAPTER 3
APPLICATION OF PART

Application of provisions of this part. §10850.

§10850. Application of provisions of this part

(a) This part does not apply in any proceeding for administration of a decedent's estate commenced before July 1, 1991.

(b) Notwithstanding its repeal, the applicable law in effect before July 1, 1991, governing the subject matter of this part continues to apply in any proceeding for administration of a decedent's estate commenced before July 1, 1991. **Leg.H.** Enacted Stats 1990 ch 79 §14 (AB 759), operative July 1, 1991. Amended Stats 1990 ch 710 §37 (SB 1775), operative July 1, 1991.

PART 8
ACCOUNTS

Chapter 1. General Provisions.
Chapter 2. When Account Required.
Chapter 3. Settlement of Account.
Chapter 4. Compelling Account.

CHAPTER 1
GENERAL PROVISIONS

Contents of account. §10900.
Production of supporting documents. §10901.
Reliance on accounting by conservator or guardian of decedent for period subsequent to death. §10902.

§10900. Contents of account

(a) An account shall include both a financial statement and a report of administration as provided in Chapter 4 (commencing with Section 1060) of Part 1 of Division 3, and this section.

(b) The statement of liabilities in the report of administration shall include the following information:

(1) Whether notice to creditors was given under Section 9050.

(2) Creditor claims filed, including the date of filing the claim, the name of the claimant, the amount of the claim, and the action taken on the claim.

(3) Creditor claims not paid, satisfied, or adequately provided for. As to each such claim, the statement shall indicate whether the claim is due and the date due, the date any notice of rejection was given, and whether the creditor has brought an action on the claim. The statement shall identify any real or personal property that is security for the claim, whether by mortgage, deed of trust, lien, or other encumbrance.

(c) The amendments to this section made by Assembly Bill 2751 of the 1995–96 Regular Session shall become operative on July 1, 1997. **Leg.H.** Enacted Stats 1990 ch 79 §14 (AB 759), operative July 1, 1991. Amended Stats 1990 ch 710 §38 (SB 1775), operative July 1, 1991; Stats 1996 ch 862 §30 (AB 2751), effective January 1, 1997, operative July 1, 1997.

Prior Law: Former Prob C §10900, similar to the present section, was added Stats 1988 ch 1199 §91, operative July 1, 1989, and repealed Stats 1990 ch 79 §13, operative July 1, 1991.

§10901. Production of supporting documents

On court order, or on request by an interested person filed with the clerk and a copy served on the personal representative, the personal representative shall produce for inspection and audit by the court or interested person the documents specified in the order or request that support an account. **Leg.H.** Enacted Stats 1990 ch 79 §14 (AB 759), operative July 1, 1991.

Prior Law: Former Prob C §10901, similar to the present section, was added Stats 1988 ch 1199 §91, operative July 1, 1989, and repealed Stats 1990 ch 79 §13, operative July 1, 1991.

§10902. Reliance on accounting by conservator or guardian of decedent for period subsequent to death

When a personal representative receives assets from the conservator of a deceased conservatee or the guardian of a deceased ward, the personal representative may incorporate by reference any accounting provided by the conservator or guardian for the decedent for the period subsequent to the date of death, and the personal representative is entitled to rely on the accounting by such other fiduciary, and shall not have a duty to independently investigate or verify the transactions reported in such an account. **Leg.H.** Added Stats 1996 ch 862 §32 (AB 2751), effective January 1, 1997, operative July 1, 1997.

Prior Law: Former Prob C §10902, similar to the present section, was enacted Stats 1990 ch 79 §14 and repealed Stats 1996 ch 862 §31, operative July 1, 1997.

Former Prob C §10902, similar to the present section, was added Stats 1989 ch 21 §26, effective May 25, 1989, operative July 1, 1989, and repealed Stats 1990 ch 79 §13, operative July 1, 1991.

CHAPTER 2
WHEN ACCOUNT REQUIRED

Court-ordered account. §10950.
Final account. §10951.
Account after authority terminated. §10952.
Account where personal representative dies, absconds, or becomes incapacitated. §10953.
When account is not required. §10954.

§10950. Court-ordered account

(a) On its own motion or on petition of an interested person, the court may order an account at any time.

(b) The court shall order an account on petition of an interested person made more than one year after the last account was filed or, if no previous account has been filed, made more than one year after issuance of letters to the personal representative.

(c) The court order shall specify the time within which the personal representative must file an account. **Leg.H.** Enacted Stats 1990 ch 79 §14 (AB 759), operative July 1, 1991.

Prior Law: Former Prob C §10950, similar to the present section, was added Stats 1988 ch 1199 §91, operative July 1, 1989, and repealed Stats 1990 ch 79 §13, operative July 1, 1991.

§10951. Final account

The personal representative shall file a final account and petition for an order for final distribution of the estate when the estate is in a condition to be closed. **Leg.H.** Enacted Stats 1990 ch 79 §14 (AB 759), operative July 1, 1991.

Prior Law: Former Prob C §10951, similar to the present section, was added Stats 1988 ch 1199 §91, operative July 1, 1989, and repealed Stats 1990 ch 79 §13, operative July 1, 1991.

§10952. Account after authority terminated

A personal representative who resigns or is removed from office or whose authority is otherwise terminated shall, unless the court extends the time, file an account not later than 60 days after termination of authority. If the personal representative fails to so file the account, the court may compel the account pursuant to Chapter 4 (commencing with Section 11050). **Leg.H.** Enacted Stats 1990 ch 79 §14 (AB 759), operative July 1, 1991.

Prior Law: Former Prob C §10952, similar to the present section, was added Stats 1988 ch 1199 §91, operative July 1, 1989, and repealed Stats 1990 ch 79 §13, operative July 1, 1991.

§10953. Account where personal representative dies, absconds, or becomes incapacitated

(a) As used in this section:

(1) "Incapacitated" means lack of capacity to serve as personal representative.

(2) "Legal representative" means the personal representative of a deceased personal representative or the conservator of the estate of an incapacitated personal representative.

(b) If a personal representative dies or becomes incapacitated and a legal representative is appointed for the deceased or incapacitated personal representative, the legal representative shall not later than 60 days after appointment, unless the court extends the time, file an account of the administration of the deceased or incapacitated personal representative.

(c) If a personal representative dies or becomes incapacitated and no legal representative is appointed for the deceased or incapacitated personal representative, or if the personal representative absconds, the court may compel the attorney for the deceased, incapacitated, or absconding personal representative or attorney of record in the estate proceeding to file an account of the administration of the deceased, incapacitated, or absconding personal representative.

(d) The legal representative or attorney shall exercise reasonable diligence in preparing an account under this section. Verification of the account may be made on information and belief. The court shall settle the account as in other cases. The court shall allow reasonable compensation to the legal representative or the attorney for preparing the account. The amount allowed is a charge against the estate that was being administered by the deceased, incapacitated, or absconding personal representative. Legal services for which compensation shall be allowed to the attorney under this subdivision include those services rendered by any paralegal performing the services under the direction and supervision of an attorney.

The petition or application for compensation shall set forth the hours spent and services performed by the paralegal. **Leg.H.** Enacted Stats 1990 ch 79 §14 (AB 759), operative July 1, 1991.

Prior Law: Former Prob C §10953, similar to the present section, was added Stats 1988 ch 1199 §91, operative July 1, 1989, and repealed Stats 1990 ch 79 §13, operative July 1, 1991.

§10954. When account is not required

(a) Notwithstanding any other provision of this part, the personal representative is not required to file an account if any of the following conditions is satisfied as to each person entitled to distribution from the estate:

(1) The person has executed and filed a written waiver of account or a written acknowledgment that the person's interest has been satisfied.

(2) Adequate provision has been made for satisfaction in full of the person's interest. This paragraph does not apply to a residuary devisee or a devisee whose interest in the estate is subject to abatement, payment of expenses, or accrual of interest or income.

(b) A waiver or acknowledgment under subdivision (a) shall be executed as follows:

(1) If the person entitled to distribution is an adult and competent, by that person.

(2) If the person entitled to distribution is a minor, by a person authorized to receive money or property belonging to the minor. If the waiver or acknowledgment is executed by a guardian of the estate of the minor, the waiver or acknowledgment may be executed without the need to obtain approval of the court in which the guardianship proceeding is pending.

(3) If the person entitled to distribution is a conservatee, by the conservator of the estate of the conservatee. The waiver or acknowledgment may be executed without the need to obtain approval of the court in which the conservatorship proceeding is pending.

(4) If the person entitled to distribution is a trust, by the trustee, but only if the named trustee's written acceptance of the trust is filed with the court. In the case of a trust that is subject to the continuing jurisdiction of the court pursuant to Chapter 4 (commencing with Section 17300) of Part 5 of Division 9, the waiver or acknowledgment may be executed without the need to obtain approval of the court.

(5) If the person entitled to distribution is an estate, by the personal representative of the estate. The waiver or acknowledgment may be executed without the need to obtain approval of the court in which the estate is being administered.

(6) If the person entitled to distribution is incapacitated, is an unborn beneficiary, is unascertained, or is a person whose identity or address is unknown, or is a designated class of persons who are not ascertained or are not in being, and there is a guardian ad litem appointed to represent the person entitled to distribution, by the guardian ad litem.

(7) If the person entitled to distribution has designated an attorney in fact who has the power under the power of attorney to execute the waiver or acknowledgment, by either of the following:

(A) The person entitled to distribution if an adult and competent.

(B) The attorney in fact.

(c) Notwithstanding subdivision (a):

(1) The personal representative shall file a final report of administration at the time the final account would otherwise have been required. The final report shall include the amount of compensation paid or payable to the personal representative and to the attorney for the personal representative and shall set forth the basis for determining the amounts.

(2) A creditor whose interest has not been satisfied may petition under Section 10950 for an account. **Leg.H.** Enacted Stats 1990 ch 79 §14 (AB 759), operative July 1, 1991. Amended Stats 1990 ch 710 §39 (SB 1775), operative July 1, 1991; Stats 2023 ch 260 §21 (SB 345), effective January 1, 2024.

Prior Law: Former Prob C §10954, similar to the present section, was added Stats 1988 ch 1199 §91, operative July 1, 1989, and repealed Stats 1990 ch 79 §13, operative July 1, 1991.

CHAPTER 3
SETTLEMENT OF ACCOUNT

Notice of hearing. §11000.
Contest of account. §11001.
Hearing on account. §11002.
Litigation expenses. §11003.
Expenses of personal representative. §11004.
Settlement of claim not properly filed. §11005.

§11000. Notice of hearing

(a) The personal representative shall give notice of the hearing as provided in Section 1220 to all of the following persons:

(1) Each person listed in Section 1220.

(2) Each known heir whose interest in the estate would be affected by the account.

(3) Each known devisee whose interest in the estate would be affected by the account.

(4) The Attorney General, at the office of the Attorney General in Sacramento, if any portion of the estate is to escheat to the state and its interest would be affected by the account.

(5) If the estate is insolvent, each creditor who has filed a claim that is allowed or approved but is unpaid in whole or in part.

(b) If the petition for approval of the account requests allowance of all or a portion of the compensation of the personal representative or the attorney for the personal representative, the notice of hearing shall so state.

(c) If the account is a final account and is filed together with a petition for an order for final distribution of the estate, the notice of hearing shall so state. **Leg.H.** Enacted Stats 1990 ch 79 §14 (AB 759), operative July 1, 1991. Amended Stats 1990 ch 710 §40 (SB 1775), operative July 1, 1991.

Prior Law: Former Prob C §11000, similar to the present section, was added Stats 1988 ch 1199 §91, operative July 1, 1989, and repealed Stats 1990 ch 79 §13, operative July 1, 1991.

§11001. Contest of account

All matters relating to an account may be contested for cause shown, including, but not limited to:

(a) The validity of an allowed or approved claim not reported in a previous account and not established by judgment.

(b) The value of property for purposes of distribution.

(c) Actions taken by the personal representative not previously authorized or approved by, the court, subject to Section 10590 (Independent Administration of Estates Act). **Leg.H.** Enacted Stats 1990 ch 79 §14 (AB 759), operative July 1, 1991.

Prior Law: Former Prob C §11001, similar to the present section, was added Stats 1988 ch 1199 §91, operative July 1, 1989, and repealed Stats 1990 ch 79 §13, operative July 1, 1991.

§11002. Hearing on account

(a) The court may conduct any hearing that may be necessary to settle the account, and may cite the personal representative to appear before the court for examination.

(b) The court may appoint one or more referees to examine the account and make a report on the account, subject to confirmation by the court. The court may allow a reasonable compensation to the referee to be paid out of the estate.

(c) The court may make any orders that the court deems necessary to effectuate the provisions of this section. **Leg.H.** Enacted Stats 1990 ch 79 §14 (AB 759), operative July 1, 1991.

Prior Law: Former Prob C §11002, similar to the present section, was added Stats 1988 ch 1199 §91, operative July 1, 1989, and repealed Stats 1990 ch 79 §13, operative July 1, 1991.

§11003. Litigation expenses

(a) If the court determines that the contest was without reasonable cause and in bad faith, the court may award against the contestant the compensation and costs of the personal representative and other expenses and costs of litigation, including attorney's fees, incurred to defend the account. The amount awarded is a charge against any interest of the contestant in the estate and the contestant is personally liable for any amount that remains unsatisfied.

(b) If the court determines that the opposition to the contest was without reasonable cause and in bad faith, the court may award the contestant the costs of the contestant and other expenses and costs of litigation, including attorney's fees, incurred to contest the account. The amount awarded is a charge against the compensation or other interest of the personal representative in the estate and the personal representative is liable personally and on the bond, if any, for any amount that remains unsatisfied. **Leg.H.** Enacted Stats 1990 ch 79 §14 (AB 759), operative July 1, 1991.

§11004. Expenses of personal representative

The personal representative shall be allowed all necessary expenses in the administration of the estate, including, but not limited to, necessary expenses in the care, management, preservation, and settlement of the estate. **Leg.H.** Enacted Stats 1990 ch 79 §14 (AB 759), operative July 1, 1991.

Prior Law: Former Prob C §11004, similar to the present section, was added Stats 1988 ch 1199 §91, operative July 1, 1989, amended Stats 1989 ch 21 §27, effective May 25, 1989, operative July 1, 1989, and repealed Stats 1990 ch 79 §13, operative July 1, 1991.

§11005. Settlement of claim not properly filed

If a debt has been paid within the time prescribed in Section 9154 but without a claim having been filed and established in the manner prescribed by statute, in settling the account the court shall allow the amount paid if all of the following are proven:

(a) The debt was justly due.
(b) The debt was paid in good faith.
(c) The amount paid did not exceed the amount reasonably necessary to satisfy the indebtedness.
(d) The estate is solvent. **Leg.H.** Enacted Stats 1990 ch 79 §14 (AB 759), operative July 1, 1991.

Prior Law: Former Prob C §11005, similar to the present section, was added Stats 1988 ch 1199 §91, operative July 1, 1989, and repealed Stats 1990 ch 79 §13, operative July 1, 1991.

CHAPTER 4
COMPELLING ACCOUNT

Sanction for failure to account. §11050.
Citation. §11051.
Punishment for contempt. §11052.

§11050. Sanction for failure to account

Subject to the provisions of this chapter, if the personal representative does not file a required account, the court shall compel the account by punishment for contempt. **Leg.H.** Enacted Stats 1990 ch 79 §14 (AB 759), operative July 1, 1991.

Prior Law: Former Prob C §11050, similar to the present section, was added Stats 1988 ch 1199 §91, operative July 1, 1989, and repealed Stats 1990 ch 79 §13, operative July 1, 1991.

§11051. Citation

(a) A citation shall be issued, served, and returned, requiring a personal representative who does not file a required account to appear and show cause why the personal representative should not be punished for contempt.

(b) If the personal representative purposefully evades personal service of the citation, the personal representative shall be removed from office. **Leg.H.** Enacted Stats 1990 ch 79 §14 (AB 759), operative July 1, 1991.

Prior Law: Former Prob C §11051, similar to the present section, was added Stats 1988 ch 1199 §91, operative July 1, 1989, and repealed Stats 1990 ch 79 §13, operative July 1, 1991.

§11052. Punishment for contempt

If the personal representative does not appear and file a required account, after having been duly cited, the personal representative may be punished for contempt or removed from office, or both, in the discretion of the court. **Leg.H.** Enacted Stats 1990 ch 79 §14 (AB 759), operative July 1, 1991.

Prior Law: Former Prob C §11052, similar to the present section, was added Stats 1988 ch 1199 §91, operative July 1, 1989, and repealed Stats 1990 ch 79 §13, operative July 1, 1991.

PART 9
PAYMENT OF DEBTS

Chapter 1. Definitions and Preliminary Provisions.
Chapter 2. General Provisions.
Chapter 3. Allocation of Debts Between Estate and Surviving Spouse.
Chapter 4. Debts That Are Contingent, Disputed, or Not Due.

CHAPTER 1
DEFINITIONS AND PRELIMINARY PROVISIONS

Article 1. Definitions.
Article 2. Proceedings Commenced Before July 1, 1988.

ARTICLE 1
Definitions

Application of definitions. §11400.
Debt. §11401.
Wage claim. §11402.

§11400. Application of definitions

Unless the provision or context otherwise requires, the definitions in this article govern the construction of this part. **Leg.H.** Enacted Stats 1990 ch 79 §14 (AB 759), operative July 1, 1991.

Prior Law: Former Prob C §11400, similar to the present section, was added Stats 1987 ch 923 §93, operative July 1, 1988, and repealed Stats 1990 ch 79 §13, operative July 1, 1991.

§11401. Debt

"Debt" means:

(a) A claim that is established under Part 4 (commencing with Section 9000) or that is otherwise payable in the course of administration.

(b) An expense of administration.

(c) A charge against the estate including, but not limited to, taxes, expenses of last illness, and family allowance. **Leg.H.** Enacted Stats 1990 ch 79 §14 (AB 759), operative July 1, 1991.

Prior Law: Former Prob C §11401, similar to the present section, was added Stats 1987 ch 923 §93, operative July 1, 1988, and repealed Stats 1990 ch 79 §13, operative July 1, 1991.

§11402. Wage claim

"Wage claim" means a claim for wages, not exceeding two thousand dollars ($2,000), of each employee of the decedent for work done or personal services rendered within 90 days before the death of the decedent. **Leg.H.** Enacted Stats 1990 ch 79 §14 (AB 759), operative July 1, 1991.

Prior Law: Former Prob C §11402, similar to the present section, was added Stats 1987 ch 923 §93, operative July 1, 1988, and repealed Stats 1990 ch 79 §13, operative July 1, 1991.

ARTICLE 2
Proceedings Commenced Before July 1, 1988

Administration proceedings commenced before July 1, 1988. §11405.

§11405. Administration proceedings commenced before July 1, 1988

(a) This part does not apply in any proceeding for the administration of a decedent's estate commenced before July 1, 1988.

(b) The applicable law in effect before July 1, 1988, governing the subject matter of this part continues to apply in any proceeding for administration of a decedent's estate commenced before July 1, 1988, notwithstanding its repeal by Chapter 923 of the Statutes of 1987. **Leg.H.** Enacted Stats 1990 ch 79 §14 (AB 759), operative July 1, 1991.

Prior Law: Former Prob C §11405, similar to the present section, was added Stats 1987 ch 923 §93, operative July 1, 1988, and repealed Stats 1990 ch 79 §13, operative July 1, 1991.

CHAPTER 2
GENERAL PROVISIONS

Priority for payment. §11420.
Immediate payment of priority debts. §11421.
Payment of debts on court order. §11422.
Interest. §11423.
Duty of personal representative to pay debts pursuant to court order. §11424.
Deposit for missing creditor. §11428.
Unpaid creditor. §11429.

§11420. Priority for payment

(a) Debts shall be paid in the following order of priority among classes of debts, except that debts owed to the United States or to this state that have preference under the laws of the United States or of this state shall be given the preference required by such laws:

(1) Expenses of administration. With respect to obligations secured by mortgage, deed of trust, or other lien, including, but not limited to, a judgment lien, only those expenses of administration incurred that are reasonably related to the administration of that property by which obligations are secured shall be given priority over these obligations.

(2) Obligations secured by a mortgage, deed of trust, or other lien, including, but not limited to, a judgment lien, in the order of their priority, so far as they may be paid out of the proceeds of the property subject to the lien. If the proceeds are insufficient, the part of the obligation remaining unsatisfied shall be classed with general debts.

(3) Funeral expenses.

(4) Expenses of last illness.

(5) Family allowance.

(6) Wage claims.

(7) General debts, including judgments not secured by a lien and all other debts not included in a prior class.

(b) Except as otherwise provided by statute, the debts of each class are without preference or priority one over another. No debt of any class may be paid until all those of prior classes are paid in full. If property in the estate is insufficient to pay all debts of any class in full, each debt in that class shall be paid a proportionate share. **Leg.H.** Enacted Stats 1990 ch 79 §14 (AB 759), operative July 1, 1991. Amended Stats 1996 ch 862 §33 (AB 2751), effective January 1, 1997.

Prior Law: Former Prob C §11420, similar to the present section, was added Stats 1987 ch 923 §93, operative July 1, 1988, and repealed Stats 1990 ch 79 §13, operative July 1, 1991.

§11421. Immediate payment of priority debts

Subject to Section 11420, as soon as the personal representative has sufficient funds, after retaining sufficient funds to pay expenses of administration, the personal representative shall pay the following:

(a) Funeral expenses.

(b) Expenses of last illness.

(c) Family allowance.

(d) Wage claims. **Leg.H.** Enacted Stats 1990 ch 79 §14 (AB 759), operative July 1, 1991.

Prior Law: Former Prob C §11421, similar to the present section, was added Stats 1987 ch 923 §93, operative July 1, 1988, amended Stats 1988 ch 113 §15.3, effective May 25, 1988, operative July 1, 1988, and repealed Stats 1990 ch 79 §13, operative July 1, 1991.

§11422. Payment of debts on court order

(a) Except as provided in Section 11421, the personal representative is not required to pay a debt until payment has been ordered by the court.

(b) On the settlement of any account of the personal representative after the expiration of four months after the date letters are first issued to a general personal representative, the court shall order payment of debts, as the circumstances of the estate permit. If property in the estate is insufficient to pay all of the debts, the order shall specify the amount to be paid to each creditor.

(c) If the estate will be exhausted by the payment ordered, the account of the personal representative constitutes a final account, and notice of hearing shall be the notice given for the hearing of a final account. The personal representative is entitled to a discharge when the personal representative has complied with the terms of the order.

(d) Nothing in this section precludes settlement of an account of a personal representative for payment of a debt made without prior court authorization. **Leg.H.** Enacted Stats 1990 ch 79 §14 (AB 759), operative July 1, 1991.

Prior Law: Former Prob C §11422, similar to the present section, was added Stats 1987 ch 923 §93, operative July 1, 1988, and repealed Stats 1990 ch 79 §13, operative July 1, 1991.

§11423. Interest

(a) Interest accrues on a debt from the date the court orders payment of the debt until the date the debt is paid. Interest accrues at the legal rate on judgments.

(b) Notwithstanding subdivision (a), in the case of a debt based on a written contract, interest accrues at the rate and in accordance with the terms of the contract. The personal representative may, by order of the court, pay all or part of the interest accumulated and unpaid at any time when there are sufficient funds, whether the debt is then due or not.

(c) Notwithstanding subdivision (a), in the case of a debt for unpaid taxes or any other debt for which interest is expressly provided by statute, interest accrues at the rate and in accordance with the terms of the statute. **Leg.H.** Enacted Stats 1990 ch 79 §14 (AB 759), operative July 1, 1991.

Prior Law: Former Prob C §11423, similar to the present section, was added Stats 1987 ch 923 §93, operative July 1, 1988, and repealed Stats 1990 ch 79 §13, operative July 1, 1991.

§11424. Duty of personal representative to pay debts pursuant to court order

The personal representative shall pay a debt to the extent of the order for payment of the debt, and is liable personally and on the bond, if any, for failure to make the payment. **Leg.H.** Enacted Stats 1990 ch 79 §14 (AB 759), operative July 1, 1991.

Prior Law: Former Prob C §11424, similar to the present section, was added Stats 1987 ch 923 §93, operative July 1, 1988, and repealed Stats 1990 ch 79 §13, operative July 1, 1991.

§11425. [Section repealed 1992]

Leg.H. Enacted Stats 1990 ch 79 §14 (AB 759), operative July 1, 1991. Repealed Stats 1991 ch 1055 §28 (SB 271). The repealed section related to payments of debts not due.

Prior Law: Former Prob C §11425, similar to the repealed section, was added Stats 1987 ch 923 §93, operative July 1, 1988, and repealed Stats 1990 ch 79 §13, operative July 1, 1991.

§11426. [Section repealed 1992]

Leg.H. Enacted Stats 1990 ch 79 §14 (AB 759), operative July 1, 1991. Repealed Stats 1991 ch 1055 §29 (SB 271). See Prob C §11465.

Prior Law: Former Prob C §11426, similar to Prob C §11465, was added Stats 1987 ch 923 §93, operative July 1, 1988, and repealed Stats 1990 ch 79 §13, operative July 1, 1991.

§11427. [Section repealed 1992]

Leg.H. Enacted Stats 1990 ch 79 §14 (AB 759), operative July 1, 1991. Repealed Stats 1991 ch 1055 §30 (SB 271). See Prob C §11463.

Prior Law: Former Prob C §11427, similar to the present section, was added Stats 1987 ch 923 §93, operative July 1, 1988, and repealed Stats 1990 ch 79 §13, operative July 1, 1991.

§11428. Deposit for missing creditor

(a) If an estate is in all other respects ready to be closed, and it appears to the satisfaction of the court, on affidavit or evidence taken in open court, that a debt has not been and cannot be paid because the creditor cannot be found, the court or judge shall make an order fixing the amount of the payment and directing the personal representative to deposit the payment with the county treasurer of the county in which the proceeding is pending.

(b) The county treasurer shall give a receipt for the deposit, for which the county treasurer is liable on the official bond. The receipt shall be treated by the court or judge in favor of the personal representative with the same force and effect as if executed by the creditor.

(c) A deposit with the county treasurer under the provisions of this section shall be received, accounted for, and disposed of as provided by Section 1444 of the Code of Civil Procedure. A deposit in the State Treasury under the provisions of this section shall be deemed to be made under the provisions of Article 1 (commencing with Section 1440) of Chapter 6 of Title 10 of Part 3 of the Code of Civil Procedure. **Leg.H.** Enacted Stats 1990 ch 79 §14 (AB 759), operative July 1, 1991.

Prior Law: Former Prob C §11428, similar to the present section, was added Stats 1987 ch 923 §93, operative July 1, 1988, and repealed Stats 1990 ch 79 §13, operative July 1, 1991.

§11429. Unpaid creditor

(a) Where the accounts of the personal representative have been settled and an order made for the payment of debts and distribution of the estate, a creditor who is not paid, whether or not included in the order for payment, has no right to require contribution from creditors who are paid or from distributees, except to the extent provided in Section 9392.

(b) Nothing in this section precludes recovery against the personal representative personally or on the bond, if any, by a creditor who is not paid, subject to Section 9053. **Leg.H.** Enacted Stats 1990 ch 79 §14 (AB 759), operative July 1, 1991. Amended Stats 1990 ch 140 §14.1 (SB 1855), operative July 1, 1991.

Prior Law: Former Prob C §11429, similar to the present section, was added Stats 1987 ch 923 §93, operative July 1, 1988, repealed Stats 1990 ch 79 §13, operative July 1, 1991, amended Stats 1990 ch 140 §14, operative until July 1, 1991, and repealed Stats 1990 ch 140 §30, operative July 1, 1991.

CHAPTER 3
ALLOCATION OF DEBTS BETWEEN ESTATE AND SURVIVING SPOUSE

When allocation may be made. §11440.
Petition for allocation. §11441.
Inventory of property of surviving spouse. §11442.
Notice of hearing. §11443.
Allocation. §11444.
Order implementing allocation. §11445.
Funeral expenses and last illness expenses. §11446.

§11440. When allocation may be made

If it appears that a debt of the decedent has been paid or is payable in whole or in part by the surviving spouse, or that a debt of the surviving spouse has been paid or is payable in whole or in part from property in the decedent's estate, the personal representative, the surviving spouse, or a beneficiary may, at any time before an order for final distribution is made, petition for an order to allocate the debt. **Leg.H.** Enacted Stats 1990 ch 79 §14 (AB 759), operative July 1, 1991.

Prior Law: Former Prob C §11440, similar to the present section, was added Stats 1987 ch 923 §93, operative July 1, 1988, and repealed Stats 1990 ch 79 §13, operative July 1, 1991.

§11441. Petition for allocation

The petition shall include a statement of all of the following:

(a) All debts of the decedent and surviving spouse known to the petitioner that are alleged to be subject to allocation and whether paid in whole or part or unpaid.

(b) The reason why the debts should be allocated.

(c) The proposed allocation and the basis for allocation alleged by the petitioner. **Leg.H.** Enacted Stats 1990 ch 79 §14 (AB 759), operative July 1, 1991.

Prior Law: Former Prob C §11441, similar to the present section, was added Stats 1987 ch 923 §93, operative July 1, 1988, and repealed Stats 1990 ch 79 §13, operative July 1, 1991.

§11442. Inventory of property of surviving spouse

If it appears from the petition that allocation would be affected by the value of the separate property of the surviving spouse and any community property and quasi-community property not administered in the estate and if an inventory and appraisal of the property has not been provided by the surviving spouse, the court shall make an order to show cause why the information should not be provided. **Leg.H.** Enacted Stats 1990 ch 79 §14 (AB 759), operative July 1, 1991.

Prior Law: Former Prob C §11442, similar to the present section, was added Stats 1987 ch 923 §93, operative July 1, 1988, and repealed Stats 1990 ch 79 §13, operative July 1, 1991.

§11443. Notice of hearing

The petitioner shall give notice of the hearing as provided in Section 1220, together with a copy of the petition and the order to show cause, if any. **Leg.H.** Enacted Stats 1990 ch 79 §14 (AB 759), operative July 1, 1991.

Prior Law: Former Prob C §11443, similar to the present section, was added Stats 1987 ch 923 §93, operative July 1, 1988, and repealed Stats 1990 ch 79 §13, operative July 1, 1991.

§11444. Allocation

(a) The personal representative and the surviving spouse may provide for allocation by agreement and, on a determination by the court that the agreement substantially protects the rights of interested persons, the allocation provided in the agreement shall be ordered by the court.

(b) In the absence of an agreement, each debt subject to allocation shall first be characterized by the court as separate or community, in accordance with the laws of the state applicable to marital dissolution proceedings. Following that characterization, the debt or debts shall be allocated as follows:

(1) Separate debts of either spouse shall be allocated to that spouse's separate property assets, and community debts shall be allocated to the spouses' community property assets.

(2) If a separate property asset of either spouse is subject to a secured debt that is characterized as that spouse's separate debt, and the net equity in that asset available to satisfy that secured debt is less than that secured debt, the unsatisfied portion of that secured debt shall be treated as an unsecured separate debt of that spouse and allocated to the net value of that spouse's other separate property assets.

(3) If the net value of either spouse's separate property assets is less than that spouse's unsecured separate debt or debts, the unsatisfied portion of the debt or debts shall be allocated to the net value of that spouse's one-half share of the community property assets. If the net value of that spouse's one-half share of the community property assets is less than that spouse's unsatisfied unsecured separate debt or debts, the remaining unsatisfied portion of the debt or debts shall be allocated to the net value of the other spouse's one-half share of the community property assets.

(4) If a community property asset is subject to a secured debt that is characterized as a community debt, and the net equity in that asset available to satisfy that secured debt is less than that secured debt, the unsatisfied portion of that secured debt shall be treated as an unsecured community debt and allocated to the net value of the other community property assets.

(5) If the net value of the community property assets is less than the unsecured community debt or debts, the unsatisfied portion of the debt or debts shall be allocated equally between the separate property assets of the decedent and the surviving spouse. If the net value of either spouse's separate property assets is less than that spouse's share of the unsatisfied portion of the unsecured community debt or debts, the remaining unsatisfied portion of the debt or debts shall be allocated to the net value of the other spouse's separate property assets.

(c) For purposes of this section:

(1) The net value of either spouse's separate property asset shall refer to its fair market value as of the date of the decedent's death, minus the date-of-death balance of any liens and encumbrances on that asset that have been characterized as that spouse's separate debts.

(2) The net value of a community property asset shall refer to its fair market value as of the date of the decedent's death, minus the date-of-death balance of any liens and encumbrances on that asset that have been characterized as community debts.

(3) In the case of a nonrecourse debt, the amount of that debt shall be limited to the net equity in the collateral, based on the fair market value of the collateral as of the date of the decedent's death, that is available to satisfy that debt. For the purposes of this paragraph, "nonrecourse debt" means a debt for which the debtor's obligation to repay is limited to the collateral securing the debt, and for which a deficiency judgment against the debtor is not permitted by law.

(d) Notwithstanding the foregoing provisions of this section, the court may order a different allocation of debts between the decedent's estate and the surviving spouse if the court finds a different allocation to be equitable under the circumstances.

(e) Nothing contained in this section is intended to impair or affect the rights of third parties. If a personal representative or the surviving spouse incurs any damages or expense, including attorney's fees, on account of the nonpayment of a debt that was allocated to the other party pursuant to subdivision (b), or as the result of a debt being misallocated due to fraud or intentional misrepresentation by the other party, the party incurring damages shall be entitled to recover from the other party for damages or expense deemed reasonable by the court that made the allocation. **Leg.H.** Enacted Stats 1990 ch 79 §14 (AB 759), operative July 1, 1991. Amended Stats 2001 ch 72 §1 (SB 668), effective January 1, 2002.

Prior Law: Former Prob C §11444, similar to the present section, was added Stats 1987 ch 923 §93, operative July 1, 1988, and repealed Stats 1990 ch 79 §13, operative July 1, 1991.

§11445. Order implementing allocation

On making a determination as provided in this chapter, the court shall make an order that:

(a) Directs the personal representative to make payment of the amounts allocated to the estate by payment to the surviving spouse or creditors.

(b) Directs the personal representative to charge amounts allocated to the surviving spouse against any property or interests of the surviving spouse that are in the possession or control of the personal representative. To the extent that property or interests of the surviving spouse in the possession or control of the personal representative are insufficient to satisfy the allocation, the court order shall summarily direct the surviving spouse to pay the allocation to the personal representative. **Leg.H.** Enacted Stats 1990 ch 79 §14 (AB 759), operative July 1, 1991.

Prior Law: Former Prob C §11445, similar to the present section, was added Stats 1987 ch 923 §93, operative July 1, 1988, and repealed Stats 1990 ch 79 §13, operative July 1, 1991.

§11446. Funeral expenses and last illness expenses

Notwithstanding any other statute, funeral expenses and expenses of last illness shall be charged against the estate of the decedent and shall not be allocated to, or charged against the community share of, the surviving spouse, whether or not the surviving spouse is financially able to pay the expenses and whether or not the surviving spouse or any other person is also liable for the expenses. **Leg.H.** Enacted Stats 1990 ch 79 §14 (AB 759), operative July 1, 1991.

Prior Law: Former Prob C §11446, similar to the present section, was added Stats 1987 ch 923 §93, operative July 1, 1988, and repealed Stats 1990 ch 79 §13, operative July 1, 1991.

CHAPTER 4
DEBTS THAT ARE CONTINGENT, DISPUTED, OR NOT DUE

"Contingent"; "Disputed"; "Not due". §11460.
Court orders providing for contingent, disputed or undue debts; Notice of hearing. §11461.
Approval of agreement. §11462.
Deposit of amount to be paid if debt becomes absolute, established, or due. §11463.
Distribution of property on assumption of liability for debt; Conditions; Statute of limitations. §11464.
Appointment of trustee to receive payment. §11465.
Distribution of property where bond provided. §11466.
Order to continue administration of estate. §11467.

§11460. "Contingent"; "Disputed"; "Not due"

As used in this chapter:

(a) A debt is "contingent" if it is established under Part 4 (commencing with Section 9000) in either a fixed or an uncertain amount and will become absolute on occurrence of a stated event other than the passage of time. The term includes a secured obligation for which there may be recourse against property in the estate, other than the property that is the security, if the security is insufficient.

(b) A debt is "disputed" if it is a claim rejected in whole or in part under Part 4 (commencing with Section 9000) and is not barred under Section 9353 as to the part rejected.

(c) A debt is "not due" if it is established under Part 4 (commencing with Section 9000) and will become due on the passage of time. The term includes a debt payable in installments. **Leg.H.** Added Stats 1991 ch 1055 §31 (SB 271).

§11461. Court orders providing for contingent, disputed or undue debts; Notice of hearing

When all other debts have been paid and the estate is otherwise in a condition to be closed, on petition by an interested person, the court may make or modify an order or a combination of orders under this chapter that the court in its discretion determines is appropriate to provide adequately for a debt that is contingent, disputed, or not due, if the debt becomes absolute, established, or due. Notice of the hearing on the petition shall be given as provided in Section 1220 to the creditor whose debt is contingent, disputed, or not due, as well as to the persons provided in Section 11601. **Leg.H.** Added Stats 1991 ch 1055 §31 (SB 271).

§11462. Approval of agreement

Notwithstanding any other provision of this chapter, if the court determines that all interested persons agree to the manner of providing for a debt that is contingent, disputed, or not due and that the agreement reasonably protects all interested persons and will not extend administration of the estate unreasonably, the court shall approve the agreement. **Leg.H.** Added Stats 1991 ch 1055 §31 (SB 271).

§11463. Deposit of amount to be paid if debt becomes absolute, established, or due

The court may order an amount deposited in a financial institution, as provided in Chapter 3 (commencing with Section 9700) of Part 5, that would be payable if a debt that is contingent, disputed, or not due, were absolute, established, or due. The order shall provide that the amount deposited is subject to withdrawal only upon authorization of the court, to be paid to the creditor when the debt becomes absolute, established, or due, or to be distributed in the manner provided in Section 11642 if the debt does not become absolute or established. **Leg.H.** Added Stats 1991 ch 1055 §31 (SB 271).

§11464. Distribution of property on assumption of liability for debt; Conditions; Statute of limitations

(a) The court may order property in the estate distributed to a person entitled to it under the final order for distribution, if the person files with the court an assumption of liability for a contingent or disputed debt as provided in subdivision (b). The court may impose any other conditions the court in its discretion determines are just, including that the distributee give a security interest in all or part of the property distributed or that the distributee give a bond in an amount determined by the court.

(b) As a condition for an order under subdivision (a), each distributee shall file with the court a signed and acknowledged agreement assuming personal liability for the contingent or disputed debt and consenting to jurisdiction within this state for the enforcement of the debt if it becomes absolute or established. The personal liability of each distributee shall not exceed the fair market value on the date of distribution of the property received by the distributee, less the amount of liens and encumbrances. If there is more than one distributee, the personal liability of the distributees is joint and several.

(c) If the debt becomes absolute or established, it may be enforced against each distributee in the same manner as it could have been enforced against the decedent if the decedent had not died. In an action based on the debt, the distributee may assert any defense, cross-complaint, or setoff that would have been available to the decedent if the decedent had not died.

(d) The statute of limitations applicable to a contingent debt is tolled from the time the creditor's claim is filed until 30 days after the order for distribution becomes final. The signing of an agreement under subdivision (b) neither extends nor revives any limitation period. **Leg.H.** Added Stats 1991 ch 1055 §31 (SB 271).

§11465. Appointment of trustee to receive payment

(a) The court may order that a trustee be appointed to receive payment for a debt that is contingent, disputed, or not due. The court in determining the amount paid to the trustee shall compute the present value of the debt, giving consideration to a reasonable return on the amount to be invested. The trustee shall invest the payment in investments that would be proper for a personal representative or as authorized in the order.

(b) The trustee shall pay the debt as provided in the order. On completion of payment, any excess in possession of the trustee shall be distributed in the manner provided in Section 11642. **Leg.H.** Added Stats 1991 ch 1055 §31 (SB 271).

§11466. Distribution of property where bond provided

The court may order property in the estate distributed to a person entitled to it under the final order for distribution, if the person gives a bond conditioned on payment by the person of the amount of a contingent or disputed debt that becomes absolute or established. The amount of the bond shall be determined by the court, not to exceed the fair market value on the date of distribution of the property received by the distributee, less the amount of liens and encumbrances. In the case of a disputed debt or in the case of a contingent debt where litigation is required to establish the contingency, the cost of the bond is recoverable from the unsuccessful party as a cost of litigation. **Leg.H.** Added Stats 1991 ch 1055 §31 (SB 271).

§11467. Order to continue administration of estate

The court may order that the administration of the estate continue until the contingency, dispute, or passage of time of a debt that is contingent, disputed, or not due is resolved. **Leg.H.** Added Stats 1991 ch 1055 §31 (SB 271).

PART 10
DISTRIBUTION OF ESTATE

Chapter 1. Order for Distribution.
Chapter 2. Determination of Persons Entitled to Distribution.
Chapter 3. Distribution of Property in Estate.
Chapter 4. Deceased Distributee.
Chapter 5. Deposit with County Treasurer.
Chapter 6. Distribution to State.
Chapter 7. Partition or Allotment of Property.
Chapter 8. Interest and Income Accruing During Administration.

CHAPTER 1
ORDER FOR DISTRIBUTION

Article 1. General Provisions.
Article 2. Preliminary Distribution.
Article 3. Final Distribution.

ARTICLE 1
General Provisions

Petition for distribution. §11600.
Notice of hearing. §11601.
Opposition to petition. §11602.
Hearing and order. §11603.
Distribution to person other than beneficiary. §11604.
Assignment of beneficiary's interest; Written agreement required; Agreement requirements. §11604.5.
Conclusiveness of order. §11605.

§11600. Petition for distribution

The personal representative or an interested person may petition the court under this chapter for an order for preliminary or final distribution of the decedent's estate to the persons entitled thereto. **Leg.H.** Enacted Stats 1990 ch 79 §14 (AB 759), operative July 1, 1991.

Prior Law: Former Prob C §11600, similar to the present section, was added Stats 1988 ch 1199 §91.5, operative July 1, 1989, and repealed Stats 1990 ch 79 §13, operative July 1, 1991.

§11601. Notice of hearing

Notice of the hearing on the petition shall be given as provided in Section 1220 to all of the following persons:
(a) Each person listed in Section 1220.
(b) Each known heir whose interest in the estate would be affected by the petition.
(c) Each known devisee whose interest in the estate would be affected by the petition.
(d) The Attorney General, at the office of the Attorney General in Sacramento, if any portion of the estate is to escheat to the state and its interest in the estate would be affected by the petition.
(e) The Controller, if property is to be distributed to the state because there is no known beneficiary or if property is to be distributed to a beneficiary whose whereabouts is unknown. A copy of the latest account filed with the court shall be delivered to the Controller with the notice. **Leg.H.** Enacted Stats 1990 ch 79 §14 (AB 759), operative July 1, 1991. Amended Stats 2017 ch 319 §83 (AB 976), effective January 1, 2018.

Prior Law: Former Prob C §11601, similar to the present section, was added Stats 1988 ch 1199 §91.5, operative July 1, 1989, and repealed Stats 1990 ch 79 §13, operative July 1, 1991.

§11602. Opposition to petition

The personal representative or any interested person may oppose the petition. **Leg.H.** Enacted Stats 1990 ch 79 §14 (AB 759), operative July 1, 1991.

Prior Law: Former Prob C §11602, similar to the present section, was added Stats 1988 ch 1199 §91.5, operative July 1, 1989, and repealed Stats 1990 ch 79 §13, operative July 1, 1991.

§11603. Hearing and order

(a) If the court determines that the requirements for distribution are satisfied, the court shall order distribution of the decedent's estate, or such portion as the court directs, to the persons entitled thereto.
(b) The order shall:
(1) Name the distributees and the share to which each is entitled.
(2) Provide that property distributed subject to a limitation or condition, including, but not limited to, an option granted under Chapter 16 (commencing with Section 9960) of Part 5, is distributed to the distributees subject to the terms of the limitation or condition.
(c) If the whereabouts of a distributee named in the order is unknown, the order shall provide for alternate distributees and the share to which each is entitled. The alternate distributees shall be the persons, to the extent known or reasonably ascertainable, who would be entitled under the decedent's will or under the laws of intestate succession if the distributee named in the order had predeceased the decedent, or in the case of a devise for a charitable purpose, under the doctrine of cy pres. If the distributee named in the order does not claim the share to which the distributee is entitled within five years after the date of the order, the distributee is deemed to have predeceased the decedent for the purpose of this section and the alternate distributees are entitled to the share as provided in the order. **Leg.H.** Enacted Stats 1990 ch 79 §14 (AB 759), operative July 1, 1991. Amended Stats 2000 ch 17 §4.6 (AB 1491).

Prior Law: Former Prob C §11603, similar to the present section, was added Stats 1988 ch 1199 §91.5, operative July 1, 1989, and repealed Stats 1990 ch 79 §13, operative July 1, 1991.

§11604. Distribution to person other than beneficiary

(a) This section applies where distribution is to be made to any of the following persons:
(1) The transferee of a beneficiary.
(2) Any person other than a beneficiary under an agreement, request, or instructions of a beneficiary or the attorney in fact of a beneficiary.
(b) The court on its own motion, or on motion of the personal representative or other interested person or of the public administrator, may inquire into the circumstances surrounding the execution of, and the consideration for, the transfer, agreement, request, or instructions, and the amount of any fees, charges, or consideration paid or agreed to be paid by the beneficiary.
(c) The court may refuse to order distribution, or may order distribution on any terms that the court deems just and equitable, if the court finds either of the following:
(1) The fees, charges, or consideration paid or agreed to be paid by a beneficiary are grossly unreasonable.
(2) The transfer, agreement, request, or instructions were obtained by duress, fraud, or undue influence.
(d) Notice of the hearing on the motion shall be served on the beneficiary and on the persons described in subdivision (a) at least 15 days before the hearing in the manner provided in Section 415.10 or 415.30 of the Code of Civil Procedure. **Leg.H.** Enacted Stats 1990 ch 79 §14 (AB 759), operative July 1, 1991.

Prior Law: Former Prob C §11604, similar to the present section, was added Stats 1988 ch 1199 §91.5, operative July 1, 1989, and repealed Stats 1990 ch 79 §13, operative July 1, 1991.

§11604.5. Assignment of beneficiary's interest; Written agreement required; Agreement requirements

(a) This section applies when distribution from a decedent's estate is made to a transferee for value who acquires any interest of a beneficiary in exchange for cash or other consideration.
(b) For purposes of this section, a transferee for value is a person who satisfies both of the following criteria:
(1) The person purchases the interest from a beneficiary for consideration pursuant to a written agreement.
(2) The person, directly or indirectly, regularly engages in the purchase of beneficial interests in estates for consideration.
(c) This section does not apply to any of the following:
(1) A transferee who is a beneficiary of the estate or a person who has a claim to distribution from the estate under another instrument or by intestate succession.
(2) A transferee who is either the registered domestic partner of the beneficiary, or is related by blood, marriage, or adoption to the beneficiary or the decedent.
(3) A transaction made in conformity with the California Financing Law (Division 9 (commencing with Section 22000) of the Financial Code) and subject to regulation by the Department of Financial Protection and Innovation.

(4) A transferee who is engaged in the business of locating missing or unknown heirs and who acquires an interest from a beneficiary solely in exchange for providing information or services associated with locating the heir or beneficiary.

(d) A written agreement is effective only if all of the following conditions are met:

(1) The executed written agreement is filed with the court not later than 30 days following the date of its execution or, if administration of the decedent's estate has not commenced, then within 30 days of issuance of the letters of administration or letters testamentary, but in no event later than 15 days prior to the hearing on the petition for final distribution. Prior to filing or serving that written agreement, the transferee for value shall redact any personally identifying information about the beneficiary, other than the name and address of the beneficiary, and any financial information provided by the beneficiary to the transferee for value on the application for cash or other consideration, from the agreement.

(2) If the negotiation or discussion between the beneficiary and the transferee for value leading to the execution of the written agreement by the beneficiary was conducted in a language other than English, the beneficiary shall receive the written agreement in English, together with a copy of the agreement translated into the language in which it was negotiated or discussed. The written agreement and the translated copy, if any, shall be provided to the beneficiary.

(3) The documents signed by, or provided to, the beneficiary are printed in at least 10-point type.

(4) The transferee for value executes a declaration or affidavit attesting that the requirements of this section have been satisfied, and the declaration or affidavit is filed with the court within 30 days of execution of the written agreement or, if administration of the decedent's estate has not commenced, then within 30 days of issuance of the letters of administration or letters testamentary, but in no event later than 15 days prior to the hearing on the petition for final distribution.

(5) Notice of the assignment is served on the personal representative or the attorney of record for the personal representative within 30 days of execution of the written agreement or, if general or special letters of administration or letters testamentary have not been issued, then within 30 days of issuance of the letters of administration or letters testamentary, but in no event later than 15 days before the hearing on the petition for final distribution.

(e) The written agreement shall include the following terms, in addition to any other terms:

(1) The amount of consideration paid to the beneficiary.

(2) A description of the transferred interest.

(3) If the written agreement so provides, the amount by which the transferee for value would have its distribution reduced if the beneficial interest assigned is distributed prior to a specified date.

(4) A statement of the total of all costs or fees charged to the beneficiary resulting from the transfer for value, including, but not limited to, transaction or processing fees, credit report costs, title search costs, due diligence fees, filing fees, bank or electronic transfer costs, or any other fees or costs. If all the costs and fees are paid by the transferee for value and are included in the amount of the transferred interest, then the statement of costs need not itemize any costs or fees. This subdivision shall not apply to costs, fees, or damages arising out of a material breach of the agreement or fraud by or on the part of the beneficiary.

(f) A written agreement shall not contain any of the following provisions and, if any such provision is included, that provision shall be null and void:

(1) A provision holding harmless the transferee for value, other than for liability arising out of fraud by the beneficiary.

(2) A provision granting to the transferee for value agency powers to represent the beneficiary's interest in the decedent's estate beyond the interest transferred.

(3) A provision requiring payment by the beneficiary to the transferee for value for services not related to the written agreement or services other than the transfer of interest under the written agreement.

(4) A provision permitting the transferee for value to have recourse against the beneficiary if the distribution from the estate in satisfaction of the beneficial interest is less than the beneficial interest assigned to the transferee for value, other than recourse for any expense or damage arising out of the material breach of the agreement or fraud by the beneficiary.

(g) The court on its own motion, or on the motion of the personal representative or other interested person, may inquire into the circumstances surrounding the execution of, and the consideration for, the written agreement to determine that the requirements of this section have been satisfied.

(h) The court may refuse to order distribution under the written agreement, or may order distribution on any terms that the court considers equitable, if the court finds that the transferee for value did not substantially comply with the requirements of this section, or if the court finds that any of the following conditions existed at the time of transfer:

(1) The fees, charges, or consideration paid or agreed to be paid by the beneficiary were grossly unreasonable.

(2) The transfer of the beneficial interest was obtained by duress, fraud, or undue influence.

(i) In addition to any remedy specified in this section, for any willful violation of the requirements of this section found to be committed in bad faith, the court may require the transferee for value to pay to the beneficiary up to twice the value paid for the assignment.

(j) Notice of the hearing on any motion brought under this section shall be served on the beneficiary and on the transferee for value at least 15 days before the hearing in the manner provided in Section 415.10 or 415.30 of the Code of Civil Procedure.

(k) If the decedent's estate is not subject to a pending court proceeding under the Probate Code in California, but is the subject of a probate proceeding in another state, the transferee for value shall not be required to submit to the court a copy of the written agreement as required under paragraph (1) of subdivision (d). If the written agreement is entered into in California or if the beneficiary is domiciled in California, that written agreement shall otherwise conform to the provisions of subdivisions (d), (e), and (f) in order to be effective. **Leg.H.** Added Stats 2005 ch 438 §1 (SB 390), effective January 1, 2006. Amended Stats 2015 ch 190 §71 (AB 1517), effective January 1, 2016; Stats 2019 ch 143 §78 (SB 251), effective January 1, 2020; Stats 2022 ch 452 §208 (SB 1498), effective January 1, 2023.

§11605. Conclusiveness of order

When a court order made under this chapter becomes final, the order binds and is conclusive as to the rights of all interested persons. **Leg.H.** Enacted Stats 1990 ch 79 §14 (AB 759), operative July 1, 1991.

Prior Law: Former Prob C §11605, similar to the present section, was added Stats 1988 ch 1199 §91.5, operative July 1, 1989, and repealed Stats 1990 ch 79 §13, operative July 1, 1991.

ARTICLE 2
Preliminary Distribution

Time for petition. §11620.
Order for distribution. §11621.
Bond. §11622.
Distribution under Independent Administration of Estates Act. §11623.
Costs of proceeding. §11624.

§11620. Time for petition

A petition for an order for preliminary distribution of all, or a portion of, the share of a decedent's estate to which a beneficiary is entitled may not be filed unless at least two months have elapsed after letters are first issued to a general personal representative. **Leg.H.** Enacted Stats 1990 ch 79 §14 (AB 759), operative July 1, 1991.

Prior Law: Former Prob C §11620, similar to the present section, was added Stats 1988 ch 1199 §91.5, operative July 1, 1989, and repealed Stats 1990 ch 79 §13, operative July 1, 1991.

§11621. Order for distribution

(a) The court shall order distribution under this article if at the hearing it appears that the distribution may be made without loss to creditors or injury to the estate or any interested person.

(b) The order for distribution shall be stayed until any bond required by the court is filed. **Leg.H.** Enacted Stats 1990 ch 79 §14 (AB 759), operative July 1, 1991.

Prior Law: Former Prob C §11621, similar to the present section, was added Stats 1988 ch 1199 §91.5, operative July 1, 1989, and repealed Stats 1990 ch 79 §13, operative July 1, 1991.

§11622. Bond

(a) If the court orders distribution before four months have elapsed after letters are first issued to a general personal representative, the court shall require a bond. The bond shall be in the amount of the distribution.

(b) If the court orders distribution after four months have elapsed after letters are first issued to a general personal representative, the court may require a bond. The bond shall be in the amount the court orders.

(c) Any bond required by the court shall be given by the distributee and filed with the court. The bond shall be conditioned on payment of the distributee's proper share of the debts of the estate, not exceeding the amount distributed. **Leg.H.** Enacted Stats 1990 ch 79 §14 (AB 759), operative July 1, 1991.

Prior Law: Former Prob C §11622, similar to the present section, was added Stats 1988 ch 1199 §91.5, operative July 1, 1989, and repealed Stats 1990 ch 79 §13, operative July 1, 1991.

§11623. Distribution under Independent Administration of Estates Act

(a) Notwithstanding Section 11601, if authority is granted to administer the estate without court supervision under the Independent Administration of Estates Act, Part 6 (commencing with Section 10400):

(1) The personal representative may petition the court for an order for preliminary distribution on notice as provided in Section 1220. Notwithstanding subdivision (c) of Section 1220, the court may not dispense with notice unless the time for filing creditor claims has expired.

(2) The aggregate of all property distributed under this section shall not exceed 50 percent of the net value of the estate. For the purpose of this subdivision, "net value of the estate" means the excess of the value of the property in the estate, as determined by all inventories and appraisals on file with the court, over the total amount of all creditor claims and of all liens and encumbrances recorded or known to the personal representative not included in a creditor claim, excluding any estate tax lien occasioned by the decedent's death.

(b) Nothing in this section limits the authority of the personal representative to make preliminary distribution under other provisions of this chapter, whether or not authority is granted to administer the estate under the Independent Administration of Estates Act, Part 6 (commencing with Section 10400). **Leg.H.** Enacted Stats 1990 ch 79 §14 (AB 759), operative July 1, 1991. Amended Stats 1990 ch 710 §41 (SB 1775), operative July 1, 1991; Stats 1991 ch 82 §30.5 (SB 896), effective June 30, 1991, operative July 1, 1991.

Prior Law: Former Prob C §11623, similar to the present section, was added Stats 1988 ch 1199 §91.5, operative July 1, 1989, and repealed Stats 1990 ch 79 §13, operative July 1, 1991.

§11624. Costs of proceeding

The costs of a proceeding under this article shall be paid by the distributee or the estate in proportions determined by the court. **Leg.H.** Enacted Stats 1990 ch 79 §14 (AB 759), operative July 1, 1991.

Prior Law: Former Prob C §11624, similar to the present section, was added Stats 1988 ch 1199 §91.5, operative July 1, 1989, and repealed Stats 1990 ch 79 §13, operative July 1, 1991.

ARTICLE 3
Final Distribution

Petition and order. §11640.
Distribution under court order. §11641.
After-acquired or after-discovered property. §11642.

§11640. Petition and order

(a) When all debts have been paid or adequately provided for, or if the estate is insolvent, and the estate is in a condition to be closed, the personal representative shall file a petition for, and the court shall make, an order for final distribution of the estate.

(b) The court shall hear and determine and resolve in the order all questions arising under Section 21135 (ademption by satisfaction) or Section 6409 (advancements).

(c) If debts remain unpaid or not adequately provided for or if, for other reasons, the estate is not in a condition to be closed, the administration may continue for a reasonable time, subject to Chapter 1 (commencing with Section 12200) of Part 11 (time for closing estate). **Leg.H.** Enacted Stats 1990 ch 79 §14 (AB 759), operative July 1, 1991. Amended Stats 2002 ch 138 §9 (AB 1784).

Prior Law: Former Prob C §11640, similar to the present section, was added Stats 1988 ch 1199 §91.5, operative July 1, 1989, amended Stats 1989 ch 21 §28, effective May 25, 1989, operative July 1, 1989, and repealed Stats 1990 ch 79 §13, operative July 1, 1991.

§11641. Distribution under court order

When an order settling a final account and for final distribution is entered, the personal representative may immediately distribute the property in the estate to the persons entitled to distribution, without further notice or proceedings. **Leg.H.** Enacted Stats 1990 ch 79 §14 (AB 759), operative July 1, 1991.

Prior Law: Former Prob C §11641, similar to the present section, was added Stats 1988 ch 1199 §91.5, operative July 1, 1989, and repealed Stats 1990 ch 79 §13, operative July 1, 1991.

§11642. After-acquired or after-discovered property

Any property acquired or discovered after the court order for final distribution is made shall be distributed in the following manner:

(a) If the order disposes of the property, distribution shall be made in the manner provided in the order. The court may, in an appropriate case, require a supplemental account and make further instructions relating to the property.

(b) If the order does not dispose of the property, distribution shall be made either (1) in the manner ordered by the court on a petition for instructions or (2) under Section 12252 (administration after discharge) if the personal representative has been discharged. **Leg.H.** Enacted Stats 1990 ch 79 §14 (AB 759), operative July 1, 1991.

Prior Law: Former Prob C §11642, similar to the present section, was added Stats 1988 ch 1199 §91.5, operative July 1, 1989, and repealed Stats 1990 ch 79 §13, operative July 1, 1991.

CHAPTER 2
DETERMINATION OF PERSONS ENTITLED TO DISTRIBUTION

Petition. §11700.
Notice of hearing. §11701.
Responsive pleading. §11702.
Attorney General as party. §11703.
Hearing; Petition by personal representative for authorization to participate. §11704.
Court order. §11705.

§11700. Petition

At any time after letters are first issued to a general personal representative and before an order for final distribution is made, the personal representative, or any person claiming to be a beneficiary or otherwise entitled to distribution of a share of the estate, may file a petition for a court determination of the persons entitled to distribution of the decedent's estate. The petition shall include a statement of the basis for the petitioner's claim. **Leg.H.** Enacted Stats 1990 ch 79 §14 (AB 759), operative July 1, 1991.

Prior Law: Former Prob C §11700, similar to the present section, was added Stats 1988 ch 1199 §91.5, operative July 1, 1989, and repealed Stats 1990 ch 79 §13, operative July 1, 1991.

§11701. Notice of hearing

Notice of the hearing on the petition shall be given as provided in Section 1220 to all of the following persons:

(a) Each person listed in Section 1220.

(b) Each known heir whose interest in the estate would be affected by the petition.

(c) Each known devisee whose interest in the estate would be affected by the petition.

(d) The Attorney General, at the office of the Attorney General in Sacramento, if any portion of the estate is to escheat to the state and its interest in the estate would be affected by the petition. **Leg.H.** Enacted Stats 1990 ch 79 §14 (AB 759), operative July 1, 1991.

Prior Law: Former Prob C §11701, similar to the present section, was added Stats 1988 ch 1199 §91.5, operative July 1, 1989, and repealed Stats 1990 ch 79 §13, operative July 1, 1991.

§11702. Responsive pleading

(a) Any interested person may appear and, at or before the time of the hearing, file a written statement of the person's interest in the estate. The written statement may be in support of, or in opposition to, the petition. No other pleadings are necessary and the written statement of each claimant shall be deemed denied by each of the other claimants to the extent the written statements conflict.

(b) If a person fails timely to file a writen statement:

(1) The case is at issue notwithstanding the failure and the case may proceed on the petition and written statements filed by the time of the hearing, and no further pleadings by other persons are necessary.

(2) The person may not participate further in the proceeding for determination of persons entitled to distribution, but the person's interest in the estate is not otherwise affected.

(3) The person is bound by the decision in the proceeding. **Leg.H.** Enacted Stats 1990 ch 79 §14 (AB 759), operative July 1, 1991.

Prior Law: Former Prob C §11702, similar to the present section, was added Stats 1988 ch 1199 §91.5, operative July 1, 1989, and repealed Stats 1990 ch 79 §13, operative July 1, 1991.

§11703. Attorney General as party

The Attorney General shall be deemed to be a person entitled to distribution of the estate for purposes of this chapter if the estate involves or may involve any of the following:

(a) A charitable trust, other than a charitable trust with a designated trustee that may lawfully accept the trust.

(b) A devise for a charitable purpose without an identified beneficiary.

(c) An escheat to the State of California. **Leg.H.** Enacted Stats 1990 ch 79 §14 (AB 759), operative July 1, 1991.

Prior Law: Former Prob C §11703, similar to the present section, was added Stats 1988 ch 1199 §91.5, operative July 1, 1989, and repealed Stats 1990 ch 79 §13, operative July 1, 1991.

§11704. Hearing; Petition by personal representative for authorization to participate

(a) The court shall consider as evidence in the proceeding any statement made in a petition filed under Section 11700 and any statement of interest filed under Section 11702. The court shall not hear or consider a petition filed after the time prescribed in Section 11700.

(b)(1) The personal representative may petition the court for authorization to participate, as necessary to assist the court, in the proceeding. Notice of the hearing on the petition shall be given to the persons identified in Section 11701 in the manner provided in Section 1220.

(2) The court may grant or deny this petition, in whole or in part, on the pleadings, without an evidentiary hearing or further discovery. A petition filed pursuant to this subdivision may be granted only upon a showing of good cause. The court shall determine the manner and capacity in which the personal representative may provide assistance in the proceeding. The court may direct the personal representative to file papers as a party to the proceeding, or to take other specified action, if deemed by the court to be necessary to assist the court. **Leg.H.** Enacted Stats 1990 ch 79 §14 (AB 759), operative July 1, 1991. Amended Stats 2013 ch 84 §1 (AB 1160), effective January 1, 2014.

Prior Law: Former Prob C §11704, similar to the present section, was added Stats 1988 ch 1199 §91.5, operative July 1, 1989, and repealed Stats 1990 ch 79 §13, operative July 1, 1991.

§11705. Court order

(a) The court shall make an order that determines the persons entitled to distribution of the decedent's estate and specifies their shares.

(b) When the court order becomes final it binds and is conclusive as to the rights of all interested persons. **Leg.H.** Enacted Stats 1990 ch 79 §14 (AB 759), operative July 1, 1991.

Prior Law: Former Prob C §11705, similar to the present section, was added Stats 1988 ch 1199 §91.5, operative July 1, 1989, and repealed Stats 1990 ch 79 §13, operative July 1, 1991.

CHAPTER 3
DISTRIBUTION OF PROPERTY IN ESTATE

Responsibility for distribution. §11750.
Receipt for distributed property. §11751.
Inventory by life tenant. §11752.
Filing receipts and discharge. §11753.
"Expense of administration of estate". §11754.

§11750. Responsibility for distribution

(a) The personal representative is responsible for distribution of the property in the estate in compliance with the terms of the court order for distribution.

(b) A distributee may demand, sue for, and recover from the personal representative or any person in possession, property to which the distributee is entitled.

(c) A distribution of property made in compliance with the terms of the court order for distribution is valid as to a person acting in good faith and for a valuable consideration. **Leg.H.** Enacted Stats 1990 ch 79 §14 (AB 759), operative July 1, 1991.

Prior Law: Former Prob C §11750, similar to the present section, was added Stats 1988 ch 1199 §91.5, operative July 1, 1989, and repealed Stats 1990 ch 79 §13, operative July 1, 1991.

§11751. Receipt for distributed property

The personal representative shall obtain the receipt of the distributee for property in the estate distributed by the personal representative. In the case of real property, the personal representative shall record the court order for distribution or the personal representative's deed or both in the county in which the real property is located. Recordation of the order or deed is deemed to be a receipt of the distributee for the property. **Leg.H.** Enacted Stats 1990 ch 79 §14 (AB 759), operative July 1, 1991.

Prior Law: Former Prob C §11751, similar to the present section, was added Stats 1988 ch 1199 §91.5, operative July 1, 1989, and repealed Stats 1990 ch 79 §13, operative July 1, 1991.

§11752. Inventory by life tenant

If personal property in the possession of a distributee is subject to possession by the distributee for life only, the personal representative shall demand an inventory of the property from the distributee. On receipt, the personal representative shall file the inventory with the court and deliver a copy to any distributee of the remainder. **Leg.H.** Enacted Stats 1990 ch 79 §14 (AB 759), operative July 1, 1991.

Prior Law: Former Prob C §11752, similar to the present section, was added Stats 1988 ch 1199 §91.5, operative July 1, 1989, and repealed Stats 1990 ch 79 §13, operative July 1, 1991.

§11753. Filing receipts and discharge

(a) Distribution in compliance with the court order entitles the personal representative to a full discharge with respect to property included in the order.

(b) The personal representative shall, before or at the time of the petition for discharge, file receipts for all property in the estate. In the case of real property, the personal representative shall file a statement that identifies the date and place of the recording and other appropriate recording information for the court order for distribution or the personal representative's deed.

(c) The court may excuse the filing of a receipt on a showing that the personal representative is unable, after reasonable effort, to obtain a receipt and that the property has been delivered to or is in the possession of the distributee. **Leg.H.** Enacted Stats 1990 ch 79 §14 (AB 759), operative July 1, 1991.

Prior Law: Former Prob C §11753, similar to the present section, was added Stats 1988 ch 1199 §91.5, operative July 1, 1989, and repealed Stats 1990 ch 79 §13, operative July 1, 1991.

§11754. "Expense of administration of estate"

Expenses of administration of the estate shall include reasonable storage, delivery, and shipping costs for distribution of tangible personal property to a distributee. **Leg.H.** Added Stats 1994 ch 806 §34 (AB 3686).

CHAPTER 4
DECEASED DISTRIBUTEE

Distribution despite death of beneficiary. §11801.
Manner of distribution. §11802.

§11801. Distribution despite death of beneficiary

(a) Except as provided in subdivision (b), the share in a decedent's estate of a beneficiary who survives the decedent but who dies before distribution shall be distributed under this chapter with the same effect as though the distribution were made to the beneficiary while living.

(b) Subject to Section 21525, distribution may not be made under this chapter if the decedent's will provides that the beneficiary is entitled to take under the will only if the beneficiary survives the date of distribution or other period stated in the will and the beneficiary fails to survive the date of distribution or other period. **Leg.H.** Enacted Stats 1990 ch 79 §14 (AB 759), operative July 1, 1991.

Prior Law: Former Prob C §11801, similar to the present section, was added Stats 1988 ch 1199 §91.5, operative July 1, 1989, amended Stats 1989 ch 21 §29, effective May 25, 1989, operative July 1, 1989, and repealed Stats 1990 ch 79 §13, operative July 1, 1991.

§11802. Manner of distribution

If a beneficiary satisfies the requirement of Section 11801, the beneficiary's share in the decedent's estate shall be distributed as follows:

(a) Except as otherwise provided in this section, distribution shall be made to the personal representative of the estate of the beneficiary for the purpose of administration in the estate of the beneficiary.

(b) If the beneficiary was issue of the decedent and died intestate while under the age of majority and not having been emancipated, distribution shall be made directly to the heirs of the beneficiary without administration in the estate of the beneficiary.

(c) If a person entitled to the beneficiary's share proceeds under Division 8 (commencing with Section 13000) (disposition of estate without administration), distribution shall be made under Division 8. **Leg.H.** Enacted Stats 1990 ch 79 §14 (AB 759), operative July 1, 1991.

Prior Law: Former Prob C §11802, similar to the present section, was added Stats 1988 ch 1199 §91.5, operative July 1, 1989, and repealed Stats 1990 ch 79 §13, operative July 1, 1991.

CHAPTER 5
DEPOSIT WITH COUNTY TREASURER

When deposit with county treasurer authorized. §11850.
Deposit of money; Sale of personal property and deposit of proceeds. §11851.
Receipt by county treasurer. §11852.
Copy of order for distribution. §11853.
Claim for property deposited in county treasury. §11854.

§11850. When deposit with county treasurer authorized

Subject to Section 11851, the personal representative may deposit property to be distributed with the county treasurer of the county in which the proceedings are pending in the name of the distributee in any of the following cases:

(a) The property remains in the possession of the personal representative unclaimed or the whereabouts of the distributee is unknown.

(b) The distributee refuses to give a receipt for the property.

(c) The distributee is a minor or incompetent person who has no guardian, conservator, or other fiduciary to receive the property or person authorized to give a receipt for the property.

(d) For any other reason the property cannot be distributed, and the personal representative desires discharge. Notwithstanding Section 11851, deposit may not be made under this subdivision except on court order. **Leg.H.** Enacted Stats 1990 ch 79 §14 (AB 759), operative July 1, 1991.

Prior Law: Former Prob C §11850, similar to the present section, was added Stats 1988 ch 1199 §91.5, operative July 1, 1989, and repealed Stats 1990 ch 79 §13, operative July 1, 1991.

§11851. Deposit of money; Sale of personal property and deposit of proceeds

(a) If property authorized by Section 11850 to be deposited with the county treasurer consists of money, the personal representative may deposit the money.

(b) If property authorized by Section 11850 to be deposited with the county treasurer consists of personal property other than money, the personal representative may not deposit the personal property except on court order. If it appears to the court that sale is for the benefit of interested persons, the court shall order the personal property sold, and the proceeds of sale, less expenses of sale allowed by the court, shall be deposited in the county treasury. If it appears to the court that sale is not for the benefit of interested persons, the court shall order the personal property deposited with the Controller, to be held subject to the provisions of Chapter 6 (commencing with Section 11900). **Leg.H.** Enacted Stats 1990 ch 79 §14 (AB 759), operative July 1, 1991.

Prior Law: Former Prob C §11851, similar to the present section, was added Stats 1988 ch 1199 §91.5, operative July 1, 1989, and repealed Stats 1990 ch 79 §13, operative July 1, 1991.

§11852. Receipt by county treasurer

The county treasurer shall give a receipt for a deposit made under this chapter and is liable on the official bond of the county treasurer for the money deposited. The receipt has the same effect as if executed by the distributee. **Leg.H.** Enacted Stats 1990 ch 79 §14 (AB 759), operative July 1, 1991.

Prior Law: Former Prob C §11852, similar to the present section, was added Stats 1988 ch 1199 §91.5, operative July 1, 1989, and repealed Stats 1990 ch 79 §13, operative July 1, 1991.

§11853. Copy of order for distribution

If money is deposited or is already on deposit with the county treasurer, the personal representative shall deliver to the county treasurer a certified copy of the order for distribution. **Leg.H.** Enacted Stats 1990 ch 79 §14 (AB 759), operative July 1, 1991.

Prior Law: Former Prob C §11853, similar to the present section, was added Stats 1988 ch 1199 §91.5, operative July 1, 1989, and repealed Stats 1990 ch 79 §13, operative July 1, 1991.

§11854. Claim for property deposited in county treasury

(a) A person may claim money on deposit in the county treasury by filing a petition with the court that made the order for distribution. The petition shall show the person's claim or right to the property. Unless the petition is filed by the person named in the decree for distribution of a decedent's estate, or the legal representative of the person or the person's estate, the petition shall state the facts required to be stated in a petition for escheated property filed under Section 1355 of the Code of Civil Procedure. On the filing of the petition, the same proceedings shall be had as are required by that section, except that the hearing shall be ex parte unless the court orders otherwise.

(b) If so ordered by the court, a copy of the petition shall be served on the Attorney General. The Attorney General may answer the petition, at the Attorney General's discretion.

(c) If the court is satisfied that the claimant has a right to the property claimed, the court shall make an order establishing the right. On presentation of a certified copy of the order, the county auditor shall draw a warrant on the county treasurer for the amount of money covered by the order.

(d) A claim for money distributed in the estate of a deceased person made after the deposit of the property in the State Treasury is governed by the provisions of Chapter 3 (commencing with Section 1335) of Title 10 of Part 3 of the Code of Civil Procedure. **Leg.H.** Enacted Stats 1990 ch 79 §14 (AB 759), operative July 1, 1991. Amended Stats 1994 ch 806 §35 (AB 3686).

Prior Law: Former Prob C §11854, similar to the present section, was added Stats 1988 ch 1199 §91.5, operative July 1, 1989, and repealed Stats 1990 ch 79 §13, operative July 1, 1991.

CHAPTER 6
DISTRIBUTION TO STATE

Distribution to State of California. §11900.
Distribution in trust for a class. §11901.
Disposition of property distributed to state. §11902.
Claims against property distributed to state. §11903.
No deposit in county treasury. §11904.

§11900. Distribution to State of California

(a) The court shall order property that is not ordered distributed to known beneficiaries to be distributed to the state.

(b) Insofar as practicable, any real property or tangible personal property shall be converted to money before distribution to the state. **Leg.H.** Enacted Stats 1990 ch 79 §14 (AB 759), operative July 1, 1991.

Prior Law: Former Prob C §11900, similar to the present section, was added Stats 1988 ch 1199 §91.5, operative July 1, 1989, and repealed Stats 1990 ch 79 §13, operative July 1, 1991.

§11901. Distribution in trust for a class

If the court orders distribution of property in the decedent's estate to the state, and the order includes words that otherwise create a trust in favor of unknown or unidentified persons as a class, the distribution shall vest in the state both legal and equitable title to the property. **Leg.H.** Enacted Stats 1990 ch 79 §14 (AB 759), operative July 1, 1991.

Prior Law: Former Prob C §11901, similar to the present section, was added Stats 1988 ch 1199 §91.5, operative July 1, 1989, and repealed Stats 1990 ch 79 §13, operative July 1, 1991.

§11902. Disposition of property distributed to state

(a) If the court orders distribution to the state, the personal representative shall promptly:

(1) Deliver any money to the State Treasurer.

(2) Deliver any personal property other than money to the Controller for deposit in the State Treasury.

(3) Cause a certified copy of the order to be recorded in the office of the county recorder of each county in which any real property is located.

(b) At the time of making a delivery of property or recordation under this section, the personal representative shall deliver to the Controller a certified copy of the order for distribution together with a statement of the date and place of each recording and other appropriate recording information. **Leg.H.** Enacted Stats 1990 ch 79 §14 (AB 759), operative July 1, 1991.

Prior Law: Former Prob C §11902, similar to the present section, was added Stats 1988 ch 1199 §91.5, operative July 1, 1989, and repealed Stats 1990 ch 79 §13, operative July 1, 1991.

§11903. Claims against property distributed to state

(a) Property distributed to the state shall be held by the Treasurer for a period of five years from the date of the order for distribution, within which time any person may claim the property in the manner provided by Title 10 (commencing with Section 1300) of Part 3 of the Code of Civil Procedure.

(b) A person who does not claim the property within the time prescribed in this section is forever barred, and the property vests absolutely in the state, subject to the provisions of Title 10 (commencing with Section 1300) of Part 3 of the Code of Civil Procedure. **Leg.H.** Enacted Stats 1990 ch 79 §14 (AB 759), operative July 1, 1991.

Prior Law: Former Prob C §11903, similar to the present section, was added Stats 1988 ch 1199 §91.5, operative July 1, 1989, and repealed Stats 1990 ch 79 §13, operative July 1, 1991.

§11904. No deposit in county treasury

No deposit of property in an estate shall be made in the county treasury by a personal representative if any other property in the estate is to be or has been distributed to the state under this chapter, but the property that would otherwise be deposited in the county treasury shall be transmitted promptly to the State Treasurer or Controller as provided in this chapter. **Leg.H.** Enacted Stats 1990 ch 79 §14 (AB 759), operative July 1, 1991.

Prior Law: Former Prob C §11904, similar to the present section, was added Stats 1988 ch 1199 §91.5, operative July 1, 1989, and repealed Stats 1990 ch 79 §13, operative July 1, 1991.

CHAPTER 7
PARTITION OR ALLOTMENT OF PROPERTY

Right to partition or allotment. §11950.
Petition. §11951.
Parties and notice; Objection to jurisdiction. §11952.
Disposition of property. §11953.
Referees. §11954.
Expenses. §11955.
Effect of division. §11956.

§11950. Right to partition or allotment

(a) If two or more beneficiaries are entitled to the distribution of undivided interests in property and have not agreed among themselves to a partition, allotment, or other division of the property, any of them, or the personal representative at the request of any of them, may petition the court to make a partition, allotment, or other division of the property that will be equitable and will avoid the distribution of undivided interests.

(b) A proceeding under this chapter is limited to interests in the property that are subject to administration and does not include other interests except to the extent the owners of other interests in the property consent to be bound by the partition, allotment, or other division. **Leg.H.** Enacted Stats 1990 ch 79 §14 (AB 759), operative July 1, 1991.

Prior Law: Former Prob C §11950, similar to the present section, was added Stats 1988 ch 1199 §91.5, operative July 1, 1989, and repealed Stats 1990 ch 79 §13, operative July 1, 1991.

§11951. Petition

(a) A petition under this chapter may be filed at any time before an order for distribution of the affected property becomes final.

(b) The petition shall:
(1) Describe the property.
(2) State the names of the persons having or claiming undivided interests.
(3) Describe the undivided interests, so far as known to the petitioner.
Leg.H. Enacted Stats 1990 ch 79 §14 (AB 759), operative July 1, 1991.

Prior Law: Former Prob C §11951, similar to the present section, was added Stats 1988 ch 1199 §91.5, operative July 1, 1989, and repealed Stats 1990 ch 79 §13, operative July 1, 1991.

§11952. Parties and notice; Objection to jurisdiction

(a) Notice of the hearing on the petition shall be given as provided in Section 1220 to the personal representative and to the persons entitled to distribution of the undivided interests.

(b) At the hearing the persons entitled to distribution of the undivided interests shall be considered the parties to the proceeding whether or not they have appeared or filed a responsive pleading. No one shall be considered as a plaintiff or as a defendant.

(c) Any objection to the jurisdiction of the court shall be made and resolved in the manner prescribed in Part 19 (commencing with Section 850) of Division 2. **Leg.H.** Enacted Stats 1990 ch 79 §14 (AB 759), operative July 1, 1991. Amended Stats 2003 ch 32 §12 (AB 167).

Prior Law: Former Prob C §11952, similar to the present section, was added Stats 1988 ch 1199 §91.5, operative July 1, 1989, and repealed Stats 1990 ch 79 §13, operative July 1, 1991.

§11953. Disposition of property

(a) The court shall partition, allot, or otherwise divide the property so that each party receives property with a value proportionate to the value of the party's interest in the whole.

(b) The court may direct the personal representative to sell property where, under the circumstances, sale would be more equitable than partition and where the property cannot conveniently be allotted to any one party. The sale shall be conducted in the same manner as other sales made during administration of an estate.

(c) Any two or more parties may agree to accept undivided interests. **Leg.H.** Enacted Stats 1990 ch 79 §14 (AB 759), operative July 1, 1991.

Prior Law: Former Prob C §11953, similar to the present section, was added Stats 1988 ch 1199 §91.5, operative July 1, 1989, and repealed Stats 1990 ch 79 §13, operative July 1, 1991.

§11954. Referees

(a) The court, in its discretion, may appoint one or three referees to partition property capable of being partitioned, if requested to do so by a party. The number of referees appointed must conform to the request of at least one of the parties.

(b) The referees shall have the powers and perform the duties of referees in, and the court shall have the same powers with respect to their report as in, partition actions under Title 10.5 (commencing with Section 872.010) of Part 2 of the Code of Civil Procedure. **Leg.H.** Enacted Stats 1990 ch 79 §14 (AB 759), operative July 1, 1991.

Prior Law: Former Prob C §11954, similar to the present section, was added Stats 1988 ch 1199 §91.5, operative July 1, 1989, and repealed Stats 1990 ch 79 §13, operative July 1, 1991.

§11955. Expenses

The expenses of partition shall be equitably apportioned by the court among the parties, but each party must pay the party's own attorney's fees. The amount charged to each party shall be included and specified in the order and, to the extent unpaid, constitutes a lien on the property allotted to the party. **Leg.H.** Enacted Stats 1990 ch 79 §14 (AB 759), operative July 1, 1991.

Prior Law: Former Prob C §11955, similar to the present section, was added Stats 1988 ch 1199 §91.5, operative July 1, 1989, and repealed Stats 1990 ch 79 §13, operative July 1, 1991.

§11956. Effect of division

(a) The partition, allotment, or other division made by the court shall control in proceedings for distribution, unless modified for good cause on reasonable notice.

(b) The proceedings leading to the partition, allotment, or other division may be reviewed on appeal from the order for distribution. **Leg.H.** Enacted Stats 1990 ch 79 §14 (AB 759), operative July 1, 1991.

Prior Law: Former Prob C §11956, similar to the present section, was added Stats 1988 ch 1199 §91.5, operative July 1, 1989, and repealed Stats 1990 ch 79 §13, operative July 1, 1991.

CHAPTER 8
INTEREST AND INCOME ACCRUING DURING ADMINISTRATION

Application of chapter. §12000.
Rate of interest. §12001.
Income and expenses of specific devise. §12002.
Interest on general pecuniary devise. §12003.

Interest on annuity. §12004.
Interest on devise for maintenance. §12005.
Remaining income to residuary or intestate distributees. §12006.
Law applicable where decedent died before July 1, 1989. §12007.
[No sections of these numbers]. §12008–12199.

§12000. Application of chapter

The provisions of this chapter apply where the intention of the testator is not otherwise indicated by the will. **Leg.H.** Enacted Stats 1990 ch 79 §14 (AB 759), operative July 1, 1991.

Prior Law: Former Prob C §12000, similar to the present section, was added Stats 1988 ch 1199 §91.5, operative July 1, 1989, and repealed Stats 1990 ch 79 §13, operative July 1, 1991.

§12001. Rate of interest

If interest is payable under this chapter, the rate of interest is three percentage points less than the legal rate on judgments in effect one year after the date of the testator's death and shall not be recomputed in the event of a change in the applicable rate thereafter. **Leg.H.** Enacted Stats 1990 ch 79 §14 (AB 759), operative July 1, 1991. Amended Stats 1992 ch 871 §14 (AB 2975).

Prior Law: Former Prob C §12001, similar to the present section, was added Stats 1988 ch 1199 §91.5, operative July 1, 1989, and repealed Stats 1990 ch 79 §13, operative July 1, 1991.

§12002. Income and expenses of specific devise

(a) Except as provided in this section, a specific devise does not bear interest.

(b) A specific devise carries with it income on the devised property from the date of death, less expenses attributable to the devised property during administration of the estate. For purposes of this section, expenses attributable to property are expenses that result directly from the use or ownership of the property, including property tax and tax on the income from the property, but excluding estate and generation-skipping transfer taxes.

(c) If income of specifically devised property is not sufficient to pay expenses attributable to the property, the deficiency shall be paid out of the estate until the property is distributed to the devisee or the devisee takes possession of or occupies the property, whichever occurs first. To the extent a deficiency paid out of the estate is attributable to the period that commences one year after the testator's death, whether paid during or after expiration of the one year period following the date of death, the amount paid is a charge against the share of the devisee, and the personal representative has an equitable lien on the specifically devised property as against the devisee in the amount paid.

(d) If specifically devised property is sold during administration of the estate, the devisee is entitled to the net income from the property until the date of sale, and to interest on the net sale proceeds thereafter, but no interest accrues during the first year after the testator's death. **Leg.H.** Enacted Stats 1990 ch 79 §14 (AB 759), operative July 1, 1991.

Prior Law: Former Prob C §12002, similar to the present section, was added Stats 1988 ch 1199 §91.5, operative July 1, 1989, and repealed Stats 1990 ch 79 §13, operative July 1, 1991.

§12003. Interest on general pecuniary devise

If a general pecuniary devise, including a general pecuniary devise in trust, is not distributed within one year after the testator's death, the devise bears interest thereafter. **Leg.H.** Enacted Stats 1990 ch 79 §14 (AB 759), operative July 1, 1991.

Prior Law: Former Prob C §12003, similar to the present section, was added Stats 1988 ch 1199 §91.5, operative July 1, 1989, and repealed Stats 1990 ch 79 §13, operative July 1, 1991.

§12004. Interest on annuity

(a) An annuity commences at the testator's death and shall be paid at the end of the annual, monthly, or other specified period.

(b) If an annuity is not paid at the end of the specified period, it bears interest thereafter, but no interest accrues during the first year after the testator's death. **Leg.H.** Enacted Stats 1990 ch 79 §14 (AB 759), operative July 1, 1991.

Prior Law: Former Prob C §12004, similar to the present section, was added Stats 1988 ch 1199 §91.5, operative July 1, 1989, and repealed Stats 1990 ch 79 §13, operative July 1, 1991.

§12005. Interest on devise for maintenance

A devisee of a devise for maintenance is entitled to interest on the amount of any unpaid accumulations of the payments held by the personal representative on each anniversary of the testator's death, computed from the date of the anniversary. **Leg.H.** Enacted Stats 1990 ch 79 §14 (AB 759), operative July 1, 1991.

Prior Law: Former Prob C §12005, similar to the present section, was added Stats 1988 ch 1199 §91.5, operative July 1, 1989, and repealed Stats 1990 ch 79 §13, operative July 1, 1991.

§12006. Remaining income to residuary or intestate distributees

Net income received during administration not paid under other provisions of this chapter and not otherwise devised shall be distributed pro rata as income among all distributees who receive either residuary or intestate property. If a distributee takes for life or for a term of years, the pro rata share of income belongs to the tenant for life or for the term of years. **Leg.H.** Enacted Stats 1990 ch 79 §14 (AB 759), operative July 1, 1991.

Prior Law: Former Prob C §12006, similar to the present section, was added Stats 1988 ch 1199 §91.5, operative July 1, 1989, and repealed Stats 1990 ch 79 §13, operative July 1, 1991.

§12007. Law applicable where decedent died before July 1, 1989

This chapter does not apply in cases where the decedent died before July 1, 1989. In cases where the decedent died before July 1, 1989, the applicable law in effect before July 1, 1989, continues to apply. **Leg.H.** Enacted Stats 1990 ch 79 §14 (AB 759), operative July 1, 1991.

Prior Law: Former Prob C §12007, similar to the present section, was added Stats 1988 ch 1199 §91.5, operative July 1, 1989, and repealed Stats 1990 ch 79 §13, operative July 1, 1991.

§§12008–12199. [No sections of these numbers]

PART 11
CLOSING ESTATE ADMINISTRATION

Chapter 1. Time for Closing Estate.
Chapter 2. Discharge of Personal Representative.

CHAPTER 1
TIME FOR CLOSING ESTATE

Time required for closing or status report. §12200.
Report of status of administration. §12201.
Citation of representative; Hearing. §12202.
Continuation of administration to pay family allowance. §12203.
Failure of personal representative to comply with order. §12204.
Sanction for failure to timely close estate. §12205.
Testamentary limitation of time for administration. §12206.

§12200. Time required for closing or status report

The personal representative shall either petition for an order for final distribution of the estate or make a report of status of administration not later than the following times:

(a) In an estate for which a federal estate tax return is not required, within one year after the date of issuance of letters.

(b) In an estate for which a federal estate tax return is required, within 18 months after the date of issuance of letters. **Leg.H.** Enacted Stats 1990 ch 79 §14 (AB 759), operative July 1, 1991.

Prior Law: Former Prob C §12200, similar to the present section, was added Stats 1988 ch 1199 §93, operative July 1, 1989, and repealed Stats 1990 ch 79 §13, operative July 1, 1991.

§12201. Report of status of administration

If a report of status of administration is made under Section 12200:

(a) The report shall show the condition of the estate, the reasons why the estate cannot be distributed and closed, and an estimate of the time needed to close administration of the estate.

(b) The report shall be filed with the court. Notice of hearing of the report shall be given as provided in Section 1220 to persons then interested in the estate, and shall include a statement in not less than 10-point boldface type or a reasonable equivalent thereof if printed, or in all capital letters if not printed, in substantially the following words: "YOU HAVE THE RIGHT TO PETITION FOR AN ACCOUNT UNDER SECTION 10950 OF THE CALIFORNIA PROBATE CODE."

(c) On the hearing of the report, the court may order either of the following:

(1) That the administration of the estate continue for the time and on the terms and conditions that appear reasonable, including an account under Section 10950, if the court determines that continuation of administration is in the best interests of the estate or of interested persons.

(2) That the personal representative shall petition for final distribution. **Leg.H.** Enacted Stats 1990 ch 79 §14 (AB 759), operative July 1, 1991.

Prior Law: Former Prob C §12201, similar to the present section, was added Stats 1988 ch 1199 §93, operative July 1, 1989, and repealed Stats 1990 ch 79 §13, operative July 1, 1991.

§12202. Citation of representative; Hearing

(a) The court may, on petition of any interested person or on its own motion, for good cause shown on the record, cite the personal representative to appear before the court and show the condition of the estate and the reasons why the estate cannot be distributed and closed.

(b) On the hearing of the citation, the court may either order the administration of the estate to continue or order the personal representative to petition for final distribution, as provided in Section 12201. **Leg.H.** Enacted Stats 1990 ch 79 §14 (AB 759), operative July 1, 1991. Amended Stats 1996 ch 563 §28 (SB 392).

Prior Law: Former Prob C §12202, similar to the present section, was added Stats 1988 ch 1199 §93, operative July 1, 1989, and repealed Stats 1990 ch 79 §13, operative July 1, 1991.

§12203. Continuation of administration to pay family allowance

(a) For purposes of this chapter, continuation of the administration of the estate in order to pay a family allowance is not in the best interests of the estate or interested persons unless the court determines both of the following:

(1) The family allowance is needed by the recipient to pay for necessaries of life, including education so long as pursued to advantage.

(2) The needs of the recipient for continued family allowance outweigh the needs of the decedent's beneficiaries whose interests would be adversely affected by continuing the administration of the estate for this purpose.

(b) Nothing in this section shall be construed to authorize continuation of a family allowance beyond the time prescribed in Section 6543.

(c) Nothing in this section limits the power of the court to order a preliminary distribution of the estate. **Leg.H.** Enacted Stats 1990 ch 79 §14 (AB 759), operative July 1, 1991.

Prior Law: Former Prob C §12203, similar to the present section, was added Stats 1988 ch 1199 §93, operative July 1, 1989, and repealed Stats 1990 ch 79 §13, operative July 1, 1991.

§12204. Failure of personal representative to comply with order

Failure of the personal representative to comply with an order made under this chapter is grounds for removal from office. **Leg.H.** Enacted Stats 1990 ch 79 §14 (AB 759), operative July 1, 1991.

Prior Law: Former Prob C §12204, similar to the present section, was added Stats 1988 ch 1199 §93, operative July 1, 1989, and repealed Stats 1990 ch 79 §13, operative July 1, 1991.

§12205. Sanction for failure to timely close estate

(a) The court may reduce the compensation of the personal representative or the attorney for the personal representative by an amount the court determines to be appropriate if the court makes all of the following determinations:

(1) The time taken for administration of the estate exceeds the time required by this chapter or prescribed by the court.

(2) The time taken was within the control of the personal representative or attorney whose compensation is being reduced.

(3) The delay was not in the best interest of the estate or interested persons.

(b) An order under this section reducing compensation may be made regardless of whether the compensation otherwise allowable under Part 7 (commencing with Section 10800) would be reasonable compensation for the services rendered by the personal representative or attorney.

(c) An order under this section may be made at any of the following hearings:

(1) The hearing for final distribution.

(2) The hearing for an allowance on the compensation of the personal representative or attorney.

(d) In making a determination under this section, the court shall take into account any action taken under Section 12202 as a result of a previous delay. **Leg.H.** Enacted Stats 1990 ch 79 §14 (AB 759), operative July 1, 1991. Amended Stats 1990 ch 710 §42 (SB 1775), operative July 1, 1991.

Prior Law: Former Prob C §12205, similar to the present section, was added Stats 1988 ch 1199 §93, operative July 1, 1989, and repealed Stats 1990 ch 79 §13, operative July 1, 1991.

§12206. Testamentary limitation of time for administration

A limitation in a will of the time for administration of an estate is directory only and does not limit the power of the personal representative or the court to continue administration of the estate beyond the time limitation in the will if the continuation is necessary. **Leg.H.** Enacted Stats 1990 ch 79 §14 (AB 759), operative July 1, 1991.

Prior Law: Former Prob C §12206, similar to the present section, was added Stats 1988 ch 1199 §93, operative July 1, 1989, and repealed Stats 1990 ch 79 §13, operative July 1, 1991.

CHAPTER 2
DISCHARGE OF PERSONAL REPRESENTATIVE

Order of discharge. §12250.
Discharge without administration. §12251.
Administration after discharge. §12252.

§12250. Order of discharge

(a) When the personal representative has complied with the terms of the order for final distribution and has filed the appropriate receipts or the court has excused the filing of a receipt as provided in Section 11753, the court shall, on ex parte petition, make an order discharging the personal representative from all liability incurred thereafter.

(b) Nothing in this section precludes discharge of the personal representative for distribution made without prior court order, so long as the terms of the order for final distribution are satisfied. **Leg.H.** Enacted Stats 1990 ch 79 §14 (AB 759), operative July 1, 1991.

Prior Law: Former Prob C §12250, similar to the present section, was added Stats 1988 ch 1199 §93, operative July 1, 1989, and repealed Stats 1990 ch 79 §13, operative July 1, 1991.

§12251. Discharge without administration

(a) At any time after appointment of a personal representative and whether or not letters have been issued, if it appears there is no property of any kind belonging to the estate and subject to administration, the personal representative may petition for the termination of further proceedings and for discharge of the personal representative. The petition shall state the facts required by this subdivision.

(b) Notice of the hearing on the petition shall be given as provided in Section 1220 to all interested persons.

(c) If it appears to the satisfaction of the court on the hearing that the facts stated in the petition are true, the court shall make an order terminating the proceeding and discharging the personal representative. **Leg.H.** Enacted Stats 1990 ch 79 §14 (AB 759), operative July 1, 1991.

Prior Law: Former Prob C §12251, similar to the present section, was added Stats 1988 ch 1199 §93, operative July 1, 1989, and repealed Stats 1990 ch 79 §13, operative July 1, 1991.

§12252. Administration after discharge

If subsequent administration of an estate is necessary after the personal representative has been discharged because other property is discovered or because it becomes necessary or proper for any other cause, both of the following shall apply:

(a) The court shall appoint as personal representative the person entitled to appointment in the same order as is directed in relation to an original appointment, except that the person who served as personal representative at the time of the order of discharge has priority.

(b) Notice of hearing of the appointment shall be given as provided in Section 1220 to the person who served as personal representative at the time of the order of discharge and to other interested persons. If property has been distributed to the State of California, a copy of any petition for subsequent appointment of a personal representative and the notice of hearing shall be given as provided in Section 1220 to the Controller. **Leg.H.** Enacted Stats 1990 ch 79 §14 (AB 759), operative July 1, 1991. Amended Stats 2007 ch 388 §1 (AB 403), effective January 1, 2008; Stats 2009 ch 8 §3 (AB 1163), effective January 1, 2010.

Prior Law: Former Prob C §12252, similar to the present section, was added Stats 1988 ch 1199 §93, operative July 1, 1989, and repealed Stats 1990 ch 79 §13, operative July 1, 1991.

PART 12
ADMINISTRATION OF ESTATES OF MISSING PERSONS PRESUMED DEAD

"Missing person" defined. §12400.
Presumption of death for purposes of administration. §12401.
Manner of administration of missing person's estate. §12402.
Jurisdiction of court. §12403.
Petition for administration. §12404.
Notice of hearing. §12405.
Determination whether person is person presumed to be dead; Search for missing person. §12406.
Appointment of personal representative and determination of date of disappearance. §12407.
Recovery of property by missing person upon reappearance. §12408.

§12400. "Missing person" defined

Unless the provision or context otherwise requires, as used in this part, "missing person" means a person who is presumed to be dead under Section 12401. **Leg.H.** Enacted Stats 1990 ch 79 §14 (AB 759), operative July 1, 1991.

Prior Law: Former Prob C §12400, similar to the present section, was added Stats 1987 ch 923 §93, operative July 1, 1988, and repealed Stats 1990 ch 79 §13, operative July 1, 1991.

§12401. Presumption of death for purposes of administration

In proceedings under this part, a person who has not been seen or heard from for a continuous period of five years by those who are likely to have seen or heard from that person, and whose absence is not satisfactorily explained after diligent search or inquiry, is presumed to be dead. The person's death is presumed to have occurred at the end of the period unless there is sufficient evidence to establish that death occurred earlier. **Leg.H.** Enacted Stats 1990 ch 79 §14 (AB 759), operative July 1, 1991.

Prior Law: Former Prob C §12401, similar to the present section, was added Stats 1987 ch 923 §93, operative July 1, 1988, and repealed Stats 1990 ch 79 §13, operative July 1, 1991.

§12402. Manner of administration of missing person's estate

Subject to the provisions of this part, the estate of a missing person may be administered in the manner provided generally for the administration of estates of deceased persons. **Leg.H.** Enacted Stats 1990 ch 79 §14 (AB 759), operative July 1, 1991.

Prior Law: Former Prob C §12402, similar to the present section, was added Stats 1987 ch 923 §93, operative July 1, 1988, and repealed Stats 1990 ch 79 §13, operative July 1, 1991.

§12403. Jurisdiction of court

(a) If the missing person was a resident of this state when last seen or heard from, the superior court of the county of the person's last known place of residence has jurisdiction for the purposes of this part.

(b) If the missing person was a nonresident of this state when last seen or heard from, the superior court of a county where real property of the missing person is located, or of a county where personal property is located if the missing person has no real property in this state, has jurisdiction for the purposes of this part. **Leg.H.** Enacted Stats 1990 ch 79 §14 (AB 759), operative July 1, 1991.

Prior Law: Former Prob C §12403, similar to the present section, was added Stats 1987 ch 923 §93, operative July 1, 1988, and repealed Stats 1990 ch 79 §13, operative July 1, 1991.

§12404. Petition for administration

(a) A petition may be filed in the court having jurisdiction under Section 12403 for the administration of the estate of a missing person.

(b) The petition may be filed by any person who may be appointed as a personal representative, other than a person described in subdivision (r) of Section 8461.

(c) In addition to the matters otherwise required in a petition for administration of the estate, the petition shall state all of the following:

(1) The last known place of residence and the last known address of the missing person.

(2) The time and circumstances when the missing person was last seen or heard from.

(3) That the missing person has not been seen or heard from for a continuous period of five years by the persons likely to have seen or heard from the missing person (naming them and their relationship to the missing person) and that the whereabouts of the missing person is unknown to those persons and to the petitioner.

(4) A description of the search or the inquiry made concerning the whereabouts of the missing person. **Leg.H.** Enacted Stats 1990 ch 79 §14 (AB 759), operative July 1, 1991.

Prior Law: Former Prob C §12404, similar to the present section, was added Stats 1987 ch 923 §93, operative July 1, 1988, amended Stats 1988 ch 1199 §93.5, operative July 1, 1989, and repealed Stats 1990 ch 79 §13, operative July 1, 1991.

§12405. Notice of hearing

Notice of hearing shall be served and published, and proof made, in the same manner as in proceedings for administration of the estate of a decedent, except that notice of hearing on the petition shall also be sent by registered mail to the missing person at his or her last known address. **Leg.H.** Enacted Stats 1990 ch 79 §14 (AB 759), operative July 1, 1991.

Prior Law: Former Prob C §12405, similar to the present section, was added Stats 1987 ch 923 §93, operative July 1, 1988, and repealed Stats 1990 ch 79 §13, operative July 1, 1991.

§12406. Determination whether person is person presumed to be dead; Search for missing person

(a) At the hearing, the court shall determine whether the alleged missing person is a person who is presumed to be dead under Section 12401. The court may receive evidence and consider the affidavits and depositions of persons likely to have seen or heard from or know the whereabouts of the alleged missing person.

(b) If the court is not satisfied that a diligent search or inquiry has been made for the missing person, the court may order the petitioner to conduct a diligent search or inquiry and to report the results. The court may order the search or inquiry to be made in any manner that the court determines to be advisable, including any or all of the following methods:

(1) Inserting in one or more suitable newspapers or other periodicals a notice requesting information from any person having knowledge of the whereabouts of the missing person.

(2) Notifying law enforcement officials and public welfare agencies in appropriate locations of the disappearance of the missing person.

(3) Engaging the services of an investigator.

(c) The costs of a search ordered by the court pursuant to subdivision (b) shall be paid by the estate of the missing person, but if there is no administration, the court in its discretion may order the petitioner to pay the costs. **Leg.H.** Enacted Stats 1990 ch 79 §14 (AB 759), operative July 1, 1991.

Prior Law: Former Prob C §12406, similar to the present section, was added Stats 1987 ch 923 §93, operative July 1, 1988, and repealed Stats 1990 ch 79 §13, operative July 1, 1991.

§12407. Appointment of personal representative and determination of date of disappearance

(a) If the court finds that the alleged missing person is a person presumed to be dead under Section 12401, the court shall do both of the following:

(1) Appoint a personal representative for the estate of the missing person in the manner provided for the estates of deceased persons.

(2) Determine the date of the missing person's death.

(b) The personal representative shall administer the estate of the missing person in the same general manner and method of procedure, and with the same force and effect, as provided for the administration of the estates of deceased persons, except as otherwise provided in this part. **Leg.H.** Enacted Stats 1990 ch 79 §14 (AB 759), operative July 1, 1991.

Prior Law: Former Prob C §12407, similar to the present section, was added Stats 1987 ch 923 §93, operative July 1, 1988, and repealed Stats 1990 ch 79 §13, operative July 1, 1991.

§12408. Recovery of property by missing person upon reappearance

(a) If the missing person reappears:

(1) The missing person may recover property of the missing person's estate in the possession of the personal representative, less fees, costs, and expenses thus far incurred.

(2) The missing person may recover from distributees any property of the missing person's estate that is in their possession, or the value of distributions received by them, to the extent that recovery from distributees is equitable in view of all the circumstances, but an action under this paragraph is forever barred five years after the time the distribution was made.

(b) The remedies available to the missing person under subdivision (a) are exclusive, except for any remedy the missing person may have by reason of fraud or intentional wrongdoing.

(c) Except as provided in subdivisions (a) and (b), the order for final distribution, when it becomes final, is conclusive as to the rights of the missing person, the rights of the beneficiaries of the missing person, and the rights of all other persons interested in the estate.

(d) If a dispute arises as to the identity of a person claiming to be a reappearing missing person, the person making the claim or any other interested person may file a petition under Section 11700, notwithstanding the limitations of time prescribed in Section 11700, for the determination of the identity of the person claiming to be the reappearing missing person. **Leg.H.** Enacted Stats 1990 ch 79 §14 (AB 759), operative July 1, 1991.

Prior Law: Former Prob C §12408, similar to the present section, was added Stats 1987 ch 923 §93, operative July 1, 1988, amended Stats 1988 ch 1199 §94, operative July 1, 1989, and repealed Stats 1990 ch 79 §13, operative July 1, 1991.

PART 13
NONDOMICILIARY DECEDENTS

Chapter 1. Definitions.
Chapter 2. Ancillary Administration.
Chapter 3. Collection of Personal Property of Small Estate by Sister State Personal Representative Without Ancillary Administration.
Chapter 4. Jurisdiction Over Foreign Personal Representative.

CHAPTER 1
DEFINITIONS

Application of definitions. §12500.
Ancillary administration. §12501.
Foreign nation. §12502.
Foreign nation personal representative. §12503.
Local personal representative. §12504.
Nondomiciliary decedent. §12505.
Sister state. §12506.
Sister state personal representative. §12507.

§12500. Application of definitions

Unless the provision or context otherwise requires, the definitions in this chapter govern the construction of this part. **Leg.H.** Enacted Stats 1990 ch 79 §14 (AB 759), operative July 1, 1991.

Prior Law: Former Prob C §12500, similar to the present section, was added Stats 1988 ch 1199 §94.5, operative July 1, 1989, and repealed Stats 1990 ch 79 §13, operative July 1, 1991.

§12501. Ancillary administration

"Ancillary administration" means proceedings in this state for administration of the estate of a nondomiciliary decedent. **Leg.H.** Enacted Stats 1990 ch 79 §14 (AB 759), operative July 1, 1991.

Prior Law: Former Prob C §12501, similar to the present section, was added Stats 1988 ch 1199 §94.5, operative July 1, 1989, and repealed Stats 1990 ch 79 §13, operative July 1, 1991.

§12502. Foreign nation

"Foreign nation" means a jurisdiction other than a state of the United States. **Leg.H.** Enacted Stats 1990 ch 79 §14 (AB 759), operative July 1, 1991.

Prior Law: Former Prob C §12502, similar to the present section, was added Stats 1988 ch 1199 §94.5, operative July 1, 1989, and repealed Stats 1990 ch 79 §13, operative July 1, 1991.

§12503. Foreign nation personal representative

"Foreign nation personal representative" means a personal representative appointed in a jurisdiction other than a state of the United States. **Leg.H.** Enacted Stats 1990 ch 79 §14 (AB 759), operative July 1, 1991.

Prior Law: Former Prob C §12503, similar to the present section, was added Stats 1988 ch 1199 §94.5, operative July 1, 1989, and repealed Stats 1990 ch 79 §13, operative July 1, 1991.

§12504. Local personal representative

"Local personal representative" means a nondomiciliary decedent's personal representative appointed in this state. **Leg.H.** Enacted Stats 1990 ch 79 §14 (AB 759), operative July 1, 1991.

Prior Law: Former Prob C §12504, similar to the present section, was added Stats 1988 ch 1199 §94.5, operative July 1, 1989, and repealed Stats 1990 ch 79 §13, operative July 1, 1991.

§12505. Nondomiciliary decedent

"Nondomiciliary decedent" means a person who dies domiciled in a sister state or foreign nation. **Leg.H.** Enacted Stats 1990 ch 79 §14 (AB 759), operative July 1, 1991.

Prior Law: Former Prob C §12505, similar to the present section, was added Stats 1988 ch 1199 §94.5, operative July 1, 1989, and repealed Stats 1990 ch 79 §13, operative July 1, 1991.

§12506. Sister state

"Sister state" means a state other than this state. **Leg.H.** Enacted Stats 1990 ch 79 §14 (AB 759), operative July 1, 1991.

Prior Law: Former Prob C §12506, similar to the present section, was added Stats 1988 ch 1199 §94.5, operative July 1, 1989, and repealed Stats 1990 ch 79 §13, operative July 1, 1991.

§12507. Sister state personal representative

"Sister state personal representative" means a personal representative appointed in a sister state. **Leg.H.** Enacted Stats 1990 ch 79 §14 (AB 759), operative July 1, 1991.

Prior Law: Former Prob C §12507, similar to the present section, was added Stats 1988 ch 1199 §94.5, operative July 1, 1989, and repealed Stats 1990 ch 79 §13, operative July 1, 1991.

CHAPTER 2
ANCILLARY ADMINISTRATION

Article 1. Opening Ancillary Administration.
Article 2. Probate of Nondomiciliary Decedent's Will Admitted to Probate in Sister State or Foreign Nation.
Article 3. Application of General Provisions.
Article 4. Distribution of Property to Sister State Personal Representative.

ARTICLE 1
Opening Ancillary Administration

Commencement of proceedings. §12510.
Venue. §12511.
Procedure. §12512.
Preference for appointment as local personal representative. §12513.

§12510. Commencement of proceedings

Any interested person, or a sister state or foreign nation personal representative, may commence an ancillary administration proceeding by a petition to the court for either or both of the following:

(a) Probate of the nondomiciliary decedent's will.

(b) Appointment of a local personal representative. **Leg.H.** Enacted Stats 1990 ch 79 §14 (AB 759), operative July 1, 1991.

Prior Law: Former Prob C §12510, similar to the present section, was added Stats 1988 ch 1199 §94.5, operative July 1, 1989, and repealed Stats 1990 ch 79 §13, operative July 1, 1991.

§12511. Venue

The proper county for an ancillary administration proceeding under this chapter is the county determined pursuant to Section 7052. **Leg.H.** Enacted Stats 1990 ch 79 §14 (AB 759), operative July 1, 1991.

Prior Law: Former Prob C §12511, similar to the present section, was added Stats 1988 ch 1199 §94.5, operative July 1, 1989, and repealed Stats 1990 ch 79 §13, operative July 1, 1991.

§12512. Procedure

Notice of an ancillary administration proceeding shall be given and, except as provided in Article 2 (commencing with Section 12520), the same proceedings had as in the case of a petition for probate of a will or appointment of a personal representative of a person who dies domiciled in this state. **Leg.H.** Enacted Stats 1990 ch 79 §14 (AB 759), operative July 1, 1991.

Prior Law: Former Prob C §12512, similar to the present section, was added Stats 1988 ch 1199 §94.5, operative July 1, 1989, and repealed Stats 1990 ch 79 §13, operative July 1, 1991.

§12513. Preference for appointment as local personal representative

If the decedent dies while domiciled in a sister state, a personal representative appointed by a court of the decedent's domicile has priority over all other persons except where the decedent's will nominates a different person to be the personal representative in this state. The sister state personal representative may nominate another person as personal representative and the nominee has the same priority as the sister state personal representative. **Leg.H.** Enacted Stats 1990 ch 79 §14 (AB 759), operative July 1, 1991.

Prior Law: Former Prob C §12513, similar to the present section, was added Stats 1988 ch 1199 §94.5, operative July 1, 1989, and repealed Stats 1990 ch 79 §13, operative July 1, 1991.

ARTICLE 2
Probate of Nondomiciliary Decedent's Will Admitted to Probate in Sister State or Foreign Nation

Proceedings governed by this article. §12520.
Petition for probate of nondomiciliary decedent's will. §12521.
Will admitted to probate in sister state. §12522.

Will admitted to probate in foreign nation. §12523.
Effect of admission of nondomiciliary decedent's will. §12524.

§12520. Proceedings governed by this article

(a) If a nondomiciliary decedent's will has been admitted to probate in a sister state or foreign nation and satisfies the requirements of this article, probate of the will in an ancillary administration proceeding is governed by this article.

(b) If a nondomiciliary decedent's will has been admitted to probate in a sister state or foreign nation, but does not satisfy the requirements of this article, the will may be probated in an ancillary administration proceeding pursuant to Part 2 (commencing with Section 8000). **Leg.H.** Enacted Stats 1990 ch 79 §14 (AB 759), operative July 1, 1991.

Prior Law: Former Prob C §12520, similar to the present section, was added Stats 1988 ch 1199 §94.5, operative July 1, 1989, and repealed Stats 1990 ch 79 §13, operative July 1, 1991.

§12521. Petition for probate of nondomiciliary decedent's will

(a) A petition for probate of a nondomiciliary decedent's will under this article shall include both of the following:

(1) The will or an authenticated copy of the will.

(2) An authenticated copy of the order admitting the will to probate in the sister state or foreign nation or other evidence of the establishment or proof of the will in accordance with the law of the sister state or foreign nation.

(b) As used in this section, "authenticated copy" means a copy that satisfies the requirements of Article 2 (commencing with Section 1530) of Chapter 2 of Division 11 of the Evidence Code. **Leg.H.** Enacted Stats 1990 ch 79 §14 (AB 759), operative July 1, 1991.

Prior Law: Former Prob C §12521, similar to the present section, was added Stats 1988 ch 1199 §94.5, operative July 1, 1989, and repealed Stats 1990 ch 79 §13, operative July 1, 1991.

§12522. Will admitted to probate in sister state

If a will of a nondomiciliary decedent was admitted to probate, or established or proved, in accordance with the laws of a sister state, the court shall admit the will to probate in this state, and may not permit a contest or revocation of probate, unless one or more of the following are shown:

(a) The determination in the sister state is not based on a finding that at the time of death the decedent was domiciled in the sister state.

(b) One or more interested parties were not given notice and an opportunity for contest in the proceedings in the sister state.

(c) The determination in the sister state is not final. **Leg.H.** Enacted Stats 1990 ch 79 §14 (AB 759), operative July 1, 1991.

Prior Law: Former Prob C §12522, similar to the present section, was added Stats 1988 ch 1199 §94.5, operative July 1, 1989, and repealed Stats 1990 ch 79 §13, operative July 1, 1991.

§12523. Will admitted to probate in foreign nation

(a) Except as provided in subdivision (b), if a will of a nondomiciliary decedent was admitted to probate, or established or proved, in accordance with the laws of a foreign nation, the court shall admit the will to probate in this state, and may not permit a contest or revocation of probate, if it appears from the order admitting the will to probate in the foreign nation, or otherwise appears, that all of the following conditions are satisfied:

(1) The determination in the foreign nation is based on a finding that at the time of death the decedent was domiciled in the foreign nation.

(2) All interested parties were given notice and an opportunity for contest in the proceedings in the foreign nation.

(3) The determination in the foreign nation is final.

(b) The court may refuse to admit the will, even though it is shown to satisfy the conditions provided in subdivision (a), where the order admitting the will was made under a judicial system that does not provide impartial tribunals or procedures compatible with the requirements of due process of law. **Leg.H.** Enacted Stats 1990 ch 79 §14 (AB 759), operative July 1, 1991.

Prior Law: Former Prob C §12523, similar to the present section, was added Stats 1988 ch 1199 §94.5, operative July 1, 1989, and repealed Stats 1990 ch 79 §13, operative July 1, 1991.

§12524. Effect of admission of nondomiciliary decedent's will

A nondomiciliary decedent's will admitted to probate under this article has the same force and effect as the will of a person who dies while domiciled in this state that is admitted to probate in this state. **Leg.H.** Enacted Stats 1990 ch 79 §14 (AB 759), operative July 1, 1991.

Prior Law: Former Prob C §12524, similar to the present section, was added Stats 1988 ch 1199 §94.5, operative July 1, 1989, and repealed Stats 1990 ch 79 §13, operative July 1, 1991.

ARTICLE 3
Application of General Provisions

Applicability of general provisions relating to estate administration. §12530.

§12530. Applicability of general provisions relating to estate administration

Except to the extent otherwise provided in this chapter, ancillary administration of a decedent's estate is subject to all other provisions of this code concerning the administration of the decedent's estate, including, but not limited to, opening estate administration, inventory and appraisal, creditor claims, estate management, independent administration, compensation, accounts, payment of debts, distribution, and closing estate administration. **Leg.H.** Enacted Stats 1990 ch 79 §14 (AB 759), operative July 1, 1991.

Prior Law: Former Prob C §12530, similar to the present section, was added Stats 1988 ch 1199 §94.5, operative July 1, 1989, amended Stats 1989 ch 21 §30, effective May 25, 1989, operative July 1, 1989, and repealed Stats 1990 ch 79 §13, operative July 1, 1991.

ARTICLE 4
Distribution of Property to Sister State Personal Representative

Order for distribution to sister state personal representative. §12540.
Sale of real property and distribution of proceeds. §12541.
Distribution where estate in sister state is insolvent. §12542.

§12540. Order for distribution to sister state personal representative

(a) If a person dies while domiciled in a sister state, the court in an ancillary administration proceeding may make an order for preliminary or final distribution of all or part of the decedent's personal property in this state to the sister state personal representative if distribution is in the best interest of the estate or interested persons.

(b) The court order shall be made in the manner and pursuant to the procedure provided in, and is subject to the provisions of, Chapter 1 (commencing with Section 11600) of Part 10. **Leg.H.** Enacted Stats 1990 ch 79 §14 (AB 759), operative July 1, 1991.

Prior Law: Former Prob C §12540, similar to the present section, was added Stats 1988 ch 1199 §94.5, operative July 1, 1989, and repealed Stats 1990 ch 79 §13, operative July 1, 1991.

§12541. Sale of real property and distribution of proceeds

If necessary to make distribution pursuant to this article, real property in the nondomiciliary decedent's estate may be sold and the court may order the proceeds to be distributed to the sister state personal representative. The sale shall be made in the same manner as other sales of real property of a decedent. **Leg.H.** Enacted Stats 1990 ch 79 §14 (AB 759), operative July 1, 1991.

Prior Law: Former Prob C §12541, similar to the present section, was added Stats 1988 ch 1199 §94.5, operative July 1, 1989, and repealed Stats 1990 ch 79 §13, operative July 1, 1991.

§12542. Distribution where estate in sister state is insolvent

If the nondomiciliary decedent's estate in the sister state where the decedent was domiciled is insolvent, distribution may be made only to the sister state personal representative and not to the beneficiaries. **Leg.H.** Enacted Stats 1990 ch 79 §14 (AB 759), operative July 1, 1991.

Prior Law: Former Prob C §12542, similar to the present section, was added Stats 1988 ch 1199 §94.5, operative July 1, 1989, and repealed Stats 1990 ch 79 §13, operative July 1, 1991.

CHAPTER 3
COLLECTION OF PERSONAL PROPERTY OF SMALL ESTATE BY SISTER STATE PERSONAL REPRESENTATIVE WITHOUT ANCILLARY ADMINISTRATION

Collection of personal property of small estate without ancillary administration. §12570.

Payment, delivery, or transfer of property to sister state personal representative. §12571.
Action against holder of property to compel payment, delivery, or transfer. §12572.
Liability of sister state personal representative who takes property under this chapter. §12573.

§12570. Collection of personal property of small estate without ancillary administration

If a nondomiciliary decedent's property in this state satisfies the requirements of Section 13100, a sister state personal representative may, without petitioning for ancillary administration, use the affidavit procedure provided by Chapter 3 (commencing with Section 13100) of Part 1 of Division 8 to collect personal property of the decedent. **Leg.H.** Enacted Stats 1990 ch 79 §14 (AB 759), operative July 1, 1991.

Prior Law: Former Prob C §12570, similar to the present section, was added Stats 1988 ch 1199 §94.5, operative July 1, 1989, and repealed Stats 1990 ch 79 §13, operative July 1, 1991.

§12571. Payment, delivery, or transfer of property to sister state personal representative

The effect of payment, delivery, or transfer of personal property to the sister state personal representative pursuant to this chapter, and the effect of failure to do so, are governed by Chapter 3 (commencing with Section 13100) of Part 1 of Division 8. **Leg.H.** Enacted Stats 1990 ch 79 §14 (AB 759), operative July 1, 1991.

Prior Law: Former Prob C §12571, similar to the present section, was added Stats 1988 ch 1199 §94.5, operative July 1, 1989, and repealed Stats 1990 ch 79 §13, operative July 1, 1991.

§12572. Action against holder of property to compel payment, delivery, or transfer

The sister state personal representative may bring an action against a holder of the decedent's property, and may be awarded attorney's fees, as provided in subdivision (b) of Section 13105. **Leg.H.** Enacted Stats 1990 ch 79 §14 (AB 759), operative July 1, 1991.

Prior Law: Former Prob C §12572, similar to the present section, was added Stats 1988 ch 1199 §94.5, operative July 1, 1989, and repealed Stats 1990 ch 79 §13, operative July 1, 1991.

§12573. Liability of sister state personal representative who takes property under this chapter

A sister state personal representative who takes property by affidavit under this chapter is not liable as a person to whom payment, delivery, or transfer of the decedent's property is made under Section 13109 or 13110 to the extent that the sister state personal representative restores the property to the nondomiciliary decedent's estate in the sister state in compliance with Section 13111. **Leg.H.** Enacted Stats 1990 ch 79 §14 (AB 759), operative July 1, 1991.

Prior Law: Former Prob C §12573, similar to the present section, was added Stats 1988 ch 1199 §94.5, operative July 1, 1989, and repealed Stats 1990 ch 79 §13, operative July 1, 1991.

CHAPTER 4
JURISDICTION OVER FOREIGN PERSONAL REPRESENTATIVE

Jurisdiction by act of foreign personal representative. §12590.
Jurisdiction by act of decedent. §12591.

§12590. Jurisdiction by act of foreign personal representative

A sister state personal representative or foreign nation personal representative submits personally in a representative capacity to the jurisdiction of the courts of this state in any proceeding relating to the estate by any of the following actions:

(a) Filing a petition for ancillary administration.

(b) Receiving money or other personal property pursuant to Chapter 3 (commencing with Section 12570). Jurisdiction under this subdivision is limited to the amount of money and the value of personal property received.

(c) Doing any act in this state as a personal representative that would have given this state jurisdiction over the personal representative as an individual. **Leg.H.** Enacted Stats 1990 ch 79 §14 (AB 759), operative July 1, 1991.

Prior Law: Former Prob C §12590, similar to the present section, was added Stats 1988 ch 1199 §94.5, operative July 1, 1989, and repealed Stats 1990 ch 79 §13, operative July 1, 1991.

§12591. Jurisdiction by act of decedent

A sister state personal representative or foreign nation personal representative is subject to the jurisdiction of the courts of this state in a representative capacity to the same extent that the nondomiciliary decedent was subject to jurisdiction at the time of death. **Leg.H.** Enacted Stats 1990 ch 79 §14 (AB 759), operative July 1, 1991.

Prior Law: Former Prob C §12591, similar to the present section, was added Stats 1988 ch 1199 §94.5, operative July 1, 1989, and repealed Stats 1990 ch 79 §13, operative July 1, 1991.

DIVISION 8
DISPOSITION OF ESTATE WITHOUT ADMINISTRATION

Part 1. Collection or Transfer of Small Estate Without Administration. Part 2. Passage of Property to Surviving Spouse Without Administration.

PART 1
COLLECTION OR TRANSFER OF SMALL ESTATE WITHOUT ADMINISTRATION

Chapter 1. Definitions.
Chapter 2. General Provisions.
Chapter 3. Affidavit Procedure for Collection or Transfer of Personal Property.
Chapter 4. Court Order Determining Succession to Property.
Chapter 5. Affidavit Procedure for Real Property of Small Value.

CHAPTER 1
DEFINITIONS

Construction of words and phrases. §13000.
Holder of the decedent's property. §13002.
"Particular item of property". §13004.
"Property of decedent"; "Decedent's property"; "Money due decedent". §13005.
"Successor of the decedent". §13006.
"Proceeding". §13007.

§13000. Construction of words and phrases
Unless the provision or context otherwise requires, the definitions in this chapter govern the construction of this part. **Leg.H.** Enacted Stats 1990 ch 79 §14 (AB 759), operative July 1, 1991.

Prior Law: Former Prob C §13000, similar to the present section, was added Stats 1986 ch 783 §24, operative July 1, 1987, and repealed Stats 1990 ch 79 §13, operative July 1, 1991.

§13002. Holder of the decedent's property
"Holder of the decedent's property" or "holder" means, with respect to any particular item of property of the decedent, the person owing money to the decedent, having custody of tangible personal property of the decedent, or acting as registrar or transfer agent of the evidences of a debt, obligation, interest, right, security, or chose in action belonging to the decedent. **Leg.H.** Enacted Stats 1990 ch 79 §14 (AB 759), operative July 1, 1991.

Prior Law: Former Prob C §13002, similar to the present section, was added Stats 1986 ch 783 §24, operative July 1, 1987, and repealed Stats 1990 ch 79 §13, operative July 1, 1991.

§13004. "Particular item of property"
(a) "Particular item of property" means:

(1) Particular personal property of the decedent which is sought to be collected, received, or transferred by the successor of the decedent under Chapter 3 (commencing with Section 13100).

(2) Particular real property of the decedent, or particular real and personal property of the decedent, for which the successor of the decedent seeks a court order determining succession under Chapter 4 (commencing with Section 13150).

(3) Particular real property of the decedent with respect to which the successor of the decedent files an affidavit of succession under Chapter 5 (commencing with Section 13200).

(b) Subject to subdivision (a), "particular item of property" includes all interests specified in Section 62. **Leg.H.** Enacted Stats 1990 ch 79 §14 (AB 759), operative July 1, 1991. Amended Stats 1991 ch 1055 §32 (SB 271).

Prior Law: Former Prob C §13004, similar to the present section, was added Stats 1986 ch 783 §24, operative July 1, 1987, and repealed Stats 1990 ch 79 §13, operative July 1, 1991.

§13005. "Property of decedent"; "Decedent's property"; "Money due decedent"
"Property of the decedent," "decedent's property," "money due the decedent," and similar phrases, include property that becomes part of the decedent's estate on the decedent's death, whether by designation of the estate as beneficiary under an insurance policy on the decedent's life or under the decedent's retirement plan, or otherwise. **Leg.H.** Added Stats 1991 ch 1055 §33 (SB 271).

§13006. "Successor of the decedent"
"Successor of the decedent" means:

(a) If the decedent died leaving a will, the sole beneficiary or all of the beneficiaries who succeeded to a particular item of property of the decedent under the decedent's will. For the purposes of this part, a trust is a beneficiary under the decedent's will if the trust succeeds to the particular item of property under the decedent's will.

(b) If the decedent died without a will, the sole person or all of the persons who succeeded to the particular item of property of the decedent under Sections 6401 and 6402 or, if the law of a sister state or foreign nation governs succession to the particular item of property, under the law of the sister state or foreign nation. **Leg.H.** Enacted Stats 1990 ch 79 §14 (AB 759), operative July 1, 1991. Amended Stats 1991 ch 1055 §34 (SB 271).

Prior Law: Former Prob C §13006, similar to the present section, was added Stats 1986 ch 783 §24, operative July 1, 1987, amended Stats 1988 ch 1199 §95, operative July 1, 1989, and repealed Stats 1990 ch 79 §13, operative July 1, 1991.

§13007. "Proceeding"
"Proceeding" means either that a petition is currently pending in this state for administration of a decedent's estate under Division 7 (commencing with Section 7000), a special administrator for the decedent's estate has been appointed in this state and is now serving, or a personal representative for the decedent's estate has been appointed in this state with general powers. "Proceeding" does not include a petition for administration which was dismissed without the appointment of a personal representative, any proceeding under Division 8 (commencing with Section 13000), or any action or proceeding in another state. **Leg.H.** Added Stats 1992 ch 871 §15 (AB 2975), effective January 1, 1993.

CHAPTER 2
GENERAL PROVISIONS

Exclusions in determining property or estate of decedent or its value. §13050.
Authority of guardian, conservator, trustee, custodian, foreign personal representative, or attorney-in-fact. §13051.
Date of valuation of property. §13052.
Application of this part. §13053.
Reference to provision of former law deemed reference to comparable provisions of Chapter 3. §13054.

§13050. Exclusions in determining property or estate of decedent or its value
(a) For the purposes of this part:

(1) Any property or interest or lien thereon that, at the time of the decedent's death, was held by the decedent as a joint tenant, or in which the decedent had a life or other interest terminable upon the decedent's death, or that was held by the decedent and passed to the decedent's surviving spouse pursuant to Section 13500, shall be excluded in determining the property or estate of the decedent or its value. This excluded property shall include, but not be limited to, property in a trust revocable by the decedent during the decedent's lifetime.

(2) A multiple-party account to which the decedent was a party at the time of the decedent's death shall be excluded in determining the property or estate of the decedent or its value, whether or not all or a portion of the sums on deposit are community property, to the extent that the sums on deposit belong after the death of the decedent to a surviving party, P.O.D. payee, or beneficiary. For the purposes of this paragraph, the terms

"multiple-party account," "party," "P.O.D. payee," and "beneficiary" are defined in Article 2 (commencing with Section 5120) of Chapter 1 of Part 2 of Division 5.

(b) For the purposes of this part, all of the following property shall be excluded in determining the property or estate of the decedent or its value:

(1) Any vehicle registered under Division 3 (commencing with Section 4000) of the Vehicle Code or titled under Division 16.5 (commencing with Section 38000) of the Vehicle Code.

(2) Any vessel numbered under Division 3.5 (commencing with Section 9840) of the Vehicle Code.

(3) Any manufactured home, mobilehome, commercial coach, truck camper, or floating home registered under Part 2 (commencing with Section 18000) of Division 13 of the Health and Safety Code.

(c) For the purposes of this part, the value of the following property shall be excluded in determining the value of the decedent's property in this state:

(1) Any amounts due to the decedent for services in the Armed Forces of the United States.

(2) The amount, not exceeding sixteen thousand six hundred twenty-five dollars ($16,625), as adjusted periodically in accordance with Section 890, of salary or other compensation, including compensation for unused vacation, owing to the decedent for personal services from any employment. **Leg.H.** Enacted Stats 1990 ch 79 §14 (AB 759), operative July 1, 1991. Amended Stats 1996 ch 563 §29 (SB 392); Stats 2011 ch 117 §3 (AB 1305), effective January 1, 2012; Stats 2019 ch 122 §4 (AB 473), effective January 1, 2020.

Prior Law: Former Prob C §13050, similar to the present section, was added Stats 1986 ch 783 §24, operative July 1, 1987, amended Stats 1989 ch 397 §39, operative July 1, 1990, and repealed Stats 1990 ch 79 §13, operative July 1, 1991.

§13051. Authority of guardian, conservator, trustee, custodian, foreign personal representative, or attorney-in-fact

For the purposes of this part:

(a) The guardian or conservator of the estate of a person entitled to any of the decedent's property may act on behalf of the person without authorization or approval of the court in which the guardianship or conservatorship proceeding is pending.

(b) The trustee of a trust may act on behalf of the trust. In the case of a trust that is subject to continuing jurisdiction of the court pursuant to Chapter 4 (commencing with Section 17300) of Part 5 of Division 9, the trustee may act on behalf of the trust without the need to obtain approval of the court.

(c) If the decedent's will authorizes a custodian under the Uniform Gifts to Minors Act or the Uniform Transfers to Minors Act of any state to receive a devise to a beneficiary, the custodian may act on behalf of the beneficiary until such time as the custodianship terminates.

(d) A sister state personal representative may act on behalf of the beneficiaries as provided in Chapter 3 (commencing with Section 12570) of Part 13 of Division 7.

(e) The attorney in fact authorized under a durable power of attorney may act on behalf of the beneficiary giving the power of attorney. **Leg.H.** Enacted Stats 1990 ch 79 §14 (AB 759), operative July 1, 1991. Amended Stats 1991 ch 1055 §35 (SB 271).

Prior Law: Former Prob C §13051, similar to the present section, was added Stats 1986 ch 783 §24, operative July 1, 1987, amended Stats 1988 ch 1199 §95.5, operative July 1, 1989, and repealed Stats 1990 ch 79 §13, operative July 1, 1991.

§13052. Date of valuation of property

In making an appraisal for the purposes of this part, the probate referee shall use the date of the decedent's death as the date of valuation of the property. **Leg.H.** Enacted Stats 1990 ch 79 §14 (AB 759), operative July 1, 1991.

Prior Law: Former Prob C §13052, similar to the present section, was added Stats 1986 ch 783 §24, operative July 1, 1987, amended Stats 1988 ch 1199 §96, operative July 1, 1989, and repealed Stats 1990 ch 79 §13, operative July 1, 1991.

§13053. Application of this part

(a) Except as provided in subdivision (b), this part applies whether the decedent died before, on, or after July 1, 1987.

(b) This part does not apply and the law in effect at the time of payment, delivery, or transfer shall apply if the payment, delivery, or transfer was made prior to July 1, 1987, pursuant to former Probate Code Sections 630 to 632, inclusive, repealed by Chapter 783 of the Statutes of 1986. **Leg.H.** Enacted Stats 1990 ch 79 §14 (AB 759), operative July 1, 1991.

Prior Law: Former Prob C §13053, similar to the present section, was added Stats 1986 ch 783 §24, operative July 1, 1987, and repealed Stats 1990 ch 79 §13, operative July 1, 1991.

§13054. Reference to provision of former law deemed reference to comparable provisions of Chapter 3

A reference in any statute of this state or in a written instrument, including a will or trust, to a provision of former Sections 630 to 632, inclusive, repealed by Chapter 783, Statutes of 1986, shall be deemed to be a reference to the comparable provisions of Chapter 3 (commencing with Section 13100). **Leg.H.** Enacted Stats 1990 ch 79 §14 (AB 759), operative July 1, 1991.

Prior Law: Former Prob C §13054, similar to the present section, was added Stats 1986 ch 783 §24, operative July 1, 1987, and repealed Stats 1990 ch 79 §13, operative July 1, 1991.

CHAPTER 3
AFFIDAVIT PROCEDURE FOR COLLECTION OR TRANSFER OF PERSONAL PROPERTY

Collection or transfer of personal property without probate. §13100.
Definitions. § 13100.5.
Furnishing affidavit or declaration. §13101.
Presenting decedent's evidence of ownership. §13102.
Inventory and appraisal of real property. §13103.
Proof of identity. §13104.
Transfer of property to successor. §13105.
Protection of transferor from liability. §13106.
Recording of affidavit or declaration where property is obligation secured by lien on real property. §13106.5.
Claim against estate in probate. §13107.
Substitution of decedent's successor in interest. §13107.5.
No pending probate proceeding; Later probate proceeding not precluded. §13108.
Liability for decedent's unsecured debts. §13109.
Transferee liability. § 13109.5.
Liability to person having superior right. §13110.
Voluntary return of transferred property. § 13110.5.
Restitution. § 13111.
Other remedies not affected. §13113.
Increase or decrease in value of property. § 13113.5.
Payment of costs and fees of public administrator and costs of coroner. §13114.
Transferred property. § 13114.5.
Chapter does not apply to real property. §13115.
Chapter supplemental to other procedures. §13116.
Interest liability excused. § 13117.

§13100. Collection or transfer of personal property without probate

Excluding the property described in Section 13050 **and any property included in a petition filed under Section 13151**, if the gross value of the decedent's real and personal property in this state does not exceed one hundred sixty-six thousand two hundred fifty dollars ($166,250), as adjusted periodically in accordance with Section 890, and if 40 days have elapsed since the death of the decedent, the successor of the decedent may, without procuring letters of administration or awaiting probate of the will, do any of the following with respect to one or more particular items of property:

(a) Collect any particular item of property that is money due the decedent.

(b) Receive any particular item of property that is tangible personal property of the decedent.

(c) Have any particular item of property that is evidence of a debt, obligation, interest, right, security, or chose in action belonging to the decedent transferred, whether or not secured by a lien on real property. **Leg.H.** Enacted Stats 1990 ch 79 §14 (AB 759), operative July 1, 1991. Amended Stats 1996 ch 86 §4 (AB 2146), ch 862 §34 (AB 2751); Stats 2011 ch 117 §4 (AB 1305), effective January 1, 2012; Stats 2019 ch 122 §5 (AB 473), effective January 1, 2020; Stats 2024 ch 331 §1 (AB 2016), effective January 1, 2025.

Prior Law: Former Prob C §13100, similar to the present section, was added Stats 1986 ch 783 §24, operative July 1, 1987, and repealed Stats 1990 ch 79 §13, operative July 1, 1991.

§ 13100.5. Definitions

The following definitions apply for the purposes of this chapter:

(a) "Transferee" means a person to whom payment, delivery, or transfer of property is made under this chapter.

(b) "Transferred property" means property that is paid, delivered, or transferred pursuant to an affidavit or declaration executed under Section 13101.

(c) "Unsecured debts" includes, but is not limited to, a decedent's funeral expenses, expenses of a decedent's last illness, and wage claims. **Leg.H.** Added Stats 2022 ch 29 §2 (AB 1716), effective January 1, 2023.

§13101. Furnishing affidavit or declaration

(a) To collect money, receive tangible personal property, or have evidences of a debt, obligation, interest, right, security, or chose in action transferred under this chapter, an affidavit or a declaration under penalty of perjury under the laws of this state shall be furnished to the holder of the decedent's property stating all of the following:

(1) The decedent's name.

(2) The date and place of the decedent's death.

(3) "At least 40 days have elapsed since the death of the decedent, as shown in a certified copy of the decedent's death certificate attached to this affidavit or declaration."

(4) Either of the following, as appropriate:

(A) "No proceeding is now being or has been conducted in California for administration of the decedent's estate."

(B) "The decedent's personal representative has consented in writing to the payment, transfer, or delivery to the affiant or declarant of the property described in the affidavit or declaration."

(5) "The current gross fair market value of the decedent's real and personal property in California, excluding the property described in Section 13050 of the California Probate Code **and any property included in a petition filed under Section 13151 of the California Probate Code**, does not exceed [Insert dollar amount specified in subdivision (g) of Section 13101 of the California Probate Code]."

(6) A description of the property of the decedent that is to be paid, transferred, or delivered to the affiant or declarant.

(7) The name of the successor of the decedent [1], as defined in Section [2] **13006,** to the described property.

(8) Either of the following, as appropriate:

(A) "The affiant or declarant is the successor of the decedent (as defined in Section 13006 of the California Probate Code) to the decedent's interest in the described property."

(B) "The affiant or declarant is authorized under Section 13051 of the California Probate Code to act on behalf of the successor of the decedent (as defined in Section 13006 of the California Probate Code) with respect to the decedent's interest in the described property."

(9) "No other person has a superior right to the interest of the decedent in the described property."

(10) "The affiant or declarant requests that the described property be paid, delivered, or transferred to the affiant or declarant."

(11) "The affiant or declarant affirms or declares under penalty of perjury under the laws of the State of California that the foregoing is true and correct."

(b) Where more than one person executes the affidavit or declaration under this section, the statements required by subdivision (a) shall be modified as appropriate to reflect that fact.

(c) If the particular item of property to be transferred under this chapter is a debt or other obligation secured by a lien on real property and the instrument creating the lien has been recorded in the office of the county recorder of the county where the real property is located, the affidavit or declaration shall satisfy the requirements both of this section and of Section 13106.5.

(d) A certified copy of the decedent's death certificate shall be attached to the affidavit or declaration.

(e) If the decedent's personal representative has consented to the payment, transfer, or delivery of the described property to the affiant or declarant, a copy of the consent and of the personal representative's letters shall be attached to the affidavit or declaration.

(f) If the decedent dies on or after April 1, 2022, the list of adjusted dollar amounts, published in accordance with subdivision (c) of Section 890, in effect on the date of the decedent's death, shall be attached to the affidavit or declaration.

(g)(1) If the decedent dies prior to April 1, 2022, the dollar amount for paragraph (5) of subdivision (a) is one hundred sixty-six thousand two hundred fifty dollars ($166,250).

(2) If the decedent dies on or after April 1, 2022, the dollar amount for paragraph (5) of subdivision (a) is the adjusted dollar amount, published in accordance with subdivision (c) of Section 890, in effect on the date of the decedent's death. **Leg.H.** Enacted Stats 1990 ch 79 §14 (AB 759), operative July 1, 1991. Amended Stats 1991 ch 1055 §36 (SB 271); Stats 1996 ch 86 §5 (AB 2146), ch 862 §35 (AB 2751); Stats 2011 ch 117 §5 (AB 1305), effective January 1, 2012; Stats 2019 ch 122 §6 (AB 473), effective January 1, 2020; Stats 2024 ch 331 §2 (AB 2016), effective January 1, 2025.

§13101. 2024 Deletes. [1] ([2] 13006 of the California Probate Code)

Prior Law: Former Prob C §13101, similar to the present section, was added Stats 1986 ch 783 §24, operative July 1, 1987, amended Stats 1987 ch 923 §94, operative January 1, 1988, Stats 1987 ch 923 §94, Stats 1988 ch 113 §15.6, effective May 24, 1988, operative May 24, 1988, and repealed Stats 1990 ch 79 §13, operative July 1, 1991.

§13102. Presenting decedent's evidence of ownership

(a) If the decedent had evidence of ownership of the property described in the affidavit or declaration and the holder of the property would have had the right to require presentation of the evidence of ownership before the duty of the holder to pay, deliver, or transfer the property to the decedent would have arisen, the evidence of ownership, if available, shall be presented with the affidavit or declaration to the holder of the decedent's property.

(b) If the evidence of ownership is not presented to the holder pursuant to subdivision (a), the holder may require, as a condition for the payment, delivery, or transfer of the property, that the person presenting the affidavit or declaration provide the holder with a bond or undertaking in a reasonable amount determined by the holder to be sufficient to indemnify the holder against all liability, claims, demands, loss, damages, costs, and expenses that the holder may incur or suffer by reason of the payment, delivery, or transfer of the property. Nothing in this subdivision precludes the holder and the person presenting the affidavit or declaration from dispensing with the requirement that a bond or undertaking be provided and instead entering into an agreement satisfactory to the holder concerning the duty of the person presenting the affidavit or declaration to indemnify the holder. **Leg.H.** Enacted Stats 1990 ch 79 §14 (AB 759), operative July 1, 1991.

Prior Law: Former Prob C §13102, similar to the present section, was added Stats 1986 ch 783 §24, operative July 1, 1987, and repealed Stats 1990 ch 79 §13, operative July 1, 1991.

§13103. Inventory and appraisal of real property

If the estate of the decedent includes any real property in this state, the affidavit or declaration shall be accompanied by an inventory and appraisal of the real property. The inventory and appraisal of the real property shall be made as provided in Part 3 (commencing with Section 8800) of Division 7. The appraisal shall be made by a probate referee selected by the affiant or declarant from those probate referees appointed by the Controller under Section 400 to appraise property in the county where the real property is located. **Leg.H.** Enacted Stats 1990 ch 79 §14 (AB 759), operative July 1, 1991.

Prior Law: Former Prob C §13103, similar to the present section, was added Stats 1986 ch 783 §24, operative July 1, 1987, amended Stats 1988 ch 1199 §96.5, operative July 1, 1989, and repealed Stats 1990 ch 79 §13, operative July 1, 1991.

§13104. Proof of identity

(a) Reasonable proof of the identity of each person executing the affidavit or declaration shall be provided to the holder of the decedent's property.

(b) Reasonable proof of identity is provided for the purposes of this section if both of the following requirements are satisfied:

(1) The person executing the affidavit or declaration is personally known to the holder.

(2) The person executes the affidavit or declaration in the presence of the holder.

(c) If the affidavit or declaration is executed in the presence of the holder, a written statement under penalty of perjury by a person personally known to the holder affirming the identity of the person executing the affidavit or declaration is reasonable proof of identity for the purposes of this section.

(d) If the affidavit or declaration is executed in the presence of the holder, the holder may reasonably rely on any of the following as reasonable proof of identity for the purposes of this section:

(1) An identification card or driver's license issued by the Department of Motor Vehicles of this state that is current or was issued during the preceding five years.

(2) A passport issued by the Department of State of the United States that is current or was issued during the preceding five years.

(3) Any of the following documents if the document is current or was issued during the preceding five years and contains a photograph and description of the person named on it, is signed by the person, and bears a serial or other identifying number:

(A) A passport issued by a foreign government that has been stamped by the United States Immigration and Naturalization Service.

(B) A driver's license issued by a state other than California.

(C) An identification card issued by a state other than California.

(D) An identification card issued by any branch of the armed forces of the United States.

(e) For the purposes of this section, a notary public's certificate of acknowledgment identifying the person executing the affidavit or declaration is reasonable proof of identity of the person executing the affidavit or declaration.

(f) Unless the affidavit or declaration contains a notary public's certificate of acknowledgment of the identity of the person, the holder shall note on the affidavit or declaration either that the person executing the affidavit or declaration is personally known or a description of the identification provided by the person executing the affidavit or declaration. **Leg.H.** Enacted Stats 1990 ch 79 §14 (AB 759), operative July 1, 1991.

Prior Law: Former Prob C §13104, similar to the present section, was added Stats 1986 ch 783 §24, operative July 1, 1987, and repealed Stats 1990 ch 79 §13, operative July 1, 1991.

§13105. Transfer of property to successor

(a) If the requirements of Sections 13100 to 13104, inclusive, are satisfied:

(1) The person or persons executing the affidavit or declaration as successor of the decedent are entitled to have the property described in the affidavit or declaration paid, delivered, or transferred to them.

(2) A transfer agent of a security described in the affidavit or declaration shall change the registered ownership on the books of the corporation from the decedent to the person or persons executing the affidavit or declaration as successor of the decedent.

(b) If the holder of the decedent's property refuses to pay, deliver, or transfer any personal property or evidence thereof to the successor of the decedent within a reasonable time, the successor may recover the property or compel its payment, delivery, or transfer in an action brought for that purpose against the holder of the property. If an action is brought against the holder under this section, the court shall award reasonable attorney's fees to the person or persons bringing the action if the court finds that the holder of the decedent's property acted unreasonably in refusing to pay, deliver, or transfer the property to them as required by subdivision (a). **Leg.H.** Enacted Stats 1990 ch 79 §14 (AB 759), operative July 1, 1991.

Prior Law: Former Prob C §13105, similar to the present section, was added Stats 1986 ch 783 §24, operative July 1, 1987, and repealed Stats 1990 ch 79 §13, operative July 1, 1991.

§13106. Protection of transferor from liability

(a) If the requirements of Sections 13100 to 13104, inclusive, are satisfied, receipt by the holder of the decedent's property of the affidavit or declaration constitutes sufficient acquittance for the payment of money, delivery of property, or changing registered ownership of property pursuant to this chapter and discharges the holder from any further liability with respect to the money or property. The holder may rely in good faith on the statements in the affidavit or declaration and has no duty to inquire into the truth of any statement in the affidavit or declaration.

(b) If the requirements of Sections 13100 to 13104, inclusive, are satisfied, the holder of the decedent's property is not liable for any taxes due to this state by reason of paying money, delivering property, or changing registered ownership of property pursuant to this chapter. **Leg.H.** Enacted Stats 1990 ch 79 §14 (AB 759), operative July 1, 1991.

Prior Law: Former Prob C §13106, similar to the present section, was added Stats 1986 ch 783 §24, operative July 1, 1987, and repealed Stats 1990 ch 79 §13, operative July 1, 1991.

§13106.5. Recording of affidavit or declaration where property is obligation secured by lien on real property

(a) If the particular item of property transferred under this chapter is a debt or other obligation secured by a lien on real property and the instrument creating the lien has been recorded in the office of the county recorder of the county where the real property is located, the affidavit or declaration described in Section 13101 shall be recorded in the office of the county recorder of that county and, in addition to the contents required by Section 13101, shall include both of the following:

(1) The recording reference of the instrument creating the lien.

(2) A notary public's certificate of acknowledgment identifying each person executing the affidavit or declaration.

(b) The transfer under this chapter of the debt or obligation secured by a lien on real property has the same effect as would be given to an assignment of the right to collect the debt or enforce the obligation. The recording of the affidavit or declaration under subdivision (a) shall be given the same effect as is given under Sections 2934 and 2935 of the Civil Code to recording an assignment of a mortgage and an assignment of the beneficial interest under a deed of trust.

(c) If a deed of trust upon the real property was given to secure the debt and the requirements of subdivision (a) and of Sections 13100 to 13103, inclusive, are satisfied:

(1) The trustee under the deed of trust may rely in good faith on the statements made in the affidavit or declaration and has no duty to inquire into the truth of any statement in the affidavit or declaration.

(2) A person acting in good faith and for a valuable consideration may rely upon a recorded reconveyance of the trustee under the deed of trust.

(d) If a mortgage upon the real property was given to secure the debt and the requirements of subdivision (a) and of Sections 13100 to 13103, inclusive, are satisfied, a person acting in good faith and for a valuable consideration may rely upon a recorded discharge of the mortgage executed by the person or persons executing the affidavit or declaration as successor of the decedent or by their successors in interest. **Leg.H.** Enacted Stats 1990 ch 79 §14 (AB 759), operative July 1, 1991.

Prior Law: Former Prob C §13106.5, similar to the present section, was added Stats 1988 ch 113 §15.7, effective May 24, 1988, operative May 24, 1988, and repealed Stats 1990 ch 79 §13, operative July 1, 1991.

§13107. Claim against estate in probate

Where the money or property claimed in an affidavit or declaration presented under this chapter is that of a deceased heir or devisee of a deceased person whose estate is being administered in this state, the personal representative of the person whose estate is being administered shall present the affidavit or declaration to the court in which the estate is being administered. The court shall direct the personal representative to pay the money or deliver the property to the person or persons identified by the affidavit or declaration as the successor of the decedent to the extent that the order for distribution determines that the deceased heir or devisee was entitled to the money or property under the will or the laws of succession. **Leg.H.** Enacted Stats 1990 ch 79 §14 (AB 759), operative July 1, 1991.

Prior Law: Former Prob C §13107, similar to the present section, was added Stats 1986 ch 783 §24, operative July 1, 1987, and repealed Stats 1990 ch 79 §13, operative July 1, 1991.

§13107.5. Substitution of decedent's successor in interest

Where the money or property claimed in an affidavit or declaration executed under this chapter is the subject of a pending action or proceeding in which the decedent was a party, the successor of the decedent shall, without procuring letters of administration or awaiting probate of the will, be substituted as a party in place of the decedent by making a motion under Article 3 (commencing with Section 377.30) of Chapter 4 of Title 2 of Part 2 of the Code of Civil Procedure. The successor of the decedent shall file the affidavit or declaration with the court when the motion is made. For the purpose of Article 3 (commencing with Section 377.30) of Chapter 4 of Title 2 of Part 2 of the Code of Civil Procedure, a successor of the decedent who complies with this chapter shall be considered as a successor in interest of the decedent. **Leg.H.** Added Stats 1991 ch 1055 §37 (SB 271). Amended Stats 1992 ch 178 §39 (SB 1496), effective January 1, 1993.

§13108. No pending probate proceeding; Later probate proceeding not precluded

(a) The procedure provided by this chapter may be used only if one of the following requirements is satisfied:

(1) No proceeding for the administration of the decedent's estate is pending or has been conducted in this state.

(2) The decedent's personal representative consents in writing to the payment, transfer, or delivery of the property described in the affidavit or declaration pursuant to this chapter.

(b) Payment, delivery, or transfer of a decedent's property pursuant to this chapter does not preclude later proceedings for administration of the decedent's estate. **Leg.H.** Enacted Stats 1990 ch 79 §14 (AB 759), operative July 1, 1991. Amended Stats 1991 ch 1055 §38 (SB 271).

Prior Law: Former Prob C §13108, similar to the present section, was added Stats 1986 ch 783 §24, operative July 1, 1987, and repealed Stats 1990 ch 79 §13, operative July 1, 1991.

§13109. Liability for decedent's unsecured debts

(a) A transferee is personally liable, to the extent provided in this section for the unsecured debts of the decedent. That debt may be enforced against the transferee in the same manner as it could have been enforced against the decedent if the decedent had not died. In any action based upon the debt, the transferee may assert any defense, cross-complaint, or setoff that would have been available to the decedent if the decedent had not died. Nothing in this section permits enforcement of a claim that is barred under Part 4 (commencing with Section 9000) of Division 7. Section 366.2 of the Code of Civil Procedure applies in an action under this section.

(b) The personal liability under subdivision (a) shall not exceed the fair market value of the transferred property at the time the affidavit or declaration is presented under this chapter, less the amount of any liens and encumbrances on the transferred property at that time, and less the amount of any payment made pursuant to subdivision (a) of Section 13110.

(c) A transferee is not liable under this section if the transferee has satisfied the requirements of Section 13109.5, 13110.5, or 13111. **Leg.H.** Enacted Stats 1990 ch 79 §14 (AB 759), operative July 1, 1991. Amended Stats 1990 ch 140 §15.1 (SB 1855), operative July 1, 1991; Stats 1992 ch 178 §40 (SB 1496), effective January 1, 1993; Stats 2022 ch 29 §3 (AB 1716), effective January 1, 2023.

Prior Law Former Prob C §13109, similar to the present section, was added Stats 1986 ch 783 §24, operative July 1, 1987, amended Stats 1988 ch 113 §16, effective May 24, 1988, operative July 1, 1988, repealed Stats 1990 ch 79 §13, operative July 1, 1991, amended Stats 1990 ch 140 §15, operative until July 1, 1991, and repealed Stats 1990 ch 140 §31, operative July 1, 1991.

§ 13109.5. Transferee liability

(a) If proceedings for the administration of the decedent's estate are commenced, a transferee is personally liable to the estate for a share of the decedent's unsecured debts.

(b) In calculating the transferee's share of liability under subdivision (a), the abatement rules provided in Part 4 (commencing with Section 21400) of Division 11 shall be applied, using all of the following assumptions:

(1) Transferred property shall be treated as if it had remained in the estate for administration.

(2) Any unsecured debts of the decedent that were paid by the transferee pursuant to Section 13109 shall be treated as if they were claims made against the decedent's estate.

(c) The personal representative shall provide a written statement of liability to the transferee, which specifies the amount that must be paid to the estate.

(d) The transferee is personally liable to the estate for the amount specified in the statement of liability. Any amount that the transferee paid pursuant to Section 13109 or 13110 shall be credited against the amount that the transferee owes the estate under this subdivision. If the amount that the transferee paid pursuant to Section 13109 or 13110 exceeds the amount specified in the written statement of liability, the estate shall reimburse the difference to the transferee. For the purposes of Section 11420, that reimbursement shall be deemed an expense of administration.

(e) The reasonable cost of proceeding under this section shall be reimbursed as an extraordinary service under Sections 10801 and 10811. The transferee is liable for the payment of that cost, which shall be separately identified in the statement of liability.

(f) A transferee is not liable under this section if the transferee has satisfied the requirements of Section 13110.5 or 13111. **Leg.H.** Added Stats 2022 ch 29 §4 (AB 1716), effective January 1, 2023.

§13110. Liability to person having superior right

(a) Except as provided in subdivision (b), a transferee is personally liable to any person having a superior right to the transferred property by testate or intestate succession from the decedent. Except as provided in subdivision (b), the personal liability established by this subdivision shall not exceed the sum of the following, less the amount of any payment made pursuant to Section 13109 or 13109.5:

(1) The fair market value of the transferred property at the time the affidavit or declaration is presented under this chapter, less the amount of any liens and encumbrances on the transferred property at that time.

(2) Income received from the property, if that income would have accrued to the estate had the property not been transferred to the transferee.

(3) If the property has been disposed of, interest on the fair market value of the transferred property from the date of disposition at the rate of 7 percent per annum. For the purposes of this paragraph, "fair market value of the transferred property" means the fair market value of the transferred property, determined as of the time of the disposition of the property, less the amount of any liens and encumbrances on the property at the time the property was paid, delivered, or transferred to the transferee.

(b) In addition to any other liability the transferee has under this section and Sections 13109, 13109.5, 13111, and 13113.5 a person who fraudulently secures the payment, delivery, or transfer of the decedent's property under this chapter is liable to the person having a superior right to that property by testate or intestate succession from the decedent for three times the fair market value of the property. For the purposes of this subdivision, the "fair market value of the property" is the fair market value of the property paid, delivered, or transferred to the person liable under this subdivision, valued as of the time the person liable under this subdivision presents the affidavit or declaration under this chapter to the holder of the decedent's property, less any liens and encumbrances on that property at that time.

(c) An action to impose liability under this section is forever barred three years after the affidavit or declaration is presented under this chapter to the holder of the decedent's property, or three years after the discovery of the fraud, whichever is later. The three-year period specified in this subdivision is not tolled for any reason.

(d) A transferee is not liable under subdivision (a) if the transferee has satisfied the requirements of Section 13110.5 or 13111. **Leg.H.** Enacted Stats 1990 ch 79 §14 (AB 759), operative July 1, 1991. Amended Stats 1991 ch 1055 §39 (SB 271); Stats 2022 ch 29 §5 (AB 1716), effective January 1, 2023.

Prior Law Former Prob C §13110, similar to the present section, was added Stats 1986 ch 783 §24, operative July 1, 1987, and repealed Stats 1990 ch 79 §13, operative July 1, 1991.

§ 13110.5. Voluntary return of transferred property

(a) If proceedings for the administration of a decedent's estate are commenced, a transferee may voluntarily return transferred property to the decedent's estate for administration.

(b) The property to be restored to the estate under this section shall be reduced or increased as provided in Section 13113.5. **Leg.H.** Added Stats 2022 ch 29 §6 (AB 1716), effective January 1, 2023.

§ 13111. Restitution

(a) If property is paid, delivered, or transferred to a transferee under this chapter, and the decedent's personal representative determines that another person has a superior right to the property by testate or intestate succession from the decedent, the personal representative may request that the transferred property be restored to the estate. Subject to subdivisions (b), (c), (d), (e), and (g) if the personal representative makes that request, the transferee is liable for all of the following:

(1) If the transferee still has the transferred property, restitution of the transferred property to the decedent's estate.

(2) If the transferee no longer has the transferred property, restitution to the decedent's estate of the fair market value of the transferred property plus interest from the date of disposition at the rate of 7 percent per annum on the fair market value of the transferred property. For the purposes of this paragraph, the "fair market value of the transferred property" is the fair market value of the transferred property, determined as of the time of the disposition of the transferred property, less the amount of any liens and encumbrances on the transferred property at the time the property was paid, delivered, or transferred to the person under this chapter.

(b) Subject to subdivision (c) and subject to any additional liability the transferee has under Sections 13109 to 13113.5, inclusive, if the transferee fraudulently secured the payment, delivery, or transfer of the decedent's property under this chapter, the transferee is liable under this section for restitution of three times the fair market value of the transferred property. For the purposes of this subdivision, the "fair market value of the transferred property" is the fair market value of the transferred property, determined as of the time the person liable under this subdivision presents the affidavit or declaration under this chapter, less the amount of any liens and encumbrances on the property at that time. Restitution provided under this subdivision shall first be used to pay the estate's cost of proceeding under this section, with the remainder paid to the person who has a superior right to the property by testate or intestate succession.

(c) The property and amount required to be restored to the estate under this section shall be reduced or increased as provided in Section 13113.5.

(d) An action to enforce the liability under this section may be brought only by the personal representative of the estate of the decedent.

(e) An action to enforce the liability under this section is forever barred three years after presentation of the affidavit or declaration under this chapter to the holder of the decedent's property, or three years after the discovery of the fraud, whichever is later. The three-year period specified in this subdivision is not tolled for any reason.

(f) In the case of a nondomiciliary decedent, restitution under this section shall be made to the estate in an ancillary administration proceeding.

(g) A transferee is not liable under subdivision (a) if the transferred property was returned to the estate under Section 13110.5. **Leg.H.** Added Stats 2022 ch 29 §8 (AB 1716), effective January 1, 2023.

Prior Law Former Prob C §13111, similar to the present section, was enacted Stats 1990 ch 79 §14 (AB 759), amended Stats 1991 ch 1055 §40 (SB 271), Stats 2015 ch 293 §18 (AB 139), Stats 2019 ch 122 §7 (AB 473), and repealed Stats 2022 ch 29 §7 (AB 1716), effective January 1, 2023.

§13112. Limitation on liability under Sections 13109 and 13110 [Repealed]

Leg.H. Enacted Stats 1990 ch 79 §14 (AB 759), operative July 1, 1991. Amended Stats 2019 ch 122 §8 (AB 473), effective January 1, 2020. Repealed Stats 2022 ch 29 §9 (AB 1716), effective January 1, 2023.

Prior Law: Former Prob C §13112, similar to the present section, was added Stats 1986 ch 783 §24, operative July 1, 1987, amended Stats 1988 ch 1199 §97.5, operative July 1, 1989, and repealed Stats 1990 ch 79 §13, operative July 1, 1991.

§13113. Other remedies not affected

The remedies available under Sections 13109 to 13111, inclusive, are in addition to any remedies available by reason of any fraud or intentional wrongdoing. **Leg.H.** Enacted Stats 1990 ch 79 §14 (AB 759), operative July 1, 1991. Amended Stats 2022 ch 29 §10 (AB 1716), effective January 1, 2023.

Prior Law Former Prob C §13113, similar to the present section, was added Stats 1986 ch 783 §24, operative July 1, 1987, and repealed Stats 1990 ch 79 §13, operative July 1, 1991.

§ 13113.5. Increase or decrease in value of property

(a) If the transferee's action or inaction increased the value of property returned to the estate or decreased the estate's obligations, the personal representative shall reimburse the transferee by the same amount. Actions or inaction that increase the value of returned property or decrease the estate's obligations include, but are not necessarily limited to, the following actions:

(1) A payment toward an unsecured debt of the decedent.

(2) A payment toward a debt secured against the returned property.

(3) A significant improvement of the returned property that increased the fair market value of the property.

(b) If the transferee's action or inaction decreased the value of property returned to the estate or increased the estate's obligations, the transferee is personally liable to the estate for that amount. Actions or inaction that decrease the value of the returned property or increase the estate's obligations include, but are not necessarily limited to, the following actions or inaction:

(1) An action or inaction that resulted in a lien or encumbrance being recorded against the property.

(2) The receipt of income from the property, if that income would have accrued to the estate had the property not been transferred to the transferee.

(c) The personal representative shall provide the transferee a written statement of any reimbursement or liability under this section, along with a statement of the reasons for the reimbursement or liability.

(d) For the purposes of Section 11420, reimbursement of the transferee under subdivision (a) shall be deemed an expense of administration.

(e) In the event that the transferee and the personal representative cannot agree on the reimbursement or liability due under this section, the transferee or personal representative may petition the court for an order determining the amount of the reimbursement or liability. In making a decision under this subdivision, the court should consider the surrounding circumstances, including whether the parties acted in good faith and whether a particular result would impose an unfair burden on the transferee or the estate. **Leg.H.** Added Stats 2022 ch 29 §11 (AB 1716), effective January 1, 2023.

§13114. Payment of costs and fees of public administrator and costs of coroner

(a) A public administrator who has taken possession or control of property of a decedent under Article 1 (commencing with Section 7600) of Chapter 4 of Part 1 of Division 7 may refuse to pay money or deliver property pursuant to this chapter if payment of the costs and fees described in Section 7604 has not first been made or adequately assured to the satisfaction of the public administrator.

(b) A coroner who has property found upon the body of a decedent, or who has taken charge of property of the decedent pursuant to Section 27491.3 of the Government Code, may refuse to pay or deliver the property pursuant to this chapter if payment of the reasonable costs of holding or safeguarding the property has not first been made or adequately assured to the satisfaction of the coroner. **Leg.H.** Enacted Stats 1990 ch 79 §14 (AB 759), operative July 1, 1991.

Prior Law: Former Prob C §13114, similar to the present section, was added Stats 1986 ch 783 §24, effective September 15, 1986, operative July 1, 1987, amended Stats 1987 ch 923 §94.1, operative January 1, 1988, Stats 1988 ch 1199 §98, operative July 1, 1989, and repealed Stats 1990 ch 79 §13, operative July 1, 1991.

§ 13114.5. Transferred property

If transferred property is returned to the estate under Sections 13110.5 or 13111, the value of that property shall be included in the total value of the estate, for all purposes. **Leg.H.** Added Stats 2022 ch 29 §12 (AB 1716), effective January 1, 2023.

§13115. Chapter does not apply to real property

The procedure provided in this chapter may not be used to obtain possession or the transfer of real property. **Leg.H.** Enacted Stats 1990 ch 79 §14 (AB 759), operative July 1, 1991.

Prior Law: Former Prob C §13115, similar to the present section, was added Stats 1986 ch 783 §24, operative July 1, 1987, and repealed Stats 1990 ch 79 §13, operative July 1, 1991.

§13116. Chapter supplemental to other procedures

The procedure provided in this chapter is in addition to and supplemental to any other procedure for (1) collecting money due to a decedent, (2) receiving tangible personal property of a decedent, or (3) having evidence of ownership of property of a decedent transferred. Nothing in this chapter restricts or limits the release of tangible personal property of a decedent pursuant to any other provision of law. This section is declaratory of existing law. **Leg.H.** Enacted Stats 1990 ch 79 §14 (AB 759), operative July 1, 1991.

Prior Law: Former Prob C §13116, similar to the present section, was added Stats 1987 ch 923 §94.3, operative January 1, 1988, and repealed Stats 1990 ch 79 §13, operative July 1, 1991.

§ 13117. Interest liability excused

If the court finds that a person to whom payment, delivery, or transfer of the decedent's property has been made under this chapter has acted reasonably and in good faith under the circumstances as known to the person, the court may, in its discretion, excuse the person from liability to pay interest, in whole or in part, under paragraph (2) of subdivision (a) of Section 13111, if it would be equitable to do so. **Leg.H.** Added Stats 2019 ch 122 §9 (AB 473), effective January 1, 2020. Amended Stats 2022 ch 29 §13 (AB 1716), effective January 1, 2023.

CHAPTER 4
COURT ORDER DETERMINING SUCCESSION TO PROPERTY

When procedure may be used. §13150.
Petition for court order determining succession to real property. §13151.

Contents of petition; Inventory and appraisal. §13152.
Notice of hearing. §13153.
Court order. §13154.
Effect of order. §13155.
Liability for decedent's unsecured debts. §13156.
Attorney's fee. §13157.

§13150. When procedure may be used

The procedure provided by this chapter may be used only if one of the following requirements is satisfied:

(a) No proceeding is being or has been conducted in this state for administration of the decedent's estate.

(b)(1) The decedent's personal representative consents in writing to use of the procedure provided by this chapter to determine that real property [1] **that was the decedent's primary residence** is property passing to the petitioners.

(2) For purposes of this chapter, "primary residence" is not limited to the decedent's residence at the time of their death. Leg.H. Enacted Stats 1990 ch 79 §14 (AB 759), operative July 1, 1991. Amended Stats 1991 ch 1055 §42 (SB 271); Stats 2024 ch 331 §3 (AB 2016), effective January 1, 2025.

§13150. 2024 Deletes. [1] of the decedent

Prior Law: Former Prob C §13150, similar to the present section, was added Stats 1986 ch 783 §24, effective September 15, 1986, operative July 1, 1987, and repealed Stats 1990 ch 79 §13, operative July 1, 1991.

§13151. Petition for court order determining succession to real property

(a) [1] If a decedent dies leaving real property **that was their primary residence** in this state and the gross value of [2] **that real property** does not exceed [3] **seven hundred fifty thousand dollars ($750,000)**, as adjusted periodically in accordance with Section 890, and 40 days have elapsed since the death of the decedent, the successor of the decedent to an interest in [4] **that** real property, without procuring letters of administration or awaiting the probate of the will, may file a petition in the superior court of the county in which the estate of the decedent may be administered requesting a court order determining that the petitioner has succeeded to that real property. [5]

(b) A successor who files a petition pursuant to subdivision (a) shall deliver a notice of the petition to each heir and devisee named in the petition pursuant to paragraph (7) of subdivision (a) of Section 13152 within five business days of filing the petition. Leg.H. Enacted Stats 1990 ch 79 §14 (AB 759), operative July 1, 1991. Amended Stats 1991 ch 1055 §43 (SB 271); Stats 1996 ch 86 §6 (AB 2146), ch 862 §36 (AB 2751); Stats 2011 ch 117 §6 (AB 1305), effective January 1, 2012; Stats 2019 ch 122 §10 (AB 473), effective January 1, 2020; Stats 2024 ch 331 §4 (AB 2016), effective January 1, 2025.

§13151. 2024 Deletes. [1] Exclusive of the property described in Section 13050, **[2]** the decedent's real and personal property in this state **[3]** one hundred sixty-six thousand two hundred fifty dollars ($166,250) **[4]** a particular item of property that is **[5]** A petition under this chapter may include an additional request that the court make an order determining that the petitioner has succeeded to personal property described in the petition.

Prior Law: Former Prob C §13151, similar to the present section, was added Stats 1986 ch 783 §24, effective September 15, 1986, operative July 1, 1987; and repealed Stats 1990 ch 79 §13, operative July 1, 1991.

§13152. Contents of petition; Inventory and appraisal

(a) The petition shall be verified by each petitioner, shall contain a request that the court make an order under this chapter determining that the property described in the petition is property passing to the petitioner, and shall state all of the following:

(1) The facts necessary to determine that the petition is filed in the proper county.

(2) The gross value of the [1] **real property that was the decedent's primary residence in this state**, as shown by the inventory and appraisal attached to the petition, does not exceed the dollar amount specified in subdivision (f).

(3) A description of the particular item of real property in this state that the petitioner alleges is property of the decedent passing to the petitioner [2] **and the facts upon which the petitioner bases the allegation** that the described [3] **real property was the decedent's primary residence**.

(4) The facts upon which the petitioner bases the allegation that the described property is property passing to the petitioner.

(5) Either of the following, as appropriate:

(A) A statement that no proceeding is being or has been conducted in this state for administration of the decedent's estate.

(B) A statement that the decedent's personal representative has consented in writing to use of the procedure provided by this chapter.

(6) Whether estate proceedings for the decedent have been commenced in any other jurisdiction and, if so, where those proceedings are pending or were conducted.

(7) The name, age, address, and relation to the decedent of each heir and devisee of the decedent, the names and addresses of all persons named as executors of the will of the decedent, and, if the petitioner is the trustee of a trust that is a devisee under the will of the decedent, the names and addresses of all persons interested in the trust, as determined in cases of future interests pursuant to paragraph (1), (2), or (3) of subdivision (a) of Section 15804, so far as known to any petitioner.

(8) The name and address of each person serving as guardian or conservator of the estate of the decedent at the time of the decedent's death, so far as known to any petitioner.

(b) An inventory and appraisal in the form set forth in Section 8802 of the [4] **real property that was the decedent's primary residence in this state** shall be attached to the petition. The appraisal shall be made by a probate referee selected by the petitioner from those probate referees appointed by the Controller under Section 400 to appraise property in the county where the real property is located. The appraisal shall be made as provided in Part 3 (commencing with Section 8800) of Division 7. [5]

(c) If the petitioner bases the petitioner's claim to the described property upon the will of the decedent, a copy of the will shall be attached to the petition.

(d) If the decedent's personal representative has consented to use of the procedure provided by this chapter, a copy of the consent shall be attached to the petition.

(e) If the decedent dies on or after April 1, 2022, the list of adjusted dollar amounts, published in accordance with subdivision (c) of Section 890, in effect on the date of the decedent's death shall be attached to the petition.

(f)(1) If the decedent dies prior to April 1, 2022, the dollar amount for paragraph (2) of subdivision (a) is one hundred sixty-six thousand two hundred fifty dollars ($166,250).

(2) If the decedent dies on or after April 1, 2022, **through March 31, 2025,** the dollar amount for paragraph (2) of subdivision (a) is the adjusted dollar amount, published in accordance with subdivision (c) of Section 890, in effect on the date of the decedent's death.

(3) If the decedent dies on or after April 1, 2025, through March 31, 2028, the dollar amount for paragraph (2) of subdivision (a) is seven hundred fifty thousand dollars ($750,000).

(4) If the decedent dies on or after April 1, 2028, the dollar amount for paragraph (2) of subdivision (a) is the adjusted dollar amount, published in accordance with subdivision (c) of Section 890, in effect on the date of the decedent's death. Leg.H. Enacted Stats 1990 ch 79 §14 (AB 759), operative July 1, 1991. Amended Stats 1991 ch 1055 §44 (SB 271); Stats 1996 ch 86 §7 (AB 2146), ch 862 §37 (AB 2751); Stats 2011 ch 117 §7 (AB 1305), effective January 1, 2012; Stats 2019 ch 122 §11 (AB 473), effective January 1, 2020; Stats 2024 ch 331 §5 (AB 2016), effective January 1, 2025.

§13152. 2024 Deletes. [1] decedent's real and personal property in this state, excluding the property described in Section 13050 **[2]**, and a description of the personal property that the petitioner alleges is property of the decedent passing to the petitioner if the requested order also is to include a determination **[3]** personal property is property passing to the petitioner **[4]** decedent's real and personal property in this state, excluding the property described in Section 13050 **[5]** The petitioner may appraise the assets that a personal representative could appraise under Section 8901.

Prior Law: Former Prob C §13152, similar to the present section, was added Stats 1986 ch 783 §24, operative July 1, 1987, amended Stats 1987 ch 923 §94.5, operative January 1, 1988, Stats 1988 ch 113 §16.5, effective May 24, 1988, operative July 1, 1988, ch 1199 §98.5, operative July 1, 1989, ch 1447 §5, and repealed Stats 1990 ch 79 §13, operative July 1, 1991.

§13153. Notice of hearing

Notice of the hearing shall be given as provided in Section 1220 to each of the persons named in the petition pursuant to Section 13152. **Leg.H.** Enacted Stats 1990 ch 79 §14 (AB 759), operative July 1, 1991.

§13154. Court order

(a) If the court makes the determinations required under subdivision (b), the court shall issue an order determining [1] **that the real property that was the decedent's primary residence,** to be described in the order, [2] is property passing to the petitioners and the specific property interest of each petitioner in the described property.

(b) The court may make an order under this section only if the court makes all of the following determinations:

(1) The gross value of the [3] **real property that was the decedent's primary residence in this state** does not exceed [4] **seven hundred fifty thousand dollars ($750,000),** as adjusted periodically in accordance with Section 890.

(2) Not less than 40 days have elapsed since the death of the decedent.

(3) Whichever of the following is appropriate:

(A) No proceeding is being or has been conducted in this state for administration of the decedent's estate.

(B) The decedent's personal representative has consented in writing to use of the procedure provided by this chapter.

(4) The property described in the order is property of the decedent passing to the petitioner.

(c) If the petition has attached an inventory and appraisal that satisfies the requirements of subdivision (b) of Section 13152, the determination required by paragraph (1) of subdivision (b) of this section shall be made on the basis of the verified petition and the attached inventory and appraisal, unless evidence is offered by a person opposing the petition that the gross value of the [5] **real property that was the decedent's primary residence in this state exceeds seven hundred fifty thousand dollars ($750,000),** as adjusted periodically in accordance with Section 890. **Leg.H.** Enacted Stats 1990 ch 79 §14 (AB 759), operative July 1, 1991. Amended Stats 1991 ch 1055 §45 (SB 271); Stats 1996 ch 86 §8 (AB 2146); Stats 2011 ch 117 §8 (AB 1305), effective January 1, 2012; Stats 2019 ch 122 §12 (AB 473), effective January 1, 2020; Stats 2024 ch 331 §6 (AB 2016), effective January 1, 2025.

§13154. 2024 Deletes. [1] (1) that real property, to be described in the order, of the decedent is property passing to the petitioners and the specific property interest of each petitioner in the described property and (2) if the petition so requests, that personal property, [2] of the decedent [3] decedent's real and personal property in this state, excluding the property described in Section 13050, [4] one hundred sixty-six thousand two hundred fifty dollars ($166,250) [5] decedent's real and personal property in this state, excluding the property described in Section 13050, exceeds one hundred sixty-six thousand two hundred fifty dollars ($166,250)

Prior Law: Former Prob C §13154, similar to the present section, was added Stats 1986 ch 783 §24, effective September 15, 1986, operative July 1, 1987, amended Stats 1988 ch 1199 §99, operative July 1, 1989, and repealed Stats 1990 ch 79 §13, operative July 1, 1991.

§13155. Effect of order

Upon becoming final, an order under this chapter determining that property is property passing to the petitioner is conclusive on all persons, whether or not they are in being. **Leg.H.** Enacted Stats 1990 ch 79 §14 (AB 759), operative July 1, 1991. Amended Stats 1991 ch 1055 §46 (SB 271).

Prior Law: Former Prob C §13155, similar to the present section, was added Stats 1986 ch 783 §24, effective September 15, 1986, operative July 1, 1987, and repealed Stats 1990 ch 79 §13, operative July 1, 1991.

§13156. Liability for decedent's unsecured debts

(a) Subject to subdivisions (b), (c), and (d), the petitioner who receives the decedent's property pursuant to an order under this chapter is personally liable for the unsecured debts of the decedent.

(b) The personal liability of any petitioner shall not exceed the fair market value at the date of the decedent's death of the property received by that petitioner pursuant to an order under this chapter, less the amount of any liens and encumbrances on the property.

(c) In any action or proceeding based upon an unsecured debt of the decedent, the petitioner may assert any defense, cross-complaint, or setoff which would have been available to the decedent if the decedent had not died.

(d) Nothing in this section permits enforcement of a claim that is barred under Part 4 (commencing with Section 9000) of Division 7.

(e) Section 366.2 of the Code of Civil Procedure applies in an action under this section. **Leg.H.** Enacted Stats 1990 ch 79 §14 (AB 759), operative July 1, 1991. Amended Stats 1990 ch 140 §16.1 (SB 1855), operative July 1, 1991; Stats 1992 ch 178 §41 (SB 1496), effective January 1, 1993.

Prior Law: Former Prob C §13156, similar to the present section, was added Stats 1986 ch 783 §24, effective September 15, 1986, operative July 1, 1987, amended Stats 1988 ch 113 §17, effective May 24, 1988, operative July 1, 1988, repealed Stats 1990 ch 79 §13, operative July 1, 1991, amended Stats 1990 ch 140 §16, operative until July 1, 1991, and repealed Stats 1990 ch 140 §32, operative July 1, 1991.

§13157. Attorney's fee

The attorney's fees for services performed in connection with the filing of a petition and obtaining a court order under this chapter shall be determined by private agreement between the attorney and the client and are not subject to approval by the court. If there is no agreement between the attorney and the client concerning the attorney's fees for services performed in connection with the filing of a petition and obtaining of a court order under this chapter and there is a dispute concerning the reasonableness of the attorney's fees for those services, a petition may be filed with the court in the same proceeding requesting that the court determine the reasonableness of the attorney's fees for those services. If there is an agreement between the attorney and the client concerning the attorney's fees for services performed in connection with the filing of a petition and obtaining a court order under this chapter and there is a dispute concerning the meaning of the agreement, a petition may be filed with the court in the same proceeding requesting that the court determine the dispute. **Leg.H.** Enacted Stats 1990 ch 79 §14 (AB 759), operative July 1, 1991.

Prior Law: Former Prob C § 13157, similar to the present section, was added Stats 1986 ch 783 §24, effective September 15, 1986, operative July 1, 1987, and repealed Stats 1990 ch 79 §13, operative July 1, 1991.

§13158. Compliance with Chapter 3 [Repealed]

Leg.H. Added Stats 1991 ch 1055 §47 (SB 271). Repealed Stats 2024 ch 331 §7 (AB 2016), effective January 1, 2025.

CHAPTER 5
AFFIDAVIT PROCEDURE FOR REAL PROPERTY OF SMALL VALUE

Filing affidavit in superior court; Inventory and appraisal. §13200.
Filing fee. §13201.
Filing; Certified copy; Recording. §13202.
Definitions. § 13202.5.
Effect of recorded affidavit. §13203.
Liability for decedent's unsecured debts. §13204.
Transferee liability. § 13204.5.
Liability to person having superior right. §13205.
Voluntary return of transferred property. § 13205.5.
Restitution. § 13206.
Other remedies not affected. §13208.
Increase or decrease in value of property. § 13208.5.
Return of transferred property. § 13209.
When procedure may be used. §13210.
Interest liability excused. § 13211.

§13200. Filing affidavit in superior court; Inventory and appraisal

(a) No sooner than six months from the death of a decedent, a person or persons claiming as successor of the decedent to a particular item of property that is real property may file in the superior court in the county in which the decedent was domiciled at the time of death, or if the decedent was not domiciled in this state at the time of death, then in any county in which real property of the decedent is located, an affidavit in the form prescribed by the Judicial Council pursuant to Section 1001 stating all of the following:

(1) The name of the decedent.

(2) The date and place of the decedent's death.

(3) A legal description of the real property and the interest of the decedent therein.

(4) The name and address of each person serving as guardian or conservator of the estate of the decedent at the time of the decedent's death, so far as known to the affiant.

(5) "The gross value of all real property in the decedent's estate located in California, as shown by the inventory and appraisal attached to this affidavit, excluding the real property described in Section 13050 of the California Probate Code, does not exceed [Insert dollar amount specified in subdivision (h)]."

(6) "At least six months have elapsed since the death of the decedent as shown in a certified copy of decedent's death certificate attached to this affidavit."

(7) Either of the following, as appropriate:

(A) "No proceeding is now being or has been conducted in California for administration of the decedent's estate."

(B) "The decedent's personal representative has consented in writing to use of the procedure provided by this chapter."

(8) "Funeral expenses, expenses of last illness, and all unsecured debts of the decedent have been paid."

(9) "The affiant is the successor of the decedent (as defined in Section 13006 of the Probate Code) and to the decedent's interest in the described property, and no other person has a superior right to the interest of the decedent in the described property."

(10) "The affiant declares under penalty of perjury under the laws of the State of California that the foregoing is true and correct."

(b) For each person executing the affidavit, the affidavit shall contain a notary public's certificate of acknowledgment identifying the person.

(c) An inventory and appraisal of the decedent's real property in this state, excluding the real property described in Section 13050, shall be attached to the affidavit. The inventory and appraisal of the real property shall be made as provided in Part 3 (commencing with Section 8800) of Division 7. The appraisal shall be made by a probate referee selected by the affiant from those probate referees appointed by the Controller under Section 400 to appraise property in the county where the real property is located.

(d) If the affiant claims under the decedent's will and no estate proceeding is pending or has been conducted in California, a copy of the will shall be attached to the affidavit.

(e) A certified copy of the decedent's death certificate shall be attached to the affidavit. If the decedent's personal representative has consented to the use of the procedure provided by this chapter, a copy of the consent and of the personal representative's letters shall be attached to the affidavit.

(f) If the decedent dies on or after April 1, 2022, the list of adjusted dollar amounts, published in accordance with subdivision (c) of Section 890, in effect on the date of the decedent's death shall be attached to the affidavit.

(g) The affiant shall deliver pursuant to Section 1215 a copy of the affidavit and attachments to any person identified in paragraph (4) of subdivision (a).

(h)(1) When the decedent dies prior to April 1, 2022, the dollar amount for paragraph (5) of subdivision (a) is fifty-five thousand four hundred twenty-five dollars ($55,425).

(2) When the decedent dies on or after April 1, 2022, the dollar amount for paragraph (5) of subdivision (a) is the adjusted dollar amount, published in accordance with subdivision (c) of Section 890, in effect on the date of the decedent's death. **Leg.H.** Enacted Stats 1990 ch 79 §14 (AB 759), operative July 1, 1991. Amended Stats 1991 ch 1055 §48 (SB 271); Stats 1996 ch 86 §9 (AB 2146); Stats 2011 ch 117 §9 (AB 1305), effective January 1, 2012; Stats 2017 ch 319 §84 (AB 976), effective January 1, 2018; Stats 2019 ch 122 §13 (AB 473), effective January 1, 2020.

Prior Law: Former Prob C §13200, similar to the present section, was added Stats 1986 ch 783 §24, operative July 1, 1987, amended Stats 1988 ch 1199 §99.5, operative July 1, 1989, ch 1447 §7, and repealed Stats 1990 ch 79 §13, operative July 1, 1991.

§13201. Filing fee

Notwithstanding any other provision of law, the total fee for the filing of an affidavit under Section 13200 and the issuance of one certified copy of the affidavit under Section 13202 is as provided in subdivision (b) of Section 70626 of the Government Code. **Leg.H.** Enacted Stats 1990 ch 79 §14 (AB 759), operative July 1, 1991. Amended Stats 2005 ch 75 §150 (AB 145), effective July 19, 2005, operative January 1, 2006.

Prior Law: Former Prob C §13201, similar to the present section, was added Stats 1986 ch 783 §24, operative July 1, 1987, and repealed Stats 1990 ch 79 §13, operative July 1, 1991.

§13202. Filing; Certified copy; Recording

Upon receipt of the affidavit and the required fee, the court clerk, upon determining that the affidavit is complete and has the required attachments, shall file the affidavit and attachments and shall issue a certified copy of the affidavit without the attachments. The certified copy shall be recorded in the office of the county recorder of the county where the real property is located. The county recorder shall index the certified copy in the index of grantors and grantees. The decedent shall be indexed as the grantor and each person designated as a successor to the property in the certified copy shall be indexed as a grantee. **Leg.H.** Enacted Stats 1990 ch 79 §14 (AB 759), operative July 1, 1991.

Prior Law: Former Prob C §13202, similar to the present section, was added Stats 1986 ch 783 §24, operative July 1, 1987, and repealed Stats 1990 ch 79 §13, operative July 1, 1991.

§ 13202.5. Definitions

For the purposes of this chapter, the following terms have the following meanings:

(a) "Transferee" means a person designated as a successor of the decedent in a certified copy of an affidavit issued under Section 13202.

(b) "Transferred property" means property transferred to a transferee pursuant to a certified copy of an affidavit issued under Section 13202.

(c) "Unsecured debts" includes, but is not limited to, a decedent's funeral expenses, expenses of a decedent's last illness, and wage claims. **Leg.H.** Added Stats 2022 ch 29 §14 (AB 1716), effective January 1, 2023.

§13203. Effect of recorded affidavit

(a) A person acting in good faith and for a valuable consideration with a person designated as a successor of the decedent to a particular item of property in a certified copy of an affidavit issued under Section 13202 and recorded in the county in which the real property is located has the same rights and protections as the person would have if each person designated as a successor in the recorded certified copy of the affidavit had been named as a distributee of the real property in an order for distribution that had become final.

(b) The issuance and recording of a certified copy of an affidavit under this chapter does not preclude later proceedings for administration of the decedent's estate. **Leg.H.** Enacted Stats 1990 ch 79 §14 (AB 759), operative July 1, 1991.

Prior Law: Former Prob C §13203, similar to the present section, was added Stats 1986 ch 783 §24, operative July 1, 1987, amended Stats 1988 ch 1199 §100, operative July 1, 1989, and repealed Stats 1990 ch 79 §13, operative July 1, 1991.

§13204. Liability for decedent's unsecured debts

(a) A transferee is personally liable to the extent provided in this section for the unsecured debts of the decedent. That debt may be enforced against the transferee in the same manner as it could have been enforced against the decedent if the decedent had not died. In any action based upon the debt, the transferee may assert any defense, cross-complaint, or setoff that would have been available to the decedent if the decedent had not died. Nothing in this section permits enforcement of a claim that is barred under Part 4 (commencing with Section 9000) of Division 7. Section 366.2 of the Code of Civil Procedure applies in an action under this section.

(b) The personal liability under subdivision (a) shall not exceed the fair market value of the transferred property at the time of the issuance of the certified copy of the affidavit under Section 13202, less the amount of any liens and encumbrances on the transferred property at that time, and less the amount of any payment made pursuant to subdivision (a) of Section 13205.

(c) The transferee is not liable under this section if the transferee has satisfied the requirements of Section 13204.5, 13205.5, or 13206. **Leg.H.** Enacted Stats 1990 ch 79 §14 (AB 759), operative July 1, 1991. Amended Stats 1990 ch 140 §17.1 (SB 1855), operative July 1, 1991; Stats 1992 ch 178 §42 (SB 1496); Stats 2022 ch 29 §15 (AB 1716), effective January 1, 2023.

Prior Law Former Prob C §13204, similar to the present section, was added Stats 1986 ch 783 §24, effective September 15, 1986, operative July 1, 1987, amended Stats 1988 ch 113 §18, effective May 24, 1988, operative July 1, 1988, repealed Stats 1990 ch 79 §13, operative July 1, 1991, amended Stats 1990 ch 140 §17, operative until July 1, 1991, and repealed Stats 1990 ch 140 §33, operative July 1, 1991.

§ 13204.5. Transferee liability

(a) If proceedings for the administration of the decedent's estate are commenced, a transferee is personally liable to the estate for a share of the decedent's unsecured debts.

(b) In calculating the transferee's share of liability under subdivision (a), the abatement rules provided in Part 4 (commencing with Section 21400) of Division 11 shall be applied, using all of the following assumptions:

(1) Transferred property under this chapter shall be treated as if it had remained in the estate for administration.

(2) Any unsecured debts of the decedent that were paid by the transferee pursuant to Section 13204 shall be treated as if they were claims made against the decedent's estate.

(c) The personal representative shall provide a written statement of liability to the transferee, which specifies the amount that must be paid to the estate.

(d) The transferee is personally liable to the estate for the amount specified in the statement of liability. Any amount that the transferee paid pursuant to Section 13204 or 13205 shall be credited against the amount that the transferee owes the estate under this subdivision. If the amount that the transferee paid pursuant to Section 13204 or 13205 exceeds the amount specified in the written statement of liability, the estate shall reimburse the difference to the transferee. For the purposes of Section 11420, that reimbursement shall be deemed an expense of administration.

(e) The reasonable cost of proceeding under this section shall be reimbursed as an extraordinary service under Sections 10801 and 10811. The transferee is liable for the payment of that cost, which shall be separately identified in the statement of liability.

(f) The transferee is not liable under this section if the transferee has satisfied the requirements of Section 13205.5 or 13206. **Leg.H.** Added Stats 2022 ch 29 §16 (AB 1716), effective January 1, 2023.

§13205. Liability to person having superior right

(a) A transferee is personally liable to any person having a superior right to transferred property by testate or intestate succession from the decedent. Except as provided in subdivision (d), the personal liability established by this subdivision shall not exceed the sum of the following, less the amount of any payment made pursuant to Section 13204 or 13204.5:

(1) The fair market value at the time of the issuance of the certified copy of the affidavit under Section 13202 of the transferred property, less the amount of any liens and encumbrances on the transferred property at that time.

(2) Income received from the property, if that income would have accrued to the estate had the property not been transferred to the transferee.

(3) If the property has been disposed of, interest on the fair market value of the transferred property from the date of disposition at the rate of 7 percent per annum. For the purposes of this paragraph, "fair market value of the transferred property" means the fair market value of the transferred property, determined as of the time of the disposition of the property, less the amount of any liens and encumbrances on the property at the time the certified copy of the affidavit was issued.

(b) In addition to any other liability the transferee has under this section and Sections 13204, 13204.5, 13206, and 13208, if the transferee fraudulently executed or filed the affidavit under this chapter, the transferee is liable to the person having a superior right to that property by testate or intestate succession from the decedent for three times the fair market value of the transferred property. For the purposes of this subdivision, the "fair market value of the transferred property" is the fair market value of the transferred property determined as of the time the certified copy of the affidavit was issued under Section 13202, less any liens and encumbrances on the transferred property at that time.

(c) An action to impose liability under this section is forever barred three years after the certified copy of the affidavit is issued under Section 13202, or three years after the discovery of the fraud, whichever is later. The three-year period specified in this subdivision is not tolled for any reason.

(d) The transferee is not liable under this section if the transferee has satisfied the requirements of Section 13205.5 or 13206. **Leg.H.** Enacted Stats 1990 ch 79 §14 (AB 759), operative July 1, 1991. Amended Stats 1991 ch 1055 §49 (SB 271); Stats 2022 ch 29 §17 (AB 1716), effective January 1, 2023.

Prior Law Former Prob C §13205, similar to the present section, was added Stats 1986 ch 783 §24, operative July 1, 1987, and repealed Stats 1990 ch 79 §13, operative July 1, 1991.

§ 13205.5. Voluntary return of transferred property

(a) If proceedings for the administration of the decedent's estate are commenced, a transferee may voluntarily return transferred property to the decedent's estate for administration.

(b) The property to be restored to the estate under this section shall be reduced or increased as provided in Section 13208.5. **Leg.H.** Added Stats 2022 ch 29 §18 (AB 1716), effective January 1, 2023.

§ 13206. Restitution

(a) If property is transferred to a transferee under this chapter, and the decedent's personal representative later determines that another person has a superior right to the property by testate or intestate succession from the decedent, the personal representative may request that the transferred property be restored to the estate. Subject to subdivisions (b), (c), (d), (e), and (g) if the personal representative makes that request, the transferee is liable for all of the following:

(1) If the transferee still has the transferred property, restitution of the transferred property to the decedent's estate.

(2) If the transferee no longer has the transferred property, restitution to the decedent's estate of the fair market value of the transferred property plus interest from the date of disposition at the rate of 7 percent per annum on the fair market value of the transferred property. For the purposes of this paragraph, the "fair market value of the transferred property" is the fair market value of the transferred property, determined as of the time of the disposition of the transferred property, less the amount of any liens and encumbrances on the transferred property at the time the certified copy of the affidavit was issued.

(b) Subject to subdivision (d), if the transferee fraudulently executed or filed the affidavit under this chapter, the transferee is liable under this section for restitution of three times the fair market value of the transferred property. For the purposes of this subdivision, the "fair market value of the transferred property" is the fair market value of the transferred property, determined as of the time the certified copy of the affidavit was issued, less the amount of any liens and encumbrances on the property at that time. Restitution provided under this subdivision shall first be used to pay the estate's cost of proceeding under this section, with the remainder paid to the person who has a superior right to the property by testate or intestate succession.

(c) Subject to subdivision (d), if the transferee made a significant improvement to the transferred property in the good faith belief that the transferee was the successor of the decedent to that property, the transferee is liable for whichever of the following the decedent's estate elects:

(1) The restitution of the transferred property to the estate of the decedent.

(2) The restoration to the decedent's estate of the fair market value of the transferred property, determined as of the time of the issuance of the certified copy of the affidavit under Section 13202, less the amount of any liens and encumbrances on the transferred property at that time, together with interest on the net amount at the rate of 7 percent per annum running from the date of the issuance of the certified copy of the affidavit.

(d) The property and amount required to be restored to the estate under this section shall be reduced or increased as provided in Section 13208.5.

(e) An action to enforce the liability under this section may be brought only by the personal representative of the estate of the decedent.

(f) An action to enforce the liability under this section is forever barred three years after the certified copy of the affidavit is issued under Section 13202, or three years after the discovery of the fraud, whichever is later. The three-year period specified in this subdivision is not tolled for any reason.

(g) The transferee is not liable under subdivision (a) if the transferred property was returned to the estate under Section 13205.5. **Leg.H.** Added Stats 2022 ch 29 §20 (AB 1716), effective January 1, 2023.

Prior Law Former Prob C §13206, similar to the present section, was added by Stats 1990 ch 79 §14 (AB 759), operative July 1, 1991; amended by Stats 1991 ch 1055 §50 (SB 271); Stats 2015 ch 293 §19 (AB 139), effective January 1, 2016; Stats 2019 ch 122 §14 (AB 473), effective January 1, 2020; and repealed by Stats 2022 ch 29 §19 (AB 1716), effective January 1, 2023.

§13207. Limitation on liability under Sections 13204 and 13205 [Repealed]

Leg.H. Enacted Stats 1990 ch 79 §14 (AB 759), operative July 1, 1991. Amended Stats 1991 ch 1055 §51 (SB 271); Stats 2019 ch 122 §15 (AB

473), effective January 1, 2020. Repealed Stats 2022 ch 29 §21 (AB 1716), effective January 1, 2023.

Prior Law Former Prob C §13207, similar to the present section, was added Stats 1986 ch 783 §24, operative July 1, 1987, and repealed Stats 1990 ch 79 §13, operative July 1, 1991.

§13208. Other remedies not affected

The remedies available under Sections 13204 to 13206, inclusive, are in addition to any remedies available by reason of any fraud or intentional wrongdoing. **Leg.H.** Enacted Stats 1990 ch 79 §14 (AB 759), operative July 1, 1991. Amended Stats 2022 ch 29 §22 (AB 1716), effective January 1, 2023.

Prior Law Former Prob C §13208, similar to the present section, was added Stats 1986 ch 783 §24, operative July 1, 1987, and repealed Stats 1990 ch 79 §13, operative July 1, 1991.

§ 13208.5. Increase or decrease in value of property

(a) If the transferee's action or inaction increased the value of property returned to the estate or decreased the estate's obligations, the personal representative shall reimburse the transferee by the same amount. Actions or inaction that increase the value of returned property or decrease the estate's obligations include, but are not necessarily limited to, the following actions:

(1) A payment toward an unsecured debt of the decedent.

(2) A payment toward a debt secured against the returned property.

(3) A significant improvement of the returned property that increased the fair market value of the property.

(b) If the transferee's action or inaction decreased the value of property returned to the estate or increased the estate's obligations, the transferee is personally liable to the estate for that amount. Actions or inaction that decrease the value of the returned property or increase the estate's obligations include, but are not necessarily limited to, the following actions or inaction:

(1) An action or inaction that resulted in a lien or encumbrance being recorded against the property.

(2) The receipt of income from the property, if that income would have accrued to the estate had the property not been transferred to the transferee.

(c) The personal representative shall provide the transferee a written statement of any reimbursement or liability under this section, along with a statement of the reasons for the reimbursement or liability.

(d) For the purposes of Section 11420, reimbursement of the transferee under subdivision (a) shall be deemed an expense of administration.

(e) In the event that the transferee and the personal representative cannot agree on the reimbursement or liability due under this section, the transferee or personal representative may petition the court for an order determining the amount of the reimbursement or liability. In making a decision under this subdivision, the court should consider the surrounding circumstances, including whether the parties acted in good faith and whether a particular result would impose an unfair burden on the transferee or the estate. **Leg.H.** Added Stats 2022 ch 29 §23 (AB 1716), effective January 1, 2023.

§ 13209. Return of transferred property

If transferred property is returned to the estate under Sections 13205.5 or 13206, the value of that property shall be included in the total value of the estate, for all purposes. **Leg.H.** Added Stats 2022 ch 29 §24 (AB 1716), effective January 1, 2023.

§13210. When procedure may be used

The procedure provided by this chapter may be used only if one of the following requirements is satisfied:

(a) No proceeding for the administration of the decedent's estate is pending or has been conducted in this state.

(b) The decedent's personal representative consents in writing to use of the procedure provided by this chapter. **Leg.H.** Added Stats 1991 ch 1055 §52 (SB 271).

§ 13211. Interest liability excused

If the court finds that a person designated as a successor of the decedent in a certified copy of an affidavit issued under Section 13202 has acted reasonably and in good faith under the circumstances as known to the person, the court may, in its discretion, excuse the person from liability to pay interest, in whole or in part, under paragraph (2) of subdivision (a) of Section 13206 or paragraph (2) of subdivision (c) of Section 13206, if it would be equitable to do so. **Leg.H.** Added Stats 2019 ch 122 §16 (AB 473), effective January 1, 2020. Amended Stats 2022 ch 29 §25 (AB 1716), effective January 1, 2023.

PART 2
PASSAGE OF PROPERTY TO SURVIVING SPOUSE WITHOUT ADMINISTRATION

Chapter 1. General Provisions.
Chapter 2. Right of Surviving Spouse to Dispose of Property.
Chapter 3. Liability for Debts of Deceased Spouse.
Chapter 3.5. Liability for Decedent's Property.
Chapter 4. Collection by Affidavit of Compensation Owed to Deceased Spouse.
Chapter 5. Determination or Confirmation of Property Passing or Belonging to Surviving Spouse.

CHAPTER 1
GENERAL PROVISIONS

Necessity of administration. §13500.
Property subject to administration. §13501.
Election of administration. §13502.
Pecuniary devise or fractional interest in property. §13502.5.
Election to transfer property to trustee. §13503.
Property held in a revocable trust. §13504.
Application of this part. §13505.
Reference in statute or written instrument to repealed statutory provision. §13506.

§13500. Necessity of administration

Except as provided in this chapter, when a spouse dies intestate leaving property that passes to the surviving spouse under Section 6401, or dies testate and by his or her will devises all or a part of his or her property to the surviving spouse, the property passes to the survivor subject to the provisions of Chapter 2 (commencing with Section 13540) and Chapter 3 (commencing with Section 13550), and no administration is necessary. **Leg.H.** Enacted Stats 1990 ch 79 §14 (AB 759), operative July 1, 1991. Amended Stats 2016 ch 50 §89 (SB 1005), effective January 1, 2017.

2016 Note: For legislative intent, see the 2016 Note following Prob C §59.

Prior Law: Former Prob C §13500, similar to the present section, was added Stats 1986 ch 783 §24, operative July 1, 1987, and repealed Stats 1990 ch 79 §13, operative July 1, 1991.

§13501. Property subject to administration

Except as provided in Chapter 6 (commencing with Section 6600) of Division 6 and in Part 1 (commencing with Section 13000) of this division, the following property of the decedent is subject to administration under this code:

(a) Property passing to someone other than the surviving spouse under the decedent's will or by intestate succession.

(b) Property disposed of in trust under the decedent's will.

(c) Property in which the decedent's will limits the surviving spouse to a qualified ownership. For the purposes of this subdivision, a devise to the surviving spouse that is conditioned on the spouse surviving the decedent by a specified period of time is not a "qualified ownership" interest if the specified period of time has expired. **Leg.H.** Enacted Stats 1990 ch 79 §14 (AB 759), operative July 1, 1991.

Prior Law: Former Prob C §13501, similar to the present section, was added Stats 1986 ch 783 §24, operative July 1, 1987, amended Stats 1987 ch 923 §96, operative January 1, 1988, Stats 1988 ch 1199 §100.5, operative July 1, 1989, and repealed Stats 1990 ch 79 §13, operative July 1, 1991.

§13502. Election of administration

(a) Upon the election of the surviving spouse or the personal representative, guardian of the estate, or conservator of the estate of the surviving spouse, all or a portion of the following property may be administered under this code:

(1) The one-half of the community property that belongs to the decedent under Section 100, the one-half of the quasi-community property that belongs to the decedent under Section 101, and the separate property of the decedent.

(2) The one-half of the community property that belongs to the surviving spouse under Section 100 and the one-half of the quasi-community property that belongs to the surviving spouse under Section 101.

(b) The election shall be made by a writing specifically evidencing the election filed in the proceedings for the administration of the estate of the deceased spouse within four months after the issuance of letters, or within any further time that the court may allow upon a showing of good cause, and before entry of an order under Section 13656. **Leg.H.** Enacted Stats 1990 ch 79 §14 (AB 759), operative July 1, 1991.

Prior Law: Former Prob C §13502, similar to the present section, was added Stats 1986 ch 783 §24, operative July 1, 1989, amended Stats 1988 ch 1199 §101, operative July 1, 1989, and repealed Stats 1990 ch 79 §13, operative July 1, 1991.

§13502.5. Pecuniary devise or fractional interest in property

(a) Upon a petition by the personal representative of a decedent and a showing of good cause, the court may order that a pecuniary devise to the surviving spouse, or a fractional interest passing to the surviving spouse in any property in which the remaining fraction is subject to the administration, may be administered under this code, except to the extent that it has passed by inheritance as determined by an order pursuant to Chapter 5 (commencing with Section 13650).

(b) Notice of this petition shall be given as provided in Section 1220 to the person designated in that section and to the surviving spouse. **Leg.H.** Added Stats 1992 ch 871 §16 (AB 2975), effective January 1, 1993.

§13503. Election to transfer property to trustee

(a) The surviving spouse or the personal representative, guardian of the estate, or conservator of the estate of the surviving spouse may file an election and agreement to have all or part of the one-half of the community property that belongs to the surviving spouse under Section 100 and the one-half of the quasi-community property that belongs to the surviving spouse under Section 101 transferred by the surviving spouse or the surviving spouse's personal representative, guardian, or conservator to the trustee under the will of the deceased spouse or the trustee of an existing trust identified by the will of the deceased spouse, to be administered and distributed by the trustee.

(b) The election and agreement shall be filed in the proceedings for the administration of the estate of the deceased spouse and before the entry of the order for final distribution in the proceedings. **Leg.H.** Enacted Stats 1990 ch 79 §14 (AB 759), operative July 1, 1991.

Prior Law: Former Prob C §13503, similar to the present section, was added Stats 1986 ch 783 §24, operative July 1, 1989, amended Stats 1988 ch 1199 §101.5, operative July 1, 1989, and repealed Stats 1990 ch 79 §13, operative July 1, 1991.

§13504. Property held in a revocable trust

Notwithstanding the provisions of this part, community property held in a revocable trust described in Section 761 of the Family Code is governed by the provisions, if any, in the trust for disposition in the event of death. **Leg.H.** Enacted Stats 1990 ch 79 §14 (AB 759), operative July 1, 1991. Amended Stats 1994 ch 1269 §61.6 (AB 2208), effective January 1, 1995.

Prior Law: Former Prob C §13504, similar to the present section, was added Stats 1986 ch 783 §24, operative July 1, 1987, amended Stats 1987 ch 128 §7, effective July 6, 1987, operative July 1, 1987, and repealed Stats 1990 ch 79 §13, operative July 1, 1991.

§13505. Application of this part

This part applies whether the deceased spouse died before, on, or after July 1, 1987. **Leg.H.** Enacted Stats 1990 ch 79 §14 (AB 759), operative July 1, 1991.

Prior Law: Former Prob C §13505, similar to the present section, was added Stats 1986 ch 783 §24, operative July 1, 1987, and repealed Stats 1990 ch 79 §13, operative July 1, 1991.

§13506. Reference in statute or written instrument to repealed statutory provision

A reference in any statute of this state or in a written instrument, including a will or trust, to a provision of former Sections 202 to 206, inclusive, of the Probate Code (as repealed by Chapter 527 of the Statutes of 1984) or former Sections 649.1 to 649.5, inclusive, or Sections 650 to 658, inclusive, of the Probate Code (as repealed by Chapter 783 of the Statutes of 1986) shall be deemed to be a reference to the comparable provision of this part. **Leg.H.** Enacted Stats 1990 ch 79 §14 (AB 759), operative July 1, 1991.

Prior Law: Former Prob C §13506, similar to the present section, was added Stats 1986 ch 783 §24, operative July 1, 1987, and repealed Stats 1990 ch 79 §13, operative July 1, 1991.

CHAPTER 2
RIGHT OF SURVIVING SPOUSE TO DISPOSE OF PROPERTY

Right of surviving spouse to dispose of real property. §13540.
Recording notice of interest in property. §13541.
Dispositions under former law not affected. §13542.
Power to dispose of decedent's community property securities. §13545.

§13540. Right of surviving spouse to dispose of real property

(a) Except as provided in Section 13541, after 40 days from the death of a spouse, the surviving spouse or the personal representative, guardian of the estate, or conservator of the estate of the surviving spouse has full power to sell, convey, lease, mortgage, or otherwise deal with and dispose of the community or quasi-community real property, and the right, title, and interest of any grantee, purchaser, encumbrancer, or lessee shall be free of rights of the estate of the deceased spouse or of devisees or creditors of the deceased spouse to the same extent as if the property had been owned as the separate property of the surviving spouse.

(b) The surviving spouse or the personal representative, guardian of the estate, or conservator of the estate of the surviving spouse may record, prior to or together with the instrument that makes a disposition of property under this section, an affidavit of the facts that establish the right of the surviving spouse to make the disposition.

(c) Nothing in this section affects or limits the liability of the surviving spouse under Sections 13550 to 13553, inclusive, and Chapter 3.5 (commencing with Section 13560). **Leg.H.** Enacted Stats 1990 ch 79 §14 (AB 759), operative July 1, 1991. Amended Stats 1991 ch 1055 §54 (SB 271); Stats 1994 ch 806 §36 (AB 3686), effective January 1, 1995.

Prior Law: Former Prob C §13540, similar to the present section, was added Stats 1986 ch 783 §24, operative July 1, 1987, and repealed Stats 1990 ch 79 §13, operative July 1, 1991.

§13541. Recording notice of interest in property

(a) Section 13540 does not apply to a sale, conveyance, lease, mortgage, or other disposition that takes place after a notice that satisfies the requirements of this section is recorded in the office of the county recorder of the county in which real property is located.

(b) The notice shall contain all of the following:
(1) A description of the real property in which an interest is claimed.
(2) A statement that an interest in the property is claimed by a named person under the will of the deceased spouse.
(3) The name or names of the owner or owners of the record title to the property.

(c) There shall be endorsed on the notice instructions that it shall be indexed by the recorder in the name or names of the owner or owners of record title to the property, as grantor or grantors, and in the name of the person claiming an interest in the property, as grantee.

(d) A person shall not record a notice under this section for the purpose of slandering title to the property. If the court in an action or proceeding relating to the rights of the parties determines that a person recorded a notice under this section for the purpose of slandering title, the court shall award against the person the cost of the action or proceeding, including a reasonable attorney's fee, and the damages caused by the recording. **Leg.H.** Enacted Stats 1990 ch 79 §14 (AB 759), operative July 1, 1991. Amended Stats 1991 ch 1055 §55 (SB 271).

Prior Law: Former Prob C §13541, similar to the present section, was added Stats 1986 ch 783 §24, operative July 1, 1987, and repealed Stats 1990 ch 79 §13, operative July 1, 1991.

§13542. Dispositions under former law not affected

The repeal of former Section 649.2 by Chapter 783 of the Statutes of 1986 does not affect any sale, lease, mortgage, or other transaction or disposition of real property made prior to July 1, 1987, to which that section applied, and such a sale, lease, mortgage, or other transaction or disposition shall continue to be governed by the provisions of former Section 649.2 notwithstanding the repeal of that section. **Leg.H.** Enacted Stats 1990 ch 79 §14 (AB 759), operative July 1, 1991.

Prior Law: Former Prob C §13542, similar to the present section, was added Stats 1986 ch 783 §24, operative July 1, 1987, and repealed Stats 1990 ch 79 §13, operative July 1, 1991.

§13545. Power to dispose of decedent's community property securities

(a) After the death of a spouse, the surviving spouse, or the personal representative, guardian of the estate, or conservator of the estate of the surviving spouse has full power to sell, assign, pledge, or otherwise deal with and dispose of community or quasi-community property securities registered in the name of the surviving spouse alone, and the right, title, and interest of any purchaser, assignee, encumbrancer, or other transferee shall be free of the rights of the estate of the deceased spouse or of devisees or creditors of the deceased spouse to the same extent as if the deceased spouse had not died.

(b) Nothing in this section affects or limits the liability of a surviving spouse under Sections 13550 to 13553, inclusive, and Chapter 3.5 (commencing with Section 13560). **Leg.H.** Added Stats 1991 ch 1055 §56 (SB 271).

CHAPTER 3
LIABILITY FOR DEBTS OF DECEASED SPOUSE

Personal liability of surviving spouse. §13550.
Limitation on liability. §13551.
Effect of commencement of proceedings for administration of estate of deceased spouse. §13552.
No liability if all property administered. §13553.
Enforcement of liability. §13554.

§13550. Personal liability of surviving spouse

Except as provided in Sections 11446, 13552, 13553, and 13554, upon the death of a married person, the surviving spouse is personally liable for the debts of the deceased spouse chargeable against the property described in Section 13551 to the extent provided in Section 13551. **Leg.H.** Enacted Stats 1990 ch 79 §14 (AB 759), operative July 1, 1991.

Prior Law: Former Prob C §13550, similar to the present section, was added Stats 1986 ch 783 §24, operative July 1, 1987, amended Stats 1988 ch 1199 §102, operative July 1, 1989, and repealed Stats 1990 ch 79 §13, operative July 1, 1991.

§13551. Limitation on liability

The liability imposed by Section 13550 shall not exceed the fair market value at the date of the decedent's death, less the amount of any liens and encumbrances, of the total of the following:

(a) The portion of the one-half of the community and quasi-community property belonging to the surviving spouse under Sections 100 and 101 that is not exempt from enforcement of a money judgment and is not administered in the estate of the deceased spouse.

(b) The portion of the one-half of the community and quasi-community property belonging to the decedent under Sections 100 and 101 that passes to the surviving spouse without administration under this part.

(c) The separate property of the decedent that passes to the surviving spouse without administration under this part. **Leg.H.** Enacted Stats 1990 ch 79 §14 (AB 759), operative July 1, 1991. Amended Stats 2022 ch 29 §26 (AB 1716), effective January 1, 2023.

Prior Law Former Prob C §13551, similar to the present section, was added Stats 1986 ch 783 §24, operative July 1, 1987, and repealed Stats 1990 ch 79 §13, operative July 1, 1991.

§13552. Effect of commencement of proceedings for administration of estate of deceased spouse

If proceedings are commenced in this state for the administration of the estate of the deceased spouse and the time for filing claims has commenced, any action upon the liability of the surviving spouse pursuant to Section 13550 is barred to the same extent as provided for claims under Part 4 (commencing with Section 9000) of Division 7, except as to the following:

(a) Creditors who commence judicial proceedings for the enforcement of the debt and serve the surviving spouse with the complaint therein prior to the expiration of the time for filing claims.

(b) Creditors who have or who secure the surviving spouse's acknowledgment in writing of the liability of the surviving spouse for the debts.

(c) Creditors who file a timely claim in the proceedings for the administration of the estate of the deceased spouse. **Leg.H.** Enacted Stats 1990 ch 79 §14 (AB 759), operative July 1, 1991.

§13553. No liability if all property administered

The surviving spouse is not liable under this chapter if all the property described in paragraphs (1) and (2) of subdivision (a) of Section 13502 is administered under this code. **Leg.H.** Enacted Stats 1990 ch 79 §14 (AB 759), operative July 1, 1991.

Prior Law: Former Prob C §13553, similar to the present section, was added Stats 1986 ch 783 §24, operative July 1, 1987, amended Stats 1988 ch 1199 §102.5, operative July 1, 1989, and repealed Stats 1990 ch 79 §13, operative July 1, 1991.

§13554. Enforcement of liability

(a) Except as otherwise provided in this chapter, any debt described in Section 13550 may be enforced against the surviving spouse in the same manner as it could have been enforced against the deceased spouse if the deceased spouse had not died.

(b) In any action or proceeding based upon the debt, the surviving spouse may assert any defense, cross-complaint, or setoff which would have been available to the deceased spouse if the deceased spouse had not died.

(c) Section 366.2 of the Code of Civil Procedure applies in an action under this section. **Leg.H.** Enacted Stats 1990 ch 79 §14 (AB 759), operative July 1, 1991. Amended Stats 1990 ch 140 §18.1 (SB 1855), operative July 1, 1991; Stats 1992 ch 178 §43 (SB 1496), effective January 1, 1993.

Prior Law: Former Prob C §13554, similar to the present section, was added Stats 1986 ch 783 §24, operative July 1, 1987, repealed Stats 1990 ch 79 §13, operative July 1, 1991, amended Stats 1990 ch 140 §18, operative until July 1, 1991, and repealed Stats 1990 ch 140 §34, operative July 1, 1991.

CHAPTER 3.5
LIABILITY FOR DECEDENT'S PROPERTY

"Decedent's property". §13560.
Liability of surviving spouse to person with superior right. §13561.
Specific liabilities of surviving spouse. §13562.
Limitations on liabilities of surviving spouse. §13563.
Availability of other remedies. §13564.
Interest liability excused. § 13565.

§13560. "Decedent's property"

For the purposes of this chapter, "decedent's property" means the one-half of the community property that belongs to the decedent under Section 100 and the one-half of the quasi-community property that belongs to the decedent under Section 101. **Leg.H.** Added Stats 1991 ch 1055 §57 (SB 271).

§13561. Liability of surviving spouse to person with superior right

(a) If the decedent's property is in the possession or control of the surviving spouse at the time of the decedent's death, the surviving spouse is personally liable to the extent provided in Section 13563 to any person having a superior right by testate succession from the decedent.

(b) An action to impose liability under this section is forever barred three years after the death of the decedent. The three-year period specified in this subdivision is not tolled for any reason. **Leg.H.** Added Stats 1991 ch 1055 §57 (SB 271).

§13562. Specific liabilities of surviving spouse

(a) Subject to subdivisions (b), (c), and (d), if proceedings for the administration of the decedent's estate are commenced, the surviving spouse is liable for:

(1) The restitution to the decedent's estate of the decedent's property if the surviving spouse still has the decedent's property, together with (A) the net income the surviving spouse received from the decedent's property and (B) if the surviving spouse encumbered the decedent's property after the date of death, the amount necessary to satisfy the balance of the encumbrance as of the date the decedent's property is restored to the estate.

(2) The restitution to the decedent's estate of the fair market value of the decedent's property if the surviving spouse no longer has the decedent's property, together with (A) the net income the surviving spouse received from the decedent's property prior to disposing of it and (B) interest from the date of disposition at the rate of 7 percent per annum on the fair market value of the decedent's property. For the purposes of this paragraph, the "fair market value of the decedent's property" is the fair market value of the decedent's property, determined as of the time of the disposition of the decedent's property, less the amount of any liens and encumbrances on the decedent's property at the time of the decedent's death.

(b) Subject to subdivision (c), if proceedings for the administration of the decedent's estate are commenced and the surviving spouse made a significant improvement to the decedent's property in the good faith belief that the surviving spouse was the successor of the decedent to the decedent's property, the surviving spouse is liable for whichever of the following the decedent's estate elects:

(1) The restitution of the decedent's property, as improved, to the estate of the decedent upon the condition that the estate reimburse the surviving spouse for (A) the amount by which the improvement increases the fair market value of the decedent's property restored, valued as of the time of restitution, and (B) the amount paid by the surviving spouse for principal and interest on any liens or encumbrances that were on the decedent's property at the time of the decedent's death.

(2) The restoration to the decedent's estate of the fair market value of the decedent's property, valued as of the time of the decedent's death, excluding the amount of any liens and encumbrances on the decedent's property at that time, together with interest on the net amount at the rate of 7 percent per annum running from the date of the decedent's death.

(c) The property and amount required to be restored to the estate under this section shall be reduced by any property or amount paid by the surviving spouse to satisfy a liability under Chapter 3 (commencing with Section 13550).

(d) An action to enforce the liability under this section may be brought only by the personal representative of the estate of the decedent. Whether or not the personal representative brings an action under this section, the personal representative may enforce the liability only to the extent necessary to protect the interests of the heirs, devisees, and creditors of the decedent.

(e) An action to enforce the liability under this section is forever barred three years after the death of the decedent. The three-year period specified in this subdivision is not tolled for any reason. **Leg.H.** Added Stats 1991 ch 1055 §57 (SB 271). Amended Stats 2015 ch 293 §20 (AB 139), effective January 1, 2016; Stats 2019 ch 122 §17 (AB 473), effective January 1, 2020.

§13563. Limitations on liabilities of surviving spouse

(a) The surviving spouse is not liable under Section 13561 if proceedings for the administration of the decedent's estate are commenced and the surviving spouse satisfies the requirements of Section 13562.

(b) The aggregate of the personal liability of the surviving spouse under Section 13561 shall not exceed the sum of the following:

(1) The fair market value at the time of the decedent's death, less the amount of any liens and encumbrances on the decedent's property at that time, of the portion of the decedent's property that passes to any person having a superior right by testate succession from the decedent.

(2) The net income the surviving spouse received from the portion of the decedent's property that passes to any person having a superior right by testate succession from the decedent.

(3) If the decedent's property has been disposed of, interest on the fair market value of the portion of the decedent's property that passes to any person having a superior right by testate succession from the decedent from the date of disposition at the rate of 7 percent per annum. For the purposes of this paragraph, "fair market value" is fair market value, determined as of the time of disposition of the decedent's property, less the amount of any liens and encumbrances on the decedent's property at the time of the decedent's death. **Leg.H.** Added Stats 1991 ch 1055 §57 (SB 271). Amended Stats 2019 ch 122 §18 (AB 473), effective January 1, 2020.

§13564. Availability of other remedies

The remedies available under Sections 13561 to 13563, inclusive, are in addition to any remedies available by reason of any fraud or intentional wrongdoing. **Leg.H.** Added Stats 1991 ch 1055 §57 (SB 271).

§ 13565. Interest liability excused

If the court finds that the surviving spouse has acted reasonably and in good faith under the circumstances as known to the surviving spouse, the court may, in its discretion, excuse the surviving spouse from liability to pay interest, in whole or in part, under paragraph (2) of subdivision (a) of

Section 13562, paragraph (2) of subdivision (b) of Section 13562, or paragraph (3) of subdivision (b) of Section 13563, if it would be equitable to do so. **Leg.H.** Added Stats 2019 ch 122 §19 (AB 473), effective January 1, 2020.

CHAPTER 4
COLLECTION BY AFFIDAVIT OF COMPENSATION OWED TO DECEASED SPOUSE

Collection of salary or other compensation by surviving spouse, guardian, or conservator; Net limitation. §13600.
Contents of affidavit; Proof of identity. §13601.
Payment by employer. §13602.
Protection of employer from liability. §13603.
Enforcement of payment. §13604.
Rights of heirs or devisees of deceased spouse not affected. §13605.
Other methods of collecting compensation not affected. §13606.

§13600. Collection of salary or other compensation by surviving spouse, guardian, or conservator; Net limitation

(a) At any time after a spouse dies, the surviving spouse or the guardian or conservator of the estate of the surviving spouse may, without procuring letters of administration or awaiting probate of the will, collect salary or other compensation owed by an employer for personal services of the deceased spouse, including compensation for unused vacation, not in excess of sixteen thousand six hundred twenty-five dollars ($16,625), as adjusted periodically in accordance with Section 890, net.

(b) Not more than sixteen thousand six hundred twenty-five dollars ($16,625), as adjusted periodically in accordance with Section 890, net in the aggregate may be collected by or for the surviving spouse under this chapter from all of the employers of the decedent.

(c) For the purposes of this chapter, a guardian or conservator of the estate of the surviving spouse may act on behalf of the surviving spouse without authorization or approval of the court in which the guardianship or conservatorship proceeding is pending.

(d) The dollar limit set forth in subdivisions (a) and (b) does not apply to the surviving spouse or the guardian or conservator of the estate of the surviving spouse of a firefighter or peace officer described in subdivision (a) of Section 22820 of the Government Code. **Leg.H.** Enacted Stats 1990 ch 79 §14 (AB 759), operative July 1, 1991. Amended Stats 2002 ch 733 §2 (AB 2059), effective September 20, 2002; Stats 2004 ch 69 §35 (SB 626), effective June 24, 2004; Stats 2011 ch 117 §10 (AB 1305), effective January 1, 2012; Stats 2012 ch 162 §140 (SB 1171), effective January 1, 2013; Stats 2016 ch 50 §90 (SB 1005), effective January 1, 2017; Stats 2019 ch 122 §20 (AB 473), effective January 1, 2020.

2016 Note: For legislative intent, see the 2016 Note following Prob C §59.

2004 Note: It is the intent of the Legislature in enacting this act to reorganize the Public Employees' Medical and Hospital Care Act and the State Employees' Dental Care Act. It is not the intent of the Legislature to make any substantive change in the law. Thus, if, in the opinion of any court or administrative officer, a different result under any provision of Part 5 (commencing with Section 22751) of Division 5 of Title 2 of, or Part 6 (commencing with Section 22950) of Division 5 of Title 2 of, the Government Code, as it read on December 31, 2003, would occur because of the enactment of this act, the provision as it read on the effective date of this act shall be followed and the result shall be as it would have been on that date. It is further the intent of the Legislature that no new or additional rights vest in any employee, annuitant, or family member nor any benefits be reduced or impaired as a result of the enactment of this act. No current or future benefits under this act shall be revised in any way because of this act. Stats 2004 ch 69 (SB 626) §40.

Prior Law: Former Prob C §13600, similar to the present section, was added Stats 1986 ch 783 §24, operative July 1, 1987, and repealed Stats 1990 ch 79 §13, operative July 1, 1991.

§13601. Contents of affidavit; Proof of identity

(a) To collect salary or other compensation under this chapter, an affidavit or a declaration under penalty of perjury under the laws of this state shall be furnished to the employer of the deceased spouse stating all of the following:

(1) The name of the decedent.
(2) The date and place of the decedent's death.
(3) Either of the following, as appropriate:
(A) "The affiant or declarant is the surviving spouse of the decedent."
(B) "The affiant or declarant is the guardian or conservator of the estate of the surviving spouse of the decedent."

(4) "The surviving spouse of the decedent is entitled to the earnings of the decedent under the decedent's will or by intestate succession and no one else has a superior right to the earnings."

(5) "No proceeding is now being or has been conducted in California for administration of the decedent's estate."

(6) "Sections 13600 to 13605, inclusive, of the California Probate Code require that the earnings of the decedent, including compensation for unused vacation, not in excess of [Insert dollar amount specified in subdivision (e) of Section 13601 of the California Probate Code] net, be paid promptly to the affiant or declarant."

(7) "Neither the surviving spouse, nor anyone acting on behalf of the surviving spouse, has a pending request to collect compensation owed by another employer for personal services of the decedent under Sections 13600 to 13605, inclusive, of the California Probate Code."

(8) "Neither the surviving spouse, nor anyone acting on behalf of the surviving spouse, has collected any compensation owed by an employer for personal services of the decedent under Sections 13600 to 13605, inclusive, of the California Probate Code except the sum of ____ dollars ($____) that was collected from ____."

(9) "The affiant or declarant requests that the affiant or declarant be paid the salary or other compensation owed by you for personal services of the decedent, including compensation for unused vacation, not to exceed [Insert dollar amount specified in subdivision (e) of Section 13601 of the California Probate Code] net, less the amount of ____ dollars ($____) that was previously collected."

(10) "The affiant or declarant affirms or declares under penalty of perjury under the laws of the State of California that the foregoing is true and correct."

(b) Where the decedent is a firefighter or peace officer described in subdivision (a) of Section 22820 of the Government Code, the affidavit or declaration need not include the content specified in paragraphs (6) to (9), inclusive, of subdivision (a). The affidavit shall instead include the following statements:

(1) The decedent was a firefighter or peace officer described in subdivision (a) of Section 22820 of the Government Code. Sections 13600 to 13605, inclusive, of the California Probate Code require that the earnings of the decedent, including compensation for unused vacation, be paid promptly to the affiant or declarant.

(2) "The affiant or declarant requests to be paid the salary or other compensation owed by you for personal services of the decedent, including compensation for unused vacation."

(c) Reasonable proof of the identity of the surviving spouse shall be provided to the employer. If a guardian or conservator is acting for the surviving spouse, reasonable proof of the identity of the guardian or conservator shall also be provided to the employer. Proof of identity that is sufficient under Section 13104 is sufficient proof of identity for the purposes of this subdivision.

(d) If a person presenting the affidavit or declaration is a person claiming to be the guardian or conservator of the estate of the surviving spouse, the employer shall be provided with reasonable proof, satisfactory to the employer, of the appointment of the person to act as guardian or conservator of the estate of the surviving spouse.

(e)(1) When the decedent dies prior to April 1, 2022, the dollar amount for paragraphs (6) and (9) of subdivision (a) is sixteen thousand six hundred twenty-five dollars ($16,625).

(2) When the decedent dies on or after April 1, 2022, the dollar amount for paragraphs (6) and (9) of subdivision (a) is the adjusted dollar amount, published in accordance with subdivision (c) of Section 890, in effect on the date of the decedent's death. The affiant or declarant shall attach the list of adjusted dollar amounts, published in accordance with subdivision (c) of Section 890, in effect on the date of the decedent's death to the affidavit or declaration. **Leg.H.** Enacted Stats 1990 ch 79 §14 (AB 759), operative July 1, 1991. Amended Stats 2003 ch 32 §13 (AB 167); Stats 2011 ch 117 §11 (AB 1305), effective January 1, 2012; Stats 2019 ch 122 §21 (AB 473), effective January 1, 2020.

Prior Law: Former Prob C §13601, similar to the present section, was added Stats 1986 ch 783 §24, operative July 1, 1987, and repealed Stats 1990 ch 79 §13, operative July 1, 1991.

§13602. Payment by employer

If the requirements of Section 13600 are satisfied, the employer to whom the affidavit or declaration is presented shall promptly pay the earnings of the decedent, including compensation for unused vacation, as provided in Section 13600, to the person presenting the affidavit or declaration. **Leg.H.** Enacted Stats 1990 ch 79 §14 (AB 759), operative July 1, 1991. Amended Stats 2011 ch 117 §12 (AB 1305), effective January 1, 2012; Stats 2019 ch 122 §22 (AB 473), effective January 1, 2020.

Prior Law: Former Prob C §13602, similar to the present section, was added Stats 1986 ch 783 §24, operative July 1, 1987, and repealed Stats 1990 ch 79 §13, operative July 1, 1991.

§13603. Protection of employer from liability

If the requirements of Section 13601 are satisfied, receipt by the employer of the affidavit or declaration constitutes sufficient acquittance for the compensation paid pursuant to this chapter and discharges the employer from any further liability with respect to the compensation paid. The employer may rely in good faith on the statements in the affidavit or declaration and has no duty to inquire into the truth of any statement in the affidavit or declaration. **Leg.H.** Enacted Stats 1990 ch 79 §14 (AB 759), operative July 1, 1991.

§13604. Enforcement of payment

(a) If the employer refuses to pay as required by this chapter, the surviving spouse may recover the amount the surviving spouse is entitled to receive under this chapter in an action brought for that purpose against the employer.

(b) If an action is brought against the employer under this section, the court shall award reasonable attorney's fees to the surviving spouse if the court finds that the employer acted unreasonably in refusing to pay as required by this chapter. **Leg.H.** Enacted Stats 1990 ch 79 §14 (AB 759), operative July 1, 1991.

Prior Law: Former Prob C §13604, similar to the present section, was added Stats 1986 ch 783 §24, operative July 1, 1987, and repealed Stats 1990 ch 79 §13, operative July 1, 1991.

§13605. Rights of heirs or devisees of deceased spouse not affected

(a) Nothing in this chapter limits the rights of the heirs or devisees of the deceased spouse. Payment of a decedent's compensation pursuant to this chapter does not preclude later proceedings for administration of the decedent's estate.

(b) Any person to whom payment is made under this chapter is answerable and accountable therefor to the personal representative of the decedent's estate and is liable for the amount of the payment to any other person having a superior right to the payment received. In addition to any other liability the person has under this section, a person who fraudulently secures a payment under this chapter is liable to a person having a superior right to the payment for three times the amount of the payment. **Leg.H.** Enacted Stats 1990 ch 79 §14 (AB 759), operative July 1, 1991.

Prior Law: Former Prob C §13605, similar to the present section, was added Stats 1986 ch 783 §24, operative July 1, 1987, and repealed Stats 1990 ch 79 §13, operative July 1, 1991.

§13606. Other methods of collecting compensation not affected

The procedure provided in this chapter is in addition to, and not in lieu of, any other method of collecting compensation owed to a decedent. **Leg.H.** Enacted Stats 1990 ch 79 §14 (AB 759), operative July 1, 1991.

Prior Law: Former Prob C §13606, similar to the present section, was added Stats 1986 ch 783 §24, operative July 1, 1987, and repealed Stats 1990 ch 79 §13, operative July 1, 1991.

CHAPTER 5
DETERMINATION OR CONFIRMATION OF PROPERTY PASSING OR BELONGING TO SURVIVING SPOUSE

Filing of petition. §13650.
Contents of petition. §13651.
Filing petition in pending proceeding. §13652.
Filing petition with petition for probate proceeding. §13653.
Effect of petition. §13654.
Notice of hearing. §13655.
Court order. §13656.
Effect of court order. §13657.
Protection of interests of creditors of business of deceased spouse. §13658.
Inventory and appraisal. §13659.
Attorney's fees. §13660.

§13650. Filing of petition

(a) A surviving spouse or the personal representative, guardian of the estate, or conservator of the estate of the surviving spouse may file a petition in the superior court of the county in which the estate of the deceased spouse may be administered requesting an order that administration of all or part of the estate is not necessary for the reason that all or part of the estate is property passing to the surviving spouse. The petition may also request an order confirming the ownership of the surviving spouse of property belonging to the surviving spouse under Section 100 or 101.

(b) To the extent of the election, this section does not apply to property that the petitioner has elected, as provided in Section 13502, to have administered under this code.

(c) A guardian or conservator may file a petition under this section without authorization or approval of the court in which the guardianship or conservatorship proceeding is pending. **Leg.H.** Enacted Stats 1990 ch 79 §14 (AB 759), operative July 1, 1991.

Prior Law: Former Prob C §13650, similar to the present section, was added Stats 1986 ch 783 §24, operative July 1, 1987, amended Stats 1988 ch 1199 §103, operative July 1, 1989, and repealed Stats 1990 ch 79 §13, operative July 1, 1991.

§13651. Contents of petition

(a) A petition filed pursuant to Section 13650 shall allege that administration of all or a part of the estate of the deceased spouse is not necessary for the reason that all or a part of the estate is property passing to the surviving spouse, and shall set forth all of the following information:

(1) If proceedings for the administration of the estate are not pending, the facts necessary to determine the county in which the estate of the deceased spouse may be administered.

(2) A description of the property of the deceased spouse which the petitioner alleges is property passing to the surviving spouse, including the trade or business name of any property passing to the surviving spouse that consists of an unincorporated business or an interest in an unincorporated business which the deceased spouse was operating or managing at the time of death, subject to any written agreement between the deceased spouse and the surviving spouse providing for a non pro rata division of the aggregate value of the community property assets or quasi-community assets, or both.

(3) The facts upon which the petitioner bases the allegation that all or a part of the estate of the deceased spouse is property passing to the surviving spouse.

(4) A description of any interest in the community property or quasi-community property, or both, which the petitioner requests the court to confirm to the surviving spouse as belonging to the surviving spouse pursuant to Section 100 or 101, subject to any written agreement between the deceased spouse and the surviving spouse providing for a non pro rata division of the aggregate value of the community property assets or quasi-community assets, or both.

(5) The name, age, address, and relation to the deceased spouse of each heir and devisee of the deceased spouse, the names and addresses of all persons named as executors of the will of the deceased spouse, and the names and addresses of all persons appointed as personal representatives of the deceased spouse, which are known to the petitioner.

Disclosure of any written agreement between the deceased spouse and the surviving spouse providing for a non pro rata division of the aggregate value of the community property assets or quasi-community property assets, or both, or the affirmative statement that this agreement does not exist. If a dispute arises as to the division of the community property assets or quasi-community property assets, or both, pursuant to this agreement, the court shall determine the division subject to terms and conditions or other remedies that appear equitable under the circumstances of the case, taking into account the rights of all interested persons.

(b) If the petitioner bases the allegation that all or part of the estate of the deceased spouse is property passing to the surviving spouse upon the will of the deceased spouse, a copy of the will shall be attached to the petition.

(c) If the petitioner bases the description of the property of the deceased spouse passing to the surviving spouse or the property to be confirmed to the surviving spouse, or both, upon a written agreement between the deceased spouse and the surviving spouse providing for a non pro rata division of the aggregate value of the community property assets or quasi-community assets, or both, a copy of the agreement shall be attached to the petition. **Leg.H.** Enacted Stats 1990 ch 79 §14 (AB 759), operative July 1, 1991. Amended Stats 1998 ch 682 §6 (AB 2069), effective January 1, 1999.

Prior Law: Former Prob C §13651, similar to the present section, was added Stats 1986 ch 783 §24, operative July 1, 1987, and repealed Stats 1990 ch 79 §13, operative July 1, 1991.

§13652. Filing petition in pending proceeding

If proceedings for the administration of the estate of the deceased spouse are pending, a petition under this chapter shall be filed in those proceedings without the payment of an additional fee. **Leg.H.** Enacted Stats 1990 ch 79 §14 (AB 759), operative July 1, 1991.

Prior Law: Former Prob C §13652, similar to the present section, was added Stats 1986 ch 783 §24, operative July 1, 1987, and repealed Stats 1990 ch 79 §13, operative July 1, 1991.

§13653. Filing petition with petition for probate proceeding

If proceedings for the administration of the estate of the deceased spouse are not pending, a petition under this chapter may, but need not, be filed with a petition for probate of the will of the deceased spouse or for administration of the estate of the deceased spouse. **Leg.H.** Enacted Stats 1990 ch 79 §14 (AB 759), operative July 1, 1991.

Prior Law: Former Prob C §13653, similar to the present section, was added Stats 1986 ch 783 §24, operative July 1, 1987, and repealed Stats 1990 ch 79 §13, operative July 1, 1991.

§13654. Effect of petition

The filing of a petition under this chapter does not preclude the court from admitting the will of the deceased spouse to probate or appointing a personal representative of the estate of the deceased spouse upon the petition of any person legally entitled, including any petition for probate of the will or for administration of the estate which is filed with a petition filed under this chapter. **Leg.H.** Enacted Stats 1990 ch 79 §14 (AB 759), operative July 1, 1991.

Prior Law: Former Prob C §13654, similar to the present section, was added Stats 1986 ch 783 §24, operative July 1, 1987, and repealed Stats 1990 ch 79 §13, operative July 1, 1991.

§13655. Notice of hearing

(a) If proceedings for the administration of the estate of the deceased spouse are pending at the time a petition is filed under this chapter, or if the proceedings are not pending and if the petition filed under this chapter is not filed with a petition for probate of the deceased spouse's will or for administration of the estate of the deceased spouse, notice of the hearing on the petition filed under this chapter shall be given as provided in Section 1220 to all of the following persons:

(1) Each person listed in Section 1220 and each person named as executor in any will of the deceased spouse.

(2) All devisees and known heirs of the deceased spouse and, if the petitioner is the trustee of a trust that is a devisee under the will of the decedent, all persons interested in the trust, as determined in cases of future interests pursuant to paragraph (1), (2), or (3) of subdivision (a) of Section 15804.

(b) The notice specified in subdivision (a) shall also be delivered as provided in subdivision (a) to the Attorney General, addressed to the office of the Attorney General at Sacramento, if the petitioner bases the allegation that all or part of the estate of the deceased spouse is property passing to the surviving spouse upon the will of the deceased spouse and the will involves or may involve either of the following:

(1) A testamentary trust of property for charitable purposes other than a charitable trust with a designated trustee, resident in this state.

(2) A devise for a charitable purpose without an identified devisee or beneficiary. **Leg.H.** Enacted Stats 1990 ch 79 §14 (AB 759), operative July 1, 1991. Amended Stats 1996 ch 563 §30 (SB 392); Stats 2017 ch 319 §85 (AB 976), effective January 1, 2018.

Prior Law: Former Prob C §13655, similar to the present section, was added Stats 1986 ch 783 §24, operative July 1, 1987, amended Stats 1987 ch 923 §98, operative July 1, 1988, Stats 1988 ch 113 §18.5, effective May 24, 1988, operative July 1, 1988, Stats 1988 ch 1199 §103.5, operative July 1, 1989, and repealed Stats 1990 ch 79 §13, operative July 1, 1991.

§13656. Court order

(a) If the court finds that all of the estate of the deceased spouse is property passing to the surviving spouse, the court shall issue an order describing the property, determining that the property is property passing to the surviving spouse, and determining that no administration is necessary. The court may issue any further orders which may be necessary to cause delivery of the property or its proceeds to the surviving spouse.

(b) If the court finds that all or part of the estate of the deceased spouse is not property passing to the surviving spouse, the court shall issue an order (1) describing any property which is not property passing to the surviving spouse, determining that that property does not pass to the surviving spouse and determining that that property is subject to administration under this code and (2) describing the property, if any, which is property passing to the surviving spouse, determining that that property passes to the surviving spouse, and determining that no administration of that property is necessary. If the court determines that property passes to the surviving spouse, the court may issue any further orders which may be necessary to cause delivery of that property or its proceeds to the surviving spouse.

(c) If the petition filed under this chapter includes a description of the interest of the surviving spouse in the community or quasi-community property, or both, which belongs to the surviving spouse pursuant to Section 100 or 101 and the court finds that the interest belongs to the surviving spouse, the court shall issue an order describing the property and confirming the ownership of the surviving spouse and may issue any further orders which may be necessary to cause ownership of the property to be confirmed in the surviving spouse. **Leg.H.** Enacted Stats 1990 ch 79 §14 (AB 759), operative July 1, 1991.

Prior Law: Former Prob C §13656, similar to the present section, was added Stats 1986 ch 783 §24, operative July 1, 1987, amended Stats 1988 ch 1199 §104, operative July 1, 1989, and repealed Stats 1990 ch 79 §13, operative July 1, 1991.

§13657. Effect of court order

Upon becoming final, an order under Section 13656 (1) determining that property is property passing to the surviving spouse or (2) confirming the ownership of the surviving spouse of property belonging to the surviving spouse under Section 100 or 101 shall be conclusive on all persons, whether or not they are in being. **Leg.H.** Enacted Stats 1990 ch 79 §14 (AB 759), operative July 1, 1991.

Prior Law: Former Prob C §13657, similar to the present section, was added Stats 1986 ch 783 §24, operative July 1, 1987, and repealed Stats 1990 ch 79 §13, operative July 1, 1991.

§13658. Protection of interests of creditors of business of deceased spouse

If the court determines that all or a part of the property passing to the surviving spouse consists of an unincorporated business or an interest in an unincorporated business which the deceased spouse was operating or managing at the time of death, the court shall require the surviving spouse to file a list of all of the known creditors of the business and the amounts owing to each of them. The court may issue any order necessary to protect the interests of the creditors of the business, including, but not limited to, the filing of (1) an undertaking and (2) an inventory and appraisal in the form provided in Section 8802 and made as provided in Part 3 (commencing with Section 8800) of Division 7. **Leg.H.** Enacted Stats 1990 ch 79 §14 (AB 759), operative July 1, 1991.

Prior Law: Former Prob C §13658, similar to the present section, was added Stats 1986 ch 783 §24, operative July 1, 1987, amended Stats 1988 ch 1199 §104.5, operative July 1, 1989, and repealed Stats 1990 ch 79 §13, operative July 1, 1991.

§13659. Inventory and appraisal

Except as provided in Section 13658, no inventory and appraisal of the estate of the deceased spouse is required in a proceeding under this chapter. However, within three months after the filing of a petition under this chapter, or within such further time as the court or judge for reasonable cause may allow, the petitioner may file with the clerk of the court an inventory and appraisal made as provided in Part 3 (commencing with Section 8800) of Division 7. The petitioner may appraise the assets which a personal representative could appraise under Section 8901. **Leg.H.** Enacted Stats 1990 ch 79 §14 (AB 759), operative July 1, 1991.

Prior Law: Former Prob C §13659, similar to the present section, was added Stats 1986 ch 783 §24, operative July 1, 1987, amended Stats 1988 ch 1199 §105, operative July 1, 1989, and repealed Stats 1990 ch 79 §13, operative July 1, 1991.

§13660. Attorney's fees

The attorney's fees for services performed in connection with the filing of a petition and obtaining of a court order under this chapter shall be determined by private agreement between the attorney and the client and are not subject to approval by the court. If there is no agreement between the attorney and the client concerning the attorney's fees for services performed in connection with the filing of a petition and obtaining of a court order under this chapter and there is a dispute concerning the reasonableness of the attorney's fees for those services, a petition may be filed with the court in the same proceeding requesting that the court determine the reasonableness of the attorney's fees for those services. If there is an agreement between the attorney and the client concerning the attorney's fees for services performed in connection with the filing of a petition and obtaining a court order under this chapter and there is a dispute concerning the meaning of the agreement, a petition may be filed with the court in the same proceeding requesting that the court determine the dispute. **Leg.H.** Enacted Stats 1990 ch 79 §14 (AB 759), operative July 1, 1991.

Prior Law: Former Prob C §13660, similar to the present section, was added Stats 1986 ch 783 §24, operative July 1, 1987, and repealed Stats 1990 ch 79 §13, operative July 1, 1991.

DIVISION 9
TRUST LAW

Part 1. General Provisions.
Part 2. Creation, Validity, Modification, and Termination of Trusts.
Part 3. Trustees and Beneficiaries.
Part 4. Trust Administration.
Part 5. Judicial Proceedings Concerning Trusts.
Part 6. Rights of Third Persons.
Part 7. Uniform Prudent Management of Institutional Funds Act.
Part 8. Payment of Claims, Debts, and Expenses from Revocable Trust of Deceased Settlor.
Part 9. Uniform Trust Decanting Act.

PART 1
GENERAL PROVISIONS

Short title. §15000.
General rule concerning application of division. §15001.
Common law as law of state. §15002.
Application of division to entities not included in definition of trusts; Exemption of substantive law of construction and resulting trusts. §15003.
Application of division to charitable trusts. §15004.

§15000. Short title

This division shall be known and may be cited as the Trust Law. **Leg.H.** Enacted Stats 1990 ch 79 §14 (AB 759), operative July 1, 1991.

Prior Law: Former Prob C §15000, similar to the present section, was added Stats 1986 ch 820 §40, operative July 1, 1987, and repealed Stats 1990 ch 79 §13, operative July 1, 1991.

§15001. General rule concerning application of division

Except as otherwise provided by statute:

(a) This division applies to all trusts regardless of whether they were created before, on, or after July 1, 1987.

(b) This division applies to all proceedings concerning trusts commenced on or after July 1, 1987.

(c) This division applies to all proceedings concerning trusts commenced before July 1, 1987, unless in the opinion of the court application of a particular provision of this division would substantially interfere with the effective conduct of the proceedings or the rights of the parties and other interested persons, in which case the particular provision of this division does not apply and prior law applies. **Leg.H.** Enacted Stats 1990 ch 79 §14 (AB 759), operative July 1, 1991.

Prior Law: Former Prob C §15001, similar to the present section, was added Stats 1986 ch 820 §40, operative July 1, 1987, and repealed Stats 1990 ch 79 §13, operative July 1, 1991.

§15002. Common law as law of state

Except to the extent that the common law rules governing trusts are modified by statute, the common law as to trusts is the law of this state. **Leg.H.** Enacted Stats 1990 ch 79 §14 (AB 759), operative July 1, 1991.

Prior Law: Former Prob C §15002, similar to the present section, was added Stats 1986 ch 820 §40, operative July 1, 1987, and repealed Stats 1990 ch 79 §13, operative July 1, 1991.

§15003. Application of division to entities not included in definition of trusts; Exemption of substantive law of construction and resulting trusts

(a) Nothing in this division affects the substantive law relating to constructive or resulting trusts.

(b) The repeal of Title 8 (commencing with Section 2215) of Part 4 of Division 3 of the Civil Code by Chapter 820 of the Statutes of 1986 was not intended to alter the rules applied by the courts to fiduciary and confidential relationships, except as to express trusts governed by this division.

(c) Nothing in this division or in Section 82 is intended to prevent the application of all or part of the principles or procedures of this division to an entity or relationship that is excluded from the definition of "trust" provided by Section 82 where these principles or procedures are applied pursuant to statutory or common law principles, by court order or rule, or by contract. **Leg.H.** Enacted Stats 1990 ch 79 §14 (AB 759), operative July 1, 1991. Amended Stats 1990 ch 710 §43 (SB 1775), operative July 1, 1991.

Prior Law: Former Prob C §15003, similar to the present section, was added Stats 1986 ch 820 §40, operative July 1, 1987, amended Stats 1987 ch 128 §8, effective July 6, 1987, operative July 1, 1987, and repealed Stats 1990 ch 79 §13, operative July 1, 1991.

§15004. Application of division to charitable trusts

Unless otherwise provided by statute, this division applies to charitable trusts that are subject to the jurisdiction of the Attorney General to the extent that the application of the provision is not in conflict with the Supervision of Trustees and Fundraisers for Charitable Purposes Act, Article 7 (commencing with Section 12580) of Chapter 6 of Part 2 of Division 3 of Title 2 of the Government Code. **Leg.H.** Enacted Stats 1990 ch 79 §14 (AB 759), operative July 1, 1991. Amended Stats 2020 ch 370 §232 (SB 1371), effective January 1, 2021.

Prior Law: Former Prob C §15004, similar to the present section, was added Stats 1986 ch 820 §40, operative July 1, 1987, and repealed Stats 1990 ch 79 §13, operative July 1, 1991.

PART 2
CREATION, VALIDITY, MODIFICATION, AND TERMINATION OF TRUSTS

Chapter 1. Creation and Validity of Trusts.
Chapter 2. Restrictions on Voluntary and Involuntary Transfers.
Chapter 3. Modification and Termination of Trusts.

CHAPTER 1
CREATION AND VALIDITY OF TRUSTS

Methods of creating trust. §15200.
Intention to create trust. §15201.
Trust property. §15202.
Trust purpose. §15203.
Trust for indefinite or general purposes. §15204.
Designation of beneficiary. §15205.
Statute of Frauds. §15206.
Oral trust of personal property. §15207.
Consideration. §15208.
Exception to doctrine of merger. §15209.
Recording of trust relating to real property. §15210.
Duration of trust for noncharitable purpose. §15211.
Trust for the care of an animal; Duration; Requirements; Use of principal and income; Designation of trustee; Accountings; Inspections. §15212.

§15200. Methods of creating trust

Subject to other provisions of this chapter, a trust may be created by any of the following methods:

(a) A declaration by the owner of property that the owner holds the property as trustee.

(b) A transfer of property by the owner during the owner's lifetime to another person as trustee.

(c) A transfer of property by the owner, by will or by other instrument taking effect upon the death of the owner, to another person as trustee.

(d) An exercise of a power of appointment to another person as trustee.

(e) An enforceable promise to create a trust. **Leg.H.** Enacted Stats 1990 ch 79 §14 (AB 759), operative July 1, 1991.

Prior Law: Former Prob C §15200, similar to the present section, was added Stats 1986 ch 820 §40, operative July 1, 1987, and repealed Stats 1990 ch 79 §13, operative July 1, 1991.

§15201. Intention to create trust

A trust is created only if the settlor properly manifests an intention to create a trust. **Leg.H.** Enacted Stats 1990 ch 79 §14 (AB 759), operative July 1, 1991.

Prior Law: Former Prob C §15201, similar to the present section, was added Stats 1986 ch 820 §40, operative July 1, 1987, and repealed Stats 1990 ch 79 §13, operative July 1, 1991.

§15202. Trust property

A trust is created only if there is trust property. **Leg.H.** Enacted Stats 1990 ch 79 §14 (AB 759), operative July 1, 1991.

Prior Law: Former Prob C §15202, similar to the present section, was added Stats 1986 ch 820 §40, operative July 1, 1987, and repealed Stats 1990 ch 79 §13, operative July 1, 1991.

§15203. Trust purpose

A trust may be created for any purpose that is not illegal or against public policy. **Leg.H.** Enacted Stats 1990 ch 79 §14 (AB 759), operative July 1, 1991.

Prior Law: Former Prob C §15203, similar to the present section, was added Stats 1986 ch 820 §40, operative July 1, 1987, and repealed Stats 1990 ch 79 §13, operative July 1, 1991.

§15204. Trust for indefinite or general purposes

A trust created for an indefinite or general purpose is not invalid for that reason if it can be determined with reasonable certainty that a particular use of the trust property comes within that purpose. **Leg.H.** Enacted Stats 1990 ch 79 §14 (AB 759), operative July 1, 1991.

Prior Law: Former Prob C §15204, similar to the present section, was added Stats 1986 ch 820 §40, operative July 1, 1987, and repealed Stats 1990 ch 79 §13, operative July 1, 1991.

§15205. Designation of beneficiary

(a) A trust, other than a charitable trust, is created only if there is a beneficiary.

(b) The requirement of subdivision (a) is satisfied if the trust instrument provides for either of the following:

(1) A beneficiary or class of beneficiaries that is ascertainable with reasonable certainty or that is sufficiently described so it can be determined that some person meets the description or is within the class.

(2) A grant of a power to the trustee or some other person to select the beneficiaries based on a standard or in the discretion of the trustee or other person. **Leg.H.** Enacted Stats 1990 ch 79 §14 (AB 759), operative July 1, 1991.

Prior Law: Former Prob C §15205, similar to the present section, was added Stats 1986 ch 820 §40, operative July 1, 1987, and repealed Stats 1990 ch 79 §13, operative July 1, 1991.

§15206. Statute of Frauds

A trust in relation to real property is not valid unless evidenced by one of the following methods:

(a) By a written instrument signed by the trustee, or by the trustee's agent if authorized in writing to do so.

(b) By a written instrument conveying the trust property signed by the settlor, or by the settlor's agent if authorized in writing to do so.

(c) By operation of law. **Leg.H.** Enacted Stats 1990 ch 79 §14 (AB 759), operative July 1, 1991.

Prior Law: Former Prob C §15206, similar to the present section, was added Stats 1986 ch 820 §40, operative July 1, 1987, and repealed Stats 1990 ch 79 §13, operative July 1, 1991.

§15207. Oral trust of personal property

(a) The existence and terms of an oral trust of personal property may be established only by clear and convincing evidence.

(b) The oral declaration of the settlor, standing alone, is not sufficient evidence of the creation of a trust of personal property.

(c) In the case of an oral trust, a reference in this division or elsewhere to a trust instrument or declaration means the terms of the trust as established pursuant to subdivision (a). **Leg.H.** Enacted Stats 1990 ch 79 §14 (AB 759), operative July 1, 1991.

Prior Law: Former Prob C §15207, similar to the present section, was added Stats 1986 ch 820 §40, operative July 1, 1987, and repealed Stats 1990 ch 79 §13, operative July 1, 1991.

§15208. Consideration

Consideration is not required to create a trust, but a promise to create a trust in the future is enforceable only if the requirements for an enforceable contract are satisfied. **Leg.H.** Enacted Stats 1990 ch 79 §14 (AB 759), operative July 1, 1991.

Prior Law: Former Prob C §15208, similar to the present section, was added Stats 1986 ch 820 §40, operative July 1, 1987, and repealed Stats 1990 ch 79 §13, operative July 1, 1991.

§15209. Exception to doctrine of merger

If a trust provides for one or more successor beneficiaries after the death of the settlor, the trust is not invalid, merged, or terminated in either of the following circumstances:

(a) Where there is one settlor who is the sole trustee and the sole beneficiary during the settlor's lifetime.

(b) Where there are two or more settlors, one or more of whom are trustees, and the beneficial interest in the trust is in one or more of the settlors during the lifetime of the settlors. **Leg.H.** Enacted Stats 1990 ch 79 §14 (AB 759), operative July 1, 1991.

Prior Law: Former Prob C §15209, similar to the present section, was added Stats 1986 ch 820 §40, operative July 1, 1987, and repealed Stats 1990 ch 79 §13, operative July 1, 1991.

§15210. Recording of trust relating to real property

A trust created pursuant to this chapter which relates to real property may be recorded in the office of the county recorder in the county where all or a portion of the real property is located. **Leg.H.** Enacted Stats 1990 ch 79 §14 (AB 759), operative July 1, 1991.

Prior Law: Former Prob C §15210, similar to the present section, was added Stats 1987 ch 1184 §10, and repealed Stats 1990 ch 79 §13, operative July 1, 1991.

§15211. Duration of trust for noncharitable purpose

A trust for a noncharitable corporation or unincorporated society or for a lawful noncharitable purpose may be performed by the trustee for only 21 years, whether or not there is a beneficiary who can seek enforcement or termination of the trust and whether or not the terms of the trust contemplate a longer duration. **Leg.H.** Added Stats 1991 ch 156 §20 (AB 1577).

§15212. Trust for the care of an animal; Duration; Requirements; Use of principal and income; Designation of trustee; Accountings; Inspections

(a) Subject to the requirements of this section, a trust for the care of an animal is a trust for a lawful noncharitable purpose. Unless expressly provided in the trust, the trust terminates when no animal living on the date of the settlor's death remains alive. The governing instrument of the animal trust shall be liberally construed to bring the trust within this section, to presume against the merely precatory or honorary nature of the disposition, and to carry out the general intent of the settlor. Extrinsic evidence is admissible in determining the settlor's intent.

(b) A trust for the care of an animal is subject to the following requirements:

(1) Except as expressly provided otherwise in the trust instrument, the principal or income shall not be converted to the use of the trustee or to any use other than for the benefit of the animal.

(2) Upon termination of the trust, the trustee shall distribute the unexpended trust property in the following order:

(A) As directed in the trust instrument.

(B) If the trust was created in a nonresiduary clause in the settlor's will or in a codicil to the settlor's will, under the residuary clause in the settlor's will.

(C) If the application of subparagraph (A) or (B) does not result in distribution of unexpended trust property, to the settlor's heirs under Section 21114.

(3) For the purposes of Section 21110, the residuary clause described in subparagraph (B) of paragraph (2) shall be treated as creating a future interest under the terms of a trust.

(c) The intended use of the principal or income may be enforced by a person designated for that purpose in the trust instrument or, if none is designated, by a person appointed by a court. In addition to a person identified in subdivision (a) of Section 17200, any person interested in the welfare of the animal or any nonprofit charitable organization that has as its principal activity the care of animals may petition the court regarding the trust as provided in Chapter 3 (commencing with Section 17200) of Part 5.

(d) If a trustee is not designated or no designated or successor trustee is willing or able to serve, a court shall name a trustee. A court may order the transfer of the trust property to a court-appointed trustee, if it is required to ensure that the intended use is carried out and if a successor trustee is not designated in the trust instrument or if no designated successor trustee agrees to serve or is able to serve. A court may also make all other orders and determinations as it shall deem advisable to carry out the intent of the settlor and the purpose of this section.

(e) The accountings required by Section 16062 shall be provided to the beneficiaries who would be entitled to distribution if the animal were then deceased and to any nonprofit charitable corporation that has as its principal activity the care of animals and that has requested these accountings in writing. However, if the value of the assets in the trust does not exceed forty thousand dollars ($40,000), no filing, report, registration, periodic accounting, separate maintenance of funds, appointment, or fee is required by reason of the existence of the fiduciary relationship of the trustee, unless ordered by the court or required by the trust instrument.

(f) Any beneficiary, any person designated by the trust instrument or the court to enforce the trust, or any nonprofit charitable corporation that has as its principal activity the care of animals may, upon reasonable request, inspect the animal, the premises where the animal is maintained, or the books and records of the trust.

(g) A trust governed by this section is not subject to termination pursuant to subdivision (b) of Section 15408.

(h) Section 15211 does not apply to a trust governed by this section.

(i) For purposes of this section, "animal" means a domestic or pet animal for the benefit of which a trust has been established. **Leg.H.** Added Stats 2008 ch 168 §2 (SB 685), effective January 1, 2009.

Former Sections: Former Prob C §15212, similar to the present section, was added Stats 1991 ch 156 §21 and repealed Stats 2008 ch 168 §1, effective January 1, 2009.

Prior Law: Former Prob C §15212, similar to the present section, was added Stats 1991 ch 156 §21 and repealed Stats 2008 ch 168 §1, effective January 1, 2009.

CHAPTER 2
RESTRICTIONS ON VOLUNTARY AND INVOLUNTARY TRANSFERS

Restraint on transfer of income. §15300.
Restraint on transfer of principal. §15301.
Trust for support. §15302.
Prohibition on compelling exercise of trustee's discretion by transferee or creditor; Liability of trustee for payment to or for beneficiary. §15303.
Where settlor is a beneficiary. §15304.
Claims for child or spousal support. §15305.
Claims for restitution for commission of felony. §15305.5.
Liability for public support. §15306.
Rights of general creditors. §15306.5.
Income in excess of amount for education and support subject to creditors' claims. §15307.
Subsequent modification of court's order. §15308.
Disclaimer not a transfer. §15309.

§15300. Restraint on transfer of income

Except as provided in Sections 15304 to 15307, inclusive, if the trust instrument provides that a beneficiary's interest in income is not subject to voluntary or involuntary transfer, the beneficiary's interest in income under the trust may not be transferred and is not subject to enforcement of a money judgment until paid to the beneficiary. **Leg.H.** Enacted Stats 1990 ch 79 §14 (AB 759), operative July 1, 1991.

Prior Law: Former Prob C §15300, similar to the present section, was added Stats 1986 ch 820 §40, operative July 1, 1987, and repealed Stats 1990 ch 79 §13, operative July 1, 1991.

§15301. Restraint on transfer of principal

(a) Except as provided in subdivision (b) and in Sections 15304 to 15307, inclusive, if the trust instrument provides that a beneficiary's interest in principal is not subject to voluntary or involuntary transfer, the beneficiary's interest in principal may not be transferred and is not subject to enforcement of a money judgment until paid to the beneficiary.

(b) After an amount of principal has become due and payable to the beneficiary under the trust instrument, upon petition to the court under Section 709.010 of the Code of Civil Procedure by a judgment creditor, the court may make an order directing the trustee to satisfy the money judgment out of that principal amount. The court in its discretion may issue an order directing the trustee to satisfy all or part of the judgment out of that principal amount. **Leg.H.** Enacted Stats 1990 ch 79 §14 (AB 759), operative July 1, 1991.

Prior Law: Former Prob C §15301, similar to the present section, was added Stats 1986 ch 820 §40, operative July 1, 1987, and repealed Stats 1990 ch 79 §13, operative July 1, 1991.

§15302. Trust for support

Except as provided in Sections 15304 to 15307, inclusive, if the trust instrument provides that the trustee shall pay income or principal or both for the education or support of a beneficiary, the beneficiary's interest in income or principal or both under the trust, to the extent the income or principal or both is necessary for the education or support of the beneficiary, may not be transferred and is not subject to the enforcement of a money judgment until paid to the beneficiary. **Leg.H.** Enacted Stats 1990 ch 79 §14 (AB 759), operative July 1, 1991.

Prior Law: Former Prob C §15302, similar to the present section, was added Stats 1986 ch 820 §40, operative July 1, 1987, and repealed Stats 1990 ch 79 §13, operative July 1, 1991.

§15303. Prohibition on compelling exercise of trustee's discretion by transferee or creditor; Liability of trustee for payment to or for beneficiary

(a) If the trust instrument provides that the trustee shall pay to or for the benefit of a beneficiary so much of the income or principal or both as the trustee in the trustee's discretion sees fit to pay, a transferee or creditor of the beneficiary may not compel the trustee to pay any amount that may be paid only in the exercise of the trustee's discretion.

(b) If the trustee has knowledge of the transfer of the beneficiary's interest or has been served with process in a proceeding under Section 709.010 of the Code of Civil Procedure by a judgment creditor seeking to reach the beneficiary's interest, and the trustee pays to or for the benefit of the beneficiary any part of the income or principal that may be paid only in the exercise of the trustee's discretion, the trustee is liable to the transferee or creditor to the extent that the payment to or for the benefit of the beneficiary impairs the right of the transferee or creditor. This subdivision does not apply if the beneficiary's interest in the trust is subject to a restraint on transfer that is valid under Section 15300 or 15301.

(c) This section applies regardless of whether the trust instrument provides a standard for the exercise of the trustee's discretion.

(d) Nothing in this section limits any right the beneficiary may have to compel the trustee to pay to or for the benefit of the beneficiary all or part of the income or principal. **Leg.H.** Enacted Stats 1990 ch 79 §14 (AB 759), operative July 1, 1991.

Prior Law: Former Prob C §15303, similar to the present section, was added Stats 1986 ch 820 §40, operative July 1, 1987, and repealed Stats 1990 ch 79 §13, operative July 1, 1991.

§15304. Where settlor is a beneficiary

(a) If the settlor is a beneficiary of a trust created by the settlor and the settlor's interest is subject to a provision restraining the voluntary or involuntary transfer of the settlor's interest, the restraint is invalid against transferees or creditors of the settlor. The invalidity of the restraint on transfer does not affect the validity of the trust.

(b) If the settlor is the beneficiary of a trust created by the settlor and the trust instrument provides that the trustee shall pay income or principal or both for the education or support of the beneficiary or gives the trustee discretion to determine the amount of income or principal or both to be paid to or for the benefit of the settlor, a transferee or creditor of the settlor may reach the maximum amount that the trustee could pay to or for the benefit of the settlor under the trust instrument, not exceeding the amount of the settlor's proportionate contribution to the trust.

(c) For purposes of this chapter, the settlor shall not be considered to be a beneficiary of an irrevocable trust created by the settlor solely by reason of a discretionary authority vested in the trustee to pay directly or reimburse the settlor for any federal or state income tax on trust income or principal that is payable by the settlor, and a transferee or creditor of the settlor shall not be entitled to reach any amount solely by a reason of that discretionary authority. **Leg.H.** Enacted Stats 1990 ch 79 §14 (AB 759), operative July 1, 1991. Amended Stats 2022 §1 (AB 1866), effective January 1, 2023.

Prior Law: Former Prob C §15304, similar to the present section, was added Stats 1986 ch 820 §40, operative July 1, 1987, and repealed Stats 1990 ch 79 §13, operative July 1, 1991.

§15305. Claims for child or spousal support

(a) As used in this section, "support judgment" means a money judgment for support of the trust beneficiary's spouse or former spouse or minor child.

(b) If the beneficiary has the right under the trust to compel the trustee to pay income or principal or both to or for the benefit of the beneficiary, the court may, to the extent that the court determines it is equitable and reasonable under the circumstances of the particular case, order the trustee to satisfy all or part of the support judgment out of all or part of those payments as they become due and payable, presently or in the future.

(c) Whether or not the beneficiary has the right under the trust to compel the trustee to pay income or principal or both to or for the benefit of the beneficiary, the court may, to the extent that the court determines it is equitable and reasonable under the circumstances of the particular case, order the trustee to satisfy all or part of the support judgment out of all or part of future payments that the trustee, pursuant to the exercise of the trustee's discretion, determines to make to or for the benefit of the beneficiary.

(d) This section applies to a support judgment notwithstanding any provision in the trust instrument. **Leg.H.** Enacted Stats 1990 ch 79 §14 (AB 759), operative July 1, 1991.

Prior Law: Former Prob C §15305, similar to the present section, was added Stats 1986 ch 820 §40, operative July 1, 1987, and repealed Stats 1990 ch 79 §13, operative July 1, 1991.

§15305.5. Claims for restitution for commission of felony

(a) As used in this section, "restitution judgment" means a judgment awarding restitution for the commission of a felony or a money judgment for damages incurred as a result of conduct for which the defendant was convicted of a felony.

(b) If the beneficiary has the right under the trust to compel the trustee to pay income or principal or both to or for the benefit of the beneficiary, the court may, to the extent that the court determines it is equitable and reasonable under the circumstances of the particular case, order the trustee to satisfy all or part of the restitution judgment out of all or part of those payments as they become due and payable, presently or in the future.

(c) Whether or not the beneficiary has the right under the trust to compel the trustee to pay income or principal or both to or for the benefit of the beneficiary, the court may, to the extent that the court determines it is equitable and reasonable under the circumstances of the particular case, order the trustee to satisfy all or part of the restitution judgment out of all or part of future payments that the trustee, pursuant to the exercise of the trustee's discretion, determines to make to or for the benefit of the beneficiary.

(d) This section applies to a restitution judgment notwithstanding any provision in the trust instrument. **Leg.H.** Added Stats 1991 ch 175 §1 (AB 534).

1991 Note: This act applies to trusts and restitution judgments in existence on January 1, 1992, regardless of the date on which the trust was created, or takes effect, or the date on which the conduct giving rise to the restitution judgment occurred. Stats 1991 ch 175 §2.

§15306. Liability for public support

(a) Notwithstanding any provision in the trust instrument, if a statute of this state makes the beneficiary liable for reimbursement of this state or a local public entity in this state for public support furnished to the beneficiary or to the beneficiary's spouse or minor child, upon petition to the court under Section 709.010 of the Code of Civil Procedure by the appropriate state or local public entity or public official, to the extent the court determines it is equitable and reasonable under the circumstances of the particular case, the court may do the following:

(1) If the beneficiary has the right under the trust to compel the trustee to pay income or principal or both to or for the benefit of the beneficiary, order the trustee to satisfy all or part of the liability out of all or part of the payments as they become due, presently or in the future.

(2) Whether or not the beneficiary has the right under the trust to compel the trustee to pay income or principal or both to or for the benefit of the beneficiary, order the trustee to satisfy all or part of the liability out of all or part of the future payments that the trustee, pursuant to the exercise of the trustee's discretion, determines to make to or for the benefit of the beneficiary.

(3) If the beneficiary is a settlor or the spouse or minor child of the settlor and the beneficiary does not have the right under the trust to compel the trustee to pay income or principal or both to or for the benefit of the beneficiary, to the extent that the trustee has the right to make payments of income or principal or both to or for the beneficiary pursuant to the exercise of the trustee's discretion, order the trustee to satisfy all or part of the liability without regard to whether the trustee has then exercised or may thereafter exercise the discretion in favor of the beneficiary.

(b) Subdivision (a) does not apply to any trust that is established for the benefit of an individual who has a disability that substantially impairs the individual's ability to provide for his or her own care or custody and constitutes a substantial handicap. If, however, the trust results in the individual being ineligible for needed public social services under Division 9 (commencing with Section 10000) of the Welfare and Institutions Code, this subdivision is not applicable and the provisions of subdivision (a) are to be applied. **Leg.H.** Enacted Stats 1990 ch 79 §14 (AB 759), operative July 1, 1991.

Prior Law: Former Prob C §15306, similar to the present section, was added Stats 1986 ch 820 §40, operative July 1, 1987, amended Stats 1989 ch 748 §2, and repealed Stats 1990 ch 79 §13, operative July 1, 1991.

§15306.5. Rights of general creditors

(a) Notwithstanding a restraint on transfer of the beneficiary's interest in the trust under Section 15300 or 15301, and subject to the limitations of this section, upon a judgment creditor's petition under Section 709.010 of the Code of Civil Procedure, the court may make an order directing the trustee to satisfy all or part of the judgment out of the payments to which the beneficiary is entitled under the trust instrument or that the trustee, in the exercise of the trustee's discretion, has determined or determines in the future to pay to the beneficiary.

(b) An order under this section may not require that the trustee pay in satisfaction of the judgment an amount exceeding 25 percent of the payment that otherwise would be made to, or for the benefit of, the beneficiary.

(c) An order under this section may not require that the trustee pay in satisfaction of the judgment any amount that the court determines is necessary for the support of the beneficiary and all the persons the beneficiary is required to support.

(d) An order for satisfaction of a support judgment, as defined in Section 15305, has priority over an order to satisfy a judgment under this section. Any amount ordered to be applied to the satisfaction of a judgment under this section shall be reduced by the amount of an order for satisfaction of a support judgment under Section 15305, regardless of whether the order for satisfaction of the support judgment was made before or after the order under this section.

(e) If the trust gives the trustee discretion over the payment of either principal or income of a trust, or both, nothing in this section affects or limits that discretion in any manner. The trustee has no duty to oppose a petition to satisfy a judgment under this section or to make any claim for exemption on behalf of the beneficiary. The trustee is not liable for any action taken, or omitted to be taken, in compliance with any court order made under this section.

(f) Subject to subdivision (d), the aggregate of all orders for satisfaction of money judgments against the beneficiary's interest in the trust may not exceed 25 percent of the payment that otherwise would be made to, or for the benefit of, the beneficiary. **Leg.H.** Enacted Stats 1990 ch 79 §14 (AB 759), operative July 1, 1991.

Prior Law: Former Prob C §15306.5, similar to the present section, was added Stats 1986 ch 820 §40, operative July 1, 1987, and repealed Stats 1990 ch 79 §13, operative July 1, 1991.

§15307. Income in excess of amount for education and support subject to creditors' claims

Notwithstanding a restraint on transfer of a beneficiary's interest in the trust under Section 15300 or 15301, any amount to which the beneficiary is entitled under the trust instrument or that the trustee, in the exercise of the trustee's discretion, has determined to pay to the beneficiary in excess of the amount that is or will be necessary for the education and support of the beneficiary may be applied to the satisfaction of a money judgment against the beneficiary. Upon the judgment creditor's petition under Section 709.010 of the Code of Civil Procedure, the court may make an order directing the trustee to satisfy all or part of the judgment out of the beneficiary's interest in the trust. **Leg.H.** Enacted Stats 1990 ch 79 §14 (AB 759), operative July 1, 1991.

Prior Law: Former Prob C §15307, similar to the present section, was added Stats 1986 ch 820 §40, operative July 1, 1987, and repealed Stats 1990 ch 79 §13, operative July 1, 1991.

§15308. Subsequent modification of court's order

Any order entered by a court under Section 15305, 15306, 15306.5, or 15307 is subject to modification upon petition of an interested person filed in the court where the order was made. **Leg.H.** Enacted Stats 1990 ch 79 §14 (AB 759), operative July 1, 1991.

Prior Law: Former Prob C §15308, similar to the present section, was added Stats 1986 ch 820 §40, operative July 1, 1987, and repealed Stats 1990 ch 79 §13, operative July 1, 1991.

§15309. Disclaimer not a transfer

A disclaimer or renunciation by a beneficiary of all or part of his or her interest under a trust shall not be considered a transfer under Section 15300 or 15301. **Leg.H.** Enacted Stats 1990 ch 79 §14 (AB 759), operative July 1, 1991.

Prior Law: Former Prob C §15309, similar to the present section, was added Stats 1986 ch 820 §40, operative July 1, 1987, and repealed Stats 1990 ch 79 §13, operative July 1, 1991.

CHAPTER 3
MODIFICATION AND TERMINATION OF TRUSTS

Presumption of revocability. §15400.
Method of revocation by settlor; Limit on modification or revocation pursuant to power of attorney. §15401.
Power to revoke includes power to modify. §15402.
Modification or termination of irrevocable trust by all beneficiaries. §15403.
Modification or termination by settlor and all beneficiaries. §15404.
Guardian ad litem. §15405.
No conclusive presumption of fertility. §15406.
Termination of trust; Trustee's powers on termination. §15407.
Trust with uneconomically low principal. §15408.
Modification or termination in changed circumstances. §15409.
Disposition of property upon termination. §15410.
Combination of similar trusts. §15411.
Division of trusts. §15412.
Effect of provision that trust may not be terminated. §15413.
Violation of rule against perpetuities. §15414.

§15400. Presumption of revocability

Unless a trust is expressly made irrevocable by the trust instrument, the trust is revocable by the settlor. This section applies only where the settlor is domiciled in this state when the trust is created, where the trust instrument is executed in this state, or where the trust instrument provides that the law of this state governs the trust. **Leg.H.** Enacted Stats 1990 ch 79 §14 (AB 759), operative July 1, 1991.

Prior Law: Former Prob C §15400, similar to the present section, was added Stats 1986 ch 820 §40, operative July 1, 1987, and repealed Stats 1990 ch 79 §13, operative July 1, 1991.

§15401. Method of revocation by settlor; Limit on modification or revocation pursuant to power of attorney

(a) A trust that is revocable by the settlor or any other person may be revoked in whole or in part by any of the following methods:

(1) By compliance with any method of revocation provided in the trust instrument.

(2) By a writing, other than a will, signed by the settlor or any other person holding the power of revocation and delivered to the trustee during the lifetime of the settlor or the person holding the power of revocation. If the trust instrument explicitly makes the method of revocation provided in the trust instrument the exclusive method of revocation, the trust may not be revoked pursuant to this paragraph.

(b)(1) Unless otherwise provided in the instrument, if a trust is created by more than one settlor, each settlor may revoke the trust as to the portion of the trust contributed by that settlor, except as provided in Section 761 of the Family Code.

(2) Notwithstanding paragraph (1), a settlor may grant to another person, including, but not limited to, his or her spouse, a power to revoke all or part of that portion of the trust contributed by that settlor, regardless of whether that portion was separate property or community property of that settlor, and regardless of whether that power to revoke is exercisable during the lifetime of that settlor or continues after the death of that settlor, or both.

(c) A trust may not be modified or revoked by an attorney in fact under a power of attorney unless it is expressly permitted by the trust instrument.

(d) This section shall not limit the authority to modify or terminate a trust pursuant to Section 15403 or 15404 in an appropriate case.

(e) The manner of revocation of a trust revocable by the settlor or any other person that was created by an instrument executed before July 1, 1987, is governed by prior law and not by this section. **Leg.H.** Enacted Stats 1990 ch 79 §14 (AB 759), operative July 1, 1991. Amended Stats 1994 ch 806 §37 (AB 3686); Stats 2012 ch 55, §1, effective January 1, 2013.

Prior Law: Former Prob C §15401, similar to the present section, was added Stats 1986 ch 820 §40, operative July 1, 1987, amended Stats 1988 ch 113 §19, effective May 24, 1988, operative July 1, 1988, and repealed Stats 1990 ch 79 §13, operative July 1, 1991.

§15402. Power to revoke includes power to modify

Unless the trust instrument provides otherwise, if a trust is revocable by the settlor, the settlor may modify the trust by the procedure for revocation. **Leg.H.** Enacted Stats 1990 ch 79 §14 (AB 759), operative July 1, 1991.

Prior Law: Former Prob C §15402, similar to the present section, was added Stats 1986 ch 820 §40, operative July 1, 1987, and repealed Stats 1990 ch 79 §13, operative July 1, 1991.

§15403. Modification or termination of irrevocable trust by all beneficiaries

(a) Except as provided in subdivision (b), if all beneficiaries of an irrevocable trust consent, they may petition the court for modification or termination of the trust.

(b) If the continuance of the trust is necessary to carry out a material purpose of the trust, the trust cannot be modified or terminated unless the court, in its discretion, determines that the reason for doing so under the circumstances outweighs the interest in accomplishing a material purpose of the trust. If the trust is subject to a valid restraint on the transfer of a beneficiary's interest as provided in Chapter 2 (commencing with Section 15300), the trust may not be terminated unless the court determines there is good cause to do so.

(c) If the trust provides for the disposition of principal to a class of persons described only as "heirs" or "next of kin" of the settlor, or using other words that describe the class of all persons who would take under the rules of intestacy, the court may limit the class of beneficiaries whose consent is necessary to modify or terminate a trust to the beneficiaries who are reasonably likely to take under the circumstances. **Leg.H.** Enacted Stats 1990 ch 79 §14 (AB 759), operative July 1, 1991. Amended Stats 2017 ch 61 §1 (SB 333), effective January 1, 2018.

Prior Law: Former Prob C §15403, similar to the present section, was added Stats 1986 ch 820 §40, operative July 1, 1987, and repealed Stats 1990 ch 79 §13, operative July 1, 1991.

§15404. Modification or termination by settlor and all beneficiaries

(a) A trust may be modified or terminated by the written consent of the settlor and all beneficiaries without court approval of the modification or termination.

(b) If any beneficiary does not consent to the modification or termination of the trust, the court may modify or partially terminate the trust upon petition to the court by the other beneficiaries, with the consent of the settlor, if the interests of the beneficiaries who do not consent are not substantially impaired.

(c) If the trust provides for the disposition of principal to a class of persons described only as "heirs" or "next of kin" of the settlor, or using other words that describe the class of all persons who would take under the rules of intestacy, the court may limit the class of beneficiaries whose consent is necessary to modify or terminate a trust to the beneficiaries who are reasonably likely to take under the circumstances. **Leg.H.** Enacted Stats 1990 ch 79 §14 (AB 759), operative July 1, 1991. Amended Stats 2017 ch 61 §2 (SB 333), effective January 1, 2018.

Prior Law: Former Prob C §15404, similar to the present section, was added Stats 1986 ch 820 §40, operative July 1, 1987, and repealed Stats 1990 ch 79 §13, operative July 1, 1991.

§15405. Guardian ad litem

For the purposes of Sections 15403 and 15404, the consent of a beneficiary who lacks legal capacity, including a minor, or who is an unascertained or unborn beneficiary may be given in proceedings before the court by a guardian ad litem, if it would be appropriate to do so. In determining whether to give consent, the guardian ad litem may rely on general family benefit accruing to living members of the beneficiary's family as a basis for approving a modification or termination of the trust. **Leg.H.** Enacted Stats 1990 ch 79 §14 (AB 759), operative July 1, 1991. Amended Stats 2023 ch 260 §22 (SB 345), effective January 1, 2024.

Prior Law: Former Prob C §, similar to the present section, was added Stats 1986 ch 820 §40, operative July 1, 1987, amended Stats 1987 ch 128 §9, effective July 6, 1987, operative July 1, 1987, and repealed Stats 1990 ch 79 §13, operative July 1, 1991.

§15406. No conclusive presumption of fertility

In determining the class of beneficiaries whose consent is necessary to modify or terminate a trust pursuant to Section 15403 or 15404, the presumption of fertility is rebuttable. **Leg.H.** Enacted Stats 1990 ch 79 §14 (AB 759), operative July 1, 1991.

Prior Law: Former Prob C §15406, similar to the present section, was added Stats 1986 ch 820 §40, operative July 1, 1987, and repealed Stats 1990 ch 79 §13, operative July 1, 1991.

§15407. Termination of trust; Trustee's powers on termination

(a) A trust terminates when any of the following occurs:
(1) The term of the trust expires.
(2) The trust purpose is fulfilled.
(3) The trust purpose becomes unlawful.
(4) The trust purpose becomes impossible to fulfill.
(5) The trust is revoked.

(b) On termination of the trust, the trustee continues to have the powers reasonably necessary under the circumstances to wind up the affairs of the trust. **Leg.H.** Enacted Stats 1990 ch 79 §14 (AB 759), operative July 1, 1991.

Prior Law: Former Prob C §15407, similar to the present section, was added Stats 1986 ch 820 §40, operative July 1, 1987, and repealed Stats 1990 ch 79 §13, operative July 1, 1991.

§15408. Trust with uneconomically low principal

(a) On petition by a trustee or beneficiary, if the court determines that the fair market value of the principal of a trust has become so low in relation to the cost of administration that continuation of the trust under its existing terms will defeat or substantially impair the accomplishment of its purposes, the court may, in its discretion and in a manner that conforms as nearly as possible to the intention of the settlor, order any of the following:
(1) Termination of the trust.
(2) Modification of the trust.
(3) Appointment of a new trustee.

(b) Notwithstanding subdivision (a), if the [1] **fair market value of the principal of a trust** does not exceed [2] **one hundred** thousand dollars [3] ($100,000) in value, the trustee has the power to terminate the trust.

(c) The existence of a trust provision restraining transfer of the beneficiary's interest does not prevent application of this section. **Leg.H.** Enacted Stats 1990 ch 79 §14 (AB 759), operative July 1, 1991. Amended Stats 2010 ch 621 §1 (SB 202), effective January 1, 2011; Stats 2018 ch 78 §1 (AB 2426), effective January 1, 2019; Stats 2024 ch 76 §1 (SB 1127), effective January 1, 2025.

§15408. 2024 Deletes. [1] trust principal [2] fifty thousand dollars [3] ($50,000)

Prior Law: Former Prob C §15408, similar to the present section, was added Stats 1986 ch 820 §40, operative July 1, 1987, and repealed Stats 1990 ch 79 §13, operative July 1, 1991.

§15409. Modification or termination in changed circumstances

(a) On petition by a trustee or beneficiary, the court may modify the administrative or dispositive provisions of the trust or terminate the trust if, owing to circumstances not known to the settlor and not anticipated by the settlor, the continuation of the trust under its terms would defeat or substantially impair the accomplishment of the purposes of the trust. In this case, if necessary to carry out the purposes of the trust, the court may order the trustee to do acts that are not authorized or are forbidden by the trust instrument.

(b) The court shall consider a trust provision restraining transfer of the beneficiary's interest as a factor in making its decision whether to modify or terminate the trust, but the court is not precluded from exercising its discretion to modify or terminate the trust solely because of a restraint on transfer. **Leg.H.** Enacted Stats 1990 ch 79 §14 (AB 759), operative July 1, 1991.

Prior Law: Former Prob C §15409, similar to the present section, was added Stats 1986 ch 820 §40, operative July 1, 1987, and repealed Stats 1990 ch 79 §13, operative July 1, 1991.

§15410. Disposition of property upon termination

At the termination of a trust, the trust property shall be disposed of as follows:

(a) In the case of a trust that is revoked by the settlor, the trust property shall be disposed of in the following order of priority:
(1) As directed by the settlor.
(2) As provided in the trust instrument.
(3) To the extent that there is no direction by the settlor or in the trust instrument, to the settlor, or his or her estate, as the case may be.

(b) In the case of a trust that is revoked by any person holding a power of revocation other than the settlor, the trust property shall be disposed of in the following order of priority:
(1) As provided in the trust instrument.
(2) As directed by the person exercising the power of revocation.
(3) To the extent that there is no direction in the trust instrument or by the person exercising the power of revocation, to the person exercising the power of revocation, or his or her estate, as the case may be.

(c) In the case of a trust that is terminated by the consent of the settlor and all beneficiaries, as agreed by the settlor and all beneficiaries.

(d) In any other case, as provided in the trust instrument or in a manner directed by the court that conforms as nearly as possible to the intention of the settlor as expressed in the trust instrument.

(e) If a trust is terminated by the trustee pursuant to subdivision (b) of Section 15408, the trust property may be distributed as determined by the trustee pursuant to the standard provided in subdivision (d) without the need for a court order. If the trust instrument does not provide a manner of distribution at termination and the settlor's intent is not adequately expressed in the trust instrument, the trustee may distribute the trust property to the living beneficiaries on an actuarial basis. **Leg.H.** Enacted Stats 1990 ch 79 §14 (AB 759), operative July 1, 1991. Amended Stats 2012 ch 55 §2 (AB 1683), effective January 1, 2013.

Prior Law: Former Prob C §15410, similar to the present section, was added Stats 1986 ch 820 §40, operative July 1, 1987, amended Stats 1987 ch 128 §10, effective July 6, 1987, operative July 1, 1987, and repealed Stats 1990 ch 79 §13, operative July 1, 1991.

§15411. Combination of similar trusts

If the terms of two or more trusts are substantially similar, on petition by a trustee or beneficiary, the court, for good cause shown, may combine the trusts if the court determines that administration as a single trust will not defeat or substantially impair the accomplishment of the trust purposes or the interests of the beneficiaries. **Leg.H.** Enacted Stats 1990 ch 79 §14 (AB 759), operative July 1, 1991.

Prior Law: Former Prob C §15411, similar to the present section, was added Stats 1986 ch 820 §40, operative July 1, 1987, and repealed Stats 1990 ch 79 §13, operative July 1, 1991.

§15412. Division of trusts

On petition by a trustee or beneficiary, the court, for good cause shown, may divide a trust into two or more separate trusts, if the court determines that dividing the trust will not defeat or substantially impair the accomplishment of the trust purposes or the interests of the beneficiaries. **Leg.H.** Enacted Stats 1990 ch 79 §14 (AB 759), operative July 1, 1991.

Prior Law: Former Prob C §15412, similar to the present section, was added Stats 1986 ch 820 §40, operative July 1, 1987, and repealed Stats 1990 ch 79 §13, operative July 1, 1991.

§15413. Effect of provision that trust may not be terminated

A trust provision, express or implied, that the trust may not be terminated is ineffective insofar as it purports to be applicable after the expiration of the longer of the periods provided by the statutory rule against perpetuities, Article 2 (commencing with Section 21205) of Chapter 1 of Part 2 of Division 11. **Leg.H.** Added Stats 1991 ch 156 §22 (AB 1577).

§15414. Violation of rule against perpetuities

Notwithstanding any other provision in this chapter, if a trust continues in existence after the expiration of the longer of the periods provided by the statutory rule against perpetuities, Article 2 (commencing with Section 21205) of Chapter 1 of Part 2 of Division 11, the trust may be terminated in either of the following manners:

(a) On petition by a majority of the beneficiaries.

(b) On petition by the Attorney General or by any person who would be affected by the termination, if the court finds that the termination would be in the public interest or in the best interest of a majority of the persons who would be affected by the termination. **Leg.H.** Added Stats 1991 ch 156 §23 (AB 1577).

PART 3
TRUSTEES AND BENEFICIARIES

Chapter 1. Trustees.
Chapter 2. Beneficiaries.

CHAPTER 1
TRUSTEES

Article 1. General Provisions.
Article 2. Cotrustees.
Article 3. Resignation and Removal of Trustees.
Article 4. Appointment of Trustees.
Article 5. Compensation and Indemnification of Trustees.

ARTICLE 1
General Provisions

Acceptance of trust by trustee. §15600.
Rejection of trust; Nonliability of person who rejects trust. §15601.
Trustee's bond; When required; Cost. §15602.
Certificate of trustee. §15603.
Appointment of nonprofit charitable corporation as trustee. §15604.

§15600. Acceptance of trust by trustee

(a) The person named as trustee may accept the trust, or a modification of the trust, by one of the following methods:

(1) Signing the trust instrument or the trust instrument as modified, or signing a separate written acceptance.

(2) Knowingly exercising powers or performing duties under the trust instrument or the trust instrument as modified, except as provided in subdivision (b).

(b) In a case where there is an immediate risk of damage to the trust property, the person named as trustee may act to preserve the trust property without accepting the trust or a modification of the trust, if within a reasonable time after acting the person delivers a written rejection of the trust or the modification of the trust to the settlor or, if the settlor is dead or incompetent, to a beneficiary. This subdivision does not impose a duty on the person named as trustee to act. **Leg.H.** Enacted Stats 1990 ch 79 §14 (AB 759), operative July 1, 1991.

Prior Law: Former Prob C §15600, similar to the present section, was added Stats 1986 ch 820 §40, operative July 1, 1987, and repealed Stats 1990 ch 79 §13, operative July 1, 1991.

§15601. Rejection of trust; Nonliability of person who rejects trust

(a) A person named as trustee may in writing reject the trust or a modification of the trust.

(b) If the person named as trustee does not accept the trust or a modification of the trust by a method provided in subdivision (a) of Section 15600 within a reasonable time after learning of being named as trustee or of the modification, the person has rejected the trust or the modification.

(c) A person named as trustee who rejects the trust or a modification of the trust is not liable with respect to the rejected trust or modification. **Leg.H.** Enacted Stats 1990 ch 79 §14 (AB 759), operative July 1, 1991.

Prior Law: Former Prob C §15601, similar to the present section, was added Stats 1986 ch 820 §40, operative July 1, 1987, and repealed Stats 1990 ch 79 §13, operative July 1, 1991.

§15602. Trustee's bond; When required; Cost

(a) A trustee is not required to give a bond to secure performance of the trustee's duties, unless any of the following circumstances occurs:

(1) A bond is required by the trust instrument.

(2) Notwithstanding a waiver of a bond in the trust instrument, a bond is found by the court to be necessary to protect the interests of beneficiaries or other persons having an interest in the trust.

(3) An individual who is not named as a trustee in the trust instrument is appointed as a trustee by the court.

(b) Notwithstanding paragraphs (1) and (3) of subdivision (a), the court may excuse a requirement of a bond, reduce or increase the amount of a bond, release a surety, or permit the substitution of another bond with the same or different sureties. The court may not, however, excuse the requirement of a bond for an individual described in paragraph (3) of subdivision (a), except under compelling circumstances. For the purposes of this section, a request by all the adult beneficiaries of a trust that bond be waived for an individual described in paragraph (3) of subdivision (a) for their trust is deemed to constitute a compelling circumstance.

(c) If a bond is required, it shall be filed or served and shall be in the amount and with sureties and liabilities ordered by the court.

(d) Except as otherwise provided in the trust instrument or ordered by the court, the cost of the bond shall be charged against the trust.

(e) A trust company may not be required to give a bond, notwithstanding a contrary provision in the trust instrument. **Leg.H.** Enacted Stats 1990 ch 79 §14 (AB 759), operative July 1, 1991. Amended Stats 2004 ch 75 §1 (AB 1883), effective January 1, 2005.

Prior Law: Former Prob C §15602, similar to the present section, was added Stats 1986 ch 820 §40, operative July 1, 1987, and repealed Stats 1990 ch 79 §13, operative July 1, 1991.

§15603. Certificate of trustee

On application by the trustee, the court clerk shall issue a certificate that the trustee is a duly appointed and acting trustee under the trust if the court file shows the incumbency of the trustee. **Leg.H.** Enacted Stats 1990 ch 79 §14 (AB 759), operative July 1, 1991.

Prior Law: Former Prob C §15603, similar to the present section, was added Stats 1986 ch 820 §40, operative July 1, 1987, and repealed Stats 1990 ch 79 §13, operative July 1, 1991.

§15604. Appointment of nonprofit charitable corporation as trustee

(a) Notwithstanding any other provision of law, a nonprofit charitable corporation may be appointed as trustee of a trust created pursuant to this division, if all of the following conditions are met:

(1) The corporation is incorporated in this state.

(2) The articles of incorporation specifically authorize the corporation to accept appointments as trustee.

(3) For the three years prior to the filing of a petition under this section, the nonprofit charitable corporation has been exempt from payment of income taxes pursuant to Section 501(c)(3) of the Internal Revenue Code and has served as a private professional conservator in the state.

(4) The settlor or an existing trustee consents to the appointment of the nonprofit corporation as trustee or successor trustee, either in the petition or in a writing signed either before or after the petition is filed.

(5) The court determines the trust to be in the best interest of the settlor.

(6) The court determines that the appointment of the nonprofit corporation as trustee is in the best interest of the settlor and the trust estate.

(b) A petition for appointment of a nonprofit corporation as trustee under this section may be filed by any of the following:

(1) The settlor or the spouse of the settlor.

(2) The nonprofit charitable corporation.

(3) An existing trustee.

(c) The petition shall include in the caption the name of a responsible corporate officer who shall act for the corporation for purposes of this section. If, for any reason, the officer so named ceases to act as the responsible corporate officer for purposes of this section, the corporation shall file with the court a notice containing (1) the name of the successor responsible corporate officer and (2) the date the successor becomes the responsible corporate officer.

(d) The petition shall request that a trustee be appointed for the estate, shall specify the name, address, and telephone number of the proposed trustee and the name, address, and telephone number of the settlor or proposed settlor, and state the reasons why the appointment of the trustee is necessary.

(e) The petition shall set forth, so far as the information is known to the petitioner, the names and addresses of all persons entitled to notice of a conservatorship petition, as specified in subdivision (b) of Section 1821.

(f) Notice of the hearing on the petition shall be given in the same manner as provided in Sections 1822 and 1824.

(g) The trustee appointed by the court pursuant to this section shall do all of the following:

(1) File the required bond for the benefit of the trust estate in the same manner provided for conservators of the estate as set forth in Section

2320. This bond may not be waived, but the court may, in its discretion, permit the filing of a bond in an amount less than would otherwise be required under Section 2320.

(2) Comply with the requirements for registration and filing of annual statements pursuant to Article 4 (commencing with Section 2340) of Chapter 4 of Part 4 of Division 4.

(3) File with the court inventories and appraisals of the trust estate and present its accounts of the trust estate in the manner provided for conservators of the estate set forth in Chapter 7 (commencing with Section 2600) of Part 4 of Division 4.

(4) Be reimbursed for expenses and compensated as trustee in the manner provided for conservators of the estate as described in Chapter 8 (commencing with Section 2640) of Part 4 of Division 4. However, compensation as trustee appointed under this section shall be allowed only for services actually rendered.

(5) Be represented by counsel in all proceedings before the court. Any fee allowed for an attorney for the nonprofit charitable corporation shall be for services actually rendered.

(h) The trustee appointed by the court under this section may be removed by the court, or may resign in accordance with Chapter 9 (commencing with Section 2650) of Part 4 of Division 4. If the nonprofit charitable corporation resigns or is removed by the court, the settlor may appoint another person as successor trustee, or another nonprofit charitable corporation as trustee under this section.

(i) The trustee appointed by the court under this section is bound by the trust instrument created by the settlor, and shall be subject to the duties and responsibilities of a trustee as provided in this code. **Leg.H.** Added Stats 1999 ch 424 §1 (SB 1090). Amended Stats 2001 ch 351 §2 (AB 479), effective January 1, 2002.

ARTICLE 2
Cotrustees

Actions by cotrustees. §15620.
Vacancy in office of cotrustee. §15621.
Temporary incapacity of cotrustee. §15622.

§15620. Actions by cotrustees

Unless otherwise provided in the trust instrument, a power vested in two or more trustees may only be exercised by their unanimous action. **Leg.H.** Enacted Stats 1990 ch 79 §14 (AB 759), operative July 1, 1991.

Prior Law: Former Prob C §15620, similar to the present section, was added Stats 1986 ch 820 §40, operative July 1, 1987, and repealed Stats 1990 ch 79 §13, operative July 1, 1991.

§15621. Vacancy in office of cotrustee

Unless otherwise provided in the trust instrument, if a vacancy occurs in the office of a cotrustee, the remaining cotrustee or cotrustees may act for the trust as if they are the only trustees. **Leg.H.** Enacted Stats 1990 ch 79 §14 (AB 759), operative July 1, 1991.

Prior Law: Former Prob C §15621, similar to the present section, was added Stats 1986 ch 820 §40, operative July 1, 1987, and repealed Stats 1990 ch 79 §13, operative July 1, 1991.

§15622. Temporary incapacity of cotrustee

Unless otherwise provided in the trust instrument, if a cotrustee is unavailable to perform the duties of the cotrustee because of absence, illness, or other temporary incapacity, the remaining cotrustee or cotrustees may act for the trust, as if they are the only trustees, where necessary to accomplish the purposes of the trust or to avoid irreparable injury to the trust property. **Leg.H.** Enacted Stats 1990 ch 79 §14 (AB 759), operative July 1, 1991.

Prior Law: Former Prob C §15622, similar to the present section, was added Stats 1986 ch 820 §40, operative July 1, 1987, and repealed Stats 1990 ch 79 §13, operative July 1, 1991.

ARTICLE 3
Resignation and Removal of Trustees

Resignation of trustee. §15640.
Liability of resigning trustee. §15641.
Removal of trustee. §15642.
Vacancy in office of trustee. §15643.
Delivery of property by former trustee upon occurrence of vacancy. §15644.
Costs and attorney's fees in proceedings for transfer of trust to successor trust company. §15645.

§15640. Resignation of trustee

A trustee who has accepted the trust may resign only by one of the following methods:

(a) As provided in the trust instrument.

(b) In the case of a revocable trust, with the consent of the person holding the power to revoke the trust.

(c) In the case of a trust that is not revocable, with the consent of all adult beneficiaries who are receiving or are entitled to receive income under the trust or to receive a distribution of principal if the trust were terminated at the time consent is sought. If a beneficiary has a conservator, the conservator may consent to the trustee's resignation on behalf of the conservatee without obtaining court approval. Without limiting the power of the beneficiary to consent to the trustee's resignation, if the beneficiary has designated an attorney in fact who has the power under the power of attorney to consent to the trustee's resignation, the attorney in fact may consent to the resignation.

(d) Pursuant to a court order obtained on petition by the trustee under Section 17200. The court shall accept the trustee's resignation and may make any orders necessary for the preservation of the trust property, including the appointment of a receiver or a temporary trustee. **Leg.H.** Enacted Stats 1990 ch 79 §14 (AB 759), operative July 1, 1991.

Prior Law: Former Prob C §15640, similar to the present section, was added Stats 1986 ch 820 §40, operative July 1, 1987, and repealed Stats 1990 ch 79 §13, operative July 1, 1991.

§15641. Liability of resigning trustee

The liability for acts or omissions of a resigning trustee or of the sureties on the trustee's bond, if any, is not released or affected in any manner by the trustee's resignation. **Leg.H.** Enacted Stats 1990 ch 79 §14 (AB 759), operative July 1, 1991.

Prior Law: Former Prob C §15641, similar to the present section, was added Stats 1986 ch 820 §40, operative July 1, 1987, and repealed Stats 1990 ch 79 §13, operative July 1, 1991.

§15642. Removal of trustee

(a) A trustee may be removed in accordance with the trust instrument, by the court on its own motion, or on petition of a settlor, cotrustee, or beneficiary under Section 17200.

(b) The grounds for removal of a trustee by the court include the following:

(1) Where the trustee has committed a breach of the trust.

(2) Where the trustee is insolvent or otherwise unfit to administer the trust.

(3) Where hostility or lack of cooperation among cotrustees impairs the administration of the trust.

(4) Where the trustee fails or declines to act.

(5) Where the trustee's compensation is excessive under the circumstances.

(6) Where the sole trustee is a person described in subdivision (a) of Section 21380, whether or not the person is the transferee of a donative transfer by the transferor, unless, based upon any evidence of the intent of the settlor and all other facts and circumstances, which shall be made known to the court, the court finds that it is consistent with the settlor's intent that the trustee continue to serve and that this intent was not the product of fraud or undue influence. Any waiver by the settlor of this provision is against public policy and shall be void. This paragraph shall not apply to instruments that became irrevocable on or before January 1, 1994. This paragraph shall not apply if any of the following conditions are met:

(A) The settlor is related by blood or marriage to, or is a cohabitant with, any one or more of the trustees, the person who drafted or transcribed the instrument, or the person who caused the instrument to be transcribed.

(B) The instrument is reviewed by an independent attorney who (1) counsels the settlor about the nature of their intended trustee designation and (2) signs and delivers to the settlor and the designated trustee a certificate in substantially the following form:

CERTIFICATE OF INDEPENDENT REVIEW

I, _____ (attorney's name), have reviewed _____ (name of instrument) and have counseled my client, _____ (name of client), fully and privately on the nature and legal effect of the designation as trustee of _____ (name of trustee) contained in that instrument. I am so disassociated from the interest of the person named as trustee as to be in a position to advise my client impartially and confidentially as to the consequences of the designation. On the basis of this counsel, I conclude that the designation of a person who would otherwise be subject to removal under paragraph (6) of subdivision (b) of Section 15642 of the Probate Code is clearly the settlor's intent and that intent is not the product of fraud, menace, duress, or undue influence.

_____
(Name of Attorney)   (Date)

This independent review and certification may occur either before or after the instrument has been executed, and if it occurs after the date of execution, the named trustee shall not be subject to removal under this paragraph. Any attorney whose written engagement signed by the client is expressly limited to the preparation of a certificate under this subdivision, including the prior counseling, shall not be considered to otherwise represent the client.

(C) After full disclosure of the relationships of the persons involved, the instrument is approved pursuant to an order under Article 10 (commencing with Section 2580) of Chapter 6 of Part 4 of Division 4.

(7) If, as determined under Part 17 (commencing with Section 810) of Division 2, the trustee is substantially unable to manage the trust's financial resources or is otherwise substantially unable to execute properly the duties of the office. When the trustee holds the power to revoke the trust, substantial inability to manage the trust's financial resources or otherwise execute properly the duties of the office may not be proved solely by isolated incidents of negligence or improvidence.

(8) If the trustee is substantially unable to resist fraud or undue influence. When the trustee holds the power to revoke the trust, substantial inability to resist fraud or undue influence may not be proved solely by isolated incidents of negligence or improvidence.

(9) For other good cause.

(c) If, pursuant to paragraph (6) of subdivision (b), the court finds that the designation of the trustee was not consistent with the intent of the settlor or was the product of fraud or undue influence, the person being removed as trustee shall bear all costs of the proceeding, including reasonable attorney's fees.

(d) If the court finds that the petition for removal of the trustee was filed in bad faith and that removal would be contrary to the settlor's intent, the court may order that the person or persons seeking the removal of the trustee bear all or any part of the costs of the proceeding, including reasonable attorney's fees.

(e) If it appears to the court that trust property or the interests of a beneficiary may suffer loss or injury pending a decision on a petition for removal of a trustee and any appellate review, the court may, on its own motion or on petition of a cotrustee or beneficiary, compel the trustee whose removal is sought to surrender trust property to a cotrustee or to a receiver or temporary trustee. The court may also suspend the powers of the trustee to the extent the court deems necessary.

(f) For purposes of this section, the term "related by blood or marriage" shall include persons within the seventh degree. **Leg.H.** Enacted Stats 1990 ch 79 §14 (AB 759), operative July 1, 1991. Amended Stats 1993 ch 293 §6 (AB 21); Stats 1995 ch 730 §9 (AB 1466); Stats 2006 ch 84 §1 (AB 2042), effective January 1, 2007; Stats 2010 ch 620 §3 (SB 105), effective January 1, 2011; Stats 2020 ch 36 §43 (AB 3364), effective January 1, 2021.

Prior Law: Former Prob C §15642, similar to the present section, was added Stats 1986 ch 820 §40, operative July 1, 1987, and repealed Stats 1990 ch 79 §13, operative July 1, 1991.

§15643. Vacancy in office of trustee

There is a vacancy in the office of trustee in any of the following circumstances:

(a) The person named as trustee rejects the trust.
(b) The person named as trustee cannot be identified or does not exist.
(c) The trustee resigns or is removed.
(d) The trustee dies.
(e) A conservator or guardian of the person or estate of an individual trustee is appointed.
(f) The trustee is the subject of an order for relief in bankruptcy.
(g) A trust company's charter is revoked or powers are suspended, if the revocation or suspension is to be in effect for a period of 30 days or more.

(h) A receiver is appointed for a trust company if the appointment is not vacated within a period of 30 days. **Leg.H.** Enacted Stats 1990 ch 79 §14 (AB 759), operative July 1, 1991. Amended Stats 2009 ch 500 §57 (AB 1059), effective January 1, 2010.

Prior Law: Former Prob C §15643, similar to the present section, was added Stats 1986 ch 820 §40, operative July 1, 1987, and repealed Stats 1990 ch 79 §13, operative July 1, 1991.

§15644. Delivery of property by former trustee upon occurrence of vacancy

When a vacancy has occurred in the office of trustee, the former trustee who holds property of the trust shall deliver the trust property to the successor trustee or a person appointed by the court to receive the property and remains responsible for the trust property until it is delivered. A trustee who has resigned or is removed has the powers reasonably necessary under the circumstances to preserve the trust property until it is delivered to the successor trustee and to perform actions necessary to complete the resigning or removed trustee's administration of the trust. **Leg.H.** Enacted Stats 1990 ch 79 §14 (AB 759), operative July 1, 1991.

Prior Law: Former Prob C §15644, similar to the present section, was added Stats 1986 ch 820 §40, operative July 1, 1987, and repealed Stats 1990 ch 79 §13, operative July 1, 1991.

§15645. Costs and attorney's fees in proceedings for transfer of trust to successor trust company

If the trustee of a trust that is not revocable has refused to transfer administration of the trust to a successor trust company on request of the beneficiaries described in subdivision (c) of Section 15640 and the court in subsequent proceedings under Section 17200 makes an order removing the existing trustee and appointing a trust company as successor trustee, the court may, in its discretion, award costs and reasonable attorney's fees incurred by the petitioner in the proceeding to be paid by the trustee or from the trust as ordered by the court. **Leg.H.** Enacted Stats 1990 ch 79 §14 (AB 759), operative July 1, 1991.

ARTICLE 4
Appointment of Trustees

Appointment of trustee to fill vacancy. §15660.
Appointment of public guardian or public administrator as trustee; Requirements; Written certification; Bond. §15660.5.

§15660. Appointment of trustee to fill vacancy

(a) If the trust has no trustee or if the trust instrument requires a vacancy in the office of a cotrustee to be filled, the vacancy shall be filled as provided in this section.

(b) If the trust instrument provides a practical method of appointing a trustee or names the person to fill the vacancy, the vacancy shall be filled as provided in the trust instrument.

(c) If the vacancy in the office of trustee is not filled as provided in subdivision (b), the vacancy may be filled by a trust company that has agreed to accept the trust on agreement of all adult beneficiaries who are receiving or are entitled to receive income under the trust or to receive a distribution of principal if the trust were terminated at the time the agreement is made. If a beneficiary has a conservator, the conservator may agree to the successor trustee on behalf of the conservatee without obtaining court approval. Without limiting the power of the beneficiary to agree to the successor trustee, if the beneficiary has designated an attorney in fact who has the power under the power of attorney to agree to the successor trustee, the attorney in fact may agree to the successor trustee.

(d) If the vacancy in the office of trustee is not filled as provided in subdivision (b) or (c), on petition of any interested person or any person named as trustee in the trust instrument, the court may, in its discretion, appoint a trustee to fill the vacancy. If the trust provides for more than one trustee, the court may, in its discretion, appoint the original number or any lesser number of trustees. In selecting a trustee, the court shall give consideration to any nomination by the beneficiaries who are 14 years of age or older. **Leg.H.** Enacted Stats 1990 ch 79 §14 (AB 759), operative July 1, 1991. Amended Stats 1992 ch 871 §17 (AB 2975), effective January 1, 1993.

Prior Law: Former Prob C §15660, similar to the present section, was added Stats 1986 ch 820 §40, operative July 1, 1987, and repealed Stats 1990 ch 79 §13, operative July 1, 1991.

§15660.5. Appointment of public guardian or public administrator as trustee; Requirements; Written certification; Bond

(a) The court may appoint as trustee of a trust the public guardian or public administrator of the county in which the matter is pending subject to the following requirements:

(1) Neither the public guardian nor the public administrator shall be appointed as trustee unless the court finds, after reasonable inquiry, that no other qualified person is willing to act as trustee or the public guardian, public administrator, or his or her representative consents.

(2) The public administrator shall not be appointed as trustee unless either of the following is true:

(A) At the time of the appointment and pursuant to the terms of the trust, the entire trust is then to be distributed outright. For purposes of this paragraph, a trust that is "then to be distributed outright" does not include a trust pursuant to which payments to, or on behalf of, a beneficiary or beneficiaries are to be made from the trust on an ongoing basis for more than six months after the date of distribution.

(B) The public administrator consents.

(3) Neither the public guardian nor the public administrator shall be appointed as a cotrustee unless the public guardian, public administrator, or his or her representative consents.

(4) Neither the public guardian nor the public administrator shall be appointed as general trustee without a hearing and notice to the public guardian or public administrator, or his or her representative, and other interested persons as provided in Section 17203.

(5) Neither the public guardian nor the public administrator shall be appointed as temporary trustee without receiving notice of hearing as provided in Section 1220. The court shall not waive this notice of hearing, but may shorten the time for notice upon a finding of good cause.

(b)(1) If the public guardian or the public administrator consents to the appointment as trustee under this section, he or she shall submit a written certification of the consent to the court no later than two court days after the noticed hearing date described in paragraph (4) or (5) of subdivision (a). The public administrator shall not be appointed as trustee under subparagraph (A) of paragraph (2) of subdivision (a) if, after receiving notice as required by this section, the public administrator files a written certification with the court that the public administrator is unable to provide the level of services needed to properly fulfill the obligations of a trustee of the trust.

(2) If the public administrator has been appointed as trustee without notice as required in paragraph (4) or (5) of subdivision (a), and the public administrator files a written certification with the court that he or she is unable to provide the level of services needed to properly fulfill the obligations of a trustee of the trust, this shall be good cause for the public administrator to be relieved as trustee.

(c) The order of appointment shall provide for an annual bond fee as described in Section 15688. **Leg.H.** Added Stats 2008 ch 237 §5 (AB 2343), effective January 1, 2009.

Prior Law: Former Prob C §15660.5, similar to present section, was added Stats 1994 ch 472 §3 and repealed Stats 2008 ch 237 §4, effective January 1, 2009.

ARTICLE 5
Compensation and Indemnification of Trustees

Trustee's compensation as provided in trust instrument; Different compensation. §15680.
Trustee's compensation where trust silent. §15681.
Court determination of prospective compensation. §15682.
Compensation of cotrustees. §15683.
Repayment of trustee for expenditures. §15684.
Trustee's lien. §15685.
Notice of increased trustee's fee. §15686.
Restrictions on dual compensation. §15687.
Payment of public guardian or public administrator and attorney. §15688.

§15680. Trustee's compensation as provided in trust instrument; Different compensation

(a) Subject to subdivision (b), and except as provided in Section 15688, if the trust instrument provides for the trustee's compensation, the trustee is entitled to be compensated in accordance with the trust instrument.

(b) Upon proper showing, the court may fix or allow greater or lesser compensation than could be allowed under the terms of the trust in any of the following circumstances:

(1) Where the duties of the trustee are substantially different from those contemplated when the trust was created.

(2) Where the compensation in accordance with the terms of the trust would be inequitable or unreasonably low or high.

(3) In extraordinary circumstances calling for equitable relief.

(c) An order fixing or allowing greater or lesser compensation under subdivision (b) applies only prospectively to actions taken in administration of the trust after the order is made. **Leg.H.** Enacted Stats 1990 ch 79 §14 (AB 759), operative July 1, 1991. Amended Stats 2008 ch 237 §6 (AB 2343), effective January 1, 2009.

Prior Law: Former Prob C §15680, similar to the present section, was added Stats 1986 ch 820 §40, operative July 1, 1987, and repealed Stats 1990 ch 79 §13, operative July 1, 1991.

§15681. Trustee's compensation where trust silent

If the trust instrument does not specify the trustee's compensation, the trustee is entitled to reasonable compensation under the circumstances. **Leg.H.** Enacted Stats 1990 ch 79 §14 (AB 759), operative July 1, 1991.

Prior Law: Former Prob C §15681, similar to the present section, was added Stats 1986 ch 820 §40, operative July 1, 1987, and repealed Stats 1990 ch 79 §13, operative July 1, 1991.

§15682. Court determination of prospective compensation

The court may fix an amount of periodic compensation under Sections 15680 and 15681 to continue for as long as the court determines is proper. **Leg.H.** Enacted Stats 1990 ch 79 §14 (AB 759), operative July 1, 1991.

Prior Law: Former Prob C §15682, similar to the present section, was added Stats 1986 ch 820 §40, operative July 1, 1987, and repealed Stats 1990 ch 79 §13, operative July 1, 1991.

§15683. Compensation of cotrustees

Unless the trust instrument otherwise provides or the trustees otherwise agree, if the trust has two or more trustees, the compensation shall be apportioned among the cotrustees according to the services rendered by them. **Leg.H.** Enacted Stats 1990 ch 79 §14 (AB 759), operative July 1, 1991.

Prior Law: Former Prob C §15683, similar to the present section, was added Stats 1986 ch 820 §40, operative July 1, 1987, and repealed Stats 1990 ch 79 §13, operative July 1, 1991.

§15684. Repayment of trustee for expenditures

A trustee is entitled to the repayment out of the trust property for the following:

(a) Expenditures that were properly incurred in the administration of the trust.

(b) To the extent that they benefited the trust, expenditures that were not properly incurred in the administration of the trust. **Leg.H.** Enacted Stats 1990 ch 79 §14 (AB 759), operative July 1, 1991.

Prior Law: Former Prob C §15684, similar to the present section, was added Stats 1986 ch 820 §40, operative July 1, 1987, and repealed Stats 1990 ch 79 §13, operative July 1, 1991.

§15685. Trustee's lien

The trustee has an equitable lien on the trust property as against the beneficiary in the amount of advances, with any interest, made for the protection of the trust, and for expenses, losses, and liabilities sustained in the administration of the trust or because of ownership or control of any trust property. **Leg.H.** Enacted Stats 1990 ch 79 §14 (AB 759), operative July 1, 1991.

Prior Law: Former Prob C §15685, similar to the present section, was added Stats 1986 ch 820 §40, operative July 1, 1987, and repealed Stats 1990 ch 79 §13, operative July 1, 1991.

§15686. Notice of increased trustee's fee

(a) As used in this section, "trustee's fee" includes, but is not limited to, the trustee's periodic base fee, rate of percentage compensation, minimum fee, hourly rate, and transaction charge, but does not include fees for extraordinary services.

(b) A trustee shall not charge an increased trustee's fee for administration of a particular trust unless the trustee first gives at least 60 days' written notice of that increased fee to all of the following persons:

(1) Each beneficiary who is entitled to an account under Section 16062.

(2) Each beneficiary who was given the last preceding account.

(3) Each beneficiary who has made a written request to the trustee for notice of an increased trustee's fee and has given an address for receiving notice.

(c) If a beneficiary files a petition under Section 17200 for review of the increased trustee's fee or for removal of the trustee and serves a copy of the petition on the trustee before the expiration of the 60-day period, the increased trustee's fee does not take effect as to that trust until otherwise ordered by the court or the petition is dismissed. **Leg.H.** Enacted Stats 1990 ch 79 §14 (AB 759), operative July 1, 1991. Amended Stats 1992 ch 178 §43.2 (SB 1496); Stats 2017 ch 319 §86 (AB 976), effective January 1, 2018.

§15687. Restrictions on dual compensation

(a) Notwithstanding any provision of a trust to the contrary, a trustee who is an attorney may receive only (1) the trustee's compensation provided in the trust or otherwise provided in this article or (2) compensation for legal services performed for the trustee, unless the trustee obtains approval for the right to dual compensation as provided in subdivision (d).

(b) No parent, child, sibling, or spouse of a person who is a trustee, and no law partnership or corporation whose partner, shareholder, or employee is serving as a trustee shall receive any compensation for legal services performed for the trustee unless the trustee waives trustee compensation or unless the trustee obtains approval for the right to dual compensation as provided in subdivision (d).

(c) This section shall not apply if the trustee is related by blood or marriage to, or is a cohabitant with, the settlor.

(d) After full disclosure of the nature of the compensation and relationship of the trustee to all persons receiving compensation under this section, the trustee may obtain approval for dual compensation by either of the following:

(1) An order pursuant to paragraph (21) of subdivision (b) of Section 17200.

(2) Giving 30 days' advance written notice to the persons entitled to notice under Section 17203. Within that 30-day period, any person entitled to notice may object to the proposed action by written notice to the trustee or by filing a petition pursuant to paragraph (21) of subdivision (b) of Section 17200. If the trustee receives this objection during that 30-day period and if the trustee wishes dual compensation, the trustee shall file a petition for approval pursuant to paragraph (21) of subdivision (b) of Section 17200.

(e) Any waiver of the requirements of this section is against public policy and shall be void.

(f) This section applies to services rendered on or after January 1, 1994. **Leg.H.** Added Stats 1993 ch 293 §6.3 (AB 21). Amended Stats 1995 ch 730 §10 (AB 1466), effective January 1, 1996.

§15688. Payment of public guardian or public administrator and attorney

Notwithstanding any other provision of this article and the terms of the trust, a public guardian or public administrator who is appointed as a trustee of a trust pursuant to Section 15660.5 shall be paid from the trust property for all of the following:

(a) Reasonable expenses incurred in the administration of the trust.

(b) Compensation for services of the public guardian or public administrator and the attorney of the public guardian or public administrator, as follows:

(1) If the public guardian or public administrator is appointed as trustee of a trust that provides for the outright distribution of the entire trust estate, compensation for the public guardian or public administrator, and any attorney for the public guardian or public administrator, shall be calculated as that provided to a personal representative and attorney pursuant to Part 7 (commencing with Section 10800) of Division 7, based on the fair market value of the assets as of the date of the appointment, provided that the minimum amount of compensation for the public guardian or the public administrator shall be one thousand dollars ($1,000). Additionally, the minimum amount of compensation for the attorney for the public guardian or the public administrator, if any, shall be one thousand dollars ($1,000).

(2) For a trust other than that described in paragraph (1), the public guardian or public administrator shall be compensated as provided in Section 15680. Compensation shall be consistent with compensation allowed for professional fiduciaries or corporate fiduciaries providing comparable services.

(3) Except as provided in paragraph (1), reasonable compensation for the attorney for the public guardian or public administrator.

(c) An annual bond fee in the amount of twenty-five dollars ($25) plus one-fourth of 1 percent of the amount of the trust assets greater than ten thousand dollars ($10,000). The amount charged shall be deposited in the county treasury. **Leg.H.** Added Stats 1997 ch 93 §3 (SB 696). Amended Stats 2002 ch 784 §581 (SB 1316); Stats 2008 ch 237 §7 (AB 2343), effective January 1, 2009.

CHAPTER 2
BENEFICIARIES

Limits on rights of beneficiary of revocable trust. §15800.
Consent by beneficiary of revocable trust. §15801.
Notice to beneficiary of revocable trust. §15802.
Rights of holder of power of appointment or withdrawal. §15803.
Notice in case involving future interest of beneficiary. §15804.
Attorney General subject to limitations on rights of beneficiaries of revocable trusts. §15805.

§15800. Limits on rights of beneficiary of revocable trust

(a) Except to the extent that the trust instrument otherwise provides or where the joint action of the settlor and all beneficiaries is required, during the time that a trust is revocable and at least one person holding the power to revoke the trust, in whole or in part, is competent, the following shall apply:

(1) The person holding the power to revoke, and not the beneficiary, has the rights afforded beneficiaries under this division.

(2) The duties of the trustee are owed to the person holding the power to revoke.

(b) Except to the extent that the trust instrument otherwise provides or where the joint action of the settlor and all beneficiaries is required, if, during the time that a trust is revocable, no person holding the power to revoke the trust, in whole or in part, is competent, the following shall apply:

(1) Within 60 days of receiving information establishing the incompetency of the last person holding the power to revoke the trust, the trustee shall provide notice of the application of this subdivision and a true and complete copy of the trust instrument and any amendments to each beneficiary to whom the trustee would be required or authorized to distribute income or principal if the settlor had died as of the date of receipt of the information. If the trust has been completely restated, the trustee need not include the trust instrument or amendments superseded by the last restatement.

(2) The duties of the trustee to account at least annually or provide information requested under Section 16061 shall be owed to each beneficiary to whom the trustee would be required or authorized to distribute income or principal if the settlor had died during the account period or the period relating to the administration of the trust relevant to the report, as applicable.

(3) A beneficiary whose interest is conditional on some factor not yet in existence or not yet determinable shall not be considered a beneficiary for purposes of this section, unless the trustee, in the trustee's discretion, believes it is likely that the condition or conditions will be satisfied at the time of the settlor's death.

(4) If the interest of a beneficiary fails because a condition to receiving that interest has not been satisfied or the trustee does not believe that the condition will be satisfied at the time of the settlor's death, the duties in paragraphs (1) and (2) shall be owed to the beneficiary or beneficiaries who would next succeed to that interest at the relevant time or period as determined under the trust instrument, as amended and restated.

(c) Incompetency, for the purposes of subdivision (b), may be established by either of the following:

(1) The method for determining incompetency specified by the trust instrument, as amended or restated.

(2) A judicial determination of incompetency. **Leg.H.** Enacted Stats 1990 ch 79 §14 (AB 759), operative July 1, 1991. Amended Stats 2021 ch 749 §1 (AB 1079), effective January 1, 2022; Stats 2022 ch 420 §42 (AB 2960), effective January 1, 2023.

Prior Law: Former Prob C §15800, similar to the present section, was added Stats 1986 ch 820 §40, operative July 1, 1987, and repealed Stats 1990 ch 79 §13, operative July 1, 1991.

§15801. Consent by beneficiary of revocable trust

(a) In any case where the consent of a beneficiary may be given or is required to be given before an action may be taken, during the time that a trust is revocable and the person holding the power to revoke the trust is competent, the person holding the power to revoke, and not the beneficiary, has the power to consent or withhold consent.

(b) This section does not apply where the joint consent of the settlor and all beneficiaries is required by statute. **Leg.H.** Enacted Stats 1990 ch 79 §14 (AB 759), operative July 1, 1991.

Prior Law: Former Prob C §15801, similar to the present section, was added Stats 1986 ch 820 §40, operative July 1, 1987, and repealed Stats 1990 ch 79 §13, operative July 1, 1991.

§15802. Notice to beneficiary of revocable trust

Notwithstanding any other statute, during the time that a trust is revocable and the person holding the power to revoke the trust is competent, a notice that is to be given to a beneficiary shall be given to the person holding the power to revoke and not to the beneficiary. **Leg.H.** Enacted Stats 1990 ch 79 §14 (AB 759), operative July 1, 1991.

Prior Law: Former Prob C §15802, similar to the present section, was added Stats 1986 ch 820 §40, operative July 1, 1987, and repealed Stats 1990 ch 79 §13, operative July 1, 1991.

§15803. Rights of holder of power of appointment or withdrawal

The holder of a presently exercisable general power of appointment or power to withdraw property from the trust has the rights of a person holding the power to revoke the trust that are provided by Sections 15800 to 15802, inclusive, to the extent of the holder's power over the trust property. **Leg.H.** Enacted Stats 1990 ch 79 §14 (AB 759), operative July 1, 1991.

Prior Law: Former Prob C §15803, similar to the present section, was added Stats 1986 ch 820 §40, operative July 1, 1987, amended Stats 1987 ch 128 §11, effective July 6, 1987, operative July 1, 1987, and repealed Stats 1990 ch 79 §13, operative July 1, 1991.

§15804. Notice in case involving future interest of beneficiary

(a) Subject to subdivisions (b) and (c), it is sufficient compliance with a requirement in this division that notice be given to a beneficiary, or to a person interested in the trust, if notice is given as follows:

(1) Where an interest has been limited on any future contingency to persons who will compose a certain class upon the happening of a certain event without further limitation, notice shall be given to the persons in being who would constitute the class if the event had happened immediately before the commencement of the proceeding or if there is no proceeding, if the event had happened immediately before notice is given.

(2) Where an interest has been limited to a living person and the same interest, or a share therein, has been further limited upon the happening of a future event to the surviving spouse or to persons who are or may be the distributees, heirs, issue, or other kindred of the living person, notice shall be given to the living person.

(3) Where an interest has been limited upon the happening of any future event to a person, or a class of persons, or both, and the interest, or a share of the interest, has been further limited upon the happening of an additional future event to another person, or a class of persons, or both, notice shall be given to the person or persons in being who would take the interest upon the happening of the first of these events.

(b) If a conflict of interest involving the subject matter of the trust proceeding exists between a person to whom notice is required to be given and a person to whom notice is not otherwise required to be given under subdivision (a), notice shall also be given to persons not otherwise entitled to notice under subdivision (a) with respect to whom the conflict of interest exists.

(c) Nothing in this section affects any of the following:

(1) Requirements for notice to a person who has requested special notice, a person who has filed notice of appearance, or a particular person or entity required by statute to be given notice.

(2) Availability of a guardian ad litem pursuant to Section 1003.

(d) As used in this section, "notice" includes other papers. **Leg.H.** Enacted Stats 1990 ch 79 §14 (AB 759), operative July 1, 1991. Amended Stats 1992 ch 178 §43.4 (SB 1496), effective January 1, 1993.

Prior Law: Former Prob C §15804, similar to the present section, was added Stats 1986 ch 820 §40, operative July 1, 1987, amended Stats 1988 ch 1199 §105.3, operative July 1, 1989, and repealed Stats 1990 ch 79 §1, operative July 1, 1991.

§15805. Attorney General subject to limitations on rights of beneficiaries of revocable trusts

Notwithstanding any other provision of law, the Attorney General is subject to the limitations on the rights of beneficiaries of revocable trusts provided by Sections 15800 to 15802, inclusive. **Leg.H.** Enacted Stats 1990 ch 79 §14 (AB 759), operative July 1, 1991.

Prior Law: Former Prob C §15805, similar to the present section, was added Stats 1987 ch 128 §12, effective July 6, 1987, operative July 1, 1987, and repealed Stats 1990 ch 79 §13, operative July 1, 1991.

PART 4
TRUST ADMINISTRATION

Chapter 1. Duties of Trustees.
Chapter 2. Powers of Trustees.
Chapter 3. Uniform Fiduciary Income and Principal Act.
Chapter 4. Liability of Trustees to Beneficiaries.
Chapter 5. Notice of Proposed Action by Trustee.
Chapter 6. California Uniform Directed Trust Act.

CHAPTER 1
DUTIES OF TRUSTEES

Article 1. Trustee's Duties in General.
Article 2. Trustee's Standard of Care.
Article 2.5. Uniform Prudent Investor Act.
Article 3. Trustee's Duty to Report Information and Account to Beneficiaries.
Article 4. Duties With Regard to Discretionary Powers.
Article 5. Duties of Trustees of Private Foundations, Charitable Trusts, and Split-Interest Trusts.
Article 6. Notice to the Attorney General of Disposal of Charitable Assets.

ARTICLE 1
Trustee's Duties in General

Duty to administer trust. §16000.
Duties of trustee of revocable trust. §16001.
Duty of loyalty. §16002.
Duty to deal impartially with beneficiaries. §16003.
Duty to avoid conflict of interest. §16004.
Relief of trustee from liability as condition for making distribution or payment prohibited. §16004.5.
Duty not to undertake adverse trust. §16005.
Duty to take control of and preserve trust property. §16006.
Duty to make trust property productive. §16007.
Duty to keep trust property separate and identified. §16009.
Duty to enforce claims. §16010.
Duty to defend actions. §16011.
Duty not to delegate. §16012.
Duty with respect to cotrustees. §16013.
Duty to use special skills. §16014.
Certain actions not violations of duties. §16015.

§16000. Duty to administer trust

On acceptance of the trust, the trustee has a duty to administer the trust according to the trust instrument and, except to the extent the trust instrument provides otherwise, according to this division. **Leg.H.** Enacted Stats 1990 ch 79 §14 (AB 759), operative July 1, 1991.

Prior Law: Former Prob C §16000, similar to the present section, was added Stats 1986 ch 820 §40, operative July 1, 1987, and repealed Stats 1990 ch 79 §13, operative July 1, 1991.

§16001. Duties of trustee of revocable trust

(a) Except as provided in subdivision (b), the trustee of a revocable trust shall follow any written direction acceptable to the trustee given from time to time (1) by the person then having the power to revoke the trust or the part thereof with respect to which the direction is given or (2) by the person to whom the settlor delegates the right to direct the trustee.

(b) If a written direction given under subdivision (a) would have the effect of modifying the trust, the trustee has no duty to follow the direction unless it complies with the requirements for modifying the trust. **Leg.H.** Enacted Stats 1990 ch 79 §14 (AB 759), operative July 1, 1991.

Prior Law: Former Prob C §16001, similar to the present section, was added Stats 1986 ch 820 §40, operative July 1, 1987, and repealed Stats 1990 ch 79 §13, operative July 1, 1991.

§16002. Duty of loyalty

(a) The trustee has a duty to administer the trust solely in the interest of the beneficiaries.

(b) It is not a violation of the duty provided in subdivision (a) for a trustee who administers two trusts to sell, exchange, or participate in the sale or exchange of trust property between the trusts, if both of the following requirements are met:

(1) The sale or exchange is fair and reasonable with respect to the beneficiaries of both trusts.

(2) The trustee gives to the beneficiaries of both trusts notice of all material facts related to the sale or exchange that the trustee knows or should know. **Leg.H.** Enacted Stats 1990 ch 79 §14 (AB 759), operative July 1, 1991.

Prior Law: Former Prob C §16002, similar to the present section, was added Stats 1986 ch 820 §40, operative July 1, 1987, and repealed Stats 1990 ch 79 §13, operative July 1, 1991.

§16003. Duty to deal impartially with beneficiaries

If a trust has two or more beneficiaries, the trustee has a duty to deal impartially with them and shall act impartially in investing and managing the trust property, taking into account any differing interests of the beneficiaries. **Leg.H.** Enacted Stats 1990 ch 79 §14 (AB 759), operative July 1, 1991. Amended Stats 1995 ch 63 §1 (SB 222), effective January 1, 1996.

Prior Law: Former Prob C §16003, similar to the present section, was added Stats 1986 ch 820 §40, operative July 1, 1987, and repealed Stats 1990 ch 79 §13, operative July 1, 1991.

§16004. Duty to avoid conflict of interest

(a) The trustee has a duty not to use or deal with trust property for the trustee's own profit or for any other purpose unconnected with the trust, nor to take part in any transaction in which the trustee has an interest adverse to the beneficiary.

(b) The trustee may not enforce any claim against the trust property that the trustee purchased after or in contemplation of appointment as trustee, but the court may allow the trustee to be reimbursed from trust property the amount that the trustee paid in good faith for the claim.

(c) A transaction between the trustee and a beneficiary which occurs during the existence of the trust or while the trustee's influence with the beneficiary remains and by which the trustee obtains an advantage from the beneficiary is presumed to be a violation of the trustee's fiduciary duties. This presumption is a presumption affecting the burden of proof. This subdivision does not apply to the provisions of an agreement between a trustee and a beneficiary relating to the hiring or compensation of the trustee. **Leg.H.** Enacted Stats 1990 ch 79 §14 (AB 759), operative July 1, 1991.

Prior Law: Former Prob C §16004, similar to the present section, was added Stats 1986 ch 820 §40, operative July 1, 1987, and repealed Stats 1990 ch 79 §13, operative July 1, 1991.

§16004.5. Relief of trustee from liability as condition for making distribution or payment prohibited

(a) A trustee may not require a beneficiary to relieve the trustee of liability as a condition for making a distribution or payment to, or for the benefit of, the beneficiary, if the distribution or payment is required by the trust instrument.

(b) This section may not be construed as affecting the trustee's right to:

(1) Maintain a reserve for reasonably anticipated expenses, including, but not limited to, taxes, debts, trustee and accounting fees, and costs and expenses of administration.

(2) Seek a voluntary release or discharge of a trustee's liability from the beneficiary.

(3) Require indemnification against a claim by a person or entity, other than a beneficiary referred to in subdivision (a), which may reasonably arise as a result of the distribution.

(4) Withhold any portion of an otherwise required distribution that is reasonably in dispute.

(5) Seek court or beneficiary approval of an accounting of trust activities. **Leg.H.** Added Stats 2003 ch 585 §1 (AB 1705), effective January 1, 2004.

§16005. Duty not to undertake adverse trust

The trustee of one trust has a duty not to knowingly become a trustee of another trust adverse in its nature to the interest of the beneficiary of the first trust, and a duty to eliminate the conflict or resign as trustee when the conflict is discovered. **Leg.H.** Enacted Stats 1990 ch 79 §14 (AB 759), operative July 1, 1991.

Prior Law: Former Prob C §16005, similar to the present section, was added Stats 1986 ch 820 §40, operative July 1, 1987, and repealed Stats 1990 ch 79 §13, operative July 1, 1991.

§16006. Duty to take control of and preserve trust property

The trustee has a duty to take reasonable steps under the circumstances to take and keep control of and to preserve the trust property. **Leg.H.** Enacted Stats 1990 ch 79 §14 (AB 759), operative July 1, 1991.

Prior Law: Former Prob C §16006, similar to the present section, was added Stats 1986 ch 820 §40, operative July 1, 1987, and repealed Stats 1990 ch 79 §13, operative July 1, 1991.

§16007. Duty to make trust property productive

The trustee has a duty to make the trust property productive under the circumstances and in furtherance of the purposes of the trust. **Leg.H.** Enacted Stats 1990 ch 79 §14 (AB 759), operative July 1, 1991.

Prior Law: Former Prob C §16007, similar to the present section, was added Stats 1986 ch 820 §40, operative July 1, 1987, and repealed Stats 1990 ch 79 §13, operative July 1, 1991.

§16008. [Section repealed 1995]

Leg.H. Enacted Stats 1990 ch 79 §14, operative July 1, 1991. Repealed Stats 1995 ch 63 §2. The repealed section related to duty to dispose of improper investments.

Prior Law: Former Prob C §16008, relating to duty of trustee to dispose of improper investments, was added Stats 1986 ch 820 §40, operative July 1, 1987, and repealed Stats 1990 ch 79 §13, operative July 1, 1991.

§16009. Duty to keep trust property separate and identified

The trustee has a duty to do the following:

(a) To keep the trust property separate from other property not subject to the trust.

(b) To see that the trust property is designated as property of the trust. **Leg.H.** Enacted Stats 1990 ch 79 §14 (AB 759), operative July 1, 1991.

Prior Law: Former Prob C §16009, similar to the present section, was added Stats 1986 ch 820 §40, operative July 1, 1987, and repealed Stats 1990 ch 79 §13, operative July 1, 1991.

§16010. Duty to enforce claims

The trustee has a duty to take reasonable steps to enforce claims that are part of the trust property. **Leg.H.** Enacted Stats 1990 ch 79 §14 (AB 759), operative July 1, 1991.

Prior Law: Former Prob C §16010, similar to the present section, was added Stats 1986 ch 820 §40, operative July 1, 1987, and repealed Stats 1990 ch 79 §13, operative July 1, 1991.

§16011. Duty to defend actions

The trustee has a duty to take reasonable steps to defend actions that may result in a loss to the trust. **Leg.H.** Enacted Stats 1990 ch 79 §14 (AB 759), operative July 1, 1991.

Prior Law: Former Prob C §16011, similar to the present section, was added Stats 1986 ch 820 §40, operative July 1, 1987, and repealed Stats 1990 ch 79 §13, operative July 1, 1991.

§16012. Duty not to delegate

(a) The trustee has a duty not to delegate to others the performance of acts that the trustee can reasonably be required personally to perform and may not transfer the office of trustee to another person nor delegate the entire administration of the trust to a cotrustee or other person.

(b) In a case where a trustee has properly delegated a matter to an agent, cotrustee, or other person, the trustee has a duty to exercise general supervision over the person performing the delegated matter.

(c) This section does not apply to investment and management functions under Section 16052. **Leg.H.** Enacted Stats 1990 ch 79 §14 (AB 759), operative July 1, 1991. Amended Stats 1995 ch 63 §3 (SB 222), effective January 1, 1996.

Prior Law: Former Prob C §16012, similar to the present section, was added Stats 1986 ch 820 §40, operative July 1, 1987, and repealed Stats 1990 ch 79 §13, operative July 1, 1991.

§16013. Duty with respect to cotrustees

If a trust has more than one trustee, each trustee has a duty to do the following:

(a) To participate in the administration of the trust.

(b) To take reasonable steps to prevent a cotrustee from committing a breach of trust or to compel a cotrustee to redress a breach of trust. **Leg.H.** Enacted Stats 1990 ch 79 §14 (AB 759), operative July 1, 1991.

Prior Law: Former Prob C §16013, similar to the present section, was added Stats 1986 ch 820 §40, operative July 1, 1987, and repealed Stats 1990 ch 79 §13, operative July 1, 1991.

§16014. Duty to use special skills

(a) The trustee has a duty to apply the full extent of the trustee's skills.

(b) If the settlor, in selecting the trustee, has relied on the trustee's representation of having special skills, the trustee is held to the standard of the skills represented. **Leg.H.** Enacted Stats 1990 ch 79 §14 (AB 759), operative July 1, 1991.

Prior Law: Former Prob C §16014, similar to the present section, was added Stats 1986 ch 820 §40, operative July 1, 1987, and repealed Stats 1990 ch 79 §13, operative July 1, 1991.

§16015. Certain actions not violations of duties

The provision of services for compensation by a regulated financial institution or its affiliates in the ordinary course of business either to a trust of which it also acts as trustee or to a person dealing with the trust is not a violation of the duty provided in Section 16002 or 16004. For the purposes of this section, "affiliate" means a corporation that directly or indirectly through one or more intermediaries controls, is controlled by, or is under common control with another domestic or foreign corporation. **Leg.H.** Enacted Stats 1990 ch 79 §14 (AB 759), operative July 1, 1991.

Prior Law: Former Prob C §16015, similar to the present section, was added Stats 1986 ch 820 §40, operative July 1, 1987, and repealed Stats 1990 ch 79 §13, operative July 1, 1991.

ARTICLE 2
Trustee's Standard of Care

Trustee's standard of care in administering trust. §16040.
Standard of care not affected by compensation. §16041.
Public guardian's deposit or investment of trust property. §16042.

§16040. Trustee's standard of care in administering trust

(a) The trustee shall administer the trust with reasonable care, skill, and caution under the circumstances then prevailing that a prudent person acting in a like capacity would use in the conduct of an enterprise of like character and with like aims to accomplish the purposes of the trust as determined from the trust instrument

(b) The settlor may expand or restrict the standard provided in subdivision (a) by express provisions in the trust instrument. A trustee is not liable to a beneficiary for the trustee's good faith reliance on these express provisions.

(c) This section does not apply to investment and management functions governed by the Uniform Prudent Investor Act, Article 2.5 (commencing with Section 16045). **Leg.H.** Enacted Stats 1990 ch 79 §14 (AB 759), operative July 1, 1991. Amended Stats 1995 ch 63 §4 (SB 222), effective January 1, 1996.

Prior Law: Former Prob C §16040, similar to the present section, was added Stats 1986 ch 820 §40, operative July 1, 1987, and repealed Stats 1990 ch 79 §13, operative July 1, 1991.

§16041. Standard of care not affected by compensation

A trustee's standard of care and performance in administering the trust is not affected by whether or not the trustee receives any compensation. **Leg.H.** Enacted Stats 1990 ch 79 §14 (AB 759), operative July 1, 1991.

Prior Law: Former Prob C §16041, similar to the present section, was added Stats 1986 ch 820 §40, operative July 1, 1987, and repealed Stats 1990 ch 79 §13, operative July 1, 1991.

§16042. Public guardian's deposit or investment of trust property

(a) Notwithstanding the requirements of this article, Article 2.5 (commencing with Section 16045), and the terms of the trust, all trust funds that come within the custody of the public guardian who is appointed as trustee of the trust pursuant to Section 15660.5 may be deposited or invested in the same manner, and would be subject to the same terms and conditions, as a deposit or investment by the public administrator of funds in the estate of a decedent pursuant to Article 3 (commencing with Section 7640) of Chapter 4 of Part 1 of Division 7.

(b) Upon the deposit or investment of trust property pursuant to subdivision (a), the public guardian shall be deemed to have met the standard of care specified in this article and Article 2.5 (commencing with Section 16045) with respect to this trust property. **Leg.H.** Added Stats 1997 ch 93 §4 (SB 696), effective January 1, 1998.

Prior Law: Former Prob C §16042, similar to present Prob C §16053, was enacted Stats 1990 ch 79 §14, operative July 1, 1991, and repealed Stats 1995 ch 63 §5.

Former Prob C §16042, similar to present Prob C §16053, was added Stats 1986 ch 820 §40, operative July 1, 1987, and repealed Stats 1990 ch 79 §13, operative July 1, 1991.

ARTICLE 2.5
Uniform Prudent Investor Act

Prudent investor rule. §16045.
Duty of trustee to comply with rule. §16046.
Standard of care. §16047.
Trustee's duty to diversify investments of trust. §16048.
Review of assets to comply with requirements of chapter. §16049.
Permissible costs. §16050.
Determination of compliance with rule. §16051.
Delegation of investment and management functions. §16052.
Terms authorizing investments permitted under chapter. §16053.
Application of article. §16054.

§16045. Prudent investor rule

This article, together with subdivision (a) of Section 16002 and Section 16003, constitutes the prudent investor rule and may be cited as the Uniform Prudent Investor Act. **Leg.H.** Added Stats 1995 ch 63 §6 (SB 222), effective January 1, 1996.

§16046. Duty of trustee to comply with rule

(a) Except as provided in subdivision (b), a trustee who invests and manages trust assets owes a duty to the beneficiaries of the trust to comply with the prudent investor rule.

(b) The settlor may expand or restrict the prudent investor rule by express provisions in the trust instrument. A trustee is not liable to a beneficiary for the trustee's good faith reliance on these express provisions. **Leg.H.** Added Stats 1995 ch 63 §6 (SB 222), effective January 1, 1996.

§16047. Standard of care

(a) A trustee shall invest and manage trust assets as a prudent investor would, by considering the purposes, terms, distribution requirements, and other circumstances of the trust. In satisfying this standard, the trustee shall exercise reasonable care, skill, and caution.

(b) A trustee's investment and management decisions respecting individual assets and courses of action must be evaluated not in isolation, but in the context of the trust portfolio as a whole and as a part of an overall investment strategy having risk and return objectives reasonably suited to the trust.

(c) Among circumstances that are appropriate to consider in investing and managing trust assets are the following, to the extent relevant to the trust or its beneficiaries:

(1) General economic conditions.
(2) The possible effect of inflation or deflation.
(3) The expected tax consequences of investment decisions or strategies.
(4) The role that each investment or course of action plays within the overall trust portfolio.
(5) The expected total return from income and the appreciation of capital.
(6) Other resources of the beneficiaries known to the trustee as determined from information provided by the beneficiaries.
(7) Needs for liquidity, regularity of income, and preservation or appreciation of capital.
(8) An asset's special relationship or special value, if any, to the purposes of the trust or to one or more of the beneficiaries.

(d) A trustee shall make a reasonable effort to ascertain facts relevant to the investment and management of trust assets.

(e) A trustee may invest in any kind of property or type of investment or engage in any course of action or investment strategy consistent with the standards of this chapter. **Leg.H.** Added Stats 1995 ch 63 §6 (SB 222), effective January 1, 1996.

§16048. Trustee's duty to diversify investments of trust

In making and implementing investment decisions, the trustee has a duty to diversify the investments of the trust unless, under the circumstances, it is prudent not to do so. **Leg.H.** Added Stats 1995 ch 63 §6 (SB 222), effective January 1, 1996.

§16049. Review of assets to comply with requirements of chapter

Within a reasonable time after accepting a trusteeship or receiving trust assets, a trustee shall review the trust assets and make and implement decisions concerning the retention and disposition of assets, in order to bring the trust portfolio into compliance with the purposes, terms, distribution requirements, and other circumstances of the trust, and with the requirements of this chapter. **Leg.H.** Added Stats 1995 ch 63 §6 (SB 222), effective January 1, 1996.

§16050. Permissible costs

In investing and managing trust assets, a trustee may only incur costs that are appropriate and reasonable in relation to the assets, overall investment strategy, purposes, and other circumstances of the trust. **Leg.H.** Added Stats 1995 ch 63 §6 (SB 222), effective January 1, 1996.

§16051. Determination of compliance with rule

Compliance with the prudent investor rule is determined in light of the facts and circumstances existing at the time of a trustee's decision or action and not by hindsight. **Leg.H.** Added Stats 1995 ch 63 §6 (SB 222), effective January 1, 1996.

§16052. Delegation of investment and management functions

(a) A trustee may delegate investment and management functions as prudent under the circumstances. The trustee shall exercise prudence in the following:

(1) Selecting an agent.
(2) Establishing the scope and terms of the delegation, consistent with the purposes and terms of the trust.
(3) Periodically reviewing the agent's overall performance and compliance with the terms of the delegation.

(b) In performing a delegated function, an agent has a duty to exercise reasonable care to comply with the terms of the delegation.

(c) Except as otherwise provided in Section 16401, a trustee who complies with the requirements of subdivision (a) is not liable to the beneficiaries or to the trust for the decisions or actions of the agent to whom the function was delegated.

(d) By accepting the delegation of a trust function from the trustee of a trust that is subject to the law of this state, an agent submits to the jurisdiction of the courts of this state. **Leg.H.** Added Stats 1995 ch 63 §6 (SB 222), effective January 1, 1996.

§16053. Terms authorizing investments permitted under chapter

The following terms or comparable language in the provisions of a trust, unless otherwise limited or modified, authorizes any investment or strategy permitted under this chapter: "investments permissible by law for investment of trust funds," "legal investments," "authorized investments," "using the judgment and care under the circumstances then prevailing that persons of prudence, discretion, and intelligence exercise in the management of their own affairs, not in regard to speculation but in regard to the permanent disposition of their funds, considering the probable income as well as the probable safety of their capital," "prudent man rule," "prudent trustee rule," "prudent person rule," and "prudent investor rule." **Leg.H.** Added Stats 1995 ch 63 §6 (SB 222), effective January 1, 1996.

§16054. Application of article

This article applies to trusts existing on and created after its effective date. As applied to trusts existing on its effective date, this article governs only decisions or actions occurring after that date. **Leg.H.** Added Stats 1995 ch 63 §6 (SB 222), effective January 1, 1996.

ARTICLE 3
Trustee's Duty to Report Information and Account to Beneficiaries

Trustee's general duty to report information to beneficiaries. §16060.
"Terms of the trust". §16060.5.
Duty to provide terms of trust to beneficiary; Exception. §16060.7.
Duty to report information about trust on request. §16061.
Duty to provide copy of terms of irrevocable trust; Determination of heirship. §16061.5.
Trustee's duty to serve notification of changes; Contents; Damages. §16061.7.
Time for contesting trust. §16061.8.
Liability of trustee. §16061.9.
Duty to account to beneficiaries. §16062.
Contents of account; Presentation. §16063.
Exceptions to duty to account to beneficiary. §16064.
Waivers as against public policy. §16068.

Exceptions to duty to account, provide terms of the trust or requested information. §16069.

§16060. Trustee's general duty to report information to beneficiaries

The trustee has a duty to keep the beneficiaries of the trust reasonably informed of the trust and its administration. **Leg.H.** Enacted Stats 1990 ch 79 §14 (AB 759), operative July 1, 1991.

Prior Law: Former Prob C §16060, similar to the present section, was added Stats 1986 ch 820 §40, operative July 1, 1987, and repealed Stats 1990 ch 79 §13, operative July 1, 1991.

§16060.5. "Terms of the trust"

As used in this article, "terms of the trust" means the written trust instrument of an irrevocable trust or those provisions of a written trust instrument in effect at the settlor's death that describe or affect that portion of a trust that has become irrevocable at the death of the settlor. In addition, "terms of the trust" includes, but is not limited to, signatures, amendments, disclaimers, and any directions or instructions to the trustee that affect the disposition of the trust. "Terms of the trust" does not include documents which were intended to affect disposition only while the trust was revocable. If a trust has been completely restated, "terms of the trust" does not include trust instruments or amendments which are superseded by the last restatement before the settlor's death, but it does include amendments executed after the restatement. "Terms of the trust" also includes any document irrevocably exercising a power of appointment over the trust or over any portion of the trust which has become irrevocable. **Leg.H.** Added Stats 1997 ch 724 §21 (AB 1172). Amended Stats 1998 ch 682 §7 (AB 2069); Stats 2000 ch 34 §2 (AB 460), effective January 1, 2001.

§16060.7. Duty to provide terms of trust to beneficiary; Exception

On the request of a beneficiary, the trustee shall provide the terms of the trust to the beneficiary unless the trustee is not required to provide the terms of the trust to the beneficiary in accordance with Section 16069. **Leg.H.** Added Stats 2010 ch 621 §2 (SB 202), effective January 1, 2011.

§16061. Duty to report information about trust on request

Except as provided in Section 16069, on reasonable request by a beneficiary, the trustee shall report to the beneficiary by providing requested information to the beneficiary relating to the administration of the trust relevant to the beneficiary's interest. **Leg.H.** Enacted Stats 1990 ch 79 §14 (AB 759), operative July 1, 1991. Amended Stats 1998 ch 682 §8 (AB 2069); Stats 2010 ch 621 §3 (SB 202), effective January 1, 2011.

Prior Law: Former Prob C §16061, similar to the present section, was added Stats 1986 ch 820 §40, operative July 1, 1987, and repealed Stats 1990 ch 79 §13, operative July 1, 1991.

§16061.5. Duty to provide copy of terms of irrevocable trust; Determination of heirship

(a) A trustee shall provide a true and complete copy of the terms of the irrevocable trust, or irrevocable portion of the trust, to each of the following:

(1) Any beneficiary of the trust who requests it, and to any heir of a deceased settlor who requests it, when a revocable trust or any portion of a revocable trust becomes irrevocable because of the death of one or more of the settlors of the trust, when a power of appointment is effective or lapses upon the death of a settlor under the circumstances described in paragraph (3) of subdivision (a) of Section 16061.7, or because, by the express terms of the trust, the trust becomes irrevocable within one year of the death of a settlor because of a contingency related to the death of one or more of the settlors of the trust.

(2) Any beneficiary of the trust who requests it, whenever there is a change of trustee of an irrevocable trust.

(3) If the trust is a charitable trust subject to the supervision of the Attorney General, to the Attorney General, if requested, when a revocable trust or any portion of a revocable trust becomes irrevocable because of the death of one or more of the settlors of the trust, when a power of appointment is effective or lapses upon death of a settlor under the circumstances described in paragraph (3) of subdivision (a) of Section 16061.7, or because, by the express terms of the trust, the trust becomes irrevocable within one year of the death of a settlor because of a contingency related to the death of one or more of the settlors of the trust, and whenever there is a change of trustee of an irrevocable trust.

(b) The trustee shall, for purposes of this section, rely upon any final judicial determination of heirship. However, the trustee shall have discretion to make a good faith determination by any reasonable means of the heirs of a deceased settlor in the absence of a final judicial determination of heirship known to the trustee. **Leg.H.** Added Stats 1997 ch 724 §22 (AB 1172). Amended Stats 1998 ch 682 §9 (AB 2069); Stats 2000 ch 34 §3 (AB 460); Stats 2010 ch 621 §4 (SB 202), effective January 1, 2011.

§16061.7. Trustee's duty to serve notification of changes; Contents; Damages

(a) A trustee shall serve a notification by the trustee as described in this section in the following events:

(1) When a revocable trust or any portion thereof becomes irrevocable because of the death of one or more of the settlors of the trust, or because, by the express terms of the trust, the trust becomes irrevocable within one year of the death of a settlor because of a contingency related to the death of one or more of the settlors of the trust.

(2) Whenever there is a change of trustee of an irrevocable trust.

(3) Whenever a power of appointment retained by a settlor is effective or lapses upon death of the settlor with respect to an inter vivos trust which was, or was purported to be, irrevocable upon its creation. This paragraph shall not apply to a charitable remainder trust. For purposes of this paragraph, "charitable remainder trust" means a charitable remainder annuity trust or charitable remainder unitrust as defined in Section 664(d) of the Internal Revenue Code.

(4) The duty to serve the notification by the trustee pursuant to this subdivision is the duty of the continuing or successor trustee, and any one cotrustee may serve the notification.

(b) The notification by the trustee required by subdivision (a) shall be served on each of the following:

(1) Each beneficiary of the irrevocable trust or irrevocable portion of the trust, subject to the limitations of Section 15804.

(2) Each heir of the deceased settlor, if the event that requires notification is the death of a settlor or irrevocability within one year of the death of the settlor of the trust by the express terms of the trust because of a contingency related to the death of a settlor.

(3) If the trust is a charitable trust subject to the supervision of the Attorney General, to the Attorney General.

(c) A trustee shall, for purposes of this section, rely upon any final judicial determination of heirship, known to the trustee, but the trustee shall have discretion to make a good faith determination by any reasonable means of the heirs of a deceased settlor in the absence of a final judicial determination of heirship known to the trustee.

(d) The trustee need not provide a copy of the notification by trustee to any beneficiary or heir (1) known to the trustee but who cannot be located by the trustee after reasonable diligence or (2) unknown to the trustee.

(e) The notification by trustee shall be served by any of the methods described in Section 1215 to the last known address.

(f) The notification by trustee shall be served not later than 60 days following the occurrence of the event requiring service of the notification by trustee, or 60 days after the trustee became aware of the existence of a person entitled to receive notification by trustee, if that person was not known to the trustee on the occurrence of the event requiring service of the notification. If there is a vacancy in the office of the trustee on the date of the occurrence of the event requiring service of the notification by trustee, or if that event causes a vacancy, then the 60-day period for service of the notification by trustee commences on the date the new trustee commences to serve as trustee.

(g) The notification by trustee shall contain the following information:

(1) The identity of the settlor or settlors of the trust and the date of execution of the trust instrument.

(2) The name, address, and telephone number of each trustee of the trust.

(3) The address of the physical location where the principal place of administration of the trust is located, pursuant to Section 17002.

(4) Any additional information that may be expressly required by the terms of the trust instrument.

(5) A notification that the recipient is entitled, upon reasonable request to the trustee, to receive from the trustee a true and complete copy of the terms of the trust.

(h) If the notification by the trustee is served because a revocable trust or any portion of it has become irrevocable because of the death of one or more settlors of the trust, or because, by the express terms of the trust, the trust becomes irrevocable within one year of the death of a settlor because of a contingency related to the death of one or more of the settlors of the trust, the notification by the trustee shall also include a warning, set out in a separate paragraph in not less than 10-point boldface type, or a reasonable equivalent thereof, that states as follows:

"You may not bring an action to contest the trust more than 120 days from the date this notification by the trustee is served upon you or 60 days from the date on which a copy of the terms of the trust is delivered to you during that 120-day period, whichever is later."

(i) Any waiver by a settlor of the requirement of serving the notification by trustee required by this section is against public policy and shall be void.

(j) A trustee may serve a notification by trustee in the form required by this section on any person in addition to those on whom the notification by trustee is required to be served. A trustee is not liable to any person for serving or for not serving the notice on any person in addition to those on whom the notice is required to be served. A trustee is not required to serve a notification by trustee if the event that otherwise requires service of the notification by trustee occurs before January 1, 1998. **Leg.H.** Added Stats 1997 ch 724 §23 (AB 1172). Amended Stats 1998 ch 682 §10 (AB 2069); Stats 2000 ch 34 §4 (AB 460), ch 592 §1 (AB 1628); Stats 2010 ch 621 §5 (SB 202), effective January 1, 2011; Stats 2017 ch 319 §87 (AB 976), effective January 1, 2018.

§16061.8. Time for contesting trust

A person upon whom the notification by the trustee is served pursuant to paragraph (1) of subdivision (a) of Section 16061.7, whether the notice is served on the person within or after the time period set forth in subdivision (f) of Section 16061.7, shall not bring an action to contest the trust more than 120 days from the date the notification by the trustee is served upon the person, or 60 days from the date on which a copy of the terms of the trust is delivered pursuant to Section 1215 to the person during that 120-day period, whichever is later. **Leg.H.** Added Stats 1997 ch 724 §24 (AB 1172). Amended Stats 2000 ch 34 §5 (AB 460), ch 592 §2 (AB 1628); Stats 2010 ch 621 §6 (SB 202), effective January 1, 2011; Stats 2017 ch 319 §88 (AB 976), effective January 1, 2018; Stats 2022 ch 30 §1 (AB 1745), effective January 1, 2023.

§16061.9. Liability of trustee

(a) A trustee who fails to serve the notification by trustee as required by Section 16061.7 on a beneficiary shall be responsible for all damages, attorney's fees, and costs caused by the failure unless the trustee makes a reasonably diligent effort to comply with that section.

(b) A trustee who fails to serve the notification by trustee as required by Section 16061.7 on an heir who is not a beneficiary and whose identity is known to the trustee shall be responsible for all damages caused to the heir by the failure unless the trustee shows that the trustee made a reasonably diligent effort to comply with that section. For purposes of this subdivision, "reasonably diligent effort" means that the trustee has delivered notice pursuant to Section 1215 to the heir at the heir's last address actually known to the trustee.

(c) A trustee, in exercising discretion with respect to the timing and nature of distributions of trust assets, may consider the fact that the period in which a beneficiary or heir could bring an action to contest the trust has not expired. **Leg.H.** Added Stats 2000 ch 34 §6 (AB 460). Amended Stats 2017 ch 319 §89 (AB 976), effective January 1, 2018.

§16062. Duty to account to beneficiaries

(a) Except as otherwise provided in this section and in Section 16064, the trustee shall account at least annually, at the termination of the trust, and upon a change of trustee, to each beneficiary to whom income or principal is required or authorized in the trustee's discretion to be currently distributed.

(b) A trustee of a living trust created by an instrument executed before July 1, 1987, is not subject to the duty to account provided by subdivision (a).

(c) A trustee of a trust created by a will executed before July 1, 1987, is not subject to the duty to account provided by subdivision (a), except that if the trust is removed from continuing court jurisdiction pursuant to Article 2 (commencing with Section 17350) of Chapter 4 of Part 5, the duty to account provided by subdivision (a) applies to the trustee.

(d) Except as provided in Section 16064, the duty of a trustee to account pursuant to former Section 1120.1a of the Probate Code (as repealed by Chapter 820 of the Statutes of 1986), under a trust created by a will executed before July 1, 1977, which has been removed from continuing court jurisdiction pursuant to former Section 1120.1a, continues to apply after July 1, 1987. The duty to account under former Section 1120.1a may be satisfied by furnishing an account that satisfies the requirements of Section 16063.

(e) Any limitation or waiver in a trust instrument of the obligation to account is against public policy and shall be void as to any sole trustee who is either of the following:

(1) A disqualified person as defined in former Section 21350.5 (as repealed by Chapter 620 of the Statutes of 2010).

(2) Described in subdivision (a) of Section 21380, but not described in Section 21382. **Leg.H.** Enacted Stats 1990 ch 79 §14 (AB 759), operative July 1, 1991. Amended Stats 1993 ch 293 §6.5 (AB 21); Stats 1998 ch 682 §11 (AB 2069); Stats 2001 ch 159 §165.5 (SB 662); Stats 2010 ch 620 §4 (SB 105), effective January 1, 2011; Stats 2011 ch 296 §244 (AB 1023), effective January 1, 2012; Stats 2016 ch 86 §250 (SB 1171), effective January 1, 2017.

Prior Law: Former Prob C §16062, similar to the present section, was added Stats 1986 ch 820 §40, operative July 1, 1987, amended Stats 1987 ch 128 §13, effective July 6, 1987, operative July 1, 1987, and repealed Stats 1990 ch 79 §13, operative July 1, 1991.

§16063. Contents of account; Presentation

(a) An account furnished pursuant to Section 16062 shall contain the following information:

(1) A statement of receipts and disbursements of principal and income that have occurred during the last complete fiscal year of the trust or since the last account.

(2) A statement of the assets and liabilities of the trust as of the end of the last complete fiscal year of the trust or as of the end of the period covered by the account.

(3) The trustee's compensation for the last complete fiscal year of the trust or since the last account.

(4) The agents hired by the trustee, their relationship to the trustee, if any, and their compensation, for the last complete fiscal year of the trust or since the last account.

(5) A statement that the recipient of the account may petition the court pursuant to Section 17200 to obtain a court review of the account and of the acts of the trustee.

(6) A statement that claims against the trustee for breach of trust may not be made after the expiration of three years from the date the beneficiary receives an account or report disclosing facts giving rise to the claim.

(b) All accounts filed to be approved by a court shall be presented in the manner provided in Chapter 4 (commencing with Section 1060) of Part 1 of Division 3. **Leg.H.** Added Stats 1997 ch 724 §26 (AB 1172), effective January 1, 1998.

2015 Note: Stats 2015 ch 629 (AB 610) §1 purported to repeal former Fam C §4007.5 effective October 8, 2015; however, the section already was repealed by its own terms on July 1, 2015.

Former Sections: Former Fam C §4007.5, similar to the present section, was added Stats 2010 ch 495 §1, effective January 1, 2011, and repealed July 1, 2015, by its own terms.

Prior Law: Former Prob C §16063, similar to the present section, was enacted Stats 1990 ch 79 §14, operative July 1, 1991, amended Stats 1996 ch 862 §38, operative July 1, 1997, and repealed Stats 1997 ch 724 §25.

Former Prob C §16063, similar to the present section, was added Stats 1986 ch 820 §40, operative July 1, 1987, amended Stats 1987 ch 128 §14, effective July 6, 1987, operative July 1, 1987, and repealed Stats 1990 ch 79 §13, operative July 1, 1991.

§16064. Exceptions to duty to account to beneficiary

The trustee is not required to account to a beneficiary as described in subdivision (a) of Section 16062, in any of the following circumstances:

(a) To the extent the trust instrument waives the account, except that no waiver described in subdivision (e) of Section 16062 shall be valid or enforceable. Regardless of a waiver of accounting in the trust instrument, upon a showing that it is reasonably likely that a material breach of the trust has occurred, the court may compel the trustee to account.

(b) As to a beneficiary who has waived in writing the right to an account. A waiver of rights under this subdivision may be withdrawn in writing at any time as to accounts for transactions occurring after the date of the written withdrawal. Regardless of a waiver of accounting by a beneficiary, upon a showing that is reasonably likely that a material breach of the trust has occurred, the court may compel the trustee to account.

(c) In any of the circumstances set forth in Section 16069. **Leg.H.** Enacted Stats 1990 ch 79 §14 (AB 759), operative July 1, 1991. Amended Stats 1992 ch 871 §18 (AB 2975); Stats 1993 ch 293 §6.7 (AB 21); Stats 2010 ch 621 §7 (SB 202), effective January 1, 2011.

Prior Law: Former Prob C §16064, similar to the present section, was added Stats 1986 ch 820 §40, operative July 1, 1987, and repealed Stats 1990 ch 79 §13, operative July 1, 1991.

§16068. Waivers as against public policy

Any waiver by a settlor of the obligation of the trustee of either of the following is against public policy and shall be void:

(a) To provide the terms of the trust to the beneficiary as required by Sections 16060.7 and 16061.5.

(b) To provide requested information to the beneficiary as required by Section 16061. **Leg.H.** Added Stats 2010 ch 621 §8 (SB 202), effective January 1, 2011.

§16069. Exceptions to duty to account, provide terms of the trust or requested information

(a) The trustee is not required to account to the beneficiary, provide the terms of the trust to a beneficiary, or provide requested information to the beneficiary pursuant to Section 16061, in any of the following circumstances:

(1) In the case of a beneficiary of a revocable trust, as provided in subdivision (a) of Section 15800, for the period when the trust may be revoked.

(2) If the beneficiary and the trustee are the same person.

(b) Notwithstanding subdivision (a), in the case of a revocable trust, if no person holding the power to revoke the trust, in whole or in part, is competent, the trustee's duties to account shall be owed to those beneficiaries specified in paragraph (2) of subdivision (b) of Section 15800. **Leg.H.** Added Stats 2010 ch 621 §9 (SB 202), effective January 1, 2011. Amended Stats 2021 ch 749 §2 (AB 1079), effective January 1, 2022.

ARTICLE 4
Duties With Regard to Discretionary Powers

Discretionary powers to be exercised reasonably. §16080.
Standard for exercise of "absolute," "sole," or "uncontrolled" powers. §16081.
Limitations on power to appoint or distribute income or principal. §16082.

§16080. Discretionary powers to be exercised reasonably

Except as provided in Section 16081, a discretionary power conferred upon a trustee is not left to the trustee's arbitrary discretion, but shall be exercised reasonably. **Leg.H.** Enacted Stats 1990 ch 79 §14 (AB 759), operative July 1, 1991.

Prior Law: Former Prob C §16080, similar to the present section, was added Stats 1986 ch 820 §40, operative July 1, 1987, and repealed Stats 1990 ch 79 §13, operative July 1, 1991.

§16081. Standard for exercise of "absolute," "sole," or "uncontrolled" powers

(a) Subject to the additional requirements of subdivisions (b), (c), and (d), if a trust instrument confers "absolute," "sole," or "uncontrolled" discretion on a trustee, the trustee shall act in accordance with fiduciary principles and shall not act in bad faith or in disregard of the purposes of the trust.

(b) Notwithstanding the use of terms like "absolute," "sole," or "uncontrolled" by a settlor or a testator, a person who is a beneficiary of a trust that permits the person, either individually or as trustee or cotrustee, to make discretionary distributions of income or principal to or for the benefit of himself or herself pursuant to a standard, shall exercise that power reasonably and in accordance with the standard.

(c) Unless a settlor or a testator clearly indicates that a broader power is intended by express reference to this subdivision, a person who is a beneficiary of a trust that permits the person, as trustee or cotrustee, to make discretionary distributions of income or principal to or for the benefit of himself or herself may exercise that power in his or her favor only for his or her health, education, support, or maintenance within the meaning of Sections 2041 and 2514 of the Internal Revenue Code. Notwithstanding the foregoing and the provisions of Section 15620, if a power to make discretionary distributions of income or principal is conferred upon two or more trustees, the power may be exercised by any trustee who is not a current permissible beneficiary of that power; and provided further that if there is no trustee who is not a current permissible beneficiary of that power, any party in interest may apply to a court of competent jurisdiction to appoint a trustee who is not a current permissible beneficiary of that power, and the power may be exercised by the trustee appointed by the court.

(d) Subdivision (c) does not apply to either of the following:

(1) Any power held by the settlor of a revocable or amendable trust.

(2) Any power held by a settlor's spouse or a testator's spouse who is the trustee of a trust for which a marital deduction, as defined in Section 21520, has been allowed.

(e) Subdivision (c) applies to any of the following:

(1) Any trust executed on or after January 1, 1997.

(2) Any testamentary trust created under a will executed on or after January 1, 1997.

(3) Any irrevocable trust created under a document executed before January 1, 1997, or any revocable trust executed before that date if the settlor was incapacitated as of that date, unless all parties in interest elect affirmatively not to be subject to the application of subdivision (c) through a written instrument delivered to the trustee. That election shall be made on or before the latest of January 1, 1998, three years after the date on which the trust became irrevocable, or, in the case of a revocable trust where the settlor was incapacitated, three years after the date on which the settlor became incapacitated.

(f) Notwithstanding the foregoing, the provisions of subdivision (c) neither create a new cause of action nor impair an existing cause of action that, in either case, relates to any power limited by subdivision (c) that was exercised before January 1, 1997.

(g) For purposes of this section, the term "party in interest" means any of the following persons:

(1) If the trust is revocable and the settlor is incapacitated, the settlor's legal representative under applicable law, or the settlor's attorney-in-fact under a durable power of attorney that is sufficient to grant the authority required under subdivision (c) or (e), as applicable.

(2) If the trust is irrevocable, each trustee, each beneficiary then entitled or authorized to receive income distributions from the trust, or each remainder beneficiary who would be entitled to receive notice of a trust proceeding under Section 15804. Any beneficiary who lacks legal capacity may be represented by the beneficiary's legal representative, attorney-in-fact under a durable power of attorney that is sufficient to grant the authority required under subdivision (c) or (e), as applicable, or in the absence of a legal representative or attorney-in-fact, a guardian ad litem appointed for that purpose. **Leg.H.** Enacted Stats 1990 ch 79 §14 (AB 759), operative July 1, 1991. Amended Stats 1996 ch 410 §1 (SB 1907), effective January 1, 1997.

Prior Law: Former Prob C §16081, similar to the present section, was added Stats 1986 ch 820 §40, operative July 1, 1987, and repealed Stats 1990 ch 79 §13, operative July 1, 1991.

§16082. Limitations on power to appoint or distribute income or principal

Except as otherwise specifically provided in the trust instrument, a person who holds a power to appoint or distribute income or principal to or for the benefit of others, either as an individual or as trustee, may not use the power to discharge the legal obligations of the person holding the power. **Leg.H.** Enacted Stats 1990 ch 79 §14 (AB 759), operative July 1, 1991.

Prior Law: Former Prob C §16082, similar to the present section, was added Stats 1987 ch 128 §15, effective July 6, 1987, operative July 1, 1987, and repealed Stats 1990 ch 79 §13, operative July 1, 1991.

ARTICLE 5
Duties of Trustees of Private Foundations, Charitable Trusts, and Split-Interest Trusts

Definitions. §16100.
Distribution under charitable trust or private foundation. §16101.
Restrictions on trustees under charitable trust, private foundation, or split-interest trust. §16102.
Exceptions applicable to split-interest trusts. §16103.
Incorporation in trust instruments. §16104.
Proceedings. §16105.
Assets subject to a charitable trust [Renumbered]. § 16106.

§16100. Definitions

As used in this article, the following definitions shall control:

(a) "Charitable trust" means a charitable trust as described in Section 4947(a)(1) of the Internal Revenue Code.

(b) "Private foundation" means a private foundation as defined in Section 509 of the Internal Revenue Code.

(c) "Split-interest trust" means a split-interest trust as described in Section 4947(a)(2) of the Internal Revenue Code. **Leg.H.** Enacted Stats 1990 ch 79 §14 (AB 759), operative July 1, 1991.

Prior Law: Former Prob C §16100, similar to the present section, was added Stats 1986 ch 820 §40, operative July 1, 1987, and repealed Stats 1990 ch 79 §13, operative July 1, 1991.

§16101. Distribution under charitable trust or private foundation

During any period when a trust is deemed to be a charitable trust or a private foundation, the trustee shall distribute its income for each taxable year (and principal if necessary) at a time and in a manner that will not subject the property of the trust to tax under Section 4942 of the Internal Revenue Code. **Leg.H.** Enacted Stats 1990 ch 79 §14 (AB 759), operative July 1, 1991.

Prior Law: Former Prob C §16101, similar to the present section, was added Stats 1986 ch 820 §40, operative July 1, 1987, and repealed Stats 1990 ch 79 §13, operative July 1, 1991.

§16102. Restrictions on trustees under charitable trust, private foundation, or split-interest trust

During any period when a trust is deemed to be a charitable trust, a private foundation, or a split-interest trust, the trustee shall not do any of the following:

(a) Engage in any act of self-dealing as defined in Section 4941(d) of the Internal Revenue Code.

(b) Retain any excess business holdings as defined in Section 4943(c) of the Internal Revenue Code.

(c) Make any investments in such manner as to subject the property of the trust to tax under Section 4944 of the Internal Revenue Code.

(d) Make any taxable expenditure as defined in Section 4945(d) of the Internal Revenue Code. **Leg.H.** Enacted Stats 1990 ch 79 §14 (AB 759), operative July 1, 1991.

Prior Law: Former Prob C §16102, similar to the present section, was added Stats 1986 ch 820 §40, operative July 1, 1987, and repealed Stats 1990 ch 79 §13, operative July 1, 1991.

§16103. Exceptions applicable to split-interest trusts

With respect to split-interest trusts:

(a) Subdivisions (b) and (c) of Section 16102 do not apply to any trust described in Section 4947(b)(3) of the Internal Revenue Code.

(b) Section 16102 does not apply with respect to any of the following:

(1) Any amounts payable under the terms of such trust to income beneficiaries, unless a deduction was allowed under Section 170(f)(2)(B), 2055(e)(2)(B), or 2522(c)(2)(B) of the Internal Revenue Code.

(2) Any amounts in trust other than amounts for which a deduction was allowed under Section 170, 545(b)(2), 556(b)(2), 642(c), 2055, 2106(a)(2), or 2522 of the Internal Revenue Code, if the amounts are segregated, as that term is defined in Section 4947(a)(3) of the Internal Revenue Code, from amounts for which no deduction was allowable.

(3) Any amounts irrevocably transferred in trust before May 27, 1969. **Leg.H.** Enacted Stats 1990 ch 79 §14 (AB 759), operative July 1, 1991.

Prior Law: Former Prob C §16103, similar to the present section, was added Stats 1986 ch 820 §40, operative July 1, 1987, and repealed Stats 1990 ch 79 §13, operative July 1, 1991.

§16104. Incorporation in trust instruments

The provisions of Sections 16101, 16102, and 16103 shall be deemed to be contained in the instrument creating every trust to which this article applies. Any provision of the instrument inconsistent with or contrary to this article is without effect. **Leg.H.** Enacted Stats 1990 ch 79 §14 (AB 759), operative July 1, 1991.

Prior Law: Former Prob C §16104, similar to the present section, was added Stats 1986 ch 820 §40, operative July 1, 1987, and repealed Stats 1990 ch 79 §13, operative July 1, 1991.

§16105. Proceedings

(a) A proceeding contemplated by Section 101(*l*)(3) of the federal Tax Reform Act of 1969 (Public Law 91-172) may be commenced pursuant to Section 17200 by the organization involved. All specifically named beneficiaries of the organization and the Attorney General shall be parties to the proceedings. Notwithstanding Section 17000, this provision is not exclusive and does not limit any jurisdiction that otherwise exists.

(b) If an instrument creating a trust affected by this section has been recorded, a notice of pendency of judicial proceedings under this section shall be recorded in a similar manner within 10 days from the commencement of the proceedings. A duly certified copy of any final judgment or decree in the proceedings shall be similarly recorded. **Leg.H.** Enacted Stats 1990 ch 79 §14 (AB 759), operative July 1, 1991.

Prior Law: Former Prob C §16105, similar to the present section, was added Stats 1986 ch 820 §40, operative July 1, 1987, and repealed Stats 1990 ch 79 §13, operative July 1, 1991.

§ 16106. Assets subject to a charitable trust [Renumbered]

Leg.H. Added Stats 2021 ch 708 §1 (AB 900), effective January 1, 2022. Amended Stats 2022 ch 28 §128 (SB 1380), effective January 1, 2023. Amended and renumbered to Cal Prob Code §16110 by Stats 2023 ch 478 §60 (AB 1756), effective January 1, 2024.

ARTICLE 6
Notice to the Attorney General of Disposal of Charitable Assets

Assets subject to a charitable trust. § 16110.

§ 16110. Assets subject to a charitable trust

(a) On and after January 1, 2025, or upon the regulations provided for in subdivision (b) taking effect, whichever occurs first, a trustee holding assets subject to a charitable trust shall give written notice to the Attorney General at least 20 days before the trustee sells, leases, conveys, exchanges, transfers, or otherwise disposes of all or substantially all of the charitable assets.

(b) On or after January 1, 2022, the Attorney General shall establish rules and regulations necessary to administer this section. **Leg.H.** Added Stats 2021 ch 708 §1 (AB 900), effective January 1, 2022. Amended Stats 2022 ch 28 §128 (SB 1380), effective January 1, 2023. Amended and renumbered from Cal Prob Code §16106 by Stats 2023 ch 478 §60 (AB 1756), effective January 1, 2024.

CHAPTER 2
POWERS OF TRUSTEES

Article 1. General Provisions.
Article 2. Specific Powers of Trustees.

ARTICLE 1
General Provisions

General powers of trustee. §16200.
Power of court to relieve trustee from restrictions on powers. §16201.
Exercise of powers subject to trustee's duties. §16202.
Application of rules governing trustees' powers. §16203.

§16200. General powers of trustee

A trustee has the following powers without the need to obtain court authorization:

(a) The powers conferred by the trust instrument.

(b) Except as limited in the trust instrument, the powers conferred by statute.

(c) Except as limited in the trust instrument, the power to perform any act that a trustee would perform for the purposes of the trust under the standard of care provided in Section 16040 or 16047. **Leg.H.** Enacted Stats 1990 ch 79 §14 (AB 759), operative July 1, 1991. Amended Stats 1995 ch 63 §7 (SB 222), effective January 1, 1996.

Prior Law: Former Prob C §16200, similar to the present section, was added Stats 1986 ch 820 §40, operative July 1, 1987, and repealed Stats 1990 ch 79 §13, operative July 1, 1991.

§16201. Power of court to relieve trustee from restrictions on powers

This chapter does not affect the power of a court to relieve a trustee from restrictions on the exercise of powers under the trust instrument. **Leg.H.** Enacted Stats 1990 ch 79 §14 (AB 759), operative July 1, 1991.

Prior Law: Former Prob C §16201, similar to the present section, was added Stats 1986 ch 820 §40, operative July 1, 1987, and repealed Stats 1990 ch 79 §13, operative July 1, 1991.

§16202. Exercise of powers subject to trustee's duties

The grant of a power to a trustee, whether by the trust instrument, by statute, or by the court, does not in itself require or permit the exercise of the power. The exercise of a power by a trustee is subject to the trustee's fiduciary duties. **Leg.H.** Enacted Stats 1990 ch 79 §14 (AB 759), operative July 1, 1991.

Prior Law: Former Prob C §16202, defining "affiliated", was added Stats 1986 ch 820 §40, operative July 1, 1987, and repealed Stats 1990 ch 79 §13, operative July 1, 1991.

§16203. Application of rules governing trustees' powers

An instrument that incorporates the powers provided in former Section 1120.2 (repealed by Chapter 820 of the Statutes of 1986) shall be deemed to refer to the powers provided in Article 2 (commencing with Section 16220). For this purpose, the trustee's powers under former Section 1120.2 are not diminished and the trustee is not required to obtain court approval for exercise of a power for which court approval was not required by former law. **Leg.H.** Enacted Stats 1990 ch 79 §14 (AB 759), operative July 1, 1991.

Prior Law: Former Prob C §16203, similar to the present section, was added Stats 1986 ch 820 §40, operative July 1, 1987, and repealed Stats 1990 ch 79 §13, operative July 1, 1991.

ARTICLE 2
Specific Powers of Trustees

Collecting and holding property. §16220.
Receiving additions to trust. §16221.
Participation in business; Change in form of business. §16222.
Investments in obligations of United States government. §16224.
Deposits. §16225.
Acquisition and disposition of property. §16226.
Management of property. §16227.
Encumbrances. §16228.
Repairs and alterations of property. §16229.
Development of land. §16230.
Leases. §16231.
Mineral leases. §16232.
Options. §16233.
Voting rights with respect to corporate shares, memberships, or property. §16234.
Payment of calls and assessments. §16235.
Stock subscriptions and conversions. §16236.
Consent to change in form of business; voting trusts. §16237.
Holding securities in name of nominee. §16238.
Deposit of securities in securities depository. §16239.
Insurance. §16240.
Borrowing money. §16241.
Payment and settlement of claims. §16242.
Payment of taxes, trustee's compensation, and other expenses. §16243.
Loans to beneficiary. §16244.
Distribution to beneficiaries under legal disability. §16245.
Nature and value of distributions. §16246.
Hiring persons. §16247.
Execution and delivery of instruments. §16248.
Actions and proceedings. §16249.

§16220. Collecting and holding property

The trustee has the power to collect, hold, and retain trust property received from a settlor or any other person until, in the judgment of the trustee, disposition of the property should be made. The property may be retained even though it includes property in which the trustee is personally interested. **Leg.H.** Enacted Stats 1990 ch 79 §14 (AB 759), operative July 1, 1991.

Prior Law: Former Prob C §16220, similar to the present section, was added Stats 1986 ch 820 §40, operative July 1, 1987, and repealed Stats 1990 ch 79 §13, operative July 1, 1991.

§16221. Receiving additions to trust

The trustee has the power to accept additions to the property of the trust from a settlor or any other person. **Leg.H.** Enacted Stats 1990 ch 79 §14 (AB 759), operative July 1, 1991.

Prior Law: Former Prob C §16221, similar to the present section, was added Stats 1986 ch 820 §40, operative July 1, 1987, and repealed Stats 1990 ch 79 §13, operative July 1, 1991.

§16222. Participation in business; Change in form of business

(a) Subject to subdivision (b), the trustee has the power to continue or participate in the operation of any business or other enterprise that is part of the trust property and may effect incorporation, dissolution, or other change in the form of the organization of the business or enterprise.

(b) Except as provided in subdivision (c), the trustee may continue the operation of a business or other enterprise only as authorized by the trust instrument or by the court. For the purpose of this subdivision, the lease of four or fewer residential units is not considered to be the operation of a business or other enterprise.

(c) The trustee may continue the operation of a business or other enterprise for a reasonable time pending a court hearing on the matter or pending a sale of the business or other enterprise.

(d) The limitation provided in subdivision (b) does not affect any power to continue or participate in the operation of a business or other enterprise that the trustee has under a trust created by an instrument executed before July 1, 1987. **Leg.H.** Enacted Stats 1990 ch 79 §14 (AB 759), operative July 1, 1991.

Prior Law: Former Prob C §16222, similar to the present section, was added Stats 1986 ch 820 §40, operative July 1, 1987, amended Stats 1987 ch 128 §16, effective July 6, 1987, operative July 1, 1987, and repealed Stats 1990 ch 79 §13, operative July 1, 1991.

§16223. [Section repealed 1995]

Leg.H. Enacted Stats 1990 ch 79 §14 (AB 759), operative July 1, 1991. Repealed Stats 1995 ch 63 §8 (SB 222). See Prob C §16047.

Prior Law: Former Prob C §16223, similar to present Prob C §16047, was added Stats 1986 ch 820 §40, operative July 1, 1987, and repealed Stats 1990 ch 79 §13, operative July 1, 1991.

§16224. Investments in obligations of United States government

(a) In the absence of an express provision to the contrary in a trust instrument, where the instrument directs or permits investment in obligations of the United States government, the trustee has the power to invest in those obligations directly or in the form of an interest in a money market mutual fund registered under the Investment Company Act of 1940 (15 U.S.C. Sec. 80a-1 et seq.) or an investment vehicle authorized for the collective investment of trust funds pursuant to Section 9.18 of Part 9 of Title 12 of the Code of Federal Regulations, the portfolios of which are limited to United States government obligations maturing not later than five years from the date of investment or reinvestment and to repurchase agreements fully collateralized by United States government obligations.

(b) This section applies only to trusts created on or after January 1, 1985. **Leg.H.** Enacted Stats 1990 ch 79 §14 (AB 759), operative July 1, 1991.

Prior Law: Former Prob C §16224, similar to the present section, was added Stats 1986 ch 820 §40, operative July 1, 1987, and repealed Stats 1990 ch 79 §13, operative July 1, 1991.

§16225. Deposits

(a) The trustee has the power to deposit trust funds at reasonable interest in any of the following accounts:

(1) An insured account in a financial institution.

(2) To the extent that the account is collateralized, an account in a bank, an account in an insured savings and loan association, or an account in an insured credit union.

(b) A trustee may deposit trust funds pursuant to subdivision (a) in a financial institution operated by, or that is an affiliate of, the trustee. For the purpose of this subdivision, "affiliate" means a corporation that directly or indirectly through one or more intermediaries controls, is controlled by, or is under common control with another domestic or foreign corporation.

(c) This section does not limit the power of a trustee in a proper case to deposit trust funds in an account described in subdivision (a) that is subject to notice or other conditions respecting withdrawal prescribed by law or governmental regulation.

(d) The court may authorize the deposit of trust funds in an account described in subdivision (a) in an amount greater than the maximum insured or collateralized amount.

(e) Nothing in this section prevents the trustee from holding an amount of trust property reasonably necessary for the orderly administration of the trust in the form of cash or in a checking account without interest. **Leg.H.** Enacted Stats 1990 ch 79 §14 (AB 759), operative July 1, 1991.

Prior Law: Former Prob C §16225, similar to the present section, was added Stats 1986 ch 820 §40, operative July 1, 1987, amended Stats 1988 ch 1199 §105.5, operative July 1, 1989, and repealed Stats 1990 ch 79 §13, operative July 1, 1991.

§16226. Acquisition and disposition of property

The trustee has the power to acquire or dispose of property, for cash or on credit, at public or private sale, or by exchange. **Leg.H.** Enacted Stats 1990 ch 79 §14 (AB 759), operative July 1, 1991.

Prior Law: Former Prob C §16226, similar to the present section, was added Stats 1986 ch 820 §40, operative July 1, 1987, and repealed Stats 1990 ch 79 §13, operative July 1, 1991.

§16227. Management of property

The trustee has the power to manage, control, divide, develop, improve, exchange, partition, change the character of, or abandon trust property or any interest therein. **Leg.H.** Enacted Stats 1990 ch 79 §14 (AB 759), operative July 1, 1991.

Prior Law: Former Prob C §16227, similar to the present section, was added Stats 1986 ch 820 §40, operative July 1, 1987, and repealed Stats 1990 ch 79 §13, operative July 1, 1991.

§16228. Encumbrances

The trustee has the power to encumber, mortgage, or pledge trust property for a term within or extending beyond the term of the trust in connection with the exercise of any power vested in the trustee. **Leg.H.** Enacted Stats 1990 ch 79 §14 (AB 759), operative July 1, 1991.

Prior Law: Former Prob C §16228, similar to the present section, was added Stats 1986 ch 820 §40, operative July 1, 1987, and repealed Stats 1990 ch 79 §13, operative July 1, 1991.

§16229. Repairs and alterations of property

The trustee has the power to do any of the following:

(a) Make ordinary or extraordinary repairs, alterations, or improvements in buildings or other trust property.

(b) Demolish any improvements.

(c) Raze existing or erect new party walls or buildings. **Leg.H.** Enacted Stats 1990 ch 79 §14 (AB 759), operative July 1, 1991.

Prior Law: Former Prob C §16229, similar to the present section, was added Stats 1986 ch 820 §40, operative July 1, 1987, and repealed Stats 1990 ch 79 §13, operative July 1, 1991.

§16230. Development of land

The trustee has the power to do any of the following:

(a) Subdivide or develop land.

(b) Dedicate land to public use.

(c) Make or obtain the vacation of plats and adjust boundaries.

(d) Adjust differences in valuation on exchange or partition by giving or receiving consideration.

(e) Dedicate easements to public use without consideration. **Leg.H.** Enacted Stats 1990 ch 79 §14 (AB 759), operative July 1, 1991.

Prior Law: Former Prob C §16230, similar to the present section, was added Stats 1986 ch 820 §40, operative July 1, 1987, and repealed Stats 1990 ch 79 §13, operative July 1, 1991.

§16231. Leases

The trustee has the power to enter into a lease for any purpose as lessor or lessee with or without the option to purchase or renew and for a term within or extending beyond the term of the trust. **Leg.H.** Enacted Stats 1990 ch 79 §14 (AB 759), operative July 1, 1991.

Prior Law: Former Prob C §16231, similar to the present section, was added Stats 1986 ch 820 §40, operative July 1, 1987, and repealed Stats 1990 ch 79 §13, operative July 1, 1991.

§16232. Mineral leases

The trustee has the power to enter into a lease or arrangement for exploration and removal of gas, oil, or other minerals or geothermal energy, and to enter into a community oil lease or a pooling or unitization agreement, and for a term within or extending beyond the term of the trust. **Leg.H.** Enacted Stats 1990 ch 79 §14 (AB 759), operative July 1, 1991.

Prior Law: Former Prob C §16232, similar to the present section, was added Stats 1986 ch 820 §40, operative July 1, 1987, and repealed Stats 1990 ch 79 §13, operative July 1, 1991.

§16233. Options

The trustee has the power to grant an option involving disposition of trust property or to take an option for the acquisition of any property, and an option may be granted or taken that is exercisable beyond the term of the trust. **Leg.H.** Enacted Stats 1990 ch 79 §14 (AB 759), operative July 1, 1991.

Prior Law: Former Prob C §16233, similar to the present section, was added Stats 1986 ch 820 §40, operative July 1, 1987, and repealed Stats 1990 ch 79 §13, operative July 1, 1991.

§16234. Voting rights with respect to corporate shares, memberships, or property

With respect to any shares of stock of a domestic or foreign corporation, any membership in a nonprofit corporation, or any other property, a trustee has the power to do any of the following:

(a) Vote in person, and give proxies to exercise, any voting rights with respect to the shares, memberships, or property.

(b) Waive notice of a meeting or give consent to the holding of a meeting.

(c) Authorize, ratify, approve, or confirm any action that could be taken by shareholders, members, or property owners. **Leg.H.** Enacted Stats 1990 ch 79 §14 (AB 759), operative July 1, 1991.

Prior Law: Former Prob C §16234, similar to the present section, was added Stats 1986 ch 820 §40, operative July 1, 1987, and repealed Stats 1990 ch 79 §13, operative July 1, 1991.

§16235. Payment of calls and assessments

The trustee has the power to pay calls, assessments, and any other sums chargeable or accruing against or on account of securities. **Leg.H.** Enacted Stats 1990 ch 79 §14 (AB 759), operative July 1, 1991.

Prior Law: Former Prob C §16235, similar to the present section, was added Stats 1986 ch 820 §40, operative July 1, 1987, and repealed Stats 1990 ch 79 §13, operative July 1, 1991.

§16236. Stock subscriptions and conversions

The trustee has the power to sell or exercise stock subscription or conversion rights. **Leg.H.** Enacted Stats 1990 ch 79 §14 (AB 759), operative July 1, 1991.

Prior Law: Former Prob C §16236, similar to the present section, was added Stats 1986 ch 820 §40, operative July 1, 1987, and repealed Stats 1990 ch 79 §13, operative July 1, 1991.

§16237. Consent to change in form of business; voting trusts

The trustee has the power to consent, directly or through a committee or other agent, to the reorganization, consolidation, merger, dissolution, or liquidation of a corporation or other business enterprise, and to participate in voting trusts, pooling arrangements, and foreclosures, and in connection therewith, to deposit securities with and transfer title and delegate discretion to any protective or other committee as the trustee may deem advisable. **Leg.H.** Enacted Stats 1990 ch 79 §14 (AB 759), operative July 1, 1991.

Prior Law: Former Prob C §16237, similar to the present section, was added Stats 1986 ch 820 §40, operative July 1, 1987, and repealed Stats 1990 ch 79 §13, operative July 1, 1991.

§16238. Holding securities in name of nominee

The trustee has the power to hold a security in the name of a nominee or in other form without disclosure of the trust so that title to the security may pass by delivery. **Leg.H.** Enacted Stats 1990 ch 79 §14 (AB 759), operative July 1, 1991.

Prior Law: Former Prob C §16238, similar to the present section, was added Stats 1986 ch 820 §40, operative July 1, 1987, and repealed Stats 1990 ch 79 §13, operative July 1, 1991.

§16239. Deposit of securities in securities depository

The trustee has the power to deposit securities in a securities depository, as defined in Section 30004 of the Financial Code, which is licensed under Section 30200 of the Financial Code or is exempt from licensing by Section 30005 or 30006 of the Financial Code. The securities may be held by the securities depository in the manner authorized by Section 775 of the Financial Code. **Leg.H.** Enacted Stats 1990 ch 79 §14 (AB 759), operative July 1, 1991.

Prior Law: Former Prob C §16239, similar to the present section, was added Stats 1986 ch 820 §40, operative July 1, 1987, and repealed Stats 1990 ch 79 §13, operative July 1, 1991.

§16240. Insurance

The trustee has the power to insure the property of the trust against damage or loss and to insure the trustee against liability with respect to third persons. **Leg.H.** Enacted Stats 1990 ch 79 §14 (AB 759), operative July 1, 1991.

Prior Law: Former Prob C §16240, similar to the present section, was added Stats 1986 ch 820 §40, operative July 1, 1987, and repealed Stats 1990 ch 79 §13, operative July 1, 1991.

§16241. Borrowing money

The trustee has the power to borrow money for any trust purpose to be repaid from trust property. The lender may include, but is not limited to, a bank holding company, affiliate, or subsidiary of the trustee. **Leg.H.** Enacted Stats 1990 ch 79 §14 (AB 759), operative July 1, 1991.

Prior Law: Former Prob C §16241, similar to the present section, was added Stats 1986 ch 820 §40, operative July 1, 1987, amended Stats 1988 ch 1341 §1, and repealed Stats 1990 ch 79 §13, operative July 1, 1991.

§16242. Payment and settlement of claims

The trustee has the power to do any of the following:

(a) Pay or contest any claim.

(b) Settle a claim by or against the trust by compromise, arbitration, or otherwise.

(c) Release, in whole or in part, any claim belonging to the trust. **Leg.H.** Enacted Stats 1990 ch 79 §14 (AB 759), operative July 1, 1991.

Prior Law: Former Prob C §16242, similar to the present section, was added Stats 1986 ch 820 §40, operative July 1, 1987, and repealed Stats 1990 ch 79 §13, operative July 1, 1991.

§16243. Payment of taxes, trustee's compensation, and other expenses

The trustee has the power to pay taxes, assessments, reasonable compensation of the trustee and of employees and agents of the trust, and other expenses incurred in the collection, care, administration, and protection of the trust. **Leg.H.** Enacted Stats 1990 ch 79 §14 (AB 759), operative July 1, 1991.

Prior Law: Former Prob C §16243, similar to the present section, was added Stats 1986 ch 820 §40, operative July 1, 1987, and repealed Stats 1990 ch 79 §13, operative July 1, 1991.

§16244. Loans to beneficiary

The trustee has the following powers:

(a) To make loans out of trust property to the beneficiary on terms and conditions that the trustee determines are fair and reasonable under the circumstances.

(b) To guarantee loans to the beneficiary by encumbrances on trust property. **Leg.H.** Enacted Stats 1990 ch 79 §14 (AB 759), operative July 1, 1991.

Prior Law: Former Prob C §16244, similar to the present section, was added Stats 1986 ch 820 §40, operative July 1, 1987, and repealed Stats 1990 ch 79 §13, operative July 1, 1991.

§16245. Distribution to beneficiaries under legal disability

The trustee has the power to pay any sum of principal or income distributable to a beneficiary, without regard to whether the beneficiary is under a legal disability, by paying the sum to the beneficiary or by paying the sum to another person for the use or benefit of the beneficiary. Any sum distributable under this section to a custodian under the California Uniform Transfers to Minors Act (Part 9 (commencing with Section 3900)) shall be subject to Section 3906. **Leg.H.** Enacted Stats 1990 ch 79 §14 (AB 759), operative July 1, 1991. Amended Stats 1996 ch 862 §39 (AB 2751), effective January 1, 1997.

Prior Law: Former Prob C §16245, similar to the present section, was added Stats 1986 ch 820 §40, operative July 1, 1987, and repealed Stats 1990 ch 79 §13, operative July 1, 1991.

§16246. Nature and value of distributions

The trustee has the power to effect distribution of property and money in divided or undivided interests and to adjust resulting differences in valuation. A distribution in kind may be made pro rata or non pro rata, and may be made pursuant to any written agreement providing for a non pro rata division of the aggregate value of the community property assets or quasi-community property assets, or both. **Leg.H.** Enacted Stats 1990 ch 79 §14 (AB 759), operative July 1, 1991. Amended Stats 1998 ch 682 §12 (AB 2069), effective January 1, 1999.

Prior Law: Former Prob C §16246, similar to the present section, was added Stats 1986 ch 820 §40, operative July 1, 1987, and repealed Stats 1990 ch 79 §13, operative July 1, 1991.

§16247. Hiring persons

The trustee has the power to hire persons, including accountants, attorneys, auditors, investment advisers, appraisers (including probate referees appointed pursuant to Section 400), or other agents, even if they are associated or affiliated with the trustee, to advise or assist the trustee in the performance of administrative duties. **Leg.H.** Enacted Stats 1990 ch 79 §14 (AB 759), operative July 1, 1991. Amended Stats 1994 ch 806 §38 (AB 3686), effective January 1, 1995.

Prior Law: Former Prob C §16247, similar to the present section, was added Stats 1986 ch 820 §40, operative July 1, 1987, and repealed Stats 1990 ch 79 §13, operative July 1, 1991.

§16248. Execution and delivery of instruments

The trustee has the power to execute and deliver all instruments which are needed to accomplish or facilitate the exercise of the powers vested in the trustee. **Leg.H.** Enacted Stats 1990 ch 79 §14 (AB 759), operative July 1, 1991.

Prior Law: Former Prob C §16248, similar to the present section, was added Stats 1986 ch 820 §40, operative July 1, 1987, and repealed Stats 1990 ch 79 §13, operative July 1, 1991.

§16249. Actions and proceedings

The trustee has the power to prosecute or defend actions, claims, or proceedings for the protection of trust property and of the trustee in the performance of the trustee's duties. **Leg.H.** Enacted Stats 1990 ch 79 §14 (AB 759), operative July 1, 1991. Amended Stats 1992 ch 871 §19 (AB 2975); Stats 2001 ch 49 §5 (SB 669), effective January 1, 2002.

Prior Law: Former Prob C §16249, similar to the present section, was added Stats 1986 ch 820 §40, operative July 1, 1987, and repealed Stats 1990 ch 79 §13, operative July 1, 1991.

§16300. [Section repealed 1999]

Leg.H. Enacted Stats 1990 ch 79 §14 (AB 759), operative July 1, 1991. Repealed Stats 1999 ch 145 §4 (AB 846). See Prob C §16320.

Prior Law: Former Prob C §16300, similar to present Prob C §16320, was added Stats 1986 ch 820 §40, operative July 1, 1987, and repealed Stats 1990 ch 79 §13, operative July 1, 1991.

§16301. [Section repealed 1999]

Leg.H. Enacted Stats 1990 ch 79 §14 (AB 759), operative July 1, 1991. Repealed Stats 1999 ch 145 §4 (AB 846). See Prob C §§16321, 16325.

Prior Law: Former Prob C §16301, similar to present C §§16321, 16325, was added Stats 1986 ch 820 §40, operative July 1, 1987, and repealed Stats 1990 ch 79 §13, operative July 1, 1991.

§16302. [Section repealed 1999]

Leg.H. Enacted Stats 1990 ch 79 §14 (AB 759), operative July 1, 1991. Repealed Stats 1999 ch 145 §4 (AB 846). See Prob C §16335.

Prior Law: Former Prob C §16302, similar to present Prob C §16335, was added Stats 1986 ch 820 §40, operative July 1, 1987, and repealed Stats 1990 ch 79 §13, operative July 1, 1991.

§16303. [Section repealed 1999]

Leg.H. Enacted Stats 1990 ch 79 §14 (AB 759), operative July 1, 1991. Repealed Stats 1999 ch 145 §4 (AB 846). The repealed section related to the meaning of principal and income.

Prior Law: Former Prob C §16303, relating to the meaning of principal and income, was added Stats 1986 ch 820 §40, operative July 1, 1987, amended Stats 1987 ch 128 §17, effective July 6, 1987, operative July 1, 1987, and repealed Stats 1990 ch 79 §13, operative July 1, 1991.

§16304. [Section repealed 1999]

Leg.H. Enacted Stats 1990 ch 79 §14 (AB 759), operative July 1, 1991. Repealed Stats 1999 ch 145 §4 (AB 846). See Prob C §§16340, 16341, 16345–16347.

Prior Law: Former Prob C §16304, similar to present Prob C §§16340, 16341, 16345–16347, was added Stats 1986 ch 820 §40, operative July 1, 1987, amended Stats 1987 ch 923 §100, operative January 1, 1988, Stats 1988 ch 1199 §106, operative July 1, 1989, and repealed Stats 1990 ch 79 §13, operative July 1, 1991.

§16305. [Section repealed 1999]

Leg.H. Enacted Stats 1990 ch 79 §14 (AB 759), operative July 1, 1991. Repealed Stats 1999 ch 145 §4 (AB 846). See Prob C §16340.

Prior Law: Former Prob C §16305, similar to present Prob C §16340, was added Stats 1986 ch 820 §40, operative July 1, 1987, amended Stats 1988 ch 1199 §106.5, operative July 1, 1989, and repealed Stats 1990 ch 79 §13, operative July 1, 1991.

§16306. [Section repealed 1999]

§16307. [Section repealed 1999]
Leg.H. Enacted Stats 1990 ch 79 §14 (AB 759), operative July 1, 1991. Repealed Stats 1999 ch 145 §4 (AB 846). See Prob C §16357.

Prior Law: Former Prob C §16307, similar to present Prob C §16357, was added Stats 1986 ch 820 §40, operative July 1, 1987, and repealed Stats 1990 ch 79 §13, operative July 1, 1991.

§16308. [Section repealed 1999]
Leg.H. Enacted Stats 1990 ch 79 §14 (AB 759), operative July 1, 1991. Repealed Stats 1999 ch 145 §4 (AB 846). See Prob C §§16350, 16352.

Prior Law: Former Prob C §16308, similar to present Prob C §§16350, 16352, was added Stats 1986 ch 820 §40, operative July 1, 1987, and repealed Stats 1990 ch 79 §13, operative July 1, 1991.

§16309. [Section repealed 1999]
Leg.H. Enacted Stats 1990 ch 79 §14 (AB 759), operative July 1, 1991. Repealed Stats 1999 ch 145 §4 (AB 846). See Prob C §§16363, 16364.

Prior Law: Former Prob C §16309, similar to present Prob C §§16363, 16364, was added Stats 1986 ch 820 §40, operative July 1, 1987, and repealed Stats 1990 ch 79 §13, operative July 1, 1991.

§16310. [Section repealed 1999]
Leg.H. Enacted Stats 1990 ch 79 §14 (AB 759), operative July 1, 1991. Repealed Stats 1999 ch 145 §4 (AB 846). See Prob C §§16361, 16362, 16364.

Prior Law: Former Prob C §16310, similar to present Prob C §§16361, 16362, 16364, was added Stats 1986 ch 820 §40, operative July 1, 1987, and repealed Stats 1990 ch 79 §13, operative July 1, 1991.

§16311. [Section repealed 1999]
Leg.H. Enacted Stats 1990 ch 79 §14 (AB 759), operative July 1, 1991. Repealed Stats 1999 ch 145 §4 (AB 846). The repealed section related to underproductive property.

Prior Law: Former Prob C §16311, relating to underproductive property, was added Stats 1986 ch 820 §40, operative July 1, 1987, and repealed Stats 1990 ch 79 §13, operative July 1, 1991.

§16312. [Section repealed 1999]
Leg.H. Enacted Stats 1990 ch 79 §14 (AB 759), operative July 1, 1991. Repealed Stats 1999 ch 145 §4 (AB 846). See Prob C §§16371–16373.

Prior Law: Former Prob C §16312, similar to present Prob C §§16371–16373, was added Stats 1986 ch 820 §40, operative July 1, 1987, and repealed Stats 1990 ch 79 §13, operative July 1, 1991.

§16313. [Section repealed 1999]
Leg.H. Enacted Stats 1990 ch 79 §14 (AB 759), operative July 1, 1991. Repealed Stats 1999 ch 145 §4 (AB 846). See Prob C §16372.

Prior Law: Former Prob C §16313, similar to present Prob C §16372, was added Stats 1986 ch 820 §40, operative July 1, 1987, and repealed Stats 1990 ch 79 §13, operative July 1, 1991.

§16314. [Section repealed 1999]
Leg.H. Enacted Stats 1990 ch 79 §14 (AB 759), operative July 1, 1991. Amended Stats 1992 ch 178 §43.6 (SB 1496). Repealed Stats 1999 ch 145 §4 (AB 846). See Prob C §16340.

Prior Law: Former Prob C §16314, similar to present Prob C §16340, was added Stats 1988 ch 1199 §107, operative July 1, 1989, and repealed Stats 1990 ch 79 §13, operative July 1, 1991.

§16315. [Section repealed 1999]
Leg.H. Enacted Stats 1990 ch 79 §14 (AB 759), operative July 1, 1991. Repealed Stats 1999 ch 145 §4 (AB 846). The repealed section related to application of changes made in certain code provisions to trusts created before July 1, 1989.

Prior Law: Former Prob C §16315, relating to application of changes made in Sections 16304 and 16305 and of Section 16314 to trust created before July 1, 1989, was added Stats 1988 ch 1199 §107.3, operative July 1, 1989, and repealed Stats 1990 ch 79 §13, operative July 1, 1991.

CHAPTER 3
UNIFORM FIDUCIARY INCOME AND PRINCIPAL ACT

Article 1. General Provisions and Definitions.
Article 2. Fiduciary Duties and Judicial Review.
Article 3. Unitrust.
Article 4. Allocation of Receipts.
Article 5. Allocation of Disbursements.
Article 6. Death of Individual or Termination of Income Interest.
Article 7. Apportionment at Beginning and End of Income Interest.
Article 8. Miscellaneous Provisions.

ARTICLE 1
General Provisions and Definitions

Citation of chapter. § 16320.
Definitions. § 16321.
Applicability of chapter. § 16322.
Applicability based on principal place of administration. § 16323.

§ 16320. Citation of chapter
This section shall be known, and may be cited, as the Uniform Fiduciary Income and Principal Act. **Leg.H.** Added Stats 2023 ch 28 §2 (SB 522), effective January 1, 2024.

Prior Law Former Prob C §16320, relating to citation of chapter, was added Stats 1999 ch 145 §5 (AB 846), effective January 1, 2000, and repealed Stats 2023 ch 28 §1 (SB 522), effective January 1, 2024.

§ 16321. Definitions
The following definitions apply for purposes of this chapter:

(a) "Accounting period" means a calendar year, unless a fiduciary selects another period of 12 calendar months or approximately 12 calendar months. The term includes a part of a calendar year or another period of 12 calendar months or approximately 12 calendar months that begins when an income interest begins or ends when an income interest ends.

(b) "Asset-backed security" means a security that is serviced primarily by the money flows of a discrete pool of fixed or revolving receivables or other financial assets that by their terms convert into money within a finite time. The term includes rights or other assets that ensure the servicing or timely distribution of proceeds to the holder of the asset-backed security. The term does not include an asset to which Section 16340, 16348, or 16353 applies.

(c) "Beneficiary" includes the following:
(1) For a trust:
(A) A current beneficiary, including a current income beneficiary and a beneficiary that may receive only principal.
(B) A remainder beneficiary.
(C) Any other successor beneficiary.
(2) For an estate, an heir, legatee, and devisee.
(3) For a life estate or term interest, a person that holds a life estate, term interest, or remainder or other interest following a life estate or term interest.

(d) "Court" means the court in this state having jurisdiction relating to a trust, estate, or life estate or other term interest described in subdivision (b) of Section 16322.

(e) "Current income beneficiary" means a beneficiary to which a fiduciary may distribute net income, whether or not the fiduciary also may distribute principal to the beneficiary.

(f) "Distribution" means a payment or transfer by a fiduciary to a beneficiary in the beneficiary's capacity as a beneficiary, made under the terms of the trust, without consideration other than the beneficiary's right to receive the payment or transfer under the terms of the trust. "Distribute," "distributed," and "distributee" have corresponding meanings.

(g) "Estate" means a decedent's estate, and includes the property of the decedent as the estate is originally constituted and the property of the estate as it exists at any time during administration.

(h) "Fiduciary" includes a trustee, personal representative, life tenant, holder of a term interest, and person acting under a delegation from a fiduciary. "Fiduciary" includes a person that holds property for a successor beneficiary whose interest may be affected by an allocation of receipts and expenditures between income and principal. If there are two or more cofiduciaries, the term includes all cofiduciaries acting under the terms of the trust and applicable law.

(i) "Income" means money or other property a fiduciary receives as current return from principal. The term includes a part of receipts from a sale, exchange, or liquidation of a principal asset, to the extent provided in Article 4 (commencing with Section 16340).

(j) "Income interest" means the right of a current income beneficiary to receive all or part of net income, whether the terms of the trust require the net income to be distributed or authorize the net income to be distributed in the fiduciary's discretion. The term includes the right of a current beneficiary to use property held by a fiduciary.

(k) "Independent person" means a person that is not:

(1) For a trust, any of the following:

(A) A beneficiary that is a distributee or permissible distributee of trust income or principal or would be a distributee or permissible distributee of trust income or principal if either the trust or the interests of the distributees or permissible distributees of trust income or principal were terminated, assuming no power of appointment is exercised.

(B) A settlor of the trust.

(C) An individual whose legal obligation to support a beneficiary may be satisfied by a distribution from the trust.

(2) For an estate, a beneficiary.

(3) A spouse, parent, brother, sister, or issue of an individual described in paragraph (1) or (2).

(4) A corporation, partnership, limited liability company, or other entity in which persons described in paragraphs (1) to (3), inclusive, in the aggregate, have voting control.

(5) An employee of a person described in paragraphs (1) to (4), inclusive.

(l) "Mandatory income interest" means the right of a current income beneficiary to receive net income that the terms of the trust require the fiduciary to distribute.

(m) "Net income" means the total allocations during an accounting period to income under the terms of a trust and this chapter minus the disbursements during the period, other than distributions, allocated to income under the terms of the trust and this chapter. To the extent the trust is a unitrust under Article 3 (commencing with Section 16330), the term means the unitrust amount determined under that article. The term includes an adjustment from principal to income under Section 16327. The term does not include an adjustment from income to principal under Section 16327.

(n) "Person" means an individual, estate, trust, business or nonprofit entity, public corporation, government or governmental subdivision, agency, or instrumentality, or other legal entity.

(o) "Personal representative" means an executor, administrator, successor personal representative, special administrator, or person that performs substantially the same function with respect to an estate under the law governing the person's status.

(p) "Principal" means property held in trust for distribution to, production of income for, or use by a current or successor beneficiary.

(q) "Record" means information that is inscribed on a tangible medium or that is stored in an electronic or other medium and is retrievable in perceivable form.

(r) "Settlor" means a person, including a testator, that creates or contributes property to a trust. If more than one person creates or contributes property to a trust, the term includes each person, to the extent of the trust property attributable to that person's contribution, except to the extent another person has the power to revoke or withdraw that portion.

(s) "Special tax benefit" means any of the following:

(1) Exclusion of a transfer to a trust from gifts described in Section 2503(b) of the Internal Revenue Code of 1986, as amended (26 U.S.C. Sec. 2503(b), as amended) because of the qualification of an income interest in the trust as a present interest in property.

(2) Status as a qualified subchapter S-trust described in Section 1361(d)(3) of the Internal Revenue Code of 1986, as amended (26 U.S.C. Sec. 1361(d)(3), as amended), at a time the trust holds stock of an S-corporation described in Section 1361(a)(1) of the Internal Revenue Code of 1986, as amended (26 U.S.C. Sec. 1361(a)(1), as amended).

(3) An estate or gift tax marital deduction for a transfer to a trust under Section 2056 or 2523 of the Internal Revenue Code of 1986, as amended (26 U.S.C. Sec. 2056 or 2523, as amended), which depends or depended, in whole or in part, on the right of the settlor's spouse to receive the net income of the trust.

(4) Exemption in whole or in part of a trust from the federal generation-skipping transfer tax imposed by Section 2601 of the Internal Revenue Code of 1986, as amended (26 U.S.C. Sec. 2601, as amended) because the trust was irrevocable on September 25, 1985, if there is a possibility of any of the following:

(A) A taxable distribution, as defined in Section 2612(b) of the Internal Revenue Code of 1986, as amended (26 U.S.C. Sec. 2612(b), as amended), could be made from the trust.

(B) A taxable termination, as defined in Section 2612(a) of the Internal Revenue Code of 1986, as amended, (26 U.S.C. Sec. 2612(a), as amended), could occur with respect to the trust.

(C) An inclusion ratio, as defined in Section 2642(a) of the Internal Revenue Code of 1986, as amended (26 U.S.C. Sec. 2642(a), as amended), of the trust that is less than one, if there is any possibility of any of the following:

(i) A taxable distribution, as defined in Section 2612(b) of the Internal Revenue Code of 1986, as amended (26 U.S.C. Sec. 2612(b), as amended), could be made from the trust.

(ii) A taxable termination, as defined in Section 2612(a) of the Internal Revenue Code of 1986, as amended (26 U.S.C. Sec. 2612(a), as amended), could occur with respect to the trust.

(t) "Successive interest" means the interest of a successor beneficiary.

(u) "Successor beneficiary" means a person entitled to receive income or principal or to use property when an income interest or other current interest ends.

(v) "Terms of a trust" means any of the following:

(1)(A) For a trust, the written trust instrument of an irrevocable trust or those provisions of a written trust instrument in effect at the settlor's death that describe or affect that portion of a trust that has become irrevocable at the death of the settlor.

(B) "Terms of a trust" includes, but is not limited to, signatures, amendments, disclaimers, and any directions or instructions to the trustee that affect the disposition of the trust.

(C) "Terms of a trust" does not include documents that were intended to affect disposition only while the trust was revocable. If a trust has been completely restated, "terms of a trust" does not include trust instruments or amendments that are superseded by the last restatement before the settlor's death, but it does include amendments executed after the restatement. "Terms of a trust" also includes any document irrevocably exercising a power of appointment over the trust or over any portion of the trust that has become irrevocable.

(2) For an estate, a will.

(3) For a life estate or term interest, the corresponding manifestation of the rights of the beneficiaries.

(w)(1) "Trust" includes both of the following:

(A) An express trust, private or charitable, with additions to the trust, wherever and however created.

(B) A trust created or determined by judgment or decree under which the trust is to be administered in the manner of an express trust.

(2) "Trust" does not include any of the following:

(A) A constructive trust.

(B) A resulting trust, conservatorship, guardianship, multiparty account, custodial arrangement for a minor, business trust, voting trust, security arrangement, liquidation trust, or trust for the primary purpose of paying debts, dividends, interest, salaries, wages, profits, pensions, retirement benefits, or employee benefits of any kind.

(C) An arrangement under which a person is a nominee, escrowee, or agent for another.

(x) "Trustee" means a person, other than a personal representative, that owns or holds property for the benefit of a beneficiary. The term includes an original, additional, or successor trustee, whether or not appointed or confirmed by a court.

(y) "Will" means a testamentary instrument recognized by applicable law that makes a legally effective disposition of an individual's property, effective at the individual's death. "Will" includes a codicil or other amendment to a testamentary instrument. **Leg.H.** Added Stats 2023 ch 28 §2 (SB 522), effective January 1, 2024.

Prior Law Former Prob C §16321, relating to definitions, was added Stats 1999 ch 145 §5 (AB 846), effective January 1, 2000, and repealed Stats 2023 ch 28 §1 (SB 522), effective January 1, 2024.

§ 16322. Applicability of chapter

Except as otherwise provided in the terms of a trust or this chapter, this chapter applies to the following:

(a) A trust or an estate.

(b) A life estate or other term interest in which the interest of one or more persons will be succeeded by the interest of one or more other persons. **Leg.H.** Added Stats 2023 ch 28 §2 (SB 522), effective January 1, 2024.

Prior Law Former Prob C §16322, relating to definitions of "accounting period," was added Stats 1999 ch 145 §5 (AB 846), effective January 1, 2000, and repealed Stats 2023 ch 28 §1 (SB 522), effective January 1, 2024.

§ 16323. Applicability based on principal place of administration

Except as otherwise provided in the terms of a trust or this chapter, this chapter applies when this state is the principal place of administration of a trust or estate or the situs of property that is not held in a trust or estate and is subject to a life estate or other term interest described in subdivision (b) of Section 16322. By accepting the trusteeship of a trust having its principal place of administration in this state or by moving the principal place of administration of a trust to this state, the trustee submits to the application of this chapter to any matter within the scope of this chapter involving the trust. **Leg.H.** Added Stats 2023 ch 28 §2 (SB 522), effective January 1, 2024.

Prior Law Former Prob C §16323, relating to definition of "fiduciary," was added Stats 1999 ch 145 §5 (AB 846), effective January 1, 2000, and repealed Stats 2023 ch 28 §1 (SB 522), effective January 1, 2024.

ARTICLE 2
Fiduciary Duties and Judicial Review

Allocation, determination, or exercise of discretion; Adjustment, § 16325.
Fiduciary decision; Remedies for abuse of discretion. § 16326.
Adjustment between income and principal. § 16327.

§ 16325. Allocation, determination, or exercise of discretion; Adjustment

(a) In making an allocation or determination or exercising discretion under this chapter, all of the following apply:

(1) A fiduciary shall act in good faith, based on what is fair and reasonable to all beneficiaries.

(2) A fiduciary shall administer a trust or decedent's estate in accordance with the trust or the will, even if there is a different provision in this chapter.

(3) A fiduciary may administer a trust or decedent's estate by the exercise of a discretionary power of administration given to the fiduciary by the trust or the will, even if the exercise of the power produces a result different from a result required or permitted by this chapter, and no inference that the fiduciary has improperly exercised the discretion arises from the fact that the fiduciary has made an allocation contrary to a provision of this chapter.

(4) A fiduciary shall administer a trust or decedent's estate in accordance with this chapter if the trust or the will does not contain a different provision or does not give the fiduciary a discretionary power of administration.

(b) A fiduciary's allocation, determination, or exercise of discretion under this chapter is presumed to be fair and reasonable to all beneficiaries. A fiduciary may exercise a discretionary power of administration given to the fiduciary by the terms of the trust, and an exercise of the power that produces a result different from a result required or permitted by this chapter does not create an inference that the fiduciary abused the fiduciary's discretion.

(c) A fiduciary shall do both of the following:

(1) Add a receipt to principal, to the extent neither the terms of the trust nor this chapter allocates the receipt between income and principal.

(2) Charge a disbursement to principal, to the extent neither the terms of the trust nor this chapter allocates the disbursement between income and principal.

(d) A fiduciary may exercise the power to adjust under Section 16327, convert an income trust to a unitrust under paragraph (1) of subdivision (a) of Section 16332, change the percentage or method used to calculate a unitrust amount under paragraph (2) of subdivision (a) of Section 16332, or convert a unitrust to an income trust under paragraph (3) of subdivision (a) of Section 16332, if the fiduciary determines the exercise of the power will assist the fiduciary to administer the trust or estate impartially.

(e) Factors the fiduciary shall consider in making the determination under subdivision (d) include all of the following:

(1) The terms of the trust.

(2) The nature, distribution standards, and expected duration of the trust.

(3) The effect of the allocation rules, including specific adjustments between income and principal, under Article 4 (commencing with Section 16340) to Article 7 (commencing with Section 16375), inclusive.

(4) The desirability of liquidity and regularity of income.

(5) The desirability of the preservation and appreciation of principal.

(6) The extent to which an asset is used or may be used by a beneficiary.

(7) The increase or decrease in the value of principal assets, reasonably determined by the fiduciary.

(8) Whether and to what extent the terms of the trust give the fiduciary power to accumulate income or invade principal or prohibit the fiduciary from accumulating income or invading principal.

(9) The extent to which the fiduciary has accumulated income or invaded principal in preceding accounting periods.

(10) The effect of current and reasonably expected economic conditions.

(11) The reasonably expected tax consequences of the exercise of the power. **Leg.H.** Added Stats 2023 ch 28 §2 (SB 522), effective January 1, 2024.

Prior Law Former Prob C §16325, relating to definition of "income beneficiary," was added Stats 1999 ch 145 §5 (AB 846), effective January 1, 2000, and repealed Stats 2023 ch 28 §1 (SB 522), effective January 1, 2024.

§ 16326. Fiduciary decision; Remedies for abuse of discretion

(a) For purposes of this section, "fiduciary decision" means any of the following:

(1) A fiduciary's allocation between income and principal or another determination regarding income and principal required or authorized by the terms of the trust or this chapter.

(2) The fiduciary's exercise or nonexercise of a discretionary power regarding income and principal granted by the terms of the trust or this chapter, including the power to adjust under Section 16327, convert an income trust to a unitrust under paragraph (1) of subdivision (a) of Section 16332, change the percentage or method used to calculate a unitrust amount under paragraph (2) of subdivision (a) of Section 16332, or convert a unitrust to an income trust under paragraph (3) of subdivision (a) of Section 16332.

(3) The fiduciary's implementation of a decision described in paragraph (1) or (2).

(b) The court may not order a fiduciary to change a fiduciary decision unless the court determines that the fiduciary decision was an abuse of the fiduciary's discretion.

(c) If the court determines that a fiduciary decision was an abuse of the fiduciary's discretion, the court may order a remedy authorized by law. To place the beneficiaries in the positions the beneficiaries would have occupied if there had not been an abuse of the fiduciary's discretion, the court may order any of the following:

(1) The fiduciary to exercise or refrain from exercising the power to adjust under Section 16327.

(2) The fiduciary to exercise or refrain from exercising the power to convert an income trust to a unitrust under paragraph (1) of subdivision (a) of Section 16332, change the percentage or method used to calculate a unitrust amount under paragraph (2) of subdivision (a) of Section 16332, or convert a unitrust to an income trust under paragraph (3) of subdivision (a) of Section 16332.

(3) The fiduciary to distribute an amount to a beneficiary.

(4) A beneficiary to return some or all of a distribution.

(5) The fiduciary to withhold an amount from one or more future distributions to a beneficiary.

(6) Upon a petition by a fiduciary for instruction, the court may determine whether a proposed fiduciary decision will result in an abuse of the fiduciary's discretion. If the petition describes the proposed decision, contains sufficient information to inform the beneficiary of the reasons for making the proposed decision and the facts on which the fiduciary relies, and explains how the beneficiary will be affected by the proposed decision, a beneficiary that opposes the proposed decision has the burden to establish that it will result in an abuse of the fiduciary's discretion. **Leg.H.** Added Stats 2023 ch 28 §2 (SB 522), effective January 1, 2024.

Prior Law Former Prob C §16326, relating to definition of "income interest," was added Stats 1999 ch 145 §5 (AB 846), effective January 1, 2000, and repealed Stats 2023 ch 28 §1 (SB 522), effective January 1, 2024.

§ 16327. Adjustment between income and principal

(a) Except as otherwise provided in the terms of a trust or this section, a fiduciary, in a record, without court approval, may adjust between income and principal if the fiduciary determines the exercise of the power to adjust will assist the fiduciary in administering the trust or estate impartially.

(b) This section does not create a duty to exercise or consider the power to adjust under subdivision (a) or to inform a beneficiary about the applicability of this section.

(c) A fiduciary that in good faith exercises or fails to exercise the power to adjust under subdivision (a) is not liable to a person affected by the exercise or failure to exercise.

(d) In deciding whether and to what extent to exercise the power to adjust under subdivision (a), a fiduciary shall consider all factors the fiduciary considers relevant, including relevant factors in subdivision (e) of Section 16325 and the application of subdivision (i) of Section 16340 and Sections 16347 and 16352.

(e) A fiduciary may not exercise the power under subdivision (a) to make an adjustment or under Section 16347 to make a determination that an allocation is insubstantial under any of the following circumstances:

(1) The adjustment or determination would reduce the amount payable to a current income beneficiary from a trust that qualifies for a special tax benefit, except to the extent the adjustment is made to provide for a reasonable apportionment of the total return of the trust between the current income beneficiary and successor beneficiaries.

(2) The adjustment or determination would change the amount payable to a beneficiary, as a fixed annuity or a fixed fraction of the value of the trust assets, under the terms of the trust.

(3) The adjustment or determination would reduce an amount that is permanently set aside for a charitable purpose under the terms of the trust, unless both income and principal are set aside for the charitable purpose.

(4) Possessing or exercising the power would cause a person to be treated as the owner of all or part of the trust for federal income tax purposes.

(5) Possessing or exercising the power would cause all or part of the value of the trust assets to be included in the gross estate of an individual for federal estate tax purposes.

(6) Possessing or exercising the power would cause an individual to be treated as making a gift for federal gift tax purposes.

(7) The fiduciary is not an independent person.

(8) The trust is irrevocable and provides for income to be paid to the settlor and possessing or exercising the power would cause the adjusted principal or income to be considered an available resource or available income under a public benefit program.

(9) The trust is a unitrust under Article 3.

(f) If paragraph (4), (5), (6), or (7) of subdivision (e) applies to a fiduciary:

(1) A cofiduciary to which paragraph (4), (5), (6), or (7) of subdivision (e) does not apply may exercise the power to adjust, unless the exercise of the power by the remaining cofiduciary or cofiduciaries is not permitted by the terms of the trust or law other than this chapter.

(2) If there is no cofiduciary to which paragraph (4), (5), (6), or (7) of subdivision (e) does not apply, the fiduciary may appoint a cofiduciary to which paragraph (4), (5), (6), or (7) of subdivision (e) does not apply, which may be a special fiduciary with limited powers, and the appointed cofiduciary may exercise the power to adjust under subdivision (a), unless the appointment of a cofiduciary or the exercise of the power by a cofiduciary is not permitted by the terms of the trust or law other than this chapter.

(g) A fiduciary may release or delegate to a cofiduciary the power to adjust under subdivision (a) if the fiduciary determines that the fiduciary's possession or exercise of the power will or may do either of the following:

(1) Cause a result described in paragraphs (1) to (6), inclusive, or (8) of subdivision (e).

(2) Deprive the trust of a tax benefit or impose a tax burden not described in paragraphs (1) to (6), inclusive, of subdivision (e).

(h) A fiduciary's release or delegation to a cofiduciary under subdivision (g) of the power to adjust pursuant to subdivision (a):

(1) Shall be in a record.

(2) Applies to the entire power, unless the release or delegation provides a limitation, which may be a limitation to the power to make any of the following adjustments:

(A) From income to principal.

(B) From principal to income.

(C) For specified property.

(D) In specified circumstances.

(3) For a delegation, may be modified by a redelegation under this subdivision by the cofiduciary to which the delegation is made.

(4) Subject to paragraph (3), is permanent, unless the release or delegation provides a specified period, including a period measured by the life of an individual or the lives of more than one individual.

(i) Terms of a trust that deny or limit the power to adjust between income and principal do not affect the application of this section, unless the terms of the trust expressly deny or limit the power to adjust under subdivision (a).

(j) The exercise of the power to adjust under subdivision (a) in any accounting period may apply to the current period, the immediately preceding period, and one or more subsequent periods.

(k) A description of the exercise of the power to adjust under subdivision (a) shall be either of the following:

(1) Included in a report, if any, sent to beneficiaries.

(2) Communicated at least annually to all beneficiaries that receive or are entitled to receive income from the trust or would be entitled to receive a distribution of principal if the trust were terminated at the time the notice is sent, assuming no power of appointment is exercised. **Leg.H.** Added Stats 2023 ch 28 §2 (SB 522), effective January 1, 2024.

Prior Law Former Prob C §16327, relating to definition of "mandatory income interest," was added Stats 1999 ch 145 §5 (AB 846), effective January 1, 2000, and repealed Stats 2023 ch 28 §1 (SB 522), effective January 1, 2024.

ARTICLE 3
Unitrust

Definitions. § 16330.
Applicability of article. § 16331.
Fiduciary authority; Beneficiary request. § 16332.
Notice requirements. § 16333.
Unitrust plan. § 16334.
Unitrust rate. § 16335.
Unitrust asset valuation. § 16336.
Unitrust plan period. § 16337.
Plan methods and standards; Special tax benefit; Fiduciary not independent. § 16338.

§ 16330. Definitions

The following definitions apply for purposes of this article:

(a) "Applicable value" means the amount of the net fair market value of a trust taken into account under Section 16336.

(b) "Express unitrust" means a trust for which, under the terms of the trust without regard to this article, income or net income shall or may be calculated as a unitrust amount.

(c) "Income trust" means a trust that is not a unitrust.

(d) "Net fair market value of a trust" means the fair market value of the assets of the trust, less the noncontingent liabilities of the trust.

(e) "Unitrust" means a trust for which net income is a unitrust amount. The term includes an express unitrust.

(f) "Unitrust amount" means an amount computed by multiplying a determined value of a trust by a determined percentage. For a unitrust administered under a unitrust plan, the term means the applicable value, multiplied by the unitrust rate.

(g) "Unitrust plan" means a plan described in Sections 16334 to 16338, inclusive, and adopted pursuant to Section 16332.

(h) "Unitrust rate" means the rate used to compute the unitrust amount under subdivision (f) for a unitrust administered under a unitrust plan. **Leg.H.** Added Stats 2023 ch 28 §2 (SB 522), effective January 1, 2024.

§ 16331. Applicability of article

(a) Except as otherwise provided in subdivision (b), this article applies to both of the following:

(1) An income trust, unless the terms of the trust expressly prohibit use of this article by a specific reference to this article or an explicit expression of intent that net income not be calculated as a unitrust amount.

(2) An express unitrust, except to the extent the terms of the trust explicitly do any of the following:

(A) Prohibit use of this article by a specific reference to this article.

(B) Prohibit conversion to an income trust.

(C) Limit changes to the method of calculating the unitrust amount.

(b) This article does not apply to a trust described in Section 170(f)(2)(B), 642(c)(5), 664(d), 2702(a)(3)(A)(ii) or (iii), or 2702(b) of the Internal Revenue Code of 1986 (26 U.S.C. Secs. 170(f)(2)(B), 642(c)(5), 664(d), 2702(a)(3)(A)(ii) or (iii), or 2702(b)).

(c) An income trust to which this article applies under paragraph (1) of subdivision (a) may be converted to a unitrust under this article regardless of the terms of the trust concerning distributions. Conversion to a unitrust under this article does not affect other terms of the trust concerning distributions of income or principal.

(d) This article applies to an estate only to the extent a trust is a beneficiary of the estate. To the extent of the trust's interest in the estate, the estate may be administered as a unitrust, the administration of the estate as a unitrust may be discontinued, or the percentage or method used to calculate the unitrust amount may be changed, in the same manner as for a trust under this article.

(e) This article does not create a duty to take or consider action under this article or to inform a beneficiary about the applicability of this article.

(f) A fiduciary that in good faith takes or fails to take an action under this article is not liable to a person affected by the action or inaction. **Leg.H.** Added Stats 2023 ch 28 §2 (SB 522), effective January 1, 2024.

§ 16332. Fiduciary authority; Beneficiary request

(a) A fiduciary, without court approval, by complying with subdivisions (b) and (f), may do any of the following:

(1) Convert an income trust to a unitrust if the fiduciary creates in a record a unitrust plan for the trust providing for both of the following:

(A) That in administering the trust, the net income of the trust will be a unitrust amount rather than net income determined without regard to this article.

(B) The percentage and method used to calculate the unitrust amount.

(2) Change the percentage or method used to calculate a unitrust amount for a unitrust if the fiduciary implements in a record a unitrust plan or an amendment or replacement of a unitrust plan providing changes in the percentage or method used to calculate the unitrust amount.

(3) Convert a unitrust to an income trust if the fiduciary implements in a record a determination that, in administering the trust, the net income of the trust will be net income determined without regard to this article rather than a unitrust amount.

(b) A fiduciary may take an action under subdivision (a) if all of the following conditions are met:

(1) The fiduciary determines that the action will assist the fiduciary to administer a trust impartially.

(2) The fiduciary sends a notice in a record, in the manner required by Section 16333, describing and proposing to take the action.

(3) No beneficiary objects to the proposed action in a writing delivered to the trustee within the period prescribed by subdivision (d) of Section 16502.

(c) If a fiduciary receives, on or before the date stated in the notice under Section 16333, an objection in a record to a proposed action, the fiduciary or a beneficiary may request the court to have the proposed action taken as proposed, taken with modifications, or prevented. A person described in subdivision (a) of Section 16333 may oppose the proposed action in the proceeding under this subdivision, whether or not the person previously consented or objected.

(d) If, after sending a notice under paragraph (2) of subdivision (b), a fiduciary decides not to take the action proposed in the notice, the fiduciary shall notify in a record each person described in subdivision (a) of Section 16333 of the decision not to take the action and the reasons for the decision.

(e) If a beneficiary requests in a record that a fiduciary take an action described in subdivision (a) and the fiduciary declines to act or does not act within 90 days after receiving the request, the beneficiary may request the court to direct the fiduciary to take the action requested.

(f) In deciding whether and how to take an action authorized by subdivision (a), or whether and how to respond to a request by a beneficiary under subdivision (e), a fiduciary shall consider all factors relevant to the trust and the beneficiaries, including relevant factors in subdivision (e) of Section 16325.

(g) A fiduciary may release or delegate the power to convert an income trust to a unitrust under paragraph (1) of subdivision (a), change the percentage or method used to calculate a unitrust amount under paragraph (2) of subdivision (a), or convert a unitrust to an income trust under paragraph (3) of subdivision (a), for a reason described in subdivision (g) of Section 16327 and in the manner described in subdivision (h) of Section 16327. **Leg.H.** Added Stats 2023 ch 28 §2 (SB 522), effective January 1, 2024.

§ 16333. Notice requirements

A notice required by paragraph (2) of subdivision (b) of Section 16332 shall be sent as required by Chapter 5 (commencing with Section 16500), including notice to a beneficiary who is a minor and to the minor's guardian, if any, and shall include all of the following:

(a) The action proposed under paragraph (2) of subdivision (b) of Section 16332.

(b) For a conversion of an income trust to a unitrust, a copy of the unitrust plan adopted under paragraph (1) of subdivision (a) of Section 16332.

(c) For a change in the percentage or method used to calculate the unitrust amount, a copy of the unitrust plan or amendment or replacement of the unitrust plan adopted under paragraph (2) of subdivision (a) of Section 16332.

(d) A statement that the person to which the notice is sent may object to the proposed action by stating in a record the basis for the objection and sending or delivering the record to the fiduciary.

(e) The date by which an objection under subdivision (d) shall be received by the fiduciary, which shall be at least 30 days after the date the notice is sent.

(f) The date on which the action is proposed to be taken and the date on which the action is proposed to take effect.

(g) The name and contact information of the fiduciary.

(h) The name and contact information of a person who may be contacted for additional information. **Leg.H.** Added Stats 2023 ch 28 §2 (SB 522), effective January 1, 2024.

§ 16334. Unitrust plan

(a) In administering a unitrust under this article, a fiduciary shall follow a unitrust plan adopted under paragraph (1) or (2) of subdivision (a) of Section 16332, or amended or replaced under paragraph (2) of subdivision (a) of Section 16332.

(b) A unitrust plan shall provide all of the following:

(1) The unitrust rate or the method for determining the unitrust rate under Section 16335.

(2) The method for determining the applicable value under Section 16336.

(3) The rules described in Sections 16335 to 16338, inclusive, that apply in the administration of the unitrust, whether the rules are either of the following:

(A) Mandatory, as provided in subdivision (a) of Section 16336 or subdivision (a) of Section 16337.

(B) Optional, as provided in Section 16335, subdivision (b) of Section 16336, subdivision (b) of Section 16337, and subdivision (a) of Section 16338, to the extent the fiduciary elects to adopt those rules. **Leg.H.** Added Stats 2023 ch 28 §2 (SB 522), effective January 1, 2024.

§ 16335. Unitrust rate

(a) A unitrust rate may not be less than 3 percent, or greater than 5 percent, unless the unitrust plan has been approved by court order. If the unitrust plan has been approved by court order, any unitrust rate may be used. Except as otherwise provided in this subdivision and in paragraph (1) of subdivision (b) of Section 16338, a unitrust rate may be either of the following:

(1) A fixed unitrust interest rate.

(2) A unitrust rate that is determined for each period, using either of the following:

(A) A market index or other published data.

(B) A mathematical blend of market indices or other published data over a stated number of preceding periods.

(b) Except as otherwise provided in subdivision (a) of Section 16335 and paragraph (1) of subdivision (b) of Section 16338, a unitrust plan may provide any of the following:

(1) A limit on how high the unitrust rate determined under paragraph (2) of subdivision (a) may rise.

(2) A limit on how low the unitrust rate determined under paragraph (2) of subdivision (a) may fall.

(3) A limit on how much the unitrust rate determined under paragraph (2) of subdivision (a) may increase over the unitrust rate for the preceding period or a mathematical blend of unitrust rates over a stated number of preceding periods.

(4) A limit on how much the unitrust rate determined under paragraph (2) of subdivision (a) may decrease below the unitrust rate for the preceding period or a mathematical blend of unitrust rates over a stated number of preceding periods.

(5) A mathematical blend of any of the unitrust rates determined under paragraph (2) of subdivision (a) and paragraphs (1) to (4), inclusive, of this subdivision. **Leg.H.** Added Stats 2023 ch 28 §2 (SB 522), effective January 1, 2024.

Prior Law Former Prob C §16335, relating to allocation of receipts and disbursements and exer- cise of discretionary power, was added Stats 1999 ch 145 §5 (AB 846), effective January 1, 2000, amended Stats 2005 ch 100 §2 (SB 754), effective January 1, 2006, and repealed Stats 2023 ch 28 §1 (SB 522), effective January 1, 2006. Derivation: (a) Former Prob C §16302, as enacted Stats 1990 ch 79 §14. (b) Former Prob C §16302, as added Stats 1986 ch 820 §40. (c) Former CC §730.02, as added Stats 1967 ch 1508 §2.

§ 16336. Unitrust asset valuation

(a) A unitrust plan shall provide the method for determining the fair market value of an asset for the purpose of determining the unitrust amount, including both of the following:

(1) The frequency of valuing the asset, which need not require a valuation in every period.

(2) The date for valuing the asset in each period in which the asset is valued.

(b) Except as otherwise provided in paragraph (2) of subdivision (b) of Section 16338, a unitrust plan may provide methods for determining the amount of the net fair market value of the trust to take into account in determining the applicable value, including all of the following:

(1) Obtaining an appraisal of an asset for which fair market value is not readily ascertainable.

(2) Exclusion of specific assets or groups or types of assets.

(3) Exceptions or modifications of the treatment of specific assets or groups or types of assets.

(4) Identification and treatment of money or property held for distribution.

(5) Use of either of the following:

(A) An average of fair market values over a stated number of preceding periods.

(B) Another mathematical blend of fair market values over a stated number of preceding periods.

(6) A limit on how much the applicable value of all assets, groups of assets, or individual assets may increase over either of the following:

(A) The corresponding applicable value for the preceding period.

(B) A mathematical blend of applicable values over a stated number of preceding periods.

(7) A limit on how much the applicable value of all assets, groups of assets, or individual assets may decrease below:

(A) The corresponding applicable value for the preceding period.

(B) A mathematical blend of applicable values over a stated number of preceding periods.

(8) The treatment of accrued income and other features of an asset that affect value.

(9) Determining the liabilities of the trust, including treatment of liabilities to conform to the treatment of assets under paragraphs (1) to (8), inclusive. **Leg.H.** Added Stats 2023 ch 28 §2 (SB 522), effective January 1, 2024.

Prior Law Former Prob C §16336, relating to adjustment between principal and income, was added Stats 1999 ch 145 §5 (AB 846), effective January 1, 2000, amended Stats 2005 ch 100 §3 (SB 754), effective January 1, 2006, and repealed Stats 2023 ch 28 §1 (SB 522), effective January 1, 2024.

§ 16337. Unitrust plan period

(a) A unitrust plan shall provide the period used under Sections 16335 and 16336. Except as otherwise provided in paragraph (3) of subdivision (b) of Section 16338, the period may be any of the following:

(1) A calendar year.

(2) A 12-month period other than a calendar year.

(3) A calendar quarter.

(4) A three-month period other than a calendar quarter.

(5) Another period.

(b) Except as otherwise provided in Section 16338, a unitrust plan may provide standards for any of the following:

(1) Using fewer preceding periods under subparagraph (B) of paragraph (2) of subdivision (a) of, or paragraph (3) or (4) of subdivision (b) of, Section 16335 if any of the following circumstances exists:

(A) The trust was not in existence in a preceding period.

(B) Market indices or other published data are not available for a preceding period.

(2) Using fewer preceding periods under subparagraph (A) or (B) of paragraph (5) of, subparagraph (B) of paragraph (6) of, or subparagraph (B) of paragraph (7) of subdivision (b) of, Section 16366, under either of the following circumstances:

(A) The trust was not in existence in a preceding period.

(B) Fair market values are not available for a preceding period.

(3) Prorating the unitrust amount on a daily basis for a part of a period in which the trust or the administration of the trust as a unitrust or the interest of any beneficiary commences or terminates. **Leg.H.** Added Stats 2023 ch 28 §2 (SB 522), effective January 1, 2024.

Prior Law Former Prob C §16337, relating to notice of proposed action, was added Stats 1999 ch 145 §5 (AB 846), effective January 1, 2000, amended Stats 2004 ch 54 §1 (SB 1021), effective January 1, 2005, and repealed Stats 2023 ch 28 §1 (SB 522), effective January 1, 2024.

§ 16338. Plan methods and standards; Special tax benefit; Fiduciary not independent

(a) A unitrust plan may include any of the following:

(1) Provide methods and standards for all of the following:

(A) Determining the timing of distributions.

(B) Making distributions in money or in kind or partly in money and partly in kind.

(C) Correcting an underpayment or overpayment to a beneficiary based on the unitrust amount if there is an error in calculating the unitrust amount.

(2) Specify sources and the order of sources, including categories of income for federal income tax purposes, from which distributions of a unitrust amount are paid.

(3) Provide other standards and rules the fiduciary determines serve the interests of the beneficiaries.

(b) If a trust qualifies for a special tax benefit or a fiduciary is not an independent person:

(1) The unitrust rate established under Section 16335 may not be less than 3 percent or more than 5 percent.

(2) The only provisions of Section 16336 that apply are subdivision (a) and paragraphs (1), (4), and (9) of, and subparagraph (A) of paragraph (5) of, subdivision (b) of that section.

(3) The only period that may be used under Section 16337 is a calendar year under paragraph (1) of subdivision (a) of Section 16337.

(4) The only other provisions of Section 16337 that apply are subparagraph (A) of paragraph (2) of, and paragraph (3) of, subdivision (b) of that section. **Leg.H.** Added Stats 2023 ch 28 §2 (SB 522), effective January 1, 2024.

Prior Law Former Prob C §16338, relating to sole remedy, was added Stats 1999 ch 145 §5 (AB 846), effective January 1, 2000, amended Stats 2005 ch 100 §8 (SB 754), effective January 1, 2006, and repealed Stats 2023 ch 28 §1 (SB 522), effective January 1, 2024.

ARTICLE 4
Allocation of Receipts

Allocation of entity distribution to income; Capital distribution determination. § 16340.

Allocation of distribution to income. § 16341.

Accounting. § 16342.

Allocation to principal. § 16343.

Allocation of property rental amounts to income. § 16344.

Allocation of interest to income; Allocation of amount received for money obligation to principal. § 16345.

Allocation of insurance proceeds. § 16346.

Reallocation of certain amounts to principal. § 16347.

Separate funds; Marital trusts. § 16348.

Allocation of liquidating assets. § 16349.

Allocation of receipts from interest in minerals, water, or other natural resources. § 16350.

Allocation of receipts from timber sales. § 16351.

Marital deduction. § 16352.

Transactions in derivatives. § 16353.
Asset-backed securities. § 16354.
Financial instruments or arrangements not addressed by chapter. § 16355.

§ 16340. Allocation of entity distribution to income; Capital distribution determination

(a) The following definitions apply for purposes of this section:

(1) "Capital distribution" means an entity distribution of money that is either of the following:

(A) A return of capital.

(B) A distribution in total or partial liquidation of the entity.

(2) "Entity" means a corporation, partnership, limited liability company, regulated investment company, real estate investment trust, common trust fund, or any other organization or arrangement in which a person owns or holds an interest, whether or not the entity is a taxpayer for federal income tax purposes. "Entity" does not include any of the following:

(A) A trust or estate to which Section 16341 applies.

(B) A business or other activity to which Section 16342 applies that is not conducted by an entity described in subparagraph (A).

(C) An asset-backed security.

(D) An instrument or arrangement to which Section 16355 applies.

(3) "Entity distribution" means a payment or transfer by an entity made to a person in the person's capacity as an owner or holder of an interest in the entity.

(b) For purposes of this section, an attribute or action of an entity includes an attribute or action of any other entity in which the entity owns or holds an interest, including an interest owned or held indirectly through another entity.

(c) Except as otherwise provided in paragraphs (2) to (4), inclusive, of subdivision (d), a fiduciary shall allocate money received in an entity distribution to income.

(d) A fiduciary shall allocate to principal all of the following:

(1) Property received in an entity distribution that is not money.

(2) Money received in an entity distribution in an exchange for part or all of the fiduciary's interest in the entity, to the extent the entity distribution reduces the fiduciary's interest in the entity relative to the interests of other persons that own or hold interests in the entity.

(3) Money received in an entity distribution that the fiduciary determines or estimates is a capital distribution.

(4) Money received in an entity distribution from an entity that is a regulated investment company or real estate investment trust if the money received is a capital gain dividend for federal income tax purposes.

(5) Money received in an entity distribution that is treated, for federal income purposes, comparably to the treatment described in paragraph (4).

(e) A fiduciary may determine or estimate that money received in an entity distribution is a capital distribution in any of the following ways:

(1) By relying without inquiry or investigation on a characterization of the entity distribution provided by or on behalf of the entity, except under either of the following circumstances:

(A) The fiduciary determines, on the basis of information known to the fiduciary, that the characterization is or may be incorrect.

(B) The fiduciary owns or holds more than 50 percent of the voting interest in the entity.

(2) By determining or estimating, on the basis of information known to the fiduciary or provided to the fiduciary by or on behalf of the entity, that the total amount of money and property received by the fiduciary in the entity distribution or a series of related entity distributions is, or will be, greater than 20 percent of the fair market value of the fiduciary's interest in the entity.

(3) If neither paragraph (1) nor (2) applies, by considering the factors in subdivision (f) and the information known to the fiduciary or provided to the fiduciary by, or on behalf of, the entity.

(f) In making a determination or estimate under paragraph (3) of subdivision (e), a fiduciary may consider the following:

(1) A characterization of an entity distribution provided by or on behalf of the entity.

(2) The amount of money or property received in either of the following:

(A) The entity distribution.

(B) What the fiduciary determines is, or will be, a series of related entity distributions.

(3) The amount described in paragraph (2) compared to the amount the fiduciary determines or estimates is, during the current or preceding accounting periods, either of the following:

(A) The entity's operating income.

(B) The proceeds of the entity's sale or other disposition of any of the following:

(i) All or part of the business or other activity conducted by the entity.

(ii) One or more business assets that are not sold to customers in the ordinary course of the business or other activity conducted by the entity.

(iii) One or more assets other than business assets, unless the entity's primary activity is to invest in assets to realize gain on the disposition of all or some of the assets.

(C) If the entity's primary activity is to invest in assets to realize gain on the disposition of all or some of the assets, the gain realized on the disposition.

(D) The entity's regular, periodic entity distributions.

(E) The amount of money the entity has accumulated.

(F) The amount of money the entity has borrowed.

(G) The amount of money the entity has received from the sources described in Sections 16346, 16349, 16350, and 16351.

(H) The amount of money the entity has received from a source not otherwise described in this paragraph.

(4) Any other factor the fiduciary determines is relevant.

(g) If, after applying subdivisions (c) to (f), inclusive, a fiduciary determines that a part of an entity distribution is a capital distribution but is in doubt about the amount of the entity distribution that is a capital distribution, the fiduciary shall allocate to principal the amount of the entity distribution that is in doubt.

(h) If a fiduciary receives additional information about the application of this section to an entity distribution before the fiduciary has paid part or all of the entity distribution to a beneficiary, the fiduciary may consider the additional information before making the payment to the beneficiary and may change a decision to make the payment to the beneficiary.

(i) If a fiduciary receives additional information about the application of this section to an entity distribution after the fiduciary has paid part or all of the entity distribution to a beneficiary, the fiduciary has no duty to change or recover the payment to the beneficiary but may consider that information in determining whether to exercise the power to adjust under Section 16327. **Leg.H.** Added Stats 2023 ch 28 §2 (SB 522), effective January 1, 2024.

Prior Law Former Prob C §16340, relating to rules after death or end of income interest, was added Stats 1999 ch 145 §5 (AB 846), effective January 1, 2000, amended Stats 2006 ch 569 §1 (AB 2347), effective January 1, 2007, and repealed Stats 2023 ch 28 §1 (SB 522), effective January 1, 2024. Derivation: (a) Former Prob C §160. (b) Former Prob C §162, as amended Stats 1941 ch 336 §1, Stats 1953 ch 986 §1, Stats 1959 ch 1882 §1, Stats 1982 ch 520 §1. (c) Former Prob C §162.5, as added Stats 1959 ch 1882 §2. (d) Former Prob C §§661, 663, 664, as added Stats 1983 ch 842 §40. (e) Former Prob C §16304, as enacted Stats 1990 ch 79 §14. (f) Former Prob C §16304, as added Stats 1986 ch 820 §40, amended Stats 1987 ch 923 §100, Stats 1988 ch 1199 §106. (g) Former Prob C §16305, as enacted Stats 1990 ch 79 §14. (h) Former Prob C §16305, as added Stats 1986 ch 820 §40, amended Stats 1988 ch 1199 §106.5. (i) Former Prob C §16314, as enacted Stats 1990 ch 79 §14, amended Stats 1992 ch 178 §43.6. (j) Former Prob C §16314, as added Stats 1988 ch 1199 §107. (k) Former CC §730.04, as added Stats 1967 ch 1508 §2, amended Stats 1968 ch 448 §1. (*l*) Former CC §730.05, as added Stats 1967 ch 1508 §2, amended Stats 1968 ch 448 §2, Stats 1983 ch 842 §4. (m) Former CC §730.06, as added Stats 1963 ch 37 §1. (n) Former CC §§1366, 1368, 1369. (o) Stats 1941 ch 898 §4. (p) Fields Draft NY CC §623. (q) Uniform Principal and Income Act §4.

§ 16341. Allocation of distribution to income

A fiduciary shall allocate to income an amount received as a distribution of income, including a unitrust distribution under Article 3 (commencing with Section 16330), from a trust or estate in which the fiduciary has an interest, other than an interest the fiduciary purchased in a trust that is an investment entity, and shall allocate to principal an amount received as a distribution of principal from the trust or estate. If a fiduciary purchases, or receives from a settlor, an interest in a trust that is an investment entity, Section 16340, 16354, or 16355 applies to a receipt from the trust. **Leg.H.** Added Stats 2023 ch 28 §2 (SB 522), effective January 1, 2024.

Prior Law Former Prob C §16341, relating to beneficiary's portion of net income, was added Stats 1999 ch 145 §5 (AB 846), effective January 1, 2000, and repealed Stats 2023 ch 28 §1 (SB 522), effective January 1, 2024. Derivation: (a)

Former Prob C §160. (b) Former Prob C §162, as amended Stats 1941 ch 336 §1, Stats 1953 ch 986 §1, Stats 1959 ch 1882 §1, Stats 1982 ch 520 §1. (c) Former Prob C §§661, 663, as added Stats 1983 ch 842 §40. (d) Former Prob C §16304, as enacted Stats 1990 ch 79 §14. (e) Former Prob C §16304, as added Stats 1986 ch 820 §40, amended Stats 1987 ch 923 §100, Stats 1988 ch 1199 §106. (f) Former CC §730.04, as added Stats 1967 ch 1508 §2, amended Stats 1968 ch 448 §1. (g) Former CC §730.06, as added Stats 1963 ch 37 §1. (h) Former CC §§1366, 1368, 1369. (i) Stats 1941 ch 898 §4. (j) Fields Draft NY CC §623. (k) Uniform Principal and Income Act §4.

§ 16342. Accounting

(a) This section applies to a business or other activity conducted by a fiduciary if the fiduciary determines that it is in the interests of the beneficiaries to account separately for the business or other activity instead of doing either of the following:

(1) Accounting for the business or other activity as part of the fiduciary's general accounting records.

(2) Conducting the business or other activity through an entity described in subparagraph (A) of paragraph (2) of subdivision (a) of Section 16340.

(b) A fiduciary may account separately under this section for the transactions of a business or other activity, whether or not assets of the business or other activity are segregated from other assets held by the fiduciary.

(c) A fiduciary that accounts separately under this section for a business or other activity:

(1) May determine the extent to which the net money receipts of the business or other activity shall be retained for any of the following purposes:

(A) Working capital.

(B) The acquisition or replacement of fixed assets.

(C) Other reasonably foreseeable needs of the business or other activity.

(2) May determine the extent to which the remaining net money receipts are accounted for as principal or income in the fiduciary's general accounting records for the trust.

(3) May make a determination under paragraph (1) separately and differently from the fiduciary's decisions concerning distributions of income or principal.

(4) Shall account for the net amount received from the sale of an asset of the business or other activity, other than a sale in the ordinary course of the business or other activity, as principal in the fiduciary's general accounting records for the trust, to the extent the fiduciary determines that the net amount received is no longer required in the conduct of the business or other activity.

(d) Activities for which a fiduciary may account separately under this section include all of the following:

(1) Retail, manufacturing, service, and other traditional business activities.

(2) Farming.

(3) Raising and selling livestock and other animals.

(4) Managing rental properties.

(5) Extracting minerals, water, and other natural resources.

(6) Growing and cutting timber.

(7) An activity to which Section 16353, 16354, or 16355 applies.

(8) Any other business conducted by the fiduciary. **Leg.H.** Added Stats 2023 ch 28 §2 (SB 522), effective January 1, 2024.

§ 16343. Allocation to principal

A fiduciary shall allocate to principal any of the following:

(a) To the extent not allocated to income under this chapter, an asset received from any of the following:

(1) An individual, during the individual's lifetime.

(2) An estate.

(3) A trust, on termination of an income interest.

(4) A payor under a contract naming the fiduciary as beneficiary.

(b) Except as otherwise provided in this article, money or other property received from the sale, exchange, liquidation, or change in form of a principal asset.

(c) An amount recovered from a third party to reimburse the fiduciary because of a disbursement described in subdivision (a) of Section 16361, or for another reason to the extent not based on loss of income.

(d) Proceeds of property taken by eminent domain, except that proceeds awarded for loss of income in an accounting period are income if a current income beneficiary had a mandatory income interest during the period.

(e) Net income received in an accounting period during which there is no beneficiary to which a fiduciary may or shall distribute income.

(f) Other receipts as provided in Article 3 (commencing with Section 16330). **Leg.H.** Added Stats 2023 ch 28 §2 (SB 522), effective January 1, 2024.

§ 16344. Allocation of property rental amounts to income

To the extent a fiduciary does not account for the management of rental property as a business under Section 16342, the fiduciary shall allocate to income an amount received as rent of real or personal property, including an amount received for cancellation or renewal of a lease. Both of the following apply to an amount received as a refundable deposit, including a security deposit or a deposit that is to be applied as rent for future periods:

(1) The amount shall be added to principal and held subject to the terms of the lease, except as otherwise provided by law other than this chapter.

(2) The amount is not allocated to income or available for distribution to a beneficiary until the fiduciary's contractual obligations have been satisfied with respect to that amount. **Leg.H.** Added Stats 2023 ch 28 §2 (SB 522), effective January 1, 2024.

§ 16345. Allocation of interest to income; Allocation of amount received for money obligation to principal

(a) This section does not apply to an obligation to which Section 16348, 16349, 16350, 16351, 16353, 16354, or 16355 applies.

(b) A fiduciary shall allocate to income, without provision for amortization of premium, an amount received as interest on an obligation to pay money to the fiduciary, including an amount received as consideration for prepaying principal.

(c) A fiduciary shall allocate to principal an amount received from the sale, redemption, or other disposition of an obligation to pay money to the fiduciary. A fiduciary shall allocate to income the increment in value of a bond or other obligation for the payment of money bearing no stated interest but payable or redeemable, at maturity or another future time, in an amount that exceeds the amount in consideration of which it was issued. **Leg.H.** Added Stats 2023 ch 28 §2 (SB 522), effective January 1, 2024.

Prior Law Former Prob C §16345, relating to time of entitlement and time when asset subject to trust, was added Stats 1999 ch 145 §5 (AB 846), effective January 1, 2000, and repealed Stats 2023 ch 28 §1 (SB 522), effective January 1, 2024. Derivation: (a) Former Prob C §160. (b) Former Prob C §162, as amended Stats 1941 ch 336 §1, Stats 1953 ch 986 §1, Stats 1959 ch 1882 §1, amended 1982 ch 520 §1. (c) Former Prob C §661, as added Stats 1983 ch 842 §40. (d) Former Prob C §663, as added Stats 1983 ch 842 §40. (e) Former Prob C §16304, as enacted Stats 1990 ch 79 §14. (f) Former Prob C §16304, as added Stats 1986 ch 820 §40, amended Stats 1987 ch 923 §100, Stats 1988 ch 1199 §106. (g) Former CC §730.04, as added Stats 1967 ch 1508 §2, amended Stats 1968 ch 448 §1. (h) Former CC §730.06, as added Stats 1953 ch 37 §1. (i) Former CC §1366. (j) Former CC §§1368, 1369. (k) Stats 1941 ch 898 §4. (l) Field's Draft NY CC §623. (m) Uniform Principal and In- come Act §4.

§ 16346. Allocation of insurance proceeds

(a) This section does not apply to a contract to which Section 16348 applies.

(b) Except as otherwise provided in subdivision (c), a fiduciary shall allocate to principal the proceeds of a life insurance policy or other contract received by the fiduciary as beneficiary, including a contract that insures against damage to, destruction of, or loss of title to an asset. The fiduciary shall allocate dividends on an insurance policy to income to the extent premiums on the policy are paid from income and to principal to the extent premiums on the policy are paid from principal.

(c) A fiduciary shall allocate to income proceeds of a contract that insures the fiduciary against loss of any of the following:

(1) Occupancy or other use by a current income beneficiary.

(2) Income.

(3) Subject to Section 16342, profits from a business. **Leg.H.** Added Stats 2023 ch 28 §2 (SB 522), effective January 1, 2024.

Prior Law Former Prob C §16346, relating to allocations to principal or income and due dates, was added Stats 1999 ch 145 §5 (AB 846), effective January 1, 2000, and repealed Stats 2023 ch 28 §1 (SB 522), effective January 1, 2024. Derivation: (a) Former Prob C §160. (b) Former Prob C §162, as amended Stats 1941 ch 336 §1, Stats 1953 ch 986 §1, Stats 1959 ch 1882 §1, Stats 1982 ch 520 §1. (c) Former

Prob C §§661, 663, as added Stats 1983 ch 842 §40. (d) Former Prob C §16304, as enacted Stats 1990 ch 79 §14. (e) Former Prob C §16304, as added Stats 1986 ch 820 §40, amended Stats 1987 ch 923 §100, Stats 1988 ch 1199 §106. (f) Former CC §730.04, as added Stats 1967 ch 1508 §2, amended Stats 1968 ch 448 §1. (g) Former CC §730.06, as added Stats 1963 ch 37 §1. (h) Former CC §§1366, 1368, 1369. (i) Stats 1941 ch 898 §4. (j) Fields Draft NY CC §623. (k) Uniform Principal and Income Act §4.

§ 16347. Reallocation of certain amounts to principal

(a) If a fiduciary determines that an allocation between income and principal required by Section 16348, 16349, 16350, 16351, or 16354 is insubstantial, the fiduciary may allocate the entire amount to principal, unless subdivision (e) of Section 16327 applies to the allocation.

(b) A fiduciary may presume an allocation is insubstantial under subdivision (a) if both of the following conditions are met:

(1) The amount of the allocation would increase or decrease net income in an accounting period, as determined before the allocation, by less than 10 percent.

(2) The asset producing the receipt to be allocated has a fair market value of less than 10 percent of the total fair market value of the assets owned or held by the fiduciary at the beginning of the accounting period.

(c) The power to make a determination under subdivision (a) may be either of the following:

(1) Exercised by a cofiduciary in the manner described in subdivision (f) of Section 16327.

(2) Released or delegated for a reason described in subdivision (g) of Section 16327, and in the manner described in subdivision (h) of Section 16327.

(d) This section does not impose a duty on the trustee to make an allocation under this section, and the trustee is not liable for failure to make an allocation under this section. **Leg.H.** Added Stats 2023 ch 28 §2 (SB 522), effective January 1, 2024.

Prior Law Former Prob C §16347, relating to undistributed income, was added Stats 1999 ch 145 §5 (AB 846), effective January 1, 2000, and repealed Stats 2023 ch 28 §1 (SB 522), effective January 1, 2024. Derivation: (a) Former Prob C §160. (b) Former Prob C §162, as amended Stats 1941 ch 336 §1, Stats 1953 ch 986 §1, Stats 1959 ch 1882 §1, Stats 1982 ch 520 §1. (c) Former Prob C §§661, 663, as added Stats 1983 ch 842 §40. (d) Former Prob C §16304, as enacted Stats 1990 ch 79 §14. (e) Former Prob C §16304, as added Stats 1986 ch 820 §40, amended Stats 1987 ch 923 §100, Stats 1988 ch 1199 §106. (f) Former CC §730.04, as added Stats 1967 ch 1508 §2, amended Stats 1968 ch 448 §1. (g) Former CC §730.06, as added Stats 1963 ch 37 §1. (h) Former CC §§1366, 1368, 1369. (i) Stats 1941 ch 898 §4. (j) Fields Draft NY CC §623. (k) Uniform Principal and Income Act §4.

§ 16348. Separate funds; Marital trusts

(a) The following definitions apply for purposes of this section:

(1) "Internal income of a separate fund" means the amount determined under subdivision (b).

(2) "Marital trust" means a trust that meets all the following criteria:

(A) The settlor's surviving spouse is the only current income beneficiary and is entitled to a distribution of all the current net income of the trust.

(B) The trust qualifies for a marital deduction with respect to the settlor's estate under Section 2056 of the Internal Revenue Code of 1986 (26 U.S.C. Sec. 2056) because of either of the following:

(i) An election to qualify for a marital deduction under Section 2056(b)(7) of the Internal Revenue Code of 1986 (26 U.S.C. Sec. 2056(b)(7)) has been made.

(ii) The trust qualifies for a marital deduction under Section 2056(b)(5) of the Internal Revenue Code of 1986 (26 U.S.C. Sec. 2056(b)(5)).

(3) "Payment" means an amount a fiduciary may receive over a fixed number of years or during the life of one or more individuals because of services rendered or property transferred to the payor in exchange for future amounts the fiduciary may receive. The term includes an amount received in money or property from the payor's general assets or from a separate fund created by the payor.

(4) "Separate fund" includes a private or commercial annuity, an individual retirement account, and a pension, profit-sharing, stock bonus, or stock ownership plan.

(b) For each accounting period, the following rules apply to a separate fund:

(1) The fiduciary shall determine the internal income of the separate fund as if the separate fund were a trust subject to this chapter.

(2) If the fiduciary cannot determine the internal income of the separate fund under paragraph (1), the internal income of the separate fund is deemed to equal 4 percent of the value of the separate fund, according to the most recent statement of value preceding the beginning of the accounting period.

(3) If the fiduciary cannot determine the value of the separate fund under paragraph (2), the value of the separate fund is deemed to equal the present value of the expected future payments, as determined under Section 7520 of the Internal Revenue Code of 1986 (26 U.S.C. Sec. 7520) for the month preceding the beginning of the accounting period for which the computation is made.

(c) A fiduciary shall allocate a payment received from a separate fund during an accounting period to income, to the extent of the internal income of the separate fund during the period, and the balance to principal.

(d) The fiduciary of a marital trust shall do all of the following:

(1) Withdraw from a separate fund the amount the current income beneficiary of the trust requests the fiduciary to withdraw, not greater than the amount by which the internal income of the separate fund during the accounting period exceeds the amount the fiduciary otherwise receives from the separate fund during the period.

(2) Transfer from principal to income the amount the current income beneficiary requests the fiduciary to transfer, not greater than the amount by which the internal income of the separate fund during the period exceeds the amount the fiduciary receives from the separate fund during the period after the application of paragraph (1).

(3) Distribute all of the following to the current income beneficiary as income:

(A) The amount of the internal income of the separate fund received or withdrawn during the period.

(B) The amount transferred from principal to income under paragraph (2).

(e) For a trust, other than a marital trust, of which one or more current income beneficiaries are entitled to a distribution of all the current net income, the fiduciary shall transfer from principal to income the amount by which the internal income of a separate fund during the accounting period exceeds the amount the fiduciary receives from the separate fund during the period. **Leg.H.** Added Stats 2023 ch 28 §2 (SB 522), effective January 1, 2024.

§ 16349. Allocation of liquidating assets

(a) For purposes of this section, "liquidating asset" means an asset whose value will diminish or terminate because the asset is expected to produce receipts for a limited time. The term includes a leasehold, patent, copyright, royalty right, and right to receive payments during a period of more than one year under an arrangement that does not provide for the payment of interest on the unpaid balance.

(b) This section does not apply to a receipt subject to Section 16340, 16348, 16350, 16351, 16353, 16354, 16355, or 16362.

(c) A fiduciary shall make allocations in the following manner:

(1) To income:

(A) A receipt produced by a liquidating asset, to the extent the receipt does not exceed 4 percent of the value of the asset.

(B) If the fiduciary cannot determine the value of the asset, 10 percent of the receipt.

(2) To principal, the balance of the receipt. **Leg.H.** Added Stats 2023 ch 28 §2 (SB 522), effective January 1, 2024.

§ 16350. Allocation of receipts from interest in minerals, water, or other natural resources

(a) To the extent a fiduciary does not account for a receipt from an interest in minerals, water, or other natural resources as a business under Section 16432, the fiduciary shall allocate the receipt in the following manner:

(1) To income, to the extent received:

(A) As delay rental or annual rent on a lease.

(B) As a factor for interest or the equivalent of interest under an agreement creating a production payment.

(C) On account of an interest in renewable water.

(2) To principal, if received from a production payment, to the extent subparagraph (B) of paragraph (1) does not apply.

(3) Between income and principal in a reasonable manner, to the extent received:

(A) On account of an interest in nonrenewable water.

(B) As a royalty, shut-in-well payment, take-or-pay payment, or bonus.

(C) From a working interest or any other interest not provided for in subparagraph (A) or (B), or paragraph (1) or (2).

(b) This section applies to an interest owned or held by a fiduciary whether or not a settlor was extracting minerals, water, or other natural resources before the fiduciary owned or held the interest.

(c) An allocation of a receipt under paragraph (3) of subdivision (a) is presumed to be reasonable if the amount allocated to principal is equal to the amount allowed by the Internal Revenue Code of 1986, as amended (Title 26 of the United States Code, as amended), as a deduction for depletion of the interest.

(d) If a fiduciary owns or holds an interest in minerals, water, or other natural resources before the effective date of this chapter, the fiduciary may allocate receipts from the interest as provided in this section or in the manner used by the fiduciary before the effective date of this chapter. If the fiduciary acquires an interest in minerals, water, or other natural resources on or after the effective date of this chapter, the fiduciary shall allocate receipts from the interest as provided in this section. **Leg.H.** Added Stats 2023 ch 28 §2 (SB 522), effective January 1, 2024.

Prior Law Former Prob C §16350, relating to allocation of receipts from entity, return of capital and trustee duties, was added Stats 2017 ch 577 §2 (AB 307), effective January 1, 2018, and repealed Stats 2023 ch 28 §1 (SB 522), effective January 1, 2024.

Former Prob C §16350, similar to the present section, was added Stats 1999 ch 145 §5 (AB 846), amended Stats 2005 ch 51 §1 (SB296), effective July 18, 2005, Stats 2013 ch 105 §1 (AB 1029), effective January 1, 2014, Stats 2014 ch 867 §1 (AB 296), effective September 30, 2014, and repealed Stats 2017 ch 577 §1 (AB 307), effective January 1, 2018.

§ 16351. Allocation of receipts from timber sales

(a) To the extent a fiduciary does not account for receipts from the sale of timber and related products as a business under Section 16342, the fiduciary shall allocate the net receipts:

(1) To income, to the extent the amount of timber cut from the land does not exceed the rate of growth of the timber.

(2) To principal, to the extent the amount of timber cut from the land exceeds the rate of growth of the timber or the net receipts are from the sale of standing timber.

(3) Between income and principal, if the net receipts are from the lease of land used for growing and cutting timber or from a contract to cut timber from land, by determining the amount of timber cut from the land under the lease or contract and applying the rules in paragraphs (1) and (2).

(4) To principal, to the extent advance payments, bonuses, and other payments are not allocated under paragraph (1), (2), or (3).

(b) In determining net receipts to be allocated under subdivision (a), a fiduciary shall deduct and transfer to principal a reasonable amount for depletion.

(c) This section applies to land owned or held by a fiduciary whether or not a settlor was cutting timber from the land before the fiduciary owned or held the property.

(d) If a fiduciary owns or holds an interest in land used for growing and cutting timber before the effective date of this chapter, the fiduciary may allocate net receipts from the sale of timber and related products as provided in this section or in the manner used by the fiduciary before the effective date of this chapter. If the fiduciary acquires an interest in land used for growing and cutting timber on or after the effective date of this chapter, the fiduciary shall allocate net receipts from the sale of timber and related products as provided in this section. **Leg.H.** Added Stats 2023 ch 28 §2 (SB 522), effective January 1, 2024.

Prior Law Former Prob C §16351, relating to distribution from trust or estate, was added Stats 1999 ch 145 §5 (AB 846), effective January 1, 2000, and repealed Stats 2023 ch 28 §1 (SB 522), effective January 1, 2024.

§ 16352. Marital deduction

(a) If a trust received property for which a gift or estate tax marital deduction was allowed and the settlor's spouse holds a mandatory income interest in the trust, the spouse may require the trustee, to the extent the trust assets otherwise do not provide the spouse with sufficient income from or use of the trust assets to qualify for the deduction, to do any of the following:

(1) Make property productive of income.

(2) Convert property to property productive of income within a reasonable time.

(3) Exercise the power to adjust under Section 16327.

(b) The trustee may decide which action or combination of actions in subdivision (a) to take. **Leg.H.** Added Stats 2023 ch 28 §2 (SB 522), effective January 1, 2024.

Prior Law Former Prob C §16352, relating to conducting business or other activity, was added Stats 1999 ch 145 §5 (AB 846), effective January 1, 2000, and repealed Stats 2023 ch 28 §1 (SB 522), effective January 1, 2024. Derivation: (a) Prob C §16309, as added Stats 1986 ch 820 §40. (b) Former CC §730.09, as added Stats 1967 ch 1508 §2. (c) Former CC §730.11, as added Stats 1953 ch 37 §1. (d) Stats 1941 ch 898 §9. (e) Uniform Principal and Income Act §9.

§ 16353. Transactions in derivatives

(a) For purposes of this section, "derivative" means a contract, instrument, other arrangement, or combination of contracts, instruments, or other arrangements, the value, rights, and obligations of which are, in whole or in part, dependent on or derived from an underlying tangible or intangible asset, group of tangible or intangible assets, index, or occurrence of an event. The term includes stocks, fixed-income securities, and financial instruments and arrangements based on indices, commodities, interest rates, weather-related events, and credit default events.

(b) To the extent a fiduciary does not account for a transaction in derivatives as a business under Section 16342, the fiduciary shall allocate 10 percent of receipts from the transaction and 10 percent of disbursements made in connection with the transaction to income and the balance to principal.

(c) Subdivision (d) applies under the following circumstances:

(1) If a fiduciary does any of the following:

(A) Grants an option to buy property from a trust, whether or not the trust owns the property when the option is granted.

(B) Grants an option that permits another person to sell property to the trust.

(C) Acquires an option to buy property for the trust or an option to sell an asset owned by the trust.

(2) The fiduciary or other owner of the asset is required to deliver the asset if the option is exercised.

(d) If this subdivision applies, the fiduciary shall allocate 10 percent to income and the balance to principal of the following amounts:

(1) An amount received for granting the option.

(2) An amount paid to acquire the option.

(3) Gain or loss realized on the exercise, exchange, settlement, offset, closing, or expiration of the option. **Leg.H.** Added Stats 2023 ch 28 §2 (SB 522), effective January 1, 2024.

§ 16354. Asset-backed securities

(a) Except as otherwise provided in subdivision (b), a fiduciary shall allocate to income a receipt from or related to an asset-backed security, to the extent the payor identifies the payment as being from interest or other current return, and to principal the balance of the receipt.

(b) If a fiduciary receives one or more payments in exchange for part or all of the fiduciary's interest in an asset-backed security, including a liquidation or redemption of the fiduciary's interest in the security, the fiduciary shall allocate to income 10 percent of receipts from the transaction and 10 percent of disbursements made in connection with the transaction, and to principal the balance of the receipts and disbursements. **Leg.H.** Added Stats 2023 ch 28 §2 (SB 522), effective January 1, 2024.

§ 16355. Financial instruments or arrangements not addressed by chapter

A fiduciary shall allocate receipts from, or related to, a financial instrument or arrangement not otherwise addressed by this chapter. The allocation shall be consistent with the principles of Sections 16353 and 16354. **Leg.H.** Added Stats 2023 ch 28 §2 (SB 522), effective January 1, 2024.

Prior Law Former Prob C §16355, relating to allocations to principal, was added Stats 1999 ch 145 §5 (AB 846), effective January 1, 2000, and repealed Stats 2023 ch 28 §1 (SB 522), effective January 1, 2024.

ARTICLE 5
Allocation of Disbursements

Disbursements from income. § 16360.
Disbursements from principal. § 16361.
Depreciation. § 16362.
Reimbursement of income. § 16363.
Reimbursement of principal; Reserve for future disbursements. § 16364.
Taxes. § 16365.
Adjustments between income and principal; Reimbursements; Offset. § 16366.

Order of distribution sources. § 16367.

§ 16360. Disbursements from income

Subject to Section 16363, and except as otherwise provided in paragraph (2) or (3) of subdivision (c) of Section 16370, a fiduciary shall disburse from income all of the following:

(a) One-half of both of the following:

(1) The regular compensation of the fiduciary and any person providing investment advisory, custodial, or other services to the fiduciary, to the extent income is sufficient.

(2) An expense for an accounting, judicial, or nonjudicial proceeding, or other matter that involves both income and successive interests, to the extent income is sufficient.

(b) The balance of the disbursements described in paragraph (1) of subdivision (a), to the extent a fiduciary that is an independent person determines that making those disbursements from income would be in the interests of the beneficiaries.

(c) Another ordinary expense incurred in connection with administration, management, or preservation of property and distribution of income, including interest, an ordinary repair, regularly recurring tax assessed against principal, and an expense of an accounting, judicial or nonjudicial proceeding, or other matter that involves primarily an income interest, to the extent income is sufficient.

(d) A premium on insurance covering loss of a principal asset or income from or use of the asset. **Leg.H.** Added Stats 2023 ch 28 §2 (SB 522), effective January 1, 2024.

Prior Law Former Prob C §16360, relating to insubstantial allocation, was added Stats 1999 ch 145 §5 (AB 846), effective January 1, 2000, and repealed Stats 2023 ch 28 §1 (SB 522), effective January 1, 2024.

§ 16361. Disbursements from principal

(a) Subject to Section 16364, and except as otherwise provided in paragraph (2) of subdivision (c) of Section 16370, a fiduciary shall disburse from principal all of the following:

(1) The balance of the disbursements described in paragraph (1) of subdivision (a) of, and subdivision (c) of, Section 16360, after application of subdivision (b) of Section 16360.

(2) The fiduciary's compensation calculated on principal as a fee for acceptance, distribution, or termination.

(3) A payment of an expense to prepare for or execute a sale or other disposition of property.

(4) A payment on the principal of a trust debt.

(5) A payment of an expense of an accounting, judicial or nonjudicial proceeding, or other matter that involves primarily principal, including a proceeding to construe the terms of the trust or protect property.

(6) A payment of a premium for insurance, including title insurance, not described in subdivision (d) of Section 16360, of which the fiduciary is the owner and beneficiary.

(7) A payment of an estate or inheritance tax or other tax imposed because of the death of a decedent, including penalties, apportioned to the trust.

(8) The following payments:

(A) A payment related to environmental matters, including:

(i) Reclamation.

(ii) Assessment of environmental conditions.

(iii) Remedying and removing environmental contamination.

(iv) Monitoring remedial activities and the release of substances.

(v) Preventing future releases of substances.

(vi) Collecting amounts from persons liable or potentially liable for the costs of activities described in clauses (i) to (v), inclusive.

(vii) Penalties imposed under environmental laws or regulations.

(viii) Other actions to comply with environmental laws or regulations.

(ix) Statutory or common law claims by third parties.

(x) Defending claims based on environmental matters.

(B) A payment for a premium for insurance for matters described in subparagraph (A).

(9) Payments representing extraordinary repairs or expenses incurred in making a capital improvement to trust property, including special assessments.

(b) If a principal asset is encumbered with an obligation that requires income from the asset to be paid directly to a creditor, the fiduciary shall transfer from principal to income an amount equal to the income paid to the creditor in reduction of the principal balance of the obligation. **Leg.H.** Added Stats 2023 §2 (SB 522), effective January 1, 2024.

Prior Law Former Prob C §16361, relating to allocation of payment and separate fund, was added Stats 2006 ch 569 §3 (AB 2347), effective January 1, 2007, amended Stats 2009 ch 152 §1 (AB 1545), effective January 1, 2010, Stats 2010 ch 71 §1 (AB 229), effective January 1, 2011, and repealed Stats 2023 ch 28 §1 (SB 522), effective January 1, 2024.

Former Prob C §16361, similar to the present section, was added Stats 1999 ch 145 §5 and repealed Stats 2006 ch 569 §2 (AB 2347), effective January 1, 2007.

§ 16362. Depreciation

(a) For purposes of this section, "depreciation" means a reduction in value due to wear, tear, decay, corrosion, or gradual obsolescence of a tangible asset having a useful life of more than one year.

(b) A fiduciary may transfer to principal a reasonable amount of the net money receipts from a principal asset that is subject to depreciation, but may not transfer any amount for depreciation:

(1) Of the part of real property used or available for use by a beneficiary as a residence.

(2) Of tangible personal property held or made available for the personal use or enjoyment of a beneficiary.

(3) Under this section, to the extent the fiduciary accounts under either of the following:

(A) Section 16349, for the asset.

(B) Section 16342, for the business or other activity in which the asset is used.

(c) An amount transferred to principal under this section need not be separately held. **Leg.H.** Added Stats 2023 ch 28 §2 (SB 522), effective January 1, 2024.

Prior Law Former Prob C §16362, relating to "liquidating asset," was added Stats 1999 ch 145 §5 (AB 846), effective January 1, 2000, and repealed Stats 2023 ch 28 §1 (SB 522), effective January 1, 2024.

§ 16363. Reimbursement of income

(a) If a fiduciary makes or expects to make an income disbursement described in subdivision (b), the fiduciary may transfer an appropriate amount from principal to income in one or more accounting periods to reimburse income.

(b) To the extent the fiduciary has not been, and does not expect to be, reimbursed by a third party, income disbursements to which subdivision (a) applies include all of the following:

(1) An amount chargeable to principal, but paid from income because principal is illiquid.

(2) A disbursement made to prepare property for sale, including improvements and commissions.

(3) A disbursement described in Section 16360.

(c) If an asset whose ownership gives rise to an income disbursement becomes subject to a successive interest after an income interest ends, the fiduciary may continue to make transfers under subdivision (a). **Leg.H.** Added Stats 2023 ch 28 §2 (SB 522), effective January 1, 2024.

Prior Law Former Prob C §16363, relating to interest in minerals, water, or other natural resources, was added Stats 1999 ch 145 §5 (AB 846), effective January 1, 2000, amended Stats 2006 ch 569 §4 (AB 2347), effective January 1, 2007, and repealed Stats 2023 ch 28 §1 (SB 522), effective January 1, 2024.

§ 16364. Reimbursement of principal; Reserve for future disbursements

(a) If a fiduciary makes or expects to make a principal disbursement described in subdivision (b), the fiduciary may transfer an appropriate amount from income to principal in one or more accounting periods to reimburse principal or provide a reserve for future principal disbursements.

(b) To the extent a fiduciary has not been, and does not expect to be, reimbursed by a third party, principal disbursements to which subdivision (a) applies include all of the following:

(1) An amount chargeable to income but paid from principal because income is not sufficient.

(2) The cost of an improvement to principal, whether a change to an existing asset or the construction of a new asset, including a special assessment.

(3) A disbursement made to prepare property for rental, including tenant allowances, leasehold improvements, and commissions.

(4) A periodic payment on an obligation secured by a principal asset, to the extent the amount transferred from income to principal for depreciation is less than the periodic payment.

(5) A disbursement described in subdivision (a) of Section 16361.

(c) If an asset whose ownership gives rise to a principal disbursement becomes subject to a successive interest after an income interest ends, the fiduciary may continue to make transfers under subdivision (a). **Leg.H.** Added Stats 2023 ch 28 §2 (SB 522), effective January 1, 2024.

Prior Law Former Prob C §16364, relating to sale of timber and related products, was added Stats 1999 ch 145 §5 (AB 846), effective January 1, 2000, amended Stats 2006 ch 569 §5 (AB 2347), effective January 1, 2007, and repealed Stats 2023 ch 28 §1 (SB 522), effective January 1, 2024.

§ 16365. Taxes

(a) A tax required to be paid by a fiduciary that is based on receipts allocated to income shall be paid from income.

(b) A tax required to be paid by a fiduciary that is based on receipts allocated to principal shall be paid from principal, even if the tax is called an income tax by the taxing authority.

(c) Subject to subdivision (d) and Sections 16363, 16364, and 16366, a tax required to be paid by a fiduciary on a share of an entity's taxable income in an accounting period shall be paid from the following:

(1) Income and principal, proportionately to the allocation between income and principal of receipts from the entity in the period.

(2) Principal, to the extent the tax exceeds the receipts from the entity in the period.

(d) After applying subdivisions (a) to (c), inclusive, a fiduciary shall adjust income or principal receipts, to the extent the taxes the fiduciary pays are reduced because of a deduction for a payment made to a beneficiary. **Leg.H.** Added Stats 2023 ch 28 §2 (SB 522), effective January 1, 2024.

Prior Law Former Prob C §16365, relating to marital deduction, was added Stats 1999 ch 145 §5 (AB 846), effective January 1, 2000, and repealed Stats 2023 ch 28 §1 (SB 522), effective January 1, 2024.

§ 16366. Adjustments between income and principal; Reimbursements; Offset

(a) A fiduciary may make an adjustment between income and principal to offset the shifting of economic interests or tax benefits between current income beneficiaries and successor beneficiaries that arises from any of the following:

(1) An election or decision the fiduciary makes regarding a tax matter, other than a decision to claim an income tax deduction to which subdivision (b) applies.

(2) An income tax or other tax imposed on the fiduciary or a beneficiary as a result of a transaction involving the fiduciary or a distribution by the fiduciary.

(3) Ownership by the fiduciary of an interest in an entity, a part of whose taxable income, whether or not distributed, is includable in the taxable income of the fiduciary or a beneficiary.

(b) If the amount of an estate tax marital or charitable deduction is reduced because a fiduciary deducts an amount paid from principal for income tax purposes instead of deducting it for estate tax purposes and, as a result, estate taxes paid from principal are increased and income taxes paid by the fiduciary or a beneficiary are decreased, the fiduciary shall charge each beneficiary that benefits from the decrease in income tax to reimburse the principal from which the increase in estate tax is paid. The total reimbursement shall equal the increase in the estate tax, to the extent the principal used to pay the increase would have qualified for a marital or charitable deduction but for the payment. The share of the reimbursement for each fiduciary or beneficiary whose income taxes are reduced shall be the same as its share of the total decrease in income tax.

(c) A fiduciary that charges a beneficiary under subdivision (b) may offset the charge by obtaining payment from the beneficiary, withholding an amount from future distributions to the beneficiary, or adopting another method or combination of methods. **Leg.H.** Added Stats 2023 ch 28 §2 (SB 522), effective January 1, 2024.

Prior Law Former Prob C §16366, relating to transactions in derivatives and option to buy, was added Stats 1999 ch 145 §5 (AB 846), effective January 1, 2000, and repealed Stats 2023 ch 28 §1 (SB 522), effective January 1, 2024.

§ 16367. Order of distribution sources

Unless otherwise provided by the governing instrument, determined by the trustee, or ordered by the court, distributions to beneficiaries shall be considered paid in the following order from the following sources:

(a) From net taxable income other than capital gains.

(b) From net realized short-term capital gains.

(c) From net realized long-term capital gains.

(d) From tax-exempt and other income.

(e) From principal of the trust. **Leg.H.** Added Stats 2023 ch 28 §2 (SB 522), effective January 1, 2024.

Prior Law Former Prob C §16367, relating to asset-backed security, was added Stats 1999 ch 145 §5 (AB 846), effective January 1, 2000, and repealed Stats 2023 ch 28 §1 (SB 522), effective January 1, 2024.

ARTICLE 6
Death of Individual or Termination of Income Interest

Death or termination of income interest; Distribution. § 16370.
Beneficiary portion of net income. § 16371.

§ 16370. Death or termination of income interest; Distribution

(a) This section applies when either of the following occurs:

(1) The death of an individual results in the creation of an estate or trust.

(2) An income interest in a trust terminates, whether the trust continues or is distributed.

(b) A fiduciary of an estate or trust with an income interest that terminates shall determine, under subdivision (g) and Article 4 (commencing with Section 16340), Article 5 (commencing with Section 16360), and Article 7 (commencing with Section 16375), the amount of net income and net principal receipts received from property specifically given to a beneficiary. The fiduciary shall distribute the net income and net principal receipts to the beneficiary that is to receive the specific property.

(c) A fiduciary shall determine the income and net income of an estate or income interest in a trust that terminates, other than the amount of net income determined under subdivision (b), under Article 4 (commencing with Section 16340), Article 5 (commencing with Section 16360), and Article 7 (commencing with Section 16375), and by doing the following:

(1) Including in net income all income from property used or sold to discharge liabilities.

(2) Paying, from income or principal, in the fiduciary's discretion, fees of attorneys, accountants, and fiduciaries, court costs and other expenses of administration, and interest on estate and inheritance taxes and other taxes imposed because of the decedent's death, but the fiduciary may pay the expenses from income of property passing to a trust for which the fiduciary claims a federal estate tax marital or charitable deduction, only to the extent that either of the following conditions is met:

(A) The payment of the expenses from income will not cause the reduction or loss of the deduction.

(B) The fiduciary makes an adjustment under subdivision (b) of Section 16366.

(3) Paying from principal other disbursements made or incurred in connection with the settlement of the estate or the winding up of an income interest that terminates, including both of the following:

(A) To the extent authorized by the decedent's will, the terms of the trust, or applicable law, debts, funeral expenses, disposition of remains, family allowances, estate and inheritance taxes, and other taxes imposed because of the decedent's death.

(B) Related penalties that are apportioned by the decedent's will, the terms of the trust, or applicable law, to the estate or income interest that terminates.

(d) A specific gift distributable under a trust shall carry with it the same benefits and burdens as a specific devise under a will, as set forth in Chapter 8 (commencing with Section 12000) of Part 10 of Division 7.

(e) A general pecuniary gift, an annuity, or a gift of maintenance distributable under a trust carries with it income and bears interest in the same manner as a general pecuniary devise, an annuity, or a gift of maintenance under a will, as set forth in Chapter 8 (commencing with Section 12000) of Part 10 of Division 7.

(f) A fiduciary shall distribute net income remaining after payments required by subdivisions (d) and (e) in the manner described in Section 16371 to all other beneficiaries, including a beneficiary that receives a pecuniary amount in trust, even if the beneficiary holds an unqualified power to withdraw assets from the trust or other presently exercisable general power of appointment over the trust.

(g) A fiduciary may not reduce principal or income receipts from property described in subdivision (b) because of a payment described in Section 16360 or 16361 to the extent the decedent's will, the terms of the trust, or applicable law requires the fiduciary to make the payment from assets other than the property or to the extent the fiduciary recovers or expects to recover the payment from a third party. The net income and principal receipts from the property shall be determined by including the amount the fiduciary receives or pays regarding the property, whether the amount accrued or became due before, on, or after the date of the decedent's death or an income interest's terminating event, and making a reasonable provision for an amount the estate or income interest may become obligated to pay after the property is distributed. **Leg.H.** Added Stats 2023 ch 28 §2 (SB 522), effective January 1, 2024.

Prior Law Former Prob C §16370, relating to disbursements from income, was added Stats 1999 ch 145 §5 (AB 846), effective January 1, 2000, and repealed Stats 2023 ch 28 §1 (SB 522), effective January 1, 2024.

§ 16371. Beneficiary portion of net income

(a) Except to the extent that Article 3 (commencing with Section 16330) applies for a beneficiary that is a trust, each beneficiary described in subdivision (f) of Section 16370 is entitled to receive a share of the net income equal to the beneficiary's fractional interest in undistributed principal assets, using values as of the distribution date. If a fiduciary makes more than one distribution of assets to beneficiaries to which this section applies, each beneficiary, including a beneficiary that does not receive part of the distribution, is entitled, as of each distribution date, to a share of the net income the fiduciary received after the decedent's death, an income interest's other terminating event, or the preceding distribution by the fiduciary.

(b) In determining a beneficiary's share of net income under subdivision (a), the following rules apply:

(1) The beneficiary is entitled to receive a share of the net income equal to the beneficiary's fractional interest in the undistributed principal assets immediately before the distribution date.

(2) The beneficiary's fractional interest under paragraph (1) shall be calculated on the aggregate value of the assets as of the distribution date without reducing the value by any unpaid principal obligation, and without regard to either of the following:

(A) Property specifically given to a beneficiary under the decedent's will or the terms of the trust.

(B) Property required to pay pecuniary amounts not in trust.

(3) The distribution date under paragraph (1) may be the date as of which the fiduciary calculates the value of the assets, if that date is reasonably near the date on which the assets are distributed.

(c) To the extent a fiduciary does not distribute under this section all the collected but undistributed net income to each beneficiary as of a distribution date, the fiduciary shall maintain records showing the interest of each beneficiary in the net income.

(d) If this section applies to income from an asset, a fiduciary may apply the rules in this section to net gain or loss realized from the disposition of the asset after the decedent's death, an income interest's terminating event, or the preceding distribution by the fiduciary. **Leg.H.** Added Stats 2023 ch 28 §2 (SB 522), effective January 1, 2024.

Prior Law Former Prob C §16371, relating to disbursements from principal, was added Stats 1999 ch 145 §5 (AB 846), effective January 1, 2000, and repealed Stats 2023 ch 28 §1 (SB 522), effective January 1, 2024.

ARTICLE 7
Apportionment at Beginning and End of Income Interest

Time of entitlement; Time when asset subject to trust. § 16375.
Allocations of income receipt or disbursement; Due dates; Periodic receipts or disbursements. § 16376.
Undistributed income. § 16377.

§ 16375. Time of entitlement; Time when asset subject to trust

(a) An income beneficiary is entitled to net income in accordance with the terms of the trust from the date an income interest begins. The income interest begins on the date specified in the terms of the trust or, if no date is specified, on the date an asset becomes subject to either of the following:

(1) The trust for the current income beneficiary.

(2) A successive interest for a successor beneficiary.

(b) An asset becomes subject to a trust under paragraph (1) of subdivision (a) as follows:

(1) For an asset that is transferred to the trust during the settlor's life, on the date the asset is transferred.

(2) For an asset that becomes subject to the trust because of a decedent's death, on the date of the decedent's death, even if there is an intervening period of administration of the decedent's estate.

(3) For an asset that is transferred to a fiduciary by a third party because of a decedent's death, on the date of the decedent's death.

(c) An asset becomes subject to a successive interest under paragraph (2) of subdivision (a) on the day after the preceding income interest ends, as determined under subdivision (d), even if there is an intervening period of administration to wind up the preceding income interest.

(d) An income interest ends on the day before an income beneficiary dies or another terminating event occurs or on the last day of a period during which there is no beneficiary to which a fiduciary may, or is required to, distribute income. **Leg.H.** Added Stats 2023 ch 28 §2 (SB 522), effective January 1, 2024.

Prior Law Former Prob C §16375, relating to adjustments and reimbursements, was added Stats 1999 ch 145 §5 (AB 846), effective January 1, 2000, and repealed Stats 2023 ch 28 §1 (SB 522), effective January 1, 2024.

§ 16376. Allocations of income receipt or disbursement; Due dates; Periodic receipts or disbursements

(a) A fiduciary shall allocate an income receipt or disbursement, other than a receipt to which subdivision (b) of Section 16370 applies, to principal if its due date occurs before the date on which either of the following occurs:

(1) For an estate, the decedent died.

(2) For a trust or successive interest, an income interest begins.

(b) If the due date of a periodic income receipt or disbursement occurs on or after the date on which a decedent died or an income interest begins, a fiduciary shall allocate the receipt or disbursement to income.

(c) If an income receipt or disbursement is not periodic or has no due date, a fiduciary shall treat the receipt or disbursement under this section as accruing from day to day. The fiduciary shall allocate to principal the portion of the receipt or disbursement accruing before the date on which a decedent died or an income interest begins, and to income the balance.

(d) A receipt or disbursement is periodic under subdivisions (b) and (c) under either of the following circumstances:

(1) The receipt or disbursement shall be paid at regular intervals under an obligation to make payments.

(2) The payor customarily makes payments at regular intervals.

(e) An item of income or obligation is due under this section on the date the payor is required to make a payment. If a payment date is not stated, there is no due date.

(f) Distributions to shareholders or other owners from an entity to which Section 16340 applies are due at one of the following times:

(1) On the date fixed by or on behalf of the entity for determining the persons entitled to receive the distribution.

(2) If a date is not fixed, on the date of the decision by or on behalf of the entity to make the distribution.

(3) If a date is not fixed and the fiduciary does not know the date of the decision by or on behalf of the entity to make the distribution, on the date the fiduciary learns of the decision. **Leg.H.** Added Stats 2023 ch 28 §2 (SB 522), effective January 1, 2024.

§ 16377. Undistributed income

(a) For purposes of this section, "undistributed income" means net income received on or before the date on which an income interest ends. "Undistributed income" does not include an item of income or expense that is due or accrued, or net income that has been added or is required to be added to principal under the terms of the trust.

(b) Except as otherwise provided in subdivision (c), when a mandatory income interest of a beneficiary ends, the fiduciary shall pay the beneficiary's share of the undistributed income that is not disposed of under the terms of the trust to the beneficiary or, if the beneficiary does not survive the date the interest ends, to the beneficiary's estate.

(c) If a beneficiary has an unqualified power to withdraw more than 5 percent of the value of a trust immediately before an income interest ends, both of the following shall apply:

(1) The fiduciary shall allocate to principal the undistributed income from the portion of the trust that may be withdrawn.

(2) Subdivision (b) applies only to the balance of the undistributed income.

(d) When a fiduciary's obligation to pay a fixed annuity or a fixed fraction of the value of assets ends, the fiduciary shall prorate the final payment as required to preserve an income tax, gift tax, estate tax, or other tax benefit. **Leg.H.** Added Stats 2023 ch 28 §2 (SB 522), effective January 1, 2024.

ARTICLE 8
Miscellaneous Provisions

Construction and application of act. § 16380.
Effect on federal Electronic Signatures in Global and National Commerce Act. § 16381.
Applicability of chapter. § 16382.
Severability of provisions. § 16383.

§ 16380. Construction and application of act

In applying and construing this uniform act, consideration shall be given to the need to promote uniformity of the law with respect to its subject matter among states that enact it. **Leg.H.** Added Stats 2023 ch 28 §2 (SB 522), effective January 1, 2024.

§ 16381. Effect on federal Electronic Signatures in Global and National Commerce Act

This chapter modifies, limits, and supersedes the Electronic Signatures in Global and National Commerce Act (15 U.S.C. Sec. 7001 et seq.), but does not modify, limit, or supersede Section 101(c) of that act (15 U.S.C. Sec. 7001(c)), or authorize electronic delivery of any of the notices described in Section 103(b) of that act (15 U.S.C. Sec. 7003(b)). **Leg.H.** Added Stats 2023 ch 28 §2 (SB 522), effective January 1, 2024.

§ 16382. Applicability of chapter

This chapter applies to a trust or estate existing or created on or after the effective date of this chapter, except as otherwise expressly provided in the terms of the trust or this chapter. **Leg.H.** Added Stats 2023 ch 28 §2 (SB 522), effective January 1, 2024.

§ 16383. Severability of provisions

If any provision of this chapter or its application to any person or circumstance is held invalid, the invalidity does not affect other provisions or applications of this chapter that can be given effect without the invalid provision or application, and to this end the provisions of this chapter are severable. **Leg.H.** Added Stats 2023 ch 28 §2 (SB 522), effective January 1, 2024.

CHAPTER 4
LIABILITY OF TRUSTEES TO BENEFICIARIES

Article 1. Liability for Breach of Trust.
Article 2. Remedies for Breach of Trust.
Article 3. Measure of Liability for Breach of Trust.
Article 4. Limitations and Exculpation.

ARTICLE 1
Liability for Breach of Trust

Breach of trust. §16400.
Trustee's liability to beneficiary for acts of agent. §16401.
Trustee's liability to beneficiary for acts of cotrustee. §16402.
Trustee's liability to beneficiary for acts of predecessor. §16403.

§16400. Breach of trust

A violation by the trustee of any duty that the trustee owes the beneficiary is a breach of trust. **Leg.H.** Enacted Stats 1990 ch 79 §14 (AB 759), operative July 1, 1991.

Prior Law: Former Prob C §16400, similar to the present section, was added Stats 1986 ch 820 §40, operative July 1, 1987, and repealed Stats 1990 ch 79 §13, operative July 1, 1991.

§16401. Trustee's liability to beneficiary for acts of agent

(a) Except as provided in subdivision (b), the trustee is not liable to the beneficiary for the acts or omissions of an agent.

(b) Under any of the circumstances described in this subdivision, the trustee is liable to the beneficiary for an act or omission of an agent employed by the trustee in the administration of the trust that would be a breach of the trust if committed by the trustee:

(1) Where the trustee directs the act of the agent.

(2) Where the trustee delegates to the agent the authority to perform an act that the trustee is under a duty not to delegate.

(3) Where the trustee does not use reasonable prudence in the selection of the agent or the retention of the agent selected by the trustee.

(4) Where the trustee does not periodically review the agent's overall performance and compliance with the terms of the delegation.

(5) Where the trustee conceals the act of the agent.

(6) Where the trustee neglects to take reasonable steps to compel the agent to redress the wrong in a case where the trustee knows of the agent's acts or omissions.

(c) The liability of a trustee for acts or omissions of agents that occurred before July 1, 1987, is governed by prior law and not by this section. **Leg.H.** Enacted Stats 1990 ch 79 §14 (AB 759), operative July 1, 1991. Amended Stats 1995 ch 63 §9 (SB 222), effective January 1, 1996.

Prior Law: Former Prob C §16401, similar to the present section, was added Stats 1986 ch 820 §40, operative July 1, 1987, and repealed Stats 1990 ch 79 §13, operative July 1, 1991.

§16402. Trustee's liability to beneficiary for acts of cotrustee

(a) Except as provided in subdivision (b), a trustee is not liable to the beneficiary for a breach of trust committed by a cotrustee.

(b) A trustee is liable to the beneficiary for a breach committed by a cotrustee under any of the following circumstances:

(1) Where the trustee participates in a breach of trust committed by the cotrustee.

(2) Where the trustee improperly delegates the administration of the trust to the cotrustee.

(3) Where the trustee approves, knowingly acquiesces in, or conceals a breach of trust committed by the cotrustee.

(4) Where the trustee negligently enables the cotrustee to commit a breach of trust.

(5) Where the trustee neglects to take reasonable steps to compel the cotrustee to redress a breach of trust in a case where the trustee knows or has information from which the trustee reasonably should have known of the breach.

(c) The liability of a trustee for acts or omissions of a cotrustee that occurred before July 1, 1987, is governed by prior law and not by this section. **Leg.H.** Enacted Stats 1990 ch 79 §14 (AB 759), operative July 1, 1991.

Prior Law: Former Prob C § 6402, similar to the present section, was added Stats 1986 ch 820 §40, operative July 1, 1987, and repealed Stats 1990 ch 79 §13, operative July 1, 1991.

§16403. Trustee's liability to beneficiary for acts of predecessor

(a) Except as provided in subdivision (b), a successor trustee is not liable to the beneficiary for a breach of trust committed by a predecessor trustee.

(b) A successor trustee is liable to the beneficiary for breach of trust involving acts or omissions of a predecessor trustee in any of the following circumstances:

(1) Where the successor trustee knows or has information from which the successor trustee reasonably should have known of a situation constituting a breach of trust committed by the predecessor trustee and the successor trustee improperly permits it to continue.

(2) Where the successor trustee neglects to take reasonable steps to compel the predecessor trustee to deliver the trust property to the successor trustee.

(3) Where the successor trustee neglects to take reasonable steps to redress a breach of trust committed by the predecessor trustee in a case where the successor trustee knows or has information from which the successor trustee reasonably should have known of the predecessor trustee's breach.

(c) The liability of a trustee for acts or omissions of a predecessor trustee that occurred before July 1, 1987, is governed by prior law and not by this section. **Leg.H.** Enacted Stats 1990 ch 79 §14 (AB 759), operative July 1, 1991.

Prior Law: Former Prob C §16403, similar to the present section, was added Stats 1986 ch 820 §40, operative July 1, 1987, and repealed Stats 1990 ch 79 §13, operative July 1, 1991.

ARTICLE 2
Remedies for Breach of Trust

Remedies for breach of trust. §16420.
Remedies for breach exclusively in equity. §16421.

§16420. Remedies for breach of trust

(a) If a trustee commits a breach of trust, or threatens to commit a breach of trust, a beneficiary or cotrustee of the trust may commence a proceeding for any of the following purposes that is appropriate:

(1) To compel the trustee to perform the trustee's duties.
(2) To enjoin the trustee from committing a breach of trust.
(3) To compel the trustee to redress a breach of trust by payment of money or otherwise.
(4) To appoint a receiver or temporary trustee to take possession of the trust property and administer the trust.
(5) To remove the trustee.
(6) Subject to Section 18100, to set aside acts of the trustee.
(7) To reduce or deny compensation of the trustee.
(8) Subject to Section 18100, to impose an equitable lien or a constructive trust on trust property.
(9) Subject to Section 18100, to trace trust property that has been wrongfully disposed of and recover the property or its proceeds.
(b) The provision of remedies for breach of trust in subdivision (a) does not prevent resort to any other appropriate remedy provided by statute or the common law. **Leg.H.** Enacted Stats 1990 ch 79 §14 (AB 759), operative July 1, 1991.

Prior Law: Former Prob C §16420, similar to the present section, was added Stats 1986 ch 820 §40, operative July 1, 1987, and repealed Stats 1990 ch 79 §13, operative July 1, 1991.

§16421. Remedies for breach exclusively in equity

The remedies of a beneficiary against the trustee are exclusively in equity. **Leg.H.** Enacted Stats 1990 ch 79 §14 (AB 759), operative July 1, 1991.

Prior Law: Former Prob C §16421, similar to the present section, was added Stats 1986 ch 820 §40, operative July 1, 1987, and repealed Stats 1990 ch 79 §13, operative July 1, 1991.

ARTICLE 3
Measure of Liability for Breach of Trust

Measure of liability for breach of trust. §16440.
Measure of liability for interest; Excuse from liability. §16441.
Other remedies not affected. §16442.

§16440. Measure of liability for breach of trust

(a) If the trustee commits a breach of trust, the trustee is chargeable with any of the following that is appropriate under the circumstances:
(1) Any loss or depreciation in value of the trust estate resulting from the breach of trust, with interest.
(2) Any profit made by the trustee through the breach of trust, with interest.
(3) Any profit that would have accrued to the trust estate if the loss of profit is the result of the breach of trust.
(b) If the trustee has acted reasonably and in good faith under the circumstances as known to the trustee, the court, in its discretion, may excuse the trustee in whole or in part from liability under subdivision (a) if it would be equitable to do so. **Leg.H.** Enacted Stats 1990 ch 79 §14 (AB 759), operative July 1, 1991.

Prior Law: Former Prob C §16440, similar to the present section, was added Stats 1986 ch 820 §40, operative July 1, 1987, and repealed Stats 1990 ch 79 §13, operative July 1, 1991.

§16441. Measure of liability for interest; Excuse from liability

(a) If the trustee is liable for interest pursuant to Section 16440, the trustee is liable for the greater of the following amounts:
(1) The amount of interest that accrues at the legal rate on judgments in effect during the period when the interest accrued.
(2) The amount of interest actually received.
(b) If the trustee has acted reasonably and in good faith under the circumstances as known to the trustee, the court, in its discretion, may excuse the trustee in whole or in part from liability under subdivision (a) if it would be equitable to do so. **Leg.H.** Enacted Stats 1990 ch 79 §14 (AB 759), operative July 1, 1991. Amended Stats 1998 ch 77 §5 (SB 1841), effective January 1, 1999.

Prior Law: Former Prob C §16441, similar to the present section, was added Stats 1986 ch 820 §40, operative July 1, 1987, amended Stats 1987 ch 128 §18, effective July 6, 1987, operative July 1, 1987, and repealed Stats 1990 ch 79 §13, operative July 1, 1991.

§16442. Other remedies not affected

The provisions in this article for liability of a trustee for breach of trust do not prevent resort to any other remedy available under the statutory or common law. **Leg.H.** Enacted Stats 1990 ch 79 §14 (AB 759), operative July 1, 1991.

Prior Law: Former Prob C §16442, similar to the present section, was added Stats 1986 ch 820 §40, operative July 1, 1987, and repealed Stats 1990 ch 79 §13, operative July 1, 1991.

ARTICLE 4
Limitations and Exculpation

Limitations on proceedings against trustee. §16460.
Exculpation of trustee; Exceptions; Conditions for effectiveness of specified provisions. §16461.
Nonliability for following instructions under revocable trust. §16462.
Consent of beneficiary to relieve trustee of liability for breach of trust. §16463.
Discharge of trustee's liability by release or contract. §16464.
Discharge of trustee's liability by subsequent affirmance. §16465.

§16460. Limitations on proceedings against trustee

(a) Unless a claim is previously barred by adjudication, consent, limitation, or otherwise:
(1) If a beneficiary has received an interim or final account in writing, or other written report, that adequately discloses the existence of a claim against the trustee for breach of trust, the claim is barred as to that beneficiary unless a proceeding to assert the claim is commenced within three years after receipt of the account or report. An account or report adequately discloses existence of a claim if it provides sufficient information so that the beneficiary knows of the claim or reasonably should have inquired into the existence of the claim.
(2) If an interim or final account in writing or other written report does not adequately disclose the existence of a claim against the trustee for breach of trust or if a beneficiary does not receive any written account or report, the claim is barred as to that beneficiary unless a proceeding to assert the claim is commenced within three years after the beneficiary discovered, or reasonably should have discovered, the subject of the claim.
(b) For the purpose of subdivision (a), a beneficiary is deemed to have received an account or report, as follows:
(1) In the case of an adult who is reasonably capable of understanding the account or report, if it is received by the adult personally.
(2) In the case of an adult who is not reasonably capable of understanding the account or report, if it is received by the person's legal representative, including a guardian ad litem or other person appointed for this purpose.
(3) In the case of a minor, if it is received by the minor's guardian or, if the minor does not have a guardian, if it is received by the minor's parent so long as the parent does not have a conflict of interest.
(c) A written account or report under this section may, but need not, satisfy the requirements of Section 16061 or 16063 or any other provision. **Leg.H.** Enacted Stats 1990 ch 79 §14 (AB 759), operative July 1, 1991. Amended Stats 1996 ch 862 §40 (AB 2751), effective January 1, 1997.

Prior Law: Former Prob C §16460, similar to the present section, was added Stats 1986 ch 820 §40, operative July 1, 1987, and repealed Stats 1990 ch 79 §13, operative July 1, 1991.

§16461. Exculpation of trustee; Exceptions; Conditions for effectiveness of specified provisions

(a) Except as provided in subdivision (b), (c), or (d), the trustee can be relieved of liability for breach of trust by provisions in the trust instrument.
(b) A provision in the trust instrument is not effective to relieve the trustee of liability (1) for breach of trust committed intentionally, with gross negligence, in bad faith, or with reckless indifference to the interest of the beneficiary, or (2) for any profit that the trustee derives from a breach of trust.
(c) Subject to subdivision (b), a provision in a trust instrument that releases the trustee from liability if a beneficiary fails to object to an item in an interim or final account or other written report within a specified time period is effective only if all of the following conditions are met:
(1) The account or report sets forth the item.
(2) The period specified in the trust instrument for the beneficiary to object is not less than 180 days, or the trustee elects to follow the procedure provided in subdivision (d).
(3) Written notice in 12-point boldface type is provided to a beneficiary with the account or report in the following form:

NOTICE TO BENEFICIARIES

YOU HAVE [insert "180 days" or the period specified in the trust instrument, whichever is longer] FROM YOUR RECEIPT OF THIS ACCOUNT OR REPORT TO MAKE AN OBJECTION TO ANY ITEM SET FORTH IN THIS ACCOUNT OR REPORT. ANY OBJECTION YOU MAKE MUST BE IN WRITING; IT MUST BE DELIVERED TO THE TRUSTEE WITHIN THE PERIOD STATED ABOVE; AND IT MUST STATE YOUR OBJECTION. YOUR FAILURE TO DELIVER A WRITTEN OBJECTION TO THE TRUSTEE WITHIN THE PERIOD STATED ABOVE WILL PERMANENTLY PREVENT YOU FROM LATER ASSERTING THIS OBJECTION AGAINST THE TRUSTEE. IF YOU DO MAKE AN OBJECTION TO THE TRUSTEE, THE THREE-YEAR PERIOD PROVIDED IN SECTION 16460 OF THE PROBATE CODE FOR COMMENCEMENT OF LITIGATION WILL APPLY TO CLAIMS BASED ON YOUR OBJECTION AND WILL BEGIN TO RUN ON THE DATE THAT YOU RECEIVE THIS ACCOUNT OR REPORT.

(d) A provision in a trust instrument that provides for a period less than 180 days to object to an item in an account or report shall be ineffective to release the trustee from liability. A trustee of a trust created by an instrument with an ineffective period may elect to be governed by the provisions of subdivision (c) by complying with the requirements of subdivision (c), except that "180 days" shall be substituted in the notice form for the ineffective period.

(e) Subject to subdivision (b), a beneficiary who fails to object in writing to an account or report that complies with the requirements of subdivision (c) within the specified, valid period shall be barred from asserting any claim against the trustee regarding an item that is adequately disclosed in the account or report. An item is adequately disclosed if the disclosure regarding the item meets the requirements of paragraph (1) of subdivision (a) of Section 16460.

(f) Except as provided in subdivision (a) of Section 16460, the trustee may not be released from liability as to any claim based on a written objection made by a beneficiary if the objection is delivered to the trustee within the specified, effective period. If a beneficiary has filed a written objection to an account or report that complies with the requirements of subdivision (c) within the specified, valid period that concerns an item that affects any other beneficiary of the trust, any affected beneficiary may join in the objection anytime within the specified, valid period or while the resolution of the objection is pending, whichever is later. This section is not intended to establish a class of beneficiaries for actions on an account and report or provide that the action of one beneficiary is for the benefit of all beneficiaries. This section does not create a duty for any trustee to notify beneficiaries of objections or resolution of objections.

(g) Provided that a beneficiary has filed a written objection to an account or report that complies with the requirements of subdivision (c) within the specified, valid period, a supplemental written objection may be delivered in the same manner as the objection not later than 180 days after the receipt of the account or report or no later than the period specified in the trust instrument, whichever is longer.

(h) Compliance with subdivision (c) excuses compliance with paragraph (6) of subdivision (a) of Section 16063 for the account or report to which that notice relates.

(i) Subject to subdivision (b), if proper notice has been given and a beneficiary has not made a timely objection, the trustee is not liable for any other claims adequately disclosed by any item in the account or report.

(j) Subdivisions (c) to (i), inclusive, apply to all accounts and reports submitted after the effective date of the act adding these subdivisions. **Leg.H.** Enacted Stats 1990 ch 79 §14 (AB 759), operative July 1, 1991. Amended Stats 2004 ch 538 §1 (AB 1990), effective January 1, 2005.

Prior Law: Former Prob C §16461, similar to the present section, was added Stats 1986 ch 820 §40, operative July 1, 1987, and repealed Stats 1990 ch 79 §13, operative July 1, 1991.

§16462. Nonliability for following instructions under revocable trust

(a) Notwithstanding Section 16461, a trustee of a revocable trust is not liable to a beneficiary for any act performed or omitted pursuant to written directions from the person holding the power to revoke, including a person to whom the power to direct the trustee is delegated.

(b) Subdivision (a) applies to a trust that is revocable in part with respect to the interest of the beneficiary in that part of the trust property. **Leg.H.** Enacted Stats 1990 ch 79 §14 (AB 759), operative July 1, 1991.

Prior Law: Former Prob C §16462, similar to the present section, was added Stats 1986 ch 820 §40, operative July 1, 1987, and repealed Stats 1990 ch 79 §13, operative July 1, 1991.

§16463. Consent of beneficiary to relieve trustee of liability for breach of trust

(a) Except as provided in subdivisions (b) and (c), a beneficiary may not hold the trustee liable for an act or omission of the trustee as a breach of trust if the beneficiary consented to the act or omission before or at the time of the act or omission.

(b) The consent of the beneficiary does not preclude the beneficiary from holding the trustee liable for a breach of trust in any of the following circumstances:

(1) Where the beneficiary was under an incapacity at the time of the consent or of the act or omission.

(2) Where the beneficiary at the time consent was given did not know of his or her rights and of the material facts (A) that the trustee knew or should have known and (B) that the trustee did not reasonably believe that the beneficiary knew.

(3) Where the consent of the beneficiary was induced by improper conduct of the trustee.

(c) Where the trustee has an interest in the transaction adverse to the interest of the beneficiary, the consent of the beneficiary does not preclude the beneficiary from holding the trustee liable for a breach of trust under any of the circumstances described in subdivision (b) or where the transaction to which the beneficiary consented was not fair and reasonable to the beneficiary. **Leg.H.** Enacted Stats 1990 ch 79 §14 (AB 759), operative July 1, 1991.

Prior Law: Former Prob C §16463, similar to the present section, was added Stats 1986 ch 820 §40, operative July 1, 1987, and repealed Stats 1990 ch 79 §13, operative July 1, 1991.

§16464. Discharge of trustee's liability by release or contract

(a) Except as provided in subdivision (b), a beneficiary may be precluded from holding the trustee liable for a breach of trust by the beneficiary's release or contract effective to discharge the trustee's liability to the beneficiary for that breach.

(b) A release or contract is not effective to discharge the trustee's liability for a breach of trust in any of the following circumstances:

(1) Where the beneficiary was under an incapacity at the time of making the release or contract.

(2) Where the beneficiary did not know of his or her rights and of the material facts (A) that the trustee knew or reasonably should have known and (B) that the trustee did not reasonably believe that the beneficiary knew.

(3) Where the release or contract of the beneficiary was induced by improper conduct of the trustee.

(4) Where the transaction involved a bargain with the trustee that was not fair and reasonable. **Leg.H.** Enacted Stats 1990 ch 79 §14 (AB 759), operative July 1, 1991.

Prior Law: Former Prob C §16464, similar to the present section, was added Stats 1986 ch 820 §40, operative July 1, 1987, and repealed Stats 1990 ch 79 §13, operative July 1, 1991.

§16465. Discharge of trustee's liability by subsequent affirmance

(a) Except as provided in subdivision (b), if the trustee, in breach of trust, enters into a transaction that the beneficiary may at his or her option reject or affirm, and the beneficiary affirms the transaction, the beneficiary shall not thereafter reject it and hold the trustee liable for any loss occurring after the trustee entered into the transaction.

(b) The affirmance of a transaction by the beneficiary does not preclude the beneficiary from holding a trustee liable for a breach of trust if, at the time of the affirmance, any of the following circumstances existed:

(1) The beneficiary was under an incapacity.

(2) The beneficiary did not know of his or her rights and of the material facts (A) that the trustee knew or reasonably should have known and (B) that the trustee did not reasonably believe that the beneficiary knew.

(3) The affirmance was induced by improper conduct of the trustee.

(4) The transaction involved a bargain with the trustee that was not fair and reasonable. **Leg.H.** Enacted Stats 1990 ch 79 §14 (AB 759), operative July 1, 1991.

Prior Law: Former Prob C §16465, similar to the present section, was added Stats 1986 ch 820 §40, operative July 1, 1987, and repealed Stats 1990 ch 79 §13, operative July 1, 1991.

CHAPTER 5
NOTICE OF PROPOSED ACTION BY TRUSTEE

Scope and effect of chapter; Proposed action described. §16500.
Persons required to receive notice; When use of notice prohibited. §16501.
Content of notice. §16502.
Objection to proposed action; Petition; Liability of trustee. §16503.
Procedures not required. §16504.

§16500. Scope and effect of chapter; Proposed action described

Subject to subdivision (d) of Section 16501, a trustee may give a notice of proposed action regarding a matter governed by Chapter 2 (commencing with Section 16200) or Chapter 3 (commencing with Section 16320) as provided in this chapter. For the purpose of this chapter, a proposed action includes a course of action or a decision not to take action. This chapter does not preclude an application or assertion of any other rights or remedies available to an interested party as otherwise provided in this part regarding an action to be taken or not to be taken by the trustee. **Leg.H.** Added Stats 2004 ch 54 §2 (SB 1021), effective January 1, 2005.

§16501. Persons required to receive notice; When use of notice prohibited

(a) The trustee who elects to provide notice pursuant to this chapter shall deliver notice pursuant to Section 1215 of the proposed action to each of the following:

(1) A beneficiary who is receiving, or is entitled to receive, income under the trust, including a beneficiary who is entitled to receive income at the discretion of the trustee.

(2) A beneficiary who would receive a distribution of principal if the trust were terminated at the time the notice is given.

(b) Notice of proposed action is not required to be given to a person who consents in writing to the proposed action. The consent may be executed at any time before or after the proposed action is taken.

(c) A trustee is not required to provide a copy of the notice of proposed action to a beneficiary who is known to the trustee but who cannot be located by the trustee after reasonable diligence or who is unknown to the trustee.

(d) Notwithstanding any other provision of this chapter, the trustee may not use a notice of proposed action in any of the following actions:

(1) Allowance of the trustee's compensation.

(2) Allowance of compensation of the attorney for the trustee.

(3) Settlement of accounts.

(4) Discharge of the trustee.

(5) Sale of property of the trust to the trustee or to the attorney for the trustee.

(6) Exchange of property of the trust for property of the trustee or for property of the attorney for the trustee.

(7) Grant of an option to purchase property of the trust to the trustee or to the attorney for the trustee.

(8) Allowance, payment, or compromise of a claim of the trustee, or the attorney for the trustee, against the trust.

(9) Compromise or settlement of a claim, action, or proceeding by the trust against the trustee or against the attorney for the trust.

(10) Extension, renewal, or modification of the terms of a debt or other obligation of the trustee, or the attorney for the trustee, owing to or in favor of the trust. **Leg.H.** Added Stats 2004 ch 54 §2 (SB 1021). Amended Stats 2016 ch 64 §1 (AB 1700), effective January 1, 2017; Stats 2017 ch 319 §91 (AB 976), effective January 1, 2018.

§16502. Content of notice

The notice of proposed action shall state that it is given pursuant to this section and shall include all of the following:

(a) The name, mailing address, and electronic address of the trustee.

(b) The name, telephone number, and electronic address of a person who may be contacted for additional information.

(c) A description of the action proposed to be taken and an explanation of the reasons for the action.

(d) The time within which objections to the proposed action can be made, which shall be at least 45 days from the delivery or receipt of the notice of proposed action.

(e) The date on or after which the proposed action may be taken or is effective. **Leg.H.** Added Stats 2004 ch 54 §2 (SB 1021). Amended Stats 2017 ch 319 §92 (AB 976), effective January 1, 2018.

§16503. Objection to proposed action; Petition; Liability of trustee

(a) A beneficiary may object to the proposed action by delivering a written objection pursuant to Section 1215 to the trustee at the address stated in the notice of proposed action within the time period specified in the notice of proposed action.

(b) A trustee is not liable to a beneficiary for an action regarding a matter governed by this part if the trustee does not receive a written objection to the proposed action from a beneficiary within the applicable period and the other requirements of this section are satisfied. If no beneficiary entitled to notice objects under this section, the trustee is not liable to any current or future beneficiary with respect to the proposed action. This subdivision does not apply to a person who is a minor or an incompetent adult at the time of receiving the notice of proposed action unless the notice is served on a guardian or conservator of the estate of the person.

(c) If the trustee receives a written objection within the applicable period, either the trustee or a beneficiary may petition the court to have the proposed action taken as proposed, taken with modifications, or denied. In the proceeding, a beneficiary objecting to the proposed action has the burden of proving that the trustee's proposed action should not be taken. A beneficiary who has not objected is not estopped from opposing the proposed action in the proceeding.

(d) If the trustee decides not to implement the proposed action, the trustee shall notify the beneficiaries of the decision not to take the action and the reasons for the decision, and the trustee's decision not to implement the proposed action does not itself give rise to liability to any current or future beneficiary. A beneficiary may petition the court to have the action taken, and has the burden of proving that it should be taken. **Leg.H.** Added Stats 2004 ch 54 §2 (SB 1021). Amended Stats 2017 ch 319 §93 (AB 976), effective January 1, 2018.

§16504. Procedures not required

This chapter does not require a trustee to use these procedures prior to taking any action. **Leg.H.** Added Stats 2004 ch 54 §2 (SB 1021), effective January 1, 2005.

CHAPTER 6
CALIFORNIA UNIFORM DIRECTED TRUST ACT

Citation of chapter; Legislative findings and declarations. § 16600.
Definitions. § 16602.
Applicability of chapter; Principal place of administration. § 16604.
Consent to trust director or directed trustee appointment. § 16605.
Inapplicability of chapter to certain powers. § 16606.
Trust director powers. § 16608.
Trust director subject to same rules as trustee under certain circumstances. § 16610.
Trust director fiduciary duty and liability. § 16612.
Directed trustee compliance; Release of liability. § 16614.
Information provided between trust directors and trustees; Liability for actions in reliance on information provided. § 16616.
Actions outside scope of trustee or trust director duties. § 16618.
Cotrustee relief from duty and liability. § 16620.
Time limitations for breach of trust action. § 16622.
Defenses in breach of trust action. § 16624.
Personal jurisdiction over trust director. § 16626.
Rules applicable to trustee also applicable to trust director for certain matters. § 16628.
Application and construction of chapter. § 16630.
Effect of chapter on federal law. § 16632.

§ 16600. Citation of chapter; Legislative findings and declarations

(a) This chapter shall be known, and may be cited, as the California Uniform Directed Trust Act.

(b) The Legislature finds and declares all of the following:

(1) This chapter governs an arrangement commonly known as a directed trust.

(2) In a directed trust, the terms of the trust grant a person other than a trustee a power over some aspect of the trust's administration.

(3) Under this chapter, this power is called a power of direction, the person that holds the power is called a trust director, a trustee that is subject to the power is called a directed trustee, and the trust is a directed trust.

(4) A directed trustee is required to take reasonable action to comply with a trust director's exercise or nonexercise of a power of direction.

(5) Except for willful misconduct, a directed trustee is liable only for its own breach of trust in executing a direction and not for the trust director's breach of trust in exercising or not exercising the power of direction. **Leg.H.** Added Stats 2023 ch 721 §3 (SB 801), effective January 1, 2024.

§ 16602. Definitions

For purposes of this chapter, the following definitions shall apply:

(a) "Breach of trust" includes a violation by a trust director or trustee of a duty imposed on that director or trustee by the terms of the trust, this chapter, or law of this state other than this chapter pertaining to trusts.

(b) "Directed trust" means a trust for which the terms of the trust grant a power of direction.

(c) "Directed trustee" means a trustee that is subject to a trust director's power of direction.

(d) "Power of direction" means a power over a trust granted to a person by the terms of the trust to the extent the power is exercisable while the person is not serving as a trustee. Power of direction includes a power over the investment, management, or distribution of trust property or other matters of trust administration. The term excludes the powers described in subdivision (a) of Section 16606.

(e) "Settlor" means a person, including a testator, who creates, or contributes property to, a trust. If more than one person creates or contributes property to a trust, each person is a settlor of the portion of the trust property attributable to that person's contribution except to the extent another person has the power to revoke or withdraw that portion.

(f) "Terms of a trust" means either of the following:

(1) The manifestation of the settlor's intent regarding a trust's provisions as expressed in the trust instrument or established by other evidence that has been admitted in a judicial proceeding.

(2) The trust's provisions as established, determined, or amended by a trustee or trust director in accordance with applicable law, the exercise of a power of appointment in accordance with applicable law, a court order, or other binding modification, including, but not limited to, under Section 15404.

(g) "Trust director" means a person that is granted a power of direction by the terms of a trust, to the extent the power is exercisable while the person is not serving as a trustee. The person is a trust director whether or not the terms of the trust refer to the person as a trust director and whether or not the person is a beneficiary or settlor of the trust. **Leg.H.** Added Stats 2023 ch 721 §3 (SB 801), effective January 1, 2024.

§ 16604. Applicability of chapter; Principal place of administration

(a) This chapter applies to a trust, whenever created, that has its principal place of administration in this state, subject to all of the following rules:

(1) If the trust was created before January 1, 2024, this chapter applies only to a decision or action occurring on or after that date.

(2) If the principal place of administration of the trust is changed to this state on or after January 1, 2024, this chapter applies only to a decision or action occurring on or after the date of the change.

(b) Without precluding other means to establish a sufficient connection with the designated jurisdiction in a directed trust, terms of the trust that designate the principal place of administration of the trust are valid and controlling if all of the following are met:

(1) A trustee's principal place of business is located in, or a trustee is a resident of, the designated jurisdiction.

(2) A trust director's principal place of business is located in, or a trust director is a resident of, the designated jurisdiction.

(3) All or part of the administration occurs in the designated jurisdiction. **Leg.H.** Added Stats 2023 ch 721 §3 (SB 801), effective January 1, 2024.

§ 16605. Consent to trust director or directed trustee appointment

Notwithstanding any other law, the consent of the public administrator, public guardian, or public conservator is required before they may be appointed to act as a trust director or directed trustee. **Leg.H.** Added Stats 2023 ch 721 §3 (SB 801), effective January 1, 2024.

§ 16606. Inapplicability of chapter to certain powers

(a) This chapter does not apply to any of the following:

(1) A power of appointment.

(2) The power to appoint or remove a trustee or trust director.

(3) The power of a settlor over a trust, to the extent the settlor has a power to revoke the trust.

(4) The power of a beneficiary over a trust, to the extent the exercise or nonexercise of the power affects the beneficial interest of the beneficiary.

(5) The power over a trust if both of the following apply:

(A) The terms of the trust provide that the power is held in a nonfiduciary capacity.

(B) The power is required to be held in a nonfiduciary capacity to achieve the settlor's tax objectives under the United States Internal Revenue Code of 1986 and regulations issued thereunder.

(b) Unless the terms of a trust provide otherwise, a power granted to a person to designate a recipient of an ownership interest in, or power of appointment over, trust property that is exercisable while the person is not serving as a trustee is a power of appointment and not a power of direction. **Leg.H.** Added Stats 2023 ch 721 §3 (SB 801), effective January 1, 2024.

§ 16608. Trust director powers

(a) Subject to Section 16610, the terms of a trust may grant a power of direction to a trust director.

(b) Unless the terms of a trust provide otherwise, a trust director may exercise any further power appropriate to the exercise or nonexercise of a power of direction granted to the trust director pursuant to subdivision (a).

(c) Unless the terms of a trust provide otherwise, trust directors with joint powers shall act by majority decision. **Leg.H.** Added Stats 2023 ch 721 §3 (SB 801), effective January 1, 2024.

§ 16610. Trust director subject to same rules as trustee under certain circumstances

A trust director is subject to the same rules as a trustee in a like position and under similar circumstances in the exercise or nonexercise of a power of direction or further power under subdivision (b) of Section 16608 regarding either of the following:

(a) A payback provision in the terms of a trust necessary to comply with the reimbursement requirements of Medicaid law in Section 1917 of the Social Security Act (42 U.S.C. Section 1396p(d)(4)(A)) and regulations issued thereunder.

(b) A charitable interest in the trust, including notice regarding the interest to the Attorney General. **Leg.H.** Added Stats 2023 ch 721 §3 (SB 801), effective January 1, 2024.

§ 16612. Trust director fiduciary duty and liability

(a) Subject to subdivision (b), with respect to a power of direction or further power under subdivision (b) of Section 16608, both of the following apply:

(1) A trust director has the same fiduciary duty and liability in the exercise or nonexercise of the power, if the power is held individually, as a sole trustee in a like position and under similar circumstances or, if the power is held jointly with a trustee or another trust director, as a cotrustee in a like position and under similar circumstances.

(2) The terms of the trust may vary the trust director's duty or liability to the same extent the terms of the trust could vary the duty or liability of a trustee in a like position and under similar circumstances.

(b) Unless the terms of a trust provide otherwise, if a trust director is licensed, certified, or otherwise authorized or permitted by law other than this chapter to provide health care in the ordinary course of the trust director's business or practice of a profession, to the extent the trust director acts in that capacity, the trust director has no duty or liability under this chapter.

(c) The terms of a trust may impose a duty or liability on a trust director in addition to the duties and liabilities under this section. **Leg.H.** Added Stats 2023 ch 721 §3 (SB 801), effective January 1, 2024.

§ 16614. Directed trustee compliance; Release of liability

(a) Subject to subdivision (b), a directed trustee shall take reasonable action to comply with a trust director's exercise or nonexercise of a power of direction or further power under subdivision (b) of Section 16608, and the trustee is not liable for the action.

(b) A directed trustee shall not comply with a trust director's exercise or nonexercise of a power of direction or further power under subdivision (b) of Section 16608 to the extent that, by complying, the trustee would engage in willful misconduct.

(c) An exercise of a power of direction under which a trust director may release a trustee or another trust director from liability for breach of trust is not effective if any of the following is true:

(1) The breach involved the trustee's or other trust director's willful misconduct.

(2) The release was induced by improper conduct of the trustee or other trust director in procuring the release.

(3) At the time of the release, the trust director did not know the material facts relating to the breach.

(d) A directed trustee that has reasonable doubt about their duty under this section may petition the court for instructions.

(e) The terms of a trust may impose a duty or liability on a directed trustee in addition to the duties and liabilities under this section. **Leg.H.** Added Stats 2023 ch 721 §3 (SB 801), effective January 1, 2024.

§ 16616. Information provided between trust directors and trustees; Liability for actions in reliance on information provided

(a) Subject to Section 16618, a trustee shall provide information to a trust director to the extent the information is reasonably related both to the powers or duties of the trustee and the powers or duties of the trust director.

(b) Subject to Section 16618, a trust director shall provide information to a trustee or another trust director to the extent the information is reasonably related both to the powers or duties of the trust director and the powers or duties of the trustee or other trust director.

(c) A trustee that acts in reliance on information provided by a trust director is not liable for a breach of trust to the extent the breach resulted from the reliance, unless by so acting the trustee engages in willful misconduct.

(d) A trust director that acts in reliance on information provided by a trustee or another trust director is not liable for a breach of trust to the extent the breach resulted from the reliance, unless by so acting the trust director engages in willful misconduct. **Leg.H.** Added Stats 2023 ch 721 §3 (SB 801), effective January 1, 2024.

§ 16618. Actions outside scope of trustee or trust director duties

(a)(1) Unless the terms of a trust provide otherwise, a trustee does not have a duty to do either of the following:

(A) Monitor a trust director.

(B) Inform or give advice to a settlor, beneficiary, trustee, or trust director concerning an instance in which the trustee might have acted differently than the trust director.

(2) By taking an action described in paragraph (1), a trustee does not assume the duty excluded by paragraph (1).

(b)(1) Unless the terms of a trust provide otherwise, a trust director does not have a duty to do either of the following:

(A) Monitor a trustee or another trust director.

(B) Inform or give advice to a settlor, beneficiary, trustee, or another trust director concerning an instance in which the trust director might have acted differently than a trustee or another trust director.

(2) By taking an action described in paragraph (1), a trust director does not assume the duty excluded by paragraph (1). **Leg.H.** Added Stats 2023 ch 721 §3 (SB 801), effective January 1, 2024.

§ 16620. Cotrustee relief from duty and liability

The terms of a trust may relieve a cotrustee from duty and liability with respect to another cotrustee's exercise or nonexercise of a power of the other cotrustee to the same extent that, in a directed trust, a directed trustee is relieved from duty and liability with respect to a trust director's power of direction under Sections 16614, 16616, and 16618. **Leg.H.** Added Stats 2023 ch 721 §3 (SB 801), effective January 1, 2024.

§ 16622. Time limitations for breach of trust action

(a) An action against a trust director for breach of trust shall be commenced within the same limitation period as for an action for breach of trust against a trustee in a like position and under similar circumstances.

(b) A report or accounting has the same effect on the limitation period for an action against a trust director for breach of trust that the report or accounting would have under Section 16460 in an action for breach of trust against a trustee in a like position and under similar circumstances. **Leg.H.** Added Stats 2023 ch 721 §3 (SB 801), effective January 1, 2024.

§ 16624. Defenses in breach of trust action

In an action against a trust director for breach of trust, the director may assert the same defenses a trustee in a like position and under similar circumstances could assert in an action for breach of trust against the trustee. **Leg.H.** Added Stats 2023 ch 721 §3 (SB 801), effective January 1, 2024.

§ 16626. Personal jurisdiction over trust director

(a) By accepting appointment as a trust director of a trust subject to this chapter, the trust director submits to personal jurisdiction of the courts of this state regarding any matter related to a power or duty of the trust director.

(b) This section does not preclude other methods of obtaining jurisdiction over a trust director. **Leg.H.** Added Stats 2023 ch 721 §3 (SB 801), effective January 1, 2024.

§ 16628. Rules applicable to trustee also applicable to trust director for certain matters

Unless the terms of a trust provide otherwise, the rules applicable to a trustee apply to a trust director regarding all of the following matters:

(a) Acceptance under Sections 15600 and 15601.

(b) Giving of a bond to secure performance under Section 15602.

(c) Reasonable compensation under Section 15681.

(d) Resignation or removal under Article 3 (commencing with Section 15640) of Chapter 1.

(e) Vacancy and appointment of a successor under Section 15660. **Leg.H.** Added Stats 2023 ch 721 §3 (SB 801), effective January 1, 2024.

§ 16630. Application and construction of chapter

In applying and construing this chapter, consideration shall be given to the need to promote uniformity of the law with respect to its subject matter among states that enact it. **Leg.H.** Added Stats 2023 ch 721 §3 (SB 801), effective January 1, 2024.

§ 16632. Effect of chapter on federal law

This chapter modifies, limits, or supersedes the Electronic Signatures in Global and National Commerce Act, 15 U.S.C. Section 7001 et seq., but does not modify, limit, or supersede Section 101(c) of that act, 15 U.S.C. Section 7001(c), or authorize electronic delivery of any of the notices described in Section 103(b) of that act, 15 U.S.C. Section 7003(b). **Leg.H.** Added Stats 2023 ch 721 §3 (SB 801), effective January 1, 2024.

PART 5
JUDICIAL PROCEEDINGS CONCERNING TRUSTS

Chapter 1. Jurisdiction and Venue.
Chapter 2. Notice.
Chapter 3. Proceedings Concerning Trusts.
Chapter 4. Testamentary Trusts Subject to Continuing Court Jurisdiction.
Chapter 5. Transfer of Trust to Another Jurisdiction.
Chapter 6. Transfer of Trust From Another Jurisdiction.

CHAPTER 1
JURISDICTION AND VENUE

Subject matter jurisdiction. §17000.
Full-power court. §17001.
Principal place of administration of trust. §17002.
Jurisdiction over trustees and beneficiaries. §17003.
Basis of jurisdiction over trust, trust property, and trust parties. §17004.
Venue. §17005.
Jury trial. §17006.

§17000. Subject matter jurisdiction

(a) The superior court having jurisdiction over the trust pursuant to this part has exclusive jurisdiction of proceedings concerning the internal affairs of trusts.

(b) The superior court having jurisdiction over the trust pursuant to this part has concurrent jurisdiction of the following:

(1) Actions and proceedings to determine the existence of trusts.

(2) Actions and proceedings by or against creditors or debtors of trusts.

(3) Other actions and proceedings involving trustees and third persons.
Leg.H. Enacted Stats 1990 ch 79 §14 (AB 759), operative July 1, 1991.

Prior Law: Former Prob C §17000, similar to the present section, was added Stats 1986 ch 820 §40, operative July 1, 1987, and repealed Stats 1990 ch 79 §13, operative July 1, 1991.

§17001. Full-power court

In proceedings commenced pursuant to this division, the court is a court of general jurisdiction and has all the powers of the superior court. **Leg.H.** Enacted Stats 1990 ch 79 §14 (AB 759), operative July 1, 1991. Amended Stats 1990 ch 710 §44 (SB 1775), operative July 1, 1991.

Prior Law: Former Prob C §17001, similar to the present section, was added Stats 1986 ch 820 §40, operative July 1, 1987, and repealed Stats 1990 ch 79 §13, operative July 1, 1991.

§17002. Principal place of administration of trust

(a) The principal place of administration of the trust is the usual place where the day-to-day activity of the trust is carried on by the trustee or its representative who is primarily responsible for the administration of the trust.

(b) If the principal place of administration of the trust cannot be determined under subdivision (a), it shall be determined as follows:

(1) If the trust has a single trustee, the principal place of administration of the trust is the trustee's residence or usual place of business.

(2) If the trust has more than one trustee, the principal place of administration of the trust is the residence or usual place of business of any of the cotrustees as agreed upon by them or, if not, the residence or usual place of business of any of the cotrustees. **Leg.H.** Enacted Stats 1990 ch 79 §14 (AB 759), operative July 1, 1991.

Prior Law: Former Prob C §17002, similar to the present section, was added Stats 1986 ch 820 §40, operative July 1, 1987, and repealed Stats 1990 ch 79 §13, operative July 1, 1991.

§17003. Jurisdiction over trustees and beneficiaries

Subject to Section 17004:

(a) By accepting the trusteeship of a trust having its principal place of administration in this state the trustee submits personally to the jurisdiction of the court under this division.

(b) To the extent of their interests in the trust, all beneficiaries of a trust having its principal place of administration in this state are subject to the jurisdiction of the court under this division. **Leg.H.** Enacted Stats 1990 ch 79 §14 (AB 759), operative July 1, 1991.

Prior Law: Former Prob C §17003, similar to the present section, was added Stats 1986 ch 820 §40, operative July 1, 1987, and repealed Stats 1990 ch 79 §13, operative July 1, 1991.

§17004. Basis of jurisdiction over trust, trust property, and trust parties

The court may exercise jurisdiction in proceedings under this division on any basis permitted by Section 410.10 of the Code of Civil Procedure. **Leg.H.** Enacted Stats 1990 ch 79 §14 (AB 759), operative July 1, 1991.

Prior Law: Former Prob C §17004, similar to the present section, was added Stats 1986 ch 820 §40, operative July 1, 1987, and repealed Stats 1990 ch 79 §13, operative July 1, 1991.

§17005. Venue

(a) The proper county for commencement of a proceeding pursuant to this division is either of the following:

(1) In the case of a living trust, the county where the principal place of administration of the trust is located.

(2) In the case of a testamentary trust, either the county where the decedent's estate is administered or where the principal place of administration of the trust is located.

(b) If a living trust has no trustee, the proper county for commencement of a proceeding for appointing a trustee is the county where the trust property, or some portion of the trust property, is located.

(c) Except as otherwise provided in subdivisions (a) and (b), the proper county for commencement of a proceeding pursuant to this division is determined by the rules applicable to civil actions generally. **Leg.H.** Enacted Stats 1990 ch 79 §14 (AB 759), operative July 1, 1991.

Prior Law: Former Prob C §17005, similar to the present section, was added Stats 1986 ch 820 §40, operative July 1, 1987, and repealed Stats 1990 ch 79 §13, operative July 1, 1991.

§17006. Jury trial

There is no right to a jury trial in proceedings under this division concerning the internal affairs of trusts. **Leg.H.** Enacted Stats 1990 ch 79 §14 (AB 759), operative July 1, 1991.

Prior Law: Former Prob C §17006, similar to the present section, was added Stats 1986 ch 820 §40, operative July 1, 1987, and repealed Stats 1990 ch 79 §13, operative July 1, 1991.

CHAPTER 2
NOTICE

General notice provisions apply. §17100.
Court order not required for notice. §17105.

§17100. General notice provisions apply

Except as otherwise provided in this division, notice in proceedings commenced pursuant to this division, or notice otherwise required by this division, is governed by Part 2 (commencing with Section 1200) of Division 3. **Leg.H.** Enacted Stats 1990 ch 79 §14 (AB 759), operative July 1, 1991.

Prior Law: Former Prob C §17100, similar to the present section, was added Stats 1986 ch 820 §40, operative July 1, 1987, and repealed Stats 1990 ch 79 §13, operative July 1, 1991.

§17102. [Section repealed 1991]

Leg.H. Enacted Stats 1990 ch 79 §14 (AB 759), operative July 1, 1991. Repealed Stats 1990 ch 710 §45 (SB 1775), operative July 1, 1991. The repealed section related to notice when address is unknown.

§17105. Court order not required for notice

A petitioner or other person required to give notice may cause notice to be given to any person interested in the trust without the need for a court order. **Leg.H.** Enacted Stats 1990 ch 79 §14 (AB 759), operative July 1, 1991.

Prior Law: Former Prob C §17105, similar to the present section, was added Stats 1986 ch 820 §40, operative July 1, 1987, and repealed Stats 1990 ch 79 §13, operative July 1, 1991.

CHAPTER 3
PROCEEDINGS CONCERNING TRUSTS

Petitioners; Grounds for petition. §17200.
Circumstances permitting petition requesting court order. §17200.1.
Commencement of proceeding. §17201.

Commencement of discovery. §17201.1.
Dismissal of petition. §17202.
Notice. §17203.
Request for special notice. §17204.
Request for copy of petition. §17205.
Authority to make necessary orders; Temporary trustee. §17206.
Intermittent judicial intervention in trust administration. §17209.
Enforcement of beneficiary's rights under charitable trust by Attorney General. §17210.
Award of costs and expenses of litigation to contest account; Personal liability of contestant, etc. §17211.

§17200. Petitioners; Grounds for petition

(a) Except as provided in Section 15800, a trustee or beneficiary of a trust may petition the court under this chapter concerning the internal affairs of the trust or to determine the existence of the trust.

(b) Proceedings concerning the internal affairs of a trust include, but are not limited to, proceedings for any of the following purposes:

(1) Determining questions of construction of a trust instrument.

(2) Determining the existence or nonexistence of any immunity, power, privilege, duty, or right.

(3) Determining the validity of a trust provision.

(4) Ascertaining beneficiaries and determining to whom property shall pass or be delivered upon final or partial termination of the trust, to the extent the determination is not made by the trust instrument.

(5) Settling the accounts and passing upon the acts of the trustee, including the exercise of discretionary powers.

(6) Instructing the trustee.

(7) Compelling the trustee to do any of the following:

(A) Provide a copy of the terms of the trust.

(B) Provide information about the trust under Section 16061 if the trustee has failed to provide the requested information within 60 days after the beneficiary's reasonable written request, and the beneficiary has not received the requested information from the trustee within the six months preceding the request.

(C) Account to the beneficiary, subject to the provisions of Section 16064, if the trustee has failed to submit a requested account within 60 days after written request of the beneficiary and no account has been made within six months preceding the request.

(8) Granting powers to the trustee.

(9) Fixing or allowing payment of the trustee's compensation or reviewing the reasonableness of the trustee's compensation.

(10) Appointing or removing a trustee.

(11) Accepting the resignation of a trustee.

(12) Compelling redress of a breach of the trust by any available remedy.

(13) Approving or directing the modification or termination of the trust.

(14) Approving or directing the combination or division of trusts.

(15) Amending or conforming the trust instrument in the manner required to qualify a decedent's estate for the charitable estate tax deduction under federal law, including the addition of mandatory governing instrument requirements for a charitable remainder trust as required by final regulations and rulings of the United States Internal Revenue Service.

(16) Authorizing or directing transfer of a trust or trust property to or from another jurisdiction.

(17) Directing transfer of a testamentary trust subject to continuing court jurisdiction from one county to another.

(18) Approving removal of a testamentary trust from continuing court jurisdiction.

(19) Reforming or excusing compliance with the governing instrument of an organization pursuant to Section 16105.

(20) Determining the liability of the trust for any debts of a deceased settlor. However, nothing in this paragraph shall provide standing to bring an action concerning the internal affairs of the trust to a person whose only claim to the assets of the decedent is as a creditor.

(21) Determining petitions filed pursuant to Section 15687 and reviewing the reasonableness of compensation for legal services authorized under that section. In determining the reasonableness of compensation under this paragraph, the court may consider, together with all other relevant circumstances, whether prior approval was obtained pursuant to Section 15687.

(22) If a member of the State Bar of California has transferred the economic interest of his or her practice to a trustee and if the member is a deceased member under Section 9764, a petition may be brought to appoint a practice administrator. The procedures, including, but not limited to, notice requirements, that apply to the appointment of a practice administrator for a deceased member shall apply to the petition brought under this section.

(23) If a member of the State Bar of California has transferred the economic interest of his or her practice to a trustee and if the member is a disabled member under Section 2468, a petition may be brought to appoint a practice administrator. The procedures, including, but not limited to, notice requirements, that apply to the appointment of a practice administrator for a disabled member shall apply to the petition brought under this section.

(c) The court may, on its own motion, set and give notice of an order to show cause why a trustee who is a professional fiduciary, and who is required to be licensed under Chapter 6 (commencing with Section 6500) of Division 3 of the Business and Professions Code, should not be removed for failing to hold a valid, unexpired, unsuspended license. **Leg.H.** Enacted Stats 1990 ch 79 §14 (AB 759), operative July 1, 1991. Amended Stats 1991 ch 992 §1 (SB 727); Stats 1993 ch 293 §7 (AB 21); Stats 1996 ch 862 §41 (AB 2751); Stats 1997 ch 724 §27 (AB 1172); Stats 1998 ch 682 §13 (AB 2069); Stats 1999 ch 175 §5 (AB 239); Stats 2003 ch 629 §8 (SB 294); Stats 2010 ch 621 §11 (SB 202), effective January 1, 2011.

Prior Law: Former Prob C §17200, similar to the present section, was added Stats 1986 ch 820 §40, operative July 1, 1987, and repealed Stats 1990 ch 79 §13, operative July 1, 1991.

§17200.1. Circumstances permitting petition requesting court order

All proceedings concerning the transfer of property of the trust shall be conducted pursuant to the provisions of Part 19 (commencing with Section 850) of Division 2. **Leg.H.** Added Stats 2001 ch 49 §7 (SB 669).

Former Sections: Former Prob C §17200.1, similar to the present section, was added Stats 1996 ch 862 §42 and repealed Stats 2001 ch 49 §6.

Prior Law: Former Prob C §17200.1, similar to the present section, was added Stats 1996 ch 862 §42 and repealed Stats 2001 ch 49 §6.

§17200.2. [Section repealed 2001]

Leg.H. Added Stats 1996 ch 862 §43 (AB 2751). Repealed Stats 2001 ch 49 §8 (SB 669). See Prob C §854.

§17201. Commencement of proceeding

A proceeding under this chapter is commenced by filing a petition stating facts showing that the petition is authorized under this chapter. The petition shall also state the grounds of the petition and the names and addresses of each person entitled to notice of the petition. **Leg.H.** Enacted Stats 1990 ch 79 §14 (AB 759), operative July 1, 1991. Amended Stats 1996 ch 862 §44 (AB 2751), effective January 1, 1997.

Prior Law: Former Prob C §17201, similar to the present section, was added Stats 1986 ch 820 §40, operative July 1, 1987, and repealed Stats 1990 ch 79 §13, operative July 1, 1991.

§17201.1. Commencement of discovery

A petitioner in a proceeding under Section 17200 may commence discovery upon a trustee in accordance with the same time periods set forth in the Civil Discovery Act (Title 4 (commencing with Section 2016.010) of Part 4 of the Code of Civil Procedure) except that the time periods shall commence to run upon service of the petition and notice of hearing upon the trustee or the trustee's appearance in the proceeding, whichever first occurs. Nothing in this section shall alter when a respondent in such a proceeding may commence discovery. **Leg.H.** Added Stats 2017 ch 32 §4 (AB 308), effective January 1, 2018.

§17202. Dismissal of petition

The court may dismiss a petition if it appears that the proceeding is not reasonably necessary for the protection of the interests of the trustee or beneficiary. **Leg.H.** Enacted Stats 1990 ch 79 §14 (AB 759), operative July 1, 1991.

Prior Law: Former Prob C §17202, similar to the present section, was added Stats 1986 ch 820 §40, operative July 1, 1987, and repealed Stats 1990 ch 79 §13, operative July 1, 1991.

§17203. Notice

(a) At least 30 days before the time set for the hearing on the petition, the petitioner shall cause notice of hearing to be delivered pursuant to Section 1215 to all of the following persons:

(1) All trustees.

(2) All beneficiaries, subject to Chapter 2 (commencing with Section 15800) of Part 3.

(3) The Attorney General, if the petition relates to a charitable trust subject to the jurisdiction of the Attorney General.

(b) At least 30 days before the time set for hearing on the petition, the petitioner shall cause notice of the hearing and a copy of the petition to be served in the manner provided in Chapter 4 (commencing with Section 413.10) of Title 5 of Part 2 of the Code of Civil Procedure on any person, other than a trustee or beneficiary, whose right, title, or interest would be affected by the petition and who does not receive notice pursuant to subdivision (a). The court may not shorten the time for giving notice under this subdivision.

(c) If a person to whom notice otherwise would be given has been deceased for at least 40 days, and no personal representative has been appointed for the estate of that person, and the deceased person's right, title, or interest has not passed to any other person pursuant to Division 8 (commencing with Section 13000) or otherwise, notice may instead be given to the following persons:

(1) Each heir and devisee of the decedent, and all persons named as executors of the will of the decedent, so far as known to the petitioner.

(2) Each person serving as guardian or conservator of the decedent at the time of the decedent's death, so far as known to the petitioner. **Leg.H.** Enacted Stats 1990 ch 79 §14 (AB 759), operative July 1, 1991. Amended Stats 1992 ch 871 §20 (AB 2975); Stats 1994 ch 806 §39 (AB 3686); Stats 1996 ch 862 §45 (AB 2751); Stats 1997 ch 724 §28 (AB 1172); Stats 2017 ch 319 §94 (AB 976), effective January 1, 2018.

Prior Law: Former Prob C §17203, similar to the present section, was added Stats 1986 ch 820 §40, operative July 1, 1987, and repealed Stats 1990 ch 79 §13, operative July 1, 1991.

§17204. Request for special notice

(a) If proceedings involving a trust are pending, a beneficiary of the trust may, in person or by attorney, file with the court clerk where the proceedings are pending a written request stating that the beneficiary desires special notice of the filing of petitions in the proceeding relating to any or all of the purposes described in Section 17200 and giving an address for receiving notice by mail. A copy of the request shall be delivered pursuant to Section 1215 to the trustee or the trustee's attorney. If personally delivered, the request shall be effective when it is delivered. If mailed or electronically delivered, the request shall be effective when it is received. When the original of the request is filed with the court clerk, it shall be accompanied by a written admission or proof of service. A request for special notice may be modified or withdrawn in the same manner as provided for the making of the initial request.

(b)(1) An interested person may request special notice in the same manner as a beneficiary under subdivision (a), for the purpose set forth in paragraph (9) of subdivision (b) of Section 17200. The request for special notice shall be accompanied by a verified statement of the person's interest.

(2) For purposes set forth in paragraphs (2), (4) to (6), inclusive, (8), (12), (16), (20), and (21) of subdivision (b) of Section 17200, an interested person may petition the court for an order for special notice of proceedings involving a trust. The petition shall include a verified statement of the creditor's interest and may be served on the trustee or the trustee's attorney in a manner described in Section 1215. The petition may be made by ex parte application.

(3) For purposes of this subdivision, an "interested person" means only a creditor of a trust or, if the trust has become irrevocable upon the death of a trustor, a creditor of the trustor.

(4) This section does not confer standing on an interested person if standing does not otherwise exist.

(c) Except as provided in subdivision (d), after serving and filing a request and proof of service pursuant to subdivision (a) or paragraph (1) of subdivision (b), the beneficiary or the interested person is entitled to notice pursuant to Section 17203. If the petition of an interested person filed pursuant to paragraph (2) of subdivision (b) is granted by the court, the interested person is entitled to notice pursuant to Section 17203.

(d) A request for special notice made by a beneficiary whose right to notice is restricted by Section 15802 is not effective. **Leg.H.** Enacted Stats 1990 ch 79 §14 (AB 759), operative July 1, 1991. Amended Stats 2004 ch 334 §1 (AB 2872); Stats 2017 ch 319 §95 (AB 976), effective January 1, 2018.

Prior Law: Former Prob C §17204, similar to the present section, was added Stats 1986 ch 820 §40, operative July 1, 1987, and repealed Stats 1990 ch 79 §13, operative July 1, 1991.

§17205. Request for copy of petition

If a trustee or beneficiary has served and filed either a notice of appearance, in person or by counsel, directed to the petitioner or the petitioner's counsel in connection with a particular petition and proceeding or a written request for a copy of the petition, and has given an address to which notice or a copy of the petition may be delivered pursuant to Section 1215, the petitioner shall cause a copy of the petition to be delivered to that person within five days after service of the notice of appearance or receipt of the request. **Leg.H.** Enacted Stats 1990 ch 79 §14 (AB 759), operative July 1, 1991. Amended Stats 2017 ch 319 §96 (AB 976), effective January 1, 2018.

Prior Law: Former Prob C §17205, similar to the present section, was added Stats 1986 ch 820 §40, operative July 1, 1987, and repealed Stats 1990 ch 79 §13, operative July 1, 1991.

§17206. Authority to make necessary orders; Temporary trustee

The court in its discretion may make any orders and take any other action necessary or proper to dispose of the matters presented by the petition, including appointment of a temporary trustee to administer the trust in whole or in part. **Leg.H.** Enacted Stats 1990 ch 79 §14 (AB 759), operative July 1, 1991.

Prior Law: Former Prob C §17206, similar to the present section, was added Stats 1986 ch 820 §40, operative July 1, 1987, and repealed Stats 1990 ch 79 §13, operative July 1, 1991.

§17207. [Section repealed 1997]

Leg.H. Enacted Stats 1990 ch 79 §14, operative July 1, 1991. Repealed Stats 1997 ch 724 §29. See Prob C §1304.

Prior Law: Former Prob C §17207, similar to present Prob C §1304, was added Stats 1986 ch 820 §40, operative July 1, 1987, and repealed Stats 1990 ch 79 §13, operative July 1, 1991.

§17209. Intermittent judicial intervention in trust administration

The administration of trusts is intended to proceed expeditiously and free of judicial intervention, subject to the jurisdiction of the court. **Leg.H.** Enacted Stats 1990 ch 79 §14 (AB 759), operative July 1, 1991.

Prior Law: Former Prob C §17209, similar to the present section, was added Stats 1986 ch 820 §40, operative July 1, 1987, and repealed Stats 1990 ch 79 §13, operative July 1, 1991.

§17210. Enforcement of beneficiary's rights under charitable trust by Attorney General

In a case involving a charitable trust subject to the jurisdiction of the Attorney General, the Attorney General may petition under this chapter. **Leg.H.** Enacted Stats 1990 ch 79 §14 (AB 759), operative July 1, 1991.

Prior Law: Former Prob C §17210, similar to the present section, was added Stats 1986 ch 820 §40, operative July 1, 1987, and repealed Stats 1990 ch 79 §13, operative July 1, 1991.

§17211. Award of costs and expenses of litigation to contest account; Personal liability of contestant, etc.

(a) If a beneficiary contests the trustee's account and the court determines that the contest was without reasonable cause and in bad faith, the court may award against the contestant the compensation and costs of the trustee and other expenses and costs of litigation, including attorney's fees, incurred to defend the account. The amount awarded shall be a charge against any interest of the beneficiary in the trust. The contestant shall be personally liable for any amount that remains unsatisfied.

(b) If a beneficiary contests the trustee's account and the court determines that the trustee's opposition to the contest was without reasonable cause and in bad faith, the court may award the contestant the costs of the contestant and other expenses and costs of litigation, including attorney's fees, incurred to contest the account. The amount awarded shall be a charge against the compensation or other interest of the trustee in the trust. The trustee shall be personally liable and on the bond, if any, for any amount that remains unsatisfied. **Leg.H.** Added Stats 1996 ch 563 §31 (SB 392), effective January 1, 1997.

CHAPTER 4
TESTAMENTARY TRUSTS SUBJECT TO CONTINUING COURT JURISDICTION

Article 1. Administration of Testamentary Trusts Subject to Continuing Court Jurisdiction.
Article 2. Removal of Trusts From Continuing Court Jurisdiction.

ARTICLE 1
Administration of Testamentary Trusts Subject to Continuing Court Jurisdiction

Application of article. §17300.
Continuing court jurisdiction. §17301.
Applicable procedures. §17302.
Effect of removal from continuing jurisdiction. §17303.
Transfer of jurisdiction over trust to different county. §17304.

§17300. Application of article

This article applies only to the following:

(a) A trust created by a will executed before July 1, 1977, and not incorporated by reference in a will on or after July 1, 1977.

(b) A trust created by a will which provides that the trust is subject to the continuing jurisdiction of the superior court. **Leg.H.** Enacted Stats 1990 ch 79 §14 (AB 759), operative July 1, 1991.

Prior Law: Former Prob C §17300, similar to the present section, was added Stats 1986 ch 820 §40, operative July 1, 1987, and repealed Stats 1990 ch 79 §13, operative July 1, 1991.

§17301. Continuing court jurisdiction

If a trust described in Section 17300 continues after distribution of the decedent's estate, the court in which the decedent's estate was administered retains jurisdiction over the trust for any of the purposes specified in Section 17200. **Leg.H.** Enacted Stats 1990 ch 79 §14 (AB 759), operative July 1, 1991.

Prior Law: Former Prob C §17301, similar to the present section, was added Stats 1986 ch 820 §40, operative July 1, 1987, and repealed Stats 1990 ch 79 §13, operative July 1, 1991.

§17302. Applicable procedures

Except as otherwise provided in this article, proceedings relating to trusts under continuing court jurisdiction are governed by this part. **Leg.H.** Enacted Stats 1990 ch 79 §14 (AB 759), operative July 1, 1991.

Prior Law: Former Prob C §17302, similar to the present section, was added Stats 1986 ch 820 §40, operative July 1, 1987, and repealed Stats 1990 ch 79 §13, operative July 1, 1991.

§17303. Effect of removal from continuing jurisdiction

This article does not apply to a trust described in Section 17300 that has been removed from continuing court jurisdiction. **Leg.H.** Enacted Stats 1990 ch 79 §14 (AB 759), operative July 1, 1991.

Prior Law: Former Prob C §17303, similar to the present section, was added Stats 1986 ch 820 §40, operative July 1, 1987, and repealed Stats 1990 ch 79 §13, operative July 1, 1991.

§17304. Transfer of jurisdiction over trust to different county

(a) At any time after final distribution of the decedent's estate, a trust described in Section 17300 may be transferred to a different county in this state as provided in this section.

(b) The petition for transfer shall set forth all of the following:

(1) The name of the county to which jurisdiction over the trust is sought to be transferred.

(2) The names, ages, and places of residence of the trustees and all beneficiaries of the trust, so far as known to the petitioner.

(3) A brief description of the character, condition, value, and location of property of the trust.

(4) A brief statement of the reasons for transfer.

(c) If, after hearing, it appears to the court that the transfer of jurisdiction to the county designated in the petition or to any other county in this state will be in the best interests of the estate, or that economical and convenient administration of the trust will be facilitated by the transfer, the court shall make an order transferring jurisdiction over the trust. Upon such order, the court clerk shall certify a copy of the order of transfer to the clerk of the court to which jurisdiction is transferred, together with copies of the instrument creating the trust, the decree of distribution, and any other documents or matters of record the court determines by order to be necessary to define the powers and duties of the trustee, or otherwise to be necessary in connection with further administration of the trust.

(d) The court to which jurisdiction is transferred may from time to time require by order the filing of certified copies of additional papers or matters of record from the court in which the decedent's estate was administered as are required.

(e) Upon the filing of a certified copy of the order of transfer, together with supporting documents, the court to which jurisdiction is transferred has the same jurisdiction over the trust as the court in which the decedent's estate was administered but for the transfer. **Leg.H.** Enacted Stats 1990 ch 79 §14 (AB 759), operative July 1, 1991.

Prior Law: Former Prob C §17304, similar to the present section, was added Stats 1986 ch 820 §40, operative July 1, 1987, and repealed Stats 1990 ch 79 §13, operative July 1, 1991.

ARTICLE 2
Removal of Trusts From Continuing Court Jurisdiction

Application of article. §17350.
Removal of trust from continuing jurisdiction where trustee is trust company. §17351.
Removal of trust from continuing jurisdiction where no trustee is trust company. §17352.
Removal by trust company as successor trustee. §17353.
Effect of change in trustees or other event on removal. §17354.

§17350. Application of article

This article applies only to trusts created by will executed before July 1, 1977, and not incorporated by reference in a will on or after July 1, 1977. **Leg.H.** Enacted Stats 1990 ch 79 §14 (AB 759), operative July 1, 1991.

Prior Law: Former Prob C §17350, similar to the present section, was added Stats 1986 ch 820 §40, operative July 1, 1987, and repealed Stats 1990 ch 79 §13, operative July 1, 1991.

§17351. Removal of trust from continuing jurisdiction where trustee is trust company

(a) If any of the trustees of a trust described in Section 17350 is a trust company, the trust shall be removed from continuing court jurisdiction as provided in this section. Within six months after the initial funding of the trust, the trustee shall give a notice of removal of the trust from continuing court jurisdiction to each beneficiary. Notice of removal shall be sent by registered or certified mail or by first-class mail, but notice sent by first-class mail is effective only if an acknowledgment of receipt of notice is signed by the beneficiary and returned to the trustee.

(b) The notice of removal of the trust from continuing court jurisdiction shall contain the following:

(1) A statement that as of January 1, 1983, the law was changed to remove the necessity for continuing court jurisdiction over the trust.

(2) A statement that Section 17200 of the Probate Code gives any beneficiary the right to petition a court to determine important matters relating to the administration of the trust.

(3) A copy of the text of Sections 17200 and 17201.

(4) A statement that each income beneficiary, as defined in Section 16325, is entitled to an annual statement of the principal and income receipts and disbursements of the trust and that any other beneficiary is entitled to such information upon written request to the trustee.

(5) The name and location of the court in the county in which it is appropriate to file a petition pursuant to Section 17200, the name and location of the court that had jurisdiction over the administration of the decedent's estate, and a statement that it is appropriate to file a petition pursuant to Section 17200 with either court.

(c) The trustee shall file with the court that had jurisdiction over the administration of the decedent's estate proof of giving notice under this section within seven months after the initial funding of the trust. **Leg.H.** Enacted Stats 1990 ch 79 §14 (AB 759), operative July 1, 1991. Amended Stats 1999 ch 145 §6 (AB 846), effective January 1, 2000.

Prior Law: Former Prob C §17351, similar to the present section, was added Stats 1986 ch 820 §40, operative July 1, 1987, and repealed Stats 1990 ch 79 §13, operative July 1, 1991.

§17352. Removal of trust from continuing jurisdiction where no trustee is trust company

(a) If none of the trustees of a trust described in Section 17350 is a trust company, the trust may be removed from continuing court jurisdiction only with approval of the court. The trustee may petition for court approval at any time, and from time to time, in the trustee's discretion.

(b) The petition for removal shall set forth the trust accounts in detail, report the trustee's acts, and show the condition of the trust estate. A copy of the trust instrument shall be attached to the petition.

(c) At the hearing the court may receive testimony from any interested person and may grant or deny the petition, or may grant the petition on such conditions as the court in its discretion deems proper.

(d) If the petition is granted, the trustee shall send the notice of removal of the trust provided in subdivision (b) of Section 17351 and file proof of service as required by subdivision (c) of Section 17351 within six months and seven months, respectively, from the date the petition is granted. A copy of the court order granting the petition shall be attached to the notice.

(e) If the petition is not granted, the trust shall continue to be administered under Article 1 (commencing with Section 17300) as if the settlor had provided in the will that the court does not lose jurisdiction of the estate by final distribution. **Leg.H.** Enacted Stats 1990 ch 79 §14 (AB 759), operative July 1, 1991.

Prior Law: Former Prob C §17352, similar to the present section, was added Stats 1986 ch 820 §40, operative July 1, 1987, and repealed Stats 1990 ch 79 §13, operative July 1, 1991.

§17353. Removal by trust company as successor trustee

If a trust company is appointed as a successor trustee of a trust which, at the time of the appointment, is subject to continuing court jurisdiction because it was not removed pursuant to Section 17352, the successor trustee shall comply with Section 17351. For the purpose of complying with Section 17351, the date of appointment of the successor trustee shall be treated as the date of initial funding of the trust. **Leg.H.** Enacted Stats 1990 ch 79 §14 (AB 759), operative July 1, 1991.

Prior Law: Former Prob C §17353, similar to the present section, was added Stats 1986 ch 820 §40, operative July 1, 1987, and repealed Stats 1990 ch 79 §13, operative July 1, 1991.

§17354. Effect of change in trustees or other event on removal

After a trust is removed from continuing court jurisdiction pursuant to this article, neither a change in trustees nor any other event causes the trust to be subject to continuing court jurisdiction under Article 1 (commencing with Section 17300). **Leg.H.** Enacted Stats 1990 ch 79 §14 (AB 759), operative July 1, 1991.

Prior Law: Former Prob C §17354, similar to the present section, was added Stats 1986 ch 820 §40, operative July 1, 1987, and repealed Stats 1990 ch 79 §13, operative July 1, 1991.

CHAPTER 5
TRANSFER OF TRUST TO ANOTHER JURISDICTION

Application of chapter. §17400.
Transfer of place of administration or property from California. §17401.
Contents of petition. §17402.
Notice and hearing. §17403.
Order granting transfer. §17404.
Manner of transfer; Discharge of trustee. §17405.

§17400. Application of chapter

(a) This chapter applies to all of the following:

(1) A trust that is subject to this division.

(2) A trust subject to Chapter 8 (commencing with Section 6320) of Part 1 of Division 6.

(3) Any other trust to which the provisions of this chapter are made applicable by statute or trust instrument.

(b) This chapter does not prevent the transfer of the place of administration of a trust or of trust property to another jurisdiction by any other available means. **Leg.H.** Enacted Stats 1990 ch 79 §14 (AB 759), operative July 1, 1991.

Prior Law: Former Prob C §17400, similar to the present section, was added Stats 1986 ch 820 §40, operative July 1, 1987, and repealed Stats 1990 ch 79 §13, operative July 1, 1991.

§17401. Transfer of place of administration or property from California

(a) The court may make an order for the transfer of the place of administration of a trust or the transfer of some or all of the trust property to a jurisdiction outside this state as provided in this chapter.

(b) Except as otherwise provided in this chapter, proceedings under this chapter are governed by this part. **Leg.H.** Enacted Stats 1990 ch 79 §14 (AB 759), operative July 1, 1991.

Prior Law: Former Prob C §17401, similar to the present section, was added Stats 1986 ch 820 §40, operative July 1, 1987, and repealed Stats 1990 ch 79 §13, operative July 1, 1991.

§17402. Contents of petition

The petition for transfer shall set forth all of the following:

(a) The names and places of residence of the following:

(1) The trustee administering the trust in this state.

(2) The trustee, including any domiciliary trustee, who will administer the trust or trust property in the other jurisdiction.

(b) The names, ages, and places of residence of the living beneficiaries, as far as known to the petitioner.

(c) Whether the trustee who will administer the trust in the other jurisdiction has agreed to accept the trust. If so, the acceptance or a copy shall be attached as an exhibit to the petition or otherwise filed with the court.

(d) A general statement of the qualifications of the trustee who will administer the trust in the other jurisdiction and the amount of fiduciary bond, if any. If the trustee is an individual, the statement shall include the trustee's age.

(e) A general statement of the nature and value of the property of any trust of the same settlor being administered in the other jurisdiction by the trustee who will administer the trust in the other jurisdiction.

(f) The name of the court, if any, having jurisdiction of the trustee in the other jurisdiction or of its accounts or in which a proceeding may be had with respect to administration of the trust or the trustee's accounts.

(g) A statement of the character, condition, location, and value of the trust property sought to be transferred.

(h) Whether there is any pending civil action in this state against the trustee arising out of the administration of the trust sought to be transferred.

(i) A statement of the reasons for the transfer. **Leg.H.** Enacted Stats 1990 ch 79 §14 (AB 759), operative July 1, 1991.

Prior Law: Former Prob C §17402, similar to the present section, was added Stats 1986 ch 820 §40, operative July 1, 1987, and repealed Stats 1990 ch 79 §13, operative July 1, 1991.

§17403. Notice and hearing

(a) At least 30 days before the time set for the hearing on the petition, the petitioner shall cause notice of the time and place of the hearing to be delivered pursuant to Section 1215 to each of the persons named in the petition at their respective addresses as stated in the petition.

(b) Any person interested in the trust, as trustee, beneficiary, or otherwise, may appear and file written grounds in opposition to the petition. **Leg.H.** Enacted Stats 1990 ch 79 §14 (AB 759), operative July 1, 1991. Amended Stats 2017 ch 319 §97 (AB 976), effective January 1, 2018.

Prior Law: Former Prob C §17403, similar to the present section, was added Stats 1986 ch 820 §40, operative July 1, 1987, and repealed Stats 1990 ch 79 §13, operative July 1, 1991.

§17404. Order granting transfer

The court may, in its discretion, grant the petition and order the trustee to transfer the trust property or to transfer the place of administration of the trust to the other jurisdiction if, after hearing, all of the following appear to the court:

(a) The transfer of the trust property to a trustee in another jurisdiction, or the transfer of the place of administration of the trust to another jurisdiction, will promote the best interests of the trust and those interested in it, taking into account the interest in the economical and convenient administration of the trust.

(b) The transfer will not violate the trust instrument.

(c) Any new trustee to whom the trust property is to be transferred is qualified, willing, and able to administer the trust or trust property under the trust instrument. **Leg.H.** Enacted Stats 1990 ch 79 §14 (AB 759), operative July 1, 1991.

Prior Law: Former Prob C §17404, similar to the present section, was added Stats 1986 ch 820 §40, operative July 1, 1987, and repealed Stats 1990 ch 79 §13, operative July 1, 1991.

§17405. Manner of transfer; Discharge of trustee

If a transfer is ordered under this chapter, the court may direct the manner of transfer and impose terms and conditions as may be just, including, but not limited to, a requirement for the substitution of a successor trustee in any pending litigation in this state. The delivery of property in accordance with the order of the court is a full discharge of the trustee in relation to all property embraced in the order. **Leg.H.** Enacted Stats 1990 ch 79 §14 (AB 759), operative July 1, 1991.

Prior Law: Former Prob C § 17405, similar to the present section, was added Stats 1986 ch 820 §40, operative July 1, 1987, and repealed Stats 1990 ch 79 §13, operative July 1, 1991.

CHAPTER 6
TRANSFER OF TRUST FROM ANOTHER JURISDICTION

Application of chapter. §17450.
Transfer of place of administration or property to California. §17451.
Venue. §17452.
Contents of petition. §17453.
Notice and hearing. §17454.
Order accepting transfer and appointing trustee. §17455.
Conditional order accepting transfer. §17456.
Administration of transferred trust; validity and construction of trust. §17457.

§17450. Application of chapter

(a) This chapter applies to a trust, or portion thereof, administered in a jurisdiction outside this state.

(b) This chapter does not prevent the transfer of the place of administration of a trust or of trust property to this state by any other available means. **Leg.H.** Enacted Stats 1990 ch 79 §14 (AB 759), operative July 1, 1991.

Prior Law: Former Prob C §17450, similar to the present section, was added Stats 1986 ch 820 §40, operative July 1, 1987, and repealed Stats 1990 ch 79 §13, operative July 1, 1991.

§17451. Transfer of place of administration or property to California

(a) The court may make an order accepting the transfer of the place of administration of a trust from another jurisdiction to this state or the transfer of some or all of the trust property in another jurisdiction to a trustee in this state as provided in this chapter.

(b) Except as otherwise provided in this chapter, proceedings under this chapter are governed by this part. **Leg.H.** Enacted Stats 1990 ch 79 §14 (AB 759), operative July 1, 1991.

Prior Law: Former Prob C §17451, similar to the present section, was added Stats 1986 ch 820 §40, operative July 1, 1987, and repealed Stats 1990 ch 79 §13, operative July 1, 1991.

§17452. Venue

(a) If the petition requests that a resident of this state be appointed trustee, the petition shall be filed in the court of the county where the proposed principal place of administration of the trust pursuant to Section 17002 is located.

(b) If the petition requests that only a nonresident of this state be appointed trustee, the petition shall be filed in the court of the county where either (1) any beneficiary resides or (2) a substantial portion of the trust property to be transferred is located or will be located. **Leg.H.** Enacted Stats 1990 ch 79 §14 (AB 759), operative July 1, 1991.

Prior Law: Former Prob C §17452, similar to the present section, was added Stats 1986 ch 820 §40, operative July 1, 1987, and repealed Stats 1990 ch 79 §13, operative July 1, 1991.

§17453. Contents of petition

The petition for transfer shall set forth all of the following:

(a) The names and places of residence of the following:

(1) The trustee administering the trust in the other jurisdiction.

(2) The proposed trustee to whom administration of the trust or trust property will be transferred.

(b) The names, ages, and places of residence of all living beneficiaries, as far as known to the petitioner.

(c) Whether administration of the trust has been subject to supervision in a jurisdiction outside this state. If so, the petition shall state whether a petition or appropriate request for transfer of place of administration of the trust or trust property to this state has been filed, if necessary, with the court in the other jurisdiction, and the status of the petition or request.

(d) Whether the trustee proposed to administer the trust in this state has agreed to accept the trust in this state. If the trustee has agreed, the acceptance shall be attached as an exhibit to the petition or otherwise filed with the court.

(e) A general statement of the qualifications of the trustee proposed to administer the trust in this state and the amount of any bond to be requested. If the trustee is an individual, the statement shall include the trustee's age.

(f) A copy of the trust instrument or a statement of the terms of the trust instrument in effect at the time the petition is filed, including all amendments thereto.

(g) A statement of the character, condition, location, and value of the trust property sought to be transferred.

(h) A statement of the reasons for the transfer. **Leg.H.** Enacted Stats 1990 ch 79 §14 (AB 759), operative July 1, 1991.

Prior Law: Former Prob C §17453, similar to the present section, was added Stats 1986 ch 820 §40, operative July 1, 1987, and repealed Stats 1990 ch 79 §13, operative July 1, 1991.

§17454. Notice and hearing

(a) At least 30 days before the time set for the hearing on the petition, the petitioner shall cause notice of the time and place of the hearing to be delivered pursuant to Section 1215 to each of the persons named in the petition at their respective addresses as stated in the petition.

(b) Any person interested in the trust, as trustee, beneficiary, or otherwise, may appear and file written grounds in opposition to the petition. **Leg.H.** Enacted Stats 1990 ch 79 §14 (AB 759), operative July 1, 1991. Amended Stats 2017 ch 319 §98 (AB 976), effective January 1, 2018.

Prior Law: Former Prob C §17454, similar to the present section, was added Stats 1986 ch 820 §40, operative July 1, 1987, and repealed Stats 1990 ch 79 §13, operative July 1, 1991.

§17455. Order accepting transfer and appointing trustee

(a) The court may, in its discretion, grant the petition and issue an order accepting transfer of trust property or the place of administration of the trust to this state and appoint a trustee to administer the trust in this state, if, after hearing, all of the following appear to the court:

(1) The transfer of the trust property to a trustee in this state, or the transfer of the place of administration of the trust to this state, will promote the best interests of the trust and those interested in it, taking into account the interest in the economical and convenient administration of the trust.

(2) The transfer will not violate the trust instrument.

(3) The trustee appointed by the court to administer the trust in this state, and to whom the trust property is to be transferred, is qualified, willing, and able to administer the trust or trust property under the trust instrument.

(4) The proper court in the other jurisdiction has approved the transfer if approval is necessary under the law of the other jurisdiction.

(b) If the court grants the petition under subdivision (a), the court shall require the trustee to give a bond, if necessary under the law of the other jurisdiction or of this state, and may require bond as provided in Section 15602. **Leg.H.** Enacted Stats 1990 ch 79 §14 (AB 759), operative July 1, 1991.

Prior Law: Former Prob C § 17455, similar to the present section, was added Stats 1986 ch 820 §40, operative July 1, 1987, and repealed Stats 1990 ch 79 §13, operative July 1, 1991.

§17456. Conditional order accepting transfer

If appropriate to facilitate transfer of the trust property or the place of administration of a trust to this state, the court may issue a conditional order appointing a trustee to administer the trust in this state and indicating that transfer to this state will be accepted if transfer is approved by the proper court of the other jurisdiction. **Leg.H.** Enacted Stats 1990 ch 79 §14 (AB 759), operative July 1, 1991.

Prior Law: Former Prob C §17456, similar to the present section, was added Stats 1986 ch 820 §40, operative July 1, 1987, and repealed Stats 1990 ch 79 §13, operative July 1, 1991.

§17457. Administration of transferred trust; validity and construction of trust

A trust transferred to this state pursuant to this chapter shall be administered in the same manner as a trust of that type created in this state. The validity of a trust and the construction of the beneficial provisions of a trust transferred to this state are not affected by this section. **Leg.H.** Enacted Stats 1990 ch 79 §14 (AB 759), operative July 1, 1991.

Prior Law: Former Prob C §17457, similar to the present section, was added Stats 1986 ch 820 §40, operative July 1, 1987, amended Stats 1987 ch 128 §19, effective July 6, 1987, operative July 1, 1987, and repealed Stats 1990 ch 79 §13, operative July 1, 1991.

PART 6
RIGHTS OF THIRD PERSONS

Chapter 1. Liability of Trustee to Third Persons.
Chapter 2. Protection of Third Persons.
Chapter 3. Rights of Creditors of Settlor.

CHAPTER 1
LIABILITY OF TRUSTEE TO THIRD PERSONS

Personal liability of trustee to third persons on contracts. §18000.
Personal liability of trustee arising from ownership or control of trust estate. §18001.
Personal liability of trustee for torts. §18002.
Liability of dissenting cotrustee to third persons. §18003.
Assertion of claims against trust. §18004.
Liability as between trustee and trust estate. §18005.

§18000. Personal liability of trustee to third persons on contracts

(a) Unless otherwise provided in the contract or in this chapter, a trustee is not personally liable on a contract properly entered into in the trustee's fiduciary capacity in the course of administration of the trust unless the trustee fails to reveal the trustee's representative capacity or identify the trust in the contract.

(b) The personal liability of a trustee on a contract entered into before July 1, 1987, is governed by prior law and not by this section. **Leg.H.** Enacted Stats 1990 ch 79 §14 (AB 759), operative July 1, 1991.

Prior Law: Former Prob C §18000, similar to the present section, was added Stats 1986 ch 820 §40, operative July 1, 1987, and repealed Stats 1990 ch 79 §13, operative July 1, 1991.

§18001. Personal liability of trustee arising from ownership or control of trust estate

A trustee is personally liable for obligations arising from ownership or control of trust property only if the trustee is personally at fault. **Leg.H.** Enacted Stats 1990 ch 79 §14 (AB 759), operative July 1, 1991.

Prior Law: Former Prob C §18001, similar to the present section, was added Stats 1986 ch 820 §40, operative July 1, 1987, and repealed Stats 1990 ch 79 §13, operative July 1, 1991.

§18002. Personal liability of trustee for torts

A trustee is personally liable for torts committed in the course of administration of the trust only if the trustee is personally at fault. **Leg.H.** Enacted Stats 1990 ch 79 §14 (AB 759), operative July 1, 1991.

Prior Law: Former Prob C §18002, similar to the present section, was added Stats 1986 ch 820 §40, operative July 1, 1987, and repealed Stats 1990 ch 79 §13, operative July 1, 1991.

§18003. Liability of dissenting cotrustee to third persons

(a) A cotrustee who does not join in exercising a power held by three or more cotrustees is not liable to third persons for the consequences of the exercise of the power.

(b) A dissenting cotrustee who joins in an action at the direction of the majority cotrustees is not liable to third persons for the action if the dissenting cotrustee expresses the dissent in writing to any other cotrustee at or before the time the action is taken.

(c) This section does not excuse a cotrustee from liability for failure to discharge the cotrustee's duties as a trustee. **Leg.H.** Enacted Stats 1990 ch 79 §14 (AB 759), operative July 1, 1991.

Prior Law: Former Prob C §18003, similar to the present section, was added Stats 1986 ch 820 §40, operative July 1, 1987, and repealed Stats 1990 ch 79 §13, operative July 1, 1991.

§18004. Assertion of claims against trust

A claim based on a contract entered into by a trustee in the trustee's representative capacity, on an obligation arising from ownership or control of trust property, or on a tort committed in the course of administration of the trust may be asserted against the trust by proceeding against the trustee in the trustee's representative capacity, whether or not the trustee is personally liable on the claim. **Leg.H.** Enacted Stats 1990 ch 79 §14 (AB 759), operative July 1, 1991.

Prior Law: Former Prob C §18004, similar to the present section, was added Stats 1986 ch 820 §40, operative July 1, 1987, and repealed Stats 1990 ch 79 §13, operative July 1, 1991.

§18005. Liability as between trustee and trust estate

The question of liability as between the trust estate and the trustee personally may be determined in a proceeding under Section 17200. **Leg.H.** Enacted Stats 1990 ch 79 §14 (AB 759), operative July 1, 1991.

Prior Law: Former Prob C §18005, similar to the present section, was added Stats 1986 ch 820 §40, operative July 1, 1987, and repealed Stats 1990 ch 79 §13, operative July 1, 1991.

CHAPTER 2
PROTECTION OF THIRD PERSONS

Protection of third person dealing with trustee. §18100.
Certification of trust; Liability of person acting in reliance thereon; Liability for damages on refusal to accept certification of trust; Recordation. §18100.5.
Application of property delivered to trustee by third person. §18101.
Protection of third person dealing with former trustee. §18102.
Effect on third person of omission of trust from grant of real property. §18103.
Effect on real property transactions where beneficiary undisclosed. §18104.
Affidavit of change of trustee; Recordation. §18105.
Recordation and indexing requirements for affidavit of change of trustee. §18106.
Recorded document establishing change of trustee as prima facie evidence; Presumption. §18107.
Copies of excerpts from original trust documents pertaining to successor trustee. §18108.

§18100. Protection of third person dealing with trustee

With respect to a third person dealing with a trustee or assisting a trustee in the conduct of a transaction, if the third person acts in good faith and for a valuable consideration and without actual knowledge that the trustee is exceeding the trustee's powers or improperly exercising them:

(a) The third person is not bound to inquire whether the trustee has power to act or is properly exercising a power and may assume without inquiry the existence of a trust power and its proper exercise.

(b) The third person is fully protected in dealing with or assisting the trustee just as if the trustee has and is properly exercising the power the trustee purports to exercise. **Leg.H.** Enacted Stats 1990 ch 79 §14 (AB 759), operative July 1, 1991.

Prior Law: Former Prob C §18100, similar to the present section, was added Stats 1986 ch 820 §40, operative July 1, 1987, and repealed Stats 1990 ch 79 §13, operative July 1, 1991.

§18100.5. Certification of trust; Liability of person acting in reliance thereon; Liability for damages on refusal to accept certification of trust; Recordation

(a) The trustee may present a certification of trust to any person in lieu of providing a copy of the trust instrument to establish the existence or terms of the trust. A certification of trust may be executed by the trustee voluntarily or at the request of the person with whom the trustee is dealing.

(b) The certification of trust may confirm the following facts or contain the following information:

(1) The existence of the trust and date of execution of the trust instrument.

(2) The identity of the settlor or settlors and the currently acting trustee or trustees of the trust.

(3) The powers of the trustee.

(4) The revocability or irrevocability of the trust and the identity of any person holding any power to revoke the trust.

(5) When there are multiple trustees, the signature authority of the trustees, indicating whether all, or less than all, of the currently acting trustees are required to sign in order to exercise various powers of the trustee.

(6) The trust identification number, whether a social security number or an employer identification number.

(7) The manner in which title to trust assets should be taken.

(8) The legal description of any interest in real property held in the trust.

(c) The certification shall contain a statement that the trust has not been revoked, modified, or amended in any manner which would cause the representations contained in the certification of trust to be incorrect and shall contain a statement that it is being signed by all of the currently acting trustees of the trust. The certification shall be in the form of an acknowledged declaration signed by all currently acting trustees of the trust. The certification signed by the currently acting trustee may be recorded in the office of the county recorder in the county where all or a portion of the real property is located.

(d) The certification of trust may, but is not required to, include excerpts from the original trust documents, any amendments thereto, and any other documents evidencing or pertaining to the succession of successor trustees. The certification of trust shall not be required to contain the dispositive provisions of the trust which set forth the distribution of the trust estate.

(e) A person whose interest is, or may be, affected by the certification of trust may require that the trustee offering or recording the certification of trust provide copies of those excerpts from the original trust documents, any amendments thereto, and any other documents which designate, evidence, or pertain to the succession of the trustee or confer upon the trustee the power to act in the pending transaction, or both. Nothing in this section is intended to require or imply an obligation to provide the dispositive provisions of the trust or the entire trust and amendments thereto.

(f) A person who acts in reliance upon a certification of trust without actual knowledge that the representations contained therein are incorrect is not liable to any person for so acting. A person who does not have actual knowledge that the facts contained in the certification of trust are incorrect may assume without inquiry the existence of the facts contained in the certification of trust. Actual knowledge shall not be inferred solely from the fact that a copy of all or part of the trust instrument is held by the person relying upon the trust certification. Any transaction, and any lien created thereby, entered into by the trustee and a person acting in reliance upon a certification of trust shall be enforceable against the trust assets. However, if the person has actual knowledge that the trustee is acting outside the scope of the trust, then the transaction is not enforceable against the trust assets. Nothing contained herein shall limit the rights of the beneficiaries of the trust against the trustee.

(g) A person's failure to demand a certification of trust does not affect the protection provided that person by Section 18100, and no inference as to whether that person has acted in good faith may be drawn from the failure to demand a certification of trust. Nothing in this section is intended to create an implication that a person is liable for acting in reliance upon a certification of trust under circumstances where the requirements of this section are not satisfied.

(h) Except when requested by a beneficiary or in the context of litigation concerning a trust and subject to the provisions of subdivision (e), any person making a demand for the trust documents in addition to a certification of trust to prove facts set forth in the certification of trust acceptable to the third party shall be liable for damages, including attorney's fees, incurred as a result of the refusal to accept the certification of trust in lieu of the requested documents if the court determines that the person acted in bad faith in requesting the trust documents.

(i) Any person may record a certification of trust that relates to an interest in real property in the office of the county recorder in any county in which all or a portion of the real property is located. The county recorder shall impose any fee prescribed by law for recording that document sufficient to cover all costs incurred by the county in recording the document. The recorded certification of trust shall be a public record of the real property involved. This subdivision does not create a requirement to record a certification of trust in conjunction with the recordation of a transfer of title of real property involving a trust. **Leg.H.** Added Stats 1993 ch 530 §2 (AB 1249). Amended Stats 2004 ch 136 §1 (AB 1848), effective January 1, 2005.

Prior Law: Former Prob C §18100.5, similar to the present section, was added Stats 1992 ch 178 §43.8, and repealed Stats 1993 ch 530 §1.

§18101. Application of property delivered to trustee by third person

A third person who acts in good faith is not bound to ensure the proper application of trust property paid or delivered to the trustee. **Leg.H.** Enacted Stats 1990 ch 79 §14 (AB 759), operative July 1, 1991.

Prior Law: Former Prob C §18101, similar to the present section, was added Stats 1986 ch 820 §40, operative July 1, 1987, and repealed Stats 1990 ch 79 §13, operative July 1, 1991.

§18102. Protection of third person dealing with former trustee

If a third person acting in good faith and for a valuable consideration enters into a transaction with a former trustee without knowledge that the person is no longer a trustee, the third person is fully protected just as if the former trustee were still a trustee. **Leg.H.** Enacted Stats 1990 ch 79 §14 (AB 759), operative July 1, 1991.

Prior Law: Former Prob C §18102, similar to the present section, was added Stats 1986 ch 820 §40, operative July 1, 1987, and repealed Stats 1990 ch 79 §13, operative July 1, 1991.

§18103. Effect on third person of omission of trust from grant of real property

If an express trust relating to real property is not contained or declared in the grant to the trustee, or in an instrument signed by the trustee and recorded in the same office with the grant to the trustee, the grant shall be deemed absolute in favor of a person dealing with the trustee in good faith and for a valuable consideration. **Leg.H.** Enacted Stats 1990 ch 79 §14 (AB 759), operative July 1, 1991.

Prior Law: Former Prob C §18103, similar to the present section, was added Stats 1986 ch 820 §40, operative July 1, 1987, and repealed Stats 1990 ch 79 §13, operative July 1, 1991.

§18104. Effect on real property transactions where beneficiary undisclosed

(a) If an interest in or lien or encumbrance on real property is conveyed, created, or affected by an instrument in favor of a person in trust but no beneficiary is indicated in the instrument, it is presumed that the person holds the interest, lien, or encumbrance absolutely and free of the trust. This is a presumption affecting the burden of proof. In an action or proceeding involving the interest, lien, or encumbrance instituted against the person, the person shall be deemed the only necessary representative of the undisclosed beneficiary and of the original grantor or settlor and anyone claiming under them. A judgment is binding upon and conclusive against these persons as to all matters finally adjudicated in the judgment.

(b) An instrument executed by the person holding an interest, lien, or encumbrance described in subdivision (a), whether purporting to be the act of that person in his or her own right or in the capacity of a trustee, is presumed to affect the interest, lien, or encumbrance according to the tenor of the instrument. This is a presumption affecting the burden of proof. Upon the recording of the instrument in the county where the land affected by the instrument is located, the presumption is conclusive in favor of a person acting in good faith and for valuable consideration. **Leg.H.** Enacted Stats 1990 ch 79 §14 (AB 759), operative July 1, 1991.

Prior Law: Former Prob C §18104, similar to the present section, was added Stats 1986 ch 820 §40, operative July 1, 1987, and repealed Stats 1990 ch 79 §13, operative July 1, 1991.

§18105. Affidavit of change of trustee; Recordation

If title to an interest in real property is affected by a change of trustee, the successor trustee may execute and record in the county in which the property is located an affidavit of change of trustee. The county recorder shall impose any fee prescribed by law for recording that document in an amount sufficient to cover all costs incurred by the county in recording the document. The affidavit shall include the legal description of the real property, the name of the former trustee or trustees and the name of the successor trustee or trustees. The affidavit may also, but is not required to, include excerpts from the original trust documents, any amendments thereto, and any other documents evidencing or pertaining to the succession of the successor trustee or trustees. **Leg.H.** Added Stats 2004 ch 136 §2 (AB 1848), effective January 1, 2005.

§18106. Recordation and indexing requirements for affidavit of change of trustee

(a) A document establishing the fact of change of trustee recorded pursuant to this chapter is subject to all statutory requirements for recorded documents.

(b) The county recorder shall index a document establishing the fact of change of a trustee recorded pursuant to this section in the index of grantors and grantees. The index entry shall be for the grantor, and for the purpose of this index, the person who has been succeeded as trustee shall be deemed to be the grantor. The county recorder shall impose any fee prescribed by law for indexing that document in an amount sufficient to cover all costs incurred by the county in indexing the document. **Leg.H.** Added Stats 2004 ch 136 §3 (AB 1848), effective January 1, 2005.

§18107. Recorded document establishing change of trustee as prima facie evidence; Presumption

A document establishing the change of a trustee recorded pursuant to this chapter is prima facie evidence of the change of trustee insofar as the document identifies an interest in real property located in the county, title to which is affected by the change of trustee. The presumption established by this section is a presumption affecting the burden of producing evidence. **Leg.H.** Added Stats 2004 ch 136 §4 (AB 1848), effective January 1, 2005.

§18108. Copies of excerpts from original trust documents pertaining to successor trustee

Any person whose interest is, or may be, affected by the recordation of an affidavit of change of trustee pursuant to this chapter may require that the successor trustee provide copies of those excerpts from the original trust documents, any amendments thereto, and any other documents which evidence or pertain to the succession of the successor trustee or trustees. Nothing in this section is intended to require or imply an obligation to provide the dispositive provisions of the trust or the entire trust and any amendments thereto. **Leg.H.** Added Stats 2004 ch 136 §5 (AB 1848), effective January 1, 2005.

CHAPTER 3
RIGHTS OF CREDITORS OF SETTLOR

Creditor's rights against revocable trust during settlor's lifetime. §18200.
Exemptions for settlor whose property is subject to creditor claims. §18201.

§18200. Creditor's rights against revocable trust during settlor's lifetime

If the settlor retains the power to revoke the trust in whole or in part, the trust property is subject to the claims of creditors of the settlor to the extent of the power of revocation during the lifetime of the settlor. **Leg.H.** Enacted Stats 1990 ch 79 §14 (AB 759), operative July 1, 1991.

Prior Law: Former Prob C §18200, similar to the present section, was added Stats 1986 ch 820 §40, operative July 1, 1987, and repealed Stats 1990 ch 79 §13, operative July 1, 1991.

§18201. Exemptions for settlor whose property is subject to creditor claims

Any settlor whose trust property is subject to the claims of creditors pursuant to Section 18200 shall be entitled to all exemptions as provided in Chapter 4 (commencing with Section 703.010) of Division 2 of Title 9 of Part 2 of the Code of Civil Procedure. **Leg.H.** Added Stats 1998 ch 682 §14 (AB 2069), effective January 1, 1999.

Prior Law: Former Prob C §18201, relating to creditor's rights against revocable trust after settlor's death, was enacted Stats 1990 ch 79 §14, operative July 1, 1991, and repealed Stats 1991 ch 992 §2.

Former Prob C §18201, relating to creditor's rights against revocable trust after settlor's death, was added Stats 1986 ch 820 §40, operative July 1, 1987, and repealed Stats 1990 ch 79 §13, operative July 1, 1991.

PART 7
UNIFORM PRUDENT MANAGEMENT OF INSTITUTIONAL FUNDS ACT

Citation of part. §18501.
Definitions. §18502.
Managing and investing an institutional fund. §18503.
Authority to appropriate for expenditure or accumulate of an endowment fund; Factors; Terms. §18504.
Delegation of management or investment function. §18505.
Release of restriction in gift instrument. §18506.
Compliance with part. §18507.
Applicability of part. §18508.
Construction with federal Electronic Signatures in Global and National Commerce Act. §18509.
Application and construction of chapter. §18510.

§18500. [Section repealed 2009]

Leg.H. Added Stats 1990 ch 1307 §4 (SB 2649), operative July 1, 1991. Repealed Stats 2008 ch 715 §3 (SB 1329), effective January 1, 2009. The repealed section related to citation of part as the Uniform Management of Institutional Funds Act. See Prob C §18501.

Prior Law: Former Prob C §18500, similar to present Prob C §18501, was added Stats 1990 ch 1307 §3, operative until July 1, 1991, and repealed Stats 1990 ch 1307 §6, operative July 1, 1991.

§18501. Citation of part

This part may be cited as the Uniform Prudent Management of Institutional Funds Act. **Leg.H.** Added Stats 2008 ch 715 §4 (SB 1329), effective January 1, 2009.

Prior Law: Former Prob C §18501, similar to present Prob C §18502, was added Stats 1990 ch 1307 §4, operative July 1, 1991, and repealed Stats 2008 ch 715 §3, effective January 1, 2009.

Former Prob C §18501, similar to present Prob C §18502, was added Stats 1990 ch 1307 §3, operative until July 1, 1991, and repealed Stats 1990 ch 1307 §6, operative July 1, 1991.

§18502. Definitions

As used in this part, the following terms shall have the following meanings:

(a) "Charitable purpose" means the relief of poverty, the advancement of education or religion, the promotion of health, the promotion of a governmental purpose, or any other purpose the achievement of which is beneficial to the community.

(b) "Endowment fund" means an institutional fund or part thereof that, under the terms of a gift instrument, is not wholly expendable by the institution on a current basis. The term does not include assets that an institution designates as an endowment fund for its own use.

(c) "Gift instrument" means a record or records, including an institutional solicitation, under which property is granted to, transferred to, or held by an institution as an institutional fund.

(d) "Institution" means any of the following:

(1) A person, other than an individual, organized and operated exclusively for charitable purposes.

(2) A government or governmental subdivision, agency, or instrumentality, to the extent that it holds funds exclusively for a charitable purpose.

(3) A trust that had both charitable and noncharitable interests, after all noncharitable interests have terminated.

(e) "Institutional fund" means a fund held by an institution exclusively for charitable purposes. The term does not include any of the following:

(1) Program-related assets.

(2) A fund held for an institution by a trustee that is not an institution.

(3) A fund in which a beneficiary that is not an institution has an interest, other than an interest that could arise upon violation or failure of the purposes of the fund.

(f) "Person" means an individual, corporation, business trust, estate, trust, partnership, limited liability company, association, joint venture, public corporation, government or governmental subdivision, agency, or instrumentality, or any other legal or commercial entity.

(g) "Program-related asset" means an asset held by an institution primarily to accomplish a charitable purpose of the institution and not primarily for investment.

(h) "Record" means information that is inscribed on a tangible medium or that is stored in an electronic or other medium and is retrievable in perceivable form. **Leg.H.** Added Stats 2008 ch 715 §4 (SB 1329), effective January 1, 2009.

Prior Law: Former Prob C §18502, relating to the expenditure of asset net appreciation for current use, was added Stats 1990 ch 1307 §4, operative July 1, 1991, and repealed Stats 2008 ch 715 §3, effective January 1, 2009. Historical derivation: (a) Former Prob C §18500, as added Stats 1990 ch 1307 §3. (b) Former Ed C §94602, as added Stats 1986 ch 820 §24.

Former Prob C §18502, relating to the expenditure of asset net appreciation for current use, was added Stats 1990 ch 1307 §3, operative until July 1, 1991, and repealed Stats 1990 ch 1307 §6, operative July 1, 1991.

§18502.5. [Section repealed 1994]

Leg.H. Added Stats 1990 ch 1307 §4 (SB 2649), operative July 1, 1991, operative until January 1, 1994. Repealed January 1, 1994, by its own terms. The repealed section related to limitation on appropriations.

Prior Law: Former Prob C §18502.5, relating to limitation on appropriations, was added Stats 1990 ch 1307 §3 and repealed Stats 1990 ch 1307 §6, operative July 1, 1991.

§18503. Managing and investing an institutional fund

(a) Subject to the intent of a donor expressed in a gift instrument, an institution, in managing and investing an institutional fund, shall consider the charitable purposes of the institution and the purposes of the institutional fund.

(b) In addition to complying with the duty of loyalty imposed by law other than this part, each person responsible for managing and investing an institutional fund shall manage and invest the fund in good faith and with the care an ordinarily prudent person in a like position would exercise under similar circumstances.

(c) In managing and investing an institutional fund, an institution is subject to both of the following:

(1) It may incur only costs that are appropriate and reasonable in relation to the assets, the purposes of the institution, and the skills available to the institution.

(2) It shall make a reasonable effort to verify facts relevant to the management and investment of the fund.

(d) An institution may pool two or more institutional funds for purposes of management and investment.

(e) Except as otherwise provided by a gift instrument, the following rules apply:

(1) In managing and investing an institutional fund, all of the following factors, if relevant, must be considered:

(A) General economic conditions.

(B) The possible effect of inflation or deflation.

(C) The expected tax consequences, if any, of investment decisions or strategies.

(D) The role that each investment or course of action plays within the overall investment portfolio of the fund.

(E) The expected total return from income and the appreciation of investments.

(F) Other resources of the institution.

(G) The needs of the institution and the fund to make distributions and to preserve capital.

(H) An asset's special relationship or special value, if any, to the charitable purposes of the institution.

(2) Management and investment decisions about an individual asset must be made not in isolation but rather in the context of the institutional fund's portfolio of investments as a whole and as a part of an overall investment strategy having risk and return objectives reasonably suited to the fund and to the institution.

(3) Except as otherwise provided by law other than this part, an institution may invest in any kind of property or type of investment consistent with this section.

(4) An institution shall diversify the investments of an institutional fund unless the institution reasonably determines that, because of special

circumstances, the purposes of the fund are better served without diversification.

(5) Within a reasonable time after receiving property, an institution shall make and carry out decisions concerning the retention or disposition of the property or to rebalance a portfolio, in order to bring the institutional fund into compliance with the purposes, terms, and distribution requirements of the institution as necessary to meet other circumstances of the institution and the requirements of this part.

(6) A person that has special skills or expertise, or is selected in reliance upon the person's representation that the person has special skills or expertise, has a duty to use those skills or that expertise in managing and investing institutional funds.

(f) Nothing in this section alters the duties and liabilities of a director of a nonprofit public benefit corporation under Section 5240 of the Corporations Code. **Leg.H.** Added Stats 2008 ch 715 §4 (SB 1329), effective January 1, 2009.

Prior Law: Former Prob C §18503, similar to present Prob C §18504, was added Stats 1990 ch 1307 §4, operative July 1, 1991, and repealed Stats 2008 ch 715 §3, effective January 1, 2009.

Former Prob C §18503, similar to present Prob C §18504, was added Stats 1990 ch 1307 §3, operative until July 1, 1991, and repealed Stats 1990 ch 1307 §6, operative July 1, 1991.

§18504. Authority to appropriate for expenditure or accumulate of an endowment fund; Factors; Terms

(a) Subject to the intent of a donor expressed in the gift instrument, an institution may appropriate for expenditure or accumulate so much of an endowment fund as the institution determines is prudent for the uses, benefits, purposes, and duration for which the endowment fund is established. Unless stated otherwise in the gift instrument, the assets in an endowment fund are donor-restricted assets until appropriated for expenditure by the institution. In making a determination to appropriate or accumulate, the institution shall act in good faith, with the care that an ordinarily prudent person in a like position would exercise under similar circumstances, and shall consider, if relevant, all of the following factors:

(1) The duration and preservation of the endowment fund.

(2) The purposes of the institution and the endowment fund.

(3) General economic conditions.

(4) The possible effect of inflation or deflation.

(5) The expected total return from income and the appreciation of investments.

(6) Other resources of the institution.

(7) The investment policy of the institution.

(b) To limit the authority to appropriate for expenditure or accumulate under subdivision (a), a gift instrument must specifically state the limitation.

(c) Terms in a gift instrument designating a gift as an endowment, or a direction or authorization in the gift instrument to use only "income," "interest," "dividends," or "rents, issues, or profits," or "to preserve the principal intact," or words of similar import have both of the following effects:

(1) To create an endowment fund of permanent duration unless other language in the gift instrument limits the duration or purpose of the fund.

(2) To not otherwise limit the authority to appropriate for expenditure or accumulate under subdivision (a).

(d) The appropriation for expenditure in any year of an amount greater than 7 percent of the fair market value of an endowment fund, calculated on the basis of market values determined at least quarterly and averaged over a period of not less than three years immediately preceding the year in which the appropriation for expenditure is made, creates a rebuttable presumption of imprudence. For an endowment fund in existence for fewer than three years, the fair market value of the endowment fund shall be calculated for the period the endowment fund has been in existence. This subdivision does not do any of the following:

(1) Apply to an appropriation for expenditure permitted under law other than this part or by the gift instrument.

(2) Apply to a private or public postsecondary educational institution, or to a campus foundation established by and operated under the auspices of such an educational institution.

(3) Create a presumption of prudence for an appropriation for expenditure of an amount less than or equal to 7 percent of the fair market value of the endowment fund. **Leg.H.** Added Stats 2008 ch 715 §4 (SB 1329), effective January 1, 2009.

Prior Law: Former Prob C §18504, relating to the authority of governing board to invest, was added Stats 1990 ch 1307 §4, operative July 1, 1991, and repealed Stats 2008 ch 715 §3, effective January 1, 2009. Historical derivation: (a) Former Prob C §18504, as added Stats 1990 ch 1307 §3. (b) Former Ed C §94604, as added Stats 1986 ch 820 §24.

Former Prob C §18504, relating to the authority of governing board to invest, was added Stats 1990 ch 1307 §3, operative until July 1, 1991, and repealed Stats 1990 ch 1307 §6, operative July 1, 1991.

§18505. Delegation of management or investment function

(a) Subject to any specific limitation set forth in a gift instrument or in law other than this part, an institution may delegate to an external agent the management and investment of an institutional fund to the extent that an institution could prudently delegate under the circumstances. An institution shall act in good faith, with the care that an ordinarily prudent person in a like position would exercise under similar circumstances, in all of the following:

(1) Selecting an agent.

(2) Establishing the scope and terms of the delegation, consistent with the purposes of the institution and the institutional fund.

(3) Periodically reviewing the agent's actions in order to monitor the agent's performance and compliance with the scope and terms of the delegation.

(b) In performing a delegated function, an agent owes a duty to the institution to exercise reasonable care to comply with the scope and terms of the delegation.

(c) An institution that complies with subdivision (a) is not liable for the decisions or actions of an agent to which the function was delegated except to the extent a trustee would be liable for those actions or decisions under Sections 16052 and 16401.

(d) By accepting delegation of a management or investment function from an institution that is subject to the laws of this state, an agent submits to the jurisdiction of the courts of this state in all proceedings arising from or related to the delegation or the performance of the delegated function.

(e) An institution may delegate management and investment functions to its committees, officers, or employees as authorized by law of this state other than this part. **Leg.H.** Added Stats 2008 ch 715 §4 (SB 1329), effective January 1, 2009.

Prior Law: Former Prob C §18505, similar to the present section, was added Stats 1990 ch 1307 §4, operative July 1, 1991, and repealed Stats 2008 ch 715 §3, effective January 1, 2009.

Former Prob C §18505, similar to the present section, was added Stats 1990 ch 1307 §3, operative until July 1, 1991, and repealed Stats 1990 ch 1307 §6, operative July 1, 1991.

§18506. Release of restriction in gift instrument

(a) If the donor consents in a record, an institution may release or modify, in whole or in part, a restriction contained in a gift instrument on the management, investment, or purpose of an institutional fund. A release or modification may not allow a fund to be used for a purpose other than a charitable purpose of the institution.

(b) The court, upon application of an institution, may modify a restriction contained in a gift instrument regarding the management or investment of an institutional fund if the restriction has become impracticable or wasteful, if it impairs the management or investment of the fund, or if, because of circumstances not anticipated by the donor, a modification of a restriction will further the purposes of the fund. The institution shall notify the Attorney General of the application, and the Attorney General must be given an opportunity to be heard. To the extent practicable, any modification must be made in accordance with the donor's probable intention.

(c) If a particular charitable purpose or a restriction contained in a gift instrument on the use of an institutional fund becomes unlawful, impracticable, impossible to achieve, or wasteful, the court, upon application of an institution, may modify the purpose of the fund or the restriction on the use of the fund in a manner consistent with the charitable purposes expressed in the gift instrument. The institution shall notify the Attorney General of the application, and the Attorney General must be given an opportunity to be heard.

(d) If an institution determines that a restriction contained in a gift instrument on the management, investment, or purpose of an institutional fund is unlawful, impracticable, impossible to achieve, or wasteful, the institution, 60 days after notification to the Attorney General and to the donor at the donor's last known address in the records of the institution, may release or modify the restriction, in whole or part, if all of the following apply:

(1) The institutional fund subject to the restriction has a total value of less than one hundred thousand dollars ($100,000).

(2) More than 20 years have elapsed since the fund was established.

(3) The institution uses the property in a manner consistent with the charitable purposes expressed in the gift instrument. An institution that releases or modifies a restriction under this subdivision may, if appropriate circumstances arise thereafter, use the property in accordance with the restriction notwithstanding its release or modification, and that use is deemed to satisfy the consistency requirement of this paragraph. **Leg.H.** Added Stats 2008 ch 715 §4 (SB 1329), effective January 1, 2009.

Prior Law: Former Prob C §18506, relating to the standard of care in investment management, was added Stats 1990 ch 1307 §4, operative July 1, 1991, and repealed Stats 2008 ch 715 §3, effective January 1, 2009. Historical derivation: (a) Former Prob C §18506, as added Stats 1990 ch 1307 §3. (b) Former Ed C §94606, as added Stats 1986 ch 820 §24.

Former Prob C §18506, relating to the standard of care in investment management, was added Stats 1990 ch 1307 §3, operative until July 1, 1991, and repealed Stats 1990 ch 1307 §6, operative July 1, 1991.

§18507. Compliance with part

Compliance with this part is determined in light of the facts and circumstances existing at the time a decision is made or action is taken, and not by hindsight. **Leg.H.** Added Stats 2008 ch 715 §4 (SB 1329), effective January 1, 2009.

Prior Law: Former Prob C §18507, relating to the release of restriction in gift instrument, was added Stats 1990 ch 1307 §4, operative July 1, 1991, and repealed Stats 2008 ch 715 §3, effective January 1, 2009. Historical derivation: (a) Former Prob C §18507, as added Stats 1990 ch 1307 §3. (b) Former Ed C §94607, as added Stats 1986 ch 820 §24.

Former Prob C §18507, relating to the release of restriction in gift instrument, was added Stats 1990 ch 1307 §3, operative until July 1, 1991, and repealed Stats 1990 ch 1307 §6, operative July 1, 1991.

§18508. Applicability of part

This part applies to institutional funds existing on or established after January 1, 2009. As applied to institutional funds existing on January 1, 2009, this part governs only decisions made or actions taken on or after that date. **Leg.H.** Added Stats 2008 ch 715 §4 (SB 1329), effective January 1, 2009.

Prior Law: Former Prob C §18508, relating to status of governing boards and duties and liabilities of directors, was added Stats 1990 ch 1307 §4, operative July 1, 1991, and repealed Stats 2008 ch 715 §3, effective January 1, 2009. Historical derivation: (a) Former Prob C §18508, as added Stats 1990 ch 1307 §3. (b) Former Ed C §94610, as added Stats 1986 ch 820 §24.

Former Prob C §18508, similar to the present section, was added Stats 1990 ch 1307 §3, operative until July 1, 1991, and repealed Stats 1990 ch 1307 §6, operative July 1, 1991.

§18509. Construction with federal Electronic Signatures in Global and National Commerce Act

This part modifies, limits, and supersedes the Electronic Signatures in Global and National Commerce Act (15 U.S.C. Sec. 7001 et seq.), but does not modify, limit, or supersede Section 101 of that act (15 U.S.C. Sec. 7001(a)), or authorize electronic delivery of any of the notices described in Section 103 of that act (15 U.S.C. Sec. 7003(b)). **Leg.H.** Added Stats 2008 ch 715 §4 (SB 1329), effective January 1, 2009.

Prior Law: Former Prob C §18509, relating to application of laws relating to the expenditure of public funds, was added Stats 1990 ch 1307 §4, operative July 1, 1991, and repealed Stats 2008 ch 715 §3, effective January 1, 2009.

Former Prob C §18509, relating to application of laws relating to the expenditure of public funds, was added Stats 1990 ch 1307 §3, operative until July 1, 1991, and repealed Stats 1990 ch 1307 §6, operative July 1, 1991.

§18510. Application and construction of chapter

In applying and construing this uniform act, consideration must be given to the need to promote uniformity of the law with respect to its subject matter among states that enact it. **Leg.H.** Added Stats 2008 ch 715 §4 (SB 1329), effective January 1, 2009.

PART 8
PAYMENT OF CLAIMS, DEBTS, AND EXPENSES FROM REVOCABLE TRUST OF DECEASED SETTLOR

Chapter 1. General Provisions.
Chapter 2. Petition for Approval and Settlement of Claims Against Deceased Settlor.
Chapter 3. Publication of Notice.
Chapter 4. Actual Notice to Creditors.
Chapter 5. Time for Filing Claims.
Chapter 6. Filing of Claims.
Chapter 7. Claims by Public Entities.
Chapter 8. Allowance and Rejection of Claims.
Chapter 9. Claims Established by Judgment.
Chapter 10. Allocation of Debts Between Trust and Surviving Spouse.
Chapter 11. Liability of Settlor's Surviving Spouse.
Chapter 12. Distributee Liability.

CHAPTER 1
GENERAL PROVISIONS

Definitions. §19000.
Property as subject to certain claims. §19001.
Construction of part. §19002.
Filing of proposed notice to creditors. §19003.
Effect of filing, publishing, and serving notice. §19004.
Payment, rejection, or contesting of claims. §19005.
Effect of filing on other trusts established by deceased settlor, and on their trustees and beneficiaries. §19006.
Liability between trusts established by same deceased settlor. §19007.
Effect of failure to hold proceedings to administer estate, to file proposed notice, and to publish notice to creditors. §19008.
Disclosure of existence or provisions of trust to creditors or beneficiaries. §19009.
Duty to initiate notice proceedings. §19010.
Prescription and adoption of designated forms by Judicial Council. §19011.
Application of part. §19012.

§19000. Definitions

As used in this part:

(a) "Claim" means a demand for payment for any of the following, whether due, not due, accrued or not accrued, or contingent, and whether liquidated or unliquidated:

(1) Liability of the deceased settlor, whether arising in contract, tort, or otherwise.

(2) Liability for taxes incurred before the deceased settlor's death, whether assessed before or after the deceased settlor's death, other than property taxes and assessments secured by real property liens.

(3) Liability for the funeral expenses of the deceased settlor.

(b) "Claim" does not include a dispute regarding title to specific property alleged to be included in the trust estate.

(c) "Creditor" means a person who may have a claim against the trust property.

(d) "Trust" means a trust described in Section 18200, or, if a portion of a trust, that portion that remained subject to the power of revocation at the deceased settlor's death.

(e) "Deceased settlor" means a deceased person who, at the time of his or her death, held the power to revoke the trust in whole or in part.

(f) "Debts" means all claims, as defined in subdivision (a), all expenses of administration, and all other proper charges against the trust estate, including taxes.

(g) "Probate estate" means a decedent's estate subject to administration pursuant to Division 7 (commencing with Section 7000).

(h) "Trust estate" means a decedent's property, real and personal, that is titled in the name of the trustee of the deceased settlor's trust or confirmed by order of the court to the trustee of the deceased settlor's trust. **Leg.H.** Added Stats 1991 ch 992 §3 (SB 727). Amended Stats 1996 ch 862 §46 (AB 2751); Stats 2007 ch 159 §8 (AB 341), effective January 1, 2008; Stats 2015 ch 48 §1 (SB 785), effective January 1, 2016.

§19001. Property as subject to certain claims

(a) Upon the death of a settlor, the property of the deceased settlor that was subject to the power of revocation at the time of the settlor's death is subject to the claims of creditors of the deceased settlor's probate estate and to the expenses of administration of the probate estate to the extent that the deceased settlor's probate estate is inadequate to satisfy those claims and expenses.

(b) The deceased settlor, by appropriate direction in the trust instrument, may direct the priority of sources of payment of debts among subtrusts or other gifts established by the trust at the deceased settlor's death. Notwithstanding this subdivision, no direction by the settlor shall alter the priority of payment, from whatever source, of the matters set forth in Section 11420 which shall be applied to the trust as it applies to a probate estate. **Leg.H.** Added Stats 1991 ch 992 §3 (SB 727). Amended Stats 2015 ch 48 §2 (SB 785), effective January 1, 2016.

§19002. Construction of part

(a) Except as expressly provided, this part shall not be construed to affect the right of any creditor to recover from any revocable trust established by the deceased settlor.

(b) Nothing in this part shall be construed as a construction or alteration of any claims procedure set forth under Part 4 (commencing with Section 9000) of Division 7. **Leg.H.** Added Stats 1991 ch 992 §3 (SB 727).

§19003. Filing of proposed notice to creditors

(a) At any time following the death of the settlor, and during the time that there has been no filing of a petition to administer the probate estate of the deceased settlor in this state of which the trustee has actual knowledge, the trustee may file with the court a proposed notice to creditors. Upon the court's assignment of a proceeding number to the proposed notice, the trustee shall publish and serve notice to creditors of the deceased settlor in the form and within the time prescribed in Chapters 3 (commencing with Section 19040) and 4 (commencing with Section 19050). That action shall constitute notice to creditors of the requirements of this part.

(b) The filing shall be made with the superior court for the county in this state where the deceased settlor resided at the time of death, or if none, in any county in this state in which trust property was located at the time of the settlor's death, or if none, in the county in this state that was the principal place of administration of the trust at the time of the settlor's death.

(c) Nothing in subdivision (a) affects a notice or request to a public entity required by Chapter 7 (commencing with Section 19200). **Leg.H.** Added Stats 1991 ch 992 §3 (SB 727). Amended Stats 2015 ch 48 §3 (SB 785), effective January 1, 2016.

§19004. Effect of filing, publishing, and serving notice

If the trustee files, publishes, and serves notice as set forth in Section 19003, then:

(a) All claims against the trust shall be filed in the manner and within the time provided in this part.

(b) A claim that is not filed as provided in this part is barred from collection from trust assets.

(c) The holder of a claim may not maintain an action on the claim against the trust unless the claim is first filed as provided in this part. **Leg.H.** Added Stats 1991 ch 992 §3 (SB 727).

§19005. Payment, rejection, or contesting of claims

The trustee may at any time pay, reject, or contest any claim against the deceased settlor or settle any claim by compromise, arbitration, or otherwise. The trustee may also file a petition in the manner set forth in Chapter 2 (commencing with Section 19020) to settle any claim. **Leg.H.** Added Stats 1991 ch 992 §3 (SB 727).

§19006. Effect of filing on other trusts established by deceased settlor, and on their trustees and beneficiaries

(a) If a trustee of a trust established by the deceased settlor files, publishes, and serves notice as provided in Section 19003 the protection from creditors afforded that trustee and trust shall also be afforded to any other trusts established by the deceased settlor and the trustees and beneficiaries of those trusts.

(b) If the personal representative of the deceased settlor's probate estate has published notice under Section 8120 and given notice of administration of the probate estate of the deceased settlor under Chapter 2 (commencing with Section 9050) of Part 4 of Division 7, the protection from creditors afforded the personal representative of the deceased settlor's probate estate shall be afforded to the trustee and to the beneficiaries of the trust.

(c) In the event that, following the filing and publication of the notice set forth in Section 19003, there shall be commenced any proceeding under which a notice pursuant to Section 8120 is required to be published, then the trustee shall have a right of collection against that probate estate to recover the amount of any debts paid from trust assets that would otherwise have been satisfied (whether by law or by direction in the deceased settlor's will or trust) by the property subject to probate proceedings. **Leg.H.** Added Stats 1991 ch 992 §3 (SB 727). Amended Stats 2015 ch 48 §4 (SB 785), effective January 1, 2016.

§19007. Liability between trusts established by same deceased settlor

Nothing in this part shall determine the liability of any trust established by the deceased settlor as against any other trust established by that settlor, except to the extent that the trustee of the other trust shall file, publish, and serve the notice specified in Section 19003 and thereafter seek a determination of relative liability pursuant to Chapter 2 (commencing with Section 19020). **Leg.H.** Added Stats 1991 ch 992 §3 (SB 727).

§19008. Effect of failure to hold proceedings to administer estate, to file proposed notice, and to publish notice to creditors

If there is no proceeding to administer the probate estate of the deceased settlor, and if the trustee does not file a proposed notice to creditors pursuant to Section 19003 and does not publish notice to creditors pursuant to Chapter 3 (commencing with Section 19040), then the liability of the trust to any creditor of the deceased settlor shall be as otherwise provided by law. **Leg.H.** Added Stats 1991 ch 992 §3 (SB 727). Amended Stats 2015 ch 48 §5 (SB 785), effective January 1, 2016.

§19009. Disclosure of existence or provisions of trust to creditors or beneficiaries

Nothing in this part shall be construed to permit or require disclosure of the existence of the trust or the contents of any of its provisions to any creditor or beneficiary except as that creditor or beneficiary may otherwise be entitled to that information. **Leg.H.** Added Stats 1991 ch 992 §3 (SB 727).

§19010. Duty to initiate notice proceedings

Nothing in this part imposes any duty on the trustee to initiate the notice proceeding set forth in Section 19003, and the trustee is not liable for failure to initiate the proceeding under this part. **Leg.H.** Added Stats 1991 ch 992 §3 (SB 727).

§19011. Prescription and adoption of designated forms by Judicial Council

(a) The Judicial Council may prescribe the form and contents of the petition, notice, claim form, and allowance or rejection form to be used pursuant to this part. The allowance or rejection form may be part of the claim form.

(b) Any claim form adopted by the Judicial Council shall inform the creditor that the claim must be filed with the court and a copy delivered pursuant to Section 1215 to the trustee. The claim form shall include a proof of delivery of a copy of the claim to the trustee, which may be completed by the claimant. **Leg.H.** Added Stats 1991 ch 992 §3 (SB 727). Amended Stats 2007 ch 159 §9 (AB 341), effective January 1, 2008; Stats 2017 ch 319 §99 (AB 976), effective January 1, 2018.

§19012. Application of part

(a) This part applies to claims against any deceased settlor who dies on or after January 1, 1992.

(b) The applicable law in effect before January 1, 1992, continues to apply to claims against any deceased settlor who dies before January 1, 1992. **Leg.H.** Added Stats 1991 ch 992 §3 (SB 727).

CHAPTER 2
PETITION FOR APPROVAL AND SETTLEMENT OF CLAIMS AGAINST DECEASED SETTLOR

Petition. §19020.
Filing petition. §19021.
Commencement of proceeding; Content of petition. §19022.
Notice of hearing to claimants. §19023.
Notice of hearing to other interested persons. §19024.
Failure to file written pleading upon notice. §19025.
Dismissal of petition. §19026.
Court orders and other actions. §19027.
Appointment of guardian ad litem. §19029.
Petitions involving charitable trusts. §19030.

§19020. Petition

At any time after the filing and first publication of notice pursuant to Chapter 3 (commencing with Section 19040), and after expiration of the time to file claims provided in that chapter, a trustee or beneficiary may petition the court under this chapter to approve either of the following:

(a) Allowance, compromise, or settlement of any claims that have not been rejected by the trustee under the procedure provided in this part and for which trust property may be liable.

(b) An allocation of any amounts due by reason of an action described in subdivision (a) to two or more trusts which may be liable for the claims. **Leg.H.** Added Stats 1991 ch 992 §3 (SB 727).

§19021. Filing petition

The petition shall be filed in that county as may be determined pursuant to Section 19003. In the event this action seeks approval of allocation to two or more trusts for which the notice proceeding in Section 19003 would prescribe superior courts for more than one county, the court located in the county so prescribed for the trustee initiating the proceeding under this chapter shall have jurisdiction. **Leg.H.** Added Stats 1991 ch 992 §3 (SB 727).

§19022. Commencement of proceeding; Content of petition

(a) A proceeding under this chapter is commenced by filing a verified petition stating facts showing that the petition is authorized under this chapter and the grounds of the petition.

(b) The petition shall set forth a description of the trust and the names of creditors with respect to which action is requested and a description of each claim, together with the requested determination by the court with respect to the claims, provided, however, that this section does not require the filing of a copy of the trust or disclosure of the beneficial interests of the trust. That petition shall also set forth the beneficiaries of the trust, those claimants whose interest in the trust may be affected by the petition, and the trustees of any other trust to which an allocation of liability may be approved by the court pursuant to the petition.

(c) The clerk shall set the matter for hearing. **Leg.H.** Added Stats 1991 ch 992 §3 (SB 727). Amended Stats 2007 ch 159 §10 (AB 341), effective January 1, 2008.

§19023. Notice of hearing to claimants

At least 30 days before the time set for the hearing on the petition, the petitioner shall cause notice of the time and place of the hearing and a copy of the petition to be served on each of the creditors whose interests in the estate may be affected by the petition in the manner provided in Chapter 4 (commencing with Section 413.10) of Title 5 of Part 2 of the Code of Civil Procedure. **Leg.H.** Added Stats 1991 ch 992 §3 (SB 727). Amended Stats 2007 ch 159 §11 (AB 341), effective January 1, 2008.

§19024. Notice of hearing to other interested persons

At least 30 days before the time set for the hearing on the petition, the petitioner shall cause notice of the time and place of the hearing, together with a copy of the petition, to be delivered pursuant to Section 1215 to each of the following persons who is not a petitioner:

(a) All trustees of the trust and of any other trusts to which an allocation of liability may be approved by the court pursuant to the petition.

(b) All beneficiaries affected.

(c) The personal representative of the deceased settlor's probate estate, if any is known to the trustee.

(d) The Attorney General, if the petition relates to a charitable trust subject to the jurisdiction of the Attorney General, unless the Attorney General waives notice. **Leg.H.** Added Stats 1991 ch 992 §3 (SB 727). Amended Stats 2015 ch 48 §6 (SB 785), effective January 1, 2016; Stats 2017 ch 319 §100 (AB 976), effective January 1, 2018.

§19025. Failure to file written pleading upon notice

(a) If any creditor, beneficiary, or trustee fails timely to file a written pleading upon notice, then the case is at issue, notwithstanding the failure.

The case may proceed on the petition and written statements filed by the time of the hearing, and no further pleadings by other persons are necessary. The creditor, beneficiary, or trustee who failed timely to file a written pleading upon notice may not participate further in the proceeding for the determination requested, and that creditor, beneficiary, or trustee shall be bound by the decision in the proceeding.

(b) The court's order, when final, shall be conclusive as to the liability of the trust property with respect to the claims at issue in the petition. In the event of a subsequent administration of the probate estate of the deceased settlor, that order shall be binding on the personal representative of the probate estate of the deceased settlor as well as all creditors and beneficiaries who had notice of the petition. **Leg.H.** Added Stats 1991 ch 992 §3 (SB 727). Amended Stats 2007 ch 159 §12 (AB 341), effective January 1, 2008; Stats 2015 ch 48 §7 (SB 785), effective January 1, 2016.

§19026. Dismissal of petition

The court may dismiss a petition if it appears that the proceeding is not reasonably necessary for the protection of the interests of the trustee or any beneficiary of the trust. **Leg.H.** Added Stats 1991 ch 992 §3 (SB 727).

§19027. Court orders and other actions

(a) The court in its discretion may make any orders and take any other action necessary or proper to dispose of the matters presented by the petition.

(b) If the court determines that the assets of the trust estate are insufficient to pay all debts, then the court shall order payment in the manner specified by Section 11420. **Leg.H.** Added Stats 1991 ch 992 §3 (SB 727).

§19028. [Section repealed 1997]

Leg.H. Added Stats 1991 ch 992 §3 (SB 727). Repealed Stats 1997 ch 724 §30 (AB 1172). See Prob C §1300.

§19029. Appointment of guardian ad litem

The court may, on its own motion or on request of a trustee or other person interested in the trust, appoint a guardian ad litem in accordance with Section 1003. **Leg.H.** Added Stats 1991 ch 992 §3 (SB 727).

§19030. Petitions involving charitable trusts

In a case involving a charitable trust subject to the jurisdiction of the Attorney General, the Attorney General may petition under this chapter. **Leg.H.** Added Stats 1991 ch 992 §3 (SB 727).

CHAPTER 3
PUBLICATION OF NOTICE

Publication and form of notice; Affidavit. §19040.
Legislative findings and declarations. §19041.

§19040. Publication and form of notice; Affidavit

(a) Publication of notice pursuant to this section shall be for at least 15 days. Three publications in a newspaper published once a week or more often, with at least five days intervening between the first and last publication dates, not counting the first and last publication dates as part of the five-day period, are sufficient. Notice shall be published in a newspaper of general circulation in the city, county, or city and county in this state where the deceased settlor resided at the time of death, or if none, in the city, county, or city and county in this state wherein trust property was located at the time of the settlor's death, or if none, in the city, county, or city and county in this state wherein the principal place of administration of the trust was located at the time of the settlor's death. If there is no newspaper of general circulation published in the applicable city, county, or city and county, notice shall be published in a newspaper of general circulation published in this state nearest to the applicable city, county, or city and county seat, and which is circulated within the applicable city, county, or city and county. If there is no such newspaper, notice shall be given in written or printed form, posted at three of the most public places within the community. For purposes of this section, "city" means a charter city as defined in Section 34101 of the Government Code or a general law city as defined in Section 34102 of the Government Code.

(b) The caption of the notice, the deceased settlor's name, and the name of the trustee shall be in at least 8-point type, the text of the notice shall be in at least 7-point type, and the notice shall state substantially as follows:

NOTICE TO CREDITORS
OF _____

_____

SUPERIOR COURT OF CALIFORNIA
COUNTY OF _____

Notice is hereby given to the creditors and contingent creditors of the above-named decedent, that all persons having claims against the decedent are required to file them with the Superior Court, at _____, and deliver pursuant to Section 1215 of the California Probate Code a copy to _____, as trustee of the trust dated _____ wherein the decedent was the settlor, at _____, within the later of four months after _____ (the date of the first publication of notice to creditors) or, if notice is mailed or personally delivered to you, 60 days after the date this notice is mailed or personally delivered to you. A claim form may be obtained from the court clerk. For your protection, you are encouraged to file your claim by certified mail, with return receipt requested.

_____
(name and address of trustee or attorney)

(c) An affidavit showing due publication of notice shall be filed with the clerk upon completion of the publication. The affidavit shall contain a copy of the notice, and state the date of its first publication. **Leg.H.** Added Stats 1991 ch 992 §3 (SB 727). Amended Stats 2007 ch 159 §13 (AB 341), effective January 1, 2008; Stats 2017 ch 319 §101 (AB 976), effective January 1, 2018.

§19041. Legislative findings and declarations

The Legislature finds and declares that to be most effective, notice to creditors should be published in compliance with the procedures specified in Section 19040. However, the Legislature recognizes the possibility that in unusual cases due to confusion over jurisdictional boundaries or oversights the notice may inadvertently be published in a newspaper which does not meet these requirements. Therefore, to prevent a minor error in publication from invalidating what would otherwise be a proper proceeding, the Legislature further finds and declares that notice published in a good faith attempt to comply with Section 19040 shall be sufficient to provide notice to creditors and establish jurisdiction if the court expressly finds that the notice was published in a newspaper of general circulation published within the city, county, or city and county and widely circulated within a true cross section of the community in which the deceased settlor resided or wherein the principal place of administration of the trust was located or the property was located in substantial compliance with Section 19040. **Leg.H.** Added Stats 1991 ch 992 §3 (SB 727).

CHAPTER 4
ACTUAL NOTICE TO CREDITORS

Creditors to whom notice shall be given. §19050.
Time for giving notice. §19051.
Form of notice. §19052.
Liability of trustee and trust estate. §19053.
Creditors to whom notice need not be given. §19054.

§19050. Creditors to whom notice shall be given

Except as provided in Section 19054, if the trustee has knowledge of a creditor of the deceased settlor, the trustee shall give notice to the creditor. The notice shall be given as provided in Section 1215. For the purpose of this section, a trustee has knowledge of a creditor of the deceased settlor if the trustee is aware that the creditor has demanded payment from the deceased settlor or the trust estate. **Leg.H.** Added Stats 1991 ch 992 §3 (SB 727). Amended Stats 2007 ch 159 §14 (AB 341), effective January 1, 2008.

§19051. Time for giving notice

The notice shall be given before expiration of the later of the following times:

(a) Four months after the first publication of notice under Section 19040.

(b) Thirty days after the trustee first has knowledge of the creditor. **Leg.H.** Added Stats 1991 ch 992 §3 (SB 727). Amended Stats 2007 ch 159 §15 (AB 341), effective January 1, 2008.

§19052. Form of notice

The notice shall be in substantially the following form:

NOTICE TO CREDITORS
OF _____

_____

SUPERIOR COURT OF CALIFORNIA

COUNTY OF _____

Notice is hereby given to the creditors and contingent creditors of the above-named decedent, that all persons having claims against the decedent are required to file them with the Superior Court, at _____, and deliver pursuant to Section 1215 of the California Probate Code a copy to _____, as trustee of the trust dated _____ wherein the decedent was the settlor, at _____, within the later of four months after _____ (the date of the first publication of notice to creditors) or, if notice is mailed or personally delivered to you, 60 days after the date this notice is mailed or personally delivered to you, or you must petition to file a late claim as provided in Section 19103 of the Probate Code. A claim form may be obtained from the court clerk. For your protection, you are encouraged to file your claim by certified mail, with return receipt requested.

_____
(Date of mailing this notice if applicable)

_____
(name and address of trustee or attorney)

Leg.H. Added Stats 1991 ch 992 §3 (SB 727). Amended Stats 2007 ch 159 §16 (AB 341), effective January 1, 2008; Stats 2017 ch 319 §102 (AB 976), effective January 1, 2018.

§19053. Liability of trustee and trust estate

(a) If the trustee believes that notice to a particular creditor is or may be required by this chapter and gives notice based on that belief, the trustee is not liable to any person for giving the notice, whether or not required by this chapter.

(b) If the trustee fails to give notice required by this chapter, the trustee is not liable to any person for that failure, unless a creditor establishes all of the following:

(1) The failure was in bad faith.

(2) The creditor did not have actual knowledge of the proceedings under Chapter 1 (commencing with Section 19000) sooner than one year after publication of notice to creditors under Section 19040, and payment would have been made on the creditor's claim if the claim had been properly filed.

(3) Within 16 months after the first publication of notice under Section 19040, the creditor did both of the following:

(A) Filed a petition requesting that the court in which the proceedings under Chapter 1 (commencing with Section 19000) were initiated make an order determining the liability of the trustee under this subdivision.

(B) At least 30 days before the hearing on the petition, caused notice of the hearing and a copy of the petition to be served on the trustee in the manner provided in Chapter 4 (commencing with Section 413.10) of Title 5 of Part 2 of the Code of Civil Procedure.

(c) Nothing in this section affects the liability of the trust estate, if any, for the claim of a creditor, and the trustee is not liable to the extent the claim is paid out of the trust estate.

(d) Nothing in this chapter imposes a duty on the trustee to make a search for creditors of the deceased settlor. **Leg.H.** Added Stats 1991 ch 992 §3 (SB 727). Amended Stats 2007 ch 159 §17 (AB 341), effective January 1, 2008.

§19054. Creditors to whom notice need not be given

Notwithstanding Section 19050, the trustee need not give notice to a creditor even though the trustee has knowledge of the creditor if either of the following conditions is satisfied:

(a) The creditor has filed a claim as provided in this part.

(b) The creditor has demanded payment and the trustee elects to treat the demand as a claim under Section 19154. **Leg.H.** Added Stats 1991 ch 992 §3 (SB 727). Amended Stats 2003 ch 32 §14 (AB 167).

CHAPTER 5
TIME FOR FILING CLAIMS

Time for filing claim. §19100.
Effect of vacancy in office of trustee. §19101.
Effect of failure to act on claim prior to expiration of time for its filing. §19102.
Conditions for allowing late filing; Conditions placed on claim; effect on prior distributions or payments. §19103.
Amendment or revision of claims. §19104.

§19100. Time for filing claim

(a) A creditor shall file a claim before expiration of the later of the following times:

(1) Four months after the first publication of notice to creditors under Section 19040.

(2) Sixty days after the date actual notice is mailed or personally delivered to the creditor. This paragraph does not extend the time provided in Section 366.2 of the Code of Civil Procedure.

(b) A reference in another statute to the time for filing a claim means the time provided in paragraph (1) of subdivision (a).

(c) This section shall not be interpreted to extend or toll any other statute of limitations, including that provided by Section 366.2 of the Code of Civil Procedure. **Leg.H.** Added Stats 1991 ch 992 §3 (SB 727). Amended Stats 2007 ch 159 §18 (AB 341), effective January 1, 2008.

§19101. Effect of vacancy in office of trustee

A vacancy in the office of the trustee that occurs before expiration of the time for filing a claim does not extend the time. **Leg.H.** Added Stats 1991 ch 992 §3 (SB 727).

§19102. Effect of failure to act on claim prior to expiration of time for its filing

A claim that is filed before expiration of the time for filing the claim is timely even if acted on by the trustee or the court after expiration of the time for filing claims. **Leg.H.** Added Stats 1991 ch 992 §3 (SB 727).

§19103. Conditions for allowing late filing; Conditions placed on claim; effect on prior distributions or payments

(a) Except as provided in subdivision (b), upon petition by a creditor or a trustee, the court may allow a claim to be filed after expiration of the time for filing a claim provided in Section 19100 if either of the following conditions are satisfied:

(1) The trustee failed to send proper and timely notice to the creditor and the petition is filed within 60 days after the creditor has actual knowledge of the administration of the trust.

(2) The creditor did not have knowledge of the facts giving rise to the existence of the claim more than 30 days prior to the time for filing a claim as provided in Section 19100, and the petition is filed within 60 days after the creditor has actual knowledge of both of the following:

(A) The existence of the facts reasonably giving rise to the existence of the claim.

(B) The administration of the trust.

(b) Notwithstanding subdivision (a), the court shall not allow a claim to be filed under this section more than one year after the date of first publication of notice to creditors under Section 19040. Nothing in this subdivision authorizes allowance or approval of a claim barred by, or extends the time provided in, Section 366.2 of the Code of Civil Procedure.

(c) The court may condition the claim on terms that are just and equitable. The court may deny the claimant's petition if a distribution to trust beneficiaries or payment to general creditors has been made and it appears the filing or establishment of the claim would cause or tend to cause unequal treatment among beneficiaries or creditors.

(d) Regardless of whether the claim is later established in whole or in part, property distributed under the terms of the trust subsequent to an order settling claims under Chapter 2 (commencing with Section 19020) and payments otherwise properly made before a claim is filed under this section are not subject to the claim. Except to the extent provided in Chapter 12 (commencing with Section 19400) and subject to Section 19053, the trustee, distributee, or payee is not liable on account of the prior distribution or payment. This subdivision does not limit the liability of a person who receives a preliminary distribution of property to restore to the trust an amount sufficient for payment of the beneficiary's proper share of the claim, not exceeding the amount distributed. **Leg.H.** Added Stats 1991 ch 992 §3 (SB 727). Amended Stats 1992 ch 178 §44 (SB 1496); Stats 2007 ch 159 §19 (AB 341), effective January 1, 2008.

§19104. Amendment or revision of claims

(a) Subject to subdivision (b), if a claim is filed within the time provided in this chapter, the creditor may later amend or revise the claim. The amendment or revision shall be filed in the same manner as the claim.

(b) An amendment or revision may not be made to increase the amount of the claim after the time for filing a claim has expired. An amendment or revision to specify the amount of a claim that, at the time of filing, was not due, was contingent, or was not yet ascertainable, is not an increase in the amount of the claim within the meaning of this subdivision. An amendment or revision of a claim may not be made for any purpose after the earlier of the following times:

(1) The time the court makes an order approving settlement of the claim against the deceased settlor under Chapter 2 (commencing with Section 19020).

(2) One year after the date of the first publication of notice to creditors under Section 19040. Nothing in this paragraph authorizes allowance or approval of a claim barred by, or extends the time provided in, Section 366.2 of the Code of Civil Procedure. **Leg.H.** Added Stats 1991 ch 992 §3 (SB 727). Amended Stats 1992 ch 178 §45 (SB 1496); Stats 2007 ch 159 §20 (AB 341), effective January 1, 2008.

CHAPTER 6
FILING OF CLAIMS

Procedure for filing claims. §19150.
Content of affidavit in support of claim. §19151.
Claims based upon written instruments; Claims secured by mortgage, deed of trust, or other recorded lien. §19152.
Adoption of claim form by Judicial Council. §19153.
Waiver of formal defect; Effect on specified equitable principles. §19154.

§19150. Procedure for filing claims

(a) A claim may be filed by the creditor or a person acting on behalf of the claimant.

(b) A claim shall be filed with the court and a copy shall be delivered to the trustee pursuant to Section 1215. Failure to deliver a copy to the trustee does not invalidate a properly filed claim, but any loss that results from the failure shall be borne by the creditor. **Leg.H.** Added Stats 1991 ch 992 §3 (SB 727). Amended Stats 2007 ch 159 §21 (AB 341), effective January 1, 2008; Stats 2017 ch 319 §103 (AB 976), effective January 1, 2018.

§19151. Content of affidavit in support of claim

(a) A claim shall be supported by the affidavit of the creditor or the person on behalf of the claimant stating:

(1) The claim is a just claim.

(2) If the claim is due, the facts supporting the claim, the amount of the claim, and that all payments on and offsets to the claim have been credited.

(3) If the claim is not due or contingent, or the amount is not yet ascertainable, the facts supporting the claim.

(4) If the affidavit is made by a person other than the creditor, the reason it is not made by the creditor.

(b) The trustee may require satisfactory vouchers or proof to be produced to support the claim. An original voucher may be withdrawn after a copy is provided. If a copy is provided, the copy shall be attached to the claim. **Leg.H.** Added Stats 1991 ch 992 §3 (SB 727). Amended Stats 2007 ch 159 §22 (AB 341), effective January 1, 2008.

§19152. Claims based upon written instruments; Claims secured by mortgage, deed of trust, or other recorded lien

(a) If a claim is based on a written instrument, either the original or a copy of the original with all endorsements shall be attached to the claim. If a copy is attached, the original instrument shall be exhibited to the trustee on demand unless it is lost or destroyed, in which case the fact that it is lost or destroyed shall be stated in the claim.

(b) If the claim or a part of the claim is secured by a mortgage, deed of trust, or other lien that is recorded in the office of the recorder of the county in which the property subject to the lien is located, it is sufficient to describe the mortgage, deed of trust, or lien and the recording reference for the instrument that created the mortgage, deed of trust, or other lien. **Leg.H.** Added Stats 1991 ch 992 §3 (SB 727).

§19153. Adoption of claim form by Judicial Council

The Judicial Council may adopt a claim form which shall inform the creditor that the claim must be filed with the court and a copy delivered to the trustee pursuant to Section 1215. Any such claim form shall include a proof of delivery of a copy of the claim to the trustee which may be completed by the creditor. **Leg.H.** Added Stats 1991 ch 992 §3 (SB 727). Amended Stats 2017 ch 319 §104 (AB 976), effective January 1, 2018.

§19154. Waiver of formal defect; Effect on specified equitable principles

(a) Notwithstanding any other provision of this part, if a creditor makes a written demand for payment within the time specified in Section 19100, the trustee may waive formal defects and elect to treat the demand as a claim that is filed and established under this part by paying the amount demanded.

(b) Nothing in this section limits application of the doctrines of waiver, estoppel, laches, or detrimental reliance or any other equitable principle. **Leg.H.** Added Stats 1991 ch 992 §3 (SB 727). Amended Stats 2007 ch 159 §23 (AB 341), effective January 1, 2008.

CHAPTER 7
CLAIMS BY PUBLIC ENTITIES

Time for filing; "Public entity". §19200.
Provision of form for notice or request; Requirements for barring claim. §19201.
Notice to State Director of Health Services. §19202.
Claims against distributees. §19203.
Effect of chapter on order of priority of debts. §19204.
Application of chapter to liability for restitution of amounts illegally acquired. §19205.

§19200. Time for filing; "Public entity"

(a) Except as provided in this chapter, a claim by a public entity shall be filed within the time otherwise provided in this part. A claim not so filed is barred, including any lien imposed for the claim.

(b) As used in this chapter, "public entity" has the meaning provided in Section 811.2 of the Government Code, and includes an officer authorized to act on behalf of the public entity. **Leg.H.** Added Stats 1991 ch 992 §3 (SB 727).

§19201. Provision of form for notice or request; Requirements for barring claim

(a) Notwithstanding any other statute, if a claim of a public entity arises under a law, act, or code listed in subdivision (b):

(1) The public entity may provide a form to be used for the written notice or request to the public entity required by this chapter. Where appropriate, the form may require the decedent's social security number, if known.

(2) The claim is barred only after written notice or request to the public entity and expiration of the period provided in the applicable section. If no written notice or request is made, the claim is enforceable by the remedies, and is barred at the time, otherwise provided in the law, act, or code.

(b)

Law, Act, or Code	Applicable Section
Sales and Use Tax Law (commencing with Section 6001 of the Revenue and Taxation Code)	Section 6487.1 of the Revenue and Taxation Code
Bradley-Burns Uniform Local Sales and Use Tax Law (commencing with Section 7200 of the Revenue and Taxation Code)	Section 6487.1 of the Revenue and Taxation Code
Transactions and Use Tax Law (commencing with Section 7251 of the Revenue and Taxation Code)	Section 6487.1 of the Revenue and Taxation Code
Motor Vehicle Fuel License Tax Law (commencing with Section 7301 of the Revenue and Taxation Code)	Section 7675.1 of the Revenue and Taxation Code
Use Fuel Tax Law (commencing with Section 8601 of the Revenue and Taxation Code)	Section 8782.1 of the Revenue and Taxation Code
Administration of Franchise and Income Tax Law (commencing with Section 18401 of the Revenue and Taxation Code)	Section 19517 of the Revenue and Taxation Code
Cigarette Tax Law (commencing with Section 30001 of the Revenue and Taxation Code)	Section 30207.1 of the Revenue and Taxation Code
Alcoholic Beverage Tax Law (commencing with Section 32001 of the Revenue and Taxation Code)	Section 32272.1 of the Revenue and Taxation Code
Unemployment Insurance Code	Section 1090 of the Unemployment Insurance Code

State Hospitals (commencing with Section 7200 of the Welfare and Institutions Code)	Section 7277.1 of the Welfare and Institutions Code
Medi-Cal Act (commencing with Section 14000 of the Welfare and Institutions Code)	Section 9202 of the Probate Code
Waxman-Duffy Prepaid Health Plan Act (commencing with Section 14200 of the Welfare and Institutions Code)	Section 9202 of the Probate Code

Leg.H. Added Stats 1991 ch 992 §3 (SB 727). Amended Stats 2007 ch 159 §24 (AB 341), effective January 1, 2008; Stats 2014 ch 144 §50 (AB 1847), effective January 1, 2015.

§19202. Notice to State Director of Health Services

(a) If the trustee knows or has reason to believe that the deceased settlor received health care under Chapter 7 (commencing with Section 14000) or Chapter 8 (commencing with Section 14200) of Part 3 of Division 9 of the Welfare and Institutions Code, or was the surviving spouse of a person who received that health care, the trustee shall give the State Director of Health Services notice of the death of the deceased settlor or surviving spouse in the manner provided in Section 215.

(b) The director has four months after notice is given in which to file a claim. **Leg.H.** Added Stats 1991 ch 992 §3 (SB 727). Amended Stats 2007 ch 159 §25 (AB 341), effective January 1, 2008.

§19203. Claims against distributees

If property in the trust is distributed before expiration of the time allowed a public entity to file a claim, the public entity has a claim against the distributees to the full extent of the public entity's claim or each distributee's share of the distributed property, as set forth in Section 19402, whichever is less. The public entity's claim against distributees includes interest at a rate equal to that specified in Section 19521 of the Revenue and Taxation Code, from the date of distribution or the date of filing the claim by the public entity, whichever is later, plus other accruing costs as in the case of enforcement of a money judgment. **Leg.H.** Added Stats 1991 ch 992 §3 (SB 727). Amended Stats 2007 ch 159 §26 (AB 341), effective January 1, 2008.

§19204. Effect of chapter on order of priority of debts

Nothing in this chapter shall be construed to affect the order of priority of debts provided for under other provisions of law. **Leg.H.** Added Stats 1991 ch 992 §3 (SB 727).

§19205. Application of chapter to liability for restitution of amounts illegally acquired

This chapter does not apply to liability for the restitution of amounts illegally acquired through the means of a fraudulent, false, or incorrect representation, or a forged or unauthorized endorsement. **Leg.H.** Added Stats 1991 ch 992 §3 (SB 727).

CHAPTER 8
ALLOWANCE AND REJECTION OF CLAIMS

Allowance or rejection of claim. §19250.
Form and content; Judicial Council prescription of form. §19251.
Payment or compromise of claim; Effect. §19252.
Claims barred by statute of limitations. §19253.
Effect of refusal or neglect to act on claim. §19254.
Effect of rejection of claim; Actions on rejected claims; Notice of pendency of action; Effect on property distributed; Court costs and litigation expenses. §19255.

§19250. Allowance or rejection of claim

When a claim is filed, the trustee shall allow or reject the claim in whole or in part. **Leg.H.** Added Stats 1991 ch 992 §3 (SB 727).

§19251. Form and content; Judicial Council prescription of form

(a) Any allowance or rejection shall be in writing. The trustee shall file the allowance or rejection with the court clerk and give notice to the claimant, together with a copy of the allowance or rejection, as provided in Section 1215.

(b) The allowance or rejection shall contain the following information:

(1) The name of the claimant.
(2) The date of the settlor's death.
(3) The total amount of the claim.
(4) The amount allowed or rejected by the trustee.
(5) A statement that the claimant has 90 days from the time the notice of rejection is given, or 90 days after the claim becomes due, whichever is later, in which to bring an action on a claim rejected in whole or in part.

(c) The Judicial Council shall prescribe an allowance or rejection form, which may be part of the claim form. Use of a form prescribed by the Judicial Council is deemed to satisfy the requirements.

(d) This section does not apply to a demand the trustee elects to treat as a claim under Section 19154. **Leg.H.** Added Stats 1991 ch 992 §3 (SB 727).

§19252. Payment or compromise of claim; Effect

The trustee shall have the power to pay any claim or portion of a claim and payment shall constitute allowance of the claim to the extent of the payment. The trustee shall have the power to compromise any claim or portion of a claim. If the trustee or the attorney for the trustee is a creditor of the deceased settlor, the trustee shall have the same powers regarding allowance, rejection, payment, or compromise set forth in this chapter. **Leg.H.** Added Stats 1991 ch 992 §3 (SB 727). Amended Stats 2007 ch 159 §27 (AB 341), effective January 1, 2008.

§19253. Claims barred by statute of limitations

(a) A claim barred by the statute of limitations may not be allowed by the trustee.

(b) The filing of a claim tolls the statute of limitations otherwise applicable to the claim until the trustee gives notice of allowance or rejection.

(c) The allowance of a claim further tolls the statute of limitations as to the part of the claim allowed until the allowed portion of the claim is paid.

(d) Notwithstanding the statute of limitations otherwise applicable to a claim, if an action on a rejected claim is not commenced or if the matter is not referred to a referee or to arbitration within the time prescribed in Section 19255, it is forever barred. **Leg.H.** Added Stats 1991 ch 992 §3 (SB 727).

§19254. Effect of refusal or neglect to act on claim

If within 30 days after a claim is filed the trustee has refused or neglected to act on the claim, the refusal or neglect may, at the option of the claimant, be deemed equivalent to the giving of a notice of rejection on the 30th day. **Leg.H.** Added Stats 1991 ch 992 §3 (SB 727).

§19255. Effect of rejection of claim; Actions on rejected claims; Notice of pendency of action; Effect on property distributed; Court costs and litigation expenses

(a) A rejected claim is barred as to the part rejected unless the creditor brings an action on the claim or the matter is referred to a referee or to arbitration within the following times, excluding any time during which there is a vacancy in the office of the trustee:

(1) If the claim is due at the time of giving the notice of rejection, 90 days after the notice is given.

(2) If the claim is not due at the time of giving the notice of rejection, 90 days after the claim becomes due.

(b) In addition to any other county in which an action on a rejected claim may be commenced, the action may be commenced in the county or city and county wherein the principal place of administration of the trust is located.

(c) The creditor shall file a notice of the pendency of the action or the referral to a referee or to arbitration with the court clerk in the trust proceeding, together with proof of giving a copy of the notice to the trustee as provided in Section 1215. Personal service of a copy of the summons and complaint on the trustee is equivalent to the filing and giving of the notice.

(d) Any property distributed by the trustee under the terms of the trust after 120 days from the later of the time the notice of rejection is given or the claim is due and before the notice of pendency of action or referral or arbitration is filed and given, excluding therefrom any time during which there is a vacancy in the office of the trustee, is not subject to the claim. Neither the trustee nor the distributee is liable on account of the distribution.

(e) The prevailing party in the action shall be awarded court costs and, if the court determines that the prosecution or defense of the action against the prevailing party was unreasonable, the prevailing party shall be awarded reasonable litigation expenses, including attorney's fees. For the purpose of this subdivision, the prevailing party shall be the trustee if the creditor recovers an amount equal to or less than the amount of the claim allowed by the trustee, and shall be the creditor if the creditor recovers an amount greater than the amount of the claim allowed by the trustee. **Leg.H.** Added Stats 1991 ch 992 §3 (SB 727). Amended Stats 1994 ch 40 §2 (AB 797), effective April 19, 1994, operative January 1, 1995; Stats 2007 ch 159 §28 (AB 341), effective January 1, 2008.

CHAPTER 9
CLAIMS ESTABLISHED BY JUDGMENT

Payment of money judgments against deceased settlor or trustee. §19300.
Establishment of validity of claim in the amount of the judgment. §19301.
Enforcement of judgment for possession or sale of trust property. §19302.
Enforcement against trust property subject to execution of lien. §19303.
Conversion of attachment liens into judgment liens. §19304.

§19300. Payment of money judgments against deceased settlor or trustee

(a) Except as provided in Section 19303, after the death of the settlor all money judgments against the deceased settlor on a claim against the deceased settlor or against the trustee on a claim against the decedent or the trust estate are payable in the course of administration and are not enforceable against property in the trust estate of the deceased settlor under the Enforcement of Judgments Law (Title 9 (commencing with Section 680.010) of Part 2 of the Code of Civil Procedure).

(b) Subject to Section 19301, a judgment referred to in subdivision (a) shall be filed in the same manner as other claims. **Leg.H.** Added Stats 1991 ch 992 §3 (SB 727).

§19301. Establishment of validity of claim in the amount of the judgment

When a money judgment against a trustee in a representative capacity becomes final, it conclusively establishes the validity of the claim for the amount of the judgment. The judgment shall provide that it is payable out of property in the deceased settlor's trust estate in the course of administration. An abstract of the judgment shall be filed in the trust administration proceedings. **Leg.H.** Added Stats 1991 ch 992 §3 (SB 727).

§19302. Enforcement of judgment for possession or sale of trust property

(a) Notwithstanding the death of the settlor, a judgment for possession of trust property or a judgment for sale of trust property may be enforced under the Enforcement of Judgments Law (Title 9 (commencing with Section 680.010) of Part 2 of the Code of Civil Procedure). Nothing in this subdivision authorizes enforcement under the Enforcement of Judgments Law against any property in the trust estate of the deceased settlor other than the property described in the judgment for possession or sale.

(b) After the death of the settlor, a demand for money that is not satisfied from the trust property described in a judgment for sale of property shall be filed as a claim in the same manner as other claims and is payable in the course of administration. **Leg.H.** Added Stats 1991 ch 992 §3 (SB 727).

§19303. Enforcement against trust property subject to execution of lien

If trust property of the deceased settlor is subject to an execution lien at the time of the settlor's death, enforcement against the property may proceed under the Enforcement of Judgments Law (Title 9 (commencing with Section 680.010) of Part 2 of the Code of Civil Procedure) to satisfy the judgment. The levying officer, as defined in Section 680.260 of the Code of Civil Procedure, shall account to the trustee for any surplus. If the judgment is not satisfied, the balance of the judgment remaining unsatisfied is payable in the course of administration. **Leg.H.** Added Stats 1991 ch 992 §3 (SB 727).

§19304. Conversion of attachment liens into judgment liens

(a) An attachment lien may be converted into a judgment lien on property in the trust estate subject to the attachment lien, with the same priority as the attachment lien, in either of the following cases:

(1) Where the judgment debtor dies after entry of judgment in an action in which the property was attached.

(2) Where a judgment is entered after the death of the defendant in an action in which the property was attached.

(b) To convert the attachment lien into a judgment lien, the levying officer shall, after entry of judgment in the action in which the property was attached and before the expiration of the attachment lien, do one of the following:

(1) Serve an abstract of the judgment, and a notice that the attachment lien has become a judgment lien, on the trustee or other person holding property subject to the attachment lien.

(2) Record or file in any office where the writ of attachment and notice of attachment are recorded or filed an abstract of the judgment and a notice that the attachment lien has become a judgment lien. If the attached property is real property, the plaintiff or the plaintiff's attorney may record the required abstract and notice with the same effect as if recorded by the levying officer.

(c) After the death of the settlor, any members of the deceased settlor's family who were supported in whole or in part by the deceased settlor may claim an exemption provided in Section 487.020 of the Code of Civil Procedure for property levied on under the writ of attachment if the right to the exemption exists at the time the exemption is claimed. The trustee may claim the exemption on behalf of members of the deceased settlor's family. The claim of exemption may be made at any time before the time the abstract and notice are served, recorded, or filed under subdivision (b) with respect to the property claimed to be exempt. The claim of exemption shall be made in the same manner as an exemption is claimed under Section 482.100 of the Code of Civil Procedure. **Leg.H.** Added Stats 1991 ch 992 §3 (SB 727). Amended Stats 2007 ch 159 §29 (AB 341), effective January 1, 2008.

CHAPTER 10
ALLOCATION OF DEBTS BETWEEN TRUST AND SURVIVING SPOUSE

Petition for order to allocate debt. §19320.
Contents of petition. §19321.
Allocations affected by value of surviving spouse's separate property, or by community or quasi-community property not administered by trust. §19322.
Notice of hearing on petition. §19323.
Allocation of debts by agreement. §19324.
Court orders on making determination under chapter. §19325.
Funeral and last illness expenses. §19326.

§19320. Petition for order to allocate debt

If it appears that a debt of the deceased settlor has been paid or is payable in whole or in part from property in the deceased settlor's trust, then the trustee, the surviving spouse, the personal representative, if any, of a deceased settlor's probate estate, or a beneficiary may petition for an order to allocate the debt. **Leg.H.** Added Stats 1991 ch 992 §3 (SB 727). Amended Stats 2015 ch 48 §8 (SB 785), effective January 1, 2016.

§19321. Contents of petition

A petition under Section 19320 shall include a statement of all of the following:

(a) All debts of the deceased settlor and surviving spouse known to the petitioner that are alleged to be subject to allocation and whether paid in whole or in part or unpaid.

(b) The reason why the debts should be allocated.

(c) The proposed allocation and the basis for allocation alleged by the petitioner. **Leg.H.** Added Stats 1991 ch 992 §3 (SB 727).

§19322. Allocations affected by value of surviving spouse's separate property, or by community or quasi-community property not administered by trust

If it appears from the petition under Section 19320 that allocation would be affected by the value of the separate property of the surviving spouse and any community property and quasi-community property not administered in the trust, and if an inventory and appraisal of the property has not been provided by the surviving spouse, the court shall make an order to show cause why the information should not be provided. **Leg.H.** Added Stats 1991 ch 992 §3 (SB 727).

§19323. Notice of hearing on petition

(a) At least 30 days before the time set for the hearing on the petition, the petitioner shall cause notice of the time and place of the hearing and a copy of the petition to be served on the surviving spouse in the manner provided in Chapter 4 (commencing with Section 413.10) of Title 5 of Part 2 of the Code of Civil Procedure.

(b) At least 30 days before the time set for the hearing on the petition, the petitioner shall cause notice of the time and place of hearing, together with a copy of the petition, to be delivered pursuant to Section 1215 to each of the following persons who are not petitioners:

(1) All trustees of the trust and of any trusts to which an allocation of liability may be approved by the court pursuant to the petition.

(2) All beneficiaries affected.

(3) The personal representative of the deceased settlor's probate estate, if any is known to the trustee.

(4) The Attorney General, if the petition relates to a charitable trust subject to the jurisdiction of the Attorney General, unless the Attorney General waives notice. **Leg.H.** Added Stats 1991 ch 992 §3 (SB 727). Amended Stats 2015 ch 48 §9 (SB 785), effective January 1, 2016; Stats 2017 ch 319 §105 (AB 976), effective January 1, 2018.

§19324. Allocation of debts by agreement

(a) The trustee, the personal representative, if any, of a deceased settlor's probate estate, and the surviving spouse may provide for allocation of debts by agreement so long as the agreement substantially protects the rights of other interested persons. The trustee, the personal representative, or the spouse may request and obtain court approval of the allocation provided in the agreement.

(b) In the absence of an agreement, each debt subject to allocation shall first be characterized by the court as separate or community, in accordance with the laws of the state applicable to marital dissolution proceedings. Following that characterization, the debt or debts shall be allocated as follows:

(1) Separate debts of either spouse shall be allocated to that spouse's separate property assets, and community debts shall be allocated to the spouses' community property assets.

(2) If a separate property asset of either spouse is subject to a secured debt that is characterized as that spouse's separate debt, and the net equity in that asset available to satisfy that secured debt is less than that secured debt, the unsatisfied portion of that secured debt shall be treated as an unsecured separate debt of that spouse and allocated to the net value of that spouse's other separate property assets.

(3) If the net value of either spouse's separate property assets is less than that spouse's unsecured separate debt or debts, the unsatisfied portion of the debt or debts shall be allocated to the net value of that spouse's one-half share of the community property assets. If the net value of that spouse's one-half share of the community property assets is less than that spouse's unsatisfied unsecured separate debt or debts, the remaining unsatisfied portion of the debt or debts shall be allocated to the net value of the other spouse's one-half share of the community property assets.

(4) If a community property asset is subject to a secured debt that is characterized as a community debt, and the net equity in that asset available to satisfy that secured debt is less than that secured debt, the unsatisfied portion of that secured debt shall be treated as an unsecured community debt and allocated to the net value of the other community property assets.

(5) If the net value of the community property assets is less than the unsecured community debt or debts, the unsatisfied portion of the debt or debts shall be allocated equally between the separate property assets of the deceased settlor and the surviving spouse. If the net value of either spouse's separate property assets is less than that spouse's share of the unsatisfied portion of the unsecured community debt or debts, the remaining unsatisfied portion of the debt or debts shall be allocated to the net value of the other spouse's separate property assets.

(c) For purposes of this section:

(1) The net value of either spouse's separate property asset shall refer to its fair market value as of the date of the deceased settlor's death, minus the date-of-death balance of any liens and encumbrances on that asset that have been characterized as that spouse's separate debts.

(2) The net value of a community property asset shall refer to its fair market value as of the date of the deceased settlor's death, minus the date-of-death balance of any liens and encumbrances on that asset that have been characterized as community debts.

(3) In the case of a nonrecourse debt, the amount of that debt shall be limited to the net equity in the collateral, based on the fair market value of the collateral as of the date of the decedent's death, that is available to satisfy that debt. For the purposes of this paragraph, "nonrecourse debt" means a debt for which the debtor's obligation to repay is limited to the collateral securing the debt, and for which a deficiency judgment against the debtor is not permitted by law.

(d) Notwithstanding the foregoing provisions of this section, the court may order a different allocation of debts between the deceased settlor's probate estate, trust, and the surviving spouse if the court finds a different allocation to be equitable under the circumstances.

(e) Nothing contained in this section is intended to impair or affect the rights of third parties. If a trustee, a personal representative, if any, of a deceased settlor's probate estate, or the surviving spouse incurs any damages or expense, including attorney's fees, on account of the nonpayment of a debt that was allocated to the other party pursuant to subdivision (b), or as the result of a debt being misallocated due to fraud or intentional misrepresentation by the other party, the party incurring damages shall be entitled to recover from the other party for damages or expense deemed reasonable by the court that made the allocation. **Leg.H.** Added Stats 1991 ch 992 §3 (SB 727). Amended Stats 2001 ch 72 §2 (SB 668), effective January 1, 2002.

§19325. Court orders on making determination under chapter

On making a determination as provided in this chapter, the court shall make an order that:

(a) Directs the trustee to make payment of the amounts allocated to the trust by payment to the surviving spouse or creditors.

(b) Directs the trustee to charge amounts allocated to the surviving spouse against any property or interests of the surviving spouse that are in the possession or control of the trustee. To the extent that property or interests of the surviving spouse in the possession or control of the trustee are insufficient to satisfy the allocation, the court order shall summarily direct the surviving spouse to pay the allocation to the trustee. **Leg.H.** Added Stats 1991 ch 992 §3 (SB 727).

§19326. Funeral and last illness expenses

Notwithstanding any other statute, funeral expenses and expenses of last illness, in the absence of specific provisions in a will or trust to the contrary, shall be charged against the deceased settlor's probate estate and thereafter, against the deceased settlor's share of the trust and shall not be allocated to or charged against, the community share of the surviving spouse, whether or not the surviving spouse is financially able to pay the expenses and whether or not the surviving spouse or any other person is also liable for the expenses. **Leg.H.** Added Stats 1991 ch 992 §3 (SB 727).

CHAPTER 11
LIABILITY OF SETTLOR'S SURVIVING SPOUSE

Bar of action upon liability of surviving spouse. §19330.

§19330. Bar of action upon liability of surviving spouse

If proceedings are commenced under this part for the settlement of claims against the trust, and the time for filing claims has commenced, any action upon the liability of the surviving spouse under Chapter 3 (commencing with Section 13550) is barred to the same extent as provided for claims under this part, except as to the following:

(a) Any creditor who commences judicial proceedings to enforce a claim and serves the surviving spouse with the complaint prior to the expiration of the time for filing claims.

(b) Any creditor who has or who secures the surviving spouse's acknowledgment in writing of the liability of the surviving spouse for the claim.

(c) Any creditor who files a timely claim in the proceedings for the administration of the estate of the deceased spouse. **Leg.H.** Added Stats 1991 ch 992 §3 (SB 727).

CHAPTER 12
DISTRIBUTEE LIABILITY

Requirements for personal liability of trust beneficiary to whom distribution has been made. §19400.

Requirements for personal liability of distributee of trust property where notice to creditors was filed and published and where creditor's identity was ascertainable. §19401.

Availability to distributee of settlor's defenses, cross-complaints, or setoffs. §19402.

Rights of good faith purchaser or encumbrancer of property. §19403.

§19400. Requirements for personal liability of trust beneficiary to whom distribution has been made

Subject to Section 366.2 of the Code of Civil Procedure, if there is no proceeding to administer the probate estate of the deceased settlor, and if the trustee does not file a proposed notice to creditors pursuant to Section 19003 and does not publish notice to creditors pursuant to Chapter 3 (commencing with Section 19040), then a beneficiary of the trust to whom payment, delivery, or transfer of the deceased settlor's property is made pursuant to the terms of the trust is personally liable, to the extent provided in Section 19402, for the unsecured claims of the creditors of the deceased settlor's probate estate. **Leg.H.** Added Stats 1991 ch 992 §3 (SB 727). Amended Stats 1992 ch 178 §46 (SB 1496); Stats 2015 ch 48 §10 (SB 785), effective January 1, 2016.

§19401. Requirements for personal liability of distributee of trust property where notice to creditors was filed and published and where creditor's identity was ascertainable

Subject to Section 19402, if the trustee filed a proposed notice to creditors pursuant to Section 19003 and published notice to creditors pursuant to Section 19040, and if the identity of the creditor was known to, or reasonably ascertainable by, the trustee within four months of the first publication of notice pursuant to Section 19040, then a person to whom property is distributed is personally liable for the claim of the creditor, without a claim first having been filed, if all of the following conditions are satisfied:

(a) The claim of the creditor was not merely conjectural.

(b) Notice to the creditor was not given to the creditor under Chapter 4 (commencing with Section 19050) and neither the creditor nor the attorney representing the creditor in the matter had actual knowledge of the administration of the trust estate sooner than one year after the date of first publication of notice pursuant to Section 19040.

(c) The statute of limitations applicable to the claim under Section 366.2 of the Code of Civil Procedure has not expired at the time of commencement of an action under this section. **Leg.H.** Added Stats 1991 ch 992 §3 (SB 727). Amended Stats 1992 ch 178 §47 (SB 1496), effective January 1, 1993.

§19402. Availability to distributee of settlor's defenses, cross-complaints, or setoffs

(a) In any action under this chapter, subject to Section 366.2 of the Code of Civil Procedure, the distributee may assert any defenses, cross-complaints, or setoffs that would have been available to the deceased settlor if the settlor had not died.

(b) Personal liability under this chapter is applicable only to the extent the claim of the creditor cannot be satisfied out of the trust estate of the deceased settlor and is limited to a pro rata portion of the claim of the creditor, based on the proportion that the value of the property distributed to the person out of the trust estate bears to the total value of all property distributed to all persons out of the trust estate. Personal liability under this chapter for all claims of all creditors shall not exceed the value of the property distributed to the person out of the trust estate. As used in this chapter, the value of the property is the fair market value of the property on the date of its distribution, less the amount of any liens and encumbrances on the property at that time. **Leg.H.** Added Stats 1991 ch 992 §3 (SB 727). Amended Stats 1992 ch 178 §48 (SB 1496), effective January 1, 1993.

§19403. Rights of good faith purchaser or encumbrancer of property

Nothing in this chapter affects the rights of a purchaser or encumbrancer of property in good faith and for value from a person who is personally liable under this section. **Leg.H.** Added Stats 1991 ch 992 §3 (SB 727). Amended Stats 2004 ch 183 §280 (AB 3082), effective January 1, 1993.

PART 9
UNIFORM TRUST DECANTING ACT

Citation of part. §19501.
Definitions. §19502.
Scope. §19503.
Fiduciary duty. §19504.
Application; Governing law. §19505.
Notice; Exercise of decanting power. §19507.
Representation. §19508.
Court involvement. §19509.
Formalities. §19510.
Decanting power under expanded distributive discretion. §19511.
Decanting power under limited distributive discretion. §19512.
Trust for beneficiary with disability. §19513.
Protection of charitable interest. §19514.
Trust limitation on decanting. §19515.
Change in compensation. §19516.
Relief from liability and indemnification. §19517.
Removal or replacement of authorized fiduciary. §19518.
Tax-related limitations. §19519.
Duration of second trust. §19520.
Need to distribute not required. §19521.
Saving provision. §19522.
Trust for care of animal. §19523.
Settlor. §19524.
Later-discovered property. §19525.
Obligations. §19526.
Uniformity of application and construction. §19527.
Petition by trustee. §19529.
Severability. §19530.

§19501. Citation of part

This part may be cited as the Uniform Trust Decanting Act. **Leg.H.** Added Stats 2018 ch 407 §1 (SB 909), effective January 1, 2019.

§19502. Definitions

For purposes of this part:

(a) "Appointive property" means the property or property interest subject to a power of appointment.

(b) "Ascertainable standard" means a standard relating to an individual's health, education, support, or maintenance within the meaning of Section 2041(b)(1)(A) or Section 2514(c)(1) of the Internal Revenue Code (26 U.S.C. Secs. 2041(b)(1)(A), 2514(c)(1)) and any applicable regulations.

(c) "Authorized fiduciary" means any of the following:

(1) A trustee or other fiduciary, other than a settlor, that has discretion to distribute or direct a trustee to distribute part or all of the principal of the first trust to one or more current beneficiaries.

(2) A special fiduciary appointed under Section 19509.

(3) A special-needs fiduciary under Section 19513.

(d) "Beneficiary" means a person that meets one of the following conditions:

(1) Has a present or future, vested or contingent, beneficial interest in a trust.

(2) Holds a power of appointment over trust property.

(3) Is an identified charitable organization that will or may receive distributions under the terms of the trust.

(e) "Charitable interest" means an interest in a trust that meets one of the following conditions:

(1) Is held by an identified charitable organization and makes the organization a qualified beneficiary.

(2) Benefits only charitable organizations and, if the interest were held by an identified charitable organization, would make the organization a qualified beneficiary.

(3) Is held solely for charitable purposes and, if the interest were held by an identified charitable organization, would make the organization a qualified beneficiary.

(f) "Charitable organization" means either of the following:

(1) A person, other than an individual, organized and operated exclusively for charitable purposes.

(2) A government or governmental subdivision, agency, or instrumentality, to the extent it holds funds exclusively for a charitable purpose.

(g) "Charitable purpose" means the relief of poverty, the advancement of education or religion, the promotion of health, a municipal or other governmental purpose, or another purpose the achievement of which is beneficial to the community.

(h) "Court" means the court in this state having jurisdiction in matters relating to trusts.

(i) "Current beneficiary" means a beneficiary that on the date the beneficiary's qualification is determined is a distributee or permissible distributee of trust income or principal. The term includes the holder of a presently exercisable general power of appointment but does not include a person that is a beneficiary only because the person holds any other power of appointment.

(j) "Decanting power" or "the decanting power" means the power of an authorized fiduciary under this part to distribute property of a first trust to one or more second trusts or to modify the terms of the first trust.

(k) "Expanded distributive discretion" means a discretionary power of distribution that is not limited to an ascertainable standard or a reasonably definite standard.

(l) "First trust" means a trust over which an authorized fiduciary may exercise the decanting power.

(m) "First trust instrument" means the trust instrument for a first trust.

(n) "General power of appointment" means a power of appointment exercisable in favor of a powerholder, the powerholder's estate, a creditor of the powerholder, or a creditor of the powerholder's estate.

(o) "Jurisdiction," with respect to a geographic area, includes a state or country.

(p) "Person" means an individual, estate, business or nonprofit entity, public corporation, government or governmental subdivision, agency, or instrumentality, or other legal entity.

(q) "Power of appointment" means a power that enables a powerholder acting in a nonfiduciary capacity to designate a recipient of an ownership interest in, or another power of appointment over, the appointive property. The term does not include a power of attorney.

(r) "Powerholder" means a person in which a donor creates a power of appointment.

(s) "Presently exercisable power of appointment" means a power of appointment exercisable by the powerholder at the relevant time.

(1) The term includes a power of appointment exercisable only after the occurrence of a specified event, the satisfaction of an ascertainable standard, or the passage of a specified time only after one of the following, respectively:

(A) The occurrence of the specified event.

(B) The satisfaction of the ascertainable standard.

(C) The passage of the specified time.

(2) The term does not include a power exercisable only at the powerholder's death.

(t) "Qualified beneficiary" means a beneficiary that, on the date the beneficiary's qualification is determined, satisfies one of the following conditions:

(1) Is a distributee or permissible distributee of trust income or principal.

(2) Would be a distributee or permissible distributee of trust income or principal if the interests of the distributees described in paragraph (1) terminated on that date without causing the trust to terminate.

(3) Would be a distributee or permissible distributee of trust income or principal if the trust terminated on that date.

(u) "Reasonably definite standard" means a clearly measurable standard under which a holder of a power of distribution is legally accountable within the meaning of Section 674(b)(5)(A) of the Internal Revenue Code (26 U.S.C. Sec. 674(b)(5)(A)) and any applicable regulations.

(v) "Second trust" means either of the following:

(1) A first trust after modification under this part.

(2) A trust to which a distribution of property from a first trust is or may be made under this part.

(w) "Second trust instrument" means the trust instrument for a second trust.

(x) "Settlor," except as otherwise provided in Section 19525, means a person, including a testator, that creates or contributes property to a trust. If more than one person creates or contributes property to a trust, each person is a settlor of the portion of the trust property attributable to the person's contribution except to the extent another person has power to revoke or withdraw that portion.

(y) "State" means a state of the United States, the District of Columbia, Puerto Rico, the United States Virgin Islands, or any territory or insular possession subject to the jurisdiction of the United States.

(z) "Terms of the trust" means the manifestation of the settlor's intent regarding a trust's provisions as expressed in the trust instrument, as may be established by other evidence that would be admissible in a judicial proceeding, or as may be established by court order or nonjudicial settlement agreement.

(aa) "Trust instrument" means a trust executed by the settlor to create a trust or by any person to create a second trust that contains some or all of the terms of the trust, including any amendments. **Leg.H.** Added Stats 2018 ch 407 §1 (SB 909), effective January 1, 2019.

§19503. Scope

(a) Except as otherwise provided in subdivisions (b) and (c), this part applies to an express trust that is irrevocable or revocable by the settlor only with the consent of the trustee or a person holding an adverse interest.

(b) This part does not apply to a trust held solely for charitable purposes.

(c) Subject to Section 19515, a trust instrument may restrict or prohibit exercise of the decanting power.

(d) This part does not limit the power of a trustee, powerholder, or other person to distribute or appoint property in further trust or to modify a trust under the trust instrument, law of this state other than this part, common law, a court order, or a nonjudicial settlement agreement.

(e) This part does not affect the ability of a settlor to provide in a trust instrument for the distribution of the trust property or appointment in further trust of the trust property or for modification of the trust instrument. **Leg.H.** Added Stats 2018 ch 407 §1 (SB 909), effective January 1, 2019.

§19504. Fiduciary duty

(a) In exercising the decanting power, an authorized fiduciary shall act in accordance with its fiduciary duties, including the duty to act in accordance with the purposes of the first trust.

(b) This part does not create or imply a duty to exercise the decanting power or to inform beneficiaries about the applicability of this part.

(c) Except as otherwise provided in a first trust instrument, for purposes of this part, the terms of the first trust are deemed to include the decanting power. **Leg.H.** Added Stats 2018 ch 407 §1 (SB 909), effective January 1, 2019.

§19505. Application; Governing law

This part applies to a trust created before, on, or after January 1, 2019, that satisfies either of the following conditions:

(a) Has its principal place of administration in this state, including a trust whose principal place of administration has been changed to this state.

(b) Provides by its trust instrument that it is governed by the law of this state or is governed by the law of this state for the purpose of any of the following:

(1) Administration, including administration of a trust whose governing law for purposes of administration has been changed to the law of this state.

(2) Construction of terms of the trust.

(3) Determining the meaning or effect of terms of the trust. **Leg.H.** Added Stats 2018 ch 407 §1 (SB 909), effective January 1, 2019.

§19507. Notice; Exercise of decanting power

(a) In this section, a notice period begins on the day notice is given under subdivision (c) and ends 59 days after the day notice is given.

(b) An authorized fiduciary may exercise the decanting power without the consent of any person and without court approval in compliance with this part.

(c) Except as otherwise provided in subdivision (h), an authorized fiduciary shall give notice of the intended exercise of the decanting power not later than 60 days before the exercise to all of the following:

(1) Each settlor of the first trust, if living or then in existence.

(2) Each qualified beneficiary of the first trust.

(3) Each holder of a presently exercisable power of appointment over any part or all of the first trust.

(4) Each person that currently has the right to remove or replace the authorized fiduciary.

(5) Each other fiduciary of the first trust.

(6) Each fiduciary of the second trust.

(7) The Attorney General, if subdivision (b) of Section 19514 applies.

(d) Unless the trust instrument provides otherwise, an authorized fiduciary shall give notice under subdivision (c) to the guardian ad litem for a qualified beneficiary who is a minor and has no representative or who is an unascertained or unborn beneficiary. If a guardian ad litem has not been appointed at the time of the notice, the authorized fiduciary shall seek the appointment of one. The court may appoint a guardian ad litem, for purposes of this section, in instances where the only matter before the court is that appointment.

(e) If an authorized fiduciary knows, or has reason to know, that a person entitled to notice under subdivision (c) is substantially unable to manage that person's own financial resources or resist fraud or undue influence, the authorized fiduciary shall give notice under subdivision (c) to that person and to the individual appointed to act on that person's behalf, including, but not limited to, an attorney-in-fact under a power of attorney. If no such individual has been appointed at the time of the notice, the authorized fiduciary shall seek the appointment of such an individual. The court may appoint a guardian ad litem, for purposes of this section, in instances where the only matter before the court is that appointment.

(f) An authorized fiduciary is not required to give notice under subdivision (c) to a person who is known to the fiduciary but cannot be located by the fiduciary after reasonable diligence.

(g) A notice under subdivision (c) shall include all of the following:

(1) A description of the manner in which the authorized fiduciary intends to exercise the decanting power, which shall include a statement as to the authorized fiduciary's reason for the proposed decanting and an explanation as to the differences between the first trust and the second trust or trusts.

(2) The proposed effective date for exercise of the power.

(3) A copy of the first trust instrument.

(4) A copy of all second trust instruments.

(5) A warning, set out in a separate paragraph in not less than 10-point bold type, or a reasonable equivalent thereof, that states the following:

"If you do not bring a court action to contest the proposed trust decanting (the proposed changes to the trust) within 59 days of this notice, you will lose your right to contest the decanting."

(h) The decanting power may be exercised before expiration of the notice period under subdivision (a) if all persons entitled to receive notice waive the period in a signed waiver.

(i) The receipt of notice, waiver of the notice period, or expiration of the notice period does not affect the right of a person to file an application under Section 19509 that asserts either of the following:

(1) An attempted exercise of the decanting power is ineffective because it did not comply with this part or was an abuse of discretion or breach of fiduciary duty.

(2) Section 19522 applies to the exercise of the decanting power.

(j) The notice required by this section shall be served by mail to the last known address, pursuant to Section 1215, or by personal delivery. **Leg.H.** Added Stats 2018 ch 407 §1 (SB 909), effective January 1, 2019. Amended Stats 2023 ch 260 §23 (SB 345), effective January 1, 2024.

§19508. Representation

(a) Notice to a person with authority to represent and bind another person under this code or a first trust instrument has the same effect as notice given directly to the person represented.

(b) Consent of or waiver by a person with authority to represent and bind another person under this code or a first trust instrument is binding on the person represented unless the person represented objects to the representation before the consent or waiver otherwise would become effective.

(c) A person with authority to represent and bind another person under this code or a first trust instrument may file an application under Section 19509 on behalf of the person represented.

(d) A settlor may not represent or bind a beneficiary under this part. **Leg.H.** Added Stats 2018 ch 407 §1 (SB 909), effective January 1, 2019.

§19509. Court involvement

(a) On application of an authorized fiduciary, a person entitled to notice under subdivision (c) of Section 19507, a beneficiary, or, with respect to a charitable interest, the Attorney General or other person that has standing to enforce the charitable interest, the court may do any of the following:

(1) Provide instructions to the authorized fiduciary regarding whether a proposed exercise of the decanting power is permitted under this part and is consistent with the fiduciary duties of the authorized fiduciary.

(2) Appoint a special fiduciary and authorize the special fiduciary to determine whether the decanting power should be exercised under this part and to exercise the decanting power.

(3) Approve an exercise of the decanting power.

(4) Determine that a proposed or attempted exercise of the decanting power is ineffective because of either of the following:

(A) After applying Section 19522, the proposed or attempted exercise does not or did not comply with this part.

(B) The proposed or attempted exercise would be or was an abuse of the fiduciary's discretion or a breach of fiduciary duty.

(5) Determine the extent to which Section 19522 applies to a prior exercise of the decanting power.

(6) Provide instructions to the trustee regarding the application of Section 19522 to a prior exercise of the decanting power.

(7) Order other relief to carry out the purposes of this part.

(b) If an application is made under subdivision (a), the burden is on the authorized fiduciary to establish that notice was given as required by Section 19507 and that the authorized fiduciary may exercise the decanting power.

(c) On application of an authorized fiduciary, the court may approve either or both of the following:

(1) An increase in the fiduciary's compensation under Section 19516.

(2) A modification under Section 19518 of a provision granting a person the right to remove or replace the fiduciary. **Leg.H.** Added Stats 2018 ch 407 §1 (SB 909), effective January 1, 2019.

§19510. Formalities

An exercise of the decanting power shall be made in a writing signed by an authorized fiduciary. The signed writing shall, directly or by reference to the notice required by Section 19507, identify the first trust and the second trust or trusts and state the property of the first trust being distributed to each second trust and the property, if any, that remains in the first trust. **Leg.H.** Added Stats 2018 ch 407 §1 (SB 909), effective January 1, 2019.

§19511. Decanting power under expanded distributive discretion

(a) For purposes of this section:

(1) "Noncontingent right" means a right that is not subject to the exercise of discretion or the occurrence of a specified event that is not certain to occur. The term does not include a right held by a beneficiary if any person has discretion to distribute property subject to the right to any person other than the beneficiary or the beneficiary's estate.

(2) "Presumptive remainder beneficiary" means a qualified beneficiary other than a current beneficiary.

(3) "Successor beneficiary" means a beneficiary that is not a qualified beneficiary on the date the beneficiary's qualification is determined. The term does not include a person that is a beneficiary only because the person holds a nongeneral power of appointment.

(4) "Vested interest" means any of the following:

(A) A right to a mandatory distribution that is a noncontingent right as of the date of the exercise of the decanting power.

(B) A current and noncontingent right, annually or more frequently, to a mandatory distribution of income, a specified dollar amount, or a percentage of value of some or all of the trust property.

(C) A current and noncontingent right, annually or more frequently, to withdraw income, a specified dollar amount, or a percentage of value of some or all of the trust property.

(D) A presently exercisable general power of appointment.

(E) A right to receive an ascertainable part of the trust property on the trust's termination that is not subject to the exercise of discretion or to the occurrence of a specified event that is not certain to occur.

(b) Subject to subdivision (c) and Section 19514, an authorized fiduciary that has expanded distributive discretion over the principal of a first trust for the benefit of one or more current beneficiaries may exercise the decanting power over the principal of the first trust.

(c) Subject to Section 19513, in an exercise of the decanting power under this section, a second trust may not do any of the following:

(1) Include as a current beneficiary a person that is not a current beneficiary of the first trust, except as otherwise provided in subdivision (d).

(2) Include as a presumptive remainder beneficiary or successor beneficiary a person that is not a current beneficiary, presumptive remainder beneficiary, or successor beneficiary of the first trust, except as otherwise provided in subdivision (d).

(3) Reduce or eliminate a vested interest.

(d) Subject to paragraph (3) of subdivision (c) and Section 19514, in an exercise of the decanting power under this section, a second trust may be a trust created or administered under the law of any jurisdiction and may do each of the following:

(1) Retain a power of appointment granted in the first trust.

(2) Omit a power of appointment granted in the first trust, other than a presently exercisable general power of appointment.

(3) Create or modify a power of appointment if the powerholder is a current beneficiary of the first trust and the authorized fiduciary has expanded distributive discretion to distribute principal to the beneficiary.

(4) Create or modify a power of appointment if the powerholder is a presumptive remainder beneficiary or successor beneficiary of the first trust, but the exercise of the power may take effect only after the powerholder becomes, or would have become if then living, a current beneficiary.

(e) A power of appointment described in paragraphs (1) to (4), inclusive, of subdivision (d) may be general or nongeneral. The class of permissible appointees in favor of which the power may be exercised may be broader than, or different from, the beneficiaries of the first trust.

(f) If an authorized fiduciary has expanded distributive discretion over part but not all of the principal of a first trust, the fiduciary may exercise the decanting power under this section over that part of the principal over which the authorized fiduciary has expanded distributive discretion. **Leg.H.** Added Stats 2018 ch 407 §1 (SB 909), effective January 1, 2019.

§19512. Decanting power under limited distributive discretion

(a) For purposes of this section, "limited distributive discretion" means a discretionary power of distribution that is limited to an ascertainable standard or a reasonably definite standard.

(b) An authorized fiduciary that has limited distributive discretion over the principal of the first trust for benefit of one or more current beneficiaries may exercise the decanting power over the principal of the first trust.

(c) Under this section and subject to Section 19514, a second trust may be created or administered under the law of any jurisdiction. Under this section, the second trusts, in the aggregate, shall grant each beneficiary of the first trust beneficial interests which are substantially similar to the beneficial interests of the beneficiary in the first trust. For purposes of this subdivision, "substantially similar" means that there is no material change in a beneficiary's beneficial interests, except as provided in subdivision (d).

(d) A power to make a distribution under a second trust for the benefit of a beneficiary who is an individual is substantially similar to a power under the first trust to make a distribution directly to the beneficiary. A distribution is for the benefit of a beneficiary if it satisfies any of the following conditions:

(1) The distribution is applied for the benefit of the beneficiary.

(2) The beneficiary is under a legal disability or the trustee reasonably believes the beneficiary is incapacitated, and the distribution is made as permitted under this code.

(3) The distribution is made as permitted under the terms of the first trust instrument and the second trust instrument for the benefit of the beneficiary.

(e) If an authorized fiduciary has limited distributive discretion over part but not all of the principal of a first trust, the fiduciary may exercise the decanting power under this section over that part of the principal over which the authorized fiduciary has limited distributive discretion. **Leg.H.** Added Stats 2018 ch 407 §1 (SB 909), effective January 1, 2019.

§19513. Trust for beneficiary with disability

(a) For purposes of this section:

(1) "Beneficiary with a disability" means a beneficiary of a first trust who the special needs fiduciary believes may qualify for governmental benefits based on disability, whether or not the beneficiary currently receives those benefits or is an individual who has been adjudicated legally incompetent.

(2) "Governmental benefits" means financial aid or services from a state, federal, or other public agency.

(3) "Special needs fiduciary" means, with respect to a trust that has a beneficiary with a disability, any of the following:

(A) A trustee or other fiduciary, other than a settlor, that has discretion to distribute part or all of the principal of a first trust to one or more current beneficiaries.

(B) If no trustee or fiduciary has discretion under subparagraph (A), a trustee or other fiduciary, other than a settlor, that has discretion to distribute part or all of the income of the first trust to one or more current beneficiaries.

(C) If no trustee or fiduciary has discretion under subparagraphs (A) and (B), a trustee or other fiduciary, other than a settlor, that is required to distribute part or all of the income or principal of the first trust to one or more current beneficiaries.

(4) "Special needs trust" means a trust the trustee believes would not be considered a resource for purposes of determining whether a beneficiary with a disability is eligible for governmental benefits.

(b) A special needs fiduciary may exercise the decanting power under Section 19511 over the principal of a first trust as if the fiduciary had authority to distribute principal to a beneficiary with a disability subject to expanded distributive discretion if both of the following conditions are satisfied:

(1) A second trust is a special needs trust that benefits the beneficiary with a disability.

(2) The special needs fiduciary determines that exercise of the decanting power will further the purposes of the first trust.

(c) In an exercise of the decanting power under this section, all of the following rules apply:

(1) Notwithstanding paragraph (2) of subdivision (c) of Section 19511, the interest in the second trust of a beneficiary with a disability may fulfill either of the following:

(A) Be a pooled trust as defined by Medicaid law for the benefit of the beneficiary with a disability under Section 1396p(d)(4)(C) of the Public Health and Welfare Code (42 U.S.C. Sec. 1396p(d)(4)(C)).

(B) Contain payback provisions complying with reimbursement requirements of Medicaid law under Section 1396p(d)(4)(A) of the Public Health and Welfare Code (42 U.S.C. Sec. 1396p(d)(4)(A)).

(2) Paragraph (3) of subdivision (c) of Section 19511 does not apply to the interests of the beneficiary with a disability.

(3) Except as affected by any change to the interests of the beneficiary with a disability, the second trust, or if there are two or more second trusts, the second trusts in the aggregate, shall grant each other beneficiary of the first trust beneficial interests in the second trusts which are substantially similar to the beneficiary's beneficial interests in the first trust. **Leg.H.** Added Stats 2018 ch 407 §1 (SB 909), effective January 1, 2019.

§19514. Protection of charitable interest

(a) For purposes of this section:

(1) "Determinable charitable interest" means a charitable interest that is a right to a mandatory distribution currently, periodically, on the occurrence of a specified event, or after the passage of a specified time and that is unconditional or will be held solely for charitable purposes.

(2) "Unconditional" means not subject to the occurrence of a specified event that is not certain to occur, other than a requirement in a trust instrument that a charitable organization be in existence or qualify under a particular provision of the United States Internal Revenue Code of 1986 on the date of the distribution, if the charitable organization meets the requirement on the date of determination.

(b) If a first trust contains a determinable charitable interest, the Attorney General has the rights of a qualified beneficiary and may represent and bind the charitable interest.

(c) If a first trust contains a charitable interest, the second trust or trusts may not do any of the following:

(1) Diminish the charitable interest.

(2) Diminish the interest of an identified charitable organization that holds the charitable interest.

(3) Alter any charitable purpose stated in the first trust instrument.

(4) Alter any condition or restriction related to the charitable interest.

(d) If there are two or more second trusts, the second trusts shall be treated as one trust for purposes of determining whether the exercise of the decanting power diminishes the charitable interest or diminishes the interest of an identified charitable organization for purposes of subdivision (c).

(e) If a first trust contains a determinable charitable interest, the second trust or trusts that include a charitable interest pursuant to subdivision (c) shall be administered under the law of this state unless any of the following occur:

(1) The Attorney General, after receiving notice under Section 19507, fails to object in a signed writing delivered to the authorized fiduciary within the notice period.

(2) The Attorney General consents in a signed writing to the second trust or trusts being administered under the law of another jurisdiction.

(3) The court approves the exercise of the decanting power.

(f) This part does not limit the powers and duties of the Attorney General under law of this state other than this part. **Leg.H.** Added Stats 2018 ch 407 §1 (SB 909), effective January 1, 2019.

§19515. Trust limitation on decanting

(a) An authorized fiduciary may not exercise the decanting power to the extent the first trust instrument expressly prohibits exercise of either of the following:

(1) The decanting power.

(2) A power granted by state law to the fiduciary to distribute part or all of the principal of the trust to another trust or to modify the trust.

(b) Exercise of the decanting power is subject to any restriction in the first trust instrument that expressly applies to exercise of either of the following:

(1) The decanting power.

(2) A power granted by state law to a fiduciary to distribute part or all of the principal of the trust to another trust or to modify the trust.

(c) A general prohibition of the amendment or revocation of a first trust, a spendthrift clause, or a clause restraining the voluntary or involuntary transfer of a beneficiary's interest does not preclude exercise of the decanting power.

(d) Subject to subdivisions (a) and (b), an authorized fiduciary may exercise the decanting power under this part even if the first trust instrument permits the authorized fiduciary or another person to modify the first trust instrument or to distribute part or all of the principal of the first trust to another trust.

(e) If a first trust instrument contains an express prohibition described in subdivision (a) or an express restriction described in subdivision (b), the authorized fiduciary shall include that provision or restriction in the second trust instrument. **Leg.H.** Added Stats 2018 ch 407 §1 (SB 909), effective January 1, 2019.

§19516. Change in compensation

(a) If a first trust instrument specifies an authorized fiduciary's compensation, the fiduciary may not exercise the decanting power to increase the fiduciary's compensation above the specified compensation unless either of the following occurs:

(1) All qualified beneficiaries of the second trust consent to the increase in a signed writing.

(2) The increase is approved by the court.

(b) If a first trust instrument does not specify an authorized fiduciary's compensation, the fiduciary may not exercise the decanting power to increase the fiduciary's compensation above the compensation permitted by this code unless either of the following occurs:

(1) All qualified beneficiaries of the second trust consent to the increase in a signed writing.

(2) The increase is approved by the court.

(c)(1) A change in an authorized fiduciary's compensation which is incidental to other changes made by the exercise of the decanting power is not an increase in the fiduciary's compensation for purposes of subdivisions (a) and (b).

(2) For purposes of this subdivision, an incidental change to an authorized fiduciary's compensation includes, but is not limited to, an increase in the compensation of the authorized fiduciary for either of the following reasons:

(A) The second trust lasts longer than the first trust.

(B) The second trust has a greater value than the first trust. **Leg.H.** Added Stats 2018 ch 407 §1 (SB 909), effective January 1, 2019.

§19517. Relief from liability and indemnification

(a) Except as otherwise provided in this section, a second trust instrument may not relieve an authorized fiduciary from liability for breach of trust to a greater extent than the first trust instrument.

(b) A second trust instrument may provide for indemnification of an authorized fiduciary of the first trust or another person acting in a fiduciary capacity under the first trust for any liability or claim that would have been payable from the first trust if the decanting power had not been exercised.

(c) A second trust instrument may not reduce fiduciary liability in the aggregate.

(d) Subject to subdivision (c), a second trust instrument may reallocate fiduciary powers among fiduciaries as permitted by the law of this state other than this part. **Leg.H.** Added Stats 2018 ch 407 §1 (SB 909), effective January 1, 2019.

§19518. Removal or replacement of authorized fiduciary

An authorized fiduciary may not exercise the decanting power to modify a provision in a first trust instrument granting another person power to remove or replace the fiduciary unless any of the following occurs:

(a) The person holding the power consents to the modification in a signed writing and the modification applies only to the person.

(b) The person holding the power and the qualified beneficiaries of the second trust consent to the modification in a signed writing and the modification grants a substantially similar power to another person.

(c) The court approves the modification and the modification grants a substantially similar power to another person. **Leg.H.** Added Stats 2018 ch 407 §1 (SB 909), effective January 1, 2019.

§19519. Tax-related limitations

(a) For purposes of this section:

(1) "Grantor trust" means a trust as to which a settlor of a first trust is considered the owner under Sections 671 to 677, inclusive, or Section 679 of the Internal Revenue Code (26 U.S.C. Secs. 671 to 677, 679).

(2) "Nongrantor trust" means a trust that is not a grantor trust.

(3) "Qualified benefits property" means property subject to the minimum distribution requirements of Section 401(a)(9) of the Internal Revenue Code (26 U.S.C. Sec. 401(a)(9)), and any applicable regulations, or to any similar requirements that refer to Section 401(a)(9) of the Internal Revenue Code (26 U.S.C. Sec. 401(a)(9)) or the regulations.

(b) An exercise of the decanting power is subject to all of the following limitations:

(1) If a first trust contains property that qualified, or would have qualified but for provisions of this part other than this section, for a marital deduction for purposes of the gift or estate tax under the Internal Revenue Code or a state gift, estate, or inheritance tax, the second trust instrument shall not include or omit any term that, if included in or omitted from the trust instrument for the trust to which the property was transferred, would have prevented the transfer from qualifying for the deduction, or would have reduced the amount of the deduction, under the same provisions of the Internal Revenue Code or state law under which the transfer qualified.

(2) If the first trust contains property that qualified, or would have qualified but for provisions of this part other than this section, for a charitable deduction for purposes of the income, gift, or estate tax under the Internal Revenue Code or a state income, gift, estate, or inheritance tax, the second trust instrument shall not include or omit any term that, if included in or omitted from the trust instrument for the trust to which the property was transferred, would have prevented the transfer from qualifying for the deduction, or would have reduced the amount of the deduction, under the same provisions of the Internal Revenue Code or state law under which the transfer qualified.

(3) If the first trust contains property that qualified, or would have qualified but for provisions of this part other than this section, for the exclusion from the gift tax described in Section 2503(b) of the Internal Revenue Code (26 U.S.C. Sec. 2503(b)), the second trust instrument shall not include or omit a term that, if included in or omitted from the trust instrument for the trust to which the property was transferred, would have prevented the transfer from qualifying under Section 2503(b) of the Internal Revenue Code (26 U.S.C. Sec. 2503(b)). If the first trust contains property that qualified, or would have qualified but for provisions of this part other than this section, for the exclusion from the gift tax described in Section 2503(b) of the Internal Revenue Code (26 U.S.C. Sec. 2503(b)) by application of Section 2503(c) of the Internal Revenue Code (26 U.S.C. Sec. 2503(c)), the second trust instrument shall not include or omit a term that, if included or omitted from the trust instrument for the trust to which the property was transferred, would have prevented the transfer from qualifying under Section 2503(c) of the Internal Revenue Code (26 U.S.C. Sec. 2503(c)).

(4) If the property of the first trust includes shares of stock in an S-corporation, as defined in Section 1361 of the Internal Revenue Code (26 U.S.C. Sec. 1361) and the first trust is, or but for provisions of this part other than this section would be, a permitted shareholder under any provision of Section 1361 of the Internal Revenue Code (26 U.S.C. Sec. 1361), an authorized fiduciary may exercise the power with respect to part or all of the S-corporation stock only if any second trust receiving the stock is a permitted shareholder under Section 1361(c)(2) of the Internal Revenue Code (26 U.S.C. Sec. 1361(c)(2)). If the property of the first trust includes shares of stock in an S-corporation and the first trust is, or but for provisions of this part other than this section would be, a qualified subchapter-S trust within the meaning of Section 1361(d) of the Internal Revenue Code (26 U.S.C. Sec. 1361(d)), the second trust instrument shall not include or omit a term that prevents the second trust from qualifying as a qualified subchapter-S trust.

(5) If the first trust contains property that qualified, or would have qualified but for provisions of this part other than this section, for a zero inclusion ratio for purposes of the generation-skipping transfer tax under Section 2642(c) of the Internal Revenue Code (26 U.S.C. Sec. 2642(c)), the second trust instrument shall not include or omit a term that, if included in or omitted from the first trust instrument, would have prevented the transfer to the first trust from qualifying for a zero inclusion ratio under Section 2642(c) of the Internal Revenue Code (26 U.S.C. Sec. 2642(c)).

(6) If the first trust is directly or indirectly the beneficiary of qualified benefits property, the second trust instrument may not include or omit any term that, if included in or omitted from the first trust instrument, would have increased the minimum distributions required with respect to the qualified benefits property under Section 401(a)(9) of the Internal Revenue Code (26 U.S.C. Sec. 401(a)(9)) and any applicable regulations, or any similar requirements that refer to Section 401(a)(9) of the Internal Revenue Code (26 U.S.C. Sec. 401(a)(9)) or the regulations. If an attempted exercise of the decanting power violates the preceding sentence, the trustee is deemed to have held the qualified benefits property and any reinvested distributions of the property as a separate share from the date of the exercise of the power and Section 19522 applies to the separate share.

(7) If the first trust qualifies as a grantor trust because of the application of Section 672(f)(2)(A) of the Internal Revenue Code (26 U.S.C. Sec. 672(f)(2)(A)), the second trust may not include or omit a term that, if included in or omitted from the first trust instrument, would have prevented the first trust from qualifying under Section 672(f)(2)(A) of the Internal Revenue Code (26 U.S.C. Sec. 672(f)(2)(A)).

(8) In this paragraph, "tax benefit" means a federal or state tax deduction, exemption, exclusion, or other benefit not otherwise listed in this section, except for a benefit arising from being a grantor trust. Subject to paragraph (9), a second trust instrument may not include or omit a term that, if included in or omitted from the first trust instrument, would have prevented qualification for a tax benefit if both of the following apply:

(A) The first trust instrument expressly indicates an intent to qualify for the benefit or the first trust instrument clearly is designed to enable the first trust to qualify for the benefit.

(B) The transfer of property held by the first trust or the first trust qualified, or, but for provisions of this part other than this section, would have qualified for the tax benefit.

(9)(A) Subject to paragraph (4), and except as otherwise provided in paragraph (7), the second trust may be a nongrantor trust, even if the first trust is a grantor trust.

(B) Subject to paragraph (4), and except as otherwise provided in paragraph (10), the second trust may be a grantor trust, even if the first trust is a nongrantor trust.

(10) An authorized fiduciary may not exercise the decanting power if a settlor objects in a signed writing delivered to the fiduciary within the notice period and either of the following conditions is satisfied:

(A) The first trust and a second trust are both grantor trusts, in whole or in part, the first trust grants the settlor or another person the power to cause the first trust to cease to be a grantor trust, and the second trust does not grant an equivalent power to the settlor or other person.

(B) The first trust is a nongrantor trust and a second trust is a grantor trust, in whole or in part, with respect to the settlor, unless either of the following apply:

(i) The settlor has the power at all times to cause the second trust to cease to be a grantor trust.

(ii) The first trust instrument contains a provision granting the settlor or another person a power that would cause the first trust to cease to be a grantor trust and the second trust instrument contains the same provision. **Leg.H.** Added Stats 2018 ch 407 §1 (SB 909), effective January 1, 2019.

§19520. Duration of second trust

(a) Subject to subdivision (b), a second trust may have a duration that is the same as, or different from, the duration of the first trust.

(b) To the extent that property of a second trust is attributable to property of the first trust, the property of the second trust is subject to any rules governing maximum perpetuity, accumulation, or suspension of the power of alienation that apply to property of the first trust. **Leg.H.** Added Stats 2018 ch 407 §1 (SB 909), effective January 1, 2019.

§19521. Need to distribute not required

An authorized fiduciary may exercise the decanting power whether or not under the first trust's discretionary distribution standard the fiduciary would have made or could have been compelled to make a discretionary distribution of principal at the time of the exercise. **Leg.H.** Added Stats 2018 ch 407 §1 (SB 909), effective January 1, 2019.

§19522. Saving provision

(a) If exercise of the decanting power would be effective under this part, except that the second trust instrument in part does not comply with this part, the exercise of the power is effective and the following rules apply with respect to the principal of the second trust attributable to the exercise of the power:

(1) A provision in the second trust instrument that is not permitted under this part is void to the extent necessary to comply with this part.

(2) A provision required by this part to be in the second trust instrument, which is not contained in the instrument, is deemed to be included in the instrument to the extent necessary to comply with this part.

(b) If a trustee or other fiduciary of a second trust determines that subdivision (a) applies to a prior exercise of the decanting power, the fiduciary shall take corrective action consistent with the fiduciary's duties. **Leg.H.** Added Stats 2018 ch 407 §1 (SB 909), effective January 1, 2019.

§19523. Trust for care of animal

(a) For purposes of this section:

(1) "Animal trust" means a trust or an interest in a trust described in Section 15212.

(2) "Protector" means either of the following:

(A) A person appointed in an animal trust to enforce the trust on behalf of the animal as described in subdivision (c) of Section 15212 or, if no person is appointed in the trust for that purpose, a person appointed by the court for that purpose.

(B) A nonprofit charitable corporation described in subdivision (e) of Section 15212 that has requested an accounting in writing.

(b) The decanting power may be exercised over an animal trust that has a protector to the extent the trust could be decanted under this part if each animal that benefits from the trust were an individual, if the protector consents in a signed writing to the exercise of the power.

(c) A protector for an animal has the rights under this part of a qualified beneficiary.

(d) Notwithstanding any other provision of this part, if a first trust is an animal trust, in an exercise of the decanting power, the second trust shall provide that trust property may be applied only to its intended purpose for the period the first trust benefited the animal. **Leg.H.** Added Stats 2018 ch 407 §1 (SB 909), effective January 1, 2019.

§19524. Settlor

A reference in this code to a trust instrument or terms of the trust includes a second trust instrument and the terms of the second trust. **Leg.H.** Added Stats 2018 ch 407 §1 (SB 909), effective January 1, 2019.

§19525. Later-discovered property

(a) For purposes of the law of this state other than this part and subject to subdivision (b), a settlor of a first trust is deemed to be the settlor of the second trust with respect to the portion of the principal of the first trust subject to the exercise of the decanting power.

(b) In determining settlor intent with respect to a second trust, the intent of a settlor of the first trust, a settlor of the second trust, and the authorized fiduciary may be considered. **Leg.H.** Added Stats 2018 ch 407 §1 (SB 909), effective January 1, 2019.

§19526. Obligations

(a) Except as otherwise provided in subdivision (c), if exercise of the decanting power was intended to distribute all the principal of the first trust to one or more second trusts, later-discovered property belonging to the first trust and property paid to or acquired by the first trust after the exercise of the power is part of the trust estate of the second trust or trusts.

(b) Except as otherwise provided in subdivision (c), if exercise of the decanting power was intended to distribute less than all the principal of the first trust to one or more second trusts, later-discovered property belonging to the first trust or property paid to or acquired by the first trust after exercise of the power remains part of the trust estate of the first trust.

(c) An authorized fiduciary may provide in an exercise of the decanting power or by the terms of a second trust for disposition of later-discovered property belonging to the first trust or property paid to or acquired by the first trust after exercise of the power. **Leg.H.** Added Stats 2018 ch 407 §1 (SB 909), effective January 1, 2019.

§19527. Uniformity of application and construction

A debt, liability, or other obligation enforceable against property of a first trust is enforceable to the same extent against the property when held by the second trust after exercise of the decanting power. **Leg.H.** Added Stats 2018 ch 407 §1 (SB 909), effective January 1, 2019.

§19529. Petition by trustee

This part does not limit a trustee's ability to petition for instructions or other approval under a trust pursuant to Chapter 3 (commencing with Section 17200) of Part 5 or to petition for modification of a trust pursuant to Chapter 3 (commencing with Section 15400) of Part 2. **Leg.H.** Added Stats 2018 ch 407 §1 (SB 909), effective January 1, 2019. Amended Stats 2019 ch 497 §212 (AB 991), effective January 1, 2020.

§19530. Severability

The provisions of this part are severable. If any provision of this part or its application is held invalid, that invalidity shall not affect other provisions or applications that can be given effect without the invalid provision or application. **Leg.H.** Added Stats 2018 ch 407 §1 (SB 909), effective January 1, 2019.

DIVISION 10
PRORATION OF TAXES

Chapter 1. Proration of Estate Taxes.
Chapter 2. Proration of Taxes on Generation-Skipping Transfer.

CHAPTER 1
PRORATION OF ESTATE TAXES

Article 1. General Provisions.
Article 2. Proration.
Article 3. Judicial Proceedings.

ARTICLE 1
General Provisions

Definitions. §20100.
Transitional provision. §20101.

§20100. Definitions

Except where the context otherwise requires, the following definitions shall govern the construction of this chapter:

(a) "Estate tax" means a tax imposed by any federal or California estate tax law, now existing or hereafter enacted, and includes interest and penalties on any deficiency.

(b) "Person interested in the estate" means any person, including a personal representative, entitled to receive, or who has received, from a decedent while alive or by reason of the death of the decedent any property or interest therein.

(c) "Personal representative" includes a guardian, conservator, trustee, or other person charged with the responsibility of paying the estate tax.

(d) "Property" means property included in the gross estate for federal estate tax purposes.

(e) "Value" means fair market value as determined for federal estate tax purposes. **Leg.H.** Enacted Stats 1990 ch 79 §14 (AB 759), operative July 1, 1991.

Prior Law: Former Prob C §20100, similar to the present section, was added Stats 1986 ch 783 §25, operative January 1, 1987, and repealed Stats 1990 ch 79 §13, operative July 1, 1991.

§20101. Transitional provision

(a) This chapter does not apply to persons interested in the estate of a decedent who died before January 1, 1987.

(b) Notwithstanding the repeal of former Article 4a (commencing with Section 970) of Chapter 15 of Division 3 of the Probate Code by Chapter 783 of the Statutes of 1986, the provisions of that former article remain applicable where the decedent died before January 1, 1987. No inference as to the applicable law in effect before January 1, 1987, shall be drawn from the enactment of this chapter. **Leg.H.** Enacted Stats 1990 ch 79 §14 (AB 759), operative July 1, 1991.

Prior Law: Former Prob C §20101, similar to the present section, was added Stats 1986 ch 783 §25, operative January 1, 1987, and repealed Stats 1990 ch 79 §13, operative July 1, 1991.

ARTICLE 2
Proration

Proration among persons interested in estate. §20110.
Manner of proration. §20111.
Allowance and charges for credits, deductions, interest, and other adjustments. §20112.
Trusts and temporary interests. §20113.
Proration of additional tax on certain qualified real property. §20114.
Excess retirement accumulations. §20114.5.
Proration of extended estate tax. §20115.
Where property not in possession of personal representative. §20116.
Reimbursement for overpayment. §20117.

§20110. Proration among persons interested in estate

(a) Except as provided in subdivision (b), any estate tax shall be equitably prorated among the persons interested in the estate in the manner prescribed in this article.

(b) This section does not apply:

(1) To the extent the decedent in a written inter vivos or testamentary instrument disposing of property specifically directs that the property be applied to the satisfaction of an estate tax or that an estate tax be prorated to the property in the manner provided in the instrument. As used in this paragraph, an "instrument disposing of property" includes an instrument that creates an interest in property or an amendment to an instrument that disposes of property or creates an interest in property.

(2) Where federal law directs otherwise. If federal law directs the manner of proration of the federal estate tax, the California estate tax shall be prorated in the same manner. **Leg.H.** Enacted Stats 1990 ch 79 §14 (AB 759), operative July 1, 1991.

Prior Law: Former Prob C §20110, similar to the present section, was added Stats 1986 ch 783 §25, operative January 1, 1987, and repealed Stats 1990 ch 79 §13, operative July 1, 1991.

§20111. Manner of proration

The proration required by this article shall be made in the proportion that the value of the property received by each person interested in the estate bears to the total value of all property received by all persons interested in the estate, subject to the provisions of this article. **Leg.H.** Enacted Stats 1990 ch 79 §14 (AB 759), operative July 1, 1991.

Prior Law: Former Prob C §20111, similar to the present section, was added Stats 1986 ch 783 §25, operative January 1, 1987, and repealed Stats 1990 ch 79 §13, operative July 1, 1991.

§20112. Allowance and charges for credits, deductions, interest, and other adjustments

(a) In making a proration of the federal estate tax, allowances shall be made for credits allowed for state or foreign death taxes in determining the federal tax payable and for exemptions and deductions allowed for the purpose of determining the taxable estate.

(b) In making a proration of the California estate tax, allowances shall be made for (1) credits (other than the credit for state death taxes paid) allowed by the federal estate tax law and attributable to property located in this state, and (2) exemptions and deductions allowed by the federal estate tax law for the purpose of determining the taxable estate attributable to property located in this state.

(c) In making a proration of an estate tax, interest on extension of taxes and interest and penalties on any deficiency shall be charged to equitably reflect the benefits and burdens of the extension or deficiency and of any tax deductions associated with the interest and penalties. **Leg.H.** Enacted Stats 1990 ch 79 §14 (AB 759), operative July 1, 1991.

Prior Law: Former Prob C §20112, similar to the present section, was added Stats 1986 ch 783 §25, operative January 1, 1987, and repealed Stats 1990 ch 79 §13, operative July 1, 1991.

§20113. Trusts and temporary interests

If a trust is created, or other provision made whereby a person is given an interest in the income of, an estate for years or for life in, or other temporary interest in, any property, the estate tax on both the temporary interest and on the remainder thereafter shall be charged against and paid out of the corpus of the property without apportionment between remainders and temporary estates. **Leg.H.** Enacted Stats 1990 ch 79 §14 (AB 759), operative July 1, 1991.

Prior Law: Former Prob C §20113, similar to the present section, was added Stats 1986 ch 783 §25, operative January 1, 1987, and repealed Stats 1990 ch 79 §13, operative July 1, 1991.

§20114. Proration of additional tax on certain qualified real property

(a) As used in this section, "qualified real property" means qualified real property as defined in Section 2032A of the Internal Revenue Code (26 U.S.C. Sec. 2032A).

(b) If an election is made pursuant to Section 2032A of the Internal Revenue Code (26 U.S.C. Sec. 2032A), the proration shall be based upon the amount of federal estate tax that would be payable but for the election. The amount of the reduction in federal estate tax resulting from an election pursuant to Section 2032A of the Internal Revenue Code (26 U.S.C. Sec. 2032A) shall reduce the tax that is otherwise attributable to the qualified real property that is the subject of the election. If the tax that is otherwise attributable to the qualified real property is reduced to zero pursuant to this subdivision, any excess amount of reduction shall reduce the tax otherwise payable with respect to the other property, this amount to be equitably prorated in accordance with Section 20111.

(c) If additional federal estate tax is imposed under subsection (c) of Section 2032A of the Internal Revenue Code (26 U.S.C. Sec. 2032A) by reason of early disposition or cessation of qualified use, the additional tax shall be a charge against the portion of the qualified real property to which the additional tax is attributable, and shall be equitably prorated among the persons interested in that portion of the qualified real property in proportion to their interests. **Leg.H.** Enacted Stats 1990 ch 79 §14 (AB 759), operative July 1, 1991.

Prior Law: Former Prob C §20114, similar to the present section, was added Stats 1986 ch 783 §25, operative January 1, 1987, and repealed Stats 1990 ch 79 §13, operative July 1, 1991.

§20114.5. Excess retirement accumulations

(a) As used in this section:

(1) A reference to Section 4980A of the Internal Revenue Code means Section 4980A of the federal Internal Revenue Code of 1986 as amended (26 U.S.C. Sec. 4980A) and also means former Section 4981A of the federal Internal Revenue Code of 1986.

(2) "Excess retirement accumulation" has the meaning given it in paragraph (3) of subsection (d) of Section 4980A.

(b) If the federal estate tax is increased under subsection (d) of Section 4980A of the Internal Revenue Code, the amount of the increase shall be a charge against the persons who receive the excess retirement accumulation that gives rise to the increase, and shall be equitably prorated among all persons who receive interests in qualified employer plans and individual retirement plans to which the excess retirement accumulation is attributable. **Leg.H.** Enacted Stats 1990 ch 79 §14 (AB 759), operative July 1, 1991. Amended Stats 2004 ch 183 §281 (AB 3082), effective January 1, 2005.

Prior Law: Former Prob C §20114.5, similar to the present section, was added Stats 1987 ch 128 §20, effective July 6, 1987, operative July 1, 1987, amended Stats 1987 ch 923 §100.5, operative January 1, 1988, Stats 1989 ch 544 §18, and repealed Stats 1990 ch 79 §13, operative July 1, 1991.

§20115. Proration of extended estate tax

Where the payment of any portion of the federal estate tax is extended under the provisions of the federal estate tax law, the amount of extended tax shall be a charge against the persons who receive the specific property that gives rise to the extension. **Leg.H.** Enacted Stats 1990 ch 79 §14 (AB 759), operative July 1, 1991.

Prior Law: Former Prob C §20115, similar to the present section, was added Stats 1986 ch 783 §25, operative January 1, 1987, and repealed Stats 1990 ch 79 §13, operative July 1, 1991.

§20116. Where property not in possession of personal representative

(a) If all property does not come into the possession of the personal representative, the personal representative is entitled, and has the duty, to recover from the persons interested in the estate the proportionate amount of the estate tax with which the persons are chargeable under this chapter.

(b) If the personal representative cannot collect from any person interested in the estate the amount of an estate tax apportioned to the person, the amount not recoverable shall be equitably prorated among the other persons interested in the estate who are subject to proration. **Leg.H.** Enacted Stats 1990 ch 79 §14 (AB 759), operative July 1, 1991.

Prior Law: Former Prob C §20116, similar to the present section, was added Stats 1986 ch 783 §25, operative January 1, 1987, and repealed Stats 1990 ch 79 §13, operative July 1, 1991.

§20117. Reimbursement for overpayment

(a) If a person is charged with or required to pay an estate tax greater than the amount prorated to that person because another person does not pay the amount of estate tax prorated to the other person, the person charged with or required to pay the greater amount has a right of reimbursement against the other person.

(b) The right of reimbursement may be enforced through the personal representative in the discretion of the personal representative, or may be enforced directly by the person charged with or required to pay the greater amount, and for the purpose of direct enforcement the person is subrogated to the position of the personal representative.

(c) The personal representative or person who has a right of reimbursement may commence a proceeding to have a court determine the right of reimbursement. The provisions of Article 3 (commencing with Section 20120) shall govern the proceeding, with changes necessary to make the provisions appropriate for application to the proceeding, and the court order determining the right of reimbursement is an enforceable judgment. **Leg.H.** Enacted Stats 1990 ch 79 §14 (AB 759), operative July 1, 1991.

Prior Law: Former Prob C §20117, similar to the present section, was added Stats 1986 ch 783 §25, operative January 1, 1987, and repealed Stats 1990 ch 79 §13, operative July 1, 1991.

ARTICLE 3
Judicial Proceedings

Who may commence proceeding. §20120.
Petition. §20121.
Notice of hearing. §20122.
Court order to effectuate proration. §20123.
Modification of court order. §20124.
Enforcement of out-of-state proration. §20125.

§20120. Who may commence proceeding

(a) The personal representative or any person interested in the estate may commence a proceeding to have a court determine the proration pursuant to this chapter.

(b) A proceeding under this article shall be commenced in the court in which the estate of the decedent was administered or, if no administration proceedings have been commmenced, in the superior court of any county in which the estate of the decedent may be administered.

(c) If proceedings for the administration of the decedent's estate are pending, a proceeding under this article shall be combined with the administration proceedings. If a proceeding is commenced at any time before final distribution, there shall be no additional filing fee. **Leg.H.** Enacted Stats 1990 ch 79 §14 (AB 759), operative July 1, 1991.

Prior Law: Former Prob C §20120, similar to the present section, was added Stats 1986 ch 783 §25, operative January 1, 1987, and repealed Stats 1990 ch 79 §13, operative July 1, 1991.

§20121. Petition

A proceeding under this article shall be commenced by filing a petition that sets forth all of the following information:

(a) The jurisdictional facts.

(b) Other facts necessary for the court to determine the proration of estate taxes. **Leg.H.** Enacted Stats 1990 ch 79 §14 (AB 759), operative July 1, 1991.

Prior Law: Former Prob C §20121, similar to the present section, was added Stats 1986 ch 783 §25, operative January 1, 1987, and repealed Stats 1990 ch 79 §13, operative July 1, 1991.

§20122. Notice of hearing

Not less than 30 days before the hearing, the petitioner shall do both of the following:

(a) Cause notice of the hearing and a copy of the petition to be delivered pursuant to Section 1215 to the personal representative and to each person interested in the estate against whom prorated amounts may be charged pursuant to paragraph (1) of subdivision (a) of Section 20123.

(b) Cause a summons and a copy of the petition to be served on each person interested in the estate who may be directed to make payment of prorated amounts pursuant to paragraph (2) of subdivision (a) of Section 20123. The summons shall be in the form and shall be served in the manner prescribed in Title 5 (commencing with Section 410.10) of Part 2 of the Code of Civil Procedure. **Leg.H.** Enacted Stats 1990 ch 79 §14 (AB 759), operative July 1, 1991. Amended Stats 2017 ch 319 §106 (AB 976), effective January 1, 2018.

Prior Law: Former Prob C §20122, similar to the present section, was added Stats 1986 ch 783 §25, operative January 1, 1987, and repealed Stats 1990 ch 79 §13, operative July 1, 1991.

§20123. Court order to effectuate proration

(a) The court, upon making a determination as provided in this article, shall make an order:

(1) Directing the personal representative to charge the prorated amounts against the persons against whom an estate tax has been prorated insofar as the personal representative is in possession of any property or interests of the persons against whom the charge may be made.

(2) Summarily directing all other persons against whom an estate tax has been prorated to make payment of the prorated amounts to the personal representative.

(b) A court order made under this section is a judgment that may be enforced against the persons against whom an estate tax has been prorated. **Leg.H.** Enacted Stats 1990 ch 79 §14 (AB 759), operative July 1, 1991. Amended Stats 1997 ch 724 §31 (AB 1172).

Prior Law: Former Prob C §20123, similar to the present section, was added Stats 1986 ch 783 §25, operative January 1, 1987, and repealed Stats 1990 ch 79 §13, operative July 1, 1991.

§20124. Modification of court order

Upon petition by the personal representative or any person interested in the estate, the court shall modify an order made pursuant to this article whenever it appears that the amount of estate tax as actually determined is different from the amount of estate tax on which the court based the order. **Leg.H.** Enacted Stats 1990 ch 79 §14 (AB 759), operative July 1, 1991.

Prior Law: Former Prob C §20124, similar to the present section, was added Stats 1986 ch 783 §25, operative January 1, 1987, and repealed Stats 1990 ch 79 §13, operative July 1, 1991.

§20125. Enforcement of out-of-state proration

(a) A personal representative acting or resident in another state may commence an action in this state to recover from a person interested in the estate, who either is resident in this state or owns property in this state, the amount of the federal estate tax, or an estate tax or death duty payable to another state, apportioned to the person.

(b) The action shall be commenced in the superior court of any county in which administration of the estate of the decedent would be proper or, if none, in which any defendant resides.

(c) For purposes of the action the apportionment by the court having jurisdiction of the administration of the decedent's estate in the other state is prima facie correct. **Leg.H.** Enacted Stats 1990 ch 79 §14 (AB 759), operative July 1, 1991.

Prior Law: Former Prob C §20125, similar to the present section, was added Stats 1986 ch 783 §25, operative January 1, 1987, and repealed Stats 1990 ch 79 §13, operative July 1, 1991.

CHAPTER 2
PRORATION OF TAXES ON GENERATION-SKIPPING TRANSFER

Article 1. General Provisions.
Article 2. Proration.
Article 3. Judicial Proceedings.

ARTICLE 1
General Provisions

Definitions. §20200.
Transitional provision. §20201.

§20200. Definitions

Except where the context otherwise requires, the following definitions shall govern the construction of this chapter:

(a) "Generation-skipping transfer tax" means a tax imposed by any federal or California generation-skipping transfer tax law, now existing or hereafter enacted, and includes interest and penalties on any deficiency.

(b) "Property" means property on which a generation-skipping transfer tax is imposed.

(c) "Transferee" means any person who receives, who is deemed to receive, or who is the beneficiary of, any property.

(d) "Trustee" means any person who is a trustee within the meaning of the federal generation-skipping transfer tax law, or who is otherwise required to pay a generation-skipping transfer tax.

(e) "Value" means fair market value as determined for generation-skipping transfer tax purposes. **Leg.H.** Enacted Stats 1990 ch 79 §14 (AB 759), operative July 1, 1991.

Prior Law: Former Prob C §20200, similar to the present section, was added Stats 1986 ch 783 §25, operative January 1, 1987, and repealed Stats 1990 ch 79 §13, operative July 1, 1991.

§20201. Transitional provision

(a) This chapter does not apply to transferees of property of a decedent who died before January 1, 1987.

(b) No inference as to the applicable law in effect before January 1, 1987, shall be drawn from the enactment of this chapter. **Leg.H.** Enacted Stats 1990 ch 79 §14 (AB 759), operative July 1, 1991.

Prior Law: Former Prob C §20201, similar to the present section, was added Stats 1986 ch 783 §25, operative January 1, 1987, and repealed Stats 1990 ch 79 §13, operative July 1, 1991.

ARTICLE 2
Proration

Proration among transferees. §20210.
Manner of proration. §20211.
Allowance and charges for credits, deductions, and interest. §20212.
Trusts and temporary interests. §20213.
Where property not in possession of trustee. §20214.
Reimbursement for overpayment. §20215.

§20210. Proration among transferees

(a) Except as provided in subdivision (b), any generation-skipping transfer tax shall be equitably prorated among the transferees in the manner prescribed in this article.

(b) This section does not apply:

(1) To the extent the transferor in a written instrument transferring property specifically directs that the property be applied to the satisfaction of a generation-skipping transfer tax or that a generation-skipping transfer tax be prorated to the property in the manner provided in the instrument.

(2) Where federal law directs otherwise. If federal law directs the manner of proration of the federal generation-skipping transfer tax, the California generation-skipping transfer tax shall be prorated in the same manner. **Leg.H.** Enacted Stats 1990 ch 79 §14 (AB 759), operative July 1, 1991.

Prior Law: Former Prob C §20210, similar to the present section, was added Stats 1986 ch 783 §25, operative January 1, 1987, and repealed Stats 1990 ch 79 §13, operative July 1, 1991.

§20211. Manner of proration

The proration required by this article shall be made in the proportion that the value of the property received by each transferee bears to the total value of all property received by all transferees, subject to the provisions of this article. **Leg.H.** Enacted Stats 1990 ch 79 §14 (AB 759), operative July 1, 1991.

Prior Law: Former Prob C §20211, similar to the present section, was added Stats 1986 ch 783 §25, operative January 1, 1987, and repealed Stats 1990 ch 79 §13, operative July 1, 1991.

§20212. Allowance and charges for credits, deductions, and interest

In making a proration required by this article:

(a) Allowances shall be made for credits, exemptions, and deductions allowed for the purpose of determining the tax payable.

(b) Interest and penalties on any deficiency shall be charged to equitably reflect the benefits and burdens of the deficiency and of any tax deductions associated with the interest and penalties. **Leg.H.** Enacted Stats 1990 ch 79 §14 (AB 759), operative July 1, 1991.

Prior Law: Former Prob C §20212, similar to the present section, was added Stats 1986 ch 783 §25, operative January 1, 1987, and repealed Stats 1990 ch 79 §13, operative July 1, 1991.

§20213. Trusts and temporary interests

If a trust is created or other provision made whereby a transferee is given an interest in income, or an estate for years or for life, or another temporary interest in property, the tax on both the temporary interest and other interests in the property shall be charged against, and paid out of, the corpus of the property without apportionment between the temporary and other interests. **Leg.H.** Enacted Stats 1990 ch 79 §14 (AB 759), operative July 1, 1991.

Prior Law: Former Prob C §20213, similar to the present section, was added Stats 1986 ch 783 §25, operative January 1, 1987, and repealed Stats 1990 ch 79 §13, operative July 1, 1991.

§20214. Where property not in possession of trustee

(a) If all property does not come into the possession of the trustee, the trustee is entitled, and has the duty, to recover from the transferees, the proportionate amount of the tax with which the transferees are chargeable under this chapter.

(b) If the trustee cannot collect from any transferee the amount of tax apportioned to the transferee, the amount not recoverable shall be equitably prorated among the other transferees who are subject to proration. **Leg.H.** Enacted Stats 1990 ch 79 §14 (AB 759), operative July 1, 1991.

Prior Law: Former Prob C §20214, similar to the present section, was added Stats 1986 ch 783 §25, operative January 1, 1987, and repealed Stats 1990 ch 79 §13, operative July 1, 1991.

§20215. Reimbursement for overpayment

(a) If a person is charged with, or required to pay, a generation-skipping transfer tax greater than the amount prorated to that person because another person does not pay the amount of generation-skipping transfer tax prorated to the other person, the person charged with or required to pay the greater amount has a right of reimbursement against the other person.

(b) The right of reimbursement may be enforced through the trustee in the discretion of the trustee, or may be enforced directly by the person charged with, or required to pay, the greater amount and, for the purpose of direct enforcement, the person is subrogated to the position of the trustee.

(c) The trustee or person who has a right of reimbursement may commence a proceeding to have a court determine the right of reimbursement. The provisions of Article 3 (commencing with Section 20220) shall govern the proceeding, with changes necessary to make the provisions appropriate for application to the proceeding, and the court order determining the right of reimbursement is an enforceable judgment. **Leg.H.** Enacted Stats 1990 ch 79 §14 (AB 759), operative July 1, 1991.

Prior Law: Former Prob C §20215, similar to the present section, was added Stats 1986 ch 783 §25, operative January 1, 1987, and repealed Stats 1990 ch 79 §13, operative July 1, 1991.

ARTICLE 3
Judicial Proceedings

Who may commence proceeding. §20220.
Petition. §20221.
Notice of hearing. §20222.
Court order to effectuate proration. §20223.
Modification of court order. §20224.
Enforcement of out-of-state proration. §20225.

§20220. Who may commence proceeding

(a) The trustee or any transferee may commence a proceeding to have a court determine the proration pursuant to this chapter.

(b) A proceeding under this article shall be commenced in the court in which the estate of the decedent was administered or, if no administration proceedings have been commenced, in the superior court of any county in which the estate of the decedent may be administered.

(c) If proceedings for the administration of the decedent's estate are pending, a proceeding under this article shall be combined with the administration proceedings. If a proceeding is commenced at any time before final distribution, there shall be no additional filing fee. **Leg.H.** Enacted Stats 1990 ch 79 §14 (AB 759), operative July 1, 1991.

Prior Law: Former Prob C §20220, similar to the present section, was added Stats 1986 ch 783 §25, operative January 1, 1987, and repealed Stats 1990 ch 79 §13, operative July 1, 1991.

§20221. Petition

A proceeding under this article shall be commenced by filing a petition that sets forth all of the following information:

(a) The jurisdictional facts.

(b) Other facts necessary for the court to determine the proration of the generation-skipping transfer tax. **Leg.H.** Enacted Stats 1990 ch 79 §14 (AB 759), operative July 1, 1991.

Prior Law: Former Prob C §20221, similar to the present section, was added Stats 1986 ch 783 §25, operative January 1, 1987, and repealed Stats 1990 ch 79 §13, operative July 1, 1991.

§20222. Notice of hearing

Not less than 30 days before the hearing the petitioner shall do both of the following:

(a) Cause notice of the hearing and a copy of the petition to be delivered pursuant to Section 1215 to the trustee and each transferee against whom prorated amounts may be charged pursuant to paragraph (1) of subdivision (a) of Section 20223.

(b) Cause a summons and a copy of the petition to be served on each transferee who may be directed to make payment of prorated amounts pursuant to paragraph (2) of subdivision (a) of Section 20223. The summons shall be in the form and shall be served in the manner prescribed in Title 5 (commencing with Section 410.10) of Part 2 of the Code of Civil Procedure. **Leg.H.** Enacted Stats 1990 ch 79 §14 (AB 759), operative July 1, 1991. Amended Stats 2017 ch 319 §107 (AB 976), effective January 1, 2018.

Prior Law: Former Prob C §20222, similar to the present section, was added Stats 1986 ch 783 §25, operative January 1, 1987, and repealed Stats 1990 ch 79 §13, operative July 1, 1991.

§20223. Court order to effectuate proration

(a) The court, upon making a determination as provided in this article, shall make an order:

(1) Directing the trustee to charge the prorated amounts against the transferees against whom the generation-skipping transfer tax has been prorated insofar as the trustee is in possession of any property or interests of the transferees against whom the charge may be made.

(2) Summarily directing all other transferees against whom the generation-skipping transfer tax has been prorated to make payment of the prorated amounts to the trustee.

(b) A court order made under this section is a judgment that may be enforced against the persons against whom a generation-skipping transfer tax has been prorated. **Leg.H.** Enacted Stats 1990 ch 79 §14 (AB 759), operative July 1, 1991. Amended Stats 1997 ch 724 §32 (AB 1172), effective January 1, 1998.

Prior Law: Former Prob C §20223, similar to the present section, was added Stats 1986 ch 783 §25, operative January 1, 1987, and repealed Stats 1990 ch 79 §13, operative July 1, 1991.

§20224. Modification of court order

Upon petition by the trustee or any transferee, the court shall modify an order made pursuant to this article whenever it appears that the amount of generation-skipping transfer tax as actually determined is different from the amount of tax on which the court based the order. **Leg.H.** Enacted Stats 1990 ch 79 §14 (AB 759), operative July 1, 1991.

Prior Law: Former Prob C §20224, similar to the present section, was added Stats 1986 ch 783 §25, operative January 1, 1987, and repealed Stats 1990 ch 79 §13, operative July 1, 1991.

§20225. Enforcement of out-of-state proration

(a) A trustee acting or resident in another state may commence an action in this state to recover from a transferee, who either is resident in this state or owns property in this state, the amount of the federal generation-skipping transfer tax, or a generation-skipping transfer tax payable to another state, apportioned to the person.

(b) The action shall be commenced in the superior court of any county in which administration of the estate of the decedent would be proper or, if none, in which any defendant resides.

(c) For purposes of the action an apportionment by the court having jurisdiction of the administration of the decedent's estate in the other state is prima facie correct. **Leg.H.** Enacted Stats 1990 ch 79 §14 (AB 759), operative July 1, 1991.

Prior Law: Former Prob C §20225, similar to the present section, was added Stats 1986 ch 783 §25, operative January 1, 1987, and repealed Stats 1990 ch 79 §13, operative July 1, 1991.

DIVISION 11
CONSTRUCTION OF WILLS, TRUSTS, AND OTHER INSTRUMENTS

Part 1. Rules for Interpretation of Instruments.
Part 2. Perpetuities.
Part 3. No Contest Clause.
Part 3.7. Presumption of Fraud or Undue Influence.
Part 4. Abatement.
Part 5. Compliance with Internal Revenue Code.
Part 6. Family Protection: Omitted Spouses and Children.
Part 7. Contracts Regarding Testamentary or Intestate Succession.

PART 1
RULES FOR INTERPRETATION OF INSTRUMENTS

Chapter 1. General Provisions.
Chapter 2. Ascertaining Meaning of Language Used in the Instrument.
Chapter 3. Exoneration; Ademption.
Chapter 4. Effective Dates.

CHAPTER 1
GENERAL PROVISIONS

Application of part. §21101.
Intention of testator. §21102.
Choice of law as to meaning and effect of disposition in instrument. §21103.
"At-death transfer". §21104.
Will to pass all property, including after-acquired property. §21105.
Direction in instrument to convert real property to money. §21107.
Abolishment of common law rule of worthier title; Grants to heirs and next of kin. §21108.
Failure of transferee to survive. §21109.
Anti-lapse statute; Substitute transferee. §21110.
Failed transfer. §21111.
Conditions regarding "issue". §21112.
Class gift to "heirs," "heirs at law," "next of kin," "relatives," "family," or the like. §21114.
Halfbloods, adoptees and persons born out of wedlock, stepchildren, and foster children. §21115.
Classification of testamentary gifts. §21117.
Satisfaction of pecuniary gift. §21118.

§21101. Application of part
Unless the provision or context otherwise requires, this part applies to a will, trust, deed, and any other instrument. **Leg.H.** Added Stats 1994 ch 806 §41 (AB 3686). Amended Stats 2002 ch 138 §10 (AB 1784).

Prior Law: Former Prob C §21101, similar to the present section, was enacted Stats 1990 ch 79 §14 (AB 759), operative July 1, 1991, and repealed Stats 1994 ch 806 §40.

Former Prob C §21101, similar to the present section, was added Stats 1987 ch 923 §101, operative January 1, 1988, and repealed Stats 1990 ch 79 §13, operative July 1, 1991.

§21102. Intention of testator
(a) The intention of the transferor as expressed in the instrument controls the legal effect of the dispositions made in the instrument.

(b) The rules of construction in this part apply where the intention of the transferor is not indicated by the instrument.

(c) Nothing in this section limits the use of extrinsic evidence, to the extent otherwise authorized by law, to determine the intention of the transferor. **Leg.H.** Added Stats 1994 ch 806 §41 (AB 3686). Amended Stats 2002 ch 138 §11 (AB 1784).

§21103. Choice of law as to meaning and effect of disposition in instrument
The meaning and legal effect of a disposition in an instrument is determined by the local law of a particular state selected by the transferor in the instrument unless the application of that law is contrary to the rights of the surviving spouse to community and quasi-community property, to any other public policy of this state applicable to the disposition, or, in the case of a will, to Part 3 (commencing with Section 6500) of Division 6. **Leg.H.** Added Stats 1994 ch 806 §41 (AB 3686). Amended Stats 2002 ch 138 §12 (AB 1784), effective January 1, 2003.

§21104. "At-death transfer"
As used in this part, "at-death transfer" means a transfer that is revocable during the lifetime of the transferor, but does not include a joint tenancy or joint account with right of survivorship. **Leg.H.** Added Stats 1994 ch 806 §41 (AB 3686). Amended Stats 2002 ch 138 §13 (AB 1784), effective January 1, 2003.

§21105. Will to pass all property, including after-acquired property
Except as otherwise provided in Sections 641 and 642, a will passes all property the testator owns at death, including property acquired after execution of the will. **Leg.H.** Added Stats 1994 ch 806 §41 (AB 3686). Amended Stats 2002 ch 138 §14 (AB 1784), effective January 1, 2003.

§21106. [Section repealed 2002]
Leg.H. Added Stats 1994 ch 806 §41 (AB 3686). Repealed Stats 2002 ch 138 §15 (AB 1784). The repealed section related to transferees as owners in common.

§21107. Direction in instrument to convert real property to money
If an instrument directs the conversion of real property into money at the transferor's death, the real property and its proceeds shall be deemed personal property from the time of the transferor's death. **Leg.H.** Added Stats 1994 ch 806 §41 (AB 3686). Amended Stats 2002 ch 138 §16 (AB 1784), effective January 1, 2003.

§21108. Abolishment of common law rule of worthier title; Grants to heirs and next of kin
The law of this state does not include (a) the common law rule of worthier title that a transferor cannot devise an interest to his or her own heirs or (b) a presumption or rule of interpretation that a transferor does not intend, by a transfer to his or her own heirs or next of kin, to transfer an interest to them. The meaning of a transfer of a legal or equitable interest to a transferor's own heirs or next of kin, however designated, shall be determined by the general rules applicable to the interpretation of instruments. **Leg.H.** Added Stats 1994 ch 806 §41 (AB 3686). Amended Stats 2002 ch 138 §17 (AB 1784), effective January 1, 2003.

§21109. Failure of transferee to survive
(a) A transferee who fails to survive the transferor of an at-death transfer or until any future time required by the instrument does not take under the instrument.

(b) If it cannot be determined by clear and convincing evidence that the transferee survived until a future time required by the instrument, it is deemed that the transferee did not survive until the required future time. **Leg.H.** Added Stats 1994 ch 806 §41 (AB 3686). Amended Stats 2002 ch 138 §18 (AB 1784), effective January 1, 2003.

§21110. Anti-lapse statute; Substitute transferee
(a) Subject to subdivision (b), if a transferee is dead when the instrument is executed, or fails or is treated as failing to survive the transferor or until a future time required by the instrument, the issue of the deceased transferee take in the transferee's place in the manner provided in Section 240. A transferee under a class gift shall be a transferee for the purpose of this subdivision unless the transferee's death occurred before the execution of the instrument and that fact was known to the transferor when the instrument was executed.

(b) The issue of a deceased transferee do not take in the transferee's place if the instrument expresses a contrary intention or a substitute disposition. A requirement that the initial transferee survive the transferor or survive for a specified period of time after the death of the transferor constitutes a contrary intention. A requirement that the initial transferee survive until a future time that is related to the probate of the transferor's will or administration of the estate of the transferor constitutes a contrary intention.

(c) As used in this section, "transferee" means a person who is kindred of the transferor or kindred of a surviving, deceased, or former spouse of the transferor, but does not mean a spouse of the transferor. **Leg.H.** Added Stats 1994 ch 806 §41 (AB 3686). Amended Stats 2002 ch 138 §19 (AB 1784); Stats 2018 ch 71 §1 (AB 1960), effective January 1, 2019.

§21111. Failed transfer

(a) Except as provided in subdivision (b) and subject to Section 21110, if a transfer fails for any reason, the property is transferred as follows:

(1) If the transferring instrument provides for an alternative disposition in the event the transfer fails, the property is transferred according to the terms of the instrument.

(2) If the transferring instrument does not provide for an alternative disposition but does provide for the transfer of a residue, the property becomes a part of the residue transferred under the instrument.

(3) If the transferring instrument does not provide for an alternative disposition and does not provide for the transfer of a residue, or if the transfer is itself a residuary gift, the property is transferred to the decedent's estate.

(b) Subject to Section 21110, if a residuary gift or a future interest is transferred to two or more persons and the share of a transferee fails for any reason, and no alternative disposition is provided, the share passes to the other transferees in proportion to their other interest in the residuary gift or the future interest.

(c) A transfer of "all my estate" or words of similar import is a residuary gift for purposes of this section.

(d) If failure of a future interest results in an intestacy, the property passes to the heirs of the transferor determined pursuant to Section 21114. **Leg.H.** Added Stats 1994 ch 806 §41 (AB 3686). Amended Stats 1996 ch 563 §32 (SB 392); Stats 2001 ch 417 §11 (AB 873); Stats 2002 ch 138 §20 (AB 1784), effective January 1, 2003.

§21112. Conditions regarding "issue"

A condition in a transfer of a present or future interest that refers to a person's death "with" or "without" issue, or to a person's "having" or "leaving" issue or no issue, or a condition based on words of similar import, is construed to refer to that person's being dead at the time the transfer takes effect in enjoyment and to that person either having or not having, as the case may be, issue who are alive at the time of enjoyment. **Leg.H.** Added Stats 1994 ch 806 §41 (AB 3686). Amended Stats 2002 ch 138 §21 (AB 1784), effective January 1, 2003.

§21113. [Section repealed 2002]

Leg.H. Added Stats 1994 ch 806 §41 (AB 3686). Repealed Stats 2002 ch 138 §22 (AB 1784). The repealed section related to transfers to a class, time of vesting, and afterborn members.

§21114. Class gift to "heirs," "heirs at law," "next of kin," "relatives," "family," or the like

(a) If a statute or an instrument provides for transfer of a present or future interest to, or creates a present or future interest in, a designated person's "heirs," "heirs at law," "next of kin," "relatives," or "family," or words of similar import, the transfer is to the persons, including the state under Section 6800, and in the shares that would succeed to the designated person's intestate estate under the intestate succession law of the transferor's domicile, if the designated person died when the transfer is to take effect in enjoyment. If the designated person's surviving spouse is living but is remarried at the time the transfer is to take effect in enjoyment, the surviving spouse is not an heir of the designated person for purposes of this section.

(b) As used in this section, "designated person" includes the transferor. **Leg.H.** Added Stats 1994 ch 806 §41 (AB 3686). Amended Stats 2002 ch 138 §23 (AB 1784), effective January 1, 2003.

§21115. Halfbloods, adoptees and persons born out of wedlock, stepchildren, and foster children

(a) Except as provided in subdivision (b), halfbloods, adopted persons, persons born out of wedlock, stepchildren, foster children, and the issue of these persons when appropriate to the class, are included in terms of class gift or relationship in accordance with the rules for determining relationship and inheritance rights for purposes of intestate succession.

(b) In construing a transfer by a transferor who is not the natural parent, a person born to the natural parent shall not be considered the child of that parent unless the person lived while a minor as a regular member of the household of the natural parent or of that parent's parent, brother, sister, spouse, or surviving spouse. In construing a transfer by a transferor who is not the adoptive parent, a person adopted by the adoptive parent shall not be considered the child of that parent unless the person lived while a minor (either before or after the adoption) as a regular member of the household of the adopting parent or of that parent's parent, brother, sister, or surviving spouse.

(c) Subdivisions (a) and (b) shall also apply in determining:

(1) Persons who would be kindred of the transferor or kindred of a surviving, deceased, or former spouse of the transferor under Section 21110.

(2) Persons to be included as issue of a deceased transferee under Section 21110.

(3) Persons who would be the transferor's or other designated person's heirs under Section 21114.

(d) The rules for determining intestate succession under this section are those in effect at the time the transfer is to take effect in enjoyment. **Leg.H.** Added Stats 1994 ch 806 §41 (AB 3686). Amended Stats 2002 ch 138 §24 (AB 1784), effective January 1, 2003.

§21116. [Section repealed 2002]

Leg.H. Added Stats 1994 ch 806 §41 (AB 3686). Repealed Stats 2002 ch 138 §25 (AB 1784). The repealed section related to the presumption that testamentary dispositions vest at testator's death.

§21117. Classification of testamentary gifts

At-death transfers are classified as follows:

(a) A specific gift is a transfer of specifically identifiable property.

(b) A general gift is a transfer from the general assets of the transferor that does not give specific property.

(c) A demonstrative gift is a general gift that specifies the fund or property from which the transfer is primarily to be made.

(d) A general pecuniary gift is a pecuniary gift within the meaning of Section 21118.

(e) An annuity is a general pecuniary gift that is payable periodically.

(f) A residuary gift is a transfer of property that remains after all specific and general gifts have been satisfied. **Leg.H.** Added Stats 1994 ch 806 §41 (AB 3686). Amended Stats 2002 ch 138 §26 (AB 1784), effective January 1, 2003.

§21118. Satisfaction of pecuniary gift

(a) If an instrument authorizes a fiduciary to satisfy a pecuniary gift wholly or partly by distribution of property other than money, property selected for that purpose shall be valued at its fair market value on the date of distribution, unless the instrument expressly provides otherwise. If the instrument permits the fiduciary to value the property selected for distribution as of a date other than the date of distribution, then, unless the instrument expressly provides otherwise, the property selected by the fiduciary for that purpose shall fairly reflect net appreciation and depreciation (occurring between the valuation date and the date of distribution) in all of the assets from which the distribution could have been made.

(b) As used in this section, "pecuniary gift" means a transfer of property made in an instrument that either is expressly stated as a fixed dollar amount or is a dollar amount determinable by the provisions of the instrument. **Leg.H.** Added Stats 1994 ch 806 §41 (AB 3686). Amended Stats 2002 ch 138 §27 (AB 1784), effective January 1, 2003.

CHAPTER 2
ASCERTAINING MEANING OF LANGUAGE USED IN THE INSTRUMENT

Giving some effect to every expression; Avoidance of intestacy. §21120.
Construction of instrument as whole. §21121.
Words given their ordinary meaning; Technical words. §21122.

§21120. Giving some effect to every expression; Avoidance of intestacy

The words of an instrument are to receive an interpretation that will give every expression some effect, rather than one that will render any of the expressions inoperative. Preference is to be given to an interpretation of an instrument that will prevent intestacy or failure of a transfer, rather than one that will result in an intestacy or failure of a transfer. **Leg.H.** Added Stats 1994 ch 806 §41 (AB 3686). Amended Stats 2002 ch 138 §28 (AB 1784), effective January 1, 2003.

Prior Law: Former Prob C §21120, similar to present Prob C §21118, was added Stats 1987 ch 923 §101, operative January 1, 1988, and repealed Stats 1990 ch 79 §13, operative July 1, 1991.

Former Prob C §21120, similar to present Prob C §21118, was enacted Stats 1990 ch 79 §14, operative July 1, 1991, and repealed Stats 1994 ch 806 §40.

§21121. Construction of instrument as whole

All parts of an instrument are to be construed in relation to each other and so as, if possible, to form a consistent whole. If the meaning of any part of an instrument is ambiguous or doubtful, it may be explained by any reference to or recital of that part in another part of the instrument. **Leg.H.** Added Stats 1994 ch 806 §41 (AB 3686). Amended Stats 2002 ch 138 §29 (AB 1784), effective January 1, 2003.

§21122. Words given their ordinary meaning; Technical words

The words of an instrument are to be given their ordinary and grammatical meaning unless the intention to use them in another sense is clear and their intended meaning can be ascertained. Technical words are not necessary to give effect to a disposition in an instrument. Technical words are to be considered as having been used in their technical sense unless (a) the context clearly indicates a contrary intention or (b) it satisfactorily appears that the instrument was drawn solely by the transferor and that the transferor was unacquainted with the technical sense. **Leg.H.** Added Stats 1994 ch 806 §41 (AB 3686). Amended Stats 2002 ch 138 §30 (AB 1784).

CHAPTER 3
EXONERATION; ADEMPTION

Specific gift subject to lien without right of exoneration. §21131.
At-death transfer of securities. §21132.
Right of recipient of an at-death transfer of specific gift. §21133.
Right of beneficiary of specific gift sold by conservator or taken in return for eminent domain award. §21134.
Conditions for treatment of gift during lifetime as satisfaction of at-death transfer. §21135.
Construction of provisions of chapter. §21139.

§21131. Specific gift subject to lien without right of exoneration

A specific gift passes the property transferred subject to any mortgage, deed of trust, or other lien existing at the date of death, without right of exoneration, regardless of a general directive to pay debts contained in the instrument. **Leg.H.** Added Stats 1994 ch 806 §41 (AB 3686). Amended Stats 2002 ch 138 §31 (AB 1784), effective January 1, 2003.

§21132. At-death transfer of securities

(a) If a transferor executes an instrument that makes an at-death transfer of securities and the transferor then owned securities that meet the description in the instrument, the transfer includes additional securities owned by the transferor at death to the extent the additional securities were acquired by the transferor after the instrument was executed as a result of the transferor's ownership of the described securities and are securities of any of the following types:

(1) Securities of the same organization acquired by reason of action initiated by the organization or any successor, related, or acquiring organization, excluding any acquired by exercise of purchase options.

(2) Securities of another organization acquired as a result of a merger, consolidation, reorganization, or other distribution by the organization or any successor, related, or acquiring organization.

(3) Securities of the same organization acquired as a result of a plan of reinvestment.

(b) Distributions in cash before death with respect to a described security are not part of the transfer. **Leg.H.** Added Stats 2002 ch 138 §33 (AB 1784), effective January 1, 2003.

Former Sections: Former Prob C §21132, similar to the present section, was added Stats 1994 ch 806 §41 and repealed Stats 2002 ch 138 §32.

Prior Law: Former Prob C §21132, similar to the present section, was added Stats 1994 ch 806 §41 and repealed Stats 2002 ch 138 §32.

§21133. Right of recipient of an at-death transfer of specific gift

A recipient of an at-death transfer of a specific gift has a right to the property specifically given, to the extent the property is owned by the transferor at the time the gift takes effect in possession or enjoyment, and all of the following:

(a) Any balance of the purchase price (together with any security agreement) owing from a purchaser to the transferor at the time the gift takes effect in possession or enjoyment by reason of sale of the property.

(b) Any amount of an eminent domain award for the taking of the property unpaid at the time the gift takes effect in possession or enjoyment.

(c) Any proceeds unpaid at the time the gift takes effect in possession or enjoyment on fire or casualty insurance on or other recovery for injury to the property.

(d) Property owned by the transferor at the time the gift takes effect in possession or enjoyment and acquired as a result of foreclosure, or obtained in lieu of foreclosure, of the security interest for a specifically given obligation. **Leg.H.** Added Stats 1994 ch 806 §41 (AB 3686). Amended Stats 2002 ch 138 §34 (AB 1784), effective January 1, 2003.

§21134. Right of beneficiary of specific gift sold by conservator or taken in return for eminent domain award

(a) Except as otherwise provided in this section, if, after the execution of the instrument of gift, specifically given property is sold, or encumbered by a deed of trust, mortgage, or other instrument, by a conservator, by an agent acting within the authority of a durable power of attorney for an incapacitated principal, or by a trustee acting for an incapacitated settlor of a trust established by the settlor as a revocable trust, the transferee of the specific gift has the right to a general pecuniary gift equal to the net sale price of the property unreduced by the payoff of any such encumbrance, or the amount of the unpaid encumbrance on the property as well as the property itself.

(b) Except as otherwise provided in this section, if an eminent domain award for the taking of specifically given property is paid to a conservator, to an agent acting within the authority of a durable power of attorney for an incapacitated principal, or to a trustee acting for an incapacitated settlor of a trust established by the settlor as a revocable trust, or if the proceeds on fire or casualty insurance on, or recovery for injury to, specifically gifted property are paid to a conservator, to an agent acting within the authority of a durable power of attorney for an incapacitated principal, or to a trustee acting for an incapacitated settlor of a trust established by the settlor as a revocable trust, the recipient of the specific gift has the right to a general pecuniary gift equal to the eminent domain award or the insurance proceeds or recovery unreduced by the payoff of any encumbrance placed on the property by the conservator, agent, or trustee, after the execution of the instrument of gift.

(c) For the purpose of the references in this section to a conservator, this section does not apply if, after the sale, mortgage, condemnation, fire, or casualty, or recovery, the conservatorship is terminated and the transferor survives the termination by one year.

(d) For the purpose of the references in this section to an agent acting with the authority of a durable power of attorney for an incapacitated principal, or to a trustee acting for an incapacitated settlor of a trust established by the settlor as a revocable trust, (1) "incapacitated principal" or "incapacitated settlor" means a principal or settlor who is an incapacitated person, (2) no adjudication of incapacity before death is necessary, and (3) the acts of an agent within the authority of a durable power of attorney are presumed to be for an incapacitated principal. However, there shall be no presumption of a settlor's incapacity concerning the acts of a trustee.

(e) The right of the transferee of the specific gift under this section shall be reduced by any right the transferee has under Section 21133. **Leg.H.** Added Stats 1994 ch 806 §41 (AB 3686). Amended Stats 2002 ch 138 §35 (AB 1784), Stats 2012 ch 195 §1 (AB 1985), effective January 1, 2013.

§21135. Conditions for treatment of gift during lifetime as satisfaction of at-death transfer

(a) Property given by a transferor during his or her lifetime to a person is treated as a satisfaction of an at-death transfer to that person in whole or in part only if one of the following conditions is satisfied:

(1) The instrument provides for deduction of the lifetime gift from the at-death transfer.

(2) The transferor declares in a contemporaneous writing that the gift is in satisfaction of the at-death transfer or that its value is to be deducted from the value of the at-death transfer.

(3) The transferee acknowledges in writing that the gift is in satisfaction of the at-death transfer or that its value is to be deducted from the value of the at-death transfer.

(4) The property given is the same property that is the subject of a specific gift to that person.

(b) Subject to subdivision (c), for the purpose of partial satisfaction, property given during lifetime is valued as of the time the transferee came into possession or enjoyment of the property or as of the time of death of the transferor, whichever occurs first.

(c) If the value of the gift is expressed in the contemporaneous writing of the transferor, or in an acknowledgment of the transferee made contemporaneously with the gift, that value is conclusive in the division and distribution of the estate.

(d) If the transferee fails to survive the transferor, the gift is treated as a full or partial satisfaction of the gift, as the case may be, in applying Sections 21110 and 21111 unless the transferor's contemporaneous writing provides otherwise. **Leg.H.** Added Stats 1994 ch 806 §41 (AB 3686). Amended Stats 2002 ch 138 §36 (AB 1784), effective January 1, 2003.

§21136. [Section repealed 2002]

Leg.H. Added Stats 1994 ch 806 §41 (AB 3686). Repealed Stats 2002 ch 138 §37 (AB 1784). The repealed section related to the rights of a beneficiary of a specific gift when the transferor enters into an agreement for sale or transfer of the specifically given property.

§21137. [Section repealed 2002]

Leg.H. Added Stats 1994 ch 806 §41 (AB 3686). Repealed Stats 2002 ch 138 §38 (AB 1784). The repealed section related to the rights of a beneficiary of a specific gift when the transferor encumbers such gift.

§21138. [Section repealed 2002]

Leg.H. Added Stats 1994 ch 806 §41 (AB 3686). Repealed Stats 2002 ch 138 §39 (AB 1784). The repealed section related to the rights of a beneficiary of a specific gift when the transferor alters his or her interest in the property.

§21139. Construction of provisions of chapter

The rules stated in Sections 21133 to 21135, inclusive, are not exhaustive, and nothing in those sections is intended to increase the incidence of ademption under the law of this state. **Leg.H.** Added Stats 1994 ch 806 §41 (AB 3686). Amended Stats 2002 ch 138 §40 (AB 1784).

CHAPTER 4
EFFECTIVE DATES

Application of part. §21140.

§21140. Application of part

This part applies to all instruments, regardless of when they were executed. **Leg.H.** Added Stats 1994 ch 806 §41 (AB 3686). Amended Stats 2002 ch 138 §41 (AB 1784), effective January 1, 2003.

PART 2
PERPETUITIES

Chapter 1. Uniform Statutory Rule Against Perpetuities.
Chapter 2. Related Provisions.

CHAPTER 1
UNIFORM STATUTORY RULE AGAINST PERPETUITIES

Article 1. General Provisions.
Article 2. Statutory Rule Against Perpetuities.
Article 3. Time of Creation of Interest.
Article 4. Reformation.
Article 5. Exclusions from Statutory Rule Against Perpetuities.

ARTICLE 1
General Provisions

Citation of chapter. §21200.
Effect of common law rule. §21201.
Application of part. §21202.

§21200. Citation of chapter

This chapter shall be known and may be cited as the Uniform Statutory Rule Against Perpetuities. **Leg.H.** Added Stats 1991 ch 156 §24 (AB 1577).

§21201. Effect of common law rule

This chapter supersedes the common law rule against perpetuities. **Leg.H.** Added Stats 1991 ch 156 §24 (AB 1577).

§21202. Application of part

(a) Except as provided in subdivision (b), this part applies to nonvested property interests and unexercised powers of appointment regardless of whether they were created before, on, or after January 1, 1992.

(b) This part does not apply to any property interest or power of appointment the validity of which has been determined in a judicial proceeding or by a settlement among interested persons. **Leg.H.** Added Stats 1991 ch 156 §24 (AB 1577).

ARTICLE 2
Statutory Rule Against Perpetuities

Property interest. §21205.
General power of appointment. §21206.
Nongeneral or testamentary power of appointment. §21207.
Effect of possibility of birth of child. §21208.
Effect of instrument language in conflict with rule. §21209.

§21205. Property interest

A nonvested property interest is invalid unless one of the following conditions is satisfied:

(a) When the interest is created, it is certain to vest or terminate no later than 21 years after the death of an individual then alive.

(b) The interest either vests or terminates within 90 years after its creation. **Leg.H.** Added Stats 1991 ch 156 §24 (AB 1577).

§21206. General power of appointment

A general power of appointment not presently exercisable because of a condition precedent is invalid unless one of the following conditions is satisfied:

(a) When the power is created, the condition precedent is certain to be satisfied or become impossible to satisfy no later than 21 years after the death of an individual then alive.

(b) The condition precedent either is satisfied or becomes impossible to satisfy within 90 years after its creation. **Leg.H.** Added Stats 1991 ch 156 §24 (AB 1577).

§21207. Nongeneral or testamentary power of appointment

A nongeneral power of appointment or a general testamentary power of appointment is invalid unless one of the following conditions is satisfied:

(a) When the power is created, it is certain to be irrevocably exercised or otherwise to terminate no later than 21 years after the death of an individual then alive.

(b) The power is irrevocably exercised or otherwise terminates within 90 years after its creation. **Leg.H.** Added Stats 1991 ch 156 §24 (AB 1577).

§21208. Effect of possibility of birth of child

In determining whether a nonvested property interest or a power of appointment is valid under this article, the possibility that a child will be born to an individual after the individual's death is disregarded. **Leg.H.** Added Stats 1991 ch 156 §24 (AB 1577).

§21209. Effect of instrument language in conflict with rule

(a) If, in measuring a period from the creation of a trust or other property arrangement, language in a governing instrument (1) seeks to disallow the vesting or termination of any interest or trust beyond, (2) seeks to postpone the vesting or termination of any interest or trust until, or (3) seeks to operate in effect in any similar fashion upon, the later of (A) the expiration of a period of time not exceeding 21 years after the death of the survivor of specified lives in being at the creation of the trust or other property arrangement or (B) the expiration of a period of time that exceeds or might exceed 21 years after the death of the survivor of lives in being at the creation of the trust or other property arrangement, that language is inoperative to the extent it produces a period that exceeds 21 years after the death of the survivor of the specified lives.

(b) Notwithstanding Section 21202, this section applies only to governing instruments, including instruments exercising powers of appointment, executed on or after January 1, 1992. **Leg.H.** Added Stats 1991 ch 156 §24 (AB 1577).

ARTICLE 3
Time of Creation of Interest

General rule. §21210.
Exercise of power to become unqualified beneficial owner. §21211.
Transfer of property to previously funded trust. §21212.

§21210. General rule

Except as provided in Sections 21211 and 21212, the time of creation of a nonvested property interest or a power of appointment is determined by other applicable statutes or, if none, under general principles of property law. **Leg.H.** Added Stats 1991 ch 156 §24 (AB 1577).

§21211. Exercise of power to become unqualified beneficial owner

For purposes of this chapter:

(a) If there is a person who alone can exercise a power created by a governing instrument to become the unqualified beneficial owner of (1) a nonvested property interest or (2) a property interest subject to a power of appointment described in Section 21206 or 21207, the nonvested property interest or power of appointment is created when the power to become the unqualified beneficial owner terminates.

(b) A joint power with respect to community property held by individuals married to each other is a power exercisable by one person alone. **Leg.H.** Added Stats 1991 ch 156 §24 (AB 1577).

§21212. Transfer of property to previously funded trust

For purposes of this chapter, a nonvested property interest or a power of appointment arising from a transfer of property to a previously funded trust or other existing property arrangement is created when the nonvested property interest or power of appointment in the original contribution was created. **Leg.H.** Added Stats 1991 ch 156 §24 (AB 1577).

ARTICLE 4
Reformation

Procedural; Conditions. §21220.

§21220. Procedural; Conditions

On petition of an interested person, a court shall reform a disposition in the manner that most closely approximates the transferor's manifested plan of distribution and is within the 90 years allowed by the applicable provision in Article 2 (commencing with Section 21205), if any of the following conditions is satisfied:

(a) A nonvested property interest or a power of appointment becomes invalid under the statutory rule against perpetuities provided in Article 2 (commencing with Section 21205).

(b) A class gift is not but might become invalid under the statutory rule against perpetuities provided in Article 2 (commencing with Section

21205), and the time has arrived when the share of any class member is to take effect in possession or enjoyment.

(c) A nonvested property interest that is not validated by subdivision (a) of Section 21205 can vest but not within 90 years after its creation. **Leg.H.** Added Stats 1991 ch 156 §24 (AB 1577).

ARTICLE 5
Exclusions from Statutory Rule Against Perpetuities

Interests excluded. §21225.

§21225. Interests excluded

Article 2 (commencing with Section 21205) does not apply to any of the following:

(a) A nonvested property interest or a power of appointment arising out of a nondonative transfer, except a nonvested property interest or a power of appointment arising out of (1) a premarital or postmarital agreement, (2) a separation or divorce settlement, (3) a spouse's election, (4) or a similar arrangement arising out of a prospective, existing, or previous marital relationship between the parties, (5) a contract to make or not to revoke a will or trust, (6) a contract to exercise or not to exercise a power of appointment, (7) a transfer in satisfaction of a duty of support, or (8) a reciprocal transfer.

(b) A fiduciary's power relating to the administration or management of assets, including the power of a fiduciary to sell, lease, or mortgage property, and the power of a fiduciary to determine principal and income.

(c) A power to appoint a fiduciary.

(d) A discretionary power of a trustee to distribute principal before termination of a trust to a beneficiary having an indefeasibly vested interest in the income and principal.

(e) A nonvested property interest held by a charity, government, or governmental agency or subdivision, if the nonvested property interest is preceded by an interest held by another charity, government, or governmental agency or subdivision.

(f) A nonvested property interest in or a power of appointment with respect to a trust or other property arrangement forming part of a pension, profit-sharing, stock bonus, health, disability, death benefit, income deferral, or other current or deferred benefit plan for one or more employees, independent contractors, or their beneficiaries or spouses, to which contributions are made for the purpose of distributing to or for the benefit of the participants or their beneficiaries or spouses the property, income, or principal in the trust or other property arrangement, except a nonvested property interest or a power of appointment that is created by an election of a participant or a beneficiary or spouse.

(g) A property interest, power of appointment, or arrangement that was not subject to the common law rule against perpetuities or is excluded by another statute of this state.

(h) A trust created for the purpose of providing for its beneficiaries under hospital service contracts, group life insurance, group disability insurance, group annuities, or any combination of such insurance, as defined in the Insurance Code. **Leg.H.** Added Stats 1991 ch 156 §24 (AB 1577). Amended Stats 1996 ch 563 §33 (SB 392).

CHAPTER 2
RELATED PROVISIONS

Selection of lives in being. §21230.
Individual described as spouse of individual alive. §21231.

§21230. Selection of lives in being

The lives of individuals selected to govern the time of vesting pursuant to Article 2 (commencing with Section 21205) of Chapter 1 may not be so numerous or so situated that evidence of their deaths is likely to be unreasonably difficult to obtain. **Leg.H.** Added Stats 1991 ch 156 §24 (AB 1577).

§21231. Individual described as spouse of individual alive

In determining the validity of a nonvested property interest pursuant to Article 2 (commencing with Section 21205) of Chapter 1, an individual described as the spouse of an individual alive at the commencement of the perpetuities period shall be deemed to be an individual alive when the interest is created, whether or not the individual so described was then alive. **Leg.H.** Added Stats 1991 ch 156 §24 (AB 1577).

PART 3
NO CONTEST CLAUSE

Definitions. §21310.
Enforcement of a no contest clause. §21311.
Construction of a no contest clause. §21312.
Application of common law. §21313.
Application of part notwithstanding a contrary provision in the instrument. §21314.
Application of part generally. §21315.

§21300. [Section repealed 2010]

Leg.H. Enacted Stats 1990 ch 79 §14 (AB 759), operative July 1, 1991. Amended Stats 2002 ch 150 §1 (SB 1878). Repealed Stats 2008 ch 174 §1 (SB 1264), effective January 1, 2009, operative January 1, 2010. The repealed section defined terms used in the part.

Prior Law: Former Prob C §21300, defining terms used in the part, was added Stats 1989 ch 544 §19 and repealed Stats 1990 ch 79 §13, operative July 1, 1991.

§21301. [Section repealed 2010]

Leg.H. Enacted Stats 1990 ch 79 §14 (AB 759), operative July 1, 1991. Repealed Stats 2008 ch 174 §1 (SB 1264), effective January 1, 2009, operative January 1, 2010. See Prob C §21313.

Prior Law: Former Prob C §21301, similar to present Prob C §21313, was added Stats 1989 ch 544 §19 and repealed Stats 1990 ch 79 §13, operative July 1, 1991.

§21302. [Section repealed 2010]

Leg.H. Enacted Stats 1990 ch 79 §14 (AB 759), operative July 1, 1991. Repealed Stats 2008 ch 174 §1 (SB 1264), effective January 1, 2009, operative January 1, 2010. See Prob C §21314.

Prior Law: Former Prob C §21302, similar to present Prob C §21314, was added Stats 1989 ch 544 §19 and repealed Stats 1990 ch 79 §13, operative July 1, 1991.

§21303. [Section repealed 2010]

Leg.H. Enacted Stats 1990 ch 79 §14 (AB 759), operative July 1, 1991. Repealed Stats 2008 ch 174 §1 (SB 1264), effective January 1, 2009, operative January 1, 2010. The repealed section related to validity of no contest clause.

Prior Law: Former Prob C §21303, relating to validity of no contest clause, was added Stats 1989 ch 544 §19 and repealed Stats 1990 ch 79 §13, operative July 1, 1991.

§21304. [Section repealed 2010]

Leg.H. Enacted Stats 1990 ch 79 §14 (AB 759), operative July 1, 1991. Repealed Stats 2008 ch 174 §1 (SB 1264), effective January 1, 2009, operative January 1, 2010. See Prob C §21312.

Prior Law: Former Prob C §21304, similar to present Prob C §21312, was added Stats 1989 ch 544 §19 and repealed Stats 1990 ch 79 §13, operative July 1, 1991.

§21305. [Section repealed 2010]

Leg.H. Added Stats 2000 ch 17 §5 (AB 1491). Amended Stats 2002 ch 150 §2 (SB 1878). Repealed Stats 2008 ch 174 §1 (SB 1264), effective January 1, 2009, operative January 1, 2010. The repealed section related to actions not constituting contest.

§21306. [Section repealed 2010]

Leg.H. Enacted Stats 1990 ch 79 §14 (AB 759), operative July 1, 1991. Amended Stats 1995 ch 730 §11 (AB 1466); Stats 2000 ch 17 §6 (AB 1491). Repealed Stats 2008 ch 174 §1 (SB 1264), effective January 1, 2009, operative January 1, 2010. The repealed section related to enforcement of no contest clause.

Prior Law: Former Prob C §21306, relating to enforcement of no contest clause, was added Stats 1989 ch 544 §19 and repealed Stats 1990 ch 79 §13, operative July 1, 1991.

§21307. [Section repealed 2010]

Leg.H. Enacted Stats 1990 ch 79 §14 (AB 759), operative July 1, 1991. Repealed Stats 2008 ch 174 §1 (SB 1264), effective January 1, 2009, operative January 1, 2010. The repealed section related to interested participant.

Prior Law: Former Prob C §21307, relating to interested participant, was added Stats 1989 ch 544 §19 and repealed Stats 1990 ch 79 §13, operative July 1, 1991.

§21308. [Section repealed 2010]

Leg.H. Added Stats 1992 ch 871 §21 (AB 2975). Repealed Stats 2008 ch 174 §1 (SB 1264), effective January 1, 2009, operative January 1, 2010. The repealed section related to tolling of statute of limitations.

§21310. Definitions

As used in this part:

(a) "Contest" means a pleading filed with the court by a beneficiary that would result in a penalty under a no contest clause, if the no contest clause is enforced.

(b) "Direct contest" means a contest that alleges the invalidity of a protected instrument or one or more of its terms, based on one or more of the following grounds:

(1) Forgery.
(2) Lack of due execution.
(3) Lack of capacity.
(4) Menace, duress, fraud, or undue influence.
(5) Revocation of a will pursuant to Section 6120, revocation of a trust pursuant to Section 15401, or revocation of an instrument other than a will or trust pursuant to the procedure for revocation that is provided by statute or by the instrument.
(6) Disqualification of a beneficiary under Section 6112, 21350, or 21380.

(c) "No contest clause" means a provision in an otherwise valid instrument that, if enforced, would penalize a beneficiary for filing a pleading in any court.

(d) "Pleading" means a petition, complaint, cross-complaint, objection, answer, response, or claim.

(e) "Protected instrument" means all of the following instruments:
(1) The instrument that contains the no contest clause.
(2) An instrument that is in existence on the date that the instrument containing the no contest clause is executed and is expressly identified in the no contest clause, either individually or as part of an identifiable class of instruments, as being governed by the no contest clause. **Leg.H.** Added Stats 2008 ch 174 §2 (SB 1264), effective January 1, 2009, operative January 1, 2010. Amended Stats 2010 ch 620 §5 (SB 105), effective January 1, 2011.

§21311. Enforcement of a no contest clause

(a) A no contest clause shall only be enforced against the following types of contests:

(1) A direct contest that is brought without probable cause.
(2) A pleading to challenge a transfer of property on the grounds that it was not the transferor's property at the time of the transfer. A no contest clause shall only be enforced under this paragraph if the no contest clause expressly provides for that application.
(3) The filing of a creditor's claim or prosecution of an action based on it. A no contest clause shall only be enforced under this paragraph if the no contest clause expressly provides for that application.

(b) For the purposes of this section, probable cause exists if, at the time of filing a contest, the facts known to the contestant would cause a reasonable person to believe that there is a reasonable likelihood that the requested relief will be granted after an opportunity for further investigation or discovery. **Leg.H.** Added Stats 2008 ch 174 §2 (SB 1264), effective January 1, 2009, operative January 1, 2010.

§21312. Construction of a no contest clause

In determining the intent of the transferor, a no contest clause shall be strictly construed. **Leg.H.** Added Stats 2008 ch 174 §2 (SB 1264), effective January 1, 2009, operative January 1, 2010.

§21313. Application of common law

This part is not intended as a complete codification of the law governing enforcement of a no contest clause. The common law governs enforcement of a no contest clause to the extent this part does not apply. **Leg.H.** Added Stats 2008 ch 174 §2 (SB 1264), effective January 1, 2009, operative January 1, 2010.

§21314. Application of part notwithstanding a contrary provision in the instrument

This part applies notwithstanding a contrary provision in the instrument. **Leg.H.** Added Stats 2008 ch 174 §2 (SB 1264), effective January 1, 2009, operative January 1, 2010.

§21315. Application of part generally

(a) This part applies to any instrument, whenever executed, that became irrevocable on or after January 1, 2001.

(b) This part does not apply to an instrument that became irrevocable before January 1, 2001. **Leg.H.** Added Stats 2008 ch 174 §2 (SB 1264), effective January 1, 2009, operative January 1, 2010.

§21320. [Section repealed 2010]

Leg.H. Enacted Stats 1990 ch 79 §14 (AB 759), operative July 1, 1991. Amended Stats 1994 ch 40 §3 (AB 797), effective April 19, 1994, operative January 1, 1995; Stats 2000 ch 17 §7 (AB 1491); Stats 2002 ch 150 §3 (SB 1878); Stats 2004 ch 183 §282 (AB 3082). Repealed Stats 2008 ch 174 §1 (SB 1264), effective January 1, 2009, operative January 1, 2010. The repealed section related to declaratory relief authorized.

§21321. [Section repealed 2010]

Leg.H. Enacted Stats 1990 ch 79 §14 (AB 759), operative July 1, 1991. Repealed Stats 2008 ch 174 §1 (SB 1264), effective January 1, 2009, operative January 1, 2010. The repealed section related to proper court.

§21322. [Section repealed 2010]

Leg.H. Enacted Stats 1990 ch 79 §14 (AB 759), operative July 1, 1991. Repealed Stats 2008 ch 174 §1 (SB 1264), effective January 1, 2009, operative January 1, 2010. The repealed section related to notice of hearing.

PART 3.5
LIMITATIONS ON TRANSFERS TO DRAFTERS AND OTHERS
[REPEALED]

§21350. [Section repealed 2014]

Leg.H. Added Stats 1993 ch 293 §8 (AB 21). Amended Stats 1995 ch 730 §12 (AB 1466); Stats 1996 ch 563 §34 (SB 392), ch 862 §47 (AB 2751); Stats 1997 ch 724 §33 (AB 1172); Stats 2003 ch 444 §1 (AB 1349). Repealed by the terms of Prob C §21355, effective January 1, 2014. The repealed section related to limitations on transfers to drafters, care custodians, and others.

§21350.5. [Section repealed 2014]

Leg.H. Added Stats 1995 ch 730 §13 (AB 1466). Repealed by the terms of Prob C §21355, effective January 1, 2014. The repealed section related to the definition of "disqualified person".

§21351. [Section repealed 2014]

Leg.H. Added Stats 1993 ch 293 §8 (AB 21). Amended Stats 1994 ch 40 §4 (AB 797), effective April 19, 1994; Stats 1995 ch 730 §14 (AB 1466); Stats 2002 ch 412 §1 (SB 1575).

§21352. [Section repealed 2014]

Leg.H. Added Stats 1993 ch 293 §8 (AB 21). Repealed by the terms of Prob C §21355, effective January 1, 2014. The repealed section related to limitations on liability.

§21353. [Section repealed 2014]

Leg.H. Added Stats 1993 ch 293 §8 (AB 21). Amended Stats 1995 ch 730 §15 (AB 1466). Repealed by the terms of Prob C §21355, effective January 1, 2014. The repealed section related to the effect of transfer failure.

§21354. [Section repealed 2014]

Leg.H. Added Stats 1993 ch 293 §8 (AB 21). Repealed by the terms of Prob C §21355, effective January 1, 2014. The repealed section related to statutory supremacy.

§21355. [Section repealed 2014]

Leg.H. Added Stats 1993 ch 293 §8 (AB 21). Amended Stats 1995 ch 730 §16 (AB 1466); Stats 2010 ch 620 §6 (SB 105), effective January 1, 2011, repealed January 1, 2014; Stats 2011 ch 296 §245 (AB 1023), effective January 1, 2012, repealed January 1, 2014. Repealed by its own terms, effective January 1, 2014. The repealed section related to applicability and repeal of the Part.

§21356. [Section repealed 2014]

Leg.H. Added Stats 1995 ch 730 §17 (AB 1466). Repealed by the terms of Prob C §21355, effective January 1, 2014. The repealed section related to the limitations period for action to establish invalidity of transfers.

PART 3.7
PRESUMPTION OF FRAUD OR UNDUE INFLUENCE

Chapter 1. Definitions.
Chapter 2. Operation and Effect of Presumption.

CHAPTER 1
DEFINITIONS

Definitions as governing construction of part. §21360.
"Care custodian"; "Health and social services". §21362.
"Cohabitant". §21364.
"Dependent adult". §21366.
"Domestic partner". §21368.
"Independent attorney". §21370.
"Related by blood or affinity". §21374.

§21360. Definitions as governing construction of part

The definitions in this chapter govern the construction of this part. **Leg.H.** Added Stats 2010 ch 620 §7 (SB 105), effective January 1, 2011.

§21362. "Care custodian"; "Health and social services"

(a) "Care custodian" means a person who provides health or social services to a dependent adult, except that "care custodian" does not include a person who provided services without remuneration if the person had a personal relationship with the dependent adult (1) at least 90 days before providing those services, (2) at least six months before the dependent adult's death, and (3) before the dependant adult was admitted to hospice care, if the dependent adult was admitted to hospice care. As used in this subdivision, "remuneration" does not include the donative transfer at issue under this chapter or the reimbursement of expenses.

(b) For the purposes of this section, "health and social services" means services provided to a dependent adult because of the person's dependent condition, including, but not limited to, the administration of medicine, medical testing, wound care, assistance with hygiene, companionship, housekeeping, shopping, cooking, and assistance with finances. **Leg.H.** Added Stats 2010 ch 620 §7 (SB 105), effective January 1, 2011.

§21364. "Cohabitant"

"Cohabitant" has the meaning provided in Section 13700 of the Penal Code. **Leg.H.** Added Stats 2010 ch 620 §7 (SB 105), effective January 1, 2011.

§21366. "Dependent adult"

"Dependent adult" means a person who, at the time of executing the instrument at issue under this part, was a person described in either of the following:

(a) The person was 65 years of age or older and satisfied one or both of the following criteria:

(1) The person was unable to provide properly for his or her personal needs for physical health, food, clothing, or shelter.

(2) Due to one or more deficits in the mental functions listed in paragraphs (1) to (4), inclusive, of subdivision (a) of Section 811, the person had difficulty managing his or her own financial resources or resisting fraud or undue influence.

(b) The person was 18 years of age or older and satisfied one or both of the following criteria:

(1) The person was unable to provide properly for his or her personal needs for physical health, food, clothing, or shelter.

(2) Due to one or more deficits in the mental functions listed in paragraphs (1) to (4), inclusive, of subdivision (a) of Section 811, the person had substantial difficulty managing his or her own financial resources or resisting fraud or undue influence. **Leg.H.** Added Stats 2010 ch 620 §7 (SB 105), effective January 1, 2011.

§21368. "Domestic partner"

"Domestic partner" has the meaning provided in Section 297 of the Family Code. **Leg.H.** Added Stats 2010 ch 620 §7 (SB 105), effective January 1, 2011.

§21370. "Independent attorney"

"Independent attorney" means an attorney who has no legal, business, financial, professional, or personal relationship with the beneficiary of a donative transfer at issue under this part, and who would not be appointed as a fiduciary or receive any pecuniary benefit as a result of the operation of the instrument containing the donative transfer at issue under this part. **Leg.H.** Added Stats 2010 ch 620 §7 (SB 105), effective January 1, 2011.

§21374. "Related by blood or affinity"

(a) A person who is "related by blood or affinity" to a specified person means any of the following persons:

(1) A spouse or domestic partner of the specified person.

(2) A relative within a specified degree of kinship to the specified person or within a specified degree of kinship to the spouse or domestic partner of the specified person.

(3) The spouse or domestic partner of a person described in paragraph (2).

(b) For the purposes of this section, "spouse or domestic partner" includes a predeceased spouse or predeceased domestic partner.

(c) In determining a relationship under this section, Sections 6406 and 6407, and Chapter 2 (commencing with Section 6450) of Part 2 of Division 6, are applicable. **Leg.H.** Added Stats 2010 ch 620 §7 (SB 105), effective January 1, 2011.

CHAPTER 2
OPERATION AND EFFECT OF PRESUMPTION

Presumption of fraud or undue influence; Costs and attorney's fees. §21380.
Inapplicability of Section 21380 to specified instruments or transfers. §21382.
When donative transfer is not subject to Section 21380; Requirements; Duties of attorney. §21384.
Inapplicability to at-death transfer between spouses. § 21385.
When donative transfer fails. §21386.
Transfer of property subject to presumption of fraud or undue influence; Liability; Notice. §21388.
Application of part notwithstanding a contrary provision in the instrument. §21390.
Applicability of part to instruments that become irrevocable on or after January 1, 2011; Legislative intent. §21392.

§21380. Presumption of fraud or undue influence; Costs and attorney's fees

(a) A provision of an instrument making a donative transfer to any of the following persons is presumed to be the product of fraud or undue influence:

(1) The person who drafted the instrument.

(2) A person who transcribed the instrument or caused it to be transcribed and who was in a fiduciary relationship with the transferor when the instrument was transcribed.

(3) A care custodian of a transferor who is a dependent adult, but only if the instrument was executed during the period in which the care custodian provided services to the transferor, or within 90 days before or after that period.

(4) A care custodian who commenced a marriage, cohabitation, or domestic partnership with a transferor who is a dependent adult while providing services to that dependent adult, or within 90 days after those services were last provided to the dependent adult, if the donative transfer occurred, or the instrument was executed, less than six months after the marriage, cohabitation, or domestic partnership commenced.

(5) A person who is related by blood or affinity, within the third degree, to any person described in paragraphs (1) to (3), inclusive.

(6) A cohabitant or employee of any person described in paragraphs (1) to (3), inclusive.

(7) A partner, shareholder, or employee of a law firm in which a person described in paragraph (1) or (2) has an ownership interest.

(b) The presumption created by this section is a presumption affecting the burden of proof. The presumption may be rebutted by proving, by clear and convincing evidence, that the donative transfer was not the product of fraud or undue influence.

(c) Notwithstanding subdivision (b), with respect to a donative transfer to the person who drafted the donative instrument, or to a person who is related to, or associated with, the drafter as described in paragraph (5), (6), or (7) of subdivision (a), the presumption created by this section is conclusive.

(d) If a beneficiary is unsuccessful in rebutting the presumption, the beneficiary shall bear all costs of the proceeding, including reasonable attorney's fees. **Leg.H.** Added Stats 2010 ch 620 §7 (SB 105), effective January 1, 2011. Amended Stats 2017 ch 56 §1 (SB 153), effective January 1, 2018; Stats 2019 ch 10 §1 (AB 328), effective January 1, 2020.

§21382. Inapplicability of Section 21380 to specified instruments or transfers

Section 21380 does not apply to any of the following instruments or transfers:

(a) Except as provided in paragraph (4) of subdivision (a) of Section 21380, a donative transfer to a person who is related by blood or affinity, within the fourth degree, to the transferor or is the cohabitant of the transferor.

(b) An instrument that is drafted or transcribed by a person who is related by blood or affinity, within the fourth degree, to the transferor or is the cohabitant of the transferor.

(c) An instrument that is approved pursuant to an order under Article 10 (commencing with Section 2580) of Chapter 6 of Part 4 of Division 4, after full disclosure of the relationships of the persons involved.

(d) A donative transfer to a federal, state, or local public entity, an entity that qualifies for an exemption from taxation under Section 501(c)(3) or 501(c)(19) of the Internal Revenue Code, or a trust holding the transferred property for the entity.

(e) A donative transfer of property valued at five thousand dollars ($5,000) or less, if the total value of the transferor's estate equals or exceeds the amount stated in Section 13100.

(f) An instrument executed outside of California by a transferor who was not a resident of California when the instrument was executed. **Leg.H.** Added Stats 2010 ch 620 §7 (SB 105), effective January 1, 2011. Amended Stats 2019 ch 10 §2 (AB 328), effective January 1, 2020.

§21384. When donative transfer is not subject to Section 21380; Requirements; Duties of attorney

(a) A donative transfer is not subject to Section 21380 if the instrument is reviewed by an independent attorney who counsels the transferor, out of the presence of any heir or proposed beneficiary, about the nature and consequences of the intended transfer, including the effect of the intended transfer on the transferor's heirs and on any beneficiary of a prior donative instrument, attempts to determine if the intended transfer is the result of fraud or undue influence, and signs and delivers to the transferor an original certificate in substantially the following form:

"CERTIFICATE OF INDEPENDENT REVIEW

I, _____ (attorney's name), have reviewed _____ (name of instrument) and have counseled the transferor, _____ (name of transferor), on the nature and consequences of any transfers of property to _____ (name of person described in Section 21380 of the Probate Code) that would be made by the instrument.

I am an "independent attorney" as defined in Section 21370 of the Probate Code and am in a position to advise the transferor independently, impartially, and confidentially as to the consequences of the transfer.

On the basis of this counsel, I conclude that the transfers to _____ (name of person described in Section 21380 of the Probate Code) that would be made by the instrument are not the product of fraud or undue influence.

_____   _____ "
(Name of Attorney)   (Date)

(b) An attorney whose written engagement, signed by the transferor, is expressly limited solely to compliance with the requirements of this section, shall not be considered to otherwise represent the transferor as a client.

(c) An attorney who drafts an instrument can review and certify the same instrument pursuant to this section, but only as to a donative transfer to a care custodian. In all other circumstances, an attorney who drafts an instrument may not review and certify the instrument.

(d) If the certificate is prepared by an attorney other than the attorney who drafted the instrument that is under review, a copy of the signed certification shall be provided to the drafting attorney. **Leg.H.** Added Stats 2010 ch 620 §7 (SB 105), effective January 1, 2011. Amended Stats 2017 ch 56 §2 (SB 153), effective January 1, 2018.

§ 21385. Inapplicability to at-death transfer between spouses

(a) An at-death transfer, as defined in Section 21104, between spouses by will, revocable trust, beneficiary form, or other instrument is not subject to Section 721 of the Family Code or any presumptions of undue influence created by that section.

(b) This section does not limit the application of any other statutory or common law presumptions of undue influence that may apply to an at-death transfer between spouses. **Leg.H.** Added Stats 2019 ch 43 §2 (AB 327), effective January 1, 2020.

§21386. When donative transfer fails

If a donative transfer fails under this part, the instrument making the donative transfer shall operate as if the beneficiary had predeceased the transferor without spouse, domestic partner, or issue. **Leg.H.** Added Stats 2010 ch 620 §7 (SB 105), effective January 1, 2011. Amended Stats 2017 ch 56 §3 (SB 153), effective January 1, 2018.

§21388. Transfer of property subject to presumption of fraud or undue influence; Liability; Notice

(a) A person is not liable for transferring property pursuant to an instrument that is subject to the presumption created under this part, unless the person is served with notice, prior to transferring the property, that the instrument has been contested under this part.

(b) A person who is served with notice that an instrument has been contested under this part is not liable for failing to transfer property pursuant to the instrument, unless the person is served with notice that the validity of the transfer has been conclusively determined by a court. **Leg.H.** Added Stats 2010 ch 620 §7 (SB 105), effective January 1, 2011.

§21390. Application of part notwithstanding a contrary provision in the instrument

This part applies notwithstanding a contrary provision in an instrument. **Leg.H.** Added Stats 2010 ch 620 §7 (SB 105), effective January 1, 2011.

§21392. Applicability of part to instruments that become irrevocable on or after January 1, 2011; Legislative intent

(a) This part shall apply to instruments that become irrevocable on or after January 1, 2011. For the purposes of this section, an instrument that is otherwise revocable or amendable shall be deemed to be irrevocable if, on or after January 1, 2011, the transferor by reason of incapacity was unable to change the disposition of the transferor's property and did not regain capacity before the date of the transferor's death.

(b) It is the intent of the Legislature that this part supplement the common law on fraud and undue influence, without superseding or interfering in the operation of that law. Nothing in this part precludes an action to contest a donative transfer under the common law or under any other applicable law. This subdivision is declarative of existing law. **Leg.H.** Added Stats 2010 ch 620 §7 (SB 105), effective January 1, 2011. Amended Stats 2017 ch 56 §4 (SB 153), effective January 1, 2018.

PART 4
ABATEMENT

Abatement subject to transferor's intent. §21400.
Purposes for which shares of beneficiaries abate. §21401.
Order of abatement. §21402.
Abatement within classes. §21403.
No exoneration by abatement of specific gift. §21404.
Contribution in case of abatement. §21405.
Transitional provision. §21406.

§21400. Abatement subject to transferor's intent

Notwithstanding any other provision of this part, if the instrument provides for abatement, or if the transferor's plan or if the purpose of the transfer would be defeated by abatement as provided in this part, the shares of beneficiaries abate as is necessary to effectuate the instrument, plan, or purpose. **Leg.H.** Enacted Stats 1990 ch 79 §14 (AB 759), operative July 1, 1991.

Prior Law: Former Prob C §21400, similar to the present section, was added Stats 1988 ch 1199 §108, operative July 1, 1989, and repealed Stats 1990 ch 79 §13, operative July 1, 1991.

§21401. Purposes for which shares of beneficiaries abate

Except as provided in Sections 21612 (omitted spouse) and 21623 (omitted children) and in Division 10 (commencing with Section 20100) (proration of taxes), shares of beneficiaries abate as provided in this part for all purposes, including payment of the debts, expenses, and charges specified in Section 11420, satisfaction of gifts, and payment of expenses on specifically devised property pursuant to Section 12002, and without any priority as between real and personal property. **Leg.H.** Enacted Stats 1990 ch 79 §14 (AB 759), operative July 1, 1991. Amended Stats 2003 ch 32 §15 (AB 167), effective January 1, 2004.

Prior Law: Former Prob C §21401, similar to the present section, was added Stats 1988 ch 1199 §108, operative July 1, 1989, and repealed Stats 1990 ch 79 §13, operative July 1, 1991.

§21402. Order of abatement

(a) Shares of beneficiaries abate in the following order:
(1) Property not disposed of by the instrument.
(2) Residuary gifts.
(3) General gifts to persons other than the transferor's relatives.
(4) General gifts to the transferor's relatives.
(5) Specific gifts to persons other than the transferor's relatives.
(6) Specific gifts to the transferor's relatives.

(b) For purposes of this section, a "relative" of the transferor is a person to whom property would pass from the transferor under Section 6401 or 6402 (intestate succession) if the transferor died intestate and there were no other person having priority. **Leg.H.** Enacted Stats 1990 ch 79 §14 (AB 759), operative July 1, 1991.

Prior Law: Former Prob C §21402, similar to the present section, was added Stats 1988 ch 1199 §108, operative July 1, 1989, and repealed Stats 1990 ch 79 §13, operative July 1, 1991.

§21403. Abatement within classes

(a) Subject to subdivision (b), shares of beneficiaries abate pro rata within each class specified in Section 21402.

(b) Gifts of annuities and demonstrative gifts are treated as specific gifts to the extent they are satisfied out of the fund or property specified in the gift and as general gifts to the extent they are satisfied out of property other than the fund or property specified in the gift. **Leg.H.** Enacted Stats 1990 ch 79 §14 (AB 759), operative July 1, 1991.

Prior Law: Former Prob C §21403, similar to the present section, was added Stats 1988 ch 1199 §108, operative July 1, 1989, and repealed Stats 1990 ch 79 §13, operative July 1, 1991.

§21404. No exoneration by abatement of specific gift

If an instrument requires property that is the subject of a specific gift to be exonerated from a mortgage, deed of trust, or other lien, a specific gift of other property does not abate for the purpose of exonerating the encumbered property. **Leg.H.** Enacted Stats 1990 ch 79 §14 (AB 759), operative July 1, 1991.

Prior Law: Former Prob C §21404, similar to the present section, was added Stats 1988 ch 1199 §108, operative July 1, 1989, and repealed Stats 1990 ch 79 §13, operative July 1, 1991.

§21405. Contribution in case of abatement

(a) In any case in which there is abatement when a distribution is made during estate administration, the court shall fix the amount each distributee must contribute for abatement. The personal representative shall reduce the distributee's share by that amount.

(b) If a specific gift must be abated, the beneficiary of the specific gift may satisfy the contribution for abatement out of the beneficiary's property other than the property that is the subject of the specific gift. **Leg.H.** Enacted Stats 1990 ch 79 §14 (AB 759), operative July 1, 1991.

Prior Law: Former Prob C §21405, similar to the present section, was added Stats 1988 ch 1199 §108, operative July 1, 1989, and repealed Stats 1990 ch 79 §13, operative July 1, 1991.

§21406. Transitional provision

(a) This part does not apply to a gift made before July 1, 1989. In the case of a gift made before July 1, 1989, the law that would have applied had this part not been enacted shall apply.

(b) For purposes of this section a gift by will is made on the date of the decedent's death. **Leg.H.** Enacted Stats 1990 ch 79 §14 (AB 759), operative July 1, 1991.

Prior Law: Former Prob C §21406, similar to the present section, was added Stats 1988 ch 1199 §108, operative July 1, 1989, and repealed Stats 1990 ch 79 §13, operative July 1, 1991.

PART 5
COMPLIANCE WITH INTERNAL REVENUE CODE

Chapter 1. General Provisions.
Chapter 2. Marital Deduction Gifts.
Chapter 3. Charitable Gifts.

CHAPTER 1
GENERAL PROVISIONS

"Internal Revenue Code" defined. §21500.
Application of part. §21501.
Effect of instrument on application of part. §21502.
Application of formula clause to federal estate tax. §21503.

§21500. "Internal Revenue Code" defined

As used in this part, "Internal Revenue Code" means the Internal Revenue Code of 1986, as amended from time to time. A reference to a provision of the Internal Revenue Code includes any subsequent provision of law enacted in its place. **Leg.H.** Enacted Stats 1990 ch 79 §14 (AB 759), operative July 1, 1991.

Prior Law: Former Prob C §21500, similar to the present section, was added Stats 1987 ch 923 §101, operative January 1, 1988, and repealed Stats 1990 ch 79 §13, operative July 1, 1991.

§21501. Application of part

(a) This part applies to a distribution made on or after January 1, 1988, whether the transferor died before, on, or after that date.

(b) A distribution made on or after January 1, 1983, and before January 1, 1988, is governed by the applicable law in effect before January 1, 1988. **Leg.H.** Enacted Stats 1990 ch 79 §14 (AB 759), operative July 1, 1991.

Prior Law: Former Prob C §21501, similar to the present section, was added Stats 1987 ch 923 §101, operative January 1, 1988, and repealed Stats 1990 ch 79 §13, operative July 1, 1991.

§21502. Effect of instrument on application of part

(a) This part does not apply to an instrument the terms of which expressly or by necessary implication make this part inapplicable.

(b) By an appropriate statement made in an instrument, the transferor may incorporate by reference any or all of the provisions of this part. The effect of incorporating a provision of this part in an instrument is to make the incorporated provision a part of the instrument as though the language of the incorporated provision were set forth verbatim in the instrument. Unless an instrument incorporating a provision of this part provides otherwise, the instrument automatically incorporates the provision's amendments. **Leg.H.** Enacted Stats 1990 ch 79 §14 (AB 759), operative July 1, 1991.

Prior Law: Former Prob C §21502, similar to the present section, was added Stats 1987 ch 923 §101, operative January 1, 1988, and repealed Stats 1990 ch 79 §13, operative July 1, 1991.

§21503. Application of formula clause to federal estate tax

(a) If an instrument includes a formula intended to eliminate the federal estate tax, the formula shall be applied to eliminate or to reduce to the maximum extent possible the federal estate tax.

(b) If an instrument includes a formula that refers to a maximum fraction or amount that will not result in a federal estate tax, the formula shall be construed to refer to the maximum fraction or amount that will not result in or increase the federal estate tax. **Leg.H.** Enacted Stats 1990 ch 79 §14 (AB 759), operative July 1, 1991.

Prior Law: Former Prob C §21503, similar to the present section, was added Stats 1987 ch 923 §101, operative January 1, 1988, and repealed Stats 1990 ch 79 §13, operative July 1, 1991.

CHAPTER 2
MARITAL DEDUCTION GIFTS

Definitions. §21520.
Sections 21524 and 21526 not applicable to estate trust. §21521.
Marital deduction gifts. §21522.
Maximum marital deduction for instrument dated before September 12, 1981. §21523.
Marital deduction gift in trust. §21524.
Survival requirement for marital deduction gift. §21525.
QTIP election. §21526.

§21520. Definitions

As used in this chapter:

(a) "Marital deduction" means the federal estate tax deduction allowed for transfers under Section 2056 of the Internal Revenue Code or the federal gift tax deduction allowed for transfers under Section 2523 of the Internal Revenue Code.

(b) "Marital deduction gift" means a transfer of property that is intended to qualify for the marital deduction. **Leg.H.** Enacted Stats 1990 ch 79 §14 (AB 759), operative July 1, 1991.

Prior Law: Former Prob C §21520, similar to the present section, was added Stats 1987 ch 923 §101, operative January 1, 1988, amended Stats 1988 ch 113 §20, effective May 25, 1988, operative July 1, 1988, and repealed Stats 1990 ch 79 §13, operative July 1, 1991.

§21521. Sections 21524 and 21526 not applicable to estate trust

Sections 21524 and 21526 do not apply to a trust that qualifies for the marital deduction under Section 20.2056(e)-2(b) of the Code of Federal Regulations (commonly referred to as the "estate trust"). **Leg.H.** Enacted Stats 1990 ch 79 §14 (AB 759), operative July 1, 1991.

Prior Law: Former Prob C §21521, similar to the present section, was added Stats 1987 ch 923 §101, operative January 1, 1988, amended Stats 1988 ch 113 §21, effective May 25, 1988, operative July 1, 1988, and repealed Stats 1990 ch 79 §13, operative July 1, 1991.

§21522. Marital deduction gifts

If an instrument contains a marital deduction gift:

(a) The provisions of the instrument, including any power, duty, or discretionary authority given to a fiduciary, shall be construed to comply with the marital deduction provisions of the Internal Revenue Code.

(b) The fiduciary shall not take any action or have any power that impairs the deduction as applied to the marital deduction gift.

(c) The marital deduction gift may be satisfied only with property that qualifies for the marital deduction. **Leg.H.** Enacted Stats 1990 ch 79 §14 (AB 759), operative July 1, 1991.

Prior Law: Former Prob C §21522, similar to the present section, was added Stats 1987 ch 923 §101, operative January 1, 1988, and repealed Stats 1990 ch 79 §13, operative July 1, 1991.

§21523. Maximum marital deduction for instrument dated before September 12, 1981

(a) The Economic Recovery Tax Act of 1981 was enacted August 13, 1981. This section applies to an instrument executed before September 12, 1981 (before 30 days after enactment of the Economic Recovery Tax Act of 1981).

(b) If an instrument described in subdivision (a) indicates the transferor's intention to make a gift that will provide the maximum allowable marital deduction, the instrument passes to the recipient an amount equal to the maximum amount of the marital deduction that would have been allowed as of the date of the gift under federal law as it existed before enactment of the Economic Recovery Tax Act of 1981, with adjustments for the following, if applicable:

(1) The provisions of Section 2056(c)(1)(B) and (C) of the Internal Revenue Code in effect immediately before enactment of the Economic Recovery Tax Act of 1981.

(2) To reduce the amount passing under the gift by the final federal estate tax values of any other property that passes under or outside of the instrument and qualifies for the marital deduction. This subdivision does not apply to qualified terminable interest property under Section 2056(b)(7) of the Internal Revenue Code. **Leg.H.** Enacted Stats 1990 ch 79 §14 (AB 759), operative July 1, 1991.

Prior Law: Former Prob C §21523, similar to the present section, was added Stats 1987 ch 923 §101, operative January 1, 1988, and repealed Stats 1990 ch 79 §13, operative July 1, 1991.

§21524. Marital deduction gift in trust

If a marital deduction gift is made in trust, in addition to the other provisions of this chapter, each of the following provisions also applies to the marital deduction trust:

(a) The transferor's spouse is the only beneficiary of income or principal of the marital deduction property as long as the spouse is alive. Nothing in this subdivision precludes exercise by the transferor's spouse of a power of appointment included in a trust that qualifies as a general power of appointment marital deduction trust.

(b) The transferor's spouse is entitled to all of the income of the marital deduction property not less frequently than annually, as long as the spouse is alive. For purposes of this subdivision, income shall be construed in a manner consistent with subdivision (b) of Section 2056 and subdivision (f) of Section 2523 of the Internal Revenue Code and shall include a unitrust payment or other allocation of income determined pursuant to a reasonable apportionment of total investment return that meets the requirements of Section 643 of the Internal Revenue Code and the regulations adopted pursuant to that statute.

(c) The transferor's spouse has the right to require that the trustee of the trust make unproductive marital deduction property productive or to convert it into productive property within a reasonable time. **Leg.H.** Enacted Stats 1990 ch 79 §14 (AB 759), operative July 1, 1991. Amended Stats 1999 ch 145 §7 (AB 846); Stats 2016 ch 140 §1 (SB 1265), effective January 1, 2017.

Prior Law: Former Prob C §21524, similar to the present section, was added Stats 1987 ch 923 §101, operative January 1, 1988, and repealed Stats 1990 ch 79 §13, operative July 1, 1991.

§21525. Survival requirement for marital deduction gift

(a) If an instrument that makes a marital deduction gift includes a condition that the transferor's spouse survive the transferor by a period that exceeds or may exceed six months, other than a condition described in subdivision (b), the condition shall be limited to six months as applied to the marital deduction gift.

(b) If an instrument that makes a marital deduction gift includes a condition that the transferor's spouse survive a common disaster that results in the death of the transferor, the condition shall be limited to the time of the final audit of the federal estate tax return for the transferor's estate, if any, as applied to the marital deduction gift.

(c) The amendment of subdivision (a) made by Chapter 113 of the Statutes of 1988 is declaratory of, and not a change in, either existing law or former Section 1036 (repealed by Chapter 923 of the Statutes of 1987). **Leg.H.** Enacted Stats 1990 ch 79 §14 (AB 759), operative July 1, 1991.

Prior Law: Former Prob C §21525, similar to the present section, was added Stats 1987 ch 923 §101, operative January 1, 1988, amended Stats 1988 ch 113 §21.5, effective May 25, 1988, operative May 25, 1988, and repealed Stats 1990 ch 79 §13, operative July 1, 1991.

§21526. QTIP election

A fiduciary is not liable for a good faith decision to make any election, or not to make any election, referred to in Section 2056(b)(7) or Section 2523(f) of the Internal Revenue Code. **Leg.H.** Enacted Stats 1990 ch 79 §14 (AB 759), operative July 1, 1991.

Prior Law: Former Prob C §21526, similar to the present section, was added Stats 1987 ch 923 §101, operative January 1, 1988, and repealed Stats 1990 ch 79 §13, operative July 1, 1991.

CHAPTER 3
CHARITABLE GIFTS

Charitable remainder unitrusts and annuity trusts. §21540.
Charitable lead trusts. §21541.

§21540. Charitable remainder unitrusts and annuity trusts

If an instrument indicates the transferor's intention to comply with the Internal Revenue Code requirements for a charitable remainder unitrust or a charitable remainder annuity trust as each is defined in Section 664 of the Internal Revenue Code, the provisions of the instrument, including any power, duty, or discretionary authority given to a fiduciary, shall be construed to comply with the charitable deduction provisions of Section 2055 or Section 2522 of the Internal Revenue Code and the charitable remainder trust provisions of Section 664 of the Internal Revenue Code in order to conform to that intent. In no event shall the fiduciary take an action or have a power that impairs the charitable deduction. The provisions of the instrument may be augmented in any manner consistent with Section 2055(e) or Section 2522(c) of the Internal Revenue Code on a petition provided for in Section 17200. **Leg.H.** Enacted Stats 1990 ch 79 §14 (AB 759), operative July 1, 1991.

Prior Law: Former Prob C §21540, similar to the present section, was added Stats 1987 ch 923 §101, operative January 1, 1988, and repealed Stats 1990 ch 79 §13, operative July 1, 1991.

§21541. Charitable lead trusts

If an instrument indicates the transferor's intention to comply with the requirements for a charitable lead trust as described in Section 170(f)(2)(B) and Section 2055(e)(2) or Section 2522(c)(2) of the Internal Revenue Code, the provisions of the instrument, including any power, duty, or discretionary authority given to a fiduciary, shall be construed to comply with the provisions of that section in order to conform to that intent. In no event shall the fiduciary take any action or have any power that impairs the charitable deduction. The provisions of the instrument may be augmented in any manner consistent with that intent upon a petition provided for in Section 17200. **Leg.H.** Enacted Stats 1990 ch 79 §14 (AB 759), operative July 1, 1991.

Prior Law: Former Prob C §21541, similar to the present section, was added Stats 1987 ch 923 §101, operative January 1, 1988, and repealed Stats 1990 ch 79 §13, operative July 1, 1991.

PART 6
FAMILY PROTECTION: OMITTED SPOUSES AND CHILDREN

Chapter 1. General Provisions.
Chapter 2. Omitted Spouses.
Chapter 3. Omitted Children.
Chapter 4. Applicability.

CHAPTER 1
GENERAL PROVISIONS

Application of part. §21600.
"Decedent's testamentary instruments"; "Estate". §21601.

§21600. Application of part

This part shall apply to property passing by will through a decedent's estate or by a trust, as defined in Section 82, that becomes irrevocable only on the death of the settlor. **Leg.H.** Added Stats 1997 ch 724 §34 (AB 1172).

§21601. "Decedent's testamentary instruments"; "Estate"

(a) For purposes of this part, "decedent's testamentary instruments" means the decedent's will or revocable trust.

(b) "Estate" as used in this part shall include a decedent's probate estate and all property held in any revocable trust that becomes irrevocable on the death of the decedent. **Leg.H.** Added Stats 1997 ch 724 §34 (AB 1172).

CHAPTER 2
OMITTED SPOUSES

Share of omitted spouse marrying spouse after execution of testamentary instruments. §21610.
Circumstances under which spouse receives no share. §21611.
Manner of satisfying share of spouse. §21612.

§21610. Share of omitted spouse marrying spouse after execution of testamentary instruments

Except as provided in Section 21611, if a decedent fails to provide in a testamentary instrument for the decedent's surviving spouse who married the decedent after the execution of all of the decedent's testamentary instruments, the omitted spouse shall receive a share in the decedent's estate, consisting of the following property in said estate:

(a) The one-half of the community property that belongs to the decedent under Section 100.

(b) The one-half of the quasi-community property that belongs to the decedent under Section 101.

(c) A share of the separate property of the decedent equal in value to that which the spouse would have received if the decedent had died without having executed a testamentary instrument, but in no event is the share to be more than one-half the value of the separate property in the estate. **Leg.H.** Added Stats 1997 ch 724 §34 (AB 1172).

§21611. Circumstances under which spouse receives no share

The spouse shall not receive a share of the estate under Section 21610 if any of the following is established:

(a) The decedent's failure to provide for the spouse in the decedent's testamentary instruments was intentional and that intention appears from the testamentary instruments.

(b) The decedent provided for the spouse by transfer outside of the estate passing by the decedent's testamentary instruments and the intention that the transfer be in lieu of a provision in said instruments is shown by statements of the decedent or from the amount of the transfer or by other evidence.

(c) The spouse made a valid agreement waiving the right to share in the decedent's estate.

(d)(1) If both of the following apply:

(A) The spouse was a care custodian, as that term is defined in Section 21362, of the decedent who was a dependent adult, as that term is defined in Section 21366, and the marriage commenced while the care custodian provided services to the decedent, or within 90 days after those services were last provided to the decedent.

(B) The decedent died less than six months after the marriage commenced.

(2) Notwithstanding paragraph (1), a spouse described by this subdivision shall be entitled to receive a share of the estate pursuant to Section 21610 if the spouse proves by clear and convincing evidence that the marriage between the spouse and the decedent was not the product of fraud or undue influence. **Leg.H.** Added Stats 1997 ch 724 §34 (AB 1172). Amended Stats 2019 ch 10 §3 (AB 328), effective January 1, 2020.

§21612. Manner of satisfying share of spouse

(a) Except as provided in subdivision (b), in satisfying a share provided by this chapter:

(1) The share will first be taken from the decedent's estate not disposed of by will or trust, if any.

(2) If that is not sufficient, so much as may be necessary to satisfy the share shall be taken from all beneficiaries of decedent's testamentary instruments in proportion to the value they may respectively receive. The proportion of each beneficiary's share that may be taken pursuant to this subdivision shall be determined based on values as of the date of the decedent's death.

(b) If the obvious intention of the decedent in relation to some specific gift or devise or other provision of a testamentary instrument would be defeated by the application of subdivision (a), the specific devise or gift or provision may be exempted from the apportionment under subdivision (a), and a different apportionment, consistent with the intention of the decedent, may be adopted. **Leg.H.** Added Stats 1997 ch 724 §34 (AB 1172), as Prob C §26112. Amended and renumbered by Stats 2003 ch 32 §17 (AB 167), effective January 1, 2004.

CHAPTER 3
OMITTED CHILDREN

Share of omitted child born or adopted after execution of testamentary instruments. §21620.
Circumstances for denial of share. §21621.
Decedent's erroneous belief. §21622.
Manner of satisfying share of omitted child. §21623.

§21620. Share of omitted child born or adopted after execution of testamentary instruments

Except as provided in Section 21621, if a decedent fails to provide in a testamentary instrument for a child of decedent born or adopted after the execution of all of the decedent's testamentary instruments, the omitted child shall receive a share in the decedent's estate equal in value to that which the child would have received if the decedent had died without having executed any testamentary instrument. **Leg.H.** Added Stats 1997 ch 724 §34 (AB 1172).

§21621. Circumstances for denial of share

A child shall not receive a share of the estate under Section 21620 if any of the following is established:

(a) The decedent's failure to provide for the child in the decedent's testamentary instruments was intentional and that intention appears from the testamentary instruments.

(b) The decedent had one or more children and devised or otherwise directed the disposition of substantially all the estate to the other parent of the omitted child.

(c) The decedent provided for the child by transfer outside of the estate passing by the decedent's testamentary instruments and the intention that the transfer be in lieu of a provision in said instruments is [1] **shown** by statements of the decedent or from the amount of the transfer or by other evidence. **Leg.H.** Added Stats 1997 ch 724 §34 (AB 1172). Amended Stats 2024 ch 80 §108.5 (SB 1525), effective January 1, 2025.

§21621. 2024 Deletes. [1] show

§21622. Decedent's erroneous belief

If, at the time of the execution of all of decedent's testamentary instruments effective at the time of decedent's death, the decedent failed to provide for a living child solely because the decedent believed the child to be dead or was unaware of the birth of the child, the child shall receive a share in the estate equal in value to that which the child would have received if the decedent had died without having executed any testamentary instruments. **Leg.H.** Added Stats 1997 ch 724 §34 (AB 1172).

§21623. Manner of satisfying share of omitted child

(a) Except as provided in subdivision (b), in satisfying a share provided by this chapter:

(1) The share will first be taken from the decedent's estate not disposed of by will or trust, if any.

(2) If that is not sufficient, so much as may be necessary to satisfy the share shall be taken from all beneficiaries of decedent's testamentary instruments in proportion to the value they may respectively receive. The proportion of each beneficiary's share that may be taken pursuant to this subdivision shall be determined based on values as of the date of the decedent's death.

(b) If the obvious intention of the decedent in relation to some specific gift or devise or other provision of a testamentary instrument would be defeated by the application of subdivision (a), the specific devise or gift or provision of a testamentary instrument may be exempted from the apportionment under subdivision (a), and a different apportionment, consistent with the intention of the decedent, may be adopted. **Leg.H.** Added Stats 1997 ch 724 §34 (AB 1172). Amended Stats 2003 ch 32 §16 (AB 167), effective January 1, 2004.

CHAPTER 4
APPLICABILITY

Applicability of part to decedent dying before January 1, 1998. §21630.

§21630. Applicability of part to decedent dying before January 1, 1998

This part does not apply if the decedent died before January 1, 1998. The law applicable prior to January 1, 1998, applies if the decedent died before January 1, 1998. **Leg.H.** Added Stats 1997 ch 724 §34 (AB 1172).

PART 7
CONTRACTS REGARDING TESTAMENTARY OR INTESTATE SUCCESSION

Contract to make will. §21700.

§21700. Contract to make will

(a) A contract to make a will or devise or other instrument, or not to revoke a will or devise or other instrument, or to die intestate, if made after the effective date of this statute, can be established only by one of the following:

(1) Provisions of a will or other instrument stating the material provisions of the contract.

(2) An expressed reference in a will or other instrument to a contract and extrinsic evidence proving the terms of the contract.

(3) A writing signed by the decedent evidencing the contract.

(4) Clear and convincing evidence of an agreement between the decedent and the claimant or a promise by the decedent to the claimant that is enforceable in equity.

(5) Clear and convincing evidence of an agreement between the decedent and another person for the benefit of the claimant or a promise by the decedent to another person for the benefit of the claimant that is enforceable in equity.

(b) The execution of a joint will or mutual wills does not create a presumption of a contract not to revoke the will or wills.

(c) A contract to make a will or devise or other instrument, or not to revoke a will or devise or other instrument, or to die intestate, if made prior to the effective date of this section, shall be construed under the law applicable to the contract prior to the effective date of this section. **Leg.H.** Added Stats 2000 ch 17 §8 (AB 1491), effective January 1, 2001.

Selected Provisions of the STANDARD GOVERNMENT CODE

of the

STATE OF CALIFORNIA

2025 EDITION

Table Showing 2024 Changes in the Government Code
Effective January 1, 2025, unless otherwise noted at end of section.

Section	Effect	Chapter	Section	Effect	Chapter
70615	Amended	631	11340.9	Amended	34

CONTENTS

Section

Title 1. General
Division 3.6. Claims and Actions Against Public Entities and Public Employees
  Part 1. Definitions
    Construction; Provisions governing 810
    "Employee" 810.2
    "Employment" 810.4
    "Enactment" 810.6
    "Injury" 810.8
    "Law" 811
    "Public entity" 811.2
    "Public employee" 811.4
    "Regulation" 811.6
    "Statute" 811.8
    State officers and trial court employees; Representation and defense; Adoption of rules of court; Effect on employment status 811.9
  Part 2. Liability of Public Entities and Public Employees
  Chapter 1. General Provisions Relating to Liability
    Article 1. Scope of Part
      Statute's inapplicability to contractual liability or nonmonetary relief 814
      Absence of implied repeal of Workers' Compensation statutes 814.2
    Article 2. Liability of Public Entities
      Absence of liability for injury except under statute; Liability as subject to statutory immunity and defenses 815
      Causes of injuries for which public entity liable; Absence of liability where employee immune 815.2
      Liability for intentional torts of elected officials; Plaintiff's recovery against assets of official; Indemnification; Defense for official during appeal 815.3
      Tortious act or omission of independent contractor; Limitation on liability . 815.4
      Liability for failure to discharge statutory duty 815.6
      Immunity from liability for National Guard activities 816
      Absence of liability for exemplary and punitive damages 818
      Adoption or failure to adopt enactment; Failure to enforce law 818.2
      Determination as to issuance, denial, suspension or revocation of license or similar authorization 818.4
      Liability of Department of Motor Vehicles to lienholder 818.5
      Failure to make any, or adequate, inspection of property 818.6
      Publication of records concerning person convicted of controlled substance violation; Use by school authorities 818.7
      Employee's misrepresentation 818.8
      Immunity from liability for advice given to small claims litigants 818.9
    Article 3. Liability of Public Employees
      Co-extensiveness with liability of private person; Defenses 820
      Exercise of discretion 820.2
      Tort liability of specified public employees 820.21
      Actions by peace officer or state or local law enforcement official deemed exercise of discretion 820.25
      Non-negligent law execution or enforcement; Absence of immunity for false arrest or imprisonment 820.4
      Good faith action under unconstitutional, invalid, or inapplicable enactment . 820.6
      Act or omission of another person; Absence of immunity from liability for own act or omission 820.8
      Vicarious liability of specified local government officials 820.9
      Adoption of, or failure to adopt, enactment; Failure to enforce enactment . 821
      Determination as to issuance, denial, suspension or revocation of license or similar authorization 821.2
      Failure to make any, or adequate, inspection of property 821.4
      Failure to restrict travel of cargo tank vehicles through tunnels 821.5
      Institution or prosecution of judicial or administrative proceeding 821.6
      Legally authorized entry on property; Limitation on exoneration 821.8
      Theft of money from employee's official custody; Absence of immunity from liability for employee's own act or omission 822
      Misrepresentations by public employees 822.2

v

TABLE OF CONTENTS

	Section
Peace officer widow, widower, heirs	823

Article 4. Indemnification of Public Employees

	Section
Duty of public entity to pay judgment, compromise, or settlement	825
Right of employee or former employee to recover amount of payment from public entity	825.2
Indemnification of public entity paying claim or judgment; When employee not liable to indemnify	825.4
When public entity may recover from employee or former employee	825.6

Article 5. Indemnification of Certain State Agents

Indemnification of health care providers defended by State	827

Chapter 2. Dangerous Conditions of Public Property
Article 1. General

"Dangerous condition"; "Protect against"; "Property of a public entity" and "public property"	830
Improvements financed by formation of special assessment district not public property	830.1
When condition not dangerous; Court's determination from evidence	830.2
Failure to provide traffic control signals, signs, or markings	830.4
Evidence not showing that public property was in dangerous condition; Happening of accident; Protective measure after injury	830.5
Liability of public entity or employee; Injury caused by construction plan or design or improvement	830.6
Failure to provide traffic signals, signs, or markings; Danger not reasonably foreseeable	830.8
Traffic signals controlled by emergency vehicle	830.9
Weather conditions affecting streets and highways; Danger not reasonably foreseeable	831
Natural condition of unimproved public property	831.2
Public beaches as in natural condition and unimproved	831.21
Liability for property damage or emotional distress off public entity's property resulting from land failure of unimproved public property; "Land failure"	831.25
Liability for injury on nondedicated road	831.3
Unpaved road providing access to fishing, hunting, or recreational areas; Trails	831.4
Public access programs by private nonprofit entities; "Public entity"; "Public employee"	831.5
Unimproved and unoccupied portions of ungranted tidelands, beds of navigable waters, etc.; Unsold portions of school lands	831.6
Liability to participant in or spectator to hazardous recreational activity	831.7
Exoneration for public entity that owns or operates dog park; Construction	831.7.5
Condition of reservoir; Condition of canals, conduits, or drains; Condition or use of unlined flood control channels or adjacent groundwater recharge spreading grounds; When exoneration from liability absent	831.8

Article 2. Liability of Public Entities

When public entity liable for injury caused by dangerous condition of property	835
What constitutes actual notice; Requisite showing of constructive notice; Admissible evidence	835.2
Conditions causing injury for which public entity not liable; Reasonable act or omission	835.4

Article 3. Liability of Public Employees

Property conditions causing injury for which employee not liable; Available immunity and defenses	840
Conditions causing injury for which employee liable; Requisite showing by plaintiff	840.2
What constitutes actual notice of dangerous condition; Requisite showing for establishment of constructive notice	840.4
Absence of liability for condition resulting in injury where act or omission creating condition was reasonable	840.6

Chapter 3. Police and Correctional Activities

"Prisoner"	844
Injury by or to prisoner	844.6
Failure to provide any or adequate police protection; Responding to alarm	845
Failure to provide prison, correctional facility, equipment, personnel, etc.	845.2
Interference with prisoner's right to judicial determination as to legality of confinement	845.4
Failure to furnish prisoner medical care	845.6

	Section
Injury from prisoner's parole or release; Injury caused by escaping or escaped prisoner, arrestee, etc.	845.8
Injury from failure to make arrest or retain person in custody	846

Chapter 4. Fire Protection

Failure to provide fire protection service	850
Failure to maintain sufficient fire protection personnel or facilities	850.2
Injury caused in fighting fires and from condition of fire fighting equipment or facilities	850.4
Act or omission of employee of public entity performing service outside fire protection area	850.6
Transportation of person injured by fire, etc.	850.8

Chapter 4.5. Unmanned Aircraft

Liability for damage by local public entity or public employee providing emergency services	853
Scope of immunity	853.1
"Unmanned aircraft"; "Unmanned aircraft system"	853.5

Chapter 5. Medical, Hospital and Public Health Activities

"Medical facility"	854
Continuity of care for individuals transitioning from developmental centers to the community; Retention of staff; Definitions applying to chapter	854.1
"Mental institution"	854.2
"County psychiatric hospital"	854.3
"Mental illness or addiction"	854.4
"Confine"	854.5
Injury by or to person committed to mental institution	854.8
Injury from failure of public entity to provide adequate equipment, personnel or facilities	855
Interference with inmate's right to judicial determination as to legality of confinement	855.2
Decision as to performance or nonperformance of disease prevention, etc.; Nonnegligent execution of decision	855.4
Injury from failure to make any or adequate physical or mental examination	855.6
Diagnosis and treatment of mental illness or addiction	855.8
Determination as to confinement for mental illness or addiction; Parole, leave of absence, or release	856
Injury or death when person confined for mental illness or addiction escapes	856.2
Failure to admit person to medical facility	856.4
Exemption from liability for participation in influenza immunization program	856.6

Chapter 6. Administration of Tax Laws

"Tax"	860
Acts or omissions not imposing liability	860.2
Inapplicability of chapter on tax refund, adjustment, etc.	860.4

Chapter 7. Use of Pesticides

Liability for injuries caused by use of "pesticide"	862

Chapter 8. Activities to Abate an Impending Peril

Legislative findings and intent	865
Exemption of local entities from liability; Avoidance of impending peril due to gradual earth movement	866
Exemption of employees	867

Chapter 21. Tort Liability Under Agreements Between Public Entities

"Agreement"	895
Joint and several liability of public entities entering into agreement	895.2
Agreement's provision for contribution or indemnification	895.4
Contribution between parties in absence of provision in agreement	895.6
Application of chapter with respect to its effective date	895.8

Part 3. Claims Against Public Entities

Chapter 1. General

Article 1. Definitions

Governing provisions	900
"Board"	900.2
"Judicial branch entity"	900.3
"Local public entity"	900.4
"State"	900.6
Date of accrual of cause of action in determining time for presenting claim	901

TABLE OF CONTENTS

	Section
Article 2. General Provisions	
Required presentation of claims against local public entities; Exceptions	905
Inverse condemnation	905.1
Required presentation of claims against state; Applicability to violations of California Whistleblower Protection Act	905.2
Claims eligible for consideration by Commission on State Mandates	905.3
Nonexclusiveness of provisions as to presentation and payment of claims	905.4
Civil liability of school district, officers, directors or employees from exposure to asbestos	905.5
Inapplicability of provisions to claims against Regents of University of California	905.6
Claims against judicial branch	905.7
Absence of additional liability	905.8
Claims against California State University	905.9
Interest on amount allowed on the claim	906
Offset of delinquent amount due for services	907
Chapter 2. Presentation and Consideration of Claims	
Article 1. General	
Person presenting claim; Contents of claim	910
Signing claim	910.2
Claim forms	910.4
Amendment of claims	910.6
Board's notice of claim's insufficiency	910.8
Waiver of defense by failure to give notice of claim's insufficiency	911
Times for presentment of claims	911.2
Notice that claim not filed timely; Contents	911.3
Application to present claim not timely filed; Time limitation	911.4
Board's grant or denial of application to present late claim	911.6
Notice of board's action on application	911.8
Time claim deemed presented where leave granted	912.2
Time for board's action on claim	912.4
Actions by Trustees of California State University on claims	912.5
Procedure in claims against local public entity	912.6
Procedure in action against judicial branch entity or judge	912.7
Procedure as to board's action on claims against State; Report and recommendations to Legislature	912.8
Notice of board's action on claim	913
Re-examination of rejected claim	913.2
Article 2. Manner of Presentation and of Giving Notice	
Delivery or mailing of claim, amendment, or application	915
Manner, time and proof of mailing claim, etc.	915.2
Delivery or mailing of notice of board action	915.4
Chapter 3. Proceedings to Determine Constitutionality of Claims Against the State	
"Omnibus claim appropriation"	920
Submission of omnibus claim appropriation to Controller	920.2
Controller's withholding payment of questioned portion of appropriation	920.4
Disbursement of disputed portion of appropriation; Proceedings to compel Controller's issuance of warrant	920.6
Reversion of withheld funds in event of Legislature's reconsideration	920.8
Chapter 4. Presentation of Claims to State Controller	
"Department"	925
Exemption of Legislature's expenses and of official salaries	925.2
Presentation of claims against state for which appropriations made or state funds available	925.4
Controller's warrant; Prerequisite audit	925.6
Warrant on approval of claim	925.8
Disapproval of claim	926
Showing for reconsideration of rejected claim	926.2
Appeal to, and reconsideration on finding by, department	926.4
Appeal to Legislature after final rejection	926.6
Federal agency's claim against credits owed by State; Certification of facts; Warrant payable to United States Treasurer	926.8
Interest on liquidated claim against another public entity	926.10
Chapter 4.5. Prompt Payment of Claims	
Citation of chapter; Legislative intent; Application of chapter	927

TABLE OF CONTENTS

	Section
Requirement of timely payment; Late payment penalties	927.1
Definitions	927.2
Submission of invoices, notice of refund or other payment due, to controller; Disputes	927.3
Maximum time for payment of undisputed invoice; Penalties	927.4
Reimbursement claims under Medi-Cal	927.5
Payment of penalties by state agencies	927.6
Payment of penalties by Controller	927.7
Additional appropriations to pay penalties	927.8
Annual report on late payment penalties paid by agencies	927.9
Payment of subcontractors and suppliers	927.10
Effect of fire season, failure to enact budget, major calamity, or criminal act	927.11
Applicability of other section	927.12
Failure to submit correct claim schedule to Controller; Penalties; Payment of claim schedule by Controller; Interest payment; Applicability	927.13

Chapter 5. Claims Procedures Established by Agreement

Provisions of state agency agreement	930
Provisions of local public entity agreement; Incorporation of ordinance or resolution	930.2
Exception as to tardy claims presented with permission	930.4
Presentation of, and determination on, claim as prerequisite to suit	930.6

Chapter 6. Claims Procedures Established by Public Entities

Governing procedure prescribed in charter, ordinance or regulation	935
Establishment of local claims board or commission; Warrant	935.2
Performance of functions of local governing body by employee; Restriction as to amount of claim allowed	935.4
Payments by state agency	935.6
Payment by Department of Transportation	935.7
Payments by Judicial Council	935.8
Payments by Trustees of California State University	935.9

Part 4. Actions Against Public Entities and Public Employees

Chapter 1. General

Article 1. Definitions

Governing provisions	940
"Board"	940.2
"Judicial branch entity"	940.3
"Local public entity"	940.4
"State"	940.6

Article 2. Construction

Claimant's right to resort to mandamus or other proceeding	942
Inapplicability to claims or actions against Regents of University of California	943
Disclaimer of additional liability	944

Chapter 2. Actions Against Public Entities

Public entity's right to sue and liability to suit	945
Application of rules of practice in civil actions	945.2
Action while charges pending; Limitation period tolled	945.3
Prohibition against suit in absence of presentation of claim and action thereon	945.4
Limitation as to time for commencing suit when claim required; Time for person sentenced to imprisonment	945.6
Applicable statute of limitations when claim presentation not required	945.8
Effect of claimant's acceptance of amount allowed, on right to maintain suit	946
Filings prerequisite to bar to sue "public agency" because of nonpresentation of claim	946.4
Judicial relief from bar to sue because of nonpresentation of claim	946.6
Settlement by state agency	948
Settlement by Judicial Council	948.1
Compromise by local governing body; Delegation of authority	949

Chapter 3. Actions Against Public Employees

Necessity for presentation of claim in order to maintain action	950
When action barred for failure to present claim or commence action within time specified	950.2
Pleading and proof excusing failure to present claim within time prescribed	950.4
Requisites for maintenance of action; Rejection; Time for commencement of suit	950.6
Invalidity of charter, ordinance or regulation requiring presentation of claim	950.8
Alleging individual liability	951

TABLE OF CONTENTS

	Section
Chapter 4. Special Provisions Relating to Actions Against the State	
Venue of action for taking or damaging property; Transfer	955
Immunity from liability for earthquake predictions	955.1
Venue of action for death or injury to person or personal property; Transfer	955.2
Venue of action by local government or agency against state	955.3
Officers on whom summons served and duty to defend imposed	955.4
Actions arising out of work performed by Department of Transportation	955.6
Actions arising out of work performed by Department of Water Resources	955.8
Service of summons in actions against judicial branch entity	955.9
Proceedings in action to partition property in which State, division or agency has a remainder or undivided fractional interest	956
Chapter 5. Special Provisions Relating to Actions Against Local Public Entities	
"Public agency"	960
Service of process in absence of filings	960.2
Order for substituted service on Secretary of State; Manner of service; Fee required	960.3
Notice to public agency by Secretary of State by registered mail; Forwarding copy of papers to Attorney General	960.4
Powers and duties of Attorney General in defense of public agency; Delegation of defense to county or district attorney	960.5
Conformity of service with "statement in the Registry of Public Agencies"	960.8
Chapter 6. Postjudgment Settlement Conference	
Request for mandatory conference by public entity; Time for conference	962

Part 5. Payment of Claims and Judgments

Chapter 1. Payment of Claims and Judgments Against the State

Designation of fund; Report to Legislature on insufficient funds to pay claims, settlements or judgments against state	965
Allowance of claim against state not exceeding specified amount	965.1
Controller's warrant; Exemption from auditing requirement	965.2
Notice of payment; Reversion	965.3
Governor's report to Legislature	965.4
Enforceability of judgment; Duration; Interest	965.5
Conditions for payment	965.6
Reports concerning preventive action	965.65
Writ of mandate; Legislative discretion	965.7
Writ of mandate to compel certification of sufficient appropriation	965.8
Application of chapter	965.9

Chapter 2. Payment of Judgments Against Local Public Entities

Article 1. General

Definitions	970
Enforceability of judgment; Duration; Calculation of interest	970.1
Duty of public entity to pay judgment in manner prescribed; Mandamus	970.2
Payment from available funds; Unappropriated funds; Appropriated funds	970.4
Deferring payment	970.5
Installment payments	970.6
Required funding	970.8
Definitions; Application of tax limitations	971
Judgments as legal investments or security	971.2

Article 2. Funding Judgments With Bonds

"Board"; "Local taxing entity"	975
Resolution for incurrence of bonded indebtedness	975.2
Publication or posting of notice of hearing	975.4
Notice accompanying copy of resolution	975.6
Conduct of hearing; Determination by board	975.8
Resolution for bond election	976
Resolution as notice of election; Publication or posting	976.2
Application of provisions governing general elections	976.4
Qualified voters	976.6
Vote authorizing board to issue bonds	976.8
Form of bonds; Denominations; Time and place for payment	977
Redemption of bonds	977.2
Signing of bonds	977.4
Sale of bonds	977.6
Action to determine validity of bonds	977.8
Exemption of bonds from taxation; Bonds as legal investments	978

TABLE OF CONTENTS

Section

Payment of bonds and interest; Property in local entity as subject to taxation; Levy of tax or assessment	978.2
Use of proceeds from sale of bonds	978.4
Resolution voiding unsold bonds	978.6
Authority provided in article as supplementary	978.8

Chapter 3.7. Procedures Applicable to State and Local Public Entities
Periodic payments on judgments by public entities	984

Chapter 4. Procedures Applicable to State and Local Public Entities
Collateral source payments in actions against public entities	985

Part 6. Insurance
"Local public entity"	989
Matters against which a local public entity may insure itself	990
Authority of Judicial Council to insure officer or attachés	990.2
Kinds of insurance that may be provided	990.4
Cost	990.6
Agreement for insurance between two or more local public entities or specified nonprofit corporations, or mutual water company and public agency	990.8
Insurance or indemnity by local public entity for health care tort claims against person rendering care without compensation	990.9
Other enactment authorizing or requiring local public entity to insure	991
Exercise of authority as not imposing liability or impairing defense	991.2

Part 7. Defense of Public Employees
Duty to provide for defense of action	995
When public entity may refuse to defend; Notification of refusal	995.2
Action against official for interference with disclosures; Liability for costs of defense	995.3
When provision for defense permitted but not required	995.4
Defense of administrative proceedings	995.6
Defense of criminal actions; Removal proceedings	995.8
Defense or indemnification of witness for public entity	995.9
Methods of providing defense	996
Refusal of entity to represent employee	996.4
Rights under this part as additional to other contractual or statutory rights	996.6

Title 2. Government of the State of California
Division 3. Executive Department
Part 1. State Departments and Agencies
Chapter 3.5. Administrative Regulations and Rulemaking
Article 1. General

Legislative findings and declarations	11340
Declarations and intent regarding establishment of Office of Administrative Law	11340.1
Office of Administrative Law; Director and deputy director	11340.2
Employment and compensation of assistants and other employees	11340.3
Recommendations on administrative rulemaking	11340.4
Adoption of guidelines, bulletins and manuals as regulations	11340.5
Petition requesting adoption, amendment, or repeal of regulation; Contents	11340.6
Procedure upon petition requesting adoption, amendment or repeal of regulation	11340.7
Electronic communications	11340.85
Inapplicable provisions	11340.9
Inapplicable provisions	11340.9
Identification numbers	11341
Authority not conferred on state agencies	11342.1
Consistency with statute; Effectuation of purpose of statute	11342.2
Regulations	11342.4

Article 2. Definitions

Governing definitions	11342.510
"Agency"	11342.520
"Building standard"	11342.530
"Cost impact"	11342.535
"Director"	11342.540
"Emergency"	11342.545
"Major regulation"	11342.548
"Office"	11342.550
"Order of repeal"	11342.560
"Performance standard"	11342.570

TABLE OF CONTENTS

	Section
"Plain English"	11342.580
"Prescriptive standard"	11342.590
"Proposed action"	11342.595
"Regulation"	11342.600
"Small Business"	11342.610

Article 3. Filing and Publication

Procedure	11343
Style of regulations; Endorsement	11343.1
Endorsement of time and date of filing and maintenance of file for public inspection	11343.2
Vehicle weight impacts and ability of vehicle manufacturers or operators to comply with laws limiting weight of vehicles to be taken into account when promulgating administrative regulations	11343.3
Effective date of regulation or order of repeal; Applicability	11343.4
Filing copies of Code of Regulations or Regulatory Code Supplement	11343.5
Rebuttable presumptions raised by filing of certified copy	11343.6
Filing and publication of regulation or order of repeal not required to be filed	11343.8

Article 4. The California Code of Regulations, the California Code of Regulations Supplement, and the California Regulatory Notice Register

Publication of Code of Regulations and Code of Regulations Supplement; Availability of regulations on internet	11344
Publication of Regulatory Notice Register	11344.1
Furnishing Code and Supplement to county clerks or delegates	11344.2
Time of publication of documents	11344.3
Sale of Code, Supplement and Regulatory Notice Register	11344.4
Rebuttable presumption raised by publication of regulations	11344.6
Authority of state agencies to purchase copies of Code, Supplement, or Register or to print and distribute special editions	11344.7
"California Administrative Code"; "California Administrative Notice Register"; "California Administrative Code Supplement"	11344.9
Identification number not required	11345

Article 5. Public Participation: Procedure for Adoption of Regulations

Purpose and applicability of article; Subsequent legislation	11346
Emergency regulations and orders of repeal	11346.1
Availability to public of copy of proposed regulation; Initial statement of reasons for proposed action	11346.2
Assessment of potential for adverse economic impact on businesses and individuals	11346.3
Adoption of regulations for conducting standardized regulatory impact analyses; Submission; Publication	11346.36
Notice of proposed action	11346.4
Increased public participation	11346.45
Contents of notice of proposed adoption, amendment, or repeal of regulation	11346.5
Duty of agency, upon request from person with certain disability, to provide narrative description of proposed regulation	11346.6
Link on website	11346.7
Hearing	11346.8
Final statements of reasons for proposing adoption or amendment of regulation; Informative digest	11346.9
Decision not to proceed with proposed action	11347
Addition to rulemaking file	11347.1
File of rulemaking; Contents and availability of file	11347.3
Rulemaking records	11348

Article 6. Review of Proposed Regulations

Definitions	11349
Review of regulations; Regulations to govern review process; Return to adopting agency	11349.1
Review of standardized regulatory impact analyses; Report; Notice of noncompliance	11349.1.5
Adding material to file	11349.2
Time for review of regulations; Procedure on disapproval; Return of regulations	11349.3
Rewriting and resubmission of regulation; Review	11349.4
Governor's review of decisions	11349.5
Review by office of emergency regulation	11349.6

	Section
Article 7. Review of Existing Regulations	
Priority review of regulations	11349.7
Repeal of regulation for which statutory authority is repealed, ineffective or inoperative	11349.8
Review of notice of repeal	11349.9
Article 8. Judicial Review	
Judicial declaration regarding validity of regulation; Grounds for invalidity	11350
Judicial declaration as to validity of disapproved or repealed regulation	11350.3
Article 9. Special Procedures	
Applicability of specified provisions to Public Utilities Commission and Workers' Compensation Appeals Board	11351
Applicability of chapter	11352
Application of chapter to water quality control policy, plans, or guidelines	11353
Effect of certain sections on court determination of applicability of chapter	11354
Application of chapter to certain policies, plans and guidelines of San Francisco Bay Conservation and Development Commission	11354.1
Applicability of articles to building standards	11356
Instructions for determining impact of proposed action on local or state agencies or on school districts	11357
Regulations relating to fire and panic safety	11359
Applicability of chapter; Adoption or revision of regulations, guidelines, or criteria	11361

Chapter 4. Office of Administrative Hearings

Article 1. General Provisions	
Chapters constituting Administrative Procedure Act	11370
"Director"	11370.1
Office of Administrative Hearings in Department of General Services; Director	11370.2
Appointment and assignment of administrative law judges and other personnel	11370.3
Determination and collection of costs	11370.4
Recommendations on administrative adjudication	11370.5
Article 2. Medical Quality Hearing Panel	
Members of panel; Published decisions; Experts	11371
Conduct of hearing by administrative law judge	11372
Conduct of proceedings under Administrative Procedure Act	11373
Facilities and support personnel for review committee panel	11373.3
Article 3. State Agency Reports and Forms Appeals	
Appeal filed by business	11380

Chapter 4.5. Administrative Adjudication: General Provisions

Article 1. Preliminary Provisions	
Administrative Procedure Act; References to superseded provisions	11400
Operative date of chapter; Applicability	11400.10
Adoption of interim or permanent regulations	11400.20
Article 2. Definitions	
Definitions governing construction of chapter	11405.10
"Adjudicative proceeding"	11405.20
"Agency"	11405.30
"Agency head"	11405.40
"Decision"	11405.50
"Party"	11405.60
"Person"	11405.70
"Presiding officer"	11405.80
Article 3. Application of Chapter	
Decision requiring evidentiary hearing	11410.10
Applicability to agencies	11410.20
Applicability to local agencies	11410.30
Adoption of chapter by exempt agency	11410.40
Applicability to specified proceedings	11410.50
Quasi-public entity	11410.60
Article 4. Governing Procedure	
Determination of procedure	11415.10
Statute to prevail over provision of chapter	11415.20
Actions by Governor to avoid loss or delay of federal funds	11415.30
Waiver of right conferred by provisions	11415.40
Procedure for decision for which adjudicative proceeding not required	11415.50
Decision by settlement	11415.60

TABLE OF CONTENTS

	Section
Article 5. Alternative Dispute Resolution	
Mediation or arbitration	11420.10
Model regulations for alternative dispute resolution	11420.20
Protection of communications	11420.30
Article 6. Administrative Adjudication Bill of Rights	
Required procedures and rights of persons affected	11425.10
Hearings open to public; Order for closure	11425.20
Specified persons not to serve as presiding officer	11425.30
Disqualification of presiding officer	11425.40
Decision to be in writing; Statement of factual and legal basis	11425.50
Decisions relied on as precedents; Index of precedent decisions	11425.60
Article 7. Ex Parte Communications	
Ex parte communications	11430.10
Permissible ex parte communications	11430.20
Permissible ex parte communication from agency that is party	11430.30
Disclosure of communication received while proceeding is pending	11430.40
Communication in violation of provisions	11430.50
Prohibited communication as grounds to disqualify presiding officer	11430.60
Agency head delegated to hear or decide proceeding	11430.70
Communication between presiding officer and agency head delegated to hear proceeding	11430.80
Article 8. Language Assistance	
"Language assistance"	11435.05
Interpretation for deaf or hard-of-hearing persons	11435.10
Provision of language assistance by state agencies	11435.15
Hearing or medical examination to be conducted in English	11435.20
Cost of providing interpreter	11435.25
Publication of list of certified interpreters	11435.30
Publication of list of certified medical examination interpreters	11435.35
Designation of languages for certification	11435.40
Application fees to take interpreter examinations	11435.45
Removal of person from list of certified interpreters	11435.50
Qualification and use of noncertified interpreters	11435.55
Party to be advised of right to interpreter	11435.60
Rules of confidentiality applicable to interpreters	11435.65
Article 9. General Procedural Provisions	
Review of decision	11440.10
Service of writing or electronic document; Notice	11440.20
Conduct of hearing by telephone, television, or other electronic means	11440.30
Proceedings involving sexual offenses; Limitations on evidence	11440.40
Benevolent gestures as admission of liability; Limitations on evidence	11440.45
Intervention; Grant of motion; Conditions	11440.50
Indication of person paying for written communication	11440.60
Article 10. Informal Hearing	
Legislative findings and declarations	11445.10
Circumstances permitting use of informal hearing procedure	11445.20
Notice of informal procedure	11445.30
Application of procedures otherwise required	11445.40
Denial of use of informal procedure; Conversion to formal hearing; Cross-examination	11445.50
Identity of witnesses or other sources	11445.60
Article 11. Subpoenas	
Application of article	11450.05
Issuance for attendance or production of documents	11450.10
Persons who may issue subpoenas; Service	11450.20
Objection to subpoena; Motion for protective order; Motion to quash	11450.30
Witness's mileage and fees	11450.40
Written notice to witness to attend; Service	11450.50
Article 12. Enforcement of Orders and Sanctions	
Grounds for contempt sanction	11455.10
Certification of facts to justify contempt sanction; Other procedure	11455.20
Bad faith actions; Order to pay expenses including attorney's fees	11455.30
Article 13. Emergency Decision	
Conduct of proceeding under emergency procedure	11460.10
Emergency decision	11460.20

	Section
Conditions for issuance of emergency decision	11460.30
Notice and hearing prior to decision	11460.40
Statement of factual and legal basis and reasons for emergency decision	11460.50
Formal or informal proceeding after issuance of emergency decision	11460.60
Agency record	11460.70
Judicial review of decision	11460.80

Article 14. Declaratory Decision

Conduct of proceeding under declaratory decision procedure	11465.10
Application; Issuance of decision	11465.20
Notice of application for decision	11465.30
Applicable hearing procedure	11465.40
Actions of agency after receipt of application	11465.50
Contents of decision; Status and binding effect of decision	11465.60
Model regulations	11465.70

Article 15. Conversion of Proceeding

Conversion into another type of proceeding	11470.10
Appointment of successor to preside over new proceeding	11470.20
Record of original proceeding	11470.30
Duties of presiding officer of new proceeding	11470.40
Adoption of regulations to govern conversion	11470.50

Article 16. Administrative Adjudication Code of Ethics

Name of rules	11475
Application	11475.10
Law governing conduct	11475.20
Definitions	11475.30
Inapplicable provisions of Code of Judicial Ethics	11475.40
Violations	11475.50
Compliance requirements	11475.60
Construction and intent	11475.70

Chapter 5. Administrative Adjudication: Formal Hearing

Definitions	11500
Application of chapter to agency	11501
Administrative law judges	11502
Accusation or District Statement of Reduction in Force	11503
Statement of issues	11504
Applicability of references to accusations to statements of issues	11504.5
Service of accusation or District Statement of Reduction in Force and accompanying papers; Notice of defense or notice of participation; Request for hearing	11505
Filing of notice of defense or notice of participation; Contents; Right to hearing on the merits	11506
Amended or supplemental accusation or District Statement of Reduction in Force; Objections	11507
Consolidated proceedings; Separate hearings	11507.3
Exclusivity of discovery provisions	11507.5
Request for discovery	11507.6
Motion to compel discovery; Order	11507.7
Time and place of hearing	11508
Notice of hearing	11509
Depositions	11511
Prehearing conference; Conduct by telephone or other electronic means; Conversion to ADR or informal hearing; Prehearing order	11511.5
Settlement conference	11511.7
Administrative law judge to preside over hearing; Disqualification; Reporting of proceedings	11512
Evidence	11513
Affidavits	11514
Official notice	11515
Amendment of accusation or District Statement of Reduction in Force after submission	11516
Contested cases	11517
Copies of decision to parties	11518
Application to correct mistake or error in decision; Modification; Service of correction	11518.5

TABLE OF CONTENTS

	Section
Effective date of decision; Stay of execution; Notice of suspension or revocation; Restitution; Actual knowledge as condition of enforcement	11519
Order of restitution for financial loss or damages	11519.1
Defaults and uncontested cases	11520
Reconsideration	11521
Reinstatement of license or reduction of penalty	11522
Judicial review	11523
Continuances; Requirement of good cause; Judicial review of denial	11524
Voting by mail	11526
Charge against funds of agency	11527
Oaths	11528
Interim orders	11529

Title 3. Government of Counties
Division 2. Officers
Part 3. Other Officers
Chapter 2. Sheriff
Article 7. Fees

	Section
Fees to be charged and collected	26720
Waiver and refund of fees	26720.5
Fees for enumerated sections	26720.9
Service or execution of process or notice; Service of writ of execution and notice of levy	26721
Unlawful detainer; Fee for service of summons, complaint, and prejudgment claim of right to possession	26721.1
Fees for service, cancellation of service, and a not-found return	26721.2
Fee for serving, executing, or processing writ or order	26722
Fee for opening safe deposit box	26723
Fee for execution of process on real property	26725
Additional parcels	26725.1
Fee for keeping property under writ; Maintaining custody under levy	26726
Copy of writ, process, paper, order, or notice	26727
Preparing and posting notices of personal property sales	26728
Additional notices	26728.1
Furnishing notice for publication	26729
Conducting or postponing sale of real or personal property	26730
Deposit of portion into special fund; Use of funds	26731
Publication of notice in newspaper	26732
Service of writ of possession of real property	26733.5
Making levy on personal property held under attachment	26734
Cancellation of service or execution of process or notice	26736
Not-found return	26738
Execution and delivery of deed or certificate of redemption	26740
Execution and delivery of certificate or deed of sale	26741
Execution and delivery of other instruments	26742
Subpoenaing witnesses	26743
Service or execution of bench warrant	26744
Fees for processing civil warrant	26744.5
Summoning trial jury	26745
Disbursement of money collected under writ of attachment, execution, possession or sale; Deposit in special fund; Use of special fund	26746
Fee for certification of correction on specified citations; Disposition of proceeds	26746.1
Transporting prisoners to county jail	26747
Expenses for inspecting, checking, releasing or other handling of property	26748
Expenses for transporting persons to hospitals, prisons, or other state institutions	26749
Fees for serving earnings withholding order; Additional fees prohibited	26750
Fee for report of repossession of vehicle; Release of vehicle by person in possession	26751

Chapter 3. County Clerk
Article 2. Fees

	Section
Fees to be charged and collected	26820
Fee for preparing copies of record, etc., on file in county clerk's office	26831
Certifying copy of paper, record, or proceeding	26833
Certificates where fee not fixed	26836
Comparing copy of paper, record, or proceeding	26837

	Section
Exemplification of record or other paper	26839
Issuance of marriage license; Disposition of fee; Fee in full for all services	26840
Filing marriage certificate	26840.1
Marriage license; Fee on issuance outside normal hours	26840.2
Fee increases for support of family conciliation court or maintenance of conciliation and mediation services	26840.3
Issuance fees for maintenance of domestic violence centers	26840.7
Filing fees for maintenance of domestic violence centers	26840.8
Increased license fees in Alameda County for governmental oversight and coordination of agencies dealing with domestic violence	26840.10
Increased license fees in Solano County for governmental oversight and coordination of agencies dealing with domestic violence	26840.11
Making record of certificate of revivor	26847
Filing bond of notary public	26849.1
Filing and indexing other papers	26850
Recording or registering license or certificate; Issuance of certificate or license and certificate	26851
Certificate to official capacity of public official	26852
Taking affidavit	26853
Fee for searching records and files	26854
Taking acknowledgment	26855
Fees for filing power of attorney for surety insurer	26855.1
Fee for filing financial statement of surety insurer; Effect of section on necessity of statement	26855.2
Fee for issuing certificate of authority of admitted surety issuer	26855.3
When fees not to be charged	26857
Matters relating to pensions	26858
Fee of commissioner of civil marriages for performing ceremony	26861

Chapter 6. Recorder

Article 3.5. Social Security Number Truncation Program

Definitions	27300
County recorder to create social security truncation program; Components of program	27301
Due diligence in locating and truncating social security numbers; Request to truncate by any person	27302
Availability of official record and public record	27303
Copy of DD214 official record	27303.5
Funding of truncation program	27304
Reporting progress to Legislature	27305
Authority of county recorder	27307

Article 5. Fees

Fees generally	27360
"Folio"	27360.5
Recording and indexing fee	27361
Documents serially incorporated or attached as separate	27361.1
Additional fee for reference to other recorded documents	27361.2
Fee for recording release of lien by state or local government	27361.3
Additional filing fee [Effective until January 1, 2026; Repealed effective January 1, 2026]	27361.4
"Page"; "Sheet"	27361.5
Margins; Quality of paper; Identification of previously recorded documents	27361.6
Substituted or copied document legible for photographic record	27361.7
Additional indexing	27361.8
Filing of preliminary notice	27361.9
Fee for certificate under seal	27364
Fee for copy of birth, death, or marriage certificate	27365
Fee for copy of other record or paper and fees for photographic, etc., reproductions	27366
Fee for searching records for birth, death, or marriage certificate	27369
Fees for reproducing map or plat in record by photographic method	27371
Fee for recording, etc., map where land subdivided	27372
Acknowledgment fee	27375
Fee for administering and certifying oaths or affirmations	27379
Fee for filing, etc., paper not required to be recorded	27380
Military discharges, etc.	27381

	Section
Fee for services rendered to State, municipality, etc.	27383
Recordation of involuntary lien	27387
Fee for Los Angeles County notification [Effective until January 1, 2030; Repealed effective January 1, 2030]	27387.1
Fee for Los Angeles County notification [Operative January 1, 2030]	27387.1
Additional recording fee; Payment to Real Estate Fraud Protection Trust Fund; Distribution	27388
Fee for recording real estate instrument, paper, or notice; Exemptions; Deposit in Building Homes and Jobs Trust Fund	27388.1
Citation of article; Definitions	27390
Authority to establish electronic recording delivery system and enter into contracts [Effective until January 1, 2027; Repealed effective January 1, 2027]	27391
Authority to establish electronic recording delivery system and enter into contracts [Operative January 1, 2027]	27391
Certification required; Approval of attorney general	27392
Adoption of regulations [Effective until January 1, 2027; Repealed effective January 1, 2027]	27393
Adoption of regulations [Operative January 1, 2027]	27393
Use of computer security auditor; Auditing electronic recording delivery system	27394
Ineligibility of individuals to be auditor or to be granted secure access to system; Fingerprinting and criminal offender record requests	27395
Monitoring the system; Action for relief from fraudulent transactions	27396
Payment of regulation and oversight costs by county; Deposit of fees into Electronic Recording Authorization Fund	27397
Contracting to be authorized submitter of records; Certification requirements	27397.5
Evaluation of system	27398
Construction with other law	27399

Title 8. The Organization and Government of Courts
Chapter 1. General Provisions

Payment of fees in criminal and civil proceedings	68092
Legislative findings; Courts providing interpreters to all parties requiring services in civil actions	68092.1
Expert witness fees	68092.5
Witness fees	68093
Grand jury	68094
Coroner's jury	68095
Compensation to government employees subpoenaed as witnesses; Reimbursement by litigant	68096.1
Payment in civil cases of mileage and fees for one day in advance; Demand; Effect of nonpayment; Exceptions	68097
Testimony by peace officers, firefighters, or certain government employees; Service of subpoena; "Tribunal"	68097.1
Salary and expenses of public employees attending as witnesses; Reimbursement	68097.2
Service of subpoena on California Highway Patrol member when CCP §1989 inapplicable	68097.3
Compensation for highway patrol members appearing as witnesses; Reimbursement to State by party seeking subpoena	68097.4
Return of peace officer for subsequent proceedings	68097.5
Reimbursement requirement of indigents	68097.55
Subpoenas for depositions of certain employees pursuant to CCP §§2025.010 et seq.	68097.6
Deposits taxable as costs by prevailing party	68097.8
Funds chargeable with fees in criminal cases	68098

Chapter 2. The Judicial Council
Article 5. The Trial Court Delay Reduction Act

Citation of article	68600
Adoption of standards of timely disposition	68603
Statistics as to compliance of superior courts and branch courts; Study; Reports	68604
Application of article	68605.5
Responsibilities and duties of judges	68607
Removal of action or proceeding from delay reduction program	68607.5
Assignments and powers of judges	68608
Rules for arbitration of uninsured motorist cases	68609.5
Training program	68610

	Section
Procedures, standards, and policies	68612
Funds	68613
Contracting out for performance of duties	68615
Minimum time periods for delay reduction rules	68616
Report	68617
Establishment of delay reduction program by superior courts; Exemptions	68620

Article 6. Waiver of Court Fees and Costs

Legislative findings and declarations	68630
Initial fee waiver	68631
"Applicant"; "Petitioner"	68631.5
Permission to proceed without paying court fees and costs	68632
Applicant for initial fee waiver required to complete Judicial Council application and financial statement; Confidentiality; Counsel	68633
Processing and determination of fee waiver applications in trial courts	68634
Processing and determination of fee waiver applications in appellate courts	68634.5
Waivers of trial court fees	68635
Granting of initial fee waiver â Notification requirement of change in financial condition; Hearing to determine status of court fee waiver; Obtaining court services in bad faith	68636
Waivers of trial court fees	68637
Issuances of abstract of judgment or writ of execution	68638
Expiration of initial fee waiver	68639
Adoption of rules allowing litigants to pay court fees in installments	68640
Adoption of rules and forms to establish uniform procedures	68641

Article 7. Ability to Pay Program

Citation of chapter	68650
Appointment of counsel for low-income parties in specified civil actions in selected courts; Civil representation programs; Funding; Donations	68651

Chapter 3. The Supreme Court

Article 2. The Chief Clerk

Fees to be collected in advance	68847

Article 4. Fees in the Supreme Court and Courts of Appeal

Filing notice of appeal in civil case; Filing petition for writ within original civil jurisdiction; Parties other than appellant or petitioner filing first document	68926
Deposit for preparation of clerk's transcript or other appeal processing or notification; Forfeiture; Additional fee	68926.1
Multiyear memorandum of understanding with superior court for court security services and operating procedures; Disputes; Resolution of disputes; Process for parties to resolve disputes	68927
Copies of records or documents; Waiver of charges for copies of opinions	68928
Comparing documents requiring certificates	68929
Certificates under seal	68930
Administering oaths for verification of claims against State	68931
Other services; Fees of notaries public	68932
Appellate Court Trust Fund; Use; Sources	68933

Chapter 5. The Superior Courts

Article 9. Official Reporters Generally

Fees	69947
Fee for reporting contested cases	69948
Reporting defaults or uncontested matters	69949
Transcription; Additional fee for special daily copy service	69951
Verbatim record; Payment by county in specified cases	69952
Verbatim record not made at public expense; Payment by parties; Deposit with clerk or reporter	69953
Fee for daily transcript requiring more than one reporter	69953.5
Compensation for transcripts prepared with computer assistance	69954

Chapter 5.8. Superior Court Fees

Article 1. Civil Fees Generally

Legislative intent; Uniform schedule of filing fees and other civil fees; Title of chapter	70600
Legislative intent; Moratorium on increases in filing fees; Exceptions; Task Force on Civil Fees	70601
Supplemental fees of certain first paper filing	70602.5
Supplemental fees of certain first paper filing; Net reduction in funding; Adoption of schedule	70602.6

TABLE OF CONTENTS

	Section
Fees in chapter to be statewide; What charges may be added; Reduction in certain distributions	70603
Fee for filing first paper in civil action or proceeding	70611
Fee for filing first paper by defendant, intervenor, respondent, or adverse party	70612
Fee for filing first paper in limited civil case; Applicability; Waiver and assessment against defendant in certain cases	70613
Additional filing fee for subsequent pleadings that increase the amount demanded	70613.5
Fee for filing first paper in limited civil case for party other than plaintiff	70614
Fees for certain appeals to superior court [Repealed effective January 1, 2032]	70615
Complex case fee; Maximum; Parties; Reimbursement; Failure to pay fees	70616
High-frequency litigant fee	70616.5
Uniform fee for filing motion, application, or paper requiring hearing subsequent to first paper; No fee for certain filings; Application to appear as counsel pro hac vice; Fee for summary judgment motion	70617
Change of venue; Fee for making up and transmission of transcript and papers; Filing fee	70618
Fee for reclassification from limited to unlimited civil case	70619
Certificate on filing notice of motion prior to filing record on appeal	70620
Fee for filing appeal in limited civil case	70621
Surcharge in Riverside County for filing specified court papers to cover costs of seismic rehabilitation of courthouses	70622
Surcharge for superior court filings in San Bernardino County to supplement Courthouse Construction Fund [Repealed effective January 1, 2026]	70624
San Francisco Courthouse Construction Fund	70625
Fees for specified court services; Use of specified equivalent amount of certain fees for civil representation program	70626
Fees for preparing copies, comparing original, and search of records	70627
Fee for exemplification of record	70628
Authentication fee	70629
Fee for permitting videoconferencing	70630
Fee for particular service or product where not prohibited	70631
Fee for handling certain funds held in trust	70632
Adoption proceedings; Proceedings to declare minor free from parental custody; Criminal actions; Services to local, state, and federal governments	70633
No fee charged for certain name changes; Sydney's Law	70635
Children's waiting rooms; Monthly allocations; Transfer of moneys; Distributions per filing fee	70640

Article 2. Fees in Probate Proceedings

Filing first petition for letters of administration and other specified probate petitions; Subsequent petitions	70650
Filing fee for objections or other papers in opposition	70651
Filing fee for petition concerning internal affairs of trust; Papers in opposition; Refunds; Applicability	70652
Filing fee for petition for appointment of conservator or guardian; Papers in opposition	70653
Filing fee for petition for appointment of guardian of person only; Papers in opposition	70654
Filing fee for petition commencing certain proceedings; Papers in opposition	70655
Filing fee for petition requesting estate of small value to be set aside; Papers in opposition	70656
Fee for filing motion, application or other paper requiring hearing subsequent to first paper	70657
Uniform filing fee for specified petitions, applications, objections or other opposition; Exceptions	70657.5
Fees for petition, application or objections to petitions or applications filed after issuance of various letters	70658
Fees for combined petitions, applications, objections or other opposition	70658.5
Payment of fees by public administrator, public guardian, public conservator, or employee of Departments of State Hospitals or Developmental Services	70659
Fee for receipt and storage of document transferred to court clerk; Reduction or waiver	70660
Fee for receipt and storage of document transferred to court clerk; Reduction or waiver	70661
Filing fee for request for special notice	70662

	Section
Fee for registering conservatorship from other state	70663

Article 3. Fees in Family Law Matters

	Section
Fee for filing first paper in proceeding under Family Code	70670
Meaning of "paper" as used in §70670(c) or (d)	70671
No filing fee for parentage or support issues where Title IV-D child support agency is providing services	70672
Members of armed forces	70673
Marriage or domestic partnership dissolution record fee	70674
Fees not to be charged to indigent petitioner for copies of specified orders	70676
Fee for filing paper requiring hearing subsequent to first paper; Fee for filing certain papers not requiring hearing	70677
Fees in proceedings regarding custody and visitation of minor children	70678

GOVERNMENT CODE
TITLE 1
GENERAL

DIVISION 3.6
CLAIMS AND ACTIONS AGAINST PUBLIC ENTITIES AND PUBLIC EMPLOYEES

PART 1
DEFINITIONS

§810. Construction; Provisions governing

(a) Unless the provision or context otherwise requires, the definitions contained in this part govern the construction of this division.

(b) This division may be referred to as the Government Claims Act. **Leg.H.** Added Stats 1963 ch 1681 §1. Amended Stats 2012 ch 759 §5 (AB 2690), effective January 1, 2013.

§810.2. "Employee"

"Employee" includes an officer, judicial officer as defined in Section 327 of the Elections Code, employee, or servant, whether or not compensated, but does not include an independent contractor. **Leg.H.** Added Stats 1963 ch 1681 §1. Amended Stats 1977 ch 745 §1; Stats 1994 ch 923 §30 (SB 1546).

§810.4. "Employment"

"Employment" includes office or employment. **Leg.H.** Added Stats 1963 ch 1681 §1.

§810.6. "Enactment"

"Enactment" means a constitutional provision, statute, charter provision, ordinance or regulation. **Leg.H.** Added Stats 1963 ch 1681 §1.

§810.8. "Injury"

"Injury" means death, injury to a person, damage to or loss of property, or any other injury that a person may suffer to his person, reputation, character, feelings or estate, of such nature that it would be actionable if inflicted by a private person. **Leg.H.** Added Stats 1963 ch 1681 §1.

§811. "Law"

"Law" includes not only enactments but also the decisional law applicable within this State as determined and declared from time to time by the courts of this State and of the United States. **Leg.H.** Added Stats 1963 ch 1681 §1.

§811.2. "Public entity"

"Public entity" includes the state, the Regents of the University of California, the Trustees of the California State University and the California State University, a county, city, district, public authority, public agency, and any other political subdivision or public corporation in the State. **Leg.H.** Added Stats 1963 ch 1681 §1. Amended Stats 2010 ch 636 §1 (SB 1046), effective January 1, 2011.

§811.4. "Public employee"

"Public employee" means an employee of a public entity. **Leg.H.** Added Stats 1963 ch 1681 §1.

§811.6. "Regulation"

"Regulation" means a rule, regulation, order or standard, having the force of law, adopted by an employee or agency of the United States pursuant to the federal Administrative Procedure Act (Chapter 5 (commencing with Section 500) of Title 5 of the United States Code) or as a regulation by an agency of the state pursuant to the Administrative Procedure Act (Chapter 3.5 (commencing with Section 11340) of Part 1 of Division 3 of Title 2). **Leg.H.** Added Stats 1963 ch 1681 §1. Amended Stats 1987 ch 1201 §14, ch 1207 §3; Stats 1988 ch 160 §50.

§811.8. "Statute"

"Statute" means an act adopted by the Legislature of this State or by the Congress of the United States, or a statewide initiative act. **Leg.H.** Added Stats 1963 ch 1681 §1.

§811.9. State officers and trial court employees; Representation and defense; Adoption of rules of court; Effect on employment status

(a) Notwithstanding any other provision of law, judges, subordinate judicial officers, and court executive officers of the superior courts are state officers for purposes of Part 1 (commencing with Section 810) to Part 7 (commencing with Section 995), inclusive, and trial court employees are employees of the trial court for purposes of Part 1 (commencing with Section 810) to Part 7 (commencing with Section 995), inclusive. The Judicial Council shall provide for representation, defense, and indemnification of those individuals and the court pursuant to Part 1 (commencing with Section 810) to Part 7 (commencing with Section 995), inclusive. The Judicial Council shall provide for that representation or defense through the county counsel, the Attorney General, or other counsel. The county counsel and the Attorney General may, but are not required to, provide representation or defense for a trial court, judge, subordinate judicial officer, court executive officer, or trial court employee if requests that assistance to fulfill its duties under this section. The fact that a justice, judge, subordinate judicial officer, court executive officer, court employee, the court, the Judicial Council, or the staff of the Judicial Council is or was represented or defended by the county counsel, the Attorney General, or other counsel shall not be the sole basis for a judicial determination of disqualification of a justice, judge, subordinate judicial officer, the county counsel, the Attorney General, or other counsel in unrelated actions.

(b) To promote the cost-effective, prompt, and fair resolution of actions, proceedings, and claims affecting the trial courts, the Judicial Council shall adopt rules of court requiring its staff to manage actions, proceedings, and claims that affect the trial courts and involve superior courts, superior court judges, subordinate judicial officers, court executive officers, or trial court employees in consultation with the affected courts and individuals. The staff's management of these actions, proceedings, and claims shall include, but not be limited to, case management and administrative responsibilities such as selection of counsel and making strategic and settlement decisions.

(c) Nothing in this section shall be construed to affect the employment status of subordinate judicial officers, court executive officers, and trial court employees related to any matters not covered by subdivision (a). **Leg.H.** Added Stats 2000 ch 447 §4.5 (SB 1533). Amended Stats 2005 ch 706 §16 (AB 1742), effective January 1, 2006; Stats 2023 ch 478 §23 (AB 1756), effective January 1, 2024.

2000 Note: The Legislature hereby declares that Section 811.9 shall not be interpreted as applicable to, nor legislative preference of, an employment status for trial court employees. The Legislature recognizes that pursuant to Chapter 850 of the Statutes of 1997, the Task Force on Trial Court Employees will make recommendations to the Legislature regarding an appropriate system of employment and governance for trial court employees. The recommendations of the Task Force on Trial Court Employees shall take effect only upon subsequent action of the Legislature. Stats 2000 ch 447 § 16.

PART 2
LIABILITY OF PUBLIC ENTITIES AND PUBLIC EMPLOYEES
CHAPTER 1
GENERAL PROVISIONS RELATING TO LIABILITY
ARTICLE 1
Scope of Part

§814. Statute's inapplicability to contractual liability or nonmonetary relief

Nothing in this part affects liability based on contract or the right to obtain relief other than money or damages against a public entity or public employee. **Leg.H.** Added Stats 1963 ch 1681 §1.

§814.2. Absence of implied repeal of Workers' Compensation statutes

Nothing in this part shall be construed to impliedly repeal any provision of Division 4 (commencing with Section 3201) or Division 4.5 (commencing with Section 6100) of the Labor Code. **Leg.H.** Added Stats 1963 ch 1681 §1.

ARTICLE 2
Liability of Public Entities

§815. Absence of liability for injury except under statute; Liability as subject to statutory immunity and defenses

Except as otherwise provided by statute:

(a) A public entity is not liable for an injury, whether such injury arises out of an act or omission of the public entity or a public employee or any other person.

(b) The liability of a public entity established by this part (commencing with Section 814) is subject to any immunity of the public entity provided by statute, including this part, and is subject to any defenses that would be available to the public entity if it were a private person. **Leg.H.** Added Stats 1963 ch 1681 §1.

§815.2. Causes of injuries for which public entity liable; Absence of liability where employee immune

(a) A public entity is liable for injury proximately caused by an act or omission of an employee of the public entity within the scope of his employment if the act or omission would, apart from this section, have given rise to a cause of action against that employee or his personal representative.

(b) Except as otherwise provided by statute, a public entity is not liable for an injury resulting from an act or omission of an employee of the public entity where the employee is immune from liability. **Leg.H.** Added Stats 1963 ch 1681 §1.

§815.3. Liability for intentional torts of elected officials; Plaintiff's recovery against assets of official; Indemnification; Defense for official during appeal

(a) Notwithstanding any other provision of this part, unless the elected official and the public entity are named as codefendants in the same action, a public entity is not liable to a plaintiff under this part for any act or omission of an elected official employed by or otherwise representing that public entity, which act or omission constitutes an intentional tort, including, but not limited to, harassment, sexual battery, and intentional infliction of emotional distress. For purposes of this section, harassment in violation of state or federal law constitutes an intentional tort, to the extent permitted by federal law. This section shall not apply to defamation.

(b) If the elected official is held liable for an intentional tort other than defamation in such an action, the trier of fact in reaching the verdict shall determine if the act or omission constituting the intentional tort arose from and was directly related to the elected official's performance of his or her official duties. If the trier of fact determines that the act or omission arose from and was directly related to the elected official's performance of his or her official duties, the public entity shall be liable for the judgment as provided by law. For the purpose of this subdivision, employee managerial functions shall be deemed to arise from, and to directly relate to, the elected official's official duties. However, acts or omissions constituting sexual harassment shall not be deemed to arise from, and to directly relate to, the elected official's official duties.

(c) If the trier of fact determines that the elected official's act or omission did not arise from and was not directly related to the elected official's performance of his or her official duties, upon a final judgment, including any appeal, the plaintiff shall first seek recovery of the judgment against the assets of the elected official. If the court determines that the elected official's assets are insufficient to satisfy the total judgment, including plaintiff's costs as provided by law, the court shall determine the amount of the deficiency and the plaintiff may seek to collect that remainder of the judgment from the public entity. The public entity may pay that deficiency if the public entity is otherwise authorized by law to pay that judgment.

(d) To the extent the public entity pays any portion of the judgment against the elected official pursuant to subdivision (c) or has expended defense costs in an action in which the trier of fact determines the elected official's action did not arise from and did not directly relate to his or her performance of official duties, the public entity shall pursue all available creditor's remedies against the elected official in indemnification, including garnishment, until the elected official has fully reimbursed the public entity.

(e) If the public entity elects to appeal the judgment in an action brought pursuant to this section, the entity shall continue to provide a defense for the official until the case is finally adjudicated, as provided by law.

(f) It is the intent of the Legislature that elected officials assume full fiscal responsibility for their conduct which constitutes an intentional tort not directly related to their official duties committed for which the public entity they represent may also be liable, while maintaining fair compensation for those persons injured by such conduct.

(g) This section shall not apply to a criminal or civil enforcement action brought on behalf of the state by an elected district attorney, city attorney, or Attorney General.

(h) If any provision of this section or the application thereof to any person or circumstances is held invalid, that invalidity shall not affect other provisions or applications of the section which can be given effect without the invalid provision or application, and to this end the provisions of this section are severable. **Leg.H.** Added Stats 1994 ch 796 §1 (AB 2508).

§815.4. Tortious act or omission of independent contractor; Limitation on liability

A public entity is liable for injury proximately caused by a tortious act or omission of an independent contractor of the public entity to the same extent that the public entity would be subject to such liability if it were a private person. Nothing in this section subjects a public entity to liability for the act or omission of an independent contractor if the public entity would not have been liable for the injury had the act or omission been that of an employee of the public entity. **Leg.H.** Added Stats 1963 ch 1681 §1.

§815.6. Liability for failure to discharge statutory duty

Where a public entity is under a mandatory duty imposed by an enactment that is designed to protect against the risk of a particular kind of injury, the public entity is liable for an injury of that kind proximately caused by its failure to discharge the duty unless the public entity establishes that it exercised reasonable diligence to discharge the duty. **Leg.H.** Added Stats 1963 ch 1681 §1.

§816. Immunity from liability for National Guard activities

A public entity is not liable for injury arising out of any activity conducted by a member of the California National Guard pursuant to Section 316, 502, 503, 504, or 505 of Title 32 of the United States Code and compensated pursuant to the Federal Tort Claims Act.

It is the intent of the Legislature, in enacting this section, to conform state law regarding liability for activities of the National Guard to federal law as expressed in Public Law 97–124. **Leg.H.** Added Stats 1982 ch 616 §1.

Prior Law: Former §816, similar to present CCP §1245.060, was added Stats 1970 ch 1099 §3 and repealed Stats 1975 ch 1240 §20, operative July 1, 1976.

§818. Absence of liability for exemplary and punitive damages

Notwithstanding any other provision of law, a public entity is not liable for damages awarded under Section 3294 of the Civil Code or other damages imposed primarily for the sake of example and by way of punishing the defendant. **Leg.H.** Added Stats 1963 ch 1681 §1.

§818.2. Adoption or failure to adopt enactment; Failure to enforce law

A public entity is not liable for an injury caused by adopting or failing to adopt an enactment or by failing to enforce any law. **Leg.H.** Added Stats 1963 ch 1681 §1.

§818.4. Determination as to issuance, denial, suspension or revocation of license or similar authorization

A public entity is not liable for an injury caused by the issuance, denial, suspension or revocation of, or by the failure or refusal to issue, deny, suspend or revoke, any permit, license, certificate, approval, order, or similar authorization where the public entity or an employee of the public entity is authorized by enactment to determine whether or not such authorization should be issued, denied, suspended or revoked. **Leg.H.** Added Stats 1963 ch 1681 §1.

§818.5. Liability of Department of Motor Vehicles to lienholder

The Department of Motor Vehicles is liable for any injury to a lienholder or good faith purchaser of a vehicle proximately caused by the department's negligent omission of the lienholder's name from an ownership certificate issued by the department. The liability of the department under this section shall not exceed the actual cash value of the vehicle. **Leg.H.** Added Stats 1985 ch 437 §2.

§818.6. Failure to make any, or adequate, inspection of property

A public entity is not liable for injury caused by its failure to make an inspection, or by reason of making an inadequate or negligent inspection, of any property, other than its property (as defined in subdivision (c) of Section 830), for the purpose of determining whether the property complies with or violates any enactment or contains or constitutes a hazard to health or safety. **Leg.H.** Added Stats 1963 ch 1681 §1.

§818.7. Publication of records concerning person convicted of controlled substance violation; Use by school authorities

No board, commission, or any public officer or employee of the state or of any district, county, city and county, or city is liable for any damage or injury to any person resulting from the publication of any reports, records, prints, or photographs of or concerning any person convicted of violation of any law relating to the use, sale, or possession of controlled substances, when such publication is to school authorities for use in instruction on the subject of controlled substances or to any person when used for the purpose of general education. However, the name of any person concerning whom any such reports, records, prints, or photographs are used shall be kept confidential and every reasonable effort shall be made to maintain as confidential any information which may tend to identify such person. **Leg.H.** Added Stats 1968 ch 182 §36. Amended Stats 1984 ch 1635 §40.

§818.8. Employee's misrepresentation

A public entity is not liable for an injury caused by misrepresentation by an employee of the public entity, whether or not such misrepresentation be negligent or intentional. **Leg.H.** Added Stats 1963 ch 1681 §1.

§818.9. Immunity from liability for advice given to small claims litigants

A court or county, its employees, independent contractors, and volunteers shall not be liable because of any advice provided to small claims court litigants or potential litigants as a public service on behalf of the court or county pursuant to the Small Claims Act (Chapter 5.5 (commencing with Section 116.110) of Title 1 of Part 1 of the Code of Civil Procedure). **Leg.H.** Added Stats 1981 ch 958 §10. Amended Stats 1990 ch 1305 §10 (SB 2627); Stats 2002 ch 806 §24 (AB 3027).

ARTICLE 3
Liability of Public Employees

§820. Co-extensiveness with liability of private person; Defenses

(a) Except as otherwise provided by statute (including Section 820.2), a public employee is liable for injury caused by his act or omission to the same extent as a private person.

(b) The liability of a public employee established by this part (commencing with Section 814) is subject to any defenses that would be available to the public employee if he were a private person. **Leg.H.** Added Stats 1963 ch 1681 §1.

§820.2. Exercise of discretion

Except as otherwise provided by statute, a public employee is not liable for an injury resulting from his act or omission where the act or omission was the result of the exercise of the discretion vested in him, whether or not such discretion be abused. **Leg.H.** Added Stats 1963 ch 1681 §1.

§820.21. Tort liability of specified public employees

(a) Notwithstanding any other provision of the law, the civil immunity of juvenile court social workers, child protection workers, and other public employees authorized to initiate or conduct investigations or proceedings pursuant to Chapter 2 (commencing with Section 200) of Part 1 of Division 2 of the Welfare and Institutions Code shall not extend to any of the following, if committed with malice:

(1) Perjury.
(2) Fabrication of evidence.
(3) Failure to disclose known exculpatory evidence.
(4) Obtaining testimony by duress, as defined in Section 1569 of the Civil Code, fraud, as defined in either Section 1572 or Section 1573 of the Civil Code, or undue influence, as defined in Section 1575 of the Civil Code.

(b) As used in this section, "malice" means conduct that is intended by the person described in subdivision (a) to cause injury to the plaintiff or despicable conduct that is carried on by the person described in subdivision (a) with a willful and conscious disregard of the rights or safety of others. **Leg.H.** Added Stats 1995 ch 977 §1 (AB 1355).

§820.25. Actions by peace officer or state or local law enforcement official deemed exercise of discretion

(a) For purposes of Section 820.2, the decision of a peace officer, as defined in Sections 830.1 and 830.2 of the Penal Code, or a state or local law enforcement official, to render assistance to a motorist who has not been involved in an accident or to leave the scene after rendering assistance, upon learning of a reasonably apparent emergency requiring his immediate attention elsewhere or upon instructions from a superior to assume duties elsewhere, shall be deemed an exercise of discretion.

(b) The provision in subdivision (a) shall not apply if the act or omission occurred pursuant to the performance of a ministerial duty. For purposes of this section, "ministerial duty" is defined as a plain and mandatory duty involving the execution of a set task and to be performed without the exercise of discretion. **Leg.H.** Added Stats 1979 ch 806 §1, effective September 19, 1979.

§820.4. Non-negligent law execution or enforcement; Absence of immunity for false arrest or imprisonment

A public employee is not liable for his act or omission, exercising due care, in the execution or enforcement of any law. Nothing in this section exonerates a public employee from liability for false arrest or false imprisonment. **Leg.H.** Added Stats 1963 ch 681 §1.

§820.6. Good faith action under unconstitutional, invalid, or inapplicable enactment

If a public employee acts in good faith, without malice, and under the apparent authority of an enactment that is unconstitutional, invalid or inapplicable, he is not liable for an injury caused thereby except to the extent that he would have been liable had the enactment been constitutional, valid and applicable. **Leg.H.** Added Stats 1963 ch 1681 §1.

§820.8. Act or omission of another person; Absence of immunity from liability for own act or omission

Except as otherwise provided by statute, a public employee is not liable for an injury caused by the act or omission of another person. Nothing in this section exonerates a public employee from liability for injury proximately caused by his own negligent or wrongful act or omission. **Leg.H.** Added Stats 1963 ch 1681 §1.

§820.9. Vicarious liability of specified local government officials

Members of city councils, mayors, members of boards of supervisors, members of school boards, members of governing boards of other local public entities, members of locally appointed boards and commissions, and members of locally appointed or elected advisory bodies are not vicariously liable for injuries caused by the act or omission of the public entity or advisory body. Nothing in this section exonerates an official from liability for injury caused by that individual's own wrongful conduct. Nothing in this section affects the immunity of any other public official.

This section shall become operative January 1, 2000. **Leg.H.** Added Stats 1997 ch 132 §2 (SB 1159), operative January 1, 2000.

Prior Law: Former Gov C §820.9, similar to the present section, was added Stats 1987 ch 1201 §15, ch 1208 §1. Amended Stats 1988 ch 490 §1; Stats 1997 ch 132 §1 (SB 1159), operative until January 1, 2000.

§821. Adoption of, or failure to adopt, enactment; Failure to enforce enactment

A public employee is not liable for an injury caused by his adoption of or failure to adopt an enactment or by his failure to enforce an enactment. **Leg.H.** Added Stats 1963 ch 1681 §1.

§821.2. Determination as to issuance, denial, suspension or revocation of license or similar authorization

A public employee is not liable for an injury caused by his issuance, denial, suspension or revocation of, or by his failure or refusal to issue, deny, suspend or revoke, any permit, license, certificate, approval, order, or similar authorization where he is authorized by enactment to determine whether or not such authorization should be issued, denied, suspended or revoked. **Leg.H.** Added Stats 1963 ch 1681 §1.

§821.4. Failure to make any, or adequate, inspection of property

A public employee is not liable for injury caused by his failure to make an inspection, or by reason of making an inadequate or negligent inspection, of any property, other than the property (as defined in subdivision (c) of Section 830) of the public entity employing the public employee, for the purpose of determining whether the property complies with or violates any enactment or contains or constitutes a hazard to health or safety. **Leg.H.** Added Stats 1963 ch 1681 §1.

§821.5. Failure to restrict travel of cargo tank vehicles through tunnels

A public entity or a public employee acting within the scope of his employment is not liable for failing to prohibit or restrict the time that cargo tank vehicles required to display flammable liquid placards may travel through a tunnel. **Leg.H.** Added Stats 1982 ch 1255 §1.

§821.6. Institution or prosecution of judicial or administrative proceeding

A public employee is not liable for injury caused by his instituting or prosecuting any judicial or administrative proceeding within the scope of his employment, even if he acts maliciously and without probable cause. **Leg.H.** Added Stats 1963 ch 1681 §1.

§821.8. Legally authorized entry on property; Limitation on exoneration

A public employee is not liable for an injury arising out of his entry upon any property where such entry is expressly or impliedly authorized by law. Nothing in this section exonerates a public employee from liability for an injury proximately caused by his own negligent or wrongful act or omission. **Leg.H.** Added Stats 1963 ch 1681 §1.

§822. Theft of money from employee's official custody; Absence of immunity from liability for employee's own act or omission

A public employee is not liable for money stolen from his official custody. Nothing in this section exonerates a public employee from liability if the loss was sustained as a result of his own negligent or wrongful act or omission. **Leg.H.** Added Stats 1963 ch 1681 §1.

§822.2. Misrepresentations by public employees

A public employee acting in the scope of his employment is not liable for an injury caused by his misrepresentation, whether or not such misrepresentation be negligent or intentional, unless he is guilty of actual fraud, corruption or actual malice. **Leg.H.** Added Stats 1963 ch 1681 §1.

§823. Peace officer widow, widower, heirs

Neither the widow, widower, nor the heirs of a peace officer, as defined in Sections 830.1, 830.2, and 830.32 of the Penal Code, shall be liable individually for any injury or death that may result from an act or omission of a peace officer that occurs in his or her line of duty, including an act or omission not directly related to the officer's death, if the officer was slain while in the line of duty. Nothing in this section shall preclude any action from being brought against the estate of the peace officer. **Leg.H.** Added Stats 1998 ch 559 §2 (AB 1865).

ARTICLE 4
Indemnification of Public Employees

§825. Duty of public entity to pay judgment, compromise, or settlement

(a) Except as otherwise provided in this section, if an employee or former employee of a public entity requests the public entity to defend him or her against any claim or action against him or her for an injury arising out of an act or omission occurring within the scope of his or her employment as an employee of the public entity and the request is made in writing not less than 10 days before the day of trial, and the employee or former employee reasonably cooperates in good faith in the defense of the claim or action, the public entity shall pay any judgment based thereon or any compromise or settlement of the claim or action to which the public entity has agreed.

If the public entity conducts the defense of an employee or former employee against any claim or action with his or her reasonable good-faith cooperation, the public entity shall pay any judgment based thereon or any compromise or settlement of the claim or action to which the public entity has agreed. However, where the public entity conducted the defense pursuant to an agreement with the employee or former employee reserving the rights of the public entity not to pay the judgment, compromise, or settlement until it is established that the injury arose out of an act or omission occurring within the scope of his or her employment as an employee of the public entity, the public entity is required to pay the judgment, compromise, or settlement only if it is established that the injury arose out of an act or omission occurring in the scope of his or her employment as an employee of the public entity.

Nothing in this section authorizes a public entity to pay that part of a claim or judgment that is for punitive or exemplary damages.

(b) Notwithstanding subdivision (a) or any other provision of law, a public entity is authorized to pay that part of a judgment that is for punitive or exemplary damages if the governing body of that public entity, acting in its sole discretion except in cases involving an entity of the state government, finds all of the following:

(1) The judgment is based on an act or omission of an employee or former employee acting within the course and scope of his or her employment as an employee of the public entity.

(2) At the time of the act giving rise to the liability, the employee or former employee acted, or failed to act, in good faith, without actual malice and in the apparent best interests of the public entity.

(3) Payment of the claim or judgment would be in the best interests of the public entity.

As used in this subdivision with respect to an entity of state government, "a decision of the governing body" means the approval of the Legislature for payment of that part of a judgment that is for punitive damages or exemplary damages, upon recommendation of the appointing power of the employee or former employee, based upon the finding by the Legislature and the appointing authority of the existence of the three conditions for payment of a punitive or exemplary damages claim. The provisions of subdivision (a) of Section 965.6 shall apply to the payment of any claim pursuant to this subdivision.

The discovery of the assets of a public entity and the introduction of evidence of the assets of a public entity shall not be permitted in an action in which it is alleged that a public employee is liable for punitive or exemplary damages.

The possibility that a public entity may pay that part of a judgment that is for punitive damages shall not be disclosed in any trial in which it is alleged that a public employee is liable for punitive or exemplary damages, and that disclosure shall be grounds for a mistrial.

(c) Except as provided in subdivision (d), if the provisions of this section are in conflict with the provisions of a memorandum of understanding reached pursuant to Chapter 10 (commencing with Section 3500) of Division 4 of Title 1, the memorandum of understanding shall be controlling without further legislative action, except that if those provisions of a memorandum of understanding require the expenditure of funds, the provisions shall not become effective unless approved by the Legislature in the annual Budget Act.

(d) The subject of payment of punitive damages pursuant to this section or any other provision of law shall not be a subject of meet and confer under the provisions of Chapter 10 (commencing with Section 3500) of Division 4 of Title 1, or pursuant to any other law or authority.

(e) Nothing in this section shall affect the provisions of Section 818 prohibiting the award of punitive damages against a public entity. This section shall not be construed as a waiver of a public entity's immunity from liability for punitive damages under Section 1981, 1983, or 1985 of Title 42 of the United States Code.

(f)(1) Except as provided in paragraph (2), a public entity shall not pay a judgment, compromise, or settlement arising from a claim or action against an elected official, if the claim or action is based on conduct by the elected official by way of tortiously intervening or attempting to intervene in, or by way of tortiously influencing or attempting to influence the outcome of, any judicial action or proceeding for the benefit of a particular party by contacting the trial judge or any commissioner, court-appointed arbitrator, court-appointed mediator, or court-appointed special referee assigned to the matter, or the court clerk, bailiff, or marshal after an action has been filed, unless he or she was counsel of record acting lawfully within the scope of his or her employment on behalf of that party. Notwithstanding Section 825.6, if a public entity conducted the defense of an elected official against such a claim or action and the elected official is found liable by the trier of fact, the court shall order the elected official to pay to the public entity the cost of that defense.

(2) If an elected official is held liable for monetary damages in the action, the plaintiff shall first seek recovery of the judgment against the assets of the elected official. If the elected official's assets are insufficient to satisfy the total judgment, as determined by the court, the public entity may pay the deficiency if the public entity is authorized by law to pay that judgment.

(3) To the extent the public entity pays any portion of the judgment or is entitled to reimbursement of defense costs pursuant to paragraph (1), the public entity shall pursue all available creditor's remedies against the elected official, including garnishment, until that party has fully reimbursed the public entity.

(4) This subdivision shall not apply to any criminal or civil enforcement action brought in the name of the people of the State of California by an elected district attorney, city attorney, or attorney general. **Leg.H.** Added Stats 1963 ch 1681 §1. Amended Stats 1972 ch 1352 §1; Stats 1979 ch 1072 §47, effective September 28, 1979; Stats 1985 ch 1373 §1; Stats 1994 ch 794 §1 (AB 2467); Stats 1995 ch 799 §1 (AB 1361).

§825.2. Right of employee or former employee to recover amount of payment from public entity

(a) Subject to subdivision (b), if an employee or former employee of a public entity pays any claim or judgment against him, or any portion thereof, that the public entity is required to pay under Section 825, he is entitled to recover the amount of such payment from the public entity.

(b) If the public entity did not conduct his defense against the action or claim, or if the public entity conducted such defense pursuant to an agreement with him reserving the rights of the public entity against him, an employee or former employee of a public entity may recover from the public entity under subdivision (a) only if he establishes that the act or omission upon which the claim or judgment is based occurred within the scope of his employment as an employee of the public entity and the public entity fails to establish that he acted or failed to act because of actual fraud, corruption or actual malice or that he willfully failed or refused to conduct the defense of the claim or action in good faith or to reasonably cooperate in good faith in the defense conducted by the public entity.

(c) If the provisions of this section are in conflict with the provisions of a memorandum of understanding reached pursuant to Chapter 12 (commencing with Section 3560) of Division 4 of Title 1, the memorandum of understanding shall be controlling without further legislative action, except that if such provisions of a memorandum of understanding require the expenditure of funds, the provisions shall not become effective unless approved by the Legislature in the annual Budget Act. **Leg.H.** Added Stats 1963 ch 1681 §1. Amended Stats 1972 ch 1352 §2; Stats 1979 ch 1072 §48, effective September 28, 1979.

§825.4. Indemnification of public entity paying claim or judgment; When employee not liable to indemnify

Except as provided in Section 825.6, if a public entity pays any claim or judgment against itself or against an employee or former employee of the public entity, or any portion thereof, for an injury arising out of an act or omission of the employee or former employee of the public entity, he is not liable to indemnify the public entity. **Leg.H.** Added Stats 1963 ch 1681 §1.

§825.6. When public entity may recover from employee or former employee

(a)(1) Except as provided in subdivision (b), if a public entity pays any claim or judgment, or any portion thereof, either against itself or against an employee or former employee of the public entity, for an injury arising out of an act or omission of the employee or former employee of the public entity, the public entity may recover from the employee or former employee the amount of that payment if he or she acted or failed to act because of actual fraud, corruption, or actual malice, or willfully failed or refused to conduct the defense of the claim or action in good faith. Except as provided in paragraph (2) or (3), a public entity may not recover any payments made upon a judgment or claim against an employee or former employee if the public entity conducted his or her defense against the action or claim.

(2) If a public entity pays any claim or judgment, or any portion thereof, against an employee or former employee of the public entity for an injury arising out of his or her act or omission, and if the public entity conducted his or her defense against the claim or action pursuant to an agreement with him or her reserving the rights of the public entity against him or her, the public entity may recover the amount of the payment from him or her unless he or she establishes that the act or omission upon which the claim or judgment is based occurred within the scope of his or her employment as an employee of the public entity and the public entity fails to establish that he or she acted or failed to act because of actual fraud, corruption, or actual malice or that he or she willfully failed or refused to reasonably cooperate in good faith in the defense conducted by the public entity.

(3) If a public entity pays any claim or judgment, or any portion thereof, against an employee or former employee of the public entity for an injury arising out of his or her act or omission, and if the public entity conducted the defense against the claim or action in the absence of an agreement with him or her reserving the rights of the public entity against him or her, the public entity may recover the amount of that payment from him or her if he or she willfully failed or refused to reasonably cooperate in good faith in the defense conducted by the public entity.

(b)(1) Upon a felony conviction for a violation of Section 1195 of this code, or of Section 68, 86, 93, 165, 504, or 518 of the Penal Code, by an elected official or former elected official of a public entity for an act or omission of that person while in office, the elected official or former elected official shall forfeit any rights to defense or indemnification under Section 825 with respect to a claim for damages for an injury arising from that act or omission.

(2) If a public entity pays any claim or judgment, or any portion thereof, either against itself or against an elected official or former elected official of the public entity, for an injury arising out of an act or omission of the elected official or former elected official of the public entity, which act or omission constituted a felony violation of Section 1195 of this code, or of Section 68, 86, 93, 165, 504, or 518 of the Penal Code, the public entity shall recover from the elected official or former elected official the amount of that payment upon the felony conviction of the elected official or former elected official for that act or omission. Upon that conviction, the public entity shall also recover from the elected official the costs of any defense to a civil action filed against the elected official for that act or omission.

(c) If the provisions of this section are in conflict with the provisions of a memorandum of understanding reached pursuant to Chapter 12 (commencing with Section 3560) of Division 4 of Title 1, the memorandum of understanding shall be controlling without further legislative action, except that if the provisions of a memorandum of understanding require the expenditure of funds, the provisions shall not become effective unless approved by the Legislature in the annual Budget Act. **Leg.H.** Added Stats 1963 ch 1681 §1. Amended Stats 1972 ch 1352 §3; Stats 1979 ch 1072 §49, effective September 28, 1979; Stats 1994 ch 797 §1 (AB 2522); Stats 1995 ch 91 §43 (SB 975).

ARTICLE 5
Indemnification of Certain State Agents

§827. Indemnification of health care providers defended by State

A provider of health care, as defined in Section 56.05 of the Civil Code, its officers, employees, agents, and subcontractors, who are defended by the Attorney General pursuant to Section 12511.5, or other legal counsel provided by the state, shall be indemnified in accordance with Section 825, subject to the same conditions and limitations applicable to state employees, except that no provider of health care shall be indemnified in a civil rights action unless the health care provider maintains insurance for professional negligence. To the extent that negligence constitutes the basis of liability of the health care provider, the provider's private insurance shall be the source of recovery. **Leg.H.** Added Stats 1995 ch 749 §3 (AB 1177), effective October 10, 1995.

CHAPTER 2
DANGEROUS CONDITIONS OF PUBLIC PROPERTY
ARTICLE 1
General

§830. "Dangerous condition"; "Protect against"; "Property of a public entity" and "public property"

As used in this chapter:

(a) "Dangerous condition" means a condition of property that creates a substantial (as distinguished from a minor, trivial or insignificant) risk of injury when such property or adjacent property is used with due care in a manner in which it is reasonably foreseeable that it will be used.

(b) "Protect against" includes repairing, remedying or correcting a dangerous condition, providing safeguards against a dangerous condition, or warning of a dangerous condition.

(c) "Property of a public entity" and "public property" mean real or personal property owned or controlled by the public entity, but do not include easements, encroachments and other property that are located on the property of the public entity but are not owned or controlled by the public entity. **Leg.H.** Added Stats 1963 ch 1681 §1.

§830.1. Improvements financed by formation of special assessment district not public property

For purposes of this chapter, seismic safety improvements or fire sprinkler improvements which are owned, built, controlled, operated, and maintained by the private owner of the building in which they are installed are not public property or property of a public entity solely because the improvements were financed, in whole or in part, by means of the formation of a special assessment district. **Leg.H.** Added Stats 1990 ch 1318 §1 (SB 2819).

§830.2. When condition not dangerous; Court's determination from evidence

A condition is not a dangerous condition within the meaning of this chapter if the trial or appellate court, viewing the evidence most favorably to the plaintiff, determines as a matter of law that the risk created by the condition was of such a minor, trivial or insignificant nature in view of the surrounding circumstances that no reasonable person would conclude that the condition created a substantial risk of injury when such property or adjacent property was used with due care in a manner in which it was reasonably foreseeable that it would be used. **Leg.H.** Added Stats 1963 ch 1681 §1.

§830.4. Failure to provide traffic control signals, signs, or markings

A condition is not a dangerous condition within the meaning of this chapter merely because of the failure to provide regulatory traffic control signals, stop signs, yield right-of-way signs, or speed restriction signs, as described by the Vehicle Code, or distinctive roadway markings as described in Section 21460 of the Vehicle Code. **Leg.H.** Added Stats 1963 ch 1681 §1.

§830.5. Evidence not showing that public property was in dangerous condition; Happening of accident; Protective measure after injury

(a) Except where the doctrine of res ipsa loquitur is applicable, the happening of the accident which results in the injury is not in and of itself evidence that public property was in a dangerous condition.

(b) The fact that action was taken after an injury occurred to protect against a condition of public property is not evidence that the public property was in a dangerous condition at the time of the injury. **Leg.H.** Added Stats 1963 ch 1681 §1.

§830.6. Liability of public entity or employee; Injury caused by construction plan or design or improvement

Neither a public entity nor a public employee is liable under this chapter for an injury caused by the plan or design of a construction of, or an improvement to, public property where such plan or design has been approved in advance of the construction or improvement by the legislative body of the public entity or by some other body or employee exercising discretionary authority to give such approval or where such plan or design is prepared in conformity with standards previously so approved, if the trial or appellate court determines that there is any substantial evidence upon the basis of which (a) a reasonable public employee could have adopted the plan or design or the standards therefor or (b) a reasonable legislative body or other body or employee could have approved the plan or design or the standards therefor. Notwithstanding notice that constructed or improved public property may no longer be in conformity with a plan or design or a standard which reasonably could be approved by the legislative body or other body or employee, the immunity provided by this section shall continue for a reasonable period of time sufficient to permit the public entity to obtain funds for and carry out remedial work necessary to allow such public property to be in conformity with a plan or design approved by the legislative body of the public entity or other body or employee, or with a plan or design in conformity with a standard previously approved by such legislative body or other body or employee. In the event that the public entity is unable to remedy such public property because of practical impossibility or lack of sufficient funds, the immunity provided by this section shall remain so long as such public entity shall reasonably attempt to provide adequate warnings of the existence of the condition not conforming to the approved plan or design or to the approved standard. However, where a person fails to heed such warning or occupies public property despite such warning, such failure or occupation shall not in itself constitute an assumption of the risk of the danger indicated by the warning. **Leg.H.** Added Stats 1963 ch 1681 §1. Amended Stats 1979 ch 481 §1.

§830.8. Failure to provide traffic signals, signs, or markings; Danger not reasonably foreseeable

Neither a public entity nor a public employee is liable under this chapter for an injury caused by the failure to provide traffic or warning signals, signs, markings or devices described in the Vehicle Code. Nothing in this section exonerates a public entity or public employee from liability for injury proximately caused by such failure if a signal, sign, marking or device (other than one described in Section 830.4) was necessary to warn of a dangerous condition which endangered the safe movement of traffic and which would not be reasonably apparent to, and would not have been anticipated by, a person exercising due care. **Leg.H.** Added Stats 1963 ch 1681 §1.

§830.9. Traffic signals controlled by emergency vehicle

Neither a public entity nor a public employee is liable for an injury caused by the operation or nonoperation of official traffic control signals when controlled by an emergency vehicle in accordance with the provisions of subdivision (a) of Section 25258 of the Vehicle Code. **Leg.H.** Added Stats 1967 ch 1037 §2.

§831. Weather conditions affecting streets and highways; Danger not reasonably foreseeable

Neither a public entity nor a public employee is liable for an injury caused by the effect on the use of streets and highways of weather conditions as such. Nothing in this section exonerates a public entity or public employee from liability for injury proximately caused by such effect if it would not be reasonably apparent to, and would not be anticipated by, a person exercising due care. For the purpose of this section, the effect on the use of streets and highways of weather conditions includes the effect of fog, wind, rain, flood, ice or snow but does not include physical damage to or deterioration of streets and highways resulting from weather conditions. **Leg.H.** Added Stats 1963 ch 1681 §1.

§831.2. Natural condition of unimproved public property

Neither a public entity nor a public employee is liable for an injury caused by a natural condition of any unimproved public property, including but not limited to any natural condition of any lake, stream, bay, river or beach. **Leg.H.** Added Stats 1963 ch 1681 §1.

§831.21. Public beaches as in natural condition and unimproved

(a) Public beaches shall be deemed to be in a natural condition and unimproved notwithstanding the provision or absence of public safety services such as lifeguards, police or sheriff patrols, medical services, fire protection services, beach cleanup services, or signs. The provisions of this section shall apply only to natural conditions of public property and shall not limit any liability or immunity that may otherwise exist pursuant to this division.

(b) This section shall only be applicable to causes of action based upon acts or ommissions occurring on or after January 1, 1988. **Leg.H.** Added Stats 1987 ch 1209 §1.

Prior Law: There was another section of this number which was added Stats 1987 ch 1201 §16 and repealed Stats 1989 ch 1360 §48.

§831.25. Liability for property damage or emotional distress off public entity's property resulting from land failure of unimproved public property; "Land failure"

(a) Neither a public entity nor a public employee is liable for any damage or injury to property, or for emotional distress unless the plaintiff has suffered substantial physical injury, off the public entity's property caused by land failure of any unimproved public property if the land failure was caused by a natural condition of the unimproved public property.

(b) For the purposes of this section, a natural condition exists and property shall be deemed unimproved notwithstanding the intervention of minor improvements made for the preservation or prudent management of the property in its unimproved state that did not contribute to the land failure.

(c) As used in this section, "land failure" means any movement of land, including a landslide, mudslide, creep, subsidence, and any other gradual or rapid movement of land.

(d) This section shall not benefit any public entity or public employee who had actual notice of probable damage that is likely to occur outside the public property because of land failure and who fails to give a reasonable warning of the danger to the affected property owners. Neither a public entity nor a public employee is liable for any damage or injury arising from the giving of a warning under this section.

(e) Nothing in this section shall limit the immunity provided by Section 831.2.

(f) Nothing in this section creates a duty of care or basis of liability for damage or injury to property or of liability for emotional distress. **Leg.H.** Added Stats 1984 ch 1071 §1. Amended Stats 1988 ch 1034 §1.

§831.3. Liability for injury on nondedicated road

Neither a public entity nor a public employee is liable for any injury occurring on account of the grading or the performance of other maintenance or repair on or reconstruction or replacement of any road which has not officially been accepted as a part of the road system under the jurisdiction of the public entity if the grading, maintenance, repair, or reconstruction or replacement is performed with reasonable care and leaves the road in no more dangerous or unsafe condition than it was before the work commenced. No act of grading, maintenance, repair, or reconstruction or replacement within the meaning of this section shall be deemed to give rise to any duty of the public entity to continue any grading, maintenance, repair, or reconstruction or replacement on any road not a part of the road system under the public entity's jurisdiction. As used in this section "reconstruction or replacement" means reconstruction or replacement performed pursuant to Article 3 (commencing with Section 1160) of Chapter 4 of Division 2 of the Streets and Highways Code. **Leg.H.** Added Stats 1981 ch 260 §1. Amended Stats 1986 ch 578 §1, effective August 26, 1986.

§831.4. Unpaved road providing access to fishing, hunting, or recreational areas; Trails

A public entity, public employee, or a grantor of a public easement to a public entity for any of the following purposes, is not liable for an injury caused by a condition of:

(a) Any unpaved road which provides access to fishing, hunting, camping, hiking, riding, including animal and all types of vehicular riding, water sports, recreational or scenic areas and which is not a (1) city street or highway or (2) county, state or federal highway or (3) public street or highway of a joint highway district, boulevard district, bridge and highway district or similar district formed for the improvement or building of public streets or highways.

(b) Any trail used for the above purposes.

(c) Any paved trail, walkway, path, or sidewalk on an easement of way which has been granted to a public entity, which easement provides access to any unimproved property, so long as such public entity shall reasonably attempt to provide adequate warnings of the existence of any condition of the paved trail, walkway, path, or sidewalk which constitutes a hazard to health or safety. Warnings required by this subdivision shall only be required where pathways are paved, and such requirement shall not be construed to be a standard of care for any unpaved pathways or roads. **Leg.H.** Added Stats 1963 ch 1681 §1. Amended Stats 1968 ch 714 §1; Stats 1970 ch 807 §2; Stats 1972 ch 1200 §2; Stats 1979 ch 1010 §1.

§831.5. Public access programs by private nonprofit entities; "Public entity"; "Public employee"

(a) The Legislature declares that innovative public access programs, such as agreements with public land trusts, can provide effective and responsible alternatives to costly public acquisition programs. The Legislature therefore declares that it is beneficial to the people of this state to encourage private nonprofit entities such as public land trusts to carry out programs that preserve open spare or increase opportunities for the public to enjoy access to and use of natural resources if the programs are consistent (1) with public safety, (2) with the protection of the resources, and (3) with public and private rights.

(b) For the purposes of Sections 831.2, 831.25, 831.4, and 831.7, "public entity" includes a public land trust which meets all of the following conditions:

(1) It is a nonprofit organization existing under the provisions of Section 501 (c) of the United States Internal Revenue Code.

(2) It has specifically set forth in its articles of incorporation, as among its principal charitable purposes, the conservation of land for public access, agricultural, scientific, historical, educational, recreational, scenic, or open–space opportunities.

(3) It has entered into an agreement with the State Coastal Conservancy for lands located within the coastal zone, as defined in Section 31006 of the Public Resources Code, with the California Tahoe Conservancy or its designee for lands located within the Lake Tahoe region, as defined in subdivision (c) of Section 66953 of the Government Code, or with the State Public Works Board or its designee for lands not located within the coastal zone or the Lake Tahoe region, on such terms and conditions as are mutually agreeable, requiring the public land trust to hold the lands or, where appropriate, to provide nondiscriminatory public access consistent with the protection and conservation of either coastal or other natural resources, or both. The conservancy or the board, as appropriate, shall periodically review the agreement and determine whether the public land trust is in compliance with the terms and conditions. In the event the conservancy or the board determines that the public land trust is not in substantial compliance with the agreement, the conservancy or the board shall cancel the agreement, and the provisions of Sections 831.2, 831.25, 831.4, and 831.7 shall no longer apply with regard to that public land trust.

(c) For the purposes of Sections 831.2, 831.25, 831.4, and 831.7, "public employee" includes an officer, authorized agent, or employee of any public land trust which is a public entity. **Leg.H.** Added Stats 1980 ch 1123 §1. Amended Stats 1980 ch 1234 §1, effective September 29, 1980, operative January 1, 1981; Stats 1984 ch 1222 §1, effective September 17, 1984; Ch 1239 §1, effective September 17, 1984; Stats 1990 ch 934 §2 (AB 3570).

§831.6. Unimproved and unoccupied portions of ungranted tidelands, beds of navigable waters, etc.; Unsold portions of school lands

Neither the State nor an employee of the State is liable under this chapter for any injury caused by a condition of the unimproved and unoccupied portions of:

(a) The ungranted tidelands and submerged lands, and the beds of navigable rivers, streams, lakes, bays, estuaries, inlets and straits, owned by the State.

(b) The unsold portions of the 16th and 36th sections of school lands, the unsold portions of the 500,000 acres granted to the State for school purposes, and the unsold portions of the listed lands selected of the United States in lieu of the 16th and 36th sections and losses to the school grant. **Leg.H.** Added Stats 1963 ch 1681 §1.

§831.7. Liability to participant in or spectator to hazardous recreational activity

(a) Neither a public entity nor a public employee is liable to any person who participates in a hazardous recreational activity, including any person who assists the participant, or to any spectator who knew or reasonably should have known that the hazardous recreational activity created a substantial risk of injury to himself or herself and was voluntarily in the place of risk, or having the ability to do so failed to leave, for any damage or injury to property or persons arising out of that hazardous recreational activity.

(b) As used in this section, "hazardous recreational activity" means a recreational activity conducted on property of a public entity that creates a substantial, as distinguished from a minor, trivial, or insignificant, risk of injury to a participant or a spectator.

"Hazardous recreational activity" also means:

(1) Water contact activities, except diving, in places where, or at a time when, lifeguards are not provided and reasonable warning thereof has been given, or the injured party should reasonably have known that there was no lifeguard provided at the time.

(2) Any form of diving into water from other than a diving board or diving platform, or at any place or from any structure where diving is prohibited and reasonable warning thereof has been given.

(3) Animal riding, including equestrian competition, archery, bicycle racing or jumping, bicycle motocross, mountain bicycling, boating, cross-country and downhill skiing, hang gliding, kayaking, motorized vehicle racing, off-road motorcycling or four-wheel driving of any kind, orienteering, pistol and rifle shooting, rock climbing, rocketeering, rodeo, self-contained underwater breathing apparatus (SCUBA) diving, spelunking, skydiving, sport parachuting, paragliding, body contact sports, surfing, trampolining, tree climbing, tree rope swinging, waterskiing, white water rafting, and windsurfing. For the purposes of this subdivision, "mountain bicycling" does not include riding a bicycle on paved pathways, roadways, or sidewalks. For the purpose of this paragraph, "body contact sports" means sports in which it is reasonably foreseeable that there will be rough bodily contact with one or more participants.

(c)(1) Notwithstanding subdivision (a), this section does not limit liability that would otherwise exist for any of the following:

(A) Failure of the public entity or employee to guard or warn of a known dangerous condition or of another hazardous recreational activity known to the public entity or employee that is not reasonably assumed by the participant as inherently a part of the hazardous recreational activity out of which the damage or injury arose.

(B) Damage or injury suffered in any case where permission to participate in the hazardous recreational activity was granted for a specific fee. For the purpose of this subparagraph, "specific fee" does not include a fee or consideration charged for a general purpose such as a general park admission charge, a vehicle entry or parking fee, or an administrative or group use application or permit fee, as distinguished from a specific fee charged for participation in the specific hazardous recreational activity out of which the damage or injury arose.

(C) Injury suffered to the extent proximately caused by the negligent failure of the public entity or public employee to properly construct or maintain in good repair any structure, recreational equipment or machinery, or substantial work of improvement utilized in the hazardous recreational activity out of which the damage or injury arose.

(D) Damage or injury suffered in any case where the public entity or employee recklessly or with gross negligence promoted the participation in or observance of a hazardous recreational activity. For purposes of this subparagraph, promotional literature or a public announcement or advertisement that merely describes the available facilities and services on the property does not in itself constitute a reckless or grossly negligent promotion.

(E) An act of gross negligence by a public entity or a public employee that is the proximate cause of the injury.

(2) Nothing in this subdivision creates a duty of care or basis of liability for personal injury or damage to personal property.

(d) Nothing in this section limits the liability of an independent concessionaire, or any person or organization other than the public entity, whether or not the person or organization has a contractual relationship with the public entity to use the public property, for injuries or damages suffered in any case as a result of the operation of a hazardous recreational activity on public property by the concessionaire, person, or organization. **Leg.H.** Added Stats 1983 ch 863 §1. Amended Stats 1995 ch 597 §1 (AB 700); Stats 2010 ch 73 §1 (AB 634), effective January 1, 2011; Stats 2011 ch 296 §109 (AB 1023), effective January 1, 2012; Stats 2014 ch 913 §17 (AB 2747), effective January 1, 2015.

§831.7.5. Exoneration for public entity that owns or operates dog park; Construction

(a) A public entity that owns or operates a dog park shall not be held liable for injury or death of a person or pet resulting solely from the actions of a dog in the dog park.

(b) This section shall not be construed to affect the liability of a public entity that exists under the law.

(c) "Public entity" has the same meaning as Section 811.2, and includes, but is not limited to, cities, counties, cities and counties, and special districts. **Leg.H.** Added Stats 2013 ch 74 §1 (AB 265), effective January 1, 2014.

§831.8. Condition of reservoir; Condition of canals, conduits, or drains; Condition or use of unlined flood control channels or adjacent groundwater recharge spreading grounds; When exoneration from liability absent

(a) Subject to subdivisions (d) and (e), neither a public entity nor a public employee is liable under this chapter for an injury caused by the condition of a reservoir if at the time of the injury the person injured was using the property for any purpose other than that for which the public entity intended or permitted the property to be used.

(b) Subject to subdivisions (d) and (e), neither an irrigation district nor an employee thereof nor the state nor a state employee is liable under this chapter for an injury caused by the condition of canals, conduits, or drains used for the distribution of water if at the time of the injury the person injured was using the property for any purpose other than that for which the district or state intended it to be used.

(c) Subject to subdivisions (d) and (e), neither a public agency operating flood control and water conservation facilities nor its employees are liable under this chapter for an injury caused by the condition or use of unlined flood control channels or adjacent groundwater recharge spreading grounds if, at the time of the injury, the person injured was using the property for any purpose other than that for which the public entity intended it to be used, and, if all of the following conditions are met:

(1) The public agency operates and maintains dams, pipes, channels, and appurtenant facilities to provide flood control protection and water conservation for a county whose population exceeds nine million residents.

(2) The public agency operates facilities to recharge a groundwater basin system which is the primary water supply for more than one million residents.

(3) The groundwater supply is dependent on imported water recharge which must be conducted in accordance with court-imposed basin management restrictions.

(4) The basin recharge activities allow the conservation and storage of both local and imported water supplies when these waters are available.

(5) The public agency posts conspicuous signs warning of any increase in waterflow levels of an unlined flood control channel or any spreading ground receiving water.

(d) Nothing in this section exonerates a public entity or a public employee from liability for injury proximately caused by a dangerous condition of property if all of the following occur:

(1) The injured person was not guilty of a criminal offense under Article 1 (commencing with Section 552) of Chapter 12 of Title 13 of Part 1 of the Penal Code in entering on or using the property.

(2) The condition created a substantial and unreasonable risk of death or serious bodily harm when the property or adjacent property was used with due care in a manner in which it was reasonably foreseeable that it would be used.

(3) The dangerous character of the condition was not reasonably apparent to, and would not have been anticipated by, a mature, reasonable person using the property with due care.

(4) The public entity or the public employee had actual knowledge of the condition and knew or should have known of its dangerous character a sufficient time prior to the injury to have taken measures to protect against the condition.

(e) Nothing in this section exonerates a public entity or a public employee from liability for injury proximately caused by a dangerous condition of property if all of the following occur:

(1) The person injured was less than 12 years of age.

(2) The dangerous condition created a substantial and unreasonable risk of death or serious bodily harm to children under 12 years of age using the property or adjacent property with due care in a manner in which it was reasonably foreseeable that it would be used.

(3) The person injured, because of his or her immaturity, did not discover the condition or did not appreciate its dangerous character.

(4) The public entity or the public employee had actual knowledge of the condition and knew or should have known of its dangerous character a sufficient time prior to the injury to have taken measures to protect against the condition.

(f) Nothing in subdivision (c) exonerates a public agency or public employee subject to that subdivision from liability for injury proximately caused by a dangerous condition of public property if all of the following occur:

(1) The person injured was 16 years of age or younger.

(2) The dangerous condition created a substantial and unreasonable risk of death or serious bodily harm to children 16 years of age or younger using the property or adjacent property with due care in a manner in which it was reasonably foreseeable that it would be used.

(3) The person injured did not discover the condition or did not appreciate its dangerous character because of his or her immaturity.

(4) The public entity or public employee had actual knowledge of the condition and knew or should have known of its dangerous character a sufficient time prior to the injury to have taken measures to protect against the condition. **Leg.H.** Added Stats 1963 ch 1681 §1. Amended Stats 1998 ch 659 §1 (AB 2023); Stats 2001 ch 756 §1 (AB 92); Stats 2008 ch 633 §1 (AB 1903), effective September 30, 2008; Stats 2012 ch 110 §1 (AB 1558), effective January 1, 2013.

ARTICLE 2
Liability of Public Entities

§835. When public entity liable for injury caused by dangerous condition of property

Except as provided by statute, a public entity is liable for injury caused by a dangerous condition of its property if the plaintiff establishes that the property was in a dangerous condition at the time of the injury, that the injury was proximately caused by the dangerous condition, that the dangerous condition created a reasonably foreseeable risk of the kind of injury which was incurred, and that either:

(a) A negligent or wrongful act or omission of an employee of the public entity within the scope of his employment created the dangerous condition; or

(b) The public entity had actual or constructive notice of the dangerous condition under Section 835.2 a sufficient time prior to the injury to have taken measures to protect against the dangerous condition. **Leg.H.** Added Stats 1963 ch 1681 §1.

§835.2. What constitutes actual notice; Requisite showing of constructive notice; Admissible evidence

(a) A public entity had actual notice of a dangerous condition within the meaning of subdivision (b) of Section 835 if it had actual knowledge of the existence of the condition and knew or should have known of its dangerous character.

(b) A public entity had constructive notice of a dangerous condition within the meaning of subdivision (b) of Section 835 only if the plaintiff establishes that the condition had existed for such a period of time and was of such an obvious nature that the public entity, in the exercise of due care, should have discovered the condition and its dangerous character. On the issue of due care, admissible evidence includes but is not limited to evidence as to:

(1) Whether the existence of the condition and its dangerous character would have been discovered by an inspection system that was reasonably adequate (considering the practicability and cost of inspection weighed against the likelihood and magnitude of the potential danger to which failure to inspect would give rise) to inform the public entity whether the property was safe for the use or uses for which the public entity used or intended others to use the public property and for uses that the public entity actually knew others were making of the public property or adjacent property.

(2) Whether the public entity maintained and operated such an inspection system with due care and did not discover the condition. **Leg.H.** Added Stats 1963 ch 1681 §1.

§835.4. Conditions causing injury for which public entity not liable; Reasonable act or omission

(a) A public entity is not liable under subdivision (a) of Section 835 for injury caused by a condition of its property if the public entity establishes that the act or omission that created the condition was reasonable. The reasonableness of the act or omission that created the condition shall be determined by weighing the probability and gravity of potential injury to persons and property foreseeably exposed to the risk of injury against the practicability and cost of taking alternative action that would not create the risk of injury or of protecting against the risk of injury.

(b) A public entity is not liable under subdivision (b) of Section 835 for injury caused by a dangerous condition of its property if the public entity establishes that the action it took to protect against the risk of injury created by the condition or its failure to take such action was reasonable. The reasonableness of the action or inaction of the public entity shall be determined by taking into consideration the time and opportunity it had to take action and by weighing the probability and gravity of potential injury to persons and property foreseeably exposed to the risk of injury against the practicability and cost of protecting against the risk of such injury. **Leg.H.** Added Stats 1963 ch 1681 §1.

ARTICLE 3
Liability of Public Employees

§840. Property conditions causing injury for which employee not liable; Available immunity and defenses

Except as provided in this article, a public employee is not liable for injury caused by a condition of public property where such condition exists because of any act or omission of such employee within the scope of his employment. The liability established by this article is subject to any immunity of the public employee provided by statute and is subject to any defenses that would be available to the public employee if he were a private person. **Leg.H.** Added Stats 1963 ch 1681 §1.

§840.2. Conditions causing injury for which employee liable; Requisite showing by plaintiff

An employee of a public entity is liable for injury caused by a dangerous condition of public property if the plaintiff establishes that the property of the public entity was in a dangerous condition at the time of the injury, that the injury was proximately caused by the dangerous condition, that the dangerous condition created a reasonably foreseeable risk of the kind of injury which was incurred, and that either:

(a) The dangerous condition was directly attributable wholly or in substantial part to a negligent or wrongful act of the employee and the employee had the authority and the funds and other means immediately available to take alternative action which would not have created the dangerous condition; or

(b) The employee had the authority and it was his responsibility to take adequate measures to protect against the dangerous condition at the expense of the public entity and the funds and other means for doing so were immediately available to him, and he had actual or constructive notice of the dangerous condition under Section 840.4 a sufficient time prior to the injury to have taken measures to protect against the dangerous condition. **Leg.H.** Added Stats 1963 ch 1681 §1.

§840.4. What constitutes actual notice of dangerous condition; Requisite showing for establishment of constructive notice

(a) A public employee had actual notice of a dangerous condition within the meaning of subdivision (b) of Section 840.2 if he had actual personal knowledge of the existence of the condition and knew or should have known of its dangerous character.

(b) A public employee had constructive notice of a dangerous condition within the meaning of subdivision (b) of Section 840.2 only if the plaintiff establishes (1) that the public employee had the authority and it was his responsibility as a public employee to inspect the property of the public entity or to see that inspections were made to determine whether dangerous conditions existed in the public property, (2) that the funds and other means for making such inspections or for seeing that such inspections were made were immediately available to the public employee, and (3) that the dangerous condition had existed for such a period of time and was of such an obvious nature that the public employee, in the exercise of his authority and responsibility with due care, should have

Sec. 840.6

discovered the condition and its dangerous character. **Leg.H.** Added Stats 1963 ch 1681 §1.

§840.6. Absence of liability for condition resulting in injury where act or omission creating condition was reasonable

(a) A public employee is not liable under subdivision (a) of Section 840.2 for injury caused by a dangerous condition of public property if he establishes that the act or omission that created the condition was reasonable. The reasonableness of the act or omission that created the condition shall be determined by weighing the probability and gravity of potential injury to persons and property foreseeably exposed to the risk of injury against the practicability and cost of taking alternative action that would not create the risk of injury or of protecting against the risk of injury.

(b) A public employee is not liable under subdivision (b) of Section 840.2 for injury caused by a dangerous condition of public property if he establishes that the action taken to protect against the risk of injury created by the condition or the failure to take such action was reasonable. The reasonableness of the inaction or action shall be determined by taking into consideration the time and opportunity the public employee had to take action and by weighing the probability and gravity of potential injury to persons and property foreseeably exposed to the risk of injury against the practicability and cost of protecting against the risk of such injury. **Leg.H.** Added Stats 1963 ch 1681 §1.

CHAPTER 3
POLICE AND CORRECTIONAL ACTIVITIES

§844. "Prisoner"

As used in this chapter, "prisoner" includes an inmate of a prison, jail, or penal or correctional facility. For the purposes of this chapter, a lawfully arrested person who is brought into a law enforcement facility for the purpose of being booked, as described in Section 7 of the Penal Code, becomes a prisoner, as a matter of law, upon his or her initial entry into a prison, jail, or penal or correctional facility, pursuant to penal processes. **Leg.H.** Added Stats 1963 ch 1681 §1. Amended Stats 1996 ch 395 §1 (SB 1493).

§844.6. Injury by or to prisoner

(a) Notwithstanding any other provision of this part, except as provided in this section and in Sections 814, 814.2, 845.4, and 845.6, or in Title 2.1 (commencing with Section 3500) of Part 3 of the Penal Code, a public entity is not liable for:

(1) An injury proximately caused by any prisoner.
(2) An injury to any prisoner.

(b) Nothing in this section affects the liability of a public entity under Article 1 (commencing with Section 17000) of Chapter 1 of Division 9 of the Vehicle Code.

(c) Except for an injury to a prisoner, nothing in this section prevents recovery from the public entity for an injury resulting from the dangerous condition of public property under Chapter 2 (commencing with Section 830) of this part.

(d) Nothing in this section exonerates a public employee from liability for injury proximately caused by his negligent or wrongful act or omission. The public entity may but is not required to pay any judgment, compromise or settlement, or may but is not required to indemnify any public employee, in any case where the public entity is immune from liability under this section; except that the public entity shall pay, as provided in Article 4 (commencing with Section 825) of Chapter 1 of this part, any judgment based on a claim against a public employee who is lawfully engaged in the practice of one of the healing arts under any law of this state for malpractice arising from an act or omission in the scope of his employment, and shall pay any compromise or settlement of a claim or action, based on such malpractice, to which the public entity has agreed. **Leg.H.** Added Stats 1963 ch 1681 §1. Amended Stats 1970 ch 1099 §5; Stats 1977 ch 1250 §2.

§845. Failure to provide any or adequate police protection; Responding to alarm

Neither a public entity nor a public employee is liable for failure to establish a police department or otherwise to provide police protection service or, if police protection service is provided, for failure to provide sufficient police protection service.

A police department shall not fail to respond to a request for service via a burglar alarm system or an alarm company referral service solely on the basis that a permit from the city has not been obtained. **Leg.H.** Added Stats 1963 ch 1681 §1. Amended Stats 1992 ch 547 §1 (AB 2611).

§845.2. Failure to provide prison, correctional facility, equipment, personnel, etc.

Except as provided in Chapter 2 (commencing with Section 830), neither a public entity nor a public employee is liable for failure to provide a prison, jail or penal or correctional facility or, if such facility is provided, for failure to provide sufficient equipment, personnel or facilities therein. **Leg.H.** Added Stats 1963 ch 1681 §1.

§845.4. Interference with prisoner's right to judicial determination as to legality of confinement

Neither a public entity nor a public employee acting within the scope of his employment is liable for interfering with the right of a prisoner to obtain a judicial determination or review of the legality of his confinement; but a public employee, and the public entity where the employee is acting within the scope of his employment, is liable for injury proximately caused by the employee's intentional and unjustifiable interference with such right, but no cause of action for such injury shall be deemed to accrue until it has first been determined that the confinement was illegal. **Leg.H.** Added Stats 1963 ch 1681 §1. Amended Stats 1970 ch 1099 §6.

§845.6. Failure to furnish prisoner medical care

Neither a public entity nor a public employee is liable for injury proximately caused by the failure of the employee to furnish or obtain medical care for a prisoner in his custody; but, except as otherwise provided by Sections 855.8 and 856, a public employee, and the public entity where the employee is acting within the scope of his employment, is liable if the employee knows or has reason to know that the prisoner is in need of immediate medical care and he fails to take reasonable action to summon such medical care. Nothing in this section exonerates a public employee who is lawfully engaged in the practice of one of the healing arts under any law of this state from liability for injury proximately caused by malpractice or exonerates the public entity from its obligation to pay any judgment, compromise, or settlement that it is required to pay under subdivision (d) of Section 844.6. **Leg.H.** Added Stats 1963 ch 1681 §1. Amended Stats 1970 ch 1099 §7.

§845.8. Injury from prisoner's parole or release; Injury caused by escaping or escaped prisoner, arrestee, etc.

Neither a public entity nor a public employee is liable for:

(a) Any injury resulting from determining whether to parole or release a prisoner or from determining the terms and conditions of his parole or release or from determining whether to revoke his parole or release.

(b) Any injury caused by:
(1) An escaping or escaped prisoner;
(2) An escaping or escaped arrested person; or
(3) A person resisting arrest. **Leg.H.** Added Stats 1963 ch 1681 §1. Amended Stats 1970 ch 1099 §8.

§846. Injury from failure to make arrest or retain person in custody

Neither a public entity nor a public employee is liable for injury caused by the failure to make an arrest or by the failure to retain an arrested person in custody. **Leg.H.** Added Stats 1963 ch 1681 §1.

CHAPTER 4
FIRE PROTECTION

§850. Failure to provide fire protection service

Neither a public entity nor a public employee is liable for failure to establish a fire department or otherwise to provide fire protection service. **Leg.H.** Added Stats 1963 ch 1681 §1.

§850.2. Failure to maintain sufficient fire protection personnel or facilities

Neither a public entity that has undertaken to provide fire protection service, nor an employee of such a public entity, is liable for any injury resulting from the failure to provide or maintain sufficient personnel, equipment or other fire protection facilities. **Leg.H.** Added Stats 1963 ch 1681 §1.

§850.4. Injury caused in fighting fires and from condition of fire fighting equipment or facilities

Neither a public entity, nor a public employee acting in the scope of his employment, is liable for any injury resulting from the condition of fire protection or firefighting equipment or facilities or, except as provided in Article 1 (commencing with Section 17000) of Chapter 1 of Division 9 of the Vehicle Code, for any injury caused in fighting fires. **Leg.H.** Added Stats 1963 ch 1681 §1.

§850.6. Act or omission of employee of public entity performing service outside fire protection area

(a) Whenever a public entity provides fire protection or firefighting service outside of the area regularly served and protected by the public entity providing that service, the public entity providing the service is liable for any injury for which liability is imposed by statute caused by its act or omission or the act or omission of its employee occurring in the performance of that fire protection or firefighting service. Notwithstanding any other law, the public entity receiving the fire protection or firefighting service is not liable for any act or omission of the public entity providing the service or for any act or omission of an employee of the public entity providing the service; but the public entity providing the service and the public entity receiving the service may by agreement determine the extent, if any, to which the public entity receiving the service will be required to indemnify the public entity providing the service.

(b) Notwithstanding any other provision of this section, any claims against the state shall be presented to the Department of General Services in accordance with Part 3 (commencing with Section 900) and Part 4 (commencing with Section 940) of Division 3.6 of Title 1. **Leg.H.** Added Stats 1963 ch 1681 §1. Amended Stats 1965 ch 1203 §1; Stats 2006 ch 538 §217 (SB 1852), effective January 1, 2007; Stats 2016 ch 31 §33 (SB 836), effective June 27, 2016.

§850.8. Transportation of person injured by fire, etc.

Any member of an organized fire department, fire protection district, or other firefighting unit of either the state or any political subdivision, any employee of the Department of Forestry and Fire Protection, or any other public employee when acting in the scope of his or her employment, may transport or arrange for the transportation of any person injured by a fire, or by a fire protection operation, to a physician and surgeon or hospital if the injured person does not object to the transportation.

Neither a public entity nor a public employee is liable for any injury sustained by the injured person as a result of or in connection with that transportation or for any medical, ambulance, or hospital bills incurred by or in behalf of the injured person or for any other damages, but a public employee is liable for injury proximately caused by his or her willful misconduct in transporting the injured person or arranging for the transportation. **Leg.H.** Added Stats 1963 ch 1681 §1. Amended Stats 1981 ch 714 §158; Stats 1992 ch 427 §45 (AB 3355).

CHAPTER 4.5
UNMANNED AIRCRAFT

§853. Liability for damage by local public entity or public employee providing emergency services

A local public entity or public employee of a local public entity shall not be liable for any damage to an unmanned aircraft or unmanned aircraft system, if the damage was caused while the local public entity or public employee of a local public entity was providing, and the unmanned aircraft or unmanned aircraft system was interfering with, the operation, support, or enabling of any of the following emergency services:

(a) Emergency medical services or ambulance transport services, including, but not limited to, air ambulance services.

(b) Firefighting or firefighting-related services, including, but not limited to, air services related to firefighting or firefighting-related services.

(c) Search and rescue services, including, but not limited to, air search and rescue services. **Leg.H.** Added Stats 2016 ch 834 §2 (SB 807), effective January 1, 2017.

§853.1. Scope of immunity

The immunity provided by this chapter is in addition to any other immunity provided to a local public entity or public employee of a local public entity under law. **Leg.H.** Added Stats 2016 ch 834 §2 (SB 807), effective January 1, 2017.

§853.5. "Unmanned aircraft"; "Unmanned aircraft system"

The following definitions shall apply to this chapter:

(a) "Unmanned aircraft" means an aircraft that is operated without the possibility of direct human intervention from within or on the aircraft.

(b) "Unmanned aircraft system" means an unmanned aircraft and associated elements, including, but not limited to, communication links and the components that control the unmanned aircraft that are required for the pilot in command to operate safely and efficiently in the national airspace system. **Leg.H.** Added Stats 2016 ch 834 §2 (SB 807), effective January 1, 2017.

CHAPTER 5
MEDICAL, HOSPITAL AND PUBLIC HEALTH ACTIVITIES

§854. "Medical facility"

As used in this chapter, unless the context otherwise requires, "medical facility" includes a hospital, infirmary, clinic, dispensary, mental institution, or similar facility. **Leg.H.** Added Stats 1963 ch 1681 §1.

§854.1. Continuity of care for individuals transitioning from developmental centers to the community; Retention of staff; Definitions applying to chapter

(a) It is the intent of the Legislature to ensure continuity of care for individuals with developmental disabilities transitioning from a developmental center to the community and to prevent the unnecessary institutionalization and hospitalization of these individuals.

(b) In the effort to achieve these goals, it is the intent of the Legislature to seek and implement recommendations that include all of the following services to retain developmental center staff as employees:

(1) Crisis management teams that provide behavioral, medical, and dental treatment, training, and technical assistance.

(2) Specialized services, including adaptive equipment design and fabrication, and medical, dental, psychological, and assessment services.

(3) Staff support in community homes to assist individuals with behavioral or psychiatric needs.

(c) As used in this chapter, the terms "mental institution" or "medical facility" also include a developmental services facility. For the purposes of this chapter "developmental services facility" means any facility or place where a public employee provides services and supports to individuals transitioning from a developmental center to the community or to individuals with developmental disabilities at risk of admission to a developmental center, an institution for mental disease, an out-of-state placement, a general acute care hospital, or an acute psychiatric hospital. **Leg.H.** Added Stats 2005 ch 538 § 1 (AB 1378), effective January 1, 2006. Amended Stats 2010 ch 717 §2 (SB 853), effective October 19, 2010; Stats 2014 ch 30 §1 (SB 856), effective June 20, 2014.

§854.2. "Mental institution"

As used in this chapter, "mental institution" means a state hospital for the care and treatment of persons with mental health disorders or intellectual disabilities, the California Rehabilitation Center referred to in Section 3300 of the Welfare and Institutions Code, or a county psychiatric hospital. **Leg.H.** Added Stats 1963 ch 1681 §1. Amended Stats 1970 ch 1099 §9; Stats 2012 ch 448 §13 (AB 2370), effective January 1, 2013, ch 457 §13 (SB 1381), effective January 1, 2013; Stats 2014 ch 144 §15 (AB 1847), effective January 1, 2015.

§854.3. "County psychiatric hospital"

As used in this chapter, "county psychiatric hospital" means the hospital, ward, or facility provided by the county pursuant to the provisions of Section 7100 of the Welfare and Institutions Code. **Leg.H.** Added Stats 1970 ch 1099 §10.

§854.4. "Mental illness or addiction"

As used in this chapter, "mental illness or addiction" means any condition for which a person may be detained, cared for, or treated in a mental institution, in a facility designated by a county pursuant to Chapter 2 (commencing with Section 5150) of Part 1 of Division 5 of the Welfare and Institutions Code, or in a similar facility. **Leg.H.** Added Stats 1963 ch 1681 §1. Amended Stats 1970 ch 1099 §11.

§854.5. "Confine"

As used in this chapter, "confine" includes admit, commit, place, detain, or hold in custody. **Leg.H.** Added Stats 1970 ch 1099 §12.

§854.8. Injury by or to person committed to mental institution

(a) Notwithstanding any other provision of this part, except as provided in this section and in Sections 814, 814.2, 855, and 855.2, a public entity is not liable for:

(1) An injury proximately caused by a patient of a mental institution.

(2) An injury to an inpatient of a mental institution.

(b) Nothing in this section affects the liability of a public entity under Article 1 (commencing with Section 17000) of Chapter 1 of Division 9 of the Vehicle Code.

(c) Except for an injury to an inpatient of a mental institution, nothing in this section prevents recovery from the public entity for an injury resulting from the dangerous condition of public property under Chapter 2 (commencing with Section 830) of this part.

(d) Nothing in this section exonerates a public employee from liability for injury proximately caused by his negligent or wrongful act or omission. The public entity may but is not required to pay any judgment, compromise or settlement, or may but is not required to indemnify any public employee, in any case where the public entity is immune from liability under this section; except that the public entity shall pay, as provided in Article 4 (commencing with Section 825) of Chapter 1 of this part, any judgment based on a claim against a public employee who is lawfully engaged in the practice of one of the healing arts under any law of this state for malpractice arising from an act or omission in the scope of his employment, and shall pay any compromise or settlement of a claim or action, based on such malpractice, to which the public entity has agreed. **Leg.H.** Added Stats 1963 ch 1681 §1. Amended Stats 1970 ch 1099 §13.

§855. Injury from failure of public entity to provide adequate equipment, personnel or facilities

(a) A public entity that operates or maintains any medical facility that is subject to regulation by the State Department of Health Services, Social Services, Developmental Services, or Mental Health is liable for injury proximately caused by the failure of the public entity to provide adequate or sufficient equipment, personnel or facilities required by any statute or any regulation of the State Department of Health Services, Social Services, Developmental Services, or Mental Health prescribing minimum standards for equipment, personnel or facilities, unless the public entity establishes that it exercised reasonable diligence to comply with the applicable statute or regulation.

(b) A public entity that operates or maintains any medical facility that is not subject to regulation by the State Department of Health Services, Social Services, Developmental Services, or Mental Health is liable for injury proximately caused by the failure of the public entity to provide adequate or sufficient equipment, personnel or facilities substantially equivalent to those required by any statute or any regulation of the State Department of Health Services, Social Services, Developmental Services, or Mental Health prescribing minimum standards for equipment, personnel or facilities applicable to a public medical facility of the same character and class, unless the public entity establishes that it exercised reasonable diligence to conform with such minimum standards.

(c) Nothing in this section confers authority upon, or augments the authority of, the State Department of Health Services, Social Services, Developmental Services, or Mental Health to adopt, administer or enforce any regulation. Any regulation establishing minimum standards for equipment, personnel or facilities in any medical facility operated or maintained by a public entity, to be effective, must be within the scope of authority conferred by law. **Leg.H.** Added Stats 1963 ch 1681 §1. Amended Stats 1978 ch 429 §49.5, effective July 17, 1978, operative July 1, 1978.

§855.2. Interference with inmate's right to judicial determination as to legality of confinement

Neither a public entity nor a public employee acting within the scope of his employment is liable for interfering with the right of an inmate of a medical facility operated or maintained by a public entity to obtain a judicial determination or review of the legality of his confinement; but a public employee, and the public entity where the employee is acting within the scope of his employment, is liable for injury proximately caused by the employee's intentional and unjustifiable interference with such right, but no cause of action for such injury shall be deemed to accrue until it has first been determined that the confinement was illegal. **Leg.H.** Added Stats 1963 ch 1681 §1. Amended Stats 1970 ch 1099 §14.

§855.4. Decision as to performance or nonperformance of disease prevention, etc.; Nonnegligent execution of decision

(a) Neither a public entity nor a public employee is liable for an injury resulting from the decision to perform or not to perform any act to promote the public health of the community by preventing disease or controlling the communication of disease within the community if the decision whether the act was or was not to be performed was the result of the exercise of discretion vested in the public entity or the public employee, whether or not such discretion be abused.

(b) Neither a public entity nor a public employee is liable for an injury caused by an act or omission in carrying out with due care a decision described in subdivision (a). **Leg.H.** Added Stats 1963 ch 1681 §1.

§855.6. Injury from failure to make any or adequate physical or mental examination

Except for an examination or diagnosis for the purpose of treatment, neither a public entity nor a public employee acting within the scope of his employment is liable for injury caused by the failure to make a physical or mental examination, or to make an adequate physical or mental examination, of any person for the purpose of determining whether such person has a disease or physical or mental condition that would constitute a hazard to the health or safety of himself or others. **Leg.H.** Added Stats 1963 ch 1681 §1.

§855.8. Diagnosis and treatment of mental illness or addiction

(a) Neither a public entity nor a public employee acting within the scope of his employment is liable for injury resulting from diagnosing or failing to diagnose that a person is afflicted with mental illness or addiction or from failing to prescribe for mental illness or addiction.

(b) A public employee acting within the scope of his employment is not liable for administering with due care the treatment prescribed for mental illness or addiction.

(c) Nothing in this section exonerates a public employee who has undertaken to prescribe for mental illness or addiction from liability for injury proximately caused by his negligence or by his wrongful act in so prescribing.

(d) Nothing in this section exonerates a public employee from liability for injury proximately caused by his negligent or wrongful act or omission in administering any treatment prescribed for mental illness or addiction. **Leg.H.** Added Stats 1963 ch 1681 §1.

§856. Determination as to confinement for mental illness or addiction; Parole, leave of absence, or release

(a) Neither a public entity nor a public employee acting within the scope of his employment is liable for any injury resulting from determining in accordance with any applicable enactment:

(1) Whether to confine a person for mental illness or addiction.

(2) The terms and conditions of confinement for mental illness or addiction.

(3) Whether to parole, grant a leave of absence to, or release a person confined for mental illness or addiction.

(b) A public employee is not liable for carrying out with due care a determination described in subdivision (a).

(c) Nothing in this section exonerates a public employee from liability for injury proximately caused by his negligent or wrongful act or omission in carrying out or failing to carry out:

(1) A determination to confine or not to confine a person for mental illness or addiction.

(2) The terms or conditions of confinement of a person for mental illness or addiction.

(3) A determination to parole, grant a leave of absence to, or release a person confined for mental illness or addiction. **Leg.H.** Added Stats 1963 ch 1681 §1. Amended Stats 1970 ch 1099 §15.

§856.2. Injury or death when person confined for mental illness or addiction escapes

(a) Neither a public entity nor a public employee is liable for:

(1) An injury caused by an escaping or escaped person who has been confined for mental illness or addiction.

(2) An injury to, or the wrongful death of, an escaping or escaped person who has been confined for mental illness or addiction.

(b) Nothing in this section exonerates a public employee from liability:

(1) If he acted or failed to act because of actual fraud, corruption, or actual malice.

(2) For injuries inflicted as a result of his own negligent or wrongful act or omission on an escaping or escaped mental patient in recapturing

him. **Leg.H.** Added Stats 1963 ch 1681 §1. Amended Stats 1970 ch 1099 §16.

§856.4. Failure to admit person to medical facility

Except as provided in Section 815.6, neither a public entity nor a public employee acting in the scope of his employment is liable for an injury resulting from the failure to admit a person to a public medical facility. **Leg.H.** Added Stats 1963 ch 1681 §1.

§856.6. Exemption from liability for participation in influenza immunization program

(a) A public entity, public employee, or volunteer, participating in the National Influenza Program of 1976, shall not be liable for an injury caused by an act or omission in the promotion of a community program or the administration of vaccine in a community program, including the residual effects of the vaccine, unless the act or omission constitutes willful misconduct.

(b) All promotions of a community program and oral and written information provided for purposes of consent to a person requesting inoculation shall contain notice of the provisions of subdivision (a) of this section. In the event the person to be inoculated is a minor, the parents or legal guardian of said minor must be informed orally or in writing of the provisions of subdivision (a) of this section and said parents or legal guardian must consent in writing to the inoculation of said minor person. The State Department of Health shall prescribe a form to be used in community programs which notifies a person of the provisions of subdivision (a) and contains a provision by which the person acknowledges that he has been so notified and understands the legal effect of the subdivision.

(c) As used in the section:

(1) "Community program" means a public program conducted by a state, city, county, or district health agency under the National Influenza Program of 1976 or a public or private organization which has entered into a contract with a state, city, county, or district health agency, with the approval of the State Department of Health, to provide services pursuant to the National Influenza Program of 1976.

(2) "Volunteer" means a licensed health professional, licensed health facility, organization, or individual participating in a community program.

(d) Notwithstanding any other provision of law, an individual authorized by the State Department of Health may administer influenza vaccine under the supervision of a licensed health professional in a community program using a jet injection apparatus. **Leg.H.** Added Stats 1976 ch 427 §1, effective July 10, 1976.

CHAPTER 6
ADMINISTRATION OF TAX LAWS

§860. "Tax"

As used in this chapter, "tax" includes a tax, assessment, fee or charge. **Leg.H.** Added Stats 1963 ch 1681 §1.

§860.2. Acts or omissions not imposing liability

Neither a public entity nor a public employee is liable for an injury caused by:

(a) Instituting any judicial or administrative proceeding or action for or incidental to the assessment or collection of a tax.

(b) An act or omission in the interpretation or application of any law relating to a tax. **Leg.H.** Added Stats 1963 ch 1681 §1.

§860.4. Inapplicability of chapter on tax refund, adjustment, etc.

Nothing in this chapter affects any law relating to refund, rebate, exemption, cancellation, amendment or adjustment of taxes. **Leg.H.** Added Stats 1963 ch 1681 §1.

CHAPTER 7
USE OF PESTICIDES

§862. Liability for injuries caused by use of "pesticide"

(a) As used in this section, "pesticide" means:

(1) An "economic poison" as defined in Section 12753 of the Agricultural Code;

(2) An "injurious material" the use of which is regulated or prohibited under Chapter 3 (commencing with Section 14001) of Division 7 of the Agricultural Code; or

(3) Any material used for the same purpose as material referred to in paragraphs (1) and (2).

(b) A public entity is liable for injuries caused by its use of a pesticide to the same extent as a private person except that no presumption of negligence arises from the failure of a public entity or a public employee to comply with a provision of a statute or regulation relating to the use of a pesticide if the statute or regulation by its terms is made inapplicable to the public entity or the public employee.

(c) Sections 11761 to 11765 of the Agricultural Code, relating to reports of loss or damages from the use of pesticides, apply in an action against a public entity under this section. **Leg.H.** Added Stats 1970 ch 1099 §17.

CHAPTER 8
ACTIVITIES TO ABATE AN IMPENDING PERIL

§865. Legislative findings and intent

The Legislature hereby finds and declares that:

(a) The gradual movement of land, such as in prehistoric slide areas, or as a result of subsidence due to the depletion of underground or subterranean supporting substances, such as minerals, petroleum sources, water, and similar substances, can result in danger to persons or property. Although the movement is gradual and expressed in terms of numbers of inches, feet or meters per day, week or year, at some point the forces that are exerted by the movement will sever underground utilities, such as water, sewer, gas, electricity or telephone services and can cause the destruction of aboveground structures whose foundations become undermined or where support is denied altogether. Unlike an earthquake or rapid rockslide or landslide, these gradual earth movements permit possible intervention to arrest the movement and avoid harm which is posed to persons or property. If there is an adequate manifestation of the problem before actual harm to persons or property, it is possible to make some determinations as to a method of remedial action which can abate the hazard. However, any undertaking to arrest the earth movement may not be successful or may have within it the potential for hastening the movement and the damages resulting from such movement. Regardless of how slight that potential for aggravating the damages, local public entities are unwilling to undertake action to alleviate the hazard if such undertaking may invite potential liability.

(b) It is the intent of the Legislature in enacting this chapter to create an incentive for local public entities, upon learning of the particular earth movement which will result in possible damage to substantial areas of property and constitute a threat of injury to persons, to undertake remedial action to abate the earth movement or protect against the danger therefrom without fear of incurring liability as a result of undertaking such action. **Leg.H.** Added Stats 1979 ch 1119 §1, effective September 28, 1979.

§866. Exemption of local entities from liability; Avoidance of impending peril due to gradual earth movement

(a) Subject to the provisions of subdivisions (b) and (c), in the event of public necessity and to avoid impending peril to persons or property as a result of gradual earth movement, a local public entity is not liable for damages for injury to persons or property resulting from such impending peril or from any action taken to abate such peril providing the legislative body of the local public entity has, on the basis of expert opinion or other reasonable basis, done all of the following:

(1) On the basis of adequate evidence such as expert opinion or otherwise, found the existence of such impending peril.

(2) Determined appropriate remedial action to halt, stabilize, or abate such impending peril.

(3) Undertaken to implement such remedial action.

As used in this chapter, "gradual earth movements" includes, but is not limited to, perceptible changes in the earth either in a subterranean area or at the surface, or both, which if not arrested or contained will over a gradual period of time result in damage to or destruction of underground or aboveground property or harm to persons. However, "gradual earth movement" does not include movement which is caused by activity undertaken by a local public entity for purposes other than the abatement of peril caused by gradual earth movement.

As used in this chapter, "local public entity" has the meaning set forth in Section 900.4.

(b) If the local public entity is unable to complete the steps described in paragraphs (1) to (3), inclusive, of subdivision (a) because of the cessation of the hazard or because such actions cannot be completed before the occurrence of the hazard sought to be avoided, or because such legislative body of such entity shall reasonably determine that such remedial action will not abate such danger, the immunity provided herein shall nevertheless apply to such actions by such local public entity.

(c) The immunity provided herein is in addition to any other immunity of the local public entity provided by law or statute, including this part, and any claim of liability based upon the impending peril or any action of the local public entity is subject to such immunities and any defenses that would be available to the local public entity if it were a private person. **Leg.H.** Added Stats 1979 ch 1119 §1, effective September 28, 1979.

§867. Exemption of employees

An employee of a local public entity is not liable for damages for injury to persons or property resulting from an impending peril or from any action taken to abate such peril pursuant to Section 866. **Leg.H.** Added Stats 1979 ch 1119 §1, effective September 28, 1979.

CHAPTER 21
TORT LIABILITY UNDER AGREEMENTS BETWEEN PUBLIC ENTITIES

§895. "Agreement"

As used in this chapter "agreement" means a joint powers agreement entered into pursuant to Chapter 5 (commencing with Section 6500) of Division 7 of Title 1 of the Government Code, an agreement to transfer the functions of a public entity or an employee thereof to another public entity pursuant to Part 2 (commencing with Section 51300) of Division 1 of Title 5 of the Government Code, and any other agreement under which a public entity undertakes to perform any function, service or act with or for any other public entity or employee thereof with its consent, whether such agreement is expressed by resolution, contract, ordinance or in any other manner provided by law; but "agreement" does not include an agreement between public entities which is designed to implement the disbursement or subvention of public funds from one of the public entities to the other, whether or not it provides standards or controls governing the expenditure of such funds. **Leg.H.** Added Stats 1963 ch 1681 §1.

§895.2. Joint and several liability of public entities entering into agreement

Whenever any public entities enter into an agreement, they are jointly and severally liable upon any liability which is imposed by any law other than this chapter upon any one of the entities or upon any entity created by the agreement for injury caused by a negligent or wrongful act or omission occurring in the performance of such agreement.

Notwithstanding any other law, if a judgment is recovered against a public entity for injury caused in the performance of an agreement, the time within which a claim for such injury may be presented or an action commenced against any other public entity that is subject to the liability determined by the judgment under the provisions of this section begins to run when the judgment is rendered. **Leg.H.** Added Stats 1963 ch 1681 §1.

§895.4. Agreement's provision for contribution or indemnification

As part of any agreement, the public entities may provide for contribution or indemnification by any or all of the public entities that are parties to the agreement upon any liability arising out of the performance of the agreement. **Leg.H.** Added Stats 1963 ch 1681 §1.

§895.6. Contribution between parties in absence of provision in agreement

Unless the public entities that are parties to an agreement otherwise provide in the agreement, if a public entity is held liable upon any judgment for damages caused by a negligent or wrongful act or omission occurring in the performance of the agreement and pays in excess of its pro rata share in satisfaction of such judgment, such public entity is entitled to contribution from each of the other public entities that are parties to the agreement. The pro rata share of each public entity is determined by dividing the total amount of the judgment by the number of public entities that are parties to the agreement. The right of contribution is limited to the amount paid in satisfaction of the judgment in excess of the pro rata share of the public entity so paying. No public entity may be compelled to make contribution beyond its own pro rata share of the entire judgment. **Leg.H.** Added Stats 1963 ch 1681 §1.

§895.8. Application of chapter with respect to its effective date

Except for Section 895.6, this chapter applies to any agreement between public entities, whether entered into before or after the effective date of this chapter. Section 895.6 applies to any agreement between public entities entered into, or renewed, modified, or extended, after the effective date of this chapter. **Leg.H.** Added Stats 1963 ch 1681 §1.

PART 3
CLAIMS AGAINST PUBLIC ENTITIES
CHAPTER 1
GENERAL
ARTICLE 1
Definitions

§900. Governing provisions

Unless the provision or context otherwise requires, the definitions contained in this article govern the construction of this part. **Leg.H.** Added Stats 1963 ch 1715 §1.

§900.2. "Board"

"Board" means:

(a) In the case of a local public entity, the governing body of the local public entity.

(b) In the case of the state, except as provided by subdivisions (c) and (d), the Department of General Services.

(c) In the case of a judicial branch entity or judge of one of those entities, the Judicial Council.

(d) In the case of the California State University, the Trustees of the California State University. **Leg.H.** Added Stats 1963 ch 1715 §1. Amended Stats 2002 ch 1007 §1 (AB 2321); Stats 2010 ch 636 §2 (SB 1046), effective January 1, 2011; Stats 2016 ch 31 §34 (SB 836), effective June 27, 2016.

§900.3. "Judicial branch entity"

A "judicial branch entity" is a public entity and means any superior court, court of appeals, the Supreme Court, the Judicial Council, or the Administrative Office of the Courts. **Leg.H.** Added Stats 2002 ch 1007 §2 (AB 2321).

§900.4. "Local public entity"

"Local public entity" includes a county, city, district, public authority, public agency, and any other political subdivision or public corporation in the State, but does not include the State. **Leg.H.** Added Stats 1963 ch 1715 §1.

§900.6. "State"

"State" means the State and any office, officer, department, division, bureau, board, commission or agency of the State claims against which are paid by warrants drawn by the Controller. **Leg.H.** Added Stats 1963 ch 1715 §1.

§901. Date of accrual of cause of action in determining time for presenting claim

For the purpose of computing the time limits prescribed by Sections 911.2, 911.4, 945.6, and 946.6, the date of the accrual of a cause of action to which a claim relates is the date upon which the cause of action would be deemed to have accrued within the meaning of the statute of limitations which would be applicable thereto if there were no requirement that a claim be presented to and be acted upon by the public entity before an action could be commenced thereon. However, the date upon which a cause of action for equitable indemnity or partial equitable indemnity accrues shall be the date upon which a defendant is served with the complaint giving rise to the defendant's claim for equitable indemnity or partial equitable indemnity against the public entity. **Leg.H.** Added Stats 1963 ch 1715 §1. Amended Stats 1968 ch 134 §1; Stats 1981 ch 856 §1; Stats 2011 ch 296 §110 (AB 1023), effective January 1, 2012; Amended Stats 2011 ch 296 §110 (AB 1023), effective January 1, 2012.

ARTICLE 2
General Provisions

§905. Required presentation of claims against local public entities; Exceptions

There shall be presented in accordance with Chapter 1 (commencing with Section 900) and Chapter 2 (commencing with Section 910) all claims for money or damages against local public entities except any of the following:

(a) Claims under the Revenue and Taxation Code or other statute prescribing procedures for the refund, rebate, exemption, cancellation, amendment, modification, or adjustment of any tax, assessment, fee, or charge or any portion of the charge, or of any penalties, costs, or related charges.

(b) Claims in connection with which the filing of a notice of lien, statement of claim, or stop notice is required under any law relating to liens of mechanics, laborers, or materialmen.

(c) Claims by public employees for fees, salaries, wages, mileage, or other expenses and allowances.

(d) Claims for which the workers' compensation authorized by Division 4 (commencing with Section 3200) of the Labor Code is the exclusive remedy.

(e) Applications or claims for any form of public assistance under the Welfare and Institutions Code or other provisions of law relating to public assistance programs, and claims for goods, services, provisions, or other assistance rendered for or on behalf of any recipient of any form of public assistance.

(f) Applications or claims for money or benefits under any public retirement or pension system.

(g) Claims for principal or interest upon any bonds, notes, warrants, or other evidences of indebtedness.

(h) Claims that relate to a special assessment constituting a specific lien against the property assessed and that are payable from the proceeds of the assessment, by offset of a claim for damages against it or by delivery of any warrant or bonds representing it.

(i) Claims by the state or by a state department or agency or by another local public entity or by a judicial branch entity.

(j) Claims arising under any provision of the Unemployment Insurance Code, including, but not limited to, claims for money or benefits, or for refunds or credits of employer or worker contributions, penalties, or interest, or for refunds to workers of deductions from wages in excess of the amount prescribed.

(k) Claims for the recovery of penalties or forfeitures made pursuant to Article 1 (commencing with Section 1720) of Chapter 1 of Part 7 of Division 2 of the Labor Code.

(*l*) Claims governed by the Pedestrian Mall Law of 1960 (Part 1 (commencing with Section 11000) of Division 13 of the Streets and Highways Code).

(m) Claims made pursuant to Section 340.1 of the Code of Civil Procedure for the recovery of damages suffered as a result of childhood sexual assault.

(n) Claims made pursuant to Section 701.820 of the Code of Civil Procedure for the recovery of money pursuant to Section 26680.

(o) Claims made pursuant to Section 49013 of the Education Code for reimbursement of pupil fees for participation in educational activities.

(p) The changes made to this section by the act that added this subdivision are retroactive and apply to any action commenced on or after the date of enactment of that act, and to any action filed before the date of enactment and still pending on that date, including any action or causes of action that would have been barred by the laws in effect before the date of enactment. **Leg.H.** Added Stats 1963 ch 1715 §1. Amended Stats 2005 ch 706 §17 (AB 1742), effective January 1, 2006; Stats 2007 ch 130 §105 (AB 299), effective January 1, 2008; Stats 2008 ch 383 §1 (SB 640), effective January 1, 2009; Stats 2010 ch 4 §4 (AB 680), effective January 1, 2011; Stats 2012 ch 776 §2 (AB 1575), effective January 1, 2013; Amended Stats 2010 ch 4 §4 (AB 680), effective January 1, 2011; Stats 2012 ch 776 §2 (AB 1575), effective January 1, 2013; Stats 2019 ch 861 §3 (AB 218), effective January 1, 2020.

§905.1. Inverse condemnation

No claim is required to be filed to maintain an action against a public entity for taking of, or damage to, private property pursuant to Section 19 of Article I of the California Constitution.

However, the board shall, in accordance with the provisions of this part, process any claim which is filed against a public entity for the taking of, or damage to, private property pursuant to Section 19 of Article I of the California Constitution. **Leg.H.** Added Stats 1976 ch 96 §1.

§905.2. Required presentation of claims against state; Applicability to violations of California Whistleblower Protection Act

(a) This section shall apply to claims against the state filed with the Department of General Services except as provided in subparagraph (B) of paragraph (2) of subdivision (b).

(b) There shall be presented in accordance with this chapter and Chapter 2 (commencing with Section 910) all claims for money or damages against the state:

(1) For which no appropriation has been made or for which no fund is available but the settlement of which has been provided for by statute or constitutional provision.

(2)(A) For which the appropriation made or fund designated is exhausted.

(B) Claims for reissuance of stale, dated, or replacement warrants shall be filed with the state entity that originally issued the warrant and, if allowed, shall be paid from the issuing entity's current appropriation or from any funds that are otherwise legally available to the entity to be used for that purpose. If an issuing entity determines that it is unable to issue a replacement warrant from its current appropriation or from any funds that are otherwise legally available to the entity to be used for that purpose, that entity may submit a request to include a claim for reimbursement of that warrant in a claims bill referenced in Section 14659.10 pursuant to a process prescribed by the Department of General Services.

(3) For money or damages on express contract, or for an injury for which the state is liable.

(4) For which settlement is not otherwise provided for by statute or constitutional provision.

(c) Claimants shall pay a filing fee of twenty-five dollars ($25), except as provided in paragraphs (1) and (2), for filing a claim described in subdivision (b), except for claims for reissuance of stale, dated, or replacement warrants as described in subparagraph (B) of paragraph (2) of subdivision (b). This fee shall be deposited into the Service Revolving Fund and shall only be available for the support of the Department of General Services upon appropriation by the Legislature.

(1) The fee shall not apply to the following persons:

(A) Persons who are receiving benefits pursuant to the Supplemental Security Income (SSI) and State Supplementary Payment (SSP) programs (Article 5 (commencing with Section 12200) of Chapter 3 of Part 3 of Division 9 of the Welfare and Institutions Code), the California Work Opportunity and Responsibility to Kids Act (CalWORKs) program (Chapter 2 (commencing with Section 11200) of Part 3 of Division 9 of the Welfare and Institutions Code), the federal Supplemental Nutrition Assistance Program (SNAP; 7 U.S.C. Sec. 2011 et seq.), or Section 17000 of the Welfare and Institutions Code.

(B) Persons whose monthly income is 125 percent or less of the current monthly poverty line annually established by the United States Department of Health and Human Services.

(C) Persons who are sentenced to imprisonment in a state prison or confined in a county jail, or who are residents in a state institution and, within 90 days prior to the date the claim is filed, have a balance of one hundred dollars ($100) or less credited to the inmate's or resident's trust account. A certified copy of the statement of the account shall be submitted.

(2)(A) For a person whose monthly income is less than one hundred dollars ($100) above the income of a person whose monthly income is 125 percent of the current monthly poverty line annually established by the United States Department of Health and Human Services, the fee assessed shall be 25 percent of the difference between their income and 125 percent of the current monthly poverty line.

(B) For a person who is sentenced to imprisonment in a state prison or confined in a county jail, or who is a resident in a state institution and, within 90 days prior to the date the claim is filed, has a balance greater than one hundred dollars ($100) and less than two hundred dollars ($200), the fee assessed shall be 25 percent of the difference between the inmate's or resident's balance and one hundred dollars ($100).

(3) Any claimant who requests a fee waiver shall attach to the application a signed affidavit requesting the waiver and verification of benefits or income and any other required financial information in support of the request for the waiver.

(4) Notwithstanding any other law, an applicant shall not be entitled to a hearing regarding the denial of a request for a fee waiver.

(d) The time for the Department of General Services to determine the sufficiency, timeliness, or any other aspect of the claim shall begin when any of the following occur:

(1) The claim is submitted with the filing fee.
(2) The fee waiver is granted.
(3) The filing fee is paid to the department upon the department's denial of the fee waiver request, so long as payment is received within 10 calendar days of the mailing of the notice of the denial.

(e) Upon approval of the claim by the Department of General Services, the fee shall be reimbursed to the claimant, except that no fee shall be reimbursed if the approved claim was for the payment of an expired warrant. Reimbursement of the filing fee shall be paid by the state entity against which the approved claim was filed. If the claimant was granted a fee waiver pursuant to this section, the amount of the fee shall be paid by the state entity to the department. The reimbursement to the claimant or the payment to the department shall be made at the time the claim is paid by the state entity, or shall be added to the amount appropriated for the claim in an equity claims bill.

(f) The Department of General Services may assess a surcharge to the state entity against which the approved claim was filed in an amount not to exceed 15 percent of the total approved claim. The department shall not include the refunded filing fee in the surcharge calculation. This surcharge shall be deposited into the Service Revolving Fund and may be appropriated in support of the department in the annual Budget Act.

(1) The surcharge shall not apply to approved claims to reissue expired warrants.
(2) Upon the request of the department in a form prescribed by the Controller, the Controller shall transfer the fees from the state entity's appropriation to the appropriation for the support of the department. However, the department shall not request an amount that shall be submitted for legislative approval pursuant to Section 14659.10.

(g) The filing fee required by subdivision (c) shall apply to all claims filed after June 30, 2004, or August 16, 2004. The surcharge authorized by subdivision (f) may be calculated and included in claims paid after June 30, 2004, or August 16, 2004.

(h) This section does not apply to claims made for a violation of the California Whistleblower Protection Act (Article 3 (commencing with Section 8547) of Chapter 6.5 of Division 1 of Title 2). **Leg.H.** Added Stats 1963 ch 1715 §1. Amended Stats 1976 ch 96 §2; Stats 2004 ch 227 §19 (SB 1102), effective August 16, 2004; Stats 2005 ch 184 §1 (AB 346), effective September 6, 2005, operative July 11, 2005; Stats 2013 ch 781 §1 (SB 496), effective January 1, 2014; Stats 2014 ch 71 §65 (SB 1304), effective January 1, 2015; Stats 2015 ch 25 §3 (SB 84), effective June 24, 2015; Stats 2016 ch 31 §35 (SB 836), effective June 27, 2016; Stats 2016 ch 344 §1 (SB 835), effective September 13, 2016; Stats 2017 ch 19 §9 (AB 111), effective June 27, 2017; Stats 2023 ch 478 §24 (AB 1756), effective January 1, 2024.

2005 Note: The amendments to Section 905.2 of the Government Code that are made by Section 1 of this act, shall become operative on July 1, 2005, or upon the enactment of the Budget Act of 2005 [Stats 2005 ch 38 (SB 77), effective July 11, 2005], whichever is later. Stats 2005 ch 184 (AB 346) § 7.

§905.3. Claims eligible for consideration by Commission on State Mandates

Notwithstanding any other law to the contrary, no claim shall be submitted by a local agency or school district, nor shall a claim be considered by the Department of General Services pursuant to Section 905.2, if that claim is eligible for consideration by the Commission on State Mandates pursuant to Article 1 (commencing with Section 17550) of Chapter 4 of Part 7 of Division 4 of Title 2. **Leg.H.** Added Stats 1977 ch 1135 §3.5. Amended Stats 1994 ch 726 §2 (AB 3069), effective September 21, 1994; Stats 2006 ch 538 §218 (SB 1852), effective January 1, 2007; Stats 2016 ch 31 §36 (SB 836), effective June 27, 2016.

§905.4. Nonexclusiveness of provisions as to presentation and payment of claims

Chapter 1 (commencing with Section 900) and Chapter 2 (commencing with Section 910) of this part shall not be construed to be an exclusive means for presenting claims to the Legislature nor as preventing the Legislature from making such appropriations as it deems proper for the payment of claims against the State which have not been submitted to the board or recommended for payment by it pursuant to Chapters 1 and 2 of this part. **Leg.H.** Added Stats 1963 ch 1715 §1.

§905.5. Civil liability of school district, officers, directors or employees from exposure to asbestos

A school district, its officers, directors, or employees shall have no civil liability in any civil action for injury, disease, death, or economic loss arising out of exposure on or after January 1, 1989, to asbestos contained in buildings owned, leased, or otherwise used by a school district, except upon proof that the injury, disease, death, or economic loss was caused by the negligence of the school district, its officers, directors, or employees. Notwithstanding the provisions of Section 815.6 of the Government Code and Section 669 of the Evidence Code, no presumption of negligence shall apply to any action under this section. This section applies only to actions against school districts, and shall not apply to any other action, including, but not limited to, actions against a manufacturer, contractor, or any person who makes, sells, distributes, furnishes, or installs asbestos-containing materials. This section shall not affect, alter, or otherwise modify the law pertaining to workers' compensation claims. This section shall not affect the right of a school district, its officers, directors, or employees to seek indemnification. **Leg.H.** Added Stats 1988 ch 1022 §1.

§905.6. Inapplicability of provisions to claims against Regents of University of California

This part does not apply to claims against the Regents of the University of California. **Leg.H.** Added Stats 1963 ch 1715 §1.

§905.7. Claims against judicial branch

All claims against a judicial branch entity for money or damages based upon an express contract or for an injury for which the judicial branch entity is liable shall be presented in accordance with Chapter 1 (commencing with Section 900) and Chapter 2 (commencing with Section 910) of this part. **Leg.H.** Added Stats 2005 ch 706 § 18 (AB 1742).

2005 Note: Section 905.7 of the Government Code, as added by Section 18 of this act, shall be effective as to causes of action that accrued on or after January 1, 2006. However, the enactment of Section 905.7 of the Government Code does not change the obligations and rights under the laws in existence at the time of accrual of judicial branch entities or of persons whose causes of action against a judicial branch entity accrued before January 1, 2006. Stats 2005 ch 706 (AB 1742) § 39.

§905.8. Absence of additional liability

Nothing in this part imposes liability upon a public entity unless such liability otherwise exists. **Leg.H.** Added Stats 1963 ch 1715 §1.

§905.9. Claims against California State University

All claims against the California State University for money or damages based upon an express contract or for an injury for which the Trustees of the California State University is liable shall be presented in accordance with Chapter 1 (commencing with Section 900) and Chapter 2 (commencing with Section 910) of this part. **Leg.H.** Added Stats 2010 ch 636 §3 (SB 1046), effective January 1, 2011.

§906. Interest on amount allowed on the claim

(a) As used in this section, "amount allowed on the claim" means the amount allowed by the Department of General Services on a claim allowed, in whole or in part, or the amount offered by the department to settle or compromise a claim.

(b) Except as otherwise provided in this subdivision, no interest is payable on the amount allowed on the claim if payment of the claim is subject to approval of an appropriation by the Legislature. If an appropriation is made for the payment of a claim described in this subdivision, interest on the amount appropriated for the payment of the claim commences to accrue 180 days after the effective date of the act by which the appropriation is enacted. **Leg.H.** Added Stats 1980 ch 215 §4. Amended Stats 2012 ch 19 §1 (SB 1504), effective June 15, 2012; Stats 2016 ch 31 §37 (SB 836), effective June 27, 2016.

§907. Offset of delinquent amount due for services

A local public entity, as defined in Section 900.4, may offset any delinquent amount due it for services rendered to any other local public entity. The offset may be charged, against any amount reciprocally owing, upon the giving of 30 days advance written notice, if no written dispute is received from the debtor within the 30-day notice period. Notices from the creditor or the debtor shall be made through certified mail.

If the offset would result in the debtor's inability to meet encumbered bonded indebtedness repayments, the debtor shall so state in a written dispute within the time period stated above.

If a dispute notice is received and the dispute is subsequently resolved in favor of the entity to whom an amount is due, interest on the principal amount from the date that amount was originally owing shall be assessed at the legal rate per annum established pursuant to Section 685.010 of the Code of Civil Procedure.

For purposes of this section, an amount reciprocally owing includes any tax revenue collected by a local public entity for disbursement to another local public entity. **Leg.H.** Added Stats 1990 ch 697 §1 (AB 3463).

CHAPTER 2
PRESENTATION AND CONSIDERATION OF CLAIMS
ARTICLE 1
General

§910. Person presenting claim; Contents of claim

A claim shall be presented by the claimant or by a person acting on his or her behalf and shall show all of the following:

(a) The name and post office address of the claimant.

(b) The post office address to which the person presenting the claim desires notices to be sent.

(c) The date, place and other circumstances of the occurrence or transaction which gave rise to the claim asserted.

(d) A general description of the indebtedness, obligation, injury, damage or loss incurred so far as it may be known at the time of presentation of the claim.

(e) The name or names of the public employee or employees causing the injury, damage, or loss, if known.

(f) The amount claimed if it totals less than ten thousand dollars ($10,000) as of the date of presentation of the claim, including the estimated amount of any prospective injury, damage, or loss, insofar as it may be known at the time of the presentation of the claim, together with the basis of computation of the amount claimed. If the amount claimed exceeds ten thousand dollars ($10,000), no dollar amount shall be included in the claim. However, it shall indicate whether the claim would be a limited civil case. **Leg.H.** Added Stats 1963 ch 1715 §1. Amended Stats 1965 ch 653 §1; Stats 1987 ch 1201 §17, ch 1208 §2; Stats 1998 ch 931 §174 (SB 2139), effective September 28, 1998.

§910.2. Signing claim

The claim shall be signed by the claimant or by some person on his behalf. Claims against local public entities for supplies, materials, equipment or services need not be signed by the claimant or on his behalf if presented on a billhead or invoice regularly used in the conduct of the business of the claimant. **Leg.H.** Added Stats 1963 ch 1715 §1.

§910.4. Claim forms

The board shall provide forms specifying the information to be contained in claims against the state or a judicial branch entity. The person presenting a claim shall use the form in order that his or her claim is deemed in conformity with Sections 910 and 910.2. A claim may be returned to the person if it was not presented using the form. Any claim returned to a person may be resubmitted using the appropriate form. **Leg.H.** Added Stats 1963 ch 1715 §1. Amended Stats 1965 ch 653 §2; Stats 2002 ch 1124 §6 (AB 3000), effective September 30, 2002, operative March 30, 2003; Stats 2004 ch 227 §20 (SB 1102), effective August 16, 2004; Stats 2005 ch 706 §19 (AB 1742), effective January 1, 2006.

§910.6. Amendment of claims

(a) A claim may be amended at any time before the expiration of the period designated in Section 911.2 or before final action thereon is taken by the board, whichever is later, if the claim as amended relates to the same transaction or occurrence which gave rise to the original claim. The amendment shall be considered a part of the original claim for all purposes.

(b) A failure or refusal to amend a claim, whether or not notice of insufficiency is given under Section 910.8, shall not constitute a defense to any action brought upon the cause of action for which the claim was presented if the court finds that the claim as presented complied substantially with Section 910 and 910.2 or a form provided under Section 910.4. **Leg.H.** Added Stats 1963 ch 1715 §1.

§910.8. Board's notice of claim's insufficiency

If, in the opinion of the board or the person designated by it, a claim as presented fails to comply substantially with the requirements of Sections 910 and 910.2, or with the requirements of a form provided under Section 910.4 if a claim is presented pursuant thereto, the board or the person may, at any time within 20 days after the claim is presented, give written notice of its insufficiency, stating with particularity the defects or omissions therein. The notice shall be given in the manner prescribed by Section 915.4. The board may not take action on the claim for a period of 15 days after the notice is given. **Leg.H.** Added Stats 1963 ch 1715 §1. Amended Stat 1970 ch 104 §2, operative January 1, 1971; Stats 2004 ch 227 §21 (SB 1102), effective August 16, 2004; Stats 2005 ch 184 §2 (AB 346), effective September 6, 2005.

§911. Waiver of defense by failure to give notice of claim's insufficiency

Any defense as to the sufficiency of the claim based upon a defect or omission in the claim as presented is waived by failure to give notice of insufficiency with respect to the defect or omission as provided in Section 910.8, except that no notice need be given and no waiver shall result when the claim as presented fails to state either an address to which the person presenting the claim desires notices to be sent or an address of the claimant. **Leg.H.** Added Stats 1963 ch 1715 §1. Amended Stats 2004 ch 227 §22 (SB 1102), effective August 16, 2004; Stats 2005 ch 184 §3 (AB 346), effective September 6, 2005.

§911.2. Times for presentment of claims

(a) A claim relating to a cause of action for death or for injury to person or to personal property or growing crops shall be presented as provided in Article 2 (commencing with Section 915) not later than six months after the accrual of the cause of action. A claim relating to any other cause of action shall be presented as provided in Article 2 (commencing with Section 915) not later than one year after the accrual of the cause of action.

(b) For purposes of determining whether a claim was commenced within the period provided by law, the date the claim was presented to the Department of General Services is one of the following:

(1) The date the claim is submitted with a twenty-five dollar ($25) filing fee.

(2) If a fee waiver is granted, the date the claim was submitted with the affidavit requesting the fee waiver.

(3) If a fee waiver is denied, the date the claim was submitted with the affidavit requesting the fee waiver, provided the filing fee is paid to the department within 10 calendar days of the mailing of the notice of the denial of the fee waiver. **Leg.H.** Added Stats 1963 ch 1715 §1. Amended Stats 1987 ch 1201 §18, ch 1208 §3; Stats 2005 ch 184 §4 (AB 346), effective September 6, 2005; Stats 2016 ch 31 §38 (SB 836), effective June 27, 2016.

§911.3. Notice that claim not filed timely; Contents

(a) When a claim that is required by Section 911.2 to be presented not later than six months after accrual of the cause of action is presented after such time without the application provided in Section 911.4, the board or other person designated by it may, at any time within 45 days after the claim is presented, give written notice to the person presenting the claim that the claim was not filed timely and that it is being returned without further action. The notice shall be in substantially the following form:

"The claim you presented to the (insert title of board or officer) on (indicate date) is being returned because it was not presented within six months after the event or occurrence as required by law. See Sections 901 and 911.2 of the Government Code. Because the claim was not presented within the time allowed by law, no action was taken on the claim.

Your only recourse at this time is to apply without delay to (name of public entity) for leave to present a late claim. See Sections 911.4 to 912.2, inclusive, and Section 946.6 of the Government Code. Under some circumstances, leave to present a late claim will be granted. See Section 911.6 of the Government Code.

You may seek the advice of an attorney of your choice in connection with this matter. If you desire to consult an attorney, you should do so immediately."

(b) Any defense as to the time limit for presenting a claim described in subdivision (a) is waived by failure to give the notice set forth in subdivision (a) within 45 days after the claim is presented, except that no notice need be given and no waiver shall result when the claim as presented fails to state either an address to which the person presenting the claim desires notices to be sent or an address of the claimant. **Leg.H.** Added Stats 1983 ch 107 §1. Amended Stats 1987 ch 1201 §19, ch 1208 §4.

§911.4. Application to present claim not timely filed; Time limitation

(a) When a claim that is required by Section 911.2 to be presented not later than six months after the accrual of the cause of action is not presented within that time, a written application may be made to the public entity for leave to present that claim.

(b) The application shall be presented to the public entity as provided in Article 2 (commencing with Section 915) within a reasonable time not to exceed one year after the accrual of the cause of action and shall state the reason for the delay in presenting the claim. The proposed claim shall be attached to the application.

(c) In computing the one-year period under subdivision (b), the following shall apply:

(1) The time during which the person who sustained the alleged injury, damage, or loss as a minor shall be counted, but the time during which he or she is mentally incapacitated and does not have a guardian or conservator of his or her person shall not be counted.

(2) The time shall not be counted during which the person is detained or adjudged to be a dependent child of the juvenile court under the Arnold-Kennick Juvenile Court Law (Chapter 2 (commencing with Section 200) of Part 1 of Division 2 of the Welfare and Institutions Code), if both of the following conditions exist:

(A) The person is in the custody and control of an agency of the public entity to which a claim is to be presented.

(B) The public entity or its agency having custody and control of the minor is required by statute or other law to make a report of injury, abuse, or neglect to either the juvenile court or the minor's attorney, and that entity or its agency fails to make this report within the time required by the statute or other enactment, with this time period to commence on the date on which the public entity or its agency becomes aware of the injury, neglect, or abuse. In circumstances where the public entity or its agency makes a late report, the claim period shall be tolled for the period of the delay caused by the failure to make a timely report.

(3) The time shall not be counted during which a minor is adjudged to be a dependent child of the juvenile court under the Arnold-Kennick Juvenile Court Law (Chapter 2 (commencing with Section 200) of Part 1 of Division 2 of the Welfare and Institutions Code), if the minor is without a guardian ad litem or conservator for purposes of filing civil actions. **Leg.H.** Added Stats 1963 ch 1715 §1. Amended Stats 1965 ch 653 §3; Stats 1970 ch 411 §1; Stats 1987 ch 1201 §20, ch 1208 §5; Stats 1999 ch 620 §1 (AB 118); Stats 2003 ch 847 §2 (AB 1151).

§911.6. Board's grant or denial of application to present late claim

(a) The board shall grant or deny the application within 45 days after it is presented to the board. The claimant and the board may extend the period within which the board is required to act on the application by written agreement made before the expiration of the period.

(b) The board shall grant the application if one or more of the following is applicable:

(1) The failure to present the claim was through mistake, inadvertence, surprise, or excusable neglect and the public entity was not prejudiced in its defense of the claim by the failure to present the claim within the time specified in Section 911.2.

(2) The person who sustained the alleged injury, damage, or loss was a minor during all of the time specified in Section 911.2 for the presentation of the claim.

(3) The person who sustained the alleged injury, damage, or loss was a minor during any of the time specified in Section 911.2 for the presentation of the claim, provided the application is presented within six months of the person turning 18 years of age or a year after the claim accrues, whichever occurs first.

(4) The person who sustained the alleged injury, damage, or loss was physically or mentally incapacitated during all of the time specified in Section 911.2 for the presentation of the claim and by reason of that disability failed to present a claim during that time.

(5) The person who sustained the alleged injury, damage, or loss was physically or mentally incapacitated during any of the time specified in Section 911.2 for the presentation of the claim and by reason of that disability failed to present a claim during that time, provided the application is presented within six months of the person no longer being physically or mentally incapacitated, or a year after the claim accrues, whichever occurs first.

(6) The person who sustained the alleged injury, damage, or loss died before the expiration of the time specified in Section 911.2 for the presentation of the claim.

(c) If the board fails or refuses to act on an application within the time prescribed by this section, the application shall be deemed to have been denied on the 45th day or, if the period within which the board is required to act is extended by agreement pursuant to this section, the last day of the period specified in the agreement. **Leg.H.** Added Stats 1963 ch 1715 §1. Amended Stats 1965 ch 653 §4; Stats 1979 ch 769 §1; Stats 1987 ch 1201 §21, 1208 §6; Stats 2021 ch 218 §1 (SB 501), effective January 1, 2022.

§911.8. Notice of board's action on application

(a) Written notice of the board's action upon the application shall be given in the manner prescribed by Section 915.4.

(b) If the application is denied, the notice shall include a warning in substantially the following form:

"WARNING

"If you wish to file a court action on this matter, you must first petition the appropriate court for an order relieving you from the provisions of Government Code Section 945.4 (claims presentation requirement). See Government Code Section 946.6. Such petition must be filed with the court within six (6) months from the date your application for leave to present a late claim was denied.

"You may seek the advice of an attorney of your choice in connection with this matter. If you desire to consult an attorney, you should do so immediately." **Leg.H.** Added Stats 1963 ch 1715 §1. Amended Stats 1970 ch 104 §3, operative January 1, 1971; Stats 1974 ch 620 §1.

§912.2. Time claim deemed presented where leave granted

If an application for leave to present a claim is granted by the board pursuant to Section 911.6, the claim shall be deemed to have been presented to the board upon the day that leave to present the claim is granted. **Leg.H.** Added Stats 1963 ch 1715 §1. Amended Stats 1965 ch 653 §6.

§912.4. Time for board's action on claim

(a) The board shall act on a claim in the manner provided in Section 912.6, 912.7, or 912.8 within 45 days after the claim has been presented. If a claim is amended, the board shall act on the amended claim within 45 days after the amended claim is presented.

(b) The claimant and the board may extend the period within which the board is required to act on the claim by written agreement made either:

(1) Before the expiration of the period.

(2) After the expiration of the period if an action based on the claim has not been commenced and is not yet barred by the period of limitations provided in Section 945.6.

(c) If the board fails or refuses to act on a claim within the time prescribed by this section, the claim shall be deemed to have been rejected by the board on the last day of the period within which the board was required to act upon the claim. If the period within which the board is required to act is extended by agreement pursuant to this section, the last day of the period within which the board is required to act shall be the last day of the period specified in the agreement. **Leg.H.** Added Stats 1963 ch 1715 §1. Amended Stats 1965 ch 653 §7; Stats 2002 ch 1007 §3 (AB 2321).

§912.5. Actions by Trustees of California State University on claims

(a) The Trustees of the California State University shall act on a claim against the California State University in accordance with the procedure that the Trustees of the California State University provide by rule.

(b) Nothing in this section authorizes the Trustees of the California State University to adopt any rule that is inconsistent with this part.

(c) If a claim for money or damages against the California State University is mistakenly presented to the Department of General Services, the Department of General Services shall immediately notify the claimant of the error and shall include information on proper filing of the claim. **Leg.H.** Added Stats 2010 ch 636 §4 (SB 1046), effective January 1, 2011. Amended Stats 2011 ch 296 §111 (AB 1023), effective January 1, 2012; Stats 2016 ch 31 §39 (SB 836), effective June 27, 2016.

§912.6. Procedure in claims against local public entity

(a) In the case of a claim against a local public entity, the board may act on a claim in one of the following ways:

(1) If the board finds the claim is not a proper charge against the public entity, it shall reject the claim.

(2) If the board finds the claim is a proper charge against the public entity and is for an amount justly due, it shall allow the claim.

(3) If the board finds the claim is a proper charge against the public entity but is for an amount greater than is justly due, it shall either reject the claim or allow it in the amount justly due and reject it as to the balance.

(4) If legal liability of the public entity or the amount justly due is disputed, the board may reject the claim or may compromise the claim.

(b) In the case of a claim against a local public entity, if the board allows the claim in whole or in part or compromises the claim, it may require the claimant, if the claimant accepts the amount allowed or offered to settle the claim, to accept it in settlement of the entire claim.

(c) Subject to subdivision (b), the local public entity shall pay the amount allowed on the claim or in compromise of the claim in the same manner as if the claimant had obtained a final judgment against the local public entity for that amount, but the claim may be paid in not exceeding 10 equal annual installments as provided in Section 970.6 only if the claimant agrees in writing to that method of payment and in such case no court order authorizing installment payments is required. If an agreement for payment of the claim in installments is made, the local public entity, in its discretion, may prepay any one or more installments or any part of an installment. **Leg.H.** Added Stats 1963 ch 1715 §1. Amended Stats 1980 ch 215 §5,

§912.7. Procedure in action against judicial branch entity or judge

The Judicial Council shall act on a claim against a judicial branch entity or judge of one of those entities in accordance with the procedure that the Judicial Council provides by rule of court. The Judicial Council may authorize any committee of the Judicial Council or employee of the Administrative Office of the Courts to perform the functions of the Judicial Council under this part. **Leg.H.** Added Stats 2002 ch 1007 §4 (AB 2321).

§912.8. Procedure as to board's action on claims against State; Report and recommendations to Legislature

Except as provided in Section 912.7, in the case of claims against the state, the board shall act on claims in accordance with that procedure as the board, by rule, may prescribe. It may hear evidence for and against the claims and, with the approval of the Governor, report to the Legislature those facts and recommendations concerning the claims as it deems proper. In making recommendations, the board may state and use any official or personal knowledge that any member may have regarding any claim. The board may authorize any employee of the state to perform the functions of the board under this part as are prescribed by the board. **Leg.H.** Added Stats 1963 ch 1715 §1. Amended Stats 1998 ch 872 §6 (AB 2771); Stats 2002 ch 1007 §5 (AB 2321); Stats 2004 ch 183 §131 (AB 3082).

§913. Notice of board's action on claim

(a) Written notice of the action taken under Section 912.5, 912.6, 912.7, or 912.8 or the inaction that is deemed rejection under Section 912.4 shall be given in the manner prescribed by Section 915.4. The notice may be in substantially the following form:

"Notice is hereby given that the claim that you presented to the (insert title of board or officer) on (indicate date) was (indicate whether rejected, allowed, allowed in the amount of $____ and rejected as to the balance, rejected by operation of law, or other appropriate language, whichever is applicable) on (indicate date of action or rejection by operation of law)."

(b) If the claim is rejected, in whole or in part, the notice required by subdivision (a) shall include a warning in substantially the following form:

"WARNING

"Subject to certain exceptions, you have only six (6) months from the date this notice was personally delivered or deposited in the mail to file a court action on this claim. See Government Code Section 945.6.

"You may seek the advice of an attorney of your choice in connection with this matter. If you desire to consult an attorney, you should do so immediately." **Leg.H.** Added Stats 1963 ch 1715 §1. Amended Stats 1970 ch 104 §4, operative January 1, 1971; Stats 2002 ch 1007 §6 (AB 2321); Stats 2010 ch 636 §5 (SB 1046), effective January 1, 2011.

§913.2. Re-examination of rejected claim

The board may, in its discretion, within the time prescribed by Section 945.6 for commencing an action on the claim, re-examine a previously rejected claim in order to consider a settlement of the claim. **Leg.H.** Added Stats 1963 ch 1715 §1.

ARTICLE 2
Manner of Presentation and of Giving Notice

§915. Delivery or mailing of claim, amendment, or application

(a) A claim, any amendment thereto, or an application to the public entity for leave to present a late claim shall be presented to a local public entity by any of the following means:

(1) Delivering it to the clerk, secretary, or auditor thereof.

(2) Mailing it to the clerk, secretary, auditor, or to the governing body at its principal office.

(3) If expressly authorized by an ordinance or resolution of the public entity, submitting it electronically to the public entity in the manner specified in the ordinance or resolution.

(b) Except as provided in subdivisions (c) and (d), a claim, any amendment thereto, or an application for leave to file a late claim shall be presented to the state by either of the following means:

(1) Delivering it to an office of the Department of General Services.

(2) Mailing it to the Department of General Services at its principal office.

(c) A claim, any amendment thereto, or an application for leave to file a late claim shall be presented to a judicial branch entity in accordance with the following means:

(1) Delivering or mailing it to the court executive officer, if against a superior court or a judge, court executive officer, or trial court employee, as defined in Section 811.9, of that court.

(2) Delivering or mailing it to the Clerk or Executive Officer of the Court of Appeal, if against a court of appeals or a judge of that court.

(3) Delivering or mailing it to the Clerk or Executive Officer of the Supreme Court, if against the Supreme Court or a judge of that court.

(4) Delivering or mailing it to the Administrative Director of the Judicial Council, if against the Judicial Council or the Administrative Office of the Courts.

(d) A claim, any amendment thereto, or an application for leave to file a late claim shall be presented to the Trustees of the California State University by delivering or mailing it to the Office of Risk Management at the Office of the Chancellor of the California State University.

(e) A claim, amendment, or application shall be deemed to have been presented in compliance with this section even though it is not delivered or mailed as provided in this section if, within the time prescribed for presentation thereof, any of the following apply:

(1) It is actually received by the clerk, secretary, auditor, or board of the local public entity.

(2) It is actually received at an office of the Department of General Services.

(3) If against the California State University, it is actually received by the Trustees of the California State University.

(4) If against a judicial branch entity or judge, it is actually received by the court executive officer, court clerk/administrator, court clerk, or secretariat of the judicial branch entity.

(f) A claim, amendment, or application shall be deemed to have been presented in compliance with this section to a public agency as defined in Section 53050 if it is delivered or mailed within the time prescribed for presentation thereof in conformity with the information contained in the statement in the Roster of Public Agencies pertaining to that public agency which is on file at the time the claim, amendment, or application is delivered or mailed. As used in this subdivision, "statement in the Registry of Public Agencies" means the statement or amended statement in the Registry of Public Agencies in the office of the Secretary of State or in the office of the county clerk of any county in which the statement or amended statement is on file. **Leg.H.** Added Stats 1963 ch 1715 §1. Amended Stats 1965 ch 653 §8; Stats 2002 ch 1007 §7 (AB 2321); Stats 2010 ch 636 §6 (SB 1046), effective January 1, 2011; Stats 2016 ch 31 §40 (SB 836), effective June 27, 2016; Stats 2017 ch 36 §4 (AB 452), effective January 1, 2018; Stats 2018 ch 92 §82 (SB 1289), effective January 1, 2019; Stats 2019 ch 329 §2 (SB 780), effective January 1, 2020; Stats 2020 ch 371 §7 (SB 1473), effective January 1, 2021.

§915.2. Manner, time and proof of mailing claim, etc.

(a) If a claim, amendment to a claim, or application to a public entity for leave to present a late claim is presented or sent by mail under this chapter, or if any notice under this chapter is given by mail, the claim, amendment, application, or notice shall be mailed in the manner prescribed in this section. The claim, amendment, application, or notice shall be deposited in the United States post office, a mailbox, sub-post office, substation, mail chute, or other similar facility regularly maintained by the government of the United States, in a sealed envelope, properly addressed, with postage paid. The claim, amendment, application, or notice shall be deemed to have been presented and received at the time of the deposit.

(b) Any period of notice and any duty to respond after receipt of service of a claim, amendment, application, or notice is extended 5 days upon service by mail, if the place of address is within the State of California, 10 days if the place of address is within the United States, and 20 days if the place of address is outside the United States. This subdivision shall not apply to the written notice set forth in Section 945.6 or the filing of a complaint after denial of a claim.

(c) As applied to this section, proof of mailing may be made in the manner prescribed by Section 1013a of the Code of Civil Procedure.

(d) If a claim, amendment to a claim, or application to a public entity for leave to present a late claim is submitted electronically, or if any notice under this chapter is given electronically, proof of electronic service may be made in a manner prescribed by Section 1013b of the Code of Civil Procedure, and proof of electronic service may be signed as provided in subparagraph (B) of paragraph (2) of subdivision (e) of Section 1010.6 of the Code of Civil Procedure. **Leg.H.** Added Stats 1963 ch 1715 §1. Amended Stats 2002 ch 1124 §7 (AB 3000), effective September 30, 2002; Stats 2011 ch 308 §7 (SB 647), effective January 1, 2012; Stats 2020 ch 371 §8 (SB 1473), effective January 1, 2021; Stats 2022 ch 215 §4 (AB 2961), effective January 1, 2023.

§915.4. Delivery or mailing of notice of board action

(a) The notices provided for in Sections 910.8, 911.8, and 913 shall be given by any of the following methods:

(1) Personally delivering the notice to the person presenting the claim or making the application.

(2) Mailing the notice to the address, if any, stated in the claim or application as the address to which the person presenting the claim or making the application desires notices to be sent or, if no such address is stated in the claim or application, by mailing the notice to the address, if any, of the claimant as stated in the claim or application.

(3) If the claim or application is submitted electronically, by sending the notice to the electronic address from which the claim or application was received unless the person presenting the claim or making the application requests notice to be sent to an alternative electronic address.

(b) No notice need be given where the claim or application fails to state either an address to which the person presenting the claim or making the application desires notices to be sent or an address of the claimant. **Leg.H.** Added Stats 1970 ch 104 §5, operative January 1, 1971. Amended Stats 2020 ch 371 §9 (SB 1473), effective January 1, 2021.

CHAPTER 3
PROCEEDINGS TO DETERMINE CONSTITUTIONALITY OF CLAIMS AGAINST THE STATE

§920. "Omnibus claim appropriation"

As used in this chapter, "omnibus claim appropriation" means an act of appropriation, or an item of appropriation in a budget act, by which the Legislature appropriates a lump sum to pay the claim of the Department of General Services or its secretary against the state in an amount that the Legislature has determined is properly chargeable to the state. **Leg.H.** Added Stats 1963 ch 1715 §1. Amended Stats 2006 ch 538 §219 (SB 1852), effective January 1, 2007; Stats 2016 ch 31 §41 (SB 836), effective June 27, 2016.

§920.2. Submission of omnibus claim appropriation to Controller

Promptly following the effective date of an omnibus claim appropriation, the board or its secretary shall submit to the Controller a claim covering the full amount of the appropriation made in the omnibus claim appropriation. Any such claim is exempt from the provisions of Chapter 4 (commencing with Section 925) of this part, and the board shall have those powers necessary to administer and disburse the omnibus claim appropriation. **Leg.H.** Added Stats 1963 ch 1715 §1.

§920.4. Controller's withholding payment of questioned portion of appropriation

If the Controller believes or has reason to believe that the payment of any portion of the omnibus claim appropriation may violate the provisions of the Constitution, he shall withhold payment of the questioned portion and shall issue his warrant for the remainder of the appropriation. The secretary, subject to the board's approval, shall promptly disburse the undisputed portion of the omnibus claim appropriation and shall promptly give notice to the Joint Legislative Budget Committee of the Controller's action concerning the withheld portion. **Leg.H.** Added Stats 1963 ch 1715 §1.

§920.6. Disbursement of disputed portion of appropriation; Proceedings to compel Controller's issuance of warrant

Unless the Joint Legislative Budget Committee within 60 days after receipt of such notice advises the board in writing that the Legislature desires to reconsider any part of the withheld portion, the board shall institute proceedings to compel the Controller to issue his warrant for the balance of the omnibus claim appropriation. The board shall prosecute any such proceeding to final determination and shall disburse the funds finally paid over to it. Funds subject to such proceedings shall continue to be available until the end of the fiscal year in which final determination of the proceeding occurs. **Leg.H.** Added Stats 1963 ch 1715 §1.

§920.8. Reversion of withheld funds in event of Legislature's reconsideration

If the Joint Legislative Budget Committee advises the board that the Legislature desires to reconsider any part of the omnibus claim appropriation withheld by the Controller, no further action shall be taken with respect to that part and the money appropriated therefor shall revert to funds from which they were appropriated, pending further legislative action. The board, however, shall institute proceedings as provided in Section 920.6 to compel payment of the remainder of the omnibus claim appropriation withheld by the Controller. **Leg.H.** Added Stats 1963 ch 1715 §1.

CHAPTER 4
PRESENTATION OF CLAIMS TO STATE CONTROLLER

§925. "Department"

As used in this chapter, "department" means the Department of General Services. **Leg.H.** Added Stats 1963 ch 1715 §1. Amended Stats 2006 ch 538 §220 (SB 1852), effective January 1, 2007; Stats 2016 ch 31 §42 (SB 836), effective June 27, 2016.

§925.2. Exemption of Legislature's expenses and of official salaries

Claims for expenses of either house of the Legislature or members or committees thereof are exempt from Section 13920 and this chapter, except Section 925.6, and claims for official salaries fixed by statute are exempt from this chapter and Section 13920. **Leg.H.** Added Stats 1963 ch 1715 §1. Amended Stats 1989 ch 592 §2.

§925.4. Presentation of claims against state for which appropriations made or state funds available

Any person having a claim against the state for which appropriations have been made, or for which state funds are available, may present it to the Controller in the form and manner prescribed by the general rules and regulations adopted by the department for the presentation and audit of claims. **Leg.H.** Added Stats 1963 ch 1715 §1. Amended Stats 2016 ch 31 §43 (SB 836), effective June 27, 2016.

§925.6. Controller's warrant; Prerequisite audit

(a) Except as otherwise provided in subdivisions (b) and (e), the Controller shall not draw their warrant for any claim until the Controller has audited that claim in conformity with law and the general rules and regulations adopted by the department, governing the presentation and audit of claims. If the Controller is directed by law to draw their warrant for any purpose, the direction is subject to this section.

(b) Notwithstanding subdivision (a), the Assembly Committee on Rules, the Senate Committee on Rules, and the Joint Rules Committee, in cooperation with the Controller, shall adopt rules and regulations to govern the presentation of claims of the committees to the Controller. The Controller, in cooperation with the committees, shall adopt rules and regulations governing the audit and recordkeeping of claims of the committees. All rules and regulations shall be adopted by January 31, 1990, shall be published in the Assembly and Senate Journals, and shall be made available to the public.

(c) Rules and regulations adopted pursuant to subdivision (b) shall not be subject to the review by or approval of the Office of Administrative Law.

(d) Records of claims kept by the Controller pursuant to subdivision (b) shall be open to public inspection as permitted by the California Public Records Act (Division 10 (commencing with Section 7920.000) of Title 1).

(e)(1) Notwithstanding subdivision (a), the Controller shall draw their warrant for any claim submitted by the Department of Housing and Community Development to advance the payment of funds to a vendor selected pursuant to Section 50897.3 of the Health and Safety Code, based on approved applicants associated with Chapter 17 (commencing with Section 50897) of Part 2 of Division 31 of the Health and Safety Code. Funds made available for advance payment pursuant to this subdivision shall not exceed 25 percent of the original amount allocated for the program described in Chapter 17 (commencing with Section 50897) of Part 2 of Division 31 of the Health and Safety Code at any given time.

(2) The vendor described in paragraph (1) shall be the fiscal agent on behalf of the Department of Housing and Community Development and shall be responsible for maintaining all records of claims for audit purposes.

(3) Unless otherwise expressly provided, this subdivision shall remain operative so long as funds are made available pursuant to Chapter 17 (commencing with Section 50897) of Part 2 of Division 31 of the Health and Safety Code or as otherwise provided under federal law. **Leg.H.** Added Stats 1963 ch 1715 §1. Amended Stats 1989 ch 592 §3; Stats 2016 ch 31 §44 (SB 836), effective June 27, 2016; Stats 2021 ch 2 §23 (SB 91), effective January 29, 2021; Stats 2021 ch 615 §135 (AB 474), effective January 1, 2022(ch 2 prevails); Stats 2022 ch 28 §51 (SB 1380), effective January 1, 2023.

§925.8. Warrant on approval of claim

If the Controller approves a claim he shall draw his warrant for the amount approved in favor of the claimant. **Leg.H.** Added Stats 1963 ch 1715 §1.

§926. Disapproval of claim

If he or she disapproves a claim, the Controller shall file it and a statement of his or her disapproval and his or her reasons with the department as prescribed in the rules and regulations of the department. **Leg.H.** Added Stats 1963 ch 1715 §1. Amended Stats 2016 ch 31 §45 (SB 836), effective June 27, 2016.

§926.2. Showing for reconsideration of rejected claim

The Controller shall not entertain for a second time a claim against the state once rejected by him or her or by the Legislature unless such facts are subsequently presented to the department as in suits between individuals that would furnish sufficient ground for granting a new trial. **Leg.H.** Added Stats 1963 ch 1715 §1. Amended Stats 2016 ch 31 §46 (SB 836), effective June 27, 2016.

§926.4. Appeal to, and reconsideration on finding by, department

Any person who is aggrieved by the disapproval of a claim by the Controller may appeal to the department. If the department finds that facts are presented justifying such action, the Controller shall reconsider his or her rejection of the claim. **Leg.H.** Added Stats 1963 ch 1715 §1. Amended Stats 2016 ch 31 §47 (SB 836), effective June 27, 2016.

§926.6. Appeal to Legislature after final rejection

After final rejection of a claim by the Controller following reconsideration, any person interested may appeal to the Legislature by filing with the department a notice of appeal. Upon receipt of such notice the department shall transmit to the Legislature the rejected claim, all papers accompanying it, and a statement of the evidence taken before the department. **Leg.H.** Added Stats 1963 ch 1715 §1. Amended Stats 2016 ch 31 §48 (SB 836), effective June 27, 2016.

§926.8. Federal agency's claim against credits owed by State; Certification of facts; Warrant payable to United States Treasurer

Whenever a governmental agency of the United States, in the collection of taxes or amounts owing to it, is authorized by federal law to levy administratively on credits owing to a debtor, it may avail itself of the provisions of this section and claim credits owing by the State to such debtor, in manner as follows:

It shall file a certification of the facts with the state department, board, office or commission owing the credit to the debtor prior to the time the state agency presents the claims of the debtor therefor to the State Controller or to the State Personnel Board. The state agency in presenting the claim of the debtor shall note thereon the fact of the filing of the certificate and shall also note any amounts owed by the debtor to the State by reason of advances or for any other purpose.

Subject to the provisions of Sections 12419.4 and 12419.5, the State Controller shall issue his warrant payable to the United States Treasurer for the net amount due the debtor, after offsetting for any amounts advanced to the debtor or by him owing to the State, or as much thereof as will satisfy in full the amount owing by the debtor to the United States as so certified; any balance shall be paid to the debtor. **Leg.H.** Added Stats 1963 ch 1715 §1.

§926.10. Interest on liquidated claim against another public entity

Any public entity as defined by Section 811.2 having a liquidated claim against any other public entity based on contract or statute of the State of California, or any person having such a claim against a public agency, shall be entitled to interest commencing the 61st day after such public entity or person files a liquidated claim known or agreed to be valid when filed pursuant to such statute or contract, and such claim is due and payable. Interest shall be 6 percent per annum. **Leg.H.** Added Stats 1971 ch 1526 §1.

CHAPTER 4.5
PROMPT PAYMENT OF CLAIMS

§927. Citation of chapter; Legislative intent; Application of chapter

(a) This chapter shall be known and may be cited as the California Prompt Payment Act.

(b) It is the intent of the Legislature that state agencies pay properly submitted, undisputed invoices, refunds, or other undisputed payments due to individuals within 45 days of receipt or notification thereof, or automatically calculate and pay the appropriate late payment penalties as specified in this chapter.

(c) Notwithstanding any other provision of law, this chapter shall apply to all state agencies, including, but not limited to, the Public Employees' Retirement System, the State Teachers' Retirement System, the Treasurer, and the Department of General Services. **Leg.H.** Added Stats 1998 ch 916 §5 (AB 2275). Amended Stats 2010 ch 719 §13 (SB 856), effective October 19, 2010.

§927.1. Requirement of timely payment; Late payment penalties

(a)(1) A state agency that acquires property or services pursuant to a contract with a business, including any approved change order or contract amendment, shall make payment to the person or business on the date required by the contract and as required by Section 927.4 or be subject to a late payment penalty.

(2) A state agency that awards a grant, as defined in subdivision (b) of Section 927.2, shall make payment to the person or business that is the recipient of the grant on the date required by the grant and as required by Section 927.4 or be subject to a late payment penalty.

(b) Except in the event of an emergency as provided in Section 927.11, effective January 1, 1999, the late payment penalties specified in this chapter may not be waived, altered, or limited by either of the following:

(1) A state agency acquiring property or services pursuant to a contract or that awards a grant.

(2) Any person or business contracting with a state agency to provide property or services or that is the recipient of a grant. **Leg.H.** Added Stats 1998 ch 916 §5 (AB 2275). Amended Stats 2000 ch 151 §1 (AB 1936); Stats 2006 ch 861 §1 (AB 2541), effective January 1, 2007.

§927.2. Definitions

The following definitions apply to this chapter:

(a) "Claim" means payment requests prepared and submitted by a state agency to the Controller for payment to the named claimant.

(b)(1) "Grant" means a signed final agreement between any state agency and a local government agency or organization authorized to accept grant funding for victim services or prevention programs administered by any state agency, or restoration activities performed by a resource conservation district.

(2) A grant defined by this subdivision is a contract and subject to this chapter.

(c) "Invoice" means a bill or claim that requests payment on a contract under which a state agency acquires property or services or pursuant to a signed final grant agreement.

(d) "Medi-Cal program" means the program established pursuant to Chapter 7 (commencing with Section 14000) of Part 3 of Division 9 of the Welfare and Institutions Code.

(e) "Nonprofit public benefit corporation" means a corporation, as defined by subdivision (b) of Section 5046 of the Corporations Code, that has registered with the Department of General Services as a small business.

(f) "Nonprofit service organization" means a nonprofit entity that is organized to provide services to the public.

(g) "Notice of refund or other payment due" means a state agency provides notice to the person that a refund or payment is owed to that person or the state agency receives notice from the person that a refund or undisputed payment is due.

(h) "Payment" means any form of the act of paying, including, but not limited to, the issuance of a warrant or a registered warrant by the Controller, or the issuance of a revolving fund check by a state agency, to a claimant in the amount of an undisputed invoice.

(i) "Reasonable cause" means a determination by a state agency that any of the following conditions are present:

(1) There is a discrepancy between the invoice or claimed amount and the provisions of the contract or grant.

(2) There is a discrepancy between the invoice or claimed amount and either the claimant's actual delivery of property or services to the state or the state's acceptance of those deliveries.

(3) Additional evidence supporting the validity of the invoice or claimed amount is required to be provided to the state agency by the claimant.

(4) The invoice has been improperly executed or needs to be corrected by the claimant.

(5) There is a discrepancy between the refund or other payment due as calculated by the person to whom the money is owed and by the state agency.

(j) "Received by a state agency" means the date an invoice is delivered to the state location or party specified in the contract or grant or, if a state location or party is not specified in the contract or grant, wherever otherwise specified by the state agency.

(k) "Required payment approval date" means the date on which payment is due as specified in a contract or grant or, if a specific date is not established by the contract or grant, 30 calendar days following the date upon which an undisputed invoice is received by a state agency.

(*l*) "Resource conservation district" means a resource conservation district established pursuant to Division 9 (commencing with Section 9001) of the Public Resources Code.

(m) "Revolving fund" means a fund established pursuant to Article 5 (commencing with Section 16400) of Chapter 2 of Part 2 of Division 4 of Title 2.

(n) "Small business" means a business certified as a "small business" in accordance with subdivision (d) of Section 14837, including certified small businesses engaged in the development, design, and construction of California's high-speed rail system pursuant to the California High-Speed Rail Act (Division 19.5 (commencing with Section 185000) of the Public Utilities Code).

(o) "Small business" and "nonprofit organization" mean, in reference to providers under the Medi-Cal program, a business or organization that meets all of the following criteria:

(1) The principal office is located in California.

(2) The officers, if any, are domiciled in California.

(3) If a small business, it is independently owned and operated.

(4) The business or organization is not dominant in its field of operation.

(5) Together with any affiliates, the business or organization has gross receipts from business operations that do not exceed three million dollars ($3,000,000) per year, except that the Director of Health Services may increase this amount if the director deems that this action would be in furtherance of the intent of this chapter.

(p) "Department of FISCal" means the organization responsible for operating and maintaining the Financial Information System for California integrating statewide accounting, budgeting, cash management, and procurement pursuant to subdivision (b) of Section 11890. **Leg.H.** Added Stats 1998 ch 916 §5 (AB 2275). Amended Stats 1999 ch 784 §8 (AB 724), effective October 10, 1999; Stats 2006 ch 861 §2 (AB 2541), effective January 1, 2007; Stats 2009 4th Ex Sess 2009–2010 ch 23 §4 (SBX4-16), effective July 28, 2009; Stats 2010 ch 719 §14 (SB 856), effective October 19, 2010; Stats 2012 ch 199 §1 (AB 2181), effective January 1, 2013; Stats 2019 ch 29 §82 (SB 82), effective June 27, 2019; Stats 2022 ch 455 §1 (AB 1776), effective January 1, 2023.

§927.3. Submission of invoices, notice of refund or other payment due, to controller; Disputes

(a) Except where payment is made directly by a state agency pursuant to Section 927.6, an undisputed invoice received by a state agency shall be submitted to the Controller for payment by the required payment approval date. A state agency may dispute an invoice submitted by a claimant for reasonable cause if the state agency notifies the claimant within 15 working days from receipt of the invoice, or delivery of property or services, whichever is later. No state employee shall dispute an invoice, on the basis of minor or technical defects, in order to circumvent or avoid the general intent or any of the specific provisions of this chapter.

(b) Except where payment is made directly by a state agency pursuant to Section 927.13, a notice of refund or other payment due received by a state agency shall be submitted to the Controller within 30 calendar days of the agency's receipt of the notice. A state agency may dispute a refund request for reasonable cause if the state agency notifies the claimant within 15 working days after the state agency receives notice from the individual that the refund is due. **Leg.H.** Added Stats 1998 ch 916 §5 (AB 2275). Amended Stats 2006 ch 861 §3 (AB 2541), effective January 1, 2007; Stats 2010 ch 719 §15 (SB 856), effective October 19, 2010.

§927.4. Maximum time for payment of undisputed invoice; Penalties

Except as otherwise provided in this chapter, to avoid late payment penalties, the maximum time from state agency receipt of an undisputed invoice to the date of payment is 45 calendar days. If payment is not issued within 45 calendar days from the state agency receipt of an undisputed invoice, late payment penalties shall be paid to the claimant in accordance with Sections 927.6 and 927.7. **Leg.H.** Added Stats 1998 ch 916 §5 (AB 2275). Amended Stats 2009 4th Ex Sess 2009–2010 ch 23 §5 (SBX4-16), effective July 28, 2009.

§927.5. Reimbursement claims under Medi-Cal

This chapter shall not apply to claims for reimbursement for health care services provided under the Medi-Cal program, unless the Medi-Cal health care services provider is a small business or nonprofit organization. In applying this section to claims submitted to the state, or its fiscal intermediary, by providers of services or equipment under the Medi-Cal program, payment for claims shall be due 30 days after a claim is received by the state or its fiscal intermediary, unless reasonable cause for nonpayment exists. With regard to Medi-Cal claims, reasonable cause shall include review of claims to determine medical necessity, review of claims for providers subject to special prepayment fraud and abuse controls, and claims that require review by the fiscal intermediary or State Department of Health Care Services due to special circumstances. Claims requiring special review as specified above shall not be eligible for a late payment penalty. **Leg.H.** Added Stats 1998 ch 916 §5 (AB 2275). Amended Stats 1999 ch 784 §9 (AB 724), effective October 10, 1999; Stats 2010 ch 719 §16 (SB 856), effective October 19, 2010.

§927.6. Payment of penalties by state agencies

(a) State agencies shall pay applicable penalties, without requiring that the claimant submit an additional invoice for these amounts, whenever the state agency fails to submit a correct claim to the Controller by the required payment approval date and payment is not issued within 45 calendar days from the state agency receipt of an undisputed invoice. The penalty shall cease to accrue on the date the state agency submits the claim to the Controller for payment or pays the claimant directly, and shall be paid for out of the state agency's support appropriation. If the claimant is a resource conservation district, certified small business, a nonprofit organization, a nonprofit public benefit corporation, or a small business or nonprofit organization that provides services or equipment under the Medi-Cal program, the state agency shall pay to the claimant a penalty at a rate of 10 percent above the United States Prime Rate on June 30 of the prior fiscal year. However, a nonprofit organization shall only be eligible to receive a penalty payment if it has been awarded a contract or grant in an amount less than five hundred thousand dollars ($500,000). If the amount of the penalty is ten dollars ($10) or less, the penalty shall be waived and not paid by the state agency.

(b) For all other businesses, the state agency shall pay a penalty at a rate of 1 percent above the Pooled Money Investment Account daily rate on June 30 of the prior fiscal year, not to exceed a rate of 15 percent. If the amount of the penalty is one hundred dollars ($100) or less, the penalty shall be waived and not paid by the state agency. On an exception basis, state agencies may avoid payment of penalties for failure to submit a correct claim to the Controller by the required payment approval date by paying the claimant directly from the state agency's revolving fund within 45 calendar days following the date upon which an undisputed invoice is received by the state agency. **Leg.H.** Added Stats 1998 ch 916 §5 (AB 2275). Amended Stats 2006 ch 861 §4 (AB 2541), effective January 1, 2007; Stats 2009 4th Ex Sess 2009–2010 ch 23 §6 (SBX4-16), effective July 28, 2009; Stats 2010 ch 719 §17 (SB 856), effective October 19, 2010; Stats 2019 ch 29 §83 (SB 82), effective June 27, 2019; Stats 2022 ch 455 §2 (AB 1776), effective January 1, 2023.

§927.7. Payment of penalties by Controller

(a) The Controller shall pay claimants within 15 calendar days of receipt of a correct claim from the state agency. If the Controller fails to make payment within 15 calendar days of receipt of the claim from a state agency, and payment is not issued within 45 calendar days from state agency receipt of an undisputed invoice, the Controller shall pay applicable penalties to the claimant without requiring that the claimant submit an invoice for these amounts. Penalties shall cease to accrue on the date full payment is made, and shall be paid for out of the Controller's funds. If the claimant is a resource conservation district, a certified small business, a nonprofit organization, a nonprofit public benefit corporation, or a small business or nonprofit organization that provides services or equipment under the Medi-Cal program, the Controller shall pay to the claimant a penalty at a rate of 10 percent above the United States Prime Rate on June 30 of the prior fiscal year, from the 16th calendar day following receipt of the claim from the state agency. However, a nonprofit organization shall only be eligible to receive a penalty payment if it has been awarded a contract or grant in an amount less than five hundred thousand dollars ($500,000). If the amount of the penalty is ten dollars ($10) or less, the penalty shall be waived and not paid by the Controller. For all other businesses, the Controller shall pay penalties at a rate of 1 percent above the Pooled Money Investment Account daily rate on June 30 of the prior fiscal year, not to exceed a rate of 15 percent. If the amount of the penalty is one hundred dollars ($100) or less, the penalty shall be waived and not paid by the Controller.

(b) The Department of FISCal shall be responsible for applicable penalties if the Financial Information System for California delays the delivery of a correct claim from the state agency to the Controller, preventing the Controller from making payment within 15 calendar days and payment is not issued within 45 calendar days from state agency receipt of an undisputed invoice. **Leg.H.** Added Stats 1998 ch 916 §5 (AB 2275). Amended Stats 2006 ch 861 §5 (AB 2541), effective January 1, 2007; Stats 2009 4th Ex Sess 2009–2010 ch 23 §7 (SBX4-16), effective July 28, 2009; Stats 2010 ch 719 §18 (SB 856), effective October 19, 2010; Stats 2019 ch 29 §84 (SB 82), effective June 27, 2019; Stats 2022 ch 455 §3 (AB 1776), effective January 1, 2023.

§927.8. Additional appropriations to pay penalties

State agencies shall avoid seeking any additional appropriation to pay penalties that accrue as a result of the agency's failure to make timely payments as required by this chapter. Any state agency that requests that the Legislature make a deficiency appropriation for the agency shall identify what portion, if any, of the requested amount is required because of any penalties imposed by this chapter. **Leg.H.** Added Stats 1998 ch 916 §5 (AB 2275).

§927.9. Annual report on late payment penalties paid by agencies

(a) Except as provided in subdivision (c), on an annual basis, within 90 calendar days following the end of each fiscal year, state agencies shall provide the Director of General Services with a report on late payment penalties that were paid by the state agency in accordance with this chapter during the preceding fiscal year.

(b) The report shall separately identify the total number and dollar amount of late payment penalties paid to small businesses, other businesses, and refunds or other payments to individuals. State agencies may, at their own initiative, provide the director with other relevant performance measures. The director shall prepare a report separately listing the number and total dollar amount of all late payment penalties paid to small businesses, other businesses, and refunds and other payments to individuals by each state agency during the preceding fiscal year, together with other relevant performance measures, and shall make the information available to the public.

(c) The reporting requirements of subdivisions (a) and (b) are not applicable to the Department of Forestry and Fire Protection. **Leg.H.** Added Stats 1998 ch 916 §5 (AB 2275). Amended Stats 2010 ch 719 §19 (SB 856), effective October 19, 2010; Stats 2013 ch 356 §4 (SB 96), effective September 26, 2013.

§927.10. Payment of subcontractors and suppliers

State agencies shall encourage claimants to promptly pay their subcontractors and suppliers, especially those that are small businesses. In furtherance of this policy, state agencies shall utilize expedited payment processes to enable faster payment by prime contractors to their subcontractors and suppliers, and shall promptly respond to any subcontractor or supplier inquiries regarding the status of payments made to prime contractors. **Leg.H.** Added Stats 1998 ch 916 §5 (AB 2275). Amended Stats 2006 ch 861 §6 (AB 2541), effective January 1, 2007.

§927.11. Effect of fire season, failure to enact budget, major calamity, or criminal act

(a) Except in the case of a contract with a resource conservation district, a certified small business, a nonprofit organization, or a nonprofit public benefit corporation, if an invoice from a business under a contract with the Department of Forestry and Fire Protection would become subject to late payment penalties during the annually declared fire season, as declared by the Director of Forestry and Fire Protection, then the required payment approval date shall be extended by 30 calendar days.

(b) No nonprofit public benefit corporation shall be eligible for a late payment penalty if a state agency fails to make timely payment because no Budget Act has been enacted.

(c)(1) If the Director of Finance determines that a state agency or the Controller is unable to promptly pay an invoice as provided for by this chapter due to a major calamity, disaster, or criminal act, then otherwise applicable late payment penalty provisions contained in Sections 927.6 and 927.7 shall be suspended, except as they apply to a claimant that is any of the following:

(A) A resource conservation district.
(B) A certified small business.
(C) A nonprofit organization.
(D) A nonprofit public benefit corporation.
(E) A small business or nonprofit organization that provides services or equipment under the Medi-Cal program.

(2) A suspension pursuant to this subdivision shall remain in effect until the Director of Finance determines that the suspended late payment penalty provisions should be reinstated.

(d) Except as provided in subdivision (b), in the event a state agency fails to make timely payment because no Budget Act has been enacted, penalties shall continue to accrue until the time that the invoice is paid. **Leg.H.** Added Stats 1998 ch 916 §5 (AB 2275). Amended Stats 2006 ch 861 §7 (AB 2541), effective January 1, 2007; Stats 2009 4th Ex Sess 2009–2010 ch 23 §8 (SBX4-16), effective July 28, 2009; Stats 2022 ch 455 §4 (AB 1776), effective January 1, 2023.

§927.12. Applicability of other section

Section 926.10 shall not apply to any contract covered by this chapter. **Leg.H.** Added Stats 1998 ch 916 §5 (AB 2275).

§927.13. Failure to submit correct claim schedule to Controller; Penalties; Payment of claim schedule by Controller; Interest payment; Applicability

(a) Unless otherwise provided for by statute, any state agency that fails to submit a correct claim to the Controller within 30 days of receipt of a notice of refund or other payment due, and fails to issue payment within 45 days from the notice of refund or other payment due, shall be liable for penalties on the undisputed amount pursuant to this section. The penalties shall be paid out of the agency's funds at a rate equal to the Pooled Money Investment Account daily rate on June 30 of the prior fiscal year minus 1 percent. The penalties shall cease to accrue on the date full payment or refund is made. If the amount of the penalty is ten dollars ($10) or less, the penalty shall be waived and not paid by the state agency. On an exception basis, state agencies may avoid payment of penalties for failure to submit a correct claim to the Controller by paying the claimant directly from the state agency's revolving fund within 45 calendar days following the agency's receipt of the notice of refund or other payment due.

(b) The Controller shall pay claimants within 15 calendar days of receipt of a correct claim from the state agency. If the Controller fails to make payment within 15 calendar days of receipt of the claim schedule from a state agency, and payment is not issued within 45 calendar days following the agency's receipt of a notice of refund or undisputed payment due, the Controller shall pay applicable penalties to the claimant. Penalties shall cease to accrue on the date full payment is made, and shall be paid out of the Controller's funds. If the amount of the penalty is ten dollars ($10) or less, the penalty shall be waived and not paid by the Controller.

(c) The Department of FISCal shall be responsible for applicable penalties if the Financial Information System for California delays the delivery of a correct claim from the state agency to the Controller, preventing the Controller from making payment within 15 calendar days and payment is not issued within 45 calendar days from the agency's receipt of a notice of refund or an undisputed payment due.

(d) No person shall receive an interest payment pursuant to this section if it is determined that the person has intentionally overpaid on a liability solely for the purpose of receiving a penalty payment.

(e) No penalty shall accrue during any time period for which there is no Budget Act in effect, nor on any payment or refund that is the result of a federally mandated program or that is directly dependent upon the receipt of federal funds by a state agency.

(f) This section shall not apply to any of the following:

(1) Payments, refunds, or credits for income tax purposes.

(2) Payment of claims for reimbursement for health care services or mental health services provided under the Medi-Cal program, pursuant to Chapter 7 (commencing with Section 14000) of Part 3 of Division 9 of the Welfare and Institutions Code.

(3) Any payment made pursuant to a public social service or public health program to a recipient of benefits under that program.

(4) Payments made on claims by the Department of General Services.

(5) Payments made by the Commission on State Mandates.

(6) Payments made by the Department of Human Resources pursuant to Section 19823. **Leg.H.** Added Stats 2010 ch 719 §20 (SB 856), effective October 19, 2010. Amended Stats 2012 ch 665 §31 (SB 1308), effective January 1, 2013; Stats 2016 ch 31 §49 (SB 836), effective June 27, 2016; Stats 2019 ch 29 §85 (SB 82), effective June 27, 2019.

2012 Note: Stats 2012 ch 665 (SB 1308) enacted the statutory changes necessary to reflect the changes made by the Governor's Reorganization Plan No. 1 of 2011.

2011 Note: 2011 Governor's Reorganization Plan No. 1 was submitted to the Legislature on June 9, 2011, and became effective September 9, 2011, pursuant to Gov C § 12080.5, and substantively operative July 1, 2012.

CHAPTER 5
CLAIMS PROCEDURES ESTABLISHED BY AGREEMENT

§930. Provisions of state agency agreement

(a) Any state agency may include in any written agreement to which the agency is a party, provisions governing the following:

(1) The presentation, by or on behalf of any party thereto, of any or all claims that are required to be presented to the board arising out of or related to the agreement.

(2) The consideration and payment of the claims described in paragraph (1).

(b) As used in this section, "state agency" means any office, officer, department, division, bureau, board, commission or agency of the state, claims against which are paid by warrants drawn by the Controller.

Leg.H. Added Stats 1963 ch 1715 §1. Amended Stats 1965 ch 653 §9; Stats 1994 ch 726 §3 (AB 3069), effective September 21, 1994.

§930.2. Provisions of local public entity agreement; Incorporation of ordinance or resolution

The governing body of a local public entity may include in any written agreement to which the entity, its governing body, or any board or employee thereof in an official capacity is a party, provisions governing the presentation, by or on behalf of any party thereto, of any or all claims arising out of or related to the agreement and the consideration and payment of such claims. The written agreement may incorporate by reference claim provisions set forth in a specifically identified ordinance or resolution theretofore adopted by the governing body. **Leg.H.** Added Stats 1963 ch 1715 §1. Amended Stats 1965 ch 653 §10.

§930.4. Exception as to tardy claims presented with permission

A claims procedure established by agreement made pursuant to Section 930 or Section 930.2 exclusively governs the claims to which it relates, except that if the procedure so prescribed requires a claim to be presented within a period of less than one year after the accrual of the cause of action and such claim is not presented within the required time, an application may be made to the public entity for leave to present such claim. Subdivision (b) of Section 911.4, Sections 911.6 to 912.2, inclusive, and Section 946.6 are applicable to all such claims, and the time specified in the agreement shall be deemed the "time specified in Section 911.2" within the meaning of Sections 911.6 and 946.6. **Leg.H.** Added Stats 1965 ch 653 §11.

§930.6. Presentation of, and determination on, claim as prerequisite to suit

A claims procedure established by agreement made pursuant to Section 930 or Section 930.2 may include a requirement that a claim be presented and acted upon as a prerequisite to suit thereon. If such requirement is included, any action brought against the public entity on the claim shall be subject to the provisions of Section 945.6 and Section 946. **Leg.H.** Added Stats 1965 ch 653 §12.

CHAPTER 6
CLAIMS PROCEDURES ESTABLISHED BY PUBLIC ENTITIES

§935. Governing procedure prescribed in charter, ordinance or regulation

(a) Claims against a local public entity for money or damages which are excepted by Section 905 from Chapter 1 (commencing with Section 900) and Chapter 2 (commencing with Section 910) of this part, and which are not governed by any other statutes or regulations expressly relating thereto, shall be governed by the procedure prescribed in any charter, ordinance, or regulation adopted by the local public entity.

(b) The procedure so prescribed may include a requirement that a claim be presented and acted upon as a prerequisite to suit thereon. If such a requirement is included, any action brought against the public entity on the claim shall be subject to Sections 945.6 and 946.

(c) The procedure so prescribed shall not require a shorter time for presentation of any claim than the time provided in Section 911.2.

(d) The procedure so prescribed shall not provide a longer time for the board to take action upon any claim than the time provided in Section 912.4.

(e) When a claim required by the procedure to be presented within a period of less than one year after the accrual of the cause of action is not presented within the required time, an application may be made to the public entity for leave to present such claim. Subdivision (b) of Section 911.4, Sections 911.6 to 912.2, inclusive, and Sections 946.4 and 946.6 are applicable to all such claims, and the time specified in the charter, ordinance, or regulation shall be deemed the "time specified in Section 911.2" within the meaning of Sections 911.6 and 946.6.

(f) Any procedure authorized to be prescribed by this section does not apply to claims of childhood sexual abuse made as described in subdivision (m) of Section 905. This subdivision is declaratory of existing law. **Leg.H.** Added Stats 1963 ch 1715 §1. Amended Stats 1965 ch 653 §13; Stats 2018 ch 153 §1 (SB 1053), effective January 1, 2019.

§935.2. Establishment of local claims board or commission; Warrant

A charter provision, or a local public entity by ordinance or resolution, may establish a claims board or commission of not less than three members to perform such functions of the governing body of the public entity under this part as are prescribed by the local public entity. A charter provision, ordinance or resolution may provide that, upon the written order of the claims board or commission, the auditor or other fiscal officer of the local public entity shall cause a warrant to be drawn upon the treasury of the local public entity in the amount for which a claim has been allowed or compromised or settled. **Leg.H.** Added Stats 1963 ch 1715 §1. Amended Stats 1965 ch 653 §14.

§935.4. Performance of functions of local governing body by employee; Restriction as to amount of claim allowed

A charter provision, or a local public entity by ordinance or resolution, may authorize an employee of the local public entity to perform those function's of the governing body of the public entity under this part that are prescribed by the local public entity, but only a charter provision may authorize that employee to allow, compromise, or settle a claim against the local public entity if the amount to be paid pursuant to the allowance, compromise or settlement exceeds fifty thousand dollars ($50,000). A charter provision, ordinance, or resolution may provide that, upon the written order of that employee, the auditor or other fiscal officer of the local public entity shall cause a warrant to be issued upon the treasury of the local public entity in the amount for which a claim has been allowed, compromised, or settled. **Leg.H.** Added Stats 1963 ch 1715 §1. Amended Stats 1965 ch 653 §15; Stats 1981 ch 317 §1; Stats 1989 ch 159 §1.

§935.6. Payments by state agency

(a) The Department of General Services may authorize any state agency to settle and pay claims filed pursuant to Section 905.2 if the settlement does not exceed one thousand dollars ($1,000) or a lesser amount as the department may determine, or to reject the claim and provide the notice required by Section 913. The department may require state agencies that it so authorizes to report annually to the department concerning the claims resolved pursuant to this section.

(b) As used in this section, "state agency" means any office, officer, department, division, bureau, board, commission, or agency of the state, claims against which are paid by warrants drawn by the Controller, but does not mean any judicial branch entity, as defined in Section 900.3, or any judge thereof. **Leg.H.** Added Stats 1963 ch 1715 §1. Amended Stats 1965 ch 1004 §2; Stats 1980 ch 215 §6; Stats 1983 ch 591 §1; Stats 1994 ch 726 §4 (AB 3069), effective September 21, 1994; Stats 2002 ch 1007 §8 (AB 2321); Stats 2007 ch 509 §1 (AB 1273), effective October 11, 2007; Stats 2016 ch 31 §50 (SB 836), effective June 27, 2016.

§935.7. Payment by Department of Transportation

(a) Notwithstanding Section 935.6, the Department of Transportation may deny or adjust and pay any claim arising out of the activities of the department without the prior approval of the Department of General Services if both of the following conditions exist:

(1) The amount claimed is equal to or less than the amount specified as the small claims court jurisdictional amount in Section 116.221 of the Code of Civil Procedure.

(2) The Director of Finance or the Director of Transportation certifies that a sufficient appropriation for the payment of the claim exists.

(b) If the department elects not to pay any claim, the department shall provide the notice required by Section 913.

(c) Any person who submits any claim arising out of any activity of the Department of Transportation shall comply with every other applicable provision of this part relating to claims against state agencies. **Leg.H.** Added Stats 1987 ch 350 §1. Amended Stats 2002 ch 1124 §8 (AB 3000), effective September 30, 2002; Stats 2003 ch 228 §11 (AB 1756), effective August 11, 2003; Stats 2012 ch 769 §1 (AB 2679), effective January 1, 2013; Stats 2016 ch 31 §51 (SB 836), effective June 27, 2016.

§935.8. Payments by Judicial Council

The Judicial Council may adjust and pay any claim arising out of the activities of a judicial branch entity or judge thereof. The Judicial Council may adopt rules of court authorizing any committee of the Judicial Council or employee of the Administrative Office of the Courts to perform the functions of the Judicial Council under this section. **Leg.H.** Added Stats 2002 ch 1007 §9 (AB 2321).

§935.9. Payments by Trustees of California State University

The Trustees of the California State University may adjust and pay any claim arising out of the activities of the California State University. The Trustees of the California State University may, by rule, authorize the Office of Risk Management at the Office of the Chancellor of the California State University to perform the functions of the Trustees of the California State University under this section. **Leg.H.** Added Stats 2010 ch 636 §7 (SB 1046), effective January 1, 2011. Amended Stats 2011 ch 296 §112 (AB 1023), effective January 1, 2012.

PART 4
ACTIONS AGAINST PUBLIC ENTITIES AND PUBLIC EMPLOYEES
CHAPTER 1
GENERAL
ARTICLE 1
Definitions

§940. Governing provisions

Unless the provision or context otherwise requires, the definitions contained in this article govern the construction of this part. **Leg.H.** Added Stats 1963 ch 1715 §2.

§940.2. "Board"

"Board" means:

(a) In the case of a local public entity, the governing body of the local public entity.

(b) In the case of the state, except as provided by subdivisions (c) and (d), the Department of General Services.

(c) In the case of a judicial branch entity or a judge thereof, the Judicial Council.

(d) In the case of the California State University, the Trustees of the California State University. **Leg.H.** Added Stats 1963 ch 1715 §2. Amended Stats 2002 ch 1007 §10 (AB 2321); Stats 2010 ch 636 §8 (SB 1046), effective January 1, 2011; Stats 2016 ch 31 §52 (SB 836), effective June 27, 2016.

§940.3. "Judicial branch entity"

A "judicial branch entity" is a public entity and means any superior court, court of appeals, the Supreme Court, the Judicial Council, or the Administrative Office of the Courts. **Leg.H.** Added Stats 2002 ch 1007 §11 (AB 2321).

§940.4. "Local public entity"

"Local public entity" includes a county, city, district, public authority, public agency, and any other political subdivision or public corporation in the State, but does not include the State. **Leg.H.** Added Stats 1963 ch 1715 §2.

§940.6. "State"

"State" means the State and any office, officer, department, division, bureau, board, commission or agency of the State claims against which are paid by warrants drawn by the Controller. **Leg.H.** Added Stats 1963 ch 1715 §2.

ARTICLE 2
Construction

§942. Claimant's right to resort to mandamus or other proceeding

Nothing in this division shall be construed to deprive a claimant of the right to resort to writ of mandate or other proceeding against the public entity or the board or any employee of the public entity to compel payment of a claim when and to the extent that it has been allowed and is required by this division to be paid. **Leg.H.** Added Stats 1963 ch 1715 §2. Amended Stats 1980 ch 215 §7.

§943. Inapplicability to claims or actions against Regents of University of California

This part does not apply to claims or actions against the Regents of the University of California nor to claims or actions against an employee or former employee of the Regents of the University of California arising out of such employment. **Leg.H.** Added Stats 1963 ch 1715 §2. Amended Stats 1965 ch 653 §16.

§944. Disclaimer of additional liability

Nothing in this part imposes liability upon a public entity unless such liability otherwise exists. **Leg.H.** Added Stats 1963 ch 1715 §2.

CHAPTER 2
ACTIONS AGAINST PUBLIC ENTITIES

§945. Public entity's right to sue and liability to suit
A public entity may sue and be sued. **Leg.H.** Added Stats 1963 ch 1715 §2.

§945.2. Application of rules of practice in civil actions
Except as otherwise provided by law, the rules of practice in civil actions apply to actions brought against public entities. **Leg.H.** Added Stats 1963 ch 1715 §2.

§945.3. Action while charges pending; Limitation period tolled
No person charged by indictment, information, complaint, or other accusatory pleading charging a criminal offense may bring a civil action for money or damages against a peace officer or the public entity employing a peace officer based upon conduct of the peace officer relating to the offense for which the accused is charged, including an act or omission in investigating or reporting the offense or arresting or detaining the accused, while the charges against the accused are pending before a superior court.

Any applicable statute of limitations for filing and prosecuting these actions shall be tolled during the period that the charges are pending before a superior court.

For the purposes of this section, charges pending before a superior court do not include appeals or criminal proceedings diverted pursuant to Chapter 2.5 (commencing with Section 1000), Chapter 2.6 (commencing with Section 1000.6), Chapter 2.7 (commencing with Section 1001), Chapter 2.8 (commencing with Section 1001.20), or Chapter 2.9 (commencing with Section 1001.50) of Title 6 of Part 2 of the Penal Code.

Nothing in this section shall prohibit the filing of a claim with the board of a public entity, and this section shall not extend the time within which a claim is required to be presented pursuant to Section 911.2. **Leg.H.** Added Stats 1981 ch 285 §1. Amended Stats 1983 ch 272 §1; Stats 1998 ch 931 §175 (SB 2139), effective September 23, 1998; Stats 2002 ch 784 §121 (SB 1316).

§945.4. Prohibition against suit in absence of presentation of claim and action thereon
Except as provided in Sections 946.4 and 946.6, no suit for money or damages may be brought against a public entity on a cause of action for which a claim is required to be presented in accordance with Chapter 1 (commencing with Section 900) and Chapter 2 (commencing with Section 910) of Part 3 of this division until a written claim therefor has been presented to the public entity and has been acted upon by the board, or has been deemed to have been rejected by the board, in accordance with Chapters 1 and 2 of Part 3 of this division. **Leg.H.** Added Stats 1963 ch 1715 §2. Amended Stats 1965 ch 653 §17.

§945.6. Limitation as to time for commencing suit when claim required; Time for person sentenced to imprisonment
(a) Except as provided in Sections 946.4 and 946.6 and subject to subdivision (b), any suit brought against a public entity on a cause of action for which a claim is required to be presented in accordance with Chapter 1 (commencing with Section 900) and Chapter 2 (commencing with Section 910) of Part 3 of this division must be commenced:

(1) If written notice is given in accordance with Section 913, not later than six months after the date such notice is personally delivered or deposited in the mail.

(2) If written notice is not given in accordance with Section 913, within two years from the accrual of the cause of action. If the period within which the public entity is required to act is extended pursuant to subdivision (b) of Section 912.4, the period of such extension is not part of the time limited for the commencement of the action under this paragraph.

(b) When a person is unable to commence a suit on a cause of action described in subdivision (a) within the time prescribed in that subdivision because he has been sentenced to imprisonment in a state prison, the time limit for the commencement of such suit is extended to six months after the date that the civil right to commence such action is restored to such person, except that the time shall not be extended if the public entity establishes that the plaintiff failed to make a reasonable effort to commence the suit, or to obtain a restoration of his civil right to do so, before the expiration of the time prescribed in subdivision (a).

(c) A person sentenced to imprisonment in a state prison may not commence a suit on a cause of action described in subdivision (a) unless he presented a claim in accordance with Chapter 1 (commencing with Section 900) and Chapter 2 (commencing with Section 910) of Part 3 of this division. **Leg.H.** Added Stats 1963 ch 1715 §2. Amended Stats 1965 ch 653 §19; Stats 1968 ch 134 §2; Stats 1970 ch 104 §6, operative January 1, 1971; Stats 1971 ch 438 §92.

§945.8. Applicable statute of limitations when claim presentation not required
Except where a different statute of limitations is specifically applicable to the public entity, and except as provided in Sections 930.6 and 935, any action against a public entity upon a cause of action for which a claim is not required to be presented in accordance with Chapter 1 (commencing with Section 900) and Chapter 2 (commencing with Section 910) of Part 3 of this division must be commenced within the time prescribed by the statute of limitations that would be applicable if the action were brought against a defendant other than a public entity. **Leg.H.** Added Stats 1963 ch 1715 §2. Amended Stats 1965 ch 653 §20.

§945.9. Claim presentation requirements for sexual assault by a law enforcement officer
(a) A claim arising out of an alleged sexual assault by a law enforcement officer if the alleged assault occurred while the officer was employed by a law enforcement agency is exempted from all state and local government claim presentation requirements.

(b) Notwithstanding any other law, the time for commencement of a claim seeking to recover damages arising out of an alleged sexual assault by a law enforcement officer, if the alleged sexual assault occurred on or after the plaintiff's 18th birthday and while the officer was employed by a law enforcement agency, shall be the later of either of the following dates:

(1) Within 10 years after the date of judgment against a law enforcement officer in a criminal case for a crime of sexual assault or a judgment against a law enforcement officer for a different crime if a crime of sexual assault was alleged and the crime for which there was a judgment against a law enforcement officer arose out of the same set of operative facts as the allegation of sexual assault in the present claim.

(2) Within 10 years after the law enforcement officer is no longer employed by the law enforcement agency that employed the officer when the alleged sexual assault occurred.

(c) Notwithstanding subdivision (b), a claim seeking to recover damages arising out of an alleged sexual assault by a law enforcement officer, if the alleged sexual assault occurred on or after the plaintiff's 18th birthday and while the officer was employed by a law enforcement agency, that has not been litigated to finality or compromised by an executed written settlement agreement and that would otherwise be barred because the applicable statute of limitations, any state or local government claim presentation deadline, or any other applicable time limit has expired, is hereby revived and may be commenced if filed within either of the following periods of time:

(1) Ten years from the date of the last act, attempted act, or assault with the intent to commit an act, of sexual assault against the plaintiff.

(2) Three years from the date the plaintiff discovers or reasonably should have discovered that an injury or illness resulted from an act, attempted act, or assault with the intent to commit an act, of sexual assault against the plaintiff.

(d) As used in this section, "sexual assault" means any of the crimes described in Section 243.4, 261, 262, 264.1, 286, 287, or 289, or former Section 288a, of the Penal Code, assault with the intent to commit any of those crimes, or an attempt to commit any of those crimes. **Leg.H.** Added Stats 2021 ch 595 §1 (AB 1455), effective January 1, 2022.

§946. Effect of claimant's acceptance of amount allowed, on right to maintain suit
Where a claim that is required to be presented to a public entity in accordance with Chapter 1 (commencing with Section 900) and Chapter 2 (commencing with Section 910) of Part 3 of this division is so presented and action thereon is taken by the board:

(a) If the claim is allowed in full and the claimant accepts the amount allowed, no suit may be maintained on any part of the cause of action to which the claim relates.

(b) If the claim is allowed in part and the claimant accepts the amount allowed, no suit may be maintained on that part of the cause of action which is represented by the allowed portion of the claim.

(c) If the claim is allowed in part, no suit may be maintained on any portion of the cause of action where, pursuant to a requirement of the board to such effect, the claimant has accepted the amount allowed in settlement of the entire claim. **Leg.H.** Added Stats 1963 ch 1715 §2.

§946.4. Filings prerequisite to bar to sue "public agency" because of nonpresentation of claim

(a) Where provision is made by or pursuant to law that no suit may be brought against a public agency as defined in Section 53050 unless and until a claim is presented to the agency, the failure to present a claim does not constitute a bar or defense to the maintenance of a suit against the public agency if, during the 70 days immediately following the accrual of the cause of action, either of the following apply:

(1) No statement pertaining to the public agency is on file, or is placed on file, in the Registry of Public Agencies in the office of the Secretary of State and of the county clerk of each county in which the public agency then maintains an office, as required by Section 53051.

(2) A statement or amended statement pertaining to the public agency is on file, or is placed on file, in the Registry of Public Agencies in the office of the Secretary of State and of the county clerk of each county in which the public agency then maintains an office, but the information contained therein is so inaccurate or incomplete that it does not substantially conform to the requirements of Section 53051.

(b) On any question of fact arising within the scope of paragraphs (1) and (2) of subdivision (a), the burden of proof is upon the public agency.

(c) This section is inapplicable where the presentation of a claim is required by a claims procedure established by agreement made pursuant to Section 930.2 unless the procedure so prescribed requires that the claim be presented to the governing body of the public agency or to a person listed in Section 53051. **Leg.H.** Added Stats 1965 ch 653 §21. Amended Stats 2019 ch 329 §3 (SB 780), effective January 1, 2020.

§946.6. Judicial relief from bar to sue because of nonpresentation of claim

(a) If an application for leave to present a claim is denied or deemed to be denied pursuant to Section 911.6, a petition may be made to the court for an order relieving the petitioner from Section 945.4. The proper court for filing the petition is a superior court that would be a proper court for the trial of an action on the cause of action to which the claim relates. If the petition is filed in a court which is not a proper court for the determination of the matter, the court, on motion of any party, shall transfer the proceeding to a proper court. If an action on the cause of action to which the claim relates would be a limited civil case, a proceeding pursuant to this section is a limited civil case.

(b) The petition shall show each of the following:

(1) That application was made to the board under Section 911.4 and was denied or deemed denied.

(2) The reason for failure to present the claim within the time limit specified in Section 911.2.

(3) The information required by Section 910.

The petition shall be filed within six months after the application to the board is denied or deemed to be denied pursuant to Section 911.6.

(c) The court shall relieve the petitioner from the requirements of Section 945.4 if the court finds that the application to the board under Section 911.4 was made within a reasonable time not to exceed that specified in subdivision (b) of Section 911.4 and was denied or deemed denied pursuant to Section 911.6 and that one or more of the following is applicable:

(1) The failure to present the claim was through mistake, inadvertence, surprise, or excusable neglect unless the public entity establishes that it would be prejudiced in the defense of the claim if the court relieves the petitioner from the requirements of Section 945.4.

(2) The person who sustained the alleged injury, damage, or loss was a minor during all of the time specified in Section 911.2 for the presentation of the claim.

(3) The person who sustained the alleged injury, damage, or loss was a minor during any of the time specified in Section 911.2 for the presentation of the claim, provided the application is presented within six months of the person turning 18 years of age or a year after the claim accrues, whichever occurs first.

(4) The person who sustained the alleged injury, damage, or loss was physically or mentally incapacitated during all of the time specified in Section 911.2 for the presentation of the claim and by reason of that disability failed to present a claim during that time.

(5) The person who sustained the alleged injury, damage, or loss was physically or mentally incapacitated during any of the time specified in Section 911.2 for the presentation of the claim and by reason of that disability failed to present a claim during that time, provided the application is presented within six months of the person no longer being physically or mentally incapacitated, or a year after the claim accrues, whichever occurs first.

(6) The person who sustained the alleged injury, damage, or loss died before the expiration of the time specified in Section 911.2 for the presentation of the claim.

(d) A copy of the petition and a written notice of the time and place of hearing shall be served before the hearing as prescribed by subdivision (b) of Section 1005 of the Code of Civil Procedure on (1) the clerk or secretary or board of the local public entity, if the respondent is a local public entity, or (2) the Attorney General, if the respondent is the state. If the petition involves a claim arising out of alleged actions or inactions of the Department of Transportation, service of the petition and notice of the hearing shall be made on the Attorney General or the Director of Transportation. Service on the Attorney General may be accomplished at any of the Attorney General's offices in Los Angeles, Sacramento, San Diego, or San Francisco. Service on the Director of Transportation may be accomplished only at the Department of Transportation's headquarters office in Sacramento. If the petition involves a claim arising out of alleged actions or inactions of a judicial branch entity, service of the petition and notice of the hearing shall be made in accordance with the following:

(1) If the petition involves a claim arising out of alleged actions or inactions of a superior court or a judge, court executive officer, or trial court employee, as defined in Section 811.9, of the court, service shall be made on the court executive officer.

(2) If the petition involves a claim arising out of alleged actions or inactions of a court of appeal or a judge thereof, service shall be made on the Clerk/Executive Officer of the Court of Appeal.

(3) If the petition involves a claim arising out of alleged actions or inactions of the Supreme Court or a judge thereof, service shall be made on the Clerk/Executive Officer of the Supreme Court.

(4) If the petition involves a claim arising out of alleged actions or inactions of the Judicial Council or the Administrative Office of the Courts, service shall be made on the Administrative Director of the Judicial Council.

(e) The court shall make an independent determination upon the petition. The determination shall be made upon the basis of the petition, any affidavits in support of or in opposition to the petition, and any additional evidence received at the hearing on the petition.

(f) If the court makes an order relieving the petitioner from Section 945.4, suit on the cause of action to which the claim relates shall be filed with the court within 30 days thereafter. **Leg.H.** Added Stats 1965 ch 653 §22. Amended Stats 1970 ch 411 §2; Stats 1987 ch 1201 §22, ch 1208 §7; Stats 1989 ch 148 §1, ch 693 §8; Stats 2001 ch 44 §9 (SB 562); Stats 2002 ch 1007 §12 (AB 2321); Stats 2017 ch 36 §5 (AB 452), effective January 1, 2018; Stats 2018 ch 92 §83 (SB 1289), effective January 1, 2019; Stats 2021 ch 218 §2 (SB 501), effective January 1, 2022.

§948. Settlement by state agency

(a) The head of the state agency concerned, upon recommendation of the Attorney General or other attorney authorized to represent the state, may settle, adjust, or compromise any pending action where the Director of Finance certifies that a sufficient appropriation for the payment of claims exists. Claims arising out of the activities of the State Department of Transportation may be paid if either the Director of Transportation or the Director of Finance certifies that a sufficient appropriation for the payment of the claim exists.

(b) If no funds or insufficient funds for the payment exist, the head of the state agency concerned, upon recommendation of the Attorney General or other attorney authorized to represent the state, may settle, adjust or compromise any pending action with the approval of the Department of Finance.

(c) As used in this section, "state agency" means any office, officer, department, division, bureau, board, commission or agency of the state claims against which are paid by warrants drawn by the Controller, but does not mean any "judicial branch entity" as defined in Section 940.3 or any judge thereof. **Leg.H.** Added Stats 1963 ch 1715 §2. Amended Stats 1965 ch 1004 §3; Stats 1980 ch 215 §8; Stats 1985 ch 778 §1; Stats 2002 ch 1007 §13 (AB 2321).

§948.1. Settlement by Judicial Council

The Judicial Council may settle, adjust, or compromise any pending action arising out of the activities of a judicial branch entity or judge thereof. The Judicial Council may adopt rules of court authorizing any committee of the Judicial Council or employee of the Administrative Office of the Courts to perform the functions of the Judicial Council under this section. **Leg.H.** Added Stats 2002 ch 1007 §14 (AB 2321).

§949. Compromise by local governing body; Delegation of authority

The governing body of a local public entity may compromise, or may delegate the authority to its attorney or an employee to compromise, any pending action. **Leg.H.** Added Stats 1963 ch 1715 §2.

CHAPTER 3
ACTIONS AGAINST PUBLIC EMPLOYEES

§950. Necessity for presentation of claim in order to maintain action

Except as otherwise provided in this chapter, a claim need not be presented as a prerequisite to the maintenance of an action against a public employee or former public employee for injury resulting from an act or omission in the scope of his employment as a public employee. **Leg.H.** Added Stats 1963 ch 1715 §2.

§950.2. When action barred for failure to present claim or commence action within time specified

Except as provided in Section 950.4, a cause of action against a public employee or former public employee for injury resulting from an act or omission in the scope of his employment as a public employee is barred if an action against the employing public entity for such injury is barred under Part 3 (commencing with Section 900) of this division or under Chapter 2 (commencing with Section 945) of Part 4 of this division. This section is applicable even though the public entity is immune from liability for the injury. **Leg.H.** Added Stats 1963 ch 1715 §2. Amended Stats 1965 ch 653 §23.

§950.4. Pleading and proof excusing failure to present claim within time prescribed

A cause of action against a public employee or former public employee is not barred by Section 950.2 if the plaintiff pleads and proves that he did not know or have reason to know, within the period for the presentation of a claim to the employing public entity as a condition to maintaining an action for such injury against the employing public entity, as that period is prescribed by Section 911.2 or by such other claims procedure as may be applicable, that the injury was caused by an act or omission of the public entity or by an act or omission of an employee of the public entity in the scope of his employment as a public employee. **Leg.H.** Added Stats 1963 ch 1715 §2. Amended Stats 1965 ch 653 §24.

§950.6. Requisites for maintenance of action; Rejection; Time for commencement of suit

When a written claim for money or damages for injury has been presented to the employing public entity:

(a) A cause of action for such injury may not be maintained against the public employee or former public employee whose act or omission caused such injury until the claim has been rejected, or has been deemed to have been rejected, in whole or in part by the public entity.

(b) A suit against the public employee or former public employee for such injury must be commenced within the time prescribed by Section 945.6 for bringing an action against the public entity.

(c) When a person is unable to commence the suit within the time prescribed in subdivision (b) because he has been sentenced to imprisonment in a state prison, the time limited for the commencement of such suit is extended to six months after the date that the civil right to commence such action is restored to such person, except that the time shall not be extended if the public employee or former public employee establishes that the plaintiff failed to make a reasonable effort to commence the suit, or to obtain a restoration of his civil right to do so, before the expiration of the time prescribed in subdivision (b). **Leg.H.** Added Stats 1965 ch 1715 §2. Amended Stats 1965 ch 653 §25; Stats 1970 ch 104 §7, operative January 1, 1971.

§950.8. Invalidity of charter, ordinance or regulation requiring presentation of claim

Any provision of a charter, ordinance or regulation heretofore or hereafter adopted by a local public entity which requires the presentation of a claim as a prerequisite to the maintenance of an action against a public employee to enforce his personal liability is invalid. **Leg.H.** Added Stats 1963 ch 1715 §2.

§951. Alleging individual liability

Notwithstanding Section 425.10 of the Code of Civil Procedure, any complaint for damages in any civil action brought against a publicly elected or appointed state or local officer, in his or her individual capacity, where the alleged injury is proximately caused by the officer acting under color of law, shall allege with particularity sufficient material facts to establish the individual liability of the publicly elected or appointed state or local officer and the plaintiff's right to recover therefrom. **Leg.H.** Added Stats 1996 ch 562 §1 (SB 1368). Amended Stats 1997 ch 17 §46 (SB 947).

Prior Law: Former §951, relating to undertaking in action against public employees, was added Stats 1963 ch 1715 §2, amended Stats 1968 ch 384 §2, and repealed Stats 1980 ch 114 §8.

CHAPTER 4
SPECIAL PROVISIONS RELATING TO ACTIONS AGAINST THE STATE

§955. Venue of action for taking or damaging property; Transfer

The proper court for trial of actions against the State for the taking or damaging of private property for public use is a court of competent jurisdiction in the county in which the property is situate.

Except as provided in Sections 955.2 and 955.3, upon written demand of the Attorney General made on or before answering, the place of trial in other actions shall be changed to Sacramento County. **Leg.H.** Added Stats 1963 ch 1715 §2. Amended Stats 1980 ch 387 §1.

§955.1. Immunity from liability for earthquake predictions

(a) The science of earthquake prediction is developing rapidly and, although still largely in a research stage, these predictions are now being initiated and are certain to continue into the future. Administrative procedures exist within the Office of Emergency Services to advise the Governor on the validity of earthquake predictions. Numerous important actions can be taken by state and local governments and special districts to protect life and property in response to earthquake predictions and associated warnings. It is the intent of this legislation to ensure that those actions are taken in the public interest by government agencies acting in a responsible manner without fear of consequent financial liabilities.

(b) The Governor may, at his or her discretion, issue a warning as to the existence of an earthquake or volcanic prediction determined to have scientific validity. The state and its agencies and employees shall not be liable for any injury resulting from the issuance or nonissuance of a warning pursuant to this subdivision or for any acts or omissions in fact gathering, evaluation, or other activities leading up to the issuance or nonissuance of a warning.

(c) Public entities and public employees may, on the basis of a warning issued pursuant to subdivision (b), take, or fail or refuse to take, any action or execute or fail or refuse to execute any earthquake or volcanic prediction response plan with relation to the warning which is otherwise authorized by law. In taking, or failing or refusing to take, such action, neither public entities nor public employees shall be liable for any injuries caused thereby or for any injuries resulting from the preparation of, or failure or refusal to prepare, any earthquake hazard or damage prediction maps, plans for evacuation of endangered areas, and other plan elements.

(d) An earthquake or volcanic warning issued by the Governor pursuant to subdivision (b) is a sufficient basis for a declaration of a state of emergency or local emergency as defined by Section 8558. Public entities and public employees shall be immune from liability in accordance with all immunity provisions applicable during such state of emergency or local emergency. **Leg.H.** Added Stats 1976 ch 1267 §1, effective September 28, 1976. Amended Stats 1979 ch 1131 §1; Stats 1984 ch 1284 §1; Stats 2010 ch 618 §18 (AB 2791), effective January 1, 2011.

See this section as modified in Governor's Reorganization Plan No. 2 §82 of 2012; Stats 2013 ch 352 §103 (AB 1317), effective September 26, 2013, operative July 1, 2013.

2013 Note: Stats 2013 ch 352 (AB 1317) enacted the statutory changes necessary to reflect the changes made by the Governor's Reorganization Plan No. 2 of 2012.

2012 Note: 2012 Governor's Reorganization Plan No. 2 was submitted to the Legislature on May 3, 2012, and became effective July 3, 2012, pursuant to Gov C § 12080.5, and substantively operative July 1, 2013.

§955.2. Venue of action for death or injury to person or personal property; Transfer

Notwithstanding any other provision of law, where the State is named as a defendant in any action or proceeding for death or injury to person or personal property and the injury or the injury causing death occurred within this State, the proper court for the trial of the action is a court of competent jurisdiction in the county where the injury occurred or where the injury causing death occurred. The court may, on motion, change the place of the trial in the same manner and under the same circumstances as the place of trial may be changed where an action is between private parties. **Leg.H.** Added Stats 1963 ch 1715 §1.

§955.3. Venue of action by local government or agency against state

Notwithstanding any provision of law, when a city, county, or city and county, or local agency is a plaintiff in an action or proceeding against the State of California, the action may be tried in any city or county, or city and county, where the city, county, or city and county, or local agency is situated.

The Attorney General may, on behalf of the State of California, before answering, move to change the place of trial to Sacramento County in accordance with the provisions of Section 397 of the Code of Civil Procedure.

For the purposes of this section, "local agency" means any governmental district, board, or agency, or any other local governmental body or corporation, or elected local public official, but shall not include the State of California or any of its agencies, departments, commissions, or boards, or elected public officials in the executive branch of the state government. **Leg.H.** Added Stats 1980 ch 387 §2. Amended Stats 1994 ch 155 §2 (AB 860), effective July 9, 1994, ch 156 §2 (SB 2127), effective July 9, 1994.

§955.4. Officers on whom summons served and duty to defend imposed

Except as provided in Sections 811.9, 955.6, 955.8, and 955.9:

(a) Service of summons in all actions on claims against the state shall be made on the Attorney General.

(b) The Attorney General shall defend all actions on claims against the state. **Leg.H.** Added Stats 1963 ch 1715 §2. Amended Stats 2002 ch 1007 §15 (AB 2321).

§955.6. Actions arising out of work performed by Department of Transportation

In actions for the taking or damaging of private property for public use within the meaning of Section 19 of Article I of the Constitution on claims arising out of work done by the Department of Transportation:

(a) Service of summons shall be made on the Attorney General or the Director of Transportation.

(b) The defense shall be conducted by the attorney for the Department of Transportation. **Leg.H.** Added Stats 1963 ch 1715 §2. Amended Stats 1980 ch 215 §10.

§955.8. Actions arising out of work performed by Department of Water Resources

In actions for the taking or damaging of private property for public use within the meaning of Section 14 of Article I of the Constitution on claims arising out of work done by the Department of Water Resources:

(a) Service of summons shall be made on the Attorney General or the Director of Water Resources.

(b) The defense shall be conducted by the legal counsel of the department, if authorized by the Attorney General pursuant to Section 127 of the Water Code; otherwise the defense shall be conducted by the Attorney General. **Leg.H.** Added Stats 1963 ch 1715 §2.

§955.9. Service of summons in actions against judicial branch entity

In actions on claims against a judicial branch entity, service of summons shall be made on:

(a) The court executive officer, in actions on claims against a superior court or a judge thereof.

(b) The Clerk/Executive Officer of the Court of Appeal, in actions on claims against a court of appeal or a judge thereof.

(c) The Clerk/Executive Officer of the Supreme Court, in actions on claims against the Supreme Court or a judge thereof.

(d) The Administrative Director of the Judicial Council, in actions on claims against the Judicial Council or the Administrative Office of the Courts. **Leg.H.** Added Stats 2002 ch 1007 §16 (AB 2321). Amended Stats 2017 ch 36 §6 (AB 452), effective January 1, 2018; Stats 2018 ch 92 §84 (SB 1289), effective January 1, 2019.

§956. Proceedings in action to partition property in which State, division or agency has a remainder or undivided fractional interest

Whenever the State has acquired by gift, under the will of a decedent or through a decree of distribution in the estate of a decedent, or otherwise than by purchase or the exercise of the power of eminent domain, a remainder interest, whether contingent or vested, in real property, or an undivided fractional interest in real property, the holder or holders of the precedent estate or of other undivided fractional interests, as the case may be may join the State as a party defendant in any action to partition said property, brought pursuant to the Code of Civil Procedure or in any action in declaratory relief brought pursuant to the Code of Civil Procedure. In the complaint in any such action the nature of the interest of the State shall be set forth and the manner in which the same was acquired and process in any such action shall be served upon the Attorney General and the Director of Finance. In any such action the Attorney General shall represent the State and may on behalf of the State execute such stipulations, disclaimers or consents as may be appropriate. **Leg.H.** Added Stats 1963 ch 1450 §2.

CHAPTER 5
SPECIAL PROVISIONS RELATING TO ACTIONS AGAINST LOCAL PUBLIC ENTITIES

§960. "Public agency"

As used in this chapter, "public agency" has the meaning given that term by Section 53050. **Leg.H.** Added Stats 1963 ch 1805 §3.

§960.2. Service of process in absence of filings

Notwithstanding any provision of law to the contrary, service of process in an action or proceeding against a public agency may be made in the manner provided in Section 960.3 if, during the 10 days immediately following the commencement of the action or proceeding, any of the following apply:

(a) No statement pertaining to the public agency is on file, or is placed on file, in the Registry of Public Agencies in the office of the Secretary of State and of the county clerk of each county in which the public agency then maintains an office, as required by Section 53051.

(b) A statement or amended statement pertaining to the public agency is on file, or is placed on file, in the Registry of Public Agencies in the office of the Secretary of State and of the county clerk of each county in which the public agency then maintains an office, but the information contained therein is so inaccurate or incomplete that it does not substantially conform to the requirements of Section 53051.

(c) A statement or amended statement pertaining to the public agency is on file, or is placed on file, in the Registry of Public Agencies in the office of the Secretary of State and of the county clerk of each county in which the public agency then maintains an office, but neither the governing body nor any officer or agent of the public agency upon whom personal service of process constitutes service upon the public agency can thereafter, with due diligence, be personally served at the address or addresses set forth in the statement. **Leg.H.** Added Stats 1965 ch 653 §27. Amended Stats 2019 ch 329 §4 (SB 780), effective January 1, 2020.

Prior Law: Former §960.2, similar to present section, was added Stats 1963 ch 1805 §3, amended Stats 1965 ch 426 §1, and repealed Stats 1965 ch 653 §26.

§960.3. Order for substituted service on Secretary of State; Manner of service; Fee required

(a) If it is shown by affidavit to the satisfaction of the court or judge that the circumstances required by Section 960.2 exist, the court or judge may make an order that service of process be made upon the public agency as provided in this section.

(b) Service of process shall be made by:

(1) Leaving two copies of the process for each public agency defendant to be served, together with two copies of the order authorizing the service, in the hands of the Secretary of State or in his or her office at Sacramento; or

(2) Mailing two copies of the process for each public agency defendant to be served, together with two copies of the order authorizing the service, to the office of the Secretary of State in Sacramento by certified or registered mail, addressee only, return receipt requested. Service shall be effective as of the day the return receipt is received from the office of the Secretary of State.

(c) Service in this manner constitutes personal service upon the public agency.

(d) A fee of fifty dollars ($50) shall be paid by the plaintiff to the Secretary of State for each public agency on which service is made in this manner. **Leg.H.** Added Stats 1965 ch 653 §28. Amended Stats 1990 ch 479 §1 (SB 2633).

§960.4. Notice to public agency by Secretary of State by registered mail; Forwarding copy of papers to Attorney General

Upon receipt of the copies of process pursuant to Section 960.3, the Secretary of State shall give notice of the service of the process to the governing body of the public agency at its principal office in this state, by forwarding to such office, by registered mail with request for return receipt, a copy of the process. If the only address disclosed by the records of the Secretary of State of the principal office of the governing body of the public agency is the county in which it is situated, then the process shall be mailed to the county seat, addressed to the public agency in care of the county clerk, or it may be mailed to any address for the public agency specified in the court order. If the process is mailed in care of the county clerk, the county clerk shall promptly send it to the public agency at its address within the county, if known to him, and if unknown shall cause the process to be posted at the courthouse of the county for 30 days. If the records of the Secretary of State disclose no address for the public agency, then the Secretary of State shall mail a copy of the process to the county clerk of either (a) the county in which the transaction or occurrence took place, or (b) the county where real property of the agency is situated, and the county clerk shall promptly send the process to the public agency at its address within the county, if known to him, or if unknown shall cause the process to be posted at the courthouse of the county for 30 days.

Upon receipt of such copies of process, the Secretary of State shall immediately forward to the Attorney General a copy of all papers served upon him. The Attorney General, upon receipt of any such process, may locate the responsible officers of the public agency involved, and the governing body of such public agency may relieve the Attorney General of any further responsibility hereunder, and may designate any other attorneys to defend said action or take such other action as they may determine. **Leg.H.** Added Stats 1963 ch 1805 §3. Amended Stats 1965 ch 653 §29.

§960.5. Powers and duties of Attorney General in defense of public agency; Delegation of defense to county or district attorney

The Attorney General, until he is relieved of further responsibility in the manner provided in Section 960.4, or until the matter has been reduced to final judgment, shall have the duty to defend such public agency by taking whatever steps he considers appropriate or necessary. The Attorney General, until he is so relieved of further responsibility, shall have full authority to bind the public agency by stipulation or admission.

The Attorney General may delegate his responsibility hereunder in any particular case, to any county counsel or district attorney willing to accept such delegation. When such responsibility has been delegated, the district attorney or county counsel, as the case may be, shall have the same power and authority with reference to the matter as is hereinabove provided for the Attorney General.

All costs and expenses, without limitation, of the Attorney General or district attorney or county counsel, pursuant to this chapter shall be a charge against the public agency in whose behalf he appears. **Leg.H.** Added Stats 1963 ch 1805 §3.

§960.8. Conformity of service with "statement in the Registry of Public Agencies"

Service of process in an action or proceeding against a public agency may be made in conformity with the information contained in the statement in the Registry of Public Agencies pertaining to that public agency which is on file at the time of that service. Service in this manner, if otherwise made in compliance with law, constitutes personal service upon the public agency.

As used in this section, "statement in the Registry of Public Agencies" means the statement or amended statement in the Registry of Public Agencies in the office of the Secretary of State or in the office of the county clerk of any county in which that statement or amended statement is on file. **Leg.H.** Added Stats 1965 ch 653 §30. Amended Stats 2019 ch 329 §5 (SB 780), effective January 1, 2020.

CHAPTER 6
POSTJUDGMENT SETTLEMENT CONFERENCE

§962. Request for mandatory conference by public entity; Time for conference

Upon entry of a verdict against a public entity in excess of one hundred thousand dollars ($100,000) in an action for personal injury or wrongful death, the public entity may, within the time set in Section 659 of the Code of Civil Procedure, request in writing a mandatory settlement conference for the purpose of discussing available methods by which the judgment shall be satisfied. The court shall then set a date for the conference. The request may be noticed with any motions pursuant to Sections 984 and 985 of the Government Code or Section 659 of the Code of Civil Procedure. At the conference the parties shall negotiate in good faith and shall review and consider structured payment plans presented by either party. The conference shall not occur until after determination of any motion for a new trial, motion for judgment notwithstanding the verdict, motion for remittitur and motion for additur, but shall occur before hearing on any motions pursuant to Sections 984 and 985.

The Judicial Council shall adopt rules providing for a reasonable extension of the time for filing the notice of appeal from a judgment on the verdict to permit a request for the mandatory settlement conference and the mandatory settlement conference itself. **Leg.H.** Added Stats 1987 ch 1204 §2.

Prior Law: There was another section of this number which was added Stats 1987 ch 1201 §23 and repealed Stats 1989 ch 1360 §49.

PART 5
PAYMENT OF CLAIMS AND JUDGMENTS
CHAPTER 1
PAYMENT OF CLAIMS AND JUDGMENTS AGAINST THE STATE

§965. Designation of fund; Report to Legislature on insufficient funds to pay claims, settlements or judgments against state

(a) Upon the allowance by the Department of General Services of all or part of a claim for which the Director of Finance certifies that a sufficient appropriation for the payment of the claim exists, and the execution and presentation of documents the department may require that discharge the state of all liability under the claim, the department shall designate the fund from which the claim is to be paid, and the state agency concerned shall pay the claim from that fund. If there is no sufficient appropriation for the payment available, the department shall report to the Legislature in accordance with Section 912.8. Claims arising out of the activities of the State Department of Transportation may be paid if either the Director of Transportation or the Director of Finance certifies that a sufficient appropriation for the payment of the claim exists.

(b) Notwithstanding subdivision (a), if there is no sufficient appropriation for the payment of claims, settlements, or judgments against the state arising from an action in which the state is represented by the Attorney General, the Attorney General shall report the claims, settlements, and judgments to the chairperson of either the Senate Committee on Appropriations or the Assembly Committee on Appropriations, who shall cause to be introduced legislation appropriating funds for the payment of the claims, settlements, or judgments.

(c) Notwithstanding subdivision (a) or (b), claims, settlements, or judgments arising out of the activities of a judicial branch entity, as defined by Sections 900.3 and 940.3, or a judge thereof may be paid if the Judicial Council authorizes payment and the Administrative Director of the Courts certifies that sufficient funds for that payment exist from funds allocated to settlement, adjustment, and compromise of actions and claims. If sufficient funds for payment of settlements or judgments do not exist, the Administrative Director of the Courts shall report the settlements and judgments to the chairperson of either the Senate Committee on Appropriations or the Assembly Committee on Appropriations, who shall cause to be introduced legislation appropriating funds for the payment of the settlements or judgments. If sufficient funds for payment of claims do not exist, the Administrative Director of the Courts shall report the claims to the Department of General Services, which shall have 90 days to object to payment. The Administrative Director of the Courts shall confer with the Director of General Services regarding any objection received during the 90-day period. If the Department of General Services withdraws the objection, or if no objection was received, the Administrative Director of the Courts shall report the claims to the chairperson of either the Senate Committee on Appropriations or the Assembly Committee on Appropriations, who shall cause to be introduced legislation appropriating funds for the payment of the claims. The Judicial Council may authorize any committee of the Judicial Council or any employee of the Administrative Office of the Courts to perform the functions of the Judicial Council under this section. The Administrative Director of the Courts may designate an executive staff member of the Administrative Office of the Courts to perform the functions of the Administrative Director of the Courts under this section. **Leg.H.** Added Stats 1963 ch 1715 §3. Amended Stats 1965 ch 1004 §4; Stats 1980 ch 212 §1, ch 215 §11; Stats 1985 ch 778 §2; Stats 1989 ch 1126 §1, effective September 29, 1989; Stats 2002 ch 1007 §17 (AB 2321); Stats 2011 ch 11 §4 (SB 80), effective March 24, 2011, ch 31 §1 (AB 119), effective June 29, 2011; Stats 2012 ch 19 §2 (SB 1504), effective June 15, 2012; Stats 2016 ch 31 §53 (SB 836), effective June 27, 2016.

2011 Note: The Governor's signing message of March 24, 2011, provides: "I am deleting the appropriation in Section 4 of this bill, which provides $1,000 General Fund to the Victims Compensation and Government Claims Board from the Restitution Fund. Sufficient appropriation authority will be provided in the Budget Bill; therefore this additional appropriation is unnecessary." The text of the appropriation appeared in subdivision (d) in the enrolled version sent to the Governor. It is reproduced below:

(d) In addition to any amounts provided in the Budget Act of 2011, one thousand dollars ($1,000) is appropriated for the 2011-12 fiscal year from the Restitution Fund to the California Victim Compensation and Government Claims Board.

§965.1. Allowance of claim against state not exceeding specified amount

The Director of General Services may allow a claim filed pursuant to subdivision (c) of Section 905.2 if the settlement amount of that claim does not exceed fifty thousand dollars ($50,000), or to reject any claim as so described. **Leg.H.** Added Stats 1994 ch 726 §5 (AB 3069), effective September 21, 1994. Amended Stats 2006 ch 538 §222 (SB 1852), effective January 1, 2007; Stats 2016 ch 31 §54 (SB 836), effective June 27, 2016.

§965.2. Controller's warrant; Exemption from auditing requirement

(a) The Controller shall draw a warrant for the payment of any final judgment or settlement against the state whenever the Director of Finance certifies that a sufficient appropriation for the payment of the judgment or settlement exists. Claims upon those judgments and settlements are exempt from Section 925.6. Claims arising out of the activities of the State Department of Transportation may be paid if either the Director of Transportation or the Director of Finance certifies that a sufficient appropriation for the payment of the claim exists.

(b) Notwithstanding subdivision (a), the Controller shall draw a warrant for the payment of any final judgment or settlement based on claims arising out of the activities of a judicial branch entity, as defined by Sections 900.3 and 940.3, or a judge thereof, whenever the Administrative Director of the Courts certifies that sufficient funds for that payment exist from funds allocated to settlement, adjustment, and compromise of actions and claims. Claims upon those judgments and settlements are exempt from Section 925.6. Claims arising out of the activities of a judicial branch entity, as defined by Sections 900.3 and 940.3, or a judge thereof, may be paid if the Administrative Director of the Courts certifies that sufficient funds for the payment exist from funds allocated to settlement, adjustment, and compromise of actions and claims. The Administrative Director of the Courts may designate an executive staff member of the Administrative Office of the Courts to perform the certification of funds pursuant to this section. **Leg.H.** Added Stats 1963 ch 1715 §3. Amended Stats 1965 ch 1004 §5; Stats 1980 ch 212 §2, ch 215 §12 (ch 215 prevails); Stats 1985 ch 778 §3; Stats 2002 ch 1007 §18 (AB 2321).

§965.3. Notice of payment; Reversion

(a) The Attorney General shall notify the Controller in writing when all claims for which an appropriation is made to the the Department of Justice or the Attorney General pursuant to subdivision (b) of Section 965 have been paid. The Controller shall, at the close of the fiscal year in which notice of payment is received from the Attorney General, cause any undisbursed balance to revert to the fund from which the appropriation was made.

(b) Whenever an appropriation exceeds the actual amount necessary to satisfy a settlement in accordance with the settlement agreement or a judgment, the excess shall revert to the fund from which the appropriation was made. **Leg.H.** Added Stats 1990 ch 1244 §1 (SB 1768), effective September 24, 1990.

1990 Note: It appears the Legislature inadvertently enacted "the the" in the first sentence of subdivision (a).

§965.4. Governor's report to Legislature

The Governor shall report to the Legislature, at each session, all judgments or settlements against the State not theretofore reported. **Leg.H.** Added Stats 1963 ch 1715 §3.

§965.5. Enforceability of judgment; Duration; Interest

(a) A judgment for the payment of money against the state or a state agency is enforceable until 10 years after the time the judgment becomes final or, if the judgment is payable in installments, until 10 years after the final installment becomes due.

(b) A judgment for the payment of money against the state or a state agency is not enforceable under Title 9 (commencing with Section 680.010) of Part 2 of the Code of Civil Procedure, but is enforceable under this chapter.

(c) Interest on the amount of a judgment or settlement for the payment of moneys against the state shall commence to accrue 180 days from the date of the final judgment or settlement.

(d) Unless another statute provides a different interest rate, interest on a tax or fee judgment for the payment of moneys against the state shall accrue at a rate equal to the weekly average one year constant maturity United States Treasury yield at the time of the judgment plus 2 percent, but shall not exceed 7 percent per annum.

(e) Subdivisions (c) and (d) shall not apply to any claim approved by the Department of General Services. **Leg.H.** Added Stats 1980 ch 215 §13. Amended Stats 1982 ch 497 §94, operative July 1, 1983; Stats 2012 ch 19 §3 (SB 1504), effective June 15, 2012; Stats 2013 ch 424 §2 (AB 748), effective January 1, 2014; Stats 2016 ch 31 §55 (SB 836), effective June 27, 2016.

§965.6. Conditions for payment

Notwithstanding any other provision of law, neither the state nor a judicial branch entity, nor any officers or employees thereof, may be required by any court in any proceeding to pay or offset a tort liability claim, settlement, or judgment for which the state or judicial branch entity is liable, unless one of the following conditions exists:

(a) The Legislature has authorized the payment or offset of the specific tort liability claim, settlement, or judgment.

(b) The Director of Finance, or the Director of Transportation for claims arising out of the activities of the Department of Transportation, has certified that a sufficient appropriation for the payment of the claim, settlement, or judgment or to provide for that offset exists. This subdivision does not apply to claims arising out of the activities of a judicial branch entity or a judge thereof.

(c) In the case of claims arising out of the activities of a judicial branch entity, as defined in Sections 900.3 and 940.3, or a judge thereof, the Administrative Director of the Courts has certified that sufficient funds for payment of the claim, settlement, or judgment, or to provide for that offset, exist from funds allocated to settlement, adjustment, and compromise of pending actions and claims. The Administrative Director of the Courts may designate an executive staff member of the Administrative Office of the Courts to perform the certification of funds pursuant to this section. **Leg.H.** Added Stats 1980 ch 215 §14. Amended Stats 1985 ch 778 §4; Stats 2002 ch 1007 §19 (AB 2321).

§965.65. Reports concerning preventive action

(a) If a request is made for certification of availability of funds, approval of a settlement, or inclusion of a claim in a claims bill pursuant to Section 948, 965, or 965.2 for a claim in excess of thirty-five thousand dollars ($35,000) against the state which arose from the activities of any state agency or employee, the agency shall report to the Director of Finance concerning any action it has taken or proposes to take to prevent the future occurrence of circumstances similar to those upon which the claim was based, including any imposition of disciplinary action.

(b) This section does not apply to a judicial branch entity, as defined in Sections 900.3 and 940.3, or claims arising out of the activities of a judicial branch entity or a judge or employee thereof. However, in the case of the categories of claims and settlements described in subdivision (a) arising out of activities of a judicial branch entity or a judge, court executive officer, or employee thereof, the Administrative Director of the Courts shall report to the Judicial Council concerning any action the Administrative Office of the Courts has taken or proposes to take to prevent the future occurrence of circumstances similar to those upon which the claim was based, including any imposition of disciplinary action. **Leg.H.** Added Stats 1990 ch 1244 §3 (SB 1768), effective September 24, 1990. Amended Stats 1992 ch 1296 §10 (SB 986), effective September 30, 1992; Stats 2002 ch 1007 §20 (AB 2321).

Prior Law: Former §965.65, similar to the present section, was added Stats 1983 ch 49 §2, effective May 27, 1983, amended Stats 1984 ch 18 §1, effective March 1, 1984, and repealed Stats 1990 ch 1244 §2 (SB 1768), effective September 24, 1990.

§965.7. Writ of mandate; Legislative discretion

(a) A writ of mandate is an appropriate remedy to compel the state, or an officer or employee of the state, to perform any act required by this chapter.

(b) Nothing in this division affects the discretion of the Legislature in determining whether or not to:

(1) Make an appropriation for the payment of a claim, compromise, settlement, or judgment or to provide an offset for a claim, compromise, settlement, or judgment.

(2) Authorize such a payment or offset. **Leg.H.** Added Stats 1980 ch 215 §15.

§965.8. Writ of mandate to compel certification of sufficient appropriation

Where any provision of this division requires a certificate of the Director of Finance or the Director of Transportation that a sufficient appropriation exists for the payment of a claim, settlement, compromise, or judgment or requires a certificate of the Director of Finance or the Director of Transportation that a sufficient appropriation exists to provide for an offset, a writ of mandate is an appropriate remedy to compel the Director of Finance or the Director of Transportation to so certify if a sufficient appropriation in fact exists for that purpose. **Leg.H.** Added Stats 1980 ch 215 §16. Amended Stats 1985 ch 778 §5.

§965.9. Application of chapter

This chapter does not apply to claims, settlements, and judgments against the Regents of the University of California. **Leg.H.** Added Stats 1980 ch 215 §17.

CHAPTER 2
PAYMENT OF JUDGMENTS AGAINST LOCAL PUBLIC ENTITIES
ARTICLE 1
General

§970. Definitions

As used in this article:

(a) "Fiscal year" means a year beginning on July 1 and ending on June 30 unless the local public entity has adopted a different fiscal year as authorized by law, in which case "fiscal year" means the fiscal year adopted by such local public entity.

(b) "Judgment" means a final judgment for the payment of money rendered against a local public entity.

(c) "Local public entity" includes a county, city, district, public authority, public agency, and any other political subdivision or public corporation in the state, but does not include the Regents of the University of California and does not include the state or any office, officer, department, division, bureau, board, commission or agency of the state claims against which are paid by warrants drawn by the Controller. **Leg.H.** Added Stats 1963 ch 1715 §3. Amended Stats 1975 ch 285 §2; Stats 1980 ch 215 §18.

§970.1. Enforceability of judgment; Duration; Calculation of interest

(a) A judgment is enforceable until 10 years after the time the judgment becomes final or, if the judgment is payable in installments, until 10 years after the final installment becomes due.

(b) A judgment, whether or not final, is not enforceable under Title 9 (commencing with Section 680.010) of Part 2 of the Code of Civil Procedure but is enforceable under this article after it becomes final.

(c) Unless another statute provides a different interest rate, interest on a tax or fee judgment against a local public entity shall accrue at a rate equal to the weekly average one year constant maturity United States Treasury yield at the time of the judgment plus 2 percent, but shall not exceed 7 percent per annum. **Leg.H.** Added Stats 1980 ch 215 §19. Amended Stats 1982 ch 497 §95, operative July 1, 1983; Stats 2013 ch 424 §3 (AB 748), effective January 1, 2014.

§970.2. Duty of public entity to pay judgment in manner prescribed; Mandamus

A local public entity shall pay any judgment in the manner provided in this article. A writ of mandate is an appropriate remedy to compel a local public entity to perform any act required by this article. **Leg.H.** Added Stats 1963 ch 1715 §3. Amended Stats 1975 ch 285 §3.

§970.4. Payment from available funds; Unappropriated funds; Appropriated funds

Except as provided in Section 970.6, the governing body of a local public entity shall pay, to the extent funds are available in the fiscal year in which it becomes final, any judgment, with interest thereon, out of any funds to the credit of the local public entity that are:

(a) Unappropriated for any other purpose unless the use of such funds is restricted by law or contract to other purposes; or

(b) Appropriated for the current fiscal year for the payment of judgments and not previously encumbered. **Leg.H.** Added Stats 1963 ch 1715 §3. Amended Stats 1975 ch 285 §4; Stats 1980 ch 215 §20.

§970.5. Deferring payment

Except as provided in Section 970.6, if a local public entity does not pay a judgment, with interest thereon, during the fiscal year in which it becomes final, the governing body shall pay the judgment, with interest thereon, during the ensuing fiscal year immediately upon the obtaining of sufficient funds for that purpose. **Leg.H.** Added Stats 1980 ch 215 §21.

§970.6. Installment payments

(a) The court which enters the judgment shall order that the governing body pay the judgment, with interest thereon, in not exceeding 10 equal annual installments if both of the following conditions are satisfied:

(1) The governing body of the local public entity has adopted an ordinance or resolution finding that an unreasonable hardship will result unless the judgment is paid in installments.

(2) The court, after hearing, has found that payment of the judgment in installments as ordered by the court is necessary to avoid an unreasonable hardship.

(b) Each installment payment shall be of an equal amount, consisting of a portion of the principal of the judgment and the unpaid interest on the judgment to the date of the payment. The local public entity, in its discretion, may prepay any one or more installments or any part of an installment. **Leg.H.** Added Stats 1963 ch 1715 §3. Amended Stats 1975 ch 285 §5; Stats 1980 ch 215 §22.

§970.8. Required funding

(a) Each local public entity shall in each fiscal year include in its budget a provision to provide funds in an amount sufficient to pay all judgments in accordance with this article.

(b) If all or any portion of the revenue used for the maintenance and operation of a local public entity (other than an entity created by an agreement described in Section 895) liable for a judgment is derived from appropriations of another local public entity, such other local public entity shall in each fiscal year appropriate funds equal to its pro rata share of an amount sufficient to permit the local public entity liable for the judgment to pay the judgment in accordance with this article. Such amount shall be paid to the local public entity liable for the judgment and shall be used by such entity to satisfy the judgment. The pro rata share of such other local public entity for each judgment is an amount bearing the same proportion to the total amount of the judgment as the revenue derived from such other local public entity for maintenance and operation during the fiscal year in which the cause of action on such judgment accrued bears to the total revenues used for maintenance and operation during such fiscal year of the local public entity liable for the judgment. For this purpose, such other local public entity shall include in its budget a provision to provide funds sufficient in amount to make the appropriation and payment required by this section. **Leg.H.** Added Stats 1963 ch 1715 §3. Amended Stats 1975 ch 285 §6; Stats 1980 ch 215 §23.

§971. Definitions; Application of tax limitations

(a) As used in this section:

(1) "Judgment resulting from a discretionary act" means a judgment arising from a liability which the local public entity has discretion to incur or not to incur and includes a judgment rendered in an eminent domain proceeding and a judgment requiring specific performance of a contractual obligation or awarding damages for failure to perform a contractual obligation.

(2) "Judgment resulting from a nondiscretionary act" means a judgment other than one described in paragraph (1) and includes a judgment founded upon tort or inverse condemnation liability.

(b) Any limitation on the amount of taxes, assessments or rates and charges that may be levied or collected by a local public entity, and any limitation on the amount of appropriations and payments that may be made by a local public entity, and any limitation on the amount of liability or indebtedness that may be incurred by a local public entity, contained in any other statute or in any charter or ordinance:

(1) Applies to the taxes, assessments, rates and charges or appropriations levied, collected or made to pay pursuant to this article a judgment resulting from a discretionary act.

(2) Does not apply to the taxes, assessments, rates and charges or appropriations levied, collected or made to pay pursuant to this article a judgment resulting from a nondiscretionary act.

(c) For the purposes of Section 2271 of the Revenue and Taxation Code, taxes levied to pay pursuant to this article a judgment resulting from a nondiscretionary act are levied to pay costs mandated by the courts. **Leg.H.** Added Stats 1963 ch 1715 §3. Amended Stats 1975 ch 285 §7; Stats 1980 ch 215 §24.

§971.2. Judgments as legal investments or security

(a) All judgments for which a local public entity is liable are legal investments for all trust funds, and for the funds of all insurance companies, banks (both commercial and savings) and trust companies, and for every other local public entity within this state, to the same extent as bonds of the local public entity liable for the judgment.

(b) Whenever any money or funds may by law be invested in or loaned upon the security of bonds of a local public entity, such money or funds may be invested in or loaned upon the security of a judgment for which such local public entity is liable; and whenever bonds of a local public entity may be used as security for the faithful performance or execution of any court or private trust or of any other act, a judgment for which such local public entity is liable may be so used.

(c) All judgments for which a local public entity is liable, to the same extent as bonds of such local public entity, are legal for use by any state or national bank or banks in the state as security for the deposit of funds of any local public entity within this state. **Leg.H.** Added Stats 1963 ch 1715 §3. Amended Stats 1975 ch 285 §8.

ARTICLE 2
Funding Judgments With Bonds

§975. "Board"; "Local taxing entity"

As used in this article:

(a) "Board" means the governing body of a local taxing entity.

(b) "Local taxing entity" means a local public entity that has the power to levy ad valorem taxes, or ad valorem assessments, upon property within the territory of the entity. **Leg.H.** Added Stats 1963 ch 1715 §3.

§975.2. Resolution for incurrence of bonded indebtedness

Whenever the board deems it necessary for the local taxing entity to incur a bonded indebtedness to fund all or any portion of an outstanding judgment against the entity, it shall by resolution state:

(a) The necessity for the indebtedness.

(b) The purpose for which the proposed debt is to be incurred.

(c) The amount of the proposed debt.

(d) The time and place for a hearing by the board on the question whether the local taxing entity should incur a bonded indebtedness to fund all or any portion of an outstanding judgment against the entity. **Leg.H.** Added Stats 1963 ch 1715 §3.

§975.4. Publication or posting of notice of hearing

Notice of the hearing shall be given by publication of a copy of the resolution pursuant to Section 6066 in a newspaper of general circulation circulated within the local taxing entity. If there is no such newspaper, the resolution shall be posted in three public places in the local taxing entity for two succeeding weeks. No other notice of the hearing need be given. **Leg.H.** Added Stats 1963 ch 1715 §3.

§975.6. Notice accompanying copy of resolution

The copy of the resolution published or posted shall be accompanied by a notice subscribed by the clerk or secretary of the local taxing entity that:

(a) The hearing referred to in the resolution will be had at the time and place specified in the resolution.

(b) At that time and place, any person interested, including persons owning property within the local taxing entity, will be heard upon the question stated in the resolution. **Leg.H.** Added Stats 1963 ch 1715 §3.

§975.8. Conduct of hearing; Determination by board

At the time and place fixed for the hearing on the resolution or at any time and place to which the hearing is adjourned, the board shall proceed with the hearing. Any person interested, including persons owning property within the local taxing entity, may appear and present any matters material to the question set forth in the resolution. Thereafter, the board shall determine whether it is necessary to incur the bonded indebtedness. The board's determination on the question of necessity is conclusive. **Leg.H.** Added Stats 1963 ch 1715 §3.

§976. Resolution for bond election

After the board has made its determination pursuant to Section 975.8, if it deems it necessary to incur the bonded indebtedness, it shall by resolution state:

(a) That it deems it necessary to incur the bonded indebtedness.

(b) The purpose for which the bonded indebtedness will be incurred.

(c) The amount of the debt to be incurred, which amount may include legal and other fees and costs incidental to or connected with the authorization, issuance and sale of the bonds, including but not limited to the costs of printing the bonds.

(d) The maximum term the bonds to be issued shall run before maturity, which term shall not exceed 40 years.

(e) The annual rate of interest to be paid, which rate shall not exceed 7 percent, payable annually or semiannually, or in part annually and in part semiannually.

(f) The proposition to be submitted to the voters.

(g) The date of the special election of the local taxing entity (which may be consolidated with any other election of the local taxing entity) at which such proposition shall be submitted to the voters; the manner of holding the election and the procedure for voting for or against the proposition. **Leg.H.** Added Stats 1963 ch 1715 §3.

§976.2. Resolution as notice of election; Publication or posting

The resolution made pursuant to Section 976 shall constitute the notice of such election and such resolution shall be published pursuant to Section 6066 in a newspaper of general circulation circulated within the local taxing entity. If there is no such newspaper, the resolution shall be posted in three public places in the local taxing entity for two succeeding weeks. No other notice of the election need be given. **Leg.H.** Added Stats 1963 ch 1715 §3.

§976.4. Application of provisions governing general elections

The board shall provide for holding the election in the same manner as

§976.6. Qualified voters

Every elector authorized to vote in general elections of the local taxing entity may vote on the proposition to authorize the bonds. **Leg.H.** Added Stats 1963 ch 1715 §3.

§976.8. Vote authorizing board to issue bonds

If two–thirds or more of the votes cast upon the proposition at the election are in favor of incurring the bonded indebtedness, the board may issue the bonds at the time or times it deems proper. **Leg.H.** Added Stats 1963 ch 1715 §3.

§977. Form of bonds; Denominations; Time and place for payment

The board shall prescribe the form of the bonds. The bonds may be issued in denominations not to exceed one thousand dollars ($1,000) and not less than one hundred dollars ($100). The board shall fix, and designate in the bonds, a time and place for payment of the bonds. **Leg.H.** Added Stats 1963 ch 1715 §3.

§977.2. Redemption of bonds

The board may provide for the redemption of bonds issued under this article before maturity at prices determined by it. A bond shall not be subject to call or redemption prior to maturity unless it contains a recital to that effect. Notice of redemption shall be published at such time and in such manner as the board may provide in the resolution providing for the issuance of the bonds. **Leg.H.** Added Stats 1963 ch 1715 §3.

§977.4. Signing of bonds

The bonds shall be signed by the presiding officer of the board and countersigned by the clerk or secretary of the local taxing entity, and the coupons shall be signed by the clerk or secretary. All signatures except that of the clerk or secretary on the bonds may be printed, lithographed or engraved. If any officer whose signature appears on the bonds or coupons ceases to be such officer before the delivery of the bonds, his signature is as effective as if he had remained in office. **Leg.H.** Added Stats 1963 ch 1715 §3.

§977.6. Sale of bonds

The local taxing entity may sell the bonds at the times or in the manner the board deems to be to the public interest. The bonds shall be sold on sealed proposals to the highest bidder after advertising for bids by publication of notice of sale pursuant to Section 6061, not less than 10 days prior to the date of sale, in a newspaper of general circulation circulating in the local taxing entity. If there is no such newspaper, the notice of sale shall be posted in three places in the local public entity for two succeeding weeks ending not less than 10 days prior to the date of sale. If satisfactory bids are received, the bonds offered for sale shall be awarded to the highest responsible bidder. If no bids are received or if the board determines that the bids received are not satisfactory as to price or responsibility of the bidders, the board may reject all bids received, if any, and either readvertise or sell the bonds at private sale. **Leg.H.** Added Stats 1963 ch 1715 §3.

§977.8. Action to determine validity of bonds

An action to determine the validity of bonds may be brought pursuant to Chapter 9 (commencing with Section 860) of Title 10 of Part 2 of the Code of Civil Procedure. **Leg.H.** Added Stats 1963 ch 1715 §3.

§978. Exemption of bonds from taxation; Bonds as legal investments

Any bonds issued by any local taxing entity under the provisions of this article have the same force, value and use as bonds issued by any municipality and are exempt from all taxation within the State.

Such bonds are legal investments for all trust funds, for the funds of all insurance companies, banks (both commercial and savings) and trust companies, for the state school funds, and for any funds which may be invested in bonds of cities, counties, school districts, or municipalities in the State. **Leg.H.** Added Stats 1963 ch 1715 §3.

§978.2. Payment of bonds and interest; Property in local entity as subject to taxation; Levy of tax or assessment

Bonds issued under this article constitute general obligations of the local taxing entity for the payment of both principal and interest of which all property in the local taxing entity subject to ad valorem taxation by the local taxing entity or subject to ad valorem assessment by the local taxing entity shall be taxed or assessed without limitation of rate or amount.

The board shall, at the time and in the manner provided by law for levying taxes or assessments, fix an ad valorem rate of tax or assessment sufficient to pay the principal of and interest on all bonds issued under this article as they become due. Such ad valorem taxes or assessments shall be in addition to all other taxes or assessments levied by the local taxing entity, and when collected shall be used for no purpose other than the payment of such bonds and the interest thereon.

Nothing in this section shall be construed to prohibit the use of other revenues of the local taxing entity for the payment of principal and interest on bonds issued under this article. **Leg.H.** Added Stats 1963 ch 1715 §3.

§978.4. Use of proceeds from sale of bonds

The proceeds from the sale of bonds issued pursuant to this article shall not be used for any purpose other than the purpose stated in the resolution authorizing the issuance of the bonds. **Leg.H.** Added Stats 1963 ch 1715 §3.

§978.6. Resolution voiding unsold bonds

The board may be resolution adopted by two–thirds vote of all its members declare that no part of a described bond issue authorized under this article which remains unsold shall be issued or sold. When the resolution takes effect, the bonds described in the resolution which remain unsold are voided. **Leg.H.** Added Stats 1963 ch 1715 §3.

§978.8. Authority provided in article as supplementary

The authority provided in this article is in addition and supplementary to any other law authorizing public entities to issue bonds to fund an outstanding indebtedness. **Leg.H.** Added Stats 1963 ch 1715 §3.

CHAPTER 3.7
PROCEDURES APPLICABLE TO STATE AND LOCAL PUBLIC ENTITIES

§984. Periodic payments on judgments by public entities

(a) As used in this section, "not insured" includes a public entity that has no liability insurance or is self–insured by itself, or through an insurance pooling arrangement, a joint powers agreement, the Local Agency Self Insurance Authority, or any other similar arrangement.

(b) If a public entity has commercial insurance as to a portion of the judgment, this section shall only apply to that portion of the judgment which is "not insured" as defined in this section.

(c) A judgment against a public entity may be ordered to be paid by periodic payments only if ordered under Section 667.7 of the Code of Civil Procedure or Section 970.6, or if the public entity has made an election under subdivision (d), or if the parties have agreed to it.

(d) If, after making any deductions pursuant to Section 985 of the Government Code, the judgment on a tort claims action against a public entity that is not insured is greater than five hundred thousand dollars ($500,000), the public entity may elect to pay the judgment in periodic payments as provided in this subdivision.

Effective January 1, 1990, the five hundred thousand dollar ($500,000) threshold amount shall be five hundred fifty thousand dollars ($550,000). Effective January 1, 1992, that amount shall be six hundred thousand dollars ($600,000). Effective January 1, 1994, that amount shall be six hundred fifty thousand dollars ($650,000). Effective January 1, 1996, that amount shall be seven hundred twenty–five thousand dollars ($725,000), and thereafter, the seven hundred twenty–five thousand dollar ($725,000) amount shall be increased 5 percent on January 1 of each year.

After any amounts reimbursed pursuant to Section 985, the judgment–debtor shall pay 50 percent of the remainder immediately, and the other 50 percent of the remainder shall be paid over a period of time to be determined by the court, not to exceed 10 years or the length of the judgment–creditor's remaining life expectancy at the time the judgment is entered, whichever is less.

(e) The following provisions apply to all judgments for periodic payment under this section against a public entity:

(1) Payments shall not terminate upon the death of the judgment–creditor.

(2) Interest at the same rate as one–year United States Treasury bills as of January 1, each year shall accrue to the unpaid balance of the judgment,

and on each January 1 thereafter throughout the duration of the installment payments the interest shall be adjusted until the judgment is fully satisfied.

(3) Throughout the term of the installment payments until the judgment is fully satisfied, the public entity shall remain liable for all payments due on the judgment and the interest.

(4) The court shall retain jurisdiction in order to enforce, amend, modify, or approve settlement of the installment payments as may be just. Upon a motion by the judgment–creditor, the court shall accelerate the installment payments if it finds any unreasonable delay in, or failure to make payments.

(5) The court, upon motion, may modify the installment payments consistent with Sections 1431 to 1431.5, inclusive, of the Civil Code to account for the insolvency or uncollectability of amounts of the judgment owed by joint tortfeasors. The defendant shall bring a motion for that adjustment under Section 1010 of the Code of Civil Procedure.

(f) Nothing in this section shall prevent the parties from agreeing to settle an action on any other terms.

(g) The Judicial Council shall adopt rules providing for a reasonable extension of the time for filing the notice of appeal from a judgment on the verdict to permit an election pursuant to this section and any hearing pursuant to subdivision (d).

(h) This section does not apply to contribution and indemnity between joint tortfeasors. **Leg.H.** Added Stats 1987 ch 1204 §3.

Prior Law: There was another section of this number which was added Stats 1987 ch 1201 §24 and repealed Stats 1989 ch 1360 §50.

CHAPTER 4
PROCEDURES APPLICABLE TO STATE AND LOCAL PUBLIC ENTITIES

§985. Collateral source payments in actions against public entities

(a) As used in this section:

(1) "Collateral source payment" includes either of the following:

(A) The direct provision of services prior to the commencement of trial to the plaintiff for the same injury or death by prepaid health maintenance organizations providing services to their members or by nonfederal publicly funded health service providers.

(B) Monetary payments paid or obligated to be paid for services or benefits that were provided prior to the commencement of trial to or on behalf of the plaintiff for the same injury or death from a provider of collateral source payments described in paragraphs (1) and (2) of subdivision (f).

(2) "Plaintiff" includes, but is not limited to, a person or entity who is entitled to make a claim under Part 2 (commencing with Section 6400) of Division 6 of the Probate Code for the collateral source benefits against the tortfeasor or alleged tortfeasor, and in the case of a minor, the minor and the minor's parent, legal guardian or guardian ad litem.

(3) "Commencement of trial" occurs as defined in paragraph (6) of subdivision (a) of Section 581 of the Code of Civil Procedure.

(b) Any collateral source payment paid or owed to or on behalf of a plaintiff shall be inadmissible in any action for personal injuries or wrongful death where a public entity is a defendant. However, after a verdict has been returned against a public entity that includes damages for which payment from a collateral source listed below has already been paid or is obligated to be paid for services or benefits that were provided prior to the commencement of trial, and the total of the collateral source payments is greater than five thousand dollars ($5,000), that amount to be increased 5 percent compounded on January 1, 1989, and each January 1 thereafter, the defendant public entity may, by a motion noticed within the time set in Section 659 of the Code of Civil Procedure, request a posttrial hearing for a reduction of the judgment against the defendant public entity for collateral source payments paid or obligated to be paid for services or benefits that were provided prior to the commencement of trial. The hearing may be noticed with any motions pursuant to Sections 962 and 984 of the Government Code or Section 659 of the Code of Civil Procedure; however, the hearing shall not occur until after the determination of any motions for a new trial, for judgment notwithstanding the verdict, for remittitur, for additur, and after any mandatory settlement conference pursuant to Section 962 of the Government Code.

(c) A defendant public entity may, by interrogatory or in writing at the trial–setting conference, request from the plaintiff a list of the names and addresses of any provider of a collateral source payment affected by this section that has provided collateral source payments directly to or on behalf of the plaintiff and the amount provided to the plaintiff from each collateral source. The plaintiff shall produce the requested list within 30 days of such request. The plaintiff shall have a continuing duty to disclose to the public entity defendant the name and address of any provider of a collateral source payment affected by this section but not disclosed in plaintiff's response if that provider pays or owes collateral source payments to or on behalf of plaintiff between the time of plaintiff's response and the commencement of trial.

The public entity shall provide written notice to each provider of a collateral source payment listed by the plaintiff or identified by defendant of the date set for any pretrial settlement conference.

The provider of a collateral source shall not be required to attend a settlement conference unless requested to do so by the court. The court may request a provider of a collateral source to attend a settlement conference or to provide written information, to be available by telephone, or to otherwise participate in the conference, and a provider of a collateral source shall waive its rights to reimbursement unless it attends or otherwise complies with the request.

(d) If the plaintiff fails or refuses to supply to the defendant public entity information as to the identity of a provider of a collateral source payment, as required by this section, the defendant public entity may, upon discovery of the identity of the provider of a collateral source payment, within five years of the date of entry of judgment, request a reduction of the judgment for payment made or for services provided prior to the commencement of trial by that source. Failure of plaintiff to provide the names of collateral source providers affected by this section and known to plaintiff, shall subject plaintiff or plaintiff's attorney to sanctions pursuant to Section 128.5 of the Code of Civil Procedure.

(e) The public entity shall also give 20 days notice to the provider of a collateral source payment of any posttrial settlement conference or hearing regarding collateral source payments under this section.

Proof of service of any notice sent pursuant to this section shall be filed with the court and a copy served on all parties to the action.

(f) At the hearing the trial court shall, in its discretion and on terms as may be just, make a final determination as to any pending lien and subrogation rights, and, subject to subdivisions (1) to (3), inclusive, determine what portion of collateral source payments should be reimbursed from the judgment to the provider of a collateral source payment, deducted from the verdict, or accrue to the benefit of the plaintiff. No provider of collateral source payments pursuant to this section shall recover any amount against the plaintiff nor shall it be subrogated to the rights of the plaintiff against a public entity defendant other than in the amount so determined by the court. The following provisions shall apply to the court's adjustments:

(1) If the court has determined that the verdict included money damages for which the plaintiff has already received payment from or had his or her expenses paid by the following collateral sources: Medi–Cal, county health care, Aid to Families with Dependent Children, Victims of Crime, or other nonfederal publicly funded sources of benefit with statutory lien rights, the court shall order reimbursement from the judgment of those amounts to the provider of a collateral source payment pursuant to this section and on terms as may be just.

(2) If the court has determined that the verdict includes money damages for which the plaintiff has already received payment from or had his or her expenses paid by the following collateral sources: private medical programs, health maintenance organizations, state disability, unemployment insurance, private disability insurance, or other sources of compensation similar to those listed in this paragraph, the court may, after considering the totality of all circumstances and on terms as may be just, determine what portion of the collateral source benefits will be reimbursed from the judgment to the provider of the collateral source payment, used to reduce the verdict, or accrue to the benefit of the plaintiff. However, nothing in this section shall create subrogation or lien rights that do not already exist.

(3) In determining the amount to be reimbursed from the judgment to a provider of a collateral source payment, or the amount by which the judgment will be reduced to account for collateral source payments, the court shall make the following adjustments:

(A) Where plaintiff has been found partially at fault, the reimbursement or reduction shall be decreased by the same percentage as the entire judgment is reduced to take into account the plaintiff's comparative fault.

(B) The court shall deduct from the reimbursement or reduction the amount of premiums the court determines were paid by or on behalf of the plaintiff to the provider of a collateral source payment.

(C) After making the adjustments described in subparagraphs (A) and (B) above, the court shall reduce that amount by a percentage equal to the percentage of the entire judgment that the plaintiff paid or owes for his or her attorney fees and costs and reasonable expenses incurred.

(g) In no event shall the total dollar amount deducted from the verdict, paid to lienholders or reimbursed to all collateral source providers, exceed one-half of the plaintiff's net recovery for all damages after deducting for attorney's fees, medical services paid by the plaintiff, and litigation costs; however, the court may order no reimbursement or verdict reduction if the reimbursement or reduction would result in undue financial hardship upon the person who suffered the injury.

(h) Unless otherwise ordered by the court, 50 percent of any amount reimbursed pursuant to this section shall be due immediately. The court may order the remaining 50 percent to be paid in installments over a period of time to be determined by the court pursuant to Section 984, not to exceed 10 years.

(i) In any case involving multiple defendants, a reduction pursuant to this section shall be proportional to the percentage of the judgment actually paid by the public entity and shall satisfy the judgment as to the portion reduced so that no other judgment debtor shall be jointly liable for the portion of the judgment reduced pursuant to this section. If, after a hearing and determination pursuant to this section, the public entity judgment debtor is required to satisfy a portion of a joint and several judgment beyond that public entity judgment debtor's several portion due to the uncollectability of a joint tortfeasor's portion, the public entity may make a motion to reduce the additional portion in an amount proportional to the determination of the court pursuant to this section.

(j) In all actions affected by this section, the court shall instruct the jury with the following language:

"You shall award damages in an amount that fully compensates plaintiff for damages in accordance with instructions from the court. You shall not speculate or consider any other possible sources of benefit the plaintiff may have received. After you have returned your verdict the court will make whatever adjustments are necessary in this regard."

(k) The Judicial Council shall adopt rules providing for a reasonable extension of the time for filing the notice of appeal from a judgment on the verdict to permit a motion for the hearing and the hearing itself.

(*l*) If the defendant public entity or defendant public employee is also a health care provider as defined in Section 3333.1 of the Civil Code, that section controls as to that defendant.

(m) This chapter does not apply to lien or subrogation rights provided in Chapter 5 (commencing with Section 3850) of Part 1 of Division 4 of the Labor Code. **Leg.H.** Added Stats 1987 ch 1201 §25, ch 1208 §8.

PART 6
INSURANCE

§989. "Local public entity"

As used in this part, "local public entity" means any public entity except a state agency covered by Section 11007.4 of the Government Code. **Leg.H.** Added Stats 1963 ch 1682 §12.

§990. Matters against which a local public entity may insure itself

Except for a liability which may be insured against pursuant to Division 4 (commencing with Section 3200) of the Labor Code, a local public entity may:

(a) Insure itself against all or any part of any tort or inverse condemnation liability.

(b) Insure any employee of the local public entity against all or any part of his liability for injury resulting from an act or omission in the scope of his employment.

(c) Insure, contract or provide against the expense of defending a claim against the local public entity or its employee, whether or not liability exists on such claim, including a claim for damages under Section 3294 of the Civil Code or otherwise for the sake of example or by way of punishment, where such liability arose from an act or omission in the scope of his employment, and an insurance contract for such purpose is valid and binding notwithstanding Section 1668 of the Civil Code, Section 533 of the Insurance Code, or any other provision of law.

(d) A hospital district may participate in a reciprocal or interinsurance exchange with the members of its medical staff as provided in Section 1284 of the Insurance Code.

Nothing in this section shall be construed to authorize a local public entity to pay for, or to insure, contract, or provide for payment for, such part of a claim or judgment against an employee of the local entity as is for punitive or exemplary damages. **Leg.H.** Added Stats 1963 ch 1682 §12. Amended Stats 1967 ch 298 §1; Stats 1971 ch 140 §1; Stats 1976 ch 1465 §2; Stats 1977 ch 904 §1.

§990.2. Authority of Judicial Council to insure officer or attachés

The Judicial Council may insure any officer or attaché of its superior courts against all or any part of the officer or attaché's liability for injury resulting from any act or omission in the scope of the officer or attaché's employment, and also may insure against the expense of defending any claim against the officer or attaché, whether or not liability exists on that claim. **Leg.H.** Added Stats 1963 ch 1682 §12. Amended Stats 1998 ch 931 §176 (SB 2139), effective September 28, 1998; Stats 2023 ch 478 §25 (AB 1756), effective January 1, 2024.

§990.4. Kinds of insurance that may be provided

The insurance authorized by this part may be provided by:

(a) Self-insurance, which may be, but is not required to be, funded by appropriations to establish or maintain reserves for self-insurance purposes.

(b) Insurance in any insurer authorized to transact such insurance in this state.

(c) Insurance secured in accordance with Chapter 6 (commencing with Section 1760) of Part 2 of Division 1 of the Insurance Code.

(d) Participation by a hospital district and its medical staff in a reciprocal or interinsurance exchange as provided in Section 1284 of the Insurance Code.

(e) Any combination of insurance authorized by subdivisions (a), (b), (c), and (d) **Leg.H.** Added Stats 1963 ch 1682 §12. Amended Stats 1976 ch 1465 §3; Stats 1977 ch 904 §2.

§990.6. Cost

The cost of the insurance authorized by this part is a proper charge against the local public entity. **Leg.H.** Added Stats 1963 ch 1682 §12.

§990.8. Agreement for insurance between two or more local public entities or specified nonprofit corporations, or mutual water company and public agency

(a) Two or more local public entities, or a mutual water company and a public agency, as authorized under subdivision (b) of Section 6525, by a joint powers agreement made pursuant to Article 1 (commencing with Section 6500) of Chapter 5 of Division 7, may provide insurance authorized by this part or for any other purpose by any one or more of the methods specified in Section 990.4. Where two or more hospital districts have joined together to pool their self-insurance claims or losses, any nonprofit corporation created pursuant to subdivision (p) of Section 32121 of the Health and Safety Code, and affiliated with a hospital district which is a party to the pool may participate in the pool.

(b) Two or more local public entities having the same governing board, or a mutual water company and a public agency, as authorized under subdivision (b) of Section 6525, may be coinsured under a master policy and the total premium may be prorated among those entities.

(c) The pooling of self-insured claims or losses among entities as authorized in subdivision (a) of Section 990.4 shall not be considered insurance nor be subject to regulation under the Insurance Code.

(d) Any liability or loss under a joint powers agreement for the pooling of self-insured claims or losses authorized by this part and provided pursuant to this section may, notwithstanding Section 620 of the Insurance Code or any other provision of law, be reinsured to the same extent and the same manner as insurance provided by an insurer.

(e) Where a joint powers agreement authorized by this part or authorized pursuant to Section 6516 provides for the pooling of self-insured claims or losses among entities, if any peril insured or covered under contract has existed, and the joint powers authority or other parties to the pool have been liable for any period, however short, the agreement may provide that the party insured or covered under contract is not entitled to the return of premiums, contributions, payments, or advances so far as that particular risk is concerned.

(f) For purposes of this section, "mutual water company" has the same meaning as the term does in Section 14300 of the Corporations Code. **Leg.H.** Added Stats 1963 ch 1682 §12. Amended Stats 1976 ch 1459 §1; Stats 1982 ch 454 §34; Stats 1986 ch 1355 §1; Stats 1996 ch 181 §1 (SB 2047); Stats 1997 ch 131 §1 (SB 1153); Stats 2015 ch 250 §1 (AB 656), effective January 1, 2016.

1997 Note: Section 990.8, as amended by Stats 1997 ch 131, shall not apply to any lawsuits filed on or before May 2, 1994. Stats 1997 ch 131 § 3.

§990.9. Insurance or indemnity by local public entity for health–care tort claims against person rendering care without compensation

Any city, county, city and county, or any other local public entity with authority to provide health care services may provide insurance or provide indemnity through self–insurance for medical or other health–care tort claims against any person who, in good faith and without compensation, renders voluntary care to low–income patients within the scope of his or her practice at a community clinic or free clinic, as those terms are defined in subdivision (a) of Section 1204 of the Health and Safety Code, serving residents within the jurisdiction of the local public entity, and who is licensed under Division 2 (commencing with Section 500) of the Business and Professions Code or under an initiative act referred to in those provisions. However, the insurance or indemnity provided pursuant to this section shall not cover liability for which there is other insurance coverage in effect. **Leg.H.** Added Stats 1993 ch 154 §1 (AB 2058).

§991. Other enactment authorizing or requiring local public entity to insure

Where an enactment, other than this part, authorizes or requires a local public entity to insure against its liability or the liability of its employees:

(a) The authority provided by this part to insure does not affect such other enactment.

(b) Such other enactment does not limit or restrict the authority to insure under this part; but, except to the extent authorized by Section 1251 of the Education Code, nothing in this part permits a school district to self–insure in any case where the school district is required to insure. **Leg.H.** Added Stats 1963 ch 1682 §12.

§991.2. Exercise of authority as not imposing liability or impairing defense

Neither the authority provided by this part to insure, nor the exercise of such authority, shall:

(a) Impose any liability upon the local public entity or its employee unless such liability otherwise exists.

(b) Impair any defense the local public entity or its employee otherwise may have. **Leg.H.** Added Stats 1963 ch 1682 §12.

PART 7
DEFENSE OF PUBLIC EMPLOYEES

§995. Duty to provide for defense of action

Except as otherwise provided in Sections 995.2 and 995.4, upon request of an employee or former employee, a public entity shall provide for the defense of any civil action or proceeding brought against him, in his official or individual capacity or both, on account of an act or omission in the scope of his employment as an employee of the public entity.

For the purposes of this part, a cross–action, counterclaim or cross–complaint against an employee or former employee shall be deemed to be a civil action or proceeding brought against him. **Leg.H.** Added Stats 1963 ch 1683 §16.

§995.2. When public entity may refuse to defend; Notification of refusal

(a) A public entity may refuse to provide for the defense of a civil action or proceeding brought against an employee or former employee if the public entity determines any of the following:

(1) The act or omission was not within the scope of his or her employment.

(2) He or she acted or failed to act because of actual fraud, corruption, or actual malice.

(3) The defense of the action or proceeding by the public entity would create a specific conflict of interest between the public entity and the employee or former employee. For the purposes of this section, "specific conflict of interest" means a conflict of interest or an adverse or pecuniary interest, as specified by statute or by a rule or regulation of the public entity.

(b) If an employee or former employee requests in writing that the public entity, through its designated legal counsel, provide for a defense, the public entity shall, within 20 days, inform the employee or former employee whether it will or will not provide a defense, and the reason for the refusal to provide a defense.

(c) If an actual and specific conflict of interest becomes apparent subsequent to the 20–day period following the employee's written request for defense, nothing herein shall prevent the public entity from refusing to provide further defense to the employee. The public entity shall inform the employee of the reason for the refusal to provide further defense. **Leg.H.** Added Stats 1963 ch 1683 §16. Amended Stats 1982 ch 1046 §1.

§995.3. Action against official for interference with disclosures; Liability for costs of defense

(a) If a state employee provides his or her own defense against an action brought for an alleged violation of Section 8547.3, and if it is established that no violation of Section 8547.3 occurred, the public entity shall reimburse the employee for any costs incurred in the defense.

(b) A public entity which does provide for the defense of a state employee charged with a violation of Section 8547.3 shall reserve all rights to be reimbursed for any costs incurred in that defense. If a state employee is found to have violated Section 8547.3, he or she is liable for all defense costs and shall reimburse the public entity for those costs. **Leg.H.** Added Stats 1984 ch 1212 §1. Amended Stats 1986 ch 353 §2; Stats 1995 ch 277 §1 (AB 1097).

§995.4. When provision for defense permitted but not required

A public entity may, but is not required to, provide for the defense of:

(a) An action or proceeding brought by the public entity to remove, suspend or otherwise penalize its own employee or former employee, or an appeal to a court from an administrative proceeding by the public entity to remove, suspend or otherwise penalize its own employee or former employee.

(b) An action or proceeding brought by the public entity against its own employee or former employee as an individual and not in his official capacity, or an appeal therefrom. **Leg.H.** Added Stats 1963 ch 1683 §16.

§995.6. Defense of administrative proceedings

A public entity is not required to provide for the defense of an administrative proceeding brought against an employee or former employee, but a public entity may provide for the defense of an administrative proceeding brought against an employee or former employee if:

(a) The administrative proceeding is brought on account of an act or omission in the scope of his employment as an employee of the public entity; and

(b) The public entity determines that such defense would be in the best interests of the public entity and that the employee or former employee acted, or failed to act, in good faith, without actual malice and in the apparent interests of the public entity. **Leg.H.** Added Stats 1963 ch 1683 §16.

§995.8. Defense of criminal actions; Removal proceedings

A public entity is not required to provide for the defense of a criminal action or proceeding (including a proceeding to remove an officer under Sections 3060 to 3073, inclusive, of the Government Code) brought against an employee or former employee, but a public entity may provide for the defense of a criminal action or proceeding (including a proceeding to remove an officer under Sections 3060 to 3073, inclusive, of the Government Code) brought against an employee or former employee if:

(a) The criminal action or proceeding is brought on account of an act or omission in the scope of his employment as an employee of the public entity; and

(b) The public entity determines that such defense would be in the best interests of the public entity and that the employee or former employee acted, or failed to act, in good faith, without actual malice and in the apparent interests of the public entity. **Leg.H.** Added Stats 1963 ch 1683 §16.

§995.9. Defense or indemnification of witness for public entity

Notwithstanding any other provision of law, upon a request made in writing to a public entity, the public entity may defend or indemnify or defend and indemnify any witness who has testified on behalf of the public entity in any criminal, civil, or administrative action. The decision of the public entity to defend or indemnify or defend and indemnify such a witness shall rest within the sound discretion of the public entity and may be based on any relevant factors, including, but not limited to, whether the provision of defense or indemnity would serve the public interest. The public entity may defend or indemnify or defend and indemnify the witness only if it is determined by the public entity that the action being brought against the witness is based directly upon the conduct which the public entity requested of the witness related to the witness' testimony or provision of evidence. The public entity has the discretion to provide a defense alone apart from indemnity, and the public entity may offer to defend or indemnify or defend and indemnify while reserving all rights to subsequently withdraw these offers upon reasonable notice.

Neither defense nor indemnification shall be provided if the testimony giving rise to the action against the witness was false in any material respect, or was otherwise not given by the witness with a good faith belief in its truth; nor shall representation or indemnification under this section be offered or promised unless the action has been commenced and the witness has requested the public entity to act for the witness' benefit under this section. The public entity shall not be liable for indemnification of a defendant witness for punitive damages awarded to the plaintiff in such an action. If the plaintiff prevails in a claim for punitive damages in an action defended at the expense of the public entity, the defendant shall be liable to the public entity for the full costs incurred by the public entity in providing representation to the defendant witness. **Leg.H.** Added Stats 1995 ch 799 §2 (AB 1361).

§996. Methods of providing defense

A public entity may provide for a defense pursuant to this part by its own attorney or by employing other counsel for this purpose or by purchasing insurance which requires that the insurer provide the defense. All of the expenses of providing a defense pursuant to this part are proper charges against a public entity. A public entity has no right to recover such expenses from the employee or former employee defended. **Leg.H.** Added Stats 1963 ch 1683 §16.

§996.4. Refusal of entity to represent employee

If after request a public entity fails or refuses to provide an employee or former employee with a defense against a civil action or proceeding brought against him and the employee retains his own counsel to defend the action or proceeding, he is entitled to recover from the public entity such reasonable attorney's fees, costs and expenses as are necessarily incurred by him in defending the action or proceeding if the action or proceeding arose out of an act or omission in the scope of his employment as an employee of the public entity, but he is not entitled to such reimbursement if the public entity establishes (a) that he acted or failed to act because of actual fraud, corruption or actual malice, or (b) that the action or proceeding is one described in Section 995.4.

Nothing in this section shall be construed to deprive an employee or former employee of the right to petition for a writ of mandate to compel the public entity or the governing body or an employee thereof to perform the duties imposed by this part. **Leg.H.** Added Stats 1963 ch 1683 §16.

§996.6. Rights under this part as additional to other contractual or statutory rights

The rights of an employee or former employee under this part are in addition to and not in lieu of any rights he may have under any contract or under any other enactment providing for his defense. **Leg.H.** Added Stats 1963 ch 1683 §16.

TITLE 2
GOVERNMENT OF THE STATE OF CALIFORNIA
DIVISION 3
EXECUTIVE DEPARTMENT

PART 1
STATE DEPARTMENTS AND AGENCIES
CHAPTER 3.5
ADMINISTRATIVE REGULATIONS AND RULEMAKING
ARTICLE 1
General

§11340. Legislative findings and declarations

The Legislature finds and declares as follows:

(a) There has been an unprecedented growth in the number of administrative regulations in recent years.

(b) The language of many regulations is frequently unclear and unnecessarily complex, even when the complicated and technical nature of the subject matter is taken into account. The language is often confusing to the persons who must comply with the regulations.

(c) Substantial time and public funds have been spent in adopting regulations, the necessity for which has not been established.

(d) The imposition of prescriptive standards upon private persons and entities through regulations where the establishment of performance standards could reasonably be expected to produce the same result has placed an unnecessary burden on California citizens and discouraged innovation, research, and development of improved means of achieving desirable social goals.

(e) There exists no central office in state government with the power and duty to review regulations to ensure that they are written in a comprehensible manner, are authorized by statute, and are consistent with other law.

(f) Correcting the problems that have been caused by the unprecedented growth of regulations in California requires the direct involvement of the Legislature as well as that of the executive branch of state government.

(g) The complexity and lack of clarity in many regulations put small businesses, which do not have the resources to hire experts to assist them, at a distinct disadvantage. **Leg.H.** Added Stats 1979 ch 567 §1, operative July 1, 1980. Amended Stats 1981 ch 865 §2; Stats 1983 ch 874 §1; Stats 1993 ch 870 §1 (SB 726), effective January 1, 1994.

§11340.1. Declarations and intent regarding establishment of Office of Administrative Law

(a) The Legislature therefore declares that it is in the public interest to establish an Office of Administrative Law which shall be charged with the orderly review of adopted regulations. It is the intent of the Legislature that the purpose of such review shall be to reduce the number of administrative regulations and to improve the quality of those regulations which are adopted. It is the intent of the Legislature that agencies shall actively seek to reduce the unnecessary regulatory burden on private individuals and entities by substituting performance standards for prescriptive standards wherever performance standards can be reasonably expected to be as effective and less burdensome, and that this substitution shall be considered during the course of the agency rulemaking process. It is the intent of the Legislature that neither the Office of Administrative Law nor the court should substitute its judgment for that of the rulemaking agency as expressed in the substantive content of adopted regulations. It is the intent of the Legislature that while the Office of Administrative Law will be part of the executive branch of state government, that the office work closely with, and upon request report directly to, the Legislature in order to accomplish regulatory reform in California.

(b) It is the intent of the Legislature that the California Code of Regulations made available on the Internet by the office pursuant to Section 11344 include complete authority and reference citations and history notes. **Leg.H.** Added Stats 1979 ch 567 §1, operative July 1, 1980. Amended Stats 1981 ch 865 §3; Stats 1983 ch 874 §2; Stats 1996 ch 501 §1 (SB 1910), effective January 1, 1997.

§11340.2. Office of Administrative Law; Director and deputy director

(a) The Office of Administrative Law is hereby established in state government in the Government Operations Agency. The office shall be under the direction and control of an executive officer who shall be known as the director. There shall also be a deputy director. The director's term and the deputy director's term of office shall be coterminous with that of the appointing power, except that they shall be subject to reappointment.

(b) The director and deputy director shall have the same qualifications as a hearing officer and shall be appointed by the Governor subject to the confirmation of the Senate. **Leg.H.** Added Stats 1979 ch 567 §1, operative July 1, 1980. Amended Stats 1980 ch 992 §1.5. See this section as modified in Governor's Reorganization Plan No. 2 § 175 of 2012; Amended Stats 2013 ch 352 §235 (AB 1317), effective September 26, 2013, operative July 1, 2013.

2013 Note: Stats 2013 ch 352 (AB 1317) enacted the statutory changes necessary to reflect the changes made by the Governor's Reorganization Plan No. 2 of 2012.

2012 Note: 2012 Governor's Reorganization Plan No. 2 was submitted to the Legislature on May 3, 2012, and became effective July 3, 2012, pursuant to Gov C § 12080.5, and substantively operative July 1, 2013.

§11340.3. Employment and compensation of assistants and other employees

The director may employ and fix the compensation, in accordance with law, of such professional assistants and clerical and other employees as is deemed necessary for the effective conduct of the work of the office. **Leg.H.** Added Stats 1979 ch 567 §1, operative July 1, 1980.

§11340.4. Recommendations on administrative rulemaking

(a) The office is authorized and directed to do the following:

(1) Study the subject of administrative rulemaking in all its aspects.

(2) In the interest of fairness, uniformity, and the expedition of business, submit its suggestions to the various agencies.

(3) Report its recommendations to the Governor and Legislature at the commencement of each general session.

(b) All agencies of the state shall give the office ready access to their records and full information and reasonable assistance in any matter of research requiring recourse to them or to data within their knowledge or control. Nothing in this subdivision authorizes an agency to provide access to records required by statute to be kept confidential. **Leg.H.** Added Stats 1995 ch 938 §14 (SB 523), operative July 1, 1997.

§11340.5. Adoption of guidelines, bulletins and manuals as regulations

(a) No state agency shall issue, utilize, enforce, or attempt to enforce any guideline, criterion, bulletin, manual, instruction, order, standard of general application, or other rule, which is a regulation as defined in Section 11342.600, unless the guideline, criterion, bulletin, manual, instruction, order, standard of general application, or other rule has been adopted as a regulation and filed with the Secretary of State pursuant to this chapter.

(b) If the office is notified of, or on its own, learns of the issuance, enforcement of, or use of, an agency guideline, criterion, bulletin, manual, instruction, order, standard of general application, or other rule that has not been adopted as a regulation and filed with the Secretary of State pursuant to this chapter, the office may issue a determination as to whether the guideline, criterion, bulletin, manual, instruction, order, standard of general application, or other rule, is a regulation as defined in Section 11342.600.

(c) The office shall do all of the following:

(1) File its determination upon issuance with the Secretary of State.

(2) Make its determination known to the agency, the Governor, and the Legislature.

(3) Publish its determination in the California Regulatory Notice Register within 15 days of the date of issuance.

(4) Make its determination available to the public and the courts.

(d) Any interested person may obtain judicial review of a given determination by filing a written petition requesting that the determination of the office be modified or set aside. A petition shall be filed with the court within 30 days of the date the determination is published.

(e) A determination issued by the office pursuant to this section shall not be considered by a court, or by an administrative agency in an adjudicatory proceeding if all of the following occurs:

(1) The court or administrative agency proceeding involves the party that sought the determination from the office.

(2) The proceeding began prior to the party's request for the office's determination.

(3) At issue in the proceeding is the question of whether the guideline, criterion, bulletin, manual, instruction, order, standard of general application, or other rule that is the legal basis for the adjudicatory action is a regulation as defined in Section 11342.600. **Leg.H.** Added Stats 1994 ch 1039 §4 (AB 2531). Amended Stats 1995 ch 938 §15 (SB 523), operative January 1, 1996; Stats 2000 ch 1060 §3 (AB 1822), effective January 1, 2001.

§11340.6. Petition requesting adoption, amendment, or repeal of regulation; Contents

Except where the right to petition for adoption of a regulation is restricted by statute to a designated group or where the form of procedure for such a petition is otherwise prescribed by statute, any interested person may petition a state agency requesting the adoption, amendment, or repeal of a regulation as provided in Article 5 (commencing with Section 11346). This petition shall state the following clearly and concisely:

(a) The substance or nature of the regulation, amendment, or repeal requested.

(b) The reason for the request.

(c) Reference to the authority of the state agency to take the action requested. **Leg.H.** Added Stats 1994 ch 1039 §5 (AB 2531), effective January 1, 1995.

§11340.7. Procedure upon petition requesting adoption, amendment or repeal of regulation

(a) Upon receipt of a petition requesting the adoption, amendment, or repeal of a regulation pursuant to Article 5 (commencing with Section 11346), a state agency shall notify the petitioner in writing of the receipt and shall within 30 days deny the petition indicating why the agency has reached its decision on the merits of the petition in writing or schedule the matter for public hearing in accordance with the notice and hearing requirements of that article.

(b) A state agency may grant or deny the petition in part, and may grant any other relief or take any other action as it may determine to be warranted by the petition and shall notify the petitioner in writing of this action.

(c) Any interested person may request a reconsideration of any part or all of a decision of any agency on any petition submitted. The request shall be submitted in accordance with Section 11340.6 and include the reason or reasons why an agency should reconsider its previous decision no later than 60 days after the date of the decision involved. The agency's reconsideration of any matter relating to a petition shall be subject to subdivision (a).

(d) Any decision of a state agency denying in whole or in part or granting in whole or in part a petition requesting the adoption, amendment, or repeal of a regulation pursuant to Article 5 (commencing with Section 11346) shall be in writing and shall be transmitted to the Office of Administrative Law for publication in the California Regulatory Notice Register at the earliest practicable date. The decision shall identify the agency, the party submitting the petition, the provisions of the California Code of Regulations requested to be affected, reference to authority to take the action requested, the reasons supporting the agency determination, an agency contact person, and the right of interested persons to obtain a copy of the petition from the agency. **Leg.H.** Added Stats 1994 ch 1994 ch 1039 §6 (AB 2531), effective January 1, 1995.

§11340.85. Electronic communications

(a) As used in this section, "electronic communication" includes electronic transmission of written or graphical material by electronic mail, facsimile, or other means, but does not include voice communication.

(b) Notwithstanding any other provision of this chapter that refers to mailing or sending, or to oral or written communication:

(1) An agency may permit and encourage use of electronic communication, but may not require use of electronic communication.

(2) An agency may publish or distribute a document required by this chapter or by a regulation implementing this chapter by means of electronic communication, but shall not make that the exclusive means by which the document is published or distributed.

(3) A notice required or authorized by this chapter or by a regulation implementing this chapter may be delivered to a person by means of electronic communication if the person has expressly indicated a willingness to receive the notice by means of electronic communication.

(4) A comment regarding a regulation may be delivered to an agency by means of electronic communication.

(5) A petition regarding a regulation may be delivered to an agency by means of electronic communication if the agency has expressly indicated a willingness to receive a petition by means of electronic communication.

(c) An agency that maintains an Internet Web site or other similar forum for the electronic publication or distribution of written material shall publish on that Web site or other forum information regarding a proposed regulation or regulatory repeal or amendment, that includes, but is not limited to, the following:

(1) Any public notice required by this chapter or by a regulation implementing this chapter.

(2) The initial statement of reasons prepared pursuant to subdivision (b) of Section 11346.2.

(3) The final statement of reasons prepared pursuant to subdivision (a) of Section 11346.9.

(4) Notice of a decision not to proceed prepared pursuant to Section 11347.

(5) The text of a proposed action or instructions on how to obtain a copy of the text.

(6) A statement of any decision made by the office regarding a proposed action.

(7) The date a rulemaking action is filed with the Secretary of State.

(8) The effective date of a rulemaking action.

(9) A statement to the effect that a business or person submitting a comment regarding a proposed action has the right to request a copy of the final statement of reasons.

(10) The text of a proposed emergency adoption, amendment, or repeal of a regulation pursuant to Section 11346.1 and the date it was submitted to the office for review and filing.

(d) A document that is required to be posted pursuant to subdivision (c) shall be posted within a reasonable time after issuance of the document, and shall remain posted until at least 15 days after (1) the rulemaking action is filed with the Secretary of State, or (2) notice of a decision not to proceed is published pursuant to Section 11347. Publication under subdivision (c) supplements any other required form of publication or distribution. Failure to comply with this section is not grounds for disapproval of a proposed regulation. Subdivision (c) does not require an agency to establish or maintain a Web site or other forum for the electronic publication or distribution of written material.

(e) Nothing in this section precludes the office from requiring that the material submitted to the office for publication in the California Code of Regulations or the California Regulatory Notice Register be submitted in electronic form.

(f) This section is intended to make the regulatory process more user-friendly and to improve communication between interested parties and the regulatory agencies. **Leg.H.** Added Stats 2000 ch 1060 §4 (AB 1822). Amended Stats 2001 ch 59 §2 (SB 561); Stats 2002 ch 389 §2 (AB 1857); Stats 2006 ch 713 §1 (AB 1302), effective January 1, 2007.

§11340.9. Inapplicable provisions

This chapter does not apply to any of the following:

(a) An agency in the judicial or legislative branch of the state government.

(b) A legal ruling of counsel issued by the Franchise Tax Board or State Board of Equalization.

(c) A form prescribed by a state agency or any instructions relating to the use of the form, but this provision is not a limitation on any requirement that a regulation be adopted pursuant to this chapter when one is needed to implement the law under which the form is issued.

(d) A regulation that relates only to the internal management of the state agency.

(e) A regulation that establishes criteria or guidelines to be used by the staff of an agency in performing an audit, investigation, examination, or inspection, settling a commercial dispute, negotiating a commercial arrangement, or in the defense, prosecution, or settlement of a case, if disclosure of the criteria or guidelines would do any of the following:

(1) Enable a law violator to avoid detection.

(2) Facilitate disregard of requirements imposed by law.

(3) Give clearly improper advantage to a person who is in an adverse position to the state.

(f) A regulation that embodies the only legally tenable interpretation of a provision of law.

(g) A regulation that establishes or fixes rates, prices, or tariffs.

(h) A regulation that relates to the use of public works, including streets and highways, when the effect of the regulation is indicated to the public by means of signs or signals or when the regulation determines uniform standards and specifications for official traffic control devices pursuant to Section 21400 of the Vehicle Code.

(i) A regulation that is directed to a specifically named person or to a group of persons and does not apply generally throughout the state. **Leg.H.** Added Stats 2000 ch 1060 §5 (AB 1822), effective January 1, 2001.

§11340.9. Inapplicable provisions

This chapter does not apply to any of the following:

(a) An agency in the judicial or legislative branch of the state government.

(b) A legal ruling of counsel issued by the Franchise Tax Board [1], State Board of Equalization, **or the California Department of Tax and Fee Administration**.

(c) A form prescribed by a state agency or any instructions relating to the use of the form, but this provision is not a limitation on any requirement that a regulation be adopted pursuant to this chapter when one is needed to implement the law under which the form is issued.

(d) A regulation that relates only to the internal management of the state agency.

(e) A regulation that establishes criteria or guidelines to be used by the staff of an agency in performing an audit, investigation, examination, or inspection, settling a commercial dispute, negotiating a commercial arrangement, or in the defense, prosecution, or settlement of a case, if disclosure of the criteria or guidelines would do any of the following:

(1) Enable a law violator to avoid detection.

(2) Facilitate disregard of requirements imposed by law.

(3) Give clearly improper advantage to a person who is in an adverse position to the state.

(f) A regulation that embodies the only legally tenable interpretation of a provision of law.

(g) A regulation that establishes or fixes rates, prices, or tariffs.

(h) A regulation that relates to the use of public works, including streets and highways, when the effect of the regulation is indicated to the public by means of signs or signals or when the regulation determines uniform standards and specifications for official traffic control devices pursuant to Section 21400 of the Vehicle Code.

(i) A regulation that is directed to a specifically named person or to a group of persons and does not apply generally throughout the state. **Leg.H.** Added Stats 2000 ch 1060 §5 (AB 1822), effective January 1, 2001. Amended Stats 2024 ch 34 §1 (SB 167), effective June 27, 2024.

§11340.9. 2024 Deletes. [1] or

§11341. Identification numbers

(a) The office shall establish a system to give a unique identification number to each regulatory action.

(b) The office and the state agency taking the regulatory action shall use the identification number given by the office pursuant to subdivision (a) to refer to the regulatory action for which a notice has already been published in the California Regulatory Notice Register.

(c) The identification number shall be sufficient information for a member of the public to identify and track a regulatory action both with the office and the state agency taking the regulatory action. No other information pertaining to the regulatory action shall be required of a member of the public if the identification number of the regulatory action has been provided. **Leg.H.** Added Stats 2000 ch 1059 §5 (AB 505), effective January 1, 2001.

§11342.1. Authority not conferred on state agencies

Except as provided in Section 11342.4, nothing in this chapter confers authority upon or augments the authority of any state agency to adopt, administer, or enforce any regulation. Each regulation adopted, to be effective, shall be within the scope of authority conferred and in accordance with standards prescribed by other provisions of law. **Leg.H.** Added Stats 1979 ch 567 §1, operative July 1, 1980. Amended Stats 1987 ch 1375 §2.

§11342.2. Consistency with statute; Effectuation of purpose of statute

Whenever by the express or implied terms of any statute a state agency has authority to adopt regulations to implement, interpret, make specific or otherwise carry out the provisions of the statute, no regulation adopted is valid or effective unless consistent and not in conflict with the statute and reasonably necessary to effectuate the purpose of the statute. **Leg.H.** Added Stats 1979 ch 567 §1, operative July 1, 1980.

§11342.4. Regulations

The office shall adopt, amend, or repeal regulations for the purpose of carrying out the provisions of this chapter. **Leg.H.** Added Stats 1981 ch 865 §19, as Gov C §11344.6. Amended Stats 1982 ch 1573 §1. Renumbered by Stats 1983 ch 797 §12.

ARTICLE 2
Definitions

§11342.510. Governing definitions

Unless the provision or context otherwise requires, the definitions in this article govern the construction of this chapter. **Leg.H.** Added Stats 2000 ch 1060 §8 (AB 1822), effective January 1, 2001.

§11342.520. "Agency"

"Agency" means state agency. **Leg.H.** Added Stats 2000 ch 1060 §8 (AB 1822), effective January 1, 2001.

§11342.530. "Building standard"

"Building standard" has the same meaning provided in Section 18909 of the Health and Safety Code. **Leg.H.** Added Stats 2000 ch 1060 §8 (AB 1822), effective January 1, 2001.

§11342.535. "Cost impact"

"Cost impact" means the amount of reasonable range of direct costs, or a description of the type and extent of direct costs, that a representative private person or business necessarily incurs in reasonable compliance with the proposed action. **Leg.H.** Added Stats 2000 ch 1059 §6.5 (AB 505), effective January 1, 2001.

§11342.540. "Director"

"Director" means the director of the office. **Leg.H.** Added Stats 2000 ch 1060 §8 (AB 1822), effective January 1, 2001.

§11342.545. "Emergency"

"Emergency" means a situation that calls for immediate action to avoid serious harm to the public peace, health, safety, or general welfare. **Leg.H.** Added Stats 2006 ch 713 §2 (AB 1302), effective January 1, 2007.

§11342.548. "Major regulation"

"Major regulation" means any proposed adoption, amendment, or repeal of a regulation subject to review by the Office of Administrative Law pursuant to Article 6 (commencing with Section 11349) that will have an economic impact on California business enterprises and individuals in an amount exceeding fifty million dollars ($50,000,000), as estimated by the agency. **Leg.H.** Added Stats 2011 ch 496 §1 (SB 617), effective January 1, 2012.

§11342.550. "Office"

"Office" means the Office of Administrative Law. **Leg.H.** Added Stats 2000 ch 1060 §8 (AB 1822), effective January 1, 2001.

§11342.560. "Order of repeal"

"Order of repeal" means any resolution, order, or other official act of a state agency that expressly repeals a regulation in whole or in part. **Leg.H.** Added Stats 2000 ch 1060 §8 (AB 1822), effective January 1, 2001.

§11342.570. "Performance standard"

"Performance standard" means a regulation that describes an objective with the criteria stated for achieving the objective. **Leg.H.** Added Stats 2000 ch 1060 §8 (AB 1822), effective January 1, 2001.

§11342.580. "Plain English"

"Plain English" means language that satisfies the standard of clarity provided in Section 11349. **Leg.H.** Added Stats 2000 ch 1060 §8 (AB 1822), effective January 1, 2001.

§11342.590. "Prescriptive standard"

"Prescriptive standard" means a regulation that specifies the sole means of compliance with a performance standard by specific actions, measurements, or other quantifiable means. **Leg.H.** Added Stats 2000 ch 1060 §8 (AB 1822), effective January 1, 2001.

§11342.595. "Proposed action"

"Proposed action" means the regulatory action, notice of which is submitted to the office for publication in the California Regulatory Notice Register. **Leg.H.** Added Stats 2000 ch 1059 §6.7 (AB 505). Amended Stats 2001 ch 59 §3 (SB 561), effective January 1, 2001.

§11342.600. "Regulation"

"Regulation" means every rule, regulation, order, or standard of general application or the amendment, supplement, or revision of any rule, regulation, order, or standard adopted by any state agency to implement, interpret, or make specific the law enforced or administered by it, or to govern its procedure. **Leg.H.** Added Stats 2000 ch 1060 §8 (AB 1822), effective January 1, 2001.

§11342.610. "Small Business"

(a) "Small business" means a business activity in agriculture, general construction, special trade construction, retail trade, wholesale trade, services, transportation and warehousing, manufacturing, generation and transmission of electric power, or a health care facility, unless excluded in subdivision (b), that is both of the following:

(1) Independently owned and operated.

(2) Not dominant in its field of operation.

(b) "Small business" does not include the following professional and business activities:

(1) A financial institution including a bank, a trust, a savings and loan association, a thrift institution, a consumer finance company, a commercial finance company, an industrial finance company, a credit union, a mortgage and investment banker, a securities broker-dealer, or an investment adviser.

(2) An insurance company, either stock or mutual.

(3) A mineral, oil, or gas broker.

(4) A subdivider or developer.

(5) A landscape architect, an architect, or a building designer.

(6) An entity organized as a nonprofit institution.

(7) An entertainment activity or production, including a motion picture, a stage performance, a television or radio station, or a production company.

(8) A utility, a water company, or a power transmission company generating and transmitting more than 4.5 million kilowatt hours annually.

(9) A petroleum producer, a natural gas producer, a refiner, or a pipeline.

(10) A manufacturing enterprise exceeding 250 employees.

(11) A health care facility exceeding 150 beds or one million five hundred thousand dollars ($1,500,000) in annual gross receipts.

(c) "Small business" does not include the following business activities:

(1) Agriculture, where the annual gross receipts exceed one million dollars ($1,000,000).

(2) General construction, where the annual gross receipts exceed nine million five hundred thousand dollars ($9,500,000).

(3) Special trade construction, where the annual gross receipts exceed five million dollars ($5,000,000).

(4) Retail trade, where the annual gross receipts exceed two million dollars ($2,000,000).

(5) Wholesale trade, where the annual gross receipts exceed nine million five hundred thousand dollars ($9,500,000).

(6) Services, where the annual gross receipts exceed two million dollars ($2,000,000).

(7) Transportation and warehousing, where the annual gross receipts exceed one million five hundred thousand dollars ($1,500,000). **Leg.H.** Added Stats 2000 ch 1060 §8 (AB 1822), effective January 1, 2001.

ARTICLE 3
Filing and Publication

§11343. Procedure

Every state agency shall:

(a) Transmit to the office for filing with the Secretary of State a certified copy of every regulation adopted or amended by it except one that is a building standard.

(b) Transmit to the office for filing with the Secretary of State a certified copy of every order of repeal of a regulation required to be filed under subdivision (a).

(c)(1) Within 15 days of the office filing a state agency's regulation with the Secretary of State, post the regulation on its internet website in an easily marked and identifiable location. The state agency shall keep the regulation on its internet website for at least six months from the date the regulation is filed with the Secretary of State.

(2) Within five days of posting, the state agency shall send to the office the internet website link of each regulation that the agency posts on its internet website pursuant to paragraph (1).

(3) This subdivision shall not apply to a state agency that does not maintain an internet website.

(d) Deliver to the office, at the time of transmittal for filing a regulation or order of repeal, a citation of the authority pursuant to which it or any part thereof was adopted.

(e) Deliver to the office a copy of the notice of proposed action required by Section 11346.4.

(f) Transmit to the California Building Standards Commission for approval a certified copy of every regulation, or order of repeal of a regulation, that is a building standard, together with a citation of authority pursuant to which it or any part thereof was adopted, a copy of the notice of proposed action required by Section 11346.4, and any other records prescribed by the California Building Standards Law (Part 2.5 (commencing with Section 18901) of Division 13 of the Health and Safety Code).

(g) Whenever a certification is required by this section, it shall be made by the head of the state agency that is adopting, amending, or repealing the regulation, or by a designee of the agency head, and the certification and delegation shall be in writing. **Leg.H.** Added Stats 1979 ch 567 §1. Amended Stats 1979 ch 1152 §12.2, operative July 1, 1980; Stats 1980 ch 204 §1, effective June 20, 1980; Stats 1981 ch 865 §5; Stats 1982 ch 749 §1, effective September 8, 1982; Stats 1983 ch 291 §1; Stats 1987 ch 1375 §3; Stats 1988 ch 1194 sec 1.2, operative January 1, 1989; Stats 2000 ch 1060 §9 (AB 1822); Stats 2002 ch 389 §3 (AB 1857); Stats 2012 ch 295 §1 (SB 1099), effective January 1, 2013; Stats 2022 ch 48 §22 (SB 189), effective June 30, 2022.

Prior Law: There was another section of this number which was added Stats 1982 ch 749 §2, to become operative January 1, 1984, and repealed Stats 1983 ch 291 §2.

§11343.1. Style of regulations; Endorsement

(a) All regulations transmitted to the Office of Administrative Law for filing with the Secretary of State shall conform to the style prescribed by the office.

(b) Regulations approved by the office shall bear an endorsement by the office affixed to the certified copy which is filed with the Secretary of State. **Leg.H.** Added Stats 1983 ch 797 §2. Amended Stats 1994 ch 1039 §12 (AB 2531), effective January 1, 1995.

Prior Law: Former Gov C §11343.1, similar to the present section, was added Stats 1979 ch 567 §1, operative July 1, 1980, and repealed Stats 1983 ch 797 §1.

§11343.2. Endorsement of time and date of filing and maintenance of file for public inspection

The Secretary of State shall endorse on the certified copy of each regulation or order of repeal filed with or delivered to him or her, the time and date of filing and shall maintain a permanent file of the certified copies of regulations and orders of repeal for public inspection.

No fee shall be charged by any state officer or public official for the performance of any official act in connection with the certification or filing of regulations pursuant to this article. **Leg.H.** Added Stats 1994 ch 1039 §14 (AB 2531), effective January 1, 1995.

Prior Law: Former Gov C §11343.2, similar to present Gov C §11346.5, was added Stats 1993 ch 870 §3, and repealed Stats 1994 ch 1039 §13.

§11343.3. Vehicle weight impacts and ability of vehicle manufacturers or operators to comply with laws limiting weight of vehicles to be taken into account when promulgating administrative regulations

Notwithstanding any other law, a state agency that is required to promulgate administrative regulations, including, but not limited to, the State Air Resources Board, the California Environmental Protection Agency, the State Energy Resources Conservation and Development Commission, and the Department of Motor Vehicles, shall take into account vehicle weight impacts and the ability of vehicle manufacturers or vehicle operators to comply with laws limiting the weight of vehicles. **Leg.H.** Added Stats 2012 ch 771 §2 (AB 1706), effective January 1, 2013.

Prior Law: Former Gov C §11343.3, similar to present Gov C § 11343.1, was added Stats 1979 ch 567 §1 and repealed Stats 1983 ch 797 §4.

§11343.4. Effective date of regulation or order of repeal; Applicability

(a) Except as otherwise provided in subdivision (b), a regulation or an order of repeal required to be filed with the Secretary of State shall become effective on a quarterly basis as follows:

(1) January 1 if the regulation or order of repeal is filed on September 1 to November 30, inclusive.

(2) April 1 if the regulation or order of repeal is filed on December 1 to February 29, inclusive.

(3) July 1 if the regulation or order of repeal is filed on March 1 to May 31, inclusive.

(4) October 1 if the regulation or order of repeal is filed on June 1 to August 31, inclusive.

(b) The effective dates in subdivision (a) shall not apply in all of the following:

(1) The effective date is specifically provided by the statute pursuant to which the regulation or order of repeal was adopted, in which event it becomes effective on the day prescribed by the statute.

(2) A later date is prescribed by the state agency in a written instrument filed with, or as part of, the regulation or order of repeal.

(3) The agency makes a written request to the office demonstrating good cause for an earlier effective date, in which case the office may prescribe an earlier date.

(4)(A) A regulation adopted by the Fish and Game Commission that is governed by Article 2 (commencing with Section 250) of Chapter 2 of Division 1 of the Fish and Game Code.

(B) A regulation adopted by the Fish and Game Commission that requires a different effective date in order to conform to a federal regulation. **Leg.H.** Added Stats 1994 ch 1039 §16 (AB 2531). Amended Stats 2000 ch 1060 §10 (AB 1822); Stats 2012 ch 295 §2 (SB 1099), effective January 1, 2013; Stats 2016 ch 546 §26 (SB 1473), effective January 1, 2017.

Prior Law: Former Gov C §11343.4, similar to present Gov C §11343.2, was added Stats 1979 ch 567 §1, operative July 1, 1980, as Gov C §11343.5, amended and renumbered by Stats 1981 ch 865 §8, and repealed Stats 1994 ch 1039 §15.

Former Gov C §11343.4, similar to the present section, was added Stats 1979 ch 567 §1, operative July 1, 1980, and repealed Stats 1981 ch 865 §7.

§11343.5. Filing copies of Code of Regulations or Regulatory Code Supplement

Within 10 days from the receipt of printed copies of the California Code of Regulations or of the California Code of Regulations Supplement from the State Printing Office, the office shall file one copy of the particular issue of the code or supplement in the office of the county clerk of each county in this state, or if the authority to accept filings on his or her behalf has been delegated by the county clerk of any county pursuant to Section 26803.5, in the office of the person to whom that authority has been delegated. **Leg.H.** Added Stats 1979 ch 567 §1, operative July 1, 1980, as Gov C §11343.6. Amended and renumbered by Stats 1981 ch 865 §9; Amended Stats 1987 ch 1375 §3.2; Stats 2000 ch 1060 §11 (AB 1822).

Prior Law: Former Gov C §11343.5 was added Stats 1979 ch 567 §1, operative July 1, 1980, and amended and renumbered Gov C §11343.4 by Stats 1981 ch 865 §8.

§11343.6. Rebuttable presumptions raised by filing of certified copy

The filing of a certified copy of a regulation or an order of repeal with the Secretary of State raises the rebuttable presumptions that:

(a) It was duly adopted.

(b) It was duly filed and made available for public inspection at the day and hour endorsed on it.

(c) All requirements of this chapter and the regulations of the office relative to such regulation have been complied with.

(d) The text of the certified copy of a regulation or order of repeal is the text of the regulation or order of repeal as adopted.

The courts shall take judicial notice of the contents of the certified copy of each regulation and of each order of repeal duly filed. **Leg.H.** Added Stats 1979 ch 567 §1, operative July 1, 1980, as Gov C §11343.7. Renumbered by Stats 1981 ch 865 §10.

Prior Law: Former Gov C §11343.6 was added Stats 1979 ch 567 §1, operative July 1, 1980, and amended and renumbered Gov C §11343.5 by Stats 1981 ch 865 §9.

§11343.8. Filing and publication of regulation or order of repeal not required to be filed

Upon the request of a state agency, the office may file with the Secretary of State and the office may publish in such manner as it believes proper, any regulation or order of repeal of a regulation not required by this article to be filed with the Secretary of State. **Leg.H.** Added Stats 1979 ch 567 §1, operative July 1, 1980, as §11343.9. Amended and renumbered by Stats 1981 ch 865 §12.

Prior Law: Former Gov C §11343.8 was added Stats 1979 ch 567 §1, operative July 1, 1980, and amended and renumbered §11343.7 by Stats 1981 ch 865 §11.

ARTICLE 4
The California Code of Regulations, the California Code of Regulations Supplement, and the California Regulatory Notice Register

§11344. Publication of Code of Regulations and Code of Regulations Supplement; Availability of regulations on internet

The office shall do all of the following:

(a) Provide for the official compilation, printing, and publication of adoption, amendment, or repeal of regulations, which shall be known as the California Code of Regulations. On and after July 1, 1998, the office shall make available on the Internet, free of charge, the full text of the California Code of Regulations, and may contract with another state agency or a private entity in order to provide this service.

(b) Make available on its Internet Web site a list of, and a link to the full text of, each regulation filed with the Secretary of State that is pending effectiveness pursuant to Section 11343.4.

(c) Provide for the compilation, printing, and publication of weekly updates of the California Code of Regulations. This publication shall be known as the California Code of Regulations Supplement and shall contain amendments to the code.

(d) Provide for the publication dates and manner and form in which regulations shall be printed and distributed and ensure that regulations are available in printed form at the earliest practicable date after filing with the Secretary of State.

(e) Ensure that each regulation is printed together with a reference to the statutory authority pursuant to which it was enacted and the specific statute or other provision of law which the regulation is implementing, interpreting, or making specific. **Leg.H.** Added Stats 1983 ch 797 §7. Amended Stats 1987 ch 1375 §3.5; Stats 1994 ch 1039 §17 (AB 2531); Stats 1996 ch 501 §2 (SB 1910); Stats 2000 ch 1060 §13 (AB 1822); Stats 2012 ch 295 §3 (SB 1099), effective January 1, 2013.

Prior Law: Former Gov C §11344, similar to the present section, was added Stats 1979 ch 567 §1, operative July 1, 1980, amended Stats 1979 ch 1203 §1, Stats 1981 ch 865 §13, ch 1091 §1, Stats 1982 ch 86 §1, effective March 1, 1982 and repealed Stats 1983 ch 797 §6.

§11344.1. Publication of Regulatory Notice Register

The office shall do all of the following:

(a) Provide for the publication of the California Regulatory Notice Register, which shall be an official publication of the State of California and which shall contain the following:

(1) Notices of proposed action prepared by regulatory agencies, subject to the notice requirements of this chapter, and which have been approved by the office.

(2) A summary of all regulations filed with the Secretary of State in the previous week.

(3) Summaries of all regulation decisions issued in the previous week detailing the reasons for disapproval of a regulation, the reasons for not filing an emergency regulation, and the reasons for repealing an emergency regulation. The California Regulatory Notice Register shall also include a quarterly index of regulation decisions.

(4) Material that is required to be published under Sections 11349.5, 11349.7, and 11349.9.

(5) Determinations issued pursuant to Section 11340.5.

(b) Establish the publication dates and manner and form in which the California Regulatory Notice Register shall be prepared and published and ensure that it is published and distributed in a timely manner to the presiding officer and rules committee of each house of the Legislature and to all subscribers.

(c) Post on its website, on a weekly basis:

(1) The California Regulatory Notice Register. Each issue of the California Regulatory Notice Register on the office's website shall remain posted for a minimum of 18 months.

(2) One or more Internet links to assist the public to gain access to the text of regulations proposed by state agencies. **Leg.H.** Added Stats 1983 ch 797 §9. Amended Stats 1987 ch 1375 §4; Stats 1994 ch 1039 §18 (AB 2531); Stats 2000 ch 1059 §7 (AB 505), ch 1060 §14.5 (AB 1822), effective January 1, 2001.

Prior Law: Former Gov C §11344.1, relating to codification of regulations, was added Stats 1979 ch 567 §1, operative July 1, 1980 and repealed Stats 1983 ch 797 §8.

§11344.2. Furnishing Code and Supplement to county clerks or delegates

The office shall supply a complete set of the California Code of Regulations, and of the California Code of Regulations Supplement to the county clerk of any county or to the delegatee of the county clerk pursuant to Section 26803.5, provided the director makes the following two determinations:

(a) The county clerk or the delegatee of the county clerk pursuant to Section 26803.5 is maintaining the code and supplement in complete and current condition in a place and at times convenient to the public.

(b) The California Code of Regulations and California Code of Regulations Supplement are not otherwise reasonably available to the public in the community where the county clerk or the delegatee of the county clerk pursuant to Section 26803.5 would normally maintain the code and supplements by distribution to libraries pursuant to Article 6 (commencing with Section 14900) of Chapter 7 of Part 5.5. **Leg.H.** Added Stats 1979 ch 567 §1, operative July 1, 1980. Amended Stats 1979 ch 1203 §2; Stats 1981 ch 865 §14; Stats 1987 ch 1375 §4.5; Stats 2000 ch 1060 §15 (AB 1822), effective January 1, 2001.

§11344.3. Time of publication of documents

Every document, other than a notice of proposed rulemaking action, required to be published in the California Regulatory Notice Register by this chapter, shall be published in the first edition of the California Regulatory Notice Register following the date of the document. **Leg.H.** Added Stats 1985 ch 1044 §9 as §11349.9. Amended and renumbered by Stats 1987 ch 1375 §23.

Prior Law: Former Gov C §11344.3, relating to furnishing Notice Register to Legislature, was added Stats 1979 ch 567 §1, operative July 1, 1980, amended Stats 1979 ch 1203 §3, Stats 1981 ch 865 §15, Stats 1982 ch 86 §2, effective March 1, 1982, and repealed Stats 1983 ch 797 §10.

§11344.4. Sale of Code, Supplement and Regulatory Notice Register

(a) The California Code of Regulations, the California Code of Regulations Supplement, and the California Regulatory Notice Register shall be sold at prices which will reimburse the state for all costs incurred for printing, publication, and distribution.

(b) All money received by the state from the sale of the publications listed in subdivision (a) shall be deposited in the treasury and credited to the General Fund, except that, where applicable, an amount necessary to cover the printing, publication, and distribution costs shall be credited to the fund from which the costs have been paid. **Leg.H.** Added Stats 1979 ch 567 §1, operative July 1, 1980. Amended Stats 1979 ch 1203 §4; Stats 1981 ch 865 §16; Stats 1987 ch 1375 §5; Stats 1988 ch 1194 §1.3, operative January 1, 1989; Stats 2000 ch 1060 §16 (AB 1822), effective January 1, 2001.

§11344.6. Rebuttable presumption raised by publication of regulations

The publication of a regulation in the California Code of Regulations or California Code of Regulations Supplement raises a rebuttable presumption that the text of the regulation as so published is the text of the regulation adopted.

The courts shall take judicial notice of the contents of each regulation which is printed or which is incorporated by appropriate reference into the California Code of Regulations as compiled by the office.

The courts shall also take judicial notice of the repeal of a regulation as published in the California Code of Regulations Supplement compiled by the office. **Leg.H.** Added Stats 1979 ch 567 §1, operative July 1, 1980, as Gov C §11343.8. Amended and renumbered Gov C §11343.7 by Stats 1981 ch 865 §11; Amended and renumbered by Stats 1983 ch 797 §5; Amended Stats 1987 ch 1375 §6; Stats 2000 ch 1060 §17 (AB 1822), effective January 1, 2001.

Prior Law: Former Gov C §11344.6 was added Stats 1981 ch 865 §19, amended Stats 1982 ch 1573 §1, and renumbered Gov C §11342.4 by Stats 1983 ch 797 §12.

Former Gov C §11344.6, relating to form of publication, was added Stats 1979 ch 567 §1, operative July 1, 1980, and repealed Stats 1981 ch 865 §18.

§11344.7. Authority of state agencies to purchase copies of Code, Supplement, or Register or to print and distribute special editions

Nothing in this chapter precludes any person or state agency from purchasing copies of the California Code of Regulations, the California Code of Regulations Supplement, or the California Regulatory Notice Register or of any unit of either, nor from printing special editions of any such units and distributing the same. However, where the purchase and printing is by a state agency, the state agency shall do so at the cost or at less than the cost to the agency if it is authorized to do so by other provisions of law. **Leg.H.** Added Stats 1979 ch 567 §1, operative July 1, 1980. Amended Stats 1981 ch 865 §20; Stats 1987 ch 1375 §6.5; Stats 2000 ch 1060 §18 (AB 1822), effective January 1, 2001.

§11344.9. "California Administrative Code"; "California Administrative Notice Register"; "California Administrative Code Supplement"

(a) Whenever the term "California Administrative Code" appears in law, official legal paper, or legal publication, it means the "California Code of Regulations."

(b) Whenever the term "California Administrative Notice Register" appears in any law, official legal paper, or legal publication, it means the "California Regulatory Notice Register."

(c) Whenever the term "California Administrative Code Supplement" or "California Regulatory Code Supplement" appears in any law, official legal paper, or legal publication, it means the "California Code of Regulations Supplement." **Leg.H.** Added Stats 1988 ch 1194 §1, operative January 1, 1989, as Gov C §11342.02. Renumbered by Stats 1994 ch 1039 §9 (AB 2531). Amended Stats 2000 ch 1060 §19 (AB 1822), effective January 1, 2001.

§11345. Identification number not required

The office is not required to develop a unique identification number system for each regulatory action pursuant to Section 11341 or to make the California Regulatory Notice Register available on its website pursuant to subdivision (c) of Section 11344.1 until January 1, 2002. **Leg.H.** Added Stats 2000 ch 1059 §8 (AB 505), effective January 1, 2001.

ARTICLE 5
Public Participation: Procedure for Adoption of Regulations

§11346. Purpose and applicability of article; Subsequent legislation

(a) It is the purpose of this chapter to establish basic minimum procedural requirements for the adoption, amendment, or repeal of administrative regulations. Except as provided in Section 11346.1, the provisions of this chapter are applicable to the exercise of any quasi-legislative power conferred by any statute heretofore or hereafter enacted, but nothing in this chapter repeals or diminishes additional requirements imposed by any statute. This chapter shall not be superseded or modified by any subsequent legislation except to the extent that the legislation shall do so expressly.

(b) An agency that is considering adopting, amending, or repealing a regulation may consult with interested persons before initiating regulatory action pursuant to this article. **Leg.H.** Added Stats 1979 ch 567 §1, operative July 1, 1980. Amended Stats 1994 ch 1039 §20 (AB 2531); Stats 2000 ch 1060 §20 (AB 1822), effective January 1, 2001.

§11346.1. Emergency regulations and orders of repeal

(a)(1) The adoption, amendment, or repeal of an emergency regulation is not subject to any provision of this article or Article 6 (commencing with Section 11349), except this section and Sections 11349.5 and 11349.6.

(2) At least five working days before submitting an emergency regulation to the office, the adopting agency shall, except as provided in paragraph (3), send a notice of the proposed emergency action to every person who has filed a request for notice of regulatory action with the agency. The notice shall include both of the following:

(A) The specific language proposed to be adopted.

(B) The finding of emergency required by subdivision (b).

(3) An agency is not required to provide notice pursuant to paragraph (2) if the emergency situation clearly poses such an immediate, serious harm that delaying action to allow public comment would be inconsistent with the public interest.

(b)(1) Except as provided in subdivision (c), if a state agency makes a finding that the adoption of a regulation or order of repeal is necessary to address an emergency, the regulation or order of repeal may be adopted as an emergency regulation or order of repeal.

(2) Any finding of an emergency shall include a written statement that contains the information required by paragraphs (2) to (6), inclusive, of subdivision (a) of Section 11346.5 and a description of the specific facts demonstrating the existence of an emergency and the need for immediate action, and demonstrating, by substantial evidence, the need for the proposed regulation to effectuate the statute being implemented, interpreted, or made specific and to address only the demonstrated emergency. The finding of emergency shall also identify each technical, theoretical, and empirical study, report, or similar document, if any, upon which the agency relies. The enactment of an urgency statute shall not, in and of itself, constitute a need for immediate action.

A finding of emergency based only upon expediency, convenience, best interest, general public need, or speculation, shall not be adequate to demonstrate the existence of an emergency. If the situation identified in the finding of emergency existed and was known by the agency adopting the emergency regulation in sufficient time to have been addressed through nonemergency regulations adopted in accordance with the provisions of Article 5 (commencing with Section 11346), the finding of emergency shall include facts explaining the failure to address the situation through nonemergency regulations.

(3) The statement and the regulation or order of repeal shall be filed immediately with the office.

(c) Notwithstanding any other provision of law, no emergency regulation that is a building standard shall be filed, nor shall the building standard be effective, unless the building standard is submitted to the California Building Standards Commission, and is approved and filed pursuant to Sections 18937 and 18938 of the Health and Safety Code.

(d) The emergency regulation or order of repeal shall become effective upon filing or upon any later date specified by the state agency in a written instrument filed with, or as a part of, the regulation or order of repeal.

(e) No regulation, amendment, or order of repeal initially adopted as an emergency regulatory action shall remain in effect more than 180 days unless the adopting agency has complied with Sections 11346.2 to 11347.3, inclusive, either before adopting an emergency regulation or within the 180-day period. The adopting agency, prior to the expiration of the 180-day period, shall transmit to the office for filing with the Secretary of State the adopted regulation, amendment, or order of repeal, the rulemaking file, and a certification that Sections 11346.2 to 11347.3, inclusive, were complied with either before the emergency regulation was adopted or within the 180-day period.

(f) If an emergency amendment or order of repeal is filed and the adopting agency fails to comply with subdivision (e), the regulation as it existed prior to the emergency amendment or order of repeal shall thereupon become effective and after notice to the adopting agency by the office shall be reprinted in the California Code of Regulations.

(g) If a regulation is originally adopted and filed as an emergency and the adopting agency fails to comply with subdivision (e), this failure shall constitute a repeal of the regulation and after notice to the adopting agency by the office, shall be deleted.

(h) The office may approve not more than two readoptions, each for a period not to exceed 90 days, of an emergency regulation that is the same as or substantially equivalent to an emergency regulation previously adopted by that agency. Readoption shall be permitted only if the agency has made substantial progress and proceeded with diligence to comply with subdivision (e). **Leg.H.** Added Stats 1979 ch 567 §1, operative July 1, 1980. Amended Stats 1979 ch 1152 §12.4, operative July 1, 1980; Stats 1980 ch 204 §2, effective June 20, 1980, ch 1238 §1, effective September 29, 1980; Stats 1981 ch 274 §7, effective August 27, 1981, ch 865 §22; Stats 1982 ch 86 §3, effective March 1, 1982; Stats 1982 ch 86 §3, effective March 1, 1982, ch 1573 §2; Stats 1983 ch 797 §13; Stats 1984 ch 287 §45, effective July 6, 1984; Stats 1985 ch 956 §10, effective September 26, 1985; Stats 1987 ch 1375 §7; Stats 1994 ch 1039 §21 (AB 2531); Stats 2000 ch 1060 §21 (AB 1822); Stats 2006 ch 713 §3 (AB 1302), effective January 1, 2007.

§11346.2. Availability to public of copy of proposed regulation; Initial statement of reasons for proposed action

Every agency subject to this chapter shall prepare, submit to the office with the notice of the proposed action as described in Section 11346.5, and make available to the public upon request, all of the following:

(a) A copy of the express terms of the proposed regulation.

(1) The agency shall draft the regulation in plain, straightforward language, avoiding technical terms as much as possible, and using a coherent and easily readable style. The agency shall draft the regulation in plain English.

(2) The agency shall include a notation following the express terms of each California Code of Regulations section, listing the specific statutes or other provisions of law authorizing the adoption of the regulation and listing the specific statutes or other provisions of law being implemented, interpreted, or made specific by that section in the California Code of Regulations.

(3) The agency shall use underline or italics to indicate additions to, and strikeout to indicate deletions from, the California Code of Regulations.

(b) An initial statement of reasons for proposing the adoption, amendment, or repeal of a regulation. This statement of reasons shall include, but not be limited to, all of the following:

(1) A statement of the specific purpose of each adoption, amendment, or repeal, the problem the agency intends to address, and the rationale for the determination by the agency that each adoption, amendment, or repeal is reasonably necessary to carry out the purpose and address the problem for which it is proposed. The statement shall enumerate the benefits anticipated from the regulatory action, including the benefits or goals provided in the authorizing statute. These benefits may include, to the extent applicable, nonmonetary benefits such as the protection of public health and safety, worker safety, or the environment, the prevention of discrimination, the promotion of fairness or social equity, and the increase in openness and transparency in business and government, among other things. Where the adoption or amendment of a regulation would mandate the use of specific technologies or equipment, a statement of the reasons why the agency believes these mandates or prescriptive standards are required.

(2)(A) For a regulation that is not a major regulation, the economic impact assessment required by subdivision (b) of Section 11346.3.

(B) For a major regulation proposed on or after November 1, 2013, the standardized regulatory impact analysis required by subdivision (c) of Section 11346.3.

(3) An identification of each technical, theoretical, and empirical study, report, or similar document, if any, upon which the agency relies in proposing the adoption, amendment, or repeal of a regulation.

(4)(A) A description of reasonable alternatives to the regulation and the agency's reasons for rejecting those alternatives. Reasonable alternatives to be considered include, but are not limited to, alternatives that are proposed as less burdensome and equally effective in achieving the purposes of the regulation in a manner that ensures full compliance with the authorizing statute or other law being implemented or made specific by the proposed regulation. In the case of a regulation that would mandate the use of specific technologies or equipment or prescribe specific actions or procedures, the imposition of performance standards shall be considered as an alternative.

(B) A description of reasonable alternatives to the regulation that would lessen any adverse impact on small business and the agency's reasons for rejecting those alternatives.

(C) Notwithstanding subparagraph (A) or (B), an agency is not required to artificially construct alternatives or describe unreasonable alternatives.

(5)(A) Facts, evidence, documents, testimony, or other evidence on which the agency relies to support an initial determination that the action will not have a significant adverse economic impact on business.

(B)(i) If a proposed regulation is a building standard, the initial statement of reasons shall include the estimated cost of compliance, the estimated potential benefits, and the related assumptions used to determine the estimates.

(ii) The model codes adopted pursuant to Section 18928 of the Health and Safety Code shall be exempt from the requirements of this subparagraph. However, if an interested party has made a request in writing to the agency, at least 30 days before the submittal of the initial statement of reasons, to examine a specific section for purposes of estimating the cost of compliance and the potential benefits for that section, and including the related assumptions used to determine the estimates, then the agency shall comply with the requirements of this subparagraph with regard to that requested section.

(6) A department, board, or commission within the Environmental Protection Agency, the Natural Resources Agency, or the Office of the State Fire Marshal shall describe its efforts, in connection with a proposed rulemaking action, to avoid unnecessary duplication or conflicts with federal regulations contained in the Code of Federal Regulations addressing the same issues. These agencies may adopt regulations different from federal regulations contained in the Code of Federal Regulations addressing the same issues upon a finding of one or more of the following justifications:

(A) The differing state regulations are authorized by law.

(B) The cost of differing state regulations is justified by the benefit to human health, public safety, public welfare, or the environment.

(c) A state agency that adopts or amends a regulation mandated by federal law or regulations, the provisions of which are identical to a previously adopted or amended federal regulation, shall be deemed to have complied with subdivision (b) if a statement to the effect that a federally mandated regulation or amendment to a regulation is being proposed, together with a citation to where an explanation of the regulation can be found, is included in the notice of proposed adoption or amendment prepared pursuant to Section 11346.5. However, the agency shall comply fully with this chapter with respect to any provisions in the regulation that the agency proposes to adopt or amend that are different from the corresponding provisions of the federal regulation.

(d) This section shall be inoperative from January 1, 2012, until January 1, 2014. **Leg.H.** Added Stats 1994 ch 1039 §23 (AB 2531). Amended Stats 1995 ch 938 §15.3 (SB 523), operative January 1, 1996; Stats 2000 ch 1059 §9 (AB 505), ch 1060 §22.5 (AB 1822); Stats 2002 ch 389 §4 (AB 1857); Stats 2010 ch 398 §1 (AB 2738), effective September 27, 2010, inoperative January 1, 2012 until January 1, 2014; Stats 2011 ch 496 §3 (SB 617), effective January 1, 2012; Stats 2012 ch 471 §2 (AB 1612), effective January 1, 2013, inoperative January 1, 2012, until January 1, 2014; Stats 2013 ch 212 §2 (SB 401), effective January 1, 2014, inoperative January 1, 2014; Stats 2014 ch 779 §1 (AB 1711), effective January 1, 2015.

2012 Note: (a) It is the intent of the Legislature that the requirements of this act only apply to state agencies that have statutory authority to propose or adopt residential building standards.

(b) It is the intent of the Legislature that this act not apply to standards developed and adopted by the State Air Resources Board, air pollution control districts, or air quality management districts. Stats 2012 ch 471 (AB 1612) § 4.

Prior Law: Former Gov C §11346.2, similar to present Gov C §11343.4, was added Stats 1979 ch 567 §1, operative July 1, 1980, amended Stats 1979 ch 1152 §12.6, Stats 1980 ch 204 §3, effective June 20, 1980, Stats 1981 ch 274 §8, effective August 27, 1981, ch 865 §23, amended Stats 1984 ch 287 §46, effective July 6, 1984, Stats 1985 ch 956 §11, effective September 26, 1985, amended Stats 1987 ch 1375 §8, and repealed Stats 1994 ch 1039 §22.

Former Gov C §11346.2, relating to availability to public of copy of proposed regulation; Initial statement of reasons for proposed action, was added Stats 2010 ch 398 §2 (AB 2738), effective September 27, 2010, operative January 1, 2012, repealed January 1, 2014 and amended Stats 2011 ch 496 § 2 (SB 617), effective January 1, 2012; Stats 2012 ch 471 §1 (AB 1612), effective January 1, 2013, ch 766 §1 (SB 1520), effective September 29, 2012, operative until January 1, 2013, ch 766 §1.5 (SB 1520), effective September 29, 2012, operative January 1, 2013, repealed January 1, 2014.

§11346.3. Assessment of potential for adverse economic impact on businesses and individuals

(a) A state agency proposing to adopt, amend, or repeal any administrative regulation shall assess the potential for adverse economic impact on California business enterprises and individuals, avoiding the imposition of unnecessary or unreasonable regulations or reporting, recordkeeping, or compliance requirements. For purposes of this subdivision, assessing the potential for adverse economic impact shall require agencies, when proposing to adopt, amend, or repeal a regulation, to adhere to the following requirements, to the extent that these requirements do not conflict with other state or federal laws:

(1) The proposed adoption, amendment, or repeal of a regulation shall be based on adequate information concerning the need for, and consequences of, proposed governmental action.

(2) The state agency, before submitting a proposal to adopt, amend, or repeal a regulation to the office, shall consider the proposal's impact on business, with consideration of industries affected including the ability of California businesses to compete with businesses in other states. For purposes of evaluating the impact on the ability of California businesses to compete with businesses in other states, an agency shall consider, but not be limited to, information supplied by interested parties.

(3) An economic impact assessment prepared pursuant to this subdivision for a proposed regulation that is not a major regulation or that is a major regulation proposed before November 1, 2013, shall be prepared in accordance with subdivision (b), and shall be included in the initial statement of reasons as required by Section 11346.2. An economic assessment prepared pursuant to this subdivision for a major regulation proposed on or after November 1, 2013, shall be prepared in accordance with subdivision (c), and shall be included in the initial statement of reasons as required by Section 11346.2.

(b)(1) A state agency proposing to adopt, amend, or repeal a regulation that is not a major regulation or that is a major regulation proposed before November 1, 2013, shall prepare an economic impact assessment that assesses whether and to what extent it will affect the following:

(A) The creation or elimination of jobs within the state.

(B) The creation of new businesses or the elimination of existing businesses within the state.

(C) The expansion of businesses currently doing business within the state.

(D) The benefits of the regulation to the health and welfare of California residents, worker safety, and the state's environment.

(2) This subdivision does not apply to the University of California, the college named in Section 92200 of the Education Code, or the Fair Political Practices Commission.

(3) Information required from a state agency for the purpose of completing the assessment may come from existing state publications.

(4)(A) For purposes of conducting the economic impact assessment pursuant to this subdivision, a state agency may use the consolidated definition of small business in subparagraph (B) in order to determine the number of small businesses within the economy, a specific industry sector, or geographic region. The state agency shall clearly identify the use of the consolidated small business definition in its rulemaking package.

(B) For the exclusive purpose of undertaking the economic impact assessment, a "small business" means a business that is all of the following:

(i) Independently owned and operated.

(ii) Not dominant in its field of operation.

(iii) Has fewer than 100 employees.

(C) Subparagraph (A) shall not apply to a regulation adopted by the Department of Insurance that applies to an insurance company.

(c)(1) Each state agency proposing to adopt, amend, or repeal a major regulation on or after November 1, 2013, shall prepare a standardized regulatory impact analysis in the manner prescribed by the Department of Finance pursuant to Section 11346.36. The standardized regulatory impact analysis shall address all of the following:

(A) The creation or elimination of jobs within the state.

(B) The creation of new businesses or the elimination of existing businesses within the state.

(C) The competitive advantages or disadvantages for businesses currently doing business within the state.

(D) The increase or decrease of investment in the state.

(E) The incentives for innovation in products, materials, or processes.

(F) The benefits of the regulations, including, but not limited to, benefits to the health, safety, and welfare of California residents, worker safety, and the state's environment and quality of life, among any other benefits identified by the agency.

(2) This subdivision shall not apply to the University of California, the college named in Section 92200 of the Education Code, or the Fair Political Practices Commission.

(3) Information required from state agencies for the purpose of completing the analysis may be derived from existing state, federal, or academic publications.

(d) Any administrative regulation adopted on or after January 1, 1993, that requires a report shall not apply to businesses, unless the state agency adopting the regulation makes a finding that it is necessary for the health, safety, or welfare of the people of the state that the regulation apply to businesses.

(e) Analyses conducted pursuant to this section are intended to provide agencies and the public with tools to determine whether the regulatory proposal is an efficient and effective means of implementing the policy decisions enacted in statute or by other provisions of law in the least burdensome manner. Regulatory impact analyses shall inform the agencies and the public of the economic consequences of regulatory choices, not reassess statutory policy. The baseline for the regulatory analysis shall be the most cost-effective set of regulatory measures that are equally effective in achieving the purpose of the regulation in a manner that ensures full compliance with the authorizing statute or other law being implemented or made specific by the proposed regulation.

(f) Each state agency proposing to adopt, amend, or repeal a major regulation on or after November 1, 2013, and that has prepared a standardized regulatory impact analysis pursuant to subdivision (c), shall submit that analysis to the Department of Finance upon completion. The department shall comment, within 30 days of receiving that analysis, on the extent to which the analysis adheres to the regulations adopted pursuant to Section 11346.36. Upon receiving the comments from the department, the agency may update its analysis to reflect any comments received from the department and shall summarize the comments and the response of the agency along with a statement of the results of the updated analysis for the statement required by paragraph (10) of subdivision (a) of Section 11346.5. **Leg.H.** Added Stats 1994 ch 1039 §24 (AB 2531). Amended Stats 2000 ch 1059 §10 (AB 505), ch 1060 §23 (AB 1822); Stats 2011 ch 496 § 4 (SB 617), effective January 1, 2012; Stats 2012 ch 766 §2 (SB 1520), effective September 29, 2012; Stats 2014 ch 779 §2 (AB 1711), effective January 1, 2015; Stats 2016 ch 346 §1 (AB 1033), effective January 1, 2017; Stats 2022 ch 478 §59 (AB 1936), effective January 1, 2023.

§11346.36. Adoption of regulations for conducting standardized regulatory impact analyses; Submission; Publication

(a) Prior to November 1, 2013, the Department of Finance, in consultation with the office and other state agencies, shall adopt regulations for conducting the standardized regulatory impact analyses required by subdivision (c) of Section 11346.3.

(b) The regulations, at a minimum, shall assist the agencies in specifying the methodologies for:

(1) Assessing and determining the benefits and costs of the proposed regulation, expressed in monetary terms to the extent feasible and appropriate. Assessing the value of nonmonetary benefits such as the protection of public health and safety, worker safety, or the environment, the prevention of discrimination, the promotion of fairness or social equity, the increase in the openness and transparency of business and government and other nonmonetary benefits consistent with the statutory policy or other provisions of law.

(2) Comparing proposed regulatory alternatives with an established baseline so agencies can make analytical decisions for the adoption, amendment, or repeal of regulations necessary to determine that the proposed action is the most effective, or equally effective and less burdensome, alternative in carrying out the purpose for which the action is proposed, or the most cost-effective alternative to the economy and to affected private persons that would be equally effective in implementing the statutory policy or other provision of law.

(3) Determining the impact of a regulatory proposal on the state economy, businesses, and the public welfare, as described in subdivision (c) of Section 11346.3.

(4) Assessing the effects of a regulatory proposal on the General Fund and special funds of the state and affected local government agencies attributable to the proposed regulation.

(5) Determining the cost of enforcement and compliance to the agency and to affected business enterprises and individuals.

(6) Making the estimation described in Section 11342.548.

(c) To the extent required by this chapter, the department shall convene a public hearing or hearings and take public comment on any draft regulation. Representatives from state agencies and the public at large shall be afforded the opportunity to review and comment on the draft regulation before the regulation is adopted in final form.

(d) State agencies shall provide the Director of Finance and the office ready access to their records and full information and reasonable assistance in any matter requested for purposes of developing the regulations required by this section. This subdivision shall not be construed to authorize an agency to provide access to records required by statute to be kept confidential.

(e) The standardized regulatory impact analysis prepared by the proposing agency shall be included in the initial statement of reasons for the regulation as provided in subdivision (b) of Section 11346.2.

(f) On or before November 1, 2013, the department shall submit the adopted regulations to the Senate and Assembly Committees on Governmental Organization and shall publish the adopted regulations in the State Administrative Manual. **Leg.H.** Added Stats 2011 ch 496 §5 (SB 617), effective January 1, 2012.

§11346.4. Notice of proposed action

(a) At least 45 days prior to the hearing and close of the public comment period on the adoption, amendment, or repeal of a regulation, notice of the proposed action shall be:

(1) Mailed to every person who has filed a request for notice of regulatory actions with the state agency. Each state agency shall give a person filing a request for notice of regulatory actions the option of being notified of all proposed regulatory actions or being notified of regulatory actions concerning one or more particular programs of the state agency.

(2) In cases in which the state agency is within a state department, mailed or delivered to the director of the department.

(3) Mailed to a representative number of small business enterprises or their representatives that are likely to be affected by the proposed action. "Representative" for the purposes of this paragraph includes, but is not limited to, a trade association, industry association, professional association, or any other business group or association of any kind that represents a business enterprise or employees of a business enterprise.

(4) When appropriate in the judgment of the state agency, mailed to any person or group of persons whom the agency believes to be interested in the proposed action and published in the form and manner as the state agency shall prescribe.

(5) Published in the California Regulatory Notice Register as prepared by the office for each state agency's notice of regulatory action.

(6) Posted on the state agency's website if the agency has a website.

(b) The effective period of a notice issued pursuant to this section shall not exceed one year from the date thereof. If the adoption, amendment, or repeal of a regulation proposed in the notice is not completed and transmitted to the office within the period of one year, a notice of the proposed action shall again be issued pursuant to this article.

(c) Once the adoption, amendment, or repeal is completed and approved by the office, no further adoption, amendment, or repeal to the noticed regulation shall be made without subsequent notice being given.

(d) The office may refuse to publish a notice submitted to it if the agency has failed to comply with this article.

(e) The office shall make the California Regulatory Notice Register available to the public and state agencies at a nominal cost that is consistent with a policy of encouraging the widest possible notice distribution to interested persons.

(f) Where the form or manner of notice is prescribed by statute in any particular case, in addition to filing and mailing notice as required by this section, the notice shall be published, posted, mailed, filed, or otherwise publicized as prescribed by that statute. The failure to mail notice to any person as provided in this section shall not invalidate any action taken by a state agency pursuant to this article. **Leg.H.** Added Stats 1979 ch 567 §1, operative July 1, 1980. Amended Stats 1979 ch 1203 §5; Stats 1981 ch 865 §24; Stats 1982 ch 1083 §3; Stats 1985 ch 1044 §1; Stats 1987 ch 1375 §9; Stats 1994 ch 1039 §25 (AB 2531); Stats 2000 ch 1059 §11 (AB 505), effective January 1, 2001.

§11346.45. Increased public participation

(a) In order to increase public participation and improve the quality of regulations, state agencies proposing to adopt regulations shall, prior to publication of the notice required by Section 11346.5, involve parties who would be subject to the proposed regulations in public discussions regarding those proposed regulations, when the proposed regulations involve complex proposals or a large number of proposals that cannot easily be reviewed during the comment period.

(b) This section does not apply to a state agency in any instance where that state agency is required to implement federal law and regulations for which there is little or no discretion on the part of the state to vary.

(c) If the agency does not or cannot comply with the provisions of subdivision (a), it shall state the reasons for noncompliance with reasonable specificity in the rulemaking record.

(d) The provisions of this section shall not be subject to judicial review or to the provisions of Section 11349.1. **Leg.H.** Added Stats 2000 ch 1059 §12 (AB 505), effective January 1, 2001.

§11346.5. Contents of notice of proposed adoption, amendment, or repeal of regulation

(a) The notice of proposed adoption, amendment, or repeal of a regulation shall include the following:

(1) A statement of the time, place, and nature of proceedings for adoption, amendment, or repeal of the regulation.

(2) Reference to the authority under which the regulation is proposed and a reference to the particular code sections or other provisions of law that are being implemented, interpreted, or made specific.

(3) An informative digest drafted in plain English in a format similar to the Legislative Counsel's digest on legislative bills. The informative digest shall include the following:

(A) A concise and clear summary of existing laws and regulations, if any, related directly to the proposed action and of the effect of the proposed action.

(B) If the proposed action differs substantially from an existing comparable federal regulation or statute, a brief description of the significant differences and the full citation of the federal regulations or statutes.

(C) A policy statement overview explaining the broad objectives of the regulation and the specific benefits anticipated by the proposed adoption, amendment, or repeal of a regulation, including, to the extent applicable, nonmonetary benefits such as the protection of public health and safety, worker safety, or the environment, the prevention of discrimination, the promotion of fairness or social equity, and the increase in openness and transparency in business and government, among other things.

(D) An evaluation of whether the proposed regulation is inconsistent or incompatible with existing state regulations.

(4) Any other matters as are prescribed by statute applicable to the specific state agency or to any specific regulation or class of regulations.

(5) A determination as to whether the regulation imposes a mandate on local agencies or school districts and, if so, whether the mandate requires state reimbursement pursuant to Part 7 (commencing with Section 17500) of Division 4.

(6) An estimate, prepared in accordance with instructions adopted by the Department of Finance, of the cost or savings to any state agency, the cost to any local agency or school district that is required to be reimbursed under Part 7 (commencing with Section 17500) of Division 4, other nondiscretionary cost or savings imposed on local agencies, and the cost or savings in federal funding to the state.

For purposes of this paragraph, "cost or savings" means additional costs or savings, both direct and indirect, that a public agency necessarily incurs in reasonable compliance with regulations.

(7) If a state agency, in proposing to adopt, amend, or repeal any administrative regulation, makes an initial determination that the action may have a significant, statewide adverse economic impact directly affecting business, including the ability of California businesses to compete with businesses in other states, it shall include the following information in the notice of proposed action:

(A) Identification of the types of businesses that would be affected.

(B) A description of the projected reporting, recordkeeping, and other compliance requirements that would result from the proposed action.

(C) The following statement: "The (name of agency) has made an initial determination that the (adoption/amendment/repeal) of this regulation may have a significant, statewide adverse economic impact directly affecting business, including the ability of California businesses to compete with businesses in other states. The (name of agency) (has/has not) considered proposed alternatives that would lessen any adverse economic impact on business and invites you to submit proposals. Submissions may include the following considerations:

(i) The establishment of differing compliance or reporting requirements or timetables that take into account the resources available to businesses.

(ii) Consolidation or simplification of compliance and reporting requirements for businesses.

(iii) The use of performance standards rather than prescriptive standards.

(iv) Exemption or partial exemption from the regulatory requirements for businesses."

(8) If a state agency, in adopting, amending, or repealing any administrative regulation, makes an initial determination that the action will not have a significant, statewide adverse economic impact directly affecting business, including the ability of California businesses to compete with businesses in other states, it shall make a declaration to that effect in the notice of proposed action. In making this declaration, the agency shall provide in the record facts, evidence, documents, testimony, or other evidence upon which the agency relies to support its initial determination.

An agency's initial determination and declaration that a proposed adoption, amendment, or repeal of a regulation may have or will not have a significant, adverse impact on businesses, including the ability of California businesses to compete with businesses in other states, shall not be grounds for the office to refuse to publish the notice of proposed action.

(9) A description of all cost impacts, known to the agency at the time the notice of proposed action is submitted to the office, that a representative private person or business would necessarily incur in reasonable compliance with the proposed action.

If no cost impacts are known to the agency, it shall state the following: "The agency is not aware of any cost impacts that a representative private person or business would necessarily incur in reasonable compliance with the proposed action."

(10) A statement of the results of the economic impact assessment required by subdivision (b) of Section 11346.3 or the standardized regulatory impact analysis if required by subdivision (c) of Section 11346.3, a summary of any comments submitted to the agency pursuant to subdivision (f) of Section 11346.3 and the agency's response to those comments.

(11) The finding prescribed by subdivision (d) of Section 11346.3, if required.

(12)(A) A statement that the action would have a significant effect on housing costs, if a state agency, in adopting, amending, or repealing any administrative regulation, makes an initial determination that the action would have that effect.

(B) The agency officer designated in paragraph (14) shall make available to the public, upon request, the agency's evaluation, if any, of the effect of the proposed regulatory action on housing costs.

(C) The statement described in subparagraph (A) shall also include the estimated costs of compliance and potential benefits of a building standard, if any, that were included in the initial statement of reasons.

(D) For purposes of model codes adopted pursuant to Section 18928 of the Health and Safety Code, the agency shall comply with the requirements of this paragraph only if an interested party has made a request to the agency to examine a specific section for purposes of estimating the costs of compliance and potential benefits for that section, as described in Section 11346.2.

(13) A statement that the adopting agency must determine that no reasonable alternative considered by the agency or that has otherwise been identified and brought to the attention of the agency would be more effective in carrying out the purpose for which the action is proposed, would be as effective and less burdensome to affected private persons than

the proposed action, or would be more cost effective to affected private persons and equally effective in implementing the statutory policy or other provision of law. For a major regulation, as defined by Section 11342.548, proposed on or after November 1, 2013, the statement shall be based, in part, upon the standardized regulatory impact analysis of the proposed regulation, as required by Section 11346.3, as well as upon the benefits of the proposed regulation identified pursuant to subparagraph (C) of paragraph (3).

(14) The name and telephone number of the agency representative and designated backup contact person to whom inquiries concerning the proposed administrative action may be directed.

(15) The date by which comments submitted in writing must be received to present statements, arguments, or contentions in writing relating to the proposed action in order for them to be considered by the state agency before it adopts, amends, or repeals a regulation.

(16) Reference to the fact that the agency proposing the action has prepared a statement of the reasons for the proposed action, has available all the information upon which its proposal is based, and has available the express terms of the proposed action, pursuant to subdivision (b).

(17) A statement that if a public hearing is not scheduled, any interested person or his or her duly authorized representative may request, no later than 15 days prior to the close of the written comment period, a public hearing pursuant to Section 11346.8.

(18) A statement indicating that the full text of a regulation changed pursuant to Section 11346.8 will be available for at least 15 days prior to the date on which the agency adopts, amends, or repeals the resulting regulation.

(19) A statement explaining how to obtain a copy of the final statement of reasons once it has been prepared pursuant to subdivision (a) of Section 11346.9.

(20) If the agency maintains an Internet Web site or other similar forum for the electronic publication or distribution of written material, a statement explaining how materials published or distributed through that forum can be accessed.

(21) If the proposed regulation is subject to Section 11346.6, a statement that the agency shall provide, upon request, a description of the proposed changes included in the proposed action, in the manner provided by Section 11346.6, to accommodate a person with a visual or other disability for which effective communication is required under state or federal law and that providing the description of proposed changes may require extending the period of public comment for the proposed action.

(b) The agency representative designated in paragraph (14) of subdivision (a) shall make available to the public upon request the express terms of the proposed action. The representative shall also make available to the public upon request the location of public records, including reports, documentation, and other materials, related to the proposed action. If the representative receives an inquiry regarding the proposed action that the representative cannot answer, the representative shall refer the inquiry to another person in the agency for a prompt response.

(c) This section shall not be construed in any manner that results in the invalidation of a regulation because of the alleged inadequacy of the notice content or the summary or cost estimates, or the alleged inadequacy or inaccuracy of the housing cost estimates, if there has been substantial compliance with those requirements. **Leg.H.** Added Stats 1979 ch 567 §1, operative July 1, 1980. Amended Stats 1979 ch 1203 §6; Stats 1981 ch 865 §25; Stats 1982 ch 327 §30, effective June 30, 1982; Stats 1983 ch 797 §15; Stats 1986 ch 879 §1; Stats 1987 ch 1375 §10; Stats 1993 ch 1046 §1 (AB 1144); Stats 1994 ch 1039 §26 (AB 2531); Stats 2000 ch 1059 §13 (AB 505), ch 1060 §24.5 (AB 1822); Stats 2002 ch 389 §5 (AB 1857); Stats 2011 ch 495 § 2 (AB 410), ch 496 § 6 (SB 617), effective January 1, 2012; Stats 2012 ch 471 §3 (AB 1612), effective January 1, 2013, ch 723 §1.5 (AB 2041), effective January 1, 2013.

§11346.6. Duty of agency, upon request from person with certain disability, to provide narrative description of proposed regulation

(a) This section shall only apply to the following proposed regulations:

(1) Regulations proposed by the Department of Rehabilitation.

(2) Regulations that must be submitted to the California Building Standards Commission that pertain to disability access compliance, including, but not limited to, regulations proposed by the State Fire Marshal, the Department of Housing and Community Development, the Division of the State Architect, and the California Commission on Disability Access.

(3) Regulations proposed by the State Department of Education that pertain to special education.

(4) Regulations proposed by the State Department of Health Care Services that pertain to the Medi-Cal program.

(b) Upon request from a person with a visual disability or other disability for which effective communication is required under state or federal law, the agency shall provide that person a narrative description of the additions to, and deletions from, the California Code of Regulations or other publication. The description shall identify each addition to or deletion from the California Code of Regulations by reference to the subdivision, paragraph, subparagraph, clause, or subclause within the proposed regulation containing the addition or deletion. The description shall provide the express language proposed to be added to or deleted from the California Code of Regulations or other publication and any portion of the surrounding language necessary to understand the change in a manner that allows for accurate translation by reading software used by the visually impaired.

(c) The agency shall provide the information described in subdivision (b) within 10 business days, unless the agency determines that compliance with this requirement would be impractical and notifies the requester of the date on which the information will be provided.

(d) Notwithstanding any other law, if information is provided to a requester pursuant to this section, the agency shall provide that requester at least 45 days from the date upon which the information was provided to the requester to submit a public comment regarding the proposed regulation. The agency shall not take final action to adopt the regulation until the requester has submitted a public comment or the extended 45-day comment period expires, whichever occurs first.

(e) The requirements imposed pursuant to subdivisions (b) to (d), inclusive, for a proposed regulation described in subdivision (a) shall apply to an agency only for purposes of that proposed regulation until the proposed regulation is filed with the Secretary of State or until the agency otherwise concludes the regulatory adoption process.

(f)(1) Not later than February 1, 2014, an agency that adopted a proposed regulation subject to the requirements of this section shall submit a report, for both the 2012 and 2013 calendar years, to the Governor, the fiscal committee in each house of the Legislature, and the appropriate policy committee in each house of the Legislature, that specifies the number of requests submitted for a narrative description of a proposed regulation, and the number of narrative descriptions actually provided pursuant to this section.

(2) The report shall be submitted to the Legislature in the manner required pursuant to Section 9795.

(3) The reporting requirement imposed by this subdivision shall become inoperative on February 1, 2018, as required pursuant to Section 10231.5.

(4) It is the intent of the Legislature to evaluate the reports submitted pursuant to this subdivision to determine whether the requirements of this section should be applied to all regulations adopted by all agencies. **Leg.H.** Added Stats 2011 ch 495 §3 (AB 410), effective January 1, 2012.

2011 Note: Nothing in this act shall be construed to limit the duty of a state agency to meet its obligations pursuant to Title II of the Americans with Disabilities Act of 1990 (42 U.S.C. Sec. 12131 et seq.) or Section 11135 of the Government Code to take appropriate steps to ensure that communications with participants and members of the public with disabilities are as effective as communications with others. Stats 2011 ch 495 (AB 410) § 4.

Prior Law: Former Gov C §11346.6, relating to the adoption of regulations differing from Code of Federal Regulations, was added Stats 1993 ch 1046 §2, and repealed Stats 1995 ch 938 §15.5, operative January 1, 1996.

§11346.7. Link on website

The office shall maintain a link on its website to the website maintained by the Small Business Advocate that also includes the telephone number of the Small Business Advocate. **Leg.H.** Added Stats 2000 ch 1059 §17 (AB 505), effective January 1, 2001.

Prior Law: Former Gov C §11346.7, similar to present Gov C §§11346.2, 11346.9, was added Stats 1979 ch 567 §1, operative July 1, 1980, amended Stats 1980 ch 204 §5, effective June 20, 1980, ch 1238 §3, effective September 29, 1980, Stats 1981 ch 865 §27; Stats 1982 ch 327 §34, effective June 30, 1982, ch 1083 §5, ch 1573 §3.5, Stats 1984 ch 1444 §4, effective September 26, 1984, Stats 1985 ch

1044 §2, Stats 1986 ch 205 §2, Stats 1987 ch 1375 §14, and repealed Stats 1994 ch 1039 §31.

§11346.8. Hearing

(a) If a public hearing is held, both oral and written statements, arguments, or contentions, shall be permitted. The agency may impose reasonable limitations on oral presentations. If a public hearing is not scheduled, the state agency shall, consistent with Section 11346.4, afford any interested person or his or her duly authorized representative, the opportunity to present statements, arguments or contentions in writing. In addition, a public hearing shall be held if, no later than 15 days prior to the close of the written comment period, an interested person or his or her duly authorized representative submits in writing to the state agency, a request to hold a public hearing. The state agency shall, to the extent practicable, provide notice of the time, date, and place of the hearing by mailing the notice to every person who has filed a request for notice thereby with the state agency. The state agency shall consider all relevant matter presented to it before adopting, amending, or repealing any regulation.

(b) In any hearing under this section, the state agency or its duly authorized representative shall have authority to administer oaths or affirmations. An agency may continue or postpone a hearing from time to time to the time and at the place as it determines. If a hearing is continued or postponed, the state agency shall provide notice to the public as to when it will be resumed or rescheduled.

(c) No state agency may adopt, amend, or repeal a regulation which has been changed from that which was originally made available to the public pursuant to Section 11346.5, unless the change is (1) nonsubstantial or solely grammatical in nature, or (2) sufficiently related to the original text that the public was adequately placed on notice that the change could result from the originally proposed regulatory action. If a sufficiently related change is made, the full text of the resulting adoption, amendment, or repeal, with the change clearly indicated, shall be made available to the public for at least 15 days before the agency adopts, amends, or repeals the resulting regulation. Any written comments received regarding the change must be responded to in the final statement of reasons required by Section 11346.9.

(d) No state agency shall add any material to the record of the rulemaking proceeding after the close of the public hearing or comment period, unless the agency complies with Section 11347.1. This subdivision does not apply to material prepared pursuant to Section 11346.9.

(e) If a comment made at a public hearing raises a new issue concerning a proposed regulation and a member of the public requests additional time to respond to the new issue before the state agency takes final action, it is the intent of the Legislature that rulemaking agencies consider granting the request for additional time if, under the circumstances, granting the request is practical and does not unduly delay action on the regulation. **Leg.H.** Added Stats 1981 ch 865 §29. Amended Stats 1981 ch 1091 §2; Stats 1982 ch 86 §4, effective March 1, 1982; Stats 1983 ch 797 §19; Stats 1987 ch 1375 §15; Stats 1994 ch 1039 §32 (AB 2531); Stats 2000 ch 1059 §16 (AB 505), ch 1060 §26.5 (AB 1822), effective January 1, 2001.

Prior Law: Former Gov C §11346.8, similar to the present section, was added Stats 1979 ch 567 §1, operative July 1, 1980, amended Stats 1979 ch 1203 §7, Stats 1980 ch 151 §1, and repealed Stats 1981 ch 865 §28.

§11346.9. Final statements of reasons for proposing adoption or amendment of regulation; Informative digest

Every agency subject to this chapter shall do the following:

(a) Prepare and submit to the office with the adopted regulation a final statement of reasons that shall include all of the following:

(1) An update of the information contained in the initial statement of reasons. If the update identifies any data or any technical, theoretical or empirical study, report, or similar document on which the agency is relying in proposing the adoption, amendment, or repeal of a regulation that was not identified in the initial statement of reasons, or which was otherwise not identified or made available for public review prior to the close of the public comment period, the agency shall comply with Section 11347.1.

(2) A determination as to whether adoption, amendment, or repeal of the regulation imposes a mandate on local agencies or school districts. If the determination is that adoption, amendment, or repeal of the regulation would impose a local mandate, the agency shall state whether the mandate is reimbursable pursuant to Part 7 (commencing with Section 17500) of Division 4. If the agency finds that the mandate is not reimbursable, it shall state the reasons for that finding.

(3) A summary of each objection or recommendation made regarding the specific adoption, amendment, or repeal proposed, together with an explanation of how the proposed action has been changed to accommodate each objection or recommendation, or the reasons for making no change. This requirement applies only to objections or recommendations specifically directed at the agency's proposed action or to the procedures followed by the agency in proposing or adopting the action. The agency may aggregate and summarize repetitive or irrelevant comments as a group, and may respond to repetitive comments or summarily dismiss irrelevant comments as a group. For the purposes of this paragraph, a comment is "irrelevant" if it is not specifically directed at the agency's proposed action or to the procedures followed by the agency in proposing or adopting the action.

(4) A determination with supporting information that no alternative considered by the agency would be more effective in carrying out the purpose for which the regulation is proposed, would be as effective and less burdensome to affected private persons than the adopted regulation, or would be more cost effective to affected private persons and equally effective in implementing the statutory policy or other provision of law. For a major regulation, as defined by Section 11342.548 proposed on or after November 1, 2013, the determination shall be based, in part, upon the standardized regulatory impact analysis of the proposed regulation and, in part, upon the statement of benefits identified in subparagraph (C) of paragraph (3) of subdivision (a) of Section 11346.5.

(5) An explanation setting forth the reasons for rejecting any proposed alternatives that would lessen the adverse economic impact on small businesses. The agency shall include, as supporting information, the standardized regulatory impact analysis for a major regulation, if required by subdivision (c) of Section 11346.3, as well as the benefits of the proposed regulation identified pursuant to paragraph (3) of subdivision (a) of Section 11346.5.

(b) Prepare and submit to the office with the adopted regulation an updated informative digest containing a clear and concise summary of the immediately preceding laws and regulations, if any, relating directly to the adopted, amended, or repealed regulation and the effect of the adopted, amended, or repealed regulation. The informative digest shall be drafted in a format similar to the Legislative Counsel's Digest on legislative bills.

(c) A state agency that adopts or amends a regulation mandated by federal law or regulations, the provisions of which are identical to a previously adopted or amended federal regulation, shall be deemed to have complied with this section if a statement to the effect that a federally mandated regulation or amendment to a regulation is being proposed, together with a citation to where an explanation of the provisions of the regulation can be found, is included in the notice of proposed adoption or amendment prepared pursuant to Section 11346.5. However, the agency shall comply fully with this chapter with respect to any provisions in the regulation which the agency proposes to adopt or amend that are different from the corresponding provisions of the federal regulation.

(d) If an agency determines that a requirement of this section can be satisfied by reference to an agency statement made pursuant to Sections 11346.2 to 11346.5, inclusive, the agency may satisfy the requirement by incorporating the relevant statement by reference. **Leg.H.** Added Stats 1994 ch 1039 §33 (AB 2531). Amended Stats 2000 ch 1060 §27 (AB 1822); Stats 2011 ch 496 § 7 (SB 617), effective January 1, 2012.

Prior Law: Former Gov C §11346.9, relating to economic impact statement, was added Stats 1983 ch 1080 §2, operative July 1, 1984, ch 1212 §1, operative July 1, 1984 and repealed December 31, 1985, by its own terms.

§11347. Decision not to proceed with proposed action

(a) If, after publication of a notice of proposed action pursuant to Section 11346.4, but before the notice of proposed action becomes ineffective pursuant to subdivision (b) of that section, an agency decides not to proceed with the proposed action, it shall deliver notice of its decision to the office for publication in the California Regulatory Notice Register.

(b) Publication of a notice under this section terminates the effect of the notice of proposed action referred to in the notice. Nothing in this section precludes an agency from proposing a new regulatory action that is similar or identical to a regulatory action that was previously the subject of a notice published under this section. **Leg.H.** Added Stats 2000 ch 1059

§17 (AB 505), ch 1060 §28 (AB 1822), effective January 1, 2001.

2000 Note: Identical versions of Section 11347 were added by 2000 chs. 1059 and 1060.

Prior Law: Former Gov C §11347, similar to present Gov C §11340.6, was added Stats 1979 ch 567 §1, operative July 1, 1980, and repealed Stats 1994 ch 1039 §34.

§11347.1. Addition to rulemaking file

(a) An agency that adds any technical, theoretical, or empirical study, report, or similar document to the rulemaking file after publication of the notice of proposed action and relies on the document in proposing the action shall make the document available as required by this section.

(b) At least 15 calendar days before the proposed action is adopted by the agency, the agency shall mail to all of the following persons a notice identifying the added document and stating the place and business hours that the document is available for public inspection:

(1) Persons who testified at the public hearing.

(2) Persons who submitted written comments at the public hearing.

(3) Persons whose comments were received by the agency during the public comment period.

(4) Persons who requested notification from the agency of the availability of changes to the text of the proposed regulation.

(c) The document shall be available for public inspection at the location described in the notice for at least 15 calendar days before the proposed action is adopted by the agency.

(d) Written comments on the document or information received by the agency during the availability period shall be summarized and responded to in the final statement of reasons as provided in Section 11346.9.

(e) The rulemaking file shall contain a statement confirming that the agency complied with the requirements of this section and stating the date on which the notice was mailed.

(f) If there are no persons in categories listed in subdivision (b), then the rulemaking file shall contain a confirming statement to that effect. **Leg.H.** Added Stats 2000 ch 1060 §29 (AB 1822), effective January 1, 2001.

Prior Law: Former Gov C §11347.1, similar to Gov C §11340.7, was added Stats 1979 ch 567 §1, operative July 1, 1980. Amended Stats 1980 ch 1238 §4, effective September 29, 1980; Stats 1991 ch 899 §2 (SB 327), effective October 12, 1991, and repealed Stats 1994 ch 1039 §35 (AB 2531).

§11347.3. File of rulemaking; Contents and availability of file

(a) Every agency shall maintain a file of each rulemaking that shall be deemed to be the record for that rulemaking proceeding. Commencing no later than the date that the notice of the proposed action is published in the California Regulatory Notice Register, and during all subsequent periods of time that the file is in the agency's possession, the agency shall make the file available to the public for inspection and copying during regular business hours.

(b) The rulemaking file shall include:

(1) Copies of any petitions received from interested persons proposing the adoption, amendment, or repeal of the regulation, and a copy of any decision provided for by subdivision (d) of Section 11340.7, which grants a petition in whole or in part.

(2) All published notices of proposed adoption, amendment, or repeal of the regulation, and an updated informative digest, the initial statement of reasons, and the final statement of reasons.

(3) The determination, together with the supporting data required by paragraph (5) of subdivision (a) of Section 11346.5.

(4) The determination, together with the supporting data required by paragraph (8) of subdivision (a) of Section 11346.5.

(5) The estimate, together with the supporting data and calculations, required by paragraph (6) of subdivision (a) of Section 11346.5.

(6) All data and other factual information, any studies or reports, and written comments submitted to the agency in connection with the adoption, amendment, or repeal of the regulation.

(7) All data and other factual information, technical, theoretical, and empirical studies or reports, if any, on which the agency is relying in the adoption, amendment, or repeal of a regulation, including any economic impact assessment or standardized regulatory impact analysis as required by Section 11346.3.

(8) A transcript, recording, or minutes of any public hearing connected with the adoption, amendment, or repeal of the regulation.

(9) The date on which the agency made the full text of the proposed regulation available to the public for 15 days prior to the adoption, amendment, or repeal of the regulation, if required to do so by subdivision (c) of Section 11346.8.

(10) The text of regulations as originally proposed and the modified text of regulations, if any, that were made available to the public prior to adoption.

(11) Any other information, statement, report, or data that the agency is required by law to consider or prepare in connection with the adoption, amendment, or repeal of a regulation.

(12) An index or table of contents that identifies each item contained in the rulemaking file. The index or table of contents shall include an affidavit or a declaration under penalty of perjury in the form specified by Section 2015.5 of the Code of Civil Procedure by the agency official who has compiled the rulemaking file, specifying the date upon which the record was closed, and that the file or the copy, if submitted, is complete.

(c) Every agency shall submit to the office with the adopted regulation, the rulemaking file or a complete copy of the rulemaking file.

(d) The rulemaking file shall be made available by the agency to the public, and to the courts in connection with the review of the regulation.

(e) Upon filing a regulation with the Secretary of State pursuant to Section 11349.3, the office shall return the related rulemaking file to the agency, after which no item contained in the file shall be removed, altered, or destroyed or otherwise disposed of. The agency shall maintain the file unless it elects to transmit the file to the State Archives pursuant to subdivision (f).

(f) The agency may transmit the rulemaking file to the State Archives. The file shall include instructions that the Secretary of State shall not remove, alter, or destroy or otherwise dispose of any item contained in the file. Pursuant to Section 12223.5, the Secretary of State may designate a time for the delivery of the rulemaking file to the State Archives in consideration of document processing or storage limitations. **Leg.H.** Added Stats 1979 ch 567 §1, operative July 1, 1980. Amended Stats 1979 ch 1203 §8; Stats 1981 ch 865 §31; Stats 1982 ch 327 §35, effective June 30, 1982; Stats 1983 ch 797 §21; Stats 1984 ch 1444 §5, effective September 26, 1984; Stats 1987 ch 1375 §16; Stats 1991 ch 899 §3 (SB 327), effective October 12, 1991; Stats 1994 ch 1039 §36 (AB 2531); Stats 1996 ch 928 §3 (SB 1507); Stats 2000 ch 1060 §30 (AB 1822); 2011 ch 496 §8 (SB 617), effective January 1, 2012.

§11348. Rulemaking records

Each agency subject to this chapter shall keep its rulemaking records on all of that agency's pending rulemaking actions, in which the notice has been published in the California Regulatory Notice Register, current and in one central location. **Leg.H.** Added Stats 2000 ch 1059 §19 (AB 505), effective January 1, 2001.

ARTICLE 6
Review of Proposed Regulations

§11349. Definitions

The following definitions govern the interpretation of this chapter:

(a) "Necessity" means the record of the rulemaking proceeding demonstrates by substantial evidence the need for a regulation to effectuate the purpose of the statute, court decision, or other provision of law that the regulation implements, interprets, or makes specific, taking into account the totality of the record. For purposes of this standard, evidence includes, but is not limited to, facts, studies, and expert opinion.

(b) "Authority" means the provision of law which permits or obligates the agency to adopt, amend, or repeal a regulation.

(c) "Clarity" means written or displayed so that the meaning of regulations will be easily understood by those persons directly affected by them.

(d) "Consistency" means being in harmony with, and not in conflict with or contradictory to, existing statutes, court decisions, or other provisions of law.

(e) "Reference" means the statute, court decision, or other provision of law which the agency implements, interprets, or makes specific by adopting, amending, or repealing a regulation.

(f) "Nonduplication" means that a regulation does not serve the same purpose as a state or federal statute or another regulation. This standard requires that an agency proposing to amend or adopt a regulation must identify any state or federal statute or regulation which is overlapped or duplicated by the proposed regulation and justify any overlap or duplica-

tion. This standard is not intended to prohibit state agencies from printing relevant portions of enabling legislation in regulations when the duplication is necessary to satisfy the clarity standard in paragraph (3) of subdivision (a) of Section 11349.1. This standard is intended to prevent the indiscriminate incorporation of statutory language in a regulation.
Leg.H. Added Stats 1979 ch 567 §1, operative July 1, 1980. Amended Stats 1981 ch 983 §4; Stats 1982 ch 1573 §4; Stats 1983 ch 797 §22; Stats 1985 ch 1044 §3; Stats 1994 ch 1039 §39 (AB 2531); Stats 2000 ch 1060 §31 (AB 1822), effective January 1, 2001.

§11349.1. Review of regulations; Regulations to govern review process; Return to adopting agency

(a) The office shall review all regulations adopted, amended, or repealed pursuant to the procedure specified in Article 5 (commencing with Section 11346) and submitted to it for publication in the California Code of Regulations Supplement and for transmittal to the Secretary of State and make determinations using all of the following standards:

(1) Necessity.
(2) Authority.
(3) Clarity.
(4) Consistency.
(5) Reference.
(6) Nonduplication.

In reviewing regulations pursuant to this section, the office shall restrict its review to the regulation and the record of the rulemaking proceeding. The office shall approve the regulation or order of repeal if it complies with the standards set forth in this section and with this chapter.

(b) In reviewing proposed regulations for the criteria in subdivision (a), the office may consider the clarity of the proposed regulation in the context of related regulations already in existence.

(c) The office shall adopt regulations governing the procedures it uses in reviewing regulations submitted to it. The regulations shall provide for an orderly review and shall specify the methods, standards, presumptions, and principles the office uses, and the limitations it observes, in reviewing regulations to establish compliance with the standards specified in subdivision (a). The regulations adopted by the office shall ensure that it does not substitute its judgment for that of the rulemaking agency as expressed in the substantive content of adopted regulations.

(d) The office shall return any regulation subject to this chapter to the adopting agency if any of the following occur:

(1) The adopting agency has not prepared the estimate required by paragraph (6) of subdivision (a) of Section 11346.5 and has not included the data used and calculations made and the summary report of the estimate in the file of the rulemaking.

(2) The agency has not complied with Section 11346.3. "Noncompliance" means that the agency failed to complete the economic impact assessment or standardized regulatory impact analysis required by Section 11346.3 or failed to include the assessment or analysis in the file of the rulemaking proceeding as required by Section 11347.3.

(3) The adopting agency has prepared the estimate required by paragraph (6) of subdivision (a) of Section 11346.5, the estimate indicates that the regulation will result in a cost to local agencies or school districts that is required to be reimbursed under Part 7 (commencing with Section 17500) of Division 4, and the adopting agency fails to do any of the following:

(A) Cite an item in the Budget Act for the fiscal year in which the regulation will go into effect as the source from which the Controller may pay the claims of local agencies or school districts.

(B) Cite an accompanying bill appropriating funds as the source from which the Controller may pay the claims of local agencies or school districts.

(C) Attach a letter or other documentation from the Department of Finance which states that the Department of Finance has approved a request by the agency that funds be included in the Budget Bill for the next following fiscal year to reimburse local agencies or school districts for the costs mandated by the regulation.

(D) Attach a letter or other documentation from the Department of Finance which states that the Department of Finance has authorized the augmentation of the amount available for expenditure under the agency's appropriation in the Budget Act which is for reimbursement pursuant to Part 7 (commencing with Section 17500) of Division 4 to local agencies or school districts from the unencumbered balances of other appropriations in the Budget Act and that this augmentation is sufficient to reimburse local agencies or school districts for their costs mandated by the regulation.

(4) The proposed regulation conflicts with an existing state regulation and the agency has not identified the manner in which the conflict may be resolved.

(5) The agency did not make the alternatives determination as required by paragraph (4) of subdivision (a) of Section 11346.9.

(e) The office shall notify the Department of Finance of all regulations returned pursuant to subdivision (d).

(f) The office shall return a rulemaking file to the submitting agency if the file does not comply with subdivisions (a) and (b) of Section 11347.3. Within three state working days of the receipt of a rulemaking file, the office shall notify the submitting agency of any deficiency identified. If no notice of deficiency is mailed to the adopting agency within that time, a rulemaking file shall be deemed submitted as of the date of its original receipt by the office. A rulemaking file shall not be deemed submitted until each deficiency identified under this subdivision has been corrected.

(g) Notwithstanding any other law, return of the regulation to the adopting agency by the office pursuant to this section is the exclusive remedy for a failure to comply with subdivision (c) of Section 11346.3 or paragraph (10) of subdivision (a) of Section 11346.5. **Leg.H.** Added Stats 1979 ch 567 §1, operative July 1, 1980. Amended Stats 1979 ch 1152 §12.8, operative July 1, 1980; Stats 1981 ch 865 §32; Stats 1982 ch 86 §5, effective March 1, 1982, ch 327 §36, effective June 30, 1982, ch 1544 §1, ch 1573 §5; Stats 1985 ch 1044 §4; Stats 1987 ch 1375 §17.5; Stats 1991 ch 794 §4 (AB 2061); Stats 1994 ch 1039 §40 (AB 2531); Stats 2000 ch 1060 §32 (AB 1822); Stats 2011 ch 496 § 9 (SB 617), effective January 1, 2012.

§11349.1.5. Review of standardized regulatory impact analyses; Report; Notice of noncompliance

(a) The Department of Finance and the office shall, from time to time, review the standardized regulatory impact analyses required by subdivision (c) of Section 11346.3 and submitted to the office pursuant to Section 11347.3, for adherence to the regulations adopted by the department pursuant to Section 11346.36.

(b) On or before November 1, 2015, the office shall submit to the Senate and Assembly Committees on Governmental Organization a report describing the extent to which submitted standardized regulatory impact analyses for proposed major regulations adhere to the regulations adopted pursuant to Section 11346.36. The report shall include a discussion of agency adherence to the regulations as well as a comparison between various state agencies on the question of adherence. The report may also include any recommendations from the office for actions the Legislature might consider for improving state agency performance.

(c) In addition to the report required by subdivision (b), the office may notify the Legislature of noncompliance by a state agency with the regulations adopted pursuant to Section 11346.36, in any manner or form determined by the office. **Leg.H.** Added Stats 2011 ch 496 §10 (SB 617), effective January 1, 2012.

§11349.2. Adding material to file

An agency may add material to a rulemaking file that has been submitted to the office for review pursuant to this article if addition of the material does not violate other requirements of this chapter. **Leg.H.** Added Stats 2000 ch 1060 §33 (AB 1822), effective January 1, 2001.

Prior Law: Former Gov C §11349.2, relating to the repeal of a regulation by a state agency, was added Stats 1979 ch 567 §1, operative July 1, 1980, amended Stats 1982 ch 1573 §6, and repealed Stats 1987 ch 1375 §18.

§11349.3. Time for review of regulations; Procedure on disapproval; Return of regulations

(a) The office shall either approve a regulation submitted to it for review and transmit it to the Secretary of State for filing or disapprove it within 30 working days after the regulation has been submitted to the office for review. If the office fails to act within 30 days, the regulation shall be deemed to have been approved and the office shall transmit it to the Secretary of State for filing.

(b) If the office disapproves a regulation, it shall return it to the adopting agency within the 30-day period specified in subdivision (a) accompanied by a notice specifying the reasons for disapproval. Within seven calendar days of the issuance of the notice, the office shall provide the adopting agency with a written decision detailing the reasons for disapproval. No regulation shall be disapproved except for failure to comply with the standards set forth in Section 11349.1 or for failure to comply with this chapter.

(c) If an agency determines, on its own initiative, that a regulation submitted pursuant to subdivision (a) should be returned by the office prior to completion of the office's review, it may request the return of the regulation. All requests for the return of a regulation shall be memorialized in writing by the submitting agency no later than one week following the request. Any regulation returned pursuant to this subdivision shall be resubmitted to the office for review within the one-year period specified in subdivision (b) of Section 11346.4 or shall comply with Article 5 (commencing with Section 11346) prior to resubmission.

(d) The office shall not initiate the return of a regulation pursuant to subdivision (c) as an alternative to disapproval pursuant to subdivision (b). **Leg.H.** Added Stats 1979 ch 567 §1, operative July 1, 1980. Amended Stats 1981 ch 865 §33; Stats 1982 ch 1236 §1; Stats 1985 ch 1044 §5; Stats 1987 ch 1375 §19; Stats 1991 ch 794 §5 (AB 2061); Stats 1992 ch 1306 §2 (AB 3511), effective January 1, 1993.

§11349.4. Rewriting and resubmission of regulation; Review

(a) A regulation returned to an agency because of failure to meet the standards of Section 11349.1, because of an agency's failure to comply with this chapter may be rewritten and resubmitted within 120 days of the agency's receipt of the written opinion required by subdivision (b) of Section 11349.3 without complying with the notice and public hearing requirements of Sections 11346.4, 11346.5, and 11346.8 unless the substantive provisions of the regulation have been significantly changed. If the regulation has been significantly changed or was not submitted within 120 days of receipt of the written opinion, the agency shall comply with Article 5 (commencing with Section 11346) and readopt the regulation. The director of the office may, upon a showing of good cause, grant an extension to the 120-day time period specified in this subdivision.

(b) Upon resubmission of a disapproved regulation to the office pursuant to subdivision (a), the office shall only review the resubmitted regulation for those reasons expressly identified in the written opinion required by subdivision (b) of Section 11349.3, or for those issues arising as a result of a substantial change to a provision of the resubmitted regulation or as a result of intervening statutory changes or intervening court orders or decisions.

(c) When an agency resubmits a withdrawn or disapproved regulation to the office it shall identify the prior withdrawn or disapproved regulation by date of submission to the office, shall specify the portion of the prior rulemaking record that should be included in the resubmission, and shall submit to the office a copy of the prior rulemaking record if that record has been returned to the agency by the office.

(d) The office shall expedite the review of a regulation submitted without significant substantive change. **Leg.H.** Added Stats 1979 ch 567 §1, operative July 1, 1980. Amended Stats 1981 ch 865 §34; Stats 1982 ch 1573 §7; Stats 1983 ch 142 §37; Stats 1985 ch 1044 §6; Stats 1987 ch 1375 §20.

§11349.5. Governor's review of decisions

(a) To initiate a review of a decision by the office, the agency shall file a written Request for Review with the Governor's Legal Affairs Secretary within 10 days of receipt of the written opinion provided by the office pursuant to subdivision (b) of Section 11349.3. The Request for Review shall include a complete statement as to why the agency believes the decision is incorrect and should be overruled. Along with the Request for Review, the agency shall submit all of the following:

(1) The office's written decision detailing the reasons for disapproval required by subdivision (b) of Section 11349.3.

(2) Copies of all regulations, notices, statements, and other documents which were submitted to the office.

(b) A copy of the agency's Request for Review shall be delivered to the office on the same day it is delivered to the Governor's office. The office shall file its written response to the agency's request with the Governor's Legal Affairs Secretary within 10 days and deliver a copy of its response to the agency on the same day it is delivered to the Governor's office.

(c) The Governor's office shall provide the requesting agency and the office with a written decision within 15 days of receipt of the response by the office to the agency's Request for Review. Upon receipt of the decision, the office shall publish in the California Regulatory Notice Register the agency's Request for Review, the office's response thereto, and the decision of the Governor's office.

(d) The time requirements set by subdivisions (a) and (b) may be shortened by the Governor's office for good cause.

(e) The Governor may overrule the decision of the office disapproving a proposed regulation, an order repealing an emergency regulation adopted pursuant to subdivision (b) of Section 11346.1, or a decision refusing to allow the readoption of an emergency regulation pursuant to Section 11346.1. In that event, the office shall immediately transmit the regulation to the Secretary of State for filing.

(f) Upon overruling the decision of the office, the Governor shall immediately transmit to the Committees on Rules of both houses of the Legislature a statement of his or her reasons for overruling the decision of the office, along with copies of the adopting agency's initial statement of reasons issued pursuant to Section 11346.2 and the office's statement regarding the disapproval of a regulation issued pursuant to subdivision (b) of Section 11349.3. The Governor's action and the reasons therefor shall be published in the California Regulatory Notice Register. **Leg.H.** Added Stats 1979 ch 567 §1, operative July 1, 1980. Amended Stats 1980 ch 1238 §5, effective September 29, 1980; Stats 1981 ch 865 §34.5; Stats 1982 ch 86 §6, effective March 1, 1982, ch 1236 §2; Stats 1983 ch 724 §1; Stats 1985 ch 1044 §7; Stats 1987 ch 1375 §20.2; Stats 1994 ch 1039 §41 (AB 2531); Stats 1995 ch 938 §15.6 (SB 523), operative January 1, 1996.

§11349.6. Review by office of emergency regulation

(a) If the adopting agency has complied with Sections 11346.2 to 11347.3, inclusive, prior to the adoption of the regulation as an emergency, the office shall approve or disapprove the regulation in accordance with this article.

(b) Emergency regulations adopted pursuant to subdivision (b) of Section 11346.1 shall be reviewed by the office within 10 calendar days after their submittal to the office. After posting a notice of the filing of a proposed emergency regulation on its Internet Web site, the office shall allow interested persons five calendar days to submit comments on the proposed emergency regulations unless the emergency situation clearly poses such an immediate serious harm that delaying action to allow public comment would be inconsistent with the public interest. The office shall disapprove the emergency regulations if it determines that the situation addressed by the regulations is not an emergency, or if it determines that the regulation fails to meet the standards set forth in Section 11349.1, or if it determines the agency failed to comply with Section 11346.1.

(c) If the office considers any information not submitted to it by the rulemaking agency when determining whether to file emergency regulations, the office shall provide the rulemaking agency with an opportunity to rebut or comment upon that information.

(d) Within 30 working days of the filing of a certificate of compliance, the office shall review the regulation and hearing record and approve or order the repeal of an emergency regulation if it determines that the regulation fails to meet the standards set forth in Section 11349.1, or if it determines that the agency failed to comply with this chapter. **Leg.H.** Added Stats 1979 ch 567 §1, operative July 1, 1980. Amended Stats 1979 ch 1203 §9; Stats 1980 ch 1238 §6, effective September 29, 1980; Stats 1981 ch 865 §35; Stats 1982 ch 1236 §3, ch 1573 §8; Stats 1983 ch 797 §23; Stats 1985 ch 1044 §8; Stats 1987 ch 1375 §20.5; Stats 1994 ch 1039 §42 (AB 2531); Stats 2000 ch 1060 §34 (AB 1822); Stats 2006 ch 713 §4 (AB 1302), effective January 1, 2007.

ARTICLE 7
Review of Existing Regulations

§11349.7. Priority review of regulations

The office, at the request of any standing, select, or joint committee of the Legislature, shall initiate a priority review of any regulation, group of regulations, or series of regulations that the committee believes does not meet the standards set forth in Section 11349.1.

The office shall notify interested persons and shall publish notice in the California Regulatory Notice Register that a priority review has been requested, shall consider the written comments submitted by interested persons, the information contained in the rulemaking record, if any, and shall complete each priority review made pursuant to this section within 90 calendar days of the receipt of the committee's written request. During the period of any priority review made pursuant to this section, all information available to the office relating to the priority review shall be made available to the public. In the event that the office determines that a regulation does not meet the standards set forth in Section 11349.1, it shall order the adopting agency to show cause why the regulation should not be repealed and shall proceed to seek repeal of the regulation as provided by this section in accordance with the following:

(a) In the event it determines that any of the regulations subject to the review do not meet the standards set forth in Section 11349.1, the office shall within 15 days of the determination order the adopting agency to show cause why the regulation should not be repealed. In issuing the order, the office shall specify in writing the reasons for its determination that the regulation does not meet the standards set forth in Section 11349.1. The reasons for its determination shall be made available to the public. The office shall also publish its order and the reasons therefor in the California Regulatory Notice Register. In the case of a regulation for which no, or inadequate, information relating to its necessity can be furnished by the adopting agency, the order shall specify the information which the office requires to make its determination.

(b) No later than 60 days following receipt of an order to show cause why a regulation should not be repealed, the agency shall respond in writing to the office. Upon written application by the agency, the office may extend the time for an additional 30 days.

(c) The office shall review and consider all information submitted by the agency in a timely response to the order to show cause why the regulation should not be repealed, and determine whether the regulation meets the standards set forth in Section 11349.1. The office shall make this determination within 60 days of receipt of an agency's response to the order to show cause. If the office does not make a determination within 60 days of receipt of an agency's response to the order to show cause, the regulation shall be deemed to meet the standards set forth in subdivision (a) of Section 11349.1. In making this determination, the office shall also review any written comments submitted to it by the public within 30 days of the publication of the order to show cause in the California Regulatory Notice Register. During the period of review and consideration, the information available to the office relating to each regulation for which the office has issued an order to show cause shall be made available to the public. The office shall notify the adopting agency within two working days of the receipt of information submitted by the public regarding a regulation for which an order to show cause has been issued. If the office determines that a regulation fails to meet the standards, it shall prepare a statement specifying the reasons for its determination. The statement shall be delivered to the adopting agency, the Legislature, and the Governor and shall be made available to the public and the courts. Thirty days after delivery of the statement required by this subdivision the office shall prepare an order of repeal of the regulation and shall transmit it to the Secretary of State for filing.

(d) The Governor, within 30 days after the office has delivered the statement specifying the reasons for its decision to repeal, as required by subdivision (c), may overrule the decision of the office ordering the repeal of a regulation. The regulation shall then remain in full force and effect. Notice of the Governor's action and the reasons therefor shall be published in the California Regulatory Notice Register.

The Governor shall transmit to the rules committee of each house of the Legislature a statement of reasons for overruling the decision of the office, plus any other information that may be requested by either of the rules committees.

(e) In the event that the office orders the repeal of a regulation, it shall publish the order and the reasons therefor in the California Regulatory Notice Register. **Leg.H.** Added Stats 1994 ch 1039 §43 (AB 2531), effective January 1, 1995.

Prior Law: Former Gov C §11349.7, relating to review of emergency regulations by agencies administer- ing them, was added Stats 1979 ch 567 §1, amended Stats 1979 ch 1203 §10, Stats 1980 ch 1238 §7, effective September 29, 1980, Stats 1981 ch 865 §36, ch 1091 §3, Stats 1982 §7, effective March 1, 1982, Stats 1982 ch 86 §7, effective March 1, 1982, ch 1236 §4, ch 1573 §9, Stats 1983 ch 797 §24, Stats 1984 ch 1115 §1, and repealed Stats 1987 ch 1375 §21.

§11349.8. Repeal of regulation for which statutory authority is repealed, ineffective or inoperative

(a) If the office is notified of, or on its own becomes aware of, an existing regulation in the California Code of Regulations for which the statutory authority has been repealed or becomes ineffective or inoperative by its own terms, the office shall order the adopting agency to show cause why the regulation should not be repealed for lack of statutory authority and shall notify the Legislature in writing of this order. In issuing the order, the office shall specify in writing the reasons for issuance of the order. "Agency," for purposes of this section and Section 11349.9, refers to the agency that adopted the regulation and, if applicable, the agency that is responsible for administering the regulation in issue.

(b) The agency may, within 30 days after receipt of the written notification, submit in writing to the office any citations, legal arguments, or other information opposing the repeal, including public comments during this period. This section shall not apply where the agency demonstrates in its response that any of the following conditions exists:

(1) The statute or section thereof is simultaneously repealed and substantially reenacted through a single piece of legislation, or where subsequent legislation evinces a specific legislative intent to reenact the substance of the statute or section. When a regulation cites more than one specific statute or section as reference or authority for the adoption of a regulation, and one or more of the statutes or sections are repealed or become ineffective or inoperative, then the only provisions of the regulation which remain in effect shall be those for which the remaining statutes or sections provide specific or general authority.

(2) The statute is temporarily repealed, or rendered ineffective or inoperative by a provision of law which is effective only for a limited period, in which case any regulation described in subdivision (a) is thereby also temporarily repealed, rendered ineffective, or inoperative during that limited period. Any regulation so affected shall have the same force and effect upon the expiration of the limited period during which the provision of law was effective as if that temporary provision had not been enacted.

(3) The statute or section of a statute being repealed, or becoming ineffective or inoperative by its own terms, is to remain in full force and effect as regards events occurring prior to the date of repeal or ineffectiveness, in which case any regulation adopted to implement or interpret that statute shall likewise be deemed to remain in full force and effect in regards to those same events.

(c) This section shall not be construed to deprive any person or public agency of any substantial right which would have existed prior to, or hereafter exists subsequent to, the effective date of this section.

(d) Thirty days after receipt of the agency's opposition material, or the close of the 30-day agency and public response period if no response is submitted, the office shall do one of the following:

(1) Inform the agency and the Legislature in writing that the office has withdrawn its order to show cause.

(2) Issue a written notice to the agency specifying the reasons for the repeal and its intent to file a Notice of Repeal of the invalid regulation with the Secretary of State. Within seven calendar days of the filing of the Notice of Repeal, the office shall provide the agency, the Governor, and the Legislature with a written decision detailing the reasons for the repeal and a copy of the Notice of Repeal, and publish the office's written decision in the California Regulatory Notice Register.

(e) The office shall order the removal of the repealed regulation from the California Code of Regulations within 30 days after filing the Notice of Repeal, if the agency has not appealed the office's decision, or upon receipt of notification of the Governor's decision upholding the office's decision, if an appeal has been filed pursuant to Section 11349.9. **Leg.H.** Added Stats 1989 ch 1170 §1, as Gov C §11349.10. Amended and renumbered by Stats 1994 ch 1039 §44 (AB 2531), effective January 1, 1995.

Prior Law: Former Gov C §11349.8, relating to dates of completion for review of titles of the California Administrative Code, was added Stats 1979 ch 567 §1, operative July 1, 1980, and repealed Stats 1987 ch 1375 §22.

§11349.9. Review of notice of repeal

(a) To initiate a review of the office's Notice of Repeal pursuant to Section 11349.8, the agency shall appeal the office's decision by filing a written Request for Review with the Governor's Legal Affairs Secretary within 10 days of receipt of the Notice of Repeal and written decision provided for by paragraph (2) of subdivision (d) of Section 11349.8. The Request for Review shall include a complete statement as to why the agency believes the decision is incorrect and should be overruled. Along with the Request for Review, the agency shall submit all of the following:

(1) The office's written opinion detailing the reasons for repeal required by paragraph (2) of subdivision (d) of Section 11349.8.

(2) Copies of all statements and other documents that were submitted to the office.

(b) A copy of the agency's Request for Review shall be delivered to the office on the same day it is delivered to the Governor's office. The office shall file its written response to the agency's request with the Governor's Legal Affairs Secretary within 10 days, and deliver a copy of its response to the agency on the same day it is delivered to the Governor's office.

(c) The Governor's office shall provide the requesting agency and the office with a written decision within 15 days of receipt of the response by the office to the agency's Request for Review. Upon receipt of the decision, the office shall publish in the California Regulatory Notice Register the agency's Request for Review, the office's response thereto, and the decision of the Governor's office.

(d) The time requirements set by subdivisions (a) and (b) may be shortened by the Governor's office for good cause.

(e) In the event the Governor overrules the decision of the office, the office shall immediately transmit the regulation to the Secretary of State for filing.

(f) Upon overruling the decision of the office, the Governor shall transmit to the rules committees of both houses of the Legislature a statement of the reasons for overruling the decision of the office. **Leg.H.** Added Stats 1989 ch 1170 §2 as Gov C §11349.11. Amended and renumbered by Stats 1994 ch 1039 §45 (AB 2531); Amended Stats 1995 ch 938 §15.7 (SB 523), operative January 1, 1996.

Prior Law: Former Gov C §11349.9, was added Stats 1985 ch 1044 §9, amended and renumbered Gov C §11344.3 by Stats 1987 ch 1375 §23.

ARTICLE 8
Judicial Review

§11350. Judicial declaration regarding validity of regulation; Grounds for invalidity

(a) Any interested person may obtain a judicial declaration as to the validity of any regulation or order of repeal by bringing an action for declaratory relief in the superior court in accordance with the Code of Civil Procedure. The right to judicial determination shall not be affected by the failure either to petition or to seek reconsideration of a petition filed pursuant to Section 11340.7 before the agency promulgating the regulation or order of repeal. The regulation or order of repeal may be declared to be invalid for a substantial failure to comply with this chapter, or, in the case of an emergency regulation or order of repeal, upon the ground that the facts recited in the finding of emergency prepared pursuant to subdivision (b) of Section 11346.1 do not constitute an emergency within the provisions of Section 11346.1.

(b) In addition to any other ground that may exist, a regulation or order of repeal may be declared invalid if either of the following exists:

(1) The agency's determination that the regulation is reasonably necessary to effectuate the purpose of the statute, court decision, or other provision of law that is being implemented, interpreted, or made specific by the regulation is not supported by substantial evidence.

(2) The agency declaration pursuant to paragraph (8) of subdivision (a) of Section 11346.5 is in conflict with substantial evidence in the record.

(c) The approval of a regulation or order of repeal by the office or the Governor's overruling of a decision of the office disapproving a regulation or order of repeal shall not be considered by a court in any action for declaratory relief brought with respect to a regulation or order of repeal.

(d) In a proceeding under this section, a court may only consider the following evidence:

(1) The rulemaking file prepared under Section 11347.3.

(2) The finding of emergency prepared pursuant to subdivision (b) of Section 11346.1.

(3) An item that is required to be included in the rulemaking file but is not included in the rulemaking file, for the sole purpose of proving its omission.

(4) Any evidence relevant to whether a regulation used by an agency is required to be adopted under this chapter. **Leg.H.** Added Stats 1979 ch 567 §1, operative July 1, 1980. Amended Stats 1981 ch 592 §1, ch 865 §37; Stats 1982 ch 86 §9, effective March 1, 1982, ch 1573 §10; Stats 1991 ch 794 §6 (AB 2061); Stats 1994 ch 1039 §47 (AB 2531); Stats 1995 ch 938 §15.8 (SB 523), operative January 1, 1996; Stats 2000 ch 1060 §35 (AB 1822); Stats 2006 ch 713 §5 (AB 1302), effective January 1, 2007.

§11350.3. Judicial declaration as to validity of disapproved or repealed regulation

Any interested person may obtain a judicial declaration as to the validity of a regulation or order of repeal which the office has disapproved pursuant to Section 11349.3, or 11349.6, or of a regulation that has been ordered repealed pursuant to Section 11349.7 by bringing an action for declaratory relief in the superior court in accordance with the Code of Civil Procedure. The court may declare the regulation valid if it determines that the regulation meets the standards set forth in Section 11349.1 and that the agency has complied with this chapter. If the court so determines, it may order the office to immediately file the regulation with the Secretary of State. **Leg.H.** Added Stats 1982 ch 1544 §2, ch 1573 §11. Amended Stats 1987 ch 1375 §23.5; Stats 1994 ch 1039 §48 (AB 2531); Stats 2000 ch 1060 §36 (AB 1822), effective January 1, 2001.

ARTICLE 9
Special Procedures

§11351. Applicability of specified provisions to Public Utilities Commission and Workers' Compensation Appeals Board

(a) Except as provided in subdivision (b), Article 5 (commencing with Section 11346), Article 6 (commencing with Section 11349), Article 7 (commencing with Section 11349.7), and Article 8 (commencing with Section 11350) shall not apply to the Public Utilities Commission or the Workers' Compensation Appeals Board, and Article 3 (commencing with Section 11343) and Article 4 (commencing with Section 11344) shall apply only to the rules of procedure of these state agencies.

(b) The Public Utilities Commission and the Workers' Compensation Appeals Board shall comply with paragraph (5) of subdivision (a) of Section 11346.4 with respect to regulations that are required to be filed with the Secretary of State pursuant to Section 11343.

(c) Article 8 (commencing with Section 11350) shall not apply to the Division of Workers' Compensation. **Leg.H.** Added Stats 1979 ch 567 §1, operative July 1, 1980, as Gov C §11445. Amended and renumbered by Stats 1980 ch 204 §6, effective June 20, 1980; Amended Stats 1982 ch 86 §10, effective March 1, 1982; Stats 1983 ch 797 §26; Stats 1987 ch 1375 §24; Stats 1994 ch 1039 §50 (AB 2531); Stats 1996 ch 14 §1 (AB 1859), effective January 1, 1997.

§11352. Applicability of chapter

The following actions are not subject to this chapter:

(a) The issuance, denial, or waiver of any water quality certification as authorized under Section 13160 of the Water Code.

(b) The issuance, denial, or revocation of waste discharge requirements and permits pursuant to Sections 13263 and 13377 of the Water Code and waivers issued pursuant to Section 13269 of the Water Code.

(c) The development, issuance, and use of the guidance document pursuant to Section 13383.7 of the Water Code.

(d) The issuance of an order pursuant to Section 116400 of the Health and Safety Code.

(e) The issuance of a notification level, response level, or definition of a confirmed detection under Section 116455 of the Health and Safety Code.

(f) The issuance of an order or directive requiring the submittal of technical reports pursuant to Section 116530 of the Health and Safety Code. **Leg.H.** Added Stats 1992 ch 1112 §1 (AB 3359). Amended Stats 2007 ch 610 §1.5 (AB 739), effective January 1, 2008; Stats 2021 ch 187 §1 (SB 776), effective January 1, 2022.

§11353. Application of chapter to water quality control policy, plans, or guidelines

(a) Except as provided in subdivision (b), this chapter does not apply to the adoption or revision of state policy for water quality control and the adoption or revision of water quality control plans and guidelines pursuant to Division 7 (commencing with Section 13000) of the Water Code.

(b)(1) Any policy, plan, or guideline, or any revision thereof, that the State Water Resources Control Board has adopted or that a court determines is subject to this part, after June 1, 1992, shall be submitted to the office.

(2) The State Water Resources Control Board shall include in its submittal to the office all of the following:

(A) A clear and concise summary of any regulatory provisions adopted or approved as part of that action, for publication in the California Code of Regulations.

(B) The administrative record for the proceeding. Proposed additions to a policy, plan, or guideline shall be indicated by underlined text and proposed deletions shall be indicated by strike-through text in documents submitted as part of the administrative record for the proceeding.

(C) A summary of the necessity for the regulatory provision.

(D) A certification by the chief legal officer of the State Water Resources Control Board that the action was taken in compliance with all applicable procedural requirements of Division 7 (commencing with Section 13000) of the Water Code.

(3) Paragraph (2) does not limit the authority of the office to review any regulatory provision which is part of the policy, plan, or guideline submitted by the State Water Resources Control Board.

(4) The office shall review the regulatory provisions to determine compliance with the standards of necessity, authority, clarity, consistency, reference, and nonduplication set forth in subdivision (a) of Section 11349.1. The office shall also review the responses to public comments prepared by the State Water Resources Control Board or the appropriate regional water quality control board to determine compliance with the public participation requirements of the Federal Water Pollution Control Act (33 U.S.C. Sec. 1251 et seq.). The office shall restrict its review to the regulatory provisions and the administrative record of the proceeding. Sections 11349.3, 11349.4, 11349.5, and 11350.3 shall apply to the review by the office to the extent that those sections are consistent with this section.

(5) The policy, plan, guideline, or revision shall not become effective unless and until the regulatory provisions are approved by the office in accordance with subdivision (a) of Section 11349.3.

(6) Upon approval of the regulatory provisions, the office shall transmit to the Secretary of State for filing the clear and concise summary of the regulatory provisions submitted by the State Water Resources Control Board.

(7) Any proceedings before the State Water Resources Control Board or a California regional water quality control board to take any action subject to this subdivision shall be conducted in accordance with the procedural requirements of Division 7 (commencing with Section 13000) of the Water Code, together with any applicable requirements of the Federal Water Pollution Control Act (33 U.S.C. Sec. 1251 et seq.), and the requirements of this chapter, other than the requirement for review by the office in accordance with this subdivision, shall not apply.

(8) This subdivision shall not provide a basis for review by the office under this subdivision or Article 6 (commencing with Section 11349) of any such policy, plan, or guideline adopted or revised prior to June 1, 1992.

(c) Subdivision (a) does not apply to a provision of any policy, plan, guideline, or revision, as applied to any person who, as of June 1, 1992, was a party to a civil action challenging that provision on the grounds that it has not been adopted as a regulation pursuant to this chapter.

(d) Copies of the policies, plans, and guidelines to which subdivision (a) applies shall be maintained at central locations for inspection by the public. The State Water Resources Control Board shall maintain, at its headquarters in Sacramento, a current copy of each policy, plan, or guideline in effect. Each regional water quality control board shall maintain at its headquarters a current copy of each policy, plan, or guideline in effect in its respective region. Any revision of a policy, plan, or guideline shall be made available for inspection by the public within 30 days of its effective date. **Leg.H.** Added Stats 1992 ch 1112 §2 (AB 3359). Amended Stats 2000 ch 1060 §37 (AB 1822), effective January 1, 2001.

§11354. Effect of certain sections on court determination of applicability of chapter

Sections 11352 and 11353 do not affect any court's determination, relating to the applicability of this chapter to any provision of a policy, plan, or guideline, in a civil action which was pending on June 1, 1992, and on that date included a challenge to a provision of a policy, plan, or guideline on the grounds that it has not been adopted in accordance with this chapter. **Leg.H.** Added Stats 1992 ch 1112 §2 (AB 3359), effective January 1, 1993.

§11354.1. Application of chapter to certain policies, plans and guidelines of San Francisco Bay Conservation and Development Commission

(a) For purposes of this section, "commission" means the San Francisco Bay Conservation and Development Commission.

(b) This chapter does not apply to any policy, plan, or guideline adopted by the commission prior to January 1, 1996, pursuant to Chapter 5 (commencing with Section 66650) of Title 7.2 of this code or Division 19 (commencing with Section 29000) of the Public Resources Code.

(c) The issuance or denial by the commission of any permit pursuant to subdivision (a) of Section 66632, and the issuance or denial by, or appeal to, the commission of any permit pursuant to Chapter 6 (commencing with Section 29500) of Division 19 of the Public Resources Code, are not subject to this chapter.

(d)(1) Any amendments or other changes to the San Francisco Bay Plan or to a special area plan pursuant to Chapter 5 (commencing with Section 66650) of Title 7.2, adopted by the commission on or after January 1, 1996, and any amendments or other changes to the Suisun Marsh Protection Plan, as defined in Section 29113 of the Public Resources Code, or in the Suisun Marsh local protection program, as defined in Section 29111 of the Public Resources Code, adopted by the commission on and after January 1, 1996, shall be submitted to the office but are not subject to this chapter except as provided in this subdivision.

(2) The commission shall include in its submittal to the office pursuant to paragraph (1) both of the following documents:

(A) A clear and concise summary of any regulatory provision adopted or approved by the commission as part of the proposed change for publication in the California Code of Regulations.

(B) The administrative record for the proceeding, and a list of the documents relied upon in making the change. Proposed additions to the plans shall be indicated by underlined text, and proposed deletions shall be indicated by strike-through text in documents submitted as part of the administrative record for the proceeding.

(3) The office shall review the regulatory provisions to determine compliance with the standards of necessity, authority, clarity, consistency, reference, and nonduplication set forth in subdivision (a) of Section 11349.1. The office shall also review the responses to public comments prepared by the commission to determine compliance with the public participation requirements of Sections 11000 to 11007, inclusive, of Title 14 of the California Code of Regulations, and to ensure that the commission considers all relevant matters presented to it before adopting, amending, or repealing any regulatory provision, and that the commission explains the reasons for not modifying a proposed plan change to accommodate an objection or recommendation. The office shall restrict its review to the regulatory provisions and the administrative record of the proceeding. Sections 11349.3, 11349.4, 11349.5, and 11350.3 shall apply to the review by the office to the extent that those sections are consistent with this section.

(4) In reviewing proposed changes to the commission's plans for the criteria specified in subdivision (a) of Section 11349.1, the office shall consider the clarity of the proposed plan change in the context of the commission's existing plans.

(5) The proposed plan or program change subject to this subdivision shall not become effective unless and until the regulatory provisions are approved by the office in accordance with subdivision (a) of Section 11349.3.

(6) Upon approval of the regulatory provisions, the office shall transmit to the Secretary of State for filing the clear and concise summary of the regulatory provisions submitted by the commission.

(e) Except as provided in subdivisions (b), (c), and (d), the adoption of any regulation by the commission shall be subject to this chapter in all respects. **Leg.H.** Added Stats 1995 ch 951 §1 (AB 1102). Amended Stats 1996 ch 124 §35 (AB 3470); Stats 2002 ch 389 §7 (AB 1857), effective January 1, 2003.

§11356. Applicability of articles to building standards

(a) Article 6 (commencing with Section 11349) is not applicable to a building standard.

(b) Article 5 (commencing with Section 11346) is applicable to those building standards, except that the office shall not disapprove those building standards nor refuse to publish any notice of proposed building standards if either has been approved by, and submitted to, the office by the California Building Standards Commission pursuant to Section 18935 of the Health and Safety Code. **Leg.H.** Added Stats 1979 ch 1152 §13.5, operative July 1, 1980, as Gov C §11446. Renumbered by Stats 1980 ch 676 §106. Amended Stats 1984 ch 677 §1; Stats 1987 ch 1375 §25; Stats 1988 ch 1194 §1.5, operative January 1, 1989; Stats 2000 ch 1060 §38 (AB 1822), effective January 1, 2001.

§11357. Instructions for determining impact of proposed action on local or state agencies or on school districts

(a) The Department of Finance shall adopt and update, as necessary, instructions for inclusion in the State Administrative Manual prescribing the methods that an agency subject to this chapter shall use in making the determinations and the estimates of fiscal or economic impact required by Sections 11346.2, 11346.3, and 11346.5. The instructions shall include, but need not be limited to, the following:

(1) Guidelines governing the types of data or assumptions, or both, that may be used, and the methods that shall be used, to calculate the estimate of the cost or savings to public agencies mandated by the regulation for which the estimate is being prepared.

(2) The types of direct or indirect costs and savings that should be taken into account in preparing the estimate.

(3) The criteria that shall be used in determining whether the cost of a regulation must be funded by the state pursuant to Section 6 of Article XIII B of the California Constitution and Part 7 (commencing with Section 17500) of Division 4.

(4) The format the agency preparing the estimate shall follow in summarizing and reporting its estimate of the cost or savings to state and local agencies, school districts, and in federal funding of state programs that will result from the regulation and its estimate of the economic impact that will result from the regulation.

(b) An action by the Department of Finance to adopt and update, as necessary, instructions to any state or local agency for the preparation, development, or administration of the state budget, or instructions to a state agency on the preparation of an economic impact estimate or assessment of a proposed regulation, including any instructions included in the State Administrative Manual, shall be exempt from this chapter.

(c) The Department of Finance may review an estimate prepared pursuant to this section for content including, but not limited to, the data and assumptions used in its preparation. **Leg.H.** Added Stats 1994 ch 1039 §51 (AB 2531). Amended Stats 2014 ch 779 §3 (AB 1711), effective January 1, 2015.

§11359. Regulations relating to fire and panic safety

(a) Except as provided in subdivision (b), on and after January 1, 1982, no new regulation, or the amendment or repeal of any regulation, which regulation is intended to promote fire and panic safety or provide fire protection and prevention, including fire suppression systems, equipment, or alarm regulation, is valid or effective unless it is submitted by, or approved in writing by, the State Fire Marshal before transmittal to the Secretary of State or the Office of Administrative Law.

(b) Approval of the State Fire Marshal is not required if the regulation is expressly required to be at least as effective as federal standards published in the Federal Register pursuant to Section 6 of the Occupational Safety and Health Act of 1970 (P.L. 91–596) within the time period specified by federal law and as provided in subdivision (b) of Section 142.4 of the Labor Code, and as approved by the Occupational Safety and Health Administration of the United States Department of Labor as meeting the requirements of subdivision (a) of Section 142.3 of the Labor Code, unless the regulation is determined by the State Fire Marshal to be less effective in promoting fire and panic safety than regulations adopted by the State Fire Marshal. **Leg.H.** Added Stats 1981 ch 1177 §1 as Gov C §11342.3. Renumbered by Stats 1994 ch 1039 §10 (AB 2531), effective January 1, 1995.

§11361. Applicability of chapter; Adoption or revision of regulations, guidelines, or criteria

This chapter does not apply to the adoption or revision of regulations, guidelines, or criteria to implement the Safe Neighborhood Parks, Clean Water, Clean Air, and Coastal Protection Bond Act of 2000 (the Villaraigosa-Keeley Act) (Chapter 1.692 (commencing with Section 5096.300) of Division 5 of the Public Resources Code), the California Clean Water, Clean Air, Safe Neighborhood Parks, and Coastal Protection Act of 2002 (Chapter 1.696 (commencing with Section 5096.600) of Division 5 of the Public Resources Code), or the Water Security, Clean Drinking Water, Coastal and Beach Protection Act of 2002 (Division 26.5 (commencing with Section 79500) of the Water Code). The adoption or revision of regulations, guidelines, or criteria, if necessary to implement those respective acts, shall instead be accomplished by means of a public process reasonably calculated to give those persons interested in their adoption or revision an opportunity to be heard. **Leg.H.** Added Stats 2000 ch 87 §5 (SB 1679), effective July 5, 2000. Amended Stats 2003 ch 240 §2 (AB 1747), effective August 13, 2003.

CHAPTER 4
OFFICE OF ADMINISTRATIVE HEARINGS
ARTICLE 1
General Provisions

§11370. Chapters constituting Administrative Procedure Act

Chapter 3.5 (commencing with Section 11340), Chapter 4 (commencing with Section 11370), Chapter 4.5 (commencing with Section 11400), and Chapter 5 (commencing with Section 11500) constitute, and may be cited as, the Administrative Procedure Act. **Leg.H.** Added Stats 1947 ch 1425 §1. Amended Stats 1961 ch 2048 §2; Stats 1981 ch 714 §176, operative until July 1, 1997; Stats 1995 ch 938 §16.5 (SB 523), operative July 1, 1997.

§11370.1. "Director"

As used in the Administrative Procedure Act "director" means the executive officer of the Office of Administrative Hearings. **Leg.H.** Added Stats 1961 ch 2048 §3. Amended Stats 1971 ch 1303 §2.

§11370.2. Office of Administrative Hearings in Department of General Services; Director

(a) There is in the Department of General Services the Office of Administrative Hearings which is under the direction and control of an executive officer who shall be known as the director.

(b) The director shall have the same qualifications as administrative law judges, and shall be appointed by the Governor subject to the confirmation of the Senate.

(c) Any and all references in any law to the Office of Administrative Procedure shall be deemed to be the Office of Administrative Hearings. **Leg.H.** Added Stats 1961 ch 2048 §4. Amended Stats 1963 ch 1786 §13, operative October 1, 1963; Stats 1971 ch 1303 §3; Stats 1985 ch 324 §13.

§11370.3. Appointment and assignment of administrative law judges and other personnel

The director shall appoint and maintain a staff of full-time, and may appoint pro tempore part-time, administrative law judges qualified under Section 11502 which is sufficient to fill the needs of the various state agencies. The director shall also appoint any other technical and clerical personnel as may be required to perform the duties of the office. The director shall assign an administrative law judge for any proceeding arising under Chapter 5 (commencing with Section 11500) and, upon request from any agency, may assign an administrative law judge to conduct other administrative proceedings not arising under that chapter and shall assign hearing reporters as required. Any administrative law judge or other employee so assigned shall be deemed an employee of the office and not of the agency to which he or she is assigned. When not engaged in hearing cases, administrative law judges may be assigned by the director to perform other duties vested in or required of the office, including those provided for in Section 11370.5. **Leg.H.** Added Stats 1961 ch 2048 §5. Amended Stats 1971 ch 1303 §3.5; Stats 1979 ch 199 §2; Stats 1984 ch 1005 §2; Stats §1985 ch 324 §14; Stats 1995 ch 938 §17 (SB 523), operative July 1, 1997.

§11370.4. Determination and collection of costs

The total cost to the state of maintaining and operating the Office of Administrative Hearings shall be determined by, and collected by the Department of General Services in advance or upon such other basis as it may determine from the state or other public agencies for which services are provided by the office. **Leg.H.** Added Stats 1961 ch 2048 §6. Amended Stats 1963 ch 1553 §1; Stats 1965 ch 462 §1; Stats 1971 ch 1303 §4.

§11370.5. Recommendations on administrative adjudication

(a) The office is authorized and directed to study the subject of administrative adjudication in all its aspects; to submit its suggestions to the various agencies in the interests of fairness, uniformity and the expedition of business; and to report its recommendations to the Governor and Legislature. All departments, agencies, officers, and employees of the state shall give the office ready access to their records and full information and reasonable assistance in any matter of research requiring recourse to them or to data within their knowledge or control. Nothing in this section authorizes an agency to provide access to records required by statute to be kept confidential.

(b) The office may adopt rules and regulations to carry out the functions and duties of the office under the Administrative Procedure Act. The regulations are subject to Chapter 3.5 (commencing with Section 11340). **Leg.H.** Added Stats 1961 ch 2048 §7. Amended Stats 1995 ch 938 §18 (SB 523), operative July 1, 1997; Stats 2002 ch 370 §3 (AB 2283).

ARTICLE 2
Medical Quality Hearing Panel

§11371. Members of panel; Published decisions; Experts

(a) There is within the Office of Administrative Hearings a Medical Quality Hearing Panel, consisting of no fewer than five full-time administrative law judges. The administrative law judges shall have medical training as recommended by the Division of Medical Quality of the Medical Board of California and approved by the Director of the Office of Administrative Hearings.

(b) The director shall determine the qualifications of panel members, supervise their training, and coordinate the publication of a reporter of decisions pursuant to this section. The panel shall include only those persons specifically qualified and shall at no time constitute more than 25 percent of the total number of administrative law judges within the Office of Administrative Hearings. If the members of the panel do not have a full workload, they may be assigned work by the Director of the Office of Administrative Hearings. When the medically related case workload exceeds the capacity of the members of the panel, additional judges shall be requested to be added to the panels as appropriate. When this workload overflow occurs on a temporary basis, the Director of the Office of Administrative Hearings shall supply judges from the Office of Administrative Hearings to adjudicate the cases.

(c) The administrative law judges of the panel shall have panels of experts available. The panels of experts shall be appointed by the Director of the Office of Administrative Hearings, with the advice of the Medical Board of California. These panels of experts may be called as witnesses by the administrative law judges of the panel to testify on the record about any matter relevant to a proceeding and subject to cross-examination by all parties, and Section 11430.30 does not apply in a proceeding under this section. The administrative law judge may award reasonable expert witness fees to any person or persons serving on a panel of experts, which shall be paid from the Contingent Fund of the Medical Board of California upon appropriation by the Legislature. **Leg.H.** Added Stats 1993 ch 1267 §51 (SB 916). Amended Stats 1994 ch 1206 §27 (SB 1775); Stats 1995 ch 938 §19.5 (SB 523), operative July 1, 1997; Stats 1998 ch 878 §56 (SB 2239), operative until January 1, 2003; Stats 2002 ch 1085 §31 (SB 1950); Stats 2005 ch 674 §21 (SB 231), effective January 1, 2006.

Prior Law: Former Gov C §11371, similar to the present section, was added Stats 1990 ch 1597 §31 and repealed Stats 1993 ch 1267 §50.

§11372. Conduct of hearing by administrative law judge

(a) Except as provided in subdivision (b), all adjudicative hearings and proceedings relating to the discipline or reinstatement of licensees of the Medical Board of California, including licensees of affiliated health agencies within the jurisdiction of the Medical Board of California, that are heard pursuant to the Administrative Procedure Act, shall be conducted by an administrative law judge as designated in Section 11371, sitting alone if the case is so assigned by the agency filing the charging pleading.

(b) Proceedings relating to interim orders shall be heard in accordance with Section 11529. **Leg.H.** Added Stats 1990 ch 1597 §32 (SB 2375). Amended Stats 1993 ch 1267 §52 (SB 916); Stats 2007 ch 588 §89 (SB 1048), effective January 1, 2008.

Prior Law: Former Gov C §11372, relating to definition of department, was added Stats 1947 ch 1175 §1, amended Stats 1947 ch 1425 §1, Stats 1961 ch 2048 §9, Stats 1971 ch 1303 §5, and repealed Stats 1979 ch 567 §2, operative July 1, 1980.

§11373. Conduct of proceedings under Administrative Procedure Act

All adjudicative hearings and proceedings conducted by an administrative law judge as designated in Section 11371 shall be conducted under the terms and conditions set forth in the Administrative Procedure Act, except as provided in the Medical Practice Act (Chapter 5 (commencing with Section 2000) of Division 2 of the Business and Professions Code)). **Leg.H.** Added Stats 1990 ch 1597 §33 (SB 2375). Amended Stats 1993 ch 1267 §53 (SB 916).

Prior Law: Former Gov C §11373, similar to present Gov C §11342.1, was repealed Stats 1979 ch 567 §2, operative July 1, 1980.

§11373.3. Facilities and support personnel for review committee panel

The Office of Administrative Hearings shall provide facilities and support personnel for the review committee panel and shall assess the Medical Board of California for facilities and personnel, where used to adjudicate cases involving the Medical Board of California. **Leg.H.** Added Stats 1990 ch 1597 §34 (SB 2375). Amended Stats 1991 ch 1091 §44 (AB 1487).

ARTICLE 3
State Agency Reports and Forms Appeals

§11380. Appeal filed by business

(a)(1) The office shall hear and render a decision on any appeal filed by a business, pursuant to subdivision (c) of Section 14775, in the event the business contests the certification by a state agency head that reporting requirements meet established criteria and shall not be eliminated.

(2) Before a business may file an appeal with the office pursuant to subdivision (c) of Section 14775, the business shall file a challenge to a form or report required by a state agency with that state agency. Within 60 days of filing the challenge with a state agency, the state agency shall either eliminate the form or report or provide written justification for its continued use.

(3) A business may appeal a state agency's written justification for the continued use of a form or report with the office.

(4) If a state agency fails to respond within 60 days of the filing of a challenge pursuant to paragraph (2), the business shall have an immediate right to file an appeal with the office.

(b) No later than January 1, 1996, the office shall adopt procedures governing the filing, hearing, and disposition of appeals. The procedures shall include, but not be limited to, provisions that assure that appeals are heard and decisions rendered by the office in a fair, impartial, and timely fashion.

(c) The office may charge appellants a reasonable fee to pay for costs it incurs in complying with this section. **Leg.H.** Added Stats 1995 ch 938 §20 (SB 523), operative July 1, 1997.

Prior Law: Former Gov C §11380, similar to present Gov C §11343, was added Stats 1945 ch 111 §1, amended Stats 1947 ch 1425 §3, Stats 1949 ch 313 §2, Stats 1953 ch 1362 §1, Stats 1959 ch 2180 §1, Stats 1974 ch 142 §1, Stats 1978 ch 131 §1, and repealed Stats 1979 ch 567 §2, operative July 1, 1980.

CHAPTER 4.5
ADMINISTRATIVE ADJUDICATION: GENERAL PROVISIONS

ARTICLE 1
Preliminary Provisions

§11400. Administrative Procedure Act; References to superseded provisions

(a) This chapter and Chapter 5 (commencing with Section 11500) constitute the administrative adjudication provisions of the Administrative Procedure Act.

(b) A reference in any other statute or in a rule of court, executive order, or regulation, to a provision formerly found in Chapter 5 (commencing with Section 11500) that is superseded by a provision of this chapter, means the applicable provision of this chapter. **Leg.H.** Added Stats 1995 ch 938 §21 (SB 523), operative July 1, 1997.

Prior Law: Former Gov C §11400, relating to codification board, was added Stats 1945 ch 111 §3 and repealed Stats 1947 ch 1175 §11, ch 1425 §17.

§11400.10. Operative date of chapter; Applicability

(a) This chapter is operative on July 1, 1997.

(b) This chapter is applicable to an adjudicative proceeding commenced on or after July 1, 1997.

(c) This chapter is not applicable to an adjudicative proceeding commenced before July 1, 1997, except an adjudicative proceeding conducted on a remand from a court or another agency on or after July 1, 1997. **Leg.H.** Added Stats 1995 ch 938 §21 (SB 523), operative July 1, 1997.

§11400.20. Adoption of interim or permanent regulations

(a) Before, on, or after July 1, 1997, an agency may adopt interim or permanent regulations to govern an adjudicative proceeding under this chapter or Chapter 5 (commencing with Section 11500). Nothing in this section authorizes an agency to adopt regulations to govern an adjudicative proceeding required to be conducted by an administrative law judge employed by the Office of Administrative Hearings, except to the extent the regulations are otherwise authorized by statute.

(b) Except as provided in Section 11351:

(1) Interim regulations need not comply with Article 5 (commencing with Section 11346) or Article 6 (commencing with Section 11349) of Chapter 3.5, but are governed by Chapter 3.5 (commencing with Section 11340) in all other respects.

(2) Interim regulations expire on December 31, 1998, unless earlier terminated or replaced by or readopted as permanent regulations under paragraph (3). If on December 31, 1998, an agency has completed proceedings to replace or readopt interim regulations and has submitted permanent regulations for review by the Office of Administrative Law, but permanent regulations have not yet been filed with the Secretary of State, the interim regulations are extended until the date permanent regulations are filed with the Secretary of State or March 31, 1999, whichever is earlier.

(3) Permanent regulations are subject to all the provisions of Chapter 3.5 (commencing with Section 11340), except that if by December 31, 1998, an agency has submitted the regulations for review by the Office of Administrative Law, the regulations are not subject to review for necessity under Section 11349.1 or 11350. **Leg.H.** Added Stats 1995 ch 938 §21 (SB 523), operative July 1, 1997. Amended Stats 1996 ch 390 §5 (SB 794), effective August 19, 1996, operative July 1, 1997.

ARTICLE 2
Definitions

§11405.10. Definitions governing construction of chapter

Unless the provision or context requires otherwise, the definitions in this article govern the construction of this chapter. **Leg.H.** Added Stats 1995 ch 938 §21 (SB 523), operative July 1, 1997.

§11405.20. "Adjudicative proceeding"

"Adjudicative proceeding" means an evidentiary hearing for determination of facts pursuant to which an agency formulates and issues a decision. **Leg.H.** Added Stats 1995 ch 938 §21 (SB 523), operative July 1, 1997.

§11405.30. "Agency"

"Agency" means a board, bureau, commission, department, division, office, officer, or other administrative unit, including the agency head, and one or more members of the agency head or agency employees or other persons directly or indirectly purporting to act on behalf of or under the authority of the agency head. To the extent it purports to exercise authority pursuant to this chapter, an administrative unit otherwise qualifying as an agency shall be treated as a separate agency even if the unit is located within or subordinate to another agency. **Leg.H.** Added Stats 1995 ch 938 §21 (SB 523), operative July 1, 1997.

§11405.40. "Agency head"

"Agency head" means a person or body in which the ultimate legal authority of an agency is vested, and includes a person or body to which the power to act is delegated pursuant to authority to delegate the agency's power to hear and decide. **Leg.H.** Added Stats 1995 ch 938 §21 (SB 523), operative July 1, 1997.

§11405.50. "Decision"

(a) "Decision" means an agency action of specific application that determines a legal right, duty, privilege, immunity, or other legal interest of a particular person.

(b) Nothing in this section limits any of the following:

(1) The precedential effect of a decision under Section 11425.60.

(2) The authority of an agency to make a declaratory decision pursuant to Article 14 (commencing with Section 11465.10). **Leg.H.** Added Stats 1995 ch 938 §21 (SB 523), operative July 1, 1997.

§11405.60. "Party"

"Party" includes the agency that is taking action, the person to which the agency action is directed, and any other person named as a party or allowed to appear or intervene in the proceeding. If the agency that is taking action and the agency that is conducting the adjudicative proceeding are separate agencies, the agency that is taking action is a party and the agency that is conducting the adjudicative proceeding is not a party. **Leg.H.** Added Stats 1995 ch 938 §21 (SB 523), operative July 1, 1997.

§11405.70. "Person"

"Person" includes an individual, partnership, corporation, governmental subdivision or unit of a governmental subdivision, or public or private organization or entity of any character. **Leg.H.** Added Stats 1995 ch 938 §21 (SB 523), operative July 1, 1997.

§11405.80. "Presiding officer"

"Presiding officer" means the agency head, member of the agency head, administrative law judge, hearing officer, or other person who presides in an adjudicative proceeding. **Leg.H.** Added Stats 1995 ch 938 §21 (SB 523), operative July 1, 1997.

ARTICLE 3
Application of Chapter

§11410.10. Decision requiring evidentiary hearing

This chapter applies to a decision by an agency if, under the federal or state Constitution or a federal or state statute, an evidentiary hearing for determination of facts is required for formulation and issuance of the decision. **Leg.H.** Added Stats 1995 ch 938 §21 (SB 523), operative July 1, 1997.

§11410.20. Applicability to agencies

Except as otherwise expressly provided by statute:

(a) This chapter applies to all agencies of the state.

(b) This chapter does not apply to the Legislature, the courts or judicial branch, or the Governor or office of the Governor. **Leg.H.** Added Stats 1995 ch 938 §21 (SB 523), operative July 1, 1997.

§11410.30. Applicability to local agencies

(a) As used in this section, "local agency" means a county, city, district, public authority, public agency, or other political subdivision or public corporation in the state other than the state.

(b) This chapter does not apply to a local agency except to the extent the provisions are made applicable by statute.

(c) This chapter applies to an agency created or appointed by joint or concerted action of the state and one or more local agencies. **Leg.H.** Added Stats 1995 ch 938 §21 (SB 523), operative July 1, 1997.

§11410.40. Adoption of chapter by exempt agency

Notwithstanding any other provision of this article, by regulation, ordinance, or other appropriate action, an agency may adopt this chapter or any of its provisions for the formulation and issuance of a decision, even though the agency or decision is exempt from application of this chapter. **Leg.H.** Added Stats 1995 ch 938 §21 (SB 523), operative July 1, 1997.

§11410.50. Applicability to specified proceedings

This chapter applies to an adjudicative proceeding required to be conducted under Chapter 5 (commencing with Section 11500) unless the statutes relating to the proceeding provide otherwise. **Leg.H.** Added Stats 1995 ch 938 §21 (SB 523), operative July 1, 1997.

§11410.60. Quasi-public entity

(a) As used in this section, "quasi-public entity" means an entity, other than a governmental agency, whether characterized by statute as a public corporation, public instrumentality, or otherwise, that is expressly created by statute for the purpose of administration of a state function.

(b) This chapter applies to an adjudicative proceeding conducted by a quasi-public entity if all of the following conditions are satisfied:

(1) A statute vests the power of decision in the quasi-public entity.

(2) A statute, the United States Constitution, or the California Constitution, requires an evidentiary hearing for determination of facts for formulation and issuance of the decision. Nothing in this section is intended to create an evidentiary hearing requirement that is not otherwise statutorily or constitutionally imposed.

(3) The decision is not otherwise subject to administrative review in an adjudicative proceeding to which this chapter applies.

(c) For the purpose of application of this chapter to a decision by a quasi-public entity:

(1) "Agency," as defined in Section 11405.30, also includes the quasi-public entity.

(2) "Regulation" includes a rule promulgated by the quasi-public entity.

(3) Article 8 (commencing with Section 11435.05), requiring language assistance in an adjudicative proceeding, applies to a quasi-public entity to the same extent as a state agency under Section 11018.

(d) This section shall be strictly construed to effectuate the intent of the Legislature to apply this chapter only to a decision by a quasi-public entity that is expressly created by statute for the purpose of administration of a state function.

(e) This section shall not apply to a decision made on authority of an approved plan of operations of a quasi-public entity that is subject to the regulation or supervision of the Insurance Commissioner. **Leg.H.** Added Stats 1997 ch 220 §9 (SB 68), effective August 4, 1997.

ARTICLE 4
Governing Procedure

§11415.10. Determination of procedure

(a) The governing procedure by which an agency conducts an adjudicative proceeding is determined by the statutes and regulations applicable to that proceeding. If no other governing procedure is provided by statute or regulation, an agency may conduct an adjudicative proceeding under the administrative adjudication provisions of the Administrative Procedure Act.

(b) This chapter supplements the governing procedure by which an agency conducts an adjudicative proceeding. **Leg.H.** Added Stats 1995 ch 938 §21 (SB 523), operative July 1, 1997.

§11415.20. Statute to prevail over provision of chapter

A state statute or a federal statute or regulation applicable to a particular agency or decision prevails over a conflicting or inconsistent provision of this chapter. **Leg.H.** Added Stats 1995 ch 938 §21 (SB 523), operative July 1, 1997.

§11415.30. Actions by Governor to avoid loss or delay of federal funds

(a) To the extent necessary to avoid a loss or delay of funds or services from the federal government that would otherwise be available to the state, the Governor may do any of the following by executive order:

(1) Suspend, in whole or in part, any administrative adjudication provision of the Administrative Procedure Act.

(2) Adopt a rule of procedure that will avoid the loss or delay.

(b) The Governor shall rescind an executive order issued under this section as soon as it is no longer necessary to prevent the loss or delay of funds or services from the federal government.

(c) If an administrative adjudication provision is suspended or rule of procedure is adopted pursuant to this section, the Governor shall promptly report the suspension or adoption to the Legislature. The report shall include recommendations concerning any legislation that may be necessary to conform the provision to federal law. **Leg.H.** Added Stats 1995 ch 938 §21 (SB 523), operative July 1, 1997.

§11415.40. Waiver of right conferred by provisions

Except to the extent prohibited by another statute or regulation, a person may waive a right conferred on the person by the administrative adjudication provisions of the Administrative Procedure Act. **Leg.H.** Added Stats 1995 ch 938 §21 (SB 523), operative July 1, 1997.

§11415.50. Procedure for decision for which adjudicative proceeding not required

(a) An agency may provide any appropriate procedure for a decision for which an adjudicative proceeding is not required.

(b) An adjudicative proceeding is not required for informal factfinding or an informal investigatory hearing, or a decision to initiate or not to initiate an investigation, prosecution, or other proceeding before the agency, another agency, or a court, whether in response to an application for an agency decision or otherwise. **Leg.H.** Added Stats 1995 ch 938 §21 (SB 523), operative July 1, 1997.

§11415.60. Decision by settlement

(a) An agency may formulate and issue a decision by settlement, pursuant to an agreement of the parties, without conducting an adjudicative proceeding. Subject to subdivision (c), the settlement may be on any terms the parties determine are appropriate. Notwithstanding any other provision of law, no evidence of an offer of compromise or settlement made in settlement negotiations is admissible in an adjudicative proceeding or civil action, whether as affirmative evidence, by way of impeachment, or for any other purpose, and no evidence of conduct or statements made in settlement negotiations is admissible to prove liability for any loss or damage except to the extent provided in Section 1152 of the Evidence Code. Nothing in this subdivision makes inadmissible any public document created by a public agency.

(b) A settlement may be made before or after issuance of an agency pleading, except that in an adjudicative proceeding to determine whether an occupational license should be revoked, suspended, limited, or conditioned, a settlement may not be made before issuance of the agency pleading. A settlement may be made before, during, or after the hearing.

(c) A settlement is subject to any necessary agency approval. An agency head may delegate the power to approve a settlement. The terms of a settlement may not be contrary to statute or regulation, except that the settlement may include sanctions the agency would otherwise lack power to impose. **Leg.H.** Added Stats 1995 ch 938 §21 (SB 523), operative July 1, 1997. Amended Stats 1996 ch 390 §7 (SB 794), effective August 19, 1996, operative July 1, 1997.

ARTICLE 5
Alternative Dispute Resolution

§11420.10. Mediation or arbitration

(a) An agency, with the consent of all the parties, may refer a dispute that is the subject of an adjudicative proceeding for resolution by any of the following means:

(1) Mediation by a neutral mediator.

(2) Binding arbitration by a neutral arbitrator. An award in a binding arbitration is subject to judicial review in the manner provided in Chapter 4 (commencing with Section 1285) of Title 9 of Part 3 of the Code of Civil Procedure.

(3) Nonbinding arbitration by a neutral arbitrator. The arbitrator's decision in a nonbinding arbitration is final unless within 30 days after the arbitrator delivers the award to the agency head a party requests that the agency conduct a de novo adjudicative proceeding. If the decision in the de novo proceeding is not more favorable to the party electing the de novo proceeding, the party shall pay the costs and fees specified in Section 1141.21 of the Code of Civil Procedure insofar as applicable in the adjudicative proceeding.

(b) If another statute requires mediation or arbitration in an adjudicative proceeding, that statute prevails over this section.

(c) This section does not apply in an adjudicative proceeding to the extent an agency by regulation provides that this section is not applicable in a proceeding of the agency. **Leg.H.** Added Stats 1995 ch 938 §21 (SB 523), operative July 1, 1997.

§11420.20. Model regulations for alternative dispute resolution

(a) The Office of Administrative Hearings shall adopt and promulgate model regulations for alternative dispute resolution under this article. The model regulations govern alternative dispute resolution by an agency under this article, except to the extent the agency by regulation provides inconsistent rules or provides that the model regulations are not applicable in a proceeding of the agency.

(b) The model regulations shall include provisions for selection and compensation of a mediator or arbitrator, qualifications of a mediator or arbitrator, and confidentiality of the mediation or arbitration proceeding. **Leg.H.** Added Stats 1995 ch 938 §21 (SB 523), operative July 1, 1997.

§11420.30. Protection of communications

Notwithstanding any other provision of law, a communication made in alternative dispute resolution under this article is protected to the following extent:

(a) Anything said, any admission made, and any document prepared in the course of, or pursuant to, mediation under this article is a confidential communication, and a party to the mediation has a privilege to refuse to disclose and to prevent another from disclosing the communication, whether in an adjudicative proceeding, civil action, or other proceeding. This subdivision does not limit the admissibility of evidence if all parties to the proceedings consent.

(b) No reference to nonbinding arbitration proceedings, a decision of the arbitrator that is rejected by a party's request for a de novo adjudicative proceeding, the evidence produced, or any other aspect of the arbitration may be made in an adjudicative proceeding or civil action, whether as affirmative evidence, by way of impeachment, or for any other purpose.

(c) No mediator or arbitrator is competent to testify in a subsequent administrative or civil proceeding as to any statement, conduct, decision, or order occurring at, or in conjunction with, the alternative dispute resolution.

(d) Evidence otherwise admissible outside of alternative dispute resolution under this article is not inadmissible or protected from disclosure solely by reason of its introduction or use in alternative dispute resolution under this article. **Leg.H.** Added Stats 1995 ch 938 §21 (SB 523), operative July 1, 1997.

ARTICLE 6
Administrative Adjudication Bill of Rights

§11425.10. Required procedures and rights of persons affected

(a) The governing procedure by which an agency conducts an adjudicative proceeding is subject to all of the following requirements:

(1) The agency shall give the person to which the agency action is directed notice and an opportunity to be heard, including the opportunity to present and rebut evidence.

(2) The agency shall make available to the person to which the agency action is directed a copy of the governing procedure, including a statement whether Chapter 5 (commencing with Section 11500) is applicable to the proceeding.

(3) The hearing shall be open to public observation as provided in Section 11425.20.

(4) The adjudicative function shall be separated from the investigative, prosecutorial, and advocacy functions within the agency as provided in Section 11425.30.

(5) The presiding officer is subject to disqualification for bias, prejudice, or interest as provided in Section 11425.40.

(6) The decision shall be in writing, be based on the record, and include a statement of the factual and legal basis of the decision as provided in Section 11425.50.

(7) A decision may not be relied on as precedent unless the agency designates and indexes the decision as precedent as provided in Section 11425.60.

(8) Ex parte communications shall be restricted as provided in Article 7 (commencing with Section 11430.10).

(9) Language assistance shall be made available as provided in Article 8 (commencing with Section 11435.05) by an agency described in Section 11018 or 11435.15.

(b) The requirements of this section apply to the governing procedure by which an agency conducts an adjudicative proceeding without further action by the agency, and prevail over a conflicting or inconsistent provision of the governing procedure, subject to Section 11415.20. The governing procedure by which an agency conducts an adjudicative proceeding may include provisions equivalent to, or more protective of the rights of the person to which the agency action is directed than, the requirements of this section. **Leg.H.** Added Stats 1995 ch 938 §21 (SB 523), operative July 1, 1997.

§11425.20. Hearings open to public; Order for closure

(a) A hearing shall be open to public observation. This subdivision shall not limit the authority of the presiding officer to order closure of a hearing or make other protective orders to the extent necessary or proper for any of the following purposes:

(1) To satisfy the United States Constitution, the California Constitution, federal or state statute, or other law, including, but not limited to, laws protecting privileged, confidential, or other protected information.

(2) To ensure a fair hearing in the circumstances of the particular case.

(3) To conduct the hearing, including the manner of examining witnesses, in a way that is appropriate to protect a minor witness or a witness with a developmental disability, as defined in Section 4512 of the Welfare and Institutions Code, from intimidation or other harm, taking into account the rights of all persons.

(b) To the extent a hearing is conducted by telephone, television, or other electronic means, and is not closed as otherwise required by law, the requirement that the meeting is open to public observation pursuant to subdivision (a) is satisfied if members of the public have an opportunity to do both of the following:

(1) At reasonable times, hear or inspect the agency's record, and inspect any transcript obtained by the agency.

(2) Be physically or virtually present at the place where the presiding officer is conducting the hearing. For purposes of this section, the term "present" can be satisfied either by providing a designated location from which members of the public can observe the meeting via a live audio or a video feed of the hearing made available to the public on the internet or by teleconference.

(c) This section does not apply to a prehearing conference, settlement conference, or proceedings for alternative dispute resolution other than binding arbitration. **Leg.H.** Added Stats 1995 ch 938 §21 (SB 523), operative July 1, 1997. Amended Stats 2021 ch 401 §11 (AB 1578), effective January 1, 2022.

§11425.30. Specified persons not to serve as presiding officer

(a) A person may not serve as presiding officer in an adjudicative proceeding in any of the following circumstances:

(1) The person has served as investigator, prosecutor, or advocate in the proceeding or its preadjudicative stage.

(2) The person is subject to the authority, direction, or discretion of a person who has served as investigator, prosecutor, or advocate in the proceeding or its preadjudicative stage.

(b) Notwithstanding subdivision (a):

(1) A person may serve as presiding officer at successive stages of an adjudicative proceeding.

(2) A person who has participated only as a decisionmaker or as an advisor to a decisionmaker in a determination of probable cause or other equivalent preliminary determination in an adjudicative proceeding or its preadjudicative stage may serve as presiding officer in the proceeding.

(c) The provisions of this section governing separation of functions as to the presiding officer also govern separation of functions as to the agency head or other person or body to which the power to hear or decide in the proceeding is delegated. **Leg.H.** Added Stats 1995 ch 938 §21 (SB 523), operative July 1, 1997.

§11425.40. Disqualification of presiding officer

(a) The presiding officer is subject to disqualification for bias, prejudice, or interest in the proceeding.

(b) It is not alone or in itself grounds for disqualification, without further evidence of bias, prejudice, or interest, that the presiding officer:

(1) Is or is not a member of a racial, ethnic, religious, sexual, or similar group and the proceeding involves the rights of that group.

(2) Has experience, technical competence, or specialized knowledge of, or has in any capacity expressed a view on, a legal, factual, or policy issue presented in the proceeding.

(3) Has as a lawyer or public official participated in the drafting of laws or regulations or in the effort to pass or defeat laws or regulations, the meaning, effect, or application of which is in issue in the proceeding.

(c) The provisions of this section governing disqualification of the presiding officer also govern disqualification of the agency head or other person or body to which the power to hear or decide in the proceeding is delegated.

(d) An agency that conducts an adjudicative proceeding may provide by regulation for peremptory challenge of the presiding officer. **Leg.H.** Added Stats 1995 ch 938 §21 (SB 523), operative July 1, 1997.

§11425.50. Decision to be in writing; Statement of factual and legal basis

(a) The decision shall be in writing and shall include a statement of the factual and legal basis for the decision.

(b) The statement of the factual basis for the decision may be in the language of, or by reference to, the pleadings. If the statement is no more than mere repetition or paraphrase of the relevant statute or regulation, the statement shall be accompanied by a concise and explicit statement of the underlying facts of record that support the decision. If the factual basis for the decision includes a determination based substantially on the credibility of a witness, the statement shall identify any specific evidence of the observed demeanor, manner, or attitude of the witness that supports the determination, and on judicial review the court shall give great weight to the determination to the extent the determination identifies the observed demeanor, manner, or attitude of the witness that supports it.

(c) The statement of the factual basis for the decision shall be based exclusively on the evidence of record in the proceeding and on matters officially noticed in the proceeding. The presiding officer's experience, technical competence, and specialized knowledge may be used in evaluating evidence.

(d) Nothing in this section limits the information that may be contained in the decision, including a summary of evidence relied on.

(e) A penalty may not be based on a guideline, criterion, bulletin, manual, instruction, order, standard of general application or other rule subject to Chapter 3.5 (commencing with Section 11340) unless it has been adopted as a regulation pursuant to Chapter 3.5 (commencing with Section 11340). **Leg.H.** Added Stats 1995 ch 938 §21 (SB 523), operative July 1, 1997.

§11425.60. Decisions relied on as precedents; Index of precedent decisions

(a) A decision may not be expressly relied on as precedent unless it is designated as a precedent decision by the agency.

(b) An agency may designate as a precedent decision a decision or part of a decision that contains a significant legal or policy determination of general application that is likely to recur. Designation of a decision or part of a decision as a precedent decision is not rulemaking and need not be done under Chapter 3.5 (commencing with Section 11340). An agency's designation of a decision or part of a decision, or failure to designate a decision or part of a decision, as a precedent decision is not subject to judicial review.

(c) An agency shall maintain an index of significant legal and policy determinations made in precedent decisions. The index shall be updated not less frequently than annually, unless no precedent decision has been designated since the last preceding update. The index shall be made available to the public by subscription, and its availability shall be publicized annually in the California Regulatory Notice Register.

(d) This section applies to decisions issued on or after July 1, 1997. Nothing in this section precludes an agency from designating and indexing as a precedent decision a decision issued before July 1, 1997. **Leg.H.** Added Stats 1995 ch 938 §21 (SB 523), operative July 1, 1997. Amended Stats 1996 ch 390 §8 (SB 794), effective August 19, 1996, operative July 1, 1997.

ARTICLE 7
Ex Parte Communications

§11430.10. Ex parte communications

(a) While the proceeding is pending there shall be no communication, direct or indirect, regarding any issue in the proceeding, to the presiding officer from an employee or representative of an agency that is a party or from an interested person outside the agency, without notice and opportunity for all parties to participate in the communication.

(b) Nothing in this section precludes a communication, including a communication from an employee or representative of an agency that is a party, made on the record at the hearing.

(c) For the purpose of this section, a proceeding is pending from the issuance of the agency's pleading, or from an application for an agency decision, whichever is earlier. **Leg.H.** Added Stats 1995 ch 938 §21 (SB 523), operative July 1, 1997.

§11430.20. Permissible ex parte communications

A communication otherwise prohibited by Section 11430.10 is permissible in any of the following circumstances:

(a) The communication is required for disposition of an ex parte matter specifically authorized by statute.

(b) The communication concerns a matter of procedure or practice, including a request for a continuance, that is not in controversy. **Leg.H.** Added Stats 1995 ch 938 §21 (SB 523), operative July 1, 1997.

§11430.30. Permissible ex parte communication from agency that is party

A communication otherwise prohibited by Section 11430.10 from an employee or representative of an agency that is a party to the presiding officer is permissible in any of the following circumstances:

(a) The communication is for the purpose of assistance and advice to the presiding officer from a person who has not served as investigator, prosecutor, or advocate in the proceeding or its preadjudicative stage. An assistant or advisor may evaluate the evidence in the record but shall not furnish, augment, diminish, or modify the evidence in the record.

(b) The communication is for the purpose of advising the presiding officer concerning a settlement proposal advocated by the advisor.

(c) The communication is for the purpose of advising the presiding officer concerning any of the following matters in an adjudicative proceeding that is nonprosecutorial in character:

(1) The advice involves a technical issue in the proceeding and the advice is necessary for, and is not otherwise reasonably available to, the presiding officer, provided the content of the advice is disclosed on the record and all parties are given an opportunity to address it in the manner provided in Section 11430.50.

(2) The advice involves an issue in a proceeding of the San Francisco Bay Conservation and Development Commission, California Tahoe Regional Planning Agency, Delta Protection Commission, Water Resources Control Board, or a regional water quality control board. **Leg.H.** Added Stats 1995 ch 938 §21 (SB 523), operative July 1, 1997.

§11430.40. Disclosure of communication received while proceeding is pending

If, while the proceeding is pending but before serving as presiding officer, a person receives a communication of a type that would be in violation of this article if received while serving as presiding officer, the person, promptly after starting to serve, shall disclose the content of the communication on the record and give all parties an opportunity to address it in the manner provided in Section 11430.50. **Leg.H.** Added Stats 1995 ch 938 §21 (SB 523), operative July 1, 1997.

§11430.50. Communication in violation of provisions

(a) If a presiding officer receives a communication in violation of this article, the presiding officer shall make all of the following a part of the record in the proceeding:

(1) If the communication is written, the writing and any written response of the presiding officer to the communication.

(2) If the communication is oral, a memorandum stating the substance of the communication, any response made by the presiding officer, and the identity of each person from whom the presiding officer received the communication.

(b) The presiding officer shall notify all parties that a communication described in this section has been made a part of the record.

(c) If a party requests an opportunity to address the communication within 10 days after receipt of notice of the communication:

(1) The party shall be allowed to comment on the communication.

(2) The presiding officer has discretion to allow the party to present evidence concerning the subject of the communication, including discretion to reopen a hearing that has been concluded. **Leg.H.** Added Stats 1995 ch 938 §21 (SB 523), operative July 1, 1997.

§11430.60. Prohibited communication as grounds to disqualify presiding officer

Receipt by the presiding officer of a communication in violation of this article may be grounds for disqualification of the presiding officer. If the presiding officer is disqualified, the portion of the record pertaining to the ex parte communication may be sealed by protective order of the disqualified presiding officer. **Leg.H.** Added Stats 1995 ch 938 §21 (SB 523), operative July 1, 1997.

§11430.70. Agency head delegated to hear or decide proceeding

(a) Subject to subdivision (b) and (c), the provisions of this article governing ex parte communications to the presiding officer also govern ex parte communications in an adjudicative proceeding to the agency head or other person or body to which the power to hear or decide in the proceeding is delegated.

(b) An ex parte communication to the agency head or other person or body to which the power to hear or decide in the proceeding is delegated is permissible in an individualized ratemaking proceeding if the content of the communication is disclosed on the record and all parties are given an opportunity to address it in the manner provided in Section 11430.50.

(c) An ex parte communication to the agency head or other person or body to which the power to hear or decide in the proceeding is delegated is permissible in an individualized determination of an application for site certification pursuant to Chapter 6 (commencing with Section 25500) of Division 15 of the Public Resources Code, that is before the State Energy Resources Conservation and Development Commission, if the communication is made by an employee of another state agency and is made for the purpose of enabling the presiding officer to effectively manage the proceeding. **Leg.H.** Added Stats 1995 ch 938 §21 (SB 523), operative July

1, 1997. Amended Stats 2010 8th Ex Sess ch 9 §4 (SBX8-34), effective March 22, 2010.

§11430.80. Communication between presiding officer and agency head delegated to hear proceeding

(a) There shall be no communication, direct or indirect, while a proceeding is pending regarding the merits of any issue in the proceeding, between the presiding officer and the agency head or other person or body to which the power to hear or decide in the proceeding is delegated.

(b) This section does not apply where the agency head or other person or body to which the power to hear or decide in the proceeding is delegated serves as both presiding officer and agency head, or where the presiding officer does not issue a decision in the proceeding. **Leg.H.** Added Stats 1995 ch 938 §21 (SB 523), operative July 1, 1997.

ARTICLE 8
Language Assistance

§11435.05. "Language assistance"

As used in this article, "language assistance" means oral interpretation or written translation into English of a language other than English or of English into another language for a party or witness who cannot speak or understand English or who can do so only with difficulty. **Leg.H.** Added Stats 1995 ch 938 §21 (SB 523), operative July 1, 1997.

§11435.10. Interpretation for deaf or hard-of-hearing persons

Nothing in this article limits the application or effect of Section 754 of the Evidence Code to interpretation for a deaf or hard-of-hearing party or witness in an adjudicative proceeding. **Leg.H.** Added Stats 1995 ch 938 §21 (SB 523), operative July 1, 1997.

§11435.15. Provision of language assistance by state agencies

(a) The following state agencies shall provide language assistance in adjudicative proceedings to the extent provided in this article:

(1) Agricultural Labor Relations Board.
(2) State Department of Alcohol and Drug Programs.
(3) State Athletic Commission.
(4) California Unemployment Insurance Appeals Board.
(5) Board of Parole Hearings.
(6) State Board of Barbering and Cosmetology.
(7) State Department of Developmental Services.
(8) Public Employment Relations Board.
(9) Franchise Tax Board.
(10) State Department of Health Care Services.
(11) Department of Housing and Community Development.
(12) Department of Industrial Relations.
(13) State Department of State Hospitals.
(14) Department of Motor Vehicles.
(15) Notary Public Section, Office of the Secretary of State.
(16) Public Utilities Commission.
(17) Office of Statewide Health Planning and Development.
(18) State Department of Social Services.
(19) Workers' Compensation Appeals Board.
(20) Division of Juvenile Justice.
(21) Division of Juvenile Parole Operations.
(22) Department of Insurance.
(23) State Personnel Board.
(24) California Board of Podiatric Medicine.
(25) Board of Psychology.

(b) Nothing in this section prevents an agency other than an agency listed in subdivision (a) from electing to adopt any of the procedures in this article, provided that any selection of an interpreter is subject to Section 11435.30.

(c) Nothing in this section prohibits an agency from providing an interpreter during a proceeding to which this chapter does not apply, including an informal factfinding or informal investigatory hearing.

(d) This article applies to an agency listed in subdivision (a) notwithstanding a general provision that this chapter does not apply to some or all of an agency's adjudicative proceedings. **Leg.H.** Added Stats 1995 ch 938 §21 (SB 523), operative July 1, 1997. Amended Stats 1996 ch 390 §5, effective August 19, 1996, operative July 1, 1997; Stats 2012 ch 440 §11 (AB 1488), effective September 22, 2012; Stats 2013 ch 76 §82 (AB 383), effective January 1, 2014.

§11435.20. Hearing or medical examination to be conducted in English

(a) The hearing, or any medical examination conducted for the purpose of determining compensation or monetary award, shall be conducted in English.

(b) If a party or the party's witness does not proficiently speak or understand English and before commencement of the hearing or medical examination requests language assistance, an agency subject to the language assistance requirement of this article shall provide the party or witness an interpreter. **Leg.H.** Added Stats 1995 ch 938 §21 (SB 523), operative July 1, 1997.

§11435.25. Cost of providing interpreter

(a) The cost of providing an interpreter under this article shall be paid by the agency having jurisdiction over the matter if the presiding officer so directs, otherwise by the party at whose request the interpreter is provided.

(b) The presiding officer's decision to direct payment shall be based upon an equitable consideration of all the circumstances in each case, such as the ability of the party in need of the interpreter to pay.

(c) Notwithstanding any other provision of this section, in a hearing before the Workers' Compensation Appeals Board or the Division of Workers' Compensation relating to workers' compensation claims, the payment of the costs of providing an interpreter shall be governed by the rules and regulations promulgated by the Workers' Compensation Appeals Board or the Administrative Director of the Division of Workers' Compensation, as appropriate. **Leg.H.** Added Stats 1995 ch 938 §21 (SB 523), operative July 1, 1997.

§11435.30. Publication of list of certified interpreters

(a) The State Personnel Board shall establish, maintain, administer, and publish annually an updated list of certified administrative hearing interpreters it has determined meet the minimum standards in interpreting skills and linguistic abilities in languages designated pursuant to Section 11435.40. Any interpreter so listed may be examined by each employing agency to determine the interpreter's knowledge of the employing agency's technical program terminology and procedures.

(b) Court interpreters certified pursuant to Section 68562, and interpreters listed on the State Personnel Board's recommended lists of court and administrative hearing interpreters prior to July 1, 1993, shall be deemed certified for purposes of this section.

(c)(1) In addition to the certification procedure provided pursuant to subdivision (a), the Administrative Director of the Division of Workers' Compensation may establish, maintain, administer, and publish annually an updated list of certified administrative hearing interpreters who, based on testing by an independent organization designated by the administrative director, have been determined to meet the minimum standards in interpreting skills and linguistic abilities in languages designated pursuant to Section 11435.40, for purposes of administrative hearings conducted pursuant to proceedings of the Workers' Compensation Appeals Board. The independent testing organization shall have no financial interest in the training of interpreters or in the employment of interpreters for administrative hearings.

(2)(A) A fee, as determined by the administrative director, shall be collected from each interpreter seeking certification. The fee shall not exceed the reasonable regulatory costs of administering the testing and certification program and of publishing the list of certified administrative hearing interpreters on the Division of Workers' Compensation' Internet Web site.

(B) The Legislature finds and declares that the services described in this section are of such a special and unique nature that they may be contracted out pursuant to paragraph (3) of subdivision (b) of Section 19130. The Legislature further finds and declares that the services described in this section are a new state function pursuant to paragraph (2) of subdivision (b) of Section 19130. **Leg.H.** Added Stats 1995 ch 938 §21 (SB 523), operative July 1, 1997. Amended Stats 2012 ch 363 §2 (SB 863), effective January 1, 2013.

2012 Notes: The Legislature finds and declares all of the following:

(a) That Section 4 of Article XIV of the California Constitution authorizes the creation of a workers' compensation system that includes adequate provision for the comfort, health and safety, and general welfare of workers and their dependents to relieve them of the consequences of any work-related injury or death, irrespective of the fault of any party and requires the administration of the workers' compensation system to accomplish substantial justice in all cases expeditiously, inexpensively, and without encumbrance of any character, all of which matters are expressly declared to be the social public policy of this state.

(b) That the current system of determining permanent disability has become excessively litigious, time consuming, procedurally burdensome and unpredictable, and that the provisions of this act will produce the necessary uniformity, consistency, and objectivity of outcomes, in accordance with the constitutional mandate to accomplish substantial justice in all cases expeditiously, inexpensively, and without encumbrance of any character, and that in enacting subdivision (c) of Section 4660.1 of the Labor Code, the Legislature intends to eliminate questionable claims of disability when alleged to be caused by a disabling physical injury arising out of and in the course of employment while guaranteeing medical treatment as required by Division 4 (commencing with Section 3200) of the Labor Code.

(c) That in enacting this act, it is not the intent of the Legislature to overrule the holding in Milpitas Unified School District v. Workers Comp. Appeals Bd. (Guzman) (2010) 187 Cal.App.4th 808.

(d) That the current system of resolving disputes over the medical necessity of requested treatment is costly, time consuming, and does not uniformly result in the provision of treatment that adheres to the highest standards of evidence-based medicine, adversely affecting the health and safety of workers injured in the course of employment.

(e) That having medical professionals ultimately determine the necessity of requested treatment furthers the social policy of this state in reference to using evidence-based medicine to provide injured workers with the highest quality of medical care and that the provision of the act establishing independent medical review are necessary to implement that policy.

(f) That the performance of independent medical review is a service of such a special and unique nature that it must be contracted pursuant to paragraph (3) of subdivision (b) of Section 19130 of the Government Code, and that independent medical review is a new state function pursuant to paragraph (2) of subdivision (b) of Section 19130 of the Government Code that will be more expeditious, more economical, and more scientifically sound than the existing function of medical necessity determinations performed by qualified medical evaluators appointed pursuant to Section 139.2 of the Labor Code. The existing process of appointing qualified medical evaluators to examine patients and resolve treatment disputes is costly and time-consuming, and it prolongs disputes and causes delays in medical treatment for injured workers. Additionally, the process of selection of qualified medical evaluators can bias the outcomes. Timely and medically sound determinations of disputes over appropriate medical treatment require the independent and unbiased medical expertise of specialists that are not available through the civil service system.

(g) That the establishment of independent medical review and provision for limited appeal of decisions resulting from independent medical review are a necessary exercise of the Legislature's plenary power to provide for the settlement of any disputes arising under the workers' compensation laws of this state and to control the manner of review of such decisions.

(h) That the performance of independent bill review is a service of such a special and unique nature that it must be contracted pursuant to paragraph (3) of subdivision (b) of Section 19130 of the Government Code, and that independent bill review is a new state function pursuant to paragraph (2) of subdivision (b) of Section 19130 of the Government Code. Existing law provides no method of medical billing dispute resolution short of litigation. Existing law does not provide for medical billing and payment experts to resolve billing disputes, and billing issues are frequently submitted to workers' compensation judges without the benefit of independent and unbiased findings on these issues. Medical billing and payment systems are a field of technical and specialized expertise, requiring services that are not available through the civil service system. The need for independent and unbiased findings and determinations requires that this new function be contracted pursuant to subdivision (b) of Section 19130 of the Government Code. Stats 2012 ch 363 (SB 863) § 1.

This act shall apply to all pending matters, regardless of date of injury, unless otherwise specified in this act, but shall not be a basis to rescind, alter, amend, or reopen any final award of workers' compensation benefits. Stats 2012 ch 363 (SB 863) § 84.

It appears the Legislature inadvertently substituted "Compensation' Internet" for "Compensation's Internet" in the second sentence of subd (c)(2)(A).

§11435.35. Publication of list of certified medical examination interpreters

(a) The State Personnel Board shall establish, maintain, administer, and publish annually, an updated list of certified medical examination interpreters it has determined meet the minimum standards in interpreting skills and linguistic abilities in languages designated pursuant to Section 11435.40.

(b) Court interpreters certified pursuant to Section 68562 and administrative hearing interpreters certified pursuant to Section 11435.30 shall be deemed certified for purposes of this section.

(c)(1) In addition to the certification procedure provided pursuant to subdivision (a), the Administrative Director of the Division of workers' Compensation may establish, maintain, administer, and publish annually an updated list of certified medical examination interpreters who, based on testing by an independent organization designated by the administrative director, have been determined to meet the minimum standards in interpreting skills and linguistic abilities in languages designated pursuant to Section 11435.40, for purposes of medical examinations conducted pursuant to proceedings of the workers' Compensation Appeals Board, and medical examinations conducted pursuant to Division 4 (commencing with Section 3200) of the Labor Code. The independent testing organization shall have no financial interest in the training of interpreters or in the employment of interpreters for medical examinations.

(2)(A) A fee, as determined by the administrative director, shall be collected from each interpreter seeking certification. The fee shall not exceed the reasonable regulatory costs of administering the testing and certification program and of publishing the list of certified medical examination interpreters on the Division of Workers' Compensation's Internet Web site.

(B) The Legislature finds and declares that the services described in this section are of such a special and unique nature that they may be contracted out pursuant to paragraph (3) of subdivision (b) of Section 19130. The Legislature further finds and declares that the services described in this section are a new state function pursuant to paragraph (2) of subdivision (b) of Section 19130. **Leg.H.** Added Stats 1995 ch 938 §21 (SB 523), operative July 1, 1997. Amended Stats 2012 ch 363 §3 (SB 863), effective January 1, 2013. Stats 2013 ch 287 § 1 (SB 375), effective January 1, 2014.

2012 Note: For legislative findings, declarations, and applicablity of Stats 2012 ch 363 (SB 863), see 2012 Notes following Gov C § 11435.30.

§11435.40. Designation of languages for certification

(a) The Department of Human Resources shall designate the languages for which certification shall be established under Sections 11435.30 and 11435.35. The languages designated shall include, but not be limited to, Spanish, Tagalog, Arabic, Cantonese, Japanese, Korean, Portuguese, and Vietnamese until the Department of Human Resources finds that there is an insufficient need for interpreting assistance in these languages.

(b) The language designations shall be based on the following:

(1) The language needs of non-English-speaking persons appearing before the administrative agencies, as determined by consultation with the agencies.

(2) The cost of developing a language examination.

(3) The availability of experts needed to develop a language examination.

(4) Other information the department deems relevant. **Leg.H.** Added Stats 1995 ch 938 §21 (SB 523), operative July 1, 1997. Amended Stats 2012 ch 360 §6 (SB 1309), effective January 1, 2013.

§11435.45. Application fees to take interpreter examinations

(a) The Department of Human Resources shall establish and charge fees for applications to take interpreter examinations and for renewal of certifications. The purpose of these fees is to cover the annual projected costs of carrying out this article. The fees may be adjusted each fiscal year by a percent that is equal to or less than the percent change in the California Necessities Index prepared by the Commission on State Finance.

(b) Each certified administrative hearing interpreter and each certified medical examination interpreter shall pay a fee, due on July 1 of each year, for the renewal of the certification. Court interpreters certified under Section 68562 shall not pay any fees required by this section.

(c) If the amount of money collected in fees is not sufficient to cover the costs of carrying out this article, the department shall charge and be reimbursed a pro rata share of the additional costs by the state agencies that conduct administrative hearings. **Leg.H.** Added Stats 1995 ch 938 §21 (SB 523), operative July 1, 1997. Amended Stats 2012 ch 360 §7 (SB 1309), effective January 1, 2013.

§11435.50. Removal of person from list of certified interpreters

The Department of Human Resources may remove the name of a person from the list of certified interpreters if any of the following conditions occurs:

(a) The person is deceased.

(b) The person notifies the department that the person is unavailable for work.

(c) The person does not submit a renewal fee as required by Section 11435.45. **Leg.H.** Added Stats 1995 ch 938 §21 (SB 523), operative July 1, 1997. Amended Stats 2012 ch 360 §8 (SB 1309), effective January 1, 2013.

§11435.55. Qualification and use of noncertified interpreters

(a) An interpreter used in a hearing shall be certified pursuant to Section 11435.30. However, if an interpreter certified pursuant to Section 11435.30 cannot be present at the hearing, the hearing agency shall have discretionary authority to provisionally qualify and use another interpreter.

(b) An interpreter used in a medical examination shall be certified pursuant to Section 11435.35. However, if an interpreter certified pursuant to Section 11435.35 cannot be present at the medical examination, the physician provisionally may use another interpreter if that fact is noted in the record of the medical evaluation. **Leg.H.** Added Stats 1995 ch 938 §21 (SB 523), operative July 1, 1997.

§11435.60. Party to be advised of right to interpreter

Every agency subject to the language assistance requirement of this article shall advise each party of the right to an interpreter at the same time that each party is advised of the hearing date or medical examination. Each party in need of an interpreter shall also be encouraged to give timely notice to the agency conducting the hearing or medical examination so that appropriate arrangements can be made. **Leg.H.** Added Stats 1995 ch 938 §21 (SB 523), operative July 1, 1997.

§11435.65. Rules of confidentiality applicable to interpreters

(a) The rules of confidentiality of the agency, if any, that apply in an adjudicative proceeding shall apply to any interpreter in the hearing or medical examination, whether or not the rules so state.

(b) The interpreter shall not have had any involvement in the issues of the case prior to the hearing. **Leg.H.** Added Stats 1995 ch 938 §21 (SB 523), operative July 1, 1997.

ARTICLE 9
General Procedural Provisions

§11440.10. Review of decision

(a) The agency head may do any of the following with respect to a decision of the presiding officer or the agency:

(1) Determine to review some but not all issues, or not to exercise any review.

(2) Delegate its review authority to one or more persons.

(3) Authorize review by one or more persons, subject to further review by the agency head.

(b) By regulation an agency may mandate review, or may preclude or limit review, of a decision of the presiding officer or the agency. **Leg.H.** Added Stats 1995 ch 938 §21 (SB 523), operative July 1, 1997.

§11440.20. Service of writing or electronic document; Notice

Service of a writing or electronic document on, or giving of a notice to, a person in a procedure provided in this chapter is subject to the following provisions:

(a) The writing, electronic document, or notice shall be delivered personally or sent by mail, electronic, or other means to the person at the person's last known address or, if the person is a party with an attorney or other authorized representative of record in the proceeding, to the party's attorney or other authorized representative. If a party is required by statute or regulation to maintain an address with an agency, the party's last known address is the address maintained with the agency.

(b) Unless a provision specifies the form of mail, service or notice by mail may be by first-class mail, registered mail, or certified mail, by mail delivery service, by facsimile transmission if complete and without error, or by other electronic means as provided by regulation, in the discretion of the sender. **Leg.H.** Added Stats 1995 ch 938 §21 (SB 523), operative July 1, 1997. Amended Stats 2021 ch 401 §12 (AB 1578), effective January 1, 2022.

§11440.30. Conduct of hearing by telephone, television, or other electronic means

(a) The presiding officer may conduct all or part of a hearing by telephone, television, or other electronic means if each participant in the hearing has an opportunity to participate in and to hear the entire proceeding while it is taking place and to observe exhibits.

(b)(1) Except as provided in paragraph (2), the presiding officer may not conduct all of a hearing by telephone, television, or other electronic means if a party objects.

(2) If a party objects pursuant to paragraph (1) to a hearing being conducted by electronic means, the presiding officer shall consider the objections and may, in the presiding officer's discretion, structure the hearing to address the party's specific objections and may require the presiding officer, parties, and witnesses, or a subset of parties and witnesses based on the specific objections, to be present in a physical location during all or part of the hearing.

(c) Subdivision (b) is not a limitation on the presiding officer transmitting the hearing by telephone, television, or other electronic means or receiving comments via electronic means from participants who are not parties or witnesses. **Leg.H.** Added Stats 1995 ch 938 §21 (SB 523), operative July 1, 1997. Amended Stats 2021 ch 401 §13 (AB 1578), effective January 1, 2022.

§11440.40. Proceedings involving sexual offenses; Limitations on evidence

(a) In any proceeding under subdivision (h) or (i) of Section 12940, or Section 19572 or 19702, alleging conduct that constitutes sexual harassment, sexual assault, or sexual battery, evidence of specific instances of a complainant's sexual conduct with individuals other than the alleged perpetrator is subject to all of the following limitations:

(1) The evidence is not discoverable unless it is to be offered at a hearing to attack the credibility of the complainant as provided for under subdivision (b). This paragraph is intended only to limit the scope of discovery; it is not intended to affect the methods of discovery allowed by statute.

(2) The evidence is not admissible at the hearing unless offered to attack the credibility of the complainant as provided for under subdivision (b). Reputation or opinion evidence regarding the sexual behavior of the complainant is not admissible for any purpose.

(b) Evidence of specific instances of a complainant's sexual conduct with individuals other than the alleged perpetrator is presumed inadmissible absent an offer of proof establishing its relevance and reliability and that its probative value is not substantially outweighed by the probability that its admission will create substantial danger of undue prejudice or confuse the issue.

(c) As used in this section "complainant" means a person claiming to have been subjected to conduct that constitutes sexual harassment, sexual assault, or sexual battery. **Leg.H.** Added Stats 1995 ch 938 §21 (SB 523), operative July 1, 1997.

§11440.45. Benevolent gestures as admission of liability; Limitations on evidence

(a) In any proceedings pursuant to this chapter or Chapter 5 (commencing with Section 11500), the portion of statements, writings, or benevolent gestures expressing sympathy or a general sense of benevolence relating to the pain, suffering, or death of a person involved in an accident and made to that person or to the family of that person shall be inadmissible as evidence of an admission of liability. A statement of fault, however, which is part of, or in addition to, any of the above shall not be inadmissible pursuant to this section.

(b) For purposes of this section:

(1) "Accident" means an occurrence resulting in injury or death to one or more persons which is not the result of willful action by a party.

(2) "Benevolent gestures" means actions which convey a sense of compassion or commiseration emanating from humane impulses.

(3) "Family" means the spouse, parent, grandparent, stepmother, stepfather, child, grandchild, brother, sister, half brother, half sister, adopted children of parent, or spouse's parents of an injured party. **Leg.H.** Added Stats 2002 ch 92 §1 (AB 2723).

§11440.50. Intervention; Grant of motion; Conditions

(a) This section applies in adjudicative proceedings of an agency if the agency by regulation provides that this section is applicable in the proceedings.

(b) The presiding officer shall grant a motion for intervention if all of the following conditions are satisfied:

(1) The motion is submitted in writing, with copies served on all parties named in the agency's pleading.

(2) The motion is made as early as practicable in advance of the hearing. If there is a prehearing conference, the motion shall be made in advance of the prehearing conference and shall be resolved at the prehearing conference.

(3) The motion states facts demonstrating that the applicant's legal rights, duties, privileges, or immunities will be substantially affected by the proceeding or that the applicant qualifies as an intervenor under a statute or regulation.

(4) The presiding officer determines that the interests of justice and the orderly and prompt conduct of the proceeding will not be impaired by allowing the intervention.

(c) If an applicant qualifies for intervention, the presiding officer may impose conditions on the intervenor's participation in the proceeding, either at the time that intervention is granted or at a subsequent time. Conditions may include the following:

(1) Limiting the intervenor's participation to designated issues in which the intervenor has a particular interest demonstrated by the motion.

(2) Limiting or excluding the use of discovery, cross-examination, and other procedures involving the intervenor so as to promote the orderly and prompt conduct of the proceeding.

(3) Requiring two or more intervenors to combine their presentations of evidence and argument, cross-examination, discovery, and other participation in the proceeding.

(4) Limiting or excluding the intervenor's participation in settlement negotiations.

(d) As early as practicable in advance of the hearing the presiding officer shall issue an order granting or denying the motion for intervention, specifying any conditions, and briefly stating the reasons for the order. The presiding officer may modify the order at any time, stating the reasons for the modification. The presiding officer shall promptly give notice of an order granting, denying, or modifying intervention to the applicant and to all parties.

(e) Whether the interests of justice and the orderly and prompt conduct of the proceedings will be impaired by allowing intervention is a determination to be made in the sole discretion, and based on the knowledge and judgment at that time, of the presiding officer. The determination is not subject to administrative or judicial review.

(f) Nothing in this section precludes an agency from adopting a regulation that permits participation by a person short of intervention as a party, subject to Article 7 (commencing with Section 11430.10) of Chapter 4.5. **Leg.H.** Added Stats 1995 ch 938 §21 (SB 523), operative July 1, 1997.

§11440.60. Indication of person paying for written communication

(a) For purposes of this section, the following terms have the following meaning:

(1) "Quasi-judicial proceeding" means any of the following:

(A) A proceeding to determine the rights or duties of a person under existing laws, regulations, or policies.

(B) A proceeding involving the issuance, amendment, or revocation of a permit or license.

(C) A proceeding to enforce compliance with existing law or to impose sanctions for violations of existing law.

(D) A proceeding at which action is taken involving the purchase or sale of property, goods, or services by an agency.

(E) A proceeding at which an action is taken awarding a grant or a contract.

(2) "Written communication" means any report, study, survey, analysis, letter, or any other written document.

(b) Any person submitting a written communication, which is specifically generated for the purpose of being presented at the agency hearing to which it is being communicated, to a state agency in a quasi-judicial proceeding that is directly paid for by anyone other than the person who submitted the written communication shall clearly indicate any person who paid to produce the written communication.

(c) A state agency may refuse or ignore a written communication submitted by an attorney or any other authorized representative on behalf of a client in a quasi-judicial proceeding, unless the written communication clearly indicates the client on whose behalf the communication is submitted to the state agency. **Leg.H.** Added Stats 1997 ch 192 §1 (SB 504).

ARTICLE 10
Informal Hearing

§11445.10. Legislative findings and declarations

(a) Subject to the limitations in this article, an agency may conduct an adjudicative proceeding under the informal hearing procedure provided in this article.

(b) The Legislature finds and declares the following:

(1) The informal hearing procedure is intended to satisfy due process and public policy requirements in a manner that is simpler and more expeditious than hearing procedures otherwise required by statute, for use in appropriate circumstances.

(2) The informal hearing procedure provides a forum in the nature of a conference in which a party has an opportunity to be heard by the presiding officer.

(3) The informal hearing procedure provides a forum that may accommodate a hearing where by regulation or statute a member of the public may participate without appearing or intervening as a party. **Leg.H.** Added Stats 1995 ch 938 §21 (SB 523), operative July 1, 1997.

§11445.20. Circumstances permitting use of informal hearing procedure

Subject to Section 11445.30, an agency may use an informal hearing procedure in any of the following proceedings, if in the circumstances its use does not violate another statute or the federal or state Constitution:

(a) A proceeding where there is no disputed issue of material fact.

(b) A proceeding where there is a disputed issue of material fact, if the matter is limited to any of the following:

(1) A monetary amount of not more than one thousand dollars ($1,000).

(2) A disciplinary sanction against a student that does not involve expulsion from an academic institution or suspension for more than 10 days.

(3) A disciplinary sanction against an employee that does not involve discharge from employment, demotion, or suspension for more than 5 days.

(4) A disciplinary sanction against a licensee that does not involve an actual revocation of a license or an actual suspension of a license for more than five days. Nothing in this section precludes an agency from imposing a stayed revocation or a stayed suspension of a license in an informal hearing.

(c) A proceeding where, by regulation, the agency has authorized use of an informal hearing.

(d) A proceeding where an evidentiary hearing for determination of facts is not required by statute but where the agency determines the federal or state Constitution may require a hearing. **Leg.H.** Added Stats 1995 ch 938 §21 (SB 523), operative July 1, 1997.

§11445.30. Notice of informal procedure

(a) The notice of hearing shall state the agency's selection of the informal hearing procedure.

(b) Any objection of a party to use of the informal hearing procedure shall be made in the party's pleading.

(c) An objection to use of the informal hearing procedure shall be resolved by the presiding officer before the hearing on the basis of the pleadings and any written submissions in support of the pleadings. An objection to use of the informal hearing procedure in a disciplinary proceeding involving an occupational license shall be resolved in favor of the licensee. **Leg.H.** Added Stats 1995 ch 938 §21 (SB 523), operative July 1, 1997.

§11445.40. Application of procedures otherwise required

(a) Except as provided in this article, the hearing procedures otherwise required by statute for an adjudicative proceeding apply to an informal hearing.

(b) In an informal hearing the presiding officer shall regulate the course of the proceeding. The presiding officer shall permit the parties and may permit others to offer written or oral comments on the issues. The presiding officer may limit the use of witnesses, testimony, evidence, and argument, and may limit or eliminate the use of pleadings, intervention, discovery, prehearing conferences, and rebuttal. **Leg.H.** Added Stats 1995 ch 938 §21 (SB 523), operative July 1, 1997.

§11445.50. Denial of use of informal procedure; Conversion to formal hearing; Cross-examination

(a) The presiding officer may deny use of the informal hearing procedure, or may convert an informal hearing to a formal hearing after an informal hearing is commenced, if it appears to the presiding officer that cross-examination is necessary for proper determination of the matter and that the delay, burden, or complication due to allowing cross-examination in the informal hearing will be more than minimal.

(b) An agency, by regulation, may specify categories of cases in which cross-examination is deemed not necessary for proper determination of the matter under the informal hearing procedure. The presiding officer may allow cross-examination of witnesses in an informal hearing notwithstanding an agency regulation if it appears to the presiding officer that in the circumstances cross-examination is necessary for proper determination of the matter.

(c) The actions of the presiding officer under this section are not subject to judicial review. **Leg.H.** Added Stats 1995 ch 938 §21 (SB 523), operative July 1, 1997.

§11445.60. Identity of witnesses or other sources

(a) If the presiding officer has reason to believe that material facts are in dispute, the presiding officer may require a party to state the identity of the witnesses or other sources through which the party would propose to present proof if the proceeding were converted to a formal or other applicable hearing procedure. If disclosure of a fact, allegation, or source is privileged or expressly prohibited by a regulation, statute, or the federal or state Constitution, the presiding officer may require the party to indicate that confidential facts, allegations, or sources are involved, but not to disclose the confidential facts, allegations, or sources.

(b) If a party has reason to believe that essential facts must be obtained in order to permit an adequate presentation of the case, the party may inform the presiding officer regarding the general nature of the facts and the sources from which the party would propose to obtain the facts if the proceeding were converted to a formal or other applicable hearing procedure. **Leg.H.** Added Stats 1995 ch 938 §21 (SB 523), operative July 1, 1997.

ARTICLE 11
Subpoenas

§11450.05. Application of article

(a) This article applies in an adjudicative proceeding required to be conducted under Chapter 5 (commencing with Section 11500).

(b) An agency may use the subpoena procedure provided in this article in an adjudicative proceeding not required to be conducted under Chapter 5 (commencing with Section 11500), in which case all the provisions of this article apply including, but not limited to, issuance of a subpoena at the request of a party or by the attorney of record for a party under Section 11450.20. **Leg.H.** Added Stats 1995 ch 938 §21 (SB 523), operative July 1, 1997.

§11450.10. Issuance for attendance or production of documents

(a) Subpoenas and subpoenas duces tecum may be issued for attendance at a hearing and for production of documents at any reasonable time and place or at a hearing.

(b) The custodian of documents that are the subject of a subpoena duces tecum may satisfy the subpoena by delivery of the documents or a copy of the documents, or by making the documents available for inspection or copying, together with an affidavit in compliance with Section 1561 of the Evidence Code. **Leg.H.** Added Stats 1995 ch 938 §21 (SB 523), operative July 1, 1997.

§11450.20. Persons who may issue subpoenas; Service

(a) Subpoenas and subpoenas duces tecum shall be issued by the agency or presiding officer at the request of a party, or by the attorney of record for a party, in accordance with Sections 1985 to 1985.4, inclusive, of the Code of Civil Procedure.

(b) The process extends to all parts of the state and shall be served in accordance with Sections 1987 and 1988 of the Code of Civil Procedure. A subpoena or subpoena duces tecum may also be delivered by certified mail return receipt requested or by messenger. Service by messenger shall be effected when the witness acknowledges receipt of the subpoena to the sender, by telephone, by mail, or in person, and identifies himself or herself either by reference to date of birth and driver's license number or Department of Motor Vehicles identification number, or the sender may verify receipt of the subpoena by obtaining other identifying information from the recipient. The sender shall make a written notation of the acknowledgment. A subpoena issued and acknowledged pursuant to this section has the same force and effect as a subpoena personally served. Failure to comply with a subpoena issued and acknowledged pursuant to this section may be punished as a contempt and the subpoena may so state. A party requesting a continuance based upon the failure of a witness to appear at the time and place required for the appearance or testimony pursuant to a subpoena, shall prove that the party has complied with this section. The continuance shall only be granted for a period of time that would allow personal service of the subpoena and in no event longer than that allowed by law.

(c) No witness is obliged to attend unless the witness is a resident of the state at the time of service. **Leg.H.** Added Stats 1995 ch 938 §21 (SB 523), operative July 1, 1997.

§11450.30. Objection to subpoena; Motion for protective order; Motion to quash

(a) A person served with a subpoena or a subpoena duces tecum may object to its terms by a motion for a protective order, including a motion to quash.

(b) The objection shall be resolved by the presiding officer on terms and conditions that the presiding officer declares. The presiding officer may make another order that is appropriate to protect the parties or the witness from unreasonable or oppressive demands, including violations of the right to privacy.

(c) A subpoena or a subpoena duces tecum issued by the agency on its own motion may be quashed by the agency. **Leg.H.** Added Stats 1995 ch 938 §21 (SB 523), operative July 1, 1997.

§11450.40. Witness's mileage and fees

A witness appearing pursuant to a subpoena or a subpoena duces tecum, other than a party, shall receive for the appearance the following mileage and fees, to be paid by the party at whose request the witness is subpoenaed:

(a) The same mileage allowed by law to a witness in a civil case.

(b) The same fees allowed by law to a witness in a civil case. This subdivision does not apply to an officer or employee of the state or a political subdivision of the state. **Leg.H.** Added Stats 1995 ch 938 §21 (SB 523), operative July 1, 1997.

§11450.50. Written notice to witness to attend; Service

(a) In the case of the production of a party to the record of a proceeding or of a person for whose benefit a proceeding is prosecuted or defended, the service of a subpoena on the witness is not required if written notice requesting the witness to attend, with the time and place of the hearing, is served on the attorney of the party or person.

(b) Service of written notice to attend under this section shall be made in the manner and is subject to the conditions provided in Section 1987 of the Code of Civil Procedure for service of written notice to attend in a civil action or proceeding. **Leg.H.** Added Stats 1995 ch 938 §21 (SB 523), operative July 1, 1997.

ARTICLE 12
Enforcement of Orders and Sanctions

§11455.10. Grounds for contempt sanction

A person is subject to the contempt sanction for any of the following in an adjudicative proceeding before an agency:

(a) Disobedience of or resistance to a lawful order.

(b) Refusal to take the oath or affirmation as a witness or thereafter refusal to be examined.

(c) Obstruction or interruption of the due course of the proceeding during a hearing or near the place of the hearing by any of the following:

(1) Disorderly, contemptuous, or insolent behavior toward the presiding officer while conducting the proceeding.

(2) Breach of the peace, boisterous conduct, or violent disturbance.

(3) Other unlawful interference with the process or proceedings of the agency.

(d) Violation of the prohibition of ex parte communications under Article 7 (commencing with Section 11430.10).

(e) Failure or refusal, without substantial justification, to comply with a deposition order, discovery request, subpoena, or other order of the presiding officer, or moving, without substantial justification, to compel

Sec. 11455.20

discovery. **Leg.H.** Added Stats 1995 ch 938 §21 (SB 523), operative July 1, 1997.

§11455.20. Certification of facts to justify contempt sanction; Other procedure

(a) The presiding officer or agency head may certify the facts that justify the contempt sanction against a person to the superior court in and for the county where the proceeding is conducted. The court shall thereupon issue an order directing the person to appear before the court at a specified time and place, and then and there to show cause why the person should not be punished for contempt. The order and a copy of the certified statement shall be served on the person. Upon service of the order and a copy of the certified statement, the court has jurisdiction of the matter.

(b) The same proceedings shall be had, the same penalties may be imposed, and the person charged may purge the contempt in the same way, as in the case of a person who has committed a contempt in the trial of a civil action before a superior court. **Leg.H.** Added Stats 1995 ch 938 §21 (SB 523), operative July 1, 1997.

§11455.30. Bad faith actions; Order to pay expenses including attorney's fees

(a) The presiding officer may order a party, the party's attorney or other authorized representative, or both, to pay reasonable expenses, including attorney's fees, incurred by another party as a result of bad faith actions or tactics that are frivolous or solely intended to cause unnecessary delay as defined in Section 128.5 of the Code of Civil Procedure.

(b) The order, or denial of an order, is subject to judicial review in the same manner as a decision in the proceeding. The order is enforceable in the same manner as a money judgment or by the contempt sanction. **Leg.H.** Added Stats 1995 ch 938 §21 (SB 523), operative July 1, 1997.

ARTICLE 13
Emergency Decision

§11460.10. Conduct of proceeding under emergency procedure

Subject to the limitations in this article, an agency may conduct an adjudicative proceeding under the emergency decision procedure provided in this article. **Leg.H.** Added Stats 1995 ch 938 §21 (SB 523), operative July 1, 1997.

§11460.20. Emergency decision

(a) An agency may issue an emergency decision for temporary, interim relief under this article if the agency has adopted a regulation that provides that the agency may use the procedure provided in this article.

(b) The regulation shall elaborate the application of the provisions of this article to an emergency decision by the agency, including all of the following:

(1) Define the specific circumstances in which an emergency decision may be issued under this article.

(2) State the nature of the temporary, interim relief that the agency may order.

(3) Prescribe the procedures that will be available before and after issuance of an emergency decision under this article. The procedures may be more protective of the person to which the agency action is directed than those provided in this article.

(c) This article does not apply to an emergency decision, including a cease and desist order or an interim or temporary suspension order, issued pursuant to other express statutory authority. **Leg.H.** Added Stats 1995 ch 938 §21 (SB 523), operative July 1, 1997.

§11460.30. Conditions for issuance of emergency decision

(a) An agency may only issue an emergency decision under this article in a situation involving an immediate danger to the public health, safety, or welfare that requires immediate agency action.

(b) An agency may only take action under this article that is necessary to prevent or avoid the immediate danger to the public health, safety, or welfare that justifies issuance of an emergency decision.

(c) An emergency decision issued under this article is limited to temporary, interim relief. The temporary, interim relief is subject to judicial review under Section 11460.80, and the underlying issue giving rise to the temporary, interim relief is subject to an adjudicative proceeding pursuant to Section 11460.60. **Leg.H.** Added Stats 1995 ch 938 §21 (SB 523), operative July 1, 1997.

§11460.40. Notice and hearing prior to decision

(a) Before issuing an emergency decision under this article, the agency shall, if practicable, give the person to which the agency action is directed notice and an opportunity to be heard.

(b) Notice and hearing under this section may be oral or written, including notice and hearing by telephone, facsimile transmission, or other electronic means, as the circumstances permit. The hearing may be conducted in the same manner as an informal hearing. **Leg.H.** Added Stats 1995 ch 938 §21 (SB 523), operative July 1, 1997.

§11460.50. Statement of factual and legal basis and reasons for emergency decision

(a) The agency shall issue an emergency decision, including a brief explanation of the factual and legal basis and reasons for the emergency decision, to justify the determination of an immediate danger and the agency's emergency decision to take the specific action.

(b) The agency shall give notice to the extent practicable to the person to which the agency action is directed. The emergency decision is effective when issued or as provided in the decision. **Leg.H.** Added Stats 1995 ch 938 §21 (SB 523), operative July 1, 1997.

§11460.60. Formal or informal proceeding after issuance of emergency decision

(a) After issuing an emergency decision under this article for temporary, interim relief, the agency shall conduct an adjudicative proceeding under a formal, informal, or other applicable hearing procedure to resolve the underlying issues giving rise to the temporary, interim relief.

(b) The agency shall commence an adjudicative proceeding under another procedure within 10 days after issuing an emergency decision under this article, notwithstanding the pendency of proceedings for judicial review of the emergency decision. **Leg.H.** Added Stats 1995 ch 938 §21 (SB 523), operative July 1, 1997.

§11460.70. Agency record

The agency record consists of any documents concerning the matter that were considered or prepared by the agency. The agency shall maintain these documents as its official record. **Leg.H.** Added Stats 1995 ch 938 §21 (SB 523), operative July 1, 1997.

§11460.80. Judicial review of decision

(a) On issuance of an emergency decision under this article, the person to which the agency action is directed may obtain judicial review of the decision in the manner provided in this section without exhaustion of administrative remedies.

(b) Judicial review under this section shall be pursuant to Section 1094.5 of the Code of Civil Procedure, subject to the following provisions:

(1) The hearing shall be on the earliest day that the business of the court will admit of, but not later than 15 days after service of the petition on the agency.

(2) Where it is claimed that the findings are not supported by the evidence, abuse of discretion is established if the court determines that the findings are not supported by substantial evidence in the light of the whole record.

(3) A party, on written request to another party, before the proceedings for review and within 10 days after issuance of the emergency decision, is entitled to appropriate discovery.

(4) The relief that may be ordered on judicial review is limited to a stay of the emergency decision. **Leg.H.** Added Stats 1995 ch 938 §21 (SB 523), operative July 1, 1997.

ARTICLE 14
Declaratory Decision

§11465.10. Conduct of proceeding under declaratory decision procedure

Subject to the limitations in this article, an agency may conduct an adjudicative proceeding under the declaratory decision procedure provided in this article. **Leg.H.** Added Stats 1995 ch 938 §21 (SB 523), operative July 1, 1997.

§11465.20. Application; Issuance of decision

(a) A person may apply to an agency for a declaratory decision as to the applicability to specified circumstances of a statute, regulation, or decision within the primary jurisdiction of the agency.

(b) The agency in its discretion may issue a declaratory decision in response to the application. The agency shall not issue a declaratory decision if any of the following applies:

(1) Issuance of the decision would be contrary to a regulation adopted under this article.

(2) The decision would substantially prejudice the rights of a person who would be a necessary party and who does not consent in writing to the determination of the matter by a declaratory decision proceeding.

(3) The decision involves a matter that is the subject of pending administrative or judicial proceedings.

(c) An application for a declaratory decision is not required for exhaustion of the applicant's administrative remedies for purposes of judicial review. **Leg.H.** Added Stats 1995 ch 938 §21 (SB 523), operative July 1, 1997.

§11465.30. Notice of application for decision

Within 30 days after receipt of an application for a declaratory decision, an agency shall give notice of the application to all persons to which notice of an adjudicative proceeding is otherwise required, and may give notice to any other person. **Leg.H.** Added Stats 1995 ch 938 §21 (SB 523), operative July 1, 1997.

§11465.40. Applicable hearing procedure

The provisions of a formal, informal, or other applicable hearing procedure do not apply to an agency proceeding for a declaratory decision except to the extent provided in this article or to the extent the agency so provides by regulation or order. **Leg.H.** Added Stats 1995 ch 938 §21 (SB 523), operative July 1, 1997.

§11465.50. Actions of agency after receipt of application

(a) Within 60 days after receipt of an application for a declaratory decision, an agency shall do one of the following, in writing:

(1) Issue a decision declaring the applicability of the statute, regulation, or decision in question to the specified circumstances.

(2) Set the matter for specified proceedings.

(3) Agree to issue a declaratory decision by a specified time.

(4) Decline to issue a declaratory decision, stating in writing the reasons for its action. Agency action under this paragraph is not subject to judicial review.

(b) A copy of the agency's action under subdivision (a) shall be served promptly on the applicant and any other party.

(c) If an agency has not taken action under subdivision (a) within 60 days after receipt of an application for a declaratory decision, the agency is considered to have declined to issue a declaratory decision on the matter. **Leg.H.** Added Stats 1995 ch 938 §21 (SB 523), operative July 1, 1997.

§11465.60. Contents of decision; Status and binding effect of decision

(a) A declaratory decision shall contain the names of all parties to the proceeding, the particular facts on which it is based, and the reasons for its conclusion.

(b) A declaratory decision has the same status and binding effect as any other decision issued by the agency in an adjudicative proceeding. **Leg.H.** Added Stats 1995 ch 938 §21 (SB 523), operative July 1, 1997.

§11465.70. Model regulations

(a) The Office of Administrative Hearings shall adopt and promulgate model regulations under this article that are consistent with the public interest and with the general policy of this article to facilitate and encourage agency issuance of reliable advice. The model regulations shall provide for all of the following:

(1) A description of the classes of circumstances in which an agency will not issue a declaratory decision.

(2) The form, contents, and filing of an application for a declaratory decision.

(3) The procedural rights of a person in relation to an application.

(4) The disposition of an application.

(b) The regulations adopted by the Office of Administrative Hearings under this article apply in an adjudicative proceeding unless an agency adopts its own regulations to govern declaratory decisions of the agency.

(c) This article does not apply in an adjudicative proceeding to the extent an agency by regulation provides inconsistent rules or provides that this article is not applicable in a proceeding of the agency. **Leg.H.** Added Stats 1995 ch 938 §21 (SB 523), operative July 1, 1997.

ARTICLE 15
Conversion of Proceeding

§11470.10. Conversion into another type of proceeding

(a) Subject to any applicable regulation adopted under Section 11470.50, at any point in an agency proceeding the presiding officer or other agency official responsible for the proceeding:

(1) May convert the proceeding to another type of agency proceeding provided for by statute if the conversion is appropriate, is in the public interest, and does not substantially prejudice the rights of a party.

(2) Shall convert the proceeding to another type of agency proceeding provided for by statute, if required by regulation or statute.

(b) A proceeding of one type may be converted to a proceeding of another type only on notice to all parties to the original proceeding. **Leg.H.** Added Stats 1995 ch 938 §21 (SB 523), operative July 1, 1997.

§11470.20. Appointment of successor to preside over new proceeding

If the presiding officer or other agency official responsible for the original proceeding would not have authority over the new proceeding to which it is to be converted, the agency head shall appoint a successor to preside over or be responsible for the new proceeding. **Leg.H.** Added Stats 1995 ch 938 §21 (SB 523), operative July 1, 1997.

§11470.30. Record of original proceeding

To the extent practicable and consistent with the rights of parties and the requirements of this article relating to the new proceeding, the record of the original agency proceeding shall be used in the new agency proceeding. **Leg.H.** Added Stats 1995 ch 938 §21 (SB 523), operative July 1, 1997.

§11470.40. Duties of presiding officer of new proceeding

After a proceeding is converted from one type to another, the presiding officer or other agency official responsible for the new proceeding shall do all of the following:

(a) Give additional notice to parties or other persons necessary to satisfy the statutory requirements relating to the new proceeding.

(b) Dispose of the matters involved without further proceedings if sufficient proceedings have already been held to satisfy the statutory requirements relating to the new proceeding.

(c) Conduct or cause to be conducted any additional proceedings necessary to satisfy the statutory requirements relating to the new proceeding, and allow the parties a reasonable time to prepare for the new proceeding. **Leg.H.** Added Stats 1995 ch 938 §21 (SB 523), operative July 1, 1997.

§11470.50. Adoption of regulations to govern conversion

An agency may adopt regulations to govern the conversion of one type of proceeding to another. The regulations may include an enumeration of the factors to be considered in determining whether and under what circumstances one type of proceeding will be converted to another. **Leg.H.** Added Stats 1995 ch 938 §21 (SB 523), operative July 1, 1997.

ARTICLE 16
Administrative Adjudication Code of Ethics

§11475. Name of rules

The rules imposed by this article may be referred to as the Administrative Adjudication Code of Ethics. **Leg.H.** Added Stats 1998 ch 95 §1 (AB 2164), effective January 1, 1999.

§11475.10. Application

(a) This article applies to the following persons:

(1) An administrative law judge. As used in this subdivision, "administrative law judge" means an incumbent of that position, as defined by the State Personnel Board, for each class specification for Administrative Law Judge.

(2) A presiding officer to which this article is made applicable by statute or regulation.

(b) This article shall apply notwithstanding any general statutory provision that this chapter does not apply to some or all of a state agency's adjudicative proceedings. **Leg.H.** Added Stats 1998 ch 95 §1 (AB 2164), effective January 1, 1999.

§11475.20. Law governing conduct

Except as otherwise provided in this article, the Code of Judicial Ethics adopted by the Supreme Court pursuant to subdivision (m) of Section 18 of Article VI of the California Constitution for the conduct of judges governs the hearing and nonhearing conduct of an administrative law judge or other presiding officer to which this article applies. **Leg.H.** Added Stats 1998 ch 95 §1 (AB 2164), effective January 1, 1999.

§11475.30. Definitions

For the purpose of this article, the following terms used in the Code of Judicial Ethics have the meanings provided in this section:

(a) "Appeal" means administrative review.

(b) "Court" means the agency conducting an adjudicative proceeding.

(c) "Judge" means administrative law judge or other presiding officer to which this article applies. Related terms, including "judicial," "judiciary," and "justice," mean comparable concepts in administrative adjudication.

(d) "Law" includes regulation and precedent decision. **Leg.H.** Added Stats 1998 ch 95 §1 (AB 2164), effective January 1, 1999.

§11475.40. Inapplicable provisions of Code of Judicial Ethics

The following provisions of the Code of Judicial Ethics do not apply under this article:

(a) Canon 3B(7), to the extent it relates to ex parte communications.

(b) Canon 3B(10).

(c) Canon 3D(3).

(d) Canon 4C.

(e) Canons 4E(1), 4F, and 4G.

(f) Canons 5A–5D. However, the introductory paragraph of Canon 5 applies to persons subject to this article notwithstanding Chapter 9.5 (commencing with Section 3201) of Division 4 of Title 1, relating to political activities of public employees.

(g) Canon 6. **Leg.H.** Added Stats 1998 ch 95 §1 (AB 2164), effective January 1, 1999.

§11475.50. Violations

A violation of an applicable provision of the Code of Judicial Ethics, or a violation of the restrictions and prohibitions on accepting honoraria, gifts, or travel that otherwise apply to elected state officers pursuant to Chapter 9.5 (commencing with Section 89500) of Title 9, by an administrative law judge or other presiding officer to which this article applies is cause for discipline by the employing agency pursuant to Section 19572. **Leg.H.** Added Stats 1998 ch 95 §1 (AB 2164), effective January 1, 1999.

§11475.60. Compliance requirements

(a) Except as provided in subdivision (b), a person to whom this article applies shall comply immediately with all applicable provisions of the Code of Judicial Ethics.

(b) A person to whom this article applies shall comply with Canon 4D(2) of the Code of Judicial Ethics as soon as reasonably possible and shall do so in any event within a period of one year after the article becomes applicable. **Leg.H.** Added Stats 1998 ch 95 §1 (AB 2164), effective January 1, 1999.

§11475.70. Construction and intent

Nothing in this article shall be construed or is intended to limit or affect the rights of an administrative law judge or other presiding officer under Chapter 10.3 (commencing with Section 3512) of Division 4 of Title 1. **Leg.H.** Added Stats 1998 ch 95 §1 (AB 2164), effective January 1, 1999.

CHAPTER 5
ADMINISTRATIVE ADJUDICATION: FORMAL HEARING

§11500. Definitions

In this chapter unless the context or subject matter otherwise requires:

(a) "Agency" includes the state boards, commissions, and officers to which this chapter is made applicable by law, except that wherever the word "agency" alone is used the power to act may be delegated by the agency, and wherever the words "agency itself" are used the power to act shall not be delegated unless the statutes relating to the particular agency authorize the delegation of the agency's power to hear and decide.

(b) "Party" includes the agency, the respondent, and any person, other than an officer or an employee of the agency in his or her official capacity, who has been allowed to appear or participate in the proceeding.

(c) "Respondent" means any person against whom an accusation or District Statement of Reduction in Force is filed pursuant to Section 11503 or against whom a statement of issues is filed pursuant to Section 11504.

(d) "Administrative law judge" means an individual qualified under Section 11502.

(e) "Agency member" means any person who is a member of any agency to which this chapter is applicable and includes any person who himself or herself constitutes an agency. **Leg.H.** Added Stats 1945 ch 867 §1. Amended Stats 1947 ch 491 §1, Stats 1977 ch 1057 §1, operative July 1, 1978; Stats 1985 ch 324 §15; Stats 1995 ch 938 §23 (SB 523), operative July 1, 1997; Stats 2013 ch 90 §2 (SB 546), effective January 1, 2014.

§11501. Application of chapter to agency

(a) This chapter applies to any agency as determined by the statutes relating to that agency.

(b) This chapter applies to an adjudicative proceeding of an agency created on or after July 1, 1997, unless the statutes relating to the proceeding provide otherwise.

(c) Chapter 4.5 (commencing with Section 11400) applies to an adjudicative proceeding required to be conducted under this chapter, unless the statutes relating to the proceeding provide otherwise. **Leg.H.** Added Stats 1995 ch 938 §24.5 (SB 523), operative July 1, 1997.

Prior Law: Former Gov C §11501, similar to the present section, was added Stats 1977 ch 122 §2, amended Stats 1978 ch 429 §50, effective July 17, 1978, operative July 1, 1978, Stats 1980 ch 992 §2, Stats 1982 ch 454 §41, Stats 1985 ch 867 §3, Stats 1988 ch 362 §1, Stats 1989 ch 886 §83, Stats 1990 ch 1256 §11. Supplemented by the Governor's Reorganization Plan No. 1 of 1991 §74, effective July 17, 1991. Amended Stats 1991 ch 359 §34, Stats 1992 ch 910 §1, Stats 1994 ch 26 §231, effective March 30, 1994, ch 627 §8, Stats 1995 ch 60 §44, effective July 6, 1995, ch 938 §24, operative January 1, 1996, Stats 1996 ch 1064 §784, operative until July 1, 1997, and repealed January 1, 1998, by its own terms.

Former Gov C §11501, similar to the present section, was added Stats 1945 ch 867 §1, amended Stats 1947 ch 491 §2, Stats 1949 ch 314 §1, Stats 1951 ch 1215 §1, Stats 1953 ch 961 §1, Stats 1955 ch 453 §1, Stats 1957 ch 1933 §1, Stats 1961 ch 104 §88, ch 2071 §88, Stats 1963 ch 1394 §1, Stats 1965 ch 1456 §2, Stats 1970 ch 346 §7, Stats 1971 ch 716 §200, Stats 1972 ch 749 §11, Stats 1973 ch 142 §17, effective June 30, 1973, operative July 1, 1973, Stats 1973 ch 1212 §13, Stats 1974 §1159 §1, Stats 1976 ch 1185 §92.5, and repealed Stats 1977 ch 122 §1.

§11502. Administrative law judges

(a) All hearings of state agencies required to be conducted under this chapter shall be conducted by administrative law judges on the staff of the Office of Administrative Hearings. This subdivision applies to a hearing required to be conducted under this chapter that is conducted under the informal hearing or emergency decision procedure provided in Chapter 4.5 (commencing with Section 11400).

(b) The Director of the Office of Administrative Hearings has power to appoint a staff of administrative law judges for the office as provided in Section 11370.3. Each administrative law judge shall have been admitted to practice law in this state for at least five years immediately preceding his or her appointment and shall possess any additional qualifications established by the State Personnel Board for the particular class of position involved. **Leg.H.** Added Stats 1945 ch 867 §1. Amended Stats 1961 ch 2048 §10; Stats 1971 ch 1303 §7; Stats 1985 ch 324 §16; Stats 1995 ch 938 §26 (SB 523), operative July 1, 1997.

§11503. Accusation or District Statement of Reduction in Force

(a) A hearing to determine whether a right, authority, license, or privilege should be revoked, suspended, limited, or conditioned shall be initiated by filing an accusation or District Statement of Reduction in Force. The accusation or District Statement of Reduction in Force shall be a written statement of charges that shall set forth in ordinary and concise language the acts or omissions with which the respondent is charged, to the end that the respondent will be able to prepare their defense. It shall specify the statutes and rules that the respondent is alleged to have violated, but shall not consist merely of charges phrased in the language of those statutes and rules. The accusation or District Statement of Reduction in Force shall be verified unless made by a public officer acting in their official capacity or by an employee of the agency before which the proceeding is to be held. The verification may be on information and belief.

(b) In a hearing involving a reduction in force that is conducted pursuant to Section 44949, 45117, or 88017 of the Education Code, the hearing shall be initiated by filing a "District Statement of Reduction in

Force." For purposes of this chapter, a "District Statement of Reduction in Force" shall have the same meaning as an "accusation." Respondent's responsive pleading shall be entitled "Notice of Participation in Reduction in Force Hearing." **Leg.H.** Added Stats 1945 ch 867 §1. Amended Stats 1947 ch 491 §3; Stats 2013 ch 90 §3 (SB 546), effective January 1, 2014; Stats 2021 ch 655 §4 (AB 438), effective January 1, 2022.

§11504. Statement of issues

A hearing to determine whether a right, authority, license, or privilege should be granted, issued, or renewed shall be initiated by filing a statement of issues. The statement of issues shall be a written statement specifying the statutes and rules with which the respondent must show compliance by producing proof at the hearing and, in addition, any particular matters that have come to the attention of the initiating party and that would authorize a denial of the agency action sought. The statement of issues shall be verified unless made by a public officer acting in his or her official capacity or by an employee of the agency before which the proceeding is to be held. The verification may be on information and belief. The statement of issues shall be served in the same manner as an accusation, except that, if the hearing is held at the request of the respondent, Sections 11505 and 11506 shall not apply and the statement of issues together with the notice of hearing shall be delivered or mailed to the parties as provided in Section 11509. Unless a statement to respondent is served pursuant to Section 11505, a copy of Sections 11507.5, 11507.6, and 11507.7, and the name and address of the person to whom requests permitted by Section 11505 may be made, shall be served with the statement of issues. **Leg.H.** Added Stats 1945 ch 867 §1. Amended Stats 1947 ch 491 §4; Stats 1968 ch 808 §1; Stats 1996 ch 124 §36 (AB 3470); Stats 1997 ch 17 §50 (SB 947), effective January 1, 1998.

§11504.5. Applicability of references to accusations to statements of issues

In the following sections of this chapter, all references to accusations shall be deemed to be applicable to statements of issues except in those cases mentioned in subdivision (a) of Section 11505 and Section 11506 where compliance is not required. **Leg.H.** Added Stats 1963 ch 856 §1.

§11505. Service of accusation or District Statement of Reduction in Force and accompanying papers; Notice of defense or notice of participation; Request for hearing

(a) Upon the filing of the accusation or District Statement of Reduction in Force the agency shall serve a copy thereof on the respondent as provided in subdivision (c). The agency may include with the accusation or District Statement of Reduction in Force any information that it deems appropriate, but it shall include a postcard or other form entitled Notice of Defense, or, as applicable, Notice of Participation, that, when signed by or on behalf of the respondent and returned to the agency, will acknowledge service of the accusation or District Statement of Reduction in Force and constitute a notice of defense, or, as applicable, notice of participation, under Section 11506. The copy of the accusation or District Statement of Reduction in Force shall include or be accompanied by (1) a statement that respondent may request a hearing by filing a notice of defense, or, as applicable, notice of participation, as provided in Section 11506 within 15 days after service upon the respondent of the accusation or District Statement of Reduction in Force, and that failure to do so will constitute a waiver of the respondent's right to a hearing, and (2) copies of Sections 11507.5, 11507.6, and 11507.7.

(b) The statement to respondent shall be substantially in the following form:

Unless a written request for a hearing signed by or on behalf of the person named as respondent in the accompanying accusation or District Statement of Reduction in Force is delivered or mailed to the agency within 15 days after the accusation or District Statement of Reduction in Force was personally served on you or mailed to you, (here insert name of agency) may proceed upon the accusation or District Statement of Reduction in Force without a hearing. The request for a hearing may be made by delivering or mailing the enclosed form entitled Notice of Defense, or, as applicable, Notice of Participation, or by delivering or mailing a notice of defense, or, as applicable, notice of participation, as provided by Section 11506 of the Government Code to: (here insert name and address of agency). You may, but need not, be represented by counsel at any or all stages of these proceedings.

If you desire the names and addresses of witnesses or an opportunity to inspect and copy the items mentioned in Section 11507.6 of the Government Code in the possession, custody, or control of the agency, you may contact: (here insert name and address of appropriate person).

The hearing may be postponed for good cause. If you have good cause, you are obliged to notify the agency or, if an administrative law judge has been assigned to the hearing, the Office of Administrative Hearings, within 10 working days after you discover the good cause. Failure to give notice within 10 days will deprive you of a postponement.

(c) The accusation or District Statement of Reduction in Force and all accompanying information may be sent to the respondent by any means selected by the agency, but no order adversely affecting the rights of the respondent shall be made by the agency in any case unless the respondent has been served personally or by registered mail as provided herein, or has filed a notice of defense, or, as applicable, notice of participation, or otherwise appeared. Service may be proved in the manner authorized in civil actions. Service by registered mail shall be effective if a statute or agency rule requires the respondent to file the respondent's address with the agency and to notify the agency of any change, and if a registered letter containing the accusation or District Statement of Reduction in Force and accompanying material is mailed, addressed to the respondent at the latest address on file with the agency.

(d) For purposes of this chapter, for hearings involving a reduction in force that are conducted pursuant to Section 44949, 45117, or 88017 of the Education Code, a "Notice of Participation" shall have the same meaning as a "Notice of Defense." **Leg.H.** Added Stats 1945 ch 867 §1. Amended Stats 1968 ch 808 §2; Stats 1970 ch 828 §1; Stats 1979 ch 199 §3; Stats 1995 ch 938 §28 (SB 523), operative July 1, 1997; Stats 2013 ch 90 §4 (SB 546), effective January 1, 2014; Stats 2021 ch 655 §5 (AB 438), effective January 1, 2022.

§11506. Filing of notice of defense or notice of participation; Contents; Right to hearing on the merits

(a) Within 15 days after service of the accusation or District Statement of Reduction in Force the respondent may file with the agency a notice of defense, or, as applicable, notice of participation, in which the respondent may:

(1) Request a hearing.

(2) Object to the accusation or District Statement of Reduction in Force upon the ground that it does not state acts or omissions upon which the agency may proceed.

(3) Object to the form of the accusation or District Statement of Reduction in Force on the ground that it is so indefinite or uncertain that the respondent cannot identify the transaction or prepare a defense.

(4) Admit the accusation or District Statement of Reduction in Force in whole or in part.

(5) Present new matter by way of defense.

(6) Object to the accusation or District Statement of Reduction in Force upon the ground that, under the circumstances, compliance with the requirements of a regulation would result in a material violation of another regulation enacted by another department affecting substantive rights.

(b) Within the time specified the respondent may file one or more notices of defense, or, as applicable, notices of participation, upon any or all of these grounds but all of these notices shall be filed within that period unless the agency in its discretion authorizes the filing of a later notice.

(c) The respondent shall be entitled to a hearing on the merits if the respondent files a notice of defense or notice of participation, and the notice shall be deemed a specific denial of all parts of the accusation or District Statement of Reduction in Force not expressly admitted. Failure to file a notice of defense or notice of participation shall constitute a waiver of respondent's right to a hearing, but the agency in its discretion may nevertheless grant a hearing. Unless objection is taken as provided in paragraph (3) of subdivision (a), all objections to the form of the accusation or District Statement of Reduction in Force shall be deemed waived.

(d) The notice of defense or notice of participation shall be in writing signed by or on behalf of the respondent and shall state the respondent's mailing address. It need not be verified or follow any particular form.

(e) As used in this section, "file," "files," "filed," or "filing" means "delivered or mailed" to the agency as provided in Section 11505. **Leg.H.** Added Stats 1945 ch 867 §1. Amended Stats 1963 ch 931 §1; Stats 1982 ch 606 §1; Stats 1986 ch 951 §20; Stats 1995 ch 938 §29 (SB 523), operative July 1, 1997; Stats 2013 ch 90 §5 (SB 546), effective January 1, 2014.

§11507. Amended or supplemental accusation or District Statement of Reduction in Force; Objections

At any time before the matter is submitted for decision, the agency may file, or permit the filing of, an amended or supplemental accusation or District Statement of Reduction in Force. All parties shall be notified of the filing. If the amended or supplemental accusation or District Statement of Reduction in Force presents new charges, the agency shall afford the respondent a reasonable opportunity to prepare his or her defense to the new charges, but he or she shall not be entitled to file a further pleading unless the agency in its discretion so orders. Any new charges shall be deemed controverted, and any objections to the amended or supplemental accusation or District Statement of Reduction in Force may be made orally and shall be noted in the record. **Leg.H.** Added Stats 1945 ch 867 §1. Amended Stats 2013 ch 90 §6 (SB 546), effective January 1, 2014; Stats 2014 ch 71 §69 (SB 1304), effective January 1, 2015.

§11507.3. Consolidated proceedings; Separate hearings

(a) When proceedings that involve a common question of law or fact are pending, the administrative law judge on the judge's own motion or on motion of a party may order a joint hearing of any or all the matters at issue in the proceedings. The administrative law judge may order all the proceedings consolidated and may make orders concerning the procedure that may tend to avoid unnecessary costs or delay.

(b) The administrative law judge on the judge's own motion or on motion of a party, in furtherance of convenience or to avoid prejudice or when separate hearings will be conducive to expedition and economy, may order a separate hearing of any issue, including an issue raised in the notice of defense or notice of participation, or of any number of issues. **Leg.H.** Added Stats 1995 ch 938 §30 (SB 523), operative July 1, 1997. Amended Stats 2013 ch 90 §7 (SB 546), effective January 1, 2014.

§11507.5. Exclusivity of discovery provisions

The provisions of Section 11507.6 provide the exclusive right to and method of discovery as to any proceeding governed by this chapter. **Leg.H.** Added Stats 1968 ch 808 §3.

§11507.6. Request for discovery

After initiation of a proceeding in which a respondent or other party is entitled to a hearing on the merits, a party, upon written request made to another party, prior to the hearing and within 30 days after service by the agency of the initial pleading or within 15 days after the service of an additional pleading, is entitled to (1) obtain the names and addresses of witnesses to the extent known to the other party, including, but not limited to, those intended to be called to testify at the hearing, and (2) inspect and make a copy of any of the following in the possession or custody or under the control of the other party:

(a) A statement of a person, other than the respondent, named in the initial administrative pleading, or in any additional pleading, when it is claimed that the act or omission of the respondent as to this person is the basis for the administrative proceeding;

(b) A statement pertaining to the subject matter of the proceeding made by any party to another party or person;

(c) Statements of witnesses then proposed to be called by the party and of other persons having personal knowledge of the acts, omissions, or events which are the basis for the proceeding, not included in subdivision (a) or (b) above;

(d) All writings, including, but not limited to, reports of mental, physical, and blood examinations and things which the party then proposes to offer in evidence;

(e) Any other writing or thing which is relevant and which would be admissible in evidence;

(f) Investigative reports made by or on behalf of the agency or other party pertaining to the subject matter of the proceeding, to the extent that these reports (1) contain the names and addresses of witnesses or of persons having personal knowledge of the acts, omissions, or events which are the basis for the proceeding, or (2) reflect matters perceived by the investigator in the course of their investigation, or (3) contain or include by attachment any statement or writing described in subdivisions (a) to (e), inclusive, or summary thereof.

For the purpose of this section, "statements" include written statements by the person signed or otherwise authenticated by the person, stenographic, mechanical, electrical, or other recordings, or transcripts thereof, of oral statements by the person, and written reports or summaries of these oral statements.

Nothing in this section shall authorize the inspection or copying of any writing or thing which is privileged from disclosure by law or otherwise made confidential or protected as the attorney's work product.

Discovery of all categories of evidence specified in this section may be conducted electronically by means prescribed by an administrative law judge. **Leg.H.** Added Stats 1968 ch 808 §4. Amended Stats 1985 ch 1328 §5; Stats 1995 ch 938 §31 (SB 523), operative July 1, 1997; Stats 2021 ch 401 §14 (AB 1578), effective January 1, 2022.

§11507.7. Motion to compel discovery; Order

(a) Any party claiming the party's request for discovery pursuant to Section 11507.6 has not been complied with may serve and file with the administrative law judge a motion to compel discovery, naming as respondent the party refusing or failing to comply with Section 11507.6. The motion shall state facts showing the respondent party failed or refused to comply with Section 11507.6, a description of the matters sought to be discovered, the reason or reasons why the matter is discoverable under that section, that a reasonable and good faith attempt to contact the respondent for an informal resolution of the issue has been made, and the ground or grounds of respondent's refusal so far as known to the moving party.

(b) The motion shall be served upon respondent party and filed within 15 days after the respondent party first evidenced failure or refusal to comply with Section 11507.6 or within 30 days after request was made and the party has failed to reply to the request, or within another time provided by stipulation, whichever period is longer.

(c) The hearing on the motion to compel discovery shall be held within 15 days after the motion is made, or a later time that the administrative law judge may on the judge's own motion for good cause determine. The respondent party shall have the right to serve and file a written answer or other response to the motion before or at the time of the hearing.

(d) Where the matter sought to be discovered is under the custody or control of the respondent party and the respondent party asserts that the matter is not a discoverable matter under the provisions of Section 11507.6, or is privileged against disclosure under those provisions, the administrative law judge may order lodged with it matters provided in subdivision (b) of Section 915 of the Evidence Code and examine the matters in accordance with its provisions.

(e) The administrative law judge shall decide the case on the matters examined in camera, the papers filed by the parties, and such oral argument and additional evidence as the administrative law judge may allow.

(f) Unless otherwise stipulated by the parties, the administrative law judge shall no later than 15 days after the hearing make its order denying or granting the motion. The order shall be in writing setting forth the matters the moving party is entitled to discover under Section 11507.6. A copy of the order shall forthwith be served by mail by the administrative law judge upon the parties. Where the order grants the motion in whole or in part, the order shall not become effective until 10 days after the date the order is served. Where the order denies relief to the moving party, the order shall be effective on the date it is served. **Leg.H.** Added Stats 1968 ch 808 §5. Amended Stats 1971 ch 1303 §8; Stats 1980 ch 548 §2; Stats 1995 ch 938 §32 (SB 523), operative July 1, 1997.

§11508. Time and place of hearing

(a) The agency shall consult the office, and subject to the availability of its staff, shall determine the time and place of the hearing. The hearing shall be held at a hearing facility maintained by the office in Sacramento, Oakland, Los Angeles, or San Diego and shall be held at the facility that is closest to the location where the transaction occurred or the respondent resides.

(b) Notwithstanding subdivision (a), the hearing may be held at any of the following places:

(1) A place selected by the agency that is closer to the location where the transaction occurred or the respondent resides.

(2) A place within the state selected by agreement of the parties.

(3) Virtually by telephone, videoconference, or other electronic means.

(c) The respondent may move for, and the administrative law judge has discretion to grant or deny, a change in the place of the hearing. A motion for a change in the place of the hearing shall be made within 10 days after service of the notice of hearing on the respondent.

(d) Unless good cause is identified in writing by the administrative law judge, hearings shall be held in a facility maintained by the office. **Leg.H.**

Added Stats 1945 ch 867 §1. Amended Stats 1963 ch 710 §1; Stats 1967 ch 17 §39; Stats 1987 ch 50 §1; Stats 1995 ch 938 §33 (SB 523), operative July 1, 1997; Stats 2005 ch 674 §22 (SB 231), effective January 1, 2006; Stats 2021 ch 401 §15 (AB 1578), effective January 1, 2022.

§11509. Notice of hearing

The agency shall deliver or mail a notice of hearing to all parties at least 10 days prior to the hearing. The hearing shall not be prior to the expiration of the time within which the respondent is entitled to file a notice of defense, or, as applicable, notice of participation.

The notice to respondent shall be substantially in the following form but may include other information:

You are hereby notified that a hearing will be held before [here insert name of agency] at [here insert place of hearing] on the ____ day of ____, 20__, at the hour of ____, upon the charges made in the accusation or District Statement of Reduction in Force served upon you. If you object to the place of hearing, you must notify the presiding officer within 10 days after this notice is served on you. Failure to notify the presiding officer within 10 days will deprive you of a change in the place of the hearing. You may be present at the hearing. You have the right to be represented by an attorney at your own expense. You are not entitled to the appointment of an attorney to represent you at public expense. You are entitled to represent yourself without legal counsel. You may present any relevant evidence, and will be given full opportunity to cross-examine all witnesses testifying against you. You are entitled to the issuance of subpoenas to compel the attendance of witnesses and the production of books, documents or other things by applying to [here insert appropriate office of agency]. **Leg.H.** Added Stats 1945 ch 867 §1. Amended Stats 1988 ch 362 §2; Stats 1995 ch 938 §34 (SB 523), operative July 1, 1997; Stats 2013 ch 90 §8 (SB 546), effective January 1, 2014.

§11511. Depositions

On verified petition of any party, an administrative law judge or, if an administrative law judge has not been appointed, an agency may order that the testimony of any material witness residing within or without the state be taken by deposition in the manner prescribed by law for depositions in civil actions under Title 4 (commencing with Section 2016.010) of Part 4 of the Code of Civil Procedure. The petition shall set forth the nature of the pending proceeding; the name and address of the witness whose testimony is desired; a showing of the materiality of the testimony; a showing that the witness will be unable or cannot be compelled to attend; and shall request an order requiring the witness to appear and testify before an officer named in the petition for that purpose. The petitioner shall serve notice of hearing and a copy of the petition on the other parties at least 10 days before the hearing. Where the witness resides outside the state and where the administrative law judge or agency has ordered the taking of the testimony by deposition, the agency shall obtain an order of court to that effect by filing a petition therefor in the superior court in Sacramento County. The proceedings thereon shall be in accordance with the provisions of Section 11189. **Leg.H.** Added Stats 1945 ch 867 §1. Amended Stats 1995 ch 938 §36 (SB 523), operative July 1, 1997; Stats 1998 ch 931 §182 (SB 2139), effective September 28, 1998; Stats 2004 ch 182 §42 (AB 3081), operative July 1, 2005.

§11511.5. Prehearing conference; Conduct by telephone or other electronic means; Conversion to ADR or informal hearing; Prehearing order

(a) On motion of a party or by order of an administrative law judge, the administrative law judge may conduct a prehearing conference. The administrative law judge shall set the time and place for the prehearing conference, and shall give reasonable written notice to all parties.

(b) The prehearing conference may deal with one or more of the following matters:

(1) Exploration of settlement possibilities.
(2) Preparation of stipulations.
(3) Clarification of issues.
(4) Rulings on identity and limitation of the number of witnesses.
(5) Objections to proffers of evidence.
(6) Order of presentation of evidence and cross-examination.
(7) Rulings regarding issuance of subpoenas and protective orders.
(8) Schedules for the submission of written briefs and schedules for the commencement and conduct of the hearing.
(9) Exchange of witness lists and of exhibits or documents to be offered in evidence at the hearing.
(10) Motions for intervention.
(11) Exploration of the possibility of using alternative dispute resolution provided in Article 5 (commencing with Section 11420.10) of, or the informal hearing procedure provided in Article 10 (commencing with Section 11445.10) of, Chapter 4.5, and objections to use of the informal hearing procedure. Use of alternative dispute resolution or of the informal hearing procedure is subject to subdivision (d).
(12) Any other matters as shall promote the orderly and prompt conduct of the hearing.

(c) The administrative law judge may conduct all or part of the prehearing conference by telephone, television, or other electronic means if each participant in the conference has an opportunity to participate in and to hear the entire proceeding while it is taking place.

(d) With the consent of the parties, the prehearing conference may be converted immediately into alternative dispute resolution or an informal hearing. With the consent of the parties, the proceeding may be converted into alternative dispute resolution to be conducted at another time. With the consent of the agency, the proceeding may be converted into an informal hearing to be conducted at another time subject to the right of a party to object to use of the informal hearing procedure as provided in Section 11445.30.

(e) The administrative law judge shall issue a prehearing order incorporating the matters determined at the prehearing conference. The administrative law judge may direct one or more of the parties to prepare a prehearing order. **Leg.H.** Added Stats 1986 ch 899 §1. Amended Stats 1995 ch 938 §37 (SB 523), operative July 1, 1997.

Prior Law: There was another section of this number, identical to this section, which was added Stats 1986 ch 597 §2 and repealed Stats 1989 ch 1360 §53.

§11511.7. Settlement conference

(a) The administrative law judge may order the parties to attend and participate in a settlement conference. The administrative law judge shall set the time and place for the settlement conference, and shall give reasonable written notice to all parties.

(b) The administrative law judge at the settlement conference shall not preside as administrative law judge at the hearing unless otherwise stipulated by the parties. The administrative law judge may conduct all or part of the settlement conference by telephone, television, or other electronic means if each participant in the conference has an opportunity to participate in and to hear the entire proceeding while it is taking place. **Leg.H.** Added Stats 1995 ch 938 §38 (SB 523), operative July 1, 1997.

§11512. Administrative law judge to preside over hearing; Disqualification; Reporting of proceedings

(a) Every hearing in a contested case shall be presided over by an administrative law judge. The agency itself shall determine whether the administrative law judge is to hear the case alone or whether the agency itself is to hear the case with the administrative law judge.

(b) When the agency itself hears the case, the administrative law judge shall preside at the hearing, rule on the admission and exclusion of evidence, and advise the agency on matters of law; the agency itself shall exercise all other powers relating to the conduct of the hearing but may delegate any or all of them to the administrative law judge. When the administrative law judge alone hears a case, the judge shall exercise all powers relating to the conduct of the hearing. A ruling of the administrative law judge admitting or excluding evidence is subject to review in the same manner and to the same extent as the administrative law judge's proposed decision in the proceeding.

(c) An administrative law judge or agency member shall voluntarily disqualify themselves and withdraw from any case in which there are grounds for disqualification, including disqualification under Section 11425.40. The parties may waive the disqualification by a writing that recites the grounds for disqualification. A waiver is effective only when signed by all parties, accepted by the administrative law judge or agency member, and included in the record. Any party may request the disqualification of any administrative law judge or agency member by filing an affidavit, prior to the taking of evidence at a hearing, stating with particularity the grounds upon which it is claimed that the administrative law judge or agency member is disqualified. Where the request concerns an agency member, the issue shall be determined by the other members of the agency. Where the request concerns the administrative law judge, the issue shall be determined by the agency itself if the agency itself hears the case with the administrative law judge, otherwise the issue shall be determined by the administrative law judge. No agency member shall withdraw voluntarily or be subject to disqualification if their disqualification would prevent the existence of a quorum qualified to act in the particular case, except that a substitute qualified to act may be appointed by the appointing authority.

(d) The proceedings at the hearing shall be reported by a stenographic reporter. However, upon the consent of all the parties, or if a stenographic reporter is unavailable and upon finding of good cause by the administrative law judge, the proceedings may be recorded electronically.

(e) Whenever, after the agency itself has commenced to hear the case with an administrative law judge presiding, a quorum no longer exists, the administrative law judge who is presiding shall complete the hearing as if sitting alone and shall render a proposed decision in accordance with subdivision (b) of Section 11517. **Leg.H.** Added Stats 1945 ch 867 §1. Amended Stats 1973 ch 231 §1; Stats 1983 ch 635 §1; Stats 1985 ch 324 §19; Stats 1995 ch 938 §39 (SB 523), operative July 1, 1997; Stats 2022 ch 48 §23 (SB 189), effective June 30, 2022.

§11513. Evidence

(a) Oral evidence shall be taken only on oath or affirmation.

(b) Each party shall have these rights: to call and examine witnesses, to introduce exhibits; to cross-examine opposing witnesses on any matter relevant to the issues even though that matter was not covered in the direct examination; to impeach any witness regardless of which party first called him or her to testify; and to rebut the evidence against him or her. If respondent does not testify in his or her own behalf he or she may be called and examined as if under cross-examination.

(c) The hearing need not be conducted according to technical rules relating to evidence and witnesses, except as hereinafter provided. Any relevant evidence shall be admitted if it is the sort of evidence on which responsible persons are accustomed to rely in the conduct of serious affairs, regardless of the existence of any common law or statutory rule which might make improper the admission of the evidence over objection in civil actions.

(d) Hearsay evidence may be used for the purpose of supplementing or explaining other evidence but over timely objection shall not be sufficient in itself to support a finding unless it would be admissible over objection in civil actions. An objection is timely if made before submission of the case or on reconsideration.

(e) The rules of privilege shall be effective to the extent that they are otherwise required by statute to be recognized at the hearing.

(f) The presiding officer has discretion to exclude evidence if its probative value is substantially outweighed by the probability that its admission will necessitate undue consumption of time. **Leg.H.** Added Stats 1992 ch 1302 §9 (AB 3107), effective September 30, 1992, operative July 1, 1995. Amended Stats 1995 ch 938 §40 (SB 523), operative July 1, 1997.

Prior Law: Former Gov C §11513, similar to the present section, was added Stats 1992 ch 1302 §8, effective September 30, 1992, operative July 1, 1993, operative until July 1, 1995, amended Stats 1993 ch 701 §1, operative January 1, 1994, operative until July 1, 1995, and repealed January 1, 1996, by its own terms.

Former Gov C §11513, similar to the present section, was added Stats 1945 ch 867 §1, amended Stats 1965 ch 299 §135, operative January 1, 1967, Stats 1972 ch 1390 §1, Stats 1977 ch 1057 §4, operative July 1, 1978, Stats 1985 ch 324 §20, ch 1328 §6, Stats 1992 ch 1302 §7, effective September 30, 1992, and repealed July 1, 1993, by its own terms.

§11514. Affidavits

(a) At any time 10 or more days prior to a hearing or a continued hearing, any party may mail or deliver to the opposing party a copy of any affidavit which he proposes to introduce in evidence, together with a notice as provided in subdivision (b). Unless the opposing party, within seven days after such mailing or delivery, mails or delivers to the proponent a request to cross-examine an affiant, his right to cross-examine such affiant is waived and the affidavit, if introduced in evidence, shall be given the same effect as if the affiant had testified orally. If an opportunity to cross-examine an affiant is not afforded after request therefor is made as herein provided, the affidavit may be introduced in evidence, but shall be given only the same effect as other hearsay evidence.

(b) The notice referred to in subdivision (a) shall be substantially in the following form:

The accompanying affidavit of (here insert name of affiant) will be introduced as evidence at the hearing in (here insert title of proceeding). (Here insert name of affiant) will not be called to testify orally and you will not be entitled to question him unless you notify (here insert name of proponent or his attorney) at (here insert address) that you wish to cross-examine him. To be effective your request must be mailed or delivered to (here insert name of proponent or his attorney) on or before (here insert a date seven days after the date of mailing or delivering the affidavit to the opposing party). **Leg.H.** Added Stats 1947 ch 491 §6.

Prior Law: Former Gov C §11514, relating to affidavits in lieu of oral evidence, was added Stats 1945 ch 867 §1 and repealed Stats 1947 ch 491 §5.

§11515. Official notice

In reaching a decision official notice may be taken, either before or after submission of the case for decision, of any generally accepted technical or scientific matter within the agency's special field, and of any fact which may be judicially noticed by the courts of this State. Parties present at the hearing shall be informed of the matters to be noticed, and those matters shall be noted in the record, referred to therein, or appended thereto. Any such party shall be given a reasonable opportunity on request to refute the officially noticed matters by evidence or by written or oral presentation of authority, the manner of such refutation to be determined by the agency. **Leg.H.** Added Stats 1945 ch 867 §1.

§11516. Amendment of accusation or District Statement of Reduction in Force after submission

The agency may order amendment of the accusation or District Statement of Reduction in Force after submission of the case for decision. Each party shall be given notice of the intended amendment and opportunity to show that he or she will be prejudiced thereby unless the case is reopened to permit the introduction of additional evidence on his or her behalf. If such prejudice is shown, the agency shall reopen the case to permit the introduction of additional evidence. **Leg.H.** Added Stats 1945 ch 867 §1. Amended Stats 2013 ch 90 §9 (SB 546), effective January 1, 2014.

§11517. Contested cases

(a) A contested case may be originally heard by the agency itself and subdivision (b) shall apply. Alternatively, at the discretion of the agency, an administrative law judge may originally hear the case alone and subdivision (c) shall apply.

(b) If a contested case is originally heard before an agency itself, all of the following provisions apply:

(1) An administrative law judge shall be present during the consideration of the case and, if requested, shall assist and advise the agency in the conduct of the hearing.

(2) No member of the agency who did not hear the evidence shall vote on the decision.

(3) The agency shall issue its decision within 100 days of submission of the case.

(c)(1) If a contested case is originally heard by an administrative law judge alone, he or she shall prepare within 30 days after the case is submitted to him or her a proposed decision in a form that may be adopted by the agency as the final decision in the case. Failure of the administrative law judge to deliver a proposed decision within the time required does not prejudice the rights of the agency in the case. Thirty days after the receipt by the agency of the proposed decision, a copy of the proposed decision shall be filed by the agency as a public record and a copy shall be served by the agency on each party and his or her attorney. The filing and service is not an adoption of a proposed decision by the agency.

(2) Within 100 days of receipt by the agency of the administrative law judge's proposed decision, the agency may act as prescribed in subparagraphs (A) to (E), inclusive. If the agency fails to act as prescribed in subparagraphs (A) to (E), inclusive, within 100 days of receipt of the proposed decision, the proposed decision shall be deemed adopted by the agency. The agency may do any of the following:

(A) Adopt the proposed decision in its entirety.

(B) Reduce or otherwise mitigate the proposed penalty and adopt the balance of the proposed decision.

(C) Make technical or other minor changes in the proposed decision and adopt it as the decision. Action by the agency under this paragraph is limited to a clarifying change or a change of a similar nature that does not affect the factual or legal basis of the proposed decision.

(D) Reject the proposed decision and refer the case to the same administrative law judge if reasonably available, otherwise to another administrative law judge, to take additional evidence. If the case is referred to an administrative law judge pursuant to this subparagraph, he or she shall prepare a revised proposed decision, as provided in paragraph (1), based upon the additional evidence and the transcript and other papers that are part of the record of the prior hearing. A copy of the revised proposed decision shall be furnished to each party and his or her attorney as prescribed in this subdivision.

(E) Reject the proposed decision, and decide the case upon the record, including the transcript, or upon an agreed statement of the parties, with or without taking additional evidence. By stipulation of the parties, the agency may decide the case upon the record without including the transcript. If the agency acts pursuant to this subparagraph, all of the following provisions apply:

(i) A copy of the record shall be made available to the parties. The agency may require payment of fees covering direct costs of making the copy.

(ii) The agency itself shall not decide any case provided for in this subdivision without affording the parties the opportunity to present either oral or written argument before the agency itself. If additional oral evidence is introduced before the agency itself, no agency member may vote unless the member heard the additional oral evidence.

(iii) The authority of the agency itself to decide the case under this subdivision includes authority to decide some but not all issues in the case.

(iv) If the agency elects to proceed under this subparagraph, the agency shall issue its final decision not later than 100 days after rejection of the proposed decision. If the agency elects to proceed under this subparagraph, and has ordered a transcript of the proceedings before the administrative law judge, the agency shall issue its final decision not later than 100 days after receipt of the transcript. If the agency finds that a further delay is required by special circumstance, it shall issue an order delaying the decision for no more than 30 days and specifying the reasons therefor. The order shall be subject to judicial review pursuant to Section 11523.

(d) The decision of the agency shall be filed immediately by the agency as a public record and a copy shall be served by the agency on each party and his or her attorney. **Leg.H.** Added Stats 1999 ch 339 §2 (AB 1692).

Prior Law: Former Gov C §11517, similar to the present section, was added Stats 1945 ch 867 §1, amended Stats 1955 ch 1661 §1, Stats 1971 ch 653 § 1, Stats 1979 ch 199 §4, Stats 1983 ch 548 §1, Stats 1985 ch 324 §21, Stats 1995 ch 938 §42, operative July 1, 1997, and repealed Stats 1999 ch 339 §1.

§11518. Copies of decision to parties

Copies of the decision shall be delivered to the parties personally or sent to them by registered mail. **Leg.H.** Added Stats 1945 ch 867 §1. Amended Stats 1947 ch 491 §7; Stats 1995 ch 938 §43 (SB 523), operative July 1, 1997.

§11518.5. Application to correct mistake or error in decision; Modification; Service of correction

(a) Within 15 days after service of a copy of the decision on a party, but not later than the effective date of the decision, the party may apply to the agency for correction of a mistake or clerical error in the decision, stating the specific ground on which the application is made. Notice of the application shall be given to the other parties to the proceeding. The application is not a prerequisite for seeking judicial review.

(b) The agency may refer the application to the administrative law judge who formulated the proposed decision or may delegate its authority under this section to one or more persons.

(c) The agency may deny the application, grant the application and modify the decision, or grant the application and set the matter for further proceedings. The application is considered denied if the agency does not dispose of it within 15 days after it is made or a longer time that the agency provides by regulation.

(d) Nothing in this section precludes the agency, on its own motion or on motion of the administrative law judge, from modifying the decision to correct a mistake or clerical error. A modification under this subdivision shall be made within 15 days after issuance of the decision.

(e) The agency shall, within 15 days after correction of a mistake or clerical error in the decision, serve a copy of the correction on each party on which a copy of the decision was previously served. **Leg.H.** Added Stats 1995 ch 938 §44 (SB 523), operative July 1, 1997.

§11519. Effective date of decision; Stay of execution; Notice of suspension or revocation; Restitution; Actual knowledge as condition of enforcement

(a) The decision shall become effective 30 days after it is delivered or mailed to respondent unless: a reconsideration is ordered within that time, or the agency itself orders that the decision shall become effective sooner, or a stay of execution is granted.

(b) A stay of execution may be included in the decision or if not included therein may be granted by the agency at any time before the decision becomes effective. The stay of execution provided herein may be accompanied by an express condition that respondent comply with specified terms of probation; provided, however, that the terms of probation shall be just and reasonable in the light of the findings and decision.

(c) If respondent was required to register with any public officer, a notification of any suspension or revocation shall be sent to the officer after the decision has become effective.

(d) As used in subdivision (b), specified terms of probation may include an order of restitution. Where restitution is ordered and paid pursuant to the provisions of this subdivision, the amount paid shall be credited to any subsequent judgment in a civil action.

(e) The person to which the agency action is directed may not be required to comply with a decision unless the person has been served with the decision in the manner provided in Section 11505 or has actual knowledge of the decision.

(f) A nonparty may not be required to comply with a decision unless the agency has made the decision available for public inspection and copying or the nonparty has actual knowledge of the decision.

(g) This section does not preclude an agency from taking immediate action to protect the public interest in accordance with Article 13 (commencing with Section 11460.10) of Chapter 4.5. **Leg.H.** Added Stats 1945 ch 867 §1. Amended Stats 1949 ch 314 §2; Stats 1976 ch 476 §1; Stats 1977 ch 680 §1; Stats 1995 ch 938 §45 (SB 523), operative July 1, 1997.

§11519.1. Order of restitution for financial loss or damages

(a) A decision rendered against a licensee under Article 1 (commencing with Section 11700) of Chapter 4 of Division 5 of the Vehicle Code may include an order of restitution for any financial loss or damage found to have been suffered by a person in the case.

(b) The failure to make the restitution in accordance with the terms of the decision is separate grounds for the Department of Motor Vehicles to refuse to issue a license under Article 1 (commencing with Section 11700) of Chapter 4 of Division 5 of the Vehicle Code, and constitutes a violation of the terms of any applicable probationary order in the decision.

(c) Nothing in this section is intended to limit or restrict actions, remedies, or procedures otherwise available to an aggrieved party pursuant to any other provision of law. **Leg.H.** Added Stats 2007 ch 93 §1 (SB 525), effective January 1, 2008.

§11520. Defaults and uncontested cases

(a) If the respondent either fails to file a notice of defense, or, as applicable, notice of participation, or to appear at the hearing, the agency may take action based upon the respondent's express admissions or upon other evidence and affidavits may be used as evidence without any notice to respondent; and where the burden of proof is on the respondent to establish that the respondent is entitled to the agency action sought, the agency may act without taking evidence.

(b) Notwithstanding the default of the respondent, the agency or the administrative law judge, before a proposed decision is issued, has discretion to grant a hearing on reasonable notice to the parties. If the agency and administrative law judge make conflicting orders under this subdivision, the agency's order takes precedence. The administrative law judge may order the respondent, or the respondent's attorney or other authorized representative, or both, to pay reasonable expenses, including attorney's fees, incurred by another party as a result of the respondent's failure to appear at the hearing.

(c) Within seven days after service on the respondent of a decision based on the respondent's default, the respondent may serve a written motion requesting that the decision be vacated and stating the grounds relied on. The agency in its discretion may vacate the decision and grant a hearing on a showing of good cause. As used in this subdivision, good cause includes, but is not limited to, any of the following:

(1) Failure of the person to receive notice served pursuant to Section 11505.

(2) Mistake, inadvertence, surprise, or excusable neglect. **Leg.H.** Added Stats 1945 ch 867 §1. Amended Stats 1947 ch 491 §8; Stats 1963

ch 931 §2; Stats 1995 ch 938 §46 (SB 523), operative July 1, 1997; Stats 2013 ch 90 §10 (SB 546), effective January 1, 2014.

§11521. Reconsideration

(a) The agency itself may order a reconsideration of all or part of the case on its own motion or on petition of any party. The agency shall notify a petitioner of the time limits for petitioning for reconsideration. The power to order a reconsideration shall expire 30 days after the delivery or mailing of a decision to a respondent, or on the date set by the agency itself as the effective date of the decision if that date occurs prior to the expiration of the 30-day period or at the termination of a stay of not to exceed 30 days which the agency may grant for the purpose of filing an application for reconsideration. If additional time is needed to evaluate a petition for reconsideration filed prior to the expiration of any of the applicable periods, an agency may grant a stay of that expiration for no more than 10 days, solely for the purpose of considering the petition. If no action is taken on a petition within the time allowed for ordering reconsideration, the petition shall be deemed denied.

(b) The case may be reconsidered by the agency itself on all the pertinent parts of the record and such additional evidence and argument as may be permitted, or may be assigned to an administrative law judge. A reconsideration assigned to an administrative law judge shall be subject to the procedure provided in Section 11517. If oral evidence is introduced before the agency itself, no agency member may vote unless he or she heard the evidence. **Leg.H.** Added Stats 1945 ch 867 §1. Amended Stats 1953 ch 964 §1; Stats 1985 ch 324 §22; Stats 1987 ch 305 §1; Stats 2004 ch 865 §34 (SB 1914).

§11522. Reinstatement of license or reduction of penalty

A person whose license has been revoked or suspended may petition the agency for reinstatement or reduction of penalty after a period of not less than one year has elapsed from the effective date of the decision or from the date of the denial of a similar petition. The agency shall give notice to the Attorney General of the filing of the petition and the Attorney General and the petitioner shall be afforded an opportunity to present either oral or written argument before the agency itself. The agency itself shall decide the petition, and the decision shall include the reasons therefor, and any terms and conditions that the agency reasonably deems appropriate to impose as a condition of reinstatement. This section shall not apply if the statutes dealing with the particular agency contain different provisions for reinstatement or reduction of penalty. **Leg.H.** Added Stats 1945 ch 867 §1. Amended Stats 1985 ch 587 §4.

§11523. Judicial review

Judicial review may be had by filing a petition for a writ of mandate in accordance with the provisions of the Code of Civil Procedure, subject, however, to the statutes relating to the particular agency. Except as otherwise provided in this section, the petition shall be filed within 30 days after the last day on which reconsideration can be ordered. The right to petition shall not be affected by the failure to seek reconsideration before the agency. On request of the petitioner for a record of the proceedings, the complete record of the proceedings, or the parts thereof as are designated by the petitioner in the request, shall be prepared by the Office of Administrative Hearings or the agency and shall be delivered to the petitioner, within 30 days after the request, which time shall be extended for good cause shown, upon the payment of the cost for the preparation of the transcript, the cost for preparation of other portions of the record and for certification thereof. The complete record includes the pleadings, all notices and orders issued by the agency, any proposed decision by an administrative law judge, the final decision, a transcript of all proceedings, the exhibits admitted or rejected, the written evidence and any other papers in the case. If the petitioner, within 10 days after the last day on which reconsideration can be ordered, requests the agency to prepare all or any part of the record, the time within which a petition may be filed shall be extended until 30 days after its delivery to him or her. The agency may file with the court the original of any document in the record in lieu of a copy thereof. If the petitioner prevails in overturning the administrative decision following judicial review, the agency shall reimburse the petitioner for all costs of transcript preparation, compilation of the record, and certification. **Leg.H.** Added Stats 1945 ch 867 §1. Amended Stats 1947 ch 491 §9; Stats 1953 ch 962 §1; Stats 1955 ch 246 §1; Stats 1965 ch 1458 §10; Stats 1971 ch 984 §1; Stats 1985 ch 324 §23; Stats 1985 ch 973 §1; Stats 1986 ch 597 §3; Stats 1994 ch 1206 §29 (SB 1775); Stats 1995 ch 938 §47 (SB 523), operative July 1, 1997; Stats 2005 ch 674 §23 (SB 231), effective January 1, 2006.

§11524. Continuances; Requirement of good cause; Judicial review of denial

(a) The agency may grant continuances. When an administrative law judge of the Office of Administrative Hearings has been assigned to the hearing, no continuance may be granted except by him or her or by the presiding judge of the appropriate regional office of the Office of Administrative Hearings, for good cause shown.

(b) When seeking a continuance, a party shall apply for the continuance within 10 working days following the time the party discovered or reasonably should have discovered the event or occurrence which establishes the good cause for the continuance. A continuance may be granted for good cause after the 10 working days have lapsed if the party seeking the continuance is not responsible for and has made a good faith effort to prevent the condition or event establishing the good cause.

(c) In the event that an application for a continuance by a party is denied by an administrative law judge of the Office of Administrative Hearings, and the party seeks judicial review thereof, the party shall, within 10 working days of the denial, make application for appropriate judicial relief in the superior court or be barred from judicial review thereof as a matter of jurisdiction. A party applying for judicial relief from the denial shall give notice to the agency and other parties. Notwithstanding Section 1010 of the Code of Civil Procedure, the notice may be either oral at the time of the denial of application for a continuance or written at the same time application is made in court for judicial relief. This subdivision does not apply to the Department of Alcoholic Beverage Control. **Leg.H.** Added Stats 1945 ch 867 §1. Amended Stats 1953 ch 962 §2; Stats 1963 ch 842 §1; Stats 1971 ch 1303 §9; Stats 1979 ch 199 §5; Stats 1985 ch 324 §24; Stats 1995 ch 938 §48 (SB 523), operative July 1, 1997, effective January 1, 1996.

§11526. Voting by mail

The members of an agency qualified to vote on any question may vote by mail or another appropriate method. **Leg.H.** Added Stats 1945 ch 867 §1. Amended Stats 1995 ch 938 §50 (SB 523), operative July 1, 1997, effective January 1, 1996.

§11527. Charge against funds of agency

Any sums authorized to be expended under this chapter by any agency shall be a legal charge against the funds of the agency. **Leg.H.** Added Stats 1945 ch 867 §1.

§11528. Oaths

In any proceedings under this chapter any agency, agency member, secretary of an agency, hearing reporter, or administrative law judge has power to administer oaths and affirmations and to certify to official acts. **Leg.H.** Added Stats 1945 ch 867 §1. Amended Stats 1969 ch 191 §1; Stats 1985 ch 324 §25.

§11529. Interim orders

(a) The administrative law judge of the Medical Quality Hearing Panel established pursuant to Section 11371 may issue an interim order suspending a license, imposing drug testing, continuing education, supervision of procedures, limitations on the authority to prescribe, furnish, administer, or dispense controlled substances, or other license restrictions. Interim orders may be issued only if the affidavits in support of the petition show that the licensee has engaged in, or is about to engage in, acts or omissions constituting a violation of the Medical Practice Act or the appropriate practice act governing each allied health profession, or is unable to practice safely due to a mental or physical condition, and that permitting the licensee to continue to engage in the profession for which the license was issued will endanger the public health, safety, or welfare. The failure to comply with an order issued pursuant to Section 820 of the Business and Professions Code may constitute grounds to issue an interim suspension order under this section.

(b) All orders authorized by this section shall be issued only after a hearing conducted pursuant to subdivision (d), unless it appears from the facts shown by affidavit that serious injury would result to the public before the matter can be heard on notice. Except as provided in subdivision (c), the licensee shall receive at least 15 days' prior notice of the hearing, which notice shall include affidavits and all other information in support of the order.

(c) If an interim order is issued without notice, the administrative law judge who issued the order without notice shall cause the licensee to be notified of the order, including affidavits and all other information in support of the order by a 24-hour delivery service. That notice shall also include the date of the hearing on the order, which shall be conducted in accordance with the requirement of subdivision (d), not later than 20 days from the date of issuance. The order shall be dissolved unless the requirements of subdivision (a) are satisfied.

(d) For the purposes of the hearing conducted pursuant to this section, the licentiate shall, at a minimum, have the following rights:

(1) To be represented by counsel.

(2) To have a record made of the proceedings, copies of which may be obtained by the licentiate upon payment of any reasonable charges associated with the record.

(3) To present written evidence in the form of relevant declarations, affidavits, and documents.

The discretion of the administrative law judge to permit testimony at the hearing conducted pursuant to this section shall be identical to the discretion of a superior court judge to permit testimony at a hearing conducted pursuant to Section 527 of the Code of Civil Procedure.

(4) To present oral argument.

(e) Consistent with the burden and standards of proof applicable to a preliminary injunction entered under Section 527 of the Code of Civil Procedure, the administrative law judge shall grant the interim order if, in the exercise of discretion, the administrative law judge concludes that:

(1) There is a reasonable probability that the petitioner will prevail in the underlying action.

(2) The likelihood of injury to the public in not issuing the order outweighs the likelihood of injury to the licensee in issuing the order.

(f) In all cases in which an interim order is issued, and an accusation or petition to revoke probation is not filed and served pursuant to Sections 11503 and 11505 within 30 days of the date on which the parties to the hearing on the interim order have submitted the matter, the order shall be dissolved.

Upon service of the accusation or petition to revoke probation the licensee shall have, in addition to the rights granted by this section, all of the rights and privileges available as specified in this chapter. If the licensee requests a hearing on the accusation, the board shall provide the licensee with a hearing within 30 days of the request, unless the licensee stipulates to a later hearing, and a decision within 15 days of the date the decision is received from the administrative law judge, or the board shall nullify the interim order previously issued, unless good cause can be shown by the Division of Medical Quality for a delay.

(g) If an interim order is issued, a written decision shall be prepared within 15 days of the hearing, by the administrative law judge, including findings of fact and a conclusion articulating the connection between the evidence produced at the hearing and the decision reached.

(h) Notwithstanding the fact that interim orders issued pursuant to this section are not issued after a hearing as otherwise required by this chapter, interim orders so issued shall be subject to judicial review pursuant to Section 1094.5 of the Code of Civil Procedure. The relief that may be ordered shall be limited to a stay of the interim order. Interim orders issued pursuant to this section are final interim orders and, if not dissolved pursuant to subdivision (c) or (f), may only be challenged administratively at the hearing on the accusation.

(i) The interim order provided for by this section shall be:

(1) In addition to, and not a limitation on, the authority to seek injunctive relief provided for in the Business and Professions Code.

(2) A limitation on the emergency decision procedure provided in Article 13 (commencing with Section 11460.10) of Chapter 4.5. **Leg.H.** Added Stats 1990 ch 1597 §35 (SB 2375). Amended Stats 1993 ch 1267 §54 (SB 916); Stats 1995 ch 938 §51 (SB 523), operative July 1, 1997; Stats 1998 ch 878 §57 (SB 2239); Stats 2013 ch 399 §3 (SB 670), effective January 1, 2014, ch 515 § 29.5 (SB 304), effective January 1, 2014; Stats 2017 ch 775 §110 (SB 798), effective January 1, 2018.

Prior Law: Former Gov C §11529, relating to citation of Administrative Procedure Act, was added Stats 1947 ch 491 §10 and repealed Stats 1947 ch 1425 §20. **2017 Note:** (a) The Legislature finds and declares both of the following:

(1) That healing arts boards may adopt regulations authorizing those boards to order a licensee on probation to cease practice for major violations and when the board orders a licensee to undergo a clinical diagnostic evaluation pursuant to the uniform and specific standards adopted and authorized under Section 315 of the Business and Professions Code.

(2) That an order to cease practice pursuant to the authority described in paragraph (1) is not governed by the provisions of Chapter 5 (commencing with Section 11500) of Part 1 of Division 3 of Title 2 of the Government Code and does not constitute disciplinary action.

(b) It is the intent of the Legislature to enact legislation in the 2017–2018 Regular Session that would prioritize patients and protection of the public from harm by authorizing the Medical Board of California to take swift and necessary action for a physician and surgeon's continued failure to comply with an order issued by the board pursuant to Section 820 of the Business and Professions Code. Stats 2017 ch 775 (SB 798) § 1.

TITLE 3
GOVERNMENT OF COUNTIES
DIVISION 2
OFFICERS

PART 3
OTHER OFFICERS
CHAPTER 2
SHERIFF
ARTICLE 7
Fees

§26720. Fees to be charged and collected

For services performed by them sheriffs shall charge and collect the fees fixed in this article. **Leg.H.** Added Stats 1947 ch 424 §1.

§26720.5. Waiver and refund of fees

Notwithstanding Section 26720, fees otherwise payable by a litigant pursuant to this article shall be waived or, if paid, refunded, in any case in which the litigant is permitted by the court to proceed in forma pauperis under rules adopted by the Judicial Council pursuant to Section 68511.3.

This section is declaratory of existing law, and the enumeration in this section of fees to be waived shall not be construed to limit the power of the court to waive fees in other instances, as permitted or required under rules adopted by the Judicial Council pursuant to Section 68511.3. **Leg.H.** Added Stats 1980 ch 1372 §4.5.

§26720.9. Fees for enumerated sections

Notwithstanding any other law, the amounts set forth in Sections 26721, 26721.1, 26725, 26728, 26734, 26742, and 26743 shall be fifty dollars ($50). **Leg.H.** Added Stats 2010 ch 4 §7 (AB 680), effective January 1, 2011, operative January 1, 2011. Amended Stats 2014 ch 470 §4 (AB 2256), effective January 1, 2015; Stats 2023 ch 29 §1 (SB 564), effective January 1, 2024.

Prior Law: Former §26720.9, similar to the present section, was added Stats 1992 ch 687 §1, operative July 1, 1993, amended Stats 2000 ch 629 §1, Stats 2010 ch 4 §6, effective January 1, 2011, and repealed January 1, 2011, by its own terms.

§26721. Service or execution of process or notice; Service of writ of execution and notice of levy

Except as provided in this article, the fee for serving or executing any process or notice required by law or the litigants to be served shall be the amount described in Section 26720.9, and there shall be no additional fee for substitute service when substitute service is authorized.

However, no fee shall be charged for serving an emergency protective order, protective order, or restraining order issued pursuant to Division 10 of the Family Code (the Domestic Violence Prevention Act) on a respondent who is in custody.

In any case where property has been levied upon and, pursuant to the levy, a copy of the writ of execution and a notice of levy are required by statute to be served either personally or by mail upon the judgment debtor or other person, no fee shall be charged for that service. **Leg.H.** Added Stats 1947 ch 424 §1. Amended Stats 1951 ch 956 §1; Stats 1961 ch 310 §1; Stats 1st Ex Sess 1966 ch 120 §7; Stats 1975 ch 368 §1; Stats 1980 ch 1372 §5; Stats 1981 ch 1034 §2; Stats 1985 ch 1296 §1; Stats 1987 ch 328 §1; Stats 1991 ch 810 §1 (AB 709); Stats 1992 ch 687 §2 (SB 1732), operative July 1, 1993; Stats 1994 ch 689 §1 (AB 3033); Stats 2000 ch 629 §2 (AB 1768).

§26721.1. Unlawful detainer; Fee for service of summons, complaint, and prejudgment claim of right to possession

In an action for unlawful detainer, the fee for service of a summons, complaint, and prejudgment claim of right to possession pursuant to Section 415.46 of the Code of Civil Procedure shall be the amount described in Section 26720.9 for all occupants not named in the summons. The fee is not refundable. **Leg.H.** Added Stats 1990 ch 1535 §4 (SB 2508). Amended Stats 2000 ch 629 §3 (AB 1768).

§26721.2. Fees for service, cancellation of service, and a not-found return

(a) For any action commenced in the superior court, the fee for the service of the summons, the complaint for which the summons is issued, and all other documents or notices required to be served with the summons and complaint, is fifty dollars ($50).

(b) The fee for cancellation of the service of a summons prior to its completion is fifty dollars ($50).

(c) The fee for making a not-found return on a summons certifying that the person cannot be found at the address specified is fifty dollars ($50). **Leg.H.** Added Stats 2006 ch 365 § 2 (SB 432), effective January 1, 2007, operative January 1, 2008. Amended Stats 2014 ch 470 §5 (AB 2256), effective January 1, 2015; Stats 2023 ch 29 §2 (SB 564), effective January 1, 2024.

Prior Law: Former § 26721.2, similar to the present section, was added Stats 2000 ch 629 §3.5, amended Stats 2003 ch 888 §3, Stats 2006 ch 365 §1, effective January 1, 2007, repealed January 1, 2008, by its own terms.

§26722. Fee for serving, executing, or processing writ or order

The fee for serving, executing, or processing any writ or order where the levying officer is required to take immediate possession of the property levied upon is one hundred twenty-five dollars ($125). **Leg.H.** Added Stats 1991 ch 810 §2 (AB 709). Amended Stats 2000 ch 629 §4 (AB 1768); Stats 2014 ch 470 §6 (AB 2256), effective January 1, 2015; Stats 2023 ch 29 §3 (SB 564), effective January 1, 2024.

Prior Law: Former §26722, relating to service or levy of attachment, execution, or order for delivery of personal property, was added Stats 1947 ch 424 §1, amended Stats 1951 ch 956 §2, Stats 1st Ex Sess 1966 ch 120 §8, and repealed Stats 1975 ch 368 §2. Historical derivation: (a) Former Pol C §4300b, as added Stats 1907 ch 282 §1, amended Stats 1921 ch 789 §1, Stats 1923 ch 15 §1, Stats 1929 ch 313 §1, Stats 1935 ch 101 §1, Stats 1937 ch 572 §1, Stats 1941 ch 1076 §1, Stats 1945 ch 981 §1. (b) Stats 1895 ch 207 p 269.

§26723. Fee for opening safe–deposit box

The fee for opening a safe-deposit box pursuant to Sections 488.460 and 700.150 of the Code of Civil Procedure is one hundred seventy dollars ($170). **Leg.H.** Added Stats 2003 ch 888 §4 (AB 394). Amended Stats 2014 ch 470 §7 (AB 2256), effective January 1, 2015; Stats 2023 ch 29 §4 (SB 564), effective January 1, 2024.

Prior Law: Former §26723, relating to fee for taking any bond or undertaking, was added Stats 1947 ch 424 §1, amended Stats 1st Ex Sess 1966 ch 120 §9, and repealed Stats 1975 ch 368 §3.

§26725. Fee for execution of process on real property

The fee for serving, executing, or processing a writ of attachment, writ of execution, writ of sale, or order on real estate, as to the initial service or posting of a continuous unbroken parcel or tract, and the fee for serving a record owner other than the defendant shall be the amount described in Section 26720.9. **Leg.H.** Added Stats 1947 ch 424 §1. Amended Stats 1951 ch 956 §3; Stats 1953 ch 1797 §1; Stats 1st Ex Sess 1966 ch 120 §11; Stats 1975 ch 368 §5; Stats 1978 ch 1419 §5; Stats 1980 ch 1372 §6; Stats 1981 ch 1034 §4; Stats 1982 ch 497 §105, operative July 1, 1983; Stats 1985 ch 1296 §2; Stats 1987 ch 328 §2; Stats 1991 ch 810 §3 (AB 709); Stats 2000 ch 629 §5 (AB 1768).

§26725.1. Additional parcels

The fee for serving or posting any additionally required notices or orders on other parcels is twenty-five dollars ($25) each. **Leg.H.** Added Stats 1975 ch 368 §6. Amended Stats 1987 ch 328 §3; Stats 1991 ch 810 §4 (AB 709); Stats 2014 ch 470 §8 (AB 2256), effective January 1, 2015; Stats 2023 ch 29 §5 (SB 564), effective January 1, 2024.

§26726. Fee for keeping property under writ; Maintaining custody under levy

(a) The fee for keeping and caring for property under a writ of attachment, execution, possession, or sale is one hundred seventy-five dollars ($175) when necessarily employed for any eight-hour period or any part thereof. If an additional keeper or keepers are required during these periods, the fee for the additional keeper or keepers shall be the same as fixed, but, in no event shall any one keeper receive more than three hundred fifty dollars ($350) during any 24-hour period when so employed.

(b) In addition to the fees provided by Section 26721, the fee for maintaining custody of property under levy by the use of a keeper is fifty dollars ($50) for each day custody is maintained after the first day.

(c) Notwithstanding any other fee charged, a keeper shall receive seventy-five dollars ($75) when, pursuant to Section 26738, a levying officer prepares a not-found return. **Leg.H.** Added Stats 2010 ch 4 §9 (AB 680), effective January 1, 2011, operative January 1, 2011. Amended Stats 2014 ch 470 §9 (AB 2256), effective January 1, 2015; Stats 2023 ch 29 §6 (SB 564), effective January 1, 2024.

Prior Law: Former §26726, similar to the present section, was added Stats 1947 ch 424 §1, amended Stats 1947 ch 685 §2, Stats 1951 ch 1114 §1, Stats 1959 ch 1620 §1, Stats 1st Ex Sess 1966 ch 120 §12, Stats 1969 ch 595 §1, Stats 1975 ch 368 §7, Stats 1978 ch 149 §1, Stats 1981 ch 1034 §6, Stats 1982 ch 497 §106, Stats 1985 ch 1296 §3, Stats 1987 ch 328 §4, Stats 1991 ch 810 §5, Stats 1998 ch 160 §1, Stats 2000 ch 629 §6, Stats 2004 ch 327 §1, Stats 2010 ch 4 §8, and repealed January 1, 2011, by its own terms.

§26727. Copy of writ, process, paper, order, or notice

The fee for a copy of any writ, process, paper, order, or notice actually made by the sheriff when required or demanded is one dollar and twenty-five cents ($1.25) per page, except that when correct copies are furnished to the sheriff for use no charge shall be made for those copies. **Leg.H.** Added Stats 1947 ch 424 §1. Amended Stats 1st Ex Sess 1966 ch 120 §13; Stats 1975 ch 368 §8; Stats 1987 ch 328 §5; Stats 1991 ch 810 §6 (AB 709); Stats 2014 ch 470 §10 (AB 2256), effective January 1, 2015; Stats 2023 ch 29 §7 (SB 564), effective January 1, 2024.

§26728. Preparing and posting notices of personal property sales

The fee for preparing and posting the initial notice of personal property sale under a writ of attachment, execution, or sale or order of court shall be the amount described in Section 26720.9. **Leg.H.** Added Stats 1947 ch 424 §1. Amended Stats 1951 ch 956 §4; Stats 1st Ex Sess 1966 ch 120 §14; Stats 1975 ch 368 §9; Stats 1980 ch 1372 §7; Stats 1981 ch 1034 §7; Stats 1982 ch 497 §107, operative July 1, 1983; Stats 1985 ch 1296 §4; Stats 1987 ch 328 §6; Stats 1991 ch 810 §7 (AB 709); Stats 2000 ch 629 §7 (AB 1768).

§26728.1. Additional notices

The fee for preparing and posting additionally required notices of personal property sales is nineteen dollars ($19) each. **Leg.H.** Added Stats 1975 ch 368 §10. Amended Stats 1987 ch 328 §7; Stats 1991 ch 810 §8 (AB 709); Stats 2014 ch 470 §11 (AB 2256), effective January 1, 2015; Stats 2023 ch 29 §8 (SB 564), effective January 1, 2024.

§26729. Furnishing notice for publication

The fee for furnishing a notice for publication is nineteen dollars ($19). **Leg.H.** Added Stats 1947 ch 424 §1. Amended Stats 1951 ch 956 §5; Stats 1st Ex Sess 1966 ch 120 §15; Stats 1975 ch 368 §11; Stats 1987 ch 328 §8; Stats 1991 ch 810 §9 (AB 709); Stats 2014 ch 470 §12 (AB 2256), effective January 1, 2015; Stats 2023 ch 29 §9 (SB 564), effective January 1, 2024.

§26730. Conducting or postponing sale of real or personal property

The fee for conducting or postponing the sale of real or personal property as required by law or the litigant is one hundred ten dollars ($110). **Leg.H.** Added Stats 1947 ch 424 §1. Amended Stats 1951 ch 1114 §2; Stats 1st Ex Sess 1966 ch 120 §16; Stats 1975 ch 368 §12; Stats 1980 ch 1372 §8; Stats 1981 ch 1034 §9; Stats 1985 ch 1296 §5; Stats 1987 ch 328 §9; Stats 1991 ch 810 §10 (AB 709); Stats 2000 ch 629 §8 (AB 1768); Stats 2014 ch 470 §13 (AB 2256), effective January 1, 2015; Stats 2023 ch 29 §10 (SB 564), effective January 1, 2024.

§26731. Deposit of portion into special fund; Use of funds

(a) Twenty-two dollars ($22) of any fee collected by the sheriff's civil division or marshal under Sections 26721, 26722, 26725, 26726, 26728, 26730, 26733.5, 26734, 26736, 26738, 26742, 26743, 26744, and 26750 shall be deposited in a special fund in the county treasury. A separate accounting of funds deposited shall be maintained for each depositor, and funds deposited shall be for the exclusive use of the sheriff's civil division or marshal.

(b) Ninety-five percent of the moneys in the special fund shall be expended to supplement the costs of the depositor for the implementation, maintenance, and purchase of auxiliary equipment and furnishings for automated systems or other nonautomated operational equipment and furnishings deemed necessary by the sheriff's civil division or marshal. Five percent of the moneys in the special fund shall be used to supplement the expenses of the sheriff's civil division or marshal in administering the funds. **Leg.H.** Added Stats 2010 ch 4 §11 (AB 680), effective January 1, 2011, operative January 1, 2011. Amended Stats 2014 ch 470 §14 (AB 2256), effective January 1, 2015; Stats 2023 ch 29 §11 (SB 564), effective January 1, 2024.

Prior Law: Former §26731, similar to the present section, was added Stats 1991 ch 810 §11, amended Stats 2000 ch 629 §9, Stats 2004 ch 327 §2, Stats 2010 ch 4 §10, and repealed January 1, 2011, by its own terms.

Former §26731, relating to advertising and posting notice of sale of real property and ship, boat, or vessel, was added Stats 1947 ch 424 §1, amended Stats 1951 ch 956 §6, Stats 1st Ex Sess 1966 ch 120 §17, and repealed Stats 1975 ch 368 §13. Historical derivation: (a) Former Pol C §4300b, as added Stats 1907 ch 282 §1, amended Stats 1921 ch 789 §1, Stats 1923 ch 15 §1, Stats 1929 ch 313 §1, Stats 1935 ch 101 §1, Stats 1937 ch 572 §1, Stats 1941 ch 1076 §1, Stats 1945 ch 981 §1. (b) Stats 1895 ch 207 p 269.

§26732. Publication of notice in newspaper

The fee for publication of a notice in a newspaper is the reasonable cost of the publication. **Leg.H.** Added Stats 1947 ch 424 §1. Amended Stats 1951 ch 1114 §3.

§26733.5. Service of writ of possession of real property

The fee for serving a writ of possession of real property on an occupant or the occupants or for posting and serving a copy on the judgment debtor is one hundred five dollars ($105). The additional fee for removing an occupant or occupants from the premises and putting a person in possession of the premises is seventy-five dollars ($75). The fee for reposting a notice to vacate shall be pursuant to Section 26721. **Leg.H.** Added Stats 1985 ch 1296 §7. Amended Stats 1987 ch 328 §10; Stats 1991 ch 810 §12 (AB 709); Stats 2004 ch 327 §3 (AB 2137); Stats 2014 ch 470 §15 (AB 2256), effective January 1, 2015; Stats 2023 ch 29 §12 (SB 564), effective January 1, 2024.

Prior Law: Former §26733.5, relating to service of writ of possession of real property in Los Angeles county, was added Stats 1980 ch 1372 §9.5 and repealed Stats 1981 ch 1034 §12.

§26734. Making levy on personal property held under attachment

The fee for making a levy on personal property already in possession of the officer who is holding it under attachment in the same action shall be the amount described in Section 26720.9. **Leg.H.** Added Stats 1947 ch 424 §1. Amended Stats 1951 ch 956 §8; Stats 1953 ch 1797 §2; Stats 1st Ex Sess 1966 ch 120 §19; Stats 1969 ch 514 §2; Stats 1975 ch 368 §15; Stats 1980 ch 1372 §10; Stats 1981 ch 1034 §13; Stats 1985 ch 1296 §8; Stats 1987 ch 328 §11; Stats 1991 ch 810 §13 (AB 709); Stats 2000 ch 629 §10 (AB 1768).

§26736. Cancellation of service or execution of process or notice

The fee for cancellation of the service or execution of any process or notice, other than a summons, prior to its completion is fifty dollars ($50). The fee provided by this section shall not be charged if a fee is charged pursuant to any other section of this article in attempting to serve or execute the process or notice. **Leg.H.** Added Stats 2010 ch 4 §13 (AB 680), effective January 1, 2011, operative January 1, 2011. Amended Stats 2014 ch 470 §16 (AB 2256), effective January 1, 2015; Stats 2023 ch 29 §13 (SB 564), effective January 1, 2024.

Prior Law: Former §26736, similar to the present section, was added Stats 1959 ch 926 §1, amended Stats 1st Ex Sess 1966 ch 120 §21, Stats 1975 ch 368 §17, Stats 1980 ch 1372 §12, Stats 1981 ch 1034 §17, Stats 1985 ch 1296 §9, Stats 1987 ch 328 §12, Stats 1991 ch 810 §14, Stats 1992 ch 687 §3, Stats 2000 ch 629 §11, Stats 2010 ch 4 §12, and repealed January 1, 2011, by its own terms.

Former §26736, relating to demand for payment on execution or delivery of property, was added Stats 1947 ch 424 §1, amended Stats 1951 ch 956 §10, ch 1114 §5, and repealed Stats 1953 ch 1797 §3.

§26738. Not-found return

The fee for making a not-found return on an affidavit and order, order for appearance, subpoena, writ of attachment, writ of execution, writ of possession, order for delivery of personal property, or other process or notice required to be served, certifying that the person or property cannot be found at the address specified is fifty dollars ($50). **Leg.H.** Added Stats 2010 ch 4 §15 (AB 680), effective January 1, 2011, operative January 1, 2011. Amended Stats 2014 ch 470 §17 (AB 2256), effective January 1, 2015; Stats 2023 ch 29 §14 (SB 564), effective January 1, 2024.

Prior Law: Former §26738, similar to the present section, was added Stats 1947 ch 424 §1, amended Stats 1951 ch 956 §11, ch 1114 §6, Stats 1953 ch 1797 §4, Stats 1963 ch 199 §1, Stats 1st Ex Sess 1966 ch 120 §22, Stats 1975 ch 368 §19, Stats 1980 ch 1372 §13, Stats 1981 ch 1034 §19, Stats 1982 ch 497 §109, Stats 1985 ch 1296 §10, Stats 1987 ch 328 §13, Stats 1991 ch 810 §15, Stats 1992 ch 687 §4, Stats 2000 ch 629 §12, Stats 2003 ch 888 §5, Stats 2010 ch 4 §14, and repealed January 1, 2011, by its own terms.

§26740. Execution and delivery of deed or certificate of redemption

The fee for the execution and delivery of a deed or certificate of redemption is nineteen dollars ($19). **Leg.H.** Added Stats 1947 ch 424 §1. Amended Stats 1951 ch 956 §12; Stats 1953 ch 1797 §5; Stats 1st Ex Sess 1966 ch 120 §24; Stats 1987 ch 328 §14; Stats 1991 ch 810 §17 (AB 709); Stats 2014 ch 470 §18 (AB 2256), effective January 1, 2015; Stats 2023 ch 29 §15 (SB 564), effective January 1, 2024.

§26741. Execution and delivery of certificate or deed of sale

The fee for executing and delivering a certificate or deed of sale is nineteen dollars ($19). **Leg.H.** Added Stats 1947 ch 424 §1. Amended Stats 1951 ch 956 §13, ch 1114 §7; Stats 1st Ex Sess 1966 ch 120 §25; Stats 1982 ch 497 §110, operative July 1, 1983; Stats 1987 ch 328 §15; Stats 1991 ch 810 §18 (AB 709); Stats 2014 ch 470 §19 (AB 2256), effective January 1, 2015; Stats 2023 ch 29 §16 (SB 564), effective January 1, 2024.

§26742. Execution and delivery of other instruments

The fee for executing and delivering any other instrument shall be the amount described in Section 26720.9. **Leg.H.** Added Stats 1947 ch 424 §1. Amended Stats 1953 ch 1797 §6; Stats 1st Ex Sess 1966 ch 120 §26; Stats 1975 ch 368 §21; Stats 1980 ch 1372 §14; Stats 1981 ch 1034 §21; Stats 1985 ch 1296 §12; Stats 1987 ch 328 §16; Stats 1991 ch 810 §19 (AB 709); Stats 1992 ch 687 §5 (SB 1732), operative July 1, 1993; Stats 2000 ch 629 §13 (AB 1768).

§26743. Subpoenaing witnesses

The fee for subpoenaing a witness, including a copy of the subpoena and any affidavit required to be served therewith, shall be the amount described in Section 26720.9. **Leg.H.** Added Stats 1947 ch 424 §1. Amended Stats 1949 ch 597 §1; Stats 1951 ch 956 §14; Stats 1st Ex Sess 1966 ch 120 §27; Stats 1969 ch 514 §4; Stats 1975 ch 368 §22; Stats 1980 ch 1372 §15; Stats 1981 ch 1034 §23; Stats 1985 ch 1296 §13; Stats 1987 ch 328 §17; Stats 1991 ch 810 §20 (AB 709); Stats 2000 ch 629 §14 (AB 1768).

§26744. Service or execution of bench warrant

The fee for serving or executing a bench warrant arising from an order of appearance issued under subparagraph (A) of paragraph (1) of subdivision (a) of Section 491.160 or subparagraph (A) of paragraph (1) of subdivision (a) of Section 708.170 of the Code of Civil Procedure is fifty dollars ($50). **Leg.H.** Added Stats 1947 ch 424 §1. Amended Stats 1961 ch 310 §2; Stats 1st Ex Sess 1966 ch 120 §28; Stats 1975 ch 368 §23; Stats 1980 ch 1372 §16; Stats 1981 ch 1034 §25; Stats 1982 ch 497 §111, ch 1198 §66, operative July 1, 1983; Stats 1985 ch 1296 §14; Stats 1987 ch 328 §18; Stats 1991 ch 810 §21 (AB 709); Stats 2006 ch 277 §4 (AB 2369), effective January 1, 2007.

§26744.5. Fees for processing civil warrant

(a) The fees for processing a warrant issued pursuant to Section 1993 of the Code of Civil Procedure shall be paid by the moving party, as follows:

(1) Fifty dollars ($50) to receive and process the warrant, which shall include the issuance and mailing of a notice advising the person to be arrested of the issuance of the warrant and demanding that the person appear in court.

(2) Fifty dollars ($50) to cancel the service of the warrant.

(3) One hundred five dollars ($105) if unable to find the person at the address specified using due diligence.

(4) One hundred twenty-five dollars ($125) to arrest the person, which shall include the arrest and release of the person on a promise to appear pursuant to Section 1993.2 of the Code of Civil Procedure.

(b) The in forma pauperis fee waiver provisions under Rules 3.50 to 3.58, inclusive, of the California Rules of Court shall apply to the collection of fees under this section. **Leg.H.** Added Stats 2010 ch 4 §17 (AB 680), effective January 1, 2011, operative January 1, 2011. Amended Stats 2014 ch 470 §20 (AB 2256), effective January 1, 2015; Stats 2023 ch 29 §17 (SB 564), effective January 1, 2024.

Prior Law: Former §26744.5, similar to the present section, was added Stats 2005 ch 474 §7, amended Stats 2007 ch 130 §126, Stats 2010 ch 4 §16, and repealed January 1, 2011, by its own terms.

Former §26744.5, relating to service or execution of bench warrant, was added Stats 1980 ch 1372 §16.5 and repealed Stats 1981 ch 1034 §26.

§26745. Summoning trial jury

The fee for summoning a trial jury of 12 or less is two dollars ($2), and for each additional juror, ten cents ($0.10). **Leg.H.** Added Stats 1947 ch 424 §1.

§26746. Disbursement of money collected under writ of attachment, execution, possession or sale; Deposit in special fund; Use of special fund

(a) In addition to any other fees required by law, a processing fee of fifteen dollars ($15) shall be assessed for each disbursement of money collected under a writ of attachment, execution, possession, or sale, but excluding any action by the local child support agency for the establishment or enforcement of a child support obligation. The fee shall be collected from the judgment debtor in addition to, and in the same manner as, the moneys collected under the writ. All proceeds of this fee shall be deposited in a special fund in the county treasury. A separate accounting of funds deposited shall be maintained for each depositor, and funds deposited shall be for the exclusive use of the depositor.

(b) The special fund shall be expended to supplement the county's cost for vehicle fleet replacement and equipment, maintenance, and civil process operations, including data systems and consultant services.

(c) A processing fee shall not be charged pursuant to this section if the only disbursement is the return of the judgment creditor's deposit for costs. **Leg.H.** Added Stats 1987 ch 1330 §1. Amended Stats 2000 ch 629 §15 (AB 1768), ch 808 §100.1 (AB 1358), effective September 28, 2000; Stats 2003 ch 888 §6 (AB 394); Stats 2010 ch 4 §18 (AB 680), effective January 1, 2011; Stats 2014 ch 470 §21 (AB 2256), effective January 1, 2015; Stats 2023 ch 29 §18 (SB 564), effective January 1, 2024.

Prior Law: Former §26746, relating to traveling in service or execution of process or notice, was added Stats 1947 ch 424 §1, amended Stats 1951 ch 956 §15, Stats 1967 ch 981 §1, and repealed Stats 1975 ch 368 §24. Historical derivation: (a) Former Pol C §4300b, as added Stats 1907 ch 282 §1, amended Stats 1921 ch 789 §1, Stats 1923 ch 15 §1, Stats 1929 ch 313 §1, Stats 1935 ch 101 §1, Stats 1937 ch 572 §1, Stats 1941 ch 1076 §1, Stats 1945 ch 981 §1. (b) Stats 1895 ch 207 p 269.

§26746.1. Fee for certification of correction on specified citations; Disposition of proceeds

(a) A twenty-five-dollar ($25) fee shall be assessed by the sheriff or marshal for certification of correction on each citation that requires inspection for proof of correction of any violation pursuant to Section 40616 of the Vehicle Code.

(b) All proceeds of the fee shall be deposited in a special fund in the county treasury. A separate accounting of funds deposited shall be maintained for each depositor, and funds deposited shall be for the exclusive use of the sheriff's civil division or marshal.

(c) Ninety-five percent of the moneys in the special fund shall be expended to supplement the costs of the depositor for the implementation, maintenance, and purchase of auxiliary equipment and furnishings for automated systems or other nonautomated operational equipment and furnishings deemed necessary by the sheriff's civil division or marshal. Five percent of the moneys in the special fund shall be used to supplement the expenses of the sheriff's civil division or marshal in administering the funds. **Leg.H.** Added Stats 2010 ch 4 §20 (AB 680), effective January 1, 2011, operative January 1, 2011. Amended Stats 2014 ch 470 §22 (AB 2256), effective January 1, 2015; Stats 2023 ch 29 §19 (SB 564), effective January 1, 2024.

Prior Law: Former §26746.1, similar to the present section, was added Stats 1991 ch 810 §22, amended Stats 2000 ch 629 §16, Stats 2010 ch 4 §19, and repealed January 1, 2011, by its own terms.

§26747. Transporting prisoners to county jail

For transporting prisoners to the county jail, the sheriff shall charge the actual cost of such transportation. **Leg.H.** Added Stats 1947 ch 424 §1.

§26748. Expenses for inspecting, checking, releasing or other handling of property

In addition to the fees provided by this article, the sheriff may collect from the litigant or person requiring his services, his actual expenses for inspection, checking, releasing, or any other handling of property under his custody, charge, or keeping pursuant to any process, writ, order, paper, or notice, and actual postal charges paid for mailing by registered mail or certified mail any notice or demand required or authorized by law to be sent by registered mail or certified mail. **Leg.H.** Added Stats 1947 ch 424 §1. Amended Stats 1953 ch 1797 §7; Stats 1957 ch 1737 §1; Stats 1975 ch 368 §25.

§26749. Expenses for transporting persons to hospitals, prisons, or other state institutions

The sheriff shall receive expenses necessarily incurred in conveying persons to and from the state hospitals and in conveying persons to and from the state prisons or other state institutions, or to other destinations for the purpose of deportation to other states, or in advancing actual traveling expenses to any person committed to a state institution who is permitted to report to an institution without escort, which expenses shall be allowed as provided by Chapter 6 (commencing with Section 4750) of Title 5 of Part 3 of the Penal Code for cases subject to that chapter, and, otherwise, by the Department of General Services and paid by the state. **Leg.H.** Added Stats 1947 ch 424 §1. Amended Stats 1951 ch 181 §1; Stats 1986 ch 1310 §1; Stats 2006 ch 538 §301 (SB 1852), effective January 1, 2007; Stats 2014 ch 144 §24 (AB 1847), effective January 1, 2015; Stats 2016 ch 31 §153 (SB 836), effective June 27, 2016.

§26750. Fees for serving earnings withholding order; Additional fees prohibited

(a) The fee for serving an earnings withholding order under the Wage Garnishment Law (Chapter 5 (commencing with Section 706.010) of Division 2 of Title 9 of Part 2 of the Code of Civil Procedure), including, but not limited to, the costs of postage or traveling, and for performing all other duties of the levying officer under that law with respect to the levy shall be forty-five-dollars ($45).

(b) Except as provided in Section 26746, the levying officer shall not charge additional fees, costs, or expenses for performing the duties under the Wage Garnishment Law (Chapter 5 (commencing with Section 706.010) of Division 2 of Title 9 of Part 2 of the Code of Civil Procedure). **Leg.H.** Amended Stats 2014 ch 470 §23 (AB 2256), effective January 1, 2015; Stats 2023 ch 29 §20 (SB 564), effective January 1, 2024.

Prior Law: Former § 26750, similar to the present section, was added Stats 1978 ch 1133 §8, operative January 1, 1980, amended Stats 1981 ch 1034 §27; Stats 1982 ch 497 §112, operative July 1, 1983, Stats 1985 ch 1296 §15, Stats 1987 ch 328 §19, ch 1330 §2, Stats 1991 ch 810 §23, Stats 2000 ch 629 §17, and Stats 2006 ch 365 §3, operative January 1, 2007, repealed January 1, 2008, by its own terms.

§26751. Fee for report of repossession of vehicle; Release of vehicle by person in possession

After possession is taken of any vehicle by or on behalf of any legal owner thereof under the terms of a security agreement or lease agreement, the debtor shall pay the sheriff a fee of fifteen dollars ($15) for the receipt and filing of the report of repossession pursuant to Section 28 of the Vehicle Code before the vehicle may be redeemed by the debtor. Except as provided herein, any person in possession of the vehicle shall not release it to the debtor without first obtaining proof of payment of the fee to the sheriff. At the request of the debtor, a person in possession of the vehicle, or the legal owner, may also release the vehicle to the debtor provided the debtor pays the fifteen dollar ($15) fee, plus an administrative fee not to exceed five dollars ($5), to the person in possession or the legal owner, who shall transmit the fifteen dollar ($15) fee to the sheriff within three business days. The failure to transmit the fee within three business days shall subject the person in possession or legal owner receiving the fee from the debtor to a fine of fifty dollars ($50). The proof of payment, or a copy thereof, shall be retained by the party releasing possession to the debtor for the period required by law, and the party releasing possession shall provide a copy of the proof of payment to the debtor upon request of the debtor. **Leg.H.** Added Stats 1993 ch 1269 §10 (AB 1972). Amended Stats 1994 ch 1114 §7 (AB 2781).

CHAPTER 3
COUNTY CLERK
ARTICLE 2
Fees

§26820. Fees to be charged and collected

The county clerk shall charge and collect the fees fixed in this article for service performed by the clerk, when not otherwise provided by law. **Leg.H.** Added Stats 1947 ch 424 §1. Amended Stats 1955 ch 862 §1; Stats 1998 ch 931 §200 (SB 2139), effective September 28, 1998; Stats 2005 ch 75 §49 (AB 145), effective July 19, 2005, operative January 1, 2006.

§26831. Fee for preparing copies of record, etc., on file in county clerk's office

The county clerk may charge a reasonable fee to cover the cost of preparing copies of any record, proceeding, or paper on file in his or her office. **Leg.H.** Added Stats 1947 ch 424 §1. Amended Stats 1949 ch 739 §10; Stats 1955 ch 1880 §1; Stats 1976 ch 822 §2; Stats 2005 ch 75 §72 (AB 145), effective July 19, 2005, operative January 1, 2006.

§26833. Certifying copy of paper, record, or proceeding

The fee for certifying to a copy of any paper, record, or proceeding on file in the office of the county clerk is one dollar and seventy-five cents ($1.75). **Leg.H.** Added Stats 1947 ch 424 §1. Amended Stats 1949 ch 739 §12; Stats 1st Ex Sess 1966 ch 120 §35; Stats 1977 ch 1257 §45, effective October 3, 1977; Stats 1980 ch 1372 §36; Stats 1982 ch 327 §74, effective June 30, 1982.

§26836. Certificates where fee not fixed

For every certificate the fee for which is not otherwise fixed, the fee is one dollar and seventy-five cents ($1.75). **Leg.H.** Added Stats 1947 ch 424 §1. Amended Stats 1980 ch 1372 §38; Stats 1982 ch 327 §76, effective June 30, 1982.

§26837. Comparing copy of paper, record, or proceeding

For comparing with the original on file in the office of the county clerk, the copy of any paper, record, or proceeding prepared by another and presented for his or her certificate, the fee is fifty cents ($0.50) a page, in addition to the fee for the certificate. **Leg.H.** Added Stats 1947 ch 424 §1. Amended Stats 1949 ch 739 §13; Stats 1955 ch 1880 §3; Stats 1st Ex Sess 1966 ch 120 §37; Stats 1969 ch 178 §1; Stats 1977 ch 1257 §46, effective October 3, 1977; Stats 1980 ch 1372 §39; Stats 2005 ch 75 §80 (AB 145), effective July 19, 2005, operative January 1, 2006.

§26839. Exemplification of record or other paper

For an exemplification of a record or other paper on file, the fee is twenty dollars ($20) and the charges allowed for copying or comparing. **Leg.H.** Added Stats 1947 ch 424 §1. Amended Stats 1949 ch 739 §15; Stats 1st Ex Sess 1966 ch 120 §38; Stats 1980 ch 1372 §41; Stats 1982 ch 327 §78, effective June 30, 1982; Stats 1993 ch 158 §9 (AB 392), effective July 20, 1993.

§26840. Issuance of marriage license; Disposition of fee; Fee in full for all services

The fee for issuing a marriage license is ten dollars ($10), to be collected at the time it is issued. One dollar ($1) of this fee shall be paid to the county recorder, one dollar ($1) of this fee shall be paid to the county clerk, and one dollar ($1) of this fee shall be paid to the State Registrar of Vital Statistics and seven dollars ($7) of this fee shall be disposed of pursuant to the provisions of Section 54 of Chapter 120, Statutes of 1966, First Extraordinary Session. In counties where the salary of the county recorder is the sole compensation allowed by law, this fee shall be paid to the county treasurer who shall credit one dollar ($1) to the county recorder and shall pay one dollar ($1) to the State Registrar of Vital Statistics. The fee provided by this section is in full for all services of the clerk and recorder in connection with the issuance of a marriage license and the filing of a certificate of registry of marriage. **Leg.H.** Added Stats 1947 ch 424 §1. Amended Stats 1947 ch 1303 §1; Stats 1st Ex Sess 1966 ch 120 §39; Stats 1967 ch 1500 §6, operative January 1, 1968; Stats 1979 ch 139 §3.

§26840.1. Filing marriage certificate

(a) The fee for filing a marriage certificate pursuant to Part 4 (commencing with Section 500) of Division 3 of the Family Code is fourteen dollars ($14), to be collected at the time an authorization for the performance of the marriage is issued or a blank authorization form is obtained from the county clerk pursuant to Part 4 (commencing with Section 500) of Division 3 of the Family Code. Four dollars ($4) of the fee shall be paid to the State Registrar of Vital Statistics. One dollar ($1) of the fee shall be paid to the county treasurer and shall be used to defray any local costs incurred pursuant to Part 4 (commencing with Section 500) of Division 3 of the Family Code.

(b) Notwithstanding subdivision (a), in addition to the amount authorized by subdivision (a) the county clerk may impose an additional amount, not to exceed three dollars ($3), if he or she determines that the additional amount is necessary to defray local costs. **Leg.H.** Added Stats 1971 ch 1244 §2. Amended Stats 1979 ch 139 §4; Stats 1981 ch 872 §3; Stats 1992 ch 163 §81 (AB 2641), operative January 1, 1994.

§26840.2. Marriage license; Fee on issuance outside normal hours

Whenever the board of supervisors of a county makes provision by ordinance for the issuance of marriage licenses outside of the normal business hours, the board may establish a fee, in addition to that provided in Section 26840, not to exceed five dollars ($5), which shall be paid to the county treasury. **Leg.H.** Added Stats 1971 ch 1527 §1. Amended Stats 1981 ch 199 §1.

§26840.3. Fee increases for support of family conciliation court or maintenance of conciliation and mediation services

(a) For the support of the family conciliation court or for conciliation and mediation services provided pursuant to Chapter 11 (commencing with Section 3160) of Part 2 of Division 8 of the Family Code, to provide all space costs and indirect overhead costs from other sources, the board of supervisors in any county may increase:

(1) The fee for issuing a marriage license, by an amount not to exceed five dollars ($5).

(2) The fee for issuing a marriage certificate pursuant to Part 4 (commencing with Section 500) of Division 3 of the Family Code, by an amount not to exceed five dollars ($5).

(b) The county shall distribute the moneys received under subdivision (a) to the court to be used exclusively to pay the costs of maintaining the family conciliation court or conciliation and mediation services provided pursuant to Chapter 11 (commencing with Section 3160) of Part 2 of Division 8 of the Family Code. **Leg.H.** Added Stats 1976 ch 1356 §1. Amended Stats 1977 ch 786 §1; Stats 1980 ch 48 §6, effective March 27, 1980; Stats 1982 ch 1071 §2; Stats 1983 ch 1277 §2; Stats 1992 ch 163 §82 (AB 2641), operative January 1, 1994 (ch 696 prevails), ch 696 §19 (AB 1344), effective September 14, 1992; Stats 1993 ch 219 §214 (AB 1500); Stats 2005 ch 75 §83 (AB 145), effective July 19, 2005, operative January 1, 2006.

§26840.7. Issuance fees for maintenance of domestic violence centers

In addition to the fee prescribed by Section 26840 and as authorized by Section 26840.3, the county clerk shall collect a fee of twenty-three dollars ($23) at the time of issuance of the license. The fee shall be disposed of by the clerk pursuant to Chapter 5 (commencing with Section 18290) of Part 6 of Division 9 of the Welfare and Institutions Code. Of this amount, four dollars ($4) shall be used, to the extent feasible, to develop or expand domestic violence shelter-based programs to target underserved areas and populations. **Leg.H.** Added Stats 1980 ch 146 §1, effective June 4, 1980. Amended Stats 1982 ch 522 §1; Stats 1984 ch 112 §1; Stats 1993 ch 420 §1 (SB 5); Stats 2006 ch 857 §1 (AB 2084), effective January 1, 2007.

§26840.8. Filing fees for maintenance of domestic violence centers

In addition to the fee prescribed by Section 26840.1 and as authorized by Section 26840.3, the person issuing an authorization for the performance of a marriage pursuant to Part 4 (commencing with Section 500) of Division 3 of the Family Code or the county clerk, upon providing a blank authorization form pursuant to Part 4 (commencing with Section 500) of Division 3 of the Family Code, shall collect a fee of twenty-three dollars ($23) at the time of providing the authorization. The fee shall be disposed of pursuant to Chapter 5 (commencing with Section 18290) of Part 6 of Division 9 of the Welfare and Institutions Code. Of this amount, four dollars ($4) shall be used, to the extent feasible, to develop or expand domestic violence shelter-based programs to target underserved areas and populations. **Leg.H.** Added Stats 1980 ch 146 §1.5, effective June 4, 1980. Amended Stats 1981 ch 872 §4; Stats 1982 ch 449 §2, ch 522 §2.5; Stats 1984 ch 112 §2; Stats 1992 ch 163 §83 (AB 2641), operative January 1, 1994; Stats 1993 ch 420 §2 (SB 5); Stats 2006 ch 857 §2 (AB 2084), effective January 1, 2007.

§26840.10. Increased license fees in Alameda County for governmental oversight and coordination of agencies dealing with domestic violence

(a) The Alameda County Board of Supervisors, upon making findings and declarations for the need for governmental oversight and coordination of the multiple agencies dealing with domestic violence, may authorize an increase in the fees for marriage licenses and confidential marriage licenses, up to a maximum increase of two dollars ($2).

(b) Effective July 1 of each year, the Alameda County Board of Supervisors may authorize an increase in these fees by an amount equal to the increase in the Consumer Price Index for the San Francisco metropolitan area for the preceding calendar year, rounded to the nearest half-dollar ($0.50). The fees shall be allocated pursuant to Section 18309 of the Welfare and Institutions Code.

(c) In addition to the fee prescribed by Section 26840.1, in Alameda County, the person issuing authorization for the performance of a marriage or confidential marriage, or the county clerk upon providing a blank authorization form pursuant to Part 4 (commencing with Section 500) of Division 3 of the Family Code, shall collect the fees specified in subdivisions (a) and (b), at the time of providing the authorization.

(d) This section shall become operative on January 1, 2015. **Leg.H.** Added Stats 2009 ch 215 §3 (AB 73), effective January 1, 2010, operative January 1, 2015.

Prior Law: Former Gov C §26840.10, similar to the present section, was added Stats 2004 ch 830 §2, amended Stats 2009 ch 215 §2, and repealed January 1, 2015, by its own terms.

§26840.11. Increased license fees in Solano County for governmental oversight and coordination of agencies dealing with domestic violence

(a) The Solano County Board of Supervisors, upon making findings and declarations for the need for governmental oversight and coordination of the multiple agencies dealing with domestic violence, may authorize an increase in the fees for marriage licenses and confidential marriage licenses, up to a maximum increase of two dollars ($2).

(b) Effective July 1 of each year, the Solano County Board of Supervisors may authorize an increase in these fees by an amount equal to the increase in the Consumer Price Index for the San Francisco metropolitan area for the preceding calendar year, rounded to the nearest one-half dollar ($0.50). The fees shall be allocated pursuant to Section 18309.5 of the Welfare and Institutions Code.

(c) In addition to the fee prescribed by Section 26840.1, in Solano County, the person issuing authorization for the performance of a marriage or confidential marriage, or the county clerk upon providing a blank authorization form pursuant to Part 4 (commencing with Section 500) of Division 3 of the Family Code, shall collect the fees specified in subdivisions (a) and (b), at the time of providing the authorization.

(d) The Solano County Board of Supervisors shall submit to the Assembly and Senate Committees on Judiciary, no later than July 1, 2009, a preliminary report and a followup report no later than July 1, 2014, containing the following information:

(1) The annual amounts of funds received and expended from fee increases for the purpose of governmental oversight and coordination of domestic violence prevention, intervention, and prosecution efforts in the county.

(2) Outcomes achieved as a result of the activities associated with the implementation of this section. **Leg.H.** Added Stats 2004 ch 830 §3 (AB 2010). Amended Stats 2009 ch 336 §1 (SB 635), effective January 1, 2010. Stats 2010 ch 520 §1 (SB 1222), effective January 1, 2011, repealed January 1, 2012; Stats 2011 ch 120 §1 (SB 154), effective January 1, 2012.

§26847. Making record of certificate of revivor

The fee for making a record of a certificate of revivor is two dollars ($2). **Leg.H.** Added Stats 1947 ch 424 §1. Amended Stats 1949 ch 739 §23.

§26849.1. Filing bond of notary public

The fee for filing, canceling, revoking, or withdrawing the bond of a notary public is seven dollars ($7).

The recording fee for the notice of cancellation, revocation, or withdrawal and any related document by the surety shall be paid to the county clerk, who shall transmit it to the county recorder. **Leg.H.** Added Stats 1949 ch 272 §11. Amended Stats 1979 ch 139 §5; Stats 1991 ch 1090 §15 (AB 1484).

§26850. Filing and indexing other papers

For filing and indexing all papers for which a charge is not elsewhere provided, other than papers filed in actions or special proceedings, official bonds, or certificates of appointment, the fee is two dollars and twenty–five cents ($2.25). **Leg.H.** Added Stats 1947 ch 424 §1. Amended Stats 1949 ch 739 §26; Stats 1982 ch 327 §79, effective June 30, 1982.

§26851. Recording or registering license or certificate; Issuance of certificate or license and certificate

For either recording or registering any license or certificate or issuing any certificate, or both, in connection with a license, required by law for which a charge is not otherwise prescribed, the fee is two dollars and twenty–five cents ($2.25). **Leg.H.** Added Stats 1947 ch 424 §1. Amended Stats 1949 ch 739 §27; Stats 1982 ch 327 §80, effective June 30, 1982.

§26852. Certificate to official capacity of public official

The fee for each certificate to the official capacity of any public official is two dollars and twenty–five cents ($2.25). **Leg.H.** Added Stats 1947 ch 424 §1. Amended Stats 1949 ch 272 §12, ch 739 §28; Stats 1st Ex Sess 1966 ch 120 §41; Stats 1979 ch 139 §6; Stats 1982 ch 327 §81, effective June 30, 1982.

§26853. Taking affidavit

The fee for taking an affidavit, except in criminal cases or adoption proceedings, is two dollars and twenty–five cents ($2.25). **Leg.H.** Added Stats 1947 ch 424 §1. Amended Stats 1st Ex Sess 1966 ch 120 §42; Stats 1980 ch 1372 §42; Stats 1982 ch 327 §82, effective June 30, 1982.

§26854. Fee for searching records and files

The fee for searching records or files is five dollars ($5) for each file. **Leg.H.** Added Stats 1947 ch 424 §1 as §16854. Amended and renumbered Stats 1947 ch 1353 §3; Stats 1980 ch 1372 §43; Stats 1982 ch 327 §83, effective June 30, 1982; Stats 1991 ch 651 §1 (SB 757).

§26855. Taking acknowledgment

The fee for taking acknowledgment of any deed or other instrument, including the certificate, is two dollars and twenty–five cents ($2.25) for each signature. **Leg.H.** Added Stats 1947 ch 424 §1. Amended Stats 1st Ex Sess 1966 ch 120 §43; Stats 1979 ch 139 §7; Stats 1982 ch 327 §84, effective June 30, 1982.

§26855.1. Fees for filing power of attorney for surety insurer

The fee for filing a power of attorney for an admitted surety insurer, or a notice of cancellation, revocation, or withdrawal of a power of attorney for an admitted surety insurer, is three dollars and fifty cents ($3.50), or, if more than one name is designated, two dollars and twenty–five cents ($2.25) for each name. **Leg.H.** Added Stats 1955 ch 800 §1. Amended Stats 1979 ch 139 §8; Stats 1982 ch 327 §85, effective June 30, 1982; Stats 1992 ch 876 §11 (AB 3296).

§26855.2. Fee for filing financial statement of surety insurer; Effect of section on necessity of statement

The fee for filing a financial statement of an admitted surety insurer is three dollars and fifty cents ($3.50), but nothing in this section shall be construed to require an admitted surety insurer to file such a statement. **Leg.H.** Added Stats 1955 ch 800 §2. Amended Stats 1957 ch 1050 §1; Stats 1979 ch 139 §9; Stats 1982 ch 327 §86, effective June 30, 1982.

§26855.3. Fee for issuing certificate of authority of admitted surety issuer

The fee for issuing a certificate pursuant to Section 995.640 of the Code of Civil Procedure is three dollars and fifty cents ($3.50). **Leg.H.** Added Stats 1955 ch 800 §3. Amended Stats 1957 ch 1050 §2; Stats 1979 ch 139 §10; Stats 1982 ch 517 §254 (ch 327 prevails), ch 327 §87, effective June 30, 1982; Stats 1983 ch 18 §23, effective April 21, 1983.

§26857. When fees not to be charged

No fee shall be charged by the clerk for service rendered to any municipality or county in the state, or to the state or national government, nor for any service relating thereto. **Leg.H.** Added Stats 1947 ch 424 §1. Amended Stats 1965 ch 456 §1; Stats 1978 ch 809 §1; Stats 1986 ch 823 §1.1; Stats 1996 ch 1023 §94 (SB 1497), effective September 29, 1996; Stats 1997 ch 850 §23 (AB 233); Stats 1998 ch 146 §2 (AB 1301), effective July 13, 1998; Stats 2005 ch 75 §92 (AB 145), effective July 19, 2005, operative January 1, 2006.

§26858. Matters relating to pensions

No fees or other compensation shall be charged by any county clerk for taking and certifying affidavits for pension claimants, the payment of a pension voucher, or any matters relating thereto under the laws of the United States. **Leg.H.** Added Stats 1947 ch 424 §1.

§26861. Fee of commissioner of civil marriages for performing ceremony

A fee of fifteen dollars ($15) may be charged for performing a marriage ceremony pursuant to Section 401 of the Family Code, which shall be paid into the county treasury. **Leg.H.** Added Stats 1973–74 ch 979 §3. Amended Stats 1974 ch 974 §1; Stats 1979 ch 139 §11, Stats 1992 ch 163 §85 (AB 2641), operative January 1, 1994.

CHAPTER 6
RECORDER
ARTICLE 3.5
Social Security Number Truncation Program

§27300. Definitions

As used in this article, the following terms have the following meanings:

(a) "Official record" means the permanent archival record of all instruments, papers, and notices as accepted for recording by a county recorder.

(b) "Public record" means a record that is in an electronic format and is an exact copy of an official record except that any social security number contained in the copied record is truncated. The public record shall have the same legal force and effect as the official record.

(c) "Truncate" means to redact the first five digits of a social security number.

(d) "Truncated social security number" means a social security number that displays only the last four digits of the number. **Leg.H.** Added Stats 2007 ch 627 §8 (AB 1168), effective January 1, 2008.

§27301. County recorder to create social security truncation program; Components of program

(a) The county recorder of each county shall establish a social security number truncation program in order to create a public record version of each official record.

(1) The program shall include both of the following components, which the recorder shall implement concurrently:

(A) For each official record recorded between January 1, 1980, and December 31, 2008, the recorder shall create in an electronic format an exact copy of the record except that any social security number contained in the copied record shall be truncated. In order to create a public record copy, the recorder shall first truncate the social security numbers in all records that already exist in an electronic format and then create an electronic version of all other records and truncate social security numbers contained in those records. Each group of records shall be handled in descending chronological order.

(B) For each official record recorded on or after January 1, 2009, the recorder shall create a copy of that record in an electronic format and truncate any social security number contained in that record.

(2) The program may include a component for each official record recorded before January 1, 1980, pursuant to which the county recorder may create a copy of that record in an electronic format and truncate any social security number contained in that record.

(b) Nothing in this article shall be construed to restrict, delay, or modify access to any official record, or modify any existing agreements regarding access to any official record, prior to the creation and availability of a public record version of that official record. A county recorder shall not charge any new fee or increase any existing fees in order to fund the social security number truncation program pursuant to this article, except as provided in subdivision (d) of Section 27361.

(c) Notwithstanding paragraph (1) of subdivision (a), a county recorder shall not be required to create a public record version of an official record if the fee authorized in Section 27304 is determined by the recorder to be insufficient to meet the cost of creating the public record version. In that case, the county recorder shall determine whether the fee is sufficient to meet the cost of creating a public record version of only a fraction of the official records described in paragraph (1) of subdivision (a). If the fee is sufficient to meet the cost of creating a public record version of a fraction of the official records, the recorder shall be required to create a public record version of that fraction only. **Leg.H.** Added Stats 2007 ch 627 §8 (AB 1168), effective January 1, 2008. Amended Stats 2017 ch 621 §1 (SB 184), effective January 1, 2018.

§27302. Due diligence in locating and truncating social security numbers; Request to truncate by any person

(a) A county recorder shall be deemed to be in compliance with the requirements of Section 27301 and shall not be liable for failure to truncate a social security number if he or she uses due diligence to locate social security numbers in official records and truncate social security numbers in the public record version of those official records. The use of an automated program with a high rate of accuracy shall be deemed to be due diligence.

(b) In the event that a county recorder fails to truncate a social security number contained in a public record, any person may request that the county recorder truncate the social security number contained in that record. Notwithstanding that a county recorder may be deemed to be in compliance with Section 27301 pursuant to subdivision (a), a county recorder that receives a request that identifies the exact location of an untruncated social security number within a specifically identified public record, shall truncate that number within 10 business days of receiving the request. The public record with the truncated social security number shall replace the record with the untruncated number. **Leg.H.** Added Stats 2007 ch 627 §8 (AB 1168), effective January 1, 2008.

§27303. Availability of official record and public record

When a public record version of an official record exists, both of the following shall apply:

(a) Upon a request for inspection, copying, or any other public disclosure of an official record that is not exempt from disclosure, a county recorder shall make available only the public record version of that record.

(b) A county recorder shall publicly disclose an official record only in response to a subpoena or order of a court of competent jurisdiction. **Leg.H.** Added Stats 2007 ch 627 §8 (AB 1168), effective January 1, 2008.

§27303.5. Copy of DD214 official record

Notwithstanding Section 27303, a county recorder may provide a copy of a DD214 official record when requested by a person listed in subdivision (b) of Section 6107 and upon certification by that person that a full social security number is required to receive benefits and he or she is authorized to receive a copy as specified in that subdivision. **Leg.H.** Added Stats 2011 ch 382 §1.4 (SB 194), effective January 1, 2012.

§27304. Funding of truncation program

(a) Each county may use funds generated by fees authorized by subdivision (d) of Section 27361 to implement a social security number truncation program required by this article.

(b) No later than June 1, 2008, the county recorder of each county shall petition the board of supervisors in that county for the authority to levy the fee authorized by subdivision (d) of Section 27361.

(c) It is the intent of the Legislature that in the interest of enabling county recorders to act expeditiously to protect the privacy of Californians, counties be permitted to seek revenue anticipation loans or other outside funding sources for the implementation of a social security number truncation program to be secured by the anticipated revenue from the fee authorized by subdivision (d) of Section 27361. **Leg.H.** Added Stats 2007 ch 627 §8 (AB 1168), effective January 1, 2008.

§27305. Reporting progress to Legislature

(a) To assist the Legislature in monitoring the progress of each county recorder's social security number truncation program, the County Recorders Association of California, no later than January 1, 2009, and annually thereafter, shall submit to the chairpersons of the Assembly Committee on Judiciary and of the Senate Committee on Judiciary, and to the Office of Privacy Protection, or any successor agency, a report on the progress each county recorder has made in complying with this article.

(b) Upon the Office of Privacy Protection making a determination that all counties have completed the component of the program described in subdivision (a) of Section 27301, the report described in subdivision (a) of this section shall no longer be required. **Leg.H.** Added Stats 2007 ch 627 §8 (AB 1168), effective January 1, 2008.

§27307. Authority of county recorder

A county recorder is authorized to take all actions required by this article notwithstanding subdivision (d) of Section 27203 or any other provision of law. **Leg.H.** Added Stats 2007 ch 627 §8 (AB 1168), effective January 1, 2008.

ARTICLE 5
Fees

§27360. Fees generally

For services performed by the recorder's office, the county recorder shall charge and collect the fees fixed in this article. **Leg.H.** Added Stats 1947 ch 424 §1. Amended Stats 2015 ch 269 §15 (SB 184), effective January 1, 2016.

2015 Note: This act shall be known, and may be cited, as the Local Government Omnibus Act of 2015. Stats 2015 ch 269 (SB 184) § 1(a).

§27360.5. "Folio"

As used in this code, the word "folio" means 100 words. Each figure, character, symbol, and initial, excluding punctuation marks, shall be regarded as a word for the purpose of computing fees by a recorder. **Leg.H.** Added Stats 1963 ch 22 §1.

§27361. Recording and indexing fee

(a) The fee for recording and indexing every instrument, paper, or notice required or permitted by law to be recorded shall not exceed ten dollars ($10) for recording the first page and three dollars ($3) for each additional page, to reimburse the county for the costs of services rendered pursuant to this subdivision, except the recorder may charge additional fees as follows:

(1) If the printing on printed forms is spaced more than nine lines per vertical inch or more than 22 characters and spaces per inch measured horizontally for not less than three inches in one sentence, the recorder shall charge one dollar ($1) extra for each page or sheet on which printing appears, except, however, the extra charge shall not apply to printed words that are directive or explanatory in nature for completion of the form or on vital statistics forms. Fees collected under this paragraph are not subject to subdivision (b) or (c).

(2) If a page or sheet does not conform to the dimensions described in subdivision (a) of Section 27361.5, the recorder shall charge three dollars ($3) extra per page or sheet of the document. The funds generated by the extra charge authorized under this paragraph shall be available solely to support, maintain, improve, and provide for the full operation for modernized creation, retention, and retrieval of information in each county's system of recorded documents. Fees collected under this paragraph are not subject to subdivision (b) or (c).

(b) One dollar ($1) of each three dollar ($3) fee for each additional page shall be deposited in the county general fund.

(c) Notwithstanding Section 68085, one dollar ($1) for recording the first page and one dollar ($1) for each additional page shall be available solely to support, maintain, improve, and provide for the full operation for modernized creation, retention, and retrieval of information in each county's system of recorded documents.

(d)(1) In addition to all other fees authorized by this section, a county recorder may charge a fee of one dollar ($1) for recording the first page of every instrument, paper, or notice required or permitted by law to be recorded, as authorized by each county's board of supervisors. The funds generated by this fee shall be used only by the county recorder collecting the fee for the purpose of implementing a social security number truncation program pursuant to Article 3.5 (commencing with Section 27300).

(2) A county recorder shall not charge the fee described in paragraph (1) after December 31, 2017, unless the county recorder has received reauthorization by the county's board of supervisors. A county recorder shall not seek reauthorization of the fee by the board before June 1, 2017, or after December 31, 2017. In determining the additional period of authorization, the board shall consider the review described in paragraph (4).

(3) Notwithstanding paragraph (2), a county recorder who, pursuant to subdivision (c) of Section 27304, secures a revenue anticipation loan, or other outside source of funding, for the implementation of a social security number truncation program, may be authorized to charge the fee

described in paragraph (1) for a period not to exceed the term of repayment of the loan or other outside source of funding.

(4) A county board of supervisors that authorizes the fee described in this subdivision shall require the county auditor to conduct two reviews to verify that the funds generated by this fee are used only for the purpose of the program, as described in Article 3.5 (commencing with Section 27300) and for conducting these reviews. The reviews shall state the progress of the county recorder in truncating recorded documents pursuant to subdivision (a) of Section 27301, and shall estimate any ongoing costs to the county recorder of complying with subdivisions (a) and (b) of Section 27301. The board shall require that the first review be completed not before June 1, 2012, or after December 31, 2013, and that the second review be completed not before June 1, 2017, or after December 31, 2017. The reviews shall adhere to generally accepted accounting standards, and the review results shall be made available to the public.

(e) Except as provided in subdivision (g) of Section 6103.8, the fee authorized by this section shall not be charged to those entities exempted from the payment of recording fees under Section 6103 or 27383. **Leg.H.** Added Stats 1947 ch 424 §1. Amended Stats 1955 ch 542 §1, operative January 1, 1956; Stats 1957 ch 954 §2, effective June 8, 1957; Stats 1971 ch 59 §1; Stats 1984 ch 1156 §1; Stats 1988 ch 344 §1; Stats 1991 ch 331 §2 (SB 21), effective August 5, 1991, ch 1168 §2.5 (AB 2142), effective October 14, 1991; Stats 1992 ch 87 §4 (AB 689), operative July 1, 1994; Stats 1997 ch 850 §26 (AB 233); Stats 1998 ch 146 §3 (AB 1301), effective July 13, 1998; Stats 2007 ch 627 §9 (AB 1168), effective January 1, 2008; Stats 2008 ch 179 §102 (SB 1498), effective January 1, 2009; Stats 2009 ch 606 §2 (SB 676), effective January 1, 2010; Stats 2021 ch 77 §14 (AB 137), effective July 16, 2021.

§27361.1. Documents serially incorporated or attached as separate

Whenever two or more instruments, papers, or notices are serially incorporated on one form or sheet, or are attached to one another, except as an exhibit marked as such, each instrument, paper, or notice shall be considered to be a separate instrument, paper, or notice for the purpose of computing the fee established by Section 27361 of this code. **Leg.H.** Added Stats 1967 ch 56 §4.

§27361.2. Additional fee for reference to other recorded documents

(a) Whenever any instrument, paper, or notice is recorded that contains references to more than one previously recorded document and requires additional indexing by the county recorder to give notice required by law, an additional fee of one dollar ($1) shall be charged for each reference to a previously recorded document, other than the first such reference, requiring additional indexing. References to group mining claims listed on a proof of labor shall be considered as only one reference when they are consecutively numbered or lettered alphabetically, and each break in consecutive numbers or letters shall be considered as an additional mine for fee purposes under this section and shall be so indexed in the index.

(b) Except as provided in subdivision (g) of Section 6103.8, the fee authorized by this section shall not be charged to those entities exempted from the payment of recording fees under Section 6103 or 27383. **Leg.H.** Added Stats 1969 ch 36 §1. Amended Stats 1971 ch 889 §1; Stats 2021 ch 77 §15 (AB 137), effective July 16, 2021.

§27361.3. Fee for recording release of lien by state or local government

(a) Notwithstanding any contrary provision of the law, the fee for recording every release of lien, encumbrance, or notice executed by the state, or any municipality, county, city, district, or other political subdivision shall be two times the fee charged to record the first page of a lien, encumbrance, or notice under subdivision (a) of Section 27361, on January 1 of the year the release is recorded if the original lien, encumbrance, or notice was recorded without fee as provided by Section 27383.

(b) No fee shall be charged for recording a release of lien, encumbrance, or notice which was recorded in error by the state, or any municipality, county, city, district, or other political subdivision if there is noted on the face of the release of lien, encumbrance, or notice a statement to that effect.

(c) Two dollars ($2) for recording each release of lien pursuant to this section shall be available solely to support, maintain, improve, and provide for the full operation for modernized creation, retention, and retrieval of information in each county's system of recorded documents. **Leg.H.** Added Stats 1974 ch 220 §1. Amended Stats 1975 ch 473 §1; Stats 1984 ch 1156 §2; Stats 1988 ch 344 §2; Stats 2019 ch 329 §11 (SB 780), effective January 1, 2020.

§27361.4. Additional filing fee [Effective until January 1, 2026; Repealed January 1, 2026]

(a) The board of supervisors of any county may provide for an additional fee of one dollar ($1) for filing every instrument, paper, or notice for record for any of the following purposes:

(1) To defray the cost of converting the county recorder's document storage system to micrographics and for restoration and preservation of the county recorder's permanent archival microfilm.

(2) To implement and fund a county recorder archive program as determined by the county recorder.

(3) To implement and maintain or utilize a trusted system, as defined by Section 12168.7, for the permanent preservation of recorded document images.

(b) The board of supervisors of any county may provide for an additional fee, other than the fees authorized in subdivisions (a) and (c), of one dollar ($1) for filing every instrument, paper, or notice for record provided that the resolution providing for the additional fee establishes the days of operation of the county recorder's offices as every business day except for legal holidays and those holidays designated as judicial holidays pursuant to Section 135 of the Code of Civil Procedure.

(c) The board of supervisors of any county may provide for an additional fee, other than the fees authorized in subdivisions (a) and (b), of one dollar ($1) for filing every instrument, paper, or notice for record provided that the resolution providing for the additional fee requires that the instrument, paper, or notice be indexed within two business days after the date of recordation.

(d) Except as provided in subdivision (g) of Section 6103.8, the fees authorized by this section shall not be charged to those entities exempted from the payment of recording fees under Section 6103 or 27383.

(e) This section shall remain in effect only until January 1, 2026, and as of that date is repealed. **Leg.H.** Added Stats 1980 ch 1002 §1, effective September 21, 1980. Amended Stats 1993 ch 710 §1 (AB 130); Stats 2019 ch 41 §3 (AB 212), effective January 1, 2020, repealed January 1, 2026; Stats 2021 ch 77 §16 (AB 137), effective July 16, 2021, repealed January 1, 2026.

§ 27361.4. Additional filing fee [Operative January 1, 2026]

(a) The board of supervisors of any county may provide for an additional fee of one dollar ($1) for filing every instrument, paper, or notice for record, in order to defray the cost of converting the county recorder's document storage system to micrographics. Upon completion of the conversion and payment of the costs therefor, this additional fee shall no longer be imposed.

(b) The board of supervisors of any county may provide for an additional fee, other than the fees authorized in subdivisions (a) and (c), of one dollar ($1) for filing every instrument, paper, or notice for record provided that the resolution providing for the additional fee establishes the days of operation of the county recorder's offices as every business day except for legal holidays and those holidays designated as judicial holidays pursuant to Section 135 of the Code of Civil Procedure.

(c) The board of supervisors of any county may provide for an additional fee, other than the fees authorized in subdivisions (a) and (b), of one dollar ($1) for filing every instrument, paper, or notice for record provided that the resolution providing for the additional fee requires that the instrument, paper, or notice be indexed within two business days after the date of recordation.

(d) Except as provided in subdivision (g) of Section 6103.8, the fees authorized by this section shall not be charged to those entities exempted from the payment of recording fees under Section 6103 or 27383.

(e) This section shall become operative on January 1, 2026. **Leg.H.** Added Stats 2019 ch 41 §4 (AB 212), effective January 1, 2020, operative January 1, 2026. Amended Stats 2020 ch 370 §155 (SB 1371), effective January 1, 2021, operative January 1, 2026; Stats 2021 ch 77 §17 (AB 137), effective July 16, 2021, operative January 1, 2026.

§27361.5. "Page"; "Sheet"

(a) As used in Section 27361, a page shall be one printed side of a single piece of paper being 8½ inches by 11 inches.

(b) A sheet shall be one printed side of a single piece of paper which is not exactly 8½ inches by 11 inches but not greater than 8½ inches by 14 inches. **Leg.H.** Added Stats 1992 ch 87 §6 (AB 689), operative July 1, 1994.

Prior Law: Former §27361.5, similar to the present section, which was added Stats 1951 ch 1309 §1, amended Stats 1955 ch 542 §2, operative January 1, 1956, and repealed Stats 1992 ch 87 §5 (AB 689), operative July 1, 1994.

§27361.6. Margins; Quality of paper; Identification of previously recorded documents

Except as otherwise provided by law or regulation, all documents submitted for recording shall have at least a ½-inch margin on the two vertical sides except in the space reserved for recording information. At least the top 2½ inches of the first page or sheet shall be reserved for recording information. The left-hand 3½ inches of the space shall be used by the public to show the name of the person requesting recording and the name and address to which the document is to be returned following recording. In the event the first page or sheet of a document does not comply with these requirements, a separate page shall be attached by the party requesting recording to the front of the document which meets these criteria and which reflects the title or titles of the document as required by Section 27324. Any printed form accepted for recordation that does not comply with the foregoing shall not affect the notice otherwise imparted by recording.

All instruments, papers, or notices presented for recordation shall be on a quality of paper and contain print of a size and color which will reproduce legibly by microphotographic or imaging processes as set forth in Sections 26205.5 and 27322.2.

Any instrument, paper, or notice presented for recordation which in any way modifies, releases, or cancels the provisions of a previously recorded document shall state the recorder identification number or book and page of the document number being modified, released, or canceled. **Leg.H.** Added Stats 1992 ch 87 §8 (AB 689), operative July 1, 1994.

Prior Law: Former §27361.6, similar to the present section, which was added Stats 1955 ch 542 §3, amended Stats 1959 ch 719 §1, Stats 1967 ch 55 §1, and repealed Stats 1992 ch 87 §7 (AB 689), operative July 1, 1994.

§27361.7. Substituted or copied document legible for photographic record

Whenever the text of a document presented for record may be made out but is not sufficiently legible to reproduce a readable photographic record, the recorder may require the person presenting it for record to substitute a legible original document or to prepare a legible copy of the first document by handwriting or typewriting and attach the same to the original as a part of the document for making the permanent photographic record. The handwritten or typewritten legible copy shall be certified by the party creating the copy under penalty of perjury as being a true copy of the original. As used in this section, the word "text" includes the notary seal, certificates, and other appendages thereto. **Leg.H.** Added Stats 1963 ch 22 §2. Amended Stats 1975 ch 252 §1; Stats 1981 ch 187 §1.

§27361.8. Additional indexing

(a) Whenever any instrument, paper, or notice is recorded that requires additional indexing by the county recorder to give notice required by law and does not refer to a previously recorded document by reference, as covered in Section 27361.2, an additional fee of one dollar ($1) shall be charged for each group of 10 names or fractional portion thereof after the initial group of 10 names.

(b) Except as provided in subdivision (g) of Section 6103.8, the fee authorized by this section shall not be charged to those entities exempted from the payment of recording fees under Section 6103 or 27383. **Leg.H.** Added Stats 1980 ch 299 §1. Amended Stats 2021 ch 77 §18 (AB 137), effective July 16, 2021.

Prior Law: Former §27361.8, relating to fee for preparing copy, was added Stats 1963 ch 22 §3, and repealed Stats 1975 ch 252 §2.

§27361.9. Filing of preliminary notice

The board of supervisors of any county may provide for an additional fee for filing every preliminary notice pursuant to subdivision (a) of Section 8214 of the Civil Code for the exclusive purpose of defraying the cost of implementing and maintaining a system to facilitate compliance with subdivision (b) of Section 8214 of the Civil Code. **Leg.H.** Added Stats 1987 ch 716 §2. Amended Stats 2010 ch 697 §34 (SB 189), effective January 1, 2011, operative July 1, 2012.

§27364. Fee for certificate under seal

The fee for each certificate under seal shall be set by the board of supervisors in an amount necessary to recover the direct and indirect costs of providing the product or service or the cost of enforcing any regulation for which the fee or charge is levied. **Leg.H.** Added Stats 1947 ch 424 §1. Amended Stats 1957 ch 869 §4; Stats 1967 ch 57 §1; Stats 1993 ch 710 §2 (AB 130).

§27365. Fee for copy of birth, death, or marriage certificate

The fee for any copy of a birth, death, or marriage certificate, when the copy is made by the recorder, is the same as is payable to a state or local registrar of vital statistics. **Leg.H.** Added Stats 1947 ch 424 §1.

§27366. Fee for copy of other record or paper and fees for photographic, etc., reproductions

The fee for any copy of any other record or paper on file in the office of the recorder, when the copy is made by the recorder, shall be set by the board of supervisors in an amount necessary to recover the direct and indirect costs of providing the product or service or the cost of enforcing any regulation for which the fee or charge is levied. **Leg.H.** Added Stats 1947 ch 424 §1. Amended Stats 1951 ch 1364 §1; Stats 1957 ch 1865 §4; Stats 1984 ch 1397 §6; Stats 1993 ch 710 §3 (AB 130).

§27369. Fee for searching records for birth, death, or marriage certificate

The fee for searching the records of his office for a birth, death, or marriage certificate is the same as is payable to a state or local registrar of vital statistics; in all other cases, for each year, fifty cents ($0.50). **Leg.H.** Added Stats 1947 ch 424 §1.

§27371. Fees for reproducing map or plat in record by photographic method

The fee for recording each map or plat where it is copied in a book of record is ten cents ($0.10) for each course, plus ten cents ($0.10) a folio for letters and figures on the map or plat.

When recording is by a photographic method the fee for recording each map or plat shall be the same as provided for under Sections 27361 and 27361.5 of this code. **Leg.H.** Added Stats 1947 ch 424 §1. Amended Stats 1951 ch 1308 §1; Stats 1957 ch 1865 §5.

§27372. Fee for recording, etc., map where land subdivided

The fee for recording or filing and indexing each map wherein land is subdivided in lots, tracts, or parcels is five dollars ($5) for the first page and two dollars ($2) for each additional page. **Leg.H.** Added Stats 1947 ch 424 §1. Amended Stats 1957 ch 1865 §6.

§27375. Acknowledgment fee

The fee for taking an acknowledgment of any instrument is seventy-five cents ($0.75). **Leg.H.** Added Stats 1947 ch 424 §1. Amended Stats 1957 ch 869 §6.

§27379. Fee for administering and certifying oaths or affirmations

The fee for administering and certifying each oath or affirmation is fifty cents ($0.50). **Leg.H.** Added Stats 1947 ch 424 §1.

§27380. Fee for filing, etc., paper not required to be recorded

The fee for filing, indexing, and keeping each paper not required by law to be recorded is three dollars ($3). **Leg.H.** Added Stats 1947 ch 424 §1. Amended Stats 1949 ch 62 §1; Stats 1957 ch 954 §3, effective June 8, 1957; Stats 1971 ch 59 §2.

§27381. Military discharges, etc.

No charge or fee shall be made for recording, indexing, or issuing certified copies of any discharge, certificate of service, certificate of satisfactory service, report of separation, or notice of separation of any soldier, sailor, marine, airman, or guardian, separated, released, or discharged from the Army, Navy, Marine Corps, Air Force, Space Force, or Coast Guard of the United States, Women's Army Corps, Women's Army Auxiliary Corps, Women's Reserve of Navy, Marine Corps, or Coast Guard, or from the Army and Navy Nurse Corps. **Leg.H.** Added Stats 1947 ch 424 §1. Amended Stats 2022 ch 379 §10 (AB 1715), effective January 1, 2023.

§27383. Fee for services rendered to State, municipality, etc.

No fee shall be charged by the recorder for services rendered to the

State, to any municipality, county in the State or other political subdivision thereof, except for making a copy of a paper or record. **Leg.H.** Added Stats 1955 ch 488 §1.

§27387. Recordation of involuntary lien

In addition to any other fee, the county recorder shall collect a fee from any lienor, other than a governmental entity, for the recordation of an abstract of judgment or other document creating an involuntary lien within the meaning of Section 27297.5 affecting title to real property. The fee shall not exceed the actual cost to the recorder of providing the notice required by Section 27297.5. **Leg.H.** Added Stats 1980 ch 1281 §4. Amended Stats 1984 ch 144 §146.

§27387.1. Fee for Los Angeles County notification [Effective until January 1, 2030; Repealed January 1, 2030]

(a) In addition to any other recording fee, the recorder, pursuant to Section 27297.6, may collect a fee from the party filing a deed, quitclaim deed, deed of trust, notice of default, or notice of sale, unless that party is a government entity. The fee shall not exceed the mailing cost of the notice specified in Section 27297.6 and the actual cost to provide information, counseling, or assistance to a person who receives the notice, not to exceed seven dollars ($7).

(b) The actual costs comprising the fee described in subdivision (a) may include administrative costs incurred by the recorder in performing the actions described in that subdivision. However, the administrative costs shall not exceed 10 percent of the total fee collected pursuant to subdivision (a).

(c) This section shall remain in effect only until January 1, 2030, and as of that date is repealed, unless a later enacted statute, that is enacted before January 1, 2030, deletes or extends that date. **Leg.H.** Added Stats 1996 ch 177 §2 (SB 1631). Amended Stats 2011 ch 141 §3 (SB 62), effective January 1, 2012, repealed January 1, 2015. Stats 2014 ch 65 §3 (SB 827), effective January 1, 2015, repealed January 1, 2020. Amended Stats 2019 ch 165 §3 (AB 1106), effective January 1, 2020, repealed January 1, 2030.

Prior Law: Former §27387.1, similar to the present section, was added Stats 1992 ch 815 §4, operative until January 1, 1996, and repealed, operative January 1, 1996, by its own terms.

§27387.1. Fee for Los Angeles County notification [Operative January 1, 2030]

(a) In addition to any other recording fee, the recorder may collect a fee from the party filing a deed, quitclaim deed, or deed of trust, other than a government entity, pursuant to Section 27297.6. The fee shall not exceed the mailing cost of the notice specified in Section 27297.6, not to exceed seven dollars ($7).

(b) This section shall become operative on January 1, 2030. **Leg.H.** Added Stats 2011 ch 141 §4 (SB 62), effective January 1, 2012, operative January 1, 2015. Amended Stats 2014 ch 65 §4 (SB 827), effective January 1, 2015, operative January 1, 2020; Stats 2019 ch 165 §4 (AB 1106), effective January 1, 2020, operative January 1, 2030.

§27388. Additional recording fee; Payment to Real Estate Fraud Protection Trust Fund; Distribution

(a)(1) In addition to any other recording fees specified in this code, upon the adoption of a resolution by the county board of supervisors, a fee of up to ten dollars ($10) shall be paid at the time of recording of every real estate instrument, paper, or notice required or permitted by law to be recorded within that county, except those expressly exempted from payment of recording fees and except as provided in paragraph (2). For purposes of this section, "real estate instrument" means a deed of trust, an assignment of deed of trust, an amended deed of trust, an abstract of judgment, an affidavit, an assignment of rents, an assignment of a lease, a construction trust deed, covenants, conditions, and restrictions Rs), a declaration of homestead, an easement, a lease, a lien, a lot line adjustment, a mechanics lien, a modification for deed of trust, a notice of completion, a quitclaim deed, a subordination agreement, a release, a reconveyance, a request for notice, a notice of default, a substitution of trustee, a notice of trustee sale, a trustee's deed upon sale, or a notice of rescission of declaration of default, or any Uniform Commercial Code amendment, assignment, continuation, statement, or termination. The fees, after deduction of any actual and necessary administrative costs incurred by the county recorder in carrying out this section, shall be paid quarterly to the county auditor or director of finance, to be placed in the Real Estate Fraud Prosecution Trust Fund. The amount deducted for administrative costs shall not exceed 10 percent of the fees paid pursuant to this section.

(2) The fee imposed by paragraph (1) shall not apply to any real estate instrument, paper, or notice if any of the following apply:

(A) The real estate instrument, paper, or notice is accompanied by a declaration stating that the transfer is subject to a documentary transfer tax pursuant to Section 11911 of the Revenue and Taxation Code.

(B) The real estate instrument, paper, or notice is recorded concurrently with a document subject to a documentary transfer tax pursuant to Section 11911 of the Revenue and Taxation Code.

(C) The real estate instrument, paper, or notice is presented for recording within the same business day as, and is related to the recording of, a document subject to a documentary transfer tax pursuant to Section 11911 of the Revenue and Taxation Code. A real estate instrument, paper, or notice that is exempt under this subparagraph shall be accompanied by a statement that includes both of the following:

(i) A statement that the real estate instrument, paper, or notice is exempt from the fee imposed under paragraph (1).

(ii) A statement of the recording date and the recorder identification number or book and page of the previously recorded document.

(D) The real estate instrument, paper, or notice is presented for recording by and is for the benefit of the state or any county, municipality, or other political subdivision of the state.

(b) Money placed in the Real Estate Fraud Prosecution Trust Fund shall be expended to fund programs to enhance the capacity of local police and prosecutors to deter, investigate, and prosecute real estate fraud crimes. After deduction of the actual and necessary administrative costs referred to in subdivision (a), 60 percent of the funds shall be distributed to district attorneys subject to review pursuant to subdivision (d), and 40 percent of the funds shall be distributed to local law enforcement agencies within the county in accordance with subdivision (c). In those counties where the investigation of real estate fraud is done exclusively by the district attorney, after deduction of the actual and necessary administrative costs referred to in subdivision (a), 100 percent of the funds shall be distributed to the district attorney, subject to review pursuant to subdivision (d). A portion of the funds may be directly allocated to the county recorder to support county recorder fraud prevention programs, including, but not limited to, the fraud prevention program provided for in Section 27297.7. Prior to establishing or increasing fees pursuant to this section, the board of supervisors may consider support for county recorder fraud prevention programs. The funds so distributed shall be expended for the exclusive purpose of deterring, investigating, and prosecuting real estate fraud crimes.

(c) The county auditor or director of finance shall distribute funds in the Real Estate Fraud Prosecution Trust Fund to eligible law enforcement agencies within the county pursuant to subdivision (b), as determined by a Real Estate Fraud Prosecution Trust Fund Committee composed of the district attorney, the county chief administrative officer, the chief officer responsible for consumer protection within the county, and the chief law enforcement officer of one law enforcement agency receiving funding from the Real Estate Fraud Prosecution Trust Fund, the latter being selected by a majority of the other three members of the committee. The chief law enforcement officer shall be a nonvoting member of the committee and shall serve a one-year term, which may be renewed. Members may appoint representatives of their offices to serve on the committee. If a county lacks a chief officer responsible for consumer protection, the county board of supervisors may appoint an appropriate representative to serve on the committee. The committee shall establish and publish deadlines and written procedures for local law enforcement agencies within the county to apply for the use of funds and shall review applications and make determinations by majority vote as to the award of funds using the following criteria:

(1) Each law enforcement agency that seeks funds shall submit a written application to the committee setting forth in detail the agency's proposed use of the funds.

(2) In order to qualify for receipt of funds, each law enforcement agency submitting an application shall provide written evidence that the agency either:

(A) Has a unit, division, or section devoted to the investigation or prosecution of real estate fraud, or both, and the unit, division, or section has been in existence for at least one year prior to the application date.

(B) Has on a regular basis, during the three years immediately preceding the application date, accepted for investigation or prosecution, or both, and assigned to specific persons employed by the agency, cases of suspected real estate fraud, and actively investigated and prosecuted those cases.

(3) The committee's determination to award funds to a law enforcement agency shall be based on, but not be limited to, (A) the number of real estate fraud cases filed in the prior year; (B) the number of real estate fraud cases investigated in the prior year; (C) the number of victims involved in the cases filed; and (D) the total aggregated monetary loss suffered by victims, including individuals, associations, institutions, or corporations, as a result of the real estate fraud cases filed, and those under active investigation by that law enforcement agency.

(4) Each law enforcement agency that, pursuant to this section, has been awarded funds in the previous year, upon reapplication for funds to the committee in each successive year, in addition to any information the committee may require in paragraph (3), shall be required to submit a detailed accounting of funds received and expended in the prior year. The accounting shall include (A) the amount of funds received and expended; (B) the uses to which those funds were put, including payment of salaries and expenses, purchase of equipment and supplies, and other expenditures by type; (C) the number of filed complaints, investigations, arrests, and convictions that resulted from the expenditure of the funds; and (D) other relevant information the committee may reasonably require.

(d) The county board of supervisors shall annually review the effectiveness of the district attorney in deterring, investigating, and prosecuting real estate fraud crimes based upon information provided by the district attorney in an annual report. The district attorney shall submit the annual report to the board on or before September 1 of each year.

(e) A county shall not expend funds held in that county's Real Estate Fraud Prosecution Trust Fund until the county's auditor-controller verifies that the county's district attorney has submitted an annual report for the county's most recent full fiscal year pursuant to the requirements of subdivision (d).

(f) The intent of the Legislature in enacting this section is to have an impact on real estate fraud involving the largest number of victims. To the extent possible, an emphasis should be placed on fraud against individuals whose residences are in danger of, or are in, foreclosure as defined in subdivision (b) of Section 1695.1 of the Civil Code. Case filing decisions continue to be at the discretion of the prosecutor.

(g) A district attorney's office or a local enforcement agency that has undertaken investigations and prosecutions that will continue into a subsequent program year may receive nonexpended funds from the previous fiscal year subsequent to the annual submission of information detailing the accounting of funds received and expended in the prior year.

(h) No money collected pursuant to this section shall be expended to offset a reduction in any other source of funds. Funds from the Real Estate Fraud Prosecution Trust Fund shall be used only in connection with criminal investigations or prosecutions involving recorded real estate documents. **Leg.H.** Added Stats 1995 ch 942 §1 (SB 537). Amended Stats 2000 ch 765 §1 (SB 762), effective September 27, 2000; Stats 2003 ch 46 §1 (AB 241); Stats 2005 ch 531 §2 (AB 901), effective January 1, 2006; Stats 2008 ch 405 §1 (SB 1396), effective January 1, 2009; Stats 2009 ch 35 §4 (SB 174), effective January 1, 2010; Stats 2012 ch 104 §2 (SB 1342), effective January 1, 2013; Stats 2015 ch 76 §1 (AB 661), effective January 1, 2016; Stats 2021 ch 77 §19 (AB 137), effective July 16, 2021.

§27388.1. Fee for recording real estate instrument, paper, or notice; Exemptions; Deposit in Building Homes and Jobs Trust Fund

(a)(1) Commencing January 1, 2018, and except as provided in paragraph (2), in addition to any other recording fees specified in this code, a fee of seventy-five dollars ($75) shall be paid at the time of recording of every real estate instrument, paper, or notice required or permitted by law to be recorded, except those expressly exempted from payment of recording fees, per each single transaction per parcel of real property. The fee imposed by this section shall not exceed two hundred twenty-five dollars ($225). "Real estate instrument, paper, or notice" means a document relating to real property, including, but not limited to, the following: deed, grant deed, trustee's deed, deed of trust, reconveyance, quit claim deed, fictitious deed of trust, assignment of deed of trust, request for notice of default, abstract of judgment, subordination agreement, declaration of homestead, abandonment of homestead, notice of default, release or discharge, easement, notice of trustee sale, notice of completion, UCC financing statement, mechanic's lien, maps, and covenants, conditions, and restrictions.

(2) The fee described in paragraph (1) shall not be imposed on any of the following documents:

(A) Any real estate instrument, paper, or notice recorded in connection with a transfer subject to the imposition of a documentary transfer tax as defined in Section 11911 of the Revenue and Taxation Code.

(B) Any real estate instrument, paper, or notice recorded in connection with a transfer of real property that is a residential dwelling to an owner-occupier.

(C) Any real estate instrument, paper, or notice executed or recorded by the federal government in accordance with the Uniform Federal Lien Registration Act (Title 7 (commencing with Section 2100) of Part 4 of the Code of Civil Procedure).

(D) Any real estate instrument, paper, or notice executed or recorded by the state or any county, municipality, or other political subdivision of the state.

(E) Any real estate instrument, paper, or notice executed or recorded to remove a restrictive covenant that is in violation of Section 12955.

(b) The county recorder shall remit quarterly, on or before the last day of the month next succeeding each calendar quarterly period, the fees, after deduction of any actual and necessary administrative costs incurred by the county recorder in carrying out this section, to the Controller for deposit in the Building Homes and Jobs Trust Fund established by Section 50470 of the Health and Safety Code, to be expended for the purposes set forth in that section. In addition, the county shall pay to the Controller interest, at the legal rate, on any funds not paid to the Controller before the last day of the month next succeeding each quarterly period.

(c) If the Department of Housing and Community Development determines that any moneys derived from fees collected are being allocated by the state for a purpose not authorized by Section 50470 of the Health and Safety Code, the county recorder shall, upon notice of the determination, immediately cease collection of the fees, and shall resume collection of those fees only upon notice that the moneys derived from the fees collected are being allocated by the state only for a purpose authorized by Section 50470 of the Health and Safety Code.

(d)(1) Subparagraph (C) of paragraph (2) of subdivision (a), as added by the act adding this subdivision, shall apply to any real estate instrument, paper, or notice executed or recorded by the federal government on or after January 1, 2018, and the fee imposed by this section shall not be imposed or billed for any real estate instrument, paper, or notice executed or recorded by the federal government in accordance with the Uniform Federal Lien Registration Act (Title 7 (commencing with Section 2100) of Part 4 of the Code of Civil Procedure) on or after that date.

(2) The Legislature finds and declares that subparagraph (D) of paragraph (2) of subdivision (a), as added by the act adding this subdivision, reflects the original intent of the Legislature in enacting this section and is therefore not a change in, but is declaratory of, existing law. Subparagraph (D) of paragraph (2) of subdivision (a), as added by the act adding this subdivision, shall apply to any real estate instrument, paper, or notice executed or recorded by the state or any county, municipality, or other political subdivision of the state on or after January 1, 2018, and the fee imposed by this section shall not be imposed or billed for any real estate instrument, paper, or notice executed or recorded by the state or any county, municipality, or other political subdivision of the state on or after that date. **Leg.H.** Added Stats 2017 ch 364 §3 (SB 2), effective September 29, 2017. Amended Stats 2018 ch 8 §2 (AB 110), effective March 13, 2018; Stats 2021 ch 359 §5 (AB 1466), effective January 1, 2022.

2017 Note: This act shall be known as the Building Homes and Jobs Act. Stats 2017 ch 364 (SB 2) § 1.

§ 27388.2. Additional county recorder fee for recording real estate instrument; Applicability of additional fee

(a) In addition to all other fees authorized by this section, a county recorder may charge a fee of two dollars ($2) for recording the first page of every real estate instrument, paper, or notice required or permitted by law to be recorded per each single transaction per parcel of real property, except those expressly exempted from payment of recording fees, as authorized by each county's board of supervisors and in accordance with applicable constitutional requirements. The funds generated by this fee shall be used only by the county recorder collecting the fee for the purpose of implementing a restrictive covenant program pursuant to Section 12956.3. "Real estate instrument, paper, or notice" means a document relating to real property, including, but not limited to, the following: deed, grant deed, trustee's deed, deed of trust, reconveyance, quit claim deed, fictitious deed of trust, assignment of deed of trust, request for notice of default, abstract of judgment, subordination agreement, declaration of homestead, abandonment of homestead, notice of default, release or discharge, easement, notice of trustee sale, notice of completion, UCC financing statement, mechanic's lien, maps, and covenants, conditions, and restrictions.

(b) The fee described in subdivision (a) shall not be imposed on any of the following documents:

(1) Any real estate instrument, paper, or notice recorded in connection with a transfer subject to the imposition of a documentary transfer tax, as defined in Section 11911 of the Revenue and Taxation Code.

(2) Any real estate instrument, paper, or notice recorded in connection with a transfer of real property that is a residential dwelling to an owner-occupier.

(3) Any real estate instrument, paper, or notice executed or recorded by the federal government in accordance with the Uniform Federal Lien Registration Act (Title 7 (commencing with Section 2100) of Part 4 of the Code of Civil Procedure).

(4) Any real estate instrument, paper, or notice executed or recorded by the state or any county, municipality, or other political subdivision of the state.

(c) A county recorder shall not charge the fee described in this section after December 31, 2027, unless the county recorder has received reauthorization by the county's board of supervisors. A county recorder shall not seek reauthorization of the fee by the board before June 1, 2027, or after December 31, 2027. Any reauthorization period shall not exceed five years. **Leg.H.** Added Stats 2021 ch 359 §6 (AB 1466), effective January 1, 2022. Amended Stats 2022 ch 420 §28 (AB 2960), effective January 1, 2023.

ARTICLE 6
Electronic Recording Delivery Act of 2004

§27390. Citation of article; Definitions

(a) This article shall be known and may be cited as the Electronic Recording Delivery Act of 2004.

(b) For the purposes of this article, the following definitions shall apply:

(1) "Authorized submitter" means a party that has entered into a contract with a county recorder pursuant to Section 27391 and is not disqualified pursuant to Section 27395.

(2) "Computer security auditor" means computer security personnel hired to perform an independent audit of the electronic recording delivery system. The computer security auditor shall be independent of the county recorder and the authorized submitter and shall not be the same contractor hired to establish or participate in a county's electronic recording delivery system or in the authorized submitter's portion of that system.

(3) "Digital electronic record" means a record containing information that is created, generated, sent, communicated, received, or stored by electronic means, but not created in original paper form.

(4) "Digitized electronic record" means a scanned image of the original paper document.

(5) "Electronic recording delivery system" means a system to deliver for recording, and to return to the party requesting recording, digitized or digital electronic records.

(6) "Security testing" means an independent security audit by a computer security auditor, including, but not limited to, attempts to penetrate an electronic recording delivery system for the purpose of testing the security of that system.

(7) "Source code" means a program or set of programs, readable and maintainable by humans, translated or interpreted into a form that the electronic recording delivery system can execute.

(8) "System certification" means the issuance of a confirmation letter regarding a county's electronic recording delivery system by the Attorney General. **Leg.H.** Added Stats 2004 ch 621 §2 (AB 578), effective September 21, 2004. Amended Stats 2016 ch 380 §2 (AB 2143), effective January 1, 2017.

2004 Note: For legislative intent, see Note following § 27399.

§27391. Authority to establish electronic recording delivery system and enter into contracts [Effective until January 1, 2027; Repealed January 1, 2027]

(a) Upon approval by resolution of the board of supervisors and system certification by the Attorney General, a county recorder may establish an electronic recording delivery system.

(b) Upon system certification, a county recorder may enter into a contract with a title insurer as defined in Section 12340.4 of the Insurance Code, underwritten title company as defined in Section 12340.5 of the Insurance Code, institutional lender as defined in paragraph (1), (2), or (4) of subdivision (j) of Section 50003 of the Financial Code, or an entity of local, state, or federal government for the delivery for recording, and return to the party requesting recording, of a digital or digitized electronic record that is an instrument to be recorded consistent with subdivision (a) of Section 27201. The contract may provide for the delivery of documents by an agent. However, the agent shall not be a vendor of electronic recording delivery systems.

(c)(1) A county recorder may enter into a contract with an authorized submitter not authorized pursuant to subdivision (b) for the delivery for recording, and return to the party requesting recording, of a digital or digitized electronic record that is an instrument to be recorded consistent with subdivision (a) of Section 27201. The contract may provide for the delivery of documents by an agent. However, the agent shall not be a vendor of electronic recording delivery systems.

(2) An authorized submitter authorized pursuant to this subdivision and any agent submitting documents on behalf of an authorized submitter pursuant to this subdivision shall provide proof of financial responsibility by providing a certificate of insurance evidencing an amount of general liability coverage reasonably adequate to protect against liability and cover potential losses. The amount of general liability coverage required by this paragraph shall be set through rule or regulation by the Attorney General in consultation with interested parties.

(d) A county recorder may refuse to enter into a contract with any party or may terminate or suspend access to a system for any good faith reason, including, but not limited to, a determination by the county recorder that termination or suspension is necessary to protect the public interest, to protect the integrity of public records, or to protect homeowners from financial harm, or if the volume or quality of instruments submitted by the requester is not sufficient to warrant electronic recordation. A county recorder may also terminate or suspend access to a system if a party commits a substantive breach of the contract, the requirements of this article, or the regulations adopted pursuant to this article.

(e) Notwithstanding Section 27321, a county recorder may require a party electronically submitting records to mail a copy of the recorded electronic document to the address specified in the instructions for mailing upon completion of recording.

(f) When a signature is required to be accompanied by a notary's seal or stamp, that requirement is satisfied if the electronic signature of the notary contains all of the following:

(1) The name of the notary.

(2) The words "Notary Public."

(3) The name of the county where the bond and oath of office of the notary are filed.

(4) The sequential identification number assigned to the notary, if any.

(5) The sequential identification number assigned to the manufacturer or vendor of the notary's physical or electronic seal, if any.

(g) This section shall remain in effect only until January 1, 2027, and as of that date is repealed. **Leg.H.** Added Stats 2004 ch 621 §2 (AB 578), effective September 21, 2004. Amended Stats 2016 ch 380 §3 (AB 2143), effective January 1, 2017, repealed January 1, 2027.

2004 Note: For legislative intent, see Note following § 27399.

§27391. Authority to establish electronic recording delivery system and enter into contracts [Operative January 1, 2027]

(a) Upon approval by resolution of the board of supervisors and system certification by the Attorney General, a county recorder may establish an electronic recording delivery system.

(b) Upon system certification, a county recorder may enter into a contract with a title insurer as defined in Section 12340.4 of the Insurance Code, underwritten title company as defined in Section 12340.5 of the Insurance Code, institutional lender as defined in paragraph (1), (2), or (4) of subdivision (j) of Section 50003 of the Financial Code, or an entity of local, state, or federal government for the delivery for recording, and return to the party requesting recording, of a digitized electronic record that is an instrument affecting a right, title, or interest in real property. The contract may provide for the delivery of documents by an agent. However, the agent shall not be a vendor of electronic recording delivery systems.

(c) A county recorder may refuse to enter into a contract with any party or may terminate or suspend access to a system for any good faith reason, including, but not limited to, a determination by the county recorder that termination or suspension is necessary to protect the public interest, to protect the integrity of public records, or to protect homeowners from financial harm, or if the volume or quality of instruments submitted by the requester is not sufficient to warrant electronic recordation. A county recorder may also terminate or suspend access to a system if a party commits a substantive breach of the contract, the requirements of this article, or the regulations adopted pursuant to this article.

(d) Notwithstanding Section 27321, a county recorder may require a party electronically submitting records to mail a copy of the recorded electronic document to the address specified in the instructions for mailing upon completion of recording.

(e) When a signature is required to be accompanied by a notary's seal or stamp, that requirement is satisfied if the electronic signature of the notary contains all of the following:

(1) The name of the notary.
(2) The words "Notary Public."
(3) The name of the county where the bond and oath of office of the notary are filed.
(4) The sequential identification number assigned to the notary, if any.
(5) The sequential identification number assigned to the manufacturer or vendor of the notary's physical or electronic seal, if any.

(f) This section shall become operative on January 1, 2027. **Leg.H.** Added Stats 2016 ch 380 §4 (AB 2143), effective January 1, 2017, operative January 1, 2027.

§27392. Certification required; Approval of attorney general

(a) No electronic recording delivery system may become operational without system certification by the Attorney General. The certification shall affirm that the proposed county system conforms to this article and any regulations adopted pursuant to this article, that security testing has confirmed that the system is secure and that the proposed operating procedures are sufficient to assure the continuing security and lawful operation of that system. The certification may include any agreements between the county recorder and the Attorney General as to the operation of the system, including, but not limited to, the nature and frequency of computer security audits. Certification may be withdrawn for good cause.

(b) The Attorney General shall approve software and other services for electronic recording delivery systems pursuant to regulations adopted as described in paragraph (7) of subdivision (b) of Section 27393. **Leg.H.** Added Stats 2004 ch 621 §2 (AB 578), effective September 21, 2004.

2004 Note: For legislative intent, see Note following § 27399.

§27393. Adoption of regulations [Effective until January 1, 2027; Repealed January 1, 2027]

(a) The Attorney General shall, in consultation with interested parties, adopt regulations for the review, approval, and oversight of electronic recording delivery systems. Regulations shall be adopted pursuant to the Administrative Procedure Act (Chapter 3.5 (commencing with Section 11340) of Part 1 of Division 3). The regulations shall comply with Section 12168.7.

(b) The regulations adopted pursuant to subdivision (a) may include, but need not be limited to, all of the following:

(1) Establishment of baseline technological and procedural specifications for electronic recording delivery systems.
(2) Requirements for security, capacity, reliability, and uniformity.
(3) Requirements as to the nature and frequency of computer security audits.
(4) A statement of a detailed and uniform definition of the term "source code" consistent with paragraph (7) of subdivision (b) of Section 27390, and as used in this article, and applicable to each county's electronic recording delivery system.
(5) Requirements for placement of a copy of the operating system, source code, compilers, and all related software associated with each county's electronic recording delivery system in an approved escrow facility prior to that system's first use.
(6) Requirements to ensure that substantive modifications to an operating system, compilers, related software, or source code are approved by the Attorney General.
(7) Procedures for initial certification of vendors offering software and other services to counties for electronic recording delivery systems.
(8) Requirements for system certification and for oversight of approved systems.
(9) Requirements for general liability coverage required by subdivision (c) of Section 27391.
(10) Requirements for fingerprinting and criminal records checks required by Section 27395, including a list of employment positions or classifications subject to criminal records checks under subdivision (f) of that section.
(11) Requirements for uniform index information that shall be included in every digitized or digital electronic record.
(12) Requirements for protecting proprietary information accessed pursuant to subdivision (e) of Section 27394 from public disclosure.
(13) Requirements for certification under Section 27397.5.

(c) The Attorney General may promulgate any other regulations necessary to fulfill his or her obligations under this article.

(d) An electronic recording delivery system shall be subject to local inspection and review by the Attorney General. The Attorney General shall furnish a statement of any relevant findings associated with a local inspection of an electronic recording delivery system, to the county recorder and the district attorney of the affected county, and to all technology vendors associated with that system.

(e) This section shall remain in effect only until January 1, 2027, and as of that date is repealed. **Leg.H.** Added Stats 2004 ch 621 §2 (AB 578), effective September 21, 2004. Amended Stats 2005 ch 22 §87 (SB 1108), effective January 1, 2006; Stats 2016 ch 380 §5 (AB 2143), effective January 1, 2017, repealed January 1, 2027.

2004 Note: For legislative intent, see Note following § 27399.

§27393. Adoption of regulations [Operative January 1, 2027]

(a) The Attorney General shall, in consultation with interested parties, adopt regulations for the review, approval, and oversight of electronic recording delivery systems. Regulations shall be adopted pursuant to the Administrative Procedure Act (Chapter 3.5 (commencing with Section 11340) of Part 1 of Division 3). The regulations shall comply with Section 12168.7.

(b) The regulations adopted pursuant to subdivision (a) may include, but need not be limited to, all of the following:

(1) Establishment of baseline technological and procedural specifications for electronic recording delivery systems.
(2) Requirements for security, capacity, reliability, and uniformity.
(3) Requirements as to the nature and frequency of computer security audits.
(4) A statement of a detailed and uniform definition of the term "source code" consistent with paragraph (7) of subdivision (b) of Section 27390, and as used in this article, and applicable to each county's electronic recording delivery system.
(5) Requirements for placement of a copy of the operating system, source code, compilers, and all related software associated with each county's electronic recording delivery system in an approved escrow facility prior to that system's first use.
(6) Requirements to ensure that substantive modifications to an operating system, compilers, related software, or source code are approved by the Attorney General.
(7) Procedures for initial certification of vendors offering software and other services to counties for electronic recording delivery systems.
(8) Requirements for system certification and for oversight of approved systems.
(9) Requirements for fingerprinting and criminal records checks required by Section 27395, including a list of employment positions or classifications subject to criminal records checks under subdivision (f) of that section.
(10) Requirements for uniform index information that shall be included in every digitized or digital electronic record.

(11) Requirements for protecting proprietary information accessed pursuant to subdivision (e) of Section 27394 from public disclosure.

(12) Requirements for certification under Section 27397.5.

(c) The Attorney General may promulgate any other regulations necessary to fulfill his or her obligations under this article.

(d) An electronic recording delivery system shall be subject to local inspection and review by the Attorney General. The Attorney General shall furnish a statement of any relevant findings associated with a local inspection of an electronic recording delivery system, to the county recorder and the district attorney of the affected county, and to all technology vendors associated with that system.

(e) This section shall become operative on January 1, 2027. **Leg.H.** Added Stats 2016 ch 380 §6 (AB 2143), effective January 1, 2017, operative January 1, 2027.

§27394. Use of computer security auditor; Auditing electronic recording delivery system

(a) To be eligible to establish an electronic recording delivery system, a county recorder shall contract with, and obtain a report from, a computer security auditor selected from a list of computer security auditors approved by the Attorney General.

(b) The Attorney General shall approve computer security auditors on the basis of significant experience in the evaluation and analysis of internet security design, the conduct of security testing procedures, and specific experience performing internet penetration studies. The Attorney General shall complete the approval of security auditors within 90 days of a request from a county recorder. The list shall be a public record.

(c) An electronic recording delivery system shall be audited, at least once during the first year of operation and periodically thereafter, as set forth in regulation and in the system certification, by a computer security auditor. The computer security auditor shall conduct security testing of the electronic recording delivery system. The reports of the computer security auditor shall include, but not be limited to, all of the following considerations:

(1) Safety and security of the system, including the vulnerability of the electronic recording delivery system to fraud or penetration.

(2) Results of testing of the system's protections against fraud or intrusion, including security testing and penetration studies.

(3) Recommendations for any additional precautions needed to ensure that the system is secure.

(d) Upon completion, the reports and any response to any recommendations shall be transmitted to the board of supervisors, the county recorder, the county district attorney, and the Attorney General. These reports shall be exempt from disclosure under the California Public Records Act (Division 10 (commencing with Section 7920.000) of Title 1).

(e) A computer security auditor shall have access to any aspect of an electronic recording delivery system, in any form requested. Computer security auditor access shall include, but not be limited to, permission for a thorough examination of source code and the associated approved escrow facility, and necessary authorization and assistance for a penetration study of that system.

(f) If the county recorder, a computer security auditor, a district attorney for a county participating in the electronic recording delivery system, or the Attorney General reasonably believes that an electronic recording delivery system is vulnerable to fraud or intrusion, the county recorder, the board of supervisors, the district attorney, and the Attorney General shall be immediately notified. The county recorder shall immediately take the necessary steps to guard against any compromise of the electronic recording delivery system, including, if necessary, the suspension of an authorized submitter or of the electronic recording delivery system. **Leg.H.** Added Stats 2004 ch 621 §2 (AB 578), effective September 21, 2004. Amended Stats 2021 ch 615 §190 (AB 474), effective January 1, 2022.

2004 Note: For legislative intent, see Note following § 27399.

§27395. Ineligibility of individuals to be auditor or to be granted secure access to system; Fingerprinting and criminal offender record requests

(a) No person shall be a computer security auditor or be granted secure access to an electronic recording delivery system if he or she has been convicted of a felony, has been convicted of a misdemeanor related to theft, fraud, or a crime of moral turpitude, or if he or she has pending criminal charges for any of these crimes. A plea of guilty or no contest, a verdict resulting in conviction, or the forfeiture of bail, shall be a conviction within the meaning of this section, irrespective of a subsequent order under Section 1203.4 of the Penal Code.

(b) All persons entrusted with secure access to an electronic recording delivery system shall submit fingerprints to the Attorney General for a criminal records check according to regulations adopted pursuant to Section 27393.

(c)(1) The Attorney General shall submit to the Department of Justice the fingerprint images and related information of persons with secure access to the electronic recording delivery system and computer security auditors for the purpose of obtaining information as to the existence and nature of a record of state or federal convictions and arrests for which the Department of Justice establishes that the applicant was released on bail or on his or her own recognizance pending trial.

(2) The Department of Justice shall respond to the Attorney General for criminal offender record information requests submitted pursuant to this section, with information as delineated in subdivision (l) of Section 11105 of the Penal Code.

(3) The Department of Justice shall forward requests from the Attorney General to the Federal Bureau of Investigation for federal summary criminal history information pursuant to this section.

(4) The Attorney General shall review and compile the information from the Department of Justice and the Federal Bureau of Investigation to determine whether a person is eligible to access an electronic recording delivery system pursuant to this article.

(5) The Attorney General shall request subsequent arrest notification service, pursuant to Section 11105.2 of the Penal Code, for all persons with secure access to the electronic recording delivery system and all computer security auditors.

(d) The Attorney General shall deliver written notification of an individual's ineligibility for access to an electronic recording delivery system to the individual, his or her known employer, the computer security auditor, and the county recorder.

(e) The Department of Justice shall charge a fee sufficient to cover the cost of processing a state or federal criminal offender record information request and any other costs incurred pursuant to this section.

(f) The Attorney General shall define "secure access" by regulation and by agreement with the county recorder in the system certification. **Leg.H.** Added Stats 2004 ch 621 §2 (AB 578), effective September 21, 2004. Amended Stats 2005 ch 520 §1 (AB 1738), effective January 1, 2006.

2004 Note: For legislative intent, see Note following § 27399.

§27396. Monitoring the system; Action for relief from fraudulent transactions

(a) The Attorney General shall monitor the security of electronic recording delivery systems statewide, in close cooperation with county recorders and public prosecutors. In the event of an emergency involving multiple fraudulent transactions linked to one county's use of an electronic recording delivery system, the Attorney General may order the suspension of electronic recording delivery systems in any county or in multiple counties, if necessary to protect the security of the system, for a period of up to seven court days. The Attorney General may seek an order from the superior court if it is necessary to extend this order.

(b)(1) The Attorney General, a district attorney, or a city prosecutor may bring an action in the name of the people of the state seeking declaratory or injunctive relief, restitution for damages or economic loss, rescission, or other equitable relief pertaining to any alleged violation of this article or regulations adopted pursuant to this article. Injunctive relief may include, but is not limited to, an order suspending a party from participation in the electronic recording delivery system, on a temporary or permanent basis.

(2) Nothing in this subdivision shall be construed to prevent the Attorney General, a district attorney, or a city prosecutor from seeking legal or equitable relief under any other provision of law. **Leg.H.** Added Stats 2004 ch 621 §2 (AB 578), effective September 21, 2004.

2004 Note: For legislative intent, see Note following § 27399.

§27397. Payment of regulation and oversight costs by county; Deposit of fees into Electronic Recording Authorization Fund

(a) A county establishing an electronic recording delivery system pursuant to this article shall pay for the direct cost of regulation and oversight by the Attorney General.

(b) The Attorney General may charge a fee directly to a vendor seeking approval of software and other services as part of an electronic recording delivery system. The fee shall not exceed the reasonable costs of approving software or other services for vendors.

(c) In order to pay costs under this section, a county may do any of the following:

(1) Impose a fee in an amount up to and including one dollar ($1) for each instrument, paper, or notice that is recorded by the county. This fee may, at the county's discretion, be limited to instruments, papers, or notices that are recorded pursuant to the electronic recording delivery system.

(2) Impose a fee upon any vendor seeking approval of software and other services as part of an electronic recording delivery system.

(3) Impose a fee upon any person seeking to contract as an authorized submitter.

(d) The total fees assessed by a county recorder pursuant to this section may not exceed the reasonable total costs of the electronic recording delivery system, the review and approval of vendors and potential authorized submitters, security testing as required by this article and the regulations of the Attorney General, and reimbursement to the Attorney General for regulation and oversight of the electronic recording delivery system.

(e) Fees paid to the Attorney General pursuant to subdivisions (a) and (b) shall be deposited in the Electronic Recording Authorization Fund which is hereby created in the State Treasury, and, notwithstanding Section 13340, is continuously appropriated, without regard to fiscal years, to the Attorney General for the costs described in those subdivisions. Moneys deposited in the Electronic Recording Authorization Account prior to the effective date of the amendments to this subdivision made during the 2015 Regular Session shall be immediately transferred to the Electronic Recording Authorization Fund. **Leg.H.** Added Stats 2004 ch 621 §2 (AB 578), effective September 21, 2004. Amended Stats 2015 ch 25 §35 (SB 84), effective June 24, 2015; Stats 2018 ch 467 §14 (SB 1498), effective January 1, 2019.

2004 Note: For legislative intent, see Note following § 27399.

§27397.5. Contracting to be authorized submitter of records; Certification requirements

(a) A county recorder may include in the county's electronic recording delivery system a secure method for accepting for recording a digital or digitized electronic record that is an instrument of reconveyance, substitution of trustee, or assignment of deed of trust.

(b) A county recorder may contract with a title insurer, as defined in Section 12340.4 of the Insurance Code, underwritten title company, as defined in Section 12340.5 of the Insurance Code, an entity of state, local, or federal government, or an institutional lender, as defined in Section 50003 of the Financial Code, or their authorized agents, to be an authorized submitter of the documents specified in subdivision (a).

(c) With respect to the electronic submission of the records described in subdivision (a), the requirements that an authorized submitter be subject to a security audit under Section 27394 and a criminal records check under Section 27395 shall not apply where the certification requirements of subdivision (d) have been met.

(d)(1) In order for subdivision (c) to apply, the county recorder and the Attorney General shall certify that the method of submission allowed under the system will not permit an authorized submitter or its employees and agents, or any third party, to modify, manipulate, insert, or delete information in the public record, maintained by the county recorder, or information in electronic records submitted pursuant to subdivision (b) of Section 27391.

(2) Certification under this section may be withdrawn by either the county recorder or the Attorney General at any time either determines that the requirements of this subdivision are not met.

(e) For purposes of this section, an agent of an authorized submitter shall not include a vendor of electronic recording delivery systems. **Leg.H.** Added Stats 2004 ch 621 §2 (AB 578), effective September 21, 2004.

2004 Note: For legislative intent, see Note following § 27399.

§27398. Evaluation of system

(a) The Attorney General shall conduct an evaluation of electronic recording delivery systems authorized by this article, and report to both houses of the Legislature on or before June 30, 2009.

(b) It is the intent of the Legislature that the evaluation include an analysis of costs, cost savings, security and real estate fraud prevention, and recommendations as to improvements and possible expansion of the provisions of this article.

(c) The evaluation shall also include a study of the feasibility of expanding the provisions of this article to cover the delivery, recording, and return of other electronic records. **Leg.H.** Added Stats 2004 ch 621 §2 (AB 578), effective September 21, 2004.

2004 Note: For legislative intent, see Note following § 27399.

§27399. Construction with other law

(a) Nothing in this article shall be construed to authorize any state agency to administer any of the processes or procedures relating to the business of the county recorders of the state in any manner not otherwise specifically set forth in this article.

(b) The authority granted in this article is in addition to any other authority or obligation under state or federal law.

(c) Nothing in this article shall be construed to repeal or affect Section 27279, 27279.1, 27279.2, 27297.6, 27387.1, or 27399.7, or the authority of the Counties of Orange and San Bernardino to act under those provisions. **Leg.H.** Added Stats 2004 ch 621 §2 (AB 578), effective September 21, 2004.

2004 Note: (a) It is the intent of the Legislature to enact legislation to develop a system to permit the electronic delivery, recording, and return of instruments affecting right, title, or interest in real property.

(b)(1) Except as set forth in subdivision (c), it is the intent of the Legislature that electronic recording be limited in its initial development to the digitized electronic delivery, recording, and return of instruments submitted by a title insurer, underwritten title company, institutional lender, as defined in paragraph (1), (2), or (4) of subdivision (j) of Section 50003 of the Financial Code, or an entity of local, state, or federal government. This will enable county recorders, county district attorneys, and the Attorney General to develop an electronic recording delivery system that will protect property owners and lenders from fraud and identity theft. It is the intent of the Legislature to consider expanding this system to cover additional submitting entities and digital electronic records based on experience with the system.

(2) It is not the intent of the Legislature in limiting electronic recordation of certain documents to digitized electronic delivery, to suggest, and no inference should be drawn, that digital documents pose a greater risk of fraud or identity theft than digitized documents.

(c) It is further the intent of the Legislature to enact legislation to permit, upon certification, a title insurer, underwritten title company, entity of local, state, or federal government, or institutional lender, as defined in subdivision (j) of Section 50003 of the Financial Code, to submit a digitized or digital electronic record that is an instrument of reconveyance, substitution of trustee, or assignment of deed of trust, without meeting specified requirements of this act because these instruments are less likely to result in consumer fraud. Stats 2004 ch 621 (AB 578) § 1.

TITLE 8
THE ORGANIZATION AND GOVERNMENT OF COURTS

CHAPTER 1
GENERAL PROVISIONS

§68092. Payment of fees in criminal and civil proceedings

Court interpreters' and translators' fees or other compensation shall be paid:

(a) In criminal cases, by the court.

(b) In civil cases, by the litigants, in proportions as the court may direct, to be taxed and collected as other costs. **Leg.H.** Added Stats 1953 ch 206 §1. Amended Stats 2010 ch 212 §10 (AB 2767), effective January 1, 2011.

§68092.1. Legislative findings; Courts providing interpreters to all parties requiring services in civil actions

(a) The Legislature finds and declares that it is imperative that courts provide interpreters to all parties who require one, and that both the legislative and judicial branches of government continue in their joint commitment to carry out this shared goal.

(b) Notwithstanding Section 26806 or 68092, or any other law, a court may provide an interpreter in any civil action or proceeding at no cost to the parties, regardless of the income of the parties. However, until sufficient funds are appropriated to provide an interpreter to every party who needs one, interpreters shall initially be provided in accordance with the priorities set forth in Section 756 of the Evidence Code. **Leg.H.** Added Stats 2014 ch 721 §3 (AB 1657), effective January 1, 2015.

§68092.5. Expert witness fees

(a) A party requiring testimony before any court, tribunal, or arbiter in any civil action or proceeding from any expert witness, other than a party or employee of a party, who is either, (1) an expert described in subdivision (b) of Section 2034.210 of the Code of Civil Procedure, (2) a treating physician and surgeon or other treating health care practitioner who is to be asked to express an opinion during the action or proceeding, or (3) an architect, professional engineer, or licensed land surveyor who was involved with the original project design or survey for which he or she is asked to express an opinion within his or her expertise and relevant to the action or proceeding, shall pay the reasonable and customary hourly or daily fee for the actual time consumed in the examination of that witness by any party attending the action or proceeding. The hourly or daily fee shall not exceed the fee charged the party who retained the expert except where the expert donated his or her services to a charitable or other nonprofit organization. A daily fee shall only be charged for a full day of attendance at a deposition or where the expert was required by the deposing party to be available for a full day and the expert necessarily had to forego all business he or she would have otherwise conducted that day but for the request that he or she be available all day for the scheduled deposition.

The party requiring the attendance shall either accompany the service of the subpoena or notice with a tender of the expert's fee based on the anticipated length of time the expert is required to remain at such place pursuant to the notice or subpoena or tender that fee at the required time of appearance. The expert's fee shall be delivered to the attorney for the party designating the expert. If the appearance of the expert takes longer than anticipated, the party serving the subpoena or notice shall pay the balance of the expert's fee within five days of receipt of an itemized statement from the expert. The party designating the expert is responsible for any fee charged by the expert for preparing for the testimony and for traveling to the place of the civil action or proceeding, as well as for any travel expenses of the expert, unless otherwise determined by the court.

(b) The service of a proper subpoena or notice accompanied by the tender of the expert witness fee described in subdivision (a) is effective to require the party employing or retaining the expert to produce the expert for testimony. If the party serving the notice or subpoena fails to tender the expert's fee under subdivision (a), the expert shall not be required to appear at that time unless the parties stipulate otherwise.

(c) If a party requiring the appearance by subpoena or notice of another party's expert witness under this subdivision deems that the hourly or daily fee of that expert for providing testimony is unreasonable, that party may move for an order setting the compensation of that expert. This motion shall be accompanied by a declaration stating facts showing a reasonable and good faith attempt at an informal resolution of each issue presented by the motion. Notice of this motion shall also be given to the expert.

In any such attempt at an informal resolution, either the party or the expert shall provide the other with (A) proof of the ordinary and customary fee actually charged and received by that expert for similar services provided outside the subject litigation, (B) the total number of times the presently demanded fee has ever been charged and received by that expert, and (C) the frequency and regularity with which the presently demanded fee has been charged and received by that expert within the two-year period preceding the hearing on the motion. Provisions (B) and (C) shall apply to actions filed after January 1, 1994.

In addition to any other facts or evidence, the expert or the party designating the expert shall provide, and the court's determination as to the reasonableness of the fee shall be based upon, (1) proof of the ordinary and customary fee actually charged and received by that expert for similar services provided outside the subject litigation, (2) the total number of times the presently demanded fee has ever been charged and received by that expert, and (3) the frequency and regularity with which the presently demanded and any other fee has been charged and received by that expert within the two-year period preceding the hearing on the motion. The court may also consider (4) the ordinary and customary fees charged by similar experts for similar services within the relevant community, and (5) any other factors the court deems necessary or appropriate to make its determination.

Upon a determination that the fee demanded by that expert is unreasonable, and based upon the evidence and factors considered, the court shall set the fee of the expert providing testimony.

(d) In the event the proceeding at which the expert witness has been notified his or her attendance is required is continued or canceled in advance of the time for which it is scheduled, such witness shall be notified of the continuance or cancellation by the party requiring his or her attendance by the quickest and most reliable means of giving notice under the circumstances. In the event such party fails to give notice as required by this subdivision, then the expert witness shall be entitled to receive the compensation specified in subdivision (a) of this section, notwithstanding his or her failure to give any testimony.

(e) An express contract entered into between a person and the party requesting or requiring the person to testify, relating to compensation, shall be enforceable and shall prevail over the provisions of this section.

(f) The deposition of an expert witness is governed by Chapter 18 (commencing with Section 2034.010) of Title 4 of Part 4 of the Code of Civil Procedure. **Leg.H.** Added Stats 1979 ch 746 §7, operative January 1, 1983. Amended Stats 1986 ch 560 §2; Stats 1988 ch 275 §1; Stats 1990 ch 771 §3 (SB 247), ch 1392 §4 (AB 3136); Stats 1993 ch 678 §2 (AB 907); Stats 2004 ch 182 §45 (AB 3081), operative July 1, 2005.

Prior Law: Former Gov C §68092.5, similar to the present section, was added Stats 1968 ch 1243 §1, amended Stats 1971 ch 1126 §1, Stats 1979 ch 746 §6 and repealed January 1, 1983, by its own terms.

§68093. Witness fees

Except as otherwise provided by law, witness' fees for each day's actual attendance, when legally required to attend a civil action or proceeding in the superior courts, are thirty-five dollars ($35) a day and mileage actually traveled, both ways, twenty cents ($0.20) a mile. **Leg.H.** Added Stats 1953 ch 206 §1. Amended Stats 1957 ch 1908 §2; Stats 1970 ch 1061 §2; Stats 1977 ch 1257 §54, effective October 3, 1977; Stats 1981 ch 184 §4; Stats 1998 ch 931 §228 (SB 2139), effective September 28, 1998; Stats 2002 ch 784 §207 (SB 1316), effective January 1, 2003.

§68094. Grand jury

Except as otherwise provided by law, witness' fees for each day's actual attendance, when legally required to attend before a grand jury, are twelve dollars ($12) a day and mileage for each mile actually traveled in attendance as such witness, one way only twenty cents ($0.20). Such per diem and mileage are discretionary and shall only be allowed upon a showing that the allowances are necessary for the expenses of the witness in attending. The court may disallow any fees to a witness unnecessarily subpoenaed. **Leg.H.** Added Stats 1953 ch 206 §1. Amended Stats 1957 ch 1908 §3; Stats 1970 ch 1061 §3.

§68095. Coroner's jury

Except as otherwise provided by law, witness' fees for each day's actual attendance, when legally required to attend, or if the witness attends voluntarily and is called to testify, before a coroner's jury, are twelve dollars ($12) a day and mileage for each mile actually traveled in attendance as a witness, one way only, twenty cents ($0.20). That per diem and mileage shall be a county charge. **Leg.H.** Added Stats 1953 ch 206 §1. Amended Stats 1957 ch 1908 §4; Stats 1970 ch 1061 §4; Stats 2003 ch 62 §161 (SB 600), effective January 1, 2004.

§68096.1. Compensation to government employees subpoenaed as witnesses; Reimbursement by litigant

(a) Any employee of a local agency who is obliged by a subpoena to attend a civil action or proceeding as a witness in litigation in a matter regarding an event or transaction that he or she perceived or investigated in the course of his or her duties, to which that local agency is not a party, shall receive the salary or other compensation to which he or she is normally entitled from that local agency during the time that he or she prepares for his or her response and appearance, during the time that he or she travels to and from the place where the court or other tribunal is located and while he or she is required to remain at that place pursuant to the subpoena. He or she shall also receive from that local agency the actual necessary and reasonable traveling expenses he or she incurred in complying with the subpoena.

(b) The party at whose request the subpoena is issued shall reimburse the local agency for the full cost incurred by the local agency in paying the employee his or her salary or other compensation and traveling expenses as provided for in this section, for each day that the employee is required to remain in attendance pursuant to the subpoena. The amount of two hundred seventy-five dollars ($275), together with the subpoena, shall be tendered to that local agency for each day that the employee is required to remain in attendance pursuant to the subpoena.

(c) If the actual expenses should later prove to be less than the amount tendered, the excess of the amount tendered shall be refunded.

(d) If the actual expenses should later prove to be more than the amount tendered, the difference shall be paid to the local agency by the party at whose request the subpoena was issued.

(e) If a court continues a proceeding on its own motion, no additional witness fee shall be required prior to the issuance of a subpoena or the making of any order directing the employee to appear on the date to which the proceeding is continued.

(f) As used in this section, "local agency" means a city, county, city and county, special district, redevelopment agency, or any other political subdivision of the state. **Leg.H.** Added Stats 1991 ch 230 §2 (SB 109). Amended Stats 1993 ch 1195 §17 (SB 405); Stats 2014 ch 170 §1 (AB 2727), effective January 1, 2015.

§68097. Payment in civil cases of mileage and fees for one day in advance; Demand; Effect of nonpayment; Exceptions

Witnesses in civil cases may demand the payment of their mileage and fees for one day, in advance, and when so demanded may not be compelled to attend until the allowances are paid except as hereinafter provided for employees of the Department of Justice who are peace officers or analysts in technical fields, peace officers of the Department of the California Highway Patrol, peace officer members of the State Fire Marshal's Office, other state employees, trial court employees, sheriffs, deputy sheriffs, marshals, deputy marshals, district attorney inspectors, probation officers, building inspectors, firefighters, and city police officers. For the purposes of this section and Sections 68097.1 to 68097.10, inclusive, only, the term "peace officer of the California Highway Patrol" shall include those persons employed as vehicle inspection specialists by the Department of the California Highway Patrol, the term "firefighter" has the definition provided in Section 50925, and a volunteer firefighter shall be deemed to be employed by the public entity for which he or she volunteers as a firefighter. **Leg.H.** Added Stats 1953 ch 206 §1. Amended Stats 1963 ch 1485 §4; Stats 1970 ch 58 §1; Stats 1972 ch 256 §1; Stats 1974 ch 986 §1, ch 1290 §1; Stats 1977 ch 593 §1.5; Stats 1992 ch 381 §1 (SB 1546), effective August 1, 1992, ch 887 §1.5 (AB 3816); Stats 1993 ch 158 §11 (AB 392), effective July 20, 1993, ch 727 §1 (AB 1522). Supplemented by the Governor's Reorganization Plan No. 1, effective July 12, 1995; Amended Stats 1996 ch 305 §34 (AB 3103); Stats 2003 ch 449 §19 (AB 1712).

§68097.1. Testimony by peace officers, firefighters, or certain government employees; Service of subpoena; "Tribunal"

(a) Whenever an employee of the Department of Justice who is a peace officer or an analyst in a technical field, peace officer of the Department of the California Highway Patrol, peace officer member of the State Fire Marshal's Office, sheriff, deputy sheriff, marshal, deputy marshal, district attorney inspector, probation officer, building inspector, firefighter, or city police officer is required as a witness before any court or other tribunal in any civil action or proceeding in connection with a matter regarding an event or transaction which he or she has perceived or investigated in the course of his or her duties, a subpoena requiring his or her attendance may be served by delivering a copy either to the person personally, or by delivering two copies to his or her immediate superior at the public entity by which he or she is employed or an agent designated by that immediate superior to receive that service.

(b) Whenever any other state employee or any employee of the trial courts is required as a witness before any court or other tribunal in any civil action or proceeding in connection with a matter, event, or transaction concerning which he or she has expertise gained in the course of his or her duties, a subpoena requiring his or her attendance may be served by delivering a copy either to the person personally or by delivering two copies to his or her immediate superior or agent designated by that immediate superior to receive that service.

(c) The attendance of any person described in subdivisions (a) and (b) may be required pursuant to this section only in accordance with Section 1989 of the Code of Civil Procedure.

(d) As used in this section and in Sections 68097.2 and 68097.5, "tribunal" means any person or body before whom or which attendance of witnesses may be required by subpoena, including an arbitrator in arbitration proceedings. **Leg.H.** Added Stats 1963 ch 1485 §5. Amended Stats 1965 ch 561 §1; Stats 1969 ch 172 §1; Stats 1974 ch 986 §2, ch 1290 §2; Stats 1977 ch 593 §2.5; Stats 1990 ch 1695 §2.5 (SB 2140); Stats 1992 ch 381 §2 (SB 1546), effective August 1, 1992, ch 887 §2.5 (AB 3816); Stats 1993 ch 158 §12 (AB 392), effective July 20, 1993, ch 727 §2 (AB 1522). Supplemented by the Governor's Reorganization Plan No. 1, effective July 12, 1995; Amended Stats 1996 ch 305 §35 (AB 3103); Stats 2003 ch 449 §20 (AB 1712), effective January 1, 2004.

§68097.2. Salary and expenses of public employees attending as witnesses; Reimbursement

(a) Any peace officer, as that term is defined in Chapter 4.5 (commencing with Section 830) of Title 3 of Part 2 of the Penal Code, any firefighter, any state employee, any trial court employee, or any county employee, who is obliged by a subpoena issued pursuant to Section 68097.1 to attend as a witness, shall receive the salary or other compensation to which he or she is normally entitled from the public entity by which he or she is employed during the time that he or she travels to and from the place where the court or other tribunal is located and while he or she is required to remain at that place pursuant to the subpoena. He or she shall also receive from the public entity by which he or she is employed the actual necessary and reasonable traveling expenses incurred by him or her in complying with the subpoena.

(b) The party at whose request the subpoena is issued shall reimburse the public entity for the full cost to the public entity incurred in paying the peace officer, firefighter, state employee, trial court employee, or specified county employee his or her salary or other compensation and traveling expenses as provided for in this section, for each day that the peace officer, firefighter, state employee, trial court employee, or specified county employee is required to remain in attendance pursuant to the subpoena. The amount of two hundred seventy-five dollars ($275), together with the subpoena, shall be tendered to the person accepting the subpoena for each day that the peace officer, firefighter, state employee, trial court employee, or specified county employee is required to remain in attendance pursuant to the subpoena.

(c) If the actual expenses should later prove to be less than the amount tendered, the excess of the amount tendered shall be refunded.

(d) If the actual expenses should later prove to be more than the amount deposited, the difference shall be paid to the public entity by the party at whose request the subpoena is issued.

shall be guidelines by which the progress of litigation in the superior court of every county may be measured. In establishing these standards, the Judicial Council shall be guided by the principles that litigation, from commencement to resolution, should require only that time reasonably necessary for pleadings, discovery, preparation, and court events, and that any additional elapsed time is delay and should be eliminated.

(b) The Judicial Council may adopt the standards of timely disposition adopted by the National Conference of State Trial Judges and the American Bar Association or may adopt different standards, but in the latter event shall specify reasons for approval of any standard which permits greater elapsed time for the resolution of litigation than that provided in the standards of the National Conference of State Trial Judges.

(c) The Judicial Council shall adopt rules effective July 1, 1991, to be used by all delay reduction courts, establishing a case differentiation classification system based on the relative complexity of cases. The rules shall provide longer periods for the timely disposition of more complex cases. The rules may provide a presumption that all cases, when filed, shall be classified in the least complex category. **Leg.H.** Added Stats 1990 ch 1232 §3 (AB 3820).

Prior Law: Former Gov C §68603, similar to the present section, was added Stats 1986 ch 1335 §1 and repealed Stats 1990 ch 1232 §2 (AB 3820).

§68604. Statistics as to compliance of superior courts and branch courts; Study; Reports

The Judicial Council shall collect and maintain statistics, and shall publish them at least on a yearly basis, regarding the compliance of the superior court of each county and of each branch court with the standards of timely disposition adopted pursuant to Section 68603. In collecting and publishing these statistics, the Judicial Council shall measure the time required for the resolution of civil cases from the filing of the first document invoking court jurisdiction, and for the resolution of criminal cases from the date of arrest, including a separate measurement in felony cases from the first appearance in superior court. The Judicial Council shall report its findings and recommendations to the Legislature in a biennial Report on the State of California's Civil and Criminal Justice Systems.

The Judicial Council shall conduct a two-year study on the stipulated continuance authorized by subdivision (c) of Section 68616. **Leg.H.** Added Stats 1990 ch 1232 §3 (AB 3820). Amended Stats 2001 ch 745 §112 (SB 1191), effective October 12, 2001.

Prior Law: Former Gov C §68604, similar to the present section, was added Stats 1986 ch 1335 §1 and repealed Stats 1990 ch 1232 §2.

§68605.5. Application of article

On and after July 1, 1992, this article shall apply to all actions and proceedings in the superior court in each county, except actions and proceedings subject to subdivision (a) of Section 68608 or subdivision (b) of Section 68609. **Leg.H.** Added Stats 1990 ch 1232 §3 (AB 3820).

§68607. Responsibilities and duties of judges

In accordance with this article and consistent with statute, judges shall have the responsibility to eliminate delay in the progress and ultimate resolution of litigation, to assume and maintain control over the pace of litigation, to actively manage the processing of litigation from commencement to disposition, and to compel attorneys and litigants to prepare and resolve all litigation without delay, from the filing of the first document invoking court jurisdiction to final disposition of the action.

The judges of the program shall, consistent with the policies of this article:

(a) Actively monitor, supervise and control the movement of all cases assigned to the program from the time of filing of the first document invoking court jurisdiction through final disposition.

(b) Seek to meet the standards for timely disposition adopted pursuant to Section 68603.

(c) Establish procedures for early identification of cases within the program which may be protracted and for giving those cases special administrative and judicial attention as appropriate, including special assignment.

(d) Establish procedures for early identification and timely and appropriate handling of cases within the program which may be amenable to settlement or other alternative disposition techniques.

(e) Adopt a trial setting policy which, to the maximum extent possible, schedules a trial date within the time standards adopted pursuant to Section 68603 and which schedules a sufficient number of cases to ensure efficient use of judicial time while minimizing resetting caused by overscheduling.

(f) Commence trials on the date scheduled.

(g) Adopt and utilize a firm, consistent policy against continuances, to the maximum extent possible and reasonable, in all stages of the litigation. **Leg.H.** Added Stats 1990 ch 1232 §3 (AB 3820).

Prior Law: Former Gov C §68607, similar to present Gov C §68608, was added Stats 1986 ch 1335 §1 and repealed Stats 1990 ch 1232 §2.

§68607.5. Removal of action or proceeding from delay reduction program

No action or proceeding may be removed from a delay reduction program because of a challenge filed under Section 170.6 of the Code of Civil Procedure. **Leg.H.** Added Stats 1990 ch 1232 §3 (AB 3820).

§68608. Assignments and powers of judges

(a) Juvenile, probate, and domestic relations cases shall not be assigned to a delay reduction program, and cases which have been assigned to a judge or judges for all purposes based on subject matter need not be assigned to the program.

(b) Judges shall have all the powers to impose sanctions authorized by law, including the power to dismiss actions or strike pleadings, if it appears that less severe sanctions would not be effective after taking into account the effect of previous sanctions or previous lack of compliance in the case. Judges are encouraged to impose sanctions to achieve the purposes of this article.

(c) This section shall become operative July 1, 1992. **Leg.H.** Added Stats 1990 ch 1232 §3 (AB 3820), operative July 1, 1992.

Prior Law: Former Gov C §68608, similar to present Gov C §68607, was added Stats 1986 ch 1335 §1 and repealed Stats 1990 ch 1232 §2.

§68609.5. Rules for arbitration of uninsured motorist cases

Each court and the Judicial Council, under subdivision (b) of Section 68619, shall adopt rules to allow for the arbitration of cases designated by the court as "Uninsured Motorist" in which an action is filed against a defendant who is an uninsured motorist and the plaintiffs claim is subject to an arbitration provision. **Leg.H.** Added Stats 1990 ch 1232 §3 (AB 3820).

Prior Law: Former Gov C §68609.5, similar to the present section, was added by Stats 1988 ch 1200 § 2, effective September 22, 1988 and repealed Stats 1990 ch 1232 §2 (AB 3820).

§68610. Training program

The Judicial Council, in conjunction with other interested groups as it determines appropriate, may prepare and administer a program, consistent with the policies and requirements of this article, for the training of judges in administering the delay reduction program. **Leg.H.** Added Stats 1990 ch 1232 §3 (AB 3820).

Prior Law: Former Gov C §68610, similar to the present section, was added Stats 1986 ch 1335 §1 and repealed Stats 1990 ch 1232 §2 (AB 3820).

§68612. Procedures, standards, and policies

Judges shall, in consultation with the bar of the county to the maximum extent feasible develop and publish the procedures, standards, and policies which will be used in the program, including time standards for the conclusion of all critical steps in the litigation process, including discovery, and shall meet on a regular basis with the bar of the county in order to explain and publicize the program and the procedures, standards, and policies which shall govern cases assigned to the program. The procedures, standards, and policies to be used in the program shall be filed, distributed, and maintained pursuant to Section 68071 and the California Rules of Court, and shall also be published for general distribution. In its discretion, the Judicial Council may assist in the development of, or may develop and adopt, any or all of such procedures, standards, or policies on a statewide basis. **Leg.H.** Added Stats 1990 ch 1232 §3 (AB 3820).

Prior Law: Former Gov C §68612, similar to the present section, was added Stats 1986 ch 1335 §1, amended Stats 1988 ch 1200 § 3, effective September 22, 1988 and repealed Stats 1990 ch 1232 §2 (AB 3820).

§68613. Funds

The Judicial Council may receive and expend on the programs established by this article any funds available from county, state, or

(e) If a court continues a proceeding on its own motion, no additional witness fee shall be required prior to the issuance of a subpoena or the making of an order directing the peace officer, firefighter, state employee, or trial court employee to appear on the date to which the proceeding is continued.

(f) For the purposes of the payment of the salary or other compensation of a volunteer firefighter pursuant to subdivision (a), a volunteer firefighter who is subpoenaed to appear as a witness in connection with a matter regarding an event or transaction that he or she has perceived or investigated in the course of his or her duties as a volunteer firefighter, shall be deemed to be entitled to reasonable compensation evidenced by the compensation paid to firefighters in jurisdictions with similar geographic and economic characteristics. However, the requirements of subdivision (a) and of this subdivision are not applicable if a volunteer firefighter will receive his or her regular salary or other compensation pursuant to the policy of his or her regular employer, for the periods during which compensation is required under subdivision (a). **Leg.H.** Added Stats 1963 ch 1485 §5. Amended Stats 1965 ch 561 §2; Stats 1969 ch 172 §2, ch 342 §2, ch 1187 §2; Stats 1974 ch 986 §3, ch 1290 §3; Stats 1977 ch 593 §3.5; Stats 1980 ch 472 §1; Stats 1986 ch 747 §1; Stats 1988 ch 588 §1; Stats 1989 ch 1416 §35; Stats 1990 ch 511 §2 (SB 163), effective August 10, 1990; Stats 1992 ch 381 §3 (SB 1546), effective August 1, 1992, ch 427 §73 (AB 3355), ch 876 §13 (AB 3296) (ch 876 prevails); Stats 1993 ch 158 §13 (AB 392), effective July 20, 1993, ch 727 §3 (AB 1522); Stats 2003 ch 449 §21 (AB 1712); Stats 2012 ch 377 §1 (AB 2612), effective January 1, 2013.

§68097.3. Service of subpoena on California Highway Patrol member when CCP §1989 inapplicable

Whenever a member of the California Highway Patrol is not subject to a subpoena pursuant to Section 1989 of the Code of Civil Procedure, he may nevertheless be required to appear as a witness before any court located in this state, in any civil action or proceeding in connection with a matter regarding an event or transaction which he has perceived or investigated in the course of his duties, by a subpoena requiring his attendance. The subpoena may be served by delivering a copy (1) to the member personally or to his immediate superior or (2) during usual office hours, at least five days prior to the date of the member's required attendance, to the person in charge of the office of the California Highway Patrol where the member filed his report of the event or transaction. **Leg.H.** Added Stats 1963 ch 1485 §7. Amended Stats 1976 ch 10 §1.

§68097.4. Compensation for highway patrol members appearing as witnesses; Reimbursement to State by party seeking subpoena

Any member of the California Highway Patrol who is obliged to appear pursuant to a subpoena issued under the provisions of Section 68097.3 as a witness, shall receive from the State the salary or other compensation to which he is normally entitled as a member of the patrol during the time that he travels to and from the place where the court is located and while he is required to remain at such place pursuant to such subpoena. He shall also receive from the State the actual necessary and reasonable traveling expenses incurred by him in complying with such subpoena.

The party at whose request a subpoena is issued pursuant to Section 68097.3 shall reimburse the State for the amount of the salary or other compensation to which the member of the California Highway Patrol involved is normally entitled from the State during the time that he travels to and from the place where the court is located and while he is required to remain at such place pursuant to such subpoena; and in addition, such party shall reimburse the State for the actual, necessary and reasonable traveling expenses incurred by the member of the California Highway Patrol in complying with such subpoena. An amount equal to the estimated amount of such salary or other compensation and expenses shall be deposited with the clerk of the court prior to the issuance of such subpoena. If the actual amount of such salary or other compensation and expenses should later prove to be more than the amount deposited, the party shall also deposit the difference with the clerk. If the actual amount should later prove to be less than the amount deposited, the excess of the amount deposited shall be refunded. All amounts received by the clerk to which the State is entitled shall be remitted to the Department of the California Highway Patrol for deposit in the State Treasury. **Leg.H.** Added Stats 1963 ch 1485 §8.

§68097.5. Return of peace officer for subsequent proceedings

No employee of the Department of Justice who is a peace officer or an analyst in a technical field, peace officer of the Department of the California Highway Patrol, peace officer member of the State Fire Marshal's office, sheriff, deputy sheriff, marshal, deputy marshal, firefighter, or city police officer shall be ordered to return by the court for subsequent proceedings beyond the day stated in the subpoena referred to in Sections 68097.1, 68097.2, 68097.3 and 68097.4, or the day upon which the witness appeared pursuant to the provisions of Section 68097.9, unless the party at whose request the subpoena was issued or the party at whose request the witness is ordered to return, shall first tender to the public entity by which the witness is employed the same sum required to be tendered for the issuance of a subpoena in the first instance. **Leg.H.** Added Stats 1963 ch 1485 §9. Amended Stats 1965 ch 561 §3; Stats 1967 ch 115 §1; Stats 1970 ch 58 §2; Stats 1974 ch 986 §4, ch 1290 §4; Stats 1977 ch 593 §4.5; Stats 1990 ch 511 §3 (SB 163), effective August 10, 1990; Stats 1992 ch 887 §3 (AB 3816). Supplemented by the Governor's Reorganization Plan No. 1, effective July 12, 1995; Amended Stats 1996 ch 305 §36 (AB 3103), effective January 1, 1997.

§68097.55. Reimbursement requirement of indigents

Notwithstanding the provisions of Section 68097.5, the court, upon good cause shown, including the fact that the party is proceeding in forma pauperis pursuant to Section 68511.3, may relieve a party of the duty to make any deposit or payment, or portion thereof, required by Sections 68096.1, 68097.1, 68097.2, 68097.3, 68097.4, and 68097.5. **Leg.H.** Added Stats 1967 ch 115 §2. Amended Stats 1980 ch 472 §2; Stats 1993 ch 93 §1 (AB 1348), effective January 1, 1994.

§68097.6. Subpoenas for depositions of certain employees pursuant to CCP §§2025.010 et seq.

Sections 68097.1, 68097.2, 68097.3, 68097.4, and 68097.5 apply to subpoenas issued for the taking of depositions of employees of the Department of Justice who are peace officers or analysts in technical fields, peace officers of the Department of the California Highway Patrol, peace officer members of the State Fire Marshal's office, sheriffs, deputy sheriffs, marshals, deputy marshals, firefighters, or city police officers pursuant to Chapter 9 (commencing with Section 2025.010) of Title 4 of Part 4 of the Code of Civil Procedure. **Leg.H.** Added Stats 1963 ch 1485 §10. Amended Stats 1970 ch 58 §3; Stats 1974 ch 986 §5, ch 1290 §5; Stats 1977 ch 593 §5.5; Stats 1992 ch 887 §4 (AB 3816). Supplemented by the Governor's Reorganization Plan No. 1, effective July 12, 1995; Amended Stats 1996 ch 305 §37 (AB 3103); Stats 2005 ch 294 §21 (AB 333), effective January 1, 2006.

§68097.8. Deposits taxable as costs by prevailing party

All deposits made pursuant to Sections 68097.2 or 68097.4 of this code, except such deposits as the party may be entitled to have refunded, shall be taxable as costs by the prevailing party. **Leg.H.** Added Stats 1963 ch 1485 §12.

§68098. Funds chargeable with fees in criminal cases

Witness' fees in criminal cases in superior courts, other than fees for expert witnesses appointed by the court for the court's needs pursuant to Section 730 of the Evidence Code, are charges against the same funds as grand jurors' fees in criminal cases. **Leg.H.** Added Stats 1953 ch 206 §1. Amended Stats 1977 ch 1257 §56, effective October 3, 1977; Stats 1998 ch 931 §229 (SB 2139), effective September 28, 1998; Stats 2012 ch 470 §48 (AB 1529), effective January 1, 2013.

CHAPTER 2
THE JUDICIAL COUNCIL
ARTICLE 5
The Trial Court Delay Reduction Act

§68600. Citation of article

This article shall be known and may be cited as the Trial Court Delay Reduction Act. **Leg.H.** Added Stats 1990 ch 1232 §3 (AB 3820).

Prior Law: Former Gov C §68600, similar to the present section, was added Stats 1986 ch 1335 §1 and repealed Stats 1990 ch 1232 §2 (AB 3820).

§68603. Adoption of standards of timely disposition

(a) The Judicial Council shall adopt standards of timely disposition for the processing and disposition of civil and criminal actions. The standards federal government or other sources which may be available for such purposes. **Leg.H.** Added Stats 1990 ch 1232 §3 (AB 3820).

Prior Law: Former Gov C §68613, similar to the present section, was added Stats 1986 ch 1335 §1 and repealed Stats 1990 ch 1232 §2 (AB 3820).

§68615. Contracting out for performance of duties

In its discretion, the Judicial Council may contract out for performance of any of the duties imposed by this article. **Leg.H.** Added Stats 1990 ch 1232 §3 (AB 3820).

Prior Law: Former Gov C §68615, similar to the present section, was added Stats 1986 ch 1335 §1 and repealed Stats 1990 ch 1232 §2 (AB 3820).

§68616. Minimum time periods for delay reduction rules

Delay reduction rules shall not require shorter time periods than as follows:

(a) Service of the complaint within 60 days after filing. Exceptions, for longer periods of time, (1) may be granted as authorized by local rule, and (2) shall be granted on a showing that service could not reasonably be achieved within the time required with the exercise of due diligence, consistent with the amount in controversy.

(b) Service of responsive pleadings within 30 days after service of the complaint. The parties may stipulate to an additional 15 days. Exceptions, for longer periods of time, may be granted as authorized by local rule.

(c) Time for service of notice or other paper under Sections 1005 and 1013 of the Code of Civil Procedure, and time to plead after service of summons under Section 412.20 of the Code of Civil Procedure, shall not be shortened, except as provided in those sections.

(d) Within 30 days of service of the responsive pleadings, the parties may, by stipulation filed with the court, agree to a single continuance not to exceed 30 days.

It is the intent of the Legislature that these stipulations not detract from the efforts of the courts to comply with standards of timely disposition. To this extent, the Judicial Council shall develop statistics that distinguish between cases involving, and not involving, these stipulations.

(e) A status conference, or similar event, other than a challenge to the jurisdiction of the court, shall not be required to be conducted sooner than 30 days after service of the first responsive pleadings, or 30 days after expiration of a stipulated continuance, if any, pursuant to subdivision (d).

(f) Title 4 (commencing with Section 2016.010) of Part 4 of the Code of Civil Procedure shall govern discovery, except in arbitration proceedings.

(g) A case shall not be referred to arbitration prior to 210 days after the filing of the complaint, exclusive of the stipulated period provided for in subdivision (d). Any rule adopted pursuant to this article shall not contravene Sections 638 and 639 of the Code of Civil Procedure.

(h) Unnamed (DOE) defendants shall not be dismissed or severed prior to the conclusion of the introduction of evidence at trial, except upon stipulation or motion of the parties. **Leg.H.** Added Stats 1999 ch 67 §10 (AB 1105), effective July 6, 1999, operative January 1, 2004. Amended Stats 2004 ch 182 §46 (AB 3081), operative July 1, 2005; Stats 2007 ch 146 §1 (AB 1264), effective January 1, 2008; Stats 2010 ch 131 §2 (AB 1894), effective January 1, 2011.

Prior Law: Former Gov C §68616, was added Stats 1993 ch 1261 §8, operative January 1, 1999. Amended Stats 1996 ch 1159 §17, operative January 1, 1999; Stats 1997 ch 892 §14, operative January 1, 1999; Stats 1999 ch 67 §9, effective July 6, 1999, and repealed Stats January 1, 2004.

Former Gov C §68616, similar to the present section, was added Stats 1990 ch 1232 §3, amended Stats 1993 ch 1261 §7, Stats 1996 ch 1159 §16, Stats 1997 ch 892 §13, operative until January 1, 1999, and repealed January 1, 1999, by its own terms.

Former Gov C §68616, relating to adoption of local rules for civil case tracking in San Diego Superior Court, was added Stats 1987 ch 238 §3, effective July 23, 1987, and repealed January 1, 1988, by its own terms.

§68617. Report

On or before October 30, 2002, the Judicial Council shall submit a report to the Legislature and the Governor regarding the effectiveness of the Centers for Complex Litigation established pursuant to the Budget Act of 1999. The report shall examine, among other things, the number of complex cases filed, the impact of the centers on case and calendar management, and the impact on the trial courts, the attorneys, and the parties, and shall make recommendations to the Legislature and the Governor. **Leg.H.** Added Stats 1999 ch 67 §11 (AB 1105), effective July 6, 1999.

§68620. Establishment of delay reduction program by superior courts; Exemptions

(a) Each superior court shall establish a delay reduction program for limited civil cases in consultation with the local bar that is consistent with the provisions of this article. In its discretion, the Judicial Council may assist in the development of, or may develop and adopt, any or all procedures, standards, or policies for a delay reduction program for limited civil cases in superior courts on a statewide basis which are consistent with the provisions of the Trial Court Delay Reduction Act.

(b) Actions and proceedings subject to the provisions of Chapter 5.5 (commencing with Section 116.110) of Title 1 of Part 1 of the Code of Civil Procedure or provisions of Chapter 4 (commencing with Section 1159) of Title 3 of Part 3 of the Code of Civil Procedure may not be assigned to or governed by the provisions of any delay reduction program established pursuant to this section.

(c) It is the intent of the Legislature that the civil discovery in actions and proceedings subject to a program established pursuant to Article 2 (commencing with Section 90) of Chapter 5.1 of Title 1 of Part 1 of the Code of Civil Procedure shall be governed by the times and procedures specified in that article. Civil discovery in these actions and proceedings is not affected by the provisions of any delay reduction program adopted pursuant to this section. **Leg.H.** Added Stats 1991 ch 90 §12 (AB 1297), effective June 30, 1991. Amended Stats 1991 ch 189 §8.5 (AB 544), effective July 27, 1991; Stats 1994 ch 587 §11 (AB 3600); Stats 1998 ch 931 §247 (SB 2139), effective September 28, 1998; Stats 2002 ch 784 §223 (SB 1316); Stats 2003 ch 62 §163 (SB 600), ch 149 §28 (SB 79) (ch 149 prevails).

ARTICLE 6
Waiver of Court Fees and Costs

§68630. Legislative findings and declarations

The Legislature finds and declares all of the following:

(a) That our legal system cannot provide "equal justice under law" unless all persons have access to the courts without regard to their economic means. California law and court procedures should ensure that court fees are not a barrier to court access for those with insufficient economic means to pay those fees.

(b) That fiscal responsibility should be tempered with concern for litigants' rights to access the justice system. The procedure for allowing the poor to use court services without paying ordinary fees must be one that applies rules fairly to similarly situated persons, is accessible to those with limited knowledge of court processes, and does not delay access to court services. The procedure for determining if a litigant may file a lawsuit without paying a fee must not interfere with court access for those without the financial means to do so.

(c) That those who are able to pay court fees should do so, and that courts should be allowed to recover previously waived fees if a litigant has obtained a judgment or substantial settlement. **Leg.H.** Added Stats 2008 ch 462 §2 (AB 2448), effective January 1, 2009, operative July 1, 2009.

§68631. Initial fee waiver

An initial fee waiver shall be granted by the court at any stage of the proceedings at both the appellate and trial court levels if an applicant meets the standards of eligibility and application requirements under Sections 68632 and 68633. An initial fee waiver excuses the applicant from paying fees for the first pleading or other paper, and other court fees and costs, including assessments for court investigations under Section 1513, 1826, or 1851 of the Probate Code, as specified in rules adopted by the Judicial Council, unless the court orders the applicant to make partial payments under subdivision (c) of Section 68632, subdivision (d) of Section 68636, or subdivision (e) of Section 68637. Under circumstances set forth in Section 68636, the court may reconsider the initial fee waiver and order the fee waiver withdrawn for future fees and costs or deny the fee waiver retroactively. At the end of the case, the court may recover fees and costs that were initially waived under circumstances set forth in Section 68637. Upon establishment of a conservatorship or guardianship, the court may collect all or part of any fees waived pursuant to this section and Section 68632 from the estate of the conservatee or ward, if the court finds that the estate has the ability to pay the fees, or a portion thereof, immediately, over a period of time, or under some other equitable agreement, without using moneys that normally would pay for the common necessaries of life for the applicant and the applicant's family. **Leg.H.** Added Stats 2008 ch 462 §2 (AB 2448), effective January 1, 2009, operative July 1, 2009. Amended Stats 2014 ch 913 §23 (AB 2747), effective January 1, 2015.

§68631.5. "Applicant"; "Petitioner"

For purposes of this article, a conservatee, ward, or person for whom a conservatorship or guardianship is sought, shall be deemed the "applicant," and the conservator, guardian, or person or persons seeking to establish the conservatorship or guardianship shall be deemed the "petitioner." In those cases, the petitioner is responsible for completing all forms and providing all information required under this article. **Leg.H.** Added Stats 2014 ch 913 §24 (AB 2747), effective January 1, 2015.

§68632. Permission to proceed without paying court fees and costs

Permission to proceed without paying court fees and costs because of an applicant's financial condition shall be granted initially to all of the following persons:

(a) An applicant who is receiving public benefits under one or more of the following programs:

(1) Supplemental Security Income (SSI) and State Supplementary Payment (SSP) (Article 5 (commencing with Section 12200) of Chapter 3 of Part 3 of Division 9 of the Welfare and Institutions Code).

(2) California Work Opportunity and Responsibility to Kids Act (CalWORKs) (Chapter 2 (commencing with Section 11200) of Part 3 of Division 9 of the Welfare and Institutions Code) or a federal Tribal Temporary Assistance for Needy Families (Tribal TANF) grant program (Section 10553.25 of the Welfare and Institutions Code).

(3) Supplemental Nutrition Assistance Program (Chapter 51 (commencing with Section 2011) of Title 7 of the United States Code) or the California Food Assistance Program (Chapter 10.1 (commencing with Section 18930) of Part 6 of Division 9 of the Welfare and Institutions Code).

(4) County Relief, General Relief (GR), or General Assistance (GA) (Part 5 (commencing with Section 17000) of Division 9 of the Welfare and Institutions Code).

(5) Cash Assistance Program for Aged, Blind, and Disabled Legal Immigrants (CAPI) (Chapter 10.3 (commencing with Section 18937) of Part 6 of Division 9 of the Welfare and Institutions Code).

(6) In-Home Supportive Services (IHSS) (Article 7 (commencing with Section 12300) of Chapter 3 of Part 3 of Division 9 of the Welfare and Institutions Code).

(7) Medi-Cal (Chapter 7 (commencing with Section 14000) of Part 3 of Division 9 of the Welfare and Institutions Code).

(8) California Special Supplemental Nutrition Program for Women, Infants, and Children (WIC Program) (Article 2 (commencing with Section 123275) of Chapter 1 of Part 2 of Division 106 of the Health and Safety Code).

(9) Unemployment compensation (Chapter 5 (commencing with Section 1251) of Part 1 of Division 1 of the Unemployment Insurance Code).

(b)(1) An applicant whose monthly income is 200 percent or less of the current poverty guidelines updated periodically in the Federal Register by the United States Department of Health and Human Services under the authority of paragraph (2) of Section 9902 of Title 42 of the United States Code or a successor statute or regulation.

(2) The Judicial Council shall annually publish a table establishing the threshold monthly household income for a fee waiver pursuant to paragraph (1) that is adjusted for household family size to be used with form FW-001.

(c) An applicant who, as individually determined by the court, cannot pay court fees without using moneys that normally would pay for the common necessaries of life for the applicant and the applicant's family. Only if a trial court finds that an applicant under this subdivision can pay a portion of court fees, or can pay court fees over a period of time, or under some other equitable arrangement, without using moneys that normally would pay for the common necessaries of life for the applicant and the applicant's family, the court may grant a partial initial fee waiver using the notice and hearing procedures set forth in paragraph (5) of subdivision (e) of Section 68634. "Common necessaries of life," as used in this article, shall be interpreted consistently with the use of that term in paragraph (1) of subdivision (c) of Section 706.051 of the Code of Civil Procedure, as that paragraph read prior to January 1, 2012.

(d) A person who files a petition for appointment of a fiduciary in a guardianship or conservatorship, or files pleadings as the appointed fiduciary of a conservatee or ward, when the financial condition of the conservatee or ward meets the standards for a fee waiver pursuant to subdivision (a), (b), or (c). **Leg.H.** Added Stats 2008 ch 462 §2 (AB 2448), effective January 1, 2009, operative July 1, 2009. Amended Stats 2011 ch 694 §2 (AB 1388), effective January 1, 2012; Stats 2014 ch 913 §25 (AB 2747), effective January 1, 2015; Stats 2022 ch 57 §6 (AB 199), effective June 30, 2022.

§68633. Applicant for initial fee waiver required to complete Judicial Council application and financial statement; Confidentiality; Counsel

(a) An applicant for an initial fee waiver under subdivision (a) of Section 68632 shall complete, under penalty of perjury, a Judicial Council application form requiring the applicant to list his or her current street address, or another address where the court can contact the applicant, occupation, employer, and the type of public benefits that he or she is receiving. At the time the application is submitted, the applicant shall not be required to provide documents supporting receipt of public benefits, to provide evidence of identity, to submit to interviews regarding the applicant's financial circumstances, to be physically present to file the application, or to fill out additional parts of the application form.

(b) An applicant for an initial fee waiver under subdivision (b) of Section 68632 shall complete, under penalty of perjury, both of the following:

(1) A Judicial Council application form requiring the applicant to provide his or her current street address, or another address where the court can contact the applicant, occupation, and employer.

(2) A financial statement showing monthly or yearly income as determined under rules, and on forms, adopted by the Judicial Council. At the time the application is submitted, the applicant shall not be required to provide documents to prove income, dependents, or expenses, to provide evidence of identity, to submit to interviews regarding the applicant's financial circumstances, to be physically present to file the application, or to fill out additional parts of the application form.

(c) An applicant for an initial fee waiver under subdivision (c) of Section 68632 shall complete, under penalty of perjury, both of the following:

(1) A Judicial Council application form requiring the applicant to provide his or her current street address, or another address where the court can contact the applicant, occupation, and employer.

(2) A financial statement showing monthly or yearly income and expenses and a summary of assets and liabilities as determined under rules, and on forms, adopted by the Judicial Council. At the time the application is submitted, the applicant shall not be required to provide documents to prove income, dependents, or expenses, to provide evidence of identity, to submit to interviews regarding the applicant's financial circumstances, or to be physically present to file the application.

(d) The clerk shall provide forms adopted by the Judicial Council pursuant to this article without charge to any person who requests those forms or indicates that he or she is unable to pay any court fees or costs. An applicant shall not be required to complete any form as part of his or her application under this article other than those forms adopted by the Judicial Council.

(e) An applicant for an initial fee waiver shall be informed that, at a later date, the court may require proof of receipt of benefits or financial information to verify eligibility, as provided in Section 68636, and that a trial court may seek reimbursement of initially waived fees under circumstances set forth in Section 68637. This notice requirement is satisfied if the information is provided on the Judicial Council fee waiver application form.

(f) Financial information provided by an applicant shall be kept confidential by the court. No person shall have access to the application except the court, authorized court personnel, and any person authorized by the applicant. No person shall reveal any information contained in the application except as authorized by law. Any hearing regarding whether to grant or deny a fee waiver request shall be held in camera, and the court shall exclude all persons except court staff, the applicant, those present with the applicant's consent, and any witness being examined. The fact that an applicant's fees and costs have been initially waived and the amount of the waived fees and costs are not confidential. The Judicial

Council shall adopt procedures to keep the financial information confidential and to consider a request seeking that confidential information.

(g) Counsel representing an applicant who is filing in a general jurisdiction civil case pursuant to an agreement that counsel will advance litigation costs shall indicate that agreement on the application form. The court shall set a hearing to determine whether or not the applicant is able to pay court fees without using moneys that normally would pay for the common necessaries of life. This subdivision does not apply if the applicant is represented by counsel for, or affiliated with, a qualified legal services project, as defined in Section 6213 of the Business and Professions Code. **Leg.H.** Added Stats 2008 ch 462 §2 (AB 2448), effective January 1, 2009, operative July 1, 2009.

§68634. Processing and determination of fee waiver applications in trial courts

(a) This section applies to the processing and determination of fee waiver applications in the trial courts.

(b) All applications for an initial fee waiver shall be accepted for filing. If an applicant submits an application without providing all required information to complete the form, the clerk may request that the applicant supply the omitted information, but shall not refuse to file the application, or refuse to file any pleadings accompanying the application, on the ground that the fee has not been paid. The clerk shall not request that the applicant furnish information that is not required on the Judicial Council fee waiver application form. At the time the application is submitted, the clerk shall not request that the applicant provide documents to support the information other than those required under Section 68633.

(c) If a person has filed an application for an initial fee waiver, the person shall be permitted to file his or her pleading or other papers immediately, without paying any fees.

(d) The court may delegate to the clerk the authority to grant applications for an initial fee waiver that meet the standards of eligibility and application requirements set forth in Sections 68632 and 68633. The court shall not delegate to a clerk the authority to deny or to partially grant an application for an initial fee waiver.

(e) The fee waiver application shall be determined without regard to the substance of the applicant's pleading or other paper filed, if any. On review of an application for an initial fee waiver the court shall take the following actions, as applicable:

(1) Grant the application if the information provided on the application establishes that the applicant meets the criteria for eligibility and application requirements set forth in Sections 68632 and 68633.

(2) Deny the application if the application is incomplete. If the application is denied on this basis, the applicant shall be given notice of the specific reason for denial and a reasonable opportunity to submit a revised application.

(3) Deny the application if the information provided on the application conclusively establishes that the applicant is not eligible for an initial fee waiver under Section 68632 on the grounds requested. If the application is denied on this basis, the applicant shall be given notice of the specific reason for denial and a reasonable opportunity to request a hearing. The applicant may submit additional information at the hearing.

(4) Set an eligibility hearing if the court has good reason to doubt the veracity of the factual statements in the application. The applicant shall be given 10 days' notice of the hearing and the specific reason the court doubts the veracity of the factual statements. The court may require that specified, reasonably available, additional information be provided concerning the truthfulness of the factual statements in the application, but shall not require submission of information that is not related to the criteria for eligibility and application requirements set forth in Sections 68632 and 68633.

(5) Set an eligibility hearing if the information provided on the application does not establish that the applicant meets the criteria for eligibility and application requirements set forth in Sections 68632 and 68633, but that information does not conclusively establish that the applicant is not eligible for an initial fee waiver on the grounds requested. The applicant shall be given 10 days' notice of the hearing and the specific reason why the court has not granted the application. The court may require that specified, reasonably available, additional information be provided, but shall not require submission of information that is not related to the criteria for eligibility and application requirements set forth in Sections 68632 and 68633.

After notice and an opportunity to be heard, the court may require an applicant under subdivision (c) of Section 68632 to pay a portion of court fees, or to pay court fees over a period of time or under some other equitable arrangement that meets the criteria of subdivision (c) of Section 68632. The court shall give a written statement of reasons if an application is denied in whole or in part.

(f) An application for an initial fee waiver is deemed granted five court days after it is filed, unless before that time, the court gives notice of action on the application as provided in subdivision (e). Any delay by the court in processing an application to initially waive court fees and costs does not count against any time limits affecting the pleadings or other papers that the applicant timely filed.

(g) If an application is denied in whole or in part, the applicant shall pay the court fees and costs that ordinarily would be charged, or make the partial payment as ordered by the court, within 10 days after the clerk gives notice of the denial, unless within that time the applicant submits a new application or requests a hearing under subdivision (e). If the applicant does not pay on time, the clerk shall void the papers that were filed without payment of the court fees and costs.

(h) A person who applies for an initial fee waiver shall indicate whether he or she has filed a prior application for an initial fee waiver in the same case within the previous six months and shall attach a copy, if one is reasonably available. **Leg.H.** Added Stats 2008 ch 462 §2 (AB 2448), effective January 1, 2009, operative July 1, 2009.

§68634.5. Processing and determination of fee waiver applications in appellate courts

(a) This section applies to the processing and determination of fee waiver applications in the appellate courts.

(b) All completed applications for a fee waiver shall be accepted for filing. If an application is submitted without all required information filled out on the form, the clerk may return the application to the applicant and request that the applicant supply the omitted information, but shall not refuse to file any paper accompanying the application on the ground that the application is incomplete or the fee has not been paid. The clerk shall not request that the applicant furnish information that is not required on the Judicial Council fee waiver application form. At the time the application is submitted, the clerk shall not request that the applicant provide documents to support the information other than those required under Section 68633.

(c) A person shall be permitted to file his or her papers immediately, even if the person does not present the filing fee, or an application for, or order granting, a fee waiver.

(d) The court may delegate to the clerk the authority to grant applications for a fee waiver that meet the standards of eligibility and application requirements set forth in Sections 68632 and 68633. The court shall not delegate to a clerk the authority to deny an application for a fee waiver.

(e) The fee waiver application shall be determined without regard to the substance of any other paper filed by the applicant. On review of an application for a fee waiver, the court shall take the following actions, as applicable:

(1) Grant the application if the information provided on the application establishes that the applicant meets the criteria for eligibility and application requirements set forth in Sections 68632 and 68633.

(2) Deny the application if the application is incomplete. If the application is denied on this basis, the applicant shall be given notice of the specific reason for denial and a reasonable opportunity to submit a revised application.

(3) Deny the application if the information provided on the application conclusively establishes that the applicant is not eligible for a fee waiver under Section 68632 on the grounds requested. If the application is denied on this basis, the applicant shall be given notice of the specific reason for denial and a reasonable opportunity to submit additional information related to the criteria for eligibility and application requirements.

(4) If the court concludes that there is a substantial evidentiary question regarding the applicant's eligibility, the court:

(A) May require the applicant to provide specified, reasonably available, additional information concerning the factual statements in the application, but shall not require submission of information that is not related to the criteria for eligibility and application requirements set forth in Sections 68632 and 68633.

(B) May set a hearing to consider evidence concerning the applicant's eligibility.

(C) Shall give a written statement of reasons if an application is denied.

(f) An application for a fee waiver is deemed granted five court days after it is filed, unless before that time, the court gives notice of action on the application as provided in subdivision (e).

(g) If an application is denied, the applicant shall pay the court fees and costs that ordinarily would be charged within 10 days after the clerk gives notice of the denial, unless within that time, the court grants a fee waiver based on a new application or additional information provided by the applicant under subdivision (e). The clerk shall notify the applicant of the consequences for failure to pay the court fees.

(h) A person who applies for an initial fee waiver shall indicate whether he or she has filed a prior application for a fee waiver in the same case and shall attach a copy, if one is reasonably available. **Leg.H.** Added Stats 2008 ch 462 §2 (AB 2448), effective January 1, 2009, operative July 1, 2009.

§68635. Waivers of trial court fees

(a) This section applies only to waivers of trial court fees.

(b) Notwithstanding any other provision of this article, a person who is sentenced to the state prison or confined in a county jail shall pay the full amount of the trial court filing fees and costs to the extent provided in this section.

(c) To apply for an initial fee waiver, a person who is sentenced to the state prison or confined in a county jail shall complete, under penalty of perjury, a Judicial Council application form giving the current address of the inmate and a statement that he or she is incarcerated, together with a statement of account for any moneys due to the inmate for the six-month period immediately preceding the application. The form shall be certified by the appropriate official of the Department of Corrections and Rehabilitation or a county jail.

(d) When the pleadings or other papers are filed, the court shall assess and, if funds exist, collect as partial payment, a partial filing fee of 20 percent of the greater of either of the following:

(1) The average monthly deposits to the inmate's account.

(2) The average monthly balance in the inmate's account for the six-month period immediately preceding the application.

(e) After the initial filing fee is partially paid, the inmate shall make monthly payments of 20 percent of the preceding month's income credited to the inmate's account. The Department of Corrections and Rehabilitation, or a county jail, shall forward payments from this account to the clerk of the court each time the amount in the account exceeds ten dollars ($10) until the filing fees are paid in full.

(f) The fees collected by the court under this section shall not exceed the amount of the fees that would be charged to a person who is not incarcerated.

(g) The court may delegate to a clerk the authority to process requests for fee waivers from inmates under this section.

(h) An inmate shall not be prohibited from filing pleadings or other papers solely because the inmate has no assets and no means to partially pay the initial filing fee. **Leg.H.** Added Stats 2008 ch 462 §2 (AB 2448), effective January 1, 2009, operative July 1, 2009.

§68636. Granting of initial fee waiver—Notification requirement of change in financial condition; Hearing to determine status of court fee waiver; Obtaining court services in bad faith

(a) After the court has granted an initial fee waiver in whole or in part, and before final disposition of the case, the person who received the initial fee waiver shall notify the court within five days of any change in financial circumstances that affects his or her ability to pay all or a portion of the court fees and costs that were initially waived.

(b) If, before or at the time of final disposition of the case, the court obtains information, including information derived from the court file, suggesting that a person whose fees and costs were initially waived is not entitled to a fee waiver, or that the person's financial condition has changed so that he or she is no longer eligible for a fee waiver, the court may require the person to appear at a court hearing by giving the applicant no less than 10 days' written notice of the hearing and the specific reasons why the initial fee waiver might be reconsidered. The court may require the person to provide reasonably available evidence, including financial information, to support his or her eligibility for the fee waiver, but shall not require submission of information that is not related to the criteria for eligibility and application requirements set forth in Sections 68632 and 68633. The court shall not conduct a hearing pursuant to this subdivision more often than once every six months.

(c) At the time of final disposition of the case, the court may give notice that a person whose fees and costs were initially waived is required to appear at a court hearing by giving the applicant no less than 10 days' written notice of the hearing. The court may require the person to provide reasonably available evidence, including financial information, to support his or her eligibility for the fee waiver, but shall not require submission of information that is not related to the criteria for eligibility and application requirements set forth in Sections 68632 and 68633.

(d) In conducting a hearing under subdivision (b) or (c), if the court determines that the person was not entitled to the initial fee waiver at the time it was granted, the court may order the waiver withdrawn retroactively. The court may order the person to pay to the court immediately, or over a period of time, all or part of the fees that were initially waived. The court shall give the person a minimum of 10 court days to begin paying the full or partial fees.

(e) In conducting a hearing under subdivision (a), (b), or (c), if the court determines that the person's financial circumstances have changed since the grant of the initial fee waiver or partial initial fee waiver, the court may order the fee waiver withdrawn prospectively from the time that the person no longer was eligible for a fee waiver. The court may order the person to pay to the court immediately, or over a period of time, all or part of the fees that were waived since the time that the person no longer was eligible for a fee waiver. The court may order the person to begin paying all or part of the court fees assessed for future activities in the case. The court shall give the person a minimum of 10 court days to begin paying the full or partial fees.

(f) If the court obtains information suggesting that a litigant whose fees and costs were initially waived is obtaining court services in bad faith, or for an improper purpose such as to harass or cause unnecessary delay, or to needlessly increase the costs of litigation, the court may give notice that the litigant is required to appear at a court hearing to consider whether limitations should be placed on court services for which fees were initially waived. **Leg.H.** Added Stats 2008 ch 462 §2 (AB 2448), effective January 1, 2009, operative July 1, 2009.

§68637. Waivers of trial court fees

(a) This section applies only to waivers of trial court fees.

(b)(1) If a party whose trial court fees and costs were initially waived is a prevailing party within the meaning of Section 1032 of the Code of Civil Procedure, the judgment or dismissal entered in favor of the party whose fees and costs were initially waived shall include an order requiring that the party against whom judgment or dismissal has been entered pay to the court the waived fees and costs. The court may refuse to enter a partial or full satisfaction of a judgment until an accompanying order requiring payment of waived fees and costs has been satisfied.

(2) A party petitioning the court to enter satisfaction of judgment shall declare, under penalty of perjury, that any order requiring payment of waived fees and costs has been satisfied.

(3) This subdivision does not apply to any of the following:

(A) Unlawful detainer cases.

(B) Family law matters, for which recovery of fees is subject to subdivisions (d) and (e).

(C) Cases in which the judgment or dismissal is entered against a party whose fees and costs were initially waived.

(c) If a party in a civil case whose trial court fees and costs were initially waived recovers ten thousand dollars ($10,000) or more in value by way of settlement, compromise, arbitration award, mediation settlement, or other recovery, the waived fees and costs shall be paid to the court out of the settlement, compromise, award, or other recovery.

(1) The court shall have a lien on any settlement, compromise, award, or other recovery in the amount of all the court fees and costs initially waived.

(2) The waived fees and costs shall first be paid to the court before the party whose fees and costs were initially waived receives anything of value under the settlement, compromise, award, or other recovery.

(3) Notice of the lien shall be given to the parties under rules and on forms adopted by the Judicial Council, and the Judicial Council shall provide by rule the procedures by which a party subject to a lien may determine the amount of the lien.

(4) The court may refuse to enter a petition for dismissal in the case until the lien is satisfied. A party filing a petition for dismissal shall declare, under penalty of perjury, that the lien has been paid, or that any settlement, compromise, award, or other recovery has a value of less than ten thousand dollars ($10,000).

(5) In a case in which an initial waiver of fees and costs was granted, or if a petition to dismiss the case is filed without the declaration, the court may issue an order to show cause why the lien should not be enforced and why the court should not enter a judgment making the parties jointly and severally liable to the court for initially waived fees and costs.

(d) If a judgment or an order to pay support is entered in a family law case, the trial court shall consider, based on the information in the court file, whether a party who did not receive a fee waiver has the ability to pay all or part of the other party's waived fees. Any order for the payment of the other party's waived fees shall be made payable only after all current support and all accrued arrears owed by the party who did not receive the fee waiver have been paid. If the court orders payment of the other party's waived fees, and the party required to pay is not present in court at the time judgment is entered, the party required to pay shall be given notice and an opportunity for a hearing to request that the court set aside the order to pay fees. A request for a hearing shall be made in writing within 30 days after service of the notice of the court order. If a request for hearing is made, the order for payment of initially waived fees shall not be enforced until after the hearing.

(e) If a judgment is entered in a family law case, the trial court shall consider, based on the information in the court file, whether a party's circumstances have changed so that it is reasonable to require a party who received an initial fee waiver to pay all or part of the fees that were initially waived. In making this determination, the court shall use the criteria for eligibility set forth in Section 68632. In considering whether a child or spousal support order constitutes a change of circumstances allowing the party to pay fees, the court also shall consider the likelihood that the support obligor will remit the payments ordered by the court. If a support order is the primary basis for the court's finding of changed circumstances, the court shall order the support obligor to pay the previously waived fees subject to the provisions of subdivision (d). When the court orders the party to pay all or part of the fees that were initially waived, the party required to pay shall be given notice and an opportunity for a hearing to request that the court set aside the order to pay fees. A request for a hearing shall be made in writing within 30 days after service of the notice of the court order. If a request for hearing is made, the order for payment of initially waived fees shall not be enforced until after the hearing. **Leg.H.** Added Stats 2008 ch 462 §2 (AB 2448), effective January 1, 2009, operative July 1, 2009.

§68638. Issuances of abstract of judgment or writ of execution

(a) The trial court may execute on any order for payment of initially waived fees and costs in the same manner as on a judgment in a civil action. The court may issue an abstract of judgment, a writ of execution, or both, for all of the following:

(1) Recovery of the initially waived fees and costs as ordered.

(2) Fees for issuing the abstract of judgment, writ of execution, or both.

(3) A twenty-five-dollar ($25) fee for administering this subdivision.

(4) An amount due to levying officers for serving and collecting on the judgment that will all be added to the writ of execution.

(b) Upon collection, the initially waived fees and costs, the fees for issuing the abstract of judgment and writ of execution, and the twenty-five-dollar ($25) administrative fee shall be remitted to the court. Thereafter, the amount due to the levying officers for serving and collecting on the judgment shall be paid. **Leg.H.** Added Stats 2008 ch 462 §2 (AB 2448), effective January 1, 2009, operative July 1, 2009.

§68639. Expiration of initial fee waiver

An initial fee waiver shall expire 60 days after the judgment, dismissal, or other final disposition of the case. **Leg.H.** Added Stats 2008 ch 462 §2 (AB 2448), effective January 1, 2009, operative July 1, 2009.

§68640. Adoption of rules allowing litigants to pay court fees in installments

The Judicial Council may adopt a rule of court to allow litigants who are not eligible for a fee waiver to pay court fees in installments. **Leg.H.** Added Stats 2008 ch 462 §2 (AB 2448), effective January 1, 2009, operative July 1, 2009.

§68641. Adoption of rules and forms to establish uniform procedures

The Judicial Council shall adopt rules and forms to establish uniform procedures to implement this article, including, but not limited to, procedures for all of the following:

(a) Considering and determining applications to proceed without paying court fees and costs at every stage of the proceedings, including at the trial and appellate levels of the court.

(b) Prescribing the court fees and costs that may be waived at every stage of the proceedings.

(c) Giving notice of lien and hearings for reconsideration and recovery of initially waived fees and costs.

(d) Collecting waived fees and costs.

(e) Requesting a hearing when an application is denied.

(f) Any other procedures necessary to implement the provisions of this article. **Leg.H.** Added Stats 2008 ch 462 §2 (AB 2448), effective January 1, 2009, operative July 1, 2009.

ARTICLE 7
Ability to Pay Program

§ 68645. Online tool for adjudication of infraction violations

The Judicial Council shall develop an online tool for adjudicating infraction violations, including ability-to-pay determinations. The Judicial Council shall implement the tool on a phased schedule and shall make this tool available statewide on or before June 30, 2024. A defendant, a designee of the defendant, or the defendant's attorney, may, upon certification, access the online tool. A defendant shall not be compelled to use this online tool. **Leg.H.** Added Stats 2021 ch 79 §8 (AB 143), effective July 16, 2021. Amended Stats 2021 ch 257 §9 (AB 177), effective September 23, 2021.

§ 68645.1. Alternatives to personal appearance

For all infraction violations for which a personal appearance is not required, a court may allow defendants to agree to forfeit bail, plead guilty or nolo contendere, request an ability-to-pay determination, or otherwise adjudicate matters through the use of technology.

(a) The date that the defendant agrees to forfeit bail, plead guilty, or plead nolo contendere shall be reported as the date of conviction for all purposes.

(b) If a defendant requests an ability-to-pay determination, the matter shall be considered adjudicated for purposes of that determination when the defendant agrees to forfeit bail or pleads guilty or nolo contendere.

(c) When a defendant agrees to forfeit bail, plead guilty or nolo contendere through the online tool, or requests an ability-to-pay determination, the defendant has appeared within the meaning of subdivision (a) of former Section 40509 and subdivision (a) of former Section 40509.5 of the Vehicle Code, and the court shall immediately file with the Department of Motor Vehicles the required certificate to recall any failure to appear notifications that have been sent for the citation. **Leg.H.** Added Stats 2021 ch 79 §8 (AB 143), effective July 16, 2021. Amended Stats 2022 ch 800 §2 (AB 2746), effective January 1, 2023.

§ 68645.15. Traffic violator school eligibility

A defendant's request for an ability-to-pay determination through the online tool shall not impact their eligibility to attend traffic violator school pursuant to Section 42005 of the Vehicle Code. **Leg.H.** Added Stats 2022 ch 191 §1 (SB 1096), effective January 1, 2023.

§ 68645.2. Deadline for offering online tool; Burden and criteria for establishment of inability to pay; Online tool payment recommendations; Language requirements

(a) By June 30, 2024, every court shall offer online ability-to-pay determinations using the tool developed by the Judicial Council. The following shall apply to ability-to-pay determinations made pursuant to this article:

(1) The defendant has the burden of establishing the inability to pay. Courts shall establish criteria for the determination of an inability to pay, and, in doing so, shall consider certain factors including, at a minimum, all of the following:

(A) Receipt of any of the public benefits listed in subdivision (a) of Section 68632.

(B) A monthly income of 125 percent or less of the current poverty guidelines, as updated periodically in the Federal Register by the United States Department of Health and Human Services pursuant to Section 9902 of Title 42 of the United States Code.

(2) The court has discretion to make an order consistent with the defendant's present and reasonably discernible future financial circumstances. Except as provided for in paragraph (4), the court is not required to make express findings as to the factors bearing on the determination or the amount it orders payable by the defendant.

(3) Based on any ability-to-pay determination, a court may do any of the following:

(A) Waive or reduce the sum of the total amount due for an infraction violation. Notwithstanding any other law, if the total amount due is reduced, the revenues collected shall be distributed on a pro rata basis.

(B) Extend the time for payment or provide for payment on an installment plan, including those amounts due after any reduction under subparagraph (A).

(C) Allow the defendant to complete community service in lieu of the total amount due. If a defendant qualifies for a reduction in the total amount due, the court may allow the defendant to complete the community service in lieu of the payment on the reduced amount.

(D) Suspend the total amount due in whole or in part.

(E) Offer an alternative disposition.

(4) The online tool shall recommend a reduction of 50 percent or more of the total amount due for all defendants who are in receipt of benefits described in subparagraph (A) of paragraph (1). The court shall make express findings if it deviates from the online tool recommendation by ordering a defendant to pay an amount greater than the recommendation pursuant to this paragraph.

(5) The online tool shall recommend a payment of no more than twenty-five dollars ($25) per month for a defendant who is eligible for a reduction pursuant to paragraph (3) and requests an installment plan.

(6) For purposes of this section, the "total amount due" is the sum of the base fine, penalty assessments, civil assessments, and fees, including mandatory fees, owed and unpaid by the defendant.

(7) As feasible, courts shall notify defendants of the result of the ability-to-pay determination within 30 days.

(8) A defendant is not required to submit bail or pay any fines or fees prior to an ability-to-pay determination.

(9) A court or county shall not charge an administrative fee to an individual for requesting an ability-to-pay determination or participating in an installment payment plan, on a nondelinquent or delinquent account, ordered pursuant to this chapter.

(10) A court or county may recover costs associated with the administration of all installment payment plans ordered under this chapter through a comprehensive collection program pursuant to subdivision (d) of Section 1463.007 of the Penal Code. Recovered costs shall not exceed thirty-five dollars ($35) per nondelinquent installment plan approved.

(b) If a court is using the online tool, paragraphs (1) to (3), inclusive, and paragraphs (6) to (10), inclusive, of subdivision (a) apply to all ability-to-pay determinations conducted through means other than the online tool, which includes paper submissions or in-person applications. When an ability-to-pay determination is made through means other than the online tool, the court shall follow the recommendations stated in paragraphs (4) and (5) of subdivision (a), but may deviate from the recommendation in paragraph (4) of subdivision (a), as provided therein.

(c) The online tool shall provide information in English, Spanish, and any other languages the Judicial Council chooses.

(d) This section does not preclude a court that has not yet adopted online ability-to-pay determinations from adopting procedures or local rules in accordance with this section, unless the Judicial Council adopts rules of court or forms for purposes of this section. **Leg.H.** Added Stats 2021 ch 79 §8 (AB 143), effective July 16, 2021. Amended Stats 2022 ch 57 §7 (AB 199), effective June 30, 2022; Stats 2023 ch 131 §100 (AB 1754), effective January 1, 2024.

§ 68645.3. Electronic verification of public benefits; Notice requirements; Determinations by clerk of the court

(a) A court may allow the online tool to electronically verify through encrypted transmittal whether the defendant receives public benefits, defined as any of the public benefits listed in subdivision (a) of Section 68632, by accessing a statewide, county, or other political subdivision of the state database, including the State Department of Social Services.

(b) The court shall obtain the defendant's consent before the online application may electronically verify benefits.

(c) The online application process shall inform the defendant of all of the following information:

(1) A defendant has the burden of establishing the defendant's inability to pay.

(2) The online verification is one of the possible means of substantiating the inability to pay.

(3) Other accepted means of verifying inability to pay.

(4) A defendant may upload other evidence in addition to or in lieu of the verification results.

(d) If the court is unable to verify that a defendant receives benefits as described in this section, the defendant may submit other evidence of an inability to pay to the court.

(e) Each court, by adopting a local rule, may authorize the clerk of the court to make ability-to-pay determinations. If a court authorizes the clerk of the court to make those determinations, both of the following apply:

(1) The determinations shall be based on specified criteria as established by the court and posted on its internet website. The criteria may include whether the defendant is receiving public benefits, including those listed in subdivision (a) of Section 68632. The court may establish criteria that waive or reduce the sum of the base fine, penalty assessments, civil assessments, and fees, including mandatory fees, owed by the defendant, by a specified amount, by a specified percentage, or by other specified criteria.

(2) If the clerk of the court denies the reduction, the defendant has the right to a review of the decision by a judicial officer in the trial court. **Leg.H.** Added Stats 2021 ch 79 §8 (AB 143), effective July 16, 2021.

§ 68645.4. Trials by declaration

(a) A court may offer trials by declaration through an online tool for all infractions for which a personal appearance is not required. If a court offers online trials pursuant to this section, all of the following shall apply, notwithstanding Section 40902 of the Vehicle Code:

(1) A defendant shall elect to have an online trial prior to the appearance date indicated on the notice to appear, unless the court grants the defendant an extension, or the court permits the defendant to have a trial at a later date.

(2) If a defendant elects to have a trial through the online tool pursuant to this section, the court shall not require the defendant to submit bail in advance, unless the court makes express findings as to why a particular defendant shall be required to submit bail.

(3) Testimony and other relevant evidence may be introduced in the form of a notice to appear, a business record or receipt, a sworn declaration of the arresting officer, and a sworn declaration by the defendant.

(4) If a defendant elects to have a trial through the online tool pursuant to this section, the defendant shall not have a right to a trial de novo.

(b) If a court elects to offer online trials pursuant to this section, it shall also make trials by written declaration available to defendants, and paragraphs (1) to (4), inclusive, of subdivision (a) shall apply to all trials by written declaration.

(c) A court may adopt local rules or forms to be consistent with this section, and the rules and forms shall govern proceedings pursuant to this section unless the Judicial Council adopts rules of court or forms for purposes of this article. **Leg.H.** Added Stats 2021 ch 79 §8 (AB 143), effective July 16, 2021. Amended Stats 2022 ch 57 §8 (AB 199), effective June 30, 2022.

§ 68645.5. Annual report

(a) No later than February 1, 2022, and annually until February 1, 2025, the Judicial Council shall provide to the Legislature a report including the following information from participating courts that have adopted online ability-to-pay determinations for infraction violations:

(1) Total number of infraction filings.

(2) Total number of ability-to-pay requests made through:

(A) The online tool.

(B) Other locally established ability-to-pay procedures.

(3) Demographic information on defendants using the online tool as reported by the defendant, including but not limited to, income level, public benefits status, race or ethnicity or both, when feasible, and ZIP Code.

(4) The total amount of initial fines and fees assessed for individuals making ability-to-pay requests.

(5) The total amount of adjusted fines and fees recommended by the online tool.

(6) The total amount of fines and fees ordered through:

(A) The online tool.

(B) Other locally established ability-to-pay procedures.

(7) Of the total amount of fines and fees ordered, the total amount collected from:

(A) Online requests.

(B) Requests via locally established ability-to-pay procedures.

(8) The number of payment plans ordered through the online tool.

(9) The number of online trials by declaration conducted in participating courts.

(b) The Judicial Council shall submit the report required pursuant to subdivision (a) in compliance with Section 9795.

(c) In the report due to the Legislature on February 1, 2023, and in addition to the information required in subdivision (a), the Judicial Council shall provide information on the first seven pilot courts, including implementation challenges, the overall effectiveness of the programs in these courts, and how those pilots informed the implementation in subsequent courts. **Leg.H.** Added Stats 2021 ch 79 §8 (AB 143), effective July 16, 2021. Amended Stats 2022 ch 57 §9 (AB 199), effective June 30, 2022.

§68645.7. Annual funding estimate

(a) On or before January 10 of each year, the Department of Finance, in consultation with the Judicial Council, shall estimate the level of funding needed to backfill the judicial branch for the amount reduced based upon the ability-to-pay determinations granted to defendants pursuant to this article. The estimate shall be developed by the Department of Finance, in conjunction with the Judicial Council, and based on the data provided to the Judicial Council by the trial courts as required in subdivision (b). The Department of Finance shall distribute the funds to the judicial branch appropriated for that purpose in the annual Budget Act or any other act approved by the Legislature. The department shall publish its estimate and transmit it to the Legislature at the time of the submission of the Governor's Budget pursuant to Section 12 of Article IV of the California Constitution.

(b) The Judicial Council shall collect data from the trial courts necessary to request funding from the Department of Finance for the purposes of subdivision (a). Only trial courts that provide data in accordance with the method required by the Judicial Council are eligible for this funding. **Leg.H.** Added Stats 2021 ch 79 §8 (AB 143), effective July 16, 2021.

CHAPTER 2.1
CIVIL LEGAL REPRESENTATION

§68650. Citation of chapter

This chapter shall be known, and may be cited, as the Sargent Shriver Civil Counsel Act. **Leg.H.** Added Stats 2009 ch 457 §6 (AB 590), effective January 1, 2010.

Prior Law: Former Gov C §68650, relating to effect of Rules of Court governing employment of trial court personnel, was added Stats 1997 ch 857 §1 and repealed January 1, 2002, by the terms of former Gov C §68656.

There was another section of this number, which was added Stats 1997 ch 869 §3 and renumbered Gov C §68660 by Stats 1998 ch 485 §95.

§68651. Appointment of counsel for low-income parties in specified civil actions in selected courts; Civil representation programs; Funding; Donations

(a) Legal counsel shall be appointed to represent low-income parties in civil matters involving critical issues affecting basic human needs in those specified courts selected by the Judicial Council as provided in this section.

(b)(1) Subject to funding specifically provided for this purpose pursuant to subdivision (e) of Section 70626 and donations provided pursuant to subdivision (e), the Judicial Council shall develop one or more programs in selected courts pursuant to a competitive grant process and a request for proposals. Programs authorized under this section shall provide representation of counsel for low-income persons, regardless of their citizenship or immigration status, who require legal services in civil matters involving housing-related matters, domestic violence and civil harassment restraining orders, probate conservatorships, guardianships of the person, elder abuse, or actions by a parent to obtain legal or physical custody of a child, as well as providing court procedures, personnel, training, and case management and administration methods that reflect best practices to ensure unrepresented parties in those cases have meaningful access to justice, and to gather information on the outcomes associated with providing these services, to guard against the involuntary waiver of those rights or their disposition by default. These programs should be designed to address the substantial inequities in timely and effective access to justice that often give rise to an undue risk of erroneous decision because of the nature and complexity of the law and the proceeding or disparities between the parties in education, sophistication, language proficiency, legal representation, access to self-help, and alternative dispute resolution services. In order to ensure that the scarce funds available for the programs are used to serve the most critical cases and the parties least able to access the courts without representation, eligibility for representation shall be limited to clients whose household income falls at or below 200 percent of the federal poverty level. Programs shall impose asset limitations consistent with their existing practices in order to ensure optimal use of funds.

(2)(A) In light of the significant percentage of parties who are unrepresented in family law matters, proposals to provide counsel in child custody cases should be considered among the highest priorities for funding.

(B) Up to 20 percent of available funds shall be directed to programs regarding civil matters involving actions under the Family Code, subject to the priority set forth in subparagraph (A). This subparagraph shall not apply to distributions made pursuant to paragraph (3).

(3) Amounts collected pursuant to subdivision (e) of Section 70626 in excess of the total amount transferred to the Trial Court Trust Fund in the 2011–12 fiscal year pursuant to subparagraph (E) of paragraph (1) of subdivision (c) of Section 68085.1 and subdivision (e) of Section 70626 shall be distributed by the Judicial Council without regard to subparagraph (B) of paragraph (2). Those amounts may be distributed by the Judicial Council as set forth in this subdivision. If the funds are to be distributed to new programs, the Judicial Council shall distribute those amounts pursuant to the process set forth in this subdivision.

(4) Each program shall be a partnership between the court, a qualified legal services project, as defined by subdivision (a) of Section 6213 of the Business and Professions Code, that shall serve as the lead agency for case assessment and direction, and other legal services providers in the community who are able to provide the services for the program. The lead legal services agency shall be the central point of contact for receipt of referrals to the program and to make determinations of eligibility based on uniform criteria. The lead legal services agency shall be responsible for providing representation to the clients or referring the matter to one of the organizations or individual providers with whom the lead legal services agency contracts to provide the service. Funds received by a qualified legal services project shall not qualify as expenditures for the purposes of the distribution of funds pursuant to Section 6216 of the Business and Professions Code. To the extent practical, the lead legal services agency shall identify and make use of pro bono services in order to maximize available services efficiently and economically. Recognizing that not all indigent parties can be afforded representation, even when they have meritorious cases, the court partner shall, as a corollary to the services provided by the lead legal services agency, be responsible for providing procedures, personnel, training, and case management and administration practices that reflect best practices to ensure unrepresented parties meaningful access to justice and to guard against the involuntary waiver of rights, as well as to encourage fair and expeditious voluntary dispute resolution, consistent with principles of judicial neutrality.

(5) The participating programs shall be selected by a committee appointed by the Judicial Council with representation from key stakeholder groups, including judicial officers, legal services providers, and others, as appropriate. The committee shall assess the applicants' capacity for success, innovation, and efficiency, including, but not limited to, the likelihood that the program would deliver quality representation in an effective manner that would meet critical needs in the community and address the needs of the court with regard to access to justice and calendar management, and the unique local unmet needs for representation in the community. Programs approved pursuant to this section shall initially be authorized for a three-year period, commencing July 1, 2011, subject to

renewal for a period to be determined by the Judicial Council, in consultation with the participating program in light of the program's capacity and success. After the initial three-year period, the Judicial Council shall distribute any future funds available as the result of the termination or nonrenewal of a program pursuant to the process set forth in this subdivision. Programs shall be selected on the basis of whether, in the cases proposed for service, the persons to be assisted are likely to be opposed by a party who is represented by counsel. The Judicial Council shall also consider the following factors in selecting the programs:

(A) The likelihood that representation in the proposed case type tends to affect whether a party prevails or otherwise obtains a significantly more favorable outcome in a matter in which they would otherwise frequently have judgment entered against them or suffer the deprivation of the basic human need at issue.

(B) The likelihood of reducing the risk of erroneous decision.

(C) The nature and severity of potential consequences for the unrepresented party regarding the basic human need at stake if representation is not provided.

(D) Whether the provision of legal services may eliminate or reduce the potential need for, and cost of, public social services regarding the basic human need at stake for the client and others in the client's household.

(E) The unmet need for legal services in the geographic area to be served.

(F) The availability and effectiveness of other types of court services, such as self-help.

(G)(i) The program's plan for providing service to all potential clients regardless of immigration status.

(ii) When renewing grants for existing programs whose lead legal services agency is prohibited from serving certain persons on account of their citizenship or immigration status, the Judicial Council shall encourage the programs to explore ways to expand access to legal services for those persons, including potential opportunities for the lead legal services agency to contract with organizations or individual providers that are not subject to the same prohibition and to include them as a member of the local advisory committee.

(iii) When selecting among new program proposals, the Judicial Council shall give additional consideration to programs that propose to establish or assist in the development of program elements that would newly provide access to legal services regardless of immigration status in that region.

(6) Each applicant shall do all of the following:

(A) Identify the nature of the partnership between the court, the lead legal services agency, and the other agencies or other providers that would work within the program.

(B) Describe the referral protocols to be used, the criteria that would be employed in case assessment, why those cases were selected, the manner to address conflicts without violating attorney-client privilege when adverse parties are seeking representation through the program, and the means for serving potential clients who need assistance with English.

(C) Describe how the program would be administered, including how the data collection requirements would be met without causing an undue burden on the courts, clients, or the providers, the particular objectives of the project, strategies to evaluate their success in meeting those objectives, and the means by which the program would serve the particular needs of the community, including how the program will provide representation to limited-English-speaking clients as well as whether and how the program will ensure that services are available to all individuals seeking services regardless of immigration status.

(7) To ensure the most effective use of the funding available, the lead legal services agency shall serve as a hub for all referrals, and the point at which decisions are made about which referrals will be served and by whom. Referrals shall emanate from the court, as well as from the other agencies providing services through the program, and shall be directed to the lead legal services agency for review. That agency, or another agency or attorney in the event of conflict, shall collect the information necessary to assess whether the case should be served. In performing that case assessment, the agency shall determine the relative need for representation of the litigant, including all of the following:

(A) Case complexity.

(B) Whether the other party is represented.

(C) The adversarial nature of the proceeding.

(D) The availability and effectiveness of other types of services, such as self-help, in light of the potential client and the nature of the case.

(E) Language issues.

(F) Disability access issues.

(G) Literacy issues.

(H) The merits of the case.

(I) The nature and severity of potential consequences for the potential client if representation is not provided.

(J) Whether the provision of legal services may eliminate or reduce the need for, and cost of, public social services for the potential client and others in the potential client's household.

(8) If both parties to a dispute are financially eligible for representation, each proposal shall ensure that representation for both sides is evaluated. In these and other cases in which conflict issues arise, the lead legal services agency shall have referral protocols with other agencies and providers, such as a private attorney panel, to address those conflicts.

(9) Each program shall be responsible for keeping records on the referrals accepted and those not accepted for representation, and the reasons for each, in a manner that does not violate privileged communications between the agency and the prospective client. Each program shall be provided with standardized data collection tools and shall be required to track case information for each referral to allow the evaluation to measure the number of cases served, the level of service required, and the outcomes for the clients in each case. In addition to this information on the effect of the representation on the clients, data shall be collected regarding the outcomes for the trial courts.

(10) A local advisory committee shall be formed for each program, to include representatives of the bench and court administration, the lead legal services agency, and the other agencies or providers that are part of the local program team. The role of the advisory committee is to facilitate the administration of the local program and to ensure that the program is fulfilling its objectives. In addition, the committee shall resolve any issues that arise during the course of the program, including issues concerning case eligibility, and recommend changes in program administration in response to implementation challenges. The committee shall meet at least monthly for the first six months of the program, and no less than quarterly for the duration of the funding period. Each authorized program shall catalog changes to the program made during the three-year period based on its experiences with best practices in serving the eligible population.

(c) The Judicial Council shall conduct a study to demonstrate the effectiveness and continued need for the programs established pursuant to this section and shall report its findings and recommendations to the Governor and the Legislature every five years, commencing June 1, 2020. The study shall report on the percentage of funding by case type and shall include data on the impact of counsel on equal access to justice and the effect on court administration and efficiency, and enhanced coordination between courts and other government service providers and community resources. This report shall describe the benefits of providing representation to those who were previously not represented, both for the clients and the courts, as well as strategies and recommendations for maximizing the benefit of that representation in the future. The report shall describe and include data, if available, on the impact of the programs on families and children. The report also shall include an assessment of the continuing unmet needs and, if available, data regarding those unmet needs.

(d) This section does not negate, alter, or limit any right to counsel in a criminal or civil action or proceeding otherwise provided by state or federal law.

(e) The Judicial Council may accept donations from public or private entities for the purpose of providing grants pursuant to this section.

Leg.H. Added Stats 2009 ch 457 §6 (AB 590), effective January 1, 2010, operative July 1, 2011. Amended Stats 2016 ch 33 §12 (SB 843), effective June 27, 2016; Stats 2019 ch 217 §2 (AB 330), effective January 1, 2020; Stats 2020 ch 370 §186 (SB 1371), effective January 1, 2021; Stats 2022 ch 486 §1 (AB 2193), effective January 1, 2023.

Prior Law: Former Gov C §68651, relating to courts' own rules to implement labor relations with recognized employee organization, was added Stats 1997 ch 857 §1and repealed January 1, 2002, by the terms of former Gov C §68656.

There was another section of this number, which was added Stats 1997 ch 869 §3 and renumbered Gov C §68661 by Stats 1998 ch 485 §96.

CHAPTER 3
THE SUPREME COURT

ARTICLE 2
The Chief Clerk

§68847. Fees to be collected in advance

The Clerk/Executive Officer of the Supreme Court shall collect in advance the fees specified in Article 4 (commencing with Section 68926) of this chapter. **Leg.H.** Added Stats 1953 ch 206 §1. Amended Stats 1963 ch 873 §1; Stats 2017 ch 36 §14 (AB 452), effective January 1, 2018.

ARTICLE 4
Fees in the Supreme Court and Courts of Appeal

§68926. Filing notice of appeal in civil case; Filing petition for writ within original civil jurisdiction; Parties other than appellant or petitioner filing first document

(a)(1) The fee for filing a notice of appeal in a civil case appealed to a court of appeal is six hundred five dollars ($605).

(2) The fee for filing a petition for a writ within the original civil jurisdiction of the Supreme Court is five hundred forty dollars ($540).

(3) The fee for filing a petition for a writ within the original civil jurisdiction of a court of appeal is six hundred five dollars ($605).

(b)(1) The fee for a party other than appellant filing its first document in a civil case appealed to a court of appeal is three hundred ninety dollars ($390).

(2) The fee for a party other than petitioner filing its first document in a writ proceeding within the original jurisdiction of the Supreme Court is three hundred ninety dollars ($390).

(3) The fee for a party other than petitioner filing its first document in a writ proceeding within the original jurisdiction of a court of appeal is three hundred ninety dollars ($390).

(c) These fees are in full, for all services, through the rendering of the judgment or the issuing of the remittitur or peremptory writ, except the fees imposed by subdivision (b) of Section 68926.1 and Section 68927. The Judicial Council may make rules governing the time and method of payment of these fees, and providing for excuse therefrom in appropriate cases. A fee may not be charged in appeals from, nor petitions for writs involving, juvenile cases or proceedings to declare a minor free from parental custody or control, or proceedings under the Lanterman-Petris-Short Act (Part 1 (commencing with Section 5000) of Division 5 of the Welfare and Institutions Code). **Leg.H.** Added Stats 1963 ch 873 §3. Amended Stats 1967 ch 17 §68; Stats 1975 ch 896 §1; Stats 1982 ch 327 §91, effective June 30, 1982; Stats 1986 ch 823 §1.2; Stats 1992 ch 1149 §2 (AB 3692), effective September 29, 1992; Stats 1999 ch 78 §55 (AB 1115), effective July 7, 1999; Stats 2003 ch 159 §15 (AB 1759), effective August 2, 2003, operative August 17, 2003; Stats 2004 ch 811 §8 (AB 3079); Stats 2011 ch 193 §2 (AB 110), effective August 30, 2011; Stats 2012 ch 41 §24 (SB 1021), effective June 27, 2012.

§68926.1. Deposit for preparation of clerk's transcript or other appeal processing or notification; Forfeiture; Additional fee

(a)(1) Upon filing a notice of appeal for which a fee is paid pursuant to Section 68926, the appellant shall deposit the sum of one hundred dollars ($100) with the clerk of the originating court. The deposit shall be credited against the amount chargeable for the preparation of the clerk's transcript or any other appeal processing or notification.

(2) The deposit shall be forfeited in the event of abandonment or dismissal of appeal prior to filing of the record in the reviewing court.

(3) The amount charged for preparation of the transcript or any deposit that is forfeited shall be distributed to the court in which it was collected.

(b) Upon filing a notice of appeal, a petition for a writ, or a petition for a hearing for which a fee is paid pursuant to subdivision (a) of Section 68926 or subdivision (a) of Section 68927, the appellant shall pay an additional fee in the amount of one hundred seventy dollars ($170). Upon filing its first document for which a fee is paid pursuant to subdivision (b) of Section 68926 or subdivision (b) of Section 68927, a party other than the appellant or petitioner is not required to pay this additional fee. The fees collected pursuant to this subdivision shall be transmitted to the State Treasury for deposit in the Appellate Court Trust Fund. **Leg.H.** Added Stats 1983 ch 493 §1. Amended Stats 1993 ch 158 §15 (AB 392), effective July 20, 1993; Stats 2003 ch 159 §16 (AB 1759), effective August 2, 2003, operative August 17, 2003; Stats 2005 ch 75 §114 (AB 145), effective July 19, 2005, operative January 1, 2006; Stats 2011 ch 193 §3 (AB 110), effective August 30, 2011.

§68927. Multiyear memorandum of understanding with superior court for court security services and operating procedures; Disputes; Resolution of disputes; Process for parties to resolve disputes

(a) The fee for filing a petition for review in a civil case in the Supreme Court after a decision in a court of appeal is five hundred forty dollars ($540).

(b) The fee for a party other than petitioner filing its first document in a civil case in the Supreme Court after a decision in a court of appeal is three hundred ninety dollars ($390).

(c) A fee may not be charged for petitions for review from decisions in juvenile cases or proceedings to declare a minor free from parental custody or control or proceedings under the Lanterman-Petris-Short Act (Part 1 (commencing with Section 5000) of Division 5 of the Welfare and Institutions Code). **Leg.H.** Added Stats 1963 ch 873 §3. Amended Stats 1967 ch 17 §69; Stats 1982 ch 327 §92, effective June 30, 1982; Stats 2003 ch 159 §17 (AB 1759), effective August 2, 2003, operative August 17, 2003; Stats 2004 ch 811 §9 (AB 3079); Stats 2005 ch 22 §107 (SB 1108), effective January 1, 2006; Stats 2011 ch 193 §5 (AB 110), effective August 30, 2011; Stats 2012 ch 41 §25 (SB 1021), effective June 27, 2012.

§68928. Copies of records or documents; Waiver of charges for copies of opinions

The fee for copies of any record or document in the office of the Clerk/Executive Officer of the Supreme Court or the Clerk/Executive Officer of a court of appeal is the prevailing commercial rate as determined by the Clerk/Executive Officer. The Supreme Court and each court of appeal may waive the charge for copies of opinions furnished to parties to the litigation and other interested persons. **Leg.H.** Added Stats 1963 ch 873 §3. Amended Stats 1967 ch 17 §70; Stats 2017 ch 36 §15 (AB 452), effective January 1, 2018.

§68929. Comparing documents requiring certificates

The fee for comparing any document requiring a certificate is five cents ($0.05) a folio, except that when the document to be compared was printed or typewritten from the same type or at the same time as the original on file and has been corrected in all respects to conform with it, such charge shall be one cent ($0.01) a folio. Such fee is in addition to the fee for the certificate. **Leg.H.** Added Stats 1963 ch 873 §3.

§68930. Certificates under seal

The fee for each certificate under seal is one dollar ($1). **Leg.H.** Added Stats 1963 ch 873 §3.

§68931. Administering oaths for verification of claims against State

There shall be no fee for administering oaths for verification of claims against the State. **Leg.H.** Added Stats 1963 ch 873 §3.

§68932. Other services; Fees of notaries public

For all other services not specified in this article the fee shall be the same as that prescribed by law for similar services by notaries public. **Leg.H.** Added Stats 1963 ch 873 §3.

§68933. Appellate Court Trust Fund; Use; Sources

(a) There is hereby established the Appellate Court Trust Fund, the proceeds of which shall be used for the purpose of funding the Supreme Court, courts of appeal, and the Judicial Council.

(b) The fund, upon appropriation by the Legislature, shall be apportioned by the Judicial Council to the courts of appeal, the Supreme Court, and the Judicial Council, as determined by the Judicial Council, taking into consideration all other funds available to each and the needs of each, in a manner that promotes equal access to the courts, ensures the ability of the courts to carry out their functions, and promotes implementation of statewide policies.

(c) Notwithstanding any other provision of law, the fees listed in subdivision (d) shall all be transmitted for deposit in the Appellate Court Trust Fund within the State Treasury.

(d) This section applies to all fees collected pursuant to Section 68926, excluding that portion subject to Section 68926.3; subdivision (b) of Section 68926.1; and Sections 68927, 68928, 68929, 68930, and 68932.

(e) The Appellate Court Trust Fund shall be invested in the Surplus Money Investment Fund and all interest earned shall be allocated to the Appellate Court Trust Fund semiannually and used as specified in this section. **Leg.H.** Added Stats 2003 ch 159 §18 (AB 1759), effective August 2, 2003, operative August 17, 2003. Amended Stats 2003 ch 757 §6 (AB 296); Stats 2023 ch 34 §8 (SB 133), effective June 30, 2023.

CHAPTER 5
THE SUPERIOR COURTS
ARTICLE 9
Official Reporters Generally

§69947. Fees

Except in counties where a statute provides otherwise, the official reporter shall receive for his services the fees prescribed in this article. **Leg.H.** Added Stats 1953 ch 206 §1.

§69948. Fee for reporting contested cases

(a) The fee for reporting testimony and proceedings in contested cases is fifty-five dollars ($55) a day, or any fractional part thereof.

(b) In San Joaquin County, the compensation for superior court reporters shall be that prescribed by Section 69993.

(c) In Madera County, the board of supervisors may, by ordinance or resolution, prescribe a higher rate of compensation for superior court reporters.

(d) In Kings County, the fee for reporting testimony and proceedings in contested cases is one hundred forty dollars ($140) a day, or any fractional part thereof.

(e) In Mariposa County, the board of supervisors may, by ordinance or resolution, prescribe the rate of compensation for superior court reporters.

(f) In Siskiyou County, the board of supervisors may, by ordinance, prescribe a higher rate of compensation for superior court reporters.

(g) In Yuba County, the board of supervisors may, by ordinance or resolution, prescribe a higher rate of compensation for superior court reporters.

(h) In Butte County, pro tempore reporters shall receive a fee of seventy-five dollars ($75) a day, or any fractional part thereof, for reporting testimony and proceedings in contested cases.

(i) In Sutter County, except as may otherwise be provided in Sections 70045.11 and 74839, the fee for reporting testimony and proceedings in contested cases is one hundred ten dollars ($110) per day, or any fractional part thereof. However, the board of supervisors may, by ordinance, prescribe a higher rate of compensation for superior court reporters.

(j) In Napa County, the board of supervisors may, by ordinance, prescribe a higher rate of compensation for superior court reporters.

(k) In Tehama County, the board of supervisors may, by ordinance, prescribe a higher rate of compensation for superior court reporters.

(*l*) In Monterey County, the fee for reporting testimony and proceedings in contested cases in any court is seventy-five dollars ($75) a day or any fractional part thereof.

(m) In Nevada County, the board of supervisors may, by ordinance, prescribe a higher rate of compensation for superior court reporters.

(n) In Calaveras County, the fee for reporting testimony and proceedings in contested cases is seventy-five dollars ($75) per day, or any fractional part thereof. However, the board of supervisors may, by ordinance, prescribe a higher rate of compensation for superior court reporters.

(o) In Placer County, the board of supervisors may, by ordinance, prescribe a higher rate of compensation for superior court reporters.

(p) In Sierra County, the board of supervisors may, by ordinance, prescribe a higher rate of compensation for superior court reporters.

(q) In Trinity County, the board of supervisors may, by ordinance, prescribe a higher rate of compensation for superior court reporters.

(r) In Humboldt County, the fee for reporting testimony and proceedings in contested cases is seventy-five dollars ($75) per day, or any fractional part thereof.

(s) In Del Norte County, the fee for reporting testimony and proceedings in contested cases is seventy-five dollars ($75) per day, or any fractional part thereof.

(t) In Alpine County, the board of supervisors may, by ordinance, prescribe a higher rate of compensation for superior court reporters.

(u) In Glenn County, the board of supervisors may, by ordinance, prescribe a higher rate of compensation for superior court reporters.

(v) In Colusa County, the fee for reporting testimony and proceedings in contested cases is one hundred twenty-five dollars ($125) per day, or any fractional part thereof.

(w) In Shasta County, the board of supervisors may prescribe a higher rate of compensation for superior court reporters.

(x) In Solano County, the fee for reporting testimony and proceedings in contested cases is ninety dollars ($90) per day, or fifty-five dollars ($55) per half day or fractional part thereof. However, the board of supervisors may, by ordinance, prescribe a higher rate of compensation for superior court reporters.

(y) In Inyo County, the board of supervisors may, by ordinance, prescribe a higher rate of compensation for superior court reporters.

(z) In Mono County, the board of supervisors may, by ordinance, prescribe a higher rate of compensation for superior court reporters. **Leg.H.** Added Stats 1953 ch 206 §1. Amended Stats 1955 ch 1303 §1; Stats 1961 ch 2061 §1; Stats 1967 ch 653 §1; Stats 1970 ch 614 §1; Stats 1975 ch 330 §1; Stats 1976 ch 1460 §2; Stats 1977 ch 224 §2, effective July 5, 1977, ch 905 §2; Stats 1978 ch 179 §2, effective June 1, 1978; Stats 1980 ch 79 §2, ch 1361 §4; Stats 1981 ch 499 §1; Stats 1982 ch 307 §1, effective June 28, 1982, ch 1033 §2; Stats 1983 ch 363 §1, effective July 25, 1983, ch 1253 §3; Stats 1985 ch 370 §1, ch 1374 §1, effective October 1, 1985; Stats 1986 ch 15 §1, effective March 11, 1986, ch 1418 §5; Stats 1987 ch 641 §1, effective September 15, 1987, ch 749 §1; Stats 1988 ch 3 §1, effective January 26, 1988; Stats 1989 ch 670 §1, effective September 22, 1989, ch 703 §2, effective and operative January 1, 1990; Stats 1990 ch 1447 §1 (SB 1818).

§69949. Reporting defaults or uncontested matters

The fee for reporting each default or uncontested action or proceeding is ten dollars ($10). If more than four defaults or uncontested matters are reported in any one day, or two or more defaults are reported in conjunction with any contested case, the fee is forty-five dollars ($45) a day, or any fractional part thereof. **Leg.H.** Added Stats 1953 ch 206 §1. Amended Stats 1961 ch 2061 §2; Stats 1967 ch 653 §1.3.

§ 69950. Transcription; Originals and copies

(a) The fee for transcription for original ribbon or printed copy is one dollar and thirteen cents ($1.13) for each 100 words, and for each copy purchased at the same time by the court, party, or other person purchasing the original, twenty cents ($0.20) for each 100 words.

(b) The fee for a first copy to any court, party, or other person who does not simultaneously purchase the original shall be twenty-six cents ($0.26) for each 100 words, and for each additional copy, purchased at the same time, twenty cents ($0.20) for each 100 words.

(c) A trial court practice and policy as to the number of words or folios on a typical transcript page shall not be unilaterally changed by a trial court. **Leg.H.** Added Stats 2021 ch 257 §11 (AB 177), effective September 23, 2021.

Prior Law Former Gov C §69950, similar to the present section, was added Stats 1953 ch 206 §1, amended Stats 1961 ch 2220 §1, amended Stats 1967 ch 1668 §1, amended Stats 1972 ch 537 §1, amended Stats 1980 ch 1350 §16, amended Stats 1986 ch 373 §2, ch 529 §13, effective July 28, 1986, amended Stats 1987 ch 56 §95, amended Stats 1990 ch 505 §11 (SB 2376), amended Stats 2002 ch 71 §4 (SB 1371), amended Stats 2012 ch 41 §37 (SB 1021), effective June 27, 2012 and repealed Stats 2021 ch 257 §10 (AB 177), effective September 23, 2021.

§ 69950.5. Legislative report on recommendations to increase uniformity in transcription rate expenditures [Repealed January 1, 2028]

(a) On or before January 1, 2024, the Judicial Council shall report to the Legislature recommendations to increase uniformity in transcription rate expenditures in California. The intent of the report shall be to not reduce the rate of pay or overall compensation to reporters or jeopardize collective bargaining agreements. The Judicial Council shall work in collaboration with key stakeholder groups, including the California Court Reporters Association, exclusively recognized employee organizations representing court reporters, and the Court Reporters Board of California.

(b) The report to be submitted pursuant to this section shall be submitted in compliance with Section 9795.

(c) This section shall remain in effect only until January 1, 2028, and as of that date is repealed. **Leg.H.** Added Stats 2021 ch 257 §12 (AB 177), effective September 23, 2021, repealed January 1, 2028.

§69951. Transcription; Additional fee for special daily copy service

For transcription, the reporter may charge an additional 50 percent for special daily copy service. **Leg.H.** Added Stats 1953 ch 206 §1. Amended Stats 2021 ch 257 §13 (AB 177), effective September 23, 2021.

§69952. Verbatim record; Payment by county in specified cases

(a) The court may specifically direct the making of a verbatim record and payment therefor shall be from the county treasury on order of the court in the following cases:

(1) Criminal matters.

(2) Juvenile proceedings.

(3) Proceedings to declare a minor free from custody.

(4) Proceedings under the Lanterman-Petris-Short Act, (Part 1 (commencing with Section 5000) of Division 5 of the Welfare and Institutions Code).

(5) As otherwise provided by law.

(b) Except as otherwise authorized by law, the court shall not order to be transcribed and paid for out of the county treasury any matter or material except that reported by the reporter pursuant to Section 269 of the Code of Civil Procedure. When there is no official reporter in attendance and a reporter pro tempore is appointed, his or her reasonable expenses for traveling and detention shall be fixed and allowed by the court and paid in like manner. When the court orders a daily transcript, necessitating the services of two phonographic reporters, the reporting fee for each of the reporters and the transcript fee shall be proper charges against the county treasury, and the daily transcript shall be pursuant to Section 269 of the Code of Civil Procedure. When the daily transcript is prepared by a single reporter, an additional fee for technological services, as set by the court with the agreement of the reporter, may be imposed. However, the total of the fee for a single reporter and the fee for technological services shall be less than the total fee for two reporters. **Leg.H.** Added Stats 1953 ch 206 §1. Amended Stats 1965 ch 2053 §2; Stats 1985 ch 1391 §1; Stats 1986 ch 823 §2.

§69953. Verbatim record not made at public expense; Payment by parties; Deposit with clerk or reporter

In any case where a verbatim record is not made at public expense pursuant to Section 69952 or other provisions of law, the cost of making any verbatim record shall be paid by the parties in equal proportion; and either party at his option may pay the whole. In either case, all amounts so paid by the party to whom costs are awarded shall be taxed as costs in the case. The fees for transcripts and copies ordered by the parties shall be paid by the party ordering them. Except as provided in Section 69952, no reporter shall perform any service in a civil action other than transcriptions until his fee for it has been deposited with the clerk of the court or with the reporter. **Leg.H.** Added Stats 1953 ch 206 §1. Amended Stats 1961 ch 2062 §3; Stats 1986 ch 823 §3.

§69953.5. Fee for daily transcript requiring more than one reporter

Notwithstanding any other provision of law, whenever a daily transcript is ordered in a civil case requiring the services of more than one phonographic reporter, the party requesting the daily transcript, in addition to any other required fee, shall pay a fee per day, or portion thereof, equal to the per diem rate for pro tempore reporters established by statute, local rule, or ordinance for the services of each additional reporter for the first day and each subsequent day the additional reporters are required. This fee shall be distributed to the court in which it was collected to offset the cost of the additional reporter. **Leg.H.** Added Stats 1986 ch 675 §1. Amended Stats 2005 ch 75 §116 (AB 145), effective July 19, 2005, operative January 1, 2006.

§69954. Compensation for transcripts prepared with computer assistance

(a) Transcripts prepared by a reporter using computer assistance and delivered on a medium other than paper shall be compensated at the same rate set for paper transcripts, except the reporter may also charge an additional fee not to exceed the cost of the medium or any copies thereof.

(b) The fee for a second copy of a transcript on appeal in computer-readable format ordered by or on behalf of a requesting party within 120 days of the filing or delivery of the original transcript shall be compensated at one-third the rate set forth for a second copy of a transcript as provided in Section 69950. A reporter may also charge an additional fee not to exceed the cost of the medium or any copies thereof.

(c) The fee for a computer-readable transcript shall be paid by the requesting court, party, or person, unless the computer-readable transcript is requested by a party in lieu of a paper transcript required to be delivered to that party by the rules of court. In that event, the fee shall be chargeable as statute or rule provides for the paper transcript.

(d) Any court, party, or person who has purchased a transcript may, without paying a further fee to the reporter, reproduce a copy or portion thereof as an exhibit pursuant to court order or rule, or for internal use, but shall not otherwise provide or sell a copy or copies to any other party or person. **Leg.H.** Added Stats 1985 ch 1391 §2. Amended Stats 1993 ch 1016 §2 (AB 1929), effective January 1, 1994.

CHAPTER 5.8
SUPERIOR COURT FEES

ARTICLE 1
Civil Fees Generally

§70600. Legislative intent; Uniform schedule of filing fees and other civil fees; Title of chapter

It is the intent of the Legislature to establish a uniform schedule of filing fees and other civil fees for the superior courts throughout the state. This chapter shall be known, and may be cited, as the Uniform Civil Fees and Standard Fee Schedule Act of 2005. **Leg.H.** Added Stats 2005 ch 75 §121 (AB 145), effective July 19, 2005, operative January 1, 2006.

§70601. Legislative intent; Moratorium on increases in filing fees; Exceptions; Task Force on Civil Fees

(a) It is the intent of the Legislature to establish a moratorium on increases in filing fees until January 1, 2008. No fee provided for in this chapter may be changed before January 1, 2008, except as may be required by the following:

(1) Legislative implementation of recommendations of the Task Force on County Law Libraries.

(2) Legislative implementation of recommendations for changes to the graduated filing fee for petitions in probate proceedings under subdivision (a) of Section 70650.

(b) The Judicial Council shall establish a Task Force on Civil Fees, including, but not limited to, representatives from the trial courts, the counties, the county law libraries, and the State Bar. On or before February 1, 2007, the task force shall make recommendations to the Judicial Council and the Legislature on the following:

(1) The effectiveness of the uniform fee structure, any operational or revenue problems, and how to address these issues.

(2) Whether a fee differential should be implemented based on the number of cases a party files in a year.

(3) A process to adjust fees in the future to accommodate inflation and other factors affecting operating costs for trial courts, county law libraries, and county programs that rely on court fees. **Leg.H.** Added Stats 2005 ch 75 §121 (AB 145), effective July 19, 2005, operative January 1, 2006. Amended Stats 2005 ch 706 §30 (AB 1742), effective January 1, 2006.

§70602.5. Supplemental fees of certain first paper filing

Notwithstanding any other law, it is the intent of the Legislature to supplement certain first paper filing fees as provided below:

(a) A supplemental fee of forty dollars ($40) shall be collected for filing any first paper subject to the uniform fee that is set at three hundred fifty-five dollars ($355) under Sections 70611, 70612, 70650, 70651, 70652, 70653, 70655, 70658, and 70670. The total fee collected under these sections, which includes the supplemental fee, shall be deposited and distributed as provided in Sections 68085.3 and 68086.1, as applicable.

(b) A supplemental fee of forty dollars ($40) shall be collected for filing any first paper subject to the uniform fee that is set at three hundred thirty dollars ($330) under Sections 70613, 70614, and 70621. The total fee collected under these sections, which includes the supplemental fee, shall be deposited and distributed as provided in Sections 68085.4 and 68086.1, as applicable.

(c) A supplemental fee of twenty dollars ($20) shall be collected for filing any first paper subject to the uniform fee that is set at two hundred five dollars ($205) under Sections 70613, 70614, 70621, 70654, and 70656 of this code, and Section 103470 of the Health and Safety Code. The total fee collected under these sections, which includes the supplemental fee, shall be deposited and distributed as provided in Section

68085.4. **Leg.H.** Added Stats 2010 ch 720 §18 (SB 857), effective October 19, 2010, inoperative July 1, 2013, repealed January 1, 2014. Amended Stats 2011 ch 193 §6 (AB 110), effective August 30, 2011; Stats 2012 ch 41 §39 (SB 1021), effective June 27, 2012.

§70602.6. Supplemental fees of certain first paper filing; Net reduction in funding; Adoption of schedule

(a) Notwithstanding any other law, a supplemental fee of forty dollars ($40) shall be collected for filing any first paper subject to the uniform fee that is set at three hundred fifty-five dollars ($355) under Sections 70611, 70612, 70650, 70651, 70652, 70653, 70655, 70658, and 70670. The total fee collected under these sections, which includes the supplemental fee, shall be deposited and distributed as provided in Sections 68085.3 and 68086.1, as applicable.

(b) The fee imposed under this section is in addition to any other fees authorized by law, including, but not limited to, the fees authorized in Section 70602.5.

(c) After the 2013-14 fiscal year, if the amount of the General Fund transfer to the Trial Court Trust Fund is decreased more than 10 percent from the amount appropriated in the 2013-14 fiscal year and is not offset by another source of revenue other than court fees so as to result in a net reduction in funding greater than 10 percent, then the amount of the supplemental fees provided in subdivision (a) shall be decreased proportionally. The Judicial Council shall adopt and publish a schedule setting the fees resulting from the decrease. **Leg.H.** Added Stats 2012 ch 41 §40 (SB 1021), effective June 27, 2012, inoperative July 1, 2015, repealed January 1, 2016. Amended Stats 2015 ch 26 §5 (SB 85), effective June 24, 2015, inoperative July 1, 2018, repealed January 1, 2019; Stats 2018 ch 45 §9 (SB 847), effective June 27, 2018, inoperative July 1, 2023, repealed January 1, 2024; Stats 2023 ch 34 §10 (SB 133), effective June 30, 2023.

§70603. Fees in chapter to be statewide; What charges may be added; Reduction in certain distributions

(a) Except as provided in this section, the fees charged for filings and services under this chapter are intended to be uniform statewide and to be the only allowable fees for those services and filings. The only charges that may be added to the fees in this chapter are the following:

(1) In a complex case, the fee provided for in Section 70616 may be added to the first paper and first responsive paper filing fees in Sections 70611, 70612, 70613, and 70614.

(2) In an unlawful detainer action subject to Section 1161.2 of the Code of Civil Procedure, a charge of fifteen dollars ($15) as provided under that section may be added to the fee in Section 70613 for filing a first appearance by a plaintiff.

(3) In Riverside County, a surcharge as provided in Section 70622 may be added to the first paper and first responsive paper filing fees in Sections 70611, 70612, 70613, 70614, 70650, 70651, 70652, 70653, 70655, and 70670.

(4) In San Bernardino County, a surcharge as provided in Section 70624 may be added to the first paper and first responsive paper filing fees in Sections 70611, 70612, 70613, 70614, 70650, 70651, 70652, 70653, 70655, and 70670. This paragraph applies to fees collected under Sections 70611, 70612, 70613, 70614, 70650, 70651, 70652, 70653, 70655, and 70670, beginning January 1, 2006.

(5) In the City and County of San Francisco, a surcharge as provided in Section 70625 may be added to the first paper and first responsive paper filing fees in Sections 70611, 70612, 70613, 70614, 70650, 70651, 70652, 70653, 70655, and 70670.

(b) Notwithstanding paragraph (1) of subdivision (c) of Section 68085.3 and paragraph (1) of subdivision (c) of Section 68085.4, when a charge for courthouse construction in the City and County of San Francisco or in the Counties of Riverside or San Bernardino is added to the uniform filing fee as provided under paragraph (3), (4), or (5) of subdivision (a), the amount distributed to the State Court Facilities Construction Fund under Section 68085.3 or 68085.4 shall be reduced by an amount equal to the charge added under paragraph (3), (4), or (5) of subdivision (a), up to the amount that would otherwise be distributed to the State Court Facilities Construction Fund. If the amount added under paragraph (3), (4), or (5) of subdivision (a) is greater than the amount that would be distributed to the State Court Facilities Construction Fund under Section 68085.3 or 68085.4, no distribution shall be made to the State Court Facilities Construction Fund, but the amount charged to the party may be greater than the amount of the uniform fee otherwise allowed, in order to collect the surcharge under paragraph (3), (4), or (5) of subdivision (a).

(c) If a filing fee is reduced by twenty-four dollars ($24) under subdivision (c) of Section 6322.1 of the Business and Professions Code, and a courthouse construction surcharge is added to the filing fee as provided under paragraph (3), (4), or (5) of subdivision (a), the amount distributed to the State Court Facilities Construction Fund under Section 68085.4 shall be reduced as provided in subdivision (b). If the amount added under paragraph (3), (4), or (5) of subdivision (a) is greater than the amount that would be distributed to the State Court Facilities Construction Fund under Section 68085.4, no distribution shall be made to the State Court Facilities Construction Fund, but the amount charged to the party may be greater than one hundred eighty-one dollars ($181), in order to collect the surcharge under paragraph (3), (4), or (5) of subdivision (a).

(d) This section shall become operative on July 1, 2013. **Leg.H.** Added Stats 2010 ch 720 §20 (SB 857), effective October 19, 2010, operative July 1, 2013.

Prior Law: Former Gov C §70603, relating to fees in chapter to be statewide; what charges may be added; reduction in certain distributions, was added Stats 2005 ch 75 §121 (AB 145), effective July 19, 2005, operative January 1, 2006 and amended Stats 2007 ch 738 §22 (AB 1248), effective January 1, 2008; Stats 2008 ch 311 §9.5 (SB 1407), effective January 1, 2009; Stats 2009 4th Ex Sess 2009–2010 ch 22 §11 (SBX4-13), effective July 28, 2009; Stats 2010 ch 720 §19 (SB 857), effective October 19, 2010, inoperative July 1, 2013, repealed January 1, 2014.

§70611. Fee for filing first paper in civil action or proceeding

The uniform fee for filing the first paper in a civil action or proceeding in the superior court, other than in a limited civil case, an adoption proceeding, a proceeding under the Probate Code, or a proceeding under the Family Code, is three hundred fifty-five dollars ($355). The fee shall be distributed as provided in Section 68085.3.

This section applies to the initial complaint, petition, or application, and the papers transmitted from another court on the transfer of a civil action or proceeding, but does not include documents filed pursuant to Section 491.150, 704.750, or 708.160 of the Code of Civil Procedure. **Leg.H.** Added Stats 1980 ch 1372 §17, as Gov C §26820.4. Amended Stats 1982 ch 454 §73 (ch 327 prevails), ch 327 §63, effective June 30, 1982 (ch 327 prevails), ch 1198 §67, ch 1364 §2.4, operative July 1, 1983; Stats 1983 ch 155 §27, effective June 30, 1983, ch 938 §6, effective September 20, 1983; Stats 1992 ch 696 §12 (AB 1344), effective September 14, 1992; Stats 1997 ch 850 §6 (AB 233); Stats 1998 ch 931 §201 (SB 2139), effective September 28, 1998; Amended and renumbered by Stats 2005 ch 75 §50 (AB 145), effective July 19, 2005, operative January 1, 2006; Amended Stats 2008 ch 311 §10 (SB 1407), effective January 1, 2009; Stats 2009 4th Ex Sess 2009–2010 ch 22 §12 (SBX4-13), effective July 28, 2009.

§70612. Fee for filing first paper by defendant, intervenor, respondent, or adverse party

(a) The uniform fee for filing the first paper in the action or proceeding described in Section 70611 on behalf of any defendant, intervenor, respondent, or adverse party, whether separately or jointly, except for the purpose of making disclaimer, is three hundred fifty-five dollars ($355). The fee shall be distributed as provided in Section 68085.3.

(b) As used in this section, the term "paper" does not include a stipulation for the appointment of a temporary judge or of a court investigator, or the report made by the court investigator. **Leg.H.** Added Stats 1947 ch 424 §1, as Gov C §26826. Amended Stats 1949 ch 55 §1, ch 272 §2, ch 739 §5; Stats 1953 ch 806 §1; Stats 1957 ch 1891 §1; Stats 1963 ch 356 §1; Stats 1st Ex Sess 1966 ch 120 §31; Stats 1974 ch 1285 §9; Stats 1975 ch 766 §9; Stats 1980 ch 1372 §28; Stats 1981 ch 109 §1; Stats 1982 ch 327 §66, effective June 30, 1982; Stats 1983 ch 1159 §13, operative July 1, 1984; Stats 1985 ch 96 §2, ch 1239 §4; Stats 1992 ch 696 §16 (AB 1344), effective September 14, 1992; Stats 1993 ch 2 §1 (AB 32), effective March 2, 1993; Stats 1998 ch 931 §203 (SB 2139), effective September 28, 1998; Amended and renumbered by Stat 2005 ch 75 §56 (AB 145), effective July 19, 2005, operative January 1, 2006; Amended Stats 2007 ch 738 §23 (AB 1248), effective January 1, 2008; Stats 2008 ch 311 §11 (SB 1407), effective January 1, 2009; Stats 2009 4th Ex Sess 2009–2010 ch 22 §13 (SBX4-13), effective July 28, 2009.

§70613. Fee for filing first paper in limited civil case; Applicability; Waiver and assessment against defendant in certain cases

(a) The uniform fee for filing the first paper in a limited civil case is three hundred thirty dollars ($330), except as provided in subdivision (b).

(b) In a case where the amount demanded, excluding attorney's fees and costs, is ten thousand dollars ($10,000) or less, the uniform fee for filing the first paper is two hundred five dollars ($205). The first page of the first paper shall state whether the amount demanded exceeds or does not exceed ten thousand dollars ($10,000).

(c) This section applies to the initial complaint, petition, or application, and any papers transmitted from another court on the transfer of a civil action or proceeding, but does not include documents filed pursuant to Section 491.150, 704.750, or 708.160 of the Code of Civil Procedure.

(d) The fee for a paper filed under this section shall be distributed as provided in Section 68085.4.

(e) The fee shall be waived in any action for damages against a defendant, based upon the defendant's commission of a felony offense, upon presentation to the clerk of the court of a certified copy of the abstract of judgment of conviction of the defendant of the felony giving rise to the claim for damages. If the plaintiff would have been entitled to recover those fees from the defendant had they been paid, the court may assess the amount of the waived fees against the defendant and order the defendant to pay that sum to the court. **Leg.H.** Added Stats 1983 ch 969 §10, as Gov C §72055, operative January 1, 1988. Amended Stats 1990 ch 56 §4 (SB 1609), effective April 20, 1990; Stats 1992 ch 696 §73 (AB 1344), effective September 14, 1992; Stats 1996 ch 942 §2 (AB 2953); Stats 1997 ch 850 §37 (AB 233); Stats 1998 ch 931 §315 (SB 2139), effective September 28, 1998; Stats 2000 ch 447 §7 (SB 1533); Stats 2001 ch 812 §18 (AB 223), Stats 2003 ch 159 §21 (AB 1759), effective August 2, 2003, operative August 17, 2003, inoperative July 1, 2006, repealed January 1, 2007. Amended and renumbered by Stats 2005 ch 75 § 126 (AB 145), effective July 19, 2005, operative January 1, 2006; Amended Stats 2008 ch 311 §12 (SB 1407), effective January 1, 2009; Stats 2009 4th Ex Sess 2009–2010 ch 22 §14 (SBX4-13), effective July 28, 2009.

Prior Law: Former Gov C §72055, similar to the present section, was added Stats 1953 ch 206 §1, amended Stats 1955 ch 604 §2, ch 955 §38, Stats 1966 1st Ex Sess ch 120 §45, Stats 1980 ch 1372 §55, Stats 1982 ch 327 §93, effective June 30, 1982, ch 497 §121, operative July 1, 1983, ch 1198 §68, ch 1364 §2.6, operative July 1, 1983, Stats 1983 ch 155 §28, effective June 30, 1983, operative July 1, 1983, ch 938 §8, effective September 20, 1983, ch 969 §9 and repealed January 1, 1988, by its own terms.

§70613.5. Additional filing fee for subsequent pleadings that increase the amount demanded

(a) Notwithstanding Section 472 of the Code of Civil Procedure, if a plaintiff or petitioner who previously was charged the filing fee under subdivision (b) of Section 70613 files an amended complaint or other initial pleading that increases the amount demanded to an amount that exceeds ten thousand dollars ($10,000) but does not exceed twenty-five thousand dollars ($25,000), so that the higher filing fee under subdivision (a) of Section 70613 would have been required if such a demand had been made in the original pleading, a fee equal to the difference between the fee for the original filing fee and the filing fee for the new amount demanded shall be charged to make up the difference between the filing fees. This fee shall be distributed to the Trial Court Trust Fund.

(b) Notwithstanding Section 472 of the Code of Civil Procedure, if a party who previously was charged the filing fee under subdivision (b) of Section 70614 files a cross-complaint, amended cross-complaint, or amendment to a cross-complaint demanding an amount that exceeds ten thousand dollars ($10,000) but does not exceed twenty-five thousand dollars ($25,000), a fee equal to the difference between the fee for the original filing fee and the filing fee under subdivision (a) of Section 70614 shall be charged to make up the difference between the filing fees. This fee shall be distributed to the Trial Court Trust Fund.

(c) The court shall not reimburse a party if the party's complaint or cross-complaint is amended to demand a lower amount that falls within the range for a filing fee lower than that originally paid. **Leg.H.** Added Stats 2007 ch 738 §24 (AB 1248), effective January 1, 2008.

§70614. Fee for filing first paper in limited civil case for party other than plaintiff

(a) The uniform fee for filing the first paper in a limited civil case on behalf of any party other than a plaintiff is three hundred thirty dollars ($330), except as provided in subdivision (b).

(b) In a case where the amount demanded, excluding attorney's fees and costs, is ten thousand dollars ($10,000) or less, the uniform fee for filing the first paper is two hundred five dollars ($205).

(c) The fees in this section do not apply to papers filed for the purpose of making disclaimer.

(d) The fee for a paper filed under this section shall be distributed as provided in Section 68085.4. **Leg.H.** Added Stats 1953 ch 206 §1, as Gov C §72056. Amended Stats 1955 ch 604 §3, ch 955 §39; Stats 1980 ch 1372 §56; Stats 1982 ch 327 §95, effective June 30, 1982; Stats 1992 ch 696 §75 (AB 1344), effective September 14, 1992; Stats 1998 ch 931 §316 (SB 2139), effective September 28, 1998. Stats 2003 ch 159 §23 (AB 1759), effective August 2, 2003, operative August 17, 2003, inoperative July 1, 2006, repealed January 1, 2007. Amended and renumbered by Stats 2005 ch 75 §128 (AB 145), effective July 19, 2005, operative January 1, 2006; Amended Stats 2008 ch 311 §13 (SB 1407), effective January 1, 2009; Stats 2009 4th Ex Sess 2009–2010 ch 22 §15 (SBX4-13), effective July 28, 2009.

§70615. Fees for certain appeals to superior court [Repealed January 1, 2032]

The fee for filing any of the following appeals to the superior court is twenty-five dollars ($25):

(a) An appeal of a local agency's decision regarding an administrative fine or penalty under Section 53069.4.

(b) An appeal under Section 40230 of the Vehicle Code of an administrative agency's decision regarding a parking violation.

(c) An appeal under Section 99582 of the Public Utilities Code of a hearing officer's determination regarding an administrative penalty for fare evasion or a passenger conduct violation.

(d) A petition under Section 186.35 of the Penal Code challenging a law enforcement agency's inclusion of a person's information in a shared gang database.

(e) An appeal under Section 22428 of the Vehicle Code of a hearing officer's determination regarding a civil penalty for an automated speed violation, as defined in Section 22425 of the Vehicle Code.

(f) An appeal under Section 22438 of the Vehicle Code of a hearing officer's determination regarding a civil penalty for an automated speed violation, as defined in Section 22435 of the Vehicle Code.

[1] **(g)** This section shall remain in effect only until January 1, 2032, and as of that date is repealed. **Leg.H.** Added Stats 2007 ch 738 §25 (AB 1248), effective January 1, 2008. Amended Stats 2016 ch 752 §1 (AB 2298), effective January 1, 2017; Stats 2017 ch 695 §2 (AB 90), effective January 1, 2018; Stats 2023 ch 808 §2 (AB 645), effective January 1, 2024, repealed January 1, 2032; Stats 2024 §2 (SB 1297), effective January 1, 2025, repealed January 1, 2032.

§70615. 2024 Deletes. [1] (f)

§ 70615. Fees for certain appeals to superior court [Operative January 1, 2032]

The fee for filing any of the following appeals to the superior court is twenty-five dollars ($25):

(a) An appeal of a local agency's decision regarding an administrative fine or penalty under Section 53069.4.

(b) An appeal under Section 40230 of the Vehicle Code of an administrative agency's decision regarding a parking violation.

(c) An appeal under Section 99582 of the Public Utilities Code of a hearing officer's determination regarding an administrative penalty for fare evasion or a passenger conduct violation.

(d) A petition under Section 186.35 of the Penal Code challenging a law enforcement agency's inclusion of a person's information in a shared gang database.

(e) This section shall become operative on January 1, 2032. **Leg.H.** Added Stats 2023 ch 808 §3 (AB 645), effective January 1, 2024, operative January 1, 2032.

§70616. Complex case fee; Maximum; Parties; Reimbursement; Failure to pay fees

(a) In addition to the first paper filing fee required by Section 70611 or 70613, a single complex case fee shall be paid to the clerk on behalf of all plaintiffs, whether filing separately or jointly, either at the time of the filing of the first paper if the case is designated as complex pursuant to the California Rules of Court, or, if no such designation was made, in each case in which a court determines that the case is a complex case pursuant to the California Rules of Court, within 10 calendar days of the filing of the court's order.

(b) In addition to the first appearance fee required under Section 70612 or 70614, a complex case fee shall be paid on behalf of each defendant, intervenor, respondent, or adverse party, whether filing separately or jointly, either at the time that party files its first paper in a case if the case is designated or counterdesignated as complex pursuant to the California Rules of Court, or, if no such designation was made, in each case in which a court determines that the case is a complex case pursuant to the California Rules of Court, within 10 calendar days of the filing of the court's order. This additional complex fee shall be charged to each defendant, intervenor, respondent, or adverse party appearing in the case, but the total complex fees collected from all the defendants, intervenors, respondents, or other adverse parties appearing in a complex case shall not exceed eighteen thousand dollars ($18,000).

(c) In each case in which the court determines that a case that has been designated or counterdesignated as complex is not a complex case, the court shall order reimbursement to the parties of the amount of any complex case fees that the parties have previously paid pursuant to subdivision (a) or (b).

(d) In each case determined to be complex in which the total fees actually collected exceed, or if collected would exceed, the limit in subdivision (b), the court shall make an order necessary to ensure that the total complex fees paid by the defendants, intervenors, respondents, or other adverse parties appearing in the case do not exceed the limit and that the complex fees paid by those parties are apportioned fairly among those parties.

(e) The complex case fee established by this section shall be one thousand dollars ($1,000), unless the fee is reduced pursuant to this section. The fee shall be transmitted to the Trial Court Trust Fund as provided in Section 68085.1.

(f) The fees provided by this section are in addition to the filing fee authorized by Section 70611, 70612, 70613, or 70614.

(g) Failure to pay the fees required by this section shall have the same effect as the failure to pay a filing fee, and shall be subject to the same enforcement and penalties.

(h) The amendments made to this section during the 2011-12 Regular Session of the Legislature do not constitute a change in, but are declaratory of, existing law. **Leg.H.** Added Stats 2003 ch 159 §8 (AB 1759), as Gov C § 28626.4, effective August 2, 2003, operative August 17, 2003, inoperative July 1, 2006, repealed January 1, 2007. Amended Stats 2003 ch 757 §3.5 (AB 296), inoperative July 1, 2006, repealed January 1, 2007; Amended and renumbered by Stats 2005 ch 75 §60 (145), effective July 19, 2005, operative January 1, 2006; Stats 2011 ch 419 §5 (SB 384), effective January 1, 2012. Stats 2012 ch 41 §41 (SB 1021), effective June 27, 2012, inoperative July 1, 2015, repealed January 1, 2016; Stats 2015 ch 26 §6 (SB 85), effective June 24, 2015, inoperative July 1, 2018, repealed January 1, 2019. Amended Stats 2018 ch 45 §10 (SB 847), effective June 27, 2018, inoperative July 1, 2023, repealed January 1, 2024; Stats 2023 ch 34 §11 (SB 133), effective June 30, 2023.

Prior Law Former Gov C §70616, relating to complex case fee, maximum, parties, reimbursement, failure to pay fees, was added Stats 2012 ch 41 §42 (SB 1021), effective June 27, 2012, operative July 1, 2015, amended Stats 2015 ch 26 §7 (SB 85), effective June 24, 2015, operative July 1, 2018, Stats 2018 ch 45 §11 (SB 847), effective June 27, 2018, operative July 1, 2023, and repealed Stats 2023 ch 34 §12 (SB 133), effective June 30, 2023.

§70616.5. High-frequency litigant fee

(a) In addition to the first paper filing fee required by Section 70611 or 70613, a single high-frequency litigant fee shall be paid to the clerk on behalf of a plaintiff who is a high-frequency litigant, as that term is defined in Section 425.55 of the Code of Civil Procedure, at the time of the filing of the first paper if the complaint alleges a construction-related accessibility claim, as those terms are defined in subdivision (a) of Section 55.3 of the Civil Code.

(b) The fee established by this section shall be one thousand dollars ($1,000). The fee shall be transmitted as provided in Section 68085.35.

(c) Failure to pay the fees required by this section shall have the same effect as the failure to pay a filing fee, and shall be subject to the same enforcement and penalties. **Leg.H.** Added Stats 2015 ch 755 §8 (AB 1521), effective October 10, 2015.

§70617. Uniform fee for filing motion, application, or paper requiring hearing subsequent to first paper; No fee for certain filings; Application to appear as counsel pro hac vice; Fee for summary judgment motion

(a) Except as provided in subdivisions (d) and (e), the uniform fee for filing a motion, application, or any other paper requiring a hearing subsequent to the first paper, is sixty dollars ($60). Papers for which this fee shall be charged include the following:

(1) A motion listed in paragraphs (1) to (12), inclusive, of subdivision (a) of Section 1005 of the Code of Civil Procedure.

(2) A motion or application to continue a trial date.

(3) An application for examination of a third person controlling defendant's property under Section 491.110 or 491.150 of the Code of Civil Procedure.

(4) Discovery motions under Title 4 (commencing with Section 2016.010) of Part 4 of the Code of Civil Procedure.

(5) A motion for a new trial of a civil action or special proceeding.

(6) An application for an order for a judgment debtor examination under Section 708.110 or 708.160 of the Code of Civil Procedure.

(7) An application for an order of sale of a dwelling under Section 704.750 of the Code of Civil Procedure.

(8) An ex parte application that requires a party to give notice of the ex parte appearance to other parties.

(9) A motion for an order determining the need for a debtor to appear for a debtor's examination under Section 708.111 of the Code of Civil Procedure.

(b) There shall be no fee under subdivision (a) or (c) for filing any of the following:

(1) A motion, application, demurrer, request, notice, or stipulation and order that is the first paper filed in an action and on which a first paper filing fee is paid.

(2) An amended notice of motion.

(3) A civil case management statement.

(4) A request for trial de novo after judicial arbitration.

(5) A stipulation that does not require an order.

(6) A request for an order to prevent civil harassment.

(7) A request for an order to prevent domestic violence.

(8) A request for entry of default or default judgment.

(9) A paper requiring a hearing on a petition for emancipation of a minor.

(10) A paper requiring a hearing on a petition for an order to prevent abuse of an elder or dependent adult.

(11) A paper requiring a hearing on a petition for a writ of review, mandate, or prohibition.

(12) A paper requiring a hearing on a petition for a decree of change of name or gender.

(13) A paper requiring a hearing on a petition to approve the compromise of a claim of a minor.

(c) The fee for filing the following papers not requiring a hearing is twenty dollars ($20):

(1) A request, application, or motion for, or a notice of, the continuance of a hearing or case management conference. The fee shall be charged no more than once for each continuance. The fee shall not be charged if the continuance is required by the court.

(2) A stipulation and order.

(3) A request for an order authorizing service of summons by posting or by publication under Section 415.45 or 415.50 of the Code of Civil Procedure.

(d) The fee for filing a motion for summary judgment or summary adjudication of issues is five hundred dollars ($500).

(e)(1) The fee for filing in the superior court an application to appear as counsel pro hac vice is five hundred dollars ($500). This fee is in addition to any other fee required of the applicant. Two hundred fifty dollars ($250) of the fee collected under this paragraph shall be transmitted to the state for deposit into the State Court Facilities Construction Fund, established in Section 70371. The remaining two hundred fifty dollars ($250) of the fee shall be transmitted to the state for deposit into the Trial Court Trust Fund, established in Section 68085.

(2) An attorney whose application to appear as counsel pro hac vice has been granted shall pay to the superior court, on or before the

anniversary of the date the application was granted, an annual renewal fee of five hundred dollars ($500) for each year that the attorney maintains pro hac vice status in the case in which the application was granted. The entire fee collected under this paragraph shall be transmitted to the state for deposit into the Trial Court Trust Fund, established in Section 68085.

(3) Fees imposed by this subdivision shall be waived when the applicant is an attorney representing a tribe in a child welfare matter under the federal Indian Child Welfare Act (25 U.S.C. Sec. 1901 et seq.).

(f) Regardless of whether each motion or matter is heard at a single hearing or at separate hearings, the filing fees required by subdivisions (a), (c), (d), and (e) apply separately to each motion or other paper filed. The Judicial Council may publish rules to give uniform guidance to courts in applying fees under this section. **Leg.H.** Added Stats 2005 ch 75 §121 (AB 145), effective July 19, 2005, operative January 1, 2006. Amended Stats 2007 ch 738 §26 (AB 1248), effective January 1, 2008; Stats 2008 ch 311 §13.5 (SB 1407), effective January 1, 2009; Stats 2010 ch 720 §21 (SB 857), effective October 19, 2010, inoperative July 1, 2013, repealed January 1, 2014; Stats 2012 ch 41 §43 (SB 1021), effective June 27, 2012, inoperative July 1, 2015, repealed January 1, 2016; Stats 2015 ch 26 §8 (SB 85), effective June 24, 2015, inoperative July 1, 2018, repealed January 1, 2019; Stats 2018 ch 45 §12 (SB 847), effective June 27, 2018, inoperative July 1, 2023, repealed January 1, 2024; Stats 2018 ch 399 §1 (AB 3047), effective January 1, 2019, inoperative July 1, 2023, repealed January 1, 2024; Stats 2021 ch 79 §31 (AB 143), effective July 16, 2021, inoperative July 1, 2023, repealed January 1, 2024; Stats 2023 ch 34 §13 (SB 133), effective June 30, 2023; Stats 2023 ch 562 §4 (AB 1119), effective January 1, 2024.

Prior Law: Former Gov C §70617, relating to uniform fee for filing motion, application, or paper requiring hearing subsequent to first paper, no fee for certain filings, application to appear as counsel pro hac vice, and fee for summary judgment motion, was added Stats 2010 ch 720 §22 (SB 857), effective October 19, 2010, operative July 1, 2013, amended Stats 2012 ch 41 §44 (SB 1021), effective June 27, 2012, operative July 1, 2015, Stats 2015 ch 26 §9 (SB 85), effective June 24, 2015, operative July 1, 2018, Stats 2018 ch 45 §13 (SB 847), effective June 27, 2018, operative July 1, 2023, Stats 2018 ch 45 §13 (SB 847), effective June 27, 2018, effective January 1, 2019, operative July 1, 2023, Stats 2018 ch 399 §2 (AB 3047), effective January 1, 2019, operative July 1, 2023, Stats 2021 ch 79 §32 (AB 143), effective July 16, 2021, operative July 1, 2023, and repealed Stats 2023 ch 34 §14 (SB 133), effective June 30, 2023.

§70618. Change of venue; Fee for making up and transmission of transcript and papers; Filing fee

When the venue in a case is changed, the fee for making up and transmitting the transcript and papers is fifty dollars ($50) and a further sum equal to the uniform fee for filing in the court to which the case is transferred. The clerk shall transmit the uniform filing fee with the papers in the case to the clerk or judge of the court to which the case is transferred. **Leg.H.** Added Stats 1947 ch 424 §1, as Gov C §26823. Amended Stats 1949 ch 739 §3; Stats 1951 ch 1553 §45; Stats 1957 ch 1579 §3; Stats 1974 ch 1285 §6; Stats 1975 ch 766 §6; Stats 1980 ch 1372 §26; Stats 1982 ch 327 §65, effective June 30, 1982; Stats 1997 ch 850 §7 (AB 233); Amended and renumbered by Stats 2005 ch 75 §54 (AB 145), effective July 19, 2005, operative January 1, 2006.

§70619. Fee for reclassification from limited to unlimited civil case

The fee for reclassification of a case from a limited civil case to an unlimited civil case under Section 403.060 of the Code of Civil Procedure is one hundred forty dollars ($140). **Leg.H.** Added Stats 2005 ch 75 §121 (AB 145), effective July 19, 2005, operative January 1, 2006.

§70620. Certificate on filing notice of motion prior to filing record on appeal

The fee for a certificate required by courts of appeal or the Supreme Court on filing a notice of motion prior to the filing of the record on appeal in the reviewing court is twenty dollars ($20). **Leg.H.** Added Stats 1947 ch 424 §1, as Gov C §26838. Amended Stats 1949 ch 272 §8, ch 739 §14; Stats 1963 ch 459 §1; Stats 1971 ch 806 §1; Stats 1980 ch 1372 §40; Stats 1982 ch 327 §77, effective June 30, 1982; Stats 1997 ch 850 §17 (AB 233); Amended and renumbered by Stats 2005 ch 75 §82 (145), effective July 19, 2005, operative January 1, 2006.

§70621. Fee for filing appeal in limited civil case

(a)(1) The fee for filing a notice of appeal to the appellate division of the superior court in a limited civil case is three hundred thirty dollars ($330), except as provided in subdivision (b).

(2) The fee for filing a petition for a writ within the original jurisdiction of the appellate division of the superior court is three hundred thirty dollars ($330), except as provided in subdivision (b).

(b) If the amount demanded in the limited civil case, excluding attorney's fees and costs, is ten thousand dollars ($10,000) or less, the fee for filing a petition for a writ or a notice of appeal to the appellate division of the superior court is two hundred five dollars ($205).

(c) The fees provided for in this section shall be distributed as provided in Section 68085.4.

(d) The Judicial Council may make rules governing the time and method of payment of the fees in this section and providing for excuse. **Leg.H.** Added Stats 1947 ch 424 §1, as Gov C §26824. Amended Stats 1949 ch 739 §4; Stats 1951 ch 1553 §46, operative January 1, 1952; Stats 1957 ch 1579 §4; Stats 1974 ch 1285 §7; Stats 1975 ch 766 §7; Stats 1977 ch 1257 §43, effective October 3, 1977; Stats 1979 ch 212 §5; Stats 1980 ch 1372 §27; Stats 1993 ch 158 §4 (AB 392), effective July 20, 1993; Stats 1998 ch 931 §202 (SB 2139), effective September 28, 1998; Amended and renumbered by Stats 2005 ch 75 §55 (AB 145), effective July 19, 2005, operative January 1, 2006; Amended Stats 2007 ch 738 §27 (AB 1248), effective January 1, 2008; Stats 2008 ch 311 §14 (SB 1407), effective January 1, 2009; Stats 2009 4th Ex Sess 2009–2010 ch 22 §16 (SBX4-13), effective July 28, 2009.

§70622. Surcharge in Riverside County for filing specified court papers to cover costs of seismic rehabilitation of courthouses

(a) In addition to the uniform filing fee authorized pursuant to Section 70611, 70612, 70613, 70614, 70650, 70651, 70652, 70653, 70655, or 70670, after giving notice and holding a public hearing on the proposal, the Board of Supervisors of Riverside County may impose a surcharge not to exceed fifty dollars ($50) for the filing in superior court of any of the following:

(1) A complaint, petition, or other first paper in a civil or probate action or special proceeding.

(2) A first paper on behalf of any defendant, respondent, intervenor, or adverse party.

(3) A petition for dissolution of marriage, dissolution of domestic partnership, legal separation, or nullity of marriage.

(4) A response to such a petition.

(5) A first paper on behalf of any party in a proceeding under Section 98.2 of the Labor Code.

(b) The county shall notify in writing the Superior Court of Riverside County and the Administrative Office of the Courts of any change in a surcharge under this section.

(c) When a surcharge under this section is imposed on a filing fee, the distribution that would otherwise be made to the State Court Facilities Construction Fund under subdivision (c) of Section 68085.3 or subdivision (c) of Section 68085.4 shall be reduced as provided in Section 70603.

(d) The surcharge shall be in an amount determined to be necessary by the board of supervisors to cover the costs of the seismic stabilization, construction, and rehabilitation of the Riverside County Courthouse, the Indio Branch Courthouse, and the family law courthouse, and collection thereof shall terminate upon repayment of the amortized costs incurred. When the amortized costs have been repaid, the county shall notify in writing the Superior Court of Riverside County and the Administrative Office of the Courts. **Leg.H.** Added Stats 1992 ch 1285 §1 (SB 1478), as Gov C §26826.1. Amended Stats 1993 ch 2 §1.5 (AB 32), effective March 2, 1993; Amended and renumbered by Stats 2005 ch 75 §57 (AB 145), effective July 19, 2005, operative January 1, 2006; Amended Stats 2006 ch 538 §331 (SB 1852), effective January 1, 2007.

§70624. Surcharge for superior court filings in San Bernardino County to supplement Courthouse Construction Fund [Repealed January 1, 2026]

(a) In addition to the uniform filing fee authorized pursuant to Section 70611, 70612, 70613, 70614, 70650, 70651, 70652, 70653, 70655, or 70670, after giving notice and holding a public hearing on the proposal, the Board of Supervisors of San Bernardino County may impose a surcharge not to exceed thirty-five dollars ($35) for the filing in superior court of (1) a complaint, petition, or other first paper in a civil, family, or probate action or special proceeding, and (2) a first paper on behalf of any defendant, respondent, intervenor, or adverse party. The county shall notify in writing the superior court and the Administrative Office of the

Courts of any change in a surcharge under this section. If a surcharge under this section is imposed on a filing fee, the distribution that would otherwise be made to the State Court Facilities Construction Fund under subdivision (c) of Section 68085.3 or subdivision (c) of Section 68085.4 shall be reduced as provided in Section 70603. This section shall apply to fees collected under Sections 70611, 70612, 70613, 70614, 70650, 70651, 70652, 70653, 70655, and 70670, beginning January 1, 2006.

(b) The surcharge shall be in an amount determined to be necessary by the board of supervisors to supplement the Courthouse Construction Fund, to be deposited in that fund and used solely for the purposes authorized for expenditures from that fund, including, but not limited to, earthquake retrofitting, renovation, and remodeling of all portions of the Central San Bernardino Courthouse in need of retrofitting, renovation, or remodeling, whether or not necessitated by the retrofitting work, including the original courthouse built in 1926 and all subsequent additions thereto. Expenditures made from the Courthouse Construction Fund that are funded from the surcharge shall be made in order of priority to ensure that all necessary earthquake retrofitting of the Central San Bernardino Courthouse will be completed. Collection of the surcharge authorized by this section shall terminate upon repayment of the amortized costs incurred, or 30 years from the sale of the bond, whichever occurs first. However, the surcharge shall not apply in instances in which no filing fee is charged or the filing fee is waived. If the amortized costs have been repaid, or 30 years have passed since the sale of the bond, the county shall notify in writing the superior court and the Administrative Office of the Courts.

(c) This section shall remain in effect only until January 1, 2026, and as of that date is repealed, unless a later enacted statute that is enacted before January 1, 2026, deletes or extends that date. **Leg.H.** Added Stats 2002 ch 367 §2 (AB 2022), as Gov C §76236. Amended and renumbered by Stats 2005 ch 75 §136 (AB 145), effective July 19, 2005, operative January 1, 2006; Amended Stats 2007 ch 738 §28 (AB 1248), effective January 1, 2008; Stats 2020 ch 210 §24 (AB 1984), effective January 1, 2021, repealed January 1, 2026.

§70625. San Francisco Courthouse Construction Fund

(a) Notwithstanding any other law, for the purpose of assisting the City and County of San Francisco in the acquisition, rehabilitation, construction, and financing of courtrooms or of a courtroom building or buildings containing facilities necessary or incidental to the operation of the justice system, the Board of Supervisors of the City and County of San Francisco may require the amounts collected pursuant to subdivision (d) to be deposited in the Courthouse Construction Fund established pursuant to Section 76100. In the City and County of San Francisco, the moneys of the Courthouse Construction Fund together with any interest earned thereon shall be payable only for the foregoing purposes and at the time necessary therefor, and for the purposes set forth in subdivision (b) and at the time necessary therefor.

(b) In conjunction with the acquisition, rehabilitation, construction, or financing of courtrooms or of a courtroom building or buildings referred to in subdivision (a), the City and County of San Francisco may use the moneys of the Courthouse Construction Fund (1) to rehabilitate existing courtrooms or an existing courtroom building or buildings for other uses if new courtrooms or a courtroom building or buildings are acquired, constructed, or financed or (2) to acquire, rehabilitate, construct, or finance excess courtrooms or an excess courtroom building or buildings if that excess is anticipated to be needed at a later time.

(c) Any excess courtrooms or excess courtroom building or buildings that are acquired, rehabilitated, constructed, or financed pursuant to subdivision (b) may be leased or rented for uses other than the operation of the justice system until such time as the excess courtrooms or excess courtroom building or buildings are needed for the operation of the justice system. Any amounts received as lease or rental payments pursuant to this subdivision shall be deposited in the Courthouse Construction Fund.

(d) In the City and County of San Francisco, a surcharge for the purpose and for the time set forth in this section may be added to the filing fees under Sections 70611, 70612, 70613, 70614, 70650, 70651, 70652, 70653, 70655, and 70670 in any civil, family, or probate action in the superior court. The surcharge shall be in an amount, not to exceed fifty dollars ($50), as set forth in a resolution adopted by the Board of Supervisors of the City and County of San Francisco. If a surcharge under this section is imposed on a filing fee, the distribution that would otherwise be made to the State Court Facilities Construction Fund under subdivision (c) of Section 68085.3 or subdivision (c) of Section 68085.4 shall be reduced as provided in Section 70603. The county shall notify in writing the superior court and the Administrative Office of the Courts of any change in a surcharge under this section. When the amortized costs that are to be repaid from this fund have been repaid, the county shall notify in writing the superior court and the Administrative Office of Courts, and the surcharge under this section shall terminate, as provided in subdivision (b) of Section 70375. **Leg.H.** Added Stats 1991 ch 189 §11 (AB 544), effective July 27, 1991, as Gov C § 76238. Amended Stats 1992 ch 427 §77 (AB 3355); Stats 2002 ch 784 §503 (SB 1316); Amended and renumbered by Stats 2005 ch 75 §137 (AB 145), effective July 19, 2005, operative January 1, 2006; Amended Stats 2010 ch 709 §6 (SB 1062), effective January 1, 2011.

§70626. Fees for specified court services; Use of specified equivalent amount of certain fees for civil representation program

(a) The fee for each of the following services is forty dollars ($40). Subject to subdivision (e), amounts collected shall be distributed to the Trial Court Trust Fund under Section 68085.1.

(1) Issuing a writ of attachment, a writ of mandate, a writ of execution, a writ of sale, a writ of possession, a writ of prohibition, or any other writ for the enforcement of any order or judgment.

(2) Issuing an abstract of judgment.

(3) Issuing a certificate of satisfaction of judgment under Section 724.100 of the Code of Civil Procedure.

(4) Certifying a copy of any paper, record, or proceeding on file in the office of the clerk of any court.

(5) Taking an affidavit, except in criminal cases or adoption proceedings.

(6) Acknowledgment of any deed or other instrument, including the certificate.

(7) Recording or registering a license or certificate, or issuing a certificate in connection with a license, required by law, for which a charge is not otherwise prescribed.

(8) Issuing a certificate for which the fee is not otherwise fixed.

(b) The fee for each of the following services is forty-five dollars ($45). Subject to subdivision (e), amounts collected shall be distributed to the Trial Court Trust Fund under Section 68085.1.

(1) Issuing an order of sale.

(2) Receiving and filing an abstract of judgment rendered by a judge of another court and subsequent services based on it, unless the abstract of judgment is filed under Section 704.750 or 708.160 of the Code of Civil Procedure.

(3) Filing an application for renewal of judgment under Section 683.150 of the Code of Civil Procedure.

(4) Issuing a commission to take a deposition in another state or place under Section 2026.010 of the Code of Civil Procedure, or issuing a subpoena under Section 2029.300 to take a deposition in this state for purposes of a proceeding pending in another jurisdiction.

(5) Filing and entering an award under the Workers' Compensation Law (Division 4 (commencing with Section 3200) of the Labor Code).

(6) Filing an affidavit of publication of notice of dissolution of partnership.

(7) Filing an appeal of a determination whether a dog is potentially dangerous or vicious under Section 31622 of the Food and Agricultural Code.

(8) Filing an affidavit under Section 13200 of the Probate Code, together with the issuance of one certified copy of the affidavit under Section 13202 of the Probate Code.

(9) Filing and indexing all papers for which a charge is not elsewhere provided, other than papers filed in actions or special proceedings, official bonds, or certificates of appointment.

(c) The fee for filing a first petition under Section 2029.600 or 2029.620 of the Code of Civil Procedure, if the petitioner is not a party to the out-of-state case, is eighty dollars ($80). Amounts collected shall be distributed to the Trial Court Trust Fund pursuant to Section 68085.1.

(d) The fee for delivering a will to the clerk of the superior court in which the estate of a decedent may be administered, as required by Section 8200 of the Probate Code, is fifty dollars ($50).

(e) An amount equivalent to twenty-five dollars ($25) of each fee collected pursuant to subdivisions (a) and (b) shall be used by the Judicial Council for the expenses of the Judicial Council in implementing and administering the civil representation program under Section 68651. **Leg.H.** Added Stats 2005 ch 75 §121 (AB 145), effective July 19, 2005, operative January 1, 2006. Amended Stats 2005 ch 706 §31 (AB 1742); Stats 2008 ch 231 §4 (AB 2193), effective January 1, 2009. Stats 2009 4th Ex Sess 2009–2010 ch 22 §17 (SBX4-13), effective July 28, 2009, ch 457 §7 (AB 590), effective January 1, 2010, inoperative July 1, 2017, repealed January 1, 2018; Stats 2012 ch 41 §45 (SB 1021), effective June 27, 2012, inoperative July 1, 2017, repealed January 1, 2018. Amended Stats 2016 ch 33 §13 (SB 843), effective June 27, 2016; Stats 2019 ch 217 §3 (AB 330), effective January 1, 2020; Stats 2022 ch 851 §6 (SB 688), effective January 1, 2023.

Prior Law: Former Gov C §70626, similar to the present section, was added Stats 2009 ch 457 §8 (AB 590), effective January 1, 2010, operative July 1, 2017, amended Stats 2012 ch 41 §46 (SB 1021), effective June 27, 2012, operative July 1, 2017, and repealed Stats 2016 ch 33 §14 (SB 843), effective June 27, 2016.

2016 Note: The Legislature hereby finds and declares all of the following:

(a) The courts provide various and diverse services to the public that are necessary for the protection of the fundamental liberties of our society.

(b) Court services are heavily subsidized by the General Fund. If the total cost were passed on to the user, it would result in prohibitively expensive fees for even minor transactions.

(c) Traditionally, funding for many court-administered programs has been linked to the filing and processing of court documents.

(d) The linking of filing fees and the allocation of amounts equivalent to specified percentages of those fees to various programs provides an accounting mechanism, as a way to estimate how much funding a program will receive and to direct that funding, and is not intended to be indicative of the actual distribution of the specific fees or the cost of the actual services provided, for which General Fund moneys are largely used. Stats 2016 ch 33 (SB 843) § 15.

§70627. Fees for preparing copies, comparing original, and search of records

The fees collected under this section shall be distributed to the court in which they were collected.

(a) The clerk of the court shall charge fifty cents ($0.50) per page to cover the cost of preparing copies of any record, proceeding, or paper on file in the clerk's office.

(b) For comparing with the original on file in the office of the clerk of any court, the copy of any paper, record, or proceeding prepared by another and presented for the clerk's certificate, the fee is one dollar ($1) per page, in addition to the fee for the certificate.

(c) The fee for a search of records or files conducted by a court employee that requires more than 10 minutes is fifteen dollars ($15) for each search. **Leg.H.** Added Stats 2005 ch 75 §121 (AB 145), effective July 19, 2005, operative January 1, 2006.

§70628. Fee for exemplification of record

For an exemplification of a record or other paper on file, the fee is fifty dollars ($50), in addition to the charges allowed for copying or comparing each page of the record or other paper. **Leg.H.** Added Stats 2005 ch 75 §121 (AB 145), effective July 19, 2005, operative January 1, 2006. Amended Stats 2013 ch 31 §7 (SB 75), effective June 27, 2013.

§70629. Authentication fee

(a) The clerk of the court shall collect a fee of fifteen dollars ($15) per signature for any document that is required to be authenticated pursuant to court order.

(b) Each document authenticated by the clerk of the court shall contain the following statement:

"_____, Clerk of the Superior Court, County of _____, State of California. Signed pursuant to court order dated _____ in the matter of _____ petitioner v. _____, respondent, Case No. ____." **Leg.H.** Added Stats 1997 ch 850 §14 (AB 233), as Gov C §26835.1. Amended Stats 2002 ch 784 §182 (SB 1316); Amended and renumbered by Stats 2005 ch 75 §78 (AB 145), effective July 19, 2005, operative January 1, 2006.

§70630. Fee for permitting videoconferencing

If the court has made videoconferencing services available, the clerk of the court shall charge a reasonable fee to cover the costs of permitting parties to appear by videoconferencing. This fee shall be deposited into the Trial Court Trust Fund. **Leg.H.** Added Stats 2005 ch 75 §121 (AB 145), effective July 19, 2005, operative January 1, 2006.

§70631. Fee for particular service or product where not prohibited

In the absence of a statute or rule authorizing or prohibiting a fee by the superior court for a particular service or product, the court may charge a reasonable fee not to exceed the costs of providing the service or product, if the Judicial Council approves the fee. The fee shall be distributed to the court in which it was collected. **Leg.H.** Added Stats 2005 ch 75 §121 (AB 145), effective July 19, 2005, operative January 1, 2006.

§70632. Fee for handling certain funds held in trust

The clerk of the court shall charge a reasonable fee for handling funds held in trust for non-court parties or entities. The amount of the fee for handling the funds shall be based on rules adopted by, or guidelines and policies authorized by, the Judicial Council under subdivision (a) of Section 77206. This fee shall be deposited into the Trial Court Trust Fund. **Leg.H.** Added Stats 2005 ch 75 §121 (AB 145), effective July 19, 2005, operative January 1, 2006.

§70633. Adoption proceedings; Proceedings to declare minor free from parental custody; Criminal actions; Services to local, state, and federal governments

(a) No fee shall be charged by the clerk for service rendered to the petitioner in any adoption proceeding except as provided in Section 103730 of the Health and Safety Code, nor shall any fees be charged for any service to the state or for any proceeding brought pursuant to Section 7841 of the Family Code to declare a minor free from parental custody or control. No fee shall be charged by the clerk for services rendered in an action to compel registration of a voter under Section 2142 of the Elections Code or to compel counting of provisional ballots under Section 14310 of the Elections Code.

(b) No fee shall be charged by the clerk for services rendered in any criminal action unless otherwise specifically authorized by law, except that the clerk may charge the fee specified in Section 70627 for making or certifying to a copy of any filed paper, record, or proceeding in a criminal action. If a criminal defendant has been granted a fee waiver or the court finds that the defendant does not have the ability to pay the fee, the court may reduce or waive the fee.

(c) Except as permitted in subdivision (b), no fee shall be charged by the clerk for service to any municipality or county in the state, to the state government, nor to the United States of America or any of its officers acting in his or her official capacity.

§70635. No fee charged for certain name changes; Sydney's Law

(a) No fee shall be charged to the petitioner in a proceeding for a change of name that meets the conditions for the exemption under subdivision (b) of Section 1277 of the Code of Civil Procedure if the action is filed on behalf of a minor.

(b) This section shall be known, and may be cited, as "Sydney's Law." **Leg.H.** Added Stats 2018 ch 818 §2 (AB 2201), effective January 1, 2019.

§70640. Children's waiting rooms; Monthly allocations; Transfer of moneys; Distributions per filing fee

(a) It is the policy of the state that each court shall endeavor to provide a children's waiting room in each courthouse for children whose parents or guardians are attending a court hearing as a litigant, witness, or for other court purposes as determined by the court. To defray that expense, monthly allocations for children's waiting rooms shall be added to the monthly apportionment under subdivision (a) of Section 68085 for each court where a children's waiting room has been established or where the court has elected to establish that service.

(b) The amount allocated to each court under this section shall be equal to the following: for each first paper filing fee as provided under Section 70611, 70612, 70613, 70614, or 70670, and each first paper or petition filing fee in a probate matter as provided under Section 70650, 70651, 70652, 70653, 70654, 70655, 70656, or 70658, the same amount as was required to be collected as of December 31, 2005, to the Children's Waiting Room Fund under former Section 26826.3 in the county in which the court is located when a fee was collected for the filing of a first paper in a civil action under former Section 26820.4.

(c) Notwithstanding any other provision of law, the court may make expenditures from these allocations in payment of any cost, excluding capital outlay, related to the establishment and maintenance of the children's waiting room, including personnel, heat, light, telephone, security, rental of space, furnishings, toys, books, or any other item in connection with the operation of a children's waiting room.

(d) If, as of January 1, 2006, there is a Children's Waiting Room Fund in the county treasury established under former Section 26826.3, the county immediately shall transfer the moneys in that fund to the court's operations fund as a restricted fund. By February 15, 2006, the county shall provide an accounting of the fund to the Administrative Office of the Courts.

(e) After January 1, 2006, the court may apply to the Judicial Council for an adjustment of the amount distributed to the fund for each uniform filing fee. A court that wishes to establish a children's waiting room, and does not yet have a distribution under this section, may apply to the Judicial Council for a distribution. Applications under this subdivision shall be made according to trial court financial policies and procedures authorized by the Judicial Council under subdivision (a) of Section 77206. Adjustments and new distributions shall be effective January 1 or July 1 of any year beginning January 1, 2006.

(f) The distribution to a court under this section per each filing fee shall be not less than two dollars ($2) and not more than five dollars ($5). **Leg.H.** Added Stats 1999 ch 115 §1 (AB 177), as Gov C §26826.3. Amended and renumbered by Stats 2005 ch 75 §59 (AB 145), effective July 19, 2005, operative January 1, 2006; Amended Stats 2005 ch 706 §32 (AB 1742), effective January 1, 2006; Stats 2007 ch 130 §135 (AB 299), effective January 1, 2008.

ARTICLE 2
Fees in Probate Proceedings

§70650. Filing first petition for letters of administration and other specified probate petitions; Subsequent petitions

(a) The uniform filing fee for the first petition for letters of administration or letters testamentary, or the first petition for special letters of administration with the powers of a general personal representative pursuant to Section 8545 of the Probate Code, is three hundred fifty-five dollars ($355).

(b) The uniform filing fee for the first objections to the probate of any will or codicil under Section 8250 of the Probate Code, or the first petition for revocation of probate of any will or codicil under Section 8270 of the Probate Code, is three hundred fifty-five dollars ($355). The uniform filing fee for the first petition for special letters of administration without the powers of a general personal representative is the fee provided in Section 70657.5. Where objections to the probate of a will or codicil or a petition for revocation of probate of a will or codicil are filed together with a petition for appointment of a personal representative described in subdivision (c) filed by the same person, only the fee provided in subdivision (c) shall be charged to that person.

(c) A fee of three hundred fifty-five dollars ($355) shall also be charged for filing each subsequent petition or objections of a type described in subdivision (a) in the same proceeding by a person other than the original petitioner or contestant. The same fee as provided in subdivision (b) shall be charged for filing each subsequent petition or objections of a type described in that subdivision in the same proceeding by a person other than the original petitioner or contestant.

(d) Notwithstanding Section 70658.5, if a petition for special letters of administration is filed together with a petition for letters of administration or letters testamentary under subdivision (a) or (c) by the same person, the person filing the petitions shall be charged the applicable filing fees for both petitions.

(e) The uniform filing fee charged under this section shall be distributed as provided in Section 68085.3. **Leg.H.** Added Stats 1974 ch 1285 §11.5, operative December 31, 1975, as Gov C §26827. Amended Stats 1975 ch 766 §11; Stats 1980 ch 1372 §30; Stats 1982 ch 327 §68, effective June 30, 1982; Stats 1988 ch 113 §8, effective May 25, 1988, operative July 1, 1988; Stats 1992 ch 696 §17 (AB 1344), effective September 14, 1992; Stats 1997 ch 850 §9 (AB 233). Stats 2003 ch 159 §9 (AB 1759), effective August 2, 2003, operative August 17, 2003, inoperative July 1, 2006, repealed January 1, 2007, ch 757 §4 (AB 296). Amended and renumbered by Stats 2005 ch 75 §61 (AB 145), effective July 19, 2005, operative January 1, 2006; Amended Stats 2007 ch 738 §30 (AB 1248), effective January 1, 2008; Stats 2008 ch 310 §1 (AB 171), effective January 1, 2009, ch 311 §15 (SB 1407), effective January 1, 2009; Stats 2009 4th Ex Sess 2009–2010 ch 22 §18 (SBX4-13), effective July 28, 2009.

§70651. Filing fee for objections or other papers in opposition

(a) The uniform filing fee for objections or any other paper in opposition to a petition described in subdivision (a) of Section 70650, other than a petition described in subdivision (c) of Section 70650, is three hundred fifty-five dollars ($355). If objections or any other paper in opposition are filed together with a petition described in subdivision (c) of Section 70650 by the same person, only the fee provided in subdivision (c) of Section 70650 shall be charged to that person.

(b) The uniform filing fee charged under this section shall be distributed as provided in Section 68085.3. **Leg.H.** Added Stats 2005 ch 75 §121 (AB 145), effective July 19, 2005, operative January 1, 2006. Amended Stats 2007 ch 738 §31 (AB 1248), effective January 1, 2008; Stats 2008 ch 310 §2 (AB 171), effective January 1, 2009, ch 311 §16 (SB 1407), effective January 1, 2009; Stats 2009 4th Ex Sess 2009–2010 ch 22 §19 (SBX4-13), effective July 28, 2009.

§70652. Filing fee for petition concerning internal affairs of trust; Papers in opposition; Refunds; Applicability

(a) The uniform filing fee for each petition concerning the internal affairs of a trust under Chapter 3 (commencing with Section 17200) of Part 5 of Division 9 of the Probate Code, or a first account of a trustee of a testamentary trust that is subject to the continuing jurisdiction of the court pursuant to Chapter 4 (commencing with Section 17300) of Part 5 of Division 9 of the Probate Code, is three hundred fifty-five dollars ($355).

(b) The uniform filing fee for each paper filed in opposition to a petition or first account of a trustee of a testamentary trust under subdivision (a) is three hundred fifty-five dollars ($355).

(c) To avoid hardship, or for other good cause, the court may direct the clerk of the court to refund all or any part of a filing fee paid under this section.

(d) This section does not apply to petitions or opposition filed concerning trusts created by court order under Article 10 (commencing with Section 2580) of Chapter 6 of Part 3 of Division 4 of the Probate Code, Article 1 (commencing with Section 3100) of Chapter 3 of Part 6 of Division 4 of the Probate Code, Article 1 (commencing with Section 3600) of Chapter 4 of Part 8 of Division 4 of the Probate Code.

(e) The uniform filing fee charged under this section shall be distributed as provided in Section 68085.3. **Leg.H.** Added Stats 2005 ch 75 §121 (AB 145), effective July 19, 2005, operative January 1, 2006. Amended Stats 2008 ch 310 §3 (AB 171), effective January 1, 2009, ch 311 §17 (SB 1407), effective January 1, 2009; Stats 2009 4th Ex Sess 2009–2010 ch 22 §20 (SBX4-13), effective July 28, 2009.

§70653. Filing fee for petition for appointment of conservator or guardian; Papers in opposition

(a) The uniform filing fee for a petition for appointment of a conservator, a guardian of the estate, or a guardian of the person and estate, pursuant to Division 4 (commencing with Section 1400) of the Probate Code, is three hundred fifty-five dollars ($355).

(b) Except as provided in subdivision (f), the uniform filing fee for objections or any other paper in opposition to a petition under subdivision (a) or (d) is three hundred fifty-five dollars ($355).

(c) If a competing petition for appointment of a guardian or conservator subject to the fee under subdivision (a) is filed together with opposition to the petition of another by the same person, the person filing the competing petition and opposition shall be charged a filing fee only for the competing petition.

(d) Notwithstanding Section 70658.5, if a petition for appointment of a temporary guardian or conservator is filed together with a petition for appointment of a guardian or conservator under subdivision (a), or a competing petition under subdivision (c) by the same person, the person filing the petitions shall be charged the applicable filing fees for both petitions.

(e) The uniform filing fee charged under this section shall be distributed as provided in Section 68085.3.

(f) No fee under this section shall be charged for objections or any other paper in opposition filed by or on behalf of the proposed conservatee, or the minor or a parent of the minor who is the subject of a guardianship proceeding. **Leg.H.** Added Stats 2005 ch 75 §121 (AB 145), effective July 19, 2005, operative January 1, 2006. Amended Stats 2007 ch 738 §32 (AB 1248), effective January 1, 2008; Stats 2008 ch 311 §18 (SB 1407), effective January 1, 2009; Stats 2009 4th Ex Sess 2009–2010 ch 22 §21 (SBX4-13), effective July 28, 2009.

§70654. Filing fee for petition for appointment of guardian of person only; Papers in opposition

(a) The uniform filing fee for a petition for appointment of a guardian of the person only, is two hundred five dollars ($205).

(b) Except as provided in subdivision (e), the uniform filing fee for objections or any other paper in opposition to a petition under subdivision (a) is two hundred five dollars ($205).

(c) If a competing petition for appointment of a guardian subject to the fee under subdivision (a) is filed together with opposition to the petition of another by the same person, the person filing the competing petition and opposition shall be charged a filing fee only for the competing petition.

(d) Notwithstanding Section 70658.5, if a petition for appointment of a temporary guardian is filed together with a petition for appointment of a guardian under subdivision (a), or a competing petition under subdivision (c) by the same person, the person filing the petitions shall be charged the applicable filing fees for both petitions.

(e) No fee under this section shall be charged for objections or any other paper in opposition filed by or on behalf of the minor or a parent of the minor who is the subject of the proceeding.

(f) The uniform filing fee charged under this section shall be distributed as provided in Section 68085.4.

(g) No other fees shall be charged for filing a paper under this section in addition to the uniform filing fee provided for in this section. **Leg.H.** Added Stats 2005 ch 75 §121 (AB 145), effective July 19, 2005, operative January 1, 2006. Amended Stats 2007 ch 738 §33 (AB 1248), effective January 1, 2008; Stats 2008 ch 311 §19 (SB 1407), effective January 1, 2009; Stats 2009 4th Ex Sess 2009–2010 ch 22 §22 (SBX4-13), effective July 28, 2009.

§70655. Filing fee for petition commencing certain proceedings; Papers in opposition

(a) The uniform filing fee for a petition that commences any of the proceedings under the Probate Code listed in subdivision (c) is three hundred fifty-five dollars ($355).

(b) The uniform filing fee for objections or any other paper filed in opposition to a petition under subdivision (a) is three hundred fifty-five dollars ($355).

(c) This section applies to petitions or opposition concerning the following proceedings:

(1) A petition for compromise of a minor's claim pursuant to Section 3600 of the Probate Code.

(2) A petition to determine succession to real property pursuant to Section 13151 of the Probate Code.

(3) A spousal or domestic partnership property petition pursuant to Section 13650 of the Probate Code, except as provided in Section 13652 of the Probate Code.

(4) A petition to establish the fact of death to determine title to real property under Section 200 of the Probate Code.

(5) A petition for an order concerning a particular transaction pursuant to Section 3100 of the Probate Code.

(6) A petition concerning capacity determination and health care decision for an adult without conservator pursuant to Section 3200 of the Probate Code.

(7) A petition concerning an advance health care directive pursuant to Section 4766 of the Probate Code.

(8) A petition concerning a power of attorney pursuant to Section 4541 of the Probate Code.

(9) A petition for approval, compromise, or settlement of claims against a deceased settlor, or for allocation of amounts due between trusts, pursuant to Section 19020 of the Probate Code.

(10) Any other petition that commences a proceeding under the Probate Code not otherwise provided for in this article.

(d) The uniform filing fee charged under this section shall be distributed as provided in Section 68085.3. **Leg.H.** Added Stats 2005 ch 75 §121 (AB 145), effective July 19, 2005, operative January 1, 2006. Amended Stats 2007 ch 738 §34 (AB 1248), effective January 1, 2008; Stats 2008 ch 311 §20 (SB 1407), effective January 1, 2009; Stats 2009 4th Ex Sess 2009–2010 ch 22 §23 (SBX4-13), effective July 28, 2009.

§70656. Filing fee for petition requesting estate of small value to be set aside; Papers in opposition

(a) The uniform filing fee for a petition requesting an order setting aside a decedent's estate of small value pursuant to Section 6602 of the Probate Code, if no estate proceeding is pending for the decedent, is two hundred five dollars ($205).

(b) The uniform filing fee for objections or any other paper filed in opposition to a petition under subdivision (a) is two hundred five dollars ($205).

(c) If a petition or objections or any other paper in opposition under this section is filed concurrently with a petition for appointment of a personal representative described in Section 70650, the petitioner or objector shall be charged only for the filing fee provided in Section 70650.

(d) The uniform filing fee charged under this section shall be distributed as provided in Section 68085.4.

(e) Except as provided in subdivision (c), no other fee shall be charged for filing a paper under this section in addition to the uniform filing fee provided for in this section. **Leg.H.** Added Stats 2005 ch 75 §121 (AB 145), effective July 19, 2005, operative January 1, 2006. Amended Stats 2008 ch 311 §21 (SB 1407), effective January 1, 2009; Stats 2009 4th Ex Sess 2009–2010 ch 22 §24 (SBX4-13), effective July 28, 2009.

§70657. Fee for filing motion, application or other paper requiring hearing subsequent to first paper

(a) Except as provided in subdivision (c), the uniform fee for filing a motion or other paper requiring a hearing subsequent to the first paper in a proceeding under the Probate Code, other than a petition or application or opposition described in Sections 70657.5 and 70658, is sixty dollars ($60). This fee shall be charged for the following papers:

(1) Papers listed in subdivision (a) of Section 70617.

(2) Applications for ex parte relief, whether or not notice of the application to any person is required, except an ex parte petition for discharge of a personal representative, conservator, or guardian upon completion of a court-ordered distribution or transfer, for which no fee shall be charged.

(3) Petitions or applications, or objections, filed subsequent to issuance of temporary letters of conservatorship or guardianship or letters of conservatorship or guardianship that are not subject to the filing fee provided in subdivision (a) of Section 70658.

(4) The first or subsequent petition for temporary letters of conservatorship or guardianship.

(b) There shall be no fee under subdivision (a) for filing any of the papers listed under subdivision (b) of Section 70617.

(c) The summary judgment fee provided in subdivision (d) of Section 70617 shall apply to summary judgment motions in proceedings under the Probate Code.

(d) Regardless of whether each motion or matter is heard at a single hearing or at separate hearings, the filing fees required by subdivisions (a) and (c) apply separately to each motion or other paper filed. The Judicial Council may publish rules to give uniform guidance to courts in applying fees under this section.

(e) No fee is payable under this section for a petition or opposition filed subsequent to issuance of letters of temporary guardianship or letters of guardianship in a guardianship described in Section 70654. **Leg.H.** Added Stats 2005 ch 75 §121 (AB 145), effective July 19, 2005, operative January 1, 2006. Amended Stats 2007 ch 738 §35 (AB 1248), effective January 1, 2008; Stats 2008 ch 311 §22 (SB 1407), effective January 1, 2009; Stats 2012 ch 41 §47 (SB 1021), effective June 27, 2012, inoperative July 1, 2015, repealed January 1, 2016; Stats 2015 ch 26 §10 (SB 85), effective June 24, 2015, inoperative July 1, 2018, repealed January 1, 2019; Stats 2018 ch 45 §14 (SB 847), effective June 27, 2018, inoperative July 1, 2023, repealed January 1, 2024; Stats 2023 ch 34 §15 (SB 133), effective June 30, 2023.

Prior Law: Former Gov C §70657, relating to fee for filing motion, application or other paper requiring hearing subsequent to first paper, was added Stats 2012 ch 41 §48 (SB 1021), effective June 27, 2012, operative July 1, 2015, amended Stats 2015 ch 26 §11 (SB 85), effective June 24, 2015, operative July 1, 2018, Stats 2018 ch 45 §15 (SB 847), effective June 27, 2018, operative July 1, 2023, and repealed Stats 2023 ch 34 §16 (SB 133), effective June 30, 2023.

§70657.5. Uniform filing fee for specified petitions, applications, objections or other opposition; Exceptions

(a) The uniform fee for filing the following petitions or applications, and objections or other opposition, is two hundred dollars ($200):

(1) Petitions or applications, or opposition, concerning the internal affairs of a trust that are not subject to the filing fees provided in Section 70650, 70651, or 70652.

(2) Petitions or applications, or objections, filed subsequent to issuance of special letters of administration or letters testamentary or of administration in decedent's estate proceedings that are not subject to the filing fee provided in subdivision (a) of Section 70658.

(3) The first or subsequent petition for special letters of administration without the powers of a general personal representative.

(b) One hundred sixty dollars ($160) of each two-hundred-dollar ($200) fee collected under subdivision (a) shall be transmitted to the state for deposit into the State Court Facilities Construction Fund, established in Section 70371.

(c) No fee is payable under this section for a disclaimer of an interest in a decedent's estate. **Leg.H.** Added Stats 2007 ch 738 §36 (AB 1248), effective January 1, 2008. Amended Stats 2008 ch 310 §4 (AB 171), effective January 1, 2009, ch 311 §23 (SB 1407), effective January 1, 2009; Stats 2021 ch 79 §33 (AB 143), effective July 16, 2021.

§70658. Fees for petition, application or objections to petitions or applications filed after issuance of various letters

(a) Except as provided in subdivision (c), the uniform fee for filing a petition or application, or objections or any other paper in opposition to a petition or application listed in this subdivision, filed after issuance of letters testamentary, letters of administration, letters of special administration to a personal representative of a decedent's estate, or letters of guardianship or conservatorship, or letters of temporary guardianship or conservatorship to a guardian or conservator, is three hundred fifty-five dollars ($355). This section shall apply to the following petitions or applications, or opposition:

(1) Petition or application for or opposition to an order directing, authorizing, approving, or confirming the sale, lease, encumbrance, grant of an option, purchase, conveyance, or exchange of property.

(2) Petition or application for or opposition to an order settling an account of a fiduciary.

(3) Petition or application for or opposition to an order authorizing, instructing, or directing a fiduciary, or approving or confirming the acts of a fiduciary.

(4) Petition or application for or opposition to an order fixing, authorizing, allowing, or directing payment of compensation or expenses of an attorney.

(5) Petition or application for or opposition to an order fixing, authorizing, allowing, or directing payment of compensation or expenses of a fiduciary.

(6) Petition or application for or opposition to an order surcharging or removing a fiduciary.

(7) Petition or application for or opposition to an order transferring or authorizing the transfer of the property of an estate to a fiduciary in another jurisdiction.

(8) Petition or application for or opposition to an order allowing a fiduciary's request to resign.

(9) Petition or application for or opposition to an order adjudicating the merits of a claim made under Part 19 (commencing with Section 850) of Division 2 of the Probate Code.

(10) Petition or application for or opposition to an order granting permission to fix the residence of a ward or conservatee at a place not within this state.

(11) Petition or application for or opposition to an order directing, authorizing, approving, or modifying payments for support, maintenance, or education of a ward or conservatee or for a person entitled to support, maintenance, or education from a ward or conservatee.

(12) Petition or application for or opposition to an order granting or denying a request under Section 2423, concerning payment of surplus income to the relatives of a conservatee, or Section 2580, concerning substituted judgment, of the Probate Code.

(13) Petition or application for or opposition to an order affecting the legal capacity of a conservatee pursuant to Chapter 4 (commencing with Section 1870) of Part 3 of Division 4 of the Probate Code.

(14) Petition or application for or opposition to an order adjudicating the merits of a claim under Article 5 (commencing with Section 2500) of Chapter 6 of Part 4 of Division 4 of the Probate Code.

(b) The uniform fee in subdivision (a) shall be distributed as provided in Section 68085.3. No other fee shall be charged for filing a paper under this section in addition to the uniform filing fee provided for in this section.

(c) The fee provided in this section shall not be charged for filing any of the following papers:

(1) A petition or application, or opposition, in a guardianship proceeding under Section 70654.

(2) A disclaimer of an interest in a decedent's estate.

(d) Two hundred five dollars ($205) of each three-hundred-fifty-five dollar ($355) fee collected under this section shall be transmitted to the Controller for deposit into the State Court Facilities Construction Fund, established in 70371. **Leg.H.** Added Stats 2005 ch 75 §121 (AB 145), effective July 19, 2005, operative January 1, 2006. Amended Stats 2007 ch 738 §37 (AB 1248), effective January 1, 2008; Stats 2008 ch 310 §5 (AB 171), effective January 1, 2009, ch 311 §24 (SB 1407), effective January 1, 2009; Stats 2009 4th Ex Sess 2009–2010 ch 22 §25 (SBX4-13), effective July 28, 2009; Stats 2021 ch 79 §34 (AB 143), effective July 16, 2021.

§70658.5. Fees for combined petitions, applications, objections or other opposition

If a petition or application, or opposition to a petition or application, described in Sections 70650 to 70656, inclusive, or Sections 70657.5 to 70658, inclusive, is filed combining requests for relief or opposition to relief that could have been stated in separate petitions or applications, or objections or other opposition, only one filing fee shall be charged under this article. If a filing combines petitions, applications, or objections, or other opposition to a petition or application, that would be subject to different filing fees under this article, the higher of the applicable filing fees shall be charged. **Leg.H.** Added Stats 2007 ch 738 §38 (AB 1248), effective January 1, 2008.

§70659. Payment of fees by public administrator, public guardian, public conservator, or employee of Departments of State Hospitals or Developmental Services

Where the public administrator, public guardian, or public conservator, or an employee of the State Department of State Hospitals or the State Department of Developmental Services is the petitioner in an official capacity in a proceeding described in Section 70650, 70653, 70657, or 70658, the fee is payable only out of the assets of the estate coming into the official's possession or control. **Leg.H.** Added Stats 1988 ch 113 §10, effective May 25, 1988, operative July 1, 1988, as Gov C §26827. Amended and renumbered by Stats 2005 ch 75 §65 (AB 145), effective July 19, 2005, operative January 1, 2006; Stats 2012 ch 440 §33 (AB 1488), effective September 22, 2012.

§70660. Fee for receipt and storage of document transferred to court clerk; Reduction or waiver

(a) The fee for receiving and storing each document transferred to the clerk of the superior court under Section 732 of the Probate Code is twenty dollars ($20).

(b) The superior court may reduce or waive the fee established pursuant to this section under either of the following circumstances:

(1) The court has assumed jurisdiction under Article 11 (commencing with Section 6180) of Chapter 4 of Division 3 of the Business and Professions Code over the law practice of the attorney with whom the document is deposited.

(2) On a showing of hardship. **Leg.H.** Added Stats 1993 ch 519 §2 (AB 209), as Gov C §26827.6. Amended Stats 2001 ch 824 §14 (AB 1700); Amended and renumbered by Stats 2005 ch 75 §66 (AB 145), effective July 19, 2005, operative January 1, 2006.

§70661. Fee for receipt and storage of document transferred to court clerk; Reduction or waiver

The fee for searching a document transferred to the clerk of the superior court under Section 732 of the Probate Code is the same as the fee under subdivision (c) of Section 70627 for searching records or files. **Leg.H.** Added Stats 1993 ch 519 §3 (AB 209), as Gov C §26827.7. Amended and renumbered by Stats 2005 ch 75 §67 (AB 145), effective July 19, 2005, operative January 1, 2006.

§70662. Filing fee for request for special notice

The filing fee for a request for special notice pursuant to Sections 1250, 2700, and 17204 of the Probate Code is forty dollars ($40). This fee shall be in addition to any other fee charged for a paper filed concurrently with a request for special notice. **Leg.H.** Added Stats 2013 ch 382 §1 (AB 1293), effective January 1, 2014, repealed January 1, 2019. Amended

Stats 2018 ch 45 §16 (SB 847), effective June 27, 2018, repealed January 1, 2024; Stats 2023 ch 34 §17 (SB 133), effective June 30, 2023.

§70663. Fee for registering conservatorship from other state

The fee for registering a conservatorship under Article 4 (commencing with Section 2011) of Chapter 8 of Part 3 of Division 4 of the Probate Code is thirty dollars ($30). The amounts collected shall be distributed to the Trial Court Trust Fund under Section 68085.1. **Leg.H.** Added Stats 2014 ch 553 §2 (SB 940), effective January 1, 2015, operative January 1, 2016.

ARTICLE 3
Fees in Family Law Matters

§70670. Fee for filing first paper in proceeding under Family Code

(a) The uniform fee for filing the first paper in a proceeding under the Family Code, other than a proceeding for dissolution of marriage or domestic partnership, legal separation, or nullity, is three hundred fifty-five dollars ($355). The fee shall be distributed as provided in Section 68085.3.

(b) The uniform fee for filing the first paper in a proceeding for dissolution of marriage or domestic partnership, legal separation, or nullity, is three hundred fifty-five dollars ($355). The fee shall be distributed as provided in Section 68085.3, except that two dollars ($2) of the funds that would otherwise be distributed to the Trial Court Trust Fund shall be transmitted to the Treasurer for deposit in the Health Statistics Special Fund.

(c) The uniform fee for filing the first paper in a proceeding under subdivision (a) on behalf of any respondent, defendant, intervenor, or adverse party, whether separately or jointly, is three hundred fifty-five dollars ($355). The fee shall be distributed as provided in Section 68085.3.

(d) The uniform fee for filing the first paper in a proceeding under subdivision (b) on behalf of any respondent, defendant, intervenor, or adverse party, whether separately or jointly, is three hundred fifty-five dollars ($355). The fee shall be distributed as provided in Section 68085.3.

(e) The fees in this section do not apply to papers filed for the purpose of making a disclaimer. **Leg.H.** Added Stats 2005 ch 75 §121 (AB 145), effective July 19, 2005, operative January 1, 2006. Amended Stats 2008 ch 311 §25 (SB 1407), effective January 1, 2009; Stats 2009 4th Ex Sess 2009–2010 ch 22 §26 (SBX4-13), effective July 28, 2009.

§70671. Meaning of "paper" as used in §70670(c) or (d)

As used in subdivision (c) or (d) of Section 70670, the term "paper" does not include any of the following:

(a) The declaration of a spouse or domestic partner filed in an order to show cause proceeding.

(b) A settlement agreement or a stipulation for judgment that is signed by a defaulted respondent and intended for incorporation in a proposed decree of dissolution of marriage or domestic partnership.

(c) A stipulation regarding the date of termination of the marital or domestic partnership status if the court has retained jurisdiction over that date.

(d) A document relating to a stipulated postjudgment modification of child support.

(e) A stipulation to modify a settlement agreement that was signed by a defaulted respondent and incorporated in a decree of dissolution if the stipulation is presented by the petitioner.

(f) A request for an order to prevent domestic violence or a responsive declaration to that request. **Leg.H.** Added Stats 2005 ch 75 §121 (AB 145), effective July 19, 2005, operative January 1, 2006.

§70672. No filing fee for parentage or support issues where Title IV-D child support agency is providing services

Notwithstanding any other provision of law, no fee shall be charged to file a first paper or any subsequent pleading or document on issues relating to parentage or support in a case in which a Title IV-D child support agency is providing services under Section 17400 of the Family Code. **Leg.H.** Added Stats 2005 ch 75 §121 (AB 145), effective July 19, 2005, operative January 1, 2006.

§70673. Members of armed forces

Notwithstanding any other provision of law, no fee shall be charged to file a respondent's appearance, stipulation if any, and waiver of rights in the action under the Service members Civil Relief Act (50 U.S.C. App. Secs. 501 to 596, inclusive) in an action for dissolution of marriage or domestic partnership, legal separation, or nullity, or to establish parentage, in any case wherein the respondent is a member of the armed forces of the United States and does not contest the action for dissolution of marriage or domestic partnership, legal separation, or nullity, or to establish parentage. **Leg.H.** Added Stats 1974 ch 39 §1, as Gov C §26857.5. Amended Stats 1996 ch 348 §1 (AB 3148); Amended and renumbered by Stats 2005 ch 75 §93 (AB 145), effective July 19, 2005, operative January 1, 2006.

§70674. Marriage or domestic partnership dissolution record fee

(a) Except as provided by Section 6103.9, and notwithstanding the fee authorized by paragraph (4) of subdivision (a) of Section 70626, a fee of ten dollars ($10) shall be paid by a public agency applicant for a certified copy of a marriage or domestic partnership dissolution record that the agency is required to obtain in the ordinary course of business. A fee of fifteen dollars ($15) shall be paid by any other applicant for a certified copy of a marriage or domestic partnership dissolution record. Five dollars ($5) of any fifteen dollar ($15) fee shall be transmitted monthly to the state for deposit into the Family Law Trust Fund as provided by Section 1852 of the Family Code. The remainder of the fees collected under this section shall be deposited into the Trial Court Trust Fund.

(b) As used in this section, "marriage or domestic partnership dissolution record" means the judgment. **Leg.H.** Added Stats 1997 ch 850 §12 (AB 233), as Gov C §26832.1. Amended and renumbered by Stats 2005 ch 75 §74 (AB 145), effective July 19, 2005, operative January 1, 2006.

§70676. Fees not to be charged to indigent petitioner for copies of specified orders

No fee shall be charged to an indigent petitioner for certified copies of any order issued pursuant to any of the following:

(a) Article 2 (commencing with Section 2045), Article 3 (commencing with Section 2047), or Article 4 (commencing with Section 2049) of Chapter 4 of Part 1 of Division 6 of the Family Code.

(b) Division 10 (commencing with Section 6200) of the Family Code.

(c) Article 2 (commencing with Section 7710), Article 3 (commencing with Section 7720), or Article 4 (commencing with Section 7730) of Chapter 6 of Part 3 of Division 12 of the Family Code. **Leg.H.** Added Stats 1979 ch 795 §11, as Gov C §26833.5, operative July 1, 1980. Amended Stats 1992 ch 163 §80 (AB 2641), operative January 1, 1994; Stats 1993 ch 219 §213.5 (AB 1500); Amended and renumbered by Stats 2005 ch 75 §76 (AB 145), effective July 19, 2005, operative January 1, 2006.

§70677. Fee for filing paper requiring hearing subsequent to first paper; Fee for filing certain papers not requiring hearing

(a) The uniform fee for filing any motion, application, order to show cause, or any other paper requiring a hearing subsequent to the first paper is sixty dollars ($60). Papers for which this fee shall be charged include the following:

(1) Papers listed in subdivision (a) of Section 70617.

(2) An order to show cause or notice of motion seeking temporary prejudgment or postjudgment orders, including, but not limited to, orders to establish, modify, or enforce child, spousal, or partner support, custody and visitation of children, division and control of property, attorney's fees, and bifurcation of issues.

(b) There shall be no fee under subdivision (a) of this section for filing any of the following:

(1) A motion, motion to quash proceeding, application, or demurrer that is the first paper filed in an action and on which a first paper filing fee is paid.

(2) An amended notice of motion or amended order to show cause.

(3) A statement to register foreign support under Section 5700.602 of the Family Code.

(4) An application to determine the judgment after entry of default.

(5) A request for an order to prevent domestic violence.

(6) A paper requiring a hearing on a petition for writ of review, mandate, or prohibition that is the first paper filed in an action and on which a first paper filing fee has been paid.

(7) A stipulation that does not require an order.

(c) The uniform fee for filing the following papers not requiring a hearing is twenty dollars ($20):

(1) A request, application, or motion for the continuance of a hearing or case management conference.

(2) A stipulation and order.

(d) Regardless of whether each motion or matter is heard at a single hearing or at separate hearings, the filing fees required under paragraph (1) of subdivision (a) and under subdivision (c) apply separately to each motion or other paper filed. If an order to show cause or notice of motion is filed as specified in paragraph (2) of subdivision (a) combining requests for relief or opposition to relief on more than one issue, only one filing fee shall be charged under this section. The Judicial Council may publish rules to give uniform guidance to courts in applying fees under this section. **Leg.H.** Added Stats 2005 ch 75 §121 (AB 145), effective July 19, 2005, operative January 1, 2006. Amended Stats 2007 ch 738 §39 (AB 1248), effective January 1, 2008. Stats 2012 ch 41 §49 (SB 1021), effective June 27, 2012, inoperative July 1, 2015, repealed January 1, 2016; Stats 2015 ch 26 §12 (SB 85), effective June 24, 2015, inoperative July 1, 2018, repealed July 1, 2019; Stats 2018 ch 45 §17 (SB 847), effective June 27, 2018, inoperative July 1, 2023, repealed January 1, 2024; Stats 2023 ch 34 §18 (SB 133), effective June 30, 2023.

Prior Law Former Gov C §70677, relating to fee for filing paper requiring hearing subsequent to first paper and fee for filing certain papers not requiring hearing, was added Stats 2012 ch 41 §50 (SB 1021), effective June 27, 2012, operative July 1, 2015, amended Stats 2015 ch 26 §13 (SB 85), effective June 24, 2015, operative July 1, 2018, Stats 2018 ch 45 §18 (SB 847), effective June 27, 2018, operative July 1, 2023, and repealed Stats 2023 ch 34 §19 (SB 133), effective June 30, 2023.

§70678. Fees in proceedings regarding custody and visitation of minor children

In addition to the fee set forth in Section 70677, a fee of twenty-five dollars ($25) shall be paid to the clerk of the court at the time of filing a motion, order to show cause, or other proceeding seeking to modify or enforce that portion of any judgment or order entered in this state or any other state which orders or awards the custody of a minor child or children or which specifies the rights of any party to the proceeding to visitation of a minor child or children. Fifteen dollars ($15) of the fee authorized in this section shall be used exclusively to pay the costs of maintaining mediation services provided under Chapter 11 (commencing with Section 3160) of Part 2 of Division 8 of the Family Code, and ten dollars ($10) of the fee shall be used exclusively to pay the costs of services provided by the family law facilitator under Section 10005 of the Family Code. **Leg.H.** Added Stats 1980 ch 48 §7, as Gov C §26862, effective March 27, 1980. Amended Stats 1997 ch 850 §24 (AB 233); Amended and renumbered by Stats 2005 ch 75 §95 (AB 145), effective July 19, 2005, operative January 1, 2006.